1994

Britannica Book of the Year

Encyclopædia Britannica, Inc.
Chicago
Auckland/London/Madrid/Manila/Paris
Rome/Seoul/Sydney/Tokyo/Toronto

Library of Congress Catalog Card Number: 38-12082
International Standard Book Number: 0-85229-600-2
International Standard Serial Number: 0068-1156

BRITANNICA BOOK OF THE YEAR

(Trademark Reg. U.S. Pat. Off.) Printed in U.S.A.

CONTENTS

The New World Disorder

BY DANIEL SCHORR

My friend Flora Lewis summed up the year 1991 in these pages, with appropriate tentativeness, as "a time of transition." She noted the fears and uncertainties that had started cropping up in the wake of the collapse of communism and the end of the Cold War. My friend Hedrick Smith saw, in 1992, the trend lines of history no longer pointing upward, but downward as explosions of ethnic and religious violence signaled a more chaotic world. His article was headlined "The Not-So-New World Order." In 1993 the trend line plunged more sharply downward. Not only did sources of instability multiply, but the international community displayed a waning capacity to cope with its many firestorms. Call this, then, "The New World Disorder."

The year opened with Czechoslovakia dividing into two states, continuing the centrifugal tendency of nation-states to fragment into state-nations. In January also, negotiations on Bosnia and Herzegovina termed "the last chance for peace" were in progress, one of many "last chances" that proved to be no chance at all. At the same time, Croatia was conducting an offensive against Serbia in which thousands were killed. In Somalia the first American soldier was killed. On Haiti, President-elect Bill Clinton reversed his promise to lift the antirefugee naval blockade that Pres. George Bush had imposed. All these sores on the body politic continued to fester during the year, and more were added, among them an attempted coup against Pres. Boris Yeltsin in Russia and civil wars in former Soviet states such as Georgia, Azerbaijan, and Moldova.

If Year Four after the collapse of communism should have brought us anything, it was surcease from nuclear peril, but that did not happen. In January, Presidents Bush and Yeltsin signed a new Strategic Arms Reduction Treaty, START II, which provided for the dismantling of a large part of the nuclear weapons stocks on both sides, but in Russia the process was delayed by economic problems. Ukraine, the world's number three nuclear power, because so many Soviet weapons had been left on its soil, dragged its feet on disposing of them. Iraq sparred with nuclear inspectors as though still reluctant to come clean about its weapons potential. And North Korea, ruled by the last unreconstructed Stalinist regime, resisted effective inspection by the International Atomic Energy Agency, suggesting the chilling prospect that it was on its way to breaking into the nuclear club. Indeed, by the end of the year, the U.S. Central Intelligence Agency had concluded that North Korea probably already had one or two nuclear devices.

Ruth Leger Sivard, a one-time U.S. government economist who produces, from her Georgetown home in Washington, D.C., a unique annual survey of the world's investment in its salvation and in its destruction, reported in November that when all current arms-reduction commitments are met, the five acknowledged nuclear powers will still have 900 times the explosive power expended in World War II. She reported also a record number of 29 "conventional" wars going on around the world, from Turkey to Peru, from Georgia to South Africa. Since the end of World War II, she noted, more than 23 million people have been killed in internal and across-border conflicts.

Particularly dismaying about 1993 was the growing sense of international helplessness in trying to quench the flames. There had been a season of high hopes after the United Nations-brokered Soviet withdrawal from Afghanistan and after the big powers, freed of the Soviet veto, had successfully assembled a coalition to fight the war in the Persian Gulf. The new secretary-general, Boutros Boutros-Ghali of Egypt, began planning for the day when an international force, free of colonial taint, would be on call to control eruptions around the world. President Clinton told the UN General Assembly that the United States, while not earmarking combat units, would make a modest contribution to a combined headquarters and provide sophisticated communications. At one heady juncture, the UN expanded its definition of "threat to peace" to apply not only to invasions but to human tragedies generating a flow of refugees in countries such as the former Yugoslavia and Somalia.

The heyday of multilateralism did not last long. Soon Boutros-Ghali found himself being jeered at in Sarajevo and Mogadishu. UN authority was eroded by lack of funds, lack of consensus, and, under the pressure of events, a cooling of America's enthusiasm about multilateral approaches.

Bosnia soon became an enormous source of frustration to President Clinton, who had denounced President Bush during the campaign as not being assertive enough and who promised forceful intervention to rescue the Bosnian Muslims. But, in trying to go beyond humanitarian aid to lifting the arms embargo on the Muslims and threatening air attacks on Serbian siege artillery, the president found himself checkmated by Western Europe and Russia. He talked for a while about taking unilateral action but was quickly persuaded by the Joint Chiefs of Staff that this was not feasible. Soon the Clinton administration retired to

---

Daniel Schorr, the last of Edward R. Murrow's legendary news team still active in daily journalism, is senior news analyst for National Public Radio. Among his most recent honours was the presentation in 1993 of the George Foster Peabody Broadcasting Award, the radio-television equivalent of the Pulitzer Prize for journalism, which cited him "for a lifetime of uncompromising reporting of the highest integrity." His books include Clearing the Air *and* Don't Get Sick in America.

(Opposite page) Photograph, Reuters/Bettmann

Secretary-General Boutros Boutros-Ghali (right) tours under the protection of United Nations peacekeeping troops on his visit to Sarajevo. The inability of the UN to intercede effectively in the war in Bosnia and Herzegovina and in other conflicts could, to a large degree, be attributed to lack of support from major member nations.
TOMAS MUSCIONICO—CONTACT

the sidelines, leaving a series of fruitless peace initiatives to UN and European mediators. Clinton called his failure to achieve consensus for intervention "the greatest single disappointment" of his first year in office. Secretary of State Warren Christopher's epitaph for American engagement was, "We are doing everything we can consistent with our national interest," and "This is a problem from Hell."

In the series of on-again, off-again negotiations about the fate of Bosnia and Herzegovina, one fact stood out sharply—whatever the final outlines of partition, Bosnia was finished as a unitary multiethnic state. This meant that, for the first time since World War II, the internationally recognized borders of a sovereign state were being changed by force—a flouting of everything collective security stands for and a precedent as menacing to the rule of law as the Italian invasion of Ethiopia and the German-Italian-supported civil war in Spain that served as harbingers of world war.

Nor would dismemberment of Bosnia necessarily end the fighting. One goes back over the history of partition arrangements—Ireland, Korea, Vietnam, India, Palestine—and notes that in each case bloody conflict ensued.

Somalia became an almost equally frustrating problem for a president threading his way through the international arena while trying to focus on problems of the economy, health, and crime at home. What started, with President Bush, as a humanitarian enterprise for U.S. forces, ensuring safe delivery of food to starving people, deteriorated into a punitive—and punishing—military expedition. Hardly realizing how the mission was changing, the Clinton administration allowed its Army Rangers to be drawn into a hunt for Somali strongman Gen. Muhammad Farah Aydid. When, in June, 24 Pakistani soldiers under UN command on a search mission were ambushed and killed, Rangers became involved in the effort to track down Aydid, with the result that 18 Americans were killed in an ambush on October 3, and a helicopter pilot was taken prisoner.

In the age of live, instantaneous global television, foreign policy tends to be video-driven, influenced by viewers' reactions to the scenes presented to them. So, ironically, U.S. forces were drawn into Somalia by televised scenes of hunger and suffering and, in effect, driven out again by pictures of an American body being dragged through the streets and an injured American pilot in hostile hands. This was, in its way, like the videotape of American hostages in terrorist hands in Lebanon that helped to push the administration of Pres. Ronald Reagan into trying to ransom them by selling missiles to Iran. In any event, Clinton, under strong congressional pressure, gave orders that the U.S. contingent first be beefed up for its own protection and then withdrawn from Somalia by March 31, 1994—the end of a second well-intentioned involvement that went sour.

Twice burned—in Bosnia and Somalia—the Clinton administration was thrice shy when it came to dealing with Haiti. In July, in negotiations on New York City's Governors Island, the military junta led by Gen. Raoul Cédras, feeling the pinch of UN sanctions, agreed to the restoration of the elected president, Jean-Bertrand Aristide, on October 30. But, when American troops arrived to fulfill technical tasks under the terms of the agreement, they became the target of an organized demonstration on the docks at Port-au-Prince, and their ship was quickly withdrawn. One could only speculate on whether the military junta had been emboldened by American faltering on Bosnia and Somalia. In any event, Cédras reneged on his promise to step down, and the introduction of some form of democratic rule to Haiti was aborted. By year's end the Clinton administration was displaying impatience with Aristide's intransigence and his unwillingness to strike a new deal with the Haitian military.

It had become all too easy to face down a mighty superpower, deeply involved in its own economic and social problems, wrestling with natural disasters like the Midwestern floods and the Southern California fires and human disasters like the assault on the Branch Davidian sect near Waco, Texas. The one deliberate use of force abroad by the Clinton administration—the missile raid in June on intelligence headquarters in Baghdad in reprisal for a supposed Iraqi attempt to assassinate former president Bush during a visit to Kuwait—was an action that stood out because of its singularity.

In the fourth year of the post-Cold War era, it seemed remarkable how little influence the sole remaining superpower exerted on the principal arenas of conflict. President Yeltsin found the West solidly supporting him as he grappled with the colossal task of converting Russia from bureaucratic governance and a command economy to representative government and a market economy. But, unable to affect the course of events, the U.S. watched with the rest of the world as Yeltsin, in September, dissolved an obstreperous Parliament, then became the target of a coup that resulted in occupation of the Parliament and City Hall buildings and almost succeeded in capturing the Ostankino television centre—probably the most crucial objective. In the end it was not the U.S., NATO, or any outside force but the Russian army that saved Yeltsin. The West watched also as Yeltsin cracked down on his opponents, arranged elections for a new Parliament—but not for a president—and cracked down on opposition parties and the media. The West was left with some doubts about Yeltsin's fealty to democracy but without any other options or any idea how to exercise those options if it had them. The lack of an acceptable alternative to Yeltsin was driven home by the appearance on the political stage of a new menace—the ultranationalist Vladimir Zhirinovsky, vaulted by the December 12 elections into the position of principal opposition leader in the new Parliament.

It seemed characteristic of the year 1993 that when long-festering conflicts showed signs of finally yielding to peaceful resolution, it was usually more because of the internal dynamics of each situation than because of outside intervention. The world's three most enduring and intractable civil conflicts were in South Africa, Northern Ireland, and the Middle East. In all three, 1993 produced stirrings of hope for peaceful outcomes. In all three, peacemakers had to cope with forces of violent resistance.

In South Africa, Nobel Peace laureates Pres. F.W. de Klerk and Nelson Mandela, president of the African National Congress, agreed in February to form a "transitional government of national unity," then began steadfastly campaigning for an election in April 1994 that would introduce majority rule to a country long ruled by apartheid. More than 13,000 persons had died in violence since February 1990, when the dismantling of apartheid began. Violence continued through 1993, mainly between ANC supporters and its rivals in the black community. It seemed not in the cards that a new South Africa would be born without further bloodshed. By year's end, however, South Africa had a new interim constitution, and apartheid was officially ended.

In Northern Ireland, where for a generation the language had been guns and bombs, it seemed a miracle that there had been talks between antagonists. Over a period of many months, the British government had maintained contacts with the Irish Republican Army and its political arm, Sinn Fein. The disclosure of the talks in November produced a political explosion, but when the dust settled, the British and Irish governments were still talking. This was a slender reed on which to base any hope of peace in this bloody conflict but, yet, the first hope in a very long time. It was bolstered when the British and Irish governments agreed on a set of principles for peace negotiations that would allow the IRA to participate and opened to the people of Northern Ireland the possibility of a referendum to decide their own fate.

The most dramatic breakthrough of the year occurred in the Middle East. Forty years of alternating wars and negotiations had failed to bridge the gulf between Israel and the Palestinians. The latest negotiating process, starting with a full-dress conference in Madrid, was plodding along with little visible result. Suddenly, on August 31, Prime Minister Yitzhak Rabin and Yasir Arafat, chairman of the Palestine Liberation Organization, stunned the world with the announcement of a preliminary agreement reached after months of secret talks in Norway. Its essence was a grant of autonomy, under PLO auspices, in the Gaza Strip and in Jericho. On September 13, President Clinton presided over the photo opportunity of the year, nudging Rabin and Arafat into a self-conscious handshake on the White House lawn. But the main credit belonged not to him but to them, both taking tremendous political risks for peace.

Eruptions of violence followed—Palestinian against Israeli, Israeli against Palestinian, Palestinian against Palestinian. But, as in South Africa, and perhaps someday in Ireland, the imperative for violence was finally being countered with an imperative for peace. The year's end found Israel and the PLO strenuously working to resolve their differences over implementation of the autonomy agreement.

During the Cold War it would have been most unlikely to see so much movement in deep-seated conflicts with so little big-power involvement. During the Cold War all conflicts, and efforts to resolve them, were measured on an index of how they fitted into East-West confrontation. For the U.S., the proxy battles with the "Evil Empire" tended to take the form of military or covert CIA action to bolster or

MOSHE MILNER—SYGMA

Colonists and right-wingers opposed to the Israeli-Palestinian accords on the West Bank and Gaza Strip battle police in Jerusalem. Despite movements toward peace in the Middle East, Northern Ireland, and South Africa, violence continued in these areas.

destabilize regimes from Vietnam to Nicaragua, from Iran to Chile. The East-West theme was gone, and perhaps with it the motivation to keep the pot boiling in Third World countries.

Now the pot was kept boiling by an outburst of ethnic, religious, and, in some cases, tribal passions. If any new unifying theme was to be found to replace communism versus capitalism, it was the threat of militant Islam. There was no doubt that what had helped bring Israel, Palestinians, and Arab states together was a shared apprehension of Iranian-based holy war, threatening all the secular states in the region alike—Israel, Egypt, Jordan, Lebanon, and, eventually, Syria. Prime Minister Rabin, visiting Washington, said that the wave of fundamentalist fervour and terror sweeping out of Iran was much more threatening than the secular radicalism of Iraq had ever been. (A pity that Israel had not realized this in 1985 when it was shipping missiles to Iran and helping to involve the Reagan administration in doing the same.)

The U.S. State Department branded Iran "the world's most dangerous state sponsor of terrorism" and called the Iranian-supported, Lebanon-based Hezbollah, or Party of God, "the most aggressive and lethal" sponsor of terrorism in the world. The name could also have been Islamic Jihad, Hamas, Muslim Brotherhood, or Islamic Salvation Front. These were all evidences of radical Islam on the march.

Shadowy, unstructured groups, including many veterans of the Afghan war who were once protégés of the CIA, sometimes clustered around mosques with radical sheikhs. In Egypt terrorists tried to assassinate the prime minister and sought to scare off foreign tourists with attacks on tour buses. In Argentina the Israeli embassy in Buenos Aires was bombed with the all-too-familiar car full of explosives. An Iranian dissident was killed in Rome.

In 1993 the Islamic holy war was transported to the United States. In January an immigrant from the Afghan border region of Pakistan, where guerrillas had once consorted with CIA agents, stood outside the agency's headquarters in Langley, Va., killed two of its employees and wounded three others, and then fled the country. Muslim militants were allegedly involved in the explosion in New York City's World Trade Center in February—the most destructive terrorist act ever perpetrated on American soil. Plans for other attacks on UN headquarters and the Lincoln Tunnel were foiled. The terrorists were connected, in one way or another, with a radical Egyptian sheikh, Omar Abdel-Rahman. He denied issuing any orders to kill but, in his Jersey City, N.J., mosque, had been heard exhorting his followers, "Hit hard and kill the enemies of God on every spot."

Other than the threat of religious fanaticism, however, the West seemed to lack any unifying theme to replace the anticommunist ideology that had guided policy making and resources allocation for a half century. In the wake of the Cold War, there were a series of corruption scandals from Italy to Japan to the U.S. As though concluding that they had taken their governments too long on trust, voters in many countries began turning against long-accepted leaders and parties.

In February, Canada's Prime Minister Brian Mulroney resigned, his approval rating at 17%, and in the October election his Conservative Party was all but swept away (plunging from 154 to 2 seats in the House of Commons). In Japan the government of Kiichi Miyazawa fell in a no-confidence vote in the parliament in June, and in the July election his Liberal-Democratic Party lost its majority. In Italy the long-ruling Christian Democrats lost heavily in municipal elections in November, and the successor to the Communists, the Democratic Party of the Left, emerged as the strongest political force. (This must have been particularly galling to veterans of the American effort, starting with the Marshall Plan in 1948 and involving years of CIA covert operations to support the Christian Democrats against the Communists.) In Germany the long-ruling Christian Democrats led by Chancellor Helmut Kohl suffered humiliating defeats in regional elections in November and December, and the former Communist Party came back strongly in eastern Germany. In December angry voters in Venezuela rejected the nation's two traditional ruling parties and elected as president Rafael Caldera, who ran as an independent.

It was as though some "political immune deficiency" virus were sweeping across much of the industrialized world. Indeed, one could hardly find an incumbent leader, President Clinton and Britain's Prime Minister John Major included, who enjoyed a majority approval rating in opinion polls. (It should be noted, however, that Clinton's standing improved to 53% in December.)

No longer afraid about a communist monolith, people seemed now to be mainly worried about economic insecurity as a recession spread across the industrial world, tempering even the economic miracles in Japan and Germany. In Germany, where economic tensions have historically expressed themselves all too quickly in political extremism, recession combined with anti-immigrant xenophobia and the burden of absorbing eastern Germany to produce a rash of skinhead violence and neo-Nazi political activity. The Central and Eastern European states of the former Soviet Bloc, finding the West more generous with verbal support than economic aid, knocked in vain at the door of the European Community. They also sought shelter in the North Atlantic alliance, which offered them something less than half the loaf of participation with a vague NATO "partnership" status.

For the U.S., slowly climbing out of its recession, the closest thing to an international ideology seemed to be international trade. In the name of trade, China was forgiven its human rights trespasses. In the name of trade, President Clinton fought and won a battle for congressional approval of the North American Free Trade Agreement. Then he went on to woo the nations of the thriving Pacific Rim at a Seattle, Wash., summit conference and to stage a full-court press for conclusion of the long-stalled General Agreement on Tariffs and Trade, which was crowned with success hours before the December 15 deadline.

It was significant that President Clinton, who campaigned for the desk in the White House with the incessantly repeated invocation of "change," shifted his emphasis to "security." As he learned from the off-year elections, "change" could be a double-edged sword for an incumbent. But, beyond that, he seemed to be addressing global anxieties when he set his sights on three forms of security—economic, health, and personal. If Americans did not respond with the enthusiasm they had shown for Pres. Franklin Roosevelt's "Four Freedoms" speech in 1941, it was, well, perhaps because they were too anxious to be lulled by words.

A paradox of 1993 was that leaders enjoying such high-tech capabilities for communicating their messages still seemed to be held, generally, in such low esteem. The "Information Highway," which broke into American consciousness in 1993, promised a new dimension of interactive communication. Whether leaders would have anything more inspiring to communicate remained to be seen.

Chronology of 1993

JANUARY

1 **Czechoslovakia now two nations.** What had been the single nation of Czechoslovakia officially became two independent states, the Czech Republic and Slovakia. Vaclav Havel, the former president of Czechoslovakia, and many others, especially ethnic Czechs, had argued vehemently against separation, but to no avail. However, once an agreement was reached on a peaceful division of the country, both sides promised to cooperate in the future. National assets were divided on a 2–1 ratio based on the Czech Republic's larger population. The International Monetary Fund chose a somewhat more precise figure in reallocating the assets and liabilities of what had been Czechoslovakia. On January 26 Havel was elected to a five-year term as president of the Czech Republic. On February 15 Michal Kovac was chosen president of Slovakia.

EC inaugurates open internal market. The 12-nation European Community (EC) began implementing the first phase of its open internal market, which, among other things, allowed individuals to transport unlimited quantities of items for personal use across national borders. The ultimate goal of the open market was to allow a free flow of people, goods, information, and currency within the EC. Some of the measures envisioned by the EC had not yet been formally adopted; others had not yet been approved by all of the individual states. Certain measures, moreover, were not scheduled to take effect until a later date. The EC market, representing some 350 million people, was expected to constitute one of the most formidable economic powers in the world. Poland was among several former Communist nations in Eastern Europe to express fears that its exports to EC nations, which were critical to its economy, would diminish significantly because it was outside the market.

3 **U.S. and Russia sign START II.** U.S. Pres. George Bush and Russian Pres. Boris Yeltsin initialed the second Strategic Arms Reduction Treaty (START II) in the Kremlin, an agreement that called for the total elimination of land-based multiple-warhead missiles and a two-thirds reduction in their respective long-range nuclear weapons. Unlike previous arms control negotiations, the details of START II were worked out in just six months. Both the U.S. and Russia agreed that START II would not take effect until all those who had signed START I had ratified the accord and complied with its provisions. Neither Ukraine nor Belarus had as yet ratified the treaty.

4 **Daniel arap Moi begins new term.** Daniel arap Moi, leader of the Kenya African National Union party, took the oath of office as president of Kenya for the fourth time. According to official tallies, he had won 37% of the popular vote in the controversial December 1992 national election. Moi's closest rival, Kenneth Matiba, leader of a faction within the opposition Forum for the Restoration of Democracy, finished second with 26% of the vote. In the National Assembly, Moi's supporters would hold 97 of the 202 seats even though 15 of Moi's 21 Cabinet ministers had been defeated when they ran for reelection. Matiba and two other leaders of the opposition repudiated the election on the grounds that it had been fraudulent. Observers noted that Moi might not have won reelection if the opposition had joined forces during the campaign.

6 **Japan's crown prince picks bride.** The Japanese press announced with great fanfare that 32-year-old Crown Prince Naruhito and Masako Owada had become engaged and would marry in early summer. An official announcement from the imperial palace was not expected for several weeks. The two met for the first time at a diplomatic reception in 1986. The 29-year-old future empress, whose father was Japan's vice minister of foreign affairs and the nation's senior career diplomat, had attended Harvard University and the Universities of Tokyo and Oxford before deciding to pursue a career in Japan's Foreign Ministry. In that capacity she had been deeply involved in delicate and highly technical trade negotiations with her U.S. counterparts.

12 **Reynolds to lead Irish coalition.** The tenure of Albert Reynolds as prime minister of Ireland was extended when the Dail (parliament) approved a new coalition government under the continued leadership of the Fianna Fail party. The Labour Party, led by Dick Spring, joined the government as a junior partner. It was the first time that the two parties had formed such a political alliance. Together they would control 101 of the 166 seats in the Dail. Reynolds began to look for political allies after the November 1992 election, when his conservative party faltered and the left-of-centre Labour Party increased its seats to 33 from 16. Because of Labour's new power, Spring was named deputy prime minister and the country's foreign minister.

Court halts the trial of Erich Honecker. A German court in Berlin dropped manslaughter charges against Erich Honecker shortly after the Constitutional Court declared that the 80-year-old former leader of East Germany was too ill to stand trial and that his continued detention would be a violation of human rights.

REUTERS/BETTMANN

On January 1 citizens of Bratislava celebrate Slovakia's birth. The Czech Republic and Slovakia separated just three years after the end of the Communist regime in Czechoslovakia.

Honecker had been accused of ordering East German guards to shoot anyone attempting to flee to West Berlin after the erection of the Berlin Wall. On January 13 a separate court in Berlin dropped charges of embezzlement related to Honecker's alleged use of public funds to build a sumptuous complex for Communist Party officials. After his release from prison, Honecker was allowed to fly to Santiago, Chile, where he was reunited with his wife and daughter on January 14.

13 **Religious strife engulfs Bombay.** More than 550 persons were reported killed in Bombay, India, during nine days of sectarian violence between Hindus and Muslims. Firemen were attacked with gasoline bombs and stones when they attempted to save burning homes, businesses, and vehicles. Policemen also came under attack when they tried to quell the riots, put an end to looting, and enforce the curfew. The police commissioner described the chaos as "incidents of madness." Order was finally restored with the help of army troops and paramilitary commandos.

Senate panel issues its final MIA report. The U.S. Senate Select Committee on POW-MIA Affairs issued its final report after a 15-month effort to determine the fate of hundreds of U.S. servicemen listed as missing in action during the Vietnam war. The panel concluded that there was no compelling evidence that any U.S. prisoner of war was still being held in Indochina. It also conceded that a small number of Americans who were listed as missing in action in Laos might have been alive and in captivity when the Paris peace accords that ended the war were signed in 1973. Sen. John Kerry, who acted as chairman of the panel, summed up its conclusions by saying: "This report does not close the issue. There is evidence, tantalizing evidence, that raises questions. But questions are not facts and are not proof."

15 **Italy apprehends Mafia leader.** The Italian police announced that plainclothes paramilitary police in Palermo, Sicily, had apprehended 62-year-old Salvatore Riina, the reputed boss of bosses of organized crime in Italy. Riina, who was unarmed, had been sought by police ever since his 1969 escape from house arrest in Bologna. In 1987 he had been tried in absentia and sentenced to life in prison after being convicted of murder and drug trafficking. He was also believed to have ordered the 1992 assassinations of two prominent prosecutors of organized crime and to have established links with such groups as the Colombian cocaine cartels. Several hundred Mafia informers were said to have contributed significantly to the government's recent successes against organized crime.

U.S. Pres. Bill Clinton and his wife, Hillary Rodham Clinton, greet visitors to the White House the day after his January 20 inauguration. Those invited to the open house represented a wide spectrum of Americans.
WALLY MCNAMEE—SYGMA

20 **Clinton becomes U.S. president.** William J. Clinton, who had been the longtime Democratic governor of Arkansas, took the oath of office as the 42nd president of the United States. In the November 1992 national election he captured 370 of 538 votes in the electoral college by winning a plurality of the popular vote in 32 states and the District of Columbia. His two major opponents had been the Republican incumbent George Bush and independent Texas billionaire H. Ross Perot. Clinton's running mate during the campaign, Sen. Albert Gore of Tennessee, took his oath as vice president shortly before Clinton was sworn in by William Rehnquist, chief justice of the United States. Justice Byron White administered the oath to Gore because retired justice Thurgood Marshall was too ill to participate.

25 **Denmark gets new government.** Poul N. Rasmussen, a 49-year-old Social Democrat, became prime minister of Denmark. His four-party coalition government included the Centre Democrats, the Radical Liberals, and the Christian People's Party. All three parties had supported the coalition that had formed Denmark's government before Prime Minister Poul Schluter resigned on January 14 after more than 10 years in office. Niels Petersen, a Radical Liberal, announced that his top priority as foreign minister would be to reverse, in a new referendum, Denmark's June 1992 rejection of the European Community's (EC's) Treaty on European Union. During a December 1992 meeting in Scotland, the EC ministers had agreed to modify the treaty to accommodate certain Danish demands.

Police kill protesters in Togo. European diplomats reported that at least 20 pro-democracy campaigners had been shot and killed by police in Lomé, the capital of Togo. The stated goal of the demonstrators was to compel the president, Gen. Gnassingbe Eyadema, to end military rule. The tiny West African nation had been under his control for 26 years. Eyadema had tried in vain to end violent antigovernment protests by legalizing opposition political parties in April 1991.

27 **Clinton delays decision on gays.** White House officials announced that President Clinton had decided to delay issuing an executive order reversing a government policy that banned homosexuals from serving in the armed forces. Although Clinton had promised during the presidential campaign that he would remove the ban if elected, he encountered vigorous opposition from the Joint Chiefs of Staff and other military personnel as well as from influential members of Congress. The issue, which was of only marginal importance compared with other critical problems facing the nation, was nonetheless certain to be hotly debated in the mass media and among individuals, both military and civilian.

28 **Israeli court backs government.** The seven-member Israeli High Court of Justice in Jerusalem ruled unanimously that the government had exercised legitimate powers in December 1992 when it deported 415 Palestinians from the occupied territories to a no-man's land in Lebanon. All the deportees were said to be actively involved with a militant Arab organization called Hamas (Islamic Resistance Movement). Such deportations had earlier been condemned by the UN Security Council as violations of international law. Shortly before the Israeli court announced its ruling, UN Secretary-General Boutros Boutros-Ghali had recommended that the council take "whatever measures are required" to enforce its demand that the Palestinians be allowed to return to their homes. On February 1 the Israeli government announced that about 100 Palestinians would be permitted to return and that the remainder would be allowed to return to their homes within a year.

FEBRUARY

4 **Help sought to topple Mobutu.** Étienne Tshisekedi, prime minister of the central African republic of Zaire, publicly pleaded for foreign help to oust Pres. Mobutu Sese Seko, who had ruled the country for 27 years. Tshisekedi was fired the next day, but it was by no means certain that Mobutu had the authority to dismiss him. Tshisekedi had been elected prime minister by a national conference in August 1992, but his five predecessors had all been appointed by

Mobutu and had served for a combined total of less than 18 months. Refusing to relinquish his post, Tshisekedi issued a plea for outside help to establish a new government. The call went out after a week of violence that erupted when soldiers in the capital city of Kinshasa were paid in new large-denomination bank notes that shopkeepers refused to accept. An estimated 1,000 people were killed when the rampaging soldiers clashed with troops loyal to Mobutu.

5 **Yeltsin faces strong opposition.** Ruslan Khasbulatov, speaker of Russia's Congress of People's Deputies, raised political tensions another notch when he told visiting Swedish Prime Minister Carl Bildt that Pres. Boris Yeltsin had "failed to cope with his duties." The two had long been on a collision course over where the ultimate power in Russia should rest. Khasbulatov, who had also publicly accused Yeltsin of acting like a dictator, was adamant in his insistence that the will of congress should prevail when the president and the congress were at loggerheads. On more than one occasion, Yeltsin had been forced to compromise because his plan to implement market reforms had been stymied by the congress. The situation was not likely to change as long as hard-line Communists, who had been elected before the demise of the Soviet Union, held the balance of power in the national legislature.

6 **Chung Ju Yung faces indictment.** Chung Ju Yung, the 77-year-old billionaire founder of one of South Korea's largest conglomerates, was officially charged with slander and with the illegal funding of his ill-fated presidential campaign. In 1992 Chung, a member of the National Assembly, had founded the United People's Party as a vehicle to gain the presidency. He was accused of slandering Kim Young Sam, who won the presidency, when he asserted that Kim had illegally received financial support from the nation's central bank. The government indictment also charged that Chung had diverted more than $60 million from his shipbuilding unit to his campaign coffers and had coerced employees into backing his party.

10 **Kuomintang chooses Lien Chan.** Leaders of the Nationalist Party (Kuomintang) in Taiwan approved Pres. Lee Teng-hui's nomination of Lien Chan as head the Republic of China's Executive Yuan. The post was equivalent to that of premier. With formal approval by the National Assembly a virtual certainty, the government in Taiwan would, for the first time, have native-born Taiwanese serving as both president and premier. The ascendency of locally born politicians was expected to diminish still further the influence of Chinese who had taken refuge in the province of Taiwan when Communist forces gained control of the mainland in 1949.

11 **Clinton nominates Janet Reno.** Janet Reno, a highly respected 54-year-old state prosecutor in Florida, was nominated by President Clinton to head the Department of Justice as U.S. attorney general. Although Reno had little experience at the federal level, she was an adept administrator and well versed in criminal law. Two earlier nominees, both women, had withdrawn from consideration amid controversies over their employment of illegal aliens for child care. On March 11 the Senate unanimously confirmed Reno's nomination by voice vote. The following day she took the oath of office and became the first woman to head the nation's highest law-enforcement agency.

12 **Historic pact in South Africa.** The South African government and the African National Congress (ANC) reached agreement on a transitional government of national unity that would end white-minority rule by April 1994. This would occur when South Africans of all races were allowed, for the first time in history, to cast ballots for a new 400-seat assembly. That body would then draw up a new constitution that would stipulate, among other things, how the new government would function. There was already agreement, however, that the nation's future president would be chosen from the party that had gained the most votes in the April 1994 assembly election. As things now stood, Nelson Mandela, the president of the ANC, was expected to fill that role.

14 **Greek Cypriots elect Clerides.** In an extremely close runoff election, Glafcos Clerides, candidate of the Democratic Rally party, defeated incumbent George Vassiliou in a race for the presidency of Cyprus. Only those living in the southern portion of Cyprus cast votes. The northern third of the island, controlled by Turkish Cypriots since 1974, had been declared a Turkish republic in 1983, but the international community refused to recognize its existence. In the first round of voting on February 7, Clerides won 37% of the popular vote and Vassiliou 44% with the strong support of the Communist Party. In the final round of voting, however, the Democratic Party, which had supported the candidacy of Paschalis Pascalides, gave Clerides the votes he needed to emerge victorious with 50.3% of the total ballots cast.

Lithuanians elect former Communist. Algirdas Brazauskas, whose Lithuanian Democratic Labour Party had won 73 of the 141 seats in the two-round October–November 1992 parliamentary elections, scored an easy victory in the presidential race by capturing 60% of the popular vote. His opponent, Stasys Lozoraitis, represented the Lithuanian Reform Movement (Sajudis), which held 30 seats in the Supreme Council (parliament). Brazauskas, the former Communist leader of Lithuania, campaigned on a promise to revitalize the nation's foundering industries by fostering closer trade relations with Russia and other former Soviet republics. One of his most urgent priorities was to secure a source of cheaper energy.

22 **UN backs trial for war crimes.** Faced with mounting evidence of unspeakable atrocities taking place in what had been Yugoslavia, the UN Security Council unanimously sanctioned

With fuel scarce, a woman gathers wood in Sarajevo, Bosnia and Herzegovina's capital. On February 22 the UN Security Council voted for formation of a war crimes court.
JON JONES—SYGMA

the formation of an international court to try those accused of committing war crimes during the civil conflict. UN Secretary-General Boutros Boutros-Ghali was asked to determine the legal structure of the proposed court. Outside observers, including members of the European Community and the U.S., roundly condemned the barbarous manner in which civilians as well as combatants were being treated. Although all parties in the civil war—Serbs, Croats, and Muslims—were taken to task for their inhumane behaviour, the severest criticism was leveled at the Serbs, whose military might was vastly superior to that of their adversaries. Whether any of those guilty of war crimes could be identified, apprehended, and brought to trial was by no means certain.

24 **Canadian prime minister resigns.** After eight and a half years in office, Brian Mulroney resigned as prime minister of Canada and as leader of the Progressive Conservative Party. With his personal popularity rating standing at a miserable 17%, Mulroney was widely believed to have tendered his resignation in order to improve his party's prospects in the next general election, which by law had to be held by November.

25 **Kim Young Sam assumes office.** Former dissident Kim Young Sam took the oath of office in Seoul as president of South Korea. Unlike his most recent predecessors, Kim had no ties to the military. During his inaugural address Kim pledged to eradicate political corruption and misconduct, which he called "the most terrifying enemies attacking the foundations of our society." Potential targets of the planned anticorruption campaign included members of Kim's own Democratic Liberal Party. The president also promised to take steps to invigorate the nation's stagnant economy and to

Emergency vehicles jam the area around the World Trade Center in New York City after a bomb exploded on February 26. Officials later charged Muslim extremists with the bombing.
ALLAN TANNENBAUM—SYGMA

work for the eventual reunification of the Korean peninsula. When Kim named his entire 26-member Cabinet on February 26, he broke with tradition by including three women. Ten days later the president summarily dismissed three of his ministers when rumours circulated that they had engaged in activities deemed unbefitting members of the new administration.

26 **New York Trade Center bombed.** A horrendous midday explosion in a parking garage on the second subterranean level beneath one of the twin World Trade Center buildings in lower Manhattan killed at least five people and left a 60-m (200-ft)-wide crater several stories deep. Because of dense smoke and the lack of electrical power, it took some six hours to evacuate an estimated 50,000 people from the building. On March 4 police arrested Mohammad Salameh, a 26-year-old Jordanian-born Palestinian, when he returned to a car-rental agency in New Jersey to reclaim the $400 deposit he had paid when he rented the van that investigators said had been used to transport the explosives to the garage. FBI agents also found evidence of bomb making when they searched Salameh's apartment. On March 10 Nidal Ayyad, a Kuwaiti-born Palestinian with a degree in chemical engineering, was arrested in New Jersey and charged with aiding and abetting the bombing. As the investigation continued, the FBI was reportedly gathering evidence against other suspects. Observers noted that the World Trade Center bombing brought violence attributed to Islamic fundamentalists to U.S. territory for the first time.

28 **Food drops aid Bosnian Muslims.** U.S. Air Force planes began air-dropping food and other supplies desperately needed by Muslims under attack from Serb forces in the former Yugoslav republic of Bosnia and Herzegovina. The unilateral U.S. mission had been ordered by President Clinton, who underscored the humanitarian nature of the operation and promised that priorities for the air deliveries would be decided "without regard to ethnic or religious affiliation." Although airlifts were admittedly an expensive and relatively ineffective way to deliver supplies, there was some hope that the use of aircraft would open up land routes that had been closed and possibly improve the prospects for a negotiated peace.

MARCH

5 **WMO reports ozone depletion.** The World Meteorological Organization reported that ozone levels over northern Europe and Canada had fallen 20% below normal. A few days later an independent Canadian study was released showing that the current ozone levels over Edmonton, Alta., and Toronto were the lowest in some 30 years. Because ozone in the atmosphere protects the Earth from the harmful effects of ultraviolet radiation emitted by the Sun, members of the European Community had agreed in December 1992 to end the production of chlorofluorocarbons (CFCs), which were a major cause of ozone depletion. They set January 1995 as their deadline. E.I. du Pont de Nemours & Co., the largest producer of CFCs, joined the campaign by announcing that by the end of 1994 it too would end its production of CFCs.

6 **Kanemaru is taken into custody.** Shin Kanemaru, widely viewed as the most powerful member of Japan's ruling Liberal-Democratic Party (LDP), was arrested by federal prosecutors in Tokyo on suspicion of income-tax evasion. Investigators, who on March 9 found millions of dollars' worth of undisclosed assets in Kanemaru's house and office, estimated that the 78-year-old veteran politician had concealed more than $10 million in income that he had allegedly used in the late 1980s to buy discount bonds. Kanemaru's arrest was but the latest item on a growing list of financial scandals plaguing the LDP and eroding confidence in the government. He was formally indicted on March 13, one day before the five-year statute of limitations was due to expire.

7 **Tentative peace in Afghanistan.** A peace plan designed to end the civil war in Afghanistan was signed in Islamabad, Pak., by eight of the rival military factions. The agreement, brokered by Pakistani Prime Minister Nawaz Sharif, was reaffirmed in Mecca, Saudi Arabia, on March 11. According to the terms of the peace accord, Afghan Pres. Burhanuddin Rabbani would remain in office and Gulbuddin Hekmatyar, the leader of the Hezb-i-Islami organization, would become prime minister. The two would then share power for 18 months until elections were held. The 14-year-old communist regime of Pres. Mohammad Najibullah had finally collapsed in April 1992. Since then, an estimated 5,000 Afghans had been killed as rival groups sought to establish control over Kabul, the capital, and over other regions of the war-ravaged country. Despite the positive outcome of the latest peace negotiations, there were a variety of reasons to wonder if the truce would be any more permanent than those that had failed in the past.

Swiss to permit high stakes in casinos. Swiss voters, who had been allowed since 1956 to engage in legal small-scale gambling, overwhelmingly approved a referendum that reversed an 1874 ban on high-stakes casino gambling. Those who favoured the change, which would benefit the nation's social security programs, pointed out that other European countries had increased government revenues significantly through such means. The Swiss government's share of the gambling profits was expected to be nearly $100 million annually.

11 **Suharto begins his sixth term.** Indonesian President Suharto took the oath of office for the sixth consecutive time one day after being unanimously reelected to another five-year term by the People's Consultative Assembly. Suharto, who had already begun relaxing government controls over many aspects of Indonesian life, had promised even greater freedom in the months ahead. Two months before the formal election, the opposition Indonesian Democratic Party had endorsed Suharto's reelection even though it had campaigned for change, including electoral reforms and the eradication of corruption in government. Try Sutrisno, who had retired as commander of the armed forces on February 17, was elected vice president. The choice of Sutrisno was reportedly dictated by high-ranking military officers.

It seemed clear that no matter what other changes came to pass, the military would remain a potent force in Indonesian politics.

12 **Bombs set off in Indian cities.** The first in a series of early afternoon bombings in western India destroyed several floors of the 29-story Bombay Stock Exchange and killed some 50 people. Within the next hour or so, bombs in other parts of the city wreaked havoc on banks, movie theatres, an airline office, and a shopping complex. Five days later, in what appeared to be an unrelated incident, two apartment buildings in Calcutta were destroyed by a bomb, with the loss of at least 80 lives. On March 19 another bomb exploded at a Calcutta train station. All told, more than 300 people were killed and more than 2,000 injured in what authorities called the worse wave of criminal violence in India's history. No individual or organization claimed responsibility for the atrocities, but on March 15 the Bombay police charged a 26-year-old Hindu and a 30-year-old Muslim with direct involvement in the bombings. Both, however, managed to escape. Political commentators publicly speculated that the terrorist acts were an attempt to destabilize the government of Prime Minister P.V. Narasimha Rao.

North Korea withdraws from NNP treaty. The North Korean government announced that it was withdrawing from the Nuclear Non-proliferation Treaty, which it had signed in 1985. Pyongyang cited Article X of the treaty, which permitted any signatory to give a 90-day notice of its intention to withdraw if it felt its "supreme interests" were being jeopardized. The aim of the international agreement was to inhibit nuclear arms sales and the spread of technology needed to manufacture nuclear weapons. The North Korean announcement came at a time when the International Atomic Energy Agency, a UN-affiliated organization, was insisting on its right to inspect several facilities in North Korea that were suspected of having acquired the capacity to produce weapons-grade plutonium. It was certain that North Korea would be immediately subjected to intense international pressure to reverse its decision and adhere to the provisions of the treaty.

13 **Australians back Labor Party.** Australian voters, obliged by law to cast ballots in the national election, returned the ruling Australian Labor Party (ALP) to power for a record fifth consecutive three-year term. The ALP was led by Paul Keating, who had succeeded in ousting Bob Hawke as party leader in December 1991. Incomplete election returns indicated that the ALP's victory over the Liberal Party–National Party coalition would increase its majority from 6 to perhaps 16 in the 147-seat House of Representatives. Numerous political pundits had expected the ALP to be unseated because the nation's economy was moribund and Australia's unemployment rate was the highest it had been since the 1930s.

President Diouf reelected in Senegal. The constitutional court in Senegal announced that Pres. Abdou Diouf had won the February 21 presidential election with 58.4% of the popular vote. Diouf, the leader of the Socialist Party and the current president of the Organization of African Unity, had ruled the West African republic since 1981. His closest rival in the eight-candidate race was the Senegalese Democratic Party candidate, Abdoulaye Wade, who officially garnered 32% of the vote. The official results were not announced earlier because the court had to respond to complaints from Diouf's opponents that the election had been rigged.

14 **Andorra opts for a new system.** Voters in Andorra, an independent principality between France and Spain, massively supported a referendum that called for the end of a seven-century-old feudal system of government and the creation of one having separate executive, legislative, and judicial branches of government. Under its new constitution, Andorra would qualify for membership in international organizations, and its citizens would be free to form political parties and labour unions. In the past the tiny country of some 57,000 people had been jointly ruled by the president of France and the Roman Catholic bishop living in a nearby Spanish town. Their roles in the new government structure would be drastically reduced.

BALDEV—SYGMA

Rescue workers remove the body of a victim of the bombing of two apartment buildings in Calcutta in mid-March. Later in the month, a bomb exploded in a Calcutta train station, and earlier, on March 12, bombs had destroyed a number of public facilities in Bombay.

20 **Rwanda moves closer to peace.** Leaders of the Rwandan Patriotic Front and rival government officials accepted two proposals that would, if implemented, merge government troops and rebel forces into a single army. The negotiations took place in Arusha, Tanzania. The Tutsi rebels had taken up arms to enforce a demand that the majority Hutu tribe stop its alleged oppression of Tutsi. A spokesman for the International Red Cross reported that the fighting had forced up to one million civilians to flee their homes.

21 **Commandos release all hostages.** Five Nicaraguan gunmen released the last of about two dozen hostages they had seized in the Nicaraguan embassy in San José, the capital of Costa Rica. After long negotiations, the commandos agreed to accept only $250,000 of the millions they had originally demanded and a guarantee of safe passage out of the country. José Manuel Urbina Lara, who had led the embassy takeover, sought and received political asylum for himself and one companion in the Dominican Republic. The three other gunmen chose a location inside Nicaragua. The gunmen's chief complaint was that Pres. Violeta Chamorro had betrayed her supporters by leaving Sandinistas in high government positions after ousting them from power in the 1990 election. Among those they demanded be discharged was Gen. Humberto Ortega, a Sandinista who commanded the nation's army.

27 **Algeria cuts official ties to Iran.** Algeria formally severed diplomatic relations with Iran for allegedly supporting the terrorists who had assassinated Algerian government and military officials in an attempt to destabilize the country. In January 1992 the military had seized power in Algeria to prevent the Front Islamique du Salut (FIS) from establishing an Islamic state. The FIS had seemed on the verge of taking over the government in December 1991 when a vast number of its candidates won parliamentary seats outright and thus avoided a runoff election. Before the final round of the elections could be held in January, the military declared an emergency, forced the president to resign, and canceled the January election showdown. The FIS was outlawed and thousands of militant extremists arrested, but others associated with the FIS had been able to carry out a successful urban campaign of assassinations. Algerian officials pointed the finger of blame at Iran.

28 **Yeltsin escapes impeachment.** During a special session of Russia's Congress of People's Deputies, Pres. Boris Yeltsin survived political attack when his adversaries were unable to persuade two-thirds of the assembly to vote for his ouster. With both factions in the power struggle constantly shifting positions and offering compromises, the country was in turmoil. Until there was

a clear-cut division of power between the president and the legislature, there would be no mutually acceptable way to resolve the impasse.

29 **Socialists battered in French vote.** After his Socialist Party suffered a stunning defeat in parliamentary elections on March 21 and 28, French Pres. François Mitterrand was forced to name a member of the opposition as prime minister. It would be the second time in 12 years that Mitterrand's Socialist government had to accept "cohabitation" with a member of the political opposition. Mitterrand chose 63-year-old Édouard Balladur, who had been named minister of finance by Prime Minister Jacques Chirac in 1986 and, like Chirac, was a member of the neo-Gaullist Rally for the Republic (RPR) party. For the Socialist Party, the election was nothing short of disastrous. The RPR and the Union for French Democracy coalition won a combined total of 460 of the 577 seats in the National Assembly, and conservative independents won an additional 24. When the dust cleared, the Socialists had lost more than 75% of the seats they had held in the previous assembly. With all eyes focused on the presidential election in 1995, the field was wide open for presidential aspirants because Balladur had said that he had no interest in joining the race.

31 **Patterson scores an easy victory.** Percival Patterson was guaranteed a full term as prime minister of Jamaica when his People's National Party captured 52 of the 60 seats in the House of Representatives while receiving 61% of the popular vote. Patterson had replaced Michael Manley when he was forced to resign in March 1992 because of poor health. The Jamaica Labour Party, led by former prime minister Edward Seaga, was severely weakened, losing 6 of the 14 seats it had previously held in the national legislature. Despite sporadic violence and reports of widespread irregularities at the polls, the turmoil was insignificant compared with the 1980 election, when some 750 people were reported killed.

Chinese leaders take part in a ceremony at the National People's Congress. At the congress, which ended March 31, Jiang Zemin (Chiang Tse-min) was chosen president of China.
REUTERS/BETTMANN

Jiang Zemin given a second position. The nearly 3,000 members of China's National People's Congress adjourned a two-week meeting after giving 67-year-old Jiang Zemin (Chiang Tse-min), the general secretary of the Communist Party of China, the additional post of president. He succeeded Yang Shangkun (Yang Shang-k'un). The legislators also reelected Li Peng (Li P'eng) to a second five-year term as premier. Although 88-year-old Deng Xiaoping (Teng Hsiao-p'ing) held no party or government posts, he continued to exercise unchallenged power to set policy and make appointments. One of his decisions had been the selection of Jiang as his successor. Jiang was also chairman of the central military commission. The fact that Jiang did not possess Deng's natural gifts for leadership and had no true power base of his own created speculation about China's future leadership.

APRIL

2 **Lesotho turns against military.** The tiny South African kingdom of Lesotho returned to parliamentary government when 74-year-old Ntsu Mokhehle took the oath of office as the nation's first civilian head of government in 23 years. In the March 27 election, Mokhehle's Basotho Congress Party (BCP) won all 65 seats in the National Assembly and complete control of the Senate. The BCP had also been victorious in the 1970 national election, but leaders of the Basotho National Party had voided the results, declared a state of emergency, and suspended the constitution. After Gen. Justin Lekhanya's successful military coup in 1986, the country was ruled by a military council.

5 **Ramos pushes electrical output.** Philippine Pres. Fidel Ramos received emergency powers for one year to deal with a dire electrical power shortage throughout the country. Manila, the capital, with a population of nearly two million people, was especially hard hit. Many businesses had to curtail their working hours, and domestic life for many was in constant turmoil. Invoking his new authority, Ramos could begin awarding contracts for new electricity-generating plants without public bids. He could also reorganize the state-owned electrical company and use gambling casino revenues to fund new desperately needed power projects.

8 **Macedonia enters United Nations.** The United Nations welcomed a new nation into the organization under the strange provisional name of the Former Yugoslav Republic of Macedonia. Greece had vigorously opposed use of the simple name Macedonia because, it said, the newly independent republic had designs on the neighbouring Greek region of Macedonia. Officials on both sides agreed to search for an appropriate permanent name. Meanwhile, by mutual consent, the new nation would not hoist its flag outside the UN headquarters or at any UN agency because Greece objected to its design. The flag's sunlike disk with 16 rays had been a symbol of Alexander the Great, who ruled Greece in the 4th century BC.

10 **Gunman murders African leader.** Chris Hani, the 50-year-old leader of South Africa's Communist Party and a charismatic member of the African National Congress (ANC), was shot and killed outside his home near Johannesburg. The police quickly arrested Janusz Walus, a Polish immigrant whose car had been seen leaving the scene of the crime. Walus was said to be a violently anticommunist member of the Afrikaner Resistance Movement, a militant group of whites opposed to black majority rule in South Africa. Black anger before and after Hani's funeral on April 19 was to a great extent muffled by ANC crowd-control marshals and by pleas for calm from Nelson Mandela, president of the ANC.

15 **Sex survey revises gay statistics.** The Allen Guttmacher Institute published the results of a national sex survey conducted by the Battelle Human Affairs Research Center in Seattle, Wash., involving 3,321 U.S. males between the ages of 20 and 39. It was the most comprehensive sex survey since the Kinsey Report of 1948 and reached conclusions that closely corresponded to similar recent surveys carried out in Great Britain, Denmark, and France. The most surprising finding, which became the focus of most news reports, was that males who described themselves as exclusively homosexual made up only 1% of the population. For decades it had been assumed that the 10% figure given by Kinsey was relatively accurate.

17 **Two police convicted in beating.** A federal jury in Los Angeles convicted two white policemen and acquitted two others on charges that they had violated the civil rights of Rodney King. In March 1991, after a wild, high-speed car chase, King was savagely beaten while being subdued by police and taken into custody. When the jury informed the court that verdicts had been reached, police and national guardsmen fanned out across the tense city. The next morning, during a live nationwide telecast, the verdicts were read one by one. The first two policemen were found guilty of violating King's civil rights; the other two were acquitted. Tensions eased almost instantly as it became clear that there would be no repetition of the horrendous riots that had erupted in 1992 when a state jury acquitted all four policemen of assault. Efforts to avoid a second trial on the grounds that the four policemen would be subjected to double jeopardy were futile because the state and federal governments represented different jurisdictions and charged the men with different crimes.

18 **Khan dismisses prime minister.** Pakistani Pres. Ghulam Ishaq Khan dismissed Prime Minister Nawaz Sharif and dissolved the National Assembly, but he did not announce a date for new elections. Sharif was ousted, as had been Prime Minister Benazir Bhutto in 1990, for alleged corruption and mismanagement. Once in office, Sharif began reversing Bhutto's socialist policies by welcoming foreign investment and selling off unprofitable state-owned enterprises. One of Sharif's more risky political maneuvers was an attempt to weaken the presidency. The incumbent, who was chosen by the Senate and by the national and four provincial legislatures, had the power to dismiss the prime minister and the national and provincial legislatures. He also appointed the chief of staff of the armed forces.

19 **Standoff in Waco ends in tragedy.** A 51-day standoff between federal agents and members of a Christian religious cult ended in tragedy when the cult compound near Waco, Texas, burned to the ground. David Koresh, the 33-year-old leader of the Branch Davidians and the cult's self-styled messiah, perished along with at least 74 others, at least 17 of whom were believed to be young children. The first act in the drama occurred on February 28 when four federal agents were shot and killed during an assault on the heavily armed compound. Earlier requests to enter the grounds to investigate charges of child abuse had been denied. After weeks of chaotic negotiations and no evidence that the talks were leading anywhere, federal agents were ordered to end the stalemate. Using special equipment, they rammed holes in the compound's walls and sprayed nonflammable tear gas through the openings. As soon as the cultists realized an assault was under way, some began racing about setting the compound ablaze. The intense heat and the extent of the conflagration were more than the firefighters could handle. Medical examiners reported that Koresh and others had been shot through the head, and many may have died by their own hand.

21 **Brazil votes to keep presidency.** In a binding national plebiscite, Brazilians overwhelmingly approved a republican form of government over a monarchy (68% to 12%) and preferred, by a margin of better than 2–1, to retain their current presidential form of government; the alternative would have been an elected parliament. In preelection surveys pollsters discovered that numerous voters had no clear understanding of the constitutional issues they were supposed to decide; some 20% of the voters, who were required by law to go to the polls, cast blank or incorrectly marked ballots. The voting went forward because the pro-monarchists and pro-parliamentarian members of the National Congress had succeeded in making the plebiscite mandatory under the 1988 constitution.

24 **Eritreans approve independence.** More than 99% of the voting citizens of the Ethiopian province of Eritrea approved a referendum calling for total independence. Isaias Afwerki, one of Eritrea's most prominent leaders, announced that formal independence would be declared on May 24, the second anniversary of the final victory of the Eritrean People's Liberation Front over Ethiopia's armed forces. The war for independence had lasted nearly 30 years and had claimed the lives of some 100,000 Eritreans. On April 22 Isaias had told reporters that he considered five years too short a time to prepare properly for civilian rule.

London rocked by huge IRA bomb. A huge bomb concealed in a parked construction truck was detonated in central London by Irish Republican Army terrorists. Because the financial district was relatively deserted on weekend mornings, only one person was killed, but more than 40 were injured. The damage to buildings over several square blocks was so severe that the chief executive of an insurance company estimated the loss at more than $1.5 billion.

A London store puts damaged goods on sale after an Irish Republican Army bombing on April 24. The terrorists targeted the City, London's financial district.

SYGMA

26 **Italy gets new prime minister.** Carlo Ciampi, the head of Italy's central bank, was named prime minister by Pres. Oscar Scalfaro. Ciampi, who became Italy's first head of government chosen from outside of Parliament, succeeded Giuliano Amato, who had resigned on April 22. Amato's Socialist Party and the long-dominant Christian Democratic Party were both caught up in a nationwide corruption scandal of such proportions that a week earlier Italian voters had angrily annulled a series of laws, including one on proportional voting, that disassembled much of the nation's current political structure.

GAMMA LIAISON

Eritrean women celebrate the victory of the April 24 referendum approving independence. The struggle by Eritreans to secede from Ethiopia had been going on for three decades.

MAY

1 **Sri Lankan president is slain.** During a May Day political rally in Colombo, Sri Lankan Pres. Ranasinghe Premadasa was killed along with most of his bodyguards and several aides when a man detonated explosives strapped to his body. A week earlier Lalith Athulathmudali, the country's leading opposition politician, had been shot and killed by an unknown gunman. Although no one came forward to take responsibility for the president's assassination, suspicion quickly focused on the Liberation Tigers of Tamil Eelam, who had used suicide assassins in the past to kill government officials. For years the Tigers had used terrorism as a weapon to reinforce their demand that the region of Sri Lanka that they called home be granted independence. The Tigers were also blamed for the murder of Indian Prime Minister Rajiv Gandhi in 1991 because he had sent Indian troops to Sri Lanka to help curb the violence of the rebel Tigers.

Despondent politician takes his life. Pierre Bérégovoy, who had been prime minister of France until the Socialists suffered a humiliating defeat in the March parliamentary elections, died after shooting himself in the head. Colleagues reported that he had been deeply depressed over charges of personal financial improprieties while he held office and was distressed by charges that his handling of the national economy had been a disaster. Earlier in his career, Bérégovoy had won respect as France's finance minister. He held the position twice as a member of Pres. François Mitterrand's Cabinet, first from 1984 to 1986 and then from 1988 to 1992.

4 **Cristiani begins to purge army.** Alfredo Cristiani, president of El Salvador, bowed to intense international pressure and began relieving 15 top army officers of their commands. Two were removed. After completing its investigation, a civilian commission had called for the dismissal of 102 officers on grounds that they had flagrantly violated human rights. Cristiani, however, apparently had tried to assuage the anger of powerful military figures by announcing that some of the officers could not be discharged until 1994 at the earliest, even though the UN-sponsored peace accord he had accepted specifically ordered a purge of certain top military personnel. Their number included Gen. René Emilio Ponce, the defense minister, whose name headed the list because allegedly, among other human rights atrocities, he had ordered the murders of six Jesuit priests in November 1989.

9 **Paraguay holds first free vote.** Politicians of various persuasions came together and agreed that, despite confirmed cases of fraud at the polls, Pres. Juan Carlos Wasmosy of the ruling Colorado Party had clearly won the first democratic election in the nation's 182-year history. Domingo Laíno, candidate of the Authentic Radical Liberal Party, garnered about 3% fewer votes than Wasmosy. Former U.S. president Jimmy Carter, whose delegation from the National Democratic Institute for International Affairs had checked nearly 2,000 polling stations, agreed that the official margin of victory was sufficient to offset any impact fraud might have played in the final tallies. The Colorado Party also won a majority in Congress and most of the state governorships, but it no longer held the country in a viselike grip. As Carter was quick to point out, opposition candidates collectively won almost 60% of the total vote.

13 **Japan's whaling plan is rejected.** The International Whaling Commission, during an annual meeting in Kyoto, Japan, rejected a proposal that would have allowed certain Japanese to engage in restricted whaling in their coastal waters. Japan proposed that four of its whaling communities be allowed to harvest 50 minke whales a year along Japan's coast to sustain their traditional culture and support their livelihood. The plan did not advocate the resumption of commercial hunting. For a number of years the regulatory body had reconsidered its position, then voted to continue the ban on limited whaling. Ten member nations supported Japan's proposal, 16 opposed it, and 6 abstained. Because there was little likelihood that the commission would lift its moratorium on commercial whaling in the foreseeable future, Norway was seriously considering withdrawing from the organization.

18 **Danes approve union with Europe.** Danish voters, who had rejected participation in the Treaty on European Union by a fraction of a percentage point in June 1992, solidly supported a revised treaty in a new referendum. Anger in some quarters was so intense after the results were announced that the police, who were generally very restrained, felt compelled to fire at leftist demonstrators, who hurled tons of cobblestones and rocks at them, barricaded a main thoroughfare, set bonfires, and smashed windows in commercial buildings. Ten or more protesters were reported to have been hit by bullets, and several dozen police officers had to be hospitalized overnight after being treated for injuries. The antigovernment riot was described as the most serious in decades. The balloting in Denmark was closely followed in other European countries because all 12 members of the European Community had to approve the treaty for it to take effect. A major objective of the treaty had been to establish a common currency by 1999. The referendum approved in Denmark, however, did not oblige the country to accept a single currency, nor did it require acceptance of a joint defense policy, European citizenship, or common immigration and judicial policies.

19 **United States recognizes Angola.** The United States officially recognized the government of Angola, in part to entice the rebel National Union for the Total Independence of Angola (UNITA) to continue peace negotiations with the democratically elected government of Pres. José Eduardo dos Santos. The U.S. decision marked a dramatic change in its relations with Angola, which had previously been ruled by a Marxist regime reinforced by thousands of Cuban troops. On May 21, when the UN-sponsored peace talks ended in failure, there was not only little immediate hope for a cease-fire but expectation that the fighting would intensify. Among many differences separating the two sides was the question of who, under a cease-fire agreement, would control the territory captured by the rebels after fighting resumed in October 1992.

20 **Britain ratifies European treaty.** Members of Britain's House of Commons ratified the Treaty on European Union by a vote of 292–112. After more than 200 hours of debate, Britain became the 12th and final member of the European Community to support greater interdependence among members of the organization. The leaders of Britain's Labour Party had urged its members to abstain when the final vote was taken, but 66 Labourities joined 41 Conservatives in casting negative votes. In a matter of weeks, the bill would be discussed in the

CARLOS CARRION—SYGMA

Supporters of Juan Carlos Wasmosy celebrate his election as the first civilian president of Paraguay in nearly four decades. In the voting on May 9, Wasmosy, of the Colorado Party, defeated two other major candidates.

Danish citizens celebrate voters' approval on May 18 of a revised Treaty on European Union. Approval by the Danes, who had rejected the original version, was vital to the treaty's success.
JERRY BERGMAN—GAMMA LIAISON

House of Lords, where the strength of the opposition was not considered a major impediment to ratification.

21 **Venezuelan president indicted.** Venezuela's Senate voted unanimously to authorize the Supreme Court to put Pres. Carlos Andrés Pérez on trial for allegedly embezzling and misappropriating some $17 million in government funds. After the vote was taken, Octavio Lepage, the president of the Senate, automatically became the nation's acting president. Within 30 days the national congress was required to elect an interim president to serve until February 1994, when Pérez's five-year term expired. As leader of Venezuela's 35-year-old civilian democracy—the oldest in South America—Pérez had taken steps to establish a free-market economy. With his indictment, there was concern at home and abroad that Pérez's policies might stagnate under his successors or even be reversed.

24 **Tibetans protest Chinese rule.** Tibetans in the capital city of Lhasa took to the streets to protest high inflation and the lifting of price controls on food, but as the crowd swelled, the march turned into an antigovernment protest with shouts of "Chinese get out of Tibet." Eyewitnesses reported that the demonstration, one of the most serious acts of political defiance in years, was quelled by salvos of tear gas. Those at the scene reported that the area was so tense that Chinese police were patrolling the streets with machine guns.

26 **Fragile peace pact in Azerbaijan.** Azerbaijan and Armenia accepted in principle a UN Security Council resolution aimed at ending the fighting over Nagorno-Karabakh, an enclave in Azerbaijan heavily populated by Christian Armenians. Nagorno-Karabakh had earlier proclaimed independence from Azerbaijan, but no nation accorded it diplomatic recognition. Russia, Turkey, and the U.S. participated in the latest peace talks in Moscow, which ended with many basic issues still unsettled. Negotiations, however, were scheduled to resume soon in Geneva.

Jordan turns its back on Iraqi leader. King Hussein of Jordan, who had supported Iraqi Pres. Saddam Hussein during the Iran-Iraq and Persian Gulf wars, told members of the national press that he could no longer support Saddam Hussein or his policies because they had deeply harmed Jordanian interests. Jordan's multiple complaints against Iraq included its harsh suppression of dissidents, especially Shi'ite Iraqis, and its refusal to abide by conditions of the Gulf war peace accord it had signed. Iraq had also halted its shipment of free oil to Jordan, an arrangement that had been acceptable to both parties as a way for Iraq to pay off old debts. Iraq had also resorted to financial manipulations to inflict severe damage on Jordanian banks and bankrupt Jordanian businessmen. By distancing himself from Saddam Hussein, the king also moved a step closer to reconciliation with other Arab nations that had joined forces with the U.S. to drive Saddam Hussein's troops out of Kuwait.

27 **Bomb devastates Uffizi Gallery.** Priceless works of art were either destroyed or damaged when a powerful car bomb exploded outside the famed Uffizi Gallery in Florence. Five persons were reported killed and 26 wounded by the blast. Authorities said they were certain that terrorists or the Mafia were responsible for the attack, but no evidence had yet been found to support this presumption. Art experts considered the Uffizi collection of 13th- to 18th-century paintings one of the finest in all of Europe. The day after the explosion, a huge crowd gathered in Florence's Piazza Santa Croce to protest the wanton destruction of Italy's cultural and artistic patrimony.

29 **Five Turks die in Germany.** Two young women and three young girls were burned to death in Solingen, Germany, when an arsonist firebombed the home their family had occupied for many years. Authorities suspected that right-wing neo-Nazi extremists had committed the murders. Three days earlier the Bundestag had voted to restrict the nation's political asylum laws, which were among the most liberal in the world. Critics of the change claimed that the vote was proof that the government had capitulated to right-wing extremists who had been carrying on a campaign of violence against foreigners. During a memorial service on June 3, the mayor of Solingen spoke for thousands of German mourners when he said: "We are horrified. We are deeply ashamed. We ask for forgiveness."

JUNE

1 **Pres. Dobrica Cosic loses office.** Members of Yugoslavia's Radical Party, with the support of Socialist members of the Federal Assembly, voted to depose Pres. Dobrica Cosic after accusing him of having violated the constitution by delaying the appointments of a prime minister and Supreme Court justices after he assumed office in June 1992. When the Chamber of Citizens voted on the evening of May 31, 75 supported Cosic's ouster, 30 opposed it, and 10 abstained. The next morning in the Chamber of Republics, the vote was 22–10 against Cosic; 4 delegates abstained and 4 were absent. Cosic had angered members of the Radical Party and other extreme Serbian nationalists when he urged ethnic Serbs in Bosnia and Herzegovina to accept a proposed international peace plan that was designed to end the horrendous slaughter of defenseless noncombatants. The most extreme partisans of Serbian nationalism, on the other hand, were urging the Bosnian Serbs to continue fighting and to seize as much territory as possible in Bosnia, which had been part of Yugoslavia before its disintegration.

3 **Norodom Sihanouk regains power.** After decades of conflict, peace finally appeared to have come to Cambodia when Hun Sen, prime minister of the Vietnamese-installed government, recognized 70-year-old Norodom Sihanouk as the head of a new coalition government. Sihanouk, who had been the nation's monarch until he was toppled in 1970, would be prime minister, supreme commander of the armed forces, and head of state. The slow process toward peace had gained momentum with the establishment of a 12-member, four-faction Supreme National

Council that by mutual agreement would rule the country under the chairmanship of Sihanouk while preparations were made for a UN-sponsored and supervised general election. After six days of voting that began on May 23, the country was still in political turmoil. The royal opposition, led by Prince Norodom Ranariddh, Sihanouk's son, finished first in the balloting; Hun Sen's party was second. Because Norodom Ranariddh and his brother Norodom Chakrapong, a ranking official in the Vietnamese-installed government, openly detested each other, their father was able to exploit their antagonism and persuade both to support his return to power. Ranariddh then changed his mind and agreed to become part of a coalition government. Both he and Hun Sen were named deputy prime ministers. The Khmer Rouge, which during Pol Pot's reign of terror in the late 1970's had caused the deaths of at least one million Cambodians, remained a menace because they had refused to lay down their arms or participate in the election, which they had no hope of winning.

5 **UN peacekeepers die in Somalia.** More than a score of Pakistani soldiers serving with the UN peacekeeping force in Somalia were slain in Mogadishu, the capital, in a series of attacks. Some died when Somalis ambushed a contingent of UN soldiers returning from a routine inspection of weapons depots controlled by Gen. Muhammad Farah Aydid, the most daring and belligerent of the local warlords. Others were killed by sniper fire at a feeding station where they were serving as security guards. U.S. helicopters responded to the murders by bombing three of Aydid's munitions dumps; they also destroyed armoured vehicles and artillery pieces. On June 6 the UN Security Council called for the "arrest and detention for prosecution, trial, and punishment" of those responsible for the attacks.

Latvians vote in parliamentary election. Latvians began casting ballots in the country's first parliamentary election since it became independent of the Soviet Union in 1991. The main issue facing the electorate during the two-day electoral process was the future status of Russian nationals who had streamed into Latvia after it was absorbed by the Soviet Union in 1940. Most Russians were not allowed to participate in the election. Latvia's Way, a centrist group under the leadership of Anatolijs Gorbunovs, won a plurality of 36 seats in the 100-seat Saeima (parliament) and 32.4% of the popular vote. Latvia's Way was expected to form a three-party coalition that included the Latvian Farmers' Union, which finished in fourth place with 12 seats in the Saeima.

6 **Guatemala elects president.** Ramiro de Léon Carpio, a crusader for human rights and a frequent critic of the military, was sworn in as president of Guatemala. The following day De Léon demanded the resignation of Defense Minister Gen. José Domingo García Samayoa and reassigned other top military commanders. On May 25 García and other high-ranking officers had backed Pres. Jorge Serrano Elías' seizure of near dictatorial powers. With the country lurching toward chaos, leading politicians, businessmen, and civic groups came together to urge a countercoup by conservative military officers. Serrano was then ousted, and the way was paved for the restoration of democracy. On June 4 the same civilian alliance that had forced the ouster of Serrano refused to accept Vice Pres. Gustavo Espina Saiguero as Serrano's successor. The following day the national Congress, which had been dissolved by Serrano, reconvened and chose De Léon to head the government.

Gonzáles wins Spanish election. Spanish Prime Minister Felipe Gonzáles was assured of another term in office when his Socialist Party won a plurality of seats in the Congress of Deputies. It was the fourth consecutive victory for the Socialists. The conservative Popular Party, however, made substantial gains under the leadership of José María Aznar and prevented the Socialists from winning an absolute majority. Early returns indicated that the Socialists had won 38.8% of the popular vote, the Popular Party 34.8%, and the United Left 9.5%. After viewing the results, Gonzáles conceded that the message from the electorate was clear: the people wanted change. Improving the situation, however, presented a difficult challenge because the country was beset with serious economic problems, including an unemployment rate exceeding 21%.

U.S. seizes ship carrying illegal aliens. Nearly 300 Chinese aliens were taken into custody by U.S. officials in New York after the ship used to smuggle them to the United States ran aground off the coast of New York City. At least six of those attempting to gain illegal entry into the U.S. drowned in the cold ocean water when they tried to reach shore in early-morning darkness. During interviews ashore, various passengers reported that the smugglers had demanded as much as $35,000 to transport each alien from Bangkok, Thailand, to New York by way of the Indian and Atlantic oceans. Until the debts were paid in full, the fate of their families back home was very precarious. Officials of the U.S. Immigration and Naturalization Service said that the agency would oppose the granting of asylum to any of the illegal immigrants. All were being held in various federal detention centres until their cases were reviewed. On June 7 the captain of the *Golden Venture* and 10 of its crew were charged in a federal district court with conspiring to smuggle illegal aliens into the country.

Skeptical Bolivian voters go to the polls. Bolivian voters went to the polls to elect a president and a congress, but many expressed their disillusionment with the electoral process. As expected, none of the presidential candidates received a majority of the popular vote, so once again the legislature was free to choose any candidate as president when it convened on August 6. On June 9, however, former dictator Gen. Hugo Banzer conceded defeat, and Gonzalo Sánchez de Lozada, who had won a plurality of the popular vote in the election, was assured of the presidency. Sánchez, who represented the Nationalist Revolutionary Movement party, had also won a plurality in the 1989 election, but he could not muster sufficient support in the backroom bargaining that followed to win the presidency. As chief executive, Sánchez was expected to invest the country's Indian population with significantly greater political power and to continue pursuing the free-market policies he had introduced in 1985 as the nation's minister of planning.

9 **Japan celebrates a royal wedding.** In a solemn Shinto ritual carried out behind the walls of the Imperial Palace in Tokyo, 33-year-old Crown Prince Naruhito and 29-year-old Masako Owada were united in matrimony. None of the 900 Japanese dignitaries in attendance, much less any of the millions who watched on television, was allowed to view the ancient ceremony, which began in the inner sanctuary of the shrine. Tradition also dictated that the reigning emperor and the empress be absent. Most of the hundreds of thousands who later cheered the newlyweds during their 30-minute ride through the streets of Tokyo were aware that, unlike any other former empress, Naruhito's bride had abandoned a highly successful professional career in the Foreign Ministry to become a member of the royal family.

13 **Woman to lead Turkish republic.** During an emergency meeting of Turkey's ruling True Path Party, an overwhelming number of delegates chose

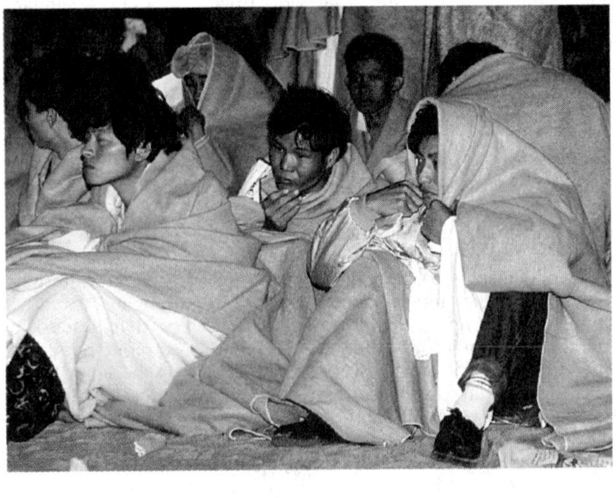

CHARLES ARRIGO—SYGMA

Chinese immigrants huddle onshore after the ship carrying them ran aground off New York City on June 6. Officials reported that many illegal immigrants from China were being smuggled into the U.S., often by criminal gangs demanding exorbitant fees.

Tansu Ciller, new head of the True Path Party and prime minister of Turkey, appears at a press conference. The ruling party named her its leader on June 13, and the following day she was named the first woman to head the Turkish government.
ABC/SYGMA

Tansu Ciller as their new party leader. She replaced Suleyman Demirel, who had vacated the post to assume the presidency after the death of Pres. Turgut Ozal on April 17. Ciller was later formally named prime minister by Demirel and was the first woman to hold the post. The True Path Party currently headed a coalition government with the Social Democratic Populist Party as a junior partner.

14 **Malawians want major changes.** A substantial majority of the Malawians who cast votes in a nonbinding referendum calling for the establishment of a multiparty democracy rejected the one-party government of Pres. Kamuzu Banda. The autocratic ruler had assumed power in the small southeastern African nation after leading it to independence from Britain in 1964. Banda's critics accused him of, among other things, imprisoning, torturing, and murdering his political foes and looting the national treasury. John Tembo, Malawi's minister of state and leader of the Malawi Congress Party, was also targeted as the power behind the throne. In October 1992 Banda had agreed to hold a referendum after a series of strikes and escalating social unrest prompted foreign donor nations to suspend $70 million in aid.

21 **High court backs Haitian policy.** The U.S. Supreme Court ruled 8–1 that the government's policy of intercepting and turning back boats ferrying Haitians to U.S. shores did not violate national or international laws even though the Haitians were not given an opportunity to present their cases for political asylum. An injunction had prevented a lower court ruling in favour of the Haitians from taking effect. The Clinton administration argued before the court that turning back the Haitians would avert a "humanitarian tragedy at sea" if tens of thousands set sail in unseaworthy boats in the hope of gaining entrance to the U.S. During the three-week period before Pres. George Bush announced the new policy in 1992, the U.S. Coast Guard had intercepted 127 boats carrying more than 10,000 Haitians. After word spread that Haitians heading for U.S. shores were being turned back without being interviewed, the dangerous voyages to the U.S. ceased almost immediately.

23 **Nigerian leader voids election.** Nigeria's military leader Gen. Ibrahim Babangida voided the June 12 presidential election and revoked his pledge to turn over power to a civilian government on August 27. It was the fourth time since 1990 that Babangida had backed away from a promise to relinquish power. A local human rights activist viewed the situation as an impending "political crisis of immeasurable, chaotic proportions." Britain responded by threatening to sever diplomatic relations with its former African colony. The U.S. also expressed outrage over Babangida's nullification of the election. It expelled Nigeria's military attaché; recalled two U.S. diplomats stationed in Lagos; summoned the Nigerian ambassador to the State Department to officially condemn Babangida's action; and suspended some $1 million in aid.

25 **Canada gets first woman leader.** Kim Campbell, who had been Canada's minister of defense, took the oath of office as the nation's first woman prime minister. She succeeded Brian Mulroney, who in February had announced his intention to turn over the reins of government after his Progressive Conservative Party chose a new leader. That was done on June 13. With her ascent to the prime ministership, Campbell not only enjoyed the powers of chief executive but, as leader of the ruling party in Parliament, also had a powerful voice in the nation's legislature. Campbell, widely viewed as a strong personality, immediately trimmed the size of her Cabinet by restructuring the ministries and reassigning responsibilities. She also made it clear that she hoped her "new approach to government" and her efforts to find solutions to Canada's economic and social problems would enhance her party's prospects of victory when general elections were held in the fall.

JULY

1 **Ruling party ousted in Belize.** After an all-night session of counting and recounting ballots, election officials in Belize declared that the United Democratic Party (UDP) had won 16 of the 29 seats in the House of Representatives. One seat was decided by a single vote, another by just three votes. The UDP's unexpected victory over the ruling People's United Party meant that Manuel Esquivel would return to power as prime minister of the small Central American nation. He would replace George Price, who had unseated him in the 1989 election.

2 **U.S. detains Sheik Abdel-Rahman.** Sheik Omar Abdel-Rahman, a 55-year-old blind Muslim cleric, was transported to a U.S. Immigration and Naturalization Service detention centre after surrendering to federal officials in Brooklyn, N.Y. The Egyptian cleric was fighting efforts to deport him to his homeland, where he faced charges of inciting his followers to acts of violence. The U.S. was also weighing evidence that could lead to an indictment of Abdel-Rahman for complicity in the bombing of the World Trade Center in February and for involvement in an alleged plot to bomb other sites in Manhattan. The chief suspects in those and other terrorist incidents regularly visited the Abu Bakr Elseddique Mosque, where the sheik held sway.

South Africa sets date for new election. South African Pres. F.W. de Klerk and Nelson Mandela, president of the African National Congress, announced in Washington, D.C., that on April 27, 1994, the nation would hold a national election in which black South Africans would be allowed to vote for the first time. Both men, following separate itineraries, later strove to convince potential investors that they would find an attractive and stable business environment in South Africa. Both men also emphasized the important role foreign capital would play in easing South Africa's difficult transition to democracy under black majority rule.

6 **Abkhazia put under martial law.** Invoking the special powers granted to him on July 2 by the country's unicameral Parliament, Georgian Pres. Eduard Shevardnadze declared a 60-day period of martial law in the Black Sea coastal region of Abkhazia. The area, already under curfew, was home to ethnic Abkhazians, who had taken up arms to enforce their declaration of independence from the central government. A UN official confirmed that as many as 1,000 Georgians may have been killed during an offensive the Abkhazians had launched south of Sukhumi, the regional capital, a few days earlier. Russia vehemently denied charges that it was supporting the separatists with arms and troops.

Egyptian militants await trial. On July 8, as part of the government's attempt to control terrorism, Egypt hanged seven men who had been convicted of attacks on foreign tourists.
FREDERIC NEEMA—SYGMA

8 **Egypt hangs Islamic extremists.** The Egyptian government hanged seven Islamic militants who had been convicted in April of involvement in six separate attacks on foreign tourists. Death sentences had also been meted out to 13 others who had been convicted of acts of terrorism. Under a 1992 anti-terrorism law, the defendants had been tried by military courts. On July 16 U.S. authorities arrested an Egyptian immigrant and charged him with having planned to assassinate Egyptian Pres. Hosni Mubarak during his visit to the U.S. in April. Two other Egyptians, who had been arrested in June for suspected involvement in the plot to blow up several sites in New York City, were also charged as coconspirators in the planned murder of Mubarak.

14 **Mexico returns smuggled Chinese.** A Mexican government official announced that for humanitarian reasons some 650 Chinese who had been detained aboard three dilapidated smuggling ships would be allowed ashore so that they could be immediately repatriated. The first flight carrying the Chinese home took off on July 17. The saga began on July 6 when the U.S. Coast Guard intercepted the ships in international waters near Mexico. Although the U.S. urged Mexico to accept and then deport the illegal aliens, Mexico initially refused to get involved even though past experience had shown that most illegal aliens arriving there intended to cross the border into the U.S. Mexico's position, at least in part, reflected the country's unwillingness "to become an arm of the U.S. immigration service." However, with conditions aboard the ships becoming more deplorable by the day, Mexico allowed the Chinese to go ashore, where arrangements were made for their speedy repatriation.

16 **U.S. asked to end Cuban embargo.** Representatives of Spain, Portugal, and 21 Latin-American nations ended their two-day Ibero-American conference in Brazil with a unanimous call for an end to the U.S. embargo on Cuba. In 1992 the U.S. Congress had, in effect, forced other nations to observe the embargo by passing a law that barred foreign merchant ships from entering U.S. ports for six months if they had docked in Cuba. Argentine Pres. Carlos Menem joined the chorus calling for an end to the embargo, but he also noted that it was unrealistic to expect the U.S. to reverse its policy until Cuban Pres. Fidel Castro embraced democratic reforms.

17 **Former Korean officials arrested.** South Korean Pres. Kim Young Sam's anticorruption campaign took on a new dimension with the arrest of two former defense ministers, who were charged with accepting bribes and kickbacks from ordnance suppliers. The former heads of the air force and navy were also arrested. The opposition Democratic Party, with the apparent approval of the government's Board of Audit and Inspection, urged the National Assembly to question former presidents Chun Doo Hwan and Roh Tae Woo if it seriously desired to get to the bottom of the scandals that had occurred during their administrations. Some legislators, attempting to circumvent the sensitive issue of interrogating former presidents, suggested that such questioning would serve no useful purpose because everything of importance was already known. On August 12 Kim hurled another thunderbolt by banning the use of false names on bank accounts, in stock trading, and in most other financial transactions. Having assets hidden away under a fictitious name clearly fostered corruption and provided a convenient way to avoid paying taxes. The true owners of an estimated $15 billion held in such accounts would now have to identify themselves.

18 **LDP loses its majority in Diet.** Japan's Liberal-Democratic Party (LDP), after 38 years of uninterrupted control of the government, lost its automatic mandate to rule when it won only 223 of the 511 seats in the lower house of the Diet (parliament). A series of financial scandals involving top leaders in the party and defections from the party by prominent legislators had severely eroded the support the LDP had so long enjoyed. On June 18 Prime Minister Kiichi Miyazawa had been forced to resign and call for new elections when 39 members of the LDP, disillusioned by their party's apparent inability or unwillingness to pursue serious reforms, joined members of the opposition in supporting a motion of no confidence in the government. Uncertainty over the makeup of Japan's new government continued until August 6, when 55-year-old Morihiro Hosokawa was elected prime minister. Even though his recently formed Japan New Party had won only 36 seats in the parliamentary election, Hosokawa was asked to form a government. He succeeded by putting together a coalition that included six other parties. The LDP's insistence that it be represented in the government, and its demand that one of its members be named speaker of the House of Representatives because the LDP had the largest representation in the Diet, fell on deaf ears. The coalition chose Takako Doi as speaker, the first woman ever to hold the post.

Pakistani leaders move to solve crisis. Pakistani Pres. Ghulam Ishaq Khan and Prime Minister Nawaz Sharif agreed to halt their interminable feuding by resigning and calling for new elections. The national and provincial legislatures were also dissolved as part of an agreement brokered by Gen. Abdul Waheed, the army chief of staff. Moeen Qureshi, a political independent, agreed to fill the political vacuum by acting as interim prime minister; Wasim Sajjad, chairman of the Senate, would be acting president. Voting for the National Assembly was scheduled for October 6, with provincial elections to follow three days later. Khan had dismissed Sharif and

HARUYOSHI YAMAGUCHI—SYGMA

Morihiro Hosokawa (centre) appears at a party function. Although the Liberal-Democrats won a plurality in the July 18 elections, Hosokawa, head of the Japan New Party, was elected by the Diet on August 6 as prime minister of a coalition government.

dissolved the National Assembly in April, but in May the Supreme Court rejected his interpretation of the president's constitutional powers, and Sharif was reinstated. In the months that followed, the two men were in constant conflict.

23 **Britain approves union treaty.** British Prime Minister John Major scored a significant political victory when the House of Commons cast a vote of confidence (339–299) on his handling of the Social Chapter of the European Community's (EC's) Treaty on European Union. That section of the treaty, which involved workers' rights, was opposed by industrial leaders and by many members of Major's Conservative Party, but it had the support of the Labour Party and Liberal Democrats, the two largest opposition parties in Parliament. Once Major had won the vote of confidence, Britain became the final member of the EC to ratify the Maastricht Treaty. A nuisance challenge to the ratification process by a member of the House of Lords was dismissed by the High Court on July 30.

29 **Demjanjuk conviction overturned.** Israel's Supreme Court overturned the conviction of John Demjanjuk, a Ukrainian-born U.S. citizen who had been sentenced to death in April 1988 for war crimes and crimes against the Jewish people and humanity. The court conceded that new evidence uncovered since the trial raised a reasonable doubt that the man who had been convicted was in fact "Ivan the Terrible," a notoriously brutal guard at the Treblinka death camp in Poland, where an estimated three-quarters of a million Jews had been put to death. Both before and after Demjanjuk was extradited to Israel to stand trial, he insisted that he was the victim of mistaken identity. During his trial the prosecution had relied heavily on the testimony of survivors of Treblinka who swore that Demjanjuk was Ivan the Terrible. During the appeal process, Demjanjuk's lawyer had presented new evidence from previously unavailable KGB files indicating that a Ukrainian named Ivan Marchenko was the infamous war criminal sought by Israel.

AUGUST

1 **Albert to be king of the Belgians.** Belgian Prime Minister Jean-Luc Dehaene informed the nation that 59-year-old Prince Albert would succeed his brother as king of Belgium. King Baudouin I, who had reigned for 42 years, had suffered a fatal heart attack in Spain on July 31. Albert's well-known reluctance to become monarch gave substance to the popular presumption that his son Philippe would one day succeed King Baudouin. The government, however, had convinced Albert that he was better qualified than his son to handle the perennial feuding between Belgium's French- and Flemish-speaking populations. When Albert II was sworn in on August 9, he was only the sixth person to occupy the throne since Belgium gained independence from The Netherlands in 1831.

2 **UN interdicts food to Liberia.** The UN special envoy to Liberia sent a letter to the government of Côte d'Ivoire ordering it to stop private relief agencies from shipping food to areas of neighbouring Liberia held by troops under the command of rebel leader Charles Taylor. The shipments, it was argued, jeopardized the implementation of a peace agreement signed by the warring factions in Geneva on July 25. Anti-Taylor forces had attacked some of the convoys in the belief that arms were being smuggled in the shipments. Several relief agencies condemned the envoy's decision on the grounds that several hundred thousand refugees, now barely surviving, would face imminent starvation if the food shipments were interdicted. Most of the refugees, including some 25,000 children, were living in a rain forest between Taylor's troops and those of a Nigerian-led West African coalition, which was supported by two other armed factions, both Liberian.

4 **Japan admits army abused women.** In one of its last official communications, the government of Japanese Prime Minister Kiichi Miyazawa issued a report acknowledging that Japan had forced some 200,000 Asian women to serve as sex partners for members of its armed forces from 1932 to the end of World War II. About half of the so-called comfort women were from Korea, which at the time was under Japanese control. Other Asian women forced to work as prostitutes in the military-controlled brothels came from China, the Philippines, and Taiwan. Dutch women seized in Indonesia were also made to serve in the "comfort stations." On August 4 a Japanese government spokesman officially apologized to all those who had "suffered immeasurable pain and incurable physical and psychological wounds as comfort women." The new government of Prime Minister Morihiro Hosokawa was reportedly considering the establishment of a fund, perhaps as much as $10 billion, to satisfy the abused women's demand for compensation.

Accord halts Rwanda civil war. Rwandan Pres. Juvénal Habyarimana and two leaders of the rebel Rwandan Patriotic Front signed a peace accord in Tanzania that was designed to end three years of civil conflict between the majority Hutu tribe and the Tutsi. The accord called for UN peacekeeping troops to replace those deployed by the Organization of African Unity. It also approved the formation of a smaller military force that integrated the mostly Tutsi rebels with government forces. During the years of fighting in the central African country, thousands of people had lost their lives, and more than one million of the nation's 7.2 million people had been forced to flee their homes.

Italy adopts a new electoral system. The Italian Parliament approved a new electoral system that allowed voters to cast ballots for specific candidates representing individual constituencies, with the victory going to the one who received the most votes. Under the previous system, voters cast ballots for a list of candidates sponsored by various political organizations. Parliamentary seats were then allotted on the basis of each party's overall showing at the polls. In the future only 25% of the seats would be distributed on the basis of party strength. Moreover, in the lower house no party would automatically be given its share of party seats unless it had won at least 4% of the popular vote. The reform, ardently

PATRICK ROBERT—SYGMA

After taking the royal oath, King Albert II of Belgium and Queen Paola greet the public. It was announced on August 1 that Albert would succeed his brother, Baudouin I.

backed by the electorate in an April referendum, would make individual politicians more accountable to their supporters, minimize proportional representation, and stifle corruption, which had become endemic in political circles. The reputations of the Christian Democratic and the Socialist parties had been especially damaged by revelations that their leadership was riddled with corruption.

10 **Ginsburg joins Supreme Court.** One week after her nomination was confirmed (96–3) by the U.S. Senate, 60-year-old Ruth Bader Ginsburg joined Justice Sandra Day O'Connor and became the second female member of the U.S. Supreme Court. She replaced Justice Byron White, who in early spring had announced his intention to resign at the end of the court's summer session. Ginsburg first took the judicial oath in the Supreme Court building and then took the federal oath of office during a nationally televised ceremony at the White House. Chief Justice William Rehnquist administered both oaths. President Clinton, who had nominated Ginsburg, remarked that the new justice would "move the court not left or right, but forward." Before her nomination Ginsburg had served for 13 years as a judge in the U.S. Court of Appeals for the District of Columbia.

11 **Germany to cut social programs.** German Chancellor Helmut Kohl and his Cabinet approved drafts of two laws that would cut the federal budget by some $45 billion over the next three years. Virtually all of the cuts would come from social programs, including unemployment compensation, social security benefits, child allowances, and payments to workers on days they were idled by bad weather. During a period of worldwide economic recession, the government was attempting to come to terms with the immense cost of rebuilding what had been Communist East Germany. Germany's leaders felt they had had no alternative but to reduce the federal budget by trimming social programs. Critics who accused the government of placing an unfair burden on the shoulders of the elderly and disadvantaged were not likely to let the issue die before national elections were held in 1994.

18 **Sudan called terrorist nation.** After an extensive investigation, the U.S. government notified The Sudan that it was being added to a list of countries sponsoring terrorism and would, as a consequence, be ineligible for any U.S. economic or military aid. Actually, no significant amount of such aid was presently being given to the Sudanese military government. The $56 million the U.S. was providing for the relief of refugees in the southern part of the country would not be affected. The U.S. complaint against The Sudan was based on evidence that it harboured such Islamic militant groups as Hezbollah, Islamic Jihad, and the Islamic Resistance Movement (Hamas), as well as the Palestinian terrorist Abu Nidal. The U.S. further claimed that The Sudan willingly allowed such groups to train on Sudanese soil for terrorist missions.

21 **Contact with Mars Observer lost.** Radio communications with the U.S. spacecraft Mars Observer suddenly ceased as the vehicle neared the end of its 11-month, 720 million-km (450 million-mi) voyage to Mars. Hope for the $1 billion attempt to map and collect geologic data on the "red planet" gradually faded when flight engineers at the Jet Propulsion Laboratory, Pasadena, Calif., tried in vain to restore radio communications. National Aeronautics and Space Administration specialists did not know with certainty why the sophisticated backup systems, designed to minimize the possibility of failure, did not respond to numerous commands from the flight-control centre. A reasonable presumption was that the spacecraft had not gone into its planned orbit around Mars. If not, it would most likely have flown past the planet and continued on into outer space.

25 **Two nations face U.S. sanctions.** The U.S. imposed trade sanctions on China and Pakistan after determining that China had violated a 1987 international agreement by selling banned technology and missile components to Pakistan. Although China had not signed the Missile Technology Control Regime (MTCR), it had promised to observe its provisions if the U.S. removed its restrictions on the export of high technology to China. U.S. law required the government to impose trade sanctions on any country found guilty of violating MTCR guidelines. Although China vehemently denied that it had violated the international agreement, the U.S. did not retreat from its announced plan to ban the export of nearly $1 billion in high-technology goods to China over the next two years.

26 **Babangida forced to resign.** After eight years of military rule, Gen. Ibrahim Babangida was forced to resign as president of Nigeria and as chairman of the Armed Forces Ruling Council. Before the resignation hundreds had been killed protesting Babangida's voiding of the outcome of the June presidential election. The antigovernment strike that began on August 12 was supported by millions of workers and brought Lagos, the former federal capital, to a standstill. With banks, stores, businesses, and government offices closed, the main thoroughfares of Lagos were virtually deserted. In other parts of the country, especially in the north, the call to strike had little effect. Nevertheless, there had never been any comparable defiance of the government in the country's 33-year history. Before stepping down, Babangida named 57-year-old Ernest Shonekan head of an interim government. How long he would remain in that position and how much power Babangida would exercise behind the scenes was a matter of conjecture. Future developments also hinged on the relationship between Shonekan and MKO Abiola, who was the undeclared winner of the June election and was expected to return to the country from London at any time.

29 **Mass murders traumatize Brazil.** The killing of four military police on August 28 was believed to have incited fellow officers to massacre 21 people in a slum area of Rio de Janeiro. The state governor called the unprovoked slaughter "an inadmissible act of revenge." Five weeks earlier hooded gunmen, widely believed to have been military police, had mercilessly shot to death seven homeless boys in downtown Rio. The children, a tiny segment of the youth population trying to survive on the streets, were looked upon as nuisance beggars, petty thieves, and drug addicts. Even though wanton killings were nothing new to Brazil, the general population was horrified by the recent murders. There had been worldwide media coverage of another act of brutality in October 1992, when heavily armed military police were called in to help quell a riot in the House of Detention in São Paulo. At least 200 inmates were killed when the police fired indiscriminately into a sea of milling inmates.

Hiding their faces to avoid revenge, street children in Rio de Janeiro attend the funeral of a friend believed killed by police. Similar senseless killings occurred on August 29.
ALEXANDRE SASSAKI—GAMMA LIAISON

31 **Russian troops leave Lithuania.** Lithuania's defense minister announced that 2,500 Russian troops, the last remnant of the former Soviet army, had left the country by rail. At one time the U.S.S.R. had had 30,000 troops stationed in the country. The final withdrawal occurred near the anniversary of the 1939 German-Soviet Nonaggression Pact, which had led to the forced incorporation of Lithuania into the Soviet Union. A dispute that threatened to delay the pullout was resolved when Lithuanian Pres. Algirdas Brazauskas agreed to postpone negotiations on compensation he contended was owed to Lithuania. The country was reportedly demanding nearly $150 billion, but Russia insisted that it too had suffered from Soviet rule and had no responsibility for compensating Lithuania or any other nations for wrongs they had endured. On September 18 the last Russian troops left Poland. Contingents of Russia's armed forces remained in the two other former Soviet Baltic republics, Estonia and Latvia.

SEPTEMBER

1 **Military dictator frees Bokassa.** Gen. André Kolingba, president of the Central African Republic, ordered the release of all the country's prisoners. Among those set free was 72-year-old Jean-Bedel Bokassa, who had seized power in 1965 and proclaimed himself emperor in 1977. His coronation had cost the impoverished nation tens of millions of dollars. In 1979 France, embarrassed by Bokassa's barbarous conduct, ousted him from its former colony but granted him residence in France. Bokassa returned home in 1986, expecting a warm welcome. Instead, he was arrested and charged with cannibalism, murder, and the theft of some $170 million in state funds. One of the most despicable of Bokassa's alleged crimes was his joyful participation in the slaughter of 100 schoolchildren who had objected to being compelled to buy their school uniforms from Bokassa's factory. Although the charge of cannibalism was never sustained in court, Bokassa was sentenced to death for other crimes. His life was spared, however, when Kolingba commuted the sentence to 10 years in prison. Kolingba's order to release all prisoners came in the wake of a humiliating defeat at the polls. Abel Goumba, the leader of the opposition, called the release an act of vengeance against the nation's electorate.

7 **South Africa embraces change.** South Africa's ruling National Party accepted a plan, approved by representatives of 23 political parties, to set up a Transitional Executive Council that would oversee preparations for the nation's first universal suffrage election in April 1994. For the first time in South Africa's history, the majority black population would have a voice in picking the nation's leaders. With virtually all political views represented in the council, differences of opinion would be resolved by compromise or, if necessary, by ballot. Meanwhile, the National Party would continue to carry out the main functions of government, with major decisions subject to a veto by 80% of the council members. On September 23 Parliament formally approved the creation of the council. The following day Nelson Mandela, leader of the African National Congress, called for an end to the economic sanctions imposed on South Africa by the international community for some 30 years.

Marcos' body returned to the Philippines. With the approval of Philippine Pres. Fidel Ramos, the body of former president Ferdinand Marcos was flown from Hawaii to Ilocos Norte, Marcos' home province, for interment on September 10. The crowd that greeted the plane was much smaller than the mass media and the Marcos family had reportedly anticipated. Marcos had left the Philippines in 1986 in the face of a popular uprising that brought Corazon Aquino to power. He died in Hawaii in 1989. Two weeks after her husband was buried in Ilocos Norte, Imelda Marcos was sentenced to 18 years in prison after being convicted of corruption. Although she was granted bail while her appeal was being prepared, the former first lady still faced some 100 other charges of corruption.

13 **Israel and the PLO sign accord.** During a ceremony in Washington, D.C., Israel and the Palestine Liberation Organization (PLO) signed an agreement that was designed to end decades of violent confrontation between Israel and its Arab neighbours. It was an event that paralleled in importance the disintegration of the Soviet Union and the tearing down of the Berlin Wall. Israeli Prime Minister Yitzhak Rabin and Yasir Arafat, official spokesman for the Palestinians and chairman of the PLO, shook hands after Israeli Foreign Minister Shimon Peres and Mahmoud Abbas, foreign policy spokesman for the PLO, had signed the "Declaration of Principles" on Palestinian self-government in occupied Gaza and the West Bank. Wrenching concessions had been made by both Rabin and Arafat to make this day possible, but both knew from years of bitter experience that there was no other path to peace in the Middle East. Both also knew that some of their followers were prepared to die if necessary to prevent peaceful coexistence between Arabs and Jews in a land both claimed was rightfully theirs. Speaking with great emotion, Rabin declared: "We the soldiers who have returned from the battle stained with blood, we who have fought against you, the Palestinians, we say to you today in a loud and clear voice: Enough of blood and tears! Enough!" Arafat remarked: "Our two peoples are awaiting today this historic hope"—a chance for true peace after generations of mutual hatred. President Clinton praised both leaders for their "brave gamble that the future can be better than the past."

Norway's ruling party wins election. Under the leadership of Norwegian Prime Minister Gro Harlem Brundtland, the Labour Party increased its plurality in the Storting (parliament) but faced growing opposition to its plan to seek membership in the European Community (EC). The agrarian Centre Party, which emerged from the election with the second largest representation in the Storting, reflected the views of most Norwegians, who, according to recent polls, wished to remain outside the EC. During the campaign Brundtland sought to mollify those voters by promising to submit the issue to a national referendum. The future of EC membership was further called into doubt when the Conservatives lost 9 of the 37 seats they had held before the election. Norway's three leading political parties were all headed by women.

16 **Hosokawa reveals economic plan.** In an effort to pull Japan out of its worst economic recession in some 20 years, Prime Minister Morihiro Hosokawa announced a $58 billion economic stimulus package. A similar effort in April by former prime minister Kiichi Miyazawa's government had envisioned an investment of more than twice that sum, but only a small portion of the money had actually been spent. Although Hosokawa characterized his program as "rather bold," many economists considered the proposed lowering of rates on electricity, gas, and imported goods, the offering of low-interest loans and tax incentives, and the launching of public works projects too insignificant to lift Japan out of its economic slump. Many businessmen, moreover, were said to be convinced that no plan would be effective unless it included a cut in income taxes, which would increase the purchasing power of the general public.

19 **Polish voters move to the left.** Apparently reacting to economic hardships brought on by the government's attempt to implement a market economy, Polish voters in large numbers turned to leftist candidates in elections to the lower house of the Sejm (parliament). The Democratic Left Alliance (SLD) won 171 of the 460 seats with 20.4% of the popular vote. It was a remarkable reversal of fortunes for the SLD, the direct successor of the communist United Workers' Party, because it had been all but obliterated in the 1989 election. The Polish Peasant Party won 132 seats with 15.4% of the vote. Prime Minister Hanna Suchocka's Democratic Union finished far back in

LES STONE—SYGMA

Encouraged by U.S. Pres. Bill Clinton (centre), Yitzhak Rabin (left), prime minister of Israel, and Yasir Arafat, chairman of the Palestine Liberation Organization, shake hands in Washington, D.C., on September 13. A few moments earlier representatives of Israel and the PLO had signed a basic agreement on Palestinian self-government in the West Bank and Gaza Strip.

third place, winning 74 seats and 10.6% of the vote. Four other parties qualified for representation in the Sejm by capturing a required minimum 5% of the vote. Among them was Pres. Lech Walesa's Non-Party Bloc to Support Reform, which captured 16 seats. Solidarity was among a score of other parties that failed to meet the 5% requirement.

21 **Prime Minister of Ukraine quits.** By a vote of 294–23, the Ukrainian parliament accepted Prime Minister Leonid Kuchma's resignation together with that of his entire Cabinet. On two previous occasions Kuchma had offered to quit. Months of confrontation with Pres. Leonid Kravchuk had paralyzed the government and intensified a national economic crisis that began when Ukraine became independent of the Soviet Union in August 1991. Kravchuk, who shrugged off Kuchma's resignation as "no tragedy," called for speedy elections to all branches of government, but there was no immediate indication when that would occur. On September 22, Kravchuk named Yefim Zvyagilsky acting prime minister but then took over government responsibilities himself after five days.

22 **Clinton offers health-care plan.** In a speech before a joint session of Congress, President Clinton set forth the basic features of his proposed national health-care program. Among numerous other things, it would guarantee affordable health coverage for all U.S. citizens and legal aliens, including the estimated 37 million Americans who were currently uninsured. The task of drafting a national health plan that would be viewed as basically fair by a large majority of Americans had been entrusted to the president's wife, Hillary Rodham Clinton, and the team she had brought together. Among those consulted during the laborious process of gathering information were physicians, hospital administrators, insurance companies, drug manufacturers, senior citizens, the handicapped and mentally ill, the unemployed, and the owners of small and large businesses, who would be expected to pay part of their employees' insurance premiums. While the task of reconciling conflicting interests of various groups or classes in society in a myriad of medical situations was mind-boggling, the problem of funding the plan was, if anything, even more daunting. Clinton proposed "managed competition" as a workable solution, but many were skeptical that the cost of such a plan could be kept within reasonable bounds. All admitted, however, that exhaustive discussions and numerous modifications of the plan would have to take place before Congress would be willing to vote the plan into law.

23 **Sydney chosen to hold Olympics.** The International Olympic Committee (IOC), after four rounds of balloting in Monte-Carlo, selected Sydney, Australia, as the site of the summer Olympic Games in the year 2000. The four other candidates, eliminated one by one after successive rounds of voting, were Istanbul; Berlin; Manchester, England; and Beijing (Peking). Because Beijing had received the most votes in each of the first three rounds, the Chinese were stunned when the IOC voted to award the games to Sydney. The disappointment was especially keen because China had waged an aggressive and expensive campaign to convince the IOC and the world at large that it deserved to serve as host for the Summer Games in 2000. On July 26 the U.S. Congress had voted (287–99) against the selection of Beijing because of its alleged violations of human rights. The IOC and China both resented this intrusion as inappropriate interference in the selection process.

Soldiers help refugees from Sukhumi board a boat that will carry them to safety. The Georgian city fell to Abkhazian secessionists on September 27.
EPA

24 **Sihanouk restored as monarch.** Norodom Sihanouk, who had first become king of Cambodia in 1941 while the country was still a French protectorate, assumed the throne for the second time. The new government, which had been installed after years of civil war, had modified the constitution so that Sihanouk could become monarch. It was an implicit acknowledgement that no other person had the prestige necessary to unite the war-weary nation. Sihanouk then named one of his sons, Norodom Ranariddh, first prime minister. His party had finished first in the May national election. In a move toward national reconciliation, Sihanouk named Hun Sen second prime minister. He had been prime minister in the former government, which had been installed by Vietnam.

27 **Sukhumi falls to secessionists.** After an 11-day offensive marked by relentless shelling from secure mountain positions, Abkhazian secessionists in the Republic of Georgia captured Sukhumi, a regional capital in the northwestern corner of the country. The fall of Sukhumi was a staggering blow to Georgian Pres. Eduard Shevardnadze, who had gone to Sukhumi and had remained to the last minute in an effort to preserve the unity of his nation. The fighting in Abkhazia had actually begun 13 months earlier when Georgian troops were ordered to oust the secessionist administration in Sukhumi. During the months of fighting that ensued, Shevardnadze repeatedly accused the Russians of aiding the rebels. Although Russia categorically denied the charge, ethnic Russians were in fact fighting on the side of the Abkhazians, with or without the approval of Moscow. Their alleged motive was revenge against Shevardnadze, who, it was claimed, shared responsibility for the breakup of the Soviet Union while he served as Soviet foreign minister under Pres. Mikhail Gorbachev. On July 27 both sides accepted a Russian-mediated cease-fire. Under terms of the accord, Georgia withdrew most of its heavy military equipment and a large portion of its army from the area. When the Abkhazians violated the cease-fire on September 17 by launching an offensive, the poorly defended city was doomed to fall. Shevardnadze acknowledged defeat, but he pledged that Georgia would one day reclaim Sukhumi—if not "tomorrow," he promised, then by the next generation.

30 **Thousands die in Indian quake.** An earthquake measuring 6.4 on the Richter scale devastated whole villages in central India in the very early hours of the morning. Nearly 3,000 people were reported killed in their sleep in the villages of Killari and Umarga, Maharashtra, when their poorly constructed homes collapsed in rubble. After daybreak, thousands of relief workers, including police and military personnel, rushed to the area over rural roads to aid those who had been injured and to bring them desperately needed supplies. Mass cremations were undertaken to prevent the spread of disease, making it impossible to determine how many lives had been lost.

OCTOBER

4 **Russian troops suppress revolt.** Government troops loyal to Russian Pres. Boris Yeltsin successfully assaulted the Parliament building in Moscow and subdued hundreds of heavily armed rebellious deputies and their supporters. Early reports indicated that 142 people were killed in what was described as the fiercest fighting in Moscow since the 1917 Bolshevik Revolution. Intense animosity between reform-minded Yeltsin and his two most powerful political foes—Vice Pres. Aleksandr Rutskoy and Parliamentary Speaker Ruslan Khasbulatov—neared the boiling point on September 21 when Yeltsin dissolved Parliament and called for new elections in December. The legislature, made up largely of hard-line communists, responded by voting to impeach Yeltsin. During the week that followed, the two sides moved inexorably toward a final, violent showdown. On October 3 Rutskoy appeared on the balcony of the barricaded Parliament building to exhort anti-Yeltsin demonstrators below to seize the Kremlin, the mayor's office, and the main broadcast facility. Faced with escalating violence in the streets, Yeltsin declared a state of emergency in Moscow and ordered elite troops to storm the building. Rutskoy and Khasbulatov were among those who surrendered.

Mogadishu raid leads to U.S. pullout. At least 12 U.S. soldiers were killed and at least 75 wounded in a 15-hour battle with the rebel forces of Somali warlord Gen. Muhammad Farah Aydid. The conflict in Mogadishu began when some 100 Rangers captured 19 of Aydid's aides in a surprise raid on his stronghold in the southern section of the city. The Rangers, forced to stay in the area when one of their 12 helicopters was shot down by Aydid's militia, were quickly surrounded by armed Somalis. Before UN reinforcements, delayed by barricades in the streets, could reach the scene, two more helicopters were downed by rockets. Videotapes showing Somalis gleefully dragging dead U.S. soldiers down a street outraged U.S. citizens, who quickly joined some members of Congress in demanding the immediate withdrawal of all U.S. troops. The original mission of preventing massive starvation, they argued, had already been successfully completed. On October 7 President Clinton promised the nation that all U.S. troops would be out by March 31, 1994. Meanwhile, he said, additional troops would be dispatched to Somalia to support those already there. He hoped that during the intervening months the area could be stabilized and that steps would be taken to establish a functioning government.

Hosni Mubarak reelected in referendum. In a national referendum, Egyptian voters overwhelmingly endorsed a third six-year term for Pres. Hosni Mubarak. The interior minister reported that fewer than 4% of those who cast ballots had opposed Mubarak's reelection. The president, who had assumed office after the 1981 assassination of Anwar as-Sadat, had reportedly won wide public support for his steadfast opposition to Islamic militants whose declared goal was the establishment of a strict Islamic state in Egypt. On October 13 Mubarak reappointed Atef Sedki prime minister.

6 **Bhutto's party wins a plurality.** Former prime minister Benazir Bhutto's Pakistan People's Party won a plurality of 86 seats in the 217-seat National Assembly, considerably fewer than she had hoped for. The Pakistan Muslim League led by Nawaz Sharif finished second with 72 seats. On July 18 Pres. Ghulam Ishaq Khan and Sharif, who at the time held the office of prime minister, agreed to end their incessant feuding by resigning and holding new elections. Because both major parties presented similar programs during the campaign, and both, according to opinion polls, were viewed as corrupt, only about 40% of the registered voters went to the polls. Monitors from some 40 foreign nations generally agreed that the election was probably the cleanest in more than 20 years. On October 19 the National Assembly elected Bhutto prime minister by a vote of 121–72. Her ability to govern would depend on the continued support of the minor parties and independents she had wooed during the weeks following the election. On November 13 members of the National Assembly, the Senate, and the four provincial legislatures elected Foreign Minister Farooq Leghari president. He defeated Wasim Sajjad by a vote of 274–168.

Study links red meat to prostate cancer. The *Journal of the National Cancer Institute* published the results of an extensive study of prostate cancer undertaken by the Harvard School of Public Health. Researchers recorded the eating habits of nearly 48,000 U.S. males over a four-year period beginning in 1986. None of the men had detectable cancer when the study began. After analyzing the data, the research team concluded that men who ate red meat five or more times a week had a significantly higher risk of developing life-threatening prostate cancer than those who ate red meat only once a week. The report was said to provide the clearest evidence thus far of a direct link between prostate cancer and the consumption of animal fat. After lung cancer, prostate cancer was the leading cause of death among U.S. males.

7 **Angolans to revive peace talks.** Angolan Pres. José dos Santos declared his willingness to resume peace negotiations with Jonas Savimbi, the rebel leader of the National Union for the Total Independence of Angola (UNITA). The statement came one day after UNITA announced that it would abide by the terms of a 1991 peace accord and accept dos Santos' victory in the September 1992 election. After a 17-month truce, UNITA had resumed fighting following its defeat at the polls. Hopes for an end to the 18-year-old civil war, which during the past year alone had claimed some 100,000 lives, were tempered by a warning from UNITA that even though it was prepared to accept the election results "if it means bringing peace to Angola," it was not prepared to relinquish control of the territory it occupied—almost 70% of Angola—in exchange for peace. On September 26 the UN Security Council had heightened pressure on UNITA by banning the sale of arms and fuel to the insurgents.

10 **Greek voters support Socialists.** The Panhellenic Socialist Movement (Pasok) party regained power in Greece by winning 170 of the 300 seats in the Chamber of Deputies (parliament).

PETER TURNLEY—BLACK STAR

The Russian Parliament building, occupied by foes of Pres. Boris Yeltsin, burns under siege from government tanks. The revolt ended on October 4 when troops stormed the building.

Somalis drag the body of a U.S. soldier through the streets of Mogadishu. Reaction at home led Pres. Bill Clinton to pledge that U.S. troops would be withdrawn by March 31, 1994.

PAUL WATSON—THE TORONTO STAR/SYGMA

Prime Minister Konstantinos Mitsotakis dissolved the parliament after 3 of the 150 members of his conservative New Democracy (ND) party had joined Political Spring, a new political entity founded by former foreign minister Antonis Samaras. The ND emerged from the election with 111 seats in the new parliament, Political Spring with 10, and the Greek Communist Party with 9. The victory of the Socialists meant that 74-year-old Andreas Papandreou would once again resume the prime ministership, which he had lost in 1989. During his previous administration he had come under fire for publicly flaunting his affair with a flight attendant half his age before divorcing his wife to marry her. He had also been charged with corruption but was acquitted in 1992. Papandreou had promised the electorate that, if elected, he would halt the privatization of public utilities and state-run industries, raise private-sector wages, and end the freeze on wage and pension increases, which had been elements of the ND's austerity program to reduce the nation's budget deficit.

14 **Poland gets new prime minister.** Pres. Lech Walesa named Waldemar Pawlak prime minister of Poland. The leftist leader of the Polish Peasant Party (PSL) was, according to a recent poll, the most popular politician in the country. The PSL, which had won 132 of the 460 seats in the September 19 elections to the Sejm (parliament), and the Democratic Left Alliance (SLD), which had won 171, had agreed on October 13 to form a coalition government. The leader of the SLD, Aleksander Kwasniewski, said at the time that he was prepared to direct the coalition caucus but that he would not join the government. Kwasniewski envisioned a government that supported a strong market economy and respected social rights.

15 **Murderers of Chris Hani to die.** Two white South African men were sentenced to death after being found guilty the previous day of the April murder of Chris Hani, the secretary-general of the South African Communist Party and a prominent black antiapartheid leader. The verdict was rendered by a white judge in Johannesburg because South African laws did not provide for jury trials. Janusz Walus, a Polish immigrant, was found guilty of fatally shooting Hani outside his home. Clive Derby-Lewis, a member of the pro-apartheid Conservative Party, was convicted of murder for supplying Walus with the gun.

20 **Noriega found guilty of murder.** Gen. Manuel Noriega, the former Panamanian strongman currently serving a 40-year sentence in Miami, Fla., for drug trafficking, was convicted by a Panamanian court of ordering the 1985 torture murder of Hugo Spadafora, a political opponent who had publicly accused Noriega of dealing in weapons and drugs. Noriega and two of his former associates were sentenced to prison for 20 years. Vociferous protests in several cities greeted the announcement on September 6 that seven other soldiers charged with complicity in the murder had been acquitted.

24 **Burundi president slain in coup.** A news report broadcast over the Burundi government radio station confirmed that Pres. Melchior Ndadaye had been slain in a military coup. Ndadaye's election in June had raised hopes that fighting between the Tutsi, who had been in power since 1962, and members of his own Hutu tribe, which constituted more than 85% of the total population, would end after more than 30 years of conflict. To that end Ndadaye had named several Tutsi to his Cabinet and had left the army under the control of Tutsi officers. On October 21, however, paratroopers stormed the presidential palace and took Ndadaye and three of his ministers captive. Steps were then taken to cut off contact with the outside world. Although former president Jean-Baptiste Bagaza, a Tutsi, had reportedly planned the coup that Lieut. Col. Jean Bikomagu allegedly carried out as commander of the army, both denied involvement when tribal violence began to engulf the country. On October 25 army generals requested Prime Minister Sylvie Kinigi, who had taken refuge in the French embassy, to form a new government. Over radio she urged army personnel to return to their barracks and promised that severe punishment would be meted out to those responsible.

25 **Canada's Liberals sweep election.** Canada's Liberal Party under the leadership of 59-year-old Jean Chrétien overwhelmed the ruling Progressive Conservative Party led by Kim Campbell by winning 177 of the 295 seats in national elections to the House of Commons. Its new total represented an increase of 98 seats. For the Conservatives, the most humiliating aspect of their defeat was the loss of all but two of the 155 seats it had held while in power. In Canada's 126-year history, no ruling party had ever been so resoundingly rejected by the voters. The Bloc Québécois, which campaigned only in its own province and was committed to independence from the Canadian federation, won 54 of the province's 75 seats. The Reform Party, based in western Canada, captured 52 seats, many of which had been held by Tories. Nine seats went to the New Democratic Party (NDP) and one to an independent. The makeup of the new House of Commons would be decidedly different from that of the previous legislature because 205 members had no previous experience in national politics. With fewer than 12 seats each, the NDP and the Progressive Conservatives lost their status as official parties and were no longer eligible for government subsidies. On November 4 Chrétien took the oath of office as Canada's 20th prime minister.

NOVEMBER

1 **Maastricht Treaty takes effect.** After years of often difficult negotiations, the Treaty on European Union, which had been individually ratified by all 12 members of the European Community (EC), officially took effect. It granted special rights and imposed new obligations on the signatories, which had committed themselves to "an ever-closer union among the peoples of Europe." The EC included Belgium, Denmark, France, the U.K., Germany, Greece, Ireland, Italy, Luxembourg, The Netherlands, Portugal, and Spain. The so-called Maastricht Treaty, named after the Dutch city where it was drafted in 1991, was an outgrowth of the Treaty of Rome, which established the Common Market in 1957. During a special meeting in Brussels just three days before the union treaty took effect, certain members of the EC expressed misgivings about some aspects of the complex agreement. There was also a perceptible lack of enthusiasm among ordinary citizens who did not feel that their interests dovetailed with those of other member nations. Some leaders were especially reluctant to accept the notion that domestic policies could, in some instances, be determined by outsiders. During the meeting in Brussels, Frankfurt, Germany, was selected as the site for the European Monetary Institute. One of the goals envisioned by the treaty was the creation of a single European currency by 1999.

Australia offers Chinese permanent home. The Australian government announced that some 19,000 Chinese who had been granted an indefinite extension of their visas following the massacre of pro-democracy demonstrators in Beijing (Peking) in 1989 would be offered permanent residence. The same privilege would be granted to the 9,500 family members who had joined them since 1989. The government also intended to review the cases of some 20,000 people who had filed applications for political asylum. About 8,000 of that number were expected to meet the government's new criteria for permanent residence. These included the ability to speak English.

2 **Islamic militants under attack.** Algerian officials reported that during the two previous days its security forces had located and killed 17 Islamic militants in an area some 65 km (40 mi) east of Algiers. In five smaller encounters a total of 11 other radical Muslims were shot and killed. During the two years that had elapsed since the Algerian government canceled the second phase of a national election that the fundamentalist Islamic Salvation Front was poised to win, an estimated 2,000 people had been killed in terrorist acts of revenge. On November 9 French police arrested 88 persons suspected of being members or supporters of the Islamic Salvation Front. Concerned that the Salvation Front might be having an unwholesome influence on the approximately three million Muslims living in France, the government said it could not accept "the use of religion as cover for political movements aimed at causing disorders."

4 **California battles raging fires.** More than 6,500 professional and volunteer firefighters, assisted by planes and helicopters dropping water and fire-retardant chemicals from the air, finally extinguished or contained the last of more than a dozen major fires that had devastated five counties of southern California. At one point various fires were raging along a 320-km (200-mi) long stretch of land reaching to the Mexican border. On October 30, four days after the first fires broke out, the worst appeared to be over. On November 2, however, the dreaded Santa Ana winds, gusting up to 110 km/h (70 mph), turned scrub vegetation into tinder as they roared into the area through the Santa Monica Mountains. Several new wildfires erupted northwest of Los Angeles, then became an inferno that sped toward the exclusive beach community of Malibu, where some 300 homes were destroyed. The J. Paul Getty Museum, which housed an art collection worth billions of dollars, was spared. According to early estimates, the fires destroyed or severely damaged at least 1,000 homes and displaced about 25,000 people. The total damage was believed to exceed $500 million. Evidence collected by fire inspectors indicated that at least half of the major fires had been set by arsonists.

6 **New Zealanders elect Parliament.** In an election so close that the decisive seat in New Zealand's national legislature was not settled until absentee ballots were tallied on November 17, the ruling National Party (NP) retained power with the barest possible majority in the 99-seat House of Representatives. Polls released just two days before the election indicated that the NP, which had held 63 seats to the Labour Party's (LP's) 29, would easily maintain its control of the government. The LP, however, emerged from the election with 45 seats; had it won the pivotal seat decided by absentee ballots, the NP would have been denied a 50th seat and a majority in the legislature. Two relatively minor parties won two seats each. Prime Minister Jim Bolger expressed satisfaction with his party's "wafer-thin" victory. Political analysts attributed the NP's decline in popularity to its austerity program, which included reductions in social services and welfare benefits.

9 **UN issues report on refugees.** Sadako Ogata, head of the United Nations agency on refugees, released a report entitled *The State of the World's Refugees—the Challenge of Protection.* It was the agency's first report on the status of refugees worldwide. The survey estimated that there were currently 19.7 million refugees living in foreign lands and an additional 24 million who had been uprooted from their homes by violence of one kind or another but remained within their national borders. The agency noted that the massive movement of refugees across international borders had "endangered the time-honoured tradition of granting asylum to those in genuine need of protection." Foreign refugees were facing mounting problems, according to the report, because "beleaguered governments are closing their doors in panic, while racist and xenophobic attitudes are dangerously on the rise." Afghanistan led the world with 4.5 million of its citizens displaced. In 1992, the year covered by the report, there were 7.2 million refugees in Asia, 5.4 million in Africa, and 3.6 million in Europe. Iran had accepted the largest number of refugees, 2.9 million from Afghanistan and 1.2 million from Iraq. Among industrial nations Germany was the most generous, having granted asylum to some 827,000 refugees.

11 **Women's war memorial dedicated.** Vice Pres. Al Gore dedicated a bronze sculpture in Washington, D.C., in honour of the 11,500 women who had served their country during the Vietnam War. Eight of their number had died in uniform. The statue, which portrayed three women assisting a wounded soldier, was placed about 90 m (300 ft) from the Vietnam Veterans Memorial wall. Gore remarked that it was the nation's way of thanking the women veterans, who, "in the tense, sometimes confusing peace" that followed the war, had not been fittingly recognized for their military service.

14 **Puerto Ricans prefer status quo.** Puerto Ricans, by a narrow margin, voted to retain the island's status as a U.S. commonwealth rather than seek union with U.S. as its 51st state. The popular vote was approximately 48.4% to 46.2%. Only 4.4% backed total independence. Gov. Pedro Rossello and his ruling New Progressive Party had campaigned for statehood. They argued that any adverse effects statehood might have on the local economy would be more than offset by various forms of federal aid. Miguel Hernández Agosto, leader of the opposition Popular Democratic Party, was among those who urged voters to retain Puerto Rico's current political status as the best way to protect the local economy, which depended in large measure on businessmen who by and large were exempted from paying U.S. federal taxes. The people were also warned that statehood would gradually erode the heritage of Spanish-speaking Puerto Ricans. In any case, Puerto Ricans were already U.S. citizens but were not obliged to pay federal income taxes. They could not, however, vote in U.S. presidential elections.

17 **House passes NAFTA legislation.** The U.S. House of Representatives voted 234–200 in favour of legislation implementing the North American Free Trade Agreement (NAFTA). The vote was crucial because rejection in the House would have killed the bill even though passage in the Senate was assured. The House vote was a major political victory for President Clinton, who began to personally lobby scores of congressmen when it appeared unlikely that the bill would pass. Twelve hours of emotional debate preceded the evening vote. Prominent Democrats, led by Majority Leader Richard Gephardt and Majority Whip David Bonier, argued on the side of most labour groups, who felt that many

A. HOLLMANN—UNHCR

An Afghan refugee settlement in Iran houses up to 30,000 people. The UN said on November 9 that Iran was home to 2.9 million persons who had fled the war in Afghanistan.

The new statue honouring U.S. women who served in the Vietnam War stands near the Vietnam Veterans Memorial wall. The memorial was dedicated on Veterans Day, November 11.

NAJLAH FEANNY—SABA

U.S. jobs would be lost to Mexico once tariffs and other trade barriers had been removed. Another vigorous opponent of NAFTA was maverick politician H. Ross Perot. Numerous Republican politicians and businessmen, on the other hand, supported Clinton's view that more U.S. jobs would be created by NAFTA than would be lost. When the final vote was taken, only 102 of 258 House Democrats voted for NAFTA, but their vote was bolstered by 132 of 175 Republicans. The Senate later approved NAFTA by a vote of 61–38. On November 22 the Mexican Senate approved NAFTA by a vote of 56–2. The pact had earlier passed the Canadian Parliament. On Jan. 1, 1994, Canada, Mexico, and the U.S. would begin the 15-year process of gradually eliminating tariffs and other trade barriers that impeded free trade across their national borders.

20 **Seattle welcomes APEC leaders.** Leaders of nations that had subscribed to Asia-Pacific Economic Cooperation (APEC) concluded their first summit in Seattle, Wash., as guests of President Clinton. Since "economies" rather than nations were the focus of attention, Taiwan and Hong Kong were members of APEC, along with Australia, Brunei, Canada, China, Indonesia, Japan, Malaysia, New Zealand, the Philippines, Singapore, South Korea, Thailand, and the U.S. The 15 economies represented nearly two billion people and half of the world's economic production. They also included the world's leading exporters. Mexico, Chile, and Papua New Guinea were due to join in 1994. Australia had taken the lead in establishing APEC in 1989, intent on devising a strategy for competing with such formidable trading blocs as the European Community and with the U.S. and Canada, which had entered into a free-trade agreement. Malaysian Prime Minister Mahathir bin Mohamad, whose anti-Western remarks often made headlines, was one of three leaders who did not attend. Australian Prime Minister Paul Keating publicly chided Mahathir for boycotting the meeting, saying that he "couldn't care less" about the prime minister's absence because "APEC is bigger than all of us."

30 **Brady handgun bill becomes law.** President Clinton signed into law the Brady Handgun Violence Protection Act, which required a five-day waiting period before anyone could purchase a handgun. During that time local law-enforcement authorities were required to check the backgrounds of prospective buyers. Minors, felons, substance abusers, and illegal immigrants would not be allowed to purchase such weapons. The legislation, informally known as the Brady bill, was named after former White House press secretary James S. Brady, who had been permanently crippled and almost killed in the 1981 attempt to assassinate Pres. Ronald Reagan. Since that time Brady and his wife, Sarah, had ceaselessly campaigned for gun control. The strongest opponents of the bill had been the National Rifle Association and its supporters. The House passed the bill on November 23, the Senate on November 24. Although many viewed the bill as little more than a feeble gesture at gun control, Brady saw it as a first step toward bringing about "the end of unchecked madness and the commencement of a heartfelt crusade for a safer and saner country."

DECEMBER

1 **Commemorations mark AIDS day.** World AIDS Day, which had been annually promoted by the World Health Organization since 1988, was observed in an estimated 180 countries. The commemorations were meant to increase awareness of the disease, to dispense information on ways to avoid it, and to make a plea for more intensive research to discover a cure for what was still an irreversible condition. The gatherings also memorialized the tens of thousands who had already succumbed to AIDS, those who were afflicted with AIDS, and those who had been diagnosed as HIV positive—that is, those infected with the virus that causes AIDS.

2 **Pablo Escobar dies in shoot-out.** Pablo Escobar, who had amassed an incredible fortune as head of an international drug cartel, was killed in a shoot-out with Colombian soldiers and police. An elite task force had traced phone calls to locate Escobar in Medellín, a city in western Colombia that was the centre of his illegal operations. Experts estimated that at one time Escobar's network had supplied about 80% of the cocaine consumed in the U.S. and that the total income from his drug sales was in the neighbourhood of $20 billion a year. About $6 billion of that amount found its way back to Colombia. Authorities had been searching for Escobar since July 1992, when he escaped from a luxurious prison where he had been held since negotiating the conditions of his surrender.

5 **Rafael Caldera wins presidency.** In an election that featured four major candidates, Rafael Caldera, running as a coalition candidate, won the presidency of Venezuela with 30.3% of the popular vote. From 1969 to 1974 he had held the same office as a member of the Social Christian Party. Political analysts attributed Caldera's victory to a general disenchantment with government reforms that promoted a free-market economy. Claudio Fermín, candidate of the Democratic Action party, finished in second place with 24.2% of the vote, and Oswaldo Alvarez, who ran as a Social Christian, finished third with 23.5%. Andrés Velásquez, who represented the leftist Radical Cause party, was preferred by 20.8% of the voters. Early analysis of the congressional races, which were decided at the same time, indicated that a pro-Caldera coalition would not control a majority of seats in the national legislature.

9 **Seoul and Tokyo yield on rice.** South Korean Pres. Kim Young Sam chose national television as the proper medium for informing the nation that he had finally agreed to open up the country's rice market to foreign imports. The statement predictably outraged the country's rice farmers and others with a vested interest in preventing foreign rice from reaching local markets. Kim explained that South Korea was doing what was necessary to help guarantee a successful conclusion to the negotiations taking place in Geneva to broaden the international General Agreement on Tariffs and Trade. On December 14 Japanese Prime Minister Morihiro Hosokawa announced that he too had reached the "regrettable" decision to allow a modest quantity of foreign rice to enter the country. The political cost Hosokawa would doubtless have to pay at home was considered unavoidable if Japan hoped to do its part to foster freer world trade.

12 **Russia faces crucial balloting.** Some 60% of those who voted throughout Russia approved a new constitution, which had been endorsed by Pres. Boris Yeltsin in early November. Yeltsin had stipulated that formal approval of the charter would require a minimum turnout of 50% of all eligible voters and approval of at least 50% of all those who cast ballots. Under the new charter, the powers of the president were significantly enhanced. Among other things, he would serve as head of state and commander in chief of the armed forces; set basic domestic and foreign policies; name the prime minister, subject to approval by the lower house of Parliament; and have

Nationalist Vladimir Zhirinovsky, who advocated restoration of the Russian empire, speaks to the press on election day. His Liberal Democratic Party won the largest percentage of votes in the December 12 elections for the Russian State Duma, the lower house of Parliament.
PATRICK ROBERT—SYGMA

authority to declare martial law and a state of emergency. The president could also veto legislation, but a two-thirds majority in the lower house would override the veto. Voters also chose a new Parliament, the makeup of which astonished almost everyone, both at home and abroad. Contrary to expectations, there was no clear endorsement of democracy or of Yeltsin's efforts to promote a market economy. On the contrary, the Liberal Democratic Party received the widest support—22.8% of the popular vote cast. Its leader was Vladimir Zhirinovsky, a Russian nationalist (some called him "fascist"), a lawyer, and a former presidential candidate very much opposed to Yeltsin's program. With Yeltsin's two most formidable political foes under arrest for leading an armed revolt in October, Zhirinovsky quickly became the focus of international media attention by making outrageous remarks that managed to offend or alarm almost everyone. He spoke, for example, of restoring the Russian empire by reclaiming part of Poland, the Baltic states, Iran, Afghanistan, and Alaska. Although Yeltsin could look for support in Parliament from such groups as Russia's Choice and the Yavlinsky-Boldyrev-Lukin bloc, it was clear that he would have no easier time dealing with the new Parliament than he had had with the one he dissolved on September 21.

Chilean voters underwrite democracy. In the country's most lopsided presidential election in 60 years, 58% of Chile's voters supported the candidacy of Eduardo Frei and his centre-left coalition. Arturo Alessandri, a representative of rightist politics and Frei's closest rival, received only 24% of the popular vote. The election demonstrated, for the third time in five years, that Chileans had resolutely turned their backs on Gen. Augusto Pinochet and other right-wing politicians. Under Pres. Patricio Aylwin, who had brought an end to Pinochet's 17-year military rule with his election victory in December 1989, an estimated one million Chileans had moved above the poverty level as the country reached the highest rate of growth and foreign investment in Latin America. Chile also had one of the region's lowest rates of inflation. After his election victory, Frei pledged to continue the policies that were transforming the country and giving its people renewed hope for the future.

13 **Hubble space telescope repaired.** U.S. astronauts aboard the space shuttle *Endeavour* returned to Earth after completing repairs on the Hubble Space Telescope. Almost immediately after the Hubble was launched into orbit in April 1990, scientists had realized that the $1.5 billion instrument was not performing according to expectations. The principal problems turned out to be a flaw in the construction of the primary mirror and malfunctions of the solar panels. On December 4, two days after blasting off from Cape Canaveral, Florida, the astronauts rendezvoused with the Hubble. Working in pairs, the crew then began a series of five space walks to retrieve the Hubble, to correct the optics of the primary mirror, to replace the solar panels, and to install new stabilizing gyroscopes. Astronomers expected to know in a matter of weeks if the repairs had given the Hubble the ability to transmit sharply focused images of objects in space as far as 15 billion light-years away—the goal NASA had in mind when the telescope was designed.

15 **GATT talks end on a high note.** Peter Sutherland, director-general of the General Agreement on Tariffs and Trade, declared in Geneva that the Uruguay round of negotiations, which had far-reaching consequences for 117 nations, had been successfully concluded after several days of marathon discussions. The announcement evoked cheers from the assembled delegates. To meet the December 15 deadline, the United States and the European Community had agreed to leave several contentious issues unresolved. Formal signing of the documents was scheduled to take place in Morocco in April 1994. The agreement, which was the broadest and most important international trade pact in history, would take effect on July 1, 1995. The Organization of Economic Cooperation and Development estimated that implementation of the accord would add more than $270 billion a year to the world economy.

28 **Tenth plane hijacked to Taiwan.** A Chinese businessman, accompanied by his wife and 11-year-old son, hijacked a Fujian Airlines plane and forced the pilot to fly to the Taipei (Taiwan) International Airport. The couple had threatened the crew with what they said was a homemade bomb. It was the year's 10th successful hijacking of a Chinese plane to Taiwan. China's Political Bureau, obviously embarrassed by the incidents, demoted the head of the nation's Civil Aviation Administration and announced that in the future all airline passengers and their baggage would be searched for items that could be used to threaten crews assigned to certain air routes.

30 **Vatican and Israel reach accord.** An uneasy relationship that had lasted for decades was dramatically transformed when Vatican City State and Israel signed an agreement in Jerusalem to establish diplomatic relations and initiate a new era of understanding and cooperation. Given the long history of conflict between Jews and the Holy See, many Israelis, as well as communities of Jews throughout the world, welcomed the opportunity to put the past behind them and recognized that the time had come for reconciliation. Israeli Deputy Foreign Minister Yossi Beilin, who signed the document for Israel, remarked, "Behind the agreement there are thousands of years of history, full of hatred, fear, and ignorance, with a few islands of understanding, of cooperation, and of dialogue." Msgr. Claudio Celli, who signed for the Vatican as undersecretary of state, called the signing a historic moment with spiritual significance for millions of people throughout the world.

MOSHE MILNER—SYGMA
On December 30 representatives of the Vatican and Israel exchange copies of an agreement establishing diplomatic relations. It was hoped that the step would help improve understanding between Roman Catholics and Jews worldwide.

People of 1993

NOBEL PRIZES

Prize for Peace

The 1993 Nobel Peace Prize was awarded jointly to two of South Africa's most prominent figures: Pres. F.W. de Klerk and Nelson Mandela, head of the African National Congress (ANC) and "the world's most famous prisoner," for their untiring efforts to bring about a peaceful transition to a nonracial democracy in a nation long and severely torn by the racial policies of apartheid. The two leaders were cited by the Norwegian Nobel Committee for their "personal integrity and great political courage. . . . South Africa has been the symbol of racially conditioned suppression. Mandela's and de Klerk's constructive policy of peace and reconciliation also points the way to the peaceful resolution of similar deep-rooted conflicts elsewhere in the world."

Both men were restrained in their responses to having won the Peace Prize. Mandela declined to comment entirely, while de Klerk ascribed the prize to a process rather than to individuals. Their wary reactions typified the pattern of their complex and mistrustful relationship as leaders of opposing camps moving toward peaceful resolutions. As the chairman of the committee made explicit, "These are not saints. They are politicians in a complicated reality, and it is the total picture that was decisive." Despite South Africa's continuing civil unrest, the committee honoured the two for setting an election date and for agreeing to create a multiracial council that would oversee the government during the elections scheduled for April 1994.

Frederik Willem de Klerk was born March 18, 1936, in Johannesburg, South Africa. He earned a law degree from Potchefstroom University in 1958 and established a successful law practice in Vereeniging, southern Transvaal. In 1972 he was elected to Parliament for the National Party (NP), and though he was rather a dull parliamentary speaker, he was distinguished by his legal talents, which led to his key roles in the ministerial portfolios of mines, social welfare, national education, energy affairs, and internal affairs. He was known for his calm and moderate, sometimes cautious, approach to sensitive political issues. As chairman of the provincial NP, he established a power base in Transvaal, the NP's largest constituency in the country, and was elected South Africa's president in September 1989. Soon after taking office, de Klerk announced a shift away from the remaining apartheid laws, and he released all political prisoners except Mandela, who was serving a life sentence on charges of conspiracy to overthrow the government by revolution as founder of *Umkhonto we Sizwe* (Spear of the Nation), the military wing of the ANC.

Nelson Rolihlahla Mandela was born July 18, 1918, in Transkei into the ruling family of the Tembu. He was expelled from the University College of Fort Hare for involvement in a student strike and fled Transkei to avoid a tribal marriage. He earned a B.A. degree by correspondence but later gained a law degree at the University of the Witwatersrand. Mandela established a law practice with Oliver Tambo, his predecessor as ANC president, and became deeply involved in political activism. He was arrested in 1952, 1956, and 1962, and in 1964 he received his life sentence. During his 27 years in prison, Mandela became a symbol of the continued struggle for freedom. After he was released from jail by de Klerk in February 1990, Mandela joined de Klerk, a former adversary, in watershed negotiations to dismantle the last vestiges of apartheid. (BONNIE OBERMAN)

Prize for Economics

Robert William Fogel of the University of Chicago and Douglass Cecil North of Washington University, St. Louis, Mo., were jointly awarded the 1993 Nobel Memorial Prize in Economic Science for their work in economic history. It was the first time the economics prize had been given to historians and the fourth year in a row that an economist from the University of Chicago had won. The two men were honoured by the Royal Swedish Academy of Sciences for "applying economic theory and quantitative methods" to historical events and were credited with founding cliometrics, a "new economic history" based on a rigorous statistical analysis of precise objective measurements. The academy also cited their creation of enormous computer databases of previously unexamined data.

North was born in Cambridge, Mass., on Nov. 5, 1920, and studied economics at the University of California at Berkeley (B.A., 1942; Ph.D., 1952). In 1950 he joined the faculty of the University of Washington, where he was professor of economics (1950–83) and department chairman (1967–79). In 1983 he left the University of Washington to teach at Washington University. A renowned theoretician, he also served as director of both the Institute for Economic Research (1960–66) and the National Bureau of Economic Research (1967–87). North developed an empirical model of early American economic history. He demonstrated that market economies are inextricably linked with social and political institutions; thus, the study of how these institutions change over time must be an integral part of economic theory. His many books include *The Economic Growth of the United States 1790 to 1860* (1961), *The Rise of the Western World: A New Economic History* (1973), and *Structure and Change in Economic History* (1981). North first brought attention to cliometrics in the early 1960s as editor of the *Journal of Economic History,* in which he published not only his own work but also that of younger colleagues, including Fogel.

Fogel, who was known for his radically new ideas, was born on July 1, 1926, in New York City. He received advanced degrees from numerous universities, including Columbia, New York City (M.A., 1960), Johns Hopkins, Baltimore, Md. (Ph.D., 1963), Cambridge (M.A., 1975), and Harvard (M.A., 1976). He first attracted attention for his theory that smaller innovations rather than giant technological breakthroughs were the backbone of industrialization and for his groundbreaking contention that the railroads had minimal impact on the growth of the American economy. The latter theory he presented in *The Union Pacific Railroad: A Case in Premature Enterprise* (1960) and *Railroads and American Economic Growth: Essays in Econometric History* (1964). In 1974 Fogel published *Time on the Cross: The Economics of American Negro Slavery,* in which he argued that rather than being self-destructive, slavery was an efficient cotton-growing system that collapsed for political, not economic, reasons. The resulting furor was so bitter and the questions the book raised were so abundant that Fogel published a four-volume defense of his work, *Without Consent or Contract: The Rise and Fall of American Slavery* (1989–92), which included a moral condemnation of slavery and clarified his prior research. In 1993 Fogel's increasingly unconventional work focused on the effects of starvation and the importance of improved nutrition on economic development.

(BONNIE OBERMAN)

Prize for Literature

Toni Morrison, a superb weaver of a web of rich stories, received her highest compliment when she was named winner of the 1993 Nobel Prize for Literature. The Swedish Academy of Letters, in awarding the $825,000 prize, proclaimed her "a literary artist of the first rank" and offered high praise for her masterful style by adding, "She delves into the language itself, a language she wants to liberate from the fetters of race. And she addresses us with the luster of poetry."

The eighth woman and the first African-American woman to win the literature prize, Morrison, a professor of creative writing at Princeton University, was hailed for such lyrical novels as *Song of Solomon* (1977), which won the National Book Critics Circle Award; *Beloved* (1987), winner of the Pulitzer Prize for fiction; and, her most

Robert W. Fogel, winner with Douglass C. North of the 1993 prize in economics, receives a congratulatory kiss from his wife, Enid. Both of the winners were economic historians and were credited with founding cliometrics.

AP/WIDE WORLD

recent work, *Jazz* (1992). She also published a book of essays, *Playing in the Dark: Whiteness and the Literary Imagination* (1992). A lesser-known novel, *Sula* (1973), was nominated for a 1975 National Book Award. In recognizing Morrison's sometimes wrenching yet poignant explorations of the African-American experience, which spanned the days of slavery to contemporary times, the academy noted that Morrison "gives life to an essential aspect of American reality" in novels of "visionary force and poetic import."

Morrison was born Chloe Anthony Wofford on Feb. 18, 1931, in Lorain, Ohio. She earned a B.A. degree (1953) in English from Howard University, Washington, D.C., and a master's degree (1955), also in English, from Cornell University, Ithaca, N.Y. For two years following her graduation, she taught English at Texas Southern University, and she began teaching at Howard in 1957. While at Howard, she married Jamaican architect Harold Morrison, with whom she had two children; they were divorced in 1964. In 1966 she moved with her children to Syracuse, N.Y., where she worked as a textbook editor for a subsidiary of Random House. During that time she began writing fiction, and one of her short stories evolved into her first novel, *The Bluest Eye* (1970). She also taught at several universities, including Yale and the State University of New York at Albany. In 1989 Morrison was named the Robert F. Goheen professor in the Council of Humanities at Princeton University.

Using folklore, mythology, and sometimes the supernatural, Morrison's work is both urgent and passionate. She employs violence to portray the struggles of troubled African-Americans attempting to survive in a racist society. The grandmother in *Sula*, for example, puts her leg in front of an oncoming train in order to collect insurance money to feed her family, and in *Beloved* a runaway slave cuts her daughter's throat rather than allow her to live in slavery. *Jazz* was a gripping and violent tale of life in Harlem during the 1920s. In her work Morrison portrays how bleak social conditions prey on the hearts and minds of the underclass. Yet, as her characters search for both individual and cultural identity, they both rage at and accept the world and mix hope with doubt and despair.

The author herself had reason to despair. A Christmas-day fire gutted her New York home in Grand View-on-Hudson, but fortunately her son escaped and her original manuscripts and papers, which were stored in the basement, were spared heavy damage. (BONNIE OBERMAN)

Prize for Chemistry

The 1993 Nobel Prize for Chemistry was awarded to Kary B. Mullis, formerly of the biotechnology firm Cetus Corp., Emeryville, Calif., and Michael Smith of the University of British Columbia. According to the Nobel committee, "The chemical methods that they have each developed for studying the DNA molecules of genetic material have further hastened the rapid development of genetic engineering. The two methods have greatly stimulated basic biochemical research and opened the way for new applications in medicine and biotechnology."

Mullis received his share of the prize for devising the polymerase chain reaction (PCR), a technique for quickly making trillions of copies of a single fragment of DNA, the genetic material of living organisms. Mullis conceived of PCR, the idea for which he said came to him during a night drive in the California mountains, while employed at Cetus. A description of the technique was first published in 1985.

Before the development of PCR, obtaining a usable quantity of a specific stretch of DNA from a large DNA molecule had been a laborious process. Once Mullis' technique became available, scientists could pick out a tiny DNA fragment from a complex brew of genetic material and repeatedly copy it, amplifying its amount enormously in just a few hours. The technique makes use of special synthetic "primers"—short pieces of DNA tailored to bind to the target DNA that is to be copied—and DNA polymerase, a bacterially derived enzyme that can assemble new DNA from

Michael Smith (left), winner with Kary B. Mullis of the prize for chemistry, receives his award from King Carl XVI Gustaf at ceremonies in Stockholm on December 10. The two chemists were cited for their work in studying DNA.

TOBBE GUSTAVSSON—REPORTAGEBILD/PHOTOREPORTERS

its building-block molecules, called nucleotides, while using the target DNA as a template. The entire process is carried out on automated bench-top equipment.

Since its introduction PCR has opened up new possibilities for gene sequencing, the determination of the order of the nucleotides that compose a gene; genetic fingerprinting, the identification of individual organisms by the distinctive patterns in their DNA; the study of evolution; and medical diagnosis. The technique has become a key tool in the ambitious international effort to map and sequence the entire genetic endowment of human beings. Using PCR on museum specimens and fossil remains, researchers have isolated DNA from plants and animals that became extinct hundreds to millions of years ago. In medicine PCR has made it possible to identify the causative agent of a patient's viral or bacterial infection directly from a tiny sample of genetic material. It has also been exploited in the search for the genetic alterations underlying hereditary diseases.

Smith received his share of the chemistry Nobel for developing the procedure known as site-directed mutagenesis and applying it to the study of proteins. With Smith's method researchers were given the tools to reprogram the genetic code—the sequence of nucleotides in a gene that provides instructions for synthesizing a specific protein from its component amino acid subunits—and, consequently, to construct proteins with new properties.

Proteins are responsible for the functions of living cells; those that serve as the biological catalysts known as enzymes have the particularly critical role of maintaining all the chemical reactions required for supporting life. The three-dimensional structure of a given protein and, hence, its function are determined by the order in which the various amino acids are linked together. By reprogramming the genetic code that specifies a particular protein, it is possible to obtain a mutated protein in which one of its amino acids has been replaced by another. Biochemical researchers had long wished to make such precise alterations in a gene in order to study how the properties of the mutated protein differ from those of the natural one. Before Smith's development researchers had resorted to inducing random mutations in DNA by exposing cells to certain chemicals or radiation and then sorting through the mutated proteins made by the cells for those of interest. Smith's process gave them the means to generate specific, customized proteins.

Smith conceived of site-directed mutagenesis in the early 1970s while working as a visiting researcher in England, and during the next few years in Vancouver he developed and refined the process. Similar in some ways to PCR, Smith's approach uses a small synthesized fragment of DNA as the starting point for the construction of an entire gene by DNA polymerase, using the natural gene as a template. The nucleotide sequence of the fragment, however, differs from the corresponding sequence of the natural gene at a single amino acid coding site, and so the new gene that is built from the fragment carries this one change. To obtain the mutated protein, researchers insert the altered genetic material, by way of an infectious carrier virus, into the DNA of a bacterium, which then makes the mutated protein as part of its normal cellular activities.

Smith's method created an entirely new means of studying proteins. By systematically changing the amino acids in a protein, researchers can determine what role each amino acid plays in directing the protein's activity or maintaining its structure. The method has found wide use in biotechnology, where scientists have sought to produce altered proteins that are more stable, more active, or more useful to medicine or industry than their natural counterparts—for example, hemoglobin variants that may serve as blood substitutes or alterations in key plant proteins that would improve the efficiency of photosynthesis in crop plants. In addition, site-directed mutagenesis may allow doctors to cure hereditary diseases by correcting the causative genetic mutation.

Mullis was born in Lenoir, N.C., on Dec. 28, 1944. He received his Ph.D. in 1972 from the University of California at Berkeley. From 1973 through 1977 he held research posts at various U.S. universities. He joined Cetus in 1979 and in 1986 became director of molecular biology at Xytronyx, Inc., San Diego, Calif. Most recently he worked as a freelance consultant based in La Jolla, Calif.

Smith, a naturalized Canadian citizen, was born in Blackpool, England, on April 26, 1932. He earned a Ph.D. from the University of Manchester in 1956. After holding a number of posts in the U.S. and Canada, Smith joined the faculty of the University of British Columbia in 1966, becoming the director of the university's biotechnology laboratory in 1987. He served as a career investigator of the Medical Research Council of Canada from 1979. Smith also provided scientific leadership for the Protein Engineering Network of Centres of Excellence (PENCE), a collaborative research effort with university, industry, and government involvement.

(CAROLYN HEMENWAY)

Prize for Physics

Two astrophysicists from Princeton University, Joseph H. Taylor, Jr., and Russell A. Hulse, were awarded the 1993 Nobel Prize for Physics for their discovery of a new type of pulsar, termed a binary pulsar, that "has opened up new possibilities for the study of gravitation," according to the Nobel committee. The pair did their prizewinning work in the 1970s while Taylor was a professor at the University of Massachusetts at Amherst and Hulse was Taylor's graduate student.

Taylor and Hulse made their discovery in 1974 while conducting a systematic search for pulsars with the large radio telescope at Arecibo, P.R. A pulsar, short for pulsating radio star, is thought to be a rapidly spinning neutron star, an extremely dense star that is composed almost entirely of neutrons and that was formed in an explosive stellar event called a supernova. The extremely intense magnetic field that surrounds a neutron star gives rise to a narrow beam of radio emission (and occasionally of other kinds of emission such as visible light or X-rays), which sweeps around the star like a beam of light from a lighthouse. When the Earth happens to lie in the path of the beam, observers detect brief, precisely timed pulses of radio waves from the star, which then is labeled a pulsar. The time between pulses corresponds to the pulsar's period of rotation.

In 1967 English astronomer Jocelyn Bell, by using a radio telescope at the University of Cambridge, detected radio signals from what would be identified as the first known pulsar. For recognizing the significance of the pulsed signals, Antony Hewish, Bell's doctoral thesis adviser and supervisor at Cambridge, was awarded the physics Nobel in 1974.

That same year Taylor and Hulse, who had already discovered dozens of ordinary pulsars, found one whose pulses were not exactly regular. The interval between pulses varied in a definite pattern, decreasing and increasing over an eight-hour period. Taylor and Hulse concluded that the pulsar must be moving alternately toward and away from the Earth; in other words, it must be in orbit around a companion body and thus part of a binary star system. From the behaviour of the pulsar's signal, the scientists were also able to deduce that the companion is another neutron star, about as heavy as the pulsar, and is located at a distance corresponding to only a few times that between the Moon and the Earth. Both bodies have a radius of some 10 km (6 mi) and a mass comparable to that of the Sun.

Taylor and Hulse's discovery of the first binary pulsar, called PSR 1913 + 16, "brought about a revolution in the field," according to the Nobel committee, because it provided a "space laboratory" in which researchers could test Einstein's general theory of relativity and alternative theories of gravity. The scientists quickly realized that, according to the general theory, the two stars' enormous interacting gravitational fields should affect the timing of the pulsar's pulses in ways large enough to measure. What they had available to them, as they pointed out in a 1975 article about their discovery, was "a nearly ideal relativity laboratory including an accurate clock in a high-speed, eccentric orbit and a strong gravitational field."

One prediction of the general theory that still awaited confirmation was the existence of gravitational waves, disturbances in space-time produced by objects moving in a gravitational field. By timing the pulses over a long period and analyzing the variations, Taylor and Hulse showed that the two stars are rotating ever faster around each other in an increasingly tight orbit. This orbital decay, signaled by a decrease in the pulsar's orbital period of about 75 millionths of a second per year, is presumed to occur because the system is losing energy in the form of gravitational waves. In fact, the rate at which the stars are spiraling together agrees with the prediction of the general theory to an accuracy of better than 0.5%. This finding, reported in 1978, not only afforded the first experimental evidence for the existence of gravitational waves but also provided powerful support for Einstein's theory of gravity over its competitors.

Taylor was born on March 24, 1941, in Philadelphia. After earning a Ph.D. in astronomy from Harvard University in 1968, he joined the University of Massachusetts faculty. From 1977 to 1981 he served as associate director of the Five-College Radio Astronomy Observatory. In 1980 Taylor moved to Princeton, where he subsequently became the James S. McDonnell distinguished university professor of physics.

In the decades after his prizewinning discovery, Taylor continued to provide experimental confirmation of the general theory by means of painstaking measurements on PSR 1913 + 16 and two other binary pulsars that his group later discovered. In 1985 Taylor's group found a new binary pulsar, designated PSR 1855 + 09, whose rotation was clocked at 186 times per second, making it the second most rapidly spinning pulsar known. Because of the speed and stability of its rotation, the pulsar and others like it, which have been termed millisecond pulsars, could provide a better time standard than even the most accurate atomic clocks.

Hulse, who was born on Nov. 28, 1950, in New York City, received a Ph.D. degree in physics in 1975 from the University of Massachusetts. After working as a postdoctoral fellow at the National Radio Astronomy Observatory, Charlottesville, Va., he changed fields from astrophysics to plasma physics and in 1977 assumed a position at the Princeton Plasma Physics Laboratory. His more recent research was associated with the Tokamak Fusion Test Reactor, an experimental facility devoted to developing usable electric power from thermonuclear fusion. (CAROLYN HEMENWAY)

Prize for Physiology or Medicine

The 1993 Nobel Prize for Physiology or Medicine was awarded to two American molecular biologists, Richard Roberts and Phillip Sharp, for their independent discovery that genes are often split; in other words, that the genetic instructions contained in DNA and used by the living cell to make proteins can be discontinuous. Before the laureates' findings, DNA research had focused primarily on bacterial cells, in which the instructions to make a given protein molecule are encoded in DNA's sequence of nucleotides, its molecular building blocks, as a single uninterrupted gene. By studying viral cells the laureates showed that this model is not generally correct. In 1977 they demonstrated that individual genes are often interrupted by long sections of DNA, since dubbed intervening sequences, or introns, that do not encode protein structure.

According to the Nobel citation, "Roberts' and Sharp's discovery has changed our view on how genes in higher organisms develop during evolution. The discovery also led to the prediction of a new genetic process, namely that of splicing, which is essential for expressing the genetic information. The discovery of split genes has been of fundamental importance for today's basic research in biology, as well as for more medically oriented research concerning the development of cancer and other diseases."

Bacterial studies conducted previously had indicated that when a gene is to be translated into its protein product, its nucleotide sequence is copied into a similar sequence in a molecule called messenger RNA. The messenger RNA, without modification, then carries its coded instructions to the cell's protein-synthesis machinery, which reads the code and uses it to assemble the protein. Scientists assumed that what they had found in bacteria also held true both for plant and animal cells and for viruses. Viruses use their genetic material to take over the protein-synthesis machinery of the cells that they infect in order to reproduce. Consequently, Roberts and Sharp reasoned that by studying how viruses make proteins in their cellular hosts, they would learn more about how the host cell makes its own proteins. Both men chose to study a common cold-causing virus, called an adenovirus, since its genome, or total endowment of genes, is contained on a single molecule of DNA and is similar in many ways to the DNA of its host cells.Their aim was to determine where in the genome different genes were located.

In the course of their experiments Roberts, who headed a team at the Cold Spring Harbor Laboratory in New York, and Sharp, whose team worked at the Massachusetts Institute of Technology (MIT), attempted to bind the adenovirus messenger RNA chemically with its DNA counterpart, matching up the nucleotides of the two molecular strands along their lengths, so as to learn which part of the viral genome had produced the messenger RNA. When the researchers used electron microscopy to visualize the matchup, to their surprise they found large loops of unbound DNA between the bound sections, indicating that substantial segments of the original viral DNA were not represented in the final messenger RNA molecule.

When Roberts and Sharp announced their findings in 1977, the news sparked an intensive search by other scientists for discontinuous gene structure in a variety of organisms. It was soon shown that split genes are common; in fact, they are now known to be the most common type of gene structure in higher organisms, including human beings.

The laureates' discovery transformed the model for understanding how proteins are synthesized from genes. Scientists now realize that in many cases the messenger RNA is first made as a large precursor molecule having the introns from the DNA represented in its structure. Then, in a process governed by enzymes, the introns are cut out and the remaining meaningful segments, called exons, spliced together in the correct order to form the final messenger RNA. Subsequent research also revealed that it is not always the same gene segments that are included in the final messenger RNA molecule. In different tissues or different developmental stages of an organism, different exon combinations may be used to produce the final RNA molecule. Thus, the same DNA region can supply information for a number of different proteins.

The discovery of split genes and gene splicing modified scientists' view of how genetic material has developed during the course of evolution. The general view is that evolution takes place by means of the accumulation of mutations, or minor alterations in the genetic material, which result in a gradual change in the overall organism. That genes are often split, however, suggests that higher organisms may also use another mechanism—the rearrangement of genetic information into new protein-coding units—to speed up evolution and to respond more flexibly to environmental challenges. Later research also suggested that introns are something more than spare DNA. They appear to serve some sort of regulatory function at least, since engineered genes from which the introns have been removed often fail to produce protein. The field of medicine has benefited from the discovery of gene splicing. For example, errors in splicing are now known to underlie a number of disorders, including beta-thalassemia, a form of anemia, and chronic myelogenous leukemia, a type of cancer of the blood.

Roberts was born on Sept. 6, 1943, in Derby, England. He obtained a Ph.D. in organic chemistry from the University of Sheffield, England, in 1968. After postdoctoral research at Harvard University, he was invited in 1972 by Nobel laureate James D. Watson to take a post as senior staff investigator at the Cold Spring Harbor Laboratory. In 1986 he became the laboratory's assistant director for research. Roberts remained at Cold Spring Harbor until 1992, when he became director of eukaryotic (nucleated cell) research at New England Biolabs, Beverly, Mass.

Sharp was born on June 6, 1944, in Falmouth, Ky., on a small farm on which his parents grew tobacco and corn. Earnings from a piece of tobacco land given to him by his parents helped pay for part of his undergraduate education at Union College, Barbourville, Ky. After receiving a Ph.D. in chemistry in 1969 from the University of Illinois at Champaign-Urbana, Sharp worked as a postdoctoral fellow at the California Institute of Technology, Pasadena, and then, in 1971–72, at Cold Spring Harbor with Watson. From 1972 to 1974 he was a senior research investigator at Cold Spring.

Sharp joined MIT in 1974. In the 1980s and early '90s he served as associate director and then director of the MIT Center for Cancer Research. In 1991 he was appointed to head MIT's department of biology, and in 1992 he became the first Salvador E. Luria professor, a chair established at MIT in honour of the 1969 Nobel laureate whose prizewinning work involved bacteriophages, viruses that infect bacteria.

(CAROLYN HEMENWAY)

BIOGRAPHIES

Akebono

In the ancient Japanese sport of sumo, no foreigner had ever been elevated to *yokozuna* (grand champion) until Hawaiian-born Chadwick Haheo Rowan, known professionally as Akebono, was promoted to that rank in January 1993. Rowan was born near Honolulu on May 8, 1969, and entered college on a basketball scholarship. In less than a year he had dropped out of school because he had arguments with his coach and found his classes boring. Setting aside a natural interest in language and culture, he finally took his father's advice and agreed to meet fellow Hawaiian Jesse Kuhaulua, who had become a sumo stablemaster in Japan. Before retiring in 1984, he was known as Takamiyama and had set a series of virtually unbeatable records as a junior champion. He persuaded Rowan to join his stable.

During his first six months in Japan, Rowan was so homesick that he cried almost every night. His Japanese was so poor he could not mix easily with his stablemates. During practice, however, Rowan showed amazing strength, but he had difficulty maintaining his balance because of his towering height (204 cm [6 ft 8 in]) and incredible weight (211 kg [466 lb]). With persistence he gradually developed the techniques and skills required for his professional debut as Akebono in March 1988. He breezed through sumo's lower ranks and junior division, setting all-time records along the way. As he worked his way up in the senior division, successes were mixed with failures. In May 1992 Akebono won his first tournament championship, a feat no one before him had ever accomplished in just 30 competitions. In time, Akebono was awarded five Emperor's Cups, four Outstanding Performance prizes, two Fighting Spirit prizes, and 487 special monetary prizes. He ended the season by winning his third consecutive, and sixth over-all, championship in the November tournament. And somewhere along the road that leads to eventual retirement, Akebono hoped to capture the elusive *zenski-yusho,* a perfect record of 15 victories in a single tournament.

Fame did not significantly alter Akebono's lifestyle. He continued to like popular and classical music, watch samurai movies, and shy away from crowds whenever possible. He knew, however, that he had to maintain the dignity and decorum expected of a *yokozuna.* Akebono still expressed pride in being an American, but he expected to reside in Japan when his career came to an end. Meanwhile, especially after the death of his father in July, he took good care of his mother and other family members in Hawaii. As he looked back on the years of rigorous training and the success that followed, Akebono knew he made the right decision. If he had stayed home, he said, he would now probably be "a bum on a beach somewhere in Hawaii."

(KAY K. TATEISHI)

NOBORU HASHIMOTO—SYGMA

Albert II

On Aug. 9, 1993, Albert II was sworn in as the sixth king of the Belgians, succeeding his childless older brother, King Baudouin (*see* OBITUARIES), Europe's longest-reigning monarch at the time of his sudden death in July. Having shown little interest in becoming the king, Albert surprised many when he chose not to abdicate in favour of his elder son, Prince Philippe. Although groomed for the throne, Philippe was thought by some in the government to be less ready than his father to act as the head of state for a Belgium troubled by a faltering economy and increasing political divisiveness between French-speaking Wallonia and Flemish-speaking Flanders. Constitutional reform in 1993 both federalized the government and curbed the power of the monarchy, but Albert, like Baudouin, remained an important symbol of unity for a nation drifting toward dissolution. The new king, speaking in French, Flemish, and German, warned of the "menaces of individual and collective egoism" during a low-key investiture interrupted by a rebellious deputy's cry of "Long live the Republic of Europe!" A similar outburst had marred Baudouin's swearing-in 42 years previously.

Albert Félix Humbert Théodore Christian Eugène Marie of Saxe-Coburg-Gotha, Prince of Belgium and Prince of Liège, was born June 6, 1934, in Brussels. His father, King Leopold III, chose house arrest over exile during the German occupation of Belgium in World War II, and the suspicion of collaboration raised by that decision eventually forced Leopold's abdication in favour of Baudouin in 1951. After being educated at home and in Geneva and Brussels, Prince Albert entered the Belgian navy in 1953. As the heir to the throne he became a member of the Belgian Senate. From 1962 until his ascension, the prince served as the honorary chairman of the Belgian Office of Foreign Trade, leading some 70 important trade missions and becoming an expert on shipping. However, that tenure was tainted by a 1979 kickback scandal involving Belgium's largest conglomerate and the construction of a hospital in Saudi Arabia. Prince Albert also served as the longtime president of the Belgian Red Cross and as a member of the International Olympic Committee.

During his brother's lengthy reign, the prince acquired a reputation as a jet-setter. He enjoyed fast cars and boats and, clad in leather, took to the road on high-powered motorcycles. In 1959 he married Paola Ruffo di Calabria, a glamorous Italian princess once refused entrance to the Vatican because she was wearing a miniskirt. With her husband's ascension to the throne, she shared the title of queen with Baudouin's widow, Fabiola. In addition to Philippe (born 1960), the royal family included a daughter, Astrid (born 1962), and another son, Laurent (born 1963).

(JEFF WALLENFELDT)

Aliev, Geidar

Some old soldiers, it seems, do not die or fade away. They just keep popping up here and there in leadership positions in various former Soviet states. In Azerbaijan, for example, Maj. Gen. Geidar Aliev, former KGB official, ex-Politburo member, and onetime chairman of the Communist Party of Azerbaijan, bounded back suddenly in 1993 as the nation's president.

Aliev's rise began in early June when Pres. Abulfez Elchibey attempted to disarm the soldiers in the city of Gyandzha and stripped Suret Guseynov, a local militia commander, of his rank for disobeying orders. Guseynov, however, denounced Elchibey and in early June ordered his troops into open rebellion. As he marched on Baku, Guseynov met little resistance. Elchibey called on Aliev, honourably rusticated to his home area, the Nakhichevan autonomous region, to go to Baku to help negotiate. The parliament quickly voted Aliev its chairman, Elchibey fled, and Aliev effectively took power as head of state. After negotiations with Guseynov, on June 30 Aliev named the maverick commander his prime minister, giving him control of the military and national security. A presidential election in October, with Aliev capturing almost 99% of the vote, legitimized his position. Not unexpectedly, Aliev took a pro-Russian tack. (Elchibey had looked toward Azerbaijan's ethnic cousins in Turkey.) He met with Russian Pres. Boris Yeltsin in Moscow in September; later that month the Azerbaijani national assembly voted to rejoin the Commonwealth of Independent States.

Geidar Ali Rza ogly Aliev was born in Nakhichevan on May 10, 1923. He entered the security service in Azerbaijan when he was 18 and in 1945 joined the Communist Party. During 1949–50 Aliyev attended the KGB Academy and he graduated from Azerbaijan State University in 1957. While holding several senior offices in the local KGB, he rose in the ranks of both the Communist Party of Azerbaijan and the Communist Party of the Soviet Union (CPSU). He was leader of the Azerbaijan S.S.R. from 1969 to 1982 and became a member of the Central Committee of the CPSU in 1971. In 1982 Aliev attained full membership in the CPSU Politburo through the graces of General Secretary Yury Andropov.

A loyal Communist, Aliev was secure in his position until after Mikhail Gorbachev took office in 1985. Aliev opposed Gorbachev's sweeping reforms, and he was removed from the Politburo in 1987, after which he dropped into obscurity. The resurrection of the resilient politician began in 1990 after Aliev put on the mantle of Azerbaijani nationalism and denounced Soviet intervention in Baku to put down anti-Armenian riots. He resigned from the Communist Party and was elected parliamentary leader of Nakhichevan, where he awaited the call from Baku.

(MARVIN MARTIN)

Aydid, Gen. Muhammad Farah

Shortly after 24 Pakistani peacekeeping troops were killed in a June 5, 1993, ambush in Somalia, the man thought to be responsible for the attack, clan leader Gen. Muhammad Farah Aydid, became the UN's first "wanted man." Posters promising a $25,000 reward for his capture rained on Mogadishu, part of a manhunt involving thousands of UN troops, including elements of the U.S. Army's counterterrorist Delta Force. Large-scale assaults on southern Mogadishu strongholds of Aydid's Habar Gadir subclan failed to result in the capture of the warlord, who went into hiding for more than 90 days. A folk hero to some for his role in the overthrow of longtime dictator Gen. Muhammad Siad Barre in January 1991, a tyrant and thief to others, Aydid was viewed by UN officials as an ally during Operation Restore Hope's efforts to relieve the suffering of those afflicted by famine. Events and policies had shifted so much in Somalia, however, that in December Aydid, the former "outlaw," was being flown to Ethiopia in a U.S. military airplane to meet with other Somali clan leaders.

Born in Italian Somaliland, Muhammad Farah Hassan was given a customary alternative surname by his mother. In Somali the name Aydid means "one with no weaknesses" or "he who will not be insulted." A shepherd in his youth, Aydid received military training in Italy and during the 1950s served as the chief of Mogadishu's colonial police. Officer training in the Soviet Union in the early '60s led to a commission in Somalia's new national army and, in 1969, to the position of chief of staff. However, Barre, a member of the Darod clan, mistrusted Aydid and jailed him for six years in the early '70s. Released and given a command during the 1977–78 war with Ethiopia, Aydid served as a military adviser until Barre, still threatened by the general's presence, named him ambassador to India in 1984. Five years later Aydid joined the opposition, eventually leading attacks that drove the dictator from Mogadishu. In the interclan warfare that followed, Aydid's Somali National Alliance faction of the United Somali Congress and another Hawiye subclan and faction of the USC, the Abgal, nearly destroyed Mogadishu as they battled to control it, with the Habar holding on to southern Mogadishu.

Meanwhile, some of Aydid's family immigrated to North America. Indeed, one of his sons, a U.S. Marine reservist, was sent to Somalia as part of the UN mission. In October 1993—after the U.S. in effect called off the manhunt following the deaths of 18 U.S. servicemen in a disastrous UN assault—the general reemerged, proposed a cease-fire, and in a press conference shortly thereafter released two captured servicemen, an American and a Nigerian. Dressed more like a businessman than a fugitive, Aydid, however, had not lost his combative resolve or his xenophobic rhetoric. (JEFF WALLENFELDT)

Balladur, Édouard

Socialist Pres. François Mitterrand named Édouard Balladur of the Gaullist Rally for the Republic (RPR) prime minister of France on March 29, 1993. Balladur headed the "cohabitation" government after the conservative parties' victory over the Socialists in the National Assembly elections of March 21 forced Mitterrand to choose a right-wing head of government. The former finance minister took office at a time when the economy of France was in recession and unemployment was quite high. Many of the measures taken by Balladur in his attempts to improve the economic picture (including a tax increase) might have made him immediately unpopular with the French populace but, amazingly, they did not. Even the devaluation of the franc in the wake of the failure of the European Monetary System and the resulting strained relations with Germany did not cause him the political embarrassment that might have been expected. Other plans that went awry included legislation intended to curb the number of illegal aliens by performing identity checks on anyone who appeared not to be a citizen and a proposal to make the central bank of France autonomous. Still, the French strongly approved of Balladur's handling of several crises, including a 16-day strike by the Air France ground staff, as well as his success in obtaining beneficial compromises at the world trade negotiations. Niggling details like rising unemployment did not seem to imperil the popularity of the aloof and aristocratic prime minister.

AP/WIDE WORLD

Balladur was born May 2, 1929, in Izmir, Turkey, into a wealthy banking family, and he grew up in Marseille after the family relocated to France in 1935. He received diplomas in law and political science, in addition to the degree conferred upon him by the prestigious École Nationale d'Administration. In 1957 Balladur began his career in public service when he joined the diplomatic service as an official in the Council of State. During the years 1964–68, he was an adviser to Prime Minister Georges Pompidou. He then went on to serve first as deputy secretary-general to the president (1969) and then as secretary-general (1974) during Pompidou's presidency. In 1977 Balladur left public service to become chairman of Générale de Service Informatique; he held the post until 1986. From 1980 to 1986 he was also president of Compagnie Européenne d'Accumulateurs. He left the private sector in 1986 to enter the National Assembly and become minister of economy, finance, and privatization in the cohabitation government of Prime Minister Jacques Chirac, a fellow member of the Gaullist RPR. (CHRISTINE SULLIVAN)

Bartoli, Cecilia

When Cecilia Bartoli attempted a concert tour in the United States in 1991, she returned to Italy with less than $1,000 in her pocket, mostly because American promoters were not willing to risk booking someone who was relatively unknown to them. By 1993, however, the mezzo-soprano had made several very successful appearances throughout the world and had released a number of best-selling recordings. She had, in fact, become the most talked-about new member of the opera world, praised for her supple voice, with its wide, even range, and for her vivaciousness as an actress in comic roles.

Opera's latest star was born in Rome on June 4, 1966. Both her parents were members of the Rome Opera chorus, and Bartoli joked that when she was a child, her baby-sitters were the likes of Rossini and Verdi. She started singing when she was a teenager, and her mother, who coached her, remained her only voice teacher. At the age of 19, she embarked on a professional career when she sang on a television show with baritone Leo Nucci. Soon after, she attracted the attention of conductors Herbert von Karajan and Daniel Barenboim, both of whom recognized her as an abundantly talented singer with a voice perfectly suited to the difficult coloratura repertoire of Mozart and Rossini.

Bartoli's roles included Rosina in Rossini's *Barber of Seville* and the title role in his *Cenerentola,* as well as Cherubino in Mozart's *The Marriage of Figaro* and Dorabella in his *Così fan tutte.* She had also begun to take on roles (Zerlina in Mozart's *Don Giovanni* and Despina in *Così fan tutte*) usually sung by sopranos. A number of her recordings, including *If You Love Me* (a collection of 18th-century Italian love songs) and collections of Rossini and Mozart arias and songs, were huge hits and appeared on the classical best-seller charts. Bartoli continued to conduct her career in a thoughtful and measured way, however, taking on new roles only when she felt ready and limiting her appearances each season. She made her U.S. stage debut (as Rosina) with the Houston (Texas) Grand Opera in April 1993, and she was scheduled to make her debut (as Despina) at the Metropolitan Opera in 1996.

(ELIZABETH LASKEY)

Birt, John

In January 1993 the British Broadcasting Corporation acquired a controversial new director general whose task was to secure the BBC's future at a time of rapid technical, cultural, and economic changes in world broadcasting. John Birt had spent most of his career in independent television, trying to wrest viewers from the BBC. Soon after arriving at his new home, he became convinced of the need to discard some of the BBC's enduring habits—something that did not endear him to every member of his new empire.

Birt was born in Liverpool on Dec. 10, 1944. He joined independent television in 1968, after graduating from the University of Oxford, and became an accomplished producer of current affairs programs. Among his achievements were a series of interviews that journalist David Frost conducted with former U.S. president Richard Nixon in 1977. During the 1970s, Birt developed a rigorous, analytic approach to television journalism that demanded—and rewarded—concentration from audiences. This style became known as "Birtism," sometimes in praise but more often in criticism.

In 1982 Birt was appointed director of programs of London Weekend Television (LWT), one of the most profitable companies in British independent television, not least because of its knack of producing light entertainment programs with mass appeal. Despite being more familiar with the more austere end of television output, Birt found little difficulty in developing this side of LWT. His mixture of experiences appealed to the governors of the BBC when they needed to appoint a new deputy director general in 1987.

Birt's arrival in 1987 provoked controversies that never died away. He argued that despite the BBC's formidable international reputation for fine programs, it was overstaffed and badly managed. Between 1987 and 1993 he oversaw a contraction in BBC staff numbers from 28,000 to 20,000 as a result of cost-saving measures and a series of decisions to buy services and some programs from outside companies. Birt's strategy of reform was, however, sidetracked for a while in February 1993 when he admitted that during his period as deputy director general he had not, in fact, been a member of the BBC staff. Rather, he had been working as a self-employed contractor, which provided some tax advantages. Despite much public criticism, Birt received support from the BBC's governors, who rejected calls for his dismissal. He embarked on the task of negotiating with the British government a new charter for the corporation to succeed the current one, which was due to expire in 1996. (PETER KELLNER)

Bishop, Bronwyn Kathleen

Bronwyn Bishop, a Liberal Party senator for the state of New South Wales, was by 1993 the choice of many Australian conservatives as their most popular personality. Following the disastrous and unexpected defeat of the conservative coalition in the March 1993 general election, Liberal Party leaders in Canberra decided to stick for the time being with their losing chieftain, John Hewson. They overlooked the clear call for new blood focused around the personality of the populist Bishop and, accordingly, throughout 1993 the conservatives were destabilized by continued rumours and suggestions of a possible leadership challenge.

Bishop was born Oct. 19, 1942, and educated at the University of Sydney. She was admitted to practice law in 1967 and was elected 20 years later to the federal Senate. She came to national prominence as a member of the Senate Estimates Committee, where her televised criticism of tax officers, including the head of the tax department, gained her wide popular support. Recognizing her charisma, Hewson tried to win her over to his camp, but he failed. Bishop rejected Hewson's offer to join the 1993 shadow cabinet in a junior capacity, and almost immediately public opinion polls confirmed the wisdom of her decision by keeping her ahead of Hewson as preferred leader of the Liberal Party. While Bishop's main target was Hewson, she did not spare Prime Minister Paul Keating. She castigated Keating, saying that his visit to meet Queen Elizabeth II in September was unconstitutional and that he should cut short his European junket, which the country could not afford, and return home to attend to the problems of the budget and the economy.

Very early, Bishop had decided to be a politician. "I wanted to have a say. Then I thought if I'm going to write the laws of the land, I really ought to understand them. So I decided to do law at university, which was a pretty unusual thing for a girl to do." Having decided to be a politician, she naturally coveted the top jobs. Australian parliamentary practice, however, demanded that party leaders hold seats in the House of Representatives. In October 1993, as if by predestination, a vacancy occurred for the safe seat of MacKellar, and immediately Bishop announced her intention to leave the Senate to seek preselection for that seat. Whether her determination would be sufficient to push her into the party's top job remained in the hands of the extraparliamentary party preselection committee in Sydney, but most Australian newspapers predicted Bishop would win MacKellar and challenge Hewson for the Liberal leadership in 1994.

(A.R.G. GRIFFITHS)

Blair, Tony

Tony Blair established himself during 1993 as the most effective of the younger generation of MPs in the U.K. Labour Party and as favourite to succeed John Smith—in due course—as party leader. Handsome, charismatic, and possessing a determination to modernize progressive politics, Blair was the Labour politician who most worried the U.K.'s Conservatives.

Anthony Charles Lynton Blair was born in Edinburgh on May 6, 1953, and educated in the city and at the University of Oxford. A barrister by profession, he entered the House of Commons in 1983 for the constituency of Sedgefield in the county of Durham. Labour MPs elected him to their shadow cabinet in 1988 at the unusually young age of 35. In November 1990 Neil Kinnock, then party leader, gave him the sensitive task of modernizing Labour's policies on industrial relations. Blair gained widespread credit for persuading both the party and the trade unions to give up the closed shop—the long-established arrangement whereby union membership was compulsory for certain jobs.

After Labour's defeat in the April 1992 general election, Blair became the most outspoken of a loose group known as "the modernizers." Given Labour's devotion to tradition and its fear of innovation, the label had a degree of ambiguity; some left-wingers employed "modernizer" as a term of abuse. Blair, however, insisted in a series of controversial speeches and newspaper articles that Labour needed to redefine its basic purpose by talking less about state control and public ownership and more about opportunity, enterprise, and community.

In July 1992 Smith was elected Labour leader and appointed Blair as shadow home secretary. Blair became responsible for the party's policies on crime—an issue on which opinion polls consistently found that voters favoured the Conservatives. Once again Blair's task was to jettison Labour's reputation for being "soft" on criminals. Once again he succeeded. He argued that the right approach was to be "tough on crime and tough on the causes of crime." He accused the Conservative government of doing too little to tackle the underlying social causes of rising crime or to provide sufficient funds for crime-prevention measures. By late 1993 Labour had overtaken the Conservatives in many people's minds as the party most widely trusted to preserve law and order.

(PETER KELLNER)

Botero, Fernando

The monumental bronze sculptures and distinctive paintings of Colombian-born artist Fernando Botero were at the centre of controversy in 1993. After an extremely popular exhibition of Botero's sculptures of exaggerated human and animal forms was mounted in late 1992 on the Champs-Élysées in Paris, a similar exhibition was held (Sept. 7–Nov. 14, 1993) on prestigious Park Avenue in New York City. The proposed site had stirred heated debate among the boulevard's wealthy residents, who objected not to Botero's work but rather to the crowds that would be flocking to see the sculptures and to the damages they might inflict on the avenue's manicured planting beds. The exhibition was mounted and damage was incurred—a vandal defaced one of the sculptures.

REUTERS/BETTMANN

Another Botero work (actually a clever forgery) caused a furor in the art world during the spring. On May 17, Christie's auction house staged a special sale featuring 11 Botero paintings. The catalog cover showcased "The Dancers," which Botero had painted in 1982. The painting of a monstrously obese couple was actually a forgery; the genuine painting belonged to a Florida collector. The embarrassed auction house quietly removed the copy. The staging of the sale and even the forged work reflected the rising popularity of both Botero's work and Latin-American art in general.

Botero was born April 19, 1932, in Medellín, Colombia. He was heavily influenced by the Spanish Colonial art that surrounded him as a child. Other influences included pre-Columbian art; the Mexican muralists, including Diego Rivera; and Spanish masters Goya and Velázquez. After graduating (1950) from the Liceo de la Universidad de Antioquia in Medellín, he had his first one-man show in Bogotá. Botero then began traveling; he studied in Madrid, where he made a living by copying paintings housed in the Prado and selling them to tourists. He later went to Paris to study the museum paintings of the old masters. In 1960 Botero moved to New York. His easily recognizable paintings of round, corpulent humans and animals became well known to the American art world. In the early '70s Botero moved to Paris and began creating sculptures in addition to painted works on canvas. During the 1980s, Botero's work became quite popular and began to command a high price in the marketplace. In 1992 one of his paintings depicting a brothel scene sold for $1.5 million, a record for a Botero at auction.

In a U.S. exhibition in late 1993, Botero's pencil and watercolour canvases repeated the familiar themes of earlier work—portrait-style images of people (especially of families), bordello scenes, still lifes, and nudes. Botero alternately resided in Paris; New York City; Cajicá, Colombia; and Pietrasanta, Italy.

(CHRISTINE SULLIVAN)

Branagh, Kenneth, and Thompson, Emma

Who was the "better half" of the acting spouses Emma Thompson and Kenneth Branagh? That would have been hard to answer in 1993, a year in which both Britons accomplished big things in film. The sandy-haired Branagh popularized Shakespeare with *Much Ado About Nothing,* a film in which he served as screenwriter, director, and star. His main costar was Thompson, who played Beatrice to his Benedick, the thorn in his side and the throb in his heart. The breezy, colourful *Much Ado* won the praise of most critics and attracted an unusually large and diverse audience. Having achieved his third success in four years, Branagh was hailed as "a one-man British film industry" and appointed to the board of the British Film Institute.

As for Thompson, she won an Academy Award for her work in *Howards End* as a pragmatic bohemian who befriends a dying woman and later marries her widower. The key element in this performance—and in her acclaimed work as a 1930s housekeeper in *The Remains of the Day* (1993)—was her strikingly large, pale blue eyes, through which she revealed more than her character could ever say. Despite her having achieved a prominence that rivaled her husband's, the couple's relationship remained—according to Thompson—one of "playful conflict."

Branagh was born in troubled Belfast, Northern Ireland, on Dec. 10, 1960, but fled to London with his working-class parents nine years later. Forced to be English at school and Irish at home, the confused Branagh sought identity in acting. He attended the Royal Academy of Dramatic Art and later, as a member of the Royal Shakespeare Company, wowed audiences with lead performances in *Hamlet* and *Henry V.* The film version of the latter earned him Oscar nominations for acting and directing. In 1989 he established his own Renaissance Theatre Company.

DAVE BENETT—ALPHA/GLOBE PHOTOS

Thompson was born in London on April 15, 1959, to actors Phyllida Law and Eric Thompson. Having a father who wore garishly checked suits and a mother who cleaned house wearing nothing at all, Thompson developed an appreciation for the ridiculous, and she parlayed it into comedy as part of the University of Cambridge's Footlights troupe. Soon after graduation she ventured into drama, distinguishing herself opposite an intriguing newcomer named Branagh in the BBC's "Fortunes of War" (1986). The two courted, clashed, and finally succumbed to marriage in 1989 after she played his queen-to-be in *Henry V.* They followed on with two more Branagh-directed films, the thriller *Dead Again* (1991), in which they played dual roles, and the sentimental comedy *Peter's Friends* (1992).

Later, screen star Thompson wryly announced that "I don't have to work with my husband anymore. And I now sleep with my Oscar." But that did not faze Branagh, who planned to step out without her, starting with the title role in *Mary Shelley's Frankenstein.*

(MICHAEL AMEDEO)

Campbell, Kim

On June 25, 1993, Kim Campbell fulfilled a lifelong ambition by becoming the first woman to serve as prime minister of Canada. Her tenure, however, was brief. Not even 4½ months after replacing (June 13) Brian Mulroney as leader of the Progressive Conservative Party, Campbell and her party suffered a crushing defeat in the October 25 general elections. The Conservatives won only two seats in the House of Commons, and Campbell herself lost her seat. Soon after Liberal leader Jean Chrétien (*q.v.*) was sworn in as the new prime minister, Campbell resigned (December 13) as leader of the Conservatives.

A political moderate in the tradition of Edmund Burke, Campbell viewed politics as the art of the possible. She was noted for her moderate, middle-of-the-road positions on issues. As minister of justice, she successfully dealt with such controversial issues as abortion, sexual abuse, and gun control.

Avril Phaedra Campbell was born March 10, 1947, in Port Alberni, B.C. After receiving a degree in political science from the University of British Columbia (1969), she attended (1970–73) the London School of Economics on a fellowship. In 1983 she obtained a law degree from the University of British Columbia. Campbell, often described as ambitious, centred her career around politics and was elected a Vancouver school trustee in 1980. As chairman (1983) and vice-chairman (1984) of the Vancouver School Board, she gained a reputation for endorsing moderate fiscal policies. In British Columbian provincial politics, Campbell was associated with the Social Credit Party. She served as key policy adviser to Premier Bill Bennett before she won a seat in the Legislative Assembly (1986). In that same year she ran for the leadership of the Social Credit Party but lost. In 1988 Campbell turned her attention to federal politics and the Progressive Conservative Party. That year she was elected to the House of Commons, representing the British Columbian riding of Vancouver Centre.

Campbell's mentor, Prime Minister Mulroney, saw her as a possible successor and fostered her career in Parliament. As a member of the Cabinet, she was named minister of state for Indian affairs and northern development (1989), minister of justice and attorney general of Canada (1990), and minister of defense and minister of veterans affairs (1993). Mulroney had brought her into the inner Cabinet in 1990 as a member of the Expenditure Review Committee. She was also placed in charge of patronage for her home province of British Columbia. In 1993 Mulroney named Campbell a member of the Operations Committee of the Cabinet, which made decisions on all major bills, communications strategies, and political planning. Even though Campbell became an international media celebrity in 1992 when a photograph was published showing her with bare shoulders and holding her lawyer's robes before her, she did not flinch over the controversy but remained steadfast in becoming Conservative Party leader. (DIANE LOIS WAY)

Cantona, Eric

Eric Cantona was sometimes described as the most talented and controversial footballer of his generation. Yet the onetime enfant terrible of France became the Gallic golden boy of English soccer, first with Leeds United in 1992 and a few months later at Manchester United.

Tall, dark, and temperamental, Cantona was a loner with a short fuse, and controversy rarely strayed from him. Born in Paris on May 24, 1966, he was discovered by the Auxerre club at age 15. He made his debut in the French First Division during 1983–84 and finally established himself in 1986–87. That same season he played for the French Under-21 team. He made the first of more than 30 appearances for the national team in August 1987, scoring against West Germany. He was transferred to Marseille for £2.2 million in 1988, and then his troubles began in earnest. He was banned from the national team for a year for openly criticizing France's coach, and he was involved in a bitter row with spectators and sent off in a charity match.

Unhappy about his behaviour, Marseille loaned him to Bordeaux and then Montpellier, where he helped to win the French Cup. After half a season at Nîmes, he was offered a trial by Sheffield Wednesday. He walked out on them, however, and in February 1992 signed for Leeds, where he became an overnight sensation and helped the team to the English League title three months later. A terrace chant of "Ooh aah, Cantona" was made into a pop record and reached number 64 in the British charts in September 1992.

Leeds was eliminated from the European Cup, and Cantona was surprisingly transferred to Manchester United in November for £1.2 million. Leeds supporters turned on their former hero. Unsold Cantona T-shirts were hastily dispatched to clothe Romanian refugees. After returning to Leeds for a match with Manchester United in February 1993, Cantona was fined £1,000 for spitting at spectators. Yet at Manchester he became even more idolized, and the United manager, Alex Ferguson, called the highly skilled forward his most influential signing. Cantona was a key factor in United's first league title in 26 years as he became the first player to win the championship with different teams in successive seasons.

But controversy continued to stalk him. In November 1993 he was banned from four European Cup matches after accusing referees of taking bribes. He also said that he would never play for France again at the Parc des Princes in Paris but then did so in the next match. On November 27, a year to the day after leaving Leeds, Cantona pledged to stay with United for the rest of his life. To celebrate he scored the only goal of the game at Coventry. (JACK ROLLIN)

Chen Kaige

Chinese movie director Chen Kaige would not likely ever forget the evening of May 24, 1993. On that date judges at the Cannes International Film Festival announced that his fifth film, *Farewell, My Concubine (Bawang bieji)*, had been chosen joint winner (with Jane Campion's *The Piano*) of the prestigious Palme d'Or (Golden Palm). The film also won the International Critics Award "for its brilliant combination of the spectacular and the intimate." No other Chinese director had ever been so honoured. The film follows the lives of two male members of the Peking Opera from their youth in the 1920s to the years after the traumatic Cultural Revolution (1966–76). The female lead was played by Gong Li and the male lead by Leslie Cheung, both established film stars in China. The film was also noteworthy for its honest depiction of homosexual love and the betrayal of loved ones and society.

The enthusiastic response the film received abroad was not matched at home. In July the Chinese government banned an already-censored version after a two-week run in Shanghai and a single showing in Beijing (Peking). Authorities cited homosexual conduct as justification for the ban. Discouraged by this rebuke, Chen set aside plans for two works on the Cultural Revolution. A month later, however, the film reopened in China with additional editing that did not substantially alter the basic story line and preserved the final scene—a suicide.

Chen, the son of teacher and filmmaker Chen Huai'ai, was born in Beijing on Aug. 12, 1952. In 1967 he was sent to the rural province of Yunnan to work on a rubber plantation. During his time among the impoverished people, Chen was indelibly impressed by the vast differences between the aspirations of the peasants and the harsh reality of their lives.

After leaving Yunnan, Chen began a five-year stint in the army, which included a brief tour in Laos. When he returned to Beijing in 1975, he elected to pursue a career in film rather than a university degree with a major in poetry. In 1978 he entered the Beijing Film Academy, which had just reopened after the Cultural Revolution. Not long after his graduation, Chen became a leading member of what became known as the "fifth generation" of Chinese filmmakers.

Chen's first film, *Yellow Earth* (*Huang tudi*), won critical acclaim after its release in 1984. It tells the story of a Communist soldier who visits a village to collect old songs. This film was followed the next year by *The Big Parade* (*Dayuebing*), which depicts young soldiers training for a military parade in Beijing. *King of the Children* (*Haizi wang*), the story of a young teacher sent to a squalid rural school "to learn from the peasants," appeared in 1987. Chen's fourth film, *Life on a String* (*Bienzou bienchang*), a 1991 release, chronicles the deeds of a blind storyteller and his blind apprentice as they roam the countryside. In all his films, Chen offered a realistic, sensitive, compassionate, and unflinching view of the lives and hopes of the Chinese people.

(JAMES HENNELLEY)

Chrétien, Jean

On Nov. 4, 1993, Jean Chrétien was sworn in as prime minister of Canada soon after his Liberal Party won a large majority of the seats in the House of Commons in the October 25 general elections. Chrétien, who for years had topped public opinion polls as one of Canada's best-liked politicians, handily won in his Quebec riding of St. Maurice. Chrétien passionately embraced a united Canada and envisioned a nation in which all Canadians would feel at home in any part of the country. His vision was endangered, however, because the Bloc Québécois, a party dedicated to Quebec independence, had emerged as the official opposition party following the elections.

Joseph-Jacques Jean Chrétien was born Jan. 11, 1934, in Shawinigan, Que. He studied law at Laval University, Quebec City, Que., and was called to the Quebec bar in 1958. Politics, however, had always attracted him. As a child he had joined his father in political activities. As a university student Chrétien served (1957–58) as vice president of the Liberal Students of Canada. He was first elected to the House of Commons in 1963 and represented his riding of St. Maurice until 1986, when he resigned to return to the practice of law. In 1990 he resumed political life when he was elected leader of the Liberal Party. Returning to the Commons as the member from the riding of Beausejour in New Brunswick, Chrétien was leader of the opposition for almost three years.

TOM HANSON—CANAPRESS

When Chrétien arrived in Ottawa in 1963, he spoke only a few words of English. He rapidly learned that language, however, and quickly rose in party ranks. He astutely outmaneuvered his fellow members to capture nine successive Cabinet posts. In those positions he distinguished himself as an incisive and shrewd administrator. In 1965 he was appointed parliamentary secretary to the prime minister. The following year he was appointed parliamentary secretary to the minister of finance, becoming minister without portfolio in 1967 and in 1977 the first French-Canadian to hold the position of minister of finance. As minister of Indian affairs and northern development (1968–74), he created 10 national parks. As minister of justice and attorney general of Canada (1980), Chrétien had the difficult task of negotiating with the provincial governments and the British government to secure the repatriation of the Canadian constitution. At the time of the Quebec referendum on independence, Chrétien was given the task of coordinating the federal government's effort to keep Quebec in the confederation. In 1984 Chrétien became deputy prime minister.

Chrétien, whom none could accuse of snobbery, cultivated the image of a rough-hewn man of the people. Self-assured, he possessed a keen political intuition. He was often underestimated by his opponents, most glaringly so in the 1993 elections, when some thought Chrétien could be defeated in his own riding. As prime minister he faced the immediate task of dealing with the burgeoning federal deficit, the economic problems of the country, and the passage of the North American Free Trade Agreement. (DIANE LOIS WAY)

Ciller, Tansu

In a year filled with extraordinary departures from the status quo, the election in 1993 of Tansu Ciller as prime minister of Turkey nonetheless ranked as remarkable. It was not so much Ciller's meteoric rise in politics or her overcoming of the opposition of Turkey's longtime leader Suleyman Demirel that made this elevation to head of state so noteworthy. Rather, what made Ciller's election revolutionary was a matter of gender. On June 25, 1993, she officially became Turkey's first woman prime minister and, perhaps even more noteworthy, the first female without a family political connection to head an Islamic country.

Ciller was born in 1946 to an affluent family in Istanbul, where she later graduated from the University of Bosporus with a degree in economics. She continued her studies in the United States, earning graduate degrees from the Universities of New Hampshire and Connecticut and attending Yale University. Ciller then returned to Turkey to teach and, at the age of 36, she became the nation's youngest full professor. Moreover, at the age of 17 she had married a man whom she persuaded to take her surname (a departure from custom almost without precedent in Turkey). Together with her husband, the owner of a chain of convenience stores and a former banker, she amassed a fortune of some $60 million through real estate speculation.

Though she was wealthy, attractive, intellectually accomplished, and professionally prominent (she was fluent in English and German and the author of nine works on economics), Ciller harboured political aspirations. She joined the ruling True Path Party (DYP) in 1990, was elected to Parliament the following year (one of eight women in the 450-seat legislative assembly), and was named economics minister in Demirel's coalition government. Although she advocated greater privatization of state-owned firms and a balanced budget, it was during her tenure as economics minister that government debt soared, inflation climbed to 65%, and the country suffered a downgrading of its international credit rating.

Despite these woes, the DYP selected Ciller as its leader at a special party conference on June 13, 1993. The office of prime minister had been vacant since Demirel's election as president in May following the death of Pres. Turgut Ozal (*see* OBITUARIES) in April. When Ciller presented her Cabinet, more than half the ministers were new, and many longtime Demirel supporters were out of policy-making positions.

As she assumed power in Turkey, Ciller's greatest challenges included dealing both with the rising tide of violence among Kurds in southeastern Turkey and with the pressing need to reduce government spending. Though Ciller faced difficult choices, she appeared ready to make tough decisions. (JEROLD L. KELLMAN)

Clarke, Kenneth Harry

In May 1993, with his government in trouble and the U.K.'s economy still struggling to escape recession, Prime Minister John Major (*q.v.*) turned to one of the most combative members of his Cabinet to restore his fortunes. He appointed Kenneth Clarke as chancellor of the Exchequer. In so doing, Major took the risk of promoting the man most likely to replace him as Conservative Party leader if his premiership foundered.

Clarke was born in Nottingham on July 2, 1940. Twenty years later he was one of a group of University of Cambridge undergraduates, including Michael Howard (*q.v.*), who became close friends and rose to positions of prominence. Clarke subsequently became a barrister (1963) before entering the House of Commons in 1970 as member for Rushcliffe, near Nottingham. He quickly established himself on the liberal, pro-European wing of his party. However, when Margaret Thatcher became prime minister in 1979, Clarke was immediately given a junior government post, working for a friend from his student days, Norman Fowler, at the Ministry of Transport.

Six years later Clarke was promoted to the Cabinet as deputy employment secretary. In 1988 he was switched to health secretary, a post that gave him a chance to prove his fighting spirit. In the autumn of 1989 he imposed a pay settlement on ambulance workers, rejecting their demands for arbitration. They went on strike, refusing to respond to all nonemergency calls. He resisted calls for compromise, and eventually the strike was abandoned. Clarke won high praise from inside his party for successfully standing firm; in particular, the Conservative right wing warmed to his style.

In November 1990, following Sir Geoffrey Howe's resignation from the Cabinet, Thatcher moved Clarke to education; four weeks later Major became prime minister and kept Clarke in the same job until April 1992, when he appointed Clarke as home secretary—one of the few Conservative opponents of capital punishment to hold the job. Following Norman Lamont's dismissal in May 1993, Clarke was appointed chancellor of the Exchequer. In his first budget, in November 1993, Clarke increased taxation, in contrast to his party's 1992 election pledge to keep taxes down. His measures were unpopular with voters, but his main concern was to please other Conservative MPs. And they, almost unanimously, welcomed the robust and confident way in which Clarke had overcome his first difficult hurdle as chancellor. (PETER KELLNER)

Clinton, Hillary Rodham

During the 1992 presidential campaign, Hillary Rodham Clinton commented that she could have stayed at home, baked cookies, and had teas rather than pursue her own legal career, a statement for which she took a lot of heat. In 1993, as leader of the Task Force on National Health Care Reform, the nation's first professional first lady proved that she preferred to take the heat on Capitol Hill rather than in the kitchen.

JEFFREY MARKOWITZ—SYGMA

Hillary Diane Rodham was born in Chicago on Oct. 26, 1947, and reared in a staunch Republican household. An early influence on her life was her church youth minister, who encouraged his students to socialize with people from other racial backgrounds and once took a group to hear (and meet) civil rights activist Martin Luther King, Jr.

Hillary graduated from high school in 1965 in the top 5% of her class and was voted most likely to succeed. She entered Wellesley (Mass.) College, majoring in political science and serving as head of the local chapter of the Young Republicans. Her political proclivities took a sharp turn in the late 1960s, when the assassinations of Malcolm X, King, and Sen. Robert Kennedy, coupled with the violence she witnessed outside the 1968 Democratic national convention, harkened her back to the teachings of her youth minister and converted her to the Democratic Party. She worked to have more black students admitted to Wellesley, wrote her senior thesis on poverty and community development, and enrolled at Yale Law School, where she met Bill Clinton (*q.v.*). In 1975 they were married, although she opted to retain her maiden name.

The couple moved to Little Rock, Ark., in 1976 when Bill was elected state attorney general. In 1978 Hillary aided Bill's campaign for governor while working at Rose Law Firm, where she was made a partner in 1980. During her husband's first term as governor, she served as head of the Rural Health Advisory Committee, which dealt with the problem of providing health care to isolated areas. After Bill lost his reelection bid, Hillary underwent an image makeover: losing weight, changing her hair and clothing style, and deciding to use her husband's last name. Bill was returned to office in 1982 and subsequently served four more terms, during which Hillary led the drive for statewide school reforms and was twice named one of the nation's top 100 lawyers.

As first lady, Hillary drew both praise and criticism for her image as independent, outspoken, and supportive. Despite a grueling presidential campaign, ongoing allegations of her husband's infidelity when he was governor, and the death of her father in April 1993, she completed an exhausting series of meetings and hearings. In September the president unveiled to the nation the fruits of his wife's labours—a proposal for the first national health-care program in the U.S. (ANTHONY L. GREEN)

Clinton, William (Bill) Jefferson

On Jan. 20, 1993, Bill Clinton was inaugurated as the 42nd president of the United States and became the first Democrat to inhabit the White House in 12 years. Having campaigned as the candidate for change, he faced high expectations from his party and the nation as well. However, in his first year as president, Bill Clinton wound up with a mixed bag of failures and successes.

Even before he was sworn in, Clinton ran into a snag when it was revealed that Zoë Baird, his nominee for attorney general, had employed an illegal immigrant couple as domestic help and failed to pay the required taxes. Less than one month after announcing the nomination, he withdrew Baird's name. Later, after a severe backlash in reaction to his effort to uphold a campaign pledge to end the ban on homosexuals in the military, Clinton wound up with a compromise policy of "don't ask, don't tell, don't pursue." However, amid these and other early setbacks, Clinton was generally praised for choosing his wife, Hillary Rodham Clinton (*q.v.*), to head the commission on national health-care reform. He was again hailed for the passage of the family-leave bill. His appointment of Ruth Bader Ginsburg (*q.v.*) to the Supreme Court also met with a favourable response.

Delivering on another campaign promise—deficit reduction—proved to be tougher. Clinton submitted his budget to Congress calling for a nearly $500 billion reduction of the national debt over five years. Although the bill had been altered somewhat from Clinton's original to ensure passage, it passed the House of Representatives by only two votes and cleared the Senate by a tiebreaking vote cast by Vice Pres. Al Gore. The president later stated that it was "just the first step in our attempts to assert control over our financial affairs, to invest in our future." Toward that end Congress passed legislation in November to implement the North American Free Trade Agreement, which Clinton signed in December. He also lobbied successfully for passage of gun-control legislation, the so-called Brady bill.

Trouble spots throughout the world threatened Clinton's concentration on domestic affairs. U.S. troops were still in Somalia—where about 30 Americans had already been killed—but Clinton set a March 1994 deadline for their return. A diplomatic settlement proved elusive in Haiti, and a proposal to send troops to Bosnia and Herzegovina was still being discussed.

Clinton was born William Jefferson Blythe IV on Aug. 19, 1946, in Hope, Ark. His father died before he was born, and he was raised by his mother and stepfather, Roger Clinton, whose last name he took at age 15. Having served five terms as governor of Arkansas, he announced his candidacy for president on Oct. 3 , 1991, and subsequently defeated Pres. George Bush in the general election in November 1992. (ANTHONY L. GREEN)

Coleman, Ornette

"I believe music is really a free thing," said Ornette Coleman, "and any way you can enjoy it, you should." When Coleman burst upon the jazz scene in 1959, there were two reasons for the sensation he caused. First, there was the intensity of the unrestrained melody and compelling, crying sound that poured from Coleman's white plastic alto saxophone. Second, there was his shocking, free approach to improvising; he abandoned the fixed harmonic patterns that had been the basis of jazz structure for its entire previous existence. "He's a fake," said some listeners; "He's a genius," said others; and the controversy over the jazz revolution that Coleman began continued into the 1990s.

In 1993, a year when Coleman seldom performed in concert, the publication of the first biographical-critical study of him and the release of his six-CD boxed set, *Beauty Is a Rare Thing,* brought Coleman back into the headlines once again. The boxed set gathered all of his 1959–61 recordings for Atlantic Records, including two works by Gunther Schuller, seven quartet pieces that had appeared only on a Japanese LP, and six tracks previously believed lost. They included recordings as influential as Louis Armstrong's and Charlie Parker's early masterpieces.

Born on March 19, 1930, in Fort Worth, Texas, Coleman began playing saxes as a teenager. Early in his career he was fired from a touring minstrel troupe and assaulted by enraged listeners on a blues tour; he also became fascinated with the unexplored harmonic and melodic possibilities of bebop. In Los Angeles, where he lived in the 1950s, and where poverty forced him to buy a plastic sax instead of a standard metal horn, he was considered eccentric. Nevertheless, he taught his harmolodic theory—"using the melody, the harmony and the rhythm all equal"—to young musicians and made his first recordings.

Coleman's New York debut, in 1959, made him an instant celebrity. A small, growing set of musicians, including John Coltrane and Miles Davis, adopted his "free jazz" principles. After years of struggle, Coleman found himself overworked, and in 1963 he retired to compose and to teach himself to play trumpet and violin, returning in 1965 as leader of a new trio. Thereafter, he alternated periods of performing and touring with long periods of composing; although several of his chamber works were recorded, only one of his orchestral works, an edited version of his symphony *Skies of America*, was released in an album.

Controversy seemed to follow Coleman's every move, and the use of his 10-year-old son in his band especially drew criticism. In the 1970s, when free jazz had become the mainstream of jazz evolution, Coleman played with the traditional musicians of a Moroccan mountain village, and then he formed an electric jazz-rock band, Prime Time. The band continued to be his principal performing medium, to the groans of critics, who relented long enough to praise his 1991 soundtrack solos in the film *Naked Lunch*; he expended most of his musical energies, however, in composing. A symphony, *The Oldest Language,* was conceived as a performance piece for ethnic players from around the world. (JOHN LITWEILER)

Denard, Robert

"Cry 'Havoc,' and let slip the dogs of war." Shakespeare's line seemed particularly appropriate on April 5, 1993, as Bob Denard, one of the world's most notorious mercenary soldiers, walked free from a Paris courtroom. For the French soldier of fortune famed for his exploits in Africa throughout the 1960s and '70s, it was a vindication of his life's work. Some observers viewed the trial as confirmation of what many had already suspected—that Denard was something more than a freelance soldier for sale to the highest bidder. Rather, as evidenced by the testimony at trial and by Denard's own admission, many of his activities had been carried out with the tacit approval of the French government.

Denard was born in France on Jan. 20, 1929. Following service with the French navy in Indochina, he joined (1952) the police force of what was then the French colony of Morocco. There Denard was convicted of taking part in an assassination attempt against French Prime Minister Pierre Mendès-France. After serving a 14-month jail term, Denard was acquitted of any wrongdoing and returned to France. In 1961, after answering a newspaper advertisement for "security men," he returned to Africa as a mercenary.

Denard first fought for the government of Moise Tshombe, who was attempting to lead the secession of the mineral-rich Katanga (now Shaba) province from the rest of the former Belgian Congo (now Zaire). Then, following a brief period of service in Yemen, Denard returned (1965) to Africa. He served in Zaire, at one point leading a force of 1,100 mercenaries, known as *les affreux* ("the terrible ones"), until he was severely wounded in 1967. With a force of some 50 mercenaries, Denard invaded the Comoros in 1978 and arrested Pres. Ali Soilih (later shot and killed while "attempting to escape"). Denard installed Ahmed Abdallah as president of the Comoros and took control of the Presidential Guard. In 1989, however, following the assassination of Abdallah and faced with the possibility of unrest in the region, the French government sent a naval task force, complete with 3,000 troops, to remove Denard and his mercenaries from the Comoros. Rather than fight the French force, Denard went into exile in South Africa.

He remained in South Africa until February 1993, when he voluntarily returned to France to face a five-year prison sentence for his 1977 role in a failed coup in Benin. Denard, arrested in Paris as he stepped off the plane, was held without bail. Within weeks of his arrest, however, both French government and military leaders spoke out on his behalf, acknowledging what Denard had maintained all along—that most of his actions had been undertaken with the knowledge and tacit approval of the government. The court overturned the original prison sentence and replaced it with a five-year suspended term. Although Denard still faced an investigation of his role in the Comoros, most observers felt that the aging mercenary would remain free.

(JOHN H. MATHEWS)

Di Pietro, Antonio

Enjoying name recognition and adulation typically accorded to rock stars and professional athletes, Antonio Di Pietro discovered in 1993 that fame had its liabilities, too. The Milan magistrate, whose Mani Pulite ("Clean Hands") anticorruption drive gave rise to graffiti testimonials ("Grazie, Di Pietro") throughout Italy, found that only with a police escort in a bulletproof car could he travel. Worse yet, the man who sought to expose and sweep away wrongdoing at the highest levels of Italy's political and business establishment was himself targeted with accusations of abuse of power.

Di Pietro was born in southern Italy in 1950. He was raised in modest circumstances and served a brief stint in Germany as a migrant factory worker before turning to a career in law enforcement. Di Pietro worked his way through night school as a police officer, earning a degree in jurisprudence. In the mid-1980s he became a magistrate, a position that in Italy functions as both a detective and a prosecutor.

In the late 1980s, Di Pietro gained a reputation for high-tech crime busting; he used computers to compile and store vast amounts of data on individuals involved in scams. By scrutinizing both these early cases and computer dossiers, Di Pietro and his associates uncovered a systematic corruption scheme in which businesspeople routinely paid bribes to receive government contracts. In early 1992 Di Pietro led the Milan sting operation that nabbed a Socialist Party leader as he accepted a payoff in exchange for a city contract. Several weeks later the accused politician began naming accomplices from far beyond the boundaries of Milan.

The scandal was vast and revealed that corruption had become routine and institutionalized in Italy. Virtually all the political parties participated in the graft, while major businesses collaborated to arrange the beneficiaries of given contracts. As the investigation gained momentum, business executives reportedly sought appointments with Di Pietro to reveal what they knew and to implicate Italy's leading politicians, all in an effort to escape arrest and imprisonment themselves. The most prominent of those fingered, former prime minister Bettino Craxi, resigned from Parliament and launched a counterattack. His claim that Di Pietro was part of a conspiracy to eradicate Italy's Socialist Party generated little support. Craxi's charge, however, that the Milan magistrate was acting like a medieval inquisitor gained resonance because Di Pietro was reportedly incarcerating untried executives and politicians with common criminals (some infected with the AIDS virus) in Milan's San Vittore prison. Though Di Pietro's methods appeared harsh to some, few sympathized with the alleged offenders, who reportedly had cost taxpayers some $20 billion over the past decade while securing inflated government contracts for themselves. (JEROLD L. KELLMAN)

Diouf, Abdou

One might have thought that being head of a fractious West African state would be a tall order, but Senegal's 1.96-m (6-ft 4-in) president, Abdou Diouf, had shown for more than a decade that he had the stature for the job. Reelected to his third successive term in March 1993, Diouf was a man in the mold of the new African statesman. He seemed less comfortable with the rough-and-tumble of party politics than with the steady security of the bureaucracy, where, as a protégé of Senegal's longtime president, poet and statesman Léopold Sédar Senghor, he got his start in government. *West Africa* magazine pointed out that a number of French politicians, such as Valéry Giscard d'Estaing and Jacques Chirac, began their political careers in government administration as well. Diouf projected a style of modesty and sincerity that masked a determination—and probably ambition—of steel. He built his distinguished career upon an image of a supertechnocrat and new-style African democrat.

MEIGNEUX—IMAPRESS/ARCHIVE PHOTOS

Diouf was born on Sept. 7, 1935, in Louga, northern Senegal, the son of a postman. He was a member of the Serer ethnic community and a devout Muslim. He read the Qur'an and attended the well-known Lycée Faidherbe in St. Louis, then still the capital of Senegal, later studying law and political science in the law faculty of the University of Dakar. In 1958 he went to Paris and studied law at the Sorbonne. Shortly after his return home in 1960, Diouf joined the civil service, and over the next four years, he was appointed to a succession of posts: regional governor, secretary-general to the government (a key post that he took over at the remarkably young age of 29 and held for three years), and minister of planning and industry. He quickly established a reputation for fair-mindedness when he oversaw the liberalization of the political system. On Feb. 28, 1970, Diouf became the country's first prime minister, a post that had only just been created through a change in the constitution. He retained that position for 11 years and upon the retirement of President Senghor and in accordance with the constitution, he succeeded to the presidency. He was elected in his own right two years later, was reelected in 1988, and won a third term in the multiparty elections in 1993.

Diouf gained international prominence as a delegate to the Organization of African Unity (OAU) in 1983, when he played a key role at the June 1983 summit meeting, and as that organization's chairman in 1985–86, when his decisive leadership and moderation restored confidence in that troubled body. He served a second term as OAU chairman in 1992–93 and he also served as chairman of the Economic Community of West African States (ECOWAS), the Islamic Conference, and the G-15 nations. With problems mounting at home, however, it seemed likely that Abdou Diouf would be concentrating his quite considerable talents on the political situation in Dakar for the remainder of his seven-year term as president. (COLIN LEGUM)

Fatialofa, Peter
On July 31, 1993, Western Samoa played an official rugby union international match against New Zealand. The contest, at Eden Park in Auckland, was the culmination of the gradual rise of the Pacific island team from comparative obscurity to a place alongside the major rugby union-playing nations. Captain and star of the team was Peter Fatialofa.

Like their counterparts in Fiji and Tonga, Samoans began rugby union play in the 1920s and quickly took to the physical, confrontational aspects of the game. But progress was spasmodic and depended a great deal on the interaction with New Zealand, traditionally one of the game's great powers. In the inaugural Rugby World Cup in 1987, Fiji and Tonga both qualified for the tournament, but Western Samoa did not. Consequently, Samoans put considerable effort into preparation for the 1991 tournament. It involved "calling home" players such as Fatialofa, who, though born in Apia, the Samoan capital, on April 26, 1959, had spent much of his life in Auckland. He had played club rugby for Ponsonby and, over an eight-year period, 72 games for Auckland, which became during that period one of the great provincial teams in world rugby.

Fatialofa—Peter Fats, as he was known—first played for Western Samoa on its 1988 tour to Wales and Ireland. A 120-kg (265-lb) furniture mover whose specialty was pianos, he proved a powerful scrummager and a formidable opponent with the ball in hand. He was appointed captain of the team in 1989 and led the country through the qualifying rounds and into the 1991 World Cup, played in Britain and France. It was then that Samoan rugby won the recognition it craved; by beating Wales and Argentina and losing only to Australia (the eventual cup winners), Fatialofa and his team qualified for the quarterfinals, where they lost to Scotland.

That tournament paved the way for Western Samoa's first international competition with New Zealand, which represented a coming-of-age for the islanders. Fatialofa captained the team in the prestigious South Pacific provincial tournament and then during the nine-match tour to New Zealand that culminated in the game at Eden Park. Although Western Samoa lost 35–13, its play on tour was generally recognized as bringing qualities of excitement and adventure to New Zealand rugby. (DAVID HANDS)

Fischer, Timothy Andrew
Tim Fischer was reelected leader of the right-of-centre National Party of Australia after the Nationals won two additional seats from the Australian Labor Party in the March 1993 general election. As chief of the progressive conservative party representing rural and regional Australia, he was seldom out of the headlines in 1993, jumping in where others feared to tread. In a speech in Western Australia, Fischer claimed that taxpayers spent about $A 1.3 billion a year on the small Aboriginal population but that this generosity was never acknowledged. He warned that people in rural areas would soon begin to resent such generosity. He particularly complained that "the poor struggling farmers couldn't get anywhere near a brand new four-wheel drive, air-conditioned vehicle, but local Aboriginal communities had plenty and replaced them every two years." Fischer also narrowly escaped a serious mauling by the press when he made statements to the effect that Australia's foreign policy was rather too anti-Arab and pro-Israel. In neither case, however, did he back away from his much-criticized convictions.

Fischer, himself a Roman Catholic, was particularly critical of Prime Minister Paul Keating's attempt to link his own Irish-Catholic heritage with support for Australia's republican movement. Fischer warned that sectarianism was never very far from the surface in Australian political life and added that Keating had been irresponsible in fanning its embers by saying that an Irish-Catholic background had led to his commitment to abolishing links with the British monarchy. Fischer felt no such allegiance. On the contrary, he spoke out against the republican movement, launching a fierce campaign urging Australians not to change the constitution without considering "the huge ramifications of making the president commander in chief of the Australian armed forces."

Fischer was born May 3, 1946, and educated at Xavier College, Melbourne. He saw military service in Vietnam as a platoon commander and transport officer in the First Royal Australian Regiment in 1967. Fischer entered the federal parliament in 1984, representing the interests of farmers and country people, after a career in New South Wales state politics, where he was National Party member in the House of Assembly. He rose through the ranks of the federal National Party and became the party's leader in 1990.

(A.R.G. GRIFFITHS)

Franco, Itamar
The anniversary of Itamar Franco's first year as president of Brazil was hardly cause for celebration in 1993. Vice President Franco had become acting president on Oct. 2, 1992, and was sworn in as president on Dec. 29, 1992, as the impeachment trial of former president Fernando Collor began. Franco's image as a quiet, down-to-earth, honest man familiar with the workings of Brazilian politics contrasted sharply with that of his slick, flashy predecessor, who was plagued by charges of corruption and inability to move reforms through the legislature. One year later, however, the corruption scandal had spread to the legislative branch. Franco seemed temperamental and indecisive—overseeing some 20 ministerial changes, including four ministers of the crucial finance portfolio. He appeared unable to tame one of "the most fragmented party systems in Latin America," and the ruling coalition seemed fragile indeed. His 14.5% approval rating was one of the worst ever. On Oct. 18, 1993, Franco offered to resign if Congress would schedule early elections (currently set for November 1994), but his offer was declined. The right feared that early elections would mean victory for the popular Workers Party; the left wanted to milk the ongoing corruption scandal; and business interests sought to avoid postponement of a debate concerning reform of the 1988 constitution. So it seemed that Franco might, in fact, serve out his term through January 1995.

Itamar Augusto Cautiero Franco was born July 28, 1931. After attending the School of Engineering of Juiz de Fora in Minas Gerais, he served (1966–74) as mayor of Juiz de Fora, which was also his hometown. He was a founding member of the Brazilian Democratic Movement (now the largest party in Congress) when it was the only opposition party permitted under military rule. Franco was a senator for 16 years, leading committees on economy and finance (1983–84) and investigating corruption (in the late 1980s). He lost a bid to be governor of Minas Gerais in 1986 but was later picked by Collor to balance the ticket and thus became vice president in 1990.

Franco was an unusual president—a private man who disliked public attention and criticism. In his first year in office he held only one scheduled news conference and Cabinet meetings on an average of one every three months. When a Rio newspaper proclaimed him "a president with a vice president's agenda," he stopped making his schedules public. He spoke only Portuguese and was an economic nationalist opposed to neoliberal market reforms. This put him at odds with the IMF among others. At a meeting of primarily Spanish-speaking Latin-American heads of state, he reportedly remained aloof and did not attend official dinners. And it was six months before he received the U.S. ambassador—despite the fact that the U.S. was Brazil's leading foreign investor and trading partner. Brazil's most widely read columnist summed up, "Itamar Franco would be a good city councilman in Juiz de Fora with his office in the corner barbershop"—not a viable option for the president of the fifth largest country in the world at a time of economic and political crisis. (ELLEN FINKELSTEIN)

Gerstner, Lou
When Lou Gerstner assumed the mantle of chief executive officer (CEO) at IBM in April 1993, he inherited what was called the toughest job in corporate America. Despite being the world's largest computer manufacturer and one of the nation's leading companies, with $60 billion in sales, IBM was reeling from losses of $5 billion in 1992. Gerstner was chosen to succeed John Akers as CEO after several of the nation's top executives declined the daunting position. Observers were surprised that a company known for its insular and traditional business methods would choose an outsider with little technological experience. But Gerstner also had the reputation of being a tough and decisive manager with a history of rebuilding corporations.

Louis Vincent Gerstner, Jr., was born in Mineola, N.Y., on March 1, 1942. He studied engineering at Dartmouth College, Hanover, N.H. (B.A., 1963), where he graduated magna cum laude. After attending Harvard University (M.B.A., 1965) he joined McKinsey & Co., a management consulting firm in New York City. By 1970 he had become one of the youngest partners in the history of the firm and distinguished himself by overhauling the bankrupt Penn Central Railway. In January 1978 he joined American Express as executive vice president and head of its travel-related services division. In his first 10 years there, the number of currencies in which the American Express credit card was issued doubled, the number of total cardholders quadrupled, and travel-related services became the most profitable division in the company. As president (1985–89) he increased corporate net income by 66%.

In March 1989 he accepted the challenge of becoming the new CEO of RJR Nabisco, which had been acquired the previous November by Kohlberg Kravis Roberts & Co. in one of the largest leveraged buyouts in corporate history. As a result of the takeover, the company was saddled with a massive $25 billion debt, with annual interest costs of $3 billion. During his four-year tenure at RJR Nabisco, Gerstner pared the debt down to $14 billion, sold off $6 billion of peripheral assets, and trimmed general expenses.

In his first six months at the helm of IBM, he faced criticism that he lacked vision by focusing on immediate cash management. He froze some long-term projects and continued the cost-cutting measures that Akers had begun in the late 1980s by ordering 35,000 additional layoffs and by reducing overhead costs and operating expenses. Gerstner also arranged an $8.9 billion write-off against company earnings—one of the largest in corporate history. Although a frequent proponent of decentralization, he rejected a proposal to break IBM into smaller divisions.

(TOM MICHAEL)

Ginsburg, Ruth Bader
On June 14, 1993, at a White House press conference held in the Rose Garden, Ruth Bader Ginsburg stood with U.S. Pres. Bill Clinton as he nominated her to replace retiring U.S. Supreme Court Justice Byron R. White. In her acceptance speech Ginsburg, a judge on the U.S. Court of Appeals since 1980 and a pioneer in equal-rights litigation, spoke of her own struggles with discrimination as a woman in the legal profession. In tribute to her mother, Celia, who had died the day before Ginsburg's high school graduation, she said, "I pray that I may be all that she would have been had she lived in an age when women could aspire and achieve and daughters are cherished as much as sons." When the U.S. Senate confirmed her nomination in late summer, this "daughter of the revolution" became the 107th justice—and only the second woman in history—to sit on the nation's highest court.

RON SACHS—ARCHIVE PHOTOS

Ruth Joan Bader was born in New York City on March 15, 1933, and raised in the Flatbush section of Brooklyn. She graduated from James Madison High School at age 17 and in the fall of 1950 entered Cornell University, Ithaca, N.Y., where she met her future husband, Martin Ginsburg. The couple married in 1954, celebrated the birth of their daughter, Jane, the following year, and in 1956 attended Harvard Law School together. There Ginsburg was one of nine women in a class of some 500 students. She moved back to New York in 1958 after her husband landed a job with a law firm there and completed her degree at Columbia Law School, tying for first-place honours in her class. Despite her meritorious achievement, not one law firm offered her a job.

After clerking for a federal judge, Ginsburg worked on an international law project that resulted in three books on Swedish legal procedure and Scandinavian law. In 1963 she started teaching at Rutgers Law School, Newark, N.J., but she hid her second pregnancy (resulting in the birth of her son, James, in 1965) because she feared that she would lose her position. In 1972 Ginsburg headed the American Civil Liberties Union's women's rights project and became Columbia's first tenured female faculty member.

A reserved but determined crusader for equal rights, Ginsburg earned a reputation as the "Thurgood Marshall of gender-equality law" after winning five of the six cases she argued before the Supreme Court in the 1970s. In addition to litigating women's issues such as gender discrimination, Ginsburg sued on behalf of men in some cases, arguing, for example, that husbands of women in the military deserve all the benefits that wives of men in the military receive.

By the summer of 1993 it was widely known that Ginsburg had an overriding interest in equal rights under the law. It was unknown to many, however, that she had a passion for opera and had planned to appear as an extra at the Washington Opera in the fall of 1993—until Clinton chose her to play a bigger, better, and much more important role. (EDWARD PAUL MORAGNE)

Girardelli, Marc

An Austrian-born Alpine ski racer who represented Luxembourg could justly claim to be the most versatile performer in his sport since becoming, in 1989, the first to end a season as the top points scorer in all four World Cup disciplines. By March 1993, at the age of 29, Marc Girardelli had achieved overall victory in the men's World Cup for a record fifth time. Those five triumphs were spread over eight years that were punctuated by a spate of injuries serious enough to discourage a lesser man, but each time he came back to prove a remarkable survivor. Once the left half of his body was so weakened that he had to undergo an exceptionally rigorous training program, embellished by weight lifting and long mountain runs.

Born on July 18, 1963, at Lustenau, Austria, and coached by his father, Helmut, Girardelli made his debut on the cup circuit at 15. In January 1993, at St. Anton, Austria, he gained his 40th cup race victory, a career achievement bettered only by Ingemar Stenmark of Sweden. Using his physical strength and unorthodox stance to telling effect, he had always made the slalom his forte and, as a result, he gained particular satisfaction from winning his first downhill race in cup competition in 1989 on the Hahnenkamm course at Kitzbühel, Austria. He promptly followed this with two more downhill victories in quick succession at Wengen, Switz., to demonstrate an unmatched all-round ability.

For one appearing not to take world championship events quite so earnestly as World Cup races, Girardelli nonetheless achieved an impressive list of championship accomplishments, beginning in 1985 at Bormio, Italy, when he was runner-up in the slalom and third in the giant slalom. He won the Alpine combination and finished second in both the slalom and giant slalom in 1987 at Crans-Montana, Switz. In 1989 he again won the combination and finished third in the slalom at Vail, Colo., and in 1991 at Saalbach, Austria, he finally won the slalom. In 1993 at Morioka, Japan, he placed second in the slalom and third in the combination. Although an Olympic gold medal so far had eluded him, he hoped to rectify the situation in 1994 at Lillehammer, Norway. In the 1992 Olympics, he finished second in the giant slalom and supergiant slalom.

A dedicated perfectionist, Girardelli said, "To top the winner's podium, you simply can't afford to make any mistake at all. It's absolutely essential to pay attention to even the smallest detail." (HOWARD BASS)

Gorecki, Henryk

Among the soul, pop, rock, and rap recordings on the British best-selling album charts in February 1993, the number six hit was a most surprising selection: *Symphony No. 3: Symphony of Sorrowful Songs* by Polish composer Henryk Gorecki, played by the London Sinfonietta, conducted by David Zinman, with soprano Dawn Upshaw. The album, reported Elektra Nonesuch, the company that issued it, was more than a British hit—by September it had sold more than half a million copies throughout the world, 150,000 in the U.S. alone; the average classical album, by contrast, sells about 15,000 copies. The success of the disc was more remarkable because Gorecki was a living, breathing composer who had spent most of his life in the sooty industrial city of Katowice in Upper Silesia, seldom leaving home. Suddenly he became an international celebrity, traveling to London, Brussels, and New York City, holding press conferences, and appearing as the subject of a British television special.

Composed in 1976, the *Symphony No. 3* hardly sounds like a conventional pop success. Its three movements are in slow lento and largo tempi and played at quiet dynamic levels. It is based on a modal canon built up from low strings; after its mourning lines slowly mount to organ-like harmonies, the soprano voice enters with pastoral melody, a delicate element of light amid otherwise dark shadows. The texts are Polish lamentations: a 15th-century monastic song, a folk song, a prayer scratched in a cell wall by a girl imprisoned by the Gestapo. The repeated orchestral lines recall, to some listeners, minimalist techniques; Upshaw's performance in particular was highly praised by critics, although praise for the *Symphony No. 3* was not universal. Some critics dismissed it as simplistic.

Two years previously only one Gorecki work, his *Monologhi* (1960), was available in the U.S.; the Zinman-Upshaw recording, however, was the fourth of the *Symphony No. 3,* and by 1993 some half dozen other works by Gorecki were available on recordings. It may be no coincidence that widespread interest in Gorecki's music appeared after Poland emerged from five decades of Nazi and then communist rule. Several of his early works were described as symbolic anticommunist protest. Elected provost of the State Higher School of Music in 1975, Gorecki resigned in protest four years later when the government refused to let Pope John Paul II visit Katowice. Gorecki's passport was withdrawn, and he said, "Thereafter, I was treated as though I was dead." Gorecki traveled to Krakow to conduct his choral work *Beatus Vir* for the pope, and he composed new works for subsequent papal visits to Poland; his *Miserere,* honoring a Solidarity leader beaten by the militia, was not performed for six years after he composed it in 1981.

Henryk Mikolaj Gorecki was born in Czernica, near Rybnik, Poland, on Dec. 6, 1933, and studied in Paris and at the Katowice Conservatory. The works of Anton von Webern, Olivier Messaien, and Karlheinz Stockhausen, previously outlawed in Poland, informed Gorecki's often atonal and violent early compositions. A change in his art came in 1963 when, challenged to write simple tunes, he created *Three Pieces in Old Style* for orchestra. Folk song, medieval music, and his Roman Catholic faith characterized his subsequent work, which frequently was based on tragic themes and was in very slow tempi. "I want to express great sorrow," Gorecki said. "The war, the rotten times under communism, our life today, the starving, Bosnia. . . . This sorrow, it burns inside me." Clearly, in 1993 the world was ready to listen. (JOHN LITWEILER)

Grisham, John

Perhaps because of Americans' fascination with the alleged illicit activities of lawyers, John Grisham's novels of legal suspense became common fixtures on the *New York Times* best-seller lists in 1993. Attorney-turned-novelist Grisham accomplished a rare feat in publishing: he completed writing four novels, *A Time to Kill* (1989), *The Firm* (1991), *The Pelican Brief* (1992), and *The Client* (1993), and had each one reach the *New York Times* best-seller lists within five years. Thus, Grisham became the fastest-selling writer of modern fiction in history.

Though often criticized for depicting one-dimensional characters and for formulating implausible plots, Grisham was generally lauded for his fast-paced, adrenaline-charged page-turners. Despite being free of gratuitous sex, violence, and gore, Grisham's novels managed to keep readers on the edge of their seats just by making heroes out of innocent people fighting corrupt government, the underworld, and immoral businessmen.

John Grisham was born in 1955 in Arkansas but grew up in Southaven, Miss. After he was admitted to the Mississippi bar in 1981, he practiced law and served (1984–89) as a Democrat in the Mississippi state legislature. Then, inspired by a trial he had observed in 1984, Grisham took three years to write his first novel, *A Time to Kill,* which deals with the legal, social, and moral repercussions when a black man is tried for the murder of two white men who raped his 10-year-old daughter. Despite good reviews for its skillfully crafted dialogue and sense of place, the novel failed to sell. Grisham vowed to "take a naked stab at commercial fiction" with his next novel, *The Firm,* about a law-school graduate who is seduced into joining a Memphis law firm that turns out to be a front for the Mafia. The film rights were sold to Paramount Pictures Corp. for $600,000, prompting a bidding war for publishing rights, which Doubleday won for $200,000. Within weeks of its release in 1991, the novel appeared on the *New York Times* best-seller list, where it stayed for nearly a year, allowing Grisham to give up his law practice and move with his family to a 28-ha (70-ac) farm in Oxford, Miss. In the meantime, *A Time to Kill* was reissued in paperback, and over three million copies were sold.

Grisham wrote his third novel, *The Pelican Brief*—about a female law student investigating the assassinations of two Supreme Court justices—in only three months. There were 5.5 million copies of the book in print by March 1993. Film rights to the novel were sold for over $1 million. Grisham's most recent novel, *The Client,* sacrificed roller-coaster suspense for humour and slapstick energy. Critics almost universally agreed that the plot, dealing with an 11-year-old boy who uncovers a mob-related murder plot, read as though it had been tailor-made for the silver screen. Indeed, the film rights to the novel were sold for $2.5 million, while the novel itself sold 2.6 million copies within 15 weeks.

(SUSAN RAPP)

Hanauer, Chip

As a boat racer, Chip Hanauer left all the other drivers in his wake. He won his seventh national championship for Unlimited hydroplanes in 1993, which tied Bill Muncey's record. His ninth victory in the Gold Cup, the equivalent of auto racing's Indianapolis 500, broke Muncey's record of eight. With 7 victories in 10 races, following his 7-for-9 mark of 1992, Hanauer had 50 victories in 15 seasons and a .376 career winning percentage, the best in hydroplane racing history.

Lee Edward Hanauer was born July 1, 1954, in Seattle, Wash., where he continued to live. As children, Hanauer and his friends would tow wooden planks behind their bicycles and pretend they were driving hydroplanes. He began racing powerboats at the age of nine, when he bought a racing boat with $250 he had earned from a paper route and baby-sitting. His mother died a few months later, leaving Chip and his brother, Scott, to live with their father, Stan, a commercial diver, who raised the family for some time on a sailboat.

At 10, Hanauer placed fifth nationally in the Junior Stock hydroplane class for 9- to 12-year-olds. He won his first American Power Boat Association (APBA) national championship at 18 in the 145 class and gained three more championships the next year. He started racing Unlimited hydroplanes, the biggest racing boats, in 1976, the year of his graduation cum laude from Washington State University. Hanauer taught emotionally disturbed children until he became a full-time powerboat racer in 1978, and he won his first race in Ogden, Utah, in 1979.

Hanauer's first big opportunity came in 1982, when he joined the *Atlas Van Lines* team to replace Muncey, who had been killed in a 1981 accident. Hanauer won five races, including a come-from-behind victory for his first Gold Cup, and ended the year with his first Unlimited national and world championships. In 1983, when he was the fastest qualifier for all 10 races and won 3 of them, he earned his first of a record six elections into the APBA's Hall of Champions.

Also a pioneer, Hanauer drove the first turbine-powered boat, which broke the one-lap record by 7 mph at 140.8 mph in 1984, and introduced the closed cockpit a year later. Currently mandatory, the closed cockpit helps prevent drowning in blow-over accidents, the type that killed Muncey, in which too much air under the front of the boat causes it to tip over backward.

When Hanauer left boats for auto racing in 1991, he finished seventh out of 127 drivers in the Firehawk Sport Class. The prestigious *Miss Budweiser* team lured him back to the water in 1992, when he set 39 records. (KEVIN M. LAMB)

Hariri, Rafiq al-

The fact that Rafiq al-Hariri, who was installed as prime minister of Lebanon on Oct. 29, 1992, was still being hailed in 1993 as his country's "Mr. Miracle" was remarkable. A rags-to-riches construction tycoon, Hariri had pledged to rebuild his war-ravaged country and to revive its moribund economy. Neither promise would be easy in a nation that had long been divided by sectarian hatreds, occupied by Syrian troops, and burdened with a gross domestic product that fell a bit short of Hariri's $4 billion net worth.

Hariri, the son of a poor Lebanese farmer, was born in 1944 in the city of Sidon. He briefly attended Beirut Arab University as a business student but left Lebanon in 1966 to go to Saudi Arabia. There he taught mathematics and worked as a part-time accountant for a Saudi contracting firm. In 1970 Hariri set up his own construction business and began amassing a fortune by building hotels, convention centres, and palaces throughout the Middle East. He later expanded his empire to include banking, real estate, and other international commercial interests. Along the way, he acquired homes all over the world, including a 26-room mansion in Washington, D.C.

Hariri also used his wealth to improve the lives of less fortunate people. In 1983 he set up the Hariri Foundation, which financed the education of thousands of Lebanese students in Europe and the United States. In addition, Hariri paid the expenses for dozens of Lebanon's rival leaders, who attended the 1989 Ta'if peace conference in Saudi Arabia.

Hariri's fortune helped him in his initial foray into politics because most Lebanese saw the multibillionaire as too rich to be corrupted, and they also trusted that his business acumen would be brought to bear on a government renowned for its lack of efficient management. His membership as a Sunni Muslim was also vitally important because by law Lebanon's prime minister must be a Sunni, just as its president must be a Christian Maronite and the speaker of the National Assembly a Shi'ite Muslim. A week after taking office, Hariri signaled his sensitivity to Lebanon's rival religions by naming a Cabinet that was equally composed of Christians and Muslims.

Hariri's agenda included the rebuilding of Lebanon into the Middle East's financial and trading capital by implementing his $10 billion plan to repair the country's infrastructure, initialing a future peace treaty with Israel, and ending terrorism, both at home and abroad. To that end Hariri disbanded the militias that once terrorized the capital and launched his plan to "go down in history as the man who rebuilt Beirut."

(JEROLD L. KELLMAN)

Hooker, John Lee

A septuagenarian known as the "Godfather of the Blues," John Lee Hooker was still a force in popular music during the early 1990s. The singer-guitarist won a Grammy award in 1990 for "I'm in the Mood," a duet with Bonnie Raitt. His album *Mr. Lucky* (1991) was also nominated for a Grammy, and *Boom Boom* (1992) was critically acclaimed. He was inducted into the Rock and Roll Hall of Fame in 1991. In 1993 he was named best traditional blues male at the W.C. Handy Blues Awards in Memphis, Tenn.

Hooker, the fourth of 11 children, was born in Clarksdale, Miss. Although most sources gave his birthdate as Aug. 22, 1917, Hooker later claimed to have changed the year from 1920 while trying to appear older as a youth. His stepfather taught Hooker to play blues guitar, and the two performed together at local fish fries. Hooker ran away from home in 1931 to Memphis, where he played with B.B. King and other future blues greats.

He moved to Cincinnati, Ohio, in 1933 and performed with various gospel acts through the early 1940s. In 1943 he left for Detroit, Mich., where he formed a band and played at local clubs. Modern Records signed him in 1948, and the next year his single "Boogie Chillen" rose to the top of the rhythm-and-blues charts. A prolific recording artist, Hooker appeared on numerous record labels—often under pseudonyms such as Texas Slim, John Lee Cooker, and Delta John—before joining Chicago-based Vee-Jay. More successes followed, including "Dimples," which was a hit in the U.K. Hooker's career took a turn in the late 1950s when he began recording acoustic blues-revival tunes. Ensuing appearances at U.S. and European folk festivals further established his folk stardom. Many of his fans in England soon turned to rock and roll, however, so Hooker adjusted again and recorded an album in 1965 with the rock band the Groundhogs. Later collaborations with rock artists led some critics to deride Hooker for abandoning his roots to attain commercial success. He scoffed at the charges, explaining that, unlike most blues artists, he was merely keeping pace with the changing character of popular music.

JACK VARTOOGIAN

Hooker's single-chord, rhythm-driven style and gravelly vocals, accompanied by the tap of his foot, inspired a generation of musicians, among them the Rolling Stones, the Animals, Led Zeppelin, Pete Townshend, and Jimi Hendrix. He recruited a group of disciples—including Raitt, Robert Cray, Carlos Santana, and George Thorogood—to record *The Healer* (1989) and made a triumphant return to the charts. The album was an international success, selling more than one million copies. Guest artists also featured prominently on *Mr. Lucky* and *Boom Boom*. Hooker's other ventures included a cameo appearance in the 1980 film *The Blues Brothers* and a collaboration with Quincy Jones on "Don't Make Me No Never Mind" for the soundtrack of *The Color Purple* (1986). (ANTHONY G. CRAINE)

Hosokawa, Morihiro

In his maiden speech before the Japanese Diet (parliament) in August, Prime Minister Morihiro Hosokawa advocated "responsible change" and promised to make Japan a country of "quality and substance." The words signaled a break with the old political order, which had sunk the nation into a quagmire of corruption and stifled reforms.

Cleaning up politics to regain public trust became the keynote of the new Cabinet; the prime minister was publicly staking his political future on the implementation of political reforms before year's end. Specifically, the new government planned to replace multimember constituencies with ones mixing single-member constituencies with proportional representation. Another goal was to tighten rules on campaign funding. Hosokawa pushed reform bills through the lower house in mid-November and scored points in his handling of foreign policy. Seeking to reassure Japan's Asian neighbours, he opened up a new era of understanding and partnership by unequivocally apologizing for Japanese "aggression and colonial rule." No other Japanese leader had ever made such a statement. Hosokawa also set out to get the derailed economy back on track by giving priority to ordinary consumers, but his attempts to deregulate and decentralize the economy met strong opposition. By year's end Hosokawa was himself admitting some disappointment in what he had been able to accomplish.

Hosokawa was born on Jan. 14, 1938, in Kumamoto prefecture. His direct ancestors were among the most famous of Japan's historical figures. After graduating in 1963 from Sophia University, a Roman Catholic institution in Tokyo, Hosokawa became a journalist with the *Asahi shimbun*. In 1971 he entered politics and became the youngest person ever elected to the (upper) House of Councillors. He served two six-year terms, spent eight years as governor of Kumamoto, then returned to national politics. Disillusioned with the scandal-ridden Liberal-Democratic Party (LDP), Hosokawa bolted the party in September 1990 and in May 1992 founded the Japan New Party (JNP). A mere two months later, he and three other members of the JNP won seats in the upper house. In the historic July 18 national elections, which ended the LDP's 38-year hold on the government, the JNP snared 36 seats in the House of Representatives. With the support of seven parties, Hosokawa was unexpectedly elected prime minister on August 6.

Although Hosokawa's rainbow Cabinet initially was given little chance of survival, the prime

REUTERS/BETTMANN

minister continued to enjoy record-high popularity ratings and a rather favourable press. The Japanese seemed somewhat awed by the aristocratic diffidence of their new leader, whose political style was perceived as a shrewd combination of new and old ways. He described himself and U.S. Pres. Bill Clinton as "leaders of the same generation, both calling for change" to meet the challenges of a world in transition.

(GERD LARSSON)

Howard, Michael

During 1993 the U.K.'s home secretary, Michael Howard, established himself as the most prominent right-wing member of Prime Minister John Major's (*q.v.*) Cabinet. In particular, Howard led a campaign to revive the reputation of the Conservative government in two areas: family values and law and order.

Howard was born on July 7, 1941, in southern Wales. He studied law at the University of Cambridge, where he formed enduring friendships with a number of other people who would become Conservative Cabinet ministers in the 1980s, such as Norman Lamont, Norman Fowler, John Gummer, and Kenneth Clarke (*q.v.*). After almost two decades as a barrister, Howard entered Parliament in 1983 as member for Folkestone & Hythe, southeast of London. Howard's talent, robust debating skills, and right-wing commitment brought him to the attention of Prime Minister Margaret Thatcher, who gave him his first ministerial job only two years later.

After the 1987 election, Howard was promoted to minister of state (the number two position) at the Department of the Environment, where he steered through Parliament controversial legislation privatizing the U.K.'s water companies. His reward was a place in Thatcher's Cabinet in January 1990 as employment secretary, a role in which he piloted through legislation that restricted trade union rights and limited workers' rights to take strike action. A prominent skeptic of European integration, Howard also played a leading role in resisting the application of the European Community's social chapter on employment rights to the U.K.

In May 1993, Major appointed Howard home secretary. He swiftly gained a reputation as a hard-liner, reversing previous policies that had sought to minimize the use of jail for young offenders. In October he announced the building of six new prisons to contain the expected increase in the numbers sentenced to jail. In the same month, at the Conservative Party's annual conference, Howard aroused controversy by stating that unemployment and poverty had nothing to do with the causes of crime—but that family upbringing did. He argued for a return to the nuclear family, on the grounds that children who were brought up by only their mothers lacked suitable adult male role models and, as a result, were more likely to turn to crime. Howard's argument infuriated the U.K.'s liberals as much as it delighted the Conservative right-wingers, who increasingly saw Howard as their standard-bearer in any future party leadership contest.

(PETER KELLNER)

Hughes, Mervyn Gregory

Mustachioed, potbellied, and encumbered with a lumbering, unathletic gait, Merv Hughes never looked the epitome of the fast bowler. But his outstanding Test record of 208 wickets for Australia (to the end of 1993) at an average of 27 told a different story. The burly cricketer, whose wholehearted commitment to the cause of his team too often turned to unacceptable verbal intimidation of his opponents, had become a far better bowler than he looked when he made his debut for Australia against India in the 1985–86 series.

Hughes was born Nov. 23, 1961, and grew up in a working-class suburb of Melbourne. He worked briefly in a factory and joined the Victoria side in 1981–82. Selected for Australia in 1985–86, he took just one wicket for 123 runs in his first Test and was quickly dropped. Recalled against England in 1986–87, he suffered badly at the hands of the all-rounder Ian Botham (who scored a record 22 runs on one over at Brisbane), and it was not until the second Test in Perth against the West Indies in the 1988–89 series that Hughes established himself as a true Test bowler, with match figures of 13 for 217. Thereafter, by sheer hard work, a willingness to experiment, persistence, and guile, he transformed himself into one of the most feared fast bowlers in Test cricket.

In 1993 he and leg spinner Shane Warne led Australia to a convincing 4–1 series win over England. Warne took 34 wickets and Hughes a heroic 31 after his fast-bowling partner, Craig McDermott, had been forced out of the series through injury. Time and again "Sumo," as he was affectionately dubbed by the British spectators because of his physical similarity to the Japanese wrestlers, produced a vital wicket when his side badly needed it. Like Botham, Hughes had an uncanny ability to make things happen from nothing, forcing the batsmen—by fair means or foul—into confrontation and into making mistakes. But he also swung the ball late, varied his line and length skillfully, and could, on his good days, be genuinely quick. His batting was erratic, huge sixes being mixed with obdurate defense, but he could be a stubborn tail-ender.

Off the field "Mad Merv" was a jovial character—a good-humoured, blunt hero to his home crowds, an infectious team member, and a popular tourist wherever he went. "I love him to death," said Australia captain Allan Border. Injury and his second knee surgery in a year ruled Hughes out of the early part of the 1993–94 season, but he was bound to be back—larger than life, with "bushwacker" mustache bristling, and mouthing his usual oaths—when England, the old foe, toured Australia in 1994–95.

(ANDREW LONGMORE)

Jordan, Michael

Leaping to unbelievable heights as usual, Michael Jordan jumped clear out of professional basketball when he retired on Oct. 6, 1993. "I don't have anything else to prove," said Jordan, who had led the National Basketball Association (NBA) in scoring the last seven seasons and had helped the 1991–93 Chicago Bulls become the first team to win three consecutive league championships since the Boston Celtics won eight in a row in the 1950s and 1960s.

He meant he had nothing left to prove in basketball. As the year ended, Jordan was training daily in hopes of playing for the Chicago White Sox of major league baseball, the sport he liked best as a child.

Jordan was one of the few team athletes to retire healthy at the peak of his career. Like Cleveland Browns fullback Jim Brown, Jordan retired at 30 after nine seasons that defined him as the greatest player in the history of his sport. His career scoring average of 32.3 was an NBA record, and some opposing coaches said he was more dangerous on defense than with the ball. In 1993 he became the first to be named Most Valuable Player of the NBA finals for three consecutive years. He was the regular-season MVP in 1988, 1991, and 1992. He captivated audiences as "Air Jordan," the powerfully high-leaping and gracefully balletic improviser performing a high-wire act with a basketball and without a wire.

No player besides 2.18-m (7-ft 2-in) centre Wilt Chamberlain had scored 3,000 points in a season before 1.98-m (6-ft 6-in), 89.8-kg (198-lb) Jordan did it in 1987, when he averaged 37.1 per game. His 32.6 average in 1993 tied Chamberlain's record of seven straight scoring titles.

Jordan was an Olympic gold medalist both in 1984 as an amateur and in 1992 on the first professional U.S. Olympic "Dream Team." He became the first U.S. athlete in a team sport to license his name and image independently of his league's licensing program. He earned more money than any other athlete in 1993 for the second straight year, *Forbes* magazine estimated—$36 million, mostly in endorsement fees. But 1993 also was a year of scandal and personal tragedy for Jordan. He admitted to losing $300,000 in golf bets to a man who accused him of losing $1,250,000, and on July 23 his father was killed on a North Carolina highway, apparently a random murder victim.

Michael Jeffrey Jordan was born Feb. 17, 1963, in Brooklyn, N.Y. In college he made the winning shot for North Carolina in the 1982 national championship game. He was all-American the next two seasons and left school after his junior year. The Bulls made him the third choice in the NBA draft, behind Houston's Hakeem Olajuwan and Portland's Sam Bowie, and he was Rookie of the Year in 1985.

(KEVIN M. LAMB)

Karan, Donna

Internationally acclaimed fashion designer Donna Karan captured the spotlight in 1993 both with her mix-and-match clothing in soft fabrics and neutral colours and with the public offering of shares—worth more than $160 million—in her

KEEBLE CAVACO & DUKA/CHICAGO TRIBUNE

company, Donna Karan Co. The nine-year-old concern was initially bankrolled with a $3 million investment, and its explosive growth provided testament to the popularity of Karan's comfortable line of fashions. Her loyal clientele responded to the simplicity of her predominately black-and-neutral-coloured designs, especially her signature bodysuits, dark tights, sarong-wrap skirts, fitted jackets, and heavy pieces of jewelry.

Karan was born Donna Faske on Oct. 2, 1948, in Forest Hills, N.Y. Her father was a tailor, and her mother was a model and a showroom sales representative in New York City's garment district. She launched a career in fashion at 14 when she lied about her age to secure a job selling clothes in a boutique. An indifferent high school student, she was accepted into New York's Parsons School of Design on the recommendation of her mother's employer, designer Chester Weinberg. After quitting school in 1968, she began working for sportswear designer Anne Klein, but she was fired after nine months. She married boutique owner Mark Karan during the brief period between her first and a second stint with Klein.

After Klein died of cancer in 1974, Karan was elevated to chief designer and made responsible for that year's Anne Klein fall collection. In 1975 Karan brought her former classmate Louis Dell'Olio into the company as a designer. The two were awarded the Coty American Fashion Critics Award in 1977 and 1981 and were later inducted into that body's Hall of Fame. The Anne Klein Co. flourished, in large part owing to Karan's marketing of a "bridge" line, a less-expensive designer line, Anne Klein II, which was christened in 1983.

In 1984 Karan used seed money provided by Tomio Taki, chairman of the American branch of a Japanese textile firm and a major partner in Anne Klein, to launch the Donna Karan Co. Karan and her second husband, sculptor Stephan Weiss, were married in 1983, and the couple served as chief executives of the firm, with Karan acting as chief designer. After the bridge line DKNY debuted in 1988, Karan's company diversified and sold blue jeans, men's wear, and a children's line in addition to accessories, hosiery, and perfume. (CHRISTINE SULLIVAN)

Kawabuchi, Saburo

During a year marked by such notable events in Japan as the defeat of the long-ruling Liberal-Democratic Party and the wedding of Crown Prince Naruhito and Masako Owada, Saburo Kawabuchi nonetheless managed to share the limelight. As chairman and chief executive of the Japan Professional Football League, known locally as the J.League, he was largely responsible for raising soccer to such a level that it began to challenge sumo and baseball in popularity. On May 15 some 60,000 people turned out to witness the kickoff of Japanese professional soccer at the National Stadium in Tokyo. The inaugural season featured 10 teams whose rosters included players from Europe and Latin America. Among the stars were Gary Lineker of England and Zico of Brazil. The opening match won a 32% share of the television audience. That figure leaped to 48% on October 28, when Japan's and Iraq's national teams met in the Asian qualifying games. A final-minute loss ended Japan's chances of competing in the World Cup for the first time.

Kawabuchi was born in Osaka, Japan, on Dec. 3, 1936. He began playing soccer in high school because he wanted the chance to visit the city of Takamatsu on the island of Shikoku, where his team was scheduled to play a match. He then attempted to quit the team, but older players recognized his potential and persuaded him to remain. As a freshman at Waseda University, Tokyo, he became a regular on what was the strongest university team in the country. The next year Kawabuchi was recruited for the national team. As centre-back, he competed in the Olympics in Rome in 1960 and in Tokyo in 1964. He also played in two qualifying games for the World Cup in Sweden in 1958 and in Chile in 1962. He continued playing with the national team even after joining Furukawa Denki, one of Japan's largest makers of electric wires and cables, and became head coach at age 35. In 1988 Kawabuchi volunteered to act as general secretary of the Japan Soccer League, which organized competitions between amateur teams sponsored by major corporations. This experience inspired the vision of a professional soccer league in Japan. In 1991 he quit his full-time job to assume leadership of the J.League. Even Kawabuchi expressed surprise at Japanese response to the J.League. In its first season, sales of TV rights, merchandise, and tickets for 180 games totaled $1 billion. A key factor behind the successful launch of professional soccer was intense coverage by the mass media. The youth of Japan especially were drawn to it because it was faster paced than baseball and, unlike sumo, unencumbered by ancient Japanese traditions. (ANDREA FORNES)

Kevorkian, Jack

In November and December 1993 Jack Kevorkian served two jail sentences on charges that he had violated the state's law against assisting in a suicide. In prison he threatened to starve himself to death to protest what he called "this immoral law." Frail and weakened by his second hunger strike, he was released from jail on Dec. 17, 1993, after promising that he would not participate in the deaths of any further terminally ill individuals. On December 18 a Wayne county Circuit Court judge ruled that Michigan's law against suicide assistance was unconstitutional, but the ruling was not binding in neighbouring Oakland county, where Kevorkian resided.

Jack Kevorkian was born in Pontiac, Mich., on May 26, 1928. He attended the University of Michigan and in 1952 graduated from the University of Michigan Medical School. Early in his professional training, Kevorkian distanced himself from the medical mainstream. As a pathology resident, he lobbied for carrying out medical experiments on death-row inmates at the hour set for their execution, then giving them lethal injections, which earned him the sobriquet "Dr. Death." Later he advocated establishing suicide clinics ("obitoria"). In the 1960s and '70s he worked as a staff pathologist at hospitals in Michigan and southern California; then in 1982 he retired from practice and began to devote full time to his mission: helping terminally ill patients end their lives.

Kevorkian gained international attention when in 1990 he enabled Janet Adkins of Portland, Ore., aged 54 and in the early stages of Alzheimer's disease, to kill herself by using his so-called Mercitron machine. Over the following 3½ years he was present at the deaths of 20 others. In response to Kevorkian's role in the death of 70-year-old Hugh Gale, the Michigan legislature passed a bill making it a felony knowingly to provide a person with the means to commit suicide or to physically assist in the act. The legislators believed that Gale may have had second thoughts after Kevorkian placed a carbon-monoxide-dispensing mask over his face. On Nov. 22, 1993, between jail sentences, Kevorkian attended the suicide of Ali Khalili. By going to Kevorkian for help, Khalili, a physician himself, seemed to be making a statement to the medical profession about its need to confront troubling ethical issues.

Physician-assisted suicide, legalized in The Netherlands in February 1993, was largely opposed by the U.S. medical establishment. Many practitioners believed that such actions violate the most basic tenet of medicine: to do no harm. Medical ethicists criticized Kevorkian for assisting in the deaths of virtual strangers and seeking publicity in order to promote his own ideas. Even some proponents of euthanasia ("mercy killing") condemned the Michigan doctor's acts.

Countering his detractors, Kevorkian claimed that he had never cared about anything but the welfare of the patient in front of him and that most U.S. doctors failed their patients by not responding to their suffering. Previously having refused to be stopped by laws, Kevorkian at the end of the year said he would no longer assist patients but would redirect his efforts toward changing those laws. (ELLEN BERNSTEIN)

Kim Young Sam

When South Korean Pres. Kim Young Sam assumed office on Feb. 25, 1993, no one was quite prepared for the whirlwind of anticorruption activity that dominated his first year in office. Before the dust settled, 10 navy and air force generals suspected of buying their promotions had been discharged from service, and two former defense ministers had been arrested for taking bribes. Because of a new law, thousands of government officials were to declare their assets, which would then be open to scrutiny. Kim's most drastic anticorruption move was to order South Koreans to use their real names in all financial transactions. Previously it had been legal to use fictitious names. Such a situation had enabled political and business figures to hide an estimated $15 billion that could not be properly taxed and could be used for improper purposes. Kim's program of reforms, however, was pushed less vigorously when investigators probed defense contracts awarded during the administrations of former presidents Chun Doo Hwan and Roh Tae Woo. The opposition Democratic Party (DP) also charged that there had been only a token investigation of Kim's own campaign finances and that the president was coddling the *chaebol,* huge business conglomerates with traditionally close government ties.

Kim was born on Dec. 20, 1927, in the southeastern province of Kyongsang, Korea. At the time, Korea was under Japanese occupation. Kim graduated from Seoul National University and served in the armed forces during the Korean War. He was elected to the National Assembly for the first of nine terms in 1954, but he resigned in protest when Pres. Syngman Rhee tried to alter the constitution. Kim also opposed the repressive administration of Pres. Park Chung Hee and was expelled from the National Assembly. He was banned from politics in 1980 because he would not moderate his relentless criticism of the government. Seven years later, with the ban removed, Kim became an unsuccessful candidate for president. Roh Tae Woo won the 1987 race with just under 36% of the popular vote, largely because Kim Young Sam and another leading dissident, Kim Dae Jung, could not agree on which of them should be the opposition candidate. Together they captured 54% of the vote—to no avail. In 1990 Kim startled political pundits by merging his political organization with that of Roh to form the Democratic Liberal Party (DLP). As the DLP's 1992 presidential candidate, Kim was swept into office with a substantial plurality.

Kim quickly set the tone of his administration by launching an anticorruption campaign and by granting amnesty to some 41,000 prisoners, including labour activists and pro-democracy demonstrators, and by wiping out the criminal records of those arrested in pro-democracy demonstrations in Kwangju in 1980. But the most serious problem by far that Kim was facing came from North Korea, where a hostile and dangerously unpredictable leader seemed determined to develop weapons of mass destruction at a time when worldwide efforts were being made to destroy existing arsenals. (JOHN LITWEILER)

Krone, Julie

Julie Krone had long established herself as the best female jockey in history before she became the first woman to win the Belmont Stakes on June 5, 1993. She was trying to be the best jockey, period, and her Belmont victory gave her mid-season U.S. rankings of third in victories and sixth in earnings. She had ranked as high as sixth, fourth, and third for total wins respectively in 1987 through 1989, when she had 368 victories, and her career high of more than $9 million in purses for 1992 ranked ninth. "Whether you're a girl or a boy or a Martian, you still have to go out and prove yourself again every day," she said.

Her Belmont victory, aboard 13-to-1 long shot Colonial Affair, made Krone the first woman to

AP/WIDE WORLD

win any of the U.S. Triple Crown races, which also include the Kentucky Derby and the Preakness. On August 20 she was the third jockey in 126 years to win five races in one day at Saratoga Race Course in Saratoga Springs, N.Y. But 10 days later at Saratoga, her season ended abruptly when her ankle was shattered in 11 places after she was thrown from her mount. She was further injured when another horse stepped on her chest and bruised her heart. Krone's career then paused with over 2,700 victories, more than double the 1,205 that had made her the winningest woman in 1988. She had won purses of $53,557,170 (from which the jockey receives 10%).

Julieanne Louise Krone was born July 24, 1963, in Benton Harbor, Mich., and grew up on a horse farm in nearby Eau Claire, Mich. Her mother, Judi, was a prizewinning show rider, and Julie was only five when she began winning horse shows in the 21-and-under division. At 14 she watched on television as 18-year-old Steve Cauthen won the 1978 Triple Crown and told her parents she was going to be a jockey. She worked for trainer Clarence Picou in the summer of 1979, and the next summer she won 20 races on Michigan's fair circuit.

After quitting high school in her senior year, Krone finished second in her first race, on Jan. 30, 1981, and won for the first time on Feb. 12, 1981, aboard Lord Farkle at Tampa Bay Downs in Florida. In 1982 and 1983 she was the leading rider at Atlantic City, N.J., and in 1987 she became the first female leading rider at major racetracks, winning at Monmouth Park and the Meadowlands, both in New Jersey. In 1987 she also won six races in one day at Monmouth and five at the Meadowlands, both tying track records. She retained the leading riding title at Monmouth through 1989 and at Meadowlands through 1990, setting the Meadowlands track record with 132 victories in 1988. In 1992 she was the leading racer at Gulfstream Park in Florida and at the Belmont spring meet. (KEVIN M. LAMB)

Kushner, Tony

In what might have been an unlikely event during the era in which the critically acclaimed play *Angels in America* is set, in 1993 *Millennium Approaches,* the first part of Tony Kushner's epic work, took four Tony awards, a Critics' Circle award, and the Pulitzer Prize for drama. In 1992 it won the London Evening Standard award.

Subtitled *A Gay Fantasia on National Themes,* Kushner's *Angels in America* evolved into two 3½-hour plays from a poem he had written in

JAY THOMPSON—CHICAGO TRIBUNE

the mid-1980s. *Millennium Approaches* opened on Broadway in May 1993 after successful productions in San Francisco, London, and Los Angeles. The second half, *Perestroika,* opened in October, with the same eight actors in their same roles. The play's controversial theme of homosexuality, AIDS, and politics during the conservative era under U.S. Pres. Ronald Reagan probably would have drawn another reaction had it been produced at that time. However, in 1993 *Millennium Approaches* was nominated for nine Tonys—more than any other play in the history of the award. Among the four that it did garner were those for best play and best direction.

The unconventional play focuses on a gay couple, one of whom has AIDS; a Mormon man coming to terms with his sexuality and his marriage; and the infamous lawyer Roy Cohn, who died of AIDS in 1986. In November the two halves of *Angels in America* were presented together onstage for the first time. In addition, the play was scheduled to be performed in many locales all over the world and was even being translated into Japanese.

Kushner was born in July 1956 in New York City, the second of three children, to parents who had a background in music. When he was still very young, the family moved to Lake Charles, La., where his father had inherited the family lumber business. He later attended Columbia University, New York City, and then did postgraduate work at New York University. Prior to the epic *Angels,* Kushner had written *A Bright Room Called Day*—his first full-length work—which was produced in San Francisco and Chicago. He had also done some directing, as well as adapting Pierre Corneille's play *L'Illusion comique*.

The end of 1993 found Kushner very busy with work on two plays, an adaptation of *The Dybbuk* and *Slavs,* as well as assisting in plans to bring *Angels in America* to the big screen in conjunction with director Robert Altman. (ANTHONY L. GREEN)

Letterman, David

In 1993 television talk-show host David Letterman finally got his wish: the chance to help tuck America into bed on weeknights in the time slot immediately following the news. He had from 1982 served as host of NBC's live "Late Night with David Letterman," which catered to a sizable, if bleary-eyed, audience of insomniacs, students, security guards, and other night owls during the hour from 12:30 to 1:30 AM Eastern Standard Time (EST). But when CBS offered him a three-year $42 million contract to be the host of a talk show at 11:30 PM EST, the hour in which many Americans watched their last television, Letterman could not resist jumping networks, despite counterbids from NBC. Critics immediately questioned whether Letterman and his ironic, abrasive, flippant antic humour would appeal to the mainstream audience of the earlier hour. Following its August debut, however, "The Late Show with David Letterman" put that concern to rest by drawing considerably more viewers than Jay Leno's "The Tonight Show," which, under late-night king Johnny Carson, had reigned for three decades as the leading U.S. late-night offering. "The Late Show" retained the elements of Letterman's NBC program, including skewering top-10 lists; sarcastic interplay between Letterman and his comic foil, bandleader Paul Shaffer; nonsensical skits, notably "Stupid Pet Tricks"; and roving cameras that captured ordinary people and placed them in the limelight. The new show's host, with his boyishly silly, gap-toothed grin, was unLetterman-like only in being unusually cordial to his guests, perhaps seeking to ensure that no one at home went to bed mad.

On his NBC show, Letterman had antagonized some notable guests; Cher, for example, was moved to curse him on camera. If Letterman's behaviour turned off some viewers, it excited the critics, who saw in his work an attempt to parody talk shows. Letterman insisted, however, that doing a funny talk show, not a parody, was his main intent.

Even as a child, Letterman, who was born April 12, 1947, in Indianapolis, Ind., had revered Carson. After cutting his teeth on television as a crazy weatherman and on comedy as a regular stand-up at the Comedy Store, a Los Angeles club for fledgling comics, he finally got to sit in Carson's chair as a "Tonight Show" guest host in 1979, the first of many such appearances. The visibility won him an NBC mid-morning show later that year, but his convention-trashing humour—exemplified by the time he sent an audience member out to fetch him coffee—failed to engage daytime viewers. He did not gain a following until he moved to "Late Night." Later, after being passed over for Carson's job, Letterman said good night to General Electric-owned NBC, giving such top-10 reasons as "I've stolen as many GE bulbs as I can fit in my garage." (MICHAEL AMEDEO)

Lim, Alfredo

When underdog Alfredo Lim overcame the odds against him to beat six opponents in Manila's March 1992 mayoral election, he faced a daunting mandate: to clean up the streets of the wayward capital. Lim, the most heavily decorated police officer in Manila's history, promised to do his best to eradicate crime, smut, and corruption from the city. After his election, the controversial mayor came to be viewed as a restorer of peace and justice but also as a strong-arm enforcer who waged vendettas to achieve his goals.

An orphan from a Manila slum, Lim joined the police force in 1951. In the years that followed, he garnered an astonishing collection of some 40 medals and 400 commendations. The nation's top cop soon became the director of the National Bureau of Investigation (NBI). Along the way, Lim gained a reputation for quick justice. As head of the NBI, Lim ordered (1990) the arrest of a notorious Manila drug lord. By the time Lim's officers had completed the short ride to headquarters, the suspect (who allegedly had reached for one of his captor's guns) was dying from a bullet wound.

Lim carried his reputation for discipline and swift retribution into the mayor's office; jaywalkers commonly stood in cages on the side of the street for up to two hours, as did offenders of the city's new antilittering and antismoking laws. Lim declared bars, nightclubs, massage parlours, and "love motels" illegal and gave owners a June 30, 1993, deadline to leave the city. While many relocated outside city limits, others stood their ground, and some 250 owners of the businesses that Lim had closed filed lawsuits and obtained restraining orders. The Lim administration also attacked such problems as garbage disposal, traffic jams, and flood control. In addition to tough antilittering laws and community street washings, Lim requested every homemaker and storekeeper to plant a tree. To solve the problem of traffic congestion, he banned provincial buses from the city. The traffic improved, though the bus operators sued; the courts sided with the mayor. For flood prevention Lim proposed a new system of ground-level canals. He also favoured penalizing the city's 400,000 squatters, saying, "Slums are not necessarily the result of poverty, but the offshoot of laxity in law enforcement." In his latest plan Lim proposed the creation of a 3,000-member police unit, recruited and trained by the mayor's office, to augment the existing police force. The new officers would be college graduates and receive the highest pay in the country. The scheme was abandoned, however, because it would destandardize officer pay; nevertheless, Lim's vision soared high. He dreamed of a city where anarchy and chaos were unknown. When asked if he would run for president in 1998, Lim replied, "All I want is to rescue Manila from decay, and then retire." (ANN BELASKI)

Limbaugh, Rush

With his 1992 book *The Way Things Ought to Be* having spent well over a year on the best-seller list and the release of his 1993 follow-up, *See, I Told You So,* receiving the largest first printing of any book in U.S. history—two million copies—there seemed to be no end in sight to the high visibility of the rotund right-wing talk-show host Rush Limbaugh. By 1993 his syndicated three-hour radio program, "The Rush Limbaugh Show," which debuted in 1988, had become the most popular talk show on radio, reaching an estimated 20 million listeners daily. This spawned in the fall of 1992 a syndicated half-hour television show that quickly climbed in the ratings.

Claiming that he had "talent on loan from God," Limbaugh filled his programs with political commentary as served up from the conservative right, satire, and a heavy dose of Limbaugh himself; he rarely, if ever, had guests, and his screened callers were among his legion of fans known as "dittoheads." Of that audience he has said, "They think I've got the truth. And I'll tell you what—they're right." His daily "truths" often enraged the many special-interest groups he targeted, including feminists, whose movement the twice-married and twice-divorced Limbaugh once said was established "to allow unattractive women easier access to the mainstream"; the homeless, the vast majority of whom, he insisted, were "demented in one way or another"; and the Democratic Party, which he claimed was "the party that can't wait to fund every abortion in the world."

Rush Hudson Limbaugh III was born in Cape Girardeau, Mo., in 1951, the elder of two sons. At the age of 16 he began working at the local radio station before and after school. After graduation from high school, he attended Southeast Missouri State University for one year and then dropped out. He left home in 1971 seeking a career in radio, but after being fired from stations in Pittsburgh, Pa., and Kansas City, Mo., he quit radio in 1978 to work in ticket sales for the Kansas City Royals professional baseball team. After five years he was back in radio as a news commentator, but he was fired for being too controversial. However, his controlled ad-lib manner was just what station KFBK in Sacramento, Calif., was looking for in 1984 to replace the outgoing Morton Downey, Jr., who exhibited a wild and often offensive style. Within a year Limbaugh had become the top radio host in Sacramento. Then in 1988 EFM Media Management signed him to a two-year contract and took him to New York City, where his national broadcast debuted on August 1.

With the popularity of his show growing, many restaurants around the country began opening "Rush Rooms," where the members of Limbaugh's "amen choir" could have their lunch and listen to his piped-in program from what he dubbed his Excellence in Broadcasting Network. Although he was a thorn in the side of many Americans, further evidence of Limbaugh's impact on radio was registered when he was inducted into the Radio Hall of Fame in November.

(ANTHONY L. GREEN)

MacKenzie, Lewis

In 1993 Canadian Maj. Gen. Lewis MacKenzie published an account of his career, *Peacekeeper: The Road to Sarajevo,* in which he recounted his harrowing experiences in 1992 as chief of staff of the United Nations peacekeeping force in former Yugoslavia. Although the purpose of the mission was to ensure a cease-fire in newly independent Croatia, the UN headquarters were located in the Bosnian capital of Sarajevo. Soon after the Republic of Bosnia and Herzegovina was created, MacKenzie found himself in the midst of warring ethnic factions. In May 1992 he created Sector Sarajevo and with his UN force set about opening the Sarajevo airport for the delivery of humanitarian aid. MacKenzie attained the status of an international celebrity by using his only weapon, the media, to try to help restore peace.

MacKenzie, the son of a career army officer, was born April 30, 1940, in Truro, Nova Scotia. He majored in philosophy at St. Francis Xavier University in Antigonish, Nova Scotia. His devotion to the military started at the age of 12, when he joined the Royal Canadian Air Cadets. MacKenzie attended the Canadian Army Command and Staff College (1970), the NATO Defense College in Rome (1977), and the United States Army War College (1983), where he studied political science. He credited his education with preparing him for the political intrigue in the Balkans.

During his 33-year career in the Canadian military, MacKenzie served with NATO forces in West Germany and with UN peacekeeping forces in the Gaza Strip, Cyprus, Vietnam, Egypt, Central America, and former Yugoslavia. In Central America he was commander of the United Nations Observer Mission (1990–91). Between peacekeeping missions MacKenzie served (1979–82) as an instructor at the Canadian Forces Command and Staff College, and he was in charge of army training at St. Hubert, Que. (1983–85). As commander of the Canadian Forces Base in Gagetown, N.B. (1988–90), he was responsible for the training of officers at the Combat Training Centre. In 1985 he was appointed director of Combat-Related Employment for Women. In 1991 he was deputy commander of the Canadian Army's Land Forces Central Area. After his return from former Yugoslavia in 1992, MacKenzie was appointed commander of the army in Ontario. In 1993 the Conference of Defence Associations Institute presented him with its Vimy Award.

The conflict in former Yugoslavia, however, followed him back to Canada. He was verbally attacked by members of the Croatian community in Canada and by factions in Bosnia. Although he tried to defend himself, as a member of the Canadian armed forces he was precluded from commenting on government policy. After criticizing the United Nations' inability to command, control, and support its peacekeeping forces, MacKenzie retired from the military in March 1993.

(DIANE LOIS WAY)

Major, John Roy

During 1993 John Major achieved the unenviable record of becoming the U.K.'s least popular prime minister in polling history. At one point only 18% of the electorate thought he was doing well in his job.

AP/WIDE WORLD

Many of Major's problems flowed from the Conservative Party's lack of unity over the issue of a united Europe. Not only were a vociferous minority of backbench Tories in Parliament hostile to his support of the Maastricht Treaty on European Union, so also, more discreetly, were some of his own Cabinet colleagues. In an unguarded moment in July, during a conversation with a television reporter when he thought the microphones had been switched off, he applied a coarse epithet to some Tory ministers—an insult that, when it was leaked to the media, did nothing to help Major's authority. Nor was Major pleased when Lady Thatcher, his predecessor as prime minister, published her memoirs in October and accused him of being an intellectual lightweight.

Speculation grew during the year that Major might be forced to resign before the end of 1994. However, he took a number of policy initiatives in order to strengthen his position. In August he launched "Operation Irma" to airlift five-year-old Irma Hadzimuratovic and other serious casualties from the former Yugoslavia. In October he joined with Irish Prime Minister Albert Reynolds in launching a fresh initiative to bring peace to Northern Ireland. In November he announced his intention to take British society "back to basics" in terms of family values and respect for law and order. Having secured parliamentary approval of British ratification of the Maastricht Treaty, he also tilted his European policy so that—in tone, at least—he seemed to accept some of his critics' arguments against economic and political union.

One part of Major's problem as prime minister was his inability to please everyone. His "back to basics" approach, like his shift on Europe, caused Thatcher to declare that he was, at last, showing his fidelity to her politics; but by the same token, some pro-Europeans became worried. In November, Thatcher's predecessor as party leader, Sir Edward Heath, voiced his opposition to Major's move to the right. As the year ended, the prime minister seemed to have won the immediate battle for survival, but doubts remained as to how long he would stay in office.

Major was born in South London on March 29, 1943, entered Parliament in 1979, and joined the Cabinet as chief secretary to the treasury in 1987. In 1989 he was foreign secretary for three months before being named chancellor of the Exchequer. He succeeded Margaret Thatcher as prime minister in November 1990. (PETER KELLNER)

Mann, Sally

By the fall of 1993, when "Sally Mann: Still Time," a 60-print photographic retrospective covering 20 years of work, opened at the Museum of Contemporary Photography in Chicago, the photographer in question had already earned a fair amount of notoriety. Mann first found herself mired in controversy after her series of black-and-white portraits, entitled "Immediate Family," was unveiled in the spring of 1992 at Houk Friedman, a gallery in New York City. Those photographs created a stir because they focused on her three children, who often appeared nude and in postures, situations, and settings that some viewers found disturbing. Some questioned whether Mann had exploited her children, while others debated about whether the images invaded the realm of child pornography. Still others lavishly praised the collection as an honest exploration of the complexities of childhood.

In "Damaged Child," one of Mann's earliest portraits in the series (begun in 1984), her eldest daughter, Jessie, appears with a swollen eye and an expression seething with recrimination, a look some interpreted as belonging to a victim of child abuse. In truth, Jessie had been bitten by a gnat. Another Mann portrait shows her oldest child, Emmett, with melted Popsicle smearing his genitals. Yet another shot depicts her youngest daughter, Virginia, sleeping nude on a urine-stained mattress with her legs flung apart.

In the introduction to her book *Immediate Family* (1992), Mann wrote that "many of these pictures are intimate . . . but most are of ordinary things every mother has seen. I take pictures when they are bloodied or sick or naked or angry." With these staged visual explorations, Mann captured some of the darker images of childhood and raised some thought-provoking issues. She was hailed for her painstaking technique, which involved mentally sketching each photograph and discarding dozens of shots before extensively labouring in the darkroom to achieve the desired effect.

Mann, who was born in 1951 in Lexington, Va., was introduced to photography by her father, Robert Munger, a physician who photographed her nude as a girl. In 1969, as a teenager, Mann took up photography in Vermont at the Putney School and then spent two years at Bennington College, where she studied under photographer Norman Sieff and met and proposed to Larry Mann, her husband of 22 years. After spending a year in Europe, she graduated (1974) summa cum laude from Hollins College, Roanoke, Va., and a year later she earned a master's degree in writing.

In 1983, using her century-old 8 × 10-in view camera, Mann started photographing 12-year-old girls. That series was showcased in her 1988 book, *At Twelve*. Another series, "Dream Sequence," explores the psychology of relationships. More recently, Mann resumed landscape photography and extended her photographic style to include more colour work. (EDWARD PAUL MORAGNE)

Mapfumo, Thomas

By 1993, in the increasingly popular realm of "world music," the music of the countries that constitute southern Africa had generated perhaps the most enthusiasm, and the Zimbabwean singer and composer Thomas Mapfumo had garnered

JACK VARTOOGIAN

more international recognition for the sounds of his country than any other musician. In Zimbabwe he was seen as both a brilliant musician and an important revolutionary figure who had rallied blacks around the independence movement through the power of his music.

Mapfumo was born in 1945 in Marondera and later moved to Salisbury (now Harare). He began his musical career when he was 16 with a band called the Cyclones. His early career with such bands as the Springfields and the Cosmic Dots featured little more than a few cover versions of Elvis Presley and Otis Redding tunes. During the early 1970s, however, when many black Zimbabweans were beginning to resist the Rhodesian regime, Mapfumo was also effecting a revolution in popular music by writing the lyrics to his songs in Shona, the language of the majority of black Zimbabweans, and incorporating traditional melodies and rhythms into his music.

One of the key elements of this style was the use of the mbira, an African hand piano with a gourd resonator fitted with a set of metal keys that were plucked with the thumbs. At first Mapfumo and his guitarist worked together to duplicate the sounds and rhythms of the mbira on the electric guitar. The intensely complicated rhythms played on the drums were meant to represent the stamping of dancers' feet. In 1976 he formed the Acid Band and with them produced a style that united pop and tradition; his lyrics were spiked with thinly veiled political messages. His first album, released in 1977, was entitled *Hokoyo!,* meaning "Watch out!" The white minority government saw Mapfumo's music as a threat and prevented it from receiving airplay on the state-controlled radio stations. His music was still heard, however, in discos and on radio broadcasts that emanated from neighbouring countries.

In late 1977, with the escalation of guerrilla warfare, security forces finally attempted to silence Mapfumo by imprisoning him for 90 days. Upon his release, he returned to writing his *Chimurenga* (Shona: "struggle") songs that became identified with the fight for freedom. When Zimbabwe won independence in 1980, Mapfumo was considered to have played no small part in the achievement. During the 1980s Mapfumo added a real mbira to his band, Blacks Unlimited, and continued to nurture and promote the traditional music of Zimbabwe. Mapfumo said that he and his band had only "scratched the surface" of Zimbabwe's musical heritage. More than a decade after independence, his music still had a sociopolitical edge and enjoyed a wider audience as a result of European and American tours in the 1980s and '90s. In his 1993 album, *Hondo* ("War"), Mapfumo's Shona lyrics still spoke of struggle—against war, the scourge of the AIDS epidemic in Africa, and the loss of traditional culture.

(ELIZABETH LASKEY)

Meciar, Vladimir

A former amateur boxer, Vladimir Meciar charged aggressively out of his corner in early 1993 as prime minister of the newly created Slovak Republic. As the year progressed, however, Meciar was sent reeling from a series of blows, most delivered by a stagnant economy that undermined his previous popularity.

Meciar was born on July 26, 1942. Educated at Comenius University in Bratislava, he served in various posts in the pro-Communist Union of Slovak Youth and apparently backed Alexander Dubcek during the "Prague Spring" of 1968. His opposition to the Communist hard-liners cost him his party membership in 1969, and he slipped into relative obscurity for the next two decades.

He reemerged as a prominent member of Public Against Violence, an anti-Communist opposition group, and became interim minister of the interior following the 1989 "Velvet Revolution." In the June 1990 elections, Public Against Violence won a clear victory in Slovakia, and Meciar became Slovak prime minister.

He was ousted from this post in April 1991, in part owing to accusations of having collaborated with the secret police during the Communist era. Instead of diminishing his power, however, Meciar's reversal boosted his popularity among Slovaks who viewed their former premier as a martyr. Out of office but riding a crest of popular acclaim, Meciar then formed the Movement for a Democratic Slovakia (HZDS). Seeing Slovak nationalism as his path to power, he pledged to stand up to Prague and its fast-paced program of free-market reforms. After the June 1992 regional parliamentary elections, the HZDS finished first and Meciar again became the Slovak prime minister.

He immediately entered into negotiations with Czech Prime Minister Vaclav Klaus over Slovakia's role in the federation. Klaus made clear that Slovakia had to choose between partnership in the rapid free-market reform movement or complete independence. Bound by his campaign pledge, Meciar chose the latter, and on Jan. 1, 1993, Czechoslovakia ended its 74-year existence and dissolved into the Czech Republic and the Slovak Republic. Meciar was now head of government in a sovereign country.

In his first year as leader of the Slovak Republic, Meciar faced a host of difficulties. A large Magyar minority turned restive. Some observers saw autocratic tendencies in the HZDS regime. More seriously, the economy stumbled as Meciar's plan for a gentle transition from socialism to capitalism did little to reduce the nation's dependence on the weakening arms industry. By midyear, unemployment had reached 11.5% and was rising, foreign investment was dropping precipitously, and no federal subsidies were forthcoming from Prague as they had previously. The HZDS government adopted an austerity budget with reduced spending for social programs. Not surprisingly, Meciar's popularity plummeted.

(JEROLD L. KELLMAN)

Meri, Lennart

The man chosen to lead Estonia as its first president since the country gained its independence from the Soviet Union was an erudite scholar who studied, documented, filmed, and burnished the memory of native Estonian history and culture.

Lennart Meri was born in Tallinn, Estonia, on March 29, 1929, in the period between the world wars when Estonia enjoyed its first, brief independence. His father, Georg Meri, was a man of letters who served the young nation as a diplomat, and the younger Meri was educated in Berlin, London, and Paris. In 1940 Georg Meri was named Estonia's first ambassador to the U.S., but while the family was preparing to leave the country, Estonia was invaded and annexed by the Soviet Union. The elder Meri, a committed nationalist, was arrested and placed in a labour camp in Moscow, while Lennart, his mother, and brother were sent into exile in Siberia. After the war the family was reunited in Soviet Estonia, where Lennart attended Tartu University and studied history.

Meri spent his professional life charting the history of the Finno-Ugric peoples, who span the former Soviet Union from the Baltic States and Finland to Siberia. He later said that he wrote books and directed film documentaries that traced the history of the native Estonian population because "it was the only way of remaining honest during the Soviet occupation period." Meri served variously at Estonian Radio, as a secretary of the Estonian Writers' Association, and as a director of the Estonian Institute.

In 1990, at the age of 60, Meri entered politics when he was named foreign minister after Estonia's first free elections. Estonia gained its independence in 1991, and Meri was appointed ambassador to Finland in April 1992. He decided to run for president later that year as head of the nationalist coalition party Isamaa (Fatherland), whose priority was to preserve Estonian culture. During the campaign, allegations surfaced that his father, who died in 1983, had served as an informant for the secret police; Meri vigorously denied the charges. Meri placed second in the elections, but no one candidate earned a majority, and the parliament, dominated by parties aligned with Meri's, elected him president on Oct. 5, 1992. Looking warily at developments in Russia in December, Meri told the *Times* that Estonia had won its independence in 1991 without bloodshed, "and this time, we mean to keep it."

(CHERYL L. COLLINS)

Molitor, Paul

Baseball fans everywhere learned what Milwaukee Brewers fans had long known when Paul Molitor won the Most Valuable Player award for the 1993 World Series. After playing in only one World Series in his 15 Milwaukee seasons, he helped the Toronto Blue Jays defeat the Philadelphia Phillies, four games to two, with 12 hits in 24 at-bats, a record-tying 10 runs scored, and 24 total bases, one shy of still another record.

Molitor left Milwaukee in 1993 because the Brewers said that their small-market resources kept them from coming close to Toronto's offer of $13 million for three years. He batted .361 in the second half of the season to finish at .332 with career highs of 22 home runs and 111 runs batted in. With a record six consecutive hits, he helped the Blue Jays defeat the Chicago White Sox in the American League Championship Series.

At 37, Molitor was the oldest player to drive in 100 runs for his first time and the oldest to exceed 20 home runs and stolen bases in one season. His 22 steals included a steal of home on the final day of the regular season. "He's 37, but he still does things like he's 25," teammate Roberto Alomar said. Molitor finished the season with a career batting average of .306 and career totals of 2,492 hits and 1,396 runs. Molitor hit with an unusually compact swing, waiting until the ball nearly reached him before he moved his hands or stepped forward. Even then, his stride was small, and he attacked the baseball with a quick stab of the bat.

Paul Leo Molitor was born Aug. 22, 1956, in St. Paul, Minn. He was all-state in baseball and basketball in high school and all-conference in both sports at the University of Minnesota in 1976 and 1977. The third choice in the 1977 baseball draft, Molitor played only 64 minor league games before batting .273 with 30 stolen bases as a rookie second baseman for the Brewers in 1978, when *The Sporting News* and *Baseball Digest* named him American League Rookie of the Year.

Because of injuries, only in two of the seasons from 1978 through 1987 did Molitor play in more than 140 games. Nevertheless, in one of those years, 1982, his 136 runs scored were the most since 1949, and he became the first batter ever with a 5-for-5 game in the World Series. From 1987 through 1993 Molitor batted over .300 six times in seven seasons. He ranked second in American League batting average in 1987 and 1993. In 1987 he hit safely in 39 consecutive games, the fifth longest major league streak since

1900, and recorded career highs of a .353 batting average and 45 stolen bases in 118 games. He most often played third base in 1982–89, but injuries had limited him after that primarily to designated hitter and, occasionally, first base.

(KEVIN M. LAMB)

Naruhito, Crown Prince, and Princess Masako
The June 9 wedding of Crown Prince Naruhito and Masako Owada in Tokyo was undoubtedly the most talked-about royal event in many years. In earlier times royal brides came from the nobility, but Naruhito followed in the footsteps of his father, Emperor Akihito, by marrying a commoner. Media from all over the world found in the courtship and marriage many telltale signs that times had changed.

The path to the wedding had been a long one. When the couple met for the first time in 1986 at a tea party, Naruhito was favourably impressed. Owada, however, was reportedly not interested in courtship. Marriage for a young woman in modern Japan would mean the loss of much of the unprecedented freedom she enjoyed. For Owada the decision was even more difficult because she would be exchanging a career in diplomacy for life in the imperial household, where the emperor's family, by tradition, lacked both privacy and autonomy. It was not until December 1992 that Owada finally decided to accept the prince's proposal.

Naruhito had persuaded his bride-to-be that her duties would be largely diplomatic in nature; he also promised to protect her for her entire life. The idea of protecting was widely interpreted to mean that he was determined to guard her from the traditional, rigid ways of the Imperial Household Agency courtiers. The newlyweds were expected to accelerate the transition to an imperial family that was more relaxed and accessible. Both, moreover, were well prepared to take advantage of the experience they had in the world beyond the palace walls.

Crown Prince Naruhito, eldest son of Emperor Akihito and Empress Michiko, was born on Feb. 23, 1960. He was the first heir to the Japanese throne to have studied abroad. During two years of researching marine transportation at Merton College, Oxford, the student prince mastered the commoners' skills of doing laundry and using a credit card. Between appearances on state occasions, the crown prince found time to play the viola and occasionally teach classes at Gakushuin University in Tokyo, where he did graduate studies.

Masako Owada, daughter of Hisashi Owada, a high-ranking official of the Ministry of Foreign Affairs, was born in Tokyo on Dec. 9, 1963. As a child she lived in the Soviet Union and in the U.S., where her father was on diplomatic missions. In 1985 she graduated from Harvard University with a major in economics. In 1986 she enrolled in Tokyo University. Having passed the diplomatic service test, she joined the Foreign Ministry in 1987. In 1990 the ministry sent her to study at Oxford. Later, as a junior diplomat, she worked long hours, compiling briefing papers on trade issues and translating tedious documents. By the time she became engaged, Owada had won wide respect for the depth of her knowledge on highly technical matters and for her skills as a diplomat.

(HIDEKO TAKAYAMA)

Netanyahu, Benjamin
In 1993 the new leader of Israel's Likud Party was conservative politician Benjamin Netanyahu, who nevertheless delighted in being compared to U.S. Pres. Bill Clinton, another particularly successful product of television-age politics. Netanyahu's stature as head of the opposition was underscored by his attempts to bring down the government of Prime Minister Yitzhak Rabin and by his vociferous opposition to the historic Israeli-Palestinian accords formalized in September by Rabin and PLO leader Yasir Arafat.

Netanyahu was born on Oct. 21, 1949. His father, Benzion Netanyahu, was a historian and a leading intellectual of the conservative revisionist movement. In 1963 the family moved to the U.S. after the elder Netanyahu was invited to teach at a

REUTERS/BETTMANN

college in Philadelphia. There Benjamin attended high school and learned the idiomatic English that would later serve him so well. He returned to Israel in 1967 to serve until 1972 as a commando in the elite, top-secret Sayeret Matcal ("Border Reconnaissance") unit, which often staged daring raids; he eventually became a captain.

In 1972 Netanyahu was on the team that successfully stormed a hijacked airliner at Ben-Gurion Airport. Later that year he commenced studies at the Massachusetts Institute of Technology (MIT), but in 1973 he returned to Israel to fight in the Yom Kippur War. After the war he finished his studies and earned an M.B.A. from MIT. It was a Sayeret raid in which he did not participate, however, that perhaps most profoundly affected his life. The 1976 raid of a hijacked airliner at Entebbe, Uganda, was led by Netanyahu's brother Jonathan, who fell as the only military casualty. Netanyahu responded by founding (1978) the Jonathan Institute, which held seminars on terrorism and drew participants from all over the world.

Netanyahu worked (1979–82) as a marketing manager for a furniture retailer before accepting an offer from Moshe Arens, the Israeli ambassador to the U.S., to join him and serve as deputy chief of mission. From 1984 to 1988 Netanyahu served as the permanent representative to the UN, and from 1988 to 1991 he was deputy minister of foreign affairs. In 1991, while serving as a deputy minister in Prime Minister Yitzhak Shamir's Cabinet, he became familiar to international television audiences. During the Gulf war he briefly interrupted a televised interview to don a gas mask during an Iraqi missile attack; at the peace talks in Madrid he forcefully articulated Israel's rejection of Palestinian demands.

After Likud fell from power, Netanyahu tried to gain control of the party and remake it in his own television-friendly image. In the first election of a Likud leader voted directly by party members instead of old-style bosses, he easily won the post that would make him prime minister if Likud were to gain power. He succeeded despite revelations that his campaign was financed mainly by U.S. businessmen, and the thrice-married Netanyahu deflected a sex scandal by publicly admitting his marital infidelity. Netanyahu was the author of *A Place Among the Nations* (1993).

(CHERYL L. COLLINS)

Ondieki, Yobes
Yobes Ondieki had not run 10,000 m on a track for 10 years when he started training for the event in February 1993. The reigning world champion at 5,000 m, he set his sights for the Bislett Games Grand Prix 10,000-m race on July 10 at Oslo, Norway, on a track where dozens of records had fallen. He prepared with three months of altitude training and three 5,000-m races through mid-June, and then he ran the 10,000 as if it were just two 5,000s.

Ondieki asked the pacesetters to run the first 5,000 m between 13 min 25 sec and 13 min 30 sec, a speed that onlookers said would leave him too weary for a strong finish. However, after a 5,000-m time of 13 min 28 sec, Ondieki led for the last third of the race and finished in 26 min 58.38 sec, shattering the 27-minute barrier that was expected to stand into the next century and shaving 9.53 seconds off a world record that had fallen by only 24 seconds during the previous 15 years.

Coming five days after fellow Kenyan Richard Chelimo had broken a four-year-old world record, Ondieki's mark made 1993 the first year since 1956 in which the 10,000-m record had been broken twice in one season. According to two widely respected comparison tables, Ondieki's was the greatest distance race ever run, from 1,500 m through the marathon.

Ondieki was born Feb. 21, 1961, in Kenya. He attended Iowa State University and afterward trained mostly in the United States. After years of injuries and bad luck, he became a world-class runner in 1988, when he finished 12th in the 5,000 m at the Olympic Games. He became a champion the next year, when he was the first man in 10 years to beat Said Aouita of Morocco at 5,000 m. He ran the world's best 5,000 times in 1989 and 1991, and his 1991 time, a personal record of 13 min 1.82 sec, was the sixth best ever. He won the 5,000 m at the 1991 world outdoor championships in Tokyo, but he finished a disappointing fifth at the distance in the 1992 Olympics at Barcelona, Spain, which took place shortly after he developed sciatica.

His strained relationship with Kenyan track and field authorities surfaced when he did not run in his country's 1993 national trials and refused to defend his 5,000-m world championship at Stuttgart, Germany, in August. He said he planned to continue running at both 5,000-m and 10,000-m distances, but he also added another goal: he planned to run his first marathon.

(KEVIN M. LAMB)

Ornish, Dean
In an age when medical science was combating heart disease with costly high-tech interventions, American physician Dean Ornish was something of a throwback. His simple, inexpensive program of lifestyle changes—which featured a low-fat, primarily vegetarian diet, moderate aerobic exercise, and daily stress management—contrasted sharply with such invasive and potentially risky treatments as bypass surgery, angioplasty, and cholesterol-lowering medication. The holistic regimen that Ornish recommended appeared not only to halt the progress of atherosclerosis (the buildup of fatty substances within the arteries) but actually to reverse it.

Despite his reluctance to being labeled a guru, Ornish continued to gain enthusiastic converts following the publication of his best-selling second book, *Dr. Dean Ornish's Program for Reversing Heart Disease: The Only System Scientifically Proven to Reverse Heart Disease Without Drugs or Surgery* (1990). Highlights of 1993 for Ornish included the publication in June of a third book, *Eat More, Weigh Less: Dr. Dean Ornish's Life Choice Program for Losing Weight Safely While Eating Abundantly;* an invitation to the White House in July; and the announcement in August that Mutual of Omaha would reimburse policyholders for the cost of participation in the program—the first time a major insurer had agreed to cover an "alternative" treatment for heart disease.

Ornish was born in Dallas, Texas, on July 16, 1953. He graduated first in his class at the University of Texas at Austin. He next went to Houston, Texas, to study at Baylor College of Medicine before moving to the Boston area for a clinical fellowship at Harvard Medical School and an internship and residency in internal medicine at Massachusetts General Hospital. Ornish first began developing his unique approach to heart disease in the late 1970s while he was still a student. In July 1984 he moved to San Francisco and began the Lifestyle Heart Trial, a controlled study of the effects of a low-fat diet and a stress-management regime on a small group of heart-disease patients. His so-called Dean Cuisine diet limited fats to 10% of total caloric intake and cholesterol to only five milligrams a day. (In contrast, the recommendations of the American Heart Association allowed up to 30% of total calories from fat and 300 mg of cholesterol daily.) In addition to giving up smoking and fatty foods, the test subjects did yoga, meditated, and participated in a support group. The results, published at the end of the decade, revealed that the effects of coronary atherosclerosis had been reversed in many patients.

Ornish attracted considerable attention for his therapeutic tactics, which also encouraged patients to "open their hearts" in the emotional sense. He believed that the stress-management aspect of his program, designed to combat social isolation as well as daily pressures, yielded untold benefits. His motivational approach complemented his skills as a fund-raiser and an adept promoter of alternative ideas. Ornish was a faculty member of the University of California School of Medicine in San Francisco and the president and director of the Preventive Medicine Research Institute in nearby Sausalito. His first book, *Stress, Diet, and Your Heart,* was published in 1982.

(TOM MICHAEL)

Orsini, Marina

Though she carefully guarded her private life from the public, Marina Orsini was distressed to find that in 1993 she was instantly recognizable on the streets of Montreal as Emilie Bordeleau, the character she portrayed in Quebec's popular television series "Les Filles de Caleb." Orsini's fans had come to love the turn-of-the-century young woman who struggled to leave her home on the farm, educate herself, and pursue a career as a teacher while eventually marrying one of her students. "Les Filles de Caleb" was a success on television in France and was seen on English-language television in Canada under the title "Emilie."

TOM HANSON—CANAPRESS

Orsini was born *c.* 1968 in Montreal, and she began a modeling career at the age of 15. She was intent, however, upon a television or film career. In 1985 Orsini auditioned for a role in the television series "Lance et Compte," a hockey saga seen in English-speaking Canada as "He Shoots! He Scores!" Though her acting experience consisted of only a few television commercials, director Jean-Claude Lord saw Orsini's potential. He cast her in the role of Suzie Lambert, sister of the main character. The series was successful, and Orsini played the part for two years. Her second television series, "L'Or et le papier," received three Gémeaux awards in 1990, including one for Orsini as best actress.

Orsini, fluent in French, English, and Italian, appeared in films in Canada, France, Switzerland, and the United States. She had roles in two Quebec-made films: *L'Emprise* (1987), directed by Michel Brault, and *La Grenouille et la baleine* (1988), directed by Lord. In 1989 she starred as the female lead in Lord's film *Eddie and the Cruisers II: Eddie Lives!* In her first live stage performance, on Radio-Canada's New Year's Eve show *Bye-Bye* (1991), she did a spoof of Quebec's rock-and-roll star Marjo—a radical departure from the demure Emilie.

Orsini, who cultivated an interest in film techniques, dreamed of spending a day behind the camera directing. As an actress she was committed to projecting a responsible image. Performers, she felt, were in a position of power because people related to them and their characters. As a result, she refused roles that did not meet her standards. Her appreciative audiences voted Orsini their favourite female personality of 1992, an honour that merited her a Métrostar award.

In 1992–93 Orsini made use of her language skills. She did her own dubbing for the English-language version of "Les Filles de Caleb," and she took lessons in the language of the Mohawk for her role in "Shehaweh," a miniseries produced for French-Canadian television. For that part she played a 17th-century Iroquois princess kidnapped by French colonists. She also revived the role of Emilie in "Blanche," the sequel to "Les Filles de Caleb."

(DIANE LOIS WAY)

Ovitz, Michael

In 1993 the middleman was alive, well, and taking his cut in Hollywood. The most powerful such person was Michael Ovitz, who, through his Creative Artists Agency (CAA), pampered, promoted, and profited from such clients as Madonna, Bill Murray, Whoopi Goldberg, Kevin Costner, Tom Cruise, Steven Spielberg, and—most dramatically in 1993—David Letterman (*q.v.*). As Letterman's agent, Ovitz negotiated an unprecedented three-year, $42 million contract for the talk-show host to leave his 12:30 AM Eastern Standard Time program at NBC for a show one hour earlier on CBS. After the signing, Letterman described his agent as "a smart, thoughtful man" and declared himself "a satisfied customer."

Later Ovitz ventured beyond the talent-agent business to advise the French bank Crédit Lyonnais on its red-inked entertainment holdings, particularly Metro-Goldwyn-Mayer, Inc. He arranged a deal in which the bank would forgive past loans to MGM, give it additional moneys to increase film production, and appoint as the studio's new chairman Frank G. Mancuso, an experienced Hollywood hand and an Ovitz friend. While Crédit Lyonnais praised its agent's counsel, the press and CAA's competitors called the deal a conflict of interest because Ovitz was both advising a studio and representing clients who might seek work there. Ovitz denied the charge all the way to the bank; his estimated 1993 income from commissions and fees amounted to a whopping $10 million. Defending the deal in a rare interview, he insisted that "Hollywood is a small, familial place," where "everyone does business with everybody else."

Ovitz was born on Dec. 14, 1946, in Encino, Calif. His parents wanted him to become a doctor but, while working part-time as a guide for Universal studios, he fell in love with the idea of pursuing a career in Hollywood. After graduating from the University of California at Los Angeles in 1968, he took a job in the mail room of the William Morris Agency, a leading talent-management firm. The aggressive and disciplined Ovitz soon worked his way up to being an agent for television talents Merv Griffin and Bob Barker. In 1975 he joined with four other disgruntled Morris agents to form CAA. Thanks to Ovitz' knack for hustling up clients, CAA was quickly transformed from a cheesy operation with card tables and folding chairs to a bustling agency with modern offices and power suits.

A short man with narrow brown eyes and a tight smile, Ovitz had a secretive, anonymous air akin to that of an underworld attorney, an image that was especially apt in the 1980s, when his success engendered a mix of respect and fear. His hard bargaining techniques and large stable of big-name talent greatly inflated Hollywood's costs, but few criticized him until he reached for a lion's share of business with the MGM deal.

(MICHAEL AMEDEO)

Paglia, Camille

The controversial academic, aesthete, and self-described feminist Camille Paglia enunciated her unorthodox views on sexuality and the development of culture and art in Western civilization in two books, *Sexual Personae: Art and Decadence from Nefertiti to Emily Dickinson* (1990) and *Sex, Art, and American Culture: Essays* (1992). Her public persona and iconoclastic views enraged many academics and feminists and titillated audiences of television talk shows and college lecture halls as well as those who read her magazine essays and op-ed contributions.

A self-styled in-your-face Italian-American rebel with working-class immigrant grandparents, Paglia was born on April 2, 1947, in Endicott, N.Y., the daughter of a professor of Romance languages. Valedictorian of her class at the State University of New York at Binghamton (B.A., 1968), she became a disciple of outspoken critic and educator Harold Bloom at Yale University, where she received a Ph.D. in 1974. A teacher of literature at Bennington (Vt.) College (1972–80) and Wesleyan University, Middletown, Conn. (1980), she was visiting lecturer at Yale (1981–83; 1984). From 1984 she was affiliated with the University of the Arts, Philadelphia (formerly the College of Performing Arts), where from 1991 she was professor of humanities.

Paglia expounded a theory, based on comparisons from Greek myths, of the duality of Western culture: the rational, orderly Apollonion aspect of society feels threatened by the Dionysian, chaotic forces of nature, which are murky and earthbound (her term is *chthonic*). An admirer of the works of Sigmund Freud, Sir James Frazier, and Charles Darwin, Paglia claimed that perversions in sexual behaviour came not from social injustice but from natural forces. For example, Paglia declared rape to be a sexual, not a violent, act, adding that women should avoid situations that might invite rape.

She posited that men develop cerebral achievement in order to separate themselves from the mother and her inexorable psychological domination. According to Paglia, "If civilization had been left in female hands, we would still be living in grass huts." Women, the keepers of the hearth, are chthonic; women writers are unable to rise to the heights of Apollonion designs to which men have access.

Paglia advocated the decriminalization of prostitution, abortion, drug usage, and pornography. She urged the revamping of the U.S. educational system by institution of a core curriculum based primarily on the classics. She also called for the abolition of such highly politicized college majors as African-American studies and women's studies.

At odds with what she called the feminist establishment, Paglia celebrated the feminism demonstrated by unsentimental, independent, "ask-no-quarter, give-no-quarter" women, such as the aviator Amelia Earhart and the actress Katharine Hepburn. A self-proclaimed bisexual who celebrated decadence in its many guises, she also professed admiration for rock stars Madonna and Keith Richards and writers Oscar Wilde and the Marquis de Sade.

(NAOMI BERNARDS POLONSKY)

Peter Rabbit

In 1993 children of all ages celebrated the 100th birthday of the world's best-known and most beloved lagomorph. The guest of honour was not only long in the tooth, he was also long in the ears. Peter Rabbit, who began his public life in Edwardian times and retained his best-seller status in the postmodern era, proved to be a contemporary centenarian. A nontrendy vegetarian, the mischievous Peter tended to ignore his mother's warnings about making forbidden, potentially fatal forays into Mr. McGregor's garden to satisfy his yen for carrots and lettuce.

Peter Rabbit was created on Sept. 4, 1893, in the pages of an illustrated letter written to a sick little boy by the British watercolourist and writer Beatrix Potter. "My dear Noel," she began, "I don't know what to write to you, so I shall tell you a story about four little rabbits whose names were Flopsy, Mopsy, Cottontail and Peter." From that letter developed the small illustrated book *The Tale of Peter Rabbit*, which Potter published privately in 1901, and which became the best-selling children's book on record. Twenty-three books and 80 million copies later, Potter's books had been translated into more than 20 languages. All the books contained Potter's watercolour illustrations, which captured the timeless, tranquil beauty of England's Lake District.

Peter himself was quite possibly the world's oldest licensed character, with 2,000 new products adorned with his likeness produced every year. The merchandising of Peter Rabbit did not begin with greedy late 20th-century entrepreneurs, however; Potter herself guided the production of her books. She patented her own Peter Rabbit doll, invented a board game featuring him, and even attempted to market Peter Rabbit wallpaper designs.

To what can Peter Rabbit's longevity be attributed? Certainly not to his costume, consisting of a little blue waistcoat with decidedly old-fashioned styling, or his bucolic and circumscribed world. Perhaps Potter's tales of Peter, couched in Edwardian sensibilities and morality, introduced young readers to the very real dangers lurking in the adult world and to actions whose consequences needed to be addressed. In Potter's animal kingdom, foxes sometimes got eaten and kittens nearly baked into puddings. Even Peter barely escaped Farmer McGregor's clutches and returned, frightened but a little wiser, to his mother's waiting, comforting embrace. And Mrs. Rabbit had at the ready a cup of chamomile tea for Peter; for his good little siblings, who never got into the scrapes that tempted Peter, she produced a supper of bread and milk and blackberries.

In addition to books about Peter Rabbit, Potter, who died in Lancashire in 1943, wrote about many other animals, including Benjamin Bunny, Peter's cousin, and the Flopsy Bunnies, Peter's nieces and nephews. "The World of Peter Rabbit and Friends," a six-part animated series that used Potter's illustrations, was created in 1992 for television broadcast and home video.

(NAOMI BERNARDS POLONSKY)

Peyron, Bruno

In 1872 the fictional Phileas Fogg traveled *Around the World in Eighty Days* by train, boat, and elephant. In 1993, more than a century after French author Jules Verne penned that adventure, French yachtsman Bruno Peyron and his four-man crew challenged Fogg's seemingly unattainable record on the high seas. Seventy-nine days, 6 hours, and 15 minutes after beginning the race for the newly created Trophée Jules Verne, Peyron's high-tech, sail-powered, 26-m (86-ft) *Commodore Explorer*, the world's largest catamaran, shattered the previous circumnavigation sailing record of 109 days set in 1990.

From January 31 to April 20, Peyron and crew survived turbulent storms, glacial and gale-force winds, 19-m (65-ft) waves, a near capsize, crew members washed overboard, and, on the 70th day, a collision with two sperm whales—the second time a hull on the vessel was damaged. As *Commodore* sailed, Peyron added more speed records to the history books—nine days to the equator, 23 days to South Africa's Cape of Good Hope, 33 days to Australia's Cape Leeuwin, and 53 days to South America's Cape Horn—and covered a historic 816 km (507 m) in a 24-hour run to complete the legendary voyage. Without stopping or receiving outside assistance, Peyron journeyed more than 27,000 nautical miles, averaging 21.12 knots/mile.

In 1990 Peyron joined the Association Tour du Monde en 80 Jours, a confederation of 15 sailors whose goal was to reenact Verne's late-19th-century voyage with the use of modern technology. Shortly thereafter, Peyron appropriated and modified the boat *Jet Services 5*, which held the crew transatlantic record (6 days 13 hours) and the 24-hour speed record.

Bruno Tristan Peyron was born on Nov. 10, 1955, in Angers, France, the oldest of two nautical world-champion brothers. Peyron was raised in La Baule in southern Brittany's Loire Valley. As a young child he fell in love with the ocean when his father and mentor, an oil-tanker captain, taught him to sail. As a teenager Peyron began pursuing a lifelong goal: "to break every speed record on all the oceans of the world." He soon matured into a regularly honoured sailor on the international offshore multihull racing circuit.

Peyron successfully crossed the Atlantic Ocean 27 times—11 of them solo. In 1987 he was awarded France's equivalent of Athlete of the Year, and from that time he ranked as the top Formula One (boats longer than 21 m [70 ft]) skipper. During 1987, while racing only against his brother, he set his first record for sailing single-handedly across the Atlantic from New York to England—11 days 11 hours 46 minutes. He improved that solo record with a transatlantic voyage of less than 10 days in July 1992.

After surpassing his fictional hero's 80-day mark, Peyron planned to produce a book and a film about his globe-circling experiences before attempting to break another one of his own sailing records.

(BEVERLY E. SORKIN)

Rasmussen, Poul Nyrup

When Prime Minister Poul Schlüter was forced from office by Denmark's ongoing "Tamilgate" affair on Jan. 14, 1993, Poul Nyrup Rasmussen, the leader of the Social Democrats, was faced not only with the challenge of forming a new government but also with the task of overseeing Denmark's key second referendum on the Maastricht Treaty. Furthermore, the country had just taken over the European Community's rotating presidency.

A scandal involving the illegal actions of the Ministry of Justice in preventing the immigration of Tamil refugees from Sri Lanka brought to an end the 10-year rule of Schlüter's Conservative-Liberal minority government. In its place Rasmussen, who had never before held high public office, formed a four-party majority coalition, enlisting the support of the seven-member Radical Liberal Party—holder of the balance of power between socialist and nonsocialist parties for some 70 years. The new prime minister's Cabinet, expanded to 24 members to accommodate wide participation by all four partners in the coalition, included eight women.

Before Rasmussen could turn his attention to the May 18 referendum on the Maastricht Treaty, Denmark's currency became the object of market speculation that threatened the country's continued participation in the European exchange-rate mechanism. Surviving that crisis, Rasmussen began the task of persuading the Danish people (especially his own party, which had voted three to two against the referendum when it was narrowly defeated in June 1992) to approve a version of the treaty that now included special exemptions for Denmark. Promising tax reform if the referendum passed, Rasmussen called those who opposed it "raving mad." The referendum, voted upon by 86% of the electorate, passed easily, but two days of rioting in Copenhagen followed. The country had, in Rasmussen's words, "taken a step toward bringing Europe closer to ordinary citizens." Maastricht was still alive, and Denmark clearly had found a capable new leader.

The son of an unskilled worker and a cleaner, Rasmussen was born on June 15, 1943, in Esbjerg, Den. He graduated from the University of Copenhagen with a degree in economics in 1971 and worked for the Danish Trade Union Council until 1986, becoming its chief economist in 1980. While serving as the managing director of the Employees Capital Pension Fund and as chairman of Lalandia Invest (1986–88), Rasmussen became deputy leader of the Social Democrats (1987) and a member of the Folketing, or parliament (1988). He served as the chairmen of the Parliamentary Committee on Commerce, Industry and Shipping from 1988 until 1992, when he became the leader of his party.

(JEFF WALLENFELDT)

Reno, Janet

On March 12, 1993, Janet Reno was sworn in as the 78th attorney general of the United States. She was the first woman to serve as the nation's top law-enforcement official and seemed to be

DAVID BURNETT—CONTACT PRESS IMAGES

one of the few bright spots in the administration of Pres. Bill Clinton, who had been dogged by political missteps and questionable nominations. An experienced and able prosecutor, Reno was also known for launching innovative programs designed to steer nonviolent drug offenders away from jail and for espousing often controversial opinions regarding the rights of criminal defendants. As the new head of the Justice Department, Reno faced considerable challenges, not the least of which was reconciling her own views on the root causes of crime and social disorder with the views of a crime-weary populace that was demanding tougher laws and harsher punishments.

Reno was born on July 21, 1938, in Miami, Fla. Her father, Henry, was a Danish immigrant who worked as a police reporter for the *Miami Herald*. Her mother, Jane, who worked as an investigative reporter for the *Miami News*, was locally known as a colourful eccentric who wrestled alligators, recited poetry, and was made an honorary princess by the Miccosukee Indians. Following her graduation from Harvard Law School in 1963, Reno worked for several law firms and for the Florida state legislature. In 1978 she was appointed state's attorney for Dade county, which encompassed the entire greater-Miami area. In this position she dealt with the 1980 bloody riots in the Liberty City section of Miami and with the greatly increased crime spurred by the booming 1980s drug trade. By reforming the juvenile justice system and aggressively prosecuting child-abuse cases, she also gained recognition as a strong advocate for the rights of children.

Reno was criticized by some in the law-enforcement community for her perceived leniency toward criminals and for her tendency to plea-bargain cases. However, her innovative ideas and vast experience as a prosecutor put her on Clinton's shortlist for attorney general. Reno's nomination followed two others: Zoë Baird and Kimba M. Wood both withdrew from consideration amid controversy about their employment of illegal immigrants as domestics.

Soon after taking office, Reno in April ordered agents of the FBI to conduct the final raid on the Branch Davidian cult compound near Waco, Texas, where weapons were reportedly being stockpiled. She received plaudits for shouldering responsibility for the ill-fated raid, which ended a 51-day standoff and left at least 75 people dead. She also drafted new legislation to broaden the federal scope of child pornography laws. Her philosophy often differed from that of the Clinton administration, and in October she annoyed the White House by threatening to force television networks to curb violence and by failing to endorse Vice Pres. Al Gore's plan to merge the Drug Enforcement Administration and the FBI. Nevertheless, by year's end the independent-minded Reno was still publicly viewed as one of the more popular figures in government.

(JOHN H. MATHEWS)

Rivera, Chita

In *Kiss of the Spider Woman,* a Latin-American prisoner attempts to while away the hours by recounting for his cell mate the stories of films that starred Aurora, a film goddess of the past who played a character known as the Spider Woman, and by imagining himself in scenes from those movies. At first the choice of Chita Rivera for that Marlene Dietrich-like character in the Broadway musical production—which, like the 1985 movie, was based on the novel by Manuel Puig—seemed unlikely to some. At 60 she was well beyond the age by which most dancers have ceased performing. In addition, in 1986 her left leg had been broken in 12 places in an automobile accident, and it was thought that she might never walk again, let alone dance. Nevertheless, critics and audiences alike lauded her performance, extolling this Broadway legend's energetic, sultry portrayal of an exotic film legend. A number of awards confirmed this reaction, among them the 1993 Tony award for best actress in a musical.

Rivera was born Dolores Conchita Figuero del Rivero on Jan. 23, 1933, in Washington, D.C. Her first performances were in shows her brother organized for production in the basement of their home. She took voice, piano, and ballet classes, and dance became her overwhelming favourite. She won a scholarship to George Balanchine's School of American Ballet in New York City and studied there for three years. In 1952 she accompanied a friend to an audition for dancers for the touring company of *Call Me Madam,* was hired, and spent 10 months on the road. Returning to New York, she replaced a principal dancer in *Guys and Dolls* on Broadway and then joined the chorus of *Can-Can.* In 1954 she left chorus work behind her and performed off-Broadway in *Shoestring Revue.* Roles in *Seventh Heaven* (1955) and *Mr. Wonderful* (1956) followed, and then she landed the part of Anita in *West Side Story* and received her first Tony award nomination. More plaudits accumulated, among them Tony nominations for Rose in *Bye Bye Birdie* (1960), Anyanka in *Bajour* (1964), and Velma in *Chicago* (1975). She also appeared as Nickie in the film version of *Sweet Charity* (1969) and toured with her highly regarded cabaret act.

Rivera finally won a Tony for her performance as Anna in *The Rink* (1984), which was written specifically for her. One critic said that she commanded the audience like "a lion tamer with a whip snap in her walk." The next year saw her back on Broadway in *Jerry's Girls.* It was during the run of the show that the career-threatening auto accident occurred. After many months of rehabilitation, she eased her way back into show business by performing her cabarat act on cruise ships. She toured with the Rockettes in *Can-Can* in 1988 and '89 before her triumphant return to Broadway in *Kiss of the Spider Woman* once again illustrated her power to ensnare an audience.

(BARBARA WHITNEY)

Roddick, Anita

Recycling waste, saving the rain forests, and stopping animal testing were unusual concerns for a business when Anita Roddick opened the first Body Shop in Brighton, England, in 1976. The natural-ingredient skin and hair products she sold were unproven oddities in the cosmetics industry. Roddick's progressive ideas found an audience, though, and the audience liked the products enough that by 1993 Body Shop International operated in 41 countries.

She was born Anita Lucia Perella on Oct. 23, 1942, in Littlehampton, West Sussex. She watched her Italian-immigrant family transform a common English café into an ostentatious American-style diner, an experience she described as "my first lesson in marketing aesthetics."

She attended Newton Park College of Education at Bath, Avon. While teaching at a secondary school, she was awarded a scholarship to study in Israel for three months. Returning to Littlehampton, she resumed teaching, but she had experienced too much of the world to contain herself in a classroom.

In the early 1970s Roddick lived a desultory existence with her husband, Gordon, and two

FRANK CAPRI—SAGA/ARCHIVE PHOTOS

daughters. A bed-and-breakfast venture peaked and crashed quickly. They had some success with a restaurant but found it too time-consuming. Roddick then had an idea. In her travels she had admired the skin and hair of women in less developed countries, who used nothing more than the plants and fruits nature provided. She also saw no need for elaborate packaging of cosmetics. In fact, why not refill customers' empty containers? So began The Body Shop.

After two funeral directors in Brighton objected to the name of her business in close proximity to their own enterprises, Roddick told it to the press. The coverage brought in customers and began a company tradition of using publicity instead of paid advertising. Within months she was scouting locations for a second store. By the late '70s she was authorizing franchises across Europe. In 1984 the company went public on the Unlisted Securities Market, and Roddick began receiving awards from the business community. In 1991 she published her autobiography, *Body and Soul.*

Roddick's desire to teach never diminished. She used The Body Shop as a source of funds and a forum to educate the public about the work of Amnesty International, the Kayapo tribe of the Brazilian rain forests, and anything else she deemed worthy. In July 1993, with sales (and the share price) hurt by the recession, the Roddicks and their company won a judgment of £276,000 in a libel suit against Britain's Channel Four, which had aired a television program that questioned their social commitment. (STEPHEN S. SEDDON)

Sampras, Pete

When Pete Sampras became the top-ranked tennis player in the world on April 12, 1993, he was swinging the same model of racket he had started using at the age of 16. When he won his second U.S. Open championship on September 12 in straight sets, he was launching the 204-km/h (127-mph) serve that he had been cultivating since the age of seven. He still had the expression between points that had earned him the nickname "Smiley" as a child. As he had said after his first Open victory three years earlier, "I want to be the same person that I was two months ago."

Sampras set men's tennis tour records in 1993 with 1,011 aces (unreachable first serves), earnings of $3,648,075, and a margin of 683 points ahead of second-ranked Michael Stich. He led the tour in aces, first-serve points, service games won, and service break points saved. He won eight tournaments, reached at least the semifinals of seven others, and led the world with a won-lost match record of 83–15, the most victories by a man since 1985. Besides his U.S. Open victory over Cédric Pioline, Sampras won his first Wimbledon championship over previously top-ranked Jim Courier on July 4.

Sampras' 1993 season followed his 70–18 match record and five championships in 1992, giving him a career total of 20 tournament wins since his first tour victory in 1990. That was the year in which he soared from 81st to 5th in the world rankings and, at the age of 19 years 28 days, became the youngest man ever to win the U.S. Open. After beating Ivan Lendl and John McEnroe, he defeated Andre Agassi in the final with his 100th ace of the seven-match tournament.

Sampras slumped slightly in 1991; he lost in the second rounds at Wimbledon and the French Open and indicated he was relieved to have the pressure removed when he lost in the U.S. Open quarterfinals. But after his Wimbledon victory in 1993, he said, "I expect myself to be a contender for every tournament I enter. If I don't win it, I'm going to be disappointed."

Peter Sampras was born Aug. 12, 1971, in Washington, D.C., the son of a second-generation Greek father and a Greek immigrant mother. He began playing tennis after the family moved to southern California when Sampras was seven. His father wanted to spare him the pressure of being a tennis prodigy and asked pediatrician Peter Fischer to coach him. Fischer had never coached before and tutored Sampras without pay. When Sampras switched from two hands to one on his backhand at 14, he started losing to players he had consistently beaten. One year later, however, he made the 1987 Boys' Junior Davis Cup team and finished second to Michael Chang in the 18-and-under U.S. tournament. He turned professional the next year, 1988, at 16.

(KEVIN M. LAMB)

Seinfeld, Jerry

In 1993 Jerry Seinfeld was again standing up on the job—and keeping countless Americans in their seats laughing. He accomplished the feat mainly through "Seinfeld," an Emmy-winning television sitcom in which he played himself: a thirtysomething stand-up comedian combing everyday life for the little absurdities that would inspire his routines. Produced and sometimes co-written by Seinfeld, the quirky, widely watched show emphasized loosely structured stories, seemingly insignificant subject matter, and a buddy system of comedy in which the Jerry character often played a straight man to his three tightly wound, loosely screwed friends. A typical episode would put the four in the middle of some peculiar development or two—the discovery of an infectious body odour in Jerry's car or even a contest to see who could go the longest without masturbating. The humour was similar to the kind that Seinfeld routinely delivered in his sold-out stand-up appearances. It was hip, clever, and generally temperate and clean, and it prompted *Playboy* to call Seinfeld "a white Bill Cosby." Yet in his routines Seinfeld sometimes seemed less like a superstar comic than a precocious kid who was playacting as one, and that endearing quality helped make him a standout among stand-ups.

Seinfeld had long been a kid with comic aspirations. Born on April 29, 1954, in Brooklyn, N.Y., he had not celebrated too many birthdays before he decided he wanted to be funny like his father, a sign maker who was also a closet comedian. By age eight Seinfeld was putting himself through a rigorous comic training, watching television day and night to study the technique of every comedian who reared his talking head.

Television never showed him what to do about stage fright, however. In 1976 he attempted to make his stand-up debut behind the open mike of a Manhattan comedy club, but his mind went blank, his body went numb, and he could only mutter a few words before slinking off the stage. Later he learned that the audience had actually liked him and, encouraged, Seinfeld resolved to try again. A career in comedy was off and limping.

After he spent years refining his act in smoky little clubs, it took Seinfeld five minutes to become a hit with his television appearance on "The Tonight Show" in 1981. Dozens of talk shows and hundreds of club and college appearances later, Seinfeld was voted the funniest male stand-up comic in 1988 at the American Comedy Awards. This success—followed by the 1990 debut of "Seinfeld" and his 1993 best-selling book *SeinLanguage,* a compilation of observations in the same vein as his stand-up routine—brought closer scrutiny by the critics, a few of whom felt his humour was "generic" or "empty." For Seinfeld the criticism hurt only when the audience did *not* laugh—a rare occurrence.

(MICHAEL AMEDEO)

Sereno, Paul

With the relish of a paleontologist unearthing a grungy but valuable fossil, Americans in 1993 blew the dust off the mystique of dinosaurs and made them into pop culture icons. The appeal of dinosaurs, especially to the young, was exemplified by cuddly Barney, TV's purple dinosaur character, and by the blockbuster movie *Jurassic Park*. To the academic world, however, the media-celebrated, "Indiana Jones" adventures of real-life paleontologist Paul Sereno made Barney and robotic movie dinosaurs look completely manufactured by comparison.

MATTHEW GILSON—UNIVERSITY OF CHICAGO

Unlike most paleontologists, who often wait a lifetime before making a significant discovery, Sereno demonstrated his astounding talent before reaching the age of 35 by seeking and locating fossils in places more experienced paleontologists had never even considered. In 1989 he announced that he and his team of co-workers had found the first well-preserved skull and complete skeleton of the oldest known dinosaur, *Herrerasaurus ischigualastensis,* in the Ischigualasto Formation near the foothills of the Andes near San Juan, Arg. Its remains led Sereno to conclude that this dinosaur was about 2.5 m (8 ft) long and had a unique double-hinged jaw that allowed it to hold struggling prey. This discovery, however, paled in comparison with Sereno's 1993 announcement that he and co-worker Ricardo Martinez had uncovered the first known skull of the most primitive dinosaur, which Sereno later named *Eoraptor lunensis*. Sereno determined that *Eoraptor* was the most primitive because it had not developed any of the specialized features found in later dinosaurs. He speculated that although it was not the common ancestor of all dinosaurs, it might be the closest complete example the world would ever get, and he said that it definitely confirmed the theory that all dinosaurs stemmed from small carnivorous bipedal prototypes. Sereno also won acclaim in the study of ancient birds. He was able to reconstruct the dinosaur-like *Sinornis,* thought to be the first bird capable of sustained flight, from 135 million-year-old remains sent to him by a Chinese colleague.

Sereno was born in Aurora, Ill., on Oct. 11, 1957, to a large family that encouraged scientific as well as artistic pursuits. As an undergraduate at Northern Illinois University, Sereno majored in both art and biology, hoping to become an anatomic illustrator. Instead, he redirected his studies and completed a graduate degree in vertebrate paleontology at Columbia University, New York City. Sereno earned his doctorate in geologic sciences at Columbia in 1987 and promptly joined the University of Chicago's department of organismal biology and anatomy as an associate professor. Feeling most at home in the field, Sereno led expeditions to Asia, Africa, and South America. On these trips he made his famous discoveries while trying to assemble a clear picture of the family tree of the ornithischian dinosaurs (*e.g.,* the stegosaurus). At the end of 1993, Sereno led an expedition to the Sahara to look for proof of the existence of a new species of plant-eating dinosaur. Scientists estimated that more than half the known species of dinosaurs had been discovered in only the past 20 years. Thanks to the expertise and luck of Sereno, there might be many more to come.

(SUSAN RAPP)

Seth, Vikram

With the publication in 1993 of *A Suitable Boy,* Vikram Seth weighed in as a heavyweight of English letters—quite literally. The massive epic of more than 1,300 pages—one of the longest works of fiction in English since the 18th century—drew immediate comparison with Seth's compatriot Salman Rushdie's *Midnight's Children.* Both books depict India shortly after the Partition and its independence from Britain, and both are panoramic in scope; however, while Rushdie's works are known for free-wheeling invention, Seth's *Boy* is a model of gentle pacing and classic English prose. More akin to Jane Austen, E.M. Forster, or Charles Dickens, Seth gives the reader an "India of the drawing room." It fondly portrays the lives of four interwoven families (complete with family trees on the endpapers) and a traditional privileged society at a time of change. The narrative—with its main plot that deals with the question of which suitor will gain the hand of Lata, a Hindu college student, and its equally important subplots—is bracketed by two weddings; its exquisite detail of daily life gives parts of the book the feel of a documentary. While secular in tone, the novel describes religious customs and rituals; the Hindu-Muslim tensions eerily prefigure the current conflict. Seth's clever wordplay and the passion and sheer magnitude of the subcontinent are controlled by the classic form, much as his earlier poetry was contained by meter and rhyme. The work made best-seller lists in India and Britain and was a Book of the Month Club selection in the U.S.

The son of a judge and a businessman, Seth was born June 20, 1952, in Calcutta. He attended the exclusive Doon School in India, then studied at Corpus Christi College, Oxford (B.A., 1975), and Stanford University (M.A., 1978). His first volume of poetry, *Mappings* (1980), was written while

DILIP MEHTA—CONTACT PRESS IMAGES

he was in China doing research for his doctoral dissertation at Nanjing (Nanking) University. *The Humble Administrator's Garden* (1985) is divided into three sections that reflect his life in China, India, and California. *From Heaven Lake* (1983), the story of his journey hitchhiking from Nanjing via Tibet to New Delhi to visit his family, won him critical acclaim and Britain's most prestigious travel-writing award. Called "the great California novel" by Gore Vidal, *The Golden Gate* (1986) is a tour de force. It follows the lives of several yuppies in Silicon Valley (touching on topics such as gay rights and the antinuclear movement) and is written entirely in metered, rhyming 14-line stanzas based on Charles Johnston's 1977 English translation of Aleksandr Pushkin's *Yevgeny Onegin.* His mastery of the verse form brought comparisons to Alexander Pope. Seth returned to live with his family in New Delhi in 1987. Other works include the 1990 collection *All You Who Sleep Tonight* and *Beastly Tales from Here and There* (1992), tetrameter couplets of animal fables from India, China, Greece, Ukraine, and Seth's own mind.

(ELLEN FINKELSTEIN)

Shalikashvili, John Malchase David

When Gen. Colin L. Powell announced that he was going to step down as chairman of the Joint Chiefs of Staff, Pres. Bill Clinton was afforded the opportunity to demonstrate that his own lack of military experience did not have to prove a barrier in selecting the best person to lead the United States armed forces into a new era. Nominee Gen. John Shalikashvili was hailed as an excellent choice, and he was unanimously confirmed by the Senate on Oct. 5, 1993. A soldier's soldier who had risen through the ranks from private to general, Shalikashvili also displayed the political acumen necessary for dealing with the drastically changed role of the United States military in the new world order.

The grandson of a tsarist general, Shalikashvili was born on June 27, 1936, in Warsaw, Poland. His father, who was originally from the Soviet republic of Georgia, served as an officer in the Polish army until its defeat by the Germans in 1939. After a period as a prisoner of war, the elder Shalikashvili enlisted in the Georgian Legion, a Nazi-organized group of ethnic Georgians formed for the purpose of freeing Georgia from Soviet rule. In 1944 the Georgian troops came under the command of the SS, the elite corps of the Nazi Party, and were transferred to Germany. That same year Shalikashvili and his mother fled Poland and settled in Germany. When Shalikashvili was 16, his family immigrated to the U.S., settling in Peoria, Ill., where he learned English, partly by watching John Wayne films. He was drafted into the army as a private in 1958 and was commissioned a second lieutenant in 1959.

Following service at a variety of domestic posts throughout the 1960s, he was sent to Vietnam in 1968. By then a major, Shalikashvili served as a senior district adviser to South Vietnamese forces. Rising steadily through the ranks, he spent most of the 1970s and '80s serving in various capacities in Europe. In 1991 Shalikashvili took command of Operation Provide Comfort—the campaign to airlift food and medical supplies to Kurdish refugees in Iraq in the aftermath of the Gulf war. Shalikashvili won praise for his leadership of the multinational force that not only helped supply the Kurds but also protected them from aggression by Saddam Hussein's Iraqi forces.

In 1992 Shalikashvili took up the post of supreme commander of the forces of NATO, dealing with the changes wrought by the end of the Cold War. The conflict in the former Yugoslavia threatened to spread throughout the Balkan region, while the collapse of the Soviet empire had created a power vacuum in that area. Shalikashvili's appointment as chairman of the joint chiefs of staff was largely due to his able response to these situations. At his confirmation hearings in September, Shalikashvili presented a more hawkish viewpoint than Powell's, but he also pledged that the future commitment of U.S. troops throughout the world would be restricted to areas where the United States had a clearly defined interest.

(JOHN H. MATHEWS)

Sheehan, Patty

The day after Patty Sheehan qualified for the Hall of Fame of women's golf, she woke up to play a practice round at 7 AM. At age 36, she said, "There's a lot of things I still want to do. I'm too young to just sit down and be a Hall of Famer."

Sheehan became the 13th member of the Ladies' Professional Golf Association (LPGA) Hall of Fame on Nov. 13, 1993, after qualifying with her 30th tour victory on March 21 with a tournament record of 17 under par at the Standard Register Ping in Phoenix, Ariz. With at least six-figure earnings in all of her full seasons, she held records of 13 years of more than $100,000 and 11 with at least $200,000. Her only year without a tour victory was 1987.

Patricia Leslie Sheehan was born Oct. 27, 1956, in Middlebury, Vt. Her father coached football running backs, baseball players, golfers, and skiers at Middlebury College. Patty first played golf at the age of two, when her father gave her a sawed-off two-iron. She was a nationally ranked junior skier at 13 but quit that sport in favour of golf at 14. Moving to Reno, Nev., Sheehan won three straight state high-school individual championships. She attended the University of Nevada for three years and won the Nevada state amateur championships in 1975–78. Transferring to California State University at San Jose, she won California's amateur title in 1978–79 and the national college championship in 1980, the year she turned professional.

After winning her first LPGA tour victory, in 1981 at the Mazda Japan Classic, Sheehan was named Rookie of the Year for that season. Within three years she won two major championships, the LPGA tournaments of 1983 and 1984. She won four tournaments in each of those years, also gaining Player of the Year honours in 1983 and the tour's lowest scoring average, 71.40, in 1984. But she did not win another major tournament for eight years.

It seemed to be Sheehan's year in 1990; she won five tournaments, posted a career-best 70.62 scoring average, shot 29 rounds in the 60s, and became the second woman ever to earn $700,000 in a season. She led the U.S. Open by nine strokes on the final, 36-hole day, and her 12-under-par score at one point made her the first golfer ever to reach 10 under par at any stage of a men's or women's U.S. Open. But she then lost the lead to Betsy King for her third second-place finish in nine Opens.

When Sheehan finally won the Open in 1992, she had to win an 18-hole play-off against college teammate Juli Inkster. A year later Sheehan made the LPGA championship her fourth major and 31st career win. (KEVIN M. LAMB)

Sihanouk, Norodom

Norodom Sihanouk was crowned king of Cambodia for the second time on Sept. 24, 1993. The decision to restore the monarchy was an admission that only Sihanouk had the prestige and authority to bring peace to a nation exhausted after years of civil war.

Sihanouk was born in Phnom Penh, Cambodia, on Oct. 31, 1922, and was educated at French schools in Vietnam, China, and France. During World War II, when Cambodia was still a French protectorate, Sihanouk became monarch (April 1941) for the first time. The Nazi-backed Vichy regime in Paris apparently believed that an overindulged teenager could be manipulated more easily than his father. After World War II, Sihanouk negotiated for Cambodia's sovereignty. France recognized that times had changed and in 1953 granted independence to Cambodia.

In 1955 Sihanouk abdicated in favour of his father and formed the People's Socialist Community, which won the national elections that year. As foreign minister and prime minister, Sihanouk characteristically sought to steer a middle course between competing ideological factions and Cold War rivalries; he established relations with China, the U.S.S.R., and the West. In 1956 he became Cambodia's permanent representative to the United Nations. Following the death of Sihanouk's father, the Cambodian constitution was amended to allow direct elections for the head of state. Sihanouk won the post easily in the June 1960 election.

By the end of 1962 the U.S. had some 11,000 military advisers in South Vietnam. In 1965, after Cambodian villages had been bombed, Sihanouk broke off relations with the U.S., which by that time had become deeply involved in the Vietnam War. In 1970, while on a foreign tour, Sihanouk was overthrown, and Lon Nol, who favoured close ties with the U.S., took charge of the government. Sihanouk then created a government in exile in Beijing (Peking) and made allies of the North Vietnamese and the rebel Khmer Rouge army in an effort to regain power. Lon Nol fled the country in April 1975 as Khmer Rouge troops advanced on the capital. When Pol Pot took over the government, Sihanouk returned to Cambodia as the head of state; one year later he resigned. He was under house arrest during Pol Pot's reign of terror. Among the estimated one million Cambodians who lost their lives were 2 of Sihanouk's sons, 3 daughters, and at least 15 grandchildren. When the Khmer Rouge were driven from power in 1979 by troops from North Vietnam, Sihanouk went into exile in China. During the next decade he helped direct the struggle against Cambodia's Vietnamese-installed government. As president of a government in exile, he embraced the Khmer Rouge and elements of the faction that had toppled him in 1970.

In 1991, after years of frustrating negotiations, the four main factions vying for power in Cambodia agreed to establish a Supreme National Council that would rule the country under the chairmanship of Sihanouk while preparations were made for a UN-sponsored and supervised election in May 1993. Even though Sihanouk's party finished in third place, he was named prime minister on June 3. One of his sons, Ranariddh, whose party had finished in first place, was named deputy prime minister, as was Hun Sen, the leader of the former Vietnamese-installed government. On September 21 the Constituent Assembly, recognizing Sihanouk's unique place in Cambodia's turbulent history over the past half century, modified the constitution and restored the monarchy. (CHERYL L. COLLINS)

Smith, Dick

Australia's answer to Leonardo da Vinci, Dick Smith continued to amaze the public with his displays of versatility when he was blown into the record books once more in 1993. In an echo of the earlier headline "The sky is the limit for Great Adventurer," Smith, who became famous for flying his Sikorsky S76A helicopter under the Sydney Harbour Bridge, swapped the fixed-wing and helicopter aircraft of his previous exploits for a hot air balloon and entered a race to cross the Australian continent west to east. The millionaire adventurer vowed that his most recent and dangerous adventure would be his last, and when he landed in northern New South Wales in June 1993, exhausted but ecstatic, Smith resolved that henceforth he would stick to being a watchdog for civil aviation interests, where he would concentrate on such issues as air-traffic control systems and the provision of rescue beacons for finding crashed aircraft.

Richard Harold Smith—aviator, filmmaker, explorer, businessman, and publisher—was born March 18, 1944, in Roseville, New South Wales. He had limited formal education at public schools and a technical high school, but his inventiveness and curiosity soon turned him into one of the signal success and survival stories in modern Australia. His astonishing entrepreneurial skills first appeared when he founded Dick Smith Electronics in 1968. By the time he sold the firm in 1982, Smith was a household name and his firm was a market leader in selling small electronic items from calculators to computers. With the proceeds of the sale, he began a new career in philanthropy, exploration, and publishing. Smith made the first solo helicopter flight around the world (1983), the first helicopter flight to the North Pole (1987), and the first flight around the world via the poles (1988). As a philanthropist he became Australia's most generous individual when he donated $A 1 million to the Smith Family (no relation) charity. In 1987 he purchased *The Australian Encyclopaedia.*

The love of his life turned out to be the quarterly magazine *Australian Geographic,* which he founded in 1986 and modeled on the U.S. publication *National Geographic.* In October 1993 Smith proudly announced that *Australian Geographic* would henceforth be printed in Australia, rather than overseas. This, said Smith, would save Australian dollars in foreign exchange revenue. In keeping with his nationalist perspective, Smith exhorted media moguls Kerry Packer and Rupert Murdoch to follow his example and to print in Australia. (A.R.G. GRIFFITHS)

Snipes, Wesley

Wesley Snipes became established as a bona fide bankable movie star in 1993, when he both shared name-above-the-title billing with two of Hollywood's biggest draws in two of the top-grossing films of the year and became one of the highest-paid actors in the motion-picture industry.

Like screen legend Sean Connery (alias James Bond), his costar in *Rising Sun* (1993), and screen superstar Sylvester Stallone (alias Rambo), his costar in *Demolition Man* (1993), Snipes's rapid ascension to this elite Hollywood echelon occurred mainly as a result of his film portrayals of action heroes who consistently outfought, outshot, and outsmarted the "bad guys." Unlike Connery and Stallone, however, Snipes rose through the ranks with one notable distinction: the actor portrayed gunslinging, karate-chopping heroes who were black.

Snipes gained recognition in 1990 when he played a musician in director Spike Lee's film *Mo' Better Blues.* He received critical acclaim in 1991 with his portrayal of Nino, a ruthless Harlem drug lord in the film *New Jack City.* That same year Snipes won notice for his performance as an architect who had an affair with his white secretary in *Jungle Fever,* also directed by Lee. In 1992, after starring roles in *White Men Can't Jump* and *The Waterdance,* Snipes played an airline security expert who battled terrorists in *Passenger 57,* which became a smash hit at the box office.

His experiences as a youth helped prepare Snipes for the diverse roles he portrayed on the silver screen. He was born in Orlando, Fla., on July 31, 1962. His parents had divorced before he was two years old, and he spent his early years in New York City's South Bronx. Snipes studied martial arts from age seven, initially because he was small for his age and needed to defend himself.

At age 12, after winning a small role in an off-Broadway production of *The Me Nobody Knows,* he decided that performing would be the focus of his future. He studied acting, music, and dance at the High School of the Performing Arts until 1977, when his mother moved the family back to Orlando. There he graduated from Jones High School. Shortly after receiving a B.A. degree from the State University of New York at Purchase, he made his motion-picture debut in *Wildcats* (1986) and appeared in a number of theatrical and television productions, including "Miami Vice" and the soap opera "All My Children."

(EDWARD PAUL MORAGNE)

Thompson, Emma

See Branagh, Kenneth, and Thompson, Emma.

U2

At a 1993 U2 concert all eyes focused on a darkened stage lit only by the flashing headlights of several suspended Trabant automobiles. Giant video monitors projected Nazi propaganda footage punctuated by staccato bursts of slogans—"The Media Is the Anti-Christ," "Everything You Know Is Wrong," "Everyone's a Racist Except You"—reminiscent of some kind of bizarre brainwashing technique. Heavy drumbeats, amplified guitar wails, warped vocals, and 450 tons of technology rocked the walls and floors of the arena like a giant heartbeat. U2 featured four members: passionate lead singer and songwriter Bono, unpretentious lead guitarist and technological wizard The Edge, bad-boy bass guitarist Adam Clayton, and James-Dean-look-alike drummer Larry Mullen, Jr. U2 staged its Zoo TV tour, the hottest concert ticket of 1992 (in the U.S.) and 1993 (in Europe and other venues), to support its critically acclaimed albums *Achtung Baby* (1991) and *Zooropa* (1993), both platinum albums. Incredibly, *Zooropa* was conceived, recorded, and released in the three-month break between the U.S. and European legs of the tour. The nihilistic sound of these albums, as well as the glitzy tour, reflected society's eager embrace of the electronic superhighway and multimedia age and highlighted the battle between humanity and technology. The disorienting songs also dealt with the void left in Europe by the fall of Communism and the Berlin Wall.

In 1976 in Dublin three high school students, Paul Hewson (born May 10, 1960), Dave Evans (born Aug. 8, 1961), and Adam Clayton (born March 13, 1960), answered an ad that was tacked to a bulletin board by Larry Mullen, Jr. (born Oct. 31, 1961), who wanted to form a garage band. The four initially named themselves Feedback,

OUTLINE

then The Hype, and finally U2 (probably after the American spy plane, though no one knew for sure). Hewson was christened Bono Vox (later shortened to Bono) after a hearing aid store in Dublin, and he in turn renamed Evans The Edge because of his tendency to stay on life's fringe, just observing. While touring the local club circuit, U2 honed their unique blend of punk rock and classic rock mixed with Gaelic influences, and in 1978 they were signed by Island Records. The intelligent lyrics layered with social and religious references and the sometimes brooding, sometimes anthemic music on their first five albums, *Boy* (1980), *October* (1981), *War* (1983), *The Unforgettable Fire* (1984), and *The Joshua Tree* (1987), gained them worldwide critical and popular acclaim and earned them a reputation as the eight-legged conscience of rock and roll. The success of *The Joshua Tree* propelled them into indisputable superstardom and won them the titles "Band of the Eighties" by *Rolling Stone* and "Rock's Hottest Ticket" by *Time*.

By the early 1990s, U2 had won several Grammy awards, sold more than 40 million albums, and been listed as one of *Forbes*' top-15 highest-paid entertainers. In an effort to shed the image they suddenly found themselves suffocating under, U2 reinvented their sound and pleasantly shocked the critics and most of their fans with the release of the two harder-edged, postindustrial albums. Whatever their musical direction, Ireland's second biggest export (next to Guinness stout) proved that artistic integrity would remain their chief hallmark. (SUSAN RAPP)

Wasmosy, Juan Carlos

In the first free elections in Paraguay's history on May 9, 1993, Juan Carlos Wasmosy was elected president. When he was sworn in for a five-year term on August 15, he also became the first civilian president since 1954. How much change this transition really signaled was unclear. The triangle—government, army, and ruling Colorado Party—that had governed Paraguay since 1947 remained intact. Yet there were fissures. In what appeared to be a vote for continuity and stability, Wasmosy, the Colorado Party candidate, won approximately 40% of the vote in the May general elections. He did not, however, have the backing of a unified party.

Wasmosy had contested the party's late December 1992 elections and had wrested the nomination from rival Luis María Argaña. A controversial Colorado Party electoral tribunal ruling on March 4, 1993, narrowly proclaimed Wasmosy the winner of the party's nomination. He was backed by then president Andrés Rodríguez, party president Blas Riquelme, and powerful forces within the military, while Argaña had the support of exiled former president Alfredo Stroessner. The Colorado Party won the largest number of seats in both chambers of Congress in the May elections, but the united opposition bloc held a majority. Meanwhile, supporters of Argaña held more seats than those of Wasmosy and vowed to follow their own agenda. The new president faced a challenge in the passage of each piece of legislation.

The 54-year-old president came to the office with little government experience; his only post had been as the minister of integration under outgoing President Rodríguez. Trained as a civil engineer at National University in Asunción, Wasmosy was known as one of Paraguay's wealthiest businessmen—a leading cotton exporter, cattle rancher, and construction magnate. He made his fortune in the 1970s with construction contracts for the Paraguayan–Brazilian Itaipú Dam, the world's largest hydroelectric dam. As president Wasmosy hoped to renegotiate the Itaipú treaty to allow Paraguay to sell to Argentina some of its shares of electricity. A solid conservative who supported market-oriented economic policies, Wasmosy favoured Paraguay's participation in Mercosur, a regional common market. He also pledged to accelerate privatization of the national airline, merchant fleet, and steel company, among others. His allegiance to the status quo was made clear by his support of Gen. Lino Oviedo, the country's military strongman, who had alarmed some with his emphatic preelection declarations that the Colorados would win.

(ELLEN FINKELSTEIN)

Wiles, Andrew John

In June 1993, at a small conference of mathematicians at the Isaac Newton Institute, Cambridge, Andrew Wiles dropped a historic bombshell. He had solved one of mathematics' oldest mysteries, Fermat's last theorem. The Princeton University professor's seven-year attack on the 350-year-old problem, one that many mathematicians had declared unsolvable, ended when on the third and final day of his lecture on elliptic curves, he announced his proof of the theorem. In December, during review of the 200-page proof for publication, a small snag was found, but the pervasive feeling among Wiles's peers was that he had indeed pulled off the seemingly impossible.

Fermat's last theorem, so called because it was the only remaining theorem of the 17th-century French mathematician Pierre de Fermat that had been neither proved nor disproved, dates to 1637. While reading a copy of the *Arithmetica* by the ancient Greek mathematician Diophantus, Fermat scribbled the theorem in the book's margin along with the note that he had a "remarkable proof" but that "the margin is too small to contain it." So began a mystery that stymied the world's greatest mathematical minds for the next three centuries. Particularly vexing for would-be solvers was the theorem's simplicity. It states that there are no positive integer solutions to $x^n + y^n = z^n$ when n is greater than two. Fermat himself eventually found a space large enough to write a proof for $n = 4$, and others elaborated proofs for specific cases of n. A universal solution, however, remained elusive until Wiles made his June announcement.

The heart of Wiles's proof relies upon the Taniyama-Weil conjecture, a difficult problem in number theory dealing with the nature of elliptic curves (equations of the form $y^2 = x^3 + ax + b$, in which a and b are constants). In 1986 Kenneth A. Ribet of the University of California at Berkeley showed that if the conjecture could be proved, a proof of Fermat's theorem would follow. Inspired by Ribet's work, Wiles laboured privately and secretly in the attic office of his Princeton home for seven years. By May 1993 he had succeeded in solving a special case of the Taniyama-Weil conjecture—enough to prove Fermat's last theorem—and he quickly signed on to speak at the Cambridge conference. After the first day's lecture, speculation swelled that Wiles had a solution to Fermat's problem. On the third day, when Wiles finally revealed the proof, he received a standing ovation from the audience.

Wiles was born April 11, 1953, in Cambridge. He had dreamed of solving Fermat's last theorem from the age of 10, when he first encountered the problem in a book. In fact, he credited the problem with inspiring his interest in mathematics and leading him to his life's work as a number theorist. Wiles, who was also married to a mathematician (they used to recite the decimal places of pi to each other), studied mathematics at Clare College, Cambridge, earning an M.A. in 1977 and a Ph.D. in 1980. He joined the mathematics faculty of Princeton University in 1980.

(JAMES HENNELLY)

Young, Steve

In 1993 Steve Young passed Joe Montana as the National Football League's best all-time passer, but he could not flee Montana's shadow. Young won his third consecutive passing championship, something no NFL quarterback had done, but many fans of his San Francisco 49ers still believed that the team had traded the wrong quarterback when it sent 37-year-old Montana to Kansas City and kept 31-year-old Young. Montana had led the 49ers to four Super Bowl victories, and Young finished the 1993 regular season looking for his first.

Young's passer rating of 101.5, after seasons of 101.8 and 107, made him the first NFL passer with three straight 100s on a scale where 100 was meant to be the realistic maximum. He also led the league a third straight season in the most important single statistic, yards per pass attempt, following averages of 9.02 and 8.62 with 8.71 in a category where 7 was above average. He led the NFL in 1993 with 29 touchdown passes, his career best, and had other career highs of 68% completed, 6.3% for touchdowns, 4,023 yd gained, 462 attempts, and 314 completions. He finished his ninth NFL season with a career passer rating of 95.7, ahead of Montana's 92.8. His 8.08 yd per attempt exceeded Montana's, and his ratio of 121 touchdown passes to 58 interceptions was also better than Montana's 257 to 130. Montana's career .635 completion percentage was still the record, but Young ranked second with .621. Young also had an NFL career rushing average of 6.1 yd per carry after 1993. For Los Angeles in the United States Football League (USFL) in 1985, he was the first professional player in history to run for 100 yd and pass for 300 in the same game.

Jon Steven Young was born Oct. 11, 1961, in Salt Lake City, Utah, and raised in Connecticut, where he was all-state in football and baseball at Greenwich High School. He was the great-great-great-grandson of Brigham Young, an early leader of the Church of Jesus Christ of Latter-day Saints (Mormons), and he was both an all-American quarterback in 1983 and a law school graduate in 1993 at Brigham Young University, Provo, Utah. Young broke 13 national college records, including his .713 completion percentage in 1983, when he was recognized as one of the top five student athletes in the U.S.

The Cincinnati Bengals intended to make Young the first pick of the 1984 NFL draft, but Young accepted the richest contract in team sports history at the time when he signed with the Los Angeles Express of the fledgling USFL. In two seasons with a bad team, he completed only 56.4% of his passes with 16 touchdowns and 22 interceptions. He bought out his contract with the hapless Express after the spring season of 1985, but his NFL rights belonged to the equally hapless Tampa Bay Buccaneers. In the two seasons there before San Francisco traded for him, Young passed for 11 touchdowns, 21 interceptions, and a .533 completion rate. (KEVIN M. LAMB)

OBITUARIES

Abe Kobo (ABE KIMIFUSA), Japanese novelist, short-story writer, and playwright (b. March 7, 1924, Tokyo, Japan—d. Jan. 22, 1993, Tokyo), created portrayals of alienation and loss of identity in modern life that reached a wide audience in postwar Japan and later throughout the world. His writings commonly depicted loss and loneliness among the desolation of urban life (one of his characters changes into a plant; another moves into a box to be free of the world). He read such Western writers as Kafka and Dostoyevsky and was often compared to the former. Abe grew up largely in Manchuria, when that part of China was under Japanese military occupation, where his father taught at a medical school. (Kobo is the rendering in Chinese of Kimifusa.) He himself graduated (1948) in medicine from the University of Tokyo, although he never practiced. His earliest published writings appeared in the 1940s, and he established a reputation with the novel *Owarishi michi no shirube ni* ("The Road Sign at the End of the Street"), published in 1948. His best-known work was the novel *Suna no onna* (1962), published in English in 1964 as *The Woman in the Dunes*. The book was translated into some 20 languages, and Abe wrote the screenplay for a prizewinning film version. In all, he published 13 novels and more than 50 short stories, as well as several stage plays and radio and television dramas. It was estimated that worldwide his books sold more than nine million copies. He won a number of awards and honours, both in Japan and abroad.

Abravanel, Maurice, U.S. conductor (b. Jan. 6, 1903, Thessaloniki, Greece—d. Sept. 22, 1993, Salt Lake City, Utah), was of Spanish-Portuguese Sephardic parentage and had his early career in the cultural ferment of Weimar Germany, but he later spent more than three decades as music director and conductor of the Utah Symphony Orchestra. Abravanel grew up in Lausanne, Switz., and gave up the prospect of medicine to study music. In 1922 he went to Berlin, where he studied performance and composition with Kurt Weill, and two years later he made his debut as a conductor. He conducted throughout Europe and in 1933 fled to Paris and was engaged as music director for George Balanchine's Les Ballets 1933. In 1936 he went to the U.S., where he became the youngest conductor in the history of the Metropolitan Opera. Abravanel then conducted musicals on Broadway, including works of Weill. In 1947 he became director of the Utah Symphony, and he remained there until 1979. Under his leadership the orchestra flourished and gained widespread recognition; among their many recordings was the first complete cycle of the symphonies of Gustav Mahler made by a U.S. orchestra. In 1982 Abravanel began an affiliation with the Berkshire Music Center, in Tanglewood, Mass. He was awarded the National Medal of Arts in 1991.

Adams, Diana, U.S. ballerina (b. March 29, 1926, Staunton, Va.—d. Jan. 10, 1993, San Andreas, Calif.), captivated audiences with her radiant beauty and spellbinding dramatic interpretations while performing with Ballet Theatre (now American Ballet Theatre; 1944–50) and the New York City Ballet (1950–63). Adams studied under her stepmother, Emily Hadley-Adams, before traveling to New York City, where she was tutored by Edward Caton, Agnes de Mille, and Antony Tudor. Adams made her stage debut on Broadway in the musical *Oklahoma!* (1943) and the following year joined Ballet Theatre, where she created the role of Cybele in Tudor's *Undertow* (1945) and had prominent roles in his *Romeo and Juliet, Numbus,* and *Jardin aux lilas*. She also was featured as Myrthe in *Giselle* and in the female leads in George Balanchine's *Theme and Variations*. Adams, tall and long legged and combining grace with athleticism, was the epitome of the perfect Balanchine dancer. She followed Balanchine to the New York City Ballet, where he featured her in *La Valse* (1951), *Opus 34* (1954), *Ivesiana* (1954), and the challenging *Agon* (1957), in which she and Arthur Mitchell created the central duet, considered by many the most significant and influential movement sequence in all of 20th-century dance. Adams also performed in films—she partnered Danny Kaye in *Knock on Wood* (1954) and worked with Gene Kelly in *Invitation to the Dance* (1956). She became a teacher at the School of American Ballet while still dancing. After retiring from the stage in 1963, she continued to teach until 1971.

Ademola, Sir Adetokunbo Adegboyega, Nigerian judge (b. Feb. 1, 1906, Abeokuta, Nigeria—d. Jan. 29, 1993, Lagos, Nigeria), was the first indigenous chief justice of the Nigerian Supreme Court (1958–72) and a cofounder of the Nigerian law school. Ademola was the son of Sir Ladapo Ademola II, the paramount ruler (1920–63) of the Egba people in southwestern Nigeria, and was educated at King's College in Lagos and Selwyn College, Cambridge. He studied law at the Middle Temple in London and was called to the bar in 1934. After returning to Nigeria, Ademola worked in the civil service, practiced law, and served as a magistrate (1939–49) and a puisne (junior) judge (1949–55). He was named to the Nigerian Supreme Court by the British authorities in 1949 and appointed chief justice of the western region in 1955. Three years later he was elevated to chief justice of the federation. Ademola retained his post after Nigeria became independent (1960) and retired from the bench in 1972. He was chosen to supervise the 1973 national census, but the controversial results were never officially accepted. He remained in public service, however, as chancellor of the University of Nigeria (from 1975) and chairman of the Commonwealth Foundation (from 1978). Ademola was knighted in 1957 and was made a privy counsellor in 1963.

Allison, Davey, U.S. race-car driver (b. Feb. 25, 1961, Hueytown, Ala.—d. July 13, 1993, Birmingham, Ala.), won 19 titles while competing on the Winston Cup tour, including the National Association for Stock Car Auto Racing's (NASCAR's) 1992 Daytona 500, the sport's premier race. He was named Rookie of the Year in 1987. Allison was the son of racing legend Bobby, who retired in 1988 after a near-fatal racing accident, and the brother of Clifford, who was killed in August 1992 during a practice run on a racetrack in Brooklyn, Mich. After joining the NASCAR circuit in 1985, Allison soon won eight titles, but he was frustrated by his uneven performances. The turning point in his career came in 1991, when Larry McReynolds became Allison's team crew chief and helped the headstrong driver curb his intensity and capture the remaining 11 of his titles. During his career Allison won $6,726,974. By his own admission, Allison's favourite race was the 1988 Daytona 500, when he placed second behind his father. In 1992 Allison sustained a concussion and broke several bones after a crash at a Pennsylvania racetrack. In typical fashion, he returned to racing the following week wearing a special cast that permitted him to operate the steering wheel and gearshift. In that season he had a 30-point lead over his nearest challenger and was poised to take the Winston Cup crown when an accident during the last race of the year dropped him to third in the final rankings. In July Allison was piloting a newly purchased helicopter and was attempting to land at the Talladega (Ala.) Superspeedway when the aircraft crashed on its left side. He died the next day.

Ameche, Don (DOMINIC FELIX AMICI), U.S. actor (b. May 31, 1908, Kenosha, Wis.—d. Dec. 6, 1993, Scottsdale, Ariz.), was a versatile performer who was at home on radio, on television, and in films but was best remembered for two standout motion-picture roles; his performance in the title role in *The Story of Alexander Graham Bell* (1939) was so riveting that Ameche became a byword for telephone, and his comedic interpretation of a septuagenarian who exhibited his alien-aided rejuvenation by break dancing in *Cocoon* (1985) earned him an Academy Award for best supporting actor. Even so, critics seemed to be most impressed with Ameche's light-comedy touches in *Heaven Can Wait* (1943), in which he portrayed a rakish hero. After attending Columbia (now Loras) College in Dubuque, Iowa, Ameche studied law before launching (1930) a radio career in Chicago. He starred on such shows as "The First Nighter," "Grand Hotel," and "The Chase & Sanborn Hour" and with Frances Langford appeared as the Bickersons, an irrepressibly feuding couple. Ameche, who sported a pencil-thin mustache, exuded a suave sophistication and charm, which made him perfectly suited to roles as a bon vivant. Ameche appeared in *Alexander's Ragtime Band* (1938), *Midnight* (1939), and *The Three Musketeers* (1939) before moving to television and starring as the ringmaster (1961–65) for "International Showtime." Film roles were scarce until he made a triumphant return in *Trading Places* (1983) as a ruthless millionaire. Ameche also appeared in *Cocoon: The Return* (1988), *Oscar* (1991), and *Folks!* (1992).

Anderson, Marian, U.S. singer (b. Feb. 27, 1897, Philadelphia, Pa.—d. April 8, 1993, Portland, Ore.), maintained a quiet dignity while transcending the racial and cultural barriers imposed on her artistry and used her rich contralto voice brilliantly to interpret the works of Schubert, Schumann, Brahms, Mahler, Verdi, and Richard Strauss as well as spirituals. Though Anderson's birth certificate stated that she was born in 1897, she maintained that her birth date was Feb. 17, 1902. She began singing in church choirs at the age of six, and by the time she graduated from high school, she was singing professionally. Anderson's application to a local music school was turned down because she was black, so friends and family financed her private voice lessons with Giuseppe Boghetti in New York City. After winning first prize in a New York Philharmonic voice competition in 1925, she secured concert and recital engagements. Her prospects soon dwindled, however, and she embarked on a series of European trips for study and then for concert tours. There the quality of her full-bodied voice and her emotive spirituals, including "My Lord, What a Morning" and "Crucifixion," enraptured audiences and prompted Arturo Toscanini to rave that a voice like hers was heard only "once in a hundred years." She gave royal command performances for the kings of Denmark and Sweden before returning to the U.S. in 1935 as a mature

UPI/BETTMANN

and experienced performer. After Anderson gave a highly successful recital at Town Hall in New York City, she was deluged with engagements. In 1939, however, because of her race, the Daughters of the American Revolution (DAR) refused to allow her to sing at Constitution Hall in Washington, D.C. In protest, first lady Eleanor Roosevelt resigned from the DAR, and it was arranged for Anderson to present a free Easter Sunday (April 9, 1939) concert at the Lincoln Memorial, where 75,000 admirers gathered to hear her renditions of Schubert's "Ave Maria" and such spirituals as "Gospel Train," "Trampin'," and "My Soul Is Anchored in the Lord." Anderson performed at the White House and at presidential inaugurations, and during World War II she finally appeared at Constitution Hall. She was past her vocal prime when she made her operatic debut, but in 1955 she became the first black to sing at the Metropolitan Opera in New York City, appearing as Ulrica in Verdi's *Un ballo in maschera* (*A Masked Ball*). Though she never accepted another operatic role, she had assumed the mantle of a trailblazer. Anderson's serene stage presence, coupled with her ability to adapt to a wide range, especially in lieder, became the hallmark of her long and distinguished career. Her autobiography, *My Lord, What a Morning,* appeared in 1956. After an extended farewell tour, she retired in 1965. Anderson was the recipient of the 1963 Presidential Medal of Freedom, a 1978 Kennedy Center Honor, and the 1986 National Arts Medal, and her image was minted on a 1980 congressional gold medal.

Antall, Jozsef, Hungarian politician (b. April 8, 1932, Budapest, Hung.—d. Dec. 12, 1993, Budapest), as prime minister of Hungary (1990–93) and the longest-serving postcommunist leader in Eastern Europe, maintained stability in the country at a time when other Eastern European countries were struggling, often violently, to introduce democracy after decades of communist repression. Antall was serving as chairman of a revolutionary committee at the Eotvos Gymnasium at the outbreak of the Hungarian Revolution of 1956, when the people overthrew the communist regime (which was reinstated seven days later by the Soviets). He was suspended from his job and banned from teaching and publishing until 1963. Earlier, he had studied humanities and political science at the Lorand Eotvos University in Budapest before working as an archivist, librarian, high-school teacher, and director of the capital's Semmelweis Medical History Museum. He prided himself on his knowledge of Hungarian history, starting with the kings. After becoming aware of the first cracks in the Communist regime, Antall joined the centre-right Democratic Forum Party, was elected party chairman in 1989 after exhibiting his skills as a negotiator in the roundtable talks that led to the March 1990 multiparty elections, and became prime minister following his party's victory in those elections. As prime minister, Antall guided Hungary on a conservative course and one that welcomed foreign investment and an alliance with Western European countries. In 1990 he was diagnosed with cancer, the disease that claimed his life.

Argyll, Margaret, Duchess of, British socialite (b. Dec. 1, 1912, Newton Mearns, Renfrewshire, Scotland—d. July 26, 1993, London, England), was an elegant society hostess and one of Britain's most celebrated beauties, but she scandalized the nation when she became embroiled in a prolonged (1959–63), sensational divorce from her second husband, Ian Campbell, the 11th Duke of Argyll. She was born Ethel Margaret Whigham, the daughter of a Scottish textile manufacturer, and was educated in an exclusive private school in New York City. A stunning brunette with flawless white skin and green eyes, she was named debutante of the year after her coming-out ball in 1930. Thereafter, newspapers chronicled every detail of her life, including her romances with Prince Aly Khan and the 7th Earl of Warwick, her glamorous marriage in 1933 to American stockbroker Charles Sweeney, and her near-fatal illness and stillborn baby the next year. As Mrs. Sweeney, she was named one of the world's best-dressed women and immortalized in Cole Porter's song "You're the Top." After an amicable divorce in 1947, she married (1951) the Duke of Argyll and set about restoring his ancestral home, Inveraray Castle. In their divorce trial the duke charged his wife with slander, forgery, and multiple adulteries, producing a photograph of the duchess in flagrante delicto with a naked man whose face was never seen and whose secret identity sparked public speculation for years afterward. In 1963 the court castigated her in a lengthy divorce judgment. She gradually lost her social position and her home, and she died in poverty. The duchess's autobiography, *Forget Not,* appeared in 1975.

Ashe, Arthur Robert, Jr., U.S. tennis player and social activist (b. July 10, 1943, Richmond, Va.—d. Feb. 6, 1993, New York, N.Y.), captured centre court when he won the men's singles title at the debut of the U.S. Open championship in 1968, becoming the first African-American man to win a Grand Slam event, one of the four major tournaments of the sport. He followed this with men's singles titles at the Australian Open in 1970 and at the All-England (Wimbledon) championship in 1975. He was a poised and eloquent spokesman for effecting social change and publicly championed his convictions with support for such causes as the antiapartheid movement in

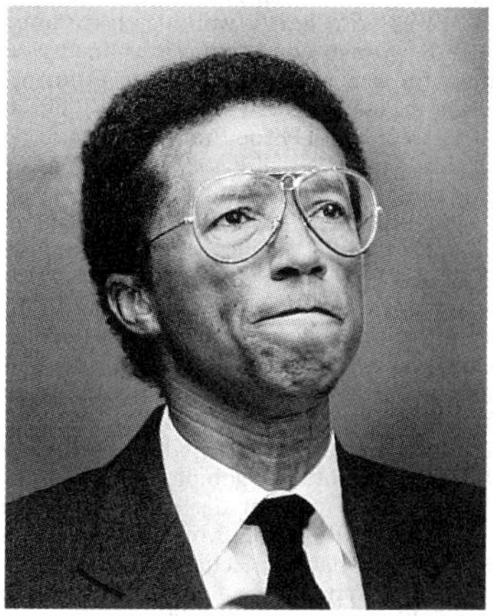

AP/WIDE WORLD

South Africa, the plight of U.S. inner-city children and Haitian refugees, and the education of people about AIDS, the disease that claimed his life. Ashe honed his tennis skills while attending the University of California at Los Angeles, which he led to the National Collegiate Athletic Association tennis championship. His powerful serves, stunning backhand, and hard-hit, topspin ground strokes helped bedevil his opponents, most notably the heavily favoured Jimmy Connors, whom Ashe, slender and tall (70.2 kg [155 lb], 1.83 m [6 ft]) yet nonetheless powerful, calmly defeated in the 1975 Wimbledon final. In 1963 Ashe had become the first black to be named to a U.S. Davis Cup team, and he compiled a 27–5 singles record from 1963 to 1978. When he served as a nonplaying captain of the Davis Cup team (1981–85), the U.S. won championships in 1981 and 1982. Though his Grand Slam and numerous professional victories (he held 33 tournament titles) and product endorsements made Ashe tennis's first black millionaire, his wealth did not impede his social activism. After three attempts Ashe was finally granted a visa to South Africa in 1973, and he became the first black to reach the final of the South African Open. In 1979, after having ranked among the top 10 players for 15 years, Ashe was stricken with the first of three heart attacks. He underwent quadruple bypass surgery in 1979 and double bypass surgery in 1983. Though his third attack did not require surgery, Ashe had announced his retirement as a player in 1980. It was reportedly through a transfusion during his second surgery that he contracted AIDS. In 1985 Ashe was inducted into the International Tennis Hall of Fame. He published an autobiography, *Off the Court* (1981), and the three-volume *A Hard Road to Glory: A History of the African-American Athlete* (1988). That year he suffered a severe bacterial infection in his head, and blood work revealed that he had AIDS. Ashe announced his condition to the public in April 1992 after he learned that a newspaper was preparing a scoop. Part of his legacy was the organization of the Arthur Ashe Foundation for the Defeat of AIDS.

Auger, Arleen, U.S. opera singer (b. Sept. 13, 1939, South Gate, Calif.—d. June 10, 1993, Leusden, Neth.), projected a commanding stage presence and was especially praised for her flexible coloratura soprano voice and subtle interpretations of works by Bach, Handel, Haydn, Monteverdi, Gluck, and especially Mozart. After graduating from California State University at Long Beach (1963), she taught elementary school and studied voice in Chicago with Ralph Errolle. Two years later in Los Angeles, she captured the I. Victor Fuchs Competition and won an audition with the Vienna Volksoper. Though she had only three songs in her repertoire, Auger so impressed one person at her audition, Josef Krips, director of the Vienna State Opera, that he offered her a contract despite her lack of stage experience and unfamiliarity with the German language. Auger made her debut (1967) there as the Queen of the Night in *Die Zauberflöte;* she later expanded her repertoire to more than a dozen roles, notably Constanze in *Die Entführung aus dem Serail* and Gilda in *Rigoletto*. She left the Vienna State Opera in 1974 but continued to expand her recital repertoire and made selective appearances in roles she felt were suitable for her rich tone; she sang Schubert and Schumann lieder and turn-of-the-century French art songs besides commissioning new song cycles by Libby Larsen and Judith Zaimont. Auger, who was more popular in Europe than in the U.S., performed at most of the European opera houses before making her New York City Opera debut in 1976. It was not until 1984 that she began to attract a serious U.S. following. The highlight of her career was her performance at the wedding of Prince Andrew and Sarah Ferguson, the Duke and Duchess of York, on July 23, 1986, when she sang Mozart's "Exsultate, Jubilate." Auger's superb coloratura technique was documented on nearly 200 recordings. She continued to perform until 1992, when the brain cancer that later claimed her life forced her retirement.

Barnhart, Clarence Lewis, U.S. lexicographer and editor (b. Dec. 30, 1900, near Plattsburg, Mo.—d. Oct. 24, 1993, Peekskill, N.Y.), devoted his life to the compilation and revision of dictionaries and, together with educational psychologist Edward Lee Thorndike, was a pioneer in creating references that were exclusively geared for school-age readers—Thorndike-Barnhart dictionaries. Soon after joining (1929) textbook publisher Scott, Foresman & Co. as an editor, Barnhart graduated (1930) from the University of Chicago, where he also undertook graduate studies (1934–37). While working at Random House, he edited the original *The American College Dictionary* of 1947. The following year Barnhart founded his own reference book company. His many impressive undertakings included the creation in 1943 of a Dictionary of United States Army Terms and the editing of the three-volume *The New Century Cyclopedia of Names* (1954; with William D. Halsey), *The World Book Encyclopedia Dictionary* (1963), and ongoing issues of *The Barnhart Dictionary Companion* (with his son David K. Barnhart).

Baudouin I (Baudouin Albert Charles Leopold Axel Marie Gustave of Saxe-Coburg-Gotha), Belgian monarch (b. Sept. 7, 1930, Stuyvenberg Castle, near Brussels, Belgium—d. July 31, 1993, Motril, Spain), as king of the Belgians from 1951, restored confidence in the monarchy after the stormy reign of his father, King Leopold III, and provided a symbol of national unity for both his Flemish- and his French-speaking subjects. During World War II, Baudouin (Dutch: Boudewijn) remained under house arrest with his father after the king surrendered to the Germans in 1940 rather than escaping to England. This capitulation brought Leopold under suspicion of collaboration, and the royal family was forced into postwar exile in Switzerland until the Belgian people voted to allow their return in July 1950. Amid continuing protests, Leopold reluctantly abdicated, and Baudouin was sworn in as acting head of state on August 11. He formally acceded to the throne on July 17, 1951. A devout Roman Catholic, he risked another constitutional crisis on April 3, 1990, when he refused to sign into law a bill permitting abortions. Parliament allowed him to step down for 24 hours while the bill was formally enacted. Because Baudouin and his Spanish wife, Queen Fabiola, were childless, he was succeeded by his younger brother, King Albert II (*see* BIOGRAPHIES).

Beck, David ("DAVE") U.S. labour leader (b. June 16, 1894, Stockton, Calif.—d. Dec. 26, 1993, Seattle, Wash.), as president of the International Brotherhood of Teamsters from 1952 to 1957, was one of the most powerful labour leaders of the time. Beck dropped out of high school at 16 to help support his family by driving a laundry truck. After service in the navy during World War I, he returned to that job and, having joined the Teamsters in 1914, began his involvement in union activities. He worked his way up from part-time organizer to become executive vice president in 1947 and then president in 1952. Under Beck's leadership the union grew to have 1.6 million members, and they were the country's best-paid unionized workers. He lost his position, however, after he invoked the Fifth Amendment more than 100 times during U.S. Senate investigations of union corruption, and in 1959, when he was convicted of federal tax-evasion and state embezzlement charges, he became the first of several Teamsters presidents who ended up in prison. He was paroled after 30 months, and he always maintained his innocence. In 1975 Pres. Gerald R. Ford granted Beck a full pardon.

Benet Goita, Juan, Spanish novelist (b. Oct. 7, 1927, Madrid, Spain—d. Jan. 5, 1993, Madrid), wrote intricate, highly allusive novels and short stories, many of them set in Región, a fictional rural province reminiscent of William Faulkner's Yoknapatawpha county. Benet, who studied at the University of Madrid, qualified as a civil engineer in 1954 and spent much of his life supervising the construction of dams and other public works in northwestern Spain. He published his first collection of stories, *Nunca llegarás a nada* ("You'll Never Amount to Anything"), in 1961. He gained critical attention, however, with *Volverás a Región* (1967; *Return to Región,* 1984), a complex novel chronicling the tragic effects of the Spanish Civil War (1936–39) on a community in that imaginary province. This book, the first in a trilogy, was followed by *Una meditación* (1969; *A Meditation,* 1982) and *Un viaje de invierno* (1972; "A Winter Journey"). His other novels include *En el estado* (1977; "In the State"), *Saúl ante Samuel* (1980; "Saul Before Samuel"), *Herrumbrosas lanzas* (1983; "Rusty Lances"), and *El caballero de Sajonia* (1991; "The Knight of Saxony"). Benet also translated Faulkner and Shakespeare into Spanish and wrote short stories, a play, and several volumes of essays.

Berberova, Nina Nikolayevna, Russian-born writer (b. Aug. 8, 1901, St. Petersburg, Russia—d. Sept. 26, 1993, Philadelphia, Pa.), was an important figure in Russian-émigré literary circles, but she did not gain wide renown for her writings until she was in her 80s. Berberova began composing poetry as a young girl and, while attending avant-garde literary meetings in St. Petersburg, she met famed poet Vladislav Khodasevich. The two left the country in 1922 and traveled in Europe—living for a time in Berlin and later on the Italian island of Capri with Maxim Gorky—before settling in Paris, then the centre of the émigré community. Berberova's short stories, which were published in Russian-language newspapers and magazines, and her novels centred on the Russian expatriate community and were largely distributed and limited to that small group. After leaving Khodasevich in 1935, Berberova worked as a journalist, translator, and typist while writing several biographies, notably one of Tchaikovsky. In 1947 she helped found the weekly *Russkaya Mysl'* ("Russian Thought"). Three years later, without a command of English, Berberova immigrated to the U.S. with only two suitcases and $75. She secured a teaching position at Yale University even though she had no diploma; she later taught (1963–71) at Princeton University. In 1969 her autobiography, *The Italics Are Mine,* was published in English, followed by the original Russian version in 1972. During the late 1980s translated collections of her extended short stories became best-sellers in France. In 1991 *The Tattered Cloak and Other Novels* was published in the U.S., and in 1993 a film based on her story "The Accompanist" was released.

Bérégovoy, Pierre Eugène, French politician (b. Dec. 23, 1925, Déville-les-Rouen, France—d. May 1, 1993, near Nevers, France), was a leader in the moderate wing of the French Socialist Party (PS), a close associate of Pres. François Mitterrand, and the author of rigorous monetary policies in his role as minister of finance (1984–86, 1988–92). During his short term as prime minister (1992–93), he was unable to stop an alarming rise in unemployment, avoid involvement in a financial scandal, or prevent the PS's defeat by a centre-right coalition in the March 1993 general election. Bérégovoy was born into a working-class family and had little formal education. He trained as a lathe operator and worked for the government-run railway during World War II. From 1950 he pursued a career with Gaz de France, the national gas company, rising to director in 1978. After serving as campaign manager in Mitterrand's successful 1981 presidential bid, Bérégovoy became chief of staff (1981–82), minister of social affairs (1982–84), and finance minister. In April 1992 he was appointed to succeed the controversial Edith Cresson as prime minister. He was a popular choice initially, but within months it was disclosed that he had accepted an interest-free loan in 1986 from businessman Roger-Patrice Pelat, who was later accused of insider trading. Although Bérégovoy denied any wrongdoing, the disclosure added to the voters' growing disillusionment with the scandal-ridden PS. Bérégovoy, apparently despondent over the party's election defeat and the lack of personal support from Mitterrand during his own troubles, committed suicide.

Bernstein of Leigh, Sidney Lewis Bernstein, BARON, British business executive (b. Jan. 30, 1899, Ilford, Essex, England—d. Feb. 5, 1993, London, England), built a small chain of music halls into the Granada Group, a vast multimedia empire that included Granada Television, one of Britain's first (and most successful) commercial television companies. Bernstein, who was the son of an immigrant property dealer, left school at the age of 15 to join the family business, and when his father died in 1922, he inherited a group of music halls and theatres. He soon took advantage of the burgeoning English movie industry by converting the theatres so they could show films, and in 1930 he opened the first of a chain of opulent Granada supercinemas. He also managed other theatrical houses, served as an adviser to the Ministry of Information during World War II, and produced three films directed by his friend Alfred Hitchcock. In 1954 he applied for one of the first four commercial television licenses in Britain, and in May 1956 Granada Television began broadcasting. By the time Bernstein retired as chairman in 1979, Granada was the only one of the original four still in operation and was a financial and critical success, with such popular series as "World in Action," "Brideshead Revisited," "Jewel in the Crown," and the long-running "Coronation Street." He was created a life peer in 1969.

Bixby, Bill, U.S. actor (b. Jan. 22, 1934, San Francisco, Calif.—d. Nov. 21, 1993, Los Angeles, Calif.), was best remembered for three starring television roles: as reporter Tim O'Hara on "My Favorite Martian" (1963–66); as the widowed father of a six-year-old boy on "The Courtship of Eddie's Father" (1969–72); and as a mild-mannered research scientist who (as a result of a laboratory accident) turned, when angered, into a raging, green-skinned monster (portrayed by bodybuilder Lou Ferrigno) on "The Incredible Hulk" (1978–82). The one-time hotel clerk and lifeguard with pleasing good looks launched a career in show business by serving as a model for automobile advertisements. After landing a bit role on a television episode of "The Many Loves of Dobie Gillis," the durable Bixby enjoyed a more than 30-year career on television and also starred on such short-lived series as "The Magician" (1973–74) and "Goodnight, Beantown" (1983–84). At the time of his death, Bixby, who also appeared in such films as *Irma La Douce* (1963) and *Under the Yum Yum Tree* (1963), was directing the television comedy series "Blossom."

Bolton, John Gatenby, British-born Australian astronomer (b. June 5, 1922, Sheffield, England—d. July 6, 1993, Buderim, Queensland, Australia), was a pioneer in the field of radio astronomy and director (1961–71) of the Australian National Radio Astronomy Observatory, where the 64-m (210-ft) Parkes radio telescope played a crucial role in the U.S. Apollo space program. Bolton studied mathematics and physics at Trinity College, Cambridge, and then served as a radar officer in the British Royal Navy (1942–46). He immigrated to Australia in 1946 and joined the staff of the Radiophysics Laboratory of the Commonwealth Council for Scientific and Industrial Research in Sydney. In 1948 Bolton's team identified the first known radio galaxies, or "radio stars," external galaxies that can be traced by the strong signals they emit at radio wavelengths. He established the Owens Valley Radio Observatory during a six-year stint teaching physics and astronomy at the California Institute of Technology (1955–61), but in 1961 he returned to Australia to oversee construction of the Parkes dish. In 1962–63, under Bolton's direction, this radio telescope played a key role in the discovery of the prototype of a family of very distant and luminous objects called quasars. Bolton later used it to pinpoint more than 8,000 extragalactic radio sources, including hundreds of quasars. In 1969 the instrument became the ear of the world when it received the radio signals transmitted by Apollo 11 from the Moon. Bolton was made Commander of the Order of the British Empire in 1981.

Brandon, (Oscar) Henry, Czech-born British journalist (b. March 9, 1916, Liberec, Bohemia, Austria-Hungary—d. April 20, 1993, London, England), as chief Washington correspondent for the British newspaper *The Sunday Times* (1950–83), gained personal access to nearly everyone of power and influence in the U.S. government and achieved a uniquely intimate perspective on Western politics throughout the 40-year cold war. Brandon was educated at the Universities of Prague and Lausanne, Switz, and moved to London in 1939. He joined *The Sunday Times* as a freelance contributor, then served as a war correspondent (1943–45), Paris correspondent (1945–46), and roving diplomatic correspondent (1947–49) before moving to Washington. A man of natural charm and discretion, Brandon cultivated close ties with U.S. presidents and Cabinet members. The extent of his political knowledge was so well known that Pres. Richard Nixon ordered his phone tapped in 1969 despite the journalist's personal friendship with Henry Kissinger, then Nixon's national security adviser. In 1983 Brandon retired from *The Sunday Times,* of which he had been associate editor from 1963, but he remained at the centre of things as a columnist for the New York Times World Syndicate and a guest scholar with the Brookings Institution (1983–93). Brandon's books include *The Retreat of American Power* (1973) and *Special Relationships* (1989). He was made Commander of the Order of the British Empire in 1985.

Brown, John Robert, U.S. judge (b. Dec. 10, 1909, Funk, Neb.—d. Jan. 22, 1993, Houston, Texas), as a federal judge (1955–67) and chief justice (1967–79) of the U.S. Court of Appeals for the 5th Circuit, played a pivotal role in championing and enforcing civil rights legislation in the South, perhaps most notably when he ordered (1962) that African-American James Meredith be enrolled in the all-white University of Mississippi over the objections of Gov. Ross Barnett. After earning (1932) a law degree from the University of Michigan, Brown joined the Houston law firm of Royston & Rayzor, specializing in maritime law. He served as chairman of the Harris county (Texas) Republican Party (1953–55) before being named to the Court of Appeals by Pres. Dwight Eisenhower just a year after the U.S. Supreme Court ended school segregation. Brown's jurisdiction, racked by violent protests against that decision, extended to Texas, Louisiana, Mississippi, Georgia, Florida, Alabama, and the Panama Canal Zone. His judicial legacy included decisions to overturn the Texas poll tax, prohibit Georgia and Alabama officials from barring blacks from voting, and overturn the conviction of two Louisiana blacks (on death row for 13 years) because black jurors were excluded from their trial. Brown, together with three other judges, was the subject of the 1981 book *Unlikely Heroes.*

Burgess, Anthony (JOHN ANTHONY BURGESS WILSON), British novelist, critic, and man of letters (b. Feb. 25, 1917, Manchester, England—d. Nov. 22, 1993, London, England), worked in a number of disciplines—fiction, music, journalism, and criticism among them—and was considered one of his generation's most clever and original writers. He wrote more than 50 books and considered himself primarily a comic writer, but he was best known for his novel *A Clockwork Orange* (1962), which portrayed a bleak, violent future in which gangs of teenagers (speaking a language Burgess invented) commit acts of violence

JERRY BAUER

to rebel against the conformity of their society. The 1971 film version of the novel, directed by Stanley Kubrick, became controversial for its violence, which was more pronounced than that in the book and was said to have inspired similar violence in gangs of youths. It eventually was withdrawn from distribution. Burgess developed an interest in music at an early age, taught himself to play the piano, and, while still in school, wrote a cello concerto and a symphony. He received (1940) a degree in English from Manchester University, served (1940–46) in the army, and became a teacher before becoming (1954) an education officer in Malaya. While there he wrote his first novels, a trilogy with a Malayan setting. Diagnosed with an inoperable brain tumour and given only a year to live in 1959, Burgess, having returned to England, began to write at an intense pace so that his wife would be provided for after his death. When the diagnosis turned out to be incorrect, he maintained that pace, writing at least one book a year. He left England for good in 1968, teaching in the U.S. until 1974 and then moving to Malta, Rome, and finally Monaco and Switzerland. Among his works—some written under the pseudonym Joseph Kell—were the comic Enderby series (1963–84); the Broadway musical *Cyrano* (1973), based on his translation of Edmond Rostand's *Cyrano de Bergerac; Earthly Powers* (1980); *The End of the World News* (1983); a number of motion-picture and television screenplays; symphonies; and his last book, *A Dead Man in Deptford* (1993). Burgess was a fellow of the British Royal Society of Literature and a Commandeur des Arts et des Lettres of France.

Burke, Kenneth, U.S. literary critic and philosopher (b. May 5, 1897, Pittsburgh, Pa.—d. Nov. 19, 1993, Andover, N.J.), studied the relationships between language, literature, culture, and power in a variety of wide-ranging and complex works; for many years his theories were often dismissed as obscure and idiosyncratic, but they later gained a renewed appreciation. Although drawn to language and literature from an early age, Burke quit college because he was disenchanted with formal education ("horrified . . . what college can do to a man of promise") and began a rigorous and expansive self-education. While working on his own stories, Burke began to formulate the ideas on literary form elaborated in his first work of criticism, *Counter-Statement* (1931). While he worked as a reviewer, editor, translator, and writer, his theoretical work gained influence, and he earned prominence in the literary critical school known as New Criticism. Burke produced a body of original and ever evolving work whose cross-disciplinary approach made them difficult for readers and reviewers to easily consume and categorize and put him out of the academic mainstream, yet late 20th-century approaches to literary criticism brought rekindled interest in and praise for his works. Burke never held a permanent university position and spent most of his life at his farm in New Jersey. Among his works are *The Philosophy of Literary Form* (1941), *A Rhetoric of Motives* (1950), and *Language as Symbolic Action* (1966).

Burkitt, Denis Parsons, Irish physician (b. Feb. 28, 1911, Enniskillen, Northern Ireland—d. March 23, 1993, England), recognized the significance of varying climatic conditions and eating habits in the incidence of cancer and certain other diseases. His most significant medical achievement was in the painstaking study of the cause of and treatment for Burkitt's lymphoma, a lethal cancer of the lymphatic system of high incidence among children in tropical Africa. Outside of medical circles, however, he was best known for his well-publicized theories on nutrition and the importance of a high-fibre diet. Burkitt matriculated at Trinity College, Dublin (B.A., 1933; M.D., 1946), and served as an army doctor during World War II. In 1946 he joined the colonial service in Uganda, where he was a government surgeon, a lecturer in surgery at Makerere University Medical School, and senior surgeon to the Ministry of Health. In the late 1950s he sent out hundreds of questionnaires to doctors and traveled some 16,000 km (10,000 mi) across Africa to study hospital records on a form of malignant facial tumour found mainly in boys under 12. His research demonstrated that Burkitt's lymphoma (as it came to be called) was endemic only in mosquito-ridden equatorial Africa and led to the discovery that the cancer was linked to the presence of the Epstein-Barr virus (the cause of acute infectious mononucleosis) in children whose immune system was depressed by chronic malaria. He later helped develop an effective chemotherapy treatment for the lymphoma. Burkitt joined the Medical Research Council (MRC) in Uganda in 1964, and two years later he transferred to the London MRC centre. In the late 1960s he turned his attention to the apparent link between dietary fibre and colon cancer. His subsequent publications, including the popular book *Don't Forget Fibre in Your Diet* (1979), triggered a new interest in nutrition and a greater emphasis on fibre in the Western diet.

Burr, Raymond William Stacey, U.S. actor (b. May 21, 1917, New Westminster, B.C.—d. Sept. 12, 1993, near Healdsburg, Calif.), created formidable and enduring television characters, including the legendary criminal lawyer "Perry Mason" (1957–66) and the wheelchair-confined San Francisco detective "Ironside" (1967–75). Prior to his television career, he portrayed a series of villains in films, most memorably the white-haired wife

AP/WIDE WORLD

killer in Alfred Hitchcock's suspense classic *Rear Window.* The actor, who specialized in portraying screen heavies, appeared as a deported gangster in *His Kind of Woman,* a crooked club owner in *Meet Danny Wilson,* and a stalker in *A Cry in the Night.* He also had a brief stint (March–August 1977) as the chief reporter and editor in chief of a newspaper and media organization in the television crime drama "Kingston: Confidential." His courtroom drama was revived in 1985 when he returned as Perry Mason, appeals court judge, for a television film; thereafter Burr made about three television films a year, most frequently appearing as lawyer Perry Mason, the role that had earned him two Emmy awards.

Cahn, Sammy (SAMUEL COHEN), U.S. lyricist (b. June 18, 1913, New York, N.Y.—d. Jan. 15, 1993, Los Angeles, Calif.), was an enormously prolific songwriter whose catchy lyrics and precise rhyming were the hallmark of such Academy Award-winning songs as "Three Coins in the Fountain" (1954), "All the Way" (1957), "High Hopes" (1959), and "Call Me Irresponsible" (1963) and helped many of his other songs become enduring standards. As a teenager Cahn played the violin in burlesque houses, adapting ribald lyrics to some of the numbers. While playing in an orchestra, he met pianist Saul Chaplin, and the two formed a songwriting partnership. Their first hit, "Rhythm Is Our Business," became the theme song of the Jimmy Lunceford orchestra; it was followed by an English-language version of the Yiddish folk song "Bei Mir Bist Du Schoen," which sold a million records for the Andrews Sisters. After moving to Hollywood, Cahn teamed up with Jule Styne. The two wrote songs for 19 films from 1942 to 1951, most unforgettably "I'll Walk Alone," "It's Magic," "Five Minutes More," "Time After Time," "Saturday Night Is the Loneliest Night of the Week," "The Things We Did Last Summer," and "Let It Snow!" They also collaborated on songs for the 1947 hit Broadway musical *High Button Shoes,* but Cahn felt more at home in Hollywood. He partnered Axel Stordahl and Paul Weston, with whom he turned out two of singer Frank Sinatra's biggest hits, "Day by Day" and "I Should Care," and joined Nicholas Brodzsky for "Be My Love," Mario Lanza's first hit. In 1956 Sinatra (who would record 89 Cahn songs) introduced Cahn to Jimmy Van Heusen; the new team turned out so much material for Sinatra that they were considered his personal songwriters. The duo wrote the title song for the film *The Tender Trap* and such all-time favourites as "High Hopes," "The Second Time Around," "My Kind of Town," "Come Fly with Me," and title songs for four Sinatra albums. They also wrote the scores for two unsuccessful Broadway musicals, *Skyscraper* (1965) and *Walking Happy* (1966), and for the film *Thoroughly Modern Millie* (1967). In 1974 Cahn published his autobiography, *I Should Care,* and starred in a one-man Broadway retrospective of his career, *Words and Music*. He became a member (1972) and president (1973) of the Songwriters Hall of Fame.

Campanella, Roy ("CAMPY"), U.S. baseball player (b. Nov. 19, 1921, Homestead, Pa.—d. June 26, 1993, Woodland Hills, Calif.), was a sensational catcher and home-run specialist for the Brooklyn Dodgers until his professional playing career ended in 1958 when he was paralyzed from the shoulders down after the car he was driving skidded into a telephone pole; he became, however,

AP/WIDE WORLD

an inspirational spokesman for the handicapped, and he coached Los Angeles Dodger players during spring training from 1978 to 1993. Campanella played semiprofessional baseball on the Nicetown, Philadelphia, sandlots before signing with the Negro leagues at age 15. After joining the Dodgers in 1948 as the major leagues' second black player (Jackie Robinson was the first), he became one of the stars of one of the greatest teams in baseball, the storied "boys of summer," who captured five National League pennants between 1949 and 1956. Campanella was named the league's Most Valuable Player in 1951, 1953, and 1955, and he displayed his hitting prowess in 1953 by slamming 41 home runs and leading the league with 142 runs batted in. He published his memoirs, *It's Good to Be Alive,* in 1959. Campanella was inducted into the Baseball Hall of Fame in 1969.

Cantinflas (MARIO MORENO REYES), Mexican comic actor (b. Aug. 12, 1911, Mexico City, Mexico—d. April 20, 1993, Mexico City), was idolized in Latin America for his uproarious film portrayals, which relied on slapstick comedy and brilliantly captured the persona of the *pobrecito* ("poor little person"). He broadened his appeal to English-speaking audiences after playing Passepartout, the loyal manservant of Phileas Fogg (David Niven), in the Academy Award-winning film *Around the World in 80 Days* (1956), but his greatest acclaim was in Spanish-speaking countries. Because his family was not pleased with his foray into show business—as a *torero bufo* (buffoonish matador) and as a master of ceremonies, acrobat, and clown at a *carpa* (Mexican tent show)—he concocted the name Cantinflas. His career as a comic was inadvertently launched when he suffered a bout of stage fright as he filled in for the master of ceremonies at a *carpa* and began flailing his arms and speaking gibberish. From his nonsensical talk was born the Spanish verb *cantinflear,* meaning to talk much and say nothing, and it was later to become one of his trademarks. Others included

UPI/BETTMANN

his pencil-thin mustache, which appeared only at the corners of his mouth; a battered hat; pants that slid down his hips; and a bowlegged, Chaplinesque walk. His satirical antics, though more biting, were often compared to those of Chaplin, who was a great admirer of Cantinflas and dubbed him the greatest comedian alive. Cantinflas made 49 films during his career and amassed a personal fortune that allowed him to live lavishly and also generously support dozens of charities, as well as contribute to the Roman Catholic Church. The diminutive actor made his film debut in 1936, and his first two full-length feature films, *Ahí está el detalle* (1941; "Here's the Point") and *Ni sangre, ni arena* (1941; "Neither Blood nor Sand"), smashed box-office records for Mexican-made films throughout Latin America. His other credits include *Romeo y Julieta* (1943; "Romeo and Juliet"), *Los tres mosqueteros* (1942; "The Three Musketeers"), and *El patrullero 777* (1978; "Patrol Car 777"). After filming *Pepe* (1960) in the U.S., he returned to Mexico, where his portrayals of a *pelado* (Mexican slum dweller) had made him a living legend. Cantinflas retired from films in 1981.

Chalmers, Floyd Sherman, U.S.-born Canadian editor, publisher, and philanthropist (b. Sept. 14, 1898, Chicago, Ill.—d. April 26, 1993, Toronto, Ont.), relied on hard work and initiative to become editor in chief of the *Financial Post* by the time he was 27 and later acquired a fortune as a major shareholder of Maclean Hunter, publisher of *Maclean's* magazine. He used his considerable wealth and organizational talents to generously support the arts in Canada. Chalmers, who grew up in Orillia, Ont., left high school to serve as an apprentice reporter at the *Toronto News*. He later joined the *Financial Post* and then stamped his editorial imprint on Maclean Hunter. He was elected a director of Maclean Publishing Co. in 1938 and was president (1952–64) and chairman of the board of directors (1964–69) of Maclean Hunter. Chalmers was especially remembered for commissioning Harry Somers to produce the opera *Louis Riel* for Canada's centennial celebration, for financing the publication of the English and French editions of the *Encyclopedia of Music in Canada,* for serving as a cofounder of the Canadian Opera Company and the Stratford Shakespearean Festival, for establishing (together with his wife, Jean) the Jean A. Chalmers Chair in Canadian Music and the Institute for Canadian Music at the Faculty of Music, University of Toronto, and for his $10 million gift to 16 arts and educational institutions in 1989. He was also chancellor of York University, North York, Ont., from 1968 to 1973 and was made a Companion of the Order of Canada in 1985.

Charteris, Leslie (LESLIE CHARLES BOWYER YIN), British-born writer (b. May 12, 1907, Singapore—d. April 15, 1993, Windsor, Berkshire, England), created the roguish Simon Templar, known as the Saint, one of the 20th century's most enduring and endearing fictional adventurers. Charteris was born in Singapore (then a British crown colony) to a British mother and a Chinese father, and he spoke Malay and Chinese before he learned English. As a child, he created his own magazine and illustrated it with stick figures he later adapted into the Saint's haloed logo. He was educated in England, but he left Cambridge after a year to write. He held a variety of odd jobs, including tin mining, pearl fishing, bartending, and professional bridge playing, and wrote his first thriller, *X Esquire* (1927). In 1928 he legally changed his name to Charteris and published his third novel, *Meet the Tiger,* which introduced the charming and debonair gentleman-thief Templar. Four years later Charteris moved to the U.S., where he became a citizen in 1946. During the 1930s and '40s, he and his modern Robin Hood delighted the public with a series of novels, short stories, and film adaptations. He also wrote other Hollywood scripts, designed comic strips, founded *The Saint Mystery Magazine* (1953–67), raised money for charity through the Saint Club, and served as a consultant on the popular TV series "The Saint" (1963–68), starring actor Roger Moore, and its two sequels. Altogether, Charteris wrote some 50 novels and story collections; translations were published in at least 15 languages.

Chavez, Cesar Estrada, U.S. migrant farm worker and labour leader (b. March 31, 1927, Yuma, Ariz.—found dead April 23, 1993, San Luis, Ariz.), was an inspirational Hispanic leader who quit his job in the fields to organize poorly paid Mexican-American migrant farm labourers into the nation's first successful union of agricultural workers, the National Farm Workers Association (NFWA), the forerunner of the United Farm Workers of America (UFW). Chavez had begun working beside his parents in the fields by the time he was 10. He sporadically attended some 65 different schools and lived in a succession of migrant worker camps before serving in the navy during World War II. After the war he returned to migrant farm work in Arizona and California. Chavez received training as an organizer from California's Community Service Organization (CSO), a creation of Saul Alinsky's Industrial Areas Foundation. He served as general director (1958–62) of the CSO before founding the NFWA in 1962. Chavez captured national attention in 1965, when he became the driving force in what became a five-year California grape pickers strike, and again in 1968, when he led a nationwide boycott of California table grapes. He remained in the public eye by fasting and by inviting arrest to dramatize his fight with both grape growers and iceberg lettuce producers. By 1970, with 17 million Americans supporting the grape boycott, growers had agreed to

MASTRO/ARCHIVE PHOTOS

sign with the union. Though the Teamsters union tried to organize field hands, they abandoned the effort in 1977. Meanwhile, the UFWA had merged with an AFL-CIO farm group to form UFWOC, the United Farm Workers Organizing Committee, AFL-CIO in 1966. That organization became the UFW in 1971. Chavez, who ruled the union with an authoritarian hand, eventually lost the support of his top aides, who resigned. Union membership also dwindled from 100,000 to some 20,000 members as it became increasingly difficult for Chavez to concentrate on organization efforts when he became involved in encounter programs, holistic medicine, vegetarianism, meditation, and faith healing. Chavez died in his sleep of natural causes.

Christoff, Boris, Bulgarian-born opera singer (b. May 18, 1914, Plovdiv, Bulg.—d. June 28, 1993, Rome, Italy), brought a commanding stage presence and a smooth, perfectly controlled bass voice to many of the great acting-singing roles in opera, notably Philip II in *Don Carlos* and the title character in *Boris Godunov,* which became his signature role. Christoff studied law in Sofia, but he was induced to pursue a singing career by King Boris, who heard him perform with the renowned Gusla Choir and arranged for him to study with the baritone Riccardo Stracciari in Rome. Christoff went to Austria during World War II, then resumed his studies in Italy, where he later became a citizen. He appeared in concert in 1946 and made a spectacular opera debut the same year as Colline in *La Bohème.* He first sang *Boris Godunov* in his 1949 debut at London's Covent Garden, and over the next 30 years he perfected his interpretation of the mad czar, recording it twice. After a delay of six years because of visa problems, he made his U.S. debut in San Francisco in 1956. Christoff's other roles included Mephistopheles (*Faust*), Prince Galitsky and Khan Konchak (*Prince Igor*), King Mark (*Tristan und Isolde*), and Henry VIII (*Anna Bolena*). As a champion of Russian vocal music, he recorded a complete set of Mussorgsky's songs, as well as songs by Borodin, Glinka, and others.

Collins, Albert, U.S. blues musician (b. Oct. 1, 1932, Leona, Texas—d. Nov. 24, 1993, Las Vegas, Nev.), was a passionate instrumentalist and singer who became known as the "Master of the Telecaster" for the distinctively pure "icy" tone he produced from his Fender Telecaster electric guitar. Collins learned piano and guitar as a teenager in Houston, Texas, and played in local clubs as a band musician and pickup guitarist for other performers. On his first record, "The Freeze" (1958), he introduced the bare-finger plucking style and D-minor open-chord tuning that became his trademarks. He followed up with successful instrumentals, including "Defrost," "Frosty," and "Sno-Cone." In the late 1960s he moved to Los Angeles, where the blues/rock group Canned Heat helped him sign with a major record label and broaden his appeal to a young white audience. Collins added vocals in the 1970s. He won the W. C. Handy Award for best blues album for *Don't Lose Your Cool* (1983) and *Cold Snap* (1986) and captured a Grammy for *Showdown* (1987), recorded with Johnny Copeland and Robert Cray. Collins' other albums include *Ice Pickin'* (1978), *Frostbite* (1980), and *Molten Ice* (1992).

Conn, William David, Jr. ("Billy"; "The Pittsburgh Kid"), U.S. boxer (b. Oct. 8, 1917, East Liberty, Pa.—d. May 29, 1993, Pittsburgh, Pa.), was on the brink of defeating Joe Louis for the heavyweight championship title by outpointing him when he brashly decided to knock out the champion but instead was knocked out by Lewis with two seconds left in the 13th round. Conn, who had lightning-quick hands and feet, was outweighed by Lewis but had nearly knocked him out in the previous round of that celebrated fight on June 18, 1941. Though a rematch was scheduled, their fight was postponed for four years, first because Conn broke his hand in a fight with his father-in-law and then because both Conn and Louis were inducted into the army. In the June 1946 rematch, Louis knocked out the agile Conn in the eighth round and thereby illustrated his famous prefight line, "He can run, but he can't hide." Earlier Conn had reigned as light-heavyweight champion, beating Melio Bettina for the title in 1939. Conn had three successful title defenses before relinquishing that crown to compete as a heavyweight. He appeared in the film *The Pittsburgh Kid* (1941), scored a few victories in 1948, and sparred in December of that year with Louis in a six-round exhibition fight in Chicago (losing on decision) before retiring. During his professional boxing career (1935–48), Conn fought in 75 bouts; he had 63 wins (14 by knockouts), 11 losses, and 1 draw. Conn was elected to the Boxing Hall of Fame in 1965.

Connally, John Bowden, Jr., U.S. politician (b. Feb. 27, 1917, Floresville, Texas—d. June 15, 1993, Houston, Texas), was an ambitious political figure who, besides helping elect Presidents Dwight D. Eisenhower, John F. Kennedy, and Lyndon B. Johnson, served as secretary of the navy in the Kennedy administration (1961), as a three-term governor of Texas (1963–69), and as secretary of the treasury (1971) under Pres. Richard M. Nixon; he was indelibly identified as the seriously wounded front-seat passenger who was riding in the presidential limousine in Dallas, Texas, when Kennedy was assassinated on Nov. 22, 1963. Connally, a tall, handsome man with an engaging yet forceful personality, was determined to transcend his impoverished childhood. After attending the University of Texas and earning a law degree, he became an aide to Johnson, who at the time was a freshman Democratic representative. Connally served in the navy during World War II but returned to the political arena to manage Johnson's brutal but successful Senate campaign in 1948. He put aside party loyalty to help Eisenhower, the Republican candidate, win the presidency in 1952 but returned to the Democratic fold to manage Johnson's ill-fated attempt to wrest the presidential nomination from Kennedy; he stayed with the ticket, however, when Kennedy named Johnson as his running mate. Though appointed secretary of the navy, he soon resigned to run for governor of Texas. It was during his first term in office that Connally (who was first sitting in the back seat with Kennedy but later in the motorcade moved to the front seat) was shot. The bullet passed through his body and resulted in scarring on his back, chest, wrist, and thigh and in a lifelong lung condition, pulmonary fibrosis, manifested by a shortness of breath during exertion. He was returned to office for two more terms. As secretary of the treasury, Connally took the U.S. off the gold standard and imposed wage-and-price controls. In 1973, shortly after Johnson died, Connally officially became a Republican. Though indicted by a Watergate grand jury in 1974 for accepting a $10,000 bribe from milk producers, he was acquitted. In 1980 Connally made an unsuccessful bid in the Republican presidential primaries. After spending more than $11 million, he had secured only one delegate. He then embarked on ventures in Texas real estate, oil, and other businesses before that state's economy collapsed in the 1980s. Connally declared personal bankruptcy in 1988 to satisfy debts of $93 million, but within a year he had emerged from that status. Shortly before his death of complications from pulmonary fibrosis, Connally completed his autobiography, *In History's Shadow.*

Craven, Daniël Hartman ("Danie"), South African rugby player and administrator (b. Oct. 11, 1910, Lindley, Orange Free State, South Africa—d. Jan. 4, 1993, Stellenbosch, Cape Province, South Africa), was at the centre of South African rugby for more than 50 years—as a player, coach, and selector; as president (1956–92) of the South African Rugby Board (SARB); and as copresident (from 1992) of the multiracial South African Rugby Football Union (SARFU). Craven first played for the national Springbok team in 1931, while he was a theology student at the University of Stellenbosch. An injury induced him to switch majors, and he eventually received doctorates in anthropology, psychology, and physical education. Although he usually played at the scrum-half position, in his 16 matches as a Springbok the versatile Craven also played fly-half, fullback, and No. 8. He made his last appearance for South Africa in 1938 and then served as director of physical education for the national defense force (1938–41) and for the South African military college (1941–46). In 1947 he returned to the University of Stellenbosch, where he remained as head of the physical education department (1947–75) and director of sport and recreation (1976–80). He was also a Springbok coach and selector until 1956. As SARB president, Craven sought to end his country's exclusion from international rugby. In 1988 he defied South African law to meet with members of the then-banned African National Congress in exile in Zimbabwe, and when the breakdown of apartheid began in 1991, he led talks between the all-white SARB and the other racially based governing bodies to form the unified SARFU. Despite ill health, Craven traveled to Europe in October 1992 to watch South Africa play against France.

Crosby, George Robert ("Bob"), U.S. bandleader (b. Aug. 25, 1913, Spokane, Wash.—d. March 9, 1993, La Jolla, Calif.), was a mediocre vocalist but was able to capitalize on the star status of his older brother Bing, a famous crooner, to secure engagements for his swing band, the Bobcats, which produced a string of hit songs, including "South Rampart Street Parade," "The Big Crash from China," and "The Big Noise from Winnetka," and was featured in more than 20 films, notably *Let's Make Music, As Thousands Cheer,* and *Pardon My Rhythm*. In 1935 Crosby fronted his own orchestra, and his Bobcats evolved from that larger group, making it the first band within a band, a major contribution to jazz. Its potent arrangements of New Orleans jazz became known as Dixieland Swing and made it one of the most interesting bands of the 1930s and '40s. Crosby also formed the short-lived Bob-o-Links, a vocal group from within his band. The Bobcats disbanded in 1942 soon after the outbreak of World War II. Later Crosby reassembled the band for special occasions and tours, performing with it for more than 40 years.

Cusack, Cyril James, Irish actor (b. Nov. 26, 1910, Durban, South Africa—d. Oct. 7, 1993, London, England), was considered the finest Irish actor of his generation; he had a subtle, economical, and finely controlled style and a brooding, melancholic air that mesmerized audiences. He was especially compelling as Covey in Sean O'Casey's *The Plough and the Stars* and as Christy Mahon in John Synge's *The Playboy of the Western World.* Cusack and his mother moved to Ireland in 1916, and with the actor Brefni O'Rourke they formed a theatrical company that toured throughout the country. Cusack made his acting debut at age seven and later claimed that he had attended nearly every school in Ireland. He earned a degree in law at University College, Dublin, but decided to pursue an acting career. He joined (1932) the Abbey Theatre in Dublin and during the following 13 years appeared in nearly 70 plays. During that time, he also occasionally appeared onstage in Britain. He then formed (1945) his own company, writing, directing, and acting in innumerable productions. Cusack joined the Royal Shakespeare Company (1963) and the National Theatre (1964) in London, continued to appear in Ireland, and traveled to Paris and to the U.S., winning critical acclaim, awards, and honorary doctorates. He also appeared on television and in such motion pictures as *Odd Man Out* (1947), *The Spy Who Came in from the Cold* (1965), *The Taming of the Shrew* (1967), *The Day of the Jackal* (1973), and *My Left Foot* (1989). Cusack was the patriarch of a theatrical dynasty; his four daughters and a grandson also became actors. In 1990 he appeared in London with three of his daughters in Chekhov's *The Three Sisters.*

Dawson, Les, British comedian (b. Feb. 2, 1934, Collyhurst, near Manchester, England—d. June 10, 1993, Manchester), was a stand-up comic and television personality whose dour, misanthropic humour was reminiscent of W.C. Fields but reflected his own northern England working-class origins. His sardonic put-downs were most often aimed at mothers-in-law, bosses, and other figures of everyday authority that his appreciative audiences could take delight in ridiculing. Dawson was the son of a struggling Manchester bricklayer and left school at the age of 14. After drifting through a series of jobs, he moved to Paris to try his hand at writing; instead, he got into show business—playing piano in a brothel. Back in England he played in working-class clubs, where he found he could make people laugh with his bawdy remarks and barbed retorts to hecklers. He became a hit on radio and on such television programs as "Opportunity Knocks," "Blackpool Night Out," his own long-running "Sez Les," "The Les Dawson Show," and the often inane quiz show "Blankety Blank." Occasionally Dawson acted in plays, most notably in a 1991 BBC production of the Argentine farce *Nona.* He also wrote several novels, and his autobiography, *A Clown Too Many,* was published in 1985.

de Mille, Agnes George, U.S. choreographer (b. Sept. 18, 1905, New York, N.Y.—d. Oct. 7, 1993, New York), changed the face of American dance by incorporating American subject matter and elements of folk dancing into her ballets, and she revolutionized musical comedy by making dance not just a spectacular diversion but an integral part of the action. Her choreography was instrumental in advancing the plot and helping to define the characters. De Mille, the daughter of

PHOTOFEST

the playwright William Churchill de Mille and the niece of the motion-picture producer-director Cecil B. DeMille, moved with her family to Hollywood in 1914. After seeing dance performances by Anna Pavlova and Ruth St. Denis, she decided to be a dancer and began taking ballet classes. Her father insisted that she be educated, however, and she attended the University of California at Los Angeles, graduating cum laude with a degree in English. She thereupon resumed her dance training and moved to New York City. De Mille soon began performing, and in 1928 she gave her first solo recital. From 1929 to 1940 she toured in the U.S. and Europe, studying, performing, and choreographing. In 1937 she danced in the premiere of Antony Tudor's *Dark Elegies* with Ballet Rambert in London. In 1940 she began choreographing for Ballet Theatre (later American Ballet Theatre) in New York City, and in 1942 she created *Rodeo* for the Ballet Russe de Monte Carlo; it proved to be her first major success. Set on a ranch, it combined square dancing and tap dancing with ballet, and de Mille herself danced the lead role of the cowgirl. After that triumph, she was invited to choreograph the Broadway musical *Oklahoma!* (1943), which ran for more than five years and reigned as one of the greatest successes in American musical comedy. Her dance choreography strengthened the story and added to the dramatic atmosphere; the "dream ballet" that ended the first act provided psychological insights into the show's main character. Other Broadway successes followed, including *Carousel* (1945), *Brigadoon* (1947), *Gentlemen Prefer Blondes* (1949), *Paint Your Wagon* (1951), *Kwamina* (1961), and *110 in the Shade* (1963). De Mille also continued to create ballets. *Fall River Legend* (1948), based on the true story of Lizzie Borden, was widely regarded as her masterpiece. In addition, she wrote extensively, with 12 books, some of them autobiographical, among her output. Even after a cerebral hemorrhage disabled her in 1975, she continued to work, choreographing *The Informer* (1988) and *The Other* (1992), writing, and lecturing. De Mille was given more than 15 honorary degrees and was elected to the Theater Hall of Fame (1973). She received two Tony awards (1947 and 1962), the Handel Medallion (1976), the Kennedy Center Career Achievement Award (1980), and the National Medal of the Arts (1986).

De Vries, Peter, U.S. writer (b. Feb. 27, 1910, Chicago, Ill.—d. Sept. 28, 1993, Norwalk, Conn.), was critically acclaimed as the author of such uproarious novels as *The Tunnel of Love* (1954), *Comfort Me with Apples* (1956), and its sequel, *The Tents of Wickedness* (1959), which showcased his acerbic wit, flair for wordplay, and mastery of puns. De Vries, who worked during the Great Depression as a taffy apple peddler, candy vending machine operator, and furniture mover before joining (1938) the Chicago-based *Poetry* magazine as an associate editor, found his widest reading audience as a staff member (1944–87) of *The New Yorker* magazine. There he wrote stories and later found his niche in the art department, putting the finishing touches on the magazine's renowned cartoon captions. His strict Calvinist upbringing found comic expression in novels that explored religious themes, notably *The Mackerel Plaza* (1958). The book humorously detailed the plight of the Rev. Andrew ("Holy") Mackerel, who faces opposition from his congregation when he announces his intention to remarry after the death of his saintly wife. His one serious novel, *The Blood of the Lamb* (1961), was an autobiographical account of the death of his young daughter from leukemia and his own struggle with religious issues. De Vries later explored feminism, gender identity, and the sexual revolution before returning to a lighter touch in *Consenting Adults; or, The Duchess Will Be Furious* (1980). His most commercially successful work, *The Tunnel of Love,* was the story of a hapless cartoonist modeled after himself; the novel was later adapted for stage and film. In 1986 De Vries curtailed his writing; he quipped, "When you know you're done, you're done."

Deming, W(illiam) Edwards, U.S. business-management expert (b. Oct. 14, 1900, Sioux City, Iowa—d. Dec. 20, 1993, Washington, D.C.), used statistical analysis to formulate quality-control methods in industrial production. His methods, advocating enlisting the cooperation of the workers in the achievement of high-quality results during the manufacturing process instead of relying on inspection at the end of the process to find flaws, were credited with the success of Japan's post-World War II economic boom. Deming earned (1928) a Ph.D. in mathematical physics from Yale University, taught physics, worked as a mathematical physicist, and was a statistical adviser, a professor of statistics, and a research consultant before being invited to Japan to teach executives and engineers his methods. Japanese companies eagerly adopted his ideas, and it was partly because of this that Japanese consumer-electronics products came to dominate the market in many parts of the world. The Deming Prize, given to companies making major advances in quality control and considered the Nobel Prize of Japanese business, was established (1951) in his honour. U.S. companies, which for many years complacently ignored Deming's methods, finally began to implement them in the 1980s. Deming continued to conduct quality-management seminars until days before his death.

Dickey, William Malcolm ("Bill"), U.S. baseball player (b. June 6, 1907, Bastrop, La.—d. Nov. 12, 1993, Little Rock, Ark.), was the outstanding catcher (1928–41) for the star-studded New York Yankees professional baseball teams that reigned seven times as World Series champions during their heyday in the 1920s and '30s, and he later briefly served as the team's manager and as a coach. Dickey's invaluable and wide-ranging knowledge of opposing batters; powerhouse hitting; ability to pull in knuckleballs, fastballs, and spitballs from pitchers; and top-notch defensive play earned him laurels as perhaps the best all-around catcher in the history of the sport. In 1929, a year after joining the Yankees, he became the starting catcher (throwing right-handed) and one of the most feared clutch hitters (batting left-handed). During his remarkable career, Dickey caught more than 100 games a season 13 times and compiled a .313 batting average with 202 home runs and 1,209 runs batted in. He was behind the plate for every inning of his 38 World Series games and had a series average of .400 (.438 in the 1932 series). After serving in the navy during World War II, Dickey returned to the Yankees in 1946 and replaced the ailing Joe McCarthy as manager for the remainder of that season. More comfortable as a coach (beginning in 1949), Dickey helped develop the skills of a struggling Yankee rookie catcher, Yogi Berra. Dickey later served as scout (1959–60) for the Yankees before retiring to sell securities in Little Rock, an occupation he continued until 1977. He was inducted into the Baseball Hall of Fame in 1954.

Doolittle, James Harold, general (ret.), U.S. Army Air Force (b. Dec. 14, 1896, Alameda, Calif.—d. Sept. 27, 1993, Pebble Beach, Calif.), was a lieutenant colonel when he commanded the strike force of B-25 bombers that on April 18, 1942, conducted a daring daylight air raid on Japan. Even though the secret mission, the first counterattack of the war, inflicted negligible damage on Tokyo, Yokohama, and other cities, it helped bolster U.S. morale following the Japanese bombing of Pearl Harbor and illustrated to Japan that the U.S. was in air-striking distance. Doolittle, who had established an unparalleled string of aviation records in the 1920s and '30s as an army pilot and as an employee of the Shell Oil Co., practiced flying B-25s on a short takeoff run in Florida be-

ARCHIVE PHOTOS

fore he led "Doolittle's Raiders" on their special mission. Sixteen B-25s carrying 80 aviators flew from the deck of the aircraft carrier *Hornet* and traveled westward. Though most of the crew had to bail out over mainland China or the Soviet Far East, 69 of them safely reached friendly lines on the Chinese mainland. Doolittle received the Medal of Honor for his execution of the mission and was soon promoted to brigadier general. His feat was the subject of the 1944 film *Thirty Seconds over Tokyo,* starring Spencer Tracy. Doolittle later commanded the 12th Air Force in Britain, the 15th Air Force in North Africa and Italy, and the 8th Air Force in attacks on Germany. After the war Doolittle returned to Shell Oil and remained active in both public- and private-sector aeronautical advisory committees. In 1989 Doolittle was the recipient of the Presidential Medal of Freedom.

Dorsey, Thomas Andrew, U.S. songwriter, singer, and pianist (b. July 1, 1899, Villa Rica, Ga.—d. Jan. 23, 1993, Chicago, Ill.), as the "father of gospel music," blended elements of soulful blues with the traditional sacred music of his religious upbringing to create a new genre called gospel, which infused an uplifting, foot-stomping sound into black congregations, primarily of Baptist and Holiness churches. Dorsey, the son of a preacher, began composing mainly secular blues songs while a teenager, and he helped support his family by singing and playing the piano. After moving to Chicago (1916), he appeared under the name Georgia Tom, became pianist for blues great Ma Rainey, and composed "hokum" songs (those peppered with risqué double entendres), notably "It's Tight like That" (1928; with guitarist Tampa Red), which eventually sold some seven million copies. In 1919 he began to write what would be the first of more than 1,000 gospel songs. One of his first successes, "If You See My Savior, Tell Him that You Saw Me" (1926), was written after a close friend died, and the hymn "Precious Lord, Take My Hand" was composed following the death of his first wife in childbirth and his infant son the following day. That song was popularized by singer Mahalia Jackson, was named by the Rev. Martin Luther King, Jr., as his favourite song, and threatened to unseat "Amazing Grace" as the anthem of African-Americans. Another famous composition was "Peace in the Valley," which was popularized by many singers, including Elvis Presley. In 1932 Dorsey, who had written hundreds of blues songs, abandoned that genre; he founded (1932) the Pilgrim Baptist Church in Chicago and served as its musical director until 1983. In 1933 he founded the National Convention of Gospel Choirs and Choruses in Chicago, of which he was president for 40 years. In 1982 he appeared in the gospel documentary *Say Amen, Somebody.*

Drew, Kenny, U.S.-born jazz pianist (b. Aug. 28, 1928, New York, N.Y.—d. Aug. 4, 1993, Copenhagen, Den.), was the centre of a largely black expatriate jazz colony that settled in Copenhagen in the 1960s. Drew began the study of classical piano at age five and attended the High School of Music and Art in New York City. He was early influenced by such pianists as Fats Waller, Teddy Wilson, and Art Tatum and, later, by Bud Powell and Thelonious Monk, and throughout his career there were elements of both swing and bebop in his playing. During the 1950s Drew accompanied and recorded with several of the major jazz artists of the time. After a brief period on the West Coast, he went to Paris in 1961, and in 1964 he settled in Copenhagen, where he became house pianist at the Montmarte Jazzhus. There he began an association with the Danish bassist Niels-Henning Orsted Pedersen, with whom he performed and recorded extensively. Drew later took up composing and orchestrating and was involved in music publishing and recording businesses. His son, Kenny Drew, Jr., also became a jazz pianist.

Drysdale, Donald Scott ("Big D"), U.S. baseball player and broadcaster (b. July 23, 1936, Van Nuys, Calif.—d. July 3, 1993, Montreal, Que.), as a star right-handed power pitcher for the Brooklyn (1956–58) and Los Angeles (1958–69) Dodgers, intimidated batters with his hopping fastball and trademark brushback pitches; he later became a sports announcer after retiring as a player. The "Big D" had a banner year in 1962, when he had 25 wins, 9 losses, and 232 strikeouts and won the Cy Young Award as the best pitcher in the National League. In 1968 he pitched 58 consecutive scoreless innings, a record that stood until 1988, when another Dodger pitcher, Orel Hershiser, pitched 59. Drysdale's specialty brushback pitches, virtually unknown in modern times because of rule changes, were responsible for hitting 154 batters, a 20th-century National League record. Drysdale, who pitched in five World Series and was named to nine All-Star teams, had a career record of 209 victories, 166 losses, 2,486 strikeouts, 49 shutouts, and a 2.95 earned run average. He was inducted into the Baseball Hall of Fame in 1984. In 1990 he published *Once a Bum, Always a Dodger.* Drysdale, who reportedly had undergone an angioplasty because of heart problems, was found dead in his hotel room after suffering a heart attack.

Duke, Doris, U.S. tobacco heiress and philanthropist (b. Nov. 22, 1912, New York, N.Y.—d. Oct. 28, 1993, Beverly Hills, Calif.), inherited most of her father's American Tobacco Co. fortune at the age of 12 and used her position as one of the world's richest women to benefit Duke University, AIDS research, animal rights, environmental and ecological causes, and historic preservation. Her personal life, however, was rife with disappointments, including failed marriages; the death of her only child, a day-old girl; and the disillusionment that followed her adoption of 35-year-old Charlene Gail Heffner in 1988. The statuesque Duke spent a large part of her life escaping from the probing eye of the public. She often fled into seclusion to luxuriously appointed homes in New Jersey, Rhode Island, California, and Hawaii, where she spent many of her later years at Shangri-La, a fantasy-inspired residence in Honolulu. Her widely publicized marriages to James Cromwell (1935–43) and Porfirio Rubirosa (1947–48) ended in divorce. At the time of Duke's death, a lawsuit filed by Heffner challenging the distribution of her estate was pending. In her will, Duke disinherited Heffner and left the bulk of her estimated $1.2 billion fortune to the newly created Doris Duke Charitable Foundation, one of the world's most richly endowed philanthropies.

Dutt, Utpal, Indian actor, director, and writer (b. March 29, 1929, Barisal, Bengal [now in Bangladesh]—d. Aug. 19, 1993, Calcutta, India), was a key figure in Bengali theatre and cinema for over 40 years. He was perhaps best known for his commitment to communist ideology and for the contemporary political dramas he produced on open-air stages in rural Bengal. Dutt was educated in Calcutta, where he founded (1947) the Calcutta Little Theatre Group. He twice toured with the Shakespearean International Theatre Company (1947–49; 1953–54) and was acclaimed for his passionate portrayal of Othello. From 1954 he wrote and directed controversial Bengali political plays, notably *Angar* (1959). He was arrested in 1965 and detained for several months because the ruling Congress Party feared that *Kallol* was provoking antigovernment protests in West Bengal. During the 1970s three of his plays drew crowds despite being officially banned. Dutt appeared in some 200 films, beginning with *Michael Madhusudan* (1950), and had considerable success as a director, particularly for *Megh* (1961), *Jhar* (1978), and *Mother* (1984). An intense, dramatic actor, he did some of his best work with the directors Satyajit Ray (*Jana Aranya*; *Agantuk*), Mrinal Sen (*Bhuban Som*; *Chorus*), and James Ivory (*Shakespeare Wallah*; *The Guru*). In 1970 Dutt won the Padma Bhusan award for best actor for *Bhuban Som.* He also published books on Shakespeare and the revolutionary theatre.

Eckstine, William Clarence ("Billy"), U.S. singer and bandleader (b. July 8, 1914, Pittsburgh, Pa.—d. March 8, 1993, Pittsburgh), was a superb stylist whose caressing bass baritone exuded the essence of romance in such standard ballads as "Everything I Have Is Yours," "Fools Rush In," and "I Apologize." Nevertheless, his velvety vocals and astonishing range were often overshadowed by his band (1944–47), one of the most artistically talented bebop configurations in the history of jazz, boasting such legendary figures as Dizzy Gillespie (*q.v.*), Charlie Parker, Sarah Vaughan, Miles Davis, Art Blakey, Fats Navarro, Gene Ammons, and Dexter Gordon. Eckstine, who was largely self-taught, not only sang but excelled as a trumpeter, valve-trombonist, and guitarist. A handsome fashion plate (he sported a jacket hung over his shoulders and a rolled shirt collar), Eckstine emerged as one of the first black male sex symbols; his popularity also crossed over to the white recording market during the 1940s. "Mr. B.," as he was affectionately known, launched his singing career in 1933 and worked in nightclubs until he was hired by Earl Hines in 1939 as a vocalist. Eckstine helped Hines recruit Gillespie and Parker and, after Eckstine left that band in 1943, they followed him when he organized his own orchestra in 1944. Eckstine's band revolutionized popular music as the first great bebop ensemble; however, dance patrons resisted the new sound, and the group was a commercial failure. Eckstine then reestablished himself as a singer and made numerous recordings, including "None but You," "Gigi," and "Passing Strangers." He also made cameo appearances in two films, *Skirts Ahoy* (1952) and *Let's Do It Again* (1975), and he toured internationally until 1992.

Elworthy, Samuel Charles Elworthy, Baron, New Zealand-born marshal (ret.) of the British Royal Air Force (b. March 23, 1911, Timaru, N.Z.—d. April 4, 1993, Christchurch, N.Z.), was in the top military ranks—as commander in chief in the Middle East (1960–63), chief of air staff (1963–67), and chief of defense staff (1967–71)—during a period when the U.K. was redefining its role in NATO and the world. Elworthy studied law at Trinity College, Cambridge (M.A., 1933), and was called to the bar (1935), but he quit to take a permanent commission in the RAF (1936). During World War II he was a highly decorated bomber pilot and leader. After the war he planned and taught bomber tactics and helped organize the military in newly independent India and Pakistan. In 1960 he was sent to Aden (now in Yemen) to stabilize the region, and it was in large part his quick, preemptive show of force in Kuwait that deterred a threatened Iraqi invasion the next year. He was promoted to marshal of the RAF in 1967. As air chief and then defense chief, Elworthy presided over a decrease in British military power, spending cutbacks, and growing concern over Soviet hegemony and the emergency in Northern Ireland. After retiring from the RAF, he was constable and governor of Windsor Castle (1971–78) and lord lieutenant of Greater London (1973–78). Elworthy was knighted in 1961 and created a life peer in 1972. He returned to private life in New Zealand in 1978.

Fellini, Federico, Italian film director (b. Jan. 20, 1920, Rimini, Italy—d. Oct. 31, 1993, Rome, Italy), created motion pictures with a landscape so unique that the term *Felliniesque* was used to describe any scene in which a hallucinatory image invaded an otherwise ordinary situation. His films were deeply personal and often portrayed people at their most bizarre. Fellini moved to Florence (1938) and then to Rome (1939), where in 1943

THE NEW YORK TIMES

he met and, four months later, married the actress Giulietta Masina, who would later star in many of his movies. With several friends he opened (1944) the Funny Face Shop, where Allied soldiers purchased photos, caricatures, portraits, and voice recordings to send home. He became acquainted with the director Roberto Rossellini there and was asked to collaborate on *Roma città aperta* (1945; *Open City*), which became the best-known example of Italian Neorealism. They collaborated further on such films as *Paisà* (1946; *Paisan*) and *Il miracolo* (1948; *The Miracle*). Fellini made his directorial debut when he codirected *Luci del varietà* (1951; *Variety Lights*) with Alberto Lattuada. His first solo effort came in 1952 with *Lo sceicco bianco (The White Sheik),* and he followed that with *I vitelloni* (1953), which won a Venice Film Festival award. For his next film, *La strada* (1954; "The Road"), Fellini won the first of his four Academy Awards for best foreign-language film. His other Oscars were for *Le notti di Cabiria* (1957; *The Nights of Cabiria*), *Otto e mezzo* (1963; *8½*), and *Amarcord* (1974; "I Remember"). *La dolce vita* (1960; "The Sweet Life") was Fellini's first "phenomenon." Starring Marcello Mastroianni—often referred to as Fellini's alter ego—it was a satire of the decadence of contemporary jet-set society and became an immediate sensation. Both the Italian government and the Roman Catholic Church attacked it, but it went on to win the Palme d'Or at the Cannes Film Festival. With *Otto e mezzo* came the style to which Fellini would remain faithful for the rest of his career: fantasy indiscriminately intermingled with reality. The film, blatantly autobiographical, portrayed a moviemaker reviewing his life in the face of self-doubts and a creative block. Then *Giulietta degli spiriti* (1965; *Juliet of the Spirits*) explored the fantasies of a bored housewife obsessed by spirits. Other notable films were *Fellini Satyricon* (1969), inspired by the ancient Roman writer Petronius; *Roma* (1972); *Amarcord,* a memoir of Fellini's youth; *Casanova* (1976); and *Ginger e Fred* (1986; *Ginger and Fred*), which centred on the reunion of former dance partners who had modeled themselves on Rogers and Astaire. In 1993 Fellini was given a special Academy Award for lifetime achievement.

Frink, Dame Elisabeth Jean, British sculptor (b. Nov. 14, 1930, Thurlow, Suffolk, England—d. April 18, 1993, Woolland, Dorset, England), was best known for her monumental figurative bronzes. Frink brought a sense of passion and energy to her naturalistic horses and birds and to larger-than-life figures of animals and naked men walking, standing, running, or mounted on massive horses. She studied at the Guildford School of Art (1947–49) and the Chelsea School of Art in London (1949–53) and had her first exhibition while she was still a student. She captured the attention of both the public and the critics with her earliest works—rough-textured warriors and menacing predatory birds, one of which was bought by the prestigious Tate Gallery in 1953. She had her first New York City exhibition in 1959. During the 1960s Frink created a series of enormous goggled heads, which were inspired by the Algerian civil war and were the first of several collections of heads honouring the victims of human oppression and brutality. She executed public commissions throughout the world, including a sculpture at the Kennedy Memorial in Dallas, Texas, and religious pieces for the Anglican cathedrals in Coventry, Salisbury, and Liverpool. She also lectured at the Chelsea and St. Martin's art schools and illustrated classic books, including Aesop's *Fables,* Chaucer's *Canterbury Tales,* and the Homeric epics. Frink was elected to the Royal Academy in 1977, made Dame Commander of the Order of the British Empire in 1982, and named Companion of Honour in 1992.

Gallo, Julio Robert, U.S. winegrower (b. March 21, 1910, Oakland, Calif.—d. May 2, 1993, near Tracy, Calif.), together with his older brother, Ernest, founded (1933) E.&J. Gallo Winery in Modesto, Calif., and built an empire by shaping American drinking tastes with inexpensive nonvintage wines. The brothers claimed to have

FRED MERTZ—THE NEW YORK TIMES

started their own business after the death of their father, Joseph Gallo, Sr., who had founded the Gallo Wine Co. in 1909. The brothers maintained that they learned wine making on their own after their father inexplicably killed their mother and then shot himself just after the end of Prohibition. With Julio serving as the wine maker and Ernest handling the marketing, the two introduced some 16 brands of wine and cornered more than 25% of the U.S. market. Some of their early offerings, including the widely popular Thunderbird, Ripple, and Boone's Farm wines, drew criticism; these inexpensive wines with a relatively high alcohol content were branded "street wines," the choice of winos and tramps. Later market entries that appealed to the suburban palate included Hearty Burgundy and Chablis Blanc. The brothers also began to aggressively market varietal and vintage wines. In 1981 the company began producing a premium-quality chardonnay, and in the 1980s it branched out into medium-priced Bartles and Jaymes wine coolers. Gallo, known as a technical innovator, pioneered the use of stainless steel wine-making vats and of computers for blending. The company, which owned nearly half of the vineyard acreage in California, reportedly had annual revenues of about $1 billion. In 1983 a third brother, Joseph, Jr., launched a cheese factory under the Gallo name, prompting the winery to sue him (1986) for trademark infringement. His countersuit charged that he had been cheated out of a one-third interest in the family business. However, the court ruled that Julio and Ernest had started their own concern when Joseph was 13 years old. The courtroom trial brought the family history under scrutiny, and their saga became the subject of the book *Blood and Wine: The Unauthorized Story of the Gallo Wine Empire* (1993). Gallo died after sustaining serious injuries in a car crash.

Gardini, Raul, Italian entrepreneur (b. June 7, 1933, Ravenna, Italy—d. July 23, 1993, Milan, Italy), turned a provincial, family-owned agribusiness into Italy's second-largest company and made himself into one of the country's richest and most admired industrialists but in 1993 was caught up in the financial corruption scandal that rocked the Italian government. After studying agriculture at the University of Bologna, Gardini went to work for Serafino Ferruzzi, a successful grain merchant. He married Ferruzzi's daughter in 1957 and took control of the business when his father-in-law died in 1979. Under Gardini, the Ferruzzi group expanded rapidly until the 1985 acquisition of the Montedison chemicals group made the newly renamed Ferruzzi-Montedison Italy's largest private-sector firm after Fiat. In 1989 Gardini launched an unsuccessful but financially lucrative attempt to take over Enimont, a joint venture with the state-owned ENI petrochemicals group. Gardini's other business ventures cost the company money, however, as did his financing of the racing yacht *Il Moro di Venezia,* which contested the 1992 America's Cup final off San Diego, Calif. In November 1991 other members of the Ferruzzi family forced him out of the debt-ridden company. Gardini was reportedly about to be arrested for corruption and bribery when he shot himself, three days after Gabriele Cagliari, the former head of ENI, committed suicide in jail.

Gesell, Gerhard A., U.S. judge (b. June 16, 1910, Los Angeles, Calif.—d. Feb. 19, 1993, Washington, D.C.), upheld citizens' rights over the power of the government while presiding over landmark legal cases, including the Watergate scandal, the Iran-contra affair, the legalization of abortion, and the release of the top-secret Pentagon Papers, a government study about the Vietnam War. Gesell graduated from Yale University in 1932 and from its law school in 1935. He served as staff lawyer and adviser (1935–41) to Chairman William O. Douglas at the Securities and Exchange Commission before joining the firm of Covington & Burling, where he specialized in antitrust and corporate law. He was appointed to the Federal District Court in Washington, D.C., by Pres. Lyndon Johnson in 1967 and gained prominence in 1969 when he struck down the District of Columbia's ban on abortion. Gesell, a decisive jurist, ruled that the *New York Times* and *Washington Post* newspapers could publish the Pentagon Papers, which the Nixon administration had tried to block. In 1974 he ruled that national security was not a valid reason for agents to have broken into the office of the psychiatrist Daniel Ellsberg (an author of the Pentagon Papers) at the Watergate complex in 1971. In the Watergate scandal Gesell ruled that the 1973 dismissal of special prosecutor Archibald Cox had been illegal and that Pres. Richard Nixon would have to surrender his secret White House tapes. He also sentenced Nixon's chief adviser on domestic affairs, John D. Ehrlichman, to 20 months to 5 years in prison for his role in the break-in. In 1989 Gesell presided over the criminal trial of Lieut. Col. Oliver North, who, as a deputy director of the National Security Council, was charged with helping to divert Iranian funds to Nicaraguan rebels in what became known as the Iran-contra affair. When a jury found North guilty of 3 of 12 charges, Gesell reasoned that North was one of the subordinates in the illegal operation and gave him a lighter-than-expected sentence—a $150,000 fine, two years of probation, and 1,200 hours of community service. Gesell remained on the bench until his death.

Gillespie, John Birks ("Dizzy"), U.S. trumpeter, composer, and bandleader (b. Oct. 21, 1917, Cheraw, S.C.—d. Jan. 6, 1993, Englewood, N.J.), was a brilliant innovator and virtuoso who expanded the harmonic structure of jazz and together with Charlie Parker ushered in bebop, a radically new jazz style that flourished during the 1940s and featured rapidly shifting rhythms, unconventional chords, use of the flatted fifth, and unrestrained tempi. Gillespie, with his goatee, thick horn-rimmed glasses, and beret, created the bebop persona, and his trademarks—a bent trumpet (which took its 45°-angle shape in 1953 after it was accidentally fallen upon), onstage clowning, and a bullfrog-cheeked playing style—made him instantly recognizable. Gillespie's musical training was fostered by his father and advanced at the Laurinburg Institute in North Carolina. He was an accomplished musician by the time he was a teenager and got his first break when he replaced (1937) his idol Roy Eldridge in Teddy Hill's band. He composed, arranged, and soloed with Hill and with Cab Calloway's band in the 1930s before performing with groups fronted by Benny Carter and Earl Hines during the early 1940s. Gillespie launched the era he coined bebop while coleader of a group on 52nd Street with bassist Oscar Pettiford. In 1944, when Billy Eckstine's (*q.v.*) band showcased Gillespie's and Parker's bebop improvisations, the distinctive style became popular. The following year Gillespie formed his own swing-era-sized big band, the first of many, and he was also associated with smaller combos,

POPPERFOTO/ARCHIVE PHOTOS

many of them in association with Parker. As one of the most important figures in the development of jazz, Gillespie influenced such modern jazz trumpeters as Miles Davis, Thad Jones, and Kenny Dorham and such saxophone soloists as John Coltrane, Benny Golson, Dexter Gordon, and James Moody. He was also credited with assimilating Afro-Cuban elements into modern jazz, as evidenced in such standard songs as "Night in Tunisia," "Manteca," and "Con Alma." In 1948, the year before bebop faded, Gillespie and his band made a highly successful tour in Europe. He continued to tour with various reorganized bands, coaxing his trumpet to the highest registers of its range and improvising in unexpected and daring situations. After entering his 70s, he assumed the mantle of elder statesman of jazz, yet he continued to tour until late 1992. Gillespie published his autobiography, *To Be or Not to Bop,* in 1979.

Gilliatt, Penelope Ann Douglass, British-born writer and critic (b. March 25, 1932, London, England—d. May 9, 1993, London), was for many years a film critic for *The New Yorker;* she also produced fiction that was noted for its sensitive, sometimes wry look at modern life. She briefly attended colleges in London and Vermont and then worked for a short time in New York City. When she won an award from the British *Vogue* for a short story, she returned to London to work for the magazine, later becoming its features editor. In 1961 she began working as a film and drama critic for *The Observer,* sharing duties with Kenneth Tynan, and in 1968 she began alternating with Pauline Kael as film critic for *The New Yorker.* During the following decade the magazine also published several of her short stories and profiles. She left *The New Yorker* in 1979 after Graham Greene complained about inaccuracies in her profile of him and another writer on Greene accused her of plagiarism. Gilliatt was perhaps best known for her screenplay for the 1971 film *Sunday, Bloody Sunday.* Based on her novel *One by One* (1965), the screenplay won awards from the British Film Writers' Guild, the National Society of Film Critics, and the New York Film Critics Circle, and it was nominated for an Academy Award. In all, she published five novels and a number of collections of stories and other short writings, as well as book-length studies of the French director Jean Renoir and actor Jacques Tati. Her second, brief marriage was to the British playwright John Osborne.

Gish, Lillian Diana, U.S. actress (b. Oct. 14, 1893, Springfield, Ohio—d. Feb. 27, 1993, New York, N.Y.), was a fragile beauty whose film heroines projected a waiflike vulnerability and virginal innocence that was belied by an indomitable spirit; her dramatic and masterful use of gestures and her expressive eyes earned her accolades as "the First Lady of the Silent Screen." Gish, who made her stage debut at the age of five, was billed as Baby Lillian. Both she and her younger sister, Dorothy, were child stars, and the two made their bow with their mother in the film *An Unseen Enemy* the same day that their friend Gladys Smith (Mary Pickford) secured them bit roles with director D.W. Griffith. Gish vaulted to stardom when she was given the lead role of Elsie Stoneman in Griffith's box-office smash hit *The Birth of a Nation* (1915), which was followed by another blockbuster, *Intolerance* (1916). She became famous for her heartrending interpretations in such sentimental Griffith melodramas as *Hearts of the World* (1918), *Broken Blossoms* (1919), *True Heart Susie* (1919), *Way Down East* (1920), and *Orphans of the Storm* (1922), the latter with her sister, whom she had directed in *Remodeling Her Husband* (1920). After amicably leaving Griffith she made *The White Sister* (1923) for Inspiration Films before joining MGM. There she made some of her best films, including *La Bohème* (1926), under the direction of King Vidor, and *The Scarlet Letter* (1926) and *The Wind* (1928), both with the Swedish director Victor Sjöström. Gish returned to the New York stage and appeared in such plays as *Camille, Uncle Vanya, Life with Father,* and *The Chalk Garden* before making her talkie

BURR VERGER—GLOBE PHOTOS

debut in *One Romantic Night* (1930) and starring in her last screen lead in *His Double Life* (1933). She earned an Academy Award nomination for her performance in *Duel in the Sun* (1947), and went on to appear in such films as *Portrait of Jennie* (1949), *The Cobweb* (1955), and *The Night of the Hunter* (1955). Her enduring career included such television films as *The Day Lincoln Was Shot, The Sound and the Fury,* and *Arsenic and Old Lace,* with Helen Hayes (*q.v.*). Gish made her final Broadway appearance in *A Musical Jubilee* (1975) and her last film appearance in *The Whales of August* (1987). She published two volumes of memoirs, *Life and Lillian Gish* (1932) and *The Movies, Mr. Griffith & Me* (1969). Gish received a special Academy Award in 1970 for her "superlative artistry," Kennedy Center honours in 1982, and a lifetime achievement tribute in 1984 from the American Film Institute.

Golding, Sir William Gerald, British novelist (b. Sept. 19, 1911, St. Columb Minor, Cornwall, England—d. June 19, 1993, Perranarworthal, Cornwall), won the 1983 Nobel Prize for Literature for his novel *Lord of the Flies* (1954; filmed 1963 and 1990) and other works, which, "with the perspicuity of realistic narrative art and the diversity and universality of myth, illuminate the human condition in the world of today." Golding was educated at Marlborough Grammar School and Brasenose College, Oxford (B.A., 1935; M.A., 1961). He published a small volume of poetry in 1934, briefly worked in a settlement house, and became a teacher (1939) at Bishop Wordsworth's School in Salisbury. He later said the idea for his best-known work was inspired by his experiences as a schoolmaster and by his service in the Royal Navy during World War II, during which he was witness to the sinking of the German battleship *Bismarck* and to the Allied landing at Normandy. After the war he returned to teaching and to writing novels. *Lord of the Flies,* his fourth attempt, was a shattering tale (set in the near future) of English schoolboys marooned on an island during an atomic war. The novel reportedly was rejected by 21 publishers before it finally appeared to lukewarm reviews. A paperback edition released in the U.S. in 1959, however, gained near-cult popularity and a financial success that allowed Golding to quit teaching. In this harrowing parable of good and evil, most of the boys gradually regress into idol worship, tribal savagery, and ritualistic murder—a reflection of the adult world beyond the island and the real world beyond the book, where civilized behaviour is a thin veneer and "man produces evil as a bee produces honey." Golding returned to this theme in later novels, notably *The Inheritors* (1955), in which the last Neanderthals are destroyed by clever, weapons-wielding Homo sapiens, and *The Spire* (1964), a tale of vainglory and obsession in a medieval clergyman. Other novels include *Pincher Martin* (1956), *Free Fall* (1959), *The Pyramid* (1967), *Darkness Visible* (1979), and *The Paper Men* (1984). *Rites of Passage* (1980) won the Booker Prize and inspired two sequels, *Close Quarters* (1987) and *Fire Down Below* (1989). Golding was made Commander of the Order of the British Empire in 1966 and was knighted in 1988.

Gormley of Ashton-in-Makerfield, Joseph Gormley, BARON, British labour leader (b. July 5, 1917, Ashton-in-Makerfield, Lancashire, England—d. May 27, 1993, Wigan, Greater Manchester, England), was the president (1971–82) of the National Union of Mineworkers; he guided the NUM through two national strikes (1972 and 1974), the second of which led to the collapse of Prime Minister Edward Heath's Conservative government. Gormley was born into a coal-mining family and went down into the pit at age 14. He was elected to the NUM's national executive committee in 1957, and four years later he was named general secretary of the Lancashire area. After losing in his bid to become national secretary, he was elected president in 1971 and promptly redirected the union to consolidate more power in that office. Although he privately opposed the strike votes in 1972 and 1974, Gormley proved to be a tough negotiator and a wily leader, securing higher wages for the miners while staving off challenges by more radical rivals within the union. In 1981 he forced Prime Minister Margaret Thatcher's government to back down on plans to close nearly two dozen pits. Gormley was also a longtime member of the Labour Party's national executive committee (1963–73) and of the Trades Union Congress general council (1973–80). He was made a life peer in 1982.

Granger, Stewart (JAMES LABLACHE STEWART), British-born motion-picture actor (b. May 6, 1913, London, England—d. Aug. 16, 1993, Santa Monica, Calif.), portrayed swashbuckling heroes, dashing adventurers, and debonair romantic leads with elegance and wit in a cinema career that spanned 35 years. Although he was at his peak in such 1950s Hollywood adventure classics as *King Solomon's Mines, Scaramouche, The Prisoner of Zenda, Beau Brummel,* and *Bhowani Junction,* Granger occasionally parodied his own screen image, as in the 1960 gold-rush comedy *North to Alaska.* He started as a bit player in British films, studied at the Webber-Douglas School of Dramatic Art, and performed in repertory theatre. He got his film break in the 1943 costume melodrama *The Man in Grey.* Tall, dark, handsome, and oozing with on-screen arrogant charm, he soon became one of Britain's biggest box-office draws. In 1950 he moved with his second wife, actress Jean Simmons, to Hollywood, where he gained equal stardom with *King Solomon's Mines.* Granger was often forced into mediocre films by his long-term contracts, and in later years he resisted the switch to unromantic character roles. After a 10-year absence from the movies, he played a suave villain in the 1978 adventure *The Wild Geese.* In the 1980s he worked in the theatre and television. Granger's autobiography, *Sparks Fly Upward,* was published in 1981.

Gray, Gordon Joseph Cardinal, Scottish prelate (b. Aug. 10, 1910, Leith, near Edinburgh, Scotland—d. July 19, 1993, Edinburgh), as spiritual leader of some 800,000 Roman Catholics in Scotland from 1969, was the first resident Scottish cardinal since the Reformation and the first cardinal ever to address the General Assembly of the Presbyterian Church of Scotland (1977). After being ordained in 1935, Gray served as a parish priest in Hawick (1941–47) and as rector of the national junior seminary in Aberdeen (1947–51). He was made archbishop of St. Andrews and Edinburgh in 1951 and was elevated to cardinal in 1969. Although he endorsed conservative theology, Gray was actively involved in church reform and the ecumenical movement that came out of the Second Vatican Council (1962–65). He was chairman of the International Commission for English in the Liturgy, which translated the Latin liturgy into English; coauthor of the Pastoral Instruction on the Media, which was drafted in 1971 by the Pontifical Commission for Social Communications; and cofounder (1955) of the National Catholic Radio and Television Centre in Middlesex, England. Gray retired from his duties as archbishop in 1985.

Grimond of Firth, Jo(seph) Grimond, BARON, British politician (b. July 29, 1913, St. Andrews, Fife, Scotland—d. Oct. 24, 1993, Kirkwall, Orkney, Scotland), led Britain's small and centrist Liberal Party from 1956 to 1967. Grimond, the son of a wealthy jute manufacturer and committed Liberal Party member, attended Eton and the University of Oxford. He earned a degree in 1935 and was called to the bar in 1937. The following year he married into the most prominent of Liberal families when he wed the granddaughter of Lord Asquith, the last leader of the Liberal Party to serve as prime minister. During World War II, Grimond served in a Scottish infantry regiment. In 1945 he was asked to stand as the party's candidate for Orkney and Shetland islands, Britain's northernmost constituency, but he lost by a narrow margin. In 1950 he ran again, but this time he won the election. After becoming leader of the party in 1956, Grimond helped raise the standing of the party, and by 1963 he had established it as a nonsocialist alternative to the Conservative Party. A strong turnout for the Labour Party in 1964, however, left the Liberals with no role to play. Grimond resigned as party leader in 1967 but continued to represent his constituency. In 1983 he moved to the House of Lords on becoming Baron Grimond. His books include *The Liberal Future* (1959), *The Common Welfare* (1978), *Memoirs* (1979), *A Personal Manifesto* (1983), and *The St. Andrews of Jo Grimond* (1992).

Gwynne, Fred(erick) Hubbard, U.S actor and writer (b. July 10, 1926, New York, N.Y.—d. July 2, 1993, Taneytown, Md.), possessed a lanky and towering physique, which, coupled with his distinctive high forehead and long-jawed, dour face, made him a natural to portray the Frankensteinian Herman Munster, a lugubrious funeral director and patriarch of the ghoulish yet kindly family on the hit television series "The Munsters" (1964–66). The Harvard-educated Gwynne, who once aspired to become a portrait painter, was for several years an advertising copywriter for the J. Walter Thomson agency and, from 1958 to 1988, wrote and illustrated a number of children's books. He made his Broadway debut as a gangster named Stinker in *Mrs. McThing* (1952), with Helen Hayes (*q.v.*), following that role with another onstage as a police officer in *Irma La Douce.* That portrayal led to Gwynne's being cast as Francis Muldoon, a bumbling New York City policeman who partnered officer Gunther Toody on the television comedy series "Car 54, Where Are You?" (1961–63). Though Gwynn was best remembered as lovable Herman Munster, he enjoyed a diverse career that encompassed serious roles, notably Big Daddy in the 1974 Broadway revival of *Cat on a Hot Tin Roof.* He also won an Obie award for best actor for his work in the off-Broadway play *Grand Magic* (1979). Gwynn's film credits include *On the Waterfront* (1954), *Munster Go Home* (1966), *The Cotton Club* (1984), *Fatal Attraction* (1987), *Pet Sematary* (1989), and *My Cousin Vinny* (1992).

Hajek, Jiri, Czech politician (b. June 6, 1913, Krhanice, Czech.—d. Oct. 22, 1993, Prague, Czech Republic), was forced from office as a Communist Party official during the 1968 Soviet crackdown and was later an activist in the dissident movement. Hajek became involved in politics while studying law at Charles University, Prague, where he joined the youth branch of the Social Democratic Party (SDP) and organized an antifascist group. These activities led to his arrest in 1939; he was interned in German camps during World War II. After the war, he served as SDP deputy to the National Assembly until 1948, when the SDP merged with the Communist Party. As a member of that party, Hajek continued to serve in the assembly (1948–58) and was promoted to various governmental and academic posts. He served as professor of international relations at Charles University (1953–55), ambassador to Britain (1955–58), deputy foreign minister (1958–62), representative to the UN (1962–65), and education minister (1965–68). In the Prague Spring of 1968, Hajek supported the reformist forces that came to power, and that year he was appointed foreign minister. When a Warsaw Pact army invaded in August, Hajek was on vacation in Yugoslavia. He traveled to the UN and denounced the invasion but resisted Western involvement. After returning to Prague he was forced to resign. Hajek returned to academic life and in 1970 was purged from the party. In 1977 Hajek was one of the original signatories of the human rights appeal known as Charter 77 and emerged as one of the group's leading spokespersons. He later formed (1988) a group to monitor the country's compliance with human rights laws. Hajek was awarded the French Legion of Honor in 1993. His writings include *The Legend of Wilson in the History of Czechoslovakia* (1953), *Munich* (1958), and *Dix Ans après* ("Ten Years After"; 1978).

Haldeman, H(arry) R(obbins) ("BOB"), U.S. political figure (b. Oct. 27, 1926, Los Angeles, Calif.—d. Nov. 12, 1993, Santa Barbara, Calif.), was best known for his role in the cover-up of the Richard M. Nixon administration's involvement in the 1972 break-in at the Democratic Party's National Committee headquarters in the Watergate complex in Washington, D.C. Haldeman was working in advertising at the J. Walter Thompson agency when he became impressed with Nixon during the House Un-American Activities Committee hearings in 1948 and offered his assistance on Nixon's 1952 vice presidential election campaign on the Republican Party ticket. Nixon refused the offer, but Haldeman finally managed to get hired for the 1956 election campaign and became a trusted aide. He served as campaign manager for Nixon's successful 1968 presidential campaign and became White House chief of staff when Nixon took office. He was extremely powerful in that position and was often referred to as "the keeper of the gate" and "the Iron Chancellor" because of his ruthlessness in limiting access to the president. On April 30, 1973, after his role in the Watergate cover-up had been revealed, Haldeman was forced to resign. In 1975 he was convicted of conspiracy, obstruction of justice, and perjury and was sentenced to 2½–8 years in prison. He was released after 1½ years and thereafter worked as a businessman and consultant.

Hall, Adelaide, U.S.-born singer (b. Oct. 20, 1901, New York, N.Y.—d. Nov. 7, 1993, London, England), was a sensational jazz improviser whose wordless rhythm singing ushered in what became known as scat singing. Her pioneering vocals were preserved on Duke Ellington's 1927 classic recording "Creole Love Call." Hall, who was educated at New York City's Pratt Institute (where her father was a music teacher), secured her first professional job in the chorus of the benchmark *Shuffle Along,* which opened (1921) at the 63rd Street Theatre, helped reestablish black show business, and featured Florence Mills, Josephine Baker, and Paul Robeson. She appeared in *Runnin' Wild* before launching a 1926 European tour as the star of *Chocolate Kiddies.* After returning to the U.S., Hall toured in vaudeville and appeared on Broadway in *Desires of 1927, Town Topics,* and *Blackbirds of 1928* before taking up permanent residence in Europe in 1934. In Paris she and her husband opened a nightclub, and they opened another such club in London, where they settled permanently. A major star in Europe, Hall achieved that status in the U.S. only when a Salute to Black Broadway was mounted in 1979 at Avery Fisher Hall in New York City and after she staged a one-woman show at Carnegie Hall. In 1989 Hall was the subject of a television film, *Sophisticated Lady,* and later her story was recounted on radio in a program entitled "Sweet Adelaide."

Hani, Martin Thembisile ("CHRIS"), South African political activist (b. June 28, 1942, Cofimvaba, South Africa—d. April 10, 1993, Boksburg, South Africa), was secretary-general (1991–93) of the South African Communist Party (SACP) and chief of staff (1987–91) of Umkhonto we Sizwe ("Spear of the Nation"), the military wing of the black-nationalist African National Congress (ANC). Hani, whose father was a migrant worker and ANC member, joined the ANC Youth League in 1957. He studied Latin and Classics at Fort Hare University (1959–61) and Rhodes University (B.A., 1962), considered entering the priesthood, and briefly prepared for a legal career, but his involvement in Umkhonto and the SACP (both from 1962) soon took precedence. He underwent military training, fought with black nationalists in Rhodesia (now Zimbabwe), and directed guerrilla operations against South Africa from Lesotho and Zambia. Hani was elected to the ANC executive council in 1974 and was named deputy commander of Umkhonto in 1982. He officially resigned as Umkhonto chief of staff in 1991, when he succeeded Joe Slovo as SACP secretary-general. Hani was foremost among the so-called Young Lions, ANC members who endorsed using violence against civilian targets, as opposed to the somewhat more moderate tactics of older leaders, such as Nelson Mandela and Oliver Tambo (*q.v.*). After the ban on the ANC was lifted in 1990, however, he participated in the negotiations for a peaceful transfer to majority rule. Hani, who had survived previous assassination attempts, was gunned down outside his home in a quiet, racially integrated suburb outside Johannesburg.

Hasluck, Sir Paul Meernaa Caedwalla, Australian politician (b. April 1, 1905, Fremantle, Australia—d. Jan. 9, 1993, Perth, Australia), was a respected Cabinet minister and the first serving party politician to be named (1969) governor-general of Australia. Hasluck, who was from a family of Salvation Army officers, obtained a master's degree from the University of Western Australia, worked as a newspaper journalist (1922–38), and taught (1939–40) at his alma mater. He joined the federal Department of External Affairs in 1941, represented his country at the 1945 conference in San Francisco that established the United Nations, and then led the first Australian UN delegation (1946). In 1949 he was elected to Parliament for the Liberal Party. As minister for territories (1951–63), Hasluck worked to prepare Papua New Guinea for self-rule and eventual independence. Later, as the head of the Ministries for Defense (1963–64) and External Affairs (1964–69), he supported Australian involvement in the war in Vietnam. In 1968 he was narrowly defeated in his bid to succeed the recently deceased prime minister, Harold Holt, as Liberal Party leader and head of government. Although his appointment as governor-general was controversial, he was widely respected, but in 1974 he refused a second five-year term. Hasluck's numerous books include *Black Australians* (1942), an insightful and progressive history of Aborigine-white relations; *The Government and the People, 1939–1945* (vol. 1, 1952; vol. 2, 1970), an official history of Australia in World War II; *Shades of Darkness: Aboriginal Affairs 1925–65* (1988); a volume of collected verse; and an autobiography, *Mucking About* (1977). Hasluck was knighted in 1969.

Hassett, (Arthur) Lindsay, Australian cricketer (b. Aug. 28, 1913, Geelong, Victoria, Australia—d. June 16, 1993, Bateman's Bay, New South Wales, Australia), was one of his country's finest batsmen for more than two decades and was Don Bradman's successor (1949) as captain of the Australia Test side. Hassett first showed his style as a 17-year-old student at Geelong College, when he scored 147 not out against a touring West Indian team. He played first-class cricket for Victoria from 1932, and he was selected to tour England with Bradman's Test side in 1938. After serving with an antiaircraft regiment during World War II, he was persuaded to lead an Australian armed services team on a postwar tour to England and India. Hassett's short stature, slim build, and mischievous nature belied his prodigious skill as a batsman, especially against spin bowling. He amassed a first-class career total of 16,890 runs (average 58.24) and 59 centuries, including 3,073 runs (average 46.56) and 10 centuries in 43 Test matches. During his tenure as captain (1949–53), he led Australia 24 times, with an enviable record of 14 wins and only 4 losses. He retired in 1953 after losing the Ashes (held by Australia since 1934) to a reinvigorated England side captained by Len Hutton. Hassett was made a Member of the Order of the British Empire in 1953.

Hawkins, Erskine, U.S. bandleader and trumpeter (b. July 26, 1914, Birmingham, Ala.—d. Nov. 11, 1993, Willingboro, N.J.), headed a popular swing band in the 1930s and '40s. He took up music as a child and graduated (1934) from Alabama State Teachers College, where he played in the student band. As the 'Bama State Collegians, this orchestra made its debut in New York City in the mid-1930s. Eventually becoming known as the Erskine Hawkins Orchestra, in 1936 it began a decade-long engagement at the Savoy Ballroom in New York; radio broadcasts and recordings during this period made it one of the most popular of all swing bands. Hawkins, who was famous for his high notes on trumpet, was often called the "20th-century Gabriel." In the 1950s he began to work with smaller groups, and during his later years he sometimes played rhythm and blues. His best-known composition, "Tuxedo Junction," referred to a suburb of Birmingham.

Hayes, Helen (HELEN HAYES BROWN), U.S. actress (b. Oct. 10, 1900, Washington, D.C.—d. March 17, 1993, Nyack, N.Y.), as the luminous first lady of the American theatre, enraptured audiences with her twinkling eyes and elfin smile and, though diminutive in stature (1.5 m [5 ft]), she exuded a majestic stage presence that made her regal performances in Maxwell Anderson's *Mary of Scotland* (1933) and Laurence Housman's *Victoria Regina* (1935) two of her most memorable roles. Hayes, who made her professional stage debut at the age of five and her Broadway bow at the age of nine, established herself as a popular light comedian with brilliant performances in *What Every Woman Knows* (1926, 1938, and 1954). After her husband, writer Charles MacArthur, coaxed her to Hollywood during the 1930s, she made her motion-picture debut starring in the tearjerker *The Sin of Madelon Claudet* (1931) and won the Academy Award for best actress. Other notable film credits include *Arrowsmith* (1931), *A Farewell to Arms* (1932), and *What Every Woman Knows* (1934). Hayes longed for the footlights, however, and resumed her stage career. She received critical acclaim for roles in Anita Loos's *Happy Birthday* (1946), Mary Ellen Chase's *Mrs. McThing* (1952), Thornton Wilder's *The Skin of Our Teeth* (1955), Tennessee Williams' *The Glass Menagerie* (1956), Jean Anouilh's *Time Remembered* (1957), and Eugene O'Neill's *A Touch of the Poet* (1958) and *Long Day's Journey into Night* (1971). Hayes, beset with dust allergies, retired from live theatre in 1971, the year after she earned a best supporting Oscar for her film performance as a dotty old woman stowaway in *Airport* (1970). She appeared in such television movies as *The Snoop Sisters* (1972) and *Victory at Entebbe* (1976) and starred as Agatha Christie's Miss Marple in *Murder Is Easy* (1982), *A Caribbean Mystery* (1983), and *Murder with Mirrors* (1985). During

DEBORAH K. OBRIEN—GLOBE PHOTOS

her more than 80-year career, Hayes was lavishly honoured. Besides her two Academy Awards, she was the recipient of three Tony awards, an Emmy award, the 1940 Best Radio Actress Award, a Grammy award for a reading of the Bill of Rights, the 1981 lifetime achievement honours from the Kennedy Center for the Performing Arts, and the 1986 Presidential Medal of Freedom. In 1955 New York City's Fulton Theater was renamed the Helen Hayes Theater and, after that structure was razed in 1982, Broadway's Little Theater was christened (1983) with her name. Among her several volumes of autobiography were *A Gift of Joy* (1965), *On Reflection* (1968), *Twice Over Lightly* (1971; with Anita Loos), and *My Life in Three Acts* (1990). Her daughter died of polio at the age of 19, and her actor-son, James, became identified with the character Danno on the television program "Hawaii Five-O."

Hearst, William Randolph, Jr., U.S. journalist and newspaper proprietor (b. Jan. 27, 1908, New York, N.Y.—d. May 14, 1993, New York), shared a 1956 Pulitzer Prize for international reporting shortly after being named editor in chief of the Hearst Corp. The privately held company had been built into a media empire by William Randolph Hearst, Sr., the flamboyant press baron. The younger Hearst, the second of five sons, spent two years at the University of California at Berkeley before joining the *New York American* as a police reporter. He was named publisher of the paper in 1936, the year before the Hearst paper became the *Journal-American* after a merger. During World War II, when Hearst was serving as a war correspondent in Europe and North Africa, he reportedly was told by his father, who was also his editor, to stop reporting on bombing missions until he had flown one. He did so, and he continued to seek the approval of his father, with whom he shared a fervent anticommunist stance. After his father died in 1951, Hearst headed a 17-man editorial committee to unravel the affairs of the chain of 18 newspapers, including the flagship *San Francisco Examiner,* and 11 magazines. As editor in chief, Hearst helped revitalize the business and scored a personal coup when he, Frank Conniff, and Kingsbury Smith secured a series of revealing interviews with four politicians in Moscow and published a series of eight articles that rightly predicted that Nikita Khrushchev would become the next leader of the Soviet Union. The series earned the trio Pulitzer Prizes. Hearst, who for 40 years wrote a politically conservative editorial column for the chain, steadfastly championed Sen. Joseph McCarthy and his 1950s communist witch-hunts. Hearst's name was also identified with that of his niece Patty, who, after being abducted by the Symbionese Liberation Army in 1974, helped them rob a bank; she was then incarcerated for seven years. In 1991 Hearst published *The Hearsts: Father and Son,* in which he acknowledged that his own career had been overshadowed by that of his father.

Hepburn, Audrey (EDDA VAN HEEMSTRA HEPBURN-RUSTON), Belgian-born U.S. actress (b. May 4, 1929, Brussels, Belgium—d. Jan. 20, 1993, Tolochenaz, Switz.), projected a doelike innocence with her large, expressive brown eyes, possessed an ethereal beauty that illuminated the screen, and created unforgettable film roles as the epitome of sophistication and glamour while paradoxically bewitching audiences and critics with her sprightly mannerisms and elfin charm; she was also renowned in later years as a tireless goodwill ambassador for UNICEF and as one of the foremost advocates for Third World children. Hepburn, who grew up in London, spent part of her childhood trapped (while on vacation) in Nazi-occupied Holland, subsisting partly on tulip bulbs as that country neared starvation at the end of World War II. After returning to London, she modeled and studied ballet and acting. Hepburn was discovered by French novelist Colette, who insisted that she star on Broadway in *Gigi* (1951). The same year, Hepburn made her American motion-picture debut in *One Wild Oat* and, two years later in her first starring role in *Roman Holiday,* she enchanted audiences with her portrayal of a high-spirited princess who falls in love with a journalist, portrayed by Gregory Peck; her performance earned her an Academy Award as best actress, and her tomboyish haircut and attire (oversize man's shirt worn with rolled-up sleeves) created a fashion rage, the first of many trends she set. She earned a Tony award for her performance in *Ondine* (1954) opposite her first husband, Mel Ferrer. Hepburn continued to delight moviegoers as a chauffeur's daughter romantically linked with William Holden and Humphrey Bogart in *Sabrina* (1954), as Natasha in *War and Peace* (1956), as a bookstore clerk turned fashion model in the musical *Funny Face* (1957), as a nun questioning her vocation in *The Nun's Story* (1959), and, in one of her most celebrated roles, as the endearing Holly Golightly in *Breakfast at Tiffany's* (1961). She made *The Children's Hour* (1962), *Charade* (1963), *My Fair Lady* (1964), *Two for the Road* (1967), and the thriller *Wait Until Dark* (1967) before retiring. Hepburn and Ferrer divorced in 1968, and she married psychiatrist Andrea Dotti the following year. After she and Dotti divorced, Hepburn and Dutch actor Robert Wolders became longtime companions. She garnered Oscar nominations for *Sabrina, The Nun's Story, Breakfast at Tiffany's,* and *Wait Until Dark.* Hepburn came out of retirement to star in *Robin*

PHOTOFEST

and Marian (1976) and appeared sporadically in films before making a final cameo as an angel in *Always* (1989). The internationally beloved Hepburn, a symbol of gentility and kindness, was posthumously awarded the Jean Hersholt Humanitarian Award after succumbing to colon cancer.

Herlihy, James Leo, U.S. novelist, playwright, and actor (b. Feb. 27, 1927, Detroit, Mich.—d. Oct. 21, 1993, Los Angeles, Calif.), specialized in portraying troubled adolescents and characters living on the fringe of society in novels brimming with gritty realism, including *All Fall Down* (1960; film 1962) and *Midnight Cowboy* (1965; film 1969). He began writing short stories after graduating from high school. He attended Black Mountain College in North Carolina, where he studied the arts, before finding a niche in the theatre. After attending (1948–50) Pasadena (Calif.) Playhouse College of the Theater, he appeared (1948–52) on West Coast stages in some 50 roles. Meanwhile, Herlihy's first play, *Streetlight Sonata,* was produced (1950) in Pasadena, followed by *Moon in Capricorn* (1953) in New York City and *Blue Denim* (1958, with William Noble), which premiered on Broadway. His brilliantly woven tales were laced with elements of the bizarre and the grotesque and contained masterful characterizations and biting dialogue. He used a diary form in such works as *A Story That Ends with a Scream, and Eight Others* (1967), which contains a profile about an institutionalized homicidal maniac, and his last novel, *The Season of the Witch* (1971), about a young woman who runs away to New York City with her homosexual next-door neighbour. Herlihy died from an overdose of sleeping pills.

Hersey, John Richard, U.S. journalist and novelist (b. June 17, 1914, Tianjin [Tientsin], China—d. March 24, 1993, Key West, Fla.), as a foreign correspondent in East Asia, Italy, and Russia for *Time* and *Life* magazines (1937–46), was acclaimed for his poignant, documentary-style reports of the most momentous events of World War II. His *A Bell for Adano* (1944), a fictionalized account of the Allied occupation of a Sicilian town, captured the Pulitzer Prize; it was followed by his masterpiece, *Hiroshima* (1946), a dispassionate yet graphic nonfiction narrative of the effects of the atomic bomb explosion on six survivors. The latter work, though first scheduled for serialization in *The New Yorker* magazine, was so compelling that the editors unprecedentedly devoted the entire Aug. 31, 1946, issue to it. Hersey, the son of missionaries, lived in China until the age of 10, when he went to the U.S. After graduating from Yale University in 1936, he worked as a private secretary to Nobel Prize-winning novelist Sinclair Lewis before securing a job with *Time*. His first book, *Men on Bataan* (1942), chronicled the heroic American efforts to hold the Philippines against the Japanese in 1941. He then published *Into the Valley* (1943), which explored from the American soldiers' perspective a skirmish during the battle between Allied and Japanese forces for control of Guadalcanal in the Solomon Islands. (Hersey himself was commended by the U.S. secretary of the navy for bravery for helping to move wounded soldiers from the line of fire on Guadalcanal.) One of his best-known war novels was *The Wall* (1950), which described the Nazi destruction of the Warsaw ghetto. That same year he began an association with his alma mater that lasted until 1984. Besides writing books of social criticism, Hersey was a sponsor of a 1965 March on Washington for Peace in Vietnam and was a member of a number of educational organizations. Some of the diverse themes of his later works included: the manipulation of gifted children in *The Child Buyer* (1960), racism in *The Algiers Motel Incident* (1968), and a Stradivarius violin in *Antonietta* (1991). His last collection of short stories, *Key West Tales,* was scheduled for 1994 publication.

Hibbert, Eleanor Alice (VICTORIA HOLT; JEAN PLAIDY), British novelist (b. 1906/1910?, London, England—d. Jan. 18, 1993, at sea between Athens, Greece, and Port Said, Egypt), published more than 200 popular romance novels under half a dozen pseudonyms. Although some critics dismissed her work as escapist trash, others recognized the deft storytelling, well-researched historic detail, and strong female characters that brought Hibbert fame, fortune, and millions of devoted readers in some 20 languages. Hibbert, who kept her birth date and most of her personal life a closely guarded secret, decided to be a novelist at an early age, but she did not publish her first book, *Beyond the Blue Mountains,* until 1947. It was the first of more than 90 historical romances written under the pen name Jean Plaidy. Her U.S. agent later suggested she write a new series of Gothic romances, the first of which, *Mistress of Mellyn,* appeared in 1960 under the nom de plume Victoria Holt. (The 32nd Victoria Holt novel, *The Black Opal,* was published posthumously.) She wrote two Jean Plaidy romances and one Victoria Holt per year until 1972, when she added *The Miracle at St. Bruno's,* the first of a 17-novel family saga published under the pen name Philippa Carr. Hibbert also wrote under her maiden name, Eleanor Burford, and the pseudonyms Elbur Ford, Kathleen Kellow, and Ellalice Tate.

Hodes, Art(hur) W., Russian-born U.S. pianist (adopted birth date Nov. 14, 1904, Nikolayev, Russia—d. March 4, 1993, Harvey, Ill.), was a blues-based jazz traditionalist who elicited a haunting melancholy sound by combining a 1920s lyrical blues approach with jazz improvisation. Hodes, who emigrated with his family when he was about six months old, chose his own birthday because the family's formal documents were lost in the move. Growing up in Chicago, he took piano lessons at Hull House, a local community centre. Hodes drew musical inspiration from the city's great black jazz and blues musicians who had come from New Orleans, La., and the South during the 1920s to play in Chicago's clubs and theatres. His two greatest influences were jazz trumpeter Louis Armstrong and blues singer Bessie Smith. Hodes performed with Bix Beiderbecke, Gene Krupa, Eddie Condon, and Wild Bill Davison before leaving Chicago in 1938 for New York City, where he was the host of a jazz radio program on WNYC; published, wrote, and edited his own monthly magazine, the *Jazz Record;* performed with the bands of Jose Marsala and Mezz Mezzrow; and recorded piano solos with his own short-lived record company. When traditional jazz lost its lustre, Hodes returned (1950) to Chicago and settled in the suburbs. He performed and toured internationally; wrote a regular column for *Downbeat,* the premier U.S. jazz magazine; and produced a series for public television called "Art's Place." Among his compositions were "Liberty Inn Drag," "Blues 'n' Booze," "Stuff and Nonsense," and "Paging Mr. Jelly." A series of strokes ended his playing career in the early 1990s, but he published his autobiography, *Hot Man,* in 1992.

Hogg-Priestly, Helen Battles Sawyer, U.S.-born Canadian astronomer (b. Aug. 1, 1905, Lowell, Mass.—d. Jan. 28, 1993, Toronto, Ont.), was an internationally recognized expert in the field of variable stars within globular star clusters, and she spent her entire professional career cataloging these stars of changing brightness in the International Astronomical Almanac. Hogg-Priestly received an undergraduate degree (1926) from Mount Holyoke College, South Hadley, Mass., before earning a Ph.D. (1931) from Radcliffe College, Cambridge, Mass., where she became interested in star clusters. In 1935 she and her first husband, Frank Hogg, became affiliated with the University of Toronto. She served as a volunteer for a year before becoming a lecturer and research assistant there in 1936, spending much of her time at the David Dunlap Observatory at Richmond Hill, Ont. She became a professor of astronomy in 1957, a post she held until her retirement in 1976, when she was named professor emeritus. Besides her many scholarly writings, including *The Stars Belong to Everyone* (1976), Hogg-Priestly popularized her subject for the general public in "The Stars," a weekly column she wrote for the *Toronto Daily Star* from 1951 to 1981 (the piece had been written by her husband from 1941 until his death in 1951). In 1985 she married Francis E.L. Priestly, who died in 1988. For her work Hogg-Priestly was awarded the Annie J. Cannon Prize of the American Astronomical Society (1950), the Rittenhouse Silver Medal (1967), and the Companion of the Order of Canada (1976). In 1984 Asteroid 2917, which was discovered in 1980, was renamed Asteroid Sawyer Hogg.

Holley, Robert William, U.S. biochemist (b. Jan. 28, 1922, Urbana, Ill.—d. Feb. 11, 1993, Los Gatos, Calif.), shared the 1968 Nobel Prize for Physiology or Medicine with H. Gobind Khorana and Marshall W. Nirenberg; the three scientists independently conducted research that helped to decipher the genetic code chemically and explain how the genetic information stored in the DNA of a cell controls the synthesis of proteins, the building blocks of cells. Holley, who began his painstaking work in 1956 while at the U.S. Department of Agriculture's Plant, Soil and Nutrition Laboratory at Cornell University, Ithaca, N.Y., determined the structure of alanine transfer RNA by purifying small amounts of the RNA isolated from more than 135 kg (300 lb) of baker's yeast. In 1965 Holley reported that "the complete nucleotide sequence of an alanine transfer RNA, isolated from yeast, has been determined. This is the first nucleic acid for which the structure is known." After earning a Ph.D. in organic chemistry (1947) from Cornell, Holley became associated with the university's state and federal agricultural stations and taught biochemistry and molecular biology (1962–66), serving at chairman of the biochemistry department from 1965 to 1966. In 1968 he became a resident fellow at the Salk Institute for Biological Studies in La Jolla, Calif., where he remained until his death. There he studied both the normal and the abnormal functions of the growth of cells in mammals, primarily focusing on the timing of cell division. The latter was crucial to understanding the growth of cancer and aided in diagnosis and treatment of that disease and others. Holley was also the recipient of the prestigious Lasker Award (1965) and of an award in molecular biology (1967) from the National Academy of Sciences.

Hollows, Frederick Cossom, New Zealand-born Australian physician (b. April 9, 1929, Dunedin, N.Z.—d. Feb. 10, 1993, Sydney, Australia), was a leader in the campaign to combat eye diseases (especially trachoma) among Aboriginal peoples and cofounder of the Aboriginal Medical Service (AMS), which established a system of community clinics. Hollows was educated in New Zealand and at the Royal College of Ophthalmology in London. In 1965 he immigrated to Australia, where he accepted a professorship at the University of New South Wales. He soon learned that thousands of Aborigines were going blind from trachoma, a treatable eye disease brought on by poor hygiene and inferior sanitation. Despite official opposition, he developed an efficient, inexpensive cure for the disease, trained a team of specialists to take the treatment to those in need, and brought restored eye health to some 30,000 affected Aborigines. In 1971 Hollows was brought in as a consultant for the first AMS clinic in Sydney. He later set up similar programs in Nepal, Vietnam, and Eritrea (then part of Ethiopia). Hollows was named Australian of the Year in 1990 and was made an Officer of the Order of Australia the next year. The Hollows Foundation was established in 1992.

Horszowski, Mieczyslaw, Polish-born U.S. pianist (b. June 23, 1892, Lwow, Poland [now Ukraine]—d. May 22, 1993, Philadelphia, Pa.), had a performing career that spanned more than nine decades; his playing was often praised for its thoughtfulness and beauty of tone. He studied first with his mother (who had studied with Karl Mikuli, a pupil of Chopin) and then, beginning at the age of seven, with the noted teacher Theodor Leschetizky. A child prodigy, Horszowski made his performing debut in 1901 in Warsaw. He settled in the U.S. at the beginning of World War II and in 1941 joined the faculty of the Curtis Institute of Music in Philadelphia, where he remained as a teacher for the rest of his life. Among his students were a number of the most prominent of present-day pianists, including Peter Serkin, Murray Perahia, and Richard Goode. Horszowski was known for his collaborations with other musicians, including the cellist Pablo Casals (at festivals in France and Puerto Rico and at the United Nations) and the violinists Joseph Szigeti and Alexander Schneider (*q.v.*). Concerts and recordings during his 90s, often featuring music of Bach, Mozart, Beethoven, Chopin, and Debussy, received widespread praise.

Houphouët-Boigny, Félix, Côte d'Ivoirian politician and physician (b. Oct. 18, 1905(?), Yamoussoukro, Côte d'Ivoire, western Africa—d. Dec. 7, 1993, Yamoussoukro, Côte d'Ivoire), had ruled Côte d'Ivoire since it emerged as an independent nation in 1960; at the time of his death, he was Africa's longest-serving head of state. He was born Dia Houphouët into a family of tribal chiefs. His family held cocoa and coffee plantations, and their relative prosperity allowed him to attend school. At the age of 11 he converted to Roman Catholicism, apparently partly because of his discomfort with human sacrifice, and changed his name from Dia ("divine healer") to Félix. He trained as an "African doctor" (the highest-level medical degree allowed a colonial) and from 1925 to 1940 worked as a physician. In 1940 he inherited plantation land in Yamoussoukro and returned there to assume the role of chief of the canton. In 1945 he was elected to the French National Assembly; the same year, he gained passage of legislation that abolished the much-hated practice of forced labour in the colonies (at that time he added Boigny, meaning "ram," to his name). His party eventually joined the ruling French coalition, and Houphouët-Boigny gained a minister's post. As other colonies started to seek independence, he argued for a French-speaking community of nations in Africa; he began supporting full independence, however, when public opinion strongly favoured it, and he helped negotiate the terms for independence. In 1960 he was elected president of the new country. He rejected the anti-Western stance and Marxist ideology that was then popular, and he was thus able to gain generous foreign-aid packages from the West. Policies that invited foreign investment and stressed agricultural, not industrial, productivity helped the annual growth of the economy for much of his early reign. Although his paternalistic style and personal authority were still widely respected, discontent grew in his later years after a sharp change in the country's economy. Attention was focused on the huge basilica he built in Yamoussoukro—Notre Dame de la Paix, completed in 1989 at an estimated cost of $200 million—although it was said to have been funded with his moneys. Houphouët-Boigny allowed multiparty elections for the first time in 1990.

PATRICK ROBERT—SYGMA

Hourani, Albert Habib, British historian (b. March 31, 1915, Manchester, England—d. Jan. 17, 1993, Oxford, England), was a foremost authority on the Middle East, director (from 1958) of the Middle East Centre at St. Antony's College, Oxford, and author of the popular best-seller *A History of the Arab Peoples* (1991). Hourani, the son of a Lebanese Christian immigrant, attended Magdalen College, Oxford, and taught for two years at the American University in Beirut, Lebanon. After working in the British Middle East office in Cairo during World War II, he returned (1948) to Oxford to take up a teaching fellowship. Hourani was instrumental in the establishment of the prestigious Middle East Centre at St. Antony's and was much admired as a visiting lecturer, notably at Harvard and the University of Chicago. He retired in 1980, but he gained unexpected popularity when his eloquent and insightful Arab history was published during the 1990–91 Persian Gulf crisis. Hourani also wrote numerous scholarly papers, published *Arabic Thought in the Liberal Age, 1798–1939* in 1962, and contributed to the *Encyclopædia Britannica.*

Howe, Irving, U.S. literary and social critic (b. June 11, 1920, New York, N.Y.—d. May 5, 1993, New York), as a founder (1953) and editor of *Dissent,* an influential left-wing journal, advocated democratic socialism but deplored the authoritarian proclivity of the American New Left, leftist totalitarianism, and the abuses of capitalism. He was best remembered for his literary criticism, notably in works on Sherwood Anderson (1951), William Faulkner (1952), and Thomas Hardy (1967). Howe spent 10 years preparing *World of Our Fathers* (1976), a probing narrative history of Eastern European Jewish immigration to the U.S., which won the National Book Award. Howe, who was raised in the Jewish tenements of New York City, graduated (1940) from City College of New York. He served four years in the army and taught at Brandeis University, Waltham, Mass. (1953–61), and Stanford University (1961–63), before returning to New York City to teach English at Hunter College of the City University of New York as professor (1963–70) and distinguished professor (1970–86). Some of his other important writings include *Politics and the Novel* (1957), *Decline of the New* (1970), the biography *Leon Trotsky* (1978), *Celebrations and Attacks: Thirty Years of Literary and Cultural Commentary* (1979), and *A Margin of Hope: An Intellectual Autobiography* (1982). Though he retired from teaching in 1986, he continued to give speeches and to write essays for *Dissent.*

Hunt, James Simon Wallis, British race car driver (b. Aug. 29, 1947—d. June 15, 1993, London, England), won the 1976 Formula One Grand Prix racing drivers' world championship by one point over his Austrian archrival, Niki Lauda. Although many people considered Hunt's title to be tarnished (Lauda missed part of the season after being seriously injured in a fiery crash), his blond good looks, irreverent charm, and flamboyant personal life made him a popular favourite and brought a glamorous image to the sport. Hunt began racing his own car in Formula Ford events in 1969. He quickly graduated to Formula Three races, where his aggressive driving and several accidents earned him the nickname "Hunt the Shunt." In 1972 he joined the Formula One circuit as a driver for Lord Alexander Hesketh. He signed with the McLaren team in 1976, and in his first season he edged out Lauda for the title when the Austrian, coming back from a near-fatal crash, refused to finish the Japan Grand Prix on a rain-soaked track. In his seven years on the Formula One circuit, Hunt won 10 victories and 14 pole positions in 92 Grand Prix races. He retired from racing in 1979 and thereafter worked as a sportswriter and BBC commentator.

Ibuse, Masuji, Japanese writer (b. Feb. 15, 1898, Loma, Hiroshima prefecture, Japan—d. July 10, 1993, Tokyo, Japan), was a master craftsman who painstakingly revised and polished his short stories, essays, poetry, and novels, notably the compelling *Kuroi ame* (1966; *Black Rain,* 1969; filmed 1989). The latter chronicled, in diary and documentary form, the aftereffects of the atomic bomb on the people of Hiroshima and especially on Yasuko, a young girl who could not marry because of her exposure to radiation. Ibuse, who initially was interested in painting, became immersed in French and Russian literature while studying at Waseda University, Tokyo. He began to write in 1918, and his first published story, *Koi* (1926; *Carp,* 1971), was followed by another fable-like tale, *Sanshouo* (1929; *Salamander,* 1966), one of his most heavily revised (first appeared in 1923 as *Yuhei,* "Confinement") and best-known stories. Another important work was the historical novel *Jon Manjiro hyoryuki* (1937; *John Manjiro, the Castaway: His Life and Adventures,* 1941). During World War II Ibuse was drafted into the army and served as a war correspondent in Thailand and Singapore. He achieved wider fame after the war with the publication of *Honjitsu kyushin* (1950; *No Consultations Today,* 1964; filmed 1952), a wry characterization of a town and the tragicomic doctor and his down-and-out patients who lived there. His antimilitary satire *Yohai taicho* (1950; *A Far-Worshiping Commander,* 1964) was also well received. Ibuse's self-deprecating humour coupled with his gift for satire ensured that his compassion for his characters would not lapse into sentimentality. In 1966 Ibuse received both the Noma Prize for Literature and the Order of Cultural Merit for *Kuroi ame.*

Jadid, Salah al-, Syrian military officer and Ba'th politician (b. 1926?, Duwayr B'abda, near Jablah, Syria—d. Aug. 19, 1993, Damascus, Syria), was leader of the country from 1966 to 1970, when he was ousted and imprisoned by rival Hafiz al-Assad, who subsequently became president. A member of the 'Alawite religious minority, Jadid entered the army after secondary school. In the 1950s, by then an officer, he joined the Ba'th Party, which was banned at the time. He was promoted to major general in 1963 and named chief of staff of the Syrian armed forces. With Assad, he led a coup in February 1966 that ousted the more moderate Ba'th leadership. For the next four years, although he held only a party post, Jadid was the effective leader of Syria. In September 1970 he sent armoured troops to Jordan in support of Palestinians fighting King Hussein and unsuccessfully tried to persuade Assad, who commanded the air force, to provide cover. When the Syrian forces suffered defeat, Assad had Jadid arrested. A man of strict principle, Jadid remained defiant, and he spent the remaining 23 years of his life under arrest, making him one of the world's longest-held political prisoners.

Janeway, Eliot, U.S. economist and writer (b. Jan. 1, 1913, New York, N.Y.—d. Feb. 8, 1993, New York), proposed the controversial and thought-provoking theory that political pressures shape economic and market trends and was dubbed "Calamity Janeway" on Wall Street because of his perpetually gloomy forecasts on the stock market. Janeway, one of the foremost political economists in the U.S., studied economics at Cornell University, Ithaca, N.Y., and did postgraduate work at the London School of Economics and Political Science. After writing a series of articles for *Nation* magazine on the looming 1937–38 inventory crisis and offering solutions to that problem, he influenced some policy-making bodies within the Franklin D. Roosevelt administration. Politically independent, Janeway criticized the economic policies of presidents from Franklin D. Roosevelt to Ronald Reagan in books, in columns he wrote for the Chicago Tribune-New York News Syndicate, and in his weekly financial newsletters, the backbone of Janeway Publishing and Research Corp., which he operated from his home. Janeway's first book, *Struggle for Survival* (1951), was followed by a series of works for the private investor—*What Shall I Do with My*

ARCHIVE PHOTOS

Money? (1970), *You and Your Money* (1972), and *Musings on Money: How to Make Dollars out of Sense* (1976)—and by two volumes that analyzed government policies, *Prescriptions for Prosperity* (1983) and *The Economics of Chaos* (1989).

Juan de Borbón (JUAN CARLOS TERESA SILVERIO ALFONSO DE BORBÓN Y BATTENBERG, CONDE DE BARCELONA), Spanish royal (b. June 20, 1913, Segovia, Spain—d. April 1, 1993, Pamplona, Spain), was pretender to the Spanish throne from the death of his father, King Alfonso XIII, in 1941 until 1977, when he formally renounced his claim in favour of his son, King Juan Carlos I. The third son of King Alfonso XIII, Don Juan (as he was always known) went into exile with his family in 1931. Two years later he succeeded to the pretendership when his eldest brother renounced the throne to marry a commoner; his second brother, who was deaf, also ceded his claim. In 1936 Don Juan tried unsuccessfully to join Gen. Francisco Franco's Nationalist forces in the Spanish Civil War. However, after the war he publicly opposed Franco's dictatorial rule and campaigned from exile for the establishment of a constitutional monarchy. In 1948 he reluctantly agreed to send his sons, Juan Carlos and Alfonso, to be educated in Spain. After refusing several times, Juan Carlos agreed in 1969 to be named as Franco's successor. Father and son were estranged until 1975, when Franco died and Juan Carlos quickly called for the constitutional monarchy his father had long sought. In May 1977, shortly before Spain's first democratic elections, Don Juan returned to his homeland and formally renounced his claim to the throne. He was given a state funeral and buried in the royal crypt alongside his father.

Kadoorie, Lawrence Kadoorie, BARON, Hong Kong industrialist (b. June 2, 1899, Hong Kong—d. Aug. 25, 1993, Hong Kong), was one of the colony's last great taipans (businessmen of enormous power and influence) and the first native of Hong Kong to be awarded a British life peerage (1981). His father, Sir Elly Kadoorie, was a Jewish immigrant from Baghdad, now in Iraq, who made a fortune in hotels, transport, and electric power in Hong Kong and Shanghai but died in a Japanese prison camp during World War II. Lawrence and his brother, Horace, survived wartime internment and returned to reclaim the family's venerable Peninsula Hotel in Kowloon. Despite a further loss of assets in Shanghai when the Chinese Communist forces took control in 1949, the brothers built a business empire that included banking and textiles, as well as the Hong Kong and Shanghai Hotel group and the New Territories Benevolent Society. The corporate centrepiece, however, was China Light and Power, Hong Kong's largest electric utility and, literally, the power behind much of the colony's economic growth. In 1985 Kadoorie negotiated a contract to build China's first nuclear power station. He retired as chairman in 1992.

Keeler, Ruby, Canadian-born U.S. actress and dancer (b. Aug. 25, 1909, Halifax, N.S.—d. Feb. 28, 1993, Rancho Mirage, Calif.), starred as a fresh-faced ingenue who would triumphantly emerge from the chorus line to replace an ailing or temperamental star in a string of lavish formulaic Depression-era musicals remembered for the colossal kaleidoscopic dance sequences orchestrated by choreographer-director Busby Berkeley. After moving with her family to New York City at the age of 4, Keeler took some dancing lessons and, at the age of 14, landed her first chorus job. She then honed her tap-dancing skills in the city's speakeasies until a Broadway producer gave her a job in the chorus of *Bye Bye Bonnie* (1927). This was followed by a featured role in *The Sidewalks of New York*. Though Florenz Ziegfeld offered her a sizable role in *Whoopee*, Keeler dropped out before rehearsals because she had met and married (1928) her first husband, Al Jolson, while on a trip to the West Coast. In 1929 she appeared for only a month in Ziegfeld's *Stage Girl*, returning to join Jolson. Keeler's film debut was in the smash hit *42nd Street* (1933), in which she played opposite Dick Powell, who starred with her in a rapid succession of extravaganzas, including *Gold Diggers of 1933, Dames, Footlight Parade, Flirtation Walk, Shipmates Forever,* and *Colleen.* In 1935 Keeler and Jolson adopted a baby boy, and she appeared with her husband in their only film together, *Go into Your Dance.* Keeler starred in *Ready Willing and Able* (1937) and *Mother Carey's Chickens* (1939) before her last starring role in *Sweetheart of the Campus* (1941). In 1940 she and Jolson were divorced, and her career fizzled out. She remarried and went into retirement before being persuaded, at the age of 60, to stage a dancing comeback in the 1971 Broadway revival of *No, No, Nanette,* which ran for 871 performances. Keeler once again retired from show business after that extraordinary success but resurfaced in cameo roles in *They Shoot Horses, Don't They?* (1969) and *Phynx* (1970).

Klos, Elmar, Czech filmmaker (b. Jan. 26, 1910, Brno, Moravia, Austria-Hungary—d. July 19, 1993, Prague, Czech Republic), collaborated with the Hungarian-born director Jan Kadar on some of the finest motion pictures in the so-called Czech New Wave, most notably *The Shop on Main Street,* which won the Academy Award for the best foreign film of 1965. Klos studied law at Charles University in Prague and began doing odd jobs in the film industry at the age of 18. At age 25 he established his own studio to write and direct documentaries and educational films; later he joined the state-owned studio in Prague as head of the creative art staff. In 1955 he helped found the Czech motion-picture academy known as FAMU, where he was professor of film history until 1969. Klos worked with Kadar on eight films, including *The Hijacking* (1952), *The Third Wish* (1958), *The Accused* (1964), and *Adrift* (1969). After the 1968 Warsaw Pact invasion of Czechoslovakia, Kadar immigrated to the U.S. Klos remained in Prague but was banned from moviemaking. He worked as a construction engineer until the postcommunist government allowed him to return to FAMU as a teacher in the 1990s.

Kopal, Zdenek, Czech-born astronomer (b. April 4, 1914, Litomysl, Bohemia, Austria-Hungary—d. June 23, 1993, Wilmslow, Cheshire, England), directed an international project, financed by the U.S. Air Force, to photograph and map the entire surface of the Moon by using the refracting telescope at the Pic du Midi Observatory in southern France. He also made important discoveries concerning the transfer of matter between close binary stars. Kopal matriculated at Charles University in Prague (B.S., 1934; D.Sc., 1937) and received fellowships to the University of Cambridge and Harvard University. He taught astronomy at Harvard (1940–48) and at the Massachusetts Institute of Technology (1947–51). In 1951 he was invited to England to head the new astronomy department at the University of Manchester. In 1958 Kopal took charge of the lunar mapping project, which increased scientific understanding of the Moon and paved the way for the National Aeronautics and Space Administration's (NASA's) Apollo lunar missions. He also worked as a special consultant to NASA, the U.S. Army, the space science division of the Jet Propulsion Laboratory in Pasadena, Calif., and private industry. Kopal was founding editor of three journals—*Icarus, Astrophysics and Space Science,* and *Moon* (later renamed *Earth, Moon and Planets*). His published works include *Numerical Analysis* (1955), *Close Binary Systems* (1959), *Physics and Astronomy of the Moon* (1962), *Mapping of the Moon* (1974), *Dynamics of Close Binary Systems* (1978), and *Mathematical Theory of Stellar Eclipses* (1990). He retired from the University of Manchester in 1981.

Kulwicki, Alan, U.S. race-car driver (b. Dec. 14, 1954, Greenfield, Wis.—d. April 1, 1993, near Bristol, Tenn.), in the closest championship points battle in stock-car history, won the National Association for Stock Car Auto Racing's (NASCAR's) 1992 Winston Cup. Kulwicki, an anomaly in the sport, was both the first champion to graduate from college and the first born north of the Mason-Dixon line. He was also the first owner-driver to win the title since Richard Petty in 1979. After graduating from the University of Wisconsin at Milwaukee with a degree in mechanical engineering, Kulwicki worked as an engineer and raced cars as a hobby before joining the NASCAR circuit in 1985. The following year he was named Rookie of the Year. A perfectionist who operated on a shoestring, he raced a single car, had a two-man crew, and served as his own chief engineer and chief mechanic. In 1988 he captured the first of five professional victories, and by the time he had signed (1991) a sponsorship agreement with Hooters Restaurant, he had established a reputation as one of the top drivers on the circuit. After winning the 1992 Winston Cup by a slim 10-point margin, Kulwicki defied tradition by taking his victory lap the wrong way around the track. At the time of his death, in a plane crash, he was in ninth place after five 1993 season races.

Kunayev, Dinmukhamed Akhmedovich, Soviet politician (b. Jan. 12, 1912 [Dec. 31, 1911, Old Style], Verny [now Almaty], Kazakhstan—d. Aug. 22, 1993, near Almaty), as first secretary of the Communist Party of Kazakhstan (1960–62; 1964–86), was the effective ruler of the Kazakh Soviet Socialist Republic for more than two decades and the highest-ranking Soviet leader of Muslim heritage. Kunayev studied metallurgy in Moscow and worked as a machinist, engineer, and administrator in the mining industry. He joined the Communist Party of the Soviet Union in 1939, and in 1942 he was named deputy chairman of the Kazakhstan Council of Ministers. After a three-year break, during which he served as president of the Academy of Sciences of Kazakhstan (1952–55), he was promoted to chairman of the republic's Council of Ministers. Kunayev, a close associate of Leonid Brezhnev, who also hailed from Kazakhstan, took control in the republic after Brezhnev ousted Nikita Khrushchev as Soviet leader in 1964. He became a candidate member of the CPSU Politburo in 1966 and was elevated to full membership in 1971. Although Kunayev's term was marked by autocratic ruthlessness and corruption, there were widespread protests when he was replaced in 1986.

Kurtzman, Harvey, U.S. cartoonist and editor (b. Oct. 3, 1924, New York, N.Y.—d. Feb. 21, 1993, Mount Vernon, N.Y.), cleverly lampooned the sacred institutions of American life as the comic genius who conceived of *Mad* magazine and its gap-toothed, freckle-faced mascot, Alfred E. Neuman. Kurtzman, who published his first cartoon at the age of 14, attended the High School of Music and Art in New York City. After contributing humour fillers for magazines, he drew the strip "Hey Look!" in a distinctively loose, thick-outlined style for Timely Comics, Inc. For EC (Entertainment Comics) publisher William Gaines, Kurtzman created two well-researched antiwar comic books, *Two Fisted Tales* and *Front Line Combat*. While recuperating from an illness, Kurtzman began illustrating a strip cartoon called "Mad," which featured his unique brand of humour and a broad range of parodies, including ones of other cartoon characters, politics, and television. The strip was a sensation, and Kurtzman was persuaded by Gaines to convert his brainchild into a magazine. Although Kurtzman edited only the first four issues of *Mad* magazine, which premiered in 1952, his distinctive imprint remained visible even after his departure. He then went to work for Hugh Hefner, the publisher of *Playboy* magazine, and produced the short-lived *Trump*, *Humbug*, and *Help* comic books before striking gold with "Little Annie Fanny," which premiered in *Playboy* in 1962. Kurtzman's satirical humour laid the foundation for such contemporary television programs as "Saturday Night Live" and "Monty Python's Flying Circus," and he helped launch other cartoonists by publishing their works in a comic book called *Nuts*. Other works include *My Life as a Cartoonist, Strange Adventures,* and *From Aargh! to Zap!*

Kusch, Polykarp, U.S. physicist (b. Jan. 26, 1911, Blankenburg, Germany—d. March 20, 1993, Dallas, Texas), was awarded the 1955 Nobel Prize for Physics for his precise work in measuring the electron's magnetic moment, a vital determination that led to revised theories about the interactions of electrons with electromagnetic radiation and to new scientific principles as a basis for quantum electrodynamics; he shared the prize with Willis E. Lamb, Jr., who independently performed related experiments on the hyperfine structure of the hydrogen atom. Kusch immigrated to the U.S. with his family in 1912 and became a citizen in 1922. He graduated (1931) from Case Institute of Technology, Cleveland, Ohio, before earning an M.A. (1933) and a Ph.D. (1936) from the University of Illinois at Urbana-Champaign, where he taught physics from 1931 to 1936. He joined Columbia University, New York City, in 1937, and there, with physicist Isidor I. Rabi, he conducted studies of the effects of magnetic fields on beams of atoms. Kusch remained associated with Columbia until 1972 except for a time during World War II, when he engaged in military research on the applications of vacuum tubes and microwave generators at Westinghouse Electric Corp. (1941–42) and Bell Telephone Laboratories (1944–46). At Columbia he served as chairman of the physics department (1949–52 and 1960–63), director of the radiation laboratory (1952–60), and academic vice president and provost (1969–72). From 1972 until his retirement in 1982, he taught at the University of Texas at Dallas.

Kutner, Luis, U.S. human rights activist (b. June 9, 1908, Chicago, Ill.—d. March 1, 1993, Chicago), achieved international prominence as a cofounder (1961), with Peter Benenson, of Amnesty International, an organization devoted to making human rights abuses public; as founder of World Habeas Corpus, dedicated to protecting people from false imprisonment; and as creator of the living will, a document that provides instructions about the use of extraordinary medical procedures to prolong human life. Kutner, who graduated (1929) from the University of Chicago, worked as a clerk for defense lawyer Clarence Darrow before setting up a law practice in 1930, specializing in human rights. He handled such highly publicized international cases as the post-World War II release of poet Ezra Pound from a mental ward and negotiations, at the behest of Pope Pius XII, for improved conditions for Jozsef Cardinal Mindszenty, who was imprisoned in Hungary. With Kutner's aid Mindszenty was later released from house arrest. In 1975 Kutner also secured the release of 730 Irish prisoners from Northern Ireland's Long Kesh prison. Nationally he gained recognition in 1949 when he won freedom for a black mechanic who had served 26 years of a life term for raping an itinerant woman, who, it was later discovered, had never been raped (a prosecutor had suppressed the vital testimony of the examining doctor). Kutner was also the author of numerous works about the law, some volumes of poetry, a novel, and a biography of Adm. George Dewey, *The Admiral* (1944; with Laurin Healy).

Lachs, Manfred, Polish educator, diplomat, and jurist (b. April 21, 1914, Stanislawow, Austria-Hungary—d. Jan. 14, 1993, The Hague, Neth.), was the longest-serving member of the International Court of Justice (1967–93; president 1973–76) and a brilliant legal scholar who had a profound influence on the development of international law after World War II. Lachs received a doctorate in law from the Jagiellonian University of Krakow (1937) and did graduate work at the Consular Academy of Vienna and the London School of Economics. After serving in the military and the Polish government in exile during the war, he applied his sharp legal mind and multilingual skills in the Polish Foreign Ministry as director of the Legal and Treaties Department (1947–60), official legal adviser to the foreign minister (1960–67), and ambassador-at-large. Lachs came to international prominence as a member of the 1945 UN War Crimes Commission, a Polish representative at the 1946 Paris Peace Conference, and a longtime delegate to the UN General Assembly. In 1966 he was elected to the World Court, where he was a respected consensus builder and advocate of moderate international cooperation. Lachs was also chairman of the General Assembly Legal Committee (1949, 1951, 1955), chairman of the UN Legal Commission for the Peaceful Uses of Outer Space (1962–67), and professor of law at the University of Warsaw (1952–93). His numerous books and papers (written in more than a dozen languages) include *War Crimes: An Attempt to Define the Issues* (1945), *The International Law of Outer Space, a Law in the Making* (1964), and *The Teacher in International Law* (1982).

Lahbabi, Mohammed Aziz, Moroccan writer and philosopher (b. Dec. 25, 1922, Fès, Morocco—d. Aug. 23, 1993, Rabat, Morocco), had influence in the Arab world through his many writings, some of which were translated into as many as 30 languages. Lahbabi was educated at the Sorbonne in Paris and received a doctorate of philosophy. He taught philosophy at Muhammad V University, Rabat, and the University of Algiers and held other academic positions, among them dean of the faculty of letters at Rabat. His writings, which combined Arab and Islamic with Western philosophical and humanistic influences, encompassed a wide variety of forms, including poetry, fiction, and nonfictional works in philosophy, economics, politics, and literary studies. He wrote in both Arabic and French. Lahbabi founded the Union of Arab Writers of the Maghreb and the review *Afaq* ("Horizons"). He was nominated for the 1987 Nobel Prize for Literature. Among his writings are *Le Personnalisme Musulman* (1964; "Muslim Personalism") and *Le Monde de demain: Le Tiers-Monde accuse* (1980; "The World of Tomorrow: The Third World Challenges").

Lamborghini, Ferruccio, Italian industrialist (b. April 28, 1916, Cento, Italy—d. Feb. 20, 1993, Perugia, Italy), founded a luxury car company that produced some of the fastest, most expensive, and sought-after sports cars in the world. Lamborghini worked as a mechanic in the Italian army during World War II, and after the war he started a tractor company to build farm implements using recycled parts from Allied army surplus and abandoned German tanks. In 1963 he opened a state-of-the-art factory to manufacture a sports car that would challenge the top-ranked Ferrari high-performance cars. The innovative Lamborghini 350GT debuted that year, and three years later the company surprised the automobile industry with the Miura, a low-slung, V-12 two-seater that could exceed 298 km/h (185 mph). By the end of the 1960s Lamborghini's luxury sports cars were in demand by sports car enthusiasts and by celebrities impressed with the cars' quality and panache. In 1973 Lamborghini sold his share of the firm and retired to a country estate in Umbria, where he established an automobile museum, cultivated grapes, and produced premium table wine.

Langmuir, Alexander, U.S. epidemiologist (b. Sept. 12, 1910, Santa Monica, Calif.—d. Nov. 22, 1993, Baltimore, Md.), created and led the Epidemic Intelligence Service (EIS) for the U.S. government and was credited with saving thousands of lives with his revolutionary work. Langmuir received his medical degree at Cornell University, Ithaca, N.Y., in 1935. He joined the United States Public Health Service in 1949, becoming the chief epidemiologist for the Communicable Disease Center (the forerunner of the Centers for Disease Control and Prevention [CDC]). In 1951 he created and headed the EIS, which was established to study and track the transmission of disease. Langmuir's vigorous training and high standards proved critical for his group's effectiveness, and the service gained renown for its "shoe-leather" detective work in the field. Langmuir served at the CDC until 1970, when he retired from public service, and taught at Harvard University until 1977. In later years he criticized the CDC's tracking of the spread of AIDS.

Lecanuet, Jean-Adrien-François, French politician (b. March 4, 1920, Rouen, France—d. Feb. 22, 1993, Neuilly-sur-Seine, France), challenged Pres. Charles de Gaulle in France's first direct presidential election in 1965 and forced an unexpected runoff between the formerly invincible de Gaulle and the Socialist candidate, François Mitterrand. Although Lecanuet, representing the centrist Popular Republican Movement (MRP), came in third, his high-profile campaign drew considerable attention, and he was credited with triggering the runoff by drawing votes from traditional de Gaulle supporters. Lecanuet received a doctorate in philosophy in 1942, and during World War II he fought with the Resistance. He was elected to the National Assembly in 1951 and spent most of the remainder of his life as an elected official there (1951–55) or in the Senate (1959–73, 1977–93). A lifelong devotee of European unity and trans-Atlantic cooperation, he served as president of the MRP (1963–65), the Democratic Centre Party (1966–76), the Centre for Social Democrats (1976–82), and the centre-right Union for French Democracy (UDF; 1978–88). Lecanuet held several Cabinet posts in the 1970s, including minister of justice (1974–76). He also served in the European Parliament (1979–88) and was the mayor of Rouen from 1968.

Leinsdorf, Erich, Austrian-born U.S. conductor (b. Feb. 4, 1912, Vienna, Austria-Hungary—d. Sept. 11, 1993, Zürich, Switz.), had some of his first successes in opera but later worked mainly with orchestras; his conducting was characterized by clarity and precision. He studied piano as a child and later the cello, music theory, and composition and graduated from the University of Vienna and State Academy of Music. He conducted at Salzburg until he left Europe in 1937 for the U.S., where he formed an association with the Metropolitan Opera. In 1943 he became music director and conductor of the Cleveland (Ohio) Orchestra, but he was almost immediately drafted into military service. From 1947 to 1956 he directed the Rochester (N.Y.) Philharmonic Orchestra, with which he made a number of recordings. After periods with the New York City Opera and the Metropolitan, in 1962 he succeeded Charles Munch as director of the Boston Symphony Orchestra. At Boston until 1969, Leinsdorf was especially known for performing many new works. He disliked administrative duties and, except for a short period with the Berlin Radio Symphony Orchestra, for the remainder of his career he served as guest conductor for many major orchestras. His appearances were noted for innovative programming, which often included new or little-known works in unusual combinations with the standard repertoire. Leinsdorf was a man of wide-ranging interests and knowledge, and he was outspoken in his views on musical and other matters. The autobiographical *Cadenza: A Musical Career* was published in 1976, and his book on conducting, *The Composer's Advocate,* in 1981.

Lewis, Reginald F., U.S. lawyer and financier (b. Dec. 7, 1942, Baltimore, Md.—d. Jan. 19, 1993, New York, N.Y.), was a partner (1970–73) in Murphy, Thorpe & Lewis, the first black law firm on Wall Street. After his $1 billion takeover in 1987 of the Beatrice Companies, a food concern, he became one of the nation's richest businessmen. Lewis, who earned a law degree from Harvard Law School in 1968, worked for the firm of Paul, Weiss, Rifkind, Wharton & Garrison after graduation. In 1973 he went into private practice with the founding of his own law firm, Lewis & Clarkson, which specialized in venture capital projects. Among his most outstanding business deals were the 1983 purchase (he led the $23 million buyout with $1 million in savings) of the McCall Pattern Co., which he then sold in 1987 to the John Crowther Group of Britain for $63 million in cash; the sale netted Lewis a $50 million personal profit. After acquiring Beatrice Companies, he formed his own concern, TLC (The Lewis Company) Beatrice International. Lewis, who amassed a personal fortune of $400 million and headed the largest company in the U.S. run by an African-American, was most proud, however, of his philanthropies to education. He donated large sums to Virginia State and Howard universities, and in 1992 he gave $3 million to Harvard Law School, making him the school's largest individual donor. Lewis died of a cerebral hemorrhage related to brain cancer.

Loy, Myrna (MYRNA WILLIAMS), U.S. actress (b. Aug. 2, 1905, Raidersburg, Mont.—d. Dec. 14, 1993, New York, N.Y.), was the cool beauty who reigned as "Queen of the Movies" (Clark Gable was "King") and first showcased her mastery of sophisticated comedy with her portrayal of the unforgettable Nora Charles in *The Thin Man* (1934), the first in a series of six engaging comedy-mystery films. Loy created the role of the "perfect wife" with her wry wit, sophisticated charm, and unflappable temperament while teaming with William Powell (as Nick Charles) as the cocktail-loving, bantering husband-and-wife detective team. Loy, who appeared in more than 100 films, was typecast in some 60 of them as an exotic, mysterious, and often Oriental femme fatale, usually in villainous roles, notably in *The Mask of Fu Manchu* (1932). She broke the mold with *The Thin Man* and its sequels. She also had starring roles with Gable in *Manhattan Melodrama* (1934; also with Powell), *Test Pilot* (1938), and *Too Hot to Handle* (1938). During World War II Loy interrupted her career to work with the American Red Cross. After returning to the screen, she gave a stirring performance as the wife of a returning veteran in the classic *The Best Years of Our Lives* (1946). In her maturing screen roles she was Cary Grant's whimsical wife in *Mr. Blandings Builds His Dream House* (1948) and the shrewd mother in *Cheaper by the Dozen* (1950), starring Clifton Webb. She also used her high profile to speak out against the communist witch-hunts during the late 1940s, and she was a longtime film adviser to Unesco. While devoting more of her time to the UN, she took on fewer film roles. She appeared on Broadway in 1973 in *The Women* and was seen on-screen in *Airport 1975* (1974). *Just Tell Me What You Want* (1980) was her last big-screen role. The following year she joined Henry Fonda to portray an aging couple reminiscing about their lives in the well-received television movie "Summer Solstice." Loy, who was married and divorced four times, received an honorary Academy Award in 1991.

McFarland, George Robert Phillips ("SPANKY"), U.S. actor (b. Oct. 2, 1928, Dallas, Texas—d. June 30, 1993, Grapevine, Texas), was the precocious rotund child star who voiced authority while portraying Spanky, the beanie-sporting leader of "Our Gang," a highly successful series of two-reel comedies featuring the antics of Spanky, Buckwheat, Stymie, Froggy, Butch, Alfalfa, and Petey the dog. McFarland started modeling when he was three and was starring in a Wonder Bread film advertisement when he was discovered by Hal Roach, who cast him to lead the gang. McFarland's career as Spanky lasted 11 years, and he also appeared in 14 feature-length films, notably *General Spanky* (1936), *Trail of the Lonesome Pine* (1936), and *The Woman in the Window* (1944), his last. When he realized that his advancing age had diminished his juvenile appeal, McFarland retired from films at the age of 16. The "Our Gang" series, which reached the height of its popularity in the 1930s, was later renamed "The Little Rascals" and shown on television. McFarland, who had worked as a salesman, as a spokesperson for Justin Boot Co., and as a restaurateur, gained renewed popularity with his now-grown fans. He made cameo appearances in the films *Moonrunners* (1975) and *The Aurora Encounter* (1986), and he appeared on television as a talk-show guest and on an episode of "Cheers" in April 1993.

Makino, Masahiro, Japanese film director (b. Feb. 29, 1908, Kyoto, Japan—d. Oct. 29, 1993, Tokyo, Japan), specialized in creating action films that featured loners as heroes, usually duty-bound samurai or gangsters avenging injustices out of a sense of personal obligation. During his career, which spanned the period from 1926 to 1972, the versatile Makino directed more than 230 films, encompassing fantasies, operettas, musical comedies, and historical epics. He was best known, however, for the special rhythm of his shooting technique, which was marked by slow-moving sentimental sequences followed by rapid-fire action. Makino was the son of Shozo Makino, one of the pioneers of the Japanese film industry. The younger Makino began acting in his father's films before he even went to school, and he later served as his father's assistant director. Makino wrote and almost entirely directed (after the director became ill) *Aoi me no ningyo* ("Blue-Eyed Doll"). His first masterpiece, *Roningai* (1928; "Street of Masterless Samurai"), was completed when he was only 20. During World War II, Makino made propaganda films, but he later returned to creating the sword-fighting classics that became his hallmark.

Mankiewicz, Francis, Canadian filmmaker (b. March 15, 1944, Shanghai, China—d. Aug. 14, 1993, Montreal, Que.), had a slender output but was considered one of the country's leading talents; his films sensitively and poignantly portrayed, in psychological depth, a child's viewpoint. Mankiewicz' parents fled Nazi Germany for France and then China, where he was born. As an infant he was taken to Montreal, where he attended university and studied geology. In 1966, however, he enrolled at the London School of Film Technique and, after returning to Canada in 1969, he made educational films and television dramas. His directorial feature-length film debut, *Le Temps d'une chasse* (1972; "Hunting Season"), chronicled a hunting weekend as viewed by a young boy and was a critical success. His second film, *Les Bons Débarras* (1980; "Good Riddance"), a Gothic tale of passion and jealousy between a mother and daughter, was widely hailed as a masterpiece and swept the 1981 Genie awards. His last film, *Les Portes tournantes* (1988; "The Revolving Doors"), was a family saga centred around a 12-year-old boy. Mankiewicz then became exclusively involved in English television. He directed the successful television dramas *Love and Hate: The Story of Colin and JoAnn Thatcher* (1989) and *Conspiracy of Silence* (1991), both of which received Gemini awards and then spellbound U.S. audiences. Mankiewicz succumbed to cancer.

Mankiewicz, Joseph Leo, U.S. director, screenwriter, and producer (b. Feb. 11, 1909, Wilkes-Barre, Pa.—d. Feb. 5, 1993, Mount Kisco, N.Y.), infused witty and often biting dialogue into his screenplays and as a motion-picture director was especially remembered for his masterful use of flashbacks and sound track narration, notably in *A Letter to Three Wives* (1949) and *All About Eve* (1950), films for which he won four Academy Awards (two each for director and screenplay). Mankiewicz launched his Hollywood career in 1929 when his brother, Herman (co-writer of *Citizen Kane)*, secured him a job as a scriptwriter for Paramount Pictures. His early writing credits included *The Mysterious Dr. Fu Manchu* (1929); *If I Had a Million* (1932), for which he coined W.C. Field's famous phrase "my little chickadee"; and *Million Dollar Legs* (1932). He was the producer of *Fury* (1936), *The Adventures of Huckleberry Finn* (1939), *The Philadelphia Story* (1940), and the first of the snappy Katharine Hepburn-Spencer Tracy vehicles, *Woman of the Year* (1942). In 1946 Mankiewicz made his directorial debut after replacing the ailing Ernst Lubitsch on *Dragonwyck* (1946), the first of many films that he both wrote and directed. Others were *Somewhere in the Night* (1946), *The Ghost and Mrs. Muir* (1947), *The Barefoot Contessa* (1954), *Guys and Dolls* (1955), and *The Quiet American* (1957), the last of which he also produced. Mankiewicz directed *House of Strangers* (1950), *No Way Out* (1950), *Five Fingers* (1952), the critically acclaimed *Julius Caesar* (1953), and *Suddenly, Last Summer* (1959) before directing and co-writing the lavish *Cleopatra*, starring Elizabeth Taylor and Richard Burton. After the failure of that film, Mankiewicz directed just a few others: *The Honey Pot* (1967), *There Was a Crooked Man* (1970), and *Sleuth* (1972), his last.

Marshall, Thurgood, U.S. judge (b. July 2, 1908, Baltimore, Md.—d. Jan. 24, 1993, Bethesda, Md.), profoundly influenced civil rights legislation, first as a lawyer and chief counsel (1938–61) for the National Association for the Advancement of Colored People (NAACP) and then as the first African-American to sit (1967–91) as a justice on the U.S. Supreme Court. Marshall, the great-grandson of a freed slave, graduated (1930) from Lincoln University, in Lincoln University, Pa., before enrolling in Howard University Law School in Washington, D.C., where he graduated magna cum laude in 1933. He had been denied admission to the University of Maryland Law School because he was black. After joining the legal staff of the NAACP (1936) and launching an attack against state segregation, Marshall triumphed in a lawsuit that forced the University of Maryland

JOSE R. LOPEZ—THE NEW YORK TIMES

to integrate. His most famous case, however, was the 1954 landmark *Brown* v. *Board of Education of Topeka,* in which racial segregation in U.S. public schools was declared unconstitutional. With his characteristic plainspoken, forthright style, Marshall won 29 of the 32 cases he argued before the Supreme Court (14 as a private lawyer and 18 as solicitor general), notably ones that eliminated racial discrimination in voting, housing, and public facilities. He had already established a reputation as "Mr. Civil Rights" when Pres. John F. Kennedy appointed him to the U.S. Court of Appeals in 1961; his confirmation, however, was stalled for nearly a year by Southern senators. After taking office in 1962, he strengthened constitutional safeguards against illegal searches and seizures in the home, struck down loyalty oaths for teachers, and curbed the power of immigration authorities to summarily deport aliens. In 1965 Pres.

Lyndon B. Johnson appointed Marshall solicitor general, and two years later he elevated him to the Supreme Court. Marshall's appointment produced a liberal majority in the conservative court, and he wrote a number of majority opinions, notably the 1969 decision in which the court ruled that private possession of pornography was not a crime and the 1972 ruling that struck down state capital punishment laws. An engaging raconteur, Marshall brought a unique and influential insight into the court, recounting his experiences in the South as a civil rights champion. Later, when Republican administrations appointed conservatives to the court, Marshall, a stalwart liberal, became known as the "great dissenter." He wrote minority opinions to a 1973 case in which the court ruled that a property tax system that unequally distributed resources did not violate the constitution and to a 1980 court ruling that stipulated that the government did not have to fund abortions for poor women. Through failing health Marshall remained on the court, but in June 1991 he announced his impending retirement (which became effective the following October), unable to wait any longer for an administration that would appoint a liberal to his seat. In 1993 two biographies appeared: *Dream Makers, Dream Breakers* by Carl T. Rowan and *Thurgood Marshall* by Michael D. Davis and Hunter R. Clark.

Maynard, Robert Clyve, U.S. journalist and newspaper publisher (b. June 17, 1937, New York, N.Y.—d. Aug. 17, 1993, Oakland, Calif.), inspired and was mentor to hundreds of minority journalists as the first African-American to gain, through sheer determination, a prominent position in U.S. publishing; he was the first black national correspondent and the first black editor and owner of a major daily newspaper. Though Maynard dropped out of school as a teenager, he remained single-minded in his pursuit of a journalistic career. He served as a cub reporter for the black weekly *New York Age* but was turned down for more than 300 jobs at white-owned papers. In 1961, however, he finally landed a job in Pennsylvania with the *York Gazette and Daily*. After making his mark there and gaining a Nieman fellowship to Harvard University, Maynard was offered a position with the *Washington Post*, where he became a national correspondent in 1967. He rose in prominence and served as the paper's ombudsman and in 1976 was chosen as one of the three who questioned Jimmy Carter and Gerald Ford in their final presidential debate. The following year he cofounded the Institute for Journalism Education in Berkeley, Calif., where hundreds of aspiring minority journalists learned their craft. Maynard believed that "this country cannot be the country we all want it to be if its story is told by only one group of citizens." In 1979 he was hired by Gannet Co. to serve as editor of the *Oakland Tribune*. In 1983, with not a penny of his own money, he bought the financially troubled paper from that company for $22 million and embarked on massive improvement efforts. Under his direction the *Tribune* garnered hundreds of awards for editorial excellence, but Maynard, battling prostate cancer, was forced to sell the unprofitable newspaper in 1992.

Mikardo, Ian, British politician (b. July 9, 1908, Portsmouth, Hampshire, England—d. May 6, 1993, Stockport, Greater Manchester, England), was one of the Labour Party's most outspoken and influential members of Parliament (1945–59; 1964–87) although he was never named to a ministerial post and remained a backbencher all his life. Mikardo, the son of Polish and Ukrainian immigrants, grew up in London's East End and spoke mainly Yiddish as a child. He worked at a variety of odd jobs until he entered politics. At the 1944 Labour Party national conference, he delivered a fiery speech demanding a return to socialist principles and successfully introduced a resolution calling for the wholesale nationalization of British industry. In the 1945 general election, Labour swept to victory, and Mikardo took the previously safe Tory seat for Reading, which he represented until he was unexpectedly ousted in 1959. He returned in 1964 as the member for Poplar, and in subsequent Labour governments he led the radical backbench opposition to Prime Ministers Harold Wilson and James Callaghan. Mikardo held many party positions, including party chairman (1970–71) and chairman of the international committee (1973–78). In 1980 he helped engineer the election of his friend and ally Michael Foot as Labour leader. A lifelong leftist, Mikardo was vice president (1978–83) and honorary president (1983–93) of the Socialist International. He retired in 1987 and published his autobiography, *Back-Bencher,* in 1988.

Mize, John Robert ("JOHNNY"; "THE BIG CAT"), U.S. baseball player (b. Jan. 7, 1913, Demorest, Ga.—d. June 2, 1993, Demorest), was a slow-moving right-handed first baseman but a powerhouse left-handed hitter whose unique, graceful swinging style earned him the moniker "the Big Cat." His heavy Southern drawl spawned the nickname "Big Jawn." Mize belted 359 home runs during a 15-year major-league career with the St. Louis Cardinals (1936–41), New York Giants (1942–49), and New York Yankees (1949–53). Mize, who as a youth also excelled in tennis, honed his legendary hand-eye coordination by batting a tennis ball against a barn with a broomstick. He was a high school baseball star and, after turning professional, he made several incredible achievements. Mize was the only major-league player to hit three home runs in a game six times, had eight pinch-hit home runs, led or tied for the lead in home runs four times (28 in 1939, 43 in 1940, 51 in 1947, and 40 in 1948), led the National League with 16 triples in 1938 and 39 doubles in 1941, and in 1947 led the majors with 138 runs batted in. Mize retired in 1953 with a .312 batting average and was inducted into the Baseball Hall of Fame in 1981.

Montoya, Carlos García, Spanish-born guitarist and composer (b. Dec. 13, 1903, Madrid, Spain—d. March 3, 1993, Wainscott, N.Y.), transformed flamenco guitar music from its traditional use as an accompaniment to Andalusian gypsy folk dancers and singers to an internationally recognized musical art form. Montoya was born into a gypsy family and studied guitar with his mother and a neighbouring barber and music teacher, Pepe el Barbero. His uncle, Ramón Montoya, was already an influential solo guitarist, and the young Carlos began accompanying flamenco singers and dancers in cafés at age 14. In the 1920s and '30s, Montoya toured Europe, Asia, and North America with various performers, including the great dancer La Argentina. When World War II broke out, he was on a U.S. tour with another dancer, La Argentinita. He settled in New York City and later became a U.S. citizen. After La Argentinita died (1945), Montoya toured on his own, playing fiery improvisational flamenco, as well as inspired adaptations of blues, jazz, and popular music, with symphony orchestras and in solo recitals. He also appeared on television and recorded some 40 albums, notably *Suite Flamenca,* a concerto he wrote and recorded with the St. Louis (Mo.) Symphony Orchestra in 1966.

Moore, Charles, U.S. architect (b. Oct. 31, 1925, Benton Harbor, Mich.—d. Dec. 16, 1993, Austin, Texas), was one of the most important and prolific advocates of the informed and eclectic style known as Postmodernism; he was influential as an architect, educator, and author. Moore graduated from the University of Michigan in 1947 and received his Ph.D. from Princeton University in 1957. He came to prominence in the 1960s as a member of the partnership that came to be known as MLTW/Moore Turnbull. In 1966 Moore gained acclaim for his Sea Ranch condominium project in California. The resort featured a style that seemed to reflect its dramatic cliff-side location and one that became popular for many suburban developments. Other important projects included the Piazza d'Italia in New Orleans, La. (1978), and the Alumni Center at the University of California at Irvine, (1983–85). Moore taught at numerous universities and served as the chairman of the architecture departments at the University of California at Berkeley (1962–65) and Yale University (1965–69); from 1985 he held the O'Neil Ford chair in architecture at the University of Texas at Austin. He wrote or cowrote 11 books, notably *Body, Memory and Architecture* (1978; with Kent Bloomer) and won the prestigious 1991 Gold Medal of the American Institute of Architects.

Moore, Garry (THOMAS GARRISON MORFIT), U.S. television personality (b. Jan. 31, 1915, Baltimore, Md.—d. Nov. 29, 1993, Hilton Head Island, S.C.), was the winsome television host whose folksy charm attracted viewers to the variety program "The Garry Moore Show" (1950–64 and 1966–67) and such quiz forums as "I've Got a Secret" (1952–64) and "To Tell the Truth" (1969–76). Moore, who was distinguished by a trademark bow tie and crew cut, quit high school to work in radio, where he met Durward Kirby, who became his sidekick and announcer on his variety show. That pioneering program helped launch the careers of such comedians as Carol Burnett, Don Knotts, and Jonathan Winters. "The Garry Moore Show," which reached the height of its popularity in the 1950s, went off the air after losing ground with its younger audience. Moore sailed around the world before the show reappeared in 1966 against "Bonanza" and was canceled because of poor ratings. Moore left television in 1977 after developing throat cancer.

Moore, Robert Frederick Chelsea ("BOBBY"), British footballer (b. April 12, 1941, Barking, Essex, England—d. Feb. 24, 1993, London, England), was the "golden boy of English soccer" and captain of the national side that defeated West Germany 4–2 in the 1966 World Cup final at Wembley Stadium in London; it was England's only World Cup championship and the high point of Moore's 19-year, 1,000-game career. Moore, an inspired defensive player, made his professional debut with West Ham United in 1958, and within months he was captain of the England Youth side. In 1964 he was named Footballer of the Year after leading West Ham to the 1963–64 FA Cup championship, and the next year he guided the club to the European Cup-Winners' Cup title. In 1973, after 544 games with West Ham, he transferred to the Fulham Football Club, where he played another 124 games before retiring in 1977. Moore played 18 games for England Youth and 8 for the Under-23s before joining the senior side in 1962 against Peru, the first of 108 games for England (90 as captain). He faced the darkest point in his career when he was falsely accused of stealing a diamond bracelet in Bogotá, Colombia, just days before the 1970 World Cup began in Mexico. Despite the bad publicity and personal strain, he played brilliantly in England's hard-fought 1–0 semifinal loss to Brazil. Moore made his last international appearance in 1974. After retiring from Fulham in 1977, he played briefly in the U.S. and managed the Oxford City club (1979–81) and Southend United (1983–86). Later he became a sports editor (1986–90) and radio commentator (1990–93). Moore was made an Officer of the Order of the British Empire in 1967.

Moores, Sir John, British entrepreneur (b. Jan. 25, 1896, Eccles, Lancashire, England—d. Sept. 25, 1993, Freshfield, Merseyside, England), parlayed a small football pools business into the U.K.'s largest private company; with a fortune estimated at over £1.5 billion, he was reputed to be the second wealthiest man in Britain and the ninth wealthiest person in the world. His Littlewoods Organisation comprised more than 120 stores and employed some 30,000 people. Moores left school at age 14 and became a post office messenger, studying telegraphy at night. At 16 he went to work for the Commercial Cable Co. and, after spending part of World War I in the Royal Navy, he was posted (1921) to an isolated cable station in Ireland. There he began importing goods to sell to co-workers. Back in England in 1923, Moores and two partners set up a football pool in Liverpool. When at first it lost money, Moores bought out his partners. With the help of family members, he persevered, however, and by 1932 he was a millionaire. He left the pools in the hands of his brother, Cecil, and launched Littlewoods Mail Order. Business boomed, and he organized a division of chain stores in 1936, with the first one opening in Blackpool the following year. During World War II he concentrated on manufacturing war equipment, eventually employing 44,000 people in 16 factories. After the war his attention returned to the retail empire, which continued to grow and thrive. Moores retired as chairman of Littlewoods in 1982 but remained president for life. He was also a notable philanthropist and art patron. Moores was made Companion of the Order of the British Empire in 1972 and was knighted in 1980.

Mori, Taikichiro, Japanese real estate tycoon (b. 1904, Tokyo, Japan—d. Jan. 30, 1993, Tokyo), was a self-made billionaire who amassed a fortune after retiring at age 55 as head of the School of Commerce at Yokohama City University and entering the family real estate concern, Mori Building Co. Mori, an unassuming mogul who neither smoked nor drank, was dedicated to redevelopment—replacing the type of buildings

AP/WIDE WORLD

(especially the wooden ones) that he saw destroyed in the earthquake of 1923 with steel-frame concrete structures. Mori transformed downtown Tokyo from a clutter of narrow lanes populated with houses, small shops, and workshops into a modern urban centre of "smart buildings" equipped with computer-driven heating systems, electronic "talking" elevators, and electric curtains. These sleek glass, concrete, and brick towers boasted foundations secured with an intricate system of rollers designed to absorb the shock of earthquakes. Mori graduated (1928) from Tokyo Shoka University (now Hitotsubashi University) and pursued an academic career before taking over the modest holdings (two buildings) of the Mori Building Co. after the death of his father in 1959. An enormous growth and economic boom in real estate fueled his progress, and he was especially successful in persuading local residents to cooperate with his development plans. At the time of his death, his company controlled 83 buildings in the centre of Tokyo, the most expensive real estate in the world. Mori was especially proud of the Ark Hills high-technology office-apartment complex he built in the centre of Tokyo during the 1980s. Another such project, Shiroyama Hills, opened in 1991. For that year and in 1992, Mori was ranked by *Forbes* magazine as the wealthiest private citizen in the world; his wealth was estimated to be $13 billion.

Mosconi, William Joseph ("WILLIE"), U.S. billiards player (b. June 21, 1913, Philadelphia, Pa.—d. Sept. 16, 1993, Haddon Heights, N.J.), reigned as world pocket billiards champion 15 times and was renowned both for his accurate, rapid-fire shots and for dismantling the image associated with the sport as one played in smoky pool parlours populated with hustlers and drunks. Though his father owned a pool hall, Mosconi was not allowed to use the cues or balls, so he practiced shooting round potatoes into the pockets with a broomstick. Mosconi's stylish dress (he always wore a jacket while playing) and finesse around the billiard table were in sharp contrast to his nemesis, hustler Rudolph ("Minnesota Fats") Wanderone, whom Mosconi easily defeated in a celebrated 1978 television match. Mosconi, who once had an incredible run (series of successful shots) of 526 balls in a 1954 exhibition game, also set numerous tournament records, including the fastest game on record with 125 points in 30 minutes. Though a stroke sidelined the champion in 1957, he soon returned to tournament play and continued to serve as a consultant to the Brunswick Corp., a sports-equipment manufacturer. He also lent his technical expertise, including the shooting of fancy shots, to the production of such films as *The Hustler* (1961) and its sequel, *The Color of Money* (1986). Mosconi was the author of *Willie Mosconi on Pocket Billiards* (1959), *Winning Pocket Billiards* (1965), and an autobiography, *Willie's Game* (1993).

Nabiyev, Rakhmon Nabiyevich, Tajik political leader (b. Oct. 5, 1930, Shaykhburhan, Khujand *rayon* (sector), Tajik S.S.R., U.S.S.R.—d. April 10–11, 1993, Khujand, Tajikistan), was a devout member of the Communist Party of the Soviet Union (CPSU) and twice (1982–85, 1991–92) head of a Tajik Communist government. Nabiyev was educated at the Tashkent Institute of Irrigation and Mechanized Agriculture and worked as an agricultural engineer in Khujand until he joined the CPSU in 1960. Thereafter he held government posts in agriculture, in the Central Committee of the Tajik Communist Party, and in the Tajikistan Council of Ministers. As Communist Party boss, he ruled the republic from April 1982 until December 1985, when he was ousted from power in a series of sweeping reforms by Soviet leader Mikhail Gorbachev. Nabiyev made a political comeback during the breakup of the Soviet Union and was elected president of independent Tajikistan in November 1991. However, he failed to prevent civil war between his hard-line Communist supporters and a coalition of pro-democratic and pro-Islamic insurgents. He was forced to resign at gunpoint in September 1992, and when the Communists regained control two months later, he was not restored to office.

Ndadaye, Melchior, Burundian banker and politician (b. March 28, 1953, Nyabihanga, Muramvya, Burundi—d. Oct. 21, 1993, Near Bujumbura, Burundi), became Burundi's president and the first member of the Hutu ethnic majority to rule after his Front for Democracy in Burundi (Frodebu) and two allied parties won two-thirds of the seats in the National Assembly in June 1993 elections. His triumph in the country's first free elections after 26 years of military rule marked the end of centuries of domination of the Hutu by the Tutsi, who initially accepted their historic defeat. Ndadaye, a banking executive, spent many years in exile in neighbouring Rwanda after the massacre of some 200,000 Hutu in 1972. After fleeing into exile, he studied at the teacher training college in Butare, Rwanda, and served as a teacher and part-time university lecturer. After returning to Burundi, Ndadaye worked at a neurological and psychiatric centre before serving as a training manager with the Savings and Credit Cooperative. After five years in that post, he took a correspondence course in banking, and in 1989 he was appointed adviser to the Rural Development Ministry. He worked at the Meridien BIAO bank from 1989 until his election as president. Ndadaye was known for his calm demeanour and for his skill in leading Frodebu through difficult times. As president he appointed a broadly based government, including a woman prime minister (a Tutsi), and he promised to work for national reconciliation and to strengthen Burundi's human rights. His reign was abruptly ended by the Tutsi, however, when he was killed in a bloody coup led by former president Jean-Baptiste Bagaza and Army Chief of Staff Col. Jean Bikomagu.

Niederland, William Guglielmo, German-born U.S. psychoanalyst (b. Aug. 29, 1904, Schippenbeil, East Prussia [now Sepopol, Poland]—d. July 30, 1993, Englewood, N.J.), was the first to formulate (1961) a "survivor syndrome," which he defined as a feeling of self-reproach and severe guilt among survivors of Nazi death camps, natural disasters, and automobile accidents and which was manifested by symptoms of insomnia, nightmares, personality changes, chronic depression, disturbances of memory, anxiety, and psychosomatic illnesses. Niederland himself was a refugee from Nazi Germany, was interned in Britain as an enemy alien, and was able to assimilate some of his own experiences into his work. He had received M.D.'s from the Universities of Würzburg, Germany, and Genoa, Italy, before obtaining another from the New York Institute of Psychoanalysis. Niederland practiced medicine in Milan and served as a ship's doctor in the Philippines before arriving in New York in 1940. In his private practice he treated more than 800 persons who had been subjected to massive cumulative trauma, and from these sessions he coined the term *survivor syndrome.* Niederland taught at the University of Tampa, Fla., served as a staff psychiatrist at Mount Sinai Medical Center in New York City, and from 1952 to 1974 was in private practice while also teaching. Niederland was intrigued with studying the psychological motives of explorers, including Columbus, and what he termed the "dark roots of creativity," an unconscious factor such as a defect or malformation that could result in "heightened bodily sensation" and spark genius. He was the author of some 200 articles and such books as *Man-made Plague: A Primer on Neurosis* (1948), *Psychic Traumatization* (1971), and *The Schreber Case: Psychoanalytic Profile of a Paranoid Personality* (1974), one of his most famous studies.

Nikolais, Alwin, U.S. choreographer, designer, and composer (b. Nov. 25, 1912, Southington, Conn.—d. May 8, 1993, New York, N.Y.), created works that combined motion with shapes, colours, and sound. He was known for high-tech multimedia dance spectacles that used slide projections, light playing on the performers' bodies, unusual fabrics and costumes, abstract props, and original, often electronic, music. Nikolais played piano for silent films in the late 1920s and then worked as a puppeteer before studying dance with protégés, including Hanya Holm, of the German dancer Mary Wigman. He began teaching and choreographing in the late 1930s. In 1948 Nikolais joined the Henry Street Settlement Playhouse in New York City, and what became his dance company grew out of activities there. His first major work, *Masks, Props, and Mobiles* (1953), featured dancers in stretch fabrics. Among later works were *Kaleidoscope* (1956), *Allegory* (1959), and *Imago* (1963). Beginning in the 1960s his company toured the U.S. and Europe and, later, other parts of the world. His work was especially popular in France, where he was artistic director of the Centre Nationale de Danse Contemporaine, in Angers, from 1979 to 1981. He received the Kennedy Center Honors and the National Medal of Arts, and the French republic made him a knight of the Legion of Honour. In 1989 his company merged with the group of longtime partner Murray Louis to form Nikolais and Murray Louis Dance. A retrospective of his work opened in New York in July 1993.

Nixon, Patricia ("PAT"; THELMA CATHERINE RYAN), U.S. first lady (b. March 16, 1912, Ely, Nev.—d. June 22, 1993, Park Ridge, N.J.), was a gracious hostess during her years in the White House and became a symbol of dignity and fortitude; she was especially remembered for her unswerving loyalty when her husband, Richard M. Nixon, was forced to resign as U.S. president (Aug. 9, 1974) amid the Watergate scandal. She was the daughter of a one-time coal miner turned farmer, who nicknamed her "Pat" in honour of her birth on the eve of St. Patrick's Day. She recalled her childhood near Los Angeles on a truck farm as one of hard work, picking crops and digging potatoes. After her mother died when she was 12 years old and her father succumbed five years later, she moved to New York City, where she worked as a secretary and as an X-ray technician. She saved enough money to return to California, and she helped finance her education at the University of Southern California by working as a motion-picture extra. After graduating cum laude in 1937, she taught typing and shorthand in Whittier, Calif., where in 1938, at rehearsals for a play, she met Richard M. Nixon, a recent law school graduate. After marrying in 1940 she bore two daughters, Tricia and Julie, and, after reconciling herself to the political life her husband had chosen, she became a stalwart campaigner for him. As first lady she entertained extensively, headed U.S. delegations, promoted education programs and volunteer work, and gathered more than 500 historical paintings for the White House collection. She was rarely seen in public after Nixon resigned, and the two moved to San Clemente, Calif., and then to New Jersey. She suffered a stroke in 1976 and another in 1983 and was in frail health for many years. She died of lung cancer.

Noonuccal, Oodgeroo (KATH WALKER; KATHLEEN JEAN MARY RUSKA), Australian Aboriginal poet and writer (b. Nov. 3, 1920, Stradbroke Island, Queensland, Australia—d. Sept. 16, 1993, Brisbane, Australia), was the first Aborigine to have her works published, and she used those works to champion the cause of civil rights for Australia's indigenous peoples. On Stradbroke Island, where she grew up, many of the ancient Aboriginal customs were still practiced, and her upbringing exposed her to native traditions. Noonuccal left school at 13 to work as a domestic and then joined the Australian Women's Army Service when World War II broke out. Her awareness of the plight of the Aborigines grew, and she became an activist for Aboriginal rights. She began to write poetry, and her first book, *We Are Going* (1964), sold out in three days. Other works of poetry, fiction, essays, and folktales followed, including *The Dawn Is at Hand* (1966), *Stradbroke Dreamtime* (1972), *Father Sky and Mother Earth* (1981), and *The Rainbow Serpent* (1988). She successfully campaigned for the passage of a referendum (1967) that for the first time gave constitutional recognition to Aborigines. She was made a Member of the Order of the British Empire in 1970, but in 1988, during celebrations of the 200 years of European settlement in Australia, she returned the honour to Queen Elizabeth II to protest the history of mistreatment of Aboriginal people. At that same time, she changed her name from Kath Walker to a traditional tribal name.

Nosaka, Sanzo, Japanese politician (b. March 30, 1892, Yamaguchi prefecture, Japan—d. Nov. 14, 1993, Tokyo, Japan), held sway for more than 70 years in the Japan Communist Party (JCP) as one of its founders in 1922, as chairman of the Central Committee from 1958 to 1982, and as honorary chairman from 1982. He was disgraced and expelled from the party as a traitor in December 1992, however, when it came to light that he had falsely accused (in a 1939 letter to the KGB in Moscow) Comintern comrade Kenzo Yamamoto and his common-law wife of spying for the *kempeitai* (Japanese military police). The two were executed by a Soviet firing squad. Nosaka, who graduated (1917) from Keio University, was studying in England when he joined the British Communist Party upon its formation in 1920, a move that precipitated his deportation. In Japan Nosaka became a trade union organizer and editor of the Communist Party's newspaper, *Musansha Shimbun.* His political agitation resulted in two imprisonments, and in 1931 he and his wife, Rye, were sent by the party to Russia, where he served as an executive member of the Comintern, the Soviet organization in charge of the international activities of the Communist Party. During World War II Nosaka was in China working with Mao Zedong (Mao Tse-tung). He also formed the Japan Liberation League and conducted propagandist activities against the Japanese army. After returning to Japan in 1946, Nosaka helped reestablish the JCP and was elected to the lower house of the Diet (parliament). He was one of the leading theoreticians of the party and professed a peaceful evolution into communism. He went underground when the U.S. occupation authorities purged communists from politics during the 1950s Cold War era. He resurfaced in 1955 as first secretary of the JCP and assumed a prominent role as the grand old man of the JCP until the age of 100, when revelations about his former activities destroyed his reputation.

Nouira, Hedi Amira, Tunisian politician (b. April 6, 1911, Monastir, Tunisia—d. Jan. 25, 1993, La Marsa, Tunisia), was the hard-line prime minister of Tunisia for a decade (1970–80) and the designated successor of the president-for-life, Habib Bourguiba, until a stroke ended his political career in March 1980. Nouira was educated in Paris and trained as a lawyer. In 1934 he was a founding member of Bourguiba's nationalist Neo-Destour Party (later renamed the Destourien Socialist Party). He became secretary of the Confederation of Tunisian Workers in 1938, but he was arrested for subversion by the French colonial authorities and held in detention in France until he was released (1940) by the German occupation forces. After returning to Tunisia, Nouira was the Neo-Destour Party's secretary-general (1942–54, 1969–80). He joined the Tunisian government as minister of commerce (1954–55) and finance (1955–58) and then served as governor of the country's newly formed central bank (1958–70). As prime minister from Nov. 2, 1970, he supervised the early stages of Tunisia's economic revival while rejecting calls for multiparty elections and ruthlessly crushing all opposition to President Bourguiba's policies. In 1974 Nouira stepped in to quash a proposed union between Tunisia and Libya.

Nureyev, Rudolf Hametovich, Soviet-born ballet dancer (b. March 17, 1938, near Irkutsk, Russian S.F.S.R., U.S.S.R.—d. Jan. 6, 1993, Paris, France), was one of the most celebrated dancers of the 20th century and the first male superstar of the ballet world since Vaslav Nijinsky. He mesmerized audiences with spectacular leaps and turns, but it was his passionate temperament and flamboyance onstage and off that made him a phenomenon. Nureyev, who was of Tatar descent, was reared in Moscow and Ufa, where he studied dance and apprenticed with the Ufa Ballet. He was an outstanding but rebellious student at the Leningrad Ballet School from 1955 to 1958, when he bypassed the corps de ballet and graduated directly to solo roles with the Kirov Ballet. Three years later, on June 17, 1961, while on tour with the Kirov in Paris, he eluded Soviet security guards and requested asylum from officials at Le Bourget airport. In the following months he performed in Paris, New York City, London, and Chicago, but he reached a turning point in 1962 when he partnered the British Royal Ballet's acclaimed ballerina Margot Fonteyn, who was 19 years his senior. Nureyev's fiery virtuosity proved to be a perfect counterpoint to Fonteyn's elegant maturity, and their long partnership rejuvenated her career and established his. Despite his association with the Royal Ballet as a "permanent guest artist" for 20 years, Nureyev was not formally affiliated with the dance company. He worked as a guest artist around the world, both as a dancer and later as a choreographer. He was equally admired in classical and modern works, including *Giselle, Swan Lake, Le Corsair, La Bayadère, Marguerite and Armand, Romeo and Juliet, Don Quixote,* and *Lucifer,* which was choreographed for him and Fonteyn by Martha Graham in 1975. In the 1970s Nureyev branched into other performing arts. He appeared on television and in motion pictures, notably *Valentino* (1977), in which he played the legendary silent-film star. He also toured the U.S. as the King of Siam in a revival of the Broadway musical *The King and I,* and he even tried his hand at conducting. Although he became an Austrian citizen in 1982, he lived mainly in Paris, where he was director (1983–89) and principal choreographer (1989–92) of the Paris Opéra Ballet. In 1989 he danced in the Soviet Union (with the Kirov) for the first time since his defection. Nureyev made his last public appearance in October 1992, taking a bow at the Paris premiere of his new production of *La Bayadère.* After his death it was revealed that he had been suffering from AIDS for several years.

MARTHA SWOPE

Ochoa, Severo, Spanish-born molecular biologist (b. Sept. 24, 1905, Luarca, Spain—d. Nov. 1, 1993, Madrid, Spain), was co-winner of the 1959 Nobel Prize for Physiology or Medicine for his work in artificially synthesizing RNA, genetic material essential to the translation into protein of the hereditary information contained in genes. Ochoa shared the prize with Arthur Kornberg, who had synthesized DNA. Ochoa graduated from the University of Málaga, Spain, at the age of 16 and entered the University of Madrid's medical school at age 17. After earning an M.D. degree in 1929, he worked for two years at the laboratory of Nobel Prize-winning biochemist Otto Meyerhof. He briefly served (1935–36) as head of the physiology research division at the medical school of the University of Madrid but left that post because he felt that research opportunities in Spain would be hindered by the civil war. He worked at various European universities before emigrating to the U.S. in 1941. Ochoa joined the staff of New York University in 1942, becoming chairman of the biochemistry department in 1954. While conducting research on high-energy phosphates in 1955, he made an accidental discovery. He found that the bacterial enzyme that he called polynucleotide phosphorylase was able to synthesize RNA from its chemical building blocks, instead of breaking down the molecule as expected; he was then able to create molecules of artificial RNA. It was for this groundbreaking work that Ochoa received the Nobel Prize. As research continued, it was confirmed that the enzyme Ochoa discovered did indeed break down RNA except under specific laboratory conditions, when the enzyme's natural

AP/WIDE WORLD

reaction ran in reverse. From the early 1970s he was associated with the Autonomous University of Madrid and, after leaving New York University in 1974, with the Roche Institute of Molecular Biology in Nutley, N.J. (1974–85).

O'Connell, Helen, U.S. singer (b. May 23, 1920, Lima, Ohio—d. Sept. 9, 1993, San Diego, Calif.), was still a teenager when she joined (1939) Jimmy Dorsey's big band, and she became an overnight sensation after recording "Green Eyes" with crooner Bob Eberly. O'Connell's cool renditions of such other songs as "Tangerine," "Amapola," "Jim," "I Remember You," and "When Arthur Murray Taught Me Dancing in a Hurry" kept her in the limelight. She also appeared with the orchestras of Artie Shaw, Woody Herman, and Glenn Miller until 1943, when she temporarily retired from show business to raise a family. O'Connell was later visible on television in the 1950s as host of "TV's Top Tunes," as a featured vocalist on the "Russ Morgan Show," as Dave Garroway's sidekick on the "Today Show," and as the star of her own twice-weekly 15-minute program, "The Helen O'Connell Show." For nine years she was also cohost, with Bob Barker, of the "Miss Universe Pageant." From 1978 to 1979 O'Connell toured with singers Rosemary Clooney, Margaret Whiting, and Rose Marie in a highly successful concert revue, "4 Girls 4."

Ozal, Turgut, Turkish politician (b. Oct. 13, 1927, Malatya, Turkey—d. April 17, 1993, Ankara, Turkey), dominated Turkish politics for nearly a decade; as prime minister (1983–89) and president (1989–93), he pushed Turkey onto the world stage through free-market economic reforms and closer commercial and political ties with the West. Ozal studied electrical engineering at Istanbul Technical University (M.S., 1950) and economics during a brief stay in the U.S. (1952–53). He oversaw the construction of hydroelectric power stations in Turkey's massive electrification program and served as a technical adviser to the Defense Ministry, the State Planning Organization (SPO), and Prime Minister Suleyman Demirel. In 1967 he was named SPO undersecretary. After Demirel was ousted in a military coup (1971), Ozal worked in the private sector and at the World Bank in Washington, D.C. (1971–73). Demirel regained power in 1975, and Ozal resumed his post at the SPO four years later. In 1980, after the military once again took control, Ozal stayed on to direct his painful but ultimately successful economic austerity program. In 1983 he formed the Motherland Party, which won the general election later that year and put him at the head of a new civilian government. By the time he became president in 1989, Ozal had revived the economy, increased external trade, strengthened Turkey's commitment to NATO, and applied to join the European Community. In 1990 he used Turkey's pivotal geographic location to command a central role in the Western-Arab alliance against Iraq's invasion of Kuwait, and after the breakup of the Soviet Union the next year, he offered his secular Muslim government as a role model for the newly independent Central Asian republics.

Parkinson, C(yril) Northcote, British historian (b. July 30, 1909, Barnard Castle, Durham, England—d. March 9, 1993, Canterbury, Kent, England), formulated "Parkinson's Law," the oft-repeated dictum "Work expands so as to fill the time available for its completion." He later discovered (as he called it) ancillary laws, including "Expenditure rises to meet income." Parkinson showed a flair for expressing serious economic and social "truths" in the form of pithy witticisms and humorous paradoxes that captured the public's fancy and made him an international celebrity. After studying history at Emmanuel College, Cambridge (B.A., 1932), and King's College, London (Ph.D., 1935), he taught at Cambridge and at a boys' school in Devon (1937–39). He later said that his laws were inspired by his experiences as an army staff officer during World War II, when he observed bureaucrats making work for each other and expanding their staffs in order to enhance their own prestige. After the war he taught naval history at the University of Liverpool. In 1950 Parkinson moved to Singapore, where he was Raffles professor of history at the University of Malaya (1950–58). In 1955 he published his first law in a dry, tongue-in-cheek article in *The Economist* magazine. He expanded his ideas in a series of books, including *Parkinson's Law, or The Pursuit of Progress* (1958), *The Law and The Profits* (1960), and *Mrs. Parkinson's Law, and Other Studies in Domestic Science* (1968). From 1958 to 1960 he was a visiting professor in the U.S.; thereafter he wrote and traveled the after-dinner lecture circuit until he retired to Kent in 1989. In addition to his more famous books, Parkinson wrote serious historical works, notably *The Evolution of Political Thought* (1958) and *Britannia Rules: The Classic Age of Naval History, 1793–1815* (1977); several novels; biographies of fictional characters such as C.S. Forester's Horatio Hornblower and P.G. Wodehouse's Jeeves; and an autobiography.

Paul, Wolfgang, German physicist (b. Aug. 10, 1913, Lorenzkirch, Germany—d. Dec. 6/7, 1993, Bonn, Germany), developed the Paul trap, an electromagnetic device that captures ions and holds them long enough for study and precise measurement of their properties. For his work he shared the 1989 Nobel Prize for Physics with Hans G. Dehmelt and Norman F. Ramsey. Paul studied physics and engineering at technological institutes in Munich and Berlin, receiving (1939) a doctoral degree from the Technical University in Berlin. During World War II he was part of a group researching a method of producing material to be used in atomic bombs, though he later opposed the possession of nuclear weapons by the German military. In 1944 he became a lecturer at the University of Göttingen, and from 1950 he was a full professor. In 1952 he also became director of the Physics Institute at the University of Bonn. In addition, Paul was involved in the development of the European Organization for Nuclear Research (CERN) in Geneva, was president of the Alexander von Humboldt Foundation (1979–89), and received a number of honorary degrees.

AP/WIDE WORLD

Peale, Norman Vincent, U.S. religious leader (b. May 31, 1898, Bowersville, Ohio—d. Dec. 24, 1993, Pawling, N.Y.), was an influential and inspirational clergyman who, after World War II, tried to instill a spiritual renewal in the U.S. with his sermons, broadcasts, newspaper columns, and books; he encouraged millions with his 1952 best-seller, *The Power of Positive Thinking*, a classic that ranked (behind the Bible) as one of the highest-selling spiritual books in history. Peale was attracted to the ministry by his father, a Methodist preacher who advised his son "that the way to the human heart is through simplicity." Later some criticized Peale for oversimplifying Christianity in his uplifting sermons and avoiding deeper confrontations with sin and guilt. Peale, who graduated from Ohio Wesleyan University, was ordained in the Methodist Episcopal Church in 1922 and continued theological studies at Boston University, where he earned bachelor of sacred theology and master of arts in social ethics

ARCHIVE PHOTOS

degrees in 1924. That year he was assigned to a small congregation in Brooklyn, N.Y., and during his three-year tenure there he built a new church and increased membership from 40 to 900. In 1927 Peale moved to the University Methodist Church in Syracuse, N.Y., and joined a select few who preached on their own radio program. Five years later Peale changed his denominational affiliation to the Dutch Reformed Church in order to accept the pastorate at the Marble Collegiate Church in New York City. His dynamic sermons helped increase church membership, and they were televised during the 1950s. In answer to the many problems facing his congregation, Peale also established a clinic and enlisted the aid of a psychiatrist to help handle parishioners' complex psychological problems. In 1951 that operation was organized as a nonprofit American Foundation of Religion and Psychiatry, with Peale acting as president. After World War II Peale published and served as editor of a weekly four-page spiritual leaflet for businessmen called *Guideposts,* which during the 1950s appeared as a monthly magazine with some two million subscribers. Peale and his wife also appeared (1952–68) on the television program "What's Your Trouble?" Among Peale's other publications are *The Art of Living* (1937), *You Can Win* (1938), *A Guide for Confident Living* (1948), and *This Incredible Century* (1991). He retired as senior pastor in 1984.

Pennel, John Thomas, U.S. pole-vaulter (b. July 25, 1940, Memphis, Tenn.—d. Sept. 26, 1993, Santa Monica, Calif.), shattered the pole-vaulting world record eight times during the 1960s, beginning in 1963 with a 4.95-m (16-ft 2¾-in) vault and a thrilling 5.20-m (17-ft ¾-in) benchmark vault, which made him the first person to clear 5.18 m (17 ft). Pennel, who competed for Northeast Louisiana State College (later Northeast Louisiana University), used the then revolutionary fibreglass pole instead of a traditional aluminum pole to accomplish his stunning feats. Though Pennel was the recipient of the 1963 Sullivan Award as the nation's top amateur athlete and was expected to take home a medal from the 1964 Olympic Games in Tokyo, he suffered injuries that prevented him from gaining a top finish (he placed 11th). Pennel placed a disappointing fifth at the 1968 Olympics in Mexico City. In 1969, however, he cleared 5.44 m (17 ft 10¼ in), a personal best. A succession of injuries forced Pennel to retire from vaulting.

Petrovic, Drazen, Croatian basketball player (b. Oct. 22, 1964, Sibenik, Yugos.—d. June 7, 1993, near Ingolstadt, Germany), won two Olympic silver medals, first for Yugoslavia (1988) and then for independent Croatia (1992), before signing on as one of the National Basketball Association's (NBA's) hottest young shooting guards. Petrovic, a 1.95-m (6-ft 5-in) powerhouse, turned down an offer from the University of Notre Dame at the age of 19 in order to remain in Europe. He played one season (1988–89) in Spain, leading Real Madrid to the 1989 European Cup title. At the end of that season, the NBA's Portland Trail Blazers bought out his contract and selected him in the players draft. In January 1991 he was traded to the New Jersey Nets, where he became one of the league's top three-point shooters, averaging 22.3 points per game in his last season. He was returning to his family's home in Zagreb after playing for Croatia in a European championship qualifying tournament in Poland when the car in which he was riding crashed into a truck on a rain-slick road between Nürnberg and Munich. Petrovic was lionized as a national hero in Croatia, where his funeral drew thousands of mourning fans.

Pharaon, Henri-Philippe, Lebanese politician and businessman (b. 1901?, Alexandria, Egypt?—d. Aug. 6, 1993, Beirut, Lebanon), was a founding father of independent Lebanon, the designer of the Lebanese national flag, and a champion of peaceful coexistence between Christians and Muslims. Pharaon was born into a wealthy Greek Catholic family and educated in Switzerland and France, where he received a law degree. He entered the parliament when Lebanon gained independence from France (1943–46). As foreign minister (1945; 1946–47), he oversaw Lebanon's role as a founding member of the Arab League. In the late 1950s he sought to mediate between the country's pro-Western and pro-Arab factions, but when he was not appointed to the compromise Cabinet, he gradually withdrew from politics. Pharaon's business interests included a major role in the port of Beirut, control of one of the country's leading banks, a fabulous art collection he acquired for the Pharaon palace in central Beirut, and one of the world's largest stables of Arabian racehorses.

Philbrick, Herbert Arthur, U.S. advertising salesman, writer, and spy (b. May 11, 1915?—d. Aug. 16, 1993, North Hampton, N.H.), infiltrated the Communist Party for the FBI while posing as a loyal member of the party and holding a job in advertising; he chronicled this deception in his best-selling 1952 autobiography, *I Led Three Lives*, which was adapted into a popular television series in 1953. Philbrick joined the Massachusetts Youth Council in the 1940s and later realized that the organization was a front for the Communist Party. After he informed the FBI of his suspicions, he was asked to remain with that group and supply information to the agency. Philbrick rose through party ranks, describing himself as "one of the most hardworking Communists in New England." Because of his inside information, Philbrick was called as a surprise witness at the 1949 conspiracy trial of 11 Communist leaders. After his testimony ensured their conviction, he recounted his spy activities in 17 serialized installments in the *New York Herald Tribune*. Philbrick then returned to advertising before working for federal nuclear regulators and finally as president of a not-for-profit educational organization.

Phoenix, River, U.S. actor (b. Aug. 23, 1970, Madras, Ore.—d. Oct. 31, 1993, Los Angeles, Calif.), secured a reputation as a promising young star with his intense portrayal of a tough youth in the 1986 film *Stand by Me*, about a group of boys who find a corpse in the woods. After debuting in *Explorers* (1985), Phoenix earned plaudits for his roles in such films as *The Mosquito Coast* (1986), *Little Nikita* (1988), *A Night in the Life of Jimmy Reardon* (1988), and *Indiana Jones and the Last Crusade* (1989). He received an Academy Award nomination for best supporting actor for his stirring performance as a gifted son of two anti-Vietnam War radicals on the lam in *Running on Empty* (1988). In *My Own Private Idaho* (1991) he portrayed a male hustler, and in *Sneakers* (1992) he appeared as a computer hacker. He was the son of Children of God missionaries, who named him River. His siblings included a brother named Leaf and sisters Summer, Liberty, and Rain. Phoenix was finishing the filming of *Dark Blood* when he collapsed and died of a massive drug overdose outside a Sunset Strip nightclub.

Pleven, René, French politician (b. April 13, 1901, Rennes, France—d. Jan. 13, 1993, Paris, France), held a succession of Cabinet posts in post-World War II France, including two brief periods as prime minister (July 1950–February 1951, August 1951–January 1952); in 1950 he sponsored the unsuccessful Pleven Plan for a unified European army, which laid the groundwork for NATO. After receiving his law degree from the University of Paris, Pleven worked as a telephone company executive in North America and England. In 1940 he joined Charles de Gaulle's Free French government in London. He was elected to the new National Assembly in 1945 and was cofounder (with François Mitterrand) and president (1946–53) of the small Democratic and Socialist Union of the Resistance, which he quit in 1958. Pleven was twice minister of defense (1949–50, 1952–54), and he was harshly criticized for failing to prevent the decisive 1954 defeat of the French army at Dien Bien Phu, Vietnam. He served briefly as foreign minister in 1958 and supported de Gaulle's reelection as president in 1965, but they later had a falling out over France's withdrawal from NATO, and Pleven joined Pres. Georges Pompidou's Cabinet as justice minister in 1969. Pleven lost his legislative seat in the 1973 elections and retired to Bretagne, where he was president of the regional council (1974–76).

Pontecorvo, Bruno, Italian-born British physicist (b. Aug. 22, 1913, Marina di Pisa, Italy—d. Sept. 25, 1993, Dubna, Russia), was a distinguished scientist who defected to the Soviet Union to study the peaceful uses of nuclear power. Pontecorvo was one of eight children born to a Jewish textile merchant. He received his doctorate from the University of Rome, where in the early 1930s he worked with Enrico Fermi. After Mussolini's government passed a series of race laws, Pontecorvo fled to Paris to continue his research. When Paris was invaded by the Germans in 1940, he made his way to the U.S. In 1943 Pontecorvo joined the Anglo-Canadian nuclear research team at Chalf River in Canada. He became a British citizen in 1948, and the following year he joined the Atomic Energy Authority research station at Harwell, England, where classified research was being conducted. While on vacation in Italy in 1950, Pontecorvo, his wife, and three children abruptly left for Stockholm. They then went to Helsinki, Fin., and were not heard from until 1955, when Pontecorvo appeared at a press conference in Moscow to promote the peaceful use of nuclear power. His disappearance had followed revelations that some highly placed scientists (including Klaus Fuchs, one of Pontecorvo's colleagues at Harwell) had given secrets to the Soviet Union and raised fears about how seriously these scientists had endangered the free world. Pontecorvo denied ever having worked on nuclear weapons research. While in the Soviet Union, he worked at the Joint Institute for Nuclear Research outside Moscow. He received numerous awards from the state, including the Lenin Prize (1963) and the Order of Lenin (1983).

Popp, Lucia, Czech-born Austrian lyric soprano (b. Nov. 12, 1939, Uhorska Ves, Czech.—d. Nov. 16, 1993, Munich, Germany), had a light, transparent voice that became weightier as she matured, allowing her to take on heavier operatic roles. She studied music at the academy in Bratislava and made her professional debut in the city in 1963 as Queen of the Night in Mozart's *The Magic Flute*. The role, which was especially well suited to her voice, was one she became closely identified with in her early career. In 1963 Popp also made her debut at the Vienna State Opera, where she formed a lifelong association and was given the honorary title *Kammersängerin* (court singer), and at Salzburg, Austria. Later in the 1960s she made debuts at London's Covent Garden and New York's Metropolitan Opera, and at Cologne, Germany, she appeared in the Mozart cycle staged by Jean-Pierre Ponnelle in the '70s. Although Popp was especially associated with Mozart and Strauss (she sang both Sophie and the Marschallin in Strauss's *Der Rosenkavalier* and recorded his *Four Last Songs* three times), she also sang Janacek, Puccini, and Wagner, appeared as soloist in Handel oratorios and Mahler symphonies, and became a noted recitalist. She made a large number of recordings. Popp died of a brain tumour.

Preil, Gabriel, U.S. poet (b. Aug. 21, 1911, Tartu [Dorpat], Estonia—d. June 5, 1993, Jerusalem, Israel), was internationally acclaimed for his introspective and lyrical poems written in Hebrew, which he deemed the language of his heart. Though he lived most of his life in the U.S., he was a powerful influence on younger Israeli poets, both with his own works and with his translations into Hebrew of such American poets as Robert Frost, Carl Sandburg, and Robinson Jeffers. Preil, who immigrated to the U.S. in 1922 and became a citizen in 1928, settled in New York City, where he attended the Rabbi Isaac Elchanan Theological Seminary and the Teachers Institute (both now part of Yeshiva University). Preil drew inspiration from the New England and New York City autumn landscapes, as evidenced in such volumes as *Nof shemesh u-khfor* (1944; "Landscape of Sun and Frost") and *Autumn Music* (1979; poems in English translation). Some of his other poems were collected in *Mapat 'erev* (1960; "Map of Evening"), *Ner mul kokhavim* (1954; "Candle Under the Stars"), and *Mi-tokh zeman va-nof* (1972; "Of Time and Place"). Among Preil's many honours were the Louis La Med award for Hebrew literature (1942), the National Jewish Book Award for poetry in Hebrew (Kovner Memorial) from the Jewish Book Council and the Jewish Welfare Board (1955 and 1962), and Israel's prestigious Bialik Prize (1992).

Premadasa, Ranasinghe, Sri Lankan politician (b. June 23, 1924, Colombo, Ceylon [now Sri Lanka]—d. May 1, 1993, Colombo), was at the centre of the Sri Lankan government for more than 25 years as leader of the national state assembly (1977–88), prime minister (1978–88), and president (1989–93). Premadasa, a Sinhalese born into the dhobi (washerman's) caste, was the first member of a low caste to lead the country, and he faced considerable resentment from high-caste political opponents. As a youth he was involved in a social movement that promoted Buddhist moral values. He joined the Ceylon Labour Party in 1949 and entered local government in Colombo the next year. In 1956 he ran unsuccessfully for the assembly as a member of the United National Party (UNP). He won a seat in 1960 but lost it when a snap election was called only four months later. When the UNP gained a majority in 1965, he was reelected and named chief government whip. As minister of local government (1968–70; local government, housing, and construction, 1977–88), he oversaw the construction of a million low-cost homes, thereby increasing his support among working-class Sinhalese. In 1987 he opposed the use of Indian troops to fight Tamil separatists in northern Sri Lanka, and there were charges that he supplied arms to the Tamils. Premadasa was often called autocratic and ruthless, but under his tight rule as president there were some signs of progress in the Tamil civil war. He was killed in a suicide bombing only eight days after Lalith Athulathmudali, a former minister of security and the founder of the opposition Democratic United National Front, was shot dead while addressing a provincial election rally.

Price, Vincent, U.S. actor (b. May 27, 1911, St. Louis, Mo.—d. Oct. 25, 1993, Los Angeles, Calif.), as the undisputed dark prince of gothic thrillers, cultivated his image as a debonair yet menacing villain with his silken voice, wicked grin, and imposing figure (he was 1.93 m [6 ft 4 in tall]); his spine-tingling performances coupled with a self-mocking air oozed of treachery in such horror classics as *House of Wax* (1953), *The Tingler* (1959), *Diary of a Madman* (1963), and *Theatre of Blood* (1973). Price, who earned a B.A. in art history and English from Yale University, obtained an advanced degree in fine arts from the University of London. After making his London stage debut in 1935, Price played Prince Albert in the West End production of *Victoria Regina*. He reprised the role on Broadway, and by the time he made his film bow in 1938, he was an established star. His early roles included some romantic leads and historical characterizations, including Sir Walter Raleigh in *The Private Lives of Elizabeth and Essex* (1939), King Charles II in *Hudson's Bay* (1941), and Cardinal Richelieu in *The Three Musketeers* (1948). His mellifluous voice and ghoulish inflections provided narration for a number of films, and his creepy tones represented a ghastly spectre in Michael Jackson's *Thriller* video. Price's most memorable villains and madman, however, emerged in films adapted from Edgar Allen Poe stories. Among them were *The House of Usher* (1960), *The Pit and the Pendulum* (1961), *The Raven* (1963), *The Haunted Palace* (1964), and *The Masque of the Red Death* (1964). Price also served as the host of the PBS series "Mystery!" and gained notice as an art connoisseur, gourmet, and author of cookbooks. He returned to the screen in *The Whales of August* (1987) and as the inventor of *Edward Scissorhands* (1990).

Pulitzer, Joseph, Jr., U.S. publisher and art collector (b. May 13, 1913, St. Louis, Mo.—d. May 26, 1993, St. Louis), was the grandson of the founder of the *St. Louis Post-Dispatch*, of which he became editor and publisher in 1955 on the death of his father; maintaining the newspaper's tradition of crusading investigative reporting, he saw the *Post-Dispatch* garner five Pulitzer Prizes, including prizes for commentary and editorial cartooning, while serving as its editor (1955–86). Pulitzer, baptized Joseph Pulitzer III, adopted the designation junior after his father dropped that identifier when his own father died. Pulitzer graduated (1936) from Harvard University with a fine arts degree and became an art connoisseur; his collection ultimately included 86 works, some of them masterpieces by such artists as Matisse, Monet, Degas, Picasso, and Miró. After graduation Pulitzer joined the *Post-Dispatch* and worked in every department before becoming editor. As chairman of Pulitzer Publishing Co. and editor of its flagship publication, the *Post-Dispatch,* Pulitzer oversaw the operation of three newspapers, seven television stations, and two radio stations and, when the company went public in 1986, he resigned as editor to devote his full attention to the publishing firm. Pulitzer's grandfather established the Pulitzer Prizes in his will (annual awards began in 1917), and 70 years later Pulitzer was given a special citation from the Pulitzer Prize board for his "extraordinary services to American journalism and letters."

Quennell, Sir Peter Courtney, British writer (b. March 9, 1905, Bickley, Kent, England—d. Oct. 27, 1993, London, England), was praised as one of the last men of letters owing to his wide-ranging knowledge, lucid style, and attention to language. By the age of 18, Quennell had published several of his poems and a book of verse, *Masques and Poems.* He attended (1923–25) the University of Oxford but did not take his studies seriously and left without a degree. Two more works, a novel and a book of verse, were not popularly received, but Quennell's wit and erudition helped gain him access to important literary circles. In 1934 he gained respect with the publication of *Byron,* the first in a series that included *Byron: The Years of Fame* (1935) and *Byron in Italy* (1941), which secured him a popular following and was one of his best-known works. Besides holding a job in an advertising agency in the late 1930s and accepting several government posts during World War II, Quennell wrote a biography, *Caroline of England* (1939), on the mistress of King George II. Quennell served as book reviewer (1943–56) of the *Daily Mail* and editor (1944–51) of *The Cornhill Magazine,* a respected literary publication. After the war he produced popular and accessible works on Shakespeare, Alexander Pope, William Hogarth, John Ruskin, and Samuel Johnson, among others. In 1951 he became coeditor of *History Today,* a post he held until 1979. Quennell also contributed to periodicals, and he edited collections of essays, memoirs, and letters. He was knighted in 1992 and produced two autobiographical volumes: *The Marble Foot* (1976) and *The Wanton Chase* (1980).

Raczynski, Count Edward Bernard André Maria, Polish diplomat (b. Dec. 19, 1891, Zakopane, Poland—d. July 30, 1993, London, England), was a central figure in the Polish government-in-exile based in London during and after World War II; he eventually served one term as president-in-exile (1979–86). Raczynski, the son of a wealthy nobleman, was educated at the London School of Economics and the Universities of Krakow and Leipzig. He joined the Polish foreign service in 1919 and was a delegate to the 1932–34 disarmament conference in Geneva. As ambassador to the court of St. James's (1934–45), he signed the Anglo-Polish pact that brought the U.K. into the war when Poland was invaded in 1939. Raczynski served in the Polish government-in-exile as foreign minister (1941–43), but he refused to join the postwar communist government established in Warsaw as a consequence of the 1945 Yalta Conference. He remained active in émigré politics as an adviser to the British government and as chairman (1940–67) of the Polish Research Centre in London. Raczynski published his wartime diaries in English in 1963 and wrote several volumes of poetry and reminiscences in Polish.

Reichenbach, François-Arnold, French filmmaker (b. July 3, 1921, Paris, France—d. Feb. 2, 1993, Neuilly, near Paris), wrote, directed, and photographed a wide range of documentary motion pictures, notably the Academy Award-winning *Arthur Rubinstein, l'amour de la vie* (1969). Reichenbach worked as a songwriter in Paris and as an art dealer in the U.S. He acquired a 16-mm camera in 1953; two years later he released his first short documentary, *Impressions de New York,* which took a special prize at the Festival of Tours in 1956. Other films followed, including *Visages de Paris* (1955), *Les Marines* (1957), and *La Douceur du village* (1963), which won a grand prize at the 1964 Cannes film festival. His first feature-length documentary, *L'Amérique insolite* (1960; *America Through the Keyhole*), won an award at Cannes in 1960 and established his international reputation. Reichenbach was particularly known for his cinema verité portraits of public individuals such as John F. Kennedy, Brigitte Bardot, Yehudi Menuhin, and Herbert von Karajan. In equally impressive films, however, he explored the lives of lesser figures, notably in *Un Coeur gros comme ça* (1961), a day-by-day account of a young Senegalese boxer in Paris, and *Houston, Texas* (1981), a close examination of the trial and execution of a convicted murderer.

Ridgway, Matthew Bunker, general (ret.), U.S. Army (b. March 3, 1895, Fort Monroe, Va.—d. July 26, 1993, Fox Chapel, Pa.), was a valiant leader and brilliant strategist who parachuted with his troops into Sicily (July 1943) during World War II, therewith planning and executing the first major airborne assault in U.S. military history. Ridgway, a 1917 graduate of the U.S. Military Academy at West Point, N.Y., served in various staff positions during World War I. By 1942 he was a brigadier general and commander of the 82nd Infantry Division, which he converted to the 82nd Airborne Division and then commanded during the Sicily campaign. Of all the generals, Ridgway saw the most combat during the war; he parachuted with his troops into Normandy during the D-Day invasion (June 6, 1944) and led his corps in action in The Netherlands, Belgium, and Germany. Ridgway was known for his ability to rally dispirited troops and was visually distinguished by the hand grenade that he wore strapped to a shoulder of his battle jacket. As commander of the U.S. 8th Army in Korea during the Chinese Communist offensive in late 1950, he energized demoralized and retreating United Nations forces and launched a counteroffensive that drove the Chinese out of South Korea. In 1951 Ridgway succeeded Gen. Douglas MacArthur, who was relieved of his command as Allied commander in the Far East. Ridgway launched the negotiations that eventually led to an armistice ending the Korean War. He replaced Gen. Dwight D. Eisenhower as supreme commander of the Allied forces in Europe in 1952, and the following year he was appointed chief of staff of the U.S. Army. Ridgway retired in 1955 as a four-star general. He published his memoirs, *Soldier,* in 1956 and another volume, *The Korean War,* in 1967.

Ridley of Liddesdale, Nicholas Ridley, BARON, British politician (b. Feb. 17, 1929, Newcastle upon Tyne, England—d. March 4, 1993, near Cheltenham, Gloucestershire, England), was a staunch supporter of free-market economic policies and one of Prime Minister Margaret Thatcher's closest political allies. Known for his sharp tongue and sharper mind, he held a series of Cabinet posts under Thatcher until he resigned under pressure in 1990 after he had denounced European union and insulted both France and Germany in a magazine interview. Ridley was born into a distinguished family. His father, the 3rd Viscount Ridley and Baron Wensleydale, was a Tory member of Parliament and the grandson of the 1st Viscount Ridley, who was a Cabinet minister under Benjamin Disraeli and Lord Salisbury; his mother was the daughter of the architect Sir Edwin Luytens, granddaughter of the former viceroy of India, and great granddaughter of the novelist Edward Bulwer-Lytton. Ridley attended Eton and studied mathematics and engineering at Balliol College, Oxford. He joined a civil engineering firm in 1950 and served as a director there (1954–70), but from an early age he sought a political career. He lost his bid for Parliament in 1955, but he won in 1959 and became the 10th Ridley to serve in the House of Commons. He held a variety of minor posts in the Ministries of Technology and Trade and Industry under Prime Minister Edward Heath, but he refused an appointment as arts minister. In 1979 Thatcher named him minister of state to the foreign office, but his abrupt outspokenness and caustic wit made him generally unsuited to foreign service. Although he alternately charmed and enraged his opponents, Ridley served Thatcher loyally as financial secretary to the treasury (1981–83) and as secretary of state for transport (1983–86), the environment (1986–89), and trade and industry (1989–90). As one of the architects of "Thatcherism," he privatized industry and instituted the first poll tax. Ridley was so closely associated with Thatcher that he was assumed to be speaking for her in *The Spectator* interview when he referred to the European Community as "a German racket" and described the French as "poodles to the Germans." The ensuing embarrassment forced him to resign and contributed to the prime minister's fall shortly thereafter. Ridley remained a gadfly on the backbench, however. He published his memoirs, *My Style of Government: The Thatcher Years,* in 1991, and he campaigned against the Maastricht Treaty until his death. He was created baron in 1992.

Ryu, Chishu, Japanese actor (b. May 13, 1906, Tamamizu, Kumamoto prefecture, Japan—d. March 16, 1993, Yokohama, Japan), was one of Japan's most enduring character actors; he was best known for his long association with the acclaimed cinema director Yasujiro Ozu, having appeared in all but two of Ozu's 54 films. Ryu was the son of a Buddhist priest and was preparing to follow his father into the temple until 1925, when he abruptly quit to join the acting school at the Shochiku film studio in Tokyo. He played mainly bit parts at first, but after playing a small role in Ozu's second motion picture, *Wakodo no yume* (1928; "The Dreams of Youth"), he joined the director's stock company of actors. Ryu's subtle characterizations, low-key acting style, and on-screen air of benevolence and melancholy were used to advantage in Ozu's films, notably *Chichi ariki* (1942; "There Was a Father"), *Banshun* (1949; "Late Spring"), *Tokyo monogatari* (1953; *Tokyo Story*), and *Samma no aji* (1962; "An Autumn Afternoon"). After Ozu's death in 1963, Ryu worked with other directors, including Akira Kurosawa in *Akahige* (1965; *Red Beard*) and *Dreams* (1990). Between 1969 and 1991 Ryu played the recurring role of a kindly temple priest in the popular "Tora-san" series of some 45 sentimental comedies.

Sabin, Albert Bruce, Polish-born U.S. physician and microbiologist (b. Aug. 26, 1906, Bialystok, Poland—d. March 3, 1993, Washington, D.C.), was a towering figure in medical research and the developer in 1955 of the first oral vaccine for polio, which was administered to millions of children in Europe, Africa, and the Americas beginning in the late 1950s. His live, weakened (attenuated) vaccine, which was dispensed on a sugar cube or in liquid, was easier to administer and provided longer protection than the killed, injected vaccine developed by Jonas Salk a year earlier. Both vaccines, however, were credited with virtually eradicating the crippling and sometimes fatal effects of poliomyelitis, or infantile paralysis, a scourge that, at its peak in 1952, paralyzed 21,000 Americans and killed 3,100. Sabin immigrated to the U.S. in 1921 with his family, and two cousins taught him enough English to make it possible for him to enter high school. Ten years later he earned an M.D. degree from New York University. He served two years as house physician at Bellevue Hospital in New York City before attending the Lister Institute of Preventive Medicine in London. After returning to New York City in 1935, he joined the staff of the Rockefeller Institute for Medical Research, where he was the first to demonstrate the growth of poliovirus in human nervous tissue outside the body. After becoming (1939) associate professor of pediatrics at the University of Cincinnati (Ohio) College of Medicine, he served as chief of the college's division of infectious diseases at the Children's Hospital Research Foundation (1939–43). During World War II he interrupted his polio research to work with the U.S. Army Medical Corps. Sabin isolated the virus that caused sandfly fever, which was epidemic among U.S. troops in Africa, and he later developed vaccines against dengue fever and Japanese encephalitis. After the war he returned to the University of Cincinnati and served as professor of research pediatrics (1946–60) and distinguished service professor (1960–71) before becoming professor emeritus in 1971. Sabin was also associated with the University of South Carolina at Charleston, the Weizmann Institute of Science in Rehovot, Israel, and the National Institutes of Health in Bethesda, Md. Though he was paralyzed (1983) with polyneuritis, an inflammation of the nerve cells, he made almost a full recovery and continued working on a measles vaccine before retiring in 1988. Sabin was elected to the National Academy of Sciences in 1951 and was the recipient of the U.S. Medals of Science (1970), Freedom (1986), and Liberty (1986).

LONDON DAILY EXPRESS/ARCHIVE PHOTOS

Sabzevari, ʿAbd al-Aʿala al-Mussawi al-, Iranian-born cleric (b. Dec. 21, 1910, Sabzevar, Iran—d. Aug. 16, 1993, an-Najaf, Iraq), was, for the last year of his life, the grand ayatollah in the Islamic holy city of an-Najaf and, thus, spiritual leader of more than 11 million Shiʿite Muslims in Iraq. After finishing his basic education in Iran, Sabzevari moved to an-Najaf to pursue advanced studies in philosophy and religious law. A pious, scholarly man, he wrote extensively, including 11 volumes of commentary on the Qur'an and more than 30 works on Islamic jurisprudence. Until 1991 Sabzevari lived quietly, teaching, writing, and directing charitable works. He was reportedly involved in the unsuccessful Shiʿite uprising in March 1991, and when Grand Ayatollah Abolqassem al-Khoei died in August 1992, Baghdad tried to prevent Sabzevari from being recognized as his successor. Iraqi Shiʿites, however, refused to accept the government's own candidate as their spiritual leader. On Dec. 9, 1993, another grand ayatollah, Muhammad Reza Golpayegani, died in Tehran. The 94-year-old Golpayegani was a distinguished teacher and educational administrator and was a senior spiritual leader in the holy city of Qom, Iran. His death, so soon after Sabzevari's, left only three living grand ayatollahs at the head of the world's 162 million Shiʿites.

Salisbury, Harrison Evans, U.S. journalist and author (b. Nov. 14, 1908, Minneapolis, Minn.—d. July 5, 1993, near Providence, R.I.), was a crack reporter for United Press (1930–48) and the *New York Times* (1949–73) and, after he returned from a five-year posting (1949–54) as the *Times*'s bureau chief in Moscow, won the 1955 Pulitzer Prize for international reporting for a series of articles he wrote chronicling events during the height of the Cold War and the death of Joseph Stalin. He also recounted historical events in such critically acclaimed epics as *The 900 Days: The Siege of Leningrad* (1969) and *The Long March: The Untold Story* (1985). During Salisbury's extraordinary career, he became the first reporter allowed into Communist Albania, North Korea, and Mongolia, and he was the first Western journalist permitted to visit Hanoi during the Vietnam war. His 1966 eyewitness accounts of the civilian and not just "surgical" bombing of sites in that country created a stir in Washington, where the Lyndon B. Johnson administration tried to discredit Salisbury's virtually irrefutable dispatches. His articles also contributed to a skepticism in the U.S. about the objective and purpose of the war. Salisbury, variously described as intrepid, indefatigable, passionately enthusiastic about his work, shrewd, reflective, and sometimes even aloof, possessed all the qualities of a "journalistic one-man band." At the *Times* he was in charge of the paper's national coverage (1962–64), and he served as assistant managing editor (1964–72) and associate editor (1972–73). His 1970 creation of the paper's op-ed page was a sensation, and the following year he was one of a group of top editors who sanctioned the publishing of the sensitive Pentagon Papers, which contained a history of U.S. involvement in Indochina from World War II until May 1968. A specialist on the Soviet Union and China, he wrote 29 books, 10 of them on Russia and some 6 on China. Among his offerings were *Russia on the Way* (1946), *Moscow Journal: The End of Stalin* (1961), *Orbit of China* (1967), *War Between Russia and China* (1969), *Tiananmen Diary: Thirteen Days in June* (1989), and *The New Emperors* (1992). His memoirs include *A Journey for Our Times* (1983) and *A Time of Change* (1988).

Sauvé, Jeanne Mathilde, Canadian journalist and politician (b. April 26, 1922, Prud'homme, Sask.—d. Jan. 26, 1993, Montreal, Que.), was a respected print, radio, and television journalist before launching a political career in 1972 and trailblazing a path for women in government; she was the first Quebec woman named (1972) to a Cabinet post, the first woman speaker of the House of Commons (1980–84), and the first woman governor-general of Canada (1984–90). Sauvé, who attended the University of Ottawa and the University of Paris, had a superb command of both English and French. She was urged by her husband, Maurice (a politician himself), to enter politics, and she represented the Montreal riding (electoral district) of Ahuntsic (1972–79) and the Quebec riding of Laval-des-Rapides (1979–84). A member of the federal Cabinet, she served as minister of state in charge of science and technology (1972–74), minister of the environment (1974–75), and minister of communications (1975–79). As speaker of the House, she was taken to task by some members of that predominately male forum for not being familiar with its many rules and procedures, yet she did manage to completely reform, in less than three years, the administration of the House. Her official swearing in as governor-general was postponed for some months because of an undisclosed illness (later identified by a close family member as Hodgkin's disease). When Sauvé did take office, the diminutive, silvery-haired federalist seemed frail. In this largely ceremonial post, Sauvé adopted a more formal approach than her predecessor. She angered some when she closed to the public the gardens and lawns of Rideau Hall, the official residence; that order was revoked by her successor.

Schaefer, Vincent Joseph, U.S. chemist (b. July 4, 1906, Schenectady, N.Y.—d. July 25, 1993, Schenectady), was conducting atmospheric research at the General Electric (GE) Research Laboratory in Schenectady when in 1946 he undertook the first systematic series of experiments to investigate the physics of precipitation. Schaefer, who struck upon a method to create a snowstorm in the laboratory, proved that he could accomplish the same feat with supercooled clouds in the free atmosphere. From an aircraft over Massachusetts, he seeded clouds with pellets of dry ice (solidified carbon dioxide) and successfully produced snow. His initiative launched the science of experimental meteorology and weather control. Schaefer dropped out of school at the age of 16 but later graduated (1928) from the Davey Institute of Tree Surgery. After joining GE he became the protégé of Nobel laureate Irving Langmuir. The two worked on studies of surface chemistry (1931–40) before undertaking defense work during World War II. They invented several useful devices to aid the military, notably gas mask filters, submarine detectors, and a machine for making smoke clouds to conceal aircraft maneuvers. After leaving GE in 1954, he served as research director of the Munitalp Foundation until 1958, when he resigned to devote his time to research and education. Schaefer joined the faculty of the State University of New York at Albany in 1959, and the following year he became a founder of the Atmospheric Sciences Research Center, which he directed from 1966 to 1976. Schaefer was the author of some 300 scientific papers and books and in 1976 received a special citation from the American Meteorological Society.

Schneider, (Abraham) Alexander, Russian-born U.S. violinist and conductor (b. Oct. 21, 1908, Vilna, Russian Empire [now Vilnius, Lithuania]—d. Feb. 2, 1993, New York, N.Y.), for many years a member of the famed Budapest Quartet, was especially known for the passion of his music making and for his devotion to teaching. He entered the Vilna Conservatory at age 10 and at age 16 went to Frankfurt am Main, Germany, to continue his studies. In 1932 Schneider became second violinist in the Budapest Quartet (two years after his elder brother, Mischa, had become the group's cellist). He was a member of the quartet until 1944 and again from 1955 until it disbanded in 1964. In the late 1930s the quartet settled in the U.S. In 1950 Schneider persuaded cellist Pablo Casals to end his retirement, in protest against the Spanish government, which was the beginning of collaborations between the two at festivals in France, Puerto Rico, Israel, and elsewhere. Also in the 1950s Schneider founded his own string quartet, which performed and recorded the Haydn quartets, and he later helped found the Chamber Orchestra of Europe and other musical organizations. His New York String Orchestra, founded in 1968, offered workshops for students and gave concerts at Carnegie Hall and the Kennedy Center.

Scott, Jay (JEFFREY SCOTT BEAVEN), U.S.-born Canadian film critic (b. Oct. 4, 1949, Lincoln, Neb.—d. July 30, 1993, Toronto, Ont.), elevated film criticism to an art with his insightful, witty, and influential reviews, which graced the pages of the Toronto-based *Globe and Mail* from 1977 until his death. Before moving to Toronto in 1977 and changing his name to Jay Scott, the aspiring writer was simultaneously studying drama and working at the *Albuquerque* (N.M.) *Journal*. There, as a feature writer, he had himself briefly committed to a hospital and wrote a prizewinning series on how the state treated the mentally ill. In 1975 he moved to Canada, where he worked as an investigative reporter for the now-defunct *Calgary Albertan* newspaper—producing, for example, a groundbreaking series on sex-change operations—besides writing film reviews. Scott, Canada's most eminent film critic and the winner of three National Newspaper Awards, died of AIDS-related infections.

Sen, Binay Ranjan, Indian diplomat (b. Jan. 1, 1898, Dibrugarh, India—d. June 12, 1993, Calcutta, India), as director general (1956–67) of the UN's Food and Agriculture Organization (FAO), drew on his experience as relief commissioner (1942–43) during a devastating famine in his native Bengal to build the FAO from a data-gathering bureaucracy into a major force against world hunger. After studying at the Universities of Calcutta and Oxford, Sen joined the Indian civil service in Bengal. In 1942 a massive typhoon, followed by Japanese bombing attacks, left parts of Bengal in ruins and brought about a famine in which some one million people died. Sen found that his efforts to distribute food were often thwarted by disorganization and official corruption. This, and his work as director general of food for all India (1943–46), convinced him that hunger and malnutrition were crucial issues in the modern world. He took his concerns to the international stage as a member of India's first delegation to the UN (1947) and as ambassador

LONDON DAILY EXPRESS/ARCHIVE PHOTOS

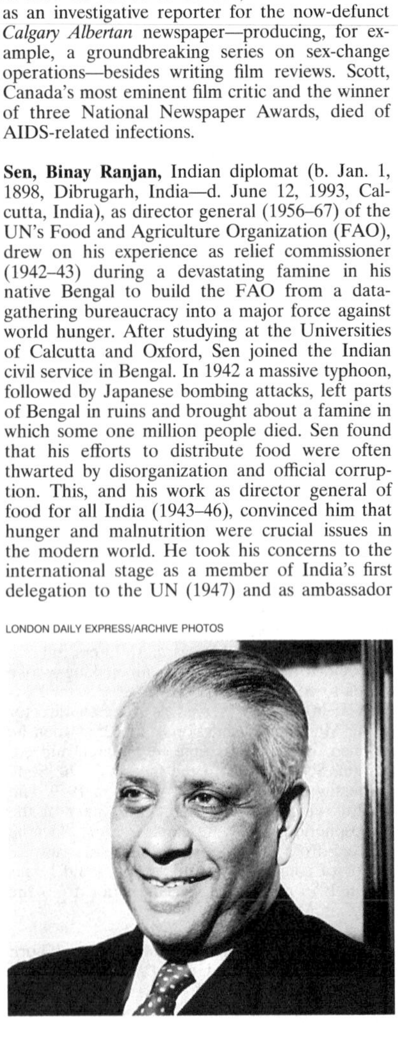

to the U.S., Italy and Yugoslavia, Japan, and Mexico. He worked on a variety of FAO projects before being named director general in 1956. In 1960 Sen announced the Freedom from Hunger campaign, which led to the 1963 World Food Congress in Washington, D.C., attended by representatives from more than 100 countries.

Sharaff, Irene, U.S. costume designer (b. 1910, Boston, Mass.—d. Aug. 16, 1993, New York, N.Y.), created stylish and sumptuous fashion designs for some 60 stage productions, 40 motion pictures, and such ballet companies as the Ballets Russes de Monte Carlo, American Ballet Theatre, and the New York City Ballet. In all, she received 15 Academy Award nominations and garnered 5 Oscars for designs for *An American in Paris* (1951), *The King and I* (1956), *West Side Story* (1961), *Cleopatra* (1963), and *Who's Afraid of Virginia Woolf* (1966); she also won a Tony award for the stage production of *The King and I*. Sharaff's leitmotiv was the use of her favourite colours—reds, oranges, and pinks. She created a fashion rage with her brilliant use of Thai silks in *The King and I* and ignited a boom in Thailand's silk industry. Sharaff initially studied painting at the New York School of Fine and Applied Arts, the Arts Students League, and the Grande Chaumière in Paris before serving as an illustrator for fashion magazines and securing a reputation for her costume and scenery designs in Eva Le Gallienne's 1932 production of *Alice in Wonderland*. Sharaff, who enjoyed a more than 50-year career, provided designs for the stage productions of *As Thousands Cheer, A Tree Grows in Brooklyn,* and *Lady in the Dark* and for such films as *Madame Curie, Meet Me in St. Louis, Guys and Dolls, Porgy and Bess,* and *Hello, Dolly!* Other credits include both the stage and film adaptations of *Funny Girl, Flower Drum Song,* and *West Side Story.* Sharaff's last stage designs were created in 1972, and her last film designs were for *Mommie Dearest* (1981).

Sheehan, George, U.S. physician, author, and running enthusiast (b. Nov. 5, 1918, Brooklyn, N.Y.—d. Nov. 1, 1993, Ocean Grove, N.J.), fueled the recreational running movement in the 1970s with a best-selling book, *Running and Being* (1978), which anointed him as the inspirational guru of runners. Sheehan's philosophy expounded on the physical, psychological, and spiritual benefits of running. While practicing medicine as a Red Bank, N.J., cardiologist, Sheehan broke his right hand when he punched a wall in a fit of temper after being unnecessarily awakened by a patient. Unable to continue playing tennis, which had been his favourite sport, the former Manhattan College outstanding miler at age 44 began pounding the pavement in lieu of lunch and in the process launched a running phenomenon. In 1969 Sheehan became the first man over the age of 50 to run the Boston Marathon in less than five hours, but he clocked his fastest marathon at the age of 61. Sheehan, a charismatic speaker who liberally quoted from the great philosophers to support his cause, gave up his medical practice in 1984 to devote himself full-time to speaking, writing, and running. He was also medical editor of *Runner's World* magazine and the author of *This Running Life* (1980), *How to Feel Great 24 Hours a Day* (1983), and *Personal Best* (1989). At the time of his death from prostate cancer, Sheehan was in the process of recording his feelings and experiences related to dying.

Shirer, William Lawrence, U.S. journalist and author (b. Feb. 23, 1904, Chicago, Ill.—d. Dec. 28, 1993, Boston, Mass.), kept extensive diaries while working for CBS as a radio broadcaster in Berlin (1937–41) and used them and volumes of confidential information retrieved from the German archives after World War II to chronicle the Nazis' rise to power under Adolf Hitler in the massive, best-selling *The Rise and Fall of the Third Reich* (1960), which won the 1961 National Book Award. After graduating (1925) from Coe College, Cedar Rapids, Iowa, Shirer was lured by Europe's mystique. He borrowed funds and worked his way there on a cattle boat. He secured a job with the *Chicago Tribune* as a copywriter and then as a foreign correspondent, and during the 1920s and '30s he sent dispatches from India, Afghanistan, and the capitals of Europe for the *Tribune* and later for the Universal News Service. While working for CBS, Shirer won several journalism awards for his impassioned commentaries. He laced his speeches with American slang in an effort to confuse the censors and convey information about the operations of the German army. After serving as bureau chief in Vienna, Shirer left CBS in 1947. He was blacklisted during the McCarthy era as a leftist sympathizer. It was then that he had time to complete *The Rise and Fall of the Third Reich*. Some of Shirer's other works include *Berlin Diary: The Journal of a Foreign Correspondent, 1934–1941* (1941), *The Collapse of the Third Republic: An Inquiry into the Fall of France in 1940* (1969), and *Gandhi: A Memoir* (1979). Shirer also published three volumes of memoirs and prior to his death had completed a book on Leo Tolstoy.

Simon, Norton, U.S. industrialist and art collector (b. Feb. 5, 1907, Portland, Ore.—d. June 2, 1993, Los Angeles, Calif.), was a savvy businessman who amassed a fortune after he parlayed a bankrupt orange-juice company into a consumer-products conglomerate, Norton Simon Inc., which boasted such prominent concerns as Hunt Food and Industries, McCall Corp., and Canada Dry Corp. He used his vast wealth to acquire one of the largest and most impressive art collections in the world, much of it housed in the Norton Simon Museum of Art in Pasadena, Calif. Simon briefly attended the University of California at Berkeley before launching a sheet-metal business. After selling the juice company, which he had renamed Val Vita Food Products, to Hunt Brothers Packing Co., he bought stock in Hunt, gained control of it in 1943, and the following year became chairman of the newly created Hunt Food and Industries. In 1969, after forming his international empire, Simon resigned as director of Norton Simon Inc. to concentrate on collecting art. His superb collection contained some 12,000 paintings and sculptures and included canvases by Gauguin, Pissarro, Matisse, Picasso, and Raphael, plus an impressive stock of Asian and Southeast Asian statuary. During the 1980s his collection was appraised at $750 million.

Sinclair, Sir Keith, New Zealand historian (b. Dec. 5, 1922, Auckland, N.Z.—d. June 20, 1993, Canada), presented the history of New Zealand from a nationalist rather than a British colonial perspective and helped to promote public awareness of a distinctly New Zealand identity and cultural heritage. His most influential book, *A History of New Zealand* (1959; revised and expanded, 1980), was widely recognized as the standard popular work on the subject. Of almost equal importance was an earlier work, *The Origins of the Maori Wars* (1957), in which he sought to place 19th-century New Zealand in its historical context and thereby provided a scholarly basis for the resurgence of Maori nationalist activism in the 1970s and '80s. Sinclair received his B.A. (1945), M.A. (1946), and Ph.D. (1954) from Auckland University College (later renamed the University of Auckland). After serving in the army (1941–44) and navy (1944–46), he returned to his alma mater as a history instructor. He was made a full professor in 1963, and 20 years later he was selected to write the official history of the university. His other scholarly works include *A Destiny Apart: New Zealand's Search for National Identity* (1986). Sinclair was also an accomplished poet and biographer, and in 1977 he won the National Book Award for his biography of former prime minister Walter Nash. Sinclair was knighted in 1985. His autobiography, *Halfway Round the Harbour,* was published shortly after his death.

Slayton, Donald Kent ("DEKE"), U.S. astronaut (b. March 1, 1924, Sparta, Wis.—d. June 13, 1993, League City, Texas), was selected in 1959 by the National Aeronautics and Space Administration (NASA) as one of the original Mercury Seven astronauts, the highly touted aviators who made solo spaceflights during the infancy of the U.S.

space program. Slayton's flight, however, was delayed for 16 years (he had been scheduled to become the second in orbit, after John Glenn) because he was found to have an irregular heartbeat. In 1975, after the ailment unaccountably disappeared, he served as pilot of the Apollo docking module in the historic Apollo-Soyuz mission, in which U.S. and Soviet spacecraft linked in space. Slayton, who joined the air force in 1942, flew 56 combat missions during World War II. After the war he earned a B.A. in aeronautical engineering (1949) from the University of Minnesota and worked for Boeing Aircraft Co. in Seattle, Wash., before being recalled to active duty in the Minnesota Air National Guard. He became a test pilot at Edwards Air Force Base in California after attending school there. When Slayton's dream of spaceflight as a Mercury Seven astronaut was crushed, he proved instrumental as chief of flight operations at the Johnson Space Center, where he directed astronaut training and chose crews for nearly all Gemini and Apollo missions. He was determined, however, to regain his health. Slayton quit smoking and started exercising and dieting. After participating in the last Apollo mission, Slayton returned to NASA in a managerial capacity, directing early tests of the space shuttle until his 1982 retirement. He then founded and directed Space Services Inc., a pioneering company that launched small satellites.

Smith, Alexis (GLADYS SMITH), U.S. actress (b. June 8, 1921, Penticton, B.C.—d. June 9, 1993, Los Angeles, Calif.), was a striking and statuesque leading lady and supporting player in Hollywood during the 1940s and '50s and made a spectacular splash on Broadway in 1971 with her performance as a cynical aging former showgirl in the Stephen Sondheim musical *Follies,* for which she won a Tony award (1972). In her most memorable film roles, she portrayed charming yet aloof and resourceful women, and she was especially effective as the "other woman." Smith played opposite some of Hollywood's most dashing leading men, including Errol Flynn in *Gentleman Jim* (1942) and *San Antonio* (1945), Cary Grant in *Night and Day* (1946), and Clark Gable in *Any Number Can Play* (1949), before retiring in 1959 when her star began to wane. She triumphantly returned to acting in *Follies* and received critical acclaim, especially for her rendition of the song "Could I Leave You." Smith later appeared in such films as *Jacqueline Susann's Once Is Not Enough* (1975) and *The Little Girl Who Lives down the Lane* (1977). She was seen on television in the role of Jessica Montfort on the hit series "Dallas" as J.R. Ewing's recurrent adversary from 1984 to 1990.

Smithson, Alison Margaret, British architect (b. June 22, 1928, Sheffield, Yorkshire, England—d. Aug. 16, 1993, London, England), with her husband, Peter, was in the forefront of New Brutalism, an architectural movement that stressed spartan functionality and a stark presentation of structure and materials, including exposed concrete and visible service conduits. She was born Alison Gill and studied at the University of Durham, where she met fellow student Peter Smithson. They were married in 1949. In 1950 they began a joint practice and a seamless partnership in which they shared credit for everything they designed or wrote. Although the Smithsons built relatively few major projects, their revolutionary Secondary Modern School at Hunstanton, Norfolk (completed 1954), was generally recognized as the first example of New Brutalism. Other significant projects included the Economist Building Group, St. James's, London (1964), and Robin Hood Gardens (1972), a low-income housing scheme in London's East End. As key figures in the radical Independent Group and Team X, the Smithsons carried even more weight for their theoretical writings, notably *Urban Structuring Studies* (1967), *Without Rhetoric: An Architectural Aesthetic* (1973), and numerous articles in *Architectural Design.* She also wrote a novel, *A Portrait of the Female Mind as a Young Girl* (1966).

Stark, Dame Freya Madeline, British travel writer (b. Jan. 31, 1893, Paris, France—d. May 9, 1993, Asolo, Italy), wrote two dozen highly personal books in which she described local history and culture as well as the everyday life she observed in her journeys, many of them to remote areas in Turkey and the Middle East where few European men and no European women had traveled before. Stark had no formal education as a child, but she moved about with her artist parents and learned French, German, and Italian before she entered the University of London in 1912. After working as a nurse in Italy during World War I, she returned to London to attend the School of Oriental Studies. In her first major book, *The Valleys of the Assassins* (1934), Stark established her style, combining practical travel tips with an entertaining commentary on the people, places, customs, and history of Persia (now Iran). Thereafter, she traveled extensively in the Middle East, Turkey, Greece, and Italy, where she made her home. During World War II she worked for the British Ministry of Information in Aden, Baghdad, and Cairo, where she founded the anti-Nazi Brotherhood of Freedom. She later visited Asia, notably Afghanistan and Nepal. Stark's other books include *The Southern Gates of Arabia* (1936), *Letters from Syria* (1942), *Alexander's Path* (1958), *The Minaret of Djam* (1970), several volumes of collected letters, and four volumes of memoirs. She was made Dame Commander of the Order of the British Empire in 1972.

Stegner, Wallace Earle, U.S. novelist (b. Feb. 18, 1909, Lake Mills, Iowa—d. April 13, 1993, Santa Fe, N.M.), redefined the notion of the West as a desirable landscape for rugged individualists, particularly stereotypical loners sporting Stetson hats, and instead celebrated the pioneering spirit of cooperation in works of fiction and nonfiction that also addressed environmental concerns. Among his first offerings was the semiautobiographical *The Big Rock Candy Mountain* (1943), which explored the illusory vision of the West as a utopia and his own father's preoccupation with searching for prosperity there by frequently moving the family. Stegner, who attended the Universities of Utah (B.A., 1930) and Iowa (M.A., 1932; Ph.D., 1935), taught creative writing at the Universities of Utah and Wisconsin and at Harvard and Stanford universities. He served as inspiration for such students turned western writers as Larry McMurtry and Thomas McGuane. During his 50-year literary career, Stegner published more than two dozen novels, historical works, and collections of stories and essays. In 1972 he won the Pulitzer Prize for fiction for *Angle of Repose,* an account of an elderly man who accepted his own hardships after learning that his pioneer grandparents had endured similar trials. Stegner won a National Book Award in 1977 for *The Spectator Bird* but refused the National Medal for the Arts in 1992 because of the political controls placed upon the National Endowment for the Arts, the agency that issued the award. Some of his other notable works include *Wolf Willow* (1962), about a cattle drive through a blinding snowstorm in Saskatchewan; *Beyond the Hundredth Meridian* (1954), a biography of Colorado River explorer John Wesley Powell; and *Where the Bluebird Sings to the Lemonade Springs: Living and Writing in the West* (1992). Stegner, who died some two weeks after sustaining injuries in a car crash, spent most of his career at Stanford, where he taught from 1945 until his 1971 retirement.

Sulzberger, C(yrus) L(eo), U.S. journalist (b. Oct. 27, 1912, New York, N.Y.—d. Sept. 20, 1993, Paris, France), as a globe-trotting foreign correspondent for the *New York Times* during World War II, traveled to more than 30 countries and developed priceless contacts with major leaders, including kings, dictators, and politicians; these connections proved invaluable to him, especially when he served as the newspaper's chief correspondent (1944–54) and author (1954–78) of its thrice-weekly "Foreign Affairs" column. Sulzberger, the nephew of Arthur Hays Sulzberger and cousin of Arthur Ochs Sulzberger, both of them former publishers of the *New York Times,* worked for the *Pittsburgh* (Pa.) *Press,* the United Press, and the *London Evening Standard* before joining his family at the *New York Times* in 1939. Sulzberger was especially distinguished for his dispatches from Yugoslavia, notably his exclusive prison-cell interview with Archbishop Alojzije Stepinac; his reportage earned him a special Pulitzer Prize in 1951. Sulzberger's experiences and views also found expression in some two dozen books, including *What's Wrong with U.S. Foreign Policy* (1959), *The Last of the Giants* (1970), and *Seven Continents and Forty Years* (1977), a memoir.

Sun Ra (HERMAN ["SONNY"] BLOUNT), U.S. jazz pianist, arranger, and composer (b. May 1914?, Birmingham, Ala.—d. May 30, 1993, Birmingham), led an ensemble whose performances were as much theatre as concert. Early in his career he played boogie-woogie, blues, and swing, and in 1946-47 he was pianist with Fletcher Henderson's orchestra. He also was active in the experimental jazz movement in Chicago and from the 1950s on, under the name Sun Ra, performed with his own group, usually called the Solar Arkestra. This multimedia ensemble included singers and dancers as well as instrumentalists who performed in elaborate costumes suggestive of astrology, ancient Egyptian mythology, science fiction, and other influences. The music, sometimes performed before a filmed background, included elements as different as gospel, bebop, and electronic effects and often featured free improvisation. Innovative percussion instruments, microtonal melodies, and aleatory elements were other features of Sun Ra's music, which was unique in the field of jazz.

Tambo, Oliver Reginald, South African political activist (b. Oct. 27, 1917, Bizana, South Africa—d. April 24, 1993, Johannesburg, South Africa), directed the activities of the black nationalist African National Congress (ANC) from exile for 30 years (1960–90); he served as ANC president

CAMERA PRESS/GLOBE PHOTOS

general from 1969 until 1991, when he was succeeded by his college friend and former law partner, Nelson Mandela. Tambo was born to peasant farmers of the Pondo tribe in a small Transkei village. He attended St. Peter's Secondary School in Johannesburg, received a scholarship to the University College of Fort Hare (B.Sc., 1941), and returned to St. Peter's to teach. In 1943 he joined the ANC, and the next year he and Mandela founded the ANC Youth League. The two young men studied law together, and in 1952 they opened a joint legal practice. Tambo rose rapidly in the ANC; he was a member of the ANC executive council from 1949, secretary-general (1955–58), and deputy president general (1958–69). He was arrested (1956) for treason, released (1957), and then banned (1959) for five years, but in 1960, when word leaked out that the ANC was to be banned, he was able to leave the country. With Mandela and others imprisoned, leadership fell to Tambo. He devoted the next 30 years to publicizing the black nationalist cause, promoting the international boycott of South Africa, and raising money and support for the armed struggle against apartheid. He returned to Johannesburg in triumph in December 1990, but he was unable to continue his executive duties because of a stroke he had suffered in 1989. In July 1991 Mandela was named ANC president general, and Tambo was elevated to honorary chairman. He died quietly of a stroke two weeks after the assassination of Chris Hani (*q.v.*), the former chief of staff of the ANC's military wing.

Tanaka, Kakuei, Japanese politician (b. May 4, 1918, Kariwa, Japan—d. Dec. 16, 1993, Tokyo, Japan), was Japan's prime minister from 1972 until late 1974, when a corruption scandal forced him to resign. Tanaka established a construction company when he was 18. After brief army service he became ill, was discharged (1941), and returned to his business, which prospered, largely because of military contracts, making him one of Japan's richest men. Tanaka was elected to the Diet (parliament) in 1947 and, rising rapidly through the

UPI/BETTMANN

ranks of the Liberal-Democratic Party, went on to serve in a number of Cabinet posts. In 1972 he staged a surprising upset victory in the battle for party leader and thus became prime minister. Shortly thereafter he normalized relations with China, and he pushed through many government projects and helped revitalize much of western Japan. In 1974, however, allegations that he had profited illegally from financial dealings made possible by his high office led to his resignation. Two years later he was arrested on charges of having accepted bribes from the Lockheed Aircraft Corp. to influence the purchase of jet airliners by All Nippon Airways. His trial lasted until 1983 and ended in conviction. He was fined and sentenced to four years in prison, but his conviction was under appeal. Tanaka continued to be politically powerful, however, and served as his party's kingmaker, influencing the choice of several successive prime ministers. The effects of a stroke in 1985 eventually caused him to retire from politics in 1990.

Tata, J(ehangir) R(atanji) D(adabhoy), Indian industrialist (b. July 29, 1904, Paris, France—d. Nov. 29, 1993, Geneva, Switz.), for more than 50 years controlled what under his leadership became India's largest industrial empire. Tata was born into one of India's wealthiest families, but his mother was French, and he spent much of his childhood in France. As a result, French was his first language. It was while on a summer vacation that he first met aviation pioneer Louis Blériot. This encounter kindled an interest in aircraft that eventually became a lifelong passion. Tata returned to India to join the family business in 1922. He gained the director's seat on the board of Tata Sons Ltd. left vacant by his father's death in 1926, and by 1938 he was chairman of the company. During his tenure Tata Sons diversified from ironworks and steelworks into chemicals, hotels, engineering, and other industries. His true interest remained airplanes, however, and in 1932 he formed Tata Airlines and piloted its inaugural flight between Karachi (then in India) and Bombay. The airline developed into the international carrier Air India. In 1953 air transport was nationalized along with other industries in India. Tata, as compensation, was offered the chairmanship of Air India, which he held until 1978. Tata also worked for and generously supported many causes. He was an early advocate of family planning (an often politically unpopular position), and in 1971 he created the Family Planning Foundation. In 1991 he received the Bharat Ratna, India's highest civilian award, and in 1992 he received the United Nations Population Award. In 1991 Tata stepped down from Tata Sons at the age of 87; the more than 80 companies that the empire comprised generated approximately $4 billion annually.

Theremin, Leon (Lev Sergeyevich Termen), Russian scientist and inventor (b. Aug. 24, 1896, St. Petersburg, Russia—d. Nov. 3, 1993, Moscow, Russia), created one of the first electronic instruments; originally called the etherophone but later renamed for its inventor, the theremin provided the eerie, otherworldly sound in numerous motion pictures, the works of several composers, and such pop recordings as "Good Vibrations" by the Beach Boys. The instrument was designed to be played without being touched—the movement of the player's hands above the antenna and near a metal loop controlled pitch and volume—and was considered to have been the first synthesizer. Theremin was educated in St. Petersburg—in physics and astronomy at the university and music at the conservatory—and took a post at the Physico-Technical Institute in that city. He invented the theremin in 1920 and demonstrated it at the Kremlin for Lenin in 1922 and in Berlin for Albert Einstein in 1927. Later in 1927 he went to New York, and the next year he patented his instrument. He continued working on inventions, creating a variety of other musical devices and developing an electronic security system for prisons. In 1938 he was forced to return to the Soviet Union and was sent to a Siberian labour camp, but during World War II he was transferred to a military laboratory, where he worked on ship- and submarine-tracking systems and remote-control systems. Theremin also invented a miniature eavesdropping device for the KGB, for which he was secretly awarded the Stalin Prize. He was released from prison and went to Moscow, where he continued as a scientist for the KGB and then became (1964) a professor of acoustics at the Moscow Conservatory. He was dismissed from that post after a *New York Times* article about him was published, and he thereafter worked as a technician at the Moscow Polytechnic Institute. Theremin was honoured at electronic music festivals in France in 1989 and at Stanford University in 1991.

Thomas, James ("Son"; "Sonny Ford"), U.S. blues musician (b. Oct. 14, 1926, Eden, Miss.—d. June 26, 1993, Greenville, Miss.), personified the classic Mississippi Delta blues tradition. Thomas was born on a farm and moved as a youth to Leland, Miss., where he laboured as a field hand, gravedigger, and factory worker. He taught himself to play the guitar by listening to the radio and played in local juke joints and barrelhouses until he made his first record in 1968. By the mid-1970s Thomas had built an international following and had taken his traditional guitar work and wry songs about hard times, women, and survival to music festivals and clubs across the U.S. and Europe. He also appeared on television and in films produced by the Center for Southern Folklore, notably the award-winning *Delta Blues Singer: James "Sonny Ford" Thomas* (1970). Thomas' albums include *Highway 61 Blues.*

Thomas, Jess, U.S. operatic tenor (b. Aug. 4, 1927, Hot Springs, S.D.—d. Oct. 11, 1993, San Francisco, Calif.), sang a number of lyric roles but became best known as a Wagnerian heldentenor. He participated in local musical activities as a child, studied psychology at the University of Nebraska (B.A., 1949) and at Stanford University (M.A., 1954), and worked as a high school counselor. A professor at Stanford, Otto Schulman, persuaded him to make opera his career. Thomas made his debut with the San Francisco Opera in 1957 and then worked for several years in Europe, mainly Germany. He sang Parsifal at Bayreuth in 1961 under Wieland Wagner and for a number of years performed with German opera companies, including those of Stuttgart, Karlsruhe, and Munich (where he was made a *Kammersänger* [court singer] of the Bavarian State Opera). His Metropolitan Opera debut (1962) was as Walther in Wagner's *Die Meistersinger von Nürnberg*. Other major roles included, in Wagner, Lohengrin and Tristan; in Strauss, Bacchus in *Ariadne auf Naxos* and the Emperor in *Die Frau ohne Schatten;* and Saint-Saëns' Sampson, Lensky in Tchaikovsky's *Eugene Onegin,* and Florestan in Beethoven's *Fidelio.* In 1966 he created the role of Octavius Caesar in Samuel Barber's *Antony and Cleopatra,* the inaugural work of the Metropolitan in its new home at Lincoln Center. He made a number of recordings. An imposing man over 1.8 m (6 ft) tall, Thomas had an athletic build that he liked to show off onstage, and he was highly regarded for the dramatic power of his acting as well as his singing.

Thomas, Lewis, U.S. physician and author (b. Nov. 25, 1913, Flushing, N.Y.—d. Dec. 3, 1993, New York, N.Y.), translated his passionate interest in and wonder at the intricate mystery of the Earth's biology into a series of finely crafted, award-winning essays that reached a wide audience. Thomas was the son of a doctor and a nurse. He graduated from Princeton University at age 19 and earned his medical degree from Harvard Medical School at 23. He went on to work at various universities, serving as researcher, educator, and administrator, as well as pathologist, pediatrician, bacteriologist, and epidemiologist. He joined the staff of New York University in 1954, and in 1966 he became dean of the School of Medicine there. In 1969 Thomas moved to Yale University, where in 1972 he became dean of the School of Medicine. From 1971 to 1980 Thomas wrote a column for the *New England Journal of Medicine* entitled "Notes of a Biology Watcher"; some of these essays were collected into a book, *The Lives of a Cell* (1974), which won the National Book Award in 1975 in the arts and letters category. From 1973 to 1980 he served as president of the Memorial Sloan-Kettering Cancer Center in New York City. Other works include *The Medusa and the Snail* (1979), *Late Night Thoughts on Listening to Mahler's Ninth Symphony* (1983), and *The Fragile Species* (1992).

Thompson, E(dward) P(almer), British historian (b. Feb. 3, 1924—d. Aug. 28, 1993, Upper Wick, Worcester, England), held academic posts early in his career but beginning in the late 1970s devoted much of his time to the antinuclear peace movement. His particular interest was the role of common people and the working class in the making of history. Thompson was the son of Methodist missionaries. He served in Italy in World War II and attended Corpus Christi College, Cambridge (B.A., 1946). He taught in the extramural department of the University of Leeds from 1948 to 1965 and at the Centre for Social History at the University of Warwick from 1965 to 1971. A Marxist from his student days, he left the Communist Party in 1956 when Soviet troops crushed the Hungarian uprising, but he remained a socialist for the rest of his life. Thompson's first book was a 1955 study of William Morris, the 19th-century socialist and leader of the Arts and Crafts Movement. His best-known work is *The Making of the English Working Class* (1963), a study of the period 1780–1832; in Thompson's words, his aim was to save English workers "from the enormous condescension of posterity." He published several other books, including *Whigs and Hunters: The Origin of the Black Act* (1975), and with his wife, Dorothy, also a historian, he founded and contributed to political journals of dissent. At the time of his death he had completed a book on William Blake—*Witness Against the Beast*—which was published posthumously.

Treurnicht, Andries Petrus, South African politician (b. Feb. 19, 1921, Piketburg, South Africa—d. April 22, 1993, Cape Town, South Africa), was a staunch advocate of South African apartheid and, as founder (1982) of the hard-line Conservative Party, led the parliamentary opposition to antiapartheid reforms. Treurnicht studied theology and philosophy at the Stellenbosch Theological Seminary and the Universities of Stellenbosch (M.A.) and Cape Town (M.A. and Ph.D.). He was a practicing minister (1946–60) in the Dutch Reformed Church until he took over as editor of the church's weekly newspaper, *Die Kerkbode.* As editor (1967–71) of the right-wing Pretoria daily paper *Hoofstad,* he promoted the ruling National Party's pro-apartheid policies. He was elected to Parliament in 1971 and came to be called "Dr. No" for his firm stand against concessions to nonwhites. Treurnicht became provincial party leader in Transvaal (1978–82) and held several Cabinet posts. He drew world attention and triggered the Soweto uprising of 1976 when, as deputy minister of Bantu administration and education (1976–78), he insisted that black children be taught in Afrikaans. In 1982 he (with about 20 others) publicly resigned from the National Party and formed the Conservative Party in order to protest plans for separate elective chambers for Asians and Coloureds. He was reelected to Parliament as a Conservative in 1983, and after the 1989 general elections he led the official opposition. Although Treurnicht sought to preserve apartheid, he disliked violence and eventually came to support the idea of a separate white state.

Triffin, Robert, Belgian-born economist (b. Oct. 5, 1911, Flobecq, Belgium—d. Feb. 23, 1993, Ostend, Belgium), warned in 1962 that without a complete overhaul the international system of fixed exchange rates established at the Bretton Woods Conference in 1944 would inevitably collapse under the weight of a "dollar glut." His warning went unheeded, however, and in 1971 U.S. Pres. Richard Nixon—faced with persistent inflation, a growing trade deficit, and a worldwide run on the weakened dollar—devalued the U.S. currency and suspended its convertibility into gold. This signaled the end of the old system and ushered in an era of floating currencies and monetary instability. Triffin matriculated at the Catholic University of Louvain (1934) and at Harvard University (M.A., 1935; Ph.D., 1938). He taught at Harvard (1939–42) and held a series of senior advisory posts with the U.S. Federal Reserve System (1942–46), the International Monetary Fund (1946–48), and the Organisation for European Economic Co-operation (1948–51). In 1951 he was named a professor of economics at Yale University. Although Triffin became a U.S. citizen in 1942, he reclaimed Belgian citizenship when he returned to Europe in 1977. A fierce supporter of European unity, he was involved in the development of the European Monetary System and was a strong advocate of the European Community's plans for a central bank. He was made a baron in 1989. Triffin's influential books include *Europe and the Money Muddle* (1957), *Gold and the Dollar Crisis* (1960), and *Our International Monetary System: Yesterday, Today and Tomorrow* (1968).

Troyanos, Tatiana, U.S. mezzo-soprano (b. Sept. 12, 1938, New York, N.Y.—d. Aug. 21, 1993, New York), was renowned for her dark, warm, emotional voice; also a skilled actress, she had a wide repertoire, much of which she recorded. Troyanos first studied piano before an interest in singing developed during her teenage years. After high school she studied at the Juilliard School, New York City, and with Hans Heinz. She then sang in summer stock and on Broadway and in 1963 made her debut with the New York City Opera. In the 1965–66 season Troyanos began a 10-year association with the Hamburg (West Germany) State Opera; among the highlights of her years there was creation of the role of Jeanne in the world premiere of Krzysztof Penderecki's *The Devils of Loudon* (1969). She had earlier gained wide European acclaim, however, as the Composer (one of the trouser roles with which she became identified) in Richard Strauss's *Ariadne auf Naxos* at the 1966 Aix-en-Provence (France) Festival. Troyanos sang the title role in Handel's *Ariodante* at the opening of the Kennedy Center in Washington, D.C., in 1971 and made her Metropolitan Opera debut in 1976 as Octavian in Strauss's *Der Rosenkavalier.* Other roles for which she was especially known include Cherubino in Mozart's *The Marriage of Figaro,* the title role in Bizet's *Carmen,* Santuzza in Mascagni's *Cavalleria rusticana,* and Countess Geschwitz in Berg's *Lulu.* In 1992 Troyanos created the role of Queen Isabella in Philip Glass's *The Voyage* at the Metropolitan. She was diagnosed with cancer only shortly before her death.

Tunkin, Grigory Ivanovich, Soviet diplomat and legal scholar (b. Oct. 13 [Sept. 30, old style], 1906, Chamovo, Russia—d. Aug. 23, 1993, Moscow, Russia), played a major role in the formation of Soviet foreign policy in the post-Stalin era, especially Nikita Khrushchev's groundbreaking policy of "peaceful coexistence." Tunkin graduated from the Moscow Law Institute (1935) and Moscow State University (Ph.D., 1938). He joined the diplomatic service in 1939 and held a succession of posts, including legal counsel to the embassies in Canada (1942–44) and North Korea (1948–51). As head of the Foreign Ministry's treaties and legal division (1952–65), he advised the government on points of international law, drafted treaties, and encouraged cooperation with the West. He also represented the U.S.S.R. at international conferences and on the UN International Law Commission (1957–66). After Khrushchev's fall from power in 1964, Tunkin left government service to head the international law department at Moscow State University. His many published works include *Foundations of Modern International Law* (1956) and *Theory of International Law* (1970).

Tweedie, Jill Sheila, British journalist and author (b. May 22, 1936, Egypt—d. Nov. 12, 1993, London, England), was a columnist for *The Guardian* from 1969 to 1988 and on that paper's women's pages was one of the first to write about such feminist subjects as the treatment of women during childbirth, bride burning in India, the circumcision of women, and rape in marriage. Her writings served as an inspiration to a generation of women and in the 1970s and '80s helped shape the debate on the role of women. With humour, warmth, and sincerity, Tweedie explored what she and her readers had in common and made thousands of them feel that they knew her and were close friends. She was 1971's Woman Journalist of the Year, and her *Letters from a Fainthearted Feminist* (1982)—a compilation of columns, all of them letters from a housewife to a militantly feminist friend—became a BBC television series. Another of Tweedie's books was *Eating Children* (1993), the first volume of her autobiography, in which she recounted—not with self-pity but with wit—the mostly unhappy, unlucky early decades of her life. Her father was cruel and scornful, and she rebelled against him most of her life. After attending finishing school in Switzerland, Tweedie moved to Canada. There she went to work for a radio station, and at age 18 she married a Hungarian count. The first of their three children died at the age of five months, and when her marriage broke down, her husband abducted the other two and disappeared; she did not find them until they were adults. She had another son by her second husband, whom she had married in 1963, and she married for a third time in 1973, this time happily. At the time of her death, she was working on her second volume of autobiography, *Frightening People.*

Twitty, Conway (HAROLD LLOYD JENKINS), U.S. singer (b. Sept. 1, 1933, Friars Point, Miss.—d. June 5, 1993, Springfield, Mo.), was a successful songwriter and rockabilly star who struck gold with the 1958 pop recording "It's Only Make Believe" and, when his star began to wane in the early 1960s, reinvented his image and used his rich, tremulous baritone to specialize in country ballads. Twitty, backed up by the Lonely Blue Boys and, later, the Twitty Birds, eventually scored more than 50 number one hits on the country charts. He was known for his lost-love classics and for his steamy love lyrics; his hits included "Tight Fittin' Jeans," "Hello Darlin'," "You've Never Been This Far Before," and "After All the Good Is Gone." During the early 1970s Twitty teamed up with Loretta Lynn, and the two produced a string of duets, notably "Louisiana Woman, Mississippi Man" and "After the Fire Is Gone," which won them a 1971 Grammy award. They also won the Country Music Association's vocal duo award for four consecutive years (1972–75). Twitty was a dynamic yet no-nonsense stage performer. He sported a succession of distinctive haircuts, ranging from a Brylcreem-laden Roman centurion look to a semi-Afro. He was also an astute businessman, and in 1982 he launched Twitty City, a popular 3.6-ha (9-ac) tourist complex in Hendersonville, near Nashville, Tenn., where he also had part ownership in a baseball team. Twitty, who created his name from the names of two towns—Conway, Ark., and Twitty, Texas—died shortly after surgery for a stomach aneurysm.

Vera (VERA NEUMANN), U.S. artist and designer (b. July 24, 1910, Stamford, Conn.—d. June 15, 1993, North Tarrytown, N.Y.), created brightly coloured scarves, bedroom and kitchen linens, and draperies and sportswear that bore her name. Vera, who had been a designer of children's furniture and murals, used only her first name after founding (1946), with her husband, George Neumann, and F. Werner Hamm, a textile expert, the Vera Companies for silk-screened prints. She created both realistic and abstract designs, and her motifs included flowers, leaves, ferns, grass, vegetables, the Sun, and ladybugs. Her designs also adorned plastics and needlepoint products. Vera served as president of the company, which became a subsidiary of Manhattan Industries in 1967 and, from 1988, a division of Salant Corp. She continued to produce designs under the Vera signature until shortly before her death. In 1972 the Smithsonian Institution in Washington, D.C. mounted an exhibit of her designs.

Walker, Edwin Anderson, general (ret.), U.S. Army (b. Nov. 10, 1909, Center Point, Texas—d. Oct. 31, 1993, Dallas, Texas), valiantly served in World War II as the leader of the "Devil's Brigade" commandos, who fought at the Anzio beachhead in Italy and in the invasion of southern France, but he later resigned (1961) from the army with the rank of major general after receiving a public admonishment for circulating right-wing literature to his troops in Germany and publicly asserting that former U.S. president Harry Truman, Eleanor Roosevelt, and former secretary of state Dean Acheson were all "definitely pink." Walker, a 1931 graduate of the U.S. Military Academy at West Point, N.Y., was decorated with the Silver Star, the Bronze Star with cluster, and the Legion of Merit for his outstanding combat record. During the Korean War he commanded the 3rd Infantry Division's 7th Regiment and served as senior adviser to the 1st Korean Corps. He later was military adviser to Chiang Kai-shek, leader of China's Nationalist government. Walker commanded the federal troops that were ordered (1957) to Little Rock, Ark., to enforce school integration. A member of the right-wing John Birch Society, Walker then began an active role in efforts to resist the civil rights movement in the South. After federal marshals were ordered to the University of Mississippi to quell riots and secure the admission of black student James Meredith, Walker was arrested on a federal warrant charging him with insurrection and seditious conspiracy. The charges were later dropped. A few months later he was the target of an unknown assassin (later identified as Lee Harvey Oswald), who fired a bullet that narrowly missed Walker's head as he sat in his study. In 1982 the pension that Walker had forfeited because he resigned rather than retired from military service was quietly reinstated by the army.

Wang Zhen (WANG CHEN), Chinese politician and military leader (b. 1908, Liuyang [Liu-yang] county, Hunan province, China—d. March 12,

1993, Guangzhou [Canton], Guangdong [Kwangtung], China), was an uncompromising hard-liner who used his position as vice president (1988–93) of China to promote Maoism. He supported Deng Xiaoping (Teng Hsiao-p'ing) in the military suppression of the student-led 1989 Tiananmen (T'ien-an-men) Square pro-democracy movement, and it was rumoured that he personally commanded the troops on June 4, the night of the massacre. Wang, who attended school for only three years, joined the Communist Party at the age of 19. He was a veteran of the Long March (1934–35), and he later led a brigade that in 1941 reclaimed an arid wasteland at Nanniwan in Shaanxi (Shensi) province and turned it into an agricultural model of self-sufficiency. After World War II, Wang fought with the Red Army against Chang Kai-shek's Kuomintang troops. After the Communist victory in 1949, he was appointed political commisar of the Xinjiang (Hsin-chiang) military area. There he and his soldiers imposed authority over the largely Turkic population, reclaimed land and developed it into state farms, and introduced Han Chinese settlers into the region. In 1955 he was promoted to general, and the following year he was made a member of the Communist Party Central Committee. He served as minister of state farms and reclamation until the Cultural Revolution (1966–76), which he survived without being purged. Wang later served as vice-premier of the state council (1975–80) and was named to the Political Bureau Central Committee in 1978. Wang also orchestrated, behind the scenes, the purge of two of China's most reform-minded leaders, Hu Yaobang (Hu Yaopang) and Zhao Ziyang (Chao Tzu-yang), dismissed as Communist Party general secretaries in 1987 and 1989, respectively. Though Wang openly opposed Deng's reformist economic policies, his criticisms were ignored, and Deng continued to institute liberal policies designed to speed economic growth in China.

Watson, Thomas J., Jr., U.S. business executive (b. Jan. 8, 1914, Dayton, Ohio—d. Dec. 31, 1993, Greenwich, Conn.), inherited the leadership of International Business Machines Corp. from his father and propelled the company into the computer age. After graduating (1937) from Brown University, Providence, R.I., Watson joined IBM as a junior salesman while his father presided at the company's helm. In 1946, after returning from service in the Army Air Forces, he quickly moved through the ranks at IBM, becoming a vice president in that year, executive vice president in 1949, and finally president in 1952 (as his father became chairman). The younger Watson ardently pushed for the company to reach beyond tabulating machines and enter the nascent computer industry. IBM finally did so, though later than its rivals; IBM's first large automated system (the IBM 701) was unveiled in 1952. In 1956 Watson became chairman when his father retired. (The elder Watson died six weeks later.) Watson's aggressive tactics and heavy outlays for research established IBM's dominance in the industry so thoroughly that the U.S. government filed an antitrust suit against the company in 1969. (The case was dropped in 1982.) By the time Watson retired in 1971, IBM's stock had increased in value by more than $36 billion from when he gained the chairmanship. Watson later—from 1979 to 1981—served as ambassador to Moscow. In his memoirs, *Father, Son & Co.* (1990; with Peter Petre), Watson detailed his often stormy relationship with his father.

White, Sir Dick Goldsmith, British intelligence official (b. Dec. 20, 1906, Kent, England—d. Feb. 20, 1993, Sussex, England), was, at the time of his death, the only person to have headed both the British internal security service, MI-5 (1953–56), and the overseas secret intelligence service, MI-6 (1956–69). White was educated at Christ Church, Oxford, and at the Universities of Michigan and California. During World War II he rose to the rank of colonel in the army and was attached to the Allied headquarters as a counterintelligence officer. After the war he joined MI-5, of which he was named director general in 1953; three years later he moved to MI-6 as the first civilian to head that agency. As the director of the British intelligence community throughout much of the cold war, White reorganized and modernized both MI-5 and MI-6. In 1967 his hitherto top secret identity at MI-6 was divulged in the *Saturday Evening Post* magazine. It was later revealed that he had long suspected Kim Philby (who defected in 1963) of being a Soviet agent and that he had known since 1964 that Sir Anthony Blunt (who was publicly unmasked in 1979) was also a counterspy. After leaving MI-6, White served as intelligence coordinator to the Cabinet (1969–72). He was knighted in 1955.

Wilson, J(ohn) Tuzo, Canadian geophysicist (b. Oct. 24, 1908, Ottawa, Ont.—d. April 15, 1993, Toronto, Ont.), helped rekindle the concept of plate tectonics with his important 1965 paper *A New Class of Faults and Their Bearing on Continental Drift,* which introduced his theory of an entirely new class of geologic faults, transform faults (boundaries of plates that slide past each other), as a third type of movement in addition to convergent plates (those moving closer together) and divergent plates (those moving apart). His theory, devised to help explain continental drift, became almost universally accepted, and he was credited with coining the term *plate* in reference to the rigid portions into which the Earth's crust is divided. Wilson's mother, Henrietta Tuzo, was an explorer and mountaineer, and her name was given to British Columbia's Mt. Tuzo in the Canadian Rockies. By the time he was out of high school, Wilson had participated in geologic field expeditions into the Canadian wilderness. When he graduated (1930) from Trinity College, University of Toronto, he was the first person at any Canadian university to earn a degree in geophysical studies. He later attended St. John's College, Cambridge (B.A., 1932), Princeton University (Ph.D., 1936), and the University of Cambridge (M.A., 1940; Sc.D., 1958). Known as an adventurer, Wilson was the first to climb the 4,000-m (12,000-ft) Mt. Hague in Montana, and he visited each continent at least once. After working with the Geological Survey of Canada (1936–39) and serving with the Royal Canadian Engineers during World War II, he became professor of geophysics at the University of Toronto, where he remained until 1974. That year he became director general of the Ontario Science Centre, which he turned into a fascinating interactive environment for children, who were encouraged by posted signs to "please touch." As director of the centre until 1985, he introduced working models, innovative demonstrations, and traveling exhibits to help make scientific study enjoyable. He published *One Chinese Moon* (1959), *IGY: Year of the New Moons* (1961), *A Revolution in Earth Science* (1967), and *Continents Adrift and Continents Aground* (1977). The Wilson mountain range in Antarctica was named in his honour.

Zappa, Francis Vincent ("Frank"), U.S. rock musician and composer (b. Dec. 21, 1940, Baltimore, Md.—d. Dec. 4, 1993, Los Angeles, Calif.), during his three-decade-long career, released over 50 albums in a variety of musical styles—from rock and jazz to avant-garde classical; *Absolutely Free* (1967) blended rock, rhythm and blues, and the music of Igor Stravinsky and Edgard Varèse. He was also known for his satiric works and for his sometimes scatological lyrics. Zappa moved to California with his family when he was 10 and during the 1950s began his musical studies. When he was in high school, he was a drummer with the Blackouts, and at 18 he switched to the guitar, having taught himself. Zappa wrote movie scores in 1960 and 1963 and in 1964 began working with the Soul Giants; the group later became the Mothers and then the Mothers of Invention. The band released its first album, the double record *Freak Out!,* in 1966. In 1967 Zappa, with a 50-piece orchestra, recorded *Lumpy Gravy* and with the Mothers of Invention spent several months in residence at the Garrick Theater in New York City's Greenwich Village. The group disbanded in 1969 but was re-formed in 1971. It was renamed Zappa in 1979. Over the years Zappa formed several record labels—among them, Bizarre, Straight, and Barking Pumpkin—and released such albums as *We're Only in It for the Money* (1967), *Uncle Meat* (1969), *Hot Rats* (1970), *Burnt Weeny Sandwich* (1970), *Sheik Yerbouti* (1979), *Shut Up 'n' Play Yer Guitar* (1981), and *Jazz from Hell* (1988), a Grammy award winner. His sound track for *200 Motels* was performed in concert with Zubin Mehta and the Los Angeles Philharmonic in 1970. His greatest commercial success came in 1982 with "Valley Girl," a parody of California slang featuring his daughter Moon Unit (his other children were named Dweezil, Ahmet, and Diva). In 1985 Zappa took up the fight against the censorship of rock lyrics, and his campaign encouraging young people to register to vote resulted in 11,000 new names on the rolls for the 1988 election.

REUTERS/BETTMANN

Zuckerman of Burnham Thorpe, Solly Zuckerman, Baron, British scientist (b. May 30, 1904, Cape Town, South Africa—d. April 1, 1993, London, England), made an improbable transition from his beginnings as a research anatomist with the London Zoological Society (1928–32) to being a trusted scientific adviser and military strategist with the British Defense Ministry (1939–46; 1960–66) and finally to his position as chief scientific adviser to the British government (1964–71). Zuckerman matriculated at the University of Cape Town and University College Hospital, London, eventually receiving doctorates in science and medicine. At the Zoological Society he studied primate physiology and wrote his groundbreaking first books, *The Social Life of Monkeys and Apes* (1931) and *Functional Affinities of Man, Monkeys, and Apes* (1933). In 1934 he switched his focus to human anatomy, which he taught at the Universities of Oxford (1934–45), Birmingham (1946–68), and East Anglia (1969–74). During World War II, Zuckerman was called on to determine the effects on the body of the shock waves from bomb blasts. He quickly became an invaluable government adviser, with strong views on everything from saturation bombing (which he opposed) to nuclear disarmament (which he endorsed) to environmental pollution. These diverse interests were reflected in his later books, notably *Scientists and War* (1966) and *Great Zoos of the World* (1980), and in his two volumes of memoirs, *From Apes to Warlords* (1978) and *Monkeys, Men, and Missiles* (1988). Zuckerman remained with the Zoological Society throughout his career, serving as secretary (1955–77) and president (1977–84). He was knighted in 1964, awarded the Order of Merit in 1968, and elevated to a life peerage in 1971, shortly after he retired from public service.

Events of 1993

Agriculture and Food Supplies

World agricultural and food production declined in 1993, according to preliminary estimates of the UN Food and Agriculture Organization (FAO). Excessive rain and flooding severely damaged feed-grain and oilseed crops in the U.S., and economic disruptions in the former Soviet Union and, to a lesser extent, Eastern Europe continued to obstruct the expansion of agricultural production and trade. The drought in southern Africa, which brought famine to much of the region in 1992, was broken, but food supplies remained scarce in several areas. Other countries in Africa were still afflicted with or not yet recovered from war or civil strife. Food-aid commitments in 1992–93 reached a record 15.1 million tons of cereals as donors responded to emergencies. The FAO published an important assessment of the likely course of the world food situation, especially as affecting the less developed countries (LDCs) through the first decade of the 21st century, that had both optimistic and sobering elements.

Trade issues affecting agriculture captured the headlines during much of the year. Agricultural issues were critical to U.S. acceptance of the North American Free Trade Agreement (NAFTA) and to the conclusion of the Uruguay round of multilateral trade negotiations under the General Agreement on Tariffs and Trade (GATT). The agricultural provisions of NAFTA had less effect on trade between the U.S. and Mexico than provisions for other sectors, but modifications of some provisions, particularly those dealing with sugar, were vital to the agreement's passage. An 11th-hour agreement resolving long-standing differences between the U.S. and the European Community (EC) on agriculture made possible the completion of the GATT negotiations and U.S. submission of the pact to Congress before expiration of the "fast-track" negotiation authority on December 15.

Food Emergencies. Reports by the FAO and the World Food Program suggested that civil warfare or its aftermath continued to be a greater threat to food security than weather in 1993, especially in Africa. In Angola internal strife brought collapse of the country's economy and marketing system, drove many farmers away from their farms, and prevented outside help from reaching famine-stricken areas. Continued fighting in The Sudan created more refugees and displaced persons at the same time that many people stricken by famine earlier were returning to their homes. Some 40,000 Sudanese were reported to have crossed into Uganda and another 60,000 into Ethiopia, Kenya, and Zaire.

Table I. Selected Indexes of World Agricultural and Food Production

(1979–81 = 100)

	Total agricultural production						Total food production						Per capita food production					
Region or country	1988	1989	1990	1991	1992	1993[1]	1988	1989	1990	1991	1992	1993[1]	1988	1989	1990	1991	1992	1993[1]
Developed countries	105	110	110	107	108	105	105	110	111	107	109	105	99	104	104	100	100	105
United States	94	102	106	105	114	106	94	103	106	104	114	106	87	95	96	94	102	94
Canada	102	114	126	126	122	121	103	115	127	127	124	122	96	105	115	113	109	106
Europe	108	110	109	108	106	104	108	110	109	109	106	104	106	107	105	105	102	100
Japan	97	99	98	91	96	87	100	102	101	94	99	89	95	96	95	88	93	84
Oceania	113	109	112	112	121	114	110	108	110	110	121	116	99	96	96	95	102	97
South Africa	106	113	103	105	82	101	105	113	104	105	81	102	87	90	81	80	60	74
Former U.S.S.R.	117	120	119	106	100	98	118	122	121	108	101	99	110	113	111	98	92	89
Less developed countries	131	135	140	144	147	148	132	136	141	144	148	150	111	113	114	144	116	114
South and East Asia[2]	129	134	136	138	143	145	130	136	137	140	144	147	111	113	112	113	114	114
Bangladesh	112	123	125	127	126	128	113	125	126	128	127	129	92	99	98	97	94	93
China	143	147	158	164	170	169	140	145	156	160	168	168	125	127	135	136	141	139
India	138	147	147	151	155	160	140	148	149	152	157	161	118	123	121	122	123	124
Indonesia	147	152	162	166	176	182	150	156	156	170	181	187	127	130	136	136	143	145
Korea, South	113	111	114	117	125	121	115	112	116	119	128	123	103	100	102	104	110	105
Malaysia	186	181	189	206	215	233	188	215	229	253	266	291	152	170	176	190	195	209
Myanmar (Burma)	130	118	119	120	129	139	132	119	121	122	131	142	112	98	98	97	102	108
Pakistan	144	153	160	171	169	180	140	150	155	161	166	174	108	111	112	113	114	116
Philippines	109	115	117	118	118	120	108	114	117	118	118	121	89	91	92	90	88	89
Thailand	125	132	125	135	131	132	124	129	120	131	125	125	109	111	103	110	104	103
Vietnam	138	145	151	155	163	167	138	145	151	154	162	166	116	119	121	122	126	126
Western Asia	129	122	138	135	141	140	130	122	138	136	142	142	103	94	102	98	99	96
Iran	144	146	167	181	189	175	144	147	169	184	192	178	104	103	114	121	123	111
Turkey	128	122	130	130	131	131	128	123	129	131	132	133	106	100	103	102	101	100
Africa[3]	126	131	132	138	134	138	127	132	133	139	135	139	100	101	98	100	94	94
Egypt	127	130	137	142	147	151	137	140	149	155	159	163	112	112	116	118	118	119
Ethiopia	105	108	111	112	114	113	108	109	112	113	115	113	88	87	87	85	84	80
Morocco	167	182	171	197	145	151	166	181	171	197	146	150	135	144	132	149	107	108
Nigeria	142	147	164	173	188	195	142	147	164	172	188	195	110	110	119	121	127	128
Sudan, The	117	94	86	113	130	125	118	92	87	115	133	129	92	70	64	83	93	88
Zaire	125	128	129	132	134	134	125	127	129	132	134	134	99	95	93	93	91	88
Latin America	121	124	125	126	129	128	123	126	127	129	132	132	104	105	104	103	104	102
Argentina	112	102	110	113	117	112	112	102	110	112	117	113	100	90	96	97	100	95
Brazil	131	138	129	133	140	143	136	143	133	137	146	148	114	119	108	110	115	115
Colombia	119	126	134	139	137	136	124	135	140	141	138	142	105	113	115	114	110	111
Mexico	117	119	125	125	129	123	116	120	126	127	134	128	97	98	100	99	102	96
Peru	131	129	116	120	112	116	134	130	119	124	117	120	112	107	95	98	90	91
Venezuela	131	132	132	135	138	133	131	132	132	136	139	137	107	105	103	103	103	100
World	118	123	125	126	128	127	118	123	126	125	128	127	103	105	106	104	104	102

[1]Preliminary. [2]Excludes Japan. [3]Excludes South Africa.
Source: Food and Agriculture Organization of the United Nations, *FAO Quarterly Bulletin of Statistics*.

Table II. World Cereal Supply and Distribution

In 000,000 metric tons

	1990–91	1991–92	1992–93	1993–94[1]
Production				
Wheat	588	542	561	560
Coarse grains	821	804	857	779
Rice, milled	351	348	351	344
Total	1,760	1,694	1,769	1,682
Utilization				
Wheat	564	559	546	563
Coarse grains	809	809	834	823
Rice, milled	346	353	355	355
Total	1,718	1,721	1,734	1,741
Exports				
Wheat	102	109	109	99
Coarse grains	88	94	88	87
Rice, milled	12	14	14	15
Total	202	216	212	201
Ending stocks[2]				
Wheat	145	129	143	140
Coarse grains	140	134	158	113
Rice, milled	59	55	52	40
Total	345	318	352	294
Stocks as % of utilization				
Wheat	25.8%	23.0%	26.2%	24.9%
Coarse grains	17.3%	16.6%	18.9%	13.8%
Rice, milled	17.2%	15.5%	14.5%	11.4%
Total	20.1%	18.5%	20.3%	16.9%
Stocks held by U.S. in %				
Wheat	16.2%	10.0%	10.0%	12.5%
Coarse grains	34.1%	25.3%	40.1%	25.1%
Stocks held by EC in %				
Wheat	11.4%	17.7%	17.6%	16.2%
Coarse grains	10.9%	13.4%	11.4%	15.9%

[1] Forecast.
[2] Series includes estimates of Chinese and Soviet stocks. Data not available for all countries, including parts of Eastern Europe and Asia.
Source: USDA, Foreign Agricultural Service, December 1993.

In Somalia the intervention of UN and U.S. troops may not have brought political stability, but it did lead to a significant improvement in the country's food situation. Relief agencies began to scale down their operations as food became more available in markets and prices fell, but the need for food for returning refugees also contributed to the necessity for continuing outside food aid.

The slow return of some 650,000 Rwandan refugees following the September peace agreement delayed the planting of 1993–94 crops and created a continuing need for food aid. Eritrea continued heavily dependent on food aid because of the large number of returning refugees with the end of conflict there. Food supplies were considered satisfactory in Ethiopia, thanks to good crops and substantial food-aid imports.

Kenya's corn crop—normally the source of substantial exports—was hard hit by drought. The country was already burdened with nearly half a million refugees from neighbouring Somalia, Ethiopia, and The Sudan. Continuing civil strife in Liberia was disastrous for food production and distribution, especially in central and northern areas, but the midyear peace agreement gave hope of expanded food relief.

Fighting also hampered food production in Sierra Leone, and relief shipments could not reach some areas, particularly those held by rebels. Political and economic turmoil left many displaced and destitute in Zaire. In Mozambique the October 1992 peace agreement and the end of the drought permitted an increase in domestic food supplies and improved relief distribution, especially to returning displaced persons.

Slow Retreat of Hunger. In November the FAO released an extensive review of the current state and future prospects for the global food situation, *Agriculture: Towards 2010*. FAO analysts started by combining the data on soil quality and terrain features—contained in the FAO-Unesco Soil Map of the World—with inventories of temperature and moisture conditions for individual countries. They then assessed how the crop yields actually achieved by the technology available under the most favourable conditions by experiment stations and farmers might be approached or reduced under the agroclimatic conditions they had mapped.

The comprehensive study reported slow but steady progress in increasing global food production and per capita food supplies. World per capita food supplies were some 18% larger than 30 years previously, and the majority of LDCs shared in the gains. The number of people chronically undernourished was estimated to have declined, from nearly 950 million 20 years earlier to some 800 million persons in 1993, and represented about one-fifth of the population in the LDCs. Many countries, however, hardly made any progress, and sub-Saharan Africa was worse off than it had been 20 or 30 years earlier.

Looking to the future, the FAO saw this combination of slow progress and the persistence of serious hunger likely to continue over the next two decades. The incidence of chronic undernutrition in LDCs could fall from about 800 million people to about 650 million, with per capita food supplies for direct human consumption growing from an average of nearly 2,500 calories per day to just over 2,700 by 2010. By comparison, per capita supplies in the developed countries were not expected to rise much above the current average of 3,400 calories. These estimates assumed world population growth of about 1.5% annually—from 5.3 billion people in 1990 to 7.2 billion by 2010. About 94% of the increase would come in the LDCs.

It was anticipated that consumption in the Middle East, North Africa, East Asia (including China), Latin America, and the Caribbean region could climb to or above 3,000 calories per day. The increase in East Asia could cut the number of malnourished dramatically (from about 250 million to about 70 million) and leave sub-Saharan Africa, at about 2,150 calories, with the largest and fastest-growing concentration of undernourished people (nearly 300 million). Population there was expected to grow 3.2% annually. Moderate gains in South Asia, approaching 2,500 calories, would leave the region with about 200 million undernourished persons.

These gains would result mainly from increased domestic production in the LDCs supplemented by some growth in food imports. They would come even in the absence of major new technological breakthroughs and despite a further slowdown in overall world agricultural production—from 2.3% annually over the past 20 years to perhaps 1.8% over the next two decades. The slower growth reflected less need for expanded production in most developed countries—and in several LDCs where consumption requirements were be-

Table III. Shipment of Food Aid in Cereals

In 000-metric-ton grain equivalent

Region and country	Average 1988–89, 1990–91	1991–92	1992–93	1993–94[1]
Australia	336	328	249	300
Canada	1,093	996	802	700
European Community	2,702	3,707	4,107	3,000
By members	951	945	953	...
By organization	1,750	2,762	3,154	...
Japan	461	387	499	400
Norway	37	72	62	40
Sweden	103	113	165	100
Switzerland	67	48	57	50
United States	6,188	7,052	8,186	6,500
Others[2]	320	383	1,008	265
Total	11,307	13,086	15,135	11,355
To less developed countries	10,331	11,137	11,823	10,000
To LIFDC[3]	8,852	10,080	9,818	...
Sub-Saharan Africa	2,886	4,390	5,227	...
To other countries	976	1,949	3,312	1,355

[1] Estimated.
[2] Included Argentina, Austria, China, Finland, India, OPEC Special Fund, Saudi Arabia, Turkey, and World Food Program, but not necessarily for all years.
[3] Low-income food-deficit countries with per capita incomes under U.S. $1,235 in 1991.
Source: FAO, *Food Outlook*, December 1993.

A barn and silos in West Quincy, Mo., stand in floodwaters. The flooding of the Mississippi and Missouri rivers and several of their tributaries during the summer of 1993 caused severe crop damage, particularly to corn (maize).
DAVID GRAHAM

coming largely satisfied—and the slow growth of effective demand in many poorer countries where consumer buying power remained weak.

In other words, the continued existence of poverty was the main reason for undernutrition, not resource constraints like inadequate land, water, or technical knowledge such as that embodied in high-yielding plant varieties. There remained, nevertheless, a strong connection between eliminating undernutrition and promoting more rapid agricultural development because the majority of the poor in LDCs still depended on agriculture for employment and income. Increasing agricultural production in many cases represented the major opportunity for increasing income and improving nutrition, particularly in countries with high concentrations of rural poverty.

The report in effect conceded that limited agricultural resources were still an obstacle to food security and that the need had not been overcome for both private and government action to achieve the potential increases in output that were identified in the report. The existence of 650 million undernourished persons implied continuing food emergencies and a need for external food aid.

Agriculture and Trade Policies. *Multilateral Trade Negotiations.* The Uruguay round of GATT negotiations begun in 1986 was finally concluded on December 15, just hours before expiration of the "fast-track" authority for U.S. congressional approval. The "now-or-never" character of the deadline contributed to resolution of agricultural issues that had dragged the negotiations out for three years. The agreement was lauded as bringing agriculture truly under international trade rules for the first time and as a major step toward greater market orientation of domestic agricultural and trade policies around the world.

Agriculture presented special obstacles because the sector was generally more heavily dependent upon domestic support policies, which were closely intertwined with trade policies. Further complications were agriculture's vulnerability to instability because of weather, the socioeconomic impact of the movement of rural people to cities, and the slow adjustment of political representation in many countries to those shifts. Domestic agricultural policies were almost completely off-limits to discussion. For instance, the U.S. had joined GATT only on the condition—"the section 22 waiver"—that it could restrict agricultural imports if they interfered, for almost any reason, with domestic support programs. Although the U.S. initially challenged internal elements of the EC's common agricultural policy (CAP) in the Tokyo round of 1979, it ultimately pulled back rather than risk gains in the reduction of barriers to industrial products.

Conditions were changing, however. The mid-1980s saw large increases in the budgetary costs of supporting domestic agricultural programs, particularly in the U.S. and the EC. Domestic agricultural prices were supported at levels that induced more production than could be absorbed in the domestic market without producer subsidies, restriction on price-undercutting imports, or export subsidies to dispose of surpluses. The cost of these programs began to make finance ministers in many countries the discreet advocates of reduced agricultural supports and freer trade, leaving agricultural ministers to bear the brunt of farmer complaints.

Not only that, the trade barriers and export-subsidy competition were generating a full menu of trade disputes—the chicken, pasta, and white wine "wars" making the most colourful headlines. These disputes threatened waves of retaliations and counterretaliations of expanding magnitudes. The major warring parties tended to be the U.S. and the EC, which rose from net importer to major exporter largely as a consequence of its CAP. Other exporters that relied less on subsidies threatened to join the fray. Many LDCs with strong tendencies toward government intervention in their economies began to see advantages to freeing up their economies and promoting freer trade as an engine of growth. All these influences gave growing support to the view that there also were advantages to be gained from a worldwide simultaneous reduction of trade-distorting policies and the internal government support policies that inspired them. However, U.S. persistence in pushing for serious reform measures, even at the risk of endangering an overall GATT agreement, was probably decisive in bringing agricultural policies under GATT.

The changes in world agriculture brought about by the agreement were major but were due to come in small increments. For the first time under GATT, commitments to reduce export subsidies, to increase import access systematically, and to reduce internal support were specified in detail. The greatest impact of the agreement would likely come from the reduction of export subsidies, which may have been the primary U.S. objective in the negotiations. Both the EC and the U.S. would make substantial reductions in such expenditures. The increase in market access accomplished by the agreement was likely to be smaller initially, but the stage was set for future reductions by the establishment of specific tariffs and the elimination of the moving target represented by nontariff barriers.

For many—especially the EC and the U.S.—the agreed-to cuts in agricultural subsidies primarily represented a freezing of subsidies at current levels brought about by domestic budgetary pressures. The plan helped deter backsliding and opened the way for future reductions. The agreement called for further negotiations in its fifth year, based on a reassessment of the agreement's accomplishments, taking into account nontrade concerns, "special and differential treatment" for LDCs, and the agreement's object of establishing a fair and market-oriented agricultural trading system. The main features of the final agreement built upon the "Dunkel text" of 1991 and the EC–U.S. "Blair House agreement" of 1992.

Export Subsidies. Except for LDCs, all parties by the end of the six-year implementation period were to have reduced budgetary outlays for export subsidies by at least 36% and the quantity of products subject to export subsidies by 21% from the average in the 1986–90 base period. No reductions would be required of the "least developed countries," but the reductions were 24% and 14%, respectively, for other LDCs. One part of the accord called for the cuts to be in equal annual installments, but another had the effect of permitting smaller cuts in the early years, as long as the target established by the 1986–90 base period was met at the end of the six years. (Parties were permitted a later base period—such as 1991–92, when subsidies were higher—for calculating the maximum level of subsidies permitted annually.) This modification accommodated the need of the EC for more time to dispose of its large stocks of surplus grain—especially wheat—and represented a key compromise that led to French, and thus EC, acceptance of the agricultural package.

Import Access. The agreement required "tariffication"—the conversion to tariffs of all nontariff barriers—and commitments to guarantee and gradually increase minimum levels of access to import markets. These barriers included the EC's variable levies, the section 22 U.S. import quotas on sugar and dairy products, the "voluntary restraints" on meat exports accepted by Australia and New Zealand to avoid triggering the U.S. meat quota, and the outright prohibition of imports by many other countries, such as Japan's ban on imported rice.

Table IV. World Production of Oilseeds and Products

In 000,000 metric tons

	1991–92	1992–93[1]	1993–94[2]
Production of oilseeds	223.5	226.6	222.9
Soybeans	106.9	116.5	111.7
U.S.	54.1	59.6	49.9
China	9.7	10.3	11.6
Argentina	11.2	11.0	12.0
Brazil	19.3	22.3	23.3
Cottonseed	36.6	31.4	30.9
U.S.	6.3	5.7	5.7
Former Soviet republics	4.4	3.7	3.9
China	9.7	7.7	6.7
Peanuts	22.3	23.1	22.7
U.S.	2.2	1.9	1.5
China	6.3	6.0	7.2
India	7.1	8.6	7.4
Sunflower seed	21.5	21.3	22.1
U.S.	1.6	1.2	1.5
Former Soviet republics	5.6	5.5	6.0
Argentina	3.8	3.1	3.5
European Community	4.0	4.1	3.7
Rapeseed	28.1	25.9	26.6
Canada	4.2	3.7	5.4
China	7.4	7.7	6.7
European Community	7.0	6.2	5.6
India	5.8	5.4	5.8
Copra	4.8	4.6	4.8
Palm kernel	3.4	3.8	4.0
Oilseeds crushed	184.2	184.1	185.6
Soybeans	91.9	96.1	97.3
Oilseed ending stocks	21.7	23.5	20.2
Soybeans	18.3	20.8	17.4
World production[3]			
Total fats and oils	72.6	...	...
Edible vegetable oils	59.2	59.8	61.8
Soybean oil	16.8	17.2	17.6
Palm oil	11.5	13.0	13.8
Animal fats	12.4	...	...
Marine oils	1.1	1.0	1.1
High-protein meals[4]	118.2	119.0	120.4
Soybean meal	72.8	76.3	77.2

[1] Preliminary.
[2] Forecast.
[3] Processing potential from crops in year indicated.
[4] Converted, based on product's protein content, to weight equivalent to soybeans of 44% protein content.
Source: USDA, Foreign Agricultural Service, December 1993.

The new tariffs initially were intended to maintain the same level of protection as had the old nontariff barriers unless reductions were negotiated elsewhere in the agreement. For developed countries these new tariffs, as well as pre-existing ones, were to be reduced over six years by an average of 36%, with a minimum of 15% for individual tariff items. The percentages were 24% and 10%, respectively, for LDCs, except for the least developed countries, which were exempt. The preagreement level of import access was supposed to be guaranteed, generally by use of tariff-rate quotas (TRQs) that charged a lower tariff on a specified volume of imports but a much higher tariff for imports in excess of that amount. All tariffs, new or old, were to be binding. Such bindings fixed tariffs at levels that could not be changed unless negotiations had provided for other forms of compensation to trading partners for the resulting reduced market access.

Just how much increased trade these reductions might actually encourage was hard to say because countries tended to adopt a wide margin of safety in setting them. Probably of more trade importance was the creation of minimum import opportunities through the use of TRQs in cases where imports were less than 5% of domestic consumption. The TRQs, initially set at 3%, were to be expanded to 5% over the six years. Special, somewhat less stringent, minimum-access commitments were agreed to by Japan and South Korea for rice. Special quantity and price-based safeguards would protect producers in importing countries from sudden surges in imports; special provisions applied in LDCs where a primary agricultural product was the predominant staple in the country's traditional diet.

Internal Support. The amount of all trade-distorting subsidies was to be reduced by 20% by the year 2000 from the 1986–88 base period for each developed country and 13.3% by the year 2005 for each LDC, except that the least developed countries needed only not exceed subsidies in the base period. For all countries, reductions since the base period were counted. As agreed at Blair House, the reduction applied to all supported commodities in aggregate, not to commodities individually. The flexibility allowed by this provision and the fact that both the EC and the U.S. had cut back supports since the base period, when they were at a peak, made it unnecessary for either to cut subsidies further.

Food and Health Safety. The agreement also recognized a government's right to apply sanitary and phytosanitary protections to human, animal, and plant life. All signatories were encouraged to adopt internationally recognized standards but were free to apply stricter standards. All such measures were to be based on scientific justification or on risk assessment.

Commodities. *Grains.* The sharp decline in the weather-ravaged U.S. coarse-grain crop was the primary cause of an expected (in December) 5% reduction in world grain production in 1993–94. Grain supplies were adequate for maintaining consumption in 1993–94 with moderate increases in international prices because of the substantial buildup of global grain stocks during 1992–93.

World wheat production in 1993–94 was little changed from 1992–93, and supplies were ample because of large carry-in stocks. Production gains in China, South Asia, and Eastern Europe roughly offset reductions in the former Soviet Union (mainly Kazakhstan), the EC, and North America. In Eastern Europe a poor 1992 wheat harvest and a lack of foreign exchange with which to import wheat contributed to an overall decline in global wheat consumption in 1992–93. Global wheat stocks increased substantially in 1992–93, with the EC again the leading stock holder.

Wheat imports by the former Soviet republics increased to about 23.7 million tons in 1992–93, assisted by various aid, credit, and barter arrangements with the U.S. and the EC, but the ability of the region to maintain imports in 1993–94 was weakened by a shaky credit record. By the end of 1993, Russia had made considerable progress in catching up on overdue grain payments to the U.S., the EC, and Canada but not sufficiently to be reinstated in the U.S. credit-guarantee program from which it had been suspended in late 1992.

The decline in global rice production in 1992–93 mainly reflected sharp declines in Chinese and Japanese output. Large stocks of rice resulting from China's bumper harvest the previous year depressed prices in an economy that as a result of economic reforms responded more to market signals. Consumer demand was weak for high-yield, low-quality rice, the production of which was encouraged by the government's previous policies. Farmers responded by switching to higher quality but lower yielding rice varieties, more profitable cash crops (*e.g.,* vegetables, fruit, and fish), and nonagricultural land uses. The result was the smallest harvested area for rice since 1969–70.

Unfavourable weather reduced Japanese rice output to the lowest level in decades and led the government to end its ban on rice imports temporarily. The need to import substantial quantities of rice may also have made it easier for the government to agree, for the first time, to permit importation of at least small quantities of rice on a regular basis under the GATT agreement. The Japanese consumer's preference for high-quality japonica rice, which normally accounted for less than 15% of a world rice market (dominated by indica rice), led to a strong run-up in prices that favoured the major suppliers of that rice, Australia and the U.S.

The 31% reduction in the U.S. corn (maize) crop was responsible for a 9% decline in world coarse-grain production in 1993–94. Overall, global coarse-grain supplies, however, were only 5% smaller because of large carry-in stocks in the U.S. resulting from the record-high U.S. corn harvest. Among major export competitors, production rose in Canada, China, Australia, and the EC. China emerged as the second largest coarse-grain exporter (mainly corn and barley), shipping 11.9 million tons in 1992–93, compared with 8.6 million for the EC and 51 million for the U.S.

Coarse-grain imports into the countries of the former Soviet Union, which averaged more than 20 million tons annually in 1989–91, were about half that in 1992–93. Besides the financial restraints on imports, the reduction of livestock subsidies, higher meat prices, and weakened consumer demand reduced meat consumption and feed-grain consumption. In October Mexico announced a reduction in corn support prices to take place over a short transition that was likely to lead to the substitution of wheat for corn plantings, particularly in irrigated areas where corn had supplanted wheat. The U.S. was expecting a substantial expansion of corn exports to that country as the combined result of this policy and Mexico's reduction of import barriers as the result of NAFTA.

Oilseeds. World oilseed output was expected to be smaller in 1993–94 because of a U.S. soybean crop greatly reduced by rain and flood damage in some areas and drought in others. A 50% reduction in producer prices for oilseeds resulting from lower price supports, together with land idling under the EC reform of the CAP, resulted in a 10% decline in EC oilseed production in 1993–94.

Table V. Livestock Numbers and Meat Production in Major Producing Countries

In 000,000 head and 000,000 metric tons (carcass weight)

Region and country	1992[1]	1993[2]	1992[1]	1993[2]
	Cattle and buffalo		Beef and veal	
World total	1,034.4	1,033.4	45.93	45.80
Canada	11.7	11.9	0.91	0.93
United States	100.9	102.1	10.61	10.66
Mexico	30.6	30.7	1.66	1.71
Argentina	55.6	55.0	2.52	2.55
Brazil	129.4	128.9	3.95	4.10
Uruguay	9.9	10.4	0.37	0.33
Western Europe	86.7	84.9	9.09	8.83
European Community	79.5	77.6	8.44	8.18
Eastern Europe	12.2	11.6	1.05	0.82
Former Soviet republics[3]	100.9	97.7	7.01	6.89
Russian Federation	52.2	49.0	3.44	3.25
Ukraine	22.5	21.5	1.65	1.55
Australia	25.7	25.7	1.84	1.77
India	271.3	271.8	1.02	1.05
China	107.6	110.0	1.80	2.00
	Hogs		Pork	
World total	754.3	759.8	65.80	66.86
Canada	10.6	10.5	1.21	1.20
United States	59.0	58.5	7.19	7.66
Mexico	11.3	12.2	0.83	0.87
Western Europe	119.1	119.2	14.93	15.27
European Community	110.0	110.0	13.82	14.16
Eastern Europe	39.9	36.4	3.57	3.13
Former Soviet republics[3]	56.9	51.8	4.97	4.55
Russian Federation	31.5	28.0	2.86	2.55
Ukraine	16.2	15.0	1.19	1.05
Japan	10.8	10.6	1.43	1.42
China	384.2	398.2	26.35	28.00
			Poultry meat[4]	
World total	...	...	38.98	40.49
United States	...	...	11.89	12.42
Brazil	...	...	2.93	3.17
European Community	...	...	7.37	7.56
Eastern Europe	...	...	0.94	0.88
Former Soviet republics[3]	...	...	2.71	2.52
Japan	...	...	1.37	1.36
China	...	...	4.54	5.10
	Sheep		Sheep, goat meat	
World total[5]	931.4	920.4	6.41	6.37
			All meat	
Total			157.11	159.53

[1] Preliminary livestock numbers at year's end. Consists of 51 countries for beef and veal, 38 for pork, 51 for poultry meat, 30 for sheep and goat meat, and roughly the same coverage for animal numbers. Includes nearly all European producers, the most significant in the Western Hemisphere, and scattered coverage elsewhere.
[2] Forecast.
[3] Former Soviet Union, comprising 12 nations, excluding its Baltic States.
[4] Ready-to-eat equivalent.
[5] Includes China.
Source: USDA, Foreign Agricultural Service, August and October 1993.

In the EC reduced domestic oilseed meal supplies and cheaper feed-grain prices—both the result of CAP reform—were resulting in less oilseed meal and more grain being fed to animals. Financial and credit problems, together with declining livestock herds were the cause in Eastern Europe and Russia. Large carry-in stocks of soybeans from bumper harvests in 1992–93 cushioned the impact of smaller oilseed supplies, but international soybean prices, which had tended slowly downward in recent years, began to strengthen in the latter half of 1993. They averaged $246 per ton (c.i.f., Rotterdam, U.S. No. 2 yellow) in 1992–93 (October–September), compared with $237 in 1991–92, and showed signs of moving higher.

Production of oilseeds with relatively high oil content—such as rapeseed, sunflower seed, and palm oil—had been growing more rapidly in recent years than those with high meal content. Efforts by many, particularly among the LDCs, to achieve self-sufficiency in vegetable oils were a major factor. The resulting increase in vegetable oil supplies contributed to lower prices and more rapid expansion of global consumption and trade than was the case for meals. Prices of most vegetable oils, except coconut and corn, recorded gains in 1992–93. Soybean oil prices began to recover in mid-1993, averaging $453 per ton (f.o.b., Rotterdam) in 1992–93, compared with $437 in 1991–92. The price of soybean meal edged up to $207 per ton (c.i.f., Rotterdam) in 1992–93.

Table VI. World Production of Dairy Products

Production of cow's milk
In 000,000 metric tons

Region and country	1991	1992[1]	1993[2]
Developed countries	362.2	347.1	337.8
United States	67.3	68.8	68.6
Canada	7.8	7.4	7.4
Western Europe	128.8	126.3	125.4
European Community	113.9	111.6	110.7
France	25.7	25.3	25.2
Germany	28.9	27.8	27.6
Italy	11.4	11.1	10.8
Netherlands, The	11.0	11.0	10.9
United Kingdom	14.5	14.4	14.4
Other Western Europe	14.9	14.7	14.7
Eastern Europe	31.5	28.2	27.3
Poland	14.5	12.7	12.3
Former Soviet republics	95.5	85.5	77.8
Baltic States	5.8	4.6	4.3
Australia/New Zealand[3]	14.7	15.4	16.2
Japan/South Africa	10.7	10.9	11.0
Less developed countries	165.0	168.0	173.0
Latin America	44.0	44.0	45.0
Brazil	14.2	14.8	15.1
Africa	12.0	11.0	11.0
Asia	109.0	113.0	117.0
China	4.6	5.0	5.5
India	28.2	29.4	30.5
World total	527.2	515.1	510.8

	Production		Year-end stocks	
Product/Region	1992[1]	1993[2]	1992[1]	1993[2]
	In 000 metric tons			
Butter[4]	6,074	5,948	932	782
EC	1,613	1,583	490	443
U.S.	619	580	206	110
Cheese[4]	11,137	11,257	1,707	1,681
EC	5,031	5,078	1,154	1,164
U.S.	2,943	3,050	213	200
Nonfat dry milk[4]	2,881	2,806	497	367
EC	1,214	1,202	274	137
U.S.	396	340	37	25

[1] Preliminary.
[2] Forecast.
[3] Year ended June 30 for Australia and May 31 for New Zealand.
[4] Butter and cheese totals include virtually all developed countries, India, Argentina, Brazil, Mexico, and Venezuela, except that Chile is included for nonfat dry milk and India is excluded from stock data for butter and cheese.
Sources: FAO, *Food Outlook*, December 1993; USDA, Foreign Agricultural Service, July 1993.

Meat and Livestock. The decline of the world cattle inventory tapered off in 1993. The U.S., where the cattle herd had been expanding since 1991, accounted for most of the gains. The largest declines were in the former Soviet Union, the result of confused market conditions and a shortage of animal feed. Dairy reforms in the EC, where cattle herds were important for both dairy and beef production, reduced cow herds in nearly all countries. In reunified Germany, the herd was to be reduced by five million head over five years. World beef output was estimated (in October) to be marginally smaller in 1993. EC government-held surplus stocks of beef continued to exceed one million tons in 1993, despite the decline in EC beef production.

The growth in global pork production slowed in 1993. The largest increases were in China and the EC. China had been encouraging the creation of large-scale modern production facilities, increasing production efficiency, and greatly reducing government intervention in marketing, but commercial production still accounted for only about 20% of all hog production. Per capita meat consumption was growing at a moderate pace in China.

The world's sheep flock, particularly in China and Australia, was increasingly being devoted to producing meat rather than wool. The trend was likely to accelerate in the U.S., where a program created to ensure wool supplies during World War II, which provided a producer premium equal to one or two times the market price, was being phased out.

The freeing up of markets in China led to a dynamic expansion of its poultry industry, aided by an inflow of foreign capital and technology. Annual production increases had been 12% or more over the past four years, and China was challenging Brazil as the second largest exporter of broiler poultry meat. The strong domestic demand for white meat in the U.S., together with a sharp reduction in sales to the former Soviet Union, freed up large quantities of inexpensive dark meat for export that embroiled the U.S., the world's leading poultry meat exporter, in several trade disputes around the world. Most Central American countries, Colombia, Venezuela, the Czech Republic, Poland, and South Africa all imposed new import restrictions that the U.S. found reason to question.

Dairy Products. World milk production was estimated by the FAO to have fallen about 1% in 1993, the third year of decline in a row. Output fell nearly 3% in the developed countries, largely because of continuing reductions in Eastern Europe and the former Soviet Union, where it fell the most because of further herd reductions and short supplies of feed and winter fodder. Output in the LDCs, however, which accounted for only about one-third of global production, rose 3%.

EC and U.S. export subsidies, larger supplies from Oceania, and a slowing of shipments to the former Soviet Union helped weaken international dairy prices. International prices for butter and nonfat dry milk (NFDM) weakened in 1993, slipping from a peak in January of $1,450 per metric ton of butter (f.o.b., North European and selected world ports) to a low of $1,250 by October–November. The former Soviet republics, however, continued as the major importer of butter, thanks to food aid and other subsidized sales. The price of NFDM—$1,725 in January and February—was down to $1,338 by December. Demand for cheese remained

ALEX QUESADA—MATRIX

Bananas in Latin America are processed for export. Led by France, Spain, and the U.K., the European Community raised tariffs on bananas from the Americas in order to favour imports from European tropical islands and former colonies.

generally strong globally, leading to further expansion of both production and consumption.

The U.S. Food and Drug Administration (FDA) perpetuated a highly charged controversy over the use of hormones in dairy cows to increase milk output when in November it approved the use of recombinant bovine somatotropin (BST). This synthetic hormone would supplement the BST produced naturally in a cow's pituitary gland. Sale of the drug was delayed until February 1994 after completion of a congressionally mandated study of the drug's social and economic impact.

FDA approval came after several extensive scientific reviews of the drug's safety begun in the early 1980s. The FDA found milk from treated cows safe to consume and indistinguishable from milk of untreated cows. The FDA did find that cows treated with BST had a slightly increased incidence of mastitis but concluded that safeguards were adequate.

A 12-month extension of the ban on BST was agreed upon in December by EC agricultural ministers, however. Their concerns were primarily economic and social. They feared the drug's use would undermine the CAP by unbalancing the supplies of both milk and meat (BST is also a livestock growth promotant) and drive many small farmers out of business in poorer regions.

Sugar. Expectations of a record-matching sugar crop in 1992–93 were not met because of unfavourable weather late in the year in parts of Asia and the poor performance of the Cuban sugar industry. A shortage of production inputs and industry breakdowns were limiting production in Cuba, Ukraine, and Russia. Cuba's sugar production fell almost 40% in 1992–93, and only a very modest recovery was in sight for 1993–94. The harvest was curtailed to permit early preparations for expanding future production. The disruption of Cuban markets in Russia and Eastern Europe had also contributed to the precipitous decline in Cuban output in recent years. Cuba's sugar exports fell from about 7 million tons annually at the end of the 1980s to about 3.8 million in 1992–93. Although the downward trend in sugar output in the former Soviet Union appeared to be reversing, supplies remained tight because of a shortage of foreign exchange with which to import sugar. Russia planned to barter fuel, fertilizer, and other supplies for two million tons of Cuban sugar in 1993–94.

U.S. growers' opposition to the NAFTA provisions dealing with sugar endangered congressional acceptance of the entire agreement. The original text allowed duty-free entry into the U.S. of a minimum of 7,250 tons or up to 25,000 tons of Mexico's net production surplus—production minus domestic consumption—during the first six years of the agreement's 14-year transition period. Limiting exports to surplus prevented the reexport of sugar Mexico might import from third countries. If Mexico achieved a production surplus in any two successive years, it could ship its entire surplus duty-free in years 7 through 14; if not, only 150,000 tons in year 7 plus annual increments of 10% thereafter would be allowed.

The revised agreement eliminated this "two-year rule" and instead permitted Mexico to ship up to 250,000 tons of its production surplus duty-free annually in years 7 through 14. Another revision limited potential Mexican exports by counting consumption of high-fructose corn syrup as part of total sugar consumption in determining the production surplus. By the end of the transition, all restrictions on sugar trade between the two countries were to be eliminated except those applying to sugar imported duty-free into the U.S. for refining and reexported under an existing U.S. program.

Coffee. Renewed attempts during the year to negotiate a new International Coffee Agreement under the designation of the International Coffee Organization (ICO) failed because of inability to agree on the allocation of export quotas and differences between consuming and producing countries over how much higher quality coffees would be available under the quotas. The treatment of sales to non-ICO members was also an issue. The ICO had had no economic provisions since export quotas were suspended in July 1989. The ICO lost its largest consumer member in September when the U.S. announced that it would not extend its membership in the ICO beyond Sept. 30, 1994, because of a lack of congressional support and the U.S. coffee industry's preference for a free market in coffee.

Table VII. World Production of Centrifugal (Freed from Liquid) Sugar

In 000,000 metric tons raw value

Region and country	1991–92	1992–93	1993–94[1]
North America	10.2	11.6	10.8
United States	6.6	7.1	6.7
Mexico	3.5	4.3	4.0
Caribbean	8.1	5.4	5.7
Cuba	7.0	4.3	4.5
Central America	2.4	2.3	2.4
Guatemala	1.1	1.1	1.2
South America	15.0	15.6	15.4
Argentina	1.6	1.4	1.1
Brazil	9.2	9.8	9.8
Colombia	1.8	1.8	1.9
Europe	21.2	21.7	21.3
Western Europe	16.7	18.2	17.7
European Community	15.7	16.9	16.7
France	4.4	4.7	4.7
Germany	4.3	4.4	4.6
Eastern Europe	4.4	3.5	3.5
Poland	1.6	1.6	1.9
Former Soviet republics	6.5	6.9	7.4
Africa and Middle East	10.9	10.0	9.8
South Africa	2.4	1.6	1.3
Turkey	2.1	2.1	2.3
Asia	38.1	33.8	34.5
China	8.5	8.3	7.4
India	15.3	12.5	13.3
Indonesia	2.3	2.3	2.1
Pakistan	2.5	2.6	2.9
Philippines	2.0	2.1	2.0
Thailand	5.1	3.8	4.2
Oceania	3.6	4.9	4.7
Australia	3.2	4.4	4.2
Totals			
Beginning stocks	21.9	24.5	22.0
As % of consumption	19.6%	21.6%	19.3%
Production	116.3	112.0	112.4
Imports[2]	28.7	27.5	28.2
Consumption	111.6	113.2	114.3
Exports[2]	30.8	28.7	28.2

[1] Preliminary.
[2] Exports do not equal imports because "Totals" are a composite of slightly differing marketing years, not all beginning in the same months.
Source: USDA, Foreign Agricultural Service, November 1993.

Table VIII. World Green Coffee Production

In 000 60-kg bags

Region and country	1991–92	1992–93[1]	1993–94[2]
North America	18,227	17,266	16,828
Costa Rica	2,530	2,400	2,375
El Salvador	2,357	2,916	2,500
Guatemala	3,549	3,584	3,000
Honduras	2,255	1,981	2,070
Mexico	4,620	3,850	4,200
South America	51,435	43,105	47,455
Brazil	28,500	24,000	28,500
Colombia	17,980	14,950	14,000
Ecuador	1,700	1,600	1,800
Africa	19,256	16,297	17,010
Cameroon	1,920	1,030	950
Côte d'Ivoire	3,967	2,500	3,700
Ethiopia	3,000	3,000	3,000
Kenya	1,505	1,217	1,250
Uganda	2,900	2,800	3,000
Zaire	1,500	1,300	1,100
Asia and Oceania	14,604	14,980	16,445
India	3,200	2,815	3,500
Indonesia	7,100	7,350	7,500
Vietnam	1,350	1,670	2,200
Total production	103,522	91,648	97,738
Exportable[3]	81,721	69,767	74,514
Beginning stocks[4]	39,221	41,031	36,003
Exports	80,064	75,172	73,464

[1] Preliminary.
[2] Forecast.
[3] Production minus domestic use.
[4] In exporting countries.
Source: USDA, Foreign Agricultural Service, December 1993.

In July coffee-producing countries began to band together to raise coffee prices. In September 28 countries representing nearly 90% of global coffee exports announced formation of the Association of Coffee Producing Countries, with headquarters in Brazil. It included all of the major coffee-producing countries (*see* Table VIII) except Mexico, India, and Vietnam. The association agreed to hold back exportable production on a scale beginning at 20% when the 20-day moving-average ICO composite price for "Other Milds and Robustas" was below 75 cents per pound. Members exporting less than 400,000 bags annually would be exempt from retention, and no decision was made about the inclusion of instant coffee in the scheme.

The indicator price, after averaging nearly 54 cents for 1992, had risen, with implementation of the scheme, to over 71 cents in mid-December. The recovery in Brazilian output gave a prospect of substantially increased global coffee production in 1993–94. Supplies in importing countries were already more than ample because of their large buildup of stocks in 1992–93.

Cocoa. World prices for cocoa beans gave indication of bottoming out in 1993 after eight consecutive years of decline. The reason was expectations of reduced global cocoa output in 1993–94 resulting from poor crop prospects in West Africa. Futures prices (New York, nearest three-month average) steadied in 1993, averaging about 43 cents per pound during the first eight months, compared with 47 cents in 1992, but began to rise in the autumn. Despite the fact that low prices discouraged new plantings and good farming practices in many countries, the impact on overall production was fairly small. The large plantings of cacao trees in Malaysia, Côte d'Ivoire, and Indonesia in the mid-1980s were just approaching their maximum harvest potential. Cocoa bean stocks were drawn down modestly again in 1992–93 when cocoa bean grindings once again exceeded production, but stocks still equaled the equivalent of a six-month global supply. Overall, cocoa consumption was restrained by continuing low consumption in the former Soviet Union and Eastern Europe.

A new International Cocoa Agreement (ICCA) was adopted in July to replace one that expired on September 30. The 1986 ICCA had attempted to maintain cocoa prices within an agreed band through operation of a buffer stock. The arrangement broke down in 1989 when large supplies severely depressed prices and the buffer stocks reached their maximum. Lengthy negotiations failed thereafter over differences between producing and consuming nations on what new, lower price band to defend, how to finance a withholding scheme, and how to handle large arrears owed by producing countries to maintain the buffer stock. The new agreement abandoned the buffer-stock concept in favour of supply management based on voluntary cuts in production by members. Implementation of the cuts, however, was postponed until February 1994 because of delays in ratification. Malaysia, Indonesia, and the U.S. were expected to remain outside the ICCA. A sell-off of the buffer stock in monthly installments to be spread over four and a half years was already under way.

Table IX. World Cocoa Bean Production

In 000 metric tons

Region and country	1991–92	1992–93	1993–94[1]
North and Central America	109	107	109
South America	474	491	476
Brazil	301	324	310
Ecuador	82	76	75
Africa	1,238	1,288	1,226
Cameroon	107	100	90
Côte d'Ivoire[2]	747	700	750
Ghana	243	315	230
Nigeria[3]	110	140	125
Asia and Oceania	481	493	524
Indonesia	200	220	250
Malaysia	217	214	210
Total production	2,302	2,379	2,335
Net production	2,729	2,355	2,312
Cocoa grindings	2,312	2,400	2,400
Change in stocks	−33	−45	−88

[1] Forecast.
[2] Includes some cocoa marketed between Ghana and Côte d'Ivoire.
[3] Includes cocoa marketed through Benin.
Source: USDA, Foreign Agricultural Service, October 1993.

Table X. World Cotton Production

In 000,000 480-lb bales

Region and country	1991–92	1992–93[1]	1993–94[1]
Production	96.0	82.5	81.9
Western Hemisphere	25.2	20.5	21.5
United States	17.6	16.2	16.3
Brazil	3.4	2.1	2.1
Europe	1.5	1.6	1.6
Former Soviet republics	11.3	9.4	9.9
Uzbekistan	6.8	6.0	6.3
Africa	5.5	6.0	5.7
Asia and Oceania[2]	52.5	54.5	52.4
China	26.1	20.7	18.5
India	9.4	10.6	10.8
Pakistan	10.0	7.1	7.3
Consumption	84.4	85.8	85.9
United States	9.6	10.3	10.3
China	19.0	21.7	21.3
India	8.7	9.4	9.7
Pakistan	6.5	6.6	6.7
European Community	5.2	5.0	4.8
Southeast Asia	4.2	4.3	4.5
Russia	4.5	2.7	2.9

[1] Estimate.
[2] Includes Middle East.
Source: USDA, Foreign Agricultural Service, December 1993.

Cotton. A modest decline in world cotton production was expected in 1993–94 despite generally better weather than the previous year. Farmers in China moved much land out of cotton and into other crops in response to poor weather, insect infestations, and deferred government payments. The recovery of Pakistani output was slowed by damage from insects and the leaf-curl virus; the government suspended cotton exports to prevent a further rise in domestic cotton prices that threatened to undermine the competitiveness of the country's textile exports. In Central Asia the long decline in acreage planted to cotton appeared to be ending, and production was expected to record the first increase since 1988.

Cotton use was rising most in countries that supplied their own cotton to manufacture and export textiles. Several countries in East Asia that traditionally relied on imported cotton to produce yarn for export had to cut back yarn production. One result was that cotton trade grew more slowly than cotton use.

Global cotton stocks, which had soared to 40.6 million bales by the end of 1991–92, fell 5% during 1992–93, and an even larger decline seemed in prospect for 1993–94. Most of the decline occurred in China's large stocks. International cotton prices remained depressed by large global carryover stocks of cotton, which at the end of 1992–93 equaled 45% of cotton use.

International prices of cotton (Northern European Cotlook Index "A"), whose most recent high in 1990–91 (August–July) averaged 82.9 cents per pound, had fallen to an average of 57.7 cents by 1992–93 and moved in a narrow band under 56 cents during early 1993–94. These continuing depressed prices led to reduced cotton plantings in Latin America, and several traditional cotton exporters there, such as Brazil, Mexico, Colombia, and some Central American countries, were increasingly importing more cotton than they exported. (RICHARD M. KENNEDY)

See also Gardening.

This article updates the *Macropædia* article The History of AGRICULTURE.

FISHERIES

According to the latest statistics compiled by the Food and Agriculture Organization (FAO) of the United Nations, the total world fish catch continued to decline, although less steeply than was evident in 1990. The record catch of 100 million metric tons in 1989 had declined to 97,245,600 metric tons in 1990; the 1991 total world catch was confirmed at 96,925,900 metric tons, a drop of just under 320,000 tons from the previous year.

A recovery in the catch of Peruvian anchovy (anchoveta) to 4,017,106 metric tons in 1991 from 3,771,577 metric tons in 1990 reversed a decline of 1,635,950 metric tons recorded from 1989 to 1990. Alaska pollock, however, continued to drop in catch from 5,736,109 metric tons in 1990 to 4,893,493 in 1991. The top 10 species landed in 1991 (in order of tonnage) were Alaska pollock, South American pilchard, anchoveta, Chilean jack mackerel, Japanese pilchard, skipjack tuna, silver carp, Atlantic herring, European pilchard (sardine), and Atlantic cod. These 10 species produced a combined total catch of 27,716,381 metric tons, compared with 29,773,392 metric tons in 1990, a decline of nearly two million metric tons. Catches of other species, including capelin, large-head hairtail, Araucanian herring, pink salmon, and Cape horse mackerel, showed significant increases but not enough to offset the deficit.

China increased its catch from 12,095,363 metric tons in 1990 to 13,134,967 in 1991, an increase of 8.6%. The republics of the former Soviet Union dropped from second to third position with a decline from 10,389,030 metric tons in 1990 to 9,216,927 in 1991. Japan moved up to second place despite the fact that its catch fell from 10,350,338 metric tons in 1990 to 9,306,827 in 1991. Both Peru and Chile benefited from the return of the anchoveta. The top 10 catching nations in 1991 were China, Japan, the former Soviet Union, Peru, Chile, the U.S., India, Indonesia, Thailand, and South Korea.

The worldwide problem of overfishing and dwindling fish stocks continued to be at the forefront of the commercial fishing agenda. One of the major areas of concern was the continued pressure being put on migratory and straddling fish stock. The latter are species that straddle a country's 200-mi exclusive economic zone (EEZ), spending part of their life cycle within the boundaries of a particular country's waters but also spending either part of the year or part of their life cycle outside that zone in international waters, where there is little effective regulation of fishing. The northern cod and groundfish stocks on the Grand Banks off Canada's Newfoundland and Labrador coasts were good examples of such species. During the past few years, Canada had campaigned relentlessly to stop what it described as illegal fishing by European Community (EC) fishermen, who were operating on the boundary of Canada's 200-mi EEZ on the Grand Banks. In 1992 Canada instituted a two-year moratorium on domestic fishing for cod along the northern coasts of Newfoundland and Labrador and called on the EC to withdraw its fleets. Northwest Atlantic Fisheries Organization (NAFO) estimates revealed that stocks of cod, redfish, flounder, and American plaice had dropped to historically low levels; by 1992 they were less than one-third of the total in 1986. Some 890,000 metric tons of these species were estimated to have been taken from NAFO-regulated waters between 1986 and 1992, some 16 times the quota set for those stocks. After the moratorium on cod was introduced, the areas affected were extended and other species included; when they would be reopened remained uncertain. The effect of this in the past three years was the loss of jobs for 40,000 fishermen and fish-processing workers in Newfoundland and Labrador. In December Canada's Federal Fisheries Minister Brian Tobin officially closed several Atlantic cod and haddock fisheries.

The survival of straddling stocks was not unique to Canada, with threats being posed on Argentina's Patagonian shelf, in the Barents Sea, in the waters off of Namibia, off the shores of Chile and Peru, on New Zealand's Challenger plateau, in the Sea of Okhotsk, and in the Bering Sea. Highly migratory fish stocks were also under extreme pressure, with species such as yellowfin, skipjack, albacore, southern and northern bluefin, and bigeye tuna all in danger.

The opportunity for countries throughout the world to take steps toward addressing these problems came in July 1993 with the first substantive session of the United Nations Conference on Straddling Fish Stocks and Highly Migratory Fish Stocks, held in New York City. The conference's mandate was to identify and assess existing problems related to the conservation and management of these two types of fish stocks, to consider means of improving cooperation between nations, and to formulate appropriate recommen-

ANDREW VAUGHAN—CANAPRESS

Canadian fishing boats hold the Russian trawler *Pioner Murmana* hostage in the port of a fishing village in Nova Scotia. The local fishermen, who had been hurt in recent years by dwindling stocks of cod and other valuable species, were protesting fishing by foreign vessels in Canadian waters.

dations. At the conclusion of the conference, a high level of agreement was reached on many subjects, and an additional two sessions were planned before the summer of 1994 to allow fulfillment of the mandate.

World fish-meal production, which had risen to 6.9 million metric tons by the end of the 1980s, fell dramatically from the 1990 figure of 6.3 million metric tons to 6.1 million metric tons in 1992. The world's major producers of fish meal were Chile, Peru, Japan, and the Scandinavian countries. All those countries, with the exception of Japan, were major exporters. Japan suffered a major drop in its output, producing more than one million tons at the end of the 1980s and dropping consistently from that time to 430,000 metric tons in 1992—a decline of 60%.

At the end of 1992 Peru experienced a remarkable increase in fish-meal production, resulting in an increase during that year to 1,370,000 metric tons, compared with 1,310,000 in 1991. This unexpected rise resulted in a dramatic downturn in the price of fish meal, which fell from $500 per metric ton on the Hamburg (Germany) market in June 1992 to $350 per metric ton in June 1993. The pattern of fish-meal imports also had changed over the past decade. In 1983 Europe dominated the import trade with more than 50% of the total imports. In 1992, however, Europe represented less than one-third of the imports, with nearly two-thirds being imported by the Far East. This dramatic change was caused largely by a rapid rise of fish-meal consumption in China.

In the late 1980s the total world production of fish oil was about 1.6 million metric tons, a figure that dropped during the early 1990s to 1,370,000 metric tons in 1990 and 1,050,000 in 1992. This decrease was principally caused by a dramatic decline in production in Japan, Peru, and Chile. The major producers and exporters of fish oil were Japan, Scandinavia, the U.S., and Chile. Exports during 1992 fell by more than 25% compared with 1989. The major importing countries remained the U.K., Germany, and The Netherlands.

Fish oil is mainly used in the production of foods such as margarine. In recent years, however, it was being used increasingly by the fish-farming industry, resulting in an estimated usage of fish oil in fish feed at about one-third of total world production. Fish-oil production by the major exporting countries during the first half of 1993 rose by about 30% compared with the same period in 1992. Peru was the main reason for this dramatic rise. Fish-oil prices varied during 1992 in response to fluctuating prices of competing vegetable oils. In June 1992 the price of fish oil in the Rotterdam market was about $375 per ton.

(MARTIN J. GILL)

This article updates the *Macropædia* article Commercial FISHING.

Table XI. World Fisheries, 1991[1]

Country	Catch in 000 metric tons		Trade in $000,000	
	Total	Inland	Imports	Exports
China	13,135.0	5,528.1	438.1	1,182.0
Japan	9,306.8	204.0	12,043.6	839.2
U.S.S.R.	9,216.9	1,030.8	162.3	837.2
Peru	6,944.2	30.0	1.0	491.1
Chile	6,002.9	6.8	5.9	1,066.9
U.S.	5,473.3	275.0	5,997.8	3,279.3
India	4,036.9	1,700.8	—	570.3
Indonesia	3,186.0	806.0	47.4	1,192.1
Thailand	3,065.2	270.0	1,050.0	2,901.4
South Korea	2,515.3	30.4	568.2	1,490.6
Philippines	2,311.8	612.4	96.1	467.7
Norway	2,095.9	0.5	307.0	2,282.2
Denmark	1,793.2	36.5	1,148.2	2,302.3
North Korea	1,700.1	100.0	—	61.4
Canada	1,529.8	50.3	675.2	2,169.1
Mexico	1,429.1	171.4	46.7	393.5
Spain	1,350.0	29.2	2,748.3	772.6
Iceland	1,050.4	0.8	14.0	1,280.0
Bangladesh	892.7	258.9	—	178.9
Vietnam	877.0	267.0	—	112.8
United Kingdom	830.6	19.2	1,911.9	1,121.9
France	812.8	46.0	2,926.0	925.6
Brazil	800.0	214.4	180.8	157.4
Myanmar (Burma)	769.2	175.2	—	26.2
Argentina	640.6	10.6	16.8	448.0
Malaysia	620.0	14.5	170.5	264.9
New Zealand	609.0	1.3	37.1	460.8
Morocco	592.9	1.4	1.2	608.9
Italy	548.2	56.7	2,689.6	249.0
Pakistan	515.5	115.9	—	110.4
South Africa	498.9	2.3	143.4	140.5
Poland	457.4	48.0	37.4	188.7
The Netherlands	443.1	4.1	977.4	1,356.2
Tanzania	400.3	345.0	—	—
Ecuador	383.6	2.4	5.8	587.6
Ghana	365.0	57.0	31.3	15.9
Turkey	364.6	47.2	24.8	61.0
Venezuela	352.8	21.3	4.6	89.5
Portugal	325.3	2.6	757.8	287.2
Senegal	319.7	17.6	38.6	233.4
Germany	300.2	46.8	2,114.7	716.0
Egypt	298.0	215.9	73.2	11.0
Iran	277.4	82.4	12.2	83.7
Nigeria	266.6	90.9	191.5	15.6
Other	7,221.7	2,129.6	5,850.0	6,498.4
World	96,925.9	15,177.2	43,546.4	38,528.4

[1]Excludes aquatic mammals, crocodiles and alligators, pearls, corals, sponges, and aquatic plants.
Source: United Nations Food and Agriculture Organization, *Yearbook of Fishery Statistics*, vols. 72 and 73.

FOOD PROCESSING

In 1993 consumers took more care in selecting their food purchases, sought more value for their money, and resented obscure label information. Any product that reduced the trouble of preparation was popular. Brand loyalty declined; in the U.S. sales of private-label products grew twice as fast as sales of national brands.

Genetic manipulation aroused ethical concerns. Environmental and religious groups were offended by the prospect of the implantation of animal genes into plants to enhance various properties and of the introduction of human genes into cows to bring the composition of their milk nearer to that of human milk. The U.S. Food and Drug Administration (FDA) in November approved a genetically engineered hormone to raise milk productivity. In December the Union of Concerned Scientists asked the FDA to delay approval of two genetically altered vegetable varieties scheduled to come onto the market in early 1994. Also at the end of the year, the FDA adopted new regulations that would require manufacturers of dietary supplements to adhere to the same strict labeling requirements as were applied to food products. The move was intended to eliminate false or exaggerated claims about the health benefits of such products.

The incidence of food poisoning rose throughout the world. The World Health Organization estimated that in 1992 some 6.5 million cases of food-borne illnesses occurred in the U.S. alone, with approximately 9,000 fatalities. The newly appointed secretary of the U.S. Department of Agriculture (USDA), Mike Espy, announced plans for new meat-inspection programs and said that irradiation might be used to destroy harmful bacteria in beef. In the U.K. one person in 20 claimed to have suffered from food poisoning during 1992.

Business Trends. Food company profits fell during the year, especially in the U.S. Restructuring was common throughout the food industry.

U.S. processors continued to invest large sums in developing substitutes for natural fats. Food processors had anticipated that sales of fat substitutes would have reached $1 billion a year by 1993, but actual sales were less than half of that because the industry failed to develop sufficiently palatable products.

The British Soft Drinks Association (BSDA) warned that brand pirating was a growing problem in the U.K. soft drink trade. Of total U.K. soft drink consumption of about 8 billion litres, dispensers accounted for some 420 million litres, and the BSDA estimated that 10% of the latter were pirated, a figure rising to 30% in some areas.

Foreign investment in Eastern Europe was stimulated by the provision of favourable credit facilities, with Hungary, the Czech Republic, Bulgaria, and Poland in the forefront. London financial analysts Coopers & Lybrand found that the former Eastern-bloc countries were in a much better position to do business than had been believed in the West. But the war in the former Yugoslavia badly hurt Bulgarian state-owned food-processing companies, which were expected to lose more than $81 million in 1993 because of lost business resulting from sanctions against Serbia and Montenegro.

China continued the rapid development of its fast-food industry. As of late 1993 the country had more than 300 instant-noodle lines producing over 200,000 metric tons per year and 60 bread lines producing 100,000 metric tons per year. Development remained at a very early stage, however.

Western Australia aimed to become a major supplier of high-quality processed foods for the rapidly growing Asian market, where consumption per head was likely to match that of Australia by the year 2000. Annual growth rates of processed food imports reached 18% in South Korea, 14% in Japan, and 12% in Hong Kong.

Technology. Interest in high-pressure technology (HPT) for sterilizing food products grew; Japan was the world leader. HPT jam and grapefruit juice were on the market there, and the Wakayama company started work on an HPT system for bulk pasteurization of fresh orange juice. The French government funded an HPT development program involving three large companies: Bongrain, BSN, and Pernod Ricard; 15 partners in Belgium, Germany, France, Spain, and the U.K. jointly proposed a three-year study of HPT. In the U.S. a pilot system was installed by ABB Autoclave Systems Inc. at Columbus, Ohio, and the same company supplied a mobile system for testing at food-plant sites in Sweden and started building a pilot plant for a European customer.

Vending-machine technology advanced with the appearance of machines incorporating freezing systems coupled with microwave cookers so that the products were heated and ready to eat. Major U.S. processors were developing complete semiautomatic restaurants. Machines were being tested that cooked ready-to-eat meals and accepted debit cards. Processors agreed that vending was poised to grow rapidly into an industry that would provide high-quality food wherever people were—at work, at play, or traveling.

Developed by Niro of Denmark, a commercial freeze concentration system was installed by a dairy in Wisconsin. The process partially converted the water content of dairy products into ice crystals, which were then removed by a centrifuge machine; it was cheaper than thermal concentration and did not degrade flavour or aroma.

New Products and Ingredients. Many new products were in the "health" category, and the main focus was on reduced fat and calorie content and increased dietary fibre. European food companies followed the lead of those in the U.S. and launched products based on olive oil, examples being a low-fat spread from Golden Vale of Ireland, a self-basting chicken product from Moy Park of the U.K., and a low-fat milk from Farmer's Best Milk of Australia.

A recent marketing trend in the U.S. was clear beverages, which appeared and were promoted as more refreshing and lower in calories than coloured drinks. American brewers introduced "clear beer," and Coca-Cola Co. and PepsiCo introduced clear versions of their traditional cola soft drinks.

First patented by the USDA, "Oatrim," a fat substitute made from oat flour and oat bran treated with enzymes, was launched in the U.S. jointly by Quaker Oats Co. and Rhône-Poulenc. A new development in which Oatrim played a part was the appearance of beverages containing soluble dietary fibre. A process for producing a liquid fibre ingredient from Oatrim was developed by the USDA, and the ingredient, suitable for incorporation into beverages without affecting flavour, was launched commercially by ConAgra and the joint Quaker Oats/Rhône-Poulenc venture.

Ahold of The Netherlands introduced thin-sliced technology (TST) meat products. These were ready-to-eat fresh meat slices formed from cheap cuts or trimmings and hardly distinguishable from sliced muscle meat. They were being sold in several countries.

Packaging. Significant growth in modified-atmosphere packaging, consisting of a flexible film pack enclosing the product in an inert gas, took place in Europe, where 14 different types of system were in use. Another fast-growing packaging material was polyvinyl chloride (PVC), a major market for which was transparent bottles for mineral water.

The world packaging industry perceived its biggest challenge as the protection of the environment and made intense efforts to develop products that would be environmentally sound. Continental PET Technologies of Florence, Ky., developed a process for incorporating layers of recycled plastic into soft-drink bottles and plastic food containers and teamed with Husky Injection Molding Systems Ltd. of Ontario to develop a molding system that would produce bottles with up to 50% recycled content. British Steel Tinplate of the U.K. launched its "ultimate can" (UC) project to achieve a 30% weight reduction of steel beverage cans by using a new steel alloy and produced 3,000 UC prototypes.

Company Developments. PepsiCo of the U.S. acquired two Spanish beverage companies for $320 million, the centrepiece of a $1 billion five-year investment plan that was expected to double PepsiCo's share of Spain's carbonated-drinks market. The Anglo-Dutch group Unilever bought the U.S. ice cream business of Kraft General Foods for an estimated $400 million, doubling the size of the group's operation in the U.S. Unilever also acquired two companies in Chile and established a joint venture in Beijing (Peking). Philip Morris, Inc., owners of Kraft General Foods, merged the latter's European operations with Jacobs Suchard to create one of the biggest food groups in Europe, worth $9 billion and employing 32,000 people.

Cadbury Schweppes of the U.K. asked its stockholders for nearly $500 million to fund the acquisition of A&W Brands of the U.S. The company also announced its entry into a joint venture to establish Cadbury as a leading chocolate confectionery brand in China, with an initial investment of $30 million to create Cadbury Beijing.

Government Action. The European Community (EC) failed to achieve fully its aim of becoming an area without inner frontiers. Some, but not all, objectives were attained. An unexpected result was that food could be moved across frontiers without any inspections, and to counter this the EC announced the establishment of a food health inspectorate.

The FDA published regulations implementing the Nutrition Labeling and Education Act. Estimates of the cost of compliance to the U.S. food industry varied widely between $1.4 billion and $10.3 billion over 20 years. The FDA also issued standards and proposals for bottled water, setting limits for some 40 possible contaminants.

(ANTHONY WOOLLEN)

See also Environment; Health and Disease; Industrial Review: *Beverages; Textiles; Tobacco.*

This article updates the *Macropædia* article FOOD PROCESSING.

Anthropology

Culture, in the words of University of Chicago anthropologist Marshall Sahlins, today "is on everybody's lips." Discussions of cultural identity, multiculturalism, cultural autonomy, and cultural diversity were taking centre stage everywhere. Entire nation-states were coming together and splitting apart along cultural demarcation lines. People who only a few years earlier had not even thought of themselves as belonging to particular ethnic groups now sought equal status as members of distinct cultures. Cultural studies, a new discipline emphasizing the roles of political domination, race, class, and gender in culture, now gave voice to the viewpoints and aspirations of these and other people considered marginalized, oppressed, or excluded. Established disciplines like history and literature, for their part, were increasingly employing the concept of culture in their studies.

The Wenner-Gren Foundation for Anthropological Research convened a four-day meeting of 15 prominent anthropologists in February 1993 to explore issues affecting the discipline's future. In essays surveying the field published in the sourcebook *Assessing Cultural Anthropology,* University of Hawaii anthropologist Robert Borofsky brought together an even larger group of distinguished scholars to discuss concerns facing the discipline. Acknowledging the wide epistemological, theoretical, and methodological gulfs that separated and divided many anthropologists, both groups nevertheless found that a unified discipline still held the best promise to realize the goal of a universal study of humankind.

The problems and possibilities of interdisciplinary research were most graphically exemplified in studies that sought to understand relationships between biology and culture. New developments in genetics, molecular biology, and the structure and chemistry of the brain promised new insights into the evolution and physiology of human behaviour. Intrigued by new discoveries in experimental psychology, University of Cambridge anthropologist Pascal Boyer explored in *The Naturalness of Religious Ideas* the ways culture and biology interact to produce strikingly similar forms of religious ideas in different cultural environments. Other investigators, such as University of California at Santa Barbara anthropologist Donald E. Brown, the author of *Human Universals,* continued to consider biological factors in their efforts to explain why human beings share so many different behavioral traits.

Such speculations were anathema to some of their colleagues. Opposed to racism, sexism, and other biologically based ideologies that use scientific methods and findings to legitimate discriminatory acts and beliefs, these scholars emphasized the possibilities for culture to modify human behaviour. Believing that culture could now control human nature, some anthropologists, such as New York University ethnologist Fred Myers, in a statement quoted in a December issue of *Science,* claimed that cultural anthropologists "regard human evolution as finished." The development and spread of new contagions like AIDS, the resurgence of old diseases like tuberculosis, and enduring problems of violence, poverty, prejudice, and environmental devastation and degradation, however, suggested that Darwinian evolutionary principles such as random mutation and natural selection still deeply influenced cultural behaviour.

Many ethnologists rejecting theories linking biology and culture further criticized what they regarded as claims of objective impartiality made by science and scientists occupying privileged positions. Inspired by postmodernist theories emphasizing the subjective cultural contexts of all knowledge systems, these scholars thought of science as an ideology no more or less valid than any other framework of belief. Increased awareness of the potential effects of cultural bias on scholarship benefited all researchers. Aware of this fact, few scientifically oriented anthropologists claimed objectivity. Most instead continued to use the scientific method of systematic, controlled experimentation to develop and test hypotheses on human behaviour.

Ethnologists stimulated by the atmosphere of experimentation suffusing the discipline were forging new lines of inquiry as they reexamined old problems in new ways. In her study *In the Realm of the Diamond Queen,* for example, University of California at Santa Cruz ethnologist Anna Lowenhaupt Tsing redirected attention to creative possibilities emerging at margins between people and cultures. Tsing had conducted fieldwork in the southeastern Borneo highland rain forest in several communities of subsistence-farming Meratus Dayak during the 1980s. Formerly regarded as isolated primitives, they were now viewed as a disadvantaged and unsophisticated minority by local Muslim Banjara neighbours and by bureaucrats in distant Jakarta. Tsing shows how Meratus people exploited their marginality to respond creatively to challenges posed by encroachments of Indonesian officials, loggers, and settlers on their lands.

Ethnologists were increasingly focusing attention on their own societies. Numerous studies addressed AIDS, gender relations, poverty, violence, and other problems. In *An Inquiry into Well-Being and Destitution,* University of Cambridge anthropologist Partha Dasgupta used findings from a wide range of disciplines to develop a cross-cultural description of poverty that could be used both to identify and to change factors perpetuating poverty. In *Vinyl Leaves,* Florida International University ethnologist Stephen M. Fjellman showed how technical wizardry and efficient organization creating artificial reality at Disney World produced an exhilarating sense of unreality he called "commodity Zen." Likening it to the state of mind frequently induced in visitors to shopping malls, Fjellman suggested that the Disney organization used commodity Zen both to make money and to affirm the values of "commodification" and "techno-corporate control."

Several innovative studies examined the social, symbolic, and political significance of what frequently were regarded as everyday objects. Working with an interdisciplinary team of art historians, historians, textile experts, and anthropologists, ethnologists Annette B. Weiner of New York University and Jane Schneider of the City University of New York showed how textiles symbolically expressed and influenced identity and power in both large- and small-scale societies in *Cloth and Human Experience*. Intrigued by the discovery that flowers were relatively unimportant in most societies in Africa, University of Cambridge professor emeritus Jack Goody published a worldwide survey assessing the aesthetic, political, and economic implications of what he called *The Culture of Flowers*.

Two events, the 1992 Columbian Quincentenary commemorating the 500th anniversary of Columbus' voyage to the Americas and the 1993 United Nations International Year for the World's Indigenous People, redirected attention to people who traditionally had been the primary subjects of anthropological inquiry. Working as individuals or through organizations like Survival International and Cultural Survival, anthropologists supported efforts of indigenous people to maintain control over their cultures, lands, and resources. Ethnobotanists helped shamans, for example, secure patents for medicinal plants they identified as part of a recently announced five-year, $12.5 million worldwide drug-search program administered through the U.S. government's National Institutes of Health. In *State of the Peoples,* other ethnologists reported on the current status of the approximately 6,000 present-day indigenous societies. A global survey sponsored and published by Cultural Survival, the document examined the wide range of problems challenging indigenous people and presented solutions proposed by them to counteract these threats. Inclusion of native perspectives in this study showed how indigenous people were increasingly working with ethnologists more as collaborators than as informants. (ROBERT S. GRUMET)

See also Archaeology.

This article updates the *Macropædia* article Human EVOLUTION.

Archaeology

Eastern Hemisphere. Reports in 1993 on archaeological excavations were far fewer than normal. Little news was yet at hand for Central and Eastern Europe, or from Africa and Asia, because of political circumstances. No excavations were done in large parts of the southwestern Asian Middle East, and work was difficult in Egypt.

In addition to the significant "rediscovery" in Russia of Heinrich Schliemann's "gold of Troy," excavated in the late 1800s and missing from a Berlin museum since the time of the Russian occupation after World War II (see *Museums*, below), it was announced that 10 volumes of critical field notes had been recovered in the Bode Museum in the former East Berlin. In the 1920s and 1930s a joint American-German effort at Medinet Habu, Egypt, recovered a remarkable series of artifacts, and their find spots and associationships were carefully recorded. It was these records—critical to historical understandings of the artifacts—that went to Berlin. Various U.S. museums also faced claims for the return of antiquities, mainly artifacts purchased from sources selling the results of illicit excavation. The Metropolitan Museum of Art in New York City, for example, yielded to a six-year legal action by Turkey for the return of the "Lydian Hoard" of gold and silver vessels and jewelry, illegally excavated and exported.

In 1988 the joint Istanbul University (Beyazit) and University of Chicago excavations at Cayonu, an early village site (*c.* 9,000 years before the present), recovered an antler haft with evidence of what appeared to be "fossilized" cloth. None of the field staff could positively identify the traces, however, and by national law artifacts may not leave Turkey. In early 1993 Gillian Vogelsang-Eastwood of the National Museum for Ethnology in Leiden, Neth., an expert on early textiles, was able to examine the haft and identified the traces as a piece of textile, probably linen. It was the oldest trace of woven textile so far recovered.

Pleistocene Prehistory. Increasingly, Greece was yielding evidence of very early prehistoric occupation (archaeology there had tended to focus almost entirely on "Classical" times). A Micoquian hand ax uncovered in Epirus expanded evidence of prehistoric sites south of Thessaly, where chopper and flake tools had previously been found. Pleistocene archaeologists were also active in both Israel and Jordan. Cave art in France and Spain received attention again through new techniques in radiocarbon dating and the analysis of the pigments of paintings. It was established that animal figures on the walls of caves, such as those at Altamira, Spain, had not always been painted at one time but could have taken as long as 700 years before completion. New radiocarbon assays at Cosquer, an underwater cave

With this contribution, Robert J. Braidwood begins his 51st year of writing about archaeology for the Britannica Book of the Year. *The editors and staff would like to extend their special thanks and cordial greetings to our esteemed colleague on this occasion.*

This clay figurine of a horse, found in ruins along the Euphrates River in Syria, is about 4,300 years old. The discovery, announced in 1993, indicated that horses had played an important role in the Middle East earlier than had been supposed.

UNIVERSITY OF CHICAGO

near Marseille, France, dated the drawings at 27,000 years, making it the earliest cave art known.

Investigations on the climatic interstadial of 11,000–12,000 years ago in Beringia (now submerged under the Bering Strait) and the way it provided for the peopling of the New World from Asia were reported. Traces of starch from an apparently domesticated variety of the taro plant on flint tools from the Solomon Islands suggested that conscious planting was being done in the Pacific as long ago as 28,000 years before the present.

The Middle East. Interest was increasing in the beginnings of a village-farming community way of life in southwestern Asia, although not in classic southern Mesopotamia or in the more desertic regions. Much more excavation was being done in the Levant—Israel, Jordan, the more westerly regions of Syria—than in the regions beyond the Euphrates. One exception, the site of Hallan Cemi on a tributary of the Tigris in southeastern Turkey, showed fascinating indications of the incipience of food production. In central Turkey a somewhat more developed but still "preceramic" village site, Asikli, was also of interest.

Pages in the development of agricultural centres and the appearance of towns continued to unfold in Turkey, Syria, Jordan, and Israel. In Turkey and upper Syria evidence of citylike centres—already apparent (*c.* 3500 BC) at Arslantepe with its linkages to the Uruk development in southern Mesopotamia—was further exposed at Hacinebi, along the southernmost stretch of the Euphrates in Turkey.

A Yale University team recovered evidence of a later (*c.* 2500 BC) climatic decline at Tell Leilan, in northern Syria, where the city reflected what must have been part of the degeneration of the Akkadian dynasty in more southerly Mesopotamia. A clay figurine of a horse discovered at Tell as-Sweyhat on the Euphrates clearly indicated that the horse was domesticated much earlier than had been believed.

The scarcity of reports of foreign work in Jordan might possibly reflect some political prudence, although archaeologists appeared to have been quite active in Israel. A joint effort between the Hebrew University of Jerusalem, the University of Madrid, and the California Institute of Technology made important architectural clearances at 2nd and early 1st millennium levels. At Tel Dan a stone fragment of *c.* 850 BC bore an inscription reading "House of David."

At year's end, with the area soon to be ceded to Palestine, Israeli archaeologists were intensifying their search for antiquities in the vicinity of Jericho.

There was much interest in Manfred Korfmann's new exposures at traditional Troy. At Bogazkoy new Hittite buildings were cleared, and outside the archaeological territory road repairs yielded an interesting inscribed bronze sword dedicated to one of the Hittite kings.

In Egypt the well-established yearly field efforts continued, and none of the archaeologists appeared to have been affected by the political unrest in that country. In the Nile delta region, tests indicated the time of the beginnings of fertile soil deposition as about 6500–5500 BC. Farming in Egypt apparently began as a consequence, with settlement from the Levant. There still were claims of earlier plant cultivation in the southern desertic regions, however.

Egyptian and German archaeologists uncovered the tomb of an army commander of pharaoh Ramses II. At Tell el-Daba in the delta, a site linked to a pharaoh of Hyksos times, the remains of scattered mural paintings were found. The style of the paintings was clearly that of the Minoan murals of Crete.

The Greco-Roman World. A very useful updating of the current understandings of Bronze Age developments on the Greek mainland was published in the *American Journal of Archaeology*. This complemented the coverage in Machteld Mellinck's "Newsletter" of the excavations dealing with the same time range in Turkey. Further surface survey work continued on Crete.

For the Classical (1st millennium BC) time range, the various national archaeological research schools were active in Greece, but little in the way of results was yet available. Excavations at sites in Turkey such as Ephesus, Pergamum, and Sardis were all well reported. At Nikopolis, Greece, site of the sea battle of Actium, ship wreckage was being recovered. Another, earlier seabed recovery was being conducted off the island of Alónnisos; the wreck was a very large, upright ship of *c.* 400 BC containing hundreds of jars that had held wine. Greek and U.S. experts were involved in the restoration of broken metopes of the Athenian Parthenon.

In Italy work in various laboratories continued on the Roman bronze statues recovered in 1992 from a wreck near Brindisi. On the island of Ischia, near Naples, detailed attention was being given to a large number of cremated skeletal remains, evidently Greek colonists, of the 8th–6th century BC.

The remains of a long wooden boat were exposed in Dover, England, while modern sewers were being enlarged.

THE ORIENTAL INSTITUTE

This fragment of woven cloth is the oldest sample of textile ever found. Verified in 1993, the 10,000-year-old cloth was discovered five years earlier at a dig in Turkey begun in 1963 by Robert J. Braidwood and colleagues from the University of Chicago and Istanbul University.

Of middle Bronze Age times, the boat was believed to have been used for cross-channel voyages. *Current Archaeology* also described work on Celtic, Roman, and Middle Age sites in Britain, Scotland, and Ireland. Recovered town remains dating from some hundred years after London was founded (*c.* AD 50) suggested about a century of near desertion, from *c.* AD 150 to 270. The decline was assumed to be economic. A fascinating attempt to present computer-assisted reconstructed views of the very old abbey of Cluny, France, destroyed during the French Revolution, was described in *Science*.

Asia, Africa, and the Pacific. Radar images from a National Aeronautics and Space Administration space shuttle yielded evidence of the track of the Silk Road from northwestern China to the Middle East and settlement remains along the route. Much archaeological news from East Asia focused on the problems of antiquity smuggling, evidently particularly troublesome in China. One extraordinary discovery in China was an underground tomb near Xian (Sian) dating to *c.* 25 BC. It had been looted twice in antiquity, but on its ceiling was a remarkable printed map of the stars and a series of constellations.

There was uncertainty about the origins of human occupation of Australia. Existing physical evidence had been determined to be at the limits of the early reach of radiocarbon dating, but thermoluminescence assays now suggested that human settlement began as early as 50,000 years ago. *Antiquity* considered the interesting circumstances for archaeological research in Australia and discussed how such efforts had changed with the growth in respect for the aboriginal peoples. (ROBERT J. BRAIDWOOD)

Western Hemisphere. Archaeological research in the Western Hemisphere in 1993 was marked by discoveries in ancient Mayan and Mexican archaeology, new evidence for the antiquity and origins of early human habitation in North America, and, for the historic period, the unearthing of fortifications built by the earliest 16th-century Spanish explorers. Traditional archaeological discoveries were matched by findings that highlight the role of archaeology in the reconstruction of environmental conditions for areas and time periods before scientific data were collected.

Environmental Archaeology. Reliable official hurricane records exist only for the past 120 years, but the use of archaeological stratigraphic records and radiocarbon determinations of storm-deposited sand in an Alabama lake has provided evidence of major hurricanes in the area every 600 years on the average. By studying the depth of sand lenses to determine relative age and their thickness to determine wind intensity, Kam-biu Liu of Louisiana State University developed a technique that may extend the record of storm activity in the Gulf States to 6,000 years before the present. A basis also may be provided for testing models of global warming that suggested that hurricanes intensify in force and frequency with rising global temperatures.

New insights into the impact of precontact cultures on the landscape helped to explode myths of the pristine nature of these environments. Working in the lowlands of Costa Rica, multidisciplinary teams discovered evidence that America's tropical forests may not be as natural and untouched by past human activity as had been thought. Buck Stanford of the University of Denver, Colo., announced the recovery from the soil of ancient charcoal dating to 1,200–2,000 years before the present, indicating that the area's "virgin" forest was once burned and cultivated. The discovery of a buried stone hearth, burial sites, tools, and food remains supported the idea that the forest inhabitants raised yucca and corn (maize) as early as AD 800. Related studies of corn pollen by Mark Bush, a paleoecologist at Duke University,

Durham, N.C., working in the Darién Gap rain forest in Panama, revealed that the area had been heavily altered by cultivation from at least 4,000 years before the present and as recently as 300 years ago. Finally, parallel studies of the traditional raised field agriculture of the ancient inhabitants of highland Mexico also cast doubts upon the environmental health of these practices, long held to represent an example of man's living in harmony with nature. A series of deep lake cores into the sediments of Lake Pátzcuaro, northwest of Mexico City, by a team headed by Sarah L. O'Hara of the University of Sheffield, England, provided evidence that farming may have induced severe environmental impacts. The investigators identified three major episodes of ancient soil erosion, with the third and most destructive dating to between AD 1200 and the arrival of the Spanish in the 16th century. Roughly contemporaneous with the time of the Aztec Empire, this period was characterized by what O'Hara described as "staggeringly high" environmental impacts and erosion rates of 208 metric tons of soil per hectare (85 tons per acre) per year.

Early Human Sites. Archaeologists working in northern Alaska reported evidence from radiocarbon datings that supported the antiquity of one of the earliest early human sites in the Northern Hemisphere. U.S. Bureau of Land Management scientists announced the initial discovery of an early Paleo-Indian site on a high mesa in 1978. In 1993 the team, under the direction of Michael Kunz, confirmed the antiquity of this find at 9,700–11,700 years before the present. In addition, the 50 bifacially flaked fluted points found there were similar to those of the Clovis complex tools found with extinct mammoth remains in the U.S. Southwest half a century earlier. They were quite different from points found at the Nenana culture complex in Alaska, which also dates to *c.* 11,000 years before the present, and showed strong cultural parallels to early stone tool industries in eastern Siberia for this time period. The discovery of these two distinctive stone tool cultures suggested that two very different Early Man groups were present in northern Alaska at the time of early immigration from Asia into the New World.

Colonial Period in North America. Researchers working under the direction of Kathleen Deagan of the Florida Museum of Natural History at Gainesville announced the discovery of Spanish fortifications that appeared to con-

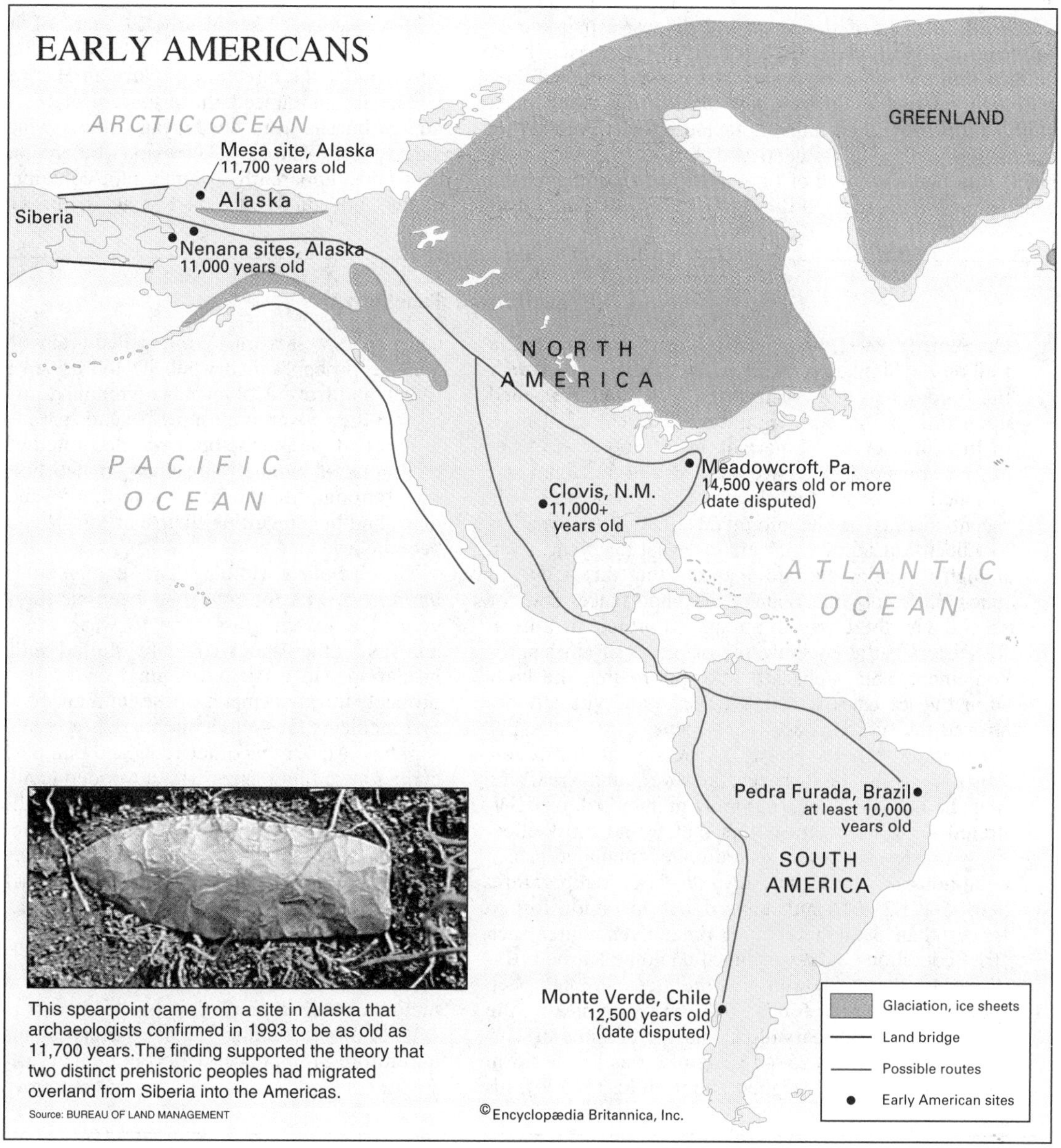

This spearpoint came from a site in Alaska that archaeologists confirmed in 1993 to be as old as 11,700 years. The finding supported the theory that two distinct prehistoric peoples had migrated overland from Siberia into the Americas.

Source: BUREAU OF LAND MANAGEMENT

This 9-m (30-ft) Mayan frieze, shown in an artist's rendering, depicts a ruler, ancestor gods, dancing figures, shells, and monsters. The frieze was found on a pyramid in Belize and was dated to between AD 800 and 900.
UCLA INSTITUTE OF ARCHAEOLOGY

firm the exact location of the earliest European settlement in Florida and the U.S. Over the summer, archaeologists excavated portions of the moat and defensive palisade of what appeared to represent a fort built by Pedro Menéndez de Avilés in 1565. Under orders to destroy Fort Caroline, a French settlement near modern Jacksonville, Menéndez built his fort around an Indian longhouse structure. He dug a moat one metre (3 ft) deep and 4 m (14 ft) wide and, inside it, a defensive wall of one-metre-wide wooden posts. This Spanish fort predated the establishment of Jamestown by four decades and the landing of the *Mayflower* at Plymouth Rock in 1620 by half a century.

Mesoamerica. After nearly 20 years of investigation at the early Classic Mayan city of Cuello in Belize, archaeologists under the direction of Norman Hammond of Boston University announced the discovery of the earliest known human burials from the Mayan culture, which appeared to date to approximately 3,000 years before the present. The new finds, apparently a family plot containing the remains of five individuals who died at about the same time, were

The Iceman Teacheth

On Sept. 19, 1991, two German hikers wandered off a trail on the Similaun Glacier in the Tyrolean Alps, near the border between Austria and Italy, and happened upon one of the most significant archaeological finds of the 20th century. Emerging from the ice was what at first appeared to be a discarded doll and then was assumed to be just another of the several relatively recent victims of the mountains that warm weather had been causing the glaciers to reveal that year. Even though it quickly became apparent that this body was much older, no one realized its importance, and for several days there was no attempt to protect it. Curiosity seekers gathered souvenirs of pieces of clothing or equipment, and haphazard attempts to free the body from the ice caused further damage and virtually destroyed the site's archaeological value.

Forensics experts at the University of Innsbruck, Austria, finally took charge, however, and—realizing that the body had been naturally mummified, or dehydrated—instituted procedures that would most effectively preserve it. It was stored under simulated glacial conditions—relative humidity: 96–98%; temperature: −6° C (21.2° F)—and allowed out for study for no longer than 30 minutes at a time. Even under such strict conditions, however, much could be learned. Radiocarbon dating showed that the "Iceman" had been sealed in the glacier for 5,200–5,300 years (making the body nearly 2,000 years older that the mummy of Tutankhamen). He was 25–40 years old, was about 1.6 m (5 ft 2 in) tall, and weighed about 50 kg (110 lb); his teeth were well worn by the milled-grain products he ate. He probably died when he fell asleep in a small trench and froze. Cold winds mummified his body, and he was then covered by snow. Scientists were surprised to find that part of the body was decorated with tattoos of groups of parallel blue lines—it had been thought that tattooing began 2,500 years later—and that humans had begun cutting their hair longer ago than had been believed.

The Iceman's clothing and equipment were also impressive. His fur robe had been carefully stitched; he had a woven grass cape to wear over the robe; and his leather shoes could be stuffed with grass for insulation. He carried two fungi on leather thongs—probably for medicinal purposes and maybe the world's first medicine kit—and a birchbark box containing food supplies. Among his other tools and equipment were a copper ax, a flint dagger with a wooden handle, a backpack with a wood frame, and a newly made and still unstrung bow made of yew. Most impressive, however, was his deerskin quiver, the oldest quiver ever found. In it were 12 unfinished shafts and 2 expertly finished arrows, the latter demonstrating that ballistic principles had been known and applied.

Some 120 researchers in Europe and the U.S. were studying microscopic pieces of the body and equipment. As work continued, it was likely that the Iceman would go on revealing details of everyday life during a heretofore little-known period in human history.

(BARBARA WHITNEY)

found in deep sediment layers dating to the earliest phase of occupation at the site, *c.* 1200–900 BC, nearly a thousand years before the time period of the previously excavated burials at Cuello.

A basalt stela measuring 1.6 × 1.2 m (6 × 4 ft), originally found in 1986 during the construction of a riverside dock near the village of Mojarra, 40 km (25 mi) inland from Veracruz on Mexico's Gulf Coast, provided key evidence for the decipherment of the earliest known readable text in the Americas. The stela depicts the figure of a standing man with an elaborate headdress, bordered on the top and sides by 21 columns of hieroglyphic writing. After two years of study, John S. Justeson, an anthropologist at the State University of New York at Albany, and Terrence Kaufman, a linguist at the University of Pittsburgh, Pa., announced the decipherment of approximately 100 of a total of 150 glyphs from this example of the epi-Olmec writing system and the identification of in excess of 30 "logograms," or image elements, depicting the warrior king, sunrise and the stars, jaguars, and a penis, which figured in the Mayan ritual of renewal for the king and his nobles. The carved stela and text were dated to AD 159. This find led some scholars to believe that the earliest Mayan scripts developed gradually over a long period of time rather than in a burst of innovation.

Finally, archaeologists working under the direction of Richard M. Leventhal of the Institute of Archaeology at the University of California at Los Angeles announced that at least one Mayan centre, the city of Xunantunich, 112 km (70 mi) west of Belize City, Belize, appeared to have survived as a vibrant urban centre for 150–200 years after other similar centres had declined or been abandoned at the end of the Classic period. Evidence came from large quantities of late Mayan ceramics that could be dated to the 10th century AD and from the excavation of a huge, well-preserved plaster frieze. The elaborate modeled and painted facade of the frieze, 9 m (30 ft) in length and found along the west side of a 13-story pyramid structure, contained the images of a ruler, ancestor gods, dancing figures, shells, and earth monsters, all of which were executed between AD 800 and 900. Leventhal suggested that this urban centre of some 10,000 inhabitants may have managed to survive precisely because of its small size at a time when the larger urban centres in the region, such as Dos Pilas, Tikal, Seibal, and Caracol, were engulfed in warfare and political decline.

(JOEL W. GROSSMAN)

See also Anthropology.

This article updates the *Macropaedia* article The Study of HISTORY: *Archaeology.*

Architecture

The architectural world in 1993 was dominated to a considerable extent by the personality of the British architect Sir Norman Foster. In December it was announced that Foster, 58, was winner of the annual Gold Medal of the American Institute of Architects (AIA), the highest honour in U.S. architecture. It was the first time since 1966 that the Gold Medal, given for lifetime achievement, had gone to an architect from outside North America.

Foster, an avid aviator, was known for glittering, crisply detailed "high-tech" metal and glass buildings, of which the best known was his Hong Kong and Shanghai Banking Corporation tower in Hong Kong. His mirror-glass Willis Faber office building in Ipswich was the only British building built since World War II to be officially listed as a historic landmark.

Foster's Carré d'Art, an art museum and library, opened in early summer in Nîmes, France, on a site opposite the Maison Carrée, a Roman temple from the 1st century AD. Critics acclaimed the new structure as a light-filled, glass-walled modern equivalent of the classical temple. During 1993 Foster was also named architect for the redevelopment of the Reichstag in Berlin, the ornate former national capitol built in 1871 and burned by the Nazis in 1933. It would house the Parliament of the newly united Germany. Foster was also picked to design the American Air Museum in Duxford, England. His uncharacteristically sober Joslyn Art Museum addition in Omaha, Neb., started construction in June.

Awards. Japanese architect Fumihiko Maki was chosen in April as winner of the $100,000 Pritzker Prize, the nearest thing in architecture to a Nobel Prize. The award was made in Prague in order to call attention to the architectural merit of that historic Central European city, one of Maki's favourites. Maki, 65, spent the years 1952–65 as a student and teacher in the U.S., then opened a practice in Japan in which he created modern buildings in bold, sculptural shapes, often finished in a surface of brushed aluminum or stainless steel that seemed bathed in light. Among the best known were the Wacoal showroom, known as the Spiral Building, in Tokyo, the Fujisawa Municipal Gymnasium, the Chiba Convention Center, the National Museum of Modern Art in Kyoto, and the Hillside Terrace Apartments in Tokyo. For the latter complex, he received the 1993 Prince of Wales Prize in Urban Design, awarded to Maki jointly with the Swiss architect Luigi Snozzi.

Other prestigious awards included the $138,000 Praemium Imperiale for architecture to Japanese architect Kenzo Tange, 79, best known for the Olympic stadia of 1964 in Tokyo and the Yamanashi Press Institute in Kofu. The AIA gave its 1993 Twenty-Five Year Award, an annual prize for an American building that had proved its worth over at least a quarter century, to the Deere & Co. Administration Building in Moline, Ill., by Eero Saarinen. It was the sixth such award, a record, to a building by Saarinen. (During the year it was announced that an earlier Saarinen winner, Dulles International Airport outside Washington, D.C., would be enlarged in the manner the architect had envisioned, by extension of the original structure by 98 m [320 ft] at each end). The Twenty-Five Year Award for 1994 was to be presented to Haystack Mountain School of Crafts in Deer Isle, Maine, by Edward Larrabee Barnes. The AIA also picked 18 American buildings for its annual Honor Awards for good architecture. Among the better known were NationsBank Plaza in Tampa, Fla., by Harry Wolf; Canal+ Headquarters in Paris by Richard Meier; Wexner Center for the Arts in Columbus, Ohio, by Peter Eisenman; Hynes Convention Center in Boston by Kallmann, McKinnell & Wood; Buckhead Branch Library in Atlanta, Ga., by Scogin Elam & Bray; and two restorations, the Rookery Building, an 1886 Chicago classic by Burnham & Root with modifications by Frank Lloyd Wright, restored by the McClier firm, and the Furness Building of 1891, originally a college library, now named for its architect, Frank Furness, in Philadelphia, restored by Venturi, Scott-Brown & Associates.

Architect Glenn Murcatt of Australia won the Alvar Aalto Medal, awarded by Finnish architects for work that, according to the citation, "fuses ingredients of modernity with elements of an indigenous rural tradition to create structures that appear . . . locally rooted and universal." The long-anticipated Walt Disney Concert Hall in Los Angeles by Frank O. Gehry, not yet built, won an award for its design from the magazine *Progressive Architecture.*

Civic Buildings. Perhaps the most widely discussed new building of the year, and one of the most admired in many years, was the United States Holocaust Memorial Museum, which opened in April on a site near the Mall in Washington, D.C. (*See* MUSEUMS.) The architect was James Ingo Freed of the New York firm Pei Cobb Freed & Partners, and the exhibits were designed by Ralph Appelbaum. The museum attempted, through its architecture, to evoke the Nazi death camps and to suggest how modern technology and efficiency could be put to perverted and even insane purposes. The exhibits, using photographs and such objects as an actual railroad car of the type used to transport victims to the camps, traced the history of the Nazi policy of extermination of the Jewish people.

Also widely publicized was a fire station in the Vitra furniture factory complex in Weil am Rhein, Germany, the first building actually built by Zaha Hadid, an architect long known as a leader of the so-called deconstructionist movement, in which buildings often appear to be exploding into sharply angled fragments. "The results are not Classical proportions and Euclidian geometries, but attenuated and tapered forms that deliver the thrill of high-speed travel without the rocket," wrote one critic. The Vitra company's "campus" included other buildings, some built and some in progress, by such international "star" architects as Gehry, Tadao Ando, Alvaro Siza, and Nicholas Grimshaw.

An addition to Milan's Lignate Airport was designed by the Italian Aldo Rossi to suggest a gateway. A Federal Judiciary Building in Washington was designed by Barnes as a simplified imitation of the historic Union Station by Daniel Burnham, which stands adjacent. The Greater Columbus Convention Center, by Eisenman, was designed in such a way that its walls looked as if they had been thrown off balance by an earthquake. On an island in Japan, Ando created a Buddhist Lotus Temple around an elliptical pool of water.

Commercial and Cultural Buildings. An American acropolis began to assume final form in San Francisco at the 35-ha (87-ac) Yerba Buena Gardens urban-renewal project. A Center for the Arts, designed by Maki and containing mostly performance spaces, opened in October. Not yet complete were the San Francisco Museum of Modern Art, by the Swiss architect Mario Botta, and the Center for the Arts Theater, by James Stewart Polshek. The adjacent Moscone Center convention facility was being extended by Freed, part of it beneath the Center for the Arts.

In Frankfurt, Germany, a new skyscraper complex for the DG Bank, by American architect William Pedersen of Kohn Pedersen Fox Associates, PC, mixed a variety of heights, shapes, and window patterns in a harmonious group. In Charlotte, N.C., the 60-story NationsBank Corporate Center and Blumenthal Performing Arts Center, by Cesar Pelli, recalled the classic towers of the Empire State Building era with its elegantly illuminated setback top. In New York, architect Kevin Roche enlarged the Jewish Museum by adding a new wing in exact imitation of the neo-Gothic style of the original. Optical laser scanners helped stone-carvers replicate details, and the new limestone was roughened by being chiseled to match the older weathered stone.

In Salem, Mass., the Salem Witch Trials Tercentenary Memorial opened with a design by architect James Cutler and artist Maggie Smith, chosen in an international competition from among 242 entries. Names and statements of victims of the witchcraft persecution were carved into stone walls, slabs, and benches to create a memorial park. A Women's Rights National Historical Park opened in Seneca Falls, N.Y., where the movement for women's rights began in 1848. In Wellesley, Mass., the new Davis Museum at Wellesley College, the first U.S. building by the noted Spanish architect Rafael Moneo, was praised as one of the best art museum interiors of recent years. Moneo was also at work on a major extension of the Houston (Texas) Art Museum.

Exhibitions, Competitions, and New Commissions. A major exhibit of the work of Italian architect Renzo Piano—one of the designers of the Pompidou Centre, which he called "a spaceship landing in the middle of Paris"—was on display at the Architectural League in New York City and later at the Menil Collection in Houston, a building originally done by Piano for which the architect was now designing an addition to display works of the painter Cy Twombly.

The Pompidou Centre itself mounted an exhibit of the avant-garde deconstructionist Vienna firm of Coop-Himmelblau. Wrote one critic: "Formal aspects of the 'open architecture' advanced by the firm's founders—fragmenting,

RICHARD BRYANT—ARCAID

The new Carré d'Art in Nîmes, France, echoes elements of the Roman-period Maison-Carrée. The museum houses contemporary art as well as a library that includes rare books and manuscripts.

breaking, dematerializing, contorting, impaling, reversing, exploding—are abundantly evident in the show's 47 alarming models." The Museum of Modern Art (MOMA) in New York City put on an exhibit of bridges, buildings, and sculptures by Spanish engineer and architect Santiago Calatrava. MOMA also showed the 10 finalist entries in a competition to design the Nara Convention Center in Japan, including the winner by Arata Isozaki. (Isozaki also won a competition in the U.S., for a sculpture garden at the Bass Museum in Miami Beach, Fla.)

In an effort to bring notice to the architecture of the Pacific region, the San Francisco Museum of Modern Art mounted a huge exhibit of the work of a young Japanese architect, Shin Takamatsu. The catalog compared Takamatsu's wildly expressive work to "the strange monuments of a religious cult" and to "overscaled mechanical models and, at times, gigantic jewelry." Architect Stanley Tigerman designed the exhibit "Chicago Architecture and Design, 1923–1993," shown at the Art Institute of Chicago.

New York City architect Peter Pran led a team that won a competition to design a new $230 million New York Police Academy in the South Bronx. Pelli proposed a pair of 85-story towers for the Kuala Lumpur City Centre in Malaysia. Rossi designed a set of office buildings in the stoplight colours of red, green, and yellow for the Disney Development Co. in the Disney town of Celebration, Fla.

Controversies. A long battle by admirers of the headquarters of the Salk Institute for Biological Sciences in La Jolla, Calif., ended in defeat in May when bulldozers razed a grove of eucalyptus trees at the entrance, making way for construction of a new wing. Designed by Louis I. Kahn and built in 1966 for polio vaccine pioneer Jonas Salk, the research complex was regarded as one of the great American buildings. Critics of the addition argued that it would harm the orchestrated sequence of movement through the grove, across a threshold, and onto a courtyard with a stunning framed view of the Pacific horizon. Salk supported the addition, but it was opposed by prominent architects and historians, including Gehry, Meier, Philip Johnson, Vincent Scully, and Robert Venturi. *New York Times* critic Herbert Muschamp called the Salk "the most sublime landscape ever created by an American architect." The addition, designed by former Kahn associates David Rhinehart and Jack MacAllister, would contain laboratories, offices, and an auditorium.

In New York City it was announced that the 1918 main post office, by McKim Mead and White, would be renovated as an Amtrak railroad passenger terminal. The post office stood directly across the street from the site of the old Pennsylvania Station, designed by the same architects, now demolished.

In Italy, after decades of trying to figure out what to do about the Leaning Tower of Pisa, engineers decided that the landmark was in imminent danger of collapse. A massive weight of lead and concrete was inserted at the high side of the tower's foundation, intended to act as a counterweight that would gradually reverse the tower's tilt. In the first three months, the tower righted itself by 0.3°.

Urban Design and Planning. Agreement appeared to have been reached on New York City's huge Riverside South project on 23 ha (56 ac) of former rail yards overlooking the Hudson River from 59th to 72nd Street in Manhattan. Developer Donald Trump in 1985 proposed a "Television City" development with 1.4 million sq m (15 million sq ft) of floor space, including the world's tallest (150 stories) building. A coalition of neighbourhood and civic groups opposed the project and formed themselves into a Riverside South Development Corp. They produced an alternate scheme of

The colours in the interior of Peter Eisenman's new convention centre in Columbus, Ohio, serve to help visitors find their way through the 54,000-sq m (580,000-sq ft) building. Used on the centre's exterior, the same colours make the building stand out vividly in its urban setting.
JEFF GOLDBERG—ESTO

about half the bulk, including 10 ha (25 ac) of new public park. The new design, although endorsed by the city and by Trump himself, was still opposed by some neighbourhood groups.

Also in Manhattan came the fourth proposal of recent years for improvements to a sleazy honky-tonk strip. Proponents of "42nd Street Now!"—including architect Robert A.M. Stern—wished to transform a block of old theatres between 7th and 8th Avenue into a Hollywood version of the Times Square of the past, with even more glitz and rooftop signs and bright lights than the original. Some of the renovations would be temporary, until the economy revived sufficiently to permit construction of the huge office towers long intended for this block.

Miami-based architects Andres Duany and Elizabeth Plater-Zyberk, designers of the influential model village of Seaside, Fla., established a group called the Congress for the New Urbanism. CNU sponsored, in October, the first of a series of symposia in support of traditional ideas about city planning. CNU promoted communities made up of closely packed neighbourhoods, as opposed to typical recent developments of superhighways and scattered suburbs, which were seen as wasteful of resources and alienating for their inhabitants.

Business and Practice. The global ecological crisis was a recurrent theme in architecture in 1993. "Designing for a Sustainable Future" was the theme of the annual convention of the AIA, held in Chicago in June. The National Audubon Society opened a new headquarters in New York City, remodeling an 1891 department store as an example of environmentally responsible design. Designed by Croxton Collaborative, the renovated structure used 62% less energy than required by New York's strict energy code. Audubon

Zaha Hadid's fire station for a furniture company in Weil am Rhein, Germany, employs such devices as a soaring canopy and dramatic angles to create its effect. Although the Iraqi-born architect had received wide recognition for her drawings, the building in Weil am Rhein was her first freestanding, permanent structure to be built.
RICHARD BRYANT—ARCAID

also argued that it was saving energy by preserving an old building rather than erecting a new one and by locating in a downtown that was well served by public transportation.

The largest U.S. retailer, Wal-Mart Stores, Inc., opened the first of a series of "Eco-marts" in Lawrence, Kan., using renewable construction materials and efficient lighting and featuring a recycling centre. Critics of Wal-Mart pointed out that goods and customers still arrived at the suburban stores by energy-consumptive vehicles, however. In the New England region, opponents in several towns succeeded in killing proposals for new Wal-Mart stores, arguing they would challenge and perhaps destroy community retail life on "Main Street."

With economic recession continuing in most countries, less was being built than in the recent past. Around the world, airports were among the few major types of buildings being built in large numbers. In the U.S. a series of new federal courthouses, some by outstanding architects, promised to become, for the 1990s, what the art museum was during the '70s and '80s: the major embodiment of civic architectural pride.

In some places the idea of architecture as a profession was being questioned. In Great Britain the government considered abolishing the requirement for testing and licensing of architects. In Spain and Germany efforts were under way to abolish fee scales set by architects, an action taken several years earlier in the U.S.

Deaths during 1993 included Reima Pietila, the most distinguished living Finnish architect, in August at age 70. Alison Smithson (*see* OBITUARIES) of Great Britain, prominent in the 1950s and '60s with her husband, Peter, as an advocate of socially responsible architecture, also died in August, at age 65. Influential Postmodernist architect Charles Moore, designer of such projects as Sea Ranch Condominium north of San Francisco, the Piazza d'Italia in New Orleans, La., and the St. Matthew's Episcopal Church in Pacific Palisades, Calif., died on December 16 at age 68. (*See* OBITUARIES.) (ROBERT CAMPBELL)

See also Engineering Projects; Industrial Review: *Building and Construction*.

This article updates the *Macropædia* article The History of Western ARCHITECTURE.

Art Exhibitions and Art Sales

If the Matisse exhibition was the leading show in 1992, then its worthy sequel in 1993 was the exhibition of paintings from the Barnes Collection in Merion, Pa. The traveling exhibition of masterpieces of Impressionist and Postimpressionist art from that little-known private collection included some of the most splendid works by Matisse anywhere. Because the Barnes Foundation did not normally lend its paintings, the traveling shows seen at the National Gallery in Washington, D.C., and the Orsay Museum in Paris in 1993 were especially notable events.

The Barnes Collection had been in the news since the early 1960s, when legal challenges to the terms of its constitution were begun. It had always limited visiting hours, and the admission fee was pegged at just $1. Colour reproduction of any work from the collection was banned, and works of art were never lent. The 1993 exhibition evolved from the decision to renovate the 1922 villa that housed the pictures, since the works of art were to be taken down in any event. (*See* Sidebar.) There was debate about whether loans should be permitted, but the financial advantages were tempting, and the need to raise some $7 million for building repairs was decisive. The show attracted some 500,000 visitors in Washington, and both the French and the Japanese provided substantial funds for the privilege of showing the paintings. (After appearing in Paris in the autumn and winter of 1993, the show would travel to Tokyo and to Philadelphia in 1994.) As a result, the first-ever colour catalog and book about the collection were published.

Albert Barnes, a physician who had made his fortune by discovering and marketing an antiseptic, began to collect in 1912 and by his death in 1951 had amassed some 2,000 works of art. The great strength of his collection was in the Impressionists and Postimpressionists, many of whose works he had acquired in the early 1920s. In 1922 Barnes set up an educational foundation and began to allow limited access to his works of art. This early attempt at public exhibition was not well received by the critics, and as a result, Barnes began to limit access severely, imposing the lending ban and the prohibition on colour reproduction. This restrictive regime continued through the 1980s during the trusteeship of his successor. Thus, the Barnes Collection remained a secret collection, its existence known but its paintings rarely seen.

During the renovation 80 works went on tour. They included several wonderful paintings, such as "The Card Players" by Cézanne and "Les Poseuses" by Seurat. In Paris the paintings could be compared with related works from the permanent collection of the Orsay Museum.

If the "bidding" that preceded the selection of venues for the Barnes show provided further evidence of what big business art exhibitions had become—with significant political and financial ramifications—comments by New York City's mayor, David Dinkins, confirmed the importance of art exhibitions in attracting the tourist dollar. The mayor announced that four exhibitions held in late 1992 had attracted a total of more than 1,750,000 visits. These included the Matisse exhibition at the Museum of Modern Art, shows devoted to Magritte and Ribera at the Metropolitan Museum of Art, and the exhibition devoted to Russian and Soviet avant-garde art at the Guggenheim Museum. The total viewing attendance was roughly equivalent to the total attendance at New York Mets baseball games during the 1992 season, and it was reported that nearly three-quarters of the visitors had come from outside New York City.

Political and economic considerations continued to be foremost in 1993. In Britain concern was expressed that the country seemed to miss out on many of the leading international blockbuster shows. British gallerygoers were obliged to travel to Paris to see the Matisse and the Barnes Collection shows, as well as the 100-work Titian show in the spring. Major reasons seemed to be the perceived lack of a satisfactory temporary exhibition space in or near central London and the reduction in sponsorship that inhibited major shows from visiting more venues. It had been hoped that the Barnes Collection might have been seen at the Royal Academy of Arts in London, but in the end the ability of Paris and Tokyo to pay large sums prevailed. The Royal Academy had approached financial and governmental institutions as well as wealthy patrons in an effort to attract the show to London, but support was not found.

The Matisse show at the Museum of Modern Art, which closed in early 1993, was the largest and grandest exhibition devoted to that artist ever, with more than 400 works on view. A substantial part of the exhibition moved on to Paris, where 130 works were on display at the Pompidou Centre from February to June. The scope, covering 1904 to 1917, was more limited than in New York. The "Bathers by a River" from the Chicago Art Institute, for many the highlight of the New York show, did not travel to Paris. The Matisse canvases from the Barnes Collection, seen in Paris later in the year, provided a fine comparison for visitors who had also seen the Matisse exhibition.

Late 19th- and 20th-century subjects remained popular for 1993 exhibitions. A charming but not so well-known group, the Nabis, was the subject of shows at the Kunsthaus in Zürich, Switz., and later at the Grand Palais in Paris. The artists of this group included Pierre Bonnard, Édouard Vuillard, and Félix Vallotton, and the last comprehensive exhibition of their work had taken place in Paris in 1955. The works of 12 artists, primarily dating from the 1890s, made up the show. The influence of Japanese printmaking on the group was illustrated by the inclusion of prints that had actually been owned by the artists. Vuillard had a particularly fine collection that included works by Hokusai and Utamaro. The show also included theatrical designs, graphic arts, and book illustrations as well as paintings.

Late works by French Impressionist Camille Pissarro were shown in Texas at the Dallas Museum of Art and later traveled to Philadelphia and London. The subject matter was the painter's series of views of French cities, including Paris, Rouen, Le Havre, and Dieppe.

An exhibition entitled "American Art in the 20th Century" was mounted at the Royal Academy in London in the autumn, having traveled there from Berlin. In London it took a slightly different form, with an associated show at the Saatchi Gallery concentrating on contemporary works. The wide range of subject matter led to criticism that the show was disjointed, and in particular there was debate as to the success of its coverage of contemporary subjects. The show focused on the third quarter of the 20th century, the period in which modern American artists had the greatest international influence. Most major figures within their respective movements were represented, including the Abstract Expressionists Jackson Pollock, Willem de Kooning, and Mark Rothko. Separate sections were devoted to artists such as Andy Warhol and Jasper Johns. The emphasis on well-known names meant that, in Berlin at least, some less-high-profile artists were poorly represented. The wide variety of style and approach was stimulating and exciting if sometimes difficult to analyze historically. Because the theme of the show was very much American art as seen from the European point of view, artists whose influence was not notable tended to be underrepresented. Surrealism, Minimalism, and Pop were present, but Conceptual and West Coast movements were not.

Another 20th-century art movement, Dada, was the subject of a major retrospective exhibition devoted to the work of Max Ernst, which was seen at the Museum of Modern Art in New York City, the Menil Collection in Houston, Texas, and the Art Institute of Chicago. Entitled "Dada and the Dawn of Surrealism," it covered the period from

"The Boat Studio," a self-portrait by Claude Monet, was included in the traveling show from the Barnes Collection that appeared in Washington, D.C., and Paris in 1993. It was the first time since 1923 that works from the collection had appeared outside their Merion, Pa., home.

"The Hunter (Catalan Landscape)" was among the works by Joan Miró included in an exhibition at the Museum of Modern Art in New York City to celebrate the centenary of his birth. Other shows were held in Spain, including a major retrospective in Barcelona.

Ernst's early expressionistic works to his influential works in Dada and Surrealism of the 1920s. Art lovers who had visited the Matisse show could contrast it with Ernst's very different approach to Modernism. The artists, though contemporaries, could hardly have been more different in outlook, style, philosophy, or technique.

Twentieth-century art was also featured in London at the Tate Gallery in a show entitled "Paris Post War: Art and Existentialism 1945 to 1955." That such an exhibition could be considered mainstream illustrated the extent to which deconstructivist criticism and philosophy had become established in the museum and art history worlds. The exhibition explored relations between painting, philosophy, and literature as well as politics and ideology. Artists represented included painter Jean Hélion and sculptors Alberto Giacometti and Germaine Richier.

A major survey exhibition of the architecture and design of the 20th-century Dutch architect Gerrit Rietveld was on view at the Central Museum in Utrecht, Neth., and later in Paris at the Pompidou Centre. Entitled "Gerrit Thomas Rietveld 1883 to 1964," the exhibition was organized by the Central Museum, which holds the most important collection of his work. The version of the show in Paris was slightly smaller than that in the architect's home city, but it included one complete room, 43 pieces of furniture, 33 architectural models, and nearly 200 drawings and photographs. Rietveld was particularly noted for furniture made of wood and metal and for interiors that show a preoccupation with geometry and simplicity of line. His most famous house was the Schroeder House in Utrecht, designed in 1924. This project was well represented in the exhibition, which would travel after Paris to Antwerp, Belgium, and possibly to the Guggenheim Museum in New York City.

Abstract Expressionism was the subject of a small show comprising 60 works on paper selected by the Metropolitan Museum of Art from its own collection. Included were examples of work by Robert Motherwell, Mark Tobey, Theodore Roszak, and Elaine de Kooning. The exhibition had been seen earlier in the year at the High Museum of Art in Atlanta, Ga.

An exhibition in Venice at the Palazzo Grassi was devoted to relatively unfamiliar works by Modigliani, an artist also well represented in the Barnes Collection. Those on show in Venice were drawn from the collection of his first patron, Paul Alexandre, who had died at the age of 87 in 1968. Alexandre was a doctor with a practice in the Montmartre district of Paris, where he met and befriended many artists, including Modigliani. He amassed a collection of 430 drawings by Modigliani, nearly half of those in existence, together with much documentary material. The Venice show covered the period from 1906 to 1914, allowing an unprecedented appreciation of Modigliani's expertise as a draftsman.

In Tokyo the National Museum of Modern Art mounted a survey show devoted to modern Japanese art. The pieces on display were selected from among the 6,000 or so works the museum had acquired since 1952. Few of them were normally on view.

In Belgium, Antwerp celebrated its year as cultural capital of Europe with a series of art exhibitions, the most important of which was devoted to the work of Jacob Jordaens. It was a complete overview of the artist's work, including 93 paintings, 6 tapestries, 67 drawings, and 31 prints. Jordaens, less well known than his great contemporaries Rubens and Van Dyck, was represented by a carefully selected group of varied and high-quality works. Religious subjects, portraits, and oil sketches were on display. Notable lenders included Eastern European collections such as the Hermitage in St. Petersburg and museums in Moscow as well as in Poland and Romania.

A show at the Cathedral of Our Lady in Antwerp comprised important carved and painted altarpieces from that city, made in the 15th and 16th centuries. It enabled visitors to appreciate how rich and varied was the interior of the cathedral before its catastrophic fire of 1533. On view were 23 retables and 25 sculpted fragments, illustrating a neglected aspect of Netherlandish art. Many of the sculptures were normally hidden away in parish churches throughout Europe and had not before been assembled. They enabled the visitor to appreciate how the church might have looked before the Reformation. During this early period Antwerp was becoming the commercial and artistic centre of northwestern Europe, an ascendancy that ended with the Reformation, when these carved wood and painted altarpieces were removed. Other exhibitions in Antwerp included "The Panoramic Dream," on view in the summer and commemorating the international expositions held in that city in 1885, 1894, and 1930, and a show devoted to contemporary European sculpture.

In France, Colmar's Unterlinden Museum, best known for the Isenheim altar by Matthias Grünewald, mounted a fascinating exhibition illustrating how artists of the 20th century have been influenced by that harrowing work of art. Artists represented included American, British, and European painters such as Pablo Picasso, Francis Bacon,

Mark Rothko, and Graham Sutherland. The 22nd Council of Europe exhibition held at the National Museum in Copenhagen was entitled "From Viking to Crusader" and focused on Scandinavian art and its European connections during the Dark Ages. Many works were lent by international collections.

An important international loan exhibition devoted to 5th-century BC Greek sculpture was seen in Washington, D.C., at the National Gallery of Art and later at the Metropolitan Museum of Art in New York City. The show was called "The Greek Miracle: Classical Sculpture from the Dawn of Democracy," with 22 key works lent by the National Archaeological Museum in Athens.

"Gates of Mystery: The Art of Holy Russia" was an exhibition comprising liturgical objects and icons borrowed from the State Russian Museum in St. Petersburg that toured the U.S. and also traveled to the Victoria and Albert Museum in London. It comprised the most important collection of medieval Russian art and icons to travel to the West in more than 60 years and included many works never before seen outside Russia. Some had survived as a result of being hidden when churches and monasteries were closed after the Revolution of 1917. Included was a famous 15th-century icon depicting Saint George and the Dragon.

In Stuttgart, Germany, the sesquicentenary of the founding of that city's Staatsgalerie was commemorated by a show of some 300 works of art commissioned between 1770 and 1830. The exhibition included many works influenced by artists working in Rome and Paris, and relatively unfamiliar artists such as Valentin Sonnenschein and Friedrich Füger were included. Realism and naturalism characterized many of the pieces on show, and documents and literary quotations illustrated the spirit of the times. Fascinating parallels were apparent between these works and the works of French artists of the period.

An unusual exhibition showing the range and quality of French painting in the 17th century, entitled "Le Grand Siècle," was on view at two French provincial museums, the Museum of Fine Arts and Archaeology in Rennes and the Fabre Museum in Montpellier. It had previously been seen at the Museum of Fine Arts in Montreal with the title "Century of Splendour." On view were approximately 130 works covering the whole of the 17th century. Most of the exhibits came from French provincial museums, but there were a few church loans and paintings by Claude Lorrain and Nicolas Poussin sent by the Louvre. That a show of this size and quality could be mounted by provincial French galleries (it was organized by those in Rennes and Montpellier) illustrated the recent renaissance of such French museums, many of which had been recently refurbished and extended and their collections restored and increased. For Parisian exhibition visitors the splendid French railroad system meant that it was possible to travel to Rennes in less time than it might take to queue for admittance to one of the major Paris shows.

The Queen's Gallery at Buckingham Palace was the venue for "A King's Purchase," a show chosen from works acquired for the royal collections by George III from the collection assembled in Venice in the mid-18th century by Joseph Smith. At the National Gallery in London, 10 of the most notable canvases from the Wellington Museum at Apsley House were on show, while that museum was closed for renovation. Paintings by Velázquez and Correggio were included.

A show devoted to Spanish cubist painter Juan Gris, a contemporary of Braque and Picasso, was seen at the Staatsgalerie in Stuttgart in the winter and at the Rijksmuseum Kröller-Müller in Otterlo, Neth., following a showing at the Whitechapel Art Gallery in London. Worthy of note were the paper cutouts and the generally monochromatic palette characteristic of the artist. (SANDRA MILLIKIN)

ART SALES

As the recession eased slightly during 1992–93, the super-rich began to buy art again, but with caution. Auctioneers' seasonal turnover, measured in dollars, changed very little compared with the previous year. Christie's recorded a 1% improvement on the 1991–92 season and Sotheby's 4%. These figures were much in line with the January-to-July sales totals announced by Paris auctioneers, which were up 3% over 1992 in terms of French francs. American collectors were the strongest art buyers over the year. Their return to the market led to a revival in the Impressionist and modern markets. In contrast, economic turmoil in Italy and Spain led their nationals to withdraw from the market, leaving many Old Master pictures unsold.

The 1980s boom had been particularly concentrated in Impressionist and modern pictures, as was the fall in prices in 1990–91. Fears that this market would not recover were put to rest in May 1993 when Sotheby's sold a Cézanne still life, "Nature morte—Les Grosses Pommes," for $28.6 million, double the presale estimate. Shortly afterward the most expensive art deal ever struck outside the auction room was announced. Walter Annenberg, the American publishing tycoon, had bought Van Gogh's "Wheat Field with Cypresses" for $57 million from the family of the Swiss arms manufacturer Emil Bührle, who died in 1956. Bührle's magnificent collection of modern masters is housed in a private museum in Zürich, Switz. Annenberg bought the picture as a gift for the Metropolitan Museum of Art in New York City, to which he had promised to bequeath his own collection.

The recovery in prices for lesser works still had a long way to go, however. The November 1992 forced sale of pictures that the flamboyant Paris dealer Alain Lesieutre had used as collateral with his bank in the boom times starkly underlined the problem. The paintings were auctioned in Paris without reserve and made between one-third and one-fifth of the prices Lesieutre had paid in 1989–90. Dubuffet's great circus picture, "La Calipette," which had set an auction record for the artist's work when Lesieutre paid £2.3 million for it in April 1990, was down to F 6 million; a Degas "Dancer" was down from F 4 million to F 1.5 million; and a Miró pastel, from F 3.2 million to F 550,000. The first signs of recovery came at the New York sales in November 1992 when Sotheby's sold one Matisse, "L'Asie," to the Kimbell Museum of Fort Worth, Texas, for $11 million and Christie's another, "Harmonie jaune," for $14,520,000—reputedly to an American businessman.

The new American confidence was also reflected in prices for flashy Victorian pictures—which had a strong following in New York City—and 19th-century paintings by American artists. The French artist James Tissot and the Dutch painter Sir Lawrence Alma-Tadema—both of whom worked in Queen Victoria's England—turned out the top runners. Tissot's sentimental "L'Orpheline"—a woman and a little girl on an autumn riverbank—made $2,970,000 at Christie's New York in February and Alma-Tadema's orgiastic Roman banquet scene, "The Roses of Heliogabulus," £1,651,500 at Christie's London in June. Their American contemporaries proved even more expensive. Childe Hassam's "Room of Flowers" made $5.5 million and a pastel of "Peonies" by William Merritt Chase, $3,962,500.

In the Old Master field, the J. Paul Getty Museum of Malibu, Calif. (whose collections were threatened by the southern California wildfires in October), managed to carry off almost all the great works on offer with little competition. Its most sensational purchase was a drawing by Michelangelo of "Holy Family with the Infant Baptist on the Rest on the Flight into Egypt," which cost £4,181,500 at Christie's in July, the highest price ever paid for a drawing. The handsome compositional sketch had been hidden away in an English country house, Great Tew in Oxfordshire, since 1836, and its existence was virtually unknown. In December 1992 the Getty Museum spent £4,950,000 on a Goya, and in May 1993 it spent £2.3 million on a landscape by the German painter Caspar David Friedrich. In between it bought, for an undisclosed sum, a Rubens "Entombment" that the American collector-dealer Alfred Bader had picked up at Christie's in December 1992 for a bargain £1,045,000.

It was a relatively quiet year for the decorative arts, broken here and there by the emergence of a particularly sensational object or collection. While prices for Georgian furniture drifted lower, the £1.8 million sale of a magnificent Regency desk made for the Marquess of Anglesey—who led the cavalry at the Battle of Waterloo—set a new auction price record for English furniture.

Islamic art, which had been in little demand since the 1991 Gulf war, staged a recovery in April. One of the earliest products of the Turkish potteries at Isnik, a blue and white candlestick made around 1480, sold for a record £617,500, while a 17th-century silk and metal thread "Polonaise" became the world's most expensive Persian carpet at £441,500. The auction market in Chinese art suffered from a lack of Japanese and American buyers, but a Hong Kong financier, Joseph Lau, set a new auction price record for Chinese ceramics when he paid $2,860,000 for a 46-cm (18-in) wine jar with a Jiajing reign mark (1796–1820) at Sotheby's New York in December 1992.

Princess Gloria von Thurn und Taxis of Germany, selling off a miscellany of unwanted silver and jewelry to shore up the family finances, struck an exceptionally strong market in October 1992. A jewel-encrusted snuffbox made for Frederick the Great of Prussia around 1770 set an auction record at Sw F 2,530,000, while the Société des Amis du Louvre spent Sw F 935,000 on a pearl and diamond tiara made for the Empress Eugénie's wedding but subsequently acquired for a Thurn und Taxis bride.

Meanwhile, the year's most sensational auction muddle was Christie's sale of an early 19th-century gilt and lacquered brass mechanical calculator by J.C. Schuster, which, although estimated at £20,000, brought £7.7 million. The successful bidder, the well-known Swiss dealer Edgar Mannheimer, told Christie's that his client did not intend to pay; the underbidder, Bernhard Korte, director of the Research Institute for Discrete Mathematics in Bonn, Germany, later revealed that his museum's price limit had been £200,000 but declined to reveal why he had continued bidding up to £7 million.

Book Sales. The recession began to be felt in the book market in 1992–93, a good two years behind other market sectors. It made owners reluctant to sell and produced a thin year; prices, especially for major rarities, were off the top, but there was no dramatic fall.

Americana was the exception to the rule, where prices actually rose and remained strong all year. On Nov. 20, 1992, Christie's set a new auction price record for American manuscript material when they sold an album kept by Caroline Wright, a friend of Abraham Lincoln and the wife of the governor of Indiana, for $1,320,000. Lincoln had copied the concluding paragraph of his second inaugural address into the album—the famous lines beginning "With malice

Deaccessioning

In the second half of the 20th century, and particularly from the 1970s on, deaccessioning, the sale by a museum of works from its permanent collection, has raised ethical questions. Faced with rising costs, museums began to consider selling art objects to fund administrative and building costs. While deaccessioning to improve the collection has not usually been controversial, selling works of art to pay running costs has caused debate.

The Museums Association of the United Kingdom defines a museum as a non-profit-making institution for the public benefit with an ethic of public service. Its policy on deaccessioning is defined by acts of Parliament that specifically prohibit disposal of items in the most important national collections. Where no specific act governs a particular collection, a museum is not permitted to deaccession without court or other legal authority. The aim of such deaccessioning should be to offer an object by exchange or gift to other institutions before sale is considered. The American Association of Museums defines a museum in similar terms. Moreover, its policy on deaccessioning is that disposal of artworks should be only for advancement of the museum's mission through improving and enhancing its collections.

Commercial and financial considerations, coupled with the often spectacular rise in the value of works of art, have put severe pressure on such policies. In 1991, for example, there was a public row in Sweden following revelations that the directors of the Göteborg Art Museum secretly intended to raise £20 million by selling Picasso's "The Harlequin's Family," one of his most important works and the museum's star and most valuable exhibit. In Britain similar controversies raged over the announcement by Royal Holloway College of the University of London that to provide for general expenses, it would sell a Turner work from its fine collection of Victorian paintings.

The Boston Museum of Fine Arts conceived a novel way to solve the problem: paintings that could not be sold might be rented out. This developed further the recent tendency for permanent collections to lend works to profit-making touring shows. The Courtauld Institute sent some of its finest works on tour a few years ago to raise funds for the conversion of its new gallery at Somerset House in London. The 1993 traveling show from the Barnes Foundation had a similar motive.

The Boston scheme envisaged the proposed opening of a "sister" museum in Nagoya, Japan, where the Museum of Fine Arts would send a semipermanent introductory exhibition. The arrangement would result in a hefty consulting fee for Boston, which, it was hoped, might quickly eliminate the museum's deficit. The arrangement, however, raised questions about the long-term loan of crucial works from permanent museum collections as well as issues of safety and conservation.

(SANDRA MILLIKIN)

This 15th-century Turkish candlestick, which commanded a record price for Islamic art, is 23 cm (9 in) tall and is decorated with leaves and flowers, with inscriptions in Arabic and Kufic script. It was the only such piece privately owned, all others being held by museums.
SOTHEBY'S

toward none; with charity for all"—and signed it. Christie's had been estimating $300,000–$400,000 before the sale. Sotheby's had a similar estimate on a single leaf inscribed with a draft of Lincoln's "house divided" speech, probably written in the winter of 1857–58, which was offered one month later and revised the manuscript record upward to $1,540,000. It was bought by the Gilder Lehrman collection, an assembly of historic Americana that investment bankers Richard Gilder and Lew Lehrman were forming.

In Sotheby's May sale of Americana, Visual Equities Inc. of Atlanta, Ga., a troubled art-investment group, offered the early printing of the Declaration of Independence for which it had paid $2.4 million two years before. This time the bidding failed to reach the $2 million low estimate, and it was sold after the sale at an undisclosed price to Kaller Historical Documents.

The only other deal that stretched into seven figures was Lord Shelburne's sale of the papers of Sir William Petty (1623–87) to the British Library, negotiated by London book dealers Bernard Quaritch. Petty was a pioneer of theoretical economics, and his survey of Ireland, which underpinned the Cromwellian land settlement, was the first scientific, district-by-district, survey of any country. Quaritch also negotiated the sale of Lord Harlech's collection of medieval manuscripts to the National Library of Wales.

Among the most expensive failures of the year was a group of 43 letters written by the Earl of Essex to Queen Elizabeth I in the 1590s. Sotheby's had expected to make £500,000, but no bidder appeared. Christie's was expecting the same kind of price for a copy of the first book printed in English, William Caxton's English translation of a text by Raoul Lefèvre entitled *The Recuyell of the Histories of Troy,* but it was also left unsold.

Named collections, as usual, made for successful sales. Christie's offered the library of the late John Sparrow, warden of All Souls College, Oxford. Although the Bodleian Library and several Oxford colleges had been allowed to pick what they wanted beforehand, the sale made 50% above estimate. The remainder of the library of the earls of Granard—most of which was burned out in the 18th century—attracted similarly enthusiastic bidding at Sotheby's. The collections of two famous book dealers reached the sale room. The private collection of the late Alan Thomas, which had never been for sale, met an enthusiastic reception. The remaining stock of E.P. Goldschmidt was more difficult to sell since it had been available to the market, but Goldschmidt's bibliographical reference library was fiercely fought over. (GERALDINE NORMAN)

This article updates the *Macropædia* articles The History of Western PAINTING; The History of Western SCULPTURE.

Astronomy

For astronomy 1993 was a year of discovery but also one of bitter disappointment. The U.S. Mars Observer spacecraft, eagerly anticipated for its ability to make the first close-up observations of Mars in 17 years, suddenly fell silent on August 21, three days before it was to go into orbit around the planet. The Hubble Space Telescope (HST) produced many new optical images of astronomical objects but was plagued by problems with pointing, power, and a flawed primary mirror. At year's end space shuttle astronauts successfully completed the most elaborate repair mission in the history of the U.S. space program to fix the telescope, although the results of their work would take weeks to evaluate. On the positive side, observations from several spacecraft provided insights into a variety of phenomena, and to cap the year two American astronomers from Princeton University, Russell Hulse and Joseph Taylor (*see* NOBEL PRIZES), were awarded the Nobel Prize for Physics for their discovery and subsequent study of a binary pulsar, a rapidly

Earth Perihelion and Aphelion, 1994

Jan. 2	Perihelion, 147,099,800 km (91,403,400 mi) from the Sun
July 9	Aphelion, 152,095,200 km (94,507,400 mi) from the Sun

Equinoxes and Solstices, 1994

March 20	Vernal equinox, 20:28[1]
June 21	Summer solstice, 14:48[1]
Sept. 23	Autumnal equinox, 06:19[1]
Dec. 22	Winter solstice, 02:23[1]

Eclipses, 1994

May 10	Sun, annular (begins 14:12[1]), the beginning visible southeast of Hawaii, Baja California, New Mexico, midwestern United States (south of Lake Michigan; near Chicago), New England, Nova Scotia, central Atlantic Ocean; the end visible in Morocco.
May 25	Moon, partial (begins 01:18[1]), the beginning visible in the midwestern and eastern United States, southeastern and south-central Canada, Mexico, Central and South America, the southern tip of Greenland, Iceland, most of Antarctica, Africa, and Europe, the southeastern North Pacific Ocean, the Atlantic Ocean, and the southwestern Indian Ocean; the end visible in the coterminous United States, most of Canada, Mexico, Central and South America, most of Antarctica, southern and western Africa, the western coast of Europe, much of the eastern Pacific Ocean, and the Atlantic Ocean.
Nov. 3	Sun, total (begins 11:05[1]), the beginning visible in the eastern Pacific (south of the Galapagos Islands), southern Peru, Bolivia (near La Paz), Paraguay, southern Brazil (near Pôrto Alegre), the southern Atlantic Ocean; the end visible near the Cape of Good Hope, south of South Africa.
Nov. 18	Moon, penumbral (begins 04:26[1]), the beginning visible in North America, Greenland, Iceland, the Arctic regions, Central and South America, Hawaii, western Africa, Europe, extreme western Asia, Antarctica, the eastern Pacific Ocean, and most of the Atlantic Ocean; the end visible in North America, Greenland, Iceland, the Arctic regions, Central America, western South America, Hawaii, northeastern Asia, eastern Australia, New Zealand, the Pacific Ocean, and the western Atlantic Ocean.

[1]Universal time.
Source: *The Astronomical Almanac for the Year 1994* (1993).

Strung out like glowing beads, Comet Shoemaker-Levy 9's fragmented nucleus presented an unusual sight when the comet was first detected in March. Astronomers believed that the comet had been shattered by Jupiter's gravitational field during its pass by the giant planet in July 1992, and they predicted that the fragments would return to Jupiter in July 1994, this time plunging to their destruction in the Jovian atmosphere.

JANE LUU, UNIVERSITY OF CALIFORNIA, BERKELEY, AND DAVID JEWITT, UNIVERSITY OF HAWAII

spinning neutron star in orbit with another star around a common centre of gravity.

Solar System. Although the solar system is dominated by the Sun and major planets, some of the more exciting revelations of 1993 involved comets and asteroids. In March a spectacular comet was discovered by Carolyn and Eugene Shoemaker of the U.S. Geological Survey, Flagstaff, Ariz., and David H. Levy of the University of Arizona. The most unusual feature about Comet Shoemaker-Levy 9 was that it looked like a string of glowing pearls. An HST photograph revealed about 20 cometary chunks spread out in a line. Calculations suggested that the comet's nucleus broke up after a near collision with the giant planet Jupiter in July 1992 and predicted that the pieces would plunge into Jupiter's atmosphere about July 20, 1994, unleashing an energy equivalent to roughly 100 million megatons of TNT.

In 1991, as the Galileo spacecraft passed near the asteroid Gaspra en route to Jupiter, it snapped the first close-up picture of an asteroid. In August 1993 Galileo passed and imaged a second asteroid, 243 Ida. An elongated object about 52 km (32 mi) across, Ida is heavily cratered, suggesting it is at least a billion years old. While passing Ida, Galileo's onboard magnetometer detected shifts in the direction of the magnetic field of the local solar wind. Since the solar wind consists of electrically charged particles blowing away from the Sun and dragging the magnetic field along with it, the measurements suggested that Ida possesses its own magnetic field, which distorts the solar wind field.

Where do comets come from? For years astronomers have postulated a comet storehouse beyond the orbit of Pluto. According to theory, objects lying in this so-called Kuiper belt would occasionally be perturbed by encounters with nearby stars, thereby hurtling fresh comets into the inner solar system. In 1992 David Jewitt of the University of Hawaii and Jane X. Luu of the University of California at Berkeley discovered an object, designated 1992 QB1, that seemed to be part of this belt. In early 1993 the two astronomers reported a second body, dubbed 1993 FW, lying

De revolutionibus

The year 1993 marked the 450th anniversary of the publication of Nicolaus Copernicus' revolutionary work *De revolutionibus orbium coelestium* (*On the Revolutions of the Celestial Spheres*). Despite the fact that the treatise concerns astronomy, it played a major role in changing the philosophical view of humankind's place in the universe and in advancing the idea that no amount of philosophical authority could dictate what one actually experienced in nature. Whereas the Greek Aristarchus had suggested 2,000 years earlier that the Sun is at the centre of the solar system, Copernicus provided the first coherent argument for a heliocentric universe—one in which, despite centuries of learned discourse to the contrary, the Earth revolves around the Sun.

It must be remembered that before the invention of the telescope, simple naked-eye observations easily could be interpreted to yield the conclusion that the Sun, Moon, and planets all move around the Earth. Still, in his mind's eye Copernicus saw the Earth spinning on its axis once each day, thus explaining the Sun's apparent motion, and also revolving around the Sun once each year, thus accounting for the heretofore bewildering back-and-forth movements of the planets.

Even the great scientist Galileo, while willing to entertain the notion that the Earth moves, did not provide a convincing case for a heliocentric point of view until 1609 when he raised his first astronomical telescope to the heavens. When he saw the moons of Jupiter and recorded their revolution about that planet, Galileo concluded that he was in fact seeing the Copernican system in miniature. His discovery of the phases of Venus provided another observation more naturally reconciled with a nonmoving Sun. Yet, for taking up the cause of heliocentrism, which was contrary to the doctrine of the Roman Catholic Church, Galileo was tried, made to recant his views, and placed under house arrest.

At his trial, after renouncing the Copernican system with its moving Earth, Galileo is said to have whispered, "And yet it moves," an event echoed in the 1967 Beatles song "The Fool on the Hill," which contains the refrain, "But the fool on the hill sees the sun going down/And the eyes in his head see the world spinning round." Not until 1992 did the church formally admit its error in forcing Galileo to deny the evidence of his own senses. (KENNETH BRECHER)

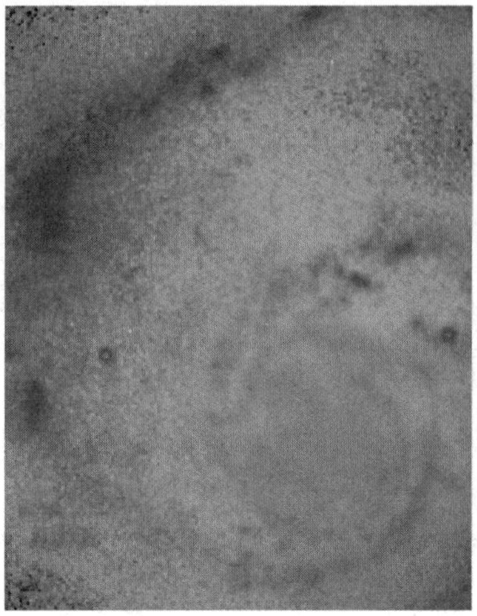

A detailed image of the central portion of M51, the Whirlpool Galaxy, made in near-infrared light (right) shows that the magnificent spiral arms so prominent in visible light (far right) wrap nearly three times around and extend much closer to the galaxy's dust-enshrouded centre than can be seen in conventional images. The finding, reported in July, challenged astronomers' theoretical understanding of the structure of spiral galaxies.

(RIGHT) DENNIS ZARITSKY, HANS-WALTER RIX, AND MARCIA RIEKE; (FAR RIGHT) T. BOROSON—NATIONAL OPTICAL ASTRONOMY OBSERVATORIES

at what may be the belt's inner edge. By October four more objects had been spotted, although these appeared to lie somewhat closer in, just outside Neptune's orbit. It may be that the latter objects are comets that have left the belt and are moving inward toward the Sun; alternately, they may be asteroids having permanent residence near Neptune.

Stars. In the early 1970s the first gamma-ray observatory satellite, SAS-2, detected a bright gamma-ray source with no obvious optical counterpart. Its discoverers called the object Geminga (Milanese Italian dialect for "it's not there"), but its nature remained a mystery until 1992 when detection of periodic X-ray and gamma-ray emission suggested that Geminga is a pulsar. In February, Italian astronomer Giovanni Bignami and co-workers reported that they had measured the proper motion of the object, from which they concluded that Geminga was the nearest pulsar to Earth detected to date. Their observations also supported the optical identification of Geminga with a very dim (25th-magnitude) star. Because of its rather young age of about 350,000 years and its close distance of about 300 light-years, astronomers speculated that Geminga may have had an effect on Earth when the pulsar formed in a supernova explosion. The solar system lies in a hot, rarefied region of interstellar space called the Local Bubble. The supernova that produced Geminga may have heated and thinned out matter in Earth's local region to form the bubble.

The enigmatic events called gamma-ray bursts were also first detected in the early 1970s. Unlike most astronomical phenomena, these bursts, which last a few seconds or less, have never been associated with any known type of object. Nonetheless, it was widely hypothesized that the events are somehow produced by neutron stars in the Milky Way. During the year the Burst and Transient Source Experiment (BATSE) aboard the Earth-orbiting Compton Gamma Ray Observatory (GRO) steadily detected such events, with more than 700 bursts reported by late 1993. From GRO data it appeared that there are really two classes of burst: those lasting only tenths of a second and those lasting tens or hundreds of seconds. One event on January 31 (dubbed the Super Bowl burst for its coincidence with the football event) was, while it lasted, 100 times brighter than Geminga. Although there was still no definitive identification of any gamma-ray burst with a star, quasar, or other known object, the distribution of the events over the sky is telling. Because their arrival directions are spread evenly over the sky, unlike the distribution of stars in the galaxy in which the Earth is immersed, gamma-ray bursts seem likely to come from outside the Milky Way.

Galaxies and Cosmology. Whether the observed expansion of the universe may someday stop, to be followed by a collapse, depends on the mass density of the universe. With a sufficiently high density the "closed" universe has enough gravitational pull to overcome the expansion. But the amount of matter seen in the form of visible stars, gas, and galaxies is insufficient to close the universe. Nonetheless, many astronomers believe that the universe is closed and have been searching for the so-called dark matter that would confirm their belief. The year saw its share of proposed "sightings" of dark matter. Early on came the announcement of the detection of dark matter in a nearby group of galaxies called the NGC 2300 group. The result was derived from the detection of X-rays from this galaxy cluster by the Röntgensatellit (ROSAT) orbiting observatory. What ROSAT saw was an X-ray glow from the region around NGC 2300, presumably emitted by hot gas filling the local intergalactic space. The ROSAT team concluded that to hold the detected hot gas within the cluster, more mass than is present in the visible galaxies is required. The team reported that if the inferred dark matter also exists in other similar groups of galaxies, it would provide enough mass to close the universe.

Several groups reported the detection of MACHOs (massive compact halo objects) lying within the outer reaches of the Milky Way. Astronomers believe that a halo consisting mainly of dark matter surrounds the Milky Way. It was proposed that if the halo consists of numerous small starlike objects, each too dim to be seen directly, their presence could be detected indirectly by their effects on the light from more distant visible stars. According to Einstein's general theory of relativity, a mass will act as a lens and bend light that passes through its gravitational field. Thus, light from a more distant star would brighten and dim if a dim foreground MACHO were to pass in front of it. In 1993 a U.S.-Australian team reported detecting the predicted telltale stellar light variations. After monitoring roughly two million stars in the nearby Large Magellanic Cloud Galaxy, the team found a star that became brighter and then dimmer over a period of about a month. By year's end three more reports of such MACHO events had appeared. The nature of the unseen objects remained elusive, although candidates included brown dwarfs, red dwarf stars, and white dwarf stars. Even though the amount of matter represented by the reported MACHOs, if extrapolated to other galaxies, was insufficient to close the universe, the observational technique did open a new channel for detecting dark matter in the universe. (*See* PHYSICS.) (KENNETH BRECHER)

See also Space Exploration.

This article updates the *Macropædia* articles The Cosmos; Galaxies; The Physical Sciences: *Astronomy;* The Solar System; Stars and Star Clusters.

Botanical Gardens and Zoos

Botanical Gardens. In 1993 botanical gardens around the world discussed ways to meet the challenges set forth by the 1992 United Nations Conference on Environment and Development in Rio de Janeiro. Chapter 15 of Agenda 21 specifically called for the implementation of *ex situ* programs for species conservation. In addition, it was expected that botanical gardens would play a pivotal role in the conference's stated aims of habitat restoration, sustainable use of biological and genetic resources, and promotion of integrated or cross-sectoral conservation programs.

The networking of botanical gardens was on the upswing. The Australian Network for Plant Conservation was advising the Kebun Raya Indonesia (the botanical gardens at Bogor, Java) on the creation of a national network and the development of a comprehensive strategy for the conservation of Indonesian flora. A conference was held in July 1992 to initiate this ambitious program and to celebrate the 175th anniversary of the Kebun Raya. In Mexico City the Asociación Mexicana de Jardines Botánicos marked its 10th anniversary in March 1993 with a meeting that looked particularly at the educational role of botanical gardens. This theme also predominated at the second International Congress on Education in Botanic Gardens in Las Palmas de Gran Canaria in May 1993. These latter two meetings testified to the remarkable vigour of the botanical garden community in the Spanish-speaking world.

In April 1993 the Center for Plant Conservation at the Missouri Botanical Garden was host to a major conference on habitat restoration and species reintroduction, two increasingly important areas of botanical garden activity, particularly in North America and Australia. The Bok Tower Gardens in Florida, for instance, were running a reintroduction program for the endangered shrub *Conradina glabra*.

The 175th anniversary of the Conservatoire et Jardin Botaniques in Geneva was celebrated with a conference on "Nature and Botanical Gardens for the 21st Century." Focusing on the activities of European gardens and again featuring the topics of conservation and education, the meeting was a particularly useful opportunity for Eastern European botanical garden managers to meet with Western European colleagues. In addition, representatives of the Swiss botanical gardens met to initiate a national network.

In May 1992 more than 60 delegates from Slovak and Czech botanical gardens attended the 25th conference of the Czechoslovak Botanic Gardens. After the breakup of the U.S.S.R., a new association, formed through collaboration between the Moscow Main Botanic Garden and Botanic Gardens Conservation International, was founded to support and coordinate the activities of facilities in Russia and neighbouring countries.

A number of projects were developing that illustrated the role of botanical gardens in promoting sustainable development. The Royal Botanic Gardens, Kew, near London, worked with the International Institute for the Environment and Development in supporting the drafting of a National Sustainable Development Strategy for the Atlantic island of Saint Helena. Another team at Kew was working closely with Brazilian colleagues on tackling environmental problems in arid northeastern Brazil and focusing particularly on the benefits of plants in the region for local people. In 1993 Kew also inaugurated new training programs on botanical garden management and plant-conservation techniques. Finally, the Conservatoire Botanique National de Porquerolles in the south of France was developing a sophisticated and imaginative program for the conservation of island plants in the Mediterranean. (Michael Maunder)

Zoos. The most important event of 1993—indeed of the past decade—was the publication of *World Zoo Conservation Strategy.* This 76-page document was conceived by the International Union of Directors of Zoological Gardens (IUDZG) and the Captive Breeding Specialist Group (CBSG) of the Species Survival Commission of the International Union for Conservation of Nature and Natural Resources. A gestation period of about two years resulted in a birth in Brussels in September.

Zoos and aquariums, with a collective annual visitation of over 600 million people, are linked by international, regional, and national associations, which together constitute one of the largest conservation networks on Earth. The IUDZG/CBSG strategy document emphasized the enormous potential of this network and listed three major areas in which zoos and aquariums could help achieve conservation goals and set their own policies and priorities:

1. By actively supporting the conservation of endangered species and their natural ecosystems. Coordinated zoo breeding programs are a necessary part of the conservation of many species, some of which will survive only with the support of a captive population. Where reintroduction or restocking is feasible, the protection of a flagship species will also help maintain other life-forms within the habitat.

2. By offering support and facilities to increase scientific knowledge that will benefit conservation. The expertise of many hundreds of zoologists and veterinarians on the staff of zoos and aquariums represents a considerable potential contribution to the understanding of the biology of species and their relationships to their surroundings. Zoo-acquired knowledge is often crucial to the stimulation of further research in the wild.

3. By promoting increased public awareness of the need for conservation, particularly via zoo education programs.

Most important, the *World Zoo Conservation Strategy* clearly stated that the conservation role of zoos and aquariums must be complimentary to, and not a substitute for, other conservation activities.

(*continued on page 112*)

MICHAEL NICHOLS—MAGNUM

Visitors to the Bronx Zoo in New York City watch prairie dogs through transparent bubbles set in the middle of their habitat. Zoos continued to remodel facilities so that visitors could observe animals in habitats that were as close as possible to natural environments.

Special Report: Zoos

Zoos Look to the 21st Century

BY LESTER E. FISHER

The role of the zoo has undergone several important changes over the centuries, but in the past 25 years critical changes have taken place that could affect the very survival of dozens of species of animals on Earth.

More than 2,000 years ago, Chinese rulers kept wild animals in private collections as part of their Garden of Intelligence. Egyptian pharaohs retained wild animals presented to them as gifts from subjects throughout Africa. For more than 400 years, European rulers kept wildlife in private collections.

The earliest European zoo, the collection at Schönbrunn Palace in Vienna, was started in 1752; it is the oldest zoo in continuous operation. Collections in Madrid (1775), Paris (1793), and London (1828) followed. Philadelphia organized a zoological society in 1856, and its zoological gardens opened in 1874. Chicago's Lincoln Park Zoo received a pair of swans from the Central Park Zoo in New York and began its operations in 1868. The animal collections were typically organized in park settings; hence the name zoological gardens. The primary role of the zoo from the mid-1800s to the mid-1900s was to afford its visitors a recreational opportunity to view interesting and unusual animals from around the world.

The Changing Role of Zoos. Most wild animals were housed in small barred enclosures built more for the public's safety than for the animals' comfort. Today in Bern, Switz., one can still see the deep bear pit that has housed European brown bears for several hundred years. It was not until the turn of the century that the exhibition of wild animals changed significantly. Carl Hagenbeck of Hamburg, Germany, created the first large, open African plains scene using moats for part of the enclosure barriers.

Following Hagenbeck's revolutionary model, many zoos began to eliminate barred enclosures. Several excellent examples of exhibits inspired by the early work of Hagenbeck can be seen today at the Denver (Colo.) Zoo and Chicago's Brookfield Zoo, where, in the 1930s, the first attempts were made in the United States to create visually interesting backdrops for the animals by using realistic artificial rock work.

For health reasons some zoos utilized tile and cement cages with glass to replace their barred enclosures. Although effective from a veterinary standpoint, these resulted in an antiseptic environment for the animals. As zoo veterinarians became better able to control the internal parasites and bacterial infections affecting captive wild animals, more appropriate cage furnishings were developed as well.

By the 1960s many zoos had built "naturalistic" moated exhibits for their hoofed animals, allowing the public an unobstructed view. Similarly, at the National Zoo in Washington, D.C., piano wire retainers were used for indoor bird exhibits, providing a relatively unobstructed view of the birds and enabling visitors to hear their songs. The enclosures could also be heavily planted to provide live green backgrounds in the avian habitats.

Even with all the visual exhibition improvements, however, the emphasis of public zoos remained on exhibition of wildlife. The next developmental phase, which began in the late 1960s, focused on conservation of wildlife and natural habitats. Discussions began in earnest when a voluntary ban on importing young orangutans was instituted in U.S. zoos in 1968. Zoo directors sought to reduce the capture of orangutans in Indonesia, which was typically accomplished through the killing of the mothers in order to secure their babies. Federal legislation in the 1970s provided further controls over the health and captive breeding of many species.

In the late 1970s new emphasis began to be placed on the educational component of zoos. The Philadelphia and New York zoos have had small science components for over 50 years, but science and research staffs in other zoos have become commonplace only in the past decade or so.

Today there are over 1,000 organized zoos and as many as 10,000 animal collections in the world. Broadly, the current objectives of the zoo community can be summarized as follows: increasing awareness of the vital need for conservation; expanding scientific knowledge to benefit conservation programs worldwide; supporting the preservation of endangered species in the wild as well as in zoos through managed, cooperative breeding programs; and supporting further field work and other research projects in conservation of natural habitats, biotypes, and ecosystems.

In short, zoos are using their unique position to heighten public and political awareness of the interdependence of all life elements on this planet.

Zoos Working Together. Scientists and administrators from institutions around the world are increasing their cooperative efforts as well. The American Association of Zoological Parks and Aquariums expanded its conservation activities with the development in 1981 of a Species Survival Plan (SSP) program to manage cooperative captive breeding programs for 72 different species at 150 zoos. Examples of animals represented in SSPs are the Bali mynah, the California condor, the lowland gorilla, Grevy's zebra, and Dumeril's boa. As a direct result of a few early SSP programs, the nene goose has been reestablished in Hawaii, the Arabian oryx in Oman, the golden lion tamarin in Brazil, and Père David's deer in China. Some 200 species are to be included in the SSP program by the year 2000.

Current aids to national and international breeding programs now include the International Species Inventory System, the *International Zoo Yearbook* species studbook, and various computer programs designed to manage captive populations and create statistical models to predict population viability. Providing adequate and appropriate space for captive specimens is also a concern. Cooperative population management, however, entails real risks of degeneration of the wild population that can take place over hundreds of years because of the increasing domesticity of the wild population and the loss of genetic variability.

New tools for captive reproduction, such as artificial insemination, cryopreservation, and biotechnology, are being developed. Many species of birds, including cranes and the California condor, are being successfully inseminated artificially. The collection and freezing of both ova and sperm of all animals is now regularly taking place, and studies continue on appropriate materials for enhancing storage and extenders for use of these gametes. The Cincinnati (Ohio) Zoo is a pioneer in cryopreservation and has already established a "frozen zoo."

Lester E. Fisher, D.V.M., is Director Emeritus of the Lincoln Park Zoo in Chicago.

Reaching out to the Public. Now regarded as a key element in furthering the goals of conservation, the educational component of the zoo's activities is growing apace. Professional educators are prominent members of the staff at most collections in the U.S., the United Kingdom, and Western Europe. Education programs serve visitors on-site and provide access to zoos through community outreach efforts. Teacher workshops are regularly held to incorporate zoo education programs into regular school curricula, and zoo experts work closely with the science faculties of most local school systems. Trained volunteers also work with zoo staff to expand the quality and quantity of education programs. Volunteers provide the manpower essential for zoos to respond to the needs of visitors numbering up to seven million a year in some cases.

Field trips to the zoo have always been a popular part of the school year, but now zoo visits are often part of the biology curriculum, directly tied to classroom studies. Many zoos maintain specialized libraries in the biological sciences and sponsor programs of lectures and audiovisual presentations by zoo staff that help promote conservation awareness in the community. Finally, in the area of community outreach, "traveling zoos" fill a unique niche. The first such program was originated in Chicago in the 1950s by zoo director and TV naturalist Marlin Perkins and took animals—and the conservation message—to hospitals, senior centres, nursing homes, schools, and and a variety of community recreation programs.

The Ethical Dimension. Even though most people throughout the world enjoy and support zoos, questions are being raised about the role of zoos and the need for a zoo today. Concern for animal rights—sometimes quite adamant—seems to be supplanting the animal welfare work of the humane societies. Beyond concerns about vivisection—the experimental use of animals by the biomedical community—which has been an issue for more than 75 years, questions are now also being raised about keeping wild animals. Some oppose the zoo as an institution, believing that wildlife should remain in a natural habitat and not be made to live in captivity.

Certainly, not all zoos have housed animals in an exemplary fashion. In some Third World countries there are zoos that are not up to standard, usually because of financial or cultural reasons; some also lack professionally trained employees. The International Union of Directors of Zoological Gardens has offered to assist zoos worldwide in efforts to upgrade facilities. In the past, roadside collections of wild animals along the U.S. highway systems often were not properly managed but, happily, state and national laws are helping make the roadside zoo disappear as a tourist attraction. The U.S. Department of Agriculture has now been charged with approving such facilities.

Redefining the Zoo. Today even the name "zoo" has been called into question. The National Zoo in Washington now prefers to call itself a biopark, the better to reflect its role in interpreting the animals and plants it exhibits. The New York Zoological Society has changed its name to NYZS/The Wildlife Conservation Society and calls its borough zoos "wildlife parks" to convey the organization's conservation mission. Other institutions will surely follow in an effort to create broader awareness of the new role of zoos in the 21st century. Regardless of the name, those who place wild animals in a captive state have a moral and ethical responsibility to provide the best care possible. This awareness, as well as responsive programs in education, conservation, and science, strongly enhances the original recreational role of zoos such that the effectiveness and relevance of zoos will continue to grow in the coming years.

(continued from page 110)

The zoo conservation strategy was launched immediately after the annual meetings of CBSG and IUDZG in Antwerp, Belgium. CBSG reported a particularly busy and productive year. Over 40 workshops and meetings were held between September 1992 and August 1993. IUDZG reported on the expansion of its activities and membership, which stood at over 130 collections and zoo associations. Two problems of immediate concern were debated at some length: the plight of zoos, animals, and professional staff in the increasing number of war-stricken areas of the world and the urgent need to help zoos in countries that lack the resources to maintain their collections at acceptable standards.

The use of naturalistic enclosures that include the means to stimulate natural behaviours has been shown to improve a zoo animal's welfare and reproductive capacity and enhance the educational value of the exhibit. In recent years many imaginative techniques had been devised to enrich an animal's environment, and the importance of such innovations was being recognized throughout the zoo community. In July the first International Conference on Environmental Enrichment was held at Metro Washington Park Zoo in Portland, Ore., and it proved to be a resounding success, with nearly 200 participants from around the world. The more naturalistic approach was also reflected in the designs of two new zoos—the Monarto Zoological Park (South Australia) and Cameron Park Zoo (Waco, Texas)—and in a number of new exhibits—Eagle Canyon at the Living Desert (Palm Desert, Calif.), the gorilla exhibit at Cleveland (Ohio) Metroparks Zoo, Habitat Africa at Chicago Zoological Park, the pygmy hippopotamus-mandrill exhibit at Melbourne (Australia) Zoo, the Qantas Aviary of the Forest at Auckland (N.Z.) Zoo, and the Bonobo Enclosure at Dierenpark Planckendael (Belgium). (P.J.S. OLNEY)

See also Environment; Gardening.

Chemistry

Superconductivity. Efforts to develop high-temperature superconductors passed a milestone in 1993 when researchers in Switzerland reported making a mercury-containing ceramic material that starts to become superconducting, losing all resistance to the flow of electricity, when cooled to about 133 K (kelvins). (To convert kelvins to degrees Celsius, subtract 273; thus, 133 K = −140° C. To convert Celsius to Fahrenheit, multiply by 1.8 and add 32.) Despite intensive worldwide research, no compound synthesized since 1988 had showed superconductivity at a temperature warmer than 127 K, a record set by a thallium-containing material. The 127-K barrier was broken by Hans R. Ott and associates at the Swiss Federal Institute of Technology, Zürich, with a mixed-metal oxide material containing mercury, barium, calcium, copper, and oxygen. Chemists and materials scientists continued to search for new compounds that become superconductors at ever higher transition temperatures, the ultimate goal being a room-temperature (about 300 K) superconductor. Such a material could revolutionize transmission of electric current by decreasing losses due to resistance and have many other practical applications.

Late in the year C.W. Chu of the University of Houston, Texas, and Manuel Nuñez-Regueiro of the National Centre for Scientific Research, Grenoble, France, described superconductivity in mercury-type compounds at temperatures above 153 K. Working independently, the groups achieved the high transition temperatures by subjecting the materials to pressures of 150,000 and 230,000 times that at sea level. According to Chu, the results suggested that certain modifications in the atomic structure of the compounds could lead to materials with similar transition temperatures that superconduct at ordinary pressures. (*See* PHYSICS.)

Inorganic Chemistry. For 50 years chemists had tried to make a stable silicon (Si) cation, a positively charged form of the element that is attached to other atoms by three bonds rather than the two, four, or five that silicon forms naturally. Despite many failures they persisted, noting, for instance, that a carbon atom will form such a triply bonded arrangement, called a carbocation. Carbon is silicon's neighbour on the periodic table, and the two elements share many properties. But triply bonded silicon, or tricoordinate silicon in the form R_3Si^+ (in which R is a generalized atom or group), proved elusive. During the year a team headed by Joseph B. Lambert of Northwestern University, Evanston, Ill., finally reported success.

The chemists cited two recent discoveries as critical for making tricoordinate silicon. One involved finding a solvent that would not react with, and instantly destroy, the cation. Aromatic hydrocarbons, especially toluene, worked well. The other was finding the proper negatively charged ion, or anion, to pair with the silicon cation. Anions that are compatible with carbocations would react with the silicon cation, transforming it back into its four-bonded form. Lambert's group finally found an anion, $(C_6F_5)_4B^-$, that did not react with silicon and was stable in toluene. Researchers believed that the cation may have important applications as a catalyst in speeding up polymerization reactions used in making adhesives, lubricants, and other silicon products.

Isomers are compounds that consist of the same collection of elements in the same atomic quantities but that differ in their molecular structure or in the arrangement of their atoms in three-dimensional space. Although identical in chemical composition, isomers have different properties. Familiar kinds of isomerism include structural isomers, distinguished by different bonding patterns, and stereoisomers, having the same bonding patterns but different spatial arrangements. During the year Boon K. Teo and Hong Zhang of the University of Illinois at Chicago reported a new type of isomerism that they termed rouletteamerism. Teo and Zhang observed the phenomenon in a newly synthesized gold-silver cluster, $\{[(C_6H_5)_3P]_{10}Au_{13}Ag_{12}Br_8\}^+$. The metal core of the cluster consists of two icosahedra with a common vertex. In one conformation four metal pentagons in the core have an "ses" or "staggered-eclipsed-staggered" configuration. In another they have an "sss" or "staggered-staggered-staggered" configuration. (*See* Figure.) The two forms are conformers, or conformational isomers, of the same molecule. They interconvert by rotation around the same chemical bond. According to the researchers, the clusters represent a new variation on rotamerism, in which conformers engage in restricted rotation around a single vertex or bond. The rotorlike motion was thought to have interesting potential for nanotechnology, the development of mechanical devices on a scale of nanometres (billionths of a metre), the size realm of individual molecules.

Chemical Synthesis. Synthetic chemists traditionally have had to use a sequence of numerous separate chemical reactions to make complex molecules. In a typical synthesis two reactants are allowed to react to form an intermediate compound. The product is isolated from solution, purified, and then used as one of the reactants in the next step of the sequence, which may yield other intermediates that also must be isolated and purified. The tediousness of the process has stimulated interest in "one-pot" syntheses, in which all the starting materials are placed in the reaction vessel and allowed to react under proper conditions of pH (acidity or alkalinity), temperature, and pressure to produce the desired product. Chemists have tried such reactions with as many as four reactants. Alexander Dömling and Ivar Ugi of the University of Munich, Germany, took the technique further by successfully completing two different one-pot syntheses involving seven reactants. Dömling and Ugi regarded it as an advance toward one-beaker syntheses of products with industrial or commercial value.

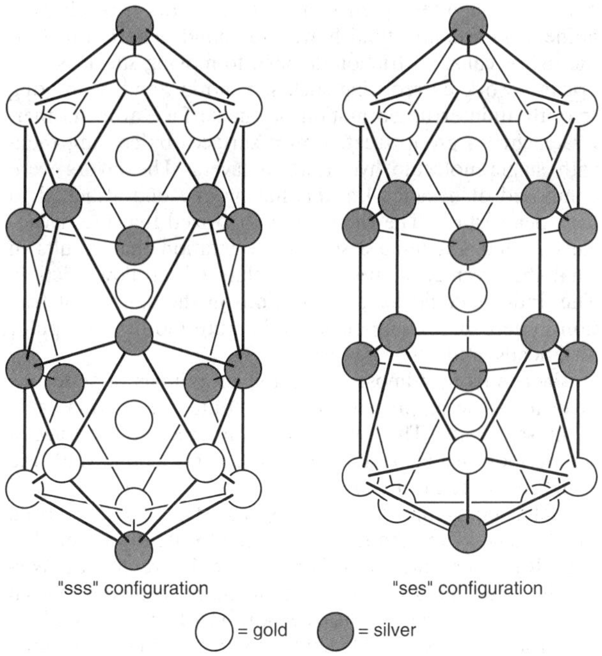

Synthesis of the largest all-hydrocarbon molecule ever made was reported by Jeffrey S. Moore and Zhifu Xu of the University of Michigan. The molecule, $C_{1398}H_{1278}$, is one of a family of stiff dendrimers, or highly branched polymers, composed of phenylacetylene units. Moore and Xu made $C_{1398}H_{1278}$ as part of an effort to construct molecules in a size range of 2,000–50,000 atomic mass units, a range long neglected by organic chemists. Their giant dendrimer was intended not to have functional properties but to explore techniques for building extremely complex branched structures. Nevertheless, researchers believed that molecules of this size could have properties useful as catalysts and sensors and in other applications.

Materials. In 1991 Sumio Iijima and associates at NEC Corp., Tsukuba, Japan, reported making carbon nanotubes, unusual all-carbon structures predicted to have remarkable mechanical and electronic properties. Nanotubes are hollow nanometre-wide tubules of carbon atoms bonded in a graphitelike structure that theoretically should have, for instance, enormous mechanical strength. Efforts to characterize nanotubes had been hindered by the lack of techniques for making pure samples of uniform-sized tubules. Original methods yielded impure mixtures of tubules of many different sizes, often with tubes nested inside others. Iijima's group and a second group headed by Donald S. Bethune of the IBM Almaden Research Center, San Jose, Calif., reported that they had found ways of making uniform batches of single nanotubes. Iijima vaporized a carbon electrode in the presence of methane, argon, and iron vapour. Bethune vaporized carbon and cobalt in a helium atmosphere.

The first experimental observation of a state of ultralow friction was reported by Jacob Israelachvili and co-workers at the University of California at Santa Barbara. They observed the phenomenon during studies of the so-called stick-slip motion of specially treated mica surfaces. Stick-slip motion is an interrupted motion that occurs in such phenomena as friction, fluid flow, and sound generation. It is the major cause of friction damage to moving surfaces. Lubricants work by reducing stick-slip motion and promoting smooth, uninterrupted motion of one surface over another. Israelachvili's group treated mica surfaces by coating them with single-molecule hydrocarbon layers. The layers were composed of hexadecyl chains having one end attached to the mica surface. The researchers theorized that the hydrocarbon chains assume a specific orientation that results in what they termed a superkinetic state of ultralow friction. The findings could have applications in the control of friction in aerospace components, miniature motors, computer disk heads, and other devices.

Biochemistry. Almost all motion in animals depends on myosin and actin, proteins that constitute the tiny filaments in muscle cells. The two proteins interact to produce a sliding motion that results in muscle contraction. With the structure of actin already known, biochemists had focused on determining the three-dimensional structure of myosin, which makes up about 60% of the protein in muscles. Ivan Rayment and co-workers of the University of Wisconsin determined the structure of the head of the myosin molecule. The head is the key portion of myosin, sticking out from the myosin filament and interacting with actin. Rayment reported that the head is an elongated, pear-shaped molecule that bends in the middle. Determination of the structure led the group to propose a new theory of muscle contraction in which myosin flexes rather than remaining rigid, as previously believed. Rayment expected that the three-dimensional structure would prove important for understanding the molecular basis of muscle contraction and the abnormalities that occur in certain diseases.

Juvenile hormone (JH) normally keeps insects in the immature larval stage until their bodies have grown enough to enter the pupal stage and complete their metamorphosis to adults. As long as JH remains docked to a specific protein receptor in the insects' cells, larvae do not mature. The pesticide industry has exploited this phenomenon by developing compounds, insect growth regulators (IGRs), that fit into the receptor and prevent maturation of mosquitoes, biting flies, and other pests that cause damage as adults. There had been, however, no comparable agent to control larvae of butterflies and moths, which cause great damage to crops and forests as caterpillars. Conventional IGRs would simply prolong the damage-causing stage of these insects.

IBM RESEARCH DIVISION

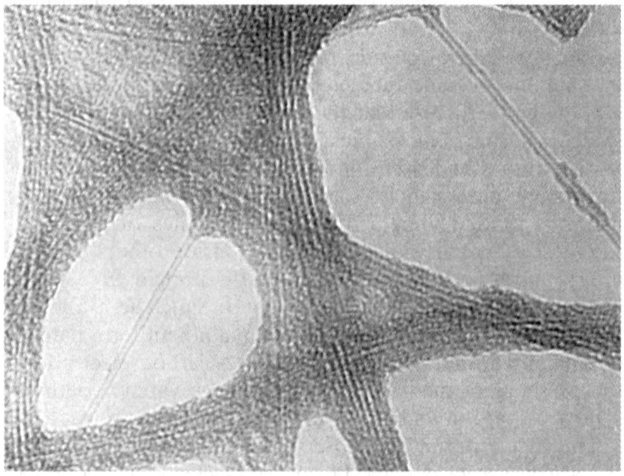

Single-walled all-carbon nanotubes about 1.2 nanometres in diameter crisscross through darker carbon debris in this electron micrograph of material synthesized by IBM researchers. Bare sections of nanotubes are visible in the lower left and upper right.

Researchers finally gave the pesticide industry the biochemical road map for synthesizing such an agent by cloning (reproducing in the laboratory) the cellular receptor for JH. The work was reported by Lynn Riddiford of the University of Washington and co-workers at the University of California at Davis and the State University of New York at Stony Brook. The researchers first made JH analogs and used them to show that caterpillar cell nuclei contain a protein that binds to JH. They isolated the protein, the JH receptor, and then isolated the gene that codes for its synthesis. Riddiford cited evidence that the JH receptor is the first known member of a family of hormone receptors that function in the nucleus of insect cells. Availability of the receptor could lead to development of rapid methods for screening potential new IGRs, including versions that cause premature metamorphosis in caterpillars.

(MICHAEL WOODS)

This article updates the *Macropædia* articles BIOCHEMICAL COMPONENTS OF ORGANISMS; CHEMICAL COMPOUNDS; CHEMICAL REACTIONS; MATTER: *Low-temperature phenomena;* The PHYSICAL SCIENCES: *Chemistry.*

Consumer Affairs

Global consumption continued to mirror the world's distribution of wealth. With more than one billion people still mired in absolute poverty in 1993, some 800 million consumers were unable to purchase sufficient amounts of food. Industrialized countries consumed 15 times as much paper, 10 times as much steel, and 12 times as much fuel per person as less developed countries. Incomes of the richest one-fifth of the world's population were, on average, more than 150 times higher than those of the poorest one-fifth.

Consumption trends were also influenced by the continuing rapid globalization of markets and the formation of regional economic blocks. The increased trade in goods and services was generally viewed as beneficial to consumers—providing them with wider choices of products at more competitive prices. On the other hand, there were also concerns that the regional "harmonization" of product safety standards and other trade requirements could lead to a significant lowering of existing consumer- and environmental-protection measures in some countries. In many countries—particularly those experiencing deepening poverty, deteriorating living standards, and reduced social spending—consumer organizations sought to ensure that basic, essential products remained within reach of low-income and marginalized consumers. Growth of the global consumer movement was especially strong in Central America, Africa, Central and Eastern Europe, and southwestern Asia.

World Consumer Rights Day, commemorated annually on March 15, provided a global platform for local campaigns by consumer organizations and other public-interest groups. A long-running consumer campaign was also renewed at the UN following the final breakdown of its previous negotiations on a draft Code of Conduct on Transnational Corporations (TNCs). The world consumer movement, led by the International Organization of Consumers Unions (IOCU), urged the UN to adopt a more acceptable and timely set of provisions to guide the foreign operations of TNCs and promote their fair treatment by host countries.

Jan. 1, 1993, marked the long-anticipated arrival of the European single market, encompassing some 345 million consumers in 12 countries of the European Community (EC). Its establishment as the world's largest trading bloc made it illegal for any EC country to restrict the passage or sale of any product manufactured or imported by another member country. The complete removal of regional trade barriers was expected to create a brighter shopping future for EC consumers. Cross-border advice centres began operating in several countries as the European Bureau of Consumers Unions and its members called for better consumer information, higher safety standards, effective and adequate redress mechanisms, and transparent, inexpensive ways for consumers to make cross-border payments.

The endurance of consumers in Central and Eastern Europe was severely tested by the continuing uphill struggle to establish functional free markets in their countries. Regional governments acknowledged the need to establish basic frameworks and legislation for consumer protection, with support from consumer organizations. Many of those groups also monitored markets for hazardous products, monopolistic pricing, and other rampant abuses while addressing dire environmental problems resulting from decades of uncontrolled industrial pollution.

In North America and Asia, the future of two regional economic alliances promised to have far-reaching consequences for consumers. The controversial North American Free Trade Agreement (NAFTA) was intended to establish a single market of more than 370 million consumers in the U.S., Canada, and Mexico. The Association of Southeast Asian Nations (ASEAN) tried to hammer out differences blocking the formation of an ASEAN Free Trade Area, which could encompass well over 1.5 billion consumers within 15 years.

The snail-paced Uruguay round of the General Agreement on Tariffs and Trade (GATT), which began in 1986, was successfully concluded before the Dec. 15, 1993, deadline. The U.S. and the EC agreed to set aside for future consideration a few unresolved issues. The trade agreement, which would have far-reaching implications for more than 100 nations, was the broadest and most important international trade pact in history and would take effect on July 1, 1995. The GATT accord was expected to infuse more than $270 billion a year into the world economy.

On a home-shopping television channel, a woman models clothing offered for sale through a toll-free telephone number. Making purchases from the home via television continued to grow in popularity during 1993, with increased participation by upscale merchandisers.

PETER FREED

The End of a Merchandising Era: Sears Closes the Big Book

When Sears, Roebuck and Co. announced in January 1993 that it would close down its mail-order catalog operation at the end of the year, the news marked the passing of one of the great icons of Americana. Over the 97 years of the Sears catalog's existence, its arrival in millions of American homes was an eagerly awaited event. The "big book," as it became known, displayed everything from lingerie to prefabricated houses in its more than 1,000 pages. Children and adults alike scanned a cornucopia of products, covetously ogling toys, fashions, firearms, and every conceivable item for the home, all at temptingly low prices. In addition, before the era of television the catalog was valued as a medium of entertainment in isolated pockets of rural America, and it was also educational. Early editions gave many a young boy his first—albeit somewhat distorted—idea of the female figure from line drawings of wasp-waisted, corseted women.

In the late 19th and early 20th centuries, before the tightening of food and drug laws and copyright standards, the catalog offered unwary consumers a cure for virtually anything that ailed them. The 1900 edition advertised "Dr. Rose's Dyspepsia Powders," "Reliable Cure for the Opium and Morphia Habit," and "Dr. Hammond's Nerve and Brain Pills," which claimed to cure "lifelessness" and "a constant feeling of dread." Few of these remedies actually worked, of course. Some customers, however, might have received powerful relief from an item in the 1897 catalog—laudanum, an opium-based sedative and headache cure.

The catalog served so well as a barometer of the lifeways and styles of the times that it would become an invaluable reference for set and costume design in theatre, film, and television. Virtually all of the catalog merchandise was illustrated—first by line drawings, then by photographs, and finally by pictures of models. Some of those models even became Hollywood stars, including Jean Arthur, Lauren Bacall, Joan Caulfield, Anita Colby, Susan Hayward, Fredric March, Norma Shearer, and Gloria Swanson. Many aspiring writers also cut their literary teeth writing Sears catalog copy, notably Edgar Rice Burroughs, author of the popular Tarzan series of books.

It all began in 1886 when a young railroad agent in North Redwood, Minn., named Richard Sears purchased a shipment of watches that was refused by a local jeweler. Sears sold them himself and soon began selling timepieces and jewelry through printed mailers that bulged into catalogs. In 1887 he moved his operation to Chicagó, where he hired Alvah C. Roebuck, an Indiana watchmaker. The chemistry of that combination exploded into one of America's great retailing success stories.

In 1893 numerous items were added to the catalog in addition to watches and jewelry, and in 1896 the company produced its first large general-merchandise catalog. Nearly 100 years later, however, with the company facing stiff competition from superdiscount stores and experiencing a plummeting market value, Sears' executives determined that it was time to restructure. The decision to strip away the financial division, coupled with the catalog's yearly after-tax losses of some $135 million–$170 million in 1990–92, sealed the fate of the big book. (MARVIN MARTIN)

Consumer organizations also requested greater participation in the setting of international food standards by the UN Food and Agriculture Organization/World Health Organization Codex Alimentarius Commission. The institution drew heavy criticism for being dominated by industry representatives from northern countries, with consumers and representatives from less developed countries having much weaker access in comparison.

Reforms in the Codex Alimentarius Commission were among some 100 recommendations made by a new consumer policy paper on food quality adopted by European and North American members of the IOCU. The paper also urged that specific controls and prohibitions be placed on some unsafe pesticides, food additives, growth hormones, veterinary drugs, and biotechnology and food-irradiation processes in order to ensure the quality and safety of consumers' food supplies.

As more people became aware of serious environmental problems linked to wasteful consumption, a large percentage appeared willing to recycle their waste and pay higher prices for so-called green products. In June the EC launched a new "eco-labeling" program that would award a seal of approval to products meeting stringent environmental criteria. Green testing—evaluating the actual environmental impact of products—became an area of increasing interest and importance for consumer groups around the world. In May consumer leaders and representatives from more than 40 countries met in The Hague to discuss strategies for advocating sustainable consumption. A global policy paper was also launched that called on developed countries to take the lead in achieving sustainable consumption patterns.

(KEVIN G. COOK)

In 1993 home-equity credit cards came under attack by Bankcard Holders of America and the Consumer Federation of America as irresponsible on the part of banks. Bankers advertised the cards as a financing tool for homeowners that combined low interest rates with federal tax deductibility. Consumer advocate groups were opposed to these credit cards because consumers could lose their homes if they did not pay off their equity card balances.

The Federal Aviation Administration continued to investigate the impact of electronic gadgets on aircraft instrumentation operations. It was found that electronic apparatuses emit electromagnetic radiation that has a range up to 3.7 m (12 ft) and can create problems for an aircraft's navigation equipment and disrupt radio signals from the airport control tower during landing. Portable phones, remote-control toys, and other radio transmitters had been banned on airplanes for many years, but most airlines allowed passengers to use cassette players, tape recorders, and laptop computers. The Federal Aviation Administration issued an advisory in February that left it to the airlines to set their own rules. At the request of pilots, a number of airlines expanded their list of electronic devices forbidden for use by passengers.

Consumers became more concerned about the hazards of going to hospitals as studies reported that nearly 30% of hospitalized patients suffered from errors in medications or adverse reactions to the drugs they were given. It was reported that 100,000 deaths a year are caused by hospital-acquired infections. More than 50% of operating-room deaths were attributed to errors in surgery and/or anesthesia. Consumer groups such as the Center for Medical Consumers believed that the privately financed Joint Commission on Accreditation of Healthcare Organizations was not effective in correcting problems because the agency received its funding from the hospitals.

The Federal Communications Commission issued rulings against "slamming"—switching customers from one long-distance phone service to another without their permission. Under the rulings, if a company sold a long-distance service over the telephone, it had to obtain a written authorization to switch the service, have the consent verified by telephone to an independent third party, or send the consumer information, including a postpaid postcard for the consumer to return if the service was not wanted.

Automobile lemon laws passed by states in earlier years came under review by consumer advocate groups in 1993. Between 1982 and 1993 every state but Arkansas and South Dakota had passed a lemon law. Most states defined a lemon as a new car that had been in the repair shop for 30 days or had been returned to the dealer for the same problem four times within the first year of ownership. Consumer advocate groups believed the laws were weak because many states allowed the automobile manufacturer to run the mandated arbitration process. In some cases it was found that manufacturers forced to take back an automobile shipped the car out of state to unsuspecting buyers in the used-car market. Of 11,000 arbitration cases handled nationally by the Better Business Bureau in 1991, 1,500 resulted in consumers' receiving a replacement car or a full refund.

From 1991 to 1993 consumer confidence in the safety of products sold in supermarkets slipped, according to the Food Marketing Institute, a trade association representing supermarkets. In 1991, 17% of those surveyed said they were completely confident the food they bought in a supermarket was safe. By 1993 only 13% were completely confident, while almost 25% were concerned about the products they bought. As a result of consumer complaints and television coverage of supermarket violations of health and safety standards, states increased their inspections of markets and publicly named those markets violating the law.

(EDWARD MARK MAZZE)

See also Economic Affairs: *World Economy;* Environment; Industrial Review: *Advertising.*

Crime, Law Enforcement, and Penology

Violent Crime. *Terrorism.* In the early months of 1993, three of the world's major cities and financial centres, New York, Bombay, and London, were each the target of devastating bombing attacks. On February 26 a 550-kg (1,210-lb) bomb, packed in a van, exploded in the parking garage of the World Trade Center in New York City, ripping a 60-m (200-ft) crater in the basement of the world's second tallest building. The blast, which killed 6 people and injured more than 1,000, caused millions of dollars of damage and severely disrupted business. Officials described it as "the most destructive terrorist attack ever on U.S. soil."

On March 12 a string of bomb explosions struck the business district of Bombay, including the 29-story building housing the Bombay Stock Exchange and another skyscraper occupied by Air-India. The attacks killed 317 people, injured more than 1,100, and caused damage exceeding $250 million in India's commercial capital. (*See* WORLD AFFAIRS [South and Central Asia]: *India.*)

On April 24 a massive bomb exploded in a truck parked in the City (financial district) of London. One person was killed by the blast and some 44 injured, while property damage amounting to almost $1 billion was inflicted on more than 100 surrounding buildings, including a 13th-century church. A little over a year earlier, also in the City, a similar bomb had produced widespread devastation. (*See* WORLD AFFAIRS [Europe]: *United Kingdom.*)

The three incidents provided a frightening demonstration of the destructive capacity of modern terrorists and of the vulnerability of large cities to such attacks. In the United States, which had in the past remained largely immune from international terrorist attacks, particular concern was expressed that those groups were shifting their attention to targets within the country. That concern was heightened as investigators into the World Trade Center bombing began rapidly to uncover a complex conspiracy among a group of Islamic fundamentalists to commit this and other acts of urban terrorism in the U.S. The mastermind of this conspiracy was alleged to be Sheikh Omar Abdel-Rahman, the spiritual leader of the fundamentalists in Egypt and elsewhere in the world.

In Northern Ireland on October 23, Irish Republican Army assassins armed with a bomb walked into a busy Belfast fish shop. The bomb exploded, probably prematurely, killing 10 people, including one of the bombers, and injuring more than 50 people. The bombing provoked an immediate wave of revenge killings by the Ulster Freedom Fighters, an outlawed Protestant extremist group. Political leaders from both sides of Northern Ireland's deeply divided sectarian society condemned the killings, which seemed intended to derail recent peace talks aimed at ending this long-standing conflict.

In June the trial began in Kuwait of 14 persons accused of a plot to assassinate former U.S. president George Bush during his visit to that country in April. Wali ʿAbd al-Hadi al-Ghazali, one of two defendants to plead guilty at the opening session of the trial, claimed that he was approached by Iraqi intelligence officers to kill Bush with a car bomb or, if this failed, by detonating a pack of explosives tied to his body. The mission failed completely because the police uncovered the plot and arrested the conspirators. On June 27, U.S. naval forces in the Red Sea and Persian Gulf launched 23 Tomahawk missiles aimed at the Iraqi intelligence service headquarters in Baghdad, where the Bush assassination plot was said to have been planned. Twenty missiles were believed to have found their target, but the strike also killed at least 8 Iraqi civilians and injured 20.

War Crimes. The continuing atrocities being perpetrated by the combatants involved in the civil war in the Balkans prompted the UN Security Council to vote in February to establish an international tribunal to try war crimes in the republics of the former Yugoslav federation. The tribunal was the first of its kind to be set up since the victorious Allies in World War II established similar bodies in Nürnberg, Germany, and Tokyo to try Nazi and Japanese leaders. In September the UN General Assembly elected candidates from 11 nations to serve as members of the new tribunal, which would try those accused of murder, rape, torture, "ethnic cleansing," and other crimes committed since the breakup of Yugoslavia. Critics suggested that the tribunal would experience great practical difficulties obtaining objective evidence of war crimes and of linking such crimes to the leaders of the various factions involved in the Yugoslav conflict.

On July 29 the Israeli Supreme Court quashed the conviction and death sentence imposed on John Demjanjuk, the former Cleveland, Ohio, autoworker who was believed to have been the Nazi death camp guard known as "Ivan the Terrible." The court said that it had found "reasonable doubt" that Demjanjuk was the sadistic killer who operated the gas ovens at the Treblinka concentration camp. The court's decision was based on new evidence from archives in the former Soviet Union. (*See* LAW.)

Drug Trafficking. At a major conference on U.S. drug policy held in Washington, D.C., in May, newly appointed U.S. Attorney General Janet Reno and other high-ranking officials raised serious questions about the nation's entire drug-interdiction apparatus, suggesting that it could well be futile to continue trying to win the war against drugs by stopping drugs from entering the country. Influential members of the U.S. Congress expressed similar concerns. According to the chairperson of the House of Representatives Judiciary Committee's Subcommittee on Crime and Criminal Justice, Rep. Charles E. Schumer (Dem., N.Y.), "The international eradication and interdiction effort has been a near total failure."

In Colombia the nation's continuing battle to combat drug traffickers, assisted by the U.S., seemed to be making little progress. A series of bombings and assassinations in Medellín, the world's cocaine centre, and Bogotá, the nation's capital, caused a wave of death and destruction. Pablo Escobar, leader of the Medellín drug cartel and at large since a July 1992 jailbreak, was killed in a December shootout with soldiers and police. (*See* WORLD AFFAIRS [Latin America and the Caribbean]: *Colombia.*)

DARIO MITIDIERI—SELECT

Officials inspect damage caused by a terrorist bombing on May 27 at the Uffizi Gallery in Florence. Five people were killed and 26 wounded, and three paintings were destroyed and several others damaged by the blast.

Murder and Other Violence. Violent crime in the U.S. increased slightly in 1992, but the overall level of crime reported to law-enforcement agencies declined 3% compared with 1991. Commenting on the crime figures, the newly appointed FBI director, Louis J. Freeh, said that "any reduction in reported crime is welcome but the amount of violent crime and other grave offenses nationwide remains intolerable."

The rate of violent crime, which included murder, forcible rape, robbery, and aggravated assault, rose by 1% during the year. There were 23,760 murders in 1992, a 4% drop from the record-setting level of 1991. Firearms were used in approximately 7 out of every 10 murders and in one in 3 of all murders, robberies, and aggravated assaults collectively. Almost half of the murder victims were related to or acquainted with their assailants. Among female murder victims almost one-third were killed by their husbands or boyfriends.

The deadly impact of the gun culture in the United States was dramatically illustrated by a National Center for Health Statistics report that gunshots now caused one in every four deaths among U.S. teenagers. Bullets killed 4,200 teenagers in 1990, the most recent year for which figures were available, compared with 2,500 in 1985. According to the National Education Association, an estimated 100,000 students carried a gun to school, while a Louis Harris poll released in July revealed that among a sample of 11- to 18-year-old students surveyed in 96 schools across the country, 15% said they had carried a handgun in the previous 30 days.

On July 1 a lone gunman walked into a San Francisco law office and opened fire with a 9-mm Uzi machine gun and a .45-calibre semiautomatic pistol. The gunman, later identified as Gian Ferri, a mortgage broker, killed eight people and injured six before fatally shooting himself. The attack, which took place on the 34th and 32nd floors of a 49-story office building in the heart of the city's financial district, was a graphic example of the violent crime that was affecting the daily lives of Americans across the nation. In Florida particular concern was expressed at the effect this violence was having on the state's highly lucrative tourist industry. Nationwide statistics on attacks on tourists were not available, but in 1992 in Florida alone 36,766 visitors, foreign and domestic, were murdered, raped, robbed, or otherwise victimized. From October 1992 to October 1993, nine foreign tourists were murdered in the state, and these deaths received extensive publicity in the U.S. and abroad. In Japan travel agents reported that bad publicity of this type was persuading Japanese tourists to vacation in safer destinations.

In England in November, the trial was held of two 11-year-old boys on charges of abduction and murder of a 2-year-old boy, James Bulger, who strayed from his mother at a crowded shopping mall in Liverpool. The abduction was filmed by an automatic security camera in the mall, and the pictures were subsequently widely broadcast on British television. The crime deeply shocked and repelled the local community. The accused boys, who were both 10 at the time of the crimes, were the youngest ever to have been charged with murder in Britain. Because angry crowds attacked the police van carrying the boys to their first court appearance in February, officials moved their trial to Preston, a town 50 km (30 mi) north of Liverpool. Both boys pleaded not guilty to all charges. In late November, however, a jury of three women and nine men found them guilty. They were sentenced to detention "at Her Majesty's pleasure," the equivalent of a life sentence in a high-security unit. Only four other youths were serving life sentences in Britain.

In Brazil and other Latin-American countries, homeless children living on the streets were reported to be the continuing victims of violence. According to UNICEF estimates, 1,000 minors were murdered each year in Brazil, while in Colombia, with one-quarter of the population, twice as many were said to be being killed. Street children were claimed to be the particular targets of police shootings in such cities as Rio de Janeiro because they represented a threat to businessmen who lost trade when customers stayed away from their stores for fear of being mugged or pickpocketed. Few of those responsible for these murders were apprehended, and fewer still successfully prosecuted.

Two women and three children died on May 29 in the German steelmaking city of Solingen when the two-story home of a Turkish family was firebombed. The attack, allegedly plotted by a group of four local skinheads known for their neo-Nazi sympathies, set off a wave of angry demonstrations across the country by Turkish residents, who formed Germany's largest group of foreign guest workers. These workers, 1.8 million of them Turks, were increasingly the object of insults and attacks in many parts of the nation. (*See* WORLD AFFAIRS [Europe]: *Germany.*)

Nonviolent Crime. *Political Crime and Espionage.* In Italy a huge web of corruption, involving some of the most senior figures in government and the world of business, continued to be uncovered. Operation Clean Hands, a far-reaching probe into Italy's culture of kickbacks, led to the notification of at least 800 people that they were under investigation for corruption, a legal step in the Italian justice system in which investigating magistrates officially declared that they intended to proceed with a trial on the basis of the evidence they had obtained. (*See* WORLD AFFAIRS [Europe]: *Italy.*)

Corruption scandals also continued to rock the foundations of the Japanese government. A wide-ranging investigation into "money politics," a system of kickbacks and payoffs involving principally the ruling Liberal Democratic Party, resulted in the arrest and detention in March of Shin Kanemaru, one of Japan's most powerful political figures. (*See* WORLD AFFAIRS [East Asia]: *Japan.*)

In August, after a New York City trial lasting five months, a jury acquitted banker and lawyer Robert Altman of four felony charges ranging from bribery to deceiving the government. All of the charges were related to Altman's affiliations with the failed and corrupt Bank of Credit and Commerce International (BCCI). The verdict was a setback for prosecutors, who seemed to face formidable barriers in bringing to justice those responsible for what was described as the biggest financial scandal in history. Altman, together with his former law partner and Washington power broker Clark Clifford, still faced trial on a range of other criminal and civil charges linked to BCCI.

Law Enforcement. In August, U.S. Pres. Bill Clinton unveiled a $3.4 billion plan to put 50,000 additional police officers on the beat, expand use of the death penalty, and curtail the availability of handguns and automatic pistols. In September the White House released the report of a task force, headed by Vice Pres. Al Gore, that made radical proposals to consolidate federal law-enforcement functions. The report noted that more than 140 federal agencies were responsible for enforcing 4,100 federal criminal laws. Most federal crimes involved several laws and fell under the jurisdictions of several agencies. A drug case, for example, could encompass violations of financial, firearm, immigration, and customs laws, as well as drug statutes. The report recommended that the federal government transfer law-enforcement functions of the Drug Enforcement Administration and the Bureau of Alcohol, Tobacco and Firearms (ATF) to the FBI.

The task force report's recommendations came at a time when the actions of both the ATF and the FBI were under intense scrutiny over their handling of a 51-day siege near Waco, Texas. The siege began on February 28 when more than 100 ATF agents stormed a heavily armed and fortified compound occupied by members of a religious cult known as the Branch Davidians. The raid went badly awry. The cult, led by David Koresh, had apparently been tipped off about the assault, and in an ensuing gun battle 10 persons were killed, including 4 ATF agents. The action resulted in a long standoff that was broken on April 19 by a new assault launched by the FBI using tear gas pumped into the compound by tanks with battering rams. In a raging fire that then broke out, at least 75 out of the 95 people believed to have been in the compound perished, including Koresh and at least 17 children. In October the U.S. Department of the Treasury issued a scathing report on the ATF's handling of the original assault, while a U.S. Department of Justice examination of the siege revealed that there had been sharp disagreements among FBI officials about how to deal with Koresh and his followers. Reno was found to have exhausted all "reasonable alternatives" in handling the matter and to have made no mistakes when she approved the FBI's final tear gas assault.

In April in Los Angeles a federal court trial, launched after the previous year's state court acquittals of four Los Angeles police officers accused of beating black motorist Rodney King—a beating that was videotaped and broadcast around the world—ended in the conviction of two of the officers of violating King's civil rights. Two officers were acquitted of similar charges. The guilty verdicts for Sgt. Stacey Koon and Officer Laurence Powell seemed to put a swift end to months of tension in Los Angeles and to fears that there would be a repeat of the riots that followed the earlier acquittal and left at least 53 persons dead and almost $1 billion in damage. In August the two convicted officers were each sentenced to 30 months' imprisonment. In another related trial, which ended in October, two men accused of beating white truck driver Reginald Denny during the Los Angeles riots were acquitted of most charges. For disfiguring Denny with a brick, Damian Williams was found guilty of simple mayhem, which carried a maximum prison term of up to eight years. His codefendant, Henry Watson, was convicted on a misdemeanour assault charge that carried a six-month prison term. Watson was released from jail, where he had already spent 17 months awaiting trial. (*See* LAW.)

Pallbearers carry the casket of two-year-old James Bulger, who was mutilated and killed after he had been kidnapped at a shopping centre in Liverpool, England. Two 11-year-old boys were convicted of the crime, one of a number of violent incidents involving children.
DAVID JONES—ASSOCIATED PRESS

Italian police claimed one of their most significant breakthroughs in the long-standing fight against organized crime with the arrest in January of the Mafia's superboss, Salvatore Riina. Riina, who had been on the run for 23 years, was captured in the Sicilian town of Palermo. (*See* WORLD AFFAIRS [Europe]: *Italy*.)

At an international police conference held at the British Police Staff College at Bramshill in June, senior police officials warned that eastern European crime syndicates would be supplying guns and drugs to the inner cities of Britain within five years. Weapons from the former Soviet army, such as AK47s, were already being found. Officials said that Britain was particularly vulnerable because it alone in Europe did not have a serious firearms problem or an armed police force or security guards. Echoing these views, the newly appointed London Metropolitan Police Commissioner, Paul Condon, predicted that the British police could be armed as a matter of routine over the next 10 to 20 years.

The United Kingdom was not the only European country to be alarmed about the impact of organized criminal activities originating from the former Soviet Union and other Eastern-bloc countries. With the removal of most of the border controls in the European Community (EC), many

GREG SMITH—SABA
Outside Waco, Texas, the compound of the Branch Davidians, a religious cult headed by David Koresh, goes up in flames on April 19. A standoff between the religious group and federal officials, which had begun on February 28 when agents attempted a raid, ended with the Branch Davidians apparently choosing death by fire over capture.

nations expressed anxieties about the way in which terrorists, smugglers, and drug dealers could move freely around Europe. A multinational police apparatus that would compensate to some degree for the loss of frontier checks within the EC was not yet in place.

In early December Austria was wracked by a series of letter bombs that were sent to journalists, government officials, and priests who aided immigrants. In one incident the mayor of Vienna suffered serious injuries to his left hand. The police believed that right-wing radicals were responsible for the attacks.

In late December four kidnappers took 11 Russian teenagers and 2 adults hostage and demanded $10 million in ransom. Four days later, after two military pilots flew them across southern Russia in a helicopter, the kidnappers released the hostages and forced the pilots to take them near Makhachkala. They were apprehended with most of the ransom money after they tried to flee on foot into the Caucasus Mountains. (DUNCAN CHAPPELL)

Prisons and Penology. *Penal Policy.* In the U.S., Pres. Bill Clinton's crime bill, announced in August 1993, broadly adopted the main features of the legislation long stalled in Congress. The Clinton package provided $3.4 billion for 50,000 additional police officers (as a "down payment" on the 100,000 promised during the campaign) and $700 million for prison construction. In an early move, the new U.S. attorney general, Janet Reno (*see* BIOGRAPHIES), ordered a review of the impact of mandatory minimum sentencing with reference to less serious drug offenses. In France tougher measures with respect to serious offenses, including drug trafficking, were approved in July 1992.

Contrasting developments were evident in many countries. A judicial reform bill passed in the Turkish legislature in November 1992 reduced the period during which suspects could be held in custody before trial and also allowed access to a lawyer during questioning. These measures did not cover terrorist cases or crimes against the state, nor were they applicable in those provinces where there was a state of emergency. Tough measures were announced in Britain, including plans for secure training centres for 12–15-year-olds. Key sections of the Criminal Justice Act of 1991 were also amended so as to give courts discretion to take account of all offenses charged as well as previous convictions.

Elsewhere, liberalizing measures included the ruling by the Barbados Court of Appeal in September 1992 that flogging by a cat-o'-nine-tails was inhuman and degrading. One of the largest amnesties occurred in South Korea, where Pres. Kim Young Sam celebrated his inauguration by releasing almost 42,000 prisoners and expunging the records of 5 million people convicted of minor crimes.

Prison Conditions. Prison populations in many parts of the world continued an upward trend. In the U.S., federal and state prison numbers rose 7% in 1992, and the jail population (persons on remand or serving sentences of less than a year) increased by 5%. The prison and jail population of 1.3 million represented an incarceration rate of 455 per 100,000 inhabitants, one of the highest of any country and, for example, 10 times as high as the rate for The Netherlands. Considerable overcrowding and severe budget pressures coexisted at all levels of government. The federal prison system was 52% over capacity, and California had one of the most crowded state systems, at 90% over capacity. In California and South Carolina new prisons remained empty because budgets did not permit the hiring of additional staff. In 14 states prison personnel were cut back, while an additional 20 states declined to add new positions despite rising prison populations. Deteriorating conditions were also widespread in many facilities for juvenile offenders.

Crowded and often unhygienic prison conditions also existed in many other countries. For example, in September the Zimbabwe government set up an inquiry into the deaths of more than 200 prisoners since the start of the year. In Greece steps were announced to repossess hotels so as to relieve prison crowding that had been caused in part by a crackdown on tax evasion. The imprisonment of many Italian politicians and business leaders gave visibility to the oft-neglected issue of the treatment of prisoners. One hundred fifty of the elite prisoners were among 2,000 persons sharing accommodation at San Vittore Prison, designed to hold 800. Some cells intended for single occupancy were holding six prisoners in summer temperatures rising to 40° C (104° F).

Serious prison riots occurred in several countries. In April at least seven prisoners were killed following a riot at Pavocito Prison on the outskirts of Guatemala City. Also in April nine prisoners and one guard died during an 11-day uprising at the Lucasville, Ohio, maximum-security prison. Although no serious injuries resulted, overnight rioting in September largely destroyed Wymott Prison in Lancashire, England. In France a national strike by prison officers took place after two of their number were killed in separate incidents over the summer. Subsequently, the Ministry of Justice agreed to establish 700 new positions.

Torture and the severe abuse of prisoners remained endemic in many countries. In China, according to Amnesty International, beatings, assaults with electric batons, shackling over periods of weeks, and suspension by the arms or feet were among the methods of torture used. In Egypt, Middle East Watch reported in February that custodial confinement was particularly abusive, and the Egyptian Human Rights Organization claimed that security police routinely tortured Islamic radicals.

Death Penalty. Amnesty International reported during the year that the death penalty remained in force in 106 countries. China, which executed about 1,000 persons in 1991, put at least 59 people to death in January in a crackdown on train and highway robbers. An additional 154 persons were executed for drug offenses on June 26, designated as International Day Against Drug Abuse and Trafficking. In Pakistan 11 convicted murderers were hanged in November 1992. The Islamic code of laws (Shari'ah) was the basis for capital punishment in several countries. For example, in Saudi Arabia, according to Amnesty International, 105 people were executed in the 12 months to June 1993, a fourfold increase over the previous 12 months.

Japan ended its three-year moratorium on executions in March, when at least three and possibly more than five people were hanged. The men had been under sentence of death for periods of up to 23 years. The South African Parliament voted in June to resume the use of the death penalty, which had been suspended since early 1990. Elsewhere in Africa, by contrast, Angola's new constitution, approved in August 1992, abolished the death penalty.

In 1993, 38 persons were executed in the U.S., bringing the total to 226 since the resumption of capital punishment in 1977. The Clinton administration's crime bill extended to 47 the number of federal capital offenses. A poll conducted in April by the Death Penalty Information Centre found that 77% of the respondents supported the death penalty but that this number fell to 56% if the alternative was imprisonment without parole for 25 years. Furthermore, almost 60% of those questioned stated that the possibility of executing innocent people caused them to have doubts about the death penalty. (ANDREW RUTHERFORD)

See also Law.

This article updates the *Macropædia* articles CRIME AND PUNISHMENT; POLICE.

Dance

North America. Unlike the rebellious innovation that dominated dance at the start of the 20th century, the stress near the closing end was beginning to be one of retrospection. The deaths in 1993 of Rudolf Nureyev, one of the most influential ballet dancers in 25 years, and Agnes de Mille, whose choreography revolutionized U.S. theatrical dance, set an unexpected tone of reflection. (*See* OBITUARIES.)

The year's most prominent planned event was the "Balanchine Celebration" put on by New York City Ballet (NYCB) to mark the 10th anniversary of the death of George Balanchine. The company founded by the late, great ballet master performed a repertoire of 73 works over an eight-week period. The results were mixed in detail but mighty in message.

Peter Martins, who inherited the directorship of the company, paid a more convincing homage to his mentor in word than in deed. If the momentum of this overly ambitious grand plan sometimes flagged, owing to inappropriate casting and inadequate dancing, it did not collapse. Such an awesome concentration of Balanchine's demanding work produced its own integrity and yielded a truly historic event.

In smaller ways other ballet companies run by dancers who once worked for Balanchine paid similar homage to the major founder of ballet in the United States. These included San Francisco Ballet (SFB) under Helgi Tomasson, Ballet Chicago under Daniel Duell, Pennsylvania Ballet under Christopher d'Amboise, Miami (Fla.) City Ballet under Edward Villella, and Pacific Northwest Ballet (PNB) under Kent Stowell and Francia Russell.

Boston Ballet under the direction of Bruce Marks, who was not from Balanchine's fold, produced an all-Balanchine program as well as new productions of two 19th-century narrative ballets, *Don Quixote* and *Sleeping Beauty,* both staged by Anna-Marie Holmes. The ever present interest in so-called story ballet resulted in a coproduction of *Swan Lake* arranged between the Atlanta (Ga.) Ballet and Cleveland (Ohio) San Jose (Calif.) Ballet.

American Ballet Theatre (ABT), the American company that put the dramatic/story ballet on the cultural map, added a production of Sir Kenneth MacMillan's *Manon* to its repertory. This three-act production was a holdover selection from the short-lived directorship of Jane Hermann. Kevin McKenzie, who was appointed in 1992, had this more-acting-than-dancing work as part of his administration's first New York season. Limited to only six weeks, ABT's shortened season at the Metropolitan Opera House displayed an almost pointed neglect of Balanchine—only his *Symphonie Concertante,* which remained from Mikhail Baryshnikov's tenure, was shown. Frederick Ashton's *Symphonic Variations* and Mark Morris' *Drink to Me Only with Thine Eyes* were among few repertory works truly worthy of the company's impressively strong classical dancers. Most impressive was Julie Kent, who made her debut as Odette/Odile in *Swan Lake*.

At the end of the year, in Los Angeles, with his new version of *The Nutcracker,* for which playwright Wendy Wasserstein reworked the Christmas scenario, McKenzie began his very own chapter of ABT history. Former ABT

Elizabeth Loscavio dances in the San Francisco Ballet's production of *Swan Lake.* The company's young ballerina received rave reviews for her performances.

JOHAN ELBERS

BEATRIZ SCHILLER

The Nikolais and Murray Louis Dance Company performs *Imago,* one of the group's best-known works. The production was part of a New York City retrospective of the work of dancer and choreographer Alwin Nikolais, who died in 1993.

dancers also assumed ballet directorships in 1993: Kirk Peterson at Hartford (Conn.) Ballet and Fernando Bujones at Ballet Mississippi.

The Joffrey Ballet, which had had a number of financial problems, began the year with the premiere of a work that elicited steady and keen interest over the following 12 months. *Billboards,* with a score by rock star Prince, comprised four sections, each by a different choreographer; the ballet worked to recapture the company's long-standing focus on youth and media trends. The result, coordinated by the troupe's artistic director, Gerald Arpino, was neither as earthshakingly innovative as company statements would have it nor as unspeakably trashy as dance doomsayers would tell it.

Dance Theatre of Harlem played an eagerly attended two-week New York season after an absence due to financial instability. Its vivid performances of Alvin Ailey's *The River* were the highlight of the run. The Alvin Ailey American Dance Theater continued, under Judith Jamison's savvy direction, to honour its founder's high standards, especially with regard to thrilling dancing and dancers.

The multimedia interests of Alwin Nikolais, the modern-dance practitioner who died in May (*see* OBITUARIES), were showcased in a miniretropsective given by the Nikolais and Murray Louis Dance Company in New York City during July. This two-week season and subsequent tour showed a modest selection of work by a dance maker whose lighting and costume permutations distinguished his dances. The season proved more instructive than anything else, showing how work once hailed as avant-garde could mellow into a footnote of 20th-century dance theatre.

For the 40th-anniversary season of his company, Merce Cunningham presented *Enter,* a full company work that had had its premiere at the Paris Opéra. Its cast of 16 included the ever riveting presence of the 73-year-old choreographer-dancer himself. This playful and ritualistic dance came into view from behind a scenic adaptation of a drawing by American composer John Cage, Cunningham's longtime collaborator, who died in 1992.

The 60th anniversary of the American Dance Festival (in Durham, N.C.) was marked by premiere works from Cunningham, Laura Dean, Paul Taylor, and Pilobolus. Taylor and Pilobolus subsequently took their works to New York City. Of these, Taylor's *Spindrift* was the more substantial. Both SFB and PNB performed *Company B,* Taylor's hit from 1992. Unfortunately, Taylor's company had to perform its mere two-week New York season to taped, rather than live, musical accompaniment. Mark Morris took his dance company to New York City in the spring with three new works. *Home,* to very "live" music by Michelle Shocked and Rob Wasserman, stood out with an edginess and elation that Morris deftly intermixed. Twyla Tharp began the year with *Cutting Up,* which she danced with Baryshnikov (who also appeared in Morris's New York season). She returned in the fall with a two-week stint of lecture demonstration-like showings and a world premiere for the Martha Graham Dance Company. *Demeter and Persephone,* the first work created for this group by a choreographer outside Graham's "fold," was a smilingly energetic essay of group and solo dancing to klezmer band music.

The buzzword *multiculturalism* best described the guiding theme of "Dancing," the eight-hour Public Broadcasting System series that aired in the spring. Unfortunately, the "politics" of that term weighed oppressively on the simple dance focus, and a would-be show about dancing often became a lame or confused travelogue about ideas of dancing.

In Canada the year had a pattern of transition. William Whitener, a former Tharp and Joffrey dancer, was appointed director of the Royal Winnipeg Ballet after his stint as director of Les Ballets Jazz in Montreal. Ballet, as such, in Canada elicited serious reevaluating amid appraisals of experimental dance theatre. Three special showcases for such nontraditional work were offered during the year: the fringe Festival of Independent Dance in Toronto, Festival International de Nouvelle Danse in Montreal, and Dancing on the Edge in Vancouver, B.C. The National Ballet of Canada (NBC) held its Erik Bruhn Prize competition and conferred top female honours on ABT's Kent. NBC also got American expatriate choreographer John Neumeier to create one of his rare works outside his home base in Hamburg, Germany. Neumeier's *Now and Then* included in its cast the young Margaret Illmann, who was cast in the lead of *The Red Shoes,* an ill-fated Broadway musical.

Other deaths during the year included ballerina Diana Adams (*see* OBITUARIES), dancer-choreographer Louis Falco, dancer Gary DeLoatch, dancer-choreographer Christopher Gillis, dancer Elise Reiman, choreographer John Butler, and the 1930s tap-dancing screen star Ruby Keeler (*see* OBITUARIES). (ROBERT J. GRESKOVIC)

Europe. For European dance the year's most noted event was the death of Rudolf Nureyev, who was mourned through public and private expressions of grief and an avalanche of worldwide media coverage. In the main, 1993 was a year of uncertainty in dance, a period of change when much of

HUGO GLENDINNING

Members of the Shobana Jeyasingh Dance Company perform one of the Indian-born choreographer's works. Jeyasingh, who lived in London, described her work as a contemporary form of bharatha natya, the principal style of Indian classical dance.

Europe was dogged by the problems of recession and wars waged in eastern parts of the continent. With audiences fluctuating and financial constraints reigning in artistic policies, dance seemed to rely either on conservatism or on promises of change.

In a surprise move it was announced that Peter Schaufuss had signed a seven-year contract, effective in August 1994, to direct the Royal Danish Ballet in Copenhagen. In his position as artistic director of the Berlin Ballet, he had been able to implement an effective policy, but German reunification had reduced funding and increased competition, and there was perhaps a certain logic that as a Dane he should return to his homeland and his artistic roots.

Less surprising was Ivan Nagy's abrupt departure from English National Ballet following a period when, despite increased box-office receipts, the company's artistic policy had been derided for moving "down-market." Nagy's successor, Derek Deane, promised a revitalized company that would focus principally on large-scale classics.

For the first time in its 63-year history, Britain's Royal Ballet found itself without a resident choreographer—following the death in 1992 of Sir Kenneth MacMillan and the resignation of David Bintley. This was reflected in a repertoire that was notably short of new creations, and (with the exception of Bintley's *Tombeaux*) the chief attractions originally had all been produced for North American companies.

Both of Britain's major modern dance companies acknowledged the need for an identity change. Rambert Dance Company, after the departure of artistic director Richard Alston at the end of 1992, remained nominally leaderless. Christopher Bruce was named as his successor, but he was not free to begin full-time work until April 1994. He made it clear that his leadership would create a company to bridge the gap between ballet and modern dance and announced that for his first season an increased number of dancers would appear in works by himself, Jiri Kylian, Ohad Naharin, and Martha Clarke. This indicated a strong affinity with Kylian's Netherlands Dance Theatre.

A viable new policy for London Contemporary Dance Theatre (LCDT) could not be conjectured so rapidly, and after the departure of Nancy Duncan in 1992, the company's founding artistic director, Robert Cohan, was effectively in charge for the year. For a company with a 25-year history, its artistic identity had reached a crisis point, and the problem was one not simply of finding an artistic director but of finding a new creative impetus.

Another company facing major change was France's Ballet du Nord, where "internal problems" led to the mid-season departure of director Jean-Paul Comelin and the cancellation of further performances of his ballets. There was talk that a new director might be appointed to give the company a more contemporary look.

Other significant directorial appointments included Carolyn Carlson to Sweden's Cullberg Ballet; Michael Denard to the Deutsche Staatsoper Berlin; Elisabetta Terabust to the ballet company of La Scala, Milan; Simon Mottram to the Royal Swedish Ballet; Anne Woolliams to the Vienna State Opera Ballet; Jean-Christophe Maillot to the Ballet de Monte-Carlo; and Vladimir Derevianko to the Staatsoper Dresden. Ray Barra was appointed caretaker director of the Berlin Ballet.

In contrast to so many breaks with the past, two pillars of European dance, Neumeier and Pina Bausch, celebrated 20 years of directing their companies. Bausch, who evolved a unique style of Postmodern Expressionism in her two decades with Germany's Tanztheater Wuppertal, was one of 20th-century dance's seminal figures. Neumeier, too, won a distinctive reputation for his work with the Hamburg Ballet through the creation of large-scale narrative ballets, often set to symphonies and choral works.

Among many companies struggling to survive, Italy's Aterballetto began what was described as a "long layoff" period. London City Ballet nearly closed, but it was saved at the last minute by sponsorship deals.

In a year that commemorated the centenary of Peter Ilich Tchaikovsky's death, there was a proliferation of *Swan Lakes, Sleeping Beauties,* and *Nutcrackers.* Notable among them was Schaufuss' complete trilogy of the Tchaikovsky classics, his parting shot for Berlin. Somewhat ironically—given that production plans are made far in advance—the swan song of his predecessor in Copenhagen, Frank Andersen, also turned out to be Tomasson's new production of *Sleeping Beauty*. Russia's two main ballet companies, the St. Petersburg Ballet (formerly the Leningrad Kirov) and Moscow's Bolshoi, continued to value the Tchaikovsky ballets and other 19th-century classics above all else. A noted Bolshoi initiative was a January–February season in London's specially converted Albert Hall; programs of "potted" classics aroused critical fury but nonetheless drew thousands of newcomers to ballet.

Among major ballet companies concerned with 20th-century "classics," there was continuing enthusiasm for certain North American choreographers. Balanchine was celebrated by the Paris Opéra Ballet (POB) with a full evening of his works and by a week-long predominantly Balanchine season by the NYCB on tour in Copenhagen. In France the POB, as in 1992, presented a triple bill of Jerome Robbins's works. The Norwegian National Ballet gave a triple bill of Glen Tetley's ballets, and the Royal Swedish Ballet presented his full-length work *The Tempest.*

Honouring European choreographers, the Stuttgart (Germany) Ballet paid homage to MacMillan's memory with a program of two ballets created for the company (*Requiem* and *Song of the Earth*). The POB featured Roland Petit's work and became the first company apart from the Cullberg Ballet to present Mats Ek's expressionist version of *Giselle*—during a period when the conventional 19th-century production was also in the repertory.

If Europeans regularly celebrated Americans, the Japanese revered Maurice Béjart, whose new full-length work *M* was performed by the Tokyo Ballet throughout a two-month European tour. Béjart was also honoured by the Japan Art Association, becoming the first choreographer to receive the prestigious Praemium Imperiale.

Reputations were upheld by Europe's modern dance leaders, including Bausch, Kylian, William Forsythe, Ek, Bruce, and Anne Teresa De Keersmaeker, all of whom produced new works. British achievements in the modern field were acknowledged in Canada with invitations to choreographers Michael Clark, Lloyd Newson, Jonathan Burrows, and Shobana Jeyasingh to present their groups at Montreal's Festival International de Nouvelle Danse. In Britain performances by the small company CandoCo—founded by Celeste Dandeker, a dancer with LCDT who broke her neck and was left paralyzed—gave an opportunity to some dancers who were in wheelchairs, provoking much debate.

Besides Nureyev, notable deaths during the year included Gret Palucca, a leading member of German Expressionist dance; Michel Renault, a former star of the POB; Paolo Bortoluzzi, an Italian dancer with Béjart's Ballet of the Twentieth Century; and three English celebrities: dancer and teacher Keith Lester, dancer-choreographer Hetty Loman, and critic Oleg Kerensky. (ANN NUGENT)

See also Music; Theatre.

This article updates the *Macropædia* article The History of Western DANCE.

Disasters

The loss of life and property from disasters in 1993 included the following:

Aviation

January 9, Near Surabaya, Indon. A plane carrying 39 passengers and 5 crew members crashed shortly after takeoff; 15 persons were killed, including 4 of the 5 crew.

January 27, Zaire. A plane that was carrying £100 million for the diamond industry crashed, and 11 passengers were killed; a teenager, apparently belonging to a crowd of looters, was shot dead by a soldier near the scene of the wreck.

January 30, Sumatra, Indon. A plane carrying Singaporean salvage workers, who were to study a ruptured supertanker that was crippled off the coast of Sumatra, slammed into a mountain during bad weather; all 16 persons aboard the craft lost their lives in the crash.

February 8, Tehran. A passenger plane carrying pilgrims to Meshed crashed shortly after takeoff when a military aircraft sliced into its tail, causing it to explode and plummet to the ground on an empty lot inside Iran's Revolutionary Guards Corps' compound; all 132 persons aboard the passenger plane were killed.

March 5, Skopje, Macedonia. A newly built Fokker 100 passenger plane fell from the sky a minute after takeoff, crashed, and then exploded; of the 97 persons aboard, at least 77 lost their lives, and some of the survivors suffered severe burns.

April 16, Near Pul-i-Khumri, Afghanistan. A helicopter carrying 15 persons, including two American journalists, crashed in a ravine near a mountain village; there were no survivors.

April 26, Near Aurangabad, India. A passenger plane carrying 118 persons crashed during takeoff after slamming into a truck on the runway and then striking high-tension wires as it sought to make its ascent; as many as 75 persons were feared dead.

April 27, Near Tashkurghan, Afghanistan. A military transport plane carrying 76 persons, including 15 members of an Afghan wrestling team, crashed in heavy fog; all aboard were killed.

April 28, Near Libreville, Gabon. A Zambian military plane carrying 30 persons crashed into the Atlantic Ocean and exploded shortly after taking off from a refueling stop; all aboard lost their lives, including most of Zambia's national soccer team, which was en route to a World Cup qualifying match against Senegal.

Early May, Nizhny Tagil, Russia. An aircraft failed to make a proper maneuver during a stunt show and crashed into a crowd of spectators; 17 persons lost their lives.

May 19, Near Urrau, Colombia. After it had been cleared for landing, a Boeing 727 carrying 132 persons crashed into the slope of a remote Andes mountainside; there were no survivors of the crash, which possibly occurred because radio navigation sites had been blown up by left-wing guerrillas the previous year.

July 1, Irian Jaya province, Indon. A domestic airliner with 43 persons aboard crashed on the beach while attempting to land; there were only 3 survivors.

July 23, Yinchuan (Yin-ch'uan), Ningxia (Ning-hsia) Hui autonomous region, China. An airliner that was attempting its second takeoff veered off the runway, crashed into a lake, and broke apart; at least 59 of the 113 persons aboard the craft were killed.

July 26, Near Haenam, South Korea. A passenger airliner crashed into a mountain in driving wind and rain after attempting, for the third time, to land at Mokpo airport; at least 66 of the some 110 persons aboard the craft were killed.

July 31, Near Kathmandu, Nepal. A commercial airliner crashed into a hillside; 18 persons lost their lives.

August 28, Southern Tajikistan. An overcrowded passenger jetliner went down shortly after takeoff from Khorog and crashed near the country's border with Afghanistan; engine failure was blamed for the crash, which claimed the lives of at least 35 persons.

November 20, Near Ohrid, Macedonia. A passenger jet crashed in the rugged mountains and exploded some seven kilometres (four miles) from Ohrid airport; 115 persons were killed, and the lone survivor was seriously injured.

November 21, Near Guatemala City, Guatemala. A twin-engine plane slammed into a fog-enshrouded mountain; 13 persons, including U.S., Canadian, and German tourists, were killed in the crash.

December 1, Near Hibbing, Minn. A commuter plane carrying 18 persons crashed into the side of a man-made hill while attempting to land in dense fog and freezing rain; all aboard perished.

December 13, Near Phong Savan, Laos. A Laotian airliner carrying 17 persons slammed into a mountain while making its landing approach to the airport; there were no survivors.

Fires and Explosions

January 19, Taipei, Taiwan. A predawn fire at a 24-hour restaurant claimed the lives of 30 persons who had access to only one of three emergency fire exits; arson was suspected after authorities found traces of what was believed to be butane gas near the entrance of the establishment.

February 14, Tangshan (T'ang-shan), China. A department store fire believed to have been sparked by welders working in the building killed at least 78 persons and injured at least 51.

March 16, Chicago. A fast-burning early-morning fire swept through a four-story single-room-occupancy transient hotel and claimed the lives of 19 residents; the roof and several walls of the structure collapsed as a result of the five-alarm fire, the origin of which remained unclear.

April 19, Nonsan, South Korea. A predawn fire in a mental hospital housing 45 patients claimed the lives of at least 34 of them, some of whom were chained or shackled to their beds.

April 28, Outskirts of Istanbul. A buildup of methane gas caused an explosion at a garbage dump, where a massive avalanche of rotting refuse descended into a valley and engulfed nearby squatter huts; at least 13 persons were known dead, and more than 30 were trapped and feared dead.

May 10, Near Bangkok, Thailand. A massive fire in a doll factory sent more than 100 fire trucks racing to the site, where as many as 800 employees tried to flee the blazing four-story structure, which collapsed as workers were evacuating the top floors; at least 187 persons were killed, and 500 were injured in the inferno, which was believed to have been fueled by the materials used to make dolls. The cause of the world's deadliest factory fire was under investigation.

June 25, Bruz, France. A fire in a three-story private psychiatric clinic claimed the lives of 16 patients and one nurse, most of whom succumbed to burns and smoke inhalation; the more than 100-year-old structure was not equipped with fire alarms, smoke detectors, or sprinkler systems, and locked exit doors and windows apparently prevented escape for at least some of the medicated patients.

August 5, Shenzhen (Shen-chen), Guangdong (Kwangtung) province, China. Two powerful explosions about an hour apart claimed the lives of at least 8 persons and possibly as many as 70 and injured more than 100; the first blast was apparently caused by a leak of nitric acid at a factory warehouse, and the second fire erupted when a nearby storage depot exploded and sent up a fireball of what was believed to be liquid petroleum gas.

August 31, Laberinto, Peru. Flames swept through a gold-mining town after a kerosene lamp in a guest house apparently sparked the fire; at least 18 persons were killed, and 7 were injured in the conflagration.

Early September, Valparaíso, Chile. A fire in a discotheque claimed the lives of 17 persons.

September 28, Near Caracas, Venezuela. A natural gas pipeline exploded beside a highway during rush-hour traffic after a telephone company crew that was laying fibre-optic cables apparently struck the pipeline; the blast ripped through a passenger bus and several cars and claimed the lives of at least 51 persons.

November 2, Quang Ninh province, Vietnam. A burst gasoline pipeline ignited in flames as a crowd tried to steal fuel from the ruptured vessel; at least 39 persons were killed, and some 60 others were injured.

November 19, Near Shenzhen, Guangdong province, China. A fire in a toy factory in the village of Kuiyong (K'uei-yung) swept through the structure as most of the 240 workers toiled behind locked windows and doors; at least 81 persons lost their lives, many of them trampled in the stampede to escape the inferno.

December 13, Fujian (Fukien) province, China. A raging fire swept through a textile factory in Fuzhou (Fu-chou) and claimed the lives of 60 workers.

December 20, Near Buenos Aires, Arg. A fire in a discotheque filled with some 500 teenagers celebrating the end of the high-school year claimed the lives of at least 17 persons. The victims were trapped behind padlocked emergency exits. Some of the young revelers initially believed that the smoke was emanating from a special-effects machine, but when the fumes became unbearable, they fled through the main entrance, the only escape.

CVELE/ZAMUR—GAMMA LIAISON

The crumpled fuselage of a jetliner lies in the mountains of southern Macedonia, where it crashed on November 20. All but one of the 116 persons aboard were killed.

Rescue workers remove bodies from a toy factory near Bangkok, Thailand, where a fire on May 10 killed at least 187 persons. It was called the deadliest factory fire in history.
KRAIPIT/SIPA

Marine

January 14, Off the coast of Germany. A Polish ferryboat carrying at least 60 persons capsized and sank in the Baltic Sea during a storm packing winds of up to 161 km/h (100 mph); at least 54 persons drowned when the hurricane-force winds shifted the vessel's cargo of trucks and railroad cars, causing the boat to keel over.

January 25, Off the coast of Trincomalee, Sri Lanka. A civilian ferry carrying some 80 to 85 passengers, double its licensed capacity, capsized in rough waters; 40 persons were killed.

February 16, Off the coast of Petit Goave, Haiti. A triple-decker ferry carrying as many as 1,500–2,000 passengers to the capital of Port-au-Prince to sell their goods capsized and sank during a rainstorm; 285 persons survived the stormy seas, some for as long as 30 hours, by clinging to floating objects.

February 28, Brazzaville, Congo. A ferry gangplank, by which hundreds of Zairean deportees were boarding, collapsed; as many as 147 persons drowned in the swift-moving Congo River.

March 15, Off the coast of Nova Scotia. A Liberian freighter loaded with ore bound for Tampa, Fla., sank while being battered by high waves in hurricane-force winds; the crew of 33 was believed to have abandoned the foundering vessel, but rescue workers recovered only the body of one sailor, an insulated immersion suit, and two damaged life rafts.

March 28, Southern Bangladesh. A fierce storm swamped an overcrowded ferry traveling from Barisal to Lalmohan; of the 250 persons aboard, 32 were known dead and at least 100 others were missing and feared drowned. The storm reportedly overwhelmed some 22 other boats, each of them carrying about 10 persons whose fates were unknown.

Mid-April, Off the coast of Spain. An Indian cargo ship sank in frigid seas; 12 persons were known dead, and 28 were missing and presumed drowned.

May 9, Northern India. A ferryboat sank in the Ganges River near Doriganj; 60 persons were feared drowned.

Mid-May, Off the coast of Mombasa, Kenya. A dhow carrying Somali refugees back to their homeland capsized; 7 persons were known drowned, and 47 were missing.

Late May, Off the coast of South Africa. A vessel carrying 20 sailors sank in rough seas; all aboard were believed lost at sea.

Late May, Off the coast of Myanmar (Burma). A ship with more than 300 persons aboard sank in the Andaman Sea; 17 persons were known dead, and 120 were missing.

July 2, Bocaue, Phil. A floating pagoda mounted on three boats and loaded with more than 500 persons participating in a religious festival collapsed in the Bocaue River; of the hundreds of women and children hurled into the murky waters, at least 310 drowned and 40 others were missing.

August 11, Vadodara, India. An overcrowded boat carrying some 35 passengers, at least 15 more than its capacity, capsized in the Sur Lake; 30 persons drowned.

Mid-August, Central Sudan. A ferryboat capsized in the Nile River; 17 persons drowned.

October 10, Off the coast of Puan, South Korea. An overcrowded ferryboat capsized and sank during a fierce storm; of the more than 360 passengers aboard, most of them tourists, only 74 survived.

November 20, Off the coast of southern Bangladesh. A ferry carrying Muslim pilgrims, mostly women, to a shrine on the island of Kutubdia sank after being rammed by a trawler; at least 45 persons were feared drowned.

December 19, Off the coast of Desaru, Malaysia. Two fishing trawlers, apparently carrying illegal immigrants, collided on the high seas; one boat sank, leaving 49 persons missing and believed drowned, and the other ship dropped its passengers on the beach and sailed away.

Mining

May 13, Secunda, South Africa. A methane gas explosion in a coal mine claimed the lives of 50 miners, and 3 were missing and feared dead.

Miscellaneous

January 1, Hong Kong. Shortly after midnight, New Year's revelers stampeded down a cobblestone hillside that was dampened with beer and party foam; at least 20 persons were trampled to death, and 69 were injured in the melee.

January, Tajikistan. A wheat crop, harvested late reportedly because of the civil war in that country, became contaminated with a deadly microorganism; at least 24 persons died when they ate bread made from the poisoned wheat, and as many as 1,600 were hospitalized with bloated stomachs.

Early February, Rift Valley, Kenya. A yellow fever epidemic claimed the lives of at least 500 persons.

February 14, Near Perm, Russia. A hydroelectric plant released hot water into a river, resulting in the deaths of 15 ice fishermen who drowned when the frozen surface of the water broke apart.

Mid-February, Northern India. The roof of a school collapsed; 24 persons were killed, and 23 children were hospitalized with serious injuries.

Late February, Near Buenos Aires. Tainted wine that had been laced with methyl alcohol, a lethal colourless liquid, killed at least 24 persons and resulted in the hospitalization of at least 75; the winery that sold the cheap white wine was ordered closed by Pres. Carlos Menem.

Late March, Yettambadi, India. Food poisoning killed at least 16 and hospitalized 630 persons who consumed the decomposed meat of animals sacrificed during a Hindu ritual.

August 13, Nakhon Ratchasima, Thailand. A six-story hotel that was under renovation to add a seventh floor collapsed in a heap of debris; more than 100 persons were killed, some 50 were missing, and 225 were injured. Officials speculated that the top three floors, which were added to the structure in 1990, may have weakened the structure or three huge water-storage tanks positioned on the roof may have contributed to the collapse of the building.

August 25–26, Assam, India. A rogue elephant stampeded through the villages of Thelamara, Muslim Char, and Butamari and trampled at least 44 persons; a few weeks later the rampaging pachyderm, which had successfully eluded hunters, killed 6 more persons in the Assam district of Sonitpur.

August 27, Qinghai (Ch'ing-hai) province, China. The dam at Gouhou (Kou-hou) reservoir inexplicably burst and unleashed a torrent of water on several villages in the vicinity; the onslaught caused the deaths of more than 1,250 persons and economic losses of more than $27 million.

Late November, Near Hyderabad, Andhra Pradesh, India. Fermented liquor adulterated with chemicals to increase its potency was blamed for the deaths of 14 persons.

Natural

Early January, Bangladesh. A brutal one-week cold wave claimed the lives of at least 34 persons, many of them destitute children and the elderly.

January 2–3, Fiji. Deadly Cyclone Kina ripped across the islands and caused widespread damage with winds swirling to 185 km/h (115 mph); at least 12 persons were known dead, hundreds of homes were destroyed, and three major bridges were washed away.

January 7–20, Southern California and Tijuana, Mexico. Two weeks of relentless pounding rain caused massive mud slides and severe flooding, which led to the deaths of at least 30 persons and left more than 1,000 homeless.

January 8, Northeastern Bangladesh. A five-minute tornado ravaged villages in Sylhet and Sunamganj districts, killed 32 persons, and left more than 1,000 injured.

January 14, Near Pasto, Colombia. The Galeras volcano erupted and trapped a team of scientists who were inside the crater collecting gas samples; of the some 70 persons believed to have been on the volcano when it erupted, at least 9, including 6 volcanologists, were killed and 7 were injured.

January 18, Ozengeli, Turkey. A thundering avalanche entombed half of the village; at least 18 persons were killed, and some 50 were buried under the snow.

Late January, Between Russia and Georgia. An avalanche in the Caucasus Mountains blocked the only pass linking the two countries; 18 persons were feared dead.

Early February, Java, Indon. Heavy rains precipitated severe flooding, which claimed the lives of at least 60 persons, destroyed thousands of homes, and forced some 250,000 persons to be evacuated.

February 2, Near Legaspi, Phil. Mayon Volcano unexpectedly spewed a gigantic plume of ash and sent tons of superheated debris tumbling down its slopes and onto farmers' fields; the minor explosion claimed the lives of 68 persons.

Mid-February, Ecuador. A week of relentless rains precipitated severe flooding in the coastal provinces, where dozens of persons were killed, thousands of hectares of banana, soya, and rice crops were destroyed, and landslides made roads impassable.

Late February, Iran. Large-scale flooding killed some 500 persons and caused some $1 billion in damages in one of the country's worst natural disasters to date.

March 12–15, Eastern U.S. A ferocious storm billed as the Blizzard of '93 produced record-breaking bitter-cold temperatures while dumping tons of snow from Alabama to Maine; spawned tornadoes in Florida, where residents were still recovering from the 1992 destruction caused by Hurricane Andrew; and generated hurricane-force winds that made projectiles of unsecured objects and whipped up tides along coastal areas, causing severe flooding. The violent "nor'easter," a low-pressure system that gained its force when arctic air collided with warm, humid air from the Gulf of Mexico, claimed the lives of at least 238 persons, including 50 in Pennsylvania and 44 in Florida; trapped some 100 hikers and several campers in North Carolina and Tennessee; and spread destruction as far north as Canada (4 deaths) and as far south as Cuba (3 deaths). Damage estimates reached $1 billion.

March 15, Northern Pakistan. Avalanches in a remote region of the country buried at least 36 persons, injured 16, crushed adobe homes in two villages, and destroyed cattle herds.

Late March, Afghanistan. A thundering avalanche of snow and ice blocked the northern end of the Salang tunnel on the main highway linking Kabul with the northern part of the country; at least 100 persons were reported to have died of exposure, and thousands were trapped on the highway without proper clothing or sufficient food.

March 29, Near Cuenca, Ecuador. Rains in a mining region caused a landslide that entombed a small community in the southern part of the country; several hundred persons were killed.

April 9, West Bengal, India. A killer tornado leveled five villages in the Murshidabad district and claimed the lives of at least 100 persons.

April 26, Northwestern Colombia. Heavy rains caused massive flooding and landslides, which blocked 24 main roads and claimed the lives of as many as 100 persons; the Tapartó River burst its banks, inundated five nearby hamlets, destroyed some 50 houses, and ravaged coffee, banana, and cane crops.

Early May, Gansu (Kansu) province, China. A menacing sandstorm that locals dubbed "the black wind" because it ominously darkened the midday skies whipped up sand and dirt and blew residents, most of them children, into water channels and pools; at least 43 fatalities were attributed to the storm.

May 3, Santiago, Chile. Heavy rain was blamed for swelling rivers that burst canal banks, unleashing a mass of water and mud that buried poorer neighbourhoods in the capital; at least 11 persons lost their lives.

May 9, Ecuador. A landslide roared down a steep slope denuded of trees, pouring thousands of tons of mud and rock on a gold-mining settlement; as many as 200 persons were feared dead.

Mid-June–August, U.S. Midwest. A stormy weather front that stagnated over the Midwest for weeks caused some of the worst flooding in U.S. history in the states of Illinois, Iowa, Kansas, Minnesota, Missouri, Nebraska, North Dakota, South Dakota, and Wisconsin when the Missouri and Mississippi rivers overflowed after reaching record crests even though volunteers tried to shore up the banks with some 75 million sandbags. "The Great Flood of '93" claimed the lives of 50 persons; caused an estimated $12 billion in damages, including $200 million to rail lines and bridges and $8 billion in crop damages; and affected additional areas in the states of Arkansas, Kentucky, and Tennessee before subsiding in August.

Mid-June, Bangladesh. Fierce storms inundated the capital city of Dhaka, causing rivers to overflow their banks and claiming the lives of nearly 200 persons, who died in the massive flooding.

Mid-June, Western El Salvador. Heavy rains precipitated a mud slide at a garbage dump; more than 20 persons were feared dead.

Early July, Himachal Pradesh state, India. Four days of relentless monsoon rains caused massive flooding, which led to the deaths of at least 175 persons.

Early July, Northeastern U.S. A searing week-long heat wave with punishing temperatures over 38°C (100°F) claimed dozens of lives—many were elderly persons whose homes had no air-conditioning—including at least 41 in Philadelphia.

July 6–7, Mexico. Hurricane Calvin whipped up dangerous winds and seas, pounded seaports and airports in Acapulco, and forced thousands from their homes; at least 28 deaths were attributed to the storm, which pummeled the country's Pacific coast.

July 12, Northern Japan. A major earthquake, measuring 7.8 on the Richter scale, and its subsequent deadly tsunamis (seismic sea waves) claimed the lives of at least 185 persons, some of whom either succumbed inside collapsed or burning buildings, were swept away and drowned, or were buried in landslides. The island of Okushiri, which was hit the hardest, was virtually destroyed.

Late July–Early August, Bangladesh, India, and Nepal. The worst monsoon rains in 40 years caused water from the Himalayan mountain ranges to burst the banks of rivers draining into low-lying plains and inundate bordering villages; thousands were killed, crops were washed away, and millions of people were affected—many of them marooned—by the massive flooding.

Late July, Hunan (Hu-nan) and Sichuan (Szechwan) provinces, China. Torrential rains unleashed massive flooding and landslides that claimed the lives of about 120 persons.

Late July–Early August, Southern Japan. Torrential downpours caused flooding and mud slides, which killed at least 40 persons and left an estimated 22 missing.

August 8, Venezuela. Tropical Storm Bret, packing ferocious winds and driving rain, caused intense flooding and mud slides, which left thousands homeless and claimed the lives of at least 100 persons, many of them buried in their hillside shanties; the capital city of Caracas was hardest hit, with many streets in slum areas resembling rivers.

Early September, Kyushu, Japan. Typhoon Yancy, the worst storm of its type in 30 years, blasted the island with winds in excess of 209 km/h (130 mph) and claimed the lives of at least 41 persons.

Early September, T'boli, Phil. A landslide buried 21 miners in their bunkhouses during a storm.

C. ANDREWS—GAMMA LIAISON

Residents of Killari, India, search the ruble of their homes destroyed in an earthquake on September 30. It was one of the most devastating earthquakes in India in half a century.

Mid-September, Nicaragua, Honduras, and Mexico. Tropical Storm Gert lashed the countries with heavy rains that caused flooding, numerous mud slides, and massive destruction of roads and highways; at least 28 persons were killed in Nicaragua and Honduras, and about 14 lost their lives when the storm ravaged Mexico.

September 30, Maharashtra state, India. An earthquake measuring 6.4 on the Richter scale, the worst in India in over 50 years, rocked the region, flattening a dozen villages and killing more than 9,700 persons who were buried when their mud-and-mortar homes entombed them as they slept; the devastation wreaked by the powerful temblor was massive, and only those who had stayed outside to celebrate the Hindu festival honouring Ganesa, the elephant-headed god, were spared. Hardest hit were the towns of Umarga, Latur, and Killari; the tragedy prompted India, for the first time in its independent history, to accept international aid.

Early October, China. The waters of the Qiantang (Ch'ien-t'ang) River swept away dozens of persons from a jetty where they had gathered to witness the cresting waves of the river's autumn peak; 19 persons were known dead, and 40 were missing.

Early October, Luzon, Phil. Tropical Storm Flo ravaged the country, burying 200 homes under mud flows, destroying over $10 million of crops and property, and killing at least 41 persons; more than 30 were missing and presumed dead.

October 8, Kodigama, Sri Lanka. Heavy rains precipitated a landslide, which thundered down a hillside and buried at least eight homes in mud; about 50 persons were feared dead.

Mid–Late October, Northern Papua New Guinea. A series of earthquakes during a 12-day period killed at least 65 persons.

October 31–November 2, Northern Honduras. Torrential rains inundated the provinces of Yoro and Colón and precipitated massive mud slides, which buried more than 1,000 homes; an estimated 400 persons lost their lives.

Late October–Early November, Southern California. A series of wildfires driven by the Santa Ana winds scorched at least 61,500 ha (152,000 ac) and claimed the lives of three persons.

November 23, South-central Vietnam. Ferocious Typhoon Kyle battered four provinces, claimed the lives of at least 45 persons, and injured at least 244; hardest hit was the province of Khanh Hoa, where 30 persons were killed, 67 were missing, and more than 1,000 homes were destroyed.

Late November–Early December, Moscow. A deep freeze that lasted longer than two weeks claimed the lives of at least 41 persons, caused more than 200 to require treatment for frostbite and exposure, and resulted in limb amputations in more than 60 persons.

Early December, Southern India. A cyclone pummeled the country's southern coastal districts and claimed the lives of at least 47 persons.

Early December, Great Britain. Hurricane-force winds, among the strongest ever recorded during December, claimed the lives of at least 12 persons, disrupted road and rail travel, and toppled trees and power lines.

December 11, Near Kuala Lumpur, Malaysia. A 12-story luxury apartment building collapsed after a landslide hit the structure; at least 56 persons were killed.

December 14, Cairo. A monumental rock broke free from a cliff, thundered down a mountain, and shattered into large boulders as it demolished several buildings; at least 25 persons were killed in the landslide.

December 16, Pakistan. An avalanche triggered by a blizzard buried 10 Pakistani soldiers on the Siachen glacier.

December 17, Dabeiba, Colombia. Severe rains sent a torrent of water through the town and unleashed a mud slide, which demolished some 25 homes; at least 22 persons were killed, about 35 were injured, and several were missing.

December 25, Oran, Alg. Heavy rains triggered mud slides that demolished the shanties of some 130 families; at least 12 persons were known dead, and 46 were injured.

Engines and passenger cars of the Sunset Limited, an Amtrak train en route to Miami, Fla., from Los Angeles, lie in Big Bayou Canot near Mobile, Ala. The accident, which occurred in the early hours of September 22 and killed 47 people, was blamed on a weakened bridge that had been damaged only moments before by a barge.

HERB WELCH—THE SUN HERALD/SIPA

December 25–26, Philippines. Typhoon Nell pummeled the islands and claimed the lives of at least 47 persons; the late-season storm was one in a series that killed more than 300 persons during the month.

Late December, Northeastern Malaysia. Week-long rains caused the worst flooding in 13 years as swollen rivers broke their banks; at least 14 deaths were attributed to the flooding, which also damaged homes and crops.

Late December, Belgium, France, Germany, Luxembourg, Spain, and The Netherlands. The worst flooding in decades inundated parts of Europe after brutal storms lashed the areas with relentless rains, causing rivers, especially the Rhine, to overflow their banks; at least seven persons were known dead, and property damage was estimated in the hundreds of millions of dollars.

Railroad

January 16, Near Kanpur, India. The Rajdhani Express train collided with a derailed 16-car freight train; the official death toll was put at 6, but another source claimed that the toll was 15, with at least 27 more injured than the officially reported 38.

January 30, Kenya. A train traveling from Mombasa to Nairobi with some 600 passengers aboard was forced off the tracks when a bridge, weakened by floodwaters, collapsed and sent the engine and five cars plummeting into the swollen Ndethia Geithia River; at least 117 persons were known dead, and more than 180 were missing in the country's worst railroad accident to date.

Late January, Liaoning (Liao-ning), China. A bus that was trying to speed through a railroad crossing was hit by an oncoming train; 66 of the 94 passengers aboard the bus were killed, and 28 were injured.

Mid-February, Southern Hungary. A train slammed into a bus at a crossing where the warning lights were burned out; 10 children were killed, and 20 were injured.

March 28, Pusan, South Korea. An overcrowded passenger train derailed when the wet ground beneath the tracks caved in following underground blasting work for an electric-cable tunnel; at least 75 persons were killed, and more than 120 were injured.

May 27, Gyumri, Armenia. A passenger train rammed into seven freight cars that had rolled down from a side bank into its path; 30 persons were killed, and 48 were injured.

Early August, Mairwa, India. A speeding passenger train derailed as it passed through Mairwa station in eastern India; 22 persons traveling on the roof of the train were killed, and 15 were injured.

September 22, Near Mobile, Ala. Amtrak's Sunset Limited, which had launched its Los Angeles-to-Miami route in April, was carrying some 210 persons and was traveling over the wood-and-steel span over Big Bayou Canot at about 3 AM when all three of its locomotives and several of its double-decker coaches plunged into the alligator- and snake-infested swamp as the 84-year-old bridge gave way, presumably because a barge had weakened the structure by unknowingly hitting it in heavy fog. The accident, the deadliest in Amtrak's history, claimed the lives of 47 persons. Rescue efforts were hampered by the fog-enshrouded darkness, but as many as 30 persons were guided to safety by one passenger, and they were then able to swim to shore, even though waters were saturated with diesel fuel and explosions were being set off by a fire emanating from one of the locomotives.

September 28, Near Rabat, Morocco. A crowded passenger train erupted in flames after being rammed from behind by a tanker train filled with naphtha, a highly combustible liquid; 14 persons perished, and 80 were injured in the fiery collision.

October 13, Near Borivli, India. A speeding train crushed some 49 women to death when, thinking that a compartment of the stationary commuter train they were on was ablaze, they panicked and jumped into the path of an oncoming rush-hour train; some 70 other women from the "Ladies Special" train were injured.

November 2, Depok, Indon. During the morning rush hour two passenger trains collided head-on; at least 69 persons were killed, and 75 were injured in the crash.

Traffic

January 3, Near Cancún, Mexico. A bus carrying 52 tourists on an excursion from Cancún to the Mayan ruins of Chichén Itzá slammed into a high-tension power pole, apparently while traveling too fast on the slippery freeway; 25 tourists lost their lives and more than 25 were injured when a transformer from the pole hit the bus, which then caught fire.

January 3, Northern Lima, Peru. A bus traveling down a winding, fog-enshrouded road tumbled off a steep cliff; at least 12 persons were killed, and some 30 were injured.

January 9, Near Santo Tomé, Arg. A triple bus crash occurred when one vehicle tried to pass another on a curve and collided head-on with an oncoming Paraguayan bus. The passing bus burst into flames as it ripped the Paraguayan bus in two, and the bus being passed collided with other vehicles; at least 60 persons were killed, and 80 were injured.

January 17, Phichit province, Thailand. Two passenger buses collided head-on in the northern province; 18 persons were killed in the crash.

January 19, Himachal Pradesh, India. A private bus plunged into a deep ravine near the village of Bathal; at least 19 persons were killed, and 3 were injured.

Early February, Lagos, Nigeria. A bus ignited apparently after its engine caught fire; some 80 persons trapped inside were burned to death.

April 26, Near Colombo, Sri Lanka. A bus plunged into a river after the bridge it was crossing collapsed; at least 30 persons were feared dead.

July 6, Italy. A tour bus carrying senior citizens plunged off a road in the Dolomites; at least 15 persons were killed, and 21 were injured.

July 16, Near Lac-Bouchette, Que. A pickup truck and a bus carrying senior citizens from a shrine crashed head-on while traveling on a winding highway; 19 persons were killed in the accident, and one person died later.

July 24, Near Avanos, Turkey. The collision of two buses resulted in the deaths of 57 persons and injuries to 34.

August 1, Near Urleasca, Rom. A tractor pulling a trailer of field workers was struck by a train when the driver of the tractor disregarded warning lights at the crossing and started to cross the tracks; 12 persons were killed, and 8 were injured in the crash.

August 3, Near Hyderabad, India. A passenger bus fell into a swollen river; 37 persons lost their lives.

August 11, Near Baldian, India. A passenger bus that swerved to avoid hitting an oncoming car fell into a mountain gorge; at least 17 persons were killed, and 30 were injured in the plunge.

September 14, Bihar, India. An overloaded bus carrying more than 100 persons crashed into a ditch near Hajipur; at least 40 persons were killed.

November 10, Near Mirambeau, France. A tanker truck traveling on the Paris-to-Bordeaux highway burst into flames after its cargo of flammable methanol was ignited by a burning tire; at least 15 persons were killed, and some 47 were injured when trucks and cars slammed into the blazing truck.

November 10, Near Canterbury, England. A tour bus carrying 46 persons skidded off a rain-slicked highway and plunged down an embankment, apparently after hitting a van and spinning out of control; 10 persons lost their lives, and more than 35 were injured.

December 11, Maharashtra state, India. A train barreled into a school bus filled with children returning from a picnic; at least 32 students and 4 adults were killed in the crash.

December 11, Maharashtra state, India. A truck loaded with farm labourers skidded off a road; 22 persons perished, and 40 were injured.

December 27, Near Curitiba, Brazil. A bus and a sports car collided on the "highway of death" after the driver of the car attempted to pass on a curve; 41 persons, including both drivers, were killed, and 84 were injured.

Late December, Near Laingsburg, South Africa. An overloaded minibus collided with a truck; 19 persons lost their lives in the crash.

Earth Sciences

GEOLOGY AND GEOCHEMISTRY

In 1993 the U.S. National Academy of Sciences published the report *Solid-Earth Sciences and Society,* which recommended priorities for future research in the field while delineating the scientific challenges facing modern society. In its outlook the report echoed a theme that was recurring more and more often within the Earth sciences at the international level, namely, the reciprocal relationship between the Earth sciences and society concerning, on the one hand, the response of society to hazardous geologic processes and environmental changes and, on the other hand, the role of industrial society in extracting, using, and discarding materials and thereby changing geologic processes. In discussing priorities the report attempted to reduce the head-on conflict between basic science and societal needs by developing a "research framework" matrix with five major scientific topics set against the understanding of scientific processes and three objectives—resources, hazards, and environmental change. Overall, the report recommended studying processes while viewing the Earth as an integrated, dynamic system rather than as a collection of isolated components divided up among different disciplines.

A top-priority scientific topic continued to be mantle dynamics. Convection within the Earth's mantle, the slow movement of the Earth's hot, solid outer 2,900 km of rock, represents the Earth's engine at work and is the driving force for many near-surface geologic features. (A kilometre is about 0.62 mi.) The process was being investigated by means of geophysical and geochemical methods and computer models.

One debate was whether convective motions are mantle-wide, causing mixing through the complete mantle down to the core-mantle boundary at a depth of 2,900 km, or whether they are defined within two discrete layers that remain physically separate, one descending to a depth of 670 km and the other from this depth down to 2,900 km. At 670 km there exists a phase transition (where a less dense rock above is compressed into a more dense rock below) that had been investigated by geochemists in high-pressure laboratory experiments. In 1993 several investigators presented models in which massive transfer of material occurs across the 670-km boundary by means of "periodic flushing" of the upper mantle into the lower mantle. The most detailed were those of Paul Tackley and co-workers of the California Institute of Technology. Their calculations in three-dimensional spherical geometry combined with the phase transition at 670 km depth revealed a flow pattern containing cylindrical plumes and flat sheets. The dynamics are dominated by the accumulation of sheets of downwelling cold material (corresponding to subducted lithospheric slabs) just above 670 km, as the material is not dense enough to penetrate more deeply. When the volume of subducted material reaches a critical amount, it initiates a catastrophic flushing event, which drains the material into the lower mantle in broad cylindrical downwellings to the core-mantle boundary. The downwelling then shuts off completely and does not recur in exactly the same place. There are corresponding hot upwellings. Several flushing events are in progress at different places in the model at the same time.

Several distinctive rock masses involved in mantle convection have been characterized by the isotopic signatures, *i.e.,* the characteristic patterns of isotopes, of mantle rock fragments (xenoliths) brought to the surface in some lavas. One signature, called HIMU, was believed to represent recycled oceanic crust in the convecting mantle, while a component dubbed EMII was believed to represent enrichment by recycled sediments. During the year Erik H. Hauri of the Woods Hole (Mass.) Oceanographic Institution and co-workers reported that the trace-element patterns of four xenoliths from oceanic islands showed that they had reacted with carbonate-rich melts within the mantle. They concluded that a mechanism must exist for the transport of carbon dioxide through subduction zones and into convecting mantle. David H. Green of Australian National University, Canberra, and colleagues commented that these results "may have provided a critical linking piece in the jigsaw of mantle dynamics," adding that minute concentrations of carbon and hydrogen can exert huge geochemical effects on the melting behaviour of the mantle. Diamond samples containing solid carbon dioxide, which must have become trapped in the diamond at depths of 220–270 km—reported during the year by Marcus Schrauder and Oded Navon of Hebrew University, Jerusalem—could also be explained by the subduction of carbon-containing sediments at least to these depths.

Whereas the biosphere is linked through the carbon cycle to mantle convection, evolution in the biosphere may be linked to objects from space. The case had been advanced for a few years that the extraterrestrial object responsible for the impact crater at Chicxulub in Mexico's Yucatán Peninsula was also responsible for the mass extinction of dinosaurs and many other creatures 65 million years ago at the end of the Cretaceous Period (denoted in rock strata by the K-T boundary). In 1993 the idea gained support from a reexamination of gravity measurements over the basin by Virgil Sharpton of the Lunar and Planetary Institute, Houston, Texas, and co-workers. They placed the scar of the crater edge at 300 km in diameter, nearly twice as wide as the previous estimate. The figure, if correct, would make the Chicxulub crater the largest impact crater known on Earth and imply an extremely devastating effect on Cretaceous life for the impact. In fact, the catastrophic-impact extinction issue was complex and contained many unresolved problems. One persistent one was that of explaining how any animals at all managed to survive a catastrophe of such magnitude.

A new method of satellite radar interferometry was providing researchers with insights into the processes account-

UNIVERSITY OF LEEDS; PHOTOGRAPHY, COURTESY OF WHOI

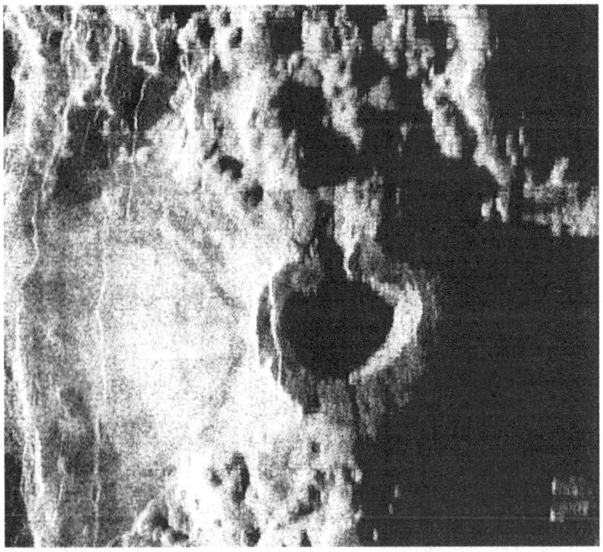

This small seafloor volcano is one of hundreds that line the crest of the Mid-Atlantic Ridge, where erupting lava is forming new ocean crust. The image, the sharpest ever made of such a formation, was taken by a sonar device towed behind a research ship.

ing for recent evidence that the Antarctic ice sheets formed and collapsed several times during the past few million years. During the year Richard Goldstein and colleagues of the Jet Propulsion Laboratory, Pasadena, Calif., applied the method to the study of fast-moving ice streams in Antarctica. A pair of radar images taken a few days apart provided a diagram that directly displayed relative surface motions for the time interval between images, with detection limits of 1.5 mm (0.06 in) for vertical motions and 4 mm (0.16 in) for horizontal motions. This information permitted measurements of rates of ice flow and mapping (with a resolution of 0.5 km) of the "grounding line," *i.e.,* the limit of ice lying on bedrock, since ungrounded ice is revealed by vertical motions of about two metres owing to tidal uplift. (A metre is about 3.3 ft.)

A possible link between the Antarctic fast ice streams and volcanoes, described during the year by Donald Blankenship of the University of Texas at Austin and Robin Bell of Lamont-Doherty Earth Observatory, Palisades, N.Y., suggested that volcanoes may affect the global climate in more than one way. The familiar atmospheric effect of volcanoes is exemplified by the millions of tons of sulfur dioxide, other gases, and dust lofted into the upper atmosphere by the 1991 eruption of Mt. Pinatubo in the Philippines—emissions that were being monitored and evaluated for their effects on global temperatures and the ozone hole. Blankenship and Bell identified an active volcano having a peak about 1.5 km beneath the ice near the head of one of the five fast-moving ice streams flowing from the centre of the West Antarctic Ice Sheet into the Ross Ice Shelf, which is afloat offshore from the grounding line. Aerial surveys across a circular depression in the ice measured its surface and thickness, and measurements of gravity and magnetic field combined with radar mapping of the ground underneath the ice sheet revealed a cone rising about 650 m above surrounding bedrock. The surface depression, about 50 m deep and 6 km in diameter, represents ice that has been melted. It was inferred that this meltwater softens the glacial sediments beneath the ice (the effect had been detected by seismology a few years earlier and confirmed by direct drilling in 1990). The subglacial layer of water-logged sediment lubricates the ice stream (50 km wide, 1 km deep, 500 km long), which is moving about 100 times as fast—up to two metres per day—as the adjacent ice sheet.

Five major ice streams make up about 90% of the outflow from the ice sheet, and their behaviour is critical to the stability or catastrophic collapse and melting of the Western Antarctic Ice Sheet. If heat from subglacial volcanoes increases the flow rates, causing retreat of the grounding line, then ice presently locked onto bedrock would be freed, perhaps leading to accelerated flow and disintegration of the ice sheet. Such a collapse would raise the sea level by about six metres, flooding many of the world's heavily populated cities. (PETER JOHN WYLLIE)

GEOPHYSICS

Sept. 30, 1993, marked the end of the 10-day festival in India honouring Ganesa, god of good fortune and new beginnings. Thousands of villagers in the southern Deccan Plateau fell into bed exhausted from the revelry; they had only hours to live. Shortly before 4 AM an earthquake of magnitude 6.4 turned thousands of mud-brick dwellings to dust and rubble, burying the inhabitants and killing more than 9,700. The epicentre was located between the major cities of Bombay and Hyderabad, nearly equidistant from the Arabian Sea and the Bay of Bengal. It was the most destructive shock to hit the region in 58 years, almost totally demolishing the villages of Killari, Latur, and Umarga.

One great earthquake, *i.e.,* an earthquake having a magnitude of 8 or greater, occurred during the year. The shock, of magnitude 8.0, struck south of Guam in the Mariana Islands on August 8, injuring 48 and causing minor damage in the centre of the island. On July 12 an earthquake of magnitude 7.8 rocked northern Japan. The quake and consequent tsunamis (seismic sea waves) killed at least 185 persons; the island of Okushiri, especially hard hit, was virtually destroyed. Residents of Klamath Falls, Ore., were surprised in mid-September by the first tremors ever recorded in the region. The activity consisted of a magnitude-5.8 shock and several large aftershocks, one of magnitude 5.5.

Several volcanic events resulted in tragedies. On February 2 the Mayon Volcano in the Philippines erupted in a series of explosions, culminating in the largest on February 12. The first blast was unexpected and sent a pyroclastic flow six kilometres down the Bonga Gully, where it spread over the fan deposited in the 1984 eruption, killing 68 persons and prompting the evacuation of tens of thousands. (One kilometre is about 0.62 mi.) Three main explosions produced towering ash clouds, the first and largest rising to 4.5 km.

The Galeras Volcano, only eight kilometres from Pasto, Colombia, a city of 300,000, has been the most active volcano in South America for the past 500 years. Accordingly it was chosen as the only South American volcano to be included in the UN International Decade of Natural Disaster Reduction program. In January a workshop comprising 50 scientists from Colombia and 40 scientists from 14 other countries was convened. Part of its program included field studies in which lava, gas, and rock samples were to be taken from the crater and temperatures, seismic activity, and other phenomena monitored. On January 14, while several scientists were in the crater and several more were on the rim, the volcano exploded, killing six; three tourists also died from the blast. In Ecuador on March 12 two volcanologists who had ascended the dome of Guagua Pichincha were killed instantly by a strong explosion.

The international Ocean Drilling Program (ODP) continued to explore the sea bottom and subsurface oceanic structures. On Leg 143 the scientific drilling ship *JOIDES Resolution* sailed from Honolulu westward above the submerged Mid-Pacific Mountains to a point approximately 18° N latitude, 180° longitude, where it occupied the first of six sites on its itinerary. The purpose of the expedition was to extract core samples of guyots and thereby discover the origin of these underwater mesas. In the 19th century Charles Darwin had outlined what he believed to be the evolutionary sequence of events leading to the formation of guyots. He postulated a progression from a volcanic island, which became surrounded by a coral reef, to the gradual erosion of the central island to leave an atoll encompassing a shallow lagoon. Modern researchers went one step further, theorizing that the lagoon gradually silts up and sinks beneath the surface as a flat-topped guyot.

The ODP team drilled two deep holes along with several shallow ones at the first site, called Allison Guyot. Cores of seafloor were obtained to a depth of 870 m through overlying limestone to a layer of abundant plant and marine-animal debris, indicating that the layer was once a marsh and reinforcing Darwin's hypothesis. (One metre is about 3.3 ft.) The next site, located about 21° N latitude, 175° E longitude, was a formation named Resolution Guyot after the drilling ship and its crew. There drilling established a single-leg depth record with a hole cored to 1,743.6 m through limestone and volcanic basalts. Two other sites were cored on the perimeter of Resolution Guyot in search of the expected reef, but none was found, suggesting an evolution different from that of Allison Guyot.

Hess Deep is located at the western extremity of the seafloor spreading centre between the Nazca and Cocos tectonic plates north of the Galápagos Islands in the eastern Pacific. It is notable because at this site the Mohorovicic discontinuity (Moho), the boundary between the Earth's crust and upper mantle, lies only a few hundred metres beneath the ocean bottom. On Leg 147 of the ODP, 13 holes were drilled and cores obtained that traversed the Moho with penetrations of less than 300 m. This core material was especially important because it represented the first direct evidence obtained from a fast-spreading mid-ocean ridge. Leg 147 was the first voyage of several to be made during the 1993–94 season in a coordinated effort to investigate the lower crust and upper mantle.

A number of organizations around the globe with goals similar to those of the ODP were exploring the subsurface structure of the continents. One, called COCORP (for Consortium for Continental Reflection Profiling) and begun in 1975 at Cornell University, Ithaca, N.Y., was funded principally by the U.S. National Science Foundation and included participants from universities, government agencies, and industry. As of 1993 it had assembled 12,000 km of seismic reflection data from across the U.S., in some areas delineating the Moho and noting its varying depths, elsewhere tracing faults to great depth and even discovering seismic reflectors in the mantle below the Moho. Since its beginnings COCORP had stimulated similar quests in as many as 30 other countries, including Canada, the U.K., France, Australia, Germany, and China. (RUTLAGE J. BRAZEE)

HYDROLOGY

For the U.S. the biggest news in hydrology during 1993 was the midyear flooding in the Midwest. Stalled weather patterns in the early and middle parts of the year produced long-term heavy rains over much of the Dakotas, Minnesota, Wisconsin, Iowa, Nebraska, Kansas, and parts of Illinois, Missouri, Colorado, and Wyoming. Coming on top of wet soils, the rains resulted in flows on the Mississippi River from April to July that broke records dating to the late 19th century. (See *Meteorology,* below).

The drought that had dogged the western U.S. came to a dramatic end over much of the area during the winter of 1992–93. High rains and a heavy snowpack in the mountains promised relief as the spring progressed. Early rains were as much as twice normal, and the snowpack in the Sierra Nevada range stood at its highest level in 50 years. Salt Lake City, Utah, reported record-high snowfall, and Yuma, Ariz., recorded rain at 840% of normal. Early in the year jubilant water officials in thirsty Los Angeles announced the end of seven years of water rationing. The end of the drought was not an unmixed blessing, however. The high rains early in the winter and melting snow in the southern Rocky Mountains later resulted in high waters and flooding in parts of Baja California and the southwestern U.S.

Heavy weather caused floods in China and Southeast Asia. Flooding that resulted from torrential summer rains in south-central China cut off road transport in the mountains. In a band from India's Punjab region across Nepal and into Bangladesh, monsoon rains in the latter part of the year brought swollen rivers and floods to low-lying lands in the major river basins. In India the overflowing Ravi and Beas rivers washed away bridges and stretches of highway. Although monsoon rains are a normal part of the mid- and late-year weather pattern, they were reported in some places to have hit with a ferocity not seen in decades.

Water-management activities during the year ranged from considerations of flood control to hydroelectric power production. After the floods in the U.S. Midwest had amply demonstrated that levees prevent floodplains from serving to control floods, the federal administration directed the U.S. Army Corps of Engineers to evaluate alternatives to levees for flood control in future planning. In the wake of flooding in India, the national government was excoriated in the press for "continuous neglect of flood prevention projects." China broke ground for what was to be the world's largest dam. Although not holding the largest reservoir or having the greatest height, the Three Gorges Dam on the Chang Jiang (Yangtze River) would be the largest hydropower producer in the world when it was finished in about a decade. Flood control was the major argument posed in favour of the structure, while siltation was expected to be the largest potential problem once the project had been completed.

Remote-sensing images taken by an Earth-orbiting satellite revealed a dry riverbed 850 km (530 mi) in length buried beneath the sands of Saudi Arabia and Kuwait. Segments of the channel had been noted previously as dry-streambed depressions known as wadis, but dunes cutting across the area had masked their identity as part of a single river system. According to Farouk El-Baz of Boston University, the so-called Kuwait River, which begins in Saudi Arabia's Hijaz Mountains, last flowed 5,000 to 11,000 years ago when the region experienced a wet period. Because the riverbed follows a geologic fault, the underlying rock might still contain water that could be accessed with wells driven hundreds of metres deep. (N. EARL SPANGENBERG)

METEOROLOGY

A combination of factors appeared to have contributed to the atmospheric circulation pattern responsible for 1993's extreme warm-season weather conditions over parts of the Northern Hemisphere. A prolonged El Niño/Southern Oscillation (ENSO) event (a pattern of anomalous oceanic and atmospheric behaviour in the tropical Pacific that appears every few years), which had begun in 1991, may have combined with natural climatic variability to produce the unusually strong and persistent upper-air pattern that dominated the April–September weather across North America and led, most disastrously, to copious rains and extensive flooding across the U.S. Midwest.

Prior to these persistent anomalies, the 1992–93 wet season in the far West provided excess precipitation that finally ended the long-term (1986–92) drought in California. (See *Hydrology,* above.) In the East a mid-March "storm of the century" dumped up to 60 cm (2 ft) of snow on the extreme southern Appalachians northeastward into lower elevations of the mid-Atlantic, where blizzard conditions were widespread but relatively short-lived. Prolonged blizzard conditions ranged from the south-central Appalachians northeastward across most of New England, where 60–150-cm (2–5-ft) snowfalls were common. At least 238 lives were lost in the storm, and an estimated $1 billion in property damage occurred.

The floods in the U.S. Midwest were preceded over much of the eastern half of the country by months of surplus precipitation, which saturated soils and set up high streamflow levels. That situation, combined with heavy spring and summer rainfall, created severe flooding throughout the northern half of the Mississippi drainage basin. Some locations in Iowa, Kansas, and Missouri measured more rain from April through July than normally fell in a full year. Many reservoirs overflowed; over two-thirds of the region's levees were overtopped or breached; and severe lowland flooding ensued. At some locations the Mississippi expanded to a width of nearly 11 km (7 mi) and the Missouri to 32 km (20 mi), while the confluence of the Mississippi and Missouri rivers shifted 32 km upstream of its previous position.

Two satellite images, one taken July 4 in the drought year of 1988 (top) and the other July 18, 1993 (bottom), give dramatic illustration of the extent of the midyear flooding in the St. Louis, Mo., area. The Mississippi River flows from the top centre of the photograph, with the Illinois River to its east, and the Missouri River flows from west to east. At some locations during the flooding, the Mississippi swelled to nearly 11 km (7 mi) in width and the Missouri to 32 km (20 mi).

PHOTOGRAPHS, EARTH OBSERVATION SATELLITE COMPANY

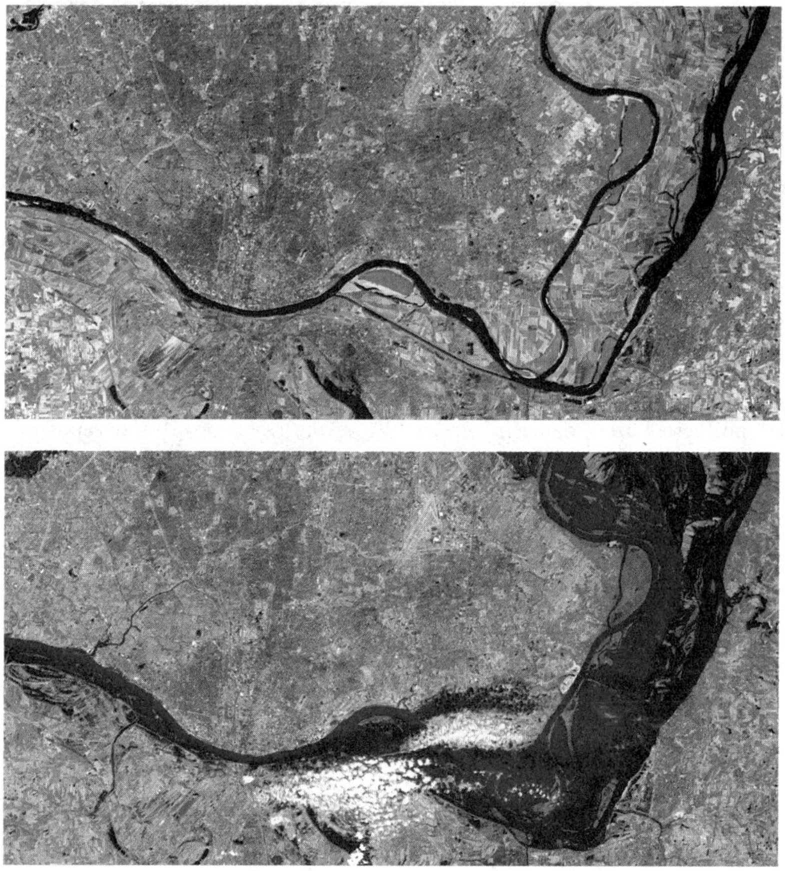

Almost 942 km (585 mi) of the Mississippi and the lower 861 km (535 mi) of the Missouri were closed to navigation for several weeks. At least 50 lives were lost owing to the flooding, and damages were estimated to be at least $12 billion.

In late October and early November, two waves of wildfires, many of them set by arsonists, raced across southern California, fueled by an abundance of dead timber and brush from six years of drought and driven by strong Santa Ana winds gusting as high as 113 km/h (70 mph). All told, the fires scorched at least 61,500 ha (152,000 ac), destroyed more than 1,000 homes, took 3 lives, and injured more than 150 people.

The 1993 Atlantic and Caribbean hurricane season adversely affected parts of northern South America, the Caribbean, and Central America. During early August resilient Tropical Storm Bret generated severe flooding across Colombia, Venezuela, Nicaragua, Costa Rica, and Honduras, killing hundreds of people and leaving thousands homeless. During mid-September heavy rains once again fell on parts of Central America, this time from Tropical Storm Gert. Thousands were left homeless from flooding, and dozens of lives were lost in Nicaragua and Honduras. As Gert emerged over the Gulf of Mexico, it strengthened into a hurricane and made landfall near Tuxpan, Mexico, with gusts to 200 km/h (120 mph). As much as 400 mm (16 in) of rain inundated the Mexican state of San Luis Potosí, producing severe flooding and mud slides that left over 100,000 individuals homeless and at least 14 dead.

Heavy precipitation also drenched much of central South America for the first two months of the year, although prolonged dryness continued in northeastern Brazil. By March sizable moisture deficits had spread through Paraguay, Uruguay, and Argentina. In contrast, unusually heavy April rains fell on Ecuador and northern Peru and covered most of central South America during May, alleviating the aforementioned moisture shortages.

Much of southern Europe and the Mediterranean began the year with very dry conditions, with some areas receiving only 10–30% of normal precipitation during the 1992–93 winter. Heavy April and May rains alleviated dryness in western Europe, but a dry July and August brought renewed moisture deficits to the region. In September and early October copious rains pelted southern Switzerland, southern France, and northern Italy, causing floods that took more than a dozen lives. In Greece, however, inadequate long-term rainfall dropped reservoir levels near Athens to dangerously low levels.

Through late July a subnormal rainy season dominated large sections of sub-Saharan Africa. In the next two months rainfall across the northern tier of the western Sahel increased significantly, with the greatest improvement across northern Senegal and southwestern Mauritania. Farther south, moisture deficits persisted throughout the rainy season across southern sub-Saharan Africa. A favourably moist rainy season through late July deteriorated during August and September across the eastern Sahel, leaving below-normal seasonal rainfall amounts in most areas. In southern Africa heavy precipitation at the start of the 1992–93 summer rainy season eased many of the drought-related effects from the previous year, but renewed moisture shortages were observed through much of the region late in the season. In late September and early October, however, heavy rains soaked southeastern sections of the region, providing a favourable start to the 1993–94 rainy season.

Monsoon rains generally began on schedule and in abundance across the Indian subcontinent. Heavy rains in late July and early August caused severe flooding in parts of

India, Nepal, and Bangladesh. The floods were one of the worst disasters on record in Nepal, with damage estimates of $20 million and possibly 3,000 deaths. Torrential warm-season rains also inundated China, Korea, and Japan. Fourteen tropical storms, most of which became typhoons, hit Japan; more than 2,500 mm (100 in) of rain inundated parts of Kyushu from June through August. Meanwhile, subnormal rainfall threatened crop production in Taiwan, and low reservoir levels forced the rationing of hydroelectric power.

Cyclone Kina, the worst storm to strike Fiji in 57 years, caused considerable damage to the South Pacific island nation in early January. In the western Pacific, Typhoon Koryn battered the Philippine island of Luzon in late June, abruptly ending a two-month dry spell and engendering landslides and floods. In early October, Tropical Storm Flo, the 25th storm to hit the Philippines in 1993, dumped copious rains on northern Luzon, damaging up to 10% of the rice crop and taking dozens of lives. In Australia the year commenced with very wet weather across New South Wales and Victoria, while large moisture deficits accumulated across Queensland through most of the 1992–93 austral summer rainy season. Torrential late January rains across northern Australia and southwestern Indonesia created flooding and forced a quarter of a million people to flee their homes. Beginning in September heavy early-season rains covered eastern and southeastern Australia and continued through October. (ELBERT W. FRIDAY, JR.)

This article updates the *Macropædia* article CLIMATE AND WEATHER.

OCEANOGRAPHY

In 1993 the World Ocean Circulation Experiment (WOCE) neared the midpoint of its 1990–97 program of observations intended to span entire ocean basins. Planning for WOCE began in the early 1980s when researchers realized that changes in ocean circulation might hold the key to predicting climate. One example of the new results that were emerging from the experiment related to the Pacific-wide distribution of carbon-14.

Cosmic rays from space continually convert a very small amount of the stable isotope carbon-12 present in the atmosphere into the radioactive isotope ^{14}C. The half-life of ^{14}C—the time it takes half the atoms in a given sample to decay—is about 5,730 years. A buried or otherwise isolated sample of carbon that has been out of contact with the atmosphere for several thousand years thus will have much less ^{14}C than a sample in contact with the atmosphere. The age of the isolated sample can be determined through measurement of its ^{14}C content. Oceanographers use ^{14}C measurements to determine the time that waters below the surface of the ocean have been away from the atmosphere. Some of the more interesting WOCE results of 1993 concerned such measurements in the Pacific Ocean.

On the basis of ^{14}C content, researchers believe that the deep water of the north Pacific has been away from the atmosphere for about 1,500 years. This water is a mixture of water that was last at the surface around Antarctica or even farther away in the far north Atlantic. The traditional view of Pacific deep circulation is that the oldest water (the water below the surface for the longest time) is to be found deep in the northwestern corner of the Pacific, but WOCE ^{14}C measurements during the year surprisingly changed this picture. The oldest Pacific waters were found at depths of thousands of metres (but not at the bottom) in two east-west transpacific bands about 1,000 km (620 mi) wide, one on either side of the equator. The water in the very northern part of the Pacific is not the oldest; its ^{14}C content suggested that it had been in contact with the atmosphere more recently than that in the transpacific bands.

The term El Niño refers to a recurring event in which the cold, nutrient-rich waters off the west coast of South America are replaced by warmer, relatively nutrient-poor water, with consequent catastrophic failure of coastal fisheries. Researchers gradually realized that El Niño is but one part of a Pacificwide pattern of oceanic and atmospheric change now called the El Niño/Southern Oscillation (ENSO). Predicting ENSO events is of global economic importance. A number of researchers had successfully predicted the 1986 and 1991 events, but predictions made in the fall of 1993 ranged widely, from another El Niño to an abnormally cold east Pacific.

One problem in developing predictive El Niño models has been that, because ENSO events typically occur only once or twice a decade, historical meteorologic records cover a fairly small number of events. Typically, ENSO events include abnormally intense rainfall at equatorial Pacific islands. During the year researchers reported that the concentration of the isotope oxygen-18 in a core of coral grown over the previous 96 years at an island in the west Pacific mirrors the index of rainfall over the central Pacific. The condensation of water vapour during atmospheric convection preferentially separates out oxygen isotopes of different weight into the rainfall; consequently, the ^{18}O content of the ocean surface water, and hence of corals growing in it, is lower during

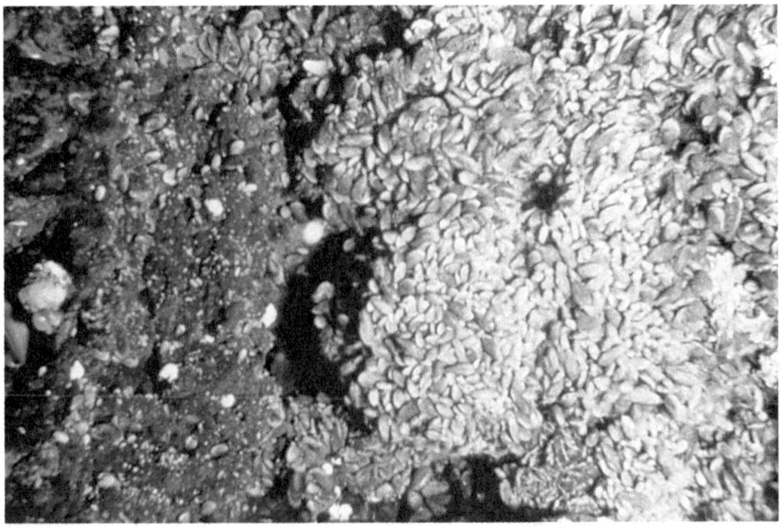

CHARLES LANGMUIR—LAMONT-DOHERTY EARTH OBSERVATORY

Yellow mussels thrive around a thermal vent, part of a newly discovered field of volcanic hot springs on the Mid-Atlantic Ridge near the Azores. The mussels feed on bacteria that metabolize sulfur from the vent.

times of abnormally intense rainfall. The coral record may actually be a better measure of rainfall averaged over the tropical Pacific than would be an island rain-gauge record because ocean currents cause the ^{18}O content of the coral to reflect rainfall conditions over a broad region rather than just where the coral grows. Such work was expected to allow researchers to look back over many more ENSO events to see if their frequency and duration have changed over time.

Relaxation of Cold War tensions provided oceanographers with an unexpected new source of data. They gained access to the U.S. Navy's global acoustic undersea surveillance system, originally designed to detect and track submarines, in order to listen for signals as diverse as whale vocalizations and seafloor volcanoes and earthquakes. The global coverage afforded by this system would provide whale researchers with a basin-scale picture of numbers and locations of whales at any given time. Earth scientists would enjoy greatly increased ability to monitor seismic activity under the ocean, particularly the frequent but relatively low-level activity that is believed to occur along with volcanism at ocean-ridge crests, the sites of seafloor spreading.

Seafloor earthquakes sometimes generate extremely destructive ocean waves called tsunamis. Because seismic waves travel faster through the Earth's crust than do the water waves of the tsunami, researchers who monitor the world for earthquakes on the seafloor or near the coast often can warn coastal residents of a possible tsunami several hours or more in advance. But they cannot tell with certainty whether a particular earthquake has, in fact, generated a large tsunami. In 1993 researchers suggested that the traditional measure of earthquake intensity underestimates the size of those earthquakes that release their energy relatively slowly and thus have hidden potential for generating tsunamis. They argued that the Nicaraguan earthquake of Sept. 2, 1992, which generated only mild ground motions at the coast but was followed by large tsunami waves, was one such slow earthquake, and they noted similar historical occurrences around the Pacific. Their work suggested that a change in the way earthquakes are monitored could provide more certain tsunami warnings than are presently available.

(MYRL C. HENDERSHOTT)

See also Disasters; Energy; Environment; Life Sciences; Mining; Space Exploration.

This article updates the *Macropædia* articles ATMOSPHERE; DINOSAURS; The EARTH; The EARTH SCIENCES; EARTHQUAKES; GEOCHRONOLOGY; The HYDROSPHERE; OCEANS; PLATE TECTONICS; RIVERS; VOLCANISM.

Economic Affairs

Economic growth in the world remained sluggish in 1993. Partial International Monetary Fund (IMF) estimates and other economic indicators available at year's end pointed to a growth rate of 2.2%. This represented a small improvement on the previous year and meant below-average growth for the fourth year running. The continuation of the global recession was largely attributable to declining growth rates in Europe (excluding the U.K.) and Japan. Falling output in these countries neutralized relatively faster economic growth in the Asian countries, the U.S., and, to a lesser extent, the U.K. Although government policy in Europe, particularly Germany, became increasingly supportive of economic growth during 1993, large public-sector deficits and the need to maintain counterinflationary policies constrained the speed of interest-rate cuts. As the change in policy in Europe came late in the year, it did not make much of an impact on the economic outcome. As 1993 drew to a close, however, there were encouraging indicators that the low point in the current economic cycle had been passed and that most countries would grow faster in 1994.

Reflecting the continuing economic adjustments in the developed world, once again those countries' overall performance lagged behind growth rates in the less developed world. Thus, the gross national product (GNP) of the developed countries rose by an estimated 1.1%, down from the previous year's anemic 1.7%. By contrast, the economies of the less developed countries (LDCs) grew by an estimated 6.1%, against 5.8% in 1992.

The strongest performance among the developed countries was in the U.S., with an estimated 2.8% gross domestic product (GDP) growth, slightly faster than the previous year. It was followed by Canada, Australia, and the U.K. By and large, these countries entered into a downturn ahead of the others and were recovering, thanks to lower interest rates in place since 1992 or earlier. In contrast, in Germany and Japan the economy went into the downturn later and was slow in emerging from it. In fairness, the German Bundesbank's policy became less restrictive in response to moderating inflationary pressures and measures introduced by the government to stabilize the public-sector deficit. However, it was not until the widening of currency bands, from 2.5% to 15%, within the European exchange-rate mechanism (ERM) in August that interest rates were reduced significantly in Germany. The wider bands meant the breakup of the old, rigid ERM, and the action implied a suspension of the Bundesbank's obligations to support the other European currencies within the ERM. (Such intervention added to the already buoyant money stock and made it harder to combat inflation.) France, Belgium, and The Netherlands all followed high-interest-rate policies aimed at maintaining the agreed value of their currencies against the Deutsche Mark within the ERM and, as a result, those countries experienced prolonged recession and rising unemployment. Japan, by contrast, pursued a progressively stimulatory fiscal and monetary policy but could not escape sliding deeper into recession. Continuing corporate and household adjustment to the steep fall in stock and asset prices in 1991 and 1992, together with attendant uncertainty and a rise in the Japanese yen, led to zero GDP growth—the worst performance since the 1974 oil crisis.

In eastern Germany the economic recovery that had started in 1992 continued, leading to an estimated GDP growth of about 6%. However, unemployment remained a serious problem. Likewise, modest growth took place in most Central and Eastern European countries, consolidating the recovery that had started in 1992. Poland, Hungary, and the Czech Republic performed better than Bulgaria and Slovakia. The latter was experiencing adjustment problems following the dissolution of Czechoslovakia. In the former Soviet Union, economic decline continued. Development in the dynamic Asian economies (Hong Kong, South Korea, Malaysia, Singapore, Taiwan, and Thailand) recovered from a slight slowdown in 1992, and GDP expanded by 6.5% (up from 5.7% in 1992). The main reason for the upturn was recovery in the U.S. and continued expansion in China, which had become an important market for their exports. In Latin America growth that had started in 1991–92 after a decade of stagnation continued in 1993 but at a slower pace than the year before.

Against the background of another year of low global economic growth, many components of demand either remained flat or declined compared with the previous year. Private consumption was the most buoyant element and expanded by an estimated 1.3% in the developed world. Even so, it grew more slowly than the previous year's 1.8%.

Table I. Real Gross Domestic Products of Selected OECD Countries

% annual change

Country	1989	1990	1991	1992	1993*
United States	2.5	1.2	−0.7	2.6	2.8
Japan	4.7	4.8	4.0	1.3	0
Germany†	3.6	5.7	1.7	1.9	−2.3
France	4.3	2.5	0.7	1.4	−1.1
United Kingdom	2.1	0.4	−2.2	−0.5	1.8
Canada	2.4	−0.2	−1.7	0.7	2.7
Italy	2.9	2.1	1.3	0.9	−0.4
All developed countries	3.2	2.3	0.5	1.7	1.1
Seven major countries above	3.1	2.3	0.4	1.8	1.30
European Community	3.5	3.0	0.8	1.1	−0.20

*Estimated.
†From 1991 figures include former East Germany.
Sources: International Monetary Fund, *World Economic Outlook*, October 1993; *The Economist.*

A relatively robust increase of nearly 3% in the U.S. and a rise of more than 2% in Canada were offset by declining private consumption in Japan as well as in Germany and other European countries. Consumer confidence appeared to have been weakened in many countries by a squeeze on purchasing power, fear of unemployment, and a desire to reduce high personal debts incurred before the recession. The weakness of domestic demand, a slackening of industrial capacity, and relatively high real interest rates reduced the incentives for business to invest. During 1993 real private nonresidential fixed investment in the developed countries was estimated to have fallen faster than the previous year (down 5.5%, compared with a 3.8% decline in 1992). Once again the U.S., reflecting its well-established recovery, went against the trend and registered an 8% gain. In Japan and Europe (except the U.K.) business investment fell. Likewise, in most developed countries the need to reduce the public-sector deficits led to cancellation or deferral of many public programs. Japan, unburdened by such constraints, went against the trend and introduced several public works programs to stimulate its flagging economy. As world trade grew by only 3% during 1993 (4.6% in 1992), external demand contributed to a smaller proportion of economic growth in the world, particularly in some developed countries such as Germany and Japan that relied heavily on exports.

Against a background of weak economic activity, high and rising unemployment, and declining oil prices, the inflation rate continued to moderate during 1993. In the industrialized world it slowed down to an annual increase of 2.7%, compared with 3.3% in the previous year. This was the best performance in more than 20 years. In the LDCs the average inflation rate accelerated to 44% from 39% in 1992, but the average was influenced by very high inflation in a few countries. The median inflation was a more modest 7%. Thanks to structural reforms and stabilization programs, inflation in most LDCs remained low. In Turkey, while inflation was stable at around 65%, it remained very high on account of fiscal deficits. Likewise, in many Central and Eastern European countries, where basic structural reforms were still being implemented to complete the transition to free-market economies, inflation remained high. In Bulgaria and Romania, for instance, it was heading for 90% and 165%, respectively, while in Poland, Hungary, and the Czech Republic and Slovakia it was more modest, between 16% and 40%. Hyperinflationary conditions were experienced in the former Soviet Union, however. While there were no reliable estimates in late 1993, the outcome was likely to be worse than the previous year's 2,000%. With the exception of Brazil, where annual inflation was running at about 900%, Latin-American countries made considerable progress in moderating their inflation rates, although they remained at around 12%. In Asia inflation was stable, between 6% and 7%, but it varied across the region. It was the highest among the relatively less developed countries such as Thailand and Malaysia, while in Singapore and Taiwan it was comparable to the European levels. China, which was experiencing rapid economic growth rates, was showing signs of overheating, with inflation in urban areas running at 10–15%.

In most developed countries unemployment continued to rise in 1993 but at a slower rate than the year before. This was partly a result of reducing interest rates too cautiously, which did succeed in keeping inflation at bay but delayed economic recovery and added to unemployment. The U.S. went against the trend of rising unemployment—the proportion of the labour force that was unemployed was 6.8% in October, compared with 7.4% a year before. Elsewhere during the year, it rose by between 0.2 and 4.6 percentage points. In the industrialized countries as a whole, unemployment rates rose from 7.9% to an estimated 8.6%. This meant that during 1993 an average of 35 million people were out of work, of which nearly 30% were in North America and 60% in Europe. Spain (with over 23%) had the highest rate of unemployment in Europe, followed by France and Italy. Because unemployment usually begins to fall well after a recovery is under way, most observers expected unemployment to continue to rise in Europe well into the second half of 1994, albeit at a slower pace. The U.S. and the U.K. were expected to see steady drops in the numbers of people out of work.

Interest rates remained stable in the U.S. and the U.K. from autumn 1992 or early 1993. In Japan rates declined to 1.75%, a historically low level. Across continental Europe, the high interest rates declined appreciably only after the European currency turmoil in August and the attendant widening of the currency bands. Despite these reductions, it could be argued that interest rates remained high in real terms, particularly against the background of continuing recession, and did not stimulate the economy sufficiently.

In contrast to an easing of monetary policy, which reduced the cost of borrowing, the fiscal stance was tightened in most developed countries. This meant increased tax burdens and reduced government spending, which were in conflict with the overall objective of encouraging economic recovery. Given the spiraling public-sector deficits, however, in the interests of sound money and financial stability, unpleasant but necessary measures were introduced. In the U.S., for example, Pres. Bill Clinton's administration put forward a complex package of tax and expenditure changes of $500 billion, which was projected to reduce the deficit over five years. In the U.K. the largest tax increase in real terms since 1945, amounting to £10.6 billion, was announced in March, but its implementation was deferred by a year so as not to stall the fragile recovery. In France and Germany supplementary budgets were introduced to cut planned public-spending levels and contain the budget deficits. Japan was the only developed country where both monetary policy and fiscal policy were relaxed during 1993. Most developed countries faced increasing public-sector spending in the years ahead as an aging population put greater demands on the social welfare systems. (*See* Special Report.)

NATIONAL ECONOMIC POLICIES

Developed Market Economies. *United States.* Revisions to the U.S. economic statistics showed that the 1990–91 recession was not as deep as had been thought previously. GDP fell by 1.6% instead of the 2.2% originally reported. Moreover, the recovery had been stronger than anticipated but still remained subdued compared with previous upturns. During 1993 economic activity gained momentum, and real GDP grew at an annualized rate of 2.8% in the third quarter, well above the anemic rates of 0.8% and 1.9% in the first and second quarters, respectively. Had it not been for the summer floods in the Midwest, growth in the third quarter would have been stronger. With economic indicators pointing to stronger activity in the closing months of the year, GDP for the year grew by an estimated 2.8%, marginally faster than in the previous year. Despite this sluggish recovery pace, the U.S. economic performance during 1993 was better than that of any other major industrial country.

Among the various factors that underpinned economic expansion in 1993, capital spending, housing investment, and consumer spending were the most potent. As corporate profitability improved sharply in response to steps taken previously that reduced payrolls and repaired balance sheets by reducing debts and scaling back loss-making activities, business confidence recovered, boosting investment in equipment and buildings by over 7%.

Housing investment strengthened as consumers were less burdened with debt payments than they had been in recent years. This was partly because they had repaid large amounts of debt and partly because low interest rates made it easier to carry existing debts. Both housing starts and permits rose strongly in the second half and, for the year as a whole, were estimated to have risen by around 8%.

Despite continuing job insecurity and higher taxes introduced by the Clinton administration, consumer spending gained strength, rising 4.2% in the third quarter, compared with 3.4% in the second and 0.8% in the first. For the year as a whole, it rose by an estimated 3%—up from 2.3% the year before. Spending on automobiles, furniture, and household goods was strong, as was spending on services. As a result of higher spending, total consumer debt outstanding rose by around 4%.

Production and capacity use both began to move up in late 1992 and continued to improve during 1993. Output reached record levels in the autumn as industrial production grew by an overall 4% during the year. Capacity utilization stabilized at 81.6% in the autumn, the highest level since October 1990.

Government spending in real terms went against the general trend and weakened. In the third quarter, for instance,

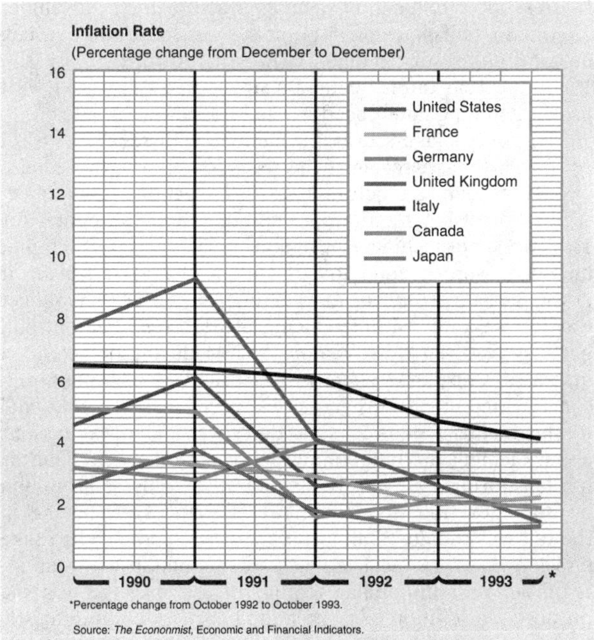

*Percentage change from October 1992 to October 1993.

Source: *The Econonmist*, Economic and Financial Indicators.

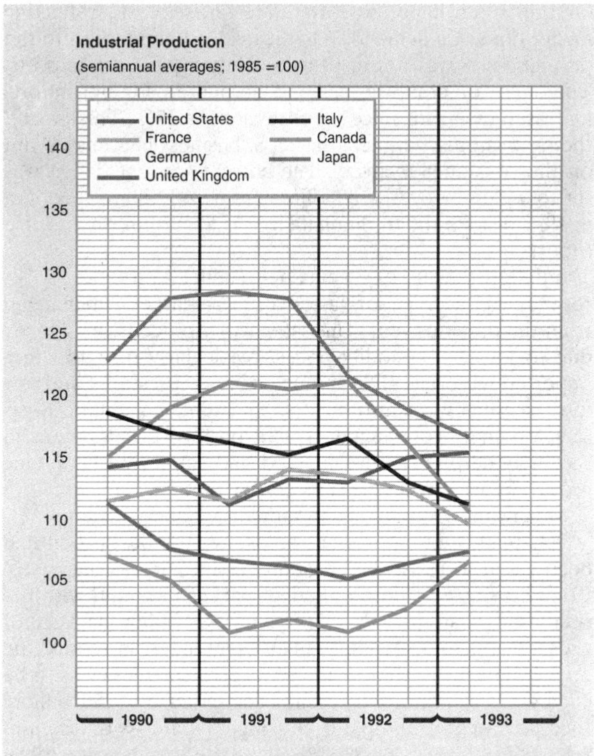

Source: International Monetary Fund, *International Financial Statistics*.

it fell by 1.1% after picking up from a 6.4% drop in the opening quarter. For the year as a whole, it declined by an estimated 2.5%. Defense spending was a notable casualty, with an 8% fall reflecting reduced defense commitment following the ending of the Cold War. Nondefense spending was static and would have declined but for higher spending by state and local authorities on buildings and highway construction.

The job market, however, was slow to respond to the economic upturn. Because of competitive pressures, U.S. companies were still reluctant to increase staff levels. Many companies continued to lay off workers or to turn increasingly to temporary and part-time employees. (*See* LABOUR-MANAGEMENT RELATIONS: *Special Report*.) Unemployment stood at 6.8% in October, down from 7.4% a year before but barely changed from the spring and summer levels. It fell to 6.5% in November and edged down to end the year at 6.4%. Most of the job gains were in the service sector rather than in manufacturing, where employment fell back a little. Productivity, which rose strongly during the recession, appeared to have run out of steam, particularly in the all-important services sector. During the second half of the year, productivity growth was negative. The sluggish labour market restrained wage increases, raising concern about the outlook for consumer spending. Average weekly earnings in the autumn were 2.7% higher than a year before. At that level they were only marginally above the inflation rate and thus did not confer a significant real increase in employee purchasing power.

In the short term, worries about unemployment were linked with the growing trade deficit, which had become a political issue. During the first nine months of the year, the trade deficit averaged $10.2 billion a month and was heading for a deficit of $125 billion, compared with $96 billion in 1992. During the same period, export growth was a modest 3.1%, owing in part to the downturn in Europe and Japan but also to the relatively high value of the dollar. Imports, on the other hand, rose by an estimated 9%, reflecting higher domestic demand. What provided ammunition to the protectionists was not just the absolute increase in imports. The share of domestic demand accounted for by imports had risen by a fifth since the recession, to 25%. This meant, the protectionists argued, that U.S. business had missed out on the consumer recovery. The current-account deficit was set to widen to over $100 billion from $66 billion recorded in 1992 despite the traditional large U.S. surplus on invisible exports.

Inflation during 1993 remained stable. Consumer prices rose by an average of just over 3%—largely unchanged from the previous year. This satisfactory outcome was partly due to lower commodity prices, particularly oil and other imported materials. The absence of wage pressures and low interest rates were also factors. The subdued inflation was seen by many commentators as a positive development in that it underpinned real demand and supported economic growth by improving business confidence.

Meanwhile, both fiscal and monetary policy remained relatively tight. During previous recoveries the tax burden had been eased to assist the economy; in 1933 it was increased. Congress passed Clinton's budget package, though with the smallest of majorities. The five-year, $500 billion package of tax increases and spending cuts was intended to reduce the budget deficit. To achieve the reduction, spending was to be cut by $255 billion and revenue increased by $240 billion. Income taxes went up for the higher paid, with the top rate rising to 36% from 31%, backdated to January 1993. Tax relief on pensions was reduced and the wage ceiling on Medicare payments removed. The corporate tax rate went up from 34% to 35%. A new gasoline tax of 4.3 cents per gallon was imposed from October 1.

Unlike previous years, there was no stimulus to the economy from lower interest rates. As the money supply was subdued and grew well within the target ranges, there was no change to the Federal Reserve Bank's (Fed's) discount rate. Thus, commercial banks' prime rates remained unchanged at 6%. Some critics thought the real rate of interest rates was too high—nearly twice as high as it had been in previous recoveries. The financial markets thought otherwise and feared the Fed might gently raise short-term rates in the new year to prevent faster growth from pushing up inflation.

Table II. Consumer Prices in OECD Countries

% change in preceding year

Country	1989	1990	1991	1992	1993*
United States	4.8	5.4	4.2	3.0	2.6
Japan	2.3	3.1	3.3	1.7	1.9
Germany†	2.8	2.7	3.5	4.0	4.2
France	3.7	3.4	3.2	2.4	2.2
Italy	6.6	6.1	6.5	5.3	5.0
United Kingdom	7.8	9.5	5.9	3.7	1.1
Canada	5.0	4.8	5.6	1.5	1.7
Austria	2.5	3.3	3.3	4.0	3.4
Belgium	3.0	3.4	3.2	2.4	3.2
Denmark	4.8	2.7	2.4	2.1	1.2
Finland	6.6	6.1	4.3	2.9	2.1
Greece	13.8	20.4	19.5	15.9	14.6
Iceland	20.3	15.9	6.8	3.6	1.4
Ireland	4.0	3.3	3.2	3.1	1.4
Luxembourg	3.3	3.7	3.1	3.2	5.0
Netherlands, The	1.1	2.5	3.9	3.7	2.0
Norway	4.6	4.1	3.4	2.3	2.2
Portugal	12.6	13.4	11.4	8.9	5.8
Spain	6.8	6.7	5.9	5.9	4.6
Sweden	6.4	10.5	9.3	2.3	4.5
Switzerland	3.2	5.4	5.8	4.0	3.5
Turkey	63.1	60.3	66.0	70.0	71.2
Australia	7.6	7.3	3.2	4.0	1.9
New Zealand	5.7	6.1	2.6	1.0	1.3
OECD Total	5.9	5.8	5.2	4.0	1.8

*Twelve-month rate of change in August 1993.
†From 1991 figures include former East Germany.
Source: OECD, *Main Economic Indicators*.

Table III. Standardized Unemployment Rates in Selected Developed Countries

(% total labour force)

Country	1989	1990	1991	1992	1993
United States	5.2	5.4	6.6	7.4	6.8*
Japan	2.3	2.1	2.1	2.2	2.7*
Germany	5.6	4.8	4.2	4.6	5.6*
France	9.4	8.9	9.4	10.3	11.8†
United Kingdom	7.2	6.8	8.7	9.9	10.2*
Canada	7.5	8.1	10.2	11.2	11.1*
Italy	12.0	10.3	9.9	10.5	11.7*
All developed countries	6.2	6.1	6.8	7.5	7.9‡
Seven major countries above	5.7	5.6	6.3	6.9	7.0‡
European Community	9.0	8.4	8.6	9.5	10.7‡

*October, national definition. †September, national definition. ‡August.
Sources: OECD, *Main Economic Indicators*, October 1993; *The Economist*.

United Kingdom. The U.K. economy pulled out of the recession during 1993 ahead of its European neighbours, but the pace of recovery remained sluggish and uneven, with some loss of momentum in the closing months of the year. It appeared that GDP had grown by about 2%, the best performance since 1989 and well above earlier estimates. The recovery was principally due to lower interest rates following the withdrawal of sterling from the ERM in September 1992. The return of economic growth had been underpinned by a rise in private consumption, higher industrial output, a modest recovery in housing activity, and improvement in corporate profitability. Inflation remained subdued, despite the sizable devaluation of sterling.

Following the ERM debacle, short-term interest rates were progressively cut and additional stimulus was provided by a package of measures introduced in the closing months of 1992. The base rate was cut a further 1% to 6% early in 1993 as new doubts emerged about the pace of the recovery. By that time the effective exchange rate had fallen by nearly 15%, giving British exporters a competitive advantage. The new chancellor of the Exchequer, Kenneth Clarke (*see* BIOGRAPHIES), had not found it necessary to change the policy stance he inherited from his predecessor, Norman Lamont. The exchange rate had remained broadly stable at close to $1.50 and DM 2.50, and in the absence of inflationary pressures, there was no change in monetary policy. Interest rates remained unchanged at 6% until November 23, when a half-percentage-point cut was sanctioned a week before Clarke's first budget. However, a further cut of 0.5–1% in the near future seemed a strong possibility in view of fiscal tightening announced in the budget a week later.

The policy makers faced a dilemma with regard to fiscal policy. Partly as a result of the recession and partly because of higher spending before the 1992 elections, the public-sector borrowing requirement spiraled, and the deficit for 1993 was approaching £50 billion, or 8% of GDP. Urgent measures were needed to control the deficit and bring it down, but the recovery at the time of the March budget was too weak to risk introducing higher taxes. Lamont had partially resolved this dilemma by introducing deferred tax increases, to become effective in April 1994. The main reason for announcing tax increases in advance was to signal to the financial markets that the government was serious about tackling the burgeoning public-sector deficit. The tax burden during 1993–94 was increased by only £500 million by nonindexation of income tax allowances. The sting in the tail was the £6.7 billion tax increase announced to take effect from April 1994, rising to £10.3 billion the year after. The most unpopular feature of the package was the proposed imposition of value-added tax (VAT) on domestic heating bills. Representing 1.5% of GDP, the forthcoming

Kiichi Miyazawa (centre), prime minister of Japan, acted as host of the meeting of the Group of Seven nations held in Tokyo in July. The leaders agreed to provide additional aid to Russia, represented at the meeting by Pres. Boris Yeltsin, and to work for lower trade barriers and faster economic growth.
AFP

changes were the biggest tax increase in real terms since 1945. The future tightening of fiscal policy was accompanied by a squeeze on public-sector spending, including a virtual pay freeze in the public sector. In his first budget (the budget date was brought forward from March 1994 to November 1993 to bring together decisions on spending and revenues), Clarke set out to reduce the public-sector deficit more quickly than had previously been planned and added another £1,750,000,000 tax to what was in the pipeline. In a bold move he also announced a £10 billion cut from previously published public-spending plans for the next three years. However, it was not immediately clear where all the cuts were coming from.

Early in the year the recovery was led by a surge in exports, reflecting the competitiveness of British products. In the opening quarter total exports rose by over 7% in real terms compared with the same period a year before, but in the summer the growth rate slowed to 3.5%. During the autumn the trade deficit fell unexpectedly, as exports strengthened and imports slowed. However, this was not sufficient to reverse the underlying deterioration. On the basis of incomplete data, export volumes were estimated to have grown by 5% for the year as a whole. Imports, on the other hand, grew steadily at an average rate of 6%. As a result, the trade gap widened and was heading for a total deficit of £14 billion, the highest since 1991.

Industrial production reflected the changes in total demand, external and domestic. Early in the year it grew strongly and was at its highest since October 1990. By autumn the growth rate had become erratic. For the year as a whole, industrial production was estimated to have grown by under 2%. There was a marginal improvement in capacity utilization and, not surprisingly, business investment remained flat. Total investment had risen by an estimated 0.6%, largely as a result of increased government investment and higher housing starts. Total construction output had fallen for the third consecutive year and declined by 1.25%.

As external demand faltered, consumer spending took over as the main engine of growth. During 1993 it rose by an estimated 2.5%, led by retail sales. The strength of consumer spending was somewhat surprising against a background of continuing job insecurity and high personal debts relative to incomes. However, consumers sensed that the worst of the recession was over. Lower interest rates meant that repayment of mortgages and other debts absorbed a lower proportion of household budgets, so a higher proportion of incomes was spent. The savings ratio, which had risen sharply in 1992 to a high of 12.5%, fell back to an average 10.5%. Car sales also rose sharply in response to lower interest rates and the abolition of the car tax in 1992. New registrations showed a year-on-year gain in excess of 12%. Partly as a result of higher car sales, total new credit increased. As new borrowing exceeded repayments, total outstanding consumer debt rose.

Another surprising feature of the U.K. economy in 1993 was an unexpected decline in unemployment, which began in February. Usually unemployment continued to rise for six to nine months after output began to recover. This reduction in the number of unemployed was, at least in part, a reaction to deep job cutting in late 1992. In November the total number of unemployed stood at 2,810,000, an unemployment rate of 10%, the lowest since August 1992.

Despite the devaluation in 1992, inflation remained subdued and was well within the government's target, thanks to low oil and other commodity prices as well as strong competition in the retail trade. In November the annual rate of inflation unexpectedly slowed down to 1.4%, the level it stood in early summer, after rising by 1.8% in the run-up to autumn. The underlying index, excluding mortgage interest repayments, slowed down to 2.8% from 3.3% and was well within the government's 1–4% target.

Given the high levels of unemployment and subdued inflation, growth in average earnings decelerated to under 3.5% in the third quarter, compared with over 4% at the beginning of the year. However, the slowdown in earnings was in response to lower inflation, not ahead of it. This meant that the real earnings of those who remained employed had risen in real terms throughout the recession. Perhaps this was the only positive feature of the longest recession since World War II.

Japan. Hopes for an upturn in the Japanese economy, which had declined for nearly two years, were short-lived. Despite stimulatory measures introduced by the government in 1992 and again in April 1993, economic recovery stalled.

Table IV. Changes in Output in the Less Developed Countries

% annual change in real gross domestic product

Area	1989	1990	1991	1992	1993*
All less developed countries	4.1	3.7	4.5	5.8	6.1
Oil-exporting countries	5.0	4.1	4.1	5.9	2.9
Non-oil-exporting countries	3.8	3.6	4.6	5.7	7.0
Africa	3.6	1.9	1.6	0.4	1.6
Asia	5.5	5.7	6.1	7.8	8.7
Middle East and Europe	3.6	4.2	2.4	7.8	3.4
Western Hemisphere	1.6	0.3	3.3	2.5	3.4

*Estimated. Source: International Monetary Fund, *World Economic Outlook*, October 1993.

A rapid rise in the value of the yen, combined with an exceptionally wet and cool summer, pushed the economy back onto a downward track. Continuing adjustment by the corporate and finance sectors (and to a lesser extent by households) to the sharp fall in stock prices and real estate prices that had occurred in 1991 and 1992 was also a drag on the economy. The net effect of this adjustment process was reduced willingness by corporations to invest and greater caution by financial institutions in lending, particularly for high-risk projects. It also reduced consumers' propensity to spend.

As a result of these adverse developments, real GNP fell by 0.5% in the second quarter, reversing a similar gain in the opening quarter. The new government of Prime Minister Morihiro Hosokawa (*see* BIOGRAPHIES), which ended 38 years of continuous Liberal-Democratic Party rule in August, acted swiftly and introduced a new packet of stimulatory measures in mid-September. The Bank of Japan quickly cut its discount rate by 0.75% to 1.75%—a larger-than-expected cut—to curb the strength of the yen and improve confidence. However, the September measures came too late to influence the outcome in 1993. On the basis of incomplete data in December, the economy remained flat for most of the second half and was heading for zero growth in 1993—the worst outcome since the oil crisis in 1974.

Against the background of sluggish economic activity and low inflationary pressures, the government and the Bank of Japan pursued expansionary policies. Since April 1992 four packages of stimulatory measures had been introduced, some spending had been brought forward into the first half of the fiscal year, and various new public-works programs had been planned. A 13.2 trillion-yen package was announced in April 1993—the largest ever introduced by a Japanese government. In addition to government spending on infrastructure projects, easier loan conditions were introduced to promote investment, together with training programs and measures to support imports and the stock market. As these proved ineffective in stimulating the economy, a further 6 trillion-yen package was announced in mid-September. Electricity and gas prices, telephone charges, and domestic airfares were also reduced.

Despite these repeated measures, which in normal times would have sparked an economic growth, most components of demand remained weak. Private consumption was only 0.6% higher in the first half of the year than a year before. Retail sales, a large component of private consumption, fell by 2.5% during the same period. A lack of confidence was instilled in consumers as their purchasing power declined. Slower growth in the economy reduced wage rises to 1% in the first half, less than the 1.4% rise in the second half of 1992. Overtime and bonuses also slowed. Summer bonuses in 1993 were 1.1% lower than a year earlier—the first reduction in over 10 years. As bonuses accounted for up to a quarter of salaries, such a reduction was a significant setback. However, as inflation remained stable at around 1.3%, it softened the blow of declining earnings somewhat by propping up their purchasing power.

Rising unemployment also made people more cautious about spending. Although unemployment in Japan, by world standards, remained very low at 2.7%, it was at the highest level in over five years. Since October 1992 the job-offer to job-seeker ratio, a key indicator for labour, had consistently declined. In September it stood at 0.69, down from a peak of 1.47 in March 1991. If unemployment had been defined in the same way as in other industrialized countries, it would have been considerably higher than the official figures suggested. Furthermore, the Japanese tradition of companies offering lifetime employment minimized layoffs. Asahi Bank estimated that Japan's true unemployment rate, if "hidden" unemployment were taken into account, was 6.5%. Judging by the moves by leading giant corporations such as Fujitsu and Nippon Telegraph & Telephone to reduce their labour force, the recession might force some change in attitudes.

Inevitably, the weakness of domestic demand and the strength of the yen were reflected in the trend of industrial production. In the year to September, industrial production was 2.6% lower than a year before. Despite an increase in shipments in the autumn, the level of inventories of finished products remained at historically high levels. The Bank of Japan's quarterly Tankan survey indicated a continued fall in business confidence in the third and the final quarter of 1993; there was little optimism for an upturn in the short term. Not surprisingly, gross fixed-capital investment was flat in the first half of the year, reflecting reduced investment in machinery and equipment. In contrast, private-housing investment and government investment picked up strongly, reflecting the effects of the government's packages.

Since 1991 Japan's trade surplus had been on the rise again as exports benefited from the recovery in the U.S. and imports weakened as the economy slowed. The strength of the yen boosted export revenues in dollar terms and depressed imports. In September exports were up 6% over the year before in dollar terms but were down 11% in yen terms, largely because of currency fluctuations. Nevertheless, in November Japan showed a 12-month trade surplus of $140 billion, up from $133 billion in 1992. This raised concerns that the trade friction with the U.S. and the European Community (EC) might further increase and heightened the dilemma faced by the policy makers. While policy makers wanted to stimulate domestic demand to pull the economy out of the recession, correction of external imbalances also required reforms that opened up the Japanese markets to imports, particularly of manufactured goods. Given the depressed state of the manufacturing industry and the softening employment market, this option would have been highly unpopular.

A related dilemma was the rapid rise in the yen since the summer. At one point it almost reached the psychologically important level of 100 yen to the dollar. This was caused by the rising current-account surplus and the turmoil in European currencies that led capital to seek refuge in the yen. In the short term a high yen was a drag on economic growth because it slowed exports and eroded the profits of export-dependent companies. In turn, these companies curtailed new investment and squeezed employees' income. Also, the influx of cheap imports reduced the profits of domestic producers. In the longer term, however, the economy would benefit from lower costs and increased competition. The business community, which sought short-term protection, seemed to have been reasonably successful in slowing the reform and deregulation necessary to open up the economy and let the long-term benefits flow through.

Germany. The recession in the German economy—the deepest in some 50 years—had not yet run its course, despite encouraging indicators as the year drew to a close. Furthermore, there were few signs that a sustained recovery was on the way. After falling for four consecutive quarters, real GDP in western Germany picked up by 0.6% in the second quarter. A similar rise in the third quarter indicated that economic activity was still sluggish. For the year as a whole, the western German economy was estimated to have declined by nearly 2%. In former East Germany, the recovery continued, and real GDP was officially estimated to have increased by 6%.

This worse-than-expected downturn was largely due to the tight monetary and fiscal policies pursued by the authorities in 1992 to dampen the inflationary pressures unleashed by unification. However, the weak recovery in the U.S. and the U.K. also played a role. Given that the money supply was growing well outside its target range and inflation was still too high, the Bundesbank's scope for sharply reducing interest rates was limited. Likewise, to prevent the budget deficit from widening further, the government was forced to introduce measures to cut its planned expenditure despite the deep recession.

However, the effect of the DM 21 billion in cuts planned for 1994 (larger cuts were agreed for 1995 and 1996) was to hold the central government's budget deficit unchanged from that of 1993, which was up sharply from the previous year. The overall public-sector deficit, inclusive of social security funds, was expected to rise to DM 160 billion, or 5% of GDP in 1993.

The thrust of the cuts was to reduce welfare support, particularly for the unemployed. In this respect it was unprecedented, as generous welfare provision had been one of the main features of the German social and economic system. Reduced spending was the only avenue open to the fiscal authorities, for there was no room for additional taxation. The tax burden had risen to 41.5% in 1993 (compared with 39.75% in the 1980s) and was set to rise further.

These cuts came soon after the so-called Solidarity Pact agreed in March between the government and the opposition. The need for this came about from the need to provide medium-term funds for eastern Germany. The principal instrument of the pact was the reintroduction of the 7.5% solidarity surcharge on personal and corporate incomes from January 1995. This lifted the threat of immediate tax increases and paved the way for spending cuts by the government.

ANDREA MOHIN—THE NEW YORK TIMES

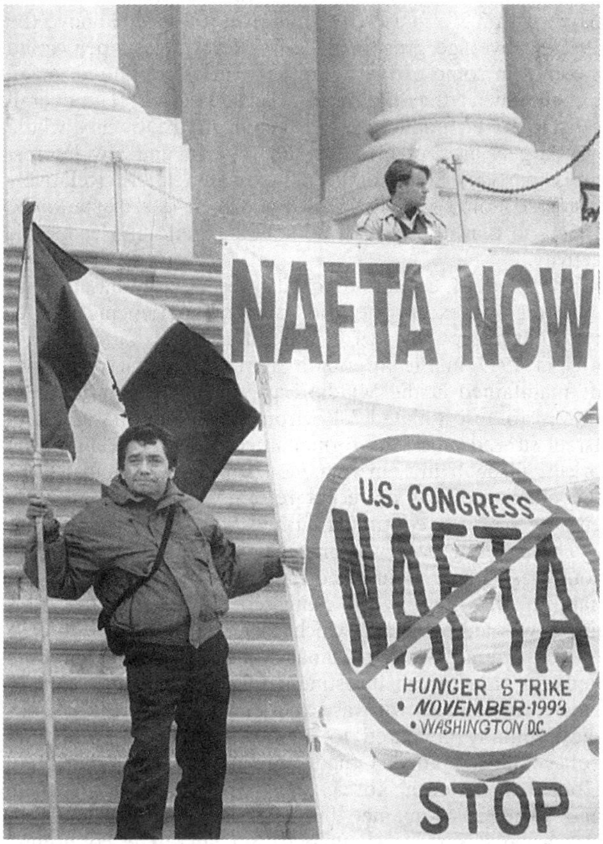

A supporter and an opponent of the North American Free Trade Agreement (NAFTA) display banners at the U.S. Capitol. Some feared a loss of manufacturing jobs to low-wage Mexico, while others argued that many U.S. industries would benefit from increased trade.

The long-awaited fall in German interest rates materialized in 1993 but only slowly, as the Bundesbank had cautiously relaxed its tough anti-inflation monetary policy following a moderation in the inflation rate, public-sector spending cuts, and widening of the ERM bands in August. The Bundesbank cut its interest rates by 0.5% on October 22. Previous cuts had been made in September, twice in July, and in April. As a result, in November both the discount and the Lombard rates were three percentage points below their summer 1992 peak.

Inflation in western Germany stabilized at around 4% during 1993. Although this was above the government's target of 3.5%, the overshoot was largely due to higher VAT rates and higher rents. The upward push from higher wage settlements, much in evidence during 1992, moderated. In eastern Germany, although the headline inflation was close to 15%, the differential was largely due to a hike in administration prices.

The recession took its toll on the manufacturing sector as domestic and foreign demand weakened. Production in the western sector, excluding construction, remained largely flat during most of 1993 but showed signs of an uplift near the end of the year. However, compared with the previous year, it was down 8%. In eastern Germany manufacturing production continued to recover and was 8% higher in the first half of the year. Capacity utilization at 78.6% in the second quarter fell to the lowest point in more than eight years. Likewise, investment in the west fell by an estimated 2% during 1993, while in the east it expanded by nearly 15%, largely as a result of robust reconstruction activity.

As employers took steps to bring the workforce in line with lower levels of activity, unemployment soared. An estimated 600,000 fewer people were employed in western Germany during the autumn compared with the same period a year earlier. The unemployment rate stood at 8.8% in October—up from the previous year's 7%. In the eastern states, despite the strength of the recovery, unemployment continued to rise, albeit at a slower rate. In September the number of unemployed stood at 1,160,000. This was below the January 1992 peak of 1,340,000 but a little higher than the figures in the spring. Unemployment remained a serious problem in former East Germany, as illustrated by the 16% unemployment rate. A further 1.5 million people were on job-creation or retraining programs or had retired early. Some estimates suggested that the true unemployment rate was close to 35%.

Private consumption followed a downward path for most of the year. Retail sales plunged by 8% in January when higher VAT rates came into force. Although it picked up gradually in the summer, it was still 2% lower in real terms than a year before. New vehicle registrations fell steeply, reversing the sharp gains seen in previous years. By contrast, in the east a modest increase of 2–3% took place in private consumption. Apart from higher VAT, consumption was held back by a lower rise in earnings. The efforts to curb inflation succeeded in moderating wage rises to 3–4%—down from the previous year's 6%.

The foreign-trade position had been complicated by the EC's move to a single market from Jan. 1, 1993. The initial estimates pointed to a sharp drop in exports owing to weakness in EC countries and the high value of the Deutsche Mark earlier in the year. However, imports were estimated to have fallen even faster because of the weakness of the economy and higher VAT rates. As a result, a trade surplus of DM 42 billion was expected, somewhat higher than the DM 33 billion recorded in 1992. The current-account deficit, on the other hand, was likely to have stabilized at around DM 40 billion after having risen in the previous two years.

France. The economic slowdown, much in evidence since the Gulf war, developed into a full-blown recession during 1993. Compared with a modest rise of 1.3% in the previous year, real GDP was estimated to have declined by 0.7% during 1993. However, thanks to the stimulus (lower interest rates and lower exchange rate) provided to the French economy by the August ERM crisis, the recession appeared to be coming to an end, as indicated by a faster rate of economic activity in the closing months of the year.

While the recession in Germany and the sluggish pace of recovery in the U.S. and the U.K. were contributory factors, what worsened the recession was the government's policy of strong currency and a sound finance. Unlike authorities in the U.K. and Italy, the French authorities resisted devaluation in September 1992 through higher interest rates and intervention in the currency markets. In the relative calm of the subsequent months, instead of taking action to stimulate the economy, which was rapidly sliding into a recession, economic policy remained focused on maintaining the franc/Deutsche Mark exchange-rate parity within the ERM. However, the high interest rates that were needed in Germany to counter the inflationary effects of unification were totally incompatible with the domestic situation in France and exacerbated the recession. They also provided new opportunities for speculators to put pressure on the franc. Despite the willingness of the French authorities to defend the currency, when the financial crisis in August 1993 pushed the franc to its floor within the ERM, they reluctantly agreed to a widening of the bands to 15%.

Clearly, the deteriorating economic situation at home and rapidly rising unemployment made it impossible to continue with the previous policy. This paved the way for lower interest rates, yet the Bank of France remained cautious and did not lower its interest rates immediately. French interest rates began falling after a reduction in the German official rates in September and October. In November the franc stood at 3.45 against the Deutsche Mark, 3.45 centimes lower than its old floor. Toward the end of the year, the French prime rate stood at 8.15%, down from a peak of 10% in early 1993 but still high in real terms.

The other plank of the newly elected conservative government's economic policy consisted of measures to check rapidly deteriorating public finances. (The 1992 budget deficit had been significantly overshot partly as a result of the recession.) This, too, was in conflict with the aim of ending the recession. Nevertheless, in June a supplementary package of measures was announced to restrict the budget deficit to F 317 billion. A state loan was issued to fund some of the additional expenditure. The loan raised F 110 billion, far above the target of F 40 billion. Ironically, the success of the loan heightened dissatisfaction among the business community, as it was not followed by any new programs to stimulate the economy.

High short-term interest rates and insufficient measures to stimulate private consumption led to a sharp rise in unemployment and declines in consumer spending, manufacturing output, and fixed-capital investment. Consumer spending was one of the weaker components of demand early in the year, reflecting a squeeze on households' real purchasing power. Consumer spending, in real terms, rose by less than 0.5% in 1993, down from the previous year's 1.7%. Lower wage rises and higher unemployment were the main factors depressing consumption. In the second half of the year, disposable incomes were cut by the arrangements introduced for the financing of Unedic, the unemployment benefit system. This siphoned off nearly F 10 billion from household incomes on an annual basis, on top of rises in indirect taxes introduced at the time of the May supplementary budget. Sales of automobiles and other durable goods were hardest hit by the slowdown in consumer spending.

Industrial production reflected the weak domestic and export demand and fell by an estimated 2.5%. This was the weakest performance since 1983. Not surprisingly, capacity utilization fell to 80% in the second half of the year—to the lowest level since early 1976. Investment also continued to fall for the second year running. It was forecast by the government to have declined by 4.2% in 1993.

Unemployment rose to a post-World War II record of 3,250,000 in September as firms cut back in the face of stagnant or falling demand. At this level 11.8% of the work force was out of work, compared with 10.5% a year earlier. Hardest hit were young workers. The unemployment rate for those under the age of 25 was 22% in the autumn. In protest against the rising tide of layoffs, low wage increases, and the government's austerity measures, several groups of workers went on strike. The strike by Air France workers received the most media coverage and resulted in a partial backdown by the government. That year-on-year inflation rate remained largely unchanged at around 2.5% was of little comfort to many consumers, as most wage settlements came in at below 3%.

Less Developed Countries. The LDCs as a group experienced another year of above-average economic growth, in contrast to the sluggish or declining pace of economic activity in the developed world. According to IMF estimates, real GDP growth in the LDCs in 1993 was around 6%, slightly faster than the previous year's 5.8%. Encouragingly, as the pace of population growth slowed somewhat, GDP growth per person accelerated to an estimated 3.8%, compared with 3.2% in 1992. At this level it was well above the 1982–92 average growth of 2.5%. Nevertheless, per capita incomes in some of the poorest countries continued to fall to below what they had been a decade earlier. The overall satisfactory economic performance of the LDCs as a whole was largely attributable to policy reforms and low interest rates, particularly on dollar-denominated loans. Relatively faster economic growth in Asia and, to a lesser extent, the U.S. also played a role by stimulating trade and economic activity.

The pace of economic activity was broadly based, with most regions, except the Middle East, experiencing a modest uplift in growth rates. The rapid upswing that got under way in 1992 in the aftermath of the Gulf war could not be maintained in the Middle East, and GDP growth there slowed to an estimated 3.4% from 7.8%. Saudi Arabia and Israel slowed most, the former in response to declining oil prices. Growth in Iran remained strong at around 5% as the positive effects of recent reforms continued. The UN embargo on Iraq continued during 1993.

The fastest growth was once again achieved by the Asian countries as they maintained their underlying economic dynamism and grew by an estimated 8.7%. Growth in this group was led by China, which achieved GDP growth close to 13%. Rapid growth in China was fueled by rising domestic demand and foreign investment following certain reforms. However, a slowdown was experienced late in the year as the economy appeared to be overheating and monetary policy was tightened. Other economies in Asia—including Hong Kong, South Korea, Singapore, Indonesia, Taiwan, and Thailand—remained buoyant as they benefited from increasing intratrade stimulated by China. The continuing recovery in the U.S. also stimulated exports from this region. India was another success story in the region, with an estimated real growth of 4.5% thanks to continuing stabilization and reform programs that included liberalization of trade and payments systems. Pakistan also experienced faster growth despite political uncertainties and foreign exchange constraints.

Economic performance in the LDCs of the Western Hemisphere remained satisfactory, and growth averaged 3.5% in 1993. A strong recovery in Brazil with growth of 4%—reversing 1992's decline of 1%—was in contrast to a moderate slowdown in Argentina, Chile, and Venezuela. Economic activity in Mexico remained sluggish, reflecting efforts to reduce the current-account deficit.

In Africa, because of adverse weather, weak demand from industrial countries, and policy imbalances, growth remained sluggish at around 1.5%. Among the larger economies, activity in Algeria contracted in 1993, while it strengthened in Kenya. Rapid inflation and fiscal imbalances led to a sharp slowdown in The Sudan. Likewise, activity in Morocco remained sluggish owing to drought and weak export markets in Europe.

The improvement in the external balances of LDCs in 1992 was short-lived, and both the trade and current-account balances widened during 1993. Exports from the LDCs increased by around 9%, with most of the increase coming from non-oil-exporting countries. The weak demand for oil reduced the volume of exports from oil-producing countries. Strong economic activity in many of the LDCs led to increased demand for imports, particularly from non-oil countries. Sluggish economic activity and declining oil prices reduced the import capacity of oil-producing countries.

According to IMF estimates, the aggregate trade deficit of the LDCs was projected to rise to $19 billion, compared with $9 billion in 1992. Owing to a fall in surpluses on services, official transfer payments, and private inflows, the aggregate current-account deficit was expected to widen to $80 billion from $62 billion in 1992. This was equal to 1.5% of the aggregate GDP. Regionally, most of the deterioration occurred in Asia, reflecting higher demand for imports arising from rapid economic growth. Large deficits also persisted in the Western Hemisphere countries, including Argentina and Mexico. The deteriorating terms of trade in some African countries also adversely affected the trade balances in that region.

The financing of the moderately wider current-account deficit did not pose any difficulties, as net financial flows (comprising official transfers, direct investments, and external borrowing) rose by an estimated $4 billion to $115 billion. Furthermore, the funding of this deficit did not lead to a rise in debt levels, as there was a strong rise in direct investment. The IMF noted that direct investment as a share of non-debt-creating flows recovered in the Western Hemisphere, dominated by Latin America, to the level prevailing before the debt crisis, around 90%. The IMF expected the proportion in Asia to have risen to 85% in 1993, compared with 50% in 1979. The main factors that encouraged greater direct investment into Latin America and Asia included sound monetary and fiscal policies, as well as privatization programs that increased the efficiency of the private sector. Measures taken to improve their creditworthiness and reduction of debt overhang were also contributory factors. The relatively less attractive conditions restricted the flow of direct capital investment to Africa, however. For the poorest countries official flows (grants and soft loans) still made up a high proportion of all inflows—up to 80%. Such flows had risen considerably in real terms over a decade, but World Bank figures showed that aid from very few countries was close to the World Bank target of 0.75% of GDP.

During 1993 the total external debt of the LDCs rose by an estimated 6% to $1,476,000,000,000. Although this increase was larger than in the previous year, total debt of the LDCs as a proportion of exports of goods and services continued the declining trend apparent since 1986 and fell to around 117.

Average inflation in the LDCs rose in 1993 to an estimated 44% from 39% in 1992, but the very high inflation rate

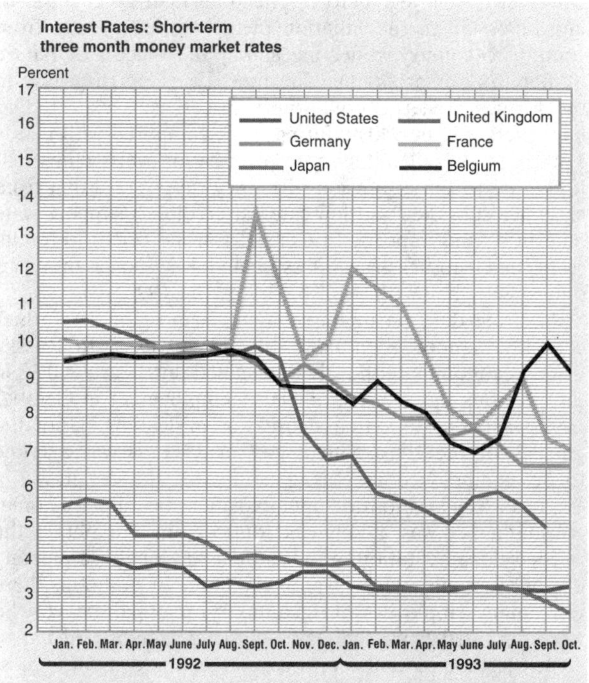

Source: International Monetary Fund, *International Financial Statistics.*

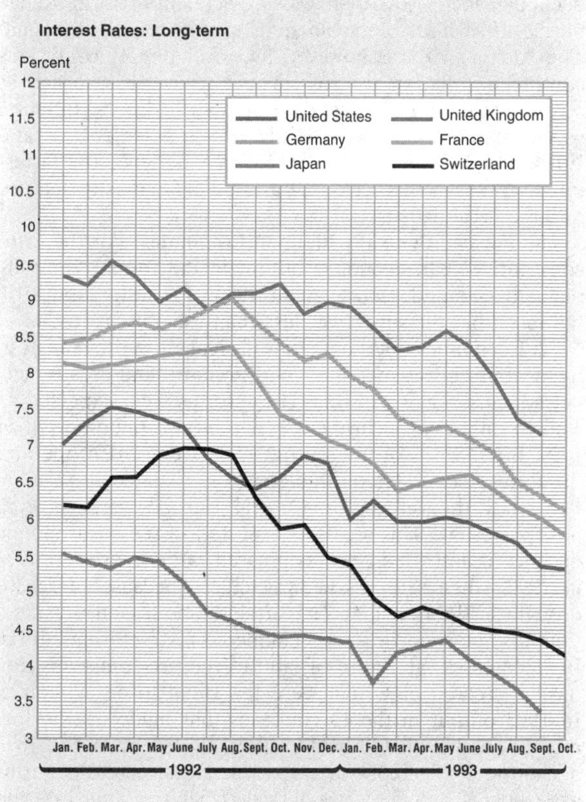

Source: International Monetary Fund, *International Financial Statistics.*

Posters advertise foreign films at a theatre in Paris. Largely because of objections from France, motion pictures were not included in the General Agreement on Tariffs and Trade (GATT), and, thus, films could continue to be subject to high duties.
JEAN-PIERRE AMET—SYGMA

in a few countries affected the average, giving a somewhat misleading impression. Median inflation, which was more representative of the underlying trends, was around 7%. Regionally, average inflation was the highest in the Western Hemisphere at 220%, up from the previous year's 166%. This increase occurred in spite of a reduction in inflation in a number of countries in that region, including Argentina, Peru, and Nicaragua. In Brazil inflation remained at very high levels. According to IMF estimates, inflation in the region, excluding Brazil, was heading for 16% and was on a moderating trend.

In Africa inflation was still high at around 36% but was declining gently. Inflation was expected to rise in Kenya during 1993 and to remain high in Algeria, Nigeria, and The Sudan. In Zaire, however, hyperinflationary conditions continued. Inflation also rose in Asia to over 8%, largely as a result of rapid economic development in China. Inflation was expected to decline slightly in the Middle East and Europe to 23%. Turkey continued to experience the fastest inflation rate in this region, at around 66%, mostly because of large fiscal deficits.

The Former Centrally Planned Economies. For the third consecutive year, economic output in the former centrally planned economies declined in 1993. The estimated 10% fall in output, however, was less than the 15% recorded in 1992. Economic conditions showed signs of improvement in many countries as measures to restructure and create market systems began to work. The reforms were expected to lead to only a small further decline in economic output in 1994, after which overall output from Central Europe and the former Soviet Union would rise.

Already the reforms in Central Europe were showing positive results. This area was expected to see an economic decline of less than 2%, compared with a drop of 9% in 1992, when setbacks in agriculture—because of severe drought in the region and uncertainty about land privatization in some countries—had hampered restructuring efforts. In some cases the return of land to the pre-communist-era owners created plots that were too small to be economic. In 1993 output in the 15 countries that made up the former Soviet Union fell by 14%, slightly less than the 18% decline in 1992. Economic progress and structural reforms were being hampered by political difficulties and, in some countries, armed conflict.

Many of the problems that existed in 1992 persisted. Economic links between the republics had stalled, as had state demand for military and other capital goods. Trade with countries outside the former Soviet Union had collapsed, and new markets had to be found. Nevertheless, progress in restructuring was beginning to be made. In September 1993, 9 of the 15 former republics signed a treaty of economic union that, if agreement on the details could be reached, would create a free-trade zone with strong monetary cooperation in the form of an exchange-rate mechanism, with currencies being linked to the Russian ruble. The treaty was not signed by the three Baltic states, but Ukraine and Turkmenistan became associate members.

Inflation continued to be a problem throughout the region. Because of this, many countries experienced a depreciation of their currencies. The average rate for the countries in transition was expected to exceed 560% in 1993, down from 786% the year before. The total figure was misleading, however, as the inflation picture varied greatly from country to country, reflecting mainly the success or failure of stabilization programs. The most dismal picture was in the former Soviet Union, where prices were expected to have increased by 940% during 1993, compared with nearly 1,300% in 1992. The high rates of inflation were almost entirely due to the expansion of money supply resulting from excessive subsidies and low-interest credits to support state enterprise and imports. In Central Europe prices were still rising much too fast, at an estimated 142% over the year, only slightly below the 162% recorded in 1992.

Accurate data on unemployment in most of the former centrally planned economies still did not exist. In Russia, where economic output had declined by nearly 40% in the previous three years, official unemployment in October 1993 was 1.3%, but that figure was misleading. Until the passage of the Employment Act of 1991, it was a crime to be unemployed in Russia, and after the act it was a disgrace. Registration for unemployment benefits was time-consuming; it was a long and difficult task to obtain the needed documentation; and the benefits, for those meeting eligibility requirements, were very little. In addition, there were many employees on involuntary or unpaid leave who were excluded from the statistics. These factors existed to some extent in several countries, and unemployment in most of the former Soviet republics remained hidden.

In the more open economies, such as Bulgaria, the Czech Republic, Hungary, Poland, Romania, and Slovakia, data were more reliable. Unemployment levels in those countries were in the range of 14% to 17%, with the exception of the Czech Republic, where the unemployed accounted for only about 3.5% of the workforce. In general, unemployment rates increased slightly faster in 1993 than in the year before. This was inevitable as the overmanned state enterprise sectors continued to shed employees and the growing private sector introduced more efficient work practices and up-to-date technology that required fewer workers. In the short term the decline in real wages and rising unemployment reduced popular support for the reform process and remained a threat to democracy.

Not surprisingly, the high rates of inflation and growing unemployment brought a deterioration in the lifestyles of many. The value of the state benefits being paid out had been eroded by high inflation. Inevitably, restructuring and reform caused temporary distortions in the economy, creating severe hardship for some people, such as the elderly and disadvantaged. The problem was how to target the benefits to those in most need without hampering the change to a market economy or stifling individual initiative. Limited progress was made in this area.

Meeting the cost of statutory benefits—family allowances, maternity leave, and sickness pay—was increasingly difficult for all governments, as the revenue from state enterprises had declined. New benefits, such as unemployment insurance, which had been unnecessary under communism, also had to be established. The communist governments had made pension promises to their citizens, which their successors would not be able to honour in years to come. Plans were being made to reform pensions, and the old pay-as-you-go systems were likely to be replaced by funded pension schemes such as existed in the U.K. and the U.S. The lack of sophistication of the region's financial markets posed a problem since pension funds needed suitable outlets for investment. The merits of various pension systems were being considered before final decisions could be taken.

The region's trade with industrialized countries continued to grow as a result of far-reaching trade-liberalization programs, but there were signs of protectionism in some of the industrialized countries. Western European countries with which a number of trade and cooperation agreements had been signed were suffering from recession and were reluctant to open their markets further to products that were particularly competitive. The EC was quick to respond to an outbreak of foot-and-mouth disease affecting livestock in the former Yugoslavia and, from April 8, 1993, imposed a temporary ban on imports of livestock, fresh meat, and dairy and meat-based products from 18 Central and Eastern European countries. Nevertheless, trade between the two regions was developing well. Exports from the Visegrad countries (Czech Republic, Hungary, Poland, and Slovakia) to countries in the Organization for Economic Cooperation and Development (OECD) rose an average 23% a year between 1989 and 1992, while imports increased by an average 30%. Since trade liberalization, however, the region's trade with the EC countries had moved from a surplus to a deficit of $3.6 billion in 1992. The overall deficit on current account of the former centrally planned countries grew from $4 billion in 1992 to a projected $15 billion in 1993. Increased financial assistance, with the rescheduling of official debt, meant an increase in financial flows to a projected $30 billion in 1993, up from $22 billion in 1992.

The shift of assets from the state to the private sector continued as privatization programs progressed. By 1993 a large number of small enterprises had been successfully privatized in most Eastern European countries, with the notable exception of Bulgaria. The main difficulty encountered was the privatization of land because of uncertainties about ownership. Most of the former Soviet republics had moved slowly to implement any privatization programs.

Privatization of the large-scale enterprises that formed the core of the command economy was proving more difficult than had been expected. Even in Hungary and Poland, which had started their reforms in 1989, problems were being encountered. In 1992 more than half of Hungary's revenue from privatization was from foreign capital. In 1993 the flow of foreign investment faltered, partly because of the recession in Western Europe and partly because it was being attracted to other destinations in Eastern Europe. In October Hungary announced plans to offer state shareholdings in 70 companies. They were designed to encourage small investors, and the government wanted to attract up to a million buyers. Toward the end of 1993 an ambitious program was getting under way in Poland to transfer a large and profit-making share of industry to private management. Nearly 400 companies were targeted for the plan, and under the Pact on State Enterprises signed late in 1993, privatization was to be accelerated. It had already brought the share of the private sector to about 45% of the Polish economy. Overall, Poland led the region, with economic growth of about 4%. In the Czech Republic 800 companies with a book value of about $5 billion were being privatized through the use of vouchers issued in November 1993. It was estimated that 40–60% of the national economy was in private ownership, and when the privatizations planned in 1993 were completed, 80% of state property would have been sold off.

Management buyouts were proving an attractive means by which management and employees could obtain significant control. By September official Russian statistics showed that 80% of 70,000 large and medium-sized enterprises (covering four million employees) had been privatized in this way. The success of such buyouts, however, was often threatened by poor management skills and inadequate financing.

The means by which countries privatized had different financial implications, and banking systems in many countries were inadequate and lacked the necessary experience in providing credit to the private sector. Efforts were being made to strengthen the balance sheets of commercial banks. In the meantime, privatization continued to erode the role of governments in setting prices and allocating resources. With a growing share of output coming from the private sector, the governments' revenues depended increasingly not only on private-sector profits but also on the development of efficient taxation systems. In the short term, large budget deficits had emerged, and the governments had little option but to increase their debt to meet current obligations.

INTERNATIONAL TRADE

World trade growth faltered in 1993 following an encouraging upturn in 1992. Although the estimates and projections available toward the end of the year were subject to a greater degree of error because of the EC single market, which led to the discontinuation of customs controls, all the indications pointed to a global slowdown. IMF projections issued in October anticipated a growth of 3%, compared with 4.6% the year before. If confirmed, this would be the slowest growth rate since 1991 and below the 1975–84 average of 3.4%.

The slowdown in world trade in 1993 was largely the result of the recession in Europe and Japan, which reduced the amount of demand. By contrast, stronger economic

(continued on page 145)

Special Report: Economic Affairs

Financial Support for the Elderly

BY JANET H. CLARK

By 1993 industrialized countries throughout the world were facing a common and growing problem—how to cope with the financial problems created by a growing proportion of elderly in their populations. Governments could no longer afford the generous welfare systems built up during the 1960s and 1970s, and in most developed countries pensions for the elderly accounted for the largest share of benefits. The problem was being compounded by the fact that workforces relative to the retired population were shrinking. This meant that there were fewer employers and employees to contribute to the national welfare systems on which increasing numbers depended for their financial livelihood.

An unprecedented growth in the pensions markets in the industrialized world and in newly industrializing countries (Hong Kong, South Korea, Singapore, and Taiwan) took place in the 1980s and early 1990s. This was the result of employer and employee concern about provision for the elderly. Longer life expectancies (the longest being 81 years for the average Japanese female) and in some countries the scaling down or capping of state pensions added to these fears. Birthrates in most of Europe had been falling since the mid-1960s.

In most of Europe, too, the cost of state social security schemes, of which pensions accounted for the largest share, had for many years been rising much faster than national income. Expenditure on health care for the elderly—largely financed by the state—was becoming increasingly onerous. The costs showed that for a typical European country 80% of state health spending was used for people over the age of 65. Governments had little choice, particularly at a time when raising the rate of taxation was not politically acceptable, but to try to shift the burden of pensions onto the private sector. The trend was expected to accelerate as more countries reassessed their benefits systems.

Growing Demographic Pressures. In 1993 the population of Europe, as in much of the rest of the industrialized world, was near stagnation. Children were no longer seen as essential in a marriage, and the development of social welfare systems reduced the economic need for having a family. Elsewhere, the less developed countries that made up most of the world's population had the opposite problem. They wanted to reduce their population growth rates.

The industrialized countries' share of the world population was shrinking rapidly. (*See* Table.) It was projected that by 2025 the 12 member countries of the European Community (EC) would have only 4% of the world population, compared with 11% in 1950 and an estimated 6.4% in 1991. The share of the U.S.'s population was also projected to fall sharply from 6.1 (1950) to 3.9% (2025), and that of Japan was expected to drop from 3.3 (1950) to 1.6% (2025). The

	1950		1991		2025†	
Area	Pop.*	%	Pop.*	%	Pop.*	%
More developed countries	832	33.1	1,219	22.6	1,412	16.3
European Community	278	11.0	346	6.4	348	4.0
United States	152	6.1	253	4.7	334	3.9
Japan	84	3.3	124	2.3	135	1.6
Less developed countries	1,684	66.9	4,165	77.4	7,234	83.7
World total	2,516	100.0	5,384	100.0	8,646	100.0

*Population in 000,000. †Projected.
Source: Eurostat Demographic Statistics 1993.

combination of low birthrates and longer life expectancy, however, meant that the proportion of those over 60 was increasing and would make up more than a quarter by 2025, compared with less than one-fifth in the early 1990s. Already the economic recession in the industrialized countries had added to the number of "pensioners." Employees over the age of 50 were being laid off and given early retirement as companies tried to cut costs. In many European countries it was possible to receive state benefits in advance of the official pension age.

Higher unemployment levels were adding to dependency ratios (the population of those over 65 to the population aged 15–64 years). These were already in the region of 20 to 25% and by the year 2035, in most major countries, would be in the range 32 to 42%. A majority of pensioners in Europe relied on the state for most of their retirement income. The individual on average earnings in France (including mandatory private), Greece, Italy, Luxembourg, Portugal, and Spain, for example, could expect to receive a state pension at retirement the equivalent of between 60% and nearly 90% of final earnings, provided that certain contribution requirements had been met. In countries where the state pension was less generous—such as Denmark, Ireland, The Netherlands, and the U.K.—and was expected to cover a smaller proportion of final earnings (24–40%), the shortfall tended to be met from a company or personal pension. In most countries higher-paid workers were less dependent on the state for retirement income.

Although pension-provision methods varied widely in industrialized countries, the aim of most state and company plans was to provide a total pension on retirement of about two-thirds of earnings at retirement. A more meaningful measure of the pension, and the degree to which it enabled the recipient's standard of living to be maintained after retirement, was to compare the take-home pension (the amount received after any income taxes owed have been deducted) with the take-home pay at retirement. An individual retiring on one and a half times the average national earnings in 1993 in the EC could expect a net total pension equivalent to 84% of net earnings. Gross pension as a percentage of gross earnings was a much lower 68%, the better take-home pension reflecting the much larger tax and other statutory deductions taken from the pay of those still working. By contrast the take-home pension for retirees in Japan and the U.S. was less than the EC average of 84%, at 79 and 67%, respectively. So, too, was the average for the seven European Free Trade Association countries, at 76%. Within Europe there were quite large national variations, with the net replacement of earnings being a very high 92% in The Netherlands, compared with 74% in Germany. Europe's generous pensions relative to earnings—at least for those with uninterrupted careers and good contribution records—were becoming unsustainable in countries where the major share of the funding was being provided by the state. These included Greece, Italy, Spain, and Portugal, where the governments needed to cut public spending to curb burgeoning public deficits. In some cases the benefits in these countries were already being scaled down. Where

Janet H. Clark is research manager for Sedgwick Noble Lowndes employee benefits consultants and author of a forthcoming book on the crisis in European labour costs.

state systems provided most of the pension, private pension schemes tended to be poorly developed. This made shifting the burden to the private sector more difficult.

The Choice Governments Faced. Governments were faced with a difficult choice in ensuring that future pensions were adequate. In many countries governments were reluctant for political reasons to abandon what was seen as their social responsibilities. But the cost of supporting generous social security systems had led to the introduction of unacceptedly high levels of taxation. Even Sweden, which had become the most highly taxed country in Europe, was forced to make reforms, notably raising the eligibility age for receiving a partial pension. The general trend was to shift responsibility to the private sector—both corporate and individual. Other moves included encouragement of workers to take later retirement, increases in contribution rates to state schemes, and a capping of earnings-related benefits. In the countries of Eastern Europe, reforms also were taking place. Pensions provided in the former centrally planned economies had quickly become totally inadequate as inflation eroded their value in the transition to a mixed economy. The state no longer had the revenue to meet its earlier promises.

In all the industrialized countries there were different types of retirement provision (both public and private) and ages at which pensions became payable. Most state systems were pay-as-you-go, under which contributions of the current workers paid for the pensions of those already retired. As the number of workers relative to the retired declined, these systems were jeopardized. Some countries, such as France, faced the prospect of more pensioners than workers by the year 2020.

Private schemes, such as those in the U.S., Canada, the U.K., Japan, and The Netherlands, tended to be funded with funds held separately from company assets. Workers and, usually, employers on their behalf made contributions that were actuarially calculated to meet the liabilities of the pension fund. The investment and management of the funds varied widely. Most notably, in Germany book reserves were allocated in the company accounts to meet pension liabilities, the risk of insolvency being covered by insurance. Most schemes were noncontributory. Companies set up a reserve in their accounts, in accordance with tax authority requirements, and claimed a tax deduction. In the U.S. some individual savings plans received tax breaks. The adequacy of such arrangements to meet future liabilities given the demographic trends was questionable.

Pension Funds Were a Powerful Force. The political and economic importance of pension funds was considerable. Europe's pension funds were estimated at about $1 trillion, with those in the U.S. being three times larger. Global pension funds were expected to rise to about $7.2 trillion by 1996. The way such investments were invested affected capital and currency markets. In Europe the U.K. not only had the largest pension fund assets but also had considerable investment freedom. Some three-quarters of assets were invested in equities, compared with under a quarter in most of continental Europe, where bond investments were much more important. The U.S., Japan, and Canada invested heavily in domestic equities and bonds. The recycling of tax-advantaged funds, which was facilitated by book reserves schemes, such as in Germany, made a major contribution to corporate growth.

Any action on the part of governments that affected pension funds, such as changes in investment regulations or taxation of pension contributions or fund assets, could have far-reaching consequences. Not only was the financial security of pensioners at stake but so too was the stability of capital and currency markets.

(continued from page 143)

activity among the LDCs was reflected in faster growth in trade. This helped to sustain the overall level of world trade. Exports from the developed countries were estimated to have remained unchanged during 1993, while the estimated volume of their total imports had grown marginally by 1.2%. The comparative figures for the LDCs were 9.4% (export growth) and 9.3% (import growth).

Germany and France were the largest contributors to the slowdown in export volume in the developed world. The relatively high value of their currencies, coupled with the recession in Europe and sluggish recovery in the U.S., resulted in an estimated decline in their export volume by 5.4% and 7.1%, respectively. The appreciating yen and dollar also contributed to a slowdown in exports from Japan and the U.S. In the U.S., domestic recovery diverted some products for the home market and further reduced exports. Significant depreciation in the lira and the pound sterling, following the withdrawal of Italy and the U.K. from the ERM in September 1992, led to relatively faster growth in their export volume—around 4% and 7%, respectively.

The continuing economic recovery in the U.S. was reflected in a strong growth in import volume, estimated at 8.8%. Although this was somewhat slower than the 10.9% rise the year before, it was comfortably ahead of the long-term projection and by far the fastest growth anywhere in the developed world. Despite the weak economy, there was a modest increase in imports into Japan. This was partly a reflection of cumulative pressure on Japan to cut its trade surplus, but it was also created by the rise in the yen and economic reforms introduced in Japan. In contrast, the deepening recession in Germany and France cut back imports by about 5% and 8%, respectively.

The level of trading activity in the former communist countries remained weak, as exports, particularly from Central and Eastern European countries, had declined because of the recession in continental Europe. In the former Soviet Union, with the exception of energy-related products, exports had continued to decline. Many of the former Soviet republics had not been successful in finding new markets for their products following the collapse of the Soviet bloc. In any event, continuing economic decline and hyperinflationary conditions reflected the slow progress in developing free-market mechanisms to replace the collapsed central planning system. Although hard currency imports had been sharply reduced, by up to 50%, this had been offset by a decline in exports. Thus, chronic trade and balance of payments problems remained.

The LDCs' trade performance was much better than that of the developed countries, given the global sluggish economic activity, but a slowdown was inevitable. However, the slowdown was more marked in imports than in exports. Thanks to China's booming economy, which provided lucrative export markets for smaller countries in southern Asia, the volume of total exports from the developed world remained largely unchanged at about 9.5%. Elsewhere there was a small drop in export volumes. In Africa the combination of declining commodity prices and weak global demand meant there was no growth in export volume. In the Western Hemisphere the growth rate was halved to 3.3%. Export volumes from the LDCs in the Middle East and Europe fell, but their performance, with an estimated 7% growth, was relatively better. On the import side, the overall volumes for the LDCs fell by an estimated one percentage point to just over 9%. Most major regions saw a marked slowdown in their imports; an exception was in Asia, where it was estimated to have remained largely unchanged at around 14%. Western Hemisphere countries experienced the sharpest decline, from 21% to 4%, as they took steps to reduce their net borrowing.

During 1993 the trend of world trade prices remained generally unfavourable to the LDCs. According to IMF estimates, the prices of nonfuel primary commodities declined by nearly 3%, the fifth consecutive annual decrease, bringing the cumulative decline since 1988 to over 17%. Weak overall demand from developed countries and mounting stocks were the main reasons behind the downward trend in commodity prices. Food prices fell by around 2%, following a drop of 1% the year before. The long-running decline in the prices of beverages came to an end as prices stabilized during 1993. Despite a rise in the price of gold, prices of metals and minerals as a whole declined steeply by 13%. As with commodities in general, weak demand and excess production were the main reasons behind it. In December oil prices were around $14.20 a barrel, which was 23% lower than at the start of the year—the lowest level in over five years. In addition to the fundamental imbalance between supply and demand, the short-term price weakness was attributable to renewed speculation that the UN would allow Iraq to resume oil exports in early 1994, thus adding to the excess supply of oil in the world.

Because of adverse currency movements, the LDCs earned less per unit of exports than in 1992. However, they benefited from a 3% fall in the prices of manufactured goods, partly because of low inflation. This favourable combination resulted in a smaller decline in the terms of trade: 1%, according to IMF estimates, compared with 1.2% in 1992 and 3.7% in 1991. The terms of trade fell most in Africa and the Middle East. The improvement in the terms of trade in the developed countries was a modest 0.6% in the wake of 1.5% the year before. The largest gain was in those countries with appreciating currencies; Japan's improvement was 7%, followed by Germany, Canada, and the U.S. The U.K. and Italy faced a decline in their terms of trade.

Considerable progress was made in trade liberalization during 1993. First, the North American Free Trade Agreement (NAFTA), concluded in December 1992, was approved by the U.S. Congress. This agreement created a free-trade area between the U.S., Canada, and Mexico—a vast area with a population of more than 370 million, slightly larger than the EC. This meant tariffs on 99% of goods traded between the U.S. and Mexico would be phased out over the next decade. It was to take another five years for some sensitive agricultural products to be traded completely freely. The scope of NAFTA was wide ranging. In addition to physical goods and products, it included financial services, telecommunications, investment, and patent protection.

The ratification of NAFTA was the logical conclusion of the close ties that already existed in the region. Canada and the U.S. had implemented their own free-trade agreement in 1989. Trade interdependency between the U.S. and Mexico was high and had risen quickly since Mexico's accession to the General Agreement on Tariffs and Trade (GATT) in 1986. This was reflected in the trade figures, which showed that over 70% of Mexico's imports came from the U.S. in 1992 and that 76% of Mexico's exports were destined for the United States. Mexican tariffs on U.S. goods had fallen from 100% in 1981 to 10% by 1993, and U.S. tariffs on Mexican goods averaged 4%. Nevertheless, hostility to NAFTA in the U.S. was strong just before Congress voted. Opponents feared that it would lead to an exodus of jobs from the U.S. and Canada into Mexico as employers scrambled to take advantage of lower wages and less-strict environmental and labour laws in Mexico.

The winning of the NAFTA battle encouraged expectations that a GATT deal between the U.S. and the EC would follow suit, enabling successful completion of the Uruguay round by the December 15 deadline. (*See* AGRICULTURE AND FOOD SUPPLIES.) Farm trade remained the issue that had prolonged the Uruguay round negotiations for seven years and repeatedly threatened to sink them. Negotiations continued at a fairly leisurely pace during most of 1993. As the deadline approached, however, France finally reached a compromise with the U.S. on agricultural subsidies it deemed necessary to pacify militant French farmers, and Japan reluctantly agreed to ease its ban on imported rice. France again threatened to derail the talks when it announced it intended to continue subsidizing the French film industry. On December 14 the U.S. and the EC "agreed to disagree" and postponed final negotiations on the toughest issues, including shipping, financial services, and entertainment. The next day the delegates of the 117 GATT member nations approved by consensus the biggest trade deal in history, although the accord had to be formally approved by all 117 national legislative bodies before it went into effect as scheduled on July 1, 1995. The agreement would create a new organization to replace GATT, reduce tariffs by an average of one-third, eliminate many import quotas in favour of less-restrictive tariffs, cut agricultural subsidies, and ensure the protection of intellectual property, including copyrights, patents, and trademarks. Estimates by the World Bank and the OECD suggested that the successful completion of the Uruguay round could add between $213 billion and $274 billion to the world economy over 10 years.

INTERNATIONAL EXCHANGE AND PAYMENTS

For the second year in succession, the international monetary scene was plagued by prolonged and, at times, intense exchange-rate instability. As in 1992, this was centred principally on the ERM of the European Monetary System (EMS). However, the dollar and the Japanese yen had also seen significant movements, mostly upward. Following the crises in September and November 1992, which forced sterling and the lira out of the system and led to devaluation of the Spanish peseta (twice) and Portuguese escudo (once), a period of relative calm prevailed. One exception to that was the devaluation of the Irish pound in January 1993 to bring it closer to the pound sterling.

In early 1993, despite a deepening recession, France and Denmark successfully defended their currencies, through a mixture of high interest rates, intervention in foreign-exchange markets, and support from the German Bundesbank. In May the escudo and the peseta were devalued again, by 6.5% and 8%, respectively. Financial markets appeared to regard these devaluations as reflecting local cost-competitive pressures rather than applying to all ERM currencies, and there was no immediate pressure within the system. During this period the markets appeared to be content with actual or expected reduction in German interest rates. There was virtually no upward pressure on the Deutsche Mark, as the Bundesbank had cut the Lombard and discount rates in February in response to moderating money-supply and wage rises. Consequently, in the spring France and other ERM countries reduced their interest rates close to the German rates.

The easing of interest rates in Europe was widely seen as the right move, as economic statistics released during the summer indicated a further deterioration in many European economies. A modest interest-rate cut by the Bundesbank on July 1 heightened expectations of further cuts before the summer holidays to stimulate economic recovery. Contrary to expectations, the Bundesbank became concerned that rapid growth in money supply and weakness of the Deutsche

Mark could add to inflationary pressures, so it decided to slow the pace of interest-rate reductions. This heightened the underlying conflict between the need to keep interest rates high in Germany to dampen inflationary pressures and the necessity for other ERM partner countries to lower their interest rates. ERM currencies came under speculative pressure as the markets came to believe that the existing exchange rates were indefensible. True to form, on July 26 the central banks in Belgium and Portugal raised interest rates and intervened in the currency markets. The markets' and ERM partners' attention focused on the Bundesbank's scheduled meeting on July 29. It was widely expected that the Bundesbank would make a significant cut in the discount rate to allow interest rates to fall across Europe and end the latest currency crises. The decision of the Bundesbank to cut its securities repurchase rate by 50 basis points but leave the crucial discount rate unchanged sent shock signals to the markets. Immediately, the Deutsche Mark and the Dutch guilder came under intense upward pressure, while the other ERM currencies were under downward pressure. Despite massive intervention and a hike in overnight interest rates to defend the currencies under attack, many of them were pushed close to or below their ERM floors. At an emergency meeting during the weekend of July 31, it became clear there was no realistic option but to abandon the rigid ERM system. It was agreed to widen the bands around the ERM central parities from 2.25% to 15%.

This provided considerable flexibility for the ERM countries to reduce their interest rates to enable a rapid economic recovery. Several countries, however, particularly France, reacted very cautiously and were reluctant to reduce their interest rates independently of Germany for fear of a drop in the value of their currencies, which, in turn, could stimulate inflationary pressures. In France significant interest-rate cuts came in September after Germany had cut its discount and Lombard rates, and France again followed the Bundesbank's lead and reduced the discount rate in October. The French authorities remained wedded to a policy of a strong currency and sound finance. In December the franc stood at 3.45 against the Deutsche Mark, representing a small devaluation of around 4%. After the widening of the ERM bands in August, relative calm returned to the European currencies.

The U.S. dollar and the yen also moved upward against the European currencies, partly in response to the ERM turmoil and partly because of interest-rate differentials. The dollar appreciated strongly against the European currencies in the early part of the year as interest rates started coming down gently in Europe. In early summer the dollar moved lower as the growth rate slowed in the U.S. and expectations of rapid interest-rate cuts in Europe were dashed. Following the widening of the ERM bands, European interest rates declined, growth in the U.S. economy strengthened, and the dollar gained ground. In December the effective exchange rate of the dollar was close to 67, compared with 65.3 at the beginning of the year, an effective appreciation of 2.6%. The yen also appreciated against other currencies during 1993 by around 20%, reflecting continuing large current-account surpluses. Against the dollar the Japanese currency strengthened from 125 yen per dollar and in September touched 100 yen per dollar. Thereafter, the weakness of the Japanese economy and expectations of interest-rate cuts weakened the yen somewhat. In December it averaged 110 yen per dollar and was still falling.

The balance of payments position around the world had reflected the sluggish demand in Europe, economic recovery in the U.S., and rising intraregional trade in Asia. Despite sluggish economic growth among the developed countries, their current-account deficits widened appreciably in 1993. IMF estimates indicated a deficit of $51 billion in 1993, up from $39 billion the year before. Most of the increase was attributable to a larger deficit in the U.S., where continuing economic recovery sucked in imports and resulted in an estimated current-account deficit of $111 billion. By contrast, export growth in the U.S. was modest, as many of its trading partners, in particular Europe and Japan, were in recession. The EC saw a modest narrowing in its deficit, reflecting weak demand. The EC countries with large deficits included Germany ($29 billion), the U.K. ($26 billion), and Italy ($21 billion). With the exception of Germany, all the

Effective Exchange Rates*
average rates, 1985 = 100

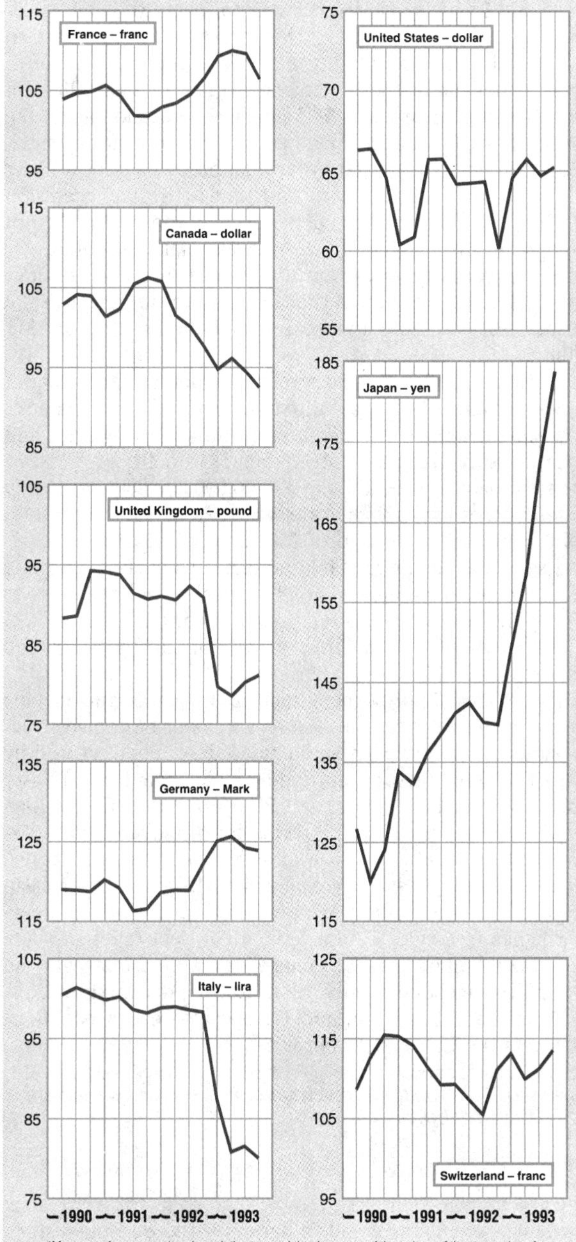

*Measure of a currency's value relative to a weighted average of the values of the currencies of the country's principal trading partners.

Source: International Monetary Fund, *International Financial Statistics*.

others were traditionally deficit-prone countries. Germany, however, started running a current-account deficit after unification in 1990. By contrast, the seemingly unstoppable rise in Japan's current-account surplus continued in 1993. Despite a rise in the value of the yen and recession in Europe, Japan's surplus was heading for $140 billion, compared with the previous year's $117 billion. Although it was the lowest rate of increase since 1990, it remained a source of friction with Japan's main trading partners, particularly the U.S.

The LDCs also experienced a widening in their current-account deficit from $62 billion in 1992 to an estimated $80 billion. A large proportion of the increase in the deficit was attributable to a larger trade deficit. The dynamic Asian economies rapidly sucked in imports of capital goods and raw materials and contributed to a widening of the region's balance of payments deficits from $4.8 billion in 1992 to over $20 billion. In Africa weak export demand and declining commodity prices led to a widening of the deficit to an estimated $9 billion, a deterioration of over 20%. The position in former communist countries in Central and Eastern Europe also deteriorated. The IMF expected the current-account deficits of those countries to rise to $4.6 billion in 1993 from the prior year's $1.5 billion. The economies of the former Soviet republics remained in a very precarious state, with declining output and hyperinflationary conditions. The hard currency exports were constrained by the recession in Europe, while imports depended on the availability of foreign aid. Ironically, if more aid were made available, this would increase their capacity to import and add to their deficit. The IMF expected the current-account deficit in the former Soviet Union to rise fourfold during 1993 to $11 billion.

Fortunately, the financing of the wider current-account deficits of the LDCs was not problematic, as net financial flows that comprise official transfers, direct investments, and external borrowing rose. IMF estimates were for a 6% rise in the total debt of the LDCs to $1,476,000,000,000—a slightly faster rate of increase than the year before. However, total debt, expressed as a ratio of the value of exports of goods and services, remained stable at 123, effectively continuing the good progress since 1986. The level of indebtedness as a proportion of GDP also improved among LDCs. In 1993 it was estimated by the IMF at 27.2%, slightly below the prior year's 28.6%.

The modest improvement seen in 1993 was due in part to lower interest rates but also to a number of debt-restructuring arrangements. These included debt relief granted by Paris Club creditors to four middle-income countries (Costa Rica, Guatemala, Jamaica, and Peru) as well as to five low-income countries (Benin, Burkina Faso, Guyana, Mauritania, and Mozambique). Russia's debt arrears and service payments due in 1993 (totaling some $15 billion) were also rescheduled by its official bilateral creditors, while commercial banks had agreed on a $35 billion debt-relief package for Brazil. Similar arrangements were entered into with the Dominican Republic and Jordan. Low or declining interest rates in the U.S., Japan, and Europe also had a beneficial effect on the LDCs' debt burden. (IEIS)

This article updates the *Macropædia* articles BANKS AND BANKING; ECONOMIC GROWTH AND PLANNING; GOVERNMENT FINANCE; INTERNATIONAL TRADE.

STOCK EXCHANGES

It was a vintage year, with double-digit gains for most stock exchanges across the world. What drove the European stock markets upward in 1993 were falling interest rates, which, it was anticipated, would boost economic recovery and company profits, while in South Asia it was the high economic growth rates and the positive outlook for corporate profits. Falling interest rates reduced the attraction of putting savings in deposit accounts and encouraged private investors to switch to equity-linked investments. This, in turn, stimulated demand for stocks and shares underpinning the high levels reached. Despite a very poor performance in Japan, overall the world stock markets gained some 20% in 1993, as measured by the Morgan Stanley Capital International Index. This led the chairman of a leading securities house in London to comment, "This has been a splendid year, not only in this country, but across the world. If you have not made money this year, you never will."

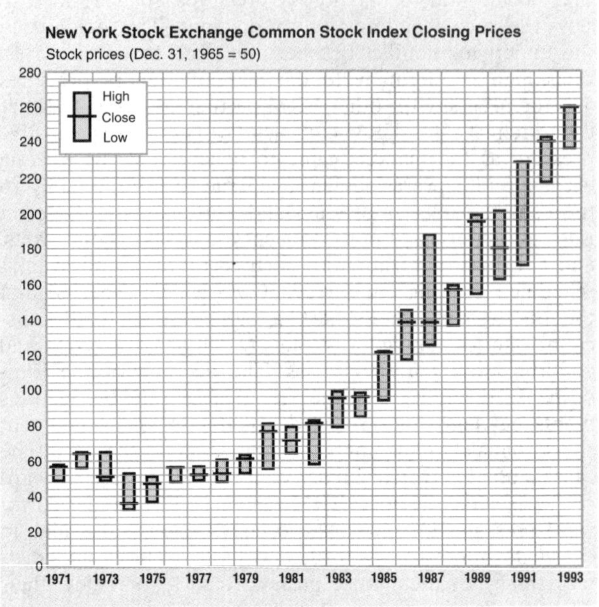

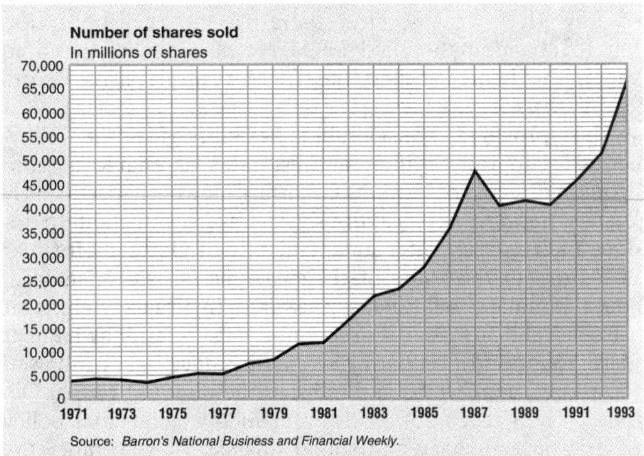

Source: *Barron's National Business and Financial Weekly.*

The rise in stock and share prices led to an upsurge in trading activity in most stock markets. In London, for instance, during the third quarter, British and Irish shares valued at £147 billion were traded. This was slightly higher than the previous record of £143 billion established in the third quarter of 1987. During the third quarter of 1993, the average volume of deals concluded rose to 40,000 bargains. Trading in overseas shares was even higher, reaching £161 billion. The activity was frantic during August following the virtual collapse of the European exchange-rate mechanism (ERM). The strong markets also encouraged companies to float or raise money on the stock exchange. During the first nine months, in the London market, rights issues raised £9.6 billion. The total for the year was expected to be £10.1 billion, which would set a new record. More than 100 companies had taken full listings on the London market.

Yields from fixed-income securities declined sharply during 1993, reflecting the downward trend in global interest rates and decelerating inflation rates. This led to a sharp rise in prices. The highest total gains (income plus price rises) from government bonds and other fixed-income securities were seen in continental Europe, with typical gains between 11% and 15%. The scope for interest-rate cuts was greatest in continental Europe following the ERM crisis in August. Until then, countries within the ERM were forced to follow the high German interest rates. (IEIS)

United States. The stock market was bullish in 1993, with the major indexes of stock prices achieving healthy gains. The Dow Jones industrial average (DJIA) rose 452.98 points, or 13.7%, to 3754.09, while the broader Standard & Poor's (S&P) 500 stock index ended the year with a 7.1% gain, up 30.74 points to 466.45. On the over-the-counter (OTC) market, the National Association of Securities Dealers automated quotation (Nasdaq) composite index closed the year up 99.85 points, or 14.8%, at 776.8, just below its all-time closing high of 787.42, set on October 15. The American Stock Exchange (Amex) market-value index climbed 77.92 points, or 19.5%, to 477.15. Spurred by a sharp drop in interest rates and by the economic recovery, investors were drawn to formerly shunned groups, such as automobile, airline, and machinery stocks. Short-term interest rates were at a 30-year low, and stock and bond prices reached record highs. Dividend declarations were up 23% in 1993, with 1,635 increases, compared with 1,333 in 1992.

The economy gained power steadily in 1993 despite major burdens imposed by federal deficit reduction, defense cutbacks, state and local fiscal problems, weak exports due to an international recession, continuing corporate downsizing, depressed commercial real estate, and relatively high corporate and personal debt. Capital spending was up 7%.

Increased business investment in capital equipment and consumer durable goods, including autos, computers, appliances, home furnishings, medical equipment, environmental technology, and the space industry, gave the economy a boost in 1993. Low interest rates were a major factor. Vigorous consumer spending and booming new car business drove the pace of recovery in the final quarter of the year. Foreign direct investment in the first nine months aggregated $21 billion, compared with slightly more than $2 billion in 1992.

The best performing groups in the DJIA in 1993 were: communications, up 69.8%; lodging, up 63.48%; heavy machinery, up 63.17%; auto manufacturers, up 62.24%; precious metals, up 59.10%; and entertainment stocks, up 54.83%. The worst performers were: footwear, down 30.24%; pollution control, down 27.53%; tobacco, down 25.56%; clothing and fabric, down 23.43%; advanced medical devices, down 21.53%; and pharmaceuticals, down 10.58%.

A major market development in 1993 was the expansion in trading of derivative securities, securitization of debt portfolios, and the development of synthetic securities, which introduced new instruments for hedging and diversification. With many economists predicting continued low inflation and low interest rates, the bullish mood prevailed all year.

In the third quarter of 1993, the government reported that net U.S. purchases of foreign securities were a record $43.3 billion, compared with $24.1 billion in the second quarter. The third-quarter figure nearly equaled the total net purchases for 1992 of almost $48 billion. Net purchases of foreign stocks in the third quarter by U.S. investors were a record $24.4 billion, compared with $13.5 billion in the second quarter. Net purchases in Western Europe jumped from $11.8 billion to $22.8 billion.

Merger and underwriting activity reached record levels in 1993. The volume of mergers announced rose nearly 80% to $275.2 billion from $153 billion a year earlier. The strong U.S. financial markets encouraged merger activity, as did the growing alliance between high-technology and entertainment companies. Wall Street recorded sales of new stocks and bonds in excess of $1.1 trillion (excluding tax-free securities such as Treasury and municipal bonds), up from $860.9 billion in 1992. Major corporations refinanced high-interest debt. Because of low interest rates on bank deposits, investors moved to stocks and bonds for higher returns. There were 6,652 U.S. stock and bond deals through mid-December, well ahead of 1992's total, according to Securities Data Co., a financial research firm.

The junk-bond market set an annual record for new issues. This was mainly because a growing number of lower-rated credits were welcomed by investors hungry for higher yields and many companies took advantage of low interest rates to issue new debt and use the proceeds to retire older, higher-cost debt. Through the end of November, the new issues of high-yield bonds totaled slightly more than $50 billion, compared with $38.2 billion for all of 1992.

Share offerings, including new issues of closed-end mutual funds, totaled $102 billion, up more than 25% from a year earlier, while the number of stock offerings rose to 931 from 760. Through the first nine months, initial public offerings (IPOs) totaled $27.6 billion, up 43% from the corresponding 1992 period. Among the various industries represented in 1993's huge class of IPOs, financial services took the biggest share, with $15.1 billion, while technology issues turned in the best overall performance in trading after the initial offerings. During the first 11 months of 1993, 622 companies went public, not counting closed-end funds. This broke the 1992 full-year record of 513. The $36 billion raised in IPOs came close to the $40 billion total for the two previous years combined.

New corporate bond issues totaled a record $433 billion in 1993. During the first nine months, municipal bond issuance rose 28% over the year-earlier period to $218.5 billion; it ended the year at $287.4 billion. Issuance of real estate investment trusts in the first nine months was $3.9 billion, more than five times the volume in all of 1992.

Table V. Selected Major World Stock Market Indexes*

Country and index	1993 range† High	1993 range† Low	Year-end close	Percent change from 12/31/92
Australia, Sydney All Ordinaries	2174	1495	2174	+40
Austria, Credit Aktien	430	300	429	+37
Belgium, Brussels BEL20	1474	1125	1473	+30
Canada, Toronto Composite	4330	3275	4330	+29
Denmark, Copenhagen Stock Exchange	367	262	366	+40
Finland, HEX General	1608	843	1582	+91
France, Paris CAC 40	2282	1772	2273	. . .
Germany, Frankfurt FAZ Aktien	852	599	848	+41
Hong Kong, Hang Seng	11,888	5438	11,888	+116
Ireland, ISEQ Overall	1889	1191	1889	. . .
Italy, Milan Banca Comm. Ital.	633	446	619	+39
Japan, Nikkei Average	21,148	16,079	17,417	+3
Mexico, IPC	2603	1504	2603	. . .
Netherlands, The, CBS All Share	281	199	281	+42
Norway, Oslo Stock Exchange	1064	670	1062	+59
Philippines, Manilla Composite	3196	1271	3196	. . .
Singapore, SES All-Singapore	629	394	629	+59
South Africa, Johannesburg Industrials	5571	4333	5596	+28
Spain, Madrid Stock Exchange	324	216	323	+51
Sweden, Affarsvarlden General	1435	879	1403	+54
Switzerland, SBC General	1014	679	1013	+47
Taiwan, Weighted Price	6071	3088	6071	+80
Thailand, Bangkok SET	1683	819	1683	+88
Turkey, Istanbul Composite	20,683	3956	20,683	. . .
United Kingdom, FT-SE 100	3462	2738	3418	+20
United States, Dow Jones Industrials	3794	3242	3754	+14
World, MS Capital International	607	489	600	. . .

*Index numbers are rounded.
†Based on daily closing price.
Source: *Financial Times*.

Table VI. U.S. Stock Market Prices

Month	Transportation (20 stocks)		Public utilities (40 stocks)		Industrials (400 stocks)		Composite (500 stocks)	
	1993	1992	1993	1992	1993	1992	1993	1992
January	374.27	340.35	159.79	149.70	504.96	493.37	435.23	416.08
February	379.57	348.31	166.41	143.06	508.91	490.89	441.70	412.56
March	376.22	346.73	170.48	139.45	517.24	484.86	450.16	407.36
April	390.85	344.98	172.27	141.61	505.00	484.53	443.08	407.41
May	386.40	356.62	167.52	147.25	513.68	470.72	445.25	414.81
June	374.77	342.07	171.65	146.79	515.73	481.96	448.06	408.27
July	379.98	334.44	176.50	153.70	508.10	487.88	447.29	415.05
August	400.98	321.77	180.06	149.97	514.17	490.88	454.13	417.93
September	397.25	323.19	186.76	155.36	517.37	493.56	459.24	418.48
October	402.75	327.46	183.50	154.28	527.13	483.33	463.90	412.50
November	...	351.64	...	152.12	...	496.09	...	422.84
December	...	363.35	...	157.18	...	509.50	...	435.64

Source: U.S. Department of Commerce, *Survey of Current Business*. Prices are Standard & Poor's monthly averages of daily closing prices, with 1941–43 = 10, except Transportation, 1982 = 100.

Table VII. U.S. Government Long-Term Bond Yields

Month	Yield (%) 1993	1992	Month	Yield (%) 1993	1992
January	7.17	7.48	July	6.34	7.40
February	6.89	7.78	August	6.18	7.19
March	6.65	7.93	September	5.94	7.08
April	6.64	7.88	October	5.90	7.26
May	6.68	7.80	November	...	7.43
June	6.55	7.72	December	...	7.30

Source: U.S. Department of Commerce, *Survey of Current Business*. Yields are for U.S. Treasury bonds that are taxable and due or callable in 10 years or more.

Table VIII. U.S. Corporate Bond Yields

Month	Yield (%) 1993	1992	Month	Yield (%) 1993	1992
January	7.91	8.20	July	7.17	8.07
February	7.71	8.29	August	6.85	7.95
March	7.58	8.35	September	6.66	7.92
April	7.46	8.33	October	6.67	7.99
May	7.43	8.28	November	...	8.10
June	7.33	8.22	December	...	7.98

Source: U.S. Department of Commerce, *Survey of Current Business*. Yields are based on Moody's Aaa domestic corporate bond index.

Wall Street underwriters had a very successful year, collecting a record $9.1 billion in underwriting fees, up 35% from the year before. Merrill Lynch & Co. was the top underwriter for a sixth year, with $192.8 billion, or 13.1% of the global market. Merrill Lynch had 16.4% of the total U.S. market, totaling $173.8 billion; Goldman, Sachs & Co. had a 12% market share, totaling $127.3 billion; and Lehman Brothers Inc. had a 10.9% market share, totaling $116 billion.

Interest rates declined in 1993, with Treasury bond yields falling from the 7.38% level at the beginning of the year to 6.41% at year's end. Yields on bank money-market accounts declined to 2.34%, down from 2.72% a year before, but the prime rate remained unchanged at 6%.

The major stock exchanges engaged in strong promotion campaigns to attract new listings. The New York Stock Exchange (NYSE) advertised its competitive advantages, as did the other major exchanges in 1993. The market value of NYSE securities was $4.5 trillion, more than four times all other U.S. markets combined. In 1993 more than $36 billion was raised in new equity capital by IPOs on the NYSE, nearly three times all other U.S. markets combined. Trading volume on the NYSE was 66,920,000,000 shares, up 30.26% from 1992's 51,380,000,000. There were 1,790 advances, 729 declines, and 41 unchanged for a total of 2,957 issues traded. In the month that ended December 15, the number of shares sold short and not yet covered rose to a record 1,240,000,000 shares. Bond volume on the NYSE in 1993 was $9,752,161,000, down 16% from the $11,629,012,000 recorded the previous year.

The NYSE chairman reported that 1993 was the greatest year ever. Forty-five companies moved over from Nasdaq to the Big Board. A record 306 companies were newly listed, up from a previous high of 251 in 1992. Of the 306, a record 191 were IPOs that raised $45.2 billion in capital. In 1992 there were 165 IPOs that yielded $34.5 billion in fresh capital. The most active stocks traded on the Big Board were: Merck, with a volume of 791,353,400 shares traded; RJR Nabisco, 773,160,700; WalMart, 758,946,300; Philip Morris, 722,235,200; Telefonos de México, 593,685,900; General Motors, 586,661,000; IBM, 579,564,800; Chrysler, 563,596,000; Citicorp, 535,185,700; and Glaxo Holdings, 483,753,600.

Volume on the Amex was up 29.3% in 1993, with 4.5 billion shares traded. Short sales reached 104.5 million in August, a record. The Amex index gained 19.52% for the year. There were 583 advances, 259 declines, and 17 unchanged for a total of 997 issues traded. The smaller exchanges similarly showed record trading activity.

Volume on Nasdaq through December 22 was 67,052,627,700, up 42.6% compared with 1992. The Nasdaq composite index ranged from a high of 787.42 to a low of 645.87 and closed the year at 776.8, a gain of 14.75% for the year. There were 1,715 advances, 1,085 declines, and 51 stock prices unchanged. In all, there were 5,284 issues traded on Nasdaq and the OTC markets. Short interest on the Nasdaq Stock Market set a record for the 11th consecutive month in mid-December, rising marginally to 672 million shares from mid-November's 671.3 million. Telecommunications and technology companies were among those with the largest short positions.

The mutual fund industry continued its explosive growth during 1993 as 1,300 new funds were offered, bringing the total number to 4,385, more than the number of company listings on the Big Board. Mutual fund assets grew to $1.8 trillion. Money-market funds made up more than 70% of all funds in 1992, but their market share dropped to 30% in 1993. They were the largest buyers of common stocks and municipal bonds. More than a third of the $200 billion that poured into U.S. mutual funds in the first nine months of 1993 went into funds that specialized in foreign investments. Gold funds did particularly well, accounting for 15 of the top 25 individual funds.

The S&P 500 composite index (Table VI) began the year at 435.23, 4.6% above the corresponding figure of 416.08 in January 1992. The index rose in February and March, dipped to 433.08 in April, and then climbed slowly to 463.9 in October, 12.5% above the corresponding month in the previous year. It closed the year at 466.45. The industrials followed a similar pattern, beginning the year at 504.96 and moving irregularly to 527.13 in October, 9% over the comparable 1992 figure. For the entire year the S&P industrials were up more than 6% at 540.19. The S&P public utilities index began the year at 159.79, rose to 186.76 by September, and then dipped to 183.5 in October for an 18.9% gain on a year-to-year basis. The utilities were up 14.12 overall at 172.58 at year's end. Transportation stocks rose from 374.27 in January to peak at 402.75 in October, a 7.6% gain for the 10-month period but 23% above the corresponding year-earlier figure. The transportation index finished the year at 425.6.

U.S. government long-term bond yields were well below prior year levels all though 1993. From a high average of 7.17% in January (Table VII), the yield slid gradually to 6.64 in April, paused in May, and resumed its decline to 5.9% in October, 23% below the corresponding 1992 figure.

Corporate bond yields (Table VIII) declined steadily throughout most of the year. From a level of 7.91% at the beginning of the year, the average slid to a low of 6.66%

in September before rising slightly in the last quarter of the year. On a year-to-year basis, the October level was nearly 20% lower than in 1992.

Trading volume in the nation's futures and options markets continued to climb toward record levels, with volume more than 9.2% above that of 1992. Some 45% of all futures and options contracts traded were interest-rate instruments, an increase of 32% above the prior year. It was a record year at the Chicago Board of Trade. Contract volume soared past its previous annual record in December as the 1993 volume hit 155 million contracts, an all-time high. Financial futures and options led the way, compared with agricultural futures and options and stock index futures and options, which had been more popular in earlier years. An attempt by the Chicago Board Options Exchange (the nations biggest stock options exchange) to take over the Philadelphia Stock Exchange (the fourth largest) was rebuffed.

U.S. stock options trading never returned to its pace set before the 1987 crash. There were 125 million stock option contracts traded in 1993, up 22% from 1992 but still nearly 24% fewer than the 164 million options traded in 1987, according to Options Clearing Corp.

The Securities and Exchange Commission (SEC) was very active in 1993 on a number of regulatory issues. It proposed several new rules to make mutual fund investing safer and easier to understand. One proposed rule called for mutual funds to disclose how much compensation each director earned from all the funds in the same family of funds. The proposals marked the SEC's first change in mutual fund proxy material since 1960. Another proposal provided that national tax-exempt money funds would be barred from investing more than 5% of their assets in any one security.

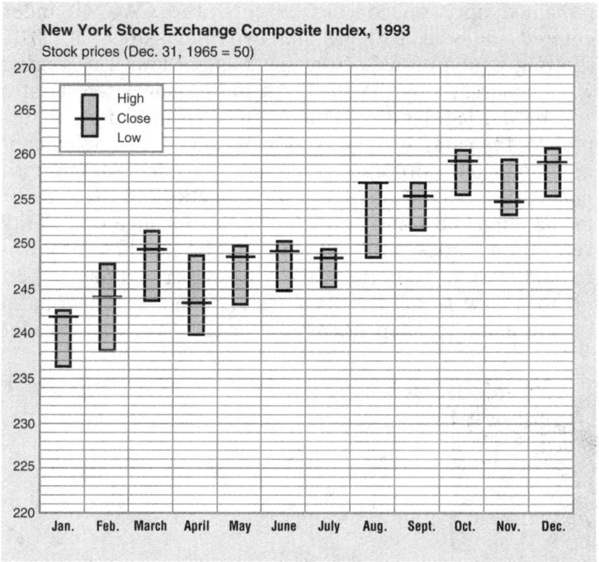

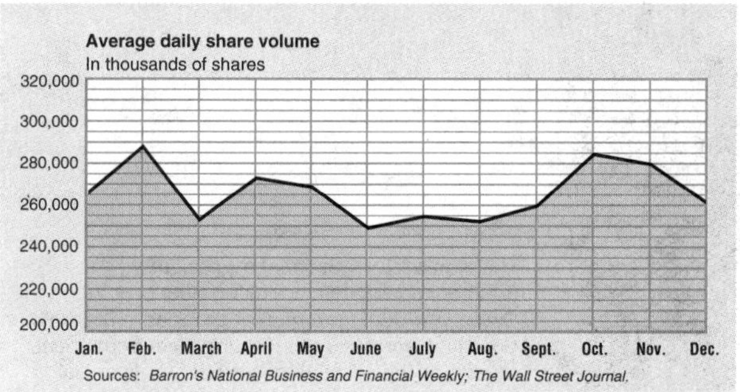

Sources: *Barron's National Business and Financial Weekly; The Wall Street Journal.*

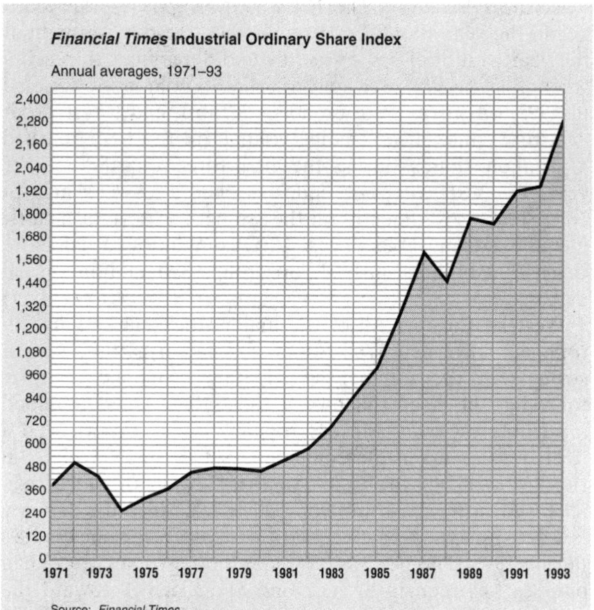

Source: *Financial Times.*

The SEC was also interested in proposals that would, for the first time, require continuing financial disclosure on the $1.2 trillion municipal bond market. While the disclosure was expected to increase costs for municipal bond issuers, it would provide bond buyers with a basis for valuation of their securities in the after market. The plan would prohibit dealers from underwriting new bonds unless the issuer agreed to continuing financial disclosure. The SEC also escalated its pressure on securities firms to change brokers' compensation and to control "cold calling"; that is, soliciting investments from people who were not clients of the firm. The adequacy of supervision of brokers was the subject of an ongoing investigation as of year's end because of what appeared to be widespread abuses in the sale of highly speculative limited partnerships.

Canada. The stock exchanges in Canada performed very well during 1993, in part because the Canadian dollar was near a six-year low relative to the U.S. dollar. The recession was easing, with an inflation rate below that of the U.S., although unemployment was still unacceptably high at more than 11%. Low inflation, a gradually improving trade balance, and commodity prices that appeared poised to rise supported the Canadian currency and bond markets. Investors bought Can$20 billion of new equity in 1993, nearly twice the $11 billion of 1992, the previous record year. Foreign purchases of Canadian securities hit Can$45.8 billion in the first nine months of 1993, three times the volume of the equivalent period in 1992. In September foreign holdings of Canadian debt hit an all-time high of Can$271.8 billion. The Canadian Dow Jones Equity Index had a yearly high of U.S.$99.72 and a low of U.S.$81.40 for a 14.03% year-to-year gain.

The composite index of the Toronto Stock Exchange (TSE), which did 78% of all the trading in Canada, rose 29% in 1993, outperforming Wall Street and many other markets abroad. Volume was never stronger. The same was true of Montreal, with 17% of the activity, the Vancouver Stock Exchange (VSE), with 3%, and the Alberta and Winnipeg exchanges, which did the rest of the business. In August the TSE 300 index passed its former record, set in 1987. For the year it set 17 new highs, including 4320.88 attained on December 30. Bullishness was accompanied by ever increasing volume. The daily average was 60 million shares, almost twice the 1992 figure. The TSE (300) composite price index began the year about 3300 and climbed steadily throughout the year with brief pauses in July and September to reach a level of 4321.43 by year's end. Toronto's gold index doubled in 1993, oil stocks were up about a third, and forest products rose some 50%. Trading volume on the VSE reached 4.4 billion shares during the first three quarters of the year. The VSE composite index reached a 52-week high of 1052.86 on November 12 on the strength of several factors, including strong gold prices. VSE companies raised more than $770 million in 1993, up from $390 million during 1992. (IRVING PFEFFER)

Western Europe. All of the major stock markets in Europe outperformed Wall Street and Japan as they surged strongly in the summer, anticipating economic recovery following the near collapse of the ERM, which heralded lower interest rates. Most European bourses experienced a further spurt up in December and set their 1993 highs in the last week of the year. An overall gain of more than 40% shown by the Euro Top-100 Index, since the January low, was matched or exceeded by many European bourses during 1993. The best performance among larger European bourses was seen in Sweden and Spain, which toward the end of the year were 54% and 51% higher, respectively, than they had been at year-end 1992. Germany, with a 41% increase over the same period, was also a good performer.

The London Stock Exchange (LSE) lagged behind its continental European counterparts, as the share prices had risen by 20% during the previous autumn after the pound withdrew from the ERM and interest rates fell by three percentage points. Thus, the *Financial Times* Stock Exchange (FT-SE 100) Index in London fluctuated narrowly in the first seven months of the year between 2800 and 2950—rising when traders sensed interest rates might be cut and retreating when hopes were dashed or company profits were disappointing. In the spring the index tested the psychologically important 3000 level on hopes of an early cut in German interest rates, but it fell back when these did not materialize. The FT-SE drifted throughout the summer, as economic activity proved to be sluggish and there was no change in policy to stimulate the economy. In August, when the German interest rates were cut, the FT-SE rose strongly, and by early September it was 10% higher than the July low. By early November the FT-SE 100 Index stood at 3200, but this level could not be sustained, and it fell back to under 3100 as the market was perceived to be ahead of the recovery in company profits. Uncertainty was injected ahead of the unified budget on November 30. In the event, the budget was a major stimulus as tax increases were less than feared and the chancellor of the Exchequer aimed to reduce the public-sector deficit more quickly than previously planned. The FT-SE 100 Index soared to its highest-ever level of 3462 and finished the year at 3418.4.

In Germany, despite the deepest recession in 50 years, investors were rewarded by a 41% gain in 1993, as measured by the FAZ Aktien Index. In the opening months of the year, the FAZ Aktien Index rose from around 600 to 650 on hopes of interest rates easing following agreement on measures to reduce the public-sector deficit. A setback in late March was followed by three months of drifting as the economic indicators worsened and company profits slumped. In the summer, as the tension within the ERM grew and the French franc fell to its floor against the Deutsche Mark, the markets anticipated a cut in interest rates and recovered. Although the Bundesbank cut the discount rate by a paltry 0.5% in early August, the market soared as investors anticipated that other European countries had more room to reduce interest rates. This, in turn, was expected to benefit German exporters. By November the FAZ index had breached the 800 level, despite disappointing news on the economic front and a cautious approach by the Bundesbank to cutting interest rates. Factors that stimulated prices in the autumn included expectations of further interest-rate cuts, restructuring by companies that would improve their competitiveness and profitability, and external demand, particularly from U.S. investors. By year's end the market had consolidated at around the 850 level.

The Paris Bourse also registered a gain (of more than 20%) during 1993. Although the Bank of France was too cautious in cutting interest rates and the old "franc fort" policy survived the revision to the ERM, investors still remained optimistic of further cuts. The CAC 40 Index entered the year strongly and by March stood at 2010, showing a gain of 13% from the January low. The market was encouraged by the small cut in German interest rates and by the legislative election results. In the spring it lost most of the gains as the recession deepened, unemployment mounted, and corporate profitability headed for an estimated 15% fall on top of a 25% decline in 1992. The desire to maintain the franc/Deutsche Mark exchange-rate parity kept interest rates artificially high and exacerbated the recession. The surge in the market in August and September, up to a new high of 2230, reflected France's freedom to pursue a more independent line in the new era of wider

THOMAS HILDEBRANDT—LEHTIKUVA/SABA

The Korea Stock Exchange, a booming Asian bourse, is housed in a striking new building in Seoul. In August the market dropped sharply when South Korean Pres. Kim Young Sam announced an end to the practice of conducting financial transactions under assumed names.

ERM bands. The market entered a volatile phase in the autumn and fluctuated between 2050 and 2230 as it was influenced by conflicting sentiments of uncertain economic outlook. Sentiments improved in December and, after setting a new high of 2282 on the 27th, the CAC 40 ended the year at 2273.

The Swiss and Austrian stock markets had risen by 47% and 37%, respectively, since the end of 1992. The purchase of equities was seen by investors as a way of gaining international exposure with limited risks. The banks and pharmaceutical companies that dominated the Swiss market were perceived to be strong beneficiaries of lower interest rates. Likewise, the strong Swiss currency was a safe haven against the turbulence in other European currencies.

The Benelux countries benefited from a combination of low inflation, declining interest rates, and projected economic recovery. The Netherlands, in particular, was seen as a Germany without the burden of the unification and finished the year with a similar gain. The Belgian market rose more modestly, with an increase of 30%.

Floating exchange rates and lower interest rates since autumn 1992 improved the export earnings of most Scandinavian countries and signaled a recovery ahead of the rest of continental Europe. Finland was the star performer, with a rise of over 90% as it continued to recover from the sharp falls caused in 1991 by the collapse of the Soviet Union. Ironically, the severity of the recession in Sweden and cost cutting in industrial sectors was expected to improve company profitability and made it attractive to the international funds. Both the Swedish and Norwegian markets rose by more than 50% during 1993, while Denmark registered a slightly smaller gain (40%).

The southern European bourses also proved sensitive to lower interest rates and currency devaluations. Spain was among the best performers in 1993, with a 51% gain as it looked relatively undervalued early in 1993 following a large decline in 1992. Investors were also encouraged by the Social Pact between the government and the unions to moderate wage rises and reform Spain's rigid labour laws. In the longer term, it was hoped that these measures would accelerate Spain's integration into the EC. Italy bounced back to a yearly high in August of 633, then fell below 600 as sentiment was adversely affected by political crises and financial scandals that refused to go away. It staged a partial recovery to end the year at 619.

Other Countries. Although most stock markets performed well in 1993, the region that caught the imagination of the investors was Asia. Its super growth prospects on the back of U.S. economic recovery and continued rapid growth in China led to a boom in most stock markets in the region except Japan. Despite a setback in November, the Philippines was one of the best performing countries, with a 150% increase since the beginning of the year. Malaysia also rose by more than 100%. Taiwan and Thailand had gains of some 80%. Singapore, too, rose strongly (59%) owing to faster economic growth and a generous budget. Hong Kong, the second most important stock market in the region, was in good form, and the Hang Seng Index rose 116% to 11888.39, despite a strong correction in the summer due to worries about the austerity program in China and the worsening relations between China and the U.K. However, the forecast of rapid economic growth in China and Hong Kong, coupled with some progress in the talks between China and Britain, pushed the market to new records.

Japan, meanwhile, suffering from weak domestic demand and strong currency, remained in a recession despite 30,000 billion yen pumped into the economy by the government in the previous 15 months in three economic packages. The poor economic outlook was reflected in the Tokyo stock market, which slumped in November, canceling earlier gains. The Nikkei Average ended the year at around 17,400, only slightly above where it started and 36% below the December 1991 peak. The market, having entered 1993 on a weak note, recovered steadily between March and June and rose by 25%. Political problems caused a modest decline in the summer, but the lost ground was made up in August and September. The larger-than-expected cut in the discount rate in late September encouraged the market, and the Nikkei briefly exceeded the 21,000 level. In late October and early November, sentiment turned bearish, and foreign investors withdrew their support. The market fell by more than 20%, close to the psychologically important support level of 16,000. What worried investors most were the potential bad debts of the banks, declining corporate profitability, and confirmation from the Economic Planning Agency that a recovery was not likely to emerge until between mid-1994 and March 1995. In December the market recovered somewhat on expectations of new economic-stimulus measures.

Commodity Prices. As the world economy experienced its fourth consecutive year of sluggish growth, it was not surprising that prices of many commodities declined or remained weak. *The Economist* Commodity Price Index of spot prices for 28 internationally traded foodstuffs, nonfood agricultural products, and metals rose by 6.8% in U.S. dollar terms during the first 11 months of the year. In sterling terms it was marginally farther ahead at 9.2%.

The price of crude oil, which was not included in *The Economist* Index, fell by around 18%. North Sea Brent, for instance, fluctuated between $19.5 and $16 for most of the year, but in December it was below $14, the lowest level in over five years. The price weakness was induced by supply exceeding the weak demand from the recession-stricken industrial countries. A mild winter and the possibility that Iraqi oil would come to the market in 1994 did not help either. In its November meeting, OPEC decided to hold its output ceiling at 24.5 million bbl a day, but output from member countries regularly exceeded the target. Production from Russia and other non-OPEC members was also rising.

The two major sectors of *The Economist* Index performed very differently. The food index rose 16% in dollar terms, while the industrials index rose by only 1%. Floods in the U.S. and frosts and droughts elsewhere reduced yields and led to a fall in output of some products. Excess stocks and problems with international price-support agreements depressed the prices of beverages. Nonfood agricultural products such as rubber were also weak. Wool prices recovered from earlier weakness as production was expected to fall at a time when demand from both Japan and Europe was on the upswing. *The Economist* Metals Index fell by 20% in dollar terms as demand fell short of production. An increase in production was especially noticeable in the countries of the former Soviet Union.

Gold came back to life in 1993 and at one point was 25% up, but the price fell back, trimming the gain to 12%. The price of gold was quiet early in 1993 at around $326 per troy ounce until two veteran speculators, George Soros and Sir James Goldsmith, stirred it up by investing in gold and gold shares. The price swiftly moved up to $405 at the end of July. As they realized most of their gains and reduced their holdings, the gold price tumbled back to $344 in September. After that, gold traded in a narrow range and at year's end stood at $390.80. Gold bugs remained optimistic and predicted that the gold price would rise to $500 once the world economy was fully out of the recession. (IEIS)

This article updates the *Macropædia* article MARKETS.

Education

Key issues in education in 1993 included financing for schools and colleges at all levels; curriculum and textbook reform; religious, ethnic, and racial questions in primary and secondary schools and, in higher education, problems of academic and administrative autonomy; and the effects of violence, including wars, on education. Problems of how to guarantee the quality of staff and facilities and international cooperative educational efforts also were discussed.

In the United States almost 64 million students were enrolled in schools in 1993, and nearly 8 million people were employed in education at all levels. Elementary and secondary enrollments rose to 48.9 million. Rapid increases in preschool and kindergarten classes brought total enrollments to 6,650,000. Minorities accounted for 31.5%, up from 26.8% in 1983.

College enrollments broke a record with 15 million—9.1 million in four-year and 5.9 in two-year schools. (*See also* 1994 BRITANNICA WORLD DATA: *Comparative National Statistics: Education*.)

Compared with other developed countries, U.S. teachers earned lower salaries, had less class-preparation time, and taught larger classes, according to a survey of 19 nations by the American Federation of Teachers. The top pay for U.S. high school teachers was $38,000, while that of Swiss teachers was $70,000. Teachers in Norway and Italy also received incomes at the low end of the scale.

A study conducted by researcher-editor C. Emily Feistritzer found that small schools (up to 300 pupils) are conducive to a good learning environment. School size was found to be more significant than class size. The researcher found three other important quality variables: high expectations of students, challenging courses, and well-managed schools. The ALEC Foundation published the report.

U.S. college graduates earned twice as much as high school graduates, but in a tough job market, the college graduates often faced difficulties in securing their first jobs and often took low-paying ones. The U.S. Bureau of Labor Statistics expected the number of graduates to outstrip the number of jobs for two more decades.

Primary and Secondary Education. *Funding.* Education costs in the U.S. were projected to reach $493 billion for the 1993–94 school year, a 50% increase (adjusted for inflation) since 1983–84. The proportion of gross domestic product devoted to education moved from 6.7% to 7.9% during the 10-year period. Without adopting an alternative, the state of Michigan eliminated property taxes as its main school revenue, and some $6.3 billion—two-thirds of the money used to support public schools—was lost. Property taxes had long been criticized as being inequitable because they provided rich districts with much more money than was available to poor districts. Eleven states had earmarked state lottery income for education, but this yielded little fiscal relief, according to a report of the Educational Research Service. On average, only 3.8% of education costs was raised through lottery earnings.

Educational Reforms. Niamh Breathnach, a former school teacher, became Ireland's first minister of education from the Labour Party and only the third woman to hold that post. She was chosen partly because of a growing consensus that more should be done to help the socially disadvantaged in a society with an unemployment rate of 20%. An initial reform to be adopted was the reduction of class size, which at more than 30 was the highest in Europe. The goal was to reduce the teacher-pupil ratio to 1:22 by 1996, to provide 500 more remedial teachers, and to offer psychological services for all schools. In addition, Ireland joined the world's growing decentralization movements by devolving more responsibility for school management from the central government to local boards of education.

Planned school reforms in Hungary led to public protests over the government's intent to postpone teachers' salary increases and to introduce legislation that would provide classes on religious education, give churches the right to establish private schools, and institute a national curriculum similar to Western European models. Primary and secondary schoolteachers in New Zealand refused to place new syllabi into practice until the government dropped its plan to give each school a bulk salary grant based on an average salary for the school rather than on individual teachers' actual wages. The scheme was viewed by teachers unions and boards of education as grossly unfair.

In China the government tacitly encouraged the establishment of private primary and middle schools on the apparent assumption that competition would raise the quality of education both in state and in private institutions. Public demand for schooling opportunities that train learners for a market economy was particularly heavy in the economically booming province of Guangdong (Kwangtung) in southern China.

ALLEN TANNENBAUM—SYGMA

Students in New York City plead for an end to violence in their school. Although it took different forms, violence in schools continued to grow throughout the world, becoming a major problem for educators.

In Spain a revolutionary approach to primary schooling was instituted under the direction of Álvaro Marchesi, a professor of developmental psychology. Two aims of the plan were to reduce the amount of curricula designed by the central government in order to focus children's studies more on their immediate environments and to replace rote memorization with meaningful understanding. Key decisions about lesson content and teaching method were thus delegated to local schools. To help implement the innovations, a broad array of new textbooks were reproduced in the nation's officially recognized languages—Castilian Spanish and the regional tongues of the Basques, Galicians, and Catalonians. Music and physical education would be provided for the youngest children, and a second language—in most cases English—would be introduced at age eight.

New Russian textbooks for teaching English reflected the nation's revised curriculum guidelines. Unlike the former texts that were laden with communist polemics, the new books featured modern language-instruction techniques without political messages, thereby conforming to the requirement of the 1992 education laws that forbade mixing political ideology and language instruction. In the past, history textbooks in Japan omitted mention of acts of aggression and cruelty committed by the nation's military units during World War II. However, revised texts issued in 1993 included accounts of unsavoury events that had been missing from earlier versions. The recent addition of such events reflected the government's response to sharp criticism from South Korea and China that Japan was attempting to distort accounts of what occurred in the 1930s and '40s in territories occupied by Japanese forces.

Educational planners in Hong Kong, anticipating the 1997 transfer of political control of the colony from Britain to China, were placing increased emphasis on studies that encouraged heightened awareness of Chinese culture and political consciousness. New textbooks were picturing China in more favourable terms than in the past. In the nearby Portuguese colony of Macau, a similar set of curriculum changes foreshadowed that territory's scheduled return to Chinese sovereignty in 1999. Efforts to censor schoolbooks and materials increased in the U.S., according to a report from People for the American Way. The civil liberties group said that the increase was a result of activism by conservative groups and the religious right. At issue were topics such as self-esteem, sexuality, drugs, and racism.

Religious Issues. National policies defining the relationship between church and state in the conduct of education were the object of controversy in France, Poland, Israel, and the U.S. France's new minister of education, François Bayrou, a devout Roman Catholic, worked with church lobbyists to pass legislation that would provide vastly increased public funds for Catholic schools. Opposing groups calculated that the plan, if put into effect, would reduce the state system's income by F 4 billion and deprive many children of the opportunity for a secular republican education. A Polish constitutional tribunal decreed that religious instruction in state schools was admissible under the law. The decision was welcomed by the Catholic majority but was criticized by nonbelievers and adherents of other faiths, who contended that crosses displayed on classroom walls were an offense to non-Catholics and that the decision would lead to prejudicial treatment of their own followers.

In Israel pressure from the ultra-Orthodox Shas political party forced Shulamit Aloni out of her post as minister of education on the charge that she had extolled Charles Darwin's version of creation in preference to the biblical version and had said it was no longer necessary to maintain Jewish dietary laws. Upon achieving independence from Ethiopia, Eritrea adopted a pragmatic socialist political philosophy that permitted all Muslim and Christian denominations to teach religious matters in schools as long as they followed a national curriculum in their secular subjects. Charges of religious discrimination were voiced by supporters of the private Islamia School in London when their application for a grant as a voluntary aided school was rejected by British authorities. Voluntary aided status would have paid all of the school's operating costs and 85% of capital spending. Britain had 4,100 Christian and 21 Jewish voluntary aided schools but none for the country's one million Muslims.

The U.S. Supreme Court granted a church access to school facilities for a religious program. The justices held that the church's access had to be equal to the use granted other community groups. Under those circumstances access did not violate the prohibition in the First Amendment to the Constitution against official "establishment" of religion, and the access upheld constitutional rights to free speech. The Supreme Court also let stand a U.S. Court of Appeals ruling that student-led prayers at graduation were permitted, while a religious figure's prayers were not. Amid much controversy a Jackson, Miss., high school principal, Bishop Knox, was dismissed in November for allowing students to read a prayer over the school intercom. A few weeks later the school board reinstated Knox but placed him on suspension without pay for the remainder of the school year.

Ethnic and Racial Questions. Since the former Yugoslav republic of Macedonia became an independent state, struggles over the control of education between the Macedonian majority and the ethnic Albanian minority had threatened to ruin the educational system and perhaps lead to general bloodshed. The issue was whether Macedonians, who made up two-thirds of the population, should control education and employ their language as the medium of instruction throughout the country or whether the Albanian minority should have the same right in the provinces they dominated. Albanians called for more secondary education in their language and a higher-learning institution of their own. In the nation's two universities, where all teaching was in Macedonian, only 5% of the students were Albanian.

German educators faced the challenge of teaching ethnic tolerance and peaceful political action to a nation experiencing a rapid escalation of attacks by neo-Nazis on foreigners and the handicapped. A study revealed that one-third of young Germans between ages 15 and 24 held racist views or were susceptible to right-wing propaganda.

In the U.S. a two-decades-old policy on using race as a key factor in assigning teachers was upheld by the Supreme Court. Involuntary transfers of teachers to maintain racial balances in individual schools had previously been held constitutional by a federal appeals court. The U.S. Census Bureau predicted that by 2010 Hispanics rather than African-Americans would be the largest minority group. The demographic changes were expected to result in calls for more Spanish-language classes and other changes. In November a federal court ruled that a University of Maryland scholarship for blacks only was constitutional because of the university's history of discrimination.

Social Issues: Violence. A survey of secondary schools in Japan reported a marked increase in truancy and bullying among pupils. Critics blamed the increase on the education system's unduly strict discipline that impelled students to keep pace with a demanding national curriculum. However, the Ministry of Education was not inclined to alter the traditional pattern of schooling that was credited with producing the highly literate citizenry considered essential for the nation's socioeconomic well-being. The government's effort to reduce bullying consisted of assigning 14,000 social welfare officers to work in schools. Teachers from four secondary schools in a Paris suburb staged a series of strikes in protest against what they claimed was the Ministry of Education's inadequate reaction to growing violence. Incidents included physical attacks on teachers, drug peddling, intimidation of classmates to get their possessions, and sexual abuse of younger students by older ones. The ministry responded by assigning national servicemen from the Defense Department to the beleaguered schools.

Surveys showed that two-thirds of the German public placed the blame for growing lawlessness on the heavy dose of violence and sex dominating TV programming. Nearly three-quarters of the population believed that a detrimental influence on young people resulted from television's removing traditional taboos from killing. In the U.S. the four major television networks agreed to include parental warnings at the beginning of violent TV shows. A study by the American Psychological Association found that by the time the average child completed elementary school, he or she had viewed 8,000 killings and 100,000 violent acts on television. Another study, released in December by the Metropolitan Life Insurance Co., showed that nearly one in four pupils and one in 10 teachers had been victims of violence on or near school property.

Vocational and Special Education. The administration of U.S. Pres. Bill Clinton unfolded its plan to reform high school vocational education, calling for cooperative school and business activities to provide students with paid work experience, mentoring, and counseling. School-based experiences would include both academic instruction and vocational training. The program would serve the 75% of American youth who did not attend college.

Early in the year Greek students and teachers conducted demonstrations principally in protest against the government's effort to promote private institutes of vocational training—fee-paying colleges for 16- to 18-year-olds—alongside currently established institutions. Demonstrators claimed that the government's attempt would be the first step toward abolishing free state education.

In an Arizona case the U.S. Supreme Court ruled that schools may provide special education students with assistance even in a parochial school. The ruling for the first time permitted a public employee—an interpreter—to serve a child whose parents had selected a religious school. The court viewed the assistance as benefiting the child and not subsidizing the religious school.

International and Regional Cooperation. Educators in Argentina, Brazil, Paraguay, and Uruguay organized to write a common regional history as part of those nations' movement toward forming a common economic market, Mercosur, by 1994–95. Side agreements between the four countries' Ministries of Education committed them to providing instruction in both Spanish and Portuguese in their schools and to setting common standards for certifying teachers. The four also formed a regional education association that had convened three conferences.

Antonio Ruberti of Italy, the European Community's (EC's) newly appointed commissioner responsible for science, research, and development, defined three goals for the immediate future: to increase the mobility of ideas and educational programs between the 12 member nations, to improve the exchange of information among Ministries of Education on the development of training policies, and to foster more rapid agreement on diploma equivalency between the community's educational institutions.

In Chile the government's satisfaction with initial results of the country's 900-Schools Project led the Ministry of Education to extend the program to 635 additional schools, thereby reaching about 15% of public primary schools and 20% of primary students. Originally funded by a grant from Denmark and Sweden, the 900-Schools Project provided Chile's most poorly equipped schools with textbooks, workbooks, libraries, training for teachers, and funds to repair buildings.

Higher Education. *Funding.* Financial struggles continued to plague higher-education institutions in various parts of the world. Funding problems endangered the continued operation of the eight Palestinian universities in the Israeli-occupied West Bank and Gaza Strip. After 1973, when the first university was established, a large portion of the institutions' funds came from Arab countries. Israel closed the universities in 1988 for nearly four years after the Palestinian *intifada,* and funds from abroad declined, particularly after the 1991 Gulf war. All eight universities had reopened by the end of 1992. The current financial crisis resulted from a combination of less funding from abroad and rapidly rising enrollments. In 1993 an estimated 17,000 students attended the eight institutions, exceeding the pre-*intifada* total because the 1993 entrants included a backlog of high school graduates from the 1988–92 period.

Pressure to admit more students into higher education motivated the Israeli government to authorize between $175 million and $250 million for construction projects over the 1993–96 period, the first significant government expenditure for buildings since 1974. The proposal was designed to cope with enrollments that had increased by 15,000 students between 1991 and 1993, partly as a result of immigration.

The threat of reduced public moneys for Australian higher education was averted when the Labor Party won a surprise victory over opposing conservative parties that had advocated cutbacks in central government support of universities and colleges. The Labor government promised to add U.S. $300 million to the universities' U.S. $4.3 billion budget, a move that could increase the enrollment in higher education by 25,000 students. The demand for higher education in Australia far exceeded the available places. In 1993 an estimated 583,000 students attended the country's 35 public universities, while 50,000 qualified applicants were unable to gain admission. Total enrollment in the university system had increased by 67% over the previous 10 years.

In the United States college costs had increased by 126% in the 1980s and by the 1990s were exceeded only by housing costs as the most expensive family budget item. In 1993 a congressionally appointed commission urged that the present patchwork system of federal aid to college students be scrapped and instead that each eligible student receive $14,000 per year. The annual aid would be adjusted on the basis of averaged college expenses. The College Board estimated that by 2010 the cost of four years in a public college would be $121,000 and in a private college $250,000. The U.S. Department of Education and congressional investigators reported that the major federal college student aid plan was the victim of large-scale fraud. The Pell Grants program was designed to help students gain job skills by attending college or trade schools. Alleged abuses in the $6.7 billion program included payments received by the schools for students not attending classes, sale of lists to permit schools to apply for grant money, awards to students who had not graduated from high school, and kickbacks to ineligible students who allowed their names to be used in applications for Pell Grants.

A key Clinton campaign theme, performing community service to earn college money, was signed into law in September. Some $1.5 billion was made available for tuition, living allowances, and health care/child day care. Initially some 20,000 college students were likely to receive benefits.

Violence continued to cripple higher education in some areas of the world, most notably in the former Yugoslavia, where Serbs, Croats, and Muslims struggled for political control. During the area's past civil strife, more than 25% of the country's scientists had fled abroad, an exodus intensified by UN economic sanctions that hampered scholars' travel and access to new books and journals. Serbian authorities ousted the rector of the University of Belgrade and forced the election of a person acceptable to the government; nearly half of the university's faculty members declined to vote in the election. Protracted war in Bosnia and Herzegovina not only closed universities but led to what critics claimed was the intentional destruction by Serbian forces of Bosnian national libraries and other repositories of historical and cultural knowledge.

Administration. Educational institutions in Europe and Asia wrestled with questions of relationships with their governments. Parliament in The Netherlands granted the nation's 14 universities and 19 vocational institutes wide-ranging academic and administrative autonomy in exchange for the introduction of a new system of quality control. Minister of Education Jo Ritzen predicted that greater efficiency would result because university officials "can see what decisions are necessary sooner and better than we at the ministry can." Whereas in the past, curricula were set by the central ministry, under the new plan each institution could introduce courses without consulting the ministry. This move to permit a greater measure of self-governance followed similar policies instituted in Sweden and Denmark.

In a break from the past, responsibility for higher education in France was removed from the Ministry of Education and assigned, along with research programs, to a new ministry headed by François Fillon, a career politician who previously specialized in military affairs but had no professional experience in education or research. Shortly after his appointment, Fillon sought to quell fears that he would promote the privatization of higher education. He told the academic community that while he favoured more autonomy for universities, he did not intend to undermine the existing national system.

Privatization was much on the minds of educators in the former communist countries of Eastern Europe and northern Asia, where private colleges were being established at a growing pace as part of their rapid shift toward a market economy. In Mongolia the number of private colleges increased from six in 1991 to 18 by 1993. Furthermore, government institutions began charging students fees and engaging in outside moneymaking ventures to help pay operating costs. Such ventures in Mongolia included renting rooms to private businesses, offering consultancy services, and managing flocks of sheep. The government in Lithuania reacted against the Soviet practice of strong central control of higher education by giving full autonomy to that country's 13 institutions of higher learning, thereby matching a policy already applied in Estonia and Latvia.

Political opposition forced the Hungarian Ministry of Education to abandon its plan to consolidate 20 universities and 50 specialized colleges into a new system that would have featured six comprehensive university centres. The plan represented a way to use scarce resources more efficiently, but it was defeated by politically influential administrators and faculty members who stood to lose their positions.

In Russia thousands of would-be entrepreneurs, including retired military personnel, attended the scores of business schools that had sprung up since 1991. Many of the new schools were extensions of departments in existing state institutions, whereas others were private enterprises. The EC allocated $2 million to support the training of future leaders

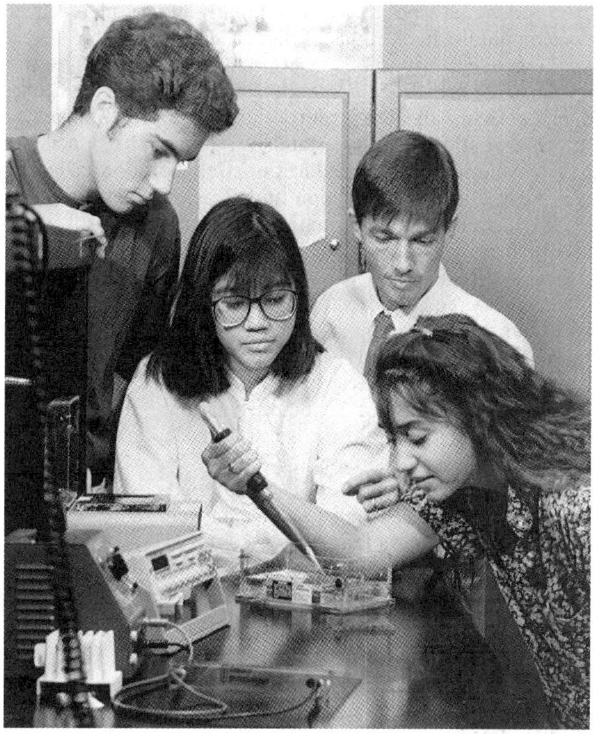

Tracey Leon Bailey (rear), 1993 Teacher of the Year, oversees the work of high school science students in Satellite Beach, Fla. Sponsored by Encyclopædia Britannica, Inc., and the Council of Chief State School Officers, the award recognizes excellence in teaching.

BOB GOLDBERG

of industry at the Institute of Management Economics and Strategic Research in Almaty, Kazakhstan. Private British and American firms also contributed funds for training the 125 postgraduate students in Kazakhstan who were earning master's degrees in business administration and economics.

Guaranteeing Quality Faculty. Appraisals of the quality of institutions were conducted in the United Kingdom and Canada. In Britain a comprehensive government assessment of higher-education research placed the University of Cambridge at the top with "world-class" ratings in 41 disciplines. The University of Oxford was second with world-class distinction in 28 fields, while University College, London, placed third with high marks in 21 areas. Britain's Association of University Teachers warned that the nation's universities would lose a great number of professors through retirement over the coming decade because more than half of the country's faculty members would be over age 50 within five years. Under existing law males must retire at age 65 and females at age 60. According to the association, the vacated positions would be difficult to fill because academic salaries were too low.

Concern for making higher-learning institutions more accountable to society stimulated officials in nearly all of Canada's 10 provinces to launch audits of their universities and colleges. Prominent among the issues being investigated were questions of the unproductive duplication of departments, students' transferring credits from one institution to another, and institutions' responsibility for service to society in the fields of business, education, engineering, and environmental science.

In the Czech Republic an assessment of a different kind took place as all 13,000 faculty members of the country's 23 public colleges and universities were required to reapply for their positions before the end of September 1993 or lose their posts. The reapplication plan provided for reviewing each individual's political and scholarly fitness to teach in postcommunist institutions of higher learning.

International Education. In a move toward increasing the scope of cooperation in higher education between Canadian, Mexican, and U.S. institutions, 270 representatives of the three nations met to establish a Trilateral Council for North American Higher Education Collaboration, a North American Distance Education and Research Network, and a clearinghouse for information on academic institutions and their programs.

Issues of regional educational standardization were raised in the EC when the European Commission warned Spain's Autonomous University of Barcelona that it had to reduce the number of veterinary students from 1,450 to 700 within two years if its graduates' qualifications were to be recognized in the EC's other 11 member nations. The university also was told to double the veterinary department's nonteaching staff and increase the budget by 500% to meet the Commission's standards. The warning was issued under a 1989 directive designed to make university degrees and certification comparable in all EC countries.

(JOEL L. BURDIN; ROBERT MURRAY THOMAS)

See also Law; Libraries.

This article updates the *Macropædia* articles History of EDUCATION; TEACHING.

Energy

During the first half of 1993, the dominant development in regard to energy was the intense political struggle waged over the energy tax proposals in U.S. Pres. Bill Clinton's budget plan. As presented to the U.S. Congress, the plan included a broad-based tax on nearly all forms of energy, with the level of the tax to be determined by the heat content of the various fuels. Each of the basic energy industries concluded that it would be disadvantaged in one or more ways by such a tax structure. Coal, with the highest energy content per unit, would be hit hardest, as the industry vehemently pointed out. The oil industry stressed the market dislocations that would result from different taxes on the various oil products. The natural gas and nuclear industries objected to their fuels' being taxed when they made little or no contribution to air pollution. The public in general made known its dislike of the increases in transportation and heating costs that would result from such taxes. In the face of such opposition, the legislation passed by Congress in August contained only a single tax of 4.3 cents per gallon on transportation fuels.

As the year began, a milestone in U.S. energy policy passed with little fanfare—the last remaining controls on the price of natural gas at the wellhead were phased out. The effect was minor—because more than 95% of all gas being sold was at prices below the legal ceilings—but it marked the end of an era that had begun in the 1950s. In May the U.S. Department of Energy said that it would voluntarily submit to the supervision of worker safety by the Occupational Safety and Health Administration.

Petroleum. For yet another year OPEC struggled vainly to achieve prices for oil at the organization's target level of $21 a barrel. As in previous years, the nub of the problem was OPEC's inability to enforce compliance by its members with the agreed-upon quotas for each country's production. At the February meeting of the organization, the quotas were adjusted to include Kuwait, which had recovered from the destruction of its oil facilities in the 1991 Gulf war. In June the total OPEC production ceiling remained unchanged, and because its quota was not significantly increased, Kuwait elected to remain outside the agreement. Price weakness intensified during the summer as total OPEC output increased in the face of no rise in demand. By the time of the OPEC meeting at the end of September, prices had fallen some $6 per barrel below the $21 target and threatened to fall as low as $10 per barrel. This possibility produced a measure of unity. A new production ceiling was agreed upon, with Kuwait this time accepting its quota, and the ceiling was set for a six-month period rather than the customary three months. Market weakness reappeared during October and November. An OPEC meeting at the end of November failed to produce any agreement on curtailing production, and on December 17 prices dropped to $13.91 per barrel, the lowest levels in nearly three years in the U.S. market and in five years in the European market.

Saudi Arabia merged its national production company with its refining and marketing company, creating the world's largest fully integrated oil firm. Venezuela approved the first oil projects with foreign oil company participation since its industry was nationalized in 1976. The projects involved development of the country's huge resources of extra-heavy crude oil in the Orinoco River basin. China agreed to the first foreign drilling onshore since the establishment of the communist regime in 1949. At year's end the Mobil Corp. announced that it and a Japanese consortium had been granted the right to drill offshore in Vietnam, while Exxon, with a consortium that included Mobil and Texaco, Inc., had been given offshore rights on Russia's Sakhalin Island. A well in the Adriatic Sea off the Italian "bootheel" established a new record water depth of 850 m (2,789 ft) for commercial production. In October, Shell Oil Co. said that it planned to drill for oil 894 m (2,933 ft) beneath the Gulf of Mexico off the coast of Louisiana.

Natural Gas and Coal. On November 1 the natural gas industry in the U.S. entered a new era as the Federal Energy Regulatory Commission's Order 636 took effect. The order completed the process, begun in 1986, of increasing competition and creating more open markets in the industry. Under the order, interstate gas pipeline companies gave up their traditional role as suppliers of gas to local distribution companies, becoming instead service companies offering transportation, storage, and other functions to all interested buyers. The distributors and large industrial users, in turn, became fully responsible for obtaining their own gas supplies, without the benefit of the pipeline's traditional backup function.

Natural gas prices in the U.S. remained generally strong throughout the year. A sharp increase during the spring brought them to near record levels. Despite a subsequent decline during the summer, prices remained above $2 per thousand cubic feet as September brought the onset of the heating season. The Venezuelan government approved the first foreign investment in that country's gas industry since nationalization. The multibillion-dollar project involved the liquefaction of gas for export. Poland granted a U.S. company the rights to develop the production of methane gas from coal by drilling wells in the coal beds of working mines as well as in unworked deposits.

Labour strikes plagued the U.S. coal industry throughout most of the year but did not lead to any supply shortages for coal users. In Britain the government began the process of privatization of the national coal industry by offering the first pits for sale.

Other Developments. Despite several severe weather incidents during the year, the energy industries fared surprisingly well. An unusually strong winter storm in March, with high winds and tornadoes along with record snowfalls and plunging temperatures from Florida through the mid-

Atlantic states, resulted in the loss of power to more than 1.2 million customers in Florida alone. Predicted cold temperatures in the wake of the storm did not materialize, however, and statewide blackouts were averted. Electric utilities in states along most of the Eastern Seaboard suffered only moderate damage. The storm caused some gas pipelines to curtail deliveries, but in this regard also the effect on customers was minor. A severe and prolonged heat wave in July (with temperatures of more than 38° C [100° F] from New York City to Memphis, Tenn.) resulted in new all-time or summer record levels of peak demand for 22 electric utility systems in the eastern half of the U.S. The historic and devastating floods produced by unending rainfall during the summer and fall in the upper Mississippi River drainage basin likewise spared electric utilities from severe damage to their systems. Some generating plants and substations were flooded out, but the effects were local, and power supplies were not affected by the flood interference with fuel shipments.

A troublesome event in nuclear energy was the action by the Ukrainian legislature in October to reverse a decision in 1991 to close the two remaining operating reactors at the Chernobyl nuclear power plant at the end of 1993. The plant was the site of the world's worst civilian nuclear disaster in 1986. The decision was based on the urgent need to rely on nuclear plants to provide the country with adequate power, despite the dismal safety record of the type of reactors at Chernobyl. In the U.S. the government announced that the uranium-enrichment business would be privatized, and the operator of the Trojan nuclear power plant near Rainer, Ore., closed the plant four years ahead of schedule rather than perform needed repairs. In October the U.S. Department of Energy announced that it was abandoning a plan to put plutonium-contaminated bomb waste in underground storage in New Mexico. In China the country's largest nuclear power plant began operations. The decision to open the plant, located about 50 km (30 mi) northeast of Hong Kong and jointly owned by a Hong Kong utility and the Chinese government, was made despite controversy over its safety. (The plant is located on a geologic fault and in an area subject to typhoons.)

Two developments in the field of unconventional energy deserve mention. In May a team of researchers in Zürich, Switz., reported the discovery of a new superconducting material that raises the temperature at which superconductivity is attainable. The previous limit was 127 degrees on the Kelvin scale, equivalent to −231° F (−146° C). The new limit was 133 K (−220° F [−140° C]). The higher temperature was made possible by the incorporation of mercury for the first time in a superconducting material. (The other elements in the new compound are barium, calcium, copper, and oxygen.) The material itself has no practical applicability; it is difficult to prepare and is toxic. It is, nevertheless, significant in widening the range of superconducting possibilities. In April the largest wind farm for electric power generation outside the U.S. began operation at Llandinam, Powys, Wales. The 103 wind turbines had a capacity of 31 MW, enough power to supply 20,000 homes.

(BRUCE C. NETSCHERT)

See also Engineering Projects; Industrial Review; Mining; Transportation.

This article updates the *Macropædia* articles ENERGY CONVERSION; FOSSIL FUELS.

SARITA KENDALL—THE NEW YORK TIMES

Employees of British Petroleum work at a drilling site in the Cusiana field in Colombia. Pumping from the field, estimated to contain two billion barrels, began in June 1993, with production divided between Colombia's state oil company and three foreign investors.

Engineering Projects

Bridges. At least five potential world-record holders were under construction in 1993. In Hong Kong the Tsing Ma Bridge, a double-decked road and rail suspension bridge, was well under way with slipforming of the giant 205-m-high concrete towers being completed and temporary cable beginning to be slung for the spinning of the giant steel cables that would span 1,377 m, the main part of the crossing between Kowloon and Lantau Island (1 m = 3.3 ft). The Tsing Ma would be the biggest two-level bridge in the world when complete but would not quite equal the record 1,410-m span of Britain's Humber Bridge.

But the Humber's record would soon fall to the East Bridge section of Denmark's Store Bælt (Great Belt), a tunnel and double bridge crossing linking Copenhagen on Zealand, Denmark's main island, to the mainland. A huge 67-span prefabricated-concrete road bridge crosses 6.1 km (3.8 mi) of water, but a 6.6-km (4.1-mi) second section was needed for the eastern half, with a 1,624-m span single-deck suspension bridge in the middle. Huge caissons for foundations were floated in during the summer of 1993, and towers were scheduled to start rising soon.

Store Bælt's world record was expected to be short-lived, as progress continued to be made on the Akashi-Kaikyo suspension bridge in Japan, which was to have a 1,990-m main span. Work began on deepwater caisson foundations in 1988, and by late 1993 the 297-m-high steel towers had been completed. The vast $2.4 billion structure would break the world record at its scheduled opening in 1998.

Meanwhile, the battle was on for the longest cable-stay bridge. The suspension bridge, in which cables are slung from tower to tower, supporting the bridge deck on vertical hangers, was the only engineering form for very long bridges, but the cable-stay design was catching up. During the past two decades its simplicity and elegance found favour worldwide, especially for middle-length bridges.

A cable-stay bridge is supported directly from the towers, using many cables that usually fan out from the tower or are strung back to it in a harp shape. Well-known examples include Florida's new Sunshine Skyway; the Vancouver (B.C.) Alex Fraser Bridge, at just over 465 m the former world record holder; and the Hamburg harbour bridge in Germany.

China in 1993 was beginning to show that it, like the rest of the Pacific Rim, was not only catching up but overtaking the world in cable-stay bridge construction. A bridge of more than 400 m in Shanghai was joined in the autumn by the opening of the Yangpu Bridge, across the Huang Pu (Huang-p'u) River, with a dramatic 602-m main span that established a new world record for length. The design was by the Shanghai Engineering Design Institute.

Because the loads in a cable-stay bridge are carried directly onto the towers, the latter have to be higher than those in a suspension bridge; this becomes a problem near airports. But cable stays do not require huge shoreside anchorage points as do suspension bridges, which take loads back along the cables to the ground. This consideration was critical for the Pont de Normandie in northern France because the Seine estuary outside Le Havre has no high sides for anchorages. Thus, the bridge has a cable-stay design with an 856-m central clear span, a new record length. Inverted Y-shaped towers more than 200 m high were completed for the bridge, which was to have a very slim deck. This would be in a stiff concrete near the towers but then would employ lightweight steel of high tensile strength to help achieve the enormous length of the central span.

The Pont de Normandie's record length would soon be topped by a new cable-stay bridge in Japan, between the main island of Honshu and densely populated Shikoku. The Tatara Bridge was under construction but was not expected to be completed until 1999. It was to have an 890-m central span.

Among other bridges being planned was a high cable-stay bridge that would form the centre of the 16.2-km (10-mi) crossing of the Øresund between Copenhagen and Malmö, Sweden. But the crossings of the Strait of Gibraltar, the Strait of Messina between Italy and Sicily, and the estuary of the Río de la Plata in Argentina were the projects that set the blood running. The Messina crossing, with a 3,300-m main span, was already in the design phase.

Proposals for a 2,000-m bridge spanning the Izmit Gulf of the Sea of Marmara in Turkey might result in a hybrid, fusing cable stay with suspension. The sections near the towers would have cables, and the middle would be suspended.

Finally, in Scotland a small cable-stay footbridge might indicate the way forward. The 63-m-main-span bridge over the River Tay at Aberfeldy Golf Club was made entirely of lightweight composites. (ADRIAN LEE GREEMAN)

Buildings. The continued expansion of the French Train à Grande Vitesse (TGV) high-speed rail network and the linking of the British network into that of mainland Europe by the Channel Tunnel was leading to some impressive rail station buildings. During the year the final phase of the rail station at the Satolas international airport in Lyon, France, was begun. The platforms were below ground, but the roof was designed to let as much natural light as possible onto the platforms and walkways. This was achieved by an elegant white concrete lattice supported on rows of tapering columns. Elongated diamond-shaped skylights set in the lattice allowed daylight in. The station extended for 400 m along the straight track, and concrete poured at the site was chosen in preference to precast concrete to keep the number of joints to a minimum and thereby enhance the visual aspects of the construction. At the centre of the platforms was a 26-m-high waiting room, a giant gliding birdlike structure in structural steel supported at three points.

In the U.K. the new Waterloo international rail terminal in London was completed. In contrast to Satolas, the superstructure was made of steel. The roof spanned a width of up to 48.5 m over five tracks and their associated platforms. Because of the plan layout and headroom requirement, an asymmetrical structure was necessary. It took the form of a three-pinned arch, made up of two bowstring trusses pinned at a crown that was offset from the centre. On the long span stainless steel decking was used, and this was placed on the outer surface of the trusses.

Construction activity was being generated by the prospect of the Olympic Games for the year 2000. Though the choice of Sydney, Australia, as the site for the Games was not announced until 1993, two of the new stadiums and associated sports halls were already under construction there, and

PETER TRIEVNOR—TIMES NEWSPAPERS LTD.

London's new Waterloo railway terminal features dramatic use of steelwork in a restricted space. The structure was praised for being both boldly modern and reminiscent of 19th-century stations.

four more were to follow. These types of buildings provided opportunities for interesting and innovative engineering solutions. For example, the water sports centre, designed to accommodate up to 12,500 spectators, had a latticed-vault diagonal roof supported by columns along one side and a long-span arch on the other to provide uninterrupted views of the main pool. The athletics centre had a cable-stayed roof suspended from two latticed steel towers that were guyed back to the ground outside the stadium.

Another contender for the Olympics had been Manchester, England, where a city centre sports arena and velodrome (cycling track) were under construction and would continue to be built even though the city lost its bid for the Games. The velodrome had a particularly interesting roof structure. A trussed steel arch with a span of 122 m extended along the centre of the building like a spine and was formed by two 4.5-m-deep lattices 21 m apart and braced by secondary lattices. Steel roof trusses with spans of up to 42 m carried the roof between the spine arch and columns at the side of the building.

The development of the Passagen site in the former East Berlin was challenging foundation engineers. Berlin had traditionally used mainly shallow foundations because of its sandy soil and high water table. The new development was to have a maximum of seven stories above ground but a basement 15 m deep. This presented problems of side support and stability of the excavation during construction. In order for the stability of the bottom of the excavation to be controlled, slurry diaphragm walls had to be built around the entire 900-m perimeter of the site down to 50 m below ground. Because of the high soil pressures on the wall after excavation had taken place, steel sheet piling was inserted in the top 20 m of the wall. Once the 1.2-m-thick concrete floor of the excavation had been completed, it was anchored by several hundred vertical ground anchors.

Turning to foundations of an older building, the second stage of temporary measures to stabilize the Leaning Tower of Pisa (Italy) began. A concrete ring had been cast around the base, and this was being loaded on the uptilted side with lead weights to encourage settlement. Adjacent to the tower field trials were being made of methods of controlling the settlement. The tower was built on clay, and when water is removed from clay it shrinks. One method of control involved passing an electrical direct current through the soil, causing the water to migrate toward the anode, thus removing it from the cathode area. This would allow settlement to be selectively located according to the disposition of the electrodes. (GEOFFREY M. PINFOLD)

Dams. To meet its population needs, China in 1993 had more than 50 large dams in various stages of construction and was adding more each year. Its expansion was directed toward energy development, to support its economic expansion. China also developed a program of providing small dams in remote undeveloped areas, not connected to its national power grid, to help to improve the living standards and to provide energy for the development of local enterprises. By 1993 there were more than 60,000 of these small plants, with a total capacity of more than 14,000 MW.

China's Manwan Dam on the Lancang Jiang (Lan-ts'ang River) was commissioned during the year. It was a 132-m-high gravity-type dam with a generating capacity of 1,250 MW. There were plans to install an additional 22,000 MW at 14 projects on the river. The first of these was to be the Dachaoshan Dam with 1,260 MW. China announced its program for the Three Gorges Dam on the Chang Jiang (Yangtze River). Work started on access roads and electricity to the site. Between 1996 and 1999 work was to begin on the diversion of the river, and by 2005 work would be in progress on the main dam. About 750,000 people would need to be resettled from the reservoir area.

Workers install turbines at the Corpus Posadas project, a joint undertaking of Argentina and Paraguay on the Paraná River. Scheduled to be completed in 1994, the dam was to include two plants for the generation of hydroelectricity.
GUSTAVO GILABERT—JB PICTURES

India was proceeding with its Narmada River project, which included the controversial Sardar Sarovar Dam. Because of World Bank requirements for India to mitigate ecological problems, the government withdrew requests for World Bank support; India sought funding from other sources and affirmed its commitment to the project. (*See* ENVIRONMENT: *National Developments: India.*)

India also was expanding developments on the upper reaches of the Ganges River, where the flow from the Himalayan mountains offered the potential for vast energy developments. The 204-m-high Lakhwar Dam, with 300 MW of capacity, was nearing completion, and the Tehri Dam, under construction on the Bhagirathi River (a Ganges tributary), would develop 1,000 MW and provide for irrigation of more than 600,000 ha (1,480,000 ac).

Thailand and Myanmar (Burma) agreed to develop eight dams along their common border rivers. The project would develop more than 6,400 MW and require an investment of $5 billion. Preliminary studies were under way.

In South Africa the government initiated construction of its second rolled-compacted-concrete (RCC) dam, the Taung Dam on the Hartz River. The dam would be 58 m high and 320 m long and have a volume content of 140,000 cu m (1 cu m = 35.3 cu ft). In Lesotho the Highlands project, in which water from Lesotho would be transferred to South Africa to support the continuing industrial expansion, was nearing completion. The Katse Dam and several reservoirs would store the water, to be transferred by means of tunnels more than 90 km (55 mi) in length.

The Egyptian government released a study of the benefits brought about by the construction of the Aswan High Dam on the Nile River. The study's conclusions were that the dam eliminated all fears of floods and reassured the availability of water releases for downstream agriculture. Industries opened up to produce iron and steel, fertilizer, brick, granite, and marble. Fish production from Lake Nasser, which was formed by the dam, represented 17–25% of the total fish production of Egypt, about 30 to 35 tons. More than 140,000 ha (345,000 ac) of land were placed under irrigation. Moreover, tourism expanded from 105,000 in 1962 to 750,000 in 1992.

In Poland construction was being resumed at the Czorsztyn Dam near Krakow, which had been under construction for 20 years. Environmental problems arose because surrounding towns did not have adequate sewage-treatment plants and the reservoir water was in danger of eutrophication (increase in the amount of dissolved nutrients that stimulate the growth of aquatic plants, resulting in the depletion of dissolved oxygen) if the pollutant inflow was not stopped. Pressure was applied to meet pollution-control standards, and the towns agreed to install modern sewage-treatment plants.

In Germany the Vohburg Dam on the Danube River was inaugurated. It was designed to generate 24 MW of power. Elsewhere in Europe, five large dams under construction in Greece would provide 750 MW, and Turkey reported that it had 150 dams in various stages of construction.

The Peruca Dam in Croatia, a 65-m-high embankment dam completed in 1960, was sabotaged by Serb rebels who placed 15 tons of explosives in the embankment. The Croatians quickly drained the dam to prevent it from failing. Thousands of people were evacuated from the valley after being alerted to the possible dam failure.

Major World Dams Under Construction in 1993[1]

Name of dam	River	Country	Type[2]	Height (m)	Length of crest (m)	Volume content (000 cu m)	Gross reservoir capacity (000 cu m)
Al-Wahda	Fez	Morocco	E	88	1,600	27,000	3,800,000
Al-Wehda	Yarmuk	Jordan/Syria	E,R	164	700	21,000	486,000
Arakhthos/Kalaritiko	Arakhthos	Greece	E	185	238	1,500	1,840,000
Bakun	Rajana	Malaysia	R	204	900	29,400	43,800,000
Banje	Devoll	Albania	E,R	100	1,350	15,000	700,000
Bekme	Greater Zab	Iraq	E,R	204	600	34,000	17,000,000
Berke	Ceyhan	Turkey	A	210	270	730	427,000
Boyabat	Kizilirmak	Turkey	G	195	675	2,300	3,557,000
Bureya	Bureya	Russia	G	140	765	3,440	20,940,000
Catalan	Ceyhan	Turkey	E	82	894	17,000	2,126,000
Chapeton	Paraná	Argentina	E,G	35	224,000	296,000	60,600,000
Chisapani	Karali	Nepal	E,R	210	850	35,000	15,000,000
Cipasang	Cimanuk	Indonesia	E,R	200	640	90,000	860,000
Corpus Posadas	Paraná	Argentina/Paraguay	E,R	65	8,474	18,200	13,000,000
Daliushu	Ningxia	China	E,R	160	680	15,000	11,000,000
Dongfeng	Wujiang	China	A	173	259	1,144	1,025,000
Ertan	Yalongjiang	China	A	240	763	4,742	5,800,000
Guayillabamba	Guayillabamba	Ecuador	A	165	413	704	105,000
Hongjiadu	Hongshui	China	E,R	178	490	9,800	4,700,000
Hrusov-Dunakiliti-Gabcikovo	Dunaj	Czechoslovakia/Hungary	E,G	29	31,500	18,340	199,000
Huites	Fuerte	Mexico	G	155	390	2,100	3,675,000
Ingapata	Paute	Ecuador	G	166	430	1,600	413,000
Kambaratinsk	Naryn	Kyrgyzstan	R	255	560	112,000	4,650,000
Kanev	Dnieper	Ukraine	E,G	40	16,479	33,000	2,620,000
Karun No. 3	Karun	Iran	A	200	831	7,600	623,000
Katse	Malibamatso	Lesotho	A	182	700	2,200	2,000,000
Katun	Katun	Russia	E,R	179	755	32,700	5,800,000
Kishau	Tons	India	E,G	253	680	9,500	2,400,000
Kumgang	North Itan	North Korea	E	150	1,120	8,760	9,250,000
La Vueltosa	Caparo	Venezuela	E	118	1,200	15,000	5,300,000
Lijiaxia	Huang He	China	A	165	382	2,340	1,630,000
Longtan	Hongshui He	China	RCC	185	790	7,610	27,280,000
Maroun	Maroun	Iran	E,R	165	350	7,490	1,200,000
Mashai	Malibamatso	Lesotho	E	155	680	14,400	3,306,000
Messochora	Acheloos	Greece	E,R	150	300	4,200	625,000
Misogawa	Kiso	Japan	E,R	150	455	8,000	61,000
Miyagase	Nakatsu	Japan	E,R	155	400	2,000	193,000
M'Jara (Wahada)	Ouegha	Morocco	E	87	1,600	25,000	4,000,000
Namakhvani I	Rioni	Georgia	A	161	460	1,200	560,000
Nukui	Takiyama	Japan	A	155	382	800	82,000
Ozluce	Peri	Turkey	E,R	150	9,400	1,075	170,000
Pati	Paraná	Argentina	E,G	36	174,900	238,180	38,000,000
Potrerillos	Mendoza	Argentina	E	146	550	17,120	860,000
Roncador	Uruguay	Brazil/Argentina	E,R	78	1,598	9,940	33,580,000
San Roque	Agno	Philippines	E	210	1,130	43,150	990,000
Sardar Sarovar	Narmada	India	G	163	1,202	7,472	9,500,000
Serra da Mesa	Tocantins	Brazil	E,R	150	1,544	12,700	54,400,000
Songwon	Chungmangang	North Korea	R	160	630	1,100	3,200,000
Tehri	Bhagirathi	India	E,R	261	575	27,032	3,540,000
Tianshenggiao	Hongshui	China	E,R	178	1,137	17,810	10,260,000
Urayama	Takiyama	Japan	G	155	400	1,730	58,000
Valea Sadului	Jiu	Romania	E,R	52	7,150	18,250	306,000
Xiaolangdi	Yellow	China	E,R	154	1,317	12,650	12,650,000
Yacyreta-Apipe	Paraná	Paraguay/Argentina	E,R	43	69,600	67,700	21,000,000
Zimapan	Moctezuma	Mexico	A	200	80	280	1,426,000
Zungeru	Kaduna	Nigeria	RCC	116	2680	5160	27,050,000
Major World Dams Completed in 1992 and 1993[1]							
Aguamilpa	Santiago	Mexico	E,R	187	642	14,000	6,950,000
Geheyan	Qingjiang	China	A	151	641	3,250	1,200,000
Kabalebo	Kabalebo	Suriname	E,R	45	1,650	3,790	19,000,000
Kayraktepe	Gaksu	Turkey	E,R	199	580	17,000	4,800,000
Kouilou	Kouilou	Congo	A	137	345	390	35,000,000
Lhakwar	Yamuna	India	G	204	454	2,871	580,000
Piedra del Aguila	Limay	Argentina	E,G,R	163	820	2,520	11,300,000
Porto Primavera	Paraná	Brazil	E,R	38	11,835	37,644	18,500,000
Thein (Rajit)	Ravi	India	E,R	160	565	14,213	3,280,000
Thissavros	Nestos	Greece	E,R	172	480	10,000	700,000
Turkwell Gorge	Turkwell	Kenya	A	153	150	170	1,641,000

[1] Having a height exceeding 150 m (492 ft); or having a volume content exceeding 15 million cu m (196 million cu yd); or forming a reservoir exceeding 14,800 × 10^6 cu m of capacity (12 million ac-ft).

[2] Type of dam: E = earth; R = rockfill; A = arch; G = gravity; RCC = roller-compacted-concrete.

(T.W. MERMEL)

The Spanish government canceled construction of two dams because of objections from environmentalists. Both were located in the Cantabrian Mountains in the northern tip of the Iberian Peninsula. The fate of the wild bears living there was an issue.

The governments of Argentina and Paraguay agreed on a plan to develop the Corpus Posadas project, which had a potential of 4,800 MW, on the Paraná River. The project involved two power plants with eight 300-MW units on each side of the river. The main purpose of the project was energy production and river navigation.

In Canada a number of dams under construction in Quebec, as part of the La Grande project, would add 5,000 MW. The Coboraca Dam in Mexico was commissioned after 10 years of construction. It had a reservoir capacity of 45 million cu m and would provide irrigation water to 2,100 ha (5,200 ac) of previously arid land.

In the U.S. more than 50 dams were under construction. Much effort was being placed on improving the safety of dams and increasing their capacities and benefits with minimum impact on the environment. The New Waddell Dam was completed in Arizona on the Agua Fria River. An earth and rock-fill dam 111 m high and 1,460 m long, it would have a 45-MW plant to be used for peaking for the Arizona power grid system. (T.W. MERMEL)

Roads. The worldwide movement toward charging motorists for the use of roads continued, with the construction of new toll roads, the application of tolls to previously free roads, and trials of "road pricing" systems under which charges are levied according to the time of day and the level of congestion on a road. Plans were announced for the first privately owned toll road in Russia. The 1,000-km superhighway would connect Moscow to Minsk, Belarus, and the Polish border (1 km = 0.62 mi). Toll expressways were also under construction or planned for a number of other Central and Eastern European countries, notably Hungary.

Brazil announced that it would allow private investment in road building and maintenance for the first time in order to improve the condition of the country's roads. Up to $1.5 billion would be needed over three years to repair 6,000 km of roads. Argentina, which had previously privatized some expressways, announced the further privatization of three radial highways in Buenos Aires. The first toll expressway in Mexico's National Highway Plan, connecting Cuernavaca to Acapulco, was completed. The 263-km route had been under construction since 1989.

A new six-lane toll highway north of Toronto was to be financed by the private sector. The project was scheduled for completion in 1996 but would have taken almost 20 years without toll revenue.

In Bangkok, Thailand, a new city centre expressway was seized by the government after a contractual dispute with the Japanese-led construction consortium. The road was to be financed by toll revenues but, as construction approached completion, the government announced that the toll rate would be only 20 baht instead of the 30 baht originally agreed upon. Bangkok was widely regarded as having some of the worst traffic jams in the world.

The growth in toll roads was accelerated by the economic difficulties being experienced in many countries and, in some cases, by decades of underinvestment in road construction and maintenance. A report published by the International Road Federation showed, however, that even without new tolls governments already made profits from road-related taxation. The report showed that in 18 European countries the combined revenue from vehicle, fuel, and usage taxes was three times the amount spent on road construction and maintenance.

A report by the World Health Organization revealed that almost two-thirds of fatal road accidents occurred in less developed countries, while deaths in industrialized countries had declined by 20% from the previous decade. The world's worst accident record was in Ethiopia, with 150 deaths per 10,000 vehicles. This compared with 2.5 deaths per 10,000 vehicles in the U.S., the world's most motorized country.

Major road-construction programs were announced in several countries. Thailand planned to embark on a seven-year highway-construction plan valued at $1.7 billion, almost half of which would be allocated to the construction of the 893-km Highway 4. China announced plans to construct a new network of highways to connect its major cities; the country had more than one million kilometres of roads, but this was not enough to cope with the expanding demand. In Sweden a 10-year infrastructure program, including the construction of 700 km of new expressways, was valued at $14 billion. Some 7,300 km of highway were planned to link the countries of the Maghreb Union in North Africa (Mauritania, Morocco, Algeria, Tunisia, and Libya). The Maghreb Motorway was to be built over a 30-year period and might be connected to Europe by a crossing of the Strait of Gibraltar. More than $6 billion of road and bridge projects were announced in Turkey, including 1,200 km of new highways.

In the U.S., massive flooding of the Mississippi and Missouri rivers caused widespread damage to roads and bridges throughout the Midwest. Most damage was caused by gravel foundations being loosened and washed away by the floodwaters.

The British government suffered a significant defeat on environmental grounds when it was forced to abandon plans to build a new road through the 8,000-year-old Oxleas Wood in South London. Construction of another environmentally sensitive project in Britain, the extension of the M3 motorway through Twyford Down, continued despite vociferous and violent protests. (RUSS SWAN)

Tunnels. The largest man-made underground cavern ever built for public use opened in May in Norway. With a freestanding roof span of 62 m, the 91-m-long and 35-m-high underground ice hockey arena at Gjøvik would seat more than 5,000 spectators and was built by Norway for the 1994 winter Olympic Games. Engineers created the cavern by removing some 140,000 cu m (4,944,100 cu ft) of gneiss rock from inside the mountain and supporting the roof with shotcrete reinforced with steel fibres and with more than 3,000 rock bolts and twin-strand cable bolts up to 6 m and 12 m long, respectively. Rock movement was monitored continuously during the drill-and-blast excavation, and settlement of the 62-m-wide roof was recorded at a maximum of 8 mm (0.31 in).

Construction on the Neue Eisenbahn Alpen Transversale (NEAT) railway tunnels project in Switzerland began with a 5-km-long and 5.2-m-diameter exploratory gallery designed to optimize geologic investigation studies. Several long tunnels totaling more than 115 km were planned for the overall NEAT project. The longest, at more than 50 km, was to be beneath the St. Gotthard Pass, with another of 38 km on the Berne-Lötschberg-Simplon line. The tunnels would pass a maximum of 2,500 m under the massive formation of the Alps and be excavated by the most advanced of full-face, hard-rock tunnel-boring machine (TBM) technology.

The Robbins Co. of Kent, Wash., a leader in the early design and continued development of full-face TBM technology, merged with the Altas Copco group of Sweden, also involved in the design and manufacture of tunneling machines. The merger provided Robbins with a stronger financial base and consolidated the TBM manufacturing industry, in which other major suppliers included Herrenknecht and Wirth of Germany, Lovat of Canada, Howden of the U.K., and Kawasaki, Mitsubishi, IHI, and other large companies in Japan.

Full-face TBMs were applied on two unusual projects during 1993. In Arizona a 4.62-m-diameter Robbins TBM started excavation of more than 10 km of access tunnels on different levels for the development of the San Manuel Mine for the Magma Copper Co. In Sweden a 5-m-diameter Atlas Copco TBM was ordered to excavate a 420-m-long test tunnel at the underground nuclear waste research laboratory on the island of Äspö off the east coast.

In Japan the first of eight 14.1-m-diameter soft-ground TBMs was factory tested before delivery to its site in Tokyo, where it was to work on the ambitious Trans-Tokyo Bay Highway. The 15-km highway comprised twin 10-km tunnels, some 15 m beneath the bed of the bay, to one of two man-made islands; from there it passed to the opposite landfall on a 5-km bridge. The tunnels in this seismically active zone were lined with precast concrete segments, which on some of the TBMs would be put in place by a fully automatic segment erector system.

Tunneling on the Lesotho Highlands Water Project in southern Africa advanced past the halfway mark, with more than 50 km of the 82-km tunnel network completed by mid-November 1993. Most of it was excavated by five TBMs of about five metres in diameter.

An original opening date of May 1993 for the Channel Tunnel between France and England was postponed to March 7, 1994. This delay was incurred despite the fact that all 147 km of tunneling required for forming the undersea rail link was completed in mid-1991, earlier than scheduled. Car-ferry operators were reportedly preparing to lower their fares in anticipation of the opening.

SSC LABORATORY

Workers are dwarfed by a section of the tunnel for the Superconducting Super Collider, under construction in Texas. In October 1993, despite pleas from a number of prominent scientists, the U.S. Congress cut off further funding for the project.

Tunneling on the final link of the three-metre-diameter London Water Ring Main project was completed in February, nine months ahead of schedule. Record-breaking rates of advance were achieved, the best being 501 m in 10 consecutive shifts of 10 hours each, achieved by a Lovat TBM working through stable London clay geology and erecting a nonbolted expanded wedge block lining of precast concrete segments. When fully operational, the 80-km loop of the Ring Main would supply more than 1.3 billion litres (343.2 billion gal) of drinking water per day to consumers.

Work on the Superconducting Super Collider project in Waxahachie, Texas, one of the largest tunneling projects in the world and certainly the largest tunneling project in the U.S., was stopped in late 1993. Continued federal funding for the 87-km underground particle accelerator was rejected by the House of Representatives and the Senate as one of several initiatives by the Clinton administration to control the huge public-spending deficit in the U.S. The rejection of further funding came in October, by which time more than $2 billion had been invested in the project and some 24 km of tunnel had been completed. (SHANI WALLIS)

This article updates the *Macropædia* articles BUILDING CONSTRUCTION; PUBLIC WORKS.

Environment

In January 1993 it was reported that a temporary secretariat would be established in Geneva to coordinate implementation of the Convention on Protecting Species and Habitats (the so-called biodiversity convention), agreed at the UN Conference on Environment and Development, nicknamed the Earth Summit, held in Rio de Janeiro in June 1992. The agreement was signed by 167 countries. Ratified by the members of the European Community (EC) in December 1992, the treaty took force on December 29.

INTERNATIONAL COOPERATION

A four-page petition sponsored by the Union of Concerned Scientists and signed by at least 1,500 eminent scientists, including nearly 100 Nobel Prize winners, was sent to government leaders throughout the world on Nov. 18, 1992. Entitled "Warning to Humanity," the paper called for more efficient use of resources, an end to activities that damage the environment, the elimination of poverty, and the granting to women of control over their own reproductive decisions.

Two weeks later a joint report by the UN Environment Program (UNEP) and the World Health Organization (WHO) warned of health problems caused by urban air pollution and urged a reduction in pollution levels. *Urban Air Pollution in Megacities of the World* described a 15-year study of the 20 cities in which 47% of the global population would be living by the year 2000. Each city had, or by then was expected to have, 10 million or more inhabitants. Mexico City was the most seriously polluted. Suspended particulate matter was serious in 11 cities. Seoul, South Korea, and Beijing (Peking) had very high levels of sulfur dioxide; Karachi, Pak., had the highest lead levels; and ozone pollution was serious in Los Angeles, Tokyo, and São Paulo, Brazil. Overall, Tokyo, New York City, and London were the cleanest cities, usually meeting WHO guidelines for four or five of the six pollutants studied.

As the Global Environment Facility (GEF) approached the end of its three-year pilot phase, representatives of

Women labourers climb a rise at the construction site of the Sardar Sarovar Dam, part of the Narmada River project in India. Both the World Bank and Indian citizens questioned the scheme, primarily because it would displace large numbers of people and, some said, harm the environment.
BALDEV—SYGMA

60 governments met in Beijing in May 1993 to discuss disagreements that had arisen over funding between European governments and the United States. European officials called for more definite commitments to the $3 billion–$4 billion the GEF was estimated to need over five years, but criticisms of secrecy and bureaucratic slowness had led the U.S. to withhold its pledged $150 million. There was also disagreement between rich and poor countries over the voting system for making decisions. Poorer countries preferred giving one vote to each participating country, while the wealthier nations were in favour of a weighted system reflecting the size of the financial contribution made by each country.

European Community. The composition of the European Commission for 1993 and 1994 was announced in December 1992. Acting environment commissioner Karel van Miert was appointed competition commissioner, and Yannis Paleokrassas became the new environment commissioner. In October 1993 Copenhagen was selected to house the new European Environment Agency.

A section of the Single European Act permitting free trade to be overruled for environmental reasons was used in October 1992 when environment ministers of the 12 member countries agreed to permit national governments to forbid the importation of toxic wastes. The agreement, which came into force in October 1993, allowed the exportation of a "green list" of less toxic wastes to countries in Eastern Europe and of any waste intended for recycling or recovery to less industrialized countries other than those receiving aid under the Lomé Convention agreement. In December 1992 environment ministers also agreed on regulations to block the importation to the EC of nonradioactive hazardous wastes.

On Nov. 25, 1992, the European Court of Justice found the British government guilty of having failed to achieve promised improvements in drinking-water quality by 1985, in contravention of the 1980 directive on drinking-water quality. Nitrate levels had been found to exceed the 50 parts per million EC limit in 28 areas. On Dec. 16, 1992, the advocate-general for the court gave a reasoned opinion that in failing to ensure clean bathing waters on beaches at Blackpool and Southport, Britain was in breach of a 1976 directive.

A survey published in Britain in July 1993 showed that the EC drinking-water directive was being breached in several countries. Some failed to supply adequate data—an action that itself was a breach—and it appeared that those providing the most complete information were most likely to be prosecuted. Britain proposed to the Commission that the drinking-water directive be revised in accordance with a draft of new WHO standards. Britain also continued to press for the new limits at talks held in September, arguing in favour of rules based on existing scientific knowledge rather than the "precautionary principle" preferred by The Netherlands, Germany, and Denmark, under which products would be banned unless they could be shown to be safe. France joined Britain in urging that pesticide rules be framed under a different directive administered by agricultural officials.

Disagreement continued on ways to meet the undertaking to reduce carbon dioxide emissions given in the UN Convention on Climate Change. A document on transport policy published in December 1992 forecast that emissions would rise about 24% between 1990 and 2000, road transport would account for 30% of all EC carbon dioxide emissions by 2010, and stabilization could not be achieved by technical improvements in fuel efficiency alone. According to another Commission forecast, emissions would be 3% higher in 2000 than they had been in 1990 because substantial reductions planned by Germany, Belgium, Denmark, and The Netherlands would be insufficient to offset increases from Ireland, Portugal, and Spain, which were industrializing.

In March 1993 ministers from Germany, Italy, The Netherlands, Denmark, Belgium, and Luxembourg, supported by the Commission, warned that reduction targets could not be met unless Britain accepted the proposed carbon and energy tax. British Environment Minister David Maclean doubted whether the tax would achieve the required reduction and stated that the two-thirds reduction to which Britain was committed would result from its planned imposition of a value-added tax (VAT) on fuel and energy. Discussions resumed in April. British Energy Minister Tim Eggar supported Maclean, and on June 28, at the end of another meeting, British Environment Secretary John Gummer said the EC tax was "all but dead," with individual countries having agreed to adopt their own measures to meet the Rio objective. At a meeting of environment ministers on October 5, the British minister of state, Tim Yeo, said that unless other member states abandoned the tax, Britain would ratify the climate change convention alone, making it impossible for EC members to hold a joint ratification ceremony.

NATIONAL DEVELOPMENTS

Bangladesh. The $5 billion Bangladesh Flood Action Plan seemed likely to founder in August because of reluctance by Western governments and the World Bank to finance the building of huge embankments on the Ganges and Brahmaputra rivers. There were doubts about the feasibility of sealing the rivers from their flood plains and fears of adverse environmental and social consequences arising from the attempt to do so.

Brazil. Two Brazilian conservationists were murdered in 1993. Paulo Vinha, a biologist who opposed the extraction of sand from beaches, dunes, and salt marshes, was found shot dead on a beach in Barro do Jucu, in Espirito Santo, on April 28. Vinha was working on a documentary film about environmental destruction. Arnaldo Ferreira, a leader of the Rural Workers' Union in Eldorado do Carajas, Amazonia, and an opponent of the logging of mahogany in tribal lands and ecological reserves, was shot dead while he slept on May 2.

Canada. The Freshwater Institute in Winnipeg, Man., reported in July that some hydroelectric reservoirs emitted as much carbon dioxide and methane as coal-fired power plants of similar capacity. The gases were produced by the decomposition of organic material inundated when the reservoirs filled.

France. The two environmentalist parties, the Greens and Ecological Generation, united to contest the March general election, fielding a single candidate in each of the 555 constituencies. Only three candidates won enough first-round votes to contest the second round, in which they were all defeated. After the election the green coalition fragmented. The Greens divided at a council meeting in August when a group opposed to an alliance with the Socialist Party formed behind Antoine Waechter. In September Ecological Generation leader Brice Lalonde, a former environment minister, declared his support for the right-wing prime minister, Édouard Balladur.

Police guarded approaches to the port of Cherbourg and naval and coastguard vessels protected the harbour when the Japanese ship *Akatsuki Maru* arrived in October 1992 to load about 1.5 tons of reactor-grade plutonium from La Hague reprocessing plant. Protesters from Greenpeace International squared off against some 2,000 French police and naval commandos. Greenpeace's inflatables were chased by harbour patrol vessels, its ship *Beluga* was towed from the harbour, and commandos boarded the *Moby Dick.* The Japanese ship sailed on November 7, accompanied by the helicopter carrier *Shikishima* and shadowed by the Greenpeace ship *Solo,* which had evaded boarding by French authorities. On Jan. 5, 1993, the *Akatsuki Mara* reached Tokai, Japan, where there were further Greenpeace demonstrations.

The Institute of Research into the Exploitation of the Sea reported in July that shellfish around the French coast were less heavily contaminated with metals and organic pollutants than they had been in 1979. High levels of cadmium, from a pond near a factory that had closed, were found off Bordeaux, and high levels of polychlorinated biphenyls (PCBs) were found at several places.

Germany. In local elections the Greens increased their share of the vote in Hesse to 11%, while the Green Alternative List won 13.5% of the vote in Hamburg. The Greens and Alliance 90, an association of civil rights campaigners from former East Germany, sealed their merger at a conference in Leipzig on May 15–16. The union encouraged the Greens to hope they might emerge as a third force in the 1994 general election.

Agriculture Minister Ignaz Kiechle reported in November 1992 that 27% of forest trees continued to be affected by pollution, a 2% increase from 1991. Although pollutant emissions had greatly decreased, forest ecosystems were responding slowly.

The national waste-recycling program caused difficulties. Lower Saxony and Rhineland-Palatinate left the scheme in June, and other federal states were considering following suit. The Dual System Deutschland (DSD) required householders to wash containers, separate them from other waste, and sort them by type, but the annual volume of accumulated recyclables, estimated at 400,000 tons, exceeded the capacity of recycling plants, and DSD was DM 500 million in debt.

The states had agreed to contribute an additional DM 160 million for servicing the debt, and on June 21 there were calls in the Bundestag (parliament) for a packaging tax to help pay the high recycling cost. On July 21 Environment Minister Klaus Töpfer said the accumulated waste would stimulate the building of recycling facilities. It was estimated that about 180,000 tons would be reprocessed in 1993 and that a new plant to be built in eastern Germany would convert 250,000 tons a year into synthetic oil.

Plans to halve 1987 emission levels of methane, nitrous oxide, nitrogen oxides, volatile hydrocarbons, and carbon monoxide by 2005 were published in August. Since 1987 carbon dioxide emissions over Germany as a whole had fallen 14.5%, and a further 25–30% reduction was considered feasible.

Greece. Plans by a consortium of British, French, and Italian companies to construct a hydroelectric and irrigation project on the Akheloos River, reported in March, were opposed by conservationists. They said that three dams and an 18-km (11-mi) tunnel from Sikia in the western Pindus Mountains to Trikala on the Plains of Thessaly would destroy a wetland that was protected under EC law and the Ramsar Convention and would partly drain the Mesolongion Lagoon.

Hong Kong. In order to reduce pollution, the government was reported in June to have started collecting chemical waste for free disposal in its own $167 million plant. The accumulation of heavy metals from two million tons of mainly untreated waste discharged daily, much of it from circuit-board manufacturing, had reached critical levels in coastal waters.

Hungary. Despite five days of protest demonstrations in October and objections from the Hungarian government, diversion of the Danube River to the Gabcikovo Dam began on Oct. 25, 1992. On April 7, 1993, Hungary and Slovakia agreed to refer their dispute over the project to the International Court of Justice, meanwhile operating a temporary water-management scheme to reconcile the Slovakian need for hydropower with Hungarian concerns about water supply and environmental effects.

India. In October 1992, 59% of the World Bank's directors voted to continue funding the controversial Sardar Sarovar Dam project on the Narmada River in India, although U.S., German, and Japanese directors were opposed. The president of the World Bank, Lewis Preston, said changes to the project made by the Indian government and the affected states justified continuing for a few months longer. In March it was reported that the Indian government would not seek further World Bank funding for the project to provide drinking water and irrigation by building 30 large, 135 medium, and about 3,000 small dams. The scheme would involve resettling about 100,000 people and flood some 121,400 ha (300,000 ac) of forest. Nearly 400 protesters were arrested on August 5 to prevent them from drowning themselves deliberately. On August 10 the government agreed to review some aspects of the scheme.

Italy. The possible cause of the large evil-smelling, mucilaginous mats that had formed in the Adriatic Sea every summer since 1989 was revealed in April. Scientists from the Institute for Water Research and the University of Milan believed they were due to zeolites and polycarboxylic acids used in place of phosphates in "green" detergents.

Russia. An explosion at the Siberia Chemical Centre plant near Tomsk on April 6 released 20 cu m (700 cu ft) of radioactive contaminated material. The accident, near the Tomsk-7 nuclear weapons site, occurred during reprocessing of a fuel element for uranium recovery. The radioactive cloud moved east, and pollution was confined to a largely unpopulated area. Residents near the plant were advised to remain indoors, and contaminated snow and soil were removed, but workers were not evacuated. As a precaution, children were evacuated from the village of Georgiyevka in the affected area.

The Ministry of Ecology and Natural Resources reported in January that 50 million Russian people were breathing air with 10 times—and 60 million breathed air with 5 times—the permitted levels of pollutants. The report also drew attention to severe pollution by ammonium nitrate in the Oka River and by phenols and heavy metals in the Ivankovsky reservoir that supplied water to Moscow, as well as to viral contamination in the Volga, Don, and Ob rivers. Toxic wastes were said to be dumped in quarries and on waste ground and radioactive wastes in ordinary waste dumps.

United Kingdom. In his March budget, Chancellor of the Exchequer Norman Lamont announced that from April 1994 fuel and energy for domestic, residential, and charity use would become liable to 8% VAT, rising to the standard 17.5% rate in April 1995. The measure was justified as a means of reducing carbon dioxide emissions, but critics pointed out that it failed to discriminate by energy source and therefore would not encourage a shift toward power-generation systems that release no carbon dioxide.

It was announced in May that in March 1994 the principal government air-pollution laboratory, the Warren Spring Laboratory, would close and its work would be merged with that of the Atomic Energy Authority Laboratory to form a National Environmental Technology Centre. Many of the 152 members of the scientific staff were not prepared to move, and it was feared that some teams would disintegrate, making it difficult to attain the declared objective of bringing the best environmental research under one roof.

In April the Marine Conservation Society gave poor water quality as the main reason for omitting more than 70 beaches from its *Heinz Good Beach Guide.* Sewage pollution was serious, and litter was also common, a finding confirmed by a report supported by WHO and published on April 16 in the *British Medical Journal.* On May 31, however, the National Rivers Authority reported that compared with 1988–90, the proportion of a sample of 416 beaches satisfying EC criteria between 1990 and 1992 increased from 57% to 64%.

Controversy continued throughout the year over plans to commission British Nuclear Fuels' (BNF) Thermal Oxide Reprocessing Plant (Thorp) at Sellafield, Cumbria. The Thorp would reprocess reactor fuel, much of it imported from Germany and Japan, returning fissionable uranium and plutonium but retaining most of the waste for disposal in Britain. Concern over planned emissions of krypton-85 that might increase the atmospheric content of this gas by 15% a year led to a commissioning delay in October 1992. BNF decided on cost grounds against installing the £50 million plant needed to remove the gas and maintained that the emissions would be 20 times lower than those allowed in its original approval granted in 1977. The Inspectorate of Pollution instructed BNF to allow eight weeks of public consultation over emission levels before taking radioactive material into the plant, and the environment minister ordered a three-month postponement of the Jan. 1, 1993, commissioning date, although BNF, trade unions, and the Department of Trade and Industry warned of the risk to existing contracts and jobs. On Nov. 16, 1992, the inspectorate published its draft permit, allowing an increase in emissions of some radioactive substances but lowering the total dose to people most exposed by reducing overall discharges. The Radioactive Waste Management Advisory Committee said that since the Thorp would convert a small volume of high-level waste into a greater volume of medium- and low-level waste, it could not be justified on waste-management grounds and reprocessing would probably prove more expensive than disposal in an underground repository. The National Radiological Protection Board agreed with this assessment.

In June 1993 Ireland and Denmark expressed concern over the discharges, and at its annual meeting the Commission of the Paris Convention on Marine Discharges from Land-Based Sources called for fresh consultations and a full environmental impact statement, to which the British government agreed. On August 4 a policy paper from the

MICHAEL LAMBERT—GAMMA LIAISON

Police arrest members of Greenpeace demonstrating at Cherbourg, France, in October 1992 against the arrival of a Japanese ship to load plutonium from a reprocessing plant. The vessel returned safely to Japan in January 1993.

Department of the Environment said a final decision on the Thorp would be delayed until December, but it dismissed health threats and fears of plutonium's falling into the wrong hands. The second round of consultation began with the publication of a favourable joint report by the inspectorate and the Ministry of Agriculture, Fisheries, and Food (MAFF), two reports by BNF also in favour of commissioning, and a government report dismissing health and environmental objections and saying economic arguments were a matter for BNF.

On August 25 the inspectorate and MAFF gave permission for trials of the separation plant using nonenriched uranium nitrate to commence on September 2. Greenpeace applied for a judicial review but was refused an order delaying the trials pending the hearing of its application. The application was refused on September 29. By October 1993 the Department of the Environment was anticipating that there would be 60,000 objections to the Thorp in addition to the 83,000 it had received in January. On October 4 about 600 protesters blocked the government offices at Whitehall. However, on December 15 the government gave Thorp the go-ahead.

United States. Shortly before he left office in January, Pres. George Bush signed an executive order establishing a National Biodiversity Center to store data from the U.S. and its territories. On February 8 President Clinton formed a White House office for ecological coordination to be led by Vice Pres. Al Gore. The new president also promised to bring the director of the Environmental Protection Agency into his Cabinet.

On the eve of Earth Day, April 21, Clinton said he would sign the biodiversity convention agreed at the 1992 Earth Summit and introduce legislation and controls to stabilize carbon dioxide emissions at their 1990 levels by the year 2000. He would require federal agencies to use ozone-friendly products, energy-saving computers, fuel-efficient vehicles, and recycled products. Agencies releasing toxic substances would have to devise plans to halve emissions by 1999 and to report emissions publicly.

In April Interior Secretary Bruce Babbitt pledged support for the California Desert Protection Act. This would create a 607,000-ha (1.5 million-ac) Mojave National Monument in East Mojave and add 526,000 ha (1.3 million ac) and 81,000 ha (200,000 ac), respectively, to the Death Valley and Joshua Tree national monuments.

Clinton announced a far-reaching forest-management plan in July that would allow logging to continue on federal land while protecting key watersheds and old-growth forests. A follow-up agreement in October would permit some logging to be resumed in Washington and Oregon in forests inhabited by the northern spotted owl.

The administration was reported in September to be planning to drop pesticide restrictions imposed under the Delaney Clause Amendment to the Federal Food, Drug and Cosmetic Act (1938), which it felt were scientifically anachronistic. New regulations would permit pesticide residues on raw and processed food if the risk from them was judged to be no more than one cancer per million people over a lifetime.

The National Science Foundation estimated in July that 64 cruises would visit Antarctica during 1993, taking at least 8,460 American tourists ashore, compared with 59 cruises and 6,400 tourists in 1992. Reversing the decision of a lower court, on January 29 the Court of Appeals for the District of Columbia ruled that the National Environmental Policy Act applied to U.S. Antarctic bases. The ruling meant that food wastes could no longer be incinerated at McMurdo Station, although all other waste was shipped out for disposal. Several U.S. federal agencies urged Clinton to contest the ruling, but in March he refused.

The oil tanker *Braer* sits on rocks off the coast of the Shetland Islands after running aground on January 5. Although the ship eventually broke up and lost all of its cargo of petroleum, environmental damage was not as severe as had been originally feared.

HODSON—GAMMA LIAISON

ISSUES OF CONCERN

Climate Change. Dust from the 1991 Mt. Pinatubo eruption and the ending of an El Niño episode of unusually warm water in the southeastern Pacific were believed to account for a worldwide fall in temperature during 1992. The British Meteorological Office reported in January that for 11 months of 1992 the global average temperature was 0.17° C (0.31° F) above the 1951–80 average, compared with 0.36° C (0.65° F) higher in 1991 and 0.39° C (0.7° F) in 1990.

Water at intermediate depth in the North Atlantic was reported in November 1992 to be cooler and less saline than in the 1960s, possibly because of increased precipitation. A study of 27,000 temperature profiles over 40 years, reported in January 1993, showed no evidence of surface warming in the Arctic Ocean and a significant temperature decrease in the western ocean between 1950 and 1990.

Ozone Layer. Record ozone depletion (up to 21%) was recorded in the winter and spring of 1992–93 between latitudes 45° and 65° in the Northern Hemisphere, although any increase in penetration of ultraviolet radiation was too small to detect. Globally, depletion was about 4% in 1993, an increase from 1992 that was attributed to changes in stratospheric chemistry and air circulation due to the Mt. Pinatubo eruption. The 1993 seasonal Antarctic depletion began earlier than usual, in September rather than October, and was particularly severe.

The fourth Montreal Protocol meeting was held in Copenhagen in November 1992. European countries advocated transferring the administration of the proposed fund, of \$240 million over three years, from Montreal Protocol officials to the GEF. The fund was intended to assist less industrialized countries in introducing technologies to eliminate use of ozone-depleting chemicals, but some refused to deal with the GEF, over which they had little control.

Agreement was reached on phasing out halons by January 1994 instead of 2000; abolishing carbon tetrachloride and methyl chloroform by January 1996 instead of 2005; reducing hydrochlorofluorocarbon (HCFC) use by 35% by 2004, 65% by 2010, and 90% by 2015; and eliminating HCFCs altogether by 2030. There was no general agreement to phase out methyl bromide, which was used as a soil fumigant to control pests, although the U.S. planned to do so by 2000 and urged other countries to adopt the same target.

Acid Rain. Negotiations under the auspices of the UN Economic Commission for Europe began in Geneva in March with the aim of establishing a protocol for the reduction of sulfur-dioxide emissions. The critical loads that sensitive ecosystems could tolerate without damage would be identified and targets calculated to reduce by at least half the difference between present acid precipitation and the critical load. Talks resumed in September, but Belgium, Britain, Denmark, France, and Spain proposed measures producing less than the required reductions, and no agreement was reached. The draft UN treaty on reducing European sulfur-dioxide emissions negotiated in May replaced the critical-load formula for 11 badly affected areas, covering 250,000 sq km (96,500 sq mi), in which less stringent targets would apply.

In December 1992 the World Bank was reported to have made a $1 million grant to help fund an international scientific network planning to map the impact of acid rain in Asia. The scientists would use the computer model developed at the International Institute for Applied Systems Analysis in Austria, which guided EC acid-rain policy.

Toxic Wastes. At the first meeting held under the Basel Convention in Piriápolis, Uruguay, in December 1992, industrial countries blocked an attempt by less industrialized countries to impose a total ban on the export to them of toxic wastes. A compromise was agreed, permitting the export of wastes intended for recycling. UNEP said that only half of the 56 signatory nations attending had ratified the convention and that 95% of the wastes under discussion were produced by countries that had not ratified.

Marine Pollution. The Greek tanker *Aegean Sea* grounded in severe weather on rocks near the Tower of Hercules, off La Coruña, Spain, early on Dec. 3, 1992. The ship broke in two, rupturing seven of its tanks. One tank exploded and the ship caught fire. Continuing bad weather hampered efforts to contain the oil, and by December 6 about (97 km) 60 mi of the Galician coast had been contaminated and the slick covered about 52 sq km (20 sq mi).

On Jan. 5, 1993, the Liberian-registered tanker *Braer* lost power in heavy seas between Fair Isle and Sumburgh Head, at the southern tip of the Shetland Islands off Scotland. Rescue attempts failed, and the ship was driven onto rocks in Quendale Bay, eventually losing all its cargo of 85,000 tons of light-crude and 5,000 tons of heavy-fuel oil. There was extensive contamination of both east and west coasts of Shetland and damage to farmed salmon. On June 17 the Ecological Steering Group studying the effects reported that the survival of wildlife was not threatened.

Scientists met in Oslo, Norway, in February under the auspices of the International Atomic Energy Agency to discuss radioactive contamination of the seas caused by the damaged reactor and warheads on the submarine *Komsomolets,* which sank in April 1989. Raising the submarine would cost $500 million. Russia could not afford this and proposed to smother the wreck in a chitin and chitosan gel, which would absorb heavy metals without compromising future plans to raise the vessel. At the meeting Russian scientists confirmed that seven reactors with their fuel rods and more than 11,000 containers of low-level waste had been dumped in the seas.

Power Lines. The Swedish National Board for Industrial and Technological Development was reported in October 1992 to have been convinced by a study carried out at the Karolinska Institute concerning a link between childhood leukemias and electromagnetic radiation from power lines. A second study, by the Swedish National Institute of Occupational Health, linked exposure to electromagnetic radiation to brain cancer and chronic lymphocytic leukemia in men.

In August Ray and Denise Studholme, who lived near Manchester, England, were granted legal aid to sue the power-supply company Norweb over the epilepsy and death from leukemia of their son, Simon. They attributed this to the electromagnetic field in his bedroom, which was 10 times higher than that linked to leukemia in the Swedish and earlier U.S. studies. (MICHAEL ALLABY)

WILDLIFE CONSERVATION

On Dec. 1, 1992, six California condors were released into the wild to join the single bird surviving from the two released the previous January. Five of seven Hawaiian crow chicks hatched in Hawaii in April 1993 were released, the first captive-hatched 'alala ever to fly in the wild. Two other chicks were transferred to the existing captive flock of 12 birds.

In November 1992 it was reported that only 2,475 black and 5,800 white rhinoceroses were believed to be left in Africa. In Zimbabwe efforts to save the rhinos from poachers appeared to be failing. A survey in Java revealed that only about 50 Javan rhinos survived. On May 29, 1993, China became the last nation to legislate against domestic trade in rhino horn, but in July undercover investigators from international conservation organizations claimed that Chinese state officials had offered to sell them one ton of rhino horn. Taiwan had also banned the sale of medicines containing rhino horn in November 1992, but six months later 19 out of 24 pharmacies in Taiwan still offered them for sale. On September 7 the standing committee of the Convention on International Trade in Endangered Species recommended that wildlife trade sanctions be taken against China and Taiwan.

Illegal trade in Asia also threatened tigers, particularly Bengal tigers in India and Siberian tigers in southeastern Russia and China. Their numbers were declining because of high levels of poaching to supply bones and skin for traditional medicine in China and South Korea. India's 20-year-old Project Tiger, whose 19 reserves were home to two-thirds of the world's remaining tiger population, came under criticism for inflating its reported figures. Project officials claimed a rise in the tiger population from 1,800 to 4,600 since 1973, but others believed that only 2,000 tigers remained in India.

The 45th annual meeting of the International Whaling Commission (IWC), which convened in Kyoto, Japan, May 10–14, upheld the ban on commercial whaling, but Norway announced that it would resume commercial whaling anyway. It killed the first of a proposed total of 296 minke whales (160 for commercial purposes and 136 for research) in June. Japan announced that it intended to catch 300 minke whales for research in the 1993–94 season. Increases were reported for some whale populations, including the southern right whale population off South Africa, humpback whales off Australia, and blue whales off California.

The Vu Quang ox (*Pseudoryx nghetinhensis*), the first newly identified large mammal in more than 50 years, is a bovid similar to a cow but with a coat like a horse and the horns of an antelope. This artist's reconstruction, published in 1993, was based on specimens of skulls, hides, and teeth found in Vietnam and led scientists to continue the search for the live animal.
KAREN PHILLIPPS

New Zealand declared a Marine Mammal Sanctuary around the Auckland Islands Nature Reserve to protect Hooker's sea lion, which was vulnerable to by-catch by squid trawl fisheries. California sea lions with gunshot wounds were washed up in record numbers on the shores. It was suspected that the animals were the victims of fishermen, who blamed the sea lions for meagre fish stocks. Increasing numbers of common seals and gray seals were being shot illegally by fishermen around the coast of Scotland.

Wolves started to make a comeback in several countries in 1993. In western Germany wolves returned after an absence of more than 140 years. In former East Germany any wolves migrating across the border from Poland in the past had been shot, but after reunification in 1991 the former West Germany's hunting regulations applied throughout the country. Wolves were recorded in France for the first time in 50 years, and in the U.S. it was reported that gray wolves had returned unaided to Yellowstone Park in Wyoming. Elsewhere in North America wolf hunting was controversial. In October Alaska authorized a kill of 80% of the wolves in a region southwest of Fairbanks. In Algonquin Provincial Park in Ontario, 35 of 75 wolves were killed when they followed deer that had migrated out of the park. The Yukon government planned to kill 150 wolves in 1993 but found fewer than they had estimated and killed only 61.

A new species of bovid—the vu quang ox (*Pseudoryx nghetinhensis*)—was described from Vietnam. Its most striking feature was the very long, almost straight, sharp horns. The animal had not yet been captured alive by scientists, but 20 specimens were obtained from hunters in Ha-tinh province along the Laos border. It was the first new mammal to be identified in more than 50 years. Among the reports of new bird species described were two species of leaf warbler from China (*Phylloscopus sichuanensis* and *P. hainanus*), an antpitta (*Grallaria kaestneri*) from Colombia, and a tyrannulet (*Phylloscartes kronei*) from Brazil. The Cebu flowerpecker (*Dicaeum quadricolor*), which had not been seen for 80 years, was rediscovered on the island of Cebu in the Philippines. The giant ibis (*Thaumatibis gigantea*) was refound in Laos after an apparent absence of 30 years. A search of Mana Island, New Zealand, found 100 goldstripe geckos (*Hoplodactylus chrysosireticus*). None had been seen for 10 years. Bulmer's fruit bat (*Aproteles bulmerae*) was reported rediscovered in Papua New Guinea, having been previously known only from a skin collected in 1975. Salim Ali's fruit bat (*Latidens salimalii*) was rediscovered in the High Wavy Mountains in southern India, where it had been last seen in 1948. In Australia the Adelaide bluetongue (*Tiliqua adelaidensis*) was believed extinct, having last been seen in 1959, but a specimen was discovered inside a road-killed snake in late 1992, and this was followed by the discovery of living individuals and the establishment of a captive-breeding population in 1993. Spanish biologists discovered 350 Mediterranean monk seals (*Monachus monachus*) in caves in the disputed border zone of Western Sahara and Mauritania, doubling the known world population.

Ornithologists spent three months in Cuba searching for the ivory-billed woodpecker (*Campephilus principalis bairdii*) but concluded that it was almost certainly extinct. In August it was reported that the last surviving individual of the cafe marron (*Ramosmania heterophylla*) on Rodrigues Island in the Indian Ocean had been damaged by persons unknown.

(JACQUI M. MORRIS)

See also Agriculture and Food Supplies; Botanical Gardens and Zoos; Energy; Life Sciences.

This article updates the *Macropædia* article CONSERVATION OF NATURAL RESOURCES.

Fashion and Dress

In 1993 a softer style for women took hold, unseating the hard-edged power dressing that had lingered since the late 1980s. Relaxed attitudes about beauty and clothing helped usher in a new freedom. It was no coincidence that the '70s held primary sway over trends for much of the year. Men's styles remained conservative, with flair added in the accessories.

Women's Fashions. Amazon supermodels with curvaceous figures had epitomized the feminine ideal since the late '80s, but they were supplanted by a brigade of waifs in 1993. Shorter, thinner, and wispier, these models were better suited to the flower-power mood of '70s styles and '90s grunge. They also appealed directly to the 20- to 30-year-olds classified as Generation X. Waif models, including Kate Moss and Amber Valletta, sparked controversy because some critics charged that their rail-thin figures encouraged eating disorders among young women.

Models over the age of 40 also regained prominence, with several well-known faces of the '70s emerging from retirement. U.S. designer Calvin Klein gave older models the biggest boost by featuring a mixture of 40-plus models as well as 18-year-old waifs in his fall runway show.

A new order also prevailed in the clothing industry, with French establishment couturiers losing ground to an avant-garde pack of Belgian and Japanese designers. The deconstructionist trend advocated by the avant-garde was too aesthetically unappealing for mass consumption, but it was embraced by a contingent of young women in France. Its torn, ragged, down-and-out look made it a cousin to grunge, a style spawned by rock bands based in Seattle, Wash. (*See* Sidebar.)

These upheavals contributed to the turmoil in the industry. Clothing sales remained weak as the recession dragged on, and many women rejected the increasingly outlandish styles presented by designers. The spring collections were built around a '70s revival that included sheer fabrics, crocheted tops, bell bottoms, elongated vests, ruffled blouses, and platform shoes. Fall was split into two camps: austere, monastic styles and romantic, dandyish looks that often verged on costumes.

In keeping with the conservative buying habits caused by the weak economy, colours were tried-and-true neutrals. For fall, black made a major resurgence, relieved now and then by chocolate brown, gray, wine, or forest green.

White blouses with ruffled collars were one of the few items that succeeded in reaching the mainstream. Teenagers wore them with jeans, while professional women paired them with suits. Vests also caught on with women of all ages, with silk, wool, or knit versions often taking the place of a blouse under blazers in spring and summer. Elongated vests sometimes substituted for jackets. During the warmer months, women of all ages wore long, '40s-style housedresses or calf-length knit tube dresses.

In keeping with the new softness, the predominant silhouette was a gently flowing A-line that flared from narrow shoulders. It was often achieved with a dress or an elongated vest and wide-legged pants.

Trousers were emphasized more than skirts as hemlines continued to descend for most of the year. Although trousers were still frowned upon in many conservative professions, they gained ground as more women began wearing pantsuits to work. Even the U.S. Senate changed its dress code to permit both sexes to wear trousers after a female senator wore them.

ANDREA RENAULT—GLOBE PHOTOS

Model Kate Moss wears one of the softer fashions that became popular in 1993. Use of very thin, frail-looking models, called waifs, was criticized by some on the grounds that it encouraged eating disorders among women.

Women who wore skirts to the office mostly favoured those with knee-length hemlines. French designers created confusion by elongating hemlines through the fall season in their ready-to-wear collections and then doing an about-face by showing microminis in their fall haute couture collections. Within weeks, New York City department stores were displaying miniskirts in their windows.

Because people were feeling unsettled by economic, environmental, and health concerns, spiritual symbols took hold in jewelry. Crosses became a preferred accessory, both on the runway and on the street. Ankhs, yin and yang symbols, and healing stones also grew in popularity.

In their fall runway shows, designers took spirituality a step further, showing clothing inspired by monks' robes, nuns' habits, and the garb of Hasidic Jews. Sober suits and high-waisted dresses best exemplified the mood. Accessories in this antifashion look were relegated either to a single cross or to rosary beads. Industrial work clothes and styles worn by turn-of-the-century immigrants also turned into fodder for designers who sought to romanticize previous eras.

The antithesis of the austere styles was the lush Edwardian look. Brocade, velvet, ruffles, and lace came together in romantic ensembles that were usually built around a frock coat, ruffled blouse, and skinny pants. Chokers, cameos, and long beads were among the preferred accessories.

Military jackets fit into the '70s inspiration for spring and carried through fall's dandyish and equestrian looks. Both jackets and coats bore gold braid, turned-back collars, epaulets, and metal buttons. Velvet was a dominant fabric for fall, exemplifying the softness and richness of the season. Panne velvet and stretch velvet appealed to younger shoppers in everything from dresses to crushable hats.

Clunky footwear was one category that spanned all the trends. The bulkier the footwear and heavier the sole, the better. Among young people, Doc Martens became so prevalent that they cut into sales of athletic shoes. Teenagers revived suede Pumas from the '70s and added their own platforms until manufacturers introduced platform versions. Platform shoes became mainstream, with teenagers opting for the more extreme five-centimetre (two-inch) platforms, and professional women wearing discreet one-and-one-quarter-centimetre (half-inch) styles. For fall, granny boots took off for all ages, pairing up perfectly with both minimalist and Edwardian styles.

Outside influences that attracted the attention of the fashion industry included a major Henri Matisse art exhibit in late 1992 and early 1993 in New York City. Matisse's cutouts later turned up as jewelry, belt buckles, prints, and appliqués. In films, the winter 1992 release of *Bram Stoker's Dracula* spawned a slew of bat-sleeved Dracula dresses and contributed to the romantic styles that came out for fall. During the summer and fall of 1993, the period costumes in *Orlando,* based on Virginia Woolf's novel, and *The Age of Innocence,* adapted from Edith Wharton's book, were also predicted to affect upcoming styles.

For young people, the rap, grunge, and rave music scenes wielded the strongest influence. In the U.S., west coast skateboarders and snowboarders also started many street trends. Teens bought clothes several sizes too big to achieve a baggy look. Headgear ranged from baseball caps to knit stocking caps, which were sometimes tied with a string near the top. Ravers wore tall, striped hats dubbed "Dr. Seuss hats" because they resembled the type of hat worn by the title character in Seuss's book *The Cat in the Hat.* Another teen fad, which was introduced by rappers, was plastic baby pacifiers worn dangling from a cord around the neck.

Cartoon characters soared in popularity with both teens and adults. Baby boomers wore clothing bearing images of Bugs Bunny or Mickey Mouse out of a sense of nostalgia, while teenagers favoured logo clothing that combined cartoon characters with colleges or athletic teams.

The '70s revival also brought back the shag hairstyle, a short, layered cut. U.S. first lady Hillary Rodham Clinton did not choose a hairdo that extreme, but she did have her pageboy cut into a short, layered style. An increasing number of black women opted for natural hairstyles that did not require chemical treatments. Short Afros, braids, and dreadlocks all gained in popularity. (LISBETH LEVINE)

Men's Fashions. In Europe as in the United States, the lingering effects of the recession continued to bite into the sales of men's clothing during 1993. The sales of boys' clothing, however, remained buoyant—so much so that in Britain some of the leading suppliers of men's outerwear, notably DAKS, introduced new lines of boys' wear for the first time. Other companies, including Aquascutum and Austin Reed, met with some success by introducing clothes that were styled especially for the young men's market and designed to be flexible enough for both formal and informal occasions.

At the other end of the age scale, men's fashions continued to be safe and sure in classic and conservative styling. Older men, however, also liked to feel that they were fashionably dressed when they wore striped and coloured shirts and ties in bold geometric or heavy floral patterns. They remained faithful to sober suits, mostly in gray or blue; beige or blue raincoats in lightweight cotton; and ¾-length camel or gray topcoats for autumn and winter.

There were also some revivals of former fashions. In business suits, for example, the slimmer silhouette returned with a slightly longer jacket, more often in a single-breasted rather than a double-breasted styling, with shorter lapels and with a higher-positioned buttonhole where the jacket fastened. Trousers were formfitting.

There was also a trend toward using more lightweight fabrics and toward coordinating jackets and trousers rather than wearing two-piece suits made from the same material. These jackets and trousers were often offered in different cloths as well as in different colours. Both linens and linen-and-cotton blends, usually in cream-coloured shades, were fashionable for both jackets and trousers.

Again, as for several years, the younger men were responsible for setting trends. Casual shirts were invariably worn outside trousers, with knitwear being longer than the jacket and sometimes tied around the waist. Caps, especially American styles, were worn at jaunty angles. At Wimbledon a tradition that had stood for centuries was broken when hatless ball boys and girls were issued blue baseball caps to protect them from the scorching heat.

Footwear trends saw a number of variations to the sandal, including a type with a single strap. The sandal remained functional and fashionable for leisure, but young men and boys favoured Reebok shoes, preferably in white. The Doc Martens boot, steeped in British tradition, was worn throughout the year.

In the annals of men's fashion history, 1993 would probably be remembered as a year of insecurity and price sensitivity. Customers took more time in making their selections, fewer clothes were finally bought, and the ones that were purchased had to be of better quality—for which higher prices were paid, sometimes reluctantly.

(STANLEY H. COSTIN)

See also Industrial Review: *Furs.*

This article updates the *Macropædia* article DRESS AND ADORNMENT.

Grunge, a Fleeting Fashion Rage

In the MTV era, music groups reign as trendsetters in the realm of clothing styles for U.S. youth. This phenomenon helped provide an explanation for the relatively short-lived explosion of grunge, which started in Seattle, Wash., and eventually echoed in Europe.

The term *grunge* originally applied to the punk-metal guitar sound of such Seattle-based bands as Nirvana, Pearl Jam, and Soundgarden, but it also became synonymous in the late 1980s with both their music and clothing styles. Before a group's music took off, band members dressed in thrift shop clothes out of economic necessity. The fickle weather of the Pacific Northwest prompted musicians to wear layers and always to have a spare flannel shirt tied around their waists.

The key components of the grunge look consisted of the ubiquitous plaid flannel shirt, thermal underwear, T-shirts with band logos, ripped jeans, and stocking caps. The favoured footwear was either combat boots, particularly Doc Martens, or Converse high-top sneakers.

While 1970s punk was antifashion, rejecting the prevailing trends, the grunge movement was "unfashion" at heart. Typical grunge dressers created their mismatched outfits by wearing whatever clothes were scattered on the floor nearest to the bed.

Some teen fans began dressing like those musicians in 1991, before trend watchers started taking notice in the summer of 1992 with the release of *Singles,* a movie about the Seattle scene. By the end of that year, grunge had become a byword. Although the style was worn by both sexes, it tended to be more popular with men.

In the spring of 1993 a few influential New York designers sent grunge-inspired women's collections down the runway. At Perry Ellis designer Marc Jacobs piled on the layers, combining a cropped vest, low-calf dress, midriff-baring T-shirt, and thermal hot pants with combat boots and a stocking cap. He tied plaid shirts around the waist, but his were made of silk, not flannel. Anna Sui and Christian Francis Roth also endorsed grunge, often mixing it with '70s elements such as rainbow stripes and butterfly appliqués.

Although the grunge styles shown on the runway were a flop with designer customers, the international media attention helped boost the popularity of the movement among teenagers. By fall major mass retailers had labeled grunge a key back-to-school trend, but by then only some younger teens were still wearing grunge styles.

The commercial hype had made grunge a dirty word in its hometown. By fall the Seattle version of grunge had already evolved. The new look was more of a blue-collar, work-clothes style. Jackets normally worn by service station attendants, sporting patches with such American good-old-boy names as Bud, Clem, and Goober soared in popularity, as did other uniform-type apparel. (LISBETH LEVINE)

Gardening

The weather was perhaps the greatest single factor affecting home gardening in the United States and Britain during 1993. In the U.S. the "Great Flood of '93" saturated the Midwest, while drought or near-drought conditions scorched the Southeast. Tomatoes, undoubtedly the most commonly grown food in home gardens, performed miserably in the areas of the country that were plagued with overabundant rainfall. The full extent of permanent damage to gardens, trees, lawns, and landscape in areas sustaining significant flood damage remained to be assessed. In Britain a wet winter and steady rainfall over a succession of months culminated in extremely heavy October rains, which resulted in severe flooding in many low-lying areas and created headaches for gardeners and farmers.

Nevertheless, more than 56 million households in the U.S. and 19 million in Britain were involved in gardening. Those who chose to make manual garden tasks easier were offered a wide range of new products, including rechargeable battery-powered lawn mowers, hedge clippers, and nylon-line weed trimmers. The new offerings were also meant to address environmental concerns about emissions from gasoline-powered lawn-maintenance equipment. Mulching mowers, though not new, recycled fine grass clippings back onto the soil surface and eliminated the need for bagging and disposing of the sheared grass. The mulching mowers' higher-than-average price tag, however, made consumers somewhat reluctant to purchase them. In an effort to cut skyrocketing water bills, manufacturers introduced water-efficient drip irrigation systems and computerized faucet timers so that gardeners would be able to conserve and regulate water usage.

Biological pest control became more widely available to home gardeners through both retail and mail-order suppliers offering a larger range of products. BioSafe, a vine-weevil-control preparation containing nematodes, was the first such product to be developed with an extended shelf life. This innovation meant that BioSafe could be sold in stores rather than by mail order only. Other biological agents were introduced for the control of red spider mite, whitefly, and caterpillars. In Britain a natural slug-control agent was developed. A naturally occurring strain of nematode isolated from the soil was found to infect and kill a range of slug species, including those known to damage agricultural and garden crops in Europe. This specific nematode, which was effective even at very low soil temperatures, posed no danger to beneficial insects and animals because it attacked only slugs. A patent was filed for the production and use of nematodes against mollusk pests.

In the U.S. a new trend developed in the sale of live plants. Specialty retail nurseries and garden centres, long the primary marketing channel for green goods (live plants), were being overtaken by such mass merchandisers as Wal-Mart, Kmart, and Home Depot. By the end of the decade, it was predicted that 60% of all green goods would be sold through mass-merchandise outlets. In the event of such a shift to serve-yourself merchandising, gardeners could expect less personal service and a reduction in the number of plant varieties available.

A host of colourful new plants were introduced during 1993. In Britain the award for Rose of the Year went to Dawn Chorus, a large-flowered hybrid tea rose. Among the best from Hilliers Nursery, one of the country's oldest family-owned concerns, were *Lavatera* Pink Frills, *Ceanothus* Blue Mount, and *Spiraea japonica* Firelight and Candlelight. In the U.S. new colour choices debuted for old garden favourites. In an effort to produce a pure white marigold, the W. Atlee Burpee Co. introduced the hybrid French Vanilla. The plant was bushier and more floriferous than open-pollinated varieties, and the creamy-white and odourless flowers were large (up to 7.6 cm [3 in] across).

Native plants are used to beautiful effect in the dry climate of southern California. The use of native flora, hardier than exotics and thus requiring less care, especially appeals to gardeners interested in preserving the diversity of local plant life.

KATHLENE PERSOFF—TIME MAGAZINE

At a British trade show in September, *Nemesia denticulata* Confetti won the new product award. This colourful perennial plant flowers for up to eight months, with delicately fragrant deep pink blooms. A compact shrub, *Hebe* Purple Pixie, was successfully marketed and came complete with a purple pot. Other new offerings included a hybrid perennial, *Limonium* Misty hybrids, bred in Japan for a Dutch grower, and the colourful and scented *Dianthus* Gipsy hybrids. For the home and conservatory, Dutch growers introduced the first variegated yucca houseplant, *Yucca variegata* Jewel. A new carrot, Fly Away, was billed as the most resistant variety yet against the pest carrot root fly. Two new Ballerina apples also debuted: Charlotte, a cooking apple, and Flamenco, a dark red dessert apple.

Fleuroselect, the European seed-testing organization, awarded gold medals to *Viola* Velour Blue, *Bellis perennis* Robella, and *Centaurea cyanus* Florence White and Florence Pink. The All-America Selections for 1993 included Rio Samba, a bright yellow hybrid tea rose tipped with flaming orange; Solitude, a grandiflora rose with scalloped outer petals of radiant orange with an orange-gold reverse; Sweet Inspiration, a floribunda rose with clusters of pink blossoms; and Child's Play, a miniature rose with white petals edged in pink. In the fruits and vegetables category, Husky Gold tomatoes won. The award winner produced shiny golden fruits that were meaty and flavourful; it was the first time in nine years that the honour was bestowed on a tomato variety. (KAY MELCHISEDECH OLSON; ADAM GERHOLD PASCO)

See also Agriculture and Food Supplies; Botanical Gardens and Zoos; Life Sciences.

This article updates the *Macropædia* article GARDENING AND HORTICULTURE.

Health and Disease

In 1993 exciting developments in the application of genetics to the diagnosis, understanding, and potential treatment of a number of diseases shared the stage with the worsening epidemics of AIDS and tuberculosis (TB). The year was also marked by growing concern not only about the emergence of previously unrecognized infectious diseases but also about the capacity of familiar—and apparently vanquished—infections to exact further human tolls.

Genetics. As scientists around the world observed the 40th anniversary of the elucidation of the molecular structure of DNA, French researchers announced that they had succeeded in constructing the first rough map of all the human chromosomes. Progress continued in the ongoing hunt for genes responsible for particular diseases. Among the disorders whose underlying genetic defects were pinpointed in 1993 were neurofibromatosis type 2, the inherited cancer syndrome known as von Hippel-Lindau disease, one type of diabetes, and a form of amyotrophic lateral sclerosis (ALS; Lou Gehrig's disease).

The crowning achievement of the year was the discovery on chromosome 4 of the gene for Huntington's disease, a hereditary neurological affliction that leads to incoordinated limb movements, mental deterioration, and, eventually, death. The search for the gene took 10 years and involved more than 50 researchers in laboratories in the U.S. and Europe. The mutation was an unusual type that so far had been found in only four other diseases: fragile-X syndrome (the most common type of inherited mental retardation), myotonic dystrophy (a kind of muscular dystrophy that affects adults), spinobulbar muscular atrophy (Kennedy's disease), and spinocerebellar ataxia type 1. Its basis is a genetic "mistake" in which a sequence of three nucleotides (the building blocks of DNA) is repeated in a manner some have likened to a stutter. Affected individuals were found to have as many as 100 of these repetitions. People who had a greater number of repetitions seemed to develop the disease earlier and had more severe cases.

Because of both the unusual nature of the mutation and the lack of knowledge about the function of the normal gene's protein product, dubbed *huntingtin* by researchers, no treatment was yet in hand. However, it was possible to identify those who would eventually get the disease. This situation could create psychological difficulties for members of affected families. Whereas previously they could only wait for signs of the disease to appear—usually in middle age—now they had the option of seeking early diagnosis through DNA analysis. If the test was positive, they would then have to cope with the news that they faced inevitable, devastating disease later in life.

Progress also occurred in the understanding of genetic factors in Alzheimer's disease. Allen Roses and colleagues at Duke University Medical Center, Durham, N.C., found that people with one variant of the gene for the cholesterol-carrying protein apolipoprotein E were at increased risk of getting late-onset Alzheimer's. (The late-developing form of the disease accounted for about 80% of U.S. cases.) The protein binds a substance called beta-amyloid, which is known to accumulate in the brains of Alzheimer's patients.

The pace of gene-therapy trials quickened considerably. Two different teams performed gene therapy in patients with cystic fibrosis (CF), introducing normal versions of the CF gene by aerosol into airway cells. Ronald Crystal of Cornell University Medical Center, New York City, used a genetically modified cold virus to carry the normal genes; James Wilson, at the University of Pennsylvania, used a slightly different method. Wilson also used gene therapy to successfully treat a few patients with familial hypercholesterolemia, an inherited disorder in which the gene for the low-density lipoprotein (LDL) receptor is defective, resulting in failure to remove LDL from the blood and allowing fatty deposits to build up in blood vessels.

Genetics researchers also published the results of studies that suggested an inherited basis for sexual orientation. Investigators at the National Cancer Institute (NCI), Bethesda, Md., linked homosexuality in men to a region on the X, or female, chromosome, the sex chromosome that males inherit from their mothers. (Women have two X chromosomes; men have one X and one Y.) The researchers first interviewed gay men, finding that they had a higher-than-expected number of homosexual relatives on the maternal side. Focusing on 40 families in which there were two gay brothers, they found that in 33 pairs the two brothers had identical regions at the tip of the X chromosome—a much higher proportion than would be expected. No specific gene was identified as predisposing to homosexuality, however, and the work done thus far would have to be confirmed by others. Moreover, the trait seemed to be paternal in some families. Nonetheless, the study was regarded as the most scientific in the field to date, and the group had already

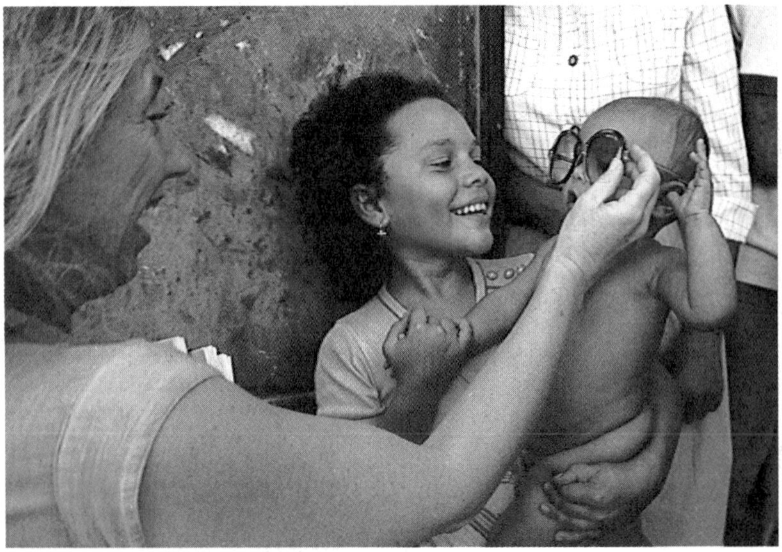

NICK KELSH

Psychologist Nancy Wexler of the Hereditary Disease Foundation in Santa Monica, Calif., plays with a Venezuelan child. In the early 1980s Wexler and other scientists began studying Venezuelan families with a history of Huntington's disease. These investigations ultimately made possible the identification, in 1993, of the gene responsible for the disorder.

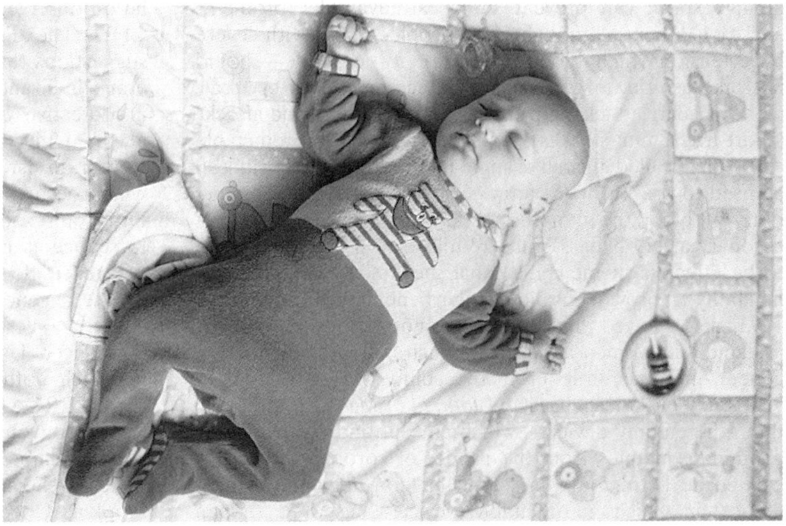

This infant has been placed on his back for sleeping, a practice recommended by European clinicians. New research confirmed earlier studies showing that placing a baby in a prone position, the practice more common in the U.S., increases the risk of sudden infant death syndrome.
OWEN FRANKEN—STOCK, BOSTON

started a study of female homosexuality. Another study of lesbians, based solely on interviews, found that in 71 identical twin pairs, 48% of the sisters were either lesbian or bisexual, compared with only 16% of 37 nonidentical twin pairs and 6% of 35 adoptive sisters.

In one of the most controversial developments of the year, Robert Stillman, a fertility specialist at George Washington University Medical Center, Washington, D.C., reported in October that he had experimentally cloned human embryos, using techniques already well known in the breeding of livestock and other animals. The report raised the possibility that identical twins could be born years, or even generations, apart. The ethical and legal dilemmas posed by such a capability would not easily be resolved.

Infectious Diseases. U.S. microbiologists reported a marked increase in cases of pulmonary TB in New York City caused by organisms resistant to the drugs normally used to treat the disease. There were also reports that the drug-resistant bacteria could reinfect patients while they were being treated (or after they were treated) for TB caused by antibiotic-sensitive strains. This finding contradicted previous beliefs that because of immunity conferred by the initial infection, reinfection occurred only very rarely. (*See* Sidebar.)

Cholera loomed large as a global health problem. In mid-1993 the World Health Organization (WHO) reported that the continuing pandemic of the disease, caused by the so-called El Tor strain of *Vibrio cholerae* (first isolated in Indonesia in 1961) had claimed more than three million victims and caused tens of thousands of deaths. In August researchers at the International Centre for Diarrhoeal Diseases Research in Bangladesh described epidemics in Bangladesh and India caused by a new strain of *V. cholerae,* prompting fears of the start of yet another pandemic, the eighth such worldwide outbreak in history.

The role of an infectious agent, the bacterium *Helicobacter pylori*, in both duodenal ulcers and gastric cancer became clearer during the year. A study carried out in Austria demonstrated that administration of antibiotics to eradicate this bacterium was followed by a marked reduction in ulcer recurrence. And a major international study strongly implicated *H. pylori* as a cause of gastric cancer. Researchers in Britain and Italy showed that in five out of six patients with one particular type of stomach cancer, elimination of the bacterium through antibiotic therapy was followed by regression of the tumour.

That new infectious diseases continue to emerge was dramatically demonstrated by the appearance in the southwestern U.S. of a mysterious, often fatal flulike illness that brought about rapid respiratory failure in young, previously healthy individuals. A number of cases were subsequently reported in other parts of the country, from California to Louisiana. An intensive investigation led to the identification of a rodent-borne hantavirus of a type not previously associated with human illness in the U.S. Authorities speculated that increased rainfall may have caused a population explosion in the white-footed mouse, which carries the organism. The virus itself was not believed to be "new."

AIDS. The AIDS epidemic continued virtually unabated, and WHO estimated that the number of those infected with HIV would reach 30 million–40 million by the year 2000. The WHO data also showed that half of new HIV infections were occurring in people 25 years old or younger. Modes of transmission varied by region. In Africa and parts of Asia, heterosexual sex was the primary factor in the spread of HIV. In the U.S., Europe, and South America, however, transmission via intravenous drug abuse and homosexual contacts still predominated.

Enormous disappointments occurred during the year when several studies, principally the collaborative British-French Concorde study, showed that use of AZT (zidovudine; Retrovir) early in the course of HIV infection was not as effective in forestalling AIDS as had been believed. A second disappointment came when a widely hailed study showing great promise for a combination therapy—concurrent use of three anti-HIV drugs—was revealed to have been flawed. Because of the initial excitement over the study, a national clinical trial of the treatment had already begun; it was apparently to continue despite the revelation.

In light of the failure of efforts to find better treatment, more experts stressed prevention. Michael Merson, head of WHO's global AIDS program, urged the spending of an additional $1.5 billion to $2.9 billion a year in less developed countries on prevention programs. "Governments can pay now or pay a much higher price later," he said. The strategies would include continued emphasis on the importance of condom use; a concerted effort to treat other sexually transmitted diseases, which potentiate the risk of contracting HIV; an increase in AIDS education programs; and the operation of needle-exchange programs for people who inject illicit drugs.

Cardiovascular Disease. The American Heart Association, in a position statement published in February, confirmed what many already believed and practiced—that taking aspirin can prevent some cardiovascular problems and treat others. Although some people—those with severe hypertension (high blood pressure), for example—should not take aspirin, in general it was recommended for treatment of heart attacks in progress, transient ischemic attacks (short-lived mini-strokes), and the type of unpredictable chest pain called unstable angina. In addition, aspirin can be used to prevent heart attacks, strokes caused by obstructions of blood flow in the brain, and early occlusion of coronary artery bypass grafts. While aspirin use was known to be effective in men, there had been some doubt about its ability to provide cardiovascular benefits in women. One 1993 study showed that aspirin does not dissolve blood clots as rapidly in women as in men, which may account for the gender difference in its protective ability.

A study in the *New England Journal of Medicine* indicated that atherectomy devices—which cut out and remove lipid-containing plaques from the insides of coronary arteries—yielded no better outcomes than balloon angioplasty techniques, in which an inflatable device is used to reopen blocked arteries. Another study showed that women who underwent angioplasty had a higher in-hospital death rate from the procedure than men.

Attention focused on the growing evidence that regular light alcohol consumption affords some degree of protection against coronary heart disease (CHD). Danish researchers demonstrated that moderate drinking is especially protective in men of a certain blood type who are at particularly high risk of developing—and dying from—CHD.

Most of the recent work on the cardiovascular benefits of regular drinking had indicated that the active agent was ethyl alcohol itself. One puzzle, however, had been the low incidence of atherosclerosis (narrowing of blood vessels caused by fatty deposits) in some regions of France where the typical diet contains considerable quantities of saturated fat. This finding was in marked contrast to the close correlation observed elsewhere between saturated fat intake and CHD. The discovery of this "French paradox" prompted suggestions that something in red wine—the preferred beverage in France—other than its alcohol content may exert a protective effect. Working in collaboration, researchers at the University of California at Davis and the Volcani Center in Israel demonstrated that phenolic compounds, which occur in red wine, could prevent oxidation of LDL. Other antioxidants had been shown in animal experiments to reduce atherosclerosis.

Cancer. Several teams were working during the year to isolate a gene—called BRCA1—whose inherited mutation confers a very high risk of developing breast and ovarian cancer. Using molecular markers and studying families in which both diseases were highly prevalent, researchers traced BRCA1 to chromosome 17. In April 1993 they fully identified women who had defective forms of the gene.

In a major breakthrough in cancer genetics, two teams of researchers, one headed by Bert Vogelstein of the Johns Hopkins Oncology Center, Baltimore, Md., and the other directed by Richard D. Kolodner of the Dana-Farber Cancer Institute, Boston, and Richard Fishel of the University of Vermont Medical School, announced in December that they had isolated a gene implicated in an extremely common type of colon cancer, hereditary nonpolyposis colorectal cancer. The gene directs the synthesis of a protein that corrects mistakes in the pairing of nucleotides. It was estimated that one in every 200 people inherits the defective form of the gene; such individuals face a 70 to 90% chance of developing colon cancer. In addition, women with the mutation are at greater risk for uterine and ovarian cancer. Scientists predicted that a test for people from families with a history of colon cancer could be ready as early as the middle of 1994, enabling presymptomatic screening for those at risk. A similar test was developed in 1993 for another hereditary condition that often leads to colon cancer.

Drug-resistant Diseases

Infectious agents continually undergo genetic change. Today, however, this process is being fostered by human behaviour and, ironically, modern medicine. One culprit is the overuse of antibiotics. Some authorities estimate that half of the antibiotics used in the U.S. are unnecessary—the drug prescribed is too powerful, is taken for longer than is necessary, or is not needed at all. Overuse and misuse can lead to the development of drug-resistant bacterial strains, which in turn require more expensive, more toxic alternative drugs.

The recent resurgence of tuberculosis is a case in point. Effective drug treatment for TB has been available in the developed world since the 1950s, but beginning in the mid-1980s, the disease staged a comeback. Its rise was attributed in part to social factors—increasing poverty, homelessness, substance abuse, and deteriorating health care systems. It was also linked to the AIDS pandemic; because of the effect of the virus on the immune system, people infected with HIV are much more susceptible than others to TB.

Treatment of TB in 1993 was complicated by the emergence of drug-resistant strains, which have more than doubled in the past 10 years. Classic uncomplicated TB can be cured with a six-month regimen of antibiotics for about $500. The cost of treatment of multiple-drug-resistant (MDR) TB may exceed $180,000. Moreover, such treatment is often ineffective. To successfully eradicate MDR strains, several drugs must be taken simultaneously and over an extended period of time. However, the population most affected by TB—the poor, the homeless, substance abusers, the immunocompromised—is the very group that has the most difficulty complying with a complex, protracted regimen. Interrupted or incomplete treatment allows the infectious organisms to mutate and multiply.

Drug resistance to TB is not an isolated phenomenon. Resistance to the antimalarial chloroquine by the most virulent malaria parasite was reported in 1961. Even more troubling is the organism's resistance, demonstrated in 1990, to a recently introduced drug that took 17 years to develop. The antiviral acyclovir has been the drug of choice for treatment of herpes simplex virus (HSV) since its approval in 1984. Prior to the AIDS pandemic, resistance to acyclovir was uncommon. However, acyclovir-resistant HSV is now found in HIV-infected patients. Resistance to AZT, used to treat HIV infection itself, appears to develop after six months of use.

These are only a few examples of the growing numbers of drug-resistant infections. The medical community and public health officials must remain vigilant if they are to keep pace. (ELLEN FINKELSTEIN)

Residents of Lin Xian (Lin Hsien), China—where diets are poor and the incidence of certain cancers is high—wait to be screened as part of a five-year clinical trial to determine if vitamin and mineral supplements can help to prevent some forms of the disease. The results, announced in 1993, showed a significant reduction in deaths from cancer as well as from other diseases.

PHILLIP TAYLOR, M.D., NATIONAL CANCER INSTITUTE; PHOTOGRAPH, THE NEW YORK TIMES

Such genetic screening techniques may someday replace the stool tests for fecal occult blood that were currently used to screen for colorectal cancer. The drawbacks of stool tests led one group of physicians during the year to call the method ineffective in detecting colon cancer, although another group concluded that regular testing decreased colon cancer deaths by 33%. Such tests were inexpensive but also inconclusive. A positive stool test would therefore have to be confirmed by further—and much more costly—studies.

In breast cancer, use of another screening test, mammography, had been controversial for women in their 40s because of doubts that such screening reduced the death rate in this age group, as it did in women over 50. Articles published and meetings held during the year did not resolve the controversy.

Can colorectal cancer be prevented by regular use of aspirin or other nonsteroidal anti-inflammatory drugs? Several studies published in 1993 suggested that it can, although another discounted this conclusion. Experts said that long-term, randomized studies involving several aspirin doses would be necessary before any specific recommendations could be made.

Cancer of the prostate gland, the second most common cancer (after lung cancer) in U.S. men, got increased attention in 1993, although major controversies continued about how to diagnose and treat it and whether small, localized prostate cancers should be treated at all. One study showed that radiation therapy was more likely to cure large, inoperable prostate tumours if the men were given hormones for two months before radiation therapy. And a major study from Harvard looked at 300 men (out of a group of more than 47,000) who had been diagnosed with prostate cancer between 1986 and 1990 and found that the intake of animal fat, especially fat from red meat, was directly correlated with the risk of developing advanced disease.

Other Developments. A major, 10-year study of nearly 1,500 persons with type I (insulin-dependent) diabetes showed that intensive treatment to control the level of blood glucose worked better than conventional treatment in reducing common complications of the disease, such as eye and kidney problems and nerve damage. The intensive regime involved taking three to five insulin injections per day or using a pump that automatically injected insulin into the bloodstream, testing of blood glucose four to seven times per day, and working closely with a medical and support team. A major drawback, however, was that the intensive regimen was difficult to adhere to and more costly than the conventional approach.

There was a step forward in the understanding of sudden infant death syndrome (SIDS), also known as crib death or, in Britain, cot death. Although several retrospective studies had indicated that babies who slept in the prone position were at increased risk of SIDS and had suggested that infants be placed on their backs or sides, many pediatricians were reluctant to make this recommendation because of uncertainty as to why the prone position should be hazardous. The new research, carried out in Australia and New Zealand, not only confirmed the higher risk of prone sleeping but also identified four contributing factors that increase risk—the use of soft (natural fibre) mattresses, swaddling, recent illness, and overheating of bedrooms.

The apparent role of vitamins and minerals, both from dietary sources and as supplements, continued to grow in importance. In one NCI study, conducted in a rural area of China where intake of fresh fruits, meat, and dairy products was limited, people who took a supplement of beta-carotene, vitamin E, and selenium for five years had a 13% lower risk of dying from cancer, a 10% reduction in the risk of death from stroke, and a 9% lower risk of death due to all causes. The group taking the supplement also experienced a 21% decline in deaths from stomach cancer, which occurs at a particularly high rate in this region.

Studies conducted in the U.S. indicated that dietary consumption of antioxidants—especially beta-carotene and vitamin E—reduces the risk of stroke in general and the thickness of the walls of the carotid arteries (which carry blood to the brain) in particular. Moreover, reports from two ongoing studies of U.S. health professionals showed that taking vitamin E supplements was associated with a significant decrease in the risk of CHD.

A number of studies had shown that women who take folic acid supplements have a reduced risk of bearing children with the congenital malformations known collectively as neural tube defects. However, it was very difficult to obtain a protective level of folic acid from the diet alone. Therefore, in 1993 the U.S. Food and Drug Administration recommended that folic acid be used to fortify common grain products so that women who become pregnant will have enough of the substance in their bodies very early in pregnancy, when the neural tube (which becomes the brain and spinal cord) begins to form.

(BERNARD DIXON; GAIL W. MCBRIDE)

MENTAL HEALTH

Two advances in the understanding of the most common of the serious mental illnesses, schizophrenia, emerged from work at King's College Hospital, London. First, a team there set out to locate the basis of the auditory hallucinations ("hearing voices") that characterize this illness. According to one view, such hallucinations occur because schizophrenics are unable to monitor their own thoughts, or "inner speech," which they therefore regard as alien.

The researchers used an imaging technique known as photon emission tomography (PET) to study 12 men both when they were and when they were not experiencing such hallucinations. The PET scans showed that blood flow in a part of the brain called Broca's area was significantly greater during hallucinations than at other times. This suggested that the production of auditory hallucinations is associated with increased activity in one of the main regions of the brain that is specialized for language.

Research by the same group also threw light on the origin of schizophrenia. Four different studies showed that exposure of pregnant women to influenza during the fifth or sixth month of gestation increased the risk of schizophrenia's appearing later in the offspring. The effect was more pronounced in female than in male children.

A collaborative survey conducted in London and Bordeaux, France, highlighted significant differences in the diagnosis of schizophrenia by British and French psychiatrists. This disparity, which reflected the greater influence of psychoanalytic ideas in France, could partially explain why first hospital admission rates in France for schizophrenia are much higher before the age of 45 but lower after that age. Particularly in light of political and economic union, which means that medical professionals in the European Community (EC) will be able to practice in any EC country, the authors of the report argued that further work was necessary to ensure that psychiatrists speak a common language.

Another disparity that came to light during 1993 was that of the prevalence of dementia in different elderly populations. A study among 85-year-olds in Göteborg, Sweden, showed that 29.8% of them were suffering from dementia. This was similar to the figure reported following a recent survey in Shanghai but contrasted with the 47.2% found by community-based screening in East Boston, Mass., and the 12.6% rate for medically diagnosed cases of dementia in Rochester, Minn. It was not yet clear whether these differences reflected regional variations in incidence or differing diagnostic criteria. In the Swedish study almost half of those with dementia appeared to have a form of the disease related to circulatory problems, which may be more amenable to treatment or prevention than Alzheimer's disease.

Reflecting increasing interest in the relationship between mind and body, a link between mental illness and the circulatory system emerged from a study carried out at the University of California at San Diego. Researchers there were interested in finding out why, according to several recent clinical trials of cholesterol-lowering drugs, benefits in the reduction of deaths from coronary heart disease were accompanied by significant increases in suicides and other violent deaths. One possible explanation was that the lowering of blood cholesterol triggered a rise in depressive illness. This turned out to be true. In men aged 70 and older, depression was three times more common in those with low cholesterol than in those with higher levels. Since health authorities now widely recommended measures to reduce blood cholesterol, the investigators were further studying the significance of this relationship and possible mechanisms responsible for it.

A Danish survey established that psychological distress late in pregnancy is associated with a heightened risk of preterm delivery, which is in turn linked with increased rates of infant death and other adverse consequences. Although there had been similar suggestions previously, this study of some 6,000 women put the matter beyond dispute, indicating the need for intervention to avoid psychological distress during pregnancy. (BERNARD DIXON)

This article updates the *Macropædia* article MENTAL DISORDERS and Their Treatment.

DENTISTRY

As Pres. Bill Clinton introduced his U.S. health reform proposal during 1993, the American Dental Association (ADA) concurred with the recommendation that a high priority be placed on children's dental services but sharply disagreed with the administration's contention that costs would limit the scope of coverage in the early years. A preliminary draft of the plan proposed coverage of children's preventive services to age 18 and preventive care for adults by the year 2,000.

A team of researchers at the University of Florida College of Dentistry was using recombinant DNA technology to construct a non-acid-producing microorganism that could be used in the mouth to replace the common oral bacterium *Streptococcus mutans,* which lives on the teeth and appears to cause most dental cavities. Replacement therapy depends on finding a bacterial strain that does not cause disease itself and that, by virtue of its presence, prevents infection by a pathogenic strain. In previous studies the team constructed an organism that effectively prevented dental cavities in animals.

Contrary to earlier reports, two studies published during the year failed to find a link between drinking fluoridated water and having an increased risk of osteoporosis, the thinning of the bones that occurs with age. Fluoridation drastically reduced dental cavities around the world and resulted in generations of people being virtually free of tooth decay. A long-term Canadian study showed that hip-fracture rates were the same in Edmonton, Alta., which had fluoride levels of one part per million, and Calgary, Alta., with a fluoride level of 0.3 ppm. A second study, conducted by the Mayo Clinic, found that hip-fracture rates in Rochester, Minn., were slightly higher prior to fluoridation of drinking water in 1960 than they were afterward.

Smoking has been linked for several decades with an increased risk of various health problems, including periodontal disease. New findings suggested that smoking not only affects the development of gum disease but also reduces the success of treatment. Research conducted at the University of Texas at San Antonio and the University of California at Los Angeles found that patients with severe gum disease who smoke at least half a pack of cigarettes daily do not respond to treatment as well as do nonsmokers. Periodontal therapy successfully eliminated bacteria associated with the disease in only 48% of the patients who were smokers, compared with a 70% success rate in the nonsmokers. It was not yet known whether a short-term cessation of smoking during the therapy would be sufficient to improve the results.

(LOU JOSEPH)

VETERINARY MEDICINE

It had long been suspected that some dogs could predict the onset of an epileptic seizure in humans, but little solid evidence had been produced. In 1993 Andrew Edney, a veterinarian in the U.K., published the results of a survey of objective accounts of such incidents. Respondents reported significant behaviour changes in dogs preceding a seizure in

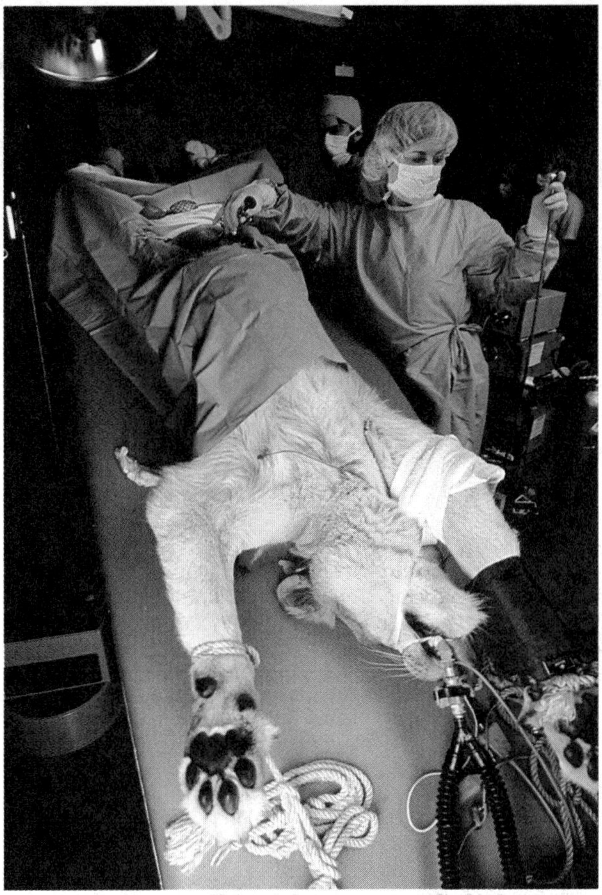

At the National Zoo in Washington, D.C., an anesthetized female lion undergoes laparoscopy in preparation for artificial insemination with sperm from a wild male. A number of zoos have undertaken innovative programs in so-called managed breeding.
M. NICHOLS—MAGNUM

their owners. The dogs barked or whined, licked the subjects' faces or hands, or sought assistance. Edney suggested that further work might make it possible to identify dogs possessing the ability, with a view toward helping people with epilepsy.

Although used for centuries, the practice of "firing" in the treatment of equine lameness—application of a hot iron to the affected area—had become discredited. Instead, several alternative treatments were suggested, including anti-inflammatory drugs such as corticosteroids. Substances that combined anti-inflammatory action with replacement of defective synovial fluid (a natural fluid that bathes the joints) also were used in treating equine lameness caused by joint disease. One such substance was sodium hyaluronate, a natural constituent of both cartilage tissue and synovial fluid. It had several drawbacks, however. The product had to be injected directly into the affected joint, which was not always easy, and it was expensive. Traditional manufacture was based on extraction of material from animal tissues. In a major advance, scientists working in the U.S. for pharmaceuticals manufacturer Bayer devised a method of producing hyaluronic acid from bacteria by a fermentation process. Not only did this reduce the cost, it enabled a product of greater purity to be produced. The new product could be administered intravenously.

An ambitious worldwide concept for an information database for practicing veterinarians was launched in 1993 by a group based in Cambridge, England. Called Vetstream, the system envisaged a "central information depot" linked by telephone line and satellite to veterinary practices. Each would have a computer terminal with core information on CD-ROMs plus a facility for continual updating. Comprehensive clinical information would be presented via text, sound, and pictures. For example, a veterinarian consulting the system about a particular heart condition would be able to see a typical cardiogram and simultaneously listen to the related heart sounds. If a surgical procedure was indicated, it could be screened in full colour, complete with commentary. (EDWARD BODEN)

See also Life Sciences: *Molecular Biology.*

This article updates the *Macropædia* articles DIAGNOSIS AND THERAPEUTICS; DISEASE; INFECTIOUS DISEASES; MEDICINE.

Industrial Review

The period since 1990 was proving a difficult time for the older industrialized economies, which had suffered from prolonged recession at home, and also for the previously centrally planned economies of Eastern Europe and the former Soviet Union, which were struggling to make the transition to a market-based system. In addition, both faced enormous competition from the dynamic Asian economies, where wages were a fraction of those in the industrial world.

In the industrialized nations in 1993, the cycle in the major economies remained desynchronized. The recession that began in North America, Australia, and the U.K. in 1990 had come to an end, and a sluggish recovery was under way. In continental Europe and Japan, however, the peak of the cycle came later, as did the recession. Toward the end of 1993, there was still no genuine indication that the trough of the recession had been reached in those economies.

The policy stance was shifting nonetheless. In the U.S., where the bias had long been pro-growth and pro-jobs, the monetary policy remained supportive of such activity. In Europe and Japan, however, there was a change. Japanese interest rates fell to record low levels, and rates in Germany declined sharply from the near-10% levels that the Bundesbank had established to counter the inflationary effects of the postunification boom.

Prodded by supragovernmental bodies such as the International Monetary Fund and the Organization for Economic Cooperation and Development, governments were coming to accept the seriousness of the unemployment problem and were seeking to stem job losses, especially in manu-

Table I. Annual Average Rates of Growth of Manufacturing Output, 1980–92

Percent

Area	1980–84	1985–89	1990	1991	1992
World[1]	1.7	4.2	0.2	0.0	0.6
Industrial countries	1.4	3.7	−1.3	−2.0	−1.7
Less industrialized countries	3.5	7.0	8.2	9.4	10.9

[1] For definition, *see* Table IV.
Source: UN, *Monthly Bulletin of Statistics.*

Table II. Manufacturing Production in Eastern Europe and the Former Soviet Union[1]

1980 = 100

Country	1988	1989	1990	1991	1992	%[3]
Bulgaria[2]	141	139	116	90	79	−12
Former Czechoslovakia	124	125	121	89	. . .	−26
Hungary	117	111	101	76	63	−17
Poland	111	109	80	70	71	1
Former Soviet Union	136	139	139	126	. . .	−9

[1] Romania not available.
[2] All industries.
[3] % change 1991–92 except Czechoslovakia and Former Soviet Union 1991–90.
Source: UN, *Monthly Bulletin of Statistics.*

facturing. It was in this sector that the need to match the low costs of the newly industrializing economies was most pronounced. Efforts to accomplish this resulted in large-scale restructuring in many companies and rapid productivity gains, especially in those countries where the recession had ended.

The slump in output experienced by the former centrally planned economies was at last beginning to come to an end, though the scale of the reduction in activity had been more extreme than many had hoped. According to official data, manufacturing output, which had been the backbone of the planned system, had dropped by about 40–50% in the more reform-minded economies, where there were signs that the bottom had been reached. In the less reformist economies, such as Russia and the other countries of the former Soviet Union, the fall in output was continuing.

Against the background of recession in the industrialized world and reconstruction in Eastern Europe, the performance of some of the economies of Asia and Latin America stood out. Particularly in East Asia, the development process had taken off, and the economies were acquiring a seemingly unstoppable momentum. For the most part, they took Japan as their model and were seeking to expand by way of manufactured exports. Capital for their enterprises was provided by Japan itself, where that nation's huge trade surplus was being channeled into mainland Asia, and from other parts of the region. The initial breakthrough achieved by the "four dragons" (Hong Kong, Singapore, South Korea, and Taiwan) was being emulated in such countries as Thailand, Malaysia, and Vietnam.

The most dramatic development, however, was in China, an economy of 1.2 billion people, where reforms were enabling private, market-based activity to develop alongside a still-restrictive political system. In a number of provinces and special enterprise zones, planning restrictions were lifted, and with capital coming in, especially from Hong Kong and Taiwan, the pace of development was rapid.

Tables I and III, which are based on UN data and exclude China, show that in the less industrialized countries as a whole, double-digit growth in manufacturing was attained in 1992, while the rest of the world continued to be in recession. In some sectors, such as base metals, chemicals, and paper and printing, double-digit growth had been the norm for the past three years. In marked contrast, the majority of sectors in the industrialized world had been in decline for three years.

There could be no clearer indication of the trend in the world economy than these summary statistics. The industrial base of the world economy was shifting away from the older industrial economies in favour of the low-cost regions of East Asia, and the trend was accelerating. This posed a major challenge to the industrial world and to the openness of the world trading system. It remained to be seen whether Europe and North America would respond positively to this challenge or seek to avoid it by protectionist measures of one form or another. (GEOFFREY R. DICKS)

Table III. Pattern of Output, 1989–92

Percent change from previous year

	World[1]				Developed countries				Less developed countries			
	1989	1990	1991	1992	1989	1990	1991	1992	1989	1990	1991	1992
All manufacturing	4	0	0	1	3	−1	−2	−2	6	8	9	11
Heavy industries	4	0	0	0	4	−1	−2	−2	6	10	10	12
Base metals	2	−1	−1	0	1	−2	−4	−3	7	10	11	15
Metal products	5	0	−1	−2	5	−1	−2	−3	4	9	7	6
Building materials, etc.	4	−1	−2	−1	3	−2	−5	−2	8	4	9	8
Chemicals	4	1	3	5	3	−2	−1	2	5	11	13	15
Light industries	3	0	1	2	2	−2	−1	−1	6	6	8	10
Food, drink, tobacco	4	3	4	4	2	0	1	0	9	9	11	13
Textiles	2	−5	−2	0	1	−8	−4	−2	3	4	3	4
Clothing, footwear	1	−5	−3	−1	−1	−7	−6	−4	6	1	4	6
Wood products	2	−1	−2	2	1	−2	−3	1	3	6	6	7
Paper, printing	4	3	2	2	3	2	0	−1	9	11	13	17

[1] Excluding Albania, China, North Korea, Vietnam, Czechoslovakia, former Soviet Union, and former Yugoslavia.
Source: UN, *Monthly Bulletin of Statistics*.

Table IV. Index Numbers of Production, Employment, and Productivity in Manufacturing Industries

1980 = 100

Area	Relative importance[1] 1980	Relative importance[1] 1992	Production 1991	Production 1992	Employment 1991	Employment 1992	Productivity[2] 1991	Productivity[2] 1992
World[3]	1,000	1,000	131	131	. . .	. . .	. . .	. . .
Industrial countries	861	785	122	120	. . .	. . .	. . .	. . .
Less industrialized countries	139	215	188	209	. . .	. . .	. . .	. . .
North America[4]	282	279	128	130	. . .	. . .	. . .	. . .
Canada	22	19	111	111	. . .	. . .	. . .	. . .
United States	260	260	136	139	92	90	148	154
Latin America[5]	79	116	166	193	. . .	. . .	. . .	. . .
Brazil	26	18	97	93	. . .	. . .	. . .	. . .
Mexico	18	18	129	132	. . .	. . .	. . .	. . .
Asia[6]	183	239	175	172	. . .	. . .	. . .	. . .
India	11	. . .	204	. . .	. . .	. . .	. . .	. . .
Japan	131	141	150	141	120	122	125	116
South Korea	6	16	342	360	. . .	. . .	. . .	. . .
Europe[7]	422	347	111	108	. . .	. . .	. . .	. . .
Austria	9	9	137	138	86	. . .	159	. . .
Belgium	13	12	123	119	. . .	. . .	. . .	. . .

Area	Relative importance[1] 1980	Relative importance[1] 1992	Production 1991	Production 1992	Employment 1991	Employment 1992	Productivity[2] 1991	Productivity[2] 1992
Denmark	5	5	135	138	99	97	136	142
Finland	6	5	117	120	79	71	148	169
France	75	62	108	108	. . .	. . .	. . .	. . .
Former West Germany	114	109	128	125	. . .	. . .	. . .	. . .
Greece	4	3	102	101	. . .	. . .	. . .	. . .
Ireland	2	3	202	222	85	. . .	238	. . .
Netherlands, The	14	14	126	128	. . .	. . .	. . .	. . .
Norway	5	4	109	111	. . .	. . .	. . .	. . .
Portugal	3	3	147	141	. . .	. . .	. . .	. . .
Spain	23	. . .	118	. . .	. . .	. . .	. . .	. . .
Sweden	13	11	112	108	80	. . .	134	. . .
Switzerland	13	12	124	123	. . .	. . .	. . .	. . .
United Kingdom	58	51	116	116	. . .	. . .	. . .	. . .
Rest of the world[8]	34	30	. . .	. . .	. . .	. . .	. . .	. . .
Oceania	15	13	109	110	. . .	. . .	. . .	. . .
South Africa	8	6	103	100	. . .	. . .	. . .	. . .

[1] The 1980 weights are those applied by the UN Statistical Office.
[2] This is 100 times the production index divided by the employment index, giving a rough indication of changes in output per person employed.
[3] Excluding Albania, China, North Korea, Vietnam, Czechoslovakia, former Soviet Union, and former Yugoslavia.
[4] Canada and the United States.
[5] South and Central America (including Mexico) and the Caribbean islands.
[6] Asian Middle East and East and Southeast Asia, including Japan, Israel, and Turkey.
[7] Excluding Albania, former Czechoslovakia, former Yugoslavia, and European countries of the former Soviet Union.
[8] Africa and Oceania.
[9] Bulgaria, Czechoslovakia, Hungary, Poland, Romania, and the former Soviet Union.
Source: UN, *Monthly Bulletin of Statistics*.

An advertisement touts the Intel microchip, found in 80% of the world's personal computers. In 1993 Intel was judged by the magazine *Financial World* to be the third most valuable brand name, an unusually high ranking for a nonconsumer product.
INTEL CORPORATION

ADVERTISING

In 1993 late-night television generated more than $400 million in advertising revenue for the four major U.S. television networks. The average advertising rates for a 30-second spot varied; "Nightline" with Ted Koppel was the highest at $45,000, followed by "The Tonight Show" starring Jay Leno at $31,000 and the "Late Show with David Letterman" at $30,000. Leading the list of the top 100 national advertisers in the U.S. in 1992 was Procter & Gamble Co., which spent $2,165,600,000. Philip Morris Companies, General Motors Corp., and Sears, Roebuck & Co. all allocated more than $1 billion for advertising in 1992. Together, the top 100 national advertisers spent more than $36 billion in 1992, with automotive companies, business and consumer services, and pharmaceutical concerns spending the most. Procter & Gamble also led ($535,-300,000) in network television advertising.

"Home Improvement" (ABC) headlined the 1993 television season by charging $325,000 for a 30-second advertising spot. "Roseanne" (ABC) was second highest with $300,000, followed by "Seinfeld" (NBC), $295,000, "Coach" (ABC), $290,000, and "NFL Monday Night Football" (ABC), $260,000. ABC boasted five of the most expensive top-10 prime-time shows. The final episode of "Cheers" (NBC) commanded $650,000 for a 30-second commercial.

Your Choice TV, a pay-per-view cable television service, showed only four minutes of commercial advertising per hour of programming, which included movies, repeat broadcasts, or cable network shows for as little as $1 a program.

Although African-American buying power represented $282 billion in annual income, large advertisers lacked information about blacks. After extensive studies were conducted, advertisers found that black consumers valued prestigious brand names more highly than other consumers did and were willing to spend more for those products. Black shoppers also paid more attention to advertising. The studies were the first aimed specifically at blacks.

During the year celebrities touched by scandal lost advertising endorsements. The most notable was singer Michael Jackson, who, amid charges of child molestation, canceled his concert tour to seek treatment for a drug addiction. PepsiCo Inc., sponsor of the tour, ended its nine-year association with the superstar. The messy marital breakup of Burt Reynolds and Loni Anderson caused both the Quaker State (motor oil) Corp. and the Florida Citrus Commission to drop Reynolds as their spokesperson. When basketball player Michael Jordan's father was missing and later found to have been murdered, McDonald's, Gatorade, Hanes apparel, Honey Gold Wheaties cereal, and Ball Park Franks all temporarily pulled ads featuring Jordan. Miller Brewing Co. also temporarily discontinued ads that playfully called for hog-tying "big-shot lawyers" after eight persons were fatally shot at a San Francisco law firm.

In France the National Assembly passed a new law requiring the media to publish advertising rate cards and purchasers of media advertising time to sign contracts before any transactions occurred. The law abolished the standard 15% agency commission on media time and, instead, required that the commissions be paid from the media to the advertiser, which could then pass the commission on to the advertising agencies. The French law intended to protect advertisers and the media from inordinate losses to advertising agencies. Beginning in January 1993, France joined Canada, Finland, New Zealand, and Norway in banning all tobacco advertising. *Fortune* magazine reported that Philip Morris planned to keep its Marlboro trade name in the French public eye, however, by means of a travel service and a clothing line bearing the Marlboro name; they would also sponsor more events. The French Grand Prix auto race was canceled because the law forbade the showing on television of cars bearing the names of tobacco company sponsors. The race was reinstated in February, *sans* advertising, but the cars were allowed to bear the colours of their sponsors. Many millions of sponsorship dollars would likely be lost because of the ban.

An advertising revolution continued to take place in China. Commercials proliferated and included products ranging from coconut milk to audio systems. Even cars of high-ranking government officials in one city displayed advertisements (free of charge) for an alcoholic product, for which a local distillery paid $78 million in taxes annually. Some 370,000 Chinese found spouses through 1.5 million personals appearing in magazines and newspapers. The country's advertising rates also increased; a 30-second spot on China Central Television appearing immediately after the evening news was $4,386 in 1993, compared with $1,750 in 1992. A 30-second advertising spot before the morning news of the Central Broadcasting Station increased to $78,950 annually. In China there were more than 16,000 advertising agencies, with 12,000 of them owned by the government. In most cases advertisers dealt directly with the media, but the government planned to stop direct advertising and to require all advertising to filter through an advertising agency, which could charge 15% more than the advertising cost. The Chinese postal bureau operated its own advertising agency, which designed and sent direct-mail advertising, 17% of China's total mail in 1992.

The provocative nonproduct ads of Italian-based clothing manufacturer Benetton continued to arouse controversy. Founder Luciano Benetton posed nude in one ad to "ask for his clothes back" for a redistribution project. Another ad displaying the genitals of men, women, and infants was rejected by all, with the exception of one French publication.

(EDWARD MARK MAZZE)

AEROSPACE

The international airline business, the biggest sector of the world aerospace industry, continued to operate at disastrously high levels of unprofitability in 1993. The International Air Transport Association, before its annual meeting in November, projected that its members would lose $2 billion during the year, bringing cumulative losses since 1990 to $13.5 billion. Nevertheless, the 1993 figure was smaller than the $4.8 billion shortfall of 1992. The reason for the continued deficit continued to be excess capacity. Ireland's Guinness Peat Aviation, the world's largest commercial-aircraft leasing firm, was saved from bankruptcy when some of its aircraft were purchased by General Electric Capital Corp. and deliveries of others from Boeing Co., McDonnell Douglas Corp., and Airbus Industrie were delayed.

Observers forecast a "new look" for Europe, with fewer but larger and more efficient airlines, mostly privatized, to compete with the three U.S. megacarriers, United, Delta, and American. Four European airlines (SAS, Swissair, KLM, and Austrian Airlines) were studying strategic alliances to compete more effectively in world markets. British Airways continued plans to invest in U.S. operator US Air despite protests by United, Delta, and American that this was unfair, while Lufthansa narrowed to United its search for a strategic partner.

The airframe companies likewise all suffered from canceled or deferred orders. U.S. Pres. Bill Clinton intervened for his nation's interests when he telephoned King Fahd of Saudi Arabia with the offer of a

Workers perform maintenance on an engine at Lockheed's Commercial Aircraft Center in San Bernardino, Calif. Like other aerospace companies hurt by cutbacks in U.S. defense spending, Lockheed continued to emphasize diversification into related businesses.

MICHAEL GRECCO—SYGMA

$6.2 billion loan, covering 85% of the financing needed to reequip the Arab country's Saudia airline with U.S. equipment.

More optimistically, Boeing (which rolled out its 1,000th 747) and McDonnell Douglas predicted that the next two decades would see a demand for some 13,000 new transport planes worth $1 billion. For the moment, however, Boeing and Martin Marietta both announced plant closings and personnel layoffs in late 1993. Meanwhile, the four-engined Airbus A340, the largest European-built transport, began scheduled services with Air France and Lufthansa. Russia's advanced transport, the Ilyushin Il-96M, was unveiled at a Moscow air show. Though fitted with U.S. avionics and engines and theoretically a competitor to the Airbus A330/A340 series and the upcoming Boeing 777, it was thought to lack credibility in the U.S. and Western Europe, and observers forecast that it would have an uphill struggle in an already oversubscribed market. Airbus Industrie (scheduled to be privatized in about 1995) was preparing to sign an agreement with Russian transport manufacturer Tupolev to build parts for its A300/320/330 series airliners. In Ukraine the Kiev-based Antonov company continued to expand its monopoly role in the global superheavy load business with its giant An-124 freighters.

Western nations continued to plan for new military strategies in the wake of geopolitical realignments and changing or diminishing threats from the former Warsaw Pact countries. The problem was how, in the wake of plunging defense needs, to maintain a skilled industrial base of design teams as a hedge against future conflicts. A partial answer was seen to be concentration on technical upgrades; for example, Western avionics companies were studying the market for upgrading Russia's MiG-21. Experts noted that new avionics for this still-effective fighter could be worth about $1 billion over a 10-year period.

In the U.S. the Department of Defense launched a major reevaluation of its needs in an effort to reduce its budget by many billions of dollars over the next four years. It recommended canceling the A/FX and multi-role fighters (two proposed new combat aircraft) and replacing them with a new plane, the joint attack fighter (for the U.S. Air Force and U.S. Navy), to be placed in service in 2012. The review counseled continuation of both the F-22, winner of the Advanced Tactical Fighter competition for a new U.S. Air Force aircraft to replace the F-15, and the U.S. Navy's F/A-18 carrier fighter. (*See* MILITARY AFFAIRS.)

Lockheed Corp. strengthened its position in the military field by purchasing General Dynamics' fighter business at Fort Worth, Texas, for $1.5 billion, thereby consolidating its already strong presence in the Western defense community. Of other programs coming under scrutiny, the U.S. Army ordered that the cost of the RAH-66 Comanche battlefield helicopter be cut by one-third.

Meanwhile, doubt was cast over the efficiency of some of the "smart" weapons that were supposed to have done so well in the Gulf war. The Tomahawk cruise missile was singled out in this context. Nonetheless, experts predicted that these small, relatively cheap but effective and difficult-to-detect devices would proliferate and perhaps become the most important offensive weapons.

Europe's top military-aircraft program, the four-nation (U.K., Germany, Italy, and Spain) European Fighter Aircraft, came under threat in late 1992 when Germany, worn down by the expenses of reunification, refused to support the mounting costs. The project was then restructured around a simpler specification and relaunched under the new name Eurofighter 2000.

Observers at the biennial Paris Air Show—in its 40th year—called for a reduction in the number of such international trade events. Thailand's first aerospace exposition, Thai Airshow 93, was held in September, while Taiwan held its second during the previous month; the Dubayy show was scheduled for November. Industry observers protested that the international aerospace industry could not continue to support such a drain on its resources, especially at a time of deep recession in both civil and military markets. The French aerospace industry association noted that its members were in a crisis situation, and figures showed that this decline had started as long ago as 1983. The sale of 60 Mirage 2000s to Taiwan in late 1992 was one of the few success stories in this field for France.

The recession problem was even more difficult for Russia's aerospace industry, delegates from which arrived at Paris searching for a new identity. Many new collaborative ventures with Western companies were agreed upon, but the core problem remained that of launching onto international markets new and competitive combat aircraft at a time of acute financial stringency in Russia. In an effort to capture sales, Russia's top military fighters, the MiG-29 Fulcrum and Su-27 Flanker, were heavily promoted at Western air shows (two MiG-29s collided in midair at a major U.K. event), and Malaysia bought a batch of MiG-29s, which would fly alongside U.S.-produced F/A-18 Hornets in that country.

(MICHAEL WILSON)

AUTOMOBILES

World car production (excluding Russia) in 1992 totaled 33,035,000, 1.3% higher than in 1991. This compared with the record world output of 34,155,000 cars in 1990. The rise reflected gains in two of the three major manufacturing blocs. European Community (EC) manufacturers increased output from 12,846,000 cars to 13,069,000 in 1992, and production in the U.S. rose from 5,439,000 in 1991 to 5,666,000 in 1992. Japanese production declined for the third successive year—9,378,000 cars in 1992, 9,753,000 in 1991, and the record 9,948,000 in 1990.

The only significant EC manufacturing nation that produced fewer cars in 1992 than in 1991 was Italy, where output fell by 9.6%. Production rose in France, Germany, Spain, and the United Kingdom. Among other manufacturing nations to record higher car production in 1992 were South Korea, Brazil, Sweden, Turkey, Argentina, and Czechoslovakia. Production declined in Australia, Belgium, Canada, India, and Romania. The year was also notable for the collapse of manufacturing in the former Yugoslavia as a result of the civil war.

In the 12 countries of the EC, new car sales rose 6.8% to a record 12,608,000. Total new car sales in 1992 in the European Free Trade Association nations were 6.4% lower, the third successive year of decline. Sales of new cars in Taiwan fell 13.6%; the South African market rose 80%; and Thailand gained 82%.

The manufacturers' contest in 1992 for leadership in the EC, the world's largest market, resulted in a clear victory for Volkswagen AG and its Spanish subsidiary SEAT, with 1,777,942 sales. France's PSA group—Peugeot and Citroën—sold 1,588,524 cars for second place, ahead of Ford of Europe's 1,503,263.

In December 1992 there was a major step in the revitalizing of car manufacturing in the U.K. after two decades of decline. Toyota rolled out its first new car from its manufacturing facility at Burnaston near Derby. Toyota planned to produce 200,000 cars a year at Derby and their engines from its second U.K. plant at Deeside by 1995. Thus, Toyota, like Nissan and Honda, became a full-fledged U.K. manufacturer for the EC market.

European manufacturers found themselves struggling during 1993 to maintain favourable profits and to avoid unfavourable press reports. In an unseemly spectacle that dragged on through the summer, José Ignacio López de Arriortua, the head of purchasing for General Motors Corp. (GM), defected to join Volkswagen as that carmaker's production chief. GM protested and filed suit, charging that López had taken production secrets with him when he left. Volkswagen faced up to its critical need to downsize and in late October announced that it would cut 8,000 of its 108,000-member workforce in Germany as well as 9,000 of the 23,500 employees of SEAT in Barcelona, Spain. VW and the Union, IG Metall, agreed on a four-day workweek with some pay cuts to avoid a threatened 30% reduction in the workforce by 1995. Necessary belt-tightening was also behind VW's withdrawal of an offer of an $878 million loan to the Skoda factory in the Czech Republic, which VW was in the process of taking over.

Italy's Fiat SpA was rocked by the arrests in February of two top corporate officials, and Chairman Gianni Agnelli made the unusual move in April of publicly acknowledging that the political corruption that was being exposed throughout Italy also had touched his company. Finally, in November the Fiat company, tightly controlled by the Agnelli family, agreed to stockholders' demands for changes in its management style.

In what would have been the biggest automotive story of the year, France's Renault SA and Sweden's AB Volvo, both suffering heavy losses, announced on September 6 that they would merge operations on Jan. 1, 1994. The plans, however, met with stiff resistance from members of Volvo's top management (chairman Pehr Gyllenhammar was forced to resign), as well as from the stockholders, who apparently were concerned about the sale of a leading Swedish company to foreign interests at what they saw as a bargain price.

The year 1993 ended with warning bells ringing loudly for most of the established world motor industry. For the European manufacturers, the new factories of the Japanese and others such as GM Europe's new facilities at Eisenach, Germany, and Fiat's at Melfi, Italy, intensified the pressure to make older plants more productive. Such improvements would be necessary to compete with the newcomers, which had advantages in quality, productivity, and cost competitiveness. (JOHN R. WEINTHAL)

United States. U.S. automakers won back some of their domestic market share in the 1993 model year ended September 30. With strong sales of minivans, trucks, Jeep utility vehicles, and its new LH-body sedans, the Chrysler Corp. posted model-year records in minivan, truck, and Jeep sales while regaining the third-place spot in car sales that it had lost in 1992, when both Honda and Toyota moved ahead of it.

For the 1993 model year, General Motors sold 2,829,745 cars for a 34% share of the market, down from sales of 2,879,371 and a 35.3% share in model year 1992. Ford Motor Co. sold 1,879,178 cars for a 22.3% share, up from 1,713,481 and a 21% share the year earlier. Chrysler sold 823,466 cars, a 9.9% share, up from 671,936 and an 8.2% share a year earlier.

Among the Japanese, Toyota sold 763,936 cars, including Lexus, down from 764,480 in 1992. Market share declined to 9.2 from 9.4%. Honda sold 730,497 cars, including Acura, for an 8.8% market share, down from 9.5% in the 1992 model year, while Nissan sold 468,955 new cars, up from 403,388 a year earlier, thanks in large part to the success of its Altima replacement for the former Stanza. Nissan's market share rose to 5.6 from 4.9%.

GM, Ford, and Chrysler sold 5,532,389 cars in the 1993 model year, and their share of the U.S. market rose to 65.7 from 64.5% the previous year. The Japanese, meanwhile, sold 2,484,092 new cars, again in large part owing to the demand for the new Altima, but their market share declined to 29.9 from 30.1% a year earlier. European car sales in the U.S. slipped to 299,683 units, primarily because of the 10% federal luxury tax on the amount of a sales transaction exceeding $30,000 and the fact that Mercedes-Benz had few entry-level 190 series models on hand in order to clear out stocks in preparation for its new C-Class replacement.

Among the top sellers, the Ford Taurus captured the number one spot by beating the Honda Accord in total car sales by 399,573 units to 343,017. In 1992 Taurus had outsold the Accord for the first time in three years to capture the title of best-selling car in the industry.

Behind Taurus and Accord for the 1993 model year were the Toyota Camry (306,586), the Honda Civic (253,086), the Chevrolet Cavalier (249,388), the Ford Escort (246,723), the Chevrolet Lumina (225,025), the Ford Tempo (214,973), the Pontiac Grand Am (211,544), and the Saturn (210,775).

Among the top-selling trucks, the full-size Ford F-Series was first with sales of 522,096, while the Chevrolet full-size C-K series truck was second at 506,290. Thus, the F-Series and C-K series outsold all makes of automobiles. Rounding out the truck-sales leaders were the compact Ford Ranger pickup (311,406), the Ford Explorer sport utility (301,668), the Dodge Caravan minivan (267,650), the Plymouth Voyager minivan (217,016), the Chevrolet compact S-10 pickup (191,033), the Jeep Grand Cherokee sport utility (190,789), the Ford Aerostar minivan (189,527), and the compact Toyota pickup (183,482). Industrywide, 8,425,596 new cars were sold, up from 8,159,644 in the prior model year, and 5,218,884 new trucks were sold, up from 4,487,654 in the previous year.

The automakers introduced a variety of new models in the fall of 1993 for the 1994 model year. At GM, Cadillac enlarged and restyled the Deville sedan (dropping the coupe) and renamed the top-of-the-line Deville, the Concours. (It had been called the Sixty Special.) Deville Concours offered Cadillac's 4.6-litre, 32-valve Northstar V-8 engine for the first time. Oldsmobile chopped 7.5 cm (3 in) off the front end of its Silhouette minivan (as did Chevrolet with its Lumina and Pontiac with its Trans Sport minivans) and added two new options, a power side-sliding door and traction control. Oldsmobile was saving its debut of a new top-of-the-line Aurora sedan for mid-1994 as a 1995 model. Buick prepared to bring out at midyear a new, longer Riviera coupe that was to be based on the all-new Oldsmobile Aurora sedan. It, too, would be a 1995 model. Pontiac, other than the minivan, added a driver-side air bag to its top-selling Grand Am compact car for the first time and added a convertible to the Firebird lineup. Chevrolet restyled the S-10 pickup truck, added a Camaro convertible, and prepared to bring out at midyear a new Impala high-performance sedan powered by the 5.7-litre Corvette V-8 engine, as well as a restyled Lumina sedan and a coupe companion to the midsize Lumina called the Monte Carlo, thus resurrecting a familiar name from Chevrolet's past.

Ford unveiled an all-new Mustang sport coupe available in regular or convertible body styles in both the base and GT models. A 3.8-litre V-6 engine was offered in

MICHAEL L. ABRAMSON

A Chrysler worker makes adjustments to a right-hand-drive Jeep Cherokee built in the U.S. for export to Japan. It was foreign-owned U.S. plants, however, that continued to expand most rapidly in the export of automobiles.

The Volkswagen plant in Wolfsburg, Germany, continued production even as the company slashed costs. VW was also troubled in 1993 by charges that José Ignacio López de Arriortua, hired away from General Motors in March, had stolen confidential GM documents.
JAN-PETER BONING

the base model and a 5-litre V-8 in the GT. For the first time, a removable hard-top option was offered on the Mustang convertible. Also for the first time, all Mustangs offered both driver- and passenger-side air bags as standard equipment. For midyear Ford planned to add a new front-wheel-drive minivan called Windstar. Ford also planned to bring out at midyear a pair of new sedans, the Ford Contour and Mercury Mystique, to replace the venerable Ford Tempo and Mercury Topaz compacts.

At Chrysler all Dodge, Plymouth, and Chrysler minivans for the first time offered dual air bags as well as the choice of an optional 3-litre V-6 engine that ran on natural gas instead of gasoline. Chrysler also prepared to bring out an all-new subcompact car, called the Neon, to replace the Dodge Shadow and Plymouth Sundance. With dual air bags as standard, Neon was designed to serve as Chrysler's attempt—like GM's Saturn—to build and sell a small car in the U.S. at a profit.

Among the changes from the imports, Honda brought out a restyled Accord sedan but said that it would not add a V-6 engine in the car until 1995; Toyota added a new V-6 and a coupe to its Camry as well as a redesigned Celica sports coupe; Acura restyled the Integra; Nissan added a driver-side air bag to its Quest minivan and also prepared to bring out newly designed Maxima sedans and 240SX coupes in mid-1994.

Among the Europeans, Mercedes-Benz replaced its entry-level 190 series with a new, larger C-Class sedan and replaced the 300 series sedan with a new E-Class line. It also changed its nomenclature to call its cars by letter and number: E300, S500, SL600, etc. Audi added a convertible to the 100 series; BMW added a convertible to the 3-Series and put dual air bags in all its cars; Jaguar added a an XJ sedan powered by a V-12 engine and offered the same engine in its XJS coupes for the first time; Porsche dropped the Carrera 4 Targa and Cabriolet; Rolls-Royce offered cellular phones as standard for the first time in all Rolls and Bentley cars and an optional TV screen in the headrest and a VCR recorder in the trunk of all Rolls-Royces for the first time; Volkswagen dropped the entry-level Fox; and Volvo eliminated its 240 series.

An escalation in the value of the Japanese yen against the U.S. dollar forced the Japanese to dramatically raise prices on their 1994 export models in the fall. Toyota raised U.S. prices by an average of 6.2%, or $957; Nissan by 5.2%, or $823; Honda by 3.3%, or $403; Mazda by 4%, or $666; and Mitsubishi by 8.4%, or $1,500. Honda kept its average down by freezing the price of the base model Accord DX at the 1993 level of $14,330.

The increases in the Japanese luxury car lines were even more pronounced. Honda's Acura line went up by 7.7%, or $1,508; Nissan's Infiniti line by 6%, or $2,072; and Toyota's Lexus line by 6.5%, or $2,424. The Lexus LS400, which started at $35,000 in 1990 when it was first introduced, was listed at $49,900 for the start of the 1994 model year.

Among the U.S. manufacturers the average price increase for 1994 was 4.6%, or $701, which compared with an average increase of 5.3%, or $912, among the Japanese. Chrysler raised prices by 5.6%, or $619; Ford by 2.1%, or $365; and GM by 5.8%, or $936. Much of the increase was accounted for by the addition of air bags and/or antilock brakes as standard equipment.

While the domestic automakers boasted about keeping prices down in comparison with the Japanese, Chrysler increased the price of its minivans by an average of $1,200 per unit. The reason for doing so was the addition of dual air bags and side-door guard beams as standard.

In Europe, Mercedes-Benz chose to price its new C-Class only $50 over the old 190 series to a base of $29,900 and lowered the price for 1994 on its new E-Class sedan by $1,300 to $42,500. Mercedes, which in 1993 said that it was going to yield the under-$40,000 luxury segment to the Japanese and focus on the $50,000 range instead, decided to change its strategy and compete once the Japanese started raising prices. Thus, the Mercedes C-Class entry-level car was priced about $1,000 less than the entry-level Lexus ES300 sedan, and its E-Class sedan was about $7,000 less than a Lexus LS400 sedan.

Among other noteworthy events of the year, Mercedes-Benz announced that it would manufacture a luxury sports utility vehicle at a plant to be built in Vance, near Tuscaloosa, Ala. Previously, BMW had announced that it would build cars in the U.S. at a plant in Spartanburg, S.C. To counter the effects of the rising value of the yen, Honda said that by 1996 all Accord and Civic cars to be sold in the U.S. would be made there. Honda also said that it was considering making at least one Acura model in the U.S. Toyota said the fluctuation in the value of the yen might force it to build at least one Lexus model in the U.S.

At Ford, Harold ("Red") Poling retired as chairman and named Alexander Trotman, president of Ford's automotive group, to succeed him. Lee A. Iacocca, former chairman of the Chrysler Corp., unexpectedly resigned from the board of directors on September 2.

Finally, GM surprised its competition by announcing that it would make 30 battery-powered Impact electric two-seater cars available to the public to test-drive starting in 1994. GM was seeking to obtain feedback from consumers as to whether they would be willing to purchase a battery-powered car in the future. (JAMES L. MATEJA)

Japan. In February, Nissan announced that it would close one of its major factories and lay off 5,000 employees in 1995 as a means of restructuring. The factory, located in Zama, southwest of Tokyo, had been manufacturing 280,000 cars annually. Mazda also announced production cuts at year's end.

Because of weakened consumer demand, new-car sales in Japan fell 7.8%, to 2,574,-229 units, in the first half of 1993 compared with the same period in 1992. It was the worst showing since 1988. The strength of the yen reduced exports. In the first fiscal half year (April–September), Toyota exported 1,748,237 units, and Nissan 900,609. These totals were 9.8 and 26.4% below the figures for the same period in the previous year. Because of both sluggish domestic demand and poor export performance, total car production between April and September was 5,514,420 units, 10.4% lower than in the same period of 1992.

In an effort to stimulate consumption, the leading automakers introduced restyled and/or new models during September and October. These included Toyota's Celica, Nissan's Skyline, Honda's Accord, and Mazda's Lantis and Eunos 800. Some successes were noted; for example, Nissan's new-car sales in September rose 1.4%, the first upward turn in 22 months. Economic conditions were expected to continue to be severe, however, and 1993 was expected to be the third consecutive year of declining new-car sales. (KAZUNORI OKANO)

BEVERAGES

Beer. Alliances, acquisitions, and segmentation all carried the day in 1993. Brewers that wished to expand their reach saw fit to reach over to somebody else's operations and form various types of partnerships.

Table V. Estimated Consumption of Beer in Selected Countries

In litres[1] per capita

Country	1989	1990	1991
Germany	142.9	143.1	142.7
Czechoslovakia	131.8	135.0	135.0
Denmark	123.4	126.2	125.9
Austria	119.3	121.3	123.7
Ireland	115.6	123.9	123.0
Luxembourg	119.3	121.4	116.1
Belgium	114.9	120.7	111.3
New Zealand	116.8	110.8	109.5
Hungary	103.0	107.0	107.0
United Kingdom	110.4	109.5	106.2
Australia[2]	111.6	108.2	101.9
Netherlands, The	87.5	87.7	88.5
United States	88.6	90.8	87.4
Finland	79.4	83.5	85.3
Canada[3]	80.6	78.3	. . .
Spain	71.7	71.8	70.9
Switzerland	69.3	69.8	70.1
Portugal	63.8	65.1	67.4
Colombia	57.7	60.7	65.0
Venezuela	61.8	63.5	63.8
Sweden	57.6	59.8	59.3
Cyprus	54.1	57.1	54.7
Japan	49.1	52.3	53.8
Norway	51.8	52.5	52.8
South Africa	52.0	*c.* 52.5	52.0

[1] One litre = 1.0567 U.S. quarts = 0.8799 imperial quart.
[2] Years ended June 30.
[3] Years ended March 31.

Table VI. Estimated Consumption of Distilled Spirits in Selected Countries

In litres[1] of pure alcohol per capita

Country	1989	1990	1991
Poland	4.5	3.8	4.5
Hungary	5.0	4.2	3.4
Cyprus	3.0	3.2	3.3
Czechoslovakia	3.4	3.3	3.3
Bulgaria	3.2	3.2	2.8
Germany	2.0	2.2	2.7
Spain	2.8	2.7	2.7
Greece	2.9	2.7	2.7
Finland	3.2	3.0	2.6
France	2.6	2.5	2.5
Canada[2]	2.3	2.2	. . .
Iceland	2.2	2.1	*c.* 2.1
United States	2.3	2.3	2.1
Netherlands, The	1.9	2.0	2.0
Japan	2.1	2.2	2.0
Cuba	1.9	2.0	2.0
Soviet Union	2.0	2.0	. . .
Romania	*c.* 2.0	*c.* 2.0	*c.* 2.0
Switzerland	1.9	1.8	1.8
Ireland	1.7	*c.* 1.7	*c.* 1.7
Sweden	1.9	1.7	1.7
United Kingdom	1.8	1.7	1.6
Yugoslavia	1.6	1.6	*c.* 1.6
New Zealand	1.4	1.6	1.6
Uruguay	1.6	1.6	1.6

[1] One litre = 1.0567 U.S. quarts = 0.8799 imperial quart.
[2] Years ended March 31.

Table VII. Estimated Consumption of Wine in Selected Countries

In litres[1] per capita

Country	1989	1990	1991
France	74.1	72.7	66.8
Portugal	53.0	50.0	62.0
Luxembourg	61.4	58.2	60.3
Italy	69.7	61.4	56.8
Argentina	54.7	54.2	52.4
Switzerland	49.5	49.4	48.7
Spain	36.9	37.4	34.3
Austria	35.2	35.0	33.7
Greece	29.9	32.8	32.4
Hungary	20.0	24.0	30.0
Chile	35.0	30.0	29.5
Uruguay	25.0	25.0	25.4
Germany	26.3	26.1	24.9
Belgium	23.0	24.9	23.9
Yugoslavia	21.1	22.1	22.1
Denmark	19.2	21.3	22.0
Bulgaria	21.8	23.4	20.4
Romania	16.9	26.0	19.0
Australia[2]	18.3	17.7	18.6
Netherlands, The	14.9	14.5	15.3
New Zealand	14.3	14.7	15.1
Czechoslovakia	13.8	13.9	13.9
Cyprus	13.6	13.5	12.6
Sweden	12.5	12.2	12.3
United Kingdom	11.6	11.6	11.5

[1] One litre = 1.0567 U.S. quarts = 0.8799 imperial quart.
[2] Years ended June 30.

Source: *World Drink Trends,* in association with Produktschap voor Gedistilleerde Dranken, Schiedam, The Netherlands.

Anheuser-Busch Companies Inc. led the way in this process, teaming up with Kirin Brewery Co. in Japan, Grupo Modelo in Mexico, and Peroni in Italy to expand distribution of its Budweiser brand. Anheuser-Busch also became the first foreign investor in China's Tsingtao. Philip Morris Inc., owner of Miller Brewing Co., bought a piece of Mexico's Femsa, a large beer and soft drink business, while Miller took on the Molson and Foster's business in the United States. Adolph Coors Co., the third largest U.S. beer maker, formed a joint venture with Australia's Lion Nathan to market Australian brews in the U.S. Lion Nathan competitor Foster's, in turn, acquired a 60% stake in Shanghai-based Huaguang Brewery. British-based Guinness PLC extended its reach into North America by buying Jamaica's Desnoes & Geddes Ltd., maker of Red Stripe.

After several years of stagnant sales, increased emphasis was being placed on less expensive beers. Though they did not provide as much profit margin for the producers, these brands at least kept the product moving out the door. The call for value also led to larger bottles.

At the other end of the spectrum, high-priced specialty beers were gathering strength in the U.S. This trend was an outgrowth of the microbrew movement of the past decade, when brewers made small, handcrafted beers by imitating European brewing styles and attracted loyal audiences. Boston-brewed Samuel Adams and San Francisco's Pete's Wicked Ale emerged as leaders in this category. The large brewers began making their own high-end specialty beers to capitalize on the trend. In 1993 Miller released Reserve Amber Ale, and Coors announced that it would extend its Christmas-season Winterfest line into a year-round rotation of seasonal beers.

In Canada a new type of beer called ice beer—named for the subfreezing temperature at which it is brewed—was introduced. Labatt Brewing Co. Ltd. and Molson Companies Ltd. brought out ice beers in the spring; by August the ices combined for 10% of the Canadian market. Another prospective innovation, clear beer, may have been ahead of its time. Miller Clear was removed from three test markets within six months of its introduction. (GREG W. PRINCE)

EDWIN TUYAY

Workers move cases of beer in a San Miguel brewery in the Philippines. Consumption of beer was increasing in parts of Asia, with both local and Western companies vying for the market.

Spirits. Europe continued to be distiller to the world. About 80 of the top 100 spirits brands worldwide were either owned or produced by European companies in 1993. Equally important, European consumption of spirits had remained stable during the past five years, down about 1% since 1987. By contrast, U.S. consumption declined by more than 10% during the same period.

Nevertheless, the U.S. spirits business, written off in recent years as a victim of changing tastes and lifestyles, showed renewed vitality in 1993, offering packages and products to meet consumer demand. Certainly that was the idea behind the onslaught of prepared cocktail products. Spurred by the debut in 1991 of Bacardi Breezers, other distillers decided to combine spirits with mixers and put them in single-serve cans and bottles. The effect was electric. Prepared cocktails were credited with boosting U.S. spirits volume in 1992, following a string of annual declines. Joining Breezer on the shelves in 1993 were such items as Jack Daniel's Country Cocktails, Jose Cuervo Margaritas to Go, and Seagram's Piña Colada Cooler.

Seagram Co. Ltd. formed a marketing, sales, and distribution operation in Poland, while it sold its French distribution outfit to the Hiram Walker subsidiary of Allied-Lyons PLC. In another noteworthy international move, Britain's Grand Metropolitan

PLC won approval from the government of India to form a joint venture in India to make and sell liquor there. Whiskey remained the spirit of choice in India, holding more than half of the market and outselling second-place rum by a two-to-one margin. Suntory moved into South Korea, selling its whiskeys via Seoul-based Dongwha Liquor. South Koreans, while moving toward beer, ranked as Asia's top spirits-consuming country, with per capita annual consumption of 6.7 litres.

A growing segment of the industry in the U.S. was the single-malt Scotch whisky business, where a number of competitors—Aberlour, Glenlivet, and Glengoyne among them—were offering a high-quality product. Brown spirits continued to outsell white ones by about a three-to-two margin in the U.S. In the U.K., Scotch whisky sales fell 5.5% from the previous year.

(GREG W. PRINCE)

Wine. World wine production in 1992, estimated at 287 million hl (one hectolitre equals 26.4 U.S. gallons), returned to its normal level after an exceptionally weak 1991 harvest (251 million hl). The first indications for 1993 suggested a smaller harvest than in 1992, notably because of spring frosts in the Mediterranean wine-growing region and because of heavy rains during the harvest in France, Switzerland, and Italy.

Despite the decline in area devoted to wine growing in the European Community (EC) countries, the potential for production remained quite high, with a 1992 EC output of 192 million hl. Italy was again the largest producer, with 68.6 million hl in 1992, followed by France (65.4 million), Spain (37.5 million), the U.S. (16.7 million), and Argentina (14.3 million).

Wine consumption increased in the United Kingdom, Denmark, and The Netherlands; stagnated in Greece and Luxembourg; decreased slightly in Germany and Belgium; and decreased sharply in France and Italy. In the other countries of Europe—apart from Scandinavia—consumption declined, as it also did in South America. In the U.S. the "French Paradox" (the name comes from a television program that discussed the possible beneficial effects of red wine in preventing cardiovascular diseases among French consumers) could explain the increase in consumption.

The world price index, established by the International Vine and Wine Office, rose 6.6 points in 1992 after a decline of 1.3 points in 1991 and an increase of 28 points in 1990. Spain, which experienced a fall in market price of 15.1 points in 1991, recovered by 14 points, and Italy's prices rose by 7.4 points. On the other hand, France, which lost 2.8 points in 1991, continued this trend with a drop of 11 points in 1992.

(YANN JUBAN)

Soft Drinks. Consolidation remained the watchword of the soft drink industry in 1993. In the most noteworthy development of the year, the world's third-largest maker of carbonated soft drinks, Cadbury Schweppes PLC, bought A&W Brands Inc., the United States' sixth-largest soft drink company. At the same time, Cadbury increased its stake in Dr. Pepper/Seven-Up Companies Inc., the third-largest soft drink producer in the U.S. and a company with the best recent growth rates in the industry. Cadbury's actions, along with a new management team (headed by Cadbury's former North American president, John Carson) at Royal Crown, fueled speculation that between them Cadbury, Dr. Pepper/Seven-Up, A&W, and RC could eventually form a solid competitor to perennial soft drink leaders Coca-Cola Co. and PepsiCo Inc.

Even without that threat, Coca-Cola and PepsiCo also had to consider the impact of supermarket house brand soft drinks that generally sold for lower prices than name brands. As sales of the private labels increased in North America, Coca-Cola closed eight plants in Canada. Coke and Pepsi continued to look abroad from their U.S. headquarters to increase profits.

Pepsi tried injecting life into the slumping diet drink market by introducing in Europe Pepsi Max, a "full-bodied" reduced-calorie cola. What plagued Pepsi in the U.S., however, was something supposedly added to its products. In June an isolated news report of a syringe found in a can of Diet Pepsi—later found to be based on erroneous information—fueled false claims of tampered-with cans across the country. It was later determined that most people filing such reports had done so fraudulently, either for profit or for a moment's attention. The company's showcase introduction, clear-cola Crystal Pepsi, appeared to be waning despite a massive advertising campaign. A similar translucent offering from Coke, Tab Clear, also failed to gather momentum.

(GREG W. PRINCE)

BUILDING AND CONSTRUCTION

In October 1993 the U.S. Department of Commerce reported that expenditures for building and construction during the first eight months of 1993, on a seasonally adjusted annual-rate basis, were higher in each month than in the comparable months of 1991 and 1992. Total outlays, on this basis, were $456 billion in August 1993, compared with $424 billion in August 1992 and $405 billion in 1991. It was reported also that the number of employees in contract construction had increased greatly during the first nine months of 1993. The preliminary figure reported for September was 4.9 million employees, compared with 4.1 million in January. Both the dollar outlays and the employment data indicated that the construction industry was contributing significantly to the economic recovery in the U.S.

The number of new housing units started in the U.S. in the second and third quarters of 1993 was higher than in the comparable quarters of 1991 and 1992. This increase was attributed to the low rates of interest on home mortgages and the need to replace housing due to the destruction of homes by Hurricane Andrew and by other violent weather conditions in the United States. Mortgage interest rates were at the lowest levels in more than two decades. The favourable financial conditions brought new home buyers into the market and caused some home owners to upgrade their housing. In many places 30-year fixed-rate mortgages could be obtained at less than 7%. The average price of new homes sold declined in 1991 and 1992, but in 1993 they rose, and in August the average price was reported to be $153,600.

The *National Economic Review* provided information on economic developments in Canada, the U.K., selected European countries, and Japan. In Canada residential construction increased in 1992 after being down the two preceding years, but it declined again in the first three months of 1993. The prospects for the remainder of the year were more favourable because housing starts and sales were up in the second quarter. Nonresidential construction also was expected to show improvement in 1993.

In the U.K., economic growth in 1993 was reported to be about 2%. It was reported also that public housing investment would be up in 1993 and down slightly in 1994, while private housing investment in 1993 would remain at the same level as in the preceding year but would increase slightly in 1994. Consumer confidence in the economy, along with governmental policies and depressed economic conditions in European and other industrialized countries, was reported to be an important factor in evaluating the private and public investment outlook. Germany was experiencing a recession in 1993, with a reported decline in production of 2% and a decline in investment of approximately 3%. Construction was the only type of investment that continued to increase there, largely because of the housing needs brought about by the reunification of the country. France also was in a recession in 1993. Investment had declined in 1991 and 1992 and was expected to fall by 4.5% in 1993. The high rate of unemployment and the uncertain economic outlook were not favourable to housing or business investment.

Japan's economy in 1993 was experiencing the lowest rate of growth in almost two decades. The outlook for private investment in housing and business in 1993 was for declines similar to those experienced in 1992. The substantial investments by the government in 1992 and 1993, however, were expected to bring about increases in private investment in 1994.

(CARTER C. OSTERBIND)

CERAMICS

In spite of a weak economy, sales in most sectors of the ceramics industry rose in 1992. This increase was attributed to a slow strengthening of the economy along with a focus on quality, customer service, and increased research and development for new products. Worldwide sales of ceramic materials and components in 1992 totaled approximately $88 billion, according to a survey by *Ceramic Industry*, an increase of approximately 10% over 1991. Captive production of advanced ceramics continued to grow. This consisted of production that was consumed within a firm as components in systems or subsystems or in their production, and so it was not reported by the U.S. Department of Commerce data and is only partially recorded in this survey.

Worldwide sales of fibre-optic components totaled $4.3 billion in 1992 and were projected to grow at a compounded average rate of approximately 20% through 1998, when they would reach $14 billion. The largest growth was expected in Eastern Europe, South America, and the Middle East. Long-haul cable installation declined in the United States, Japan, and Germany, but growth of the market in local distribution systems more than offset the fall. Worldwide growth in sales for local distribution systems was expected to increase at a rate of more than 30% through 1998.

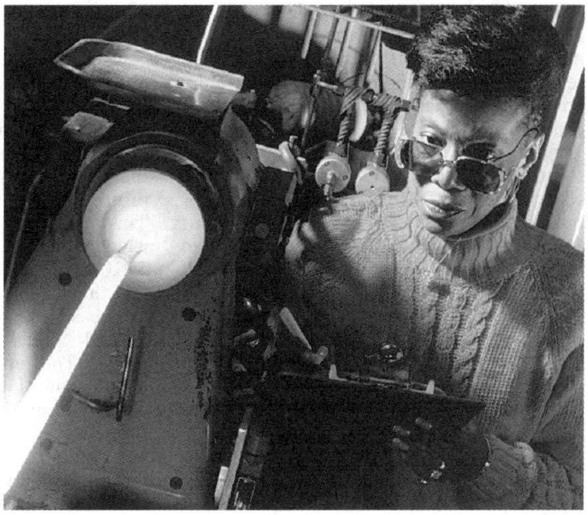

A worker produces fibre-optic cable at an AT&T factory in Atlanta, Ga. Sales of cable and other fibre-optic components were expected to increase through the 1990s.
ANN STATES—SABA

Sales of advanced ceramics were approximately $15 billion in 1992, similar to 1991 sales. Electronic ceramics accounted for 60% of the total. This sector included electronic substrates, electronic packages, capacitors, ferrites, piezoelectrics, and sensors. The market for aluminum nitride electronic substrates, which have a higher thermal conductivity than aluminum oxide, was expected to grow because of the greater heat load that had to be removed from advanced electronic components. Cost, however, continued to be a major factor limiting its use. The current price of aluminum nitride powder was approximately $50 per pound, compared with $2–$5 per pound for aluminum oxide. Dow Chemical Co. recently announced plans to construct a global aluminum nitride powder manufacturing facility that could produce up to 1,135,000 kg (2.5 million lb) per year. An initial production rate of 45,400 kg (100,000 lb) per year was scheduled to begin in late 1996. This large-scale plant was expected initially to reduce the powder cost by 50% to $25 per pound, with further decreases as production levels increased. According to the U.S. Advanced Ceramics Association, worldwide production of aluminum nitride powder in 1993 was 300 metric tons per year, and the market for aluminum nitride powder was expected to increase to $550 million by the year 2000.

The reduction in defense spending in the U.S. was having a significant effect on the current and future markets for advanced ceramics. The defense industry had been a major factor in the development of advanced ceramics because of unique properties that enabled system designers to develop sophisticated military hardware. By 1993 companies had been forced to reevaluate their advanced ceramics programs. This led to a stronger focus on the reduction of manufacturing costs in order to open up new markets in the civilian sector.

U.S. shipments of refractor materials in 1992 equaled the 1991 level at $1,950,000,000; worldwide sales were $6 billion. Refractory ceramic fibre insulation, used for industrial furnace lining, represented about 13% of the market for refractories. Since refractories are closely tied to steel production, shipments were expected to grow in 1993, and improved sales were expected owing to an increase in economic activity in the durable-goods sectors.

Porcelain enamel sales showed a strong increase in 1992 despite the sluggish economy. This rise was attributed to an upturn in appliance sales, a strong emphasis on quality and customer satisfaction, and the introduction of new products. Sales by companies in the United States were approximately $6 billion, an increase of more than 15% for the year.

Sales of whiteware (including tile, dinnerware, sanitaryware, and electrical porcelain) increased approximately 10% in 1992 to more than $9 billion on a worldwide basis. The strong performance of this sector in a slow economy was attributed to a focus on customer satisfaction and research to develop new products such as low-water-consumption toilets. (DALE E. NIESZ)

CHEMICALS

For world chemical producers, 1994 loomed as a lustreless year. Sales were not expected to decline, but neither were they expected to increase. In the fall of 1993, unlike the case in the autumn of 1991 and 1992, few industry people spoke with confidence about the coming 15 months. Even in the United States, where faint recovery signs could be seen, optimism was tempered by the industry's massive layoffs and corporate restructurings.

As expected, corporate profits in individual countries were largely affected by the health of their particular market economies. Early data indicated that the major U.S. companies, after more than two years of unremitting cost cutting, in 1993 managed about a 10% gain in profits, although sales were up only 3%. Some improvement in profits took place in the U.K., but companies in France, Germany, and Japan found the dismal economies of those nations dragging many of them into a second year of profit declines and, sometimes, actual losses.

In 1993 several product trends were developing that seemed sure to carry into 1994. World sulfur markets were in disarray because environmental rules requiring fuel and exhaust cleanup produced so much "recovered" sulfur that prices for this element neared giveaway levels in much of the U.S. and Canada. Competition forced prices to be low nearly everywhere else in the world.

Oil and gas price drops presented makers of petrochemicals—dominated by the familiar plastics—with attractive potentials that they were unable to realize because of overcapacity and recession-shrunken markets. The markets for chlorine and sodium hydroxide shifted sharply from the conditions of just two years earlier, with chlorine now in high demand (although facing a clouded future because of environmental pressures) and sodium hydroxide languishing. These two materials are produced in nearly equal amounts from the same electrochemical cells filled with sodium chloride brine. But they are seldom market equals, and through 1993 U.S. chlorine prices rose to their highest levels ($180 per ton) in five years. Demand was keyed to rising building-product markets, particularly to polyvinyl chloride (PVC) plastic. Sodium hydroxide, about $50 per ton in late 1993, had reached $275 per ton in 1991, when chlorine was at about $25 per ton.

Synthetic fibres, an estimated 9 billion kg (20 billion lb) per year world business (4.1 billion kg [9 billion lb] per year in the U.S. alone), was an industry marked by frantic producer scrambles. For example, the huge Imperial Chemical Industries (ICI) in the U.K. and the Du Pont Co. in the U.S. swapped facilities, with Du Pont concentrating on nylon and ICI on acrylic fibres.

Synthetic fibres are often primary products of countries that are developing their chemical industries. In 1992, for example, China hiked its fibres output 9%, and Taiwan lifted its production by 5%.

One of the most important technological advances in the manufacture of the familiar polyethylene plastics was the first commercial production (by Dow Chemical Co. and Exxon Chemical Co. in the U.S. and Mitsui in Japan) of plastics using what are termed "single-site" or "metallocene" catalysts. The U.K.'s BP Chemicals was among rivals expected to enter this business soon. With the new catalysts, polymers could be tailored very precisely for specific properties.

The employment picture for the world chemical industry, once one of the brighter scenes in manufacturing, had been discouraging for the past three years and might have hit a low point in 1993. Weak sales forced plant shutdowns that affected production workers. That was accompanied by corporate reorganizations that trimmed professional, executive, and administrative personnel.

In 1992 chemical industry employment was down 2.2% in the European Community (EC), off 0.1% in the U.S., and up just 1% in Japan. No development in any part of the world pointed to higher employment in 1993. An encouraging aspect in the U.S. was in research and development, where research spending rose 7%, much of it being intensively market oriented.

Production volumes in the EC rose 2.7% in 1992, with Western Europe overall (EC plus Switzerland, Finland, Norway, Sweden, and Austria) up 2.6%. France, where chemical production increased 5.5% in 1992, took important steps toward its long-talked-of privatization of the chemical industry, with the state-held 43% of Rhône-Poulenc the first to be offered to the public. As 1993 progressed, however, and the economy worsened, hopes dwindled for a high price on the Rhône-Poulenc stock. In Germany, where major chemical companies had experienced decades of steady growth, there was only a 1% gain in 1992, and declines were expected for 1993 and 1994.

The U.S. production volume in 1992 was up 5.5%, while Australia rose 5.3% and Canada 5%. Some optimism concerning 1994 was expressed for the apparently recovering U.S. and Canada, but industry observers wondered if Australia could avoid the recession fever infecting Japan. Japan's volume in 1992 declined 0.3%. In contrast, South Korea's statistical office showed that that nation had increased its chemical output 12%, while Taiwan upped its output 9%. In China there was wide, varied growth. No chemical industry segment increased by less than 5%, and plastics grew by 19%.

Eastern Europe experienced its third year of substantial declines in 1992. Russia's production volume fell 20%, while Hungary was down 13.6%, Romania off 14.1%, Ukraine down 13.1%, and Belarus down 15.7%. Czechoslovakia dipped a relatively mild 5.5%, and Poland actually gained 6.8%.

International chemical trade was vigorous, up some 6% in 1992. Countries, such as the U.S., with comparatively healthy economies, however, found themselves losing export markets to more hard-pressed exporters that offered lower prices.

(J. ROBERT WARREN)

ELECTRICAL

Manufacturers of power station equipment were benefiting in 1993 from the recent deregulation of natural gas. Restrictions on the burning of this fuel in plants generating electric power had recently been relaxed in most countries. This focused attention on power plants that burned natural gas because they were smaller and cheaper than those that burned coal. Electricity producers in the developed and less developed countries were, therefore, abandoning their large, expensive coal-fired plants in favour of gas units.

During 1992 the demand for gas plant technology rose sharply; the global market in 1993 was forecast by General Electric (GE) to be $5.7 billion of the $13.4 billion total worldwide power station equipment market. GE had a head start in the expanding gas market because a decade earlier it alone had predicted the rush to gas and had begun to revise its manufacturing plans. By September 1993 it was able to claim 40% of the world market for installed or ordered gas-fired electricity-generation plants.

The world's largest manufacturer of power plant equipment in 1992 was Asea Brown Boveri (ABB), with revenue in its power systems businesses alone of $15,898,000,000, up 2.3% from 1991. ABB said that demand for its gas-fired power plants was driven by the customers' need for low investment costs, short construction times, low emission levels, and high efficiency. The company continued to support coal technology, however; it invested heavily in developing more efficient coal-burning techniques.

ABB's total revenue in 1992 was $29,615,000,000, an increase of 2.5% over 1991; however, earnings, at $1,110,000,000, were down 3.7% from the previous year. Employment was reduced 14,000 in 1992, leaving a total workforce of 213,407 at the end of the year. Percy Barnevik, chief executive of ABB, said that 1992 "was a year of truth for ABB, since we were confronted with the longest and deepest recession in 45 years." He expected profits in 1993 to be the same as for 1992. However, Barnevik did not let recession get in the way of investment. In 1992, ABB spent $2.4 billion on research and development, 8% of revenue and over twice as much as the company's total earnings.

The world's second largest company in terms of sales of power system equipment was Siemens, with net sales in its power businesses of DM 12,138,000,000 (about $7,586,000,000). Total sales of the German firm for the year ended Sept. 30, 1992, were DM 78,509,000,000 (about $49,068,000,000), 8% above 1990–91; net income of DM 1,955,000,000 (about $1,222,000,000) was 9% over the previous year. In the six months to March 31, 1993, new orders fell by 4% to DM 40.9 billion (about $25,563,000,000), but sales increased by 3% to DM 37 billion (about $23,125,000,000). By July 1993 the decline in orders had increased to 6%, and Heinrich von Pierer, president and chief executive, said that the company would shed 16,000 workers during the year, bringing the total workforce to below 400,000.

Third behind ABB and Siemens in the size of power plant sales, General Electric's power systems business had an income in 1992 of $6,371,000,000. Total revenue for all of GE's electrical manufacturing activities (excluding its Aircraft Engines, Broadcasting, and GE Capital Services businesses) was $29,523,000,000, up 3% from 1991.

The fourth largest firm in power plant sales was the Anglo-French GEC Alsthom. For the year ended March 31, 1993, sales of power plant equipment (excluding transport, marine, and industrial equipment) totaled ECU 4,478,000,000 (about $5,268,000,000), up 6% from the previous year.

The power systems business of Westinghouse Electric Corp. had an operating revenue in 1992 of some $2.8 billion. The company had experienced continuing financial problems, and in 1992 it decided to divest itself of its financial services and several other businesses. The 1992 sales of the continuing operations only, excluding broadcasting, were $7,594,000,000, down 0.8% from the previous year; however, operating profit, at $587 million, was up 28%. In November 1992, Westinghouse announced its intention to sell its control business. This was acquired by Eaton Corp. for $1.1 billion in September 1993. Eaton manufactured vehicle components and electrical and electronic components, employed 38,000 worldwide, and had an income in 1992 of $3.9 billion.

Merlin Gerin (part of the French Schneider Group) manufactured high-power transmission plant and power station controls but not power-generation plant equipment. Its sales totaled F 20,519,000,000 (about $3,651,000,000) in 1991.

In the former Soviet Union, the Siemens power plant division, KWU, acquired in mid-1993 a 10% share in Russia's largest industrial turbine manufacturer, AO Kaluzhsky Turbiny Zavod in Kaluga. Siemens said that one of its first actions would be to improve the Russian production facilities.

(T.C.J. COGLE)

FURNITURE

After the furniture industry-supported North American Free Trade Agreement was approved in the U.S. Congress in November 1993, home-furnishing businesses anticipated some $1 billion in increased sales by 1995.

The march toward internationalism and expanding markets combined with optimistic projections that the year would end with substantially increased domestic business was promising to make 1993 the year the industry turned around. Revenues were projected to reach $17,822,000,000 by 1994. This figure was a 9.9% increase over 1992, which closed higher than projected at $16,356,000,000 and marked the third year in a row that sales had moved upward.

The styles that were introduced in the United States were emphatically homegrown. The emergence of casual, country, western, and lodge styles heralded a slogan to "Buy American!" Multicoloured denim sofas were hyped by Bernhardt Industries Inc., while Lexington promoted De Cristofaro, a garden-variety style that emphasized farm life and such fun American leisure symbols as kites. Century Furniture Co. introduced Jim Peed's "Country Cousins," which featured elements of cottage, mission, low country, and Victorian styles. Hickory Furniture Co. unveiled reproductions based on the furnishings in Mount Vernon, George Washington's Virginia home. More sophisticated and/or international designs such as Classic-Contemporary and British Empire remained visible but were overshadowed.

The lists of the top manufacturers and retailers prepared by *Furniture/Today* remained basically the same as in 1992, with the top three furniture manufacturers occupying the same positions. First was Masco Home Furnishings with $1,534,000,000 in sales, followed by Broyhill/Lane with $910 million and La-Z-Boy with $661 million. One major change was the drop of Thomasville Furniture Industries, Inc., from fifth to seventh place. Klaussner had the largest growth spurt at 32.3%. The top three retailers were still Levitz ($901.3 million), Ethan Allen Home Interiors ($597.5 million), and Swedish-based IKEA ($475.6 million).

Manufacturers La-Z-Boy and Ethan Allen emerged as trendsetters by also retailing their own products, a concept known as vertical marketing. Manufacturers' galleries, including single-product specialty stores, multiproduct stores, and single-product and multiproduct independently operated establishments, continued to expand and were projected to occupy 2,787,000,000 sq m (30 million sq ft) of space by 1997, a 50% increase.

A consumer study developed by the Wirthin Group for the American Furniture Manufacturers Association and the Home Furnishings Council indicated that attention to quality and consumer needs would improve sales.

Though the rising cost of wood affected both pricing and the way in which furniture was constructed, large-scale beds of the "Paul Bunyan" type made a discreet return. Discounters continued to plague traditional retailers, and some closed-to-the-public design centres even rethought their marketing strategies. Such new avenues for furniture distribution as catalogs and warehouse stores continued to proliferate. An all-industry voluntary fire-safety program known as UFAC (Upholstered Furniture Action Council) inspired Europeans to create EUFAC.

(ABBY CHAPPLE)

FURS

Demand for furs continued to show improvement in 1993 following an initial surge in 1992 and after a two-year decline. The slow but gradual economic recovery in the U.S. coaxed middle- and upper-income consumers to relax the tight grip on their purse strings, and colder fall and winter weather prompted many to embrace furs. Retail sales in the U.S. were expected to end the year about 15% higher than 1992's $1.1 billion estimated total. Canada's fur industry, which hit rock bottom in 1992, experienced a magnificent rebound. Total exports rose 38% and U.S. exports jumped 75%.

Pelt prices staged a dramatic recovery during the year, largely as a result of sharp cutbacks in production. An oversupply of pelts, which had developed since 1987, brought about the collapse of the industry's price structure and resulted in a huge five-year loss. The strongest comeback was made in mink prices, which advanced as much as 50% for some types during the year. Though mink ranchers received a 13.2% increase in pelt prices, the amount was not enough to cover their production costs. As a result, the number of mink farms in operation shrank another 16%.

Besides stronger sales in the U.S., Germany, and other established markets, broader worldwide pelt demand surfaced in South Korea, China, and Russia.

Meanwhile, the U.S. industry—which had already undergone severe attrition—shrank further. A late-year report issued by the U.S. International Trade Commission listed only 200 fur-manufacturing establishments, compared with 236 the previous year and 341 in 1989. The survey also counted some 1,000 factory workers, about half the number that were employed in 1989.

At the same time, imports of fur apparel into the U.S. began rising again after plunging from a 1987 peak of $477 million. Commerce Department figures showed that imports were running more than 50% ahead of 1992; the year's total was expected to reach some $200 million, compared with $122 million in 1992.

Antifur activities by animal activists were muted for most of the year. The reduced impact of the antifur movement was attributed to the strident measures, including the use of violence, by some of the militants. While media coverage of the antifur activists decreased, legal actions against them rose. Vandals were jailed, and grand jury investigations were under way against several of the movement's leaders. The European Community banned imports of furs from any country that used leghold traps to capture animals; 70% of the beaver pelts from New York had been exported to Europe. (SANDY PARKER)

GAMES AND TOYS

Nothing stands still for long in the games and toy business, a fact that was again confirmed in 1993. During the year Mattel Inc. announced that it was to merge with Fisher-Price Inc., thus creating a $2.5 billion corporation to challenge Hasbro Inc., which, since it acquired Tonka Corp in 1991, had stood alone at the top of the pack. The deal—a stock swap for Fisher-Price shareholders—combined the $800 million-plus Fisher-Price line with Mattel's billion-dollar Barbie and confirmed Mattel's approach of having toys with worldwide popularity at the heart of its business: Barbie, Fisher-Price, Disney toys, and Hot Wheels accounted for 85% of the corporation's sales, a marked contrast to Hasbro, where no single brand totaled more than 5% of the company's sales.

Teenagers play Mortal Kombat, the most popular new video game in 1993. One version of the game featured exceptionally gruesome violence that delighted many young players but disturbed parents.
KAREN WOLLINS

Worldwide, the toy and game market—plus video—was estimated in 1993 to be worth $60 billion at retail prices. Of that total, the Toys "Я" Us chain of stores controlled about 13% of all sales, with turnover for the year expected to end up at around $8 billion. Toys "Я" Us continued its aggressive merchandising in 1993. The company gained business from the defunct Child World and Lionel Leisure chains in the U.S. and opened its first stores in countries as far afield as Austria, Portugal, and Belgium, all the time strengthening its power base in the U.K., France, Germany, and, of course, Japan. It planned to move into Scandinavia in 1994, but local governments and businesses successfully blocked its entry into Italy.

China cemented its position in 1993 as the main source of toy production, surviving the arrival of a new administration in the U.S. with its most-favoured-nation status intact, but the future was less than certain. The toy industry continued to favour MFN for China, but political considerations could yet prevail, with a fire that killed 80 workers at a Chinese toy factory in November doing little to soothe matters.

In Europe recession took its toll in France and Germany, but recovery began slowly in the U.K. A product called Ondamania–Slinky by any other name—took the French and Spanish markets by storm but failed when it went to the U.K. Idéal Loisirs, Europe's biggest private toy company after LEGO System A/S, bought Majorette to add die-cast toys to its line, and Hasbro bought the Petra fashion doll from Plasty in Germany.

Theme parks were the subject of considerable news coverage throughout the year. LEGO announced plans to open an amusement park in Carlsbad, Calif.; the firm had opened its first park in 1968 in its native Denmark. Meanwhile, another famous park, Euro Disney, fell into all sorts of trouble with a staggering $1 billion loss for the year, taking everyone by surprise. France, everyone agreed, was a mistake as a location for the park. At the year's end it was not known whether Disney would pull out of the theme park business in Europe.

The top toys of the year in the U.S. came from Hasbro and Mattel. They included action figures and dinosaurs based on the film *Jurassic Park* from Hasbro's Kenner unit, Mattel's Hollywood Hair Barbie, Street Fighter action figures from the Hasbro toy unit, Talking Barney from Playskool, and the American Girl line of dolls, each with its own book, from the Pleasant Co. But the year ended with new characters coming out of nowhere: Mighty Morphin Power Rangers, made by Bandai America.

Throughout the year Sega Enterprises Ltd. and Nintendo Co. Ltd. were battling for supremacy in the video-game market. Hit game of the year was Mortal Kombat, and Sega overtook Nintendo in the game's 16-bit cartridge format and kept its lead in the compact disc (CD) version. On that front Nintendo was not expected to launch a machine until 1994. The 3DO Co. introduced an advanced games machine that used a 32-bit cartridge.

Alfred Butts, the inventor of Scrabble, died in April. More than 100 million sets of the world's most popular word game had been sold, in 24 languages, since Butts devised it in the 1930s.

(JONATHAN M. SALISBURY)

GEMSTONES

By mid-1993 signs of economic recovery in the Western world were still unevenly spread, although retail sales of gemstones in the United Kingdom steadily improved for several successive months. Jewelers at the top end of the market were still doing quite well. The shakeout of small, mainly new firms seemed to have slowed, leaving the field to the long-established companies. In general, compared with the sales of consumer durables, fine jewelry sales were somewhat better, and most major chains stayed in business.

Treatment of coloured stones continued to headline the gemstone news. A treatment used on ruby and sapphire stones to enhance colour, eliminate some unsightly inclusions, and lighten dark colours was partly summarized in a useful new book, though most of the details were still kept secret by the practitioners. Though various gemstone regulatory bodies met several times during the year, no general agreement was reached on whether treatment of the gemstones should be disclosed to the customer. The number of methods used to enhance the colour of emerald also increased; this stone previously had been oiled, but the danger of the oil's being lost during cleaning processes had made the practice unpopular. The newly established methods of filling some of the inclusions in emerald were said to be undetectable and permanent, though many senior gemologists disagreed with that assessment. Overall, the question of treatment was unlikely to be settled quickly. There was no doubt that some stones, especially sapphires from Montana, were permanently improved by heating.

More gem minerals were appearing on the market from Russia's Ural Mountains, but some rubies from eastern Africa were of widely varied quality. The prospect of Siberia's achieving independence from Russia caused concern in diamond circles. A green transparent zoisite joined the ranks of the rarer gemstones, and fine rhodochrosite was discovered at the Sweet Home Mine in Colorado. Some "Burmese" gemstones appeared on the market since limited access to the northern gem-producing region of Myanmar was again possible. A 51.33-carat diamond, not of top colour, sold for $4,732,500, and a top-quality cultured pearl necklace fetched $1,157,500.

(MICHAEL O'DONOGHUE)

GLASS

The glass industry continued to experience difficulties in many of the world's leading industrialized nations. Production capacity continued to exceed demand, despite restructuring and plant closing. Eastern European industrial privatization progressed, and Western European manufacturers were showing increased interest in setting up subsidiaries in Central and Eastern European countries. Exports to Western markets rose in all sectors of the industry despite the recession, and export sales prices increased owing to better access to market information.

Container manufacturers continued to modernize their production facilities, particularly in the areas of process monitoring and control, in order to compete in a highly competitive packaging market. However, production capacity in the U.S. container industry continued to exceed demand. Shipments in the U.S. rose 1.5% in 1992 and were forecast to climb 2.5% in 1993 to 289.8 million gross units. According to the Glass Packaging Institute, 33% of all glass containers made and sold in the U.S. were recycled in 1992.

Throughout 1992 the European glass container industry operated in a sharply worsening climate, with the economy in decline. Production fell by 0.4% in 1992 to 15.3 million metric tons, contrasting with the period 1982–92, during which production rose by one-third. The container industry was working toward recycling and recovery targets set by proposed European Community packaging legislation. Glass, compared with some other packaging materials, was well placed, since collection systems had been in use for some time; the average recycling rate of glass in Europe in 1992 was 49%.

The world's flat glassmaking capacity had been underutilized, which had intensified competition and put pressure on selling prices. Float glass prices in 1992 fell to 1982 levels, some 30% lower than when the recession began. The indications that the worst of the recession was over in the U.S. and U.K. had not yet been reflected in the demand for float glass, which had been partially offset by economic deterioration in the rest of Europe. Although higher sales volumes were achieved in the U.S. market, these were offset by lower prices. Shipments jumped 6.7% in 1992 and were expected to increase 3.6% in 1993, fostered by continued growth in the residential construction and automotive sectors. However, European markets suffered from both lower sales volumes and prices. Attempts to increase prices in Europe failed as imports predominantly from the U.S. undercut them.

Higher sales volumes were achieved in the worldwide fibreglass-reinforcement and auto-replacement glass sectors. However, these gains also were offset by lower prices. Demand for fibreglass for building insulation was maintained. There was sustained growth in fibreglass production in Southeast Asia and Japan, and an annual growth of 4–5% was predicted for continuous fibreglass for the industry as a whole in 1993.

The lead crystal industry throughout the industrialized world continued to suffer because of increasing environmental and health and safety legislation and competition from cheap imports. Manufacturers were deciding whether to continue using lead or to develop an alternative.

(HEIDI C.D. BROWN)

INSURANCE

Worldwide sales of private insurance approached an estimated $1.5 trillion in 1993. Although sales growth throughout the world had been stagnant in recent years, Europe, Latin America, and Asia (excluding Japan) registered annual increases of 7–10%. U.S. market share was about 42%, while Japan was 12%, Germany 10%, and the U.K. 6%. Highest per capita expenditures for insurance were approximately $3,000 in Switzerland and $2,000 in the U.K. and the U.S.

In contrast to the U.S. proposals for increased government involvement in health insurance, other countries were reducing their insurance roles. For example, New Zealand's Life Insurance Office was sold; Italy proposed to sell its government insurer that was the largest provider of life insurance; Tasmania ended its 25-year-old state monopoly of insurance; and India and China were studying ways to encourage private insurance to replace or compete with their state-owned insurance monopolies. The global reinsurance market was relatively calm, but increased costs for property coverages were expected for year-end renewals, especially in Europe.

In the U.K., insurance companies reported a return to profitability for general (non-life) insurance as a result of greater selectivity and increased rates. Life insurers continued their gains but faced problems with government proposals to require disclosure of commissions and with banks and building societies that were setting up their own life insurance companies. Steep rises in automobile and household insurance rates, attributable to higher claims costs, encouraged consumers to search for lower premiums. Lloyd's of London continued to be beset by a sea of troubles. The latest data, for 1990 on its three-year accounting system, showed a loss of £2.9 billion. This topped the all-time losses of the previous two years. Losses for 1991 and 1992, though smaller, were also expected. The number of individual underwriting members had fallen to 19,467 by January 1993 and was continuing to decline. Lloyd's planned to maintain the £9 billion underwriting capacity by attracting limited-liability corporate capital in 1994 for the first time. Meanwhile, many legal actions were in progress against members' agents and against underwriting agents who managed Lloyd's syndicates, which had fallen from 400 in 1990 to 240 in 1993.

For U.S. property-liability insurers, net written premiums rose to $120 billion for the first half of 1993, up almost 5% compared with the same period of the previous year. The combined ratio of losses and expenses to premiums was down 1%, to 107%. Net income increased to $12 billion, with underwriting losses of $9 billion offset by $21 billion of investment gains. Catastrophe losses, based on those separate losses exceeding $5 million of insured property damage, fell to $4 billion. The floods in the Midwest, which attracted the most attention in the news, caused an estimated $12

ANDREW FAULKNER—SIPA

Flames and smoke from burning houses fill the sky above Malibu, Calif., in November. The Malibu fires and similar blazes in other parts of southern California in 1993 destroyed hundreds of expensive homes and represented a major loss for insurance companies.

billion in damages, but fewer than 10% of those were covered by insurance. Losses after midyear included July windstorms that caused $655 million of insured damages, a tragic Amtrak train crash in September with $300 million in claims, and spectacular firestorms in southern California that burned at least 61,500 ha (152,000 ac) and destroyed hundreds of high-valued homes. Reinsurers were still staggering from the record hurricane losses of 1992 that drove up the combined ratio to 118% and reduced the number of U.S. reinsurers by 10%, to 71. Overall, property-liability insurers faced declining interest income on reinvestments and increased balance-sheet problems unless underwriting losses decreased.

U.S. Pres. Bill Clinton's proposal for health-care reform overshadowed every other event in U.S. life and health insurance in 1993, setting off a major political battle for survival of private health insurance. Counterproposals viewed with skepticism the viability of Clinton's plan for employer-mandated universal coverage in "regional health alliances." Midyear surveys of health insurance premiums for large employers showed 8% increases, a decline from 11% the year before but still rising at more than twice the general rate of inflation. Critics of the president's plan also warned of decreased Medicare-Medicaid coverage, new sin taxes, the demise of flexible-benefit employee plans, and a very limited role for health insurers and agents.

The sale of variable insurance products was exceptionally strong during the first half of 1993. (Variable insurance bases its reserves and policy amount payable on investments devoted primarily to common stocks; in a period of inflation the value of the stocks will increase, and so will the amounts payable on the contract, thus counterbalancing decreases in purchasing power.) The Life Insurance Marketing and Research Association reported increased sales of 81% for variable life insurance. A Tillinghast survey noted variable universal life insurance increases of 29% to $750 million and individual variable annuity sales up 42% to $16 billion. Total variable annuity sales were expected to reach $40 billion, more than double those just two years earlier. (DAVID L. BICKELHAUPT)

IRON AND STEEL

The general economic revival for 1993 in the industrialized countries occurred only in North America, the U.K., and Australia, which started moving slowly out of the recession. In most of the other industrialized countries, including Japan, gross domestic product (GDP) stagnated, and the countries of the European Community (EC) experienced a decrease in their GDP. As a result, steel consumption in the industrialized economies in 1993 was expected to be 6% lower than had been estimated a year earlier, reaching only 297 million metric tons of finished steel products.

For 1994 only little change could be expected. While the U.S. and the EC countries hoped for a strengthening of the steel market in the second half of that year, with increases of about 3% for each, Japan anticipated a further fall in demand, by nearly 4%, to 74 million metric tons of finished steel products. Thus, total consumption in the industrialized countries in 1994 would only slightly exceed that of 1993, by 1.4%, to reach 301 million metric tons.

The countries of Central and Eastern Europe as well as the republics of the former Soviet Union continued on a downward trend economically. Steel consumption there in 1993 was estimated to have declined to 16 million metric tons, compared with past peak levels of 40 million metric tons; in the former Soviet Union, where steel consumption amounted to 140 million metric tons before the political changes occurred, it could, at best, reach 75 million metric tons in 1993. The outlook for 1994 was for some improvement in Poland, the Czech Republic, and Hungary, where the private sector was expanding rapidly. In the former Soviet Union the economies of the successor republics were in a dire state of disorganization and of disruption of trading relations. Thus, there was little hope for improvement in 1994, and it was estimated that steel consumption would decline further to 65 million metric product tons.

The steel markets in the less developed countries showed increased strength in 1993, and consumption in those countries rose by more than 5% to 135 million metric product tons. This trend was expected to continue in 1994, especially in Latin America, where the liberalized and privatized economies were making steady progress and where steel use was forecast to expand by 5.9%, reaching 29 million metric tons of finished steel. The other principal growth area was expected to be Southeast Asia, mainly supported by the dynamic economies of South Korea, Taiwan, Malaysia, and, more recently, India. Steel consumption in this region was projected to exceed 90 million tons in 1994, an increase of more than 6% over 1993.

The economic progress of the East Asian countries was much enhanced by the newest leap forward of the Chinese economy; the continuing strong growth of China's gross national product by as much as 14% during the first half of 1993 was accompanied by an equally vigorous expansion of steel consumption, estimated at 82 million metric tons in 1993, 12 million tons, or 17%, more than in 1993. For 1994 some slowdown of economic growth was likely as the restrictive

Table VIII. World Production of Crude Steel

In 000 metric tons

Country	1988	1989	1990	1991	1992	1993 First 9 months	Percent change 1993/92
World	780,062	786,182	769,991	733,734	722,284	[1]	[1]
Soviet Union/CIS	163,037	160,096	154,414	132,666	118,302	72,867	−14.7
Japan	105,681	107,908	110,339	109,649	98,132	76,030	+4.4
U.S.	90,650	88,834	89,723	79,203	84,322	64,961	+3.8
China	59,430	61,590	66,349	70,436	80,037	66,339	+13.1
Germany[2]	41,023	41,073	38,434	42,169	39,711	28,385	−9.1
Italy	23,760	25,213	25,510	25,007	24,842	19,419	+2.2
Brazil	24,657	25,055	20,567	22,617	23,895	18,802	+5.4
France	19,122	19,335	19,015	18,434	17,961	13,033	−6.5
Poland	16,873	15,094	13,625	10,439	9,835	7,439	−0.6
Czech Republic	15,379	15,465	14,775	12,071	11,140	7,884	−7.6
U.K.	18,950	18,740	17,841	16,474	16,212	12,615	+2.2
South Korea	19,118	21,873	23,125	26,001	28,054	24,432	+20.9
Romania	14,314	14,415	9,754	7,092	5,372	4,015	−3.1
Canada	14,866	15,458	12,281	12,987	13,933	10,886	+5.5
India	14,309	14,608	14,963	16,394	18,117	13,907	+4.5
Spain	11,886	12,765	12,935	12,867	12,182	9,394	−1.9
Belgium	11,217	10,948	11,414	11,331	10,330	7,629	−3.9
South Africa	8,837	9,337	8,619	9,358	9,061	6,454	−5.3
Mexico	7,779	7,851	8,726	7,883	8,436	6,765	+7.9
Australia	6,387	6,735	6,676	6,141	6,877	5,677	+10.8
North Korea	6,830	6,930	7,000	7,000[3]	7,000[3]	—	—
Turkey	7,982	7,799	9,322	9,336	10,343	8,488	+14.6
Taiwan	8,288	9,047	9,747	10,957	10,705	11,212	+37.8
Netherlands, The	5,518	5,681	5,412	5,171	5,439	4,483	+10.2
Yugoslavia	4,485	4,500	3,608	2,497	1,633	—	—
Austria	4,560	4,717	4,291	4,186	3,953	3,013	−1.9
Sweden	4,779	4,692	4,454	4,248	4,358	3,284	+3.7
Hungary	3,582	3,315	2,866	1,862	1,533	1,253	+10.5
Luxembourg	3,661	3,721	3,560	3,379	3,068	2,462	+9.4
Venezuela	3,646	3,196	2,998	3,119	3,441	2,542	−3.9
Argentina	3,652	3,908	3,657	2,992	2,661	2,035	+2.9
Bulgaria	2,880	2,899	2,180	1,703	1,522	—	—
Finland	2,798	2,921	2,860	2,890	3,077	2,413	+5.5
Indonesia	2,054	2,383	2,892	3,000[3]	3,100	—	—
Egypt	2,025	2,114	2,235	2,541	2,524	709	+31.2

[1]1993 figures not yet available. [2]Includes the former East Germany from 1991. [3]Estimate.
Source: International Iron and Steel Institute.

Table IX. World Production of Pig Iron

In 000 metric tons

Country	1988	1989	1990	1991	1992
World	538,164	544,826	531,835	504,781	459,637
Soviet Union/CIS	114,559	113,928	110,167	90,953	85,396
Japan	779,295	80,197	80,229	79,985	73,144
China	557,040	58,200	62,606	64,280	73,438
U.S.	450,572	50,677	49,666	44,123	47,378
Germany[1]	232,453	32,777	30,097	30,969	28,548
Brazil	223,454	24,363	21,141	22,695	23,152
France	114,786	15,071	14,415	13,646	13,051
Italy	111,375	11,795	11,882	10,862	10,461
India	111,714	12,074	12,645	14,176	15,126
Poland	19,929	9,167	8,423	6,355	6,348
U.K.	113,056	12,638	12,319	11,883	11,351
Czech Republic	9,706	9,911	9,667	8,479	8,039
Romania	8,941	9,051	6,355	4,525	3,135
Canada	9,498	10,139	7,346	8,268	8,621
South Korea	112,578	14,846	15,339	18,510	19,323
Belgium	9,184	8,923	9,416	9,353	8,524
Australia	5,723	6,084	6,127	5,633	6,384
South Africa	6,171	6,543	6,257	6,968	6,498
North Korea	5,900	5,900	5,900	6,000[2]	6,000[2]
Spain	4,691	5,535	5,482	5,588	5,076
Netherlands, The	4,994	5,163	4,960	4,696	4,849
Taiwan	5,487	5,780	5,491	5,561	5,292
Mexico	3,639	3,230	3,645	3,039	3,404
Turkey	4,462	3,508	4,827	4,594	4,489
Austria	3,665	3,823	3,452	3,439	3,074
Yugoslavia	2,916	2,898	2,313	1,266	824
East Germany	2,786	2,732	2,159	—	—
Luxembourg	2,519	2,684	2,645	2,463	2,255
Sweden	2,492	2,638	2,736	2,812	2,735
Hungary	2,093	1,954	1,708	1,311	1,176
Finland	2,173	2,284	2,283	2,331	2,451
Argentina	1,596	2,248	2,003	1,437	971

[1]Includes the former East Germany from 1991.
[2]Estimate.
Source: International Iron and Steel Institute.

policies pursued by the government began to be felt; consequently, steel consumption could remain at about the 1993 level.

Steel production showed trends largely similar to those observed for demand. Output of the industrialized countries, having fallen by 11 million metric tons, or 3%, in 1992, continued to decline in most of the EC countries (−3% over the first nine months). In North America and, more recently, also in Japan, crude steel production started to rise again, though from a rather low level.

Central and Eastern European output was sharply reduced in 1992, by as much as 26%; in 1993 the decrease was much less (3.3%), and it could come to a halt in 1994. The republics of the former Soviet Union continued on a downward trend; crude steel production there dropped by about 6% in 1992, and a reduction of almost 15% was expected for 1993. China had already in 1992 expanded its crude steel output to reach 80 million metric tons (a rise of 12%) as new capacities were commissioned; in 1993 an additional 10 million tons were likely to be added, an increase of more than 13%.

Steel production in the less developed countries continued to rise; in 1992 it increased 5%, and in 1993 it was expected to increase again to a total of 127 million metric tons of crude steel (up 8.5%). Most of the increase came from Southeast Asia (mainly South Korea and Taiwan), but Latin-American steelmakers also significantly increased their output.

Given the continuing decrease in demand and fierce competition, steel prices failed to improve over 1992, remaining as much as 35% below their prerecession (1989–90) level. Efforts to reduce production capacities, particularly for flat products, continued in the EC countries, where a voluntary reduction by 30 million metric tons of capacity was sought; other industrialized countries also closed down a number of installations or at least refrained from expanding capacities.

International steel-trade disputes and defensive measures continued during 1993. Part of the 84 antidumping and countervailing duty cases filed by U.S. steelmakers in 1992 against competitors in more than 20 countries were recognized by the International Trade Commission, and countervailing duties were imposed.

(D.F. ANDERSON)

MACHINERY AND MACHINE TOOLS

Machine tools are customarily defined as power-driven machines, not portable by hand, that are used to shape or form metal by cutting, impact, pressure, electrical techniques, or a combination of these processes. This broad category of manufacturing equipment is often subdivided into metal-cutting types and metal-forming types.

Preliminary figures for 1992 indicated that Japan was again the world's largest producer of machine tools, with production worth $8.4 billion. Other leading producers included Germany, with production worth $7.7 billion; Italy, $3.1 billion; the United States, $3 billion; China, $1.8 billion; Switzerland, $1.7 billion; and Russia, the United Kingdom, and Taiwan, each with production worth about $1 billion.

In 1992 Germany was the biggest exporter of machine tools, having shipped machines worth $4.7 billion, while Japan was the second largest, with exports worth $3.5 billion. Italy and Switzerland each exported about $1 billion worth.

The nations with the largest value of consumption of machine tools (consumption signifies the number of machines newly installed in factories and is, therefore, a gauge of industrialization or of modernization) included Japan, with consumption in 1992 worth $5.4 billion; Germany, $4.9 billion; the U.S., $3.7 billion; China, $2.5 billion; Italy, $2.3 billion; and France, $1.7 billion. South Korea, the U.K., and Russia each had totals between $1.4 billion and $1 billion.

Regarding the machine-tool industry in the U.S., exports reached a new high in 1992 for the third straight year, exceeding $1.2 billion. Exports had increased in each of the past nine years and had nearly tripled since 1984; they accounted for about 40% of total U.S. production in 1992. This percentage had increased in each of the past seven years. Mexico, Canada, and South Korea provided the three largest export markets for the U.S. in 1992, receiving, respectively, $250 million, $165 million, and $140 million worth of machine tools.

U.S. machine-tool imports fell in 1992 for the fourth straight year—to $1.9 billion. These imports came primarily from Japan, with shipments worth $850 million; from Germany, with shipments worth $340 million; and from Switzerland and Taiwan, each of which shipped about $110 million worth.

(JOHN B. DEAM)

MICROELECTRONICS

Because of increased demand for the chips used in personal computers and related applications, projected worldwide sales of semiconductors rose in 1993 by 29% to $77.3 billion, according to the Semiconductor Industry Association (SIA). North America led the world's major semiconductor markets with 1993 shipments of $24.8 billion, a growth rate of 34.5%. This was the first time since 1985 that the North American market was larger than Japan's. The largest gain, 35.6%, was once again shown by the Asian Pacific market, including Korea, Taiwan, and Singapore, with shipments of $14.4 billion. The world market was expected to reach $100 billion by 1996.

A devastating fire at the Sumitomo Chemical Co. in Niihama, Japan, in July created a major shortage of the semiconductor epoxy resin used in the casing of many computer chips. Estimates of Sumitomo's share of the semiconductor resin market ran as high as 60%.

Motorola, Inc., the second-largest producer of computer chips in the United States, introduced its new PowerPC family of microprocessors, which it developed jointly in conjunction with IBM Corp. and Apple Computer. It was positioned in the same market as the Intel Corp.'s new Pentium chip (*see* below) but would sell at about one-half the price.

Both Motorola and Texas Instruments, Inc., announced that they planned to build $1 billion research and semiconductor-manufacturing plants in Texas.

The Intel Corp., in 1993 the world's largest chip producer, officially introduced its new processor, the Pentium. In a break with tradition, the chip was not called the 586 (after its predecessors, the 386 and 486). Using a technology referred to as submicron [0.8 micron (micrometer)], the Pentium consisted of 3.1 million transistors, more than twice as many as the 486. In addition, the Pentium would support not only DOS/Windows as did its predecessors but also other multitasking operating systems, such as Microsoft's NT Operating System, UNIX, and IBM's OS/2. Operating at 66 MHz, the Pentium microprocessor ran at speeds more than twice as fast as the 486 chips. Hitachi announced a room-temperature single-electron memory chip in December.

A new law, the Television Decoder Circuitry Act, specified that all new 13-in and larger televisions sold in the United States after July 1993 had to include a microchip able to decode closed-captioned programs. This was expected to lead to expanded use of these chips to provide for "smarter" TVs in the home.

Driven by the personal and mobile communications markets, as well as the emerging "multimedia" computers, a new market developed for low-cost digital signal processing (DSP) chips. These chips were being used to augment workstations, portable computers, and personal communicators by performing specific processing tasks. Applications for DSP chips included providing modem and fax capabilities for laptop and pen-based personal computers, music synthesis, speech recognition, and text-to-speech/speech-to-text conversions.

(THOMAS E. KROLL)

NUCLEAR INDUSTRY

Data for 1992, released by the International Atomic Energy Agency in 1993, revealed that there were 424 nuclear power units in operation in 29 countries, with a total capacity of 330,651 MW. This was a net growth of four units and a rise of 4,040 MW in total capacity compared with the previous year. There were 72 units under construction in 19 countries. Nuclear plants produced a total of 2,027.4 TWh (terawatt hours; one terawatt equals one trillion watts) of electricity during 1992. More than half of the national production of electricity was by nuclear power in France (72.9%); in Lithuania it was about 60% and in Belgium, 59.9%.

In March the government of the Czech Republic announced that construction of the Temelin plant would be resumed. The project, started in 1985 during the former Czechoslovak Communist regime, had been held up pending a decision on it by the new government. Fuel for the two Skoda-built VVER-1000 reactors (the pressurized-water reactor [PWR] design from the former Soviet Union) was to be supplied by Westinghouse Electric Corp. This would be the first time that a Soviet-designed reactor would use Western-supplied fuel. Under another contract, Westinghouse was to supply the instrumentation and control equipment for Temelin.

China's second nuclear unit, the 900-MW Guangdong 1 unit at Daya Bay, started operation during the year. Designed by the French firm Framatome, the project was to be financed largely by the sale of electricity to Hong Kong, which would receive some 70% of the output from the station.

The Narora 1 unit in India was put out of action for a large part of the year by a fire that gutted the turbine hall. Although not affecting the nuclear equipment, the fire destroyed much cabling associated with emergency electrical supplies, requiring activation of the primary and secondary shutdown systems.

A World Bank study concluded that Ukraine could afford to shut down the Chernobyl units still in operation. The Ukrainian government was concerned that the loss of the units would place too heavy a burden on the local population because of the cost of the increased coal imports that would be necessary. Three PWR-type VVER units were under construction in the region.

In a bizarre incident at Three Mile Island in Pennsylvania, a man described as a former mental patient drove his station wagon onto the island, crashed through a gate onto the site, and finally rammed through a door into the turbine building. The resulting inquiry by the U.S. Nuclear Regulatory Commission (NRC) concluded that no serious harm had been done to the plant, but as a result of the security questions raised, the NRC introduced upgraded physical barriers to surround U.S. nuclear plants. These had to be able to stop a truck from crashing through the barriers as far as the plant building. Cost estimates for the upgrade ranged from $500,000 to $2 million per station.

Two five-year contracts were signed for work on advanced light-water reactors (ALWR) by the Advanced Reactor Corp., a consortium of 16 U.S. utilities. One, for $158 million, was with Westinghouse, and the other, for $100 million, was with General Electric Co. (GE). The contracts were for the development of the first-of-a-kind-engineering for Westinghouse's AP600 (advanced 600-MW PWR) and GE's 1,350-MW advanced boiling-water reactor (ABWR).

ABB Combustion Engineering signed a long-term collaboration agreement with Stone and Webster Engineering to develop the System 80+ ALWR. ABB would supply the nuclear steam supply system and Stone and Webster the balance of the plant. The NRC's schedules for completing the final design approvals of four ALWR designs increased by between 9 and 17 months during the year, causing considerable dismay and criticism among the firms bidding for the contracts. In March, meanwhile, the local authorities at the Tsuruga nuclear sites in Japan approved the first ALWR project in the world, a two-unit advanced PWR with a total rating of 2,700 MW, which were to be a joint Westinghouse-Mitsubishi design.

The full-power license issued to Comanche Peak 2, near Glen Rose, Texas, by the NRC in April marked the end of an era in the U.S. nuclear industry. This unit was the last to be ordered by a privately owned utility that survived to reach full power.

Three steam generators were replaced at Virginia Power's North Anna 1 plant in world-record time 14 days ahead of schedule, with half the expected cumulative radiation dose to the workers and for $50 million less than the $185 million budget. The new Westinghouse steam generators were replaced in 51 days during a normal 96-day outage for refueling and maintenance.

The United States Department of Energy's proposed budget for nuclear power, published in the spring, was not encouraging for many of the new concepts previously being funded. Federal financing was to be cut for gas and sodium cooler reactors, with a proposed overall reduction of some 45% from the previous year. Some of the proposed cuts were rejected by the House of Representatives later in the year, allowing work to continue on the gas turbine modular helium reactor, for example, but terminating funding on the GE advanced liquid-metal reactor and the SP-100 space reactor.

The British government's review of the future of the coal industry provided two important reassurances for the nationalized nuclear operator, Nuclear Electric. The government accepted the favourable assessment of the costs of running the country's oldest nuclear plants, the Magnox stations, and also accepted the case for continuing the nuclear levy until its phasing out by 1999. But the government declared that it would examine critically any request for extension of the life of an aging Magnox plant. Later in the year, it was announced that the Trawsfynydd Magnox station in Wales, which shut down early in 1991 for investigation of pressure vessel embrittlement, would be decommissioned.

The U.K. government planned a complete review of the industry within the next year. Nuclear Electric welcomed this decision in the light of improving nuclear unit performance and the progress with the Sizewell B project, Britain's first PWR station, which was running "months ahead of schedule and under budget."

Retubing of the CANDU pressurized heavy-water reactor (PHWR) unit 4 at Pickering A on the shores of Lake Ontario east of Toronto was completed in a record time of 18 months, compared with 5 years, 4 years, and 23 months for units 2, 1, and 3, respectively. Ontario Hydro withdrew its 25-year supply-and-demand plan in the face of a growing surplus of capacity. The plan, published at the end of 1989, was based on economic and population growth figures that did not come to pass. It originally called for 10 new CANDU units.

The start-up of Siemens' mixed-oxide fuel fabrication plant in Hanau, Germany, was delayed when three of the six operating licenses were ruled illegal by the State Court. The commissioning of the plant was expected to be held up, possibly for two years, pending appeals by Siemens.

The reactivation of the Superphénix fast-breeder reactor at Creys-Malville, France, was delayed by the French government, awaiting the publication of a report on the use of the reactor to consume plutonium and other actinides. The conclusions of the public hearings, held in the autumn, were also awaited, and new measures were demanded to protect against sodium fires. These measures were scheduled for completion in March 1994.

The AEA Technology Prototype Fast Reactor at Dounreay in Scotland was to be closed in March 1994, and the British government also decided to withdraw funding from the European Fast Reactor. German support for that project also appeared to have waned by the end of the year.

(RICHARD A. KNOX)

PETER MARLOW—MAGNUM

The Thorp reprocessing plant at Sellafield, England, stands finished, awaiting government permission (which came in mid-December) to begin operation. A slowdown in the development of nuclear power in Europe resulted partly because reprocessing had become uneconomical.

PAINTS AND VARNISHES

Paint manufacture may well be a global business, but multinationals experienced distinctly variable performances in 1993. The American components reported better financial results than the European holdings, while those in the Asian Pacific Rim fared best of all. Paint giants Germany and Japan both reeled under the recession.

With a growth rate of 15%, China's Pearl River Delta emerged as the world's fastest-growing region. In China paint production neared one million metric tons, and the increase in demand for high-tech coatings such as automotive finishes could run as high as 47%. Emertung Coatings, an Australian joint venture with a Hong Kong company, was quick to spot the opportunity of expanding into the promising Vietnamese market.

In the coatings world, 1993 would be remembered as the year when Akzo of The Netherlands merged with Nobel Industries of Sweden to form the world's largest paint manufacturer, ahead of ICI. ICI, meanwhile, had become a highly specialized paint business, concentrating on three core areas only—architectural, automotive, and packaging coatings—in all of which the company had a dominant global presence.

Intercontinental joint ventures were popular. Courtaulds Coatings of the U.K. and Nippon of Japan established a common Europewide coil coatings operation. Akzo and Dexter of the U.S. forged a two-part deal involving a European joint venture in aerospace finishes on the one hand and a transfer of Dexter's American coil coatings business to Akzo in exchange for Akzo's American aerospace coatings on the other.

Joint ventures were also used for global marketing. Herberts of Germany entered into two such intercontinental agreements—one with Dai Nippon Toryo for automotive coatings and the other with Croda to distribute automotive repair paints in Australia.

Technological innovation followed in the footsteps of environmental legislation. Volatile organic compound (VOC) control continued as the major environmental issue, and compliant coatings were the favourite research topic. Europe had opted largely for the development of waterborne coatings, while powder coatings were more popular in the U.S., where companies were particularly attracted by the absence of solid waste—an important consideration for an industry liable for hefty waste-disposal costs.

The North American paint industry was preoccupied with aerosol restrictions, with the removal of old lead paint, and, of course, with waste. In Europe VOC control was still the major concern. European Community legislation on the classification, labeling, and packaging of chemicals was implemented in the U.K. in the form of the Chemical Hazard and Information Packaging (CHIP) regulations, which required data sheets for all industrial paints.

(HELMA JOTISCHKY)

PHARMACEUTICALS

Even before 1993 drew to a close, it brought down a deluge of bad news on the heads of U.S. pharmaceutical industry executives. The image of the big companies as blue-chip, inevitably profitable cash cows for investors was smashed. The first blow was delivered by Pres. Bill Clinton's national health plan, which presented a real threat to industry profits, research expenditures, and even current detailing practices (the means by which companies encourage prescribing among physicians and hospitals). A proposed new national health board would be empowered to investigate "unreasonable" prices; manufacturers would be required to rebate 15% for each drug paid for by Medicare; the government would have the authority to bargain down prices of new drugs before they could be paid for under Medicare; and most Americans would henceforth join health plans that would provide clout to bring down drug prices generally and encourage generic drug use.

In expectation of some or all of these effects, stock prices of Merck & Co. and other blue-chip manufacturers sustained a hammering in the late spring, losing as much as one-third of their market value. Replacement of top executives at Merck, Glaxo, Upjohn, Eli Lilly & Co., and other big firms also may have been in part a manifestation of the hard times experienced by the industry. So wide a swath through top company jobs had not been cut in recent memory.

Such a major downsizing by big U.S. corporations was also difficult to recall. In October, Eli Lilly announced that it would trim 4,000 from its workforce, only weeks after Bristol-Myers Squibb said that it would offer early retirement to 2,600 workers. Lilly's cuts were expanded to include major reductions in its European operations, and it eliminated another 2,000 domestic jobs by restricting use of temporary and contract workers and consultants. Marion Merrell Dow reported plans to lay off 1,100 to 1,300, and Procter & Gamble said it would lay off 12% of its workforce over four years, some in its pharmaceutical operation. Other personnel cutbacks involved 3,000 at Johnson & Johnson, 2,250 at Searle, 1,500 at Upjohn, about 600 at Ciba-Geigy, and 2,800 (in addition to 2,700 already under way) at Warner-Lambert Co.

Beginning in late 1992 large pharmaceutical houses began to buy up generic-drug manufacturers, whose products had begun to represent a major source of competition. Copley Pharmaceuticals agreed to be acquired by Hoechst Celanese, and Marion Merrell Dow acquired the generic business of the Rugby-Darby Group. Merck acquired Medco Containment Services, Inc., a mail-order pharmacy and managed-care drug company, in November. In a radical move, SmithKline Beecham PLC broke with industry norms in November 1993 when it offered U.S. pharmacy customers a rebate for its Tagamet (cimetidine) ulcer medicine—essentially bringing brand-name price competition to the prescription-drug market.

The final blow to the industry came in mid-October, when seven big U.S. drug manufacturers and one mail-order pharmacy were taken to court by 20 drugstores for price-fixing and antitrust violations. The manufacturers were accused of illegal discrimination by refusing to grant equal discounts on drugs provided to health maintenance organizations, hospitals, mail-order prescription houses, and clinics. (The National Association of Retail Druggists said the discount offered to some hospitals could be as much as 82% for some drugs.) Drug companies insisted that they should have the right to charge different prices to various classes of buyers. (DONALD A. DAVIS)

PLASTICS

Although it was calculated that world consumption of plastics topped 100 million metric tons in 1993 for the first time, with a growth rate from 1992 of 3–4%, in all developed countries the industry had a very poor year, and no respite was expected until late 1994 at the earliest. There were tentative signs of economic recovery in the U.S., but in Europe (except the U.K.) the recession deepened sharply, particularly in Germany, where the weakening performance set the pace for low demand for plastics throughout the area.

The Asia-Pacific region (except Japan) showed a marked exception to this gloomy picture, mainly because of the dynamic performance of the fledgling polymer industries in Thailand, Singapore, Taiwan, Malaysia, Indonesia, and, most important, China, with its huge potential. Southeast Asia led the world with double-digit plastics growth in 1993, and multinational firms increasingly sought stakes in the area through licensing and joint manufacturing ventures. One estimate was that the region's demand for polyolefins was growing 4–6% faster than that in the world as a whole and, thus, by the year 2000 its share should increase to nearly a third, compared with the present 28%—surpassing Europe and almost equaling North America. Furthermore, Asia was expected to become increasingly self-sufficient in the production of plastics.

The roots of the trouble elsewhere, especially in Europe, continued to lie in massive overcapacity for producing the "commodity" thermoplastics—polyolefins (polyethylene and polypropylene), polyvinyl chloride, and polystyrene. This overcapacity along with weak demand and substantial imports caused prices in Europe to remain very low, with near-zero or even negative profit margins for the material suppliers. The consequent potential for real industrial disaster was increasingly recognized as the year progressed. Although generally regarded as no more than palliative moves, with the really tough decisions still to come, there were some mergers and exchanges in 1993. Neste of Finland and Statoil of Norway combined their petrochemical activities to create the largest European polyolefins manufacturer, ranking fifth on the world scene. Also, Hoechst and Wacker-Chemie of Germany merged their polyvinyl chloride businesses.

Interest in high-performance specialty polymers continued to weaken with the continuing downturn in such sectors as defense and aerospace. There was instead an accelerating move toward the "monomaterial" concept; *i.e.,* the use of single or compatible polymers not only in a specific item, such as a package, but in complete assemblies, especially in the automotive field. This trend especially favoured versatile polypropylene, which continued to be the fastest growing of the commodity plastics (at about 5% per annum), with 1993 world production estimated at 14.5 million metric tons; this, however, was far less than polyethylene (32.5 million metric tons) and polyvinyl chloride (18.5 million metric tons). Polyethylene terephthalate was again a star performer among the low-tonnage thermoplastics, with demand for it in the film, sheet, and transparent semirigid bottle markets still rising steadily.

The continuing emphasis on recycling used plastics was a powerful incentive toward monomaterial use because it would reduce some of the problems of handling mixed waste. Germany was the leader in its tough legislation on compulsory recycling, but its reluctance to allow the incineration of plastics for energy recovery resulted in the creation of increasingly large amounts of waste for which no economic use could be found. (ROBIN C. PENFOLD)

PRINTING

The world's printing-equipment-manufacturing industries went through a major slump period in 1993. Only toward the end of the year, boosted by the results of the Ipex graphic arts show in England and Japan's Igas exhibition, did orders begin to pick up.

The genuinely digital printing press arrived. Indigo (Israel) claimed to have sold about 300 units to business-forms-printing groups in North America and Japan. Web-fed Xeikon (Belgium) sold 50 offset units to the largest U.S. printing group, R.R. Donnelley & Sons, which also ordered the first of the "Sunday Press" extra-high-speed web offset presses from Heidelberg Harris. The M-3000 press series was "gapless" and had a continuous blanket. It was a main challenger to gravure presses designed to cope economically with split runs. Semicommercial web presses from Germany, France, and the U.K., combining the cost advantages of newsprinting with good colour options, began to be installed in Europe and Southeast Asia as well as North Africa. Weber Colour in Switzerland put the first three Rotoman 2000 machines into production and, like Monarch Litho in California, installed batteries of MAN Roland 700 sheetfed offset machines.

Sony Corp. developed the Gravuan system for engraving plastic gravure printing plates from a PC paginator. Automated robotic offset plate change became de rigueur on new machine models, and Mitsubishi (Japan) also introduced that system to commercial web printing. German manufacturers Heidelberg and MAN Roland installed robotized paper-handling systems for sheetfed offset in France and The Netherlands.

Computer press controls became universal, and telecommunications links with manufacturers were introduced to allow diagnostics of press troubles. Production-control systems were evaluated to give customers direct information about the progress of their work by linking into press-control systems.

Frequency-modulated (random or crystal and diamond) screening for colour reproduction, new "universal" offset printing plates, and direct-to-plate imaging pointed to the day soon when most reproduction work for printing would be handled in-house by printers and even their customers and designers.

New printing plate (offset) capacity was opened in the U.S., the U.K., Germany, India, and Japan, causing price drops.

(W. PINCUS JASPERT)

RUBBER

The debate over the continuance of the International Natural Rubber Agreement (INRA) heated up during 1993 as producing and consuming countries questioned the merits of the United Nations-sponsored price-support agreement. The agreement, which was intended to stabilize natural rubber prices and guarantee adequate supplies, was scheduled to expire at the end of the year but could be renewed for two years. INRA set up a pricing mechanism whereby natural rubber would be bought should prices drop below the must-buy mark and sold when they rose above another predetermined level. Because of the depressed prices for natural rubber over the past few years, the pricing mechanism of INRA dropped the must-buy price by 5% over the objections of the producing countries. This disagreement put a hold on buying from January to September, when the buffer stock manager purchased almost 18,000 metric tons and brought the buffer stock to about 200,000 tons. Early in the year the Association of Natural Rubber Producing Countries (ANRPC) said that it wanted either a new agreement or no agreement at all and hinted at cutbacks in production to boost prices. Toward the end of the year, however, the ANRPC appeared interested in renegotiating even with the lower must-buy price.

The number of major plant closings was slight. Michelin continued its heavy workforce reduction by eliminating nearly 3,000 jobs in France and 2,500 each in Spain and North America. In addition, Michelin's U.S. subsidiary, Uniroyal-Goodrich, issued a formal notice that it planned to close its Fort Wayne, Ind., tire plant. Uniroyal-Goodrich closed its Kitchener (North), Ont., plant at the end of 1992, shifting about 400 of the plant's 1,200 workers to its Kitchener (South) facility, which would receive $79.3 million in investment though 1997. Michelin also sold its retail tire subsidiary, Tire Kingdom, and its synthetic rubber subsidiary, Ameripol Synpol. Ameripol Synpol, the world's largest producer of styrene butadiene rubber, was purchased by Gantrade Corp. of Montvale, N.J.

Pirelli Group suffered from the aftereffects of its attempt to merge with Continental A.G. Owing nearly $270 million from its stock maneuverings, Pirelli announced that it would sell off its nontire businesses. During 1993, Pirelli divested its hydraulic hose operations in Belgium to Mark IV Industries. It also sold its profiles plant in Italy and its I.T.R. S.p.A. hose business to Saing S.p.A. The company dropped passenger tire production at its plant in Burton upon Trent, England, laying off 700.

Continental cut 2,500 jobs, mostly in Germany. Continental phased out truck tire production at its Sarregeumines, France, plant, eliminating 180 jobs, and its General Tire subsidiary withdrew from the front tire farm market and eliminated 340 jobs at its Mayfield, Ky., plant. Goodyear reduced its workforce by 1,000 worldwide during the year, not including almost 200 workers idled at its Philippsburg, Germany, plant. Other significant closings during the year involved Mexico's Euzkadi Tire, closing its Mexico City tire plant, and Freudenberg Group, closing an automotive and machinery components plant in Germany.

The opening of Michelin's new state-of-the-art tire facility in Clermont-Ferrand, France, was among the new investments in 1993. The Michelin plant was said to produce the same number of tires as a plant 10 times its size. Pirelli kept active in China by completing a 300,000-per-year truck and bus tire facility in Qingdao (Tsingtao) and closing deals for a 1.4 million-a-year radial tire production facility in Beijing (Peking) and a 800,000-a-year radial tire plant on Hainan (Hai-nan) Island.

Goodyear and India's Ceat agreed to build a $150 million tire facility in Aurangabad, India. The production of the radial tire and bias earthmover tire plant was expected to reach three million tires annually by 1998. Goodyear also announced that it would spend $22 million to expand its radial tire plant in Malaysia and $34 million to increase medium radial truck tire production by 35% at its Topeka, Kan., plant. Goodyear's subsidiary, Kelly-Springfield, was spending $21.8 million to increase radial light truck capacity at its Fayetteville, N.C., plant. Bridgestone announced a $110 million expansion at its Warren county, Tenn., plant that would increase truck tire production by 76% and a 63% expansion at its bias tire facility in Indonesia.

The International Rubber Study Group (IRSG), which is devoted to collecting worldwide data on the rubber industry, found itself on shaky ground in 1993, and there was speculation that the 50-year-old group might not make it through 1994. Canada withdrew from the IRSG in 1993, and Nigeria, Italy, and Côte d'Ivoire did not pay their annual dues. Russia paid its 1991–92 dues but still owed for two years.

(DONALD SMITH)

SHIPBUILDING

The world order book, comprising ships under construction and ships on order on which construction had not begun, showed a large decrease compared with 1992. The second-quarter figures issued by Lloyd's

STUART FRANKLIN—MAGNUM

A Japanese car carrier, built for a Norwegian company, is launched. Japan continued in 1993 as the largest shipbuilding nation, with almost one-third of the world's output, followed by two other Asian neighbours–South Korea and China.

Register showed the total volume of tonnage in the world order book to be 35,052,-973 gt (gross tons), a decrease of 6,355,621 gt from the same quarter of 1992.

The total order book was made up of 16,724,962 gt of ships under construction and 18,328,010 gt of ships on order. The decreased figure for the world order book was due to a large decrease—5,354,492 gt—in ships on order. The downward trend was reinforced by a 1,001,129-gt decline of ships under construction.

There were significant changes in the types of ships being built and on order. The second-quarter figures from Lloyd's Register revealed a major decline for oil tankers. The total world order book for this type of ship was 13,944,466 gt, a startling decrease of 6,128,139 gt. Significantly, much of this was due to a decrease in orders on which construction had not begun, totaling 5,203,-969 gt. The world order book for bulk carriers and general cargo ships, at 8,982,488 gt and 6,506,333 gt, respectively, was little changed.

In terms of percentage of the total world order book in 1993, tankers represented 39.8%, bulk carriers 25.6%, and general cargo 18.6%. Of the general cargo total, 56.2% represented container ship tonnage. Liquefied-gas carriers accounted for 2.8 million gt of the total order book, equal to a capacity of 3.7 million cu m (1 cu m = 35.3 cu ft).

Continuing concern about the vulnerability of bulk carriers to side structural failures led to the introduction of a structural condition survey by London underwriters in 1991. As a result, various condition and structural surveys were requested by underwriters on selected vessels at the time of renewal or inception of insurance policies to ensure that the vessels were seaworthy. As many as 80% of the ships examined required repairs and attention to various defects. These structural condition surveys were a direct result of underwriters' loss of confidence in the traditional inspections by ship-classification societies.

The largest ship completed during the June quarter was the 301,824-dwt (deadweight ton) tanker *Chios,* built in South Korea for the Livanos Group. The biggest ship built in Japan was the 290,927-dwt tanker *Ocean Guardian* for Amoco Corp., while the largest European-built ship was the 298,900-dwt tanker *Elisabeth Maersk,* built in Denmark. The biggest dry-cargo ships completed in the second quarter were three 150,000-dwt bulk carriers: *Cape Kestrel, Anangel Pride,* and *Anangel Solidarity*.

In Japan the Techno-Superliner research-project team built two model ships for sea tests. Research was also being conducted on fuel-cell ship propulsion and superconducting electromagnetic ship propulsion.

The second-quarter figures again showed Japan as the leading shipbuilding country, with a 31.4% share of the world order book. Japan's order book of 10,998,066 gt was 3,809,654 gt more than shipbuilding giant South Korea, which captured 7,188,412 gt of the world order book, followed by China with 1,869,588 gt and Germany with 1,658,-831 gt. The next 13 places were shared by 11 European countries, Brazil, and Taiwan. Croatia continued to advance in the world shipbuilding table with an order book of 677,095 gt, placing ahead of both Ukraine and Spain. (EDWARD CROWLEY)

TELECOMMUNICATIONS

On the road to the "information superhighway," 1993 was the year of partnerships and mergers between cable, entertainment, and telecommunications companies. The largest merger was the proposed $33 billion acquisition of the largest U.S. cable provider—Tele-Communications, Inc. (TCI)—by Bell Atlantic Corp., one of the original regional Bell companies formed by the breakup of AT&T in 1984. AT&T had earlier proposed a $12.6 billion purchase of McCaw Cellular Communications, Inc., joining the biggest long-distance provider with the largest cellular telephone service company. In March Sprint Corp. completed its purchase of the Centel Corp. for $4.7 billion, forming a $10.4 billion corporation and the only large telecommunication company providing local-exchange, long-distance, and cellular service. In December Southwestern Bell Corp. and Cox Cable of Atlanta, Ga., announced plans to form a $4.9 billion joint telephone-cable network.

Employees of a telephone company and a cable television company install their equipment on the same fibre-optic network. In the U.S. mergers between such companies made the headlines in 1993.
ROB CRANDALL

British Telecom agreed to purchase a 20% interest in MCI, the second largest long-distance provider in the U.S., for $4.3 billion. U S West, Inc., invested $2.5 billion in Time Warner, Inc., and BellSouth Corp. put up $1.5 billion for the QVC home shopping network to use in its bid against Viacom, Inc., for control of the Paramount Communications entertainment conglomerate. Novell, Inc., bought the rights to the popular UNIX operating system and its development arm, UNIX Systems Laboratories, from AT&T for $350 million in Novell stock. In Germany three corporate giants—the Mannesmann engineering group, RWE Energie, and the Deutsche Bank—joined in a bid in December to challenge the telecommunications monopoly of state-owned Deutsche Telekom.

U.S. Pres. Bill Clinton chose Reed Hundt to head the Federal Communications Commission (FCC). The FCC, reacting to the U.S. Congress and the Cable Act of 1992, ordered cable companies to reduce their fees by $1 billion and roll them back to the October 1992 level. At the same time, local stations were allowed to negotiate compensation from the cable providers for retransmitting their signals. Many cable companies scaled down their basic services to include only local broadcast stations and the local access channels, and in some parts of the country a number of subscribers found that their rates actually increased. The FCC also ruled that businesses would now be able to retain their toll-free 800 numbers even though they changed carriers, resulting in fierce marketing among the long-distance companies.

In order to provide microwave spectrum availability for a new type of cellular communication, called personal communications services (PCS), the FCC announced that it would evict current users in the 2-GHz (gigahertz) band. All incumbents now had to negotiate with the PCS provider that would be assigned the spectrum on the basis of the results of an auction.

The Radio Broadcast Data System (RBDS) was introduced in 1993. This technology allowed an unused FM band, called the subcarrier band, to transmit digital signals along with the regular broadcast. Installed in both car and home radios would be a device to decode the digital signal. These decoded signals would allow broadcasters to provide ancillary information along with their regular broadcasts. Among the features of RBDS signals would be the ability to provide the call letters of the station, the name of a song and the artist performing it, weather reports, stock quotations, and emergency notices, and the signals would also allow the radio to scan for preselected, specific types of programming.

Motorola's $3,370,000,000 Iridium, a satellite-linked digital cellular network that would provide worldwide fax, paging, voice, and data services, added new partners during the year, such as Russia's Khrunichev Enterprise and a consortium of 20 Japanese companies, including Sony, Mitsubishi, and Kyocera. The project was seen to be especially important to less developed countries that lacked the infrastructure needed to provide wire-based telecommunications.

In the courts U.S. District Judge T.S. Ellis ruled in favour of Bell Atlantic's position that the 1984 Cable Act, which prevents telephone companies from providing cable-TV services in areas where they sell telephone services, inhibits their First Amendment rights to free speech. Chicago-based Ameritech Corp. took the same issue to court in Chicago and Detroit, Mich.

In January it was charged that there might be evidence of a link between brain cancer and cellular phones. The disclosure brought the stock prices of cellular telecommunications companies down. Although no direct link was found, more study was proposed. (THOMAS E. KROLL)

TEXTILES

As with other industries, textiles continued to suffer from the effects of a major world slump, and there were few signs of recovery in 1993. Machinery suppliers to the industry explained that barring a major improvement, they would probably not be able to regain even very low levels of activity. A number of European companies had to close. Others sought protection by concluding joint-venture agreements with companies in Asia, where engineering standards were often extremely high and labour costs were only a fraction of those in Europe. Much the same description applied to the textile industry, where Western manufacturers became involved in joint ventures by providing development capital and know-how to their new partners.

World textile makers pinned great hopes on new microfibres—man-made fibres that were vastly finer than anything ever before available. Softer and more luxurious materials could now be produced, and it was thought that mass production of a leather/suede substitute, which would be much softer and would incorporate easy-care properties such as wash and wear, was on the horizon. Microfibres were far more expensive than traditional fibres, however, and the amount of dyestuff required for obtaining a particular depth of shade was much greater.

"Rationalization"—or coming to terms with excess capacity among the fibre producers in developed countries—prompted certain large companies to give up fibre making completely, as they felt unable to compete effectively in what had become a commodity market. Other companies turned their attention to products with special characteristics, such as modified polyester fibres designed to transmit fluids. Others moved toward making fibres with properties that made them ideal for demanding applications in aerospace, electronics, and medicine.

A new cellulosic fibre known as lyocell, with properties that made it superior to cotton, was introduced. It was based on cellulose, which generated virtually zero effluent.

Polypropylene, a man-made fibre that is attractive to manufacturers because it is based on propylene—a waste gas from oil refineries—was witnessing a worldwide overproduction. In an attempt to tackle these difficulties and seek ways to avoid possible market collapse, the United Nations Industrial Development Organization convened a meeting of more than 100 experts from 35 countries in Tehran in November to try to help less developed countries absorb excess capacity through development of downstream petrochemical industries.

(PETER LENNOX-KERR)

Wool. Prices in the 1992–93 selling season declined further. The Australian Wool Corporation's market indicator fell to 381 cents (Australian) per kilogram (1 kg = 2.2 lb) on April 28, and prices in real terms were the lowest in 50 years. After fluctuating without clear trend from April to September, the market began to gather strength. The forecast of the Australian wool clip in 1993–94 was revised substantially downward. Production in New Zealand, South Africa, and South America also fell as farmers reacted to uneconomic prices. Demand at the same time gradually improved. A steady recovery in prices in September and October was accompanied by much sharper rises affecting superfine merinos and carpet wools as special shortages were revealed. By November the wool market as a whole was, unexpectedly, on a rising trend, and fears about the weight of stockpile wool receded.

In the spring the Australian government announced measures to find long-term solutions to the wool crisis. In August a review committee recommended the disposal of the four million-bale stockpile by fixed schedule rather than by the flexible policy adopted by the Australian Wool Realisation Commission. It was also recommended that the commission be replaced by a new wool organization, Wool International, with "a clear commercial focus." There was great concern in most wool-using countries, expressed through the International Wool Textile Organization, with stockpile disposal by fixed schedule causing particular anxiety. (H.M.F. MALLETT)

Cotton. Like other natural-product industries—cotton textiles were about to be transformed. Thanks to genetic engineering, it had become possible to introduce into the large cotton molecule specific features that could completely change it. A gene from the indigo plant was grafted to cotton DNA to produce a naturally blue cotton suitable for processing into the denim fabric used to make blue jeans. Dyeing would not be necessary. In the U.S. a far-reaching patent was granted to a single company that would effectively control this new type of cotton as well as other variants that might emerge from further genetic engineering. This was a highly controversial matter, and it raised serious legal and ethical questions.

The main cotton-producing areas were China and the United States, followed by India, Central Asia, Pakistan, and Brazil; total growing area is about 32 million ha (80 million ac), yielding some 550–600 kg/ha (490–535 lb/ac). World production of cotton in 1992 was estimated at 17,970,000 metric tons, down almost 3 million from the previous year, and it was predicted that output would hold at that level for at least two more seasons. With cotton consumption by textile industries exceeding production by about one million kilograms per year, stocks were likely to be reduced and prices somewhat stabilized.

In China cotton production in 1993–94 was expected to fall because of inflation-adjusted procurement prices as well as pest problems. Drought in India had an adverse effect on the crop. Pakistan had problems in the previous season with leaf-curl virus, but this was expected to be overcome, and production in the current season was likely to move toward some two million metric tons. The situation in Central Asia was somewhat confused, and problems were reported in developing independent exporting businesses. Likewise, Eastern Europe, once a major consumer of cotton, witnessed a decline, but there were clear signs of stabilization, and those mills still operating were profitable and increasing their output.

(PETER LENNOX-KERR)

Silk. The world silk market continued to deteriorate in 1993 for a number of reasons: the global recession, the difficulties hard-currency countries had in obtaining export orders, the continuing decline in popularity of the kimono in Japan, and a continuing flood of cheap silk garments from China and Hong Kong. Only in China itself with its rapidly rising prosperity was demand good; stocks of raw silk were reported to be low. Despite this, China cut its official price for 3A 20/22 to $30 per kilogram in December 1992. Later, even this price was undermined by goods smuggled out to Hong Kong. Beijing (Peking) tried to counteract by further discounting. By July 1993 the position appeared to be stabilizing as the unofficial RMB rate against the dollar came closer to the official rate. However, the provincial branches were obtaining more autonomy and becoming more difficult for Beijing to control.

Brazil's silk industry continued to modernize, and raw silk of excellent quality was produced. Sellers followed China's prices downward. Other countries—*e.g.,* Paraguay, South Africa, and Romania—continued to nurture emerging silk production.

A bright spot was a growing fashion for silk noil yarn for use in knitwear. Bottlenecks in supply were thought to augur well for the future of silk demand generally in 1994.

Raw silk production figures for 1992 in metric tons were:

China	54,500
India (1991–92)	11,600
Japan	5,100
Brazil	2,296

Total world production in 1991 was estimated at 76,526 metric tons.

(ANTHONY H. GADDUM)

TOBACCO

A crisis loomed in 1993 as favourable weather helped farmers produce, for the first time in years, far more tobacco than

JIM JIRU—THE NEW YORK TIMES

Women work in a Czech cigarette factory modernized as a result of investments from Philip Morris. Western tobacco companies were looking to countries of the former Soviet bloc for growth.

the world needed or was prepared to add to already plentiful stocks. World production, estimated at nearly 7.4 billion kg (16,280,000,000 lb), was some 15% above foreseeable demand; in a normal year supply and demand differed by 1 or 2%. Farm prices for tobacco slumped in free markets throughout the world, causing planters to curb their plans for 1994.

Smoking, predominantly of cigarettes, rose in 1993 by some 1.3%. As usual, an increase in Third World consumption more than offset losses in regions sensitive to antismoking campaigns. Tobacco imports were affected when a new U.S. law limited the foreign-tobacco content of U.S.-made cigarettes to 25%. The import limit aroused the ire of Third World producing nations and would undoubtedly face a challenge at world trade talks. More than 40% of the tobacco used by U.S. manufactures was imported, and it was as much as 40% less expensive than domestic tobacco. As a result, other countries affected by the curb would secure fresh markets, perhaps at the expense of U.S. exports.

In the U.S., Philip Morris Companies stunned the market in April by substantially reducing the price of Marlboro cigarettes, the world's best-selling brand. The move was made to stave off competition from discount brands, but the lost revenues in sales apparently were a factor in Philip Morris' decision, announced in November, to slash 14,000 jobs and close or idle 40 factories. RJR Nabisco Holdings Corp. followed suit a few weeks later. Ever increasing tobacco taxes, including the massive increases proposed in the U.S. on cigarettes, cigars, snuff, and other tobacco products to fund a national health care plan, steered smokers to lower-priced brands. There was also a fresh surge in illegal imports. In Canada 20% of all sales were contraband.

Transnational tobacco groups, predominantly U.S. ones, moved into Eastern Europe and the former Soviet Union as state enterprises were slowly privatized. Post-communist countries used Western cigarette blends, acquired manufacturing efficiency, and cautiously introduced Western brands.

In Germany, where loose tobacco was less heavily taxed, sales rose for tobacco rolls (cylinders of cut tobacco, which were easily inserted into hulls of cigarette paper). Cigar production continued to fall, but all-natural brands gained popularity in Europe. (MICHAEL F. BARFORD)

TOURISM

The prolonged recession pared tourism growth in 1993, but the sector fared better than such industries as consumer durables and automobiles. Even unemployed and part-time workers preferred to reduce the length of their holidays, forgo the use of travel agencies, or vacation at home as alternatives to postponing travel. Businesses economized by combining trips, trading down (especially from five- to four-star hotels), teleconferencing, and negotiating discounts with travel agencies. The youth market was squeezed as college graduates faced uncertain job prospects. The latter group, however, was not only growing, but its members were increasingly prosperous and self-reliant.

Though the number of people flying was inexorably rising, actual passenger growth remained one or two percentage points below what was forecast. Worldwide tourism offered a similar scenario; upward movement continued, though at a slower pace. Worldwide international arrivals, which had reached 482 million in 1992, were expected to grow by 3.8% in 1993 to reach 500 million. Worldwide international tourism receipts rose by 9.3% in 1993 to $324.1 billion (compared with $296.4 billion in 1992).

Most tourism-related businesses felt the chill from the winds of the economic recession. Hotels imposed tighter cost controls, programmed seasonal closures, divested themselves of surplus real estate, and converted to more profitable brand names. Indeed, during 1992–93 hotels and motels showed some of the highest share price gains on U.S. stock exchanges. Many of the world's 762 scheduled airlines, however, were unprofitable and saddled with excess capacity. Losses in 1992 peaked at $4.8 billion and were expected to reach $2 billion in 1993. Government moves to reduce subsidies to publicly owned airlines were met, as exemplified by French carrier Air France in October, with protests, strikes, and political compromise to save jobs. Still, each airline passenger actually cost the carrier $15. Such new computer reservation systems as Amadeus and Galileo helped travel agencies increase employee productivity and expand services without adding to the payroll. Tour operators continued to prosper by offering packages tailored to the market's straitened financial circumstances. Market leaders such as the United Kingdom's Thomson Holidays cut prices by 6% in anticipation of a higher volume. Tour operators predicted a market growth of 5% in 1994 as the world economy moved slowly out of recession.

Regionally, international travel to Africa steadily grew. Major tourist countries such as Morocco and Tunisia saw hotel reservations increase by 7 and 4%, respectively. Rwanda's mountain gorillas, a top tourist attraction, helped tourism become the nation's second highest earner of foreign exchange. Seychelles also secured a position as a popular ecotourism destination, with a 21% surge in arrivals.

Table X. Major Tourism Earners and Spenders

In $000,000

Major earners	Receipts	
	1982	1992
United States	11,293	53,861
France	6,991	25,000
Spain	7,126	22,181
Italy	8,339	21,577
United Kingdom	5,531	13,683
Austria	5,695	13,250
Germany	5,392	10,982
Switzerland	3,015	7,650
Hong Kong	1,446	6,037
Mexico	3,682	5,997
Canada	2,416	5,679
Singapore	1,916	5,204
Netherlands, The	1,545	5,004
Thailand	1,038	4,829
Belgium	1,578	4,053
Major spenders	**Expenditure**	
United States	12,394	39,872
Germany	16,223	37,309
Japan	4,116	26,837
United Kingdom	6,237	19,831
Italy	1,731	16,617
France	5,157	13,910
Canada	3,188	11,265
Netherlands, The	3,406	9,330
Taiwan	...	7,098
Austria	2,744	6,895
Sweden	1,895	6,794
Belgium	2,191	6,603
Mexico	3,205	6,108
Switzerland	2,216	6,088
Spain	1,008	5,542

Source: World Tourism Organization, Madrid, 1994.

The United States had an estimated 12% increase in 1993 tourism industry earnings, for a total of $60 billion. Canada's tourism was steady, while Mexico lifted foreign travel spending by 5%. In the Caribbean, tourist arrivals increased by 17% in Antigua and 13% in Grenada. Barbados (6%), Bermuda (7%), and Jamaica (10%) all had a surge in hotel reservations. In Latin America, Chile (6%), Guatemala (8%), and Paraguay (8%) experienced tourism growth.

Tourist arrivals in China grew by 21%. The Philippines began the year on an upbeat note (20%), while Hong Kong (4%), Singapore (7%) and New Zealand (8%) all performed positively in 1993. While Indonesia posted a 7% growth in its tourism earnings, Australia marked time under a recessionary cloud. Japan's rising yen made

SUSAN GREENWOOD—THE NEW YORK TIMES

A worker in Miami changes license plates to make it less easy for criminals who prey on tourists to identify the vehicle as a rental car. Several foreign visitors to Florida were victims of crime during the year.

it an increasingly expensive destination, resulting in a 3% decline in arrivals and a 6% fall in receipts. Sri Lanka's tourism recovery continued, with tourist arrivals increasing by 25%. Maldives received 6% more visitors in accommodation. Ethnic conflicts in India hurt tourism. Conservationists, however, welcomed a Supreme Court judgment banning industries from polluting and damaging India's prized Taj Mahal.

Despite the liberalization offered by the single market, European tourism was strongly influenced by poor economic prospects and high unemployment in 1993. France, Germany, Greece, The Netherlands, and Portugal showed little change compared with 1992, while Austria (1%) and Switzerland (3%) posted small declines.

The troubled Euro Disney theme park near Paris reached its yearly target of 11 million visitors but failed to achieve profitability. The site, which posted a $930 million loss in November, suffered from poor weather, few overnight stays, and a lack of French enthusiasm. There was speculation in the press in November that the attraction might be forced to close if agreement with creditor banks could not be reached by March 1994. Cyprus' hoteliers welcomed fewer visitors in early 1993, though Turkey showed a small increase in arrivals. Following three devaluations of the peseta, Spain emerged as the star of 1993, with arrivals 3% ahead of those in the record 1992 Seville Expo year.

The signing of Israeli-Palestinian accords offered a welcome break for Middle East tourism. Israel showed a 12% increase in tourism, and Syria was 17% ahead of 1992 receipts. Egypt's industry was threatened by violence directed at tourists, and hotel reservations plummeted by 14% during the first half of the year.

Violence against tourists also brought unwelcome media publicity to Egypt and the U.S., and especially Florida, where nine foreign visitors were killed near some of the state's most popular resorts. WTO's General Assembly held on the island of Bali, Indonesia, in October adopted resolutions condemning violence against tourists and calling upon governments to take corrective action. (PETER SHACKLEFORD)

Lumber at a terminal in Vancouver, B.C., awaits export. Largely because of a decrease in U.S. production attributed to the setting aside of large tracts of forests for environmental protection, the price of lumber increased dramatically in 1993.

THOMAS KITCHIN—FIRST LIGHT

WOOD PRODUCTS

Launched in Toronto on Oct. 3, 1993, against a backdrop of concern about world timber supplies, the embryonic Forest Stewardship Council (FSC) took centre stage in the conservation debate. The council's underlying aim was to promote voluntary timber certification on a national basis and to ensure that only timber from sustainable forests was cut and traded on the world market. The FSC would act as an independent agency to accredit certification bodies, which would verify that producers were obtaining timber from forests managed under FSC guidelines. The council and its guiding principles provoked international controversy, especially among producers concerned about the cost of certification.

Earlier in the year the International Tropical Timber Organization (ITTO) sustained pressure from those tropical hardwood producers supporting ITTO to both extend and increase the scope of the International Tropical Timber Agreement (slated to expire on March 31, 1994) to include nontropical temperate and boreal timber, which together made up 90% of the world's resources. Consumer countries also vehemently demanded that Target 2000, an objective for trading only timber from sustainable forests by the year 2000, be written into an extended agreement. Producers hotly contested the measure.

As many world markets stirred from recession, demand for wood products showed a small but noticeable upturn with a corresponding improvement in prices. In the U.S., hardwood product exports in 1992 reached a record $1.9 billion, but an inherent decline in log sales continued in 1993.

The log trade, predominantly in Southeast Asia, was in major conflict with tropical conservation values. Voracious markets such as Japan, where annual housing starts continued to rise, maintained a high demand for lumber. Malaysia lifted its ban on log exports from Sabah in the spring following an appeal from Japanese buyers and against the wishes of the Sabah state government, which then issued its own ban. By August, however, stringent measures to halt or restrict log exports from Malaysia, Papua New Guinea, Myanmar, and Cambodia had sent principal buyers—Japan, China, Korea, and Taiwan—scrambling for suppliers. Africa was earmarked for secondary rather than primary species. Criticism of harvesting policy was not limited to tropical areas. Canada continued to defend clear-cutting where appropriate as a fundamental management technique and firmly rejected charges of overcutting. From 1982 to 1991 the country's standing timber in commercial forests increased by 554 million cu m (1 cu m = 35.3 cu ft), but in British Columbia's vulnerable coastal forests, cutting rates were adjusted. The U.S. also revised its felling policy. The West Coast harvest was expected to fall 30% by 1995, with a drop of 20% in Alaska.

Concern deepened about timber production in the former Soviet Union, where 57% of the world's softwood inventory was concentrated. Commercial logging there fell by 30% from 400 million cu m in 1990. The emerging states of Russia and Latvia, however, made major strides. Russia annually felled some 280 million cu m of timber, compared with an estimated annual growth of 600 million cu m. Latvia led the way in establishing (with Lithuania and Estonia) the Baltic Wood Exporters Association.

Demand for wood fibre was increasingly met by timber from plantation forests, which accounted for some 4% of world forest cover and 10% of world fibre resource.

A demand for wood-based board products continued to grow in 1993, although the product mix shifted. Oriented strand board continued to take a market share from plywood, necessitating a step-up in North American production. Canadian producers welcomed the mid-December ruling by a joint U.S.-Canadian trade panel that punitive tariffs on billions of dollars of Canadian softwood lumber by the U.S. Commerce Department were not appropriate. A ruling by the Commerce Department was required in early January.

(JEAN CLARK CAMERON KLOOS)

See also Agriculture and Food Supplies; Consumer Affairs; Economic Affairs; Energy; Information Processing and Information Systems; Labour-Management Relations; Mining; Photography; Television and Radio; Transportation.

This article updates the *Macropædia* articles BEVERAGE PRODUCTION; BUILDING CONSTRUCTION; DRESS AND ADORNMENT; ELECTRONICS; ENERGY CONVERSION; FORESTRY AND WOOD PRODUCTION; INDUSTRIAL GLASS AND CERAMICS; Chemical Process INDUSTRIES; Extraction and Processing INDUSTRIES; Manufacturing INDUSTRIES; Textile INDUSTRIES; INSURANCE; MARKETING AND MERCHANDISING; PRINTING, TYPOGRAPHY, AND PHOTOENGRAVING; TELECOMMUNICATIONS SYSTEMS; TOOLS.

Information Processing and Information Systems

The world of computing got smaller in 1993 in terms of both new ultrasmall computing systems and the downsizing of giant computer corporations. Yet for all its shrinkage, the computing industry also reached out in a big way. The new, small computers were equipped with wireless networking systems, and home and office computers were offered the promise of networking with other computers nationwide on a "data superhighway."

Technology. This reaching out also occurred on the software level. One of the most popular programs for the IBM personal computer (PC) and its compatible machines was Lotus Development Corp.'s Notes, a new version of which was marketed in 1993. Notes is a "groupware" product, allowing groups of employees on a network, for instance, to produce a report jointly. Windows for Workgroups, a version of the popular Windows software, also debuted during the year, and there were plans for groupware that would link people working in their homes.

Another popular new product of 1993 also promoted connections between PC users. Named for its designer—the personal computer memory card industry association—the PCMCIA card was about the size of a business card and about 10 times as thick. When inserted into a special slot in a pocket-size computer, such as the Hewlett-Packard 95LX, it provided the PC with special functions such as extra memory. With a small radio built into it, a pocket computer could communicate with other pocket PCs or with local area networks (LANs). A PCMCIA card for the latter function was announced during the year by Proxim, Inc.; the card's speed was 40 times slower than that of most LANs.

While pocket computers were not new in 1993, a new type of handheld PC was introduced. Called the personal digital assistant (PDA), this palm-size computer was notable for having no keyboard. Instead, users wrote on its plastic screen with a special pen, and software then converted

JAMES KEYSER—TIME MAGAZINE

An electronic "poster" with likenesses of a kidnapping victim and the suspect appears on a computer screen. This application, designed to assist law-enforcement officials in California, was just one of thousands of ways in which computer users worldwide were networking.

the handwriting to type. PDAs were introduced in 1993 by AT&T, Tandy Corp., and Apple Computer Inc., which called its product the Newton.

One problem with these PDAs was that there was no standard pen-based operating system; therefore, they could not interchange software as could standard PCs. Another consideration was that, because they were battery-operated and inexpensive—Apple's Newton started at about $700—they did not have the processing power needed to keep up with fast writers or to translate their writing with perfect accuracy. Still another hurdle for PDAs was that there was no way to route the messages they created through the nation's computer networks. However, a consortium called General Magic, which included Apple and Sony Corp., announced that it was developing the software needed to accomplish this.

The best way to send messages from a PDA or any portable computer is without connecting any wires at all. The few means available to do this were expensive, but during the year the U.S. Federal Communications Commission (FCC) created "personal communications service," a cellular-like scheme having frequencies that could be used for wireless data links.

Business. While connectivity was the major theme in computer hardware, the theme for the business of computers was continued upheaval. In fact, the year's biggest business story may have been the nearly $5 billion loss reported by IBM Corp., the largest corporate loss ever. In its aftermath, IBM's longtime chairman, John Akers, was replaced by Louis Gerstner, Jr., the former chairman of RJR Nabisco. (*See* BIOGRAPHIES.) At Apple longtime chairman John Sculley was replaced by Michael Spindler, the company's former chief of European operations, while Shigechika Takeuchi, president of Apple's Japanese subsidiary, resigned in November.

IBM's primary line of business was mainframe computers. From 1990 to 1992, however, its share of the world mainframe market dropped from 58% to 52%. IBM's 1993 financial statement revealed that the corporation's mainframe revenue had declined 12% and that all hardware sales were off 20%.

Another corporate crisis took place at NeXT Computer, Inc., a firm launched in 1985 by Apple cofounder Steve Jobs. Poor sales of its sole product, a workstation for education and engineering, caused the company to cease production and lay off about half of its 2,800 employees.

Also reporting a major loss was Borland International, Inc., once expected to be the third player in a PC software triumvirate with Microsoft Corp. and Lotus Development Corp. Borland experienced a third-quarter decline of $63 million and laid off 15% of its 2,200-employee workforce. It also began selling its financial analysis software for about $100, a fifth of the price of similar programs from Microsoft and Lotus.

Not every information-industry company shrank in 1993. AT&T decided to merge with the nation's largest independent cellular company, McCaw Cellular. And, in the largest U.S. communications merger ever, Bell Atlantic, a regional Bell telephone company, announced that it would buy cable television conglomerate TCI, Inc., which owned 1,200 local networks, for $21 billion. Bell Atlantic did not plan to operate the TCI networks within its own service area, but it would be allowed to use TCI lines outside its region to carry telephone calls. This would put it in competition with other "Baby Bells," a development the U.S. Department of Justice had not envisioned when it forced the breakup of AT&T in the early 1980s.

The proposed Bell Atlantic/TCI merger demonstrated how the computer and telecommunications businesses were merging. Cable TV by 1993 was capable of serving 95% of U.S. homes and businesses, and during the year it also became a medium for carrying corporate computer data, thanks to a new technology developed by Digital Equipment Corp.

As a result, cable TV companies could compete with telephone companies, which in turn wanted to get into the cable TV business in order to finance the laying of fibre-optic cable to homes. Unlike the copper-wire phone network, fibre-optic cable could carry movies and hundreds of television channels.

The Bell Atlantic/TCI merger would create the sort of "data superhighway" that the U.S. government was championing as a means to reduce costs in such industries as health care. According to one estimate, improved telecommunications would save the health-care industry $36 billion a year. Such a network could also be used to connect students with remote databases. The government wanted private industry to build the data superhighway, but it did plan to invest in research and development and to ease the market restrictions that might otherwise prevent a merger such as Bell Atlantic's.

Already the regulatory barriers were crumbling. In 1992 the FCC began allowing phone companies to carry information services such as dial-up versions of want ads, which a home computer could search in seconds by looking for key words.

Networks. The planned fibre-optic network would not be the first offered by phone companies to improve data communications between homes and small businesses. In 1993 an integrated services digital network (ISDN) was being installed throughout the U.S. using the copper-wire network. ISDN allowed a home computer to send and receive information at rates 10 times faster than the fastest home computer modems, and one consumer group claimed that it offered 80% of what fibre-optic networks would offer but at 10% of the cost. The telephone industry said its ISDN installations were going faster than expected and that by the end of 1994, 62% of lines would have the service, not the 55% it had expected by then.

Another existing computer network caught the public imagination in 1993. Noncommercial in nature and without any central management or, for the most part, funding, Internet was simply a linkup of diverse computer networks, most of them academic or research institutions. In 1993, however, publication after publication, including *Harper's* magazine, featured stories on the electronic mail (E-mail) sent back and forth in Internet's specialized forums—electronic bulletin boards that focused on everything from AIDS research to stamp collecting. One reason Internet was gaining popularity was that several software companies introduced programs in 1993 to make it easier to use, and several on-line information services opened gateways into this "network of networks."

As networking spread, it was likely to bring about changes in how the public thought about electronic versions of what was now received on paper. In what might someday be seen as a landmark case, a federal judge ruled during the year that E-mail generated by the U.S. president's office is as much a historical record as paper documents and cannot be erased when an administration changes.

(EDWARD S. WARNER)

Developments in Japan. The year 1992 was a difficult one for computer manufacturers and software houses in Japan because of a combination of saturated international markets and the prolonged recession. The production of computers and related equipment in 1992 (January–December) amounted to 5,616,700,000,000 yen, a 7.7% decrease from 6,083,400,000,000 yen in 1991.

Investment in information equipment declined especially sharply in the financial and security industries, but this belt-tightening mood also spread to manufacturing. Most vendors predicted little or no recovery in 1993. According to the statistics based on the Ministry of International Trade and Industry's New Survey on Computers Deliveries, the total number of deliveries of computers in 1992 was 2,712,505, and the value of the deliveries was 3,794,300,000 yen. Both the numbers and the value of the deliveries decreased from the preceding year.

Included in this survey were all types of hardware—general-purpose computers, minicomputers, office computers and distributed processing processors, workstations, and PCs. In terms of the value of the deliveries, general-purpose computers ranked first with a 48.1% share, followed by personal computers (24.7%), and office computers/distributed processing processors (13.8%).

According to a survey by JEIDA (Japan Electronic Industry Development Association), the shipment of personal computers in fiscal 1991 totaled 2,310,000 in terms of central processing units, down 13.2% from the preceding year. They totaled 1,172,900,000,000 yen in monetary value, down 7.1%. Influenced by the worsening economic environment, shipments decreased from the previous year for the first time since the survey began in fiscal 1981.

(YUJI YAMADORI)

This article updates the *Macropædia* articles COMPUTERS; INFORMATION PROCESSING AND INFORMATION SYSTEMS.

Labour-Management Relations

International. In 1993 recession was a dominant force in nearly all of the industrialized market economies, even in Japan and Germany, where it was necessary to go back a long way to find such economic malaise. Unemployment was high in most countries—averaging over 10% in the countries of the European Community (EC).

The main concerns of governments in regard to labour were how to counter the high unemployment, how to ensure that increases in labour costs did not damage national competitiveness or stimulate inflation, and how to restrain the high costs of social security. Governments in Belgium, Greece, Ireland, Italy, Portugal, and Spain engaged in talks with labour unions and employers, with a view toward resolving these problems.

Created on the basis of two existing international teachers organizations, a new international trade secretariat, Education International, with charter members including 210 organizations from 114 countries and representing about 18 million people in the education sector, was launched in Stockholm in January. It was expected to move to Brussels in 1994.

In the EC, progress was made on two contentious proposals, the directives on working time and the European works council. The directive on working time was approved by the European Parliament after a second reading on November 23. Among other things, it prescribed, in general terms, rest periods, a normal maximum working week of 48 hours, and four weeks of paid vacation each year. Night workers were limited to an average of eight hours per shift. In regard to the second proposal, the United Kingdom continued its opposition to the works council directive, but in November the other 11 ministers decided to move forward with it under the procedure laid out in the Maastricht Treaty, whereby a proposal could be approved by 11 governments; it would then be operative throughout the Community except in the U.K.

An EC directive of 1977 guaranteeing employment rights for workers affected by mergers and acquisitions had repercussions in Britain during the year. As put into British law by the Transfer of Undertakings (Protection of Employment) Regulations, 1981, it was assumed that the directive applied to the private sector. However, recent judgments by the European Court of Justice suggested that it could also apply to the public sector. The matter was important for Britain because of the ongoing program for the privatization of many public services—it being assumed that in many cases private contractors would be inhibited from taking over services if they had to continue to employ the existing workforce and observe the wages and working conditions provided by the public employer. The British government's response was to insert a clause in the Trade Union Reform and Employment Rights Bill, enacted in July, bringing the U.K. in line with the European Court's decisions.

In January the U.S.-owned domestic appliance group Hoover, faced with a need to close either its factory in Scotland or one in the Dijon region of France, chose to transfer the production of the French plant to Scotland after workers there had agreed to a wage freeze and a ban on strikes . The French workers and their government reacted angrily, arguing that what was involved was a British attempt to compete on low labour costs and unfair government aid. At the same time, however, in an unusual move, the Swiss chocolate manufacturer Nestlé announced that it planned to transfer part of its operations from Scotland to France.

Britain. The Trade Union Reform and Employment Rights Act was enacted in July. It covered a wide variety of subjects, of which some of the most important concerned an individual's right to join the union of his or her choice, specific authorization to be required for deduction from paychecks of union dues, written notice to be required seven days before official industrial action was taken, a "citizen's right" to restrain unlawfully organized strikes, and the abolition of the remaining wages councils (bodies dating back to 1909 that set legally enforceable minimum hourly rates of pay in particular industries). Unions representing local government, health service, and other public employees merged on July 1 to form Britain's biggest trade union, UNISON, with some 1.4 million members.

The British trade union movement had long sought to advance its members' interests through support for the Labour Party, which it had founded and substantially financed and on the policies of which it exercised a powerful influence. In recent years, however, the party leadership had come to see this close link as an electoral disadvantage and sought to distance itself from the unions and to decrease union influence in its policy making. A proposed reform of party voting procedures met with strong opposition from powerful unions, but at the annual conference in September the leadership managed (by a small majority) to achieve its objective. Even so, it was estimated that the unions would still wield 70% of the total number of votes at the conference.

United States. In March the U.S. government announced the establishment of the Commission for the Future of Worker-Management Relations, to be chaired by former secretary of labour John Dunlop, emeritus professor, Harvard University. The commission would, among other things, examine the application of labour law and the history of labour-management cooperation.

The North American Free Trade Agreement was signed by Pres. Bill Clinton on December 8. There had been considerable antagonism toward the pact among the unions, based on their fear that large numbers of jobs would be lost to low-wage Mexico. To assuage fears of unfair practices, in September the Clinton administration negotiated a side agreement with Canada and Mexico creating a commission composed of the labour ministers of all three countries, serviced by a secretariat. The unions were unimpressed.

Potentially the most important event of the year for labour relations—the negotiations between the "big three" automobile manufacturers and the United Auto Workers—passed almost without incident. The union targeted Ford Motor Co. for the first negotiation, which yielded a three-year agreement that provided increased pay and retirement benefits and renewed layoff provisions. The company secured an arrangement providing for lower pay for beginning workers. Similar contracts were later reached with Chrysler Corp. and General Motors Corp.

A series of six-year deals between the United Steelworkers and major steel producers included restricted pay increases, strengthened job-security measures, improvements in pensions, flexibility in manpower utilization, and—the surprising innovation—a union representative to serve on the company board and participate in joint meetings with management on corporate actions that affected employees.

Continental Europe. The economic situation in Germany was poor, particularly in the former East Germany, where unemployment was high and productivity still fell far short of levels in the western states. This led the engineering employers federations in the east to terminate the agreements made in 1991, under which basic wage parity with the west was to have been achieved in April 1994. A 26% installment toward parity was due on April 1, 1993, in place of which the employers offered 9%. The union, IG Metall, responded first with warning strikes and then with large-scale strikes

(*continued on page 204*)

MANFRED VOLLMER

Members of IG Metall, the largest labour union in Germany, strike to protest the cancellation of wage and vacation contracts. A number of German employers were attempting to get concessions from union workers, whose pay and benefits were among the highest in the world.

The Changing U.S. Workforce

BY MARY H. COOPER

When the latest recession in the U.S. officially ended in March 1991, workers had reason to hope for better times. Mindful that unemployment, which had risen to 6.7% from 5.5% during the nine-month downturn, traditionally falls during an economic recovery, unemployed workers were optimistic about their job prospects. Usually factory managers, service providers, and other employers would begin calling furloughed workers back to their old jobs and start hiring new employees to meet the growing demand for their goods and services.

Weak U.S. Recovery. The sluggish recovery, however, was a disappointment to those who had counted on history's repeating itself. The recovery was unexpectedly anemic, undermined in large part by the cuts in defense spending that accompanied the end of the Cold War. During the early months of 1992, unemployment actually rose to 7.8%, earning this upturn a reputation as the "jobless recovery."

The news, however, was not all bad. By mid-1993 almost two million new jobs had been added to the U.S. economy, and by August unemployment had fallen to 6.7%. But those optimistic statistics belied a more dismal trend: fewer laid-off workers were being called back to their old jobs because those jobs had disappeared for good. In addition, the kinds of positions workers had to choose from were in many ways less attractive than those offered in the past. Well-paid, full-time manufacturing jobs with generous benefits—the backbone of the U.S. postwar economy and the road to the middle class for millions of Americans—were scarce. Many unemployed workers had to settle instead for part-time or temporary positions with relatively low pay and often no benefits. By 1993 as many as 37 million Americans—more than a quarter of the workforce—held part-time or temporary jobs. All indicators pointed to the trend toward such "contingent" work as continuing well into the 1990s.

Corporations Restructure. The change in the quality and quantity of jobs available in the U.S. occurred because of a widespread and profound restructuring of U.S. industry, a movement that had been under way since the early 1980s. Faced with growing competition from foreign producers, U.S. companies were forced either to become more efficient or to go out of business. In searching for ways to save money, corporate giants of virtually every industrial sector automated assembly operations, weeded out unnecessary layers of management, sold off less productive divisions, and transferred operations to countries where workers are paid low wages. The effects of this corporate restructuring on U.S. workers have been wage and salary freezes, cuts in fringe benefits, and, in many cases, unemployment. The Congressional Budget Office reported that on an annual average, two million full-time workers lost their jobs during the 1980s.

Mary H. Cooper is a staff writer for The CQ Researcher *at Congressional Quarterly and the author of* The Business of Drugs *(1990).*

Unfortunately for the country's 118 million workers, the restructuring continued into the 1990s, affecting a broad range of industries. In 1993, well into the recovery, a succession of corporate giants announced that they would lay off tens of thousands of employees. The list included such household names as computer manufacturer IBM (85,000 workers), automaker General Motors (80,000), retailer Sears, Roebuck & Co. (50,000), aerospace manufacturer Boeing (30,000), consumer-goods producer Procter & Gamble (15,000), and telephone company U.S. West (9,000). Tens of thousands of government workers also joined the jobless rolls, victims of budget-cutting efforts at the federal, state, and local levels.

More Americans were being squeezed out of the traditional "core" workforce—full-time employees making a decent living at one job that offered health insurance, pension coverage, paid vacation, and other fringe benefits. Typically, core workers also enjoyed some degree of job security, with the implicit promise that as long as they performed their jobs competently, they would remain with the firm, perhaps advancing in rank and income, until retiring with a comfortable pension. In the past when companies went out of business, many full-time, permanent workers found new jobs offering equivalent earnings and benefits.

Contingent Workforce Emerges. Unemployed workers now face less promising prospects. In a quest to trim labour costs, companies increasingly have hired temporary or part-time workers to do the jobs once performed by permanent staff. Once hired mainly for low-skilled "McJobs" by fast-food restaurants, telemarketing firms, and other service providers, these so-called contingent workers are now found at virtually all skill levels and in all industries. Many are clerical workers contracted through temporary-help agencies such as Manpower Inc. to take care of paperwork backlogs. But these clerical "Kelly Girls," who once made up the bulk of the temporary workforce, are now joined by managers hired on a consultant basis to reorganize departments, by professional freelance writers called on to prepare executives' speeches, and by blue-collar workers brought in to meet surges in demand for hot product lines.

Nevertheless, the shift toward contingent work has benefited some workers. Married women who want to supplement family income with a part-time job, for example, are finding more suitable openings available to them than in the past. Skilled professionals and managers, who felt tied down in corporate staff positions, also have thrived on the independence they can achieve as self-employed consultants.

But for most contingent workers, the costs have far outweighed the benefits. Although a few might later be hired as permanent employees, most temporary workers have to look for new work once the current job has been completed. Typically, both temporary and part-time workers also receive lower wages and salaries than permanent, full-time staffers. The Congressional Budget Office found that more than a third of the laid-off workers who had found new jobs during the current recovery made less than 80% of their former earnings. Consequently, many contingent workers are forced to hold down more than one job to make ends meet or work longer hours in an attempt to maintain their standard of living. Because contingent workers rarely receive fringe benefits of any kind, they are heavily represented among the 37 million Americans who lack health insurance.

The benefits of a contingent workforce to employers are obvious: lower labour costs and greater flexibility in shifting jobs to other locations or changing operations in other ways that might be resisted by permanent workers. Outside temporary workers also can be a source of useful information, bringing expertise from former jobs to innovate operations.

Hiring temporary workers to meet current demand for goods and services also helps an employer hedge against a sudden downturn during periods of sluggish growth.

But even for employers, contingent workers have posed new problems. With little or no prospects for permanent work or advancement, these workers have few incentives to demonstrate loyalty by putting in extra hours to complete a deadline, for example, or to be especially gracious to a new client. Hiring temporary workers to fill out a staff of core workers also can create morale problems, with contingent workers resentful of the two-tier wage system that pays them less for the same work and with permanent staffers apprehensive about their own job security.

International Labour Woes. American workers are not alone in suffering the consequences of mounting competition in the global economy. In an effort to eliminate barriers to internal trade, the 12 member states of the European Community are encountering equally wrenching problems resulting from corporate downsizing and automation. Europe's average unemployment rate stood at 10.5% in July, while the jobless rate ran as high as 16% in Spain and 12% in France. Critics of Europe's highly regulated economies have complained that unemployment rates have remained so much higher on the Continent, in part, because of government protections granted to workers. Though these protections have helped prevent a shift to a contingent workforce in most countries, there is mounting evidence that European companies are being forced to take drastic measures to remain competitive.

The German auto industry, suffering its worst slump since World War II because of the recession and growing competition from less expensive Japanese models, experienced an 18% drop in sales in 1993. The chairman of Daimler-Benz AG, Edzard Reuter, announced a $776 million loss during the first half of 1993 and stated that "there is no room for protected species and taboos if production locations in Germany are to remain competitive." Daimler executives announced that 40,000 jobs (20% of staff) would be eliminated by the end of 1994. The problems associated with the changing international labour market have reached such proportions that U.S. Pres. Bill Clinton called for a special "jobs summit" in early 1994. The meeting is expected to bring together labour experts and policy makers from all the leading industrialized nations.

The Outlook. Meanwhile, the Clinton administration has proposed new initiatives to help U.S. workers make the transition to a more competitive global economy. Labor Secretary Robert Reich, for example, promoted a national system of apprenticeship programs to train youths in a variety of skills, such as computer programming, that are expected to be in growing demand. Contingent workers also would benefit from President Clinton's health reform proposal, announced in September. If passed by the U.S. Congress, the health plan will extend insurance coverage to all Americans. Several lawmakers also introduced bills aimed at improving the conditions of contingent workers. Rep. Patricia Schroeder (Dem., Colo.), sponsored a measure that would offer part-time workers federal pension protection under the Employee Retirement Income Security Act.

In the short term, however, there appears to be little encouragement for workers seeking the kinds of permanent, well-paid jobs that Americans have come to expect. As trade barriers continue to fall, companies will continue to come under competitive pressure to automate, downsize, and cut labour costs. And as long as the economic recovery remains sluggish, few employers appear likely to expand their core workforce greatly. As a result, contingent work seems likely to remain a significant source of employment.

(continued from page 202)

in the east. The dispute was resolved on May 14, when the engineering employers of Saxony reached agreement with the union on the basis of delaying parity until July 1996 after staged interim increases. A "hardship" clause permitted individual enterprises to make a case to the employers federation and the union jointly that they could not meet the contractual obligation and should be allowed to pay less in order to save jobs. Essentially a decision would be made by a joint arbitration body. Parallel agreements were made in the other eastern states, and a similar settlement was made in the steel industry in the east. In September the engineering employers in the western states served formal notice of termination of their agreements with IG Metall on pay and holidays. The union reacted angrily and later put forward its own claim for pay raises of up to 6% and a moratorium on job cuts.

The economic situation in France was also difficult throughout the year, and unions were much preoccupied with responding to job cuts, privatization plans, and the new government's objective of achieving greater employment flexibility. A significant dispute arose in October when unions struck against a plan by the state-owned airline, Air France, that envisioned the loss of 4,000 jobs by the end of 1994. The major Paris airports—and at times other airports—were almost paralyzed by striking ground staff blocking the runways and, for a time, the main access roads. After a difficult week the government, which at first had described the airline's plan as indispensable, announced that a new recovery plan would be negotiated.

There was considerable legislative activity in Italy during the year. In January a decree law on pensions foreshadowed a gradual increase in retirement age from 60 to 65 for men and 55 to 60 for women. Favourable early-retirement arrangements for civil servants were to be phased out over 10 years. A second law placed public-sector employment under civil law and established an agency that would act as the bargaining agent for the state as employer.

The three-year-long talks in Italy on a new collective bargaining structure and worker representation culminated in agreement on July 3. The agreement provided that each year the government, unions, and employers should devise a policy that would limit inflation and favour economic development and employment. In collective bargaining, national agreements concerning wages for each business sector would be made for two years and those for working conditions for four years.

The Swedish economy provided a bleak background to industrial relations. Reporting on the situation in March, a government-appointed commission, headed by the eminent economist Assar Lindbeck, announced a 113-point program that stated unequivocally that wages should be decided at one level only—that of the business enterprise. The commission also suggested that professional lawyers would be more appropriate to serve on labour courts than the employer and union lay members who currently served with the legally qualified chairpersons. (R.O. CLARKE)

See also Economic Affairs: *World Economy;* Industrial Review.
This article updates the *Macropædia* article WORK AND EMPLOYMENT.

Law

International Agreements. In a dramatic close to the year, the seven-year negotiations in the Uruguay round of the General Agreement on Tariffs and Trade (GATT) came to a successful conclusion on December 15, just in time to meet the deadline firmly set by GATT Director-General Peter Sutherland and needed for "fast track" ratification by the U.S. Congress. Agreement was reached after an intense final round of negotiations involving the U.S. and the European Community (EC, from November 1 the European Union). The text was to be presented for formal signature by April 15, 1994, and would come into force (ratifications permitting) on July 1, 1995.

The treaty was exceptional in several ways and did not merely extend the existing system of tariff reductions, antidumping measures, and dispute settlement—although it did do all that as well. First, it created a new international body, the World Trade Organization (WTO), some 40-odd years after the proposal to create an International Trade Organization (ITO) as part of the UN specialized agency system, which was never accepted. GATT, a substitute for the ITO, in fact developed into an organization in its own right, and so organizationally there was unlikely to be any dramatic change. However, the WTO would have stronger powers than GATT, particularly in determining disputes and enforcement procedures, and subtle changes of power balance were likely to emerge.

Second, the treaty extended the GATT system to cover, for the first time, agriculture, textiles, and some services. Negotiation of various services had always been a problem, and some important sectors of the agreement (telecommunications, shipping, and audiovisual and financial services) were in the end excluded altogether. Services had never been subject to customs duties, and their inclusion in the new treaty marked a radical extension of GATT rules into unknown legal territory.

Third, an important legislative text was included, setting basic principles and rules for intellectual property rights. These rules went farther, albeit less deep, than the great world conventions on patents, trademarks, and copyright administered by the World Intellectual Property Organization and contained controversial provisions that had not been agreed to at those specialized levels. Also, because they were part of the GATT package, they would be binding on many less developed countries that were not party to the great conventions. This, then, was the fourth aspect of the agreement; it contained legislation on substantive private law, which formed part of the domestic legal system of nearly every state in the world. It marked, in a particularly acute manner, the increasing globalization of private law. Again, the legal and constitutional implications had not been examined, in particular the practical impossibility of amending or repealing the rules once adopted.

Against that background most other events in international law in 1993 seemed pallid even though some of them were fully as complex and pregnant with significance for the future. In Europe integration through the EC reached a new stage of complexity. Three treaties that were concluded the previous year or earlier finally completed their ratification processes. The Maastricht Treaty on European Union (1992) finally came into force on November 1 after a second, positive Danish referendum, a year-long ratification battle in the U.K. Parliament followed by an unsuccessful constitutional challenge in the English High Court in July (*Ex parte Lord Rees-Mogg*), and an extremely thorough analysis in October by the German federal Constitutional Court in *Brunner* v. *The European Union Treaty.*

At the same, time the European Economic Area (EEA) Treaty (1992) also completed its reratification following the amendments necessitated by the Swiss withdrawal after its negative referendum on Dec. 6, 1992, in time to come into force on Jan. 1, 1994. The Schengen Treaty (1990), in spite of last-minute threats by France to abstain from ratifying

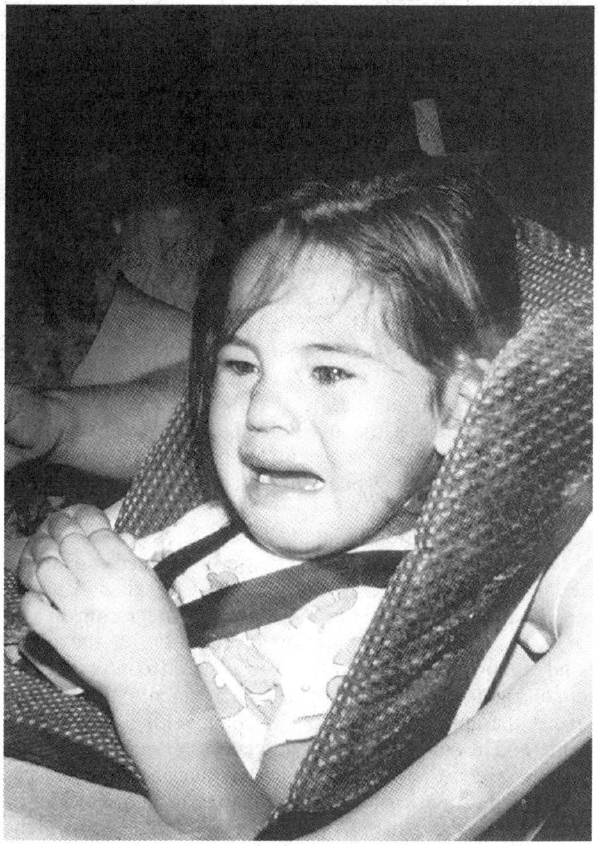

"Baby Jessica," the centre of legal attention in 1993, expresses her displeasure. After an unsuccessful appeal to the U.S. Supreme Court, her adoptive parents were forced to return her to her natural parents, even though her birth mother had given her up for adoption.
AP/WIDE WORLD

because of Dutch liberalism with regard to drug imports, was finally ratified by its nine member states and came into force on December 1, with a delay to Feb. 1, 1994, for the full freeing of border crossing.

The result of these three treaties was that, from the end of the year, the old common market would extend to 17 Western European states (the 12 EC members and 5 European Free Trade Association [EFTA] states, excluding Switzerland and Liechtenstein), with the whole corpus of existing EC law (including antitrust and free movement of both goods and people) now applying also to Austria and the four Nordic EFTA states and internal border controls between nine of the EC member states (all except the U.K., Ireland, and Denmark) being abolished.

The European Union Treaty itself was full of innovations, including terminology. The European Economic Community (EEC) lost the "Economic" and was changed to the European Community (EC) and the old term EC (European Communities [later Community]) now became EU (European Union). The European Court of Justice could for the first time award damages against a recalcitrant member state, but in return the member states regained some of their powers from the Community through the principle of subsidiarity. New legislative procedures were introduced to increase the involvement of the European Parliament. In 1996 a new revision conference was to be held, at which further developments would be negotiated.

By then the context would be very different—and not only because of the EEA, which toward the end of the year had set up the EFTA Surveillance Authority in Brussels to enforce the Community antitrust rules in the EFTA countries and also its separate EFTA Court in Geneva. The negotiations for full EC membership of Austria, Sweden, Finland, and Norway reached an advanced stage. Extension of the main principles of EC law to the Central and Eastern European states began under the association agreements. Poland had already begun the task of adapting its laws to fit with EC law.

On the regional level, in January Latvia and Lithuania signed an agreement on economic cooperation intended to lead to a free-trade agreement, and all three Baltic states also signed a defense cooperation agreement establishing a permanent Baltic defense council. In August a free-trade agreement was duly reached between the three Baltic states, and throughout the year the Swedish government fought hard in its EC membership negotiations to keep the free-trade agreement that it already had with the Baltic states. In February Hungary, Poland, and Ukraine signed a regional cooperation agreement establishing a Carpathian-Euroregion Council, while Bulgaria signed a partial free-trade agreement with EFTA.

New movements were hinted at in the Vienna Declaration of October 8–9, concluding the first-ever Council of Europe summit, which seemed to position the Council of Europe to take a more active role in European integration in the future. The Vienna Declaration of June 25, on the other hand, followed a less-than-successful world conference on human rights, which failed to reach agreement on such matters as the appointment of a UN commissioner for human rights and revealed serious divergences of view on human rights between the developed and less developed nations.

In North America a similar culmination and expectancy occurred as the North American Free Trade Agreement (NAFTA) obtained ratification from all three countries (Canada, the U.S., and Mexico) to come into force on Jan. 1, 1994. It, too, had judicial problems when in July a U.S. district court ordered that the agreement not be ratified until an environmental-impact assessment of its effects had been made and submitted to Congress. This ruling, which would have caused a serious delay, was reversed on appeal, however. The new system built upon the preexisting U.S.-Canada Free Trade Agreement, which itself had begun to produce litigation under its dispute-resolution procedure. One joint panel set up under that procedure ruled in May that U.S. import duties to counteract alleged low stumpage fees borne by Canadian loggers had been wrongly levied.

Even while NAFTA was thus progressing, a possible extension was under consideration. Chile, which entered into a free-trade agreement with Mexico in 1992, was promised negotiations toward a free-trade agreement with the U.S., although they would not start until after NAFTA was in force. A new free-trade agreement was concluded in December between Mexico, Venezuela, and Colombia, and another one the same month between Colombia and Chile. These followed another agreement signed in February between Venezuela, Colombia, and the Central American Common Market. In March Venezuela, Colombia, Ecuador, and Bolivia agreed to establish a free-trade zone from January 1994. In April the Managua Agreement on Economic Unity was signed by El Salvador, Guatemala, Honduras, and Nicaragua with the aim of improving their existing free-trade zone, increasing institutional links, and moving toward political and economic unity. The older and more political Organization of American States agreed to amend its charter to include among its aims the elimination of extreme poverty and also to allow suspension of a member whose democratic government was overthrown by force.

On the other side of the ocean, in March the Association of Southeast Asian Nations instituted a joint cooperation committee with India, and in January it brought into force the Asian Free Trade Association (AFTA) comprising Brunei, the Philippines, Indonesia, Malaysia, Singapore, and Thailand.

International Courts. International adjudication systems became more prominent during the year as well, with the International Court of Justice (ICJ) continuing its recent busy trend. New cases included the dispute between Hungary and Slovakia over the Hungarian rescission, on environmental grounds, of an agreement to divert and dam the Danube River to provide hydroelectric power and an action by Bosnia and Herzegovina alleging genocide against the rump Yugoslavia. In the latter case, filed with the court in March, an interim order was issued in April under the Genocide Convention of 1948 requiring Yugoslavia to take all measures to prevent genocide and in particular to ensure that any military, paramilitary, or irregular armed units directed or supported by it and any organizations and persons subject to its control did not commit acts of genocide. The court held that for the purposes of an interim order it would recognize (as had the UN) the legitimate status of Pres. Alija Izetbegovic as Bosnian head of state. It was interesting that, in view of the awkwardness in nomenclature concerning the remaining parts of the former Yugoslavia, the defendant was described, and accepted, as the "Federal Republic of Yugoslavia (Serbia and Montenegro)." A second application was filed in July against the use of genocide to procure the dismemberment, annexation, and incorporation of Bosnia and Herzegovina. The court issued a further order in September reaffirming its April order, denying the additional remedies sought in July, and refusing a Yugoslav counterclaim.

The dispute between Nauru and Australia over pre-independence phosphate extraction on the island was settled in August with Australia agreeing to pay $75 million in compensation. A more traditional ICJ case was that between Denmark and Norway over fishery limits in the North Atlantic—between Greenland (Danish) and Jan Mayen Island (Norwegian). Greenland's 200-mi limit was closer to Jan Mayen than the median line, and the disputed area (the overlapping part) was divided by the court so that each party obtained half the fishing grounds, with the nonfishery parts going to Norway in a rough proportion of 2 to 1.

The court's new activity was signaled by its setting up, for the first time, of a special chamber—for environmental cases. The regular partial renewal of the court's membership took place in November with, in particular, Judge Shigeru Oda of Japan being reelected. January saw the death of Manfred Lachs (*see* OBITUARIES), the longest-serving judge (26 years) on either of the world courts, ICJ president in 1973–76, and a highly influential figure in international law.

The other two great international courts were both suffering from serious growing pains. The Court of Justice of the EC was becoming more and more worried at the incessant delays in delivering judgment and reporting of its judgments (more than two years) and the continual problem of multilingualism and language equality. In a further attempt to reduce response time, the EC Council agreed to its request to transfer to the Court of First Instance all direct action brought by private parties (except antidumping cases, which some member states opposed transferring for protectionist reasons).

The European Court of Human Rights (ECHR) had also recorded a marked increase in caseload such that it, and its "filter," the European Commission of Human Rights, had in practice become full-time courts. In October the member states of the Council of Europe at the Vienna summit agreed at last to reform the whole apparatus and to replace it with a single court sitting in chambers and applying its own screening procedure. The Council of Europe was mandated to prepare a protocol to the European Convention on Human Rights to that effect for signature in May 1994.

Perhaps the most important decision handed down by the ECHR during the year was *Castells* v. *Spain*. A Spanish court had convicted an opposition member of the parliament of the criminal offense of "insulting parliament" on the basis of a newspaper article he had written. The government defended this action as "necessary in a democratic society," as permitted by the European Convention on Human Rights. In a relatively strongly worded opinion, the ECHR held that this defense could not stand. It restated its view that freedom of expression is an essential foundation of a democratic society and that freedom of the press and freedom of political debate must be protected.

Other significant ECHR cases included *Megyeri* v. *Germany,* holding that failure to appoint a lawyer to assist a mental patient in proceedings relating to his detention violated the Convention; *Olson* v. *Sweden,* holding that restrictions on parents with regard to access to their children placed in foster homes, particularly their denial of the right to have these prohibitions judicially reviewed, violated the Convention; and *Ludi* v. *Switzerland,* holding that, while Swiss law permitting the tapping of a telephone of a person suspected of illegally dealing in drugs interfered with the accused's private life, it did not violate the Convention because it was necessary in a democratic society for the prevention of crime.

Finally, apart from the setting up by EFTA of the new EFTA Court of Justice in Geneva, due to begin operating in January 1994, the other Vienna Conference in June rejected the idea of a new UN court of human rights and instead recommended that the International Law Commission be asked to examine the possibility of creating a permanent international criminal court. In May the UN Security Council did in fact resolve to establish an ad hoc war crimes tribunal under chapter VII of the UN Charter to deal with events in Bosnia and Herzegovina and based on a report by the UN secretary-general.

Although newsworthy cases seldom make a lasting contribution to the development of law as an institution, they often have political and social consequences that are immediate and sometimes far-reaching. Such was the acquittal on war-crime charges of John Demjanjuk by the Supreme Court of Israel, which made news throughout the world. The Ukrainian-born Demjanjuk immigrated to the U.S. in 1951 and was employed as an autoworker in Cleveland, Ohio. He first started making news in 1977 when he was charged with having lied on his immigration papers. The U.S. Department of Justice charged that in reality he was a Soviet soldier who had defected to join the Nazis and who had run the gas chambers at the Treblinka concentration camp in Poland. He admitted lying but denied that he was a Nazi or involved in any way at Treblinka. During a five-week trial in Cleveland in 1981, five Treblinka survivors identified him as "Ivan the Terrible," a brutal guard at that camp who was personally responsible for many deaths. Demjanjuk was convicted of lying and was about to be ordered deported to Ukraine when the Israeli government intervened and requested that he be extradited to Israel to stand trial for war crimes. After a 14-month trial, he was convicted in April 1988 and sentenced to death. He appealed the decision to the Supreme Court. Pending the appeal, information was supplied by the former Soviet Union to the effect that 32 Nazis who had been captured by the Soviets after the war had identified the real Ivan the Terrible as another man named Ivan Marchenko. Meanwhile, the federal appellate court in Ohio ordered the case reopened when it learned that the U.S. Justice Department had some knowledge concerning Marchenko and the possibility that his identity had been confused with that of Demjanjuk but had withheld this evidence from the defense and the court. Because of these developments, the Supreme Court of Israel released Demjanjuk, stating that there was reasonable doubt as to whether he, or someone else, had committed the alleged war crimes. It declined to order him tried on other charges.

U.S. Court Decisions. The trials for those accused of the crimes committed against Rodney King and Reginald Denny in Los Angeles also made headlines. Both crimes had been video recorded and played out many times on television screens everywhere. King, a black motorist, had been brutally beaten by four white police officers, who claimed that their action was necessary because he was resisting arrest. They were subsequently charged with aggravated assault. Because of the publicity that attended the case, owing to repeated showings on TV of an account of the beating filmed by an amateur photographer near the scene, the case was transferred from Los Angeles to one of its suburbs, where the four officers were acquitted by a jury with no black members. This decision sparked a serious riot in April 1992 resulting in a number of deaths and injuries as well as major property damage. One person injured in the riot was Denny, a white truck driver who happened to be passing through the riot area when he was assaulted by two black men who kicked, beat, and stomped on him and smashed his head with a brick. The assault had been videotaped from news helicopters hovering above.

The U.S. Constitution prohibits "double jeopardy," but a little-used and little-known exception to the principle exists, permitting a federal prosecution of a defendant who has been acquitted in a state court when the facts create both a state and a federal crime. Apparently yielding to great political pressure, the U.S. Department of Justice invoked this exceptional rule and indicted in federal court the police officers who had been acquitted in state court of assaulting King. The case was tried in Los Angeles, where a year after the riots a racially mixed jury found two of the defendants guilty on April 17. Meanwhile, another racially mixed jury in a state court in Los Angeles found the defendants in the Denny case guilty of six less-serious charges, acquitting them of attempted murder.

Another newsworthy case involved "Baby Jessica," who was called Anna Schmidt by her natural parents, who were not married at the time of her birth. Her mother gave her up for adoption, and later her natural parents married and sought to recover their daughter from the adoptive parents. The case was complicated by the fact that the natural parents lived in Iowa and the adoptive parents in Michigan. The adoptive parents won in the Michigan district court but lost on an appeal. Ultimately, they were bound by an Iowa Supreme Court ruling ordering the child to be returned to her natural parents.

Along similar but more bizarre lines, another case ended in a loss by the natural parents. Kimberly Mays and Arlena Twigg were born on the same day at Hardee Memorial Hospital in Wauchula, Fla., in 1978. The circumstances were unclear, but somehow the two babies were handed over to the wrong mothers. This mixup was not discovered until 10 years later, when Arlena died and tests showed that she was the Mayses' daughter, not the Twiggs'. The Twiggs then sought custody of their biological daughter but were defeated in a Florida state court, which, nevertheless, gave them visitation rights. Unhappy with the visitation aspect of the decree, Kimberly, now a teenager, brought a successful action against her natural parents to "divorce" herself from them in every way.

U.S. Supreme Court Decisions. Probably the most important decision handed down by the high court in 1993 was *Shaw* v. *Reno,* which was concerned with racial gerrymandering. The 1990 census showed that North Carolina had enjoyed a growth in population and was, therefore, entitled to an additional seat in the U.S. House of Representatives. It was necessary, as a result, to reapportion the state and establish 12 congressional districts to replace the 11 that had existed previously. North Carolina's new plan included one majority-black congressional district, but the Department of Justice rejected it because blacks constituted about 20% of the state's population and proportionately, therefore, should be represented by two blacks. The General Assembly of North Carolina then redrew the district lines to establish two districts that had black majorities. Because the black population was relatively dispersed, the General Assembly established two black-majority districts that, when drawn on a map, were very irregular in shape. Although the Justice Department approved this reapportionment plan, numerous North Carolinians did not, and they and the Republican Party brought an action alleging that the plan constituted an unconstitutional political gerrymander in violation of the equal protection clause of the 14th Amendment to the Constitution. In a 5–4 decision the U.S. Supreme Court agreed with this contention.

Other Supreme Court cases of importance handed down in 1993 included: *TXO Production Corp.* v. *Alliance Resources Corp.,* holding that a $10 million jury award for punitive damages was not excessive even though the injury amounted to only $19,000; *Lamb's Chapel* v. *Center Moriches Union Free School District,* holding that a public school board violated the First Amendment's free-speech provision by denying access to school premises outside of school hours to a church seeking to exhibit a film dealing with family issues; *Church of the Lukumi Babalu Aye* v. *City of Hialeah,* holding that a city ordinance that prohibited animal sacrifice in a religious ceremony was unconstitutional because it violated the First Amendment's free-exercise-of-religion clause; *Wisconsin* v. *Mitchell,* holding that a state, without violating the Constitution, may increase the length of a prison sentence when the accused has committed a racial "hate crime"; and *Bray* v. *Alexandria Women's Health Clinic,* holding that obstructing access to an abortion clinic did not constitute a cause of action for conspiracy to deprive a person of his or her civil rights under the Civil Rights Act.

(NEVILLE MARCH HUNNINGS; WILLIAM D. HAWKLAND)

See also Crime, Law Enforcement, and Penology; World Affairs: *United Nations.*

This article updates the *Macropædia* articles CONSTITUTIONAL LAW; INTERNATIONAL LAW.

Libraries

Librarians suffered from a crisis of identity in 1993. Were they custodians of books? Were they providers of information? Were they exploiters of information? Were they partners in the diffusion or pursuit of knowledge? An article in the British *Daily Telegraph* claimed, "It's goodbye to the tweed skirt and cardi and hello to the silk and sarong-clad librarian of the Nineties," but also acknowledged that librarians "do need to change our image."

Libraries across the United States continued to report service cutbacks and layoffs as a result of the poor economy. Particularly hard-hit was California, where the state's 1993–94 budget forced county governments to transfer $2.6 billion in property taxes to schools. Typical of the cuts was the County of Los Angeles Public Library, which lost $29.4 million, half of its budget; this forced two-day-a-week service at 43 of its 87 branches, a reduction by half of operating hours at the others, and the loss of some 200 staff positions. The Baltimore County (Md.) Public Library cut 23 staff positions and closed nine branches in February. The picture was brighter in New York City, where branch public libraries offered six-day-a-week service for the first time since 1947, and a last-minute rally by city and state officials saved the troubled New-York Historical Society library from closing. Public library circulation in the U.S. increased by 3% in 1992, while expenditures rose by 7%, according to the annual University of Illinois survey.

Two of the nation's leading library education programs were imperiled when the administration at the University of California at Los Angeles announced that its graduate library school would be eliminated and the University of California at Berkeley graduate library school suspended admissions pending an administrative review of the program. In the face of protests from alumni and other supporters, however, both universities announced measures that raised hopes that the programs would be continued in some form.

The Library of Congress received criticism from Chief Justice William H. Rehnquist and others over its decision to release the papers of Justice Thurgood Marshall to the public shortly after his death. The library also came under attack for its minority-hiring-and-promotion practices, which were the subject of House subcommittee hearings in March.

Former president Jimmy Carter addressed the American Library Association's 112th annual conference, which drew 17,165 registrants to New Orleans, La., in June. In August Hunter College Pres. Paul LeClerc was named president and chief executive officer of the New York Public Library. Chicago Public Library Chief Librarian Carla Hayden resigned in May to become director of the Enoch Pratt Free Library in Baltimore, Md. The refurbished Los Angeles Central Library reopened October 3, seven years after a devastating arson fire.

In spite of the uncertainties in the profession, libraries continued to be built. One significant project was the extension of the Carnegie Central Library in Dunfermline, Scotland, birthplace of U.S. steel baron and philanthropist Andrew Carnegie. Opened in 1879, this library was the first of Carnegie's more than 2,800 benefactions. The extension included a new children's library, a local history collection, and an exhibition area, as well as a £7,000 information retrieval system.

Two gargantuan buildings, the British Library and the Bibliothèque de France, were also in the process of construction. The British Library had been discussed since 1962 and planned since the 1969 report of the Dainton Committee. Construction on the building, which the public first saw in August 1993 when the scaffolding was removed, would be completed in 1996—27 years after the Dainton Report, eloquent testimony to the "enthusiasm" of the British government for the new library. The project had been affected by several changes of policy, including government vacillation over the increasing costs of a building intended mainly for scholars and totaling £450 million. Criticism of the architecture by the likes of Prince Charles (he had said it looked like "an academy for secret police") was also not helpful. The building was expected to house 12 million books, with reading rooms, an exhibition area, laboratories, offices, lecture theatres, and seminar rooms. Below ground would be four basements, the depth of an eight-story building, with 300 km (186 mi) of shelving, galleries, a shop, and a restaurant.

The soaring entrance hall of the new British Library building in London shows the imaginative use of different shapes by architect Colin St. John Wilson. The long-delayed and often-criticized project was not scheduled to be completed until 1996.
STEPHEN MARKESON—TIMES NEWSPAPERS LTD.

The Bibliothèque de France was initiated in 1988 and was also planned to come into service in 1996. The new library was viewed as one way of dealing with the accommodation problems of the Bibliothèque Nationale in the centre of Paris as well as of changing the traditional ways of a national library. The new facilities were designed to fill the gaps in existing collections, reinforce the areas of excellence of the Bibliothèque Nationale, and introduce the most modern library technologies. Users would be able to consult the catalog of the library or the French Union Catalogue's 13 million titles. The focus was to be on the needs of scholars, but much-needed services would also be provided to the general public. Collections were to be divided into four subject areas—science and technology; literature and art; social sciences; and history, philosophy, and the humanities. The library would seat 4,000 readers and feature an open-access collection of up to 400,000 volumes and 5,000 periodical titles. Almost 400 km (250 mi) of shelving was planned, and the building would also include exhibition centres and a conference centre comprising a 350-seat auditorium, a lecture room, and six smaller meeting rooms.

Elsewhere in the world the emphasis continued to be on developing collections and, especially, the skills of the staff. In Africa, schools of information science had been operating for a few years in Ibadan, Nigeria, and Addis Ababa, Eth., through the efforts of Unesco, the Canadian International Development Research Centre, and the respective national governments. Schools of Library and Information Science continued to flourish at the University of Botswana, Gaborone, and at Moi University, Eldoret, Kenya. Francophone schools, such as those at Dakar, Senegal, and Rabat, Morocco, had also gone beyond the traditional concepts of custodial librarianship and branched out into information science. Efforts were being made to establish a Consortium of African Information Science Schools to include Anglophone and Francophone schools. The work of the Asian Institute of Technology near Bangkok, Thailand, was well-established in the field, as was the School of Library and Information Studies of the Malaysian Institute of Technology, which recently celebrated its 25th anniversary.

(GORDON FLAGG; P. HAVARD-WILLIAMS)

This article updates the *Macropædia* article LIBRARIES AND LIBRARY SCIENCE.

Life Sciences

ZOOLOGY

Cannibalistic salamanders, social structures of frogs and pilot whales, and warm-blooded fish were all involved in zoological advances in 1993. In addition, studies of the fossil record challenged traditional theories regarding the origin of avian flight and the ancestry of humans.

Studies on cannibalism in salamanders and on the social structure of whales provided support for theories of kin selection, the tendency to favour genetic relatives over unrelated individuals, by revealing situations in which animals modify their behaviour when they belong to a genetically related family unit. The larval young in some populations of tiger salamanders (*Ambystoma tigrinum*) are known to become cannibalistic, feeding on other tiger salamanders. The cannibals grow larger than noncannibalistic larvae and develop specialized structures in the mouth that aid in eating other salamanders. Cannibalism occurs most frequently when larvae develop under crowded conditions. David W. Pfennig of Cornell University, Ithaca, N.Y., and James P. Collins of Arizona State University discovered that tiger salamanders reared in genetically unrelated groups are more likely to develop into cannibals than are salamanders raised in groups of siblings. They conducted experiments in which similar-sized larvae were placed in various groups, some being all siblings and some being unrelated. All larvae were of similar size so that variation in body size could not be used by the larvae as a cue to whether individuals were related. The investigators hypothesized that larval salamanders release chemical cues that can be used to distinguish close kin, which have a similar "smell," from unrelated larvae.

Kin-selection theory was also supported by evidence that individual organisms can increase their own genetic success by curtailing breeding and possibly helping their relatives. In a study of the biology of long-finned pilot whales in the Faeroe Islands, southeast of Iceland, Bill Amos of the University of Cambridge and colleagues Christian Schlötterer and Diethard Tautz of the University of Munich, Germany, found that males exhibit atypical behaviour. Pilot whales form large social groups called pods. The investigators used molecular techniques to establish that pod members were closely related, forming an extended family. A pod normally has more adult females than males and may number more than 100 individuals. In most mammalian species in which females live in groups, genetic inbreeding is avoided when male offspring disperse from their homesite before they become breeding adults. Pilot whale males remain with their family pod, yet genetic studies revealed that males in a pod rarely or never breed with the females, who might be their mothers or sisters. Mating is presumably carried out when

A larval tiger salamander (*Ambystoma tigrinum*) devours another larva of the same species. Researchers reported in 1993 that cannibalism develops more often among tiger salamanders reared in genetically unrelated groups than among those reared in groups of siblings, providing support for the theory of kin selection.
DAVID PFENNIG

different pods encounter each other in the ocean. Whether or how the nonbreeding males contribute to the welfare of their relatives in a pod remained to be learned, but defense from marine predators or assistance in a communal feeding effort was suggested. Ironically, the cohesive family structure of long-finned pilot whales makes them prey to human whale hunters. In the early 1990s about 1,700 of the whales were killed each year because pods could easily be herded into coastal areas.

Evidence of the way in which mating systems can develop in the best interest of an individual but not necessarily of the species was presented by Godfrey R. Bourne of Florida Atlantic University in studies of the mating system of a tropical frog, *Sinax rubra,* in Guyana. If given a choice, females, regardless of body length, select smaller male mating partners, usually about 80% of their own size. Experiments revealed that this size ratio of female to male produced the highest rate of fertilization of a female's eggs. During mating, a male frog clasps a female and releases sperm while she deposits eggs in the water. A male frog that is larger than the female is not in the proper position for the sperm to reach all of the eggs; thus, he fertilizes significantly fewer. Males smaller than the optimal size do not have enough sperm to fertilize all the eggs. Therefore, to maximize egg fertilization and have the highest reproductive success, a female needs a mate of the proper size and so chooses one accordingly.

A larger male frog, however, often displaces the smaller one that is chosen by the female and ends up mating with her instead. Competition between a small male that is preferred by the female and a large male intruder can reduce female reproductive success because fewer eggs are fertilized. On the other hand, the breeding success of the larger male is enhanced. Smaller males sometimes successfully mate by remaining quiet but alert for approaching females. When a female passes by on her way to check out a calling male, a small, silent "satellite" male may intercept her and mate. This competition among males can reduce the reproductive success of a particular female but ensure the propagation of a particular male's genes.

Most of the world's fish species, along with reptiles and amphibians, are ectotherms, or cold-blooded animals, having body temperatures corresponding to that of their surroundings. Endothermic, or warm-blooded, animals have the ability to elevate body temperature internally. The trait is characteristic of mammals and birds as well as some sharks and certain marine fish, including mackerels, tunas, and billfishes (*e.g.,* marlins and swordfish). Two contrasting theories exist to explain what selection pressures were influential in the evolution from ectothermy to endothermy. One theory proposes that endothermy arose following selection for a capability to maintain stable body temperatures across a broad range of environmental temperatures, permitting exploitation of varying thermal conditions. The other proposes that endothermy evolved in response to selection for an increase in aerobic capacity (ability to use oxygen) associated with higher metabolism and a more active lifestyle.

Barbara A. Block and colleagues of the University of Chicago used techniques of molecular genetics to establish the phylogenetic relationships among ectothermic fish species and the three groups of endothermic fishes. They found mackerels, tunas, and billfishes each to be more closely related to ectothermic species than to each other, documenting that endothermy evolved independently in the three different groups. In some species, such as the butterfly mackerel and swordfish, warming is restricted to the central nervous system and retina. The phylogenetic distribution and variable expression of endothermy among the fish groups led the researchers to conclude that endothermy in fishes evolved in response to the advantages of expanding into habitats of varied temperatures, not to a requirement of increased aerobic capacity.

A new living species of large mammal, the first such in more then 50 years, was identified from a physical examination and molecular analysis of skulls, teeth, and skins collected from a largely unexplored rain forest in Vietnam's mountainous central neck. The animal itself, however, had yet to be seen alive by the scientists involved at the time their findings were published. John MacKinnon of the Asian Bureau for Conservation, Hong Kong, and colleagues of the Vietnamese Ministry of Forestry placed the animal in the Bovidae family, which includes cattle, goats, sheep, and antelopes, and described it as weighing about 100 kg (220 lb) as an adult and having a rich brown coat with white and black markings and sharp, straight horns up to 52 cm (20 in) in length. The new bovid, called the "forest goat" or "spindle horn" by local Vietnamese hunters, was given the name *Pseudoryx nghetinhensis*.

Two major theories have been proposed for the evolution of flight in birds. One is that flight evolved in ground-dwelling animals that were preadapted for flight. The other is that flight originated in tree-dwelling species. On the basis of fossils from the Late Jurassic (150 million years ago), *Archaeopteryx* is the generally accepted predecessor of flying birds and the focus of most theoretical discussions on the origin of avian flight. During the year Alan Feduccia of the University of North Carolina lent credence to the origin of flight from tree-dwelling forms by means of a study that compared the claw geometry of *Archaeopteryx* with that of modern birds. The claw curvature of the ancient bird was shown to be similar to that of modern birds that perch in trees or climb tree trunks rather than to that of ground-dwelling birds, suggesting that this earliest known feathered ancestor of birds was arboreal. (See *Ornithology,* below.)

Among the most controversial evolutionary interpretations from the fossil record are those surrounding the relationships between humans and other primates. David R. Begun of the University of Toronto examined fossil hominids from Hungary estimated to be 10 million years old. He concluded that they may be the closest known relatives of chimpanzees, gorillas, and humans. In addition, his findings supported the view that humans are more closely related evolutionarily to chimpanzees than either are to gorillas, a position held by many molecular biologists.

(J. WHITFIELD GIBBONS)

Entomology. The fossil record of Insecta, the most diverse class of living animals, has received less attention in the English-language scientific literature than many other major animal groups. Part of the reason lies with the perception that insect fossils are rare. Refuting that notion, a study by Conrad C. Labandeira of the Smithsonian Institution, Washington, D.C., and J. John Sepkoski, Jr., of the University of Chicago revealed that insect diversity has exceeded that of four-limbed vertebrates since Carboniferous times (about 325 million years ago). The investigators compiled geochronological records for 1,263 insect families, relying on extensive fossil records reported in German, Russian, and Chinese literature. Objectives of the study were to determine the fossil diversity and rates of evolution of insects and to relate these data to the worldwide development of angiosperms (flowering plants) that originated in the Cretaceous Period (about 125 million years ago). One conclusion was that the high diversity and radiation of modern insect families began nearly 100 million years before flowering plants first appeared, rather than after and in response to their appearance. The researchers also concluded that the increasing diversity of insect families has persisted over geologic time because of low extinction rates rather than because of high rates of evolution during particular periods.

The merit in using fossilized material to interpret evolutionary relationships is often controversial. A study reported during the year, however, demonstrated the utility of using extinct insects to resolve a dilemma regarding the relationships between major groups of organisms. An Australian termite, *Mastotermes darwiniensis* (order Isoptera), had long been considered the most primitive isopteran and the "missing link" between cockroaches and termites. To establish the relationship between termites and roaches, Rob DeSalle, Ward Wheeler, and David Grimaldi of the American Museum of Natural History, New York City, and John Gatesy of Yale University used molecular techniques to examine and compare DNA sequences from the genes of *M. darwiniensis* and other living species of insects as well as an extinct termite *(M. electrodominicus)* from the Dominican Republic. The fossil, preserved in amber 25 million–30 million years old, yielded what was at the time the oldest DNA extracted from a fossil. (In mid-1993 scientists reported recovering DNA from a weevil encased in amber 120 million–135 million years old.) The investigators concluded that termites, including the genus *Mastotermes,* are a monophyletic group (all derived from the same common ancestor) that evolved independently from the roaches.

Most flies (order Diptera) emit and hear low-frequency (100–500 Hz) sounds that travel short distances, whereas crickets emit high-frequency (usually above three kilohertz) sounds audible at much greater distances. Daniel Robert and Ronald R. Hoy of Cornell University and John Amoroso of the University of Florida reported the discovery of a parasitoid fly (genus *Ormia*) having an ear capable of detecting high-frequency sounds made by crickets (genus *Gryllus*). Male field crickets produce far-reaching high-frequency sounds to attract females; however, female parasitoid flies are also attracted to the calling males, on or near which they deposit larvae that burrow into the host cricket. The cricket dies within 10 days, by which time the larvae have developed into pupae that emerge. The newly discovered hearing organ (tympanic ear) in the fly is anatomically and functionally characteristic of a cricket's and represents an instance of convergent evolution that allows the fly to exploit the mating behaviour of its host.

James T. Cronin and Donald R. Strong of the University of California at Davis conducted experiments to examine egg-laying patterns of a parasitoid, the fairyfly wasp (*Anagrus delicatus*), in relationship to its plant hopper host, *Prokelisia marginata*. Plant hoppers, the most abundant herbivorous insects in the Atlantic and Gulf coastal marshes of North America, both feed and lay eggs on salt marsh cord grass (*Spartina alterniflora*). The female wasp seeks out and lays its eggs only in the eggs of plant hoppers. The investigators measured the time the wasps took to search grass leaves for plant hopper eggs and then to deposit their eggs. They discovered that the wasps spent more than an hour on a plant once plant hopper eggs had been located. Although other plant hopper eggs were available to parasitize, a female wasp laid only a few of her eggs before leaving to search other plants, thus distributing her eggs among different leaves of grass. Such behaviour stood in contrast to the traditional view that parasitoids minimize the time invested in egg-laying activity. The researchers found that 20–30% of the cord grass leaves in the habitat aged and died during the approximately 24 days required for parasitoid larval development, resulting in deaths of the eggs of both species of insects. One conclusion was that, although wasp egg-laying rates are lower than can be achieved, the strategy of spreading eggs among several grass patches increases the probability that at least some offspring survive.

(ANNE R. GIBBONS)

This article updates the *Macropædia* article INSECTS.

Ornithology. The ability of captive African gray parrots (*Psittacus erithacus*) to mimic human speech and other sounds is well known, but observations of wild populations in West Africa had not indicated that they practice vocal mimicry naturally; that is, of the kind commonly seen in such birds as mockingbirds and starlings. However, analysis of a sound recording of a gray parrot in Zaire revealed the unmistakable reproduction of sounds from nine bird species and one kind of bat, the first evidence of sound copying by gray parrots in the wild. Furthermore, additional tapes of wild gray parrots in Gabon and Côte d'Ivoire suggested that such impressionism may be widespread.

That American blue jays eat large numbers of acorns in autumn and bury many more for winter consumption has long interested ornithologists, for although these nuts contain unpalatable tannins known to upset the digestive

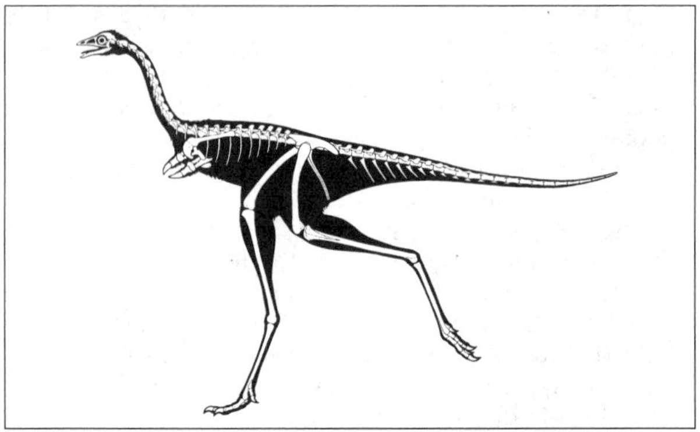

Fossils of *Mononychus olecranus* show a number of interesting structures, including stubby forelimbs, each with a single claw. Paleontologists continued to debate the place of the 75 million-year-old *Mononychus* in the development of birds from reptiles.
MICK ELLISON

enzymes of other animals that consume them, blue jays appear to suffer no harm. Carter Johnson of South Dakota State University discovered that jays eating acorns that had been invaded by acorn weevil larvae suffered no weight loss provided that each bird consumed with the nuts roughly 100 larvae a day. By comparison, other jays that ate only pristine, uninfested nuts did lose weight.

An individual Clark's nutcracker, another hoarder, may hide 30,000 conifer seeds in 6,000 separate holes in the forest floor. The birds successfully retrieve many of the seeds, displaying an excellent spatial memory, but Alan Kamil of the University of Massachusetts at Amherst and J.P. Balda of Northern Arizona University found in experimenting with some birds' orienting ability that the birds relocated seeds whether or not they approached each cache from the same direction as when burying the seeds. Thus, instead of relying on direction as an aid to memory, the nutcrackers may generate a kind of "cognitive map."

In the U.K., where the breeding biology of common bird species probably has been more widely studied than in other countries, egg-laying dates for 33 species of the 82 studied showed a trend, over the 30 years to 1990, toward earlier laying. Among the species the advance varied from one to 22 days, with a mean of 8 days. One contributory cause could be global warming.

The dunnock, or hedge sparrow, a small dun-coloured European perching bird (passerine), was the subject of a 10-year study by N.B. Davies of the University of Cambridge published as *Dunnock Behaviour and Social Evolution*. Within a population of dunnocks, nearly every conceivable mating system can be found. Some males monopolize the sexual favours of two females, while others have but one mate and still others share either one or two females with another male. Why then, when most birds are monogamous or nearly so, do dunnocks have such a variable mating system?

In broad outline Davies' finding is that the dunnock's mating system is a product both of a variable ecology and of conflict between individuals. A female will defend a territory large enough to satisfy her nutritional requirements. Males then defend territories that enclose female territories and, in so doing, control the reproductive opportunities of the females. Some territories are so large, however, as to require two males to defend the one or two occupant females. Thus commences one of the many conflicts. A female prefers both males to mate with her so that both stay and feed the offspring. In contrast, each male prefers to monopolize the female. Thus, the dominant male attempts to guard the female and keep his weaker rival at bay. The female, preferring the attention of both males, attempts to find the weaker male, who will be enticing her at a distance from a bush. It is the female's task to elude the dominant male. Once she has done so, he will flit about frantically looking for the pair so as to break them up.

Knowledge of *Archaeopteryx,* the most well-known ancient fossil bird, comes from a half-dozen specimens found in Bavarian rocks about 150 million years old. A somewhat younger fossil bird, *Sinornis satensis,* which dates from about 135 million years ago, had been known from only two specimens, one from Spain and one from Mongolia, until a third, more complete specimen, found in China, was described in the early 1990s. It was the only one of the three to be found with intact hand bones, which reveal the transition from reptilian forelimb to avian flight wing. Furthermore, the specimen displays a grooved wrist bone, which would have enabled this early bird to fold its wing back as modern birds can. On the other hand, *Sinornis* also shows a short, toothed reptilian snout and a lizardlike pelvis. In 1993 a still younger fossil bird, 75 million years old, was described from two partial skeletons unearthed in Mongolia. The species was flightless, having had stubby arms ending in a large single claw, and may have evolved from an earlier flying form, as did rheas, emus, and ostriches. Named *Mononychus olecranus,* meaning "one claw, elbow head," the fossil bird appeared more closely related to modern birds than to *Archaeopteryx*. (See *Zoology,* above.)

An average of two to three fully scientifically defensible discoveries of new bird species are made each year, adding to the approximately 9,250 living species known. In the past two years new discoveries included two warblers from China: the Chinese leaf warbler (*Phylloscopus sichuanensis*), distinguished from its closest relative, *P. chloronotus,* by its very different song and calls, and the Hainan leaf warbler (*P. hainanus*), a distinctively deep-yellow species.

A summary of the results of an exceptionally long-term study (more than 40 years) of the fulmar, a seagoing petrel, revealed that males most commonly do not first breed until they are 10 years old and females, 12 years. The fulmar's mean adult life span appeared to be about 34 years, and the oldest known individual died at about age 46.

(JEFFERY BOSWALL)

This article updates the *Macropædia* article BIRDS.

MARINE BIOLOGY

Against the background of a prediction by the Intergovernmental Panel on Climate Change in 1990 that the global sea level is set to rise at the rate of 50–90 cm per 100 years, a Bermudian study in 1993 revealed that coastal areas of mangrove were being lost even at the current lower rates of 28 cm per 100 years. (A centimetre is about 0.4 in.) Mangrove fringes were shown to have kept up, by peat accumulation, only with mean sea level rises of 9–19 cm per 100 years. From 1983 to 1990 salt marshes in the Mississippi River delta were lost to the sea by coastal submergence at the rate of 50 sq km (19.3 sq mi) per year. In response, U.S. scientists investigated the potential for creating new salt marsh habitats on dredged material on which smooth cordgrass (*Spartina alterniflora*) had been transplanted. Initially, the transplanted marshes had lower sediment concentrations, fewer crustaceans, and greater *Spartina* densities than those of natural marshes but, given time, transplanted marshes could function as natural marshes.

Waters of the Antarctic (or Southern) Ocean generally exhibit a low production of phytoplankton (the plant and plantlike component of plankton) and a low standing phytoplankton crop despite uniquely high nutrient content. South African studies of this so-called Antarctic Paradox demonstrated locally enhanced primary productivity associated with water stabilization by ice-melt water around Bouvet Island and the South Sandwich Islands in the far South Atlantic Ocean. Joint U.S. and U.K. studies showed that numbers of Antarctic fur seals (*Arctocephalus gazella*) and macaroni penguins (*Eudyptes chrysolophus*) correlated positively with the density of Antarctic krill (*Euphausia superba*), posing important new questions as to how swimming (and flying) predators locate and aggregate near concentrations of marine prey.

U.S. researchers showed that both natural assemblages and cultures of phagotrophic nanoflagellates (the tiniest flagellates that ingest nutrients in the form of particles) consume and digest a variety of marine viruses, necessitating changes in current concepts of microbial processes in the sea. A Norwegian study concluded that decline of some blooms (rapidly formed dense populations) of the coccolithophorid microalga *Emilian huxleyi* was attributable to infection by viruses and consequent lysis (disintegration) of the algal cells. The same workers reported from Norwegian and Danish waters unusual viruslike particles with tails. The heads measure 340–400 nanometres (billionths of a metre), six to seven times larger than most marine viruses, and the tails are 2.2–2.8 micrometres (millionths of a metre) long. They may be new giant viruses whose host is unknown. Very large single-celled organisms, first discovered in the mid-1980s in the gut of a surgeonfish (*Acanthurus nigrofuscus*) and assumed to be protozoans, were shown by U.S. researchers using RNA analysis to be giant bacteria, the largest known to date. Measuring a half millimetre (0.02 in) in length, the reclassified organisms challenged scientists to explain how bacterial-cell architecture and nutrient-transport systems can support cells so large.

A U.K. experiment conducted from the RRS *Discovery* from April to August 1989 as part of the Joint Global Ocean Flux Study (JGOFS) observed the south-to-north development of the spring phytoplankton bloom in the North Atlantic. As recently reported by investigators, the start of the bloom was correlated with the onset of water stratification, and seasonal succession commenced with diatoms, followed by coccolithophores, flagellates, and dinoflagellates. German studies detailed the distribution of zooplankton (the animal and animal-like component of plankton) at two sites in the temperate northeast Atlantic from the surface down to 4,500 m (14,800 ft). Downward from about 2,000 m (6,600 ft) above the seafloor, the depth-related decline in numbers of organisms and biomass was arrested. This characteristic was partly attributed to an upward flux of organic material, which was now recognized as a general feature in the deep ocean but the intensity and constancy of which was still poorly understood.

Trilobite larvae (so called for their resemblance to the extinct trilobites) of the horseshoe crab *Limulus polyphemus* were found overwintering in densities of 1,000–10,000 individuals per square metre (about 11 sq ft) at depths greater than 15 cm in the intertidal sands of Delaware Bay on the U.S. east coast. Hitherto it had been assumed that all such larvae emerge in summer. This previously unrecorded life-history phenomenon might indicate a physiological tolerance that has contributed to the success of this ancient species over geologic time. Larval behaviour of scleratinian corals (*Manicina areolata*) off Panama and of fish species on Caribbean reefs was shown to exhibit remarkable lunar periodicity associated particularly with the timing of new moons. Synchrony of behaviour has advantages, but the adaptive significance of new moon timing remained to be explained. (ERNEST NAYLOR)

This article updates the *Macropædia* articles CRUSTACEANS; FISHES; MOLLUSKS; etc.

BOTANY

Every four or six years, scientists assemble at an International Botanical Congress. The purpose of the gathering is to exchange research information and to pass resolutions that will guide research efforts in the future. In 1993 the 15th such meeting took place in Yokohama, Japan, the first ever to be held in Asia; both Crown Prince Naruhito and Princess Masako (*see* BIOGRAPHIES) of Japan attended the opening ceremonies. The formal sessions were preceded by meetings focusing on plant nomenclature, and field trips were offered both before and after the meeting. The more than 3,000 scientists who attended heard symposium talks from botanists representing more than 30 nations on a range of topics, from the evolution of maize (corn) and pattern formation in flowers and shoots to global ecology and forestry.

The majority of the earliest botanical books that still exist, either in museums or rare-book libraries, are the result of the intensive study of plants by those who have since been labeled herbalists. These botanist-physicians collected plants, made drawings, and described each plant by its "virtues"; that is, by its usefulness to humans for treating diseases and disorders. Their writings and illustrations appeared in collected works called herbals, which date back to the Middle Ages. Interest in medicinal and other uses of plants eventually developed into the present subdiscipline called economic botany and more recently into ethnobotany, which is the study of plant uses by indigenous peoples such as those who exist today in parts of Africa, South America, and the South Pacific. As a result of the work of the herbalists of yesterday and the ethnobotanists of today, many medicinal properties of plant extracts have been discovered. One of the more recent is taxol, a compound made by evergreens of the genus *Taxus,* which has been shown to be active against several kinds of cancer.

The biological activity of taxol was first investigated in the late 1960s and early 1970s, when the compound was shown to disrupt the cell-division cycle (mitosis). Because the hallmark of cancer is uncontrolled cell proliferation, the compound appeared promising as an agent for slowing or halting tumour growth, and the desirability of producing it in quantity for medical research stirred the interest of both botanists and chemists. Taxol was first isolated from the inner bark of the Pacific yew tree (*Taxus brevifolia*). Unfortunately, the chemical is present in the bark in very low concentrations, and stripping the bark kills the tree, a limited resource in old-growth forests of the northwestern U.S. and Canada.

Recently a close chemical relative of taxol, deacetylbaccatin III, was isolated from leaves of the European yew tree (*Taxus baccata*). The discovery was important because it provided chemists with a chemical that could be converted to an active substance similar to taxol; furthermore, because the leaves regrow on the plant, the trees do not die following harvest. Of perhaps even greater significance was a report in 1993 that taxol is produced by a fungus found growing as a parasite on the bark of a species of yew tree in Montana. The finding suggested the possibility of producing taxol in large fermentation tanks similar to the way penicillin is produced from the fungus *Penicillium notatum.* Meanwhile, other laboratories were engaged in devising chemical analogues of taxol that might prove as good as or better than the original compound in clinical trials—another sign of the growing enthusiasm for this family of drugs, first discovered in plants.

The range of studies that used *Arabidopsis thaliana* as the experimental organism of choice continued to expand during the year. The small plant, which until recently had been known only as an inconspicuous weed, was fast becoming an invaluable tool for research in plant genetics, plant physiology, plant developmental biology, and plant molecular biology. *Arabidopsis* belongs to the mustard family, which includes such important crops as cabbage, broccoli, cauliflower, rape seed, and bok choy. The information explosion centring on *Arabidopsis* partially explained why this organism was chosen for a multinational genome research project, similar in direction to the much more publicized human genome effort.

Because the plant is small, up to 30 cm (12 in) in height, it can be grown in large numbers in small spaces. Its diminutive seeds can be germinated in quantity in a single petri dish, making it easy to screen for plants having genetic mutations. By 1993 mutant plants had been isolated for a long list of characters. The small genome (total genetic endowment) for *Arabidopsis* was estimated to be about 100 million nucleotide bases, which are the molecular building blocks of DNA, which carries the genetic code. Compared with the human genome (estimated to be about three billion bases), this organism presents a much simpler model and allows for the analysis of defective as well as normal genes, using all of the power of modern biotechnology. Many of the mutations so far discovered are in so-called homeotic genes, resulting in disturbed patterns of development such that flower parts appear in incorrect locations. For example, flower petals become stamens (pollen-producing male organs), or stamens become carpels (ovule-bearing female structures). Using such developmental mutants, scientists were achieving a deeper understanding of the ways in which genes are regulated (switched on and off) at appropriate times. (PHILIP D. REID)

MOLECULAR BIOLOGY

Red blood cells, or erythrocytes, are specialists in carrying molecular oxygen (O_2) from the lungs to the tissues of the body and for carrying carbon dioxide (CO_2) in the opposite direction. Hemoglobin, which is responsible for the red colour of blood, is the oxygen-carrying protein in erythrocytes. Carbonic anhydrase is the enzyme that, by catalyzing the conversion of carbon dioxide to another chemical species, allows the blood to take up carbon dioxide rapidly from the tissues and release it rapidly in the lungs. Hemoglobin uses atoms of iron for reversibly binding oxygen, whereas carbonic anhydrase uses atoms of zinc at its catalytic centre.

All of the carbonic anhydrase in blood is found in the erythrocytes. It is significant that there is none of the enzyme in the blood plasma, the liquid portion of the blood. Indeed, in 1992 it was discovered by Eric D. Rousch and Carol A. Fierke of the Duke University Medical Center, Durham, N.C., that blood plasma contains a protein that strongly inhibits carbonic anhydrase. The inhibitor ensures that any carbonic anhydrase that might leak from the erythrocytes into the plasma will be rapidly inactivated. Why must carbonic anhydrase activity be restricted to the erythrocytes?

Answering this question requires an understanding of the structure and function of hemoglobin. This protein is a tetramer, composed of four iron-containing, oxygen-binding subunits (called hemes) chemically bonded to a large protein unit (globin). Each subunit is 500 times larger than the molecule of oxygen that it carries. The reasons why hemoglobin must be a tetramer and as large as it is reveal an intricate choreography of chemical events that ensure that, whereas hemoglobin meets the body's need for oxygen, it simultaneously assists in eliminating carbon dioxide. They also reveal how much complexity underlies even seemingly simple physiological processes and how perfection of a function can be approached by stepwise refinements of imperfect mechanisms.

The efficient transport of oxygen and of carbon dioxide depends on the modulation of the affinity of hemoglobin for oxygen by five different factors. Their roles will be discussed separately and then the individual strands woven together.

One modulating factor is the cooperative interaction among hemoglobin's subunits in binding oxygen. The affinity of the tetrameric hemoglobin for oxygen is less than would be expected for a comparable monomeric protein; *i.e.,* one containing a single heme subunit. For example, compared with myoglobin, a protein found in red muscle fibre, hemoglobin has only 1/26 the affinity for oxygen. Myoglobin functions well in its roles of storing oxygen in red muscle and increasing the rate of oxygen diffusion, but its affinity for oxygen is so great that it would be useless as a carrier of oxygen in the blood, for it would not release oxygen to the tissues. On the other hand, although the amount of oxygen bound by myoglobin increases in direct proportion to the concentration of oxygen (to the limit of one bound O_2 molecule per monomeric molecule of myoglobin), the amount of oxygen bound by hemoglobin increases exponentially as the 2.8th power of the concentration of oxygen (to the limit of four O_2 molecules per tetrameric molecule of hemoglobin). Hence, at low concentrations of oxygen, doubling its concentration would only double the amount bound by myoglobin but would increase the amount bound by hemoglobin 5.6-fold.

It is the cooperativeness among hemoglobin's subunits that accounts for its exponential response to changes in oxygen concentration. The essence of the cooperativeness is that binding of a molecule of oxygen to one subunit makes it easier for a second molecule of oxygen to bind to a neighbouring subunit; the binding to the second causes a further increase in affinity for O_2 at the third subunit; and so on. This cooperativeness depends on a change in the shape of the subunit upon binding of oxygen. Because the subunits are tightly packed together in the hemoglobin tetramer, a change in shape of one subunit induces a comparable change in shape of its neighbours and thus an increase in their affinity for oxygen.

The second modulating factor is acidity, or the concentration of protons (hydrogen ions, or H^+). When a subunit of hemoglobin binds oxygen, it not only changes shape but also becomes a stronger acid and releases a proton. The oxygenation of one subunit of hemoglobin (HHb^+) to form oxyhemoglobin (HbO_2) can be expressed by the following equilibrium:

(1) $$HHb^+ + O_2 \rightleftarrows HbO_2 + H^+.$$

The balance of this reaction can be shifted forward or in reverse by a change in the concentrations of either reactants or products. Raising the concentration of O_2 favours the forward direction and the binding of O_2, whereas raising the concentration of H^+ (increasing the acidity) favours the reverse direction and the release of O_2.

The effect of acidity on the binding of oxygen to hemoglobin was first reported by the Danish physiologist Christian Bohr in 1904 and is now called the Bohr effect. Bohr knew that working muscles become acidified and so understood that his discovery was physiologically significant. One source of acidification is lactic acid, a metabolic product made by muscle cells in extracting energy from glycogen. The other is carbon dioxide, which is hydrated (combined with a molecule of water [H_2O]) under the catalytic influence of carbonic anhydrase to make the bicarbonate ion (HCO_3^-), accompanied by the release of a proton. This reaction can be expressed by the following equilibrium:

(2) $$CO_2 + H_2O \rightleftarrows HCO_3^- + H^+.$$

As the erythrocytes pick up carbon dioxide from the tissues, the hydration of CO_2 via carbonic anhydrase generates acid (H^+). The increase in H^+, in turn, drives reaction (1) in reverse, thus favouring the release of O_2. Once the erythrocytes reach the lungs, their release of CO_2 via the reverse of reaction (2) diminishes H^+ and so drives reaction (1) forward, favouring the uptake of O_2. That the release of carbon dioxide in the lungs facilitates the binding of oxygen to hemoglobin was appreciated by the British physiologist J.S. Haldane in 1914.

There is another important aspect to the effect of acidity on the oxygenation of hemoglobin via reaction (1), one having to do with buffering, or minimizing changes in the acidity of the blood. As shown in reaction (2), carbon dioxide entering the blood from the tissues is hydrated by carbonic anhydrase in the erythrocytes with the release of protons. The protons could seriously acidify the blood traversing the tissues were it not for the fact that they are at the same time being taken up by oxyhemoglobin as it releases oxygen—the reverse of reaction (1). Conversely, in the lungs the loss of carbon dioxide from the blood would seriously deplete H^+ but for the fact that the hemoglobin present is releasing protons as it binds oxygen—reaction (2). Loss of carbon dioxide thus helps drive the oxygenation of hemoglobin in the lungs, while gain of carbon dioxide drives the release of oxygen from oxyhemoglobin in the tissues. The involvement of protons in both reactions (1) and (2) provides the basis for this synergism while simultaneously allowing the transport of large amounts of potentially dangerous acid without significant changes in the acidity of the blood.

The third factor contributing to the modulation of the affinity of hemoglobin for oxygen is carbon dioxide. Not all of the carbon dioxide that enters the blood from the tissues is hydrated via reaction (2). Some of it reacts directly and reversibly with hemoglobin and in so doing diminishes hemoglobin's affinity for oxygen. This reaction provides another mechanism through which the release of oxygen is favoured in tissues, where carbon dioxide is high, and the binding of oxygen is favoured in the lungs, where carbon dioxide is low.

The chloride ion (Cl^-) is the fourth modulating factor for hemoglobin. The hemoglobin molecule contains binding sites for chloride, and the binding of chloride decreases hemoglobin's affinity for oxygen. The significance of the chloride effect is enhanced by changes in chloride concentration within the erythrocyte during the respiratory cycle. As blood passes through the tissues, chloride rushes into the erythrocytes, facilitating the release of oxygen. When the blood enters the lungs, chloride leaves the erythrocytes, favouring the binding of oxygen. Carbon dioxide is the agent that drives these movements of chloride, and it does so in the following way. In the tissues carbon dioxide diffuses into the erythrocytes, where carbonic anhydrase converts it into bicarbonate while freeing a proton—reaction (1). Whereas the proton is taken up by the hemoglobin as it releases oxygen via reaction (2), the bicarbonate remains free in solution. As the concentration of bicarbonate rises, it diffuses from the erythrocyte by way of specialized channels in the cell membrane. Because electrical neutrality must be maintained, for each negatively charged bicarbonate that diffuses out of the erythrocyte, some other negatively charged ion must go the other way. That compensating ion is chloride, the most abundant negatively charged ion in blood plasma.

This shift of bicarbonate out of the erythrocytes when they are in the tissues and into the erythrocytes when they are in the lungs, with chloride always moving in the opposite direction, has long been known as the chloride shift, or the isohydric shift. It was earlier understood as a necessary consequence of the confinement of carbonic anhydrase to the erythrocyte. It can now be seen as yet another adaptation that aids delivery of oxygen from hemoglobin to the tissues and uptake of oxygen by hemoglobin in the lungs.

The final factor involved in the modulation of hemoglobin is a compound called 2,3-diphosphoglycerate (DPG). DPG has long been known to be required in catalytic amounts as a cofactor for the action of the enzyme phosphoglyceromutase (PGM). That enzyme is required for the metabolism of the sugar glucose, which occurs in erythrocytes. It had not been clear, however, why erythrocytes contain much higher concentrations of DPG than do other cells. This seeming anomaly was clarified in the early 1970s by Reinhold and Ruth Benesch of Columbia University, New York City, who showed that hemoglobin contains a binding site for DPG and that occupancy of that site markedly decreases the affinity of hemoglobin for oxygen.

In the absence of DPG, hemoglobin would be a poor carrier of oxygen because it would hold oxygen so tightly as to prevent its significant release to the tissues. DPG, by binding to the oxygen-free form of hemoglobin but not to oxyhemoglobin, competes with oxygen in the erythrocytes for binding to hemoglobin. In so doing it decreases the affinity of hemoglobin for oxygen just enough to make it an effective carrier of oxygen from the lungs to the tissues. One of the adaptations of the human body to the modestly lower oxygen levels encountered at high altitudes is an increase in the concentration of DPG in erythrocytes. This increase provides more complete release of oxygen from hemoglobin in the tissues without significantly compromising the degree to which hemoglobin is oxygenated in the lungs.

Given the foregoing background, one is now able to understand why carbonic anhydrase activity in the blood must be restricted to the erythrocytes and why an inhibitor of carbonic anhydrase is needed in the blood plasma. If carbonic anhydrase were present in the plasma, then protons and bicarbonate would be formed in the plasma from carbon dioxide as blood passed through the tissues. The bicarbonate would then diffuse into the cells, and chloride would have to move out to maintain electrical neutrality. Loss of chloride from the cells would decrease the binding of chloride to hemoglobin, which would increase hemoglobin's affinity for oxygen at the very time when a decrease in affinity would be desirable to assist the release of oxygen to the tissues. Conversely, in the lungs bicarbonate leaving the erythrocytes would exchange with chloride moving in; again, this exchange would decrease the affinity of hemoglobin for oxygen just when the opposite was desirable.

It is thus clear that the binding of chloride to hemoglobin, with concomitant decrease in affinity of hemoglobin for oxygen, can have physiologically useful effects only when the hydration of carbon dioxide is restricted to the erythrocytes. The presence of carbonic anhydrase inside the erythrocytes, and of an inhibitor of carbonic anhydrase outside these cells, guarantees such an outcome.

In the end, given all the things that hemoglobin accomplishes, one wonders not why this exquisite molecule needs to be so much bigger than the oxygen that it carries but rather how so small a molecule can do so much.

(IRWIN FRIDOVICH)

See also Botanical Gardens and Zoos; Earth Sciences; Environment.

This article updates the *Macropædia* articles AGRICULTURE; Animal BEHAVIOUR; BIOCHEMICAL COMPONENTS OF ORGANISMS; The BIOLOGICAL SCIENCES; BIOSPHERE; CANCER; CONSERVATION OF NATURAL RESOURCES; DISEASE; The Theory of EVOLUTION; The Principles of GENETICS AND HEREDITY; MAMMALS; REPRODUCTION AND REPRODUCTIVE SYSTEMS; SENSORY RECEPTION.

Literature

The 1993 Nobel Prize for Literature was awarded to Toni Morrison (*see* NOBEL PRIZES), an American novelist who had been instrumental, proclaimed London's *Daily Telegraph,* in "breaking the male domination of Black American literature." She was only the eighth woman to win the prize, and her victory was unexpected. When Morrison's name was announced, Christopher Bigsby, professor of American Studies at the University of East Anglia, declared, "She is certainly one of the most interesting novelists writing in the United States today." But, he added, "After the award to Derek Walcott last year, it strikes me that there is an element of the 'politically correct' about it." Walcott, a West Indian poet, had also been recognized as black. It was agreed that Morrison's finest novel was *Beloved,* a tragic story of black slaves in 19th-century America. She had been described in the *New York Times* as "the nearest thing America has to a national novelist." The Swedish Academy announced that the honour was given to her for her depiction of black America in novels "characterized by visionary force and poetic import" that give life to "an essential aspect of American reality."

In France the barbarities of the 19th century were commemorated by the publication of *Germinal,* Émile Zola's grim novel about striking coal miners. The work was sold at newsstands and published in the form of a broadsheet newspaper with headlines. It was one of several editions available to accompany an ambitious new film version of *Germinal,* which was studded with an all-star cast and directed by Claude Berri.

France's Prix Goncourt was awarded to a Lebanese-born novelist, Amin Maalouf, for his novel *Le Rocher de Tanios.* It was the second time in six years that this important French prize had gone to an Arab. The novelist David Malouf, who was favoured to win, was runner-up for the Booker Prize for Fiction in the U.K. with his novel *Remembering Babylon.* An Arab born in Australia, Malouf was also admired for his libretto to Michael Berkeley's new opera, *Baa Baa Black Sheep*—a study of Rudyard Kipling's childhood and his fascination with imperial India. It was noted that among the principal candidates for the Booker Prize, only Tibor Fischer had been born in Britain.

JAMES KEYSER—TIME MAGAZINE

Toni Morrison

ENGLISH

United Kingdom. General dismay was expressed at the death of E.P. Thompson (*see* OBITUARIES), a left-wing historian and peace campaigner. Thompson was "one of the most important writers, historians, and polemicists of the Modern Age and a central figure in English left-wing culture and politics for almost half a century." Two new books by the versatile author appeared during the year. One was *Alien Homage,* an account of the Indian poet Rabindranath Tagore and his relationship with Thompson's father. The other was *Witness Against the Beast,* a study of William Blake as a political thinker and ally of Thomas Paine.

The novelist Salman Rushdie was honoured by the organizers of the annual Booker Prize for Fiction in English. His novel *Midnight's Children,* which won the prize in 1981, was adjudged the "Booker of Bookers"—the best of the 25 "literary novels" awarded the prize since 1969. The news of Rushdie's honour was not received with general approbation. Cambridge scholar John Casey held that Rushdie was an inadequate storyteller; Rushdie's admirers had been challenged to remember the "plot" of *Midnight's Children*—to report "how the book *ends*"—and none had been able to answer. Casey concluded that the Booker Prize (and other literary prizes) claimed and received too much respect—since English novelists had lost "confidence in what the novel can do, of its being part of politics and history."

Casey's arguments were widely supported in a year fertile with sneers at English novelists and suspicion of Asian contenders. Allan Massie, a former candidate for the prize, declared that "the whole game of the serious novel"—or the "literary" novel—might be over. His long article in the *Daily Telegraph* was headed "Death on the Shelf: Have English novelists lost the plot?"—again referring to the literary novelists' failure to tell stories. Massie observed that the latest list of the Best Young Novelists (promoted by *Granta*) had made "no impression on anyone beyond the literary world." Other societies, other cultures, might still produce great novels because the writers were "confident that people want to learn" and that there was "a society on the march: properly guided, it could reach a satisfactory destination." That confidence was lacking in contemporary Britain, and "one feels the game is up: the novel, that beautiful and flexible art form, is on the way out."

Despite this despair, two critical studies were published and well received, both discussing contemporary fiction. One was *The Modern British Novel* by Malcolm Bradbury; the other was *After the War: The Novel and English Society Since 1945* by D.J. Taylor. Both were clearly engaged with their subject—and indeed polemical. In the *London Review of Books,* Patrick Parrinder described Bradbury as a "self-conscious progressive," while Taylor, a younger man, was a "self-conscious reactionary."

Roddy Doyle

DAVE BENETT—ALPHA/GLOBE

Fiction. Vikram Seth (*see* BIOGRAPHIES), the most charming of the Indian writers currently popular in Britain, was much applauded for his 1,000-page novel *A Suitable Boy.* As the title might suggest, the novel concerned a girl seeking a husband—a middle-class girl of 19, living in northern India in 1950. This was just three years after Partition, when India was preparing for its first general election. The scene was set, as Pico Iyer pointed out in the *Times Literary Supplement,* "not during the tumult of Independence, but in the uncertain interregnum that came after." The love story was entwined with "a wide variety of interlinked characters and stories," said John Lanchester in the *London Review of Books,* and displayed a knowledge of Indian politics, law, economics, and religion, all expressed in a lucid prose. "The resulting structural clarity is remarkable," said Lanchester. But the book might be thought too "mild-mannered," suspected Iyer: "Can an epic be built on charm alone?"

Another ambitious and admired novelist, surprisingly passed over by the Booker Prize judges, was the cosmopolitan Irishman Brian Moore. His novel *No Other Life,* although set in a Caribbean island resembling Haiti, was taken by Terry Eagleton in the *London Review of Books* to be a kind of strategy for rationalizing Moore's reluctance to live in Ireland—Moore was an atheistic member of a Belfast Catholic family. His new novel concerned a poor orphan from the hills who had been trained by the local priests for a brilliant career in the church but stood for election as president of the island after the death of a (Papa Doc Duvalier-like) dictator and finally became part of the island's mythology. The most nightmarish part of the story, according to John Banville in the *Times Literary Supplement,* concerned the priest-politician's visit to his dying mother, who had lost her faith. "There is no other life," she said. Eagleton took this phrase, the book's title, to mean also that there was no hope for "change on earth"—reform or revolution; he deplored Moore's apparent pessimism.

Other novels by respected authors disappointed critics and prize committees. William Boyd's *The Blue Afternoon* was a complicated narrative that began in Los Angeles in 1936 and moved back in time to the Philippines in 1902. The central figure was an elderly man who had been imprisoned for 20 years, after being convicted for committing gruesome serial murders. The man recounts his life story to a woman he claims as his daughter. Though the mutilated corpses were realistically described, no clue was offered as to whether the man was guilty of the crimes. In the *London Review of Books,* Ronan Bennett complained, "To set up a mystery and then wilfully refuse to explain it is to frustrate and irritate the reader." He was unsure whether the novel was an attempt at "a knowing, Post-Modernist send-up" of thrillers or had tried to tell a story but failed. Anita Brookner published *A Family Romance,* the story of a grave, cultivated London spinster and her extrovert aunt—"a Parisienne, with a voracious appetite for life, messy, solipsistic, guiltlessly dependent," as described by *Times Literary Supplement* reviewer Aisling Foster, who added, "The effect is as diverting as attendance at a family gathering where an aged maiden aunt whispers the biographies and peccadilloes of every passing guest." Allan Massie's "comedy of morals," *These Enchanted Woods,* presented another melancholy account of contemporary British life. After a woman, married into the sombre world of the Scottish landed gentry, chances to meet her former lover, an aggressive businessman, she resumes their relationship amid a cast of melancholy Scots and Londoners. A.N. Wilson, a keen churchman turned militant unbeliever, expressed his divided feelings in *The Vicar of Sorrows.* The story was of a contented clergyman without faith who falls in love with a free-living, nomadic girl and comes to accept a strange, new religious faith, leading him to madness and death. The seriousness of Wilson's intention was indicated by his unusual lack of self-assurance and the solemnity of his literary references.

None of these novels was short-listed for the Booker Prize, an institution that was severely criticized during the year. The chairman of the judges, Lord Gowrie, asserted that his team had been looking for "passion" in the contestants' novels; it was widely felt that they had not found it. They selected as their prizewinner a book about an engaging Irish child, *Paddy Clarke Ha Ha Ha* by Roddy Doyle, a Dublin schoolmaster whose previous Irish comedies had proved quite popular and had been adapted as films. Another contender was Tibor Fischer, a Hungarian born in England in 1959. His black comedy *Under the Frog* chronicled the Russian suppression of the Hungarian rebellion of 1956. Canadian-born Michael Ignatieff, a London television commentator, was also a candidate. His novel *Scar Tissue* was a stern description and discussion of the death of the narrator's mother (both are nameless) from a neurological disease. Chicago-born Carol Shields also represented Canada. Her novel, *The Stone Diaries,* was described in the *Daily Telegraph* as the story of "a woman who looks back over a life rich in episode, but devoid of emotional involvement, in an attempt to find substance in her character." More characteristic of Commonwealth literature was *Crossing the River* by Caryl Phillips, who was born in the West Indies, was raised in Britain, and became a teacher at a U.S. college. The work was a complex narrative about the descendants of an 18th-century man who sold his three children into slavery. Australian David Malouf was similarly preoccupied with imperial history. His novel *Remembering Babylon* was the story of a boy living in the last century who had been lost in the Australian bush and brought up by Aborigines.

Biography. The most discussed biography, and perhaps the greatest commercial success, was *The Downing Street Years* by Baroness Thatcher, the former prime minister, who was deposed by her own Conservative Party. It was flanked by the memoirs of two of her ministerial colleagues: *The Turbulent Years: My Life in Politics* by Kenneth Baker and *Diaries* by Alan Clark. They were all reviewed together, rather sardonically, by another ministerial colleague, Tristan Garel-Jones, who had been highly involved in the maneuvers within the party to remove Thatcher from office. It was his assessment that Clark had played a walk-on part and that Baker was a leading man, while Thatcher was "the stage, the script and even the play itself." He cautioned against trusting the two men and remarked that "Margaret Thatcher had found a method of making money—and mischief too." Conservative reviewers of the three books seemed more condemnatory than writers from the opposition benches. One keen Conservative, Sir Peregrine Worsthorne, wrote of the "tastelessness" of Baker's account: "On more than one occasion Mr. Baker falls beneath Mr. Clark's low standards." Worsthorne was so excited by the Conservative Party's intrigues, however, that he concluded, "No lack of literary skill can prevent Mr. Baker's truthful account of the political assassination of Mrs. Thatcher from being unputdownable." Less partisan readers conceded that Thatcher's book, at least, was rather well written.

STEVE VOTE

David Malouf

Among other studies of recent politicians was Philip Ziegler's biography of the former Labour prime minister Harold Wilson. It was the third on Wilson to appear within 18 months. As a result, more attention was paid to John Campbell's biography of Wilson's opponent, Edward Heath, the Conservative prime minister whose enthusiasm for European cooperation had helped to make him a formidable critic of fellow Conservative Thatcher. Campbell's careful biography drew attention to the redeeming virtues of this stubborn, rather awkward politician. Peter Paterson published a biography of one of Wilson's most embarrassing ministers, the late George Brown. The very title of *Tired and Emotional: The Life of Lord George Brown* was a joke, for the first three words had been a catchphrase, originally a euphemism for Brown's habitual drunkenness. Jeremy Paxman wrote in *The Independent* that "of all the recent political biographies this is the most entertaining read." A more serious labour politician, Harold Laski, was rediscovered and commemorated in two long biographies, one by Michael Newman and another by Isaac Kramick and Barry Sheerman. Laski was a brilliant teacher and lecturer, most influential between 1931 and 1945—inspiring not only British students but "especially those from America and what was not yet called the Third World," as E.J. Hobsbawm put it, reviewing the biographies in the *London Review of Books*. "Except by his former students, he was soon forgotten. . . . And yet, would the greatest and most humane reforming administration of the century have come about without him?"

Among the nonpolitical biographies, the most compelling was the life of the poet Philip Larkin, written by Andrew Motion. Larkin's letters had been published in 1992 and evoked considerable disquiet among readers, especially those who had most enjoyed and admired Larkin's poems. The letters seemed to present a very small-minded man, the epitome of "political incorrectness"; the biography in no way allayed readers' distaste. "I read it with growing admiration for the author," wrote the playwright Alan Bennett in the *London Review of Books,* "and, until his pitiful death, mounting impatience with the subject." Bennett found that Larkin's poems remained unscathed by the biographical revelations, such as they were, and held that it had been a sound "marketing strategy" to publish the letters first; the letters might help sell the life, but the life would not sell the letters. Another biography of particular interest to the literary world was *Rebecca's Vest* by Karl Miller, the founder and former editor of the *London Review of Books,* and previously an editor with the *Spectator,* the *New Statesman,* and the *Listener.* The memoir (its title derived from Sir Walter Scott's *Ivanhoe*) did not dwell on his literary life in London but told of his childhood and youth in Scotland, where his parents split up and left him to the care of his aunts, and then his experience of dandified Cambridge of the 1950s, furnishing some explanation of his career as a writer, editor, and teacher.

(D.A.N. JONES)

United States. *Fiction.* Not the best of times but not the worst either, the year 1993 in American fiction turned out be as much a time of testing for new and younger writers as it was a period dominated by

E. Annie Proulx
JERRY BAUER

established masters. The latter, however, were represented mainly by reprints and old material. Such was the case at least with William Styron's *A Tidewater Morning,* a slender volume comprising three short stories published in magazines in the previous decade. Critical reception was respectful, with few reviewers pointing out that Styron, still considered in the conventional wisdom to be one of the giants of contemporary American letters, had not published a full-length work of fiction since the novel *Sophie's Choice* nearly 15 years before.

Too Far from Home, an omnibus collection of the prose of Paul Bowles (edited by poet Daniel Halpern), contained only one new story, from which the volume took its title. But with the inclusion of the complete text of Bowles's 1949 masterwork, *The Sheltering Sky,* and a dozen of his marvelous stories as well as travel essays, sections from a memoir, and journals and letters, the book offered the kind of retrospective pleasure that seemed markedly absent in the Styron collection.

The new novel by the African-American Louisiana realist Ernest Gaines, *A Lesson Before Dying,* told the story of a killing and its aftermath in a rural Louisiana parish in the 1950s. It won the underrated Gaines new appreciation and turned readers' attention toward some of his impressive earlier accomplishments. Philip Roth's mock-confessional novel *Operation Shylock,* by contrast, did not do as well either with reviewers or in the bookstores. For all of its frenetic energy and wild comedy based on the motifs of the doppelgänger and Jewish nationalism, the book fell short of complete success as a narrative.

T.C. Boyle, a younger writer with a rising reputation, came out with a new novel, *The Road to Wellville,* which, however, also did not win much favour with the reading public. Among Boyle's peers it fell to Virginia writer Richard Bausch, with his new novel, *Rebel Powers,* and Michigan-based Charles Baxter, with his second novel, *Shadow Play,* to win good critical attention. Both writers explored with fine effect the fragmentation of the American family. Susan Richards Shreve's *The Train Home* was a romantic variation on the desires of a middle-class woman.

Among other writers in mid career who published fiction in 1993 with varying degrees of success were Madison Smartt Bell, whose *Save Me, Joe Louis* again displayed the author's obsession with the world of the criminal; Ishmael Reed, who brought out a sharp satire on academia, racism, and American mores in *Japanese by Spring;* and Bob Shacochis and Richard Powers, who published long convoluted novels—*Swimming in the Volcano* and *Operation Wandering Soul,* respectively—both of which were nominated for best fiction in the National Book Awards.

Octogenarian Harriet Doerr, who won the American Book Award for first fiction for her novel *Stones for Ibarra,* came out with a second work, *Consider This, Señora,* which was also set in Mexico and done in pastels. Reviewers loved it. Reception was more equivocal for David Leavitt's historical tour de force *While England Sleeps.* The author came under heavy attack for his unacknowledged borrowing from the Spanish Civil War memoirs of British poet Stephen Spender and for his candid portrayal of homoerotic love.

After the great success of his memoir *Stop-Time* in the late '70s, writer-jazz pianist-teacher Frank Conroy produced only one slim collection of stories. After a long hiatus he came out in 1993 with *Body & Soul,* a charmingly composed novel of education in the mode of Dickens (and the spirit of Hollywood of the '40s) about the rise of a poor young pianist and composer from New York City. E. Annie Proulx published *The Shipping News,* the sweetly told saga of a gentle newsman from New York state who makes a new life in the cold clime of Newfoundland. Proulx was the recipient of several prizes (*see* below). Wilton Barnhardt made a walloping success with his second novel, *Gospel,* about two American religious scholars, one an old, retired, but still randy professor and the other a young female graduate student, and their quest across Europe and Africa for a fabled lost biblical text.

An African-American photographer from Pittsburgh, Pa., named Albert French made an impressive debut with *Billy,* the powerful re-creation of a crime committed in rural Mississippi in 1937. Charlotte Watson Sherman, a young African-American woman from Seattle, Wash., published a lyrical exploration of black identity in the northwestern woods, called *One Dark Body.* A novel in stories called *Scissors, Paper, Rock* was journalist Fenton Johnson's touching first book. Theatrical producer Eric Blau told the story of a Hollywood producer of horror films who wants to make an epic about Zionist Theodore Herzl in *The Beggar's Cup.* Among story collections of new writers Thom Jones's *The Pugilist at Rest* made the biggest splash for its nine evocative stories, many of them focusing on the Vietnam War and its aftermath.

Nonfiction. In *To Feel These Things,* Leonard Michaels composed startling sentences and evocative essays on everything from smoking to going to the movies. Equally intriguing were the thoughts and revelations in *The Sixties,* the final volume of the late Edmund Wilson's notebooks. The young Delmore Schwartz could be heard in *Delmore Schwartz and James Laughlin: Selected Letters,* the correspondence between the enfant terrible of post-World War II American poetry and his publisher. The young John Cheever was heard from again in *Glad Tidings: a Friendship in Letters,* the correspondence of Cheever and writer friend John D. Weaver between 1945 and 1982 (Weaver was the editor of the volume).

Several senior American men of letters published volumes of their essays. Gore Vidal brought out *United States: Essays 1952–1992* and master critic John W. Aldridge *Classics and Contemporaries.* Novelist E.L. Doctorow offered his selected essays under the title *Jack London, Hemingway, and the Constitution.* Chicago writer Richard Stern added *One Person and Another,* assorted reviews and essays on literary subjects. John Leonard put in with *The Last Innocent White Man in America,* and Ishmael Reed presented a polemical collection of essays called *Airing Dirty Laundry.* In these lively volumes everything from politics to race to sex to baseball came under sharp scrutiny. Among poets writing criticism, Adrienne Rich's *What Is Found There: Notebooks on Poetry and Politics* soared above the rest.

In the realm of memoir, Donald Hall's *Life Work* recounted his experience with the life of writing and the advent of a serious illness. In *Extra Innings* septuagenarian novelist and critic Doris Grumbach continued the exploration of aging that she had begun several years earlier with *Coming into the End Zone.* The volume concludes with a spare but moving meditation on the nature of home. Home and family stood out as motifs in James Conaway's affecting memoir *Memphis Afternoons* and in the sturdy and intelligent essays by Scott Russell Sanders in *Staying Put.* Clark Blaise focused on the paternal in *I Had a Father* and Diana Trilling on her marriage to the late literary critic Lionel Trilling in *The Beginning of the Journey.*

PHIL ROACH—PHOTOREPORTERS

Gore Vidal

Cornel West
TED THAI—TIME MAGAZINE

The major biographies of the year brought to life both literary and political figures. In *W.E.B. Du Bois: Biography of a Race,* historian David Levering Lewis embraced the worlds of literature and society in an important study. Stanley Weintraub, in *Disraeli,* produced a portrait of a political figure who was also a writer of fiction. Novelist Erica Jong portrayed the work and mind of Henry Miller in *The Devil at Large.* The life and work of the French novelist and dramatist Jean Genet was accorded full treatment in novelist Edmund White's *Genet: A Biography.* Thomas Powers chose as his subject physicist Werner Heisenberg and his connection to the events of World War II in *Heisenberg's War.* James E.B. Breslin, a literary critic with an interest in modern poetry, took on as his subject a major American painter in *Mark Rothko: A Biography.* Deborah Baker kept poetry in the forefront in *In Extremis: The Life of Laura Riding.*

Journalist Frank Browning explored the paradoxes of homosexual life in *The Culture of Desire.* In his book-length essay *A Place at the Table,* Bruce Bawer argued forcibly for recognizing homosexuals as a valuable segment of American society. Allan Bloom wrote a meditation on eros, tracing its origins and impact in the West in *Love & Friendship.* Social historian Richard Slotkin published *Gunfighter Nation: The Myth of the Frontier in Twentieth-Century America.*

Theology professor and critic Cornel West explored in *Race Matters* issues in the life of the black intellectual and the American citizen at large. John McPhee put together his latest magazine pieces in *Assembling California.* Novelist James Howard Kunstler traced the evolution of the modern American concept of urban planning in *The Geography of Nowhere.* In *Talk* National Public Radio's special correspondent Susan Stamberg brought together incisive and entertaining interviews over several decades with people from all walks of life. NPR commentator and poet Andrei Codrescu recorded the events of an idiosyncratic cross-country journey in *Road Scholar.*

Poetry. Poet and MacArthur fellow Jim Powell brought out *Sappho: A Garland,* new translations of the poems and fragments of the 6th-century BC poet from the Mediterranean island of Lesbos. The power of Sappho's poetry resonates throughout the brief 25 pages of this new rendering of her work. Twenty-one living American poets offered their versions of the cantos in *Dante's Inferno* (edited by Daniel Halpern). In *The Lost Book of Paradise,* translator David Rosenberg presented his imaginative translation of Genesis. John Hollander edited the impressive new two-volume Library of America edition of *American Poetry, the Nineteenth Century.*

Numerous volumes of new contemporary poetry made their appearance. The voice of Mark Strand in his linked poems in *Dark Harbor* made another attempt at transcendence. Bringing together 35 years of work in *The Owl in the Mask of the Dreamer,* longtime Alaska hand John Haines broke through the mask with a certain urgency, as in the title poem, which treats the history of sculpture. James Schuyler in his *Collected Poems* spoke in a more natural voice. Four female speakers make up the linked choruses in Margaret Gibson's *The Vigil.*

A.R. Ammons offered *Garbage,* a book-length poem on the subject of American trash and its implications. In *The Museum of Clear Ideas,* Donald Hall included some long poems that employ images from his beloved baseball. Among more conventional lyric collections worth noticing were Lawrence Raab's *What We Don't Know About Each Other,* Rosanna Warren's *Stained Glass,* and Mark Doty's passionate vision of America besieged by AIDS, *My Alexandria.*

Adrienne Rich was represented by her *Collected Early Poems, 1950–1970.* Sherod Santos published a sequence of poems and prose called *The City of Women;* Susan Ludvigson came out with *Everything Winged Must Be Dreaming,* Frederick Seidel with *My Tokyo,* the African-American poet Ai with *Greed,* and Jack Marshall with *Sesame.*

Prizes and Awards. Toni Morrison (see *Introduction,* above; NOBEL PRIZES) won the Nobel Prize for Literature. The Pulitzer for fiction went to novelist and story writer Robert Olen Butler for his collection of stories about Vietnamese Americans in Louisiana called *A Good Scent from a Strange Mountain.* The PEN/Faulkner Prize was awarded to novelist Proulx for her novel *Postcards.* Proulx's novel *The Shipping News* won the National Book Award for fiction and the Heartland Prize, as well as the prestigious Aer Lingus Prize of Ireland. A.R. Ammons won the National Book Award for poetry, and Gore Vidal took the nonfiction prize for his collected essays. Barbara Kingsolver won the *Los Angeles Times* prize for fiction for her novel *Pigs in Heaven,* and Mark Doty won for poetry.

(ALAN CHEUSE)

CORNELL UNIVERSITY; PHOTOGRAPH, CHRIS HILDRETH

A.R. Ammons

Canada. Two big literary guns came out blazing in 1993, Margaret Atwood with *The Robber Bride,* a highwaywoman in many guises—smuggler, émigré, child prostitute—and mistress of psychological terror, and Timothy Findley with *Headhunter,* which echoed Joseph Conrad's *Heart of Darkness* in its journey through darkest Toronto. Short-listed for the Booker Prize, however, was a less well-known author, Carol Shields, for *The Stone Diaries: The Life of Daisy Goodwill,* a novel built from the gritty details of everyday living. Grit, and plenty of it, was required by the women in Gail Scott's *Main Brides, Against Ochre Pediment and Aztec Sky,* which took place in the span of a summer afternoon and evening.

In *The Bookseller,* Matt Cohen portrayed a writer manqué, now dealing in used books, who strove to approach his brother, a successful doctor, although always indirectly, through other people. Nino Ricci's *In a Glass House,* the second novel in an intended trilogy, moved from Italy to Canada to Africa as it chronicled a young immigrant's search for himself. A woman's search for a mate, after the bloody winnowing of World War I, was at the heart of Hugh Hood's ninth volume of his planned 12-volume New Age series, *Be Sure to Close Your Eyes.*

Many kinds of distances—temporal, spatial, and, above all, psychological—were explored in Jane Urquhart's *Away* through the portrayal of several generations of Irish immigrants in Canada, while Audrey Thomas, in *Graven Images,* delved into the past to find many a familiar artifact of human life. In *Scar Tissue,* Michael Ignatieff, also short-listed for the Booker Prize, traced the effects on her family of a mother's disintegration from Alzheimer's disease. The novel probed depths of resentment until it found the source of healing.

Notable first novels included Linda Leith's *Birds of Passage,* in which the collapse of communism in Hungary mirrored the breakup of a marriage in Canada. In Catherine Bush's *Minus Time,* a daughter's adolescent struggle for freedom and maturity was set against her mother's career as an astronaut. Greg Hollingshead's *Spin Dry* took its readers for a funny wild ride through suburban mysteries. Metaphors of movement also played a role in his short stories in *White Buick,* a vehicle for presenting a colourful mix of characters.

Mavis Gallant, in her latest collection of stories, *Across the Bridge,* shuttled her readers back and forth across the fine line between ordinary goodness and ordinary evil, revealing the horror that can unexpectedly erupt from lives of limited expectations, while Evelyn Lau's *Fresh Girls and*

Margaret Atwood
JERRY BAUER

Other Stories uncovered the same dreary wickedness in more grotesque forms. Barry Callaghan offered little comfort in *When Things Get Worst.* Mark Frutkin's *In the Time of the Angry Queen* was an exuberant mélange of eccentrics engaged in playing games from chess to blindman's buff.

Among noteworthy poetry publications were Leonard Cohen's *Stranger Music: Selected Poems and Songs,* chosen from works written between 1956 and 1992, and Irving Layton's *Fornalutx,* a collection of some of his less well-known poems of frustration and bitter desire. Marilyn Bowering's *Love as It Is* illuminated true passion in the light of love as it is not, and, from a more detached position, Raymond Souster, in *Old Bank Notes,* pondered values as observed in the vaults of the old Imperial Bank in Toronto.

Collections for adults by two well-known children's authors were Dennis Lee's *Riffs,* variations on a theme of illicit love, and Sheree Fitch's *In This House Are Many Women.*

George Bowering was represented with two collections of poetry, elegiacally in *The Moustache: Remembering Greg Curnoe* and quirkily in *George Bowering Selected: Poems 1961–1992.* Judith Fitzgerald also came forth with *Walkin' Wounded,* which included a cycle of baseball poems and "Habit of Blues," a prose poem meditating on the fate of a novelist, the late Juan Butler. Two posthumous works by bp Nichol were published, *Truth: A Book of Fictions* and *First Screening.* (ELIZABETH WOODS)

FRENCH

Many important French intellectuals from the postwar period were honoured in 1993, among them Roland Barthes, Raymond Aron, Jacques Lacan, and Claude Lévi-Strauss. The first volume in the *Oeuvres complètes* of Roland Barthes, who died in 1980, appeared, bringing together all of his works published between 1942 and 1965 as well as a few previously unpublished ones. This volume permitted a better understanding of the originality of the author of *Mythologies.* Completely enclosed within his own system, Barthes used different languages in an attempt to approach both the text and, beyond that, an understanding of himself. Raymond Aron, whose intellectual development was traced by Nicolas Baverez, was shown as having been more preoccupied with politics than literature—in contrast to Sartre, for example (with whom Aron kept up a lifelong and passionate debate), who thought it possible to reconcile the two. In her essay *Jacques Lacan, esquisse d'une vie, histoire d'un système de pensée,* Elisabeth Roudinesco described with competence the path of the man who was to become for so many a master. Most notably, she showed that Lacan had yielded to Freud in two ways—through his studies of medicine, neurology, and psychiatry and his espousal, for a time, of surrealism. Finally, mention must be made of *L'Apport Freudien,* a collective work under the direction of Pierre Kaufmann, offering a new approach to the principal concepts of psychoanalysis.

In his *Regarder, écouter, lire,* Claude Lévi-Strauss invited the reader to roam with him through the arts. As he evoked Nicolas Poussin, Jean-Baptiste-Siméon Chardin, Maurice Ravel, Arthur Rimbaud, and Denis Diderot, he also sketched a self-portrait and unfolded his thought. Michael Panoff's *Les Frères ennemis* explored similarities and differences between Lévi-Strauss and Roger Caillois. Both men had problematic literary careers, but Lévi-Strauss came to be considered a profound thinker and the founder of a particular school of thought, while Caillois now passed for an inspired if unclassifiable dabbler. Denis Hollier's *Les Dépossédés* discussed Caillois as well as Henry Bataille, André Malraux, Jean-Paul Sartre, and Michel Leiris, all of whom were fascinated by a world that had no place for them but that demanded from them the sacrifice of their art.

Still in the realm of nonfiction, Geneviève Bollème's work, *Parler d'écrire,* examined the manner in which writers since the advent of literary journalism have talked about themselves and their activity. The book dealt at length with Marguerite Duras, who—as her last two works, *Ecrire* and *Le Monde extérieur,* bear witness—analyzed herself in depth. Also published were a collection of critical articles by Duras' husband, Dionys Mascolo, *À la recherche d'un communisme de pensée,* and a polemical text, *Haine de la philosophie.*

FREDERIC REGLAIN—GAMMA LIAISON

Amin Maalouf

The 21st and final volume of Marcel Proust's *Correspondance* was published, leading up to 1922; it had been edited by the recently deceased Philip Kolb. The volume showed Proust concerned with the books that he still had to deliver to his publisher, Gallimard. He admitted to Jacques Rivière a doubt that he would be able to finish his work. The *Correspondance* between Gustave Flaubert and Guy de Maupassant (the centenary of whose death was also celebrated in 1993) revealed the great affection uniting these two writers (at times one could imagine Flaubert to be Maupassant's father).

Among notable novels in 1993, *L'Invention du monde* by Olivier Rolin distinguished itself by its audacity and originality. Rolin describes one day on Earth: March 21, 1989. The raw material for the book was provided by some 500 periodicals in 31 languages. One of Rolin's intentions in writing this "book of all possible books" was to create a song of praise for literature in general. In *Les Jours ne s'en vont pas longtemps,* Angelo Rinaldi assembled a gallery of characters who displayed certain personality traits that are borrowed from members of the Parisian literary world. One was reminded, perhaps too quickly, of Marcel Proust. In *Des hommes illustres,* Jean Rouaud continued the family saga begun in *Les Champs d'honneur* (1990 winner of the Prix Goncourt); all of the grace of the first novel, however, had disappeared, ceding place to a style that was heavy and annoying. In *La Boucle,* Jacques Roubaud practically invented a language, assisted by the possibilities offered by the computer, in order to relate his childhood memories. He plunged into the labyrinth of his memory to write a book of rare density. The same theme was evoked, soberly, by Jean-Loup Trassard in *L'Espace antérieur.* Two young women, Christine Lapostolle and Lydie Salvayre, authored two particularly successful books on difficult subjects: *Le Grand large,* on suicide, and *La Médaille,* on the world of the factory.

The Prix Goncourt was awarded to Amin Maalouf, a French writer of Lebanese origin, for *Le Rocher de Tanios,* a sort of oriental fairy tale blending history and legend. Set in the 1830s, the novel showed a vengeful spirit passed on from generation to generation. The Prix Médicis was awarded to Emmanuèle Bernheim for *Sa femme,* a short text discussing jealousy and phantasms in a dry, sterile manner. Nicolas Bréhal received the Prix Renaudot for *Les Corps célestes,* the story of a friendship, and Marc Lambron received the Prix Fémina for *L'Oeil du silence,* a novel based on the life of Lee Miller, a fashion photographer for *Vogue* and the companion of Man Ray. (FRANÇOIS POIRIÉ)

Canada. Established French-Canadian novelists continued to do excellent work. Michel Tremblay published a sequel to his 1986 novel, *Le Coeur découvert,* the story of a homosexual liaison between Jean-Marc and Mathieu. The new novel, *Le Coeur éclaté,* described the breakup of their relationship, with Jean-Marc going off to Key

West in order to dull the pains of separation (insiders were aware of the novel's autobiographical dimension). Jacques Godbout's *Le Temps des Galarneau* was the sequel—after 26 years—to the author's most popular novel, *Salut Galarneau!*

A host of new novelists were vying for the reading public's attention. Stéphane Bourguignon's *L'Avaleur de sable,* written in a pungent and jerky style, showed the slow disintegration of a man who lost the woman he loved and tried to find reasons to go on living. Monique Proulx received the most critical plaudits in 1993. The film version of her 1987 novel, *Le Sexe des étoiles,* was released concurrently with her new novel, *Homme invisible à la fenêtre*. Its narrator, a paraplegic, commented on the human condition in a stingingly alive language.

There also was a copious outpouring of French-Canadian poetry in 1993. Two volumes in particular were worth noting: Madeleine Gagnon's *La Terre est remplie de langage* and Serge-Patrice Thibodeau's *Le Cycle de Prague*. Gagnon was adept at exploiting the tension between things as such and the symbolic meaning with which language invests them. A poet of growing reputation was Louise Dupré, whose *Noir déjà* treated themes like time and death.

Works belonging to genres often thought to be minor became publishing success stories. Readers of theatrical literature enthusiastically received Gilbert Dupuis's *Kushapatshikan,* a play criticizing present-day society. Dominique Demers, prominent author of children's literature, published *Les Grands Sapins ne meurent pas*. The year's most provocative contribution to the essay was François Ricard's *La Génération lyrique,* which examined the baby-boom generation of the '40s. (PIERRE HÉBERT)

GERMAN

At the beginning of the year, Germans were startled to learn that two of the former East Germany's most respected writers, Christa Wolf and Heiner Müller, had collaborated—however briefly—with the Communist secret service. At the same time, the writer Botho Strauss provoked a lively debate with his declaration of faith in right-wing values to the extent of endorsing violence and xenophobia. The political left, which had its origins in the radical upheaval of the late 1960s, appeared to be well on the defensive.

A number of literary works reflected the changing political climate, including a turning away from politics. The narrator of Ulrich Woelk's novel *Rückspiel* embodied the indifference of the contemporary generation to political questions. The title, "Return Game," referred to the unification of Germany, implying a possible revival of Nazism, as well as to the backlash against the 1960s. Helmut Krausser's cult novel *Melodien* unfolded its vast historical panorama from the time of the Renaissance to the present day in a replay of the myth of Orphic melodies invested with the power to transform humankind and the world. Swiss author Adolf Muschg's *Der rote Ritter* was a more sober assessment of myth. Employing the Parsifal story, he showed that myth must be abandoned when it is taken over by ideology. Hanna Johansen's charming collection of "tales and laments," *Über den Himmel,* joined fantasy and science. Wolfgang Hilbig's kafkaesque *"Ich,"* remarkable

Adolf Muschg
JERRY BAUER

for being told from the point of view not of the victim but of the spy (both writers), recognized a relationship between writing and surveillance. In his diary of 1992, *Am Sonnenhang,* Reiner Kunze launched a number of accusations against fellow writers; the public theme, however, was juxtaposed with private ones, in particular the death of his father.

Aging and mortality were leitmotivs of the year. Hermann Peter Piwitt's moving *Die Passionsfrucht* told of the *amour fou* of an aging German artist for a young Italian woman painter. In her customary ironic manner Gabriele Wohmann described three sisters growing old with dignity and humour (*Bitte nicht sterben*). Martin Walser's *Ohne einander* developed the author's long-standing preoccupation with sexual rivalry and the struggle of each against all, combining these themes with a wicked attack on a prominent literary critic. A complementary theme was the evocation of childhood, idyllic in the case of Johannes Schenk's *Dorf unterm Wind,* set in the north German village of Worpswede at the end of World War II, and darker in Gert Hofmann's ironically titled *Das Glück,* a child's-eye view of the breakup of a marriage, in which both parents appear helpless. More radically, Ludwig Harig's *Die Hortensien der Frau von Roselius* called into question the reliability of memory, suggesting that fantasy plays an equally important part in reconstructing the past. In Gerhard Köpf's *Papas Koffer* the narrator's search for Ernest Hemingway's lost papers became simultaneously the quest for his own youth.

Christoph Hein disappointed his readers with his first postunification novel, *Das Napoleon-Spiel,* the story of a millionaire lawyer who decides to kill a complete stranger. The equation of moneymaking with murder and of murder with the campaigns of a Napoleon may have produced interesting results, but the narration was tedious. Two writers whose literary origins were in the proletarian, documentary tradition turned to stories of crisis and flight—in Austrian Franz Innerhofer's *Um die Wette Leben* to Italy, in Ludwig Fels's *Bleeding Heart* to Tangiers.

There were a number of novels addressing political and social issues. Friedrich Christian Delius' *Himmelfahrt eines Staatsfeindes,* a roman à clef on the events of the year of terror, 1977, remained dedicated to political consciousness-raising, implying the symbiosis of terrorism and state security. Otto F. Walter's *Die verlorene Geschichte,* the stream-of-consciousness story of an illiterate neo-Nazi Swiss construction worker who accidentally befriends an illegal immigrant from Thailand, had its obvious topicality, as did Uwe Saeger's *Landschaft mit Dornen,* which depicted teenage violence in a small town in eastern Germany. Michael Kleeberg's picaresque *Proteus der Pilger* and Wolfgang Hegewald's *Die Zeit der Tagediebe* were bizarre satires on the development of post-World War II German society. A new topic for writers from the former German Democratic Republic was the gay scene in Berlin, evoked both in Friedrich Kröhnke's *P 14* and in Mario Wirz's AIDS novel, *Es ist spät, ich kann nicht atmen*.

Two novels of special interest were *Das Leben ist eine Karawanserei* by Emine Sevgi Ozdamar, a Turkish author writing in German, and Edgar Hilsenrath's *Jossel Wassermanns Heimkehr*. The former introduced the wider German public to the customs, history, and culture of the many Turks living in their midst, while the latter evoked the lives of Jews in Eastern Europe; the individual stories were set against the impending Holocaust.

In his elegant and thought-provoking travel diary, *Fliegende Pfeile,* Peter Rosei brought to life places such as Paris, London, Istanbul, Crete, and Canada. Of the many volumes of poetry published during the year, Heinz Czechowski's *Nachtspur,* Wulf Kirsten's *Stimmenschotter,* and Richard Wagner's *Heisse Maroni* were especially noteworthy. (J.H. REID)

SCANDINAVIAN

Denmark. The year 1992 witnessed the appearance of some first-class writing. Peer Hultberg continued in his established manner in the highly acclaimed *Byen og verden,* a work of sometimes humorous, often biting, sketches of provincial life. Knud Holten's *Der var engang* was a fantastic picaresque novel of development. Juliane Preisler's *Dyr* was a psychological thriller about loneliness, obsession, and manipulation. Ib Michael's *Den tolvte rytter* recalled his earlier success, *Vanillepigen,* and incorporated perspectives spanning the 16th to the 20th century.

Historical novels came from Hans Lyngby Jepsen, with his *Men fuglene flyver* about the Holy Roman emperor Frederick II (1194–1250), and Helle Stangerup, with her *Sankt Markus nat,* a carefully researched novel set during the Danish Reformation.

Some trilogies were completed: Suzanne Brøgger rounded off her *Crème fraîche* and *Ja* with *Transparence,* while Leif Davidsen completed his "Russian" novels with *Den troskyldige russer,* a thriller set in Russia after the fall of the Soviet Union. Villy Sørensen concluded his memoirs with a third and final volume, *Perioder, 1961–74.*

Significant posthumous publications were Christian Kampmann's *Skilles og mødes*, a novel concerned with a mother fixation, bisexuality, and AIDS, and Thorkild Hansen's *Artikler fra Paris 1947–52*, a collection of lively observations and reflections that also shed light on Hansen's subsequent writings.

The late Henrik Bjelke's *Skandalens sted* was a volume of essays in which the author argued for stylistic excellence, presenting excerpts from the works of writers of particular importance to himself.

There was distinguished poetry as well. Death was a motif in Pia Tafdrup's *Krystalskoven*, while travel and departure were the subject of Henrik Nordbrandt's masterly *Støvets tyngde*. Thorkild Bjørnvig celebrated his 75th birthday with a new volume entitled *Siv vand og måne*. A newcomer was Kirsten Hammann, whose first collection of poems, *Mellem tænderne*, showed a linguistic brilliance, dark humour, and bite rarely found in Danish literature. Her latest publication, *Vera Vinkelvir,* a cross between a prose poem and a novel, had the same mixture of humour and pessimism.

(W. GLYN JONES)

Norway. Weighty in every sense was Ketil Bjørnstad's documentary novel *Historien om Edvard Munch.* This literary biography of Norway's leading painter marshaled extensive primary documentation with impressive sensitivity. Contemporary Norway was dissected by Jan Kjærstad's brilliant and humorous novel *Forføreren,* centred upon a leading television personality, and by Ingvar Ambjørnsen's witty *Utsikt til paradiset,* in which a desperately lonely good-for-nothing spends his time observing the goings-on in a block of flats opposite his own. Provincial towns provided the backdrop to Knut Faldbakken's thriller-style novel *Ormens år* and Edvard Hoem's *Engelen din, Robinson.* Rural Norway in the period around 1918 was convincingly brought to life in *Julie* by Anne Karin Elstad. In Finn Carling's *Dagbok til en død* a widow in a diary to her deceased husband lays bare the complex relationships within her family. Unique in its kaleidoscopic succession of hypnotic visual fragments was Tor Ulven's plotless novel *Avløsning.* Among short stories, Øystein Lønn's collection *Thranes metode* was distinguished for its Pinteresque style.

The thriller continued to flourish. Fredrik Skagen's *Nemesis* focused on an international conference on atomic waste held in Trondheim, with countries hungry for nuclear weapons attempting to secure expertise from the former Soviet Union. Gunnar Staalesen's *Begravde hunder biter ikke* unfolded a bloodcurdling plot against the backdrop of a keenly observed Oslo.

The keynote of Jan Erik Vold's collection of poems *Ikke* was social satire and of Lars Saabye Christensen's *Den akustiske skyggen* serious humour. With its 526 posthumous poems, Ernst Orvil's *Siste dikt* marked a worthy farewell from a productive poet.

In an annus mirabilis for biographies, pride of place could but go to Tordis Ørjasæter for her well-researched *Menneskenes hjerter: Sigrid Undset—en livshistorie.* Haagen Ringnes drew an intimate, revealing portrait of a many-faceted central character in 20th-century Norwegian cultural life in his *Johan Borgen, Har vi ham nå?* Tom Lotherington's *Wildenvey—et dikterliv,* besides being a frank account of the colourful life of the Don Juan of Norwegian poets, took the reader lightheartedly into the world of the artistic and intellectual elite of the first half of the 20th century. Published posthumously, Per Amdam's *Bjørnstjerne Bjørnson 1832–1880* was a reminder of a sad loss to Norwegian scholarship. (TORBJØRN STØVERUD)

Sweden. In the fiction of 1993 the past frequently illuminated the present. For example, a male response to contemporary feminism may, perhaps, be perceived in Stewe Claeson's *Pigan i Arras,* in which the husband of Saint Birgitta (1303–73) was shown taking second place, even when sick, to her religious preoccupations. Carina Burman's epistolary novel *Min salig bror Jean Hendrich* was a cheerful spin-off from research about the poet Johan Henrik Kellgren (1751–95), while Agneta Pleijel's *Fungi* ingeniously contrasted Schopenhauer's pessimism with his student the naturalist F.W. Junghahn's belief in the underlying harmony of creation. Lars Gustafsson's *Historien med hunden,* set in Austin, Texas, was a metaphysical thriller about the existence—or nonexistence—of God (and the indubitable existence of evil). Lars Andersson's *Vattenorgel* featured several well-known members of late 19th-century artistic circles faced with historical change, and Björn Ranelid's *Mitt namn skall vara Stig Dagerman* was a fictitious autobiography of the brilliant author Dagerman, who committed suicide at a young age in 1954. Authentic memoirs were published by major writers grappling with sickness and the shadow of death: Sven Delblanc's *Agnar;* Tomas Tranströmer's *Minnena ser mig;* Göran Tunström's *Under tiden;* and Jan Myrdal's *Inför nedräkningen.*

Kjell Espmark continued his searing investigation of modern Sweden in *Lojaliteten,* narrated by a nonagenarian worker lamenting the compromises of social democracy and the decline of the welfare state. Ola Larsmo's *Himmel och jord må brinna* presented workers' struggle for rights by juxtaposing 1909, 1917, 1976, and 1990. Kerstin Ekman's impressive *Händelser vid vatten* was both a crime story and a psychological study of an isolated community faced with social change. Ingrid Sjöstrand's *Isranunkel* was an episodic domestic variant of social change spanning 50 years. Two young women writers, Maria Fröjdh in *Blåeld* and Åsa Lundegård in *Nöd och lust,* wrote accomplished novels exclusively focused on family and sexual relationships with a positive outcome, while Mare Kandre accorded the devil sympathetic treatment in a playful alternative creation story, *Djävulen och Gud.* This stood in contrast to their male contemporaries, who produced works in a darker vein. Robert Kangas' *Fjärde budet* showed the brutalization of an unwanted child, and Magnus Dahlström's *Nedkomst* appeared as callously provocative in its cruelty.

Jesper Svenbro's learned and humorous verse in *Samisk Apollon och andra dikter* won plaudits, as did newcomer Henrik Nilsson's collection, *Utan skor.*

(KARIN PETHERICK)

ITALIAN

Literature stood no chance against the competition of reality in 1993. No fiction could beat the appeal of daily newspapers and TV news bulletins with their relentless stories of financial empires tumbling down, well-known magnates biting the dust, powerful political parties crumbling, and mighty politicians of all stripes standing accused of corruption and complicity with organized crime. There was, predictably, a flurry of instant books by journalists, sociologists, and magistrates dissecting the scandals of the day and assessing the threat they posed to national unity, but these books were more talked about than bought or read. To stimulate a flagging market, some publishers introduced the "supereconomical" paperback offering integral classics, from Epicurus to Freud, for less than the price of a cup of coffee.

Meanwhile, new literature continued to be published in quantity and quality not significantly different from in the past. Some works of fiction turned out to be strangely attuned to the apocalyptic mood sweeping across the country. By far the most compelling was *Il cardillo addolorato* by Anna Maria Ortese, a well-established though still somewhat underrated writer. Set at the end of the 18th century and written in a rich, transparent style, this remarkable novel told the story of three young men from Northern Europe who go to Naples and remain trapped there by the bewitching coldness of a mysterious young woman; the real protagonist, however, was the goldfinch of the title, whose haunting, magical singing time and again announces the defeat of reason and love and the triumph of a dark inhuman power over all human calculations and projects. It was a measure of the author's artistic achievement that her pervasive use of irony in respect to characters and events only served to increase the tension and suspense of the fiction. The same device achieved the opposite effect in Aldo Busi's *Vendita galline Km 2,* a rambling and occasionally witty monologue, ostensibly by a dead lesbian, in which the art of social gossiping was elevated to breathtaking new heights. Also dead was the narrator, as well as most of the other voices, in Roberto Pazzi's *Le città del dottor Malaguti,* an elegant, captivating story in which fantasy and reality cooperated to explore and expose, with a mixture of compassion and contempt, the sick rituals of a beautiful provincial city that, rather cleverly, was identified as Ferrara only in the novel's last word. More decidedly gloomy and enigmatic was Franco Ferrucci's *Fuochi,* a series of episodes in the sentimental journey of a young man, ending with his choosing at once love and death. What was intriguing and unsettling about this unusual book were its apparent contradictions: the sensuality of its language and the insubstantiality of its temporal and spatial settings, its rhapsodic structure and

GRAZIA IPPOLITO—FRANCA SPERANZA

Anna Maria Ortese

style, and the coherence and unity of the theme of death that inspired it. Equally dark in mood, but more clearly contemporary in setting, were the six short stories in Elisabetta Rasy's *Mezzi di trasporto,* six solitary journeys by six different means of transport into the same unpredictable, but generally inhospitable and degraded, contemporary world.

The year saw the return to fiction writing, after a silence of over 30 years, of Domenico Rea, one of the most forceful and expressive Neapolitan writers of the 1940s and '50s. In setting, subject, and style his *Ninfa plebea*—the story of a young woman's progression from the gutter to the altar—appeared still to belong to that literary period, despite its having acquired a new lexical explicitness that might not have been acceptable then.

Much more successful was *Bagheria,* Dacia Maraini's autobiographical account of her childhood in Sicily in the late '40s, an evocation of the island's natural beauty and, at the same time, an impassioned denunciation of its more recent moral and environmental devastation. Set at the opposite end of the country and covering the period from World War II to the present, were the stories of *Il silenzio* by Gina Lagorio, a book of classic beauty and maturity, in which a woman comes to terms with her solitude, still finding in the world of nature and society plenty of reasons for loving life.

Finally, most notable among new writers who made their mark during the year was Paolo Maurensig. His novel, *La variante di Lüneburg,* was the compelling story of two chess masters, one a Jew and the other a former Nazi officer, who, beyond the war and the concentration camp of Bergen-Belsen, continue to seek one another in order to play out one last deadly game. This book seemed to encapsulate all the main features of the most recent and distinguished Italian narrative: on the one hand, the search for a rich, lucid, and effective language, far from both extremes of banality and literary pompousness; on the other, the sense that literature can only reveal, but not resolve, the mystery that lies at the heart of history and reality. (LINO PERTILE)

SPANISH

Spain. The coveted Planeta Prize, traditionally awarded each year to a Spaniard for the best pseudonymously submitted manuscript of fiction, went to the Peruvian novelist Mario Vargas Llosa (whose application for Spanish citizenship was approved in July); his *Lituma en los Andes* is a story of political violence and social regression—laced with Dionysian overtones—in a contemporary Andean setting. Runner-up in the Planeta competition was essayist Fernando Savater's first attempt at extended fiction, *El jardín de las dudas,* a lively epistolary exchange between Voltaire and an enlightened French noblewoman exiled to the benighted latitudes of 18th-century Madrid.

José Luis Sampedro and Antonio Gala both appeared regularly on best-seller lists all year long. *El águila bicéfala,* Gala's collection of meditations on the eternal riddle of love, prepared readers for his denser work, *La pasión turca,* which probed the complex passions of a middle-class Spanish woman driven to extremes by self-destructive love for a duplicitous Turk.

Mario Vargas Llosa
DIANNE WALKER—GAMMA LIAISON

Sampedro published two collections of short stories—*Mar al fondo* (1992) and *Mientras la tierra gira*—as well as the concluding volume of an ambitious trilogy (*Los círculos del tiempo*); focused on the antimonarchist uprising of 1808 and the proclamation of the Second Republic in 1931, *Real sitio* offered an intimate, two-tiered drama set against a historical background of political intrigue and national upheaval.

Critics lavishly praised Juan Marsé's ninth novel, *El embrujo de Shanghai,* in which the contrasts between a dreary neighbourhood in postwar Barcelona and the exotic atmosphere of Shanghai in 1948 underscore the gulf between the innocence of Marsé's adolescent narrator and the grim reality of a treacherous adult world. Francisco Umbral exposed the twisted values and perverse milieu of an idealistic young fascist in *Madrid 1940;* in Arturo Pérez-Reverte's riveting thriller for bibliophiles, *El club Dumas,* a rare-book dealer unravels the mystery of a diabolical 12th-century manuscript; and *Días contados,* by Juan Madrid, graphically depicted the seamy side of life in the capital's rough Malasaña district. Fans of Antonio Muñoz Molina welcomed his first collection of short stories, *Nada del otro mundo.*

Two milestones bracketed the literary year: the sudden death of Juan Benet in January (*see* OBITUARIES) and the award in December of the Cervantes Prize, the highest honour in Hispanic letters, to the prolific novelist Miguel Delibes.

(ROGER L. UTT)

Latin America. The major writers in Latin America in 1993 were the Mexican Carlos Fuentes and the Peruvian Mario Vargas Llosa. Fuentes published both a novel and a book of essays. In his well-constructed novel, *El naranjo, o los círculos del tiempo,* the author returned to some of his lifelong themes, such as the implications for the present of the conquest of the Americas and the circularity of time. The five stories in this volume not only expressed Fuentes' most immediate sensual pleasures but also contained his oldest memories. In his essays, *Geografía de la novela,* he covered a broad range of literary and cultural topics. In typical Fuentes fashion, he discussed Juan Goytisolo in the context of Cervantes, and Cervantes in the context of Goytisolo.

In Vargas Llosa's novel *Lituma en los Andes,* a minor character from previous novels, Lituma, becomes the protagonist. In this well-narrated work, Vargas Llosa considered how the forces of rationality and irrationality function in an impoverished society. The novel had its origins in the author's firsthand experience with Peruvian politics. Vargas Llosa also published an autobiographical account of his recent unsuccessful candidacy for the presidency of Peru, *El pez en el agua.* During the year Vargas Llosa publicly renounced any future participation in Peruvian politics and accepted Spanish citizenship.

The Argentine writer Mempo Giardinelli joined Fuentes and Vargas Llosa among the recipients of the Rómulo Gallegos Prize. (Vargas Llosa was awarded this prestigious prize in 1967 and Fuentes 1977). Giardinelli's outstanding recent novel, *Santo Oficio de la memoria,* was generally considered the primary reason for his receiving this prize.

In Mexico the major novelists to publish, besides Fuentes, were Igancio Solares, Luis Arturo Ramos, and René Aviles Fabila. *El gran lector* by Solares continued in the author's vein of historical novels. It was the critical portrayal of a Mexican president who evinces qualities of several former Mexican heads of state. Ramos' fourth novel, *La casa del ahorcado,* is a satirical work about the protagonist's impotence. Avilés Fabila continued his long writing career with an essaylike novel about a writer who considers suicide, *Réquiem por un suicida.*

Colombian writers who published outstanding books were Ricardo Cano Gaviria, Germán Espinosa, Juan Manuel Silva, and Felipe Agudelo Tenorio. Cano Gaviria, who had already written essays and fiction, published a well-crafted epistolary novel set in the 1920s, *Una lección de abismo.* The author of several historical novels, Espinosa wrote yet another historical work, *Los ojos del basilisco.* The poet Silva published his first novel, *La tramposa de la patasola,* a work dealing with violence and the construction of myths in Colombia. Agudelo Tenorio, also a poet, published his first novel, under the title of *Las raíces de los cielos.*

Two of the most noteworthy books in Venezuela were *Pieles de leopardo* by Humberto Mata and *Yo soy la rumba* by Angel Gustavo Infante. *Pieles de leopardo* was a volume of short fiction that found its unity in the stories' common themes. In *Yo soy la rumba,* Infante used the theme of music to reconstruct life in Venezuela in the 1960s.

Both established and new writers published important books in the Southern Cone. In Chile, novelist Jorge Edwards published his first set of stories since the 1960s, *Fantasmas de carne y hueso.* Jaime Collyer's third novel appeared, *Gente al acecho,* and Sergio Gómez wrote his first volume of short stories, *Adiós, Carlos Marx, nos vemos en el cielo.* The most notable books to appear in Argentina were *El Dock* by Matilde Sánchez, *Prontuario* by David Viñas, *Cuando digo Magdalena* by Alicia Steimberg, *Acerca de Roderer* by Guillermo Martínez, *El ojo de la patria* by Osvaldo

Soriano, and *Paredón Paredón* by Gabriel Báñez.

Vargas Llosa was not the only writer in Peru to publish memoirs. Fiction writer Julio Ramón Ribeyro came forth with *La tentación del fracaso,* and novelist Alfredo Bryce Echenique wrote *Permiso para vivir: (antimemorias).* The Peruvian Miguel Gutiérrez published a lengthy and complex novel in three volumes, *La violencia del tiempo.* A further Peruvian novel of note was *País de Jauja* by Edgardo Rivera Martínez. (RAYMOND LESLIE WILLIAMS)

PORTUGUESE

Portugal. The annual Foreign Fiction Award for the best foreign novel in English translation was awarded by *The Independent* to José Saramago for *The Year of the Death of Ricardo Reis.* It was the first time that this coveted literary prize had distinguished a Portuguese author.

The most original novel of the year was *A Barragem* by Júlio Moreira, a writer who had attracted growing attention for his uncommon choice of themes and unusual ways of handling them. The situations described in this narrative were real enough, but they took place in an imaginary realm that conferred on them the quality of a universal allegory. The idea of clandestine human relationships and their frailty in an insecure environment was explored in the changing voices of the narrator, a method that communicated a sense of fear and of an imminent apocalypse. The aura of doom was enhanced by the characters' visit to the city condemned to be flooded by the finished dam.

Three literary prizes were awarded to Helena Marques—one of them the prestigious Great Prize for Fiction by the Association of Portuguese Authors—for her first novel, *O último cais.* Turning her back on the current fashion of experimentalism, Marques produced a narrative of deceptive simplicity, a love story that exposed human weaknesses and ill-assorted passions in a close-knit community of her native Madeira. The strong characters of this novel were women who slowly but firmly broke through the geographic and social insularity of their lives. Their silent liberation mirrored the restlessness of their menfolk, who discover through them their own identity and the complex security of love. A perceptive study of changing moods, the novel gives a moving picture of life that is tempered in its romantic shades by a quiet and aesthetic acceptance of death. (L.S. REBELO)

Brazil. In 1993 many works of regional fiction appeared. Antônio Olinto's *Sangue na floresta* was set in the contemporary Amazon region. Myriam Campello's semi-autobiographical Carioca novel *São Sebastião Blues* viewed the infighting for prizes and recognition among the city's literary cliques. Edla van Steen's *Madrugada,* set in São Paulo, was a novel about the death of the city as viewed through the death of four people; it was awarded the Coelho Neto Prize by the Brazilian Academy of Letters. The distinguished poet Décio Pignatari turned to fiction in his bildungsroman of life in São Paulo, *Panteros*. The dramatist Maria Adelaide Amaral's first novel, *Aos meus amigos*, was a roman à clef about the suicide of Décio Bar, a poet of her late-1960s university generation. Luiz Antônio de Assis Brasil began a new trilogy of life in Rio Grande do Sul—from the end of the second empire through the era of Getúlio Vargas—with the novel *Perversas famílias*. Also of note was new fiction by Ana Miranda, João Gilberto Noll, and Esdras do Nascimento. Antônio Callado's collection of five stories, *O homem cordial e outros contos*, reflected his personal concerns about Brazil and may be viewed as sketches for his major novels.

Waly Salamão returned to his unique form of poetry with *Armarinho da miudezas,* which reflects native Bahian traditions. Sebastião Uchoa Leite and Felipe Fortuna published new volumes of poetry. Adão Ventura, the noted black poet from Minas Gerais, published *Texturaafro,* which once again treated the theme of the black race both in Brazil and in Africa. Also of interest was the National Library's creation of a magazine, *Poesia sempre,* to promote Brazilian and foreign poetry as well as to provide a forum for debate about the poetic art.

The most interesting theatrical event of the year was the International Festival of the Theatre of the Oppressed, which staged works by dramatists from all over the world, including Brazil's founder of the Theatre of the Oppressed, Augusto Boal.

Other cultural milestones included the celebration of the 25th anniversary of the *tropicália* movement, which was accompanied by the publication of Hebert Fonseca's *Esse cara,* a collection of documents about and interviews with Caetano Veloso, one of the movement's founders. Also celebrating its 25th year was the Brazilian Children's Book Foundation. Of special interest to literary scholars was the publication of the undoctored *Memórias do cárcere* by Graciliano Ramos as Cadeia. (IRWIN STERN)

RUSSIAN

In his acceptance speech after receiving the medal of honour for literature from the National Arts Club in New York City, Aleksandr Solzhenitsyn commented on the relationship between the current situation in Russia and the state of the country's literature: "The new age has clearly begun, both for Russia and for the whole world. Russia lies utterly ravaged and poisoned; its people are in a state of unprecedented humiliation, and are on the brink of perishing physically, perhaps even biologically. Given the current conditions of national life, and the sudden exposure and ulceration of wounds amassed over the years, it is only natural that literature should experience a pause. The voices that bring forth the nation's literature need time before they can begin to sound once again."

The debate about the path and direction of Russian literature had not only a cultural but also a political and economic dimension as, once again, literature and politics became intertwined. As Solzhenitsyn was about to return to Russia (he was scheduled to arrive in May 1994), the role of the writer and the place literature was to hold in his homeland remained unclear. Criticized by some as being out of touch with the new Russia, Solzhenitsyn maintained the view that "a writer must not disunite his people, not adapt to some party, faction, or political movement, but a writer must as far as possible unite his people."

While Russian literature stopped at the crossroads, literary discussions gave way to literary quarrels. In 1992 the first Russian Booker Novel Prize, awarded to Mark Kharitonov for his novel *Linii sud'by* ("Lines of Fate") precipitated controversy. The judges, promoting the postmodernist trend in Russian literature, passed over Lyudmila Petrushevskaya, who had been widely favoured to win the prize for *Vremya: noch'* ("The Time: Night"). Meanwhile, young writers continued their attacks on the older, established writers, accusing them of holding back the younger generation. Bulat Okudzhava, a frequent target of these attacks, characterized them as "ordinary confrontations between fathers and sons," complicated by political and cultural uncertainties. "How, may I ask, can I give up my place in favour of some young person? What place? The one behind my writing desk?"

Yet Russian writers were also growing weary of intrigues and constant questions about the chaos and disarray in which they had to work. When asked to define the situation of a writer in a market economy, Joseph Brodsky responded: "A writer writes." For Petrushevskaya politics influenced Russian literature not in terms of the quality of the writing but in the opportunity and experience of being published. When asked about the lack of demand for serious literature, Okudzhava responded that serious writers should not try to compete with the authors of the detective stories, pornography, and occult literature that filled bookstores. "It's time writers got used to the new situation," he commented, believing that gradually some publishing houses would begin working on Western principles, publishing works of literary value along with books for which there was a greater demand.

Literary agencies in the West had begun to promote Russian writers. Edvard Radzinsky's *Zhizn' i smert' Nikolaya II* (*The Last Tsar*), for example, became an American best-seller. At the same time, literary awards, previously limited to Western writers, were bestowed on Russian writers as well. Germany introduced the Pushkin Prize, an international award given to Russian writers for of a body of work. In 1991 the Pushkin Prize was awarded to Andrey

JERRY BAUER

Fazil Iskander

Bitov, in 1992 to Petrushevskaya, and in 1993 to Fazil Iskander. In England the Booker committee awarded the first Russian Booker Novel Prize in 1992 in the hope of stimulating greater interest in Russian literature and of helping it through the transition to the commercial realities of Western-style publishing.

The efforts to draw Russia into the international literary community were also reflected in 1993 in the Eighth International Moscow Book Fair, held after a two-year hiatus. It was significant that on July 9, 1993, Russian Pres. Boris Yeltsin signed a law on copyright and related rights aimed at preventing book piracy, which had grown rapidly with the advent of private publishing enterprises. The instability of Russia's book market and the piracy on the part of some book publishers also led to the founding of "Authors and Publishers Against Piracy," with Iskander as its chairman.

Western colleges and universities, traditionally a haven for U.S. writers and intellectuals, opened their doors to Russian writers, offering them temporary affiliations. Not only Brodsky but also Tatyana Tolstaya, Yevgeny Yevtushenko, and Petrushevskaya, to mention only a few, were guest lecturers or artists-in-residence at U.S. universities.

In 1993, Russian literature experienced a great loss with the death of Yury M. Lotman, founder of the Moscow-Tartu school of semiotics and a pioneer in the field of cultural semiotics. Widely translated abroad, Lotman's works created an entire field of study that became known as the structural-semiotic approach to culture.

(EDWARD J. CZERWINSKI; AGNIESZKA PERLINSKA)

EASTERN EUROPEAN

Although faces in the political arena of Central and Eastern Europe seemed to be changing faster than the weather, the profile of the literary establishment remained virtually unchanged. Nowhere was this more apparent than in Poland. The 88-year-old Julian Stryjkowski received the prestigious Jan Parandowski Prize for lifetime achievement. His most recent work, *Milczenie* ("Silence"), dealt with the search for moral orientation. Zbigniew Herbert, forsaking poetry for the moment, issued a volume of prose that included six sketches and 10 "apocrypha." *Martwa natura z wędzidłem* (*Still Life with a Bridle,* 1991) contained reminiscences and ruminations of his tour of Holland. The novelist Tadeusz Konwicki offered his readers six film screenplays, including *Ostatni dzień lata* ("The Last Day of Summer"), which gave the volume its title. Ryszard Kapuscinski's *Imperium* ("Empire") was a sociological and political exploration of the Soviet Union on the eve of its dismemberment. Gustaw Herling-Grudzinski's latest diaries and political observations, *Wyjście z milczenia* ("An Exit from Silence") and *Dziennik pisany nocą, 1989–1992* ("Diary Written by Night, 1989–1992"), further illustrated the writer's lifelong concern for truth in the face of repression and presented a forthright appraisal of Poland's place in world politics.

The southern Slavs continued to produce excellent literary works despite the restrictions imposed by a continuing war. Milorad Pavic, best known for his *Dictionary of the Khazars* (1988), delighted readers with *The Inner Side of the Wind* (translated by Christina Pribicevic-Zoric). Charles Simic continued his translations of Serbian poetry, this time with *The Horse Has Six Legs: An Anthology of Serbian Poetry* and Novica Tadic's *Night Mail: Selected Poems.* The anthology was the culmination of 30 years of translating some of Serbia's finest poets, including Ivan V. Lalic, Vasko Popa, Momcilo Nastasijevic, and Nina Zivancevic.

The Macedonian Sande Stojcevski's *A Gate in the Cloud,* ably translated by David Bowen *et al.,* contained over 50 of the poet's best lyrics. The ubiquitous Simic (in collaboration with Milne Holton and Jeffrey Folks) translated Meto Jovanovski's *Faceless Men and Other Macedonian Stories.*

Don D. Wilson translated the brilliant poetry of Bulgaria's Petya Dubarova, *Here I Am, in Perfect Leaf Today.* Barely 17 when she died in 1979, Dubarova nonetheless deserved a place among Bulgaria's finest poets. Blaga Dimitrova, Bulgaria's popular vice president, was represented with two works, *Noshten dnevnik* ("Night Diary"), a collection of 70 poems written during the period 1989–92, published in Sofia; and *The Last Rock Eagle,* a translation of several of her poems, published in London.

Hungary's Istvan Orkeny, best known as a playwright, was also a superb prose stylist. His latest volume, *Levelek egypercben* ("One-Minute Letters"), contained letters, short stories, and fairy tales, written with delicate humour and an eye for the grotesque in everyday reality. Ivan Mandy's *Huzatban* ("In the Draft"), a collection of shorter and longer pieces, displayed the 75-year-old writer's refinement and exquisite style. Laszlo Krasznahorkai's *Az urgai fogoly* ("The Prisoner of Urga") won praise for its verisimilitude and delicately balanced style.

Perhaps the finest anthology of Eastern European poetry published after the fall of communism was the appropriately titled *Shifting Borders,* which contained some of the region's best poetry of the 1980s. Compiled and edited by Walter Cummins, the anthology, translated by both poets and translators, also included the poetry of the Baltic republics and Romania. Norman Manea's *October, Eight O'Clock,* translated by Cornelia Golna and others, returned to the theme of the Holocaust.

The past remained the subject of painful probing in the Czech Republic and Slovakia. *Good-bye, Samizdat: Twenty Years of Czechoslovak Underground Writing,* edited by Marketa Goetz-Stankiewicz, was a collection of dazzling texts on cultural, sociopolitical, and philosophical themes by some of the finest Czech and Slovak thinkers. Michal Viewegh was fast becoming the most acclaimed writer of the young generation. *Báječná léta pod psa* ("Glorious Lousy Years") was the story of characters too decent to become communists but too cowardly to become dissidents. His third novel, *Nápady laskavého čtenáře* ("Ideas of a Kind Reader"), poked gentle fun at several literary contemporaries. Oldrich Danek's play *Jak snadné je vládnout aneb Karel IV* ("How Easy Is It to Reign, or Charles IV") pursued the eternally vital theme of the individual's moral responsibility to society. The hero of Pavel Reznicek's surrealistic novel *Vedro* ("Oppressive Heat") turned out to be "oppressive heat" itself, an element endowed with comic human traits. Jaroslav Putik's novel *Proměny mladého muže* ("Transformations of a Young Man") focused on the generation that experienced the German occupation, World War II, and a totalitarian system.

(EDWARD J. CZERWINSKI; AGNIESZKA PERLINSKA)

JEWISH

Hebrew. The main event in Hebrew literature in 1993 was the publication of S. Yizhar's novel *Tzalhavim* ("Shining Lights"), a remarkable account of the author's youth as well as of Israel's early days. Other noteworthy works of fiction were Aharon Appelfeld's *Timyon* ("Abyss"), Amnon Navot's *Lokhdei Arikim* ("Gladiator [Studebaker], or a Note on the Military Police"), and Nathan Shaham's collection of stories, *Naknikivot Hamot* ("Hot Hot Dogs"). The most popular novels in 1993 were Sammy Michael's *Victoria* ("Victoria") and Eli Amir's *Mafri'ach haYonim* ("Farewell, Baghdad"), both of which examined Jewish life in Iraq against the background of the Zionist struggle to establish a Jewish state in Palestine. A first novel was published by Tsruya Shalev, *Rakadti Amadti* ("Dancing Standing Still"), and Gadi Taub was acclaimed for his first collection of short stories, *Ma Haya Kore Lu Ha'yeenu Shokhehim et Dov* ("What Would Have Happened Had We Forgotten Dov"). As poetry had been losing ground to fiction in Israeli literature in recent years, several poets turned to prose. Among works of fiction published by established poets were Maya Bejerano's collection of short stories, *Hasimla haKh'hula veSokhen ha-Bitu'ach* ("The Blue Dress and the Insurance Agent"), Nurit Zarchi's postmodernist-oriented stories, *Oman haMaseikhot* ("The Mask Maker"), and Asher Reich's autobiographical novel, *Zikhronot shel Hole Shikheha* ("Memories of an Amnesiac"). Novelist Yitzhak Averbuch Orpaz was the only writer going against the trend, publishing his first book of poems, *Litzlo'ach et haMe'a* ("To Cross the Century").

Notable books by veteran poets included Mordechai Geldman's *A'vin* ("Eye") and Israel Eliraz' *Pe Karu'a* ("A Torn Mouth"). First books of poetry were penned by Tamir Greenberg (*Dyokan Atzmi Im Qvant ve-Hatul Met;* "Self Portrait with Quantum and Dead Cat"), Zvika Shternfeld (*Hamarkiza miGovari;* "The Marquise of Govari"), and Shimon Shloush (*Tola Havui shel Asham;* "A Hidden Worm of Guilt").

One of the most intriguing critical studies was Amos Oz's reading of Agnon's fiction, *Shtikat haShama'vim: Agnon Mishtomen Al Elohim* ("The Silence of Heaven: Agnon's Fear of God"). Other important scholarly works were Hillel Barzel's book on the poetry of S. Tchernichovsky, Ziva Shamir's examination of the poetry of Yonatan Ratosh, Yigal Schwartz's monograph on Aaron Reuveni, and Hannan Hever's controversial discussion of Avraham Ben Yitzhak's poetry.

The prestigious Israel Prize was awarded to the literary scholars and critics Dan Miron and Gershon Shaked.

(AVRAHAM BALABAN)

Yiddish. The first issue of a new post-Soviet Yiddish monthly journal, the first since the demise of *Sovetish heymland* ("Soviet Homeland"), appeared in Moscow under the title of *Di yidishe gas* ("The Jewish Street"), edited by Aron Vergelis.

Mordkhe Schaechter's *Yidish tsvey* ("Yiddish Two") provided a groundbreaking and authoritative perspective on current Yiddish language usage, idiom, and style.

Yisroel Khaym Biletski's magisterial *Uri Tsvi Grinberg der yidish-dikhter* ("Uri Tsvi Grinberg: The Yiddish Poet") was a robust celebration of a major expressionist poet. A finely textured and capacious issue of *Di goldene keyt* ("The Golden Chain") explored the remarkable literary achievement of Avraham Sutskever. Khave Turniansky's stimulating volume, *Di yidishe literatur in nayntsetn yorhundert* ("Yiddish Literature in the 19th Century"), was a colourful sampling of the disparate strands from which contemporary writing was woven. Lili Berger's nuanced miscellany, *Ekhos fun a vaytn nekhtn* ("Echoes of a Distant Yesterday"), included Bible stories, essays, and sketches.

Three notable memoirs made their appearance. Avraham Karpinovitsh's portrait of his natal city, *Vilne mayn Vilne* ("Vilna, My Vilna"), was lovingly captured in 10 short stories. Sutskever's urbane and entertaining *Baym leyenen penimer* ("Reading Faces") ranged over many aspects of his long career. Ida Taub's intimate and moving *Ikh klem fun benkshaft* ("I Grieve from Homesickness") captured the voice of many whom the century had displaced.

In her autobiographical novel, *Khanes Shef un rinder* ("Khane's Sheep and Cattle"), Shire Gorshteyn approached her task of describing leading figures within the Soviet Jewish intelligentsia with fervour and candour. Yoysef Kerler's *Abi gezunt* ("As Long as You're Healthy") took the reader inside his remarkable life of persecution, exile, and safe haven in Israel.

Three noteworthy works of historical research appeared. Heshl Klepfish documented the impact of the century's cataclysms on communities and values in *Oyf historishe vegn* ("On Historic Paths"). Shmuel Rozhansky's *1492 . . . 500 yor nokhdem* ("1492 . . . 500 Years Later") recorded conscience, courage, and suffering in a haunting collection of materials charting the expulsion of the Jewish community from Spain and its multifaceted aftermath. Boris Sandler's *Der inyen numer 5390* ("Case Number 5390") was an arresting piece of analysis based on the author's research in the KGB archives of Chisinau, Moldova.

(THOMAS E. BIRD)

CHINESE

The year 1993 began with great promise and ended with the self-inflicted death of Gu Cheng (Ku Ch'eng), one of China's most accomplished poets. Much of the year's literary output had a provocative quality; as a result, a number of novels were banned for offensive contents, and many works written in China were published first abroad.

Established novelists were particularly prominent in 1993, some of them lending their prestige and talent to television dramas. Mo Yan (Mo Yen), whose historical novel *Honggaoliang* (*Red Sorghum*) appeared in English and other Western languages, published a collection of stories that broke new ground in form and rhetorical effects. Wang Meng, who was dismissed from his post as minister of culture in the wake of the 1989 Tiananmen (T'ien-an-men) Square massacre, saw his novel *Lianaide jijie* ("A Season for Falling in Love"), the first volume of a planned trilogy on intellectuals in post-Mao Zedong (Mao Tse-tung) China, published in China.

Also appearing during the year were English translations of Su Tong's (Su T'ung's) *Dahongdenglong gaogaogua* (*Raise the Red Lantern*), the film version of which had already won international acclaim, and Liu Heng's *Heidexue* (*Black Snow*), a novel of urban squalor and life on the edges of society. Liu continued to broaden the scope of his oeuvre with the delayed publication of his novel about the Cultural Revolution, *Shaoyaosong* ("In Praise of Leisure"), and the appearance of his most recent work, *Tangde bairimeng* ("Old River Daydreams"), a historical novel in a daringly innovative form.

In recent years the mainland literary scene had been dominated by young writers, most of them with ties to film and television. In 1993, however, a number of established middle-aged novelists published major works that showed that they, too, could win the attention of an increasingly young and sophisticated readership. Li Rui (Li Jui), one of the country's most respected fiction writers, published *Jiuzih* ("Old Sites"), a bloody, convoluted, and riveting historical novel that spans the entire 20th century. Jia Pingwa (Chia P'ing-wa), whose earlier novel *Fuzao* (*Turbulence*) had won prizes as well as readers in China and the West because of its upbeat approach to economic and political reform, turned to the more sensational theme of illicit sex, graphically described, in *Feidu* (*The Ruined Capital*), a novel of half a million words. In Shanghai, Zhu Lin (Chu Lin), who had already incurred the wrath of the literary establishment, showed that she remained unrepentant with the publication of *Wu* ("Witch"), a huge, rambling, and racy novel of rural superstitions and the dark side of life in the Chinese countryside.

Literary activity on the island of Taiwan was most notable for its relatively undistinguished output. However, Taiwanese booksellers continued to be the first to publish new work by popular young mainland writers such as Ge Fei (Ke Fei), who published not only a collection of stories entitled *Xiangyu* ("Encounters") but also his first novel, *Diren* ("Enemy"). In typical avant-garde fashion, the novel weaves a rhetorical landscape in a tale that frequently seems to offer little more than implied questions. Other mainland writers whose work first appeared in Taiwan were Yu Hua (Yü Hua) (*Xiaji taifeng;* "Summer Typhoon") and Ye Zhaoyan (Yeh Chao-yen) (*Zuihouyichede nanmin;* "The Last Carload of Refugees").

(HOWARD C. GOLDBLATT)

JAPANESE

Shūsaku Endō, internationally renowned for his historical novels *Chimmoku* ("Silence," 1966) and *Samurai* ("Samurai," 1980), set his new novel, *Fukai kawa* ("Deep River") in contemporary Japan and India. The central figure Ōtsu, unsuccessful in becoming a Catholic priest, decides to go to India after concluding that he cannot adjust to life in a French seminary. There he lives alone by the shore of the sacred Ganges and is engaged in the Hindu crematory service as a voluntary helper; Hindu belief in metamorphosis becomes a theme. Although Ōtsu remains a Catholic, the reader suspects that Endō, the author, was drawn to Asiatic paganism.

Saiichi Maruya's *Onnazakari* ("Woman in Her Prime") was a high-spirited novel about an attractive career woman who also has amorous relationships.

Natsuki Ikezawa
SHINCHO-SHA

Natsuki Ikezawa's ambitious novel *Mashiasu Giri no shikkyaku* ("The Downfall of Macias Giri") won the prestigious Tanizaki Prize. Its setting is a small island in the southern Pacific, supposedly a mandatory territory of prewar Japan. The protagonist, Macias Giri, is a clever and energetic political activist who secures a political dictatorship over the island. When his efforts to modernize his territory fail, he kills himself. The fantastic atmosphere of the tropical South and the spectacular career of Macias reflect the author's interest in Latin-American fiction, especially in the "magical realism" of the works of Gabriel García Márques.

There were two fine collections of short stories by women authors—Atsuko Anzai's *Kokuchō* ("Blackbird") and Keiko Iwasaka's *Yodogawa ni chikai machi kara* ("Town by the Yodo River"). The former is concerned with various cases of adultery, the latter with the author's childhood memories of downtown Osaka.

Two remarkable biographies also appeared—Jun Etō's *Sōseki to sono jidai* ("The Life and Times of Sōseki Natsume"), on Japan's most important modern novelist, and Kunie Iwahashi's *Shigure Hasegawa* ("Shigure Hasegawa"), on a pioneer for feminine art in pre-World War II Japan. Shoichi Saeki's *Daisezokuka no jidai to bungaku* ("Great Secularization and Literature") provided a new perspective on the complicated relationship between religion and literature in Japan and suggested the deep-rootedness of Shintoism in Japanese mentality.

Shuntaro Tanigawa's *Sekenshirazu* ("Unworldly"), a collection of poetry in a coloquial and detached style, was awarded the newly inaugurated prize commemorating the poet Sakutarō Hagiwara (1886–1942).

(SHOICHI SAEKI)

See also Libraries; Publishing.

This article updates the *Macropædia* article The History of Western LITERATURE and articles on the literatures of the various languages.

An unlikely looking conqueror, Andrew Wiles of Princeton University nevertheless apparently vanquished one of the most notorious of mathematical dragons when he announced a proof of Fermat's last theorem at a conference of mathematicians in June. Although verifying his 200-page paper would take some time—and by year's end a potential trouble spot indeed had turned up—many scholars sensed that Wiles had dispatched the 350-year-old theorem, a proof for which Pierre de Fermat had claimed to possess but had never written out.

PRINCETON UNIVERSITY; PHOTOGRAPH, DENISE APPLEWHITE

Mathematics

The outstanding mathematical event of the year, of the decade, and perhaps even of the century was the announcement in June 1993 of a proof for Fermat's last theorem by Andrew Wiles (*see* BIOGRAPHIES)—a quiet, rather diffident Englishman working at Princeton University. Mathematics has several notorious unsolved problems, and the puzzle posed by the French number theorist Pierre de Fermat over 350 years ago is one of the most notorious of them all.

Number theory—the study of the deeper properties of whole numbers—goes back to Diophantus of Alexandria, who flourished about AD 250 and wrote a book called the *Arithmetica.* It included a completely general construction for Pythagorean triples: three whole numbers that can represent the lengths of the sides of a right triangle by satisfying the Pythagorean equation $x^2 + y^2 = z^2$. Examples are $3^2 + 4^2 = 5^2$ and $5^2 + 12^2 = 13^2$.

Some time around 1637 Fermat wondered what would happen if squares are replaced by cubes or higher powers. In other words, are there any solutions in whole numbers of the "Fermat equation" $x^n + y^n = z^n$ if n is three or more? He found none, and in his copy of the *Arithmetica* he made the most famous marginal note in the history of mathematics: "To resolve a cube into the sum of two cubes, a fourth power into two fourth powers, or in general any power higher than the second into two of the same kind, is impossible; of which fact I have found a remarkable proof. The margin is too small to contain it." This statement became known as his "last" theorem, because for many years it was the only assertion of his that had been neither proved nor disproved by his successors. In 1847 the German mathematician Ernst Kummer invented the theory of "ideal numbers" and proved Fermat's last theorem for all powers up to 100, except for 37, 59, and 67. By early 1993 similar methods had proved all cases up to the four millionth power—but none of these efforts suggested a way to prove the theorem for all powers.

Meanwhile, in 1922, the English mathematician Leo Mordell had noticed a curious connection between geometry and number theory. If instead of looking at whole-number solutions of an equation, one looks at all solutions, the results can be visualized as a geometric surface, which has a number of holes—like the hole in a doughnut. He observed that if the number of holes in this surface is two or more, then the corresponding equation seems to have only finitely many integer solutions. This idea became known as the Mordell conjecture, and it was proved in 1983 by the young German mathematician Gerd Faltings. It implies that Fermat's last theorem is nearly true: there are only finitely many solutions for any given power n greater than two. This comes close, but Fermat had conjectured that there are no solutions at all.

The final resolution of the puzzle rests on a beautiful idea that lies at the heart of modern number theory, that of an elliptic curve, an equation of the form $y^2 = x^3 + ax + b$, in which a and b are constants. The number theory of elliptic curves is very well understood. Some unsolved problems still exist, however, and the biggest is called the Taniyama-Weil conjecture. It states that every elliptic curve can be described in terms of modular functions—esoteric relatives of trigonometric sines and cosines.

Early in the 1980s Gerhard Frey of the University of the Saarland, Saarbrücken, Germany, made a crucial connection between Fermat's last theorem and elliptic curves. Suppose, for the sake of argument, that there does exist a solution to the Fermat equation. If some logical contradiction can be deduced from this supposition—any contradiction—then the hypothetical solution cannot exist, and Fermat's last theorem must be true. Frey considered a particular elliptic curve defined in terms of such a hypothetical solution and discovered that it would have an extremely unlikely combination of properties. In 1986 Kenneth Ribet of the University of California at Berkeley proved that if the Taniyama-Weil conjecture is true, then Frey's elliptic curve not only is unlikely but also cannot exist at all.

Everything thus rested on the Taniyama-Weil conjecture, and Wiles decided to tackle this very difficult key problem in number theory. In a 200-page paper he marshaled enough powerful mathematical machinery to prove one special case of the Taniyama-Weil conjecture, valid for "semistable" elliptic curves, and that was enough to imply Fermat's last theorem. At year's end a prepublication review of the paper uncovered a possible snag, but Wiles expressed confidence that he could clear it up in the near future. A number of his colleagues, too, stated that it would be premature to conclude that Wiles's proof was in trouble. (IAN STEWART)

This article updates the *Macropædia* articles GEOMETRY; NUMBER THEORY.

Military Affairs

Military and defense topics of special importance in 1993 included the proliferation of weapons of mass destruction, the breakup of the massive military machine of the former Soviet Union, and the expansion of United Nations peacekeeping operations.

Proliferation. The spread of weapons of mass destruction and the systems to deliver such weapons, especially shorter-range Theater Ballistic Missiles (TBM), was widely discussed in 1993. The threat was highlighted by the tests in North Korea of Rodong-1 TBM, which were capable of delivering warheads to South Korea and Japan, plus that country's possible imminent acquisition of nuclear weapons. North Korea, one of the few surviving communist dictatorships, had 1,127,000 military personnel, with an army of 1 million, with 3,700 battle tanks (700 more than previous estimates) and 2,500 armed personnel carriers (APC). The air force of 82,000 had 730 combat aircraft, mostly older Chinese and Russian types; the navy had 45,000 personnel.

Because of this large force poised to attack South Korea—which had happened once before—successive U.S. administrations had added a nuclear deterrent by declaring that the U.S. would, if necessary, use tactical nuclear weapons to halt a North Korean attack. North Korean Pres. Kim Il Sung, however, appeared to believe that this threat might be foiled if his country could build nuclear weapons and TBM to deliver them. In 1993 North Korea conducted repeated tests of its TBM. Moreover, by the end of the year some military analysts feared that they had built a few nuclear weapons, perhaps as many as three (although other observers were skeptical that North Korea could have produced enough plutonium to make a bomb). Suspicions flared when the Pyongyang government refused to allow the International Atomic Energy Agency (IAEA) to inspect two undeclared nuclear waste dumps near its Yongbyon "radiochemical laboratory."

There were other concerns as well. Pyongyang was exporting TBM to other countries, including Iran, and some 15–20 other countries were known to be interested in acquiring weapons of mass destruction. Concern in the United States about proliferation was so great that U.S. Secretary of Defense Les Aspin announced a major new Counterproliferation Defense Initiative on December 7. The plan suggested opposing these threats by developing improved defenses against TBM, such as upgrades to the U.S. land-based Patriot antitactical ballistic missile (ATBM) system.

On March 24 Prime Minister F.W. de Klerk revealed that South Africa had manufactured six nuclear weapons between 1974 and 1990 but that all six had been dismantled in 1990–91. South Africa thus became the first country to manufacture and then give up nuclear weapons. China conducted a nuclear test in early October, ignoring calls for a moratorium on tests and raising the possibility of renewed testing by other nuclear nations. Some progress was registered during the year as well in the area of eliminating chemical weapons. Representatives of 130 nations met in Paris in January to sign a treaty calling for the destruction within 10 years of stockpiles and factories to produce chemical weapons. It was the first international agreement to ban an entire class of weapons.

Arms Control after the Soviet Breakup. Proliferation of a different sort was taking place in the former Soviet Union, which dissolved in December 1991 to be replaced by 15 independent states, 4 of which—Russia, Ukraine, Belarus, and Kazakhstan—retained nuclear weapons on their territories. During 1993 these new states were in the process of taking over physical control of the nuclear and conventional forces.

The U.S.-Soviet arms-control negotiations had been replaced by negotiations between the U.S. and Russia, plus Belarus, Kazakhstan, and Ukraine. Two U.S.-Soviet arms-control agreements had recently been concluded: the formal July 31, 1991, Strategic Arms Reduction Treaty (START I) and an informal agreement on reciprocal nuclear force reductions, START II. Cuts would be made in two stages. In the first, to be completed by 1999, strategic forces would be reduced to an overall total of 3,800–4,250 warheads, of which only 1,200 warheads could be multiple independently targeted reentry vehicle (MIRV) on intercontinental ballistic missile (ICBM) and 2,160 submarine-launched ballistic missile (SLBM) warheads. In stage two, to be completed by 2000–2003, strategic forces would be reduced to an overall total of 3,000–3,500 warheads. All MIRV on ICBM would be eliminated and a maximum of 1,750 SLBM allowed. All nuclear weapons would be withdrawn from Belarus, Kazakhstan, and Ukraine. The agreed START II cuts would eliminate some 70% of pre-START nuclear warheads, going much further than START I, which had cut U.S. and Soviet warheads by about 25% to 30%. On December 8 at Whiteman Air Force Base, Missouri, the U.S. destroyed the

JOHN FICARA—SYGMA

Demonstrators express support for a change in U.S. policy that had officially banned homosexuals from serving in the armed forces. Pres. Bill Clinton proposed dropping the ban but, after opposition from congressional and military leaders, he compromised on a number of points.

first of the 500 underground missile silos to be eliminated under START. Also in early December, the U.S. proposed to Russia that the two nuclear powers target their missiles away from each other's territory.

Russia remained the largest single military power in Europe, but its future defense policy and the degree of central control over the military forces were uncertain. Russian troops to a greater or lesser extent were involved militarily in Moldova, Abkhazia, Nagorno-Karabakh, and Tajikistan. Aggressive statements by Foreign Ministry officials and the startling showing of the jingoistic Vladimir Zhirinovsky in the December elections added to the nervousness of Russia's neighbours.

The Russian Strategic Deterrent Forces embraced the rocket, naval, and aviation forces. The 144,000 troops and modern ICBM systems of the Strategic Rocket Forces included 92 rail-mobile SS-24, 260 road-mobile SS-25 (plus 80 originally deployed in Belarus), and 198 SS-18 heavy ICBM (plus 104 in Kazakhstan). The Strategic Naval Forces had 10,000 personnel, manning 52 nuclear-fueled ballistic submarines (SSBN) carrying 788 SLBM, all based in Russian ports. Strategic Aviation Forces had 19,000 personnel and included 20 Blackjack-A Tu-160 bombers (based in Ukraine) and 89 Tu-95 Bear-H, each carrying 8 air-launched cruise missiles (ALCM) based in Kazakhstan and Ukraine, plus 66 older Tu-95. General purpose forces included an army with one million personnel, organized into 18 tank, 61 motor rifle (mechanized), 15 artillery/missile, and 5 airborne divisions of 11,100–13,500 men each. Equipment included some 25,000 tanks, 22,000 armoured infantry fighting vehicles (AIFV), and 24,000 artillery pieces. The air force had about 170,000 personnel with 3,600 combat aircraft. The air defense troops formed a separate service with some 230,000 personnel, 2,200 fighter aircraft, and 7,000 surface-to-air missile (SAM) launchers at 900 fixed sites. The navy had 300,000 personnel, 169 principal surface combatants, and 153 tactical submarines.

By year's end all effective Russian forces and equipment had been withdrawn from the former Czechoslovakia, Hungary, Lithuania, Mongolia, and Poland and were being withdrawn from Germany and the Baltic states (albeit slowly). The only significant overseas deployments of Russian forces, other than in republics of the former Soviet Union, were 2,200 troops in Cuba and 1,000 in Libya. The attempt to form Russian and local Commonwealth of Independent States Joint General Purposes Forces (CIS-JGPF) on the territories of Belarus, Ukraine, Moldova, and Armenia appeared to be coming apart by year's end.

Ukraine was vitally concerned about national security issues (especially Russia) and its economic situation, and throughout the year it attempted to bargain nuclear weapons for economic and security guarantees. In July Ukraine claimed ownership of the former Soviet strategic and tactical nuclear weapons on its territory. In November Ukraine signed START I but made its accession conditional upon compensation and security guarantees. In December, however, Ukrainian Pres. Leonid Kravchuk announced that Ukraine would give up much of the nuclear forces on its territory, including all 46 of the new SS-24 silo-based ICBM. He also said that Ukraine had already deactivated 17 missiles and would dismantle 3 more by year's end.

Meeting in Massandra, Crimea, in early September, the Ukrainian president and Russian Pres. Boris Yeltsin apparently agreed that Ukraine would sell its half control of the Black Sea Fleet (which totaled about 350 ships and 70,000 sailors) in exchange for a partial write-off of its debt to Moscow for oil and gas. When he got back to Kiev, however, Kravchuk ran into strident criticism and had to renege on the deal, so by year's end it was still unclear which government controlled which units of the fleet. Ukraine's Parliament adopted a military doctrine in October, declaring that "Ukraine will consider its potential adversary to be a state whose consistent policy constitutes a military danger to Ukraine." Large military forces were deployed, with ground forces of 217,000 personnel and 5,700 main battle tanks and an air force of 171,000 personnel and some 900 combat aircraft. Plans to create a new service, the Air Defense Troops, by merging the air defense forces with the air force seemed to have been shelved at the end of December.

Belarus deployed military forces totaling 102,600 personnel (to be cut to 90,000 by 1995), mainly ground forces of 50,500 personnel, with 3,287 main battle tanks, and an air force of 14,100 personnel and 341 combat aircraft. Belarus signed the Nuclear Non-proliferation Treaty in February. The Defense Ministry reported on December 22 that 27 of the mobile strategic SS-25 missiles had been withdrawn to Russia, where some were thought to have been redeployed. The remaining missiles were to be withdrawn by 1996.

Local press reports in mid-December hinted that agreement was near on the withdrawal of Russia's 14th Army from the Transdniester area of Moldova. Until October the flamboyant head of the Russian force, Col. Aleksandr Lebed, had been playing an increasingly political role in the heavily Russian-populated area. The main military and diplomatic concern of the three Baltic states was the continued presence of Russian (ex-Soviet) troops on their territories. At the beginning of the year these comprised an estimated 7,000 troops in Estonia, 17,000 in Latvia, and 4,300 in Lithuania; the last Russian troops were withdrawn from Lithuania at the end of August. All three Baltic states were establishing small national armed forces (2,000–7,000 personnel) during the year. Estonia appointed Col. Aleksander Einseln, a U.S. citizen, as chief of staff of its Defense Forces on May 4.

Azerbaijan, which had to cope with internal divisions in its armed forces as well as the war with Armenia, deployed the largest military forces in the Transcaucasian area—up to 38,900 troops, as well as some 12,000 claimed for the Karabakh People's Defense units. Armenia, with armed forces personnel totaling some 20,000, more or less supporting the 20,000 troops of the Nagorno-Karabakh region, made significant gains in its war with Azerbaijan over the mountainous, mainly Armenian enclave. In addition to occupying Nagorno-Karabakh, it also seized key access routes to it from Azerbaijan proper. Both Armenia and Azerbaijan had Russian troops on their territory. Georgia planned to deploy some 20,000 troops of its own, with Russian forces of one ground army and one air army on its territory. The breakaway Georgian province of Abkhazia, with some 4,000 troops of its own and with sometime support of more-or-less irregular Russian units, succeeded in expelling the Georgian army.

Each of the five former Soviet Union republics in Central Asia had significant numbers of former Soviet military forces on their territory. These were, in principle, to have joined the CIS-JGPF under joint control with Russia, but the independent republics were taking control over their forces and forming national armies. Kazakhstan had an army of 44,000 with 1,400 battle tanks plus an air force of some 140 fighter, ground-attack (FGA)/fighters. Russia retained control of Kazakhstan's air defense force of 80 fighters as well as the 50 strategic bombers and the 104 SS-18 ICBM deployed at two sites in the country. Kazakhstan ratified the Nuclear Non-proliferation Treaty on December 13, during the visit to Almaty of U.S. Vice Pres. Al Gore, and the U.S. agreed to provide $84 million in denuclearization aid.

Kyrgyzstan had an army of 12,000 personnel and 240 battle tanks. Turkmenistan's military forces, which included an army of 28,000 personnel and 900 battle tanks and an air force (including air defense) of 80 FGA and 85 fighter aircraft, were under joint Turkmen/Russian control. Uzbekistan had an army of 38,000 personnel and 210 battle tanks and an air force of 70 FGA. In Tajikistan, however, a small Russian army of 8,500 personnel with 200 battle tanks had intervened to enable the communist-dominated government to regain control of Dushanbe, the capital, from the democratic and Islamic opposition groups. Over 500,000 Tajiks became refugees, and many crossed into Afghanistan, from where opposition groups launched attacks on Russian forces. During 1993 these attacks increased, and Russia threatened to attack opposition bases in Afghanistan.

Peacekeeping and Relief Operations. The year saw the increasing deployment of United Nations peacekeeping and relief forces, which had begun in earnest in 1991. These were detachments of national military forces, usually operating under UN command. Table I lists current UN peacekeeping operations (for details of the main missions, *see* WORLD AFFAIRS: *United Nations* and the separate country reports). In 1993 the UN also sent missions to, or produced reports about, Uganda/Rwanda; Kosovo, Sandjak, and Vojvodina (Yugoslavia); Georgia; Estonia; and Moldova. Table II lists the countries that supplied more than 1,500 troops to UN peacekeeping operations (which totaled 80,146) in 1993.

Despite the burgeoning deployment of UN peacekeeping forces, the continued interest of Secretary-General Boutros Boutros-Ghali in increasing the missions, and the apparent willingness of the major world powers to pass the responsibility for "fire fighting" to the international organization, there were serious questions about the viability of the program. The U.S. military was especially insistent that its forces be committed to combat only by their president. The casualties inflicted on UN forces in Somalia, including 24 Pakistani and 18 Americans killed in separate, carefully targeted attacks, raised pointed questions about the role of UN forces, their command, and their effectiveness. Similarly, the UN "blue helmet" units in Bosnia proved too small and ineffectual to have much impact on the progress of the peace. Some countries began to withdraw their troops from UN forces in Cyprus because of lack of progress.

On another front, the UN was experiencing critical problems financing the expensive peacekeeping activities, and Boutros-Ghali spent a great deal of time in 1993 passing the hat. There was no line item in the UN budget for peacekeeping operations, nor was there any provision for the organization to take out loans. The peacekeeping budget, which had to rely on separate assessments to member governments, reached $1.4 billion in 1993, of which $1.2 billion was in arrears.

Table I. UN Peacekeeping Operations Active in 1993
(troop strengths vary and should be considered approximate)

Location	Acronym	Troops	Begun
Palestine	UNTSO	224	1948
India/Pakistan	UNMOGIP	38	1949
Cyprus	UNFICYP	1,519	1964
Israel/Syria	UNDOF	1,116	1974
Lebanon	UNIFIL	5,277	1978
Iraq/Kuwait	UNIKOM	319	1991
Angola	UNAVEM II	103	1991
El Salvador	ONUSAL	380	1991
Western Sahara	MINURSO	327	1991
Bosnia/Croatia	UNPROFOR I	10,216	1992
Cambodia	UNTAC	19,628	1992
Somalia	UNOSOM	20,854	1992
Bosnia (Sarajevo)	UNPROFOR II	9,480	1992
Mozambique	ONUMOZ	6,164	1993
Macedonia	UNPROFOR M	1,000	1993

Sources: IISS, *The Military Balance 1993–1994; The Independent,* July 6, 1993.

Table II. Countries Contributing the Largest Numbers of Troops to UN Peacekeeping Missions in 1993
(troop strengths vary and should be considered approximate)

Country	Troops	Country	Troops
France	8,096	Indonesia	2,042
Pakistan	6,027	Ghana	1,935
United States	4,353	Netherlands, The	1,916
Italy	3,648	Poland	1,852
Canada	3,210	Uruguay	1,801
United Kingdom	3,205	Belgium	1,785
India	2,820	Nepal	1,751
Bangladesh	2,629	Nigeria	1,625
Malaysia	2,216		

Source: *The Independent,* July 6, 1993

NATO. In 1993 the NATO alliance continued to assist the evolution of democratic governments in Eastern Europe, Russia, and the other states formed from the Soviet Union. At the same time, NATO maintained lower levels of defense forces, at lower states of readiness, but with enhanced mobility and flexibility. Some alliance members, notably the U.S., the U.K., and France, also continued to help enforce the terms of the UN cease-fire in Iraq.

NATO continued to reduce levels of conventional forces through the 1990 Conventional Forces in Europe (CFE) Treaty. Many NATO countries foresaw force cuts well below CFE Treaty levels, however. Under the treaty, for example, the U.S. was limited to 250,000 troops, but their forces already stood well below these levels—183,000 personnel—and cuts to 100,000 by 1996 seemed likely.

Gen. George Joulwan, formerly commander of U.S. forces in Latin America, replaced Gen. John Shalikashvili as NATO chief commander in Europe. The defense ministers of the NATO countries met at Travemünde, Germany, on October 20–21. Among other topics, they discussed the desire of Poland, the Czech Republic, Hungary, Slovakia, and Ukraine to join. Germany supported an accelerated schedule for affiliation, but other NATO nations, led by the U.S., were more reluctant, and the final formulation was that the Eastern European states would join a "Partnership for Peace" and be offered membership "sooner rather than later," in the words of Secretary Aspin, but would have to do without the desired security guarantees for the present. Russian President Yeltsin underscored his opposition to any expansion of NATO membership in the East in a meeting with NATO Secretary-General Manfred Wörner in December.

Steps were taken during 1993 to form the Eurocorps, an integrated European army of 30,000–40,000, under the aegis of the Western European Union, the security and defense arm of the European Community. Troops and equipment from the U.K., The Netherlands, France, Belgium, Germany, and Spain that had been identified for service with NATO would be attached to the WEU for use in possible future peacekeeping operations.

United States. The issue of homosexuals in the armed forces made headlines in the U.S. throughout the year. The new president, Bill Clinton, was forced to back away from a campaign pledge to drop the 50-year ban on homosexuals serving in the military when he immediately ran into opposition within the military establishment and on Capitol Hill. Finally in December, after congressional hearings and a Pentagon report, a vague compromise policy was adopted. Dubbed "don't ask, don't tell, don't pursue," it would allow gays and lesbians to serve in the armed forces but not to engage in overt homosexual activity.

Details of the drinking, debauchery, and sexual assault of dozens of women by U.S. Navy and Marine aviators at the 1991 convention of the Tailhook Society were documented in a report from the Pentagon released on April 23. The incident was presumably put to rest with the formal censure of three admirals and administrative actions against 29 other officers for failing to stop the offenses. In another incident in June, Air Force Maj. Gen. Harold N. Campbell was disciplined for making disparaging remarks about his commander in chief.

Among the key appointments of the year, on July 3 President Clinton nominated Prof. Sheila E. Widnall as secretary of the air force, the first woman to head a military service in the U.S. Gen. Colin L. Powell, chairman of the Joint Chiefs of Staff, retired on September 30 and was replaced by Gen. John M. Shalikashvili. (*See* BIOGRAPHIES.) On December 16 former CIA deputy director and retired four-star admiral Bobby Ray Inman was designated as secretary of defense, to replace Aspin, who had announced his resignation one day earlier.

The U.S. all-volunteer armed forces in 1993 totaled 1,729,700 personnel. Under the Bottom Up Defense Review (BUDR) announced in late January, further cuts were to be made in the 1995 base force proposed by the Bush administration to a level of 10 active army divisions (down from 12), a navy retaining 12 aircraft carriers and 346 major surface combatants (down from 451), and an air force of 13 active fighter wing equivalents (down from 15), each with 72 combat aircraft. The U.S. Marine Corps would remain at three divisions and three air wings. The BUDR would cut total active forces to some 1.4 million personnel. Defense spending for fiscal 1993 was almost $258.9 billion. In October Aspin announced a thorough review of the 45-year-old U.S. nuclear weapons strategy, to be completed early in 1994. Amid allegations that some tests in the Strategic Defense Initiative had been rigged, the controversial "Star Wars" program was officially terminated on May 13, to be replaced by a new Ballistic Missile Defense Organization.

Other aspects of Secretary Aspin's reorganization to mark the end of the Cold War included the creation of new Pentagon posts in the area of human rights, arms proliferation, and conversion of military industries. In April the Pentagon dropped most restrictions on women's engaging in aerial and naval combat, and later in the year legislation was signed lifting the ban on women's serving aboard naval combat vessels. A total of 203,100 women were serving in the U.S. armed forces in 1993.

The new Air Combat Command (ACC) had taken over responsibility from the Strategic Air Command for U.S. strategic nuclear programs. The elderly B-52 bomber force declined to 36 B-52Gs and 94 B-52Hs. All 36 B-52Gs had been converted to deliver conventional weapons, including the Harpoon air-to-surface missile (ASM) for antishipping missions. The 94 B-52Hs carried AGM-86B ALCM. Deployment of the advanced cruise missile (ACM), with low-observable ("stealth") technology, continued. Only 20 new B-2 stealth bombers would be built.

The U.S. land-based, fixed-silo ICBM force was to be reduced in accordance with START I and II. The 507 silo-based Minuteman III ICBM would be converted to single warheads instead of 3 MIRV. All 50 MX Peacekeeper ICBM would be eliminated, and all 450 elderly Minuteman II ICBM in fixed silos were to be retired and were stood down from alert status, as were strategic bombers. Under START II the ACC would retain 94 modern Rockwell B-1B strategic bombers, but these would be converted to deliver conventional weapons. In addition, START II limited the U.S. and Russia to 1,750 warheads deployed on submarine-launched ballistic missiles (SLBM). The U.S. ballistic missile nuclear submarine (SSBN) force was reduced to 23, carrying 480 SLBM. Six of the 14 modern Ohio-class SSBN each carried 24 Trident II/D-5 SLBM, while the other eight carried 24 Trident I/C-4s. Plans for the newer, more capable Trident II/D-5 SLBM to replace the Trident I/C-4s on the other eight Ohio-class SSBN had been scrapped, and Trident II/D-5 deployment would be limited to 250-428 SLBM. Older SSBN included five Franklin class (80 Trident I/C-4s) and four Madison class (64 Trident I/C-4s). All nuclear submarine-launched cruise missiles (SLCM) had been replaced with conventionally armed SLCM on the 21 nuclear attack/cruise missile submarines (SSGN) equipped with SLCM. Plans called for a total of over 2,300 conventionally armed BGM-109A Tomahawk sea-launched cruise missiles to be deployed.

The U.S. Navy in mid-1993 totaled 161 principal surface combatants, 66 nuclear-powered attack submarines (SSN), and 510,600 personnel. These provided 12 active carrier battle groups (CVBG), each carrier having an air wing of some 70 aircraft plus escorting surface vessels and SSN. Of the total of 13 aircraft carriers, 7 were nuclear-powered CVN and 6 were conventionally powered. Modern aircraft included 428 F-14A/D/A plus Tomcat fighters, 474 F/A-18A Hornet fighter/ground attack (FGA) planes, 461 A-6 Intruder/Prowler strike, and 110 E-2C Hawkeye electronic warfare/airborne early warning, plus 375 P-3B/C Orion maritime reconnaissance/anti-submarine warfare (ASW) aircraft. The 9 nuclear and 43 conventionally powered guided-weapons (G) cruisers (CGN/CG) included 25 modern Ticonderoga-class (CG-47 Aegis) equipped with the Aegis/Standard fleet air defense radar/missile system. Other major surface combatants included 38 destroyers and 59 frigates. The Marine Corps, with 183,000 personnel, was organized into three divisions, each with its own air wing. Modern aircraft included 288 F18-A/D Hornet FGA, 35 A-6 Intruder strike, and 219 AV-8A/C Harrier vertical/short takeoff and landing (V/STOL) FGA.

The 499,900-strong U.S. Air Force had approximately 3,451 combat aircraft plus some 1,452 in storage. Among modern types were 824 F-15-A/D Eagle fighters, 1,910 F-16 Falcon FGA, and 55 F-117 stealth FGA, plus 34 E-3 Sentry airborne warning and control systems (AWACS). Most of the 275 F-111 A-F medium bombers were being retired.

The U.S. Army, which comprised 586,200 personnel, formed eight heavy and two airborne divisions—three armoured, four mechanized, one infantry, one air assault, and one airborne—plus two light infantry divisions. Modern armour included 7,828 Abrams M-1/1A1 tanks and 6,329 M-2/3 Bradley armoured infantry fighting vehicles (AIFV), plus some 6,402 M-60/60A1 and M60-A3 tanks and 12,346 M-113 armoured personnel carriers (APC).

United Kingdom. The defense budget for 1993 totaled £23.5 billion. Modernization of the U.K.'s national nuclear forces continued with the deployment of the first of four Vanguard-class SSBN carrying 16 U.S. Trident II SLBM with U.K. warheads, to replace the three SSBN carrying U.S. Polaris A-3 SLBM with U.K. Chevaline warheads. The U.K. would also retain a substrategic nuclear capability. In November, however, it was announced that Britain would limit its deployment of Trident missiles, partly to cut costs and partly to keep in step with the U.S. and Russia, which were sharply reducing their nuclear arsenals.

The army of 134,600 had 426 new Challenger and 700 Chieftain battle tanks, plus 682 Warrior AIFV and 3,585 APC. The Royal Air Force, with 80,900 personnel, had about 688 combat aircraft. The Royal Navy had 59,300 personnel, with 13 SSN and 40 principal surface combatants. Royal Marine personnel totaled some 7,600.

Germany. The German armed forces faced continued problems in retiring or absorbing former East German armed forces personnel, safeguarding and destroying their equipment, and restructuring the unified force, more than

Approximate Strengths of Selected Regular Armed Forces of the World

Country	Military personnel in 000s			Warships[1]			Jet aircraft[3]			
	Army	Navy	Air Force	Aircraft carriers/ cruisers	Submarines[2]	Destroyers/ frigates	Bombers and fighter-ground attack	Fighters/ recon-naissance	Tanks[4]	Defense expenditure as % of 1992 GNP
I. NATO[5]										
Belgium	54.0	4.4	17.3	—	—	3 FFG	72 FGA	35, 15 R	334	1.8
Canada[6]	20.0	12.5	20.6	—	3	4 DDG, 7 FFH, 8 FF	180 F, 18 MR	—	114	2.0
Denmark	16.9	4.5	6.3	—	5	3 FFG	63 FGA	—	462	2.0
France[7]	241.0	65.4	90.6	2 CVS	8, 6 SSN, 5 SSBN	4 DDG, 35 FFG	155 B, 586 F/FGA	51 R, 32 MR	1,013	3.4
Germany	287.0	31.2	90.0	—	20	3 DDG, 3 DD, 8 FF	675 F/FGA	43 R, 19 MR	7,778	2.4
Greece	113.0	19.5	26.8	—	10	4 DDG, 4 DD, 4 FF	271 FB	72, 10 R	2,640	5.6
Italy	223.3	43.6	76.0	1 CVV, 1 CGH	8	4 DDGH, 12 FFH, 10 FF	320 FGA	18 MR	1,210	2.0
Netherlands, The	73.3	17.9	12.0	—	5	4 DDG, 13 FF	166 F/FGA	19 R, 2 MR	743	2.4
Norway	12.9	8.3	8.2	—	12	5 FFG	60 FGA	22 F, 6 MR	261	3.3
Portugal	27.2	12.5	11.0	—	3	3 FFG, 8 FF	59 FB	6 MR	209	2.9
Spain	138.9	32.0[8]	29.8	1 CVV	8	9 FFG, 6 FF	52 FGA	90, 8 R, 7 MR	838	1.7
Turkey	370.0	50.0	60.0	—	15	14 DD, 4 FFG, 7 FF	602 FGA	20, 74 R	4,835	4.7
United Kingdom	134.6	59.3[8]	80.9	3 CVV	2, 13 SSN, 3 SSBN	12 DDG, 26 FFG	23 B, 230 FGA	29 R, 29 MR	1,126	4.0
United States	586.2	693.6[8]	449.9	7 CVN, 6 CV, 9 CGN, 13 CG, 7 LHA, 5 LPH, 11 LPD, 28 LSD/T	66 SSN, 23 SSBN, 21 SSGN,	7 DDG, 31 DD, 51 FFG, 8 FF	205 SB, 237 B, 4,050 FGA/F	162 R, 375 MR/ASW	15,120	5.3
II. NON-NATO EUROPE										
Albania	60.0	2.0	11.0	—	2	—	22 FGA	70	900	2.3
Armenia	20.0	—	—	—	—	—	6 F/FGA	3	160	2.5
Austria	46.0	—	6.0	—	—	—	30 FGA	24	169	0.9
Azerbaijan	38.9	2.1	1.6	—	—	—	47 F/FGA	—	286	. . .
Belarus	50.5	—	29.7	—	—	—	156 FGA	208 F, 51 R	3,287	4.5
Bosnia and Herzegovina[9]	60.0	50.0	80.0	—	—	—	—	—	330	. . .
Bulgaria	52.0	3.0	21.8	—	2	1 FF	76 FGA	152, 70 R	2,209	5.7
Croatia	95.0	0.3	4.6	—	—	—	—	—	200	24.1
Czech Republic	71.9	—	35.6	—	—	—	107 FGA	97	1,573	. . .
Finland	27.3	2.5	3.0	—	—	—	—	86	230	1.9
Georgia	20.0	—	—	—	—	—	—	—	—	3.2
Hungary	60.5	—	17.5	—	—	—	—	59, 11 R	1,331	3.5
Ireland	11.2	1.0	0.8	—	—	—	—	—	—	1.2
Moldova	3.8	—	2.1	—	—	—	—	31 F	—	2.1
Poland	188.5	19.2	79.8	—	3	1 DDG, 1 FF	124 FGA	232, 29 R	2,850	2.3
Romania	161.0	19.0	23.1	—	—	1 DDG, 5 FF	89 FB	285, 22 R	2,869	2.9
Slovakia	33.0	—	14.0	—	—	—	41 FGA	97, 8 R	935	. . .
Slovenia	13.0	—	—	—	—	—	—	—	123	1.9
Sweden[10]	43.5/729.0	9.8	11.5	—	12	—	74 FGA	221, 50 R	338	2.5
Switzerland[10]	20.0/565.0	—	3.0/60.0	—	—	—	86 FGA	127, 18 R	785	1.6
Ukraine	217.0	—	171.0	—	—	—	115 B, 184 FGA	509 F, 87 R	5,700	3.8
Yugoslavia[11]	100.0	7.5	29.0	—	5	4 FF	188 FGA	126, 71 R	640	27.8
III. RUSSIA										
Russia	1,000.0	320.0	544.0[12]	2 CVV 3 CGN, 1 26 CG	70, 50 SSN, 32 SSBN, 28 SSGN, 5 SSG	24 DDG, 114 FF	170 SB, 488 B, 2,125 FGA	3,400, 445 R, 95 MR	25,000	9.9
IV. MIDDLE EAST AND NORTH AFRICA; SUB-SAHARAN AFRICA; LATIN AMERICA[6]										
Algeria	105.0	6.7	10.0	—	2	3 FF	50 FGA	129, 3 R	960	2.7
Egypt	310.0	20.0	100.0	—	2	4 FF	126 FGA	340, 20 R	3,157	6.0
Iran	320.0	18.0	15.0	—	—	3 DD, 5 FF	140 FGA	115, 8 R	700	. . .
Iraq[13]	350.0	2.0	30.0	—	—	—	6 B, 130 FB	180, 5 R	2,300	. . .
Israel[10]	134.0/598.0	10.0/10.0	32.0/37.0	—	3	—	590 FGA/F	14 R	3,960	11.1
Jordan	90.0	0.6	10.0	—	—	—	62 FGA	32	1,141	11.2
Kuwait	9.0	1.2	2.5	—	—	—	32 FGA	15	159	62.4
Lebanon[14]	40.0	0.5	0.8	—	—	—	—	. . .	350	5.0
Libya	40.0	8.0	22.0	—	5	3 FF	5 B,111 FGA	206, 12 R	2,300	. . .
Morocco	175.0	7.0	13.5	—	—	1 FF	29 FGA	15	284	4.0
Oman	20.0	3.5	3.5	—	—	—	20 FGA	—	73	17.5
Qatar	8.0	0.7	0.8	—	—	—	6 FGA	12	24	. . .
Saudi Arabia	68.0	11.0	18.0	—	—	4 FFG, 4 FF	99 FGA	102, 10 R	696	11.8
Sudan	68.0	1.8	3.0	—	—	—	28 FGA	17	320	15.8
Syria	300.0	8.0	100.0	—	3	2 FF	170 FGA	302, 6 R	4,500	. . .
Tunisia	27.0	5.0	3.5	—	—	—	15 FGA	—	84	3.3
United Arab Emirates	53.0	2.0	2.5	—	—	—	23 FGA	22, 8 R	125	14.6
Yemen	60.0	1.5	3.0	—	—	—	46 FGA	47	1,275	9.3

half of them professionals. Despite these difficulties, Germany was emerging as the largest military power in Europe. Under the CFE Treaty, German armed forces would be limited to a total of 345,000 personnel by 1996 but were to be reduced to 300,000. No non-German NATO forces would be stationed on the territory of the former East Germany. Russian forces stationed there, now reduced to some 58,000 personnel, were to be withdrawn by 1994, but Germany continued to pay their occupation costs.

In 1993 Germany's army comprised 12 divisions (six armoured, three armoured infantry, one mountain, and one airborne), to be reorganized and reduced to 6 divisions by the end of 1994. Armour included 2,122 new Leopard 2 (253 to be upgraded) and 2,007 Leopard 1A1 battle tanks, plus 327 T-72M and 1,455 T-54/-55 former East German tanks in store. The air force had 617 combat aircraft, including 237 new Tornadoes and 24 new MiG-29s, plus 193 older Phantom F-4s. The navy had 14 major surface combatants, together with 115 naval combat aircraft, including 101 Tornado attack/reconnaissance aircraft.

France. Modernization of France's national nuclear forces continued, with five SSBN operational and three on order. All carried the M-4 SLBM. Prestrategic (tactical) nuclear forces were mainly the ASMP air-to-surface missile. Military personnel totaled 411,600 (241,400 in the army). Equipment included 1,000 AMX-30 battle tanks, 816 AMX-10P/PC Milan AIFV, and about 4,000 APC. These were organized in the equivalent of four armoured and two mechanized infantry divisions, plus a Rapid Action Force for overseas intervention of five light divisions. The air force had 796 combat aircraft. The navy's 42 major surface combatants included 2 small carriers, 4 destroyers with SAM (DDG),

Country	Military personnel in 000s			Warships[1]			Jet aircraft[3]			
	Army	Navy	Air Force	Aircraft carriers/ cruisers	Submarines[2]	Destroyers/ frigates	Bombers and fighter-ground attack	Fighters/ recon-nais-sance	Tanks[4]	Defense expenditure as % of 1992 GNP
Angola[15]	35.0	4.0	6.0	—	—	—	49 FGA	15	200	49.5
Kenya	20.5	1.4	2.5	—	—	—	10 FGA	—	80	2.8
Madagascar	20.0	0.5	0.5	—	—	—	12 FGA	—	—	1.1
Mozambique	45.0	1.0	4.0	—	—	—	43 FGA	—	100	10.2
Nigeria	62.0	7.3	9.5	—	—	1 FFG, 1 FF	57 FGA	—	157	0.7
South Africa	47.0	4.5	10.0	—	3	—	116 FGA	14	250	3.0
Tanzania	45.0	1.0	3.5	—	—	—	—	24	65	3.6
Zaire	25.0	1.3	1.8	—	—	—	8 FGA/F	—	60	2.9
Zimbabwe	47.0	—	1.2	—	—	—	23 FGA	12	40	4.3
Argentina	40.4	21.5	8.9	—	2	6 DDG, 7 FFG	6 B, 94 FGA/F	9 MR	266	1.7
Brazil	196.0	50.0[9]	50.7	1 CVS	4	6 DDH, 13 FFG	73 FGA	18	—	0.7
Chile	54.0	25.0[9]	12.8	—	4	4 DDG, 2 DDH, 4 FFG, 2 DD	48 FGA	15	171	2.7
Colombia	120.0	13.0[9]	7.0	—	2	4 FFG	28 FGA	—	—	2.4
Cuba	145.0	13.5[9]	15.0	—	3	3 FF	20 FGA	106	1,575	5.0
El Salvador	28.0	0.5	2.0	—	—	—	—	—	—	1.7
Mexico	130.0	37.0[9]	8.0	—	—	3 DD	—	11	—	. . .
Nicaragua	13.5	0.5	1.2	—	—	—	—	—	130	10.9
Peru	75.0	25.0[9]	15.0	2 CA	9	2 DDG, 4DD, 4 FFG	13 B, 30 FGA	24	300	3.8
Venezuela	34.0	11.0[9]	7.0	—	2	6 FFH	65 FGA/F	—	70	3.6
V. SOUTH AND CENTRAL ASIA; EAST ASIA AND OCEANIA[6]										
Australia	28.6	15.3	19.3	—	5	3 DDG, 5 FFG, 3 FF	18 B, 52 FB	19 MR, 4 R	103	2.4
Bangladesh	93.0	7.5	6.5	—	—	1 FFG, 3 FF	43 FGA	23	70	1.3
China	2,300.0	260.0[9]	470.0	—	39, 1 SSG, 5 SSN, 1 SSBN	18 DDG, 33 FFG, 5 FF	630 B, 600 FGA	4,600, 300 R, 20 MR	8,000	5.0
India	1,100.0	55.0	110.0	2 CVV	15, 1 N	5 DDG, 3 FFH, 14 FF	374 FGA	334, 20 R, 39 MR	3,400	2.5
Indonesia	202.9	44.0[9]	24.0	—	2	12 FFH, 4 FF	40 FGA	14	—	1.4
Japan	149.9	43.1	44.7	—	13	7 DDG, 24 FFH, 31 FF	94 FGA	230, 10 R, 93 MR	1,200	1.0
Kazakhstan/CIS	44.0	—	—	—	—	—	140 FGA/F	80 F, 55 R	1,400	. . .
Korea, North	1,000.0	45.0	82.0	—	25	1 FFG, 2 FF	80 B, 334 FGA	360	3,700	25.7
Korea, South	520.0	60.0[9]	53.0	—	—	5 DDG, 4 DD, 7 FFG, 22 FF	238 FGA	96, 28 R	1,800	3.8
Laos	33.0	0.5	3.5	—	—	—	29 FGA	—	30	. . .
Malaysia	90.0	12.0	12.5	—	—	2 FFG, 2 FFH	33 FGA	17, 4 R	—	4.8
Mongolia	20.0	—	1.2	—	—	—	—	12	650	5.9
Myanmar (Burma)	265.0	12.0	9.0	—	—	—	12	—	46	3.1
New Zealand	4.8	2.3	3.7	—	—	4 FFH	20 FGA	6 MR	—	1.6
Pakistan	510.0	22.0	45.0	—	6	1 DDH, 5 FFG, 6 FF	126 FGA	210, 12 R, 4 MR	1,890	7.7
Philippines	68.0	23.0[9]	15.5	—	—	1 FF	—	7	—	2.2
Singapore	45.0	4.5	6.0	—	—	—	881 FGA	38, 8 R	—	5.4
Taiwan	312.0	60.0[9]	70.0	—	4	8 DDH, 14 DD, 1 FFH 10 FF	418 FGA	6 R, 32 MR	509	4.8
Thailand	190.0	62.0	43.0	—	—	4 FFG, 5 FF	30 FGA	44	153	2.7
Turkmenistan/CIS	28.0	—	—	—	—	—	—	85 F	900	. . .
Vietnam	700.0	42.0[9]	115.0	—	—	1 FFG, 5 FF	65 FGA	175	1,300	. . .
Uzbekistan/CIS	38.0	—	—	—	—	—	70 FGA	30 F	210	. . .

Note: Data exclude paramilitary, security, and irregular forces. Naval data exclude vessels of less than 100 tons standard displacement. Figures are for June 1992. Because of substantive changes in national forces and reassessments of evidence, data may not be comparable with previous editions.

[1]Aircraft carrier (CV); aircraft carrier, nuclear (CVN); aircraft carrier, small (CVS); V/STOL and helicopter carrier (CVV); general purpose amphibious assault ship (LHA); amphibious transport dock (LPD); amphibious assault ship (helicopter) (LPH); dock/tank landing ship (LSD/T); battleship (BBG); heavy cruiser (CA); guided missile cruiser (CG); guided missile cruiser, nuclear (CGN); helicopter cruiser (CAH); destroyer (DD); guided missile destroyer (DDG); frigate (FF); guided missile frigate (FFG); helicopter frigate (FFH); N denotes nuclear powered.

[2]Nuclear-powered attack submarine (SSN); ballistic missile submarine (SSB); guided (cruise) missile submarine (SSG); coastal (C); N denotes nuclear powered.

[3]Bombers (B), fighter, ground attack (FGA), strategic bombers (SB), reconnaissance fighters (R); maritime reconnaissance (MR). Data include jet combat aircraft from all services including naval and air defense. MR also includes propeller-driven ASW and ECM aircraft; data exclude light strike/counterinsurgency (COIN) aircraft.

[4]Main battle tanks (MBT), medium and heavy, 31 tons and over.

[5]Only states with significant military forces are listed.

[6]Of Canada's other military personnel, approximately 25,000 are not identified by service.

[7]French forces were withdrawn from NATO command structure in 1966, but France remains a member of NATO.

[8]Includes marines.

[9]The fighting in Bosnia makes force estimates uncertain for Bosnia and Herzegovina.

[10]Second figure is fully mobilized strength.

[11]Figures refer to force levels for Federal Republic of Yugoslavia composed of Serbia/Montenegro.

[12]Figure includes the Strategic Rocket Forces (144,000), Strategic Aviation (19,000), and the Air Defense Force (230,000), all separate services.

[13]Losses in Operation Desert Storm cause remaining force estimates to be uncertain.

[14]Lebanon's civil war and division mean that there are both national forces and militias plus 30,000 Syrian troops in occupation and Palestinian groups.

[15]Opposition UNITA forces total some 40,000 personnel.

Sources: International Institute for Strategic Studies, 23 Tavistock Street, London, *The Military Balance 1993–1994, Strategic Survey 1992–93.*

and 34 frigates as well as 13 attack submarines (5 nuclear).

Eastern Europe. The armed forces of the rump Yugoslavia (comprising Serbia and Montenegro) included some 136,500 personnel, including an army of some 100,000 with some 640 battle tanks. The air force of 29,000 had 480 combat aircraft, mostly older Soviet types, including 108 MiG-21 fighters, but these aircraft were effective in the continuing fighting in Bosnia and Herzegovina and Croatia. By the end of 1993, Serb forces controlled almost one-third of the territory of Croatia. The governments of Croatia and Bosnia and Herzegovina defended their territories with national militias, as did the former Yugoslav republic of Slovenia, which lay outside the battle zones.

Poland had military forces totaling 287,500, including a 188,500-strong army with 2,545 main battle tanks and a 79,800-strong air force with 468 combat aircraft. The creation of the Czech Republic and Slovakia on Jan. 1, 1993, was accompanied by the division of the former Czechoslovak army. The forces inherited by the Czech Republic numbered 106,500 personnel, including an army of 41,900 with 1,543 tanks and an air force of 36,600 with 226 combat aircraft (mostly MiG-21/-21U/-23 FGA). Slovakia, the smaller and less populous part of the former Czechoslovakia, received armed forces totaling 47,000, including an army of 33,000 (935 tanks) and an air force of 14,000 (146 combat aircraft).

Middle East. The military balance in the Middle East remained heavily influenced by the defeat of Iraq in the 1991 Gulf war. Strongman Saddam Hussein had lost most of his military capability to threaten neighbouring countries but retained sufficient armed forces to continue his rule by terror. Iraqi armed forces personnel totaled perhaps 382,000, including an army of some 350,000 with an estimated 2,200

Japanese tanks carry out maneuvers during a large military exercise in October. Concern over the development of a nuclear weapons capability by North Korea set off a debate in Japan over the country's military preparedness.
LIAU CHUNG REN—ASIAWEEK

battle tanks and 700 AIFV. The air force of 30,000, including 15,000 air defense personnel, had some 130 FGA and 180 fighters. UN economic sanctions against Iraqi remained in force. The UN Special Commission succeeded in verifying the destruction of declared stocks of tactical ballistic missiles and the means of manufacturing them and, despite Iraqi obstruction, located some undeclared manufacturing capabilities.

Iran was reemerging as a major regional military power, with armed forces totaling 473,000 personnel, including an army of some 320,000 personnel with some 700 battle tanks and 900 AIFV/APC, plus 120,000 personnel in the Revolutionary Guard Corps. The air force of 15,000 personnel had some 293 combat aircraft. Iran also appeared to have purchased Chinese M-9 and North Korean improved Scud TBM and to be purchasing North Korean Rodong 1 missiles. Since Iran had over 100 Scud TBM and some Scud-C TBM, it was acquiring a significant rocket force, and some observers were concerned that it could tilt the regional military balance.

Jordan's small but effective army (85,000) had 1,131 battle tanks, and the air force (11,000) had 62 F-5E/F and 32 Mirage F-1BJ/CJ/EJ FGA. Syria's armed forces personnel totaled 408,000, with an army of approximately 300,000 organized into six armoured plus three mechanized and one Republican Guard divisions. Equipment included 1,400 battle tanks and 2,250 AIFV. The air defense command had 60,000 personnel manning 95 batteries with Soviet SAM. The 40,000-strong air force had some 639 combat aircraft.

Israel was still capable of deterring major attacks by Syria, but it increasingly relied on thinly veiled threats of massive retaliation with its nuclear weapons, estimated to include up to 100 warheads and Jericho 1 and 2 SSM (surface-to-surface missiles). It remained the region's strongest military power, especially in the quality of its personnel and weapons, but its defense burden, which topped $6.8 billion for 1993, was difficult to support, even with massive aid from the U.S.

Libya's forces remained numerically large, totaling 70,000 personnel with 2,300 battle tanks (1,200 in storage) and 409 combat aircraft (many in storage). Egypt's conversion from Soviet to Western equipment was completed. The army of approximately 310,000 was equipped with 80 M-1A1 Abrams and 1,447 U.S. M-60A1/-3 plus 20 Ramses II (modified Soviet T-54/-55s). The 30,000-strong air force had 546 combat aircraft. In mid-February the United Arab Emirates announced that they would be purchasing 400 Leclerc battle tanks, choosing the French equipment over the U.S. Abrams M-1A2 and the British Vickers Challenger 2.

South and Central Asia. With the breakup of the former Soviet Union, military analysts recognized a new geostrategic area, South and Central Asia, consisting of the five former Soviet Central Asian republics (Kazakhstan, Kyrgyzstan, Tajikistan, Turkmenistan, and Uzbekistan—discussed above) plus Afghanistan, Pakistan, India, Bangladesh, Sri Lanka, Nepal, and Myanmar (Burma).

In Afghanistan, following the fall of Kabul, the major mujahideen groups took over the military equipment of the former government, including 1,200 battle tanks. Conflict between Pakistan and India remained a danger because of continued civil unrest in Kashmir and Hindu-Muslim religious clashes in India. Such a conflict could potentially escalate to the use of nuclear weapons, since Pakistan and India both appeared to have a limited number of such devices. Pakistan's armed forces totaled 577,000, mainly an army of 510,000 with some 2,000 battle tanks. The air force comprised 45,000 personnel and 393 combat aircraft. India continued to be the major regional military power, with armed forces totaling some 1,265,000 personnel. The 1.1 million-strong army had some 3,400 battle tanks. The air force of 110,000 had 707 combat aircraft, and the navy of 55,000 had 24 surface combatants and 15 submarines.

East Asia and Oceania. Evidence of the growing importance of the Pacific Rim countries was provided in July when 17 countries, including the U.S., Russia, Japan, China, Canada, Australia, New Zealand, and South Korea, met to launch the Asian Regional Forum to work together on defense and stability for the region.

Chinese armed forces in 1993 were being reduced from a total personnel strength of about three million but were still the largest in the area. New estimates of China's nuclear stockpile had grown, but it remained small, with limited numbers of comparatively old, vulnerable delivery systems. These included about 14 ICBM (CSS-3/-4), 90 CSS-2 intermediate-range ballistic missiles (IRBM), and one Xia-class SSBN with 12 CSS-N-3 (J-1) SLBM (modified DF-3s). The army had 2.3 million personnel but fewer than 8,000 battle tanks, while the 470,000-strong air force's 4,970 combat aircraft were mostly modifications of old Soviet models. The navy of 260,000 had 56 major surface vessels plus 45 tactical submarines. Vietnam remained the second largest military power in the area. The end of most economic and military aid from the Soviet Union, however, had forced the government to end its military intervention in Cambodia and Laos and cut its armed forces to a total of 857,000 personnel. The army of 700,000 had approximately 1,300 main battle tanks, and the 15,000-strong air force had approximately 240 combat aircraft, including 175 MiG-21 fighters.

Japan's 1993 defense expenditure was $34.7 billion. Armed forces personnel were being reduced from a total of 237,-700, including an army of 149,900 with 1,200 battle tanks. The air force had 44,700 personnel and 438 combat aircraft, including 73 Japanese-made F-1 FGA and 158 F-15J/DJ Eagle and 72 Phantom F-4 fighters. The 43,100-strong navy had 7 DDG, 55 frigates, and 15 tactical submarines. Taiwan's armed forces, totaling 442,000 personnel, continued to provide a credible defense against China. The army, with 312,000 personnel, had 309 battle tanks, and the 70,000-strong air force had 484 combat aircraft. Defense spending in 1993 totaled $10.4 billion.

South Korea deployed large military forces: 633,000 military personnel, with an army of 520,000 (1,800 battle tanks and 2,000 AIFV) and a navy of 60,000. The air force of 53,000 had 445 combat aircraft, mostly newer American types. The U.S. maintained a large infantry division in South Korea, with 26,000 personnel, and 2 air force wings, with 9,500 personnel and 84 combat aircraft.

Caribbean and Latin America. Russian support for local antigovernment insurgencies, largely funneled through Cuba, had ended with the fall of the U.S.S.R. In Nicaragua the democratically elected president, Violeta Chamorro, had reversed the Soviet and Cuban-backed military buildup, and armed forces personnel had been reduced and stabilized at some 15,200 volunteers. In El Salvador the cease-fire agreed to by the government and the Farabundo Martí National Liberation Front (FMLN) was holding. The FMLN had completed its demobilization by the end of 1992, and the El Salvador army was reduced to 28,000. The capture in September 1992 by the Peruvian armed forces (numbering 115,000) of Abimael Guzman, leader of the Sendero Luminoso (Shining Path), had reduced terrorist attacks somewhat, but the Maoist guerrillas still numbered 5,000–8,000.

These developments highlighted the isolation of Cuba's Pres. Fidel Castro as one of the last Stalinist-style communist leaders. Cuba retained disproportionately large armed forces by regional standards, totaling 173,500 personnel, including an army of 145,000 with 1,575 battle tanks and an air force of some 15,000 and 140 combat aircraft. All overseas Cuban military deployments had ended. Russia had cut almost all aid to Cuba, and Russian forces were down to 2,200 personnel, one-fifth of peak levels (the U.S. maintained 2,300 troops at Guantánamo Bay).

Africa South of the Sahara. Some long-running wars in Africa seemed to be winding down in 1993, but other conflicts, such as the vicious war in Liberia, continued, and racial violence broke out anew in still other countries such as Rwanda and Burundi. Broadly, there seemed to be a collapse of the limited authority of central governments and a spread of anarchy and warlordism, as in Ethiopia and Somalia.

The civil war in Ethiopia had ended in 1991, but no national military force had been formed afterward. The Tigré People's Liberation Front (TPLF), the largest rebel group, with some 100,000 military personnel, had taken over much of the former government's military equipment. The Oromo Liberation Front opposed and often fought with the TPLF. Similarly, in Somalia no national armed forces had been formed after the 1991 revolution, and military equipment and power had been taken over by clans, the traditional source of power. The government in Angola had armed forces totaling some 45,000 and 230 battle tanks. These were to have been merged with the 40,000 troops of the opposition Union for the Total Independence of Angola following a cease-fire and UN supervised elections, but the agreement collapsed. Both sides accused the other of employing South African mercenaries.

South Africa remained the dominant military power in the region but continued streamlining its armed forces, keeping step with Prime Minister de Klerk's political liberalization. Troops numbered 67,500, including an army of 47,000 in 10 area commands (plus a separate Walvis Bay command) with 250 battle tanks and 1,500 Ratel AIFV, a navy of about 4,500, and an air force of 10,000 with 245 combat aircraft.

(ROBIN RANGER)

See also Space Exploration.

This article updates the *Macropædia* article The Technology of WAR.

Mining

For the world's mining industry, uncertainty dominated 1993: about the timing and strength of recovery in the industrialized economies and how this would affect product demand and commodity prices; about the level of raw materials exports from the former Soviet Union; about the implications for minerals supply and demand of China's rapidly expanding economy; and about the future of South Africa, another of the world's leading mineral suppliers. In a climate of growing protectionism, there was also some uncertainty about the future pattern of world commodity trade.

The leading Western economies played a less dominant role in 1993 than in previous years. The high cost of reunification plunged Germany into recession; Japan had yet to recover; and there was only a modest improvement in the U.S. The most impressive growth occurred in the newly industrializing nations of Southeast Asia.

For the former Soviet Union and its previous trading partners in Eastern Europe, the transition from a planned to a free-market economy was proving extremely difficult. The notion of private ownership and capital was often not well understood, and as a result many of those countries were finding themselves in a twilight zone where there was neither plan nor market. The collapse of these economies and the contraction of their defense industries sharply reduced domestic demand for raw materials, leaving a substantial surplus available for export. This was seized upon as a ready means of securing the vital foreign exchange needed to pay for the cost of modernizing industries in order to make them competitive. As the mining industry was only too well aware, Russia's exports led to major imbalances of supply and demand in global markets and contributed to the low prices for a number of metals.

China's path differed from that of the former Soviet Union in that its leaders had not responded to calls for democracy, preferring instead to concentrate on economic development. In that, they proved remarkably successful. During the first half of 1993, the nation's gross domestic product (GDP) grew by 13%. The booming economy and major industrialization program caused demand to outpace domestic supply for a number of key commodities; consequently, imports, especially of copper, soared early in the year. China also emerged during the year as the world's biggest gold consumer for the first time.

South Africa's destiny hung in the balance as progress toward democratic government and a multiracial society faced direct opposition from a minority of white extremists and obstruction by Inkatha, the large Zulu group, which believed that it would lose influence under a new government likely to be led by the African National Congress. The ANC played down earlier talk of nationalization, but this remained a major concern for South Africa's large mining firms.

Meanwhile, South Africa's gold-mining industry continued to dominate world production, with an output of more than 600 metric tons per year. However, declining ore grades, rising costs, and a low gold price rendered several mines unprofitable, and more than 100,000 jobs had been lost over the past three years as the industry sought to improve productivity.

While rapid economic growth continued in East and Southeast Asia and a modest expansion took place in Latin America, for the less developed countries as a whole there was little or no growth. They had lost one-sixth of their commodity-export earnings during the past two years because of falling commodity prices. For sub-Saharan Africa the earnings loss was almost 25%, and per capita incomes remained below 1970 levels.

Privatization became a key feature of the minerals sector in the less developed countries. Mexico led the way in Latin America, having already privatized its copper-mining industry. In 1993 Peru invited bids for the purchase of the assets of its two state-owned base-metals-mining entities, Minero Peru and Centromin, while in Chile state-owned copper giant Codelco began looking into a number of legally available privatization schemes to generate additional capital. In Africa Ghana privatized part of the state gold-mining sector and sought to reduce its interest in Ashanti Goldfields Corp., the country's main mineral-export earner. Zambia was examining ways and means of privatizing Zambia Consolidated Copper Mines, the country's main source of export income.

Exploration. For the mining industry one of the most significant consequences of the end of the Cold War was that few countries in the world were now off limits to exploration. Indeed, the great majority, including several of the newly independent former Soviet republics, were doing their utmost to encourage foreign companies to explore. Even Cuba relaxed its restrictions.

The favourable return on investment kept gold to the fore as the preferred exploration and development target, although there was a welcome resurgence of interest in base metals. Latin America proved to be an increasingly attractive region, especially for North American mining companies. More than 100 foreign mining companies were actively exploring Mexico, mainly for gold, and a discovery in Venezuela triggered a minor gold rush there. Chile, however, was the clear winner. Copper and gold were the main targets there, and with major new deposits poised for development, the country was likely to retain its position as the world's leading copper exporter for many years.

On the other side of the Pacific Rim, Indonesia was a major focus for exploration, and PT Freeport Indonesia, which operated a huge opencut copper mine in Irian Jaya, was leading the way. Its total reserves were approaching one billion metric tons of ore containing 1.5% copper plus significant amounts of gold. Further major discoveries were being made.

In sub-Saharan Africa civil strife, political instability, and poor infrastructure deterred exploration in a number of countries where the geologic potential was unquestioned; examples included Angola and Mozambique. However, Botswana, Namibia, and Zimbabwe enjoyed a good measure of success, and in West Africa, Ghana stood out as a country where government efforts to revitalize the economy and encourage foreign investment in the minerals sector proved successful. Major gold-exploration programs were under way there, and interest was spilling over into Mali, Guinea, and Côte d'Ivoire.

Australia and Canada lost ground because of continuing problems concerning land access and unclear regulations, although both remained among the world's top mineral producers. Their problem, if one existed, lay in the future. Canada's resources were huge, but its ore reserve base was diminishing and, increasingly, exploration funding was being directed offshore. The decision in June to block development of the large Windy Craggy copper-gold-cobalt deposit in the remote northwest of British Columbia by creating a new national park did little to inspire confidence within the industry that the federal government understood the importance of mining to the economy and to the communities in remote areas.

Nevertheless, some major companies were persevering, and the Noranda group, which spent more than Can$100 million on exploration in 1992, mainly in Canada, reported major base and precious metals mineral discoveries. Canada's diamond potential, however, attracted far more publicity. Sparked by a significant discovery at Lac de Gras in the Northwest Territories by Dia Met Minerals, Canada witnessed the biggest claimstaking rush in its history. "Diamond fever" extended into Saskatchewan, Ontario, and Alberta and, although the majority of ventures were highly speculative, the activity was a boon to the exploration service companies in an otherwise lean period. Results from the original discovery suggested that Canada might well join the ranks of diamond-producing countries within a few years.

In Australia in December Parliament confirmed a 1992 High Court ruling that would give Aboriginals the right to file claims for title to lands on the continent and on the Torres Strait islands. Mining companies feared that ownership of established facilities could be challenged and that the law would inhibit new ventures. The government, however, said it expected the number of Aboriginal claims to be small and limited mostly to vacant crown land.

Much exploration interest in Australia was focusing on base metals targets in northern Queensland. Claims by gold-mining companies in 1991 that the introduction of a gold tax would kill exploration and deter investment proved untrue. Annual gold output remained close to record levels of 240 metric tons, and the industry was enjoying a major new surge in exploration.

In the U.S. mineral exploration continued to be hampered by environmental concerns, and protracted public inquiries and onerous permission procedures were the result. Also, congressional bills proposing substantial reforms to the 1872 Mining Law with regard to hard rock minerals on federal land raised a storm of protest from the industry, especially the proposal to introduce royalties. Miners claimed that the reforms threatened the future of mining in the U.S., whereas critics of the law as it stood argued that land was being "given away" and that it allowed mining to take place with insufficient regulation of environmental effects.

Commodities. Since 1991 Russia and China had exerted major influences on the mineral commodity markets, probably affecting Western economies to an extent they were never able to achieve at the height of the Cold War. Russia's exports of base metals, in particular, led to major supply-and-demand imbalances on global markets. When exports jumped initially in 1991, there were doubts that they could be sustained once stockpiles had been depleted, but the government gave a high priority to the raw materials sector, and so high levels of exports continued. Many high-cost Western producers closed down mines, and others were operating at reduced capacity in a bid to return the markets to balance. Nickel and aluminum were especially vulnerable. In October Inco, the world's biggest nickel producer, announced a 16% production cut in a bid to reduce the oversupply. In August the European Community (EC) had imposed import quotas on Russian aluminum at the behest of high-cost European producers. This move was criticized by the industry as a whole.

Against the general downtrend, China's appetite for copper bolstered the price of that metal through late 1992 and early 1993, but copper prices crashed to three-year lows when China withdrew from the market in April in an attempt to cool the national economy. Exports of those metals and materials in surplus, however, were being maintained at a high rate. This had a severe impact on the markets for a host of minor metals and minerals and was particularly serious for tin and tungsten. China's tin exports contributed to a plunge in tin prices and to the landmark decision by Malaysia Mining Corp., once the world's biggest producer, to withdraw permanently from tin mining.

On the London Metal Exchange, the world's leading terminal market for base metals, inventories grew steadily through 1993 under the influence of depressed demand and large shipments from Russia, and by the end of September total stocks had climbed above four million metric tons for the first time ever. Through the use of the futures and options markets, there were various attempts to defy the oversupply and to support metal prices artificially by restricting the availability of metal. This led to volatile trading conditions and absurd situations in the copper and zinc markets, where cash prices were forced up in spite of substantial stock surpluses.

In the precious metals markets, gold was subject to considerable speculative activity, and in the early summer it soared to $400 per ounce, only to fall rapidly again in August. The sale of substantial quantities by central banks from their reserves at the end of 1992 called gold's traditional role into question. It certainly appeared to have declined in importance as a haven for funds at times of international crisis, and even the turmoil in Moscow in early October failed to move the price.

In the energy sector coal remained the world's main source of electricity generation. China was the leading producer, with annual output exceeding one billion metric tons, but international coal trade continued to be dominated by Australia and the U.S. However, the removal of sanctions could allow South Africa to increase its market share, and such emerging producers as Colombia and Indonesia were proving to be strong competitors. Europe was increasingly reliant on imports as deep-mined-coal production continued to decline in Germany and, most sharply, in Britain, where the newly privatized electricity-supply industry turned increasingly to natural gas.

Uranium producers witnessed a further fall in prices. The changed mood toward nuclear power prevented the nuclear industry from expanding at the expected rate, causing many projects to be delayed. Canada increased its dominance as the leading producer and had an ample resource base to sustain its position. The ailing U.S. uranium industry, meanwhile, continued to contract.

Environment and Safety. In Eastern Europe environmental damage as a result of past mining was severe. Previously, there had been few or no regulations to protect the environment, and in eastern Germany, for example, there were vast tracts of ground that needed to be reclaimed as a result of lignite mining. Even more environmental damage was done there by uranium mining. In Russia the cleanup of mining and smelting operations was of concern but, given the current economic problems, it was unrealistic to expect that this would be given top priority except in the most extreme cases and without some external assistance. One such case was the airborne sulfur dioxide from nickel smelters on the Kola Peninsula. A Finnish company, Outokumpu, was providing the technology to modernize and clean up those operations.

Reliable figures on accidents in the mining industry remained difficult to obtain. A stringent health and safety regime supported by legislation and, more important, rigorously enforced was a goal that had yet to be achieved in many countries. Reports from China indicated that its mining industry continued to be one of the most hazardous in the world, but safety standards regarded as adequate in mines in many less developed countries would not be tolerated elsewhere.

Much of the research and development in the mining sector had environmental as well as cost benefits. The rapid growth of solvent extraction and electrowinning to mine and produce copper, for example, not only reduced costs substantially but also, by dispensing with the need to produce copper concentrates, bypassed the smelting step with obvious advantages in terms of sulfur emissions.

(ROGER ELLIS)

See also Earth Sciences; Energy; Industrial Review: *Gemstones; Iron and Steel.*

This article updates the *Macropædia* article Extraction and Processing INDUSTRIES.

RICK ALTMAN—THE STOCK MARKET

Aluminum ingots are piled up in a warehouse. With manufacturing of military hardware greatly reduced in post-Cold War Russia, that country continued to export large amounts of metals, leading to a glut in supplies and new price lows for many Western companies.

Motion Pictures

Hollywood in 1993 continued to dominate international screens and the loyalty of audiences throughout the world to an extent that threatened the survival of smaller national cinemas. At the Venice Festival in September, a conference of major filmmakers from throughout the world met to discuss this issue. U.S. artists proved as alarmed as the rest by the cultural implications of American dominance, but none perceived a solution to an imbalance that ultimately reflected Hollywood's economic strength, marketing skills, and technical superiority. A small victory was won through the new General Agreement on Tariffs and Trade (GATT), which excluded films and television programs from global tariff cuts. Business news was dominated by the efforts of various firms to buy or merge with Paramount Communications Inc.

English-Speaking Cinema. *United States.* Confirming Hollywood's command of world audiences, Steven Spielberg's *Jurassic Park* supplanted the same director's *E.T.—The Extraterrestrial* as the most profitable film of all time. Audiences mesmerized by the extraordinary technical effects that brought prehistoric animals to life seemed untroubled by the film's weak script and poor characterizations. Other top box-office films of the year included *The Fugitive,* based on a vintage television series and directed by a first-time filmmaker, Andrew Davis; Wolfgang Petersen's thriller about a foiled presidential assassination, *In the Line of Fire;* Sydney Pollack's adaptation of John Grisham's best-selling novel *The Firm;* and Adrian Lyne's predictable *Indecent Proposal.* Meanwhile, audiences proved increasingly resistant to star vehicles mechanically concocted for visceral appeal, such as Marco Brambilla's *Demolition Man,* starring Sylvester Stallone and Wesley Snipes (*see* BIOGRAPHIES) and John McTiernan's *The Last Action Hero* with Arnold Schwarzenegger. Another Stallone vehicle, Renny Harlin's *Cliffhanger,* was more favourably accepted.

Artistically, the outstanding U.S. film of the year was Robert Altman's *Short Cuts,* which adapted a group of minimalist short stories by Raymond Carver to construct an apocalyptic fresco of fin de siècle human life, viewed in the microcosm of greater Los Angeles. A different reflection on contemporary American nightmares was Joel Schumacher's *Falling Down,* about an urban dweller who suddenly revolts with violence against the frustrations of daily existence.

The year was generally a good one for comedy. Ivan Reitman's *Dave,* a striking departure from the director's earlier teen extravaganzas, was a political fable in the manner of Mark Twain or Frank Capra, about a simple guy who doubles for the president. In *Manhattan Murder Mystery,* a story of New York socialites caught up in a crime investigation, Woody Allen returned to pure comedy, without philosophical pretensions. Chris Columbus succeeded with Robin Williams cross-dressing as a nanny in *Mrs. Doubtfire.*

Joe Dante's *Matinee* appealingly parodied 1960s horror movies, comparing the fantasy fear on the screen with America's real-life traumas in the Cuban missile crisis. Harold Ramis' *Groundhog Day* dealt with the frustrations and romance of a TV weatherman reliving the same day over and over in a small town in Pennsylvania. In Nora Ephron's *Sleepless in Seattle,* the romantic couple did not meet one another until the end of the movie. Barry Sonnenfeld's *Addams Family Values* continued the saga of the macabre clan, and the satiric *Tim Burton's the Nightmare Before Christmas* displayed masterful animation.

Several actors made notable debuts as directors. In *The Man Without a Face,* in which he also starred, Mel Gibson surmounted a naive script through basic sincerity and instinctive skill. Robert De Niro's *A Bronx Tale,* based on Chazz Palminteri's autobiographical novel, related a boyhood in a Bronx Italian community. De Niro himself played a father trying to extricate his son from the influence of the paternalistic local Mafia boss. Forest Whitaker's first film, *Strapped,* dealt with the hazards of life in a contemporary black community.

Adaptations from other sources included Martin Scorsese's sumptuous and elegant adaptation of Edith Wharton's *The Age of Innocence* and David Cronenberg's disappointing screen version of David Henry Hwang's play *M. Butterfly.* The Australian John Duigan directed a sensitive adaptation of Jean Rhys's *Wide Sargasso Sea.* Philip Kaufman's adaptation of Michael Crichton's best-seller *Rising Sun* took care to portray the Japanese business community in the U.S. in a more flattering light than the original.

A notable example of international production was Agnieszka Holland's *The Secret Garden,* based on Frances Hodgson Burnett's classic children's book. Though U.S.-financed, the film had a Polish director and British cast and was shot in England. Steven Soderbergh made a richly evocative film, adapted from A.E. Hochner's biographical

A dinosaur inspects an automobile in director Steven Spielberg's *Jurassic Park,* which replaced his *E.T.—The Extraterrestrial* as the biggest moneymaker of all time. The film's creatures were generated by computer.

King of the Hill, about a young boy growing up in the Depression era.

Other films of the year meriting mention included Brian De Palma's *Carlito's Way,* with Al Pacino as a Puerto Rican gangster constantly frustrated in his attempts to go straight; Anthony Minghella's well-observed and charming romantic comedy *Mr. Wonderful;* Clint Eastwood's *A Perfect World,* a chase thriller with Eastwood himself in a lead role; Ronald F. Maxwell's conscientious four-hour epic of the Civil War, *Gettysburg;* and the American-Asian director Wayne Wang's adaptation of Amy Tan's best-seller *The Joy Luck Club,* about the difficult relationships of American Chinese mothers and daughters.

Notable films by African-American directors included *Menace II Society,* an unremittingly violent picture of black gang life in Los Angeles, directed by the 21-year-old twin brothers Allen and Albert Hughes; Ayoka Chenzira's feature debut with an independent production, *Alma's Rainbow,* an affectionate and lively portrait of three New York City women; Mario Van Peebles' creation of a black western pastiche in *Posse;* and John Singleton's following of his *Boyz N the Hood, Poetic Justice,* an inner-city love story.

Notable films released late in the year included Steven Spielberg's *Schindler's List,* a powerful true story about a German factory owner in Nazi-occupied Poland who saved his Jewish workers from the Holocaust; Oliver Stone's *Heaven and Earth,* the final movie in his Vietnam trilogy; Jonathan Demme's *Philadelphia,* a drama centred on an AIDS-stricken lawyer; Stephen Surjik's sequel *Wayne's World 2;* Lasse Hallström's *What's Eating Gilbert Grape,* about a quirky household in small-town Iowa; Richard Attenborough's poignant love story *Shadowlands;* Fred Schepisi's satirical *Six Degrees of Separation,* based on the John Guare play; and Alan J. Pakula's political thriller *The Pelican Brief,* from the novel by John Grisham.

At the annual awards ceremony of the Academy of Motion Picture Arts and Sciences in Los Angeles in March, Clint Eastwood's *The Unforgiven* took the Oscars for best film, best director, best supporting actor (Gene Hackman), and best editing. The best actor was Al Pacino in *Scent of a Woman,* and the best actress was Emma Thompson in James Ivory's *Howards End,* which also won awards for screenplay adaptation (Ruth Prawer Jhabvala) and art direction (Luciana Arrighi, Ian Whitmore). The best supporting actress was Marisa Tomei in *My Cousin Vinny. Indochine* (France) was adjudged the best foreign-language film, and Neil Jordan's *The Crying Game* received the award for best original screenplay. Federico Fellini received an honorary Academy Award in recognition of his lifetime achievement; and Audrey Hepburn and Elizabeth Taylor each received the Jean Hersholt Humanitarian Award. Sadly, before the end of the year both Fellini and Hepburn had died. (*See* OBITUARIES.)

Great Britain. Despite the grave economic plight of the British motion-picture industry, the variety and accomplishment of British filmmakers achieved international attention. Internationally financed, the biggest production of the year was Richard Attenborough's film biography *Chaplin. The Remains of the Day,* an adaptation of Kazuo Ishiguro's novel paralleling British domestic life and international politics in the years between World Wars I and II, again displayed Ivory's talent for evoking the culture of a particular time and place. Ivory's career-long partner and producer, Ismail Merchant, meanwhile, made a distinguished feature debut with the British-Indian coproduction *In Custody,* based on a novel by Anita Desai about a disillusioned, drunken poet.

Kenneth Branagh returned to Shakespeare, injecting great comic energy into *Much Ado About Nothing,* costarring his wife, Emma Thompson. (*See* BIOGRAPHIES.) Other directors dealt courageously with issues of present-day Britain. Mike Leigh's *Naked* portrayed the desperate frustration of an intelligent young man unemployed and homeless. Ken Loach's *Raining Stones* was a kindly, pessimistic comedy of the unemployed of the depressed industrial north. Stephen Frears's *The Snapper* was a more optimistic portrait of working-class Dublin. Antonia Bird's gifted first feature, *Safe,* was a compassionate tragedy about the homeless young. Gurinder Chadha's *Bhaji on the Beach* touched lightly on issues of family, race, and feminism in a story of a group of Indian women on a day's outing in the seaside resort of Blackpool, England.

Australia. Australia's outstanding success was Jane Campion's haunting *The Piano,* set in New Zealand in the early colonial period and evoking the passionate romance of a mute woman. The film shared the Palme d'Or at the Cannes Film Festival. Rolf de Heer also attracted international attention with *Bad Boy Bubby,* a grotesque horror comedy about a man incarcerated from childhood by his crazy mother and suddenly launched into the world, with bizarre but unexpected results.

The Nostradamus Kid, by well-known critic and journalist Bob Ellis, was a lively nostalgic reminiscence; Richard Lowenstein's *Say a Little Prayer* was a touching account of the relationship of a lonely little boy and a twentyish drug addict.

Canada. Extensive production throughout English-speaking Canada resulted in a number of excellent and varied works, including Atom Egoyan's intriguing low-budget *Calendar,* in which the director and his wife play a couple in marital breakup; David Wellington's *I Love a Man in Uniform,* a sinister tale about a mild bank clerk transformed by a policeman's uniform; François Girard's *Thirty-two Short Films About Glenn Gould,* a portrait of the enigmatic musical genius presented in a collage of scenes, documentary and acted, their structure based on the Goldberg Variations; and Paul Shapiro's *The Lotus Eaters,* a shrewd, likable picture of the pleasures and pretenses of family life on a British Columbian island in the 1960s.

From Quebec's French-language cinema, Paule Baillargeon directed *Le Sexe des étoiles,* a tender drama about the effect upon a sensitive young girl of her father's transformation into a transsexual. Robert Morin's *Requiem pour un beau sans-coeur* adopted an original narrative style in relating the rise and fall of a small-time crook.

Europe. Outside the still culturally distinctive national productions of Britain, France, Italy, and Scandinavia, a number of European features of 1993 deserve particular mention. These include, from Belgium, Stijn Coninx' *Daens,* a sumptuous period piece about a 19th-century priest dedicated to fighting industrial exploitation; from Greece, the veteran Michael Caccoyannis' sprightly sex comedy, *Up, Down and Sideways,* observing changing mores through the adventures of a middle-aged woman and her gay son; from Germany, the Yugoslav director Dusan Makavejev's comic elegy for the vanished pomp and illusions of Eastern European communism, *Gorilla Bathes at Noon;* from Portugal, 85-year-old Manoel de Oliveira's modern *Madame Bovary, Abraham Valley;* from Spain, a new Pedro Almodovar farrago, *Kika,* about crazy characters in contemporary Madrid; from Turkey, Ohan Oguz' *Whistle if You Come Back,* the story of a friendship between two outcasts—a dwarf and a transvestite—and Yavuz Ozkan's *Two Women,* which examines issues of power and politics through the story of the rape of a high-class prostitute by an influential politician.

France. The biggest production of the year was Claude Berri's massive and spectacular but pedestrian adaptation

In *The Piano,* by Australian filmmaker Jane Campion, Ada (Holly Hunter) gives her neighbour Baines (Harvey Keitel) a lesson. The film, a story of passion set in 19th-century New Zealand, shared the Palme d'Or with *Farewell, My Concubine* at the Cannes Film Festival.
MIRAMAX

of Émile Zola's *Germinal.* Other established directors at work during 1993 included Eric Rohmer, with *L'Arbre, le maire et la mediathèque,* a playful exercise about the battle between politicians and ecologists. Costa-Gavras returned to the French studios with *La Petite Apocalypse,* a comedy about people from the former Communist nations adapting to free-market economies.

Blue, the first episode of Krzysztof Kieslowski's *Red, White and Blue* trilogy, set in Paris, dealt with the efforts of a woman to reshape her life after the death of her husband and revelations about their marriage. Patrice Leconte's *Tango* provided an ironic study of macho malehood. Coline Serreau's comedy *La Crise* targeted the French middle class in an era of social breakdown. The central figure in Aline Issermann's *L'Ombre du doute* was a small girl facing the disbelief of family and authorities when she charges her father with abuse.

Italy. Older directors espoused historical subjects. Franco Zeffirelli's *Sparrow* was an ungripping tale of a 19th-century novice briefly distracted by love, and Paolo and Vittorio Taviani's *Fiorile* used a time-machine device to survey two centuries of Italian history, seen through the fortunes of an unlucky Tuscan family.

The fight against organized crime provided the theme for Ricky Tognazzi's taut and polished *La scorta,* Margarethe von Trotta's *Il lungo silenzio,* and Giuseppe Ferrara's *Giovanni Falcone,* an earnest but disappointing re-creation of historical events. More intimate contemporary themes concerned Silvio Soldini in *Un anima divisa in due,* a keenly observed story of a store detective's infatuation with a Gypsy girl, and Francesca Archibugi's *Il grande cocomero,* about the therapeutic relationship of a disturbed child and a young neurologist.

Scandinavia. Notable Swedish films included Suzanne Osten's *Talk! It's So Dark,* a compelling dialogue between an émigré Jewish psychiatrist and a young Swedish Nazi, and Ake Sandgren's *The Slingshot,* adapting the humorous impressionistic memoirs of a 1920s boyhood by the Jewish socialist Roland Schutt. A former physician, Nils Mamors of Denmark, created a tragic portrait of a depressive, *Pain of Love,* while the Icelandic director Oskar Jonass revealed a developed sense of comedy in *Remote Control*—an escalation of comic horrors beginning with a stolen TV remote control.

In Finland disciples of the leading director Aki Kaurismaki made creditable debuts: Veikko Aaltonen with *The Prodigal Son,* a thriller involving a sadomasochistic relationship; Kari Paljakka with *Goodbye, Trainmen,* a study of the friendship of two young men, one of whom succumbs to an aimless life; and Christian Lindblad with *Ripa Hits the Skids,* an improbably likable portrait of the decline and fall of an unsavoury failed filmmaker.

Eastern Europe. The film industries of the former Communist countries were all undergoing the crisis of transformation to a free market. Dominant themes were the problems of adjustment and reexamination of the recent past. Poland's greatest director, Andrzej Wajda, returned to the Polish uprising of 1944 with *The Ring of the Crowned Eagle*—this time liberated from the pressures that conditioned his great classics of the 1950s. From Slovakia, Juraj Jakubisko's *Its Better to Be Healthy and Wealthy than Poor and Ill* treated the problems of living in post-Communist society with wayward humour.

Commonwealth of Independent States. Production, shrinking fast from the boom of 1991, ranged wildly from sex comedies (Nikolay Dostal's *Small Giant, Big Sex*) to Elena Tsiplakova's perceptive observation of personal histories of workers and inmates in an orphanage, *In Thee I Trust.* Among the year's most memorable films was an autobiographical drama, *And the Wind Returneth,* by the returning émigré Mikhail Kalik—a sad saga of life as a Russian Jew from the 1930s to the 1960s and a career in films constantly frustrated by censorship.

Hungary. In a generally lean year for Hungarian cinema, Ildiko Szabo's outstanding *Child Murders* created a memorable character in a 12-year-old whose air of maturity and worldly wisdom conceal an emotional hunger that leads to catastrophic results. A child was also the central figure in Andras Jeles' powerful drama of the odyssey of a Jewish family in World War II, *Why Wasn't He There?*

Latin America. Argentine directors continued to examine the horrors of the junta years. Notable among these inquests were Lita Stantic's *A Wall of Silence* and Marcelo Pineyro's debut feature *Tango Feroz—the Legend of Tanguite,* which reconstructed the life and death of a popular singer who fell victim to the terror.

Mexican directors revealed a taste for filmed biographies, including those of a 1950s film star, *Miroslav* (director Alejandro Pelayo Rangel); the 17th-century California missionary *Kino* (director Felipe Cazals); and the 16th-century *Bartolomé de Las Casas* (director Sergio Olhovich). An outstanding film on a contemporary theme was Francisco Athie's debut work, a ferocious portrayal of Mexican slum life, *Lolo.* Also noteworthy was Alfonso Arau's domestic drama *Like Water for Chocolate.*

Middle East and North Africa. Production throughout North Africa remained sporadic. Among the most notable films of the year was a first feature by Malik Lakhdar-Hamina from Algeria, *Automne: Octobre à Alger,* about corruption and fundamentalist oppression in Algeria during the 1980s. A promising first film from Egypt, Khalid al-Haggar's *Little Dreams,* looked at the disenchantment of a generation with the myth of Pres. Gamal Abdel Nasser through the experiences of a young boy in the 1967 Six-Day War.

In *Life According to AGFA,* Assi Dayan used a modest bar in Israel, during 12 hours of one night, as a microcosm of a threatened society. Mohamed Malas' *The Night* was a distinguished drama from Syria relating, with dignity and without malice, the grave impact of the creation of the state of Israel on some hapless Arab peoples.

Far East. *China.* The new generation of Chinese directors favoured intimate, human dramas: Sun Jou's *Heartstrings,* about the relationship of a 10-year-old Peking (Beijing) Opera player and his grandfather; Li Shaohong's *Family Portrait,* which chronicles the reunion of a married man and the newly orphaned young son of his failed previous marriage; Ning Ying's *For Fun,* an endearing story of a group of aged Peking Opera veterans who get together to form an amateur opera group; and Huang Jianxin's *Stand Up, Don't Bend Over,* a mosaic of life in a contemporary apartment block.

Though officially disapproved, the year's most outstanding films resulted from coproduction with Hong Kong. These included Tian Zhuangzhuang's *The Blue Kite,* which traced the tribulations of one small backyard community in the turbulent years between the death of Stalin and the first nightmare of the Cultural Revolution; Wang Haoshuai's *Days,* chronicling the decline and ultimate collapse of a marriage under the social pressures of contemporary China; and the co-winner of the Cannes Film Festival Palme d'Or, Chen Kaige's (*see* BIOGRAPHIES) *Farewell, My Concubine,* which surveyed the troubled history of China from the 1920s to the end of the Cultural Revolution through the fortunes and loves of two actors of the Peking Opera.

Taiwan. A coproduction with the U.S., Ang Lee's *The Wedding Banquet,* shared the main prize at the Berlin Film Festival and went on to achieve major international success. Its story of a young Chinese homosexual living with an American man but hustled into a marriage of convenience with a Chinese girl to satisfy family custom, was told with enormous humour and charm. In *The Puppet Master,* Hou Hsiao-hsien examined, through the memoirs of an old puppet artist, the history of Taiwan under Japanese colonial rule.

Japan. Three of Japan's great veterans made films in 1993. At 82, Akira Kurosawa conceived a quiet, low-key study of one man's life from World War II to the present, *Not Yet.* At 78, Kon Ichikawa experimented with new high-definition video techniques for *Fusa,* a haunting tale based on a 16th-century classic love story. Finally, 81-year-old Kaneto Shindo directed a touching adaptation of an erotic classic, *The Strange Story of Oyuki.*

Among younger Japanese filmmakers, the independent director Shinji Somai tackled the previously taboo subject of divorce in *Moving.* Maruhachi Shinoda's *In Fading Memory,* a recollection of a first romance in the 1960s, was an assured and sensitive first feature.

India. Of the most notable productions of the year, Goutam Ghose's *Boatman of the River Padma* was a sensitive adaptation of Manik Bannerji's Bengali classic about coexistence between traditionally opposed religious communities, and Girish Karnad's *The Flowering Tree* was a loyal adaptation of a Karnataka folktale. An original subject, Shyam Benegal's *The Seventh Horse of the Sun* was a complex, three-episode film in which a young man relates romantic stories of his boyhood, adolescence, and young manhood.

Africa. Film activity in Africa was scattered but vital. From Burkina Faso, Idrissa Ouedraogo's *Samba Traore* adapted a familiar Western theme: a young fugitive fleeing from his own crime and guilt. A likable fable, S. Pierre Yameogo's *Wendemi, Child of the Good God* was the story of a young man in search of his identity.

From Burundi, Leonce Ngabo's *Gito the Ungrateful,* a coproduction with France and Switzerland, provided a lively comic satire on the pretensions of young, macho, foreign-educated men. From Côte d'Ivoire, Roger Gneon M'Bala's *In the Name of Christ* tackled the sensitive subject of religion through the story of a fake religious leader who starts a new cult. A Senegalese-French coproduction, Moussa Touré's *Touba Bi* was a sophisticated and endearing portrait of cultural clash, through the story of a Senegalese filmmaker in Paris. (DAVID ROBINSON)

Nontheatrical Films. Every few years a documentary comes along that stands out heads above all else. During 1993 *Ishi, the Last Yahi* was that film. Made by Jed Riffe and Pamela Roberts (Rattlesnake Productions) of Berkeley, Calif., it is the story of the last "wild" native American Indian, who was found and studied by anthropologists for three years until his death in 1915. The film won honours in one German and three U.S. competitions.

At Ekofilm in Ostrava, Czech Republic, the grand prix winner was *Decade of Decision,* made for the 1992 Earth Summit in Brazil. It shows the pressures on people to adjust to a changing world aggravated by poverty, wasteful consumption, and bad policies. Narrated by Walter Cronkite, it was produced by Meg Maguire of Maguire/Reeder for the Population Crisis Committee in Washington, D.C.

Another film receiving accolades was the Best of Festival winner at the U.S. International Film and Video Festival in Chicago, *Extreme Skiing 3, The Scot Schmidt Story.* Written and directed by Brian Sisselman, it is a profile of one of the recognized personalities in the world of "extreme skiing." (THOMAS W. HOPE)

See also Photography; Television and Radio.

This article updates the *Macropædia* article MOTION PICTURES.

PHOEBE A. HEARST—MUSEUM OF ANTHROPOLOGY, UNIVERSITY OF CALIFORNIA AT BERKELEY

Ishi, who was studied by anthropologists in the early 20th century, was said to have been the last "wild" Native American. The documentary film *Ishi, the Last Yahi,* by Jed Riffe and Pamela Roberts, won a number of awards during the year.

Museums

The destruction and damage of museums, monuments, and historic zones in armed conflicts and terrorist attacks continued into 1993. The Olympic Village museum of sport in the hills above Sarajevo, Bosnia and Herzegovina, was burned to the ground by withdrawing Serb forces. In November the 16th-century bridge at Mostar, long a symbol of peaceful multiculturalism in the Bosnian city, was destroyed by Croat shelling. In Croatia proper, significant progress was made in reopening collections damaged in the fighting, although a comprehensive review published in September 1993 reported the loss of over 40 of the republic's museums. An even more alarming development was the apparently motiveless attack on one of the world's oldest and greatest art museums, the Uffizi Gallery in Florence, which was more than 400 years old. On May 27, a powerful car bomb exploded without warning in a parking area immediately to the rear of the main building, causing extensive damage to the structure and collections, although only three works were totally lost. Unesco moved to strengthen relevant international law on destruction of cultural objects and published a major study on the problem in September.

The fate of collections lost in World War II suddenly became an issue again during 1993. In the West much of the cultural property looted by the Nazis from occupied countries had been returned as part of the postwar peace process, but the same was not true for the former Eastern bloc, and many unanswered questions remained. Improving relations between East and West led to announcements by the Russian Ministry of Culture that more than 60% of the Franz Koenigs collection of outstanding Old Master drawings seized by the Nazis from the Boymans Museum in Rotterdam, Neth., were safe in Moscow's Pushkin Museum of Fine Arts. The Pushkin also held, apparently intact, the 8,000 archaeological objects and an estimated 60,000 documents and letters of Heinrich Schliemann, the controversial 19th-century excavator of Troy, that had been missing from the Berlin Museum since 1945. Both Germany and Turkey filed claims to the collection. At the same time, Russia was demanding that Western governments investigate the fate of the estimated 200,000 items looted from the former Soviet Union by Nazi Germany, including Peter the Great's "Amber Room" from the Imperial Summer Palace.

After several years of worldwide recession, the pace of creating and building new museums was declining, and many institutions seemed to be having difficulty keeping afloat. In Great Britain, for example, the entries in the annual Museums Association *Yearbook* showed that, probably for the first time since 1945, more museums closed than opened. Several U.S. museums experienced financial difficulties; a near-million-dollar deficit at the Cleveland (Ohio) Museum of Art and a $3.5 million cutback in county funding at the Los Angeles County Museum of Art forced the end of several planned exhibitions and services and necessitated staff cuts. A nationwide study in 1988–91 by the Business Committee for the Arts showed that corporate patronage had dropped by 18% from its 1988 level. This trend was apparent in 1993 when the IBM Corp. announced that it would close its IBM Gallery of Science and Art after 10 years of operation in that company's New York City headquarters.

Still, a number of significant new museum projects and building programs came to fruition. The Dallas (Texas) Museum of Art opened its new Nancy and Jake Harmon Building to focus on the arts of the Americas, an unusual attempt to juxtapose European-influenced North American art and pre-contact Central and South American objects. The Michael C. Carlos Museum at Emory University, Atlanta, Ga., opened a new addition to its 1919 beaux arts museum. The Birmingham (Ala.) Museum of Art became the largest municipal museum in the Southeast when it reopened after a two-year closure for expansion.

Other notable gallery opening or reopening events in the U.S. included the new Norman Rockwell Museum in Stockbridge, Mass.; significant expansion of the New Orleans (La.) Museum of Art; the new medieval galleries at the Philadelphia Museum of Art; the redesigned west wing of the Brooklyn Museum; new gallery space and a restoration of the 1886 Romanesque Great Hall at the Cincinnati (Ohio) Art Museum; renovation of the Denver (Colo.) Art Museum in honour of its centennial; the new Frederick R. Weisman Art Museum at the University of Minnesota; nine new galleries at the Palmer Museum of Art at Pennsylvania State University; and the renovated David and Alfred Smart Museum of Art at the University of Chicago.

The most important museum opening in 1993, however, was certainly that of the United States Holocaust Memorial Museum in Washington, D.C.; ceremonies in April were led by Pres. Bill Clinton, with Jewish leaders from around the world and many European heads of state and government in attendance. The striking museum building, which cost $168 million to construct, was financed by private donations and built on land donated by the federal government near the Mall, Washington's main museum area. The exhibits constitute the largest collection in the Western Hemisphere of materials pertaining to the Nazi campaign to exterminate Jews. By year's end more than one million visitors had crowded into the museum, and officials took the unusual step of requesting people to postpone their visits if possible. (*See* RELIGION: *Judaism*.) A smaller Holocaust memorial museum opened in Los Angeles earlier in the year.

In New York City the Jewish Museum reopened on its 100th anniversary and significantly expanded its gallery space. The former Center for African Art changed its name to the Museum for African Art and opened a new facility in lower Manhattan. In nearby Hartford, Conn., the Wadsworth Atheneum opened the Fleet Gallery, the first permanent space in any mainstream U.S. gallery devoted to African-American art. The Freer Gallery of Art, part of the Smithsonian Institution in Washington, D.C., reopened after a 4½-year refurbishing that added much new storage and gallery space, including a new underground gallery linking the Freer to the Arthur M. Sackler Gallery, the Smithsonian's other Asian art museum, which itself received an anonymous $2.8 million benefaction in 1993. A new Sackler museum was also opened in Beijing (Peking) in May.

In Europe the museum event of the year was the relaunching in November, to mark its bicentennial, of one of the continent's oldest, the Louvre Museum in Paris. The large area of underground circulation and public service areas, with architect I.M. Pei's controversial glass pyramid over the new public entrance, now linked the old familiar (now extensively refurbished) museum; the restored Richelieu wing; the remains of the medieval castle; and completely new underground museum, commercial (*e.g.,* fashion industry), and public parking facilities. Elsewhere in Paris, the Grand Palais was closed in November for repairs.

The revolutionary management structure for French national museums devised by former culture minister Jack Lang also evoked much interest. A new semipublic body, the Etablissement du Musée du Louvre, was created to take over the museum's assets and manage all types of income generated by them. The body was directed by an administrative council and headed by an executive president, a professionally trained curator who combined the tradition-

The opening of the Richelieu wing (right), formerly government offices, adds exhibition space to the Louvre. Under the direction of architect I.M. Pei, the extensive project to expand and renovate the Louvre was completed on the 200th anniversary of the museum.
OWEN FRANKEN

ally distinct roles of director and chairman of the board of trustees. Similar changes were made at other national museums in Paris, including the Orsay Museum and the Pompidou Centre.

Innovation elsewhere was generally on a more modest scale: a new national maritime museum in Auckland, N.Z.; the challenging St. Mungo Museum of Religions in Glasgow, Scotland, a city long known for its deep sectarian divisions; and the remarkable Casa de Pontal museum in Rio de Janeiro, a private initiative by the creator of its unique collection of Brazilian popular folk art.

Museums also continued to innovate in their approaches to their public missions and to intermuseum cooperation. One remarkable example was the national project "Quest for a Swedish History," possibly the most ambitious coordinated investigation and presentation of history ever attempted by a nation's museums, launched in May 1993. Involving both the State Historical Museum and the nearby Nordic Museum in Stockholm as well as more than 40 regional and local museums throughout the country, the project aimed to rediscover the history of the nation and communicate it to the whole of the population. Another unprecedented partnership was formed between the Whitney Museum of American Art in New York City and the San Jose (Calif.) Museum of Art. Usually able to display only about 3% of its holdings, the Whitney would now send portions of its collections for display in the new wing of the San Jose Museum.

In the United States the new administration, with apparent bipartisan support, proposed to reinstate the tax break for donations to museums to allow the current market value of the art work to be the basis for calculating its value for tax purposes. Since 1986 such donations had been evaluated at their original purchase price.

(PATRICK J. BOYLAND; JOSHUA B. KIND)

See also Art Exhibitions and Art Sales.
This article updates the *Macropædia* article MUSEUMS.

Music

Classical. Amid a continuing economic slowdown in 1993, there was no shortage of furrowed brows among managers of orchestras and opera companies. What was surprising was the relatively small number of outright foldings and cancellations. Covent Garden postponed a projected new production of Fromental Halévy's *La Juive,* substituting eight performances of *La Bohème,* and La Monnaie in Brussels postponed Judith Weir's *Missa e combattimento;* frustrated at cancellation of plans for a new home for the Canadian Opera Company, Brian Dickie resigned as the Toronto company's general director. However, amid widespread worry about its fiscal viability, the New York City Opera put on a happy face for its 50th birthday, presenting a festival of three world premieres on succeeding nights—Ezra Laderman's *Marilyn* (based on the life of Marilyn Monroe), Lukas Foss's *Griffelkin,* and Hugo Weisgall's *Esther*. In both the U.K. and the U.S. a steady stream of major new orchestral works had first performances, and despite growing talk of a glut in the recordings market, each month brought a veritable flood of new releases, reissues, and repackagings.

It was not a big year for anniversaries. The centenary of Tchaikovsky's death and the 50th anniversary of Rachmaninoff's might have made more of a splash if both composers had not already been so secure in the performing repertory. The Grieg sesquicentenary was marked by a 24-disc recorded survey of the composer's output on the Victoria label, and *Gramophone* magazine gave its Record of the Year award to a Grieg recital by mezzo-soprano Anne Sofie von Otter. The two record labels most closely associated with the late Leonard Bernstein—Sony Classical and Deutsche Grammophon—observed his 75th birthday with a torrent of reissues; perhaps the most important were video releases of Bernstein's justly renowned "Young People's Concerts." The 80th anniversary of Benjamin Britten's birth occasioned a month-long Britten Festival in London, directed by Mstislav Rostropovich, and publication of a revelatory biography by Humphrey Carpenter.

A number of significant conductorial appointments were announced: Jukka-Pekka Saraste to the Toronto Symphony Orchestra (effective in 1994), Michael Tilson Thomas to the San Francisco Symphony (1995), Sir Colin Davis to the London Symphony (1995, succeeding Tilson Thomas), Charles Dutoit to the NHK Orchestra in Tokyo (1996), and Vjekoslav Sutej to the Houston (Texas) Grand Opera (1994). In addition, Antonio de Almeida took over as music director of the Moscow Symphony Orchestra, Sian Edwards at the English National Opera, and Graeme Jenkins as artistic director of the Dallas (Texas) Opera. Among notable departures were those of Eduardo Mata from the Dallas Symphony Orchestra, Amelia Friedman from the Bath (England) Festival, and John Williams from the Boston

Pops. Baritone Dietrich Fischer-Dieskau retired from performing, and mezzo-soprano Christa Ludwig began a series of farewell recitals.

The Pulitzer Prize for music went to Christopher Rouse's trombone concerto, and the Grawemeyer Award (presented by the University of Louisville, Ky.) to Karel Husa for his cello concerto. Rostropovich was among the winners of the 1993 Japanese Praemium Imperiale awards for lifetime achievement in the arts. Winners of the three top prizes in the Van Cliburn piano competition were Simone Pedroni (Italy), Valery Kuleshov (Russia), and Christopher Taylor (U.S.). First prize in the 10th Robert Casadesus piano competition went to Amir Katz from Israel.

Deaths included those of conductors Erich Leinsdorf and Maurice Abravanel, violinist-conductor Alexander Schneider, pianist Mieczyslaw Horszowski (at age 100), sopranos Arleen Auger and Lucia Popp, mezzo-soprano Tatiana Troyanos, contralto Marian Anderson, and bass Boris Christoff. (*See* OBITUARIES.) Twenty years after the death of Czech conductor Karel Ancerl, his remains were transported from Toronto to Visehrad Cemetery in his native land.

Opera. The Finnish National Opera opened a new house in Helsinki, and the Opéra de Lyon (France) inaugurated a bold new home set within and above the walls of an 1831 theatre. With Glyndebourne's theatre under construction, the British company's productions were transferred to the Royal Festival Hall in London and the new Symphony Hall in Birmingham. The Metropolitan Opera in New York City, one of the last holdouts against above-the-stage projections of translations, announced that a system of seat-back video screens would be installed to serve the same purpose.

In addition to the three new operas presented by New York City Opera—actually, Foss's was a revision of a work dating to 1955—world premieres included Michael Berkeley's *Baa Baa Black Sheep* (Cheltenham [England] Festival), Jonathan Harvey's *Inquest of Love* (English National Opera), Kevin Volans' *The Man Who Strides the Wind* and Julian Grant's *A Family Affair* (both by the English National Opera's Contemporary Opera Studio), Wilfried Hiller's *Der Rattenfänger* (Dortmund [Germany] Opera), Libby Larsen's *Mrs. Dalloway* (Lyric Opera, Cleveland, Ohio), and Daron Hagen's *Shining Brow* (Madison [Wis.] Opera). *The Cave,* a new "documentary video music theatre" work by Steve Reich and video artist Beryl Korot, was premiered at the Vienna Festival, after which it traveled to Berlin, Amsterdam, and New York City. In England the BBC's Channel 4 inaugurated a series of specially commissioned television operas with Orlando Gough's *The Empress of Newfoundland,* Peter Blagvad's *Camera,* and Stewart Copeland's *Horse Opera.* A hybrid form, the play with incidental music, was revived with a London performance of Euripides' *The Bacchae,* with music by Iannis Xenakis.

Karlheinz Stockhausen's *Tuesday of Light* was given its first staged performance by the Leipzig (Germany) Opera, and the Santa Fe (N.M.) Opera presented the first professional U.S. stagings of Kurt Weill's *The Protagonist* and *The Tsar Has His Photograph Taken.* Debussy's early and incomplete *Rodrigue et Chimène* was orchestrated by Edison Denisov and presented by the Opéra de Lyon. The same composer's *Pelléas et Mélisande* was mounted in unusual new productions by the opera companies of Amsterdam and Seattle (Wash.), the former directed by Peter Sellars and set in a villa-fortress in California, the latter with decor by the glass artist Dale Chihuly.

Verdi's *Stiffelio* was revived at Covent Garden (in an Elijah Moshinsky production set in Montana) and at the Metropolitan Opera in New York (using the newly published critical edition). Other notable revivals included Jean-Baptiste Lully's *Phaëton* (Opéra de Lyon), Gounod's *Philémon et Baucis* (Teatro Coccia, Novarra, Italy), Spohr's *Faust* (Bielefeld, Germany), Alexander Zemlinsky's *The Birthday of the Infanta* (Spoleto Festival, Charleston, S.C.), and Sir Michael Tippett's *Midsummer Marriage* (New York City Opera). The Lyric Opera of Chicago inaugurated a new *Ring,* directed by August Everding and designed by John Conklin, with Zubin Mehta conducting. The young Italian mezzo-soprano Cecilia Bartoli caused quite a stir in her stage debut in the U.S., in a Houston (Texas) Grand Opera production of Rossini's *Barber of Seville* (*see* BIOGRAPHIES).

Orchestras. For all the long-standing predictions of the imminent demise of the symphony, at least three major essays in the form had high-profile premieres: Alfred Schnittke's Sixth (by the National Symphony Orchestra of Washington, D.C., on tour in Moscow), Witold Lutoslawski's Fourth (by the Los Angeles Philharmonic, with the composer conducting), and Ellen Taaffe Zwilich's Third (by the New York Philharmonic). Other notable premieres included Peter Lieberson's viola concerto (Toronto Symphony Orchestra), Husa's violin concerto (New York Philharmonic), Geoffrey Burgon's trumpet concerto (City of London Festival), Deb-

BEATRIZ SCHILLER

Placido Domingo sings the role of the minister in a production of Verdi's *Stiffelio* at the Metropolitan Opera. Nineteenth-century censors were successful in banning the work, which is about marital infidelity, but there were revivals in 1993 in New York City and London.

orah Mollison's violin concerto (New London Orchestra), John Adams' chamber symphony (The Hague), and Robin Holloway's Second Concerto for Orchestra (BBC Symphony Orchestra, London). The tone poem seemed very much alive and well, too, with new contributions by Anthony Powers (*Terrain,* introduced by the BBC Welsh Symphony Orchestra), York Höller (*Aura,* Chicago Symphony Orchestra), John Casken (*Darting the Skiff,* Northern Sinfonia at Cheltenham), and Shulamit Ran (*Legends,* Chicago). Major new works for chorus and orchestra included *Requiem for the Victims of the Mafia,* a collective work by seven young Italian composers (Marco Tutino, Lorenzo Ferrero, Carol Galante, Paolo Arcà, Matteo D'Amico, Giovanni Sollima, and Marco Betta) premiered at Palermo Cathedral, and in England the octogenarian George Lloyd's *Symphonic Mass* (Brighton Festival) and Dmitry Smirnov's *A Song of Liberty* (Leeds Festival).

A topic of much discussion—and controversy—among orchestra professionals and critics in the U.S. was a study by the American Symphony Orchestra League. Addressing long-standing problems of graying audiences and shaky fiscal conditions, it advocated a rejection of traditional, European-based models in favour of new and distinctively American approaches to programming and promotion.

Festivals. The Edinburgh Festival featured the young Scottish composer James MacMillan, with a schedule including first performances of his trumpet concerto, *Epiclesis,* and two music-theatre works, *Tourist Variations* and *Visitatio Sepulchri.* The Venice Biennale turned its attention to Luigi Nono; the Helsinki Biennale, to Lutoslawski. A Czech Festival at London's South Bank Centre included two operas by composers incarcerated at the Nazi concentration camp at Theresienstadt (now Terezin)—Viktor Ullman's *The Emperor of Atlantis* and Hans Krasa's *Brundibar.* Among the features of the Vienna Festival was a series of concerts devoted to music dating from the year 1913; it opened with a re-creation of the notorious "scandal concert" given by Arnold Schoenberg in March of that year, including works of Mahler, Zemlinsky, Webern, and Berg as well as Schoenberg's own *Chamber Symphony.* With the guidance of composer Bright Sheng, the San Francisco Symphony mounted a "Wet Ink" festival of recent music, with a special focus on composers of the Pacific Rim. In London the Royal Academy of Music presented a five-day festival of works by 57 living British composers who had studied at the institution; among them were more than 50 world premieres. Toronto mounted a huge international choral festival, called "The Joy of Singing." Finally, the little town of Spillville, Iowa, marked the 100th anniversary of Antonin Dvorak's summer sojourn there with its own Dvorak festival.

Recordings. Decca (London) inaugurated an Entartete Musik series, devoted to works by composers who ran afoul of Adolf Hitler. The first two releases were devoted to long-forgotten operas—Erich Wolfgang Korngold's *Das Wunder der Heliane* and Ernst Krenek's *Jonny spielt auf.* A parallel series of recordings on the Channel Classics label began to explore smaller-scale works by other composers of the musical diaspora. One of the more interesting recent developments in the record industry was a prolific reissuing of prestereo recordings, even going back to acoustic recordings from early in the century. With new techniques of digital remastering, even some quite aged performances came up sounding surprisingly fresh. EMI completed a three-volume, nine-CD reissue of all of Edward Elgar's electrical recordings, revelatory performances quite unlike the norm today and many of them sounding astonishingly good. BMG marked the 50th anniversary of Rachmaninoff's death with a boxed 10-CD reissue of all his recorded performances, as both pianist and composer. Such recordings, newly refurbished, together with Robert Philip's book *Early Recordings and Musical Style* (1992), deserve to spark major reconsideration of present-day performance practices in music from earlier years in the 20th century. Pearl weighed in with four volumes devoted to "Singers of Imperial Russia," another prizewinner in the annual *Gramophone* magazine awards. Among recent "authenticist" recordings the most interesting was surely John Eliot Gardiner's period-instruments account of the Berlioz *Symphonie fantastique,* recorded by the Orchestre Révolutionnaire et Romantique in the Paris Conservatoire hall where it was first performed. The same forces also recorded Berlioz' recently rediscovered *Messe solennelle* and Verdi's *Quattro pezzi sacri.* But the most astonishing success in the classical record industry continued to be an Elektra Nonesuch release of Polish composer Henryk Gorecki's *Symphony No. 3;* by the end of the year it had sold more than 600,000 copies worldwide and reached number six even on the British pop-music charts. (*See* BIOGRAPHIES.) (SCOTT CANTRELL)

Jazz. The divisions between repertory and neoclassic, or revival, jazz on the one hand and the more exploratory kinds of jazz on the other continued to trouble the American jazz community during 1993. When early in the year Lincoln Center presented the New York City Ballet in *Jazz,* choreographed by Peter Martins, much of the acclaim for the work went to its music, which was composed by trumpeter Wynton Marsalis and played by his 11-piece band. During the summer the third annual Jazz at Lincoln Center series began, with Marsalis returning as artistic director; his "Jazz for Young People" programs; concerts of new works commissioned from Marsalis, pianists Marcus Roberts and Geri Allen, and trumpeters Roy Hargrove and Terence Blanchard; and a 30-city tour by the Lincoln Center Jazz Orchestra, directed by Roberts, were among the offerings. Since most of those commissioned to compose for the series were protégés or associates of Marsalis, charges of narrowness of focus erupted.

The Smithsonian Institution in Washington, D.C., began a three-and-a-half-year project with a concert series of Duke Ellington's works, played by the Smithsonian Jazz Masterworks Orchestra, and an Ellington film festival, along with an exhibit portraying Ellington's life with interactive videos that opened in New York and was set to tour other American cities. A Broadway production of William Shakespeare's *Timon of Athens,* with Ellington's incidental music, the Alvin Ailey Dance Theater's performances of *The River* and *The Mooch,* also with Ellington's music, and a concert of his orchestral works by the Brooklyn Philharmonic Orchestra with the Mercer Ellington band were part of the celebration. The Lila Wallace–Reader's Digest Fund, which in the 1990s emerged as a leading supporter of jazz, aided the events.

Meanwhile, there was no comparable forum for the works of more modern-styled jazz composers. The Art Ensemble of Chicago and the Deutsche Kammerphilharmonie presented new compositions by German composers and Art Ensemble members in concerts in Germany, and in the U.S. the Brooklyn Philharmonic, directed by Dennis Russell Davis and with drum soloist Max Roach, performed *Mix for Orchestra* by Henry Threadgill. Apart from the musical qualities of the performances, they were reminders that these composers and others, such as Muhal Richard Abrams, Anthony Braxton, and Ornette Coleman (*see* BIOGRAPHIES), had created further large-scale orchestral works that had been neither recorded nor performed in concert since their premieres. Although a few important composers managed to have their works performed by re-forming big bands, the need remained for repertory bands that could meet the challenges of the large body of music by jazz composers who incorporated the rhythmic-harmonic-sonic discoveries of free jazz.

Jazz festivals hardly abated in 1993, despite the erratic global economy. Issues of artistic control and financing made almost as much news as the music at the Chicago Jazz Festival, while the important new music festival at Victoriaville, Que., took a hiatus. The nine-day Vancouver, B.C., festival became North America's largest new music event, with musicians from as far away as Australia and Germany. Despite alarms over continued government funding, the Berlin Jazz Festival continued to present a variety of jazz, while its adjunct, the Total Music Meeting, concentrated on free improvisation. At the Verona, Italy, festival the 1960s Experimental Band, including the Art Ensemble, Braxton, Threadgill, and other ex-Chicagoans, held a reunion, with new music composed by the band's leader-founder Abrams.

With the pace of traditional and swing reissues slowing, the rerelease of postwar jazz albums on CD was newsworthy; they included 100 titles from the Savoy label, including 1940s Charlie Parker and Fats Navarro masterpieces, and the ESP-Disk catalog from the 1960s, including masterpieces by Coleman and Albert Ayler. The discovery of previously unheard music was crucial in the 1957 Thelonious Monk Quartet with John Coltrane *At the Five Spot* (Blue Note); *Beauty Is a Rare Thing* (Rhino/Atlantic), a five-CD set of Coleman's 1959–61 classics plus previously unissued tracks; and *The Art Ensemble 1967/68* (Nessa), a five-CD set of the earliest and in many ways best work by the Art Ensemble of Chicago players. Among notable new recordings were *It's Got to Be Funky* (Columbia), Horace Silver's first album in a decade; *Dance with the Ancestors* (Chameleon) by the Ethnic Heritage Ensemble; *Touchin' on Trane* (FMP) by Charles Gayle, William Parker, and Rashied Ali; the Globe Unity Orchestra's *20th Anniversary* (FMP), from 1986; and Benny Carter's *Legends* (MusicMasters). Two valuable artists who had died the previous year had their final recording projects issued in 1993: multisaxophonist Charles Tyler's *Mid Western Drifter* (Adda) and *Folly Fun Music Magic* (Adda) and Hal Russell's solo *Hal's Bells* (ECM) and *The Hal Russell Story* (ECM), with his NRG Ensemble.

While the arrivals of such young musicians as saxophonists James Carter, Joshua Redman, and Eric Alexander were impressive, the loss of important older musicians in 1993 was keenly felt, including bandleader Bob Crosby, blues-gospel singer-songwriter Thomas A. Dorsey (Georgia Tom), pianist-bandleader Art Hodes, Afro-Cuban jazz pioneer Mario Bauza, pianist Kenny Drew, tenor saxophonist Bob Cooper, and singer Billy Eckstine. Sun Ra, who had maintained his Arkestra for four decades, died during the year, and tenor saxophonist John Gilmore announced plans to continue the band, playing Ra's many compositions. The most notable artist to die in 1993 was Dizzy Gillespie, trumpeter and bandleader, who had been a pioneer of bebop, in small groups with alto saxophonist Charlie Parker and in the big band he formed in the 1940s. (*See* OBITUARIES.)

Especially valuable among the year's books were the biography *Beyond Category: The Life and Genius of Duke Ellington* by John Edward Hasse and *The Duke Ellington Reader,* an anthology edited by Mark Tucker.

(JOHN LITWEILER)

Popular. In 1993 popular music continued to search for new directions, often in contradictory ways, as some musicians experimented with the latest computerized technology while others favoured returning to acoustic styles. Once again, it was established artists who tended to dominate the music business.

The most startling exponents of the high-tech approach were the Irish band U2 (*see* BIOGRAPHIES), now widely accepted as the most successful rock band of the late 1980s and the '90s. They toured extensively during 1993, and their new album, *Zooropa,* which was in some ways a spin-off from their best-seller of the previous year, *Achtung Baby,* showed the band continuing to experiment and even improvise, with unexpected results. The album reflected their current fascination with the theme of technology and information saturation, and the opening track had lyrics that consisted of a string of advertising slogans. During some concerts they telephoned politicians from the stage or used live satellite links so that singer Bono could talk directly to victims of starvation and fighting in the besieged Bosnian city of Sarajevo—a device that some found moving and others regarded as exploitation.

Peter Gabriel, on tour for the first time in six years, was another established artist mixing music and technology in a new way. His live shows used high-tech devices, from trees that appeared to grow onstage to a miniature camera, strapped to his head, that transmitted close-ups of his face onto a screen behind the stage. Gabriel revealed plans to build a "music theme park" in Barcelona, Spain. It consisted of a trailer that housed a video screen and seats "programmed to dance," moving in time with the music and the images on the screen. At the same time he was promoting such high-tech entertainment, Gabriel was also helping to encourage music from the Third World through the WOMAD (World of Music Arts and Dance) organization. The effort started in Britain in 1982 but was now launched in North America with a series of concerts at which Gabriel performed alongside African, Asian, and Latin-American artists, many of whom recorded for his Real World label.

The widening interest in global folk styles was matched by a move to more acoustic styles by some rock artists. The MTV channel promoted a series of "Unplugged" concerts, which led to a batch of successful albums following the initial triumph of Eric Clapton's acoustic debut. Artists from Rod Stewart to 10,000 Maniacs recorded for the series, but the best was by the veteran star Neil Young, whose career had spanned everything from folk-country to hard rock. He continued the gentler approach shown on his *Harvest Moon* with treatment of such old favourites as "Like a Hurricane." Young was just one of the pop music old guard to prove that age did not matter much in the 1990s music market. Mick Jagger, singer with the Rolling Stones, celebrated his 50th birthday with the release of his best solo album to date, *Wandering Spirit,* that showed that neither his image nor musical style had changed drastically during his 30-year career.

Another veteran who took advantage of the continuing market for nostalgia was Lou Reed, who joined forces once again with John Cale, Sterling Morrison, and Maureen Tucker for the most unexpected reunion of the year, the return of the Velvet Underground. When the band first played together in New York in the late 1960s, they never reached a mass audience. Only when they split up did their raw, energetic style and bleak lyrics begin to make a profound impact on other musicians, and they began to acquire legendary status. It was appropriate that David Bowie, who was both influenced by the Velvet Underground and largely responsible for their posthumous fame, also made a comeback during the year. His *Black Tie White Noise* album, which dealt in part with his marriage to the Somali model Iman, was coproduced by Nile Rodgers and was his most successful recording in 10 years.

The old boys of rock still held a powerful influence, but

Pearl Jam was the latest of several Seattle, Wash., bands to top the alternative-rock charts in the 1990s. Their debut album, *Ten,* sold some six million copies, and *Vs.*, the album they released in 1993, sold nearly one million copies in the first week alone.
NEAL PRESTON—OUTLINE

there were new contenders. In Britain the most successful new band of the year, Suede, showed that the influence of Bowie still continued, while in the U.S. the continuing success of Nirvana showed how mainstream rock had been influenced by the noisy excesses of the hard-core movement. This three-piece band from Seattle, Wash., mixed melodic pop with sonic overkill and became the leaders of the grunge movement, with influence extending to films and fashion. The continuing importance of Seattle in the new rock scene (compared by some to the role of Liverpool in the 1960s) was shown by the success of another local band, Pearl Jam, whose debut album, *Ten,* outsold Nirvana's *Nevermind* and who released a best-selling second album during the autumn. Meanwhile, megastar Michael Jackson was in seclusion after accusations of child molestation and consequent nervousness on the part of his corporate sponsors and recording companies.

In the mainstream pop field the best newcomers ranged from the Californian girl group 4 Non Blondes, with their well-crafted bluesy, quirky songs, to the European dance material of Ace of Base, whose *Happy Nation* album showed that they could be the 1990s answer to Abba. Reggae also made a comeback during the year, thanks to the continuing success of Britain's UB40, with their best-selling *Promises and Lies* album, and the international success of Jamaican artists like Shabba Ranks and Chaka Demus and Pliers, who had hits with their reggae-soul fusions "Tease Me" and "She Don't Let Nobody." The new reggae revival even spread to Africa; the most successful South African artist of the year was Lucky Dube, whose style was largely influenced by Bob Marley. (ROBIN DENSELOW)

See also Dance; Motion Pictures; Television and Radio; Theatre.
This article updates the *Macropædia* article The History of Western MUSIC.

Philately and Numismatics

Stamps. Two major philatelic organizations collapsed in 1993. The British Philatelic Federation (BPF) went bankrupt, and the British Philatelic Trust assumed some of its international obligations. In the U.S. the Philatelic Foundation (of New York) ceased trading in April following severe financial losses and alleged administrative irregularities. Interim arrangements were made for the foundation's moneymaking Expert Committee to continue functioning.

A strong market for rare stamps and postal history continued, with several auction records set during the year. At Christie's first sale in Singapore, the Indhusophon collection of stamps and covers from Siam (Thailand) realized S$3,410,000, against an estimate of S$1.4 million. At Christie's (New York), sale of the Ryohei Ishikawa collection of U.S. stamps and covers from the period 1847–69 realized almost $9.3 million. At Sotheby's (London), £4,370 was paid for an unused King Edward VII 2*d* Tyrian plum found in a mixture bought by mail order. A 6*d* dull purple King Edward VII "Inland Revenue" overprint was sold at Sotheby's for £33,000, a record for a 20th-century British stamp. Harmers (London) sold a used 1847 Mauritius 1*d* "Post Office" for a record £180,000. Superior Galleries of Beverly Hills, Calif., sold a Moon cover (flown in Apollo II in 1969) for $26,400. At a Stanley Gibbons sale in Melbourne, Australia, the unissued New Zealand 1949 3*d* Royal Visit stamp made $A 10,200.

Sotheby's reopened the stamp department in its New York galleries after a 10-year gap with the sale of the Otto Kallir collection of aviation history, with realizations totaling $1,104,165; two Montgolfier autographed letters and other contemporary documents (1777–90) made $63,000 (estimate, $12,000). Cavendish Philatelic Auctions (Derby, England) realized £436,000 for the Bill Hart collection of Natal and Boer War postal history; a Mafeking Siege cover of 1890 made £15,400 (estimate £1,200), and a Natal cover of 1858 with three 1*d* buff embossed stamps sold for £7,700 (estimate, £300). In Lugano, Switz., Guido Craveri Harmers S.A. realized Sw F 100,000 (estimate, Sw F 30,000) for five colour trials of the Great Britain "Seahorses" during the Shaida sale.

The Scottish Philatelic Society in Edinburgh, to mark its centenary, served as host for the planned BPF Congress. Six invitees signed the Roll of Distinguished Philatelists: Istvan Gazda, the first Hungarian signatory; Otto Hornung (U.K.), specialist in classic Turkish stamps and postal history; Hiroyuki Kanai (Japan), noted collector of Mauritius classics; Knud Mohr (Denmark), specialist in Danish postal history; Mary Ann Owens (U.S.), sixth woman and first thematic (topical) collector to sign the roll; and Brig. Diljit Singh Virk (India), of the Indian Army Post Office and author on the subject. The Congress Medal was awarded to Derick Ray of Cambridge and the Lichtenstein Medal of the Collectors Club (of New York) to Robert P. Odenweller.

At Polska '93, held in Poznan, Poland, the major awards were: FIP Grand Prix d'Honneur, Raymond Casey (U.K.), for Russian postal history; Grand Prix International, Peng Hian Tay (Singapore), for Burma 1814–54; and Grand Prix National, Maciej Miszczak (Poland), preadhesive Poland and classic stamps.

The National Postal Museum opened in Washington, D.C., in the old Post Office Building as part of the Smithsonian Institution. The National Postal Museum in London acquired a pen-and-ink self-portrait of William Mulready, Royal academician, designer of the 1840 envelopes and wrappers. (KENNETH F. CHAPMAN)

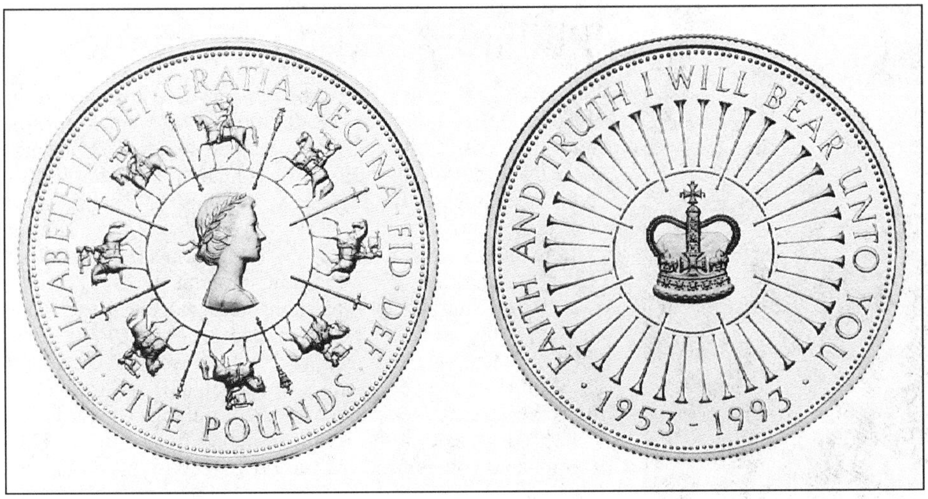

This 1993 Coronation Crown commemorates the 40th anniversary of the crowning of Queen Elizabeth II. It was one of a number of such coins issued by the British Royal Mint during the year.
THE BRITISH ROYAL MINT

Coins and Paper Money. The production of new types of currency accelerated during 1993 in the wake of numerous political and economic changes worldwide. Russia's central bank demonetized pre-1993 ruble notes in an attempt to curb inflation. The July 24 announcement gave citizens just two weeks to redeem their old bills, but Pres. Boris Yeltsin extended the exchange period to August 31 for larger denomination notes and to December 31 for notes worth 10 rubles or less. Russia and five other former Soviet republics agreed in September to keep the ruble as a common currency, but the agreement later came apart. Estonia and Lithuania, among others, issued their own money. The division of Czechoslovakia on January 1 into two countries, the Czech Republic and Slovakia, led to the creation of separate currencies denominated in koruna.

Some of the former Yugoslav republics continued to produce coins or paper money, and a variety of local issues circulated in war-torn Bosnia and Herzegovina. The government of Yugoslavia printed 10 billion-dinar notes in an attempt to keep up with the country's hyperinflation. Inflation also hurt Brazil, which released 500,000-cruzeiro notes. Brazilian officials discussed a reform plan that would remove three zeros from bank notes in circulation. On January 1, Mexico introduced coins and paper money based on a "new peso" that was worth 1,000 old pesos. The new 10- and 20-peso coins contained some silver.

The Pobjoy Mint in England made coins for the new nation of Eritrea, which gained its independence from Ethiopia on May 24. The British Royal Mint struck coins for the U.K. and 17 other countries honouring the 40th anniversary of the coronation of Queen Elizabeth II, while Japan minted millions of coins marking the June wedding of Crown Prince Naruhito and Masako Owada. In August, Ruth Hubbard became the first woman mint master of the Royal Canadian Mint, succeeding Maurice A.J. Lafontaine.

Worldwide sales of gold bullion coins spurted nearly 30% in the first half of 1993 compared with the same period in 1992 as the price of gold bullion advanced. The Gold Institute reported that Austria issued nearly 600,000 troy ounces of gold bullion coins in 1992, more than any other country. The U.S. American Eagle was the most popular silver bullion coin in 1992 for the seventh consecutive year. Also in 1993, the U.S. Mint sold to collectors three coin types commemorating the 50th anniversary of World War II and three others honouring the Bill of Rights.

The U.S. rare-coin market advanced 4.5% in the 12 months ended August 31, according to a *Coin World* survey that monitored nearly 17,000 coin values. The nine-coin "King of Siam" proof set—which included one of 15 known 1804 U.S. silver dollars—sold at auction in February for $1,815,000. In October another of the 1804 dollars brought $522,500 at auction and one of five known 1913 U.S. Liberty nickels, $962,500. The two coins had been owned by Reed Hawn of Texas. In April, Swiss police recovered another of the 1804 dollars that had been stolen in 1967 from the Willis H. du Pont family. In late 1993 Merrill Lynch & Co. liquidated its two rare-coin limited partnerships, which placed millions of dollars' worth of ancient coins on the market.

Meanwhile, people in many parts of the world—especially Europe—used electronic money cards to pay for phone calls, vending-machine products, and other small purchases. Some experts predicted that the cards eventually would make coins obsolete because they allowed consumers to deduct the cost of items from a prepaid credit balance stored on the card. (ROGER BOYE)

This article updates the *Macropædia* article COINS AND COINAGE.

Photography

Advances in film technology outpaced innovations in camera design in 1993 with the introduction of significantly improved emulsions for colour transparencies and prints. For the camera industry the segment of the market showing the most vigorous growth was that for 35-mm single-use cameras. Culturally it was a record-breaking year for the price paid for a single photograph at auction. Richard Avedon's highly touted and widely praised autobiography dominated the photographic cocktail-table-book category.

Photo Equipment. Captiva, Polaroid's newest system of instant photography, reached the U.S. in 1993. Originally code-named Joshua and first shown at Germany's Photokina exhibition in late 1992, Captiva was a compact, folding single-lens-reflex (SLR) camera that used a 10-exposure Vision 95 film cartridge loaded with ISO 600 fine-grained film. Weighing 740 g (26 oz) and measuring 5.7 × 8.3 × 17.8 cm ($2\frac{1}{4} \times 3\frac{3}{4} \times 7$ in) when folded, the camera was designed to compete with conventional 35-mm point-and-shoot compacts in terms of size and ease of operation. It produced unconventionally small colour prints—about the size of a credit card—on a white backing. The Captiva featured a 107-mm *f*/12 lens, shutter speeds from $\frac{1}{4}$ to $\frac{1}{180}$ second, a wink-light autofocus system, and built-in flash.

After the impressive number of innovative, high-technology 35-mm SLR cameras introduced in 1992, including the

Nikon N90, the Canon EOS A2E, and the Maxxum 9xi, 1993 was a relatively quiet year for SLR design. A new player in the field, the lens manufacturer Sigma, introduced its first SLR camera, the Sigma SA-300. Made in Sigma's own factory, it was a multifeatured autofocus model with a unique Sigma SA dual lens mount that had an inner bayonet for most lenses and an outer one to minimize vignetting with wide-aperture lenses and telephotos. The camera accepted SA-mount Sigma lenses with built-in motors to control autofocus and lens aperture, had shutter speeds from 30 seconds to 1/4,000 second, and included a pop-up flash.

The population explosion of compact 35-mm point-and-shoot cameras continued with new entries ranging from basic fixed-focus types to sophisticated, elegantly designed luxury models. Manufacturers competed in attempts to increase the focal range of built-in zoom lenses while retaining compactness and offering attractive features. Cameras with midrange zooms from 35 or 38 mm to 70, 80, or 90 mm were widely available, and an increasing number of cameras had zooms that reached a focal length of 105, 110, or 115 mm. In the latter category was Canon's stylish Sure Shot Z115 with an anodized-aluminum-clad body, a 38–115-mm *f*/3.6–8.5 lens focusing to 41 cm (16 in), and a 4–1/1,200-second shutter. The Pentax IQZoom 280-P was the first compact to offer a 28–80-mm *f*/3.5–*f*/8 zoom range. The Ricoh Shotmaster Zoom 105 Plus went a step further with a 28–105-mm zoom capacity, achieved with a converter lens that could be placed behind the camera's basic 38–105-mm *f*/3.6–5.5 lens to give 28-mm coverage, but at the cost of slowing the lens to *f*/8. Among new fixed-focal-length models was Nikon's ultracompact Lite-Touch, claimed to be the smallest and lightest autofocus point-and-shoot yet made. The Lite-Touch weighed only 170 g (6 oz) with battery, came with a 28-mm *f*/3.5 lens, and provided shutter speeds from 1/4 to 1/450 second. The generously wide-angle lens lent itself well to making panoramic-format pictures, which one could take at any point on a roll by turning a switch.

During a year when camera sales were mostly slack, by far the fastest-growing segment of the camera industry was the single-use type. These cardboard-encased, plastic 35-mm fixed-focus models were purchased preloaded with film. After the roll was exposed, both camera and film were turned over to a photofinisher, who processed the film and returned the camera to the manufacturer for recycling or disposal. Very popular among casual snapshooters, for special occasions, or as a substitute when a conventional camera was left behind, some 22 million single-use cameras were sold in the U.S. alone in 1992, with higher sales expected in 1993.

Kodak updated its Fun Saver and Fun Saver with Flash single-use models. The new cameras were slimmed to 29 mm (slightly more than an inch) thick and given a large grip, an optical viewfinder, and a bubble magnifier for the film counter. Both came loaded with a 27-exposure roll of Kodak Gold Ultra 400 film. Kodak also introduced a Fun Saver portrait camera whose hinged flap diffused the flash to soften the lighting and lessen the chance of red-eye. Fuji redesigned its QuickSnap line of general-purpose, flash, panoramic, and waterproof models, loading them with Super G 400 film and providing 27 rather than 24 exposures.

For films it was another year of extraordinary modifications and improvements that resulted in greater sharpness, finer grain, and rich colour at higher speeds. Kodak introduced two new families of E-6 Ektachrome colour transparency film. Lumiere, designed for professionals, was available in ISO 50 and 100 speeds and in warm (designated X) or neutral colour balance. The films incorporated T-grain emulsion technology in every imaging layer and were

In Sebastião Salgado's photograph, men covered in mud work at an opencut gold mine in Brazil. An exhibition of the photographer's work began touring during the year, and the collection *Workers: An Archaeology of the Industrial Age* was published on the U.S. Labor Day.
SEBASTIAO SALGADO—MAGNUM

claimed to have exceptional sharpness, low granularity, accurate flesh tones, and improved "pushability" (extension of sensitivity by special processing). Elite, designed for general consumers, was available in ISO 50, 100, and 200 speeds and provided increased sharpness, improved skin tones, and brilliant colour. (Elite 400 was the existing Ektachrome 400 under a new name.) An ISO 50 Ektachrome for underwater use had an increased sensitivity to red light to compensate for the blue filtering effect of water. A new Kodak colour print film, Gold Ultra 400, offered excellent sharpness, improved exposure latitude, and rich colour saturation at ISO 400. Konica announced new Konica Color Super XG 100, 200, and 400 to replace its Super-SR series.

Cultural Trends. The New York Metropolitan Museum of Art's department of photography, established in 1992, produced its first major exhibition, "The Waking Dream: Photography's First Century." It won enthusiastic critical and public response when it opened in New York City before going on tour. The 253 pictures from the Gilman Paper Co. collection traced the evolution of photography from its primitive beginnings in 1839 to its maturing as a sophisticated creative medium some 100 years later.

"John Heartfield: Photomontages" opened at New York City's Museum of Modern Art with a display of that artist's use of photographs, headlines, and other graphic elements to create savage satires attacking fascist brutality in Europe in the 1930s. The National Portrait Gallery, Washington, D.C., presented a retrospective exhibition covering 80 years of work by Harlem's great Afro-American photographer James VanDerZee. In a more contemporary vein at the California Museum of Photography, Riverside, was "Documentary Fictions/Digital Truths: New Photographs by Pedro Meyer," in which the noted Mexican photographer used computer imaging to create effects of magic realism.

"In Human Effort," an exhibition of pictures by Brazilian-born Sebastião Salgado at the Tokyo National Museum of Modern Art, was the first in the history of Japan's national

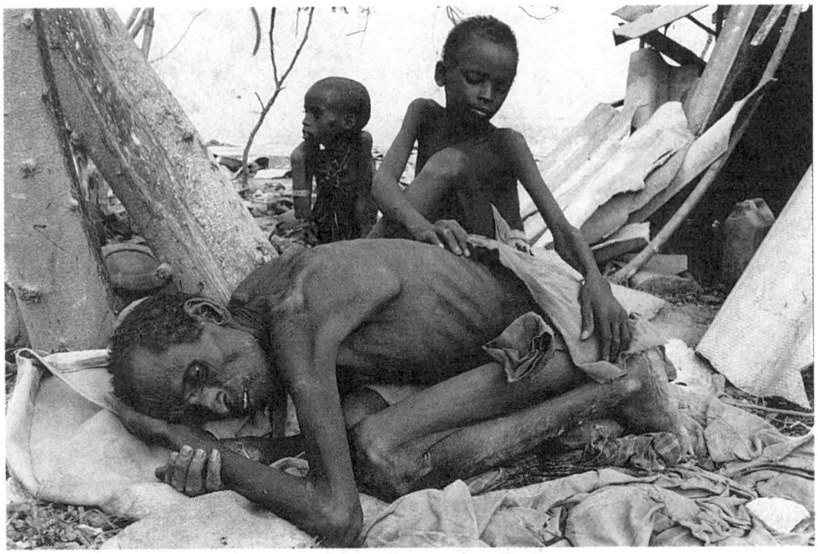

In a photograph taken in Somalia by James Nachtwey, sons watch as their father dies near the hut they have patched together. Nachtwey won a number of awards in 1993 for his photography in Somalia and in South Africa.
JAMES NACHTWEY—MAGNUM

museums to display works of an individual photographer. "The Photographs of Shoji Ueda," shown at the Tokyo Station Gallery, illustrated through numerous vintage prints the "modernism, realism, attitude, and vision" of this creative photographer. Other major exhibitions included "Love You, Tokyo" at the Setagaya (Tokyo) Museum, featuring renowned photographers Kineo Kuwabara and Nobuyoshi Araki.

Avedon's *An Autobiography* was launched amid a major media blitz in national magazines and on television shows. The sumptuously produced book gave a fascinating, highly personal survey of this influential, multifaceted photographer's lifework to date in fashion, reportage, portraiture, and photomontage. Richard Lorenz in *Imogen Cunningham: Ideas Without End* presented a revisionist view of the late long-lived member of California's famed Group *f*.64. Using 179 Cunningham photographs, many never before published, he asserted that she was not only a photographer in the "straight" tradition of Edward Weston and Ansel Adams but also a radical experimentalist. Adams, too, was presented in an unaccustomed guise as a colour photographer in *Ansel Adams in Color* with 50 colour transparencies selected by Harry Callahan. *The Permanence and Care of Color Photographs* by Henry Wilhelm with Carol Brower, decades in the making, provided an exhaustive and authoritative account of this important subject.

It was a record-breaking year for prices paid at auction for single photographs. The previous world record of $181,000 in 1992 for "Girl with Leica" by Alexander Rodchenko was toppled by $193,895 paid for Man Ray's "Glass Tears" at Sotheby's in London in mid-1993. This, in turn, was surpassed at a later auction of rare Alfred Stieglitz prints at the Pace/MacGill Gallery, New York City, where a 1920 photograph by Stieglitz, "Georgia O'Keeffe: A Portrait—Hands and Thimble," sold for an extraordinary $398,500.

The Pulitzer Prize for spot news photography went to William Snyder and Ken Geiger of the *Dallas* (Texas) *Morning News* for images of the Summer Olympics in Barcelona, Spain. Winning a Pulitzer for the third straight year, the Associated Press took the prize for feature photography, awarded for 20 images by 10 staff photographers documenting Bill Clinton's U.S. presidential campaign. At the 50th Pictures of the Year competition sponsored by the National Press Photographers Association and the University of Missouri School of Journalism, James Nachtwey of Magnum was named Magazine Photographer of the Year for his reportage from Somalia. Carol Guzy of the *Washington* (D.C.) *Post* won the Newspaper Photographer of the Year award for her portfolio. At the 36th Annual World Press Photo competition, the Press Photo of the Year had two recipients, Nachtwey for photography in South Africa and Marc Asnin of Saba Pictures for an ongoing documentation of the life of his "Uncle Charlie." At the International Center of Photography's 1993 awards program, recipients included Avedon for the Master of Photography Award and Stefan Lorant, famed photographic editor from the early days of modern photojournalism, for the Lifetime Achievement Award. The W. Eugene Smith Grant in Humanistic Photography was yet another award received by Nachtwey for his coverage of Somalia. (ARTHUR GOLDSMITH)

See also Motion Pictures.
This article updates the *Macropædia* article PHOTOGRAPHY.

Physics

The year 1993 began with a note of excitement for astrophysicists and cosmologists following release of results of new observations indicating that the stars, dust, and other observable matter in space represent less than 10% of all the mass in the universe. The results, which augmented other recent findings, supported a long-held belief among cosmologists that the universe holds a great deal of undetected "dark matter" and spurred the search for answers to what that matter could be.

The idea that as much as 90% of all matter is nonluminous is founded mainly on measurements of the rate at which galaxies rotate and on analyses of the way in which they move about in clusters. The new evidence emerged from satellite data, taken by the Earth-orbiting ROSAT X-ray observatory, of the distribution and temperature of intergalactic gas clouds in a small cluster of galaxies known as NGC 2300. This information, together with the assumption that the gas is confined by gravity to remain in the vicinity of the group, allowed ROSAT's team of scientists to estimate the total mass of NGC 2300. They concluded that visible matter could account for only about 4% (with an upper limit of 15%) of the total mass. Previous estimates had given much higher values but had been based on observations of gas clouds in rich galaxy clusters where additional gas ejected as jets from the galaxies themselves complicates the interpretation.

The new results rekindled much speculation as to the physical nature of the dark matter. One idea was that the missing mass may be hidden in starlike or planetlike objects that reside mainly in a halo of matter surrounding a galaxy and that, for various reasons, do not emit enough light to be detectable. Black holes may be an example since they are collapsed stars so massive that the gravitational attraction near them is too great to allow light to escape. Large stray planets and stellar remnants that have ceased to shine are other possibilities. The term *MACHO* (for massive compact halo object) gained popularity in some quarters to describe this candidate class of dark matter.

Some physicists preferred a less prosaic explanation for dark matter. Guided by predictions from the big bang theory of the birth of the universe and the present rate of cosmic expansion, they proposed that ordinary matter, such as that which forms planets, stars, and other cosmic objects, accounts for only a small fraction of the total mass of the universe and that a sea of hitherto undetected elementary particles filling the cosmos provides the remainder. A wide variety of particles with different exotic properties were suggested, often with correspondingly bizarre names. Axions, magnetic monopoles, and WIMPs (for weakly interacting massive particles) fell into a category known as "cold" dark matter, which would clump together readily, while at the other extreme lay "hot" dark matter, which would be dispersed more uniformly throughout the universe.

The one thing on which dark-matter researchers were agreed was that any resolution of the problem would have to come from experimental observation. Accordingly, three teams of researchers began an intensive search for MACHOs by a method first suggested by Princeton University astrophysicist Bohdan Paczynski. The technique involves studying the systematic variations in the light intensity of millions of distant bright stars over several years. The principle of the technique is that, were a MACHO to pass through the line of sight to a distant star, the object's gravitational field would focus the light from the star, rather like a lens, and terrestrial observers should see a momentary enhancement in the star's brightness.

Meanwhile, the search for dark-matter particles also began, but closer to home. For example, an experiment was set up in a tunnel at the Stanford High Energy Physics Laboratory that used a large germanium detector sensitive to the ionization produced when an atomic nucleus is struck by a WIMP or other dark-matter particle. A great deal of attention was focused on these searches, and with good reason: dark matter enters into many of the theories of the origin of the universe and its present large-scale structure, and also into models of gravity and other fundamental forces between particles. Thus, the dark-matter hunters were poised to shed light into many a murky corner of theoretical physics. (*See* ASTRONOMY.)

The year saw a revival of interest in superconductivity, the strange property possessed by a small number of materials whereby below a certain transition temperature, typically only a few degrees above absolute zero (zero kelvin, or 0 K), they entirely lose all resistance to the flow of electric current. (To convert kelvins to degrees Celsius, subtract 273; thus, 0 K = −273° C. To convert Celsius to Fahrenheit, multiply by 1.8 and add 32.) Superconductors had taken centre stage in physics several years earlier with the discovery of a new class of superconducting ceramic compounds—mixed metal oxides characterized by crystal structures containing sheets of copper and oxygen atoms—that become superconducting at temperature values as high as five times the previous record. These new so-called high-temperature superconductors appeared to hold great technological promise, as they could function as resistance-free conductors at temperatures maintained by liquid nitrogen (which boils at 77 K), a coolant that is relatively easy and cheap to obtain. After the initial discovery there ensued a period of frantic research wherein the superconducting transition temperature was quickly pushed up to 125 K, but thereafter scientists made no further progress in the quest for higher transition temperatures. Worse, theoretical efforts failed to yield any consensus on what mechanism caused the superconductivity in the new materials, and attempts to make practical devices out of them ran into serious difficulties because of their brittle, ceramic texture.

During 1993 encouraging progress was made in each of these problematic areas, and it seemed that the high-temperature-superconductor wagon once again had started to roll. A new compound in the family, incorporating mercury atoms, was discovered that becomes superconducting near 135 K at atmospheric pressure and at temperatures around 150 K when subjected to high pressures. The crystal structure of the new compound is relatively simple, suggesting that it may be a better material to use for fundamental investigations of the physical properties of high-temperature superconductors. Furthermore, in preliminary work the material appeared to perform well when subjected to magnetic fields, a behaviour encouraging for applications in the superconducting-magnet industry. (*See* CHEMISTRY.)

Rapid improvements in techniques for manufacturing high-temperature superconductors into forms suitable for practical devices were made in 1993. Methods were developed for converting the brittle materials into flexible wires, and several companies began selling wires 100 m (330 ft) long for use as underground power-transmission cables. Even more promising results came in the area of thin films, in which high-temperature superconductors offer great potential for faster and smaller electronic circuits and highly sensitive detectors of magnetic fields. The use of conventional metal conductors in such devices is limited by the

AMERICAN SUPERCONDUCTOR, WESTBOROUGH, MASSACHUSETTS

A metal tape containing threads of a ceramic high-temperature superconductor is spooled for use as magnet winding. Although the grainy, brittle nature of ceramic superconductors and their sensitivity to strong magnetic fields initially had slowed practical applications, technical advances in fabricating long wires and tapes of the materials were putting significant commercial uses within reach.

amount of heat generated in the metal films: the smaller the conducting channels are made, the greater is their resistance to current flow. Superconductors avoid problems of heating because they have zero resistance, so designers can pack channels more closely together and thereby reduce the size of microelectronic components. Because circuits are smaller, a signal takes less time to travel from one point to another, and so operation of the device is faster. Several companies began marketing devices incorporating high-temperature superconductors, including high-frequency microwave circuitry and detectors of very weak magnetic fields.

Numerous theories had been proposed to explain high-temperature superconductivity, most of which were too unspecific, or abstract, to be open to direct test by experiment. The only feature common to all the ideas was that superconductivity occurs when the electrons responsible for electrical conduction become bound in pairs. In high-temperature superconductors the binding force responsible for this coupling remained a mystery. By 1993 there remained among the theories only a small number of serious contenders and, more significantly, the architects of these theories had begun to build into them sufficient detail that predictions could be made for measurable properties, allowing a direct evaluation of the models. This evolution of theoretical work brought greater focus to the experimental measurements, and many physicists believed that a solution to the problem was close at hand. The less optimistic, however, pointed to historical precedent, noting that all the major advances in the field of superconductivity had occurred via either chance or intuition. Irrespective of their perspective, most scientists agreed that the year had been a turning point for the field. (*See* CHEMISTRY.)

(ANDREW T. BOOTHROYD)

This article updates the *Macropædia* articles The COSMOS; MATTER: *Low-temperature phenomena;* SUBATOMIC PARTICLES; The PHYSICAL SCIENCES: *Physics.*

Populations and Population Movements

DEMOGRAPHY

At midyear 1993 world population stood at 5,505,914,000, according to estimates prepared by the Population Reference Bureau. This represented an increase of about 90 million over the previous year, but the rate of increase dropped slightly from 1992. Every day 386,920 babies were born and 140,250 persons died, leading to a daily world population increase of 246,670. The overall rate of growth was estimated to have declined slightly from about 1.68% in 1992 to about 1.64% in 1993. New data from censuses in the following 21 countries were made public in 1993:

Country	Year of census	Population
Antigua and Barbuda	1991	66,687
Belize	1991	189,392
Bolivia	1992	6,344,396
Burundi	1990	5,139,073
Canada	1991	27,296,855
Côte d'Ivoire	1988	10,815,694
El Salvador	1992	5,047,925
French Guiana	1990	114,808
Ireland	1991	3,525,719
Luxembourg	1991	384,062
Malaysia	1991	17,566,982
Maldives	1990	213,215
Marshall Islands	1988	43,380
Norway	1990	4,247,546
Papua New Guinea	1990	3,529,538
Paraguay	1992	4,123,550
South Africa	1991	30,986,920
Spain	1991	38,425,679
Sweden	1990	8,587,353
Switzerland	1990	6,873,687
Tanzania	1988	23,174,336

Preparation for the 1994 International Conference on Population and Development intensified as regional preparatory conferences were held all over the world. The newly elected administration of Pres. Bill Clinton changed the U.S. approach to global population issues, reversing the Reagan administration's "Mexico City" policy of withholding funds from private organizations overseas that provided abortion services and recommending restoration of funds withheld from the UN Fund for Population Activities.

Less Developed Countries. The reliability of world demographic figures depends heavily on the availability and completeness of data from the less developed countries (LDCs), where nearly all world population growth took place but where data collection was often difficult. In 1993 an additional 85 million people were added to the population of the LDCs, compared with 5 million in the more developed countries (MDCs). Globally, women averaged about 3.3 children in their lifetime—down from 4.7 in 1970. They averaged 3.7 in the LDCs and 1.8 in the MDCs. Life expectancy at birth was 63 years for males and 67 years for females. The infant mortality rate in 1993 stood at 70 infant deaths per 1,000 live births worldwide—14 in the MDCs and 77 in the LDCs.

In 1993 evidence mounted that a decline in fertility in African countries may have begun. The Demographic and Health Survey in Rwanda reported that the birthrate had dropped to an average total fertility rate (TFR) of 6.2 children per woman, down from 8. (The TFR is the average number of children a woman will have during her lifetime, assuming that the rate of childbearing in a given year remains constant.) Zimbabwe and Kenya also had registered notable drops in fertility, as had the North African states of Algeria, Morocco, and Tunisia. The most recent UN projections showed Africa's 1993 population rising from the present 677 million to 3 billion late in the next century, assuming, however, that fertility in Africa would drop to 2.1 children by about 2040–45.

In Latin America the TFR in 1993 stood at a relatively low 3.2 children per woman. This region had experienced a drop in the birthrate that was not entirely anticipated, lowering population projections from those of earlier years. Brazil, Latin America's most populous country, had a TFR of 2.6 children per woman, while Mexico, the second largest, reported a TFR of 3.4, down from 6 in 1970.

World's 25 Most Populous Urban Areas[1]

		City proper		Metropolitan area	
Rank	City and Country	Population	Year	Population	Year
1	Tokyo, Japan	8,129,377	1992 est.	29,200,000	1990 est.
2	New York City, U.S.	7,322,564	1990 cen.	18,087,251	1990 cen.
3	Seoul, South Korea	10,612,577	1990 cen.	17,588,000	1989 est.
4	Osaka, Japan	2,603,272	1992 est.	16,210,000	1990 est.
5	São Paulo, Brazil	9,480,427	1991 cen.	15,199,423	1991 cen.
6	Mexico City, Mexico	9,815,795	1990 cen.	14,991,281	1990 cen.
7	Los Angeles, U.S.	3,607,700	1993 est.	14,531,529	1990 cen.
8	Shanghai, China	7,496,509	1990 cen.	13,341,896	1990 cen.
9	Bombay, India	9,925,891	1991 cen.	12,596,243	1991 cen.
10	Buenos Aires, Arg.	2,960,976	1991 cen.	12,582,321	1991 cen.
11	London, U.K.	6,377,900	1991 cen.	12,275,600	1989 est.
12	Calcutta, India	4,399,819	1991 cen.	11,021,915	1991 cen.
13	Beijing, China	5,769,607	1990 cen.	10,819,407	1990 cen.
14	Rio de Janeiro, Brazil	5,336,179	1991 cen.	9,600,525	1991 cen.
15	Paris, France	2,156,766	1991 est.	9,319,000	1990 cen.
16	Moscow, Russia	8,747,000	1991 est.	9,003,000	1991 est.
17	Tianjin, China	4,574,689	1990 cen.	8,785,402	1990 cen.
18	Cairo, Egypt	6,663,000	1991 est.	8,761,927	1986 cen.
19	Nagoya, Japan	2,162,007	1992 est.	8,432,000	1990 est.
20	Delhi, India	7,206,704	1991 cen.	8,419,084	1991 cen.
21	Jakarta, Indonesia	[2]	[2]	8,259,266	1990 cen.
22	Chicago, U.S.	2,783,726	1990 cen.	8,065,633	1990 cen.
23	Manila, Philippines	1,876,194	1990 cen.	7,832,000	1990 cen.
24	Karachi, Pakistan	5,208,132	1981 cen.	7,702,000	1990 est.
25	Tehran, Iran	[2]	[2]	6,773,000	1990 est.

[1]Ranked by population of metropolitan area.
[2]Administrative unit within which a separate city proper is not distinguished.

Asia. The 3.3 billion population of the largest continent accounted for 59% of the world total in 1993. China (the world's most populous country, with 1,178,000,000 inhabitants) rekindled the controversy over its stringent population-control program when it announced a very low 1992 birthrate: 18.2 births per 1,000 population, down from 23.3 in 1987. This implied that China's TFR had dropped to only 1.9 children per woman, well below "replacement level" fertility, the approximately two children per couple needed to replace successive generations.

Japan's TFR dropped to 1.49 in 1992, a rate comparable to those of the European countries with the lowest birthrates. Survey data reported by the Mainichi newspapers showed that many young Japanese couples were now limiting their family size owing to the high living costs and cramped housing. A very slow decline in fertility was suggested by sample birthrate data from India. A nationwide fertility survey was conducted in 1993, and prerelease reports suggested a larger drop in the birthrate than had been expected. India's population in 1993 stood at 897 million, with a growth rate of 2.1% per year.

Europe. Very low birthrates in Europe continued in 1993, prompting concern about population decline. In Northern Europe women averaged 1.9 children each; in Western Europe, 1.5. This trend, in conjunction with concern about a rising immigrant population, resulted in debates throughout Europe over the role immigration should play in national demographic change. New data in 1993 showed that Russia was experiencing a population decrease resulting from a very sharp drop in the birthrate. In 1992 there were only 10.7 births and 12.2 deaths per 1,000 population. A birthrate lower than the death rate was also reported in Ukraine, the second most populous former Soviet republic.

United States. The population of the U.S. stood at 258,233,000 on July 1, 1993, including armed forces overseas. This represented an increase of 9,108,000 since the 1990 census. From July 1, 1992, to July 1, 1993, the population increased by 1.08%.

The National Center for Health Statistics (NCHS) reported a provisional 4,084,000 U.S. births in 1992, continuing the slow decrease from 4,110,907 in 1991 and 4,158,212 in 1990. The crude birthrate fell from 16.7 births per 1,000 population in 1990 to 15.9 in 1992. Detailed fertility data for 1991, released by NCHS in 1993, showed that the TFR had dropped from its recent peak of 2.081 in 1990 to 2.073, and the unexpected increase in the birthrate at the end of the 1980s had come to an end.

NCHS also released its most detailed TFR for U.S. ethnic groups, allowing an in-depth analysis of national fertility patterns in 1990. The highest rate, 3.2, was found among Mexican-Americans and Hawaiians; the lowest rate, 1.1, was that of Japanese-Americans. Non-Hispanic whites, who made up about three-fourths of the population, recorded a TFR of 1.9. A record 1,213,769 births in 1991 were to unmarried women. Overall, 29.5% of births were outside marriage in 1991, also a record high.

There were 2,177,000 deaths provisionally reported in the U.S. in 1992, compared with 2,165,000 in 1991. The crude death rate in 1992 remained the same as in 1991, 8.5 deaths per 1,000 population. The age-adjusted death rate for the year ended in February 1993 was again the lowest in the country's history, 501.5 deaths per 100,000 standard population, down from 514.8 for the previous 12-month period. The 15 major causes of death accounted for 86% of all deaths in the 12-month period ended in February 1993, the same as the previous similar period. HIV infection (AIDS) jumped to the 8th leading cause of death, up from 11th in 1990.

Causes of death in the United States (year ended February 1993)		Estimated rate per 100,000 population
1.	Diseases of the heart	284.9
2.	Malignant neoplasms	203.9
3.	Cerebrovascular diseases	57.0
4.	Chronic obstructive pulmonary diseases	36.1
5.	Accidents and adverse effects	35.2
6.	Pneumonia and influenza	30.9
7.	Diabetes mellitus	20.0
8.	HIV infection	11.8
9.	Suicide	11.5
10.	Homicide and legal intervention	10.6
11.	Chronic liver disease and cirrhosis	9.9
12.	Nephritis, nephrotic syndrome, and nephrosis	9.2
13.	Septicemia	7.9
14.	Atherosclerosis	6.8
15.	Certain conditions originating in the perinatal period	6.5

In the U.S., life expectancy at birth reached a record high of 75.5 years in 1991. Infant mortality reached another new low of 8.3 infant deaths per 1,000 live births in the 12-month period ended in March 1993. A wide gap in U.S. infant mortality between whites and blacks continued through 1991, the latest year for which data were available.

There were 2,351,000 marriages in the U.S. in the 12-month period ended in March 1993, slightly down from the 2,384,000 during the same period in 1992. The marriage rate was 9.2 per 1,000 population, down from 9.4 in the period ended in March 1992. The number of divorces in 1993 compared with 1992 was almost stationary: 1,206,000 and 1,203,000, respectively.

Legal immigration to the U.S. reached a new postwar high in fiscal year 1992 as the impact of increased levels of immigration under the Immigration Act of 1990 were felt. There were 810,635 legal immigrants during fiscal year 1992, up from 704,005 in fiscal year 1991. (CARL V. HAUB)

See also World Data.

INTERNATIONAL MIGRATION

In 1993 Austria, Britain, France, Germany, and the United States all passed laws tightening controls and limiting the rights of asylum-seekers and refugees or began the process of passing such laws. The European Community interior ministers meeting in June in Copenhagen agreed upon a series of measures including stricter monitoring of short-stay visitors and expulsion of those found to have entered or remained unlawfully and exclusion of such migrants on the grounds of public policy or national security.

In the U.S. the year was marked by increasing anti-immigrant sentiment. Politicians such as Gov. Pete Wilson of California focused on the issue, laying the blame for much of his state's straitened economy on illegal immigrants. Wilson demanded that the U.S. government "reverse the rewards" for illegal immigrants by ending their medical and educational benefits and called for a constitutional amendment to deny citizenship for their American-born children. In this atmosphere Pres. Bill Clinton reversed his campaign pledge on Haitian refugees. On January 14, as president-elect, Clinton announced that he would continue the Bush administration's policy of forcibly repatriating Haitian boat people, and as president he sent a flotilla of U.S. Coast Guard ships to turn back Haitian refugees. In June he announced a number of immigration reforms—similar to those being adopted in Western Europe (*see* Sidebar)—designed to tighten controls. These included "expedited exclusion," which provides for dealing with asylum requests within a few days; enforcement of the idea of "country of first asylum"; and withholding of work authorization from all but those who have been granted asylum.

In July, through its Asylum and Immigration (Appeals) Act, the United Kingdom added restrictions to immigration rules. The act removed the right of appeal for those refused admission to enter Britain for a short stay. The law required refugees to seek asylum in the first "safe" country they reached. Amnesty International claimed the new law would increase the number of asylum-seekers expelled by Britain because they did not travel directly there from the country where they feared for their lives but via another country. The "safe" third country rule was upheld by a High Court decision on October 8. In April the Court of Appeal ruled that housing authorities, in order to pass judgment on applications for council (government-subsidized) housing, were entitled to determine whether homeless applicants were illegal entrants. The government later ordered local-government housing officials to carry out immigration passport checks on applicants for council housing.

The new French government of Prime Minister Édouard Balladur pushed a number of laws through Parliament designed, in the words of Minister of Interior Charles Pasqua, to achieve "zero immigration." The measures included the ending of the automatic right to nationality by birth, the requirement that a foreigner marrying a French citizen wait two years instead of the current six months before obtaining citizenship, and permission for the police to carry out random identity checks without judicial control. In August France's Constitutional Council rejected eight of the 53 articles in the immigration act passed by Parliament on the grounds that they deprived foreigners of basic rights.

In December 1992, after much soul-searching, Germany's opposition Social Democratic Party agreed to proposals, which had been pushed by the Christian Democratic-led government for years, to tighten immigration laws and limit the rights of asylum-seekers. The new laws that came into effect on July 1 provided that anyone who entered Germany via a "safe" third country—notably Poland and the Czech Republic—would be sent back there. Because all of Germany's neighbours had been categorized as "safe," however, it was virtually impossible for anyone claiming asylum to enter by land. Walther Koisser, an official of the UN High Commissioner for Refugees in Bonn, said that he believed there would be a chain reaction to the refugee problem as a result. Germany would "return" asylum-seekers to the safe country through which they had passed, which would send them back to the Balkans or to one of the countries of the former U.S.S.R.—all without any real test of whether they had a genuine case for receiving political asylum.

(LOUIS KUSHNICK)

REFUGEES

As of mid-1993 there were an estimated 18.2 million refugees worldwide, and a further 24 million persons were thought to be displaced within their own countries.

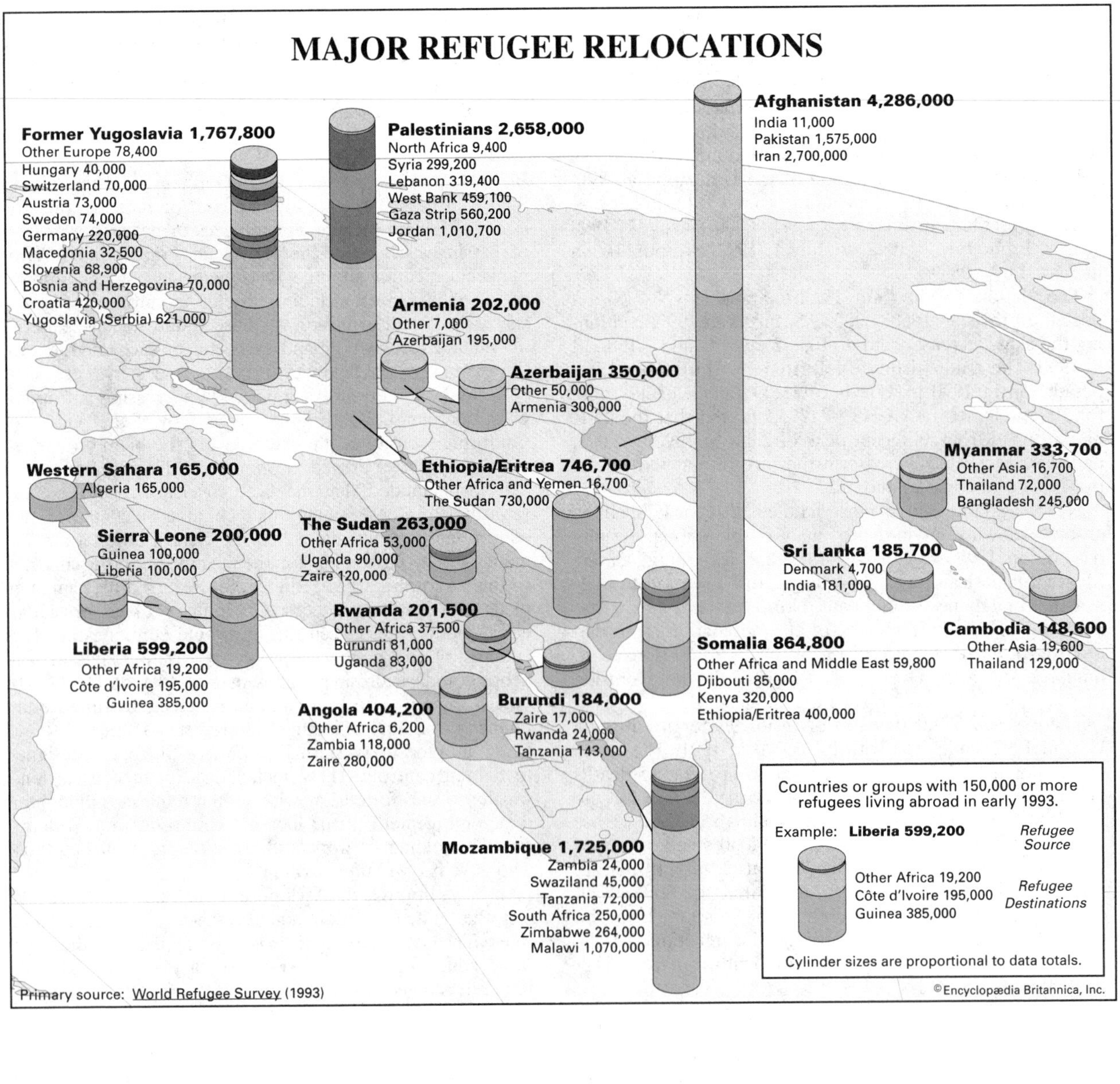

Asylum in the U.S.

In January the U.S. Coast Guard formed a flotilla around Haiti to stop refugees from fleeing to the United States. In the same month, Zoë Baird's nomination as attorney general was scrapped because she had employed an illegal immigrant as a nanny. In June a federal judge ruled that some 270 HIV-positive Haitians already granted political asylum had to be released from an "HIV prison camp" at Guantánamo Bay. In June seven Chinese died when the smuggler ship *Golden Venture* ran aground near New York City with about 300 people crammed aboard. In August a Brazilian became the first person to be granted asylum in the U.S. because of his fear of persecution as a homosexual. Immigration policy is front-page and controversial. Americans are schizophrenic on the subject—proud of the Statue of Liberty's beckoning to the "huddled masses" yet afraid of too many foreigners worsening a stagnant economy.

Pres. Bill Clinton in late July proposed reforms to the system, including "expedited exclusion" for those seeking asylum. Current U.S. law grants political asylum to people with a "well-founded fear" of persecution in their country of origin. About 140,000 requests are granted each year. A request for asylum may take months or years to process; some 10,000 requests occur each month, and in mid-1993 there were 300,000 applications backlogged. Clinton's proposal would grant Immigration and Naturalization Service officials at the point of entry the ability to judge the "justifiableness" of fear of persecution within a few days; the person denied asylum would then be deported. Immigrant rights and civil liberties advocates cautioned that this would deny "due process and meaningful judicial review to legitimate asylum seekers."

Meanwhile, the U.S. government was attempting to circumvent the asylum process. On June 21 the Supreme Court upheld 8–1 the government's policy of intercepting Haitian refugee boats while in international waters and forcibly repatriating the Haitians without screening them for asylum. In a similar move in July, the U.S. Coast Guard guided three ships smuggling would-be Chinese asylum-seekers from international waters to Mexican ports and persuaded the Mexican government to repatriate them.

The granting of asylum has always been political. During the Cold War, the majority of those who received asylum came from Soviet-bloc countries, while those seeking asylum from governments friendly to the U.S. (such as El Salvador) were denied. More recently, of those Chinese applying for asylum an incredible 85% had received it, while fewer than one-third of the 40,000 Haitians who fled their country after the 1991 coup had been granted asylum.

(ELLEN FINKELSTEIN)

The office of the United Nations High Commissioner for Refugees (UNHCR), under its mandate of protecting refugees throughout the world, continued to implement a three-pronged strategy of preparedness, prevention, and solutions.

During 1993 the African continent continued to be plagued by refugee crises. There were approximately 6 million refugees in Africa—one-third of the world's refugee population—while an estimated 15 million Africans had become internally displaced persons. Successive emergencies affected millions of drought victims, refugees, returnees, and internally displaced persons in the Horn of Africa, Angola, Benin, Ghana, Guinea, Kenya, Liberia, Malawi, Mozambique, Sierra Leone, and The Sudan. Most of the refugees and returnees in Africa were located in countries facing major economic problems and were often in the most remote, poorest, and least developed areas of those countries. Such countries were often unable to absorb the extra burden of refugees or returnees, and may not even have been able to provide essential services to their own citizens who were already experiencing hardship and suffering. In western Africa some 42,000 persons, mostly Tuareg refugees from Mali, had sought refuge in Mauritania between 1991 and mid-1993. In view of reported improvement in the situation in Mali following a government accord with rebel forces, some Tuareg began to return, and a voluntary repatriation program was envisaged for the latter half of 1993.

Southeast Asia saw a dramatic decrease in refugee populations as a result of the continuing implementation of the Comprehensive Plan of Action for Indo-Chinese Refugees. The plan led to a remarkable decline in the number of Vietnamese departing clandestinely from their homeland and the successful completion of the voluntary repatriation of 363,061 Cambodian refugees from camps in Thailand. In southern Asia, Bangladesh and Nepal were coping with influxes of Muslim refugees from Myanmar and Hindu refugees from Bhutan, respectively. Farther south, the return home of over 100,000 Sri Lankan Tamils sheltered in the Indian state of Tamil Nadu continued into 1993; some 36,000 were repatriated with UNHCR assistance.

The number of displaced persons in southwestern Asia continued to be among the largest in the world. In Tajikistan an estimated 500,000 persons had been uprooted (within Tajikistan as well as in Afghanistan, Kyrgyzstan, Kazakhstan, and Uzbekistan) as a result of civil war. The fall of the Najibullah regime in Afghanistan in April 1992 gave some 6 million Afghan refugees cause to hope for a durable solution to their plight, and by August 1993 some 1.9 million Afghans had in fact repatriated. To some extent, however, the numbers of returned Afghan refugees were offset by others who fled to neighbouring countries to escape the continued fighting at home.

In the former Yugoslavia, where incidents of targeted killing and depopulation, known as "ethnic cleansing," had led to large-scale population movements (there were some 3.6 million refugees and internally displaced persons in July 1993), UNHCR had assumed the role of lead agency for UN humanitarian relief. The conflict between Armenia and Azerbaijan, notably over the enclave of Nagorno-Karabakh, led to the displacement of an estimated 800,000 Azerbaijanis and 330,000 Armenians.

Through the International Conference on Central American Refugees, the consolidation of durable solutions for Central American refugees continued, including the first organized return of Guatemalan refugees from Mexico in January 1993. The numbers of Haitian asylum-seekers declined. Steady progress was also registered through voluntary repatriation for Chilean and Surinamese refugees.

(UNHCR)

This article updates the *Macropædia* article POPULATION.

Publishing

Newspapers. The year 1993 was the year that secured the future of *The Observer* newspaper; founded in London in 1791, it was the world's oldest Sunday newspaper, but it had been reporting heavy losses and suffering a decline in circulation to about 500,000 copies a week. The broadsheet paper, renowned worldwide for its liberal, left-of-centre stance, was bought in May by the Guardian Media Group, publishers of the daily *Guardian* newspaper, which had similar editorial values. The deal was viewed as undeniably logical and sensible, one likely to secure this influential paper's long-term survival and eventual editorial revival.

The Observer's sale and relaunch took place against the background of a recession in Europe, where competition both for readers (by adding extra bulky sections) and for advertising revenue was intense. The British publishing industry spent the year conducting a vigorous "Don't Tax Reading" lobby to prevent the government from introducing a 17.5% value-added tax (VAT) on the sales prices of books, magazines, and newspapers, all currently zero rated (*i.e.,* no tax added). They warned that the VAT would have a disastrous impact on the industry—by driving up prices, cutting sales, and leading to closures of vulnerable titles and heavy job cuts—and won considerable popular support for this stance. In November the chancellor of the Exchequer bowed to pressure and left publishing untouched in his annual budget statement to Parliament.

Rupert Murdoch's News Corp. Ltd. dominated events in the British newspaper market by introducing unprecedented price cuts. In June he reduced the price of *The Sun,* the largest-selling daily (sales 3.8 million), by 5 pence to 20 pence, making it 7 pence cheaper than its closest rival, *The Daily Mirror.* This was followed, in September, by a reduction in the cover price of *The Times* from 45 pence to 30 pence, making it the cheapest of the four broadsheet dailies. This policy, which was attacked by both rivals and industry pundits, who believed it devalued the standing of this august newspaper, was vindicated by a leap in sales of nearly 90,000 (to 440,291 in September). These reductions, however, cut the company's U.K. income by 30%, prompting complaints from other newspapers that Murdoch was engaging in unfair tactics because of the conglomerate's size. The harsh climate put a fierce squeeze on *The Independent* and *The Independent on Sunday* (both relaunched in the autumn). As the year ended, there was talk of an imminent takeover bid for the papers, which had attracted investment from Italy's *La Repubblica* and Spain's *El País.*

In January a government report stated that press self-regulation carried out by the industry's Press Complaints Commission and newspaper in-house ombudsmen had failed. Tougher legal sanctions were called for, including creation of a powerful statutory tribunal able to impose fines and new rights-to-privacy laws to outlaw the use of surveillance devices, photographs, and recordings on private property. The report was heavily influenced by the series of lurid reports and photographs about the failed marriages of Britain's royals. The Palace had lobbied for curbs, but the government seemed reluctant to act, wary of the constitutional implications of imposing state controls on press freedom. The British debate was being monitored closely in Germany, where politicians were increasingly worried by hostile media coverage of their private lives.

In Russia Pres. Boris Yeltsin raised eyebrows in October when he closed down 15 newspapers but agreed that *Pravda,* the historic organ of the Communist Party, and *Sovetskaya Rossiya,* the voice of the Russian ultranationalists, could continue publication under new names and editors. Opposition papers were also banned in Tajikistan in December; Azerbaijan instituted military censorship in December; and the board and editors of Croatia's last remaining independent newspaper, *Slobodna Dalmacija,* were forced out in May. Meanwhile in war-stricken Sarajevo, *Oslobodjenje,* the 50-year-old daily, struggled to produce its 10,000 copies against appalling odds. Produced by a staff made up of Serbs, Croats, and Muslims—Bosnia and Herzegovina's three warring groups—the paper had appeared every day since the war broke out in April 1992.

In the U.S., advertising continued to rebound modestly from the long recession, and newspaper circulation remained more or less stable. Still, the industry was not growing as fast as many others competing for investors' attention, and prospects were not encouraging. Americans no longer considered newspapers to be their primary source of news, and many publishers were worried that large numbers of potential customers, especially young people, simply did not read newspapers at all. Meanwhile, the long-term outlook for advertising was uncertain, as advertisers faced an explosion of cable television channels, specialized magazines, direct mail, event sponsorships, and other means of reaching consumers.

To ensure prosperity in this gloomy future, newspapers plunged headlong into electronic media. Publishers in St. Louis, Mo.; Chicago; San Jose, Calif.; Atlanta, Ga.; and several other cities introduced electronic versions of their newspapers available on-line to readers with home computers. Others, including such major dailies as the *Los Angeles Times* and Long Island (N.Y.)-based *Newsday,* announced plans to inaugurate electronic services in 1994. In many cases these new ventures offered more than the content of the newspaper as sold by newsdealers; they also carried texts of speeches and documents, school lunch menus, proceedings of local government bodies, social notes, and other text that the paper did not have room for in its printed version. Freed from the cumbersome burdens of presses and ink, these electronic newspapers could in some cases "scoop" their paper versions by offering breaking news earlier.

One form of electronic news delivery had already become a major moneymaker for many newspapers: audiotext, also known as voice service, in which a computer system allowed callers to dial a phone number and obtain information from a prerecorded menu of options. Nearly one-third of American newspapers had some form of audiotext system in operation in 1993. Offerings included news, weather, stock market quotes, home mortgage rates, sports results, lottery numbers, and soap-opera plot summaries. Initially, newspapers profited from a small fee for every call, but increasingly they offered the services free to callers and charged advertisers to have their commercials broadcast during the call.

To some journalists the growth of such alternative revenue sources was a troubling departure from a newspaper's primary mission. As *New York Daily News* editor James Willse said in the *American Journalism Review,* "It's wonderful that we are able to supply our readers with sports scores on demand and statistics going back to 1938. But the real reason we are protected by the First Amendment—and the Home Shopping Network isn't—is that we have to do good. We shine light in dark places, find out things people don't want us to find out. I would hate to see people get too seduced by the technology and forget that."

Some of the year's notable new ventures did not involve technology. The *Chicago Tribune,* recognizing a major demographic shift in that city, launched *¡Exito!,* a Spanish-language weekly. The *Wall Street Journal,* affirming Texas' long-awaited recovery from the decline of its oil and real estate industries, added a weekly section devoted to coverage of business in the Lone Star State. The *New York Times* concluded the largest single newspaper purchase in history when it bought Affiliated Publications Inc., owner of the *Boston Globe,* for $1.1 billion in cash and stock.

The year's most dramatic newspaper transaction, however, involved the *New York Post,* a tabloid founded in 1801. The paper effectively changed hands three times during the year, endured two staff rebellions, and nearly went out of business altogether before being rescued by media magnate Murdoch. The saga began when the *Post*'s bankrupt owner sold it to a little-known financier, who in turn lost control to a real estate developer. When that owner tried to fire editor Pete Hamill, a popular local columnist known for his working-class leanings, the staff commandeered the paper and published a remarkable 20-page tirade against the new proprietor. Amid the chaos, Murdoch offered to resume control of the *Post,* which he had sold in 1988 after eight unprofitable years of ownership. But Murdoch, too, ran into staff opposition. Eventually he managed to oust a recalcitrant journalists' union and resume publishing. Murdoch did not face an easy time of it; the paper had lost half of its one million circulation in a decade and was leaking money heavily, as were the city's two other tabloids, the *New York Daily News* and the *New York Newsday.*

PAUL LOWE—NETWORK/MATRIX

Sitting amid the ruins of Sarajevo, Bosnia and Herzegovina, a man reads *Oslobodjenje.* The newspaper, which often provided the only news from the outside world, continued to publish despite loss of staff members and shortages of paper, as well as power outages.

The 1993 Pulitzer Prize for Public Service was awarded to the *Miami* (Fla.) *Herald* for coverage of Hurricane Andrew. Other Pulitzers went to Jeff Brazil and Steve Berry of the *Orlando* (Fla.) *Sentinel* (investigative reporting) for uncovering alleged abuses by a county sheriff's squad; the *Los Angeles Times* (spot news reporting) for coverage of the riots following the acquittal of four policemen in the beating of black motorist Rodney King; John F. Burns of the *New York Times* and Roy Gutman of *Newsday* (international reporting) for coverage of the Balkans conflict; David Maraniss of the *Washington Post* (national reporting) for articles on the life and political record of Bill Clinton; Paul Ingrassia and Joseph B. White of the *Wall Street Journal* (beat reporting) for coverage of management turmoil at General Motors Corp.; George Lardner, Jr., of the *Washington Post* (feature writing) for an investigation into the murder of his daughter; Mike Toner of the *Atlanta Journal and Constitution* (explanatory journalism) for articles on the overuse of pesticides and antibiotics; *Miami Herald* columnist Liz Balmaseda (commentary); *Washington Post* book reviewer Michael Dirda (criticism); Stephen R. Benson of the *Arizona Republic* (editorial cartooning); the Associated Press (feature photography) for images of Clinton's presidential campaign; and William Snyder and Ken Geiger of the *Dallas* (Texas) *Morning News* (spot news photography) for coverage of the 1992 summer Olympic Games in Barcelona, Spain. The award was Snyder's third Pulitzer. No prize was awarded for editorial writing.

In one remarkably principled action, the *Seattle* (Wash.) *Times* became the largest U.S. newspaper to ban all tobacco advertising from its pages. The move put the *Times* at odds with civil libertarians, the tobacco lobby, and most of the newspaper industry. The Newspaper Association of America supported the right to advertise cigarettes and other products that were not illegal to use. The *Times* described its action in terms of morality and consistency. "These ads were designed to kill our readers," said *Times* president H. Mason Sizemore, "so we decided to refuse them."

In Canada the ruling of the judge in the Karla Homolka murder case raised questions about freedom of the press. Ontario Court Justice Francis Kovacs banned press coverage of "the circumstances of the deaths of any person referred to during the trial of the defendant," but Canadian citizens flocked to neighbouring U.S. cities to buy newspapers carrying stories of the trial. It was not even clear that the provincial judge's authority to muzzle the press extended beyond Ontario. (MAGGIE BROWN; DONALD MORRISON)

Magazines. Although magazines made numerous technological advances in 1993, these technologies did not seem likely soon to replace magazines on paper. *Wired,* the new voice for multimedia fans that debuted in January, pointed out that only a handful of publishers had so far turned to CD-ROMs. Computer screens might be fine for reference data, but it was not clear that magazines were as accessible on database as on paper. Only 10% of Americans owned computers, and *Newsweek,* the first mass circulation title to experiment with a quarterly version on a CD-ROM, on a disc cost about $100 for four issues. Some 3,000 specialized periodicals were available on-line with full text, although rarely with illustrations and advertisements. The cost—from $50 to $300 an hour to read or print out—was prohibitive for most casual readers.

The economic roller coaster for magazines seemed to be on the upside in 1993. Circulation increased; advertising pages were up; and there were more new titles and fewer closings than in previous years. Among the new ventures were *Family Life,* aimed at helping the 30- to 40-year-old parents; *Out,* a national magazine for gays and lesbians; *The*

National Times, an opinion journal; *Esquire Sportsman* for the upper-income outdoor person; *The Journal of Martial Arts,* an academic view of a television mania; and *Biblion* for book lovers. On the downside, *House and Garden,* a leading decorating magazine, went under after 92 years.

Directed at young parents, a new brood of family magazines made rapid headway in 1993. *Family Life,* a bimonthly for parents of children aged 3 to 12, was launched by the founder of *Rolling Stone* and joined a number of other publications in this fast-growing field, including *Child, Family Fun, Parenting,* and *Parents.*

The failure or success of a commercial magazine often is determined by the art director; an attractive layout or a redesign can recharge an old title. *Time, Newsweek, Esquire,* and *Out* had new designs in 1993. Scholarly journals slowly followed suit. In 1993, for example, *Foreign Affairs,* the bimonthly publication of the Council on Foreign Relations, received a face-lift with a glossy cover and a new logo.

Most magazines wait a long time to win the National Magazine Award, the coveted "Oscar" of the industry. Three-year-old *Lingua Franca,* however, beat out all other magazines with circulations below 100,000 in 1993. The lively gossip and shoptalk about academic life appealed to general readers as well as academics. Among others in the winner's circle were *The New Yorker* for fiction and feature writing, *Harper's Bazaar* for design, the electrical engineers' *IEEE Spectrum* for its reporting on nuclear safeguards, and *Newsweek* for general excellence.

Two major bibliographies appeared in 1993. *Journals of Dissent and Social Change,* published by California State University at Sacramento, described some 4,500 periodicals that covered alternative lifestyles. *The Right Guide* offered information on some 500 organizations that published right-wing magazines.

The major legal decision of the year came in early summer when a jury found that Janet Malcolm, *The New Yorker* writer, had libeled a psychoanalyst by putting words in his mouth. Fabricated or distorted quotations set the jury against the writer. The judge declared a mistrial after the jurors said that they were in deadlock over what damages to award. A new trial for Malcolm, but not the magazine, was ordered by a federal judge for some time in 1994. The case was likely to be a landmark in shaping libel law.

The Economist, the weekly international magazine published in the U.K. (circulation: 510,000), celebrated its 150th anniversary and appointed both a new editor, Bill Emmott, formerly the magazine's business editor, and a new chief executive officer, Marjorie Scardino. Emmott succeeded Rupert Pennant-Rea, who, in an unusual move, was chosen as the deputy governor of the Bank of England. The magazine's overall editorial stance, espousing a free-market economy, remained unchanged. Recognized as a major success story in the publishing industry and selling especially well to professionals and decision makers around the globe, *The Economist* had been notably successful in fostering a market in the U.S. (210,000 copies a week). The appointment of Scardino, an American, as CEO acknowledged her role in developing that crucial market and pointed the direction of future development. Across the Atlantic, Robert Lewis, the former managing editor of *Maclean's,* Canada's leading newsweekly, was appointed editor of the magazine, which had a circulation of some 600,000.

Emboldened by the increase in affluent readership following unification, three challengers to the established German weekly news magazines *Der Spiegel* (circulation: 1,150,000) and *Die Zeit* (470,000) appeared on the newsstands early in the year. *Focus,* the splashiest of the three, was published in full colour by the influential Burda Verlag in Munich and was made to resemble U.S. newsweeklies such as *Time* and *Newsweek.* The Hamburg publisher Gruner & Jahr dusted off *Wochenpost,* a weekly newspaper published in eastern Berlin since 1954, and distributed it nationally beginning in January, and in that same month Hoffmann & Campe, another Hamburg publisher, launched *Die Woche,* targeted at the more refined of the traditional weeklies, *Die Zeit.*

(WILLIAM A. KATZ; MAGGIE BROWN)

Books. The controversy over the Net Book Agreement in the U.K. rumbled on inconclusively in 1993, the most recent rumours being that it would be abolished in the November budget. In Belgium a parliamentary bill to introduce resale price maintenance received the support of French-speaking booksellers, but it was opposed by Flemish merchants, who argued for the freedom to discount up to 15%.

Meanwhile, the value-added tax (VAT) on books in Spain was lowered to 3%, and members of the European Parliament voted in favour of zero rating for books as well as net pricing throughout the European Community (EC). The fight against the VAT on books also was waged in Poland.

Controversy also was stirred up by new evidence that relatively cheap U.S. editions of books were entering the U.K. via other EC countries where the publisher of the U.K. edition did not have exclusive EC rights. As this practice was bound to damage sales of the U.K. edition, there were moves afoot to renegotiate the allocation of rights. Meanwhile, in Australia the Prices Surveillance Authority announced that it intended once again to scrutinize the prices of imported books, and there was pressure to change the 1991 Copyright Amendment Act on the grounds that it had so far created more problems than it had solved. In other copyright matters, the EC issued a directive to extend copyright protection to 70 years after death, operative from July 1994. Russia introduced a new copyright law in August 1993.

Over the financial year to June 1993, the majority of European book publishers prospered, with operating profits up significantly. There was renewed merger and takeover activity. The Dutch publishing firms Kluwer and Backhuys acquired Distribuciones de la Ley of Spain and Margraf Verlag of Germany, respectively, whereas Mondadori of Italy acquired the residual 30% of Grijalbo of Spain. In May 1993 Headline Book Publishing of the U.K. agreed to buy the much larger Hodder & Stoughton, thereby creating the second largest independent publisher, after Macmillan. The biggest merger by far involved Reed International and Elsevier of The Netherlands, which took place on Jan. 1, 1993. This exemplified the shift toward multinationalism via the unifying factor of the English language. In July, Reed Elsevier acquired 96% of Editions Techniques, the largest general publisher in France, and went on to pay $417 million in cash for Official Airlines Guide of the U.S., which Reed had been pursuing since 1987.

The trend toward multinationalism was also exemplified by the creation of an international consortium of 16 publishers at the end of 1992, led by Orion in the U.K. and Basic Books in the U.S. The marketing of books was evolving in other respects as well. In the U.K. 65% of children's books were now sold through supermarkets. Also in the U.K., book-club members acquired the same socioeconomic profile as retail customers, thereby greatly increasing competition among these outlets. Clubs offering paperbacks were particularly successful in eroding the traditional boundary between clubs and bookstores, especially where they imposed no obligation upon members to buy any books. Another innovation was the practice of giving out free as promotions offprints of chapters from potential best-sellers. (PETER J. CURWEN)

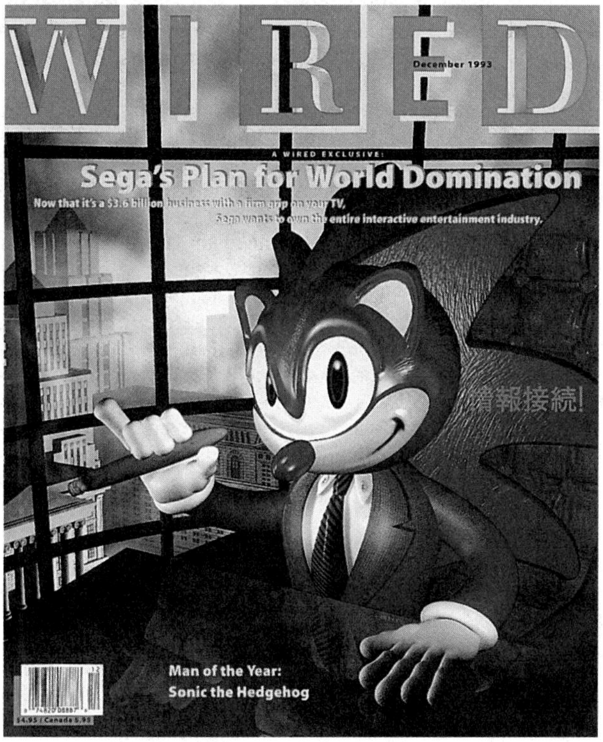

Sonic the Hedgehog, the lead character of Sega's popular videogames, graces the cover of *Wired.* A dramatically designed and colourful new magazine, *Wired* sought out the expanding number of fans of multimedia as its audience.

WIRED MAGAZINE; ILLUSTRATION BY JIM LUDTKE

Politics dominated the publishing industry in the United States in 1993. Random House and Simon & Schuster joined forces to copublish the joint memoir of James Carville and Mary Matalin, presidential campaign strategists for Bill Clinton and George Bush, respectively, and who were also romantically linked. The book, reportedly sold for $900,000, was to be coedited by the publishing houses. Simon & Schuster also bought the memoirs of Virginia Kelley, President Clinton's ailing mother. Bush signed with Alfred Knopf to write a book, coauthored by former national security adviser Gen. Brent Scowcroft, on American foreign policy and his administration, while former first lady Barbara Bush sold her memoirs to Macmillan.

Former vice president Dan Quayle's memoirs were to be copublished by HarperCollins and its Christian book subsidiary, Zondervan. Former secretary of state James Baker sold the memoirs of his years with George Bush to G.P. Putnam, while Times Books/Random House bought a proposal from Marlin Fitzwater to write about his years as press secretary to Presidents Ronald Reagan and George Bush. Lynne Cheney, former chairman of the National Endowment for the Humanities, signed with Simon & Schuster to write about political correctness on college campuses and its effect on the country.

A pro-Bush political commentator also got into the fray. Rush Limbaugh (*see* BIOGRAPHIES), a right-wing radio and television talk-show host, signed a deal for "several million" with Pocket Books for a work of nonfiction titled *See, I Told You So*. His first book, *The Way Things Ought to Be*, was the fastest-selling hardcover in history, and the new book jumped onto the best-seller list as soon as it was released. Gen. Colin Powell, former chairman of the Joint Chiefs of Staff, turned out to be the biggest winner of all; his memoirs were sold to Random House for $6.5 million. After former president Ronald Reagan, this was the second largest advance paid for a book by a former government official.

Sen. Edward M. Kennedy was again unwillingly dragged into the media spotlight with the publication of Joe McGinniss' controversial book *The Last Brother,* a supposed biography. Besides scathing reviews, two major controversies greeted the book's publication. Because he was unable to obtain Kennedy's cooperation, McGinniss invented his subject's personal thoughts. Even though he admitted to blurring fact and fiction, McGinniss insisted that his work was nonfiction. McGinniss found himself in hot water again when biographer William Manchester accused him of plagiarizing *The Death of a President,* his 1967 book about the senator's brother, John F. Kennedy.

Another attribution controversy centred around the Crown book *A Rock and a Hard Place* by Anthony Godby Johnson. The book was reportedly the autobiography of an abused teenager who had AIDS. Johnson's adoptive mother was protecting him so strenuously that neither his agent nor his editor had ever met him, sparking hypotheses that Johnson did not exist. Later a reporter was granted a face-to-face interview with Johnson and came away convinced that the boy she had met was Johnson. Hoax charges were also leveled at *The Diary of Jack the Ripper: The Discovery, the Investigation and the Authentication*. The alleged diary of the infamous murderer was pulled from publication by Warner Books after its authenticity was questioned by experts.

Popular television personality Oprah Winfrey shocked her publisher, Knopf, when she withdrew her much-anticipated autobiography from publication without warning. She would say only that a memoir at this point in her life would be "premature." Hoping to fill the "celebrity tell-all" slot she left was singer and actress Dolly Parton, who signed a seven-figure book deal with HarperCollins.

Allan R. Folsom, a virtually unknown first novelist, won a $2 million advance for his thriller *The Day After Tomorrow*. The deal, which would include an additional payment of $500,000 if net sales reached 400,000 copies, was unprecedented for a book by an unknown author. Anne Rice, best-selling author of *Interview with the Vampire* and *The Vampire Lestat*, signed with her publisher, Knopf, to write three more installments in her Vampire Chronicle series for a reported advance of $17 million. She also received $1.5 million from Knopf for three-year paperback renewal rights to *Interview with the Vampire*.

There were several mergers and divestitures of publishing companies. Paramount Communications purchased Macmillan Publishing Co. for $552.8 million, then was the object of spirited bidding by QVC and Viacom to create a multi-billion-dollar multimedia giant. Grove Press and Atlantic Monthly Press also merged, leading the way to massive lay-offs of the Grove Press staff. So-called boutique publishing took some major hits as well; Random House closed down editor Joni Evans' Turtle Bay division. Simon & Schuster did the same to editor Ann Patty's Poseidon Press.

Toni Morrison, critically praised and best-selling author, won the 1993 Nobel Prize for Literature (*see* NOBEL PRIZES). Author of six novels that chronicle the black experience in America, she was the first African-American woman to be so honoured. The 1993 Pulitzer Prize for Fiction went to Robert Olen Butler for his novel *A Good Scent from a Strange Mountain* (Holt), and the nonfiction award was given to Garry Wills for *Lincoln at Gettysburg: The Words That Remade America* (Simon & Schuster). Best-sellers for 1992, as reported by *Publishers Weekly*, were, in fiction, *Dolores Claiborne* by Stephen King (1,317,364), *The Pelican Brief* by John Grisham (1,313,437; *see* BIOGRAPHIES), and

Gerald's Game by King (1,196,765); in nonfiction they were *The Way Things Ought to Be* by Limbaugh (2.1 million), *It Doesn't Take a Hero: The Autobiography* by Gen. H. Norman Schwarzkopf (1,180,000), and *How to Satisfy a Woman Every Time* by Naura Hayden (1,050,000). Total book sales in the U.S. in 1992 rose 4.4% to $16.8 billion, according to the Association of American Publishers. U.S. book exports in 1992 rose 9% to $1,640,000,000. The increase was double that of 1991. (BETH S. LEVINE)

See also Literature.

This article updates the *Macropædia* article PUBLISHING.

Race and Ethnic Relations

The year 1993 was characterized by racial and ethnic conflicts throughout the world, ranging from "ethnic cleansing" in Bosnia and Herzegovina and other parts of the former Yugoslavia, new and continuing conflicts in various parts of the former Soviet Union, increasing levels of racist violence in Western Europe, particularly in Britain and Germany, and continuing violence in the Indian subcontinent and South Africa. There were, however, some positive developments, including the Israeli-Palestinian accords and the agreements in South Africa designed to create a multiracial democracy.

Western Europe. In Britain the new commissioner of the Metropolitan Police, Paul Condon, declared that the police had a pivotal role in combating the growth of the political far right. In a speech at a conference on fairness on February 28, he stressed that police officers had to be "totally intolerant" of racially motivated attacks and of those who used racial hatred for political ends. There were 12 murders with racial overtones during the year. In July, Peter Lloyd, minister of state in the Home Office, told the Home Affairs Select Committee of the House of Commons that racial attacks could be as much as 20 times higher than the reported level. Although the British Crime Survey registered 7,793 attacks in 1993, 78% higher than the 1988 figure, the number could be as high as 140,000. This increasing level of violence was exacerbated in the East End of London in September when the candidate of the neo-Nazi British National Party was elected to a local council seat. His racist supporters celebrated by hurling bottles at anti-Nazi protesters.

An analysis of the Labour Force Survey found well-qualified Indian, African Asian, and Chinese men to be as likely as white men to hold professional jobs. The situation for people from the Afro-Caribbean, Bangladeshi, and Pakistani communities, however, did not improve. For the period 1988–90 unemployment rates were: white 7%, Afro-Caribbean 14%, Pakistani 22%, and Bangladeshi 24%.

Racial discrimination in professionals' training and employment also continued during the year. The Commission for Racial Equality announced in January 1993 that it would undertake a formal investigation of the Bar's law school, where blacks had three times the failure rate of whites in 1992. In March 1993 a study published in the *British Medical Journal* revealed that when 23 hospitals received identical curricula vitae for fictitious doctors, some with Asian-sounding names and others with Anglo-Saxon names—all with the same age, medical education, experience, and qualifications—of the 18 names chosen for interviews, 12 had English names and 6 had Asian names.

In February, 417,289 Austrian citizens, 7.4% of the country's voters, signed a petition sponsored by Jörg Haider, leader of the right-wing Freedom Party, to force the Federal Assembly to debate a halt to immigration. Haider's plan called for an immediate stop to immigration until the economy improved, identity passes for foreigners seeking work, and a 30% limit on the number of foreign schoolchildren allowed to attend classes.

That same month in France, Jacques Chirac, leader of the Rally for the Republic, blamed unemployment on immigrants. "Today there are five million excluded from the world of work and we can't accept any more people in France. It is vital to us, and in line with moral principles, to have policies which defend our territory as well as a policy of solidarity and generosity towards countries of immigration."

On his first day as French prime minister, Édouard Balladur promised to crack down on "illegal immigrants" and change the nationality law to require immigrants' children to apply for French citizenship—a measure long demanded by the extreme right. On that premise police repeatedly raided the Goutte d'Or and other districts of Paris in search of suspected illegal immigrants. Four youths were killed

ISOPRESS—SIPA

Refugees from Burundi crowd a camp in neighbouring Rwanda. An attempted coup in October, in which Burundi's first Hutu president, Melchior Ndadaye, was killed, precipitated violence between the Hutu and the minority Tutsi that sent many people fleeing into exile.

by police in seven days. The new minister of the interior, Charles Pasqua, announced the government's goal as one of "zero immigration." He won approval in the Federal Assembly for such measures as allowing police to demand proof of identity without any justification and empowering the public prosecutor to order police sweeps in any area and for any length of time.

In Germany 17 deaths in racist- and fascist-related violence occurred in 1992, and at least 20 people were killed in the first 10 months of 1993, including 5 German-born Turks. They were killed in a firebombing in Solingen on May 29, days after the passage of tighter asylum laws. The Solingen murders elicited widespread antifascist and antiracist marches and demonstrations as well as criticism of Chancellor Helmut Kohl's government both by antiracists in Germany and by the Turkish government.

The national police intelligence office calculated that of the 41,900 Germans belonging to right-wing organizations, 6,400 were "militant and violence-prone." These figures did not include the 25,000 members of the right-wing party the Republicans. The police identified 2,584 proven acts of violence by right-wingers in 1992, a 74% increase over 1991.

The published findings of a parliamentary investigative committee into the violence in Rostock in August 1992 revealed that an oral agreement had existed between the head of police operations and the racist and fascist mob. The police chief had instructed his men "to pull back for half an hour," leaving the mob free to set fire to a refugee hostel occupied mainly by Romanian Gypsy refugees and Vietnamese. The outcome of the trials of 25 neo-Nazis arrested at Rostock resulted in prison terms of a maximum of eight months, suspended sentences, or probation orders. In February 1993 the interior minister of Mecklenburg-West Pomeria, Christian Democrat Lother Kupfer, was forced to resign after voicing "a certain understanding" for the actions of the Rostock rioters.

South Africa. The joint awarding of the 1993 Nobel Prize for Peace to South Africa's Nelson Mandela and Pres. F.W. de Klerk inspired hope in South Africa. The agreement of September 9—to establish a multiparty transition council of some 24 members with authority to oversee the operations of the police, the army, and the civil service—laid the groundwork for the African National Congress (ANC) call to end economic sanctions and provided the basis for elections scheduled for April 27, 1994. Major threats to a peaceful transition to multiracial democracy included the withdrawal of right-wing groups from constitutional talks, a newly established right-wing umbrella organization comprising neo-Nazi groups primed for violence, and a continuing and increasing level of violence, particularly in black areas. It was estimated that more than 10,500 people had been killed since Feb. 2, 1990, when President de Klerk repudiated apartheid and legalized the ANC. The July death toll of 582 was the second worst monthly figure, the 709 deaths in August 1990 having been the worst.

United States. In June the U.S. Supreme Court ruled in the racially divisive case of *Shaw* v. *Reno*. In a 5–4 decision the court permitted a group of white voters to challenge the bizarre configuration of North Carolina's 12th Congressional District, which had been created after the 1990 census to remedy past discrimination. The new district carved a 227-km (141-mi) meandering path through eight counties with concentrated black populations and thus helped ensure the election of an African-American lawmaker. This decision was seen as a threat to overturn the philosophical bases of the 1965 Voting Rights Act and the 1982 amendments to the act. One amendment barred any voting practice or procedure that resulted in members of minority groups having "less opportunity than other members of the electorate to participate in the political process and to elect representatives of their choice." The court did not, however, order a redistricting. This increasing controversy over the interpretation of the Voting Rights Act—opportunity or outcome—was an issue in the defeat of Lani Guinier, Pres. Bill Clinton's nominee for assistant attorney general in charge of civil rights. A right-wing media campaign, portraying her as a "quota queen" determined to undermine the principles of majority rule, succeeded in forcing Clinton to withdraw the nomination and thus prevented Guinier from explaining and defending her position.

The resonances of the Los Angeles riots of 1992, which followed the acquittal of police in the beating of African-American motorist Rodney King, continued to affect U.S. race relations. Sgt. Stacey C. Koon and Officer Laurence M. Powell, however, were convicted in a federal court of violating King's civil rights. They were sentenced to two and one-half years in prison by a federal judge, who declared that King had provoked their violence and that they had already suffered from widespread vilification and from prolonged judicial proceedings (*see* LAW). Damian Williams, a young black man, was convicted of beating three Hispanics, one Asian, and a white during the Los Angeles riots. He was given a maximum 10-year sentence for felony mayhem by a judge who admonished, "It is intolerable in this society to attack and maim people because of their race." A report from the Southern Poverty Law Center in December suggested that the number of racially motivated crimes by blacks in the U.S. was soaring.

There was evidence during the year of continuing discrimination by the nation's leading mortgage lenders. A computerized nationwide study by Essential Information Inc. suggested—on the basis of Federal Reserve Board data of 1,250,000 mortgage loan applications from 1990 and 1991—that 49 mortgage lenders in 16 major cities had engaged in racial redlining. A *Wall Street Journal* analysis of the records of the Equal Employment Opportunity Commission found that among whites, Hispanics, Asian-Americans, and African-Americans, only the latter group suffered a net job loss during the 1990–91 economic downturn and that some of the nation's largest corporations shed African-American employees at a disproportionate rate. The National Center for Health Statistics reported that whites born in 1991 were expected to outlive African-Americans by an average of seven years. (LOUIS KUSHNICK)

Religion

Religion and violence were linked in several prominent incidents in 1993, including a shoot-out in Texas, a bombing in New York City, and rioting in India. But in the midst of conflict, interfaith understanding made progress, too. Homosexuality, the role of women, financial problems, and church-state relations provided challenges for religious groups during the year.

The fiery demise of the Branch Davidian compound in Waco, Texas, that claimed the lives of David Koresh and at least 74 of his followers—preceded by a shoot-out in which four federal agents were killed—focused attention on how to define and deal with cults. The Seventh-day Adventist Church took pains to disassociate itself from the Koresh group, noting that the latter began as a sect in 1959 when it left a group that had itself earlier broken away from the Adventists. (See *Seventh-day Adventist Church,* below.) A statement issued after the Waco events by 16 religious and civil liberties groups, including the American Civil Liberties

Union and the National Council of Churches, said, "Under the religious liberty provisions of the First Amendment, government has no business declaring what is orthodox or heretical, or what is a true or false religion."

Islamic fundamentalism came into the limelight again when followers of Sheik Omar Abdel-Rahman were indicted on conspiracy charges in the February bombing of the World Trade Center in New York, in which six people were killed and 1,000 injured. Abdel-Rahman's insistence on the use of the Qur'an to govern Islamic societies and his advocacy of violence to overthrow Muslim leaders who disagree were criticized by a number of mainstream Islamic scholars, and several major mosques had refused to grant him a forum even before the bombing. (*See* WORLD AFFAIRS: *Middle Eastern Affairs:* Special Report.)

Members of an extremist Hindu movement called the Shiv Sena attacked Muslim neighbourhoods in Bombay and touched off riots that left hundreds dead in January. In August a bomb destroyed the Madras office of another militant Hindu group, killing at least 10 people and injuring 4. Indian Prime Minister P.V. Narasimha Rao was widely criticized for failing to take strong action against Hindus following the violence in Bombay. (See *Hinduism,* below.)

Some of India's interfaith conflicts made their way to the Parliament of the World's Religions, a nine-day gathering held in Chicago that drew representatives of Baha'i, Buddhist, Christian, Confucian, Hindu, Jain, Jewish, Muslim, Native American, Shinto, Sikh, Taoist, Unitarian, and Zoroastrian groups. At an early session, a Sikh from Punjab denounced Hindus for persecuting his faith, touching off a shouting match that ended only when police arrived. Some Zen Buddhists objected to prayers offered to God, saying that they "can practice religion with or without God." Orthodox Christians walked out to protest the involvement of neopagans and other groups that "profess no belief in God or a supreme being." Four Jewish organizations withdrew as sponsors to protest an appearance by Nation of Islam Minister Louis Farrakhan, whom they accused of having promoted religious intolerance.

Despite these problems, the parliament ended with an address in which the Dalai Lama, the exiled Tibetan Buddhist leader, stressed the common teachings—compassion, forgiveness, and love—of the major faiths and with the signing of a "Global Ethic" statement that condemned environmental destruction, hunger, poverty, sexual discrimination, and violence, especially "aggression and hatred in the name of religion."

Catholic-Jewish relations got a boost when one of Israel's two chief rabbis, Israel Meir Lau, spiritual leader of Israel's Jews of European descent, met with Pope John Paul II at the Vatican in September and when the Vatican recognized the state of Israel in December. The Evangelical Lutheran Church in America asked its ecumenical affairs department to prepare a statement addressed to the Jewish community repudiating "the anti-Judaic rhetoric and violent recommendations" of Martin Luther.

The Presbyterian Church (U.S.A.) voted to endorse the Consultation on Church Union (COCU) plan for mutual recognition of ministers and joint celebration of communion, becoming the third of its nine member denominations and the first large mainline body to take the step. In St. Louis, Mo., in July, two other COCU members, the Christian Church (Disciples of Christ) and the United Church of Christ, held joint national meetings for the first time. The Evangelical Lutheran Church in America voted to work toward a 1997 deadline for achieving full communion with the Presbyterian Church (U.S.A.), Reformed Church in America, and United Church of Christ.

An ecumenical celebration of the 400th anniversary of the (Lutheran) Church of Sweden drew the participation of Ecumenical Patriarch Bartholomew I of Constantinople; Edward Cardinal Cassidy, president of the Pontifical Council for Promoting Christian Unity; and Bishop John Hind of the Church of England. A conference in Santiago de Compostela, Spain, sponsored by the Faith and Order Commission of the World Council of Churches (WCC) drew 400 participants. WCC General Secretary Konrad Raiser called for "a new ecumenical reality" that would go beyond official theological dialogues. Greek Orthodox Archbishop Stylianos of Australia, who chaired the Orthodox delegation to the meeting, said the Orthodox participants were "deeply offended" by some comments made at the gathering, apparently referring to remarks in favour of ordination of women and shared communion.

The Presbyterian Church (U.S.A.) approved a three-year churchwide study on whether to ordain practicing homosexuals while retaining its ban on allowing them to serve as clergy, elders, and deacons. The action at the church's General Assembly in Orlando, Fla., touched off a demonstration by more than 60 people, including the Rev. Jane Spahr, a lesbian whose clergy appointment by a congregation in Rochester, N.Y., was overturned by the denomination's highest court in 1992. Leaders of the National Council of Churches (NCC) made plans for a discussion involving representatives of its 32 member churches and of homosexual groups, including the Universal Fellowship of Metropolitan Community Churches, which had tried unsuccessfully for more than a decade to gain membership or observer status in the NCC. Mel White, an evangelical writer who ghostwrote books for the Rev. Jerry Falwell and Pat Robertson, announced his homosexuality when he was installed as dean of the 1,200-member Cathedral of Hope in Dallas, Texas, which describes itself as the world's largest gay and lesbian congregation. (*See* Special Report.)

The Anglican dioceses of Vermont and Toronto elected women bishops in 1993; only one woman had previously been elected to such a position in the worldwide Anglican Communion. The Mennonite Church chose Donella M. Clements as its moderator, making her the first woman to hold its top position. The Christian Reformed Church (CRC), which had debated ordination of women for several years, voted at its synod to allow local congregations to decide the matter for themselves. Although another synod would have to ratify the resolution before it could be implemented, the action touched off immediate protests by conservatives, including a group of Korean-American church leaders who formed a breakaway body that included more than a third of the CRC's 47 Korean-language congregations. A week before the CRC synod met, the General Assembly of the Presbyterian Church in America, a smaller, evangelical church body, urged the CRC to repent over its "departure from the Scriptures in its doctrine and practice." The Church of England's 1992 decision to open the priesthood to women led some opponents, including the retired bishop of London, to join the Roman Catholic Church.

A growing number of cases involving sexual misconduct of Catholic clergy prompted Pope John Paul II to set up a panel of Vatican and U.S. Catholic Church experts to determine how best to handle such matters under church law, while the U.S. bishops established their own eight-member committee on the matter. The pope won cheers from 186,000 youths who attended a week-long international gathering in Denver, Colo., but surveys found that many Catholic teens took issue with the church's teachings on abortion, birth control, and homosexuality. In an encyclical

(continued on page 264)

Special Report: Religion

Homosexuality and the Churches

BY MARTIN E. MARTY

Sexuality, always a troubling issue in religion, has become the centre of controversy in American religious bodies in recent decades. Whereas struggles over civil rights, protest over the Vietnam war, and debate over economic issues earlier tore such bodies apart, the elements of "the sexual revolution"—changes in understanding of gender roles, women's rights, marriage and divorce, abortion and contraception, cohabitation and sexual license—have now become dominant. None has more threatened the peace of churches or occupied more of the attention of their seminaries, task forces, and denominational assemblies, however, than has homosexuality. Churches and synagogues have wrestled with the ordination of announced gays and lesbians to the ministry, religious understanding of homosexual rights, blessing of "gay marriage," and legitimation or condemnation of lifestyles associated with homosexuality.

Controversy Intensifies. The intensified controversy resulted from numerous factors. First, acknowledgement of homosexuality was part of the general sexual revolution, about which religious organizations could not be silent. Too, the issue came up in the lives of the members of church congregations and thus had to be addressed. In addition, the scriptures and traditions of all religions had much to say on the subject, and these pronouncements could not be avoided in the face of the social and cultural changes of the late 20th century. Further, activism in gay and lesbian communities found expression in formally organized interest groups in many denominations, and they would not be silent in order to keep the peace in the churches.

Scientific debates over whether homosexual tendencies are genetically transmitted (and thus part of "fate") or culturally acquired (and thus a matter of choice) also had implications for the religious debate. More conservative counselors often argued that homosexuals can change their orientation and that they must in any case be celibate lifelong. Religious activists saw it to be the duty of churches to address society, but society itself was torn over the homosexual issue. Finally, AIDS, often associated with homosexuality, particularly in the U.S., was manifest in the priesthood, the ministry, and the lay life of congregations, eliciting moral condemnation from some religious agencies and spokespersons but sympathy and alertness from others.

Conservatives and Liberals Disagree. As a result, religious bodies were polarized. The more conservative Roman Catholic, Orthodox, and evangelical and fundamentalist Protestant bodies drew upon several biblical texts and historic taboos or proscriptions to denounce all homosexual expression. The more liberal elites in Catholicism and mainstream Protestantism, as in Reform and Conservative Judaism, spoke up for homosexual rights in society, interpreted scriptures more generously, and advocated a more open acceptance of the ministry and participation of declared homosexuals at all levels of religious organization. Between them—as between aggressive pro-life and pro-choice religious forces in the abortion controversy—were the vast majority of church and synagogue members. This majority gave evidence that their minds were not made up; they were in transition, reexploring the texts, reexamining the traditions, watching the scientific and political debates, and trying to do justice both to their own understanding and to the creative challenge represented by fellow believers who were "out of the closet" about their homosexuality.

At issue for many was biblical interpretation. All sides agreed that both the Hebrew scriptures—the Christians' Old Testament—and the New Testament almost never addressed the subject, even though the religious scene of the ancient world gave the writers reason to do so. The majority agreed that few of the texts (Genesis 18:20, 19:4–11; Leviticus 18:22, 20:13; Deuteronomy 23:18; Romans 1:24–27; I Corinthians 6:9; I Timothy 1:10) addressed homosexuality in terms informed by what shows up in modern laboratory or clinical findings or in the social sciences. One side argued that those wary of homosexual expression (often described overly simply and in inflaming terms as "homophobic") were being selective and legalistic in their interpretation of texts. But because such opponents did not seek enforcement of other "Mosaic" legislation from biblical times, it was asked why they should concentrate on a verse or two in Leviticus that seemed to apply here. Conservatives, on the other hand, accused those who would affirm homosexual practice, or who at least would not condemn it, of twisting interpretation of scripture. As they read them, two or three passages explicitly forbade homosexual actions. Especially difficult was Romans 1:24–27, which to conservative interpreters was a simple denunciation of such actions. To bystanders the two parties were fighting to a draw, unable to resolve the issue or even to understand each other.

Despite the deadlock, the issue continued to receive publicity. Roman Catholicism, already stung by revelations of child abuse by priests, was sometimes charged with exacerbating the situation by insisting on an all-male celibate clergy and too often of attracting men of abnormal sexual proclivities. Those who advocated more liberal views of homosexual expression charged that such an accusation was unfair to gay men since, after all, heterosexual men in the clergy of Protestant denominations, where ministers were free to marry, sometimes abused women and children. The death of a number of clergy from AIDS brought visibility to the presence of gay priests and observations that there were an inordinate number of closeted and uncloseted gays drawn to the priesthood in a church whose leadership condemned the homosexual outlook and lifestyle.

In Protestantism, warfare was carried on through books and pamphlets, and there was conflict among caucuses on all sides, debate over what was taught in seminaries, and heated and open controversy on the floor of denominational conventions. When Paul H. Sherry, president of the United Church of Christ, joined caucuses from mainstream Protestant churches and the Universal Fellowship of Metropolitan Community Churches (a gay-based group) in a gay and lesbian rights march in Washington, D.C., on April 25, 1993, the Christian Life Commission of the Southern Baptist Convention and the Christian Coalition, headed by Pat Robertson, condemned the participants outright.

Denominational Responses to Homosexuality. A sampling of denominational actions shows the depth of feeling. The largest Protestant body, the Southern Baptist Convention, meeting in Houston, Texas, on June 15–17, issued vehement and unprecedented condemnations of Pres. Bill Clinton

Martin E. Marty is Fairfax M. Cone distinguished service professor of the history of modern Christianity at the University of Chicago and a senior editor of The Christian Century.

and Vice Pres. Al Gore, both members of the Convention, because the new administration gave signs of supporting homosexual rights in the military and elsewhere. The ultraconservative Presbyterian Church in America, in its summer Assembly in Columbia, S.C., showed an extremely rare kind of intrusion into another body's life when it asked the Christian Reformed Church, also quite conservative, to repent of its "departure from the Scriptures in doctrine and practice" over issues like tolerance for homosexuality.

At the General Assembly of the larger and mainstream Presbyterian Church (U.S.A.), held in Orlando, Fla., on June 2–9, no other topic attracted as much notice and heat as did homosexuality. In 1991 the church had said in an "authoritative" statement that homosexuality is "not God's wish for humanity." The statement was not strong enough for the antigay forces but was violently denounced by those on the other side. The flagship Presbyterian school, Princeton Theological Seminary, did not clarify the situation when it issued two competing documents. One, signed by the president and a hundred others, opposed homosexual expression, while the second asked for "rethinking," keeping open the possibility of changing the church body's view. Presbyterians have analogues to the militant secular ACT UP movement, Presbyterians for Lesbian and Gay Concerns (and even one called Presbyterian ACT UP), who pressed for the licensing of openly practicing gay and lesbian ministers for ordination. The delegates responded by chartering a churchwide study.

It could be said that the only denominations to escape controversy in the summer of 1993 were those that did not meet—not all do every year—or that evaded and postponed the issue through resolutions to rethink it. Nowhere were there signs that the issue was quieting. It is also useful to note that the movement to ordain gays and lesbians and the endorsements of homosexual lifestyles had originally been chiefly promoted by elected and appointed officers, seminary professors, task forces, and denominational elites. When lay reaction, and even strong backlash, developed against their expressions and moves, there was muffling and retreat in the leadership, which feared denominational schism or at least disruption at a time when all groups were already suffering some membership losses for other reasons.

No Easy Answers. To the homosexual rights forces, such strategic delay and reconsideration looked like a denial of the religious message. Using analogies to the civil rights movement, comparisons that nonactivists were less ready to make, they argued that the prophetic voice of church and synagogue dare not count ballots or listen to polls but rather must respond to the divine call and reinterpret the ancient texts. They were met by others who were sure that the call did not include affirmation of homosexuality—though "we must love the homosexual persons"—and that the religious texts were too clear to be reinterpretable.

Between those two camps were the majority of members. Some of these believers gave signals that they wished the issue would simply go away. Many followed the quiet promptings of their hearts, no matter what partisans or texts might say. Still others voted for rethinking and hoped the result would be that which would serve the will of God and the rights and needs of people. What the results of reconsiderations, postponements, confrontations, and rethinking would be no one could foresee. They could know only that some day there had to be reckoning and resolution. The new moderator of the Presbyterian Church (U.S.A.), David Lee Dobler, said, "I believe that the middle will hold on this." He and his kind would be given little peace by activists—"voices on the edges," he called them—on both sides, who were not to be satisfied by a middle way.

(continued from page 262)

titled *Veritatis splendor,* Latin for "The Splendour of Truth," John Paul said opposition to church teaching "cannot be seen as a legitimate expression of Christian liberty" and urged that clergy who violated official doctrines be removed from their positions. (See *Roman Catholic Church,* below.)

In November the Rev. Gordon L. Summers of the Moravian Church was sworn in as president of the NCC. Financial problems prompted several denominations, including the Evangelical Lutheran Church in America, Presbyterian Church (U.S.A.), and Southern Baptist Convention, to make more budget cutbacks. However, the WCC ended up in the black for the second year in a row, and three former U.S. presidents, Jimmy Carter, Gerald Ford, and Ronald Reagan, agreed to serve as honorary cochairmen of a drive to raise $10 million for the faith and order work of the National and World Councils of Churches.

U.S. Pres. Bill Clinton drew criticism from his own denomination, the Southern Baptist Convention, which opposed his policies on abortion and homosexual rights and urged him to "affirm biblical morality in exercising his public office." Earlier Clinton had invited leaders from 15 denominations in the NCC to meet with him in the White House, signaling a greater openness to mainline denominations than had been the case in the Reagan and Bush administrations. Leaders of the NCC, the U.S. Catholic Conference, and the Synagogue Council of America met in Washington, D.C., in June and issued a 4,000-word statement seeking to initiate "a fresh debate over the renewal of the general welfare" in the United States. The statement said the welfare of the weakest members of society was "a crucial moral test" of the common good. (*See* Special Report.) Most religious leaders and associations applauded Clinton's signing on November 16 of the Religious Freedom Restoration Act, which reinstated significant restrictions on the government's ability to regulate religious practices.

In a unanimous ruling, the U.S. Supreme Court upheld the right of the Santeria religious group to sacrifice animals during worship services, saying that no religion or religious practice may be "singled out for discriminatory treatment" even if its activities were viewed as "abhorrent" by most people. In an Arizona case, the high court ruled 5–4 that government-funded sign language interpreters may be provided for deaf parochial school students because such aid benefits the child and not the school. A unanimous decision in a New York case said religious groups must be allowed to use public schools after hours if such access was accorded to other community groups.

Massachusetts' highest court overturned the 1990 manslaughter convictions of a Christian Science couple whose son died after they relied on spiritual rather than medical healing. The 6–1 ruling said David and Ginger Twitchell had "reasonably believed" they could rely solely on spiritual treatment without fear of prosecution. But a Minneapolis, Minn., jury returned a $5.2 million verdict against a woman who relied solely on spiritual healing while her 11-year-old son was dying from diabetes and against six other defendants, including a Christian Science congregation. The verdict was the first time that civil damages had been assessed against the church in connection with its teachings on spiritual healing.

In a widely discussed book titled *The Culture of Disbelief,* Yale law professor Stephen L. Carter said religion "often thumbs its nose at what the rest of the society believes is right" and that such dissent is necessary to preserve a healthy democracy. Carter said that "a religion is, at its heart, a way of denying the authority of the rest of the world." (DARRELL J. TURNER)

PROTESTANT CHURCHES

Anglican Communion. One hundred top Anglican leaders met in Cape Town, South Africa, in January 1993 to wrestle with a daunting list of issues, including threats to the communion's unity posed by the 13 provinces that had ordained women. The archbishop of Canterbury, the Most Rev. George Carey, presided at the meetings, while the archbishop of Cape Town, the Most Rev. Desmond M. Tutu, acted as host to this first-ever joint meeting between the communion's primates and the Anglican Consultative Council, which represented churches in 163 countries. The international gathering followed a November 1992 meeting of Southern Africa's Anglican bishops, who condemned South African political leaders over "growing and shocking tolerance of corruption, lies, and murder in political life." Criticizing both the South African government and the African National Congress, the bishops decried the "moral deterioration in South African society." Meanwhile, the sixth assembly of the All-Africa Conference of Churches (AACC) conferred the first AACC peace award upon two Mozambican churchmen, Anglican Bishop Dinis Sengulane of the Lebombo diocese and Roman Catholic Archbishop Jaime Gonçalves, in recognition of their contribution to the peace process in Mozambique.

The Church of England continued to grapple with the aftermath of its November 1992 decision to ordain women. Parliament approved the decision in November 1993. England's Roman Catholic bishops promised a "generous and understanding" welcome to Church of England members who could not accept the decision and chose to leave. Among the first to do so was Graham Leonard, the retired bishop of London, a longtime opponent of women's ordination. Carey told an ecumenical gathering in Belgium that "hopes for organic unity seem to have faded" between Anglicans and Roman Catholics.

U.S. Episcopalians were surprised by a membership gain for the second straight year, reversing a steady decline that began in 1966. In June the diocese of Vermont elected the Rev. Mary Adelia McLeod as its bishop, the first woman bishop to lead a U.S. diocese and only the second woman Anglican bishop worldwide. In November the Anglican Church of Canada elected Victoria Matthews of Toronto as its first woman bishop.

A conference in August on "Shaping Our Future: A Grassroots Forum on Episcopal Structures" attracted more than 1,000 participants from 96 dioceses. Participants ranging from traditionalists to liberal activists gathered in St. Louis, Mo., to discuss changes in the church's structure and organization in order to focus more effectively on its mission. (DAVID E. SUMNER)

Baptist Churches. The largest black Baptist religious group in the nation and probably in the world, the National Baptist Convention, USA, met in New York City's Madison Square Garden, beginning Sept. 8, 1993, for its 113th annual gathering. First organized in 1880, the National Baptist Convention had more than 33,000 churches and was the third-largest Protestant denomination in the U.S. Discussions at the New York convocation showed that the organization was moving away from its conservatism of a few years earlier—when the leadership opposed, for instance, the methods of Martin Luther King, Jr.—toward more progressive positions such as voicing opposition to the Gulf war. The organization was now focusing more attention on issues such as "economic empowerment" of blacks, ways congregations can deal with AIDS, and strategies for halting the waste of young black lives through crime, poverty, and lack of opportunity.

National Baptist Convention president Theodore J. Jemison was again the subject of controversy. Some members questioned the wisdom of building a $12 million headquarters in Nashville, Tenn.; the organization had $4 million of the debt still outstanding. In 1992 Jemison had been charged with perjury in the rape trial of boxer Mike Tyson.

Among white Baptists, the Cooperative Baptist Fellowship, an organization of moderates, reacted to the tensions and battles resulting from a fundamentalist takeover of the Southern Baptist Convention and met to draw up and adopt a new constitution. Former U.S. president Jimmy Carter endorsed and pledged financial support for the group, and he gave the keynote address at the meeting. Carter, a lifelong Southern Baptist and deacon in his home church in Plains, Ga., said he valued his Southern Baptist heritage but regretted the denomination's bitter internal politics during the past 14 years.

The Baptist World Alliance reported that the number of Baptists was growing in the Middle East, where Bible distribution was seen as a major evangelism tool. Continuing persecution of evangelicals was, however, still being reported in the region.

(NORMAN R. DE PUY)

Christian Church (Disciples of Christ). The Rev. Richard L. Hamm, 45, a Nashville, Tenn., church official, was elected in July 1993 as the Christian Church's youngest-ever chief executive. He assumed a six-year term as general minister and president of the Indianapolis, Ind.-based denomination. His election was a highlight of the first Common Gathering of the Disciples General Assembly and the General Synod of the United Church of Christ in July. The mainline churches had enjoyed a unique "ecumenical partnership" since 1985.

The climax of the historic event in St. Louis, Mo., was an address, broadcast live across the United States, by the Anglican archbishop of Cape Town, Desmond M. Tutu.

The assembly took note of the disastrous flooding in the U.S. Midwest and voted $30,407 to support local relief efforts. In all, the Disciples of Christ contributed more than $575,500 toward flood relief.

Earlier in the year, general minister and president C. William Nichols called for U.S. Pres. Bill Clinton to lift the ban on gays in the military, while the assembly came out in favour of civil rights for gays and lesbians, supported the establishment of a national health plan in the U.S., and called for peace and an end to ethnic cleansing in the Balkans. In other church-wide activities, the Rev. Patricia Tucker Spier, a Tipton, Ind., pastor and former missionary to Japan, was elected president of the Division of Overseas Ministries.

(CLIFFORD L. WILLIS)

Churches of Christ. In 1993 it was reported that 80 Churches of Christ had been established in the former U.S.S.R. in the past two years. More than 100 volunteer and seasoned preachers spent all or part of 1993 in missionary efforts. World Christian Broadcasting sent weekly messages across all the former Soviet Union as well as into China. The North Atlanta, Ga., church sent 40 workers to Siberia to strengthen the church there and evangelize, while the Highland church in Memphis, Tenn., sent extensive medical supplies to Kiev, Ukraine. International Christian University of Vienna was accredited in Ukraine and began classes in Kiev. Christians from Zagreb, Croatia, and Belgrade, Yugos., met in Kaposvar, Hung., to pray for peace. The first religious campaign in Cuba since 1959 targeted nine cities and reported 94 baptisms.

The National Crusade for Christ met at the Los Angeles Convention Center for one week in July, with 7,500 attending the first day. "One Nation Under God," a nationwide direct mail and advertising campaign that reached 102 million households in the U.S. in 1992, sent 11 million copies of "Good News Is for Sharing" to Canadian households and 1.2 million to households in the Caribbean in 1993.

(M. NORVEL YOUNG)

Church of Christ, Scientist. Mary Baker Eddy's *Science and Health with Key to the Scriptures,* named by the Women's National Book Association as one of the books by women whose words had changed the world, was the focal point of the 98th annual meeting of the members of the First Church of Christ, Scientist, held in Boston in June. Virginia Harris, chairman of the Christian Science board of directors and publisher of Mrs. Eddy's writings, said of the Christian Science textbook, "*Science and Health* is itself a journey, a spiritual journey of understanding God, and of coming to know ourselves as God's treasured children." Nathan Talbot, outgoing president of the Mother Church, announced the list of officers, which included Dieter K. Förster of Bad Soden, Germany, who would serve as president for 1993–94.

In the financial report to members, the board of directors announced that the balanced budget presented at the 1992 annual meeting had been met and that the pension reserve income was more than adequate to cover all payments to retired employees. Although challenges remained, the report pointed out, the church's financial condition had improved since 1992. (See *Introduction,* above.) (M. VICTOR WESTBERG)

Church of Jesus Christ of Latter-day Saints. By the end of 1993 there were 20,000 LDS congregations in the world. The internationalization of the faith continued with the sending of higher-education missionaries to Mongolia, health specialists to Bulgaria, and welfare aid to Somalia. Moreover, a 15-year program for small-scale agriculture was inaugurated in Mexico, and meetinghouses were completed in Swaziland and Belize.

As the church was celebrating the centennial of the completion of the Mormon Temple in Salt Lake City, Utah, officials announced the dedication of the completed temple in San Diego, Calif.; the construction of temples in Bountiful and American Fork, Utah; Orlando, Fla.; St. Louis, Mo.; Hartford, Conn.; and Preston, England; and the acquisition of sites for temples in Bogotá, Colombia; Guayaquil, Ecuador; Hong Kong; and Spain.

The elegant 10-story church-owned Hotel Utah in Salt Lake City was renovated to become an administrative headquarters and public gathering place and was renamed the Joseph Smith Memorial Building. In view of the illness of the church's 94-year-old president, Ezra Taft Benson, some officials advocated the establishment of emeritus status for aging apostles.

Weary of its one-party (Republican) image and wishing to see Utah more equally represented by Republicans and Democrats, church officials began preaching the benefits of political diversity. Late in 1993 actions were initiated to discipline militant feminists and vocal intellectual and doctrinal dissenters.

For the first time in 100 years, a Mormon official was invited to speak at the World Parliament of Religions, held in Chicago in the summer. (LEONARD J. ARRINGTON)

Jehovah's Witnesses. At a time when "hate thy neighbour" seemed the trend, the international convention of Witnesses held in Moscow stood in vivid contrast. More than 23,000 delegates from around the world attended; 1,489 were baptized. Later 64,714 Witnesses convened in Kiev, Ukraine, where 7,402 were baptized—the largest number ever immersed on one occasion. During the summer, 45 conventions were held elsewhere in Eastern Europe and Eurasia, with nearly 11,000 attending in four cities of former Yugoslavia alone.

In a move to stop what Judge S.K. Martens of the European Court of Human Rights called "the rise of fierce religious intolerance which is sweeping over our modern world," the court on May 25 made a landmark decision exonerating the Witnesses. Greece was found guilty of intolerance when it arrested Witnesses for "proselytism." In upholding the European Convention of Human Rights, which states that "everyone has the right to freedom of thought, conscience and religion," the court ruled that this implies "the freedom 'to manifest [one's] religion.' Bearing witness in words and deeds is bound up with the existence of religious convictions." Judge Martens added: "Whether or not somebody intends to change religion is no concern of the State's and . . . all religions and beliefs should, as far as the State is concerned, be equal." (MILTON HENSCHEL)

Lutheran Communion. Two of the five largest North American Lutheran denominations chose successors to leaders retiring in 1993—Telmor Sartison as bishop of the Evangelical Lutheran Church in Canada and Karl Gurgel of the Wisconsin Evangelical Lutheran Synod. The Evangelical Lutheran Church in America assembly established "diaconal ministers" as a new category of rostered ministry, approved statements on racism and the care of the earth, committed more resources to rural ministry, and approved a timetable that would allow the 1997 assembly to vote on "full communion" with the Episcopal Church and three U.S. Reformed denominations. In October a study group released a draft statement on sexuality that prompted controversy.

In the middle of the year, the Council of the Lutheran World Federation (LWF) met in Norway. After heated debate it approved a resolution on the situation in the former Yugoslavia that observed that "in this sinful world the threat of the use of military action seems unavoidable, in order to protect human life, to limit killing, and to avoid even greater suffering." It added that "military force can only be the last resort after all other means have been exhausted."

Steps were taken toward resolving leadership conflicts in church bodies in Indonesia and the Philippines. Lutherans in El Salvador held their first congress. In Tanzania, Lutheran representatives from across Africa met with people from international organizations for a consultation on ethics and the economy. The Japan Evangelical Lutheran Church marked its centennial by expressing "deep repentance" for its role during World War II. Lutherans in The Netherlands took further steps in a long process to unite with the two main (and much larger) Reformed church bodies there. Latvian Lutherans chose a new archbishop.

The Church of Sweden, the largest Lutheran church body in the world, marked the 400th anniversary of the formal end of the Reformation period in Sweden and Finland. In September the international Lutheran-Roman Catholic Joint Commission announced that it had found a large measure of consensus on the doctrine of "justification." Differences on this issue were a major reason the two communions separated in the 16th century. Earlier the LWF Council had also endorsed a consultation with Seventh-day Adventists.

Led by the Lutheran Church—Missouri Synod, about two dozen church bodies—many quite small—announced formation of the International Lutheran Council, committed to "the inspired and infallible Holy Scriptures." Five ILC members—in Nigeria, South Korea, Papua New Guinea, the Philippines, and India—also belonged to LWF, but most ILC members were critical of LWF positions and actions.

(THOMAS HARTLEY DORRIS)

Methodist Churches. Figures released in 1993 by the World Methodist Council showed a 16% rise in membership over the preceding five years and a 12% rise in the total Methodist community, including young people and adherents. The areas of significant growth were Africa, Asia, and South America. There was a 1% drop in membership in North America and an 8% drop in Europe, although the overall Methodist community had risen slightly in both areas. World membership was over 29 million and the total world community over 60 million. Following disclosures at the Executive Committee in 1992 that the World Fund of the World Methodist Council, which covered the Council's administrative expenses, was likely to be running at an annual deficit, the wealthier of the 68 member churches were urged to increase their contributions significantly.

The Fifth International Seminar on Evangelism was held at Cliff College, Sheffield, England, in January 1993. During Pentecost 1993 approximately 2,000 Kingdom Missions were organized by Methodist churches worldwide as a contribution to the Decade of Evangelism. The Evangelisch-methodistiche Kirche, previously divided into two episcopal areas for the former East and West Germany, agreed to unite under a single head, Bishop Walter Klaiber.

The Roman Catholic–Methodist international commission that had been in existence for 25 years met in Vienna and worked on developing a common understanding of Revelation. The Anglican-Methodist Commission, which had held meetings in Jerusalem and Dublin, discovered large areas of agreement; discussions were continuing on the historic episcopate. The preparatory commission of the Methodist and Orthodox churches sent a formal proposal to the World Methodist

ELLEN BINDER—THE NEW YORK TIMES

Converts receive baptism at a world convention of Jehovah's Witnesses in Moscow in July. The religious body held numerous meetings in Europe and Asia during the summer of 1993.

Council and the 15 autocephalous Orthodox churches to set up an international commission to meet annually in 1997–2000.

The World Methodist Historical Society held an international conference in Cambridge, England, in July 1993 to coincide with the centenary celebrations of the British Wesley Historical Society. In September the Consultative Conference of European Methodist Churches met in Herrnhut, Germany. Discussions between the British Church and the Central Conferences in Europe of the United Methodist Church and clergy in Ireland, Italy, Portugal, and Spain resulted in 1993 in a proposal for a European Methodist Council.

(JOHN C.A. BARRETT)

Pentecostal Churches. American Pentecostal leaders held a historic "summit" meeting of leaders in January 1993 in Phoenix, Ariz., in an effort to heal the divisions between black and white Pentecostals that had existed since the formation of the Pentecostal Fellowship of North America (PFNA) in 1948. In October the annual PFNA session voted to disband if necessary in order to build a bridge to the Church of God in Christ, the predominately black church that was the largest Pentecostal denomination in the U.S.

In August the Assemblies of God elected Thomas Trask to succeed retiring General Superintendent Raymond Carlson. Also in August the International Pentecostal Holiness Church reelected B.E. Underwood general superintendent, while in June the Pentecostal Church of God reelected James Gee to lead the church.

Oral Roberts retired in January as president of Oral Roberts University in Tulsa, Okla., and was succeeded by his son, Richard Roberts. Also in January, Paul Morton, pastor of the Greater St. Stephen Full Gospel Baptist Church in New Orleans, La., organized the nationwide "Full Gospel Baptist Fellowship," made up mostly of pastors in the National Baptist Church, the largest African-American denomination in the country. In September 1,500 Roman Catholic Charismatics gathered in Assisi, Italy, for an international leaders retreat led by Raneiro Cantalamessa, preacher to the papal household. At the end of the retreat, Pope John Paul II greeted the group and praised Catholic charismatics for adding many new vocations to the church.

The Society for Pentecostal Studies met in November in Guadalajara, Mexico, its first convocation outside the U.S.

(VINSON SYNAN)

Reformed, Presbyterian, and Congregational Churches. During 1993 interchurch consultations and articles identified a number of significant concerns for and among the Reformed churches. As they strove for independence—and a new interdependence—Reformed, Presbyterian, and Congregational churches from Africa, Asia, and Latin America sought more contact and exchanges. The World Alliance of Reformed Churches (WARC) continued to grow and help provide these networking opportunities; membership expanded to 188 churches in 90 countries.

High on the agenda of churches of Reformed heritage was the need for a just resolution of the global debt crisis, which compounds the poverty in many nations. Churches registered alarm at the growing racism in Europe, and popular and legal resistance to migration from the South to the North mobilized churches in Europe and North America to public demonstrations of support for minorities and migrant labour populations.

Questions related to the acceptance of homosexuals in the Christian community riveted the attention of the Presbyterian Church (U.S.A.). The 1993 General Assembly reaffirmed its commitment to full civil rights for gays and lesbians and called for continuing study of the possibility of their ordination.

Throughout Central and Eastern Europe, efforts to secure the return of church properties confiscated by former Communist regimes remained at the centre of concern for Reformed churches. In Romania and Russia, churches sought to influence the drafting of new laws that would ensure equal treatment for minority religious groups.

The heresy of the theological justification of apartheid was the focus of a WARC consultation convened in March 1993 for branches of the Dutch Reformed Church (DRC) family in southern Africa. The South African Dutch Reformed Church had been in suspended membership in the alliance since 1982 because of its theological support of apartheid. Leading representatives of the church agreed that its renunciation of the theology of apartheid had to be exhibited in word and deed. DRC union with the Dutch Reformed Mission Church, the Dutch Reformed Church in Africa, and the Reformed Church in Africa—churches that had been created to divide believers of the Reformed tradition on lines of race—was recognized as essential to demonstrate a genuine renunciation of the theological justification of apartheid. The executive committee of the WARC agreed to wait at least two years before considering reinstatement of the DRC to regular membership.

One of America's best known clergymen, the Rev. Norman Vincent Peale, died in December (*see* OBITUARIES).

(SARAH STEPHENS)

Religious Society of Friends. New leadership took over the Friends World Committee for Consultation (FWCC) in late 1992, with Thomas F. Taylor assuming the office of general secretary in the world office in London and Asia Bennett becoming executive secretary of the FWCC Section of the Americas. Bennett, who represented Friends at the meeting of secretaries of the Christian World Communions in October 1992 in Washington, D.C., found that large Christian bodies were struggling with the same dilemmas that perplexed the Religious Society of Friends: the balance between faith and works, the pull between evangelical and liberal agendas, the right response to questions of sexual orientation, and the role of women.

The unrest in Kenya continued into 1993, causing the internal displacement of many people in Quaker regions. Responding to this need, FWCC Africa Section's Committee for Peace and Social Concerns, organized by Kenyan Friends, continued to provide relief funds and temporary housing in one of the affected areas.

(THOMAS F. TAYLOR)

Salvation Army. A new world leader was elected by the Salvation Army's High Council when it met in April 1993: Commissioner Bramwell H. Tillsley, a Canadian, who had been serving as chief of staff at International Headquarters in London. General Tillsley told the press that the Army should have the courage to speak out on social issues such as poverty, homelessness, pornography, drugs, and child abuse. "There is a crying need in our world today for men and women of integrity," he said.

Two years after it resumed activities in the former Soviet Union, the Salvation Army commissioned and ordained its first Russian officers. Outgoing general Eva Burrows, who had ordered the Army's return to Russia after an enforced 70-year absence, flew to Moscow to commission 10 officers, including a pediatrician, a psychologist, a lawyer, a professor, and a former Red Army colonel. In addition to its rapidly expanding spiritual and welfare work in the Russian cities of St. Petersburg and Moscow, the Army extended its work into Moldova, Georgia, and Ukraine.

General Burrows also strengthened the Army's ties with China. Following meetings in Beijing (Peking), she reported, "The potential for the growth of God's Kingdom in China is even beyond our imagining. Hallelujah!" (MARGARET KIRK)

Seventh-day Adventist Church. Celebrating 100 years of Adventism in southern Asia, the Annual Council of the world church met in Bangalore, India, in 1993. The church at first grew very slowly there, but in recent years India had become a fruitful field for growth, and membership in 1993 approached 200,000. The church in India was also moving toward financial strength; the centenary year saw the first conference, Mizoram, achieve self-support.

The church took major steps toward developing a satellite communication network. Live telecasts were beamed to Adventist churches from Moscow, Toronto, and São Paulo, Brazil. Regular satellite programming was scheduled to begin in 1994.

Through its relief arm, Adventist Development and Relief Agency (ADRA), the church was active in more than 90 countries on behalf of the poor, the homeless, and the dispossessed. In Bosnia, ADRA served as the conduit for all mail as well as relief supplies to Sarajevo, while in Somalia it set up a medical clinic to augment its feeding program.

The siege and subsequent inferno at a ranch near Waco, Texas, brought Adventists into national attention in many countries. David Koresh had once been a member of the Seventh-day Adventist Church and had targeted Adventists for recruitment. The church dissociated itself from Koresh's teachings and practices and made it clear that the Branch Davidians had no connection with the Seventh-day Adventist Church.

As of Dec. 31, 1992, Adventists had a presence in 204 countries and a total membership of 7,498,653.

(WILLIAM G. JOHNSSON)

Unitarian (Universalist) Churches. Meeting in Budapest, a global summit of Unitarian leaders in 1993 laid the groundwork for establishing a World Unitarian Council. For the first time, a member of the U.S. clergy was starting work in Moscow and St. Petersburg.

The strongest organization within the global picture was North America's Unitarian Universalist Association (UUA). Its 32nd annual General Assembly, held June 24–29, drew 2,998 registrants to Charlotte,

N.C., to discuss "Universalism: For Such a Time as This" and to celebrate Universalism's 200-year history. The Rev. John A. Buehrens was elected president. The General Assembly passed resolutions urging congregations to include the word "Universalist" in some manner in their official name, affirming the right of women to have access to abortion-counseling services, supporting the rights of indigenous peoples, affirming environmental justice, and condemning violence against women.

The year 1993 marked the introduction of a new hymnal, *Singing the Living Tradition,* and the start of a $10 million capital funds campaign, of which over 60% was already pledged.

The General Assembly of Unitarian and Free Christian Churches, representing Great Britain and Northern Ireland, adopted a long-range strategic plan, "Unitarian Vision 2001." A ceremony to mark the ending of a marriage and a blessing of a same-sex partnership were part of a new book of life ceremonies for special occasions. Issued by the London Unitarian headquarters, the book received the 1993 Spiritual Social Inventions Award of the (U.K.) Institute for Social Inventions.

Celebrating the 100th anniversary of the World Parliament of Religions (Chicago, 1893), the International Association for Religious Freedom met in Bangalore, India, on August 14–18. It was composed of 60 member groups from every continent.

(JOHN NICHOLLS BOOTH)

The United Church of Canada. On behalf of the United Church of Canada, moderator Stanley McKay called for government action in 1993 on such issues as the Balkan conflict and the North American Free Trade Agreement and its impact on agriculture. He expressed support for the Lubicon people in northern Alberta and offered United Church support to the prime minister in dealing with economic reform.

Work continued on the development of a new hymnal and worship book. The committee overseeing the book's development circulated a sampler of representative hymns, psalms, and prayers in anticipation of publication in November 1995.

The recommendations of a consultants' report on financial and information systems occupied the attention of the national office staff. When fully operational in 1994, the new systems would allow the church to redirect up to $1 million annually to nonadministrative programs and enable more efficient and accurate information sharing. Some of the denomination's 13 conferences (regional administrative units) were experimenting with new organizational structures. The success of these experiments could lead to a total restructuring of the current four-tier organizational system, which had been functioning since the denomination's inception in 1925.

In 1993 four United Church ministers filed lawsuits against the denomination, two of its conferences, four presbyteries (other local administrative units), and up to 20 staff and volunteer officeholders. The suits were filed in response to the denomination's process of dealing with sexual harassment charges levied against the four. The suits (seeking millions of dollars in damages) were in court and would evolve through 1994.

The United Church suffered a major loss in the sudden death on October 9 of its senior executive officer, the Rev. Howard M. Mills, general secretary of the General Council. Mills had served the church faithfully in that office since 1987.

(DOUGLAS L. FLANDERS)

United Church of Christ. For the 1.6 million-member United Church of Christ, the year 1993 was characterized by intensive efforts toward church identity and renewal, the strengthening of ecumenical commitments in the United States and around the world, and the deepening of domestic and international social witness.

In July the General Synod of the United Church of Christ and the General Assembly of the Christian Church (Disciples of Christ) met jointly for the first time (see *Christian Church,* above). At the General Synod meeting, the UCC delegates approved a Statement of Commitment that called for the church to be attentive to the Word, inclusive of all people, responsive to God's call, and supportive of one another.

Other resolutions of the Synod made the UCC "a multiracial and multicultural church," encouraged the participation of children in the full worship life of the church, including communion, called for an end to discrimination against gays and lesbians, endorsed a publicly financed approach to health care reform, and called for a cease-fire and an end to ethnic cleansing in the former Yugoslavia. The General Synod also discussed a new church hymnal being developed, proposed church structural changes, and approved a $30 million fund campaign. Many delegates assisted in flood relief along the Midwest rivers.

Paul H. Sherry and Doris R. Powell were reelected unanimously for four-year terms as president and treasurer, respectively, of the church. Victor Melendez was elected moderator of the General Synod and Donna Debney and Anthony Taylor as assistant moderators.

In January 1993 the president of the church led a delegation of UCC church leaders to Hawaii to apologize to the native Hawaiian people for the participation of some UCC forebears in the overthrow of the Hawaiian monarchy in 1893 and to reach for reconciliation as the church moved toward a new century.

(PAUL H. SHERRY)

ROMAN CATHOLIC CHURCH

The year 1993 was marked by speculation about Pope John Paul II's state of health after his cancer operation on July 15, 1992. The Vatican dismissed the rumours as alarmist and, as if to prove them wrong, the pope did not relax his strenuous round of visits. February saw him in Benin and Uganda, where he announced the start of an African synod on April 10, 1994. African theologians regretted that it would take place in Rome and feared it would be manipulated.

On his way back from this, his 10th visit to Africa, John Paul paused in The Sudan, a country under a Muslim fundamentalist regime where Christians had been severely persecuted. The papal visit was seen as a diplomatic exercise that won only a temporary respite for the Christians.

The papal visit to Spain in mid-June came tactfully after the elections in which the Socialist Felipe González Márquez, an agnostic, had narrowly defeated José María Aznar, a devout Catholic. The pope opened the neo-Gothic Cathedral de la Almudena in Madrid (begun in 1911) and went to the Seville world's fair to conclude the Columbus quincentenary.

One visit John Paul was unable to make was to Sarajevo, capital of Bosnia and Herzegovina, once the epitome of good Christian-Muslim relations. In January he did the next-best thing by inviting Bosnian Muslims to Assisi to an ecumenical meeting, where they told their story movingly and dramatically. The Vatican also tried to stay in touch with the Serbian Orthodox Church, and in August Godfried Cardinal Danneels, president of Pax Christi, went to Belgrade, Yugos., to meet Patriarch Pavle. Despite the difficulty of being evenhanded, it was generally agreed that John Paul tried to restrain the Catholic Croats and that the Bosnian Muslims found in him a friend, though an ineffectual one.

In August the pope made visits, postponed from the previous year, to Jamaica and to Yucatán state, Mexico, to conclude the Columbus quincentenary celebrations. In Yucatán the pope apologized to the Indian peoples for their centuries of oppression. The main purpose of this journey, however, was to attend the World Youth Day festival at Denver, Colo., on August 12–15, the first time the event had been held in the U.S. After a noncommittal first meeting with Pres. Bill Clinton, the pope delivered his main message, on the need to assert an objective moral order against any "privatization" of morality.

Though it was not realized at the time, John Paul was in effect giving a preview of the theme of his next encyclical, *Veritatis splendor,* scheduled to appear October 5, though it was dated August 6, the 15th anniversary of the death of Pope Paul VI. An early draft was leaked by German sources in July, so the encyclical was widely discussed before it appeared. It was concerned with fundamental moral principles and the need to "form consciences" so the morally good could be perceived. The encyclical did not, as some had feared, declare infallible *Humanae vitae,* the 1968 encyclical banning artificial birth control, though it accorded the earlier statement such a high degree of authority that dissent from it was not allowed. It included an appeal to bishops to be especially vigilant in the supervision of moral teaching. Coincidentally, an Anglican–Roman Catholic International Commission report on moral questions suggested a remarkable convergence of method between the two churches. The only moral question disputed in official documents was artificial contraception.

Charges of sexual abuse were brought against a number of U.S. churchmen late in the year. In November a former seminary student filed suit against Joseph Cardinal Bernadin of Chicago, claiming sexual abuse in the 1970s, but the National Conference of Catholic Bishops rallied in support of the cardinal. Three weeks later, however, a former priest was sentenced to a long prison term in Massachusetts for sexually abusing children in his parish in the 1960s; the Franciscan Order reported that 11 friars in California had been guilty of molesting seminary students; and at year's end the Archdiocese of Santa Fe, N.M., claimed that it was facing bankruptcy be-

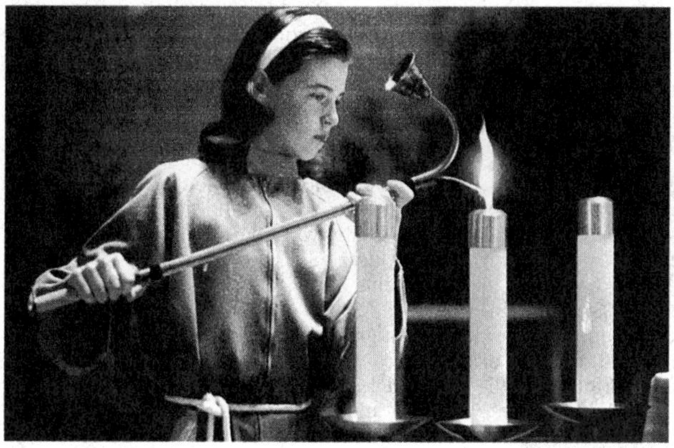

An altar girl lights candles before mass in a church in suburban Chicago. The role of women continued to be one of the most difficult issues for Roman Catholics throughout the world.

EDUARDO CONTRERAS—THE CHICAGO TRIBUNE

cause of expenses connected with the legal defense of priests charged with abuse of their parishioners.

The church lost a major spokesman for ecumenism with the death in July of the Scotsman Gordon Cardinal Gray (*see* OBITUARIES).

John Paul visited the Baltic republics early in September, where he warned against the dangers of chauvinist nationalism—by which he meant past anti-Semitism and present anti-Russian feelings. He paid tribute to "the historic importance and glorious tradition of the Orthodox Church." But his outstretched hand was not grasped. The Russian Orthodox Church was still smarting at the loss of western Ukraine, where four million people had reverted to the Uniate Church. A law proposed in May would have restricted "foreign" missionaries in Russia. Pres. Boris Yeltsin refused to sign it, however, and it got lost in his quarrels with the parliament.

The Vatican established full diplomatic relations with Israel on December 30, clearing a path for reconciliation between the two that had begun with the Second Vatican Council in 1965. A papal visit to Jerusalem in 1994 was widely anticipated.

In March there was a restructuring of the European Bishops' Council, which had been judged "too Western." Its new president, Archbishop Miroslav Vlk of Prague, was host of an enlarged symposium that was received in Hradcany Castle by Pres. Vaclav Havel. The meeting became stormy, however, as Jolanta Babiuch, a Warsaw sociologist, charged that the Polish church was losing the faithful because of its triumphalism and its attempted alliance with the rich and powerful. The Polish bishops denied this, but the September 19 election, when former Communists made a dazzling comeback, proved them wrong. (*See* WORLD AFFAIRS [Europe]: *Vatican City*.)

(PETER HEBBLETHWAITE)

THE ORTHODOX CHURCH

The issue of religious freedom and the status of the Russian Orthodox Church as the national church of the Russian people came to the fore when Parliament passed a law on July 31, 1993, requiring the registration of foreign missionaries so as to limit proselytism. Pres. Boris Yeltsin did not sign the law as passed, returning it to Parliament with recommendations reflecting international human rights agreements. In October the crisis between President Yeltsin and Parliament was mediated by Patriarch Aleksey II. Two unusual moves were taken by the Russian Orthodox Church in 1993: the establishment of a church bank to finance church projects and the announcement on February 12 of the founding of an Orthodox University in Moscow.

A rare Greater Synod of the Ecumenical Patriarchate of Constantinople was called by Ecumenical Patriarch Bartholomew I on July 30–31 to discuss the uncanonical activities of the patriarch of Jerusalem, Diodoros, who had been seeking to establish his own jurisdiction in Australia. Representatives acted to discipline the patriarch, and within days the Jerusalem patriarchate announced its withdrawal from the disputed area.

In the process of being reestablished, the Orthodox Church in Albania faced ethnic tensions. Several Greek nationals among the clergy were expelled by the government. Nevertheless, the building of new churches, the establishment of a seminary, and other new programs continued apace.

In Greece troubled relations between the Orthodox Church and the state continued as a Greek court restored three bishops to diocesan positions they had lost with the return of democracy in 1974. The Holy Synod, led by Archbishop Seraphim of Athens, opposed the decision and refused to conform to it, provoking new calls for a review of the relationship of church and state in that predominantly Orthodox country.

With the division of Czechoslovakia into two nations, the Czech Republic and Slovakia, the Orthodox Church there implemented a plan for ministering to its divided flock. The chief hierarch, Metropolitan Diodoros, would be known as metropolitan of the Czech Republic and Slovakia. In the meantime, in Slovakia the government further denied the Orthodox adequate space for worship and confiscated Orthodox churches and turned them over to the Eastern rite church.

Representatives of the (predominantly Russian) Orthodox Archdiocese of Western Europe met in Paris on May 31 and elected Archimandrite Sergey Konovalov archbishop, following the death of Archbishop George on April 6. Orthodox theologian and priest Boris Bobrinskoy was elected dean of St. Sergius Institute, Paris, on June 23.

Patriarch Mstyslav Skrypnyk of the Ukrainian Orthodox Church—Kiev patriarchate died on June 11 in Grimsby, Ont., at age 95. Volodymyr Romanyuk, a former prisoner in Soviet labour camps, was made patriarch in Kiev in October. The jurisdiction was established in 1990 when Ukrainians in large numbers severed relations with the Ukrainian Church under the Moscow patriarchate, headed by Metropolitan Vladimir of Kiev.

(STANLEY S. HARAKAS)

ORIENTAL ORTHODOX CHURCH

Patriarch Paulos of the Ethiopian Orthodox Church visited ecumenical leaders in Geneva in 1993 to seek assistance for his church, which suffered persecution during the Ethiopian communist regime.

Armenian Orthodox Patriarch-Catholicos Vasken I met on January 21 with Patriarch Aleksey II of Moscow. They issued a declaration calling for openness and understanding between Christians and Muslims in the conflict in Nagorno-Karabakh. Vasken I also met in Montreux, Switz., with Sheikh-ul-Islam Pashazadeh, the chief religious leader of the Caucasian Muslims, urging the political authorities of both Armenia and Azerbaijan to resolve the conflict peacefully.

In mid-March, during a meeting of Muslims and Christians in Cairo, Pope Shenouda III, leader of the Coptic Oriental Orthodox Church headquartered in Egypt, publicly condemned the continuing violence of Muslim fundamentalists against Christians. In May representatives of the Oriental Orthodox Church and the World Alliance of Reformed Churches met in Egypt to initiate a dialogue between the two traditions. Plans were made for a second meeting in 1994 in The Netherlands.

(STANLEY S. HARAKAS)

JUDAISM

Although the U.S. Jewish community—and particularly its political and financial leaders—found ample room to congratulate itself for certain successes in 1993, the organized community was facing a decline in the number of Jews and in the practice of Judaism.

The opening in April of the U.S. Holocaust Memorial Museum in Washington, D.C., was the culmination of a 48-year quest to memorialize the six million European Jews killed by the Nazis. The museum, a compilation of materials of the period, established the Holocaust as fact and symbol in the life of Jews and other Americans. (*see* MUSEUMS.) The Holocaust, wrote the *Baltimore* (Md.) *Jewish Times*, had been a "quasi-religion" for almost five decades, especially in the period before the 1967 Israeli-Arab War, when it seemed that the events of Europe might repeat themselves in the Middle East as Israel's neighbours threatened to wipe it off the map.

In the aftermath of the November 1992 annual meeting of the General Assembly of the Council of Jewish Federations in New York, leaders began to face the demographic challenge of a population shrinking because of aging and marriages outside of Judaism. Shoshana Cardin, of the National Jewish Center for Learning and Leadership, chastised Jewish leaders, saying that they had practiced "checkbook Judaism," trying to do with cash what they could not do with their own children—create a generation of Jews willing to practice the faith. Accordingly, observing spiritual law, studying religious texts, and attending synagogue were coming to be emphasized as more important than giving money to Israel. Several communities—including Houston, Texas; Hartford, Conn.; Cleveland, Ohio; New York;

and Los Angeles—formed special forums in which synagogues and Jewish community federations could exchange ideas and resources to improve the spiritual component of Jewish public life. The alliances were a dramatic departure from the familiar organization of the Jewish community.

If rhetoric heralded a revival in the religious life of the Jewish community, several institutions noted for their commitment to Judaism still suffered from a lack of support. College centres of the Hillel Foundation, established to provide a cultural and religious home for young Jews, suffered financial distress in a year in which American Jews donated at least $1 billion to support Jewish community federations and Israel. In March 1993 the *Baltimore Jewish Times* reported that two organizations, one that helped recently arrived Russian Jewish émigrés learn more about Judaism and another that sought to counter messianic Jews and their proselytizing, were closing or experiencing severe cutbacks because of inadequate financial support.

The crisis of identity raised an additional issue: whether concerns about assimilation would have a reactionary effect, pushing more Jews toward the strict laws of Orthodox Judaism. This familiar argument was taken up anew by the Chief Rabbi of England, Jonathan Sacks. A year earlier Sacks had argued that conciliation with an "open society" and subsequent attempts to abandon religious observance had left Jews and Judaism too weak to battle assimilation: "Jews did not keep Torah in order to survive as Jews," he said. "They survived as Jews in order to keep Torah. But the two are inextricable."

Far from debates over identity and assimilation was the New York-based Lubavitch community, a Hasidic sect organized around Rabbi Menachem Schneerson, whom they considered a holy man. Although fewer than 1% of the world's Jews were Lubavitch, Schneerson's influence was disproportionately great. In 1993 in particular he made headlines when some of his followers encouraged him to declare himself the Messiah, an idea that outraged many Jews. Although Schneerson had earlier suffered a stroke that left him partially paralyzed and unable to speak, the messianics scheduled a satellite television hookup on January 31 so that he could reveal himself as the Messiah before an international audience. The rabbi, however, did not do so.

(NOAM NEUSNER)

BUDDHISM

Buddhism entered India's politico-religious tumult during 1992–93 as the Buddha Gaya Mahabodhi Vihar All-India Action Committee agitated for exclusive control of the site of Buddha's Enlightenment. Protesting Hindu control of Bodh Gaya's management and Hinduization of the Buddhist cult at the international Buddhist centre, the primarily Dalit Committee, led by Japanese-born Arya Nagarjun Surai Sasai, marched from Bombay to Bodh Gaya in September–October 1992, lobbied, and staged a sit-in in May 1993.

Tamang leaders met in Darjeeling, India, during March to launch a campaign of posters, processions, and petitions aimed at securing scheduled tribe status for the large Tibeto-Burman Buddhist community spread throughout India's northern states and Nepal. In the same month, Ladakhi Buddhists demanded a role in settling the Kashmir problem, while a pan-Himalayan Buddhist organization called on India's government to challenge China by recognizing the Tibetan government-in-exile.

Despite arrests of pro-independence monks and nuns during March and May, Tibetans continued to protest Chinese oppression. Defying Chinese objections, Thailand allowed the Dalai Lama to join other Nobel laureates in Bangkok, Thailand, in February to protest continued Burmese imprisonment of Daw Aung San Suu Kyi. Reports of imprisonment and torture of dissident Buddhist monks continued to filter out of Myanmar.

Throughout the year Vietnamese Buddhists protested Hanoi's persecution of the opposition Unified Buddhist Church. Buddhist monks threatened self-immolation during confrontations in January; in February a Paris-based human rights organization charged that one monk had been tortured to death while another eight were being imprisoned in an effort to force them to support the state-backed Vietnamese Buddhist Church. In July Vietnamese demonstrators at European Community headquarters demanded religious freedom. The state-backed Asian Buddhist Conference for Peace issued a declaration from Hanoi in March that affirmed "the vitality of Vietnamese Buddhism" after advocating global nuclear disarmament, expressing solidarity with Cambodian Buddhists, condemning Khmer Rouge massacres of Vietnamese civilians, and calling for Korean reunification.

During 1992–93 Sri Lankan Buddhism celebrated its 2,300th anniversary. Archaeologists meanwhile announced the discovery of the ashes of Arhant Mahinda, traditional apostle of Sri Lankan Buddhism. Government festivities were spoiled by the assassination in May of the celebration's architect, Pres. Ranasinghe Premadasa.

A 34-m (112-ft)-tall bronze statue of Buddha, one of the largest in the world, was unveiled in December at the Po Lin monastery in Hong Kong. The Buddhist world lost one of its most articulate spokesmen in July with the death of Bhikkhu Buddhadasa of Thailand.

(FRANK E. REYNOLDS; JONATHAN S. WALTERS)

HINDUISM

The year 1993 began amid the turmoil generated by the destruction on Dec. 6, 1992, of the medieval mosque in Ayodhya, Uttar Pradesh, by Hindu militants, who believed the building was originally an ancient Hindu temple marking the birthplace of the god Rama. The ensuing bloody clashes between Hindus and Muslims throughout the nation claimed at least 2,000 lives within a few weeks, most of them Muslims. In Bombay riots resulted in the death of more than 600 Muslims, well over 550 alone during nine days within the first two weeks of January. Hundreds of Muslims were arrested in Ayodhya as they attempted to conduct prayers at the site of the destroyed mosque. On March 12 a series of bomb explosions in Bombay linked to a Muslim criminal element killed over 200, wounded more than 1,200, and badly damaged the headquarters of the Shiv Sena, the most powerful and radical Hindu organization in the city.

Prime Minister Narasimha Rao had promised the construction of both a temple and a mosque in Ayodhya outside the disputed area. On February 25, in defiance of a government ban, the fundamentalist Hindu Bharatiya Janata Party (BJP) attempted to hold a rally in New Delhi. Anticipating the worst, the government arrested or detained over 60,000 Hindus and sealed off New Delhi with barricades. Scuffles with the police led to the arrest of nearly 5,000, including 110 BJP members of Parliament.

On July 25 the government introduced two highly controversial bills intended to divorce politics from religion. The proposed legislation included a constitutional amendment declaring equal respect by the state for all religions and a prohibition on the state's professing, practicing, or propagating any particular religion. In response to the bombing of the headquarters of a militant Hindu organization in Madras on August 8, the Tamil Nadu state government banned all religious processions.

On August 29 and September 3, respectively, the Sri Venugopalaswamy and the Sri Yoga Ramachandraswamy temples near Vellore in Tamil Nadu state were reconsecrated in an ancient ceremony (*kumbhabhishekam*) after having fallen into disrepair through centuries of neglect. The temples were adorned with new images of the gods, the original ones having been either looted or damaged by vandals. The restoration of the temples drew attention once more to the deteriorating condition of India's religious monuments. Of the more than one million monuments in the country, only 5,000 were protected as nationally significant, and the Archaeological Survey of India operated on a $10 million annual allocation. Many of the ancient shrines had poor security, inviting not only occupation by squatters but also theft of images to supply a thriving international market in Indian antiquities. On September 1, for example, police recovered from the jungle near Lucknow, Uttar Pradesh, a 9th-century image of Vishnu, valued at nearly $200,000, which had been removed from an unguarded temple in the area.

(PATRICK H. SULLIVAN)

ISLAM

Significant trends in Islam of recent years remained valid in 1993: the increasing spread of fundamentalism, continuing warfare and violence in many Muslim areas, notably Palestine and Somalia, and Islam's sustained growth accompanied by visible manifestations of its presence. Terrorist plots in New York involving the World Trade Center and the United Nations building evoked an emotional reaction by some of the U.S. public and media against Arabs and Muslims and highlighted the need to educate the public to avoid stereotypes and distinguish Muslims in general from political terrorists. Both the United States and Europe saw instances of hate crimes against Muslims and acts of desecration against mosques.

The growing power of Islamic fundamentalism, often erupting into terrorist actions, continued to be felt in a number of Muslim nations. (*See* WORLD AFFAIRS: *Middle East and North Africa:* Special Report.) In Algeria the death toll climbed to more than a thousand since mid-1992 as sporadic fighting became almost endemic. Tunisia and Morocco suffered the same problems,

The Great Hassan II Mosque, which opened in August 1993, towers over Casablanca, Morocco. The third largest mosque in the world, it has a green laser beam directed eastward toward Mecca. The mosque cost $500 million, raised through a subscription drive conducted by King Hassan II.
REUTERS/BETTMAN

although with fewer casualties. In Egypt some of the violence was turned against foreigners as terrorist groups tried to upset the government by discouraging tourism and choking off the substantial income it brought. Radical fundamentalist reformers also attacked moderate and secular Muslim writers and intellectuals in these countries, as well as in Turkey, for holding antifundamentalist views.

Muslims in Bosnia began fighting among themselves during the fall. The civil war in Tajikistan continued as well, with outside support from Afghanistan, itself still reeling from 14 years of war and civil violence. In various locations in India, Muslims and Hindus clashed in bloody violence; the most serious encounter was in Bombay in January. Fighting continued in The Sudan and in a number of other northern and sub-Saharan African countries with large Muslim populations.

In the United States public awareness of the increasing Islamic presence was on the rise. There were claims that Muslims in the U.S. were undercounted. A total population figure of over four million, and still rising, seemed quite likely. Capt. Abdul-Rasheed Muhammad was appointed as the first chaplain for the estimated 2,500 Muslims in the U.S. Army. Media stereotyping of Muslims and Arabs remained a serious and important concern during the year. A conference held in Kansas City, Mo., in September was attended by some 7,000 American Muslims, both from immigrant families and African-American converts, who were concerned about anti-Muslim attitudes, principally, but not entirely, resulting from the bombing of the World Trade Center.

Islamic growth was underscored by the construction of two large mosques—one in Caracas, Venezuela, which was the largest in Latin America, and one in Casablanca, Morocco, which boasted the tallest minaret in the world. An Islamic society, formed recently in southern Spain by Spaniards claiming descent from the Moors resident in Spain before 1492, continued to flourish and reported developing an Islamic centre and attracting an increasing number of converts. (REUBEN W. SMITH)

WORLD RELIGIOUS STATISTICS

One hundred years passed between the 1893 World's Parliament of Religions at Chicago and the 1993 Parliament of the World's Religions in the same city. During the century massive religious shifts took place. Adherents of Christianity grew from 550 million to 1.9 billion yet remained at virtually the same percentage level throughout (34% of the world). Adherents of the other world religions increased even faster, however. Islam expanded from 12.4% of the world in 1893 to 18.2% today. Even more significant was the arrival of virtually universal religious pluralism; almost all faiths spread out of their homelands by emigration and today have widespread diasporas, many, in fact, having become worldwide religions.

(DAVID B. BARRETT)

This article updates the *Macropædia* articles The Buddha and BUDDHISM; CHRISTIANITY; EASTERN ORTHODOXY; HINDUISM; Muhammad and the Religion of ISLAM; JUDAISM; PROTESTANTISM; The Study and Classification of RELIGIONS; ROMAN CATHOLICISM; and *Micropædia* entries on the various denominations.

Adherents of All Religions by Seven Continental Areas, Mid-1993

	Africa	Asia	Europe	Latin America	Northern America	Oceania	Eurasia	World	%	Countries
Christians	341,208,000	300,383,000	409,653,000	443,056,000	241,147,000	22,686,000	111,618,000	**1,869,751,000**	33.5	270
Roman Catholics	128,167,000	130,102,000	260,034,000	412,366,000	97,892,000	8,229,000	5,711,000	**1,042,501,000**	18.7	259
Protestants	91,070,000	85,764,000	73,206,000	17,550,000	97,176,000	7,537,000	10,071,000	**382,374,000**	6.9	246
Orthodox	29,771,000	3,847,000	35,777,000	1,793,000	6,062,000	577,000	95,733,000	**173,560,000**	3.1	105
Anglicans	28,013,000	744,000	32,629,000	1,322,000	7,404,000	5,734,000	1,000	**75,847,000**	1.4	158
Other Christians	64,187,000	79,926,000	8,007,000	10,025,000	32,614,000	609,000	102,000	**195,470,000**	3.5	118
Muslims	284,844,000	668,298,000	13,633,000	1,400,000	3,332,000	104,000	42,761,000	**1,014,372,000**	18.2	184
Nonreligious	2,578,000	721,113,000	57,542,000	18,444,000	24,718,000	3,572,000	84,907,000	**912,874,000**	16.4	236
Hindus	1,569,000	746,512,000	707,000	916,000	1,285,000	369,000	2,000	**751,360,000**	13.5	94
Buddhists	22,000	332,143,000	273,000	561,000	565,000	26,000	412,000	**334,002,000**	6.0	92
Atheists	336,000	167,217,000	16,669,000	3,343,000	1,336,000	549,000	52,402,000	**241,852,000**	4.3	139
Chinese folk religionists	14,000	140,661,000	60,000	76,000	123,000	21,000	1,000	**140,956,000**	2.5	60
New-Religionists	22,000	121,693,000	50,000	550,000	1,439,000	10,000	1,000	**123,765,000**	2.2	27
Tribal religionists	70,000,000	28,654,000	1,000	971,000	41,000	69,000	0	**99,736,000**	1.8	104
Sikhs	28,000	19,318,000	232,000	8,000	257,000	9,000	1,000	**19,853,000**	0.4	21
Jews	359,000	6,264,000	1,475,000	1,132,000	6,850,000	100,000	1,973,000	**18,153,000**	0.3	134
Shamanists	1,000	10,591,000	2,000	1,000	1,000	1,000	257,000	**10,854,000**	0.2	11
Confucians	1,000	6,204,000	2,000	2,000	26,000	1,000	2,000	**6,230,000**	0.1	6
Baha'is	1,591,000	2,774,000	91,000	830,000	370,000	79,000	7,000	**5,742,000**	0.1	220
Jains	56,000	3,847,000	15,000	4,000	4,000	1,000	0	**3,927,000**	0.1	11
Shintoists	0	3,332,000	1,000	1,000	1,000	1,000	0	**3,336,000**	0.1	4
Other religionists	461,000	12,714,000	1,475,000	3,701,000	491,000	4,000	337,000	**19,183,000**	0.3	182
Total Population	**703,090,000**	**3,291,718,000**	**501,881,000**	**474,996,000**	**281,986,000**	**27,602,000**	**294,681,000**	**5,575,954,000**	**100.0**	**272**

NOTES:

Continents. These follow current UN demographic terminology. UN practice began in 1949 by dividing the world into 5 continents, then into 18 regions (1954), then into 8 major continental areas (called macro regions in 1987) and 24 regions (1963), and 7 major areas and 22 regions (1988). (*See* United Nations, *World Population Prospects 1990,* with populations of all continents, regions, and countries covering the period 1950–2025.) The table above therefore now combines its former columns "East Asia" and "South Asia" into one single continental area, "Asia" (which excludes Eurasia [or European Asia], our provisional new term for the former U.S.S.R.).

Countries. The last column enumerates sovereign and nonsovereign countries in which each religion or religious grouping has a significant following.

Rows. The list of religions is arranged by descending order of magnitude of global adherents in 1993 (last two columns but one); similarly for categories within "Christians."

Adherents. As defined and enumerated for each of the world's countries in *World Christian Encyclopedia* (1982), projected to mid-1993, adjusted for recent data.

Christians. Followers of Jesus Christ affiliated with churches (church members, including children: 1,726,420,000) plus persons professing in censuses or polls though not so affiliated.

Other Christians. Catholics (non-Roman), marginal Protestants, crypto-Christians, and adherents of African, Asian, black, and Latin-American indigenous churches.

Muslims. 83% Sunnites, 16% Shi'ites, 1% other schools. Up to 1990 the former ethnic Muslims in the U.S.S.R. who had embraced Communism were not included as Muslims in this table. After the collapse of Communism in 1990–91, these ethnic Muslims are once again enumerated as Muslims where they have returned to Islamic profession and practice.

Nonreligious. Persons professing no religion, nonbelievers, agnostics, freethinkers, dereligionized secularists indifferent to all religion.

Hindus. 70% Vaishnavites, 25% Shaivites, 2% neo-Hindus and reform Hindus.

Buddhists. 56% Mahayana, 38% Theravada (Hinayana), 6% Tantrayana (Lamaism).

Atheists. Persons professing atheism, skepticism, disbelief, or irreligion, including antireligious (opposed to all religion).

Chinese folk-religionists. Followers of the traditional Chinese religion (local deities, ancestor veneration, Confucian ethics, Taoism, universism, divination, some Buddhist elements).

New-Religionists. Followers of Asian 20th-century New Religions, New Religious movements, radical new crisis religions, and non-Christian syncretistic mass religions, all founded since 1800 and mostly since 1945.

Jews. Estimates of the Jewish population worldwide differ widely; for detailed discussion of a more narrowly defined "core" Jewish population, see the annual "World Jewish Populations" article in the American Jewish Committee's *American Jewish Year Book.*

Confucians. Non-Chinese followers of Confucius and Confucianism, mostly Koreans in Korea.

Other religionists. Including 70 minor world religions and a large number of spiritist religions, New Age religions, quasi religions, pseudo religions, parareligions, religious or mystic systems, religious and semireligious brotherhoods of numerous varieties.

Total Population. UN medium variant figures for mid-1993, as given in *World Population Prospects 1990* (New York: UN, 1991), pages 136–142. (DAVID B. BARRETT)

Social Security and Welfare Services

With a Democratic administration in the White House for the first time in 12 years, the U.S. moved boldly in the area of social welfare in 1993. Elsewhere in the world social security and welfare programs continued to be affected by adverse economic conditions and governments' concern over future population pressures. Despite some signs of economic recovery in the industrialized world, unemployment levels remained high, and more attention was focused on the rapidly increasing numbers of sickness beneficiaries and disability pensioners. Added to these problems were migration pressures, particularly in Western Europe, as people sought relief from the desperate conditions and poverty in their home countries. Central and Eastern European countries made progress in the reform of their social protection schemes, but increasing levels of poverty were evident as the real value of benefits fell further and unemployment increased. In less developed countries governments still looked for ways of improving coverage and benefit levels as well as overcoming serious financial imbalances.

The U.S. and Canada. Soon after taking office, U.S. Pres. Bill Clinton appointed his wife, Hillary Rodham Clinton (*see* BIOGRAPHIES), to head the Task Force on National Health Care Reform. In September, after months of hearings, the president announced a plan for overhauling the health care system, based on the principle of "health security to all Americans" in the form of lifetime health insurance.

While details of the plan were sketchy and disagreement arose over many aspects, there was general agreement that something had to be done. The U.S. was spending more than $900 billion on health care in 1993, or 14.7% of its gross national product (GNP). At the same time, according to the Census Bureau, an estimated 37.4 million Americans, about one-fourth of them children, did not have health insurance. Virtually all other industrialized countries provided some form of national health care for their citizens while spending a lower percentage of GNP on that care.

Two of the boldest proposals in the Clinton plan were aimed at containing the costs of the fastest-growing government entitlement programs—Medicaid, the joint federal-state health insurance plan for the poor, and Medicare, which provided health insurance for the elderly. The proposal called for cutting $114 billion, or 16%, of the money that otherwise would be spent on Medicaid between 1996 and 2000. Projected growth for Medicare would be reduced by $124 billion, or 20%, over the same five-year period, mainly by a slowdown in the rise of payments to doctors and hospitals.

The need for welfare reform in the U.S. was also pointed up by data that appeared in 1993. The Census Bureau reported that the number of poor Americans had reached 36.9 million, or 14.5% of the total population, in 1992. That was an increase of 1.2 million over the previous year and the highest figure since 1962. It included 14.6 million children, more than one of every five. The official poverty level in 1992 was $14,335 for a family of four and $7,143 for a single person. The problem of welfare reform also was put in the hands of a task force, which conducted a series of hearings around the country and gave President Clinton its recommendations at the end of the year.

Many states did not wait for the federal government to act. According to the National Governors' Association, more than a dozen states tightened regulations or set up

Americans with Disabilities Act (ADA)

By all odds it was not the biggest liability case in legal history, but the Equal Employment Opportunity Commission (EEOC) suit against Chicago-based AIC Security Investigations, Ltd., and its owner, Ruth Vrdolyak, was watched with consuming interest by the U.S. business community; it was the first case brought to trial under the relatively new Americans with Disabilities Act (ADA). The jury found that the company's discharge of AIC executive Charles H. Wessel because of his diagnosis of brain cancer was intentionally discriminatory. The verdict could have resounding implications for corporate America.

U.S. Pres. George Bush signed the ADA into law on July 26, 1990. The act provided civil rights protections to individuals with disabilities and guaranteed them equal opportunity in public accommodations, employment, transportation, state and local government services, and telecommunications. Some 43 million disabled people were affected by the law. The employment provisions applied to employers with 25 or more employees beginning July 26, 1992; those with 15–24 employees would have to be in compliance from July 26, 1994. The public accommodations provisions were generally effective beginning Jan. 26, 1992. They required that necessary changes be made to afford access by persons with disabilities to all public facilities, including restaurants, theatres, day-care centres, parks, institutional buildings, and hotels.

The greatest number of ADA violation charges made thus far were employment-related. By Aug. 31, 1993, the number of claims amounted to more than 14,000. Back impairments were the most frequent disability cited, accounting for about 18.5% of the total; mental illness, with 10%, was next. The violation most frequently charged by claimants was dismissal from their jobs—49% of the cases; second was failure to provide reasonable accommodations (22%).

In assessing their difficulties with compliance, many business leaders pointed to the confusion caused by vague language and definitions used in the act. For instance, employers were required to make "reasonable accommodation" for disabled job applicants or employees at the workplace, yet an accommodation need not be made if it would bring "undue hardship" to the employer's business. Discrimination was prohibited against "qualified" individuals with disabilities. A disabled person need only be able to handle the "essential functions" of a job with or without "reasonable accommodation."

Employers also quarreled with the broad definition of *disability,* which would include, for instance, alcoholics as long as they could perform the essential functions of the job. Such prospects sent employers scrambling to rewrite job descriptions in a way that clearly defined what was essential and what was not.

(MARVIN MARTIN)

welfare-to-work programs aimed at making clients self-sufficient, and additional states were planning new programs.

Federal and state spending on Aid to Families with Dependent Children (AFDC), the major welfare program, grew to $25,783,000 in 1993, and the number of families receiving aid hovered around the five million level. However, it was reported that financially strapped states had sharply reduced their "safety net" programs for the poor in 1992 for the second straight year. For example, 44 states cut or froze AFDC benefits, and 26 of the 27 states that provided supplemental benefits to poor, elderly, and disabled recipients of Social Security income also cut or froze those benefits.

President Clinton pushed for greater social investment in his budget plan, but he got only part of what he requested. One of the most significant expansions was in the Earned Income Tax Credit (EITC) for low- and moderate-income working families with children. Families with two or more children and a full-time minimum-wage earner would receive increased credits to bring them up to the poverty level. In addition, EITC would be extended for the first time to about 4.5 million very low-income workers without children. Elsewhere in Clinton's budget request were plans to set up a child-immunization program and establish a family-preservation program to help troubled families stay together. The Food Stamp program was expanded to cover more of the working poor, and some benefits were increased. The number of food stamp recipients reached an all-time high of 27,375,000 in March 1993.

The compromise budget enacted by Congress included cuts of $55.8 billion in Medicare and $7 billion in Medicaid over the next five years. About one-eighth of Social Security recipients—those with the highest incomes—would have to pay taxes on more of their Social Security benefits. Congress repassed the Family and Medical Leave Act that had been vetoed by Pres. George Bush in 1992, and it was signed by President Clinton. The law allowed workers to take up to 12 weeks of unpaid leave during any 12-month period because of the birth or adoption of a child; the need to care for a seriously ill child, spouse, or parent; or the worker's own serious illness. Congress also enacted a scaled-down, $1.5 billion version of Clinton's National Service initiative. It would provide tuition grants of $4,725 a year (for up to two years) and subsistence wages to some 100,000 college and trade-school students over the next three years. In return, the students would perform community service.

ALAN S. WEINER—THE NEW YORK TIMES

Workers landscape a cemetery in Georgia as part of a state program called the Peach Corps, which links community service with college tuition credit. U.S. Pres. Bill Clinton won congressional approval in 1993 for a national service program.

Canada also embarked on health-care reform during 1993. In addition to developing a National Action Plan involving more effective resource management and reducing medical school enrollments by 10%, the government established an Institute for Health Information to collect more standardized data and to inform people about their roles and responsibilities in the area of health care. In January the Child Tax Benefit replaced family allowances and the former child benefits provided through the tax system. It comprised a single monthly payment and was calculated on the basis of family income and number of children. Canada also took steps to reduce unemployment payments and tighten eligibility criteria.

Western Europe. A number of European governments took action in 1993 to curtail expenditures on their pension systems. Major changes were announced in France—indexation of pensions was to be reduced from twice yearly to annually, and the insurance period for maximum pension was to be gradually increased from 150 to 160 quarters, while pension levels would be determined on the basis of earnings over the highest 25 years rather than the highest 10. Italy introduced legislation to provide for a complementary retirement pension scheme. Greece changed its definition of pensionable earnings and simplified the benefit formula to reduce the longer-term level of pensions. Both Greece and Portugal intended to phase in an increase to 65 years in the retirement age for women, while Portugal also planned to reduce the level of benefits for new pensioners. Austria made changes effective July 1993 primarily designed to encourage people to continue working at least until the normal retirement age through the introduction of a bonus system for those remaining in the workforce after age 60 (55 for women) and the introduction of a partial pension for older workers employed on a part-time basis. Finland introduced employee contributions for the first time for employment-related pensions as well as providing incentives for older workers to stay in employment, if only on a part-time basis.

European Community countries were encouraged to focus their attention on flexible retirement provisions. On June 30, 1993, the European Council approved a resolution requesting member states to develop their employment and social security policies to promote greater flexibility for employees in their transition to retirement. Despite high levels of unemployment, member states were also preoccupied with the aging of their populations and were looking at ways of keeping older workers in employment and utilizing their skills and experience to offset potential skill shortages and reduce the strain on social security funds in the future.

Significant changes were still occurring within European health insurance systems as costs continued to escalate. Following a major reform in 1992, Germany announced further amendments, which took effect from Jan. 1, 1993, designed to achieve savings through reduced rates of reimbursement and increased pharmaceutical co-payments. France sought to contain costs by increasing daily hospital charges and reducing reimbursement rates for outpatient care. The changes came into effect on Aug. 1, 1993. In Belgium there were proposals to introduce a substantially higher schedule of co-payments, part of which would be refunded through the personal tax system at the end of each year. Spain restricted the range of pharmaceuticals covered by state subsidies, having made significant changes to its sickness insurance in 1992 by shifting the cost of benefits for the first two weeks to employers.

More industrialized countries became concerned about the increasing numbers of people of workforce age receiving social security payments. The U.K. introduced more rigorous conditions for the receipt of unemployment benefits to reduce the extent of fraud and abuse and also introduced initiatives to help beneficiaries return to work. Showing concern over increasing expenditures on invalidity benefits, the government introduced measures in April 1993 to achieve substantial savings through better targeting of medical examinations and improved administrative procedures.

Tighter procedures for people with disabilities were introduced in The Netherlands. New beneficiaries received lower benefits and only on a temporary basis, with the amount and duration varying according to age. Other countries also had to make changes in their unemployment insurance programs to cope with increased costs. France and Denmark increased contribution rates, and Switzerland agreed to extend the duration of payments but reduced the level from 80 to 70% of previous earnings for those without dependents. Sweden reduced payments and tightened eligibility conditions. France and Germany both introduced tough new laws in an attempt to stop the flow of immigrants who were either working illegally or relying on state assistance while they sought asylum. At the end of the year Germany cut a number of social welfare programs.

Central and Eastern Europe. Albania, Belarus, and Estonia introduced new systems of social security in 1993, while other countries in the region focused on implementing the legislation they had recently introduced. Major problems still confronted the social security systems of these countries, however. Poverty levels were rising as more and more people became unemployed during the process of economic restructuring, and eligibility conditions were tightened in many countries for disability and early-retirement pensions. In addition, high levels of inflation persisted, particularly in food prices, resulting in declining real values of both wages and benefits. It was evident that there was an urgent need for transition measures, but very few of these countries had been able to implement viable social assistance schemes. Furthermore, the new social insurance schemes would require effective administrative processes, which would, in turn, require investment in modern technology and intensive training of staff to ensure that both employees and employers complied with the new arrangements.

Industrialized Asia and the Pacific. Like the countries of Western Europe, Japan was considering an increase in the retirement age for its Employees' Pension Insurance system from 60 to 65 years to align it with the National Pension system. Other measures to keep older employees in the workforce were proposed, including the introduction of a partial pension to enable employees to combine part-time work with retirement. Australia announced its intention to phase in an increase in the retirement age for women to 65, the same as for men, in the context of an overall strategy to increase national savings and reduce reliance on the state pension system. In July 1993 Singapore introduced legislation requiring companies to increase the minimum retirement age from 55 to 60 years, with further increases likely in the future.

Emerging and Less Developed Countries. There were few major changes in these areas during 1993, and the problems of inadequate coverage and financial imbalance still predominated. Further progress was made in upgrading and computerizing the administration of social security systems, in many cases a necessary first step to extending coverage to the self-employed and employees in the rural and informal sectors. Colombia proposed a savings and pension scheme for old-age, disability, and survivor pensions, similar to schemes that had already been introduced in some other Latin-American countries. Argentina considered legislation for a major reform to take effect in 1994, while Mexico announced increases in contribution rates and reductions in benefits. In Africa and Asia some countries considered proposals to convert their provident funds into pension schemes and extend coverage to health care, but in general there were only incremental changes to existing arrangements, such as increases in contributions and earnings ceilings as well as adjustments to benefits to compensate partially for the effects of inflation.

The government in China focused its attention on the reforms in social security that were needed to cope with the transition to a market economy and the rapid aging of the country's population. Like the countries of Central and Eastern Europe, China was looking at ways of overcoming the significant problems of poverty in the short term while introducing a sustainable social security system for both rural and urban areas in the longer term.

(DAVID M. MAZIE; JUDITH E. RAYMOND)

See also Education; Health and Disease; Industrial Review: *Insurance*.

This article updates the *Macropædia* article SOCIAL WELFARE.

PETER SIBBALD

People gather for a meal at the Daily Bread Food Bank in Toronto. Amid continuing economic difficulties and cutbacks in government social programs in 1993, facilities for the needy in Canada and a number of other countries experienced increased demands on their resources.

Russia's unmanned supply spacecraft Progress M-18 (lower left) separates from the *Mir 1* space station. The separation freed a docking place for another craft at the upper left end of the station.
NPO ENERGIA LTD., VIRGINIA

Space Exploration

The United States experienced a frustrating year in space exploration in 1993 as several key satellites were lost, space shuttle launches were delayed five times, and the space station was drastically cut in size. In addition, a daring project to pioneer a new launch vehicle was killed before its final test flight. In December, however, an ambitious mission to repair the Hubble Space Telescope was completed successfully.

Manned Flight. The first manned mission of 1993, by *Endeavour* (STS-54, January 13–19), deployed the sixth Tracking and Data Relay Satellite (TDRS 6) and a two-stage rocket to boost it to a geostationary orbit (one in which it would remain over the same place on the Earth's surface). *Endeavour* also carried a diffuse X-ray spectrometer to scan the heavens in search of broad, faint X-ray sources. The crew included commander John Casper, pilot Donald McMonagle, and mission specialists Gregory Harbaugh, Susan Helms, and Mario Runco, Jr. Harbaugh and Runco walked in space to test equipment for maneuvering around the space station during construction. Inside, Runco and other crew members used toys to demonstrate physics principles as they talked with students at elementary schools.

Discovery (STS-56, April 8–17) carried the second in the Atmospheric Laboratory for Applications and Science (ATLAS-2) series to monitor yearly changes in 30 to 40 gases, including ozone, in the Earth's middle atmosphere. The crew comprised commander Kenneth Cameron, pilot Stephen Oswald, and mission specialists Kenneth Cockrell, Michael Foale, and Ellen Ochoa (the first Hispanic woman in space). The launch was postponed once, at T-11 seconds, by computer malfunction, and while in flight there was an hours-long blackout during which virtually all the data sent from the shuttle were lost. The crew deployed and retrieved (April 11–13) a Spartan satellite carrying a coronascope and an ultraviolet telescope to study the Sun's outer atmosphere.

Columbia (STS-55, April 26–May 6) carried Spacelab D-2 after two launch delays due to equipment problems, including an on-pad shutdown after ignition. The crew included commander Steven Nagel, pilot Terence Henricks, flight engineer Charles Precourt, mission specialists Bernard Harris and Jerry Ross, and payload specialists Hans Schlegel and Ulrich Walter (both of Germany). Among the passengers were 240 tadpoles and 240 fish larvae flown to test how their bodies adjusted to weightlessness in space. Most died in orbit. The crew and scientists on the ground also operated a robot to test teleoperations techniques that could allow remote, unmanned operations. The mission was extended a day to allow additional experiments. When bad weather at the Kennedy Space Center in Florida delayed their landing another day, the crew had to fly with most of the cabin lights out in order to conserve power. This mission brought the shuttle program's cumulative flight time to one year.

The commercially developed Spacehab module was first flown in *Endeavour* (STS-57, June 21–July 1), the crew of which consisted of commander Ronald J. Grabe, pilot Brian Duffy, flight engineer Nancy Sherlock, and mission specialists G. David Low, Janice Voss, and Peter ("Jeff") Wisoff. Spacehab, which added working space similar to that in the main cabin, was to fly twice a year, largely with National Aeronautics and Space Administration (NASA)-sponsored experiments. *Endeavour* also chased down the European Retrievable Carrier (EURECA), a satellite deployed in August 1992 by *Atlantis* to carry out automated materials experiments. A space walk by Low and Wisoff tested techniques for the Hubble Space Telescope repair mission and secured one of EURECA's antennae.

Two satellites were deployed and one retrieved by *Discovery* (STS-51, September 12–22). Members of the crew were commander Frank Culbertson, pilot William Readdy, flight engineer Daniel W. Bursch, and mission specialists James Newman and Carl Walz. On the first day the crew deployed the Advanced Communications Technology Satellite (ACTS), which was designed to experiment with communications in the radio spectrum. The next day the crew released Germany's Orbiting Retrievable Far and Extreme Ultraviolet Spectrometer (ORFEUS) to operate autonomously until September 19, when it was retrieved for return to Earth.

ORFEUS also carried a movie camera to film the shuttle in space. Newman and Walz walked in space to test additional techniques and tools for the Hubble repair mission.

Toward the end of the year, *Columbia* carried the second Space Life Sciences mission (STS-58; October 18–November 1). The crew consisted of commander John Blaha, pilot Rick Searfoss, mission specialists Rhea Seddon, Bill McArthur, David Wolf, and Shannon Lucid, and payload specialist Martin Fettman (the first veterinarian in space). Also aboard were 48 rats, six of which were sacrificed and dissected the day before landing to preserve subtle changes in their inner ears that might be lost after their return to Earth. Another 15 had blood and fluid samples withdrawn during the mission. Several were injected with erythropoietin to stimulate the production of red blood cells and counter the anemia that plagues long-duration space travelers. Most experiments used the crew as test subjects. In one, bungee cords pulled a subject to the deck while electrodes measured changes in the body's reaction to falling. In another, the subject placed his or her head in a rotating dome painted with dots while a TV camera recorded how the eye compensated for the perceived motion. Wolf set a record for the fastest heart rate—196 beats per minute—in space as he pedaled on a bicycle ergometer. The two-week mission was the longest flown by a shuttle.

In a mission regarded by many as NASA's biggest challenge since the Apollo landings on the Moon, *Endeavour* was launched from Cape Canaveral on December 2 to repair the Hubble Space Telescope. The crew consisted of commander Richard Covey, pilot Kenneth Bowersox, and mission specialists Tom Akers, Jeffrey Hoffman, Story Musgrave, Claude Nicollier, and Kathryn Thornton. During a record five space walks, Hoffman and Musgrave alternated with Akers and Thornton to correct the Hubble's flawed vision, which had been caused by improper grinding and polishing of its primary mirror. They replaced faulty gyroscopes and worn solar panels, repaired a computer, and, most important, installed a new wide-field planetary camera and a device containing 10 tiny mirrors to compensate for the defective primary mirror. On December 10 the Hubble was released into space, and on December 13 Endeavour returned to the Kennedy Space Center. Donald K. ("Deke") Slayton, 69, died June 13 of a brain tumour. He had been grounded in 1962 by a heart arrhythmia but finally flew on the Apollo-Soyuz Test Project in 1975. (*See* OBITUARIES.)

In the face of severe budget problems, the European Space Agency (ESA) in September canceled its plans to develop a small shuttlecraft with the Russian space agency. ESA had earlier reduced its Hermes shuttlecraft program to a project to develop a suit for space walks, an Apollo-style crew capsule, and an automated transfer vehicle.

Russia continued to operate its *Mir 1* space station. On February 4 cosmonauts aboard *Mir* released an aluminum-coated plastic film mirror that unfurled to a diameter of 20 m (65 ft). Mirrors several kilometres wide were proposed to illuminate cities and increase daylight for crops. Cosmonauts Anatoly Solovyev and Sergey Abdeyev returned to Earth aboard Soyuz TM-15 on February 1 after having spent six months aboard *Mir.* Their primary duties included a number of space walks to rejuvenate the seven-year-old station and extend its life. They were replaced on January 26 by Gennady Manakov and Aleksandr Poleshchuk, launched aboard Soyuz TM-16. After placing a docking target on *Mir* for the U.S. shuttle *Atlantis* to use during a planned 1995 visit, Manakov and Poleshchuk returned to Earth on July 22.

The plans by NASA to build a permanently manned space station were sharply curtailed yet again, and the craft even lost its Reagan-era name, *Freedom,* as the U.S. moved to add Russia to the international team that comprised ESA, the Canadian Space Agency, and Japan's National Space Development Agency. Soon after taking office, U.S. Pres. Bill Clinton ordered NASA to examine three redesign options intended to bring the station's price down from more than $30 billion to a range of $9 billion to $16 billion.

NASA was unable to reduce the price as low as Clinton wanted, and on June 17 the president selected a combination of two options. The new design eliminated five of the major truss elements that served as the station's backbone and used a 14-m (47-ft)-long common module for laboratory, habitat, and docking. Russia's Soyuz TM spacecraft

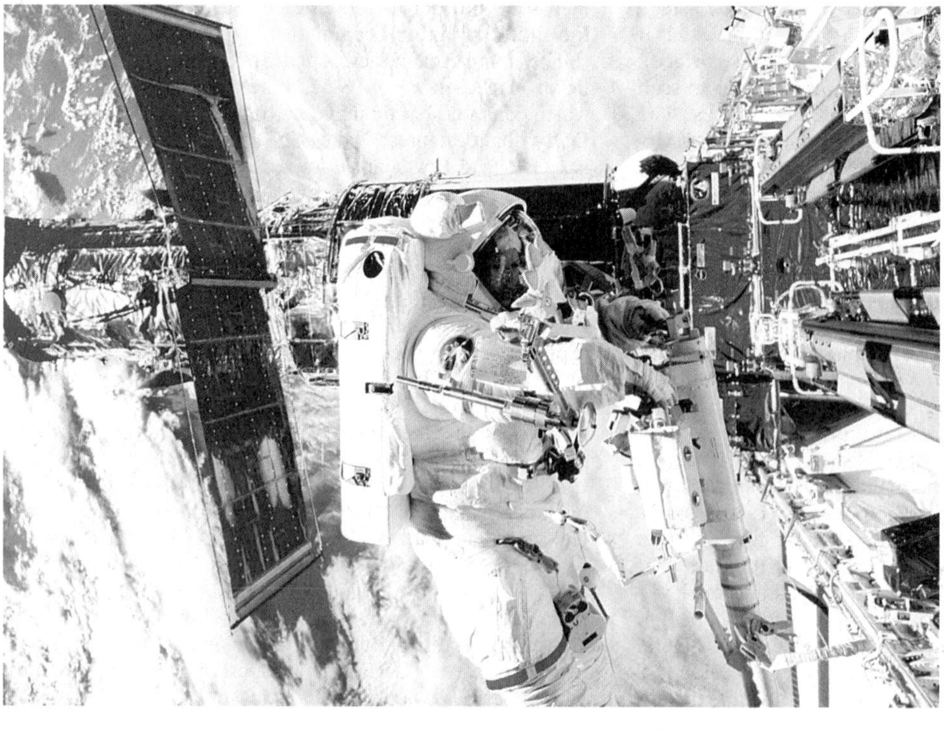

NASA

Kathryn Thornton, a member of the *Endeavour* crew, inspects equipment used to work on the Hubble Space Telescope. The space shuttle astronauts installed new optics to correct the telescope's flawed mirror and made other repairs.

would be used as a lifeboat. The first element of space station *Alpha* was to be launched in October 1997.

More changes were portended on September 2 when U.S. Vice Pres. Al Gore and Russian Prime Minister Viktor Chernomyrdin signed an agreement that would join the U.S. and Russian space station programs. In the first phase, NASA would start using *Mir* for a fee of $100 million a year. NASA would receive up to two man-years of crew time and joint development of life-support and electrical power systems and a new space suit. In the second phase, NASA's *Alpha* design would be adjusted to use Russia's *Mir 2,* now under construction, as the core module and habitat. On December 16 the U.S. and Russia formally became partners and announced that a Russian astronaut would fly in the shuttle *Discovery* in six weeks.

To streamline its management, NASA canceled contracts with its four principal space station contractors and renegotiated a new single contract, which was won by Boeing Defense and Space Group. The U.S. Congress canceled NASA's project to build an advanced solid rocket motor to help the shuttle boost modules for the station.

Planetary Probes. What was to be the year's premier planetary event became an embarrassing spell of silence as Mars Observer failed to check in after starting preparations to orbit Mars. The spacecraft's radio was shut down on August 21 to protect it while gas lines were opened and propellant tanks pressurized for the burn to insert the craft into orbit. But hours later the spacecraft failed to reestablish contact with Earth controllers. NASA worked for five days to summon the spacecraft and then listened until August 30, hoping that it would go into a "safe mode" programmed into the probe in case contact was lost. Nothing was ever heard. Mars Observer was to have mapped the surface of Mars in great detail over a period of one Martian year.

Frustration continued with the Galileo spacecraft as it coasted on the final leg of its journey to Jupiter. Galileo's high-gain antenna had refused to open because dry lubricant had slipped away during the long prelaunch wait. Extensive thermal and mechanical hammering by ground controllers failed to spring it loose, and so scientists started planning to retrieve pictures and data at much lower rates than expected. On August 28 Galileo took about 150 images of asteroid Ida as it zipped past at a distance of 2,400 km (1,490 mi) and a speed of 44,800 km/h (28,000 mph). Galileo was scheduled to arrive at Jupiter in 1995.

At Venus the Magellan spacecraft neared the end of its life mainly because of reduced funding. Flight controllers commanded it to lower its orbit by a series of delicate braking passes through the upper atmosphere of Venus. This yielded data on the density of the Venusian atmosphere. In its lower orbit Magellan would allow scientists to map Venus' gravity field with greater detail.

Possibly the first detection of interstellar dust was made by the Ulysses solar-polar spacecraft. Instruments indicated that dust struck Ulysses at 30 km per second (19 mi per second) as it arced above the solar system's equator.

Two robot tests demonstrated remote exploration techniques. On January 1 NASA's eight-legged Dante tried to explore the inside of Mt. Erebus, Antarctica's only active volcano. The test ended after Dante moved just a few metres and broke the fibre-optic cable connecting it to a ground station that linked it to operators in Greenbelt, Md. Additional tests were planned in 1994. A Russian Marsokhod was driven a few metres across the rugged Kamchatka Peninsula in August by operators at McDonnell Douglas' Huntington Beach, Calif., facilities. They were linked by a communications satellite and used a virtual reality system to produce three-dimensional images of the terrain.

An intriguing probe of the Moon and asteroid 1620 Geographos was to be launched in January 1994 by the Ballistic Missile Defense Organization with the use of a low-cost Clementine probe, a cheaper way of observing those bodies than launching dedicated targets for the spacecraft's miniature sensors. A Clementine 2 mission was being considered for an October 1994 launch to make up for part of the Mars Observer loss.

Launch Vehicles. The year's bright spot in launch vehicles was the DC-X, which demonstrated technologies for a single-stage vehicle that would be launched into orbit and then land vertically. In a series of three tests in August through October, the DC-X was launched to altitudes of a few hundred metres and successfully landed. Congress cut funding, however, before the team could attempt the most demanding final flight, which would have taken the DC-X to an altitude of 8,500 m (28,000 ft), made a U-turn, and returned to the landing site.

Efforts to develop small launchers for small satellites picked up momentum during the year as NASA contracted the Universities Space Research Association (USRA) to launch three satellites atop older Minuteman missiles that were being retired by the military. USRA would have to hold three launches within three years to demonstrate this "quicker, cheaper" approach. Early in the year Russia demonstrated a similar approach by orbiting a satellite with an old SS-25 missile. Lockheed Missiles & Space Co. formed a partnership with Russia's Khrunichev Enterprise to market the Russian Proton rocket; other U.S. companies teamed with Russian counterparts to market rocket engines that included descendants of the Sputnik 1 launch engine. The U.S. market was opened to Russian launch vehicles under an agreement related to the space station plan.

Efforts by India to gain cryogenic (very low-temperature) space-rocket technology from Russia were thwarted by U.S. objections that this would enhance India's nuclear weapons program. On September 20 India's first Polar Satellite Launch Vehicle failed to place a remote-sensing satellite in a high-enough orbit. Also, South Africa announced that it had discontinued its Arniston satellite launcher as part of the dismantling of its nuclear bomb program.

During the year three major satellites were lost because of launch mishaps: a navy communications satellite on March 26 when its Atlas-Centaur second stage misfired; an ocean surveillance satellite on August 2 when a booster on its Titan IV launch vehicle burned through and destroyed the vehicle; and the Landsat 6 Earth observation satellite on October 5 shortly after it separated from its Titan II launcher (the Titan was not considered responsible for this loss). In addition, contact was lost with the National Oceanic and Atmospheric Administration's Nova 11 advanced polar-orbiting weather satellite on August 21. Plans to launch the Commercial Experiment Transporter (COMET) were postponed by cost overruns.

Unmanned Satellites. Scientists announced that the Cosmic Background Explorer (COBE) satellite had produced the strongest evidence yet for the big bang theory of the creation of the universe. COBE's observations in the infrared spectrum revealed that the universe had the same temperature in every wavelength it observed and in every direction.

Germany's ROSAT, carrying an X-ray telescope, indicated that the universe might have enough "dark matter" to halt its expansion. On February 20 Japan launched the Asuka satellite carrying U.S. and Japanese instruments to examine stars in the X-ray region of the spectrum. The Hubble Space Telescope returned a number of interesting scientific finds despite its problems. These included an apparent collision between two galaxies and new estimates of the masses of Pluto and its moon, Charon.

(DAVE DOOLING)

See also Astronomy; Earth Sciences; Industrial Review: *Aerospace; Telecommunications;* Military Affairs; Television and Radio.

This article updates the *Macropædia* articles EXPLORATION: *Space Exploration;* TELESCOPES.

Sports and Games

AERIAL SPORTS

The realization of an 11-year-old girl's transcontinental flying dream and two more frustrating setbacks in the round-the-world hopes of a balloonist marked the year 1993 for better and worse in aerial sports. Victoria Van Meter of Meadville, Pa., became the youngest pilot ever to fly across the United States east to west and the youngest female ever to fly across the continent when she piloted a single-engine Cessna 172 from Augusta, Maine, to San Diego, Calif. Her flight, lasting from September 20 to 23 with four refueling stops, took her more than 4,640 km (1 km = 0.62 mi) through good but occasionally turbulent weather. "I got sick a little," she said. She was accompanied by her flight instructor, Bob Baumgartner, but did all the flying and navigating herself. The east–west crossing is the most difficult because it is against prevailing head winds.

Larry Newman, who had crossed both the Atlantic and Pacific oceans by balloon, had plans for a 35,200-km round-the-world helium balloon flight in 1993, starting at Reno, Nev., but was frustrated by failed launch attempts in January and again in November. The "Earthwinds Hilton" was a two-balloon craft consisting of a helium-filled top balloon and a compressed-air-filled bottom balloon, which acted as ballast; the hourglass-shaped craft had a height of 90 m (300 ft). On January 12 it was blown 16 km backward off course to the California-Nevada border, brushed the top of a mountain, and crash-landed in a snow-filled valley. On November 6 two members of Newman's inspection crew were preparing another launch from Reno when anchor bolts broke and the craft began ascending prematurely, compelling the two men to rip open the craft's enormous helium balloon to prevent a takeoff.

At the 11th world hot-air-balloon championships at Larochette, Luxembourg, August 12–22, U.S. competitors swept the first four places: Alan Blount, 15,414 points; Owen Keown, 15,188 points; Joe Heartsill, 14,812 points; and David Levin, 14,622 points.

William Bussey of the U.S. set a Class AX-8 hot-air-balloon world distance record of 1,215.9 km and a world duration record of 29 hr 14 sec with a flight in a Colt 105A from Amarillo, Texas, to Milbank, S.D., on January 25. On January 13, Jetta Schantz of the U.S. achieved a women's AX-7 world distance record of 468.9 km, flying her Raven S55A from Tulsa, Okla., to Gillett, Ariz.

Despite rain on opening day and threatening skies thereafter, the 23rd world gliding championships were held June 13–26 at Borlange, Sweden. In the standard-class competition, Andrew Davis of the U.K. was first with 7,285 points, followed by Eric Borgmann of The Netherlands with 7,059 and Poland's Tomasz Rubaj with 7,002. Gilbert Gerbaud and Eric Napoleon of France tied for first in the 15-m class contest with 8,220 points. Just behind in third was Wolfgang Janowitsch of Austria with 8,216 points. Janusz Centka of Poland won the open-class event with 9,897 points, beating out Sweden's Goran Ax with 9,525 and the U.K.'s Brian Spreckley with 9,391.

A free distance (using up to three turning points) world record for single-place gliders of 1,353 km was set by Raymond Linskey of New Zealand on January 12, flying a Nimbus 2B from Omarama Airfield to Alesandra Airfield in his country. On May 6, Hans Werner Grosse of Germany, flying with his wife, Karin, set world records for multiplace motorglider distance and distance-to-a-goal with a 1,078-km flight from Lübeck, Germany, to Rennes, France, in a Schleicher Ash 25 E.

Ingrid Koehler of Germany, in a Ventus CM, set women's distance and distance-to-a-goal single-place motorglider world records on June 14 with a 540-km flight from Tonopah, Nev., to Burley, Idaho. Austria's Karl Rabeder, in a DG-400, set single-seater motorglider straight-line distance and distance-to-a-goal world records with a 1,040-km flight from Omarama, N.Z., to Araroa Airfield, N.Z., on January 25.

From January 4 to 7 at Hendrik Verwoerd Dam, in South Africa, Germany's Klaus Holighaus flew a Nimbus 4M to set a world single-place motorglider triangular course distance record of 1,400 km. A world paragliding record for distance over a triangular course was achieved on May 17 at Mautstelle Loserstrasse, Austria, by that country's Christian Heinrich in a Nova Sphinx. He flew 90 km.

At the increasingly popular Oshkosh (Wis.) Experimental Aircraft Association show, held July 29–August 4, Jon Sharp set a new 3-km straight-line world speed record of 446.8 km/h (277.7 mph) in his "Nemesis" International Formula 1 air racer. More than 800,000 persons and 12,000 aircraft were present at the show.

In parachuting, the 10th world formation sky diving championships were held October 23–31 at Eloy, Ariz. In the eight-way competition, the U.S. was first with 169 points, France second with 168, and Russia third with 133. In the four-way contest, France won first with 190 points, the U.S. second with 182, and Denmark third with 169.

(MICHAEL D. KILIAN)

AUTOMOBILE RACING

Grand Prix Racing. International Formula One racing continued in 1993 under the prevailing rules, contested by non-turbocharged gasoline-burning single-seat cars of the highest technical ingenuity. However, this was to be the last such season because beginning in 1994 electronic aids for drivers would be forbidden in order to assist the less-wealthy teams and to try to promote closer competition.

The season opened at Kyalami, South Africa, where Alain Prost of France in a Williams-Renault beat Ayrton Senna of Brazil in a McLaren-Ford. The tour then moved to Interlagos, Brazil, where Prost led until the rains came, where-

Formula One Grand Prix Race Results, 1993

Race	Driver	Average speed (km/h)	Car
South African GP	A. Prost	186.362	Williams FW15C-Renault V10
Brazilian GP	A. Senna	166.566	McLaren MP4/8-Ford HBV8
European GP	A. Senna	166.603	McLaren MP4/8-Ford HBV8
San Marino GP	A. Prost	122.799	Williams FW15C-Renault V10
Spanish GP	A. Prost	200.221	Williams FW15C-Renault V10
Monaco GP	A. Senna	138.832	McLaren MP4/8-Ford HBV8
Canadian GP	A. Prost	189.661	Williams FW15C-Renault V10
French GP	A. Prost	186.225	Williams FW15C-Renault V10
British GP	A. Prost	216.024	Williams FW15C-Renault V10
German GP	A. Prost	233.854	Williams FW15C-Renault V10
Hungarian GP	D. Hill	170.292	Williams FW15C-Renault V10
Belgian GP	D. Hill	217.788	Williams FW15C-Renault V10
Italian GP	D. Hill	239.140	Williams FW15C-Renault V10
Portuguese GP	M. Schumacher	199.745	Benetton B193B-Ford HBV8
Japanese GP	A. Senna	185.612	McLaren MP4/8-Ford HBV8
Australian GP	A. Senna	173.183	McLaren MP4/8-Ford HBV8

WORLD DRIVERS' CHAMPIONSHIP: Prost 99 points, Senna 73 points, Hill 69 points

CONSTRUCTORS' WORLD CHAMPIONSHIP: Williams-Renault 168 points, McLaren-Ford 84 points, Benetton-Ford 72 points, Ferrari 28 points

British driver Nigel Mansell crosses the finish line in the Nazareth 200 to clinch the 1993 IndyCar championship. The 1992 Formula One champion, Mansell became the first driver to win the two titles back to back and only the third to win both.
MIKE POWELL—ALLSPORT

upon Senna went ahead to score McLaren's 100th victory. Damon Hill, the son of the late British champion Graham Hill, finished second in a Williams-Renault. For the third event of the season, the Donington Park circuit in Britain held its first Grand Prix since 1938. Senna won again in the rain, before an enormous crowd, and Hill finished second. In the Imola Grand Prix at San Marino, Prost proved that his old skills had not deserted him. He finished first in wet conditions, ahead of Michael Schumacher of Germany in a Benetton-Ford.

In the Spanish race at Barcelona, a great scrap ensued between Hill and his teammate Prost until Hill's engine expired 24 laps from the finish. Prost and Senna then finished first and second. In the traditional street race around the closed public roads of Monaco, Senna won for the fifth straight year, followed closely by Hill.

In the Canadian Grand Prix at Montreal, Prost recovered his winning form. Schumacher finished second. Great Britain got its racing treat when the tour went to Silverstone in July. The expected battle between the two bitter rivals, Prost and Senna, ended with the latter running out of fuel one lap from the flag, and Prost won again. Schumacher finished second.

At the French Grand Prix over the Magny-Cours course, also in July, the two Williams-Renaults dominated, Prost leading Hill home by the narrowest of margins. The German race, run over the Hockenheim course, was won by the seemingly unstoppable Prost after Hill suffered the bitterest of defeats when a tire blew two laps from victory. Second place was taken by Schumacher.

In Hungary, Hill finally gained his first victory, convincingly beating Riccardo Patrese of Italy in a Benetton-Ford. Hill then won again, taking the Belgian race from Schumacher, and then in the Italian Grand Prix at Monza, he won for the third time in a row. Jean Alesi of France in a Ferrari V12 finished second. At Estoril for the Portuguese event, Schumacher won from Prost. By finishing second, Prost clinched the 1993 world drivers' championship.

In the second-to-last race of the year, the Japanese Grand Prix was contested at the Suzuka circuit. Senna won the race in changing weather conditions that required frequent changes from wet-track to slick tires. Prost finished second.

Prost would have liked a victory in the Australian Grand Prix, the last event of the tour and also his final race—he had announced his retirement—but it was Senna who triumphed. Prost was second. It had been a satisfactory season, with the technically sophisticated cars demonstrating remarkable powers of acceleration, braking, and road clinging. Williams-Renault easily won the constructors' world championship. British former world champion driver James Hunt died in June at age 45. (*See* OBITUARIES.)

Rallies and Other Races. Almost as intense as Formula One racing were the international rallies, which usually consisted of several days of driving. Toyota Celica Turbos took the top two places in the Swedish Rally, and in Portugal two Ford Escort RS Cosworths triumphed. The prestigious East African Trust Bank Safari Rally, toughest of all, was a victory for Toyota, with four Celica Turbos leading the way home. A Ford Escort then triumphed over the Toyotas in the Tour of Corsica, and the Acropolis Rally was won by Ford. Juha Kankkunen of Finland won the world drivers' championship.

International sports-car racing was somewhat in the doldrums in 1993, and there was a fear that the Le Mans 24-hour race might be canceled. The event, first held in 1923, survived, however, with French Peugeot 905 Evo Ics taking the first three places. The Formula 3000 racing car champion driver was Olivier Panis of France.

(WILLIAM C. BODDY)

U.S. Racing. The stunning success of Nigel Mansell, 1992 Formula One champion, in his first year in U.S. IndyCar competition highlighted a year in which virtuosity and tragedy shared centre stage. The 40-year-old Englishman, driving a Lola-Ford Cosworth for Newman-Haas Racing, edged 1993 Indianapolis 500 winner Emerson Fittipaldi for the Championship Auto Racing Teams (CART) championship. Mansell won 5 of 17 races, including his debut at Surfers Paradise, Australia, and also was third on his rookie try at Indianapolis. His season winnings were $2,526,953—unprecedented for a first-year competitor in any kind of U.S. auto racing. Fittipaldi, a former Formula One champion himself before moving from his native Brazil to the U.S. racing scene, was the leading driver of a Chevrolet-powered car.

Fittipaldi averaged 253.103 km/h (157.207 mph) for the 500 miles of Indianapolis and earned $1,155,304 for the victory. Four Lola-Cosworths followed him in the standings in a race where 12 different drivers held the lead and a record 10 finished the entire 200 laps. Earning $681,303 for second place was Arie Luyendyk of The Netherlands, whose qualifying speed of 350.587 km/h (223.967 mph) had earned him the pole position.

Two fatal aviation accidents overshadowed the National Association for Stock Car Auto Racing (NASCAR) Winston Cup season, which featured an exciting duel between two stock-car virtuosos, newly crowned Dale Earnhardt and Rusty Wallace. Alan Kulwicki, defending NASCAR champion, and Davey Allison died in separate mishaps. (*See* OBITUARIES.) Earnhardt, in a Robert Childress-owned Goodwrench Chevrolet, outsteadied Wallace in a Pontiac, although Wallace won 10 of 30 Winston Cup races to Earnhardt's 6.

Dale Jarrett won the Daytona 500 before a record crowd of 153,000, overtaking Earnhardt on the last turn before the finish line. His average speed was 249.505 km/h (154.972 mph). Earnhardt won three other classic Winston Cup races: the Coca-Cola 600 at Charlotte, N.C.; the Pepsi 400 at Daytona Beach, Fla.; and the Diehard 500 at Talladega, Ala. Chevrolet edged Ford and Pontiac for the Winston Cup manufacturers' trophy in the closest contest in years—191, 190, 189.

The Camel GT prototype series passed into racing history as the International Motor Sports Association (IMSA) decreed a new category of less-expensive open-cockpit racers for 1994. For the 1993 season IMSA meanwhile coped with the withdrawal of factory teams from Nissan, Jaguar, and Mazda and the announcement by Toyota that it, too, was in its final year. The Toyota Eagles of Dan Gurney dominated the final Camel GT season, with Juan Fangio II repeating as champion and teammate P.J. Jones finishing second. The Toyotas won both of IMSA's Florida crown-jewel races, the Rolex 24 Hours of Daytona and the 12 Hours of Sebring.

Scott Sharp in the American Equipment Racing Chevrolet Camaro won his second-straight Sports Car Club of America (SCCA) Trans-Am drivers crown as Chevrolet won its fourth manufacturers' cup in a row. Ford Mustang's Ron Fellows finished second. (ROBERT J. FENDELL)

BADMINTON

Indonesia and South Korea posted strong showings at the 1993 world championships in Birmingham, England. This biannual tournament features two events—a team world championship for the Sudirman Cup and competition for individuals.

South Korea successfully defended its Sudirman Cup title against Indonesia the same way it had won it in 1991—by dominating the doubles events. First, Park Joo Bong and Gil Young Ah won the mixed doubles 15–2, 15–7 over Aryono Miranat and Eliza; then Kim Hak Kyun lost 11–15, 7–15 to Ardy Wiranata in men's singles, and Bang Soo Hyun lost 6–11, 6–11 to Susi Susanti in women's singles; Gil Young Ah and Chung So Young fought off two match (and title) points in the second game before defeating Lili Tampi and Finarsih 6–15, 17–15, 15–11 in women's doubles; finally, inevitably, Park Joo Bong and Kim Moon Soo clinched the Sudirman Cup by emphatically beating Ricky Subagja and Rudy Gunawan 15–10, 15–6 in men's doubles.

Indonesia, however, regrouped to take three titles in the individual events. Joko Suprianto beat compatriot Hermawan Susanto 15–5, 15–11 for the men's singles title; Susanti again triumphed over South Korea's Bang in women's singles 7–11, 11–9, 11–3; and Subagja and Gunawan defeated Malaysia's Cheah Soon Kit and Soo Beng Kiang 15–11, 15–3 in men's doubles. In women's doubles there was an all-China final as Nong Qunhua and Zhou Lei defeated Chen Ying and Wu Yuhong 15–5, 15–10. European dominance of mixed doubles continued as Denmark's Thomas Lund and Sweden's Catrine Bengtsson beat Denmark's Jon Holst-Christensen and Grete Mogensen 10–15, 15–6, 15–12.

(WARREN K. EMERSON)

BASEBALL

Major league baseball added two expansion teams for the 1993 season, and an attendance record was broken for the seventh time in nine years. With the new Colorado Rockies and Florida Marlins creating interest, and also tight division races, more than 70 million customers paid to watch regular-season games.

World Series. The Toronto Blue Jays won the World Series for the second consecutive year, thereby becoming the first repeat champions since the 1977–78 New York Yankees. The Blue Jays beat the Philadelphia Phillies four games to two, the last victory occurring at Toronto's SkyDome. The triumph thus enabled the Blue Jays to clinch the title for the first time ever in Canada. They had won their 1992 crown in Atlanta, Ga.

The Blue Jays won the opening game 8–5 at Toronto on October 16. The Phillies jumped to a 2–0 lead in the first inning against Juan Guzman, Toronto's ace pitcher, but Philadelphia starter Curt Schilling was no problem for the hard-hitting Blue Jays. They scored three runs in the seventh inning on a run-scoring double by Devon White and another double by Roberto Alomar for two runs. Al Leitner, who relieved Guzman, was credited with the victory.

In the second game at Toronto the next night, however, the Phillies scored five runs in the third inning against Toronto veteran Dave Stewart and held on to win 6–4. Jim Eisenreich's three-run home run was the big hit for the Phillies. Terry Mulholland started and pitched 5⅔ innings toward the victory.

The series moved to Philadelphia's Veterans Stadium on October 19, and the Blue Jays scored three runs in the first inning against Danny Jackson and cruised to a 10–3 conquest. Alomar, Toronto's brilliant second baseman, had four hits, and Paul Molitor (*see* BIOGRAPHIES) had three, including a home run. Pat Hentgen was the winning pitcher.

The next evening the Blue Jays and Phillies engaged in the wildest World Series game ever. The Phillies twice mounted a five-run lead only to have the Blue Jays explode for six runs in the eighth and gain a 15–14 decision that gave them a 3–1 lead in games. Many records were broken in the marathon, including length of the game; at 4 hours 14 minutes, it was the longest in World Series history. The teams combined for 31 hits, the pivotal one being a two-run triple by White in the eighth inning to bring in the tying and winning runs. Duane Ward of Toronto retired the last four Philadelphia batters for the save.

To avert elimination in the best-of-seven series, the Phillies needed a strong pitching performance on October 21. Schilling was up to the assignment. While Philadelphia's other tired arms were resting, he hurled a five-hit, complete-game 2–0 triumph.

The series returned to Toronto on October 23 for the sixth game, and the Blue Jays forged a 5–1 lead against Mulholland after five innings. Stewart, a free agent acquired from Oakland, was regarded as one of the best clutch pitchers in baseball. However, he was knocked out in the seventh inning when the Phillies scored five times, three on a home run by Len Dykstra. The Phillies, trying to force a seventh and deciding game, held their 6–5 lead entering the bottom of the ninth inning. Philadelphia reliever Mitch Williams, however, quickly unraveled. He walked Rickey Henderson, Toronto's leadoff batter, on four pitches. With one out, Molitor singled. Joe Carter, the Blue Jays' cleanup hitter and slugging right fielder, then drilled Williams' 2–2 pitch over the left-field wall for a dramatic three-run homer to give the Blue Jays an 8–6 conquest and their championship. Ward was credited with the victory.

Molitor, an off-season free-agent acquisition from the Milwaukee Brewers, was voted Most Valuable Player for the World Series. He batted .500 for six games, with 12 hits in 24 at bats including 2 doubles, 2 triples, and 2 home runs.

Championship Series. The Blue Jays won their second consecutive American League pennant by defeating the Chicago White Sox four games to two in the championship series. The Phillies upset the highly favoured Atlanta Braves four games to two to secure their first National League pennant since 1983.

The Blue Jays opened the American League series in Chicago's new Comiskey Park on October 5 with a 7–3 triumph behind Guzman. Molitor had 4 of Toronto's 17 hits, 13 of which came against White Sox ace Jack McDowell. The next afternoon Stewart raised his career play-off record to 7–0 with a 3–1 victory.

The White Sox, however, rebounded with two straight victories in Toronto on October 8 and 9. Chicago's Wilson Alvarez worked a complete-game 6–1 victory in the third game. In game four Lance Johnson batted in four runs and Frank Thomas hit a mammoth home run off Todd Stottlemyre to propel the White Sox to a 7–4 triumph. The Blue Jays beat McDowell again, 5–3 on October 10, behind Guzman's pitching and three hits by Alomar. The Blue Jays then eliminated the White Sox at Chicago on October 12 by winning 6–3 as Stewart recorded another victory. Stewart was named the Most Valuable Player for the series.

The Phillies began their postseason by beating the Braves 4–3 in 10 innings at Philadelphia on October 6. Kim Batiste, whose ninth-inning error helped Atlanta tie the game, won it with a run-scoring single. The Braves swamped Philadelphia 14–3 the next day behind four home runs and strong pitching by Greg Maddux and then pounded out a 9–4 victory on October 9 in Atlanta with Tom Glavine as the winning pitcher.

On October 10, Jackson lifted the Phillies to a 2–1 victory with $7\frac{2}{3}$ innings of excellent pitching. The Phillies scored twice in the fourth inning off Atlanta's John Smoltz. The next day the Phillies gained a 3–0 lead behind Schilling only to have it vanish on a stirring three-run rally by the Braves in the ninth. Then in the top of the 10th, Dykstra smashed a solo home run and the Phillies held on for a 4–3 decision. On October 13 in Philadelphia, Mickey Morandini's two-run triple and Dave Hollins' two-run homer supported Mulholland's efforts in the Phillies' 6–3 clincher. Schilling was named Most Valuable Player of the series.

FOCUS ON SPORTS

Texas Rangers hurler Nolan Ryan, who retired from baseball in 1993 after 27 years in the major leagues, throws one of his last pitches. During his career Ryan pitched 7 no-hitters and 12 one-hitters and had a phenomenal 5,714 strikeouts, all records.

Final Major League Standings, 1993

AMERICAN LEAGUE

East Division				
Club	W.	L.	Pct.	G.B.
Toronto	95	67	.586	–
New York	88	74	.543	7
Baltimore	85	77	.525	10
Detroit	85	77	.525	10
Boston	80	82	.494	15
Cleveland	76	86	.469	19
Milwaukee	69	93	.426	26

West Division				
Club	W.	L.	Pct.	G.B.
Chicago	94	68	.580	–
Texas	86	76	.531	8
Kansas City	84	78	.519	10
Seattle	82	80	.506	12
California	71	91	.438	23
Minnesota	71	91	.438	23
Oakland	68	94	.420	26

NATIONAL LEAGUE

East Division				
Club	W.	L.	Pct.	G.B.
Philadelphia	97	65	.599	–
Montreal	94	68	.580	3
St. Louis	87	75	.537	10
Chicago	84	78	.519	13
Pittsburgh	75	87	.463	22
Florida	64	98	.395	33
New York	59	103	.364	38

West Division				
Club	W.	L.	Pct.	G.B.
Atlanta	104	58	.642	–
San Francisco	103	59	.636	1
Houston	85	77	.525	19
Los Angeles	81	81	.500	23
Cincinnati	73	89	.451	31
Colorado	67	95	.414	37
San Diego	61	101	.377	43

Regular Season. The National League West staged one of the best races in baseball history. The Braves trailed the San Francisco Giants by $9\frac{1}{2}$ games as late as August 7 and then charged to first place. Entering the last day of the regular season, however, the teams were tied. The Braves won their third consecutive division title by beating Colorado at home, while the Giants were defeated by the Los Angeles Dodgers in Los Angeles. The Braves finished with a brilliant mark of 104–58, only one game better than the Giants.

John Olerud of the Blue Jays, after hovering near the .400 level for part of the summer, ended the season with a .363 batting average to lead the American League. Teammates Molitor (.332) and Alomar (.326) followed him. Andres Galarraga of Colorado, like Olerud, was at .400 in early July, and Galarraga then won the National League batting title with a .370 average. Tony Gwynn of the San Diego Padres finished second at .358.

Juan Gonzales of the Texas Rangers led the American League with 46 home runs, one more than Ken Griffey, Jr., of the Seattle Mariners. Barry Bonds, who signed with the Giants as a free agent from the Pittsburgh Pirates, led the National League with 46 home runs.

McDowell had 22 victories, the most in the American League. John Burkett of San Francisco and Glavine led the National League with 22 victories each. Toronto's Ward and Jeff Montgomery of the Kansas City Royals paced the American League's relief pitchers with 45 saves each. Randy Myers of the Chicago Cubs led the National League with 53.

Chicago captured three of the four postseason awards in the American League, with Thomas as Most Valuable Player, Gene Lamont as Manager of the Year, and McDowell as winner of the Cy Young Award for best pitcher. The league's Rookie of the Year was Tim Salmon of California. For the National League, Bonds was voted Most Valuable Player, Dusty Baker of San Francisco was Manager of the Year, Maddux won the Cy Young Award, and Mike Piazza of Los Angeles was Rookie of the Year.

The Rockies and Marlins both avoided last place in their first season. Colorado won 67 games and finished sixth in

New York Yankee pitcher Jim Abbott cheers the final out of his 4–0 no-hitter against the Cleveland Indians on September 4. Abbott, who won the gold medal game in the 1988 Olympics, had a highly successful career despite being born without a right hand.
MICHAEL PONZINI—SPORTS ILLUSTRATED

the National League West while establishing a league single-season attendance record with 4,483,350.

The American League won its sixth consecutive All-Star Game, beating the National League 9–3 in Baltimore on July 13. Kirby Puckett of the Minnesota Twins was named Most Valuable Player of the game. New York Yankee Jim Abbott, who was born without a right hand, pitched a no-hitter on September 4. George Brett of Kansas City and Nolan Ryan of Texas, both of whom appeared destined for baseball's Hall of Fame, retired.

Other Developments. Pending approval of the players, major league owners devised a realignment plan to be implemented starting with the 1994 season. Each league of two divisions would be rearranged to include three divisions each with an extra round of postseason play-offs featuring the six division winners plus the second-place team in either league with the best record. (ROBERT WILLIAM VERDI)

Latin America. Puerto Rico's Crab Pickers, from the town of Santurce, won the 23rd Caribbean Series in February in Mazatlán, Mexico. This was the first time Santurce had taken Latin America's top baseball prize. Another Puerto Rican team, the Mayagüez Indians, had won in 1992.

The Crab Pickers did not have an easy time in the series. After the regular six-game round-robin, they were tied for first place with the Dominican Republic's Cibao Eagles. Each team had four victories and two defeats. The tie-breaking game was tense through the fifth inning, when the score was 5–5. A two-run homer in the sixth inning, however, put the Puerto Ricans on top, and two additional runs in the bottom of the eighth clinched the game and the title for Puerto Rico. Mexico's Mexicali Eagles finished third in the series, and Venezuela's Zulia Eagles were last.

In the summer the Tabasco Olmecs took the AAA Mexican League after beating the Owls of the Two Laredos (Nuevo Laredo, Mexico, and Laredo, Texas) four games to one in the championship series. The Owls had gone down to defeat in the final series in 1992 as well.

As expected, Cuba took the gold medal in the Caribbean and Central American Games, held in the summer in Puerto Rico. The Cuban national team easily beat Mexico in the final game 11–1. (SERGIO SARMIENTO)

Japan. The Seibu Lions of the Pacific League and Yakult Swallows of the Central League met in the Japan Series for the second year in a row, and the Swallows defeated the defending champions, who had won the postseason contest six times in the last seven years, four games to three. Swallow hurler Kenjiro Kawasaki, winner of the fourth and seventh games, was voted the Most Valuable Player of the series.

In the first two games, played at Seibu Stadium in Tokorozawa, the Swallows' prowess in batting dominated. In the opener they collected 12 hits, including a three-run homer by Jack Howell, for an 8–5 victory. In the second game the Swallows knocked out Lion pitcher Kuo Tai-yuan with eight hits and four runs in the first three innings and eventually won the game 5–2.

In the third game, played at Tokyo's Jingu Stadium, the Lions' pitching excelled in a 7–2 victory, while the Swallows won the fourth 1–0. The Lions took the next two games 7–2 and 4–2 to tie the series at three. In the seventh and final game, Swallow cleanup man Katsumi Hirosawa hit a three-run home run in the top of the first inning, but Lion cleanup hitter Kazuhiro Kiyohara followed with a two-run homer to make the score 3–2. Then Kenjiro Kawasaki and short reliever Shingo Takatsu did their job and kept the opponents scoreless for the rest of the game, while the Swallows scored one more run in the eighth.

In the Central League, Swallow catcher Atsuya Furuta, who hit .308, was voted the Most Valuable Player. The league's Rookie of the Year award went to Swallow hurler Tomohito Ito, whose record was seven wins against two losses. The Pacific League's Most Valuable Player was Lion left-handed pitcher Kimiyasu Kudo, who won 15 games against 3 losses. Lion pitcher Kendo Sugiyama, who pitched in 54 games and won 7, lost 2, and earned 5 saves, was voted the Rookie of the Year in the Pacific League.

(TOSHIHIKO SUZUKI)

BASKETBALL

United States. *College.* Losing a second straight bid for the National Collegiate Athletic Association (NCAA) championship in 1993 proved more than twice as painful for the University of Michigan's "Fabulous Five." The Wolverines reached the final game of the NCAA tournament for the second year in a row only to fall short once more. A year earlier Duke had routed them 71–51. This time the Big Ten team lost to another Atlantic Coast Conference (ACC) member, North Carolina, in a 77–71 heartbreaker.

A mental error in the closing seconds by Chris Webber, the leader of Michigan's sophomore-studded lineup, enabled the Tar Heels to hang on. It was Webber's last game with "Fab Five" teammates Jalen Rose, Juwan Howard, Jimmy King, and Ray Jackson because the 2.05-m (6-ft 9-in) centre-forward had elected to drop out of school and enter the National Basketball Association (NBA) draft.

The thrilling finish in the New Orleans Superdome gave North Carolina's coach, Dean Smith, his second national title. The only major college coaches to win more were John Wooden of UCLA with 10, Kentucky's Adolph Rupp with 4, and Indiana's Bobby Knight with 3.

With Michigan trailing 73–71 in the final minute, Webber rebounded a missed free throw by Pat Sullivan of North Carolina. He dribbled downcourt and into the right corner. Then, inexplicably, Webber signaled for a time-out although the Wolverines had none left to take. The penalty for this mistake was a two-shot technical foul and possession of the ball for North Carolina. Fittingly, Donald Williams sank both free throws with 11 seconds to go, assuring the Tar

Heels their first NCAA crown since Michael Jordan's basket won the title for them 11 years earlier on the same court.

Regardless of their loss, Webber and his teammates pulled off a remarkable feat by reaching the title game in both of their seasons together. For most teams, led by seniors, reaching the Final Four just once is a dream that seldom comes true. Under Coach Steve Fisher the Wolverines peaked at tournament time. On a mission to erase the 1992 humiliation by Duke, they survived two overtime scares to reach the last step on their climb. They wanted a rematch with Duke, but the Blue Devils' quest for their third straight NCAA crown ended in the second round of the Midwest Regional with an 82–77 loss to California.

North Carolina also had to play an extra period in getting past Cincinnati 75–68 in the East Regional final. Smith's team joined Michigan, Kansas, and Kentucky in New Orleans, La., for the April 3 semifinals. The Tar Heels ousted Kansas 78–68, while Michigan overcame a four-point deficit in overtime to get past Kentucky 81–78.

That set up a championship duel two nights later between the nation's premier basketball conferences. The ACC prevailed for the third straight year after a hotly contested final. The Tar Heels's 2.13-m (7-ft) centre, Eric Montross, battled Webber under both baskets, although it was Williams' game-high 25 points and four clutch free throws at the end that made the difference. Amazingly, Williams duplicated his semifinals performance—25 points and five of seven baskets from the three-point range—to be named Most Valuable Player of the Final Four.

When the 1993–94 season began, a rules change had been made to speed up play and reduce excessive fouling in the final minutes. The NCAA men's basketball committee voted to cut the shot clock from 45 to 35 seconds, although the women's rules group elected to stay with the 30-second clock it had used since 1969.

Other significant rules changes would stop the clock after baskets in the final minute of regulation time or overtime and eliminate automatic turnovers on closely guarded players who did not pass or dribble within five seconds. The new rules package was not as radical as the introduction of the 45-second shot clock in 1985, which virtually eliminated stalling tactics.

In women's basketball, Sheryl Swoopes poured in an NCAA tournament final-game record 47 points, sparking Texas Tech to the national championship with an 84–82 victory over Ohio State. The 1.83-m (6-ft) Swoopes even topped the men's NCAA finals mark of 44 points, set by UCLA's Bill Walton in 1973. A sellout crowd of 16,141 in Atlanta, Ga., marveled at the moves and shooting touch of the transfer student from South Plains College, Levelland, Texas. Along with Swoopes's talent, her outgoing personality contributed to the growth of interest in the women's game.

Professional. The Chicago Bulls proved that the third time really was the charm by defeating the Phoenix Suns in six games to capture the 1993 NBA championship. It put the Bulls in select company as the first NBA team to string together three titles since the Boston Celtics pulled off the hat trick (as part of a run of eight consecutive championships) in 1964–66.

As always, Michael Jordan (*see* BIOGRAPHIES) was the driving force behind this coup. The 1.98-m (6-ft 6-in) guard spurred the Bulls through the 82-game regular season and into the play-offs with sheer force of will fueling his explosive blend of ability and desire. Even though Jordan and teammate Scottie Pippen went to training camp late, drained from helping the U.S. Olympic men's basketball "Dream Team" win the gold medal, in the end it made no difference. As usual, the regular-season grind served merely to whet Jordan's appetite for the "Three-Peat" he coveted.

But when the crucial moment came in the final play-off series, at the end of the sixth game in Phoenix, Ariz., it was veteran John Paxson who wore the laurel leaves. Paxson's three-point basket in the closing seconds broke the Suns' backs and their fans' hearts, sweeping the Bulls from behind to a 99–98 decision and wrapping up the best-of-seven title series with a 4–2 edge for Chicago.

RICHARD MACKSON—SPORTS ILLUSTRATED

Eric Montross shoots over the outstretched hand of Chris Webber (4) in North Carolina's 77–71 win over Michigan in the National Collegiate Athletic Association championship game. North Carolina got help in the final seconds when Michigan star Webber received a technical foul for calling a time-out his team did not have.

NBA Final Standings, 1992–93

EASTERN CONFERENCE

Team	Won	Lost
Atlantic Division		
*New York	60	22
*Boston	48	34
*New Jersey	43	39
Orlando	41	41
Miami	36	46
Philadelphia	26	56
Washington	22	60
Central Division		
*Chicago	57	25
*Cleveland	54	28
*Charlotte	44	38
*Atlanta	43	39
*Indiana	41	41
Detroit	40	42
Milwaukee	28	54

WESTERN CONFERENCE

Team	Won	Lost
Midwest Division		
*Houston	55	27
*San Antonio	49	33
*Utah	47	35
Denver	36	46
Minnesota	19	63
Dallas	11	71
Pacific Division		
*Phoenix	62	20
*Seattle	55	27
*Portland	51	31
*L.A. Clippers	41	41
*L.A. Lakers	39	43
Golden State	34	48
Sacramento	25	57

*Gained play-off berth.

Ironically, New York Knicks coach Pat Riley had copyrighted the term *Three-Peat.* The Bulls had eliminated the Knicks in a bruising six-game Eastern Conference final series, but Riley, the NBA's Coach of the Year, stood to reap a handsome profit on sales of Three-Peat merchandise.

When the Bulls capitalized on the Suns' stage fright to jump ahead 2–0 in the final play-off, the outcome of the head-to-head matchup between close friends Jordan and Phoenix superstar Charles Barkley, who had been named the league's Most Valuable Player, was assured. The Bulls also positioned themselves for a fourth straight title soon after this one by signing 2.1-m (6-ft 11-in) European superstar Toni Kukoc to a lucrative long-term contract.

In the midst of Jordan's triumph, tragedy soon turned the cheers to shocked silence. A nationwide wave of sympathy followed the news that James Jordan, Michael's father, had been murdered in North Carolina, apparently in late July. Then, in October, the superstar stunned his fans around the world when he announced his retirement.

(ROBERT G. LOGAN)

World Basketball. The year was a busy one for European basketball, with a number of tournaments throughout the continent. The major event of the year was the final round of the 28th European championships for men, for which Germany acted as host. For the first time, owing mainly to the number of new Eastern European nations, 16 teams contested the final round. The tournament favourite was Croatia, which, as part of the former Yugoslavia, had supplied most of the team that had won the title in 1991. However, Croatia was defeated by Russia in the semifinals. In the other semifinal Germany defeated Greece. A capacity crowd of 10,000 in Munich then watched an enthralling final that resulted in a dramatic 71–70 win for the home nation—the winning point coming from a Christian Welp free throw with four seconds left on the clock.

The finals of the 24th European championships for women were held in Perugia, Italy. In the final Spain defeated France 82–76 to win the championship for the first time. The European champions at cadet (under 16) level were Greece in the men's competition and Russia in the women's. Placing second in both competitions was Spain.

Two world championship titles were also contested during the year. The first world championship for men 22 and under was played in Valladolid, Spain, and was won by the U.S., with France as runner-up. In the third world championship for junior women at Seoul, South Korea, Australia was victorious, with Russia in second place.

The 13th African championship for women was won by Senegal, which defeated Kenya 89–43 in the final. In the first Asian championship for men 22 and under, held in Seoul, Taiwan defeated Korea 80–77 in the final.

The major club competition during the 1992–93 European season, the European championship for men's clubs, was won by Limoges (France). In a thrilling final at Athens, Limoges defeated Benetton Treviso (Italy) 59–55. In other European competitions Aris Salonika (Greece) won the European Cup by beating Efes Istanbul (Turkey), and CB Dorna Valencia (Spain) retained the Women's European Champions Cup with a victory over Como (Italy).

In South America the 35th men's championship, played in Guarantigueta, Brazil, was won by the host nation 82–76 over Argentina in the final. In the club competitions Unimed from Brazil won the ninth South American championship for women's clubs, defeating fellow Brazilians Leite Moca in the final round; the 31st men's championship was won by Atenas (Argentina) 76–73 over Franca (Brazil) in the final.

Off the court the basketball world mourned the death of Drazen Petrovic (*see* OBITUARIES), who died in a car accident near Ingolstadt, Germany, on June 7.

(MARK HANNEN)

BILLIARD GAMES

Carom Billiards. The World Billiard Association (BWA) 1992 World Cup for three-cushion billiards was won by defending champion Torbjorn Blomdahl of Sweden. After a slow start on the six-city international tour, Blomdahl won three of the last four events to claim his third title. At the tour's Japan Open World Cup in Tokyo, Blomdahl set a new world record, averaging 2.204 points per inning (PPI) for the tournament. Belgium's Raymond Ceulemans, 21-time world titlist, was runner-up, with Sang Chun Lee of the United States third.

Rini van Bracht of The Netherlands captured his second European championship in three-cushion billiards at Corbeil, France, defeating Germany's Maximo Aguirre 3–2 in the final. Van Bracht, who won his first European crown in 1984, averaged 1.231 PPI for the event, while runner-up Aguirre posted a PPI of 0.958. Paul Stoobants of Belgium finished third.

Blomdahl and Ceulemans met in the finals of the Briljant championship in Rotterdam, Neth., where Blomdahl made the tournament high run of 23 points on his way to a 50–35 victory in 20 innings. He set a new world record for tournament PPI average, 2.252, breaking the mark he had set in the Tokyo World Cup tour event earlier in the year.

The Efes Pilsen Open Grand Prix three-cushion tournament in Istanbul was won by Dick Jaspers of The Netherlands, who defeated Lee 3–2 in the final match. Lee, ranked second in the world to Blomdahl, garnered his fourth U.S. national three-cushion championship, held in 1993 in San Jose, Calif. He was undefeated (7–0) and had the high average of 1.489 PPI in the round-robin finals. Lee also had the tournament high run of 17 points as well as the best game (50 points in 27 innings: 1.852 PPI).

Pocket Billiards. The 1990s seemed certain to be remembered as one of pocket billiard's most tumultuous decades. Reminiscent of the power struggles that had fragmented boxing's structure and strained its credibility with much of the public, pocket billiards became the object of surprisingly intense battling between various industry groups. Each contended that it could and would provide the necessary wisdom, guidance, and control to lead pocket billiards into the next century and realize its full potential as a mass-market, big-dollar sport. While the tussles continued behind the scenes, an increase in televised events and in the variety of playing sites generated some guarded optimism among followers of the game.

Johnny Archer of Twin City, Ga., did his best to "unify" the various groups and sanctioning bodies by trying to win

Stephen Hendry lines up a shot in professional snooker's world championship, which he took from Jimmy White 18 frames to 5. It was Hendry's third world championship in four years, all won over White.
ROSS PARRY PICTURE AGENCY

everything, and he came very close. The 24-year-old World Pool-Billiard Association (WPA) champion went unbeaten to win the 1993 McDermott Masters IX in Las Vegas, Nev.; lost his first match but went on to win the Third Annual Bicycle Club Invitational 9-Ball Tournament in Bell Gardens, Calif.; and, when the WPA threatened loss of playing status to any members who entered the first Professional Billiard Tour Association World 9-Ball Championship in Las Vegas, not only ignored the edict (along with some 110 others) but also won the event. Add to that his tour money-winning lead, his number one world ranking, and several regional titles, and the result was the 1992 Player of the Year award for Archer from both major billiard publications.

The officially sanctioned WPA World 9-Ball Championship was held in Königswinter, Germany, on December 7–12. Chao Feng-pang of Taiwan won the men's title, while Loree Jon Jones of the U.S. captured the women's.

In other major men's events, the 1993 Billiard Professionals of America (BPA) Los Angeles Open overall title went to Mark Tadd; the 1992 U.S. 9-Ball Open in Chesapeake, Va., was won by Tom Kennedy; the 1993 Challenge of Champions in Las Vegas went to Allen Hopkins; and Ed Kelly was victorious in the 1993 One-Pocket Super Tournament in Reno, Nev.

Women's Player of the Year honours for 1992 were split between two top tour performers: Vivian Villarreal of San Antonio, Texas, and Ewa Mataya of Grand Ledge, Mich. Villarreal defeated Mataya to win the 1992 Women's Professional Billiard Association (WPBA) Nationals in Milwaukee, Wis. Robin Bell of Cypress, Calif., won the 1992 U.S. 9-Ball Open in Chesapeake, Va.; Villarreal took the 1993 McDermott Masters in Las Vegas; and Gerda Hofstätter of Austria won the 1993 European 9-Ball Championship in Oslo, Norway.

The Association of College Unions–International (ACU–I) 1993 Collegiate Pocket Billiard Championships were held at the University of California at Irvine. Max Eberle of James Madison University, Harrisonburg, Va., won the men's division, and Carla Swails of the College of Southern Idaho took the women's title.

The Billiard Congress of America inducted two new members into its Hall of Fame. They were Irish-born inventor, author, manufacturer, player, promoter, and patron of the sport Michael Phelan (1817–71) and the legendary undisputed "King of Bank Pool," Eddie ("The Knoxville Bear") Taylor (born in 1918).

Aficionados and casual fans alike were saddened at the passing of the best known of the sport's great stars, Willie Mosconi. One of the finest pocket billiards players in history, he was 15-time world champion beginning in 1941, when he burst upon the scene with a record-smashing tournament victory. (*See* OBITUARIES.) (BRUCE H. VENZKE)

Snooker. Stephen Hendry of Scotland retained the world professional snooker championship in May 1993 after defeating Jimmy White of England by 18 frames to 5 in the final at Sheffield, England. Hendry's 9–3 victory over Steve Davis of England at the Dubai Classic final in October was preceded by the 10–6 defeat of Davis in the Sky International final in April at Plymouth, England, and by his 9–5 victory over James Wattana of Thailand at the Wembley (England) Masters final in February. Davis, however, won the European Open championship at Antwerp, Belgium, in February with a 10–4 victory over Hendry in the final and triumphed in two more finals: the British Open at Derby, England, in March, when he defeated Wattana 10–2; and the Irish Masters in March in County Kildare, where he achieved a 9–4 victory over Alan McManus of Scotland. Wattana defeated Davis 9–6 in the world match play final at Doncaster, England. In November 17-year-old Ronnie O'Sullivan of England became the youngest winner ever of a world-ranking tournament when he defeated Hendry to take the U.K. championship. (SYDNEY E. FRISKIN)

BOWLING

World Tenpins. The international bowling season of 1992–93 began in Venezuela as young athletes from 25 countries gathered in Caracas for the second world tenpin youth championships. Boys' singles was won by Angelo Constantino of the Philippines with a record score of 1,313. Lee Dong Hee of South Korea finished second with 1,306. Constantino and his younger brother, Norberto, also won the boys' doubles for the Philippines with a score of 2,473. Qatar placed second with 2,453.

In another close contest Cristina Kortright of Puerto Rico won the girls' singles by defeating Nikki Brandolino of the U.S. 1,206–1,204. Venezuela won the girls' doubles with 2,330, and South Korea was second with 2,250. Champion of the mixed foursomes was the U.S. with 4,754, Finland placing second with 4,630.

Anthony Chapman of the U.S. won the boys' masters tournament for the 16 top bowlers in the team events, defeating South Korea's See Kook 414–380 in the final. In the girls' masters Finland's Jaana Puhakka defeated Tammy Turner of the U.S. 408–338.

Malmö, Sweden, was the site for the European championships in June. The tournament was notable in that every tournament record was broken. The winners of men's events were: singles, Patrick Boman of Sweden, 1,434; doubles, Finland, 2,760; trios, Sweden, 3,785; teams of 5, Finland, 6,318; 24 games all-events, Raymond Jansson, Sweden, 5,259; and masters, Achim Grabowski, Germany, 425–413, over Thomas Leandersson of Sweden. South Africa's George Jagga bowled the first perfect (300) game in the tournament's history.

For the women the winners were: singles, Anu Peltola, Finland, 1,284; doubles, Great Britain, 2,504; trios, Sweden, 3,692; and teams of 5, Great Britain, 6,016. The all-events' champion was Asa Larsson of Sweden with 5,001. The two-game play-off was between Larsson and Pauliina Aalto of Finland, with Aalto triumphing as the champion 439–413.

(YRJÖ SARAHETE)

U.S. Tenpins. Walter Ray Williams, Jr., dominated the professional bowling scene in 1993, just as he had reigned over the nation's horseshoe-pitching stars in other years. Williams, 34, won an astonishing seven Professional Bowlers Association (PBA) championships and held a wide lead in earnings ($296,370 to his nearest opponent's $174,528) and in average score per game (223 to 220.6). The right-hander from Stockton, Calif., appeared certain to succeed Dave Ferraro as PBA Player of the Year.

One of the other highlights of the year was the 300 game by Mike Aulby of Indianapolis, Ind., in the title match of the Wichita, Kan., Open against a 279 by David Ozio of Vidor, Texas. The perfect score gave Aulby, PBA Player of the Year in 1985, his second title of 1993.

George Branham III of Indianapolis won the 29th annual Firestone Tournament of Champions in Akron, Ohio, by defeating Parker Bohn III of Freehold, N.J., 227–214. This was the last time the tournament was sponsored by Firestone. The 1994 meet would be known as the General Tire Tournament of Champions.

There was a three-way tie for the Regular Division doubles championship in the American Bowling Congress (ABC) tournament in Tulsa, Okla. The co-winners, with a score of 1,498, were: Terry Saccone and Dave Callery of Cincinnati, Ohio; Darrin Lindsey and Rick Fangman of Waterloo, Iowa; and Ron and Randy Wilde of Green Bay, Wis. Other champions were: team, Bruegger's Bagels No. 1, Albany, N.Y., 3,537; singles, Dan Bock, Owatonna, Minn., 798; all-events, Jeff Nimke, Kenosha, Wis., 2,254.

A mother and daughter from Toronto, Gloria and Karen Collura, won the Open Division doubles crown in the Women's International Bowling Congress (WIBC) tournament in Baton Rouge, La., with a score of 1,304. Other Open winners included: singles, Kari Murph, Dayton, Ohio, and Karen Collura, 747; team, Strike Zone Pro Shop, Rolling Meadows, Ill., 2,978; all-events, Anne Marie Duggan, Edmond, Okla., 1,990. Jan Schmidt of Rochelle, Ill., captured the WIBC Queens Tournament in Baton Rouge with a 201–163 victory over Pat Costello of Lantana, Fla.

In the women's U.S. Open, sponsored by the Bowling Proprietors Association of America, Dede Davidson of San Jose, Calif., scored a 213–194 victory over Dana Miller-Mackie of Fort Worth, Texas, in the final.

(JOHN J. ARCHIBALD)

BOXING

The heavyweight division continued to be in turmoil in 1993, with three fighters claiming to be world champion. The chaos was increased by the World Boxing Organization's (WBO's) persistence in creating the most unlikely titleholders. In addition, a big upset took place when Evander Holyfield (U.S.), who had lost the World Boxing Council (WBC), World Boxing Association (WBA), and International Boxing Federation (IBF) titles to Riddick Bowe (U.S.) in November 1992, regained the WBA and IBF titles by outpointing Bowe at Las Vegas, Nev., one year later. Apart from the unexpected result, this fight would always be remembered for the bizarre interruption when a parachutist crashed into the canopy above the ring in the seventh round. The incident caused a 20-minute delay and injuries and panic among ringsiders.

Pernell Whitaker (left) lands a punch against Julio César Chávez in their World Boxing Council welterweight championship match. Most observers thought that Whitaker had a clear win and were stunned when judges declared the match a draw.

HOLLY STEIN—ALLSPORT

Bowe had obstructed the unifying of the heavyweight title after taking the WBC, WBA, and IBF versions of the title from Holyfield in 1992 by defying the WBC's order to defend his championship against Lennox Lewis (England). Subsequently, Lewis was crowned WBC champion without even putting on a pair of boxing gloves. Lewis, ordered to defend this title against the veteran Tom Tucker (U.S.), dutifully obeyed and won a dull contest in Las Vegas. While it did little for his prestige, it added greatly to his bank account, and he followed this by defending against the British veteran Frank Bruno at Cardiff, Wales. This fight took place on a damp cold night in the open air at 1 AM (British time) to coincide with peak viewing time on U.S. cable television. The referee stopped the fight in the seventh round, and although Lewis beat the 32-year-old Bruno, he was not impressive. He was behind on points until he produced the punch that dismissed Bruno, who was making his third unsuccessful challenge for a world crown. Lewis earned £4 million for his efforts.

Having spurned the WBC version of the title, Bowe did little to confirm the belief that he was the world's best heavyweight, taking on less than moderate challengers in defense of his WBA and IBF titles. His first victim was 34-year-old Michael Dokes (U.S.), a former champion long past his prime, who was battered to defeat in the first round. Bowe's next opponent, 36-year-old Jesse Ferguson (U.S.), was an unjustified challenger; the odds against him were quoted at 42–1. He was flattened in the second round at Washington, D.C., another multimillion-dollar payday for Bowe to add to the $7 million he reportedly earned against Dokes. While the IBF did not ban this bout, it declined to recognize it as a championship contest.

Though Bowe became richer, he paid for his lack of dedication and rocketed to 127 kg (280 lb). He trained down to 112 kg (246 lb) for the return with Holyfield, but he was far heavier than in their first meeting, and Holyfield appeared to be fitter. The contest was a triumph for the 31-year-old Holyfield, five years older than Bowe and nearly 14 kg (30 lb) lighter. He had reversed his only defeat, and he became the third champion, after Floyd Patterson and Muhammad Ali, to regain a lost heavyweight title. Holyfield's victory was good news for Lewis. A match in 1994 between the two for the WBA, IBF, and WBC titles was far more likely than one between Bowe and Lewis, as the managements of the latter could not agree to financial terms.

The fight with Lewis would have to wait, however, as the IBF and WBA ruled that Holyfield's next defense had to be against top-ranked challenger Michael Moorer (U.S.). At year's end the champion was reportedly offered $20 million to fight a rematch with Bowe, but Holyfield rejected the deal because he would have had to relinquish his titles or risk having them stripped if he failed to face Moorer.

The WBO lived up to its reputation of being out of step with rival bodies by ignoring both Holyfield and Bowe and choosing to recognize a lesser performer in Michael Moorer (U.S.); when Moorer did not bow to its wishes, the WBO matched Tommy Morrison (U.S.) with the 44-year-old George Foreman (U.S.) for the title. Morrison clearly outpointed his aging rival over 12 rounds. What followed was outrageous even for the WBO to tolerate. Morrison chose to defend his title against the mediocre Mike Williams (U.S.), who had appeared as an opponent of Morrison in the film *Rocky V*. Now they were to appear in the ring for real with the so-called world title at stake. An hour before the contest, Williams declined to take a drug test, and the fight was canceled. However, a crowd of 12,000 plus a large television audience had to be entertained. Someone spotted Tim Tomashek (U.S.), an unrated heavyweight, at ringside, and he was persuaded to rescue a desperate promoter and television presenter by stepping in with Morrison. The WBO accepted the practically unknown 28-year-old from Green Bay, Wis., who offered no serious opposition; the fight was ended by the ring physician in the fourth round.

Taking on yet another little-known challenger in 29-year-old Michael Bentt (U.S.), ranked only ninth by the WBO, Morrison came crashing down to Earth when flattened by Bentt in 1 min 33 sec of the first round at Tulsa, Okla., in October. Bentt, born in London, immigrated to the U.S. when only six. He achieved a good amateur record but was knocked out in the first round in his professional debut. He then gained 10 wins against almost anonymous opponents and became WBO champion in his 12th professional contest.

With television continuing to pour millions of dollars into any fight that carried a world title label, there was no shortage of people scheduling such bouts. Among them the WBA, WBC, IBF, and WBO recognized nearly 70 world champions. With three other bodies also trying to get in the act, there were 90 fighters claiming to be world champions. Not so many years earlier, there had been only eight world champions.

Despite so many irrational decisions, the WBO increased its influence in Europe, particularly in the British Isles, which by the end of 1993 claimed four of the organization's titles. This was proving very lucrative to British boxers and promoters. Chris Eubank (England), having retained the WBO super middleweight crown against several moderate challengers, faced Nigel Benn (England), the WBC super middleweight champion, over 12 rounds at Manchester. The contest ended in a draw, and so each fighter retained his title. The fight attracted 42,000, with Benn collecting £1 million and Eubank £800,000. It was seen by 16 million people on one British TV channel.

The promoter Don King, who had dominated the world heavyweight competition since persuading Pres. Mobutu Sese Seko of Zaire to stage the George Foreman–Muhammad Ali clash in Kinshasa in 1974, was copromoter of the Eubank-Benn bout. King had controlled the heavyweight division until Mike Tyson (U.S.) was jailed following a rape charge in 1992. With Bowe's management strongly opposed to King, the promoter no longer controlled the heavyweight division but remained active because of his worldwide television connections.

The outstanding boxer of the year was Julio César Chávez (Mexico), the WBC light welterweight champion. He remained undefeated after 90 contests over 13 years. Mexico's best pugilist ever had over the years held three world titles at different weights. But, when bidding for his fourth crown in September, most experts considered him extremely fortunate to be given a draw against Pernell Whitaker (U.S.), the WBC welterweight champion. The highly skilled and elusive Whitaker defied the aggressive Mexican, and Chávez was lucky not to lose his undefeated record. He remained a hero among his countrymen, and a world-record paying attendance of 132,899 had seen him retain the light welterweight title against Greg Haugen (U.S.) at the Aztec Stadium in Mexico City in February.

Other outstanding champions included Azumah Nelson (Ghana), who continued as WBC super featherweight champion though he was deemed fortunate to earn a draw with up-and-coming Jesse Leija (U.S.). Myung Woo Yuh (South Korea) retained the WBA light flyweight crown but, having won 38 of 39 contests over 16 years, announced his retirement. Virgil Hill (U.S.) successfully defended the WBA light heavyweight championship for the 14th time when he stopped Saul Montana (Mexico) in 10 rounds in November,

World and European Boxing Champions

as of Dec. 31, 1993

Division	WBC[1]	WBA[2]	IBF[3]	WBO[4]	Europe
Heavyweight	L. Lewis (England)	E. Holyfield (U.S.)	E. Holyfield (U.S.)	M. Bentt (U.S.)	H. Akinwande (England)
Cruiserweight	A. Wamba (France)	O. Norris (U.S.)	A. Cole (U.S.)	N. Giovanni (Arg.)	M. Duran (Italy)
Light heavyweight	J. Harding (Australia)	V. Hill (U.S.)	H. Maske (Germany)	L. Barber (U.S.)	E. Smulders (Neth.)
Super middleweight	N. Benn (England)	M. Nunn (U.S.)	J. Toney (U.S.)	C. Eubank (England)	V. Nardiello (Italy)
Middleweight	G. McClellan (U.S.)	J.D. Jackson (U.S.)	R. Jones (U.S.)	C. Pyatt (England)	A. Cardamone (Italy)
Light middleweight	S. Brown (U.S.)	J. Vásquez (Arg.)	G. Rosi (Italy)	V. Phillips (U.S.)	J. Castillejo (Spain)
Welterweight	P. Whitaker (U.S.)	C. España (Venezuela)	F. Trinidad (P.R.)	E. Loughran (Ireland)	G. Jacobs (Scotland)
Light welterweight	J.C. Chávez (Mexico)	J. Coggi (Arg.)	C. Murray (U.S.)	Z. Padilla (U.S.)	C. Merle (France)
Lightweight	M. González (Mexico)	O. Nazarov (Russia)	F. Pendleton (U.S.)	G. Parisi (Italy)	J. Mendy (France)
Super featherweight	A. Nelson (Ghana)	G. Hernández (U.S.)	J. Molina (P.R.)	Jimmi Bredahl (Den.)	J. Yoma (France)
Featherweight	K. Kelley (U.S.)	E. Rojas (Venezuela)	T. Johnson (U.S.)	S. Robinson (Wales)	S. Haccoun (France)
Super bantamweight	T. Patterson (U.S.)	W. Vásquez (P.R.)	K. McKinney (U.S.)	D. Jiménez (P.R.)	—
Bantamweight	Y. Yakushiji (Japan)	J. Jones (U.S.)	O. Canizales (U.S.)	R. Del Valle (P.R.)	V. Belcastro (Italy)
Super flyweight	J.L. Bueno (Mexico)	K. Onizuka (Japan)	J. Borboa (Mexico)	Johnny Bredahl (Den.)	—
Flyweight	Y. Arbachakov (Russia)	D. Griman (Venezuela)	A. Pohan (Indon.)	J. Matlala (South Africa)	L. Camputaro (Italy)
Light flyweight	M. Carbajal (U.S.)	L. Gámez (Venezuela)	M. Carbajal (U.S.)	J. Camacho (P.R.)	—
Strawweight	R. López (Mexico)	C. Porpaoin (Thailand)	R. Vorapin (Thailand)	vacant	—

[1]World Boxing Council. [2]World Boxing Association. [3]International Boxing Federation. [4]World Boxing Organization.

but Hill was criticized because it was thought he had faced too many unimpressive challengers. Ricardo López (Mexico) continued to dominate the WBC strawweight division, as did Genaro Hernandez (U.S.) the WBA super featherweight and Michael Carbajal (U.S.) the WBC and IBF light flyweight. One of the brightest of the champions was Julio Borboa (Mexico), who won and defended the IBF super flyweight title twice.

Professional boxing increased throughout Europe, mainly because the countries of Eastern Europe, where it had been banned, were now joining the chase. The European Boxing Union at its last congress accepted affiliation from Russia, Ukraine, Romania, and Latvia and gave provisional membership to Poland and Bulgaria. World title matches also were held in China and elsewhere in Asia. Good attendances and large television audiences were reported.

Boxing in the U.S. saw the end of an era when the management of New York City's Madison Square Garden announced that it was ending participation in the sport. The first arena (1874) was a converted railroad station at Madison Square; Tex Rickard promoted the first million-dollar fights there in the 1920s. The Garden, which later moved to different sites, was regarded as the most famous boxing locale in the world. In the future tournaments might be held there occasionally but only if arranged by an outside promoter. (FRANK BUTLER)

CHESS

Politics and money dominated chess in 1993 after Nigel Short, the English challenger for the world title, suggested to Garry Kasparov in February that the Kasparov-Short world-title match be conducted outside the control of the official world chess organization, Fédération Internationale des Échecs. Long-standing tensions between top players and FIDE Pres. Florencio Campomanes bubbled to the surface when Short won his final elimination round against Jan Timman of The Netherlands by a score of 7.5–5.5 in their scheduled match of 14 games at Linares, Spain, in late January.

Los Angeles had long been designated as the site of Kasparov's match with his new challenger, but the area's economic downturn and riots had led to the withdrawal of the city in late 1992. New bids for the match were submitted by several cities, and Manchester, England, was declared successful. Within three days of the announcement, Short, unhappy at the prize fund of just over £1 million, conferred with Kasparov. The two then agreed to break away from FIDE, setting up a Professional Chess Association to receive new bids in London.

The breakaway, after further bidding and controversy, was confirmed, despite little support from other leading grand masters. Those with a sense of history realized that there was a risk that world chess could reach a position similar to that before 1946, when the world title was viewed as a personal possession and the holder of the title could accept or reject challenges as he or she saw fit.

After the intentions of Kasparov and Short were determined to be firm, FIDE stripped Kasparov of his world title (in late March) and withdrew its services to both players. This was expressed by the organization's refusal to publish their rating numbers in its half-yearly rating list. As a result, Anatoly Karpov, world champion from 1975 to 1985, headed the ratings with 2760, well ahead of the rest. In accordance with FIDE regulations, he was then invited to play a FIDE world championship match against Timman, who ranked only 34th on the list.

Thus, the dispute resulted in rival world title matches, with Kasparov-Short being played in London, financed by

Garry Kasparov plays Nigel Short in their unofficial championship chess match. Although official world championship play between Anatoly Karpov and Jan Timman was under way at the same time, it was the unofficial match, won by Kasparov, that gained the most attention.
CHRIS COLE—ALLSPORT

The Times newspaper, ultimate winner of the bidding process, and Karpov-Timman to be contested in two parts, starting in The Netherlands. Both matches began in the first week of September. The London contest was run at the quicker time limit of 40 moves in two hours, as opposed to the Karpov-Timman match, which used the traditional 40 moves in 2½ hours.

In London, Kasparov took an early 3.5–0.5 lead over Short when the latter played too ambitiously at the start. Internal tensions in Short's camp led to the loss of his long-time supporter Lubosh Kavalek (U.S.), and the outcome of the match was practically settled when Kasparov took an 8.5–3.5 lead after 12 games. Despite gaining a number of promising positions, Short did not win a game until the 16th encounter. After 20 games the score was 12.5–7.5, and the remaining four games of the scheduled 24 were not played, although Kasparov and Short met in four quick-play games (score 4–0 in favour of Kasparov) and three games with nominated 19th-century openings (1.5 each) to meet contractual commitments to the media.

The Karpov-Timman contest was closer, as Timman was down only 5–4 near the end of the Dutch half of the event, but he seemed to have been more badly affected than Karpov by the realization that there had been no prize fund raised in The Netherlands and that the second half of the match was without a venue after Oman withdrew its bid. This situation was finally rectified when Indonesia agreed to serve as host for the second half of the match, which started two weeks later than the scheduled start in Oman. Timman's defenses collapsed during this half of the competition, and he lost games 14, 15, and 16 to concede the match by 12.5–8.5. Thus, chess was left in the same position as professional boxing, with rival world champions.

FIDE staged its Interzonal competition for the 1993–95 world title qualifiers in Biel, Switz. A huge contest for 73 players over 13 rounds in the second half of July produced 10 qualifiers, who, with seeded players, were to play elimination matches at Wijk aan Zee, Neth., in January 1994. The pairings were: Timman–Joel Lautier, France; Boris

A great curiosity occurred in January at a tournament in Wijk aan Zee, Neth.; Anatoly Karpov, despite winning the contest, lost a game to Larry Christiansen of the U.S. in only 12 moves.

White L. Christiansen	Black A. Karpov	White L. Christiansen	Black A. Karpov
1 d4	Nf6	7 e4	cxd4
2 c4	e6	8 Nxd4	Nc6
3 Nf3	b6	9 Nxc6	Bxc6
4 a3	Ba6	10 Bf4	Nh5
5 Qc2	Bb7	11 Be3	Bd6?
6 Nc3	c5	12 Qd1	Black resigned

Gelfand, Belarus–Michael Adams, England; Gata Kamsky, U.S.–Paul van der Sterren, The Netherlands; Valery Salov, a Russian living in Spain–A. Khalifman, a fellow Russian; Viswanathan Anand, India–Artur Yusupov, a Russian living in Germany; Vladimir Kramnik, Russia–Leonid Yudasin, a Russian living in Israel. One of the surprising losers at Biel was Judit Polgar, the 17-year-old Hungarian prodigy who won the Hastings tournament in January jointly with Yevgeny Bareyev of Russia and later that month beat veteran Boris Spassky in a match in Budapest.

The eclipse of the former Soviet school of chess, owing to the discontinuance of government subsidies and to the number of former Soviet citizens living abroad and in the process of qualifying for other countries, was demonstrated when the world team championship at Lucerne, Switz., on October 23–November 3 produced a decisive U.S. win, ahead of Ukraine, with Russia in third place of the 10 countries in contention. Four of the U.S. team of six had learned their chess in the former Soviet Union.

The strongest tournament of the year was at Linares, where Kasparov scored 10 points out of 13 to defeat Anand and Karpov by a point and a half.

A great loss in 1993 was the death in New York City of Reuben Fine, a leading grand master of the period 1935–50 and author of such useful books as *Modern Chess Openings* (1939) and *Basic Chess Endings* (1941). The British Chess Federation award for Book of the Year went to *The Oxford Companion to Chess* (new edition of 1992).

(BERNARD CAFFERTY)

CONTRACT BRIDGE

Europe in 1993 continued to make progress in contract bridge, relative to the rest of the world, but strong measures were being taken by the American Contract Bridge League (ACBL) to regain its leading place in the game. For the second consecutive time, Europeans were the finalists in the Bermuda Bowl world open team championship. Held in Santiago, Chile, it was contested by 16 teams that had been successful in zonal eliminations. In the final, consisting of 160 boards, The Netherlands defeated Norway by 350 international match points (imps) to 316. The winners were Enri Leufkens, Berry Westra, Wubbo de Boer, Bauke Muller, Piet Jansen, and Jan Westerhof; with an average age of 32 they were the youngest-ever winning team. Jaap Trouwborst was nonplaying captain. The losing semifinalists were Brazil and U.S. II.

In the Venice Cup women's series the United States won for the fourth straight time, beating Germany by 304.5 imps to 240. The winners were Karen McCallum, Jill Meyers, Sharon Osberg, Sue Picus, Kerri Sanborn, and Kay Schulle, with Jo Morse the nonplaying captain. The losing semifinalists were Sweden and Argentina.

The world junior team championship for the Ortiz-Patino Trophy was dominated by Europe. The winner was Germany, represented by Guido Hopfenheit, Roland Rohowsky, Marcus Joest, and Klaus Reps, with Michael Gromoller the nonplaying captain. They beat Norway by 254.5 imps to 203.

Membership in the World Bridge Federation (WBF) grew to 97 national contract bridge organizations, 37 of them belonging to the European Bridge League (EBL), which also received new applications from Andorra, Armenia, Georgia, Malta, and Ukraine. EBL membership rose to more than 385,000 registered players, nearly half the world's total and an increase of almost 67,000 since the beginning of 1992.

The WBF awarded China its first world championships, the 1995 Bermuda Bowl and Venice Cup series; they were to be played in Beijing (Peking). This recognized the exceptional growth of the Chinese Bridge Federation since it was first recognized by the WBF in 1980. At 50,000, its membership was the highest in the Far East Bridge Federation.

Computer bridge showed dynamic growth, with several programs allowing participation by modem in tournaments and even in private games. The ACBL agreed in principle to sanction a new computer network to run games on the same basis as ACBL-affiliated clubs.

Bee Gale Schenken, of the most famous married combination since Ely and Josephine Culbertson, died on October 5 at age 77. Until Howard Schenken, known as "the expert's expert," died in 1979 at age 73, the couple had offered a standing challenge to any husband-and-wife pair in North America. The bridge world mourned the loss on December 11 of Samuel M. Stayman, 84, one of the world's greatest players and a prominent administrator of contract bridge organizations. His name was best known for the Stayman Convention, an artificial bidding device for no-trump play used by nearly all players.

(ALBERT G. DORMER)

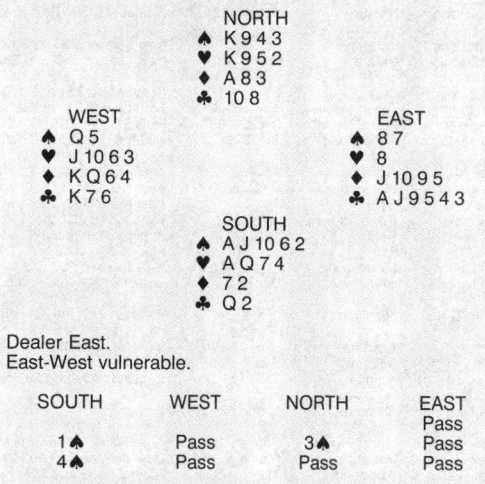

The narrowing gap between male and female experts was exemplified by a notable deal in the world team championships, where identical hands were played in both the open and the women's series. Two players displayed the same perfect technique. In the Venice Cup the declarer, South, was Kerri Shuman Sanborn, whom many considered the leading woman player in the U.S.

NORTH
♠ K 9 4 3
♥ K 9 5 2
♦ A 8 3
♣ 10 8

WEST
♠ Q 5
♥ J 10 6 3
♦ K Q 6 4
♣ K 7 6

EAST
♠ 8 7
♥ 8
♦ J 10 9 5
♣ A J 9 5 4 3

SOUTH
♠ A J 10 6 2
♥ A Q 7 4
♦ 7 2
♣ Q 2

Dealer East.
East-West vulnerable.

SOUTH	WEST	NORTH	EAST
			Pass
1♠	Pass	3♠	Pass
4♠	Pass	Pass	Pass

Opening lead: ♦K.

On the opening diamond lead, Sanborn played low in dummy, East contributing the jack. This encouraged West to play a second diamond, as the declarer had hoped. Sanborn won the second diamond with the ace, drew two rounds of trumps, and ruffed dummy's remaining diamond. She cashed the ace of hearts—a key play—and led a club. The defenders could take two club tricks and finish in either hand, but they would make no more tricks. If East were left on lead, she would have to play a club or a diamond. Declarer would then ruff in one hand and throw a losing heart from the other hand. If West were left on play, she could lead a heart but only at the cost of her heart trick.

In the Bermuda Bowl open event, Eric Rodwell followed the same sequence of play. Both Rodwell and Sanborn were winners of previous world team championships.

CRICKET

The return of South Africa to full-time Test cricket and the arrival of Zimbabwe as the ninth Test-playing nation made 1992–93 probably the busiest season in the history of the game. There were 38 Tests played in 14 different series in the 12 months ended Sept. 30, 1993, and, though some of the cricket was of questionable quality, the fourth Test between Australia and West Indies in Adelaide, Australia, would go down as one of the greatest Test matches ever. West Indies won by just one run, the narrowest winning margin in Test cricket history, after Australia had inched its way from an almost impossible position to the verge of a victory that would have given the Australians their first series win over the West Indies since 1975–76. The Australian captain, A.R. Border, who a month later became the highest run-scorer in Test cricket, was particularly disappointed by the defeat, but he had the satisfaction of leading his side to a handsome 4–1 series win against England in the summer and retaining the Ashes for the second time.

England had a disastrous year, losing eight and winning just one of its 10 Tests. It was no surprise when G.A. Gooch, who passed D.I. Gower to become the most prolific English Test batsman and recorded his 100th first-class hundred during the season, resigned as captain after the fourth Test against Australia and was replaced by M.A. Atherton. In contrast, India enjoyed something of a revival after a long barren spell, with a 3–0 series win over England and comfortable victories over Zimbabwe and Sri Lanka. Its only defeat came in the first Test series played in South Africa in 22 years and, in V.G. Kambli and A.R. Kumble, the Indians produced two of the most exciting young cricketers of the year. Kambli became only the third batsman, after Sir Donald Bradman and W. Hammond, to score double centuries in consecutive Tests, and Kumble's 21 wickets in three Tests were largely responsible for England's defeat.

B.C. Lara, a flamboyant, diminutive left-hander, and C.E.L. Ambrose, a towering fast bowler, also showed themselves to be worthy successors to the tradition of great West Indian cricketers, with the former making a faultless 277 against the Australians in Sydney and the latter taking 33 wickets at an average of 16.42, including 19 in the last two Tests, as the West Indies won the series 2–1. For Australia the ebullient M.G. Hughes (*see* BIOGRAPHIES) took 20 wickets at 21.60, and D.C. Boon, perhaps the most consistent Test scorer of the year, made 490 runs at 61.25.

England began the winter with a crushing defeat in India and ended it by losing to Sri Lanka. The England batsmen could never come to terms with the Indian spinners, and its bowlers provided no more than gentle practice for Kambli and 19-year-old S.R. Tendulkar, another prodigiously talented batsman, who gave M. Azharuddin a welcome change of fortune as the Indian captain. The England team was constantly troubled by illness, and by the end of the tour morale was so low that Sri Lanka had little difficulty in winning its first Test against England by five wickets. Only G.A. Hick, who topped both bowling and batting averages for the touring side, enhanced his reputation. But worse was to come.

Back home in the summer, England was systematically humiliated by a tough, well-organized, and well-led Australian side. After heavy defeats in three of the first four Tests, Gooch handed over the captaincy to Atherton of Lancashire, who salvaged some respect by captaining En-

Test Series Results, September 1992–September 1993

Test	Host country	Ground	Date	Scores	Result
1st	Zimbabwe	Harare	Oct. 18–22	Zimbabwe 456 and 146 for 4; India 307	Match drawn
1st	Zimbabwe	Bulawayo	Nov. 1–5	New Zealand 325 for 3 dec and 225 for 5 dec; Zimbabwe 219 and 197 for 1	Match drawn
2nd	Zimbabwe	Harare	Nov. 7–12	New Zealand 335 and 262 for 5 dec; Zimbabwe 283 and 137	New Zealand won by 177 runs
1st	South Africa	Durban	Nov. 13–17	South Africa 254 and 176 for 3; India 277	Match drawn
2nd	South Africa	Johannesburg	Nov. 26–30	South Africa 292 and 252; India 227 and 141 for 4	Match drawn
3rd	South Africa	Port Elizabeth	Dec. 26–29	India 212 and 215; South Africa 275 and 155 for 1	South Africa won by 9 wkt
4th	South Africa	Cape Town	Jan. 2–6	South Africa 360 and 130 for 6; India 276 and 29 for 1	Match drawn
1st	Australia	Brisbane	Nov. 27–Dec. 1	Australia 293 and 308; West Indies 371 and 133 for 8	Match drawn
2nd	Australia	Melbourne	Dec. 26–30	Australia 395 and 196; West Indies 233 and 219	Australia won by 139 runs
3rd	Australia	Sydney	Jan. 2–6	Australia 503 for 9 dec and 117 for 0; West Indies 606	Match drawn
4th	Australia	Adelaide	Jan. 23–26	West Indies 252 and 146; Australia 213 and 184	West Indies won by 1 run
5th	Australia	Perth	Jan 30–Feb. 1	Australia 119 and 178; West Indies 322	West Indies won by an innings and 25 runs
1st	Sri Lanka	Moratuwa	Nov. 27–Dec. 2	New Zealand 288 and 195 for 5; Sri Lanka 327 for 6 dec	Match drawn
2nd	Sri Lanka	Colombo	Dec. 6–9	Sri Lanka 394 and 70 for 1; New Zealand 102 and 361	Sri Lanka won by 9 wkt
1st	New Zealand	Hamilton	Jan. 2–5	Pakistan 216 and 174; New Zealand 264 and 93	Pakistan won by 33 runs
1st	India	Calcutta	Jan. 29–Feb. 2	India 371 and 82 for 2; England 163 and 286	India won by 8 wkt
2nd	India	Madras	Feb. 11–15	India 560 for 6 dec; England 286 and 252	India won by an innings and 22 runs
3rd	India	Bombay	Feb. 19–23	England 347 and 229; India 591	India won by an innings and 15 runs
1st	Sri Lanka	Colombo	March 13–18	England 380 and 228; Sri Lanka 469 and 142 for 5	Sri Lanka won by 5 wkt
1st	New Zealand	Christchurch	Feb. 25–28	Australia 485; New Zealand 182 and 243	Australia won by an innings and 60 runs
2nd	New Zealand	Wellington	March 4–8	New Zealand 329 and 210 for 7; Australia 298	Rain
3rd	New Zealand	Auckland	March 12–16	Australia 139 and 285; New Zealand 224 and 201 for 5	New Zealand won by 5 wkt
1st	India	Delhi	March 13–17	India 536; Zimbabwe 322 and 201	India won by an innings and 13 runs
1st	West Indies	Port of Spain	April 16–18	West Indies 127 and 382; Pakistan 140 and 165	West Indies won by 204 runs
2nd	West Indies	Bridgetown	April 23–27	West Indies 455 and 29 for 0; Pakistan 221 and 262	West Indies won by 10 wkt
3rd	West Indies	St. John's	May 1–6	West Indies 438 and 153 for 4; Pakistan 326	Match drawn
1st	England	Manchester	June 3–7	Australia 289 and 432 for 5 dec; England 210 and 332	Australia won by 179 runs
2nd	England	London (Lords)	June 17–21	Australia 632 for 4 dec; England 205 and 365	Australia won by an innings and 62 runs
3rd	England	Nottingham	July 1–6	England 321 and 422 for 6 dec; Australia 373 and 202 for 6	Match drawn
4th	England	Leeds	July 22–26	Australia 653 for 4 dec; England 200 and 305	Australia won by an innings and 148 runs
5th	England	Birmingham	Aug. 5–9	England 276 and 251; Australia 408 and 120 for 0	Australia won by 8 wkt
6th	England	London (Oval)	Aug. 19–23	England 380 and 313; Australia 303 and 229	England won by 161 runs
1st	Sri Lanka	Kandy	July 17–22	Sri Lanka 24 for 3	Rain
2nd	Sri Lanka	Colombo	July 27–Aug. 1	India 366 and 359 for 4 dec; Sri Lanka 254 and 236	India won by 235 runs
3rd	Sri Lanka	Colombo	Aug. 4–9	Sri Lanka 351 and 352 for 6; India 446	Match drawn
1st	Sri Lanka	Moratuwa	Aug. 25–30	Sri Lanka 331 and 300 for 6 dec; South Africa 267 and 251 for 7	Match drawn
2nd	Sri Lanka	Colombo	Sept. 6–10	Sri Lanka 168 and 119; South Africa 495	South Africa won by an innings and 208 runs
3rd	Sri Lanka	Colombo	Sept. 14–19	South Africa 316 and 159 for 4; Sri Lanka 296 for 9 dec	Match drawn

gland to its first win in 19 Tests against Australia in the final Test at The Oval. Boon, with 555 runs, and M.E. Waugh (550 runs) headed the Australian batting, and Hughes (31 wickets), gave strong support to S.R. Warne, who led the side with a decisive 34 wickets. Only Gooch, with 673 runs, and newcomer G.P. Thorpe made centuries for England.

South Africa's first home series in two decades, against India, produced some very dull cricket, epitomized by the final day of the fourth Test, on which only 111 runs were scored. South Africa won the third Test to take the series 1–0. A. Donald confirmed his position as one of the fastest bowlers in the world by taking 12 wickets in the match, and in the first Test, Tendulkar became the first victim of the newly introduced television replay. K. Wessels, the South African captain, who once played for Australia, became the first player to score Test hundreds for two different countries. South Africa also beat Sri Lanka to mark a successful first full year back in Test cricket. New Zealand defeated Zimbabwe and drew with Australia 1–1 in a three-Test series but lost to Sri Lanka and Pakistan. Zimbabwe drew its first-ever Test with India before losing the return match heavily in Delhi.

The series between West Indies and Pakistan was widely regarded as the unofficial championship of Test cricket. But, after a long hard schedule, the Pakistan team, captained for the first time by Wasim Akram, proved no match for the home team, for whom D.L. Haynes, with two centuries in the first two Tests, was outstanding. In domestic cricket, Middlesex won the first four-day championship in England, while one-day trophies were won by Warwickshire (NatWest), Derbyshire (Benson and Hedges), and Glamorgan (Sunday League). New South Wales won the Sheffield Shield in Australia, and Northern Districts took the Shell Trophy in New Zealand. (ANDREW LONGMORE)

CYCLING

Cycling's most prized record, for distance covered in one hour, was broken twice in seven days in 1993 by riders from Britain. On July 17 Graeme Obree of Scotland covered 51.596 km at the Olympic Hall velodrome in Hamar, Norway, to beat the record of 51.151 km set in 1984 by Francesco Moser of Italy. Six days later, on July 23, England's Christopher Boardman, the Olympic pursuit champion, set a new mark in Bordeaux, France, with a distance of 52.270 km. No cyclist from Britain had held the record since it was first recognized in 1893.

1993 Cycling Champions

Event	Winner	Country
WORLD CHAMPIONS—TRACK		
Men		
Sprint	G. Neiwand	Australia
Individual pursuit	G. Obree	Britain
Kilometre time trial	F. Rousseau	France
40-km points	E. De Wilde	Belgium
Team pursuit	B. Aitken, S. O'Grady, T. O'Shannessy, B-J. Shearsby	Australia
Keirin	G. Neiwand	Australia
Motor paced	J. Veggerby	Denmark
Tandem sprint	R. Chiappa, F. Paris	Italy
Women		
Sprint	T. Dubnicoff	Canada
Individual pursuit	R. Twigg	U.S.
30-km points	I. Haringa	The Netherlands
WORLD AMATEUR CHAMPIONS—ROAD		
Men		
Individual road race	J. Ullrich	Germany
100-km team time trial	R. Brasi, G. Contri, R. Fina, G. Salvato	Italy
Women		
Individual road race	L. van Moorsel	The Netherlands
50-km team time trial	S. Bubenkova, A. Koliaseva, V. Polhanova, O. Sokolova	Russia
WORLD PROFESSIONAL CHAMPION—ROAD		
Individual road race	L. Armstrong	U.S.
WORLD CHAMPIONS—CYCLO-CROSS		
Amateur	H. Djernis	Denmark
Professional	D. Arnould	France
MAJOR PROFESSIONAL ROAD-RACE WINNERS		
Tour de France	M. Indurain	Spain
Tour of Italy	M. Indurain	Spain
Tour of Spain	T. Rominger	Switzerland
Tour of Switzerland	M. Saligari	Italy
Milan–San Remo	M. Fondriest	Italy
Tour of Flanders	J. Museeuw	Belgium
Paris–Roubaix	G. Duclos-Lassalle	France
Liège–Bastogne–Liège	R. Sorensen	Denmark
Amstel Gold	R. Järmann	Switzerland
Leeds Classic	A. Volpi	Italy
Championship of Zürich	M. Fondriest	Italy
San Sebastian Classic	C. Chiappucci	Italy
Paris–Nice	A. Zülle	Switzerland
Ghent–Wevelgem	M. Cipollini	Italy
Flèche Wallonne	M. Fondriest	Italy
Dunkirk 4-Day	L. Desbiens	France
Grand Prix of Frankfurt	R. Sorensen	Denmark
Tour of Britain	P. Anderson	Australia
*Milk Race	C. Lillywhite	Britain
*Tour DuPont	R. Alcala	Mexico

*Mixed professional and amateur

Obree's ride came less than 24 hours after his unsuccessful attempt to break the record on the same track; he covered 50.69 km. He achieved the record on a self-built bicycle that included parts from a domestic washing machine and a handlebar section from a child's bike. He returned to the Hamar track in August to win the world 4,000-m pursuit title. The world record for this event fell three times in two

BRUNO BADE—VANDYSTADT/ALLSPORT

Graeme Obree of Scotland wins the 4,000-m pursuit at Hamar, Norway, in August with a record time of 4 min 20.894 sec. Riding a homemade bicycle, Obree broke his own record, set earlier in the semifinals.

days. Philippe Ermenault of France beat his own mark, set at Bordeaux in July, with a time of 4 min 23.283 sec in the first round. Obree clocked 4 min 22.668 sec in the semifinals before beating Ermenault in the final in 4 min 20.894 sec.

The Hamar tournament marked the first time that professionals and amateurs raced against each other in an open world track program. Two other world records fell in this competition, to Rebecca Twigg of the U.S., who won her fifth women's 3,000-m pursuit title in 3 min 37.347 sec, and to Australia, which defeated Olympic champion Germany in the final to win the team pursuit for the first time in 4 min 3.840 sec. Tanya Dubnicoff won Canada's first women's sprint title, and Denmark claimed its first motor-paced victory through Jens Veggerby. Gary Neiwand of Australia won both the men's sprint and keirin championships.

The road race championships were contested in Oslo, Norway. The professional title was won by Lance Armstrong of the U.S. He defeated Spain's Miguel Indurain, who had earlier finished first in both the national tour of Italy, for the second year, and of France, for the third successive year. Indurain won the opening time-trial stage of the three-week Tour de France, the major event on the professional calendar, at Le Puy-du-Fou. He lost the lead two days later but, after the lead had changed hands four times during the next six days, he regained the yellow jersey by winning the 59-km time trial around Lac de Madine in northern France. He then went on to finish the race 4 min 59 sec ahead of overall runner-up Tony Rominger of Switzerland. Third place went to Zenon Jaskula, who became the first rider from Poland to win a stage. (JOHN R. WILKINSON)

FIELD HOCKEY

Australia won the Champions Trophy for the sixth time with a 4–0 victory over Germany in the final of the annual tournament for six nations, held in Kuala Lumpur, Malaysia, in July 1993. The Netherlands finished third, followed by Pakistan, Spain, and Malaysia. The Africa Cup was won in February by South Africa in a round-robin competition at Nairobi, Kenya, where Egypt was second and Kenya third. In June the Irish Hockey Union celebrated its centenary with a four-nation tournament in Dublin. Germany prevailed, The Netherlands taking second place, England third, and Ireland fourth. In July India gained the Alps Cup in Vienna by defeating Austria 2–1 in the final.

South Korea won the Intercontinental Cup at Poznan, Poland, with a 1–0 triumph over Spain in the final. Third was India, and fourth Argentina. Australia defeated England 5–2 at Reading and continued its success by winning a four-nation tournament in September at Hamburg, Germany, where Pakistan was second, The Netherlands third, and Germany fourth.

In women's hockey Australia retained the Champions Trophy at Amstelveen, Neth., in August, finishing ahead of The Netherlands, Germany, South Korea, Spain, and Great Britain. In April Scotland won the four-nation tournament in Cardiff, Wales, with Ireland in second place, England third, and Wales fourth. Germany won the four-nation tournament at Glasgow, Scotland, with Scotland in second place, England third, and France fourth. In the overall placing for the Prince Takamado Cup at Osaka, Japan, South Korea finished first, Australia second, Japan third, and Spain fourth. At the fourth Intercontinental Cup in July at Philadelphia, Germany defeated Argentina 2–1 in the final. Canada finished third, followed by Russia, the U.S., India, Scotland, New Zealand, Japan, Belgium, Italy, and France.

Indoors, Germany won the European championship for the seventh time successively, in London in January. England was second. (SYDNEY E. FRISKIN)

FOOTBALL

Association Football (Soccer). The qualifying competition for the 1994 World Cup finals in the U.S. was the highlight of association football in 1993. Among the early qualifiers for the 1994 finals were Greece, making its initial appearance in the finals, and Russia, for the first time as an independent nation. The others scheduled to play in their first World Cup finals were Nigeria and Saudi Arabia.

The growth of member countries in UEFA, the European soccer organization, continued with further additions from the eastern regions, bringing the total membership to 45 with two associate members. These two came from Czechoslovakia, the latest country to be divided on ethnic lines, as the Czech Republic and Slovakia. However, its national team continued for World Cup purposes as the RCS (Representation of Czechs and Slovaks).

At the club level the increase of 13 in the number of competing clubs provided an enlarged entry for both the Champions' Cup and Cup-Winners' Cup. The 1993–94 Champions' Cup was contested by 42 clubs, while 43 entrants competed for the Cup-Winners' Cup, and the usual 64 teams vied for the UEFA Cup. Among the new entries were clubs from Albania, Belarus, Croatia, and Moldova. Wales was represented for the first time in the Champions'

Table I. Association Football National Champions

Nation	League winners	Cup winners
Albania	Partizani	Partizani
Argentina	Newell's Old Boys	
Armenia	Shirak	Ararat
Austria	FK Austria	Innsbruck
Belarus	Dynamo Minsk	Neman
Belgium	Anderlecht	Standard Liege
Bolivia	Bolivar	
Brazil	Palmeiros	Internacional
Bulgaria	Levski	CSKA Sofia
Chile	Cobreloa	Unión Español
Colombia	Atlético Junior	
Costa Rica	unresolved	
Croatia	Croatia Zagreb	Rajduk Split
Cyprus	Omonis	Apoel
Czechoslovakia	Sparta Prague	FC Kosice
Denmark	FC Copenhagen	Odense
Ecuador	El Nacional	
El Salvador	Luis Angel Firpo	
England	Manchester United	Arsenal
Estonia	Norma Tallinn	Nikol
Faeroe Islands	B36 Tottir	KI
Finland	HJK Helsinki	Mypa
France	Marseille*	Paris St. Germain
Georgia	Dynamo Tbilisi	Dynamo Tbilisi
Germany	Werder Bremen	Bayer Leverkusen
Greece	AEK Athens	Panathinaikos
Guatemala	Aurora	
Honduras	Olimpia	
Hungary	Honved	Ferencvaros
Iceland	IA Akranes	Valur
Ireland	Cork City	Shelbourne
Israel	Better Jerusalem	Maccabi Haifa
Italy	AC Milan	Torino
Latvia	Skonto Riga	RAF Jelgava
Lithuania	Ekranas	Zalgiria
Luxembourg	Avenir Beggen	Avenir Beggen
Malta	Floriana	Floriana
Mexico	Atlante	
Moldova	Zimbrul	Tiligul
Netherlands, The	Feyenoord	Ajax
Northern Ireland	Linfield	Bangor
Norway	Rosenborg	Rosenborg
Paraguay	Cerro Corá	Olimpia
Peru	Alianza	
Poland	Lech Poznan	Katowice
Portugal	Porto	Benfica
Romania	Steaua Bucharest	Uni Craiova
Russia	Spartak Moscow	Torpedo Moscow
San Marino	Tre Fiori	Tre Fiori
Scotland	Rangers	Rangers
Slovenia	Olimpija	Olimpija
Spain	Barcelona	Real Madrid
Sweden	AIK Stockholm	Degerfors
Switzerland	Aarau	Lugano
Turkey	Galatasaray	Galatasaray
Ukraine	Dynamo Kiev	Dynamo Kiev
Uruguay	Peñarol	River Plate
Venezuela	Caracas	
Wales	Cwmbran	Cardiff City
Yugoslavia (Serbia and Montenegro	Partizan Belgrade	Red Star Belgrade

*Marseille was subsequently stripped of its title.

Cup. The formula for the Champions' Cup again featured a league system for the last eight teams.

European Cup-Winners' Cup. Parma of Italy achieved its first European prize with a well-merited 3–1 win over the Belgian club Antwerp, another first-time finalist, at Wembley on May 12. There was a noticeable clash of styles, with Parma's attractive pattern-weaving proving more rewarding than Antwerp's more direct methods. The Italians took the lead after nine minutes. Antwerp goalkeeper Stevan Stojanovic misjudged Luigi Apolloni's corner kick, and the ball fell to Lorenzo Minotti, who volleyed into the roof of the rigging. The lead lasted two minutes before Daniele Zoratto's clearance hit Alex Czerniatynski. He showed smart reflexes in channeling the ball through to Francis Severeyns, who shrugged off a challenge to hit a cross shot under goalkeeper Marco Ballotta. But at the half-hour mark, Parma restored its lead. Georges Grun found Marco Osio on the edge of the penalty area. He crossed for Alessandro Melli to head in at 2–1. After that, it was not until the 83rd minute that Parma added to its score. Grun delivered a high ball that beat the offside trap, and Stefano Cuoghi was able to commit Stojanovic before slipping the ball past him.

UEFA Cup. Juventus of Italy won its second UEFA Cup trophy in four years, easily overcoming Germany's Borussia Dortmund 6–1 on aggregate scores. In Dortmund on May 5, the early exchanges gave little indication of the ultimate result. To the delight of most of the crowd, Michael Rummenigge put the Germans ahead after only two minutes. Thereafter, the Italians dominated. Dino Baggio tied the score in the 27th minute, and the unrelated Roberto Baggio, who was later named European Player of the Year, made it 2–1 four minutes later, then scored again after 74 minutes to win the match 3–1. In Turin two weeks later, Dino Baggio emulated his namesake with two goals, scoring in the fifth minute and five minutes before halftime. Andreas Moller added a third goal for Juventus in the 65th minute. Victory provided Juventus with its third UEFA Cup success, a record for the competition.

European Champions' Cup. Marseille became the first French club to win one of the three major European trophies, beating AC Milan of Italy 1–0 on May 26 in Munich, Germany. The Italians could not complain about the result, having had chances to score before Marseille struck with two minutes remaining in the first half. Daniele Massaro, preferred to Jean-Pierre Papin of France in the Milan attack, wasted three openings before the crucial goal was scored. That took place when Abedi Pele took a corner on the right, swinging the ball into the goal area, where Basile Boli rose above the Milan defense to glance a header into the far corner of the net. Papin was brought off the substitute bench in the 54th minute, but the match was already falling away from Milan's control. For Marseille coach Raymond Goethals it was a twilight achievement at the age of 72, but the celebration was short-lived. In the wake of serious bribery scandals, UEFA stripped Marseille of the European title and imposed a ban on entry for 1993–94. The team's millionaire president, Bernard Tapie, sought Swiss court action and obtained reinstatement, but threats of further sanctions by UEFA and the Fédération Internationale de Football Association (FIFA) against French national and club teams forced him to drop the lawsuit. The French Federation subsequently suspended three players and a club official and declared the club's national league title for 1992–93 void.

In Scotland the Rangers again were in dominating form, winning all three domestic trophies, including their 43rd league championship. In Poland, however, Legia Warsaw was deprived of its title when match-fixing allegations were proved against it. AC Milan had a season of contrasting fortune. After extending an unbeaten run in Italian league matches to 58, it suffered loss of confidence and a lengthy injury list. Its margin of championship success was reduced to just four points at the season's end. Milan's Gianluigi Lentini, the world's most expensive signing of the previous year at £13 million, had the misfortune to suffer severe injuries in a car crash, though he was expected to make a full recovery and attempt a comeback. But all 18 members and five officials of the Zambian national team were wiped out in an airplane crash. (*See* DISASTERS.) Meanwhile, the U.K. saw the deaths of two former champions: Bobby Moore (*see* OBITUARIES), the national hero who led England to its only World Cup title, in 1966, and at year's end Danny Blanchflower, who, in a 16-year playing career (1949–64), led Tottenham Hotspur to two FA Cups and a European Cup-Winners' Cup, played for Northern Ireland in the 1958 World Cup, and was twice named Footballer of the Year.

African countries continued to improve, with Nigeria beating Ghana, the defending champions, 2–1 in the World Under-17 Cup in Japan. This tournament was used to try out the controversial kick-in as a replacement for the throw-in. It led to more direct assaults on goal but wasted time and did nothing to improve the quality of play. Japan launched its first professional league; heavily sponsored by major local companies, it included former international players from around the world. Drawn matches were eliminated, first by sudden-death overtime and then on penalty kicks if no winner emerged. The games drew sizable crowds.

North America. Prospects for a successful World Cup in 1994 were enhanced when the US '93 Cup tournament drew a total of some 280,000 for its six matches. The largest crowd, 62,126, watched Germany beat England 2–1 in the first international ever to be played indoors on natural grass, at the Pontiac (Mich.) Silverdome in the Detroit suburbs. Within the U.S. the American Professional Soccer League carried on with seven teams, playing a 24-match schedule before the play-offs. (JACK ROLLIN)

Latin America. Qualifying for the 1994 World Cup tournament was the main concern in Latin America in 1993. Mexico was the first country to qualify, in May, after easily winning the classification tournament of the North American, Central American, and Caribbean Football Federation (Concacaf). Four months later Colombia surprised everyone and finished first in the South American Confederation's group A after beating Argentina twice—once in Barranquilla (Colombia), 2–1, and once more in Buenos Aires with a humiliating score of 5–0. Brazil recovered from a shaky start and took first place in group B. Bolivia provided the biggest surprise by finishing second in group B and knocking out two-time world champion Uruguay to qualify. Argentina finally got its berth for the World Cup by edging Australia in a consolation round.

In spite of its troubles in the World Cup qualifying tournament, Argentina demonstrated in Ecuador in June that it remained a major soccer powerhouse when it won the America Cup for the 14th time (in 33 attempts). This tournament, played since 1916, opened its doors for the first time to teams outside South America as Mexico and the U.S. were invited to participate. The Argentines edged Mexico, the surprise team of the competition, 2–1 in the final match. Colombia took third place after defeating the Ecuadoran hosts 1–0.

Brazil's São Paulo, however, continued to dominate club competition in Latin America. In May it successfully defended the Libertadores de América Cup after defeating Chile's Universidad Católica in a two-game series (with scores of 5–1 and 0–2). On December 12, moreover, it beat

AC Milan 2–1 in the Inter-Continental Cup. This made São Paulo the unofficial world club champion for the second year in a row.

In July Mexico took the Gold Cup, contested for by Concacaf's national teams, by defeating the U.S. 4–0 in the championship game. Costa Rica's Saprissa was the surprising winner of Concacaf's club competition.

(SERGIO SARMIENTO)

Rugby Football. *Rugby Union.* The 1992–93 season started with South Africa—eager to take part in as much international activity as possible after being banned from official international competition for eight years—making a tour of France and England in October and November 1992. The season ended with South Africa touring Australia in August 1993.

On the French section of the 1992 tour, the Springboks played nine matches, including two international contests against France. They won the first of the internationals 20–15 at Lyon but lost the second 29–16 in Paris. The English leg embraced four games, and the South Africans were well beaten 33–16 by England at Twickenham in the only international match.

At the same time of the year, the Australians toured Ireland and Wales, playing 13 matches altogether, including an international against each country. They defeated Ireland 42–17 in Dublin and Wales 23–6 at Cardiff. In accordance with the tradition of touring teams, they ended their tour by playing the Barbarians at Twickenham. They won that match 30–20.

The Five Nations Championship, played as always during the first three months of the new year, was won in 1993 by France even though they were beaten 16–15 by England, the favourites, at Twickenham in their first match. France went on to defeat Scotland 11–3 in Paris, Ireland 21–6 in Dublin, and Wales 26–10 in Paris. After their victory over the French, England lost 10–9 to Wales at Cardiff and 17–3 to Ireland in Dublin, but they beat Scotland 26–12 at Twickenham. Scotland started with a 15–3 win over Ireland at Murrayfield in Edinburgh and also defeated Wales 20–0 there. Ireland's 19–14 victory over Wales at Cardiff meant that they shared second place with England and Scotland in the championship table. Wales finished alone in last place.

The main event of the year was the 13-match tour of New Zealand by the Lions (England, Scotland, Ireland, and Wales combined) in May, June, and July 1993. The Lions, captained by Gavin Hastings, the Scotland fullback, won seven of their matches but were beaten 2–1 in the three-match test series. New Zealand won the first test narrowly 20–18 in Christchurch; the Lions won the second 20–7 in Wellington; and the All Blacks won the decisive third test 30–13 in Auckland. The New Zealanders went on to win the Bledisloe Cup—competed for between them and Australia—by defeating the Australians 25–10 at Dunedin.

France made a short tour of South Africa in June and July 1993 and won their two-match test series 1–0. They drew 20–20 with South Africa at Durban in the first test and won the second 18–17 in Johannesburg.

Rugby League. Great Britain and Australia reached the World Cup final, which was staged at Wembley, London, on Oct. 24, 1992. Australia won the final 10–6. In March 1993 Great Britain beat France 48–6 at Carcassonne. It was the most points the British had ever scored in a match on French soil. The following month at Leeds, they again defeated the French, this time 72–6, a world-record score for a full test match.

(DAVID FROST)

U.S. Football. *College.* Florida State University won the national championship of college football by defeating Nebraska 18–16 in the Orange Bowl at Miami, Fla., on Jan. 1, 1994. Florida State's victory gave the Atlantic Coast Conference champions a won-lost record of 12–1. The Seminoles had a 5–1 record against teams ranked in the top 25 and became the fifth team since World War II to lead the country in both points scored and points allowed, with regular-season averages of 43.2 and 9.4, respectively.

The only undefeated team in Division I-A was Auburn (11–0), which was ineligible for a bowl game or the championship because it was on probation for having violated recruiting rules. The selection of the champion by writers' and coaches' ballots intensified the outcry for a play-off system because Notre Dame (11–1) was ranked second in spite of its 31–24 victory over Florida State on November 13. The Seminoles passed the Fighting Irish in the polls when Boston College beat Notre Dame the next week, and they stayed ahead when both teams won their bowl games, Notre Dame by 24–21 over Texas A&M in the Cotton Bowl.

Third-ranked Nebraska (11–1) won the Big Eight. Auburn was ranked 4th in the writers' poll but was not considered in the coaches' poll, and so the teams ranked 4th through 10th

FOCUS ON SPORTS

Quarterback Charlie Ward (17), winner of the Heisman Memorial Trophy, leads Florida State in his team's matchup with Notre Dame. Although Notre Dame won the game 31–24, at the end of the season Florida State was voted the number one college team.

in the coaches' poll were ranked 5th through 11th by the writers. Big East winner West Virginia (11–1) was the only undefeated championship contender with Nebraska after the regular season but fell to sixth in the coaches' poll after losing 41–7 to fourth-ranked Florida in the Sugar Bowl. Florida (11–2) won the Southeast Conference by defeating Alabama (8–3) in a play-off game.

Fifth-ranked Wisconsin (10–1–1) shared the Big Ten championship with number 10 Ohio State (10–1–1) and won the Rose Bowl 21–16 against Pacific Ten champion UCLA (8–4). The Big Ten also produced seventh-ranked Penn State (10–2), which won 31–13 over Tennessee (9–2–1) in the Citrus Bowl; it was coach Joe Paterno's 15th bowl victory, tying him with Paul ("Bear") Bryant for the record. The eighth and ninth teams, respectively, were Southwest Conference winner Texas A&M (10–2) and Arizona (10–2).

Florida State quarterback Charlie Ward won the Heisman Memorial Trophy, the Maxwell Award, and the Walter Camp Player of the Year Award—all honouring the best college football player in the U.S. Ward led the nation with the highest percentage of completions (64.5) and the lowest percentage of interceptions (1.05, with four). He also won both awards for the best quarterback, the Davey O'Brien Award and the Johnny Unitas Golden Arm Award.

The outstanding lineman honours went to Outland Trophy winner Rob Waldrop, an Arizona nose tackle, and Vince Lombardi Award winner Aaron Taylor, a Notre Dame offensive tackle. Nebraska's Trev Alberts won the Butkus Award for the best linebacker and Alabama's Antonio Langham the Jim Thorpe Award for the best defensive back. Texas Tech's Byron Morris led the country with 22 touchdown runs and 12.18 points per game in winning the Doak Walker Award for the best running back.

Marshall Faulk of San Diego State led the nation with 144 points and 2,174 all-purpose yards but played in 12 games and lost the per-game titles to players with 11-game schedules. LeShon Johnson of Northern Illinois was the all-purpose leader with 189.3 yd per game and the rushing leader with a season total of 1,976 yd. Tennessee's Charlie Garner had the best rushing average, 7.3 yd per carry. The team rushing leader, Army, gained 298.5 yd per game.

Nevada gained the most passing yards and total yards with per-game averages of 397.5 and 569.1, respectively. Nevada quarterback Chris Vargas' totals of 4,265 yd passing, 34 touchdown passes, and 4,332 yd total offense all led the country, and teammate Bryan Reeves tied UCLA's J.J. Stokes with 17 touchdown catches. The leading passer was Trent Dilfer of Fresno State, with his top-ranked average of 9.84 yd per attempt helping him accumulate the most efficiency points, 173.1. Tulsa's Chris Penn was the leading receiver with both 105 catches and 1,578 yd. Ryan Yarborough of Wyoming had the best receiving average, 22.6 yd per catch.

Mississippi led in total defense with a yield of 234.5 yd per game. Arizona allowed only 30.1 yd per game and 0.9 yd per carry for the best rushing defense, and Texas A&M was the pass-defense leader with an efficiency rating of 74.99. Texas A&M also allowed the fewest touchdowns, 10, and had both individual kick-return leaders, Leeland McElroy with 39.3 yd per kickoff return and Aaron Glenn with 19.4 yd per punt return. Orlanda Thomas' nine interceptions for Southwestern Louisiana led the country. UCLA recovered the most turnovers, 39, and Notre Dame's 10 turnovers lost were the fewest.

Judd Davis of Florida won the Lou Groza Award for placekicking but finished behind Alabama's Michael Proctor, with 22 field goals, and California's Doug Brien, with an .833 percentage (15 for 18) on at least 1.5 tries per game. Chris MacInnis of Air Force led all punters with a 47.0-yd average.

Other division I-A conference champions were Southwestern Louisiana (8–3) in the Big West and Ball State (8–3–1) in the Mid-American. In the Western Athletic conference Fresno State (8–4), Wyoming (8–4), and Brigham Young (6–6) tied for first.

The undefeated teams in Division I-AA were Pennsylvania (10–0) of the Ivy League, Boston University (12–0) of the Yankee Conference, and independent Troy State (11–0–1). Other conference winners in the division for less ambitious programs were Southern (11–1) in the Southwestern Athletic, Howard (11–1) in the Mid-Eastern Athletic, Georgia Southern (10–2) in the Southern, Montana (10–2) in the Big Sky, McNeese State (10–2) in the Southland, and Dayton (9–1) in the Pioneer League.

Professional. The Dallas Cowboys became only the fifth defending Super Bowl champion in 14 years to win a division championship the next year in the National Football League (NFL) when they finished the 1993 regular season with a won-lost record of 12–4. The Cowboys had won the 1992 NFL championship by defeating the Buffalo Bills 52–17 in Super Bowl XXVII at Pasadena, Calif., on Jan. 31, 1993.

Buffalo, the first team to play in three consecutive Super Bowls, lost all three and threatened to go to a fourth by matching Dallas' 1993 record, the NFL's best. The Houston Oilers also finished 12–4 with a winning streak of 11 games, the NFL's longest in 21 years, to gain first place in the Central Division of the American Conference (AFC). Buffalo and Dallas won the Eastern divisions of the AFC and National Conference (NFC), respectively. Kansas City won the AFC Western Division for the first time in 22 years, and Detroit won the NFC Central for the first time in 10 years. San Francisco in the NFC West was the only team besides Dallas to repeat as a division champion.

Detroit and the New York Giants improved their records by five games from 1992, the best gains in the league. Other teams making the play-offs in 1993 that had not done so in 1992 were Denver, the Los Angeles Raiders, and Green Bay, the latter for the first time since 1982. Minnesota and Pittsburgh joined the Giants, the Raiders, Denver, and Green Bay as wild-card teams, those with the three best runner-up records in each conference. Washington's record dropped the farthest, five games. The other 1992 play-off teams that did not return were Miami, San Diego, Philadelphia, and New Orleans, which became the third team since 1970 to miss the play-offs after a 5–0 start.

Table II. NFL Final Standings, 1993

AMERICAN CONFERENCE	W	L	T	NATIONAL CONFERENCE	W	L	T
Eastern Division				Eastern Division			
*Buffalo	12	4	0	*Dallas	12	4	0
Miami	9	7	0	*New York Giants	11	5	0
New York Jets	8	8	0	Philadelphia	8	8	0
New England	5	11	0	Phoenix	7	9	0
Indianapolis	4	12	0	Washington	4	12	0
Central Division				Central Division			
*Houston	12	4	0	*Detroit	10	6	0
*Pittsburgh	9	7	0	*Minnesota	9	7	0
Cleveland	7	9	0	*Green Bay	9	7	0
Cincinnati	3	13	0	Chicago	7	9	0
				Tampa Bay	5	11	0
Western Division				Western Division			
*Kansas City	11	5	0	*San Francisco	10	6	0
*Los Angeles Raiders	10	6	0	New Orleans	8	8	0
*Denver	9	7	0	Atlanta	6	10	0
San Diego	8	8	0	Los Angeles Rams	5	11	0
Seattle	6	10	0				

*Qualified for play-offs.

The season was the NFL's first with a collectively bargained system of unrestricted free agency, and the most prominent player to change teams was defensive end Reggie White, whose 13 sacks for Green Bay tied New Orleans' Renaldo Turnbull for the NFC lead. Kansas City had two likely Hall of Famers who were cast off late in their careers, free-agent halfback Marcus Allen and traded quarterback Joe Montana. The 1994 season was to be the first with team salary caps tied to television revenues, and the caps were higher than anticipated after the Fox network outbid CBS by $25 million a year, leaving CBS without an NFL contract for the first time after 38 years.

NFL scoring, at 18.7 points per team per game, was the lowest since the 18.3 average in 1978, the last season before new rules made passing easier. San Francisco led the NFL with both 402.2 yd and 29.6 points per game and led the NFC in passing yards. Miami was the NFL leader with 272.1 yd passing per game and the AFC leader in total yardage.

The top defensive teams in the NFL were the Giants, allowing 12.8 points per game, and Minnesota, with an average yield of 275.3 yd. New Orleans allowed the fewest passing yards, 162.9 per game, and Houston had the best defense against the run, allowing an average of 79.6 yd per game, and the most pass interceptions, 26. Buffalo's defense led the league with 24 fumble recoveries and 47 turnovers.

At the other extreme, Atlanta's 24.1 points allowed per game were the NFL's worst, and Cincinnati scored the fewest points, 11.7 per game. Chicago gained the fewest total and passing yards; Indianapolis gained the fewest rushing yards and gave up the most total and rushing yards; and San Diego gave up the most passing yards. Houston lost a league-high 45 turnovers.

San Francisco's Steve Young (*see* BIOGRAPHIES) became the first NFL quarterback ever to lead the league in passing for three straight seasons with 101.5 rating points, which also made him the first to clear 100 three consecutive times. Young's 29 touchdown passes and average gain of 8.71 yd per pass were league highs. Teammate Jerry Rice led the NFL with 1,503 yd receiving, a record eighth consecutive season with at least 1,000. Rice led the league with 16 touchdowns and tied Atlanta's Andre Rison with 15 on pass receptions.

Troy Aikman's completion percentage of .691 led the NFL, and his Dallas team threw a league-low six interceptions. Pittsburgh's Neil O'Donnell had the NFL's lowest interception rate, with seven for 1.4%. Denver's John Elway led the AFC with a passer rating of 92.8 and the NFL with 4,030 yd passing. Vinny Testaverde's 21-for-23 passing for Cleveland against the Los Angeles Rams set a single-game record for completion percentage at 91.3%.

Green Bay wide receiver Sterling Sharpe broke his own record with 112 catches, becoming the first to catch more than 100 in consecutive years. The Raiders' James Jett averaged 23.4 yd per catch, the most for anyone with at least 30 catches.

Dallas' Emmitt Smith was the fourth player ever to lead the league three consecutive years in rushing, with 1,486 yd. His 1,900 yd from scrimmage and 5.3 yd per carry also led the league. Marcus Allen led the NFL with 12 rushing touchdowns and the AFC with 15 total touchdowns. Buffalo's Thurman Thomas led the AFC with 1,315 yd rushing and 1,702 yd from scrimmage. Neil Smith of Kansas City had the most sacks with 15.

Two kickers broke the record for consecutive field goals, first New Orleans' Morten Anderson with 25 and then San Diego's John Carney with 29. Raiders kicker Jeff Jaeger led the league with 132 points, two more than NFC leader Jason Hanson of Detroit. Pittsburgh's Gary Anderson had the best field-goal percentage, .933 on 28 for 30. Greg Montgomery of Houston led punters with a 45.6-yd average. Tyrone Hughes of New Orleans had the best punt return average, 13.6 yd.

The NFL granted franchises for its expansion to 30 teams in 1995. The newcomers would be the Jacksonville (Fla.) Jaguars and the Carolina Panthers of Charlotte, N.C.

Canadian Football. The Edmonton Eskimos in 1993 won their 11th Canadian Football League (CFL) championship, and their first since 1987, when they defeated the Winnipeg Blue Bombers 33–23 in the Grey Cup game at Calgary, Alta., on November 28. The game's Most Valuable Player was Edmonton quarterback Damon Allen, whose brother, Marcus, was an NFL star.

Calgary quarterback Doug Flutie was the first player to win a Most Outstanding Player award for a third consecutive season. Defending champion Calgary had the league's best regular-season record, 15–3, to win the Western Division but lost in the play-offs to Edmonton (12–6), the second-place Western team. In winning the Eastern Division, Winnipeg (14–4) was led by Most Outstanding Canadian David Sapunjis, the CFL receiving leader with a league-record 103 catches.

Flutie set a CFL record with 44 touchdown passes and led the league with a passer rating of 96.6, 416 completions, and 6,092 yd passing. The leading runners were Mike Richardson with 925 yd rushing for Winnipeg and Mike Oliphant with 1,572 yd from scrimmage for Sacramento, a new expansion franchise and the CFL's first team in the United States.

(KEVIN M. LAMB)

GOLF

The golfing wheel of skill, as opposed to fortune, turned decisively back to the United States in 1993. The partial supremacy that Europe had enjoyed through the 1980s was ended as Americans dominated competition on a number of fronts. They retained the Ryder Cup at the Belfry, winning on British soil for the first time since 1981; won the World Cup for the second successive year; regained the Alfred Dunhill Cup; held very easily on to the Walker Cup; and, in the hands of Corey Pavin, recaptured the Suntory World Matchplay Championship for the first time since 1979.

Europe, on the other hand, could claim only limited success. Nick Faldo of the U.K. remained, as he had been all year, at the head of the Sony world rankings, while Bernhard Langer of Germany won the Masters Tournament at the Augusta (Ga.) National Golf Club for the second time in his career.

Two of the world's four major championships, the United States Open and the Professional Golfers' Association of America (PGA) tournament were also won by Americans—Lee Janzen and Paul Azinger, respectively. In the British Open, however, there was a welcome return to form by Greg Norman of Australia.

The major confrontation between the U.S. and Europe was in the Ryder Cup, where each was represented by the best 12 players from their respective professional tours. Since 1983 the tournament had been very evenly contested, with the U.S. winning three times, Europe twice, and one match tied. During this period the overall points tally was Europe 85½, U.S. 82½; in five of those six matches, no more than two points separated the two sides.

This was again the case in 1993, with the U.S. winning 15–13 and the result in doubt until the final hour. Europe had enjoyed a one-point lead at the end of the first day, increased it to three halfway through the second, but by nightfall was back to just a one-point lead with 12 singles matches to come.

Europe's ultimate defeat was to a large extent due to the failure of its best players to win a single point. Faldo and Ian Woosnam both halved their games against, respectively, Azinger and Fred Couples, but Severiano Ballesteros, against Jim Gallagher, Langer, against Tom Kite, and Jose-Maria Olazabal, against Raymond Floyd, at 51 the oldest player to have appeared in the match, all lost.

This said a great deal for the American resolve under the captaincy of Tom Watson. Even so, Europe was still tantalizingly close to victory, the two turning points being the three-hole lead Barry Lane lost to Chip Beck with only five holes to play, followed by Costantino Rocca of Italy, who was one up with two to play, also losing to Davis Love.

It is worth stating that there was no prize money in the biennial Ryder Cup. Conversely, there was £1 million at stake in the Alfred Dunhill Cup, a medal match-play event annually held at St. Andrews, Scotland. Yet the latter, contested by teams of three from all parts of the world, remained very much the subsidiary competition. Couples and Payne Stewart were again on duty for the U.S., supplemented by the big-hitting John Daly. They headed their qualifying group and, in bitterly cold October weather, defeated Sweden in the semifinals and then England, the defending champion, by 2–1 in the final. The strong man of the side was Couples, who won all five of his games and was 15 under par for 90 holes—remarkable golf in such conditions.

In much higher temperatures at Lake Nona, Orlando, Fla., a month later, Couples was in fine fettle for the Heineken World Cup (originally the Canada Cup) and, with Love, retained the trophy they had won a year earlier in Madrid. Between them, they were 20 under par for the four rounds, with both players' scores counting in the tournament's format, and they won by five shots from Zimbabwe, which was represented by Nick Price and Mark McNulty.

Among the spectators at the World Cup, held in his hometown, was Pavin, who a few weeks earlier had won the Toyota World Matchplay championship at Wentworth, Surrey, England. In the final he defeated Faldo, the favourite, by one hole. In the earlier rounds he had beaten Peter Baker of England, Price of Zimbabwe, and Colin Montgomerie of Scotland. Against Faldo, Pavin was two up with three holes to play but lost both the 16th and 17th in the 36-hole match. However, on the 18th Faldo hit his second shot into a bush and lost the hole to Pavin's par five. Pavin was the first U.S. winner of the tournament since Bill Rogers in 1979.

This was far from being Faldo's only disappointment in a frustrating year. Though he kept his place at the head of the world rankings, the major honours eluded him, and he was even overtaken in Europe's last tournament of the year, the Volvo Masters, by Montgomerie in the race to become the year's leading money winner. Faldo had led in this competition since the British Open in July, but Montgomerie, a consistent player who had earlier in the year won the Dutch Open, rose from fifth to first place by taking the Volvo Masters in impressive style. He had official earnings of £613,682 for the year. There was also something of a surprise on the U.S. tour as Price, the 1992 PGA champion, won four tournaments, three of them in a row, to finish as leading money winner with $1,478,557.

Faldo's biggest disappointment was his failure to retain his British Open championship at Royal St. George's, Sandwich, Kent, though in most years his golf would have been good enough to have done so. Tied with Pavin for first place with 18 holes to play, he then shot a 67 and still lost by two strokes. This was the result of some exceptional golf by Norman, whose last round of 64 was the lowest ever by a British Open champion. He was also the first British Open champion to break 70 in every round—66, 68, 69, 64 for a record aggregate of 267—as he took golf on to what Faldo described as "a new level."

Greg Norman takes a shot in the 1993 British Open, which he won with a 13-under-par score of 267, the lowest ever in the event. A top player for many years but with a reputation for choking, Norman previously had won only one major championship, also the British Open, in 1986.
STEPHEN MUNDAY—ALLSPORT

Norman's only previous major tournament victory had been in the British Open of 1986, but he nearly added a third, losing the PGA at the Inverness Golf Club near Toledo, Ohio, only in a play-off to Azinger after they had tied at 272 for the 72 holes. It was Azinger's first major title. Defeat for Norman meant that he had now lost play-offs for the Masters, U.S. Open, British Open, and the PGA. Faldo was third in the PGA, a stroke behind, and was an accumulative 22 under par for that event and the British Open without winning either.

Langer's second victory in the Masters at Augusta National was impressively gained as he won by four strokes from Beck of the U.S. Langer had scores of 68, 70, 69, 70 for an 11-under-par total of 277. Janzen, one of the more promising U.S. players, broke 70 in all four rounds of the U.S. Open at the Baltusrol Golf Club in Springfield, N.J., and with a total of 272 won by two strokes from Stewart.

The U.S. gained an overwhelming 19–5 triumph in the Walker Cup at Interlachen Country Club in Edina, Minn. It was the biggest margin of victory since the format was changed in 1965 from 36-hole matches to 18. The youngest amateur team ever selected by Great Britain and Ireland was overwhelmed by the more experienced U.S. players.

One of the outstanding American contributions in the Walker Cup came from John Harris, who at the age of 41 was making his first appearance in the tournament. A week later he achieved the even-greater distinction of winning the U.S. amateur championship at the Champions Golf Club near Houston, Texas, where he beat Danny Ellis by five and three. Among the players defeated in the earlier rounds was Iain Pyman, a member of the British Walker Cup team. He had won the British amateur championship at Royal Portrush, Northern Ireland, when he defeated Paul Page at the first extra hole of an outstanding final.

Lauri Merten won the U.S. Women's Open championship at the Crooked Stick Golf Club in Carmel, Ind., with rounds of 71, 71, 70, 68 for a 72-hole total of 280, one stroke ahead of Donna Andrews and Helen Alfredsson. But the leading money winner on the Ladies' Professional Golf Association (LPGA) tour was Betsy King with $595,992.

Karen Lunn of Australia had the double distinction of winning both the Weetabix British Women's Open at Woburn, Bedfordshire, England, and leading the Women Professional Golfers' European Tour (WPGET) money list. In the Open she had rounds of 71, 69, 68, 67 for a total of 275, eight strokes ahead of Brandie Burton of the U.S. Lunn's earnings for the year on a tour that was affected by the recession amounted to £81,266.

Jill McGill won the U.S. women's amateur championship when she defeated Sarah Ingram in the final by one hole at San Diego, Calif. The British women's amateur title went to Catriona Lambert, the Scottish champion, who beat Kirsty Speak of England by three and two at Royal Lytham and St. Annes, Lancashire.

Patty Sheehan (*see* BIOGRAPHIES), winner of the Mazda LPGA championship in Bethesda, Md., became the 13th golfer to be inducted into the LPGA Hall of Fame.

(MICHAEL WILLIAMS)

GYMNASTICS

The United States gained the number one ranking in women's gymnastics in 1993 after winning five medals in the world championships in Birmingham, England. U.S. gymnasts Shannon Miller and Dominique Dawes, both 16, won a total of five medals, three golds for Miller and two silvers for Dawes. Romania won one gold, three silver, and two bronze medals, and the other medals went to Belarus (one gold) and Ukraine (one bronze).

Miller's best performances were 9.825 points in the floor exercise, 9.825 on the uneven parallel bars, and 9.787 on the vault, which helped her clinch all-around honours. In addition, Miller and Dawes placed first and second, respectively, on the uneven parallel bars, and Dawes was nosed out for the gold medal on the balance beam by Lavinia Milosovici of Romania.

The silver medalist in the women's all-around was Romania's Gina Cogean, 15. She had been a member of the second-place Romanian team in the 1992 Olympics. The bronze medalist was Tatyana Lyssenko of Ukraine, the Olympic champion in 1992 on the balance beam.

CHRIS COLE—ALLSPORT

Shannon Miller performs in the world gymnastics championships, which were held in Birmingham, England, in April. The U.S. athlete won three gold medals, including all-around honours.

Of the 21 medals in the men's competition, gymnasts from former Soviet republics earned five golds, two silvers, and three bronzes. The individual star was Vitali Sherbo of Belarus, who added three gold and two silver medals to the six golds that he had won in the 1992 Olympics. Sherbo's unusually large winning margin in the all-around over Sergey Charkov of Russia was more than 0.5 point. Charkov had returned to world championship competition after an absence of five years following surgery to repair gymnastics injuries, and he did win the gold on the horizontal bar. Andreas Wecker of Germany was the second most successful men's competitor, winning silver medals on the pommel horse and still rings and a bronze in the all-around. Neil Thomas became the first Briton ever to win a medal in the world championships when he placed second in the floor exercise.

Valery Belensky, sixth in the men's all-around, competed under the flag of the International Gymnastic Federation because his republic of Azerbaijan had not been recognized by the federation. He had won the all-around crown in the 1990 World Cup competition.

Under new rules, from 1993 there would be no "team" prize in the world championships. Moreover, each nation would be limited to a maximum of two entries in the finals of the individual apparatus events.

(CHARLES ROBERT PAUL, JR.)

HORSE RACING

Thoroughbred Racing and Steeplechasing. *United States and Canada.* Suspense surrounded the voting for the 1993 horse of the year and also for virtually all of the divisional champions as many outstanding performers emerged but few horses dominated during an eventful season of competition. All of the champion Thoroughbreds of 1993, selected by ballot among representatives of the Thoroughbred Racing Association, *Daily Racing Form,* and the National Turf Writers Association, were to be honoured at the Eclipse Awards dinner in New Orleans, La., on Feb. 4, 1994.

Several strong horse of the year candidates—Kotashaan, Lure, and Star of Cozzene—came from the ranks of turf racing. The French-bred Kotashaan captured six of his nine starts in the United States while competing exclusively over the grass. His victories included the Breeders' Cup Turf and four other Grade I stakes, bringing his 1993 earnings to $1,984,100. Star of Cozzene won 6 of his 11 starts on the turf, including the Arlington Million and the Man o' War. He also finished second four times and earned $1,620,744 for the year. Lure gained six wins in eight grass-course starts and $1,212,323 in earnings. His biggest accomplishment was winning the Breeders' Cup Mile for the second straight year.

Both Kotashaan and Star of Cozzene were sold to Japanese owners late in the year. On November 28 the two horses met in the Japan Cup, a $1\frac{1}{2}$-mi event, in which Kotashaan finished second after jockey Kent Desormeaux misjudged the finish line. Star of Cozzene ran fifth.

The champion two-year-old colt would be decided between Dehere and Brocco. Dehere won four straight stakes, including the Hopeful and Champagne, before finishing a disappointing eighth to Brocco in the Breeders' Cup Juvenile, a race in which Dehere hemorrhaged. Brocco won the Breeders' Cup Juvenile by a commanding five lengths but then lost to Valiant Nature in the Hollywood Futurity in his final start of the year.

The three-year-old-colt division was headed by Triple Crown race winners Sea Hero, which captured the Ken-

Major Thoroughbred Race Winners, 1993

Race	Won by	Jockey
United States		
Acorn	Sky Beauty	M. Smith
Arlington Million	Star of Cozzene	J. Santos
Beldame	Dispute	J. Bailey
Belmont	Colonial Affair	J. Krone
Breeders' Cup Juvenile	Brocco	G. Stevens
Breeders' Cup Juvenile Fillies	Phone Chatter	L. Pincay, Jr.
Breeders' Cup Sprint	Cardmania	E. Delahoussaye
Breeders' Cup Mile	Lure	M. Smith
Breeders' Cup Distaff	Hollywood Wildcat	E. Delahoussaye
Breeders' Cup Turf	Kotashaan	K. Desormeaux
Breeders' Cup Classic	Arcangues	J. Bailey
Champagne	Dehere	C. McCarron
Charles H. Strub Stakes	Siberian Summer	C. Nakatani
Coaching Club American Oaks	Sky Beauty	M. Smith
Florida Derby	Bull Inthe Heather	W. Ramos
Futurity	Holy Bull	M. Smith
Gulfstream Park Handicap	Devil His Due	H. McCauley
Haskell Invitational	Kissin Kris	J. Santos
Hollywood Derby	Explosive Red	C. Nakatani
Hollywood Futurity	Valiant Nature	L. Pincay, Jr.
Hollywood Gold Cup	Best Pal	C. Black
Hollywood Turf Cup	Fraise	C. McCarron
Hollywood Turf Handicap	Bien Bien	C. McCarron
International	Buckhar	J. Cruguet
Jockey Club Gold Cup	Miner's Mark	C. McCarron
Kentucky Derby	Sea Hero	J. Bailey
Kentucky Oaks	Dispute	J. Bailey
Man o' War	Star of Cozzene	J. Santos
Meadowlands Cup	Marquetry	K. Desormeaux
Metropolitan	Ibero	L. Pincay, Jr.
Mother Goose	Sky Beauty	M. Smith
Oak Tree Invitational	Kotashaan	K. Desormeaux
Pacific Classic	Bertrando	G. Stevens
Philip H. Iselin	Valley Crossing	C. Antley
Pimlico Special	Devil His Due	H. McCauley
Preakness	Prairie Bayou	M. Smith
Santa Anita Derby	Personal Hope	G. Stevens
Santa Anita Handicap	Sir Beaufort	P. Valenzuela
Spinster	Paseana	C. McCarron
Suburban	Devil His Due	H. McCauley
Super Derby Invitational	Wallenda	H. McCauley
Travers	Sea Hero	J. Bailey
Turf Classic	Apple Tree	M. Smith
Whitney	Brunswick	M. Smith
Wood Memorial	Storm Tower	R. Wilson
Woodward	Bertrando	G. Stevens
England		
One Thousand Guineas	Sayyedati	W. Swinburn
Two Thousand Guineas	Zafonic	P. Eddery
Derby	Commander in Chief	M. Kinane
Oaks	Intrepidity	M. Roberts
St. Leger	Bob's Return	P. Robinson
Coronation Cup	Opera House	M. Roberts
Ascot Gold Cup	Drum Taps	L. Dettori
Eclipse Stakes	Opera House	M. Kinane
King George VI and Queen Elizabeth Diamond Stakes	Opera House	M. Roberts
Sussex Stakes	Bigstone	D. Boeuf
International Stakes	Ezzoud	W. Swinburn
Dubai Champion Stakes	Hatoof	W. Swinburn
France		
Poule d'Essai des Poulains	Kingmambo	C. Asmussen
Poule d'Essai des Pouliches	Madeleine's Dream	C. Asmussen
Prix du Jockey-Club	Hernando	C. Asmussen
Prix de Diane	Shemaka	G. Mosse
Prix Royal-Oak	Raintrap	P. Eddery
Prix Ganay	Vert Amande	D. Boeuf
Prix Lupin	Hernando	C. Asmussen
Grand Prix de Paris	Fort Wood	S. Guillot
Grand Prix de Saint-Cloud	User Friendly	G. Duffield
Prix Vermeille	Intrepidity	T. Jarnet
Prix de l'Arc de Triomphe	Urban Sea	E. Saint-Martin
Grand Critérium	Lost World	O. Peslier
Ireland		
Irish Two Thousand Guineas	Barathea	M. Roberts
Irish One Thousand Guineas	Nicer	M. Hills
Irish Derby	Commander in Chief	P. Eddery
Irish Oaks	Wemyss Bight	P. Eddery
Irish St. Leger	Vintage Crop	M. Kinane
Irish Champion Stakes	Muhtarram	W. Carson
Italy		
Derby Italiano	White Muzzle	J. Reid
Gran Premio del Jockey-Club	Misil	L. Dettori
Germany		
Deutsches Derby	Lando	A. Tylicki
Grosser Preis von Baden	Lando	A. Tylicki
Preis der Privatbankiers Merck, Finck & Co.	Kornado	M. Rimmer
Europa Preis	Monsun	A. Tylicki
Australia		
Melbourne Cup	Vintage Crop	M. Kinane

tucky Derby; Prairie Bayou, champion of the Preakness; and Colonial Affair, which won the Belmont. Sea Hero was awarded the $1 million Triple Crown bonus, making him the leading money-winning Thoroughbred of 1993, with earnings of $2,484,190. His only other win in nine starts during the year was the Travers, and he thus became the first colt in more than half a century to win that race and the Kentucky Derby.

The ill-fated colt Prairie Bayou established his class early in the season with several stakes wins and then finished second to Sea Hero in the Kentucky Derby. He went on to post an impressive victory in the Preakness before going on to the Belmont and suffering a fatal injury. He had won five of his eight starts and more than $1.4 million.

Colonial Affair, the Belmont winner ridden by Julie Krone (*see* BIOGRAPHIES), finished second to Miner's Mark in the Jockey Club Gold Cup later in the year. Miner's Mark, which defeated older horses in the Gold Cup, became a contender for championship honours with the win.

The battle for the champion older horse of 1993 was between Devil His Due and Bertrando. Devil His Due, a four-year-old, won four major handicaps from March to July, including the Gulfstream Park Handicap, the Pimlico Special, and the Suburban, earning just under $2 million. He then lost five straight races. Bertrando, runner-up in the Breeders' Cup Classic, was the second leading money-winning Thoroughbred of 1993, with earnings of $2,227,800. His three wins in nine starts included the Woodward, in which he galloped home by 13½ lengths, and the Pacific Classic.

The biggest upset in Breeders' Cup history took place on November 6 at Santa Anita when the five-year-old Arcangues scored a two-length victory in the $3 million Classic at odds of 133–1. It was his only start in the U.S. in 1993 and his first race over the dirt.

The champion three-year-old filly appeared destined to be decided between Sky Beauty, which dominated competition on the East Coast, and Hollywood Wildcat, her West Coast counterpart. Sky Beauty won the New York filly Triple Crown (Acorn, Mother Goose, and Coaching Club American Oaks) and then captured the Alabama for her fifth win in six starts. Hollywood Wildcat, winner of several major stakes in California, scored her biggest claim to the award in her division when she defeated older champion Paseana by a nose in the Breeders' Cup Distaff, a race in which Sky Beauty finished fifth.

Leaders in the two-year-old-filly division included Sardula, winner of the Hollywood Starlet, and Phone Chatter, which defeated Sardula by a head after a stretch-long chase in the Breeders' Cup Juvenile Fillies. By virtue of her three major-stakes wins during the year, including the Spinster, Paseana was expected to repeat as champion older mare in spite of her loss in the Breeders' Cup Distaff.

Honours for champion turf female were clinched by Flawlessly for the second straight year. Her four wins in five starts included a win in the Matriarch Stakes for the third straight year.

Even though Meafara finished second in the Breeders' Cup Sprint for the second consecutive year, she did win four of eight starts and seemed to be the leader of the competition for champion sprinter of 1993.

Mike E. Smith, with more than $13 million and a record 61 major stakes victories, led all the nation's jockeys in purse winnings in 1993, while Russell Baze emerged the leader in races won for the second straight year. Robert Frankel topped the nation's trainers in purse winnings, dethroning perennial champion D. Wayne Lukas, who had won the honour for 10 straight seasons.

Peteski, winner of the Canadian Triple Crown and conqueror of some of the finest American-based horses of 1993 in the Molson Export Million Stakes, was named Canada's horse of the year. He also won a Sovereign Award as Canada's champion three-year-old male.

Sovereign Awards also went to Comet Shine (two-year-old male), Term Limits (two-year-old filly), Deputy Jane West (three-year-old filly), Cozzene's Prince (older male), Dance For Donna (older female), Hero's Love (turf horse), and Apelia (sprinter). Individual achievement Sovereigns were won by Roger Attfield (outstanding trainer), Robert Landry (outstanding jockey), and Kinghaven Farms (outstanding breeder). (JOHN G. BROKOPP)

Europe and Australia. For the second straight year, the English Derby winner was sold to a Japanese breeder before the end of the season. Commander in Chief, which also won the Irish Derby, followed the 1992 English Derby winner, Dr. Devious, to Japan. The Japanese also bought the Italian Derby winner, White Muzzle. And although they failed to buy the Prix du Jockey-Club (French Derby) winner, Hernando, that colt's owner, Stavros Niarchos, did accept their offer for his top three-year-old miler, Kingmambo, winner of two major stakes races in France and another in England.

Opera House, conqueror of White Muzzle and Commander in Chief by 1½ lengths and a short head in the King George VI and Queen Elizabeth Diamond Stakes at Ascot in July, was another that was to begin his stud career in Japan in 1994. Sheikh Muhammad, who raced Opera House, had also leased his 1989 Prix du Jockey-Club and Irish Derby winner, Old Vic, to a Japanese stud. But that arrangement was for one year only.

All this activity was taking place at a time when business in Japan was entering a recession. But that nation's Thoroughbred racing and breeding industries were responding to pressure, particularly from the United States, to offer greater opportunities to foreign-bred horses. Japanese racing was the richest in the world in 1993, and its ruling body, the Japan Racing Association, was determined to be ready to face an influx of horses from all the principal breeding nations. For that reason, it was encouraging Japanese breeders to purchase many of the world's best horses.

The abiding memory from the season in Britain was sure to be the two false starts for the Grand National steeplechase. Only 9 of the 39 horses responded to signals of the second false start. The remainder set off and, although many riders realized the problem and pulled up at halfway, 12 continued on the second circuit and 7 completed the course. The race was declared void, and more than £60 million (about $90 million) had to be returned to backers.

Commander in Chief did not reappear after his Ascot defeat, but Opera House and White Muzzle met again in the Prix de l'Arc de Triomphe at Longchamp on October 3. They appeared to have the race between them until Urban Sea, a 37–1 long shot, swept past them during the final furlong. Urban Sea, a filly whose owners were from Hong Kong and Taiwan, beat White Muzzle by a neck. Opera House was half a length farther back in third, and the English Oaks winner, Intrepidity, stayed on to finish fourth in a field of 23.

Urban Sea, which was attempting the distance (1½ mi) for the first time, was a daughter of the Kentucky-based Miswaki, a horse that competed at much shorter distances but was also responsible for Misil, the best horse seen in Italy for some years. Misil won the Gran Premio del Jockey Club (1½ mi) two weeks after finishing an unlucky seventh in the Arc. He was also a close second to Opera House in the Eclipse Stakes and to the surprising Breeders' Cup Classic winner, Arcangues, in the Prix d'Ispahan. By November Misil, too, was in Japanese ownership.

The human star of European racing was undoubtedly André Fabre, whose Chantilly stable housed the winners of 34 of the 107 Group I race winners in France, including Arcangues. Fabre also won the English Two Thousand Guineas with Zafonic, the English Oaks with Intrepidity, the Irish Oaks with Wemyss Bight, and the Turf Classic with Apple Tree.

Vintage Crop wrote a new chapter in the history of international racing when he won the Melbourne Cup by three lengths from Te Akau Nick on November 3. Also winner of the Irish St. Leger, the seven-year-old gelding was the first horse trained in the Northern Hemisphere to win Australia's greatest race. (ROBERT W. CARTER)

Harness Racing. In winning a $75,000 leg of the Driscoll Series at the Meadowlands in New Jersey in June, four-year-old pacing gelding Staying Together became harness racing's fastest race miler. His 1 min 48.4 sec broke the previous record of 1 min 49.4 sec set in 1992 at the Meadowlands by Artsplace and equaled the world's fastest time-trial clocking set by Matt's Scooter as a three-year-old in 1988. Staying Together, trained by Robert McIntosh and

AL TIELEMANS—SPORTS ILLUSTRATED

In the turn for home in the Preakness Stakes, Prairie Bayou (left) begins the move that led to his victory. Three weeks later, in the Belmont Stakes, the horse suffered a fractured foreleg and had to be destroyed.

regularly driven by William O'Donnell for Canadian owner Robert Hamather, won the $205,000 Driscoll final in 1 min 49.4 sec. He appeared to have assured himself of Horse of the Year honours when in October he won the $396,810 Breeders Crown for aged pacers and then completed his campaign by winning the $200,000 Fraser Memorial at Northlands Park in Edmonton, Alta. His 21 victories in 26 starts gave the son of Panorama earnings of just over $1.1 million in 1993.

In August Cambest, a five-year-old son of Cam Fella, became the fastest harness horse of all time with an electrifying 1-min 46.2-sec time trial at Springfield, Ill. William O'Donnell drove the pacer for trainer Fred Grant to demolish the 1-min 48.4-sec record held jointly by Matt's Scooter and Staying Together.

Presidential Ball established an all-age world record on a ⅝-mi track when Jack Moiseyev guided the three-year-old son of Cam Fella to win the $197,472 final of the Miller Memorial at Rosecroft Raceway in Maryland in 1 min 50.6 sec in May. Trained by Bill Robinson for Canadian owner Tony Chiaravalle, Presidential Ball also won the $1 million North America Cup at Greenwood Raceway in Toronto in a track-record 1 min 51 sec and the $1 million Meadowlands Pace at the Meadowlands in 1 min 50 sec. Later the same month, Presidential Ball suffered only his second defeat of the year when archrival Life Sign (driven by John Campbell) won the $301,760 final of the Art Rooney Memorial at Yonkers Raceway, N.Y., in 1 min 52.2 sec on a half-mile track, with Riyadh nosing Presidential Ball out of second.

At Delaware, Ohio, in September, Life Sign turned in the performance of his career to win the coveted Little Brown Jug. Driven brilliantly by Campbell, he prevailed in back-to-back heats of 1 min 52 sec (a world record) over a track dulled by afternoon showers. The son of Abercrombie completed his year by winning the $300,000 Breeders Crown for three-year-old pacing colts at Freehold, N.J., in October, pushing his career earnings past $1.8 million.

Driven by Ron Pierce, the three-year-old colt American Winner in August at the Meadowlands won the $1 million Hambletonian with a 1-min 53.2-sec elimination-heat victory before romping home over archrival Pine Chip in the final with a 1-min 53.4-sec clocking. The time was a world record for two heats by a three-year-old trotter, and the first effort represented the fastest-ever Hambletonian heat win. Soon afterward, American Winner finished first in a $92,500 division of the Zweig Memorial at Syracuse, N.Y., in 1 min 52.6 sec, the second fastest trotting race mile of all time, behind Mack Lobell's 1 min 52.2 sec at Springfield in 1987. Attempting to become the first trotting Triple Crown winner since his sire, Super Bowl, in 1972, American Winner lost to Pine Chip in the Kentucky Futurity after breaking stride repeatedly in the second heat. Pine Chip had won the $532,000 World Trotting Derby at Du Quoin, Ill., in straight heats in September and in October added the $300,000 Breeders Crown three-year-old trot.

Queen L, a seven-year-old mare, wheeled 17 rivals in the final stage to win the Prix d'Amerique over 1⅝ mi at Vincennes, France, in January. The 1993 Elitlopp, run at Solvalla, Sweden, in June, was won by Sea Cove, a seven-year-old stallion owned and trained in Germany and bred in Canada.

New Zealand-bred seven-year-old gelding Franco Tiger, trained in Victoria by Glenn Tippet for Eric Anderson, was a clear-cut winner of the 1992–93 Inter-Dominion Grand Circuit title, winning four of the eight events. The $NZ 300,000 New Zealand Cup, run November 9 at Addington, Christchurch, was won by Chokin, a five-year-old pacer recording his 19th win in 26 starts. (RONALD W. BISMAN)

ICE HOCKEY

North America. Off the ice the National Hockey League (NHL), the major league in the United States and Canada, underwent reshaping before and during the 1992–93 season. On the ice the Montreal Canadiens won the Stanley Cup play-offs, ending the Pittsburgh Penguins' two-year reign, but the year's most intriguing and most productive player was the Penguins' 27-year-old centre and captain, Mario Lemieux.

NHL. In 1992 dissident club owners forced out John Ziegler as the league president, named Gil Stein as a temporary replacement, and chose Gary Bettman as the league's first commissioner. On Feb. 1, 1993, Bettman, the National Basketball Association's 40-year-old senior vice president and general counsel, took office as the NHL commissioner. Stein later left the NHL, and Bettman started to remodel the league.

Bettman supervised a realignment of divisions for the 1993–94 season, with new division names as well. The Tampa Bay Lightning and the Ottawa Senators started play in 1992 as expansion teams, and future franchises were awarded to Anaheim, Calif., and Miami, Fla., for $50 million each, raising the league total to 26 teams. National television coverage improved.

In the Dale Hunter case, Bettman showed that he would try to reduce unnecessary roughness and thus make the game more attractive to television. In a play-off game, when Hunter of the Washington Capitals rammed into Pierre Turgeon of the New York Islanders from the blind side seconds after Turgeon had scored, Turgeon suffered a shoulder separation. The league suspended Hunter for 21 games, representing the first quarter of the 1993–94 season. It was the NHL's longest suspension for an on-ice incident.

1992–93 Season. From October 1992 to April 1993, each team played 84 regular-season games (up from 80). Pittsburgh ended the season with 17 consecutive victories—a league record—and then a tie. It recorded the league's best record—56 victories, 21 losses, and 7 ties for 119 points. The other division champions were the Boston Bruins (109 points), the Chicago Blackhawks (106), and the Vancouver Canucks (101).

ROBERT BECK—SPORTS ILLUSTRATED

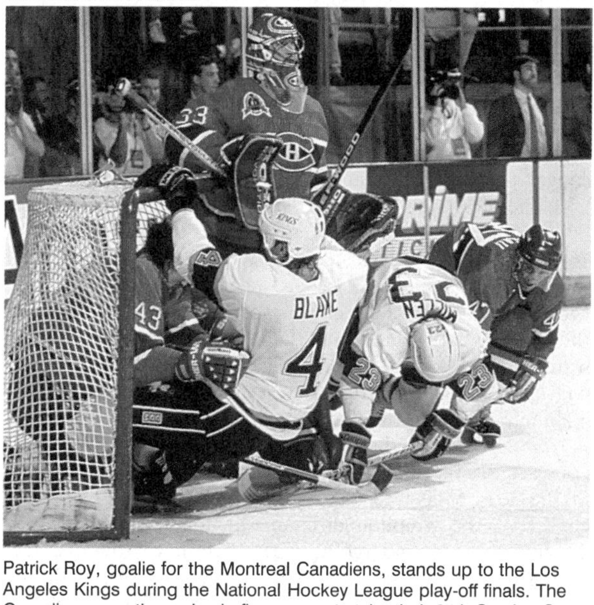

Patrick Roy, goalie for the Montreal Canadiens, stands up to the Los Angeles Kings during the National Hockey League play-off finals. The Canadiens won the series in five games to take their 24th Stanley Cup, and Roy was named Most Valuable Player of the play-offs.

Table I. NHL Final Standings, 1993

	Won	Lost	Tied	Points
Prince of Wales Conference				
PATRICK DIVISION				
*Pittsburgh	56	21	7	119
*Washington	43	34	7	93
*New York Islanders	40	37	7	87
*New Jersey	40	37	7	87
Philadelphia	36	37	11	83
New York Rangers	34	39	11	79
ADAMS DIVISION				
*Boston	51	26	7	109
*Quebec	47	27	10	104
*Montreal	48	30	6	102
*Buffalo	38	36	10	86
Hartford	26	52	6	58
Ottawa	10	70	4	24
Clarence Campbell Conference				
NORRIS DIVISION				
*Chicago	47	25	12	106
*Detroit	47	28	9	103
*Toronto	44	29	11	99
*St. Louis	37	36	11	85
Minnesota	36	38	10	82
Tampa Bay	23	54	7	53
SMYTHE DIVISION				
*Vancouver	46	29	9	101
*Calgary	43	30	11	97
*Los Angeles	39	35	10	88
*Winnipeg	40	37	7	87
Edmonton	26	50	8	60
San Jose	11	71	2	24

*Gained play-off berth.

Table II. World Ice Hockey Championships, 1993

Pool A	Pool B	Pool C
Russia	Great Britain	Latvia
Sweden	Poland	Ukraine
Czech Republic	Netherlands, The	Kazakhstan
Canada	Denmark	Slovenia
Germany	Japan	Hungary
United States	Romania	North Korea
Finland	China	Australia
Italy	Bulgaria	Belgium
Austria		South Korea
France		Spain
Norway		Israel
Switzerland		South Africa

Montreal (102 points) had the sixth highest total and became one of the 16 teams to qualify for the play-offs. The New York Rangers, who had the best regular-season record the year before, finished last in their division with 79 points and did not reach the play-offs. The Minnesota North Stars also did not gain the play-offs, and after the season they moved to Dallas, Texas, after 26 years in the Minneapolis-St. Paul area.

In the play-offs Montreal swept by the Quebec Nordiques (4 games to 2), the Buffalo Sabres (4–0), and the Islanders (4–1). The surprising Los Angeles Kings also advanced to the finals by upsetting the Calgary Flames (4–2), the Vancouver Canucks (4–2), and the Toronto Maple Leafs (4–3).

In the cup finals Montreal won three consecutive games in overtime and took the title four games to one. Montreal's 16–4 play-off record included 12 victories by one goal. Of those one-goal games, 11 were decided in overtime, and Montreal won 10 of them. The cup was Montreal's 24th, the most by any NHL team. The victory was especially rewarding for Jacques Demers, in his first season as Montreal coach, and goalie Patrick Roy, who was voted the Most Valuable Player in the play-offs.

Honours. Before the season Lemieux signed a seven-year contract for $42 million, the highest in NHL history. Early in the season he was found to have Hodgkin's disease, a cancer of the lymph nodes, and he missed 7 weeks and 23 games while undergoing 22 radiation treatments. Despite that, he returned and won the scoring title with 160 points in 60 games and received the Art Ross Trophy as scoring champion, the Hart Memorial Trophy as the NHL's most valuable player, and the Bill Masterton Trophy for dedication and sportsmanship. The other scoring leaders were Teemu Selanne of the Winnipeg Jets and Aleksandr Mogilny of Buffalo in goals (76 each) and Adam Oates of the Boston Bruins in assists (97).

Wayne Gretzky, Lemieux's predecessor as the league's outstanding player, missed almost the first half of the season with a herniated disk in the upper back. The Los Angeles Kings' centre scored 65 points in 45 games, by far his lowest output. But a healthier Gretzky became the leading scorer in the play-offs with 40 points in 24 games, including a record eight hat tricks (three goals in a game).

Chris Chelios of Chicago won the Norris Memorial Trophy as the best defenseman, Ed Belfour of Chicago the Vezina Trophy for goaltending, Doug Gilmour of Toronto the Selke Trophy as the best defensive forward, Turgeon of the New York Islanders the Lady Byng Memorial Trophy for sportsmanship and gentlemanly play, Selanne the Calder Memorial Trophy as rookie of the year, and Pat Burns of Toronto the Jack Adams Award as coach of the year. The all-star team consisted of Roy in goal, Ray Bourque of Boston and Chelios on defense, Lemieux at centre, and Luc Robitaille of Los Angeles and Selanne on wing.

(FRANK LITSKY)

International. A young Russian team, including only five players who had competed the previous year, won the 57th world championship by defeating Sweden, the defending champion, 3–1 in the Pool A final before a crowd of 10,500 in Munich, Germany. For the second year a 12-team pool had been split into two round-robin groups, played this time in Germany on April 18–May 2 at Dortmund and Munich. The first stage produced eight quarterfinalists. In the semifinals, which provided the best hockey of the tournament, the Czech Republic was beaten by Sweden, and Canada, thus far undefeated, lost to the Russians.

The first semifinal found the Czechs reeling from a Swedish goal by Charles Berglund in just 63 seconds, but Jiri Dolezal and Radek Toupal hit back for a 2–1 Czech lead at the first interval. Ulf Dahlen evened the score with the only goal of the middle session, and a third goal for Sweden from Mikael Renberg seemed enough for a Scandinavian victory until a last-minute equalizer by Drahomir Kadlec sent the game into sudden-death overtime. The issue was settled by Thomas Rundqvist, at 33 the oldest player on either side, with a shot that Petri Briza, the Czech goaltender, partially saved, only to turn and helplessly watch the puck trickle over the line for a 4–3 defeat.

The second semifinal was hardly less absorbing. Shayne Corson's opener for Canada after seven minutes was answered four minutes later by Dmitry Yuskevich. Early in the second period, Dave Manson and Corson scored power-play goals 12 seconds apart to put Canada 3–1 in front, but the Russians rose impressively to the challenge with goals from German Titov, Konstantin Astrakhantsev, Vyacheslav Bykov, and Andrey Khomutov to gain a 5–3 advantage at the second break. Eric Lindros briefly revived Canada's fading hopes, but scores by Valery Karpov and Titov sealed a 7–4 victory that prompted an admission from the Canadian coach, Mike Keenan, that "Russia outplayed us substantially."

In the final, Titov put Russia ahead after 99 seconds, jumping over the Swedish goaltender, Tommy Soderstrom, to slide the puck home. Andrey Nikoliskin increased the lead in the eighth minute after taking a pinpoint pass from Karpov. The Swedish forwards then pressed hard, but Andrey Trefilov, the Russian goalie who played in Canada for the Calgary Flames, withstood the onslaught and, in the 28th minute, Khomutov netted Russia's third score. Renberg prevented Trefilov's shutout with Sweden's lone goal midway through the final period.

The Czechs took the bronze medal by defeating Canada 5–1 in a third-place play-off. Switzerland was relegated to Pool B after placing fourth the previous year. The aggregate attendance at the 41 Pool A games was 226,379. The pool's top scorer was Lindros, with 17 points from 11 goals and 6 assists. Next best were veteran Khomutov, 12, and two more Canadians, Corson and Manson, 10 apiece. Briza was nominated best goaltender of the tournament. The award of best defender was given to Yuskevich, and Lindros was elected the best forward.

An eight-team Pool B, at Eindhoven, Neth., on March 25–April 4, was the only section of the world championship decided by a straightforward round-robin and provided the sensation of the championship when Great Britain convincingly won promotion to Pool A after an absence of 31 years from the sport's elite. Britain not only topped Pool B at its first attempt, following promotion from Pool C the previous season, but did so by winning all seven of its matches.

Including a rich vein of Canadians who had gained British nationality, the team never faltered after defeating its most dangerous rival, runner-up Poland, 4–3 in the opening game. Kevin Conway achieved the distinction of scoring the winning goal in three of the matches. World champion in 1936, twice runner-up, and twice bronze medalist, the nation that had pioneered the sport suffered a demise in the mid-1960s because of a lack of suitable rinks. The 1993 achievement was a culmination of a determined renaissance over the past decade.

Pool C, contested by 12 teams, was won by Latvia, with Ukraine runner-up and Kazakhstan third. Latvia gained promotion to Pool B, switching with Bulgaria.

Malmö IF of Sweden captured the European Cup, contested by national club champions, by beating Dynamo Moscow of Russia 4–3 in the final at Düsseldorf, Germany, on Dec. 30, 1992. Jokerit Helsinki of Finland finished third by defeating Lions Mediolanum of Italy 4–2.

(HOWARD BASS)

ICE SKATING

A drift toward opening top figure skating competitions to previously recognized professional performers was significantly indicated by the declared readiness of the International Skating Union to consider applications for reinstatement. Among former world titleholders hoping to take advantage of this new situation in 1994 were Katarina Witt of Germany; Elaine Zayak, Brian Boitano, and Christopher Bowman of the U.S., and Britain's Jayne Torvill and Christopher Dean. Gaining reinstatement would allow them and other professionals to compete again in world championships and the Olympic Games.

In speed skating the sprint event claimed particular attention in 1993. After it had taken 13 years to lower the world 500-m record by just one second, another two-tenths of a second were taken off in one season.

Figure Skating. In addition to the demands of technical skill and artistry, the ability to perform under pressure was clearly demonstrated in the women's world championships, in Prague on March 7–13, when a 15-year-old Ukrainian appeared not to have any nerves while winning the gold medal in her first appearance at the tournament until she cried with emotion while watching her high marks flash on the scoreboard. Oksana Baiul, first of the major contenders to skate in the final round, effectively put stress on her rivals with a cleverly expressed, very sound performance to a tuneful medley from film musicals. It was a sensational endorsement of a remarkable silver medal-winning display eight weeks earlier in her international debut at the European championships in Helsinki, Fin.

In striking contrast, the more experienced U.S. skater, Nancy Kerrigan, second in 1992 in Oakland, Calif., had become a firm favourite after leading in the technical portion of the competition. She began her long free-skating program uncertainly, however, touching her hand down on an opening triple toe Salchow and turning an intended triple Lutz into a single. Obviously feeling the tension, Kerrigan dropped to fifth in the final standings. It was the first time since 1969 that U.S. women skaters had not won a medal in the world championships.

Runner-up Surya Bonaly of France, the European champion, produced her customary high standard of jumps and spins, but artistic shortcomings cost her the gold medal. Lu Chen of China finished third, and Yuka Sato of Japan was fourth.

A model of unflappable coolness, Canada's Kurt Browning returned triumphantly from his series of back injuries to claim his fourth men's crown in five years. Although he included two great axels among his five triple jumps, a reduction in the number of his customary multiple leaps was amply compensated by majestic showmanship when depicting Humphrey Bogart as Rick from the classic film *Casablanca.* His energy-conserving interlude midway through his rendition portrayed humorous nonchalance with hands in pockets, an original touch that probably clinched the gold medal, the French judge responding with a perfect score of six.

Browning was outjumped by his compatriot Elvis Stojko, who landed eight triples, but Stojko's presentation suffered by comparison. Aleksey Urmanov of Russia placed third.

A second gold medal for Canada was achieved by Isabelle Brasseur and Lloyd Eisler in the pairs competition, breaking an eight-year Soviet/Russian monopoly. Their powerful overhead lifts and triple throws, interpreting Sergey Rachmaninoff music superbly, proved too good for the German runners-up, Mandy Wötzel and Ingo Steuer. Russia's Yevgeniya Shiskova and Vadim Naumov finished third.

A Russian eclipse in the dancing never looked likely, however. Maya Usova and Aleksandr Zhulin led a national clean

ANTON WANT—ALLSPORT

Fifteen-year-old Oksana Baiul of Ukraine performs in the world figure skating championships held in Prague in March. Baiul took first place over older, more established skaters.

sweep with a hypnotic blues free dance of dramatic power, comfortably ahead of their compatriots Oksana Gritschuk and Yevgeny Platov in second and Anjelika Krylova with Vladimir Fedorov in third.

Speed Skating. Falko Zandstra of The Netherlands, the previous year's runner-up, captured the overall title in the men's world championship at Hamar, Norway, on February 13–14. Johann Olav Koss of Norway, the 1991 winner, finished second ahead of Rintje Ritsma of The Netherlands. Gunda Niemann of Germany retained her women's crown on home ice in Berlin on February 6–7. Emese Hunyady of Austria was runner-up for a second successive year, followed by another German, Heike Warnicke.

In the separate world sprint championships, at Ikaho, Japan, on February 27–28, Igor Zhelezovsky of Belarus won the men's event for a record sixth time, and Ye Qiaobo retained the women's title for China. When Dan Jansen of the U.S. established a new world record for the 500-m sprint on March 21 at Calgary, Alta., his time of 36.02 sec bettered the figure he had set 14 months earlier by an astonishing 0.39 sec. At Heerenveen, Neth., Koss reduced the men's world 5,000-m record to 6 min 36.57 sec.

In the world short-track championships, at Beijing (Peking) on March 26–28, Marc Gagnon and Nathalie Lambert, both of Canada, claimed, respectively, the men's and women's overall titles. Italy, however, won the men's and women's team relays. (HOWARD BASS)

LAWN BOWLS

Though lawn bowls is played with skill by both sexes in all five continents and can produce champions from teenagers to septuagenarians, it was the young who were taking over at the top in 1993. Youthful muscles can produce a sensitivity of touch that more experienced players find difficult to match.

In England in 1993 Amy Gowshall, aged 14, skipped her mother to a national pairs championship, and at the international level Richard Corsie of Scotland proved himself the bowler of the year when he won the Mazda International Jack High Tournament in Australia; about two months earlier he had become the world indoor champion for the third time in five years at Preston (England). The world indoor pairs title also went to younger players when David Bryant (now 62) and world outdoor champion Tony Allcock of England were beaten by the younger combination of fellow England internationals Gary Smith and Andy Thomson.

In August, Cameron Curtis of Australia, just out of his teens, won in the singles and placed second in the pairs at the Pacific Games in Vancouver, B.C. Australia took the gold medal in the men's events and, despite a singles success for Carmen Anderson of Norfolk Island, New Zealand produced the best women's team. In other outdoor international matches during the year, South Africa celebrated its return to the world arena by defeating test teams of England's men and Scotland's women in April. In another test series, in New Zealand, the host team overcame Australia. (DONALD J. NEWBY)

MOTORBOATING

The American Power Boat Association (APBA) offered another season of racing for all types of boats in 1993. The big Unlimited hydroplanes were again dominated by Chip Hanauer (*see* BIOGRAPHIES), who chalked up another stellar season driving *Miss Budweiser* to a national title and an unprecedented nine APBA Gold Cup victories. Finishing second in the national standings was *Kellogg's Frosted Flakes,* piloted by Mike Hanson, and Mark Tate in *Winston Eagle* followed.

At the end of the inboard season, the winners were Gordon Jennings in K-Racing Runabout, Brad Mosier in the 4-Litre class and Grand National Hydro, Bill Morrison in the 2.5-Litre Modified, Greg Borschke in the 1-Litre Stock, Frank Richardson in the Grand Prix, Mark Weber in the 5-Litre class, Randy Haas in the 6-Litre class, Ann Fitzgerald in the 2.5-Litre Stock, Brian Ohlis in the Super Stock, and Tom and Tommy Thompson in the Jersey Speed Skiffs.

National champions were crowned in the Offshore category after competition near Galveston, Texas. Sweeping the title in Pro Outboard was Bill Westberry in *Spirit of Houston,* and in Offshore A *Frank's Marine,* driven by Frank Eiroa, took home the honours. The Stock Outboard title went to *Mobil 1* with second-year champion driver Robert Loeffler. Dan Weinstein in *Powerplay Racing* won the title in Offshore B, and Mac Seelig did the same in his Offshore C rig *Harrah's/Zubaz 777.* Allan Dunteman took the Modified championship in *Agitator,* and Stuart Hayin, driving *Recovery,* became champion in the Open class. The Super Vee title went to *INXS* and Ted Sabareese, and the Super Cat laurels were worn by Allan Feingold and *Apache Kid.*

In the U.S. Title Series outboard competition, winners of the eight classes were Jack Kuglar in RBH, Doug Hall in the 700-cc hydroplane, Tom Brinkman in the 250-cc runabout, Dan Kirts in both the 350-cc and 500-cc hydroplanes, Eddie Thirlby in the 500-cc runabout, Peter Crowley in the 250-cc hydroplane, and Jim Kirts in the 350-cc runabout.

The International Outboard Grand Prix series awarded three titles. Tim Seebold swept the series with a win at each tour stop to take the championship in the SST-140 class. The new SST-45 overall winner was David Dewald. With four first-place finishes in a row, Bill Seebold dominated the Champ Boat class. (MICHELE WESTON)

POLO

The highest-level polo played in the world, the Argentine Open, held at Buenos Aires on Nov. 27, 1993, was marred by unusually heavy rains and the absence of one of the best teams because of a suspension handed down by the Argentine Association. As a result, the overall competition was not of the usual high standards, and the final between Indios Chapaleufu and La Martina provided a lacklustre game, with the four Heguy brothers (Bautista, Gonzalo, Horacio, and Marcos) of Indios Chapaleufu winning their third straight Open championship 14–10.

At the U.S. Open, at Indio, Calif., in October, 10-goaler Memo Gracida led his team to victory and thus won his 11th Open title, a record for any player. The team Gehache, consisting of Gracida, his brother Rubin, Mike Azzaro, and Glen Holden, defeated Fish Creek 11–10, with the final goal a penalty shot by Memo Gracida. Cellular One, led by Adam Lindemann, won the Rolex Gold Cup at Palm Beach, Fla., 14–4 over Michelob.

In England the Queens Cup at Guards Polo Club was won by Urs Schwarzenbach's Black Bears 10–8 over Kerry Packer's Ellerston White. The Open championship for the Gold Cup was taken home by the Alcatel team of Peter Webb, Gabriel Donoso, Pici Alberdi, and Nacho Gonzales 9–8 over Ellerston Black. The climax of the season, the Coronation Cup, was won by England 8–3 over Chile. (ALLAN D. SCHERER)

RODEO

Once again proving himself the greatest cowboy of his era, Ty Murray of Stephenville, Texas, captured his fifth consecutive all-around cowboy world championship, based upon season earnings in two or more standard rodeo events. Murray competed in saddle bronc riding, bareback riding, and bull riding, qualifying in all three events for the $2.7 million National Finals Rodeo (NFR) held Dec. 3–12, 1993, in Las Vegas, Nev. World championships in seven standard Professional Rodeo Cowboys Association (PRCA) and Women's Professional Rodeo Association (WPRA) events are awarded on the basis of regular-season earnings plus money earned at the season-ending NFR and the National Finals Steer Roping (NFSR).

Murray took the lead in bull riding in mid-March and held on at the NFR to claim the world championship and $124,659. In addition to winning the first single-event championship of his six-year career in the PRCA, Murray claimed the NFR bareback riding award for the highest aggregate score (769 points) for 10 rides. His season earnings in all three events totaled $297,896, a new PRCA record.

Bobby Hurley of Clarksville, Ark., and Allen Bach of Merced, Calif., stunned the team-roping world by winning the last 5 rounds at the 10-round NFR. Hurley, who entered the NFR ranked fourth in the world, won the world championship in the event with $86,858.

Charmayne Rodman of Galt, Calif., claimed her 10th consecutive WPRA barrel-racing world title, staving off the challenge of newcomer Kristie Peterson of Elbert, Colo. Peterson, who at one time trailed Rodman by only $8,236, seemed destined to unseat the reigning queen of barrel racing until a tipped barrel in the ninth round cost her the NFR average—and the world title. Rodman ended the season with $103,610, including $16,317 for the NFR barrel-racing average award.

In bareback riding, Deb Greenough of Red Lodge, Mont., overcame challenges by former world champions Marvin Garrett and Clint Corey, as well as four-time Canadian champion Robin Burwash, to win his first world title. Greenough, a third-generation rodeo cowboy, concluded the season with $128,740.

In saddle bronc riding another Montana cowboy, Dan Mortensen of Manhattan, fought back the challenge of Craig Latham, of Texhoma, Texas, to win his first world championship. Mortensen ended the year with $150,062.

Steve Duhon of Opelousas, La., earned his third world title in steer wrestling. He dropped 10 steers in 49.3 seconds to win the NFR average. The $26,104 prize boosted his earnings to $113,450. Calf roper Joe Beaver of Huntsville, Texas, successfully defended his 1992 world title, capturing his fifth championship with $118,787 in season earnings.

At the National Finals Steer Roping, November 26–27 in Guthrie, Okla., Guy Allen of Vinita, Okla., gained his eighth world title, with $52,322. Roy Cooper of Childress, Texas, won the NFSR average award.

(GAVIN FORBES EHRINGER)

ROWING

Canada and Great Britain, with four titles each, were the most successful nations in world rowing in 1993. They were followed by France—with its first successes since 1962—and Germany, which each won three titles. China and Romania each took two championships, while the remaining winners were Australia, Austria, New Zealand, Spain, and the U.S.

In the world championships at Roudnice, Czech Republic, only two of the reigning champions and four of the 1992 Olympic gold medalists retained their titles. The standard of competition was high, with a dozen of the 23 events being decided by less than two seconds and only three by more than three seconds.

Great Britain took the honours in men's events by retaining its Olympic titles in coxed and coxless pairs and then adding its first win in world lightweight single sculls. Steve Redgrave and his Olympic partner, Matthew Pinsent, defeated Germany by 1.53 sec in coxless pairs, while the Searle brothers repeated their Olympic triumph over the Abbagnale brothers of Italy in coxed pairs by 2.09 sec. There was drama in the lightweight singles when Peter Haining lost his lead after hitting a marker buoy 40 strokes from the finish. He dropped to third place before fighting back to capture the title by 1.32 sec.

The French rowers won two titles, their best performance in 31 years. They beat Poland by 2.09 sec in coxless fours and Norway more comfortably by 3.73 sec in double sculls. In addition to the two British pairs, the only other reigning Olympic champions to win world titles were the Romanian coxed four and the German quadruple scullers. Germany retained its world eights title after holding off Romania by 2.25 sec, with the U.S. another 2.14 sec behind.

Canada won men's titles in lightweight eights and heavyweight single sculls, while Spain took the lightweight coxless pairs. The most exciting finishes came in the lightweight coxless fours and double sculls. The U.S. held off Switzerland by 0.72 sec in fours, and Australia denied Switzerland the double sculls title by 0.09 sec.

In the women's events there was another tight finish when China defeated the U.S. in coxless fours by 0.66 sec. China also won the quadruple sculls by a comfortable 4.24 sec over Germany. Canada also took two titles, in the single and double sculls, while Great Britain won the coxless fours after finishing second in the two preceding years. In coxed fours France beat Australia to gain its third title in the championships, and Germany took its third gold medal in the single sculls. New Zealand collected its third gold medal in double sculls, while Romania scored its second success by 1.54 sec over the U.S. in eights.

Germany dominated the world junior championships at Arungen, Norway, by winning all but 2 of the 14 titles. Australia and Norway were the remaining gold medalists, while 13 other nations shared the silver and bronze medals. Italy took six and Romania four, but no other country managed more than three.

At the Henley Royal Regatta in England, there were five overseas winners. The Grand Challenge Cup (eights) and the Diamond Sculls went to Germany; Brisbane (Australia) Boys' College won the Princess Elizabeth Cup (eights); and a double triumph for the U.S. was recorded by Harvard University in the Britannia Cup (coxed fours) and Brown University in the Ladies Plate (eights). In the 139th University Boat Race, Cambridge recorded its 70th win in the series—two more than Oxford. (KEITH OSBORNE)

SAILING

In his Farr 60 *Ragamuffin,* veteran campaigner Syd Fischer won the ocean race from Sydney on the Australian mainland to Hobart in Tasmania. This was the 24th time that he had competed in this classic event. Grant Dalton's Farr-designed maxi, *New Zealand Endeavour,* placed second.

Three multihull yachts competed in the round-the-world race for the Jules Verne trophy. *ENZA* of New Zealand (with some British help) was the revamped Nigel Irens-designed catamaran *Formulatag,* and the two French boats were *Commodore Explorer* and the trimaran *Charal,* which had been rerigged. All three set out at about the same time and made very good time, sailing nearly 800 km (500 mi) during some 24-hour periods. However, those speeds, of 15–20 knots, can be dangerous. On February 16 *Charal* ran into a submerged object or ice, severely damaging its starboard float, and on February 26 *ENZA* also struck a submerged object, shattering a dagger board and causing serious structural damage to the hull. Both boats were able to limp back to South Africa after making emergency repairs.

1993 World Class Boat Champions

Class	Winner	Class	Winner
Cadet	José De La Fuente (Argentina)	420	Bros Luciani (Italy)
Contender	Stuart Jones (United Kingdom)	505	Ian Barker (United Kingdom)
Dragon	Jesper Bank (Denmark)	Hobie 16	Shaun Ferry (South Africa)
Enterprise	Homi Motivalla (India)	J-24	Ken Read (United States)
Europe (men)	Olivier Backes (France)	Laser II	Roger Ford (United Kingdom)
Europe (women)	Dorte Jensen (Denmark)	Moth	Toby Collyer (United Kingdom)
Flying Dutchman	Jorgen Boysen-Moller (Denmark)	Optimist	Ramon Oliden (Argentina)
Flying Junior	K. Taragi (Japan)	Solo	Geoff Calveth (United Kingdom)
470	Jordi Calafat (Spain)	2.4 metre	Patrick Forsgren (Sweden)

Commodore Explorer, piloted by Bruno Peyrou (*see* BIOGRAPHIES), kept going in spite of being slowed by damage to the rigging and sails that was suffered in the southern oceans. After 79 days and some 6 hours, it crossed the finish line to beat the 80-day mark by a few hours.

The Vendée Globe Challenge, a nonstop solo race around the world, had more than its share of bad luck. Mike Plant lost his life while sailing across the Atlantic to enter the race. The huge ballast bulb fell off the yacht's carbon fibre keel, indicating that the boat most likely capsized with a sudden, violent movement. Then, soon after the event started, Nigel Burgess was killed. Sailing these boats proved to be a risky sport, particularly at night.

The Admiral's Cup series of events for ocean racers was contested off the southern coast of England in July and August. Early in the series the tides and wind were strong, and the courses were set in The Solent, the rocky channel between the English mainland and the Isle of Wight. Thus, it was not surprising that many keels were damaged, and Ireland's small-boat entry hit the Gurnard Ledge rocks so hard that the keel was wrenched off and the yacht sank quickly. Nobody was hurt, but the yacht was destroyed. The Irish tried to replace the yacht for subsequent races, but the rules did not allow this.

Among other mishaps the champion one-tonner *Brava* lost its mast, and the boats of the two top-scoring teams had a major collision, causing Australia's *Ragamuffin* and Italy's *Mandrake* so much damage that neither was able to compete in the high-scoring Fastnet race that concluded the series. Once again the Fastnet results produced a surprising team winner of the cup. This time it was the Germans who triumphed, scoring 279.13 points during the 12-day competition to 278.88 for Australia.

New Zealanders made an impressive showing again in the first leg of the 1993–94 Whitbread Round-the-World Race, which was launched at Southampton, England, on September 25. Dalton's maxi, *New Zealand Endeavour*, finished the first leg to Punta del Este, Uruguay, ahead of the pack, while Chris Dickson's *Tokio* (Japan-New Zealand) took the first-leg honours in the Whitbread-60 class. *Tokio* then ceded first place, however, to *Intrum Justitia* (Europe), which shaved two and a half days off the second-leg record and arrived in Freemantle, Australia, on December 9. *Endeavour*, with a broken mast, slipped to second among the maxis. (ADRIAN JARDINE)

SKIING

With another Olympic Winter Games scheduled for February 1994, only two years after the last competition—to adjust the four-year cycle so that summer and winter Olympic meetings were never again held the same year—the 1993 skiing season required major contenders to maintain peak form in readiness for another assault on the cherished honours. Improved commercial sponsorship enabled season-long World Cup series to thrive in Alpine racing, the various Nordic events, and freestyle skiing. All these sports also separately staged their own world championships.

Alpine Skiing. The outstanding performer in the 27th Alpine World Cup series was Marc Girardelli of Luxembourg, who at 29 became the first man to win the overall title for a fifth time, his general competence in all four disciplines once more proving too good for the specialists (*see* BIOGRAPHIES). Girardelli thus edged one title ahead of Switzerland's Pirmin Zurbriggen and Italy's Gustavo Thoeni. He demonstrated his versatility by placing third in the giant slalom, fifth in the supergiant slalom, sixth in the downhill, and 13th in the slalom. The overall runner-up was Norway's Kjetil André Aamodt, who was top scorer in both the giant and supergiant slalom. Franz Heinzer of Austria, the best downhiller, finished third. Sweden's Thomas Fogdoe won the slalom.

Anita Wachter of Austria, second in the giant slalom and fourth in both the slalom and supergiant slalom, took the women's overall title after being threatened until the very last race by the German runner-up, Katja Seizinger, winner of both the downhill and the supergiant slalom. Carole Merle of France won the giant slalom and finished third overall. The Swiss veteran Vreni Schneider won the slalom, achieving four race victories in only eight starts.

In the world championships, on February 3–14 at Morioka-Shizukuishi, Japan, Aamodt stressed his consistency with victories in both the slalom and the giant slalom. Urs Lehmann of Switzerland won the downhill, and Norway's Lasse Kjus took the Alpine combination. Weather conditions at the meeting were so difficult that for the first time in the history of the championships, one of the events, the men's supergiant slalom, had to be canceled. Merle won the women's giant slalom, Karin Buder of Austria took the slalom, and Kate Pace of Canada was victorious in the downhill. Two Germans, Miriam Vogt and Seizinger, claimed the Alpine combination and the supergiant slalom, respectively.

Nordic Events. The 14th Nordic World Cup series for men's cross-country racing was retained by Bjorn Dählie of Norway, with Vladimir Smirnov of Kazakhstan second and another Norwegian, Vegard Ulvgang, third. The women's series was narrowly captured by Lyubov Yegorova from her fellow Russian Yelena Vyalbe, the defending champion. Stefania Belmondo of Italy finished third. The separate Nordic Combination World Cup was won by Kenji Ogiwara of Japan, and the Jumping World Cup was taken by an Austrian, Andreas Goldberger.

At the world championships, on February 18–28 at Falun, Sweden, Dählie gained three cross-country gold medals, for the 15 km and 30 km and as one of the winning Norwegian quartet in the team relay. Another Norwegian, Sture Sivertsen, was first home in the 10 km, and the grueling 50 km went to Torgny Mogren of Sweden. The winning jumpers were Espen Bredesen of Norway in the 115 m and Mashiko Harada of Japan in the 90 m. Ogiwara won the Nordic combination and also helped his Japanese national team to triumph in the combination team event. Norway gained the jumping team title.

Belmondo claimed two of the five women's cross-country gold medals, retaining the 30-km title and also winning the 10 km. Vyalbe recaptured the 15 km she had first won in 1991, and the 5 km went to Larisa Lazutina, who joined Vyalbe to capture Russia's third gold, in the team relay.

Freestyle Skiing. Interest in freestyle skiing increased during the year, thanks largely to its spectacular appeal on

Carole Merle fixes her concentration on the next gate in the women's giant slalom at the world Alpine skiing championships, which were held in Morioka-Shizukuishi, Japan, in February. The French skier captured first place in the event.

MIKE POWELL—ALLSPORT

television. The 14th Freestyle World Cup series provided a second successive men's combined title for Trace Worthington of the U.S. Rune Kristiansen of Norway finished second, and Jean-Luc Brassard of Canada was third. The women's crown was captured by another Canadian, Katherina Kubenk, followed by Maja Schmid of Switzerland and Britain's Jilly Curry.

In the freestyle world championships, on March 6–14 at Altenmarkt, Germany, Sergey Shapletsov of Russia narrowly defeated Worthington for the men's crown, with Hugo Bonatti of Austria third. Kubenk won the women's title, with Natalia Orekhova taking the silver for Russia, and Kristean Porter the bronze for the U.S. (HOWARD BASS)

SQUASH RACKETS

In October 1992 Susan Devoy released her stranglehold on women's squash championships when she announced her retirement immediately after winning her fourth world title. The scramble for supremacy in 1993 then began. The winner was Michelle Martin from Brisbane, Australia. She won the British Open in April, defeating Suzanne Horner (England) 9–7, 9–0, 9–4 in the final. She then crossed the world to Japan, where she took the inaugural JSM SuperSquash title, and then emphasized her preeminence in the World Open at Johannesburg, South Africa, in September, beating fellow Australian Liz Irving 9–2, 9–2, 9–1 in the final.

In men's competition Jansher Khan of Pakistan won his second British Open 9–6, 9–5, 6–9, 9–2 over Chris Dittmar of Australia and his fifth World Open. The latter, staged in Karachi, Pak., in November, was notable for the amazing third comeback from retirement of Jahangir Khan of Pakistan. After more than nine months away from competition, he reached the final; in that match he lost to Jansher Khan 14–15, 15–9, 15–5, 15–6. It was Jahangir Khan's ninth World Open final, of which he won six. In the world team championships, which followed the individual matches, Jahangir helped Pakistan to a 3–0 win over an injury-ridden Australia to regain the title that country last held in 1987.

(ANDREW SHELLEY)

SWIMMING

After the 1992 Olympic Games, during which nine world records in swimming were set, a letdown was expected in 1993, but no one anticipated that there would be just one new mark in a 50-m, Olympic-size pool, the men's 100-m breaststroke. On August 3, Karoly Guttler of Hungary swam the distance in 1 min 0.95 sec, breaking the record of 1 min 1.29 sec set by Norbert Rozsa of Hungary in the 1991 world championships. Most of the U.S. and European Olympic medalists retired or took a year's break from hard training. Forty-nine countries participated in the World University Games at Buffalo, N.Y., held in July. The U.S. dominated with 28 medals, including 14 gold, but 15 other countries won at least one medal.

The 1993 FINA (Fédération Internationale de Natation Amateur) Swimming World Cup for 25-m pools was contested in a number of countries, beginning in Shanghai on January 5–6 and ending in Milan on February 21. In Shanghai swimmers from 10 countries competed, and in Beijing (Peking) the countries represented increased to 13. Franziska van Almsick, a 14-year-old from Berlin, set three women's world records, twice in the 100-m freestyle; the first was on January 6 at Shanghai with a time of 53.46 sec, and the second on January 10 at Beijing, 53.33 sec. The third world record was achieved January 9 in Beijing, where van Almsick won the 200-m freestyle in 1 min 55.84 sec.

In men's 25-m pool competition, Jani Sievinen of Finland lowered the world record in the 200-m individual medley on three occasions, achieving his final mark of 1 min 55.59 sec in the World Cup tournament at Malmö, Sweden, on February 10. A day earlier Sievinen had set a world record of 4 min 7.10 sec for the 400-m individual medley. On February 6 in Paris, Danyon Loader of New Zealand set a world record of 1 min 54.58 sec in the 200-m butterfly. He lowered the mark to 1 min 54.50 sec on February 9 at Malmö and then to 1 min 54.21 sec at Gelsenkirchen, Germany. At Sheffield, England, on February 17, Mark Foster of the U.K. established a 50-m freestyle world record of 21.60 sec. At Sheffield on April 12, Jeff Rouse of Fredricksburg, Va., set a new mark of 51.43 sec in the 100-m backstroke. On July 2 at the Brazilian championships in Santos, Gustavo Borges lowered the 100-m freestyle mark to 47.94 sec, and on July 7 the Brazilian quartet of Borges, Fernando Scherer, José Carlos Souza, and Teofilo Ferreira established a world record of 3 min 13.97 sec for the 4 × 100-m freestyle relay. On July 14 at Auckland, N.Z., Kieren Perkins of Australia set the first of his two world records. In the 1,500-m freestyle he bettered his previous mark by 5.88 sec from 14 min 32.40 sec to 14 min 26.52 sec, and on July 25 at Sydney, Australia, he set a world record of 7 min 34.90 sec in the 800-m freestyle. At the Australian winter championships in Melbourne in August, Philip Rogers set new marks of 59.07 sec in the 100-m breaststroke and 2 min 7.80 sec in the 200-m breaststroke.

At the inaugural short-course (25-m) world championships held in Palma de Mallorca, Spain, on December 2–5, only two new men's world records were set. The Brazilian team bettered their earlier record in the 4 × 100-m freestyle relay with a new time of 3 min 12.11 sec, and the U.S. set a new world record of 3 min 32.57 sec in the 4 × 100-m medley relay. The women, however, shattered the world record in 11 of the 16 races held. Nine of those 11 records were set by the Chinese, including three new marks in team relays: 3 min 35.97 sec in the 4 × 100-m freestyle, 7 min 52.45 sec in the 4 × 200-m freestyle, and 3 min 57.73 sec in the 4 × 100-m medley. Individual Chinese swimmers took an additional seven races, six in world-record times. Li Jingyi won the 50-m freestyle in 24.23 sec and broke van Almsick's record in the 100-m freestyle with a time of 53.01 sec. He Cihong set a new mark of 2 min 6.09 sec in the 200-m backstroke. Dai Guohong swept to victory with world-record times in three events: 1 min 6.58 sec in the 100-m breaststroke, 2 min 21.99 sec in the 200-m breaststroke, and 4 min 29.00 sec in the 400-m individual medley. Two U.S. women broke through the Chinese domination of world records, however. Angel Martino took the 100-m backstroke in a record 58.50 sec, and Allison Wagner set a new mark of 2 min 7.79 sec in the 200-m individual medley.

More than 1,000 swimmers from 36 countries competed in the 21st European swimming championships at Sheffield, England. Ten new countries—Belarus, Croatia, the Czech Republic, Estonia, Latvia, Lithuania, Moldova, Russia, Slovakia, and Ukraine—competed for the first time. Van Almsick won six gold medals and one silver. Her victories were in the 50-m, 100-m, and 200-m freestyle and as a member of three winning relays; she gained her silver in the 100-m butterfly. In winning the 100-m freestyle, van Almsick set a European record of 54.57 sec, 0.16 sec below the mark of 54.73 sec set by Kristin Otto in the world championships of 1986. Krisztina Egerszegi of Hungary, a triple gold medal winner at the 1992 Olympic Games, became the first swimmer ever to earn four titles in individual events in a single European championship. She won the 100-m backstroke in 1 min 0.83 sec, the 200-m backstroke in 2 min 9.12 sec, the 200-m butterfly in 2 min 10.71 sec, and the 400-m individual medley in 4 min 39.55 sec.

In the men's events, Olympic champion Aleksandr Popov of Russia won the 50-m freestyle in 22.27 sec, the 100-m freestyle in 49.15 sec, and the 4 × 100-m freestyle and 4 × 100-m medley relays to gain a total of four gold medals. Antti Kasvio of Finland won the 200-m freestyle in 1 min 47.11 sec and the 400-m freestyle in 3 min 47.81 sec. Tamas Darnyi of Hungary, a double world record holder, survived the toughest test of his eight-year unbeaten streak in the 400-m individual medley at major meets. Pressed by Sievinen, Darnyi won the event in 4 min 15.24 sec. Sievinen won the 200-m individual medley in 1 min 59.50 sec, a tournament record. Darnyi did not compete in the event. Russia won all three men's relays, and Germany won all three women's relays. A total of 12 tournament records were set in the 32 events. Germany collected 21 medals, including 11 gold; Russia finished second with 19, including 7 gold. Twenty-one nations won at least one medal.

Diving. Eighty divers from 18 countries competed in the 24th International at Fort Lauderdale, Fla., on May 6–9. In the women's events, Simona Koch of Germany won the 1-m springboard; Irina Lashko of Russia took the 3-m springboard; and Svetlana Khokhlova of Russia won the 10-m platform. Winners in the men's competition were Wang Yijie of China in the 1-m springboard, Lan Wei of China in the 3-m springboard, and Vladimir Timoshinin of Russia in the 10-m platform.

SIMON BRUTY—ALLSPORT

Karoly Guttler of Hungary sets a new world record in the men's 100-m breaststroke at the European championships held in August in Sheffield, England. His time of 1 min 0.95 sec, the only world record in a 50-m pool in 1993, lowered a mark that had stood since 1991.

World Swimming Records Set in 1993 in 50-m Pools

Event	Name	Country	Time
MEN			
100-m breaststroke	Karoly Guttler	Hungary	1 min 0.95 sec

World Swimming Records Set in 1993 in 25-m Pools

Event	Name	Country	Time
MEN			
50-m freestyle	Mark Foster	U.K.	21.60 sec
100-m freestyle	Gustavo Borges	Brazil	47.94 sec
800-m freestyle	Kieren Perkins	Australia	7 min 34.90 sec
1,500-m freestyle	Kieren Perkins	Australia	14 min 26.52 sec
4 × 100-m freestyle relay	Brazilian national team		3 min 13.97 sec
4 × 100-m freestyle relay	Brazilian national team		3 min 12.11 sec
100-m backstroke	Jeff Rouse	U.S.	51.43 sec
100-m breaststroke	Philip Rogers	Australia	59.07 sec
200-m breaststroke	Philip Rogers	Australia	2 min 07.80 sec
200-m butterfly	Danyon Loader	New Zealand	1 min 54.58 sec
200-m butterfly	Danyon Loader	New Zealand	1 min 54.50 sec
200-m butterfly	Danyon Loader	New Zealand	1 min 54.21 sec
200-m individual medley	Jani Sievinen	Finland	1 min 56.84 sec
200-m individual medley	Jani Sievinen	Finland	1 min 56.62 sec
200-m individual medley	Jani Sievinen	Finland	1 min 55.59 sec
400-m individual medley	Jani Sievinen	Finland	4 min 07.10 sec
4 × 100-m medley relay	U.S. national team		3 min 32.57 sec
WOMEN			
50-m freestyle	Li Jingyi	China	24.23 sec
100-m freestyle	Franziska van Almsick	Germany	53.46 sec
100-m freestyle	Franziska van Almsick	Germany	53.33 sec
100-m freestyle	Li Jingyi	China	53.01 sec
200-m freestyle	Franziska van Almsick	Germany	1 min 55.84 sec
4 × 100-m freestyle relay	Chinese national team		3 min 35.97 sec
4 × 200-m freestyle relay	Chinese national team		7 min 52.45 sec
100-m backstroke	Angel Martino	U.S.	58.50 sec
200-m backstroke	He Cihong	China	2 min 06.09 sec
100-m breaststroke	Dai Guohong	China	1 min 06.58 sec
200-m breaststroke	Dai Guohong	China	2 min 21.99 sec
200-m individual medley	Allison Wagner	U.S.	2 min 07.79 sec
400-m individual medley	Dai Guohong	China	4 min 29.00 sec
4 × 100-m medley relay	Chinese national team		3 min 57.73 sec

Divers from China swept all six events as 20 countries competed in the eighth FINA World Diving Cup at Beijing from May 28 to June 1. Tan Shuping won both the women's 1-m and 3-m springboard events, and Chi Bin took the women's 10-m platform. Winners of the men's events were Lan in the 1-m springboard, Yu Zhuocheng in the 3-m springboard, and Xiong Ni in the 10-m platform.

German and Russian divers dominated the 21st European championships at Sheffield, England, from July 30 to August 8. Koch won the 1-m springboard; Brita Baldus of Germany dominated the 3-m springboard; and Khokhlova won the 10-m platform. In the men's 1-m springboard, Peter Boehler of Germany was the winner. Jan Hempel of Germany took the men's 3-m springboard, and Dmitry Sautin of Russia won the 10-m platform.

Synchronized Swimming. Ten countries competed at the sixth Synchronized Swimming World Cup, contested in Lausanne, Switz., on July 7–10. Becky Dyroen-Lancer of the U.S. won the solo event and teamed with Jill Sudduth to take the duet. The U.S. won the team championship, defeating Canada 191.757 to 190.456.

In December, Sylvie Frechette of Canada was belatedly awarded a gold medal for individual synchronized swim for the 1992 Olympic Games. Frechette was originally denied the gold because a judge was not allowed to correct a mistyped score. (ALBERT SCHOENFIELD)

TABLE TENNIS

At the 42nd world championships in Göteborg, Sweden, Jean-Philippe Gatien became the first Frenchman to win the world men's singles championship when he defeated Jean-Michel Saive (Belgium) in the final game 21–18. Jan-Ove Waldner (Sweden), ranked number one in the world, lost to Saive in the semifinals. For the first time since the 1950s, no

1993 Table Tennis World Rankings

MEN	WOMEN
1. Jan-Ove Waldner (Sweden)	1. Deng Yaping (China)
2. Jean-Philippe Gatien (France)	2. Qiao Hong (China)
3. Jean-Michel Saive (Belgium)	3. Hyun Jung Hwa (South Korea)
4. Ma Wenge (China)	4. Li Bun Hui (North Korea)
5. Kim Taek Soo (South Korea)	5. Gao Jun (China)
6. Wang Tao (China)	6. Chen Zihe (China)
7. Jörgen Persson (Sweden)	7. Chen Jing (Taiwan)
8. Jörg Rosskopf (Germany)	8. Chai Po Wa (Hong Kong)
9. Li Gun Sang (North Korea)	9. Yu Sun Bok (North Korea)
10. Andrzej Grubba (Poland)	10. Jing Jun Hong (Singapore)

Asian player reached the semifinals. Sweden captured the men's team event; China was second, followed by Germany and North Korea.

In the five other events, no European reached the finals. Hyun Jung Hwa (South Korea) beat Chen Jing (Taiwan) to win the women's singles crown. Wang Tao and Liu Wei (China) captured the mixed doubles, and Wang and Lü Lin (China) won the men's doubles championship. The women's doubles title went to Liu and Qiao Yunping (China). In the women's team event, China placed first, North Korea second, South Korea third, and Hong Kong fourth.

The 1995 world championships, previously planned for Belgrade, Yugos., were reassigned to Tianjin (Tientsin), China. At its annual meeting the International Table Tennis Federation banned the use of liquid glues on racquets following complaints that the substances were toxic. The computer-ranking system introduced in 1991 proved to be widely popular and would continue to be used extensively.

(TONY BROOKS)

TENNIS

A number of anniversaries were celebrated in 1993, including the 100th women's championships at Wimbledon. But the year was overshadowed by the stabbing of Monica Seles of Yugoslavia on the last day of April while she was competing in the Citizen Cup tournament in Hamburg, Germany. Seles, the world's number one female player at the time, was wounded in the back during a break in play in a match against Magdalena Maleeva of Bulgaria. A male spectator was arrested after the incident. He told police that he wanted to see Steffi Graf of Germany restored to the number one position. Many tennis professionals and fans were outraged when the assailant received only a two-year suspended sentence in October.

Seles, who had defeated Graf in the final of the Australian Open, missed the three other Grand Slam championships while recovering from her injury at a clinic in Colorado. Graf replaced her as the French Open champion and consequently as the world's top-ranked woman player. Graf also successfully defended her Wimbledon singles title in July and went on to win the United States Open in September.

The Australian Open final, between Seles and Graf on the rubberized concrete of Flinders Park, Melbourne, in January, ended with Seles winning a stirring contest 4–6, 6–3, 6–2. Thus, Seles, at the age of 19, equaled Graf's feat of winning the Australian championship three years in a row and also scored her eighth success in nine Grand Slam finals. The Australian Open was the 100th Grand Slam tournament of the open era, which began in 1968.

It was hoped that Andre Agassi a winner at Wimbledon the previous July, would make his first appearance in Melbourne, but an attack of bronchitis caused the American to withdraw. Goran Ivanisevic of Croatia, the runner-up to Agassi at Wimbledon, bowed out on the eve of the tournament after tests revealed a stress fracture to his right foot. Then Boris Becker of Germany, the 1991 champion, was eliminated in his opening match, losing in five sets to Anders Jarryd of Sweden, a qualifier ranked number 151 in the world.

Stefan Edberg of Sweden, who had been halted by a torn stomach muscle in the fourth set of his Australian Open final against Ivan Lendl of the U.S. in 1990, continued to experience physical difficulties at Flinders Park. A spasm in the lower back during his third-round match caused concern, and Edberg, seeded second in the tournament, wore a body belt as a precaution while advancing to the final to meet Jim Courier of the U.S., the defending champion and top-ranked player in the world. Straight-set victories against Arnaud Boetsch of France, Christian Bergstrom of Sweden, and Pete Sampras (*see* BIOGRAPHIES) of the U.S., the third seed, confirmed Edberg's fitness, though neither he nor Courier bargained for being barbecued on the day of the final.

With the temperature on centre court touching 67° C (152° F), there was a suggestion that the stadium's retractable roof be closed to protect the players. Courier and Edberg declined. Courier, who repeated the previous year's win against Edberg, celebrated a 6–2, 6–1, 2–6, 7–5 victory by taking the customary dive into the Yarra River.

CLAUS BERGMANN—CONTI PRESS

Monica Seles receives aid after being stabbed by a deranged Steffi Graf fan during a tennis tournament in Hamburg, Germany, in April. The wounding forced Seles, winner of the earlier Australian Open and ranked number one at the time of the incident, to withdraw from the remaining Grand Slam tournaments.

Pete Sampras completes a backhand shot during play at Wimbledon, where he beat Jim Courier 7–6, 7–6, 3–6, 6–3 in an all-American men's final held on July 4. In what was his best year in professional tennis, Sampras also later won a total of eight titles.
CHRIS COLE—ALLSPORT

Neither Courier nor fellow Americans Sampras, Agassi, and John McEnroe were inclined to return to Melbourne two months later to defend the Davis Cup, and the U.S., for whom David Wheaton and Brad Gilbert were selected for the singles matches, lost 4–1. The Davis Cup finals were won by Germany and dominated by Michael Stich, whose decisive 6–4, 6–2, 6–2 victory over Australia's Richard Fromberg clinched the cup for Germany. Stich also beat Jason Stoltenberg, then teamed up with Patrick Kühnen to win the doubles. Stoltenberg was also bested by Marc Göllner, who had lost to Fromberg earlier, however, for Germany's only loss. With a 6–1, 6–4 win over Magnus Gustafsson of Sweden in the European Community championships in Antwerp, Belgium, Sampras sewed up his world number one slot even though a week later he lost the final match of the ATP Tour championship in Frankfurt, Germany, to Stich.

Sergi Bruguera of Spain provided the surprise of the French Open. The 22-year-old, seeded 10th, defeated Sampras in four sets in the quarterfinals and mesmerized his friend Andrey Medvedev in the semifinals, defeating the 18-year-old Ukrainian 6–0, 6–4, 6–2. He then ended Courier's string of 20 consecutive wins at Roland Garros stadium by defeating the Floridian in a four-hour final 6–4, 2–6, 6–2, 3–6, 6–3. Bruguera, trailing 0–2 in the final set and showing signs of fatigue, made a courageous recovery and capitalized on his opponent's unusually error-prone forehand.

The women's singles competition in the French Open was marked by an extraordinary comeback. Mary Joe Fernandez of the U.S. was down 1–6, 1–5, and 30–40 in the seventh game, with Gabriela Sabatini serving for a place in the semifinals. The Argentinian double-faulted, and Fernandez saved an additional four match points and went on to win the match 1–6, 7–6, 10–8. In the third and deciding set of the final, against Graf, Fernandez broke Graf's serve to take a 4–3 lead. However, the weight of 10 previous defeats by Graf then seemed to diminish Fernandez' confidence, and the German won 4–6, 6–2, 6–4.

At Wimbledon in June and July, Sampras ended Agassi's defense of the championship in four sets in the quarterfinals, using a serve that was truncated to compensate for a wrist injury. Sampras then secured his place in the final by defeating Becker in straight sets, while Courier dismantled Edberg's second serve to win in four sets. It was the first time since 1927, when seeding was first introduced, that the top four seeds had all qualified for the semifinals.

The pace and accuracy of Sampras' second serve was decisive in a power-dominated final. Neither player broke his opponent's serve until the ninth game of the second set. After winning the first two sets on the breaks, Sampras overcame the loss of the third set and stood firm against increasing weariness to defeat Courier 7–6, 7–6, 3–6, 6–3.

Jana Novotna's first appearance in the final was unforgettable. Having defeated Martina Navratilova of the U.S., the nine-time champion, in the semifinals, Novotna led Graf 4–1 and 40–30 in the final set. Then the Czech's nerve deserted her, and she was unable to recover after double-faulting. Graf thus won her fifth Wimbledon title 7–6, 1–6, 6–4.

Sampras and Graf maintained their form and added the U.S. Open singles titles to their Wimbledon championships. Five seeds in the men's singles lost in the opening round. The casualties were Agassi, number 16, who lost in five sets to Thomas Enqvist of Sweden; Bruguera, number 5, who was defeated by a Spanish compatriot, Javier Sánchez; Michael Stich of Germany, number 6, who lost to Henrik Holm of Sweden; Petr Korda of the Czech Republic, number 9, who was defeated by Wayne Ferreira of South Africa; and the injured Lendl, number 13.

Edberg, seeded third for his attempt to win the title for a third consecutive year, fell in the second round to Karel Novacek of the Czech Republic, and Ivanisevic, seeded 11th, was also eliminated at this stage, by Carlos Costa of Spain. Mats Wilander interrupted two years of retirement and advanced to the third round. The Swedish former world number one was then defeated by Cedric Pioline, the 15th seed from France, who provided the surprise of the championships by eliminating Courier, the number one seed, in the fourth round. Becker, the fourth seed, disappeared along with Courier, losing to Magnus Larsson of Sweden.

Pioline, a 24-year-old who did not have a professional singles title to his name, advanced to the final only to be outclassed by Sampras, the number two seed, 6–4, 6–4, 6–3. On reaching the final, Sampras was guaranteed a return to number one in the rankings, replacing Courier. It was Sampras' second triumph in the U.S. Open. In 1990 he had become the youngest winner of the tournament 28 days after his 19th birthday.

The women's singles also saw some surprises as Jennifer Capriati of the U.S., the seventh seed, lost to the unseeded Leila Meskhi of the Republic of Georgia in the opening round. Navratilova, the third seed, was defeated by Helena Sukova of the Czech Republic in the fourth round, the point at which Novotna, the eighth seed, also departed, losing to the unseeded Kimiko Date of Japan. Sukova, the 12th seed, overcame the second seed, Arantxa Sánchez Vicario of Spain in the semifinals but was unable to unsettle Graf in the final. The German, who responded fiercely when challenged by Sabatini in the quarterfinals and Manuela Maleeva-Fragnière in the semifinals, capitalized on Sukova's missed opportunities in the opening games of the final, winning 6–3, 6–3. Three weeks later, after winning a tour event in Leipzig, Germany, Graf decided to have surgery to eradicate a problem caused by a bone spur in her right foot.

There was consolation for Sukova in the doubles events at the U.S. Open. She partnered Sánchez Vicario to win the women's tournament, ending the Grand Slam prospects of

Gigi Fernandez of the U.S. and Natalia Zvereva of Belarus in the semifinals. Sukova also won the mixed doubles title, with Todd Woodbridge of Australia. The Australian's men's doubles triumph at Wimbledon, where Woodbridge was partnered with Mark Woodforde, brought Woodbridge's success rate in men's doubles finals to 20, breaking the record set by John McEnroe in 1980.

Sánchez Vicario was unbeaten in five singles matches in the Federation Cup in Frankfurt, Germany, in July as Spain won the trophy for the second time in three years. She lost again to Graf (1–6, 4–6, 6–3, 1–6) in the final of the Virginia Slims championships in November, however. Graf ended the year in the number one slot for the first time since 1990. (JOHN ROBERTS)

TRACK AND FIELD SPORTS

The world championships, held every two years, easily developed as the most notable track and field event of 1993. Held in Stuttgart, Germany, in August, the tournament survived the early threat of a boycott by athletes who demanded that a share of television revenues be put toward prize money. Eventually the International Amateur Athletic Federation placated the athletes after private negotiations and the offer of meet sponsor Mercedes-Benz to give new automobiles to all of the winners. As at the previous year's Olympic Games, the U.S. men led the overall standings, taking 15 medals, 8 of them gold. Kenya remained in second place with nine medals. For the first time the U.S. women led the medal standings. Altogether they took 11 (5 gold), while the Russian women won 10 overall.

Men's World Championships. Two world records fell, and another was tied in Stuttgart. Britain's Colin Jackson capped a near-perfect season by running the 110-m hurdles in 12.91 sec, breaking Roger Kingdom's record by 0.01 sec. In the relay races U.S. sprinters were at their best. In the qualifying heats of the 4 × 100 m, Jon Drummond, Andre Cason, Dennis Mitchell, and Leroy Burrell shocked themselves when their "easy" effort yielded a clocking of 37.40 sec, tying the record set in the Olympics. In the final the foursome attempted to better their new mark but ended up with 37.48 sec, the third-fastest time in history.

The 4 × 400 m saw what may have been the greatest relay effort of all time. The U.S. squad of Andrew Valmon, Quincy Watts, Butch Reynolds, and Michael Johnson combined to slash 1.45 sec from the old world record with their time of 2 min 54.29 sec. Johnson's split of 42.94 sec was the fastest ever recorded.

Johnson preceded that performance with an impressive win in the 400 m. His time was 43.65 sec, the third-fastest ever. It was the first time he had contested the event in an international championship, though he had been undefeated in it since 1988.

Sergey Bubka of Ukraine redeemed his poor showing in the 1992 Olympics by winning the pole vault as expected. He cleared 6 m (19 ft 8¼ in), becoming the only athlete, male or female, to have won at each of the four world championships held so far. Werner Günthör of Switzerland won the shot put with a toss of 21.97 m (72 ft 1 in), his third straight gold medal in the world championships.

A number of Olympic champions managed to win in Stuttgart. British sprinter Linford Christie, at age 33, proved that his Olympic victory had not been a fluke when his 9.87-sec 100-m performance missed the world record by only 0.01 sec. Kevin Young of the U.S. won the 400-m hurdles in 47.18 sec, and Mike Conley, also of the U.S., dominated the triple-jump field with his 17.86-m (58-ft 7¼-in) effort. Javier Sotomayor of Cuba won the high jump with a leap of 2.40 m (7 ft 10½ in), and Andrey Abduvaliyev of Tajikistan overcame a lacklustre year following the Olympics to win the hammer throw with 81.64 m (267 ft 10 in).

A U.S. athlete who had been an early Olympic favourite until he met disaster at the U.S. trials, decathlete Dan O'Brien, gained success in 1993. After a victory at the U.S. championships, he won the gold medal in Stuttgart with his score of 8,817 points, the sixth-best performance in history.

African dominance in the distance runs continued to increase. Kenyans won three events. Newcomer Paul Ruto took the 800 m in 1 min 44.71 sec. World record holder Moses Kiptanui defended his steeplechase title with a run of 8 min 6.36 sec. Ismael Kirui, only 18 years old, crushed the opposition at 5,000 m with a scintillating time of 13 min 2.75 sec, the fastest ever run in a championship meet.

Algeria produced a champion in Noureddine Morceli, who won the 1,500 m in 3 min 34.24 sec. Haile Gebresilasie of Ethiopia won the 10,000 m in 27 min 46.02 sec after a blazing last-lap battle with Moses Tanui of Kenya. Namibia had its first winner ever, Frank Fredericks, who won the 200 m in 19.85 sec, an African record.

The marathon was still an African domain even though a U.S. runner, Mark Plaatjes, won in 2 hr 13 min 57 sec. Plaatjes was a refugee from South Africa who had recently been granted U.S. citizenship.

Other Men's Competition. For much of the year, Bubka dominated the headlines with his persistent chasing of records in the pole vault. He set indoor marks of 6.14 m (20 ft 1¾ in) and 6.15 m (20 ft 2 in). They were his 33rd and 34th lifetime records, both higher than his outdoor mark. He eventually won the overall Grand Prix title, with a $130,000 prize for the season-long series.

Some top athletes skipped the world indoor championships in Toronto in March in order to concentrate on training or to put pressure on the organizers to award prize money. O'Brien highlighted the meet by winning the heptathlon—the indoor counterpart to the decathlon—with a record 6,476 points.

Outdoors, Noureddine Morceli ran undefeated in the middle distances. Prior to the world championships, he confirmed his strength with near-record runs in the 1,500 m (3 min 29.20 sec) and 3,000 m (7 min 29.24 sec). After the championships he broke the mile record with a startling run of 3 min 44.39 sec in Rieti, Italy. That was the biggest lowering of the mark (1.93 sec) since Jim Ryun's first record in 1966.

The 10,000-m record also dipped below a historic barrier. First, Richard Chelimo of Kenya broke the standard by 0.32 sec in July in Stockholm. Five days later fellow Kenyan Yobes Ondieki (*see* BIOGRAPHIES) became the first man to cover that distance in less than 27 min with his time of 26 min 58.38 sec in Oslo, Norway.

Sotomayor high jumped over the 8-ft barrier for the second time, raising his own world record to 2.45 m (8 ft ½ in) in Salamanca, Spain, in July. In the javelin Jan Zelezny of the Czech Republic twice set a new record, first with a throw of 95.54 m (313 ft 5 in) in Pietersburg, South Africa, in April. He followed his world championships win with a record toss of 95.66 m (313 ft 10 in) in Sheffield, England, in August.

Women's World Championships. Since 1988 women's world records had been rare, but Sally Gunnell of the U.K. reversed the trend in Stuttgart. Racing Sandra Farmer-Patrick of the U.S. over the 400-m hurdles, Gunnell caught her just at the finish in 52.74 sec, with Farmer-Patrick (52.79 sec) also under the old mark. In the triple jump—a new event for an international championship—newcomer Ana Biryukova of Russia leaped 15.09 m (49 ft 6¼ in) to win the gold unexpectedly and break the record.

Gail Devers of the U.S. made history by winning the sprint/hurdle double that she had attempted unsuccessfully in the Olympics. First she won the 100 m in 10.82 sec, later enduring a storm of controversy when runner-up Merlene Ottey of Jamaica (also 10.82 sec) insisted that she was the true champion. Ottey had to wait several days before she finally won her first gold medal in global competition, a quest that had frustrated her for 13 years. She triumphed in the 200 m in 21.98 sec, much to the delight of the Stuttgart crowd.

Devers returned to win the 100-m hurdles—the event in which she fell just before the finish in the Olympics—with a lifetime best of 12.46 sec. She also ran on the 4 × 100-m relay for the U.S., which narrowly lost to the Russians as both teams set national records of 41.49 sec. The U.S. won the 4 × 400-m relay in 3 min 16.71 sec, anchored by Jearl Miles, who earlier had won the 400 m in a lifetime best 49.82 sec.

Germany's Heike Drechsler won the long jump with a distance of 7.11 m (23 ft 4 in), regaining the title she had last won as a teenager 10 years earlier. Mozambique's Maria Mutola overpowered her 800-m rivals in 1 min 55.43 sec, her 1.67-sec margin of victory the largest ever in a world final.

Jackie Joyner-Kersee did not enjoy the luxury of a big margin. She scored 6,837 points in the heptathlon to regain the title she had lost two years earlier. Her 40-point bulge over Sabine Braun of Germany was the closest finish she had endured since 1984.

In the marathon Junko Asari of Japan won in 2 hr 30 min 3 sec, leading her teammates to a 1–3–11 finish. That underscored the rise of the Japanese women to primacy among the world's marathoners, a position put in jeopardy by the sudden explosion of the Chinese.

The Chinese distance runners went to Stuttgart shrouded in mystery but soon asserted their place at the top of the world's hierarchy. In the 3,000 m three Chinese ran away from undefeated favourite Sonia O'Sullivan of Ireland to sweep the medals. Qu Yunxia won in 8 min 28.71 sec, finishing with the fastest closing rush ever recorded by a woman. In the 10,000 m two Chinese easily triumphed over the best the rest of the world had to offer. Wang Junxia won in 30 min 49.30 sec after another unbelievably fast finish. In the 1,500 m Liu Dong won in 4 min 0.50 sec, crushing her competition on the last lap. The ensuing excitement and controversy was only a prelude to the biggest development of the year in the sport.

Table I. World 1993 Outdoor Records—Men

Event	Competitor and country	Performance
Mile	Noureddine Morceli (Algeria)	3 min 44.39 sec
10,000 m	Richard Chelimo (Kenya)	27 min 7.91 sec
10,000 m	Yobes Ondieki (Kenya)	26 min 58.38 sec
110-m hurdles	Colin Jackson (U.K.)	12.91 sec
4 × 100-m relay	U.S. (Drummond, Cason, Mitchell, Burrell)	37.40 sec*
4 × 400-m relay	U.S. (Valmon, Watts, Reynolds, Johnson)	2 min 54.29 sec
High jump	Javier Sotomayor (Cuba)	2.45 m (8 ft ½ in)
Javelin	Jan Zelezny (Czech Republic)	95.54 m (313 ft 5 in)
Javelin	Jan Zelezny (Czech Republic)	95.66 m (313 ft 10 in)

Table II. World 1993 Outdoor Records—Women

Event	Competitor and country	Performance
1,500 m	Qu Yunxia (China)	3 min 50.46 sec
3,000 m	Zhang Linli (China)	8 min 22.06 sec
3,000 m	Wang Junxia (China)	8 min 12.19 sec
3,000 m	Wang Junxia (China)	8 min 6.11 sec
10,000 m	Wang Junxia (China)	29 min 31.78 sec
20,000 m	Izumi Maki (Japan)	1 hr 6 min 48.8 sec
400-m hurdles	Sally Gunnell (U.K.)	52.74 sec
Triple jump	Yolanda Chen (Russia)	14.97 m (49 ft 1½ in)
Triple jump	Ana Biryukova (Russia)	15.09 m (49 ft 6¼ in)

*Equals record.

Wang Junxia sets a world record in the 3,000 m at the Chinese National Games in Beijing (Peking) in September, where she also set a new mark in the 10,000 m. She was one of a group of Chinese women who achieved spectacular success in distance running in 1993.

FOREST ANDERSON—SPORTS ILLUSTRATED

China's National Games. In mid-September in Beijing (Peking), the Chinese women unleashed a powerful display of distance running that was unprecedented in the history of track and field. On the first day, Wang slashed more than 41 seconds from the 10,000-m record, becoming the first woman to break 30 minutes with her 29-min 31.78-sec performance. Even more shocking, she ran the last 5,000 m of that race faster than the 5,000-m world record, and the last 3,000 m faster than the record at that distance—a nine-year-old mark that many had considered unbeatable.

On the fourth day, Qu shattered the record for 1,500 m with a startling run of 3 min 50.46 sec. Wang (3 min 51.92 sec) also broke the record. Unbelievably, a total of seven Chinese broke the 4-minute barrier in that race. Only two other women in the world had done so all year. On the fifth day, in the qualifying heats of the 3,000 m, Zhang Linli broke the record with a run of 8 min 22.06 sec. Teammate Zhang Lirong also bettered the old mark. Just 14 minutes later, Wang broke the record (as did teammates Qu and Ma Liyan) with a run of 8 min 12.19 sec.

On the sixth and last day, Wang shattered the 3,000-m mark again, clocking 8 min 6.11 sec. All told, six women exceeded the old world records a total of 14 times. Adding to the shock was the depth of performance in every race. Dozens of Chinese, many of them unheard of before 1993, achieved world-class performances as national records fell in every running event. The Chinese angrily denied charges that the performances were aided by a systematic national doping program. Many international experts responded with deep skepticism.

Cross Country and Marathon Running. Lynn Jennings of the U.S. failed in her attempt to win a fourth straight world cross country title, placing third behind Albertina Dias of Portugal and Catherina McKiernan of Ireland. In the men's race Kenyans took the first five places. Kenya won all four team titles available at the meet, three with perfect scores.

In marathon running the most notable race took place in April in Boston, where Cosmas N'Deti of Kenya won in 2 hr 9 min 33 sec over South Korea's Kim Jae Ryong (2 hr 9 min 43 sec). Olga Markova, who had been a favourite in the Olympics until the Russians decided to leave her off their team, attempted a record pace but had to slow down. She still clocked an impressive victory, nonetheless, at 2 hr 25 min 27 sec.

In early April the Chinese served as host for a race in Tianjin (Tientsin), in which eight women ran under 2 hr 27 min; seven of them had never raced the distance before. Because of the unprecedented speed with which winner Wang finished the race (2 hr 24 min 7 sec), the course was widely thought to be short. After Beijing's national games, however, most experts decided that Wang was indeed capable of such a feat.

The men's and women's winners of other major marathons in 1993 included: Rotterdam, Neth., Dionicio Ceron (Mexico) 2 hr 11 min 6 sec and Anne van Schuppen (The Netherlands) 2 hr 34 min 15 sec; London, Eamonn Martin (U.K.) 2 hr 10 min 50 sec and Katrin Dörre (Germany) 2 hr 27 min 9 sec; and New York, Andrés Espinosa (Mexico) 2 hr 10 min 4 sec and Uta Pippig (Germany) 2 hr 26 min 24 sec. (JEFF HOLLOBAUGH)

VOLLEYBALL

As the year following the 1992 Olympic Games, 1993 was expected by many to be slow and uneventful; nonetheless, the world of volleyball continued to grow. The $3 million World League for men, consisting of two six-team divisions and contested from mid-May to early August, completed its fourth season. Defending Olympic gold medalist Brazil captured the championship over Russia, and three-time reigning champion Italy settled for third-place honours after beating Cuba. The U.S. finished ninth but defeated runner-up Russia. Bryan Ivie and Bob Samuelson of the U.S. were members of the victorious World League all-star squad, which defeated Brazil at the World Gala in August.

The $1 million women's World Grand Prix was inaugurated in 1993. The winner was 1992 Olympic champion Cuba, which defeated Brazil in the championship match. China beat Korea to gain third place; the U.S. women placed seventh. In 1994 the World Grand Prix would expand to 12 teams in round-robin play after utilizing 8 teams in 1993.

For the U.S. 1993 marked a transition period as many of the veterans retired or took their volleyball skills to the beach. However, the growth of the sport throughout the nation was cause for optimism for the future.

Qualification for the 1994 world championships took place during autumn, and the U.S. men's and women's teams both qualified for the event. The men were among 16 teams that would vie for the world title in Greece, while the women's championships, also with 16 teams, were to be held in Brazil.

Beach volleyball received a huge boost during the year when the International Olympic Committee added two-person volleyball to the competition schedule for the 1996 Olympic Games. (RICHARD S. WANNINGER)

WEIGHT LIFTING

Ukraine and China captured team honours in, respectively, the men's and women's world weight-lifting championships, held in November 1993 in Melbourne, Australia. The International Weightlifting Federation had revised the weight classifications slightly to encourage more world records, an effort to compensate for the slowdown in new marks caused by strict testing for drug abuse in recent years. Six world marks were established in the men's total lifts, while the women accounted for eight world records in nine weight divisions.

Bulgaria won four titles in the total lift (combined total of snatch and clean-and-jerk lifts), leading off with 1992 Olympic Games champion Ivan Ivanov in the 54-kg (118.8-lb) class. In the women's competition China won six total lift gold medals, with four of the winners being teenagers.

In addition to Ivanov, other 1992 Olympic champions winning gold medals were Pyrros Dimas of Greece, in the 82.5-kg (181.5-lb) class; Viktor Tregubov of Russia in the 91.8-kg (201.9-lb) class; and Turkey's Naim Suleymanoglu, perhaps the greatest lifter for his weight in the history of the sport, in the 64-kg (140.8-lb) class.

Ukraine won the men's team honours in spite of winning only one gold, one silver, and one bronze medal. Among the other champions were Germany's super heavyweight Ronnie Weller, with a world record total lift of 442 kg (972.4 lb), and Timur Taimazov of Ukraine, victor in the 108-kg (237.6-lb) class.

For the first time the women's championships were held in conjunction with the men's. The Chinese women's team swept the day with six gold medals and two silvers in the total lifts. Taiwan won three gold medals, and Bulgaria accounted for the other championship.

(CHARLES ROBERT PAUL, JR.)

WRESTLING

The World Cup, held in Chattanooga, Tenn., on April 2–3, 1993, was a freestyle dual meet competition. The U.S. finished first with 8 points, followed by Russia with 6 points, Canada with 4, Cuba with 2, and Japan with 0.

The U.S. won the freestyle world championships, held in Toronto on August 25–28, for the first time. The U.S. scored 75 points and gained three gold medals and two silvers. Bruce Baumgartner set a U.S. record by winning his 10th world title. Russia placed second with 52 points, winning one gold, two silver, and two bronze medals. Rounding out the top five were Turkey with 51 points, South Korea with 39, and Cuba with 38.

The Greco-Roman world championships, in Stockholm on September 16–19, were won by Russia with 75 points and four gold medals, three silvers, and one bronze. Cuba finished second with 51 points and three golds and one bronze. Sweden had 43 points, Poland 34 points, and Germany 28 points.

The 63rd U.S. collegiate championships took place in Ames, Iowa, on March 18–20. Iowa won its 14th team title, scoring 123.75 points to Penn State's 87.5 and Nebraska's 79.5. Iowa crowned two champions and had five other All-Americans. (JOHANNA SCHNEIDER)

This article updates the *Macropædia* article Major Team and Individual SPORTS and *Micropædia* entries on the various sports.

World Wrestling Champions, 1993

Weight class	Freestyle	Greco-Roman
48 kg (105.5 lb)	A. Vila (Cuba)	W. Sánchez (Cuba)
52 kg (114.5 lb)	V. Jordanov (Bulgaria)	R. Martínez (Cuba)
57 kg (125.5 lb)	Terry Brands (U.S.)	A. Manukjan (Armenia)
62 kg (136.5 lb)	Tom Brands (U.S.)	S. Martinov (Russia)
68 kg (149.5 lb)	A. Fallah (Iran)	I. Duguchlev (Russia)
74 kg (163 lb)	Park Jang-Soon (S. Korea)	N. Alamanza (Cuba)
82 kg (180.5 lb)	S. Ozturk (Turkey)	M. Yerllkaya (Turkey)
90 kg (198 lb)	A. Jadidl (Iran)	G. Koguchavilli (Russia)
100 kg (220 lb)	L. Khabelov (Russia)	M. Ljungberg (Sweden)
130 kg (286 lb)	B. Baumgartner (U.S.)	A. Karelin (Russia)

Sporting Record

ARCHERY

FITA Outdoor World Target Archery Championships

year	men's individual		men's team		women's individual		women's team	
	winner	points	winner	points	winner	points	winner	points
1985	R. McKinney (U.S.)	2,601	South Korea	7,660	I. Soldatova (U.S.S.R.)	2,595	U.S.S.R.	7,721
1987	V. Esheyev (U.S.S.R.)	329	West Germany	891	Ma Xiangjun (China)	330	U.S.S.R.	884
1989	S. Zabrodsky (U.S.S.R.)	332	U.S.S.R.	985	Kim Soo Nyung (S.Kor.)	338	South Korea	995
1991	S. Fairweather (Austl.)	334	South Korea	998	Kim Soo Nyung (S.Kor.)	333	South Korea	1,030
1993	Park Kyung Mo (S.Kor.)	113	France	249	Kim Hyo Jung (S.Kor.)	104	South Korea	236

ATHLETICS

IAAF World Cup—men

	100 metre	*200 metre*	*400 metre*	*800 metre*	*1,500 metre*
1985	B. Johnson (Amer.)	R. Caetano da Silva (Amer.)	M. Franks (U.S.)	S. Koskei (Africa)	O. Khalifa (Africa)
1989	L. Christie (Gr.Brit.)	R. Caetano da Silva (Amer.)	R. Hernandez (Amer.)	T. McKean (Gr.Brit.)	A. Bile (Africa)
1992	L. Christie (Gr.Brit.)	R. Caetano da Silva (Amer.)	S. Bada (Africa)	D. Sharpe (U.K.)	M. Suleiman (Asia)

	5,000 metre	*10,000 metre*	*Steeplechase*	*110-m hurdles*	*400-m hurdles*
1985	D. Padilla (U.S.)	W. Bulti (Africa)	J. Kariuki (Africa)	T. Campbell (U.S.)	A. Phillips (U.S.)
1989	S. Aouita (Africa)	S. Antibo (Europe)	J. Kariuki (Africa)	R. Kingdom (U.S.)	D. Patrick (U.S.)
1992	F. Bayesa (Africa)	A. Abebe (Africa)	P. Barkutwo (Africa)	C. Jackson (U.K.)	S. Mateta (Africa)

	4 × 100-m relays	*4 × 400-m relays*	*Triple jump*	*High jump*	*Pole vault*
1985	United States	United States	W. Banks (U.S.)	P. Sjoberg (Europe)	S. Bubka (U.S.S.R.)
1989	United States	Americas	M. Conley (U.S.)	P. Sjoberg (Europe)	P. Collet (Europe)
1992	United States	Africa	J. Edwards (U.K.)	Y. Sergeyenko (UT)	I. Potapovich (UT)

	Long jump	*Shot put*	*Discus throw*	*Hammer throw*	*Javelin throw*
1985	M. Conley (U.S.)	U. Timmermann (E.Ger.)	G. Kolnootchenko (U.S.S.R.)	Yu. Tamm (U.S.S.R.)	U. Hohn (E.Ger.)
1989	L. Myricks (U.S.)	U. Timmermann (E.Ger.)	J. Schult (E.Ger.)	H. Weis (Europe)	S. Backley (Gr.Brit.)
1992	I. Pedroso (Amer.)	M. Stulce (U.S.)	T. Washington (U.S.)	T. Gécsek (Europe)	J. Zelezny (Europe)

	Team
1985	United States
1989	United States
1992	Africa

IAAF World Cup—women

	100 metre	*200 metre*	*400 metre*	*800 metre*	*1,500 metre*
1985	M. Göhr (E.Ger.)	M. Koch (E.Ger.)	M. Koch (E.Ger.)	C. Wachtel (E.Ger.)	H. Korner (E.Ger.)
1989	S. Echols (U.S.)	S. Moller (E.Ger.)	A. Quirot (Amer.)	A. Quirot (Amer.)	P. Ivan (Europe)
1992	N. Voronova (UT)	M.-J. Pérec (Europe)	J. Miles (U.S.)	M. Mutola (Africa)	Y. Podkopayeva (UT)

	3,000 metre	*10,000 metre*	*100-m hurdles*	*400-m hurdles*	*4 × 100-m relays*
1985	U. Bruns (E.Ger.)	A. Cunha (Europe)	C. Oschkenat (E.Ger.)	S. Busch (E.Ger.)	East Germany
1989	Y. Murray (Europe)	K. Ullrich (E.Ger.)	C. Oschkenat (E.Ger.)	S. Farmer-Patrick (U.S.)	East Germany
1992	D. Tulu (Africa)	D. Tulu (Africa)	A. López (Amer.)	S. Farmer-Patrick (U.S.)	Asia

	4 × 400-m relays	*High jump*	*Long jump*	*Shot put*	*Discus throw*
1985	East Germany	S. Kostadinova (U.S.S.R.)	H. Daute Drechsler (E.Ger.)	N. Lisovskaya (U.S.S.R.)	M. Optiz (E.Ger.)
1989	Americas	S. Costa (Amer.)	G. Chistyakova (U.S.S.R.)	Zhihong Huang (Asia)	I. Wyludda (E.Ger.)
1992	Americas	I. Quintero (Amer.)	H. Drechsler (Ger.)	B. Laza (Amer.)	M. Marten (Amer.)

	Javelin throw	*Team*
1985	O. Gavrilova (U.S.S.R.)	East Germany
1989	P. Felke (E.Ger.)	East Germany
1992	T. Sanderson (U.K.)	Unified Team

For records of previous years, *see* the entry SPORTING RECORD in the *Micropædia*.

World Marathon Cup

year	men	women
1985	A. Salah (Djib.)	K. Dörre (E.Ger.)
1987	A. Salah (Djib.)	Z. Ivanova (U.S.S.R.)
1989	K. Metaferia (Eth.)	S. Marchiano (U.S.)
1991	Y. Tolstikov (U.S.S.R.)	R. Mota (Port.)
1993	R. Nerurkar (U.K.)	Wang Junxia (China)

Q. Watts (left) and B. Reynolds (United States): World Track-and-Field Championships—men's 4 X 400-m relay (1993)

MIKE POWELL—ALLSPORT

World Track-and-Field Championships—men

event	1991	1993
100 m	C. Lewis (U.S.)	L. Christie (U.K.)
200 m	M. Johnson (U.S.)	F. Fredericks (Namib.)
400 m	A. Pettigrew (U.S.)	M. Johnson (U.S.)
800 m	B. Konchellah (Kenya)	P. Ruto (Kenya)
1,500 m	N. Morceli (Alg.)	N. Morceli (Alg.)
5,000 m	Y. Ondieki (Kenya)	I. Kirui (Kenya)
10,000 m	M. Tanui (Kenya)	H. Gebresilasie (Eth.)
steeplechase	M. Kiptanui (Kenya)	M. Kiptanui (Kenya)
110-m hurdles	G. Foster (U.S.)	C. Jackson (U.K.)
400-m hurdles	S. Matete (Zambia)	K. Young (U.S.)
marathon	H. Taniguchi (Japan)	M. Plaatjes (U.S.)
20-km walk	M. Damilano (Italy)	V. Massana (Spain)
50-km walk	A. Potashov (U.S.S.R.)	J.A. Garcia (Spain)
4 × 100-m relay	United States (A. Cason, L. Burrell, D. Mitchell, C. Lewis)	United States (J. Drummond, A. Cason, K. Mitchell, L. Burrell)
4 × 400-m relay	Great Britain (R. Black, D. Redmond, J. Regis, K. Akabusi)	United States (A. Valmon, Q. Watts, B. Reynolds, M. Johnson)
high jump	C. Austin (U.S.)	J. Sotomayor (Cuba)
pole vault	S. Bubka (U.S.S.R.)	S. Bubka (Ukr.)
long jump	M. Powell (U.S.)	M. Powell (U.S.)
triple jump	K. Harrison (U.S.)	M. Conley (U.S.)
shot put	W. Günthör (Switz.)	W. Günthör (Switz.)
discus throw	L. Riedel (Ger.)	L. Riedel (Ger.)
hammer throw	Y. Sedykh (U.S.S.R.)	A. Abduvaliyev (Tajik.)
javelin throw	K. Kinnunen (Fin.)	J. Zelezny (Cz.Rep.)
decathlon	D. O'Brien (U.S.)	D. O'Brien (U.S.)

S. Gunnell: World Track-and-Field Championships—women's 400-m hurdles (1993)
TONY DUFFY—ALLSPORT

World Track-and-Field Championships—women

event	1991	1993
100 m	K. Krabbe (Ger.)	G. Devers (U.S.)
200 m	K. Krabbe (Ger.)	M. Ottey (Jam.)
400 m	M.-J. Pérec (Fr.)	J. Miles (U.S.)
800 m	L. Nurutdinova (U.S.S.R.)	M. Mutola (Mozam.)
1,500 m	H. Boulmerka (Alg.)	Liu Dong (China)
3,000 m	T. Dorovskikh (U.S.S.R.)	Qu Yunxia (China)
10,000 m	L. McColgan (U.K.)	Wang Junxia (China)
100-m hurdles	L. Narozhilenko (U.S.S.R.)	G. Devers (U.S.)
400-m hurdles	T. Ledovskaya (U.S.S.R.)	S. Gunnell (U.K.)
marathon	W. Panfil (Pol.)	Asari Junko (Japan)
10-km walk	A. Ivanova (U.S.S.R.)	S. Essayeh (Fin.)
4 × 100-m relay	Jamaica (D. Duhaney, J. Cuthbert, B. McDonald, M. Ottey)	Russia (O. Bogoslovskaya, G. Malchugina, N. Voronova, I. Privalova)
4 × 400-m relay	U.S.S.R. (T. Ledovskaya, L. Dzhigalova, O. Nazarova, O. Bryzgina)	United States (G. Torrence, M. Malone, N. Kaiser-Brown, J. Miles)
high jump	H. Henkel (Ger.)	I. Quintero (Cuba)
long jump	J. Joyner-Kersee (U.S.)	H. Drechsler (Ger.)
shot put	Huang Zhihong (China)	Huang Zhihong (China)
discus throw	T. Khristova (Bulg.)	O. Burova (Russia)
javelin throw	Xu Demei (China)	T. Hattestad (Nor.)
heptathlon	S. Braun (Ger.)	J. Joyner-Kersee (U.S.)

W. Günthör: World Track-and-Field Championships—men's shot put (1993)
GRAY MORTIMORE—ALLSPORT

Boston Marathon

year	men	h:min:s	women	h:min:s
1989	A. Mekonnen (Eth.)	2:09:06	I. Kristiansen (Nor.)	2:24:33
1990	G. Bordin (Italy)	2:08:19	R. Mota (Port.)	2:25:23
1991	I. Hussein (Kenya)	2:11:06	W. Panfil (Pol.)	2:24:18
1992	I. Hussein (Kenya)	2:08:14	O. Markova (Russia)	2:23:43
1993	C. N'Deti (Kenya)	2:09:33	O. Markova (Russia)	2:25:27

New York Marathon

year	men	h:min:s	women	h:min:s
1989	J. Ikangaa (Tanzania)	2:08:01	I. Kristiansen (Nor.)	2:25:30
1990	D. Wakiihuri (Kenya)	2:12:39	W. Panfil (Pol.)	2:30:45
1991	S. Garcia (Mex.)	2:09:28	L. McColgan (Scot.)	2:27:23
1992	W. Mtolo (S.Afr.)	2:09:29	L. Ondieki (Austl.)	2:24:40
1993	A. Espinosa (Mex.)	2:10:04	U. Pippig (Ger.)	2:26:24

World Cross-Country Championship—men (12,000 m)

year	individual	team
1989	J. Ngugi (Kenya)	Kenya
1990	K. Shah (Mor.)	Kenya
1991	K. Shah (Mor.)	Kenya
1992	J. Ngugi (Kenya)	Kenya
1993	W. Sigei (Kenya)	Kenya

World Cross-Country Championship—women (5,000 m)

year	individual	team
1989	A. Sergent (Fr.)	U.S.S.R.
1990	L. Jennings (U.S.)	U.S.S.R.
1991	L. Jennings (U.S.)	Kenya
1992	L. Jennings (U.S.)	Kenya
1993	A. Dias (Port.)	Kenya

AUTOMOBILE RACING

Indy Car Champions

year	driver
1988	D. Sullivan
1989	E. Fittipaldi
1990	A. Unser, Jr.
1991	Mi. Andretti
1992	B. Rahal
1993	N. Mansell

Indianapolis 500

year	winner	avg. speed in mph
1989	E. Fittipaldi	167.581
1990	A. Luyendyk	185.984
1991	R. Mears	176.457
1992	A. Unser, Jr.	134.479
1993	E. Fittipaldi	157.207

A. Prost: World Championship of Drivers winner (1993)

REUTERS/BETTMANN

International Cup for Formula One Manufacturers

year	car	year	car
1988	McLaren/Honda	1991	McLaren/Honda
1989	McLaren/Honda	1992	Williams/Renault
1990	McLaren/Honda	1993	Williams/Renault

World Championship of Drivers

year	winner	car
1989	A. Prost (Fr.)	McLaren/Honda
1990	A. Senna (Braz.)	McLaren/Honda
1991	A. Senna (Braz.)	McLaren/Honda
1992	N. Mansell (U.K.)	Williams/Renault
1993	A. Prost (Fr.)	Williams/Renault

Le Mans 24-hour Grand Prix d'Endurance

year	car	drivers
1989	Mercedes-Benz	J. Mass, M. Reuter, S. Dickens
1990	Jaguar	J. Nielsen, P. Cobb, M. Brundle
1991	Mazda	V. Weidler, J. Herbert, B. Gachot
1992	Peugeot	Y. Dalmas, M. Blundell, D. Warwick
1993	Peugeot	G. Brabham, C. Bouchut, E. Helary

Monte-Carlo Rally

year	car	driver, codriver
1989	Lancia	Biasion, Siviero
1990	Lancia	Auriol, Occelli
1991	Toyota Celica	Sainz, Moya
1992	Lancia Delta Integrale	Auriol, Occelli
1993	Toyota Celica	Auriol, Occelli

Toyota Celica—D. Auriol and B. Occelli: Monte-Carlo Rally (1993)

PASCAL RONDEAU—ALLSPORT

National Association for Stock Car Auto Racing (NASCAR) Winston Cup Champions

year	winner	year	winner
1988	B. Elliott	1991	D. Earnhardt
1989	R. Wallace	1992	A. Kulwicki
1990	D. Earnhardt	1993	D. Earnhardt

BADMINTON

World Badminton Championships

year	men's singles	women's singles	men's doubles	women's doubles
1985	Han Jian (China)	Han Aiping (China)	Park Joo Bong, Kim Moon Soo (S.Kor.)	Han Aiping, Li Lingwei (China)
1987	Yang Yang (China)	Han Aiping (China)	Li Yongbo, Tian Bingyi (China)	Lin Ying, Guan Weizhen (China)
1989	Yang Yang (China)	Li Lingwei (China)	Li Yongbo, Tian Bingyi (China)	Lin Ying, Guan Weizhen (China)
1991	Zhao Jianhua (China)	Tang Jiuhong (China)	Park Joo Bong, Kim Moon Soo (S.Kor.)	Guan Weizhen, Nong Qunhua (China)
1993	J. Suprianto (Indon.)	S. Susanti (Indon.)	R. Subagja, R. Gunawan (Indon.)	Nong Qunhua, Zhou Lei (China)

All-England Championships—singles

year	men	women
1989	Yang Yang (China)	Li Lingwei (China)
1990	Zhao Jianhua (China)	S. Susanti (Indon.)
1991	A. Wiranata (Indon.)	S. Susanti (Indon.)
1992	Liu Jun (China)	Tang Jiuhong (China)
1993	H. Arbi (Indon.)	S. Susanti (Indon.)

Uber Cup (women)

year	winner	runner-up
1983–84	China	England
1985–86	China	Indonesia
1987–88	China	S.Korea
1989–90	China	S.Korea
1991–92	China	S.Korea

Thomas Cup (men)

year	winner	runner-up
1983–84	Indonesia	China
1985–86	China	Indonesia
1987–88	China	Malaysia
1989–90	China	Malaysia
1991–92	Malaysia	Indonesia

BASEBALL

World Series*

year	winning team	losing team	results
1989	Oakland Athletics (AL)	San Francisco Giants (NL)	4–0
1990	Cincinnati Reds (NL)	Oakland Athletics (AL)	4–0
1991	Minnesota Twins (AL)	Atlanta Braves (NL)	4–3
1992	Toronto Blue Jays (AL)	Atlanta Braves (NL)	4–2
1993	Toronto Blue Jays (AL)	Philadelphia Phillies (NL)	4–2

*AL—American League; NL—National League.

Toronto Blue Jays: World Series (1993)

RICK STEWART—ALLSPORT

Japan Series*

year	winning team	losing team	results
1989	Yomiuri Giants (CL)	Kintetsu Buffaloes (PL)	4–3
1990	Seibu Lions (PL)	Yomiuri Giants (CL)	4–0
1991	Seibu Lions (PL)	Hiroshima Tōyō Carp (CL)	4–3
1992	Seibu Lions (PL)	Yakult Swallows (CL)	4–3
1993	Yakult Swallows (CL)	Seibu Lions (PL)	4–3

*CL—Central League; PL—Pacific League.

BASKETBALL

National Basketball Association (NBA) Championship

season	winner	runner-up	results
1988–89	Detroit Pistons	Los Angeles Lakers	4–0
1989–90	Detroit Pistons	Portland Trail Blazers	4–1
1990–91	Chicago Bulls	Los Angeles Lakers	4–1
1991–92	Chicago Bulls	Portland Trail Blazers	4–2
1992–93	Chicago Bulls	Phoenix Suns	4–2

Division I National Collegiate Athletic Association (NCAA) Championship—men

year	winner	runner-up	score
1989	Michigan	Seton Hall	80–79
1990	UNLV	Duke	103–73
1991	Duke	Kansas	72–65
1992	Duke	Michigan	71–51
1993	North Carolina	Michigan	77–71

World Amateur Basketball Championship—men

year	winner	runner-up
1984	United States	Spain
1986	United States	U.S.S.R.
1988	U.S.S.R.	Yugoslavia
1990	Yugoslavia	U.S.S.R.
1992	United States	Croatia

World Amateur Basketball Championship—women

year	winner	runner-up
1984	United States	South Korea
1986	United States	U.S.S.R.
1988	United States	Yugoslavia
1990	United States	Yugoslavia
1992	Unified Team	China

Division I National Collegiate Athletic Association (NCAA) Championship—women

year	winner	runner-up	score
1989	Tennessee	Auburn	76–60
1990	Stanford	Auburn	88–81
1991	Tennessee	Virginia	70–67
1992	Stanford	Western Kentucky	78–62
1993	Texas Tech	Ohio State	84–82

National Invitation Tournament (NIT) Championship

year	winner	runner-up	score
1989	St. John's	St. Louis	73–65
1990	Vanderbilt	St. Louis	74–72
1991	Stanford	Oklahoma	78–72
1992	Virginia	Notre Dame	81–76
1993	Minnesota	Georgetown	62–61

Chicago Bulls: NBA Championship (1993)

WALTER IOOSS JR.—SPORTS ILLUSTRATED

BILLIARDS

WPA World Nine-ball Championships

year	men's champion	women's champion
1990	E. Strickland (U.S.)	R. Bell (U.S.)
1991	E. Strickland (U.S.)	R. Bell (U.S.)
1992	J. Archer (U.S.)	F. Stark (Ger.)
1993	Chao Feng-pang (Taiwan)	L.J. Jones (U.S.)

World Three-Cushion Championship

year	winner
1989	T. Blomdahl (Swed.)
1990	L. Dielis (Belg.)
1991	R. Ceulemans (Belg.)
1992	T. Blomdahl (Swed.)
1993	T. Blomdahl (Swed.)

World Professional Snooker Championships

year	winner
1988	S. Davis
1989	S. Davis
1990	S. Hendry
1991	J. Parrott
1992	S. Hendry
1993	S. Hendry

BOWLING

ABC Bowling Championships—Regular Division

year	singles	score	all-events	score
1989	P. Tetreault	813	G. Hall	2,227
1990	R. Hochrein	791	M. Neumann	2,168
1991	E. Deines	826	T. Howery	2,216
1992	Blatchford, Youker (tie)	801	M. Tucker	2,158
1993	D. Bock	798	J. Nimke	2,254

FIQ World Bowling Championship—men

year	singles	pairs	triples	fives
1979	G. Bugden (U.K.)	Australia	Malaysia	Australia
1983	T. Cariello (U.S.)	Australia	Sweden	Finland
1987	P. Rolland (Fr.)	Sweden	United States	Sweden
1991	Ying Chieh Ma (Taiwan)	United States	United States	Taiwan

WIBC Bowling Championship—Open Division

year	singles	score	all-events	score
1989	L. Anderson	683	N. Fehr	1,911
1990	Carter, Miller-Mackie (tie)	705	C. Norman	1,984
1991	D. Kuhn	773	D. Kuhn	2,036
1992	P. Ann	680	M. Tokimoto	1,928
1993	K. Collura, K. Murph (tie)	747	A.M. Duggan	1,990

FIQ World Bowling Championship—women

year	singles	pairs	triples	fives
1979	L. de la Rosa (Phil.)	Philippines	United States	United States
1983	L. Sulkanen (Swed.)	Denmark	West Germany	Sweden
1987	E. Piccini (Mex.)	United States	United States	United States
1991	M. Beckel (Ger.)	Japan	Canada	South Korea

Professional Bowlers Association (PBA) Firestone Tournament of Champions

year	champion
1989	D. Ballard
1990	D. Ferraro
1991	D. Ozio
1992	M. McDowell
1993	G. Branham

BOWLS

World Lawn Bowls Championships

year	singles	pairs	triples	fours	team
1984	P. Bellis (N.Z.)	United States	Ireland	England	Scotland
1988	D. Bryant (Eng.)	New Zealand	New Zealand	Ireland	England
1992	T. Allcock (Eng.)	Scotland	Israel	Scotland	Scotland

BOXING

World heavyweight champions —no weight limit

WBA
Mike Tyson (U.S.; 3/7/87)
James Douglas (U.S.; 2/11/90)
Evander Holyfield (U.S.; 10/26/90)
Riddick Bowe (U.S.; 11/13/92)
Evander Holyfield (U.S.; 11/6/93)

WBC
James Douglas (U.S.; 2/11/90)
Evander Holyfield (U.S.; 10/26/90)
Riddick Bowe (U.S.; 11/13/92)
stripped of title in 1992
Lennox Lewis (U.K.; 12/14/92)

IBF
Mike Tyson (U.S.; 8/1/87)
James Douglas (U.S.; 2/11/90)
Evander Holyfield (U.S.; 10/25/90)
Riddick Bowe (U.S.; 11/13/92)
Evander Holyfield (U.S.; 11/6/93)

World cruiserweight champions —top weight 195 pounds

WBA
Taoufik Belbouli (Fr.; 3/25/89)
declared vacant in 1989
Robert Daniels (U.S.; 11/28/89)
Bobby Czyz (U.S.; 3/8/91)
vacant
Orlin Norris (U.S.; 11/6/93)

WBC
Evander Holyfield (U.S.; 4/9/88)
gave up title in 1988
Carlos de Léon (P.R.; 5/17/89)
Massimiliano Duran (Italy; 7/27/90)
Anaclet Wamba (Fr.; 7/20/91)

IBF
Glenn McCrory (U.K.; 6/3/89)
Jeff Lampkin (U.S.; 3/22/90)
gave up title in 1991
James Warring (U.S.; 9/7/91)
Alfred Cole (U.S.; 7/30/92)

World light heavyweight champions —top weight 175 pounds

WBA
Virgil Hill (U.S.; 9/5/87)
Thomas Hearns (U.S.; 6/3/91)
Iran Barkley (U.S.; 3/21/92)
gave up title in 1992
Virgil Hill (U.S.; 9/92)

WBC
Dennis Andries (U.K; 2/2/89)
Jeff Harding (Australia; 6/24/89)
Dennis Andries (U.K.; 7/28/90)
Jeff Harding (Australia; 9/11/91)

IBF
Slobodan Kacar (Yugos.; 12/21/1985)
Bobby Czyz (U.S.; 9/6/86)
Charles Williams (U.S.; 10/29/87)
Henry Maske (Ger.; 3/20/93)

World super middleweight champions —top weight 168 pounds

WBA*
Fulgencio Obelmejias (Venez.; 5/23/88)
Baek In-chul (S.Kor.; 5/27/89)
Christophe Tiozzo (Fr.; 3/30/90)
Victor Cordoba (Pan.; 4/5/91)
Michael Nunn (U.S.; 9/12/92)

WBC†
Sugar Ray Leonard (U.S.; 11/7/1988)
gave up title in 1990
Mauro Galvano (Italy; 12/15/90)
Nigel Benn (U.K.; 10/3/92)

IBF
Lindell Holmes (U.S.; 1/27/90)
Darrin Van Horn (U.S.; 5/18/91)
Iran Barkley (U.S.; 1/10/92)
James Toney (U.S.; 2/13/93)

*Super middleweight division first recognized by WBA in 1987. †Super middleweight division first recognized by WBC in 1988.

World middleweight champions —top weight 160 pounds

WBA
Sumbu Kalambay (Italy; 10/23/87)
stripped of title in 1989
Mike McCallum (Jam.; 5/13/89)
stripped of title in 1991
Reggie Johnson (U.S.; 4/22/92)
John David Jackson (U.S.; 10/2/93)

WBC
Iran Barkley (U.S.; 6/6/88)
Roberto Duran (Pan.; 2/24/89)
stripped of title in 1990
Julian Jackson (U.S.; 11/24/90)
Gerald McClellan (U.S.; 5/8/93)

IBF
Frank Tate (U.S.; 10/10/87)
Michael Nunn (U.S.; 7/28/88)
James Toney (U.S.; 5/10/91)
gave up title in 1993
Roy Jones (U.S.; 5/22/93)

World junior middleweight champions —top weight 154 pounds (also called super welterweight)

WBA
Gilbert Dele (Fr.; 2/23/91)
Vinny Pazienza (U.S.; 10/11/91)
gave up title in 1992
Julio César Vásquez (Arg.; 12/22/92)

WBC
Gianfranco Rosi (Italy; 10/2/87)
Donald Curry (U.S.; 7/8/88)
René Jacquot (Fr.; 2/11/89)
John Mugabi (Uganda; 7/8/89)
Terry Norris (U.S.; 3/31/90)
Simon Brown (U.S.; 12/18/93)

IBF
Buster Drayton (U.S.; 6/4/86)
Matthew Hilton (Can.; 6/27/87)
Robert Hines (U.S.; 11/4/88)
Darrin Van Horn (U.S.; 2/4/89)
Gianfranco Rosi (Italy; 7/16/89)

World welterweight champions —top weight 147 pounds

WBA
Mark Breland (U.S.; 2/4/89)
Aaron Davis (U.S.; 7/8/90)
Meldrick Taylor (U.S.; 1/19/91)
Crisanto España (Venez.; 10/31/92)

WBC
Marlon Starling (U.S.; 2/4/89)
Maurice Blocker (U.S.; 8/19/90)
Simon Brown (Jam.; 3/18/91)
James McGirt (U.S.; 11/29/91)
Pernell Whitaker (U.S.; 3/6/93)

IBF
Simon Brown (Jam.; 4/23/88)
gave up title in 1991
Maurice Blocker (U.S.; 10/4/91)
Felix Trinidad (P.R.; 6/19/93)

World junior welterweight champions —top weight 140 pounds (also called super lightweight)

WBA
Loreto Garza (U.S.; 8/17/90)
Edwin Rosario (P.R.; 6/15/91)
Akinobu Hiranaka (Japan; 4/10/92)
Morris East (Phil.; 9/9/92)
Juan Martin Coggi (Arg.; 1/12/93)

WBC
René Arrendondo (Mex.; 5/6/86)
Tsuyoshi Hamada (Japan; 7/24/86)
René Arrendondo (Mex.; 7/22/87)
Roger Mayweather (U.S.; 11/12/87)
Julio César Chávez (Mex.; 5/13/89)

IBF
Julio César Chávez (Mex.; 3/17/90)
gave up title in 1991
Rafael Pineda (Colom.; 12/7/91)
Pernell Whitaker (U.S.; 7/18/92)
gave up title in 1993
Charles Murray (U.S.; 5/15/93)

World lightweight champions —top weight 135 pounds

WBA
Pernell Whitaker (U.S.; 8/11/90)
gave up title in 1992
Joey Gamache (U.S.; 6/13/92)
Tony Lopez (U.S.; 10/24/92)
Dingaan Thobela (S.Af.; 6/26/93)
Olzubek Nazarov (Russia; 10/30/93)

WBC
Julio César Chávez (Mex.; 10/29/88)
gave up title in 1989
Pernell Whitaker (U.S.; 8/20/89)
gave up title in 1992
Miguel González (Mex.; 8/24/92)

IBF
Vincent Pazienzia (U.S.; 6/7/87)
Greg Haugen (U.S.; 2/6/88)
Pernell Whitaker (U.S.; 2/20/89)
gave up title in 1992
Fred Pendleton (U.S.; 1/10/93)

World junior lightweight champions —top weight 130 pounds (also called super featherweight)

WBA
Brian Mitchell (S.Af.; 9/27/86)
gave up title in 1991
Joey Gamache (U.S.; 6/28/91)
gave up title in 1991
Genaro Hernandez (U.S.; 11/22/91)

WBC
Hector Camacho (U.S.; 8/7/83)
gave up title in 1984
Julio César Chávez (Mex.; 9/13/84)
gave up title
Azumah Nelson (Ghana; 2/29/88)

IBF
Juan Molina (P.R.; 10/7/89)
Tony Lopez (U.S.; 5/20/90)
Brian Mitchell (S.Af.; 9/13/91)
gave up title in 1992
Juan Molina (P.R.; 2/22/92)

World featherweight champions —top weight 126 pounds

WBA
Eusebio Pedroza (Pan.; 4/15/78)
Barry McGuigan (N.Ire.; 6/8/85)
Steve Cruz (U.S.; 6/23/86)
Antonio Esparragoza (Venez.; 3/6/87)
Park Yung Kyun (S.Kor.; 3/30/91)
Eloy Rojas (Venez.; 12/93)

WBC
Jeff Fenech (Australia; 3/7/88)
gave up title in 1990
Marcos Villasana (Mex.; 6/2/90)
Paul Hodkinson (U.K.; 11/13/91)
Gregorio Vargas (Mex.; 4/28/93)
Kevin Kelley (U.S.; 12/93)

IBF
Jorge Paez (Mex.; 8/4/88)
gave up title in 1991
Troy Dorsey (U.S.; 6/3/91)
Manuel Medina (Mex.; 8/12/91)
Tom Johnson (U.S.; 2/26/93)

World junior featherweight champions —top weight 122 pounds (also called super bantamweight)

WBA
Jesus Salud (U.S.; 12/11/89)
stripped of title in 1990
Luís Mendoza (Colom.; 9/11/90)
Raul Pérez (Mex.; 10/7/91)
Wilfredo Vásquez (P.R.; 3/27/92)

WBC
Pedro Decima (Arg.; 11/5/90)
Kiyoshi Hatanaka (Japan; 2/3/91)
Daniel Zaragoza (Mex.; 6/14/91)
Thierry Jacob (Fr.; 3/20/92)
Tracy Patterson (U.S.; 6/23/92)

IBF
José Sanabria (Venez.; 5/21/88)
Fabrice Benichou (Fr.; 3/10/89)
Welcome Ncita (S.Af.; 3/10/90)
Kennedy McKinney (U.S.; 12/2/92)

World bantamweight champions —top weight 118 pounds

WBA
Khaokor Galaxy (Thai.; 7/9/89)
Luisito Espinosa (Phil.; 10/18/89)
Israel Contreras (Venez.; 10/19/91)
Eddie Cook (U.S.; 3/15/92)
Eliecer Julio (Colom.; 10/10/92)
Junior Jones (U.S.; 10/23/93)

WBC
Greg Richardson (U.S.; 2/25/91)
Joichiro Tatsuyoshi (Japan; 9/19/91)
vacant
Victor Rabañales (Mex.; 3/30/92)
Byun Jong-Il (S.Kor.; 3/28/93)
Yasuei Yakushiji (Japan; 12/22/93)

IBF
Shingaki Satoshi (Japan; 4/15/84)
Jeff Fenech (Austl.; 4/26/85)
vacant
Kelvin Seabrooks (U.S.; 5/16/87)
Orlando Canizales (U.S.; 7/9/88)

World junior bantamweight champions —top weight 115 pounds (also called super flyweight)

WBA
Watanabe Jiro (Japan; 4/8/82)
stripped of title in 1984
Khaosai Galaxy (Thai.; 11/21/84)
gave up title in 1991
Katsuya Onizuka (Japan; 4/10/92)

WBC
Gilberto Román (Mex.; 3/30/86)
Jesús Rojas (Colom.; 8/9/87)
Gilberto Román (Mex.; 4/8/88)
Nana Konadu (Ghana; 11/7/89)
Moon Sung Kil (S.Kor.; 1/20/90)
José Luis Bueno (Mex.; 11/93)

IBF
Chang Tae-il (S.Kor.; 5/17/87)
Ellyas Pical (Indon.; 10/17/87)
Juan Polo Pérez (Colom.; 10/14/89)
Robert Quiroga (U.S.; 4/21/90)
Julio Borboa (Mex.; 1/16/93)

E. Holyfield (right): WBA and IBF heavyweight champion (1993)
RICHARD MACKSON—SPORTS ILLUSTRATED

World flyweight champions —top weight 112 pounds

WBA
Leopard Tamakuma (Japan; 7/29/90)
Elvis Alvarez (Colom.; 3/14/91)
Kim Yong Kang (S.Kor.; 6/1/91)
Aquiles Guzmán (Venez.; 9/26/92)
David Griman (Venez.; 12/92)

WBC
Kim Young Kang (S.Kor.; 7/24/88)
Sot Chitalada (Thai.; 6/3/89)
Muangchai Kittikasem (Thai.; 2/15/91)
Yury Arbachakov (Russia; 6/23/92)

IBF
Rolando Bohol (Phil.; 1/16/88)
Duke McKenzie (U.K.; 10/5/88)
Dave McAuley (U.K.; 6/7/89)
Rodolfo Blanco (Colom.; 6/11/92)
Phichit Sithbangprachan (Thai.; 11/29/92)

World junior flyweight champions —top weight 108 pounds

WBA
Yuh Myung Woo (S.Kor.; 12/8/85)
Hiroki Ioka (Japan; 12/17/91)
Yuh Myung Woo (S.Kor.; 11/18/92)
gave up title in 1993
Leo Gamez (Venez.; 10/21/93)

WBC
Humberto González (Mex.; 6/25/89)
Rolando Pascua (Phil.; 12/19/90)
Melchor Cob Castro (Mex.; 3/25/91)
Humberto González (Mex.; 6/4/91)
Michael Carbajal (U.S.; 3/13/93)

IBF
Choi Chong Hwon (S.Kor.; 12/7/86)
Tacy Macalos (Phil.; 11/6/88)
Muangchai Kittikasem (Thai.; 5/2/89)
Michael Carbajal (U.S.; 7/29/90)

World mini-flyweight champions —top weight 105 pounds (also called strawweight)

WBA
Kim Bong Jun (S.Kor.; 4/16/89)
Choi Hi Yong (S.Kor.; 2/2/91)
Ohashi Hideyuki (Japan; 10/14/92)
Chana Porpaoin (Thai.; 2/10/93)

WBC
Napa Kiatwanchai (Thai.; 11/13/88)
Choi Jum Hwan (S.Kor.; 11/12/89)
Ohashi Hideyuki (Japan; 2/7/90)
Ricardo López (Mex.; 10/25/90)

IBF
Nico Thomas (Indon.; 6/17/89)
Eric Chavez (Phil.; 9/21/89)
Falan Lookmingkwan (Thai.; 2/21/90)
Manny Melchor (Phil.; 9/6/92)
Ratanapol Vorapin (Thai.; 12/10/92)

CHESS

World Chess Championships—men

year	winner	runner-up
1986	G. Kasparov (U.S.S.R.)	A. Karpov (U.S.S.R.)
1987	G. Kasparov (U.S.S.R.)	A. Karpov (U.S.S.R.)
1990	G. Kasparov (U.S.S.R.)	A. Karpov (U.S.S.R.)
1993	A. Karpov (Russia)	J. Timman (Neth.)

World Chess Championships—women

year	winner	runner-up
1984	M. Chiburdanidze (U.S.S.R.)	I. Levitina (U.S.S.R.)
1986	M. Chiburdanidze (U.S.S.R.)	E. Akhmilovskaya (U.S.S.R.)
1988	M. Chiburdanidze (U.S.S.R.)	N. Ioseliani (U.S.S.R.)
1991	Xie Jun (China)	M. Chiburdanidze (U.S.S.R.)

Olympiads—men

year	winner	runner-up
1986	U.S.S.R.	United Kingdom
1988	U.S.S.R.	United Kingdom
1989	U.S.S.R.	Yugoslavia
1992	Russia	Uzbekistan

Olympiads—women

year	winner	runner-up
1984	U.S.S.R.	Bulgaria
1986	U.S.S.R.	Hungary
1988	Hungary	U.S.S.R.
1992	Georgia	Ukraine

CONTRACT BRIDGE

Bermuda Bowl

year	winner	runner-up
1987	United States	United Kingdom
1989	Brazil	United States
1991	Iceland	Poland
1993	Netherlands	Norway

World Contract Bridge Pair Championship

year	open winners	women's winners	mixed winners
1986	Jeff Meckstroth, Eric Rodwell (U.S.)	Jacqul Mitchell, Amalya Kearse (U.S.)	Pam Wittes, John Wittes (U.S.)
1990	Marcelo Branco, Gabriel Chagas (Braz.)	Kerri Shuman, Karen McCallum (U.S.)	Peter Weichsel, Juanita Chambers (U.S.)

World Team Olympiad

year	open winner	open runner-up	women's winner	women's runner-up
1988	United States	Austria	Denmark	United Kingdom
1992	France	United States	Austria	United Kingdom

CRICKET

All-time First-class Test Cricket Standings (as of Sept. 30, 1993)

	England			Australia			South Africa			West Indies			New Zealand		
	wins	draws	losses	w	d	l	w	d	l	w	d	l	w	d	l
England v.	—	—	—	89	80	105	46	38	18	24	37	43	33	35	4
Australia v.	105	80	89	—	—	—	29	13	11	30	21*	26	11	10	7
South Africa v.	18	38	46	11	13	29	—	—	—	0	0	1	19	6	2
West Indies v.	43	37	24	26	21*	30	1	0	0	—	—	—	8	12	4
New Zealand v.	4	35	33	7	10	11	2	6	19	4	12	8	—	—	—
India v.	14	36	30	8	18*	24	0	3	1	6	30	26	12	13	6
Pakistan v.	7	31	14	9	13	12	†			7	12	12	14	16	3
Sri Lanka v.	1	1	3	0	3	4	0	2	1	†			1	6	4
Zimbabwe v.	†			†			†			†			0	1	1

	India			Pakistan			Sri Lanka			Zimbabwe		
	w	d	l	w	d	l	w	d	l	w	d	l
England v.	30	36	14	14	31	7	3	1	1	†		
Australia v.	24	18*	8	12	13	9	4	3	0	†		
South Africa v.	1	3	0	†			1	2	0	†		
West Indies v.	26	30	6	12	12	7	†			†		
New Zealand v.	6	13	12	3	16	14	4	6	1	1	1	0
India v.	—	—	—	4	33	7	5	4	1	1	1	0
Pakistan v.	7	33	4	—	—	—	6	5	1	†		
Sri Lanka v.	1	4	5	1	5	6	—	—	—	†		
Zimbabwe v.	0	1	1	†			†			—	—	—

*Including one tie. †No matches.

World Cup

year	result			
1975	West Indies	291–8	Australia	274
1979	West Indies	286–9	England	194
1983	India	183	West Indies	140
1987	Australia	253–5	England	246–8
1992	Pakistan	249–6	England	227

CURLING

World Curling Championship—men

year	winner	runner-up
1989	Canada	Switzerland
1990	Canada	Scotland
1991	Scotland	Canada
1992	Switzerland	Scotland
1993	Canada	Scotland

World Curling Championship—women

year	winner	runner-up
1989	Canada	Norway
1990	Norway	Scotland
1991	Norway	Canada
1992	Sweden	United States
1993	Canada	Germany

Canada: World Curling Championship-men (1993)
MICHAEL BURNS

CYCLING

Tour de France

year	winner	km
1989	G. LeMond (U.S.)	3,215
1990	G. LeMond (U.S.)	3,399
1991	M. Indurain (Spain)	3,935
1992	M. Indurain (Spain)	3,983
1993	M. Indurain (Spain)	3,700

Cycling World Track Championships—women (amateur)

year	sprint	3-km pursuit
1989	E. Salumae (U.S.S.R.)	J. Longo (Fr.)
1990	C. Young (U.S.)	J. Longo (Fr.)
1991	I. Haringa (Neth.)	P. Rossner (Ger.)
1992	E. Salumae (Est.)	P. Rossner (Ger.)
1993	T. Dubnicoff (Can.)	R. Twigg (U.S.)

Cycling World Road-Racing Championships

year	men (amateur)	men (professional)	women (amateur)
1989	J. Halupczok (Pol.)	G. LeMond (U.S.)	J. Longo (Fr.)
1990	M. Gualdi (Italy)	R. Dhaenens (Belg.)	C. Marsal (Fr.)
1991	V. Pjaksinski (U.S.S.R.)	G. Bugno (Italy)	L. van Moorsel (Neth.)
1992	F. Casartelli (Italy)	G. Bugno (Italy)	K. Watt (Austl.)
1993	J. Ullrich (Ger.)	L. Armstrong (U.S.)	L. van Moorsel (Neth.)

Cycling World Track Championships—men

year	sprint (amateur)	sprint (professional)	pursuit (amateur)	pursuit (professional)	motor-paced (amateur)	motor-paced (professional)
1990	B. Huck (E.Ger.)	M. Hübner (E.Ger.)	Ye. Berzin (U.S.S.R.)	V. Ekimov (U.S.S.R.)	R. Königshofer (Austria)	W. Brugna (Italy)
1991	J. Fiedler (Ger.)	not awarded	J. Lehmann (Ger.)	F. Moreau (Fr.)	R. Königshofer (Austria)	D. Clark (Austl.)
1992	not held	M. Hübner (Ger.)	not held	M. McCarthy (U.S.)	C. Podlesch (Ger.)	P. Steiger (Switz.)
1993*	G. Niewand (Austl.)		G. Obree (U.K.)		J. Veggerby (Den.)	

*From 1993 professionals and amateurs competed in the same event.

FENCING

World Fencing Championships—men

year	individual			team		
	foil	épée	sabre	foil	épée	sabre
1988	S. Cerioni (Italy)	A. Schmitt (W.Ger.)	J.-F. Lamour (Fr.)	U.S.S.R.	France	Hungary
1989	A. Koch (W.Ger.)	M. Pereira (Spain)	G. Kirienko (U.S.S.R.)	U.S.S.R.	Italy	U.S.S.R.
1990	P. Omnès (Fr.)	T. Gerull (W.Ger.)	G. Nebald (Hung.)	Italy	Italy	U.S.S.R.
1991	I. Weissenborn (Ger.)	A. Shuvalov (U.S.S.R.)	G. Kirienko (U.S.S.R.)	Cuba	U.S.S.R.	Hungary
1992	P. Omnès (Fr.)	E. Srecki (Fr.)	B. Szabo (Hung.)	Germany	Germany	Unified Team
1993	A. Koch (Ger.)	P. Kolobkov (Russia)	G. Kirienko (Russia)	Germany	Italy	Hungary

World Fencing Championships—women

year	individual foil	team foil	individual épée	team épée
1989	O. Velitchko (U.S.S.R.)	West Germany	A. Straub (Switz.)	Hungary
1990	A. Fichtel (W.Ger.)	Italy	T. Chappe (Cuba)	West Germany
1991	G. Trillini (Italy)	Italy	M. Horvath (Hung.)	Hungary
1992	G. Trillini (Italy)	Italy	not held	not held
1993	F. Bortolozzi (Italy)	Germany	O. Jermakova (Est.)	Hungary

FIELD HOCKEY

World Cup Field Hockey Championships—men

year	winner	runner-up
1986	Australia	England
1990	The Netherlands	Pakistan

World Cup Field Hockey Championships—women

year	winner	runner-up
1986	The Netherlands	West Germany
1990	The Netherlands	Australia

FOOTBALL

FIFA World Cup

year	result			
1982	Italy	3	West Germany	1
1986	Argentina	3	West Germany	2
1990	West Germany	1	Argentina	0

European Cup-Winners' Cup

season	result			
1988–89	Barcelona	2	Sampdoria (Italy)	0
1989–90	Sampdoria (Italy)	2	Anderlecht (Belg.)	0
1990–91	Manchester United	2	Barcelona	1
1991–92	Werder Bremen (Ger.)	2	AS Monaco	0
1992–93	Parma (Italy)	3	Royal Antwerp	1

Libertadores de América Cup

year	winner (country)	runner-up (country)	scores
1989	Nacional of Medellín (Colom.)	Olímpia (Paraguay)	0–2, 2–0, 5–4*
1990	Olímpia (Paraguay)	Barcelona (Ecuador)	2–0, 1–1
1991	Colo Colo (Chile)	Olímpia (Paraguay)	0–0, 3–0
1992	São Paulo (Braz.)	Newell's Old Boys (Arg.)	0–1, 1–0, 3–2*
1993	São Paulo (Braz.)	Universidad Catolica (Chile)	5–1, 0–2

*Winner determined in penalty shootout after tiebreaking game.

The European Cup of Champion Clubs

season	result			
1988–89	A.C. Milan	4	Steaua Bucharest	0
1989–90	A.C. Milan	1	Benfica (Port.)	0
1990–91	Red Star Belgrade*	0	Marseille	0
1991–92	Barcelona	1	Sampdoria (Italy)	0
1992–93	Olympique Marseille	1	A.C. Milan	0

*Won on penalty kicks.

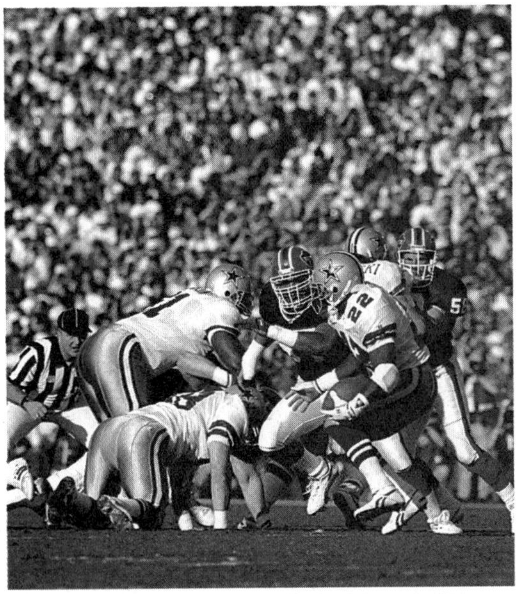

Dallas Cowboys: Super Bowl (1993)

FOCUS ON SPORTS

U.S. Football—professional

Super Bowl

	season	result			
XXIII	1988–89	San Francisco 49ers (NFC)	20	Cincinnati Bengals (AFC)	16
XXIV	1989–90	San Francisco 49ers (NFC)	55	Denver Broncos (AFC)	10
XXV	1990–91	New York Giants (NFC)	20	Buffalo Bills (AFC)	19
XXVI	1991–92	Washington Redskins (NFC)	37	Buffalo Bills (AFC)	24
XXVII	1992–93	Dallas Cowboys (NFC)	52	Buffalo Bills (AFC)	17

U.S. Football—college

Rose Bowl

season	result			
1988–89	Michigan	22	Southern California	14
1989–90	Southern California	17	Michigan	10
1990–91	Washington	46	Iowa	34
1991–92	Washington	34	Michigan	14
1992–93	Michigan	38	Washington	31
1993–94	Wisconsin	21	UCLA	16

Orange Bowl

season	result			
1988–89	Miami (Fla.)	23	Nebraska	3
1989–90	Notre Dame	21	Colorado	6
1990–91	Colorado	10	Notre Dame	9
1991–92	Miami (Fla.)	22	Nebraska	0
1992–93	Florida St.	27	Nebraska	14
1993–94	Florida St.	18	Nebraska	16

France: Five Nations Championship (1993)
HOWARD BOYLAN—ALLSPORT

Sugar Bowl

season	result			
1988–89	Florida St.	13	Auburn	7
1989–90	Miami (Fla.)	33	Alabama	25
1990–91	Tennessee	23	Virginia	22
1991–92	Notre Dame	39	Florida	28
1992–93	Alabama	34	Miami (Fla.)	13
1993–94	Florida	41	West Virginia	7

Cotton Bowl

season	result			
1988–89	UCLA	17	Arkansas	3
1989–90	Tennessee	31	Arkansas	27
1990–91	Miami (Fla.)	46	Texas	3
1991–92	Florida State	10	Texas A&M	2
1992–93	Notre Dame	28	Texas A&M	3
1993–94	Notre Dame	24	Texas A&M	21

U.S. College Football National Champion

season	champion
1988–89	Notre Dame
1989–90	Miami (Fla.)
1990–91	Colorado* Georgia Tech*
1991–92	Miami (Fla.)* Washington*
1992–93	Alabama
1993–94	Florida St.

*Tied.

Canadian football—professional

Grey Cup

year	result			
1988	Winnipeg Blue Bombers (EFC)	22	British Columbia Lions (WFC)	21
1989	Saskatchewan Roughriders (WFC)	43	Hamilton Tiger-Cats (EFC)	40
1990	Winnipeg Blue Bombers (EFC)	50	Edmonton Eskimos (WFC)	11
1991	Toronto Argonauts (EFC)	36	Calgary Stampeders (WFC)	21
1992	Calgary Stampeders (WFC)	24	Winnipeg Blue Bombers (EFC)	10
1993	Edmonton Eskimos (WFC)	33	Winnipeg Blue Bombers (EFC)	23

Rugby Union football

Record of International Test matches 1871 to Aug. 31, 1993

	England			Scotland			Ireland			Wales			British Isles		
	wins	draws	losses	wins	draws	losses	wins	draws	losses	wins	draws	losses	wins	draws	losses
England v.	—	—	—	54	17	39	61	8	37	39	12	48	—	—	—
Scotland v.	39	17	54	—	—	—	55	4	45	42	2	53	—	—	—
Ireland v.	37	8	61	45	4	54	—	—	—	33	6	57	—	—	—
Wales v.	48	12	39	53	2	42	57	6	33	—	—	—	—	—	—
British Isles* v.	—	—	—	—	—	—	—	—	—	—	—	—	—	—	—
South Africa v.	6	1	3	5	0	3	8	1	1	6	1	0	20	6	14
New Zealand v.	13	0	3	14	2	0	11	1	0	12	0	3	24	3	5
Australia v.	12	0	6	7	0	7	8	0	6	8	0	8	3	0	14
France v.	24	7	38	31	3	30	36	5	25	28	3	36	—	—	—

	South Africa			New Zealand			Australia			France		
	wins	draws	losses	wins	draws	losses	wins	draws	losses	wins	draws	losses
England v.	3	1	6	3	0	13	6	0	12	38	7	24
Scotland v.	3	0	5	0	2	14	7	0	7	30	3	31
Ireland v.	1	1	8	0	1	11	6	0	8	25	5	36
Wales v.	0	1	6	3	0	12	8	0	8	36	3	28
British Isles* v.	14	6	20	5	3	24	14	0	3	—	—	—
South Africa v.	—	—	—	20	2	16	22	0	10	13	5	5
New Zealand v.	16	2	20	—	—	—	66	5	26	23	0	5
Australia v.	10	0	22	26	5	66	—	—	—	9	2	12
France v.	5	5	13	5	0	23	12	2	9	—	—	—

*The British Isles ("British Lions") is a combined team from the four "Home Unions" (England, Ireland, Scotland, and Wales).

Five Nations Championship

year	result
1989	France
1990	Scotland*
1991	England*
1992	England*
1993	France

*Grand Slam winner.

World Cup

year	result			
1987	New Zealand	29	France	9
1991	Australia	12	England	6

Rugby League football

World Cup

year	result			
1972	Great Britain	10*	Australia	10
1975†	Australia‡			
1977†	Australia	13	Great Britain	12
1988	Australia	25	New Zealand	12
1992	Australia	10	Great Britain	6

*Great Britain won on match points. †Called International Championship from 1975 to 1977. ‡Championships played without a grand final match; England was the runner-up.

B. Langer: Masters Tournament (1993)

JOHN IACONO—SPORTS ILLUSTRATED

L. Merten: U.S. Women's Open champion (1993)

JACQUELINE DUVOISIN—SPORTS ILLUSTRATED

GOLF

British Open Tournament—men

year	winner
1989	M. Calcavecchia (U.S.)
1990	N. Faldo (U.K.)
1991	I. Baker-Finch (Austl.)
1992	N. Faldo (U.K.)
1993	G. Norman (Austl.)

United States Open Championship—men

year	winner
1989	C. Strange (U.S.)
1990	H. Irwin (U.S.)
1991	P. Stewart (U.S.)
1992	T. Kite (U.S.)
1993	L. Janzen (U.S.)

Masters Tournament

year	winner
1988	S. Lyle (Scot.)
1989	N. Faldo (U.K.)
1990	N. Faldo (U.K.)
1991	I. Woosnam (U.K.)
1992	F. Couples (U.S.)
1993	B. Langer (Ger.)

U.S. Professional Golfers' Association (PGA) championship

year	winner
1989	P. Stewart (U.S.)
1990	W. Grady (Austl.)
1991	J. Daly (U.S.)
1992	N. Price (Zimb.)
1993	P. Azinger (U.S.)

British Amateur Championship—men

year	winner
1989	S. Richardson (U.K.)
1990	R. Muntz (Neth.)
1991	R. Willison (U.K.)
1992	S. Dundas (U.K.)
1993	I. Pyman (U.K.)

United States Amateur Championship—men

year	winner
1989	C. Patton (U.S.)
1990	P. Mickelson (U.S.)
1991	M. Voges (U.S.)
1992	J. Leonard (U.S.)
1993	J. Harris (U.S.)

Women's British Open Championship

year	winner
1989	J. Geddes (U.S.)
1990	H. Alfredsson (Swed.)
1991	P. Grice-Whittaker (U.K.)
1992	P. Sheehan (U.S.)
1993	K. Lunn (Austl.)

Ladies' British Amateur Championship

year	winner
1989	H. Dobson (U.K.)
1990	J. Hall (U.K.)
1991	J. Morley (U.K.)
1992	P. Pedersen (Den.)
1993	C. Lambert (U.K.)

United States Women's Open champions

year	winner
1989	B. King (U.S.)
1990	B. King (U.S.)
1991	M. Mallon (U.S.)
1992	P. Sheehan (U.K.)
1993	L. Merten (U.S.)

United States Women's Amateur Championship

year	winner
1989	V. Goetze (U.S.)
1990	P. Hurst (U.S.)
1991	A. Fruhwirth (U.S.)
1992	V. Goetze (U.S.)
1993	J. McGill (U.S.)

Ladies' Professional Golf Association (LPGA) champions

year	winner
1989	N. Lopez (U.S.)
1990	B. Daniel (U.S.)
1991	M. Mallon (U.S.)
1992	B. King (U.S.)
1993	P. Sheehan (U.S.)

Team events

Walker Cup—men (amateur)

year	result
1985	United States 13, Britain and Ireland 11
1987	United States 16½, Britain and Ireland 7½
1989	Britain and Ireland 12½, United States 11½
1991	United States 14, Britain and Ireland 10
1993	United States 19, Britain and Ireland 5

World Cup—men (professional)

year	winner
1989	Australia (P. Fowler and W. Grady)
1990	Germany (B. Langer and T. Giedeon)
1991	Sweden (A. Forsbrand and P.-U. Johansson)
1992	United States (F. Couples and D. Love III)
1993	United States (F. Couples and D. Love III)

Ryder Cup—men (professional)

year	result
1985	Europe 16½, United States 11½
1987	Europe 15, United States 13
1989	Europe 14, United States 14
1991	United States 14½, Europe 13½
1993	United States 15, Europe 13

Curtis Cup—women (amateur)

year	result
1984	United States 9½, Britain and Ireland 8½
1986	Britain and Ireland 13, United States 5
1988	Britain and Ireland 11, United States 7
1990	United States 14, Britain and Ireland 4
1992	Britain and Ireland 10, United States 8

GYMNASTICS

World Gymnastics Championships—men

year	all-around team	all-around individual	horizontal bar	parallel bars
1989	U.S.S.R.	I. Korobchinsky (U.S.S.R.)	Li Chunyang (China)	V. Artemov (U.S.S.R.)* Li Jing (China)*
1991	U.S.S.R.	G. Misutin (U.S.S.R.)	R. Buechner (Ger.)* Li Chunyang (China)*	Li Jing (China)
1992	not held	not held	G. Misutin (CIS)	Li Jing (China)* V. Voropayev (CIS)*
1993	not held	V. Sherbo (Bela.)	S. Charkov (Russia)	V. Sherbo (Bela.)

year	pommel horse	rings	vault	floor exercise
1989	V. Mogilny (U.S.S.R.)	A. Aguilar (W.Ger.)	J. Behrend (E.Ger.)	I. Korobchinsky (U.S.S.R.)
1991	V. Belenky (U.S.S.R.)	G. Misutin (U.S.S.R.)	You Ok Youl (S.Kor.)	I. Korobchinsky (U.S.S.R.)
1992	Pae Gil Su (N.Kor.)* V. Sherbo (CIS)* Li Jing (China)*	V. Sherbo (CIS)	You Ok Youl (S.Kor.)	I. Korobchinsky (CIS)
1993	Pae Gil Su (N.Kor.)	Y. Chechi (Italy)	V. Sherbo (Bela.)	G. Misutin (Ukr.)

*Tied.

World Gymnastics Championships—women

year	all-around team	all-around individual	balance beam
1989	U.S.S.R.	S. Boginskaya (U.S.S.R.)	D. Silivas (Rom.)
1991	U.S.S.R.	K. Zmeskal (U.S.)	S. Boginskaya (U.S.S.R.)
1992	not held	not held	K. Zmeskal (U.S.)
1993	not held	S. Miller (U.S.)	L. Milosovici (Rom.)

year	uneven parallel bars	vault	floor exercise
1989	Fan Di (China)* D. Silivas (Rom.)*	O. Dudnik (U.S.S.R.)	S. Boginskaya (U.S.S.R.)* D. Silivas (Rom.)*
1991	Kim Gwang Suk (N.Kor.)	L. Milosovici (Rom.)	C. Bontas (Rom.)* O. Chusovitina (U.S.S.R.)*
1992	L. Milosovici (Rom.)	H. Onodi (Hung.)	K. Zmeskal (U.S.)
1993	S. Miller (U.S.)	Y. Piskun (Bela.)	S. Miller (U.S.)

*Tied.

Y. Chechi: Men's rings world gymnastics champion (1993)
CHRIS COLE—ALLSPORT

L. Milosovici: Women's balance beam world gymnastics champion (1993)
CHRIS COLE—ALLSPORT

HORSE RACING

2,000 Guineas

year	horse	jockey
1989	Nashwan	W. Carson
1990	Tirol	M. Kinane
1991	Mystiko	M. Roberts
1992	Rodrigo de Triano	L. Piggott
1993	Zafonic	P. Eddery

The Derby

year	horse	jockey
1989	Nashwan	W. Carson
1990	Quest for Fame	P. Eddery
1991	Generous	A. Munro
1992	Dr Devious	J. Reid
1993	Commander in Chief	M. Kinane

The St. Leger

year	horse	jockey
1989	Michelozzo	S. Cauthen
1990	Snurge	R. Quinn
1991	Toulon	P. Eddery
1992	User Friendly	G. Duffield
1993	Bob's Return	P. Robinson

Triple Crown champions—British

year	winner
1915	Pommern
1917	Gay Crusader
1918	Gainsborough
1935	Bahram
1970	Nijinsky

The Kentucky Derby

year	horse	jockey
1989	Sunday Silence	P. Valenzuela
1990	Unbridled	C. Perret
1991	Strike the Gold	C. Antley
1992	Lil E. Tee	P. Day
1993	Sea Hero	J. Bailey

The Preakness Stakes

year	horse	jockey
1989	Sunday Silence	P. Valenzuela
1990	Summer Squall	P. Day
1991	Hansel	J. Bailey
1992	Pine Bluff	C. McCarron
1993	Prairie Bayou	M. Smith

Commander In Chief: The Derby (1993)
SPORTING PICTURES LTD.

The Belmont Stakes

year	horse	jockey
1989	Easy Goer	P. Day
1990	Go and Go	M. Kinane
1991	Hansel	J. Bailey
1992	A.P. Indy	E. Delahoussaye
1993	Colonial Affair	J. Krone

Triple Crown champions—U.S.

year	horse
1946	Assault
1948	Citation
1973	Secretariat
1977	Seattle Slew
1978	Affirmed

Harness racing

The Hambletonian Trot

year	horse	driver
1989	Park Avenue Joe*	R. Waples
	Probe*	W. Fahy
1990	Harmonius	J. Campbell
1991	Giant Victory	J. Moiseyev
1992	Alf Palema	M. McNicholl
1993	American Winner	R. Pierce

*Tied.

Australian Thoroughbred racing

Melbourne Cup

year	horse	jockey
1989	Tawrrific	R.S. Dye
1990	Kingston Rule	D. Beadman
1991	Let's Elope	S. King
1992	Subzero	G. Hall
1993	Vintage Crop	M. Kinane

ICE HOCKEY

The Stanley Cup

season	winner	runner-up	games
1988–89	Calgary Flames	Montreal Canadiens	4–2
1989–90	Edmonton Oilers	Boston Bruins	4–1
1990–91	Pittsburgh Penguins	Minnesota North Stars	4–2
1991–92	Pittsburgh Penguins	Chicago Black Hawks	4–0
1992–93	Montreal Canadiens	Los Angeles Kings	4–1

World Hockey Championships

year	winner
1989	U.S.S.R.
1990	Sweden
1991	Sweden
1992	Sweden
1993	Russia

M. Usova (left) and A. Zhulin: World ice dancing champions (1993)
ANTON WANT—ALLSPORT

ICE SKATING

World figure skating champions—women

year	winner
1989	M. Ito (Japan)
1990	J. Trenary (U.S.)
1991	K. Yamaguchi (U.S.)
1992	K. Yamaguchi (U.S.)
1993	O. Baiul (Ukr.)

World figure skating champions—pairs

year	winners
1989	Ye. Gordeeva, S. Grinkov (U.S.S.R.)
1990	Ye. Gordeeva, S. Grinkov (U.S.S.R.)
1991	N. Mishkutenok, A. Dmitriev (U.S.S.R.)
1992	N. Mishkutenok, A. Dmitriev (UT)
1993	I. Brasseur, L. Eisler (Can.)

World figure skating champions—men

year	winner
1989	K. Browning (Can.)
1990	K. Browning (Can.)
1991	K. Browning (Can.)
1992	V. Petrenko (UT)
1993	K. Browning (Can.)

World ice dancing champions

year	winners
1989	M. Klimova, S. Ponomarenko (U.S.S.R.)
1990	M. Klimova, S. Ponomarenko (U.S.S.R.)
1991	I. Duchesnay, P. Duchesnay (Fr.)
1992	M. Klimova, S. Ponomarenko (UT)
1993	M. Usova, A. Zhulin (Russia)

World all-around speed-skating champions—men

year	winner
1989	L. Visser (Neth.)
1990	J.O. Koss (Nor.)
1991	J.O. Koss (Nor.)
1992	R. Sighel (Italy)
1993	F. Zandstra (Neth.)

World all-around speed-skating champions—women

year	winner
1989	C. Moser (E.Ger.)
1990	J. Börner (E.Ger.)
1991	G. Kleeman (Ger.)
1992	G. Niemann (Ger.)
1993	G. Niemann (Ger.)

World Speed-skating Sprint Championships

year	men	women
1989	I. Zhelezovsky (U.S.S.R.)	B. Blair (U.S.)
1990	Ki Tae Bae (S.Kor.)	A. Hauck (E.Ger.)
1991	I. Zhelezovsky (U.S.S.R.)	M. Garbrecht (Ger.)
1992	I. Zhelezovsky (UT)	Ye Qiaobo (China)
1993	I. Zhelezovsky (Bela.)	Ye Qiaobo (China)

World Short-Track Speed-skating Championships—overall winners

year	men	women
1989	M. Daignault (Can.)	S. Daigle (Can.)
1990	Lee Joon-ho (S.Kor.)	S. Daigle (Can.)
1991	W. O'Reilly (U.K.)	N. Lambert (Can.)
1992	Ki Hoon Kim (S.Kor.)	So He Kim (S.Kor.)
1993	M. Gagnon (Can.)	N. Lambert (Can.)

JUDO

World Judo Championships—men

year	open weights	60 kg	65 kg	71 kg
1985	Y. Masaki (Japan)	S. Hosokawa (Japan)	Y. Sokolov (U.S.S.R.)	Keun Ahn Byung (S.Kor.)
1987	N. Ogawa (Japan)	Kim Jae Yup (S.Kor.)	Y. Yamamoto (Japan)	M. Swain (U.S.)
1989	N. Ogawa (Japan)	A. Totikashvili (U.S.S.R.)	D. Becanovic (Yugos.)	T. Koga (Japan)
1991	N. Ogawa (Japan)	T. Koshino (Japan)	G. Quellmalz (Ger.)	T. Koga (Japan)
1993	R. Kubacki (Poland)	R. Sonada (Japan)	Y. Nakamura (Japan)	Yung Chung Hoon (S.Kor.)
year	78 kg	86 kg	95 kg	+ 95 kg
1985	N. Hikage (Japan)	P. Seisenbacher (Austria)	H. Sugai (Japan)	Chul Cho Yong (S.Kor.)
1987	H. Okada (Japan)	F. Canu (Fr.)	H. Sugai (Japan)	G. Verichev (U.S.S.R.)
1989	Kim Bying Ju (S.Kor.)	F. Canu (Fr.)	K. Kurtanidze (U.S.S.R.)	N. Ogawa (Japan)
1991	D. Lascau (Ger.)	H. Okada (Japan)	S. Traineau (Fr.)	S. Kosorotov (U.S.S.R.)
1993	Chun Ki Young (S.Kor.)	Y. Nakamura (Japan)	A. Kovacs (Hung.)	D. Douillet (Fr.)

World Judo Championships—women

year	open weights	48 kg	52 kg	56 kg
1986	I. Berghmans (Belg.)	K. Briggs (U.K.)	D. Brun (Fr.)	A. Hughes (U.K.)
1987	Fengliang Gao (China)	Zhang Yun Li (China)	S. Rendle (U.K.)	C. Arnaud (Fr.)
1989	E. Rodriguez (Cuba)	K. Briggs (U.K.)	S. Rendle (U.K.)	C. Arnaud (Fr.)
1991	Zhuang Xiaoyan (China)	C. Nowak (Fr.)	A. Giungi (Italy)	M. Blasco (Spain)
1993	B. Maksymow (Poland)	R. Tamura (Japan)	R. Verdecia (Cuba)	N. Fairbrother (U.K.)
year	61 kg	66 kg	72 kg	+72 kg
1986	D. Bell (U.K.)	B. Deydier (Fr.)	I. de Kok (Neth.)	Fengliang Gao (China)
1987	D. Bell (U.K.)	A. Schreiber (W.Ger.)	I. de Kok (Neth.)	Fengliang Gao (China)
1989	C. Fleury (Fr.)	E. Pierantozzi (Italy)	I. Berghmans (Belg.)	Fengliang Gao (China)
1991	F. Eickoff (Ger.)	E. Pierantozzi (Italy)	Kim Mi Jong (S.Kor.)	Moon Ji Yoon (S.Kor.)
1993	G. van de Cavaye (Belg.)	Cho Min Sun (S.Kor.)	Leng Chin Hui (China)	J. Hagn (Ger.)

R. Tamura (right): World judo champion—women's 48 kg (1993)
GRAY MORTIMORE—ALLSPORT

RODEO

Men's World All-Around Rodeo Championship

year	winner	year	winner
1988	D. Appleton	1991	T. Murray
1989	T. Murray	1992	T. Murray
1990	T. Murray	1993	T. Murray

ROWING

World Rowing Championship—men

year	single sculls	min:s	double sculls	min:s	coxed pairs	min:s
1989	T. Lange (E.Ger.)	6:58.14	R. Thorsen, L. Bjoenness (Nor.)	6:23.40	G. Abbagnale, C. Abbagnale (Italy)	6:54.81
1990	Yu. Jensen (U.S.S.R.)	7:22.15	C. Zerbst, A. Jonke (Austria)	6:56.37	G. Abbagnale, C. Abbagnale (Italy)	6:48.30
1991	T. Lange (Ger.)	6:41.29	H.-J. Zwolle, N. Rienks (Neth.)	6:06.14	G. Abbagnale, C. Abbagnale (Italy)	7:34.39
1992	T. Lange (Ger.)	6:51.40	S. Hawkins, P. Antonie (Austl.)	6:17.32	J. Searle, G. Searle (U.K.)	6:49.83
1993	D. Porter (Can.)	6:59.03	Y. Lamarque, S. Barathay (Fr.)	6:24.69	J. Searle, G. Searle (U.K.)	7:01.50

year	coxless pairs	min:s	coxed fours	min:s	coxless fours	min:s	eights	min:s
1989	T. Jung, U. Kellner (E.Ger.)	6:39.95	Romania	6:14.90	East Germany	6:06.94	West Germany	5:43.88
1990	T. Jung, U. Kellner (E.Ger.)	7:07.91	East Germany	6:46.73	Australia	5:52.20	West Germany	5:26.62
1991	S. Redgrave, M. Pinsent (U.K.)	6:21.35	Germany	5:58.96	Australia	6:29.69	Germany	5:50.98
1992	S. Redgrave, M. Pinsent (U.K.)	6:27.72	Romania	5:59.37	Australia	5:55.04	Canada	5:29.53
1993	S. Redgrave, M. Pinsent (U.K.)	6:37.11	Romania	6:14.64	France	6:04.54	Germany	5:37.08

World Rowing Championships—women

year	single sculls	min:s	double sculls	min:s	quadruple sculls	min:s
1989	E. Lipa (Rom.)	7:27.96	J. Sorgers, B. Schramm (E.Ger.)	7:01.71	East Germany	6:16.62
1990	B. Peter (E.Ger.)	7:24.10	K. Boron, B. Schramm (E.Ger.)	8:18.63	East Germany	6:14.08
1991	S. Laumann (Can.)	8:17.58	K. Boron, B. Schramm (Ger.)	6:44.71	Germany	6:55.85
1992	E. Lipa (Rom.)	7:25.54	K. Boron, K. Köppen (Ger.)	6:49.00	Germany	6:20.18
1993	J. Thieme (Ger.)	7:26.00	P. Baker, B. Lawson (N.Z.)	7:03.42	China	6:21.07

year	coxless pairs	min:s	coxless fours	min:s	eights	min:s
1989	K. Haaker, J. Zeidler (E.Ger.)	7:26.97	East Germany	6:45.81	Romania	6:07.92
1990	S. Werremeier, I. Althoff (W.Ger.)	8:28.37	Romania	7:51.68	Romania	5:59.26
1991	M. McBean, K. Heddle (Can.)	6:57.42	Canada	6:25.43	Canada	6:28.20
1992	M. McBean, K. Heddle (Can.)	7:06.22	Canada	6:30.85	Canada	6:02.62
1993	C. Gosse, H. Cortin (Fr.)	7:24.74	China	6:42.06	Romania	6:18.88

The Diamond Challenge Sculls

year	winner	min:s
1989	V. Chalupa (Dukla Praha, Czech.)	7:23*
1990	EFM Verdonk (Koru, N.Z.)	8:21
1991	W. Van Belleghem (Belg.)	†
1992	R. Henderson (Leander R.C.)	7:44
1993	T. Lange (Ger.)	7:39

*New record. †Not rowed out.

Grand Challenge Cup

year	winner	min:s
1989	Hansa Dortmund (W.Ger.)	5:58
1990	Hansa Dortmund (W.Ger.)	6:36
1991	Leander and Star R.C.	6:22
1992	University of London	6:04
1993	Dortmund, Ger.	6:11

K. Ogiwara: World Nordic Skiing champion—ski jump combined (1993)

ALAIN GROSCLAUDE—VANDYSTADT/ALLSPORT

SKIING

World Nordic Skiing Championships—men

year	10-km	15-km	30-km	50-km	relay
1988		M. Deviatiarov (U.S.S.R.)	A. Prokurorov (U.S.S.R.)	G. Svan (Swed.)	Sweden
1989		G. Svan (Swed.)	V. Smirnov (U.S.S.R.)	G. Svan (Swed.)	Sweden
1991	T. Langli (Nor.)	B. Daehlie (Nor.)	G. Svan (Swed.)	T. Mogren (Swed.)	Norway
1992	V. Ulvang (Nor.)	B. Daehlie (Nor.)	V. Ulvang (Nor.)	B. Daehlie (Nor.)	Norway
1993	S. Sivertsen (Nor.)	B. Daehlie (Nor.)	B. Daehlie (Nor.)	T. Mogren (Swed.)	Norway

World Nordic Skiing Championships—women

year	5-km	10-km	15-km	20-km	30-km	relay
1988	M. Matikainen (Fin.)	V. Ventsene (U.S.S.R.)		T. Tikhonova (U.S.S.R.)		U.S.S.R.
1989	not held	E. Vialbe (U.S.S.R.)	M. Matikainen (Fin.)		E. Vialbe (U.S.S.R.)	Finland
1991	T. Dybendahl (Nor.)	E. Vialbe (U.S.S.R.)	E. Vialbe (U.S.S.R.)		L. Yegorova (U.S.S.R.)	U.S.S.R.
1992	M. Lukkarinen (Fin.)	L. Yegorova (UT)	L. Yegorova (UT)		S. Belmondo (Italy)	Unified Team
1993	L. Lazutina (Russia)	S. Belmondo (Italy)	E. Vialbe (Russia)		S. Belmondo (Italy)	Russia

World Nordic Skiing Championships—ski jump

year	70-m hill	90-m hill	120-m hill	team jump	combined	team combined
1988	M. Nykänen (Fin.)	M. Nykänen (Fin.)		Finland	H. Kempf (Switz.)	West Germany
1989	J. Weissflog (E.Ger.)	J. Puikkonen (Fin.)		Finland	T.E. Elden (Nor.)	Norway
1991	H. Kuttin (Austria)	F. Petek (Yugos.)		Austria	F.-B. Lundberg (Nor.)	Austria
1992		E. Vettori (Austria)	T. Nieminen (Fin.)	Finland	F. Guy (Fr.)	Japan
1993		M. Harada (Japan)	E. Bredeson (Nor.)	Norway	K. Ogiwara (Japan)	Japan

World Alpine Skiing Championships—slalom

year	men's slalom	men's giant slalom	men's supergiant	women's slalom	women's giant slalom	women's supergiant
1988	A. Tomba (Italy)	A. Tomba (Italy)	F. Piccard (Fr.)	V. Schneider (Switz.)	V. Schneider (Switz.)	S. Wolf (Austria)
1989	R. Nierlich (Austria)	R. Nierlich (Austria)	M. Hangl ((Switz.)	M. Svet (Yugos.)	V. Schneider (Switz.)	U. Maier (Austria)
1991	M. Girardelli (Lux.)	R. Nierlich (Austria)	S. Eberharter (Austria)	V. Schneider (Switz.)	P. Wiberg (Swed.)	U. Maier (Austria)
1992	F.C. Jagge (Nor.)	A. Tomba (Italy)	K.A. Aamodt (Nor.)	P. Kronberger (Austria)	P. Wiberg (Swed.)	D. Compagnoni (Italy)
1993	K.A. Aamodt (Nor.)	K.A. Aamodt (Nor.)	not held	K. Buder (Austria)	C. Merle (Fr.)	K. Seizinger (Ger.)

World Alpine Skiing Championships—downhill

year	men	women
1988	P. Zurbriggen (Switz.)	M. Kichl (W.Ger.)
1989	H. Tauscher (W.Ger.)	M. Walliser (Switz.)
1991	F. Heinzer (Switz.)	P. Kronberger (Austria)
1992	P. Ortlieb (Austria)	K. Lee-Gartner (Can.)
1993	U. Lehmann (Switz.)	K. Pace (Can.)

World Alpine Skiing Championships—combined

year	men	women
1988	H. Strolz (Austria)	A. Wachter (Austria)
1989	M. Girardelli (Lux.)	T. McKinney (U.S.)
1991	S. Eberharter (Austria)	C. Bournissen (Switz.)
1992	J. Polig (Italy)	P. Kronberger (Austria)
1993	L. Kjus (Nor.)	M. Vogt (Ger.)

Alpine World Cup

year	men	women
1989	M. Girardelli (Lux.)	V. Schneider (Switz.)
1990	P. Zurbriggen (Switz.)	P. Kronberger (Austria)
1991	M. Girardelli (Lux.)	P. Kronberger (Austria)
1992	P. Accola (Switz.)	P. Kronberger (Austria)
1993	M. Girardelli (Lux.)	A. Wachter (Austria)

Nordic World Cup

year	men	women
1989	G. Svan (Swed.)	E. Vialbe (U.S.S.R.)
1990	V. Ulvang (Nor.)	L. Lazutina (U.S.S.R.)
1991	V. Smirnov (U.S.S.R.)	E. Vialbe (U.S.S.R.)
1992	B. Daehlie (Nor.)	E. Vialbe (Russia)
1993	B. Daehlie (Nor.)	L. Yegorova (Russia)

SQUASH RACKETS

British Open Championships—men

year	winner
1988–89	Jah. Khan (Pak.)
1989–90	Jah. Khan (Pak.)
1990–91	Jah. Khan (Pak.)
1991–92	Jan. Khan (Pak.)
1992–93	Jah. Khan (Pak.)

British Open Championships—women

year	winner
1988–89	S. Devoy (N.Z.)
1989–90	S. Devoy (N.Z.)
1990–91	L. Opie (U.K.)
1991–92	S. Devoy (N.Z.)
1992–93	M. Martin (Austl.)

World Open Championships—men

year	winner
1989	Jan. Khan (Pak.)
1990	Jan. Khan (Pak.)
1991	R. Martin (Austl.)
1992	Jan. Khan (Pak.)
1993	Jan. Khan (Pak.)

World Open Championships—women

year	winner
1989	M. Le Moignan (U.K.)
1990	S. Devoy (N.Z.)
1991	not held
1992	S. Devoy (N.Z.)
1993	M. Martin (Austl.)

SWIMMING

World Swimming Championships—men

	freestyle				
year	50 m	100 m	200 m	400 m	1,500 m
1978		D. McCagg (U.S.)	B. Forrester (U.S.)	V. Salnikov (U.S.S.R.)	V. Salnikov (U.S.S.R.)
1982		J. Woithe (E.Ger.)	M. Gross (W.Ger.)	V. Salnikov (U.S.S.R.)	V. Salnikov (U.S.S.R.)
1986	T. Jager (U.S.)	M. Biondi (U.S.)	M. Gross (W.Ger.)	R. Henkel (W.Ger.)	R. Henkel (W.Ger.)
1991	T. Jager (U.S.)	M. Biondi (U.S.)	G. Lamberti (Italy)	J. Hoffmann (Ger.)	J. Hoffmann (Ger.)

	backstroke		breaststroke		butterfly	
	100 m	200 m	100 m	200 m	100 m	200 m
1978	B. Jackson (U.S.)	J. Vassallo (U.S.)	W. Kusch (W.Ger.)	N. Nevid (U.S.)	J. Bottom (U.S.)	M. Bruner (U.S.)
1982	D. Richter (E.Ger.)	R. Carey (U.S.)	S. Lundquist (U.S.)	V. Davis (Can.)	M. Gribble (U.S.)	M. Gross (W.Ger.)
1986	I. Polyansky (U.S.S.R.)	I. Polyansky (U.S.S.R.)	V. Davis (Can.)	J. Szabo (Hung.)	P. Morales (U.S.)	M. Gross (W.Ger.)
1991	J. Rouse (U.S.)	M. Lopez Zubero (Spain)	N. Rozsa (Hung.)	M. Barrowman (U.S.)	A. Nesty (Suriname)	M. Stewart (U.S.)

	individual medley		team relays		
	200 m	400 m	4 × 100-m freestyle	4 × 200-m freestyle	4 × 100-m medley
1978	G. Smith (Can.)	J. Vassallo (U.S.)	United States	United States	United States
1982	A. Sidorenko (U.S.S.R.)	R. Prado (Braz.)	United States	United States	United States
1986	T. Darnyi (Hung.)	T. Darnyi (Hung.)	United States	East Germany	United States
1991	T. Darnyi (Hung.)	T. Darnyi (Hung.)	United States	Germany	United States

	diving		
	1-m springboard	3-m springboard	platform
1978		P. Boggs (U.S.)	G. Louganis (U.S.)
1982		G. Louganis (U.S.)	G. Louganis (U.S.)
1986		G. Louganis (U.S.)	G. Louganis (U.S.)
1991	E. Jongejans (Neth.)	K. Ferguson (U.S.)	Sun Shuwei (China)

World Swimming Championships—women

	freestyle				
year	50 m	100 m	200 m	400 m	800 m
1978		B. Krause (E.Ger.)	C. Woodhead (U.S.)	T. Wickham (Austl.)	T. Wickham (Austl.)
1982		B. Meineke (E.Ger.)	A. Verstappen (Neth.)	C. Schmidt (E.Ger.)	K. Linehan (U.S.)
1986	T. Costache (Rom.)	K. Otto (E.Ger.)	H. Friedrich (E.Ger.)	H. Friedrich (E.Ger.)	A. Strauss (E.Ger.)
1991	Zhuang Yong (China)	N. Haislett (U.S.)	H. Lewis (Austl.)	J. Evans (U.S.)	J. Evans (U.S.)

	backstroke		breaststroke		butterfly	
	100 m	200 m	100 m	200 m	100 m	200 m
1978	L. Jezek (U.S.)	L. Jezek (U.S.)	J. Bogdanova (U.S.S.R.)	L. Kachushite (U.S.S.R.)	J. Pennington (U.S.)	T. Caulkins (U.S.)
1982	K. Otto (E.Ger.)	C. Sirch (E.Ger.)	U. Geweniger (E.Ger.)	S. Varganova (U.S.S.R.)	M.T. Meagher (U.S.)	I. Geissler (E.Ger.)
1986	B. Mitchell (U.S.)	C. Sirch (E.Ger.)	S. Gerasch (E.Ger.)	S. Hörner (E.Ger.)	K. Gressler (E.Ger.)	M. Meagher (U.S.)
1991	K. Egerszegi (Hung.)	K. Egerszegi (Hung.)	L. Frame (Austl.)	E. Volkova (U.S.S.R.)	Qian Hong (China)	S. Sanders (U.S.)

	individual medley		team relays		
	200 m	400 m	4 × 100-m freestyle	4 × 200-m freestyle	4 × 100-m medley
1978	T. Caulkins (U.S.)	T. Caulkins (U.S.)	United States		United States
1982	P. Schneider (E.Ger.)	P. Schneider (E.Ger.)	East Germany		East Germany
1986	K. Otto (E.Ger.)	K. Nord (E.Ger.)	East Germany	East Germany	East Germany
1991	Lin Li (China)	Lin Li (China)	United States	Germany	United States

	diving		
	1-m springboard	3-m springboard	platform
1978		I. Kalinina (U.S.S.R.)	I. Kalinina (U.S.S.R.)
1982		M. Neyer (U.S.)	W. Wyland (U.S.)
1986		Gao Min (China)	Chen Lin (China)
1991	Gao Min (China)	Gao Min (China)	Fu Mingxia (China)

S. Bruguera: French Open–men's singles (1993)

GARY M. PRIOR—ALLSPORT

TABLE TENNIS

World Table Tennis Championships—men

year	St. Bride's Vase (singles)	Iran Cup (doubles)	Swaythling Cup (team)
1987	Jiang Jialiang (China)	Chen Longcan, Wei Qingguang (China)	China
1989	J.-O. Waldner (Swed.)	J. Rosskopf, S. Fetzner (W.Ger.)	Sweden
1991	J. Persson (Swed.)	P. Karlsson, T. Von Scheele (Swed.)	Sweden
1993	J.-P. Gatien (Fr.)	Wang Tao, Lu Lin (China)	Sweden

World Table Tennis Championships—women

year	G. Geist Prize (singles)	W.J. Pope Trophy (doubles)	Corbillon Cup (team)
1987	He Zhili (China)	Hyun Jung Hwa, Yang Young Ja (S.Kor.)	China
1989	Qiao Hong (China)	Qiao Hong, Deng Yaping (China)	China
1991	Deng Yaping (China)	Gao Jun, Chen Zihe (China)	Korea
1993	Hyun Jung Hwa (S.Kor.)	Liu Wei, Qiao Yunping (China)	China

World Table Tennis Championships—mixed

year	Heydusek Prize
1985	Cai Zhenhua, Cao Yanhua (China)
1987	Hui Jun, Geng Lijuan (China)
1989	Yoo Nam Kyu, Hyung Jung Hwa (S.Kor.)
1991	Wang Tao, Liu Wei (China)
1993	Wang Tao, Liu Wei (China)

Table Tennis World Cup

year	winner
1989	Ma Wenge (China)
1990	J.-O. Waldner (Swed.)
1991	J. Persson (Swed.)
1992	Ma Wenge (China)
1993	Z. Primorac (Croatia)

TENNIS

All-England (Wimbledon) Tennis Championships—singles

year	men	women
1989	B. Becker (W.Ger.)	S. Graf (W.Ger.)
1990	S. Edberg (Swed.)	M. Navratilova (U.S.)
1991	M. Stich (Ger.)	S. Graf (Ger.)
1992	A. Agassi (U.S.)	S. Graf (Ger.)
1993	P. Sampras (U.S.)	S. Graf (Ger.)

All-England (Wimbledon) Tennis Championships—doubles

year	men	women
1989	J. Fitzgerald, A. Jarryd	J. Novotna, H. Sukova
1990	R. Leach, J. Pugh	J. Novotna, H. Sukova
1991	J. Fitzgerald, A. Jarryd	L. Savchenko, N. Zvereva
1992	J. McEnroe, M. Stich	G. Fernandez, N. Zvereva
1993	T. Woodbrige, M. Woodforde	G. Fernandez, N. Zvereva

United States Open Tennis Championships—singles

year	men	women
1989	B. Becker (W.Ger.)	S. Graf (W.Ger.)
1990	P. Sampras (U.S.)	G. Sabatini (Arg.)
1991	S. Edberg (Swed.)	M. Seles (Yugos.)
1992	S. Edberg (Swed.)	M. Seles (Yugos.)
1993	P. Sampras (U.S.)	S. Graf (Ger.)

United States Open Tennis Championships—doubles

year	men	women
1989	J. McEnroe, M. Woodforde	M. Navratilova, H. Mandlikova
1990	P. Aldrich, D. Visser	M. Navratilova, G. Fernandez
1991	J. Fitzgerald, A. Jarryd	P. Shriver, N. Zvereva
1992	J. Grabb, R. Reneberg	G. Fernandez, N. Zvereva
1993	K. Flach, R. Leach	A. Sánchez Vicario, H. Sukova

Davis Cup

year	winner
1989	West Germany
1990	United States
1991	France
1992	United States
1993	Germany

French Open Tennis Championships—singles

year	men	women
1989	M. Chang (U.S.)	A. Sánchez Vicario (Spain)
1990	A. Gomez (Ecu.)	M. Seles (Yugos.)
1991	J. Courier (U.S.)	M. Seles (Yugos.)
1992	J. Courier (U.S.)	M. Seles (Yugos.)
1993	S. Bruguera (Spain)	S. Graf (Ger.)

French Open Tennis Championships—doubles

year	men	women
1989	J. Grabb, P. McEnroe	L. Savchenko, N. Zvereva
1990	S. Casal, E. Sánchez	J. Novotna, H. Sukova
1991	J. Fitzgerald, A. Jarryd	G. Fernandez, J. Novotna
1992	J. Hlasek, M. Rosset	G. Fernandez, N. Zvereva
1993	L. Jensen, M. Jensen	G. Fernandez, N. Zvereva

Australian Open Tennis Championships—singles

year	men	women
1989	I. Lendl (Czech.)	S. Graf (W.Ger.)
1990	I. Lendl (Czech.)	S. Graf (W.Ger.)
1991	B. Becker (Ger.)	M. Seles (Yugos.)
1992	J. Courier (U.S.)	M. Seles (Yugos.)
1993	J. Courier (U.S.)	M. Seles (Yugos.)

Australian Open Tennis Championships—doubles

year	men	women
1989	R. Leach, J. Pugh	M. Navratilova, P. Shriver
1990	P. Aldrich, D. Visser	J. Novotna, H. Sukova
1991	S. Davis, D. Pate	P. Fendick, M.J. Fernandez
1992	T. Woodbridge, M. Woodforde	A. Sánchez Vicario, H. Sukova
1993	D. Visser, L. Warder	G. Fernandez, N. Zvereva

Federation Cup

year	winner	runner-up	results
1989	United States	Spain	3–0
1990	United States	U.S.S.R.	2–1
1991	Spain	United States	2–1
1992	Germany	Spain	2–1
1993	Spain	Australia	3–0

VOLLEYBALL

World Volleyball Championships

year	men	women
1984	United States	China
1986	United States	China
1988	United States	U.S.S.R.
1990	Italy	U.S.S.R.
1992	Brazil	Cuba

Silver Bullet: Transpacific Race (1993)
GERI CONSER

WRESTLING

World Wrestling Championships—Freestyle

year	48 kg	52 kg	57 kg	62 kg	68 kg
1988	T. Kobayashi (Japan)	M. Sato (Japan)	S. Beloglazov (U.S.S.R.)	J. Smith (U.S.)	A. Fadzaev (U.S.S.R.)
1989	J. Kim (S.Kor.)	V. Jordanov (Bulg.)	S. Yeung (N.Kor.)	J. Smith (U.S.)	B. Bovdayev (U.S.S.R.)
1990	A. Martinez (Cuba)	M. Torkan (Iran)	A. Puerto (Cuba)	J. Smith (U.S.)	A. Fadzaev (U.S.S.R.)
1991	V. Orudzhev (U.S.S.R.)	Z. Jones (U.S.)	S. Smal (U.S.S.R.)	J. Smith (U.S.)	A. Fadzaev (U.S.S.R.)
1992	Park II (N.Kor.)	Li Hak (N.Kor.)	A. Puerto (Cuba)	J. Smith (U.S.)	A. Fadzaev (UT)
1993	A. Vila (Cuba)	V. Jordanov (Bulg.)	Terry Brands (U.S.)	Tom Brands (U.S.)	A.A. Fallah (Iran)

year	74 kg	82 kg	90 kg	100 kg	130 kg
1988	K. Monday (U.S.)	Han Myang Woo (S.Kor.)	M. Khadartsev (U.S.S.R.)	V. Puscasu (Rom.)	D. Gobedzhishvili (U.S.S.R.)
1989	K. Monday (U.S.)	E. Jabraylov (U.S.S.R.)	M. Khadartsev (U.S.S.R.)	A. Atavov (U.S.S.R.)	A.R. Soleimani (Iran)
1990	R. Sofiyadi (Bulg.)	J. Lohyna (Czech.)	M. Khadartsev (U.S.S.R.)	L. Khabelov (U.S.S.R.)	D. Gobedzhishvili (U.S.S.R.)
1991	A. Khadem (Iran)	K. Jackson (U.S.)	M. Khadartsev (U.S.S.R.)	L. Khabelov (U.S.S.R.)	A. Schroder (Ger.)
1992	Park Jang (S.Kor.)	K. Jackson (U.S.)	M. Khadartsev (UT)	L. Khabelov (UT)	B. Baumgartner (U.S.)
1993	Park Jang (S.Kor.)	S. Ozturk (Tur.)	A. Jadidi (Iran)	L. Khabelov (Russia)	B. Baumgartner (U.S.)

World Wrestling Championships—Greco-Roman style

year	48 kg	52 kg	57 kg	62 kg	68 kg
1988	V. Maenza (Italy)	J. Ronningen (Nor.)	A. Sike (Hung.)	K. Madzhidov (U.S.S.R.)	L. Dzhulfalakyan (U.S.S.R.)
1989	O. Kucherenko (U.S.S.R.)	A. Ignatenko (U.S.S.R.)	E. Iwanov (Bulg.)	K. Madzhidov (U.S.S.R.)	C. Passarelli (W.Ger.)
1990	O. Kucherenko (U.S.S.R.)	A. Ignatenko (U.S.S.R.)	R. Yildiz (Ger.)	M. Oliveras (Cuba)	I. Doguchiev (U.S.S.R.)
1991	Duk Yong Gooun (S.Kor.)	R. Martínez (Cuba)	R. Yildiz (Ger.)	S. Martynov (U.S.S.R.)	I. Doguchiev (U.S.S.R.)
1992	O. Kucherenko (UT)	J. Ronningen (Nor.)	An Han Bong (S.Kor.)	A. Pirim (Tur.)	A. Repka (Hung.)
1993	W. Sánchez (Cuba)	R. Martínez (Cuba)	A. Manukjan (Arm.)	S. Martinov (Russia)	I. Doguchiev (Russia)

year	74 kg	82 kg	90 kg	100 kg	130 kg
1988	Kim Young Nam (S.Kor.)	M. Mamiashvili (U.S.S.R.)	A. Komchev (Bulg.)	A. Wronski (Pol.)	A. Karelin (U.S.S.R.)
1989	D. Turlykhanov (U.S.S.R.)	T. Komaromi (Hung.)	M. Bullmann (E.Ger.)	G. Himmel (W.Ger.)	A. Karelin (U.S.S.R.)
1990	M. Iskandarian (U.S.S.R.)	P. Farcas (Hung.)	M. Bullmann (Ger.)	S. Demiaschkievish (U.S.S.R.)	A. Karelin (U.S.S.R.)
1991	M. Iskandarian (U.S.S.R.)	P. Farcas (Hung.)	M. Bullmann (Ger.)	H. Milian (Cuba)	A. Karelin (U.S.S.R.)
1992	M. Iskandarian (UT)	P. Farcas (Hung.)	M. Bullmann (Ger.)	H. Milian (Cuba)	A. Karelin (UT)
1993	N. Alamanza (Cuba)	M. Yerlikaya (Tur.)	G. Koguchavilli (Russia)	M. Ljungberg (Swed.)	A. Karelin (Russia)

YACHTING

America's Cup

year	winning yacht	owner	skipper	losing yacht	owner
1977	*Courageous* (U.S.)	Courageous syndicate	T. Turner	*Australia* (Australia)	A. Bond and syndicate
1980	*Freedom* (U.S.)	Maritime College at Fort Schuyler Foundation, Inc.	D. Conner	*Australia* (Australia)	A. Bond and syndicate
1983	*Australia II* (Australia)	A. Bond and syndicate	J. Bertrand	*Liberty* (U.S.)	Maritime College at Fort Schuyler Foundation, Inc.
1987	*Stars & Stripes* (U.S.)	Sail America syndicate	D. Conner	*Kookaburra III* (Australia)	K. Parry and syndicate
1988	*Stars & Stripes* (U.S.)	Sail America syndicate	D. Conner	*New Zealand* (New Zealand)	M. Fay
1992	*America*³ (U.S.)	America³ Foundation	B. Koch	*Il Moro di Venezia* (Italy)	Compagnia della Vela di Venezia

Bermuda Race

year	winning yacht	owner
1984	*Pamir*	F. Curren, Jr.
1986	*Silver Star*	D. Clarke
	and *Puritan*	D. Robinson
1988	*Congere*	B. Koeppel
1990	*Denali*	L. Huntington
1992	*Constellation*	U.S. Naval Academy

Transpacific Race

year	winning yacht	owner
1985	*Montgomery Street*	D. Denning
1987	*Merlin*	D. Campion
1989	*Silver Bullet*	J. DeLaura
1991	*Chance*	R. McNulty
1993	*Silver Bullet*	J. DeLaura

Admiral's Cup

year	winning team
1985	West Germany
1987	New Zealand
1989	United Kingdom
1991	France
1993	Germany

Television and Radio

On Oct. 13, 1993, Bell Atlantic Corp., one of the nation's largest telephone companies, announced that it would pay $30 billion for Tele-Communications Inc. (TCI), the nation's largest operator of cable systems, and an affiliated cable programming company. The combination of the firms' financial might, skills, and technologies was likely to speed the advent of interactive video and information services. Most places would be served by two networks, according to Bell Atlantic chairman and chief executive officer Ray Smith. "They will provide voice and data and video and interactive services, and there will be fierce competition based on value and reliability," he said.

The Bell Atlantic–TCI merger, which was subject to government approval and was not expected to be completed until late 1994, was the largest in a series of matchups between telephone and cable companies in 1993. U.S. West Communications Inc. invested $2.5 billion in Time Warner Entertainment, owner of cable systems and Home Box Office (HBO) and Cinemax. Southwestern Bell Corp. bought two large cable systems in suburban Washington, D.C., and launched a joint venture with Cox Enterprises Inc. The same day the Bell Atlantic–TCI deal was announced, BellSouth Corp. said it would invest up to $1 billion in Prime Cable. It later put up $1.5 billion to back the bid of cable programmer QVC Network Inc. for Paramount Communications Inc.

All the companies shared the belief that consumers were ready for video-based interactive services. They included video-on-demand (ordering a movie or program from a menu of thousands for immediate viewing), home shopping and banking, electronic yellow pages, video games, the long-promised picture phone, and others.

Organization. While the electronic media's future was being invented, their present slowly expanded. According to the U.S. Federal Communications Commission's (FCC's) July 1993 count, 1,682 TV stations and 12,815 radio stations vied for the attention of the American public. Of the radio stations, 7,680 were found in the FM band and 5,135 in the AM. Although most of the 92.1 million homes with television sets could receive broadcast TV signals off the air, 55.8 million, or 60.6%, chose to get them—along with an ever growing array of cable programming services—through cable, according to the A.C. Nielsen Co.

Almost lost in all the talk about the consolidation of the telephone and cable industries in 1993 was the imminent arrival of a new TV medium, direct broadcast satellite (DBS). Hughes Aircraft's DirecTV and Hubbard Broadcasting's United States Satellite Broadcasting planned to begin beaming cable and other video services via satellite to subscribers with "dish" antennas just 46 cm (18 in) in diameter. The service was expected to reach most homes, but consumers would have to pay $700 for the home-reception equipment before subscribing.

Over the objection of Pres. George Bush, Congress had passed a law in 1992 regulating cable rates. But implementing the law proved difficult for the FCC. Although the agency promised that cable subscribers would save up to $1.5 billion, many found their cable bills went up after the new regulations went into effect in September. The FCC explained to Congress and angry consumer groups that cable operators were able to increase some rates as long as they reduced others and kept total revenues down. A hasty survey revealed that 70% of subscribers did get a break on their cable fees.

After a long legal and regulatory battle, the big-three networks were on the verge of entering the lucrative program-rerun business. In November a federal judge lifted consent decrees that had barred them from acquiring a financial stake in the comedies and dramas that appeared on their prime-time schedules. As a result, they could look forward to a share of the profits from reruns. FCC rules continued to prohibit the networks from actually selling shows to stations in the U.S., but those were scheduled to expire in late 1995.

Broadcasters across Europe faced the continuing effects of the economic recession coupled with increased competition. They also feared that U.S. programs would become dominant in their continent, a fear that resulted in a campaign—successful for the moment at least—by broadcasters and producers to exclude audiovisual productions from the provisions agreed upon under the General Agreement on Tariffs and Trade (GATT).

Under the terms of the Television Directive of the European Community (EC), quota systems to protect domestic television production were maintained. But there were protests from Earth-bound broadcasters that quotas were not imposed on satellite channels and particularly not on the U.K.-based British Sky Broadcasting (BSkyB) services operated by Rupert Murdoch's News International.

TIMOTHY WHITE—ABC

Members of the cast of "NYPD Blue" pose on location. Steven Bochco's new television series, like his "Hill Street Blues" and "L.A. Law," was popular with viewers and critics, but watchdog groups criticized it for its language and occasional nudity.

The French government threatened to lodge a formal complaint against the U.K. government with the European Commission over Britain's alleged failure to implement EC legislation requiring television channels to broadcast a minimum of 50% of European content. The subject of the complaint was the U.K.'s licensing of two of Ted Turner's U.S.-originated satellite channels—the feature-film service TNT and the Cartoon Network.

In the U.K. the advertising-funded Independent Television (ITV) companies were divided over how to meet the threat of takeovers from overseas. The larger ITV companies sought government approval to allow them to merge with their smaller regional neighbours as a protection from such takeovers. The regional companies, in turn, sought an extension of the moratorium on company mergers that was due to expire at the end of 1993.

The BBC also faced the threat of upheaval, with the government considering renewal of the corporation's royal charter and the future of the licensee fee system. The introduction by the BBC's newly appointed director general, John Birt (*see* BIOGRAPHIES), of a radical measure to improve efficiency and introduce programming "of high quality and originality" provoked widespread controversy, not least from within the BBC itself. One of its best-known broadcasters, Mark Tully, the longtime correspondent in India, launched a well-publicized attack on the Birt proposals.

Throughout Europe broadcasters faced cutbacks and restructuring. The Dutch public service channel NOS was warned that its 100 million-guilder annual government subsidy could be cut if its audience share fell below the current 50%. The Belgian public broadcaster RTBF, facing a possible BF 1 billion loss, shed 500 jobs and halted investment in films and high-cost productions.

The Spanish public station RTVE cut 2,700 jobs in an effort to offset accumulated losses of 150 billion pesetas. In response, the government agreed to a subsidy of 29 billion pesetas—its first since 1982.

But all was not gloom in Europe. A survey by the Carat advertising group revealed that spending on television advertising had been growing faster than the continent's gross domestic products, up 360% during the previous 12 years. This was due in large part to deregulation and privatization.

Fears that the centre-right government in France would introduce a radical upheaval of broadcasting appeared to be unfounded. Instead the new communications minister, Alain Carignon, made modest proposals that included increasing the limit of share ownership in television from 25 to 49%, extending station licenses from 10 to 15 years, and granting an extra F 140 million for public broadcasters in 1994.

Satellite and cable channels continued their steady growth throughout Europe. The U.S. broadcaster NBC acquired control of the U.K.-based Super Channel service from its Italian owners, and U.S. cable operators expanded their holdings in Europe to such new markets for pay-TV as Hungary and Turkey.

As the year drew to a close, however, most attention turned to Asia following Rupert Murdoch's $525 million acquisition of the Hong Kong-based pan-Asian satellite service STAR TV. Other major media companies such as Pearson in the U.K. and the U.S. operators Cable News Network (CNN) and HBO prepared to follow with major Asian expansions.

In China a government decree restricted the sale and installation of domestic satellite receiver dishes. Six of China's major stations, serving an audience of 55 million, formed the City Network Corp., a move seen as a significant step to a general updating and restructuring of the nation's broadcasting industry.

Following the Israeli-Palestinian accords, a Palestine Television Authority was set up in the West Bank town of Ramallah with a $3 million grant from the French government and the promise of additional funding from the EC and Japan.

Programming. Just as U.S. viewers were becoming comfortable with Fox as the fourth broadcast network, two major Hollywood studios, Warner Brothers and Paramount, competed to create the fifth. They chased after the same independent TV station groups in hopes of signing them on as affiliates. Some observers picked Warner Brothers to prevail because of its early start and its affiliation agreements with two large station groups, Tribune Broadcasting and Gaylord Broadcasting. But others gave it to Paramount on the strength of its popular "Star Trek" series and its partnership with the Chris-Craft station group.

Reaction from the established networks to the would-be competitor ranged from apprehension—they relied on Warner Brothers and Paramount to produce much of their prime-time programming—to disdain. Neither one had "even the potential distribution to compete with us," said one network executive.

It was unclear what impact a bidding war for Paramount might have on its network plans. Viacom Inc., a major program syndicator and cable programmer, agreed to buy the studio in September for about $8.2 billion. But QVC Network Inc., a cable home-shopping network headed by former Paramount and Fox executive Barry Diller, decided that it wanted Paramount and began bidding aggressively for it. By year's end the price had reached $10.8 billion.

CBS demonstrated that its triumph in the 1991–92 prime-time season was no fluke. With a 13.3 rating and a 22 share, it outpaced ABC (12.4/20) and NBC (11/18) during the 1992–93 season, according to the A.C. Nielsen Television Index. (A rating is the percentage of the 92.1 million homes with television sets; a share is the percentage of homes with sets on during a program's time slot.)

CBS was helped by some comparatively new entries, notably the comedies "Love & War" and "Hearts Afire." But it was the perennial favourites that powered the network: "60 Minutes," "Murphy Brown," and "Murder, She Wrote."

Celebrating its 25th anniversary in a two-hour special on November 14, "60 Minutes" was the season's top-rated show (21.9/36). ABC's "Roseanne" placed second (20.7/31), and ABC's "Home Improvement" was third (19.4/29). In November it was announced that the cable audience had declined for the first time since its explosive growth in the 1980s. For the first seven weeks of the new season that began on September 20, cable's prime-time rating was 13.4, as compared with 13.7 for the same period in 1992. By contrast, the combined rating for the four networks (ABC, CBS, NBC, and Fox) rose from 43.8 to 44.6 during the same period, reversing a long decline.

After an 11-year run on NBC, the ensemble comedy "Cheers" signed off with a two-hour special on May 20. The show scored a 45.5 rating and 64 share—big numbers, but good for only 13th place on the all-time list of most-watched shows. The last episode of "M*A*S*H" in 1983 continued to top the list with a 60.2 rating and 77 share.

Portraying with gritty realism the lives of two New York City detectives, "NYPD Blue" was the 1993–94 season's top-rated new drama. It broke into the top 20 shows, despite (or perhaps because of) rough language, partial nudity, and a campaign by a fundamentalist religious group to persuade ABC affiliates not to air it and advertisers not to support it.

Only two other new series—both comedies—did better than "NYPD Blue" in the ratings. But NBC's "Frasier" and ABC's "Grace Under Fire" benefited from strong programs

Today's News, Tomorrow's TV Show

Television's habit of exploiting real-life events was more pervasive—and more immediate—in 1993 than ever before. Dramatic, sensational news stories had always been fair game for the entertainment industry, but the transition from news item to movie or TV screen generally took several years. More recently the TV networks seemed to initiate the rush to acquire rights and begin production within minutes after the event had occurred. In fact, in the case of the siege of the Branch Davidian compound near Waco, Texas, by U.S. federal agents, filming began while the story was still unfolding.

The TV networks had whetted the audience's appetite with such reality-based fare as "America's Most Wanted," "Rescue 911," "Hard Copy," and "I Witness Video," and in the 1992–93 season they sought to satisfy all possible hunger for such entertainment. Of the 115 movies and miniseries the three major networks produced, nearly half were based on fact. Many were ratings successes; those networks' separate movies about Amy Fisher, who shot the wife of her lover, attracted an audience of about 100 million in December 1992–January 1993.

Of course, it was inevitable that some participants in dramatic news stories—heroes and victims alike—would seek to benefit monetarily from their ordeals. It began to appear as if agents were being called before ambulances, and very large amounts of money were being negotiated. (Even the "Doonesbury" comic-strip character Duke got into the act, staging an avalanche in hopes of selling the rights to his dramatic "rescue.") Reality-based stories were still cost-effective, however. It was cheaper to re-create events than to find original ideas, and less promotion was needed because the stories had already been hyped by the headlines.

As the '93–'94 season began, the trend appeared to be continuing. There was one sign, however, of some resistance. Early in the season one TV movie—"Based on an Untrue Story"—was a spoof.

(BARBARA WHITNEY)

that preceded them. The former followed "Seinfeld" (*see* BIOGRAPHIES); the latter, "Home Improvement."

HBO, cable's top pay-TV network, walked off with 17 Emmy awards in September, more than any of the broadcast networks. HBO's original movies carried the day, with *Stalin* alone winning four awards. The broadcast networks collectively still won more than twice as many awards as the cable networks, however—42 to 20. NBC received 16 awards, CBS 14, and ABC 12. "Seinfeld" was the top comedy series, and Ted Danson of "Cheers" and Roseanne Arnold of "Roseanne" took the prizes for lead comic actor and actress. CBS's "Picket Fences" was singled out as the best dramatic series, and its leading actor and actress, Tom Skerritt and Kathy Baker, won the awards for lead dramatic performances.

David Letterman (*see* BIOGRAPHIES) emerged as the king of late-night television. Emanating from New York's Ed Sullivan Theater, "The Late Show with David Letterman" debuted on CBS on August 30 and quickly established itself as the top-rated late-night show. The "Tonight Show," which NBC had handed to Jay Leno after Johnny Carson said good-bye in May 1992, struggled to keep pace.

"Saturday Night Live" alumnus Chevy Chase was the year's major casualty in the late-night wars. He premiered on Fox on September 7 and drew a good-sized audience but also some of the nastier reviews in memory. "This new model Chevy is an Edsel," wrote TV critic Tom Jicha. Ratings went downhill, and after just 29 airings the show was off the air.

Dozens of new cable networks—some real, some little more than a business plan—vied for places on U.S. cable systems. Most of them targeted narrow audiences—the History Network, the Golf Channel, Romance Classics, the Military Channel, the Television Food Network, and America's Talking. An exception to this rule was FX, a proposed general-entertainment network from Fox and its affiliates.

PATRICK TYLER—THE NEW YORK TIMES

Satellite dishes dot apartment buildings in Beijing (Peking). In October the government banned the dishes, used by many Chinese to receive the Hong Kong-based Star TV service, which offered programming such as the BBC, CNN, and MTV.

Although the largest cable operators planned to use digital technology to increase channel capacity, the expansion would not come fast enough to accommodate all the new networks. Cable networks owned by broadcasters had an advantage in obtaining cable carriage. Cable systems traditionally carried the signals of most local TV stations without having to pay for them. But the 1992 Cable Act, which went into effect in 1993, stated that TV stations could now charge cable systems for their signals. Most cable operators refused to pay, but some agreed to provide cable carriage of local and national networks owned by the stations.

Agreeing to share some of the rewards and risks of televising the national pastime, Major League Baseball formed a joint venture with ABC and NBC to broadcast a series of regular-season games and an expanded slate of postseason action. (Another round of play-offs was to create up to 20 additional postseason games). The six-year partnership—the Baseball Network—was to begin at the start of the 1994 season. The baseball owners approved the venture after it became clear that no broadcast network was willing to pay anywhere near the $1.1 billion that CBS had for a four-year pact that ended with the last pitch of the 1993 World Series. CBS lost hundreds of millions of dollars on the deal.

ESPN in September signed a new six-year contract with baseball, agreeing to pay $250 million for an extensive regular-season cable schedule. This was about half of what the cable sports network paid for its original four-year package, which generated $160 million–$200 million in losses through the 1993 season.

Sports and media watchers were startled in mid-December when it was announced that the Fox Network had outbid (possibly by as much as $100 million) CBS for the rights to broadcast National Football Conference games beginning in 1994. This would be the first regular sports programming by the Murdoch-owned network. Unlike baseball and football, basketball had been a moneymaker on national TV, and the two new contracts the National Basketball Association signed with NBC and Turner Broadcasting Systems in 1993 underscored the fact. Both four-year deals represented big increases. NBC would pay $750 million plus 50% of the advertising revenues in excess of $1,060,000,000. Turner, which telecast games on its TNT cable network, would pay $350 million and 50% of the revenue in excess of that amount.

The stark pictures of war, revolution, and terror overshadowed much of current affairs programming on networks throughout the world. In Russia during the failed coup, it was the Ostankino television station itself that became a key target for both the insurgents, who attempted to seize the Moscow studios, and the military loyal to Pres. Boris Yeltsin. Elsewhere the graphic pictures of war and suffering from conflicts as far apart as Bosnia and Somalia touched the world's conscience. In the United Kingdom it was the image of one injured and desperate five-year-old Bosnian child, Irma Hadzimuratovic, that resulted in widespread demands that frontiers be opened to allow the sick and wounded refugee children to be airlifted and admitted for medical treatment. This demand was taken up by the public in many other European countries.

In view of the growing impact of television news pictures on the public, it was perhaps strange that ITV in the U.K. decided to move its long-running evening news program "News at Ten" to an earlier off-peak time slot. The proposal brought protests from politicians and public alike. Prime Minister John Major voiced his disapproval, and the regulatory authority, the Independent Television Commission, vetoed the move.

In another significant legal action, the U.K. Court of Appeal overturned an injunction preventing the commercial Channel 4 network from screening excerpts from Stanley Kubrick's controversial feature film *A Clockwork Orange* without the consent of the copyright owner, Time Warner Entertainment. The film had been withdrawn from public exhibition for almost 20 years. The court gave Channel 4 permission to show limited excerpts on grounds of "fair dealing."

In Italy coverage of the country's political corruption scandals, the economic crisis, and the war in nearby former Yugoslavia switched viewing habits away from the traditionally popular game shows and entertainment to current affairs and news. The audience ratings research organization Auditel, which together with a Milan advertising agency, M&CS, monitored the output of state broadcaster RAI's three channels and the three private networks of the Finninvest group, discovered an increase of more than 100 hours of news during the first quarter of the year compared with the same period in 1992. Game and variety shows were down by a third, and sports on the RAI Uno network declined 30%.

The newly appointed president of RAI, Claudio Demattè, announced proposals to increase the quality of the programming and canceled two of the network's most popular prime-time entertainment shows, "Biberon" and "Saluti e Baci," which had been watched by an audience of 10 million viewers on Saturday nights. Demattè claimed that the production budget of 10 million lire was "excessive" at a time of economic recession.

The general election in Spain resulted in a similar swing of viewing habits toward current affairs programming, attracting the largest audiences since private television was introduced in 1990. The televised debates between Prime Minister Felipe González and his opponents boosted audiences for the two private channels, Tele 5 and Antena 3, to a total of some 13 million viewers.

The economic recession also had a significant impact on program production in France, where a report by the Centre National de Cinematographie revealed an 18% decrease in the production of drama, animation, and documentaries across all TV networks during 1992. Spending also dropped by 13% to F 4,720,000,000—the first decline ever recorded. This was due in part to the bankruptcy of La Cinq network in 1992 but also resulted from a shift of programming into entertainment shows by the surviving channels.

U.S. Attorney General Janet Reno (*see* BIOGRAPHIES) during the year warned TV programmers that if they did not curb the violence on television, the government would step in early in 1994 with stiff regulations. Such regulations, she told a Senate panel in October, would not conflict with the First Amendment. TV executives were at a loss as to how to respond to Reno's ultimatum. They had already promised to limit gratuitous violence and to air advisories before violence-laden shows. Some were privately saying that they looked forward to testing Reno's First Amendment opinion in court. Those seeking to regulate TV violence had a model for doing it—the FCC's regulation of broadcast indecency, which had been upheld by the U.S. Supreme Court. The regulation did not ban indecent programming but restricted it to times when few children are in the audience—late at night.

Talk continued to be the talk of radio. Radio personalities offering nothing but information, interviews, strong opinion, or barbed satire threatened to wrest the medium from music, which had dominated the airwaves since the 1950s. More than 1,000 stations boasted a talk or news and talk format in 1993, according to the *Broadcasting & Cable Yearbook.* Country music, however, with 2,651 adherents, was still the most common format.

"Shock jock" Howard Stern delights in offending almost everyone. Although radio stations carrying his program were fined heavily by the Federal Communications Commission during the year, Stern and other "politically incorrect" radio and television stars enjoyed enormous popularity.

TED THAI—TIME MAGAZINE

The popularity of talk may have even stopped the migration of the audience from AM to FM. According to radio analyst Jim Duncan, AM's share of radio listenership in 1993 nudged up to 25.6% in 1993 from 25.4% in 1992.

Howard Stern and Rush Limbaugh (*see* BIOGRAPHIES) led the gab attack, attracting millions of listeners through national syndication and earning themselves a *Time* magazine cover in October. Stern's popularity was confirmed with the October publication of his autobiographical *Private Parts*. It raced to number one on the *New York Times* best-seller list. A book signing by Stern in New York City drew 10,000 people and forced police to close off Fifth Avenue. Stern received unwanted attention from the FCC. By the year's end the agency had fined stations that carried the Stern show $1.2 million for allegedly indecent programming. At the very end of the year, the FCC decided to delay action on bids by Infinity Broadcasting Corporation, which employed Stern, to purchase three more radio stations until the complaints against Stern's program were resolved. The delay could cost Infinity millions of dollars in financial penalties. (MARTIN JACKSON; HARRY A. JESSELL; LAWRENCE B. TAISHOFF)

Amateur Radio. The FCC had taken several steps during the past few years to open up ham radio to more users. In 1993 it liberalized some previous restrictions. Gone was the strict prohibition against doing business on amateur radio. In its place was "greater flexibility," allowing operators to use ham radios for "public service projects and personal matters."

The new rules contained many gray areas, but the FCC said that licensees could now use their radios for personal communications as long as they did not overdo it—for example, try to substitute it for a cellular telephone—or use it for "pecuniary benefit." "You can order a pizza," said one FCC official, "but the pizza shop still can't give directions to the delivery boy in his car."

The FCC earlier had moved to make ham radio more accessible by eliminating the Morse-code requirement for licenses that allow for local communications. According to the American Radio Relay League, as of September there were 628,629 licensed ham operators, and more than a third of those held no-Morse-code licenses.

(HARRY A. JESSELL; LAWRENCE B. TAISHOFF)

See also Industrial Review: *Advertising; Telecommunications;* Motion Pictures; Music.

This article updates the *Macropædia* article BROADCASTING.

Theatre

Great Britain and Ireland. After years of crying wolf, in 1993 the British theatre finally seemed to face the wolf at the door. The theatre was in a parlous state, with closures imminent around the country. Most theatres had large deficits. The Lyric, Hammersmith, a famous auditorium rehoused in a new building in 1979, launched a public appeal for funds to stay open beyond spring 1994. Important repertory theatres in Liverpool, Bristol, and Plymouth were all threatened. The director of the Royal National Theatre (RNT), Richard Eyre, supported a nationwide campaign to protest Arts Council cuts in the subsidized theatre. The British theatre remained a very close-knit society, and feelings ran deep that the government was impervious to its plight.

The best defense of all was mounted by good work, and the RNT hit the heights with *The David Hare Trilogy,* a culmination of five years' effort and the high-water mark of Eyre's tenancy. The subjects were the church and the hunger for faith in *Racing Demon* (1990); the law, prisons, and the reactive instinct for radicalism in *Murmuring Judges* (1991); and the background of politics and the packaging of socialism in the new piece, *The Absence of War.* Hare's new play used the events of the 1992 general election in Britain to define the tragedy of George Jones—easily identified in some respects as Neil Kinnock, the defeated Labour leader—who could no longer heave his heart into his mouth. John Thaw was lauded for his magnificent, rasping portrayal of George, an impetuous Cockney bachelor whose political fire is extinguished in a campaign devised to make him seem sober and responsible. The trilogy played to packed houses and great public acclaim, though most critics and some politicians were guarded in their expressions of approval.

Just as popular, and with a more predictably appreciative critical response, Tom Stoppard returned to top form with *Arcadia,* another big hit for the National. Stoppard's play was a fireworks display of coincidence and collision in a 19th-century Derbyshire country house, involving Byron, landscape gardening, and romantic love. The acting of Felicity Kendal, Rufus Sewell, Harriet Walter, and Bill Nighy was inspired in Trevor Nunn's fine direction. *Arcadia* was voted best play in the *Evening Standard* (ES) Awards.

The National's other big successes were Nicholas Hytner's revival of Richard Rodgers and Oscar Hammerstein II's *Carousel,* which moved to the West End at the end of the year; an irresistible production by John Caird of Sir Arthur Pinero's *Trelawny of the Wells;* a definitive production by Declan Donnellan of Stephen Sondheim's *Sweeney Todd,* which moved from the Cottesloe auditorium to the larger Lyttelton; and a sensational British premiere, directed by Stephen Daldry, of Sophie Treadwell's 1928 Expressionist drama *Machinal,* in which Fiona Shaw (ES best actress) triumphed as a suppressed and murderous stenographer.

The Royal Shakespeare Company (RSC) in Stratford-upon-Avon and London responded with sellout seasons of Kenneth Branagh (*see* BIOGRAPHIES) as an intensely romantic and royal Hamlet, Robert Stephens as a titanic, emotionally overwhelming King Lear, and Alec McCowen as a well-received Prospero in *The Tempest.* In the RSC's Barbican, Antony Sher laid a strong claim to be the actor of the year in both *Tamburlaine* (from the 1992 Stratford season) and as Henry Carr in the athletic, surreal revival by Adrian Noble of Stoppard's *Travesties.*

The new plays policy of the RSC was less successful. In London there was a misfired collaboration between the

American Richard Nelson and the Moscow Art Theatre of *Misha's Party,* and in Stratford, McCowen played Edward Elgar in David Pownall's *Rondo,* a piece that aimed to uncover the dark side of the composer in the manner of Peter Shaffer's *Amadeus* but failed.

There was another *King Lear* at the Royal Court, with Tom Wilkinson and a brilliant Fool (Andy Serkis), whose mysterious demise was explained by political marginalization; his vision of perfidious Albion expressed itself in subversive sloganeering, and the poor fool was hanged, for once, because he had fallen foul of a state over which Lear had ceded control. This was seen by many as an ingenious and original solution to the chief problem of the play. Images of refugeeism, inspired by the tragic events in former Yugoslavia, were pointedly incorporated.

Another outstanding Shakespearean performance was given in the West End by Mark Rylance as Benedick in *Much Ado About Nothing* at the Queen's, directed by the notable new director and designer team of Matthew Warchus and Neil Warmington. Rylance's Benedick was a humourless Belfast Protestant, and Janet McTeer presented an unusually physical and contemporary Beatrice.

The box-office jackpot was hit by Maggie Smith, at last reclaiming Lady Bracknell from the memories of Edith Evans in a faithful revival of Oscar Wilde's *The Importance of Being Earnest* at the Aldwych. Smith provided a whirlwind performance in dove-grey silk, armour-plated in a carapace of social pretension and defensiveness that swung her round immediately to the suitability of Cecily (Claire Skinner) as a match for Algernon (Richard E. Grant) when the girl's wealth became known.

The musical theatre came down to a straight contest between the Broadway hit *City of Angels* and Andrew Lloyd Webber's new blockbuster, *Sunset Boulevard,* with book and lyrics by Christopher Hampton and Don Black. Although *Sunset* did not show signs of being as big a hit as *Phantom of the Opera* or *Cats,* it was a solid achievement with spectacular designs by John Napier to match the spectacular performances of Patti LuPone and Kevin Anderson in the old Gloria Swanson and William Holden cinema roles. Nunn's *Sunset* production was compared unfavourably by most critics with Michael Blakemore's work on *City of Angels,* which won the ES best musical award but failed to attract any significant public interest. No one disputed *City's* wit or intelligence, and the lyrics of David Zippel, in particular, were justly noted.

The Savoy Theatre reopened after the fire of 1990 with a completely refurbished interior that gloriously re-created the silver-liner, Art Deco luxuriance of the 1929 Basil Ionides design. The first residents were the English National Ballet, followed by the one-sided world chess championship between Gary Kasparov and Nigel Short and a lacklustre revival of Noël Coward's 1951 *Relative Values,* an indifferent comedy, with Susan Hampshire.

American actor and director Sam Wanamaker, who devoted more than 20 years to rebuilding Shakespeare's Globe Theatre, died in December just months after the project's first stage was unveiled. Wanamaker had founded the Globe Playhouse Trust in 1971 to raise money for the reconstruction, which was scheduled to be completed in 1995.

Two regular West End heavyweights scored in 1993: Peter Shaffer and Alan Ayckbourn. Shaffer's *The Gift of the Gorgon* dealt with terrorism and passion in an adventurous fusion of classical terminology and current despair. Judi Dench was the fraught widow of a dead, disappointed playwright (Michael Pennington in flashback) whose son mediated their anguish in the form of a biographical quest. It was Shaffer's most moving play since *Amadeus.* Ayckbourn's *Time of My Life* centred on a family birthday party in three different time zones and was likewise his best play for some time. It was expertly acted by Gwen Taylor and Anton Rodgers, though it fell victim to summertime indifference and the retreat from the West End of anything like a predictable or reliable audience.

The audience for new work was otherwise healthy at the Royal Court, at the National, and on the fringe. Martin Crimp's *The Treatment* and Terry Johnson's *Hysteria* were both intelligent, skillful new pieces at the Court from the post-Hare generation of playwrights. In the first, fiction and reality clashed in the media world of "facilitators" in New York City's TriBeCa district; in the second, Sigmund Freud and Salvador Dalí were enmeshed in a Stoppardian fracas with the daughter of one of Freud's patients. Ken Campbell's *Jamais Vu* (ES best comedy) at the RNT, Riverside Studios, and Vaudeville completed a trilogy by the storytelling genius, which had become a classic of imaginative fantasy and inspired comedy.

Mike Leigh's *It's a Great Big Shame!* at Joan Littlewood's old haunt in Stratford East, an unusual domestic drama set in two different centuries, made a big impression and offered an alternative view of sexual violence to that promulgated in Leigh's brilliant new film, *Naked.* The Gate in Notting Hill was refurbished and relaunched with Valle-Inclan's *Bohemian Lights,* in which the action was moved backward from Madrid in 1920 to Dublin on the eve of the Easter Rising in 1915.

The Gate's preeminence on the fringe was shared by the Almeida in Islington, which initiated acclaimed productions of Terence Rattigan's *The Deep Blue Sea;* Aleksandr Griboyedev's *Chatsky,* brilliantly translated by Anthony Burgess (*see* OBITUARIES); Thomas Bernhard's *The Showman,* starring Alan Bates; and the world premiere of Harold Pinter's *Moonlight,* his first "full-length" (75 minutes) play in many years. This last, a nocturnal idyll in which a retired civil servant, dying in bed, is attended by his wife, haunted by the ghost of his daughter, and spurned by his two sons, gave

DONALD COOPER

Patti LuPone as has-been star Norma Desmond and Kevin Anderson as screenwriter Joe Gillis dance in the stage musical adaptation of Billy Wilder's classic film *Sunset Boulevard.* The musical, the latest work of Andrew Lloyd Webber, opened in London to favourable reviews.

a tremendous opportunity to Ian Holm, who returned in glory to the stage (ES best actor). The Rattigan and Pinter plays transferred to the West End.

In the regions the impetus was maintained at the West Yorkshire Playhouse in Leeds, the Birmingham Rep, the Glasgow (Scotland) Citizens (where Rupert Everett appeared in Wilde's *The Picture of Dorian Gray,* released by director Philip Prowse into AIDS-age pertinence), the Salisbury Playhouse, and the Leicester Haymarket. Manchester was scheduled to be the Arts Council's City of Drama in 1994, and the Royal Exchange boasted visits from Vanessa Redgrave and Tom Courtenay in new plays by Mikhail Shatrov and Ronald Harwood.

The Abbey Theatre in Dublin replaced its controversial artistic director, Garry Hynes, with Patrick Mason, who directed Brian Friel's 1990 hit, *Dancing at Lughnasa,* and Friel's new, less-successful *Wonderful Tennessee.* A pall was cast over the Dublin Festival by the death of Cyril Cusack (*see* OBITUARIES), but one of his daughters, Niamh Cusack, triumphed in *A Doll's House* at the Gate. Garry Hynes bid farewell to the Abbey with a fierce and poetical revival of Tom Murphy's 1968 *Famine.* Other Irish plays that made an impression were Vincent Woods's *At the Black Pig's Dyke* and Bill Morrison's *Love Song for Ulster* trilogy, both seen at the Tricycle in Kilburn, north London.

The second Edinburgh Festival of director Brian McMaster was one of the strongest for drama in living memory. The Deutsches Theatre of Berlin took its severe, brilliantly acted production of Heinrich von Kleist's *The Broken Jug.* But the real impact was made by the star U.S. directors: Robert Wilson with his German student company in Gertrude Stein's *Doctor Faustus Lights the Lights* and Peter Sellars with his Gulf war update of Aeschylus' *The Persians.* In addition, Peter Stein took his tumultuous Salzburg Festival production of *Julius Caesar* (with 200 extras) to an exhibition hall near Edinburgh's airport, and Robert Lepage stunned music and drama critics alike with his Canadian Opera Company versions of Bela Bartok's *Bluebeard's Castle* and Arnold Schoenberg's *Erwartung.*

Lepage returned to Britain with his Theatre Répère, Québec, production of *Coriolan* (*Coriolanus*), seen at the Nottingham Playhouse as part of that theatre's 30th anniversary. The theatre had opened on Dec. 11, 1963, with Tyrone Guthrie's production of the same play, starring John Neville, Leo McKern, and Ian McKellen.

Much was made of the fact that the British theatre as a whole depended on just such events in the regions to feed the national theatre. In accepting the ES best director award for *Tamburlaine,* Terry Hands, the former artistic director of the RSC who began his career at the Liverpool Everyman, warned politicians and the Arts Council that flagship companies like the RSC and the RNT would not be flagships for much longer if economic cuts killed off the fleet.

Belgium and France. Belgium registered a difficult year as the national debt topped $350 billion, the government resigned, and the king died, but Antwerp was still the cultural capital of Europe for 1993. In the year that European frontiers were abolished, the idealism of the Maastricht Treaty was mocked by the destruction of Sarajevo, Bosnia and Herzegovina, and by the rise of the nationalist right all over the continent. The premiere of *Sarajevo* in Antwerp's magnificently restored Bourla Theatre, therefore, had a special poignancy.

Sarajevo was a tapestry of a former city in a former country, conceived by the director Haris Pasovic and coproduced in Stockholm, Antwerp, and Hamburg, Germany. In a walled, partially tiled corrida reminiscent of the set for Ariane Mnouchkine's *Les Atrides,* an architectural student sought the "silver soul" of Sarajevo. There was no onstage representation of violence, nothing even to compare with the documentary evidence of rape and abuse that appeared throughout the year in print and on television. Goran Stefanovski's text veered between the banal and the sporadically moving; it was really just an outline, or a series of hints. Precious principles of coexistence were represented by Sufi clowns, Turkish outlaws, anarchists, priests of four religions, and even 1984 Winter Olympians, as well as a postman, a fireman, a taxi driver, a soldier, and a journalist. The airport (and the sky) was closed for lovers wanting to escape. A Bosnian casserole recipe ended in tears. A cellist was raped by her neighbour. The performance was revealed as the dream of a wounded girl.

The Parisian theatre was electrified by Matthias Langhoff's revival of Eugene O'Neill's 1924 *Desire Under the Elms* at Nanterre Amandiers. Langhoff described his production as "*un film sur scene,*" deliberately mixing realism with artifice. Langhoff's unconventional set design was a fully inhabited hillocky warren sealed in a transparent cylindrical gauze, plowed by a real horse, populated with two real cows and several chickens, and serviced by a practical water pump under an audience-encircling sky flecked with blood-red clouds.

O'Neill's stage directions, which describe everything from the "sinister maternity" of the two large elms to the wall-melting sexual intensity between Ephraim Cabot's youngest son, Eben, and Cabot's new wife, Abbie, were delivered on tape by the gravelly, authoritative voice of Alain Cuny. Meanwhile, Françoise Morvan's text recast O'Neill's stilted Irish American in a coarse, often impenetrable, Breton patois (the show was a coproduction with the Théâtre National de Bretagne at Rennes). Overall, Langhoff made a poetic and flattering production of an interesting but difficult play.

(MICHAEL COVENEY)

U.S. and Canada. The devastation that AIDS continued to inflict on the United States generally, and in the theatre world in particular, was reflected by the plays that dominated not only Broadway and off-Broadway but also U.S. regional theatres in 1993. Thus, the stage year was realistic and reflective, in contrast to the hyperactive, star-studded, and ultimately unproductive previous year.

All of this was reflected in Broadway's most acclaimed play, *Millennium Approaches,* which marked as spectacular a New York debut of any American playwright as could be recalled. Moreover, it was only the first part of a seven-hour, two-play cycle called *Angels in America*. The work by Tony Kushner (*see* BIOGRAPHIES) was a drama about nothing less than a perceived crisis in American life. With AIDS as its central metaphor, *Angels in America,* subtitled *A Gay Fantasia on National Themes,* mixed characters as diverse as middle American conservatives, East Coast liberals, and Roy Cohn—the power broker and lawyer who castigated homosexuals even as he lay dying of AIDS. A sprawling work in alternating naturalistic and surreal scenes, *Millennium Approaches* had its premiere in San Francisco in 1991 and was then produced in London before being granted a commercial New York showing. That was all because of the chilly Broadway attitude toward adventurous drama.

After winning most of the year's prizes, *Millennium Approaches* was joined, in alternating performances with the same cast, by the acclaimed second part, *Perestroika*. This was an even better play, more cohesive than the first. The characters that had been established in *Millennium Approaches* began to intertwine in dreamlike scenes of accumulating power. *The Kentucky Cycle,* which won the 1992 Pulitzer Prize, reached Broadway in November. The six-

An angel appears in *Millennium Approaches,* the first part of Tony Kushner's seven-hour drama *Angels in America* (subtitled *A Gay Fantasia on National Themes*), which won a number of awards in 1993. The second part, *Perestroika,* opened on Broadway later in the year.
JOAN MARCUS

hour, two-part epic of American history starred Stacy Keach in four different roles.

Alongside these, the season's other plays were an ordinary lot, although the popular *The Sisters Rosensweig* (with Jane Alexander and Madeline Kahn) projected a contemporary sensibility by deftly mixing the funny and the serious-minded. It had been a long time since a woman playwright had achieved such status as Wendy Wasserstein, whose earlier *The Heidi Chronicles* won many of the prizes in 1989. Late in the season Alexander left the play to take over as director of the National Endowment for the Arts amid general expressions of acclaim for Pres. Bill Clinton's choice.

As for the traditional, Broadway-style comedy, it had virtually disappeared, the exception being the annual Neil Simon entry. His 1993 model, *Laughter on the 23rd Floor,* was a reminiscence of a youth well spent as a writer on the legendary team— including Woody Allen, Mel Brooks, and Carl Reiner—that wrote the Sid Caesar television shows in the 1950s. Although this was less a play than two and a half hours of gags, there was also no mistaking the old-fashioned style of the play. In March, Simon converted his charming movie *The Goodbye Girl* into a charmless musical (lyrics by David Zippel, music by Marvin Hamlisch). Despite its attractive stars, Bernadette Peters and Martin Short, it was a lacklustre version of the kind of musical comedies that had had their day. It was Simon's first musical failure, after such successes as *Sweet Charity* and *Promises, Promises*.

In the 1990s, however, hit musicals needed to be more contemporary in style, and the year brought no blockbuster examples. *Tommy,* based on the 1969 rock album by The Who, looked flashy enough to be an MTV video, but despite some breathless reviews, the show was perhaps too much like a video to do sell-out business with audiences who preferred the theatre's human qualities. In fact, *The Kiss of the Spider Woman* came as close to a smash hit as the season got. It won the Tony award for Best Musical, as well as acting awards for Canadian actor Brent Carver and perennial Broadway favourite Chita Rivera. (*See* BIOGRAPHIES.) That was remarkable for a musical about homosexuals and revolutionaries in and out of a Latin-American prison.

The *New York Times* complained that Martin Starger's production *The Red Shoes*, which opened on December 16 at the Gershwin Theatre with nearly $8 million in investments, was "looking pretty and going no place slowly." Actually, it went no place quickly, closing on the 19th, one of the costliest Broadway failures ever.

The New York theatre was ever hungry for not a mere hit musical but a smash hit like *Phantom of the Opera* or *Les Misérables*. First, all eyes were turned east to London for the premiere of Andrew Lloyd Webber's latest, *Sunset Boulevard*. Then eyes turned westward to the Los Angeles stage, where the Lloyd Webber show, with actress Glenn Close starring and winning raves, began its journey to Broadway (scheduled to arrive in late 1994).

Following the trend of recent years, New York's institutional theatres took up the dramatic slack—not the old institutions, such as Lincoln Center, the Circle in the Square, and the Joseph Papp Public Theater, but the younger set, including the Manhattan Theatre Club and the Roundabout Theatre. While the former specialized in new plays, such as Terrence McNally's unique *The Perfect Ganesh* (another AIDS-related play), Roundabout grasped the public taste in revivals with spirited productions of Eugene O'Neill's *Anna Christie* with Natasha Richardson and Liam Neeson and the musical *She Loves Me*. The Manhattan Theatre Club staged the premiere of Arthur Miller's latest, *The Last Yankee,* simultaneously with the Young Vic in London.

Tony Randall's beleaguered National Actors Theatre finally won a modicum of credibility with Shakespeare's *Timon of Athens*. Some years earlier director Michael Langham had mounted it beautifully for the Stratford (Ont.) Festival. He virtually replicated that production for Randall's company, using the same Duke Ellington music he had then commissioned. With Brian Bedford giving the performance of a career as Timon, the National Actors Theatre at last won critical praise.

The lights were dimmed on Broadway in March when Helen Hayes, first lady of the American theatre, died at age 92. (*See* OBITUARIES.)

Off-Broadway, like Broadway, was reflecting the devastating effect that AIDS had had on the theatre. *Jeffrey,* by

MARTHA SWOPE

Brent Carver (left), in the role of a homosexual obsessed with movies, and Anthony Crivello, as a revolutionary, share a jail cell in *Kiss of the Spider Woman.* The award-winning musical, which also starred Chita Rivera, continued to be a hit on Broadway in 1993.

Paul Rudnick, was about the dilemma faced by a homosexual who was attracted to a man infected with the virus. By setting this situation in the form of a comedy, the playwright achieved a cutting, ironic, and life-affirming tone.

The regional theatres remained cautious despite the change in national politics, as if dubious about a reversal of decades of artistic inhibition and subsidy cutbacks. American artists were definitely the rule, and in Washington, D.C., Arena Stage set the example, with a schedule dominated by such national favourites as Tennessee Williams, George Gershwin, and Thornton Wilder. However, in theatres from Providence, R.I., to San Francisco, there seemed to be a healthy stretching toward the brighter, more contemporary American playwrights, such as McNally (*Lips Together, Teeth Apart*), David Mamet (*Speed-the-Plow*), and Jon Robin Baitz (*Three Hotels*). Chicago remained a beehive of theatre activity, with a dozen or so theatres, from the established Goodman to innovative smaller institutions such as the Remains Theater and Interplay.

Across the northern border, the subsidy situation was not much better. The Stratford Festival remained the pride of Canada and the only world-class repertory theatre on the continent. Nonetheless, even though government aid to the arts was a part of the Canadian culture, the cutbacks at Stratford were severe. Between that and, perhaps, a weariness with Shakespeare after four decades of specializing in his work, the festival was diversifying its fare. Thus, while the "Shakespeare" had been taken out of the Stratford Shakespeare Festival, there still was Shakespeare at Stratford. In 1993 there were productions on the main (Festival Theatre) stage of *Antony and Cleopatra, A Midsummer Night's Dream,* and *King John*. But *The Importance of Being Earnest* and the Broadway musical *Gypsy* were also mounted on that stage.

(MARTIN GOTTFRIED)

See also Dance; Music.

This article updates the *Macropædia* article The History of Western THEATRE.

Transportation

Despite the introduction of the single European market on January 1 and the progress on the North American Free Trade Agreement, the ongoing uncertainty over the General Agreement on Tariffs and Trade and continuing world recession in 1993 resulted in subdued levels of both passenger and freight movements. The lack of financial performance in some transport sectors led to a revised interest by many governments in the privatization of state-owned transport assets.

Major infrastructure projects, many involving water crossings, continued to progress. Interest in and demand for well-integrated and interconnecting services were driven by increasing congestion on highways and at airports, as well as growing concern about the quality of the air and the environment in general. The European Community (EC) issued a White Paper highlighting the dilemma in balancing accessibility with environmental standards and addressing the need for sustainable mobility. (JOHN H. EARP)

AVIATION

Another exceptionally tough trading year for the world airline industry saw passenger numbers rise an average of 5.7% but the profit made per seat—the yield—decline as wild discounting took place in vicious fare wars between some of the big carriers and as businesses traded down from first class to executive class and from executive to economy class in their efforts to save corporate costs.

As a result, the airlines within the International Air Transport Association (IATA) lost a record $4.8 billion in 1992, bringing their total loss in the three years to the end of 1992 to $11.5 billion—a sum greater than all the profits made since international scheduled services began.

At the same time that it continued to fly through turbulent economic weather, the industry was assailed by fresh demands for taxes by governments. The airlines were fined considerable sums for bringing in inadmissable passengers and were faced in the U.S. with the need to carry out random drug and alcohol testing (at a cost of several million dollars a year) and with a fuel tax on domestic air transportation set to begin in 1995.

The trend toward increased taxation was one of the problems recognized by the U.S. Presidential Commission To Insure a Strong, Competitive Airline Industry, which reported in August 1993 after hearing evidence on the industry's ills from the airlines and many other interested parties. The commission also recommended that the U.S. move quickly to set up a satellite-based national air traffic control and communications system and that the airlines' international liability regime be modernized. A similar inquiry was established in Brussels by the European Commission and was due to issue its report as the year ended.

For 1993 the airlines' losses were tentatively forecast at about $2 billion—still disastrous but a considerable improvement on 1992 as world business moved painfully out of recession and as deep cost cutting began to produce a fitter,

GEORGES MERILLON—GAMMA LIAISON

Union employees of Air France picket a runway at Orly Airport in Paris. The French carrier faced stiff resistance from workers and was ultimately forced to back down when, like other branches of the French transportation industry, it attempted to implement cost-cutting policies.

leaner industry. Since the crisis hit, the airlines had reduced direct employment by some 80,000, canceled or deferred 1,000 new aircraft deliveries, cut out many marginal routes, concentrated on their core business through subcontracting, reduced the number of first-class seats while enhancing conditions for travelers in business class, and looked for critical mass through mergers and alliances.

As the year ended, the increasingly wide range of intercarrier agreements included deals between Northwest and KLM, Continental and Air Canada, Air France and Continental, USAir and British Airways (BA), Delta and Swissair, American and Canadian International, and Lufthansa and United—all with the aim of producing "seamless" air transport globally. These accords forced the U.S. and other governments to confront key issues, such as ownership, control, and competition law.

In Europe, where KLM, Scandinavian Airlines System, Swissair, and Austrian Airlines engaged in difficult—and eventually fruitless—negotiations toward a joint airline, the third and final EC liberalization package was introduced as 1993 began. By the close of the year, the package had had little real impact on reducing fares, although there had been an increase in competition on some trunk routes between capital cities as airlines took up the freedoms offered by the package to start services against the established national carriers. Merger talks collapsed in November when the four airlines failed to agree on a U.S. partner.

In January the two-year legal battle between BA and Virgin Atlantic appeared to be over when BA agreed to pay more than £600,000 in libel damages to Virgin plus court costs of up to £3 million. In October, however, Virgin founder Richard Branson filed an antitrust suit against BA in U.S. federal court.

Labour unions at the two largest U.S. carriers led the news at year's end. A short-lived strike by flight attendants at American just before Thanksgiving disrupted hundreds of flights and sent thousands of passengers scrambling to find alternatives. Less than a month later United agreed to an employee-buyout plan. Also at year's end, the U.S. Federal Aviation Administration announced new regulations that would specify procedures for pilots of commuter aircraft and large private airplanes to follow in order to be certain that the wings of their craft were completely ice-free before takeoff.

In the aerospace sector Boeing, Airbus Industrie, and all the other big manufacturers engaged in extensive staff layoffs and lower production rates to reflect the belt-tightening among the airlines. However, planning continued for the next generation of airliners, including an 800-seat subsonic and a 350-seat supersonic. At least one carrier, Singapore Airlines, one of the leading airlines in the Southeast Asian region (where passenger growth was expected to be up to 10.5% a year), urged them to get on with the job.

IATA, too, took a more sanguine view, forecasting an average annual growth in passenger traffic of 6.6% and in air freight of 7.2% between 1993 and 1997 and predicting that the world jet fleet would rise from 8,000 aircraft to 10,800 by the year 2000. Worries remained over where the money would come from, however. (ARTHUR REED)

SHIPPING AND PORTS

It seemed that much of the attention of the shipping industry in 1993 was focused on two major events, both insurance related. In April officers at Lloyd's of London presented a new business plan for the recovery of the troubled insurance market, which had lost nearly £3 billion during the 1990 year of account. The business plan addressed past problems and proposed plans for the future. One of the proposals was that limited-liability companies should be admitted to membership, bringing corporate capital to the market.

The other insurance-related event was the U.S. Oil Pollution Act of 1990 (OPA '90), which came into force on Feb. 18, 1993, and which was applicable to vessels that stored, handled, or transported oil. The act was a direct result of the *Exxon Valdez* oil-spill disaster, for which the Exxon Corp. paid a settlement of some $1 billion. OPA '90 imposed unlimited liability on shipowners trading to the U.S. for any oil-pollution incidents, and the insurance coverage available came nowhere near the *Exxon Valdez* total.

The safety of bulk carriers remained another important issue, and John Parker, chairman of the U.K.'s Harland and Wolff shipyard, proposed that large bulk carriers have their cargo capacity reduced as a safety measure rather than rely on age-based limits. The Commission of the European Community was working on a plan to make port state control inspections mandatory outside European waters and earmarked funding from its 1994 budget to help finance the initiative.

Port developments included plans to build the largest container terminal in the U.S., costing around $300 million, for American President Lines in Los Angeles. In Vietnam a large new container port was to be built on the Saigon River near Ho Chi Minh City by a partnership that included Singapore's Neptune Orient Lines and Mitsui of Japan.

The total tonnage of the world fleet stood at 457.8 million gross tonnage (gt), an increase of 13.5 million gt over 1992. The tonnage in the total order book for registration other than in the country of build rose by 690,979 gt in the June quarter of 1993 to a figure of 25,899,219 gt (73.9% of the total world order book), including 7,579,925 gt for Liberia, 6,835,520 gt for Panama, 1,636,766 gt for Norway, and 886,500 gt for The Bahamas. (EDWARD CROWLEY)

FREIGHT AND PIPELINES

World recession and reduced global trading resulted in record losses in many of the largest container ship operators in 1993, causing consolidation within the industry. Although growth rates for total movements slackened, other changes included faster rates of annual growth in specials, notably in reefers (refrigerated trailers) at 25.2% and high cubes (27.9%). The Pacific Rim ports accounted for more than 40% of the world share of container traffic. Singapore, with 7,970,000 20-ft equivalent units (TEU), and Hong Kong, with 7,560,000 TEU in 1992, continued to outperform all other ports, the latter assisted by CITOS (computer integrated terminal operations system). In July 1993, Singapore recorded an all-time monthly record of 796,500 TEU, beating the previous record of 773,000 set by Hong Kong in August 1992.

Rotterdam, Neth., remained Europe's busiest container port, with over four million TEU, and it was stimulating the development of specialist freight villages and other transport facilities, including "piggyback" rail transport. In the U.S. double stacking played a large role in freight transport, with over 1.6 million TEU of double stack container traffic originating in the U.S.

Projections for 1993 showed a slight increase in pipeline construction over 1992, with 26,466 km (16,449 mi) of facilities being installed worldwide. The U.S. continued to dominate the field, with over 40% of new construction and more than 3,060,000 km (1.9 million mi) of long-distance pipelines and gas-distribution lines. In the former U.S.S.R., lack of spending was holding back domestic consumption and pipeline exports to Eastern Europe.

In the Middle East, Aramco remained on a five-year gas-pipeline expansion plan, and other major constructions continued in Iran-Turkey, with a study of a 6,500-km (4,000-mi) gas-line link to Greece. Engineering work was under way on the Algerian section of the 1,400-km (870-mi) Maghreb–Europe gas line, which included dual lines across the Strait of Gibraltar. In South America the $2 billion gas pipeline linking Santa Cruz, Bolivia, to São Paulo, Brazil, received top priority.

ROADS AND TRAFFIC

Although worldwide figures for car manufacturing showed declines for yet another year (European figures showed a drop of two million in sales), the total ownership of vehicles and the total vehicle mileage continued to grow against a background of highway congestion and increasing evidence of environmental pollution. Despite the continuing interest and investment in urban public-transport systems, the sheer convenience and benefit of using an automobile meant that efforts by most governments to stem car use were having little effect in urban areas.

Road pricing was slowly gaining ground as a means of both raising revenue on intercity roads and controlling congestion in urban areas. The technology for this continued to be developed in both the European DRIVE project and the U.S. intelligent vehicle highway system (IVHS) schemes. The boost that the planning of U.S. cities received from the government was somewhat muted by the lack of the promised fuel tax increases.

Urban and interurban facilities continued to be provided, although their provision was targeted at key links in the highway network, especially bridges and tunnels for water crossings. In Europe, as the Channel Tunnel and Store Bælt projects moved toward completion, attention turned toward the planning of a road and rail link between Copenhagen and Malmö, Sweden, under the Øresund Sound and a bridge and tunnel link across the Fehmarn Belt linking Denmark to Germany. The French authorities commenced work on the Somport Tunnel linking France to Spain.

In urban areas tunneling of roads was also being pursued for purely environmental reasons. Six road tunnels forming part of the Boston Central Artery Project and using new jacking methods that would save $60 million and one year of construction time were proposed.

BOOT (build, own, operate, transfer) schemes were much in evidence, especially in Australia following the successful completion of the Sydney Harbour Tunnel. The approach was extended to provide an underground car park for the Sydney Opera House, with a 50-year concession agreement.

INTERCITY RAIL

Although 1993 rail freight volumes were down, increasing passenger traffic continued to sustain worldwide confidence in the growth and development of railways. Greater emphasis was being placed on technical compatibility of systems and provision of third-party access to national systems. There was renewed interest in privatization of rail networks in such widespread locations as New Zealand, Argentina, Pakistan, Germany, and the U.K. Japan temporarily shelved its privatization efforts.

High-speed trains and networks were being planned or extended in many countries. In France the Train à Grande Vitesse (TGV) extended to La Rochelle, and the new TGV Nord line opened to traffic. The TGV Est and Méditerranée lines were to go ahead, and a high-speed line from Lille to Brussels was under construction. There were plans for high-speed link eastward both in Germany and in Poland and one in China to link Beijing (Peking) to Shanghai. European railways in Sweden, Denmark, and Germany agreed upon a common technical basis for further development. Japan and

The French TGV (Train à Grande Vitesse), which uses steel wheels running on standard rails, reaches speeds up to 320 km/h (200 mph). The high-speed trains were chosen for a route being planned to connect major cities in Texas.

STEPHANIE COMPOINT—SYGMA

Germany continued to experiment with the use of maglev (magnetic levitation) vehicles for intercity transport.

The Japanese railways successfully tested their WIN train at over 350 km/h (220 mph) and were testing the STAR 21 to 400 km/h (250 mph). They were also developing a tilting train. Germany developed its first double-decker passenger coach stock.

Freight services also made advances. The Rotterdam (Neth.)–Milan shuttle was one of four trains acting as guinea pigs for transit monitoring using the Argos satellite system. Germany was expanding its premium Inter Cargo freight service to serve its industrial heartland, and a European "Qualitynet" service introduced the hub-and-spoke concept to freight operations. China completed the second stage of its Dagin heavy long-haul coal line. Studies in France confirmed the feasibility of an ambitious plan for truck motorways on rails.

URBAN MASS TRANSIT

The keynote address to the 50th International Union of Public Transport world congress, held in Sydney, Australia, in May 1993, highlighted the role that public transport had in providing sustainable development and balancing urban mobility and environmental standards. It also underlined the need to shift resources into urban transit at a time when France, for example, was considering suppressing its pioneering *versement transport* (transport payroll tax) for urban areas.

Worldwide metro and light rail transit (LRT) systems continued to abound. Los Angeles opened its new Metro Red Line at the end of January and its Metrolink commuter line to Riverside in June and planned to open the fully automated minimetro Green Line in 1995. Metro extensions opened in 1993 were reported from as far afield as Berlin, Calcutta, Lisbon, Naples, Shanghai, and Tokyo. A host of other cities, including Amsterdam, Cairo, Mexico City, and Omsk, Russia, were constructing new LRT or metro extensions, while other cities planned new or further lines to existing networks. The New York (City) Metropolitan Transportation Authority announced a plan to introduce its first braille subway map for the visually impaired.

Trams were also making a revival. Brussels, Strasbourg, France, and Leiden, Neth., reintroduced them to combat congestion, while Guangzhou (Canton), China, was studying how to convert an old air-raid shelter into a 5-km (3.1-mi) underground tramway. Brazil still led the way with innovative approaches to bus use, exemplified by its six-door buses carrying 270 passengers on its "direct route tube" system. Germany introduced an H-Bahn (Hangesbahn; suspended railway), an automated transit system, in Dortmund. In downtown Hong Kong the world's longest escalator system, measuring 800 m (2,625 ft) and comprising 20 escalators and three moving sidewalks, operated at a cost of some HK$208 million. (JOHN H. EARP)

See also Energy; Engineering Projects; Environment; Industrial Review: *Aerospace; Automobiles.*

This article updates the *Macropædia* article TRANSPORTATION.

World Affairs

The trends that had emerged in world affairs in 1992 continued to prevail even more clearly in 1993: the era of the Cold War giving way not to a new world order—however modestly interpreted—but to a spread of local conflicts and the inability and unwillingness of the international community to deal with them. As always, there were some exceptions and countercurrents. The most dramatic was, no doubt, the handshake in Washington between Prime Minister Yitzhak Rabin of Israel and Palestine Liberation Organization (PLO) chairman Yasir Arafat. This was a true psychological breakthrough, a first mutual recognition, but it was no more than a first step on a long road providing for limited self-rule in the Gaza and Jericho region. There was strong resistance among some Palestinian factions, a lack of enthusiasm among Arab states such as Syria, and no willingness to lift the anti-Israel boycott. There was resistance in Israel, too, but less powerful.

The other part of the world where negotiations for a peaceful arrangement made some progress was South Africa—the agreement on a multiparty "transitional executive council." The award of the Nobel Prize for Peace to Nelson Mandela and F.W. de Klerk was widely welcomed. But their negotiations took place against the background of the murder of thousands—mainly internecine warfare among black groups—and the prospects for a more or less orderly transition to a new South Africa in which there would be collaboration between blacks and whites remained as yet a distant dream.

Elsewhere, local conflicts and dangers to world peace continued to prevail, and it was perhaps typical for the general lethargy that the former attracted more publicity (and generated more passion) than the latter, far more deadly ones. The proliferation of nuclear weapons and the irresponsible disposal of nuclear waste constituted an enormous danger to humankind, yet the buildup of means of mass destruction in countries such as North Korea and Iran continued without effective counteraction even contemplated. Russia continued to dump its hazardous waste into the ocean irrespective of the long-term consequences, and China resumed its nuclear tests. These were the main threats; still, attention was focused on sideshows such as Somalia, Haiti, and the former Yugoslavia—human tragedies no doubt, but on an infinitely smaller scale. Since Europe had turned its back on

World Affairs: Contents

For your convenience this article groups the countries of the world by the geopolitical regions to which they belong. Certain related topics, such as United Nations, Dependent States, and various regional affairs articles (*e.g.,* Latin-American Affairs), are also included. An alphabetical list of these topics appears below, indicating the page where each may be found. Articles on the various countries update the *Macropædia* articles of the same name (except where otherwise noted), as do the more extensive statistical treatments in the *World Data* section, arranged alphabetically beginning on page 546.

the Balkans, and since Africa was no more willing to deal with the situation in Somalia than Latin America was with Haiti, the burden fell on the United Nations and the United States, where resistance to "interventionism" was, however, increasingly vocal. The fear that American lives might be in danger or that the nation might get entangled in Vietnam-style quagmires created a climate in which American action became nearly impossible. The situation in Washington was not helped by the appointment of key foreign-policy officials whose competence was not above doubt. An absence of a clear foreign-policy concept was matched by the inability to articulate political action. The media became increasingly influential in dictating the U.S. foreign agenda, but their priorities tended to change weekly.

Initiatives aimed at creating greater free-trade zones encountered considerable resistance. While the U.S. completed negotiations in August with Mexico and Canada on "supplemental agreements" to the North American Free Trade Agreement, aiming to appease various domestic lobbies, such as organized labour and environmentalists, but also certain powerful business lobbies, opposition persisted in many quarters. Similarly, European initiatives scheduled to advance the cause of political unity, as well as social integration and the liberalization of world trade (the Uruguay round of talks under the General Agreement on Tariffs and Trade), failed to make significant progress.

Separatist trends in Eastern Europe and the former Soviet Union continued; Czechoslovakia separated into Slovakia and the Czech Republic on Jan. 1, 1993. Elsewhere, armed conflict ensued along ethnic lines (in Georgia, Tajikistan, Armenia-Azerbaijan). Russia was shaken by the conflict between Pres. Boris Yeltsin and the antireform parliament that culminated in Moscow in October with the victory of Yeltsin's forces, but success soured somewhat after the December parliamentary elections.

Elsewhere in Europe and Asia, elections usually went against the ruling parties. In France the Socialist Party suffered a decisive defeat in March; in Italy and Germany local elections reflected the weakening of the major traditional parties. In Italy as the result of a series of financial scandals, the whole political system was put into jeopardy. In Japan the Liberal-Democratic Party lost its parliamentary majority for the first time in 38 years, while in Pakistan the movement headed by Benazir Bhutto emerged victorious after years in opposition.

To some extent this worldwide trend against the governments in power (which also included Greece, Poland, Spain, the U.K., and other countries) was triggered by the worldwide recession. Another factor, particularly in Western Europe, was the growing presence of foreign workers and illegal immigrants, which fueled a latent xenophobia.

Among the positive developments toward domestic peace should be mentioned the negotiations in Cambodia, which led to the drafting of a new constitution and the crowning of Norodom Sihanouk as king. Also noteworthy was the improvement in relations between Vietnam and its neighbours as well as with its former antagonists, China and the U.S.

As in previous years, international terrorism was spearheaded by Muslim fundamentalist groups within the Arab world (Egypt, Algeria, Tunisia) as well as in Europe and the U.S. Iran acted as both principal paymaster and provider of weapons and logistic support. No end was in sight to the civil wars in Afghanistan, Angola, and The Sudan; cease-fires were concluded, only to be violated again and to be followed by renewed fighting. Ethnic strife flared up, or continued, in India, Turkey, Northern Ireland, and Burundi.

Seen in the general context of the post-Cold War period, 1993 brought no major political or military disaster, and the performance of the world economy (excepting only China), while sluggish, was not worse than expected. Measured by the high hopes of a new, more civilized and peaceful, world order and growing prosperity, however, it was a dismal year with only sporadic progress to register. For a few moments the pulse of history seemed to quicken—as during the Palestinian-Israeli meeting—but then in many other parts of the world, the example failed to have an impact, and there was no spectacular breakthrough toward the brave new world often invoked but still as distant as ever.

(WALTER LAQUEUR)

This article updates the *Macropædia* article 20th-Century INTERNATIONAL RELATIONS.

UNITED NATIONS

Calls on the United Nations for more peacekeeping forces rose dramatically, and some of the troops were authorized, for the first time, to enforce order, not just monitor peace agreements. The UN's estimated expenditures rose to $3.6 billion, but where the funds would come from remained a mystery. "Demands made upon the United Nations are not being matched by resources to do the job," said Secretary-General Boutros Boutros-Ghali. A Ford Foundation panel suggested in February that governments charge peacekeeping costs to national military budgets and authorize the UN to charge interest on arrears. (*See* MILITARY AFFAIRS.)

MALANCA—SIPA

A member of the UN peacekeeping force searches a Somali man on the streets of Mogadishu. During the year the U.S. began transferring responsibility for maintaining order in Somalia to a UN force that included troops from more than 20 countries.

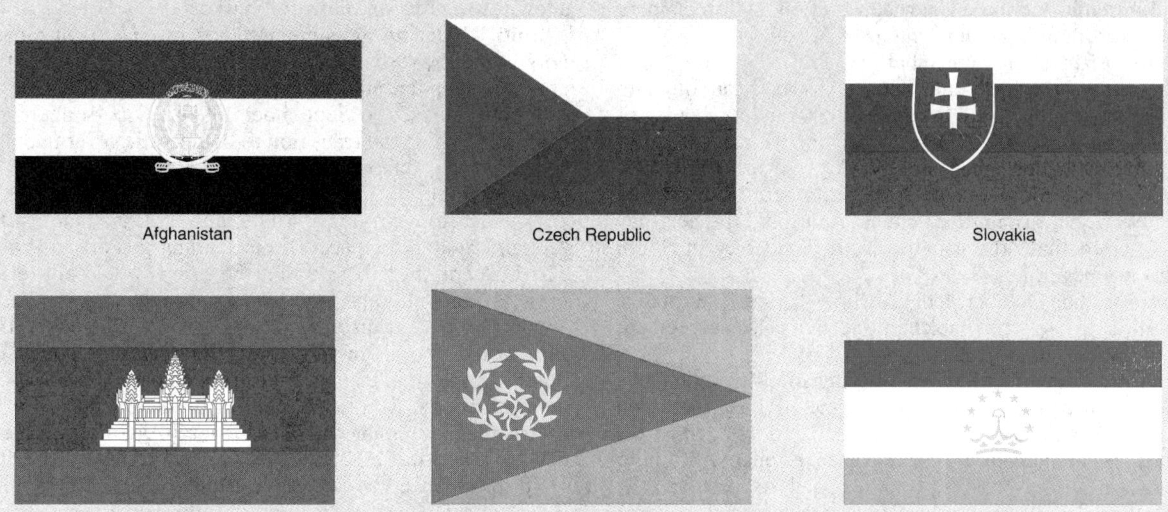

Afghanistan — Czech Republic — Slovakia

Cambodia — Eritrea — Tajikistan

Members continued paying dues late; only 18 met the January 31 deadline. The United States on October 6 redeemed the pledge made by Pres. Bill Clinton the previous week and paid $533 million ($233 million in dues and $300 million for field operations). The U.S. remained the largest debtor, however, still owing $284 million in dues and $188 million for peacekeeping.

The former Yugoslav republic of Macedonia joined the UN in April, despite Greek protests that the name Macedonia rightfully belonged to a Greek province. The other new members in 1993 were Andorra, the Czech Republic, Eritrea, Monaco, and the Slovak Republic, bringing the membership total to 184.

Somalia. Under a Security Council resolution adopted unanimously on March 26, a 26-nation UN Operation in Somalia (UNOSOM II) assumed operational command on May 4. It was the first UN force established under Chapter VII of the Charter and was thereby authorized to employ force to disarm Somali warlords and to ensure that relief supplies reached needy people.

In January and March representatives of 15 Somali factions at UN-sponsored conferences in Ethiopia agreed to disarm and start rebuilding the country politically. On June 5 forces of Gen. Muhammad Farah Aydid (*see* BIOGRAPHIES), head of the Somali National Alliance, broke the cease-fire and ambushed and killed 24 Pakistani UN peacekeepers. The next day the Security Council called on states to restore a national government and imprison those responsible for the killings—namely, Aydid.

In mid-June U.S. gunships and attack helicopters pounded Aydid's headquarters and armouries, destroying much weaponry and a radio station, and in August the U.S. sent 400 Army Rangers to capture Aydid, but they failed. Then, after 18 U.S. soldiers died in combat on October 3, the idea of capturing Aydid receded. The Rangers withdrew from Somalia on October 19, and on November 7 Aydid warned that if American troops returned to the streets of Mogadishu, he might break the cease-fire again. On November 16 the Security Council accepted a suggestion Aydid had made on September 13 that it appoint a special commission to examine charges against him, effectively canceling its June resolution.

Friction between the U.S. and the UN over Somali policy and the deaths of U.S. servicemen led Clinton to set March 31, 1994, as his deadline for withdrawing U.S. troops from Somalia, one year earlier than the Security Council had authorized on September 22. On November 18 the Council extended the UNOSOM mandate to May 1994. Boutros-Ghali reportedly believed that the U.S. was turning him and the UN into scapegoats for the disastrous October raid, though it had been conceived and executed by the U.S. alone. In any case, the Somali experience cooled U.S. enthusiasm for Boutros-Ghali's 1992 proposal to create an international standing army, and the U.S. seemed increasingly unwilling to have its troops serve under UN commanders.

The UN managed during the year to get food supplies distributed in Somalia, possibly saving one million lives, and restored order in most of the country, though strife in Mogadishu remained intense. On November 24 the UN began, whenever possible, to use armed vehicles to protect UN civilian personnel in the capital. A conference on Somali reconstruction met in Addis Ababa (November 29–December 12) but failed to agree on how to compose a transitional council to help restore legitimate government in the country.

Former Yugoslavia. Despite continuing peacemaking efforts, successive cease-fire agreements did not hold in the civil war in former Yugoslavia. Observers estimated that Serbs had killed 200,000 of their Muslim countrymen, expelled more than two million from their towns and villages in the name of "ethnic cleansing," and destroyed the cities of Vukovar and Sarajevo by blockade, shelling, and sniping.

Attacks on UN personnel, the shelling of convoys, vehicle thefts, and countless delays at roadblocks hampered relief efforts, and the UN frequently had to suspend them. Nonetheless, the UN Protection Force (UNPROFOR) escorted relief convoys throughout the year in order to get humanitarian aid to hundreds of thousands of starving people under siege, and the Security Council twice unanimously extended its mandate (June 30 and October 4).

Cambodia. Despite violence by both the government and Khmer Rouge forces, UN-supervised elections in Cambodia took place as scheduled between May 23 and 28, with 90% of the 4.7 million voters whom the UN had registered casting ballots. The UN declared the elections "free and fair," and on September 21, by a vote of 113–5–2, Cambodia's National Assembly adopted a new constitution and proclaimed Prince Norodom Sihanouk king. (*See* BIOGRAPHIES.)

South Africa. On September 23, Pres. F.W. de Klerk made the first visit by any South African head of state to UN headquarters. He asked Nelson Mandela, leader of the African National Congress, to support the lifting of economic sanctions against South Africa in view of the new interim constitution. Mandela obliged when he addressed the UN Special Committee Against Apartheid the next day and asserted that "the countdown to democracy in South Africa has begun."

Rwanda. On October 4 the Security Council adopted a resolution to assist in implementing the peace agreement signed in Rwanda in August.

Iraq. For most of the year, Iraq ingeniously denied UN inspectors access to its nuclear facilities. Allied forces on January 13 launched a "restrained and modest" air strike against Iraqi command posts and radar installations. Under threats of further attacks, Iraq dropped its ban on UN flights into Iraqi territory but then rapidly imposed other restrictions. Continuing aggravations and reports that Iraqi aircraft and surface-to-air missiles were violating flight-exclusion zones led the U.S. to respond with a Tomahawk cruise missile attack on January 17 against a Baghdad industrial area. On June 27 the U.S. told the Security Council that it had launched another missile attack against Iraqi Intelligence Service headquarters the day before as "self-defence" against an Iraqi attempt to murder former U.S. president George Bush during his visit to Kuwait City in April.

On September 16 the UN sent helicopters equipped to detect atomic radiation emanating from possible secret nuclear weapons sites in Iraq. These aircraft intensified the hunt for weapons by the special UN commission charged with disarming Iraq, and on September 27 between 50 and 100 UN inspectors began the largest of 63 inspections of Iraqi weapons sites, "declared and undeclared," since the end of the Gulf war. (Intelligence sources suggested that Iraq was hiding 200 Scud missiles.) On September 24 Iraq allowed the UN to activate monitoring cameras previously installed at two missile test sites.

On November 16 and 20, Iraqis protested UN demarcation of the Kuwait-Iraqi frontier by briefly marching into Kuwait, but in a letter to the Security Council on November 26, Iraq accepted all the UN's international monitoring requirements. It hoped thereby to persuade the Council to allow it to sell its oil on world markets.

Haiti. Under an agreement signed on July 3 on Governors Island, N.Y., by Lieut. Gen. Raoul Cédras, the Haitian army commander, and the Rev. Jean-Bertrand Aristide, the president deposed in September 1991, UN personnel were supposed to help the transition to democratic government by separating the police force from the army. On October 11, however, 40 or 50 "toughs" protected by police prevented a U.S. troop ship carrying 194 U.S. and 25 Canadian instructors and military engineers from landing at Port-au-Prince. The U.S. and the UN said that the troops would not return until Haitian military authorities guaranteed their safety. When Cédras and his unelected government indicated that they would not resign as agreed, the Security Council imposed an international oil and arms embargo, enforced by an international fleet, to take effect on October 16.

Aristide, addressing the 48th General Assembly on October 28, asked the UN to impose a total trade embargo on Haiti to force Cédras out. He said that he would not return or ask the Haitian parliament to approve an amnesty for his opponents until they surrendered power, although the Governors Island agreement called for an amnesty beforehand. The General Assembly on December 6 called for Aristide's return to office and the restoration of democracy and human rights in Haiti.

Human Rights. In April and September the International Court of Justice ordered authorities in the former Yugoslavia to stop committing genocide and not to back "military, paramilitary or irregular armed units" that might be committing such acts in Bosnia. On February 22 and May 25 the Security Council established a UN War Crimes Tribunal to prosecute persons responsible for violations of international humanitarian law committed in the former Yugoslavia since 1991. On September 17 the General Assembly elected 11 judges, who held their first meeting (on procedural matters) at The Hague on November 17.

The Commission on Human Rights condemned The Sudan and Iraq on March 10 for employing terror against people and arbitrarily executing them. It also called for an inquiry into other human rights violations in The Sudan and requested monitors in Iraq to check on reports of "massive" human rights abuses. During the year it levied serious criticisms at Afghanistan, Equatorial Guinea, Haiti, Iran, Israel

CHRIS RAINIER—JB PICTURES

A convoy of UN trucks carries Bosnian Muslims from Srebrenica, Bosnia and Herzegovina, at the end of March. The refugees had been trapped for 11 months as rebel Serbs laid siege to the city.

(in southern Lebanon), Myanmar (Burma), and Togo. On March 12 the commission adopted a resolution expressing its "deep concern" at human rights violations in East Timor, mainly against Roman Catholics by the predominantly Muslim Indonesian police and armed forces. The commission criticized Cuba for refusing to admit a UN special investigator. Nonetheless, the General Assembly on November 3 condemned the U.S.-led embargo against Cuba by a vote of 88–4. The U.S. was joined by Albania, Israel, and Paraguay in voting against the measure.

On October 12 a mob of 300 protesters in Hinche, Haiti, threatened a UN observer team, smashed a UN vehicle, and aroused concern for the safety of observers in a joint UN-Organization of American States mission monitoring human rights in Haiti.

Warring factions in the three-year civil war in Liberia signed a peace accord on July 25, but the truce did not last. On September 17 a three-member investigating panel blamed troops for massacring more than 400 refugees, including 103 infants, in the town of Harbel. On September 22 the Security Council established a UN Observer Mission in Liberia to monitor the cease-fire.

Libya ignored an October 1 deadline for turning over two suspects in the bombing of Pan American Airlines Flight 103 over Lockerbie, Scot., in 1988 and for cooperating with a French investigation into the bombing of a French airliner over Niger in 1989. Libya said on September 29 that it would not object to the men's being tried in Scotland for the bombing, in which 270 people died, if the suspects themselves consented. The men's lawyers advised them, however, not to leave Libya. On December 1 a Security Council decision taken November 11 froze Libya's overseas assets, barred sales to Libya of oil-refining and pipeline equipment, restricted commercial air links, and required member states to reduce the size of Libyan diplomatic missions and close all Libyan airline offices.

A UN "Commission on the Truth," investigating violations of human rights during the 12-year civil war in El Salvador, held active and retired military officers responsible for the killing of thousands of civilians, including Archbishop Oscar Arnulfo Romero (in 1980), and on March 15 called for the government to dismiss them and bar them from holding leadership posts for at least 10 years. The commission considered 22,000 cases of alleged violence and suggested that former U.S. officials (specifically former UN ambassador Jeanne Kirkpatrick and former secretary of state Alexander M. Haig, Jr.) who had denied or justified some of the Salvadoran government's worst violence and had supported giving the country $6 billion in aid during the 1980s were either cynical or badly misinformed. On October 31 the commission accused government death squads of committing over a dozen political killings during 1993. The General Assembly on December 20 established a new office of High Commissioner on Human Rights.

Weapons. Representatives of more than 120 nations signed a treaty in Paris on January 15 banning the production, stockpiling, and use of chemical weapons, which were to be destroyed within 10 years of the treaty's coming into force (Jan. 15, 1995, at the earliest).

The International Atomic Energy Agency (IAEA) on December 6 called North Korea's offer to allow only limited inspections of nuclear installations inadequate for ensuring that it had abandoned its nuclear weapons program. The secretary-general visited North Korea in December, presumably hoping to persuade the government to accept IAEA standards. (*See* MILITARY AFFAIRS.)

(RICHARD N. SWIFT)

This article updates the *Macropædia* article UNITED NATIONS.

COMMONWEALTH OF NATIONS

When leaders met for the biennial Commonwealth heads of government meeting in Limassol, Cyprus, on Oct. 21–25, 1993, it became apparent how much progress the member countries had made in moving away from military and one-party rule since their 1991 meeting in Harare, Zimbabwe. Although Nigeria had annulled its June 1993 election and Sierra Leone remained under military government, five countries (Guyana, Ghana, Kenya, Lesotho, and Zambia) had become more democratic. Tanzania, Malawi, and Nigeria were in the throes of change, and Sierra Leone's leader, Capt. Valentine Strasser, told the summit he would hand over to civilian rule within three years. By 1993 the Harare Declaration of 1991 was seen to have been more than just fine words. Human rights were increasingly to the fore, and, with help from the Commonwealth, political reform continued in several countries.

Commonwealth teams observed elections in Kenya (December 1992), Lesotho, Seychelles, and Pakistan. The Kenya group's report attracted some criticism for calling the election "a giant step on the road to multiparty democracy" despite having found the election process seriously flawed. The Commonwealth had not monitored the December 1992 parliamentary elections in Ghana because the main opposition parties boycotted the poll, saying that the presidential elections the previous month, declared free and fair by Commonwealth observers, had been rigged.

A team from 11 countries found the election that took Lesotho from military to civilian rule on March 27 to have been fairly carried out, although one party swept all 65 parliamentary seats. In Seychelles a 12-member Commonwealth group said the voters in the presidential and parliamentary elections in July had "cast their ballots openly, freely and fairly." The 15-member team sent to Pakistan for the elections that returned Benazir Bhutto's party to power in October found polling well carried out but the military presence at polling stations sometimes intrusive.

Bhutto briefly attended the Limassol summit within hours of her election as prime minister, and some new leaders at the meeting were the product of the democratic reforms. The secretary-general, Emeka Anyaoku, pointed to the fact that the Commonwealth had in the past "remained vulnerable to the charge of hypocrisy—the allegation that while it advocated democratic freedoms globally, it condoned their absence amongst its own membership." He said, "Only at Harare was the nettle finally grasped."

Just how firmly it had been grasped was shown in Limassol when the leaders still deferred the entry of Cameroon, which had applied to join in 1991. It was now offered admission in 1995 "provided that the current efforts to establish a democratic system, consistent with the Harare Commonwealth Declaration, would by then have been completed." South Africa, which had withdrawn in 1961, however, was offered a return to membership "at the earliest possible opportunity." For the first time in decades, South Africa had ceased to be a contentious issue in the Commonwealth, which lifted economic sanctions on September 24. The observer mission to South Africa, put in place in late 1992, was to remain there until after the 1994 elections. The summit also arranged for a strong Commonwealth team to monitor the polling and laid plans for Commonwealth countries to help train administrators.

In Limassol the five-year term of office of the secretary-general was reduced to four years from Jan. 1, 2001, although Anyaoku was asked to stay on for another five years from 1995. Thereafter, no secretary-general would serve more than two terms.

(DEREK INGRAM)

COMMONWEALTH OF INDEPENDENT STATES

(CIS) In the course of the year, if it had not been so earlier, Russia became the dominant force in the Commonwealth of Independent States. The CIS armed forces became the collective name for military contingents from various CIS states, and Russia also promoted a collective security pact. In October Azerbaijan and Georgia requested membership in the CIS. Russia intervened decisively in Tajikistan and Georgia, and Foreign Minister Andrey Kozyrev asserted Russia's right to a special role in the "near abroad," the former Soviet republics. During the armed rebellion of October 3–4, no CIS state sided with the Russian Parliament against Pres. Boris Yeltsin, and most came out strongly in his support.

The uprising strengthened the position of the Russian military and its desire to play a more important role in the "near abroad." The last Russian troops left Lithuania in September, but negotiations for withdrawal from Latvia and Estonia were proving difficult. Eduard Shevardnadze's desperate position in Georgia led to an appeal for military assistance in October, and Russia became the arbiter of the Georgian leader's fate. Abkhazia, Adzharia, and South Ossetia became virtual Russian protectorates. Russian army and air force units were stationed in Tajikistan and participated in fighting with rebels. The Azerbaijan Popular Front accused the Russian military of assisting the opposition and paving the way for the return of Geidar Aliev (*see* BIOGRAPHIES) as president. Fighting continued between Azeri and Armenian forces near the Iranian border after the Armenian occupation of Nagorno-Karabakh. The long-running dispute between Russia and Ukraine over the Black Sea Fleet first appeared to have been resolved in September when Ukraine traded the fleet for the cancellation of debts, but the agreement appeared to be unraveling later in the year. (*See also* MILITARY AFFAIRS.) In December the 12 CIS members, concerned about renewed Russian nationalism, declined Yeltsin's request for special status for Russians living on their territories.

The September 24 agreement of nine republics to establish an economic union aimed at "gradually building a common economic space on the basis of market relations." The agreement envisaged, for instance, the promotion of joint-owned enterprises (as a way of paying for Russian energy and raw materials) and a multicurrency clearing system administered by an Interstate Bank (which was established in mid-December). The arrangement would lead to a monetary union with currencies floating against the ruble. Because of the size of its economy, Russia controlled about 70% of the votes in the new union. (MARTIN MCCAULEY)

POLITICAL PARTIES

The following table is a general guide to the principal political parties and coalitions of the world. All countries that were independent on Dec. 31, 1993, are included, except the Vatican City State. Parties are included in most instances only if represented in elected parliaments (in the lower house in bicameral legislatures). Figures in the column "Parliamentary representation" indicate the number of seats obtained in the last general election (figures in parentheses are those of the penultimate one) and exclude nonelective seats and seats still undecided. If only a portion of the seats were at stake in the last general election, the figure given indicates the total number of seats held by each party after the election. The date of the most recent election follows the name of the country.

The capital letters in the column "Affiliation" show the relative positions of the parties within the political spectrum of each country. The key chosen is as follows: F-fascist; ER-extreme right; R-right; CR-centre right; C-centre; CL-centre left; SD-social democratic; S-socialist; L-non-Marxist left; K-Communist; and EL-extreme left. In addition, within some countries there are political organizations that exist chiefly to advance a special interest as distinct from a political orientation. These are represented by lower-case letters as follows: x-parties that have repudiated former Communist affiliation; e-parties based on distinct regional, ethnic, or linguistic identity; r-religious fundamentalist; g-environmental, or Green; and p-parties based largely on personalities.

The numbers in the column "Voting strength" indicate proportions of the valid votes cast for the respective parties. (MELINDA C. SHEPHERD)

Political Parties

Country / Name of party	Affiliation	Voting strength (%)	Parliamentary representation	
Afghanistan				
Interim parliament since January 1993	—	—	250	
Albania (March 1992)				
Democratic Party	CR	62.1	92	(75)
Social Democratic Party	SD	4.4	7	—
Socialist Party	x	25.7	38	(169)
Other	—	7.8	3	(6)
Algeria				
Interim government since January 1992	—	—	—	
Andorra (December 1993)				
Agrupament Nacional Democratic	CR	26.4	8	
Others and independents	—	73.6	20	
Angola (September 1992)				
Popular Liberation Movement of Angola–Labour Party (MPLA–PT)	x	53.7	129	(203)
National Union for the Total Independence of Angola (UNITA)	—	34.1	70	—
Others	—	12.2	21	—
Antigua and Barbuda (March 1989)				
Antigua Labour Party	C	63.8	15	(16)
United National Democratic Party	C	31.0	1	—
Barbuda People's Movement	—	...	1	—
Barbuda National Party	—	...	—	(1)
Argentina (October 1993)				
Movement for Dignity and Independence	R	5.8	7	(3)
Union of the Democratic Centre	CR	2.6	5	(10)
Justicialist National Movement (Peronist)	—	42.3	126	(119)
Radical Civic Union	CL	30.0	83	(85)
Provincial parties	e	10.4	38 (Provincial parties and Others together)	(19)
Others	—	8.9		(18)
Armenia (May–July 1990)				
Supreme Soviet	—	—	260	
Australia (March 1993)				
National	R	8.2	16	(14)
Liberal	C	33.6	49	(55)
Labor	L	38.2	80	(78)
Others and independents	—	20.0	2	(1)
Austria (October 1990)				
Freedom Party	R	16.6	33	(18)
People's Party	C	32.0	60	(77)
Socialist Party	SD	42.8	80	(80)
Greens	Lg	4.8	10	(8)
Azerbaijan (September–October 1990)				
Supreme Soviet	—	—	349	
Bahamas, The (August 1992)				
Progressive Liberal Party	C	...	15	(31)
Free National Movement	C	...	34	(16)
Others	—	...	0	(2)
Bahrain				
Consultative Council (advisory body)	—	—	—	
Bangladesh (February 1991)				
Bangladesh Nationalist Party	CR	31	166	(18)
National Party (coalition)	—	11	35	(251)
Awami League	SD	31	89	—
Islamic Assembly	r	12	21	(5)
Others	—	15	19	(25)
Barbados (January 1991)				
Democratic Labour Party	C	49	18	(24)
Barbados Labour Party	L	44	10	(3)
Belarus (March 1990)				
Supreme Soviet	K	—	272	
Belgium (November 1991)				
Vlaams Blok	ERe	6.6	12	(2)
Volksunie	Re	5.9	10	(16)
Front Démocratique	Re	1.5	3	(3)
Liberals: Flemish	CR	11.9	26	(25)
Liberals: French	CR	8.2	20	(23)
Social Christians: Flemish	C	16.7	39	(43)
Social Christians: French	C	7.8	18	(19)
Socialists: Flemish	SD	12.0	28	(32)
Socialists: French	SD	13.6	35	(40)
Greens: Flemish	g	4.9	7	(6)
Greens: French	g	5.1	10	(3)
Others	—	7.3	7	(3)
Belize (June 1993)				
United Democratic Party	R	48.8	16	(13)
People's United Party	C	51.2	13	(15)
Benin (February 1991)				
Union of the Forces of Progress (formerly sole party)	—	...	0	
21 other parties	—	...	64	
Bhutan				
National Assembly, no parties	—	—	100	
Bolivia (June 1993)				
Civic Solidarity Union	R	...	20	—
Nationalist Revolutionary Movement	CR	...	52	(40)

Political Parties

Country Name of party	Affiliation	Voting strength (%)	Parliamentary representation	
Patriotic Accord (coalition)	—	...	35	(71)
Conscience of the Fatherland	CL	...	13	(9)
Free Bolivia Movement	L	...	7	—
Others	—	...	3	(10)
Bosnia and Herzegovina (December 1990)				
Party of Democratic Action	e	...	86	
Serbian Democratic Party	e	...	72	
Croatian Democratic Union	e	...	44	
Democratic Party of Socialists	x	...	20	
Others	—	...	18	
Botswana (October 1989)				
Botswana Democratic Party	C	65.0	31	(29)
Botswana People's Party	L	...	—	(1)
Botswana National Front	L	27.7	3	(4)
Brazil (October 1990)				
Rightist parties	CR	...	243	
Party of the Brazilian Democratic Movement and allies	CL	...	146	
Leftist parties	L	...	95	
Others	—	...	14	
Brunei				
Legislative Council (nonelected)	—	—	—	
Bulgaria (October 1991)				
Union of Democratic Forces	CL	34.4	110	(144)
Bulgarian Socialist Party	x	33.1	106	(211)
Movement for Rights and Freedom	e	7.5	24	(23)
Bulgarian Agrarian People's Union	—	3.9	0	(16)
Other parties and independents	—	21.1	0	(6)
Burkina Faso (May 1992)				
Organization for Popular Democracy-Labour Movement	L	...	78	
Allied parties	—	...	6	
Opposition parties	—	...	23	
Burundi (June 1993)				
Burundi Democratic Front	—	71.4	65	
Unity for National Progress	—	21.4	16	
Others	—	7.2	—	
Cambodia (May 1993)				
Funcinpec	CR	45.5	58	
Buddhist Liberal Democratic Party	L	3.0	10	
Cambodian People's Party	x	38.2	51	
Others	—	13.3	1	
Cameroon (March 1992)				
People's Democratic Movement and allied party	—	...	94	(180)
Opposition parties	—	...	86	—
Canada (October 1993)				
Reform	R	18.1	52	—
Progressive Conservative	CR	16.1	2	(170)
Liberal	C	41.6	177	(82)
New Democratic	SD	6.6	9	(43)
Bloc Québécois	e	13.9	54	—
Others and independents	—	3.7	1	(0)
Cape Verde (January 1991)				
Movement for Democracy	—	68.5	56	—
African Party for the Independence of Cape Verde	—	31.5	23	(83)
Central African Republic (August–September 1993)				
Central African People's Liberation Party	—	...	34	
Others	—	...	51	
Chad				
Transitional government since March 1991	—	—	—	
Chile (December 1993)				
Independent Democratic Union	ER	...	15	(11)
National Renovation and allied party	R	...	31	(29)
Right-wing independents	R	...	4	(8)
Christian Democratic Party	C	...	37	(38)
Leftist parties	CL–L	...	32	(28)
Left-wing independent	L	...	1	(6)
China (September 1992–March 1993)				
National People's Congress	K	...	2,977	
Colombia (October 1991)				
Social Conservative Party	R	...	15	(68)
National Salvation Movement	R	...	12	—
New Democratic Force	R	...	12	—
Liberal Party	C	...	86	(112)
Democratic Alliance–April 19 Movement	L&EL	...	15	(1)
Patriotic Union	EL	...	2	(15)
Others	—	...	19	(1)
Comoros (December 1993)				
Federal Assembly	—	...	42	(42)
Congo (May–October 1993)				
Presidential Coalition	—	...	65	(69)
Opposition Coalition	—	...	57	(49)
Others	—	...	3	(7)
Costa Rica (February 1990)				
Social Christian Unity Party	CR	51.3	29	(25)
National Liberation Party	L	47.2	25	(29)
Others	—	1.5	3	(3)
Côte d'Ivoire (November 1990)				
Democratic Party	—	...	163	(175)
Popular Front	SD	...	9	—
Others and independents	—	...	3	—
Croatia (August 1992)				
Croatian Party of Rights	ERe	6.4	5	
Croatian Democratic Union	e	41.5	85	
Croatian People's Party	C	6.9	6	
Croatian Social-Liberal Party	CL	18.3	14	
Party of Democratic Changes	x	5.8	11	
Others and independents	—	20.6	17	
Cuba (February 1993)				
Communist Party	K	...	589	(499)
Cyprus				
Greek Zone (May 1991)				
Democratic Rally	R	35.8	20	(19)
Democratic Party (DIKO)	CR	19.5	11	(16)
Socialist Party (EDEK)	CL	10.9	7	(6)
Progressive Party of the Working People	K	30.6	18	(15)
Turkish Zone (December 1993)				
National Unity Party	—	30	17	
Others	—	70	33	
Czech Republic (June 1992)				
Association for the Republic–Czech Republican Party	ER	6.0	14	
Governing coalition	R&CR	41.9	105	
Czech Social Democratic Party	SD	6.5	16	
Liberal Social Union (coalition)	L	6.5	16	
Left Bloc	x	14.1	35	
Moravia/Silesia regional party	e	5.9	14	
Others	—	19.1	0	
Denmark (December 1990)				
Progress	ER	6.4	12	(16)
Conservative	R	16.0	30	(35)
Liberal (Venstre)	CR	15.8	29	(22)
Christian People's	CR	2.3	4	(4)
Radical Liberal (Radikale Venstre)	C	3.5	7	(10)
Centre Democrats	C	5.1	9	(9)
Social Democrats	SD	37.4	69	(55)
Socialist People's	S	8.3	15	(24)
Faeroe Islands and Greenland	—	—	4	(4)
Djibouti (December 1992)				
Popular Rally for Progress	—	74.6	65	(65)
New Democratic Party	—	25.4	0	—
Dominica (May 1990)				
Dominica Freedom Party	CR	49.4	11	(15)
Dominica United Workers' Party	C	23.5	6	—
Labour Party	L	26.9	4	(5)
Independents		...	0	(1)
Dominican Republic (May 1990)				
Social Christian Reformist Party	CR	...	40	(56)
Dominican Revolutionary Party	L	...	32	(48)
Dominican Liberation Party	L	...	44	(16)
Others	—	...	4	—
Ecuador (May 1992)				
Conservative Party	R	...	6	(3)
Republican Unity Party	CR	...	12	—
Social Christian Party	CR	...	21	(16)
Popular Democracy	C	...	5	(7)
Roldosist Party	—	...	13	(13)
Democratic Left	SD	...	7	(14)
Others	—	...	13	(19)
Egypt (November–December 1990)				
New Wafd Party	R	(Boycotted)		(35)
National Democratic Party	CR	79.6	348	(346)
Socialist Labour Party and allies	L	(Boycotted)		(60)
National Progressive Unionist	L	1.4	6	(0)
Independents	—	...	83	(7)
El Salvador (March 1991)				
Nationalist Republican Alliance (Arena)	R	44	39	(30)
National Conciliation Party	CR	9	9	(7)
Christian Democratic Party	C	28	26	(23)
Democratic Convergence	L	12	8	—
Others	—	7	2	(0)
Equatorial Guinea (November 1993)				
Democratic Party of Equatorial Guinea	—	...	68	(41)
Principal opposition parties	—	(Boycotted)		—
Others	—	...	12	—
Eritrea				
Transitional government from May 1993	—	—	—	
Estonia (September 1992)				
Pro Patria coalition	CR	...	29	—
Estonian Popular Front	C	...	15	(43)
Estonian National Independence	C	...	10	—
Moderates	CL	...	12	—
Safe Haven	—	...	17	—
Others	—	...	18	(62)
Ethiopia				
Transitional government since July 1991	—	—	—	
Fiji (May 1992)				
Fijian Political Party	e	...	30	
Other Fijians	e	...	7	
National Federation (Indian)	e	...	14	
Other Indians	e	...	13	
Other parties	—	...	6	
Finland (March 1991)				
National Coalition Party	R	19.0	40	(53)
Swedish People's	e	5.4	12	(12)
Centre Party	C	24.4	55	(40)
Christian Union	C	3.0	8	(5)
Rural Party	C	4.8	7	(9)
Social Democratic	L	21.7	48	(56)
Left-Wing Alliance	S	9.9	19	(20)
Green Union	g	6.7	10	(4)
Others	—	5.2	2	(1)
France (March 1993)				
National Front	ER	12.4	0	(1)
Rally for the Republic (RPR)	R	20.4	247	(127)
Other right-wing parties	R	4.7	24	(16)
Union for French Democracy (UDF)	CR	19.1	213	(129)
Socialist Party	S	17.6	54	(260)
Other left-wing parties	L	4.5	16	(16)
Communist Party	K	9.2	23	(27)
Environmentalist parties	g	7.6	0	—
Other	—	4.5	0	(1)
Gabon (September 1990)				
Democratic Party	—	...	66	(111)
Progress Party	—	...	19	—
Rally of Woodcutters	—	...	17	—
Others	—	...	18	—
Gambia, The (April 1992)				
People's Progressive Party	S	...	25	(31)
Others	—	...	11	(5)
Georgia				
Legislature suspended September 1993	—	—	—	
Germany (December 1990)				
Christian Social Union	R	7.1	51	
Christian Democratic Union	CR	36.7	268	
Free Democratic Party	C	11.0	79	
Social Democratic Party	SD	33.5	239	
Party of Democratic Socialism	x	2.4	17	
Greens/Alliance '90	g	5.1	8	
Others	—	4.2	0	
Ghana (December 1992)				
National Democratic Congress	—	...	189	
Others	—	...	11	
Greece (October 1993)				
Political Spring	CR	4.9	10	—
New Democracy	CR	39.3	111	(152)
Panhellenic Socialist Movement (Pasok)	S	46.9	170	(124)
Progressive Left Coalition	L&K	2.9 }	0	(21)
Communist Party	K	4.5 }	9	
Others	—	1.5	0	(3)
Grenada (March 1990)				
Grenada United Labour Party	R	28.3	4	(1)
National Democratic Congress	C	34.6	7	(6)
National Party	C	17.4	2	(5)
New National Party	C	17.2	2	(3)
Guatemala (November 1990)				
National Advancement Party	R	17.3	12	
Solidarity Action Movement	CR	24.1	18	
Christian Democratic Party	C	17.5	28	
National Centre Union	C	25.7	41	
Others and independents	—	15.4	17	
Guinea				
Transitional government since January 1991	—	—	—	
Guinea-Bissau (June 1989)				
African Party for the Independence of Guinea and Cape Verde	—	...	150	
Guyana (October 1992)				
United Force	CR	1.2	1	(2)
People's National Congress	Se	43.6	27	(42)
People's Progressive Party	Se	52.3	35	(8)
Working Peoples Alliance	L	1.7	2	(1)
Haiti (December 1990–January 1991)				
National Front for Change and Democracy (coalition)	CL	...	27	
Others	—	...	54	
Honduras (November 1993)				
National Party	R	42	55	(71)
Liberal Party	CR	53	71	(55)
Others	—	5	2	(2)
Hungary (March–April 1990)				
Independent Smallholders	R	11.1	43	
Hungarian Democratic Forum	CR	42.7	165	
Christian Democratic Party	CR	5.4	21	
Alliance of Free Democrats	CL	23.8	92	
Federation of Young Democrats	L	5.4	21	
Hungarian Socialist Party	x	8.5	33	
Others and independents	—	2.6	10	
Iceland (April 1991)				
Independence Party	R	38.6	26	(18)
Citizens' Party	R	1.2	0	(7)

Political Parties

Country / Name of party	Affiliation	Voting strength (%)	Parliamentary representation	
Progressive (Farmers') Party	C	18.9	13	(13)
Social Democratic Party	SD	15.5	10	(10)
People's Alliance	x	14.4	9	(8)
Women's Alliance	—	8.3	5	(6)
Others	—	3.1	0	(1)
India (May 1991–February 1992)				
Bharatiya Janata	Rr	...	121	(88)
Congress (I)	C	...	245	(192)
Janata Dal	CL	...	58	(141)
Communist parties	K	...	49	(43)
Others	—	...	72	(59)
Indonesia (June 1992)				
Golkar (Functional Groups)	—	68	281	(299)
United Development Party	r	17	63	(61)
Indonesian Democratic Party	—	15	56	(40)
Iran (April–May 1992)				
Consultative Assembly, no parties since 1987	—	...	270	
Iraq (April 1989)				
Ba'th Party	—	64	250 (Ba'th Party and Others together)	
Others	—	36		
Ireland (November 1992)				
Fianna Fail (Republican)	C	39.1	68	(77)
Fine Gael (United Ireland)	C	24.5	45	(55)
Progressive Democrats	C	4.7	10	(5)
Labour Party	L	19.3	33	(16)
Democratic Left	S	2.8	4	(7)
Green Alliance	g	1.4	1	(1)
Others	—	8.2	5	(5)
Israel (June 1992)				
Moledet	ER	2.4	3	(2)
Tzomet	R	6.4	8	(2)
United Torah Judaism	r	3.3	4	(7)
Shas	Rr	4.9	6	(6)
Likud	R	24.9	32	(40)
National Religious (Mafdal)	CRr	5.0	6	(5)
Labour	SD	34.6	44	(39)
Meretz	SD	9.6	12	(10)
Arab (Democracy)	e	1.6	2	(1)
Hadash	K	2.4	3	(4)
Others	—	4.9	0	(4)
Italy (April 1992)				
Italian Social Movement	F	5.4	34	(35)
Northern League	Re	8.7	55	—
Italian Liberal Party	CR	2.8	17	(11)
Christian Democratic Party	C	29.7	206	(234)
Republican Party	CL	4.4	27	(21)
Social Democratic Party	SD	2.7	16	(17)
Socialist Unity Party	S	13.6	92	(94)
Democratic Party of the Left	x	16.1	107	(177) (Democratic Party of the Left and Communist Refoundation Party together)
Communist Refoundation Party	K	5.6	35	
Green List	g	2.8	16	(13)
Others	—	10.9	41	(45)
Jamaica (March 1993)				
Jamaica Labour Party	CL	...	8	(15)
People's National Party	L	...	52	(45)
Japan (July 1993)				
Liberal-Democratic Party	R	36.7	225	(275)
Shinseito (Japan Renewal)	R	10.1	55	—
Japan New Party	R	8.1	36	—
New Party Sakigake	R	2.6	13	—
Komeito (Clean Government)	C	8.1	52	(45)
Democratic Socialist Party	SD	3.5	15	(14)
United Social Democratic Party	SD	0.7	4	(4)
Social Democratic Party	S	15.4	70	(136)
Japan Communist Party	L	7.7	15	(16)
Independents	—	7.1	27	(22)
Jordan (November 1993)				
Islamic Action Front	r	...	16	(20)
Independent Islamic fundamentalists	r	...	5	(12)
Tribal/traditional candidates	C	...	49	(17) (Tribal/traditional candidates and Independent centrists together)
Independent centrists	C	...	3	
Leftists	L	...	7	(11)
Kazakhstan				
Legislature dissolved December 1993	—	—	—	
Kenya (December 1992)				
Kenya African National Union	—	...	100	(188)
Forum for Restoration of Democracy (2 wings)	—	...	62	—
Democratic Party	—	...	23	—
Others	—	...	3	—
Kiribati (May 1991)				
House of Assembly	—	...	39	
Korea, North (April 1990)				
Korean Workers' Party	K	99.8	687	
Korea, South (March 1992)				
United People's Party	—	17.3	31	
Democratic Liberal Party	—	38.5	149	
Democratic Party	—	29.2	97	
Others and independents	—	15.0	22	
Kuwait (October 1992)				
Government supporters	—	...	19	
Fundamental opposition	r	...	19	
Liberal opposition	—	...	12	
Kyrgyzstan (February 1990)				
Supreme Soviet	—	—	350	
Laos (December 1992)				
Lao People's Revolutionary Party and allies	K	...	85	(79)
Latvia (June 1993)				
Ultranationalist parties	ER	18.8	21	—
Latvia's Way Union; Latvian Farmers' Union (together)	CR	43.0	48	—
Popular Front	—	2.6	0	(131)
Harmony for Latvia	CL	12.0	13	—
Equal Rights	CL	5.8	7	—
Communist Party	K	(banned)		(59)
Others	—	17.8	11	(11)
Lebanon (August–October 1992)				
Christian members	—	...	64	
Muslim/Druze members	—	...	64	
Lesotho (March 1993)				
Basotho Congress Party	—	...	65	
Others	—	...	0	
Liberia				
Interim government since December 1993	—	—	—	
Libya				
Military government since Sept. 1, 1969	—	—	—	
Liechtenstein (October 1993)				
Progressive Citizens' Party	CR	41.3	11	(12)
Fatherland Union	C	50.1	13	(11)
The Free List	g	8.5	1	(2)
Lithuania (October–November 1992)				
Christian Democrats and allies	R	...	18	
Reform Movement (Sajudis)	CR	19	29	
Social Democratic Party	SD	...	8	
Democratic Labour Party	x	45	74	
Others	—	...	12	
Luxembourg (June 1989)				
Christian Social People's Party	CR	32	22	(25)
Democratic (Liberal) Party	C	18	11	(14)
Socialist Workers' Party	SD	27	18	(21)
Communist Party	K	4	1	(2)
Five-Sixths Action Committee	—	...	4	(0)
Green parties	g	...	4	(2)
Macedonia (November–December 1990)				
Democratic Party for Macedonian National Unity	Ce	...	37	
Government parties	CL–x	...	79	
Others	—	...	4	
Madagascar (June 1993)				
Living Forces coalition	—	...	75	
Others	—	...	59	
Malawi (June 1992)				
Malawi Congress Party	—	...	136	(112)
Malaysia (October 1990)				
Muslim Unity Movement	CR	...	15	—
National Front (Barisan Nasional)				
United Malays National Organization	e	54.2 (United Malays National Organization and Allied parties together)	71	(83)
Allied parties	e		56	(65)
Democratic Action Party	SD	...	20	(24)
Others and independents	—	...	18	(5)
Maldives (November 1989)				
Citizens' Assembly	—	...	40	
Mali (February–March 1992)				
Alliance for Democracy in Mali	—	48.4	76	
Others	—	51.6	40	
Malta (February 1992)				
Nationalist Party	R	51.8	34	(35)
Labour Party	SD	46.5	31	(34)
Marshall Islands (November 1991)				
House of Representatives	—	—	33	
Mauritania (March 1992)				
Democratic and Social Republican Party	R	85	67	
Others and independents	—	15	12	
Mauritius (September 1991)				
Mauritian Social Movement and allies	CL	...	59	(49)
Opposition parties	CL	...	3	(13)
Mexico (August 1991)				
National Action Party (PAN)	CR	17.7	89	(101)
Institutional Revolutionary Party (PRI)	C	61.4	320	(261)
Democratic Revolutionary Party	L	8.3	41	(138) (Democratic Revolutionary Party and Others together)
Others	—	12.5	50	
Micronesia (March 1993)				
Congress, no parties	—	...	14	
Moldova (February–March 1990)				
Supreme Soviet	K	...	380	
Monaco (January 1993)				
National and Democratic Union	—	...	0	(18)
Campora list	—	...	15	—
Others	—	...	3	(0)
Mongolia (June 1992)				
Mongolian People's Revolutionary Party	x	56.9	71	(33)
Others	—	43.1	5	(20)
Morocco (June–September 1993)				
Constitutional Union	CR	...	54	(83)
National Democratic Party	CR	...	24	(24)
Berber parties	CRe	...	76	(47)
National Assembly of Independents	C	...	41	(61)
Democratic Bloc	CL–EL	...	120	(85)
Others and independents	—	...	18	(6)
Mozambique (November–December 1986)				
Mozambique Liberation Front (Frelimo)	K	...	250	(210)
Myanmar				
Military government since September 1988	—	—	—	
Namibia (November 1989)				
Democratic Turnhalle Alliance	C	28.6	21	
South West Africa People's Organization (SWAPO)	L	57.3	41	
United Democratic Front	—	5.6	4	
Others	—	8.5	6	
Nauru (November 1992)				
Presidential supporters	p	—	9	
Presidential opponents	p	—	9	
Nepal (May 1991)				
National Democratic parties	R	12	4	
Nepali Congress Party	C	38	110	
Communist parties	K	36	82	
Others and independents	—	14	9	
Netherlands, The (September 1989)				
Christian Democratic Appeal	CR	35.3	54	(54)
People's Party for Freedom and Democracy	CR	14.6	22	(27)
Democrats 66	CL	7.9	12	(9)
Labour Party	SD	31.9	49	(52)
Greens	g	4.1	6	(3)
Others	—	6.2	7	(5)
New Zealand (November 1993)				
New Zealand First	—	8.3	2	—
National Party	CR	35.2	50	(67)
Labour Party	CL	34.7	45	(29)
Alliance Party (coalition)	L	18.3	2	(1)
Nicaragua (February 1990)				
National Opposition Union	CR	54.7	51	
Sandinista National Liberation Front	L	40.8	39	
Others	—	4.5	2	
Niger (February 1993)				
Government Coalition	—	...	50	
Former government party	—	...	29	
Others	—	...	4	
Nigeria				
Military government since November 1993				
Norway (September 1993)				
Progress Party	R	6.3	10	(22)
Conservative Party	R	16.9	28	(37)
Christian People's Party	CR	7.9	13	(14)
Centre (Agrarian) Party	CR	16.8	32	(11)
Labour Party	SD	37.0	67	(63)
Socialist Left	S	7.9	13	(17)
Others	—	7.2	2	(1)
Oman				
Consultative Council (advisory body)	—	—	—	
Pakistan (October 1993)				
Religious parties	Rr	...	10	(6)
Pakistan Muslim League (Nawaz)	—	41.0	72	(105) (Nawaz and Junejo together)
Pakistan Muslim League (Junejo)	—	...	6	
Pakistan People's Party	—	38.0	86	(45)
Mohajir Qaumi Movement	e	(Boycotted)		(15)
Other and independents	—	...	27	(30)
Panama (May 1989–January 1991)				
Antimilitarist Opposition Democratic Alliance	p	...	55	
National Liberation Coalition	p	...	12	
Papua New Guinea (June 1992)				
House of Assembly	—	—	108	(109)
Paraguay (May 1993)				
Colorado Party	R	43.0	38	(48)
Authentic Radical Liberal Party	CL	35.1	33	(19)
National Encounter coalition	—	17.1	9	—
Others	—	4.8	0	(5)
Peru (November 1992)				
Christian Popular Party	R	7.7	8	(60) (Christian Popular Party, Liberal Party and Popular Action together)
Liberal Party	R	—	—	
Popular Action	CR	(Boycotted)		
New Majority–Change 90	—	38.6	44	(32)
American Popular Revolutionary Alliance	CL	(Boycotted)		(52)
Others	—	53.7	28	(36)
Philippines (May 1992)				
National People's Coalition	R	...	48	
Liberal Party	C	...	15	

Political Parties

Country / Name of party	Affiliation	Voting strength (%)	Parliamentary representation	
National Union of Christian Democrats	—	...	51	
Democratic Filipino Struggle	—	...	87	
Poland (September 1993)				
Confederation for an Independent Poland	R	5.8	22	(46)
Non-Party Bloc to Support Reform	R	5.4	16	—
Democratic Union	CL	10.6	74	(62)
Labour Union	L	7.3	41	(4)
Democratic Left Alliance	x	20.4	171	(60)
Polish Peasant Party	x	15.4	132	(48)
German minority organizations	e	—	4	(7)
Others	—	35.1	0	(233)
Portugal (October 1991)				
Social Democratic Party	C	50.4	135	(148)
Socialist Party	L	29.3	72	(60)
Communist alliance	K	8.8	17	(31)
Other parties	—	11.5	6	(11)
Qatar				
Consultative Council (advisory body)	—	—	—	
Romania (September 1992)				
Romanian National Unity Party	ERe	7.7	30	
Greater Romania	e	3.9	16	
Democratic Convention of Romania	CR	20.0	82	
Democratic National Salvation Front	x	27.7	117	
National Salvation Front	x	10.2	43	
Hungarian Democratic Union	e	7.5	27	
Others	—	23.0	13	
Russia (December 1993)				
Liberal Democratic Party	F	22.8	64	
Russia's Choice	CR	15.4	70	
Russian Party of Unity and Accord	CR	6.8	19	
Yavlinsky–Boldyrev–Lukin bloc	C	7.8	23	
Civic Union	C	1.9	1	
Women of Russia	C	8.1	23	
Democratic Party	C	5.5	14	
Russian Movement for Democratic Reforms	CL	4.1	4	
Communist Party	K	12.3	48	
Agrarian Union	K	7.9	33	
Cedar	g	0.8	0	
Other parties	—	6.6	16	
Independents elected from constituency lists	—	—	129	
Rwanda				
Transitional government from November 1993	—	—	—	
Saint Kitts and Nevis (November 1993)				
People's Action Movement	CL	33.6	4	(6)
Nevis Reformation Party	CL	8.5	1	(2)
St Kitts–Nevis Labour Party	L	43.8	4	(2)
Concerned Citizens' Movement	—	10.9	2	(1)
Saint Lucia (April 1992)				
United Workers' Party	C	56.3	11	(9)
St. Lucia Labour Party	CL	43.5	6	(8)
Saint Vincent and the Grenadines (May 1989)				
New Democratic Party	C	66.3	15	(9)
St. Vincent Labour Party	L	30.3	0	(4)
San Marino (May 1993)				
Christian Democrats	CR	41.4	26	(27)
Socialist Party	S	23.7	14	(7)
Progressive Democratic Party	x	18.6	11	(18)
Popular Democratic Alliance	—	7.7	4	—
Other parties	—	8.6	5	(8)
São Tomé and Príncipe (January 1991)				
Party of Democratic Convergence	C	54.37	33	—
Movement for Liberation	L	30.53	21	(40)
Others	—	15.10	1	—
Saudi Arabia				
Consultative Council (advisory body)	—	—	—	
Senegal (May 1993)				
Socialist Party	SD	56.6	84	(103)
Senegalese Democratic Party	—	30.2	27	(17)
Let Us Unite Senegal	EL	4.9	3	—
Other parties	—	8.3	6	—
Seychelles (July 1993)				
People's Progressive Front	L	56.5	32	(23)
Others	—	43.5	11	—
Sierra Leone				
Military government since May 1992	—	—	—	
Singapore (August 1991)				
People's Action Party	CR	61	77	(80)
Democratic Party	CL	12	3	(1)
Workers' Party	L	14	1	(0)
Slovakia (June 1992)				
Slovak National Party	Re	7.9	15	
Christian Democratic Movement	CR	8.9	18	
Movement for a Democratic Slovakia	—	37.3	74	
Democratic Left	x	14.7	29	
Hungarian minority coalition	e	7.4	14	
Others	—	23.8	0	
Slovenia (December 1992)				
Slovenian National Party	ER	9.9	12	
Christian Democrats	CR	14.5	15	
People's Party	—	8.8	10	
Associated List coalition	—	13.6	14	
Democratic Party	C	5.0	6	
Liberal Democratic Party	CL	23.7	22	
Social Democratic Party	SD	3.3	4	
Greens of Slovenia	g	3.7	5	
Others	—	17.5	0	
Solomon Islands (May 1993)				
Government Alliance	p	...	24	
Opposition party	p	...	23	
Somalia				
No effective government since January 1991	—	—	—	
South Africa				
Transitional government since September 1993	—	—	—	
Spain (June 1993)				
Popular Party	R	34.8	141	(107)
Democratic and Social Centre	C	1.7	0	(14)
Basque Nationalist Party	Ce	1.2	5	(5)
Canary Islands coalition	Ce	0.9	4	—
Convergence and Union (Catalan)	CLe	5.0	17	(18)
Socialist Workers' Party	S	38.7	159	(175)
United Left	L&K	9.6	18	(17)
Herri Batasuna (Basque radicals)	ELe	0.9	2	(4)
Others	—	7.2	4	(10)
Sri Lanka (February 1989)				
United National Party	SD	...	125	(140)
Freedom Party	SD	...	67	(8)
Tamil groups	e	...	23	(18)
Communists and others	—	...	10	(2)
Sudan, The				
Transitional government since February 1992	—	—	—	
Suriname (May 1991)				
National Democratic Party	—	21.8	12	(3)
Front for Democracy and Development (four-party coalition)	—	54.2	30	(42)
Democratic Alternative '91	—	16.7	9	—
Swaziland (September–October 1993)				
House of Assembly, no parties	—	—	55	
Sweden (September 1991)				
New Democracy	R	6.8	24	—
Christian Democrats	R	7.2	27	(0)
Moderate (Conservative) Party	R	22.1	80	(66)
Centre (Agrarian) Party	CR	8.6	31	(42)
People's (Liberal) Party	C	9.2	33	(44)
Social Democrats	S	38.2	138	(156)
Left (Communist) Party	L	4.5	16	(21)
Greens	g	3.4	0	(20)
Switzerland (October 1991)				
Swiss Car Party	R	5.1	8	(2)
Christian Democrats	R	18.3	36	(42)
Liberal Party	R	3.0	10	(9)
Swiss People's	CR	11.9	25	(25)
Radical Democrats	C	21.0	44	(51)
Social Democrats	SD	18.5	41	(41)
Green Party	g	6.1	14	(9)
Others	—	16.1	22	(21)
Syria (May 1990)				
National Progressive Front				
Ba'th Party	—	...	134	
Other parties	—	...	32	
Independents	—	...	84	
Taiwan (December 1992)				
Nationalist (Kuomintang)	—	53	94	(72)
Democratic Progressive Party	—	31	52	(21)
Others and Independents	—	16	15	(8)
Tajikistan (March 1990)				
Supreme Soviet	—	—	230	
Tanzania (October 1990)				
Revolutionary Party of Tanzania (CCM)	—	...	204	(169)
Thailand (September 1992)				
Pro-military parties:				
Thai Nation	—	21.4	77	
National Development	—	16.7	60	
Others	—	1.1	4	
Pro-democracy parties:				
Democrat	—	21.9	79	
New Aspiration	—	14.2	51	
Righteous Force	—	13.1	47	
Solidarity	—	2.2	8	
Others	—	9.4	34	
Togo				
Ad hoc government from January 1993	—	—	—	
Tonga (February 1993)				
Pro-Democracy Party	—	...	6	(6)
Others	—	...	3	(3)
Trinidad and Tobago (December 1991)				
People's National Movement	C	45.1	21	(3)
National Alliance for Reconstruction (four parties)	C	24.4	2	(33)
United National Congress	L	29.1	13	—
Tunisia (April 1989)				
Government party	—	80.5	141	(125)
Others	—	19.5	0	—
Turkey (October 1991)				
Nationalist Labour Party	ER }	16.9	19	—
Welfare Party	Rr }		43	(0)
True Path Party	CR	27.0	178	(59)
Motherland Party	CR	24.0	115	(292)
Social Democratic Populist	CL }	20.8	66	(99)
People's Labour Party	e }		22	—
Democratic Left Party	CL	10.8	7	(0)
Turkmenistan				
Assembly	—	—	—	
Tuvalu (September 1993)				
Supporters of prime minister	p	—	6	
Opponents	p	—	6	
Uganda (February 1989)				
National Resistance Council	—	—	210	(98)
Ukraine (March 1990)				
Supreme Soviet	—	...	450	
United Arab Emirates				
Federal National Council (advisory body)	—	—	—	
United Kingdom (April 1992)				
Democratic Unionists	Re	0.3	3	(3)
Conservative Party	CR	41.9	336	(375)
Liberal Democrats	CL	17.9	20	(22)
Labour Party	L	34.4	271	(229)
Scottish National Party	e	1.9	3	(3)
Plaid Cymru (Welsh Nationalists)	e	0.5	4	(3)
Ulster Unionists	—	0.8	9	(9)
Social Democratic and Labour Party (Northern Ireland)	CLe	0.6	4	(3)
Sinn Fein (Northern Ireland)	ELe	0.2	0	(1)
Other	—	1.5	1	(2)
United States (November 1992)				
Republican	CR	...	175	(167)
Democratic	C	...	259	(267)
Other	—	...	1	(1)
Uruguay (November 1989)				
Civic Union	R	...	0	(2)
National (Blanco) Party	C	...	39	(36)
Colorado Party	C	...	30	(40)
New Space	SD	...	9 }	(21)
Broad Front	L	...	21 }	
Other	—	...	0	(2)
Uzbekistan (February 1990)				
Supreme Soviet	—	—	500	
Vanuatu (December 1991)				
Union of Moderate Parties	CR	...	19	(20)
National United Party	CR	...	10	—
Vanua'aku Pati	—	...	12	(26)
Others	—	...	5	(0)
Venezuela (December 1993)				
COPEI (Social Christians)	CR	26.6	52	(67)
Democratic Action	S	28.2	55	(97)
Movement to Socialism	L	12.8	25	(18)
Others	—	32.3	63	(19)
Vietnam (July 1992)				
National Assembly	—	...	395	
Western Samoa (April 1991)				
Human Rights Protection Party	—	...	30	(27)
National Development Party	—	...	14	(19)
Independents	—	...	3	(1)
Yemen (April 1993)				
Yemeni Alliance for Reform	Rr	...	62	
General People's Congress	—	...	122	
Yemeni Socialist Party	K	...	56	
Other parties	—	...	12	
Independents	—	...	49	
Yugoslavia (December 1992)				
Serbian Radical Party	Fe	24.4	34	(33)
Serbian Democratic Movement	C	18.7	20	—
Democratic Party	C	6.5	5	—
Socialist Party of Serbia	xe	34.2	47	(73)
Democratic Party of Socialists of Montenegro	xe	3.0	17	(23)
Democratic Community (Hungarian)	e	2.4	3	(2)
Others	—	10.8	12	(6)
Zaire				
Ad hoc governments from 1992	—	—	—	
Zambia (October 1991)				
Movement for Multiparty Democracy	—	75.8	125	—
United National Independence	—	24.2	25	(125)
Zimbabwe (March 1990)				
Zimbabwe African National Union	S	75.4	117	
Zimbabwe African National Union/Ndonga	—	0.9	1	
Zimbabwe Unity Movement	—	16.6	2	

Africa South of the Sahara

AFRICAN AFFAIRS

The subcontinent's 48 states experienced a year of promise and disappointment. A new state, Eritrea, was born in May; three serious violent conflicts were halted with cease-fire agreements (Rwanda, Liberia, and Mozambique); but three others (Somalia, Angola, and The Sudan) saw an intensification of fighting. The movement toward democracy kept up its momentum but with only four changes of government (Lesotho, Madagascar, Central African Republic, and, briefly, Burundi). Despite grave violence, South Africa's negotiations for a postapartheid society stayed on course with agreement on an interim government and elections based on a universal franchise, but countries like Zaire and Togo remained bogged down in controversy. Good rains broke the century's severest drought and promised hope for economic recovery, but this was slowed down by the international economic recession. In many East African and Sahelian countries, a serious plague of locusts destroyed new crops.

Political Developments. Despite setbacks and growing violence, South Africa's two major political forces, the ruling National Party of Pres. F.W. de Klerk and Nelson Mandela's African National Congress, accepted the principles for a democratic constitution and agreed to hold the country's first-ever national elections in April 1994. (*See* NOBEL PRIZES.) The international sanctions against South Africa were ended in October. Rwanda made uneasy progress toward breaking centuries of ethnic conflict between the minority Tutsi and the majority Hutu. A military challenge by a Tutsi-led rebellion was checked by a cease-fire and an agreement to hold multiparty elections. Following the elections Burundi witnessed a bloody Tutsi-led reaction, however, and the country's first Hutu president, Melchior Ndadaye (*see* OBITUARIES), was killed in a coup attempt in October. Military rule ended in Lesotho, and elections resulted in a landslide victory for the veteran radical Ntsu Mokhehle. In the Central African Republic, the military-led regime was defeated in free elections. A return to multiparty elections in Kenya saw the reelection of Pres. Daniel arap Moi's party. Under international pressure, Malawi's president for life, Hastings Kamuzu Banda, agreed to abandon his single-party rule. The promised ending of military rule in Nigeria ended in anticlimax when the junta refused to accept the choice of a new civilian president, MKO Abiola; their refusal plunged the country into a crisis that was only partly eased by the resignation of Pres. Ibrahim Babangida. One of Africa's elder statesmen, Pres. Félix Houphouët-Boigny of Côte d'Ivoire, died in December. (*See* OBITUARIES.)

Persistent Conflicts. The nearly 20-year civil war in Angola continued with increased violence after Jonas Savimbi, leader of the National Union for the Total Independence of Angola (UNITA), rejected the election results that had ended in victory for Pres. José Eduardo dos Santos' Popular Movement for the Liberation of Angola. The United Nations condemned UNITA's action, declared military and economic sanctions against it, and called on Savimbi to end the fighting and accept the election results. A cease-fire in the other former Portuguese colony, Mozambique, was arranged between the government and its challenger, the Mozambique National Resistance. Arrangements were made for free elections and the disarming of both armies under UN military supervision.

The bitter civil war in Liberia between the interim government led by Amos Sawyer and the National Patriotic Front of Liberia led by Charles Taylor was halted in July when a cease-fire was agreed to and a coalition government was formed. The agreement was brokered by the Economic Community of West African States, whose 11,000-strong force had operated as a peacekeeping force. The long drawn-out negotiations for a democratic constitution in Zaire continued to be frustrated by Pres. Mobutu Sese Seko's refusal to accept the designated prime minister, Étienne Tshisekedi, with the result that two parallel governments came into existence. However, agreement was finally reached on principles for holding multiparty elections.

Horn of Africa. Civil war continued unabated in The Sudan and Somalia, while the normally tranquil Djibouti witnessed serious armed conflict between the governing Issas and the minority Afars. Negotiations remained stalled in The Sudan between the Islamic fundamentalist regime in Khartoum and its several opponents. The war lost its character as a struggle between a mainly Muslim north and a predominantly Christian and animist south when the Sudan People's Liberation Army itself became divided, and the two major Muslim sects, the Ansars and Khatmia, entered into a loose alliance with the southerners.

The civil war in Somalia became internationalized when a UN-led peacekeeping operation (UNOSOM-II) was drawn deeper into the conflict and ended up in a declaration of war against a major claimant to power, Gen. Muhammad Farah Aydid (*see* BIOGRAPHIES), after his supporters had killed 24 Pakistani members of UNOSOM-II and a dozen American soldiers. After a failure to capture Aydid, a standoff was declared in a new effort to achieve a negotiated settlement.

The promising new development in the Horn was the achievement of Eritrea's independence in May after almost

MARK PETERS—SIPA

F.W. de Klerk (left), president of South Africa, and Nelson Mandela, leader of the African National Congress, shake hands after reaching an agreement in November on an interim constitution that would end white-minority rule. Elections were set for April 1994.

30 years of armed struggle. Ethiopia, to which Eritrea had formerly been linked, accepted Eritrea's breakaway, and the two countries signed a treaty of cooperation that, inter alia, guaranteed Ethiopia's free access to its two lost Red Sea ports, Mitsiwa and Aseb.

The Organization of African Unity (OAU). The 29th summit of heads of state and government met in Cairo in June under the chairmanship of Egypt's president, Hosni Mubarak. Eritrea was admitted as the 52nd member, and its president, Isaias Afwerki, aroused controversy by trenchant criticism of the OAU's past failures. A major departure of policy was marked by the adoption of a mechanism for conflict prevention, management, and resolution that would enable the OAU to play a more active role in dealing with conflicts in the continent.

The mechanism would primarily seek to anticipate and prevent conflicts. The central organ would be composed of heads of state drawn from different parts of the continent who would themselves meet at least once a year; there were to be twice-yearly meetings at ministerial levels, and monthly talks at ambassadorial levels. The main responsibility for the work of the mechanism was entrusted to OAU Secretary-General Salim Ahmad Salim, who was reelected. The OAU was also active in trying to mediate in conflicts in Somalia and Zaire and was successful in helping to settle the conflict in Rwanda.

Inter-African Relations. All the major countries ended the OAU's diplomatic and economic boycott of South Africa and established formal relations. The OAU also indicated its readiness to admit South Africa as a member after a new government was elected. Meanwhile, South Africa obtained observer status in regional organizations such as the Southern African Development Community. Kenya and Zimbabwe played a leading role in helping to broker an agreement between the warring groups in Mozambique. The Sudan's relations with Kenya became strained over its complaints that the Moi government was supporting the rebels, but its major disagreement was with Egypt because of a border dispute. Cairo also accused Khartoum of supporting Islamic fundamentalists who crossed the border to attack tourists. Kenya was drawn into conflict with the warring Somali factions because of its alleged support for the ousted president, Muhammad Siad Barre. After years of tension Uganda and Kenya established good relations. Zaire was widely accused of giving support to UNITA and was strongly criticized by the Angolan government. Relations became strained between Togo and Ghana because of the latter's supposed support for opponents of Pres. Gnassingbe Eyadema. After having reached a point of near-war, Mauritania and Mali again established good relations. Sierra Leone was dragged into the civil war in Liberia when rebel forces began to operate from its territory.

International Relations. The decision by Pres. George Bush in 1992 to send a U.S. force to Somalia to ensure the safe conduct of food was initially welcomed by most African governments, but after the situation deteriorated in 1993, there was increasing criticism of the U.S. role. However, there was virtually no criticism of Washington when it declared The Sudan to be a terrorist state. Although The Sudan, backed by the Arab League, reacted strongly to Washington's decision, its regime sought to repair relations.

Israel again began to play an active role in the continent after a number of African governments ended their diplomatic boycott of Jerusalem. Iran pursued an activist policy, seeking to allay suspicions that it was engaged in promoting the cause of Islamic fundamentalism in the continent—an accusation strongly made by Tanzania. China, Taiwan, and the two Koreas pursued a low-key policy on the continent. Japan increased its trading interest in Africa and doubled its economic aid budget. France continued its colonial policy of interventionism in the continent and played a major role in the elections in the Central African Republic, which led to the defeat of its military leader. It also sent troops to support the government of Rwanda and found itself unwillingly involved in the fighting in Djibouti. France and Britain were both active in persuading governments like those in Kenya and Malawi to abandon single-party rule and to improve their human rights record. With the collapse of the U.S.S.R., Russian influence shrank to zero in the continent. The Nordic countries continued to be the largest donors of aid to the continent but in some cases suspended aid to countries like Kenya because of perceived abuse of human rights.

Economic Affairs. Sub-Saharan Africa's economic situation continued to deteriorate despite strenuous efforts to foster recovery and in spite of the fact that almost all countries had been implementing structural adjustment programs in cooperation with the International Monetary Fund (IMF). The international recession affected African exports to industrialized countries, resulting in lower commodity prices and weaker markets, which, in turn, led to a deterioration in the terms of trade and to a consequent increase in the balance of payments deficit. Internal factors also contributed to the decline, but the IMF and other authorities agreed that the huge debt burden of sub-Saharan countries was a major contributory factor to the region's failure to grow.

The region's gross domestic product (GDP) grew by only 1.8% in 1992, the same as in the previous year, and was not expected to have improved much in 1993. With an average population increase of 3%, this amounted to negative growth. At the same time, per capita consumption, investment, and exports had continued to grow faster since 1991.

Despite the growth in exports and because of lower prices, the region's current account deficit reached almost 10% of GDP, necessitating increased borrowing to finance domestic needs. Interest arrears mounted to $14 billion, more than three times the level of 1987—and this was despite debt forgiveness for the poorest of the region's countries.

African concerns were that assistance to other areas of the world would diminish the amount of development aid provided by industrialized countries. However, Edward Jaycox, the World Bank's vice president for Africa, insisted that the continent would continue to enjoy top priority. He added that a different kind of relationship for the continent was envisaged for the future—one that stressed education, full use of African personnel, and strong local institutions.

(COLIN LEGUM)

ANGOLA

A republic, Angola is located on the Atlantic coast in southwestern Africa. The small exclave of Cabinda is separated from Angola by a strip of Zaire. Area: 1,246,700 sq km (481,354 sq mi). Pop. (1993 est.): 10,916,000. Cap.: Luanda. Monetary unit: New kwanza, with (Oct. 4, 1993) a par value of 4,000 New kwanzas to U.S. $1 (free rate of 6,080 New kwanzas = £1 sterling) and a black market rate estimated at 50,000 New kwanzas to U.S. $1 (76,000 New kwanzas = £1 sterling). President in 1993, José Eduardo dos Santos; prime minister, Marcolino Moco.

For the people of Angola, 1993 was a tragic year, and it was a deeply frustrating one for those, like the members of the UN observer force, who were striving to encourage peaceful political progress. In January a military offensive by government troops appeared to be achieving rapid success at the expense of the rebels of the National Union for the Total Independence of Angola (UNITA), who had refused

A UNITA soldier guards what is left of a building. Government forces and UNITA rebels, who refused to accept the MPLA victory in Angola's 1992 elections, were engaged in bloody fighting throughout much of the year.
STEPHEN DUPONT/KATZ—SABA

to accept the clear-cut victory of the Popular Movement for the Liberation of Angola (MPLA) in the September 1992 elections and had resorted to arms to assert their own claims. After only a week the government announced that no city of any significance remained under UNITA's control. Foreign observers were skeptical, and Jonas Savimbi, the UNITA leader, fulfilled his promise to strike where it hurt by seizing the important oil-distribution centre of Soyo in the northwest on January 20. The loss of the town seriously threatened the country's oil sales. As the struggle intensified in the field and in the media, each force again claimed the other was recruiting white South African mercenaries.

The two sides agreed to a meeting in Addis Ababa, Eth., at the end of January, but nothing came of the talks. Fighting continued in many areas and raged fiercely for control of the rebel capital, Huambo, which fell to UNITA on March 7. An appeal by the UN special representative, Margaret Anstee, for a truce to enable humanitarian supplies to be distributed in regions of greatest need fell on deaf ears, and a warning to UNITA to cease fighting by February 17, issued by Portugal, Russia, and the U.S., all of which had special observer status in Angola, was equally unavailing.

Further talks held in Abidjan, Côte d'Ivoire, in April foundered because of UNITA's refusal to withdraw from the cities, towns, and other areas occupied since fighting resumed in October 1992. Although the decision taken by the U.S. on May 19 to recognize the MPLA government gave a boost to the morale of Pres. José dos Santos' regime, it was equally ineffective in promoting peace. Once again the UN called for the cooperation of the warring parties to help in the distribution of aid to those desperately in need by setting up air and land corridors; this proposal also collapsed because of UNITA's intransigence.

In such circumstances the announcement of the state budget in April, with its promise to mobilize resources to reduce the difficulties faced by people suffering as a result of the war, seemed almost an irrelevance. Soyo had been recaptured but fell once again on May 24 to a small UNITA force after minimal resistance. Nonetheless, in February, Italy was prepared to go ahead with a plan to finance an oil terminal in the Cabinda enclave, while the oil companies Chevron and Elf proposed to expand their operations in the same area. In July the Luanda government also announced that it was ready to award two new contracts for oil exploration to Exxon and Royal Dutch/Shell.

At the end of June, Alioune Blondin Beye took over as UN special representative. Shortly afterward, on August 9, Britain lifted its embargo on the supply of arms to Angola, but few arms were forthcoming, except by purchase from the former Eastern bloc countries. Fighting increased anyway as both factions sought control of the central highlands before the onset of heavy rain. An offer of a cease-fire by UNITA in September was rejected. UN-brokered talks in Lusaka, Zambia, in November–December seemed close to success but then fell apart again. The continuing struggle swelled the number of displaced persons to some two million—about a fifth of the whole population—and an agreement by the World Food Programme to carry out a six-month emergency operation to meet their needs had to be limited to what were deemed to be safe areas near Luanda, Lubango, and Lobita. (KENNETH INGHAM)

This article updates the *Macropædia* article SOUTHERN AFRICA: *Angola.*

BENIN

The republic of Benin is on the southern coast of West Africa, on the Gulf of Guinea. Area: 112,680 sq km (43,500 sq mi). Pop. (1993 est.): 5,091,000. Cap.: Porto-Novo (executive offices remain in Cotonou). Monetary unit: CFA franc, with (Oct. 4, 1993) a par value of CFAF 50 to the French franc and a free rate of CFAF 283.25 to U.S. $1 (CFAF 429.12 = £1 sterling). President in 1993, Nicéphore Soglo.

Increasing rancour developed between the press and the government of Benin's Pres. Nicéphore Soglo during 1993. Edgar Kaho, publisher of the independent *Le Soleil,* was jailed after being convicted of libeling the president's wife, Rosine. In July the president, who had remained officially above party politics, announced that he would join the Renaissance Party of Benin. Soglo lost his majority in the National Assembly in October, but two weeks later 11 groups rallied behind the president and formed the African Assembly for Progress and Solidarity.

Pope John Paul II visited Benin in February and met with religious leaders, including a delegation of voodoo priests. On February 8 the International Voodoo Art and Culture Festival opened in Ouidah. Clashes between Muslims and voodoo followers in Porto-Novo in April resulted in 2 deaths and 24 injuries.

In January diplomatic relations with South Africa were established, and the first Israeli ambassador since 1974 arrived. The annual summit of the Economic Community of West African States (ECOWAS) was held in Cotonou on July 22–24. Benin's economy remained weak; Japan and the Nordic Development Fund were major aid donors.

(NANCY ELLEN LAWLER)

This article updates the *Macropædia* article WESTERN AFRICA: *Benin.*

BOTSWANA

A landlocked republic of southern Africa, Botswana is a member of the Commonwealth. Area: 581,730 sq km (224,607 sq mi). Pop. (1993 est.): 1,406,000. Cap.: Gaborone. Monetary unit: pula, with (Oct. 4, 1993) a free rate of 2.54 pula to U.S. $1 (3.84 pula = £1 sterling). President in 1993, Sir Ketumile Masire.

Remarkably for this troubled region, Botswana managed again in 1993 to maintain a low profile. The country had minimum internal unrest, a democratic system, and elections held regularly since independence in 1966. Yet, despite its relative prosperity (a per capita gross national product of $2,590), Botswana had some special problems of poverty. At the end of 1992 accusations of serious human rights abuses were leveled against wildlife personnel and the Botswana Wildlife and National Parks Department for their treatment of the Masarwa, a small, nomadic people of the Kalahari. Since the mid-1980s the Masarwa and other rural poor had been placed in designated "Remote Area Settlements" as part of a government plan to counteract the impact upon them of severe drought conditions.

Exports continued to be dominated by diamonds (80%), but through the recession-hit 1980s Botswana managed an average annual gross domestic product (GDP) growth rate of 9.8%. For two years, however, the economy had experienced a considerable downturn, with GDP falling 6.5% in 1991–92 (compared with 13.4% the previous year). This was principally the result of international recession, which affected the demand for Botswana's primary exports.

(GUY ARNOLD)

This article updates the *Macropædia* article SOUTHERN AFRICA: *Botswana.*

BURKINA FASO

Burkina Faso is a landlocked country of West Africa. Area: 274,400 sq km (105,946 sq mi). Pop. (1993 est.): 9,780,000. Cap.: Ouagadougou. Monetary unit: CFA franc, with (Oct. 4, 1993) a par value of CFAF 50 to the French franc and a free rate of CFAF 283.25 to U.S. $1 (CFAF 429.12 = £1 sterling). President (chairman) of the Popular Front in 1993, Capt. Blaise Compaoré; prime minister, Youssouf Ouedraogo.

Economic aid poured into Burkina Faso in 1993 as international organizations signaled their approval of the nation's implementation of the Structural Adjustment Program. Grants for rural development were received from various UN agencies, the World Bank, the International Monetary Fund, and the European Community. The Paris Club of creditor nations wrote off 50% of Burkina Faso's debt in recognition of its efforts to reduce state spending and its 5% annual growth rate. Domestically, however, the hardships caused by the Structural Adjustment Program resulted in protests by students and trade unions.

The political scene remained calm. Seventeen of Burkina Faso's 27 parties had seats in the National Assembly, although the ruling Organization for Popular Democracy–Labour Movement held 78 of the 107 seats. In June, Pres. Blaise Compaoré attempted unsuccessfully to mediate between Togo's Pres. Gnassingbe Eyadema and the opposition coalition in talks to resolve that country's political crisis. Progress was made, however, in negotiations between Burkina Faso and Côte d'Ivoire to delineate their common border.

(NANCY ELLEN LAWLER)

This article updates the *Macropædia* article WESTERN AFRICA: *Burkina Faso.*

BURUNDI

Burundi is a landlocked republic of central Africa. Area: 27,816 sq km (10,740 sq mi). Pop. (1993 est.): 5,665,000. Cap.: Bujumbura. Monetary unit: Burundi franc, with (Oct. 4, 1993) a free rate of FBu 244.49 to U.S. $1 (FBu 370.40 = £1 sterling). Presidents in 1993, Maj. Pierre Buyoya and, from June 2 to October 21, Melchior Ndadaye; prime ministers, Adrien Sibomana and, from July 10, Sylvie Kinigi.

On April 17, 1993, Pres. Pierre Buyoya signed decrees setting June for Burundi's first democratic elections under its new multiparty constitution. Buyoya was expected to win easily but was defeated by the leader of the opposition Democratic Front in Burundi (Frodebu), Melchior Ndadaye (*see* OBITUARIES), the first Hutu to become head of state. Although the presidential elections passed without violence, they were followed by demonstrations in Bujumbura by disgruntled Tutsi (who constituted some 14% of the population but had always dominated the government). Frodebu won a large majority in the June 29 legislative elections, and Ndadaye created a carefully balanced government of 8 Tutsi and 14 Hutu, with a woman, Sylvie Kinigi (a Tutsi), as prime minister. All was for naught, however: Ndadaye was killed in an attempted coup by Tutsi on October 21; Kinigi sought refuge in the French embassy; and waves of ethnic violence followed, first against the Tutsi, then against the Hutu. Thousands were killed and entire villages were burned; the UN said that some 800,000 refugees had fled. Constitutionally, presidential power passed to the National Assembly leader pending new elections, but by year's end the situation remained unclear. Silvestre Ntibantunganya, the new Frodebu leader, seemed most likely to succeed Ndadaye as president.

(GUY ARNOLD)

This article updates the *Macropædia* article CENTRAL AFRICA: *Burundi.*

CAMEROON

A republic of western central Africa, Cameroon lies on the Gulf of Guinea. Area: 475,442 sq km (183,569 sq mi). Pop. (1993 est.): 13,103,000. Cap.: Yaoundé. Monetary unit: CFA franc, with (Oct. 4, 1993) a par value of CFAF 50 to the French franc and a free rate of CFAF 283.25 to U.S. $1 (CFAF 429.12 = £1 sterling). President in 1993, Paul Biya; prime minister, Simon Achidi Achu.

Cameroon Pres. Paul Biya's embattled government outmaneuvered its opponents in June 1993 by convening a Grand National Debate on Constitutional Reform rather than the Sovereign National Conference, as demanded by the Social Democratic Front (SDF) of John Fru Ndi, who refused to attend. In March antigovernment marchers were arrested in three cities, and demonstrations considered to have potential for violence were banned. The opposition was further weakened by the Cameroon Anglophone Movement's continuing insistence on the reestablishment of federalism before it would support the SDF's call to convene the National Conference.

The economy remained in crisis despite three years of lower budgets, cuts in civil service salaries, and replacement of university grants with fees. Student protests shut down the University of Yaoundé on January 20. Civil servants, unpaid for months, demonstrated in June. Capital investments were virtually frozen, money remained scarce, and export earnings suffered owing to low world prices. The government continued to press its application for membership in the Commonwealth. In an attempt to resolve long-standing border conflicts, a joint Cameroon-Nigeria boundary commission met on August 10. (NANCY ELLEN LAWLER)

This article updates the *Macropædia* article WESTERN AFRICA: *Cameroon.*

CAPE VERDE

The republic of Cape Verde occupies an island group in the Atlantic Ocean about 620 km (385 mi) off the west coast of Africa. Area: 4,033 sq km (1,557 sq mi). Pop. (1993 est.): 350,000. Cap.: Praia. Monetary unit: Cape Verde escudo, with (Oct. 4, 1993) a free rate of 73.66 escudos to U.S. $1 (111.60 escudos = £1 sterling). President in 1993, Antonio Mascarenhas Monteiro; prime minister, Carlos Veiga.

In January 1993 Prime Minister Carlos Veiga announced that the privatization of a range of industries in Cape Verde was to be carried out over the next four years and a reform program to liberalize the economy was to be drawn up for immediate implementation. The prime minister insisted that the program would be indigenous and not one designed on Cape Verde's behalf by either the World Bank or the International Monetary Fund. As part of his economy measures, he also announced that the civil service was to be reduced by half. In a major Cabinet reshuffle in March, the foreign minister, Jorge Carlos Fonseca, was dismissed without explanation; he was replaced by Manuel Casimiro de Jesus Chantre. Reports of a coup attempt in August were vehemently denied by Pres. Mascarenhas Monteiro's permanent undersecretary.

Although Cape Verde had a per capita gross national product of $890 (which was considerably higher than that of a number of other African states), the country was permanently dependent upon aid to maintain it. The adverse balance of trade was running at between 85 and 90%, and exports consisted mainly of bananas and fish (tuna).

(GUY ARNOLD)

This article updates the *Macropædia* article WESTERN AFRICA: *Cape Verde.*

CENTRAL AFRICAN REPUBLIC

The Central African Republic is a landlocked state in central Africa. Area: 622,436 sq km (240,324 sq mi). Pop. (1993 est.): 2,998,000. Cap.: Bangui. Monetary unit: CFA franc, with (Oct. 4, 1993) a par value of CFAF 50 to the French franc and a free rate of CFAF 283.25 to U.S. $1 (CFAF 429.12 = £1 sterling). Presidents in 1993, Gen. André Kolingba and, from September 27, Ange-Félix Patassé; prime ministers, Timothée Malendoma, Enoch Lakoue from February 26, and, from October 25, Jean-Luc Mandaba.

On Aug. 22, 1993, Pres. André Kolingba of the Central African Republic joined the growing list of African military dictators defeated at the polls. Former prime minister Ange-Félix Patassé received nearly 38% of the vote in the first round and 52.47% in the second round of the oft-postponed presidential elections against longtime opposition leader, Prof. Abel Goumba. Kolingba attempted to invalidate the first round by announcing laws changing both the electoral code and the membership of the Supreme Court. Protests from the opposition and pressure from France, which immediately suspended all aid, forced Kolingba to withdraw the decrees. On September 1, the 12th anniversary of his coming to power, Kolingba, in a move widely seen as retaliation for his electoral defeat, declared a total amnesty for all prisoners, including former president Jean-Bedel Bokassa, jailed in 1986 for cannibalism, murder, and embezzlement. The year of political confusion did little to assuage the country's economic woes. The government virtually ceased to function as civil servants, unpaid for seven months, went on a prolonged strike. Students and soldiers held numerous protests during the year. (NANCY ELLEN LAWLER)

This article updates the *Macropædia* article CENTRAL AFRICA: *Central African Republic.*

CHAD

Chad is a landlocked republic of central Africa. Area: 1,284,000 sq km (495,755 sq mi). Pop. (1993 est.): 6,118,000. Cap.: N'Djamena. Monetary unit: CFA franc, with (Oct. 4, 1993) a par value of CFAF 50 to the French franc and a free rate of CFAF 283.25 to U.S. $1 (CFAF 429.12 = £1 sterling). President in 1993, Col. Idriss Déby; prime ministers, Joseph Yodoyman, Fidèle Moungar from April 7 to October 28, and, from November 6, Delwa Kassire Koumakoye.

On Jan. 15, 1993, Pres. Idriss Déby formally opened the national conference, a move that represented the next step in the process of the democratization of Chad. The conference was suspended after four days, however. At the end of the month, while Déby was out of the country, a coup on behalf of the former president, Hissène Habré, was attempted but failed. An alleged coup plot was foiled in October, and rebel leader Col. Abbas Koty was shot dead. The national conference selected its presidium (February 11) and elected Adoum Maurice El-Bongo, the trade union leader, chairman. By this time 40 opposition parties, 20 other organizations, and 6 rebel movements were due to make declarations to the conference, although the rebel Movement for Democracy and Development continued fighting in the Lake Chad region. In March 15,000 people from southern Chad fled into the Central African Republic following massacres by government troops. The national conference set up a special court to try former president Habré. On April 7 the conference adopted a transitional charter and elected Fidèle Moungar as the transitional prime minister. Moungar appointed a Cabinet in June, but it resigned after a vote of no confidence in October; the former minister of justice, Delwa Kassire Koumakoye, was elected prime minister.

(GUY ARNOLD)

This article updates the *Macropædia* article WESTERN AFRICA: *Chad.*

COMOROS

The Islamic republic of the Comoros is an island state in the Indian Ocean off the east coast of Africa. Area: 1,862 sq km (719 sq mi), excluding the island of Mayotte, which continued to be a de facto dependency of France. Pop. (1993 est.; excluding Mayotte): 516,000. Cap.: Moroni. Monetary unit: Comorian franc, with (Oct. 4, 1993) a par value of CF 50 to the French franc and a free rate of CF 283.25 to U.S. $1 (CF 429.12 = £1 sterling). President in 1993, Said Mohamed Djohar; prime ministers, Ibrahim Abderamane Halidi, Said Ali Mohamed from May 26 to June 19, and, from June 20, Ahmed Ben Cheikh Attoumane.

The final outcome of the November 1992 elections was a stalemate in the Federal Assembly, and on Jan. 1, 1993, Pres. Said Mohamed Djohar appointed Ibrahim Abderamane Halidi prime minister of the Comoros. Halidi announced an 11-member coalition government on January 6 that included himself as trade and economics minister, Said Athoumane Said Ahmed of the Mitsamiouli Party as foreign minister, and the president's son, Anis Djohar, as secretary-general to the government. On April 25, death sentences were passed on nine people who had taken part in the coup attempt of September 1992 (they included two sons of the former president, Ahmed Abdallah, who had been assassinated in November 1989). These sentences were later commuted to prison terms.

In May, following a no-confidence vote, President Djohar appointed Said Ali Mohamed prime minister and asked him to form a new government. Another political crisis erupted in June when the president dissolved the Federal Assembly and appointed a new interim prime minister following a motion of censure. After three postponements by Djohar, elections were held throughout December amid great violence, rule changes, and other irregularities; the president's supporters reportedly won 21 of the 42 seats in the Federal Assembly. (GUY ARNOLD)

This article updates the *Micropædia* article COMOROS.

CONGO

A republic, Congo is in central Africa on the Atlantic Ocean. Area: 342,000 sq km (132,047 sq mi). Pop. (1993 est.): 2,775,000. Cap.: Brazzaville. Monetary unit: CFA franc, with (Oct. 4, 1993) a par value of CFAF 50 to the French franc and a free rate of CFAF 283.25 to U.S. $1 (CFAF 429.12 = £1 sterling). President in 1993, Pascal Lissouba; prime ministers, Claude Antoine Dacosta and, from June 23, Jacques Yhombi-Opango.

Political tensions increased in Congo after the May 2, 1993, legislative elections. Pres. Pascal Lissouba's Pan-African Union for Social Democracy took 62 of the 125 seats. Violence erupted in June following a runoff election. Protesting Lissouba's appointment of former military ruler Jacques Yhombi-Opango as prime minister, opposition leader Bernard Kolelas set up a rival government. Twenty were killed and many more injured in violent demonstrations early in July. Fears of a possible military coup intensified when Lissouba dismissed army chief Gen. Jean-Marie Mokoko on July 16 after the general reportedly called the new National Assembly an "illegal" government. Following a series of armed attacks on civilians by rival militia, a state of emergency was proclaimed. On July 29 government representatives met with opposition leaders in Libreville, Gabon, agreeing to ratify the results of the May elections and hold a runoff. Ethnic-tinged violence continued through the year's end, however, and 60 lives were lost in Brazzaville in mid-December. In addition to its electoral woes, the government remained nearly bankrupt. Congo's civil servants were to receive only seven months' pay in 1993.

(NANCY ELLEN LAWLER)

This article updates the *Macropædia* article CENTRAL AFRICA: *Congo.*

CÔTE D'IVOIRE

A republic of West Africa, Côte d'Ivoire lies on the Gulf of Guinea. Area: 322,463 sq km (124,504 sq mi). Pop. (1993 est.): 13,459,000. Cap.: Abidjan; capital designate, Yamoussoukro. Monetary unit: CFA franc, with (Oct. 4, 1993) a par value of CFAF 50 to the French franc and a free rate of CFAF 283.25 to U.S. $1 (CFAF 429.12 = £1 sterling). Presidents in 1993, Félix Houphouët-Boigny and, from December 7, Henri Konan Bédié; prime ministers, Alassane Ouattara and, from December 11, Daniel Kablan Duncan.

Despite improvements in cocoa and coffee prices, the economy of Côte d'Ivoire made only modest gains in 1993. The world's leading cocoa exporter faced increased competition from rising Asian production. Relations with the World Bank remained cool over dissatisfaction with progress toward reduction of Côte d'Ivoire's international debt of some $18 billion. It was announced that 10 more state-controlled enterprises, including the railroad, would be privatized.

The structural adjustments led to progress in reducing the budget deficit, mainly by cuts in civil service and military salaries and in student grants. The result was continued labour unrest, including a mutiny of 45 members of the elite Republican Guard in March. On April 19 police used tear gas to disperse 3,000 protesting university students. In response, students and faculty launched a four-month strike; it ended on August 21 when the government agreed to most demands and promised to pay salary arrears. Tensions remained high. Twenty-four students went on a hunger strike, and two journalists from the independent newspaper *Bonsoir* were arrested, accused of spreading a rumour that one of the students had died.

Talks with Burkina Faso in June over the delineation of the frontier were apparently successful. In September the sealed border with Liberia was reopened to allow convoys of humanitarian aid to leave Côte d'Ivoire. A relatively smooth transition—but accompanied by a sharp drop in world cocoa prices—followed the death, on December 7, of Félix Houphouët-Boigny, Ivoirian president since independence in 1960. (*See* OBITUARIES.)

(NANCY ELLEN LAWLER)

This article updates the *Macropædia* article WESTERN AFRICA: *Côte d'Ivoire.*

DJIBOUTI

The republic of Djibouti is in the Horn of northeastern Africa on the Gulf of Aden. Area: 23,200 sq km (8,950 sq mi). Pop. (1993 est.): 565,000 (excluding about 130,000 Somali refugees). Cap.: Djibouti. Monetary unit: Djibouti franc, with (Oct. 4, 1993) a par value of DF 178.17 to U.S. $1 (free rate of DF 270.82 = £1 sterling). President in 1993, Hassan Gouled Aptidon; prime minister, Barkat Gourad Hamadou.

Although the Popular Rally for Progress won the elections in December 1992, taking all 65 seats with 76.71% of the votes cast, 51% of the voters failed to cast their votes.

Fighting between government troops and forces of the Afar Front for the Restoration of Unity and Democracy (FRUD) around the northeastern town of Tadjoura in December 1992 and January 1993 left dozens dead and hundreds wounded. On February 4 Pres. Hassan Gouled Aptidon reshuffled the government but reappointed Barkat Gourad Hamadou prime minister. New ministries were created for Planning, Lands, and Cooperation; Economy and Trade; and Transport, Tourism, and Communications, raising the total number to 18. A careful ethnic balance was struck in the Cabinet with the appointment of eight Issas, seven Afars, one Arab, one Issaq, and one Gadaboursi.

In February government forces attacked FRUD positions in the southwest of the country, and they regained control of the entire south by driving the rebels from positions they had held for a year. In the May 7 elections President Hassan Gouled was reelected with 60.76% of the vote, defeating four rivals in the first round over protests that the election had been neither free nor fair. (GUY ARNOLD)

This article updates the *Macropædia* article EASTERN AFRICA: *Djibouti.*

EQUATORIAL GUINEA

The republic of Equatorial Guinea consists of Río Muni, on the Atlantic coast of West Africa, and the offshore islands of Bioko and Annobon. Area: 28,051 sq km (10,831 sq mi). Pop. (1993 est.): 377,000. Cap.: Malabo. Monetary unit: CFA franc, with (Oct. 4, 1993) a par value of CFAF 50 to the French franc and a free rate of CFAF 283.25 to U.S. $1 (CFAF 429.12 = £1 sterling). President in 1993, Brig. Gen. Teodoro Obiang Nguema Mbasogo; prime minister, Silvestre Siale Bileka.

In 1993, for the second year, the United Nations Commission for Human Rights condemned violations of human rights in Equatorial Guinea and urged Pres. Teodoro Obiang Nguema Mbasogo to set up an independent judiciary. The government was also suspected of having instigated a death threat against the U.S. ambassador, John Bennett, known for his staunch advocacy of human rights. A government decree freeing all political prisoners came into effect on March 30. It was issued under a National Democratic Pact signed by the government and the Joint Opposition Platform, which represented the legalized opposition parties. Also in March, the exiled opposition movements—the Christian Democratic Progress Party, led by Severo Moto, and the Guinean Popular Union, led by Armengol Engonga—signed a merger agreement in Madrid. Lieut. Pedro Motu Mamiaka, a member of the opposition Popular Union, was arrested in August and died in prison under suspicious circumstances. On July 16 the president announced that the first-ever legislative elections would be held on September 12. The 12 opposition parties threatened to boycott the elections, however, and outside backers refused to finance them because of continuing violations of human rights. The elections were eventually postponed to November 21. The president's party, the Democratic Party of Equatorial Guinea, won easily, but an alliance of opposition parties boycotted, voter turnout was low (about 20%), and international observers called polling procedures "a travesty."

(GUY ARNOLD)

This article updates the *Macropædia* article WESTERN AFRICA: *Equatorial Guinea*.

ERITREA

Eritrea is in the Horn of Africa, on the Red Sea. Area: 117,400 sq km (45,300 sq mi). Pop. (1993 est.): 3,421,000 (including about 750,000 Eritrean refugees, of whom 500,000 are in The Sudan). Cap.: Asmera. Monetary unit: Ethiopian birr, with (Oct. 4, 1993) a par value of 5 birr to U.S. $1 (free rate of 7.60 birr = £1 sterling). President from May 24, 1993, Isaias Afwerki.

Eritrea, formerly the northernmost region of Ethiopia, became independent on May 24, 1993, after a referendum on April 23–25 had produced an overwhelming majority for independence. This was the culmination of a process under way since the Eritrean People's Liberation Front (EPLF) had seized the capital, Asmera, in May 1991 and of a conflict that had first broken out in 1961. Some 1,018,000 voters were registered for the referendum, of whom 800,000 were in Eritrea itself, 150,000 in The Sudan, 40,000 in Ethiopia, and 28,000 in the U.S. Voting took place amid widespread celebration; 98.2% of those eligible went to the polls, and no fewer than 99.8% of them voted for independence; there was no organized campaign for a "no" vote, and only 1,882 votes were cast against independence. The vote was monitored by large numbers of observers from the UN, the Organization of African Unity (OAU), and various countries.

At independence the previous provisional government of Eritrea was replaced by a transitional government that was to remain in office for four years, pending the promulgation of a constitution. In effect, therefore, power remained in the hands of the EPLF, and the introduction of any multiparty political system was postponed. With the addition of 60 more members, 11 of whom had to be women, the Central Committee of the EPLF was transformed into a National Assembly. EPLF leader Isaias Afwerki was elected president by the National Assembly and installed a 24-member State Council, which was composed of equal numbers of Christian and Muslim members.

Independence was recognized by Ethiopia and other countries, and Eritrea was admitted to the UN and the OAU. At the OAU summit in June, however, Isaias bitterly criticized the organization, which had long upheld the sanctity of African nations' existing frontiers and thus legitimized Ethiopian control of Eritrea.

(CHRISTOPHER S. CLAPHAM)

This article updates the *Micropædia* article ERITREA.

ETHIOPIA

The landlocked republic of Ethiopia is in the Horn of northeastern Africa. Area: 1,133,882 sq km (437,794 sq mi). Pop. (1993 est.): 52,078,000. Cap.: Addis Ababa. Monetary unit: birr, with (Oct. 4, 1993) a par value of 5 birr to U.S. $1 (free rate of 7.60 birr = £1 sterling). Interim president in 1993, Meles Zenawi; acting prime minister, Tamirat Laynie.

The Ethiopian People's Revolutionary Democratic Front (EPRDF) regime installed in 1991 remained in power in 1993 but under conditions of increasing strain. On January 4 a demonstration by Addis Ababa University students, protesting a visit by UN Secretary-General Boutros Boutros-Ghali to discuss independence for the northern region of Eritrea, was violently dispersed; though the government acknowledged only one death, eyewitness accounts put the number much higher. Eritrea became independent in May. The university was closed and its president and vice presidents dismissed. In April more than 40 members of the university's academic staff were also summarily dismissed, including several of the most noted scholars. During the same month, members of five parties representing various southern peoples were expelled from the Council of Representatives (the interim legislature established in 1991); in March in Paris they had participated in a conference with exiled opposition leaders that had issued a statement critical of the regime. The president of the opposition All Amhara People's Organization, Asrat Woldeyes, was jailed on charges of inciting violence.

Despite these incidents, the government attempted to convince its external backers, notably the United States, that its program for multiparty constitutional democracy was still on course. A constitutional commission was established in April, and a constitutional symposium attended by numerous foreign speakers was held in May. However, the national legislative elections that had been promised for 1993 were postponed. Some 400 officials of the former regime of Lieut. Col. Mengistu Haile Mariam, imprisoned since 1991, were released on bail, but the expected trials of leading figures in that regime, which had been guilty of massive human rights violations, were again deferred. A critical U.S. Department of State report on human rights in Ethiopia in 1992 drew attention to violations by the EPRDF and also by other movements, including the Oromo Liberation Front and the Islamic Front for the Liberation of Oromia.

Although there was no serious challenge to the regime's control, violent clashes between EPRDF forces and opposition movements took place in several parts of the country. Opposition came from Amharas in the former Gonder region; Oromos in Harerge, Welega, and western Shoa; and Somalis in the Ogaden. There were also protests against ill-treatment of people in Sidamo by the EPRDF. The EPRDF forces, dominated by the Tigre People's Liberation Front (TPLF), appeared to be increasingly overstretched, and the first hints of dissension within the previously tightly disciplined TPLF emerged in August, when several members were jailed on corruption charges; this was widely interpreted as an attempt to muzzle dissent over the government's political strategy.

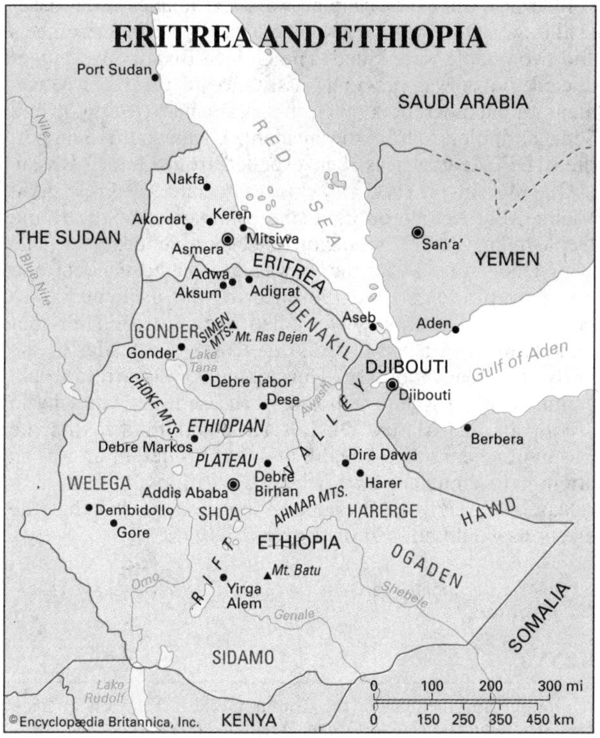

Although some four million Ethiopians continued to depend on relief aid, good rains in 1992 and generally settled political conditions helped prevent any famine emergency, except in the Somali-inhabited Ogaden, which was affected both by floods and by the conflicts in Somalia. Market-oriented agricultural policy reforms also encouraged peasant farmers, although the government continued to postpone a decision on the vital issue of land ownership. Some 44,000 Ethiopian refugees were repatriated from Kenya in March, while fighting in Djibouti in July led some 50,000 Djiboutians to seek refuge in Ethiopia. In figures issued late in 1992, nearly 4,000 cases of AIDS were reported; actual numbers were thought to exceed 20,000, however, with several hundred thousand people estimated to be infected with HIV, the human immunodeficiency virus.

(CHRISTOPHER S. CLAPHAM)

This article updates the *Macropædia* article EASTERN AFRICA: *Ethiopia.*

GABON

Gabon is a republic of central Africa, on the Atlantic Ocean. Area: 267,667 sq km (103,347 sq mi). Pop. (1993 est.): 1,280,000. Cap.: Libreville. Monetary unit: CFA franc, with (Oct. 4, 1993) a par value of CFAF 50 to the French franc and a free rate of CFAF 283.25 to U.S. $1 (CFAF 429.12 = £1 sterling). President in 1993, Omar Bongo; prime minister, Casimir Oyé-Mba.

Protesting the disparity between living conditions in the capital and those in the regional towns, thousands of demonstrators took to the streets in central and southern Gabon during April 1993, demanding the installation of running water and electricity and the paving of roads. The following month, the African Development Bank announced that it would loan CFAF 44 billion for improvement of Gabon's internal road system and the promotion of small industry in rural areas. In April France announced that it would provide CFAF 1,130,000,000 for the development of market garden and livestock companies, which it hoped would serve as models for 200 agro-industrial enterprises to be set up around major cities. The Omar Bongo University, Libreville, was closed on June 14 after disturbances broke out during the administration of the annual examinations. In September, 10 opposition newspapers were suspended for failing to request authorization to publish.

On December 5, like many other African states, Gabon held its first multiparty elections. Pres. Omar Bongo was returned with slightly over 51% of the vote, but opposition leader Paul Mba Abessole, a Roman Catholic priest, claimed victory and formed a rival government. International observers said that the elections were badly disorganized and provided ample opportunity for fraud.

(NANCY ELLEN LAWLER)

This article updates the *Macropædia* article CENTRAL AFRICA: *Gabon.*

GAMBIA, THE

A republic and member of the Commonwealth, The Gambia extends from the Atlantic Ocean along the lower Gambia River in West Africa; it is surrounded by Senegal. Area: 10,689 sq km (4,127 sq mi). Pop. (1993 est.): 1,033,000. Cap.: Banjul. Monetary unit: dalasi, with (Oct. 4, 1993) a free rate of 9.33 dalasis to U.S. $1 (14.14 dalasis = £1 sterling). President in 1993, Sir Dawda Jawara.

The Gambia abolished the death sentence on April 7, 1993. Vice Pres. Saihou S. Sabally said the move was in keeping with The Gambia's commitment to human rights and pointed out that of 87 death sentences passed since independence, only one had been carried out. Another influx of refugees from the troubled Casamance province in neighbouring Senegal took place in March. In April, Ousman Manjang and Hamidou Drammeh, leaders of the Movement for Justice in Africa party, banned for 12 years after the abortive coup of 1981 and legalized again only in November 1992, returned to The Gambia, where they were expected to reactivate the party.

Achievements in agriculture, the basis of the economy, continued to fall short of potential. A $17.2 million project was launched to improve agricultural services for 550,000 rural Gambians over five years. The International Development Association was providing a credit of $12.3 million, the International Fund for Agricultural Development $3.6 million, and The Gambia itself $1.3 million. In June, Gambia Airways announced a new weekly service between Banjul and London in addition to its West African services. In August a £1 million agreement with the British Overseas Development Administration was concluded for teacher training in The Gambia, with particular emphasis on English and mathematics.

(GUY ARNOLD)

This article updates the *Macropædia* article WESTERN AFRICA: *The Gambia.*

GHANA

A republic of West Africa and member of the Commonwealth, Ghana lies on the Gulf of Guinea. Area: 238,533 sq km (92,098 sq mi). Pop. (1993 est.): 15,636,000. Cap.: Accra. Monetary unit: cedi, with (Oct. 4, 1993) a free rate of 659.97 cedis to U.S. $1 (999.85 cedis = £1 sterling). Chairman of the Provisional National Defense Council and, from January 7, president, Jerry John Rawlings.

On Jan. 7, 1993, the Fourth Republic of Ghana was inaugurated before representatives of 78 countries and international organizations. With 189 out of 200 seats in the House of Parliament, the National Democratic Congress began the year in a position of apparently overwhelming strength, although only 29% of the electorate had actually voted in the

December 1992 legislative elections. Justice D.F. Annan was unanimously elected speaker of the new Parliament, and the new Cabinet was sworn in on March 22. The opposition, however, claimed that the Parliamentary Appointments Committee had been lax in its examination of appointments, although it did reject two proposed ministers. Twenty-one of the 35 nominees had previously served under the former executive body, the Provisional National Defense Council. The admission by Pres. Jerry Rawlings that the absence of any opposition in Parliament was a setback for democracy was immediately seized upon by Adu Boahen, the leader of the New Patriotic Party, who called for new elections.

By 1993 Ghana still had a per capita income of only $400 despite real economic advances over the previous few years. The country's good reputation with the World Bank and donors facilitated obtaining the aid it sought—$2.1 billion to cover two years' import requirements. (GUY ARNOLD)

This article updates the *Macropædia* article WESTERN AFRICA: *Ghana.*

GUINEA

The republic of Guinea is located in West Africa, on the Atlantic Ocean. Area: 245,857 sq km (94,926 sq mi). Pop. (1993 est.): 7,418,000 (excluding more than 600,000 refugees from Liberia and Sierra Leone). Cap.: Conakry. Monetary unit: Guinean franc, with (Oct. 4, 1993) a free rate of GF 806.39 to U.S. $1 (GF 1,222 = £1 sterling). President in 1993, Gen. Lansana Conté.

Pro-democracy demonstrations continued in Guinea through much of 1993. After three people died and scores were injured in protests in Conakry and Dinguiraye in late May, fears that senior military officers would try to intervene in the democratization process swept the country. In apparent response, a group of officers published an open letter backing the transition process and expressing anger at the neglect shown families of soldiers killed and wounded in Liberia. On July 4 thousands rallied across the nation to demand that Pres. Lansana Conté open a dialogue on democracy and appoint a national electoral commission. Votes in the December 5 elections were cast for parties along regional/ethnic lines and amid some violence. Conté of the Unity and Progress Party took 50.9% of the votes over Alpha Condé of the Rally of the People of the Left (RPG) with 20.8% and Mamadou Ba of the Union for a New Republic (UNR) with 13.1%.

The economy remained weak, despite nine years of structural adjustment and economic reform. Although the gross domestic product was growing at 4.5% and cuts were made in both the inflation rate and budget deficit, the Guinean franc continued to lose ground against the dollar and the French franc. Unemployment continued to rise following privatization of many state enterprises and large reductions in the size of the civil service. (NANCY ELLEN LAWLER)

This article updates the *Macropædia* article WESTERN AFRICA: *Guinea.*

GUINEA-BISSAU

A republic of West Africa, Guinea-Bissau lies on the Atlantic Ocean. Area: 36,125 sq km (13,948 sq mi). Pop. (1993 est.): 1,036,000. Cap.: Bissau. Monetary unit: Guinea-Bissau peso, with (Oct. 4, 1993) a free rate of 4,964 pesos to U.S. $1 (7,520 pesos = £1 sterling). President in 1993, João Bernardo Vieira; prime minister, Carlos Correia.

Large-scale army desertions at the end of 1992, because of appalling living conditions, served to emphasize the poor state of Guinea-Bissau's economy. Senegalese army units bombarded what they claimed were Casamance rebel bases in the São Domingos area of Guinea-Bissau in December, and two people were killed. The Guinea-Bissau government denied that it was providing assistance to the rebel Movement of Democratic Forces in Casamance (MDFC), and Senegal apologized for the incident. Diamacoune Senghor, the MDFC leader, was then expelled from Guinea-Bissau.

On March 17, 1993, a close associate of Pres. João Vieira, Maj. Robalo de Pina (the commander of the Rapid Deployment Force), was shot dead by a subordinate. The army chief of staff said that it was an isolated incident and not a coup attempt, but the effect of the incident was to postpone the elections, which had been set for later that month. In May, however, João da Costa, the leader of the Party for Renovation and Development, was arrested and confined to a psychiatric hospital, accused of complicity in a coup plot in March. Da Costa's lawyer insisted that he was in excellent mental health and that his detention was an attempt to eliminate him from the elections; he was later released. On July 10 President Vieira announced that the elections would be held on March 27, 1994.

(GUY ARNOLD)

This article updates the *Macropædia* article WESTERN AFRICA: *Guinea-Bissau.*

KENYA

A republic and member of the Commonwealth, Kenya is in eastern Africa, on the Indian Ocean. Area: 582,646 sq km (224,961 sq mi), including 11,230 sq km of inland water. Pop. (1993 est.): 28,113,000. Cap.: Nairobi. Monetary unit: Kenya shilling, with (Oct. 4, 1993) a free rate of 68.75 shillings to U.S. $1 (104.15 shillings = £1 sterling). President in 1993, Daniel arap Moi.

No sooner did the results of the Kenyan presidential and legislative elections, held on Dec. 29, 1992—the first multiparty balloting in 26 years—begin to emerge than opposition groups launched an attack on the conduct of the elections. The report of a Commonwealth observer team acknowledged that there had been irregularities favouring Pres. Daniel arap Moi and his Kenya African National Union (KANU) party but concluded that the overall result largely reflected the views of the electorate. The results made it clear that although a considerable majority voted against Moi, his victory was due not to fraud but to the opposition's having nominated three candidates to challenge him.

Having thus met one condition for the resumption of international financial aid—multiparty elections—Moi then addressed the second requirement. On February 12 the government agreed to drastic economic reforms, including the devaluation of the currency by 25%. When, however, a month later the government called upon its foreign creditors to resume payment of their monthly £27 million aid package, the request was turned down. Moi responded by scrapping the reform program on the grounds that it had already caused widespread hardship in the country. On the heels of devaluation, inflation had soared to 50%, and many businesses were threatened with bankruptcy or large-scale layoffs. Under pressure from donor countries, the International Monetary Fund reacted cautiously, while the same countries suggested that the UN or some other international agency try to persuade Moi to reconsider his decision.

Japan, meanwhile, had signed an agreement worth 86 million shillings, the bulk of which would be used to increase food production and finance the purchase of fertilizers. Later Japan provided 23 million shillings to improve transport, education, and communications. In April the government closed the private Trade Bank, which had experienced recurring liquidity problems. At the beginning of May, a

Kenyan Pres. Daniel arap Moi receives congratulations after being sworn in on Jan. 4, 1993, for another five-year term. Moi, president of Kenya since 1978, won a plurality of votes in the elections held in December 1992.
JOEL STETTENHEIM—SABA

national strike calling for the release of detained union leaders led to rioting in Nairobi.

Later in the month, in response to an offer of £57 million from the World Bank and an agreement with the IMF, the government announced a new set of economic reforms, including another devaluation of the currency and the lifting of import restrictions. In July, Finance Minister Musalia Mudavadi assured foreign donors that his country was committed to servicing its debt even though doing so took 30% of the GDP. A month later, against a background of financial scandals and following the resignation of the governor of the central bank, Mudavadi announced that there would be an inquiry into the operations of that bank and other financial institutions. Additional aid grants were announced by Germany and Japan in October, and the government announced that the shilling would be allowed to float against world currencies.

Sporadic fighting continued in the western highland districts. The opposition claimed that Kalenjin warriors, men of Moi's own ethnic group, covertly encouraged by the government, were attacking Kikuyus and other groups. Raids continued through the autumn, with as many as 2,000 dead. In November, following a series of counterattacks, five Kikuyu leaders were arrested, further evidence, some charged, of a government-supported policy of "ethnic cleansing."

(KENNETH INGHAM)

This article updates the *Macropædia* article EASTERN AFRICA: *Kenya.*

LESOTHO

A constitutional monarchy of southern Africa and member of the Commonwealth, Lesotho forms a landlocked enclave within South Africa. Area: 30,355 sq km (11,720 sq mi). Pop. (1993 est.): 1,903,000. Cap.: Maseru. Monetary unit: loti (plural: maloti), at par with the South African rand, with (Oct. 4, 1993) a free rate of 3.45 maloti to U.S. $1 (5.23 maloti = £1 sterling). King, Letsie III; chairman of the Military Council to April 1993, Maj. Gen. Elias Phisoana Ramaema; prime minister from April 2, Ntsu Mokhehle.

In January 1993 the government of Lesotho announced that elections, postponed from November 1992, would be held on March 27. Wrangles about the future of the monarchy led King Letsie III to declare that he was willing to step down in favour of his father, deposed king Moshoeshoe II.

The elections gave a landslide victory to the Basotho Congress Party (BCP) of Ntsu Mokhehle, which took all 65 National Assembly seats. In some constituencies the BCP secured up to five times as many votes as the former ruling Basotho National Party (BNP), with up to 80% of the 700,000 voters taking part. UN and Commonwealth monitors reported that the elections had generally been free and fair, although both the defeated BNP and the military claimed they had been rigged. The BCP renounced socialism and declared its readiness to accept a mixed economy.

REUTERS/BETTMANN

A man casts his ballot in Maseru on March 27 in the first free legislative elections to be held in Lesotho since 1970. Multiparty elections such as these, which ended seven years of military rule in Lesotho, were held for the first time in several African states in 1993.

Mokhehle was sworn in as prime minister on April 2, and King Letsie III swore allegiance to the new constitution. The new prime minister made various gestures of reconciliation to the opposition parties, but in May the opposition BNP rejected a government offer of two seats in the Senate, insisting that the government was illegitimate. Deposed king Moshoeshoe continued to maintain his right to return to the throne. (GUY ARNOLD)

This article updates the *Macropædia* article SOUTHERN AFRICA: *Lesotho.*

LIBERIA

The republic of Liberia is located in West Africa, on the Atlantic Ocean. Area: 99,067 sq km (38,250 sq mi). Pop. (1993 est.): 2,844,000 (including Liberian refugees temporarily residing in surrounding countries estimated to number more than 1,000,000). Cap.: Monrovia. Monetary unit: Liberian dollar, at par with the U.S. dollar, with a free rate (Oct. 4, 1993) of L$1.52 to £1 sterling. President of the interim government in 1993, Amos Sawyer.

Fighting at the end of 1992 between units of the newly reinforced ECOMOG (the peacekeeping forces of the Economic Community of West African States—ECOWAS) and Charles Taylor's National Patriotic Front of Liberia (NPFL) resulted in an estimated 3,000 dead and 8,000 wounded. The leaders of seven ECOWAS countries meeting at Abuja, Nigeria, gave ECOMOG carte blanche to impose a cease-fire by force. This followed U.S. pressures that included the withdrawal of its ambassador from Burkina Faso to protest that country's alleged support for Taylor. In January ECOMOG launched an apparently successful offensive against the NPFL forces in and around Monrovia. In February another 5,000 ECOMOG troops arrived in Liberia and captured Lofa county in the north of the country, an area deemed vital to Taylor.

On June 6 a brutal massacre of refugees at Carter Camp just outside Harbel town left some 600 dead (many of them mutilated). A UN panel of inquiry reporting in September laid the blame on units of the Armed Forces of Liberia. In yet another peace bid, three groups—Amos Sawyer's Interim Government of National Unity, Taylor's NPFL, and, for the first time, Alhaji Kromah's United Liberation Movement of Liberia for Democracy (supporters of former president Samuel Doe)—met in Cotonou, Benin, in July. They agreed on a cease-fire from August 1 and the setting up of a Council of State (transitional government) composed of five representatives of the warring factions. The arrangement broke down in November, however, when Taylor and Sawyer provocatively replaced their councillors; Sawyer named Philip Banks to replace the head-of-state-in-waiting, Bismarck Kuyon. At follow-on talks in Cotonou, the sides could not agree on ministerial assignments.

(GUY ARNOLD)

This article updates the *Macropædia* article WESTERN AFRICA: *Liberia.*

MADAGASCAR

The republic of Madagascar occupies the island of the same name and minor adjacent islands in the Indian Ocean off the southeast coast of Africa. Area: 587,041 sq km (226,658 sq mi). Pop. (1993 est.): 13,255,000. Cap.: Antananarivo. Monetary unit: Malagasy franc, with (Oct. 4, 1993) a free rate of FMG 1,824 to U.S. $1 (FMG 2,764 = £1 sterling). Presidents in 1993, Didier Ratsiraka and, from March 9, Albert Zafy; prime ministers, Guy Razanamasy and, from August 9, Francisque Ravony.

Barely failing to obtain an overall majority in the first round of Madagascar's presidential elections in November 1992, Albert Zafy won convincingly in the runoff on Feb. 10, 1993, over incumbent Didier Ratsiraka; he took 66.62% of the votes cast. His victory had been assured in January when Francisque Ravony, the first deputy prime minister, deserted Ratsiraka, launched the Committee for the Support of Democracy and Development in Madagascar, and spearheaded the campaign to elect Zafy. The election brought an end to Ratsiraka's 17-year period of rule after a long struggle with Zafy's Committee of Active Forces.

The newly elected president pledged his readiness to maintain the unitary constitution, which had been approved by referendum in 1992. In accordance with the constitution, President Zafy resigned his post as chairman of the National Union for Democracy and Development in May. A month later the Committee of Active Forces had an easy win in the elections for the legislature, although there was considerable violence at the polls and 30–40% abstention by voters. Ravony was elected prime minister on August 9, and he announced his Cabinet appointments on August 27.

In a fresh approach to foreign affairs, President Zafy in April announced the recognition of Israel, South Africa, and South Korea. Under Ratsiraka's Marxist regime, Madagascar had withdrawn from the franc zone and turned for economic investment to the Eastern bloc (although without much success). The quality of life in Madagascar generally had deteriorated following the withdrawal from its affairs of the World Bank, the IMF, and France. (GUY ARNOLD)

ROGER JOB—GAMMA LIAISON

Supporters of rebel Charles Taylor display the skull of a war victim. The United Nations brought about a cease-fire, effective August 1, that for the time being put an end to Liberia's brutal three-year civil war.

MALAWI

A republic and member of the Commonwealth, Malawi is a landlocked state in eastern Africa. Area: 118,484 sq km (45,747 sq mi). Pop. (1993 est.): 10,581,000 (including about 1.1 million Mozambican refugees). Cap.: Lilongwe (legislature meets in Zomba). Monetary unit: Malawi kwacha, with (Oct. 4, 1993) a free rate of 4.35 kwacha to U.S. $1 (6.60 kwacha = £1 sterling). President in 1993, Hastings Kamuzu Banda.

After numerous hesitations, due to opposition parties' distrust of the government and fears of intimidation, the Malawi electorate overwhelmingly voted on June 14, 1993, for the introduction of a multiparty political system. The referendum had been postponed from March in order to give monitoring organizations time to ensure a fair vote. Would-be reformers feared that they might be cheated out of victory because Pres. Hastings Kamuzu Banda refused to share power with opposition parties. Banda's power gradually eroded, however, and in October a presidential council headed by Gwanda Chakuamba took over the government while Banda, a nonagenarian, was recovering from brain surgery in a South African hospital. In a special meeting of the National Assembly on November 17 to prepare for democratic elections, Banda was declared no longer "president for life" and lost his privilege of nominating deputies to the assembly. In December Banda declared himself fully recovered and fit to lead his party into the May 1994 elections.

In April, Minister of Finance Louis Chimango presented his budget and bemoaned the effects of the prolonged drought and the withholding of development aid by donor countries pressuring the government to accept a multiparty system. He was more optimistic about the economic outlook, however, and steady rain meant that the threat of food shortages had been removed. (KENNETH INGHAM)

This article updates the *Macropædia* article SOUTHERN AFRICA: *Malawi.*

MALI

Mali is a landlocked republic of West Africa. Area: 1,248,574 sq km (482,077 sq mi). Pop. (1993 est.): 8,646,000. Cap.: Bamako. Monetary unit: CFA franc, with (Oct. 4, 1993) a par value of CFAF 50 to the French franc and a free rate of CFAF 283.25 to U.S. $1 (CFAF 429.12 = £1 sterling). President in 1993, Alpha Oumar Konaré; prime ministers, Younoussí Touré and, from April 12, Abdoulaye Sekou Sow.

Schools and universities were temporarily closed following a massive demonstration on April 5, 1993, when politically disaffected university students rioted in Bamako. Several public buildings, including the National Assembly, and numerous cars were set afire by the demonstrators. Four days after the disturbances, in which one student was killed and 45 others were wounded, Prime Minister Younoussí Touré resigned. A few days later Pres. Alpha Oumar Konaré named Minister of Defense Abdoulaye Sekou Sow prime minister. The Cabinet was reshuffled again on November 7.

Former president Moussa Traore and three of his top-ranking officers were sentenced to death on February 12 for their roles in the deaths of 106 people in the March 1991 antigovernment demonstrations. In May their appeal to the Supreme Court was denied.

In February, Mali agreed to incorporate 600 members of the Tuareg Unified Movements and Forces of the Azawad into the Malian army. The merging of the two forces officially marked the end of the Tuareg northern rebellion. By late summer more than 1,000 Tuareg refugees had reportedly returned voluntarily from Mauritania, Niger, and Algeria, with thousands more expected to follow.

(NANCY ELLEN LAWLER)

This article updates the *Macropædia* article WESTERN AFRICA: *Mali.*

MAURITANIA

The republic of Mauritania is on the Atlantic coast of West Africa. Area: 1,030,700 sq km (398,000 sq mi). Pop. (1993 est.): 2,171,000. Cap.: Nouakchott. Monetary unit: ouguiya, with (Oct. 4, 1993) a free rate of 112.98 ouguiya to U.S. $1 (171.17 ouguiya = £1 sterling). President in 1993, Col. Maaouya Ould Sidi Ahmed Taya; prime minister, Sidi Mohamed Ould Boubacar.

On May 29, 1993, the National Assembly granted unconditional amnesty to all military and security personnel convicted of violent actions that had resulted in the deaths of several hundred black Mauritanians between April 15, 1990, and April 15, 1991. The following day, police used tear gas to disperse hundreds of angry demonstrators in Nouakchott who were protesting the passage of the bill. Tensions between Moors and black Mauritanians remained high. Hamdi Ould Mouknass, leader of the opposition Union of Democratic Forces–New Era, was arrested on June 24, reportedly two days before a scheduled press conference.

Despite the restoration of full diplomatic relations with Senegal and the reopening of the border in 1992, more than 50,000 Mauritanian refugees who had fled to Senegal depended upon aid from international organizations. An additional 8,000 refugees from the conflict were expected to provide for themselves as a result of previous aid programs.

The burden of international debt continued to depress the economy. In January, Japan provided 1,480,000,000 yen to restructure and reschedule debts owed to it. The Paris Club reduced Mauritania's debt by 50%.

(NANCY ELLEN LAWLER)

This article updates the *Macropædia* article WESTERN AFRICA: *Mauritania.*

MAURITIUS

The republic of Mauritius, a member of the Commonwealth, occupies an island in the Indian Ocean about 800 km (500 mi) east of Madagascar and includes the island dependencies of Rodrigues, Agalega, and Cargados Carajos Shoals. Area: 2,040 sq km (788 sq mi). Pop. (1993 est.): 1,103,000. Cap.: Port Louis. Monetary unit: Mauritian rupee, with (Oct. 4, 1993) a free rate of Mau Rs 17.64 to U.S. $1 (Mau Rs 26.73 = £1 sterling). President in 1993, Cassam Uteem; prime minister, Sir Anerood Jugnauth.

The government predicted a continuing growth rate of 6.5% for 1993 and 1994 following steady growth of the economy in 1992. The economic plan, geared to account for shifts in market forces, relied on three prongs of development growth: sugar, tourism, and the production of textiles in the export-processing zones. The minister of economic planning and development, Swaley Kasenally, stressed that the plan also encompassed such social services as welfare, health, and training.

In pursuit of its market-economy policies, the government offered citizens interest-free loans to enable them to cash in on the thriving Mauritius stock exchange. Workers could obtain loans of up to Mau Rs 10,000 to buy shares in the government's National Investment Trust, which floated 40 million shares valued at Mau Rs 10 each. Loans would be repaid over a 10-month period. By mid-1993 the economy was showing signs of slowing down, with the rate of growth reduced to a still-healthy 5.2%. This decline was almost entirely due to reduced sugar output; the industry was expected to experience a 5% negative growth rate for 1993. On the other hand, the tourist sector showed a healthy 9% growth rate, as did the water-and-electricity-distribution sector, with a 10% growth rate.

On August 18 Prime Minister Anerood Jugnauth of the Mauritian Socialist Movement dismissed coalition partner Paul Berenger of the Mauritian Militant Movement (MMM) as foreign minister because he claimed that Berenger had constantly criticized the government. An expected political crisis did not follow, however, and Kasenally of the MMM replaced Berenger as foreign minister. (GUY ARNOLD)

This article updates the *Micropædia* article MAURITIUS.

MOZAMBIQUE

The republic of Mozambique is located in eastern Africa, on the Indian Ocean. Area: 812,379 sq km (313,661 sq mi). Pop. (1993 est.): 15,243,000 (excluding Mozambican refugees estimated to number about 1.3 million before repatriation began in June). Cap.: Maputo. Monetary unit: metical, with (Oct. 4, 1993) a free rate of 4,415 meticais to U.S. $1 (6,689 meticais = £1 sterling). President in 1993, Joaquim Chissanó; prime minister, Marío de Graça Machungo.

Although inflation had reached 50% in December 1992, the economic situation looked brighter in 1993 after Finance Minister Eneas Comiche announced early in the year that the government's total income for the previous year had exceeded the targeted figure by 1%. Unfortunately, serious tax evasion had led to a 3% shortfall in revenue. In spite of fears that the needs of better-publicized areas of distress might distract potential donors from offering assistance, financial aid from a number of sources was readily available. The OPEC International Development Fund offered a loan of $8.5 million to help in the rehabilitation of hospitals in Maputo and Beira. Shortly afterward, Denmark provided a loan of 146 million kroner to finance health and agricultural programs and to assist in the training of journalists. Britain followed suit with a grant of £7 million of humanitarian aid, which was principally for food but also included seeds and tools to foster agricultural production.

Serious efforts were made to revive the production of cashew nuts, the country's second most valuable export. The undertaking was greatly assisted by a healthy demand for the nuts and by an additional $30 million in aid granted in April by the African Development Bank to assist in a five-year rehabilitation program. In an attempt to improve the living conditions of 20,000 poorer people in suburban districts of Maputo, the government launched a project to create jobs. The plan was financed in conjunction with the Italian government and the International Monetary Fund.

The optimism following the October 1992 agreement signed between the government and the Mozambique National Resistance (Renamo) gradually eroded because of delays in fulfilling the terms of the accord. In February, Aldo Ajello, the UN's special representative in Mozambique, suggested that the first multiparty general elections, scheduled for October 1993, be postponed until June 1994. His proposal had the support of the government, Renamo, and other opposition parties. The elections commission outlined in the peace agreement had not yet been appointed, and he urged that it be brought into force. Mutual recriminations between Pres. Joaquim Chissanó and Afonso Dhlakama, leader of Renamo, did nothing to speed the process. Twelve smaller opposition parties joined together as a united front and called for a transitional coalition government to lead the country to elections. The plan was rejected by the government as undemocratic. Ajello announced that two election funds totaling $30 million had been set up; one would be used to subsidize Renamo, and the other would be made available to other opposition parties.

Another casualty of the prevailing uncertainty was the UN plan to repatriate more than a million refugees, who had fled the country during the civil war. When the troops promised by the UN to oversee the peace process arrived in May, other obstacles arose. Renamo had not demobilized its forces in preparation for the creation of a unified army as had been agreed. Elections could not take place until these terms were implemented, and Ajello postponed elections until October 1994. Although the UN made provision for the repatriation of 24,000 refugees from Swaziland, the continuing distrust between the government and the opposition, together with the absence of basic services and the reputed presence of more than two million land mines, discouraged many refugees in other countries from returning home. Despondent aid workers began to predict that elections would not be held until 1995.

UN Secretary-General Boutros Boutros-Ghali met in Maputo with Chissanó and Dhlakama on October 20 and announced an agreement on the creation of a 20-member multiparty election commission as well as a schedule for the demobilization of paramilitary forces. The government and Renamo themselves reached agreement and began the disarmament process on December 1. (KENNETH INGHAM)

This article updates the *Macropædia* article SOUTHERN AFRICA: *Mozambique.*

NAMIBIA

A republic and member of the Commonwealth, Namibia is in southern Africa, on the Atlantic Ocean; it surrounds the 1,124-sq km jointly administered (with South Africa) area of Walvis Bay. Area: 823,994 sq km (318,146 sq mi). Pop. (1993 est.): 1,537,000. Cap.: Windhoek. Monetary unit: Namibian dollar, at par with the South African rand (also legal currency), with (Oct. 4, 1993) a rate of Nam$3.45 to U.S. $1 (Nam$5.22 = £1 sterling). President in 1993, Sam Nujoma; prime minister, Hage Geingob.

In a four-day poll with an 80% turnout in December 1992, the South West Africa People's Organization (SWAPO) convincingly won regional and local elections. In the course of 1993 the leader of the Democratic Turnhalle Alliance (DTA), Dirk Mudge, announced his retirement, and the president of the South West African National Union, Vekuii Rukoro, resigned and was replaced by Hitjevi Veii. On June 6, Pres. Sam Nujoma was the first tropical African head of state to be received by U.S. Pres. Bill Clinton.

During the year Namibia became a member of the Preferential Trade Area for East and Southern Africa. In September the country introduced its own currency, the Namibian dollar. Namibia continued to experience the effects of the severe drought and harvest failure of 1992 and was the recipient of World Food Program aid. The foreign aid component of the budget was projected at R 91 million. In July farmers with 100 trucks staged a demonstration in Windhoek against new taxes. In September generous tax incentives for manufacturers were announced.

A Labour Advisory Council with representation from government, business, and labour was established, but the National Union of Namibian Workers complained that it was underrepresented on the body. During the year a farmworkers union was launched. Consolidated Diamond Mines laid off 1,000 workers with the agreement of the Mineworkers Union of Namibia and asked the government to take up shareholding. The government took over a fish factory at a low cost to save 580 jobs.

A presidential commission investigated allegations that a tribal authority had allocated farms to top civil servants and a deputy minister. In July police used tear gas to break up a clash allegedly between two rival tribal groups in Katima Mulilo in Caprivi. Joint Namibian–South African administration of Walvis Bay was initiated in January, and in August the South African multiparty negotiating forum resolved that Walvis Bay should be handed over to Namibia beginning March 1, 1994. (MARTIN LEGASSICK)

This article updates the *Macropædia* article SOUTHERN AFRICA: *Namibia.*

NIGER

Niger is a landlocked republic of West Africa. Area: 1,287,000 sq km (497,000 sq mi). Pop. (1993 est.): 8,516,000. Cap.: Niamey. Monetary unit: CFA franc, with (Oct. 4, 1993) a par value of CFAF 50 to the French franc and a free rate of CFAF 283.25 to U.S. $1 (CFAF 429.12 = £1 sterling). Presidents in 1993, Gen. Ali Saibou and, from March 27, Mahamane Ousmane; prime ministers, Amadou Cheiffou and, from April 17, Mahamadou Issoufou.

Niger's 15-month transition to multiparty democracy was completed in 1993 elections described by 130 international observers as a model for Africa. Economist Mahamane Ousmane, the candidate of the coalition Alliance of the Forces of Change, won the second round of the March 27 presidential elections, taking 54.5% of the vote. The new government took steps to extend the three-month truce, declared by the Tuareg Liberation Front of Air and Azawad on March 19, promising to lift the state of emergency in the north, reestablish free movement across the Algerian border, and provide financial aid for returning refugees. The truce was renewed again in the autumn, but in mid-November France apparently decided to suspend its mediation mission.

Following months of strikes by students, the academic year was declared null and void in May, and student demonstrations in November turned violent. Soldiers mutinied in four cities in July over cuts in the defense budget. On August 23 members of the parliamentary opposition organized protests in Niamey and other cities over alleged violations of the new constitution. (NANCY ELLEN LAWLER)

This article updates the *Macropædia* article WESTERN AFRICA: *Niger.*

NIGERIA

A republic and member of the Commonwealth, Nigeria is located in West Africa, on the Gulf of Guinea. Area: 923,768 sq km (356,669 sq mi). Pop. (1993 est.): 91,549,000. Cap.: Abuja. Monetary unit: naira, with (Oct. 4, 1993) a free rate of 29.78 naira to U.S. $1 (45.12 naira = £1 sterling). Head of state to Aug. 26, 1993: Maj. Gen. Ibrahim Babangida (various titles); interim president from August 26 to November 17, Ernest Shonekan; chairman of the Provisional Ruling Council from November 17, Gen. Sani Abacha.

On Jan. 4, 1993, the Transitional Council and the National Defense and Security Council (NDSC) were inaugurated. They were scheduled to exist until August, when a democratically elected president would assume office. The chairman of the Transitional Council was Chief Ernest Adegunle Shonekan, but real power remained in the hands of Maj. Gen. Ibrahim Babangida as president of the NDSC. On January 5 the National Electoral Commission (NEC) barred all previous presidential candidates and all members of the two disbanded political parties from campaigning for the office, and then the process of screening some 250 presidential candidates began.

At the end of March the Social Democratic Party (SDP) chose Moshood Kashimawo Olawale ("MKO") Abiola as its presidential candidate, and the National Republican Convention (NRC) selected Bashir Othma Tofa. The presidential elections were held as scheduled on June 12, and Abiola clearly emerged as the front-runner. However, an application to the High Court by the Association for a Better Nigeria called for a delay in elections while it filed suit to extend military rule. On June 16 publication of the results was postponed, but two days later the Campaign for Democracy (in Lagos), in defiance of the court order, released what it said were the election results, which gave Abiola an outright win in 19 of the 30 states. On June 23 the NDSC announced that the elections had been annulled "so as to protect our legal system and the judiciary from being ridiculed and politicized both nationally and internationally." The U.S. reacted by describing the annulment as "outrageous," on the grounds that the elections had been seen as free and without serious irregularities, and both the U.S. and Britain then restricted aid to Nigeria. Abiola proclaimed that he was the president of Nigeria and urged the country to back him against the military, while the Campaign for Democracy called for civil disobedience to force the NDSC to rescind its annulment. Babangida, however, issued regulations that banned both Abiola and his rival Tofa from taking part in a new election.

Supporters of MKO Abiola attend a campaign rally in preparation for elections on June 12. When Abiola won what were called the fairest elections in Nigeria's history, Maj. Gen. Ibrahim Babangida and the NDSC voided the results and prevented him from taking office.
SCOTT PETERSON—GAMMA LIAISON

Unrest followed, including a strike in Lagos and a week of civil disobedience, and tanks were called out before order was restored. On July 6 the government issued an ultimatum to the SDP and NRC either to agree to a nonelected interim national government or to face new elections. Both parties agreed to participate in an interim administration, though the SDP insisted that it should be headed by Abiola; he declined on the grounds that it would be no more than military rule by proxy.

On July 16 the NEC announced plans for new elections, but these were abandoned almost at once, and on July 31 President Babangida announced that an interim government would take office on August 27. On August 26 Babangida "stepped down" as president and handed power over to a nonelected interim national government, dominated by handpicked Babangida loyalists, that was to run the country until March 31, 1994. Chief Shonekan was named head of this administration. Meanwhile, many in Nigeria demanded that power be given to Abiola, who, however, on August 4 had fled to London, from where he denounced the new arrangement. Protests and strikes in August brought Lagos and Ibadan to a standstill.

On November 17 the military seized power again, this time in the person of the defense minister, Gen. Sani Abacha. He sent Shonekan packing and disbanded the federal and local governmental institutions established under Babangida, who left for Egypt. Abacha lifted curbs on the media and issued the usual round of promises about moves toward democracy. He established a Provisional Ruling Council, mostly made up of military men but with a few civilians, including one close ally of Abiola. The closest thing Nigeria had to a democratically elected head of state, Abiola was uncharacteristically silent about whether he would cooperate with the new regime. International reaction to the coup was almost uniformly negative, but Nigerians and their politicians were generally philosophical about the prospects for more military rule. (GUY ARNOLD)

This article updates the *Macropædia* article WESTERN AFRICA: *Nigeria.*

RWANDA

The landlocked republic of Rwanda is situated in central Africa. Area: 26,338 sq km (10,169 sq mi). Pop. (1993 est.): 7,584,000. Cap.: Kigali. Monetary unit: Rwanda franc, with (Oct. 4, 1993) a free rate of RF 143.89 to U.S. $1 (RF 218 = £1 sterling). President in 1993, Maj. Gen. Juvénal Habyarimana; prime ministers, Dismas Nsengiyaremye and, from July 18, Agathe Uwilingiyimana.

Much of 1993 was spent attempting to end the civil war that had erupted in October 1990 when the rebel Rwandan Patriotic Front (FPR) launched an offensive against the government. In January, Pres. Juvénal Habyarimana repudiated a power-sharing agreement almost as soon as it had been signed, leading to continued ethnic clashes between the Hutu of the ruling National Republican Movement for Democracy and Development (MRNDD) and the predominantly Tutsi FPR. Severe fighting in February affected one million people, a majority of whom fled toward the capital of Kigali from the north or into neighbouring Tanzania. France moved to protect some 400 French nationals living in Rwanda by reinforcing an existing garrison there. Another massacre by the FPR was reported in mid-November.

Peace talks continued amid the fighting until August 4, when a peace accord was signed by President Habyarimana and Col. Alex Kanyarengwe of the FPR. The pact, which would be added to the constitution, called for a transitional government open to the FPR, elections in June 1995, and the repatriation of some 650,000 refugees. In November a UN peacekeeping force arrived to help oversee the implementation of the agreement.

In July Habyarimana named Agathe Uwilingiyimana of the opposition Republican Democratic Movement (MDR) as the new prime minister. (GUY ARNOLD)

This article updates the *Macropædia* article CENTRAL AFRICA: *Rwanda.*

SÃO TOMÉ AND PRÍNCIPE

The republic of São Tomé and Príncipe comprises two main islands and several smaller islets that straddle the Equator in the Gulf of Guinea, off the west coast of Africa. Area: 1,001 sq km (386 sq mi). Pop. (1993 est.): 125,000. Cap.: São Tomé. Monetary unit: dobra, with (Oct. 4, 1993) a free rate of 238.26 dobras to U.S. $1 (360.96 dobras = £1 sterling). President in 1993, Miguel Trovoada; prime minister, Norberto José d'Alva Costa Alegre.

The year 1993 was dominated by economic problems as São Tomé and Príncipe continued to chart a new direction following the nation's first democratic elections in 1991. The International Monetary Fund (IMF) demanded a pay freeze on government workers until 1994 as well as a one-third reduction of the 5,000-member government workforce, whose salaries swallowed one-third of the state budget. The dobra's value dropped by 80% in 1992. Cocoa remained the mainstay of the economy.

France, one of São Tomé's largest aid donors, provided F 75 million to finance a number of projects in agriculture, water, and energy, including the rehabilitation of two cocoa plantations, and to support balance of payments. The International Bank of São Tomé and Príncipe, a joint venture with two Portuguese banks and the government, was incorporated during the year. It began operations with capital of $1.8 million. The European Community (EC) supplied a grant worth ECU 1.3 million to improve the country's road infrastructure and in particular to facilitate the movement of agricultural products from the south to the capital of São Tomé. The EC also agreed to provide ECU 3.9 million to renovate the water-supply system for 40,000 people living in the capital. (GUY ARNOLD)

This article updates the *Macropædia* article CENTRAL AFRICA: *São Tomé and Príncipe.*

SENEGAL

The republic of Senegal is located in West Africa, on the Atlantic Ocean; it surrounds the country of The Gambia. Area: 196,712 sq km (75,951 sq mi). Pop. (1993 est.): 7,899,000. Cap.: Dakar. Monetary unit: CFA franc, with (Oct. 4, 1993) a par value of CFAF 50 to the French franc and a free rate of CFAF 283.25 to U.S. $1 (CFAF 429.12 = £1 sterling). President in 1993, Abdou Diouf; prime minister, Habib Thiam.

Senegal withdrew its troops in January 1993 from the ECOMOG operation in Liberia in order to provide security for its own presidential elections on February 21. An absolute majority of all votes cast gave incumbent Abdou Diouf (*see* BIOGRAPHIES) victory over seven opponents. On May 15, six days after Diouf's Socialist Party took 84 of the National Assembly's 120 seats in the legislative elections, gunmen assassinated Babacar Seye, vice president of the Constitutional Council. Abdoulaye Wade, leader of the opposition Senegalese Democratic Party (PDS), and several associates including deputy Mody Sy were arrested in connection with the killing. A group calling itself the People's Army claimed responsibility; Wade was released two days later. The PDS charged that police had tortured Sy, and it organized a mass demonstration on July 27 demanding his release. On October 1, Wade and others were rearrested and charged with complicity in the murder.

Separatists in southern Casamance province killed at least 40 people in the spring. As many as 300 rebels may have died in an army action near the Guinea-Bissau border on April 18 and another 20 near Ziguinchor in late June. Tourism in the area, once Senegal's main source of foreign exchange, had virtually ended.

Talks between the government and the Confederation of Senegalese Workers broke down in October over the former's refusal to lower prices on basic foodstuffs, part of the new austerity program designed to reduce Senegal's projected CFAF 60 billion budget deficit. The union threatened more demonstrations as a result of the imposition of new taxes and the projected 15% reduction in civil service wages. (NANCY ELLEN LAWLER)

This article updates the *Macropædia* article WESTERN AFRICA: *Senegal.*

SEYCHELLES

A republic and member of the Commonwealth, the Seychelles consists of about 100 islands widely scattered over the western Indian Ocean. The main island of Mahé is 1,800 km (1,100 mi) from the east coast of the African continent. Area: 455 sq km (176 sq mi). Pop. (1993 est.): 71,300. Cap.: Victoria. Monetary unit: Seychelles rupee, with (Oct. 4, 1993) a free rate of SR 5.06 to U.S. $1 (SR 7.67 = £1 sterling). President in 1993, France-Albert René.

In April, Pres. France-Albert René reshuffled his Cabinet, relinquishing the portfolio of defense, which he gave to James Michel, and taking community development in place of industry, which he gave to Esme Jumeau. Michel continued as minister of finance and information; however, he had given up his post as chief of staff of the armed forces the previous November as part of the process of separating the military from the ruling Seychelles People's Progressive Front (FPPS). The constitutional commission, which had had its draft constitution rejected in a November 1992 referendum, was reconvened in January. The opposition Democratic Party, which had withdrawn from the commission in September 1992, agreed to take a full part again.

On May 7 the 22-member commission unanimously adopted a draft constitution to be put to a referendum in June, and both the FPPS and the Democratic Party called upon the electorate to approve it. In the referendum 73.6% voted for the constitution. The new constitution institutionalized multiparty politics; it provided for a 33-member National Assembly that included appointed members in proportion to votes cast for parties. On July 23 elections under this new constitution confirmed René and his FPPS in power. On August 3 a new Cabinet was announced, and René relinquished all his ministerial portfolios.

(GUY ARNOLD)

This article updates the *Micropædia* article SEYCHELLES.

SIERRA LEONE

A republic of West Africa and member of the Commonwealth, Sierra Leone lies on the Atlantic Ocean. Area: 71,740 sq km (27,699 sq mi). Pop. (1993 est.): 4,491,000. Cap.: Freetown. Monetary unit: leone, with (Oct. 4, 1993) a free rate of 546.01 leones to U.S. $1 (827.20 leones = £1 sterling). President in 1993, chairman of the Supreme Council of State, and head of state, Capt. Valentine E.M. Strasser; vice chairman (and head of government), Lieut. Solomon Anthony James Musa and, from July 5, Lieut. Julius Maada Bio.

In January 1993 Britain canceled £4 million in aid to Sierra Leone to protest the execution of 26 alleged coup plotters on Dec. 30, 1992. Britain maintained that they had been summarily executed without a fair trial. On July 5, Pres. Valentine Strasser dismissed Lieut. Solomon Anthony James Musa as vice chairman and head of government. He was replaced by Lieut. Julius Maada Bio, who was also a member of the Supreme Council of State. Musa sought refuge in the Nigerian embassy in Freetown and was later granted asylum in Britain. Though he had helped Strasser stage the April 1992 coup, he had been criticized for repressive measures and for harbouring ambitions to become head of state. Another group of four more men was detained on October 14 as alleged mercenaries planning a coup.

The 1993–94 budget increased to 485 billion leones from 395 billion leones in 1992–93. Most of the budget increase was earmarked for health and education. The government planned to sell the majority state-owned National Diamond Mining Co. to private interests. Plans were also announced to curb illegal diamond mining, which, if successful, would generate substantial additional revenue. The government, which had promised to return the country to civilian rule within a year, set a new target date of 1996.

(GUY ARNOLD)

This article updates the *Macropædia* article WESTERN AFRICA: *Sierra Leone*.

SOMALIA

Situated in the Horn of northeastern Africa, Somalia lies on the Gulf of Aden and the Indian Ocean. Area: 637,000 sq km (246,000 sq mi). Pop. (1993 est.): 8,050,000 (including Somali refugees in neighbouring countries estimated to number more than one million). Cap.: Mogadishu. Monetary unit: Somali shilling, with (Oct. 4, 1993) a free rate of 2,601 Somali shillings to U.S. $1 (3,940 Somali shillings = £1 sterling). Somalia had no functioning government in 1993.

The international military force operating under United Nations auspices landed in Somalia in late 1992. (*See also* WORLD AFFAIRS: *United Nations: Somalia*.) Operation Restore Hope rapidly established control over much of the south. By the end of March 1993, security and food deliveries were much improved, but the UN troops had not accomplished the essential task of disarming the militias of the various leaders, dubbed "warlords" by the media, each drawing support from one or more of the Somali clans.

Despite a cease-fire agreement, fighting broke out again in February between the two factions of the former United Somali Congress, whose conflict was laying Mogadishu in ruins. These were headed respectively by the self-declared interim president, Ali Mahdi Muhammad of the Abgal subclan, and the formidable Gen. Muhammad Farah Aydid (*see* BIOGRAPHIES) of the Habar Gadir subclan, each faction leading an alliance of other groups. Still other clans were clashing elsewhere in the country.

Under the aegis of the UN, two Reconciliation Conferences were held in Addis Ababa, Eth., in January and March. Representatives of 15 militia groups and others agreed to a cease-fire and disarmament of the militias, as well as the setting up of a Transitional National Council to be "the repository of national sovereignty" and regional councils. The Somali National Movement from the northern region, which had declared itself the independent "Republic of Somaliland" in 1991, sent observers as well.

On May 4 the UN handed over control to a much-reduced force, the UN Operation in Somalia (UNOSOM II), supervised by U.S. Adm. Jonathan Howe, who replaced Ismat Kittani as UN special envoy. The peace process appeared to be well under way when, on June 5, 24 Pakistani UN soldiers were killed in an ambush by Aydid's men. On June 17 the UN ordered Aydid's arrest. From this point the situation in Mogadishu became a conflict between UNOSOM and Aydid's forces. Aydid, allegedly receiving support from The Sudan and Iran, evaded capture and even strengthened his position, claiming to represent the Somali nation against a "colonialist" aggressor. Somali factions opposed to Aydid, however, tended to side with the UN.

There were large numbers of Somali casualties, many of them civilians, and UN forces were accused of human rights abuses. On July 12 four foreign journalists were killed by a pro-Aydid crowd. By October the UN forces had lost 74 men; on October 3, 18 U.S. soldiers were killed in a gun battle and a number of others captured, prompting a reevaluation in Washington of the prudence of U.S. involvement in Somalia.

General Aydid proposed a cease-fire in October, and on November 16 the UN Security Council voted to countermand the order for his arrest. Instead, they appointed a

Somalis express their opposition to UN attempts, led by U.S. forces, to capture warlord Gen. Muhammad Farah Aydid. As the UN's original humanitarian mission turned toward establishing civil authority and when violence against its troops escalated, the U.S. began making plans to withdraw.
DON ELDON—SYGMA

new commission of inquiry to determine responsibility for the attacks on UN peacekeeping forces.

By year's end there were a few tentative signs of a return to normalcy. District councils had been set up, and in Mogadishu the police and the judicial system were reestablished. Observers were encouraged when Aydid attended a conference of clan leaders in Ethiopia in mid-December after having refused to attend a UN-sponsored humanitarian aid meeting earlier. Several countries had begun withdrawing their troops from the UN contingent, and all U.S. forces were to leave Somalia by March 1994.

(VIRGINIA R. LULING)

This article updates the *Macropædia* article EASTERN AFRICA: *Somalia.*

SOUTH AFRICA

The Republic

South Africa occupies the southern tip of Africa, with the Atlantic Ocean to the west and the Indian Ocean to the east. It includes the 1,124-sq km exclave of Walvis Bay surrounded by Namibia (temporarily jointly administered with Namibia from November 1992, Walvis Bay is to be administered by Namibia only from March 1994) and partially surrounds the four republics of Bophuthatswana, Ciskei, Transkei, and Venda (whose reincorporation into South Africa was pending in late 1993). Area: 1,123,226 sq km (433,680 sq mi). Pop. (1993 est.): 33,071,000. (Area and population figures exclude the four republics.) Executive cap., Pretoria; judicial cap., Bloemfontein; legislative cap., Cape Town. Monetary unit: South African rand, with (Oct. 4, 1993) a financial rate of R 4.17 to U.S. $1 (R 6.32 = £1 sterling) and a commercial rate of R 3.45 to U.S. $1 (R 5.23 = £1 sterling). State president in 1993, Frederik W. de Klerk.

The Republic. *Domestic Affairs.* The main event of 1993 in South Africa was the rapprochement between the governing National Party (NP) and the African National Congress (ANC). Agreement was reached at a multiparty negotiating forum on the holding of the first one-person one-vote national elections in South Africa's history, by proportional representation, on April 27, 1994. A Transitional Executive Council to supervise those elections was enacted by Parliament in November and convened on December 7.

The elections, to be held under an interim constitution, were to establish a 400-member Parliament that would also serve as a body to draw up a final constitution for the country. The constitution-making body would be bound by constitutional principles already agreed upon, including a strong emphasis on federalism. The interim constitution, approved by the South African Parliament on December 22, provided that the new government would be composed of representatives of all parties securing more than 5% of the vote, referred to by the ANC as a "government of national unity." On the basis of agreements reached between the NP government and the ANC in February, this government would serve for up to five years.

Huge anger was felt in African townships at the assassination of Chris Hani (*see* OBITUARIES), secretary-general of the South African Communist Party (SACP), on Easter Saturday, April 10. On April 14 one and a half million persons were estimated to have taken part in rallies, marches, and other forms of protest, some erupting into violence. Janusz Walus, a Polish immigrant, and Clive Derby-Lewis, leading member of the Conservative Party (CP), were found guilty of the assassination and sentenced to death in October. Township political violence continued, particularly in Natal and on the East Rand, and rose after the announcement of the election date.

The role of state forces in past and present state violence continued to be controversial. The Goldstone Commission issued a series of reports on different aspects of the violence, and Justice Richard Goldstone said that there was strong circumstantial evidence of security force involvement in current political violence. Following revelations in 1992 that there had been a signal from military officials ordering the "permanent removal from society" of Matthew Goniwe, who with three others was killed on June 27, 1985, the inquest was reopened. The inquest was told that the words of the signal meant long-term detention and not death. Leading military officers testifying at the inquest refused to answer questions on the grounds of self-incrimination. The inquest adjourned in October until February 1994.

The multiparty negotiating forum, comprising 26 groups and including for the first time the CP and Afrikaner Volksunie (AVU) and the Pan-Africanist Congress (PAC), reconvened in April. An innovation was the requirement that at least one woman be a part of each delegation. On June 25 the World Trade Center, where the negotiations were being held, was invaded by protesting members of the Afrikaner Weerstandsbeweging (AWB) and other white right-wing elements. On July 2 the Inkatha Freedom Party (IFP), the KwaZulu government, and the Conservative Party walked out of the negotiations upon the setting of an election date, claiming that their standpoint was not reflected in the agreements. In October the governments of Ciskei and Bophuthatswana also left the forum.

Since late 1992 the IFP, the CP, and the governments of Ciskei and Bophuthatswana had been grouped in the Concerned South Africans Group (COSAG). In October COSAG was supplanted by the Freedom Alliance. Besides the CP, the IFP—which was joined by several prominent white politicians during the year—and the Bophuthatswana and Ciskei governments, the Freedom Alliance included the AVU and the Afrikaner Volksfront (AVF), launched in May, headed by former South African Defence Force (SADF) chief Gen. Constand Viljoen, and involving the Conservative Party and AWB. Andries Treurnicht, leader of the CP, died in April (*see* OBITUARIES) and was succeeded by Ferdi Hartzenberg.

The Freedom Alliance argued that the agreements reached by the multiparty negotiating forum were insufficiently federalist and did not provide for the self-determination of the Afrikaner people in a "volkstaat" (people's state). They favoured a negotiated agreement among political leaders on a final constitution before an election. The IFP demanded a regional constitution agreed by Natal-KwaZulu. The Freedom Alliance sought separate negotiations with government as a bloc and threatened defiance of the agreements reached at the multiparty forum. The ANC argued that the Freedom Alliance represented discredited apartheid structures and minorities attempting to hold the country to ransom. Three-way talks in late December seemed to have found a compromise.

Opening Parliament in January, Pres. F.W. de Klerk announced further measures dismantling apartheid, including the intention to establish a single nonracial education system in which, however, there would be "differentiated" education based on religious and cultural values and mother tongue. The end of compulsory military service for white males was announced in August. The National Party secured a majority in the (Indian) House of Delegates, appointed three nonwhites to its Cabinet in February, and relaunched itself as a multiracial political party. De Klerk stated that he "deeply regretted" apartheid and spoke in June at a rally in Pietersburg attended by a number of Northern Transvaal chiefs supporting the NP.

In March the government for the first time admitted that South Africa had developed a nuclear capability but claimed that its six bombs had been dismantled in 1989. It also announced the renunciation of its missile-delivery capability. A new board, chaired for the first time by a black woman, was selected after public hearings to govern the South African Broadcasting Corporation. There were further official reports claiming mismanagement and corruption in government departments. In September the South African government took control of the finances of the self-governing territory of Lebowa, claiming that its 1992–93 budget of R 3.6 billion had been overspent by R 772 million.

Oliver Tambo, chairman of the ANC, died in April (*see* OBITUARIES) and was succeeded by Thabo Mbeki. In July a highway shoot-out between police and bodyguards of Walter Sisulu, deputy president of the ANC, resulted in the death of one of the bodyguards. A third investigation into abuses in ANC guerrilla camps in exile, chaired by Sam Motsuenyane, concluded that the security department had exercised uncontrolled power. The ANC called for establishment by government of a "commission of truth" to investigate abuses of power by state officials as well.

The Appeal Court in June quashed the conviction of Winnie Mandela, former wife of Nelson Mandela, on four charges of being accessory to assault and confirmed her conviction on four counts of kidnapping but substituted a fine for a jail sentence for these offenses. She was elected chair of the Witwatersrand region of the South African National Civic Organization (SANCO) in June and president of the ANC Women's League in December.

The PAC, in talks with the government, refused to suspend its armed struggle. Its military wing, the Azanian People's Liberation Army (APLA), had from November 1992 attacked a series of targets, including white farms and white-patronized restaurants. The government alleged that such incidents included the killing of 11 worshipers at St. James Church in Cape Town on July 25. In March the Goldstone Commission said there was "little doubt" that APLA was using the Transkei as a springboard for these attacks. On May 25, 75 leading PAC members were arrested in police raids, though few were charged. In October the SADF raided an alleged APLA base in the Transkei, killing five teenagers.

Foreign Affairs. In an important speech at the United Nations in September, Nelson Mandela, president of the ANC, called for the lifting of remaining sanctions against South Africa in view of the negotiated agreements reached for transition to a democratic government and encouraged foreign investment to reconstruct the country. Mandela and President de Klerk, who each made a number of foreign visits during the year, were awarded the Nobel Peace Prize (*see* NOBEL PRIZES), as well as a Liberty Medal by the U.S. government. Mangosuthu Gatsha Buthelezi, president of the IFP, also made foreign visits.

Mandela's speech accelerated the lifting of economic sanctions by the UN General Assembly on October 8 and the normalization of South Africa's relations with the rest of the world. The country extended its missions abroad and was readmitted to the International Monetary Fund (IMF). China held a trade fair in South Africa, and a mission of the Southern African Development Community (SADC) was opened in South Africa for the first time. United Nations, Commonwealth, and European Community monitoring of peace agreements in South Africa continued.

The South African government continued to be diplomatically involved in the civil wars in Angola and Mozambique, apparently assisting in attempts at peacemaking. Accusations of logistic assistance to the National Union for the Total Independence of Angola (UNITA) in the civil war in Angola from South African soil were made by the Popular Movement for the Liberation of Angola (MPLA) government, though it accepted that the South African government was not involved in this. There was evidence that former SADF personnel were serving as mercenaries in Angola on both sides in the civil war. South Africa did not follow the U.S. in recognizing the MPLA government. As regards Mozambique, Foreign Minister Pik Botha admitted that South Africa had supported the Mozambique National Resistance (Renamo) in the past, but Mozambican Pres. Joaquim Chissanó accepted that this was no longer the case.

Economy. Recession continued into its fifth year, though there were signs of recovery. In 1992 gross domestic product (GDP) fell by 2.1%, a figure worsened by the drought, and gross domestic fixed investment by 12%. The central bank estimated that 288,000 jobs had been lost since the start of the recession and that 46% of the economically active population was unemployed in the formal sector.

Despite the recession, tight monetary policies continued. Money supply was growing at 3.95% per annum in June (below the 6%-per-annum target.) The bank rate was cut from 14 to 13% in February and to 12% in late October. Further cuts were inhibited by capital outflows uncovered by the surpluses on the current account of the balance of payments. Foreign exchange reserves fell from R 11.2 billion, worth two months of imports, at the end of 1992 to R 7,030,000,000 in August 1993. An eight-year repayment schedule for settlement of the country's outstanding foreign debt was negotiated in September. An $850 million loan from the IMF for drought relief, the first for some time, was secured toward the end of the year.

Annual inflation (which had averaged 14.6% per annum through the 1980s) fell to 9.6% in December 1992, rose to 11% per annum in April, and fell again to 10% in June. International uncertainties led to a temporary boom in the gold price, from a bottom of $326 on March 10 to over $400 in July.

The government's 1992–93 budget deficit (projected at 4.1%) turned out to be 8.6% of GDP. The 1993–94 budget deficit was projected at 6.8%. The budget increased the value-added tax from 10% to 14%, with exemptions on basic foodstuffs. Social service spending made up 44% of the budget, but interest on state debt (17%) was the second largest single component. Racial parity in state pensions was to be applied from September 1. A National Economic Forum, with representation from government, business, and labour, held its first plenary session in June.

To the end of September, strikes amounted to 2.4 million man-days, in comparison with 3.1 million for the comparable period in 1992 and 2 million in 1991. Some 70,000 teachers struck for better salary increases and against retrenchments, while a classroom revolt of school students secured the suspension of an increase in matriculation-examination fees. Members of the Police and Prisons Civil Rights Union marched in a protest demonstration in Johannesburg in August and struck in the Eastern Cape later in the year. Farm and domestic workers' rights were included in industrial legislation for the first time.

An academic economist estimated that 88% of the country's wealth was in the hands of 5% of the population, and 10% of the population earned 45% of its income. Operation Hunger stated that nine million South Africans suffered from malnutrition.

SELWYN TAIT—GAMMA LIAISON

Demonstrators in Pretoria protest the assassination on April 10 of Chris Hani, head of the South African Communist Party and a leader in the African National Congress. The killing was one of a number of violent acts against both blacks and whites during the year.

Bophuthatswana

The republic of Bophuthatswana consists of seven discontinuous, landlocked geographic units, entirely surrounded by South Africa except for one unit that borders Botswana on the northwest. Area: 44,000 sq km (16,988 sq mi). Pop. (1993 est.): 2,564,000. Cap.: Mmabatho. Monetary unit: South African rand. President in 1993, Kgosi (Chief) Lucas Mangope.

Ciskei

Bordering the Indian Ocean in the south, Ciskei is surrounded on land by South Africa. Area: 7,760 sq km (2,996 sq mi). Pop. (1993 est.): 897,000. Cap.: Bisho. Monetary unit: South African rand. Chairman of the Military Committee and of the Council of State in 1993, Brig. Joshua Oupa Gqozo.

Transkei

Bordering the Indian Ocean and surrounded on land by South Africa, Transkei comprises three discontinuous geographic units, two of which are landlocked and one of which borders Lesotho. Area: 43,653 sq km (16,855 sq mi). Pop. (1993 est.): 3,664,000. Cap.: Umtata. Monetary unit: South African rand. Head of the Military Council in 1993, Gen. Harrison Bantubonke Holomisa.

Venda

The landlocked republic of Venda is located in extreme northeastern South Africa. Area: 7,176 sq km (2,771 sq mi). Pop. (1993 est.): 590,000. Cap.: Thohoyandou. Monetary unit: South African rand. Head of state in 1993, Brig. Gabriel Ramushwana.

The Homelands. The questions of financial support received by these areas from South Africa, and of their reincorporation into South Africa, remained controversial. The Ciskei and Bophuthatswana governments rejected reincorporation until a final constitution was agreed for South Africa. The Transkei and Venda governments declared their willingness to be reincorporated into a democratic South Africa.

In February the auditor-general tabled a report criticizing government for failing to implement financial order in the Transkei, Bophuthatswana, Venda, and Ciskei states, which had failed to keep spending within guidelines. In the 1992–93 financial year these territories received South African government aid of R 6.2 billion. Outstanding loans to Transkei, Venda, and Ciskei amounted to R 3.3 billion at the end of the 1991–92 financial year.

International bodies called on the Bophuthatswana government to repeal its Internal Security Act because of violations of human rights. Following police occupation of the University of Bophuthatswana on April 27, all university-level institutions were closed indefinitely. The government tried to sack the vice-chancellor when he attempted to reopen the campus in July and deployed troops.

The Ciskei government indemnified 69 security force members implicated in the September 1992 Bisho massacre. In August Ciskei Pres. Joshua Oupa Gqozo appeared at an inquest in the Supreme Court and was found responsible for the deaths of political opponents Charles Sebe and Mangwana Guzana in 1991. His trial began in November. Relations between the South African government and Transkei were tense during the year, with blockades mounted by South African security forces. In March Pres. Harrison Bantubonke Holomisa rejected the Goldstone Commission's claim that the APLA used the Transkei as a springboard, arguing that this was based solely on evidence from the South African security forces. He also released documents claiming implication of the SADF in plans to murder former Ciskei ruler Lennox Sebe. In October, to widespread condemnation, the SADF raided a house in Umtata, killing five teenagers, claiming it was an attack on an APLA base. In June Transkei riot police stormed the Education Department to end an eight-day sit-in by teachers calling for the resignation of the minister of education; Holomisa said that he regretted the incident. (MARTIN LEGASSICK)

This article updates the *Macropædia* article SOUTHERN AFRICA: *South Africa.*

SUDAN, THE

A republic of North Africa, The Sudan has a coastline on the Red Sea. Area: 2,503,890 sq km (966,757 sq mi). Pop. (1993 est.): 25 million. Executive cap., Khartoum; legislative cap., Omdurman. Monetary units: Sudanese pound, with (Oct. 4, 1993) a free rate of Lsd 129.05 to U.S. $1 (Lsd 195.52 = £1 sterling), and (from May 1992) the Sudanese dinar (a new unit of currency circulating in parallel with the Sudanese pound at a rate of 1 dinar = Lsd 10). President of the Revolutionary Command Council for National Salvation, president (from October 16), and prime minister during 1993, Lieut. Gen. Omar Hassan Ahmad al-Bashir.

Having dismissed a UN General Assembly resolution in December 1992 expressing deep concern over human rights violations in The Sudan, the government was under criticism from many quarters, external as well as internal, throughout 1993. During his February visit to The Sudan, Pope John Paul II sternly rebuked the authorities for their harsh treatment of the Christian minority. On August 6 the International Monetary Fund (IMF), which earlier in the year had declared The Sudan to be an "uncooperative state," suspended membership in the organization because it had not paid its arrears of contributions and because it refused to take the IMF's advice on how to improve the country's economy. Twelve days later the U.S. listed The Sudan as a supporter of international terrorism, which barred it from receiving any nonhumanitarian aid from the U.S. The British ambassador was expelled on December 30 after the archbishop of Canterbury pointedly did not stop in Khartoum during his four-day visit to The Sudan. Relations with Egypt were also strained as the result of a border dispute in the oil-rich Hala'ib region near the Red Sea.

Not all the sufferings of the Sudanese people were the result of government actions. Fierce fighting between rival factions within the southern rebel forces caused many to seek sanctuary in Uganda. The fighting brought aid operations to a virtual standstill. The government contributed to the disaster, however, by launching a large-scale attack on the rebels in Western Equatoria province in August. The UN relief organization trying to function in the area protested strongly. The military also prevented the International Red Cross from undertaking a vast emergency operation, even though the government had approved the plans. The government's efforts to secure supplies from Iran in April were unsuccessful. On October 16 the military junta disbanded and appointed its leader, Omar al-Bashir, president of the country. (KENNETH INGHAM)

SWAZILAND

Swaziland is a landlocked monarchy of southern Africa and a member of the Commonwealth. Area: 17,364 sq km (6,704 sq mi). Pop. (1993 est.): 814,000. Administrative cap., Mbabane; royal and legislative cap., Lobamba. Monetary unit: lilangeni (plural: emalangeni), at par with the South African rand, with (Oct. 4, 1993) a free rate of 3.45 emalangeni to U.S. $1 (5.23 emalangeni = £1 sterling). King, Mswati III; prime ministers in 1993, Obed Dlamini, Andreas Fakudze (acting) from October 25, and, from November 4, Jameson Mbilini Dlamini.

Swaziland held its first multiparty elections in September 1993, which resulted in the prime minister, Obed Dlamini, failing to win a seat in Parliament (he was given a seat in the Senate, however). In June Swaziland signed an agreement with Pretoria to allow the secondment of South African judges, magistrates, and prosecutors to serve in Swaziland's courts. In August a number of opposition leaders were sought by the police—allegedly for distributing seditious pamphlets. They included Kislon Shongwe, the president of the People's United Democratic Movement, who reputedly took refuge in the U.K. High Commission.

According to the Food and Agriculture Organization, some 150,000 Swazis suffering from the effects of the disastrous drought of 1992 would require food aid during 1993. The Swazi National Disaster Task Force chairman, Ben Sibandza, asked for further government aid for those hardest hit, mostly in eastern and southern Swaziland. Nearly 500,000 residents of the country were fed in what was the worst drought in memory. The livestock population was now secure, however, although the drought wiped out half the country's cattle in 1992. (GUY ARNOLD)

This article updates the *Macropædia* article SOUTHERN AFRICA: *Swaziland.*

TANZANIA

The republic of Tanzania, a member of the Commonwealth, consists of Tanganyika, on the east coast of Africa, and Zanzibar, just off the coast in the Indian Ocean, which includes Zanzibar Island, Pemba Island, and small islets. Area: 942,799 sq km (364,017 sq mi). Pop. (1993 est.): 26,542,000. Cap.: government in process of being transferred from Dar es Salaam; legislature meets in Dodoma, the new capital. Monetary unit: Tanzania shilling, with (Oct. 4, 1993) a free rate of 445.74 shillings to U.S. $1 (675.30 shillings = £1 sterling). President in 1993, Ali Hassan Mwinyi; prime minister, John Malecela.

Early in 1993 Pres. Ali Hassan Mwinyi instituted a number of Cabinet changes by creating new portfolios and by transferring existing ministers to other posts. The first significant innovation was the creation of the new post of deputy prime minister, to which on January 24 the minister of home affairs, Augustine Lyatonga Mrema, was appointed; he also retained his old portfolio. On April 13 a new Ministry of Legal and Constitutional Affairs was established, headed by Samuel Sitta. Meanwhile, on January 28 Ahmed Hassan Diria, minister of foreign affairs and international relations, had exchanged portfolios with Joseph Clemence Rwegasira, minister of labour and youth development.

The new deputy prime minister soon became prominent when he announced that three Sudanese nationals who were Muslim teachers at a school in Morogoro had been expelled on April 25 for promoting Islamic fundamentalism and plotting to stage a holy war in order to install an Islamic regime. The government's action was an indication of its concern over the disturbances created by Muslims in many parts of the country, which had led to the arrest earlier in April of more than 50 people, including Kasim ibn Juma, imam of a mosque in Dar es Salaam; they were charged with incitement and with holding illegal demonstrations.

On January 10 Zanzibar confirmed that it had joined the Organization of the Islamic Conference (OIC) but stressed that it would keep political and religious issues apart and that its union with mainland Tanzania would not be threatened by this action. Mwinyi gave his support to Zanzibar on January 28, arguing that the island had joined the OIC for economic rather than political ends. Some of the mainland legislators were not so accommodating, however. Zanzibar, they claimed, had violated the country's constitution, which prohibited any part of Tanzania from joining such an association. Previously, mainland legislators had, for the most part, favoured a strong union and had looked askance at Zanzibar's special constitutional status. In light of recent events, however, 58 of them introduced a bill in August for a separate government for the mainland similar to that enjoyed by Zanzibar. In a closed session of the legislature later in the month, former Tanzanian president Julius Nyerere argued strongly that such a proposal was neither logical nor cost-effective and that if it were to be adopted, it would lead to the collapse of the union. Following the meeting, Pres. Salmin Amour of Zanzibar promised that his government would withdraw from the OIC, and on the mainland the vote was deferred, but many thought it was too late to halt the drift toward dissolution.

The economy continued to cause problems. On March 12 it was announced that 30,000 government employees would be laid off by the end of the 1993–94 financial year, and in July, in an attempt to alleviate the difficulties faced by the industrial sector, the government decided to raise taxes on imported goods that were also produced in the country. The first high-level diplomatic contacts with South Africa since 1964 marked a significant advance in external relations.

(KENNETH INGHAM)

This article updates the *Macropædia* article EASTERN AFRICA: *Tanzania.*

TOGO

A republic of West Africa, Togo is situated on the Bight of Benin. Area: 56,785 sq km (21,925 sq mi). Pop. (1993 est.): 3,810,000. Cap.: Lomé. Monetary unit: CFA franc, with (Oct. 4, 1993) a par value of CFAF 50 to the French franc and a free rate of CFAF 283.25 to U.S. $1 (CFAF 429.12 = £1 sterling). President in 1993, Gen. Gnassingbe Eyadema; prime minister, Joseph Kokou Koffigoh.

Pres. Gnassingbe Eyadema of Togo began the year by first firing and then reappointing the increasingly unpopular Prime Minister Joseph Koffigoh. On January 25 police killed at least 20 demonstrators awaiting the arrival of the foreign ministers of France and Germany, who were to help restart the stalled democratization process. The European Community immediately suspended all aid. Five days later the army loyal to Eyadema rampaged through Lomé, attacking the homes of opposition leaders. France and the U.S. cut off all aid after negotiations to secure the army's neutrality in the electoral process broke off in February. At least 300,000 Togolese were refugees in Benin and Ghana.

A failed military coup resulted in a purge of the army. In April and May the offices and presses of three opposition newspapers were destroyed. After several postponements and months of negotiations, the presidential elections were finally held on August 25. Five major opposition candidates withdrew. Only 36% of the electorate participated, but Eyadema received 96.5% of the votes cast. In November parliamentary elections were postponed until January 1994.

(NANCY ELLEN LAWLER)

This article updates the *Macropædia* article WESTERN AFRICA: *Togo.*

UGANDA

A landlocked republic and member of the Commonwealth, Uganda is located in eastern Africa. Area: 241,040 sq km (93,070 sq mi), including 44,000 sq km of inland water. Pop. (1993 est.): 17,741,000. Cap.: Kampala. Monetary unit: Uganda shilling, with (Oct. 4, 1993) a priority rate of 1,171 shillings to U.S. $1 (1,774 shillings = £1 sterling). President in 1993, Yoweri Museveni; prime minister, George Cosmas Adyebo.

External support for Uganda's economic development remained strong in response to what was seen to be the government's adherence to the structural adjustment program approved by the International Monetary Fund (IMF). In its annual report, published on March 9, the UN Conference on Trade and Development listed Uganda among those of the poorest less developed countries that, as a result of their comparatively stable economies, had achieved higher growth rates and had increased their per capita incomes.

Japan led the way in offering aid to Uganda in 1993 with a loan of $50 million, repayable over 30 years, and soon afterward the Consultative Group for Uganda pledged financial support to the tune of $825 million in the 1993–94 financial year. Still later, the minister of state for finance, Moses Kintu, signed an agreement with the director of

ANTONIN KRATOCHVIL—DOT

On July 31, in a ceremony combining ancient customs and modern conveniences, Ronald Muwenda Mutebi is crowned kabaka (ruler) of the kingdom of Buganda. Uganda's constitution had been amended to allow Buganda and three other tribal kingdoms to restore traditional rulers.

the U.S. Agency for International Development in Uganda under the terms of which $25 million would be spent over a six-year period in an attempt to increase and diversify nontraditional agricultural exports. Germany offered DM 20 million in addition to the DM 50 million already granted for road maintenance.

Another promising sign for Uganda's economy was the increase noted in the future price of coffee. Since the breakdown of the international quota system in 1989, Uganda, along with other coffee-producing countries, had suffered heavy losses in its earnings from the export of coffee. At a meeting in Kampala in August, African coffee producers agreed to join a scheme inaugurated earlier in the year by Latin-American growers to withhold 20% of their output from the world market. Although the scheme would not take effect until October 1, the result of the announcement was instantaneous; future prices rose immediately by 19%. In July the minister of finance, Joshua Mayanja-Nkangi, demonstrated his confidence in the country's future by announcing in his budget the proposed expenditure of 430 billion shillings on recurrent costs and more than 400 billion on development.

The approval of Western countries was surprising in view of Pres. Yoweri Museveni's continued rejection of a multiparty political system, although he tolerated the existence of political parties provided they did not campaign in the pursuit of office. On February 16 hopes of a change were raised when the government announced a plan to elect, on the basis of universal adult suffrage, a constituent assembly of 180 members to draft a new constitution. Yet on May 24 Museveni again made clear his opposition to any multiparty system. In late November, March 28, 1994, was selected as the date for the legislative elections.

In July another important step was taken when the constitution was amended to allow for the restoration of traditional rulers in the four former kingdoms of the south and southwest. On July 31, in one of the more potentially controversial of the responses to the government's measure, Ronald Muwenda Mutebi was officially installed as kabaka of Buganda. It had been Buganda's attempt to insist upon its separate identity that had been at the root of many of the country's troubles in the years immediately following independence and, although Museveni insisted that the traditional rulers had only a cultural role to play, many observers were concerned that ethnic loyalties might once again come into conflict with loyalty to Uganda.

Early in February, Pope John Paul II visited Uganda and aroused criticism by maintaining that abstinence from sexual intercourse was the sole solution to the country's AIDS problem. Although the spread of AIDS was Uganda's most serious concern, the government was also aware that, as in many other African countries, university education was facing a crisis. Low salaries and a lack of resources for research were among the main reasons for this.

(KENNETH INGHAM)

This article updates the *Macropædia* article EASTERN AFRICA: *Uganda*.

ZAIRE

The republic of Zaire is located in central Africa with a short coastline on the Atlantic Ocean. Area: 2,345,095 sq km (905,446 sq mi). Pop. (1993 est.): 42,473,000. Cap.: Kinshasa. Monetary unit: zaïre, with (Oct. 4, 1993) a free rate of 8,751,200 zaïres to U.S. $1 (13,258,000 zaïres = £1 sterling). President in 1993, Mobutu Sese Seko; first state commissioners (prime ministers), Étienne Tshisekedi plus, from March 18, Faustin Birindwa.

Attacked by critics inside and outside Zaire, Pres. Mobutu Sese Seko continued in 1993 to play a game of survival by using well-tried tactics with a confidence that gave the impression it was his opponents who were embattled rather than himself. On January 15 a general strike called by the opposition coalition, the Sacred Union, virtually shut down Kinshasa. A few days later Mobutu paid his troops with 5 million-zaïre notes, which Prime Minister Étienne Tshisekedi, who was anxious to challenge the president's control of the economy, immediately condemned as inflationary and, therefore, worthless. In response to the prime minister's warning, shopkeepers in most towns refused to accept them. The disgruntled troops rioted, and for more than a week the capital was subjected to looting and violence in the course of which many lives were lost, including that of the French ambassador. Mobutu sent his presidential guard to crush the revolt, their loyalty ensured by their being paid in hard currency. They were eventually effective in restoring a semblance of order, although skirmishing between rival groups continued. Outside Kinshasa the soldiers were not so easily restrained. In a number of towns businessmen, terrorized by threats of looting or even death, were forced to collect large sums of money in small-denomination notes to pay off the troops.

In a joint communiqué issued on February 3, the U.S., France, and Belgium called upon Mobutu to transfer his power to Tshisekedi, who had been elected by a national pro-democracy conference in August 1992 and who had appealed to the three countries to intervene militarily. Mobutu, who had frequently employed rioting troops to disconcert his opponents, contemptuously responded by accusing Tshisekedi of being incapable of forming a government and by calling upon the self-elected transitional parliament, the High Council of the Republic (HCR), to submit the name of a new prime minister. Tshisekedi replied that since Mobutu had not appointed him, he could not dismiss him. He was supported by the HCR, which rejected Mobutu's order. But the members of the HCR themselves were harassed by impoverished troops, who on February 24 blocked the streets leading to the parliament building and demanded that the 5 million-zaïre notes be officially recognized.

A roundtable session called by Mobutu on March 9 to resolve the conflict was boycotted by the Sacred Union, which had already decided three days earlier that it would attend only a conference summoned by the HCR. Mobutu reacted by appointing Faustin Birindwa prime minister, thus leaving the country with two prime ministers. On April 2, Birindwa announced the membership of his Cabinet, which included another former prime minister, Nguza Karl-I-Bond, who became deputy prime minister responsible for defense. Mobutu, meanwhile, ordered troops to search the houses of leading members of the opposition, ostensibly to recover government property. The Sacred Union, renamed the Innovative Forces of the Sacred Union (FONUS), called a one-day strike in Kinshasa to protest against the appointment of Birindwa. The European Community also refused to recognize the new prime minister. The party supporting Mobutu, the Popular Movement for Renewal (MPR), then called on Birindwa's government to break off diplomatic relations with the U.S., France, and Belgium, accusing those countries of pursuing a policy of neocolonialism.

Birindwa took the initiative in May by designating July 30 as the day on which a constitutional referendum would be held, to be followed three months later by general elections. Tshisekedi's government immediately called for a boycott of the referendum. Meanwhile, serious developments were taking place in the southeast of the country. In September 1992 a governor appointed by Mobutu in Shaba province had launched a campaign to rid the province of many thousands of members of Tshisekedi's Kasai tribe. By 1993 the campaign had spread to North Kivu province, resulting, it was reported, in more than 1,000 deaths. In mid-December it was reported that Shaba province (which had seceded once before, after Congolese independence in 1960) had declared its autonomy under its former name of Katanga. The two Kasai provinces—loyal to Tshisekedi, who was still considered prime minister—were reportedly thinking of following suit.

On July 5, Mobutu banned Tshisekedi's party, the Union for Democracy and Social Progress, but Birindwa also came under criticism from the MPR for failing to make progress. A meeting between Mobutu's representatives and the Sacred Union, scheduled for August 13, did not take place because the president's men did not turn up. On September 5, Tshisekedi was unanimously appointed head of a new opposition group that called itself the Democratic Forces of Congo-Kinshasa. Five days later talks began between Mobutu's representatives and members of the opposition; after 20 days of discussion, they resulted in an agreement to put an end to parallel institutions and to adopt a single constitutional text for the transition period. The talks hit a snag in October, however, and the UN special envoy left Kinshasa without a protocol having been signed.

The apparently unending political turmoil had a disastrous impact upon the economy. On October 21 the government attempted to introduce a new currency with a value of 1 new zaïre to 3 million old zaïres, but the monetary structure promptly collapsed, and scattered rioting broke out yet again. In June the World Food Program had begun assisting vulnerable groups, especially children, in Kinshasa.

(KENNETH INGHAM)

This article updates the *Macropædia* article CENTRAL AFRICA: *Zaire*.

ZAMBIA

A landlocked republic and member of the Commonwealth, Zambia is in eastern Africa. Area: 752,614 sq km (290,586 sq mi). Pop. (1993 est.): 8,504,000. Cap.: Lusaka. Monetary unit: kwacha, with (Oct. 4, 1993) a free rate of 350.66 kwacha to U.S. $1 (531.25 kwacha = £1 sterling). President in 1993, Frederick Chiluba.

An excellent corn (maize) crop—18 billion bags, 8 billion more than Zambia required for internal consumption—promised a speedy recovery from some of the worst effects of the 1992 drought. The growers' reluctance to sell at low government prices, however, coupled with the government's lack of cash to buy even at the price it was offering, threatened many producers with bankruptcy and left the country reliant upon heavily subsidized imported grain. Nevertheless, there was a widespread feeling among donor countries that Zambia was handling its structural adjustment program satisfactorily, and further help was made available from a number of quarters. The U.S., Germany, and the U.K. wrote off substantial portions of Zambia's debts. Japan, Zambia's biggest source of aid, made a grant of 6 billion kwacha to buy fertilizer to be distributed to peasant farmers. The International Monetary Fund also promised to seek further aid from the Paris Club in April. Minister of Defense Benjamin Mwila, responding to criticism of the large defense budget, found some justification from the need to send troops to the Angolan border to resist incursions from the National Union for the Total Independence of Angola rebels.

Early in March, Pres. Frederick Chiluba declared a state of emergency and detained a number of opposition leaders after the discovery of an alleged plot to overthrow the government. Many of the detainees were released on bail, and the state of emergency was lifted on May 25, but not before Chiluba had dismissed four senior ministers. One of them, Guy Scott, minister of agriculture, insisted that he was still a loyal supporter of the Movement for Multiparty Democracy (MMD), but another, Arthur Wina, minister of education, was critical of what he saw as the government's failure to check corruption and drug dealing. Wina and nine other members resigned from the party and were later joined by a further defector. Together they founded a new National Party (NP). The MMD itself expelled five other party members, including Scott. The National Party was later joined by members of another opposition party, the United Democratic Party, which was dissolved (its leader, Enoch Kavindele, defected back to Chiluba one week later, however), and by two former members of the United National Independence Party. The November by-elections, following upon the resignation of four MMD MPs, proved quite alarming for Chiluba; the NP won four of the eight seats contested, and the MMD took only three.

(KENNETH INGHAM)

This article updates the *Macropædia* article SOUTHERN AFRICA: *Zambia*.

ZIMBABWE

A republic and member of the Commonwealth, Zimbabwe is a landlocked state in eastern Africa. Area: 390,757 sq km (150,872 sq mi). Pop. (1993 est.): 10,687,000. Cap.: Harare. Monetary unit: Zimbabwe dollar, with (Oct. 4, 1993) a free rate of Z$6.52 to U.S. $1 (Z$9.87 = £1 sterling). President in 1993, Robert Mugabe.

As Zimbabwe began its slow recovery from the effects of the drought in 1992, it was concern for the economy that took precedence over all other aspects of national life. Indicators were contradictory. The collapse of the world chrome market forced the closing in June of the Sengwa colliery, which had been designated to supply fuel to the ferrochrome industry. As a result, construction of a Z$20 million road linking the mine to the country's main transport system was abandoned, as had the plan by the national railways to purchase a number of 30-ton trucks to carry the ore. On the other hand, an increase in the world price of gold, coupled with the depreciation in value of the Zimbabwe dollar, led to increased efforts in the production of gold, the country's third largest foreign currency earner.

By the middle of 1993 the rate of inflation had fallen to 25% from the peak of 50% reached in August 1992, and a number of projects were proposed to improve the economic situation. The Wankie Colliery Co. planned to supply gas to the country's thermal power station at Hwange, thereby saving Z$20 million a year on imported fuel. Retrenchment in the army and its merger with the air force promised a reduction in personnel of 10,000 over the next five years while making the army more suited to the mobile role it was intended to play. One sphere in which Zimbabwe's military commitment had already been reduced was Mozambique. In March the troops that had been defending the transport links and fuel pipeline from the coast to the Limpopo River were withdrawn after the arrival of United Nations forces to replace them.

More important in the overall economic picture was the announcement by Finance Minister Bernard Chidzero on April 27 of trade-liberalization measures aimed at encouraging foreign investment. Chief among them was the phasing out of capital-repatriation restrictions on foreigners investing in companies quoted on the Zimbabwe stock exchange or buying primary issues of government bonds and stocks. This was a total reversal of the government's former policy and was seen as an indication of Pres. Robert Mugabe's commitment to the structural-adjustment program designed by the International Monetary Fund and the World Bank.

Chidzero's optimistic budget announced in July was received with some skepticism by foreign businessmen and economic commentators. While, as the minister indicated, considerable savings could be made as a result of the reduction in drought-relief payments, the decline in industrial production during the first five months of the year, together with the problems faced by the tobacco and beef industries, made his prediction of a 4% growth in gross domestic product (GDP) seem unduly hopeful. Barclays Bank of Zimbabwe thought a figure of 3.2% more realistic. Despite, too, a 14% proposed rise in defense spending and increases of 12.6% in education and 9% in health, the minister forecast a fall in overall government spending as a percentage of GDP.

In July important changes were promised with a view to liberalizing agricultural marketing, but these were offset by the concern that was vocally expressed by white farmers who felt gravely threatened by the earlier announcement that the government intended to appropriate 70 commercial farms under the terms of the Land Acquisition Act in order to hand them over to African peasant farmers; the owners, most of whom were white, were to be compensated at rates established by the government. This action was seen as a breach of an earlier promise to acquire only derelict and underutilized land, and it was also believed to pose a threat to the government's hopes of encouraging foreign investment in Zimbabwe. The argument that it was uneconomical to replace commercial farms with smallholdings had less foundation because peasant growers of corn (maize), the country's staple crop, had certainly proved themselves capable of matching the productivity of white-owned farms. When some white farmers objected to the government action, they were warned that their land might be taken without any compensation.

On March 28, Enoch Dumbutshena, a former chief justice, was elected leader of a new political group calling itself the Forum Party. The party brought together intellectuals, businessmen, the Shona and Ndebele tribal groupings, and a number of white liberals. It announced its adherence to the principle of unfettered market economics and aimed to boost investment and provide more jobs. If elected to office in 1995, the party planned to privatize most state-funded companies, including the media. Thus, there was now an alternative government-in-waiting, Dumbutshena declared, but in 1993 there was little evidence that the new party posed a serious challenge to the ruling Zimbabwe African National Union (Patriotic Front; ZANU[PF]).

In the field of external relations, there were a number of contrasting moves. Fearing a trade war with South Africa following that country's decision that it would not exempt an import duty on Zimbabwean textile products, President Mugabe was forced in February to abandon his attempts to restrict contact with South Africa, and he invited the South African trade minister to Harare for talks. A few days later, and as a result of the fruitful cooperation between Zimbabwean and U.S. troops in Somalia the previous month, 26 U.S. soldiers arrived to spend 45 days training with a Zimbabwean commando battalion. At the other end of the spectrum, President Mugabe was invited in October by Yasir Arafat, chairman of the Palestine Liberation Organization, to be the first foreign head of state to visit him in Jericho and the Gaza Strip in 1994 after the Israelis had withdrawn from those areas. (KENNETH INGHAM)

This article updates the *Macropædia* article SOUTHERN AFRICA: *Zimbabwe*.

Middle East and North Africa

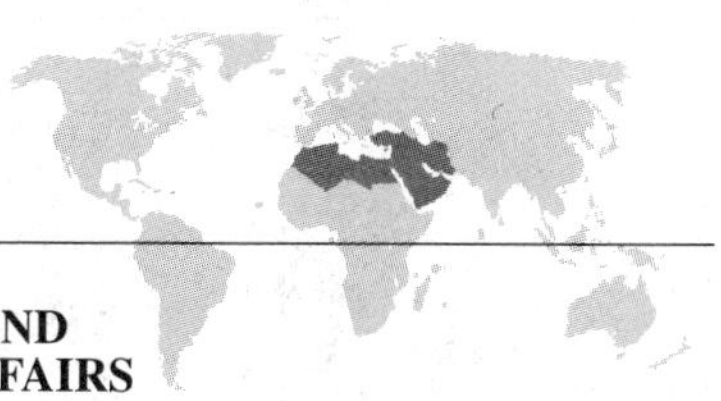

MIDDLE EASTERN AND NORTH AFRICAN AFFAIRS

The bilateral agreement between Israel and the Palestinians for self-government in parts of the Israeli-occupied territories was signed by Israeli Foreign Minister Shimon Peres and Palestine Liberation Organization (PLO) representative Mahmoud Abbas in a historic ceremony on the U.S. White House lawn on Sept. 13, 1993. The accord was the most significant breakthrough in the Middle East peace process since the U.S.-brokered peace between Egypt and Israel in 1979. The Israeli concessions in the agreement came in return for PLO recognition of Israel, but the deal contained nothing for the hundreds of thousands of Palestinians expelled by Israel in 1948 and their descendants.

The year began with the prospects for the success of the peace process, started in Madrid in 1991, apparently blighted by Israel's harsh tactics over 415 Palestinian deportees stranded in the no-man's-land between Israel and Lebanon. It ended with PLO units preparing to take over security duties in the Gaza Strip and Jericho in the West Bank, although the December 13 deadline for withdrawal by the Israelis from the Gaza Strip and Jericho was missed.

PLO leader Yasir Arafat and Israeli Prime Minister Yitzhak Rabin met on October 6 in Cairo for their first face-to-face negotiating session. They met again on December 12 but only to confirm that the deadline for Israeli withdrawal should be extended by 10 days. In talks in Paris, which ended on December 23, Israel reportedly offered to expand the Palestinian autonomous area in Jericho from 91 to 155 sq km (35 to 60 sq mi), a considerable advance to the Palestinian demand for 207 sq km (80 sq mi). However, there was little sign of progress on the main issue that plagued the talks, namely the question of who would have authority at the frontier crossings between the future Palestinian self-ruled areas, which bordered both Jordan and Egypt.

Arab-Israeli Relations. The groundwork on the historic Declaration of Principles between Israel and the PLO was undertaken largely at secret talks between negotiators in a lonely farmhouse in the Norwegian countryside outside Oslo. Although assisted by low-key Norwegian intermediaries, they achieved the accord in direct talks, without the participation or knowledge of any of the powerful outsiders from the U.S., Europe, or the moderate Arab states.

The declaration ceremony in Washington included a symbolic handshake between Rabin and Arafat, but it was met with predictable anger from radicals. The Palestinian fundamentalist group Hamas, which had more support in Gaza than Arafat's Fatah group, announced that it would wage civil war if the deal went through.

The agreement offered the Palestinians a chance to elect their own "interim self-government authority," or council. This would take control over taxation, health, education, welfare, tourism, and other sectors to be negotiated later. The military withdrawal was a key element that would start with the Gaza Strip and Jericho but would continue in 1994 with the Israeli military's withdrawal from "populous areas" in the West Bank.

The leader of the Palestinian delegation to the multilateral peace talks, Haider Abdel-Shafi, described the agreement as less than the bare minimum. Among the issues that remained outstanding were the status of Israeli settlements, which were not to be discussed until permanent status talks

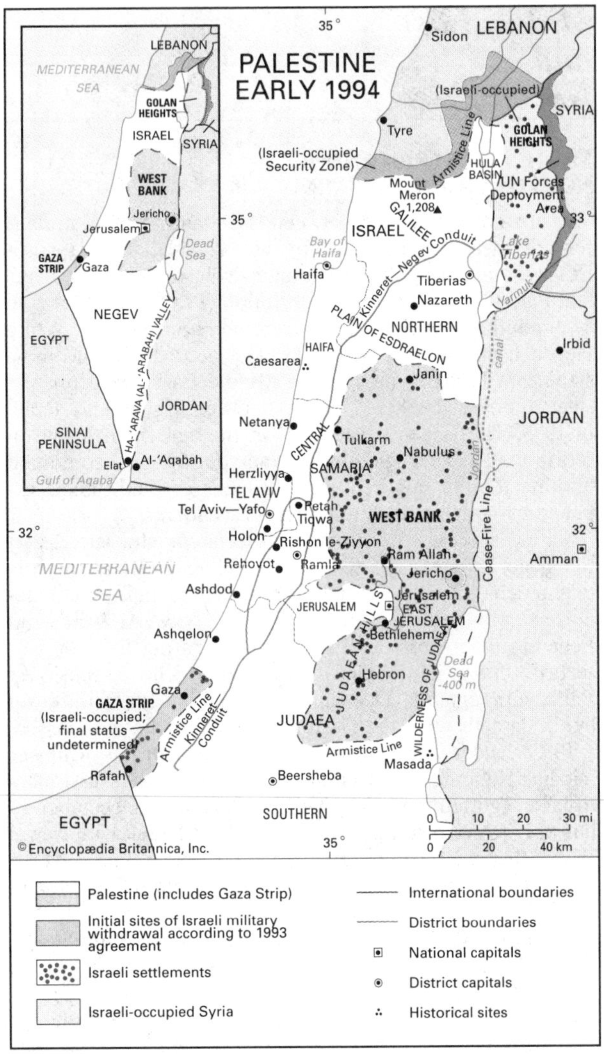

started in 1996, and sovereignty over East Jerusalem, although Palestinians living there would be allowed to vote in the interim council elections on July 15, 1994. The deal also made no mention of compensation for refugees expelled in 1948 from their homes and property.

The agreement was, however, welcomed by the international community, and the World Bank had drafted a $3 billion development plan for the occupied territories by the beginning of October. This prompted pledges of financial assistance totaling nearly $2 billion from donors at a Washington conference on October 1. An ad hoc liaison group was created by the conference; it comprised the U.S., Canada, the European Community (EC), Japan, Russia, Norway, and Saudi Arabia. The Palestinians, Israel, Egypt, and Jordan were associate members. The World Bank was to act as the secretariat for the new group created after heated debate between the U.S. and the EC over its final form.

In contrast with these amounts of aid pledged, the PLO produced its own $12 billion development plan for the West Bank and Gaza. In financing the projects, the PLO's usual bankers in the Gulf states were likely to prove reticent in light of the PLO's support for Iraq in the Kuwait crisis of 1990–91.

Among Arab states the Syrian reaction was the most important, with Pres. Hafez al-Assad meeting Arafat on September 5, after which it was made clear that Assad neither "approved or rejected" the peace deal. Although the veteran Syrian leader remarked bitterly to the Egyptian daily *Al Akhbar* that "no-one had gained except Israel," his neutrality provided a boost to the peace process. Pres. Hosni Mubarak of Egypt was predictably positive and played a significant role in the buildup to the accord, although this was not acknowledged in the speech making in Washington on September 13.

In a much more low-key ceremony at the U.S. State Department on September 14, Jordan and Israel concluded an agreement on an agenda listing various issues for bilateral negotiation. The focus then switched to what commentators called "the Syrian track," although little progress was made in 1993. Syria was in no hurry to conclude a deal with Israel on the future of the Golan Heights, although its stated position was to exchange full peace with Israel for total Israeli withdrawal from the Golan.

On April 14 Mubarak met Rabin at a summit that resulted in agreement on a number of issues: Israel accepted the return of up to 50 Palestinians deported before the outbreak of the *intifada* (uprising) in December 1987; Faisal al-Husseini, leader of the Palestinians in the occupied territories, was allowed to join the Washington peace talks; and Rabin agreed to the setting up of a Palestinian police force, which subsequently began undergoing training in Jordan. Egypt also kept the momentum for peace going when Israel's Peres met his Egyptian counterpart, Amr Moussa, and Mubarak in Cairo and Alexandria on July 4–5. Immediately afterward, Mubarak flew to Damascus to brief Assad. Egypt's mediator role also took on an important dimension when the Arab League met for a special meeting at the end of July to consider an Israeli attack on southern Lebanon. On July 31 a cease-fire was agreed on, and the crisis failed to derail the peace process.

Rabin agreed on February 1, after mediation by the U.S. government, to allow the return of 101 of the 415 Palestinian deportees expelled from Israel into southern Lebanon on Dec. 17, 1992, and that all the others could return by the end of 1993. The U.S. agreed to find host countries for the detainees in the meantime. Two days later, however, Rabin told the Israeli Knesset (parliament) that Israel retained the right to make further expulsions.

The ninth round of bilateral negotiations between Israel and the Arabs opened in Washington on April 27 and broke up in mid-May with both sides blaming each other for the stalemate. Infighting between members of the Palestinian delegation inhibited progress, but Israel's decision to close off the West Bank and Gaza Strip on March 30 added to tensions. The closure decision followed the murder of two Israeli police officers at Hadera, Israel, on March 30, bringing to 17 the number of Israelis killed since December 1992. Multilateral talks on regional economic issues convened in Rome on May 4, with Israel succeeding in persuading the EC and the U.S. to provide up to $100 million in emergency aid to the occupied territories.

When the 10th round of bilateral talks took place between June 15 and July 1 and once again ended inconclusively, there was no public indication of progress toward an accord. On June 7 Peres had asserted that Israel was "a stroke of a pen" away from a deal with Jordan and Syria. Speaking to settlers near the Golan Heights, Israeli Finance Minister Avraham Shohat said there would be no new long-term investments in the area.

The 11th round of bilateral talks, which opened in Washington on August 31, were overshadowed by the announcement on August 30 of the Norwegian-brokered deal. Lebanon's foreign minister, Fares Bouez, reacted by com-

(continued on page 378)

Special Report: Middle Eastern Affairs

Islamic Fundamentalism

BY JOHN L. ESPOSITO

From the Iranian revolution of 1978–79 to the bombing of the New York World Trade Center in 1993, Islamic fundamentalism has become an issue of international attention and concern. It is a broad-based but diverse religious movement that has swept across much of the Muslim world, from North Africa to Southeast Asia, during the past two decades. Contemporary Islamic fundamentalism has manifested itself in personal and political life, from greater emphasis on religious observances such as prayer, fasting, Islamic dress, and family values to the reassertion of Islam in politics.

The term *Islamic fundamentalism,* while commonly used, is regarded by many as misleading. The term *fundamentalism* is laden with Christian presuppositions and Western stereotypes, and it implies a monolithic threat. More useful terms are *Islamic revivalism* and *Islamic activism,* which are less value-laden and have roots within a tradition of political reform and social activism.

Historical Perspective. Muslim belief and history have provided the sources for the worldview of Islamic activists. A Muslim's duty is obedience and submission (*islam*) to the will of God. However, the submission incumbent upon the Muslim is not mere passivity or acceptance of a set of dogmas or rituals; rather, it is submission to the divine command, to strive (*jihad*) to actively realize God's will in history. Thus, the Qur'an declares that Muslims are God's vicegerents, or representatives, on Earth; that God has given creation to humankind as a divine trust; and that realization of God's will leads to eternal reward or punishment.

The Muslim's obligation to realize God's will is communal as well as individual. The Islamic community/state serves as the dynamic vehicle for realization of the divine mandate in society, as an example to other peoples of the world. Islamic activists believe that religion is integral to every aspect of life: prayer, fasting, politics, law, and society. This belief is reflected not only in Islam's doctrine of *tawhid* (oneness of God, or monotheism) but also in the development of the Islamic state and Islamic law.

In the first Islamic state at Medina in the 7th century, Muhammad served as both prophet and political leader of the Islamic community/state. Islamic law, the Shar'iah, was rooted in divine revelation, the Qur'an, and Sunna (example, or model behaviour, of the Prophet). Law provides the blueprint for Muslim society, a comprehensive mode of life that includes laws regulating prayer and almsgiving as well as family, criminal, commercial, and international transactions.

Belief in the divinely ordained nature and mission of the community was validated and reinforced by Muslim success and power. Within 100 years of Muhammad's death, the original Islamic community, through expansion and conquest, became an empire more extensive than any other the world had known. In time the Islamic world extended from Arabia west to North Africa and Spain and east to Indonesia. Success and power were regarded as both signs of divine guidance and the rewards for the community's fidelity.

Origins of Contemporary Revivalism. Current Islamic revivalism builds on a considerable legacy of reform. During the 18th and 19th centuries, religio-political movements occurred across the Islamic world in response to political fragmentation and economic, social, and moral decline. A common theme was the need to purify Islam through the suppression of foreign (un-Islamic) practices and to return to the fundamentals of Islam—the Qur'an and model of Muhammad and the early Muslim community. In the first half of the 20th century, there emerged the Muslim Brotherhood in Egypt and the Jamaat-i-Islami (Islamic Society) in South Asia, both of which became prototypes of today's Islamic movements. Their legacy includes the belief that Islam affects public policy as much as private worship and the objective of establishing effective organizations to implement an Islamic system of government and law.

During the 1970s contemporary Islamic revivalism emerged. The personal aspect was reflected in increased emphasis upon religious observances (mosque attendance, Ramadan fast, outlawing of alcohol and gambling), the proliferation of religious literature, and the birth of new associations or movements that sought to "Islamize" the population.

At the same time, Islam dramatically reemerged in public life. Throughout the Muslim world Islamic symbols, slogans, ideology, and actors became prominent fixtures in politics. Religion was used both by incumbent governments and by opposition movements to reinforce their legitimacy and mobilize popular support. Libyan leader Col. Muammar al-Qaddafi's *Green Book* of Islamic socialism and use of Islam internationally; Gen. Zia ul-Haq's 1977 coup d'état in Pakistan and his call for the establishment of an Islamic system of government; Ayatollah Khomeini's Iranian revolution of 1978–79; the seizure of the Grand Mosque in Mecca by militants in 1979; Pres. Anwar as-Sadat's appeal to Islam in Egyptian politics, his legitimation of the 1973 war with Israel as a jihad, and his assassination in 1981 by religious extremists; the Afghan resistance (by mujahideen, or holy warriors) to the Soviet invasion and occupation throughout the 1980s—all were instances of Islam reasserting itself.

The causes of the resurgence are varied. Widespread failures (the 1967 Arab-Israeli war, Malay-Chinese riots in 1969, Bangladesh's war of succession from Pakistan in 1971, and the Lebanese civil war in the mid-1970s) served as catalysts. As a result of such events, Muslims experienced a sense of impotence and loss of self-esteem, as well as disillusionment with the West and with governments that failed to respond to the needs of their societies. The 1973 Arab-Israeli war and Arab oil embargo and the Iranian revolution of 1978–79 produced a newfound sense of pride and power.

The negative effects of modernization are equally important in understanding the Islamic resurgence. They include massive migration from villages and rapid urbanization of overcrowded cities; the breakdown of traditional family, religious, and social values; and the adoption of a Western lifestyle, enthusiastically pursued as a symbol of modernity but also criticized as a source of moral decline and spiritual malaise, corruption, unemployment, and maldistribution of wealth.

For the vast majority of Muslims, the resurgence of Islam is a reassertion of cultural identity, formal religious obser-

John L. Esposito is Professor of Religion and International Affairs and Director of the Center for Muslim-Christian Understanding at Georgetown University, Washington D.C. He is the author of several books on Islam, including The Islamic Threat: Myth or Reality? *and* Islam: The Straight Path.

vance, family values, and morality. The establishment of an Islamic society is seen as requiring a personal and social transformation that is a prerequisite for true Islamic government. Effective change is to come from below through a gradual social transformation brought about by implementation of Islamic law.

On the other hand, a significant minority views the societies and governments in Muslim countries as hopelessly corrupt. They believe that un-Islamic societies and their leaders are no better than infidels and that the religious establishment has been co-opted by the government. Such critics believe that both established political and religious elites must be overthrown and a new Islamically committed leadership chosen and Islamic law imposed. These radical revolutionary groups, though relatively small in membership, have proved effective in political agitation, disruption, and assassination. They have not, however, been successful in mobilizing the masses.

Extremists and Activists. Much of the 1980s was dominated by fear of Iran and its threat to export revolution and by images of extremist organizations that used violence, hostage taking, and terrorism. By the late 1980s and early 1990s, however, Islamic movements were diverse rather than a monolithic threat. A minority of radical extremists, with names like Islamic Jihad, the Party of God, the Islamic Liberation Front, and the al-Jama'a al-Islamiya (Islamic Group), have continued to exist in many parts of the Muslim world. Groups like Egypt's al-Jama'a al-Islamiya battle the government and attack and kill Coptic Christians and foreign tourists, and other extremists are alleged to be behind the World Trade Center bombing. However, Islamic activism is also a social and political force operating within the system. Islamically inspired organizations run schools, clinics, hospitals, banks, and publishing houses and offer a wide array of social welfare services. A new generation of elites, modern educated but Islamically rather than secularly oriented, can be found among physicians, lawyers, engineers, teachers, and social workers seeking to implement Islamic alternatives or visions in society.

At the same time, calls for political democratization have brought both greater liberalization and repression. Where governments have opened up their political systems, Islamic organizations have participated in elections and emerged as the leading opposition, as in Egypt, Tunisia, and Jordan. In Algeria the Islamic Salvation Front swept municipal and parliamentary elections in the early 1990s and seemed poised to come to power when the Algerian military intervened. The successes of Islamic movements in electoral politics have led governments such as those in Algeria, Tunisia, and Egypt to engage in political repression, charging that religious extremists threaten to "hijack democracy," to use the political system to come to power and then impose their will and undermine the stability of society. Iran and The Sudan are often cited to support concerns about democracy and pluralism, in particular as governments that deny the rights of minorities and women.

Some experts counter that many governments whose political legitimacy is tenuous and supported by a heavy reliance on security forces will only tolerate "risk-free democracy" (a political liberalization that does not threaten their power and rule) and that the indiscriminate suppression of Islamists may contribute to radicalization and extremism. While some governments and experts identify Islamic fundamentalism as a major threat to the stability of their societies and to global politics, others point out that it is important to distinguish between authentic populist movements that are willing to participate within the system and rejectionists who seek to topple governments through violent revolution.

(continued from page 376)
plaining that the Palestinians had failed to explain their plan at a late-August meeting in Beirut. Subsequently, a 12th round of talks scheduled for late October was canceled.

The personal standing of Arafat within the Palestinian movement came under fire, with some of his colleagues accusing him of selling out to Israel. Arafat claimed a convincing victory after two days of debate at the PLO central council, which ended in Tunis on October 12. The vote in favour of the accord was 63–8 with 9 abstentions. Among those who abstained was Farouk Qaddoumi, head of the PLO political department.

Following the September accord, U.S. and Israeli officials pressed for the ending of the 43-year-old Arab boycott of Israel. At a meeting between U.S. Secretary of State Warren Christopher and Arab ministers in New York City at the beginning of October, the Gulf states refused to give way, while Jordan's Crown Prince Hassan said lifting the boycott would be "economic suicide." Subsequently, a meeting of Arab boycott officials was canceled.

Regional Considerations. The Arab Islamic fundamentalist movement became a more significant force in 1993 but without achieving a breakthrough in terms of popular mobilization. The most dramatic operation in which the fundamentalists were implicated was the February 26 bombing of the World Trade Center in New York City, blamed on followers of the Egyptian divine Sheikh Omar Abdel-Rahman, who was being held in the U.S. for alleged immigration offenses. On January 25 Mubarak said that extremism was threatening all aspects of life in Egypt.

Saudi Arabia was at the forefront of Arab anger at the harsh treatment of Muslims by Serbs in occupied parts of Bosnia and Herzegovina. Speaking on June 1, King Fahd claimed that the world community was wavering and argued that only a firm stance against the Serbs would stop the extermination of the Bosnian Muslim people. The 21 foreign ministers at the Organization of Islamic Conference meeting in Karachi, Pak., on April 27 voted for a resolution calling for the UN to use all necessary means to stop the genocide of Muslims in Bosnia.

The signatories of the 1991 Damascus Declaration—Egypt, Syria, and the Gulf Cooperation Council (GCC) states (Saudi Arabia, Kuwait, Bahrain, Qatar, the United Arab Emirates, and Oman)— met in Abu Dhabi, U.A.E., on June 12–13 and renewed their condemnation of Iraq's continued threat to the region. However, they failed to take any practical measures to implement the economic program included in the declaration. The Abu Dhabi statement demanded increased ties with Iran based on the principles of noninterference in domestic affairs, but it reaffirmed the U.A.E.'s sovereignty over the disputed islands of Abu Musa and the uninhabited Greater and Lesser Tunbs. The eight states postponed a decision on Lebanon's application to join.

It was reported on April 20 that Iran had restored the status quo on Abu Musa, dropping any restrictions on the movement of third-country nationals, which had been imposed in 1992. The U.A.E. claimed the restrictions violated a 1971 deal under which the two states shared administrative responsibilities for the islands but maintained their sovereignty claims.

GCC heads of state, meeting for the annual summit in Saudi Arabia on December 20, discussed a broad range of economic issues, including tariffs, property, commercial arbitration, and the airline industry, according to the GCC undersecretary for economic affairs, Abdullah al-Quwaiz. The common tariff system was a key element in agreeing to a free-trade accord with the EC, but the GCC failed to settle the issue at a meeting of finance ministers in late October. Following its December 1992 summit meeting, the GCC's founding secretary-general, Abdullah Bishara, retired. He was succeeded on April 1 by a U.A.E. diplomat, Sheikh Fahim al-Qassimi. On April 15 Qassimi led GCC officials in a meeting of the EC-GCC joint cooperation committee to seek progress on the free-trade accord. This was followed by a formal EC-GCC foreign ministers meeting at the European Commission's headquarters on May 11, but there were few indications of major progress.

On September 22 GCC trade ministers recommended that all six states join the General Agreement on Tariffs and Trade, of which only Kuwait was a member, although earlier in 1993 Saudi Arabia had applied to join. Quwaiz said on September 22 that Bahrain, Qatar, and the U.A.E. were considering membership. In a separate regional meeting in Amman, Jordan, on June 12, electricity officials from Egypt, Iraq, Jordan, Syria, and Turkey agreed to a program to connect their electricity grids by the year 2002.

North African Affairs. Conservative Arab states in North Africa viewed with alarm the rising Islamic challenge in Algeria. On February 7 the Algerian regime extended its state of emergency indefinitely, although a demonstration on March 22 against Islamic violence in Algeria attracted 100,000 people. The kidnapping in Algeria of three French diplomats for a week in October sparked an exodus of expatriates, and the murder in December of 12 Croatian and Bosnian workers brought the foreign death toll to 23 since September.

Morocco was boosted by a weakening of the nationalist Polisario Front in Western Sahara, although a meeting took place between Polisario officials and the Moroccan government on July 17–19 at El Aaiun in the disputed territory. The talks failed, however, to resolve the issue of voter eligibility in the proposed UN-sponsored referendum on the future of the ex-Spanish colony.

The four-year-old Arab Maghreb Union (AMU) remained paralyzed by political differences between Algeria, Morocco, Tunisia, Mauritania, and Libya. There was disagreement among the five partners over the Kuwait crisis in 1990–91, and this was heightened when Libya's AMU colleagues decided to follow the UN ruling on sanctions against Libya for its alleged role in the destruction of an airliner over Lockerbie, Scotland, in 1988.

The visit by Rabin to Rabat, Morocco, in September, on his way home from signing the accord with the PLO, was seen as an acknowledgement of Morocco's moderation and patient diplomacy. King Hassan, however, declined to follow up an Israeli invitation to visit Jerusalem. In a creative appointment on November 13, the Moroccan government named a Jewish Moroccan, Serge Berdugo, as tourism minister, the only Jewish minister in an Arab government.

On May 13 at Ain Beni Mathar, Morocco, a ceremony took place to mark the beginning of work on the Maghreb-Europe gas pipeline linking Algeria and Europe via Morocco. Relations between Algeria and Morocco were not judged sufficiently good, however, for heads of state to attend.

New UN sanctions, including a freeze on foreign assets, went into force against Libya on December 1 following a vote in the UN Security Council on November 11 after four months of lobbying by the U.K., the U.S., and France. On August 13 the three countries had given Libya a deadline of October 1 to comply with UN Resolutions 731 and 748, but this ultimatum passed without compliance by the Libyans. Tripoli's response to the tougher sanctions was as contradictory as ever. While Col. Muammar al-Qaddafi threatened to burn Libya's oil fields and ports in a gesture of defiance to the West, Maltese mediators said Libya was willing to let a U.K. or U.S. judge preside at the trial of the alleged Lockerbie bombers.

Tunisia and Morocco harboured hopes of closer ties with the EC. In Tunisia's case negotiators were seeking a comprehensive cooperation accord to improve substantially on the financial protocols and quota agreements that determined links across the Mediterranean. Morocco had abandoned its hopes of joining the EC but was seeking an improved economic accord. (JOHN WHELAN)

ALGERIA

Algeria is a republic of North Africa on the Mediterranean Sea. Area: 2,381,741 sq km (919,595 sq mi). Pop. (1993 est.): 27,029,000. Cap.: Algiers. Monetary unit: Algerian dinar, with (Oct. 4, 1993) an official rate of 19.20 dinars to U.S. $1 (29.09 dinars = £1 sterling). Chairman of the High State Council in 1993, Ali Kafi; prime ministers, Belaid Abdessalam and, from August 21, Redha Malek.

The Algerian government had to grapple with continued social tension throughout 1993 in the wake of the 1992 removal of Pres. Chadli Bendjedid's government by the army and its replacement by the High State Council (HSC), headed by Ali Kafi. Violence continued at levels similar to those of 1992, when more than 210 security personnel were

MERILLON/TURPIN—GAMMA LIAISON

Masked commandos ride a bus in Algiers. The Algerian government also was using troops to guard roads and public buildings against terrorist attacks by Islamic fundamentalists.

killed. By October 1993 around 1,000 Islamist sympathizers had died, 3,800 were before the special security courts, and 240 had been condemned to death. Despite the renewal of the state of emergency on February 9, attacks continued against prominent figures. On February 13 the defense minister, Khalid Nezzar, narrowly escaped assassination, and on August 22 former prime minister Kasdi Merbah was killed. A spate of killings of Algerian intellectuals led to a mass protest demonstration in Algiers on March 22, the same day on which 18 soldiers were massacred in their barracks at Bougzoul.

Despite government claims that the killings were the responsibility of the banned Islamic Salvation Front (FIS), the public continued to believe that others were involved, including independent Islamic groups, factions within the regime, and the clandestine secular opposition. The government's inability to end the violence only increased its unpopularity, despite a call for "dialogue" by Kafi in January with a promise that there would be constitutional reform later in the year. Neither dialogue nor reform occurred, however, as the major political parties resolutely remained opposed to the regime.

Instead, Prime Minister Belaid Abdessalam remained dedicated to a course of economic centralism, refused to reschedule Algeria's massive foreign debt (estimated at $24.4 billion), and showed a willingness to incur a heavy budget deficit to cover increased security and social service costs. Abdessalam was forced from office on August 21 by the HSC and replaced by a new administration led by Redha Malek, the former foreign minister and a member of the HSC. Malek reversed the policies of his predecessor toward debt rescheduling, maintained a resolute opposition to the Islamist movement, rejected dialogue, and relied on renewed repression. Nezzar—seen as the strongman of the regime—retired from government for health reasons in July, although he retained his position on the HSC.

On March 27 diplomatic relations with Iran were severed, and Algeria withdrew its ambassador from The Sudan on the grounds that both countries were aiding the Islamist movement. Algeria also joined with Tunisia and Egypt in a common front against regional Islamist influences at a meeting in Cairo in late June. Relations with Morocco declined during the year as a result of remarks made by King Hassan criticizing the suspension of the electoral process in Algeria. Support for Western Sahara improved as a result, although by the end of the year it appeared that Algeria had reluctantly accepted that Morocco would win control there.

(GEORGE JOFFÉ)

This article updates the *Macropædia* article NORTH AFRICA: *Algeria.*

BAHRAIN

The monarchy (emirate) of Bahrain consists of a group of islands in the Persian Gulf between the Qatar Peninsula and Saudi Arabia. Area: 695 sq km (268 sq mi). Pop. (1993 est.): 486,000. Cap.: Manama. Monetary unit: Bahrain dinar, with (Oct. 4, 1993) a free rate of 0.37 dinar to U.S. $1 (0.57 dinar = £1 sterling). Emir in 1993, Isa ibn Sulman al-Khalifah; prime minister, Khalifah ibn Sulman al-Khalifah.

The new 30-member consultative council met for the first time on Jan. 16, 1993, under its chairman, former transport minister Ibrahim Humaidan, in what was seen as a tentative step toward democracy. Among the councillors appointed by the emir, mainly from the business community, were a number of former members of the elected National Assembly that had been dissolved in 1975. Following the creation of the new council, the emir granted an amnesty to eight political prisoners and awarded pardons to 11 exiles in a gesture aimed at healing differences within the nation, which was evenly divided between Sunni and Shi'ite Muslims. Diplomats said that the consultative council gave further legitimacy to the monarchical regime and helped reinforce its image as a stable, tolerant centre for the Gulf region, specializing in banking, aluminum, ship repairs, oil refining, and petrochemicals.

Ali ibn Khalifah ibn Sulman al-Khalifah, a son of the prime minister, was appointed transport and communications minister to replace Humaidan. At the end of 1993, there were seven posts held by the ruling al-Khalifah family in the 17-member Cabinet.

Bahrain asserted its territorial claim against Qatar in regard to their long-running dispute over ownership of islands, sandbanks, and reefs by declaring in a government decree of April 20 a territorial-waters claim of 12 nautical miles. In an adjacent area of another 12 nautical miles, the government said that it "will exercise its rights to sovereignty as prescribed in international law."

(JOHN WHELAN)

This article updates the *Macropædia* article ARABIA: *Bahrain.*

CYPRUS

An island republic and member of the Commonwealth, Cyprus is in the eastern Mediterranean Sea. Island area: 9,251 sq km (3,572 sq mi). Island pop. (1993 est.): 764,000. Area of the Turkish Republic of Northern Cyprus (TRNC), proclaimed unilaterally (1983) in the occupied northern third of the island (controlled by Turkish Cypriots since 1974): 3,355 sq km (1,295 sq mi); pop. (1993 est.): 178,000. Cap.: Nicosia. Monetary unit: Cyprus pound, with (Oct. 4, 1993) a free rate of £C 0.49 to U.S. $1 (£C 0.75 = £1 sterling). Presidents in 1993, George Vassiliou and, from February 28, Glafcos Clerides. President of TRNC in 1993, Rauf Denktash.

The year 1993 in Cyprus was symbolized by the main international event on the island, the Commonwealth summit conference in October. Like the Commonwealth itself, Cypriot politics were long on rhetoric and history and short on achievement. The division of the island would reach the 20-year mark in 1994, and although talks at unification continued, there were strong forces to maintain the status quo.

Greek Cypriot Pres. George Vassiliou, who had started in office by promising a settlement of the dispute with the Turkish Republic of Northern Cyprus (TRNC) within six months, ended his term in defeat after five years on February 14 by losing a second-round election runoff to veteran conservative campaigner Glafcos Clerides. The campaign was dominated by a single issue, the UN "set of ideas" for reunification. These would reduce Turkish Cypriot territory from 38% of the island to about 28%. Cyprus would become a federal nation, with freedom of movement but limited settlement rights between the Greek and Turkish zones. During the campaign Clerides, leader of the right-wing Democratic Rally, claimed that Vassiliou had sold out and would not be able to amend the UN proposals, particularly on the issue of returning 200,000 Greek Cypriots to their lost homes in the occupied north. Vassiliou, seeking his second term, accepted the UN ideas, with negotiated amendments, as a basis for a settlement. Enough voters agreed with Clerides to hand him victory by less than 0.5% of the 393,375 ballots cast in a nearly 100% turnout.

Amid growing international impatience with the Cypriots, on May 11 Russia used its first veto in the UN since 1984 to block a resolution calling for the costs of the Cyprus peacekeeping force to be divided among all UN members instead of relying on voluntary donations. Canada then pulled out its troops from the force. They were replaced by an Argentine contingent.

Clerides and Denktash met on May 24. Confidence-building measures were the main topic, amid speculation that Denktash would return the deserted border town of Varosha-Famagusta to Greek Cyprus as a goodwill gesture. But when Denktash tried to wrest an implied recognition of the TRNC from Clerides, the talks were doomed. By the end of the year, the Cyprus problem was back on a familiar track—no progress, no concessions.

The Commonwealth conference gave Denktash another opportunity to dig his heels in. He said that the basis for a settlement in Cyprus was destroyed by the final Commonwealth communiqué, which he called "biased." The communiqué demanded the speedy withdrawal of Turkey's 35,000 troops and 50,000 mainland settlers from the north. It also demanded the return of 180,000 Greek Cypriots to their homes there.

Important political developments took place in the north late in the year. In a dispute with Prime Minister Dervis Eroglu, who advocated a harder line against the Greek Cypriots, Denktash dissolved the TRNC parliament on October 20 and called for elections on December 12, more than a year and a half before they were due. A coalition government was being formed in late December.

(THOMAS O'DWYER)

EGYPT

A republic of North Africa, Egypt has coastlines on the Mediterranean and Red seas. Area: 997,739 sq km (385,229 sq mi). Pop. (1993 est.): 57,109,000. Cap.: Cairo. Monetary unit: Egyptian pound, with (Oct. 4, 1993) a free rate of LE 3.32 to U.S. $1 (LE 5.03 = £1 sterling). President in 1993, Hosni Mubarak; prime minister, Atef Sedki.

Islamic militants carried out a new wave of political violence and attacks on tourists as Pres. Hosni Mubarak faced renewed pressure for reform from both the establishment and the legitimate opposition. Abroad the president played a central role in the Middle East peace process, while a new three-year program was agreed with the International Monetary Fund (IMF), providing further evidence of Egypt's progress toward liberalization of the economy.

On October 4 a nationwide presidential referendum endorsed Mubarak for a third six-year term. A major campaign by the ruling National Democratic Party left Cairo plastered in "Yes, to Mubarak" posters, and the president, who was the only candidate, duly received 96% of the valid votes cast. However, only about 19 million Egyptians, or some 33% of the total population, bothered to register for what was seen by many as a foregone conclusion.

The day after the referendum, the president promoted the defense minister, Gen. Muhammad Hussain Tantawi, to the rank of field marshal—only the fifth Egyptian army commander to receive this honour in 40 years. Nevertheless, Mubarak declined to name a vice president—and, therefore, heir apparent—at the beginning of his third term. The government's alliance with the military remained strong, with Tantawi stating on October 11 that the armed forces were ready to intervene as a last line of defense against the regime's increasingly violent Islamic opponents.

During his inauguration on October 13, the president promised the People's Assembly "new blood," but when his new Cabinet was announced, it was hallmarked by continuity rather than change. Prime Minister Atef Sedki, in office since 1986, was retained and became the longest serving Egyptian prime minister since Gamal Abdel Nasser's coup in the 1950s. Eleven new ministers joined the 34-member Cabinet, but the key portfolios of foreign affairs, defense, interior, finance, petroleum, and information were untouched.

Among the major ministerial changes were the appointments of Ismail Hassan, a seasoned commercial banker, as the new central bank governor with Cabinet rank; Atef Obeid as minister for the public business sector and environmental affairs; Mahmoud Muhammad Mahmoud as minister of economy and foreign trade; and Mamdouh Beltagui as tourism minister. The latter promotion was at the expense of Fouad Sultan, a popular figure with the business community, who was fired from the top job at tourism.

Domestic Affairs. The new government quickly affirmed its determination to continue iron-fisted policies against fundamentalist-inspired violence, which had led to the killing of more than 200 people in 18 months and a severe slump in tourism. Although attacks on Coptic Christians diminished, assaults on tourists intensified in 1993. On June 8 a bomb was thrown at a tourist bus in Giza's Pyramid Road, killing an Egyptian and wounding five foreigners and nine Egyptians. Later in the year a gunman shot dead two Americans and one Frenchman as they dined at Cairo's expatriate-managed Semiramis Hotel. In March, the bloodiest month for militant attacks, 45 people were killed (including at least 29 killed by security forces) in bomb attacks, raids,

STERN/BLACK STAR

An image of Hosni Mubarak, running for his third term as president of Egypt, adorns a coffee shop in Cairo. Despite opposition by Islamic militants and by others who charged the president with stifling democratic reforms, 96% of voters said "yes" to six more years of Mubarak.

and shootouts between religious extremists and the security forces; about 700 suspects were rounded up. On March 29, al-Jama'a al-Islamiya, an extremist group, claimed responsibility for an explosion at the pyramid of Chephren. In a fax to news organizations on March 5, it warned investors "to liquidate their investments in Egypt at the earliest opportunity," as they could become a target. A second fax sent on March 30 warned tourists and investors to quit Egypt before it was too late.

On March 20, Egypt's Nobel Prize-winning novelist Naguib Mahfouz published a warning to the government in an Italian newspaper, which was widely quoted in the local press. He urged the authorities to heed demands for democratic reforms and said growing corruption in government was making Egyptians respond favourably to extremists.

On April 18 the interior minister, Muhammad ʿAbd al-Halim Moussa, was sacked in what was seen as a signal to militants that there would be no negotiated truce. Moussa had embarrassed the government by sanctioning mediation efforts with the militants through the efforts of a television evangelist, Sheikh Muhammad Mitwalli ash-Sharaawi. His successor, Hassan Muhammad al-Alfi, a former governor of Asyut, promised a new approach through tougher police action. On August 18 terrorists detonated a bomb as Alfi's motorcade neared the Interior Ministry—the second abortive attempt to assassinate a member of the Egyptian government. In April guerrillas had ambushed the minister of information, Muhammad Safwat ash-Sharif, who was slightly wounded. The August bomb killed 5 people and wounded 16, including Alfi. It was carried out by the Vanguards of Conquest, a hitherto unknown extremist splinter group. Prime Minister Sedki escaped injury in a car-bomb attack on November 25, which killed a schoolgirl and wounded 21 others. On December 29 government forces arrested a number of militants thought to be planning the assassination of officials.

The government also cracked down on the more moderate Islamic movement, represented by the banned Muslim Brotherhood, by rushing through new laws restricting trade unions. In elections to the journalists union on March 21, a Mubarak supporter was elected chairman, defeating an Islamic candidate. Nevertheless, a government appeal for constitutional parties to unite against extremists was supported by only 5 of Egypt's 11 political parties and 10 of the 22 unions. The Muslim Brotherhood and its proxy, the Socialist Labour Party, were excluded from the appeal.

On August 14 government policy suffered a setback when a civil judge acquitted Islamic fundamentalist suspects of the 1990 murder of parliamentary speaker Rifaat al-Mahgoub because evidence allegedly had been extracted under torture. By the end of October, however, the mass trials by the military courts—denounced by the London-based human rights organization Amnesty International as a "travesty of justice"—had passed at least 30 death sentences.

On May 24 the 1993–94 budget was passed by the People's Assembly with a 4.5% rise in total expenditure, less than half the rate of inflation. Egypt managed in 1992–93 to cut its budget deficit to a little over the IMF target of 3.5–4%. Expenditure on food subsidies was to be cut, but the prime minister stressed that there would be no rise in the price of bread. On September 20 the IMF approved a three-year fund facility program for Egypt, backed by about $569 million, but with $17 billion in international reserves Egypt was not expected to draw down the funds. Having received the IMF loan, Egypt was free to enter the second stage of its 1991 Paris Club debt-restructuring agreement. To achieve the IMF deal, Egypt accepted preconditions that included further steps on economic reform.

Foreign Affairs. Egypt's support for the Middle East peace process was a major boost for U.S. Pres. Bill Clinton, although Cairo felt slighted at the lack of recognition of its mediation role. Egyptian mediation efforts also extended to its western neighbour, Libya. In November Jordan's King Hussein visited Cairo for talks with Mubarak, ending the three years of bitter relations that had begun with the Persian Gulf crisis in 1990.

On May 9–16, Mubarak undertook a tour of the Gulf Co-operation Council (GCC) states in an effort to isolate Iran, which Egypt accused of backing Islamic extremist groups. Mubarak claimed he had details of Iranian "mobilizations" of warships around Port Sudan, 100 km (160 mi) south of the disputed Hala'ib border area, and threatened to strike immediately if the warships used the port. The GCC states, however, were nervous about offending Iran and declined to give explicit public support. Mubarak was more successful in cutting off Gulf state funds for the militants in Egypt, as Saudi Arabia and the United Arab Emirates issued decrees banning nongovernmental Muslim charities from sending money abroad.

The 29th summit of the Organization of African Unity (OAU) took place in Cairo on June 28–30, presided over by Mubarak as the new OAU chairman—the second time in 10 years. At the meeting Mubarak met the Sudanese president, Lieut. Gen. Omar Hassan Ahmad al-Bashir, and agreed to halt a war of words with the Sudanese government. On June 22, The Sudan had ordered Egypt to close its consulates in Port Sudan and al-Ubbayid as tension mounted over Egypt's military warning to The Sudan over movements in the Hala'ib border area.

On July 4, Egypt requested the extradition from the U.S. of Sheikh Omar Abdel-Rahman, the spiritual mentor of al-Jama'a al-Islamiya, over alleged involvement in violence in 1989. Sheikh Omar was arrested in the U.S. on July 2 on immigration charges. Fourteen men with links to the sheikh were also indicted in the U.S. in connection with the February 26 bombing of the World Trade Center in New York City and other crimes. Lawyers queried the validity of Cairo's request, as Egypt's only extradition treaty with Washington dated to 1874. (JOHN WHELAN)

IRAN

The Islamic Republic of Iran is in southwestern Asia on the Caspian and Arabian seas and the Persian Gulf. Area: 1,638,057 sq km (632,457 sq mi). Pop. (1993 est., including about 2.3 million Afghan refugees): 60,768,000. Cap.: Tehran. Monetary unit: Iranian rial, with (Oct. 4, 1993) a free rate of 1,587 rials to U.S. $1 (2,404 rials = £1 sterling). *Rahbar* (spiritual leader) in 1993, Ayatollah Sayyed Ali Khamenei; president, Hojatolislam Hashemi Ali Akbar Rafsanjani.

Presidential elections were held on June 11, 1993. Of the 128 candidates initially nominated, only 4 were endorsed by the 12-man Council of Guardians, including Pres. Hashemi Rafsanjani; Ahmad Tavakkoli, editor of *Resalat* newspaper; Abdullah Jasbi of the Supreme Council of the Cultural Revolution; and Rajabali Taheri, a former revolutionary guard commander. Though Rafsanjani conducted a low-key campaign, he emerged as the winner, capturing 63.2% of the votes. A turnout of only 57.6% of the electorate, compared with 68.3% in the 1989 presidential election, indicated a measure of voter apathy. Rafsanjani would serve his second and final four-year term as president under the existing constitutional arrangements.

It was expected that Rafsanjani would use his election victory to reassert his authority on the regime, to press for greater economic growth, and to open up the country to

Their faces uncovered, Iranian women eat in a restaurant in Tehran. Despite indications that some Islamic restrictions had eased, the government remained under the firm control of fundamentalists.
JEAN GUAM—MAGNUM

the outside world. A major Cabinet reshuffle did not occur, however, and on August 8 a list of 23 Cabinet members was sent to the Majlis (parliament) for approval. Of the five new candidates proposed for the Ministries of Defense, Culture, Interior, Health, and Housing, none represented serious changes in either policies or the political balance between reformists and hard-liners within the regime. The nomination of the minister of economy and finance, Mohsen Nurbakhsh, was rejected by the Majlis and was seen as a repudiation of his failed economic policies. On completion of the new Cabinet, it was clear that there would not be a sweeping political or economic reorientation and that the country would continue to drift as a result of the unresolved competition between reformists and hard-liners.

Foreign policy also suffered from a lack of clear direction as a result of deep political ambivalence about the desirability of more diplomatic and commercial involvement with the international community. Iran discounted a change in the U.S. outlook toward Iran under Pres. Bill Clinton, and by April the accusation by U.S. Secretary of State Warren Christopher that Iran was an "outlaw" nation had ensured that relations would remain distant. Alleged Iranian support for the Islamic government in The Sudan and for Islamic revivalist groups in Egypt, Algeria, Lebanon, and the West Bank added to friction between Iran and the U.S. Claims that Iran was involved in terrorism, including the attempted murder of the Norwegian publisher of Salman Rushdie's *Satanic Verses,* gave rise to further suspicions that Iran remained active in international terrorism. As a result, the U.S. threatened to isolate Iran (and Iraq) through a policy of dual containment. Meanwhile, the Rushdie issue remained an obstacle in relations with both the United Kingdom and the European Community as Rushdie launched a more active public campaign to have the 1989 death sentence against him rescinded.

On May 25, Iran attacked opposition Mujahedin-e Khalq army bases in Iraq. After a three-year lull, some small progress was made toward reopening negotiations with Iraq on UN Resolution 598, which outlined the terms for ending the eight-year Iran-Iraq war. A deputy foreign minister from Iran visited Baghdad in mid-October for talks on prisoner exchanges and other matters. Conflict subsided between Iran and the United Arab Emirates over the status of Abu Musa island and the two islands of Greater and Lesser Tunb, all seized by Iran in 1971. Iranian participation in the annual hajj to Mecca in May was vetoed by Saudi Arabia. A limited measure of cooperation between Iran and other Gulf oil-producing nations occurred during the September OPEC ministerial meeting in Geneva. Iran later projected a less popular image, however, by taking a strong line against the Israeli-Palestinian accords of September 13 and by promising to give assistance to Palestinian groups opposing the pact.

The government faced a growing economic crisis in 1993. Though oil production rose to 3.7 million bbl and exports increased to more than 2.6 million bbl, international oil prices fell. Annual oil revenues were $13.5 billion, lagging behind a forecast target of $16 billion. The country's growing trade deficit soared to $3 billion, and foreign debt climbed to $30 billion. Economic growth fell off markedly to some 3% in real terms; per capita income languished at $2,000, the lowest level since the 1979 revolution; and the Iranian rial weakened against most hard currencies.

(KEITH S. MCLACHLAN)

IRAQ

A republic of southwestern Asia, Iraq has a short coastline on the Persian Gulf. Area: 435,052 sq km (167,975 sq mi). Pop. (1993 est.): 19,435,000. Cap.: Baghdad. Monetary unit: Iraqi dinar, with (Oct. 4, 1993) an official rate of 0.31 dinar to U.S. $1 (free rate of 0.47 dinar = £1 sterling); a truer value of the dinar was on the black market, where in late September about 90 dinars = U.S. $1 (about 137 dinars = £1 sterling). President in 1993, Saddam Hussein; prime ministers, Muhammad Hamzah az-Zubaydi and, from September 5, Ahmad Husayn Khudayir as-Samarrai.

Pres. Saddam Hussein celebrated his 56th birthday on April 28, 1993, with an ancient Babylonian-style procession, parading in a gold carriage drawn by six black horses. The folk dancing, military march past, and air-force flyover were seen as signs of Baghdad's defiance of the international community. Two days later the U.S. State Department named Iraq—with Iran, Syria, Cuba, Libya, and North Korea—as a country that sponsors "state terrorism."

Tension erupted in the Shatt al-Arab waterway in April when an Iraqi gunboat seized an Iranian vessel, although details of the incident were not reported until July. In mid-July, Iraq also was reported to the UN by Saudi Arabia for "border provocation" when its troops opened fire on Saudi border positions. On November 24 the speaker of the Iraqi parliament, Saadi Mahdi Salih, said Iraq would not agree to long-term monitoring of its military industries without guarantees that compliance would result in the UN Security Council's lifting sanctions.

Tensions with the U.S. rose in mid-January when the Iraqis were given until January 15 to dismantle six police posts close to the Kuwaiti border. In the final hours of U.S. Pres. George Bush's term of office, Tomahawk cruise missiles once again hammered the Iraqi capital, with attacks on a factory in a Baghdad suburb suspected as being part of the government's nuclear-weapons-building capability. The al-Rashid Hotel, home to visiting foreign journalists, was also hit, and three civilians were killed. The U.S. subsequently said the hotel had not been a target and blamed the civilian deaths on Iraqi interception of a missile. In a blatantly political gesture, Hussein declared a "cease-fire" on the day before Pres. Bill Clinton's inauguration. By January 23 hostilities had temporarily ceased. At the end of June, however, U.S. warships fired 23 missiles on Baghdad in a bid to destroy the Iraqi intelligence-service headquarters. Six civilians were killed when three missiles strayed off their target, but the Clinton administration said the attack had been a success in "crippling Iraq's intelligence capability." By November 14 the Iraqi government was claiming that its intelligence headquarters had been rebuilt. The attack was in apparent retaliation for an alleged Iraqi plot to assassinate Bush while he was on a visit to Kuwait. The Kuwaiti government claimed to have evidence of three separate conspiracies to kill Bush—two by car bombs and one by a suicide bomber. U.S. investigators confirmed the allegations, which were based on the interrogation of 16 suspects.

On August 2, the third anniversary of Iraq's seizure of Kuwait and called the Yom al-Nidaa (Day of Calling), Iraqi newspapers issued belligerent and unrepentant statements aimed at destabilizing Kuwait. *Al-Thawra* said in an editorial that Kuwait had always been part of Iraq and that this fact could not be subject to negotiation. Kuwait's response was to proceed with building border defenses. On November 18, and again two days later, Iraqi farmers and other workers demonstrated at Umm Qasr against the border fortifications. Iraq continued to hold Britons convicted of illegally entering Iraq through the Kuwaiti border but released Kenneth Beaty, a U.S. oil worker, after he had served six months of an eight-year jail sentence for an identical offense.

On November 15 the British government released photographs of villages destroyed in the marshlands of southern Iraq. Evidence continued to mount of a deliberate strategy by the Baghdad government to drain the marshlands in a bid to extinguish Shi'ite rebel strongholds. It was reported that thousands of marsh Arabs had fled to nearby villages and into Iran. The Iraqi nuclear researcher Hussain Shahristiani, who had defected to the West, alleged that on September 26 Iraqi security forces had killed hundreds in a chemical weapons attack on villages in the south.

Although the government remained in control of the country, a car bomb exploded in Baghdad on August 4. The president's son Uday Hussein escaped an assassination attempt in May, and an attempt on the president's life was reported in June. (JOHN WHELAN)

ISRAEL

A republic of southwestern Asia, Israel is situated on the Mediterranean Sea. Area: 20,700 sq km (7,992 sq mi), not including territory occupied in the June 1967 war. Pop. (1993 est.): 5,451,000. Cap.: Jerusalem (but *see* Israel table in *World Data* section). Monetary unit: New (Israeli) sheqel, with (Oct. 4, 1993) a free rate of 2.84 sheqalim to U.S. $1 (4.30 sheqalim = £1 sterling). Presidents in 1993, Chaim Herzog and, from March 24, Ezer Weizman; prime minister, Yitzhak Rabin.

Soon after his Labour-dominated coalition won power in the summer of 1992, Prime Minister Yitzhak Rabin embarked on a mission to redraw the political map of the Middle East; his plan assumed an altogether new dimension in 1993 when he finalized historic accords with Palestine Liberation Organization (PLO) leader Yasir Arafat on September 13 in Washington, D.C.

Barely six months after assuming office, Rabin had established his political authority in a manner the country had not witnessed since the golden days of its first prime minister, David Ben-Gurion, some 45 years earlier. With diplomatic patience, political insight, and a deliberate sense of purpose, Rabin subdued hostilities with the Likud and right-wing opposition parties and pacified his quarrelsome religious and left-wing coalition partners. He needed both to maintain his working majority in the Knesset (parliament). Rabin accomplished this feat despite persistent Palestinian and Arab demands for concessions deemed unacceptable by Israel, repeated acts of Palestinian terrorism, and cool relations with both the United Nations and the European Community (EC). Relations with the U.S. remained undefined during the transition of presidential leadership from George Bush to Bill Clinton. However, during a March 15 meeting in Washington, D.C., between Clinton and Rabin, the basis for renewed cordial relations was established.

Although many secret meetings with Arab leaders had taken place over the years, usually through the mediation of third parties, there had been no such rapprochement at any time with the Palestinians. Further, none of these meetings had produced tangible results. The stalemate continued

SHYAM BHATIA—THE OBSERVER

On the lookout for government patrols, Shi'ite rebels stand guard in the marshes of southern Iraq. The Iraqi government continued to drain the marshes, thus removing the rebels' cover.

A Palestinian motorcade in Gaza celebrates the accords reached with Israel in September. The agreements guaranteed Israel's security and provided for Palestinian self-rule in the Gaza Strip and in the West Bank town of Jericho.
ALLEN TANNENBAUM—SYGMA

into 1993 despite the ongoing "peace process" talks that were launched in October 1991 in Madrid and moved to Washington.

A number of seemingly unrelated developments, however, introduced a new dimension into Israeli policy making. It had become evident to Rabin by late February 1993 that no real progress was being made in Washington with the Syrians and the Palestinians. Virtual agreement had been reached with Jordan, but King Hussein was not prepared to settle with Israel until parallel agreements had been made with Syria and the Palestinians.

In some ways Rabin's unique style accentuated the deadlock. Unlike the former prime minister, Yitzhak Shamir, Rabin wanted to talk, negotiate, offer concessions, and make peace with Syria, Jordan, and the Palestinians. The impact on the Arab negotiators was dramatic. They could no longer blame Israel for being inflexible. As a result, they were unsure how to respond. The Syrians became more extreme; the West Bank Palestinian leaders insisted on referring all substantial decisions to Arafat, who presided in Tunis, Tunisia.

As a result, Prime Minister Rabin and Foreign Minister Shimon Peres decided, together with a small number of trusted officials, that it was time to open backdoor negotiations with Arafat. Rabin reasoned that since decisions were being made by Arafat in Tunis and not by the Palestinian leaders in Jerusalem, it made more sense to deal with the source of power. There was another, perhaps more compelling, reason for dealing directly with Arafat. The PLO leader was in dire trouble: he was publicly abused and written off by many of his former friends and supporters; important officials had resigned or withdrawn from his organization; and his administration and PLO institutions were financially bankrupt and could no longer meet their commitments.

Arafat, never before so vulnerable, looked in vain for help from the Arab states and from his own ranks. Rabin's secret initiative offered him and the Palestinians a lifeline that could save him and the Palestinian cause. The price was peace with Israel. Both Rabin and Arafat understood that the negotiations would have to be both secretly conducted and concluded with the help of a trusted and credible third party. Information would have to be withheld from all except those who had need to know. Washington, Jerusalem, and Cairo, notorious sources of news leaks, would not be informed. The invaluable and discreet third party was Norwegian Foreign Minister Johan Jorgen Holst and a few hand-picked members of his staff.

During negotiations total secrecy and strict confidentiality was maintained. Rabin delegated Peres to oversee the Israeli interests, and Arafat nominated one of his veteran political advisers, Mahmoud Abbas, known as Abu Mazen, to take charge for the Palestinians. The meetings were conducted at a country house provided by the Norwegian Foreign Ministry, and the staff and facilities were furnished by the foreign minister. Both the U.S. and Israeli governments were unaware of the talks. The Palestinian, Arab, and Israeli delegations, deadlocked in negotiations in Washington, had no inkling either until the first rumours surfaced in the Israeli and Palestinian media following comments by one of Arafat's disgruntled "political advisers," Bassam Abu Sharif, whose advice Arafat had neither sought nor taken.

For five months, from April to the end of August, Israeli and Arab politicians and diplomats argued in Washington while the Norwegian-sponsored talks were secretly taking place in Oslo. There once-deadly foes—the Israeli and PLO leaders—fashioned a new order in Arab-Israeli relations.

Rabin's firmness of purpose and Arafat's desperate political need overcame the last-minute threat to the peace talks. The pro-Iranian Hezbollah fundamentalists launched rocket attacks, possibly with Syrian support, against northern Israel with the evident intention of derailing an Israeli-Palestinian agreement. Rabin ordered a fearsome retaliation in kind. Some 300,000 southern Lebanese were temporarily displaced and fled north before returning to their villages. The northern front became relatively quiet. Syria's attempt to assert a predominant position on its own terms had been suppressed by Israel's military response. The time had come to announce Israel's secret negotiations with the PLO.

The existence of the talks was revealed in late August. The climax to those clandestine meetings occurred on September 13. In Washington, with President Clinton as host, Rabin and Arafat met and shook hands. Peres and Abbas signed the Declaration of Principles, which outlined the process and timing of self-rule for the Palestinians. By the end of October, detailed negotiations for the implementation of the Gaza-Jericho agreement and phased Israeli withdrawal from the West Bank were under way. The discussions for Palestinian autonomy, including the civilian takeover of municipal and policing functions, were held in Taba, Egypt.

Though the taboo blocking negotiations between the leaders of Israel and the PLO had been broken, acceptance of the Israeli-PLO accords by those in occupied areas and in surrounding regions would take time. After the accords went into effect on October 13, Israel pledged to release more than 10,000 Palestinians still held in Israeli jails. In an opening gesture Israel freed Salim al-Zreii, the longest-held prisoner (23 years). Soon afterward hundreds of others were given their freedom. Later that month Israel eased long-standing travel restrictions, allowing Palestinians in the occupied territories to enter Israel, Jerusalem in particular. In December the last 200 Palestinians exiled to Lebanon in 1992 were allowed to return.

In November Teddy Kollek, mayor of Jerusalem for 28 years, was soundly defeated in elections by hard-liner Ehud Olmert, a member of the opposition Likud. The defeat of Kollek was viewed as a rebuke to Rabin, who had urged the octogenarian to run for office, even though Kollek had planned to retire.

Tensions heightened in the occupied territories following the signing of the September 13 accords, and three moderate Palestinians were assassinated. The most notable victim, Assad Saftawi, a close associate of Arafat, was murdered by two masked Palestinian gunmen on October 21. Israeli settlers in the occupied areas voiced their displeasure by rioting in the West Bank and Gaza Strip. On November 9 Rabin met with three leaders representing the settlers. He promised not to abandon them when Palestinian self-rule took effect.

The international response to the Israeli-Palestinian accords was dramatic and swift. The U.S. pledged some $2 billion; $400 million was promised by EC donors; and the World Bank vowed to raise $475 million annually for 10 years.

Efforts to meet the December 13 deadline for implementing the accords were unsuccessful, however. Key issues included Israel's insistence on controlling the borders with Jordan and Egypt and the question of the size of the Jericho area to be under Palestinian control. Talks continued, nonetheless, and progress was reported at the end of the year.

Earlier in the year the Knesset elected as Israel's seventh president 69-year-old Ezer Weizman, a nephew of Israel's first president and chief of the country's air force during the 1967 Six-Day War. Weizman, a forthright advocate of peace and a supporter of Rabin, had played an important role in making peace with Egypt in 1979.

In March the Likud elected Benjamin ("Bibi") Netanyahu (*see* BIOGRAPHIES) its new leader. It was a difficult inauguration for the new party head, who vociferously opposed the Israeli-Palestinian accords even though Rabin's initiative had produced a favourable response at home and abroad.

As the year closed, Israel began to savour the dividends of making peace with the PLO. New areas of the world economy, hitherto closed as a result of the Arab economic boycott, were beginning to open. India led the way, and China followed. On his way home from an official visit to Beijing (Peking), Rabin made an unannounced visit to meet with Indonesian President Suharto in Jakarta. Indonesia boasted the largest Muslim population in the world. Agreements were in the negotiation stages with important European-U.S. multinationals and with several Arab Gulf states. In mid-November Peres announced that a peace agreement with Jordan was close to being initialed. After 45 years Israel had emerged from the economic isolation precipitated by the Arab boycott, and it was the only country to enjoy and benefit from a free-trade agreement with both the EC and the United States. For all practical purposes the Arab boycott, which had done so much damage to Israel, remained little more than a polite fiction by the end of 1993. At the opening of the 1993 General Assembly, for the first time since Israel became a member of the United Nations, no Arab delegation challenged its membership.

On November 7, some 500 years after the expulsion of Jews from Spain by King Ferdinand and Queen Isabella, Spain's King Juan Carlos and Queen Sophia visited Israel as part of a policy of reconciliation. On December 29 the Vatican and Israel announced that they would establish diplomatic relations. (JON KIMCHE)

JORDAN

A constitutional monarchy, Jordan is located in southwestern Asia and has a short coastline on the Gulf of Aqaba. Area: 88,946 sq km (34,342 sq mi). Pop. (1993 est.): 3,764,000. Cap.: Amman. Monetary unit: Jordan dinar, with (Oct. 4, 1993) an official rate of 0.69 dinar to U.S. $1 (1.04 dinars = £1 sterling). King, Hussein I; prime ministers in 1993, Sharif Zaid ibn Shaker and, from May 29, ʿAbd as-Salam al-Majali.

Muslim fundamentalists retained the largest bloc of deputies in parliamentary elections on Nov. 8, 1993, but suffered a decline in the number of seats they held. Widespread speculation that King Hussein would postpone the election to prevent it from becoming a referendum on the Arab-Israeli peace process proved unfounded.

Voters elected 16 candidates to the 80-member parliament from the Islamic Action Front (IAF), the political wing of the Muslim Brotherhood, down from 22 in 1989. The outcome gave a moral victory to King Hussein, who had followed a policy of accommodating Muslim extremists within the political system rather than excluding them, as in Algeria and Egypt. Political parties had been legalized in 1992 after a 35-year ban.

Although some 20 parties contested the election, the majority of elected deputies were tribal and centrist, without party ties. Only six candidates from non-IAF parties won seats, prompting King Hussein to say at a postelection press conference on November 9 that he hoped the next time there would be fewer parties. Fundamentalist candidates performed well in Jordan's nontribal urban areas of Amman and az-Zarqa, where high unemployment and poverty made them perfect breeding grounds for radicalism. Jordan's first woman parliamentarian, Toujan Faisal, was an activist branded by fundamentalists as an apostate. (For tabulated results, see *Political Parties,* above.)

Turnout was 68% of the about 1.2 million-member electorate, which voted on a "one person, one vote" system following a new electoral law that was introduced after the dissolution of the House of Deputies on August 4. Ten days before polling, a ban on political rallies was rescinded. By polling day the kingdom was festooned with posters, banners, and campaign leaflets, but manifestos consisted mostly of little more than slogans calling for national unity, Arab unity, a free Palestine, and democracy for all.

The parliament opened again on November 23 to consider a draft budget of 1.5 billion dinars. The assembly was expected to support government policies, especially the peace process, although the peace process was rejected by the IAF. U.K.-educated ʿAbd as-Salam al-Majali had been appointed on May 29 to head a caretaker government of 26 ministers after the resignation of Prime Minister Sharif Zaid ibn Shaker. Sami Qammuh was named as finance minister to replace Basil Jardaneh. The new Cabinet contained two Christians and six Jordanians of Palestinian origin. Majali was named again in the Cabinet announced December 1.

On September 14, Jordan signed an agreement with Israel to cover future talks, taking into account the Israeli-Palestinian accords signed the previous day. Jordanian hopes of a huge "peace dividend" were without foundation, but in the improved climate U.S. Pres. Bill Clinton on September 15 released grant aid frozen since 1992.

Children carry posters of an Islamic fundamentalist candidate at a preelection rally in Amman. In the vote on November 8, Jordan's first multiparty elections since 1956, moderate candidates supporting peace talks with Israel won an overwhelming majority.
REUTERS/BETTMANN

In another hopeful sign, Israeli Foreign Minister Shimon Peres met Crown Prince Hassan for talks on October 1 with Clinton in Washington, D.C. As the year ended, Jordan was close to signing an agreement with the Palestine Liberation Organization that would give the central bank of Jordan wide-ranging monetary responsibilities in the occupied territories during the transitional period of Palestinian self-rule.

On June 25, King Hussein left the U.S. after a visit that included cordial talks with Clinton and a health checkup at the Mayo Clinic. Observers pointed to an improvement in bilateral relations, which had been soured by Jordan's support for Iraq during the Gulf war. A young Jordanian of Palestinian origin, Mohammad Salameh, was charged with bombing the World Trade Center in New York City on February 26, and on March 1 the U.S. government warned its nationals not to travel to Jordan. King Hussein had earlier expressed dismay at U.S. attacks on Baghdad, Iraq, and said he would work to break Iraq's isolation in the Arab world. Jordan continued to mend fences with the other Gulf states, welcoming back the Qatari ambassador. Only Kuwait continued to reject any dialogue with Amman.

(JOHN WHELAN)

KUWAIT

A constitutional monarchy (emirate), Kuwait is in the northeastern Arabian Peninsula, on the Persian Gulf. Area: 17,818 sq km (6,880 sq mi). Pop. (1993 est.): 1,433,000. Cap.: Kuwait City. Monetary unit: Kuwaiti dinar, with (Oct. 4, 1993) an official rate of 0.30 dinar to U.S. $1 (0.45 dinar = £1 sterling). Emir, Sheikh Jabir al-Ahmad al-Jabir as-Sabah; prime minister in 1993, Crown Prince Sheikh Saad al-Abdullah as-Salim as-Sabah.

Kuwait's elected National Assembly assumed a greater importance in domestic policy in 1993 as the government continued to rebuild the emirate's economic and military power following the Iraqi invasion crisis of 1990–91. The government remained implacably opposed to reconciliation with Iraq or its Arab supporters, including Jordan, Yemen, and the Palestine Liberation Organization, and started work on border fortifications that would include the deployment of 1.3 million Iraqi land mines recovered after the Gulf war. In March the armed forces chief of staff, Gen. Sheikh Jabir al-Khaled as-Sabah, resigned in the face of continued criticism of his failure to defend Kuwait against Iraqi attack.

On February 3 the UN Security Council agreed on the deployment of a single battalion of troops to Kuwait, which resulted in the dispatch of 750 Argentine soldiers. The U.S. sent troops and the U.K. a token force. Early in the year Kuwait confirmed the purchase of 236 U.S. tanks and $200 million worth of Patriot surface-to-air missiles, providing further evidence of its weapons buildup.

In a major policy statement on March 7, the Kuwaiti government reacted with some irritation to reconciliation initiatives with Iraq started by Qatar, saying that it was not even looking for a mediator. On June 20 the exiled Iran-based leader of the Supreme Assembly for Islamic Revolution in Iraq, Muhammad Baqir al-Hakim, was accorded full diplomatic honours while on a visit to Kuwait, underlining the government's support of political opponents of Iraqi Pres. Saddam Hussein. On April 12 the speaker of the National Assembly, Jassem as-Saadoun, claimed that he had been attacked by two Iraqi delegates while attending a parliamentary conference in India. On April 26, 14 alleged Iraqi terrorists were arrested near the border with arms and explosives, including a 250-kg (550-lb) booby-trapped bomb.

The National Assembly also probed widely into domestic affairs. In February it passed a bill requiring full disclosure of investments by government-owned companies where the state's holding was more than 25% of the equity. In early June the government agreed to relax its secondary trade boycott against Israel, allowing foreign companies that did business with Israel to trade with Kuwait but not allowing direct links with Israeli companies.

Kuwait's oil production rose to 2,160,000 bbl a day by September, continuing the remarkable recovery since the invasion. Oil Minister Ali Ahmad al-Baghli was put in a difficult position, however, with Kuwait exceeding OPEC's quotas for most of the year. (JOHN WHELAN)

This article updates the *Macropædia* article ARABIA: *Kuwait.*

LEBANON

A republic of southwestern Asia, Lebanon is situated on the Mediterranean Sea. Area: 10,230 sq km (3,950 sq mi). Pop. (1993 est.): 2,909,000 (including Palestinian refugees estimated to number more than 300,000). Cap.: Beirut. Monetary unit: Lebanese pound, with (Oct. 4, 1993) a free rate of LL 1,711 to U.S. $1 (LL 2,593 = £1 sterling). President in 1993, Elias Hrawi; prime minister, Rafiq al-Hariri.

Despite the biggest Israeli attack on southern Lebanon since the 1982 invasion, on July 25, and a Cabinet crisis in August, the recovery of Lebanon from 16 years of civil war continued in 1993 and suffered no major setbacks. Prime Minister Rafiq al-Hariri (*see* BIOGRAPHIES), who held dual Saudi and Lebanese citizenship, pushed ahead with an ambitious plan to rebuild Beirut, with invitations on November 1 for Arab and Lebanese investors to subscribe $650 million. In March a 10-year reconstruction-and-revival plan for Lebanon, designed to cost $10 billion, was unveiled. Hariri began a diplomatic offensive to the Gulf states to secure funding, but only $1 billion was secured, with the addition of a $175 million World Bank loan approved in March.

Between April and May the government ordered the suspension of two daily newspapers and one television station and the prosecution of a third newspaper. The most prominent, the left-wing daily *As-Safir,* was closed on May 12 after publishing leaked confidential details of Israeli proposals to the Lebanese negotiating team involved in the multilateral Middle East peace talks.

Political reconciliation between the Muslim and Christian leaderships in Lebanon was under strain in May and early June, while a Christian Maronite minister, George Efrem, in the key Ministry of Electricity and Water Resources, was all but sacked. He was given a new post in a reshuffle, but some weeks later he was ousted from the government after filing a lawsuit against the prime minister.

On May 20 further controversy was caused when Hariri filled 72 civil service posts, which evoked allegations of cronyism. The most significant nomination was Riyad Salameh, a vice president of Merrill Lynch & Co., as governor of the Banque du Liban (Lebanon's central bank). Many ministers claimed that the Cabinet had not been consulted about these appointments.

The Cabinet crisis that boiled over during the summer was put to an end only on August 26, when Syria's vice president announced during a visit to Beirut that the Hariri government had Syria's full backing. Nevertheless, his statement that the Lebanese Cabinet would stay "until the year 2000" upset some parliamentarians.

On August 18, Syria and Lebanon formally agreed to establish a permanent secretariat for the Higher Council (called for in a bilateral treaty signed in May 1991). Nasri Khoury, a Maronite from al-Matn, was nominated secretary-general. The council, whose decisions would be binding, comprised senior ministers and parliamentarians and would meet once a year. On September 16, Syria and Lebanon signed accords on health, transport, agriculture, and socioeconomic affairs.

During the summer, attacks by Hezbollah guerrillas on Israel and its client South Lebanon Army led to a sudden escalation of violence. On July 25, Israel launched its largest artillery, naval, and air strike since 1982. The attack lasted six days and left more than 130 dead, 500 wounded, and 300,000 homeless from 75 villages. A cease-fire on July 31 was followed by Lebanese action to revoke all gun permits in the south and by the deployment of an army battalion to help maintain peace. Arab League ministers meeting in Damascus, Syria, at the end of July pledged $500 million to help repair the damage.

Lebanon's relations with the United States were dented when a military court in Beirut ruled on April 24 that the persons responsible for a 1983 truck-bomb attack on the U.S. embassy in Beirut were covered by a 1991 amnesty. Two days later the U.S. offices of Lebanon's flag carrier, Middle East Airlines, were ordered to close. Stepping into the crisis, the Lebanese government then lodged an appeal in the military court, asking for an exception to be made for crimes against political leaders and foreign diplomats.

(JOHN WHELAN)

LIBYA

A socialist country of North Africa, Libya lies on the Mediterranean Sea. Area: 1,757,000 sq km (678,400 sq mi). Pop. (1993 est.): 4,573,000. Cap.: Tripoli (policy-making body meets in Surt). Monetary unit: Libyan dinar, with (Oct. 4, 1993) a free rate of 0.29 dinar to U.S. $1 (0.45 dinar = £1 sterling). De facto chief of state in 1993, Col. Muammar al-Qaddafi; secretary of the General People's Congress (nominal chief of state), Zentani Mohammad Zentani; secretary of the General People's Committee (premier), Abu Zaid Umar Dourda.

The year 1993 was a difficult one for Libyan leader Col. Muammar al-Qaddafi and his people. The governments of the United States, the United Kingdom, and France, with the approval of the United Nations, imposed embargoes on Libyan trade and air traffic because Libya would not surrender two countrymen—ʿAbd al-Basset Ali Muhammad al-Meghrabi and al-Amin Khalifa Fahimah—who were suspected of planting a bomb on the Pan Am flight that exploded over Lockerbie, Scotland, in December 1988 and resulted in the deaths of 270 persons.

In early September there were signs that the Libyan authorities would allow the suspects to face trial in Scotland, but Britain ultimately rejected the initiative because it was not explicit about how the suspects would be handed over and because there was no mention of Libyan cooperation with a judicial investigation of the explosion of a French jetliner over Niger in September 1989, resulting in the deaths of 171 persons. At the end of September, new and tougher sanctions were imposed on Libya. The air and arms embargo was extended to include a ban on oil-refinery equipment and transport, but not oil-drilling equipment, and some Libyan financial assets were frozen. These measures were taken despite intensive activity in Tunisia and Paris, where the Libyan ambassador to Tunis, Abedelati al-Obeidi, discussed the issue with French officials in Paris and with the secretary-general of the United Nations, Boutros Boutros-Ghali.

On November 11, however, the UN Security Council voted to tighten further the sanctions against Libya, freezing the country's overseas assets and banning sales of oil equipment. The resolution was supported by all members of the Council except China and the three Islamic members—Djibouti, Pakistan, and Morocco—which abstained. The tougher measures went into effect on December 1.

The embargo affected many aspects of daily life and had a serious impact on the Libyan economy. The volume of movements to and from the country was reduced by the absence of direct flights to Libya, and those movements that did take place were subject to great inconvenience.

ESAIS BAITEL—GAMMA LIAISON

Israeli troops in southern Lebanon fire on positions held by the pro-Iranian fundamentalist group Hezbollah. The action was taken in retaliation for rocket attacks Hezbollah had made on settlements in northern Israel.

Some roundabout itineraries included land or sea journeys via Tunisia, Egypt, or Malta to enter the country.

The economy continued to be weighed down with difficulties. There were not enough funds either to sustain the existing infrastructure or to further urgent development of natural resources. The government had to consider borrowing money from the African Development Bank to fund the next stage of the Great Man-Made River, an ongoing project to pipe water to Libya's most densely settled area on the Al-Jifarah Plain.

Domestic politics continued to be dominated by Qaddafi, who indicated during the year that he was concerned over the problems of neighbouring countries, where radical Islamic groups were posing a threat to the government. In April he made the rather ambiguous announcement that the implementation of some of the regulations of the Shariʿah (Islamic law) were being contemplated. It appeared that Qaddafi was both placating religious opponents of his regime and forcing the public to confront the realities of a radical Islamic government, already confident that the majority of the population was opposed to a revival of radical Islam. Qaddafi put down a revolt by army units in October.

In keeping with his policy of reconciliation with the international community, the Libyan leader was generally reticent regarding the peace agreement between the Palestinians and Israelis. He safely placed himself, however, among those Arab leaders who insisted on more immediate concessions for Palestinians. (J.A. ALLAN)

This article updates the *Macropædia* article NORTH AFRICA: *Libya.*

MOROCCO

A constitutional monarchy of North Africa, Morocco has coastlines on the Atlantic Ocean and the Mediterranean Sea. Area: 458,730 sq km (177,117 sq mi). Pop. (1993 est.): 26,494,000. (Area and population figures refer to Morocco as constituted prior to the purported division of Western Sahara between Morocco and Mauritania and the subsequent Moroccan occupation of the Mauritanian zone in 1979.) Cap.: Rabat. Monetary unit: dirham, with (Oct. 4, 1993) a free rate of 9.04 dirhams to U.S. $1 (13.70 dirhams = £1 sterling). King, Hassan II; prime minister in 1993, Mohamed Karim Lamrani.

The domestic scene in Morocco during 1993 was dominated by the parliamentary elections. The first round of the elections (for the 222 directly elected seats) took place on June 25 and resulted in a win for the left-wing Socialist Union of Populist Forces (USFP), which obtained 48 seats. The Democratic Bloc, an alliance of the USFP, the Independence Party (Istiqlal), the Party of Progress and Socialism, and the Organization for Democratic and Popular Action, won 99 of the 222 seats. The remainder were largely captured by the five loyalist parties. (For tabulation results, see *Political Parties,* above.) In the indirect elections for the remaining 111 seats, held on September 17, the loyalist parties radically improved their position, with the USFP picking up only four additional seats. The USFP was still expected to form a new government.

In early October, however, the USFP announced that it would not form a government, apparently because the party perceived that it either would have to form a coalition or would be a minority government. Furthermore, the USFP leader, ʿAbd ar-Rahman al-Yousifi, resigned his post as a protest against electoral fraud. Relations with the Royal Palace were strained as a result. The new government was eventually drawn from the ranks of the loyalist parties, thus signaling that Morocco was ultimately concerned about political continuity rather than radical experiment. Continuity was also emphasized by the opening of the Hassan II Mosque in Casablanca—the largest in the world outside Saudi Arabia—at an estimated cost of $500 million.

Despite problems created by a poor harvest (with consequent declines in economic growth and increases in imports and the current account deficit), Morocco continued to attract international attention as a good investment risk. Receipts from the privatization program exceeded the $214 million target figure as the first large-scale foreign purchases began.

The Western Sahara issue continued to dominate foreign affairs, especially as Morocco's relations with Algeria remained strained. The Polisario Front demonstrated its continued fighting ability with a military parade in Tindouf on May 20 and its willingness to negotiate during meetings in El Aaiun with Moroccan officials over procedures for the planned referendum. The major problem continued to be the voting lists to be used, with the Polisario Front insisting on the 1974 Spanish census of the Western Sahara as the guide and Morocco demanding inclusion of an additional 120,000 Sahrawis, who they said had been forced out of the territory by Spain. The UN, which was providing a monitoring force, MINURSO, tried to revive negotiations with a visit by Secretary-General Boutros Boutros-Ghali in June and later announced preparations for a new census.

(GEORGE JOFFÉ)

This article updates the *Macropædia* article NORTH AFRICA: *Morocco.*

OMAN

The sultanate of Oman occupies the southeastern part of the Arabian Peninsula, facing the Persian Gulf, the Gulf of Oman, and the Arabian Sea. A small part of the country lies to the north and is separated from the rest of Oman by the United Arab Emirates. Area: 306,000 sq km (118,150 sq mi). Pop. (1993 est.): 1,698,000. Cap.: Muscat. Monetary unit: rial Omani, with (Oct. 4, 1993) a par value of 0.38 rial to U.S. $1 (free rate of 0.58 rial = £1 sterling). Sultan and prime minister in 1993, Qabus ibn Saʿid.

Oman and Yemen symbolically achieved even closer relations with the opening on June 1 of their first border post at Mazyouna in Oman province. During the event, presided over by Qais ibn ʿAbd al-Munim az-Zawawi, Oman's deputy prime minister for financial and economic affairs, the two governments announced their intention to build a new town at the border post and to inaugurate a free-trade zone for use by businesses from both countries.

Oman's decision to proceed with plans for a $9 billion liquefied natural gas project at Bimmah on the east coast north of Sur and some 200 km (124 mi) south of the capital was in anticipation of an expected economic boom in the period preceding Sultan Qabus ibn Saʿid's silver jubilee in November 1995. Sultan Qabus improved his popularity with tribesmen by making a monthlong tour of the interior beginning on January 26 and by gaining better recognition for Oman in the Arab world. Oman was the host nation of an April meeting attended by heads of Arab aid funds and development banks.

The Indian prime minister, P.V. Narasimha Rao, visited Muscat during June to discuss joint ventures, including hydrocarbons projects and fertilizer plants in Oman. On March 13 the two governments had signed a memorandum of understanding for a submarine oil pipeline. The South African foreign minister, Pik Botha, was received in mid-April.

On January 28, British Prime Minister John Major concluded a military procurement contract with the sultanate, which purchased 18 Challenger II main battle tanks and ancillary equipment valued at $208 million. On June 22 the agreement was formally signed by both Oman's Defense Ministry secretary Saif ibn Muhammad al-Batashi and representatives of the British manufacturers, Vickers P.L.C. In February Oman announced plans to purchase French naval vessels. (JOHN WHELAN)

This article updates the *Macropædia* article ARABIA: *Oman*.

QATAR

A monarchy (emirate) on the Arabian Peninsula, Qatar occupies a desert peninsula and nearby small islands on the west coast of the Persian Gulf. Area: 11,427 sq km (4,412 sq mi). Pop. (1993 est.): 539,000. Cap.: Doha. Monetary unit: Qatar riyal, with (Oct. 4, 1993) a free rate of 3.61 riyals to U.S. $1 (5.47 riyals = £1 sterling). Emir and prime minister in 1993, Sheikh Khalifah ibn Hamad ath-Thani.

In May 1993 a border agreement, which had been struck by Qatar and Saudi Arabia on Dec. 20, 1992, was the subject of amicable talks held in the capital of Doha between Emir Sheikh Khalifah ibn Hamad ath-Thani and Saudi Defense Minister Prince Sultan ibn ʿAbd al-Aziz as-Saʿud. The meeting reportedly ended hostilities between the two desert states. Qatar continued, however, to maintain an independent line in foreign policy, which was sometimes at odds with other Gulf Arab partners. In April the Qatari government became the first Arab state to receive a visit by South African Foreign Minister Pik Botha, symbolizing the end of the Arab boycott of South Africa.

The territorial dispute with Bahrain over ownership of the Hawar Islands soured Qatari relations with its neighbour. The matter, however, was scheduled for a hearing at the International Court of Justice at The Hague on Feb. 28, 1994.

The North Field gas project, Qatar's most ambitious industrial scheme, took another step forward on January 31 when Mobil Oil Corp. purchased a 10% stake in the Qatar Liquefied Gas Co., assuring a wider market for its products. J.P. Morgan, the leading New York investment bank, was appointed financial adviser to the project and was given a mandate to advise on borrowing requirements.

In October Qatar was host to round-robin soccer matches between the six Asian Zone nations (Iran, Iraq, North Korea, Japan, Saudi Arabia, and South Korea) attempting to qualify for the 1994 World Cup in the U.S.

(JOHN WHELAN)

This article updates the *Macropædia* article ARABIA: *Qatar*.

SAUDI ARABIA

The kingdom of Saudi Arabia occupies four-fifths of the Arabian Peninsula, with coastlines on the Red Sea and the Persian Gulf. Area: 2,240,000 sq km (865,000 sq mi). Pop. (1993 est.): 17,419,000. Cap.: Riyadh. Monetary unit: Saudi Arabian riyal, with (Oct. 4, 1993) an official rate of 3.76 riyals to U.S. $1 (5.69 riyals = £1 sterling). King and prime minister in 1993, Fahd.

Political reform, pro-Western policies from the government, and the formation of a fundamentalist civil rights movement were dominant themes in Saudi Arabia in 1993 as economic recovery continued following the aftermath of the Kuwait invasion crisis of 1990–91.

In July Abdullah ibn Amr Nassif, a former dean of King Abdul Aziz University, Jiddah, was named vice chairman of the *majlis ash-shura* (Consultative Council) to preside over the 60-member advisory body. The other members (whose names were also published) were appointed by King Fahd and drawn from the ranks of tribal and religious leaders, the professions, academics, and businessmen. One-third of the all-male *majlis* were former civil servants, but observers noted that none of the 5,000 princes from the ruling as-Sʿaud family had been included. Only one Shiʿite was identified as a member of the council, which officially opened on December 29.

In proceeding with the council, King Fahd was seen as having begun to fulfill the pledge made in 1962 by Faysal when he was crown prince. On August 20 a law was published covering the operations of the council and laying down formal rules for the conduct of the Council of Ministers (Cabinet). Among other provisions, the law specified a four-year term of office for ministers, although extensions were possible.

The king also divided the existing Ministry of Pilgrimage Affairs and Religious Trusts into two ministries. Mahmoud ibn Muhammad Safar was named minister of pilgrimage affairs, while the existing minister retained responsibility for religious endowments. Observers interpreted this change as a sign of the government's determination to strengthen the official religious establishment against the challenge posed by fundamentalists. It also recognized the growing complexity of handling the annual pilgrimage (hajj), when Muslims pour into the kingdom to visit the holy cities of Medina and Mecca. The Saudi government had adopted a quota system for pilgrims from different countries in order to reduce the possibility of thousands of radicals infiltrating the holy places.

The 1993 hajj season passed off quietly, with the Saudi authorities taking a tough line against political demonstrations. Nevertheless, police were forced to ban a planned demonstration by Iranian pilgrims on May 27. On June 1 demonstrators managed to assemble and shout anti-Israel and anti-American slogans.

In a further round of political reforms, on September 16 King Fahd issued a decree confirming the internal organization of the kingdom into 13 regions under governors (emirs). The decree created councils for each governorate with a mandate "to monitor development and advise the government."

Despite these changes, King Fahd for the first time in his reign faced a challenge from within the establishment. On May 9 academics and religious leaders belonging to the Committee for the Defense of Legitimate Rights—an organization with a religious manifesto—called on the government to "safeguard the legitimate rights of the Shariʿah." (In 1992 members of the committee had put their names to a petition calling for reform of the government and a return to Islamic values.) Three days later, as the crisis escalated, the 20-member Supreme Council of ulema (religious elders), headed by the blind divine Sheikh Abdel-Aziz ibn Baz, declared the committee's declaration to be "illegal" and reminded Saudis of the "duty of all Muslims to obey the king and the ulema."

On May 13 five men, all religious conservatives from within the establishment but associated with the committee, were dismissed from their jobs: Muhammad ibn al-Masa'ari of King Saud University, Riyadh; Abdullah al-Hamid and Abdullah at-Tuwaijari, both of the Islamic University of Imam Muhammad ibn Saud, Riyadh; Hamad as-Sulaifeh of the Ministry of Education; and Abdullah al-Jubrin, who worked for a religious organization for Islamic research. Jubrin, however, resigned from the committee on May 20 and declared his loyalty to the government. On May 15 Masa'ari, who was the most prominent of the rebels, was arrested, and religious police subsequently detained Hamid and Tuwaijari. A group of 60 academics signed a petition to the king in August demanding the release of detained members of the committee.

Saudi Arabia's human rights record also came under attack from the London-based organization Amnesty International, which said in a critical report that capital punishment by beheading with a single stroke of a sword had been carried out on 105 people in 1992–93—four times as many as the previous year, when U.S. and allied soldiers were in the kingdom as part of Operation Desert Storm.

King Fahd permitted the U.S. to operate air strikes against Iraq in January during the last days of Pres. George Bush's administration, with sorties being flown from military bases at az-Zahran, Riyadh, at-Ta'if, and Khamis Mushayt. Relations with the U.S. remained cordial after the inauguration of Pres. Bill Clinton. King Fahd gave his support for the agreement signed by the Palestine Liberation Organization and Israel on September 13 in a move that helped to give further momentum to the peace process.

On January 28 U.K. Prime Minster John Major confirmed an order from the Saudi government for 48 Tornado aircraft as part of the al-Yamamah project signed in 1988. Prince Charles met King Fahd in Jiddah on November 7 in an effort to strengthen business ties between the two states. Saudi foreign policy retained a strong pro-Western and anti-Iraqi line, with Crown Prince Abdullah welcoming a delegation from the opposition London-based Iraqi National Congress, an umbrella organization of Iraqi underground groups, on May 26.

Within OPEC, Saudi Arabia maintained a moderate stance by accepting an unchanged oil output quota of eight million barrels a day on September 29. Saudi Arabia was the only country to volunteer no increase. Its share of total OPEC production (22.7 million bbl a day) was its lowest since August 1990, but Saudi Arabia enjoyed an economic boom produced by sustained government spending. Bank profits increased and liquidity increased in the nascent Saudi stock market.

The London-based Center for Global Energy Studies, which was founded by Sheikh Ahmed Zaki Yamani, said in a report in October that the kingdom would easily be able to expand its theoretical capacity of 9.6 million bbl a day to 10 million bbl a day by 1994 if the government chose. Nevertheless, the report's author said the government would need to invest at least $18 billion before 2000 to reach and maintain its 10 million bbl a day capacity. He said there was little possibility of new fields, such as the giant Shaybah field near the United Arab Emirates border, because of their remoteness and lack of infrastructure.

In October the Saudi Arabian national soccer team delighted its supporters throughout the kingdom by qualifying for the first time to play in the finals of the World Cup in the U.S. in 1994. (JOHN WHELAN)

This article updates the *Macropædia* article ARABIA: *Saudi Arabia.*

SYRIA

A republic of southwestern Asia, Syria is on the Mediterranean Sea. Area: 185,180 sq km (71,498 sq mi). Pop. (1993 est.): 13,398,000. Cap.: Damascus. Monetary unit: Syrian pound, with (Oct. 4, 1993) a par value (essential rate) of LS 11.22 to U.S. $1 (LS 17.05 = £1 sterling) and a nonessential rate of LS 21.50 to U.S. $1 (LS 32.68 = £1 sterling). President in 1993, Gen. Hafez al-Assad; prime minister, Mahmoud Zuabi.

Syria retained reservations about the Israeli-Palestinian accords concluded in September 1993. Pres. Hafez al-Assad agreed to withhold any active opposition to the plans to allow limited self-rule for the Palestinians in parts of the occupied territories but rejected lifting the Arab boycott of Israel. On September 20 Assad was quoted as saying that the only winner from the Israeli-Palestinian agreement was Israel, but six days later at a meeting with Pres. Hosni Mubarak of Egypt, he modified his position. In December he agreed to resume peace talks in early 1994. After Assad promised to help trace seven Israeli soldiers missing in Lebanon since the 1980s, the U.S. announced that it would relax sanctions against Syria.

An extraordinary meeting of the Arab League took place in Damascus at the end of July after Israel attacked southern Lebanon on July 25. Despite the cease-fire agreed on July 31, Assad met the central command of the National Progressive Front on August 5 for a briefing on the security situation. It was the first time the president had convened the ruling party's politburo since the 1973 Arab-Israeli war. On May 11 Assad approved the 1993 budget with a total expenditure of LS 123,020,000,000, up from LS 93,040,000,000 in 1992.

On May 20, after a meeting in Qatar, a new mandate was agreed for the Damascus Declaration alliance of Egypt, Syria, and the six conservative Gulf Cooperation Council states, comprising Saudi Arabia, Kuwait, Oman, Qatar, Bahrain, and the United Arab Emirates. It was agreed that cooperation would focus on economic assistance rather than on mutual defense. Some $6.5 billion had been subscribed by the Gulf states to fund the agreement.

On April 29 the Arab Boycott of Israel biannual meeting took place in Damascus and announced a ban on a company from Bulgaria and the former Yugoslavia. The meeting was a sign of Syria's continued hostility to Israel despite the peace process. On February 12 the European Parliament voted to reject the European Community's fourth financial protocol 1992–96 with Syria for ECU 148 million because of continued concerns over Syria's human rights record.

Syria maintained close ties with Iran as a counterbalance to its hostility to Iraq. On January 3–5 Vice Pres. ʽAbd al-Halim ibn Said Khaddam took part in a meeting in Tehran of the joint Iranian-Syrian Higher Committee. Two weeks later Turkish Prime Minister Suleyman Demirel visited Damascus, and the two governments said a joint agreement on shared water resources would be concluded by the end of 1993—the first time a date had been announced. Assad gave an assurance that Syria would not allow Turkish Kurdish Workers' Party guerrillas to operate from its territory. Turkey, Iran, and Syria held a foreign ministers meeting in Damascus in February and agreed that they would work to preserve the territorial integrity of Iraq.

On August 18 Syria and Lebanon formally agreed to establish a permanent secretariat for the Higher Council, which had been constituted under a bilateral treaty signed between the two governments in May 1991. A month later the two countries signed four accords on economic cooperation. Syria continued to have a vital influence on the internal political affairs of its neighbour—on August 26 the Syrian vice president's backing for the government of Prime Minister Rafiq al-Hariri in Lebanon was crucial to its survival after a sharp internal crisis.

In April and May the government stepped up its campaign against the underground drug industry in Syria. In April the People's Council passed legislation calling for the death penalty for drug dealers and smugglers. In late March a public execution was staged of five men convicted in al-Hasakah of having set fire to a jail, killing 57 inmates.

Former interior minister Muhammad Rabah at-Tawil died in May less than a year after his release from prison. Tawil was arrested after Assad seized control of the government in 1970 and served 22 years in detention. Seventeen other senior Baʽth Party officials and civil servants and 50 other individuals were still in prison. (JOHN WHELAN)

TUNISIA

A republic of North Africa, Tunisia lies on the Mediterranean Sea. Area: 164,150 sq km (63,378 sq mi). Pop. (1993 est.): 8,530,000. Cap.: Tunis. Monetary unit: Tunisian dinar, with (Oct. 4, 1993) a free rate of 1.01 dinars to U.S. $1 (1.53 dinars = £1 sterling). President in 1993, Gen. Zine al-Abidine Ben Ali; prime minister, Hamed Karoui.

Tunisian political life throughout 1993 continued to be bedeviled by the problem of political representation. At the end of the preceding year, on December 6, Pres. Zine al-Abidine Ben Ali had called a meeting of leaders in the Constitutional Democratic Assembly (RCD), which was effectively Tunisia's single political party and controlled all seats in the Chamber of Deputies, in order to try to create a basis for multiparty democracy. The meeting discussed reforms of the RCD to be presented for approval at the movement's second congress in July 1993. That congress, held July 29–31, heard calls for the five legal opposition parties to be allowed to participate in the National Assembly and for the adoption of a new electoral law. The legislative elections were scheduled for March 1994, and in November President Ben Ali said that the legal opposition would be allowed to sit in the parliament. Presidential elections would also take place in March 1994, and at the RCD's July congress Ben Ali was nominated again as the RCD's candidate.

Tunisia's opposition to Islamists was echoed in foreign affairs when in late June, just before an Organization of African Unity conference in Cairo, President Ben Ali met with his Egyptian and Algerian counterparts to organize resistance to the regional spread of Islamist movements. The meeting condemned the role of The Sudan in the spread of those movements. In an ironic counterpart to that meeting, the British government granted the major Tunisian Islamist leader, Rachid Ghannouchi, political asylum in midyear, despite Tunisian protests.

Tunisia also tried to repair its links with the Persian Gulf states, damaged in 1990–91 over the Iraqi invasion of Kuwait. Foreign Minister Habib Ben Yahia made the first formal visit by a senior Tunisian minister to Kuwait since the 1990–91 crisis in the hope of reviving Kuwaiti investment interest in Tunisia. In a final legacy of the Gulf war, Tunisia continued to hold aircraft on behalf of Iraq. As a result of the agreement between the Palestine Liberation Organization and Israel in September, the Tunisian government held discussions with PLO officials over the future status of the organization in Tunisia, where it had been based since being expelled from Lebanon in 1982–83.

The Tunisian economy continued to improve throughout the year. The growth rate of the gross domestic product, which reached 8.4% in 1992, was expected to be maintained, despite low levels of foreign investment and continuing current account deficits. (GEORGE JOFFÉ)

This article updates the *Macropædia* article NORTH AFRICA: *Tunisia*.

TURKEY

A republic of Asia Minor and southeastern Europe, Turkey has coastlines on the Aegean, Black, and Mediterranean seas. Area: 779,452 sq km (300,948 sq mi), including 23,764 sq km in Europe. Pop. (1993 est.): 59,869,000. Cap.: Ankara. Monetary unit: Turkish lira, with (Oct. 4, 1993) a free rate of 12,073 liras to U.S. $1 (18,291 liras = £1 sterling). Presidents in 1993, Turgut Ozal to April 17, Husamettin Cindoruk (acting) from April 17 to May 16, and, from May 16, Suleyman Demirel; prime ministers, Suleyman Demirel to May 16, Erdal Inonu (acting) from May 16, and, from June 25, Tansu Ciller.

Pres. Turgut Ozal, the author of Turkey's rapid economic development in the 1980s, died on April 17, 1993. (*See* OBITUARIES.) He was succeeded by his erstwhile opponent, Prime Minister Suleyman Demirel. On June 13 Demirel was replaced in the leadership of the centre-right True Path Party by Tansu Ciller (*see* BIOGRAPHIES), an academic economist, and on the following day she was named Turkey's first woman prime minister. She proceeded to reconstitute the coalition, while changing most of the ministers belonging to her own party.

Changes at the top made little impression on Turkey's pressing problem of terrorism. On January 24 the country's best-known radical newspaper columnist, Ugur Mumcu, was assassinated by Islamic fundamentalists in Ankara. Hundreds of thousands of mourners turned his funeral on January 27 into the biggest-ever demonstration in defense of the secular republic. On July 2 a mob of Sunni fanatics set fire to a hotel in Sivas in which the Turkish writer Aziz Nesin, who had published excerpts of Salman Rushdie's *The Satanic Verses* in his newspaper, was staying. Nesin escaped, but 36 people, most of them Shi'ite intellectuals, perished in the fire.

It was the terror campaign of the separatist Kurdish Workers' Party (PKK), however, that claimed most victims. Hopes were raised when the Damascus, Syria-based PKK leader Abdullah ("Apo") Ocalan declared a unilateral truce, which began on March 20; on May 24, however, a PKK band murdered 33 unarmed soldiers and 5 civilians in an ambush in the mountains of the southeast. The security forces then intensified their operations, while the PKK mounted new attacks, many of them directed against their civilian Kurdish opponents. The PKK launched a coordinated series of attacks on Turkish diplomatic offices and businesses in Germany, Switzerland, France, and Denmark on June 24. On October 22 PKK snipers killed the southeast regional gendarmarie commander, Gen. Bahtiyar Aydin, in the township of Lice. The security forces responded massively, leaving the town in ruins. In November a Turkish military court handed down sentences, including 15 death sentences and 14 for life imprisonment, against 145 PKK members and other Kurdish separatists. Most of those sentenced were at large. Later, in December, the government carried out raids and air strikes on Kurdish positions inside Iraq. The worsening security situation led to the replacement of the ministers of defense and the interior.

The Islamic opponents of the PKK were also active. On September 4 they murdered a radical member of the parliament, Mehmet Sincar of the New Democracy Party (formerly the People's Labour Party).

Turkish diplomacy had little to show for its efforts in 1993. In spite of the visit paid to Syria by Prime Minister Demirel in January and of constant contacts with Iran, PKK terrorists continued to operate from both countries, as well as from the Kurdish safe haven in northern Iraq. Turkish pleading for firmer action in defense of Bosnian Muslims was ineffective. The Turkish government did not intervene when Armenians enlarged their conquests in Azerbaijan or when the pro-Turkish president of Azerbaijan, Abulfez Elchibey, was ousted in June.

A visit to the Turkic republics by President Ozal a few days before his death and a visit to Moscow by Prime Minister Ciller on September 9 sought to promote trade links with the former Soviet states but had little impact on political developments. Ciller's trip to Germany on September 20 served to improve relations after the murder of Turkish workers by German neo-Nazis. Turkey's pressing need for foreign finance was discussed when Prime Minister Ciller went to Washington, D.C., on October 15. In Brussels work continued on the implementation of a full customs union between Turkey and the European Community in 1995.

Inflation in Turkey rose to 68% by the end of September. The country's foreign-trade gap nearly doubled from $5 billion to $9.3 billion by the end of August. The Social Democrats prevented any significant progress in privatization, even though Ciller had identified it as one of her main objectives. (ANDREW MANGO)

UNITED ARAB EMIRATES

Consisting of Abu Dhabi, Ajman, Dubayy, al-Fujayrah, Ra's al-Khaymah, ash-Shariqah, and Umm al-Qaywayn, the United Arab Emirates is a federation of seven largely autonomous emirates located on the eastern Arabian Peninsula. Area: 83,600 sq km (32,300 sq mi). Pop. (1993 est.): 1,986,000. Cap.: Abu Dhabi. Monetary unit: United Arab Emirates dirham, with (Oct. 4, 1993) a free rate of 3.69 dirhams to U.S. $1 (5.57 dirhams = £1 sterling). President in 1993, Sheikh Zaid ibn Sultan an-Nahayan; prime minister, Sheikh Maktum ibn Rashid al-Maktum.

Diplomacy to settle the seizure by Iran in 1992 of Abu Musa and Greater and Lesser Tunb, three islands near the Strait of Hormuz, stumbled over the insistence by the United Arab Emirates (U.A.E.) that the dispute be submitted to international arbitration. The Iranian foreign minister visited the U.A.E. in May, and the two countries announced the resumption of talks.

In January the appointed Federal National Council was reestablished by Pres. Sheikh Zaid ibn Sultan an-Nahayan and announced that plans to build a permanent federal capital on the Abu Dhabi–Dubayy border had been abandoned. In a meeting with Islamic scholars to mark the end of Ramadan (holy month of fasting), Pres. Sheikh Zaid issued a strong statement against religious extremism, indicating growing concern at the spread of Islamic fundamentalism.

On October 9, 13 former officials of the failed Bank of Credit and Commerce International (BCCI) went on trial in Abu Dhabi on charges of forgery and false accounting. The Abu Dhabi ruling family, principal shareholder in BCCI, filed a $9 billion civil suit against the 13 in December.

Dubayy tightened contract proposals for buyers of its crude oil after a contract with 31 buyers broke down in June, causing panic in the Dubayy oil market. On November 7 a major air show opened in Dubayy; it was attended by 450 companies from 33 countries. The U.S. reached agreement at the end of the year on quotas for the imports of textiles from the United Arab Emirates. (JOHN WHELAN)

This article updates the *Macropædia* article ARABIA: *United Arab Emirates.*

YEMEN

A republic of the southwestern Arabian Peninsula, Yemen has coastlines on the Red Sea, the Gulf of Aden, and the Arabian Sea. Area: 531,869 sq km (205,356 sq mi), including 59,770 sq km of undemarcated area bordered by Saudi Arabia claimed by the former Yemen Arab Republic (North Yemen). Pop. (1993 est.): 12,519,000. Cap.: San'a'. Monetary unit: Yemen rial, with (Oct. 4, 1993) a par value of 16.50 rials to U.S. $1 (free rate of 25.08 rials = £1 sterling); a truer value of the rial was on the black market, where in October about 46 rials = U.S. $1 (about 70 rials = £1 sterling). President in 1993, Gen. Ali Abdallah Salih; prime minister, Haidar Abu Bakr al-Attas.

A major political crisis erupted in August 1993 when Vice Pres. Ali Salim al-Beidh declared that he would boycott meetings in the capital, San'a', and remain in his southern power base of Aden. The announcement followed a visit to the U.S., where he was apparently warned of a plot to kill him in San'a'. Prime Minister Haidar Abu Bakr al-Attas supported the vice president's call for political and economic reforms as well as improved security. Beidh claimed that more than 150 members of his Yemeni Socialist Party (YSP) had been killed in ongoing political violence.

On April 27, Yemen went to the polls in a general election that resulted in Pres. Ali Abdallah Salih's General People's Congress' becoming the largest single party, with 122 seats in the 301-member House of Representatives. The election was contested by 3,267 candidates from 21 parties. In the north the contests were largely between the fundamentalists and Salih's GPC, while in the south the YSP dominated. (For tabulated results, see *Political Parties,* above.)

On May 30, Salih formed a 31-member coalition Cabinet with representatives from all the major parties, including six ministers from the fundamentalist al-Islah and one pro-Iraqi Ba'thist. Despite Salih's stated commitment to political reform, the government's cohesion remained fragile. The defense forces chief of staff, Col. Abdullah Hussein al-Bushiri, resigned, citing personal differences with the new defense minister and lack of progress in amalgamating the armed forces of the former North and South Yemen.

A U.S. diplomat, kidnapped by tribesmen at the end of November, was released a few days later.

While suffering from political upheavals and harassment by tribesmen, Western companies continued the search for oil, with Canadian Occidental bringing the Masila block on stream in July, boosting Yemen's overall production to 300,000 bbl a day. (JOHN WHELAN)

This article updates the *Macropædia* article ARABIA: *Yemen.*

HUTCHINSON LIBRARY

A freighter docks at Port Rashid, near Dubayy town. The port and the Jebel Ali free-trade zone made the United Arab Emirates a major distribution centre between East and West.

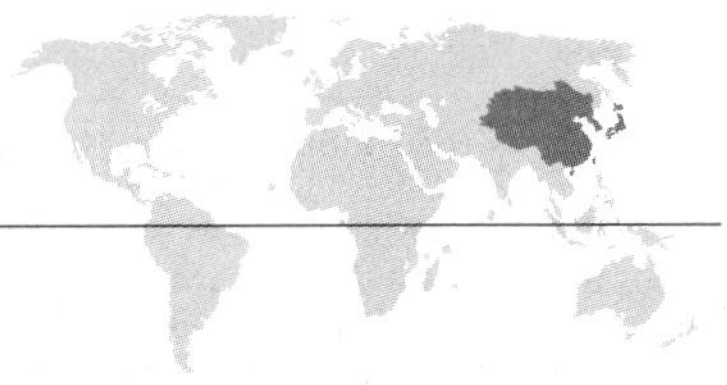

East Asia

CHINA

The People's Republic of China is situated in eastern Asia, with coastlines on the Yellow Sea and the East and South China seas. Area: 9,572,900 sq km (3,696,100 sq mi), including Tibet and excluding Taiwan. (See *Taiwan,* below.) Pop. (1993 est., excluding Taiwan): 1,179,467,000. Cap.: Beijing (Peking). Monetary unit: renminbi yuan, with (Oct. 4, 1993) an official rate of 5.78 yuan to U.S. $1 (8.76 yuan = £1 sterling). Presidents in 1993, Yang Shangkun (Yang Shang-k'un) and, from March 27, Jiang Zemin (Chiang Tse-min); premier, Li Peng (Li P'eng).

As the era of Deng Xiaoping (Teng Hsiao-p'ing) was drawing to a close, the contradictions associated with the profound social transformation of the past 15 years threatened to undermine national unity and the political stability that many Chinese felt was the foundation of the nation's rapid economic growth and rising international stature. Toward the end of 1993, the Communist Party of China (CPC) unveiled an economic reform program aimed at accelerating the transformation of China into a market economy without threatening the prosperity, power, and privileged position of the central and local Communist Party elite. At almost the same time, a diplomatic initiative undertaken by the new administration of U.S. Pres. Bill Clinton presented China's leaders with an opportunity to work together with the U.S. to reverse a troublesome downward spiral in Sino-American relations. Nonetheless, Clinton made it clear that a renewal of China's most-favoured-nation trade status depended on an improvement in its observance of human rights. China's international reputation had been damaged by its poor human rights record, a fact brought forcefully home in September when the International Olympic Committee awarded the summer Olympic Games in the year 2000 to Sydney, Australia, rather than to Beijing (Peking).

Politics and the Economy. In early 1992, Deng personally reenergized China's economic reform program by touring booming coastal southeastern China and lauding its progress. On November 2 the publication of volume 3 of Deng's selected works marked a further step in his apotheosis from an 89-year-old political leader into a textual deity of "socialism with Chinese characteristics." Earlier in the year, Deng's youngest daughter, Deng Rong (Teng Jung), softened and humanized the portrait of the tough-minded and unsentimental politician in an admiring biography.

Deng's waning energy focused attention on the still unresolved problem of political succession. A heart attack suffered by 64-year-old Premier Li Peng (Li P'eng) in April, not long after his reelection in office by the National People's Congress (NPC) in March, sidelined him for seven weeks, but by early summer he had resumed a full schedule of activities. An indication of Li's unpopularity was evident when 300 NPC delegates failed to support his reelection. In June, Vice Premier Zhu Rongji (Chu Jung-chi), a no-nonsense technocrat much admired in the West, replaced Li Guixian (Li Kuei-hsien) as governor of the Bank of China, the country's central bank. His immediate task was to cool off China's overheated economy.

Jiang Zemin (Chiang Tse-min) improved his paper credentials as Deng's main putative successor by adding the title of state president to his positions as CPC general secretary and chairman of the party's Central Military Commission. His actual sphere of domestic political power, however, was restricted to propaganda and general political exhortation. It was Jiang, for example, who kicked off the party's midsummer anticorruption campaign, inveighing against officials who charged fees for what were supposed to be free public services and for establishing businesses from which they profited by abusing their authority. So vast was the scale of corruption that even the application of the death sentence to particularly venal officials was unlikely to have more than a marginal effect. Jiang's credentials as a world statesman were slightly improved by his attendance at the Seattle, Wash., summit of the Asia-Pacific Economic Cooperation forum in November, where he also met privately with Clinton. The two men reportedly discussed China's growing trade surplus with the U.S., its observance of human rights, and its sale of weapons to other countries. Serious doubts persisted, however, about Jiang's influence over Chinese military leaders, a substantial number of whom apparently viewed him as a weak and ineffectual leader. Qiao Shi (Ch'iao Shih), a member of the Political Bureau Standing Committee and one who also hoped to inherit Deng's mantle, acquired some international exposure by touring Southeast Asia in his capacity as head of the NPC.

The decorous jostling for political position among China's central party and governmental leaders was partially overshadowed by the ongoing devolution of power from the centre to the provinces, counties, and municipalities, a result of China's continuing economic and social transformation. When the centre supported further economic reform in early 1992 by relaxing controls, there was a renewed pell mell rush toward market-driven prosperity in the dynamic coastal provinces. Periodic attempts to reassert central control to dampen inflation and protect tax revenues threatened growth. The localities thus functioned as the engine of growth and the centre as the brake. As a result, China's forward motion over a dozen years had been rapid but often herky-jerky.

In his report to the NPC in March, Li Peng announced a plan to restructure the State Council by cutting government staff by 25% over a three-year period and by reducing the number of government ministries and commissions from 86 to 59. Earlier attempts to put the Chinese state on a diet had proved futile. The state bureaucracy of nearly 40 million persons had increased by one million annually, much faster

REUTERS/BETTMANN

Jiang Zemin (Chiang Tse-min, left), general secretary of the Communist Party of China, congratulates Premier Li Peng (Li P'eng) on his speech to delegates attending the National People's Congress in March. Li was reelected premier, and Jiang was given the additional post of president.

A young woman chooses makeup in a Chinese department store. With the economy booming, the expanding middle class in China quickly developed a taste for Western products not formerly available.
GREG GIRARD—CONTACT

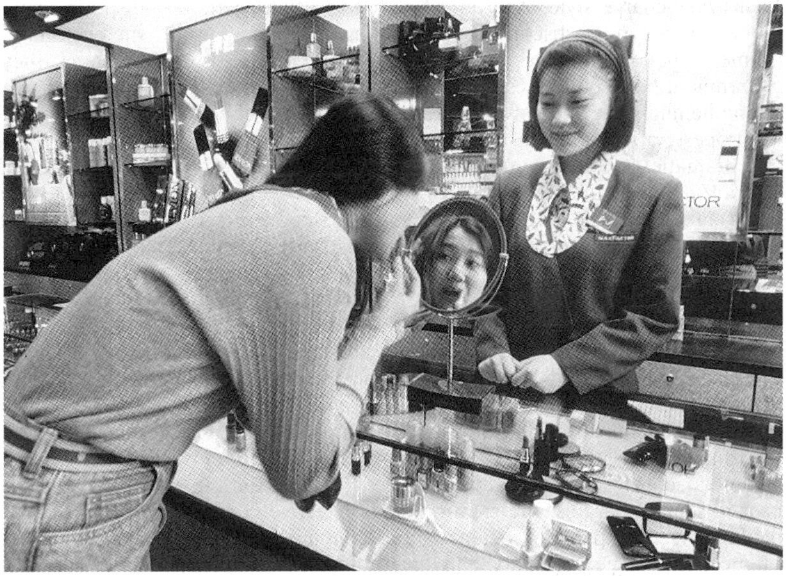

than the rate of population growth. Administrative expenditures consumed 40% of the central government's revenues.

China's protracted war against political opposition continued during the year. Well-known political prisoners were treated as a valuable commodity to be released in carefully calibrated quantities to satisfy Western (primarily U.S.) demands for visible progress in human rights. Freed from prison in February after serving most of a four-year sentence, Tiananmen (T'ien-an-men) student leader Wang Dan (Wang Tan) expressed a desire to make money because he viewed prosperity as a prerequisite for the democratization of China. On the eve of the annual U.S. debate over China's trade status, Beijing released Xu Wenli (Hsü Wen-li), who had served 12 years for his role in the democracy movement of 1978–79. China's most famous political prisoner, 43-year-old Wei Jingsheng (Wei Ching-sheng), was released in September on the eve of the International Olympic Committee vote. Wei, unbowed and unrepentant, planned to write his prison memoirs, but he was warned that publication of such material was forbidden. Meanwhile, new prisoners took the place of the old. Veteran human rights activist Fu Shenqi (Fu Shen-ch'i) was sentenced to three years for speaking to foreign reporters. Bai Weiji (Pai Wei-chi), his wife, Zhao Lei (Chao Lei), and others were given long sentences for leaking documents to a Western journalist. In most other countries the material would never have been considered state secrets. Chinese officials sought to refute Western critics of their harsh penal system by depicting Chinese prison conditions as almost cushy. They also accused the U.S. of gross hypocrisy in attacking China for exporting goods made by prison labour because a number of U.S. states, notably California, were vigorously promoting prison exports.

More worrisome to the CPC were demonstrations in Lhasa, Tibet, in late May. As many as a thousand protesters chanting anti-Chinese, pro-independence slogans had to be silenced by a show of force. The Tibet issue was so sensitive that China felt compelled to block the Dalai Lama from addressing the UN-sponsored World Conference on Human Rights in Vienna in June. Muslim discontent surfaced in October in remote Qinghai (Tsinghai) province when crowds in the provincial capital of Xining (Hsi-ning) attacked government offices and police over the publication of a book they considered offensive to their faith. In addition, worker strikes and some 200 small-scale but occasionally violent peasant protests against corrupt and rapacious local officials reportedly occurred in more than a dozen Chinese provinces. Rural discontent over a widening gap between urban and rural living standards accelerated migration to urban areas. Perhaps 100 million unregistered job hunters crowded into the cities, straining the resources and capacity of municipal governments. None of these developments signaled an imminent social explosion, but they justified high-level anxiety. Acknowledging a multiplicity of rural problems, Jiang pledged that the CPC would rebuild its disintegrated network of local party organizations in the countryside. Chinese society was also being stratified in other ways. The older Communist elite discreetly enjoyed their special privileges behind curtained car windows, in unmarked special stores, and in off-limits resorts. The new class of affluent urban entrepreneurs, as well as officials on the take, flaunted their wealth, indulging in an overtly bourgeois lifestyle that contrasted sharply with that of ordinary workers and salaried professionals. Sexual mores that questioned traditional values and concepts, sharply rising suicide rates, and increased incidence of mental illness accompanied social change.

Unable to do much more than shake their fists at the rising tide, China's cultural commissars nevertheless sought to guard public morals. They banned public showing of Chen Kaige's (Ch'en K'ai-ke's; *see* BIOGRAPHIES) politically subversive homoerotic film *Farewell, My Concubine,* which shared the Palme d'Or at the Cannes Film Festival, but reluctantly reversed themselves under international pressure. Actually, the literary and political writings of dissidents as well as video and audio cassettes continued to circulate rather freely inside China.

Deng generally favoured high economic growth with the attendant risk of instability over the more cautious approach preferred by some of his colleagues. In the first half of 1993, China's gross domestic product (GDP) grew at the phenomenal rate of 13.9%. Industrial production increased by over 25%; imports soared; and the money supply expanded by nearly 50%, while the Chinese yuan–U.S. dollar exchange rate fell from 7.4 to 10.6 on China's foreign currency swap markets. The budgetary deficit grew as government spending increased by 12.5% while revenues increased only 3.5%.

It was in this context that the Central Committee issued a 16-point document aimed at cooling down the economy. Zhu Rongji was entrusted with its implementation.

In his take-charge style, Zhu quickly moved to tighten the money supply by restricting credit, cutting back on government spending, increasing savings through compulsory government bond purchases, slashing capital purchases, and strengthening price controls that still remained. The effects on property prices and construction activity were immediate and dramatic. In Hainan province real-estate prices quickly fell 50%. Before the full effects of this austerity program could take hold, however, the party leadership reversed itself, opting for growth over stability. At its third plenum, in November, the 14th Central Committee adopted a comprehensive resolution entitled "CPC Central Committee Decision Concerning Some Questions Regarding the Establishment of a Socialist Market Economic System." Among the changes envisioned in the lengthy document were the economic modernization of state-owned enterprises and their gradual conversion into joint-stock companies, the establishment of a modern tax system based on income and value-added taxes to guarantee adequate revenue for the central state apparatus, the creation of an effective central banking system capable of regulating the economy by means of macroeconomic monetary and financial policies rather than by state administrative orders, and the establishment of a comprehensive system of social security to cushion the shock of large-scale urban unemployment as inefficient state industries merged or folded. The new tax plan was scheduled to go into effect on Jan. 1, 1994.

China's dynamic economic growth attracted foreign investment at a rate several times greater than in 1992. In the first three quarters, contracts totaling $83 billion in direct foreign investment were signed. Several hundred million dollars' worth of Chinese bonds were snapped up on the New York and London bond markets, and corporate and institutional money managers hastened to add Chinese investments to their portfolios. According to Chinese statistics, foreign trade shot up 17.7% between January and September, with imports surging 29.9% to $68.2 billion and exports growing at a more modest 6.6% to $61.2 billion. China consequently faced its first foreign-trade deficit since 1989.

As if to confirm that China had come of age economically, the International Monetary Fund asserted in its 1993 World Economic Outlook that China's economy was far larger than had previously been calculated and that in absolute terms it was surpassed only by the U.S. and Japan. The upward revaluation of China's GDP by a factor of seven came about through comparison of the purchasing power of the local currency in a local setting with the purchasing power of other currencies in their local settings—instead of calculation of GDP in U.S. dollars on the basis of market exchange rates. Under this newer method, called purchasing power parity, China's GDP in 1992 exceeded $2.8 trillion instead of the previously accepted $440 billion, and its per capita GDP was $2,470 instead of $370.

Foreign Relations. China continued the generally successful courtship of its Asian neighbours, playing its economic trump card to expand trade and investment with the Association of Southeast Asian Nations states as well as South Korea and Japan. The latter became China's major trading partner, surpassing Hong Kong, which was a special case. China bitterly denounced Hong Kong Gov. Chris Patten for proposing what were actually quite moderate changes in the British colony's electoral system before China's takeover in 1997, but it continued to discuss with the British how to structure the legislative elections in 1995.

During his September visit to Beijing, Indian Prime Minister P.V. Narasimha Rao and Li Peng signed a landmark agreement to maintain peace along the Line of Actual Control in the long-disputed border areas pending a final disposition of the conflicting claims. It seemed likely that the eventual territorial settlement would leave things pretty much as they were. Both sides pledged to refrain from the use or threat of force, to provide prior notification of military exercises, and to open up additional border passes to trade. The danger of a Sino-Indian war was at its lowest point in 35 years.

Shortly after the signing of the Middle East peace accords between Israel and various Palestinian organizations, China played host to Palestine Liberation Organization chairman Yasir Arafat and Israeli Prime Minister Yitzhak Rabin. China and Israel had a long history of covert cooperation in military technology transfers, although the value and content of such exchanges were in dispute. Elsewhere in the Middle East, China signed a deal to build a 300-MW nuclear power plant in Iran, and it maintained an active interest in the strife-torn neighbouring post-Soviet republics of Central Asia.

The November visit to Beijing of Russian Defense Minister Pavel Grachev produced a five-year military cooperation agreement that would increase Chinese capabilities in such fields as rocketry and antisubmarine warfare. Russia's hopes of maintaining even a weak position in Asia depended on good neighbourly relations with China.

The U.S. remained a very large thorn in China's side. In May, Clinton extended China's most-favoured-nation (MFN) status for another year, but he attached a series of human rights conditions that China had to meet before renewal in 1994. MFN was, in fact, a misnomer because all but a very few countries enjoyed the status. In August, Washington banned the export of certain high-technology equipment to China, alleging that the Chinese export of M-11 missile components to Pakistan violated provisions of the Missile Technology Control Regime, which Beijing had promised to respect. China rejected the charge. In August the U.S. shadowed a Chinese freighter that was reportedly transporting precursor chemicals for mustard and nerve gas to Iran. After a search of the ship's cargo failed to uncover evidence of such chemicals, Chinese Foreign Minister Qian Qichen (Ch'ien Ch'i-ch'en) blasted the U.S. for acting like "a self-styled world cop who tramples upon international law and norms of international relations." China also denounced the U.S. Congress for opposing the selection of Beijing as an Olympic site. On July 26, at the urging of Rep. Tom Lantos, the House had opposed the selection of Beijing by a vote of 287–99. Washington also threatened to slash quotas for Chinese textile imports unless Beijing curbed cheating via third-country reexports.

Clinton's reassessment of U.S. policy toward China in September held out some hope of arresting negative developments. High-level contacts between U.S. and Chinese officials, which the U.S. had cut off after the Tiananmen massacre, were restored late in the year. The November meeting between Jiang and Clinton in Seattle was brief and not immediately consequential. Even the resumption of Sino-American dialogue on diverse matters, including military-security affairs and human rights, promised no early resolution of differences. Nonetheless, discussions were better than mutual denunciations.

Chinese leaders calculated that U.S. economic interests in China would weigh heavier in the balance than concern about democracy, human rights, or Tibet. They eagerly courted the U.S. business community, which wanted a large slice of the China pie. But it would take considerable legerdemain for Clinton to circumvent his own human rights criteria for extending MFN status. A burgeoning U.S. trade deficit with China, on the order of $23 billion, did not make things easier.

Crown Prince Naruhito and Masako Owada wear court robes of the Heian era (794–1185) for their marriage in a Shinto ceremony on June 9. The new princess was educated at Harvard University and the Universities of Tokyo and Oxford and had worked in Japan's Foreign Ministry, specializing in U.S. trade issues.
HARUYOSHI YAMAGUCHI—SYGMA

In sum, uncertainties about the political succession, growing rifts between coastal and interior China, social tensions, and the vacuum of values left by the decay of Marxism-Leninism continued to cloud China's future. But the bright lights of the booming cities and the unprecedented prosperity enjoyed by the adaptable Communist elite and the protocapitalist nouveaux riches diverted attention away from the stormy passage that China was still likely to traverse on its voyage from a dying socialism to an as yet unknowable and unnameable new system. (STEVEN I. LEVINE)

JAPAN

A constitutional monarchy in the northwestern Pacific Ocean, Japan comprises an archipelago with four main islands (Hokkaido, Honshu, Kyushu, and Shikoku), the Ryukyus (including Okinawa), and lesser adjacent islands. Area: 377,750 sq km (145,850 sq mi). Pop. (1993 est.): 124,612,000. Cap.: Tokyo. Monetary unit: yen, with (Oct. 4, 1993) a free rate of 105.78 yen to U.S. $1 (160.25 yen = £1 sterling). Emperor, Akihito; prime ministers in 1993, Kiichi Miyazawa and, from August 9, Morihiro Hosokawa.

During 1993 Japan experienced political turmoil but not quite a revolution when the Liberal-Democratic Party (LDP) was ousted after 38 years in power. A coalition of seven dissident LDP factions and opposition parties elected Morihiro Hosokawa prime minister. (*See* BIOGRAPHIES.) Despite record-high approval ratings, Hosokawa faced formidable obstacles: a shaky coalition riven by policy differences, a stubborn recession aggravated by appreciation of the yen and deepened by unseasonable weather, and an eventual challenge in another general election. Japan's current account surplus, which in 1992 had soared to over $117 billion, or about 3% of gross national product (GNP), was increasingly criticized abroad, particularly by the U.S. By year's end, however, Japan's trade surplus appeared to be on the decline.

Domestic Affairs. Late in 1992 Prime Minister Kiichi Miyazawa appointed his second LDP Cabinet, reshuffling positions to defuse criticism of a "money-politics" scandal involving a major trucking company and Shin Kanemaru, the LDP's chief power broker. Kanemaru had been forced to resign as head of the faction that had ties to former prime minister Noboru Takeshita. Miyazawa named Masaharu Gotoda justice minister and point man in the Sagawa Kyubin affair. Yohei Kono became chief Cabinet secretary and the ailing Michio Watanabe deputy prime minister and foreign minister. Watanabe resigned in April and was replaced by Kabun Muto.

On January 22 the 150-day regular session of the Diet opened with the LDP focusing attention on the economy and the need for political reform. Opposition parties and dissident LDP members went on the offensive, blaming the government for the latest scandal and criticizing Miyazawa's management of the economy.

On June 18, hours after the (lower) House of Representatives passed a motion of no confidence in the prime minister, Miyazawa called a snap general election. He had lost the vote (255–220) because 39 members of the LDP had deserted him. On June 19, 10 LDP members defected and founded Sakigake (Harbinger, or Pioneer, Party) with Masayoshi Takemura as leader. On June 23 Tsutomu Hata, a former finance minister and founding member of the Takeshita faction, quit the LDP and formed the Japan Renewal Party (JRP), with the support of Ichiro Ozawa, a former LDP secretary-general. Hata announced, "Our party was formed to expedite a new wind, a new voice, a new system." He became the "public face" of the reformers because Ozawa had been closely linked to Kanemaru. The LDP had counted 274 members in the lower house before 56 defected in a single week.

During a two-week period in late June, public support for the Miyazawa Cabinet had dropped from 43.6 to 28.6%—the lowest level since 1989. Voters appeared to have lost confidence in all political parties. In the Tokyo Metropolitan Assembly election on June 27, the LDP barely held its own, winning 44 seats; Komeito (Clean Government Party), a major opposition group, took 25; and the Social Democratic Party of Japan (SDPJ), hitherto leaders of the opposition, won only 14. The surprising results were due to another rash of LDP defections.

Morihiro Hosokawa, the descendant of a samurai family and the grandson of Prince Fumimaro Konoe (prime minister in 1937–39 and 1940–41), had launched the Japan New Party (JNP) in May 1992. By July Hosokawa and three other members of the JNP had been elected to the (upper) House of Councillors. In the 1993 Tokyo election, the JNP won 20 seats. With one in 10 voters favouring the new party, the media began to refer to the "JNP boom." It was not the JNP, however, that laid the foundation stones for a new regime. On June 27 Hata met with the leaders of four opposition parties: the SDPJ, Komeito, the Democratic Socialist Party (DSP), and the United Social Democratic Party (USDP). The goal was to work toward electoral reform and corruption-free politics in the Diet. LDP hardliner and Ozawa archrival Seiroku Kajiyama asked voters whether they preferred continued stability under LDP rule or an unstable coalition government.

The July national election produced quite mixed results. The LDP remained the largest party in the lower house, but it failed to retain its absolute majority. Miyazawa's resignation as president of the LDP on July 22 coincided with Kanemaru's first court appearance on tax-evasion charges. Cabinet secretary Yohei Kono was then chosen to lead the party. On July 29 seven parties agreed to form an anti-LDP, noncommunist coalition and to field Hosokawa as their candidate for prime minister. At the time, lower house seats (total 512) were apportioned as follows (with prior strength): LDP 225 (227); SDPJ 70 (134); JRP 55 (36); Komeito 52 (45); JNP 35 (0); DSP 15 (13); Sakigake 13 (10); USDP 4 (4); Japan Communist Party (JCP) 15 (16); independents 27 (12); vacancies 0 (15). In the upper house (total 252), the representation was: LDP 99; SDPJ 73; JRP 8; Komeito 24; JNP 4; DSP 11; JCP 11; minor party backed by Rengo (Japan Trade Union Confederation) 10; vacancies 12.

On August 6 Hosokawa was elected prime minister when he received 262 of 503 votes cast. Kono, president of the LDP, garnered 224; Tetsuzo Fuwa, chairman of the JCP, received 15. In the upper house, Hosokawa was confirmed when he received 132 votes, with 93 votes being cast for Kono. Just before the critical vote, Takako Doi, who had been the first woman to head a major party (the SDPJ), became the first female to be elected speaker of the House. Doi's acceptance of the post tended to stabilize the coalition. That same day Hosokawa named six heads of the other coalition parties to his Cabinet: Hata (JRP) foreign minister and deputy prime minister); Takemura (Sakigake) chief Cabinet secretary; Sadao Yamahana (SDPJ) minister without portfolio in charge of political reform; Koshiro Ishida (Komeito) director of the Management and Coordination Agency; Keigo Ouchi (DSP) Health and Welfare Ministry; and Satsuki Eda (USDP) director of the Science and Technology Agency. Three women also received portfolios: Ryoko Akamatsu as minister of education, Manae Kubota as director of the Economic Planning Agency, and Wakako Hironaka as director of the Environment Agency. Although Yamahana accepted a Cabinet post, he resigned as chairman of the SDPJ. The task of rebuilding the SDPJ was turned over to Tomiichi Murayama, head of the party's Diet Administration Committee.

In his first policy address to the Diet on August 23, Hosokawa pledged to overhaul the economy in order to boost domestic demand and cut Japan's huge current account surplus. In addition, he urged a new plan to balance direct and indirect taxes and noted that electoral reform would include a ban on corporate donations. Turning to foreign relations, Hosokawa expressed "remorse and apologies" for the Pacific conflict, a statement of great importance to Japan's Asian neighbours. Ties with the U.S. would remain the hub of Japanese foreign policy. The new prime minister revealed an easy public style, particularly before TV cameras, which was unusual for Japanese leaders. He also appeared without the maroon lapel badge that signified Diet status. On August 15, the 48th anniversary of Japan's surrender ending World War II, he did not visit Yasukuni Shrine, which memorializes the nation's war dead. The decision of a prime minister to visit or not visit the shrine had strong nationalistic and political overtones. One month after its establishment, the Hosokawa Cabinet received a record-high 71% public-approval rating.

The coalition Cabinet passed its first test on August 28 when it approved a plan for electoral reform. The current lower house, based on multiseat constituencies, would be reduced from 512 to 500 members (250 from single-seat constituencies, 250 national seats based on proportional representation). Each voter would cast two votes—one for a district candidate, one for a national party. The LDP planned to introduce a rival plan of its own.

The Imperial Family. On June 9 in Tokyo, Crown Prince Naruhito (*see* BIOGRAPHIES) married Masako Owada, a career woman from the Foreign Ministry. Emperor Akihito and Empress Michiko began an unprecedented four-day visit to Okinawa on April 23 to pay respect to nearly 200,000 soldiers and civilians killed in the Pacific war. After the empress collapsed on October 20, her 59th birthday, the only medical information made public was the fact that she could not speak.

The Economy. In the face of intense pressure from the opposition, the Miyazawa Cabinet pushed a $603 billion budget (fiscal year 1993) through the lower house on March 7.

TORIN BOYD

Japanese citizens demonstrate against government corruption. Tainted by numerous scandals involving payoffs by businesses to politicians, the Liberal-Democratic Party finally lost control of the government in 1993 for the first time in 38 years.

About 5% of expenditures was earmarked for public works to stimulate the economy. On the eve of the new fiscal year (March 31), the upper house likewise approved the budget.

Despite stimulation, the gross national product (GNP) in fiscal 1992 had grown an anemic 0.8% in real terms, the lowest rate since 1974. The GNP further shrank (−0.5%, or −2% in annual terms) during the April–June quarter. Growth was affected by a decline in exports (−5.4%), a result of the yen's appreciation. Japan's 11 major commercial banks all posted declines in pretax profits as they struggled with problem loans. On April 13 the government unveiled a $115 billion stimulus package, the largest in history, to offset one of the nation's worst economic slumps since World War II. The Hosokawa Cabinet added a set of measures on September 16 to reduce economic regulations and to pass along the benefits of the yen's appreciation to Japanese consumers. The prime minister thus ignored Ozawa's demand to slash income taxes in half.

Foreign Affairs. In Tokyo's first contact with the new administration in Washington on February 11, Pres. Bill Clinton urged Foreign Minister Watanabe to try to cut Japan's $46 billion trade surplus with the U.S. Watanabe responded that the Super 301 trade clause being considered by Congress (allowing unilateral retaliation against unfair trade practices) "is not a good approach." In any case, the Finance Ministry announced that Japan's total current account surplus (fiscal 1992) had surged almost 40% to a record $126 billion (trade surplus, $136 billion). Three factors were driving up the yen's value against the dollar: Japan's trade surplus; the dollar's weakness, reflecting cuts in U.S. interest rates; and international coordination in raising the yen's value to cut the surplus.

Emerging from his first meeting with Miyazawa in Washington on April 16, Clinton told reporters that he wanted "specific results" in the trade arena. Miyazawa replied that good relations could not be realized with "managed trade" or under threat of "unilateralism." On July 10, after the meeting of the Group of Seven major industrial nations (G-7) in Tokyo, Japan and the U.S. agreed on a "framework" for trade relations. Tokyo would accept "objective criteria" to gauge market access. Miyazawa and Clinton referred to "tangible, measurable progress" in the negotiations and reaffirmed the agreement in a meeting at the UN in New York on September 28. On December 14 Hosokawa announced that he had made the "regrettable" decision to allow the importation of a modest amount of rice. Despite vigorous opposition at home, Hosokawa felt it was a concession Japan had to make to foster freer international trade.

During the year Japan made a significant effort to assuage the feelings of victims of the Pacific war. On March 11 Miyazawa offered an apology to Philippine Pres. Fidel Ramos for the forced prostitution of Filipinas during the conflict. Tokyo also welcomed the unusual concession of Kim Young Sam, South Korea's newly elected president, not to seek compensation for some 150,000 "comfort women" who had been forced into frontline brothels by the Imperial Japanese Army. Kim said this decision made Seoul "morally superior" in its relations with Tokyo. On August 4, after much delay, Japan's chief Cabinet secretary publicly admitted that his nation's military had been in control of such women during the war. On August 15, the anniversary of Japan's defeat, an *Asahi shimbun* editorial commented on Hosokawa's public admission that Japan had engaged in a "war of aggression." It said, "It took the Japanese government 48 years to admit what people abroad have been saying all along."

Meanwhile, South Korea's foreign minister and Miyazawa agreed to continue efforts to resolve the issue of North Korea's suspected development of nuclear arms. Miyazawa called Pyongyang's decision to withdraw from the Nuclear Non-proliferation Treaty and to block inspections of its nuclear facilities "a great security threat." On June 12 Pyongyang announced a delay in abandoning the treaty. North Korea was the only Asian country that had no diplomatic relations with Japan.

Japan had established normal relations with the U.S.S.R. in 1956, but a formal peace treaty with its successor, Russia, remained hung up over a territorial dispute. It involved four small islands in the southern Kurils, occupied by Russia but claimed by Japan. Tokyo threatened to limit aid to Moscow until the issue was resolved. In April, before the Tokyo summit, the G-7 ministers, whose number included the Japanese minister, hammered out a $40 billion aid package for Russia. Miyazawa informally met Pres. Boris Yeltsin on July 8 at the "G-7 plus 1" summit, but it was apparent that the president's precarious position at home precluded any territorial concession. After two postponed official visits, a cautious Yeltsin arrived in Tokyo on October 11. To save face, minor agreements were announced, but Tokyo offered no increase in aid to Russia, and Moscow no plan to solve the territorial problem.

On February 19 UN Secretary-General Boutros Boutros-Ghali completed a five-day visit to Tokyo. At a banquet in his honour, the secretary-general hinted that such nations as Japan, Germany, and Brazil needed to assume greater roles in the world organization. The emerging new world order, he added, required a "democratized" UN. Japan concluded this to mean that it should have a permanent seat on the Security Council. Speaking to the UN General Assembly in New York on September 27, Hosokawa advocated an expanded Council. He promised to "participate constructively," but he stopped short of openly proposing that Japan be given a permanent seat.

On April 27 the Cabinet approved the second deployment of Self-Defense Forces (SDF) on UN-organized peacekeeping operations. In mid-May contingents departed for Maputo, Mozambique, where they were to remain until general elections were held. On September 12, after a year in Cambodia, a 600-man engineering battalion from the Ground SDF completed its UN assignment and closed its base at Takeo. Altogether over 1,200 SDF personnel had served in Japan's first UN peacekeeping operation.

(ARDATH W. BURKS)

KOREA, DEMOCRATIC PEOPLE'S REPUBLIC OF

A socialist republic of northeastern Asia on the northern half of the peninsula of Korea, the Democratic People's Republic of Korea (North Korea) borders the Sea of Japan, the Yellow Sea, and the Republic of Korea at roughly the 38th parallel. Area: 122,762 sq km (47,399 sq mi). Pop. (1993 est.): 22,646,000. Cap.: Pyongyang. Monetary unit: won, with (Oct. 4, 1993) a free rate of 2.13 won to U.S. $1 (3.23 won = £1 sterling). President in 1993, Marshal Kim Il Sung; chairman of the Council of Ministers (premier), Kang Song San.

On March 12, 1993, North Korea announced that it would withdraw from the Nuclear Non-proliferation Treaty effective June 12. The news sent shock waves around the world because no nation had ever threatened to renege on an international agreement to control the spread of nuclear weapons. Pyongyang's decision was a direct response to the International Atomic Energy Agency's (IAEA's) insistence that it be allowed to inspect North Korea's nuclear facilities. The agency suspected that North Korea was violating the treaty by separating plutonium for possible use in nuclear weapons. Claiming that the IAEA's demand was a violation of its sovereignty, Pyongyang refused.

The IAEA had given Pyongyang one month to approve visits to two nuclear-waste-disposal sites at the Yongbyon nuclear complex, 90 km (56 mi) north of the capital. The IAEA team that had inspected some of the facilities in 1992 and examined small amounts of plutonium taken from the site concluded that North Korea was probably reprocessing more plutonium than it had earlier admitted.

The North's decision to withdraw from the Non-proliferation Treaty came while the U.S. and South Korea were conducting their annual Team Spirit military exercises. Pyongyang called the maneuvers a rehearsal for nuclear war and put its forces on a "semiwar" footing. In response to the North's decision, South Korean Pres. Kim Young Sam imposed economic sanctions on Pyongyang. The IAEA's March 31 deadline passed without compliance. The agency then made a formal complaint to the UN Security Council. Because China had made it clear that it would oppose sanctions, the Council passed a resolution on May 11 calling on Pyongyang to reconsider its actions.

On April 9 the North Korean government appointed Kim Jong Il chairman of the National Defense Commission, the nation's top military post. Placing the son (and presumed successor) of Pres. Kim Il Sung in complete charge of the military increased suspicions that he was orchestrating the nuclear confrontation. Tensions increased in late May when North Korea successfully tested an intermediate-range missile in the Sea of Japan. The Rodong 1 missile, with a range of 1,000 km (600 mi), was capable of reaching most Japanese cities.

To defuse the crisis, a series of meetings were held in New York between Robert Gallucci, U.S. assistant secretary of state, and Kang Sok Chu, North Korea's first deputy minister for foreign affairs. On June 11, hours before North Korea's deadline for withdrawing from the treaty, Pyongyang agreed to suspend its withdrawal and to continue talks with the U.S. After further meetings in Geneva, North Korea agreed to discuss site inspections with the IAEA. When the discussions proved fruitless, the IAEA passed another resolution in September pressuring Pyongyang to permit access to its nuclear complex. (JOSEPH L. NAGY)

This article updates the *Macropædia* article KOREA: *North Korea*.

KOREA, REPUBLIC OF

A republic of northeastern Asia on the southern half of the peninsula of Korea, the Republic of Korea (South Korea) borders the Sea of Japan, the Korea Strait, the Yellow Sea, and the Democratic People's Republic of Korea at roughly the 38th parallel. Area: 99,274 sq km (38,330 sq mi). Pop. (1993 est.): 44,042,000. Cap.: Seoul. Monetary unit: won, with (Oct. 4, 1993) a free rate of 814.40 won to U.S. $1 (1,234 won = £1 sterling). Presidents in 1993, Roh Tae Woo and, from February 25, Kim Young Sam; prime ministers, Hyun Soong Jong, Hwang In Sung, and, from December 16, Lee Hoi Chang.

Kim Young Sam, the first South Korean president in more than 30 years with no ties to the military, wasted little time carrying out his campaign pledge to battle corruption. Only weeks after being sworn in on Feb. 25, 1993, Kim launched one of the most comprehensive anticorruption campaigns in the nation's history. Before the year was out, he had purged thousands of bureaucrats, military leaders, and businessmen; released thousands of political prisoners; launched wide-ranging investigations into administrative abuses; and initiated sweeping financial reforms. In the process he earned record-high public-approval ratings.

A longtime opposition leader before his Reunification

South Korean Pres. Kim Young Sam addresses the National Assembly. The first president of South Korea in 32 years without ties to the military, Kim instituted reforms that included ethics guidelines for officeholders and business people, tighter control of the military, and an end to the practice of using false names in financial transactions.
REUTERS/BETTMANN

Democratic Party and Kim Jong Pil's New Democratic Republican Party merged with the ruling Democratic Justice Party in 1990 to form the Democratic Liberal Party, Kim began his quest for a "clean and just society" by revealing his own net worth—$2.1 million—and pledging never to accept political donations during his five-year term. He then called on all 161 ruling party lawmakers to disclose their personal assets. The subsequent revelations sparked such public outrage that several high-ranking legislators, including the speaker of the National Assembly, Park Jyun Kyu, were forced to resign. In May the National Assembly passed a law requiring all of its members, some 7,000 government officials, and senior military officers to reveal their assets.

Kim's Cabinet was a mix of political veterans and newcomers. He appointed the party's chief policy maker, former general Hwang In Sung, prime minister. Hwang was given the task of reviving the country's sagging economy. Another key appointment was the naming of Lee Hoi Chang, a Supreme Court judge, to head the Board of Audit and Inspection (BAI), which was to spearhead the president's anticorruption drive. Kim set a precedent by appointing Kim Deok, an academic, head of the powerful Agency for National Security Planning, which in the past had been accused of persecuting political dissidents.

The president's vigorous ethics campaign so upset conservatives within the ruling party that they hit back. On March 8 Kim was forced to fire three newly appointed ministers after reports surfaced of past misdeeds. Justice Minister Park Hee Tae was said to have used unfair means to get his daughter into a university; Health Minister Park Yang Shil was accused of real-estate speculation; and Construction Minister Huh Jae Hyung was accused of "irregularities." In addition, Seoul Mayor Kim Sang Chul was fired for involvement in illegal land development. The embarrassing revelations, however, did nothing to slow down the president's efforts.

The military was one of Kim's main targets. During his first month in office he replaced the army chief of staff and the head of military intelligence. Next came investigations into the military's procurement program and into charges of payoffs for military promotions. In time, 13 officers, including five air force generals, the former air force chief of staff, and seven other officers, were arrested on charges of receiving payoffs for promotions. The Defense Ministry later released the 13 from jail, but it announced that all would be discharged from active service. In a separate probe, the BAI investigated the procurement of weapons systems. Former air force chief of staff Gen. Chung Yong Ho charged that the government of former president Roh Tae Woo may have accepted bribes to switch a $5.2 billion contract for fighter planes from McDonnell Douglas Corp. to General Dynamics. The National Assembly investigated the matter in September, but no formal charges were made.

The BAI soon extended its investigation to all military procurement programs, including the purchase of submarines, tanks, and other equipment. In October two former navy chiefs, Kim Chul Woo and Kim Chong Ho, were sentenced to six years in jail for accepting bribes for defense contracts and for selling promotions. Other casualties of the anticorruption campaign included Chief Justice Kim Duck Joo and Kim Hyo Eun, the national police chief; both resigned in September after disclosing their assets.

Kim further tightened his hold on the military by removing top generals with ties to former military regimes. In April he dismissed two three-star generals who had headed army units linked to the 1979 coup that brought Chun Doo Hwan to power. In May he fired Gen. Lee Pil Sup, the chairman of the joint chiefs of staff, and two other senior generals for their involvement in the 1979 coup.

The administration's other major concern was the economy. The growth rate had slipped to 4.7% in 1992, the lowest in a decade. In May the government released its five-year economic-reform plan. Its goal was to cut government red tape and replace most government controls with free-market mechanisms by 1997. The program, among other things, called for deregulation of interest rates and the phasing out of subsidized government loans to industry by private banks.

Kim dropped his biggest financial bombshell on August 12 when he announced on national television that anonymous or false-name financial transactions would become illegal. The use of false-name accounts allowed business conglomerates to funnel millions of dollars into the ruling party coffers. It also contributed to corruption by allowing officials to speculate in the stock and real-estate markets. It was, moreover, a handy way to avoid income taxes. The reform was considered a keystone in Kim's anticorruption campaign.

On December 9 Kim announced that he had agreed to allow foreign rice imports as part of the General Agreement on Tariffs and Trade. Other countries had also made concessions in order to improve the world's economy by removing or lowering international trade barriers. The move led to Prime Minister Hwang's resignation and a major Cabinet reshuffle. (JOSEPH L. NAGY)

This article updates the *Macropædia* article KOREA: *South Korea*.

MONGOLIA

A landlocked republic between Russia and China in eastern Asia, Mongolia was formerly known as Outer Mongolia. Area: 1,566,500 sq km (604,800 sq mi). Pop. (1993 est.): 2,256,000. Cap.: Ulaanbaatar (Ulan Bator). Monetary unit: tugrik, with (Oct. 4, 1993) a free rate of 397.10 tugrik to U.S. $1 (601.60 tugrik = £1 sterling). President in 1993, Punsalmaagiyn Ochirbat; prime minister, Puntsagiyn Jasray.

Domestic politics in 1993 was dominated by the country's first-ever presidential election, held on June 6, in which Punsalmaagiyn Ochirbat was returned to office. The result was a resounding defeat for the Mongolian People's Revolutionary Party (MPRP), the reformed communist party, despite its commanding position in the Great Hural (assembly). Angered by his strong constitutional stand, the MPRP had abandoned support for the incumbent in favour of a hard-line ideologist, Lodongiyn Tudev. Ochirbat, a former MPRP member, received the nomination of the opposition parties, the National Democrats (a new alliance) and Social Democrats. The MPRP vote split, and Ochirbat won the election by 592,622 votes to 396,870.

The election was part of an administrative and legislative reform package initiated by the 1992 constitution. Among other changes, the criminal code, adopted in 1986, was amended to abolish crimes against state security and reduce the number of crimes punishable by execution, although in general the length of prison terms was increased. In the face of rising crime, President Ochirbat ordered the establishment of a special council, which would initially concentrate on measures to deal with public drunkenness and alcoholism.

The outcome of the election reflected growing dissatisfaction with hardships, including shortages and rising prices, stemming from the MPRP's policies on privatization and monetary control. Moreover, the period March–July was marked by a series of natural disasters. Heavy snowfall in the west, steppe fires in the east, snow and dust storms in central regions, and flooding in the north caused loss of human life and took a heavy toll of livestock.

The government's efforts to meet the strict terms for financial reform required by the International Monetary Fund were rewarded in April by the restoration of standby credit suspended in 1992. The tugrik was devalued at the beginning of 1993 and then floated on May 28. A new 500-tugrik note bearing the portrait of Genghis Khan was put into circulation. The third meeting of donor countries, held in Tokyo in September, agreed on another aid-and-loan package for Mongolia worth $150 million for medium- and long-term projects in 1994, including a $41 million loan from Japan for the rehabilitation of Mongolian railways.

By means of further liberalization measures, including the new foreign-investment law that came into force in July, Mongolia was hoping to attract capital from abroad, particularly into the mining sector. Both President Ochirbat, who visited Moscow in January to sign a new treaty with Russia, and Prime Minister Puntsagiyn Jasray, who visited the U.S. in June, assured businessmen of Mongolia's political and financial stability and encouraged them to participate in joint ventures. (ALAN J.K. SANDERS)

TAIWAN

Taiwan, which consists of the island of Taiwan and surrounding islands off the coast of China, is the seat of the Republic of China (Nationalist China). Area: 36,179 sq km (13,969 sq mi), including the island of Taiwan and its 86 outlying islands, 22 in the Taiwan group and 64 in the Pescadores group. Pop. (1993 est.): 20,926,000. (Area and population figures include the Quemoy and Matsu groups, which are administered as an occupied part of Fujian [Fukien] province.) Cap.: Taipei. Monetary unit: New Taiwan dollar, with (Oct. 4, 1993) a free rate of NT$26.91 to U.S. $1 (NT$40.78 = £1 sterling). President in 1993, Lee Teng-hui; presidents of the Executive Yuan (premier), Hau Pei-tsun and, from February 10, Lien Chan.

The fire of partisan politics kept the political pot boiling furiously in the Republic of China in Taiwan throughout 1993 as support for the ruling Kuomintang (KMT) continued to erode. Challenges both from inside and outside the KMT tested the leadership of Pres. Lee Teng-hui, who was also chairman of the KMT. On February 10 the National Assembly approved Lee's choice of Lien Chan to head the Executive Yuan, a post equivalent to that of premier. Lien had earned a doctorate in political science at the University of Chicago and had served as provincial governor of Taiwan. With his appointment the two top government posts, for the first time, were held by native-born Taiwanese.

Critical of what they viewed as Lee's weakening commitment to the concept of a united China, a small group of mostly second-generation mainlanders in the KMT formed an intraparty faction in May called the New KMT Alliance and then bolted the KMT in August to form the Chinese New Party. Coming out in favour of direct talks with China and the establishment of direct transportation links between Taiwan and mainland China, leaders of the Chinese New Party said they hoped to shock the KMT into undertaking long-overdue reforms.

At its 14th National Party Congress in August, Lee was reelected chairman of the KMT by a large majority in the first such secret ballot, and his supporters garnered 151 of the 210 seats on the Central Committee. Four vice-chairmen were added to the party hierarchy, two of whom supported Lee and two who did not. Notwithstanding Lee's victory, party leaders felt their grip on power was imperiled. KMT leaders were finding it increasingly difficult to enforce party discipline, and on the eve of Taiwan's off-year local elections, the KMT Central Standing Committee expelled 19 party members for running without the KMT's official endorsement or for supporting candidates fielded by opposition parties.

Encouraged by dissension in the KMT ranks and buoyed by its gains in the 1992 Legislative Yuan elections, the opposition Democratic Progressive Party (DPP) had high hopes of victory in the November local elections. The KMT, however, increased its share of mayoral and county magistrate offices from 14 to 15; the DPP slipped from 7 to 6; and Independents took 2. For the KMT the downside of the election was their loss of popular support, which slipped from 53 to 47%. The DPP's share edged upward from 38 to 41%, indicating that for the first time, the electorate might be viewing the DPP as a plausible governing alternative to the KMT rather than as just a party of protest.

With rare bipartisan support, Lee launched a futile bid for Taiwan to rejoin the UN. It had lost its seat in 1971 when the UN withdrew its recognition and transferred it to the People's Republic of China. Direct talks between representatives of Taiwan and China took place in April and November on issues related to their expanding economic relations. Indirect trade via Hong Kong was estimated at $10 billion, although Taiwan exports to the mainland were temporarily slowed by Beijing's (Peking's) midyear austerity program. In September the U.S. sold 41 Harpoon antiship missiles to Taiwan in the largest deal since then president George Bush had authorized the sale of 150 F-16s a year earlier.

Taiwan's export-driven economy expanded by a very respectable 6% in 1993. A shortage of capital, caused in part by massive private investments on the Chinese mainland, led to the scaling back and prolongation of Taiwan's massive infrastructure development plans. Responding to enormous U.S. pressure, Taiwan passed additional legislation in April to protect intellectual property rights, particularly regarding computer software. However they made their money, the residents of Taiwan continued to live increasingly well as the island's projected 1993 per capita gross national product rose to an estimated $10,600. (STEVEN I. LEVINE)

South and Central Asia

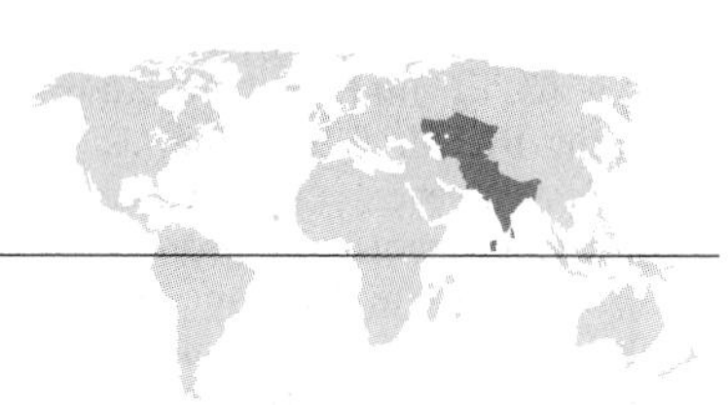

AFGHANISTAN

Afghanistan is a landlocked Islamic republic in central Asia. Area: 652,225 sq km (251,825 sq mi). Pop. (1993 est.): 20,269,000 (excluding Afghan refugees estimated to number about 1.5 million in Pakistan and 2.3 million in Iran). Cap.: Kabul. Monetary unit: afghani, with (Oct. 4, 1993) a free rate of 1,520 afghanis to U.S. $1 (2,304 afghanis = £1 sterling). President in 1993, Burhanuddin Rabbani; prime minister, Gulbuddin Hekmatyar (designated on March 8, sworn in on June 17).

Afghanistan marked the first anniversary of the fall of the communist regime and the birth of an Islamic government, but in general the country had little to celebrate in 1993. One year after a rebel coalition triumphantly ousted the communist president, Mohammad Najibullah, and declared an Islamic government on April 28, 1992, Afghanistan remained a battleground, with rival factions fighting for power and pounding the capital with rockets. An estimated 10,000 people were killed, 750,000 were displaced, and many neighbourhoods in Kabul were devastated. Most UN officials and foreign diplomats left Afghanistan. Although the fighting lessened somewhat in the latter half of 1993, it was still unclear if the nation, which withstood 14 years of civil war, ultimately would be governable. Meanwhile, Najibullah, who had received a promise of safe passage from the UN when it negotiated his abdication, remained in the UN office in Kabul, suffering from a kidney ailment. The UN had been unable to secure his freedom.

Continuing hostilities also delayed the homecoming of an estimated 3.8 million refugees in Iran and Pakistan, the largest refugee population in the world. The UN believed it would take until the end of 1995 for the 1.5 million Afghans remaining in Pakistan to return home.

In early January a national assembly of tribal and religious leaders confirmed the acting president, approved the creation of a parliament and a new army, and set a strict Islamic path for Afghanistan. Despite allegations of vote buying, bribery, and threats of renewed civil war, the assembly voted to keep Burhanuddin Rabbani as president. The 53-year-old Islamic scholar was sworn in on January 2. Five of the 10 main rebel groups denounced the council as unrepresentative, however, and described Rabbani's reelection as a declaration of war. The 1,335-member assembly further ordered that only Muslims work for the government, banned all non-Muslim organizations, and declared that radio and television had to conform to Islamic law.

Despite continuing fighting among the various rebel leaders—principally between government forces under Defense Minister Ahmed Shah Masood and Hezb-i-Islami faction troops loyal to fundamentalist Gulbuddin Hekmatyar—a 22-member Cabinet was named on May 20. Hekmatyar was designated prime minister in March after his forces captured Masood's ministry building in Kabul, which Hezb-i-Islami troops had been shelling for a year.

Acceding to Hekmatyar's demands, the May cease-fire agreement called for the Defense Ministry to be run by a commission under President Rabbani. Other Cabinet posts were divided among the 10 major rebel groups, including Mohammad Yunus Khalis' breakaway faction of the Hezb-i-Islami, which had boycotted all past agreements. Afghanistan's minority Shi'ites, allies of Hekmatyar who

People in Kabul carry on with their daily lives amid the ruins of civil war. During 1993 Afghanistan continued to suffer from fighting between rival groups, much of it occurring in the capital city.
T.A. DAVIS

had been demanding greater representation, were given the Finance and Health ministries.

Hekmatyar ventured into Kabul in mid-June for the first time since 1992. On June 17 he was formally sworn in as prime minister in a low-key ceremony in a village outside Kabul, the capital. The state-controlled Kabul radio reported on September 27 that the Afghan leadership, after five days of negotiations, had approved an interim constitution and that elections would be held in 1994.

On the international front Afghanistan made efforts to win support and money from Islamic nations. Prime Minister Hekmatyar visited Tehran in August and returned with a pledge that Iran would help repair roads destroyed in the war and help Afghanistan look for oil and gas. In the same month, Afghanistan said that it would not return Stinger missile launchers supplied by the U.S. to anti-Soviet rebels during the 1978–92 Afghan war. Washington wanted to buy back the antiaircraft weapons to keep them from falling into the hands of terrorists.

Afghanistan, the world's largest opium grower, according to the UN, produced an estimated 2,000 tons in 1992. This was a concern not only for the West, where the production fueled the illegal heroin trade, but also at home, where it was estimated that 15% of all adult Afghan males age 15–40 were addicted to hard drugs. (DILIP GANGULY)

BANGLADESH

A republic and member of the Commonwealth, Bangladesh is in the northeastern part of the Indian subcontinent, on the Bay of Bengal. Area: 148,393 sq km (57,295 sq mi). Pop. (1993 est.): 115,075,000. Cap.: Dhaka. Monetary unit: taka, with (Oct. 4, 1993) an official rate of 39.49 taka to U.S. $1 (59.83 taka = £1 sterling). President in 1993, Abdur Rahman Biswas; prime minister, Khaleda Zia.

Bangladesh served as host to a seven-nation summit of South Asian leaders in April 1993 to improve the image of a nation perhaps best known for its grim battle against hunger, disease, overpopulation, cyclones, floods, and political violence. These factors often caused the otherwise fertile country of 115 million people to be one of the poorest in the world. For Prime Minister Khaleda Zia, the summit of India, Pakistan, Sri Lanka, Bhutan, Nepal, Maldives, and Bangladesh came as a showpiece for projecting her country's potential.

Twenty-two years after its independence from Pakistan, Bangladesh in 1993 had some success stories to tell. During the year the economy grew by 5%, up 1.4%. The annual per capita income also increased to $210 in 1993 from $170 in 1990. Meanwhile, the rate of inflation, which had been as high as 61% in 1974, came down to 9.3% in 1990 and further down to 3% in 1993. Although the population kept rising, the rate of growth was cut to 2.03% in 1993 from an average 3%. The use of contraceptives increased to 40%, compared with 7.7% 18 years earlier.

The production of grain, mainly rice, was estimated at a record 19.6 million tons in 1993. This was only 200,000 tons less than the nation needed to gain self-sufficiency in food grains. To many people the 1993 figures might appear meaningless in a predominantly agrarian nation where more than 55% of the population lived below the poverty line (meaning they could not afford two meals a day) and half of the labour force was either unemployed or underemployed. But it showed great progress from the early 1970s, when the world termed the newly independent Bangladesh a basket case for its almost negative economic growth, total dependence on foreign aid, and growing population.

Although Zia, whose Bangladesh Nationalist Party had swept the 1992 elections, was successful in projecting a better image of her country, her battle to remain in power continued throughout 1993. A new challenge came from Islamic fundamentalists, who staged several street protests to overthrow the democratically elected government.

The opposition Awami League led a series of strikes and antigovernment rallies throughout the year. On January 24, bombs exploded at a rally of Awami League leader Sheik Hasina Wajeb, who said it was an attempt on her life. Two days later a dawn-to-noon nationwide strike paralyzed the country. The opposition staged more nationwide strikes in July and August to protest alleged government corruption.

To add to the woes, 27,000 nurses went on strike in August to protest the appointment of a bureaucrat to head their administration. The strike was called off a week later.

On the international front, Dhaka's relations with Malaysia, India, China, and Pakistan improved with growing trade relations. On January 10 repatriation of stranded Pakistanis began with the airlifting of 300 Muslims who had chosen Pakistan as their homeland. About 500,000 Urdu-speaking Muslims lived in Bangladeshi camps awaiting repatriation to Pakistan.

The issue of Muslim refugees from Myanmar (Burma), however, strained Yangon-Dhaka relations. On March 20 soldiers from Myanmar attacked a Bangladesh border village, killing one man and wounding five others. On May 12

UN High Commissioner for Refugees Sadako Ogata visited Bangladesh and toured refugee camps. Over 250,000 Muslims had fled to Bangladesh to avoid persecution in military-ruled Myanmar.

Former Bangladesh president Hussain Mohammad Ershad remained in prison in 1993 and faced 19 more charges, ranging from corruption to possession of illegal arms. Ershad was ousted on Dec. 6, 1990, after a series of street protests against his rule. He was convicted on three different counts and sentenced to up to 10 years in prison.

(DILIP GANGULY)

BHUTAN

The monarchy of Bhutan is a landlocked state situated in the eastern Himalayas between China and India. Area: 47,000 sq km (18,150 sq mi). Pop. (1993 est.): 1,546,000 (official projection based on 1980 census includes some 600,000–700,000 Nepalese residents purportedly declared stateless by the Bhutanese government in late 1990, more than 80,000 of whom are now refugees in Nepal). Cap.: Thimphu. Monetary unit: ngultrum, at par with the Indian rupee (which is also in use), with (Oct. 4, 1993) a free rate of 31.15 ngultrums to U.S. $1 (47.19 ngultrums = £1 sterling). Druk gyalpo (king) in 1993, Jigme Singye Wangchuk.

Four years after trying to quash an uprising by its Nepalese minority, Bhutan was still unable to solve its most pressing problem in 1993. Nepalese activists, who professed to be waging a prodemocracy campaign against an absolute monarchy, asserted that 53% of Bhutan's residents were Nepalese. The government claimed that barely a third were Nepalese and that all others were illegal aliens from India and Nepal. Some 80,000 Nepalese who had fled Bhutan were sheltered in camps on the Nepal-Bhutan border.

A Nepalese delegation visited Bhutan in July to discuss the refugee issue, although a meeting in April between King Jigme Singye Wangchuk and Nepalese Prime Minister Girija Prasad Koirala had ended in failure. The two discussed setting up a joint committee to determine the citizenship of the refugees, but nothing more was accomplished. The International Red Cross visited Bhutan in January to investigate alleged violations of human rights and appalling living conditions in prisons. After increasing incidents of piracy of Buddhist statues and antiques, Bhutan planned to enact special laws to deal with antiques smugglers. Bhutan also donated a Himalayan bear to the Kuwaiti zoo to help repair the damage done by Iraqi troops during the Gulf war.

(DILIP GANGULY)

INDIA

A federal republic of southern Asia and member of the Commonwealth, India is situated on a peninsula extending into the Indian Ocean with the Arabian Sea to the west and the Bay of Bengal to the east. Area: 3,166,414 sq km (1,222,559 sq mi), including the Indian-administered portion of Jammu and Kashmir. Pop. (1993 est): 896.6 million, including Indian-administered Jammu and Kashmir. Cap.: New Delhi. Monetary unit: Indian rupee, with (Oct. 4, 1993) a free rate of Rs 31.15 to U.S. $1 (Rs 47.19 = £1 sterling). President in 1993, Shankar Dayal Sharma; prime minister, P.V. Narasimha Rao.

Domestic Affairs. During 1993 Indian politics was dominated by the fallout from two events that had occurred the previous year: the destruction of the Babri Mosque in Ayodhya and the scandal in the stock market. There were an escalation of activity by Hindu fundamentalists, a growing sullenness among Muslims, and interreligious riots in many cities. While a joint parliamentary committee was investigating the "scam" (the popular term for the stock market scandal), the principal actor, Harshad Mehta, contended that he had personally given Rs 10 million to Prime Minister P.V. Narasimha Rao, who promptly denied the charge. His political savvy and the people's weariness over the prospects of another midterm election enabled Rao to survive the combined onslaught of the opposition parties. The government won a vote on the budget (248–197) in May and defeated a no-confidence motion (265–251) in July. Indians would also associate 1993 with its worst earthquake in half a century; some 10,000 people lost their lives.

Hindu-Muslim riots that broke out in Bombay on January 6 claimed 557 lives in the first week; the estimated Rs 40 billion in property damage included the destruction of 10,000 homes. There were also disturbances in Ahmadabad and other cities.

On January 7 the president issued an ordinance for the acquisition of 27.4 ha (67.7 ac) of land in Ayodhya around the site of the demolished Babri Mosque. The ordinance also called for the setting up of two trusts, one to rebuild the mosque and the other to build a temple for Lord Rama to satisfy Hindus. The ordinance also requested the Supreme Court to decide whether there was evidence that a Rama temple had stood on the site before the mosque was built. The ordinance was later adopted by Parliament.

L.K. Advani, M.M. Joshi, Ashok Singhal, and other Hindu leaders who had been arrested in December 1992 were released on January 10. A tribunal that reviewed the ban imposed on the Rashtriya Swayamsevak Sangh (RSS), the Bajrang Dal, and the Vishwa Hindu Parishad (VHP) upheld the ban only in respect to the VHP. The tribunal, however, was of the view that the demolition of the mosque had been carefully planned. The Hindu parties had organized interstate marches to mobilize popular support. In October the Central Bureau of Investigation filed cases against Advani, Joshi, Bal Thackeray (head of the Shiv Sena), and others for planning the demolition.

The government came out with a bill to separate politics from religion. After strong protests from avowedly Hindu and Muslim political parties, it was referred to a select committee of Parliament. The joint parliamentary committee investigating the scam did not issue its final report, but its interim report blamed weaknesses in the governmental system rather than any individual for failure to exercise necessary supervision. Another committee that investigated the dimensions of the scam determined that the total loss was of the order of Rs 40,242,000,000.

KAMAL SAHAI—ASIAWEEK PICTURES

Mohammed Altaf Alamgir (masked), who advocates unification of Kashmir with Pakistan, walks with members of his militant group. The Indian government continued to try to control separatist movements in Jammu and Kashmir state, which was contested with Pakistan.

The union Cabinet was reshuffled on January 17. Dinesh Singh was inducted as minister for external affairs and Pranab Mukherjee as minister of commerce. A few days earlier, Madhavrao Scindia had resigned as minister for civil aviation. Early in March the minister of defense, Sharad Pawar, assumed the new post of chief minister of Maharashtra.

The Mandal Commission's recommendations that 27% of the jobs in the central government and public-sector undertakings be reserved for backward classes (above the 22.5% for designated castes and tribes) came into effect in September. The government had earlier, following a Supreme Court directive, identified the "creamy layer" in these classes who would not be eligible for the benefit.

The Supreme Court acquired a new chief justice, M.N. Venkatachaliah. One of the most important rulings of the court was that the chief justice of India should have primacy in the choice of judges for the state high courts and the Supreme Court. In another judgment, the court held that free education was a right only up to 14 years of age and that in professional colleges 50% of seats could be filled by candidates prepared to pay higher fees. There could be no quota for families, castes, or communities that might have set up colleges. An impeachment motion against Justice V. Ramaswami, the first against a Supreme Court judge, failed to secure a majority in May.

To meet domestic and external allegations of widespread violence and brutality by the police and security forces, the government announced the appointment of a human rights commission. While the threat of militancy in Punjab had generally ebbed, the same could not be said of the state of Jammu and Kashmir. An encounter in Sopore claimed 50 lives in January. There was a serious confrontation with the separatists in October. The army cordoned off the Hazratbal Mosque in Srinagar and demanded the surrender of the armed militants who had taken refuge there. The militants laid down their weapons only on November 16. There were demonstrations against the action of the army. The Border Security Force fired on a crowd in Bijbihara on October 22, killing 43 people. There were also politically motivated explosions in Calcutta in March (60 deaths), in Bombay in April (33 deaths), and at the office of the RSS in Madras in August (11 deaths).

Several states changed their governors, including Maharashtra, West Bengal, Tamil Nadu, Uttar Pradesh, Rajasthan, Madhya Pradesh, Orissa, Himachal Pradesh, and Mizoram. Elections were held in Manipur, Tripura, and Meghalaya. The Left Front led by the Communist Party of India (Marxist) returned to power in Tripura with a strong majority. The president gave assent to two constitutional amendment bills (the 72nd and 73rd), both of which had been passed by Parliament in the second half of 1992. They were intended to enhance the governing powers of village councils (parchayats) and municipalities.

The districts of Latur and Osmanabad in Maharashtra were devastated by an earthquake in the pre-dawn hours of September 30. Although it measured a modest 6.4 on the Richter scale, the death toll was heavy; some 10,000 were believed to have died, substantially fewer than the 35,000 figure that appeared in early unofficial reports. In addition, an estimated 140,000 were rendered homeless. Conservationists stepped up their campaign against the Sardar Sarovar dam project in western India across the Narmada River. India formally withdrew its request for an installment of $180 million of a World Bank loan because it considered the conditions unacceptable. As many as 184 industries around the Taj Mahal in Agra were ordered closed by the courts in order to reduce damage to the monument from pollution. A surface-to-surface missile, Prithvi, was successfully launched in June, as was also the Insat-2B satellite in July, but the Polar Satellite Launch Vehicle failed to put the Indian remote sensing satellite IRS-IE into orbit in September.

The Economy. The union government's budget, presented on February 27, outlined a series of measures to further liberalize the economy. The rupee was made fully convertible on trade accounts, and import duty on capital goods was substantially reduced. Excise duty was abolished on coffee and tea. Asserting that "the sense of crisis is behind us," the finance minister, Manmohan Singh, declared that his objectives were to restructure trade and industrial policies, encourage efficiency through greater domestic competition, allow producers to have access to imports at reasonable rates of duty, encourage foreign investment, upgrade technology, and integrate the Indian economy with the world economy. The budget envisaged total receipts (revenue plus capital) of Rs 1,270,090,000,000 and total expenditure of Rs 1,313,230,000,000 (including Rs 412,510,000,000 for development). The total budgetary deficit was placed at Rs 43,140,000,000. The allocation for defense was Rs 191.8 billion. Nationalized banks were allowed to raise up to 49% of capital from the public. The maximum interest rate on bank deposits was reduced from 12 to 11% and the maximum lending rate on commercial advances from 18 to 17%.

In the first six months of the fiscal year (April–September), exports registered a 27% increase. This, along with increased foreign investments and the accumulation of $500 million in gold through bond sales, helped raise foreign exchange reserves to $7.2 billion by October. The inflation rate, which had reached 17% by August 1991, stood at 8.5% on November 16. Industrial production was still sluggish, but a satisfactory monsoon held prospects for another good harvest in 1993–94. During the previous fiscal year, production had risen 8%. A growth rate of 4.5% was forecast for the year. Because of pressure from farming interests, a subsidy was reinstated on nonnitrogenous fertilizers. Licensing of cars, air conditioners, refrigerators, and a whole range of domestic appliances was abolished in April. Foreign investment commitments were placed at $3 billion over an 18-month period. Some of the collaboration agreements were in the power sector. Coca-Cola reentered India. The International Monetary Fund reported that the Indian economy was the sixth largest in the world.

Foreign Affairs. When Prime Minister Narasimha Rao visited China in September, both countries agreed to regard actual control of disputed areas as a workable basis for settling border disputes, and to reduce forces along the border. In July, Russia responded to U.S. pressure and suspended its agreement with India for the supply of cryogenic rocket technology. There was consternation that U.S. Pres. Bill Clinton had included Kashmir in the list of countries affected by religious strife and civil war. In his October congratulatory message to Benazir Bhutto on her election as prime minister of Pakistan, Rao hoped that outstanding issues between the two countries would be settled peacefully through negotiations. India repeatedly maintained that the Kashmir militants received arms and support from the Inter Services Intelligence of Pakistan.

The prime minister's visit to Iran was of special importance. Other countries that he visited were Thailand, Uzbekistan, Kazakhstan, Oman, Bhutan, South Korea, and Bangladesh. Pres. Shankar Dayal Sharma paid state visits to Greece, Hungary, Iran, Turkey, Ukraine, and the U. K. in July. Among important statesmen to visit India during the year were Pres. Boris Yeltsin of Russia, Prime Minister John Major of the U.K., Chancellor Helmut Kohl of Germany, and the kings of Bhutan, Nepal, and Sweden. Following the visit of Israeli Foreign Minister Shimon Peres, India lifted its 47-year-old trade sanctions against Israel. In November India and the U.K. signed an extradition treaty during the visit of the British foreign minister, and diplomatic relations with South Africa were reestablished during a visit by that country's foreign minister. (H.Y. SHARADA PRASAD)

KAZAKHSTAN

A republic of Central Asia, Kazakhstan borders Russia on the west and north, China on the east, Kyrgyzstan on the southeast, Uzbekistan and the Aral Sea on the south, and Turkmenistan and the Caspian Sea on the southwest. Area: 2,717,300 sq km (1,049,200 sq mi). Pop. (1993 est.): 17,186,000. Cap.: Almaty (formerly Alma-Ata). Monetary unit: Russian ruble (the monetary systems of Kazakhstan and Russia were unified on Sept. 23, 1993), with (October 4) a free rate of 1,165 rubles = U.S. \$1 (1,765 rubles = £1 sterling). President in 1993, Nursultan Nazarbayev; prime minister, Sergey Tereshchenko.

During 1993 Kazakhstan continued to enjoy a reputation as one of the more democratic of the new states of Central Asia on the basis of its relatively free press, commitment to rapid privatization, and encouragement of foreign investment. Pres. Nursultan Nazarbayev and his government maintained a monopoly over political decision making, arguing that in Kazakhstan's multiethnic environment democratization would have to be a protracted process. A wide spectrum of political parties was allowed to function, on the understanding that they would not engage in extremist rhetoric or seek to upset the ethnic status quo. Most of these groups were tiny and had no real influence, though the Socialist Party, the People's Congress Party, and the People's Unity Union sought to become genuine opposition parties. The independence of Kazakhstan's Constitutional Court was an encouraging sign that democratic principles were taking root; on several occasions the court ruled presidential or government decrees unconstitutional.

The lack of a common Kazakhstani national consciousness transcending ethnic loyalties caused considerable concern to the country's leadership, and in June, Nazarbayev created a special presidential council of intellectuals, scientists, and government officials to find ways to create a "national ideology." While many Russians identified themselves fully as loyal citizens, others were disturbed by the rising level of Kazakh ethnic assertiveness and the increasing "Kazakhization" of official positions.

In early September, Nazarbayev achieved a long-cherished goal with the creation of an economic union of members of the Commonwealth of Independent States. Immediately prior to this agreement, Kazakhstan joined with Uzbekistan and Russia in establishing a single currency zone.

Kazakhstan had signed a number of international agreements committing itself to giving up the strategic nuclear missiles it inherited from the Soviet Union. In mid-December Nazarbayev and U.S. Vice Pres. Al Gore signed an agreement that committed the U.S. to funding denuclearization. In another significant move, the parliament approved the Nuclear Non-proliferation Treaty by a vote of 283-1 on December 13.

In the spring a package of legislation was adopted by the national legislature to speed up privatization, but while small establishments were quickly sold, privatization of housing and larger enterprises proceeded very slowly. Many foreign-owned businesses and joint ventures opened in Almaty, and in June an ambitious scheme involving six foreign partners was initiated to explore the petroleum potential of the northeastern shelf of the Caspian Sea. (BESS BROWN)

This article updates the *Macropædia* article CENTRAL ASIA: *Kazakhstan.*

KYRGYZSTAN

A landlocked republic of Central Asia, Kyrgyzstan borders Kazakhstan to the north, China to the southeast, Tajikistan to the south and west, and Uzbekistan to the west. Area: 198,500 sq km (76,600 sq mi). Pop. (1993 est.): 4,526,000. Cap.: Bishkek. Monetary unit: som (introduced May 10, 1993), with (October 4) a free rate of 5.83 som = U.S. \$1 (8.83 som = £1 sterling). President in 1993, Askar Akayev; prime minister, Tursunbek Chyngyshev.

Kyrgyzstan was among those states that suffered most as a result of the disruption of the relationships with other former Soviet republics. The country's president, physicist Askar Akayev, was steadfast in his commitment to creating a democratic state, but economic problems and wrangling between Kyrgyzstan's political parties complicated the realization of his goal. Consequently, on Nov. 29, 1993, the president called for a late January 1994 referendum on his rule. Akayev's most vocal opposition came from the reconstituted Communist Party of Kyrgyzstan, which increasingly dominated the national legislature and opposed his reforms at every opportunity. The Communists played a leading role in forcing an investigation of a Kyrgyz-Canadian joint venture in gold mining. Akayev, fearful that needed investment would be frightened off, appealed for an end to political infighting.

In May, under pressure from the International Monetary Fund, Kyrgyzstan became the first Central Asian state to introduce its own currency, the som, and to withdraw from the Commonwealth of Independent States (CIS) ruble zone. Uzbekistan and Kazakhstan reacted immediately by suspending trade. At least in the short run, the introduction of the som only worsened Kyrgyzstan's already catastrophic economic situation. Kyrgyzstan joined the newly established CIS economic union in September but declared its intention to keep its own currency. (BESS BROWN)

This article updates the *Macropædia* article CENTRAL ASIA: *Kyrgyzstan.*

MALDIVES

A republic and member of the Commonwealth in the Indian Ocean, Maldives consists of about 1,200 small islands southwest of the southern tip of India. Area: 298 sq km (115 sq mi). Pop. (1993 est.): 237,000. Cap.: Male. Monetary unit: rufiyaa, with (Oct. 4, 1993) a free rate of 11.89 rufiyaa to U.S. \$1 (18.01 rufiyaa = £1 sterling). President in 1993, Maumoon Abdul Gayoom.

In October 1993, Pres. Maumoon Gayoom was reelected in a landslide to another five-year term. The victory, Gayoom's fourth, underscored the country's political stability.

Maldives' rate of growth during the 1991–93 National Development Plan was at a healthy level of 8%. Apart from the overseas sale of frozen fish (the country's main export industry) and certain essential imports, the government pursued an open market policy. In January 1993, 25% of the shares in the state-owned Bank of Maldives were offered to the public. The islands also continued to attract tourists; 240,000 visitors arrived in 1992.

The main political-economic government concern was the continued rise in ocean levels, which threatened to submerge the islands. Maldives obtained a wide range of aid commitments, notably from main donors China and Japan and from the U.S. and Kuwait, both of which recognized Maldives' "support" for Kuwait during the 1990–91 Gulf war. (GUY ARNOLD)

This article updates the *Micropædia* article MALDIVES.

NEPAL

A constitutional monarchy, Nepal is a landlocked country in the Himalayas between India and the Tibetan Autonomous Region of China. Area: 147,181 sq km (56,827 sq mi). Pop. (1993 est.): 19,264,000. Cap.: Kathmandu. Monetary unit: Nepalese rupee, with (Oct. 4, 1993) a free rate of NRs 46.09 to U.S. $1 (NRs 69.83 = £1 sterling). King, Birendra Bir Bikram Shah Dev; prime minister in 1993, Girija Prasad Koirala.

The United Nepal Communist Party and allied smaller communist parties, which had helped transform this Himalayan nation from an absolute monarchy to a democracy in 1990, led several strikes and street protests in 1993 in an effort to unseat the elected government.

The conflict between the communists, the largest opposition group in Parliament (82 of the 205 seats), and the Nepali Congress Party of Prime Minister Girija Prasad Koirala began on May 16 with a road accident in which two prominent communists were killed. An official investigation blamed driver negligence for the deaths, but the communists insisted that the men had been killed by the government.

In June, July, and September, the communists led general strikes and protests in Kathmandu and two neighbouring towns. Police opened fire on protesters, and at least 12 people were killed. The events in 1993 were the first major street violence since the 1990 popular antimonarchy uprising, which forced King Birendra to surrender his absolute power.

On the international front, Nepal's king and queen visited China in September. This was King Birendra's seventh visit to China since ascending the throne in 1972. Beijing (Peking) remained Nepal's biggest source of foreign aid, and in 1993 China helped Nepal build highways, industries, and hydroelectric power plants. (DILIP GANGULY)

PAKISTAN

A federal republic and a member of the Commonwealth, Pakistan is in the northwestern part of the Indian subcontinent, on the Arabian Sea. Area: 796,095 sq km (307,374 sq mi), excluding the 83,716-sq km Pakistani-controlled section of Jammu and Kashmir. Pop. (1993 est., including some 1.9 million Afghan refugees and 3 million residents of Pakistani-controlled Jammu and Kashmir): 127,962,000. Cap.: Islamabad. Monetary unit: Pakistan rupee, with (Oct. 4, 1993) a free rate of PRs 29.60 to U.S. $1 (PRs 44.85 = £1 sterling). Presidents in 1993, Ghulam Ishaq Khan (interim), from July 18, Wasim Sajjad, and, from November 14, Farooq Ahmed Leghari; prime ministers, Nawaz Sharif to April 18, Balakh Sher Mazari to May 26, Nawaz Sharif to July 18, Moeen Qureshi to October 19, and, from October 19, Benazir Bhutto.

None of Pakistan's political parties scored an outright victory in the October 6 elections to the 217-seat National Assembly, but the 86 seats captured by the Pakistan People's Party (PPP) represented a plurality of the 201 contested seats. The Pakistan Muslim League, led by Prime Minister Nawaz Sharif, finished second with 72 seats. The remaining 43 seats were divided among independents and members of other parties. The PPP's victory meant that its leader, Benazir Bhutto, would once again occupy the office of prime minister. The party's control of the government, however, was so fragile that Bhutto would have to tread carefully to avoid pitfalls that could send the country tumbling into another political crisis.

The election marked an impressive comeback for Bhutto, who in 1988 had become the first woman to head a modern Muslim state, only to be ousted on charges of corruption after less than two years. The ballot was Pakistan's third in five years of turbulent politics. The voter turnout of 40% was several percentage points lower than polls in 1988 and 1990, reflecting dissatisfaction with politicians who had failed to form stable, effective governments capable of serving their five-year terms.

Benazir Bhutto, named prime minister of Pakistan for the second time, appears with her ally and the new president, Farooq Ahmed Leghari. Bhutto became head of a coalition government after her Pakistan People's Party won a plurality in the October parliamentary elections.
AFP

The campaign for the 1993 elections was tumultuous in a country that had bounced between democracy and military rule throughout its 46 years of independence. Twenty-seven people were massacred in an election-related gun battle.

The year's political turbulence began on April 18 when Pres. Ghulam Ishaq Khan dismissed Nawaz Sharif's 30-month-old government on charges of corruption, maladministration, and nepotism. On May 26, however, the nation's Supreme Court ruled that President Khan had overstepped his constitutional authority and restored Sharif's ousted government. Then, after months of political feuding, Khan and Sharif resigned simultaneously on July 18. They were replaced by, respectively, Wasim Sajjad and Moeen Qureshi.

Prior to the election, on August 19, Prime Minister Qureshi announced sweeping economic reforms aimed at resuscitating Pakistan's flagging economy. The nation was staggering through social and economic problems—annual income in 1993 averaged $400 a person; the literacy rate remained about 25%; and many children never went to school. Pakistan's population increased by 3.2% in 1993, one of the highest rates in the world. Pledges of $1.5 billion in new loans from the International Monetary Fund and the World Bank helped the country stave off bankruptcy.

The cost of servicing Pakistan's $18 billion foreign debt was expected to be about $1.5 billion. The 6% economic growth rate projected for 1993 was likely to be closer to 3%. In an austerity drive during the year, Pakistan closed embassies in Hungary, Mexico, Germany, Yugoslavia, Tanzania, Namibia, and Somalia. Information centres in Australia, Italy, Kuwait, Canada, Saudi Arabia, Sri Lanka, and Kenya were also closed. In a single stroke of the pen, Qureshi imposed taxes on Pakistan's powerful feudal landlords, something no government before his had risked doing.

On August 25 the United States imposed trade sanctions on Pakistan, charging that it had received missile technology from China in violation of an international arms control agreement. At issue was U.S. evidence suggesting that China transferred to Pakistan technology for the M-11 surface-to-surface missile, the export of which violated the Missile Technology Control Regime. (DILIP GANGULY)

SRI LANKA

A republic and member of the Commonwealth, Sri Lanka occupies an island in the Indian Ocean off the southeast coast of peninsular India. Area: 65,610 sq km (25,332 sq mi). Pop. (1993 est.): 17,616,000. Legislative cap., Sri Jayawardenepura Kotte; administrative cap., Colombo. Monetary unit: Sri Lanka rupee, with (Oct. 4, 1993) a free rate of SL Rs 48.56 to U.S. $1 (SL Rs 73.57 = £1 sterling). Presidents in 1993, Ranasinghe Premadasa until May 1 and, from May 7, Dingiri Banda Wijetunga; prime ministers, Dingiri Banda Wijetunga and, from May 7, Ranil Wickremasinghe.

Pres. Ranasinghe Premadasa (*see* OBITUARIES) was assassinated on May 1, 1993, by a suspected Tamil separatist suicide bomber who rode a bicycle into the president as he watched a May Day parade in Colombo. Premadasa had made relentless efforts to stem the bloodshed in Sri Lanka caused by secessionist insurrections. On May 7 Parliament unanimously elected Prime Minister Dingiri Banda Wijetunga, an ally of Premadasa, president; Wijetunga then appointed Ranil Wickremasinghe prime minister.

After his election President Wijetunga made fresh peace overtures to the Liberation Tigers of Tamil Eelam, the major separatist group battling for an independent Tamil homeland in the north and east of the nation, but little progress was made. Tamils, who formed 18% of Sri Lanka's 17.6 million population, claimed they were discriminated against by the majority Sinhalese, who controlled the government, the military, and a vast majority of the nation's businesses.

A 45-member parliamentary committee appointed to find a solution to the decade-old ethnic conflict recommended two separate councils for the north and east and a quasi-federal system to meet the rebel demand for an independent homeland. The rebels rejected the offer, and in late September 9,000 government troops mounted a major offensive against them. A Tamil rebel sea base in Kilali on the Jaffna Peninsula was captured on October 1, and the government troops destroyed 120 boats. The capture of Kilali was a major setback for the rebels, who had used it as a base from which to reach the mainland. At least 114 government soldiers and 200 rebels were killed in the offensive, the largest in two years. Despite the loss of Kilali, most of the Jaffna Peninsula remained under the control of Tamil rebels.

The Sri Lankan army on August 23 opened 21 centres to induct more than 10,000 soldiers to fight the Tamil rebels. To expand the army by 10 infantry battalions, the government lowered its recruitment standards. The new soldiers would reinforce the 42 battalions deployed mainly against Tamil rebels. By late 1993 Sri Lanka's mainly Sinhalese army had lost more than 4,250 soldiers, including those killed during a Tamil attack on a military base in mid-November.

On August 17 Haniffa Mohamed, the speaker of the Parliament, named an 18-member parliamentary committee to look into constitutional reforms. Sri Lanka's present constitution, adopted in 1978, had long been criticized by the opposition, who said that it gave too much power to the president and too little to Parliament. The committee would have to submit proposals well ahead of the next presidential elections, scheduled for December 1994. (DILIP GANGULY)

TAJIKISTAN

A landlocked republic of Central Asia, Tajikistan borders Kyrgyzstan on the north, Uzbekistan on the north and west, Afghanistan on the south, and China on the east. Area: 143,100 sq km (55,300 sq mi). Pop. (1993 est.): 5,705,000. Cap.: Dushanbe. Monetary unit: pre-1993 Russian ruble, with (Oct. 4, 1993) a free rate of 1,165 rubles to U.S. $1 (1,765 rubles = £1 sterling). Chief of state in 1993 (chairman of the National Assembly and acting president), Imomali Rakhmonov; prime ministers, Abdumalek Abdulajanov to December 18 and, from late December, Abdujalil Samadov.

The civil war that ravaged Tajikistan in the last six months of 1992 wound down in January 1993 with a government of former Communist officials installed in Dushanbe determined to silence, if not physically destroy, the anti-Communist opposition that had briefly dominated the country's government the previous year. Tens of thousands of Tajiks, mostly sympathizers of the Islamic Renaissance Party, fled into Afghanistan between late December 1992 and February 1993 to escape attacks by armed supporters of the Dushanbe government, over whom the new leadership appeared to have minimal control.

From the moment of its arrival in Dushanbe, the new government began persecuting the groups that had made up the anti-Communist coalition in 1992—the Islamic Renaissance Party, the Western-oriented Democratic Party, the Tajik nationalist Rastokhez ("Rebirth") Party, and the Lale Badakhshon movement, which sought independence for the

P. BARTHOLOMEW—GAMMA

Mourners accompany the body of slain Sri Lankan Pres. Ranasinghe Premadasa to cremation ceremonies in Colombo. His assassination on May 1 was attributed to a Tamil separatist.

Russian soldiers stationed along Tajikistan's border with Afghanistan buy supplies from a local merchant. Russian troops were being used primarily to prevent incursions by Tajik Islamic fundamentalist rebels operating from Afghanistan.
REUTERS/BETTMANN

Gorno-Badakhshan autonomous oblast in the Pamirs. The opposition press was closed down, and Tajik nationalist control of the broadcast media was ended. Some liberal journalists were arrested and others went into exile. The four opposition organizations were formally banned in June. Their leaders were charged, largely in absentia, with armed insurrection against the constitutional order and with waging war against the established government. Most opposition leaders fled to Afghanistan, Iran, or Russia, where they attempted to continue their resistance to the pro-Communist forces in power in Dushanbe.

Although it was able to gain control of most of the country in early 1993, the new government remained heavily dependent on military assistance from other Commonwealth of Independent States (CIS) countries, primarily Russia and Uzbekistan, to counter continued insurgency inside Tajikistan by armed supporters of the Islamic Renaissance Party and attacks from Tajik oppositionists in Afghanistan and their Afghan supporters. Fighting continued into the summer between government troops and small groups of resistance fighters who took refuge in the mountains east of the capital. The government also had limited success in enforcing its will on Gorno-Badakhshan, where the leadership continued to sympathize with the opposition.

The main threat to the regime in Dushanbe was, however, the attacks from Afghanistan. Fighting on the border occurred almost daily throughout the year, with casualties on both sides. One such attack, in which 25 Russian troops were killed, was widely believed to have been the reason for the firing of Russian Security Minister Viktor Barannikov in July. While most assaults involved small handfuls of Tajik opposition fighters and Afghan helpers, in September and October incursions by groups of up to 400 men were reported by Russian border guards stationed on the Tajik-Afghan border.

Return of the Tajik refugees in Afghanistan became a major concern for Tajikistan's leadership, who feared with some justification that the refugees would come under the influence of Afghan Islamic fundamentalists. Tajikistan's head of state, National Assembly Chairman Imomali Rakhmonov, sought United Nations help and even courted the Kabul government in an effort to get the refugees back. By year's end, however, few had proved willing to accept government assurances of their safety should they return to their homes.

By the end of 1993, Tajikistan was the only former Soviet republic still using Soviet (*i.e.,* pre-1993) rubles as its single authorized currency. Dependent on Russian military aid and with the Tajik economy virtually destroyed by the civil war, the country's leadership believed that it had no alternative but to join Russia in a new economic union that had been spurned by the other CIS states. In return, Russia promised to provide assistance to keep Tajikistan's economy from complete collapse. (BESS BROWN)

This article updates the *Macropædia* article CENTRAL ASIA: *Tajikistan.*

TURKMENISTAN

A republic of Central Asia, Turkmenistan borders Uzbekistan on the northeast, Kazakhstan on the northwest, the Caspian Sea on the west, Iran on the southwest, and Afghanistan on the southeast. Area: 488,100 sq km (188,500 sq mi). Pop. (1993 est.): 4,294,000. Cap.: Ashgabat (formerly Ashkhabad). Monetary unit: Russian ruble, with (Oct. 4, 1993) a free rate of 1,165 rubles to U.S. $1 (1,765 rubles = £1 sterling). President in 1993, Saparmurad Niyazov.

The dominant factor in Turkmenistan's political life in 1993 was the personality cult of Pres. Saparmurad Niyazov. Foreign human rights groups were critical of the treatment accorded the Turkmen opposition; when important foreign guests visited Turkmenistan, opposition leaders were routinely placed under house arrest. All information media remained a government monopoly. Niyazov ensured his popularity by providing all citizens with free electricity and water, and foreign investors were attracted by the political stability achieved through Niyazov's benevolent authoritarianism that so distressed Turkmen intellectuals and human rights activists.

Turkmenistan was very successful in attracting foreign assistance for its gas industry and in 1993 began expanding its petroleum industry, which had stagnated in the last years of the U.S.S.R. because of Moscow's reluctance to invest in the region. An important source of gas for other Commonwealth of Independent States (CIS) countries, Turkmenistan proved a hard bargainer in its demands on its trading partners, forcing Caucasian and Central Asian consumers to agree to steep price increases or barter exchanges that primarily benefited the Turkmen side.

Niyazov said that he did not contemplate taking Turkmenistan out of the CIS, but he was vehemently opposed to the creation of an economic union, which he considered an infringement of his independence in dealing with foreign states. When the union was created in September, however, Turkmenistan became an associate member. At the beginning of November the country left the ruble zone and introduced its own currency, the manat, with Niyazov's portrait on the bills. (BESS BROWN)

This article updates the *Macropædia* article CENTRAL ASIA: *Turkmenistan.*

UZBEKISTAN

A republic of Central Asia, Uzbekistan borders the Aral Sea to the north, Kazakhstan to the north and west, Turkmenistan to the southwest, Afghanistan to the south, and Tajikistan and Kyrgyzstan to the east. Area: 447,400 sq km (172,700 sq mi). Pop. (1993 est.): 21,901,000. Cap.: Tashkent (Uzbek: Toshkent). Monetary unit: Russian ruble (the monetary systems of Uzbekistan and Russia were unified on Sept. 17, 1993), with (Oct. 4, 1993) a free rate of 1,165 rubles to U.S. $1 (1,765 rubles = £1 sterling). President in 1993, Islam Karimov; prime minister from January 8, Abdulhashim Mutalov.

Political power in 1993 remained firmly in the hands of Pres. Islam Karimov and his People's Democratic Party, the name adopted by the former Communist Party of Uzbekistan. The crackdown on all political opposition, begun in 1992, continued throughout 1993; this included a ban on all opposition publications. Foreign criticism of the government's human rights record was ignored or rebuffed.

The Uzbek nationalist Birlik (Unity) Movement, the most influential opposition group, had its activities banned for the first three months of the year while alleged legal violations by its members were investigated by the state prosecutor. Both Birlik and the Erk (Freedom) Party were effectively prevented from registering as political parties and hence from functioning legally.

The Uzbek opposition also faced harassment in the form of physical assaults and arrests on trumped-up charges of insulting the president or seeking to overthrow the constitutional order. Some of the oppositionists who were put on trial in 1993 were granted amnesty after sentencing, but six who were accused of having sought to organize an alternate parliament under the name Melli Majlis (Popular Assembly) were sentenced to terms of 10–15 years in labour camps. Physical intimidation was also used against former vice president Shukrulla Mirsaidov, who had clashed with Karimov over economic reform.

Karimov rejected rapid introduction of a market economy as a danger to the country's stability. In 1993 the government began to take tentative steps toward privatization of some state assets, but the president insisted that the pace would have to be slow in order to avoid potentially explosive social dislocation. He had a certain amount of justification for his concerns, as the severe social problems, including widespread unemployment, that accumulated in Uzbekistan in the last years of Soviet rule remained unsolved. During 1993 government officials announced that Uzbekistan was considering introducing its own currency; in September, however, it opted for the economic union and inclusion in a new ruble zone.

To prevent the penetration into Uzbekistan of Islamic fundamentalism from Tajikistan, or from Afghanistan via Tajikistan, Karimov became the most vocal supporter of Commonwealth of Independent States intervention in the Tajik civil war. He sent his new army to help Tajikistan's government put down the Islamic resistance and to attempt to seal the Tajikistan-Afghanistan border to Tajik opposition groups armed and trained by Afghan fundamentalists. On October 12 a law reinstating the Latin alphabet for the Uzbek language went into effect. (BESS BROWN)

This article updates the *Macropædia* article CENTRAL ASIA: *Uzbekistan.*

Southeast Asia

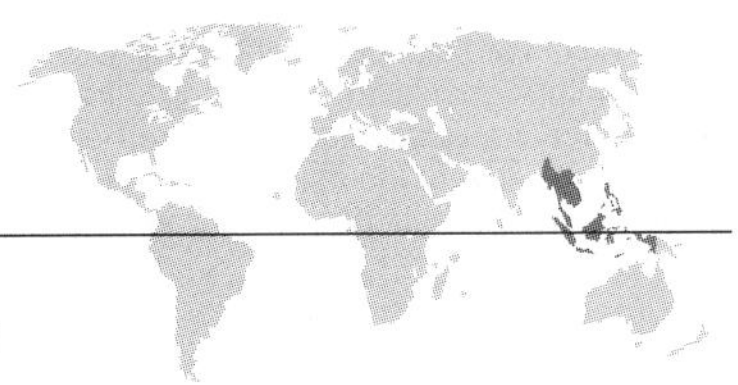

SOUTHEAST ASIAN AFFAIRS

Regional cooperation in the post-Cold War era continued to preoccupy Southeast Asian nations, although trade had drawn equal to or surpassed security as the key debating point in 1993. This was due in part to the new administration of U.S. Pres. Bill Clinton, which demanded market-opening measures and "fair trade" by Asian countries. There were also concerns about the fate of the Uruguay round of the General Agreement on Tariffs and Trade (GATT). All nations in the region supported a successful conclusion to the GATT talks, but the potential for failure was widely recognized. There was much discussion of future courses of action within the Association of Southeast Asian Nations (ASEAN), grouping Brunei, Indonesia, Malaysia, the Philippines, Singapore, and Thailand. Malaysian Prime Minister Datuk Seri Mahathir bin Mohamad continued to press for an East Asian Economic Caucus (EAEC), which would include Asian nations and territories from Japan to Indonesia but would exclude Australia and New Zealand. Australia and the U.S. had since 1989 promoted the forum on Asia-Pacific Economic Cooperation (APEC), which would include the ASEAN nations, Japan, South Korea, China, Taiwan, and Hong Kong plus Australia, New Zealand, and countries on the eastern side of the Pacific, thus far the U.S. and Canada.

The U.S. assistant secretary of state for East Asian and Pacific affairs, Winston Lord, signaled a change of approach in March by voicing support for regional forums for both political and security issues. The administration of former president George Bush had put more emphasis on bilateralism. Lord indicated that the U.S. would take an active role in promoting APEC and joining discussions about regional defense.

Other U.S. officials expressed support for the new security meetings being conducted under the aegis of the ASEAN postministerial conference after the annual meeting of ASEAN foreign ministers. Clinton later proposed that an APEC ministerial meeting planned for Seattle, Wash., in November be upgraded to an informal summit. An advisory "eminent persons group" suggested that the grouping be renamed the Asia Pacific Economic Community.

The ASEAN foreign ministers conference, held in Singapore in July, proved decisive on both the political and security fronts. The EAEC issue, pitting Malaysia against Indonesia, which supported APEC, was resolved when ministers agreed that EAEC would become a caucus within APEC. While some believed that EAEC had been effectively buried, others saw the change as a grouping of Asian nations within APEC to form a counterweight to non-Asian nations, particularly the U.S. Malaysia, however, remained cool to APEC, and Mahathir announced that he would not personally attend the Seattle summit. It proved to be the first meeting of all the major nations of the Pacific.

The ASEAN conference followed a preparatory meeting in Singapore in May. For the first time, senior officials of the six-member grouping held talks on security with key officials from the seven dialogue partners of the postministerial conference. These were the U.S., Japan, Australia, New Zealand, Canada, South Korea, and the European Community. Backing a position originally taken by Japan, the group concluded that there was a need to find "means for consultations on regional political and security issues." The ASEAN foreign ministers then took the watershed decision in July to set up the ASEAN Regional Forum. It was to be composed of their six members and the seven dialogue partners plus Russia, China, Vietnam, Laos, and Papua New Guinea. It would have its first meeting in Bangkok, Thailand, in 1994. In effect, the Southeast Asians had created an Asia-wide venue for discussion. At the postministerial conference, U.S. Secretary of State Warren Christopher called for stronger efforts to stop the spread of weapons of mass destruction in Asia.

Southeast Asian nations remained concerned about Chinese territorial claims in the South China Sea, especially to the Spratly Islands. At a high-level informal workshop held in August, Indonesian Foreign Minister Ali Alatas proposed more formal government-to-government talks on the islands. China rejected the idea, but during a visit to Malaysia and Singapore, Chinese Defense Minister Chi Haotian (Ch'ih Hao-t'ien) reiterated Beijing's (Peking's) pledge not to use military force to resolve the issue. Russia, meanwhile, was becoming a source of cheap arms. Malaysia bought 18 MiG-29 fighter aircraft from Moscow in a deal hotly contested by the U.S.; the $600 million compromise included the purchase of eight U.S. F/A-18D aircraft. Russia also raised some regional eyebrows by telling Vietnam it wished to maintain its naval base at Cam Ranh Bay under a Soviet-era agreement expiring in 2000.

The massive $3 billion UN effort to pacify the warring parties in Cambodia and hold credible elections in May proved to be a remarkable success, despite predictions of a new civil war and despite at least 21 fatalities among the 20,800 UN personnel supplied by 32 countries. Worries about a renewal of hostilities receded after the election when soldiers of the Marxist Khmer Rouge began defecting in increasing numbers. In August copremiers Norodom Ranariddh and Hun Sen visited Vietnam. The two sides largely avoided such divisive issues as border disputes and the return of some 30,000 ethnic Vietnamese who had fled Cambodia early in the year amid Khmer Rouge attacks. The UN Transitional Authority in Cambodia was able to wind down operations on schedule in September when Ranariddh's father, former ruler Prince Norodom Sihanouk, was restored as king under a new constitution. All UN personnel were scheduled to leave by November. Elections in Cambodia were supposed to be a key point in the U.S. "road map" leading to the normalization of relations with Vietnam. The unresolved issue of U.S. prisoner-of-war and missing-in-action cases, however, led Clinton to continue the long-standing trade embargo against Vietnam. Clinton had eased up somewhat in July by allowing the International Monetary Fund and the World Bank to grant loans to Hanoi. In February, French Pres. François Mitterrand became the first Western head of state to visit Hanoi since the communist republic was formed.

Controversies over human rights continued to dog relations between Southeast Asia and the West. In preparation for the World Conference on Human Rights held in Vienna in June, Asian nations met in Thailand in March to produce the Bangkok Declaration. This upheld the principle of noninterference in the internal affairs of other nations and argued that while human rights were universal, "various historical, cultural, and religious backgrounds" could not be disregarded. ASEAN countries, notably Malaysia and Singapore, maintained the pressure in Vienna for a wider definition of human rights, including economic rights. In Southeast Asia the U.S. put considerable pressure on Indonesia by threatening trade action over alleged violations of workers' rights. In August, Washington blocked the sale by Jordan to Indonesia of U.S.-supplied F-5 fighter planes, citing concern over human rights in East Timor. The U.S. also began assessing whether it was taking a sufficiently strong line against the ruling military junta in Myanmar (Burma). In February several Nobel Peace Prize laureates, including the Dalai Lama, South African Bishop Desmond Tutu, and former Costa Rican president Oscar Arias, flew to Bangkok to demand the release of Myanmar opposition leader and fellow laureate Aung San Suu Kyi, who had been detained under house arrest since 1989. The group was denied entry to Myanmar.

Relations between Malaysia and the Philippines warmed in January when Fidel Ramos arrived in Kuala Lumpur. He was the first Philippine head of government to make an official state visit in 25 years. The two sides agreed to set up a joint commission to expand ties and settle outstanding issues, including a Philippine claim to the Malaysian state of Sabah in northern Borneo. The two agreed to establish "extension offices" for their respective embassies, in Sabah for the Philippines and in Mindanao for Malaysia. This seemed to implicitly recognize Sabah as part of Malaysia, but Ramos said that settling the Philippine claim would be "a long, step-by-step process."

Meeting in Manila in August, the six nations along the Mekong River—China, Myanmar, Thailand, Laos, Cambodia, and Vietnam—agreed on a list of projects that, if approved by the Asian Development Bank, would upgrade road and other links. In October stock markets in the region reached seemingly stratospheric levels before declining. Growth levels continued at their characteristically high rates. Southeast Asian Chinese business groups were increasingly attracted by investment opportunities in China. The battle for Asian television screens heated up as global media tycoon Rupert Murdoch bought Hong Kong-based STAR TV, a multichannel satellite service reaching 38 countries.

(BERTON WOODWARD)

BRUNEI

The sultanate of Brunei is located on the northern coast of the island of Borneo, on the South China Sea. Area: 5,765 sq km (2,226 sq mi). Pop. (1993 est.): 275,000. Cap.: Bandar Seri Begawan. Monetary unit: Brunei dollar, with (Oct. 4, 1993) a free rate of B$1.58 to U.S. $1 (B$2.40 = £1 sterling). Sultan and prime minister in 1993, Sir Muda Hassanal Bolkiah Mu'izzadin Waddaulah.

A widening diplomacy in Asia highlighted 1993 for Brunei. The tiny oil-rich nation opened relations with Laos in July and Myanmar (Burma) in September. The sultan was planning to make his first official visit to China late in the year. The country sent 12 policemen to join the UN force in Cambodia, Brunei's first venture in international peacekeeping. In January, Japanese Prime Minister Kiichi Miyazawa visited as part of a Southeast Asian tour. Later the two countries renewed their expiring 20-year agreement on the supply of Brunei's entire output of liquefied natural gas to Japan.

With an eye to increasing bilateral trade, which had been minimal, Malaysian Prime Minister Mahathir bin Mohamad visited. The two sides also agreed to set up a joint border committee to discuss boundary disputes involving the Limbang salient, Sarawak, and offshore economic zones.

With Hong Kong's return to Chinese sovereignty looming in 1997, Brunei announced that it would end its 30-year-old practice of using off-duty judges from the British-administered territory for its High Court and Court of Appeals. Judges would henceforth be hired. Open dissent continued to be extremely rare in the feudally run state.

In April, however, it was reported that unsigned documents complaining of corruption and incompetence in government were circulating. The circulars did not criticize the sultan, who was generally seen as popular. (BERTON WOODWARD)

This article updates the *Macropædia* article SOUTHEAST ASIA: *Brunei.*

CAMBODIA (KAMPUCHEA)

A constitutional monarchy of Southeast Asia, Cambodia occupies the southwestern part of the Indochinese Peninsula, on the Gulf of Thailand. Area: 181,916 sq km (70,238 sq mi). Pop. (1993 est.): 9,287,000. Cap.: Phnom Penh. Monetary unit: riel, with (Oct. 4, 1993) an official rate of 3,500 riels to U.S. $1 (5,320 riels = £1 sterling). Chairman of the Supreme National Council (until June 1993) and head of state, Prince Norodom Sihanouk, who became king on September 24; coequal prime ministers from June to September, Norodom Ranariddh and Hun Sen; from September 21, first prime minister, Norodom Ranariddh, and second prime minister, Hun Sen.

Prospects for holding the May 1993 general election seemed gloomy as political and ethnic violence increased. The Khmer Rouge not only ignored the January 31 deadline to choose to participate in the election but continued to refuse to cooperate with the United Nations Transitional Authority in Cambodia's (UNTAC's) effort to disarm all factions and register voters as stipulated in the 1991 Paris peace treaty.

UNTAC reported that 200 people were killed in the months before the election. It attributed 131 deaths to the Khmer Rouge, whose massacres of local ethnic Vietnamese caused thousands to flee to Thailand. At least 15 other murders were blamed on the government, which had targeted workers of opposition parties, particularly Prince Norodom Ranariddh's United National Front for an Independent, Neutral, Peaceful, and Cooperative Cambodia (Funcinpec). The nation's problems were exacerbated when the value of the riel was halved in March, and food prices rose dramatically. Moreover, the $880 million in aid promised by the international community was slow in coming.

Implementation of the provisions of the peace treaty, however, remained on schedule. Some 370,000 refugees from Thai border camps were back in Cambodia by the end of April. About 4.7 million voters—95% of those estimated to be of age—had registered, and 20 parties had signed up. More than 4.2 million voters turned out for a mainly peaceable six-day election in late May. Funcinpec won 58 National Assembly seats, the Phnom Penh government's Cambodian People's Party (CPP) 51, Son Sann's Buddhist Liberal Democratic Party 10, and Moulinaka, a Funcinpec offshoot, 1.

In early June, Prince Norodom Sihanouk formed a coalition government with Ranariddh and the CPP's Hun Sen as deputy prime ministers, but he dissolved it a day later after being accused of staging a "coup." The CPP at first rejected the election result, claiming there had been irregularities, and in mid-June a party faction led by Prince Norodom Chakrapong, a son of Sihanouk and half brother of Ranariddh, declared much of eastern Cambodia an autonomous zone. The breakaway movement collapsed within days, however, and was viewed as a bargaining ploy by the CPP. The National Assembly met on June 14 and gave "full and special powers" to Sihanouk as head of state, and by early July Funcinpec and the CPP had set up an interim government with Ranariddh and Hun Sen as prime ministers. Son Sann was appointed National Assembly president.

The Khmer Rouge continued attacks on UNTAC forces and mounted operations against the CPP, capturing the famous Preah Vihear temple on the northern border in early July, but two weeks later, after talks in Phnom Penh, they announced that their army would join a united national army and that their officials would join the government. The U.S. warned that it would cut off aid if this happened. In August and December government forces launched successful offensives against the Khmer Rouge, and Washington announced that it would provide aid worth $10 million over the next five years. The new government established friendly relations with Vietnam in late August.

Norodom Sihanouk acknowledges greetings from the Cambodian people. On September 24, following a UN-sponsored settlement of Cambodia's civil war, Sihanouk returned to the throne, which he had occupied as both king (1941–55) and prince (1960–70).

JASON BLEIBTREU—SYGMA

On September 21 the National Assembly ratified changes in the constitution that restored the monarchy. The king would "reign but not rule" and had power to make appointments, but only in consultation with ministers or senior civil servants. Sihanouk was officially installed on September 24. Ranariddh became first prime minister and Hun Sen second prime minister. In November UNTAC was disbanded.

The International Committee on the Reconstruction of Cambodia pledged $1 billion in aid, and the International Monetary Fund (IMF) approved a $9 million loan after Cambodia cleared $52 million in arrears. The IMF also promised to finance balance of payments needs for at least three years. (JUDITH L. CLARKE)

This article updates the *Macropædia* article SOUTHEAST ASIA: *Cambodia.*

INDONESIA

A republic of Southeast Asia, Indonesia consists of the major islands of Sumatra, Java, Kalimantan (Indonesian Borneo), Celebes (Indonesian: Sulawesi), and Irian Jaya (West New Guinea) and more than 13,000 smaller islands and islets. Area: 1,919,317 sq km (741,052 sq mi). Pop. (1993 est.): 188,216,000. Cap.: Jakarta. Monetary unit: rupiah, with (Oct. 4, 1993) a free rate of 2,088 rupiah to U.S. $1 (3,163 rupiah = £1 sterling). President in 1993, Suharto.

Months before the 1,000-member People's Consultative Assembly chose the country's two top officials in March, President Suharto was widely expected to seek and win a sixth five-year term. Attention consequently focused on the vice presidency, a pivotal post should Suharto step aside in midterm or not seek another term in 1998. The president was thought to favour retaining Sudharmono, a Muslim who had long served to counterbalance the military's clout. In February, however, the head of the armed forces' faction in the House of People's Representatives (parliament) nominated Try Sutrisno, a popular general who had just retired as commander in chief of the armed forces. Sutrisno was close to Muslim leaders and to Benny Murdani, the defense minister. He was also said to be a person who could be trusted to show concern for Suharto's family in the future and protect their vast financial interests. Following tradition, both men were elected unopposed.

The sweeping Cabinet reshuffle that followed was partly attributed to the president's misgivings about the way the military had openly backed Sutrisno. Murdani and Home Minister Rudini, another ex-general, were replaced. Gen. Edi Sudradjat, who had replaced Sutrisno as armed forces chief in February, took over the Defense Ministry. When he gave up the more powerful armed forces post in May, there was speculation that the way was possibly being paved for army commander Wismoyo, Suharto's brother-in-law, to become chief of the armed forces. The president's hold on power was also strengthened in October when three-term Information Minister Harmoko, a Suharto ally, was elected the first civilian chairman of Golkar, the country's most powerful political organization. The powerful "superminister" for finance, industry, and the economy; the finance minister; and the central bank governor were also replaced in March. The new economic team was seen as a boost to Research and Technology Minister B.J. Habibie. The German-trained engineer and other technologists favoured more sophisticated, higher-value industries rather than the labour-intensive export enterprises promoted by a group of U.S.-trained technocrats known as the "Berkeley Mafia." Suharto, nonetheless, chose two key advisers who were identified with the technocrats.

The country's image abroad was a cause for concern because its human rights record had come under attack during a human rights conference in Vienna and was repeatedly criticized by the U.S. In November 1992 government troops had captured Xanana, an alias used by José Alexandre Gusmão, a top rebel in East Timor, a former Portuguese colony. Although Indonesia had seized the territory in 1975, the annexation was still being challenged by the United Nations. In August, Suharto reduced Gusmão's life sentence to 20 years, with the possibility of parole in 2005. Jakarta also eased restrictions on the Petition of 50, a group of prominent critics. In July the president met with one of its key figures, lifted a travel ban on all but 11 of the dissidents, and established a national council on human rights. In August, citing human rights concerns, Washington vetoed Jordan's planned sale of U.S.-made F-5 fighter jets to Indonesia. It also threatened to withdraw certain trade privileges unless the conditions of Indonesian workers improved. Just before a visit of U.S. officials in September, the government reorganized the official labour federation, but it continued to block two independent unions.

Falling interest rates helped business recover and made the Jakarta Stock Exchange one of the region's biggest gainers. Worries about the financial health of banks, however, persisted following the collapse of medium-sized Bank Summa in December 1992. In June an anonymous report, allegedly leaked by a government office, listed hundreds of millions of dollars in delinquent loans supposedly held by state banks. The report also asserted that certain business groups, some connected to the Suharto family, were major debtors. About the same time, 300 businessmen with large loans were barred from going abroad. According to one report, the head of the state receivership agency concluded that 90% of all bad bank loans—estimated at over $1 billion—were held by government institutions. Policy makers also fretted over a slowdown in foreign investment just when the government was trying to curb external borrowing. Still, the economy managed moderate growth of about 5.5%.

(RICARDO L. SALUDO)

LAOS

A landlocked republic, Laos is in the northern part of the Indochinese Peninsula. Area: 236,800 sq km (91,429 sq mi). Pop. (1993 est.): 4,533,000. Cap.: Vientiane. Monetary unit: kip, with (Oct. 4, 1993) an official rate of 720 kip to U.S. $1 (1,094 kip = £1 sterling). President in 1993, Nouhak Phoumsavan; prime minister, Gen. Khamtai Siphandon.

The 85-member National Assembly, elected in December 1992, met in February with a mandate to make "fundamental changes" in society. But the sweeping transformation that followed, or rather continued, owed little to the legislature. The communist Lao People's Revolutionary Party, though wholly committed to abolishing the command economy, remained firmly in control. It would stay in power "forever," a party official said after the election. Pres. Nouhak Phoumsavan and Prime Minister Khamtai Siphandon proceeded apace with the creation of a full-scale market economy.

A government official visiting Bangkok, Thailand, in August was able to report that the sale of state-owned factories to private enterprise was virtually complete. A Thai firm had acquired the national telephone system and television broadcasting facilities. A senior World Bank official called this transformation truly amazing. In August a nine-man committee was set up to fight rising corruption.

Neighbouring Thailand was by far the largest source of foreign investment, although firms from the U.S., Japan, and France also injected capital. Thai ventures that won approval included hotels, gas stations, industrial estates, mining operations, and cement marketing. Thai commercial banks opened many branches, while the Bank of Thailand taught the Laotian central bank how to regulate a market economy. Work also continued on a new investment law. In June, Thai Prime Minister Chuan Leekpai signed a memorandum of understanding on development of energy resources. Electricity, the country's most profitable export, was set to expand enormously with the harnessing of hydropower on tributaries of the Mekong River. A study in May indicated that seven new power stations could increase the country's current generating capacity of 195 MW to 2,690 MW within eight years. In addition, a Thai company agreed to develop a 150-MW lignite-fired plant.

The Friendship Bridge across the Mekong—which linked Vientiane, the Laotian capital, and the Thai port city of Nong Khai—neared completion. A gift of the Australian government, the bridge was designed to accommodate future railroad lines. Studies were also under way for a highway crossing Laos from Thailand to a Vietnamese port. In July Cambodian officials offered alternative access to the sea for Laotian exports. Relations with the U.S. remained good. Laotian authorities cooperated fully as the U.S. continued its search for the remains of 514 servicemen still listed as missing in action during the Vietnam War. The reluctance of Vientiane to accept back tens of thousands of Hmong who had fled the country after the Communist takeover had become a source of friction with several countries. Thailand, for example, reported that some 35,000 Hmong refugees were still living within its borders. (ROBERT WOODROW)

This article updates the *Macropædia* article SOUTHEAST ASIA: *Laos.*

MALAYSIA

A federal constitutional monarchy of Southeast Asia and member of the Commonwealth, Malaysia consists of the former Federation of Malaya at the southern end of the Malay Peninsula (excluding Singapore) and Sabah and Sarawak on the northern part of the island of Borneo. Area: 330,442 sq km (127,584 sq mi). Pop. (1993 est.): 19,077,000. Cap.: Kuala Lumpur. Monetary unit: ringgit, with (Oct. 4, 1993) a free rate of 2.55 ringgit to U.S. $1 (3.87 ringgit = £1 sterling). Paramount ruler in 1993, with the title of *yang di-pertuan agong,* Tuanku Azlan Muhibbudin Shah ibni al-Marhum Yusuff Ghafarullahu-Lahu Shah; prime minister, Datuk Seri Mahathir bin Mohamad.

The principal political issues in 1993 were constitutional amendments that stripped the nine hereditary rulers of legal immunity in purely personal matters and the triennial elections of the preeminent New United Malays National Organization (UMNO). In late 1992 the Sultan of Johore allegedly assaulted a hockey coach. It was merely the latest of many such allegations, one involving the killing of a golf caddie. The sultan, however, enjoyed immunity and could not be prosecuted. That prompted Prime Minister Datuk Seri Mahathir bin Mohamad to challenge the royals once again. In 1983 the king had been deprived of his veto power over legislation, and in 1992 the rulers were rebuked for interfering in politics and business.

When the rulers refused to give their required consent for laws directly affecting them, Mahathir proposed withdrawing privileges not guaranteed by law. In February the rulers accepted revised amendments. Later, when the Sultan of Kelantan objected, a UMNO legislator questioned his claim to the throne. Under amendments approved in March, any ruler could be tried by a special court. The decision of the court would be final and could not be appealed. But a convicted ruler could be pardoned by the Conference of Rulers after it had considered the attorney general's written opinion. A ruler sentenced to more than one day in prison would lose his crown, which would then go to his designated successor unless the ruler received a "free pardon" from the Conference of Rulers.

With Mahathir running unchallenged as UMNO president, all attention focused on the deputy president, who traditionally became deputy premier. Mahathir initially suggested that Ghafar Baba be retained to preserve unity, but he did not bar Finance Minister Anwar Ibrahim from becoming a candidate. After four decades in UMNO, Ghafar enjoyed grassroots support, but Anwar won key Cabinet endorsements and backing from party treasurer Daim Zainuddin, whose supporters controlled major newspapers. By October Anwar, who had been jailed in 1974 as an activist, had obtained nearly all of the 153 possible nominations, thereby guaranteeing a victory in November.

Tensions continued between the federal government and Sabah, the Borneo state ruled by Parti Bersatu Sabah (PBS), an opposition party in Parliament. Kuala Lumpur pursued corruption charges against Joseph Pairin Kitingan, the head of PBS. In January log exports from Sabah were banned, cutting its budgeted revenues by nearly half and creating problems for logging, transport, and equipment firms. After the Supreme Court voided a Sabah law barring its legislators from switching parties, the state assembly passed a measure allowing dismissal of lawmakers who "betray their mandate." The founder of the United Sabah National Organization (USNO) accepted an invitation to join UMNO, but his son, the leader of USNO, formed a coalition with its rival PBS. The federal government then revoked USNO's registration, but USNO filed an appeal. On the whole, the parliamentary opposition seemed divided, especially over royal immunity and the imposition of *hudud,* Muslim punishment that included amputation of hands for repeated theft and stoning for adultery.

Fueled by lower interest rates and surging exports, the economy turned in faster-than-expected growth of 8.5–9%, up from 8% in 1992. Inflation was moderated by curbs in consumer spending and a slowdown in direct foreign investment. The stock market set records through much of the year. Malaysia hoped to attract more capital into small and medium-sized industries and increase local content in manufacturing. It reduced to 35% (from 51%) the minimum equity Malays or other bumiputra (indigenous people) had to own for ventures to be favoured as bumiputra enterprises.

Malaysia supported Muslim concerns in the Middle East and the Balkans and offered to send 1,500 soldiers to Bosnia and Herzegovina. It continued to push for an East Asian Economic Caucus, but Mahathir refused to attend the September Asia-Pacific Economic Cooperation forum in Seattle, Wash. He was the only national leader to boycott the gathering of 15 "Pacific economies."

(RICARDO L. SALUDO)

This article updates the *Macropædia* article SOUTHEAST ASIA: *Malaysia.*

MYANMAR (BURMA)

Myanmar (Burma until May 26, 1989) is a republic of Southeast Asia with coastlines on the Bay of Bengal and the Andaman Sea. Area: 676,577 sq km (261,228 sq mi). Pop. (1993 est.): 44,613,000. Cap.: Yangon (Rangoon). Monetary unit: kyat, with (Oct. 4, 1993) a free rate of 6.25 kyats to U.S. $1 (9.48 kyats = £1 sterling). Chairman of the State Law and Order Restoration Council in 1993, Gen. Than Shwe.

Myanmar's ruling military junta in 1993 ignored calls from the U.S., the European Community, the UN, and Australia to release pro-democracy leader and Nobel Peace Prize winner Aung San Suu Kyi. Instead, they extended her house arrest on July 20 for a fifth year. They did, however, allow a visit with her British husband, Michael Aris. In January the junta opened a constitutional convention of 700 delegates, mostly chosen by the junta. The delegates promised to usher in multiparty democracy, but they also approved measures that would allow the military to participate actively in government and to take over in emergencies. In principle, at least, there would be an executive president chosen by an electoral college, a two-chamber parliament, and power sharing between the central government and 14 regional governments. Freedom of expression and worship also would be guaranteed. Observers, however, viewed the entire process as a sham because the military had jailed or otherwise barred key victors in the 1990 election from taking part in the constituent assembly.

Amnesty International reported that more than 40 people had been arrested for political reasons in 1993. It urged the immediate release of two dissidents sentenced in October to long prison terms for their political activities. Ma Thida, a novelist, and Aung Khin Sint, a convention delegate, were named "prisoners of conscience" by Amnesty International, which already had given the designation to Suu Kyi. In May Foreign Minister U Ohn Gyaw had criticized the West for trying to impose its human rights standards on Myanmar and for not helping to stem the production of illegal drugs. The country's minister for national planning and economic

Wa soldiers march in the mountains of eastern Myanmar (Burma). Leaders of the Wa, a small minority group that produced almost all of Myanmar's opium, were seeking both an autonomous state within the country and foreign economic assistance to bring a halt to the opium trade.
FALISE/GENIER

development said his country could not effectively eradicate poppy growing and crack down on drug manufacturing without foreign assistance. (DILIP GANGULY)

This article updates the *Macropædia* article SOUTHEAST ASIA: *Myanmar.*

PHILIPPINES

Situated in the western Pacific Ocean off the southeast coast of Asia, the republic of the Philippines consists of an archipelago of about 7,100 islands. Area: 300,076 sq km (115,860 sq mi). Pop. (1993 est.): 64,954,000. Cap.: Manila (lower house of the legislature meets in Quezon City). Monetary unit: Philippine peso, with (Oct. 4, 1993) a free rate of 27.57 pesos to U.S. $1 (41.78 pesos = £1 sterling). President in 1993, Fidel V. Ramos.

Pres. Fidel V. Ramos began restructuring the Philippine armed forces and police in 1993. He sought to adapt them to a security situation that was changing because a two-decade-old Communist insurgency had waned and rebel military officers were believed to have abandoned attempts to overthrow the government.

The Communist Party of the Philippines was also at odds over its future course. Its Manila regional committee, with some 40% of the party's estimated 24,000 members, broke in mid-July with the central committee headed by José Maria Sison, the exiled party founder. The strife demoralized the party's dwindling guerrilla force, the New People's Army. Guerrilla clashes with authorities became less frequent. Insurgency-related deaths, which numbered 2,121 in 1992, declined to 523 in the first half of 1993, and some 1,000 insurgents surrendered during that period.

Ramos, a career military officer before he became president, ordered the armed forces to turn over counterinsurgency responsibilities to the National Police by 1995. The armed forces, which had focused on Communist guerrillas and the military rebels, began retraining for external defense, although the Philippines faced no foreign threat.

On April 24 the entire leadership of the 98,000-man National Police was fired after an investigation of corruption. Ramos, who had headed a predecessor organization, approved the forced retirement of 23 police generals and the reassignment to innocuous jobs of some 175 other officers. With crime still a major problem, the legislature reinstated the death penalty in December. Ramos reported on June 30 that it had made considerable progress against all sorts of illegal activities, including automobile hijacking, drug trafficking, and illegal logging.

Ramos also launched a campaign to control the private armies of local politicians and wealthy provincial landowners. According to police, 562 private armies terrorized the countryside. The secretary of interior and local government, Rafael Alunan, accused them of "the most gruesome and heinous crimes in the annals of our society." Efforts to disband them had been ineffectual.

EDWIN TUYAY—ASIAWEEK PICTURES

Pres. Fidel Ramos (centre) of the Philippines examines a model of the proposed redevelopment of Subic Bay. After the U.S. closed its naval base in 1992, local leaders began to promote the area as an international business and trading centre.

Ramos' goal of ending electricity shortages by the end of 1993 was set back by problems in contracting for new generators. With many Manila area businesses getting reduced power or no power at all from 11 AM until 7 PM, factories operated at reduced capacity and the economy slumped. This contributed to the highest unemployment rate in metropolitan Manila in 50 years. Small businesses increased imports of small generators—an inefficient way of producing electricity—by 63% in early 1993. Ramos announced on May 30 that a $2.5 billion nuclear power plant, completed in 1985 but standing idle for political and environmental reasons, would be converted to nonnuclear electrical production at a cost of $600 million.

Ramos told Congress on July 26 that the Philippines' 2.3% rate of population growth impeded efforts to improve the quality of life and strained resources to provide jobs, education, housing, health clinics, and other social services. Ramos, a Protestant, also endorsed a family-planning program based on choice that was intended to reduce the growth rate to below 2% by 1998. Predictably, the Roman Catholic Church, to which most Filipinos belong, attacked the program as working "toward the destruction of the Filipino family."

The body of ousted former president Ferdinand E. Marcos, who died in Hawaii in 1989, was taken back to the Philippines on September 7 and entombed three days later at Batac in northern Luzon. The government had feared disruptive demonstrations, but only small crowds turned out. Imelda Marcos, the former first lady, was convicted September 24 of two charges of corruption and sentenced to prison for 9 to 12 years on each charge. She planned an appeal. (HENRY S. BRADSHER)

SINGAPORE

Singapore, a republic of Southeast Asia and member of the Commonwealth, occupies a group of islands, the largest of which is Singapore, at the southern extremity of the Malay Peninsula. Area: 639 sq km (247 sq mi). Pop. (1993 est.): 2,876,000. Monetary unit: Singapore dollar, with (Oct. 4, 1993) a free rate of S$1.58 to U.S. $1 (S$2.40 = £1 sterling). Presidents in 1993, Wee Kim Wee and, from September 1, Ong Teng Cheong; prime minister, Goh Chok Tong.

During most of 1993, Singaporeans were preoccupied with questions about national leadership. Both of Prime Minister Goh Chok Tong's deputies, Ong Teng Cheong and Lee Hsien Loong, had learned in November 1992 that they had lymphatic cancer. Lee, a retired brigadier general and the son of longtime prime minister Lee Kuan Yew, had been the odds-on favourite to succeed Goh as prime minister. When he began chemotherapy, he had little choice but to give up his demanding second post as minister of trade and industry. Doctors reported in April that Lee was free of the cancer, but he continued to restrict his activities on the advice of his physicians.

Ong, however, was able to remain on the job because his ailment had been diagnosed as a lower-grade cancer. In August he became Singapore's first directly elected president by winning 57.4% of the vote in a national election. Unlike his predecessor, Ong would have veto power over financial and budget policies and the right to vet key appointments. Initially it appeared that no one would challenge Ong, but Chua Kim Yeow, a 67-year-old retired civil servant, made a token contest. He conceded that Ong was "a far superior candidate." Given such a scenario, political observers were surprised that Chua received 40.4% of the total vote. Some interpreted the returns as a sign of disenchantment with the long-ruling, paternalistic People's Action Party (PAP).

Nonetheless, Lee's withdrawal to the sidelines and the election of Ong, who was considered friendly to Goh, were seen as strengthening the prime minister's position as he worked in the shadow of the immensely influential Lee Kuan Yew, who held the post of senior minister in the Cabinet. After winning a December 1992 by-election with a strong majority, Goh showed a new willingness to disagree publicly with Lee Kuan Yew. Goh also replaced Lee in the powerful post of PAP secretary-general.

Meanwhile, the political opposition was in relative disarray. Infighting in the Singapore Democratic Party, which held three of the four opposition seats in Parliament, led Chiam See Tong to resign as leader of the party. Chee Soon Juan, who had opposed the PAP in the December by-election, took over as acting secretary-general. He later went on a 10-day hunger strike to protest his dismissal as a lecturer at the National University of Singapore.

In March the government introduced legislation raising the retirement age to 60 from 55 because of the growing labour shortage. It also prohibited people under 18 from buying cigarettes or smoking in public. The economy made a strong comeback during the year, growing at a rate of 10%. (BERTON WOODWARD)

This article updates the *Macropædia* article SOUTHEAST ASIA: *Singapore*.

THAILAND

Thailand is a constitutional monarchy in Southeast Asia, on the Andaman Sea and the Gulf of Thailand. Area: 513,115 sq km (198,115 sq mi). Pop. (1993 est.): 57,829,000. Cap.: Bangkok. Monetary unit: baht, with (Oct. 4, 1993) a free rate of 24.93 baht to U.S. $1 (37.78 baht = £1 sterling). King, Bhumibol Adulyadej; prime minister in 1993, Chuan Leekpai.

Internal differences within the five-party coalition government of Prime Minister Chuan Leekpai kept the political climate unsettled throughout 1993. Moreover, the opposition parties in the National Assembly, despite their own differences, were able to maintain constant pressure on the government. In mid-September the Social Action Party (SAP), a member of the ruling coalition with 21 seats in the 360-seat lower house, announced plans to merge with four opposition parties. Chuan met the crisis by persuading the smaller Seritham opposition party to replace SAP in the coalition.

The government came under constant pressure to find a permanent solution to Bangkok's notorious and worsening traffic problems. The Education Ministry entered the picture when it decreed that school classes would start at 7:30 AM to shorten the time children wasted in buses. The fact that some commuters were spending five hours a day in traffic raised fears that foreign investors would be tempted to look elsewhere when confronted with such chaotic conditions. The king and queen separately called for urgent action to relieve congestion. An acrimonious dispute over the tolls to be levied and the sharing of revenues from a $1.1 billion privately funded 32-km (20-mi) city expressway had kept the 22.8-km (14-mi) completed portion closed until a court, responding to the anger and frustration of drivers, ordered the road opened on September 2. Banks that had financed the project were unhappy with the government's "high-handed" action. Another expressway and three private-sector rapid-transit systems were bogged down in disputes over financing, routing, and revenue sharing. Four other new arterial highways were going ahead.

Ethnic Malay separatists in the southernmost provinces were active again for the first time since the 1970s. Early in August, 35 government schools in Muslim districts were

Government troops on patrol question a man in southern Thailand near the border with Malaysia. In 1993 Muslim and Malay-speaking separatists turned again to violence against the Thai government.
ASIAWEEK PICTURES

burned in a well-coordinated attack. There were charges that the arson was the work of non-Muslim opponents of Chuan out to destabilize the government. Ambushes of government troops and shootings at buses and trains added to the tension. During a visit to Bangkok, Malaysian Prime Minister Mahathir Mohamad categorically assured the Thais that Malaysia did not offer sanctuary to border rebels.

Following the Cambodian elections in May and the establishment of a government on September 24, Thailand was forced to reevaluate its long-standing policy of not taking sides in the conflict. International pressure on Thailand to abandon its tacit support for the Khmer Rouge and threats from Phnom Penh to curtail Thai commercial interests led Foreign Minister Prasong Soonsiri to insist that Thailand would not tolerate border crossings by militants opposed to the new Cambodian government. Thailand continued to resist international pressure to limit commercial contacts with the repressive military regime in Myanmar (Burma). In February the Dalai Lama and several other winners of the Nobel Peace Prize were allowed to visit Bangkok to pressure the Myanmar junta to release Aung San Suu Kyi from house arrest. On July 20 the activist for human rights learned that she would remain under arrest for a fifth year.

Two tragedies focused international attention on lax enforcement of building codes. In May at least 187 workers were burned to death in a doll factory outside Bangkok, and in August more than 100 died when a hotel in the provincial town of Korat collapsed.

The economy performed well despite the volatile political climate and recession in Thailand's major export markets. A gross domestic product growth of 7.5% seemed likely for the year. Disputes with the U.S. over copyright protection cooled off after Thai police cracked down on software and video pirates, thereby diminishing the likelihood of retaliation. As a member of the Association of Southeast Asian Nations Free Trade Agreement, Thailand began reducing tariffs on manufactured goods imported from neighbouring countries. The strategy of "economic growth triangles," which linked neighbouring countries together, was given enthusiastic government support. Tourism began to revive toward the end of the year, thanks mostly to visitors from other parts of Asia. (ROBERT WOODROW)

This article updates the *Macropædia* article SOUTHEAST ASIA: *Thailand.*

VIETNAM

The socialist republic of Vietnam occupies the eastern part of the Indochinese Peninsula in Southeast Asia and is bounded on the south and east by the South China Sea. Area: 329,566 sq km (127,246 sq mi). Pop. (1993 est.): 70,902,000. Cap.: Hanoi. Monetary unit: dong, with (Oct. 4, 1993) a free rate of 10,672 dong to U.S. $1 (16,168 dong = £1 sterling). President, Le Duc Anh; prime minister, Vo Van Kiet.

The pace of economic growth accelerated during 1993. The value of the dong stabilized, and inflation fell to an annual rate of 4%. Compared with the same period a year earlier, foreign investment more than doubled in value during the first five months of the year. Most important of all was a July 2 decision by the U.S. to no longer stand in the way of International Monetary Fund (IMF) loans to Vietnam. This change in policy led to new grants and loans by the IMF, other international bodies, and bilateral donors. A series of visits abroad by Prime Minister Vo Van Kiet and other Vietnamese officials also improved bilateral relations. At the same time, however, authorities had difficulty coping with domestic corruption and dissidence.

The U.S. decision in late 1992 to allow American companies to set up offices in Vietnam was a signal from Washington that it would eventually end its embargo. A number of U.S. enterprises carried forward or completed plans for joint ventures with the Vietnamese even though direct investments and direct trade were still forbidden by U.S. law. The largest foreign investor remained Taiwan, which counted among its new projects a $300 million joint venture with Ho Chi Minh City authorities in September to build a new town. In the first five months of the year, however, Hong Kong headed the list of investors in Vietnam with a total of $423.9 million; Taiwan was second with $284.1 million and South Korea third with $221.4 million. Between 1987 and October 1993, Vietnam had approved a total of 747 foreign investment projects worth $6.6 billion. Altogether, the government would need $15 billion–$20 billion from overseas investors over the next decade as part of its overall capital requirement of $40 billion–$50 billion.

After careful deliberations, a group of nations headed by France and Japan arranged a $55 million grant and $85 million in loans to Vietnam, which it then used to pay off its arrears to the IMF. In October the IMF announced that it was granting new loans of $223 million. A short time later, the World Bank announced $320 million in loans from the International Development Agency. Vietnam also paid off its $13.5 million debt to the Asian Development Bank, which later announced that it had approved a grant of $568,000 for technical assistance and a loan of $76 million. After talks with the international lending bodies, Vietnam began selling off some of its state-owned enterprises and closed down others that were incurring mounting losses. In April the government began to implement a new pay scale for civil servants, who would as a consequence receive higher salaries in cash. The change was expected to increase the budget deficit from 3.8 trillion dong in 1992 to 9 trillion dong in 1993. Meanwhile, the country's industrial output increased 10–11% over the previous year. The unprecedented $20 million trade surplus in 1992 turned into a $200 million deficit in 1993.

French Pres. François Mitterand's visit to Hanoi in February was the first by a Western leader since 1975. Mitterand announced that French aid would reach $65 million in 1993, twice the amount France had provided in 1992. Relations with Laos were strengthened during Laotian leader Khamtai Siphandon's visit to Hanoi in March. In May, Prime Minister Vo Van Kiet visited South Korea. Before departing, Kiet was informed that South Korea would provide Vietnam with $50 million worth of low-interest loans. The two countries had normalized relations in late 1992. Kiet then went to Australia, where he was promised $A 100 million in aid. In June and July he visited Germany, France, and Britain, where he received additional pledges of aid. Kiet also made a trip to Cuba.

Vietnam established relations with Israel in July and with Venezuela in August. Late that month the two coequal prime ministers of Cambodia visited Hanoi. The two countries strengthened their bonds by setting up commissions on border demarcation and immigration. In November Pres. Le Duc Anh became the first Vietnamese head of state since 1955 to visit China. Economic issues were the principal topic of conversation between the president and the Chinese prime minister. Relations with the U.S. improved, in great part because Vietnam assisted U.S. personnel in six new searches for the remains of U.S. soldiers still listed as missing in action during the Vietnam War. In July, Winston Lord, an assistant secretary of state, led the highest-level U.S. delegation to Vietnam since the end of the war. A reciprocal visit to Washington was undertaken by Deputy Prime Minister Phan Van Khai in October. Relations with China remained prickly. Beijing (Peking) reacted to Vietnam's 1992 limits on trade with China by placing retaliatory restrictions on imports from Vietnam. Vietnam then eased tensions by removing the restrictions, imposing higher taxes, and tightening border controls. Early in the year China detained a number of Vietnamese ships off Hong Kong, and in September the two countries exchanged complaints over a Chinese oil rig in the Gulf of Tonkin. In October China and Vietnam formally agreed to speed up border negotiations and not to use force in their border disputes. In 1993 more Vietnamese returned than left the country. Late in the year there were still some 73,000 Vietnamese in Asian camps even though 50,000 had been voluntarily repatriated since 1989.

During the January plenum of the Communist Party of Vietnam, wide disagreements surfaced over how to deal with declining recruitment. The number of new members had dropped to 36,000 in 1991 from a regular enrollment of about 100,000 a year up to 1987. The delegates also discussed such "negative phenomena" as party and official corruption, opposition groups, and writers. Events during the year showed how serious these problems were. In August the party called for the trial of the former energy minister, who had been dismissed in October 1992 for corruption, and in September the marine products minister was charged with corruption. In March a group of dissidents led by intellectual Doan Viet Hoat received long jail sentences for publishing a newspaper that advocated multiparty democracy. In Ho Chi Minh City police foiled a plot or plots to set off bombs in February and March. Four overseas Vietnamese were given long jail sentences, while 6 others and 10 local residents received shorter sentences. Disputes between the government and Buddhist monks who opposed an officially sponsored church flared into violent protests in Hue and Vung Tau, and several monks were arrested. Four Buddhist monks and five others were sentenced to prison terms of six months to four years in mid-November for the Hue disturbances. (JUDITH L. CLARKE)

This article updates the *Macropædia* article SOUTHEAST ASIA: *Vietnam.*

GREG DAVIS—TIME MAGAZINE

Billboards along the Saigon River advertise Japanese products. With the U.S. government slow to lift its trade embargo against Vietnam, most business investment was coming from Southeast Asian and European countries.

Europe

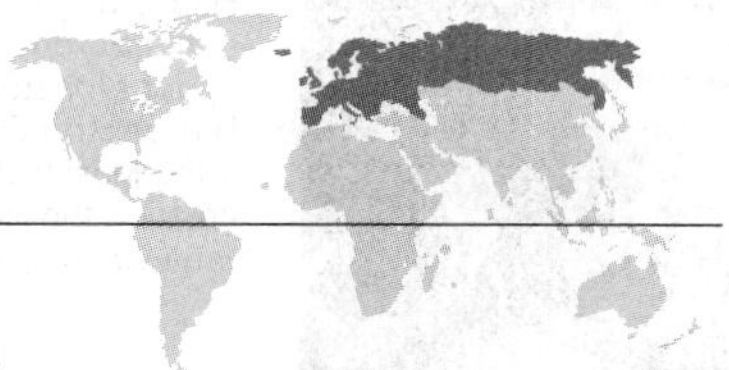

EUROPEAN AFFAIRS

Western Europe. After a long period of uncertainty and introspection, the European Community (EC)—or the European Union, as it became known after the Maastricht Treaty on European Union entered into force on November 1—ended 1993 on a positive note. The special summit in Brussels at the end of October confirmed the treaty. The European Union now was responsible for decisions on common foreign-policy concerns, security matters, and judicial cooperation, while the European Commission remained the legal body of the EC.

Jubilation was not unbounded, however, and deep doubts remained about the EC's ability to achieve economic and monetary union within the Maastricht timetable. Britain and Italy had withdrawn their currencies from the European exchange-rate mechanism (ERM) in September of the previous year, and by early 1993 many people had already begun to wonder if the ERM was not too rigid. There were doubts about the ability of the EC member states to achieve sufficient economic cohesion in view of persistent recession and rising unemployment. Nor was it encouraging that Germany was not rushing to abandon the Deutsche Mark in favour of a European currency.

Denmark assumed the rotating presidency of the EC in January. The new European Commission met for the first time in that month, but for a two-year limited session. Jacques Delors was confirmed as EC president, while former British Cabinet minister Sir Leon Brittan assumed a new role as commissioner for external economic affairs and was put in charge of the General Agreement on Tariffs and Trade (GATT) negotiations.

Economic Affairs Commissioner Henning Christophersen announced that the European Commission was revising downward its overoptimistic forecasts for average growth in the year to 0.8%. He blamed the reduction, in part, on Germany's forecast of no growth for 1993. In an atmosphere of increasing economic crisis, the European Commission began holding bilateral meetings with each member state to discuss wage cuts, fiscal consolidation, and the possible switching of government spending to capital projects to increase jobs.

Some signs of the financial crisis that was to hit the ERM later in the year were already becoming apparent. Christophersen warned speculators in January that runs on the Danish krone, French franc, and Irish punt could prove expensive as the economic fundamentals of the countries were put in order. As January closed, finance ministers approved an ECU 8 billion balance of payments loan to Italy. Conditions attached to the loan required the country to reduce its debt-to-GNP (gross national product) ratio, limit government borrowing, and implement government reforms of public spending in such areas as health, pensions, and the civil service.

Brittan condemned the United States for unwarranted and heavy-handed action to impose swinging tariffs on steel imports. He said that the EC steel producers had scrupulously respected the antidumping agreement that ran for 10 years until its expiration at the end of March 1992. The issue was the first skirmish in a series of trade disputes that were to mar the GATT negotiations and perpetuate doubts that the December 15 target date for a Uruguay-round agreement would be realistic. Within a few days Brittan was reacting strongly again, this time to a decision by Washington to prevent federal agencies from awarding contracts to EC companies. The move was seen as "strike two" for the U.S. government's new administration in its first two weeks, and the EC was left concerned about possible protectionist policies developing across the Atlantic.

The GATT talks dominated the EC's political agenda throughout the year. In March Delors met U.S. Pres. Bill Clinton in an attempt to cool down the various long-running disputes over telecommunications and public procurement that were hampering a GATT deal. The visit by the EC president came just one week after the U.S. called off negotiations with the Commission on the long-running disputes. In the end both Clinton and Delors expressed a desire to find a "mutually satisfactory solution." Clinton announced that he would be seeking the consent of Congress for an extension to the end of the year of the "fast-track" negotiating mandate in the GATT negotiations.

In April the Community turned its attention to the former Soviet Union. At the two-day Group of Seven (G-7) meeting in Tokyo, Christophersen announced a further package of EC assistance to the former Soviet republics of about $3 billion but warned that despite the massive injection of aid, far more would have to be done. Meanwhile, the EC agreed that its role should be to set an example to its eastern neighbours with the promise of opening EC markets while warning them that in return they must gradually remove state protection. The Commission made it clear that it would not hesitate to use its powers to defend EC industry from breaches of multilateral trading standards, such as the dumping of cheap imports by Eastern competitors.

By the end of April, the U.S. and the EC were pulling back from the brink of an all-out trade war after reaching a partial agreement on public procurement contracts. At the same time, the Commission's ninth annual report on U.S. barriers to trade described the situation as "highly unsatisfactory." Although the EC trade deficit with the U.S. had fallen from $16.7 billion to $9 billion, there had been no significant reduction in the number of U.S. trade barriers facing EC firms. The report also expressed concern about the U.S. legislation that had had an impact on trade outside U.S. territory, such as the Cuban Democracy Act, and it highlighted EC efforts to negotiate a deal on multilateral free trade. In talks in Tokyo in April, the Commission expressed concern about the European Community's growing trade deficit with Japan. At $31.2 billion in 1992, the deficit had reached a level that was potentially explosive, the Commission said, unless measures were taken to reverse the trend.

In May, in their second referendum on the Maastricht Treaty, 56.8% of the Danes voted "yes." In accordance with a plan worked out at the Edinburgh EC summit in December 1992, Denmark had been allowed to opt out of the single-currency and defense arrangements of the treaty. Delors said that the Danish reversal on the 50.7% "no" vote in 1992 gave the EC the stimulus needed to pull it out of a period of gloom and inaction.

The Danish government announced that initiatives for growth and employment would be at the top of the agenda at the midyear EC summit, for which it would serve as host in Copenhagen. The plan was timely, coming as it did at a time when the Community's economy was shrinking for the first time since 1975, according to the current-year report of the European Commission. The issue of unemployment continued to resonate in EC gatherings throughout the year.

The German government had always insisted that neither the strains of unification nor internal controversy over the Maastricht Treaty would lead to any wavering of its com-

Heads of government and heads of state of the European Community nations line up for a photograph at their meeting in Brussels on October 29. On November 1 the Maastricht Treaty came into force, creating the European Union.
WILLIAM STEVENS—GAMMA LIAISON

mitment to the EC. The German question came to a head at the end of July at a special meeting of the European Monetary Committee, made up of central bank governors and representatives of national governments. Germany and its powerful Bundesbank were the targets of bitter recriminations as the ERM was effectively dismantled and the currency exchange fluctuation bands were expanded to 15%. Only Germany and The Netherlands elected to keep their currencies within the original 2.5% band, giving rise to concern that Germany was becoming the nucleus of a Deutsche Mark zone in a two-speed Europe.

The troubled Maastricht Treaty successfully weathered the parliamentary process in the U.K., but Prime Minister John Major was badly damaged by the political deals he had been forced to make with opponents on the right of his Conservative Party. Germany was the last country to ratify the accords; the Constitutional Court gave its somewhat tentative approval in October.

Belgian Foreign Minister Willy Claes told the EC leaders who had gathered in Brussels on October 29 to ratify the Maastricht Treaty that "there is no reason to be euphoric"; indeed, there was none. The tally of progress on European unity for 1993 was mixed at best: reluctant agreement on Maastricht, disagreement with the U.S. and Eastern Europe on trade matters, and nonagreement among EC members on currency issues. Further questions of changing the administrative structure and possibly the voting procedures (which gave proportionately more weight to smaller countries) of EC bodies were becoming urgent, and the possibility of four new members—Austria, Finland, Norway, and Sweden (Switzerland voted during the year not to pursue its application)—joining the EC in 1995 was looming as well. The Brussels meeting did manage to resolve the contentious issue of awarding sites for various new European agencies. The European Monetary Institute, the core of a future central bank, went to Frankfurt, Germany. Among the other assignments were Copenhagen as the site of the European Environment Agency and The Hague as the headquarters for the Europol Drugs Agency.

By November, German economic forecasts were being revised upward, introducing a cautious and qualified note of economic optimism to the entire Community. Delors, however, was less sanguine as, in a series of speeches, he warned of the danger that the EC would become "an English-style free-trade area" and complained that Community leaders were not doing enough to promote economic growth and employment.

The year ended with perhaps the greatest failure of the European movement still unresolved: the tragic lack of cohesion over the former Yugoslavia. Deep divisions within the EC and between the EC and the U.S. had by this time become open and public. There were also sharp disagreements over the lifting of the arms embargo on Bosnia and Herzegovina and demands advanced by some EC countries for limited air strikes against the Serbs and later the Croats. The clear message from Clinton, was that the EC needed to get its act together. Faced with a clear signal that U.S. interest in European security was diminishing, this key pillar of the Maastricht Treaty was given new impetus. In December most of the EC members—led by Germany, France, and the U.K.—announced plans to establish diplomatic relations with The Former Yugoslav Republic of Macedonia, despite the protests of Greece, which was due to assume the EC presidency on Jan. 1, 1994.

The Western European Union (WEU) played an increasingly important role as the forum for a future European security and defense policy. In November the full European Army Corps of 50,000 French, German, and Belgian soldiers was formed. It was intended to provide the basis of a European army answerable to the EC through the WEU but also to be available to NATO.

The Council of Europe expanded to 32 members during the year to become the only body encompassing both Eastern and Western European countries. In answer to calls from countries with sizable minority problems, such as Slovakia and Romania with their large ethnic Hungarian populations, the organization decided to focus on the problems of minorities at a summit in Vienna in October. The decision reflected a general view that a more positive approach to the problems of minorities earlier on would have helped to avoid the conflict in Bosnia. The Vienna summit also concentrated on plans to assist Eastern European countries with their democratization programs. (JOHN PALMER)

Central and Eastern Europe. When measured by the criterion of whether democracy was enhanced, the year in Central and Eastern Europe was a rather gloomy one. Indeed, while the trends were not catastrophic, there was little doubt that the high hopes that had accompanied the fall of communism in 1989 would not soon be realized. The currents noted in previous years—the significance of nationalism and the slow pace of transformation from a centrally planned to a market economy—persisted, with some minor variations. But new, alarming trends were added to the negative factors of the previous few years.

Perhaps most important, it was evident that "postcommunism" was not a transitional phenomenon but had established itself as a permanent feature of the political landscape. The political structures of these states would be determined by the communist legacy for many years to come. Equally, the patterns established by the new postcommunist elites in response to their experience of communism had made their impact on the way in which political business was conducted.

The systems were elitist in the sense that the new leaders behaved with limited regard to public opinion, continued to engage in complex moral and ideological debates while tending to neglect bread-and-butter issues, and looked for scapegoats when things went wrong. Furthermore, they tended to be inefficient in the actual organization and management of government and to believe that the issuing of regulations was sufficient to solve problems.

The response on the part of a growing section of the population was to look for radical alternatives. The most striking success in this respect was the extraordinarily high vote achieved by the former communists in Poland, which became the largest single party in the Sejm (parliament). This development appeared to confirm the precedent set by neighbouring Lithuania, where the former communists first gained a parliamentary majority toward the end of 1992 and then won the presidential election in early 1993. The former communists in Hungary could hope to perform successfully in the 1994 elections, while their counterparts in Slovakia and the Czech Republic were maintaining strong positions.

To be fair, the former communists insisted that their commitment to democracy—Western style—was sincere and that they would fully respect the domestic and international obligations assumed by their predecessors. There was no suggestion of any deviation from this position in either Lithuania or Poland. The shift in emphasis that they sought was in the direction of slowing down privatization, defending the welfare state against cuts in the state budget, and diluting the right-wing's moralizing rhetoric.

The right, indeed, appeared increasingly to be something of a threat to democracy. It made little secret of the fact that it had no time for the procedural or substantive niceties demanded by a democratic order. While few right-wingers espoused authoritarianism openly, the basic assumptions of liberal democracy were undoubtedly rejected by the right in favour of populist-nationalist collectivism, which in some cases (Poland, Slovenia) could be tinged with clericalism.

Their key feature, however, was a combination of populism and nationalism. For the populist the true relationship is that between the leader and the people, for the authentic leader has the innate ability to understand and articulate the wishes of the people. This political position is ultimately incompatible with democracy, but it has been attractive to those who find the complexity of modern life too much to cope with and are ready to listen to a message promising greater simplicity. Furthermore, it seems to be a standard feature of populism to promise more than the populist leader can deliver. Politically vulnerable and unsophisticated populations, left in that state by communism, were increasingly impatient with what they saw as the needless obfuscations of democratic politics.

This message was dangerous enough in itself, but it was turned into a far more volatile cocktail by the addition of nationalism. While not all nationalists are populists, it is hard to conceive of a nonnationalist populism, given that the constituency of the populist—the people—is bound to be the nation under modern conditions. Where political institutions are well established and public opinion understands the need for procedures, emotional appeals of this kind can be diluted. The problem in the postcommunist world was precisely that institutions were weak and lacked popular credibility. Sections of the population tended to be suspicious of the entire paraphernalia of democracy, making them vulnerable to political adventurers.

What exacerbated this complex of problems was that the nationalist agitation of one country was bound to have an impact on its neighbours, not least because of the continuing presence of ethnic minorities with attachments in the neighbouring state. In these circumstances it was extremely easy to whip up nationalist fervour and to undermine potential compromise solutions. Several such interstate disputes were in danger of entering into a subacute or acute phase, notably the dispute between Slovakia and Hungary over the ethnic minority in southern Slovakia, the Greek minority in Albania, the Polish minority in Lithuania, the Turkish minority in Bulgaria, and the Albanian minority in Macedonia.

Behind all these disputes there loomed the awful example of former Yugoslavia, where the dissolution of the state was accompanied by extreme violence and unspeakable cruelty. The war of Yugoslav succession influenced the situation in two directions. On the one hand, it was warning of what could happen if ethnic violence were to get out of hand; on the other, it encouraged ethnic entrepreneurs in the belief that they, too, could emulate the precedents set in Bosnia and Herzegovina and proceed with genocide or ethnic cleansing against local minorities. The situation in the Balkans was especially tense, as a series of interrelated ethnic and frontier disputes, all connected with the ambitions of Serbia to dominate the region, were a potential threat to stability. Indeed, the Balkan crisis carried added dangers because it involved Greece and Turkey, both of which were members of NATO, while Greece was also a member of the European Community.

Another source of mounting concern to the Central and Eastern European states was the resurgence of Russia. As the initial shock of the collapse of the Soviet Union wore off and, equally, the Western powers seemed mesmerized by the Yugoslav war and the apparently insoluble problem of reestablishing stability in the Balkans, the rise of Russia was rather weakly welcomed by the West because it relieved it of the responsibility of peacekeeping in a highly volatile area. The Russian government, after the initial shock had worn off, formulated the doctrine of the "near abroad," the territory of the former Soviet Union, where, in effect, Moscow had the right to involve itself in the affairs of nominally independent states. Anxiety in Central and Eastern Europe mounted when Russia sought to veto the approaches they were making to NATO, as this looked very like a revival of the Soviet empire. The West watched this process helplessly. (GEORGE SCHÖPFLIN)

See also Economic Affairs; Military Affairs.

ALBANIA

A republic in the western Balkan Peninsula of southeastern Europe, Albania is situated on the Adriatic Sea. Area: 28,748 sq km (11,100 sq mi). Pop. (1993 est.): 3,422,000. Cap.: Tirane. Monetary unit: lek, with (Oct. 4, 1993) a free rate of 109.20 leks to U.S. $1 (165.44 leks = £1 sterling). President in 1993, Sali Berisha; prime minister, Aleksander Meksi.

Having begun its difficult transition from paralysis to democracy in March 1992, Albania in 1993 entered a new, postemergency period. A relative economic recovery was manifested by an 8% growth in gross national product, the highest in Eastern Europe; inflation was brought down to a monthly rate of 1.3%; and the agricultural sector showed new vitality as a result of privatization. The pace of recovery was acknowledged by international bodies such as the International Monetary Fund, the World Bank, and the European Bank for Reconstruction and Development.

By 1993 the Albanian government had gone beyond its former passive approach to a more active program to stabilize the economy. Serious unemployment, the high cost of living, and the slow rate of foreign investment were the major problems. Albania's economic situation remained precarious, and the country would still have to rely on foreign aid to ensure the successful completion of the reform process. Nonetheless, the period of total reliance on foreign emergency aid gradually gave way to a situation that began to attract foreign investment and saw the beginnings of Albanian economic cooperation with the outside world.

Former Communist leader Ramiz Alia, almost all former Politburo members, and the Socialist Party leader Fatos Nano were under arrest in 1993 awaiting trial on charges of abuse of office. Ties with the European Community and other international bodies, as well as with such neighbouring countries as Turkey and Italy, improved, and Albania joined the Organization of the Islamic Conference. Tirane even expressed interest in joining NATO. Pope John Paul II made a historic visit in April. (The last pope to travel to Albania—in 1464—died en route.) Relations with Greece deteriorated, however, as a result of Albania's expulsion of an Orthodox cleric and Greece's subsequent deportation of thousands of illegal Albanian migrant workers. The shooting of Albanian citizens on the Macedonian and Serbian borders and the continued violation of human rights of the ethnic Albanian population in the Serbian province of Kosovo served to further undermine Albania's efforts at peaceful regional cooperation. (LOUIS ZANGA)

This article updates the *Macropædia* article BALKAN STATES: *Albania.*

ANDORRA

A landlocked parliamentary coprincipality of Europe, Andorra is in the Pyrenees Mountains between Spain and France. Area: 468 sq km (181 sq mi). Pop. (1993 est.): 61,900. Cap.: Andorra la Vella. Monetary units: French franc and Spanish peseta. Coprinces: the president of the French Republic and the bishop of Urgel, Spain; chief executive in 1993, Oscar Ribas Reig.

On March 14, 1993, the citizens of Andorra voted overwhelmingly to adopt their first constitution, thus ending a system of government that had run on feudal lines for 715 years. The vote was 74.2% in favour and 25.8% against as 75.7% of the 9,123 eligible voters turned out. (Some 80% of Andorra's population consisted of foreign residents.) For the first time, Andorra would gain full sovereignty, with the right to establish an independent judicial system and set foreign policy. The constitution maintained the principality's unique system of coprinces, or joint sovereignty by the president of France and the bishop of Urgel, Spain, but with greatly reduced powers. It provided for the election of the parliament by universal suffrage and permitted the formation and membership by Andorran citizens of political parties and trade unions. The government was empowered for the first time to raise revenue through income taxes.

The new constitution took effect on May 4, having previously been signed by Pres. François Mitterrand of France and Joan Marti Alanis, the bishop of Urgel. On June 3 Andorra signed a treaty of friendship and cooperation with France and Spain, which recognized its sovereignty. On July 28 Andorra became the 184th member of the UN. In the general election on December 12, Oscar Ribas Reig's party won the most seats (8) in the 28-seat parliament. Ribas Reig was expected to form a new coalition government.

(ANNE ROBY)

This article updates the *Micropædia* article ANDORRA.

ARMENIA

A landlocked republic of Transcaucasia, Armenia borders Georgia to the north, Azerbaijan to the east, Iran to the south, the Azerbaijani exclave of Nakhichevan to the southwest, and Turkey to the west. Area: 29,800 sq km (11,500 sq mi). Pop. (1993 est.) 3,550,000. Cap.: Yerevan. Armenia claims the predominantly Armenian-populated Nagorno-Karabakh region, which has been part of Azerbaijan since 1923. Monetary unit: Russian ruble, with (Oct. 4, 1993) a free rate of 1,165 rubles = U.S. $1 (1,765 rubles = £1 sterling). The dram, the new national currency, was introduced on November 22 at a rate of 14.50 dram = U.S $1 (22.04 dram = £1 sterling). President in 1993, Levon Ter-Petrosyan; prime ministers, Khosrow Arutyunyan and, from February 2, Hrant Bagatyan.

Armenia enjoyed relative political stability in 1993 despite severe economic hardships and waning popular support for the leadership of Pres. Levon Ter-Petrosyan, repeatedly accused by the opposition of incompetence and authoritarian methods. In early February, Prime Minister Khosrow

PASCAL LE SEGRETAIN—SYGMA

In Yerevan a woman walks between rows of trees whose branches have been cut off for use as fuel. During the year Armenia continued to suffer shortages of electricity.

Arutyunyan was dismissed in a disagreement over the 1993 budget. The standoff in Parliament between Ter-Petrosyan's ruling Armenian Pan-National Movement and the eight opposition parties continued throughout the year, delaying adoption of the budget and of a law on citizenship and the drafting of a new constitution. An opposition demand in September for new parliamentary elections to be held in March 1994 was rejected.

Foreign policy continued to be dominated by the war over Nagorno-Karabakh. Despite mediation efforts by the Conference on Security and Cooperation in Europe and by the U.S., Turkey, and Russia acting jointly, little progress was made toward a political settlement. Relations with Turkey, Russia, and Iran deteriorated following the summer offensive in southern Azerbaijan by Karabakh Armenian forces, for which all three countries blamed Yerevan, and Armenia's political isolation increased.

Acute shortages of electricity, resulting from the 1989 closure of the Medzamor nuclear power station, paralyzed industry and urban transport during the winter months; in early March only 50 of 400 major enterprises were working. Repeated sabotage of the gas supply pipeline from Georgia compounded the damage, leaving homes in Yerevan without heat or hot water for extended periods.

Economic relations were strained by the Russian central bank's decision in July to withdraw from circulation all pre-1993 banknotes. Although Armenia initially reiterated its readiness to remain within the ruble zone, on November 22 a new national currency, the dram, was introduced.

(ELIZABETH FULLER)

This article updates the *Macropædia* article TRANSCAUCASIA: *Armenia.*

AUSTRIA

The federal republic of Austria is a landlocked state of Central Europe. Area: 83,859 sq km (32,378 sq mi). Pop. (1993 est.): 7,938,000. Cap.: Vienna. Monetary unit: Austrian Schilling, with (Oct. 4, 1993) a free rate of 11.42 Schillings to U.S. $1 (17.31 Schillings = £1 sterling). President in 1993, Thomas Klestil; chancellor, Franz Vranitzky.

Negotiations began on Feb. 1, 1993, on Austria's full membership in the European Community (EC). Areas for discussion included Austria's agricultural policy, land titles, and neutrality; maintaining the country's high social and environmental standards; and, above all, ensuring that the Transit Treaty between Austria and the EC remained in force until the year 2004. Austria was to hold a referendum on the issue and could accede to the EC as early as Jan. 1, 1995.

The economy was expected to contract by about 2% in 1993. Austria also experienced a massive fall in exports, a rapid decline in industrial production, and a series of failures of large enterprises. Particularly affected were steel, iron, chemical, paper, and textile production, where state-owned heavy industry saw losses of several billion Schillings. Unemployment reached its highest level in 40 years, with an average of 130,000 people out of work in 1993. Struggling to restructure itself under acute pressure from Eastern European markets, with their lower wage and price structures, Austrian industry badly needed an upturn in the economy.

All sides clamoured for subsidies in order to stem a tide of bankruptcies that caused losses exceeding 35 billion Schillings by the end of the third quarter. These demands put pressure on the 1994 budget, originally to have been an austerity plan but in the event having to include a 3% deficit. Even worse, the national debt crossed the significant billion-Schilling threshold in March. The lean year of 1993 was also characterized by further privatization of state property, curtailment of social services, and rising taxes. With the increase in the capital gains tax to 22%, very low interest, and rising inflation rates, many bank depositors found that they were losing money.

As a result, the two major political parties, the social-democratic Austrian Socialist Party and the Christian-democratic Austrian People's Party, suffered heavy losses in regional elections in Niederösterreich, Salzburg, and Graz. The winners at the ballot box were the right-wing Austrian Freedom Party (FPÖ), the Greens, and the splinter parties. Nationalism and the radical right also grew stronger in Austria, as was the case elsewhere in Europe. The FPÖ launched a rather unsuccessful antiforeigner petition drive at the end of January, and at the same time, a number of laws regulating the status of foreigners were rescinded. Action groups such as "SOS–Our Fellow Man" and "Laws, Not Foreigner Bashing" staged a large "sea of light" candlelight demonstration, in which some 200,000 persons participated. In early February five dissidents under FPÖ deputy head Heide Schmidt left the party to found the Liberal Forum and set up a separate parliamentary faction. This group, in turn, joined the Liberal International, from which the FPÖ resigned in order to avoid likely expulsion. In December right-wing extremists were blamed for a series of letter-bomb attacks, one of which injured the mayor of Vienna.

In June, after decades of tension caused by Austria's refusal to accept any responsibility for Nazi crimes, the pro-Arab policies of former chancellor Bruno Kreisky, and the outrage over the election of Kurt Waldheim as federal president, the country's relations with Israel began an entirely new chapter. During the first visit to Israel by an Austrian head of state, Chancellor Franz Vranitzky acknowledged Austria's collective responsibility for the victims of Nazi crimes. Various agreements were signed that greatly broadened cooperation between the two countries.

A number of former officials—including Chancellor Fred Sinowatz, Foreign Minister Leopold Gratz, and Interior Minister Karl Blecha—faced trial in June for alleged involvement in the illegal export of arms to Iran; only Blecha was convicted. The largest conference in UN history—and the first World Conference on Human Rights in 25 years—took place in June as delegates from 171 countries gathered in Vienna.

(ELFRIEDE DIRNBACHER)

AZERBAIJAN

A republic of Transcaucasia, Azerbaijan borders Russia on the north, the Caspian Sea on the east, Iran on the south, Armenia on the west, and Georgia on the northwest. The 5,500-sq km exclave of Nakhichevan to the southwest is separated from Azerbaijan proper by a strip of Armenia. Area (including Nakhichevan): 86,600 sq km (33,400 sq mi). Pop. (1993 est.): 7,398,000. Cap.: Baku (Azerbaijani: Baky). Monetary unit: manat, with (Oct. 4, 1993) a par value of 10 Russian rubles to 1 manat (free rates of 116.50 manat = U.S. $1 and 176.50 manat = £1 sterling). Presidents in 1993, Abulfez Elchibey to June 24 and, acting from June 24 and official from October 10, Geidar Aliev; prime ministers, Rakhim Guseynov to January 26, Ali Masimov to April 28, Panakh Guseynov to June 7, and, from June 27, Suret Guseynov.

High-level corruption, oppression of the political opposition, failure to counter plummeting living standards, and, above all, Armenian territorial and military gains in Nagorno-Karabakh combined to erode popular support for the leadership of pro-Turkish Pres. Abulfez Elchibey during spring 1993. Suret Guseynov, a leading army commander, was dismissed in February amid rumours he was planning a coup. In June his men deflected an attack on their headquarters by government forces and occupied Gyandzha, Azerbaijan's second city. Guseynov then demanded the resignation of Prime Minister Panakh Guseynov and parliament chairman Isa Gambarov and marched unchallenged on Baku, precipitating Elchibey's flight into internal exile. Nakhichevan parliament chairman Geidar Aliev (*see* BIOGRAPHIES) was elected parliament chairman and then acting president. Aliev strengthened his position by holding a referendum in August in which the population overwhelmingly expressed their lack of confidence in Elchibey. In October, Aliev was elected president with 98.8% of the vote.

In April Armenian forces occupied Kelbadzhar, effectively consolidating control of the region between the western border of Nagorno-Karabakh and the Armenian-Azerbaijani frontier and displacing tens of thousands of refugees. Karabakh forces later took advantage of the political turmoil in June–July to occupy Agdam. A UN Security Council resolution calling on the Armenians to withdraw from occupied territory gave new momentum to the stalled Conference on Security and Cooperation in Europe (CSCE) negotiations on a political settlement of the conflict. Successive drafts of a timetable for demilitarization, although accepted by both the Armenian and Azerbaijani governments, were rejected by the Armenian authorities in Stepanakert. A CSCE Conference late in the year failed to break the impasse.

Aliev distanced himself from the CSCE Karabakh mediation effort, possibly under Russian pressure, and embarked upon direct talks with the Karabakh Armenian authorities, which resulted in the signing in late July of a cease-fire agreement in Nagorno-Karabakh but did not prevent a new Armenian offensive south of the enclave in August. Iran deployed troops along its border with Azerbaijan to prevent tens of thousands of Azerbaijani refugees from entering its territory and subsequently financed camps and humanitarian aid for them within Azerbaijan. In November Nagorno-Karabakh parliament chairman Karen Baburyan proposed withdrawing from occupied Azerbaijani territory south and east of Nagorno-Karabakh in return for official recognition by Azerbaijan of the enclave's independence.

Aliev's advent to power signaled the end of Turkey's privileged relationship with Azerbaijan and a rapprochement with Russia and Iran. In early September Aliev traveled to Moscow for talks with Russian Pres. Boris Yeltsin and leading government officials on political and economic cooperation. Later that month, after several postponements, the Azerbaijani National Assembly voted in favour of Azerbaijan's rejoining the Commonwealth of Independent States. A visit to Baku in October by Iranian Pres. Ali Akbar Rafsanjani likewise focused on economic cooperation, specifically in the oil sector.

Economic decline continued; hopes for recovery in 1994 were predicated on Western investment in the oil sector. A draft agreement with eight Western companies on joint exploitation of three offshore oil fields, suspended by Aliev in June, was renegotiated on terms more favourable to Azerbaijan. (ELIZABETH FULLER)

This article updates the *Macropædia* article TRANSCAUCASIA: *Azerbaijan*.

BELARUS

A landlocked republic of Eastern Europe, Belarus borders Latvia on the north, Russia on the north and east, Ukraine on the south, Poland on the west, and Lithuania on the northwest. Area: 207,600 sq km (80,200 sq mi). Pop. (1993 est.): 10,353,000. Cap.: Minsk. Monetary unit: Belarusian rubel, with (Oct. 4, 1993) a free rate of 2,330 rubels = U.S. $1 (3,530 rubels = £1 sterling). Chairman of the Supreme Soviet in 1993, Stanislau Shushkevich; prime minister, Vyacheslau Kebich.

In 1993 Belarus embarked on a difficult transitional path to economic reform that was highlighted by significant drops in output and labour productivity. The Supreme Soviet, elected in 1990 and composed mainly of former Communists, forestalled any significant moves toward a market economy.

One crucial and unresolved economic problem was reliance on energy imports from Russia (comprising 90% of Belarus' oil and gas supplies), which were curtailed periodically throughout the year because of unpaid debts. In 1993 a heated but unresolved debate was held on the question of whether Belarus should revive its nuclear energy program, abandoned in 1988. New Belarusian rubel banknotes printed in Germany were not yet in circulation. Instead, the zaichik (named after the hare on the rubel bill) had been in use since May 1992. In July, when Russia began to recall Russian ruble banknotes, the Belarusian rubel dropped in value, and by August it had fallen to 50% of the Russian ruble. In late August the official rubel-to-ruble exchange rate was fixed at 2:1, and on November 24 the zaichik was declared the sole legal currency. A bilateral Russian-Belarusian commission met on December 17 to stabilize the exchange rate and prepare for currency union.

Political life was dominated by the conflict between Prime Minister Vyacheslau Kebich and Supreme Soviet Chairman Stanislau Shushkevich, primarily over the question of joining a military and security union with Russia. Belarus also agreed to enter an economic union in September and to form a monetary union with Russia (again over the protests of Shushkevich) in November. The most powerful grouping in Parliament was the reactionary Belarus Faction, which opposed economic reforms and favoured closer integration with Russia. A reflection of the conservative nature of the ruling government was the reactivation of the old Communist Party of Belarus early in 1993, now one of two Communist parties in the republic.

In February Belarus voted to adhere to the Nuclear Nonproliferation Treaty and ratified the Strategic Arms Reduction Treaty (START I). Some 80 SS-25 ICBMs were under Russian control and were to be transferred to Russia by the end of 1994. In many spheres Belarus appeared to have entered the Russian orbit, although not without opposition. In the summer the Association of Belarusian Students picketed the Parliament building to demand a date for a referendum on fixing new parliamentary elections and to declare Belorussian the sole official language in the republic. In August a bomb was detonated in a central square of Minsk, ostensibly by a right-wing extremist faction that sought the restoration of the U.S.S.R.

The Belarusian Popular Front, which formed a political party to contest the 1994 elections, bitterly contested Parliament's course and accused it of failing to deal with major issues. The declining economy saw a large rise in joblessness, with projections as high as 700,000 unemployed by the start of 1994. The consequences in Belarus of the 1986 Chernobyl atomic power plant disaster in neighbouring Ukraine were another concern; for example, the number of thyroid cancers among children was rising dramatically, and as much as 40% of the republic's territory was contaminated by radioactive cesium. (DAVID R. MARPLES)

BELGIUM

A federal constitutional monarchy, Belgium is situated on the North Sea coast of northwestern Europe. Area: 30,528 sq km (11,787 sq mi). Pop. (1993 est.): 10,072,000. Cap.: Brussels. Monetary unit: Belgian franc, with (Oct. 4, 1993) a free rate of BF 35.15 to U.S. $1 (BF 53.25 = £1 sterling). Kings, Baudouin I and, from August 9, Albert II; prime minister in 1993, Jean-Luc Dehaene.

Exactly 289 days after the conclusion of the so-called Saint-Michael's agreements between the Social Christian and Socialist coalition parties, the two houses of Parliament approved the constitutional changes that would turn Belgium into a federal state. The required two-thirds majority was obtained with the help of the Green parties and the Flemish nationalist Volksunie. In exchange for this support, the coalition parties agreed that ministers would henceforth resign their seats in Parliament and that they would support the introduction of much-criticized "eco-taxes" on various types of wrappings and newsprint. At the request of the Volksunie, residual powers were transferred to the language communities and geographic regions.

A statement by the Flemish regional minister-president, Luc Van den Brande, claiming that confederalism would be the next step in the transformation of Belgium prompted strong reaction since it was considered a move toward separatism. King Baudouin's invitation to Van den Brande to explain his views was criticized in certain Flemish circles. A demonstration in Brussels against the separatist trend drew large public support. The discussion nevertheless continued concerning unjustifiable transfers of financial resources from Flanders to Wallonia, in particular in the social security sector.

The budgetary situation further deteriorated, and in March it caused a crisis within the government, prompting Prime Minister Jean-Luc Dehaene to tender his resignation, which King Baudouin refused to accept. Acting as a mediator between the coalition parties, Dehaene achieved an agreement on measures to reduce the deficit by BF 113 billion. A decision was also reached on the privatization of a number of public companies. These included the National Savings and Loan Bank, shares of which were acquired by the Belgian-Dutch insurance group Fortis, providing the government with new financial resources.

Meanwhile, the crisis made further inroads in the economy. The number of bankruptcies in Belgium increased dramatically. Among the most serious was the loss of the last Belgian ship-repair firm. The country's largest retail chain store reduced its workforce by one-quarter (4,600 people), while the multinational petrochemical company Solvay reported a loss for only the second time in its 130-year history. On the other hand, the Société Générale de Belgique holding company sold the country's major cement producer, CBR (with subsidiaries in Europe and North America), to one of its German competitors, Heidelberger, for nearly $1 billion.

Faced with the consequences in employment and social security of the ever expanding recession, Dehaene conceived the idea of a "social pact" to which employers, trade unions, and the government would subscribe. Unemployment at the end of August stood at 13.4% of the active population. In the event, the government's austerity plan, released on November 17, triggered a one-day general strike that brought the country to a virtual standstill.

Compulsory military service was abolished in 1993, and the number of reservists was scaled down to 30,000. The Army Command feared it would become impossible for Belgium to meet its NATO commitments. The Belgian contingent in Somalia was due to be withdrawn in December.

The death of King Baudouin (*see* OBITUARIES) at his vacation home in Motril, Spain, provoked an outpouring of emotion that showed the extent of the support he enjoyed among the population. Tens of thousands paid a last homage, at the same time underlining their desire to maintain the country's unity. He was succeeded by his younger brother, who was sworn in as King Albert II (*see* BIOGRAPHIES) on August 9. (JAN R. ENGELS)

Special Report: Bosnia and Herzegovina

Bosnia and Herzegovina in Historical Perspective

BY IAN D. ARMOUR

The roots of the "Bosnian question" as a Balkan and European problem go back at least 150 years, when the competing claims of Serb and Croat nationalists to either the whole or parts of Bosnia and Herzegovina emerged. Insofar as, for much of this period, Bosnia and Herzegovina was subsumed within supranational states such as the Ottoman Empire, the Habsburg monarchy, and the successive versions of Yugoslavia, the most extreme "solution" to the problem—civil war leading to partition—had been averted. Nor was it necessary, until recently, for the Muslim population to define itself as anything other than one of three communities or to seek its own separate territory. Paradoxically, the independence of Bosnia and Herzegovina was no sooner proclaimed, in early 1992, than its constituent nationalities started tearing it to pieces.

Since the Slavs first arrived in the Balkan Peninsula, settling in the river valleys south of the Danube only in the early 7th century, there had been conflicting claims as to who settled where first. It is probable that the first wave of Slavs was a mass of undifferentiated tribes; only later did the arrival of additional peoples, whose names were recorded, give to the lands they occupied specific names. Two such peoples, invited to settle within Byzantine territory by the Emperor Heraclius (reigned 610–641), were the Croats and

Ian D. Armour is a freelance researcher and writer. He is coauthor, with Ian Porter, of Imperial Germany 1890–1918 *(London: Longman, 1991).*

Hung with automobile tires for protection, Mostar's renowned 16th-century stone bridge shows severe damage from mortar shells. Croatian shelling in early November completed the destruction of the bridge, which had served as a physical and symbolic link between the eastern (Muslim) and western (Croatian) parts of the city.
NIGEL CHANDLER—SYGMA

the Serbs. Because the earliest recorded Croat and Serb territories were never wholly contiguous, it is possible that the core of what later became known as Bosnia, a territory centring on the headwaters of the River Bosna, was originally settled by that first, undifferentiated wave of Slavs. All claims, therefore, are conjectural. In view of the persistence with which Croat and Serb nationalists claim Bosnia and Herzegovina as "theirs," however, and refer to the present-day Muslims as mere "Islamicized" Croats and Serbs, it is worth pointing out that while the vast majority of Bosnia and Herzegovina's population is undoubtedly of Slav origin, no one group can claim undisputed seniority.

For centuries there was nothing in the area corresponding to a modern "state." Individual tribes maintained their hold over local territory, and gradually some tribes won control over neighbouring areas, usually by fighting for it. The first identifiable principalities, all of whose origins are obscure, were Croatia, between the Sava and Drava rivers; Bosnia to the southeast; Hum (Herzegovina), south of Bosnia; Zeta, corresponding roughly to modern Montenegro; and Raska, centred on the town of Ras in what is now the Sandzak of Novi Pazar and the core of the later Serbia.

All these medieval principalities underwent drastic and usually short-lived expansion and contraction. Medieval Croatia, at its greatest extent in the late 11th century, extended as far south as the Vrbas River in west-central Bosnia. Raska, for a time, controlled much of Hum and parts of Bosnia. Each claimed suzerainty over its neighbours, a situation complicated by the interest of Hungary in both Croatia (which it ruled after 1102) and Bosnia. Greatest of all of these principalities, but for a very brief period, was the Serbian empire of Stephen Dusan (reigned 1331–55), which stretched from Herzegovina to northern Greece and the Aegean.

After emerging as a distinct principality in the 12th century, Bosnia too enjoyed a strong dynasty under King Tvrtko I (1353–91), who established his dominion over the Dalmatian littoral. But medieval Bosnia had no sooner reached its apogee than it was conquered by the Ottoman Turks in the 1460s. Herzegovina, which had broken away from Bosnian rule, was conquered by 1482.

In contrast to most of the other Christian populations taken over by the Ottoman Empire, many of the Bosnian Slavs, and especially the landowners, converted to Islam since under Ottoman law only Muslims could own property. Those who remained Christian either emigrated or were relegated to peasant status, free to exercise their religion but in all other respects a subject people. As the Ottoman Empire declined in the 18th and 19th centuries, this Christian underclass suffered increasingly from the exactions of their landlords and the misrule of local despots. The fact that the peasantry was also Serb or Croat, in addition to being Orthodox or Catholic, assumed even greater importance in an age of nationalism.

By the 1860s nationalists in both the autonomous Principality of Serbia (still officially subject to the sultan) and the Kingdom of Croatia (part of Hungary, within the Habsburg Empire) regarded Bosnia and Herzegovina as rightfully theirs. Not only were these claims mutually exclusive, but both Croats and Serbs also assumed that the large Muslim element, being originally Slav, could be reclaimed for either Catholicism or Orthodoxy.

The waters were further muddied by the involvement of the Habsburg monarchy. The imperial Foreign Ministry in Vienna was adamant that Bosnia and Herzegovina was never to be abandoned to Serbia; this would have created a large South Slav state on the monarchy's southern frontier, which could have exerted an attractive power over Austria-Hungary's own South Slavs. After 1867, when Hungary achieved home rule within the monarchy, Hungarian politicians for several years pursued the opposite goal. By encouraging the Serbian government to think that it could, with Hungarian assistance, acquire at least part of Bosnia and Herzegovina, the Hungarians hoped to win Serbia over for close economic and political ties to the monarchy. This improbable project was abandoned in 1871, but not before it had reinforced suspicion on both sides.

Count Gyula Andrassy, the principal promoter of this scheme, became the Austro-Hungarian foreign minister in 1871 and thereafter pursued the old policy of keeping Serbia out of Bosnia. Thus, when the Christians first of Herzegovina and then of Bosnia rose in revolt in 1875, provoking a prolonged international crisis, it was Austria-Hungary and not Serbia that occupied the provinces.

The Austro-Hungarian takeover of Bosnia and Herzegovina, which was administered by the Habsburgs until 1918, gave mortal offense to Serb nationalists everywhere. Despite bringing law and order to a previously anarchic part of the Balkans and developing the infrastructure and industry, Habsburg rule (entrusted largely to Hungarians) left much else unchanged. The exploitative relationship between Muslim landowners and Christian peasants remained, and political organization was not permitted until 1908, when Austria-Hungary formally annexed Bosnia from the Ottomans. Above all, the Serbian population, in 1910 still the largest ethnic group, was marginalized as potentially treasonable, while Catholic Croats tended to be favoured. In this climate of simmering nationalist tension, it is not surprising that it was a young Bosnian Serb, Gavrilo Princip, who assassinated Archduke Francis Ferdinand in Sarajevo in 1914, an act that provided the occasion for war between Austria-Hungary and Serbia and, by extension, World War I.

The war proved the Habsburg monarchy's undoing, and when, in 1918, it collapsed and was dismembered, Bosnia and Herzegovina was taken over by a triumphant Serbia in the name of the new Kingdom of Serbs, Croats, and Slovenes. Upon the withdrawal of Habsburg authority, communal violence at once flared up in Bosnia, with the Muslim landowners especially targeted. One of the most important changes of the post-1918 period was the gradual expropriation of Muslim estates, with land being parceled out to the peasants. The result was a concentration of the Muslim population in the urban centres.

The problem with the new Yugoslav state was that it was in reality a Greater Serbia, with a centralist constitution that ensured that all important decisions were taken by a government in Belgrade dominated by Serbs. Bosnia's position in this respect was neither better nor worse than that of the other provinces, but in 1929 King Alexander, having established a royal dictatorship, redrew the internal administrative boundaries on purely geographic lines. The state was also renamed Yugoslavia in a vain attempt to minimize nationalist antagonisms and build loyalty to a supranational ideal. Within a decade the attempt foundered on the rocks of continuing Serb domination and Croat separatism. An agreement in 1939 redrew the map yet again, this time assigning most of Herzegovina and southeastern Bosnia to Croatia, with the rest subsumed in Serbia. No account was taken of the Muslim population.

Two years later Yugoslavia was invaded and partitioned by the Axis powers. Bosnia and Herzegovina went to the Nazi puppet Independent State of Croatia, and in the civil war that ensued, the three ethnic communities were pitted against one another as never before. The worst offenses were undoubtedly perpetrated against the Serb Orthodox population by the Croat Ustase regime, often aided by Muslims, but reprisals were carried out with similar savagery first by the royalist Serb Chetniks, then by Josip Broz Tito's communist Partisans. Half a century later the memory of these horrors lives on and is used by all sides as justification for fresh atrocities. Chetnik and Ustase have resurfaced as abusive terms for Serb and Croat, respectively.

The postwar communist dictatorship solved the problems of Bosnia and Herzegovina temporarily by driving them underground. For the first time, Bosnia and Herzegovina existed as one of six equal federated republics. Nationalist divisions were explicitly ignored as incompatible with socialism. The Yugoslav constitution of 1974, however, which devolved considerable autonomy to the republics, in the end made matters worse because the republics increasingly adopted nationalist policies. Only in Bosnia and Herzegovina was this a contradiction in terms. Instead, the situation there was complicated by the recognition, enshrined in the 1974 constitution, of the Muslims as a separate nationality. Henceforth, in the maelstrom of competing nationalism that Yugoslavia became after Tito's death in 1980, some sort of ethnic conflict looked more and more likely. This was confirmed when in the first free elections, held in November 1990, the three communities split along firm ethnic lines. Even this, however, though ominous, might not necessarily have proved unworkable. It was the decision of the government in Sarajevo to proclaim independence from Yugoslavia that, by unleashing the full hysteria of Serb nationalism, rendered war inevitable.

BOSNIA AND HERZEGOVINA

A republic of the western Balkans, Bosnia and Herzegovina borders Croatia on the north, southwest, and south, the Adriatic Sea on the south (via a narrow extension), and Yugoslavia on the east. Area: 51,129 sq km (19,741 sq mi). Pop. (1993 est. based on prewar projection): 4,422,000. Cap.: Sarajevo. De facto monetary unit: Yugoslav new dinar, with (Oct. 4, 1993) a free rate of 104.24 new dinars to U.S. $1 (157.92 new dinars = £1 sterling); Bosnia has no national currency and has not been supplied with dinars by Yugoslav authorities since June 1992. President in 1993, Alija Izetbegovic; prime ministers, Mile Akmadzic to August and, from October 25, Haris Silajdzic.

The year began with a joint European Community–United Nations initiative for Bosnia named after the two chief negotiators, Lord Owen and Cyrus Vance, which was presented to the UN Security Council by Secretary-General Boutros Boutros-Ghali on February 2. The Vance-Owen plan proposed dividing the republic into 10 autonomous provinces, largely based on nationality and with guarantees for a balanced representation of minority groups in each area. The Serbs (33% of the total population in 1991) would get about 46% of the republic's territory, the Muslims (with 44% of the population) about 30%, and the Croats (18%) about 24%. The Bosnian Croat leadership accepted the plan; the Muslims were unhappy but did not reject it outright; and the Bosnian Serbs accepted it subject to ratification by their self-styled parliament—which it declined to do.

At a meeting in Washington that marked the abandonment of the Vance-Owen plan, representatives of the U.S., Russia, Britain, France, and Spain proposed a new 13-point plan for "safe areas" based on the Vance-Owen plan and linked to provision of international policing and humanitarian aid. On June 4 the Security Council established six "safe areas" for the Muslims, mainly in eastern and central Bosnia. UN troops supervising them were empowered to retaliate if attacked, and on June 18 the UN decided to dispatch 7,600 soldiers to protect the zones.

The Bosnian government rejected the idea of "safe areas" as both unjust and unviable. Meanwhile, its forces started an offensive against Croat troops, in central Bosnia, who had taken some mixed regions allocated to the Croats under the old Vance-Owen plan. The Muslims made considerable headway against the Croats, although the latter managed to hold on to the strategic city of Mostar, where Croatian shelling destroyed the 16th-century bridge that had connected the Muslim and Croat parts of the city. The Serbs, meanwhile, continued to besiege Sarajevo.

In September, Lord Owen and Thorvald Stoltenberg (who had replaced Cyrus Vance) led another round of negotiations centring on the concept of Bosnia as a union of three republics, each of which could later join other states. The interested parties met on the British warship *Invincible* on the Adriatic, but the attempt to reach a settlement failed when the Muslims demanded more territory from the Serbs and access to the sea from the Croats. In the end, the mainly Muslim assembly in Sarajevo rejected the proposed settlement, partly because the U.S. failed to provide assurances of military presence to protect the settlement. Another initiative, associated with the German and French foreign ministers, offered the Serbs the gradual lifting of economic sanctions in return for territorial concessions demanded by the Muslims. But the Serbs, increasingly torn by internal divisions in Bosnia (an anti-Karadzic rebellion among army units in Banja Luka in September was put down with difficulty), refused to oblige. Meanwhile, Fikret Abdic, a local Muslim leader, denounced the Sarajevo officials as intransigent and made a separate deal with the Serbs and Croats.

International negotiators met again in late December, but a proposed cease-fire failed, and fighting continued.

(K.F. CVIIC)

This article updates the *Macropædia* article BALKAN STATES: *Bosnia and Herzegovina.*

BULGARIA

The republic of Bulgaria is on the eastern Balkan Peninsula of southeastern Europe, along the Black Sea. Area: 110,994 sq km (42,855 sq mi). Pop. (1993 est.): 8,466,000. Cap.: Sofia. Monetary unit: lev, with (Oct. 4, 1993) a free rate of 26.14 leva to U.S. $1 (39.60 leva = £1 sterling). President in 1993, Zhelyu Zhelev; prime minister, Lyuben Berov.

The government of Prime Minister Lyuben Berov was kept in power in 1993 by support in the National Assembly from the Movement for Rights and Freedoms (MRF), a mainly Turkish party; the Bulgarian Socialist Party; and the New Union for Democracy, a breakaway section of the Union of Democratic Forces (UDF). An angry UDF consistently accused the government of backtracking on reform and of wishing to restore socialism. In support of this they pointed to government interference with the media (from which a number of antiregime figures were removed), the reinstatement of some former communists to official posts, the refusal to remove the Soviet war memorial in Sofia, and the slowing down of economic reform. The chief UDF demand was for the holding of new general elections.

Matters came to a head during June when UDF deputy Edvin Sugarev went on a hunger strike in an effort to force Pres. Zhelyu Zhelev's resignation. Large antigovernment and anti-Zhelev demonstrations ensued, and at the end of the month Vice Pres. Blaga Dimitrova resigned, claiming that some form of dictatorship was imminent.

Berov's position was more threatened, however, by growing discontent among the Turkish minority and, therefore, in the MRF. Ethnic Turkish tobacco growers complained bitterly about the level of government-fixed purchase prices. On September 17 the National Assembly annulled the controversial 1992 census results for two areas in southwest Bulgaria that allegedly reported exaggerated numbers of Turkish residents. The MRF protested that the Turks were being denied the right to choose their ethnic identity; there were echoes of the communist regime's attempts in the 1980s to bulgarize the Turkish population.

The country was much affected by the UN-sponsored embargo on trade with and through the rump Yugoslavia. By midsummer Bulgarians were claiming that their country had lost over $1.3 billion in the first six months of the year, and the country was having difficulties resuming payment of its foreign debt obligations.

The Berov government had already caused the International Monetary Fund (IMF) concern by announcing that the budget deficit for 1993 would be between 8 and 10%, far above the IMF ceiling for creditworthy states. The IMF also questioned government spending and the slowing pace of economic reform and privatization. By September, in the critical agrarian sector, no more than a quarter of the claims for land restitution had been met, despite government promises that the majority of claims would be settled by the end of the year. In December some 20,000 miners staged a prolonged strike to protest anticipated layoffs caused by the closure of unprofitable mines. After 26 days the government was forced to guarantee back pay to strikers and jobs to those who were laid off.

August 1993 saw the 50th anniversary of the death of King Boris III. The occasion was marked by the reburial of what was alleged to be his heart in Rila Monastery and by a visit to Bulgaria by his widow, who had left the country in 1946.

(RICHARD J. CRAMPTON)

This article updates the *Macropædia* article BALKAN STATES: *Bulgaria.*

CROATIA

A republic of the northwestern Balkans, Croatia is an elongated crescent-shaped country to the north, west, and southwest of Bosnia and Herzegovina. Its extensive Adriatic coastal region on the southwest includes nearly 1,200 islands and islets. Area: 56,538 sq km (21,829 sq mi). Pop. (1993 est.) 4,821,000. Cap.: Zagreb. Monetary unit: Croatian dinar (or kuna), with (Oct. 4, 1993) a free rate of 7,181 dinars to U.S. $1 (10,879 dinars = £1 sterling). President in 1993, Franjo Tudjman; prime ministers, Hrvoje Sarinic and, from March 29, Nikica Valentic.

Croatia's main preoccupations in 1993 were the refugee problem (Muslim and Croat refugees arriving from Bosnia and Herzegovina) and concern about the Croat territories—nearly one-third of the whole country—remaining under Serb control. On January 22, Croatian forces recaptured territory near the port city of Zadar and the site of the destroyed Maslenica bridge. Three days later the UN Security Council condemned the action and asked that Croatian troops withdraw; at the same time, the UN demanded that the Serb militia return the heavy weapons they had seized from UN stores to the UN forces stationed in Serb-occupied

JASMIN KPRAN—GAMMA LIAISON

Citizens of Zagreb stand before a monument to victims of the siege of Vukovar, from which Croatians were expelled after the devasted city fell to Serbs in 1991. As elsewhere in the former Yugoslavia, Croatia continued to deal with large numbers of internal refugees, as well as with others displaced by the fighting.

regions of Croatia. On January 27 Croatian forces began shelling the Peruca hydroelectric dam, and they captured it the next day. Rebuilt by the Croats after the January action, the Maslenica bridge was sunk by Serb artillery fire on August 2, then rebuilt again. On October 4 the Security Council extended by another six months the mandate of the 14,000-strong UN force stationed in Croatia.

Throughout 1993, talks were held about the reopening of the Zagreb-Belgrade highway, the Zagreb-Split railway, and the Rijeka-Zagreb oil pipeline, all three passing through territory under Serb control, but they led to no agreement. Local cease-fires negotiated with the Serbs in eastern Croatia around Osijek on November 11 and in central Croatia near Karlovac on November 14 held, however.

In the February 7 local and regional council and parliamentary elections, the ruling right-wing Croatian Democratic Union (HDZ) party of Pres. Franjo Tudjman won a commanding 37 seats in the upper chamber, but it lost in 7 out of 21 counties and in over half of all towns. During the spring and the summer of 1993, there were a number of challenges to Tudjman's leadership, notably from the increasingly self-confident ultranationalist right of his party. At the HDZ congress in October, however, Tudjman outmaneuvered his critics, imposed a "centrist" leadership on the party, and was himself reelected party leader.

In a referendum held in the self-declared Serb Republic of Krajina (the Serb-occupied areas of Croatia) on June 19–20, 98.6% of those who voted said "yes" to the idea of a union with the Serbs of Bosnia and Herzegovina and with "other Serb states." In the elections on December 12 for the president of the Krajina, Milan Babic, an outright opponent of any reintegration into Croatia, beat Milan Martic, an ally of Serbian Pres. Slobodan Milosevic.

The Croatian dinar was devalued by 21% and pegged to the Deutsche Mark in October as part of a package of economic-stabilization measures designed above all to bring inflation under control. The strict monetarist measures undertaken by the government of Nikica Valentic, however, led to an overvalued dinar that stifled growth and accelerated the outflow of scarce foreign currency. (K.F. CVIIC)

This article updates the *Macropædia* article BALKAN STATES: *Croatia*.

CZECH REPUBLIC

The Czech Republic is a landlocked state of central Europe. Area: 78,864 sq km (30,450 sq mi). Pop. (1993 est.): 10,332,000. Cap.: Prague. Monetary unit: koruna, with (Oct. 4, 1993) a free rate of 28.75 koruny to U.S. $1 (43.56 koruny = £1 sterling). President from Feb. 2, 1993, Vaclav Havel; prime minister, Vaclav Klaus.

The Czech Republic began its first year of existence without Slovakia with high hopes that, having left behind what it saw as a burden, it would be able to integrate into Europe at a very early stage. Indeed, the prime minister, Vaclav Klaus, hinted that the Czech Republic might be able to join the European Community (EC) within a few years, an idea that was completely unrealistic. The Czech Republic was rapidly given membership in all the international organizations of which Czechoslovakia had been a member, but that did not in itself take it any closer to the cherished goal of full membership in the EC and NATO.

Domestically, Klaus was unassailable. Although he commanded only just over a third of the votes in the 1992 election, he dominated the political scene, and the opposition seemed quite incapable of exercising effective criticism of him and his policies. He successfully constructed a conservative four-party coalition in the parliament with an absolute majority. This consisted of Klaus's own party, the Civic Democratic Party, plus the Civic Democratic Alliance, the Christian and Democratic Union–Czech People's Party, and the Christian Democratic Party. Despite expectations of fragility within the coalition, it held together reasonably effectively and was unimpressed by the weak showing of the opposition. The coalition was largely united on a policy of rapid movement toward the creation of a market through privatization and, of course, integration into Europe.

The economic strategy was not quite as successful as it appeared, however. Economic conditions remained favourable in the Czech Republic during the year. Unemployment was very low at about 3.5%; inflation was under control; and the overall performance of the economy was fairly solid. This was achieved, however, at the cost of delaying major structural reform.

The Czech Republic had inherited a fully industrialized economy from communism, but one that was seriously obsolete in many branches. Launching a reequipment program would require massive inputs of capital; many uneconomic factories would have to be closed and resulting unemployment dealt with. When viewed from this perspective, the low level of unemployment indicated that serious reform of the economy had still to begin. In the interim the Czech Republic was ready to exploit its great natural advantage in tourism—the attractiveness of Prague—and to switch to a service-based economy.

Restructuring seemed to be a move that Klaus was not ready to contemplate, despite his high-profile free-market and monetarist rhetoric. Presumably, he reasoned that public opinion would not tolerate the social fallout from rapid restructuring of the kind that had been pursued by Poland. This left the Czech Republic in the odd position of proclaiming one economic strategy, that of marketization, and actually pursuing another, that of continued state subsidies for ailing industries.

For the time being, the opposition was divided and incapable of putting together a shared platform. The former communists, indeed, were themselves split on whether to move toward full acceptance of democratic norms or to adhere to traditional communist principles.

Klaus's dominance of the political scene even exceeded that of Vaclav Havel, who was much better known internationally. Havel, having been president of Czechoslovakia until July 1992, was elected president of the Czech Republic in January 1993. He was known to be unhappy with the division of Czechoslovakia, and he reemerged into the political limelight only after the split had taken place. His role in Czech politics, however, was one of influence rather than power. (GEORGE SCHÖPFLIN)

This article updates the *Macropædia* article CZECH AND SLOVAK REPUBLICS: *Czech Republic*.

DENMARK

A constitutional monarchy of north-central Europe, Denmark lies between the North and Baltic seas. Area: 43,094 sq km (16,639 sq mi), excluding the Faeroe Islands and Greenland. Pop. (1993 est.): 5,187,000. Cap.: Copenhagen. Monetary unit: Danish krone, with (Oct. 4, 1993) a free rate of 6.57 kroner to U.S. $1 (9.96 kroner = £1 sterling). Queen, Margrethe II; prime ministers in 1993, Poul Schlüter and, from January 25, Poul Nyrup Rasmussen.

Denmark mended its fences with the European Community (EC) in 1993 following the dramatic Danish rejection the previous summer of the Maastricht Treaty on closer European political union. The year also saw the return to power of the opposition Social Democratic Party at the head of a four-party centre-left majority coalition after a decade of minority Conservative-Liberal rule under veteran prime minister Poul Schlüter.

Denmark's six-month term in the EC's rotating presidency was marred shortly after it got under way in January when a long-running political scandal came to a head. Prime Minister Schlüter resigned on January 14 after a judicial inquiry accused him of deliberately misleading the Folketing (parliament) regarding measures that were taken to prevent Tamil refugees from Sri Lanka from entering Denmark. In addition, the 6,000-page report, released after a 32-month investigation, blamed Schlüter for failing to recognize that Ministry of Justice restrictions on immigrants had been illegal. Schlüter's former minister of justice, Erik Ninn-Hansen, faced impeachment charges over the scandal.

After 11 days of a political vacuum, Poul Nyrup Rasmussen (*see* BIOGRAPHIES), leader of the Social Democrats, Denmark's biggest political party, formed a new coalition along with three small centrist groupings, the Radical Liberal Party, the Centre Democrats, and the Christian People's Party. Denmark's first majority coalition since 1971, the new government had a one-seat majority in the 179-seat Folketing.

The most pressing task of the new administration was to clarify Denmark's future role in Europe. May 18 was set as the date for the country's second Maastricht referendum. A major campaign was launched to secure a resounding "yes" from the "Euro-skeptical" Danish electorate. A complex accommodation arrangement approved by Denmark's 11 EC partners at the summit in Edinburgh in December 1992 would permit the Danes to opt out of plans for a common EC currency, joint defense, union citizenship, and supranational legal cooperation—aspects of the Maastricht Treaty unpalatable to the Danish electorate. Despite support from seven of the eight parties represented in the Folketing, powerful industrial and agricultural lobbies, and virtually the entire press, the exemption deal met major opposition from grassroots organizations. In the event, the May referendum ended with 56.8% of doubting Danes voting rather reluctantly for Maastricht with the opt-out clauses while 43.2% opposed the treaty. The outcome sparked two nights of riots—called the worst in Danish history—involving disenchanted squatter youths and police in Copenhagen's Nørrebro working-class district.

The new government also addressed the issue of tax reform, Denmark being the EC country with the highest level of income tax. The plan aimed to reduce taxes broadly to 38–58% of income, compared with the current 52–68%, in the period 1994–98. Revenue lost through cuts in the country's exceptionally high marginal tax rates was to be offset by "green" levies on gasoline, motor vehicles, energy, and water consumption, coupled with increased social security contributions.

The Danish economy—showing a solid balance of payments, foreign trade surpluses, and ultralow inflation—continued to perform remarkably well throughout the year despite the general European recession, currency turmoil within the European exchange-rate mechanism, high interest rates, and sluggish growth in gross domestic product. The government identified unemployment—at around 12% of the workforce, its highest point since the 1930s—as Denmark's most serious problem.

Autumn saw the marking of the 50th anniversary of the miraculous evacuation rescue by Danish fishermen of 7,000 Jews from roundup and deportation by Nazi occupiers during World War II. That feat had earned Denmark the eternal gratitude of the international Jewish community.

(CHRISTOPHER FOLLETT)

ESTONIA

A republic of northern Europe, Estonia borders the Baltic Sea on the west and north. Area: 45,226 sq km (17,462 sq mi). Pop. (1993 est.): 1,536,000. Cap.: Tallinn. Monetary unit: kroon, with (Oct. 4, 1993) a par value of 8 krooni to DM 1 (free rates of 12.93 krooni = U.S. $1 and 19.58 krooni = £1 sterling). President in 1993, Lennart Meri; prime minister, Mart Laar.

The free-market philosophy of the government and the positive climate for business won international acclaim for Estonia in 1993. In spite of the collapse of several banks beginning in 1992, the currency remained stable, foreign investment grew noticeably, privatization progressed, and foreign trade shifted decisively to the West and away from Russia (down to 20% of the total).

Progress continued in the restoration of civil society. Accepting revisions suggested by a team of European experts, Pres. Lennart Meri (*see* BIOGRAPHIES) signed Estonia's controversial law on aliens in July. Elections to municipal and rural district councils were held on October 17. A number of judges, including Supreme Court justices, were appointed. In November the interior minister was fired for failing to cope with crime, the government's leading domestic worry.

Estonia was admitted to the Council of Europe on May 14. Regional affairs were pursued primarily through the new Council of Baltic Sea States. The key issue in foreign relations was the continued presence in the country of Russian military forces, which Moscow, in disregard of the UN General Assembly resolution of Nov. 25, 1992, had yet to withdraw. Despite Moscow's blustering to the contrary during the summer of 1993, by year's end it appeared that Russian forces might soon depart.

Uncertainties beset the relationships between President Meri and the Cabinet and Parliament. Elected to his post by a broad-based governing coalition, Meri refused to promulgate a number of important laws passed by Parliament. More serious was his tendency to overreach his constitutional powers in defense and foreign affairs. The opposition failed to unseat Prime Minister Mart Laar in November, when only 21% of the members of Parliament supported a motion of no confidence. (TÕNU PARMING)

This article updates the *Macropædia* article BALTIC STATES: *Estonia.*

FINLAND

The republic of Finland is in northern Europe, on the Gulf of Bothnia and the Gulf of Finland. Area: 338,145 sq km (130,559 sq mi). Pop. (1993 est.): 5,058,000. Cap.: Helsinki. Monetary unit: Finnish markka, with (Oct. 4, 1993) a free rate of 5.82 markkaa to U.S. $1 (8.82 markkaa = £1 sterling). President in 1993, Mauno Koivisto; prime minister, Esko Aho.

In March 1993, Pres. Mauno Koivisto, who turned 70 in November, announced that he would retire in March 1994 after completing two successive six-year terms in office. The news prompted all the major political parties, several smaller parties, and a few popular movements to nominate candidates for the post, which carried sweeping powers, including responsibility for the formulation and monitoring of foreign policy. The expected scenario of a close presidential race between a few prominent politicians was upset in the spring when a civil servant, Martti Ahtisaari, won the nomination of the opposition Social Democratic Party in a primary open to all voters. His victory was viewed as a reflection of popular disenchantment with long-serving politicians. As the 1994 elections approached, polls showed that Ahtisaari maintained a clear lead over all other rivals, including Paavo Väyrynen of the Centre Party and Raimo Ilaskivi of the National Coalition (Conservative) Party.

Though action against politicians on ethical grounds was rare in Finland, the high court of impeachment, which had not convened since 1961, found Kauko Juhantalo, a former trade and industry minister, guilty of abuse of office and of having solicited a bribe from Skopbank, the commercial arm of an association of savings banks. Juhantalo, who received a one-year suspended prison sentence, intended to retain his parliamentary seat.

On the domestic scene Finland continued to be blighted by a recession, which was prolonged as a result of Koivisto's advocacy of an overvalued Finnish markka, a policy he maintained until the currency was floated in September 1992. By late 1993 the markka had stabilized against major currencies at a level at least 25% below its rate of two years earlier. Diminished demand also contributed to the lingering recession. Household disposable income fell as a result of higher taxes, a freeze on wages, and unemployment. Some 500,000 persons, somewhat less than 20% of the workforce, were unemployed at the end of the year. The government predicted that the unemployment figure would not fall to 15% until the second half of the decade. The inflation rate, however, fell to about 2%. There was a loss of exports to Russia, and the government borrowed heavily from abroad while maintaining that the rising surplus in visible trade would balance the deficit in the current account within the next few years.

The government continued to reduce public services to help reduce expenditures under the national budget. Overall spending rose, however, under supplementary budgets, which were used to offset the effects of rising unemployment and to provide financing for banks hit by the recession. The Savings Bank of Finland received some $6 billion before being sold later in the year to four commercial banks for about $2 billion.

In foreign affairs Finland was quick to express support for Pres. Boris Yeltsin during the September leadership struggle in neighbouring Russia, which had traditionally been one of Finland's primary security concerns. Though Koivisto and other Finnish leaders repeatedly remarked that they did not fear a military threat from Russia, they expressed concern about a possible armed forces buildup just across the 1,270-km (800-mi) border after the withdrawal of Russian troops from parts of Eastern Europe.

Finland, which hoped to join the European Community (EC) in 1995, stated that it would accept the Maastricht Treaty on European Union. Finland also agreed to a joint foreign and security policy but wished to retain its military neutrality and an independent defense. Finland's admission into the EC would depend, however, on EC assurances that special provisions would be made for Finland's heavily subsidized Arctic and sub-Arctic farming.

(EDWARD M. SUMMERHILL)

FRANCE

A republic of western Europe, France includes the island of Corsica in the Mediterranean Sea and has coastlines on the English Channel, the Mediterranean, and the Atlantic Ocean. Area: 543,965 sq km (210,026 sq mi). Pop. (1993 est.): 57,690,000. Cap.: Paris. Monetary unit: franc, with (Oct. 4, 1993) a free rate of F 5.67 to U.S. $1 (F 8.58 = £1 sterling). President in 1993, François Mitterrand; prime ministers, Pierre Bérégovoy and, from March 29, Édouard Balladur.

" '93? A terrible year!" Thus, one commentator, swept up by a series of historical events, paraphrased the great novelist Victor Hugo to depict the France, not of 1793 but of 1993. There was, of course, the switch from left to right in the March general elections, but more than this it was the symbolic death of the left with the suicide of Pierre Bérégovoy (*see* OBITUARIES), one month after losing his post as prime minister, that struck the public and would mark a year in which tragedy was never far away.

Domestic Affairs. The year began where 1992 left off—in scandals scorching a Socialist government on its last legs. After former prime minister Laurent Fabius and two of his ministers were sent before the High Court of Justice in the "affair of the contaminated blood" (in which hundreds of persons with hemophilia had received transfusions of HIV-tainted blood), nothing worse could happen in the eyes of the public, but the multiplication of the scandals touching politicians and others close to power continued right up to the elections. The case against Fabius and the others ended unsatisfactorily; the High Court ruled it had passed the three-year statute of limitations. The opposition and the press criticized the sale of Adidas by Bernard Tapie (who had been reappointed minister of urban affairs) to a group of holding companies made up of many public companies, as well as the sale of Yves Saint-Laurent, presided over by Pierre Bergé (a confidant of Pres. François Mitterrand), to the public company Elf-Sanofi. There were other scandals that were minor in appearance but annoying for the administration. These included the publication by Jacques Attali, Mitterrand's former special councillor, of his memoirs, entitled *Verbatim,* which sparked accusations of plagiarism by Nobel laureate Elie Wiesel, and the national security services' illegal phone tapping of a journalist from the newspaper *Le Monde* and other media representatives. In February longtime French mercenary Bob Denard (*see* BIOGRAPHIES) surrendered to authorities in Paris.

But the scandal that appeared to be fatal for the left was the otherwise minor infraction of a loan to Bérégovoy. When he was named prime minister in 1992, Bérégovoy had pledged himself to revivify the spirit of a left dispirited about its chances in the 1993 legislative elections. To accomplish this task he made the fight against corruption his main issue, but then he himself was touched by scandal. It turned out that he had benefited from an interest-free loan of a million francs in 1986 in order to buy an apartment. However, more than the loan, which had been declared and was thus not fraudulent, it was the lender that posed a problem: Roger-Patrice Pelat, an intimate friend of Mitterrand and one of the people implicated in the 1989 insider-trading scandal that blemished the takeover of American Can Co. by state-owned Péchiney. When the news became known, protesters disrupted every meeting of the prime minister, angrily reminding him of the loan. The left probably would have lost the elections after 12 years in power even without this shabby scandal, but for Bérégovoy, one of those rare Socialists actually to be reelected, it was "his" scandal that cost his friends the election. On May 1 the former trade-union worker killed himself on the banks of a canal. The echo caused by the suicide of a "man of the people" who had become prime minister was enormous, and a fight developed over the responsibility of judges and journalists in Bérégovoy's death.

The Socialist Party (PS) had prepared for defeat in the general elections in March, but it turned out to be a rout. In the first round the PS lost half the votes, in terms of percentage, that it had received in the 1988 elections. In the second round the conservative parties of the right won a crushing victory, with 485 of the National Assembly's 577 seats. The Gaullist Rally for the Republic (RPR) took the largest number (247), followed by the centre-right Union for French Democracy (UDF) with 213. The PS and its allies fell from a majority of 277 in the old parliament to only 67 in the new. (For tabulated results, see *Political Parties,* above.) Mitterrand named as the new prime minister the original theoretician of "cohabitation," former finance minister Édouard Balladur of the RPR. (*See* BIOGRAPHIES.)

The changing of the majority party in the legislature, however, did little to halt the revelation of scandals, which continued undiminished. The public was losing interest in this spectacle until the summer, when a new "Tapie affair" danced into the limelight. Tapie found himself embroiled in a scandal concerning the Olympique Marseille association football (soccer) team he owned. His club, which had just brought to France its first European championship, was accused of bribing players on the Valenciennes club in order to ensure victory in the French championship. Marseille players and managers were put in prison, and the judge in the case attempted to corner Tapie, who, to defend himself, offered as a witness a former Socialist Cabinet minister. At year's end the National Assembly lifted Tapie's parliamentary immunity, opening the possibility of a judicial inquiry. In November Jacques Médecin, the former mayor of Nice who in 1992 was convicted *in absentia* of misusing public funds, was finally arrested in Uruguay.

Prudently, the new prime minister stayed out of these affairs, preferring to devote himself entirely to what he called "the rectification of France." His popularity for many months surpassed 60%, a figure not reached by a prime minister since the days of Pres. Charles de Gaulle. Even more than his politics, however, Balladur was appreciated for his courteous, discreet, honest, and frank style. Beginning immediately in May, he put forth a number of reforms on the economic level as well as on the more symbolic level of social problems. The efforts were aimed at limiting the budget deficit, pushing forward with privatizations, and enacting new, tougher laws concerning identification documents, political asylum, and the nationalities code. The conservative section of the electorate, influenced by Jean-Marie Le Pen's extreme right-wing National Front, took heart from these measures. The left, crushed by the magnitude of its defeat, had almost no reaction at all.

Rather than finding his opposition on the left, Balladur was challenged from the right. A certain competition developed between the prime minister and Jacques Chirac, leader of the RPR. Chirac, who could have claimed the post of prime minister, was discouraged by the bad experience of the first attempt at "cohabitation" in 1986–88 and had decided to let his lieutenant take care of the day-to-day duties so that he could devote himself to preparations for the 1995 presidential elections. But polls showed that more and more people had a strong preference for Balladur, rather than Chirac, to succeed Mitterrand.

After the government backed off from its belt-tightening plans for Air France—following a 16-day strike in October in which strikers went so far as to occupy the runways, blocking all air traffic into Paris for many days—the press began to criticize Balladur for his "retreats." The prime minister had in many instances preferred a strategic retreat rather than risking a confrontation with the public, more than 70% of whom expected a social explosion. This approach was certainly at work in the matter of adjustment of student grants, which had brought the universities to the boiling point.

While Balladur was "rectifying" France, former prime minister Michel Rocard was attempting to "reconstruct the left," beginning with the PS. Taking advantage of the disarray following the historic defeat, Rocard organized the rank and file; an unscheduled party congress was held in July, at which he was elected by a large majority. Nevertheless, polls gave him only a slim chance of winning the next presidential elections. Even Mitterrand, who had little regard for Rocard, said that such a victory would require "a miracle."

The Economy. The symbolic level of three million unemployed was broken in 1993, and the increase was astonishing—from 2.9 million in 1992 to over 3.4 million. In addition to the usual disastrous effects on younger workers, this plague had now, for the first time, reached older, more senior staff. The huge rise in unemployment was accompanied by some remarkable phenomena. In May the laid-off founder of a computer company, using the pseudonym H.B. (for "human bomb"), took hostage a teacher and children attending a day-care centre in the suburbs of Paris before being struck down by the police. One company reserved taxis so that laid-off workers would leave the premises within the hour. Large public corporations announced the layoff of 13,500 workers on the same day that Balladur's government presented its five-year employment plan. In November, with unemployment holding steady at 12%, the Senate approved a controversial scheme to create a 32-hour workweek with a commensurate cut in pay.

There were many attacks on the franc in 1993, despite the often-reaffirmed government policy of a "strong franc." In July speculation hit the franc and the European exchange-rate mechanism (ERM) at the same time. Only a decision permitting an increase in the fluctuation margins for currencies within the ERM allowed Balladur to save face by proclaiming that "the value of the franc will be preserved." Two days later the franc lost a full 3% of its value against the Deutsche Mark, although it eventually recovered.

The new prime minister considered the general economic situation to be "the worst since 1945." First there was the recession, and then production fell 0.8%. Tempted to place responsibility for this disastrous situation on the preceding administration, the new government immediately began to assemble a "commission of inquiry." Bérégovoy's suicide on the eve of the publication of the commission's report, however, necessitated an end to the debates. Balladur's economic-recovery program distinguished itself first of all by budgetary restrictions aimed at reducing the budget deficit to F 317 billion. The 1994 budget foresaw a deficit of only F 300 billion coupled with an ambitious prediction for growth of 1.4%. An offering of state bonds was enormously successful; instead of the F 40 billion expected, the government received a record F 110 billion. In May the government announced plans to privatize 21 state-owned companies, including Air France and the auto manufacturer Renault. The privatizations began under the most auspicious conditions; Banque National de Paris (BNP), the second largest French bank, attracted some 2.8 million bidders, nearly three times what BNP's directors had expected.

The year was also marked by the death of Francis Bouygues, founder and president of the worldwide leader in the construction business, the Bouygues Group, and the first French television channel, TF1.

Foreign Affairs. Since the narrow victory of the "yes" votes in the 1992 referendum on the Maastricht Treaty, French opinion, formerly so passionately pro-European, had turned skeptical—indeed, in certain sectors it was decidedly hostile—blaming Europe for all of France's troubles. The opening of a single market on Jan. 1, 1993, was greeted with general indifference. The announcement of the transfer of a Hoover factory from Dijon to Scotland incited a wave of protests, which the government joined by criticizing what it called "social dumping." Still, the overwhelming majority of the French political class remained firmly pro-European, from Mitterrand, who had made the construction of a unified Europe his final goal, to Balladur, who took up arms

Édouard Balladur (left), named prime minister of France in March after conservatives had won a landslide victory in legislative elections, shakes hands with Pierre Bérégovoy, his Socialist predecessor. Despondent over the failure of his policies and at charges of financial misconduct, Bérégovoy committed suicide on May 1.
ELODIE GREGOIRE—REA/SABA

against those of his right-wing colleagues who had chosen "another policy."

In spite of cohabitation and the monetary tensions, the French-German axis was still intact and remained the engine of Europe. The transformation, due to the Maastricht Treaty, of the European Community (EC) into the European Union (EU), however, did not provide the awaited boost to the building of Europe. Mitterrand tried to provide a social objective for the EU by proposing a European loan of ECU 100 billion (F 700 billion) to finance large public-works projects in order to reduce unemployment.

French fears of a unified Europe were magnified when it came to the General Agreement on Tariffs and Trade (GATT). After the so-called Blair House compromise, the left and the right had opposed what they described as an intolerable attack, launched by the U.S., on French agriculture, and French farmers still had not accepted the new EC common agricultural policy (CAP) passed in Brussels. Bérégovoy's government committed itself to a policy that was, in general, hostile to GATT's agricultural compromises. The agriculture minister went so far as to threaten a French veto. Balladur's government opened a second front, calling for a "cultural exception" in order to protect French cinema and television. Mitterrand succeeded in getting a resolution in favour of the "cultural exception" adopted at the summit of Francophone countries held on Mauritius. The fervour that developed around these topics led to caution against this increasing protectionism and extreme nationalism.

Despite its frequently reaffirmed interest in the Middle East, France remained absent from the process leading to the Israeli-Palestinian accords. Yasir Arafat's visit to Paris, where he was received as a head of state a few weeks after his historic handshake in Washington, D.C., with Yitzhak Rabin, did not change this. French impotence was even more disquieting in the matter of Algeria. The assassination of two of the 25,000 French living in Algeria, and the kidnapping of three more, by fundamentalist groups in the former colony was troubling. The three hostages were finally released with an ultimatum from their captors that all French citizens had to leave Algeria within a month. At year's end Switzerland lodged a formal protest after the French government refused to extradite two Iranians suspected of killing a Swiss political figure and returned the men to Tehran. (CHRISTIAN SAUVAGE)

See also *Dependent States,* below.

GEORGIA

A republic of Transcaucasia, Georgia borders Russia on the north and northeast, Azerbaijan on the southeast, Armenia and Turkey on the south, and the Black Sea on the west. Area: 69,700 sq km (26,900 sq mi). Pop. (1993 est.): 5,493,000. Cap.: Tbilisi. Monetary unit: coupon (transitional currency introduced April 5, 1993, at par with the Russian ruble, became sole legal tender as of August 20), with (October 1993) a free rate of 31,500 coupons = U.S. $1 (47,800 coupons = £1 sterling). De facto head of state and chairman of Parliament in 1993, Eduard Shevardnadze; prime ministers, Tengiz Sigua, Eduard Shevardnadze (acting) from August 6, and, from August 20, Otar Patsatsia.

Developments in Georgia in 1993 were dominated by the war in Abkhazia and its repercussions on domestic politics. A large-scale offensive by Abkhazian and Russian forces in March failed to capture Sukhumi. In May, Georgian head of state Eduard Shevardnadze and Russian Pres. Boris Yeltsin concluded an agreement, to which Abkhazian Parliament chairman Vladislav Ardzinba later acceded, on a cease-fire, which, however, never took hold. A second Abkhazian attack on Sukhumi in July was paralleled by strong Russian diplomatic pressure on Georgia to agree to a settlement. Under the terms of a cease-fire agreement signed on July 27, Georgian government forces and heavy artillery withdrew from Sukhumi, leaving the town defenseless when the Abkhazians launched an offensive. After 11 days of fierce fighting, Georgian government troops abandoned Sukhumi in late September. Abkhazian forces then consolidated control over the entire region, precipitating the exodus of up to 200,000 ethnic Georgian refugees. In November, Ardzinba called for the deployment of UN observers along the frontier to preclude any attempt by Georgian forces to regain military control of Abkhazia. UN-sponsored talks on a political settlement that would guarantee Abkhazia's autonomy within Georgia resulted in a peace accord, signed on December 1, to include deployment of UN peacekeeping forces. On December 19 the two sides effected the first prisoner exchange.

In early May, Shevardnadze forced the resignation of maverick Defense Minister Tengiz Kitovani, who had reportedly twice planned to oust him. Preoccupied by the fighting in Abkhazia, the Georgian Parliament failed either to draft and debate the legislative foundations of a

Ethnic Georgians flee the war in Abkhazia. Separatists, with unofficial Russian military support, made strong gains during the year against Georgian government troops, but after later political developments Russian forces came to the aid of Georgia.

JAMES HILL—COLORIFIC

sovereign law-based state or to form a working majority. Shevardnadze took advantage of these failings to demand ever greater executive powers, alienating radical deputies, who demanded his resignation. In August the government had to resign after Parliament rejected three consecutive draft budgets. One month later Shevardnadze himself resigned after deputies rejected as "dictatorial" his proposal to restructure the Cabinet of Ministers and impose a state of emergency. He retracted this decision only on condition that Parliament declare a two-month state of emergency and recess for three months.

The domestic instability encouraged former president Zviad Gamsakhurdia, who since his ouster in January 1992 had lived in exile in Chechnia, to attempt a comeback. His private army occupied and then retreated from towns in western Georgia throughout August and September. In October they launched a major offensive and came close to taking Kutaisi, Georgia's second city, before being beaten back by Georgian government troops with Russian support. It was later reported that Gamsakhurdia had shot himself on December 31.

The debacle in Abkhazia had a major impact on Russian-Georgian relations. Negotiations on a series of bilateral treaties collapsed in February after Russia pegged them to a peaceful solution of the Abkhazian conflict. Unofficial Russian military participation in the attack on Sukhumi in September elicited from Shevardnadze accusations that Russia had betrayed Georgia, but it did not deter him from subsequently committing Georgia to membership in the Commonwealth of Independent States. This concession won him logistic support and the deployment of Russian troops to guard roads and railroads against attack by Gamsakhurdia's forces, but it also outraged radicals in Parliament, who vowed to vote against ratification.

The war in Abkhazia exacerbated economic and social collapse. In October industry was functioning at less than 25% of capacity, and unemployment stood at 50%. The introduction in April of coupons intended as a parallel currency with the ruble failed to curb inflation. Originally traded at parity with the ruble, the coupon fell in value to 7:1 in August, 27:1 in October, and 66:1 in mid-December.

(ELIZABETH FULLER)

This article updates the *Macropædia* article TRANSCAUCASIA: *Georgia.*

GERMANY

Germany is in central Europe, on the North and Baltic seas. Area: 356,733 sq km (137,735 sq mi). Pop. (1993 est.): 81,187,-000. Cap. designate, Berlin; seat of government, Bonn. Monetary unit: Deutsche Mark, with (Oct. 4, 1993) a free rate of DM 1.62 to U.S. $1 (DM 2.46 = £1 sterling). President in 1993, Richard von Weizsäcker; chancellor, Helmut Kohl.

Economic difficulties in Germany in 1993 fueled widespread popular disillusionment with the mainstream parties in government and the opposition. The protest vote rose sharply in the two elections in the western states. Public disenchantment was strengthened by a rash of scandals, which claimed senior victims from all the main parties. The government's hope of an upturn in the economy in the second half of the year failed to be realized. Foreign affairs were dominated by the controversy over Germany's new international security role; while the opposition Social Democratic Party (SPD) argued for a strict interpretation of the Constitution to ban German participation in any military actions outside the NATO area, the government kept pushing for a broader role. Late in the year, Germany became the last of 12 members of the European Community (EC) to complete its ratification process for the Maastricht Treaty, but Chancellor Helmut Kohl found it hard to inject new momentum into a Community in some disarray. For all these reasons, the celebration of German unity on October 3 was muted, and political leaders warned against faintheartedness, pessimism, and a return to nationalist thinking.

The Economy. The sharp economic downturn that had begun the previous year struck Germany in 1993 with a harshness far exceeding even the gloomiest forecasts. Within two months of the beginning of the year, the government conceded that western Germany was in the worst recession since World War II, while the east still showed no signs of nearing self-reliant growth. Unemployment shot up as the key sectors of German industry slashed their workforce to reduce costs. Unable to avoid the problem of paying for unification, the federal government in Bonn was obliged to make two efforts at belt-tightening, calling upon Germans to adapt to the harsh new times.

In its New Year report, the Federation of German Industry said its members were facing a "crisis of confidence" as successive associations in the steel, auto, chemical, and machine-tool sectors came out with grim predictions of plunging outputs and sharp job cuts. The sense of shock in Europe's most powerful economy was captured by Helmut Werner, the chairman-elect of the luxury car maker Mercedes-Benz, who attacked the very ethos of Germany's postwar industrial thinking by denouncing "overengineering." He said Germany was in danger of pricing itself out of markets by trying to produce perfect products, regardless of cost, in the misguided belief that people would always pay more for a "Made in Germany" label. This call for a fundamental change in thinking to emphasize lower-cost production, coming from a symbol of German industry, soon began to be echoed by other manufacturers.

By early February the new economics minister, Günter Rexrodt, finally had broken with the government line that things were not as bad as they seemed; he spoke of the "worst recession since the war." The strains within the economy broke to the surface on February 18 when engineering-sector employers in eastern Germany, egged on by their western counterparts, scrapped the existing wage contracts—the first time this had happened in modern German history. Pointing to the extremely difficult economic situation, the employers tore up a 1991 contract under which basic wages in eastern Germany were increased annually and were to reach full parity with western levels during 1994. On April 1 engineering workers in the east were due to get a 26% pay raise, which would bring their wages to 87% of the western level. With productivity roughly one-third of western levels, many firms operating in the east said such a wage increase would put them out of business. The employers offered instead a wage rise of up to 9% and no equalization commitment. IG Metall, Germany's most powerful trade union, said the very principle of collective bargaining was at stake and prepared for strikes.

The workers began striking in early May—their first legal industrial action in 60 years. The conflict escalated until a deal was finally struck on May 14, with the unions claiming victory. Although equalization with wage levels in the western states was delayed until the end of 1996 and the pay settlement was a little less than the original 26%, the unions expressed satisfaction that the principle of wage contracts had been preserved. Employers described the settlement as a "painful compromise." The workers in IG Metall had little time to celebrate, however, because on May 25 their leader and Germany's best known unionist, Franz Steinkühler, resigned over dubious stock dealings.

One of the factors eroding popular confidence in the main parties was the seemingly endless arguments about possible new ways of financing the rising costs of unification. Virtually every week produced a suggestion about a new tax or contribution increase, which then disappeared without a trace, leaving a mood of growing uncertainty. In March the government finally agreed on the so-called Solidarity Pact, by which it hoped to restore order to public finances. This compromise postponed the real pain, however, since the reintroduction of a special income tax surcharge would take place only in 1995. Even before the much-debated Solidarity Pact reached the statute books, it was overtaken by events. Finance Minister Theo Waigel conceded that the federal deficit in 1993 would be nearer DM 70 billion than the DM 43 billion originally forecast in December. With the recession hitting tax revenues and sharply increasing unemployment payments, the government faced a spending crisis. The question of real cuts, which the Solidarity Pact had evaded, was back on the agenda as the government braced itself for more argument and protest over its next belt-tightening project, the so-called Consolidation Program.

Watching these developments with alarm was the Bundesbank, Germany's powerful, independent central bank. Its calls for strict control of public finances became increasingly urgent, and it made plain that the government's failure to cut spending radically was a major factor in preventing a lowering of Germany's high interest rates. This battle between the Bundesbank and the government in Bonn, as it tried to enforce fiscal rectitude through its tight monetary policy, became one of the dominant tests of strength, even if conducted largely behind the scenes. The repercussions, moreover, went far beyond the country's borders because the interest rates of all countries in the European exchange-rate mechanism (ERM) were effectively dictated by Germany's. Desperate to give relief to their own recession-struck economies, other European governments piled pressure on the Bundesbank to cut rates quickly, but with little success. The tension within the system built up, eventually leading to currency speculation in August and the widening of the ERM's currency bands from 2.5% to 15%, for which the Bundesbank received much of the blame. In late April, Rexrodt revised the government's forecast of a 1% decline in western German gross domestic product in 1993, saying it now expected a 2% drop.

In mid-August, in its second attempt to control ballooning public spending, the Bonn government gritted its teeth and agreed on a DM 22 billion savings package. With the Bundesbank effectively blocking increased borrowing, for the first time the Consolidation Program included wide-ranging cuts in social benefits. The gravity of the situation was underlined in early September when Kohl, presenting

REGIS BOSSU—SYGMA

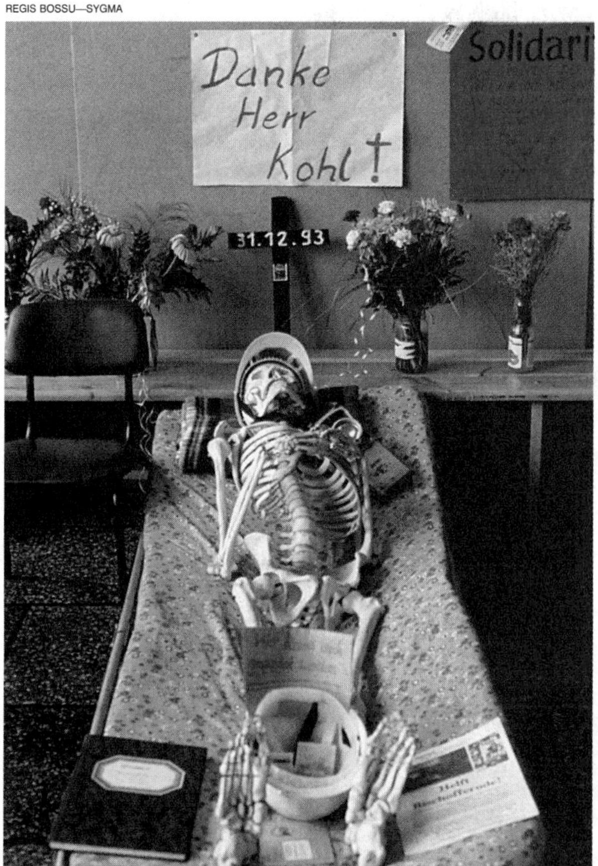

A skeleton and a sign reading "Thanks, Mr. Kohl" express the anger of miners on a hunger strike in Bischofferode, Germany, in July. The government of Chancellor Helmut Kohl later submitted legislation that would reduce social benefits for the German people.

to the Bundestag (parliament) his "Report on Safeguarding Germany's Economic Future," said, "Old habits must be questioned and new priorities created." The scheme called for a new flexibility and dynamism in a society grown complacent during years of prosperity. By November unemployment in western Germany had reached a postwar high of 2,490,000, or 7.8%, up from 2 million at the end of 1992; in the east 1,150,000 people were out of work.

At the beginning of October, at an imposing ceremony in Frankfurt pointing to the power of the institution, the Bundesbank's president during the past two turbulent years, Helmut Schlesinger, handed over the post. His successor, Hans Tietmeyer, was a man regarded as more European in orientation and more politically sensitive than the inflexible Schlesinger.

Government and Politics. The year opened on a sour note for the government with the resignation on January 3 of Economics Minister Jürgen Möllemann, overcome by a scandal concerning his promotion of a relation's product with several big supermarket chains. His departure provoked a shake-up at the top of the smallest governing coalition party, the centrist Free Democratic Party (FDP), where Möllemann had been one of the front-runners to succeed Otto Graf Lambsdorff as chairman. The field was now left effectively clear for Klaus Kinkel, the foreign minister, to take over the job as FDP leader. Rexrodt, a businessman turned politician, became the new economics minister.

The municipal elections in the state of Hessen on March 7 offered dramatic evidence of popular disgruntlement over politics and politicians. While the main parties, the SPD and the Christian Democratic Union (CDU), both lost support, there was a sharp rise in the protest vote, with the Greens receiving 11% and the far-right Republicans getting 8.3%. In Frankfurt, the major city with the highest proportion of foreigners in Germany, the Republicans polled 10%. The results sparked anguished soul-searching among the political establishment.

CHARLES CARATINI—SYGMA

Flowers and banners mark the house in Solingen where five Turks died in May in a fire apparently set by neo-Nazis. Violence against foreigners increased in Germany during the year, leading Chancellor Helmut Kohl to accede to demands to ease restrictions on citizenship.

A number of political scandals claimed several important victims in May. Björn Engholm, leader of the SPD, resigned from all his political offices on May 3 after admitting that he had lied to a parliamentary investigating committee. Engholm had won power as prime minister of Schleswig-Holstein after the exposure of a dirty-tricks campaign by his conservative rival before the 1987 election. At the time, Engholm said he learned of the smear tactics just before the election, but now it turned out that he had known earlier. Engholm's departure came at a disastrous time for the SPD, which remained severely at odds with itself over most important issues and completely unable to capitalize on the centre-right government's difficulties. On May 6 Günther Krause, the CDU transport minister, resigned because of a series of minor scandals. These began with revelations that taxpayers had financed his house move in 1991 and that a cleaning woman he employed had been paid partly out of state funds. Krause's exit removed from the Cabinet the most prominent eastern German politician, who at one time had been a rising star enjoying Kohl's patronage.

Max Streibl, the conservative prime minister of Bavaria, announced on May 12 that he would be stepping down, a victim of the so-called Amigo affair, in which he had accepted free holidays and flights from a Bavarian aircraft manufacturer. This sparked a bitter struggle for his job between the two leading personalities in the Bavarian Christian Social Union (CSU)—Waigel, the federal finance minister, and Edmund Stoiber, the CSU chairman. In the end Stoiber prevailed, obliging a deeply disillusioned Waigel to go back to the task of trying to restore order to Germany's public finances. The scandals had by now touched all the main parties. Political *Verdrossenheit* (listlessness) dominated opinion polls and public discussion.

In an unexpectedly high turnout in mid-June, SPD members elected Rudolf Scharping, the prime minister of Rhineland-Palatinate, to replace Engholm as party leader. No sooner had the main opposition party begun to put its house in order than the government was plunged into turmoil again after a botched attempt to arrest two suspected members of the Red Army Faction movement. One suspected terrorist and a member of the elite GSG-9 antiterrorist squad died in the shoot-out at Bad Kleinen. On July 4 CDU Interior Minister Rudolf Seiters resigned and was replaced by Manfred Kanther. Two days later Germany's state prosecutor, Alexander von Stahl, was dismissed.

In mid-September Kohl, having said he wanted Germany's next president to come from the east, threw his weight behind a virtual unknown, Steffen Heitmann, the CDU justice minister from Saxony. The new president, who would replace Richard von Weizsäcker, was to be elected by a special Federal Assembly in May 1994. With some plain speaking about Germany's need to put its past behind it, Kohl's openly conservative candidate rapidly became the focus of national controversy. Although it was a partner in the governing coalition, the centrist FDP refused to support Heitmann and in October nominated its own candidate, Hildegard Hamm-Brücher. Heitmann withdrew from the race on November 25. Public annoyance with the continued political squabbling was again demonstrated at elections in the city-state of Hamburg on September 19. Support for the main parties again plunged, while a curious protest grouping, the Statt Partei ("Instead Party"), formed just three months previously, won 5.6% of the vote and eight seats. The Greens jumped from 7 to 13%.

Other Domestic Affairs. On January 12 a Berlin court dropped manslaughter charges against Erich Honecker, the former communist leader of East Germany, in connection with the shoot-to-kill policy that had claimed hundreds of lives at the Berlin Wall and on the inner-German border. A Berlin court had ruled it would be inhumane to continue to detain Honecker, aged 80 and diagnosed as terminally ill with liver cancer. On January 13 Honecker flew to join his wife and daughter in Santiago, Chile. On September 16 three former East German ministers were jailed for between four and a half and seven and a half years for their part in the shootings at the Berlin Wall. The former head of the Stasi secret police, Erich Mielke, was also declared physically unfit to be tried. In late October, however, Mielke was sentenced to six years' imprisonment in a separate case concerning the killing of two policemen in 1931.

Bundestag deputies had to run the gauntlet of several thousand protesters on May 26 as the government parties, supported by the opposition SPD, finally ended years of wrangling and amended the constitution to tighten Germany's open-door law on asylum. Germany had taken in 440,000 asylum-seekers in 1992, 79% of the EC total, mostly from Eastern Europe. The economic and social strains of the uncontrolled influx were blamed for the rise of the extreme right as well as for acts of racist violence. The new law enabled asylum-seekers from "safe" countries, which included most of Eastern Europe, to be sent back immediately. It came into effect on July 1 and brought about an immediate drop in the number of entries.

Any hope that this long-awaited political action would banish the spectre of xenophobic violence was brutally shattered in the early hours of May 29 when five Turks—two women and three children—died after the house in Solingen in which they lived was set afire. The worst incident of violence against foreigners since World War II, the attack provoked waves of protests among Germany's 1.8 million-strong Turkish community. In a speech to the Bundestag in June, Kohl spoke for the first time of a possible loosening of Germany's strict citizenship laws, enabling dual citizenship in special cases. At year's end four youths were arrested in connection with the attack. Earlier in December two young neo-Nazis were convicted of a similar 1992 firebombing in which a woman and two children died.

In the autumn health officials tried to stop panic over fears that large numbers of people may have contracted AIDS from contaminated blood plasma. Germans who had received blood during operations since 1982 were advised to undergo an AIDS test. A scandal ensued, affecting the Health Ministry, and at least two private companies were accused of selling contaminated blood products.

Foreign Affairs. On a visit to Bonn in early January, UN Secretary-General Boutros Boutros-Ghali appealed for Germany to find a way around its constitutional restrictions and play a full part in international security missions. German medical troops were already involved in a UN humanitarian mission in Cambodia, and the German air force was taking part in mercy flights to Sarajevo, Bosnia and Herzegovina. The question of doing more in areas outside the purely humanitarian became ever more pressing and controversial as the government considered letting German airmen take part in airborne warning and control system (AWACS) aerial surveillance missions over Bosnia.

The AWACS issue became the focus of stormy debate. The Defense Ministry and the majority CDU/CSU, opposed at every step of the way by the SPD, sought to force back the restrictions and gain the needed two-thirds parliamentary majority. The FDP said that because participation in such military missions contravened the constitution, German airmen would have to pull out. Because Germans made up one-third of the 18 AWACS crews, however, their departure would have jeopardized the entire mission. NATO stepped up the pressure; NATO Secretary-General Manfred Wörner called German approval decisive. Amid considerable political confusion in Bonn, the governing parties finally agreed only to disagree, and the issue was referred to the Constitutional Court. On April 8, in a preliminary ruling, the judges rejected the objections of the FDP and SPD, saying that they would "tolerate" German participation, but they refused to give a formal constitutional ruling on the matter, handing it back to the parties.

No sooner were German airmen on the AWACS missions than the UN appealed for further military help, this time in Somalia. In late April, again over SPD opposition, the Bundestag approved a humanitarian mission. A month later an advance team arrived at Beledweyne, a so-called pacified area well away from Mogadishu and the fighting. There Germans were to help with logistics and supplies for other nations' troops. As the violence escalated in Somalia and the U.S. notably took a more aggressive stance, the debate in Germany became clamorous, and popular opinion began to swing against keeping troops there in such changed circumstances. The SPD appealed to the Constitutional Court, but the government strongly backed the mission, and more troops flew out in late July, eventually bringing the German contingent to 1,700.

While anxious about Somalia, German public opinion reflected great frustration at the lack of much tougher policies towards Serbia over Bosnia. At the EC summit in Copenhagen in June, the chancellor argued unsuccessfully for sending arms to the Bosnian Muslims. Later, in August, Germany supported the U.S. in its campaign to win alliance support for air strikes against Serbia, but this initiative foundered on French and British opposition.

In October, Germany became the last of the 12 EC members to complete ratification of the Maastricht Treaty after the Constitutional Court rejected several objections. In giving their ruling, however, the judges said that the movement toward European economic and monetary union could not be automatic, as Kohl had originally viewed it, and that future moves would be acceptable only if explicitly approved by Parliament. At a special EC summit in late October, the chancellor tried again to revive some momentum in the European unification process, which had fallen into considerable disarray over the year. Kohl acknowledged, however, that he had misjudged popular enthusiasm, and he began to talk more about the continued importance of the nation-state within the European process. At the special summit, Frankfurt was named as the site for the future European central bank. (JOHN EISENHAMMER)

GREECE

The republic of Greece occupies the southern part of the Balkan Peninsula and several adjoining island groups in southeastern Europe, in and between the Ionian and Aegean seas. Area: 131,957 sq km (50,949 sq mi). Pop. (1993 est.): 10,310,000. Cap.: Athens. Monetary unit: drachma, with (Oct. 4, 1993) a free rate of 234.28 drachmas to U.S. $1 (354.94 drachmas = £1 sterling). President in 1993, Konstantinos Karamanlis; prime ministers, Konstantinos Mitsotakis and, from October 13, Andreas Papandreou.

An abruptly called election on Oct. 10, 1993, brought the Panhellenic Socialist Movement (Pasok) of Andreas Papan-

Andreas Papandreou and his wife, Dimitra, are greeted by supporters after his Panhellenic Socialist Movement won the October 10 elections in Greece. Papandreou, who was acquitted in 1992 of criminal charges, had served as prime minister from 1981 until mid-1989.

ARIS PHILLIPPE—CONTRAST PRESS

dreou back into power, barely four years after it was booted out under a cloud of suspicion and scandal. The premature poll was prompted by defections that deprived the ruling New Democracy (ND) conservatives of their parliamentary majority of two. Prime Minister Konstantinos Mitsotakis was forced to resign after a long period of harassment by adversaries, both inside and outside the party, who questioned his integrity, assailed his bold economic reforms, and thwarted attempts for a reasonable settlement on Macedonia. After his defeat, the 74-year-old Cretan politician resigned the leadership of the ND party, which he had held for nine years.

The Mitsotakis government's downfall, six months before elections were due, came as a sequel to the summary dismissal of Antonis Samaras from the post of foreign minister in 1992 over a disagreement about Greece's policy on Macedonia. Samaras, who was being coached by Mitsotakis as his successor, quit the ND and set up his own party on June 30, 1993, calling it Political Spring. One month later he urged his ND friends to defect over a completely different issue—the partial privatization of the nation's decrepit telephone system (OTE) and the transfer of its management to foreign experts. The legislature approved the bill, but five ND deputies loyal to Samaras quit the party, two withdrawing their confidence from the government.

The OTE affair became a turning point in the ND's economic reform program, which relied heavily on the privatization of insolvent state enterprises to slash government deficits and reduce inflation. The stiffest opposition came from the trade unions eager to safeguard the status of state employees—most of them hired under the party spoils system rather than on merit.

The Mitsotakis government's perseverance in enforcing an unpopular austerity program yielded significant results. Inflation dropped to 12.8% (as of September), the lowest in two decades; the overstaffed civil service was severely trimmed; pension funds were reorganized; the labour market was freed from crippling regulations; and foreign reserves reached their highest level—more than $6 billion. However, hopes that tax evasion would be discouraged by a reduction in tax rates were dashed by the end of 1993. The government's revenue dropped sharply, eroding an anticipated primary budget surplus of $4 billion designed to defray in part the massive internal debt. European and international organizations commended the government's efforts highly but pressed for tighter financial discipline as they released lavish European Community (EC) funds for major public works—ranging from a subway system in Athens to a new international airport and from vital highway networks to gigantic irrigation projects. In view of this promising record, the EC viewed with misgiving Pasok's election victory. In one of his first policy statements, the new prime minister pledged that he would scrap the privatization program.

In foreign affairs the Mitsotakis government acted defensively. Greece blocked efforts by the former Yugoslav republic of Macedonia to gain recognition as the independent nation of Macedonia, which was also the name of the main northern Greek province, by soliciting support from fellow members in the EC. When Macedonia applied for United Nations membership at the end of 1992, Greece, in order to stall such recognition, accepted UN mediation under veteran U.S. diplomat Cyrus Vance. In the interim it was agreed to call the new state The Former Yugoslav Republic of Macedonia.

Throughout the year friction continued with Greece's other Balkan neighbours. A crisis point was reached in June when Albania deported a Greek priest, accusing him of instigating the union of northern Epirus (southern Albania) with Greece. Greece retaliated with massive expulsions of Albanian refugees. Efforts by Prime Minister Mitsotakis to continue improving relations with Turkey stumbled on the latter's reluctance to pressure the Turkish Cypriots to agree to a UN-sponsored solution of the long-standing dispute on Cyprus.

Strangely enough, Macedonia figured minimally in the Greek election campaign. The main rival parties chose to emphasize the sins of their opponents rather than sing their own virtues. A boon for Pasok was the electoral system introduced by Mitsotakis in 1990, while he was still under the shock of his own failure to secure a working majority in Parliament despite his party's 47% share of the vote. Pasok, before stepping down, had devised a system that made it practically impossible for its conservative rival to win anything but the slimmest majority. The irony was that in 1993 Pasok polled exactly the same percentage of votes (47%), winning 170 of the 300 seats, compared with ND's 151 for the same vote proportion in 1990. This time ND trailed behind its rival by more than seven points, returning 111 deputies. Samaras' Political Spring finished third with 5% of the vote and won 10 seats, while the Stalinist Communist Party of Greece took just over 4% and elected 9 deputies.

As the new Pasok government under Papandreou took over on October 13, two questions emerged: whether Papandreou, who had made a miraculous recovery from serious heart surgery five years earlier, could safely assume the arduous workload of the EC presidency that rotated to

Greece on Jan. 1, 1994, and whether his government would run its full four-year term. Since Pres. Konstantinos Karamanlis' five-year term would end in May 1995, his successor would have to be elected by the legislature on a three-fifths majority, or at least 180 votes. Failing that, elections would have to be proclaimed, and the new legislature could then choose a president even on a 151–149 majority. Unless Papandreou could secure additional support in the legislature in favour of Pasok's own presidential candidate, elections would become inevitable. (MARIO MODIANO)

HUNGARY

A republic, Hungary is a landlocked state in central Europe. Area: 93,033 sq km (35,920 sq mi). Pop. (1993 est.): 10,296,000. Cap.: Budapest. Monetary unit: forint, with (Oct. 4, 1993) a free rate of 96.50 forints to U.S. $1 (146.20 forints = £1 sterling). President in 1993, Arpad Goncz; prime ministers, Jozsef Antall and, from December 12, Peter Boross.

Viewed from the inside, Hungary appeared to be highly turbulent during 1993, but viewed from the outside matters seemed relatively stable. The contest for power between government and opposition continued, and the broad rules of parliamentary democracy, despite many exceptions, were sustained. As the year progressed, the shadow of the 1994 election began to loom, and essentially much of the autumn was spent in preparing for the coming polls.

Early in the year the leading party in the governing coalition, the Hungarian Democratic Forum, finally faced up to the mounting challenge that the radical right inside the party was launching and took the step of forcing the right-radicals out of the Forum. Prime Minister Jozsef Antall, who died in December (*see* OBITUARIES), accepted that the radicals, led by Istvan Csurka, were threatening to destabilize the party and thereby the government coalition itself. At its congress in January, Antall was reelected chairman of the Forum, and with this authority he was able to confront the radicals' challenge.

Csurka then went on to establish his own parliamentary grouping, Hungarian Justice, which offered his particular populist-nationalist critique of what the government was doing. The core of the populist argument was that the end of communism had represented an opportunity to create a new, revolutionary order, in which there would be justice and plenty for all. The populists rejected the slow-speed transformation—the platform on which the Forum had won its victory in 1990—pursued by the government and demanded thoroughgoing changes. They rejected both capitalism and communism and pressed for a genuinely right-wing system derived from the national essence. These formulas were vague but were thought to have something of a following in the country.

While the government rejected this part of the populist program, it had no qualms about adopting another aspect of it—control of the media, especially radio and television. Few topics in Hungarian politics generated as much heat as this one. The government by and large rejected all media criticism as biased and favouring the opposition. It was deaf to counterarguments that in a democratic system the role of the media was precisely to be as critical as possible of the exercise of power.

The government campaigned steadily to bring the electronic media under its direct supervision. It eventually achieved this by threatening to cut state funding and forcing the withdrawal of the independent chairmen of the television and radio at the beginning of the year. As the year went on, journalists not prepared to back the government were gradually forced out, and programs were tailored to the government's wishes, much to the opposition's vocal dismay.

The opposition, for its part, found itself in a rather contradictory position. The coalition was clearly weakening—partly as a result of general exhaustion, partly through the erosion of the parties making up the government (the Smallholders had already split in 1992), and partly through what eventually proved to be the prime minister's fatal illness. The coalition was lacking in a sense of direction and, perhaps even more significant, it proved incapable of introducing and sustaining a coherent economic policy.

Antall's death in December did not produce any serious crisis. Interior Minister Peter Boross, effectively his deputy, succeeded him without any upset. The continuity that the Forum had always declared as its policy was evidently sustained in this instance.

In parliamentary terms, by the end of the year the opposition was close to being able to outvote the coalition, but it seemed unwilling to do so, mostly because it was afraid of the outcome of early elections. The main opposition

LASZLO BELICZAY—THE NEW YORK TIMES

Citizens gather to honour the memory of Miklos Horthy, leader of Hungary from 1920 to 1944, who died in exile in Portugal in 1957 but was reburied in his hometown of Kenderes in September. Opinion on Horthy, who collaborated with Adolf Hitler for part of World War II, was sharply divided between those who saw him as a traitor and those who regarded him as a patriot.

party, the Alliance of Free Democrats, was making a poor showing in the public opinion polls, and the Federation of Young Democrats was no nearer to being able to translate its popularity in the polls into concrete votes.

In foreign affairs there was only one important change, and that came toward the end of the year—the possibility of the return of a resurgent, nationalist Russia to Central and Eastern Europe. This alarmed Hungary considerably, but the counterbalancing that it sought from the West was not forthcoming. Indeed, Western inaction was on occasion replaced by what was perceived as active discrimination against the postcommunist states, such as the European Community's ban on agricultural exports from Hungary in the spring. Hungarian spokesmen, together with their Polish and Czech counterparts, issued a number of warnings to the West concerning the likely negative outcome of such neglect. Hungary's relations with its neighbours remained largely unchanged. They were good with Austria, Ukraine, Slovenia, and Croatia and were poor with Slovakia, Romania, and Serbia, the three countries with sizable Hungarian minorities.

The country's economy tended to stagnate during the year, although given the size of the gray or shadow economy, which was not included in the official statistics, one could not be absolutely certain. What the statistics did show, however, was a growing budget deficit that the government seemed unable to control. This was a clear indication that market conditions were still a long way from operating effectively, inasmuch as the bulk of the deficit derived from subsidies to uneconomic enterprises. In mid-December Ameritech Corp. and Deutsche Bundespost Telekom agreed to invest $437.5 million each to acquire a 30% interest in the state telephone company.

Many companies would have gone bankrupt had a market been operating, but that not only would have given rise to serious social problems with higher unemployment but would also have weakened the government's patronage and power that it exercised through the subsidies. The habit of maintaining subsidies made Budapest unpopular with the International Monetary Fund, which warned that these habits would have to be curbed if Hungarians expected further standby credits. (GEORGE SCHÖPFLIN)

ICELAND

Iceland is an island republic in the North Atlantic Ocean, near the Arctic Circle. Area: 102,819 sq km (39,699 sq mi). Pop. (1993 est.): 264,000. Cap.: Reykjavík. Monetary unit: Icelandic króna, with (Oct. 4, 1993) a free rate of 69.25 krónur to U.S. $1 (104.92 krónur = £1 sterling). President in 1993, Vigdís Finnbogadóttir; prime minister, Davíd Oddsson.

Following a deep recession in 1992, Iceland's economy remained stagnant during 1993, with gross domestic product (GDP) unchanged from the previous year. Declining export prices caused the terms of foreign trade to deteriorate and, thus, national income in real terms was estimated to have declined by 2% from 1992. Unemployment rose to an average of 4.5% for the first half of the year, the highest level since World War II. Inflation, on the other hand, remained low by previous standards, averaging 4% for the year. The deficit on current account remained moderate, estimated at under $100 million, some 1.5% of GDP.

The main cause of the continued recession was the limit imposed on the fish catch for conservation reasons. The stock of fish in the ocean around Iceland had declined considerably in recent years owing to overfishing and inclement weather. This was particularly true of cod, the most important species, the catch of which had declined by nearly 30% since 1982–83. The cod catch limit for one year beginning in September 1993 was, therefore, reduced by 25% from the previous 12 months to 165,000 tons. Consequently, growth prospects for the Icelandic economy for the next several years were dim. Official forecasts indicated that GDP might decline by 2–3% in 1994.

To meet the contraction in the economy and limit its impact on export industries and the balance of payments, the government devalued the currency by 6% in November 1992 and by 7.5% in June 1993. In addition, it shifted a number of taxes from businesses to households in order to improve business profitability.

In January, following more than two years of intense and sometimes acrimonious debate, Iceland ratified the agreement whereby the member nations of the European Free Trade Association (EFTA) would join the European Community (EC) to establish a European Economic Area (EEA). The process was made extremely difficult by Switzerland's refusal to join the other EFTA nations in ratification and by Spain's declaration that it could not accede to the EEA agreement after Switzerland's rejection.

In conjunction with the EEA agreement, Iceland concluded a fisheries accord with the EC whereby vessels from EC countries would be allowed to catch up to 3,000 tons of redfish in Icelandic waters; in turn, Iceland would be given the right to catch up to 30,000 tons of capelin in EC waters.

Iceland continued its ban on whaling but resigned from the International Whaling Commission in 1992 in protest against the commission's intentions to enforce a ban on all whaling rather than determine where whaling could be safely pursued without endangering individual species. Thereafter, the U.S. government hinted to both Iceland and Norway that it would apply trade sanctions should either country seek to resume commercial whaling. Norway nevertheless went ahead and allowed limited whaling, and Icelandic officials strongly hinted in the second half of 1993 that they would consider the resumption of limited commercial whaling during the 1994 summer season.

Owing to overfishing in the sea surrounding Iceland, Icelandic vessels began an intensive search for fishing possibilities in distant waters. They found a small gap in the Barents Sea outside the economic zones of the former Soviet Union and Norway and started fishing there in mid-1993 under protest from Norway, which considered the area to be within its sphere of influence.

(BJÖRN MATTHÍASSON)

IRELAND

The republic of Ireland, separated from Great Britain by the North Channel, the Irish Sea, and St. George's Channel, shares its island with Northern Ireland to the northeast. Area: 70,285 sq km (27,137 sq mi). Pop. (1993 est.): 3,516,000. Cap.: Dublin. Monetary unit: Irish pound (punt), with (Oct. 4, 1993) a free rate of £Ir 0.69 to U.S. $1 (£Ir 1.05 = £1 sterling). President in 1993, Mary Robinson; prime minister, Albert Reynolds.

Following the Nov. 25, 1992, election and after an unprecedented seven-week delay, the Fianna Fail party reconciled its differences with the Labour Party and formed a coalition government. Albert Reynolds, leader of Fianna Fail, was then reelected prime minister on Jan. 12, 1993. The negotiations took place against end-of-year reports from the treasury that confirmed the worst financial showing in five years, with government borrowing reaching 2.7% of national output. The coalition government announced the creation of three new government departments, promised that creation of jobs would be a priority, and pledged a major concentration on social issues.

The new political partnership was not allowed the luxury of a honeymoon period. Unemployment rose swiftly to 302,000, and business dealings were so adversely affected by the fall in the value of the pound sterling that special assistance packages had to be devised to help industry weather the crisis. Despite assurances that it would not happen, a decision to devalue the Irish pound by 10% was taken at the end of January in an effort to protect it from further speculative attack. This resulted in an increase in the national debt and debt-servicing costs.

The budget, which the government had promised would be the toughest since the foundation of the state, proved to be something of an anticlimax. The coalition opted for a package of measures designed to slow, rather than halt, the rise in the level of unemployment. In March the government invited the opposition parties to join in a National Economic and Social Forum to promote consensus on economic and social policy and develop initiatives to tackle unemployment. By the end of the year, the situation had barely changed, however, and criticism of the coalition partners for failing to address this issue adequately was increasing. The grim economic news was not lightened by the crisis at Aer Lingus, the national airline, which had incurred huge debts and was reportedly losing more than £Ir 1 million a week. A controversial government plan to guarantee the company's long-term survival foresaw widespread layoffs opposed by the trade unions—and the ending of regular stopovers at Shannon Airport during the winter months.

On the positive side, Ireland benefitted from a grant of £Ir 7.8 billion, spread over seven years, from the European Community's Cohesion Fund. This subvention was in addition to generous structural funds that had already been made available by the EC to support general infrastructure programs. The latter included a number of highly controversial interpretative centres, situated in areas of outstanding natural beauty, that drew fire from environmentalists and resulted in court action to halt construction in some cases. Included in the spending plans for the Cohesion Fund were the completion of ring roads around Dublin, construction of a tunnel under the River Lee in Cork, upgrading of rail links, and reopening of a canal waterway from Dublin to the west of Ireland. Each project was specifically intended to help decrease unemployment.

The effective collapse of the European exchange-rate mechanism in August forced the government to revise its financial targets, which had been based on the Maastricht Treaty. The minister of finance, Bertie Ahern, acknowledged that plans to move toward a single European currency before the end of the decade had been dealt a serious blow and that it would now be difficult to maintain the Irish pound (floating for the first time on foreign exchange markets) at a relatively stable level.

Former EC commissioner Peter Sutherland, an Irishman, was appointed director general of the General Agreement on Tariffs and Trade (GATT) in June. He immediately ran into opposition from the Irish government, which backed the French in their opposition to the proposed GATT farm deal calling for a 21% cut in EC farm export subsidies. The plan would have had serious consequences for Ireland's £Ir 1.5 billion beef industry, although an Irish government report found that in the long term the proposed world trade agreement would be in Ireland's economic interests.

In Northern Ireland, faced with an apparent stalemate and with interparty talks stalled, the leader of the Social Democratic and Labour Party, John Hume, took the initiative and began talks with Sinn Fein leader Gerry Adams. Hume chose to report directly to the Irish government on terms of an agreement that would embrace a cessation of violence from the Provisional wing of the Irish Republican Army in return for the involvement of Sinn Fein in all-party talks. Evaluating the prospects for peace engaged the government during October, but with unionist politicians unenthusiastic, the outlook was not promising.

Pres. Mary Robinson paid the first-ever courtesy call by an Irish head of state on a British monarch when she had tea with Queen Elizabeth II at Buckingham Palace in May. A later visit by the president to Northern Ireland, during which she shook hands with Adams, angered unionists.

A more acceptable example of north-south cooperation was highlighted when an Irish team conquered Mt. Everest on the same day as the president's historic visit with the queen. The leader of the expedition, Dawson Stelfox, was a Belfast architect, and the deputy leader, Frank Nugent, was a project manager from Dublin.

In order to fight the spread of AIDS, a new Family Planning Bill, providing for the sale of condoms through public vending machines, passed through the Dail (parliament) in June without a single dissenting vote. A bill decriminalizing homosexuality and designed to lift the 132-year-old prohibition on homosexual acts also had a smooth passage through the Dail and was widely welcomed.

Four of the most important paintings (estimated to be worth £Ir 40 million) stolen from the Beit collection at Russborough House in County Wicklow in 1986 were recovered in Antwerp, Belgium, in September.

(MAVIS ARNOLD)

See also *United Kingdom,* below.

ITALY

A republic of southern Europe, Italy occupies the Apennine Peninsula, Sicily, Sardinia, and a number of smaller islands in the Mediterranean Sea. Area: 301,302 sq km (116,333 sq mi). Pop. (1993 est.): 57,235,000. Cap.: Rome. Monetary unit: Italian lira, with (Oct. 4, 1993) a free rate of 1,589 lire to U.S. $1 (2,407 lire = £1 sterling). President in 1993, Oscar Luigi Scalfaro; prime ministers, Giuliano Amato and, from April 29, Carlo Ciampi.

Among the highlights of 1993 were the gradual disappearance of a governing old guard discredited beyond recall by charges of corruption, the consolidation of the fractious Northern League under Umberto Bossi, and electoral reforms that prepared the ground for a political change. Up and down the peninsula, a new generation of magistrates broadened the so-called Operation Clean Hands, an investigation of suspect public figures begun in Milan in February 1992 by the magistrate Antonio Di Pietro. (*See* BIOGRAPHIES.) Di Pietro became something of a national hero as the probing reached higher levels and exposed as corrupt almost in its entirety a system of power in force since World War II. Almost a whole political class fell into disgrace, as well as industrialists and senior judges. Some 2,500 people had been fingered as the year ended, including five former prime ministers and about 200 members of Parliament. They were variously accused of having accepted illicit funds for political parties and of bribery, extortion, embezzlement, and fraud. Billions of dollars were involved, and most traditional political parties were implicated. The most tarnished turned out to be the Socialist Unity Party (PSU), which had always finished in third place in postwar elections behind the Christian Democrats (DC) and the Communists, now called the Democratic Party of the Left (PDS). Few of the accused stood trial, partly because of a slow-moving judiciary.

The first career ended was that of Bettino Craxi, former prime minister and pugnacious leader of the Socialists for 17 years. He resigned from the latter post in February after being accused in January of pocketing a bribe of $25 million in exchange for public works contracts, one of 20 separate charges eventually brought against him. He robustly dismissed all the charges as part of a smear campaign. His party deputy, Claudio Martelli, minister of justice for two years, also stepped down, over an alleged slush fund in Switzerland. Giorgio La Malfa, leader of the Republican Party, bowed out in February, and the chief of the small Liberal Party, Renato Altissimo, resigned in March, the month in which prison officers complained of a lack of space for the many without clean hands. In May Franco Nobili was arrested; he had been head of the state holding company IRI, which controlled most public-sector industries. In October the general manager of the automobile manufacturer Fiat, Cesare Romiti, came under scrutiny, as did Carlo De Benedetti, chairman of Olivetti.

A month earlier, Diego Curto, the deputy chief judge on the Milan civil bench and a prolific author, had become the first sitting judge to be actually jailed (in Brescia), for his confessed part in the biggest single case of high-level corruption yet exposed by the magistrates. At its centre was alleged to be an industrialist, Raul Gardini, well-known in Italy as a yachtsman. In July he took his life with a pistol shot after learning that arrest was imminent. (*See* OBITUARIES.) Former chairman of the chemical corporation Ferruzzi, he was wanted for fraud, corruption, and bribing mainly Christian Democrat and Socialist leaders to the tune of some $80 million. According to the magistrates, the money had been paid to the leaders for their cooperation in the creation, survival, and profitable liquidation of Enimont, a giant joint venture between the state petrochemical giant ENI and private firms controlled by Gardini. It failed, burdened with debts, in 1990 after the government had duly bought out its private component, Montedison, at a price inflated by some 20%. The scheme was revealed by the imprisoned Giuseppe Garofano, a former chairman of Montedison arrested earlier in Geneva. Gardini's suicide, the 10th since the start of Clean Hands, came during the same week that Gabriele Gagliari, former chairman of ENI, took his life in a prison cell in Milan.

By this time magistrates in Palermo had turned their attention to still-murkier matters by accusing Giulio Andreotti, the preeminent veteran of Italian politics, of collusion with the Mafia. Andreotti, seven times prime minister, Europe's longest-serving politician, and long considered invulnerable as the shrewdest of survivors, disclosed the charges against him in March. In his statement he said that he was "very hurt" in view of harsh anti-Mafia measures enacted under his leadership. In April, Parliament's anti-Mafia commission implied that Andreotti was the Mafia's agent in Rome. It found that Salvatore Lima, a former Christian Democratic mayor of Palermo who was murdered in 1992, had been linked to the Mafia and that Andreotti had been Lima's "political contact." Days later, Mafia turncoats were quoted as alleging that Mafia boss Salvatore ("Toto") Riina (*see* below) had once been seen planting a kiss on Andreotti. In June Andreotti came under suspicion of involvement in the murder in Rome of an "inconvenient" journalist (Carmine Pecorelli) in March 1979. Andreotti denied all the charges, questioning the reliability of charges based on the testimony of Mafia informers. A Senate committee voted in April to strip him, as senator for life, of immunity to prosecution. Few Italians found themselves astonished. Andreotti's nickname for years had been "The Godfather."

Having lost seven of his ministers to judicial inquiry, Prime Minister Giuliano Amato, after 10 months in office, resigned in April. His successor was Carlo Azeglio Ciampi, former governor of the Bank of Italy and the first nonpolitician to run Italy in the 20th century. He was chosen by Pres. Oscar Luigi Scalfaro specifically to lead a transitional team of technocrats that would pick its way through a world clearly falling apart and enact reforms before the general elections that were scheduled for spring 1994.

An initial reform passed by Parliament (in March) aimed at curing the chronic instability of town councils; for the first time, citizens were to elect their mayors directly by name, and the winners would pick 60% of their town councils. In June the voters in 145 towns rejected the candidates of the most corrupt parties, and in the north they gave a triumph to the untainted Northern League of Umberto Bossi, an astute, rough-hewn demagogue with a "North-for-Northerners" slogan, a tactical hankering for secession, and a real ear for impatience over what happened to northern money in wasteful Rome. Already the country's fourth-largest party with 80 parliamentarians after the national elections of April 1992, the League won local control of Italy's industrial heartland by a three-to-one majority. It took over Milan and 15 other northern cities, though not Turin. The PDS

LIVIO ANTICOLI—GAMMA LIAISON

Mario Segni (right), leader of the campaign for approval of a referendum on reform of the Italian government, celebrates victory with his colleagues. Voters approved a number of measures, including majority elections for most of the Senate, the ending of patronage jobs in certain government agencies and industries, and the establishment of an environmental oversight agency.

did well in central Italy (Ancona and Siena, for example) and altogether gained 73 new mayors. A new left-wing anti-Mafia party, La Rete (The Network), won footholds in the south. The Christian Democrats were able to elect only nine mayors, their worst showing in 40 years, and the Socialists won only two. Thus, the traditional mold of Italian politics lay shattered. But Bossi's success caused some concern and visions of national disruption. "The Senator," as he was called, failed to assuage anxiety when he threatened a northern tax revolt and a parliamentary walkout unless his call for early general elections was accepted.

Even more radical reform had been achieved on April 18–19 when 82.7% of voters in a referendum called for the majority of the Senate (238 senators out of 315) to be elected directly by the numbers of votes cast rather than by proportional representation. In response to another of the eight questions, voters also chose to end state funding of political parties. As intended, the referendum was interpreted as a demand for an overall change in the voting laws, in answer to which Parliament in August adopted a modified British-style electoral system for both houses. In both the Chamber of Deputies and the Senate, 75% of the seats would go to the winners by direct vote, while 25% would be handed out on a percentage basis. This was a reward for the past loyalty of small coalition allies, which feared extinction otherwise. The reform finally put to rest the proportional-representation system introduced after World War II essentially to keep the Communists out of power; the cost, however, had been political fragmentation and thus instability, responsible for 52 different governments since 1948.

Five terrorist bombs that went off in Rome, Milan, and Florence in May and July were widely seen as attempts to block reform by creating a climate of tension. The worst blast was on May 27 in Florence, where five people were killed and a wing of the famous Uffizi Gallery damaged. It was reopened in record time 24 days later. Nobody claimed responsibility for the bombing.

There had been gasps earlier over the arrest of Riina, described as the Mafia boss of bosses. After 23 years at large, he was picked up in January by a police patrol as he slowly drove through Palermo. Few could believe that this rather pudgy 62-year-old man with blurred speech was the most-wanted person in Italy, sought for some 50 murders, drug trafficking, and extortion. In October he was sentenced to life for the killing of two Mafia members.

Significant in foreign affairs was a clash in July between Italy on the one hand and the United States and the United Nations on the other over strategy and coordination in Somalia. While the commander of Italy's 2,600 troops in Somalia, Gen. Bruno Loi, advocated a degree of negotiation with local warlords, the UN command sought to disarm them. The dispute became acute with calls, resisted by Italy, for General Loi's removal. In December Italy announced that all of its troops would be withdrawn by the end of March 1994. (DEREK WILSON)

LATVIA

A republic of northern Europe, Latvia is on the eastern shore of the Baltic Sea. Area: 64,610 sq km (24,946 sq mi). Pop. (1993 est.): 2,596,000. Cap.: Riga. Monetary unit: lats (permanent currency introduced March 5, 1993; it became sole legal tender when the Latvian ruble [former transition currency] was phased out October 18), with (Oct. 4, 1993) a free rate of 0.61 lats to U.S. $1 (0.92 lats = £1 sterling). Leadership in 1993: (until July 7–8) chairman of the Supreme Council, Anatolijs Gorbunovs; prime minister, Ivars Godmanis; (after July 7–8) president, Guntis Ulmanis; chairman of the Saeima (parliament), Anatolijs Gorbunovs; prime minister, Valdis Birkavs.

On June 5–6, 1993, Latvia held its first free elections to the Saeima (parliament) since 1940. Three-fourths of the 100 deputies were right of centre, in part because, with voting limited only to citizens of Latvia on June 17, 1940, and their descendants, about 34% of current residents, primarily Slavs, could not vote. On July 6 the Saeima elected former Supreme Council chairman Anatolijs Gorbunovs its chairman, and on July 7 Latvian Farmers' Union (LZS) candidate Guntis Ulmanis Latvia's president. Latvia's Way and LZS formed a coalition government on July 20, headed by Prime Minister Valdis Birkavs.

Many of Latvia's domestic and foreign concerns were driven by its demographic situation—only 52% of the population were ethnic Latvians. The Saeima discussed, but did not yet adopt, a citizenship law, a requirement for Latvia's admission into the Council of Europe. Russia had frequently accused Latvia of discrimination against Russian-speaking residents—a charge Latvia officially denied—and tied resolution of the question to the withdrawal of its troops from Latvia. Russia called Latvian demands that all troops leave by the end of 1993 impossible. In November 1993 Russia proposed leaving by September 1994 but only on condition that it retain its radar station at Skrunda for six more years and that social rights be guaranteed for military pensioners. Latvia refused and continued to seek international help to get Russian troops out sooner.

After successfully reducing inflation by a tight fiscal policy, Latvia introduced its currency, the lats, on March 5. The standard of living had deteriorated. Industrial production continued to decrease in 1993 because of dependence on Russia for fuel and as its main export market. The official rate of unemployment rose to 5.5% but would be significantly higher if hidden unemployment were added.

(SAULIUS A. GIRNIUS)

This article updates the *Macropædia* article BALTIC STATES: *Latvia.*

LIECHTENSTEIN

A landlocked constitutional monarchy of central Europe, Liechtenstein is united with Switzerland by a customs and monetary union. Area: 160 sq km (62 sq mi). Pop. (1993 est.): 30,100. Cap.: Vaduz. Monetary unit: Swiss franc, with (Oct. 4, 1993) a free rate of Sw F 1.42 to U.S. $1 (Sw F 2.15 = £1 sterling). Sovereign prince, Hans Adam II; head of government in 1993, Hans Brunhart and, from May 26, Markus Büchel.

General elections were held in the principality on Feb. 7 and Oct. 24, 1993. In the February elections the right-wing Progressive Citizens' Party (FBP), which had governed in coalition since 1938 with the centrist Fatherland Union (VU), won a plurality of seats in the parliament. When the new government, headed by FBP leader Markus Büchel, was given a no-confidence vote in the parliament in September, Prince Hans Adam II, Liechtenstein's reigning monarch, dissolved the legislature and ordered October elections. In that election the VU regained a parliamentary plurality, leading the way for the VU's Mario Frick to take over as head of government. The transition to a new government, however, would not take place until Jan. 1, 1994.

A dispute with former Czechoslovakia, begun in 1992, continued to brew in 1993. Prince Hans Adam II demanded compensation for Czechoslovakia's 1945 confiscation of his ancestral home and estates (some 1,600 sq km [617 sq mi]). The prince estimated the value of his property at some $1 billion, but he indicated that he would settle for Sw F 300 million before taking his case to the International Court of Justice in The Hague. (KAREN M. SPARKS)

This article updates the *Micropædia* article LIECHTENSTEIN.

Pope John Paul II, followed by Lithuanian Pres. Algirdas Brazauskas, arrives in Vilnius on September 4 in his first visit to a country of the former U.S.S.R. The pontiff then traveled to the other Baltic republics, Latvia and Estonia.
GIANNI GIANSANTI—SYGMA

LITHUANIA

A republic of northern Europe, Lithuania is on the southeastern shore of the Baltic Sea. Area: 65,301 sq km (25,213 sq mi). Pop. (1993 est.): 3,753,000. Cap.: Vilnius. Monetary unit: litas (permanent currency introduced June 25, 1993; it became sole legal tender on July 20, the day the Lithuanian coupon [former transitional currency] was phased out), with (Oct. 4, 1993) a free rate of 4.23 litas to U.S. $1 (6.41 litas = £1 sterling). Chairman of the Supreme Council and acting president and then, from February 25, president, Algirdas Brazauskas; prime ministers, Bronislovas Lubys and, from March 10, Adolfas Slezevicius.

Despite the return to power of the former Communists, reorganized into the Lithuanian Democratic Labour Party (LDLP), internal and foreign policy changed little in 1993. The groundwork for the two most important foreign policy achievements of the year—Lithuania's acceptance as a member of the Council of Europe on May 14 and the withdrawal of Russian troops from the republic on August 31—had been laid by the previous right-wing parliament.

The LDLP's chairman, Algirdas Brazauskas, won the presidential elections on February 14. He appointed Adolfas Slezevicius prime minister; at its third congress the LDLP elected Slezevicius as party chairman on April 17. The Homeland Union was founded on May 1 on the basis of the defeated and dispirited Sajudis organization and became the most formidable conservative force in Lithuania.

Lithuania made little progress in converting to a market economy. The government's new regulations for privatization of state-owned enterprises halted the whole process. Although trade with the West increased slightly, Lithuania's economy remained excessively dependent on Russia. The high cost of fuel, purchased from Russia at world prices, made Lithuanian products too expensive for domestic markets and for most foreign customers. Industrial production continued to decline. Agricultural production increased, but many farmers were unable to sell their products to food processors because high prices decreased demand.

The standard of living also continued to decline. More than two-thirds of the average salary was spent on food, and many people were unable to pay for utilities. A tight monetary policy set the stage for the introduction of the national currency, the litas, on June 25.

(SAULIUS A. GIRNIUS)

This article updates the *Macropædia* article BALTIC STATES: *Lithuania.*

LUXEMBOURG

Luxembourg is a landlocked constitutional monarchy in western Europe. Area: 2,586 sq km (999 sq mi). Pop. (1993 est.): 392,000. Cap.: Luxembourg. Monetary unit: Luxembourg franc, at par with the Belgian franc, with (Oct. 4, 1993) a free rate of Lux F 35.15 to U.S. $1 (Lux F 53.25 = £1 sterling). Grand duke, Jean; prime minister in 1993, Jacques Santer.

The government announced in January 1993 a new regulation creating a fund to hold money confiscated from narcotics traffickers and money launderers. Because of a loophole in the previous money-laundering law, a Court of Appeals judge had ruled that $36 million in alleged cocaine profits had to be returned to its owners.

Luxembourg came under pressure in April from its European Community partners to introduce a withholding tax on savings and investments. In particular, France, Belgium, and Germany, upset with the flight of capital to banks in Luxembourg, urged EC Tax Commissioner Christiane Scrivener to set a 15% minimum withholding tax, which would be levied on the interest on investments throughout the EC. Luxembourg expressed concern that introducing the withholding tax would lead to an easing of the strict banking-secrecy regulations that attract foreign capital to the country.

EC ministers meeting in Luxembourg on June 1 approved a measure to limit the workweek to 48 hours. The directive also set standards for paid vacations, workday breaks, and time off. The 48-hour workweek limit would affect only Britain, Ireland, and Denmark, because the other EC nations already met that standard. Britain, which opposed the measure as economically harmful, challenged its legality in the European Court of Justice. (ANNE ROBY)

MACEDONIA

A landlocked republic of the central Balkans, Macedonia borders Yugoslavia to the north, Bulgaria to the east, Greece to the south, and Albania to the west. Area: 25,713 sq km (9,928 sq mi). Pop. (1993 est.): 2,063,000. Cap.: Skopje. Monetary unit: denar (sole legal tender from May 7, 1993), with (Oct. 4, 1993) an official rate of 27 denars to U.S. $1 (41.04 denars = £1 sterling). President in 1993, Kiro Gligorov; prime minister, Branko Crvenkovski.

In 1993 Macedonia managed to achieve what had eluded it in 1992: in April it was granted membership in the United

Soldiers are sworn into the Macedonian army. Although the country was admitted to the UN in April under the provisional name The Former Yugoslav Republic of Macedonia, Greece continued to refuse to recognize the name Macedonia or the republic's flag, which showed the symbol of Alexander the Great.
RUSSELL LIBMAN—SIPA

Nations, albeit under the compromise name of The Former Yugoslav Republic of Macedonia. By the end of the year, all members of the European Union except Greece had taken steps to establish diplomatic relations with Macedonia. Relations with Serbia remained tense, however. Serbia strongly criticized the election of a new patriarch of the Macedonian Orthodox Church, said in Belgrade to be an anti-Serb Macedonian nationalist. Relations with Albania deteriorated after a number of border incidents.

In November, Pres. Kiro Gligorov and the government narrowly averted being toppled in the parliament by the ultranationalist Internal Macedonian Revolutionary Organization (VMRO), which was pressing for the exclusion of ethnic Albanians from the country's coalition government. Then the Interior Ministry announced that arms manufactured in Albania had been seized in Skopje and two other cities. The deputy minister of health, an ethnic Albanian, who had allegedly kept ammunition in his office, disappeared, but six other suspects were arrested.

Macedonia's economy, despite UN sanctions imposed on its main trading partner, Yugoslavia, maintained a degree of stability. Still, inflation reached a monthly rate of 70–80% by the end of the year; industrial production for the year was 33% lower than in 1992; and severe drought reduced agricultural output by about one-third. (K.F. CVIIC)

This article updates the *Macropædia* article BALKAN STATES: *Macedonia.*

MALTA

The republic of Malta, a member of the Commonwealth, comprises the islands of Malta, Gozo, and Comino in the Mediterranean Sea between Sicily and Tunisia. Area: 316 sq km (122 sq mi). Pop. (1993 est.): 363,000. Cap.: Valletta. Monetary unit: Maltese lira, with (Oct. 4, 1993) an official rate of 0.38 lira to U.S. $1 (0.57 lira = £1 sterling). President in 1993, Censu Tabone; prime minister, Eddie Fenech Adami.

In June 1993 the Commission of the European Community (EC) gave a positive opinion on Malta's three-year-old application to join the union. Malta had the qualifications for full membership in the EC, but various economic reforms and certain legislative measures were required. The EC proposed intensive dialogue with Malta so that the process of change would start immediately, and discussions began in July.

Omar Muhammad Ali Rezzaq, convicted in the 1985 hijacking of an Egyptian airliner that led to some 60 deaths, completed his prison term in February and left Malta. The U.S. government strongly condemned the release, but Malta insisted that it had to act in accordance with the law. In July Rezzaq was arrested in Nigeria and taken to Washington, D.C., to stand trial.

The Maltese lira was devalued by 10% when the budget for 1993 was announced. A capital gains tax was later introduced. In January, Shell Oil Co. and NIMIR (a Saudi Arabian firm) were granted a concession to explore for oil to the south of Malta. An agreement was signed in July with the Istituto Scientifico ed Ospedale San Raffaele to establish a hospital to complement St. Luke's, which was the only one on the island. The Council of Europe made 12 million liri available to help guarantee that the effort to establish a new medical facility would be successful.

Italy undertook to follow up its aid to Malta with a fourth agreement to provide financial, economic, and technical assistance. The president of Malta paid state visits to Australia, New Zealand, and Italy during the year. Local councils were created by new legislation, and the first elections were held in November. (ALBERT GANADO)

MOLDOVA

A landlocked republic of the extreme northeastern Balkans, Moldova borders Ukraine on the north, northeast, and southeast and Romania on the west. Area: 33,700 sq km (13,000 sq mi). Pop. (1993 est.) 4,362,000. Cap.: Chisinau. Monetary unit: ruble, with (Oct. 4, 1993) a free rate of 1,165 rubles = U.S. $1 (1,765 rubles = £1 sterling). President in 1993, Mircea Snegur; prime minister, Andrei Sangheli.

Moldova failed during 1993 to regain sovereignty over its eastern region on the left bank of the Dniester, controlled by Russia's 14th Army and the unrecognized "Dniester republic" led by local Russian residents. Although Russians form only the third-largest ethnic group in the region, after Moldovans and Ukrainians, and the region itself is separated from Russia by Ukraine, local secessionist leaders and the 14th Army command publicly broached their intention to join the region with the Russian Federation. Bilateral negotiations concerning the 14th Army remained deadlocked as Russia conditioned a future withdrawal on a political resolution of the conflict, while the breakaway republic demanded full state attributes. Moldova offered the region local autonomy short of sovereignty. In the south a tentative agreement on local autonomy defused the confrontation with the other breakaway region, the "Gagauz republic."

Prohibitive Russian import tariffs on goods from Moldova forced it to join the Commonwealth of Independent States and the Economic Union in order to regain access to Moldova's main market and to Russian fuels. Economic conditions deteriorated, particularly in the cities, and inflation of the Moldovan coupon accelerated. Chisinau's reform programs were approved and supported with loans by the International Monetary Fund and the World Bank.

During the year Moldova continued distancing itself from Romania, confirming the choice of the government and the native majority for independent statehood over unification. Most non-Moldovans west of the Dniester, where a large majority of the Russians and of the other nonindigenous populations reside, demonstrated acceptance or support of Moldovan independence. (VLADIMIR SOCOR)

This article updates the *Macropædia* article BALKAN STATES: *Moldova.*

MONACO

A sovereign principality on the northern Mediterranean coast, Monaco is bounded on land by the French département of Alpes-Maritimes. Area: 1.95 sq km (0.75 sq mi). Pop. (1993 est.): 30,500. Monetary unit: French franc, with (Oct. 4, 1993) a free rate of F 5.67 to U.S. $1 (F 8.58 = £1 sterling). Chief of state, Prince Rainier III; minister of state in 1993, Jacques Dupont.

On May 25, 1993, the principality of Monaco applied for membership in the United Nations after Minister of State Jacques Dupont visited New York City for talks with UN Secretary-General Boutros Boutros-Ghali and members of the Security Council. Monaco had held observer status at the United Nations since 1955. On May 28 Monaco and newly independent Eritrea were admitted to UN membership, bringing the total number of member states to 183.

The Vatican announced on April 5 that it had declared legitimate Princess Caroline's children from her second marriage to Stefano Casiraghi, who had died in a speedboat accident in 1990. Her first marriage to Philippe Junot of France, whom she had divorced in 1980, was annulled by the Vatican in 1992. Caroline's three children by Casiraghi—Andrea, Pierre, and Charlotte—had been technically disqualified from the succession in Monaco because they were born before the church recognized Caroline's 1983 marriage to Casiraghi. (ANNE ROBY)

This article updates the *Micropædia* article MONACO.

NETHERLANDS, THE

A constitutional monarchy of northwestern Europe, The Netherlands, a Benelux country, is on the North Sea. Area: 41,526 sq km (16,033 sq mi). Pop. (1993 est.): 15,302,000. Cap., Amsterdam; seat of government, The Hague. Monetary unit: Netherlands guilder, with (Oct. 4, 1993) a free rate of 1.82 guilders to U.S. $1 (2.76 guilders = £1 sterling). Queen, Beatrix; prime minister in 1993, Ruud Lubbers.

On Jan. 12, 1993, Defense Minister Relus ter Beek presented a list of priorities for restructuring the military. A 44% reduction in manpower was foreseen by 2002. Land forces would be reduced by 54% and the navy by 25%. The main task of the armed forces was defined as "peacekeeping crisis control"; Dutch troops would participate only in international peacekeeping operations that were initiated by the United Nations or in the context of European alliances.

On January 28 the lower house of Parliament passed a bill on new disability benefits, ending a debate that had begun in 1991. The Labour Party, a member of the ruling coalition, acceded in the vote only after Prime Minister Ruud Lubbers threatened to bring down the Cabinet. A compromise was reached to retain the existing benefit level (70% of full income), but new benefits would depend on individual circumstances, and allowances would be somewhat lower than before. The new arrangements were necessary because the growing number of disabled people—900,000, or one-seventh of the workforce—had overburdened the Dutch economy. A parliamentary inquiry in May–June 1993 examined allegations that on a large scale workers laid off during the economic recession of the 1980s got disability benefits to which they were not entitled, but the inquiry found no proof of such irregularities.

Following 20 years of sharp national debate on the issue of euthanasia, on February 9 Parliament voted in favour of a bill that would permit physicians to assist in suicide under strict medical and ethical conditions. In late November the Senate voted 37–34 in favour of a carefully worded bill that did not legalize euthanasia but set forth guidelines indicating what doctors could do without fear of criminal prosecution. For one thing, patients would have to ask repeatedly to die before the doctor could intervene. The bill was expected to become law in 1994.

On June 4 Elske ter Veld, secretary of state for social affairs, resigned after an emotional debate. She had been an active proponent of social welfare, sometimes going beyond the program of the Labour Party, and her departure caused serious rifts in the party faction in Parliament. She was replaced by Jacques Wallage, a former secretary of state in the Department of Education.

Roel in 't Veld, the new secretary of state for education, in turn had to resign on June 17, having been in office for only eight days. He was accused of abuse of his position while he was a professor at the Erasmus University of Rotterdam. Job Cohen, rector of the University of Limburg at Maastricht, took over as education secretary on June 30.

In her speech on "Prinsjesdag," the traditional ceremonial opening of the parliamentary year on the third Tuesday in September, Queen Beatrix stressed the alarming rate of unemployment in The Netherlands. Joblessness was on the rise for the first time since 1988, and near-term projections were gloomy, with a postwar record high foreseen in 1994. Other topics for government consideration in late 1993 were the stabilization of the deficit, maintenance of social security, and a general reduction of the costs of labour.

(KLAAS J. HOEKSEMA)

See also *Dependent States,* below.

NORWAY

A constitutional monarchy of northern Europe, Norway occupies the western part of the Scandinavian Peninsula, with coastlines on the Skagerrak, the North Sea, the Norwegian Sea, and the Arctic Ocean. Area: 323,878 sq km (125,050 sq mi), excluding the Svalbard Archipelago and Jan Mayen Island. Pop. (1993 est.): 4,308,000. Cap.: Oslo. Monetary unit: Norwegian krone, with (Oct. 4, 1993) a free rate of 7.10 kroner to U.S. $1 (10.76 kroner = £1 sterling). King, Harald V; prime minister in 1993, Gro Harlem Brundtland.

The minority Labour government, headed by Prime Minister Gro Harlem Brundtland, captured 67 seats in the Sept. 13, 1993, parliamentary election to retain power for a new four-year term. By propelling the anti-EC agrarian Centre Party to the status of main opposition party, the election, more than anything else, demonstrated the strong resistance of Norwegians to membership in the European Community

(EC). Led by Anne Enger Lahnstein, the Centre Party overtook the pro-EC Conservatives, led by Kaci Kullman-Five, who suffered their worst-ever election. (For tabulated results, see *Political Parties,* above.)

In March the European Commission approved Norway's application to join the EC, and accession negotiations began in earnest in September. Norway had rejected membership in a divisive referendum in 1972, and some opinion polls consistently showed that a large majority of Norwegians still opposed membership. Other polls, however, showed that a majority supported the application, illustrating just how confused and divided over membership the electorate was. Brundtland's government planned a new membership referendum by 1996 if negotiations with the EC over the highly sensitive issues of fisheries, agriculture, and petroleum were satisfactory. Many Norwegians feared that EC membership would cause them to lose their hard-won sovereignty, limit control over local natural resources, and force massive cuts in lavish agriculture subsidies. International Monetary Fund figures showed that subsidies made up 77% of the value of agricultural output, compared with the EC average of 49%. Both neighbouring Sweden and Finland were negotiating on EC membership alongside Norway, and there was a widely held view that if their referenda were held successfully before Norway's vote, they could have a positive influence on Norwegian public opinion.

Labour's hold on power was in part due to a belief in government stability with Brundtland at the helm. It was also helped by clear signs of economic recovery. In 1992 gross domestic product (GDP) grew by 3.3%. Even excluding petroleum and shipping revenues, the economy grew by 2%, and much the same performance was expected in 1993. Inflation looked set to rise slightly to 2.75% for the year as a whole, but at its mid-1993 level of 2.3% it was the lowest in Norway for three decades, and the lowest in Europe. The Bank of Norway cut its key overnight lending rate no fewer than 12 times between January and September, lowering it from 11 to 5.5%. The real jobless rate grew steadily throughout the year to slightly above 8% of the workforce, compared with 7.6% in 1992.

The persistent six-year banking crisis showed signs of abating, with the country's two biggest commercial banks, Christiania Bank and Den norske Bank (DnB), forecasting a return to profit in 1993. Since 1987 the government had injected an estimated 30 billion kroner to prop up the banking sector. Meanwhile, UNI Storebrand, the country's biggest insurer, was freed from public administration in August and relisted on the Oslo Stock Exchange after having collapsed in 1992 under the weight of 3.8 billion kroner in debt used to finance a failed raid on Skandia Forsakrings, Sweden's biggest insurer.

In April, Foreign Minister Thorvald Stoltenberg handed over his Cabinet seat to Johan Jörgen Holst, the defense minister, so that he could replace Cyrus Vance as joint mediator with Lord Owen of negotiations between the warring factions in the former Yugoslavia.

In August, Norway disclosed that it had played the role of a "back channel" mediator between Israel and the Palestine Liberation Organization. A declaration of principles shaped and initialed in Oslo in August led to the signing of the historic Middle East peace agreement in Washington in September.

All of Norway was in the final throes of gearing up to host the Winter Olympics, to be held in Lillehammer, north of Oslo, in February 1994. (KAREN L. FOSSLI)

See also *Dependent States,* below.

POLAND

A republic of eastern Europe, Poland is on the Baltic Sea. Area: 312,685 sq km (120,728 sq mi). Pop. (1993 est.): 38,521,000. Cap.: Warsaw. Monetary unit: zloty, with (Oct. 4, 1993) a free rate of 19,657 zlotys to U.S. $1 (29,780 zlotys = £1 sterling). President in 1993, Lech Walesa; prime ministers, Hanna Suchocka and, from October 26, Waldemar Pawlak.

The ex-communists and their allies were returned to power in 1993 in Poland's second fully democratic general election. This sea change in the politics of the new democracy was brought about by a combination of political misjudgment on the part of the incumbent coalition and an unashamed propaganda pitch by the left-wing parties to capitalize on the economic discontent among the electorate.

The year began on an upbeat as most of the 300,000 striking coal miners ended their 22-day protest and returned to the pits on January 4. By a narrow vote Prime Minister Hanna Suchocka succeeded in getting an austerity budget through the Sejm (parliament) in February against stiff resistance from the Solidarity parties. In what was seen as a reversal for the prime minister and a portent of a split in the coalition, however, the Sejm voted on March 18 to halt the government's plan to privatize some 600 state enterprises. In late April the Sejm reversed itself and voted to continue the privatization program, but it was too late for Suchocka. The Solidarity trade union called strikes among teachers and public health workers in May and eventually succeeded in forcing a vote of confidence.

NTB/PHOTOREPORTERS

This farmhouse near Oslo was one of the places where delegates from Israel and the Palestine Liberation Organization met secretly to work out a declaration of principles that led to the signing of a peace agreement in September. The initial contacts were made with the help of the Norwegian Institute for Applied Social Science, which was studying living conditions in the West Bank and the Gaza Strip.

Russians leave a train in Warsaw on their way to sell consumer goods at Polish street markets. The resale of Russian products usually brought at least a small profit, but the Polish government was increasingly restricting trade in such goods as tobacco and alcohol.
CLAUS REISINGER—BLACK STAR

Suchocka resigned on May 28. Pres. Lech Walesa asked her to remain in a caretaker capacity and then set September 19 as the date for new elections. The centrists and rightists were routed by two left-wing parties formerly allied with the communists: the Democratic Left Alliance (SLD) of Aleksander Kwasniewski, with 20.4% of the vote, and the Polish Peasant Party (PSL), led by Waldemar Pawlak, with 15.4%. Suchocka's centrist Democratic Union received 10.6%.

On October 14 Pawlak was asked to form a government. Propped up by the eminence grise Kwasniewski, who chose to stay out of the Cabinet, Pawlak put together a PSL-SLD coalition, but he awarded the sensitive portfolios of foreign, internal, and defense affairs to persons outside the coalition. The SLD retained control of the Finance and Privatization ministries, which provided some assurance to those concerned with the fate of Poland's hard-won reforms. The government handily won a vote of confidence in the Sejm (310–83, with 24 abstentions) on November 10.

Walesa cast himself in the role of defender of the democratic and economic gains he claimed the Suchocka government had handed to its successor. He continued his enigmatic style of dealing with the government by issuing a less-than-resounding endorsement of the new prime minister: "I wish Pawlak well, but in my opinion he will not stand up to the job."

One potential area of conflict seemed to have been avoided as the Sejm seemed likely to ratify the concordat with the Vatican. On the other hand, any attempt to reverse abortion legislation (in January the Sejm approved strictly limited access to abortions but did not ban the procedure completely, as the leadership of Poland's Roman Catholic Church had sought) or remove "Christian values" clauses from media legislation could change this situation. The church won a victory in April when a constitutional tribunal dismissed a challenge by the government ombudsman questioning the legality of compulsory teaching of religion in Polish schools. The perception of growing church influence in state affairs undoubtedly played a role in the defeat of the pro-church parties in the September elections, and Prime Minister Pawlak went on the attack in October by making it clear that he did not support Poland's strict abortion law.

Economic problems were certain to claim most of the attention of the Pawlak government, and holding the line on a budget deficit of 5% seemed likely to prove especially difficult. Unemployment officially stood at 2.9 million—15.4% of the working population. Although personal savings rose and consumption of consumer durables expanded, poverty was reported to have overtaken one-third of households. Poland's 4% growth in gross domestic product for the year was, in large measure, due to the expansion of the private sector. The annual inflation rate was down to 38%, and Poland successfully weathered the introduction of value-added and personal income taxes. The 6% decline in exports, accompanied by the 25% growth in imports, was likely to persuade the new government toward a more protectionist policy, particularly for agricultural produce.

Issues of security, European integration, and refugees dominated Poland's foreign affairs in 1993. Political uncertainty and hard-line rhetoric in Russia, as well as the modest successes in reinvigorating the Commonwealth of Independent States, kept Polish politicians' attention concentrated on the country's eastern borders. President Walesa deflected an overture from Ukrainian Pres. Leonid Kravchuk to join in a regional security arrangement that would exclude Russia. The last troops of the former U.S.S.R. left Polish soil on September 18, the 54th anniversary of the Red Army's invasion. During his visit in Poland in late August, Russian Pres. Boris Yeltsin struck a conciliatory note on the question of Poland's joining NATO, although later statements were less accommodating.

Some progress, but mostly setbacks, was recorded in Poland's quest for closer integration with Western Europe. The general agreement of the NATO countries at their summit in October to extend opportunities for cooperation to Eastern European countries while putting off the timetable for membership was a disappointment for Poland. In February Warsaw yielded to pressure from Bonn to take back third-country immigrants entering Germany illegally from Poland, and on May 7 a formal agreement was signed. A spat with the European Community over imports of meat in April underlined the protectionist EC attitudes and fears in the West of cheaper Polish products flooding the market. Even with the $47.2 billion foreign debt, however, Poland's relatively robust economy continued to meet the lending criteria of international development banks and creditor organizations. The European Bank for Reconstruction and Development announced plans in October to lend the country $1 billion to support privatization and another $200 million to recapitalize a large insurance company.

(GEORGE KOLANKIEWICZ)

PORTUGAL

A republic of southwestern Europe, metropolitan Portugal is on the Atlantic coast of the Iberian Peninsula, which it shares with Spain. Area: 92,389 sq km (35,672 sq mi), including the Azores and Madeira island groups/archipelagoes in the Atlantic. Pop. (1993 est.): 9,823,000. Cap.: Lisbon. Monetary unit: Portuguese escudo, with (Oct. 4, 1993) a free rate of 167.26 escudos to U.S. $1 (253.40 escudos = £1 sterling). President in 1993, Mario Soares; prime minister, Anibal Cavaco Silva.

Tension between Pres. Mario Soares and Prime Minister Anibal Cavaco Silva intensified during the summer of 1993 after Soares vetoed a Social Democrat (PSD)–sponsored bill that drastically restricted the right of political asylum. Conflict between Soares and Cavaco Silva over the issue continued during the following months.

Midway through its term the PSD was struggling with the implementation of difficult and unpopular reforms to the national health service and the education system. The situation was not improved by the lacklustre performance of Finance Minister Jorge Braga de Macedo or the unpopularity of Minister of Agriculture Arlindo Cunha. Even the charismatic Cavaco Silva was suffering in the opinion polls. The opposition accused the PSD of trying to stifle criticism and of packing the high ranks of the civil service with its members. According to a Socialist Party report, 90% of middle-ranked and senior employees in the Ministries of Health, Education, Agriculture, Industry, and Public Works belonged to the PSD.

The president of the Court of Auditors was effectively prevented from criticizing the government when the Assembly voted that he could only coordinate the work of his members without voicing an opinion himself. During the year the Court of Auditors issued scathing reports concerning the government's 1991 accounts and its financial mismanagement at the Belém cultural centre in Lisbon.

In August the former governor of Macao was acquitted of taking bribes from a German firm while bids were being submitted for a new airport in the colony. The presiding judge in the case took the unusual (and perhaps illegal) step of announcing that he had voted against acquittal. The prosecution said that it would appeal the case.

Portugal's Social and Economic Council was unable to make progress on a wage pact when it met in July, although after the meeting the General Union of Workers indicated that it was still willing to reach some sort of agreement. The larger, Communist-dominated labour union, Intersindical, was ineffective in protesting both the imposition of a 5–6% ceiling on pay increases for government workers and the raising of the retirement age for women to 65. On August 4 the minimum legal age of employment was lowered to 14. The labour unions protested against the legislation, claiming that it violated the recommendations of the International Labour Organization. Public response was also hostile despite the fairly widespread use of child labour.

A plan to spend 100 billion escudos to offset the negative consequences for Portugal of the European Community's (EC's) common agricultural policy was announced in June. The plan involved the retirement of 6,591 farmers and the transfer of their land to others, as well as the reforestation of 155,000 ha (383,000 ac). Refinancing, with EC aid, of 150 billion escudos of unpaid farm-sector debt was also unveiled. The farm plan called for preferential interest rates for new loans, an additional 8 billion escudos for drought relief, and a moratorium on loans contracted by farmers in 1992 to tide them over the effects of severe drought. Special support for farmers in the Alentejo region, which was hardest hit by the drought, was also given.

The government also announced spending of 300 billion escudos on the health service over the next seven years. EC grants would help pay for part of the plan, which would introduce a mixed health insurance scheme that would allow a much larger role for the private sector.

In October the Cabinet began preparation of the 1994 budget. Portugal was planning to introduce a system under which nonresidents would be refunded their withholding taxes on bond holdings within one day. Portugal's bond markets underwent sweeping reforms during the year, with the goal of raising foreign investment in them from 5% of the total to 25–30%. (MICHAEL WOOLLER)

See also *Dependent States,* below.

ROMANIA

A republic on the Balkan Peninsula in southeastern Europe, Romania has a coastline on the Black Sea. Area: 237,500 sq km (91,699 sq mi). Pop. (1993 est.): 22,789,000. Cap.: Bucharest. Monetary unit: leu, with (Oct. 4, 1993) a free rate of 940.50 lei to U.S. $1 (1,425 lei = £1 sterling). President in 1993, Ion Iliescu; prime minister, Nicolae Vacaroiu.

The relative stability that characterized the period of government of Theodor Stolojan was maintained in 1993 under his successor as prime minister, Nicolae Vacaroiu, who, in the wake of a general election, was asked to form an administration by Pres. Ion Iliescu in November 1992. Vacaroiu continued to apply the economic reform measures recommended by the World Bank and the International Monetary Fund in the early part of 1993, although both institutions expressed concern in the summer that the pace of privatization had slackened and threatened to withhold supplementary credits.

An association agreement, signed on February 1, marked the beginning of Romania's integration into the European Community's political and economic structures. Tariffs and quotas on most of Romania's industrial exports to the EC were abolished, and those that remained were to be progressively eliminated over the following six years. At the EC summit in Copenhagen in June, a decision was taken to invite Romania, along with the other associate member states, to consultative minisummits to be held twice a year.

ANDREI ILIESCU—THE NEW YORK TIMES

Citizens of Cluj try to claim profits from a pyramid scheme. It was estimated that Romanians, desperate to escape impoverishment but lacking experience in the workings of a modern economy, had put 30–50% of their savings in the scheme.

In order to bring Romanian fiscal policies into line with EC practice, a value-added tax (VAT) was introduced on July 1. Further landmarks in Romania's success in casting off its image of political turbulence and authoritarian government were its admission on September 28 to the Council of Europe's parliamentary assembly and the U.S. Senate's decision to grant Romania most-favoured-nation trade status on October 21.

The confusion surrounding the introduction of the VAT was symptomatic of many of the problems besetting the management of the economy. Although its application was limited to food and was fixed at a rate of 18%, shopkeepers took advantage of a government decision to abolish a ceiling on profit margins, which came into force on the same day, to raise food prices by up to 80%. Coming on top of the elimination of subsidies on May 1 on bread, milk, electricity, gas, and gasoline and an increase in customs duties from 5 to 20%, this price hike helped to create an inflation rate in consumer prices calculated by the Bank of Romania and by Western institutions to have reached 300% by the end of the year (the figure for 1992 was 210%). The growing discrepancy between prices and incomes fueled wage demands and led to a wave of strikes in August led by the miners in the Jiu Valley. The actions paralyzed the coal mining and railway industries, but the government successfully resisted the strikers' demands. Nevertheless, the labour unrest reflected the high social cost of the reform program. Unemployment, standing at one million, or 9.3% of the working population, in September, showed only a small increase over 1992 and reflected the government's policy of diverting its foreign credits to keep the mammoth heavy industrial plants afloat instead of using the moneys for restructuring. Economic performance maintained its downward spiral and was estimated to have fallen by 22% compared with 1992.

Progress in privatization remained checkered. Although a legal framework for privatization was put in place in 1991, the political will to carry it out remained weak. This was largely due to the government's dependency for a parliamentary majority on the ultranationalist Party for National Unity of the Romanians and the Greater Romania Party, both of which opposed any significant privatization involving foreign capital. Outright ownership of land was denied to foreign companies, and more than 30% of the land confiscated under the Communists remained in the hands of the state. No new measures of significance were taken to return nationalized property to its original owners. The restrictions, coupled with the continued incoherence in fiscal legislation and its arbitrary application, kept foreign investment, which was largely restricted to joint ventures, to about $680 million by June 1993—a modest level in comparison with most of the other former Communist states of eastern Europe. The number of joint ventures rose in 1993 to 25,000 but most were small units, often shops set up by businessmen from Lebanon, Syria, and Turkey. A pyramid investment scheme called Caritas, set up in 1992, attracted up to 50% of the population's private savings before it reached a point in November when it could no longer make promised payments. Some four million people had handed over money to Caritas in the hope of making mind-boggling profits.

Caritas was also a manifestation of the search by large sections of the population for a miraculous cure for the economic malaise. Another was the phenomenon of crowds of more than 150,000 people lining up in Bucharest in October to touch the relics of an Orthodox saint said to have miraculous properties. The economic problems were matched by a growing breakdown of law and order that was particularly evident in the armed holdups of buses by gangs of thieves in the province of Moldova. Reported crime rose by more than 400% in 1993 compared with 1992. Racial attacks also showed an increase. Resentment between Romanians and Hungarians on the one hand and Romas (Gypsies) on the other exploded in Transylvania in late September when, after a Roma knifed a Romanian, the villagers lynched three Romas and torched 13 houses. The attack was but one of 16 incidents involving violence against Romas for which no arrests were made.

There were only cosmetic changes in the political scene. The ruling Democratic National Salvation Front changed its name to the Party of Social Democracy in Romania at its annual conference in July, and in the same month one of the main opposition parties, the Civic Alliance, split.

(DENNIS J. DELETANT)

This article updates the *Macropædia* article BALKAN STATES: *Romania*.

RUSSIA

Russia is a federal republic occupying eastern and northeastern Europe and all of northern Asia. Area: 17,075,400 sq km (6,592,800 sq mi). Pop. (1993 est.): 148 million. Cap.: Moscow. Monetary unit: ruble, with (Oct. 4, 1993) a free rate of 1,165 rubles = U.S. $1 (1,765 rubles = £1 sterling). President in 1993, Boris Yeltsin; prime minister, Viktor Chernomyrdin.

Pres. Boris Yeltsin began 1993 in retreat but ended it in partial triumph. The year offered dramatic scenes of confrontation between Yeltsin and the conservative parliament, reached its apotheosis in October with the storming of the White House (the parliament building), and saw its denouement in the December vote on a new constitution and a new parliament for Russia.

Politics and Government. Yeltsin's attempt to browbeat the seventh Congress of People's Deputies (December 1992) into submission backfired. In a series of collisions over policy, the congress whittled away the president's extraordinary powers, which it had granted him in late 1991. The legislature, marshaled by Speaker Ruslan Khasbulatov, began to sense that it could block and even defeat the president. The tactic it adopted was gradually to erode presidential control over the government. Blocked by the legislature, the president called a referendum on a new constitution for April 11.

The eighth Congress of People's Deputies opened on March 10 with a strong attack on the president by Khasbulatov, who accused Yeltsin of acting unconstitutionally. The congress voted to amend the constitution, strip Yeltsin of many of his powers, and cancel the scheduled April referendum. The president stalked out of the congress. Vladimir Shumeyko, first deputy prime minister, declared that the referendum would go ahead, but on April 25.

The parliament was gradually expanding its influence over the government. On March 16 the president signed a decree that conferred Cabinet rank on Viktor Gerashchenko, chairman of the central bank, and three other officials; this was in accordance with the decision of the eighth congress that these officials should be members of the government. The congress's ruling, however, had made it clear that as ministers they would continue to be subordinate to the parliament.

The president's response was dramatic. On March 20 he declared that he intended to introduce a "special regime." He bitterly attacked the parliament, accusing the deputies of trying to restore the communist order. Vice Pres. Aleksandr Rutskoy condemned Yeltsin's grab for special powers, and the Constitutional Court ruled that Yeltsin had indeed acted unconstitutionally.

Communist opponents (left) and supporters (right) of Boris Yeltsin demonstrate in Moscow in March, when the Congress of People's Deputies narrowly failed to vote the Russian president's ouster. With the support of the military, Yeltsin crushed an armed uprising against him in October, dismissed the parliament, and scheduled elections, including a vote on a new constitution, for December, but the world was shocked when reform parties were outpolled by communist and nationalist groups.

(LEFT) VLADIMIR SICHOV—SIPA; (RIGHT) EAST NEWS/SIPA

The ninth congress, which opened on March 26, began with a virulent attack on Yeltsin by Khasbulatov. Yeltsin conceded that he had made mistakes and appealed for a compromise, but he was rejected contemptuously by the congress. The legislators could not muster a two-thirds majority to impeach the president, however, falling 72 short of the 689 votes necessary. When it became known that Khasbulatov had attempted to cut a deal with the president that involved abandoning the April 25 referendum and simultaneous elections for president and the parliament in November 1993, the congress turned on him, and one-third of the deputies voted in favour of his removal. The referendum would go ahead, but the congress voted that in order to win, the president would need to obtain 50% of the whole electorate, not 50% of those who voted. The Constitutional Court supported Yeltsin and ruled that the president required only a simple majority on two issues: confidence in him, and economic and social policy; he would need the support of half the electorate in order to call new parliamentary and presidential elections.

Yeltsin's gamble paid off in the referendum of April 25. With a surprisingly high voter turnout of 64.5%, fully 58.7% expressed confidence in the president and 53% in his economic and social policies, 49.5% were in favour of early presidential elections, and 67.2% supported early parliamentary elections. Although this permitted the president to declare that the population supported him, not the parliament, he lacked a constitutional mechanism to implement his victory. As before, the president had to appeal to the people over the heads of the legislature.

In an attempt to outmaneuver the parliament, Yeltsin convened a constitutional assembly in June. After much hesitation the Constitutional Committee of the Congress of People's Deputies decided to participate. Some 700 representatives adopted a draft constitution on July 12 that envisaged a bicameral legislature and the dissolution of the congress. The Supreme Soviet, the standing parliament, immediately rejected the draft and declared that the Congress of People's Deputies was the supreme lawmaking body and hence would decide on the new constitution. Because the new constitution would dissolve the congress, there was little likelihood that it would vote itself into oblivion.

The parliament was active in July, while the president was on vacation, and passed a raft of decrees that revised economic policy in order "to end the division of society." It also launched investigations of key advisers of the president, accusing them of corruption. The president returned in August and declared that he would deploy all means, including circumventing the constitution, to achieve new parliamentary elections.

The president launched his offensive on September 1 when he temporarily suspended Rutskoy as vice president. Two weeks later he declared that he would agree to early presidential elections provided the parliament also called elections. The parliament ignored him. Yeltsin then brought economist Yegor Gaidar back into the government as a deputy prime minister and minister for the economy. Predictably the Supreme Soviet rejected this appointment. On September 21 the president dissolved the Congress of People's Deputies and the Supreme Soviet and set new elections to a two-chamber parliament for December 11–12. According to the new plan, the lower house would have 450 deputies and be called the State Duma, the pre-1917 name of the Russian legislature. The Federation Council, which would bring together representatives from the 89 subdivisions of the Russian Federation, would play the role of an upper house.

The reaction of the Supreme Soviet was instantaneous. During an all-night session, chaired by Khasbulatov, it declared the president's decree null and void. Rutskoy was proclaimed president and took the oath on the constitution. He dismissed Yeltsin and key ministers Pavel Grachev (defense), Nikolay Golushko (security), and Viktor Yerin (interior). Russia now had two presidents and two ministers of defense, security, and interior. It was dual power in earnest.

Yeltsin received strong backing from leaders of the Western democracies and the other Soviet successor states. The Congress of People's Deputies adopted a hostile position; Khasbulatov, especially, was uncompromising. The Russian

Orthodox Church acted as host to desultory discussions between representatives of the parliament and the president. The political impasse developed into an armed conflict in the afternoon of October 3 after Moscow police failed to control a demonstration near the White House. The crowd, urged on by Rutskoy and Khasbulatov, who had barricaded themselves inside, sacked the mayor's office and routed the troops inside. Demonstrators then marched toward Ostankino, the television centre. A pitched battle ensued that resulted in many fatalities.

Khasbulatov called for the storming of the Kremlin. The military equivocated for several hours about how to respond to the president's call for action. Army tanks began to shell the White House on October 4. By late afternoon the charred upper floors of the building bore eloquent testimony to the viciousness of the conflict. Hostilities were stopped several times to allow some of those in the White House to leave, but Rutskoy and Khasbulatov stayed to the bitter end before surrendering.

The "second October Revolution" had lasted one day and cost perhaps 200 lives. It had been a close call. Yeltsin owed his victory to the military, the former KGB, and Ministry of Interior forces—not to support from the regions. The instruments of coercion had gained the most, and they would expect Yeltsin to reward them in the future. General Grachev became a key political figure.

The president moved quickly to consolidate his position. Many political parties and newspapers that had supported the parliament were banned, and Yeltsin called on those regional councils that had opposed him—by far the majority—to disband. Valery Zorkin, chairman of the Constitutional Court, was forced to resign, and the court was suspended. The prosecutor general was also removed and was replaced by a pro-Yeltsin lawyer. The chairman of the Federation of Independent Trade Unions, formerly dominated by trade unions, was also sacked, and the president took the opportunity to deprive trade unions of their administration of the social security system.

"Russia needs order," Yeltsin told the people in a television broadcast in November in introducing his new draft constitution, which was to be put to a referendum on December 12. The new basic law would confer enormous powers upon the president. The bicameral legislature, to sit for only two years, was restricted in crucial areas. The president could choose the prime minister even if the parliament objected and could appoint the military leadership without parliamentary approval. He would head and appoint the members of a new, more powerful Security Council. If a vote of no confidence in the government was passed, the president would be enabled to keep it in office for three months and could dissolve the parliament if it repeated the vote. He could veto any bill passed by a simple majority in the lower house, after which a two-thirds majority would be required for the legislation to be passed. The president could not be impeached for contravening the constitution. The central bank would become independent, but the president would need the approval of the State Duma to appoint the bank's governor, who would thereafter be independent of the parliament. Most political observers regarded the draft constitution as shaped by and for Yeltsin but unlikely to survive him.

Twenty-one parties and blocs garnered the requisite 100,000 signatures to qualify for participation in the December 12 election. Eight, including the Constitutional Democratic Party–Party of Popular Freedom led by Mikhail Astafyev and the Russian National People's Union headed by Sergey Baburin, were disqualified. Both these nationalist leaders were virulent opponents of the president. Russia's Choice, headed by Gaidar, was touted as the most democratic; the Yavlinsky-Boldyrev-Lukin bloc and the Russian Party of Unity and Accord were also broadly in favour of market reform; the Civic Union was the industrialists' lobby and keen on steady progress toward the market; and the Communist Party and the Agrarian Union opposed the market route.

Yeltsin won half a victory on December 12. The draft constitution was approved by approximately 60% of the voters (on a turnout of about 53%). The parliament elected on the same day, however, produced no clear majority in favour of the market economy and democracy. The most popular group, however, proved to be the Liberal Democratic Party (whose program was neither liberal nor democratic). Its leader, Vladimir Zhirinovsky, opposed almost everything that Yeltsin stood for, and in the weeks following the elections, he managed to offend and alarm many people in Russia and abroad with his Russian-chauvinistic declarations. (For tabulated election results, see *Political Parties,* above.)

The Economy. Russian gross domestic product (GDP) declined by 12% in 1993, after an approximate 20% drop in 1992. Industrial output was down by 16.4%, compared with 18.8% the year before. The harvest was 100 million tons, down 7 million from 1992. The budget deficit for the year was 10% of GDP. Another survey stated that the bottom 10% of the population had experienced an improvement in their standard of living. Unemployment, officially, was very low, at somewhat over 1% of the labour force. Workers were kept in employment by the liberal credit policy of the central bank, which provided huge subsidies to ailing enterprises. Negative rates of interest were charged, the normal practice throughout the commercial banking sector. The largest commercial banks were all tied to a particular branch of the economy and serviced their branch. The policies of the central bank led to many confrontations with the government, especially the Ministry of Finance, headed by Boris Fedorov. The latter regarded stabilization and the reduction of the budget deficit as top priorities, but bank chairman Gerashchenko disagreed, stating that industrial chaos and monopolies rendered these policies inoperative. At year's end inflation had reached 20% a month.

In July the central bank decreed that pre-1993 rubles were no longer legal tender, setting in motion panic attempts to change currency in the allotted time. Inflation increased as other republics sought to transfer vast amounts of rubles to Russia to circumvent the decree. The central bank estimated that Russian companies were holding $15.5 billion in Western accounts, eloquent testimony to their lack of confidence in the Russian economy. Not surprisingly, foreign investment was very modest. The promised aid from the International Monetary Fund was not forthcoming because it was contingent on economic reform and stabilization in Russia proceeding toward agreed targets. The European Community offered Russia trade concessions and a possible free-trade zone in 1998.

Russia and nine other former Soviet republics signed a treaty of economic union on September 24. Six states opted to stay within the ruble zone and have their fiscal monetary policy decided by Russia. By November, however, this union was unraveling after Russia insisted that its partner states transfer their gold and hard-currency reserves to the central bank. In December the CIS Interstate Bank was established to facilitate CIS trade transactions, with 5 billion rubles contributed as initial working capital. Russia's prorated share was 50%.

Foreign Affairs. Yeltsin and Foreign Minister Andrey Kozyrev concentrated on cultivating the Group of Seven states throughout the year, and their support proved important during the October showdown. In April Yeltsin and U.S. Pres. Bill Clinton declared themselves very satisfied after their summit in Vancouver, B.C. The U.S. extended a $1.6 billion aid package. In October Yeltsin made a successful visit to Japan and apologized for the treatment by the U.S.S.R. of Japanese prisoners of war during World War II, and he all but affirmed that the unfulfilled 1956 agreements on the contested Kuril Islands, by which Russia would return two of the islands, were still valid.

(MARTIN MCCAULEY)

SAN MARINO

The republic of San Marino is a landlocked enclave in northeastern Italy. Area: 61 sq km (24 sq mi). Pop. (1993 est.): 24,100. Cap.: San Marino. Monetary unit: Italian lira, with (Oct. 4, 1993) a free rate of 1,589 lire to U.S. $1 (2,407 lire = £1 sterling). The republic is governed by two *capitani reggenti,* or coregents, appointed every six months by a popularly elected Great and General Council. Executive power rests with the Congress of State, headed by the coregents and composed of three secretaries of state and seven ministers.

In 1993, during a historic first-ever visit, UN Secretary-General Boutros Boutros-Ghali praised San Marino as an exemplary republic whose independence of national spirit was tempered by deep concern for the world community. This official visit to the world's second smallest republic culminated with the conferment on the secretary-general of the Collar of the Knights of San Marino.

An important indication of national stability was furnished by the results of the spring elections. The Great and General Council, elected every five years, once more contained a majority of Christian Democrats and Socialists. However, following the balloting, controversy arose over a 1982 law that allowed nonresident voters to be reimbursed for travel to San Marino to cast their vote. Disappointed opposition parties called for the repeal of the law, which, they claimed, not only favoured government parties but also discriminated against women.

The University of San Marino launched a new master course in science and technology as part of a plan to enrich the activities of the five-year-old institution. Its programs in the humanities had already achieved international renown. The country also witnessed the live broadcast by national television of its own inaugural celebration.

(GREGORY O. SMITH)

This article updates the *Micropædia* article SAN MARINO.

SLOVAKIA

Slovakia is a landlocked state in central Europe. Area: 49,035 sq km (18,933 sq mi). Pop. (1993 est.): 5,329,000. Cap.: Bratislava. Monetary unit: Slovak koruna, with (Oct. 4, 1993) a free rate of 31.79 koruny to U.S. $1 (48.16 koruny = £1 sterling). President from March 2, 1993, Michal Kovac; prime minister, Vladimir Meciar.

Slovakia's first year of independence in 1993 was one of bewilderment, economic fluctuation, and painful adjustment after Czechoslovakia split into two nations. Because it had fairly poor relations with neighbouring Czech Republic and Hungary, Slovakia was relatively isolated and suffered from the weakness of its democratic institutions.

As far as relations with Prague were concerned, expectations in Bratislava had always been unrealistic about the extent to which the Czechs would maintain shared institutions from the past. The drastic differentiation insisted on by Prague was a severe shock to the new state. At Czech insistence, for example, the common currency argument rapidly dissolved, as an indirect result of which bilateral trade fell sharply. The Czechs insisted on frontier controls, and there were disputes over the division of Czechoslovakia's assets.

As far as Hungary was concerned, there were two main issues—the fate of the ethnic Hungarian minority (about 11% of the population) in Slovakia and the construction of the Gabcikovo-Nagymaros dam on the Danube, which the Hungarians saw as an environmental threat. The Slovak leadership made matters worse by its inexperience. It began by proclaiming that Slovakia would pursue a foreign policy independent of its neighbours and would not seek early integration into Europe, but it had to revise this fairly rapidly once the realities of its political and economic weakness had made themselves felt. Unemployment was high, the budget deficit was growing, foreign currency reserves were being depleted, foreign investment was low, and the economy deteriorated further. The rate of inflation, however, remained steady.

This state of affairs was paralleled in politics, in that the democratic structures were ignored or undermined by the dominant political figure in Slovakia, Vladimir Meciar, the prime minister. (*See* BIOGRAPHIES.) Meciar had emerged as the leading Slovak politician in the 1992 elections as head of the Movement for a Democratic Slovakia, and he took the country to independence. He proved to be a rather authoritarian figure who clamped down on many expressions of criticism and opposition, however. The media were one of his early targets. He had little time for the opposition in general, and he sought to counterbalance the effects of his declining popularity by intensifying Slovak nationalism, thereby exacerbating the Hungarian problem.

(GEORGE SCHÖPFLIN)

This article updates the *Macropædia* article CZECH AND SLOVAK REPUBLICS: *Slovakia.*

SLOVENIA

A republic of the extreme northwestern Balkans, Slovenia borders Austria to the north, Hungary to the east, Croatia to the southeast and south, the Adriatic Sea to the southwest, and Italy to the west. Area: 20,256 sq km (7,821 sq mi). Pop. (1993 est.): 1,997,000. Cap.: Ljubljana. Monetary unit: tolar, with (Oct. 4, 1993) a free rate of 115.48 tolarji to U.S. $1 (174.95 tolarji = £1 sterling). President in 1993, Milan Kucan; prime minister, Janez Drnovsek.

Slovenia strengthened its domestic political and economic stability in 1993 while continuing its opening to the West, in particular by forging new links with the European Community (EC), NATO, and Germany. On January 25 the Slovene National Assembly voted 60–25 to confirm a new coalition government made up of the Liberal Democrats, the strongest party in the Dec. 6, 1992, election, and the Christian Democrats, the second largest party. Janez Drnovsek, leader of the Liberal Democrats; was reconfirmed as prime minister; Lojze Peterle, leader of the Christian Democrats, became foreign minister.

The relative domestic political calm was upset by the seizure of a 120-ton consignment of arms at the airport in Maribor in July under the terms of the UN arms embargo covering the entire area of former Yugoslavia. An investigation was ordered by the government, which led to the arrest of seven persons. On September 24 the Ministry of Interior Affairs announced that the arms, in a deal of which the former minister of interior affairs was cognizant, had been destined for the Muslim-led government in Bosnia and Herzegovina. On October 2 the office of the president denied allegations that he had known about arms sales to Bosnia. On October 7 the head of the intelligence service resigned in connection with the affair.

In October it was officially revealed that Slovenia was looking after 29,000 refugees from former Yugoslavia, not 70,000 as had been previously claimed. On November 23 the National Assembly adopted tighter regulations on naturalization, requiring, among other things, a 10-year residence period (5 years of that time continuous).

In April in Luxembourg, Slovenia signed a so-called asymmetrical agreement with the EC under which Slovenia's exports would gain virtually unlimited access to EC markets while exports from the EC to Slovenia would remain subject to certain restrictions. Slovenia's relations with Croatia became tense in December when Slovenia announced the closure, "sometime in 1994," of the jointly financed and operated Krsko nuclear station because of Croatia's alleged failure to fulfill its financial obligations.

Slovenia's main trading partners in 1993 were Germany, Italy, France, and Austria. Its gross domestic product grew by 1% compared with 1992. Total exports were 4.8% lower than in 1992; imports in 1993 grew by 10.8% compared with 1992. About 55% of Slovenia's total foreign trade was with the countries of the EC. The inflation rate in 1993 was 33%. Industrial production in the January–November 1993 period was 3.4% lower than in the first 11 months of 1992. Unemployment in the January–October 1993 period was 14.9%, higher than in the first 10 months of 1992.

(K.F. CVIIC)

This article updates the *Macropædia* article BALKAN STATES: *Slovenia*.

SPAIN

A constitutional monarchy of southwestern Europe with coastlines on the Bay of Biscay, the Atlantic Ocean, and the Mediterranean Sea, Spain shares the Iberian Peninsula with Portugal; it includes the Balearic and Canary island groups, in the Mediterranean and the Atlantic, respectively, and enclaves in northern Morocco. Area: 504,783 sq km (194,898 sq mi). Pop. (1993 est.): 39,141,000. Cap.: Madrid. Monetary unit: Spanish peseta, with (Oct. 4, 1993) a free rate of 130.86 pesetas to U.S. $1 (198.25 pesetas = £1 sterling). King, Juan Carlos I; prime minister in 1993, Felipe González Márquez.

In the June 1993 elections, the Socialist Workers' Party (PSOE) of Prime Minister Felipe González Márquez won a plurality (159) of the 350 seats in the Congress of Deputies but fell 17 seats short of winning an overall parliamentary majority. A strong showing by the conservative Popular Party (PP), which won 141 seats and was led by José María Aznar, demonstrated the vulnerability of the ruling PSOE, which had been wracked by party infighting, a corruption scandal, and voter discontent over the country's intractable social and economic problems. (For tabulated results, see *Political Parties,* above.) Following a July 9 parliamentary vote of confidence, González, backed by his own party and Basque and Catalan nationalists, was returned to office for a fourth consecutive term. It was the first time since sweeping into office in 1982 that he had found himself heading a minority government.

The fragile state of the PSOE was underscored in October when regional presidential elections were held in the northwestern autonomous region of Galicia. Manuel Fraga Iribarne of the PP scored an overwhelming victory over the Socialists. It was the PSOE's worst defeat there since González came to power nationally. Fraga was also the founder of the PP (originally the Popular Alliance) and was widely believed to be the power behind Aznar, to whom he had relinquished leadership.

The early elections, initially scheduled for the fall, had been called by González partly in an effort to mend a fracture in the PSOE. Relations between supporters of González and the left-wing followers of Alfonso Guerra, deputy secretary-general of the PSOE, had worsened following the March release to the Supreme Court of a government auditors' report, which confirmed that in 1989–91 two senior party officials had operated front companies known as Filesa and Time Export and had been paid some 1 billion pesetas for consultancy services that were never rendered. The two had accepted tax-free payoffs from both domestic and foreign companies, apparently in exchange for government contracts. González accepted the resignations of the two officials and assumed direct control of the PSOE hierarchy in an attempt to reestablish himself as party leader. The PSOE had traditionally operated with González controlling the government and Guerra the PSOE structure. The prime minister's continuing political drift toward the centre, however, soured the arrangement. As a result, Guerra had been forced out of the government in 1991. González also insisted that the PSOE take full responsibility for the "Filesa Affair." José María Benegas, the PSOE organizational secretary and an ally of Guerra, offered to shoulder the blame as the third-highest-ranking official, but he was miffed by the lack of party loyalty. In a compromise agreement with the PSOE executive committee, González was given wider powers over the running of the election campaign in exchange for withdrawing his threat to step down unless a senior party official took responsibility for the party corruption and resigned.

During an emergency debate in the lower house on March 2, González presented a $2.5 billion package designed to combat unemployment. The provisions included spending on infrastructure, investment in small- and medium-scale enterprises, and measures to relax employment laws to help create new jobs. During the elections all the political parties and leading unions endorsed the creation of a pact for moderate salaries and labour reforms in exchange for employer guarantees not to initiate firings or massive layoffs. Prior to the July 27 first round of talks on the proposed accord, González struck a deal with the unions. He agreed not to amend the recently passed strike law if the unions would support the pact. Agreement on the measures, which included complex proposals for wages, pensions, labour reforms, and cuts in unemployment, could not be reached by the September 20 deadline. There was hope, however, that the pact would go into effect in 1994 as planned.

There was concern that the extra spending called for in the accord would boost the budget deficit, and reports of such deterioration circulated in early 1993. During the first four months, the budget deficit grew 13.7% over the 1992 figure. On May 13 the peseta was devalued 8%, the third depreciation of the currency in eight months. The move allowed the government to reduce official interest rates by 1.5 points to 11.5% on May 14 and to make further reductions to 11.25% on May 25 and 11% on July 2. A month later the government abandoned the remnants of its strong-currency, high-interest-rate policy. By September 3 official interest rates had fallen to 10%, the lowest level since the 1970s.

The country's unemployment rate of 22% was the worst in Western Europe. As a result of a looming budgetary crisis, the government was forced to call an emergency session of the Cortes (parliament) on August 5 to confront the crisis. Later that month the government was again urged to present a coherent economic policy and a credible budget by September 30.

The Basque terrorist organization Euzkadi ta Azkatasuna (ETA) continued to attack military and civilian targets during the year. ETA's July 5 kidnapping and holding for ransom of Julio Iglesias Zamora, the head of the Ikusi

Spanish Prime Minister Felipe González Márquez throws flowers as another Socialist candidate applauds at a rally leading up to the June 6 elections. Although the Socialists lost ground to the conservative Popular Party, they retained power.
REUTERS/BETTMANN

engineering company, gave impetus to a peace movement in the Basque country and Catalonia. Supporters of ETA clashed with peace campaigners during the mid-August annual fiestas in San Sebastian and Bilbao. Eighty persons were injured and 16 others were arrested. Bombs found in Barcelona on August 15 had allegedly been left by ETA. They represented the first such bomb attacks in the region since shortly before the 1992 Olympic Games. Though one bomb was deactivated, two others exploded in crowded restaurants, and five persons were wounded. In response, thousands of people in the region, including former U.S. president George Bush, who was on vacation in Catalonia, protested the action by wearing a special blue ribbon that had become the official badge of the peace movement. In early August, French and Basque police worked in coordination to arrest eight suspected ETA members for blackmailing 30 Basque companies and collecting over 1 billion pesetas in so-called revolutionary taxes to finance ETA's operations. Later that month the press reported that a new four-person ETA leadership had begun operations under the protection of radical left-wing groups based in Paris. In October ETA was suspected in the death of a Spanish air force general, who was shot while approaching his car.

In mid-October González announced that his government had reached an agreement with Catalan nationalists over concessions for the autonomous region. The accord meant that the prime minister could expect parliamentary backing for his austerity budget. (MICHAEL WOOLLER)

SWEDEN

A constitutional monarchy of northern Europe, Sweden occupies the eastern side of the Scandinavian Peninsula, with coastlines on the North and Baltic seas and the Gulf of Bothnia. Area: 449,964 sq km (173,732 sq mi). Pop. (1993 est.): 8,727,000. Cap.: Stockholm. Monetary unit: Swedish krona, with (Oct. 4, 1993) a free rate of 8.07 kronor to U.S. $1 (12.23 kronor = £1 sterling). King, Carl XVI Gustaf; prime minister in 1993, Carl Bildt.

It was apparent that Swedes would not be sorry to see the end of 1993. It was the third consecutive year of the country's deepest economic slump in more than 50 years. By many measures the crisis was worse in 1993 than in either of the two previous years, although there were firm signs that the bottom of the cycle had been reached by year's end.

There were two main problems: rapidly rising unemployment and a budget deficit that in relative terms was the largest in the Western world. Unemployment—including those involved in training schemes— reached 13% in 1993, a level that would have been unthinkable even two years earlier. It cruelly exposed the famed generosity of the Swedish welfare state and the centre-right coalition government's inability to fund it in a harsh economic climate.

The crisis forced the government to abandon its tax-cutting plans and switch its emphasis to cutting costs. At the centre of the program was a plan to reduce the budget by 81 billion kronor over five years. The government ruled out any attempt to stimulate the economy, such as a general cut in the value-added tax, on the grounds that the country could not afford it. There were still doubts about whether the government was doing enough to come to grips with the difficulties, and this, together with the sheer size of Sweden's borrowing requirement, weighed on the financial markets for much of the year. The result was a gradual weakening of the Swedish krona, which proved highly beneficial for the country's big multinational exporters. However, they were unable to exploit fully their newfound competitiveness because of the continuing recession in many of Sweden's main European markets, particularly Germany. In December the automaker Volvo A.B., yielding to intense pressure from share holders, canceled plans to merge its car and truck operations with Renault S.A. of France.

The economic problems made 1993 a difficult year for the four-party coalition government led by Prime Minister Carl Bildt. In the spring the coalition's survival was seriously threatened when New Democracy, a populist party outside the government, looked set to vote against it in a vote of confidence triggered by a row over the budget. In the end the crisis was averted following concessions from the government that brought tacit support for its policies from New Democracy for the rest of the year.

Sweden began negotiations to join the European Community (EC) in February, taking its place alongside Norway, Finland, and Austria in the enlargement discussions. Unlike some of its fellow applicants, Sweden chose not to strike an aggressive stance on any particular issue, although it was clear it was looking for sympathetic treatment in some areas, such as agriculture and alcohol policy. (Like Norway and Finland, Sweden had for many years operated an alcohol monopoly it wanted to retain on health grounds.) Membership in the EC was backed by all the major political parties, as well as the vast majority of business leaders.

Sweden had already signed up for the European Economic Area, the free-trade agreement between the EC and the seven-nation European Free Trade Association that was scheduled to take effect some time in 1994. The country was then to join the EC in January 1995, but the timetable would be tight. The negotiations had to be completed early in 1994, and a referendum had to be held specifically on the membership issue. Political leaders would have to work hard if they were going to persuade a skeptical population that the EC was worth joining. Opinion polls in 1993 showed a solid majority against membership.

Sweden's application to join the EC reflected a country in transition from semi-isolation on the fringes of Europe to full integration in it. The sense of uncertainty this had caused was enhanced by other changes within the country, such as the scaling back of the welfare state and the rise in unemployment. Some Swedes unfairly confused the two, blaming the EC integration process for cuts in services. Unemployment also brought with it increased social and racial tensions in a country with little experience of either.

(CHRISTOPHER BROWN-HUMES)

SWITZERLAND

A landlocked federal state in west central Europe, Switzerland consists of a confederation of 26 cantons (6 of which are demi-cantons). Area: 41,284 sq km (15,940 sq mi). Pop. (1993 est.): 6,996,000. Administrative cap., Bern; judicial cap., Lausanne. Monetary unit: Swiss franc, with (Oct. 4, 1993) a free rate of Sw F 1.42 to U.S. $1 (Sw F 2.15 = £1 sterling). President in 1993, Adolf Ogi.

Uncertainty about the future was widespread in Switzerland during 1993, with unemployment continuing to rise and drug addicts often being blamed for street crime. Even so, by comparison with their neighbours, the Swiss, certainly those outside the cities, had reason to feel their country could still be categorized as peaceful and, despite the prevailing recession, basically prosperous. As such, it remained a magnet for refugees, with many of them entering illegally before applying for political asylum.

The shock waves caused by the hairbreadth rejection—50.3% of votes in a nationwide referendum on Dec. 6, 1992—of the government's draft agreement on entering the European Economic Area (EEA), which would group the 12 members of the European Community (EC) and the 7 countries of the European Free Trade Association (EFTA), including Switzerland, soon subsided. There followed efforts by industrial chiefs, business leaders, and government ministers to persuade anti-EEA voters that the country's best prospects would ultimately be realized by full EC membership. A second vote was expected but not before 1996 at the earliest.

In the meantime, the government went ahead with measures to curtail the damage, which included a year's delay in bringing the EEA into operation. At EC headquarters in Brussels, Swiss representatives sought to convince officials that the unexpected result was no more than a passing aberration and in no way a change of heart. Their endeavours resulted in the EC foreign ministers' agreeing on Nov. 8, 1993, to pursue bilateral negotiations with Switzerland on transport (particularly the long-standing Swiss refusal to allow 40-ton trucks to transit their territory), joint research projects, removal of the restriction on EC agricultural products, and points arising from the EEA's entry into force early in 1994. Pro-Europeans could interpret this as showing the country was discreetly coming back on track. They were encouraged, too, by the approval in a November referendum of the government's proposal to introduce a value-added tax (VAT), initially at 6.5%, which would replace the 6.2% sales tax and yield an estimated additional $550 million for the federal treasury.

While the VAT was a step toward bringing Switzerland into line with EC practice, it was primarily one of a series of measures to increase revenue and cut spending because of a record $4.7 billion deficit in the 1994 budget. State employees, including those of the post office and railways, were informed that salaries could no longer be wholly index-linked (inflation was down to 3.4%), thus setting a precedent for the private sector.

By far the main preoccupation, however, was unemployment, which rose, as recession persisted, toward the 200,000 mark in a labour force of 3.5 million. The Geneva region, with 7% out of work, was particularly badly hit. Even if the figure was well below the European average, the impact was profound in a country where full employment had come to be regarded as virtually assured. With their members' real earnings falling for the second year in succession, trade unions were in no mood for compromise in their annual negotiations on setting wage levels under the collective labour contracts. These, incorporating index-linked increases, dated from the 1937 no-strike agreement that hitherto had ensured industrial peace.

Talk of strikes was in the air as winter set in, with demonstrators, though in no great numbers, taking to the streets bearing banners with demands such as "A halt to deterioration in conditions of work and life." Local government elections in Geneva in November produced a clear swing to the right, with the Socialists deprived of representation in the seven-member city council for the first time since 1945.

In November, Defense Minister Kaspar Villiger publicly expressed interest in U.S. Defense Secretary Les Aspin's suggestion that neutral countries, as well as former Warsaw Pact states, might consider an association with NATO amounting to something less than full membership.

(ALAN MCGREGOR)

UKRAINE

A republic in eastern Europe, Ukraine borders Russia to the north and east, the Black Sea to the south, Romania and Moldova to the southwest, and Hungary, Slovakia, and Poland to the west. Area: 603,700 sq km (233,100 sq mi). Pop. (1993 est.): 52,344,000. Cap.: Kiev. Monetary unit: karbovanets (Ukrainian coupon), with (Oct. 4, 1993) a free rate of 16,827 karbovantsy = U.S. $1 (25,493 karbovantsy = £1 sterling). President in 1993, Leonid Kravchuk; prime ministers, Leonid Kuchma to September 22 and, until September 27 Yefim Zvagilsky; vacant thereafter.

Ukraine began 1993 in a state of "economic crisis" that grew more severe with time: inflation approached 50% per month; and the 1992 deficit of 1,325 trillion karbovantsy was still on the rise; and Russia reduced oil and gas supplies and raised its prices close to world levels. The Cabinet of Ministers created an extraordinary committee, headed by Prime Minister Leonid Kuchma, which introduced an emergency plan to prevent economic collapse, advocating strict limits on the growth of the money supply, rapid privatization, and incentives for foreign investment. By August, however, the currency had begun a "free fall," dropping from under 6,000 to the dollar on August 12 to 19,000 one week later.

Industrial output also fell sharply in the summer, partly because of a miners' strike that began in the Donbass coalfields in early June and soon spread to other industries. The workers' action became political in nature, with demands for pay raises to match increases in the cost of living, calls for economic autonomy for the Donbass or its transfer to Russia, and demands for a confidence vote in the government and presidency. Pres. Leonid Kravchuk responded with economic concessions and called for new elections for both Parliament and the presidency. Viktor Pynzenyk, Kravchuk's deputy prime minister with responsibility for economic reform, resigned in late August, claiming that the conservative Parliament was making economic reforms impossible.

By late autumn Ukraine appeared to have come full circle, returning to state control after a brief "market" experiment. Kravchuk accepted Kuchma's resignation and took over the government himself. New laws were established to fix prices for wholesale and retail goods. Critical problems in the energy sector were also resolved in a controversial fashion when on October 21 Parliament lifted the 1990 moratorium on commissioning new nuclear reactors. On the same day, Parliament decided not to shut down the Chernobyl atomic power plant by the end of 1993 as originally scheduled, a decision that provoked warnings from the European Community and the International Atomic Energy Agency about safety problems with Ukraine's reactors.

About 34% of Ukraine's electricity was being produced by nuclear power. That percentage was likely to increase (even though potentially serious accidents had occurred at several of its nuclear power stations) because Russian oil and gas had to be purchased with precious hard currency.

Ukraine's strategic nuclear weapons elicited world concern as well. Parliament equivocated over whether to ratify the START I Treaty, and there was an extended debate about whether Ukraine's 46 SS-24 strategic missiles were even covered by that treaty in the original Lisbon Protocol. Ukraine insisted that disarmament could not take place without international guarantees of its security. On November 18, Parliament voted to ratify the START I Treaty and the Lisbon Protocol, with the reservation that Article 5, which committed Ukraine to joining the nonproliferation treaty as a nonnuclear state, would not apply. Moreover, ratification was made conditional on adequate compensation for the delivery of the tactical nuclear warheads delivered to Russia in 1992, foreign compensation to cover the costs of disarmament, and security guarantees of Ukraine's existing borders—none of which was immediately forthcoming. However, by year's end Ukraine had dismantled 17 of the SS-24s as a show of good faith.

Territorial issues were perhaps Ukraine's main political concern and were the focal point of relations with Russia. Kravchuk and Russian Pres. Boris Yeltsin held several meetings during the year, the most significant of which was at Massandra in the Crimea on September 3. Yeltsin declared (without contradiction from Kravchuk) after the meeting that Ukraine had agreed to sell its half of the Black Sea Fleet to Russia and that Ukraine would permit Russia to dismantle nuclear weapons currently in the country in return for uranium extracted from their warheads. The accord was not ratified by the Ukrainian Parliament, however, and the affair diminished Kravchuk's credibility in the country. Parliament later approved a military doctrine, which called for a reduction in the size of Ukraine's army from more than 525,000 troops to 450,000 by 1995.

In July, Russia laid claim to the Crimean city of Sevastopol (on the grounds that it was not included in the 1954 treaty that ceded Crimea to Ukraine), thereby exacerbating an already tense situation in the peninsula, which had a large Russian majority and was the home port of the Black Sea Fleet. Crimean separatists added to Kiev's woes.

Ukraine faced other threats to its current territory as well. Ruthenians tried to establish a provisional government in Transcarpathia; Donetsk province expressed a desire to join the Russian Federation; and Romania maintained its claim to parts of Bessarabia and the Chernovtsy (Romanian: Cernauti) region.

By October the Kravchuk government had laid the groundwork for a future regime based on stronger central control. Economic recovery, however, proved elusive. Kravchuk had become the sole figure in political life, though Kuchma remained popular. Neither the Rukh nor any of the 29 political parties registered by year's end had presented a viable alternative economic program or fielded a potential rival for the presidency. Indeed, a feature of 1993 was the political decline of "democratic" candidates. On October 5 the Ministry of Justice officially registered the Communist Party of Ukraine, with a reported membership of 128,000. The election bill approved by Parliament in November established 450 single-mandate electoral districts. Ukraine's "first past the post" election law would likely favour the Communists, who had a powerful organization in the eastern cities that should ensure that their candidates received a plurality of the votes. (DAVID R. MARPLES)

JAMES HILL—THE NEW YORK TIMES

Coal miners, working at a mine in Donetsk, ride an elevator to the surface. The miners went on strike in June to demand better pay and increased autonomy for the eastern Donbass region of Ukraine, where a majority of the people were ethnic Russians.

UNITED KINGDOM

A constitutional monarchy in northwestern Europe and member of the Commonwealth, the United Kingdom comprises the island of Great Britain (England, Scotland, and Wales) and Northern Ireland, together with many small islands. Area: 244,110 sq km (94,251 sq mi), including 3,218 sq km of inland water but excluding the crown dependencies of the Channel Islands and Isle of Man. Pop. (1993 est.): 58,080,000. Cap.: London. Monetary unit: pound sterling, with (Oct. 4, 1993) a free rate of £0.66 to U.S. $1 (U.S. $1.52 = £1 sterling). Queen, Elizabeth II; prime minister in 1993, John Major.

Domestic Affairs. For the first seven months of 1993, the U.K.'s domestic politics were dominated by the struggle of Prime Minister John Major (*see* BIOGRAPHIES) to secure Parliament's approval of his bill on the Maastricht Treaty on European Union. He finally succeeded, but at considerable political cost. The ruling Conservative Party was seen as divided, and Major's own leadership was widely criticized, not least within his own party. With the country's economy struggling to recover from recession, few people were surprised when the Conservatives lost votes in the county elections held in May. What was noteworthy, however, was the unprecedented size of the swing against the party in those contests and in two parliamentary by-elections.

The European Communities (Amendment) Bill was meant to commit the U.K. to the Maastricht Treaty. The treaty, agreed among the 12 European Community (EC) leaders in 1991, had given the U.K. the right to opt out of two components: monetary union and the "social chapter," which sought to establish basic employment rights across the EC. Major faced domestic opposition on two fronts. The Labour Party and most of the smaller parties wanted the U.K. to endorse the social chapter; on the other hand, a minority of up to 40 of the 334 Conservative members of Parliament (MPs) disliked the Maastricht Treaty altogether.

As a tactical maneuver, the Conservative rebels decided to back Labour demands for a separate parliamentary vote on the social chapter. After a series of arcane procedural disputes, Foreign Secretary Douglas Hurd was forced to give way. Matters came to a head on July 22. MPs had two proposals before them. Labour's resolution, endorsing the social chapter, was defeated by one vote. Then the government's resolution (which merely asked MPs to "take note" of its policy on the social chapter) was also defeated, 324–316, with 23 Tories voting against their own government. Major immediately announced that a debate would be held the following day on a motion of confidence linked to the Maastricht Treaty and threatened to hold a general election if he lost. With the Conservatives trailing badly in the opinion polls, many of the party's MPs seemed likely to lose their seats. The rebels surrendered and voted for the confidence motion. The U.K. finally ratified the treaty on August 2.

The impression of an administration being buffeted by events was reinforced by actions in other areas. In October 1992, Michael Heseltine, president of the Board of Trade, had declared that 31 of British Coal's 50 remaining collieries would be closed. Faced with a public outcry and resistance by some Conservative MPs, Heseltine had to delay the closures pending a wide-ranging review. On March 25, 1993, Heseltine said that 12 of the 31 collieries would be reprieved for the time being. He declined, however, to tackle the underlying reason why so many pits were uncompetitive: the fact that gas and nuclear power received preferential treatment under the government's energy policy. As a result, stocks of unsold coal built up. It soon became clear that the 12 reprieved pits could not attract sufficient customers in the prevailing market conditions. On October 20, Timothy Eggar, the energy minister, announced that they would be closed after all and that further closures would be needed. By the mid-1990s, Britain would have only about 15 working collieries, compared with 211 as recently as 1981.

The government also took controversial action with respect to another state-run industry: the railways. On November 5 a bill to privatize many of British Rail's services passed into law. The intention was not to sell BR in its entirety but rather to invite private companies to tender for individual routes or groups of routes. The government's hope was that an injection of private-sector finance and management skills would increase efficiency and expand consumer choice. Critics of the bill (including BR's management) argued that services would decline and prices would rise. Ministers were undeterred by these critics or by opinion-poll evidence that 70% of electors opposed the measure.

Cabinet ministers faced even greater trouble over plans to introduce standard nationwide tests for all 14-year-old children at state schools. This reform was linked to the intentions of John Patten, the education secretary, to publish "league tables" showing the exam results of all schools in the state sector. His plans faced criticism from two groups: government advisers, who complained that the proposed

SIMON WALKER—TIMES NEWSPAPERS LTD.

Tourists peer through a fence at Buckingham Palace. To help raise money for the repair of Windsor Castle, which was damaged by fire in 1992, Queen Elizabeth II opened the palace in August and September, for the first time allowing visitors to see the State Apartments and their collection of artwork and furnishings.

tests were over-complicated, bureaucratic, and time-consuming; and all of the unions and professional associations representing head teachers and classroom teachers, who complained both about the rigidity of the tests and about the plan for league tables. Backed by most parent groups, the unions voted to boycott the new tests, scheduled for June. Very few tests were conducted, and no league tables could be published. Patten asked the new chief curriculum adviser, Sir Ron Dearing, to sort out the mess. When Dearing reported back in August, he endorsed many of the criticisms and proposed radical cuts in the testing program for future years. Patten accepted recommendations and expressed hope that an accommodation could be reached with teachers groups before the next examinations, scheduled for June 1994.

On June 21, Heseltine, possibly the most charismatic member of the Cabinet, suffered a heart attack, which put him out of action at a time when the prime minister needed all the morale-raising support he could muster. Three days later Michael Mates, a junior minister for Northern Ireland, was forced to resign from the government over allegations that he had acted unwisely in relation to Asil Nadir, a fugitive businessman who had fled to Northern Cyprus while on bail facing criminal charges. Mates confirmed press reports that he had given Nadir a watch inscribed "Don't let the buggers get you down." Major was embarrassed not only by Mates's resignation but also by the charge that Nadir had used stolen money to make donations totaling £440,000 to the Tories. Sir Norman Fowler, the Conservative Party chairman, promised that the party would repay any money that proved to be stolen. By the end of the year, however, proof was still elusive, and none of the money had been repaid.

Further unsolicited aggravation was caused in October by the publication of Baroness Thatcher's much-anticipated book about her 11½ years as Prime Minister Margaret Thatcher, *The Downing Street Years*. Media reports of the memoirs concentrated on her criticism of Major's period as her chancellor of the Exchequer. She also castigated Major for being lukewarm toward her during her struggle to remain prime minister in November 1990. Thatcher herself attracted criticism, however, for the way her memoirs found shortcomings in almost all her erstwhile colleagues and none in herself. Although the book attracted enormous publicity and broke British publishing sales records, Major seemed to emerge from the episode with his reputation somewhat less tarnished than Thatcher's.

Labour Party leader John Smith devoted much of his energies in 1993 to a battle over the role of trade unions inside the party. He believed that Labour would win greater public support if the party were seen to be controlled more by its own members and less by the unions. Specifically, he proposed that unions should cease to have any votes in the selection of Labour's parliamentary candidates. Despite opposition from the leaders of two of Britain's unions, Smith's plan was approved by a narrow margin at Labour's annual conference in Brighton in September.

Of possibly equal long-term significance were signs of increasing local cooperation between the Labour Party and the Liberal Democrats (LDP). In the local elections in May, the Conservatives lost control of 15 of the 16 county councils they had previously held. In most cases no single party gained control, and in most of these counties Labour and the LDP reached some kind of power-sharing agreement. These coalitions were widely seen as a possible prelude to power sharing at Westminster should a future general election leave no single party with an outright majority. Meanwhile, the LDP was able to claim to wield more power than the Conservatives in Britain's county halls. Its success in the county elections was underscored by record-breaking victories in by-elections in Newbury (Berkshire) and Christchurch (Dorset), two southern England constituencies that had returned Conservative MPs with large majorities in the April 1992 general election. These LDP victories reduced the Conservatives' overall majority in the House of Commons from 21 to 17 and added to Major's problems of governing with a small majority.

The year saw pressure mount for new measures to protect the privacy of individuals from media intrusion. In January a government-appointed committee reported that voluntary self-regulation by the press had failed and called for a statutory press-complaints commission. In March an all-party committee of MPs also advocated the creation of a new commission, backed by an ombudsman, with the power to fine newspapers, order corrections, and award compensation. In July the Lord Chancellor published a consultation paper on privacy; this favoured a right of privacy enforceable through the civil courts. Pressure built up still further in November after the *Sunday Mirror* and *Daily Mirror,* two mass-circulation newspapers, published photographs taken secretly of the Princess of Wales exercising at a private gymnasium.

In an attempt to avoid new laws, most tabloid papers, including the Mirror group, announced that they would tone down their reporting of the royal family. They took as their occasion an announcement on December 3 by the Princess of Wales that she was withdrawing from public life in order to spend more time with her sons, Harry and William. The Princess made it clear that her decision had been provoked, in part, by the aggressive and intrusive attention of the tabloid press.

Economic Affairs. After two years of contraction, the U.K. economy grew by around 2% in 1993. The increase, which was well above the 1.25% growth predicted early in the year, was the first calendar-year rise since 1990. This brought some relief to the government, but it was not enough to cause a significant reduction in unemployment, which remained at 2.8 million–3 million, or more than 10% of the labour force, throughout the year. Other economic indicators were more favourable. On January 26 the Bank of England reduced its base rate to 6%, the lowest since 1977, while an additional cut to 5.5% in November brought the rate to its lowest level in 21 years. In June annual inflation fell to 1.2%, the lowest since 1964. Following sterling's departure from Europe's exchange-rate mechanism (ERM) in September 1992, the pound remained broadly stable throughout 1993, at around DM 2.50 and $1.50.

In his March budget, Chancellor of the Exchequer Norman Lamont announced that the U.K.'s public-sector borrowing requirement for 1992–93 had risen to £36.5 billion, and it was projected to climb to £50 billion, or 8% of gross domestic product (GDP), in 1993–94. He introduced a package of tax increases, some designed to take effect immediately (reduced income tax allowances and higher excise duties on gasoline, alcohol, and tobacco) and some to take effect over the following two years (including reduced tax relief on mortgages for home ownership and the extension of the value-added tax to cover domestic fuel).

Lamont's budget attracted the criticism that it was, in general, unwise to raise taxes when the economy was still in the early stages of recovery and, specifically, wrong to impose a value-added tax on domestic fuel, which would have a disproportionate effect on poorer households. This controversy added weight to the view, already widespread within the Conservative Party, that Lamont was a liability as chancellor. He was criticized for his handling of the econ-

Mourners accompany the bodies of a mother, father, and child killed in an October bombing in Belfast by the Irish Republican Army. Although there were talks during the year between the governments of the U.K. and Ireland, the violence in Northern Ireland continued, with a number of people on both sides killed.

JOHN GILES—PRESS ASSOCIATION

omy in the buildup to "Black Wednesday"—the day sterling left the ERM—and, more generally, for his lacklustre performances in the House of Commons and on television. On May 27, Major bowed to this pressure and sacked Lamont, replacing him with Kenneth Clarke. (*See* BIOGRAPHIES.)

In his first budget, on November 30, Clarke increased taxes yet again, mainly by reducing tax allowances. He declared that his aim was to accelerate the reduction in government borrowing and bring the U.K.'s public-sector finances back into balance by the end of the decade. The combined impact of the two 1993 budgets was to raise taxes by £14 billion, or more than 2% of GDP—the biggest single-year rise in taxation in peacetime. However, by setting out his austere policy with some panache, Clarke managed in the first instance to avoid the kind of criticisms from within his party that had engulfed Lamont.

Foreign Affairs. Throughout 1993 the U.K. continued to send humanitarian aid to the former Yugoslavia and to resist calls for other forms of military intervention. More British troops were sent to assist the distribution of aid supplies; their numbers grew from 1,800 in August 1992 to almost 3,000 by late 1993. The government continued to support an arms embargo against all local armies, including that of Bosnia and Herzegovina. This policy brought the U.K. into conflict with the German and U.S. governments. In April, Hurd told Parliament, "We should not pretend that, from outside, we can ensure a solution. Even a prolonged military commitment by the international community could not guarantee that."

In August the British government began "Operation Irma" to airlift casualties from the former Yugoslavia who were in urgent need of medical treatment. The operation was named after Irma Hadzimuratovic, a five-year-old girl whose plight was reported on British television and immediately attracted massive public sympathy. She was taken to London's Great Ormond Street Hospital for treatment for meningitis and an operation to remove shrapnel. Altogether 21 war victims were taken to the U.K.

The U.K. and China remained deadlocked in negotiations over the future of Hong Kong. In March, Chris Patten, the governor of the colony, published a bill to amend the structure of its Legislative Council to ensure that it was more representative of the people of Hong Kong. He announced that elections would be held in 1995 and sought China's commitment to respect the results and not disband the council when sovereignty of the colony reverted to China in 1997. China refused to give that undertaking. It argued that Patten's proposal infringed previous agreements between the U.K. and China. Talks between the two countries resumed in April but made little progress, and relations were strained at the end of the year.

Just before Christmas, immigration officials refused entry to 28 Jamaican tourists and flew them back to Kingston. The Home Office denied that the evictions were racially motivated and that the action indicated plans to impose visa requirements on Jamaican visitors in the future.

Northern Ireland. On April 23, Sir Patrick Mayhew, the U.K.'s Northern Ireland secretary, launched a new initiative to bring peace to the province. He proposed a "substantial" transfer of power from London to local politicians and the creation of a select committee of MPs at Westminster to monitor those powers retained by the U.K. government. Mayhew ruled out any joint Anglo-Irish responsibility for Northern Ireland.

Meanwhile, two separate series of private dialogues were established with a view to ending 25 years of conflict. Both were kept secret for some months; details began to emerge only toward the end of 1993. One dialogue was between John Hume, the leader of the Social Democratic and Labour Party—a nonviolent, nationalist party composed mainly of Roman Catholics—and Gerry Adams, the president of Sinn Fein, the political wing of the Irish Republican Army (IRA). The second dialogue was between the IRA and the British government. This took place through intermediaries; when its existence was disclosed in November, Major insisted that its purpose was not to negotiate but to clarify existing policies. Major said that the dialogue had started in February 1993 following the receipt of a message from the IRA that it regarded the conflict as over and sought advice on how to end it. The IRA disputed this interpretation of its February message.

Both dialogues contributed to a belief in London and Dublin that new opportunities existed to bring an end to the conflict. On December 15 in London, Major and Albert Reynolds, prime minister of the Irish Republic, launched a joint peace initiative. They agreed that Northern Ireland could be reunited with the republic if—and only if—majorities in both Ulster and the republic voted for reunification. They also agreed that if the IRA ended its campaign of violence, it could join full negotiations three months after a cease-fire.

The Major-Reynolds initiative was supported by the main opposition parties in London and Dublin, by Hume, and by the Official Ulster Unionists. It was opposed by the Democratic Unionists, led by Ian Paisley. However, the key to the initiative's success lay with the IRA. It embarked on a series of internal discussions; by the end of 1993 it had not announced whether it would accept or reject the proposals.

Terrorist actions by both the IRA and Protestant paramilitary groups continued throughout 1993. The IRA won few friends with a midday bomb attack on a busy shopping centre in Warrington, Cheshire, in March in which two local boys were killed. Five weeks later another IRA bomb attack caused damage worth £1 billion to buildings in the City of London.

Within Northern Ireland a spate of killings culminated in October with 23 deaths from terrorism in a single week. These included 10 deaths (including the man who planted the bomb) from an IRA attack on a Belfast fish-and-chip shop and seven deaths when two members of the Protestant Ulster Freedom Fighters opened up machine-gun fire in a Londonderry bar frequented by both Catholics and Protestants. (PETER KELLNER)

See also *Commonwealth of Nations,* above; *Dependent States,* below.

VATICAN CITY STATE

The independent sovereignty of Vatican City State is surrounded by but is not part of Rome. As a state with territorial limits, it is properly distinguished from the Holy See, which constitutes the worldwide administrative and legislative body for the Roman Catholic Church. Area: 44 ha (109 ac). Pop. (1993 est.): 1,800. As sovereign pontiff, John Paul II is the chief of state. Vatican City is administered by a pontifical commission of five cardinals headed by the secretary of state, in 1993 Angelo Cardinal Sodano.

In 1993, a year dominated by international activity, Pope John Paul II's first-ever visit to Albania highlighted Vatican diplomacy. During the spring visit, the pope ordained four Albanian bishops in an effort to strengthen the church's pastoral role in a country that had long regarded the church with hostility.

The Vatican expressed concern for the troubled Balkans by repeatedly calling for an end to hostilities in Bosnia and Herzegovina and by making a substantial donation to the UN secretary-general for the support of Bosnian refugees. The president of Slovenia also visited the Vatican.

As part of his apostolic mission, the pope made his 10th visit to Africa and toured in Benin, Uganda, and The Sudan. In August he made brief visits to Jamaica and Mexico en route to Denver, Colo., where he met with U.S. Pres. Bill Clinton and joined some 400,000 celebrants at the World Youth Day festivities.

Bishops from as far away as Madagascar and Papua New Guinea visited the Vatican, and many distinguished visitors, including the patriarch of the Ethiopian Orthodox Church and Jerusalem's Ashkenazi chief rabbi were received by the pontiff. In September the Vatican sent a representative to Beijing (Peking) to attend the Chinese National Athletic Games. Roger Cardinal Etchegaray was the highest-ranking church official to visit China since 1949. In Jerusalem on December 30, after 17 months of negotiations, Israel and the Vatican signed an agreement to establish diplomatic relations, although some of the legal details still had to be worked out.

On the domestic front the Vatican was assailed by an increasing deficit, which was exacerbated by the need to finance a newly created pension fund for some 2,000 Vatican lay employees. In October the Holy See agreed to help Milan magistrates determine if the Vatican bank had been used to disguise bribes to Italian officials. In November the 73-year-old pope fell during a Vatican audience and suffered a fractured shoulder joint and a dislocated shoulder. (GREGORY O. SMITH)

See also RELIGION: *Roman Catholic Church.*

This article updates the *Micropædia* article VATICAN CITY.

YUGOSLAVIA

A federal republic comprising the republics of Serbia and Montenegro, Yugoslavia borders Hungary to the north, Romania to the northeast, Bulgaria to the southeast, Macedonia and Albania to the south, the Adriatic Sea to the southwest, and Croatia and Bosnia and Herzegovina to the west. Area: 102,173 sq km (39,449 sq mi). Pop. (1993 est.): 10,561,000. Cap.: Belgrade. Monetary unit: Yugoslav new dinar, with (Oct. 4, 1993) a free rate of 104.24 new dinars to U.S. $1 (157.92 new dinars = £1 sterling); hyperinflation has caused major ongoing devaluations since the beginning of 1992. Presidents in 1993, Dobrica Cosic until June 1 and, from June 25, Zoran Lilic; prime minister, Radoje Kontic.

Many observers might think it remarkable, but the Socialist (former Communist) regime of Slobodan Milosevic, president of Serbia since 1989, managed to maintain and even consolidate its power in 1993. To be sure, it was helped by the hugely popular territorial conquests, constantly glorified by the state-controlled mass media in Serbia, and applauded by Belgrade-backed Serbs in Croatia and Bosnia and Herzegovina, even in the teeth of widespread but ineffectual international disapproval. Milosevic's political strength overcame growing economic hardship and hyperinflation. In August Yugoslavia reached a monthly inflation rate of 1,880%; in December it was about 300,000% and still rising. UN-imposed economic sanctions continued to hit Yugoslavia hard, but thanks to its porous borders with Albania, Bulgaria, and Macedonia plus the tacit support of its close ally, Greece, it continued to import sufficient quantities of essentials such as oil and to export enough goods (including arms) to cover about 80% of the cost of its imports.

Following earlier extensive purges of its officer corps, on August 26 the Yugoslav Army (the former Yugoslav Na-

RON HAVIV—SABA

Zeljko Raznatovic, known as "Arkan," holds up a live tiger cub as he stands before his comrades in the Serbian terrorist group the Tigers. Wanted by Interpol for crimes that included murder, Raznatovic failed to win reelection to parliament as head of the Serbian Unity Party.

tional Army) was placed under the control of Gen. Momcilo Perisic, a Milosevic loyalist and veteran of the wars in Croatia and Bosnia. In June Milosevic secured the elimination from his post as president of Yugoslavia a strong Serb nationalist and his erstwhile ally, the writer Dobrica Cosic, who had attempted to exercise his powers as commander in chief by independently summoning army generals to see him.

Serbia's divided opposition proved unable to offer a serious challenge to Milosevic. The police broke up a popular demonstration in Belgrade on June 1 and severely beat and subsequently arrested Vuk Draskovic, the charismatic leader of the opposition Serbian Renewal Movement. In October a series of clashes over the policy toward Bosnia occurred between Milosevic and his erstwhile protégé and ally Vojislav Seselj, leader of the semifascist Serbian Radical Party. Seselj, a Bosnian Serb and bitter enemy of Radovan Karadzic, Milosevic's man in Bosnia, accused Milosevic and Karadzic of plotting to sell out in Bosnia in exchange for the lifting of international sanctions against Yugoslavia. When Seselj called for a vote of no confidence in the government, Milosevic dissolved the parliament and called new elections. During the campaign Seselj was portrayed in the state-controlled media as a war criminal guilty of serious atrocities in the war in Croatia in 1991 and Bosnia in 1992. Milosevic's main ally in the campaign was Zeljko Raznjatovic, who aligned his Party of Serbian Unity with Milosevic's Serbian Socialist Party. Better known by his nom de guerre, Arkan, Raznjatovic had been a deputy from Kosovo since December 1992, but he was also notorious in Europe as a criminal and a spy for the Yugoslav security service who had reportedly enriched himself in the wars in Croatia and Bosnia. In the event, however, Milosevic failed to achieve a majority, winning only 123 of the 250 seats at stake in the December 19 polling.

Throughout the year pressure was maintained—on the whole successfully—by Belgrade against the political opposition in Kosovo, the 90% ethnic Albanian province fully reintegrated into Serbia. Aware of the local Albanians' weakness against the Serbs as well as of the inability of Albania to come to their rescue, the moderate Kosovar leadership under its unofficial president, Ibrahim Rugova, put up no serious opposition. Belgrade's confidence over Kosovo was demonstrated by its decision earlier in the year to expel the international monitoring group stationed there since 1992 at the request of the Conference on Security and Cooperation in Europe. This decision provoked Western protests but no retaliation. The Milosevic regime also managed to maintain political control in the volatile Sandzak, an area with a Muslim majority next door to Bosnia.

In the second half of the year, the Milosevic regime ran into increasing political trouble in Montenegro, Serbia's small but strategically important federal partner. As early as March, Montenegro's president, Momir Bulatovic, had demonstrated a tendency toward independent action by taking into the new government members of the opposition Liberal Alliance, which had been critical of Milosevic's policy of curtailing Montenegro's autonomy. As part of its policy of diversifying Montenegro's foreign relations, Bulatovic visited Albania in September. Soon afterward, a large convoy carrying food for Montenegro was halted on the Montenegrin-Serbian border, causing an upsurge of anti-Serbian feeling. A week earlier the Liberal Alliance, with 13 seats in the 85-seat Montenegrin parliament, had left the coalition in protest against Montenegro's subordinate relationship with Serbia. The People's Party (14 seats) proposed a vote of no confidence in the government. (K.F. CVIIC)

This article updates the *Macropædia* article BALKAN STATES: *Yugoslavia*.

North America

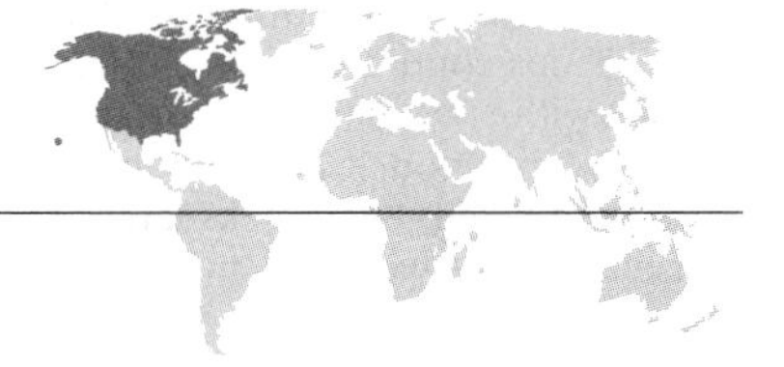

CANADA

Canada is a federal parliamentary state and member of the Commonwealth covering North America north of conterminous United States and east of Alaska. Area: 9,970,610 sq km (3,849,-674 sq mi). Pop. (1993 est.): 28,149,000. Cap.: Ottawa. Monetary unit: Canadian dollar, with (Oct. 4, 1993) a free rate of Can$1.34 to U.S. $1 (Can$2.03 = £1 sterling). Queen, Elizabeth II; governor-general in 1993, Ramon Hnatyshyn; prime ministers, Brian Mulroney, Kim Campbell from June 25, and, from November 4, Jean Chrétien.

Domestic Affairs. Canada changed its government in a national election on Oct. 25, 1993. The Liberal Party swept into power, capturing 177 of the 295 seats in the House of Commons, more than twice the number it had held at the dissolution of Parliament. More extraordinary was the collapse of the Progressive Conservative Party, which had governed Canada since 1984. From 155 members in the Commons, it was reduced to a corporal's guard of only 2 members, one from New Brunswick and one from Quebec. A party dedicated to securing the independence of Quebec, the Bloc Québécois, captured 54 of the French-speaking ridings in the province to become the official opposition in Parliament. The Reform Party, a protest movement coming from the western provinces, won almost as many seats as the Bloc, having drawn away support from the Conservatives in Ontario and the western provinces. Although the Canadian political scene was left in a confused state by the election, it was significant that a party strongly committed to maintaining the country's federal structure had won a solid victory at the polls.

Preparations for the election were set in motion when Prime Minister Brian Mulroney, leader of the Progressive Conservatives, announced his retirement on February 24. In the search for a successor, a 46-year-old Vancouver lawyer, Kim Campbell (*see* BIOGRAPHIES), soon became the front-runner. Campbell was a new face on the Canadian political scene: a woman from the West, who was intelligent and articulate in both English and French. Although her federal political experience dated only from 1988, she had risen rapidly in Mulroney's Cabinet, having served as minister of justice and, briefly, as minister of national defense. Public opinion polls suggested that her prospects of leading the party to a third election victory were good. Deterred by Campbell's sudden popularity, more experienced ministers in the Mulroney Cabinet decided not to challenge her for the leadership. In the end one principal rival emerged: Minister of the Environment Jean Charest, a bilingual, 34-year-old lawyer from Sherbrooke, south of Montreal. The five candidates who eventually entered the race crisscrossed the country seeking delegate support before the leadership convention in Ottawa on June 9–13. At the convention Campbell won a narrow victory on the second ballot, gathering 1,817 votes to Charest's 1,630. She became the second woman to lead a national political party in Canada, the first being Audrey McLaughlin, who had been chosen leader of the New Democratic Party (NDP) in 1989. Campbell was sworn in as Canada's first woman prime minister on June 25.

The new prime minister's first move was to reduce the size of the 35-member Mulroney Cabinet to 25 through eliminating or merging departments. Her Cabinet consisted of 18 holdovers from the Mulroney government and 7 new

With his wife, Aline, Jean Chrétien celebrates the sweeping victory of the Liberal Party in the elections on October 25. Chrétien replaced Kim Campbell of the Progressive Conservative Party, which won only two seats in the House of Commons, as Canada's prime minister.
MOE DOIRON—SYGMA

faces. The new administration went to the people with a blunt message: the annual national deficit of $35 billion threatened to undercut all the operations of government; if social and economic programs were to be continued, the deficit had to be drastically reduced. Campbell pledged to eliminate the operating deficit in five years but offered few hints of how she would deal with Canada's worrisome unemployment rate, which stood at more than 11% of the labour force. The Campbell administration was burdened by the unpopularity of Mulroney and the government he had led for nine years. The Mulroney policy of free trade with the U.S. and the sweeping tax on goods and services he instituted were unpopular with many Canadians. Campbell defended these measures while claiming that her government would be more accountable to the popular will. She wished, as a commentator put it, to change the face of the Mulroney government without changing the governing party. In the event, her attempt proved futile.

The real danger to the Progressive Conservatives came from two regional parties that threatened to cut into traditional bases of support. Mulroney had enlisted the backing of nationalists from Quebec in constructing a nationally based party and leading it to victory in 1984. In 1993 the nationalists were being drawn to a new political movement, the Bloc Québécois, founded in 1990 by a lieutenant of Mulroney's. Lucien Bouchard had broken with the Conservatives over the Mulroney government's constitutional proposals. As the election approached, the Bloc consisted of eight members of Parliament, most of them disgruntled Conservative MPs whom Bouchard had persuaded to leave the party. The Bloc promised to speak out for Quebec's interests in the federal Parliament and to promote the long-term goal of a separate state for Quebec. Early in the campaign, polls showed it eroding Conservative support in the province's French-speaking constituencies, a shift in allegiance that Campbell and Charest tried vainly to prevent.

The other challenge to the Progressive Conservatives came from the Reform Party, which attracted considerable interest in Alberta and British Columbia. Founded in 1987 by Preston Manning, an evangelical Christian from Alberta, Reform sought to mobilize those Canadians who felt that the old-line parties had let them down. It campaigned for a leaner government and questioned the constant attention that it believed Ottawa lavished on Quebec. The Reform Party claimed that there should be no "special status" for Quebec; instead, Canada should be maintained on its original model of 10 equal provinces. In its worries over immigration and crime in society, Reform echoed some of the themes of the populist movement led by H. Ross Perot in the U.S. Early in the campaign the Reform Party threatened to become a "spoiler" in the national election.

The Liberals, the official opposition when Parliament was dissolved, saw their chance in 1993. Their leader, Jean Chrétien (*see* BIOGRAPHIES), was an experienced political figure who had first entered Parliament in 1963 and had held a number of senior Cabinet posts under Prime Minister Pierre Trudeau. A committed federalist, Chrétien had campaigned hard against the sovereignty option in the Quebec referendum in 1980. Although he promised a government that would be fiscally responsible, he emphasized the creation of jobs as his highest priority. In contrast to the Conservatives, the Liberals presented a full statement of proposals to meet Canada's economic and social problems.

The third national party, the social-democratic NDP, faced a bleak prospect in the 1993 campaign. Although they held 43 seats in Parliament, their image was tarnished by the unpopularity of NDP governments in the two large provinces of Ontario and British Columbia. McLaughlin, the party leader, had failed to arouse enthusiasm among voters, even within the traditionally friendly trade-union movement.

On October 25 the Liberal wave began in the Maritime Provinces, where the party captured all but one of the region's 32 seats. Liberals went on to take 19 of the 75 seats in Quebec, all but one of Ontario's 99 seats (unprecedented in the province's history), and 12 of Manitoba's 14 seats, but it did less well in the three provinces to the west. Chrétien won his seat in a strongly nationalist region of Quebec. Altogether the Liberals' 177 seats gave them a solid majority in the new Parliament. Campbell lost her seat in Vancouver, as did all the members of the Cabinet except Charest, who retained one of the party's only two seats. Under Campbell's brief leadership the party had suffered the most humiliating defeat for a governing party in Canada's political history. The Conservatives won only 16.1% of the popular vote, compared with 43% they had won in the previous election five years before. The Liberals' popular vote amounted to 41.6%, almost 10 points higher than their showing in 1988.

In Quebec the Bloc captured more than 50% of the popular vote, winning a total of 54 seats. This was the second highest standing recorded by a party in the election and gave Lucien Bouchard the official position of leader of the opposition. Reform was not far behind, winning 22 seats in Alberta and 24 in British Columbia, which, with scattered other seats, gave it a contingent of 52 members in the new House. The NDP won only 9 ridings, all in the West and in the Yukon, where McLaughlin held on to her seat.

It was doubtful whether any Conservative leader could have avoided defeat in the 1993 election. The Mulroney government had sunk to less than a 20% approval rating in the polls, and Campbell was unable to project a new image for the party. She conducted a weak campaign, at one point saying that the 47 days leading up to the vote were insufficient to discuss serious issues such as social policy. Her party's message lacked substance, and her political judgment was frequently called into question during the campaign. In contrast, the veteran Chrétien conducted a shrewd campaign that touched on the questions, such as unemployment, that were of concern to the average voter. On December 13, Campbell stepped down as party leader.

Chrétien was sworn in as Canada's 20th prime minister on November 4. He appointed 22 members to his Cabinet to represent the regions of the country. Ten members came from Ontario and five were from Quebec. Five members of the Cabinet had served under Trudeau before 1984, and there were five others who had first been elected in the recent election. The most important economic portfolios went to moderate figures who were respected in the business community: finance to Montreal businessman Paul Martin and international trade to Toronto magazine publisher Roy MacLaren. Chrétien's partner in opposition, Sheila Copps from Hamilton, Ont., became deputy prime minister and minister of the environment. The external affairs portfolio (renamed *foreign* affairs) went to André Ouellet, a veteran Quebec minister. Chrétien also appointed eight junior ministers, called secretaries of state, with responsibility for specific areas such as training and youth, Asia-Pacific affairs, and science, research, and development. The secretaries of state would not sit at the Cabinet table but would be responsible to the senior minister appointed in their field of interest. In a move that stunned Canada's defense establishment, in mid-December Chrétien abruptly removed the chief of defense staff, Adm. John Anderson, who had been involved in two major scandals during the Campbell government, and replaced him with Gen. John de Chastelain, the ambassador to the U.S., who had himself held the defense job until January 1993.

Chrétien's task in governing with a deeply divided House of Commons was formidable. He would have to balance his government's initiatives against the opposition of two parties that held radically different views of the destiny of Canada. Reform was impatient with the attention paid to Quebec, yet the Bloc's role was to press forward Quebec's interests. Chrétien's standing as a spokesman for French Canada was weakened by the failure of his party to win any seats in French-speaking ridings.

Four provinces also held elections in 1993. In Prince Edward Island, a Liberal government under Premier Catherine Callbeck won all but one of the 32 seats in the legislature in an election on March 29. Premier Clyde Wells and a Liberal government were returned in Newfoundland on May 3. Nova Scotia swung to the Liberals on May 25, when a new administration under John Savage replaced the Progressive Conservatives, who had held power for 15 years. Thus, all four provinces in the Atlantic region were controlled by Liberal governments. The Conservatives held on to power in Alberta on June 15, when a new leader, Ralph Klein, was successful in bringing a new image to a party that had been in office for 22 years.

Despair and Suicide at Davis Inlet: When Ancient Folkways Collide with the 20th Century

The Canadian public was jolted into the reality of a festering social problem in January 1993 by the televised videotape of six 12- to 14-year-old Innu children at Davis Inlet attempting suicide by inhaling gasoline fumes from plastic bags. When discovered, the youths fought off attempts to be rescued and screamed that they wanted to die. In fact, suicidal activity was not uncommon among the Innu of Davis Inlet, which had become a virtual primer in communal self-destruction, with rampant solvent inhaling and alcoholism amid unseemly poverty and squalor. One local source estimated that some 25% of the community's 500 residents had attempted suicide.

The publicizing of the suicide incident brought long overdue attention to the settlement off the coast of Labrador. In 1967 the Newfoundland government had convinced the Mushuau Innu ("the people of the barrens") to move from their traditional home on the Labrador mainland to a Davis Inlet island in the hope that they could establish a fishing industry there. The Innu had been nomadic caribou hunters for some 6,000 years—with their pride, traditions, and spirituality tied to the land of their ancestors—and on Davis Inlet their social fabric soon fell apart.

The difficulties of transition were complicated even more by failed government promises to provide fresh water and sewerage systems. The government built houses, but they were tiny shacks that housed 15 to 20 members of an extended family. Most dwellings had only wood stoves for heat and were without plumbing. Still the government provided cable television, snowmobiles, and plastic-wrapped packaged goods, which only emphasized the cultural clash between aboriginal nomad and 20th-century mass society. The results were those that sometimes accompany attempts to reorder traditional societies: unemployment, poverty, alcoholism, drug addiction, domestic violence, suicide, and child abuse.

After the suicide attempt brought Davis Inlet into the spotlight, journalists flocked there from Canada, the U.S., and elsewhere. It was pointed out, however, that the conditions at Davis Inlet were representative of problems among native communities across Canada and elsewhere. The six youths and other inhalant users, some as young as eight, were airlifted to a treatment centre in Alberta. After six months they were released and placed temporarily in a wilderness camp at Sango Bay, near the traditional Innu hunting grounds, where the entire community hoped to relocate. In the meantime, outside counselors and government aid brought some improvements to Davis Inlet. Nevertheless, the village leaders, headed by Chief Katie Rich, remained adamant on moving to Sango Bay, where they felt they would be closer to their spiritual roots. Frustrations and tempers were still running high at the end of the year.

(MARVIN MARTIN)

The Economy. The first six months of 1993 saw Canada slowly emerging from the recession that had begun in 1990. The annual growth rate in the economy, based on first-quarter performance, was estimated at 3.8%, a rate that was not sustained in later months. Gross domestic product (GDP), on a seasonally adjusted annual basis, was estimated at $709.2 billion in market prices at the end of June. GDP had climbed above the level it had attained on the eve of the recession. Exports to the United States were strong, helped by a reviving U.S. economy, a Canadian dollar that had fallen 12% against its American counterpart in the year and a half before May, and a more competitive Canadian export sector. Unemployment still remained distressingly high. In December 1,565,000 Canadians were out of work, a figure representing some 11.2% of the labour force. Inflation remained under control, the consumer price index standing at 1.9% in October. Under these conditions commercial lending rates dropped to their lowest level in almost 20 years.

Finance Minister Donald Mazankowski presented a pre-election stand-pat budget on April 26. There were no new taxes and only marginal decreases in spending. Total federal expenditures for 1993–94 would reach $159.5 billion. The deficit was estimated at $32.6 billion, about $3 billion less than that reached in the previous fiscal year. Slower revenues later forced the minister to revise his deficit figure upward. Mazankowski announced a shrinking of the public service, with 16,500 jobs to be eliminated over the next five years. Grants to organizations and interest groups would be cut, as would subsidies to the rail passenger network, VIA Rail, and to the Canadian Broadcasting Corporation. Defense spending would be held to a growth of only 1.6% a year for the next five years.

Foreign Affairs. Peacekeeping constituted a major theme in Canada's foreign policy in 1993. The amount of money Canada had spent on peacekeeping activities in the former Yugoslavia approached $1 billion in 1993, or almost 20 times the amount spent on humanitarian aid. The 1,200 troops the country had sent to Croatia in March 1992 were transferred to central Bosnia in February to escort relief supplies past Serbian lines to Muslim communities. In Somalia the 900 men of the Airborne Regiment helped in the distribution of emergency relief and attempted to restore law and order in the capital, Mogadishu. In February and March the deaths of four Somali civilians cast a shadow on Canada's image as a leading peacekeeper. Four Canadian soldiers were later charged with torture and negligence and two with second-degree murder in connection with the deaths. Questions were also raised in late December when 11 Canadian "blue helmets" were captured and mock-executed by drunken Serbs in Bosnia. In June, 415 Canadian troops left Cyprus after 29 years of patrolling the buffer zone between Greek and Turkish Cypriots. Former prime minister Joe Clark, retired from the federal Cabinet, was appointed a UN mediator to attempt to resolve the long-standing confrontation.

Canada approved the North American Free Trade Agreement (NAFTA) on June 23, the first of the three countries (U.S., Mexico, and Canada) to ratify the arrangement. The implementing measure, passed after an all-night debate in the House of Commons, amended 22 Canadian statutes dealing with trade. Appropriately, the approval came during the final week of Mulroney's tenure in office. Mulroney had been responsible for Canada's joining the NAFTA negotiations in 1991. The Liberal Party threatened to look carefully at NAFTA's terms after it came to power, and year-end negotiations with Mexico and the U.S. brought three small concessions to Chrétien and put the pact back on track.

(D.M.L. FARR)

UNITED STATES

The United States of America is a federal republic composed of 50 states. Area: 9,372,571 sq km (3,618,770 sq mi), including 205,856 sq km of inland water but excluding the 156,492 sq km of the Great Lakes that lie within U.S. boundaries. Pop. (1993 est.): 258,233,000. Cap.: Washington, D.C. Monetary unit: U.S. dollar, with (Oct. 4, 1993) a free rate of U.S. $1.52 to £1 sterling. Presidents in 1993, George Bush and, from January 20, Bill Clinton.

William Jefferson ("Bill") Clinton (*see* BIOGRAPHIES) swept into the White House in 1993 on a wave of high expectations. As the candidate of "change," a word he used often during his presidential campaign against incumbent George Bush, President Clinton was committed to a dramatic reversal of the economic and political stagnation he had blamed on 12 years of conservative Republican rule. Within weeks of the January 1993 inauguration, however, Clinton's new administration was wobbling badly, the victim of ineptitude, bad judgment, and a knack for needless controversy. Fortunately for Clinton, the freshman jitters were eventually dispelled, and the 42nd president of the United States finished the year with an impressive record of accomplishment. According to *Congressional Quarterly*, for instance, he succeeded in moving more legislation through Congress in his first year than any other president since Dwight Eisenhower in 1952. And he did not have to use his veto power even once, a feat not seen since Richard Nixon's first year in 1969.

The Presidency. President Clinton's start was one of the shakiest in recent history. Among his first acts was his declaration that he would seek an end to the U.S. military's long-standing ban on homosexuals in the ranks. Though the move was popular among gays and many other Americans and Clinton had promised it during the election campaign, few Washington analysts thought he would move on such a potentially explosive issue so quickly. Indeed, Clinton's declaration put him at odds with top military leaders and with a number of key civilians who had oversight responsibilities for the armed forces. Chief among the latter was Sen. Sam Nunn, the Georgia Democrat who headed the Senate Armed Services Committee. After heated debate, Clinton managed to gain support for a compromise measure under which homosexual servicemen and servicewomen could remain in the military if they did not openly declare their sexual preference, a policy that quickly became known as "don't ask, don't tell." Yet military officers were overwhelmingly opposed to that approach, fearing that the mere presence of homosexuals in the armed forces would undermine morale. The policy was further undermined by discrimination suits that upheld the right of gays to serve in the military without fear of discrimination. The controversy helped send Clinton's approval ratings plunging to the lowest levels ever recorded for a first-year president and distracted the administration as it struggled to assemble its initial legislative agenda.

The White House also encountered exasperating difficulty in filling a number of high-level positions in the new government. Two successive nominations for the job of attorney general, the nation's top law-enforcement officer, were derailed by disclosures involving the hiring of domestic help. Zoë Baird, a Connecticut insurance lawyer, was accused by Republicans of not having paid proper payroll taxes for a child-care worker; though the offense was minor and the taxes were eventually paid, she withdrew after being accused of impropriety. Kimba Wood, a federal judge in New York, was reported to have hired an undocumented foreigner for her household; though the practice was not illegal at the

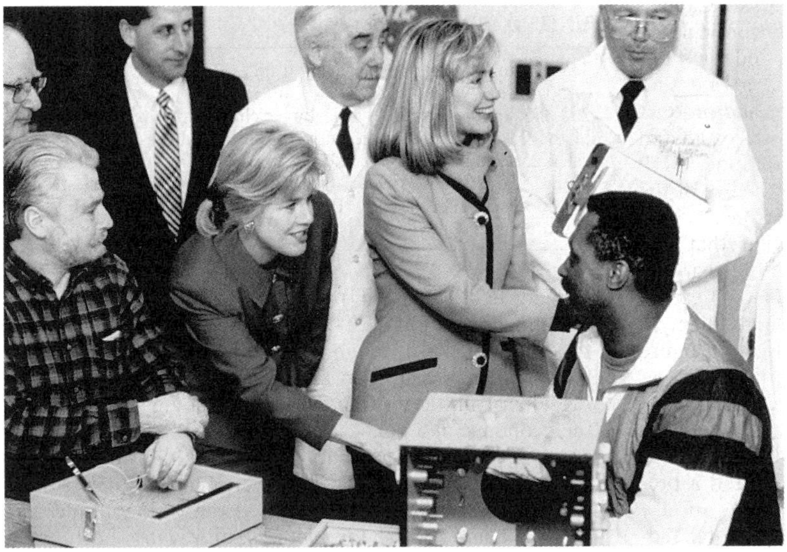

Hillary Rodham Clinton (right) and Tipper Gore visit a medical centre in Philadelphia. The president's wife headed a commission established to study reform of the U.S. health-care system.
DAVID R. SWANSON—GAMMA LIAISON

time and Wood had kept abreast of payroll taxes, she too was forced to withdraw. The job eventually went to Janet Reno, the state's attorney for Dade county, Fla. (*See* BIOGRAPHIES.) The Baird and Wood incidents angered many women, who felt that such accusations would not have been brought up in connection with a male candidate. Indeed, Ron Brown, the former Democratic National Committee chairman whose nomination as commerce secretary sailed through Congress, admitted later—to no ill effect on his appointment—that he, too, had been less than punctilious in hiring domestic help.

One other female nominee was sidelined by Republican opposition, though in this case ostensibly for ideological reasons. Lani Guinier, a law professor at the University of Pennsylvania, withdrew from consideration as the Justice Department's top civil rights official after conservatives objected to what they described as Guinier's radical positions on voting rights and related issues. Though Guinier's supporters protested that her views had been distorted and were hardly controversial, Clinton chose not to stand by her.

And so it went throughout the early months of the administration. The White House would announce a nomination, Republican opposition would coalesce, and the candidate would withdraw. The failure rate was remarkable for a Democratic president whose party controlled both houses of Congress. Clinton was widely criticized for his timidity in confronting the Republicans. One crucial problem for him was an unusual degree of cohesion among the opposition. Far from being in disarray after losing the White House, the Republicans were lining up en bloc against administration initiatives. Conservative Republicans hinted that they were simply giving Clinton appointees the same sort of harassment they felt that three Republican nominees for the Supreme Court, Robert Bork, Douglas Ginsburg, and Clarence Thomas, had suffered at the hands of Democrats during the Reagan-Bush years (Bork and Ginsburg withdrew; Thomas eventually won confirmation, but only after televised hearings into allegations that he had sexually harassed a colleague, Anita Hill). The Democrats, meanwhile, were just as independent-minded as ever. Under long-standing House and Senate rules designed to limit abuses by the majority, a determined minority could prevent appointments and legislation from even coming to a vote. The Republicans acted cohesively enough to take advantage of those rules; the Democrats were too fractious to stop them. As a consequence, Clinton began to look ineffective.

One of the president's first major pieces of legislation, an economic stimulus plan, was killed by a Republican filibuster. Clinton's next big initiative, a deficit-reduction package, ran into an early blitz of opposition from Republicans and from various special interests. That was not surprising, given its content: substantial tax increases and modest spending cuts that would affect many industries and individuals adversely. After months of wrangling, a watered-down version of the measure passed with the narrowest of margins; Vice Pres. Al Gore, in his role as president of the Senate, cast the tie-breaking vote.

The package was expected to cut $500 billion from the federal budget deficit over five years. It included stiff tax increases for upper-income Americans, a slight boost in the corporate tax rate, and a 4-cent-a-gallon (1 gal = 3.8 litres) increase in the federal excise on gasoline. Americans barely noticed the latter, since a softness in global petroleum prices and notoriously low U.S. petroleum taxes had helped keep U.S. gasoline among the world's cheapest—about 25–30 cents a litre. The spending cuts ranged widely across the federal budget, though no serious reductions were made in such major and sacrosanct items as social security and Medicare.

As the months wore on, Clinton began to gain expertise at wooing and arm-twisting. He succeeded in gaining adoption of his $1.5 billion national service plan, under which 100,000 young Americans would earn cash and credits toward college tuition by working in public service jobs. By autumn, when he faced one of the biggest tests of his administration, he was ready to wheel and deal. The issue was congressional approval of the North American Free Trade Agreement. NAFTA had been painstakingly negotiated by administrations of Ronald Reagan and George Bush, and Clinton had declared his support for it during the 1992 election campaign. The treaty would reduce tariffs between the U.S., Canada, and Mexico on a wide array of products and, in effect, create the world's largest free-trade zone. Business executives and economists supported the measure by a wide margin, confident that it would spur trade and thus prosperity in all three countries. Trade union leaders, environmentalists, and a variety of other interest groups opposed the measure, fearing, among other things, that it would prompt U.S. companies to move their operations to Mexico, where wages were lower than in the U.S. and Canada and environmental standards less rigorous.

(continued on page 468)

The Oregon Trail Revisited

"Westward Ho!" went out the cry from the wagon master, and some 120 wagons began their creaking 3,200-km (2,000-mi) journey to the great uncharted "Oregon Country," a stretch of territory then controlled by Britain. The year was 1843, and it was the largest single wagon train ever assembled, consisting of about 1,000 intrepid pioneers and 5,000 head of livestock. Its westward trek from Independence, Mo., marked what was to become the official opening of the Oregon Trail and the westward movement that created a single nation from the Atlantic to the Pacific, a fulfillment of what some termed "our Manifest Destiny."

In 1993 the United States celebrated the sesquicentennial anniversary of the Oregon Trail. All of the states through which the trail passed—Missouri, Kansas, Nebraska, Wyoming, Idaho, and Oregon—planned a series of events and exhibits to commemorate the anniversary, including wagon rides of various lengths along the trail. At least one wagon train set out to go the entire length of the trail, ending in the Columbia River region of Oregon. In 1978 the Oregon National Historic Trail had been designated by Congress.

Adventurous automobile travelers could approximate much of the pioneers' route by road, viewing along the way some 480 km (300 mi) of still discernible ruts and some 125 historic sites. They could "relive" some of the pioneers' experiences, but their trip would take only a tolerable two weeks or less rather than up to six months. Observing some of the bleak landscapes and rugged terrain from a car window, the traveler might well wonder why anyone would knowingly set out by ox-drawn wagon on a 3,200-km journey fraught with danger and hardship.

The emigrants, as they were called, came from every segment of American society. Many were farmers, but their numbers included tradesmen, businessmen, journalists, adventurers, missionaries, gamblers, and miners. They were motivated by a variety of reasons, but the big surge that began in 1843 was strongly instigated by depressed economic conditions that then gripped the nation. The hard times played out against the siren song of Manifest Destiny. Publications—such as John C. Frémont's *Topographical Report*—that painted enticing pictures of lush, available western lands put thousands on the trail. Outbreaks of cholera and malaria in the Midwest caused others to flee westward. Some—like the Mormons—were escaping religious persecution. And still others, like the "Forty-niners" off to seek gold in California, went for the sheer adventure.

For whatever reason emigrants took to the trail, most at some point along the way came to wonder at their decision. A CBS report on Sept. 7, 1993, called the Oregon Trail the longest graveyard in the world, estimating that almost 11 persons per kilometre died along the route. Although emigrants feared Indian attacks, these turned out to be of minor consequence. Rather it was disease—which they had hoped to leave behind—that was the main killer. Cholera alone claimed some 5,000 lives in 1850. Accidents involving firearms and hazardous river crossings took their toll, and a few deaths were attributed to Indian attacks, starvation, and severe weather.

By late September 1843, that first large wagon train of pioneers had reached Oregon, and farmers were claiming land along the Willamette and Columbia rivers. They were followed by more than 300,000 emigrants, constituting the largest mass migration in history. The route's decline was signaled largely by completion of the railway that connected the two coasts in 1869. However, as late as the early 1900s, occasional wagons could still be seen rumbling along the trail.

(MARVIN MARTIN)

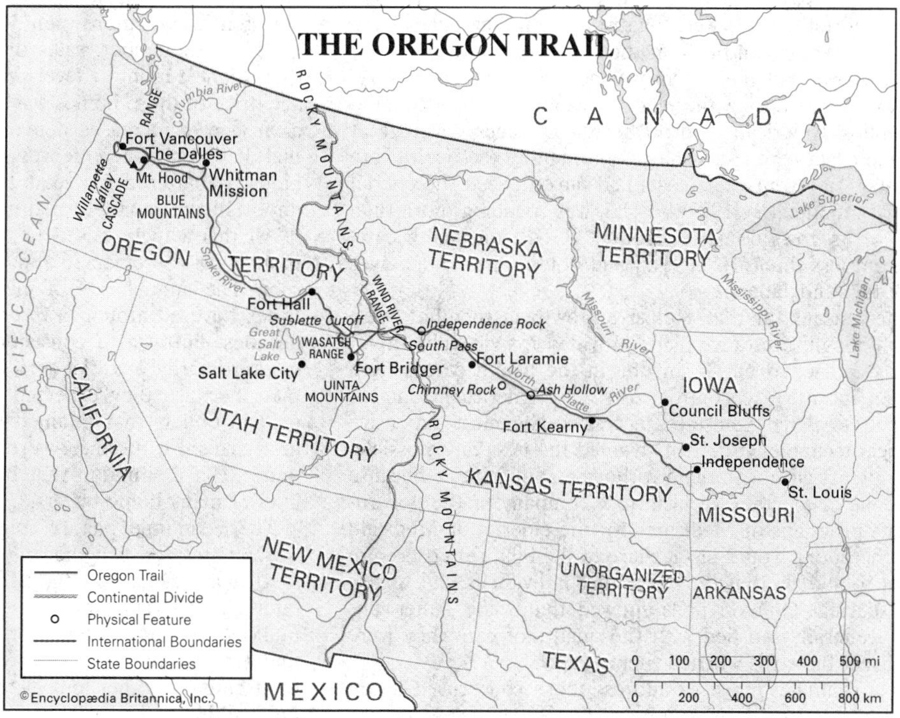

(continued from page 466)

Prominent among NAFTA's opponents was H. Ross Perot, the Texas billionaire who a year earlier had made a run for the presidency. Perot's prediction that the measure would produce "a giant sucking sound" as U.S. jobs were lost to Mexico became a rallying cry of the treaty's critics. As the congressional vote on the agreement approached, chances of passage seemed dim. In apparent desperation, the White House accepted Perot's proposal that he and Vice President Gore debate the issue on national television. They appeared together on interviewer Larry King's Cable News Network talk show, and Gore was credited by many pundits and pollsters with having got the better of his challenger. In any case, public opinion began to swing toward the treaty. Meanwhile, Clinton was wooing legislators with intimate dinners at the White House and promises of federal largesse for their home districts. In the end Clinton prevailed, and NAFTA was passed by both houses.

The victory provided the president with a measure of momentum that had previously eluded him. Capitalizing on it, he successfully pressed for the passage of a major anticrime bill that included a controversial waiting period on handgun purchases. He also intervened decisively a month later to end a strike by American Airlines flight attendants that threatened to disrupt travel over the Thanksgiving holiday weekend. By year's end it appeared that Clinton, a newcomer to Washington whose previous job had been governor of Arkansas, had figured out how to do business in the nation's capital.

Health Care. Perhaps the most important initiative of the new administration, health care, had not yet been formally debated by Congress by the end of 1993, but it nonetheless carried the potential for dramatically changing the way many Americans lived. Unlike most industrial countries, the individualistic, free-enterprise U.S. did not have a comprehensive government health care system. Instead, Americans made do with a patchwork of private insurers, employer-paid insurance, private doctors, private and tax-supported hospitals, and government subsidies for the poor and the elderly. For years the system worked satisfactorily. Though infant mortality rates were relatively high, Americans were generally healthy, and U.S. medical technology was the envy of the world. Yet the system was not without its critics. As Clinton noted during the election campaign, an estimated 37 million Americans had no health insurance coverage at all, and costs were rising sharply throughout the health care industry. In recent years costs had far outpaced the overall rate of inflation. By 1992 the U.S. was spending more than 14% of its gross domestic product (GDP) on health care, up from less than 6% in 1965 and double the percentages in Britain and Japan.

The reasons for that explosive growth in spending were clear enough; insurance plans provided for virtually unlimited coverage, so hardly anyone in the health care system had an incentive to control costs, and Americans found it difficult to deny themselves access to the most expensive medical technology. Patients wanted the best care possible, and doctors gave it to them without regard to price because someone else, either an insurance company or the government's programs of Medicare (for the elderly) or Medicaid (for the poor), would pay a share of the bill. Yet costs were rising so steeply that the share that individuals had to pay was soaring. Opinion polls showed that while Americans were generally satisfied with the quality of care they were receiving, the costs worried them deeply.

In a dramatic move to address those concerns, Clinton unveiled a thorough overhaul of the U.S. health care system. The plan, which had been formulated under the supervision of first lady Hillary Rodham Clinton (*see* BIOGRAPHIES), had three basic elements: universal coverage for all Americans; employer mandates, under which companies would pay 80% of their workers' health insurance premiums; and a system of controls on medical costs. The plan had other details certain to be altered in the expected give-and-take with Congress and interest groups. For instance, the proposal would cover mental health costs, which could prove unacceptably expensive. Likewise, the plan called for a national health board that would enforce price controls, a notion that doctors and hospitals opposed and that economists called unworkable. Another feature of the plan, the creation of giant health alliances that would purchase coverage from private insurers on behalf of nearly all people in a particular region, was so radical that it faced months of study and debate, as well as a likelihood of being dropped.

Amendment 27 to the U.S. Constitution (ratified May 7, 1992)

No law, varying the compensation for the services of the Senators and Representatives, shall take effect, until an election of Representatives shall have intervened.

The Economy. The pall of gloom that had hung over the U.S. economy for years was lifting. The recovery had actually begun during the Bush administration, but public perception did not catch up with reality until late in 1993. Most measures of business and consumer confidence were rising, and the stock markets hit new highs several times during the year.

Signs of renewed vigour were almost everywhere. Consumer spending in the third quarter was up 4.2% from a year earlier. Investment in plant and equipment hit levels not seen since 1984. Unemployment dropped from 7% at the beginning of the year to 6.4% in December, and an average of 150,000 new jobs were created every month (despite a number of highly publicized mass layoffs announced by leading companies). GDP, the total amount of goods and services produced in the country, rose at an inflation-adjusted rate of more than 3%, about the same pace as in 1992. In September, sales of new single-family homes hit their highest monthly level since December 1986. The average price of those homes was up 7.9% from a year earlier, a clear sign of increased demand in a sector of the economy that had long been depressed. Even the American auto industry, battered for years by declining profits and rising imports from Japan, turned in its best year since 1989.

All this activity raised fears that inflation might return, though prices remained remarkably stable throughout the year. The annual rate of increase of the Consumer Price Index hovered around 3%, one of the lowest levels in two decades. Partly as a consequence, interest rates remained extraordinarily low (lenders were willing to charge lower rates because they expected that the loans would be repaid in dollars that retained their value). Fixed-rate home mortgages, for instance, were carrying annual interest rates under 7%, a situation that had not prevailed in the adult lives of many home buyers.

The economic picture might have been even brighter were it not for two major natural disasters. In the summer, heavy rains sent the Missouri, Mississippi, and other midwestern rivers surging over their banks. More than two million hectares (five million acres) of farmland were inundated; hundreds of cities and towns were flooded; and thousands of homes and factories were swept away. In the fall, wildfires devastated southern California, burning at least 61,500 ha (152,000 ac) and forcing 25,000 people from their homes. Damage from the two disasters totaled in the billions of dollars, and economists figured that the resulting dislocation may have shaved half a percentage point off the increase in GDP. Some of that was expected to be regained in 1994 as money spent to restore the damage flowed into the economy.

Social Issues. The year brought some major advances for women in the U.S. as they continued to gain important posts in business and government. Congress approved President Clinton's appointment of Ruth Bader Ginsburg (*see* BIOGRAPHIES), a New York law professor, to the Supreme Court, where she became the second woman on the nine-member panel. In addition, Congress enacted 30 major bills related to women and family issues, compared with 5 in 1989, according to the Congressional Caucus for Women's Issues. Prominent among the new laws was the Family and Medical Leave Act, which provided up to 12 weeks of job-guaranteed leave for workers to care for themselves or sick family members or to have or adopt a baby. The caucus, which at year's end comprised the 7 female members of the Senate and the 47 congresswomen (both numbers were up sharply from the previous legislative session), nonetheless failed in an effort to repeal a measure that banned Medicaid funds from being used for abortions.

Despite the inauguration of a Democratic president committed to reproductive rights, foes of abortion continued their campaign of disruption and intimidation against clinics where the procedure was performed. The administration loosened some federal restrictions on terminating pregnancies, but abortion foes hoped to make it difficult for women to obtain them. In response, abortion rights advocates sought the intervention of local authorities and the courts. In one closely watched case, abortion rights advocates sought to have clinic blockaders prosecuted under the 1970 Racketeer Influence and Corrupt Organizations (RICO) Act, which was normally used against organized crime. The Supreme Court was expected to rule on the matter in 1994. The court had previously upheld the broadening of RICO to prosecute commodity traders and gang members, although in 1993 the justices ruled that federal courts may not stop abortion clinic blockades by invoking an 1871 civil rights law.

A number of well-publicized incidents had the effect of polarizing popular opinion along gender lines. One was the disclosure that Sen. Robert Packwood, a veteran Oregon Republican, may have made sexual advances against more than two dozen women over 20 years and tried to intimidate some of his alleged victims into silence. Women in Congress demanded Packwood's resignation, and the Senate launched an investigation. At year's end Packwood hinted that he might resign.

In December Secretary Hazel O'Leary announced that the Department of Energy would investigate reports that a number of major medical institutions and U.S. government research laboratories had exposed civilians to radiation without having fully informed them of the nature of the experiments. More than 1,000 subjects were involved in various programs dating from the late 1940s to the early 1970s.

Crime. A perennial concern among Americans, crime became almost a national obsession in 1993. Highly publicized reports of gang- and drug-related violence, carjackings that ended in death, innocent bystanders killed in gun battles, children bringing guns to school for protection, and foreign tourists killed during robberies in Florida all fanned the flames of public concern. In one typical survey nearly 90% of those polled said they believed that the country's crime problem was growing, and nearly half reported that there was more crime in their neighbourhoods than a year earlier.

That fear of crime was seemingly at odds with reality. FBI statistics indicated a 4% drop in overall reported crime in 1992, and major cities reported declines in several categories of violent crime, including murder, rape, and robbery. Yet many Americans did not believe such reports, and their concerns led to a number of dramatic steps toward making their localities safer. Sharon Pratt Dixon, the mayor of Washington, D.C., asked the Clinton administration to provide National Guard troops to help police the city's more crime-ridden precincts (the request was denied). Voters in several states approved stiffer sentences for many crimes, as well as money to build more prisons.

Criminal justice and public safety had long been a matter of state and local responsibility in the U.S., with only a modest federal role. As the clamour for relief from crime rose, however, Washington was listening. Congress passed

JIM WILSON—THE NEW YORK TIMES

With U.S. Pres. Bill Clinton (fifth from left) as host, leaders of the countries of the Asia-Pacific Economic Cooperation forum meet at an Indian longhouse near Seattle, Wash. The November discussions among Pacific Rim nations centred on trade issues.

the Clinton administration's crime bill, which went far beyond previous measures. It lengthened the list of offenses that could be prosecuted by federal authorities, including, as critics of the measure noted with derision, the murder of a federal chicken inspector. On a more positive note, the bill also provided funds to hire 100,000 new police. The most remarkable feature was the bill's inclusion of a long-standing proposal to require a five-day waiting period for the purchase of a handgun. That measure was known as the Brady bill, after James Brady, the White House press secretary who was seriously injured in the 1981 attack on Ronald Reagan. Brady, confined to a wheelchair and unable to resume his duties, campaigned hard for the bill, but it was fiercely opposed by the National Rifle Association (NRA), one of Washington's most formidable interest groups. Even supporters of the Brady bill conceded that it was unlikely to have a major effect on crime, but they welcomed its passage as a step toward more limits on the easy availability of handguns in the U.S. and as a major setback for the NRA.

The agency responsible for federal criminal enforcement, the U.S. Justice Department, was widely criticized for the way it handled a standoff near Waco, Texas, between federal agents and heavily armed members of a religious cult known as the Branch Davidians and their charismatic leader, David Koresh. Four agents of the Bureau of Alcohol, Tobacco and Firearms were killed in an ill-planned attempt to storm the cult's 31-ha (77-acre) compound. That raid led to a nationally televised 51-day siege and a fiery conflagration after which it was discovered that some 75 people inside the compound, including at least 17 children, had died; a number had been shot. Nearly all the deaths appeared to have been caused by the Branch Davidians, but the report concluded that federal officials handled the situation ineptly.

Foreign Affairs. With an administration focused on its domestic policy agenda, international matters receded into the background of public attention. One reason was that since the fall of the Berlin Wall in 1989 and the general collapse of communism around the world, the Cold War no longer served as a framework for U.S. foreign policy and as a focus for public anxiety about the possibility of superpower confrontation. Another reason was that the international conflicts that did occupy the year's headlines in Somalia, the Balkans, Haiti, and the Middle East were mostly protracted regional affairs and were maddeningly resistant to the application of U.S. power.

In Somalia, for instance, the U.S. began pulling out the more than 25,000 troops it had sent a year earlier to help ensure the distribution of relief supplies to a populace suffering from starvation and from the depredations of feuding warlords. U.S. forces were surprised to encounter hostility from the very people they had been sent to save. When an angry crowd of Somalis attacked a United Nations convoy, American helicopters fired into the crowd, killing and wounding more than 100 people. Then troops under the control of a leading warlord, Muhammad Farah Aydid (*see* BIOGRAPHIES), whom the U.S. had been trying to capture, killed 18 Americans in a gun battle. President Clinton quickly announced a pullout of all remaining U.S. forces by March 1994. In an ironic twist to the unhappy American experience in Somalia, the U.S. not only dropped its attempt to seize Aydid but gave him preferential treatment and passage on a U.S. plane to attend peace talks in neighbouring Ethiopia.

In the Balkans, President Clinton indicated his willingness to send U.S. troops to help maintain order if warring factions in Bosnia and Serbia could settle their differences. The offer was not taken up, in part because the conflict dragged on and European countries could not agree on a role for themselves and the U.S. On other matters Europe and the U.S. did appear to be in agreement. Among them was an American proposal to expand the membership of NATO possibly at some time in the future to include states of the Warsaw Pact, a now-defunct alliance of former Soviet-bloc states. That was an astonishing development, given the four decades of enmity between the two blocs. In addition, after years of sometimes desultory talks, the U.S. and Europe resolved most of their differences on trade and in December concluded an agreement under the General Agreement on Tariffs and Trade. (*See* ECONOMIC AFFAIRS.)

In Haiti the U.S. found itself in the position of supporting exiled Pres. Jean-Bertrand Aristide but unable to arrange his return. Haitian army commander Raoul Cédras, who ousted Aristide after the former Roman Catholic priest was democratically elected in 1990, refused to yield power. Cédras did participate in a UN-brokered agreement that would allow Aristide to take office, and the U.S. and Canada promised to send a small contingent of lightly armed troops to help police the arrangement. Yet when the U.S. troop ship arrived in Haiti, a violent mob of army-backed civilians refused to let it dock, and the troops returned home. Clinton ordered six American ships into the region to enforce a UN arms and oil embargo against Haiti. Meanwhile, forces loyal to Cédras continued to intimidate and even murder their opponents with impunity.

In the Middle East, where the U.S. had long played a major role, Clinton presided over the historic meeting in Washington of Palestine Liberation Organization chief Yasir Arafat and Israeli Prime Minister Yitzhak Rabin. The two leaders met for the signing of an agreement allowing an unprecedented measure of Palestinian autonomy in the Israeli-occupied West Bank and Gaza Strip. The U.S. had little directly to do with arranging the agreement, and at one point late in the year, Rabin asked the U.S. to refrain from direct involvement in Israel's talks with the Palestinians.

As the year came to a close, President Clinton shifted U.S. attention to North Korea. That country, ruled by the reclusive Kim Il Sung and dedicated to a brand of highly regimented Stalinist communism, was refusing to allow international inspections of its nuclear energy facilities. American policy makers, concerned that Kim was developing a nuclear weapons program, indicated that the U.S. might take military action if Kim's government did not comply with the inspection. North Korea declared that it was prepared to endure war or economic sanctions; in response, the U.S. said it would increase its military activities in South Korea, Kim's neighbour and bitter foe. Tensions eased somewhat when North Korea said that it might allow some inspections and that it would turn over the remains of U.S. soldiers killed four decades earlier in the Korean War.

The book was finally closed on one of the country's most enduring political scandals: the Iran-contra affair. The final report of the special prosecutor investigating the matter indicated that former presidents Reagan and Bush were far more complicit than they had asserted. The scandal involved the sale of arms to Iran and the diversion of the resulting profits to provide arms for the contra rebels fighting the leftist government of Nicaragua in the 1980s. Though the Reagan and Bush administrations publicly favoured the contras, Congress had banned military support for them. The report, by prosecutor Lawrence Walsh, concluded that Reagan had set the stage for the illegal activities and that Bush was less than truthful when he declared that he was "out of the loop" and not kept informed about the matter. Neither man, however, was said to be guilty of a crime.

(DONALD MORRISON)

See also *Dependent States,* below.

State and Local Affairs

Two months into his presidency, onetime governor Bill Clinton met with 100 state legislative leaders in the state dining room at the White House. "I'd be hypocritical," he told them, "if I changed my position just because I am no longer governor." The president would not be the first hypocrite in high office, but state officials were hopeful that the new administration understood their problems and was more inclined to do something about them. Indeed, there was evidence of progress in at least two areas where states had felt strangled. The National Performance Review, established for the purpose of "reinventing government," made recommendations to alleviate the burden of unfunded mandates, the method by which Washington makes state governments institute or maintain various programs without providing money to run them. In addition, federal waivers were more forthcoming, allowing states to experiment in such areas as welfare and health-care reform. There was, finally, a consensus among state leaders that an era of partnership had begun, that they could participate in making government responsive and effective, and that having a soul mate in the White House certainly could not hurt.

Party Strengths. The November elections brought few changes in state party strength, primarily because there were not many races. But the returns were a tonic for the Republican Party one year after losing the White House. In addition to winning important mayoral races in New York City and Los Angeles, the Republicans captured the only two gubernatorial contests, New Jersey and Virginia. The results were widely interpreted as a continuation of the protest vote by voters angry about high taxes and soaring crime rates.

In New Jersey incumbent Democrat James Florio was defeated by Republican Christine Todd Whitman, the first woman to be elected governor in the state. Her slim victory was seen less as an affirmative endorsement than a rejection by voters angry with Florio over his $2.8 billion tax increase in 1990. Whitman capitalized on the antitax backlash by pledging to reduce state income taxes by 30% over three years, a pledge even many Republicans believed she would be unable to redeem. Her victory celebration was immediately overshadowed by allegations of campaign dirty tricks.

In Virginia conservative Republican George Allen trounced former state attorney general Mary Sue Terry to succeed the Democratic governor, Douglas Wilder, who by law was barred from running for another term. A former congressman and son of the late coach of the Washington Redskins football team, the 41-year-old Allen put Terry on the defensive with a platform stressing family values and economic development and striking a hard line on law and order. Terry's moderate stance on most issues was ultimately regarded as too liberal by a conservative electorate in which fundamentalist Christian voters demonstrated surprising strength.

Despite the loss of two governorships, Democrats remained in control of 28 statehouses, compared with 20 Republicans and 2 independents. Legislative strength was essentially unchanged; the Democrats continued to control both houses of the legislature in 25 states, while Republicans held 9 and 15 others were split. (Nebraska has a unicameral, nonpartisan legislature.)

Rudolph Giuliani appears with his wife after his election as mayor of New York City. Having risen to prominence on his reputation as a tough federal prosecutor, Giuliani was one of several Republicans who won important elections in November.
WESLEY BOCXE—JB PICTURES

In New York City a bitter mayor's race saw incumbent Democrat David Dinkins ousted by Republican Rudolph Giuliani, a former federal prosecutor. Winning by approximately 45,000 votes, Giuliani became the first Republican to defeat an incumbent Democratic mayor in 60 years and the first Republican mayor since 1974.

Four other veteran big-city mayors left office voluntarily during the year. Democrat Tom Bradley was succeeded by Republican businessman Richard Riordan in Los Angeles. In Detroit, Mich., Coleman Young was succeeded by Dennis Archer, a former state Supreme Court justice. City councilman Bill Campbell won a runoff to succeed Mayor Maynard Jackson in Atlanta, Ga., and in Minneapolis, Minn., City Council president Sharon Sayles Belton became the city's first black and first female mayor, succeeding Donald Fraser. Popular black incumbent mayors in Cleveland, Ohio, and Seattle, Wash., were reelected by comfortable margins. Acting mayor Thomas Menino became Boston's first Italian-American mayor and the first non-Irish-American to lead the city in more than 60 years.

Government Structures, Powers. The 1996 presidential-selection process was significantly reshaped by the legislative action of two large states to move their presidential primaries forward. California's delegate-rich primary was changed from the first Tuesday in June to the last Tuesday in March, while in Ohio the primary was shifted from May to the same Tuesday in March as the Illinois and Michigan primaries. Political experts concluded that the glut of primary contests in March would virtually ensure an early end to nomination battles for the presidency.

In dozens of referendums and ballot initiatives, voters signaled their disaffection by imposing term limits on state and municipal officeholders, turning down various tax-increase proposals, and insisting upon tougher measures to fight crime in the streets.

Voters in Maine approved a measure limiting state legislators and elected officials to a maximum of four consecutive two-year terms. An eight-year limit was imposed on the mayor and other top elected officials in New York City. Seven states planned ballot initiatives on term limits in 1994, and several others were expected to do likewise.

In New Jersey a constitutional amendment was approved allowing voters to recall any elected official, including representatives and senators. The constitutionality of such action by states against federal officials, however, remained in doubt.

A desire to curb the spending authority of legislators was demonstrated by Washington state voters, who approved an initiative limiting future increases in government spending to the rates of population growth and inflation. A related but more stringent measure to roll back state taxes and spending to 1992 levels was rejected as too draconian.

A widely publicized ballot measure in Washington showed that voters overwhelmingly supported a so-called Three Strikes You're Out proposition requiring mandatory life sentences (in prison) for felons convicted three times. Similar proposals were expected to be on the ballot in California and a few other states in 1994. Staten Island, one of the five boroughs of New York City, voted to declare its independence and secede. The action could not proceed without the approval of the state legislature and the governor.

Finances. A modest national recovery from recession, combined with sizable spending cuts in 1991 and 1992, made it a bit easier for beleaguered states to balance their budgets. Higher revenue collections as a result of economic growth compensated in part for the ongoing revolt by voters resistant to expanding state taxes. The National Conference of State Legislatures estimated that state tax changes would generate a net increase of $4.1 billion in the 1994 fiscal year, a modest increase from 1993.

Taxes were raised in 22 states, 26 had no significant change, and 2 states reduced taxes. Personal income taxes rose in 12 states, corporate taxes in 11, and sales and use taxes in 10. Arizona, Maine, Mississippi, and Vermont were the only states to reduce personal income taxes. Major income tax increases were implemented in New York, which postponed a scheduled reduction in tax rates; Illinois, which made a 1989 increase permanent; and Ohio, which added a new top rate.

Users of cigarette and tobacco products were hit hard by a sixfold increase in taxes levied by 16 states. Sixteen states increased taxes on health-care providers, and 15 states raised waste and environmental taxes. Michigan effectively repealed its state inheritance tax. Several jurisdictions raised revenues by broadening their tax bases. Alaska imposed a salmon-marketing tax. New Hampshire began taxing hospital rooms and meals. Illinois repealed its controversial "granny tax" on nursing homes, but Ohio imposed a similar levy. Arkansas enacted a tax on gross receipts from bingo. New York imposed a surcharge on area code 900 telephone calls, while Ohio began taxing carbonated beverages.

States required to submit proposed tax increases before the voters were for the most part disappointed. Taxpayers in Oregon and Montana voted down attempts to enact sales taxes, leaving those states, along with Alaska, Delaware, and New Hampshire, as the only five states without a sales tax. In Washington, however, voters rejected a bid to roll back $1 billion in alcohol and tobacco taxes enacted in 1992 to fund comprehensive health-care reform. A companion measure was adopted that would tie future tax increases to the rate of inflation and population growth. In recession-wracked California, where major spending cuts were enacted for the second year to balance the budget and avert a fiscal crisis, voters nevertheless approved a half-cent hike in the sales tax, with proceeds earmarked for law enforcement and fire fighting. Texas voters decreed that any future proposed state income tax be submitted to a plebiscite.

Education. In big cities and small towns alike, there was grim evidence that U.S. schools were falling apart after years of neglect. In New York City one million students were left stranded as 115 schools were unable to start the school year because of possible asbestos contamination. Some schools were closed for nearly three months, and more than 300 others operated with some of their facilities closed indefinitely. A study by the American Association of School Administrators disclosed that nearly one-third of the country's 84,000 schools were more than 50 years old and another 43% were more than 30 years old.

Illinois approved a $410 million bailout plan for the state's debt-ridden public schools; the funding crisis forced Chicago to cancel the first week of classes in the country's third largest school system.

Declining confidence in the performance of educational bureaucracies prompted some jurisdictions to try radical approaches in search of reform. The Minneapolis school board hired a private consulting firm to take over management of the city's 75 schools and $220 million budget. California turned over control of the country's largest public school system to a businessman specializing in rescuing troubled corporations by aggressive cost cutting.

California voters decisively rejected Proposition 174, a plan to give every student a $2,600 voucher that could be used to help pay tuition at private schools. Supporters argued that the measure would improve educational quality by forcing all schools to compete for students; opponents, led by the state teachers union, said it would be the death knell for public education. The voucher concept appeared to be gathering support nationwide; bills similar to that in California were pending in the Pennsylvania legislature and in Jersey City, N.J.

Acting just days before a June 1 court deadline that would have cut off state funds to school districts, Texas ended nearly 25 years of wrangling and approved a plan to slash the disparity on spending per student between rich and poor districts. The 100 wealthiest districts would be required to lower their taxable property base per student, with the excess transferred by one of four methods to poorer jurisdictions. Three previous wealth-sharing plans had been invalidated by state courts.

Financing systems were in flux elsewhere as well. The Massachusetts Supreme Court ordered the state to create a new school financing plan not pegged to property taxes. In Michigan, Gov. John Engler signed legislation eliminating property taxes as a source of school funding.

Virginia attempted to stem violence in the schools with a law requiring parents registering children for school to disclose whether the youngsters had ever been expelled from another jurisdiction. The names of juveniles convicted on weapons or drug offenses would also have to be disclosed to school superintendents.

Health and Welfare. Unwilling or unable to wait for national health-care reform, legislatures in 40 states considered health-care proposals, and many instituted reforms of their own with federal approval. Maryland changed state insurance laws to make coverage affordable for small businesses and established a Health Care Access and Cost Commission to write a standard benefit plan. In Tennessee a five-year demonstration project called TennCare would take one million Medicaid recipients and 500,000 uninsured residents and cover them all in a single insurance program. Participants would choose from managed-care networks. Costs such as premiums and deductibles would be based on income levels, and preventive services would be free. Hawaii decided to combine its three public health programs into one managed-care system. Known as Hawaii Health Quest, the plan would create one large purchasing pool. Quest participants would then be offered a choice of enrollment in a managed-care system.

Florida instituted reform using the theory of managed competition, the idea that when businesses pool their purchasing power, they can obtain health insurance at reasonable prices. The plan called for 11 purchasing alliances across the state, including businesses with up to 50 employees, state workers, and Medicaid recipients.

Maine became the first state to pass legislation shielding doctors from malpractice suits provided they agreed to adhere to state-approved guidelines. The "medical liability demonstration project" covered only four specialties—obstetrics and gynecology, radiology, anesthesiology, and emergency medicine. Doctors helped write the checklist of explicit treatment protocols, and more than 90% of eligible physicians enrolled in the project.

For the first time since New York began releasing tens of thousands of the less seriously ill patients from state mental hospitals in the mid-1950s, officials found a way to allocate funds to care for the mentally ill in the communities in which they live. For years, thousands of former patients had to fend for themselves with little if any public aid, and many became homeless. The new plan would use about $200 million to provide rehabilitation and vocational training and to care for the homeless.

Maryland began a primary prevention initiative program that rewarded welfare clients with small bonuses for getting physical exams and prenatal care. The project withheld $25 from welfare parents whose children did not get regular checkups and immunizations and were not regularly attending school. Arkansas passed the "home infusion therapy" law, the first of its kind in the nation, enabling patients to receive intravenous drugs at home. Providing this service for AIDS sufferers or patients requiring continuous medication could cut $9 million a year in Medicaid costs.

Michigan allocated more than half the funds in its family-planning programs to providing Norplant in its clinics. Norplant, a synthetic hormone released by thin capsules surgically implanted in a woman's arm, effectively prevents conception for up to five years. Lawmakers in 13 other states who attempted programs requiring Norplant for poor or drug-addicted women had been met with charges of genocide and social engineering.

DAVE SCHLABOWSKE—TIME MAGAZINE

Reacting to the brutal murder of a young girl, citizens in Milwaukee, Wis., sign a petition to ban handguns. A number of states voted restrictions on firearms in 1993, and in November the U.S. Congress passed the so-called Brady bill, which mandated a waiting period for the purchase of handguns.

Vermont, Florida, and Wisconsin appropriated an idea offered by Clinton during his presidential campaign to put a time limit on welfare benefits. Vermont imposed a 30-month limit with the guarantee of a job with either the government or a not-for-profit agency. In Wisconsin, where the plan would be tried in only two counties, there was no job guarantee, but officials said that training, child care, and other assistance would be provided.

Abortion. Violence against abortion clinics escalated, culminating in the shooting death of a Florida doctor outside his office. Clinics in Texas, Florida, Idaho, and Montana were destroyed, and facilities in other states were vandalized. Connecticut and Colorado passed laws protecting access to abortion clinics, and more than 20 similar bills were introduced in a dozen other states. Congress voted to make it a federal crime to attack abortion facilities and to assault or obstruct people who use them.

The Clinton administration announced that the Medicaid program would be instructed to pay for abortions for low-income women who were victims of rape. The U.S. Supreme Court let stand a Mississippi law requiring women under 18 to obtain both parents' permission before having an abortion.

Law and Justice. The national disgust over crime turned to national embarrassment after the widely publicized slayings of several foreign tourists in Florida. A special session of the state legislature voted without dissent to ban possession of firearms by juveniles and to make parents responsible if their children were caught with a gun. Virginia passed a law limiting individuals to the purchase of one handgun per month. According to the Bureau of Alcohol, Tobacco and Firearms, 26% of traceable guns seized in New York City and 36% of those in Washington, D.C., were bought in Virginia. Indeed, in New York City, 90% of the guns seized were purchased out of state. Law-enforcement officials in New York state established a three-member gun-tracing operation to coordinate joint investigations with federal officials and police departments in other states to curb gun trafficking.

Connecticut joined New Jersey and California to become the third state to pass a comprehensive ban on assault weapons. Owners of the newly banned weapons had to register them and provide proof that they had been purchased before the law took effect on October 1. Both houses of the New Jersey legislature voted to overturn the state's ban on assault weapons, but Republicans in the legislature failed to override the Democratic governor's veto.

The West Virginia Supreme Court invalidated 10 years' worth of blood tests used in criminal cases when it was discovered that the state police serologist had lied about test results in such a way as always to win a conviction. The court's ruling opened the way for new trials for at least 134 prisoners, many convicted of murder or rape. The serologist's work aroused suspicion during a 1987 rape case when the first DNA sample to be admitted in a state court proved that the defendant could not have been guilty.

In the first action of its kind by a state, Vermont passed a sweeping no-smoking law. The first stage, begun in July 1993, affected all public buildings and some private concerns such as stores and video arcades. In July 1995 the ban would apply to restaurants, bars, and hotels. Florida became the only state after New York to legalize breast-feeding in public. The law amended Florida's statutes on lewd and lascivious behaviour and indecent exposure.

Ethics. Gov. Guy Hunt of Alabama was convicted on a felony charge for violating a state ethics law. He was accused of appropriating $200,000 from an inaugural fund for personal use. Hunt became the fourth governor in U.S. history to be convicted of a felony while in office. He resigned immediately after his conviction; his appeal was denied. Gov. David Walters of Oklahoma became the state's first sitting governor found guilty of a crime when he admitted accepting an illegal contribution during his 1990 campaign.

A special session of the Kentucky legislature created a Legislative Ethics Commission and introduced tough new campaign finance laws, both the result of an ongoing FBI probe into public corruption. The investigation focused on an expansion of gambling in the racing industry. The former speaker of the house was convicted of racketeering and extortion; five former legislators were convicted on various charges; and a sitting senator was indicted.

Prisons. Debate over the politics of imprisonment intensified as evidence mounted that the get-tough era of minimum mandatory and harsher sentences plus more prison construction was simply too costly and did nothing to lower the crime rate. North Carolina, Arkansas, and Kansas considered new sentencing policies as well as the placement of nonviolent criminals in nonprison settings, and at least seven other states were moving in that direction.

Many states were ordered by federal courts to relieve overcrowding by releasing prisoners early or finding new space for them. In Arizona drunk drivers were moved into tents to open up cells for more dangerous criminals. Though states allocated $15 billion to run corrections departments, Arkansas eliminated 1,000 prison jobs, 13 other states also cut jobs, and 20 states were unable to add new jobs.

More death sentences and less public money available added up to a severe shortage of lawyers representing inmates on death row. One-third of California's 350 death row prisoners did not have lawyers, and 48 of the 376 inmates in Texas were not represented. As many as 40% of all death sentences were typically reversed by federal and state courts.

Gambling. Expansion of South Dakota's $1 billion gambling industry was halted, thanks to the efforts of a small-town grandmother. Her fierce opposition to gambling forced the legislature to schedule a special-ballot referendum in which voters reversed legislation that would have dramatically raised the stakes in the historic Black Hills town of Deadwood. The legislation, known unofficially as the "Costner bill," had given actor Kevin Costner and his brother the go-ahead to build a $65 million casino resort and would have raised the betting limit from $5 to $100. Most farming counties east of the Missouri River opposed the expansion, while voters in the western part of the state supported the measure. Deadwood's part-time mayor expressed his town's deep resentment, saying, "Obviously, we do dance to the east river tune."

Nearly 70 Indian tribes in 20 states took in about $6 billion in gambling revenue. New York agreed to let the St. Regis Mohawk tribe open a casino on the Canadian border, the state's second, and Connecticut signed an agreement with the Mashantucket Pequot Indians permitting slot machines at their casino in Ledyard in exchange for a minimum $100 million yearly contribution to a state fund for poor cities.

Environment. Almost half the states missed the deadline imposed by the Clean Air Act requiring them to submit plans to the Environmental Protection Agency for reducing air pollution from stationary sources. California, Illinois, and Indiana were warned they could face sanctions for not enacting laws for stringent pollution inspections for cars.

A Michigan ban went into effect prohibiting the disposal of yard wastes from all government facilities into landfills or municipal incinerators. The ban, which applied to weeds, grass clippings, shrubs, leaves, and branches, would not apply to homeowners until 1995.

Equal Rights. A lower court's injunction against Colorado's controversial Amendment 2 was upheld in the state Supreme Court and later ruled unconstitutional. Approved by voters the previous year, the law would have invalidated existing gay rights laws and prohibited new ones. In Cincinnati, Ohio, and Lewiston, Maine, voters repealed local antidiscrimination laws against homosexuals. In Portsmouth, N.H., voters rejected an antidiscrimination law. Hawaii's Supreme Court struck down a ban on marriage by same-sex couples.

A largely ignored 1972 federal civil rights law received renewed attention. The law, Title IX, required colleges and universities to provide equal opportunity for men and women to participate in intercollegiate sports. In California a lawsuit was settled against the state university system when it was agreed that women at the 20 member campuses would be offered basically the same varsity sports opportunities as men by the 1998–99 academic year. Florida passed a "female sports equity law," requiring sports programs for men and women to be equal or risk fines. The National Collegiate Athletic Association scheduled a conference for January 1994 to address what it called "gender-equity guidelines."

Although Wisconsin bars housing discrimination on the basis of marital status, the state's highest court ruled that a landlord could refuse to rent to unmarried couples. The court asserted that "living together is 'conduct,' not 'status,' " and that public policy in Wisconsin promoted marriage.

Consumer Protection. Twenty-three states, including New York, Connecticut, Virginia, Florida, and California, joined forces to investigate whether major cable television companies were taking advantage of loopholes in a new federal law. The law was designed to control prices, but many consumers saw their bills rise. The subsequent disclosure of an internal memo from one cable company prompted a swift investigation. "We cannot be dissuaded from the charges simply because customers object," it said. "The best news of all is we can blame it on reregulation and the government. Let's take advantage of it!"

(MELANIE ANNE COOPER)

Latin America and the Caribbean

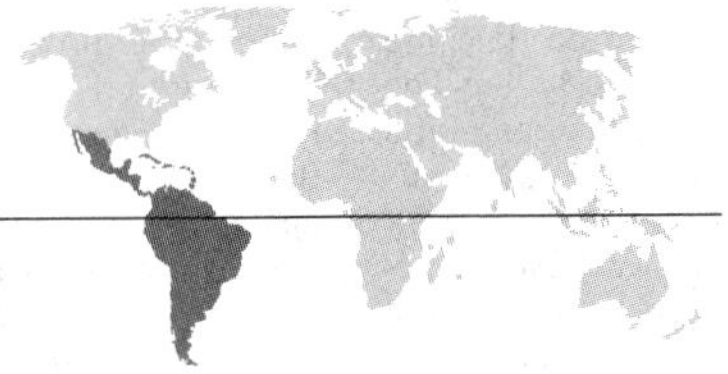

LATIN-AMERICAN AFFAIRS

Political Developments. The year 1993 was a mixed one for Latin America and the Caribbean. On February 24, for the first time since the 1959 revolution, Cubans had the opportunity to vote directly for 589 members of the country's National Assembly as well as for provincial bodies. While those standing were not required to be members, all candidates were supporters of the ruling Communist Party. In Jamaica, Prime Minister Percival J. Patterson of the People's National Party called a general election for March 30, some 11 months before it was due. The timing reflected favourable poll ratings for the PNP over the main opposition Jamaica Labour Party following a period of relative economic stability. As expected, Patterson, who had taken over from Michael Manley in 1992, was reelected in a landslide. A similar snap general election (15 months ahead of time) called in Belize for June 30 did not produce a winning outcome for George Price's People's United Party. The opposition United Democratic Party led by Manuel Esquivel won, benefiting from Price's failure to persuade the British authorities to maintain defense forces in Belize.

From early in the year, it became clear that the government of Jorge Serrano Elías in Guatemala was unlikely to deliver improvements in human rights. On May 25, Serrano suspended the constitution and closed both Congress and the Supreme Court. Serrano was forced to step down on June 1. Elections were quickly convened by Congress, with members voting to install Ramiro de León Carpio as president on June 6. Within three months, however, there was a further crisis in the wake of de León's calls for members of Congress to resign amid allegations of corruption. There followed a period of legal wrangling over reform, with a referendum called for November 28 although the poll was subsequently suspended. Elections in Honduras on November 28 were won by the Liberal Party's Carlos Roberto Reina. Rifts were reopened over human rights issues in El Salvador, where, in March, Pres. Alfredo Cristiani proposed an amnesty for military personnel named in a UN report as perpetrators of atrocities during the country's civil war. By November, evidence of a resurgence of death squads was being investigated by the UN after an increase in killings of members of the left-wing Farabundo Martí National Liberation Front. Pres. Violeta Chamorro's government in Nicaragua appeared increasingly vulnerable as members of the National Opposition Union, which had backed her, withdrew support, putting the former ruling Sandinistas in a stronger bargaining position.

The attempt to reinstate the exiled president of Haiti, Jean-Bertrand Aristide, was not successful. In March the administration of U.S. Pres. Bill Clinton made clear that it would not issue a formal ultimatum to the Haitian military regime. Soon after, during April, the UN proposed a formula to resolve the crisis, and there were indications that the military-backed prime minister would resign to allow for democratic government. In late August Aristide's prime minister designate, Robert Malval, was endorsed by the legislature in Haiti, with a view to Aristide's return by October 30. Despite the dispatch of a U.S. troopship in early October, the deadline passed amid increasing signs that support for Aristide's return was waning, and Malval subsequently announced his resignation.

Allegations of corruption wracked the governments of Venezuela and Brazil. In Venezuela, Pres. Carlos Andrés Pérez was forced to leave office in May following allegations of embezzlement. Octavio Lepage briefly took over, but Ramón José Velásquez was subsequently agreed upon by Congress as interim president. A law approved by Congress in August helped Velásquez push through economic legislation. Repeated speculation that a military coup was in the offing (two failed coups had taken place in February and November 1992) was not borne out, although the political climate was tense. In the presidential and congressional elections on December 5, a veteran politician and former president, Rafael Caldera, standing as an independent but backed by a coalition of minority parties in the National Convergence, defeated the Social Christian (COPEI) candidate, Oswaldo Alvarez Paz. In Brazil a national plebiscite on April 21 retained the presidential system and republican form of government. Having replaced Pres. Fernando Collor de Mello in October 1992 after Congress had voted to impeach him for corruption, the Itamar Franco government suffered a setback in October 1993 when a former treasury official made allegations of widespread corruption. The work of a congressional inquiry contributed to delays in revising the 1988 constitution.

AFP

The leaders of five of the six Group of Rio nations enjoy a lighthearted moment at their summit in Santiago, Chile, in October. From left to right are Presidents César Gaviria Trujillo, Colombia; Itamar Franco, Brazil; Patricio Aylwin Azócar, Chile; Gonzalo Sánchez de Lozada, Bolivia; and Carlos Salinas de Gortari, Mexico.

The ruling Peronist (Justicialist National Movement) party in Argentina did well in the congressional elections on October 3, helping to reinforce Pres. Carlos Menem's bid for constitutional reform that would include a provision to allow him to run for a second consecutive term in 1995. A referendum on the issue was called for November 21, but it was suspended following an accord with the opposition Radical Civic Union, whose leader, Raúl Alfonsín, agreed to cooperate with the National Congress to secure a two-thirds majority for the reform in the Chamber of Deputies.

General elections in Bolivia were held on June 6, with Gonzalo Sánchez de Lozada of the Nationalist Revolutionary Movement winning some 34% of the vote, compared with 21% for the ruling Patriotic Accord led by a former general, Hugo Banzer Suárez. The new president took office on August 6 following his confirmation by two-thirds of Congress. Juan Carlos Wasmosy (*see* BIOGRAPHIES) of the Colorado Party became Paraguay's first democratically elected president on August 15, having been elected on May 9. In elections in Chile on December 11, the Christian Democrat Eduardo Frei, the presidential candidate of the ruling Concertación centre-left coalition, won by a wide margin.

The administration of Alberto Fujimori in Peru continued to reap dividends from having captured Sendero Luminoso (Shining Path) guerrilla leader Abimael Guzman in 1992. Municipal elections held on January 29 returned a large number of independents and were relatively peaceful. A new constitution was endorsed by a slim majority of 53% to 47% in a referendum held on October 31. In Colombia the year was marked by repeated outbursts of drug-related violence, scandals, and politically motivated killings. In December government forces killed Pablo Escobar, leader of the Medellín drug cartel, who had escaped from prison in July 1992.

Economic Affairs. Gross domestic product was expected to grow in 1993 by about 3%, similar to the rate for 1992, partly underpinned by still strong growth rates in Chile (up to 6%) and Argentina (7%) and by more moderate rates in the 3–5% range in other countries, including Brazil (4.5%), which registered a significant recovery in the first half of 1993 after several years of stagnant to negative results. In November the annual growth forecast for Mexico was officially revised down to 1.1% from 2.5–3%, with performance being impaired by uncertainty arising from delays in completing the North American Free Trade Agreement (NAFTA) with the U.S. and Canada. After side accords on labour and the environment were negotiated, NAFTA was ratified by the U.S. Congress in November, paving the way for it to go into operation on Jan. 1, 1994.

With the exception of Brazil, where monthly inflation was running at over 35% in November, inflation remained largely under control, with the regional average projected at 19% for the year, down from 25% in 1992. Both Mexico and Argentina succeeded in bringing annual inflation rates down to below 10% for the first time in many years, reflecting in large measure the success of efforts to control public-sector accounts, keeping them in balance or surplus, and the stability of exchange rates. Of the major economies, Brazil and Venezuela were expected to run sizable deficits, keeping upward pressure on inflation.

The regional trade balance appeared likely to register a deficit of at least $14 billion in 1993, after an $11 billion deficit in 1992, partly because of reduced surpluses in Brazil and Colombia and a reversal of Chile's usual surplus (a deficit of some $800 million was predicted). Poor world prices and weak world demand for many export commodities hampered growth in export revenues from their 1992 level of $127 billion, while overvalued exchange rates in some countries, combined with a more liberal trade regime, favoured import growth well above the $137 billion of 1992.

The aggregate amount of outstanding foreign debt remained high at some $465 billion at the end of 1992, with servicing costs put at some $62 billion during 1993 ($2 billion less than in the previous year). Of the largest debtors, Argentina managed to complete its Brady deal (the reduction of debt through refinancing) with commercial creditors. Brazil, despite having reached a similar Brady deal in July 1992, was unable to complete the agreement by the deadline of Nov. 30, 1993, owing largely to domestic political problems. The deadline was then extended until mid-April 1994.

On regional trade, the Clinton administration pronounced in favour of encouraging a trading bloc along the lines of former president George Bush's Enterprise for the Americas Initiative. The ratification of NAFTA in late November put in place one of the key pieces in this strategy, with Colombia, Venezuela, and Mexico agreeing in December to sign a free-trade pact in January 1994. Uruguay's Pres. Luis Alberto Lacalle expressed the view, however, that a hemisphere-wide bloc was inappropriate in the short run, with emphasis better placed on subregional groups of the kind already being developed. The Southern Cone Common Market (Mercosur) involving Argentina, Brazil, Paraguay, and Uruguay, which aimed to have arrangements for integration in place by the end of 1994, suffered a number of further setbacks during the course of 1993, in large measure related to the widening differences in economic management between Argentina and Brazil. A decision in July by the Caribbean Community and Common Market (Caricom) to increase trade and technical cooperation with Cuba was not well received by the U.S. (SUSAN M. CUNNINGHAM)

ANTIGUA AND BARBUDA

A constitutional monarchy and member of the Commonwealth, Antigua and Barbuda comprises the islands of Antigua, Barbuda, and Redonda in the eastern Caribbean Sea. Area: 442 sq km (171 sq mi). Pop. (1993 est.): 66,000. Cap.: Saint John's. Monetary unit: Eastern Caribbean dollar, with (Oct. 4, 1993) a par value of EC$2.70 to U.S. $1 (free rate of EC$4.10 = £1 sterling). Queen, Elizabeth II; governors-general in 1993, Sir Wilfred E. Jacobs and, from June 10, James Carlisle; prime minister, Vere Cornwall Bird.

The government remained adamant, when the 1993–94 budget was presented in March 1993, that a personal income tax would not be reintroduced into Antigua and Barbuda in the foreseeable future. Finance Minister Molwyn Joseph forecast a 2.5% growth rate for the year.

Civil servants received support from the High Court in March when the judges ruled that legislation barring government employees from publishing political information or expressing political views was illegal. In April government authorities cracked down on foreign drug couriers, who had increasingly been using Antigua and Barbuda as a transshipment point. New laws were introduced allowing confiscation of the assets of those found guilty of trafficking.

In August a controversial book by American author Robert Coram accused the government of "corruption." Such accusations did not inhibit the members of the governing Antigua Labour Party from electing Foreign Affairs Minister Lester Bird as their new political leader. Bird would take over from his father, 83-year-old Vere Bird, who was scheduled to step down before the general election in March 1994. In June, James Carlisle was sworn in as the new governor-general. (DAVID RENWICK)

This article updates the *Macropædia* article The WEST INDIES: *Antigua and Barbuda.*

ARGENTINA

The federal republic of Argentina occupies the eastern section of the Southern Cone of South America, along the Atlantic Ocean. Area: 2,780,400 sq km (1,073,518 sq mi). Pop. (1993 est.): 33,507,000. Cap.: Buenos Aires. Monetary unit: peso, with (Oct. 4, 1993) an official rate of 1 peso to U.S. $1 (1.52 pesos = £1 sterling). President in 1993, Carlos Saúl Menem.

Domestic Affairs. In 1993 Argentina continued to prosper under the framework for stability provided by the April 1991 "convertibility plan." Drawn up by Economy Minister Domingo Cavallo, the plan engendered ongoing advantages for the administration of Pres. Carlos Menem and his Peronist party, the Justicialist National Movement. The success of Cavallo's economic management contributed to a favourable result for the Peronists and their allies among the provincial parties in the midterm elections for 127 of 259 seats in the Chamber of Deputies held on October 3. The Justicialists won some 42% of the 13.2 million votes cast, compared with 30% for the main opposition party, the Radical Civic Union (UCR). The Union of the Democratic Centre (UCeDe), which was among the parties supporting the government, took only 2.6% of the vote, while other district party allies gained about 10%.

The Justicialists did especially well in the city of Buenos Aires, where, contrary to eve-of-poll surveys showing the UCR ahead by up to five percentage points, it won, helped by the campaign led by former defense and economy minister (and close associate of President Menem) Erman González. The party also exceeded expectations in its stronghold of Buenos Aires province, taking over 50% of the vote, up to 15 points more than had been forecast on the basis of opinion surveys. As the country's largest electoral district, Buenos Aires province accounted for some 20 of the 127 seats contested. The strength of support for the ruling party in the country's economic heartland (with the main exception of Córdoba, where there was well-entrenched support for the UCR) appeared to vindicate the reform and liberalization policies pursued by Menem.

Menem's bid for reelection, necessitating a change in the 1853 constitution, was renewed during 1993 after being shelved temporarily in 1992. The move had initially met with resistance from the UCR (and from some Justicialists) despite Menem's efforts to broaden the government's reform agenda. Although the Justicialists and their allies increased their number of seats in the Chamber of Deputies as a result of the October elections, the total fell short of the two-thirds majority required for amending the constitution. Proposals for reform (including the reelection of the president for a second consecutive term but for a reduced period of four years) were finally agreed to by Menem and Raúl Alfonsín, former president and leader of the UCR, in November and approved by the Chamber of Deputies and the Senate the next month.

The opening of government files late in the year showed that more than a thousand Nazi war criminals, many more than previously thought, had entered Argentina. Rioting by disgruntled public workers who had not been paid forced Menem to return home in mid-December from a state visit to the Vatican.

The Economy. Stability, with good growth and low inflation, was sustained during 1993 following an 8.7% growth in gross domestic product to $226 billion and consumer price inflation of 17.5% in 1992. Growth for 1993 was officially projected in the 6–7% range, while annual inflation appeared likely to register below 10%. Industrial output was expected to increase at a slower rate than the 7.8% of 1992, and in the agricultural sphere, flood damage during May (especially in the province of Buenos Aires) affected the output of certain crops. The exchange rate remained firm, with the central bank's buy-and-sell rates effectively held at 0.99 peso and 1 peso per U.S. dollar as part of the strategy devised under the April 1991 convertibility plan, whereby the bank was required to back issues of currency with its international reserves.

Modifications to economic policy in 1993 were less marked than in previous years. During early January government authorities announced an incentive program for export companies. The key feature of the program was lower import tariffs (as low as 2% rather than 22%, rising in stages over a seven-year period to 22%) on goods that would be further processed and exported. On May 1 President Menem used the opportunity of his annual state of the nation address to outline the goals of the administration during the remainder of his term and to announce selected measures for the economy. Amplified by Cavallo, they included a number of actions: exemption of most foreign capital goods

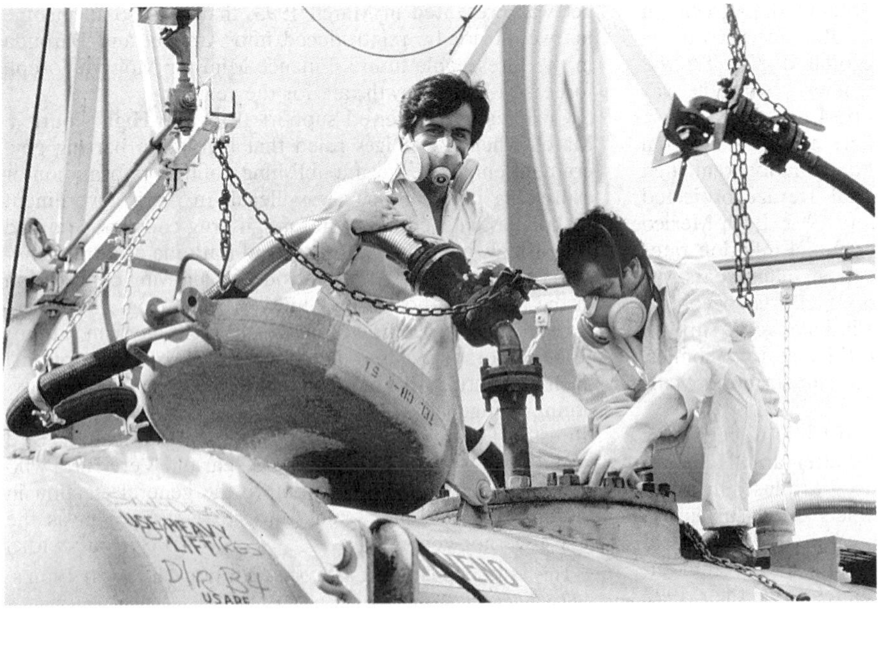

RAFAEL WOLLMANN—GAMMA LIAISON

Workers are engaged in operations at YPF, Argentina's state-run oil company. As a part of Argentina's economic reform, a portion of the company was sold to private investors in 1993.

from import duties; tax rebates of 15% for purchases of domestically produced capital goods; a cut in top loan rates by the state-owned Banco de la Nacion from 17 to 16% per year for dollar-denominated loans and from 1.8 to 1.6% per month for peso loans; increased lending to small and medium-sized farms and companies; exemption from a 1% asset tax for certain industrial sectors; and easier payment terms for those firms that were in arrears on tax and social security debts.

Among other legislative reforms, the government succeeded in winning legislative approval for its long-delayed social-security-reform bill when the Senate voted the bill through on September 23 (the Chamber of Deputies had passed it in May). The bill would allow for the voluntary establishment of private pensions as an alternative to the government scheme. A new labour-reform bill was introduced, with expected opposition from the main labour confederation being partly defused by the offer of consultation prior to presentation of the bill to the legislature. In late June some $3,040,000,000 of stock in the state oil concern, YPF, was put up for sale. (SUSAN M. CUNNINGHAM)

BAHAMAS, THE

A constitutional monarchy and member of the Commonwealth, The Bahamas comprises an archipelago of about 700 islands in the North Atlantic Ocean just southeast of the United States. Area: 13,939 sq km (5,382 sq mi). Pop. (1993 est.): 266,000. Cap.: Nassau. Monetary unit: Bahamian dollar, with (Oct. 4, 1993) a par value of B$1 to U.S. $1 (free rate of B$1.52 = £1 sterling). Queen, Elizabeth II; governor-general in 1993, Clifford Darling; prime minister, Hubert Ingraham.

A Commission of Inquiry, which began hearings in February 1993 into allegations of corruption and misuse of funds at the national airlines (Bahamasair), was also investigating the Bahamas Telecommunications Corporation and the Bahamas Hotel Corporation.

In May an agreement was signed for the establishment of an industrial park for U.S., European, and Asian high-tech companies in the free zone at Freeport on Grand Bahama. The park was to be operated by Grand Bahama International Teleport Ltd. Despite a forecast by the Bahamas Hotel Employers' Association that the industry was likely to register a gross operating loss for the first time in 1993, the construction of another 500-room hotel on Grand Bahama was announced in June. Signaling its intention to develop a local securities market to match the country's international financial role, in June the government appointed a task force to do feasibility studies.

The Inter-American Development Bank granted a $31.8 million loan for a new Bahamas Electricity Corporation project in the Family Islands.

Illegal Haitian immigrants were a major preoccupation of the authorities during the year. As of June, 571 Haitians had been detained, with most of them being deported. (DAVID RENWICK)

This article updates the *Macropædia* article The WEST INDIES: *The Bahamas*.

BARBADOS

The constitutional monarchy of Barbados, a member of the Commonwealth, occupies the most easterly island in the southern Caribbean Sea. Area: 430 sq km (166 sq mi). Pop. (1993 est.): 260,000. Cap.: Bridgetown. Monetary unit: Barbados dollar, with (Oct. 4, 1993) a par value of BDS$2.01 to U.S. $1 (free rate of BDS$3.06 = £1 sterling). Queen, Elizabeth II; governor-general in 1993, Dame Nita Barrow; prime minister, Erskine Sandiford.

The Barbados central bank, which had predicted real economic growth of 1–2% in 1993, later revised that to no growth at all. Barbadians had hoped for an improvement after three continuous years of economic decline. In May it was announced that one of the few economic sectors continuing to do well—cruise tourism—would be further enhanced by a $3 million extension to the Bridgetown cruise terminal. Cruise tourists now spent about $20 million a year in Barbados. The future of the sugar industry, on the other hand, remained in doubt. When the sugar crop began winding down in June, production stood at only about 48,000 metric tons, a 62-year low. The sugar industry remained in receivership, and a new management company for the industry had not yet got off the ground.

In August government, labour, and business achieved agreement on a two-year income and prices policy, necessary for improving relations with international lending agencies. There was to be a pay freeze until April 1995, and price increases would be restrained.

In August 43-year-old Owen Arthur took over as leader of the opposition Barbados Labour Party, replacing the ailing Henry Forde. (DAVID RENWICK)

This article updates the *Macropædia* article The WEST INDIES: *Barbados*.

BELIZE

A constitutional monarchy and member of the Commonwealth, Belize is on the Caribbean coast of Central America. Area: 22,965 sq km (8,867 sq mi). Pop. (1993 est.): 204,000. Cap.: Belmopan. Monetary unit: Belize dollar, with (Oct. 4, 1993) a par value of BZ$2 to U.S. $1 (free rate of BZ$3.04 = £1 sterling). Queen, Elizabeth II; governors-general in 1993, Dame Minita Gordon and, from November 17, Colville Young; prime ministers, George Cadle Price and, from July 3, Manuel Esquivel.

Because of improved relations between Belize and Guatemala since 1991, the U.K. announced in May 1993 that the British garrison staffed in Belize for 45 years would be withdrawn. This would give Belize formal responsibility for its own defense starting Jan. 1, 1994. Britain would remain available for consultation in the event of a military threat from Guatemala.

This announcement and the military-backed coup in Guatemala on June 1 were major issues in the general elections called for June 30 (more than a year before they were due) by the People's United Party (PUP). Nevertheless, the United Democratic Party (UDP) won 16 seats out of 29 in the House of Representatives. Manuel Esquivel of the UDP was elected prime minister and later asked for the resignation of longtime governor-general Dame Minita Gordon, a move criticized by the PUP. The PUP was defeated for only the second time since its foundation in 1950.

Despite Guatemala's claim that it would continue to recognize Belizean independence, Esquivel announced that the new UDP government would suspend all partial agreements with Guatemala until a final agreement was signed ending Guatemala's claim on Belize. (INES T. BAPTIST)

This article updates the *Macropædia* article CENTRAL AMERICA: *Belize*.

BOLIVIA

Bolivia is a landlocked republic in central South America. Area: 1,098,581 sq km (424,164 sq mi). Pop. (1993 est.): 7,715,000. Administrative cap., La Paz; judicial cap., Sucre. Monetary unit: boliviano, with (Oct. 4, 1993) a free rate of 4.33 bolivianos to U.S. $1 (6.56 bolivianos = £1 sterling). Presidents in 1993, Jaime Paz Zamora and, from August 6, Gonzalo Sánchez de Lozada Bustamente.

Bolivia held presidential and congressional elections in June 1993. The principal presidential contenders were Gonzalo Sánchez de Lozada of the Nationalist Revolutionary Movement (NRM); Hugo Banzer Suárez of Nationalist Democratic Action and leader of the Patriotic Accord; Max Fernández, a brewery owner and head of Civic Solidarity Union; and Carlos Palenque of Conscience of the Fatherland and a talk-show host. Sánchez de Lozada won 34% of the vote, while his party fell short of the 79 seats required for an absolute majority in Congress. Sánchez de Lozada's opponents conceded defeat before a second ballot was called.

Among the reasons for the NRM victory was disillusion with the previous government's inability to capitalize on the economic stability introduced in 1985 by Sánchez de Lozada himself. Inflation fell to 11% in 1992 (with 9% forecast for 1993); gross domestic product grew by 3.4%; and net reserves stood at over $200 million. In contrast, the trade deficit, at $561 million in 1992, was the worst in a decade. The main causes were the termination of a fixed-price agreement on gas sales to Argentina and declining nontraditional exports. It was expected that the target of 3.2% for the public-sector deficit set by the International Monetary Fund would be exceeded, threatening a rescheduling agreement with the Paris Club of creditor nations. In addition, the UN and the World Bank stated that Bolivia still had the highest percentage of rural poverty in the world and that per capita income, at $700, was 20% lower in 1993 than in 1980. This indicated that economic stability had not benefited the poorest sectors. On March 1, members of the Bolivian Labour Federation began a hunger strike and a general strike for salary increases.

The cocaine trade remained a major contributor to the economy, although U.S. and Bolivian antinarcotics agencies claimed some success in limiting the cultivation of coca and the illegal export of coca paste and cocaine.

In the key mining sector, Comibol, the state-owned mining corporation, closed two mines as international metal prices fell but also opened new facilities. Negotiations collapsed between the government and Lithco of the U.S. on the exploitation of the world's largest lithium deposit. The government's failure to define clear rules for joint ventures and privatization eroded hopes for renewed foreign investment. Sánchez de Lozada unveiled a plan for capitalization of state companies, rather than privatization, that would involve selling 49% of selected enterprises to private investors, who would then help restore efficiency before the government stake was distributed to the Bolivian people.

In April, Gen. Luís García Meza, who, as dictator in 1980, had been associated with cocaine trafficking, was sentenced to prison for 30 years in absentia, having jumped bail in 1989. (BEN BOX)

BRAZIL

Brazil is a federal republic in eastern South America on the Atlantic Ocean. Area: 8,511,996 sq km (3,286,500 sq mi). Pop. (1993 est.): 156,493,000. Cap.: Brasília. Monetary unit: cruzeiro real (introduced August 2 to replace the cruzeiro at the rate of 1 cruzeiro real = 1,000 cruzeiros), with (Oct. 4, 1993) a free rate of 128.47 cruzeiros reais to U.S. $1 (194.64 cruzeiros reais = £1 sterling). President in 1993, Itamar Franco.

Domestic Affairs. Late in 1992 Itamar Franco (*see* BIOGRAPHIES) replaced Fernando Collor de Mello as president of Brazil when the latter resigned during his impeachment trial. Franco was sworn in to complete the remainder of Collor's five-year term, which was to run to January 1995. Early in 1993 Franco managed to galvanize cross-party support from the great majority of members of Congress—who had supported the impeachment of Collor for his alleged involvement in a multimillion-dollar corruption and influence-peddling scheme—for legislative measures needed to help overcome a fiscal crisis.

In late January, Congress approved a package of partial tax reforms and the modernization-of-ports bill. On January 20 the introduction of a tax of 0.25% on checks and related bank transfers was approved. This aimed to raise some $7 billion of additional revenues in a full year, but obstacles to implementation prevented it from going into effect until the end of August. Only a few weeks after its introduction, the Supreme Court suspended collection pending a review of its constitutionality, which was due to be completed by the end of the year.

To help win support for the fiscal measures, Franco had to assure members of key parties (especially the Party of the Brazilian Democratic Movement [PMDB] and the Workers Party [PT]) that a portion of new revenues would be deployed in social projects in the spheres of housing and education. Finance Minister Paulo Haddad had incorporated such provisions in his plans for the economy, but they were delayed until late April owing to his resignation on March 1. His successor, Eliseu Resende, retained the basic outlines of the plan, which was announced on April 24, but also emphasized the use of funds originally designated for privatization to finance social projects. The Resende plan included a $2.6 billion low-income-housing program, public works projects, an emergency food-distribution plan, reduced import tariffs on medicines, and subsidies to agriculture.

Following a decline in gross domestic product (GDP) of 0.9% in 1992, the government's underlying aim was to reflate the economy modestly so as to provide growth of about 3.5% in 1993. Although initially well received, the plan faced implementation difficulties and required a revision of the budget, which had been approved only one month earlier. Resende's stay in office proved short, his resignation coming in the third week of May after allegations that he had been involved in influence-peddling activities. On October 17 a former senior treasury official accused more than 30 politicians, including some members of the Cabinet, of corruption and unleashed a new congressional inquiry.

Brazil's national plebiscite on the form and system of government took place as planned on April 21. Two-thirds of the 50 million voters who cast valid ballots favoured retaining the presidential system, and a six-to-one majority also voted to keep the republican form of government.

Revision of the constitution was scheduled to begin after Oct. 5, 1993. Despite efforts of some groups (led by the PT and the Democratic Labour Party [PDT]) to prevent it, the review did begin on October 7. Deliberations during the remainder of that month were dominated by procedural issues and amendment proposals, with long-term fiscal reforms (including changes in the allocation of federal funds to state and municipal governments) being among the priorities.

Fernando Henrique Cardoso of the Social Democrat Party (PSDB) was nominated to the post of finance minister (having previously been foreign minister) after Resende's departure in late May. Cardoso moved in the following months to appoint other PSDB members to senior posts both within his ministry and to other key agencies such as the National Development Bank and the central bank. Cabinet posts were reshuffled during August and September, triggered initially by the failure of the Socialist Party (PSB) to support the government in a crucial vote on a revised wage bill; the government later won a majority in the vote on the bill. The PSB relinquished several Cabinet

Prices posted in a Rio de Janeiro supermarket show the effects of Brazil's hyperinflation. In midyear the government introduced the cruzeiro real, a new currency that dropped three zeroes from the old one. The move had no effect on the country's inflation rate, but it did make calculations easier.

JOHN MAIER—THE NEW YORK TIMES

posts, providing Franco with an opportunity to bring in the Progressive Reform Party and widening his base of political power.

Incidents of violence continued to mar life in Brazil in 1993. In July three military policemen were arrested and charged with the killing of seven homeless boys in Rio de Janeiro, and a month later 33 policemen were apprehended for the murder of 21 people in a Rio shantytown. Also in August illegal Brazilian gold miners in remote Amazonas state reportedly killed 73 members of the Yanomamö Indian tribe, although later reports significantly reduced the number of deaths and placed the killings across the border in Venezuela.

The Economy. It became evident during the first quarter of 1993 that a recovery was under way, industrial output having begun to improve in late 1992, helped by lower domestic interest rates. Industrial output for the first quarter of 1993 increased 8% over the same period of 1992, largely because of even larger rises in the consumer durables sector, where there was buoyant vehicle production. GDP grew about 5.5% during the first half of 1993, led by a 10.9% increase for manufacturing.

Despite the efforts of successive finance ministers to stabilize the economy and bring the public-sector accounts into balance without resorting to such drastic measures as price and wage freezes, inflation continued on an upward curve, increasing from more than 27% in January to about 30% in June and 35% in October. The draft budget for 1994 was made available in early August 1993, but the events of October made it necessary for Cardoso to revise this with a view to reducing a projected deficit of some $25 billion.

Legislation was signed on September 8 to separate the accounts of the central bank and the treasury (the move also permitted the transfer of $52 billion held in government debt instruments from the bank to the treasury), paving the way for the central bank to deal with monetary and exchange-rate policy while the treasury handled fiscal policy. Further progress was made with privatization, with the entire steel sector having been disposed of by the end of September. A number of petrochemical concerns were scheduled to be auctioned in November.

The external accounts position continued to be positive. By the end of September, the nine-month trade surplus had reached $10.3 billion, with exports close to $29 billion and imports $18.6 billion. (SUSAN M. CUNNINGHAM)

CHILE

The republic of Chile extends along the Pacific coast of the Southern Cone of South America. Area: 756,626 sq km (292,135 sq mi), not including Chile's Antarctic claim. Pop. (1993 est.): 13,542,000. Cap.: Santiago (national); Valparaíso (legislative). Monetary unit: Chilean peso, with (Oct. 4, 1993) a free rate of 407.95 pesos to U.S. $1 (618.05 pesos = £1 sterling). President in 1993, Patricio Aylwin Azócar.

Sept. 11, 1993, was declared a national holiday to commemorate 20 years since the military coup led by Gen. Augusto Pinochet Ugarte in 1973, which overthrew the socialist alliance of Salvador Allende Gossens. A monument with an eternal flame was erected close to the Moneda presidential palace, and a 10-peso copper coin was minted for the occasion. Troubled by human rights abuses, thousands of protesters clashed with the police in Santiago; two people were killed and about 100 injured, some by gunfire.

Pres. Patricio Aylwin Azócar attempted to speed up delayed investigations of some 200 active cases (600–800 more pending) of human rights abuses by the military, but his bill was rejected in the Chamber of Deputies in July. The sticking point for the left-wing opposition was the stipulation that trials should be held in secret, with anonymity guaranteed for members of the military called as witnesses. Aylwin had hoped that the bill would encourage more evidence to emerge, but its rejection meant that no legislation would be passed before the presidential elections.

Critics within the military declared that human rights trials were a waste of time anyway, as an amnesty in 1978 had agreed that no incidents occurring before 1978 would be considered. However, President Aylwin was determined to locate the remains of over 1,000 people who had disappeared after detention during the military regime. In November two generals were sentenced to prison for ordering the assassination of opposition leader Orlando Letelier in Washington, D.C., in 1976. It was the first time that the courts had sentenced senior army officers to prison for rights abuses.

In the presidential elections held on December 11, Eduardo Frei, the candidate of the ruling Concertación centre-left coalition won a decisive victory. Frei was a 45-year-old Christian Democrat whose father had been president from 1964 to 1970. The leading opposition party was the Union for Chilean Progress, a right-wing coalition of three parties whose candidate was 69-year-old Arturo Alessandri.

Democratic powers were still circumscribed by the armed forces, partly as a result of a new constitution introduced in 1980 by General Pinochet, which remained largely in force. The constitution allowed Pinochet, as commander of the armed forces, to appoint nine nonelected senators to Congress, likely to weight it heavily in favour of the right wing. The ruling Concertación was stuck in a vicious circle, as it could not gain control of Congress without changing the constitution, which could not be done without having a two-thirds majority in Congress. Despite overwhelming support for Concertación, it did not gain a sufficient majority in the December parliamentary elections to outweigh the right wing in the balance of power.

Chile's status as Latin America's most stable economy was upset by forecasts of its first trade deficit in 12 years, predicted to total more than $500 million by the end of 1993. Reasons given for the deficit were that a 6% increase in gross domestic product had led to a surge in import consumption and foreign investment. Imports were estimated to total $10.9 billion, a rise of some 18% over 1992. Foreign investment exceeded $400 million in 1992, according to the Chilean central bank, a rise from $10 million in 1988. Lower world prices and strong foreign competition in copper, fish meal, pulp, and fruit—all key industries—were also blamed for the trade imbalance. Consumer spending remained high as wages and employment levels continued to rise. Inflation was forecast to total 12% by the end of 1993, against 12.7% at the end of 1992. (HUW CLOUGH)

COLOMBIA

A republic in northwestern South America, Colombia has coastlines on the Caribbean Sea and the Pacific Ocean. Area: 1,141,748 sq km (440,831 sq mi). Pop. (1993 est.): 33,951,000. Cap.: Bogotá. Monetary unit: Colombian peso, with (Oct. 4, 1993) a free rate of 804.95 pesos to U.S. $1 (1,220 pesos = £1 sterling). President in 1993, César Gaviria Trujillo.

On Jan. 1, 1993, the government announced a 25% increase in the minimum wage, bringing the basic monthly income to $100. Approximately three million workers received the basic salary, which had remained constant in real terms since the mid-1980s. Economic activity was steady throughout 1993, with a 4% increase in real gross domestic product forecast by the end of the year. This growth was matched by a persistently high inflation rate, however, predicted to average 24%.

The economy was boosted by new oil production in the Llanos foothills, 160 km (100 mi) northeast of Bogotá. Significant oil deposits were discovered there in July 1991, and when the main Cusiana field was declared commercial in mid-1993, the state oil company, Ecopetrol, acquired a 50% stake. The government estimated that the new oil fields could yield $2.5 billion a year by 1997, but it offered assurances that an oil boom would not lead to dependence on one industry, as had occurred in other oil-producing states in the region, such as Venezuela and Mexico. Oil revenue would also be used to develop the general infrastructure and social programs.

On December 2 Pablo Escobar, leader of the Medellín drug cartel, was shot dead, along with a bodyguard, as they were trying to escape from the roof of a house where hundreds of policemen and soldiers had trapped them. He had made a spectacular escape from prison in July 1992 and since that time had made several unsuccessful attempts to negotiate a surrender with authorities. Throughout 1993 the war between the drug cartels and the government had continued unabated, with Escobar reportedly ordering the assassination of rivals in an attempt to maintain his power. However, the police slowly tightened the net around Escobar, exposing his safe houses and arresting his top bodyguards.

Exploiting Escobar's imprisonment and subsequent refuge from justice, the rival Cali cartel increased its illegal drug activities. U.S. drug-enforcement authorities estimated that Cali controlled over 80% of drugs smuggled into the U.S. In what was seen largely as a publicity exercise, the Cali cartel announced in May that it would give up all illegal business activities if allowed to come out of hiding and, by implication, be pardoned for all crimes to date.

Government action against guerrilla organizations continued. A state of emergency, originally imposed in November 1992, was renewed in February 1993 and again in May for a further 90 days. The government offered to renew talks with the guerrillas in March but only if they agreed to a unilateral cease-fire, a condition that was rejected. Violence occurred throughout the year, and the army claimed that from November 1992 to May 1993 over 1,200 rebels had been either captured or killed. Rigorous new legal measures

CARLOS ANGEL—GAMMA LIAISON

The body of Pablo Escobar lies on a roof in Medellín, where he was shot and killed by government forces on December 2. Leader of the Medellín drug cartel and accused of widespread murder and violence, Escobar had escaped from prison in July 1992.

and financial rewards were also introduced to try to bring an end to guerrilla activity. Judges' salaries were increased and extra safeguards provided for their protection. Awards were offered for the arrest of the leaders of the two main guerrilla groups: Manuel Marulanda Vélez of the Revolutionary Armed Forces of Colombia and Manuel Pérez of the National Liberation Army. Some 10,000 more soldiers and 8,000 more police were recruited as part of a general increase of intelligence and counterinsurgency operations.

(HUW CLOUGH)

COSTA RICA

The Central American republic of Costa Rica has coastlines on the Caribbean Sea and the Pacific Ocean. Area: 51,100 sq km (19,730 sq mi). Pop. (1993 est.): 3,199,000. Cap.: San José. Monetary unit: Costa Rican colón, with (Oct. 4, 1993) a free rate of 144.73 colones to U.S. $1 (219.26 colones = £1 sterling). President in 1993, Rafael Angel Calderón Fournier.

Political parties in Costa Rica spent 1993 preparing for the February 1994 presidential and congressional elections. The ruling Social Christian Unity Party (PUSC) chose as its presidential candidate Miguel Angel Rodríguez. The opposition National Liberation Party (PLN) selected José María Figueres, the son of the former president. The PUSC maintained its leadership in the municipal council elections on May 1 and in the internal congressional elections, but in national politics its popularity fell. Despite healthy growth of 7.8% in gross domestic product in 1992, a lower public-sector deficit, rising exports, and falling unemployment, incomes slumped, leading to labour unrest and strikes.

On March 8, five armed Nicaraguans seized the Nicaraguan embassy in San José and took 25 hostages, including the ambassador. They demanded a $6 million ransom and the dismissal of the Nicaraguan armed forces commander, Humberto Ortega, and the minister of the presidency, Antonio Lacayo. All hostages were eventually released, and the kidnappers' leader, José Manuel Urbina Lara, a former contra, was granted asylum in the Dominican Republic.

On April 26, five Costa Rican gunmen seized 19 Supreme Court justices and 5 assistants, demanding a $20 million ransom and safe passage to Brazil. Pres. Rafael Angel Calderón Fournier declared that the government would not pay ransom. On April 29 the hostages were released and the gunmen were arrested. The trial of former president Luís Alberto Monge and 18 other former PLN leaders charged with embezzlement and misappropriation of a disaster relief fund in 1983–85 opened on May 17.

Stone Container Corp. of Chicago, which had a 10,125-ha (25,000-ac) plantation of gmelina, a fast-growing nonnative tree, was reported to be preparing to build the largest chip mill in Central America on the Osa Peninsula. Conservationists expressed fears that secondary forests and wetlands would be threatened, as would the Dulce Gulf, a breeding ground for whales, dolphins, and many species of fish.

(SARAH CAMERON)

This article updates the *Macropædia* article CENTRAL AMERICA: *Costa Rica*.

CUBA

The socialist republic of Cuba comprises the island of Cuba and several thousand smaller islands and cays in the Caribbean Sea. Area: 110,861 sq km (42,804 sq mi). Pop. (1993 est.): 10,892,000. Cap.: Havana. Monetary unit: Cuban peso, with (Oct. 4, 1993) an official rate of 0.75 peso to U.S. $1 (1.14 pesos = £1 sterling). President of the Councils of State and Ministers in 1993, Fidel Castro Ruz.

The majority of Cubans continued to face economic hardships in 1993. Severe weather, moreover, added to their misery. January rains ruined the sugar harvest, and a hurricane in March and flooding in June forced the evacuation of 60,000 people. The sugar export crop, which accounted for 65% of all foreign exchange earnings in 1992, was down by 40% in 1993, the lowest level in 30 years. Other export crops (*e.g.,* citrus and tobacco) and domestic staples (*e.g.,* bananas and cassava) were ruined. Many farms, factories, and warehouses also incurred damage.

The government actively recruited outside trading and investment partners to prevent overreliance on any one source of financial aid. Foreign groups promised to invest some $500 million over a period of several years to support such things as tourism, mining, light industry, agribusiness, and electronics. Nevertheless, falling local demand led to a further decline in imports, forecast at $1.7 billion in 1993, compared with $2.2 billion in 1992 and $8 billion in 1989. Continued fuel shortages caused frequent power blackouts and transport problems. Petty theft, prostitution, and black marketeers became more common, while the gulf separating those who had dollars from those who did not continued to widen.

A mysterious neural disease that caused muscular disorders and, in about 10% of the cases, blindness affected some 50,000 people. The European Commission helped fight the disease by donating $6 million. The government distributed $40 million worth of multivitamins to the entire population to improve general health and to increase resistance to the disease even though officials denied that the illness was due to malnutrition.

The dire state of the economy and a chronic shortage of foreign exchange forced the government to embrace a new policy in 1993. In July it announced that Cuban citizens would be allowed to possess U.S. dollars and other convertible currencies and to spend them in special shops. The U.S. administration stated that the current $300-per-quarter limit on remittances would not be relaxed, although it was generally accepted that this would be difficult to police. On July 26, in his Moncada anniversary speech, Castro also stated that more Cubans living abroad would be allowed to visit their relatives in Cuba. These moves increased the risk of social unrest because they favoured dissidents with exiled relatives in Florida over the party faithful, who worked for the state and had no access to dollars.

The mood of reform intensified in August when four key economic ministers were replaced. Alfredo Jordán Morales was appointed minister for agriculture, Nelson Torres Pérez minister for sugar, Gen. Silvano Colas Sánchez minister of communications, and José Luis Rodríguez García minister of finance.

A small step toward establishing a mixed economy was taken in September when Castro signed a decree authorizing limited private enterprise in some 100 trades, crafts, and services. Entrepreneurs would be allowed to benefit directly from their work and negotiate prices with their clients, but they would not be allowed to employ other people. It was expected that small family businesses similar to those found in Vietnam and China would soon appear. Taxi drivers, carpenters, mechanics, decorators, cooks, and computer programmers would be able to run their own businesses, but graduates, especially doctors and company managers, would be barred from private enterprise.

There was no relaxation of the U.S. trade and financial embargo on Cuba, but relations improved and were considerably less confrontational. There were frequent suggestions in the press and in business circles that the embargo be lifted. After Pres. Bill Clinton took office, the anti-Castro

In a Cuban pharmacy a woman shops for medicinal herbs, sold as a substitute for drugs no longer available. As Cuba continued to suffer from the U.S.-led embargo and the collapse of the Soviet bloc, the government made moves toward a mixed economy during the year.
CINDY KARP—BLACK STAR

Cuban-American National Foundation was less influential in government circles. The House of Representatives voted to cease funding for TV Martí, the U.S. government's anti-Castro television station. The U.S. State Department's new guidelines for telecommunications companies allowed telephone links to Cuba. This small breach in the economic embargo would allow Cuba to receive half of future telephone revenues, although its estimated $80 million share of earlier telecommunications revenues remained frozen in an escrow account in New York. After U.S. and Cuban coast guard officials met to discuss the rise in illegal immigrants reaching the U.S., immigration personnel from both sides agreed that 20,000 Cubans would be allowed to enter the U.S. each year, the level agreed to in 1984 but suspended in 1985. Contacts on military matters had become so amicable that the U.S. kept Cuba informed of its naval exercises in the area. In September the two countries cooperated in an antidrug operation. Acting on information passed on by a U.S. counternarcotics patrol, the Cuban coast guard seized a boat in Cuban waters. U.S. drug agents flew to Cuba to take custody of the two Americans suspected of smuggling cocaine. It was the first time Cuba had returned a boat and its crew to the U.S. for prosecution on narcotics charges.

In a much-publicized incident in December, Alina Fernández Revuelta, daughter of Castro, escaped to Spain and then was granted asylum in the U.S. Castro allowed his granddaughter to join her mother several days later.

(SARAH CAMERON)

This article updates the *Macropædia* article The WEST INDIES: *Cuba*.

DOMINICA

An island republic within the Commonwealth, Dominica is in the eastern Caribbean Sea. Area: 750 sq km (290 sq mi). Pop. (1993 est.): 73,900. Cap.: Roseau. Monetary unit: Eastern Caribbean dollar, with (Oct. 4, 1993) a par value of EC$2.70 to U.S. $1 (free rate of EC$4.10 = £1 sterling). Presidents in 1993, Clarence Augustus Seignoret and, from October 25, Crispin Sorhaindo; prime minister, Eugenia Charles.

Prime Minister Dame Eugenia Charles reaffirmed in May 1993 that the Dominica Freedom Party's (DFP's) policy of selling off state enterprises would stand, regardless of criticism from various quarters. Another controversial government policy, that of selling citizenship to Asian businessmen as a means of encouraging much-needed investment, seemed to be working. A government spokesman said that the "vast majority" of the 466 people who had become Dominican citizens between August 1991 and April 1993 were Taiwanese. It was estimated that this policy had brought some $5.8 million into the economy.

As elsewhere in the Caribbean, the governing party in Dominica moved in 1993 to make provision for the orderly replacement of an aging leader. In August the external affairs minister, Brian Alleyne, defeated three other candidates to become the new head of the DFP. He would take over from Dame Eugenia when she retired prior to the general election scheduled for May 1995. Dame Eugenia had led the party since its founding in 1968. Also during 1993, former left-wing radical Rosie Douglas consolidated his position as new leader of the opposition Labour Party of Dominica. He inherited the post from his brother, Michael, who died of cancer in 1992.

(DAVID RENWICK)

This article updates the *Macropædia* article The WEST INDIES: *Dominica*.

DOMINICAN REPUBLIC

The Dominican Republic covers the eastern two-thirds of the Caribbean island of Hispaniola, which it shares with Haiti. Area: 48,443 sq km (18,704 sq mi). Pop. (1993 est.): 7,634,000. Cap.: Santo Domingo. Monetary unit: Dominican peso, with (Oct. 4, 1993) a free rate of 12.91 pesos to U.S. $1 (19.55 pesos = £1 sterling). President in 1993, Joaquín Balaguer.

Political campaigning intensified in 1993 in anticipation of the presidential elections in 1994. Although Pres. Joaquín Balaguer several times denied that he would be seeking reelection, rumours of his candidacy continued to spread despite his age, blindness, and failing health. During the year he spent two weeks in a hospital in Miami, Fla., recovering from an operation and then spent an additional period of convalescence in the Dominican Republic.

The main opposition party, the left-wing Dominican Revolutionary Party, announced the candidacy of its leader, José Francisco Peña Gómez. Polls showed him to be the most likely to win. At a meeting in August, he said that he would share power and proposed electoral reform to prohibit repeated presidential terms. He accused the ruling Social Christian Reformist Party of mounting a racist campaign against him, calling him a Haitian, and also of raising fears of a French-sponsored campaign to unite the Dominican Republic and Haiti.

In March the state-owned Rosario Dominicana temporarily closed down its gold-mining activities and suspended 70% of its employees. Costs of production had greatly exceeded sale prices; output was declining; and the company was carrying a high level of debt. The closing did not affect plans to open the Pueblo Viejo mine, where deposits were valued at more than $6 billion. (SARAH CAMERON)

This article updates the *Macropædia* article The WEST INDIES: *Dominican Republic.*

ECUADOR

The republic of Ecuador is in western South America, on the Pacific Ocean. Area: 272,045 sq km (105,037 sq mi), including the Galápagos Islands. Pop. (1993 est.): 10,985,000. Cap.: Quito. Monetary unit: sucre, with (Oct. 4, 1993) an official rate of 1,813 sucres to U.S. $1 (2,746 sucres = £1 sterling) and a free rate of 1,933 sucres to U.S. $1 (2,929 sucres = £1 sterling). President in 1993, Sixto Durán Ballén.

A massive landslide at the end of March 1993 in the southern province of Azuay caused the country's worst-ever natural disaster, with damages estimated in excess of $100 million. The initial death toll was put at 32, but subsequent rescue teams estimated that several hundred victims were buried beneath debris. Thousands of homes were destroyed, and communication was cut off between Quito and Guayaquil. The Paute River became dammed, and the resulting backwater flooded hundreds of hectares of surrounding land.

In January public- and private-sector workers received wage increases equivalent to a 30% raise over the year. Despite these increases a wave of labour unrest spread across the country, including lockouts and strikes. Farmworkers staged mass demonstrations in reaction to rumours that social security was to be privatized or even eliminated. Further protests occurred in March, organized by trade unions campaigning against the privatization of industries. Congress, however, approved a privatization law in October.

Pres. Sixto Durán Ballén continued to face union opposition to his economic policies. By mid-1993 opinion polls were giving the president only a 20% popularity rating as accusations rose that the poor were being left even poorer. Credit agreements with the International Monetary Fund expired in December 1992 and, in order for the arrangements to be renewed, a target inflation rate of 25–30% was set for the end of 1993. For 1992 the consumer price index rose 60.2% overall.

In August the army began a human rights program, the first of its kind for the military in Latin America. Approximately 6,000 officers and troops began training in human rights, democratic values, and regional security. If the pilot scheme proved successful, it would be incorporated into the training of all 85,000 members of the armed forces. The program was drawn up with the Latin American Human Rights Association and approved by the United Nations and the Organization of American States. (HUW CLOUGH)

EL SALVADOR

The republic of El Salvador is situated on the Pacific coast of Central America. Area: 21,041 sq km (8,124 sq mi). Pop. (1993 est.): 5,517,000. Cap.: San Salvador. Monetary unit: Salvadoran colón, with (Oct. 4, 1993) a free rate of 8.64 colones to U.S. $1 (13.08 colones = £1 sterling). President in 1993, Alfredo Cristiani.

In March a United Nations Truth Commission report was published on the atrocities of El Salvador's 12-year-old civil war. It found that senior army officers were responsible for ordering the murder of thousands of civilians. It named the defense minister, Gen. René Emilio Ponce, together with four other senior officers, as responsible for the murders of six Jesuit priests and their cook and her daughter in 1989; the late Roberto d'Aubuisson, leader of the right-wing Nationalist Republican Alliance (Arena), for the murder of Archbishop Oscar Romero in 1980; and the U.S.-trained Atlacatl battalion for the massacre of hundreds of civilians at El Mozote in 1981. The commission recommended the officers' dismissal and urged that they be barred from public office for 10 years and prohibited from ever gaining military or security responsibilities.

The Legislative Assembly subsequently passed an amnesty for all those who had committed murder and other crimes during the war. This provoked the UN secretary-general to accuse the government of reneging on the peace settlement and to criticize Pres. Alfredo Cristiani for not sending an envoy to New York with a timetable for implementing proposals in the commission's report. The army high command angrily denounced "international pressures," while the U.S. said it would withhold further military aid until the purge of officers had been completed. By the end of June, changes had been announced in the high command and in other key posts, with the defense minister, the deputy defense minister, and the chief of staff all pushed into retirement.

AP/WIDE WORLD

A monument commemorates the men, women, and children killed in 1981 at El Mozote and nearby hamlets during El Salvador's civil war. A UN commission report issued in 1993 concluded that a group trained in the U.S. had been responsible for the massacre.

The political parties named their candidates for the March 1994 presidential elections. The ruling Arena party chose Armando Calderon Sol, who was president of the party and mayor of San Salvador. The Democratic Convergence chose Rubén Zamora, vice president of the Legislative Assembly. Fidel Chávez Mena was nominated by the Christian Democrats even though he had failed to win in the 1989 elections. (SARAH CAMERON)

This article updates the *Macropædia* article CENTRAL AMERICA: *El Salvador.*

GRENADA

A constitutional monarchy within the Commonwealth, Grenada (with its dependency, the Southern Grenadines) is in the eastern Caribbean Sea. Area: 344 sq km (133 sq mi). Pop. (1993 est.): 91,000. Cap.: Saint George's. Monetary unit: Eastern Caribbean dollar, with (Oct. 4, 1993) a par value of EC$2.70 to U.S. $1 (free rate of EC$4.10 = £1 sterling). Queen, Elizabeth II; governor-general in 1993, Reginald Palmer; prime minister, Nicholas Brathwaite.

Public employees received the news in January 1993 that 700 of them would lose their jobs as part of the effort to reduce government spending. The alternative was an austerity program imposed by the International Monetary Fund, something Prime Minister Nicholas Brathwaite and the National Democratic Congress government had been trying for years to avoid.

Grenada's ailing economy was given a boost in April when the announcement was made that a $30 million, 300-room resort hotel and marina were to be built on Hog Island. The tourist trade, however, continued to be so bedeviled by the rising crime rate that government spokesmen expressed fears that officials in the United States would issue a negative travel advisory.

The government attempted to improve the climate for investment in May when it had the Trade Disputes, Arbitration and Inquiry Act amended by Parliament. An independent tribunal would be able to make "binding and final" rulings to bring labour disputes to an end when the country's economic interests were threatened.

In June Grenada moved in concert with Indonesia to force up the world price of its main commodity export by destroying 700 metric tons of nutmegs. The artificial shortfall so created was meant to get the nutmeg price back to about $3,000 a ton. (DAVID RENWICK)

This article updates the *Macropædia* article The WEST INDIES: *Grenada.*

GUATEMALA

A republic of Central America, Guatemala has coastlines on the Caribbean Sea and the Pacific Ocean. Area: 108,889 sq km (42,042 sq mi). Pop. (1993 est.): 9,713,000. Cap.: Guatemala City. Monetary unit: quetzal, with (Oct. 4, 1993) a free rate of 5.83 quetzales to U.S. $1 (8.83 quetzales = £1 sterling). Presidents in 1993, Jorge Serrano Elías and, from June 6, Ramiro de León Carpio.

Political, economic, and social policies pursued by the government of Pres. Jorge Serrano Elías had alienated nearly everybody by 1993, and the country was in disarray. The Christian Democrats and the National Centre Union withdrew their support in Congress, leaving the government without a majority. Amid growing unrest, on May 25 President Serrano suspended the constitution, dissolved Congress and the Supreme Court, and imposed press censorship.

International and domestic condemnation for his self-coup was immediate. After only a few days, Serrano was ousted by a combination of military, business, and opposition leaders. Congress chose Ramiro de León Carpio, previously the human rights ombudsman and one of the officials arrested by former president Serrano, as successor.

This spectacular choice led initially to great optimism, but it was short-lived. On July 3, while traveling in El Quiche with bodyguards, family, and friends, the president's cousin and ally, Jorge Carpio Nicolle, was shot dead, apparently in an attempt to destabilize the new government. The new ombudsman, Jorge García Laguardia, was himself threatened with death after calling into question the police investigation. On August 26 President de León requested the resignation of Congress, along with top members of the judiciary, to allow constitutional reforms designed to purge corruption. In an attempt to settle the issue, he scheduled a referendum for November 28, but the Supreme Court canceled it. It was later agreed that a referendum on reform proposals would be held at the end of January.

On January 20, 2,400 refugees returned to Guatemala from Mexico. They were among some 45,000 people, largely

MARK DOWNEY

Busloads of refugees return to Guatemala from Mexico. These highland Indians had fled their homes in the early 1980s to escape a government military campaign against leftist guerrillas.

A demonstrator in Port-au-Prince kicks an automobile carrying an American diplomat. U.S.-led attempts to reinstate the deposed president, Jean-Bertrand Aristide, who had been overthrown by the Haitian military in 1991, were unsuccessful.
AFP

Maya, who had been displaced in the country's 32-year civil war. Talks between the government and leftist guerrilla groups aimed at ending the war took place during the year but did not reach a settlement. The new government continued the economic policies of its predecessor, under the guidance of the International Monetary Fund. This caused disillusionment among the popular movements and opposition from the media. (SARAH CAMERON)

This article updates the *Macropædia* article CENTRAL AMERICA: *Guatemala.*

GUYANA

A republic and member of the Commonwealth, Guyana is situated in northeastern South America, on the Atlantic Ocean. Area: 215,083 sq km (83,044 sq mi). Pop. (1993 est.): 755,000. Cap.: Georgetown. Monetary unit: Guyana dollar, with (Oct. 4, 1993) an official rate of G$126 to U.S. $1 (G$191.52 = £1 sterling). President in 1993, Cheddi Jagan; prime minister, Sam Hinds.

While the People's Progressive Party settled down to run the country after its October 1992 election victory, the People's National Congress (PNC), which had been in power for 28 years, was finding it difficult in 1993 to adjust to opposition. In March, Hamilton Green, the former prime minister, sued the PNC leadership for violating his constitutional rights by expelling him from the party. Green later moved to form his own group, Forum for Democracy. In April the PNC's problems were further compounded when its leader, former president Desmond Hoyte, had to be rushed to New York City for a triple bypass heart operation.

There was good economic news, however. What would eventually be Guyana's largest gold mine began producing in February. The Canadian-owned Omai mine was expected to hit peak production of 280,000 troy ounces within a year or two. The British government, meanwhile, wrote off Guyana's entire official debt, amounting to $80.5 million. In the same month, the Paris Club of creditor nations also forgave Guyana $40 million of bilateral debt and rescheduled the rest over 23 years. In July the government announced that 16 state enterprises would be considered for divestment, among them Guysuco (sugar) and Linmine (bauxite).

Discussions continued in October on a possible settlement of Venezuela's long-standing claim to two-thirds of Guyana's territory. (DAVID RENWICK)

HAITI

The republic of Haiti occupies the western one-third of the Caribbean island of Hispaniola, which it shares with the Dominican Republic. Area: 27,700 sq km (10,695 sq mi). Pop. (1993 est.): 6,902,000. Cap.: Port-au-Prince. Monetary unit: gourde, with (Oct. 4, 1993) a free rate of 12 gourdes to U.S. $1 (18.24 gourdes = £1 sterling). President in 1993, Jean-Bertrand Aristide (in exile); head of military government, Lieut. Gen. Raoul Cédras; prime ministers, Marc L. Bazin to June 8 and, from August 30, Robert Malval.

Haitian affairs were dominated in 1993 by generally unsuccessful efforts, notably by new U.S. Pres. Bill Clinton, to stem the tide of refugees from that impoverished country and to return to power its democratically elected president, the Rev. Jean-Bertrand Aristide. The Clinton government announced a $1 billion international aid package for Haiti if democracy was restored but threatened fiercer economic sanctions if no progress toward Aristide's reinstatement was made. At the same time, the United Nations and its special envoy, Dante Caputo, stepped up efforts to resolve the crisis. In February army commander Gen. Raoul Cédras agreed to the deployment of several hundred human rights observers in the country. By June international pressure had still failed to make the unelected government relinquish power. The Organization of American States called for an extension of its embargo to cover all oil supplies and air links. On June 23 the UN Security Council signaled its loss of patience by instigating a worldwide ban on oil and arms shipments to Haiti. This proved to be the catalyst for talks, which began on June 27 on Governors Island, N.Y. Accords were signed between the army and Aristide on July 3.

A 10-stage plan for Aristide's return on October 30 included the suspension of the oil embargo once an Aristide-nominated prime minister had been installed, and Robert Malval, a publisher, was appointed. General Cédras was to leave office on October 15, and the powerful Port-au-Prince police chief, Lieut. Col. Michel François, would be replaced.

Still, violence was unchecked. In September, Antoine Izméry, a businessman, was dragged from church and shot by *attachés,* plainclothes affiliates of François's police force; on October 14, Justice Minister Guy Malary was murdered in his office. Both supported Aristide's return. Opponents of Aristide threatened Malval's choice of Cabinet members as well as UN personnel in Haiti, and a dockside protest in October forced a U.S. ship with UN soldiers aboard to retreat from Haitian waters. Since neither Cédras nor François surrendered office as agreed, the UN reimposed the oil and arms embargo. Malval announced that he would resign on December 15, but he agreed to stay on as acting prime minister. (BEN BOX)

This article updates the *Macropædia* article The WEST INDIES: *Haiti.*

HONDURAS

A republic of Central America, Honduras has coastlines on the Caribbean Sea and the Pacific Ocean. Area: 112,088 sq km (43,277 sq mi). Pop. (1993 est.): 5,148,000. Cap.: Tegucigalpa. Monetary unit: lempira, with (Oct. 4, 1993) a free rate of 6.91 lempiras to U.S. $1 (10.47 lempiras = £1 sterling). President in 1993, Rafael Leonardo Callejas.

In the general elections held on Nov. 28, 1993, Carlos Roberto Reina of the Liberal Party (PL) defeated the candidate of the ruling National Party (PN), Oswaldo Ramos Soto. Reina, a former president of the Inter-American Court of Human Rights, vowed to attack corruption in the government and to curb the influence of the armed forces.

The Honduran armed forces came under pressure for reform in 1992–93 as a result of U.S. and domestic criticism of human rights abuses. The military was implicated in a variety of scandals, including murder, corruption, drug trafficking, and car theft. There were also allegations that the telephone lines of the president, public officials, businessmen, labour leaders, journalists, and foreign diplomats were routinely tapped by the military, not only for security reasons but also to protect their far-reaching business interests. In March 1993 the military agreed to put the National Department of Investigations (DNI) under civilian control by January 1994. The opposition called for the sale of Honduras' squadron of 12 F-5 supersonic fighters, which the U.S. sold to Honduras for providing territory for the Nicaraguan contra bases.

In the first three months of 1993, over 90 children disappeared in Tegucigalpa. It was rumoured that a clandestine hospital on the Atlantic coast was trafficking in children's organs. In April, after the bodies of two children were found with obvious signs of organ removal, Pres. Rafael Leonardo Callejas appointed a commission to investigate. Health officials declared a national alert on June 16 after 15 new cases of cholera had been detected in two days.

(SARAH CAMERON)

This article updates the *Macropædia* article CENTRAL AMERICA: *Honduras.*

JAMAICA

A constitutional monarchy within the Commonwealth, Jamaica occupies an island in the Caribbean Sea. Area: 10,991 sq km (4,244 sq mi). Pop. (1993 est.): 2,472,000. Cap.: Kingston. Monetary unit: Jamaica dollar, with (Oct. 4, 1993) a free rate of J$27.15 to U.S. $1 (J$41.13 = £1 sterling). Queen, Elizabeth II; governor-general in 1993, Howard Cooke; prime minister, Percival J. Patterson.

The Jamaican electorate gave Prime Minister Percival J. Patterson and his People's National Party a convincing mandate in March 1993, with a 52–8 seat victory in the general election. Patterson was facing the polls for the first time as party leader, having succeeded the veteran Michael Manley in March 1992. The defeated Jamaica Labour Party promptly said that it would boycott Parliament in protest against the "fraudulent" conduct of the election, including the "partisan" role of the police. Party leader Edward Seaga called off the boycott in July after a new police chief had been appointed and the government promised to strengthen the electoral system.

In June the government presented its first budget, amounting to J$40.2 billion. The budget contained a large new tax package, including an increase in the general consumption tax from 10 to 12.5%. It also provided J$4 billion for funding foreign exchange transactions undertaken by the Bank of Jamaica. Bank officials had earlier been dismissed for mismanagement of foreign exchange operations, and the bank governor himself subsequently resigned, as did Finance Minister Hugh Small.

Heavy rain in May severely affected the agricultural sector, particularly sugar. In July it was announced that on the basis of the findings of three foreign prospecting companies, Jamaica stood a good chance of becoming a gold producer.

(DAVID RENWICK)

This article updates the *Macropædia* article The WEST INDIES: *Jamaica.*

MEXICO

A federal republic of North America, Mexico has coastlines on the Pacific Ocean, the Gulf of Mexico, and the Caribbean Sea. Area: 1,958,201 sq km (756,066 sq mi). Pop. (1993 est.): 89,955,000. Cap.: Mexico City. Monetary units: Mexican (old) peso, with (Oct. 4, 1993) a free rate of 3,122 pesos to U.S. $1 (4,730 pesos = £1 sterling), and the Mexican new peso (currency circulating alongside the Mexican [old] peso from January 2 for a period of 2½ years at the rate of 1 new peso = 1,000 [old] pesos). President in 1993, Carlos Salinas de Gortari.

The North American Free Trade Agreement (NAFTA), between Mexico, Canada, and the U.S., moved toward ratification in 1993 with the introduction of various amendments. One such pact, agreed upon in August, would allow trade sanctions to be taken against NAFTA members who broke their national laws on various issues, including wage levels, the environment, labour standards, and human rights. In November the U.S. Congress and Mexican Senate approved the treaty.

The territory covered by NAFTA member nations would be the largest free-trade zone in the world, populated by 370 million consumers, with a combined gross national product of $6.4 trillion. The agreement had its critics, however, both in Mexico and among prominent U.S. politicians. NAFTA opponents in the U.S. Congress raised concerns about Mexico's one-party dominance, corruption, and human rights and labour rights abuses. Anti-NAFTA groups also emerged within Mexico. According to Carlos Heredía of the progressive policy group Development Gap, many Mexicans were worried that NAFTA would serve only to reinforce the current political system.

Uncertainty over NAFTA depressed economic growth in Mexico throughout the year. After a 2.6% growth in gross domestic product in 1992, there was only a 1.4% expansion in the first half of 1993. Though interest rates were kept high, at 8%, as a lure to attract foreign capital, such investment declined sharply from the 1992 total. Inflation, however, was forecast to fall from the 1992 level of 11.9% to 8.5% by the end of 1993.

At the beginning of October, Pres. Carlos Salinas de Gortari announced economic measures agreed upon in the annual pact between the government, labour unions, and the private sector. These included a cut in corporate and employment taxes and an increase in the minimum wage (at the time, equivalent to $5.45 a day) by more than 15%. Radical agricultural reforms were announced in October, offering direct cash grants to farmers instead of the previous system of price supports. Industrial privatization schemes

A worker inspects gas ranges at a General Electric appliance factory in Mexico. Attracted primarily by the lower labour costs incurred there, a number of U.S. manufacturing companies had established plants in Mexico in recent years.
KEITH DANNEMILLER—SABA

continued, with new regulations introduced in May for the opening up of the electricity sector to private companies. During the same month, similar opportunities were announced for private investment in maritime port authorities. The management of Mexico City's water system was handed over to private consortia in June in a $2 billion contract.

The Ministry of Health released data on cholera throughout the country. A total of 6,000 cases were reported nationwide in 1993, with 108 deaths from the disease. A media campaign was launched, concentrating on proper sewage treatment, boiling of drinking water, and avoidance of fried food bought from street stalls.

Water and sewage control across Mexico was reviewed by the government as part of a $50 million environmental campaign. The government introduced legislation forcing companies to prevent or clean up their waste spillages. Budgeted for 1993 was $230 million to improve the sewerage and drinking-water systems for towns north and south of the U.S. border as part of the so-called Integrated Environmental Border Program. It was estimated that some $1.6 billion would be spent on pollution-control equipment by 1994.

The year began badly for the ruling Institutional Revolutionary Party (PRI), with a series of political embarrassments. A private dinner party, attended by President Salinas and leading ministers, was held in February for 30 wealthy business figures in order to raise funds for the forthcoming PRI election campaign. Each guest was asked to make a donation of about 75 million pesos, in return for which business concessions were granted. One guest, television magnate Emilio Azcárraga, was said to have offered three times that sum. In an attempt to defuse the public outcry when the story leaked, PRI announced that it would accept only a maximum of 1 million pesos from each guest. Later Genaro Borrego Estrada, the PRI chairman, was moved to a new position as the head of the Mexican social security department, widely regarded as a demotion that was punishment for his role in the event.

Also in February allegations were made by a Mexican representative of IBM Corp. that government officials had tried to extort bribes from the firm in connection with a $21.7 million contract for upgrading Mexico City's airport. The claims were swiftly proved false in an official investigation, but the accusations remained in the news for some time, providing further bad publicity.

In several state elections PRI won comfortably, apparently unaffected by the above-mentioned scandals. Guillermo Mercado Romero won for PRI in Baja California Sur, normally a stronghold of the right-wing National Action Party (PAN); Hidalgo, Quintana Roo, Guerrero, and Yúcatán were also taken easily by PRI candidates.

Presidential elections were scheduled for August 1994. The major parties began preparations with internal reorganizations at their annual conferences. PAN chose a new leader in March; Carlos Castillo Peraza replaced Luís Álvarez. Castillo Peraza announced a change in the party's traditionally conservative image, calling for extra care for the poor. A new party, the Democratic Forum Party (PFD), a Christian Democratic movement headed by Pablo Emilio Madero, was formed in March. The emergence of PFD effectively weakened PAN, from which several leading members departed to join the new party. Cuauhtémoc Cárdenas Sólorzano retained his leadership of the leftist Democratic Revolutionary Party (PRD), reckoned to be the most serious threat to PRI's political domination.

Because the constitution prohibited the president of the republic from holding two consecutive terms of office, in November the PRI announced the successor to Salinas. The choice was Luis Donaldo Colosio Murrieta, secretary of social development in the Salinas government and one of the president's closest associates.

Electoral reforms were approved at the end of August. These included a ceiling to be set on financial contributions to party funds, increased independence of electoral institutes, and regulation of access to the media by canvassing parties. Also, as of 1999, the offspring of a foreign-born Mexican parent would be allowed for the first time to run for the presidency. This last reform was greeted with mixed feelings by PAN, whose most popular candidate, Vicente Fox, would thus not be eligible for the 1994 elections.

(HUW CLOUGH)

NICARAGUA

A republic of Central America, Nicaragua has coastlines on the Caribbean Sea and the Pacific Ocean. Area: 131,779 sq km (50,880 sq mi). Pop. (1993 est.): 4,265,000. Cap.: Managua. Monetary unit: córdoba oro, with (Oct. 4, 1993) an official rate of 6.17 córdobas oro to U.S. $1 (9.35 córdobas oro = £1 sterling). President in 1993, Violeta Barrios de Chamorro.

Members of Nicaragua's leftist National Dignity Command hold a news conference after capturing leaders of the conservative National Opposition Union. The hostages were later set free when the rightist 3-80 Front released its own hostages, including two legislators.
ARTURO ROBLES—JB PICTURES

Pres. Violeta Chamorro found her tenure increasingly threatened in 1993. Bands of contras and Sandinistas, which had been fighting intermittently since 1991, became more active. In May, President Chamorro decreed a 30-day suspension of constitutional guarantees in the north and central departments. On July 21 a group called the Revolutionary Workers and Campesinos Front (FROC), mostly former members of the Sandinista army but also including some contras, attacked and held Estelí for a day, killing 45 people and wounding 100. Another group, the 3-80 Front, said that it would not disarm until the government dismissed Gen. Humberto Ortega, chief of the armed forces since 1979, and restructured the National Assembly.

A new crisis broke on August 19 when a delegation to Quilalí, including two Sandinista deputies, was taken hostage by the 3-80 Front, which demanded the dismissal of General Ortega and of the minister of the presidency, Antonio Lacayo. In retaliation, on August 20 the National Dignity Command took over the headquarters of the National Opposition Union (UNO) coalition in Managua and captured party leaders, including Vice Pres. Virgilio Godoy. An agreement was then negotiated between representatives of the government, the Sandinista National Liberation Front (FSLN), and UNO for the simultaneous release of all hostages. Over the next few days, groups were released, the last on August 25. President Chamorro subsequently announced that General Ortega would be replaced as army chief in 1994.

On September 20 the National Transport Commission, representing private bus owners and truck and taxi drivers, began a nationwide strike to protest against gasoline price increases and a new tax on vehicle ownership. Two people were killed and several injured as police tried to dislodge armed strikers blocking traffic in Managua. On September 22 the government agreed to suspend the taxes temporarily, paving the way for negotiations with the strikers.

(SARAH CAMERON)

This article updates the *Macropædia* article CENTRAL AMERICA: *Nicaragua.*

PANAMA

A republic of Central America, Panama lies between the Caribbean Sea and the Pacific Ocean on the Isthmus of Panama. Area: 75,517 sq km (29,157 sq mi). Pop. (1993 est.): 2,563,000. Cap.: Panama City. Monetary unit: balboa, at par with the U.S. dollar, with a free rate (Oct. 4, 1993) of 1.52 balboas to £1 sterling. President in 1993, Guillermo Endara Galimany.

As political parties geared up for presidential elections in May 1994, opinion polls in late 1993 indicated that the front-runner was Ruben Blades, the U.S.-based performer of salsa music. His party, Papa Egoró ("Mother Earth" in an indigenous language), aimed to provide an alternative to traditional Panamanian oligarchies. Support for Blades underlined general dissatisfaction with Panamanian society. The polls also suggested a high level of indecision, despite the fact that the elections would be fully democratic for the first time in 25 years.

At the end of 1992, accusations and counteraccusations of drug-related corruption were exchanged between several senior government officials. Involved were the director general of customs, Rodrigo Arosemena; the attorney general, Rogelio Cruz; and his deputy, Ariel Alvarado. All three were arrested, but they were released for lack of evidence.

On February 19 Pres. Guillermo Endara Galimany signed the Belize Declaration, designed to limit the trafficking and consumption of narcotics in Central America. Since the U.S. overthrow of Gen. Manuel Noriega in 1989, Panama's role as a centre for money laundering and the transshipment, production, and use of drugs had grown rather than diminished. Related to this was an increase in crime, especially among minors. In January politicians demanded stronger measures to combat armed robbery and murder, but the police claimed that they had inadequate resources for tackling the problem.

In September seven people accused of the 1985 murder of Hugo Spadafora, a former guerrilla and opponent of Noriega, were acquitted. The trial's outcome inspired five days of protests. In October, however, Noriega and two former soldiers were found guilty of the crime. Earlier, in April, a proposed amnesty bill for political prisoners, mostly from 1989, exposed deep political divisions. The government faced popular protests during the year from six indigenous groups demanding title to their land, as well as strikes by transport, banana, and public-sector workers and by teachers.

(BEN BOX)

This article updates the *Macropædia* article CENTRAL AMERICA: *Panama.*

PARAGUAY

Paraguay is a landlocked republic of central South America. Area: 406,752 sq km (157,048 sq mi). Pop. (1993 est.): 4,613,000. Cap.: Asunción. Monetary unit: guaraní, with (Oct. 4, 1993) a free rate of 1,772 guaraníes to U.S. $1 (2,685 guaraníes = £1 sterling). Presidents in 1993, Gen. Andrés Rodríguez and, from August 15, Juan Carlos Wasmosy.

In what were considered to be the first free multiparty elections in Paraguay's history, held on May 9, 1993, Colorado Party candidate Juan Carlos Wasmosy (*see* BIOGRAPHIES) won the presidency. He took approximately 40% of the vote, followed by Domingo Laíno of the Authentic Radical Liberal Party, Guillermo Caballero Vargas of the newly formed National Encounter and the favourite in preelection polls, and three other candidates. Wasmosy, who had taken the nomination of the Colorado Party from Luis María Argaña in a disputed election, thus extended the rule of the governing party and also became the first civilian president of Paraguay since 1954.

Wasmosy's win reflected in part strong support from the outgoing president, Gen. Andrés Rodríguez, and the military. Shortly before the elections the government raised the minimum wage, and Rodríguez called on public-sector employees to vote for the Colorado Party candidate, amid suggestions by some that a win by the opposition would put their jobs in jeopardy. Teachers were used to mobilize the rural vote. A prominent military man, Gen. Lino Oviedo, made the widely publicized statement that the armed forces and the Colorado Party would rule Paraguay forever. Some fraud and irregularities were reported during the voting; among other problems, the military prevented emigrants living in Argentina and Brazil, who normally would support the opposition, from entering Paraguay to vote. Nonetheless, observers from the National Democratic Institute for International Affairs, including former U.S. president Jimmy Carter, and the Organization of American States judged the outcome to be fair.

The new president favoured a free-market economy, advocating the privatization of businesses and the extension of free trade. It was thought, however, that Wasmosy might have difficulties with Congress since the Colorado Party had failed to win control of either house and all parties were troubled by factional fighting. (MICHAEL WOOLLER)

PERU

The republic of Peru is located in western South America, on the Pacific Ocean. Area: 1,285,216 sq km (496,225 sq mi). Pop. (1993 est.): 22,916,000. Cap.: Lima. Monetary unit: nuevo sol, with (Oct. 4, 1993) a free rate of 2.10 nuevos soles to U.S. $1 (3.19 nuevos soles = £1 sterling). President in 1993, Alberto Fujimori; prime ministers, Oscar de la Puente Raygada and, from August 28, Alfonso Bustamente y Bustamente.

In municipal elections on Jan. 29, 1993, independent candidates won the majority of council seats throughout the country. The results highlighted the general sense of mistrust of traditional parties and established institutions fostered by Pres. Alberto Fujimori since he seized power in April 1992.

Throughout 1993 President Fujimori's attempts to end terrorism, eradicate corruption, and liberalize the economy met with a large measure of success but not unqualified support. Opinion polls suggested that over 60% of Peruvians thought Fujimori should be allowed to achieve his goals. A new constitution, drawn up by the Democratic Constituent Congress (CCD) in July and August, was approved in a referendum on October 31. The new constitution changed electoral rules to permit the president to stand for reelection, reduced the legislature to one 120-seat chamber, changed the judicial system, and introduced the death penalty for convicted terrorists. It also legitimized many of the economic reforms introduced by Fujimori, such as the cutting of import tariffs, privatization, and the institution of rules governing foreign investment.

Foreign concern was expressed over the restriction of press freedom, while the local press association complained of harassment by politicians. President Fujimori defended his authoritarian measures as necessary for the restoration of state efficiency. Opponents claimed that the resulting extension of presidential power, reflected in the new constitution, weakened the country by not replacing the military, state, and judicial institutions eliminated.

The capture of the leaders of Sendero Luminoso (Shining Path; Abimael Guzman) and the Movimiento Revolucionario Tupac Amaru (MRTA; Victor Polay) in 1992 did not halt terrorist violence. Shining Path car bombed the U.S. embassy in Lima in July, and its followers massacred 55 Ashaninka Indians in Junín department in August. Throughout the year there were many other bomb attacks and killings. Guzman was alleged by President Fujimori in September to have offered a peace plan; the president quoted the letter to the United Nations, and then Guzman read from the letter on television. Shining Path's operational leadership rejected the claim, saying that the guerrillas' opposition would continue and accusing President Fujimori of falsification. MRTA, badly affected by arrests and the surrender of important figures under the government's extended amnesty program, was thought by the military to be a spent force by October.

Allegations that the murder of one professor and nine students from La Cantuta University in July 1992 had been carried out by a military death squad were studied by two commissions. A CCD human rights subcommittee laid the blame on the army; a government coalition report said that terrorists had perpetrated the crime. After President Fujimori had accepted the latter, the case was sent to a military tribunal. The CCD committee demanded the case's removal to civilian courts after the bodies of the victims were found in a grave near Lima in July.

In February the U.S. administration linked financial aid to human rights and democracy, but Peru's economy and finance and justice ministers, on a visit to Washington, assured the U.S. that concerns about the treatment of political prisoners and harassment of human rights groups would be addressed. This freed a multilateral bridging loan, arranged

VERA LENTZ—BLACK STAR

Pres. Alberto Fujimori dances at ceremonies marking the opening of a new school. Polls showed that a majority of Peruvians approved of the president's policies, which were seen as antidemocratic but effective in bringing stability to the nation.

by the U.S. and Japan, that allowed Peru to pay off arrears to the International Monetary Fund and the World Bank. These two agencies then activated credits valued at $1.4 billion over three years and $1,030,000,000, respectively, and the IMF also restored borrowing rights. In June Peru sought $100 million from international sources to help alleviate poverty, estimated to affect 60% of the population. While gross domestic product was forecast to grow by 3.5% in 1993, compared with a 2.8% fall in 1992, real GDP per capita continued to decline. Nevertheless, inflation was successfully reduced from 409.5% in 1991 to 72.5% in 1992 and an estimated 50% by mid-1993. (BEN BOX)

SAINT KITTS AND NEVIS

A constitutional monarchy and member of the Commonwealth, St. Kitts and Nevis comprises the islands of St. Kitts and Nevis in the eastern Caribbean Sea. Area: 269 sq km (104 sq mi). Pop. (1993 est.): 41,800. Cap.: Basseterre. Monetary unit: Eastern Caribbean dollar, with (Oct. 4, 1993) a par value of EC$2.70 to U.S. $1 (free rate of EC$4.10 = £1 sterling). Queen, Elizabeth II; governor-general in 1993, Sir Clement Arrindell; prime minister, Kennedy Alphonse Simmonds.

In elections on November 29 the ruling People's Action Movement (PAM) lost its majority in the National Assembly. Followers of the Labour Party, which won a majority of the vote but the same number of seats as PAM, subsequently rioted, leading the government to declare a state of emergency.

In June the government received an infusion of capital for its development program from an unusual source—the Kuwaiti Investment Fund, which had extended its reach to the Eastern Caribbean. For a project to double the country's water-storage capacity, U.S. $6.6 million would be made available. Another loan agreement was successfully concluded in October, this time with the World Bank's International Development Association (IDA). The IDA extended $20 million for a 27.4-km (17-mi) road program in St. Kitts and seaport rehabilitation in Nevis.

Like most other territories in the region, St. Kitts and Nevis had a drug-transshipment problem, and in August it signed a narcotics-control agreement with the U.S. whereby the U.S. agreed to provide $137,500, part of which would go toward the purchase of a high-speed boat. In the same month, the government strengthened the Proceeds of Crime Act, which permitted the forfeiture of the property of those found guilty of trafficking and money laundering.

(DAVID RENWICK)

This article updates the *Macropædia* article The WEST INDIES: *Saint Kitts and Nevis.*

SAINT LUCIA

A constitutional monarchy and member of the Commonwealth, St. Lucia is the second largest of the Windward Islands in the eastern Caribbean Sea. Area: 617 sq km (238 sq mi). Pop. (1993 est.): 136,000. Cap.: Castries. Monetary unit: Eastern Caribbean dollar, with (Oct. 4, 1993) a par value of EC$2.70 to U.S. $1 (free rate of EC$4.10 = £1 sterling). Queen, Elizabeth II; governor-general in 1993, Stanislaus A. James; prime minister, John Compton.

In March 1993 St. Lucia cracked down on the money laundering and organized fraud associated with the drug trade by providing heavier fines and prison terms for those found guilty of such offenses. At the same time, the regulations governing offshore banking were tightened.

In May the country added to its already considerable port infrastructure when a new U.S. $14.8 million deepwater container terminal, one of the most modern in the Caribbean, was opened at Vieux Fort. A free zone was to be established, with a view to making the area a major Caribbean transshipment centre.

The tourism industry took a major step in June when the former Cunard La Toc hotel reopened as the 273-room, all-inclusive Sandals La Toc after a U.S. $20 million renovation. Not everyone in St. Lucia was happy with the all-inclusive concept. In August the government was persuaded to appoint a committee to investigate the impact these hotels were having on the local hotel and restaurant sector. The St. Lucia Hotel and Tourism Association reported that its smaller members had suffered a 76% falloff in business in the wake of the rapid growth of all-inclusive hotels.

(DAVID RENWICK)

This article updates the *Macropædia* article The WEST INDIES: *Saint Lucia.*

SAINT VINCENT AND THE GRENADINES

A constitutional monarchy within the Commonwealth, St. Vincent and the Grenadines comprises the islands of St. Vincent and the northern Grenadines in the eastern Caribbean Sea. Area: 389 sq km (150 sq mi). Pop. (1993 est.): 109,000. Cap.: Kingstown. Monetary unit: Eastern Caribbean dollar, with (Oct. 4, 1993) a par value of EC$2.70 to U.S. $1 (free rate of EC$4.10 = £1 sterling). Queen, Elizabeth II; governor-general in 1993, David Jack; prime minister, James Fitz-Allen Mitchell.

A major development program on Union Island in the Grenadines, expected to cost U.S. $100 million, was announced in March 1993. It involved the construction of a luxury hotel, a 300-berth marina, and a number of private villas. Prime Minister James Mitchell brushed aside protests over the government's decision to grant 99-year leases to investors in beachfront property. He insisted that the uncertainty over the future of the country's chief export, bananas, in the European Community left little alternative to the encouragement of tourism and property investment. St. Vincent and the Grenadines became the recipient of a U.S. $3.3 million loan from the Kuwaiti Investment Fund in June for the purchase of a generator for the St. Vincent Electricity Services.

The Criminal Procedure Code Act was amended by the House of Assembly in August. It raised the minimum age for application of the death penalty from 16 to 18. The government still had no plans to abolish the death penalty, however, despite pressure from international human rights organizations. (DAVID RENWICK)

This article updates the *Macropædia* article The WEST INDIES: *Saint Vincent and the Grenadines.*

SURINAME

The republic of Suriname is in northern South America, on the Atlantic Ocean. Area: 163,820 sq km (63,251 sq mi), not including a 17,635-sq km area disputed with Guyana. Pop. (1993 est.): 405,000. Cap.: Paramaribo. Monetary unit: Suriname guilder, with (Oct. 4, 1993) a par value of 1.79 guilders to U.S. $1 (free rate of 2.72 guilders = £1 sterling). President in 1993, Ronald Venetiaan; prime minister, Jules Adjodhia.

On April 5, 1993, Minister of Defense Siegfried Gilds appointed Col. Arthy Gorré as commander of the national army in an effort to restore discipline and democratic values in the army. The appointment led to mutiny and a threat of a new coup by some military factions. On May 12 the National Assembly sanctioned the appointment of Gorré and at the same time asked rebellious officers to resign. A few days later deputy commander Ivan Graanoogst, Badrissein Sital, and Chas Mijnals announced their resignation. All three had been important participants in the military regime of Dési Bouterse.

On August 1 The Netherlands stopped its financial support to Suriname. This action followed a European Community report concluding that the government of Pres. Ronald Venetiaan had failed to restructure the economy and had caused a high rate of inflation.

On August 8 Arti Jesserun, deputy chairman of the Suriname National Party, and Dilip Sardjoe, treasurer of the Progressive Reform Party (PRP; a Hindustani party), resigned their offices after they were accused of having taken bribes from Dutch trade companies. On November 8 Jaggernath Lachmon of the PRP escaped an attack, and shortly thereafter Sardjoe's property suffered damage.

(KLAAS J. HOEKSEMA)

TRINIDAD AND TOBAGO

A republic and member of the Commonwealth, Trinidad and Tobago consists of two islands in the Caribbean Sea off the coast of Venezuela. Area: 5,128 sq km (1,980 sq mi). Pop. (1993 est.): 1,249,000. Cap.: Port of Spain. Monetary unit: Trinidad and Tobago dollar, with (Oct. 4, 1993) a free rate of TT$5.48 to U.S. $1 (TT$8.30 = £1 sterling). President in 1993, Noor Mohammad Hassanali; prime minister, Patrick Manning.

Nucor Corp., a leading U.S. steel company, agreed in January 1993 to establish the world's first commercialized iron carbide plant at the Point Lisas industrial estate in central Trinidad. It was designed to produce 320,000 metric tons a year for export to the firm's plants in the U.S.

In March the government began its privatization program in earnest when it sold its 51% interest in the Fertilisers of Trinidad and Tobago's (Fertrin) ammonia plant and its 100% holding in the Trinidad and Tobago Urea Co. for U.S. $175 million. The government was to sell at least 28 of the 32 corporations in which it had 100% interest.

The Trinidad and Tobago dollar was made freely convertible and allowed to float on the foreign exchange market in April. A depreciation of 26% against the U.S. dollar immediately took place. The measure was designed to create confidence in the Trinidad and Tobago dollar, attract investment, and encourage exports.

In June a major expansion of methanol capacity was announced under which two German firms bought 31% of the state-owned Trinidad and Tobago Methanol Co. The plant was to be expanded so as to produce an additional 550,000 metric tons a year, enabling the country to produce over 1.6 million metric tons of methanol by 1996, making Trinidad and Tobago the world's largest methanol exporter.

In August Prime Minister Patrick Manning, along with four other Caribbean leaders, met U.S. Pres. Bill Clinton in Washington, D.C., to explain that the Caribbean Community policy of forging closer links with Cuba could be accommodated within the framework of overall U.S. policy.

(DAVID RENWICK)

This article updates the *Macropædia* article The WEST INDIES: *Trinidad and Tobago.*

URUGUAY

A republic of eastern South America, Uruguay lies on the Atlantic Ocean. Area: 176,215 sq km (68,037 sq mi). Pop. (1993 est.): 3,149,000. Cap.: Montevideo. Monetary unit: peso uruguayo (introduced March 1, eventually to replace the Uruguayan new peso at the rate of peso uruguayo = 1,000 new pesos), with (Oct. 4, 1993) a free rate of 4.17 pesos uruguayos to U.S. $1 (6.32 pesos uruguayos = £1 sterling). President in 1993, Luis Alberto Lacalle.

Attempts by Pres. Luis Alberto Lacalle to reform the Uruguayan economy in 1993 continued to be resisted by political opponents as well as by various interest groups. Labour unions called a number of strikes during the year, and pensioners were active in opposing reform of the troubled state pension system. Efforts to reform civil service failed, as did Lacalle's plan to privatize state companies, a policy that had been soundly rejected by the electorate in a December 1992 referendum. The president's difficulties were partly attributed to the fact that his National (Blanco) Party lacked a majority in Congress, but his problems were compounded by dissension among the Blancos as well as among the opposition parties. Further, polls showed that only one-fifth or so of the people gave the president positive ratings.

The case of a secret agent made news in 1993. Eugenio Berrios Sagredo, a former agent of Chile's secret police, had been connected to the murders of two Chileans in Washington, D.C., in 1976. He disappeared in 1991, thought to have been kidnapped by a Chilean, Argentine, and Uruguayan military operation and held in Atlántida, a resort town in Uruguay. Berrios escaped in late 1992 and reported his situation to the local police, who returned him to the military. When news of the events was leaked to members of Congress, the police official responsible was dismissed, over the objections of the military. President Lacalle was forced to cut short an official trip to Europe and return home to deal with the resulting government crisis on June 11. As part of the resolution, it was agreed that any member of the military charged in the affair would be tried by court-martial, rather than in the civil courts. Berrios, after having been thought dead, later appeared at the Uruguayan consulate in Milan.

(MICHAEL WOOLLER)

VENEZUELA

A republic of northern South America, Venezuela lies on the Caribbean Sea. Area: 912,050 sq km (352,144 sq mi). Pop. (1993 est.): 20,609,000. Cap.: Caracas. Monetary unit: bolívar, with (Oct. 4, 1993) a free rate of 97.39 bolívares to U.S. $1 (147.54 bolívares = £1 sterling). Presidents in 1992, Carlos Andrés Pérez to May 21, Octavio Lepage (acting) from May 21, and, from June 5, Ramón José Velásquez (interim).

Having survived two unsuccessful coup attempts in 1992, Pres. Carlos Andrés Pérez was forced to leave office in May 1993. The Supreme Court ruled that there was sufficient evidence for Pérez to be tried for corruption, and following months of political disquiet, he was suspended. The charges involved the embezzlement of $17.2 million worth of secret government funds intended for security and defense but allegedly used by Pérez and two former Cabinet ministers to buy dollars at the preferential exchange rate. The dollars were then sold on the free market and the resulting $10 million profit used for political campaigning. While Pérez denied the accusations, it was his own policies of freeing the judiciary from political ties, proposing greater independence for the central bank (which provided foreign exchange receipts as evidence), and encouraging political debate that contributed to his impeachment. Similarly under investigation for corruption was Pérez' predecessor, Jaime Lusinchi, but on different charges.

To replace Pérez, the chairman of the Senate, Octavio Lepage, was sworn in as acting president, but he held office for only two weeks, as Congress, at the beginning of June, voted Sen. Ramón José Velásquez interim president until February 1994. Velásquez was permitted to appoint a Cabinet without influence from any political party in order to tackle the many social and economic problems facing

Citizens in Caracas celebrate the decision of the government in May to try Pres. Carlos Andrés Pérez on charges of misusing public funds. The president, who had promoted free-market economic reforms, charged that his impeachment was motivated by politics, but many observers claimed that Venezuelan government officials had long been involved in corruption.

C. ANGEL—GAMMA LIAISON

Venezuela and to ensure the holding of presidential, congressional, and state assembly elections on December 5.

The first half of the year was marred by demonstrations and riots surrounding both Pérez' impeachment and the rerunning of gubernatorial elections in the states of Sucre and Barinas. In each case the ruling Democratic Action (AD) Party had refused to concede defeat in December 1992 polls, but it suffered heavy defeats in the rescheduled March elections. There were also strikes and unrest over economic policy, which was causing hardship for many sectors of society.

Velásquez's task was not eased by a series of bombings in Caracas, beginning in July, that were aimed at destabilizing the country. One attack was specifically blamed on people trying to manipulate the stock market. Also blamed were drug racketeers, who targeted judges. In a subsequent development, Velásquez himself was implicated in a conspiracy to free a prominent narcotics trafficker, but his involvement was categorically disproved.

Political uncertainty prevailed up to the eve of the elections. Rumours of possible coup attempts surfaced throughout the year, the latest at the beginning of December. Concern was such that the U.S. sent its assistant secretary for inter-American affairs, Alexander Watson, to Caracas to underline the dangers of Venezuela's failing to maintain democracy. The elections proceeded, however, and were won by former president Rafael Caldera, who stood as an independent leading a broad coalition called National Convergence (CN). His main rivals, out of 17 candidates, were Claudio Fermín of Pérez' AD Party, Oswaldo Alvarez Paz of the Social Christian Party (COPEI), and Andrés Velásquez of the left-leaning Radical Cause. Caldera, who had been president from 1969 to 1974, was the founder of COPEI in the 1940s, but he broke from the party before the 1993 campaign. Seventeen small parties, including left-wing groups of which Caldera was formerly a fierce opponent, made up the CN. Just as Caldera's success disrupted the AD/COPEI domination of Venezuelan politics of more than four decades, so congressional elections appeared to have ended the two-party division of seats. Given Caldera's narrow majority, a Congress comprising many different parties would require him to make alliances to govern effectively.

High on Caldera's agenda was modification of the free-market reforms instituted by Pérez. In fact, all of the main contenders adopted firm positions for or against the economic adjustment and austerity measures. Although Caldera demanded changes in the policies, he stressed to the private sector and foreign investors that he did not oppose the free market itself or privatization. However, the privatization program, which interim president Velásquez favoured, was suspended in November until after the new president's inauguration in 1994. Velásquez continued many of Pérez' unpopular policies but also obtained special powers to pass by decree several economic measures that Congress had previously been unable to ratify. These included tackling the deficit, opening up banking to foreign involvement within wider financial reform, tax reform to raise revenues, the introduction of a sales tax and a tax on the assets of private companies, and assistance to the agricultural sector.

Political unrest did not deter foreign investment in the oil and gas industry, notably the approval of the multibillion-dollar Cristóbal Colón liquefied natural gas project, or in mining. The Canadian company Placer Dome discovered the largest gold deposit yet found in Bolívar state, Venezuela's traditional gold-mining area. Generally, however, overseas investors were wary of committing themselves to Venezuela at this time.

Growth in gross domestic product showed a real deficit of over 2% in January–June compared with the first half of 1992. For the year as a whole, forecasts ranged from 1 to 4% growth, compared with an initial prediction of 5% and with 7.3% growth in 1992. The imposition of a 10% value-added tax in October was expected to contribute to a rise in inflation to some 40% for the year. Weak international oil prices were a principal cause of the deficit, but they did not threaten the strength of international reserves, which were bolstered by high interest rates. Nevertheless, high interest rates and continuing low oil prices would restrict Caldera's plans for curtailing austerity, at the same time cutting government spending.

Despite the fiscal deficit, President Velásquez' government sought funds to compensate the thousands of Caraqueños who lost their homes or were injured when Tropical Storm Bret hit the capital in August. The majority were slum dwellers, among the poorest of society. In another major disaster, at least 51 people died at the end of September when a gas pipe exploded beside one of the capital's highways. (BEN BOX)

Oceania

OCEANIAN AFFAIRS

Environmental issues dominated the 1993 meeting of the South Pacific Forum, which was held in Nauru in August. For the first time in many years, the Forum was attended in person by the heads of governments of all 15 Forum members. After the completion of its own deliberations, the Forum met with representatives of the "dialogue partners"—Canada, the European Community, France, Japan, China, the U.K., and the U.S. Separate, informal talks were held with the representatives of Taiwan, in line with the "one China" policy adopted by most Forum members.

The Forum was particularly concerned with the difficulty in finding a basis for sustainable development in a region that was prone to natural disasters, was likely to suffer further environmental damage as a consequence of global warming, especially from rising sea levels and more frequent cyclonic storms, and was experiencing high levels of population growth. In an earlier address to the UN General Assembly, Sir Baddeley Devesi, deputy prime minister of Solomon Islands, had declared that the Framework Convention on Climate Change from the 1992 "Earth Summit" in Rio de Janeiro did not take sufficient account of global warming and called for the negotiation of meaningful protocols under the convention. The region's own climate and sea-level surveillance program, funded by Australia ($A 6.9 million over a five-year period), had established monitoring stations in the Cook Islands, Fiji, Kiribati, Marshall Islands, Papua New Guinea, Tonga, Tuvalu, Vanuatu, and Western Samoa.

The government leaders also addressed issues relating to the expansion of trade in the region, particularly with reference to the South Pacific Regional Trade and Economic Cooperation Agreement, which governed preferential access to Australian and New Zealand markets for the small island states. Subsequent discussions focused on the "rules of origin," which specified that 50% of the value of goods must have been created in the exporting country. This posed particular difficulties for the garment-manufacturing industries in many Pacific Islands countries, especially Fiji, where much of the value lay in imported fabric. The Forum also expressed a strong desire to see the major trading nations reach an early agreement on the Uruguay round of talks under the General Agreement on Tariffs and Trade.

Late in 1992 Forum members had protested Japan's plans to ship plutonium from Europe and to allow the vessel to pass through the exclusive economic zones of member states without warning them of the vessel's passage. The president of Nauru referred to "the public risks and burdens" that were imposed on small island states by large and powerful neighbours. In taking this stand he was also drawing attention to the Forum's earlier criticism of nuclear testing by France and the destruction of chemical weapons at Johnston Atoll by the U.S. At its meeting in August, the Forum welcomed the moratorium on nuclear tests by the U.S., Russia, and France and invited the U.S., the U.K., and France to sign protocols to the South Pacific Nuclear Free Zone Treaty (Treaty of Rarotonga). Many Forum members joined in the wider regional protest against Russia's dumping of liquid nuclear waste in the North Pacific. The protest succeeded in persuading Russia to suspend its dumping program in October 1993. In light of all of these developments, and further proposals put by waste companies to member states (notably Kiribati, the Marshall Islands, and Tonga) for the storage or destruction of toxic materials, the South Pacific Regional Environment Program took steps to develop a regional convention to ban the importation and movement of hazardous waste.

During the Forum meeting, Nauru announced that it had reached a negotiated settlement with Australia for $A 107 million in respect of environmental damage caused by phosphate mining on the island during the period of Australian administration under League of Nations and UN trusteeship. As a condition of the settlement, Nauru agreed to withdraw its damages action then before the International Court of Justice. Australia announced it would seek to have the settlement costs shared by the U.K. and New Zealand, the other trustee powers.

At the beginning of 1993, Australia, New Zealand, and France reached agreement on procedures to ensure the better coordination of disaster relief and on the establishment of more reliable weather reporting for the region. The Joint Commercial Commission, proposed by U.S. Pres. George Bush during his meeting with island leaders in 1990, was formally established, with headquarters in Hawaii.

In February the Summit of Small Pacific Islands States (a subgrouping of Forum members), attended by the Cook Islands, Kiribati, Nauru, Niue, and Tuvalu (with French Polynesia as an observer), met at Funafuti, Tuvalu. Discussions focused on the development of marine resources, with particular reference to the prospects for black pearl cultivation, the harvesting of bêche de mer (trepang), and the development of mullet farming.

The Melanesian Spearhead Group (Papua New Guinea, Solomon Islands, and Vanuatu) held its seventh summit in July. The possibility of Fiji's joining the Spearhead in the future was left open, as was membership for New Caledonia once it had attained "a certain degree of autonomy."

Ati George Sokomanu was elected the new secretary-general of the South Pacific Commission. The vacancy arose because the original appointee had died before taking office, and some governments, notably Australia, wanted applications reopened. The appointment was controversial because Sokomanu, a former president of Vanuatu, had been removed from office after being implicated in a failed coup. Upon his election, Sokomanu exacerbated a tense situation by criticizing Australia for its "colonial club mentality." The outgoing secretary-general, Atanraoi Baiteke of Kiribati, observed that in some Pacific Islands countries the "pace of development was too fast and causing social unrest." He categorized development as "a malady, a sickness first of the individual spirit and then the very soul of one's nation."

The South Pacific Festival of Arts, held in Rarotonga, Cook Islands, over eight days in October 1992, drew more than 2,000 performers from 23 countries. Performances were held at 12 venues on Rarotonga, with the central focus on the new $NZ 11.6 million cultural centre built for the occasion. A major attraction was a number of oceangoing canoes, some of which had been sailed to Rarotonga by traditional forms of navigation. (BARRIE MACDONALD)

AUSTRALIA

A federal parliamentary state (formally a constitutional monarchy) and member of the Commonwealth, Australia occupies the smallest continent and includes the island state of Tasmania. Area: 7,682,300 sq km (2,966,200 sq mi). Pop. (1993 est.): 17,729,000. Cap.: Canberra. Monetary unit: Australian dollar, with (Oct. 4, 1993) a free rate of $A 1.55 to U.S. $1 ($A 2.35 = £1 sterling). Queen, Elizabeth II; governor-general in 1993, Bill Hayden; prime minister, Paul Keating.

Prime Minister Paul Keating and his wife, Annita, greet supporters after the Labor Party won the Australian elections on March 13. Annita Keating, born in The Netherlands, had figured prominently in the campaign and had helped in Australia's bid to bring the 2000 Olympics to Sydney.
REUTERS/BETTMANN

Domestic Affairs. The Australian Labor Party (ALP), which had governed Australia for 10 years, was reelected for a record fifth term in elections held on March 13, 1993. From his suburban Sydney electorate of Bankstown, Prime Minister Paul Keating appeared on television with his wife, Annita, to a tumultuous welcome and proclaimed, "This is the sweetest victory of all." Although the victory was sweet, it was not crushing. (For tabulated results, see *Political Parties,* above.) While the government increased its majority in the House of Representatives, it failed to win control of the Senate, where two independent Greens representing environmentalist causes held the balance of power.

The new Keating administration was announced on March 24. Keating and former prime minister Bob Hawke put aside their differences for the occasion after Keating paid tribute to Hawke's outstanding record of four election victories. The ALP described the Cabinet as "baby-boomers"—only two ministers were over 50 years old. Gareth Evans remained minister for foreign affairs in the new government.

Although he had led them to an unexpected defeat, opposition leader John Hewson was reelected leader of the Liberal Party. Hewson appointed a shadow ministry that included five women, a record number. No previous federal government opposition had had so many women on its front bench. Meanwhile, one of the toughest and most popular women in the party, Sen. Bronwyn Bishop (*see* BIOGRAPHIES), was being touted as a future challenger for the Liberal leadership. The National Party also reelected its leader, Tim Fischer (*see* BIOGRAPHIES).

Keating scored a public relations triumph with his high-profile support of Sydney's bid to serve as host to the Olympic Games in the year 2000. Keating took the gamble of being in Monaco when the result of the voting by the International Olympic Committee was announced, and he experienced an immediate leap in popularity. Annita Keating, who had moved from The Netherlands to Australia 20 years earlier, took the unprecedented step of making a speech to help Sydney's presentation and used her own European origins to the best advantage. In the end, Sydney beat Beijing (Peking) by only two votes.

While the prime minister outpointed Hewson at the moment of joy when the decision was announced, he lost ground in the propaganda battle over the issue of whether Australia should become a republic. Almost immediately after the venue for the 2000 Olympics was announced, Keating used the Sydney victory to increase the pressure to change Australia to a republic and to replace the existing flag (with the British Union Jack in the corner) with a new ensign. It was unacceptable to him that Queen Elizabeth II would open the Olympics and that a flag featuring the Union Jack would be unfurled at the opening ceremony. In Britain suggestions that the queen might not open the Games caused an uproar in some quarters.

To try to gain the initiative, Keating set up a Republican Advisory Committee of eminent Australians. Its chairman was the prominent attorney Malcolm Turnbull, and it included former Liberal New South Wales premier Nick Greiner and television news presenter Mary Kostakidis. In October the Turnbull committee produced a 530-page report at a cost of $A 600,000, in which they found that Keating's proposed minimalist republic could easily be achieved. At that point Hawke weighed into the debate, saying that Australia was increasingly overgoverned, that a minimalist republic as proposed by Keating was impossible, and that the ALP should be aiming for the abolition of the states. Hewson seized on Hawke's remarks, saying that Keating had a secret agenda to scrap the states and the Senate as well as the flag in his republican push.

Much debate also centred on the High Court's "Mabo" decision to recognize a form of native title to land. The Mabo decision recognized customary law and traditions as a source of Australian law. It established a new entitlement to land, grounded not in established statutes but in the place of Aboriginal and Torres Strait Islander peoples as the original owners of the continent. On September 2 Keating released a draft of proposed legislation to deal with problems that arose from the ruling. A federal tribunal was to grant compensation for loss of title and was to be required to take into account factors that reflected the special significance of the land to indigenous people, besides economic and public interest. Both houses of Parliament passed the legislation on December 22. Keating called the decision "a turning point for all Australians." The native title law was to take effect on Jan. 1, 1994, but tribunals to hear claims would be set up only some months later.

Foreign Affairs. While Foreign Minister Gareth Evans tried to keep the focus of Australian diplomacy on the country's role in the United Nations, Australia's participation in UN peacekeeping activities, and national support for the

International Year of Indigenous Peoples, the Foreign Affairs Department was faced with the perennial difficulty caused by the prime minister's forays into personal diplomacy. Keating set out to put his stamp on his new administration by making highly publicized overseas trips. In some cases, as with his journeys to South Korea and China, Keating's diplomatic efforts were a success; in others the results were not so clear-cut.

In June Keating made official visits to South Korea and China, both major economic partners of Australia. (South Korea was Australia's third largest export market, and China was the ninth largest.) In Seoul, Keating made an arrangement under which Australian and South Korean companies and research institutes were to be encouraged to cooperate in commercializing information, semiconductors, raw materials, energy, resources, and food-processing technologies. Of South Korea's complaint about the trade imbalance between the two countries (2.5 to 1 in Australia's favour) and antidumping laws, Keating noted that it was necessary to look at global trade balances.

In China, Keating attended to the conclusion of a number of major investments in China by Australian companies, including Carton United's investment in a brewery in Shanghai and Cadbury Schweppes's in a chocolate-making factory in Beijing. Coinciding with the visit, the Australia and New Zealand Banking Group Ltd. received approval to open the first Australian bank in Shanghai. Keating also had discussions on possible integration of the Australian wool and Chinese textile industries in the hope that joint ventures would help diminish Australia's wool stockpile.

Keating's main foreign affairs focus was on cementing Australia's relations with the U.S. He formed a strong positive personal opinion of U.S. Pres. Bill Clinton when they met in Washington, D.C., and he was particularly encouraged and impressed by Clinton's invitation for Australia to attend the meeting of Asia-Pacific Economic Cooperation (APEC) leaders in Seattle, Wash. Clinton proposed that a meeting of APEC leaders take place in Tokyo on July 7 before the start of the Group of Seven summit, and Keating was delighted to have the opportunity to participate on Australia's behalf. During Keating's visit to Washington, D.C., Clinton assured him that the U.S. Export Enhancement Program would not be used to undermine Australia's interests. Keating also held talks with U.S. Trade Representative Mickey Kantor in an attempt to coordinate Australian-U.S. strategy on resolving the Uruguay round of the General Agreement on Tariffs and Trade.

While Keating was justifiably proud of his achievements in helping Australia's diplomatic and trade prospects in Washington through talks with Clinton, he was naturally apprehensive about the following stages of his grand tour, involving visits to the U.K., Ireland, France, and Monaco. Accordingly, in a stroke of bravado, he barraged the British press with insults before taking off from the U.S. On the eve of his arrival in London, he described England's popular press as being driven to an orgy of insults by his impending arrival. While addressing the Asia Society in New York City, Keating said that he was going from a country that barely noticed the presence of an Australian prime minister to one in which he was described as a barbarian "bent on taking Australia towards some hellish Japanese future."

As it turned out, apart from describing Annita Keating as "a former air-hostess," the criticism was muted. Much attention was focused on the prime minister's talks on Australian republicanism with Queen Elizabeth at Balmoral Castle. Despite the long-standing convention that conversations at Balmoral remain confidential, the queen gave Keating permission to reveal their content.

During a three-day visit to Ireland, Keating rediscovered his Irish roots in the small village of Tynagh, County Galway, the home of his ancestors. This happy occasion was more successful than his fruitless talks with Irish Prime Minister Albert Reynolds. Keating lectured Reynolds about the Irish approach of expanding industrial exports while maintaining high agricultural protection. In return, Reynolds criticized Australia's attitude toward East Timor, saying that Australia was too uncritical of Indonesia.

The prime minister took the occasion of a visit to the World War I battlefields of northern France to launch an attack on the French government for its agricultural policies. After a memorial service at the small village of Villers Bretonneux to commemorate the 45,000 Australians killed during World War I, Keating said that the flower of many countries' youth was lost in France, unselfishly, for the greater good of France. Referring to attempts by the French government to renegotiate the Blair House agreement limiting the application of subsidies on rural export produce, Keating said, "It is time for the French to reassess themselves and magnanimously be a part of the world rather than sitting out there by themselves thinking that the world owes them a living." The outspoken historian Geoffrey Blainey commented that Keating had blundered by telling the French that Australia had lost 10% of its population in World War I. Blainey pointed out that the correct figure was 1% and added that Keating's impetuous statements about the two world wars were becoming his hallmark.

As was becoming common, Australia's relations with Japan were damaged by repeated claims and counterclaims about Japanese World War II atrocities and Australian war crimes. The Returned and Services' League (RSL) of former servicemen and servicewomen was in the thick of the debate, which was hosed down by the Foreign Affairs Department. The RSL continued its pressure on the government to support the traditional Commonwealth connection with the U.K. and to force Japan to apologize for its treatment of Australian soldiers in World War II. The new national president of the RSL, Maj. Gen. William James, said that Japan's leaders had fallen short of adequate contrition. In a counterclaim a Japanese scholar alleged that women in Japan had been raped with the approval of the Allied high command at the same time as Japanese military figures were being tried for war crimes.

The Economy. The Australian economy showed promising signs of recovery in 1993, not the least being the stabilizing of low inflation and the bull run on the stock exchange. However, unemployment remained stubbornly high, and Treasurer John Dawkins' failure to get his budget smoothly through the Senate precipitated what newspapers called the greatest constitutional crisis since 1975 and led the U.S. ratings agency Moody's to warn about the future direction and strength of the economy. The problems for the government began in the 1993 election campaign when the prime minister promised tax cuts and, imitating U.S Pres. George Bush's "read my lips" speech, spelled out that the tax cuts would never be reneged because they were "l-a-w." The tax cuts were not to be delivered, however, by Dawkins, who, when he presented his budget in August, said that it was not negotiable. The budget was dismissed by the financial press as a "brutal tax-and-grab" exercise, which increased gasoline prices by up to 10 cents a litre (38 cents a gallon) and cigarettes by 12% over a two-year period. Many consumer goods, such as refrigerators and televisions, were to cost more after an increase in wholesale tax. Other imposts were to be earlier and larger repayments by higher education students charged for their education, while lump-sum payments on unused annual and long-service leaves were to be taxed as normal income. In addition, the pension age for women was to be increased from 60 to 65 years over a 20-year period. The most controversial aspects of the budget were the decisions to defer the second round of promised tax cuts until 1998 and to increase the tax on wine. Dawkins estimated that the deficit would be $A 16 billion, compared with $A 14.6 billion in fiscal 1992–93.

The major defeat for the government came over its proposed increase in wine taxes. Brian Croser, the president of the Winemakers' Federation of Australia, described the government's policy of high taxes on productive sectors of the national economy as a disaster. Croser said that the proposed wine-tax increase had shown him the amazing proliferation of political and bureaucratic self-interest and the total disregard for regional economies and that Canberra was totally divorced from the realities of job and wealth creation.

The government faced not only negative expressions of public opinion but also a failure to command a majority in the upper house. Senators hostile to the budget held the treasurer and prime minister hostage, forcing changes and backdowns to the "nonnegotiable" budget. Even after months of negotiations, Dawkins was unable to get his budget past the Senate, where the Australian Democrats and two Greens held the balance of power. Green Sen. Dee Margetts refused to rule out ending the budget's progress in the Senate and forcing the government to a double dissolution and an early election. The Greens wanted to see big cuts in defense spending, the removal of income tax cuts to higher income earners, and a government backdown on increases in wine taxes. After intense pressure from the hospitality industries, Dawkins watered down the tax on fringe-benefit payments to executives staying away from home and reduced the proposed tax increase on wine to get his budget through the Senate.

It had been a difficult period of unexpected stress. Faced with over a month of frustration, the treasurer, when releasing the third version of his budget on September 21, almost broke down. With prominent bags under his eyes and shaking with emotion, Dawkins said that he had contemplated retirement and considered resigning when his budget crumbled, and he wondered whether shuttling back and forth between Fremantle, Western Australia, and Canberra was worth it. In the end Dawkins did resign, abruptly and without further clarification, on December 17 "to pursue other interests—what, I don't know."

The prime minister himself also felt the heat over the budget debacle and terminated question time in the House of Representatives on October 5, walking out of the chamber to chanting, screaming, boos, and howls from the opposition. Hewson claimed that Keating was cracking under the pressure and was totally out of control. "He decided to crash through," said Hewson, "but he just crashed." He continued, "He can certainly dish it out in politics, but he can't take it." For his part, Keating explained that his unusual action was taken to draw public attention to the opposition's disruption, which was aiming to tear away at the government's legitimacy.

The government raised extra funds by selling a further 19% of the Commonwealth Bank but decided to postpone the float of the remaining 75% of QANTAS (25% was owned by British Airways). Explaining the delay in selling QANTAS, Finance Minister Ralph Willis said the government had been advised that it would get more for the airline when the market picked up after QANTAS had been given more time to smooth its merger with Australian Airlines.

(A.R.G. GRIFFITHS)

See also *Dependent States,* below.

FIJI

The republic of Fiji occupies an island group in the South Pacific Ocean. Area: 18,274 sq km (7,056 sq mi). Pop. (1993 est.): 762,000. Cap.: Suva. Monetary unit: Fiji dollar, with (Oct. 4, 1993) a free rate of F$1.54 to U.S. $1 (F$2.34 = £1 sterling). Presidents in 1993, Ratu Sir Penaia Ganilau (died December 15) and Ratu Sir Kamisese Mara (acting from December 15); prime minister, Sitiveni Rabuka.

Prime Minister Sitiveni Rabuka surprised observers in December 1992 when he called for a government of national unity, with the aim of smoothing over ethnic and political divisions. Despite interparty talks, however, little progress was made.

In June members of the predominantly Indian Fiji Labour Party walked out of Parliament over Rabuka's failure to fulfil promises made at the time of his appointment. In a conciliatory gesture the government established a constitutional review committee that included opposition members of Parliament. In December the government was defeated on its budget when a group of parliamentarians crossed the floor. Prime Minister Sitiveni Rabuka responded by calling a general election for early in the new year. Fiji lost its president, Ratu Sir Penaia Ganilau, who died in Washington, D.C., on December 15.

The government maintained the economic direction of its predecessor, taking further steps to deregulate the economy, reduce government spending, and promote growth. The deficit was held to 2.5% of gross domestic product, compared with 3.4% in 1992, and a 10% value-added tax was introduced. Cyclones Joni and Kina caused more than 20 deaths in early 1993 and destroyed four major bridges.

It was estimated that ethnic Fijians outnumbered Indians by some 30,000 in June 1992. Over the preceding two years, 90% of all emigrants from Fiji had been Indian, 42% of them in professional, skilled, and managerial occupational categories.

(BARRIE MACDONALD)

This article updates the *Macropædia* article PACIFIC ISLANDS: *Fiji.*

KIRIBATI

A republic in the western Pacific Ocean and member of the Commonwealth, Kiribati comprises the former Gilbert Islands, Banaba (Ocean Island), the Line Islands, and the Phoenix Islands. Area: 811 sq km (313 sq mi). Pop. (1993 est.): 76,900. Cap.: Bairiki, on Tarawa. Monetary unit: Australian dollar, with (Oct. 4, 1993) a free rate of $A 1.55 to U.S. $1 ($A 2.35 = £1 sterling). President (*beretitenti*) in 1993, Teatao Teannaki.

Kiribati continued its efforts to strengthen the private sector in 1993, announcing plans to privatize hotels on South Tarawa and Kiritimati Atoll (Christmas Island), the national supply company (a major importer and distributor of building materials and other hardware), and the commercial marine venture on Kiritimati. The government also advanced its planning for accelerated development and resettlement on Kiritimati, which accounted for more than half of the country's land but only 5% of the population.

Penalties on vessels encroaching into the Kiribati exclusive economic zone added substantially to fisheries-related revenue. A South Korean bunker vessel that was arrested twice in 1991 and declared forfeit by the courts was renamed *Phoenix Islander* and added to the Kiribati fleet. Another vessel was seized and released after a negotiated fine of $A 330,000 had been paid. Under the South Pacific Forum Fisheries Agency multilateral fishing treaty with the U.S., Kiribati received payments of $A 5.7 million.

At a regional Asia-Pacific symposium on climate change, the representative from Kiribati issued a call for detailed studies on the implications of global warming for atoll populations. Planning was advanced for a national coordination centre for communications and disaster that would be built in Kiribati with assistance from Australia.

(BARRIE MACDONALD)

This article updates the *Macropædia* article PACIFIC ISLANDS: *Kiribati.*

MARSHALL ISLANDS

A republic in the central Pacific Ocean, the Marshall Islands comprises two 1,300-km (800-mi)-long parallel chains of coral atolls. Area: 181 sq km (70 sq mi). Pop. (1993 est.): 52,100. Cap.: Majuro. Monetary unit: U.S. dollar, with (Oct. 4, 1993) a free rate of U.S. $1.52 to £1 sterling. President in 1993, Amata Kabua.

The Marshallese government claimed in 1993 that changes in trade arrangements and federal funding programs after the implementation of the Compact of Free Association with the U.S. had cost $50 million, for which compensation of $30 million had been sought from the U.S. Proposals to develop a new antinuclear missile shield raised the possibility of a substantial increase in U.S. defense spending and in the number of military personnel at the missile-testing facility on Kwajalein. By late 1993 the U.S. had paid $101 million for damage caused by radiation. Most of the funds went to islanders from Bikini, Enewetak, Rongelap, and Utirik who were directly affected by nuclear tests conducted in the 1940s and 1950s.

Asian Development Bank funding was secured in 1993 for fishing, education, and water-supply projects. Sea and air surveillance brought increased revenues from fishing, but an attempt to extend the Marshall Islands' exclusive economic zone to Wake Island was rejected by the U.S.

A "resource recovery system" that would incinerate imported toxic waste on Likiep Atoll aroused national and international opposition but remained under consideration. Another proposal, to use imported petroleum-contaminated soil to build a causeway on Kwajalein, was rejected.

(BARRIE MACDONALD)

This article updates the *Macropædia* article PACIFIC ISLANDS: *Marshall Islands.*

MICRONESIA, FEDERATED STATES OF

A republic in the western Pacific Ocean, the Federated States of Micronesia comprises more than 600 islands and islets in the Caroline Islands archipelago. Area: 701 sq km (271 sq mi). Pop. (1993 est.): 103,000. Cap.: Palikir, on Pohnpei. Monetary unit: U.S. dollar, with (Oct. 4, 1993) a free rate of U.S. $1.52 to £1 sterling. President in 1993, Bailey Olter.

In 1993, during its third year of independence, the Federated States of Micronesia continued to build international links. In July Micronesia became a member of the International Monetary Fund and its agencies and paid $1.2 million for a membership levy and subscription. Late in 1992 Pres. Bailey Olter visited China; he reaffirmed Micronesia's commitment to a single-China policy and signed a cooperation agreement. Olter also received the new Spanish ambassador, thus renewing historical and cultural links with a former colonial power in the region.

Continuing drought in the district of Chuuk (formerly Truk) in the latter part of 1992 brought relief assistance from the U.S. and necessitated water shipments from Guam. Thirty-four islanders from the district of Kosrae (formerly Kusaie) pressed for compensation from the U.S. for health problems, which they charged stemmed from exposure to nuclear radiation. The men claimed that they were hired by the U.S. to clean up at Bikini after the conclusion of nuclear testing in the 1950s. The U.S. government stated that it had no medical or work records for the claimants. Under the Compact of Free Association, non-Marshallese could not claim compensation from the $270 million fund set aside for the Marshall Islands, but they could submit a direct claim to the U.S.

(BARRIE MACDONALD)

This article updates the *Macropædia* article PACIFIC ISLANDS: *Micronesia.*

NAURU

An island republic within the Commonwealth, Nauru lies in the Pacific Ocean about 1,900 km (1,200 mi) east of New Guinea. Area: 21 sq km (8 sq mi). Pop. (1993 est.): 10,000. Cap.: Government offices in Yaren district. Monetary unit: Australian dollar, with (Oct. 4, 1993) a free rate of $A 1.55 to U.S. $1 ($A 2.35 = £1 sterling). President in 1993, Bernard Dowiyogo.

In 1993 Nauru celebrated the 25th year of its independence by serving as host for the South Pacific Forum. Bernard Dowiyogo, president of Nauru, was chairman of the Forum, the annual meeting of the leaders of governments of self-governing countries in the South Pacific. The public relations aspect of the Forum was not entirely successful, however. A group of Nauruan women used the arrival of the local political leaders to protest against what they saw as the gross mismanagement of their small republic's phosphate wealth. They attached banners to the sides of cars reading "Wealth belongs to the ministers." The protests were in response to events that included the resignation of the Australian manager of the Nauru Phosphate Trust, Geoffrey Chatfield, in May 1993. In his resignation letter Chatfield complained that various government organizations kept bleeding the trust, which he alleged showed an overall decline in value following unwise investments in foreign real estate.

Shortly before the Pacific Forum talks began, Australian Prime Minister Paul Keating made an offer to settle out of court a claim for damages that Nauru had been pursuing for four years in the International Court of Justice. Nauru had sought $A 110 million to rejuvenate the island, 80% of which was uninhabitable because of phosphate mining. Australia agreed to pay Nauru $A 57 million within 12 months, and to provide an additional $A 2.5 million annually for 20 years.

(A.R.G. GRIFFITHS)

This article updates the *Macropædia* article PACIFIC ISLANDS: *Nauru.*

NEW ZEALAND

New Zealand, a constitutional monarchy and member of the Commonwealth in the South Pacific Ocean, consists of North and South islands and Stewart, Chatham, and other minor islands. Area: 270,534 sq km (104,454 sq mi). Pop. (1993 est.): 3,520,000. Cap.: Wellington. Monetary unit: New Zealand dollar, with (Oct. 4, 1993) a free rate of $NZ 1.82 to U.S. $1 ($NZ 2.76 = £1 sterling). Queen, Elizabeth II; governor-general in 1993, Dame Catherine Tizard; prime minister, Jim Bolger.

In 1993, for the first time in 65 years, a New Zealand general election failed at the first night's counting to give a majority to any party to form a government. After the November 6 polling, the National Party (NP), led by Prime Minister Jim Bolger, had 49 seats to the Labour opposition's 46. Two new parties—an Alliance of various small parties and a conservative breakaway from the NP, New Zealand First—won two seats each. The NP lost 20 seats to Labour, which itself lost one seat to each of the new parties.

Jim Anderton, a former Labour MP, was the outstanding personality of the campaign. His Alliance Party almost magically bound together such parties as the Social Credit Political League (renamed the Democratic Party), the conservationists, and Anderton's own New Labour Party.

Bolger declared the NP's intention of continuing to govern despite the stalemate, and the leaders of all minority parties involved declared their interest in preserving stability and finding common ground to enable a constructive form of government to continue. Gov.-Gen. Dame Catherine Tizard, another former Labour MP, said she would have no need to talk to any party leader until after 200,000 absentee and other special votes were counted.

When the results of the counting of absentee and special votes were announced on November 17, one seat had changed hands, giving the NP a bare majority of 50 to Labour's 45. (For tabulated results, see *Political Parties,* above.) Despite the government's slim victory, one Cabinet minister lost his seat in the casualty list. He was Maurice McTigue, a low-profile immigration and labour relations minister, who was downed by a former Labour agriculture minister, Jim Sutton, for the Timaru seat. Finance Minister Ruth Richardson, in an electorate of sharply altered boundaries, had a majority of 5,441 votes cut to 653. A strict monetarist, she was the first (November 29) to be dismissed from among a number of ministers discarded when National's new Cabinet needed to reflect the attitudes of other party leaders.

On the same day, the country voted in a referendum on its form of government, and on this issue voters called by 53.8 to 46.2% for their long-standing first-past-the-post system to be replaced by mixed member proportional (MMP) representation—a system calling for interparty consultation. A previous referendum had preferred MMP to other proportional systems. The new government was expected to accept the MMP system, work out details, and have the next general elections decided by it.

Under the MMP system the old 99-member Parliament would expand to 120 members—64 elected and 56 appointed from party lists. The public interest in an alternative system seemed to reflect disenchantment with a single-chamber system's lightning pace with new legislation, petty party rivalry, and casual attitudes to manifesto promises, as well as the level of unemployment (less than 10%) in an era of restructuring.

The NP government had gone to the country largely on restructuring initiated by its Labour predecessor's finance minister, Sir Roger Douglas, architect of deregulation and privatization reforms that were recognized in other countries more than in New Zealand. Labour fell apart over the Douglas reforms; National had carried on with them, breaking down industrywide union contracts into plant-centred ones based on voluntary unionism.

Registered unemployment fell to its lowest level in two years, though it remained almost 40,000 higher than when the NP government took office in 1990. National and Labour both used the figures in the election campaign. A household labour-force survey (the official measure) also trended down, and in June it stood at 9.9% of the workforce. The budget announced in July provided for a deficit of $2,278,000,000, which would be reduced to $1,130,000,000 in 1995–96 and produce a surplus the following year.

Foreign Minister Dan McKinnon said in May that New Zealand would not seek to leave the Commonwealth, even though Prime Minister Paul Keating in neighbouring Australia had decided that his country should do so.

(JOHN A. KELLEHER)

See also *Dependent States,* below.

PAPUA NEW GUINEA

A constitutional monarchy and member of the Commonwealth, Papua New Guinea is situated in the southwestern Pacific Ocean and comprises the eastern part of the island of New Guinea, the islands of the Bismarck, Kiriwina (Trobriand), Louisiade, and D'Entrecasteaux groups, Muyua (Woodlark) Island and other nearby islands, and parts of the Solomon Islands, including Bougainville. Area: 462,840 sq km (178,704 sq mi). Pop. (1993 est.): 3,918,000. Cap.: Port Moresby. Monetary unit: kina, with (Oct. 4, 1993) a free rate of 0.99 kina to U.S. $1 (1.50 kinas = £1 sterling). Queen, Elizabeth II; governor-general in 1993, Wiwa Korowi; prime minister, Paias Wingti.

Amid uproar and dismay in the Papua New Guinea Parliament, Prime Minister Paias Wingti outmaneuvered his political opposition by resigning on Sept. 23, 1993, and being reelected almost simultaneously. This legitimate strategy saved him and his Cabinet from facing a vote of no confidence in the foreseeable future. The nation's constitution restricted the number of no-confidence motions that could be made in a 12-month period.

Wingti, who first became prime minister in 1985 after leading a no-confidence motion against Michael Somare, made a deliberate effort in 1993 to turn the direction of the nation's foreign policy focus toward Asia. He argued, following visits to Singapore, Malaysia, and Indonesia, that the challenge for Papua New Guinea was to find its place in the Asia-Pacific regional economy of the 21st century.

Wingti's main obstacles to his dream were not simply the difficulty in attracting investors to Papua New Guinea but also in guaranteeing physical security for foreign nationals and local citizens. Accordingly, because of the problems with law enforcement that continued to trouble the nation in 1993, he announced a system of national registration. Papua New Guineans traveling from their homes to anywhere in the country would be required to carry identification that included their names and addresses. (A.R.G. GRIFFITHS)

This article updates the *Macropædia* article PACIFIC ISLANDS: *Papua New Guinea.*

SOLOMON ISLANDS

A constitutional monarchy and member of the Commonwealth, the Solomon Islands comprises a 1,450-km (900-mi) chain of islands and atolls in the western Pacific Ocean. Area: 28,370 sq km (10,954 sq mi). Pop. (1993 est.): 349,000. Cap.: Honiara. Monetary unit: Solomon Islands dollar, with (Oct. 4, 1993) a free rate of SI$3.22 to U.S. $1 (SI$4.87 = £1 sterling). Queen, Elizabeth II; governor-general in 1993, Sir George Lepping; prime ministers, Solomon Mamaloni and, from June 18, Francis Billy Hilly.

After the general election in May 1993, Francis Billy Hilly became prime minister, replacing Solomon Mamaloni. Although Mamaloni controlled the largest parliamentary grouping, he did not command a majority in the newly expanded 47-seat Parliament and lost by 24 votes to 23. The new government, called the National Coalition Partners, was an alliance of seven groups opposed to Mamaloni, who put up a lengthy legal battle in an attempt to prevent Hilly from taking office.

The civil war on neighbouring Bougainville, which was trying to secede from Papua New Guinea, caused tension between the two nations despite agreements to normalize relations. Mamaloni's government was seen as supporting the Bougainville rebels, while Papua New Guinean forces made incursions into Solomon territory, killing and injuring civilians and causing significant property damage. In November Amnesty International reported torture and murder by Papua New Guinean military forces against secessionists.

After a period of economic instability, gross domestic product grew by 8% in 1992, largely because of an 80% increase in log production. The government was obliged to prop up ailing Solomon Airlines and offer for sale its 70% shareholding. (BARRIE MACDONALD)

This article updates the *Macropædia* article PACIFIC ISLANDS: *Solomon Islands.*

TONGA

A constitutional monarchy and member of the Commonwealth, Tonga comprises about 170 islands split into three main groups in the Pacific Ocean east of Fiji. Area: 780 sq km (301 sq mi). Pop. (1993 est.): 99,100. Cap.: Nuku'alofa. Monetary unit: pa'anga, with (Oct. 4, 1993) a free rate of 1.56 pa'anga (T$) to U.S. $1 (2.35 pa'anga = £1 sterling). King, Taufa'ahau Tupou IV; prime minister in 1993, Baron Vaea.

The February 1993 general elections provided the opportunity for pro-democracy reformers to challenge the royal establishment. Under the constitution the king and 11 members of his Cabinet occupied 12 permanent seats in the 30-member Parliament, while the hereditary nobles and the commoners each elected 9 members. Of the nine vacant seats contested, pro-democracy candidates won six. Pro-democracy leader 'Akolisi Pohiva maintained that all seats should be decided by popular ballot, with the king appointing a Cabinet from among those elected. The government, however, vigorously defended the existing system.

On July 4 the kingdom celebrated the 75th birthday of King Taufa'ahau Tupou IV and the 25th anniversary of his reign.

Faced with continuing recession, the government cut spending by restricting the use of three patrol vessels (donated by Australia) to reduce the costs of fuel and maintenance. The overall budget of T$ 51.7 million allocated T$ 34.3 million for such development projects as fisheries, agriculture, tourism, and infrastructure. A gross domestic product growth of 4% was projected for 1993–94. The king also proposed that a study be conducted on the feasibility of a major land-reclamation and oil-refinery project on Tongatapu.

BILL MORTON—PACIFIC ISLANDS MONTHLY

In 1993 Tongan voters elected a new legislature, which meets in this building in Nuku'alofa. Pro-democracy candidates, who are committed to fundamental changes in the Tongan government, made a strong showing in the February voting.

In October, Roman Catholic Bishop Patelisio Finau, who had campaigned for social justice and political reform, died while visiting Niue. (BARRIE MACDONALD)

This article updates the *Macropædia* article PACIFIC ISLANDS: *Tonga.*

TUVALU

A constitutional monarchy within the Commonwealth, Tuvalu comprises nine main islands and their associated islets and reefs in the western Pacific Ocean. Area: 24 sq km (9 sq mi). Pop. (1993 est.): 9,500. Cap.: Fongafale, on Funafuti Atoll. Monetary unit: Australian dollar, with (Oct. 4, 1993) a free rate of $A 1.55 to U.S. $1 ($A 2.35 = £1 sterling). Queen, Elizabeth II; governor-general in 1993, Toaripi Lauti; prime ministers, Bikenibeu Paeniu and from December 10, Kamuta Laatasi.

Long-simmering tensions between Tuvalu and the United Kingdom, its former colonial power, surfaced at the end of 1992 when Britain's minister of state for foreign and commonwealth affairs criticized Tuvalu's economic policy and, in particular, public-service pay increases. In response, Prime Minister Bikenibeu Paeniu maintained that the British government had not adequately prepared the island nation for independence and did not appreciate Tuvalu's development priorities. He noted that the pay increases did not even cover inflation and that, with the salaries for top public servants at no more than $A 11,000, Tuvalu lagged significantly behind its neighbours. Tuvalu's financial projections showed a surplus of $A 1.5 million on a budget of $A 1.8 million for 1993, and further surpluses were expected through 1996.

Following a general election in mid-1993, the Parliament was deadlocked over its selection of prime minister. After Parliament had twice failed to resolve the issue, Gov.-Gen. Toaripi Lauti dissolved Parliament on September 22 and scheduled a new general election for November 25. Kamuta Laatasi was elected prime minister on December 10. (BARRIE MACDONALD)

This article updates the *Macropædia* article PACIFIC ISLANDS: *Tuvalu.*

VANUATU

The republic of Vanuatu, a member of the Commonwealth, comprises 12 main islands and some 60 smaller ones in the southwestern Pacific Ocean. Area: 12,190 sq km (4,707 sq mi). Pop. (1993 est.): 160,000. Cap.: Vila. Monetary unit: vatu, with (Oct. 4, 1993) a free rate of 123.03 vatu to U.S. $1 (186.39 vatu = £1 sterling). President in 1993, Fred Timakata; prime minister, Maxime Carlot Korman.

There was a period of political instability at the end of 1992 when former prime minister Walter Lini's National United Party, a junior coalition member in the ruling Union of Moderate Parties of Prime Minister Maxime Carlot Korman, dismissed six officials, including two Cabinet ministers, and Lini temporarily withdrew his support. A Cabinet reshuffle followed, with the prime minister assuming the foreign affairs portfolio. Carlot Korman managed to survive with a tenuous parliamentary majority but had further troubles in August 1993 when Lini's party withdrew from the government. The minister of finance resigned in November, leaving the government in a precarious position.

Controversy of another kind followed the passing late in 1992 of legislation that would have allowed the minister of finance to revoke a business license without reason or appeal. The acting high commissioner for Australia was expelled for expressing opposition to the legislation, which was subsequently overturned by the Supreme Court.

A bilingual television service was established in Vanuatu in 1993. Most programming would be based on a mixture of French material and English-language programs from New Zealand. (BARRIE MACDONALD)

This article updates the *Macropædia* article PACIFIC ISLANDS: *Vanuatu.*

WESTERN SAMOA

A constitutional monarchy and member of the Commonwealth, Western Samoa occupies an island group in the South Pacific Ocean. Area: 2,831 sq km (1,093 sq mi). Pop. (1993 est.): 163,000. Cap.: Apia. Monetary unit: Western Samoa tala, with (Oct. 4, 1993) a free rate of 2.55 tala to U.S. $1 (3.87 tala = £1 sterling). Head of state (*O le Ao o le Malo*) in 1993, Malietoa Tanumafili II; prime minister, Tofilau Eti Alesana.

The economy was still recovering from the effects of serious cyclones in each of the previous three years, but after declines in gross domestic product in both 1991 and 1992, growth of 4% was anticipated for 1993. Exports, at 14 million tala, were at their lowest level for decades, while imports remained high because of postcyclone reconstruction. In the agriculture sector, domestic supplies as well as exports had been affected by cyclone damage and a serious outbreak of taro blight. In light of all these difficulties, the Yazaki automotive wiring plant assumed particular importance. It accounted for 80% of export earnings in 1992 and, with 1,400 workers, was the largest employer after the government.

Western Samoa introduced its first full broadcasting facility in 1993, with both local programs and satellite transmissions from New Zealand. There was concern over new libel legislation that could force journalists to reveal sources in defamation cases and could restrict the publication of court evidence concerning third parties to an action.

There was some tension within the ruling Human Rights Protection Party when three members were expelled. Prime Minister Tofilau Eti Alesana offered to resign, but he was asked by his colleagues to remain in office.

(BARRIE MACDONALD)

This article updates the *Macropædia* article PACIFIC ISLANDS: *Western Samoa.*

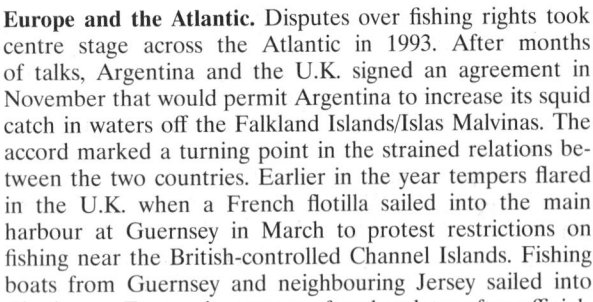

Dependent States

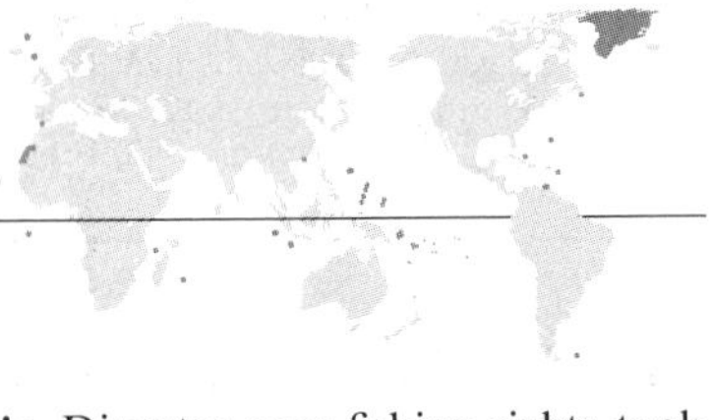

Europe and the Atlantic. Disputes over fishing rights took centre stage across the Atlantic in 1993. After months of talks, Argentina and the U.K. signed an agreement in November that would permit Argentina to increase its squid catch in waters off the Falkland Islands/Islas Malvinas. The accord marked a turning point in the strained relations between the two countries. Earlier in the year tempers flared in the U.K. when a French flotilla sailed into the main harbour at Guernsey in March to protest restrictions on fishing near the British-controlled Channel Islands. Fishing boats from Guernsey and neighbouring Jersey sailed into Cherbourg, France, in protest a few days later after officials repudiated the informal agreement reached by the local fishermen.

In June the International Court of Justice ruled that the waters between Greenland and the Norwegian island of Jan Mayen should be divided equally between Denmark and Norway, but the dispute with Iceland and Russia over Norway's self-declared 200-nautical-mile protective zone around Svalbard remained at issue. Meanwhile, the collapse of the fisheries industry in the Faeroe Islands triggered the resignation of the Faeroese government in April and forced Denmark to increase its aid to the colony to help stave off economic disaster.

In March Britain officially met with Spain for the first time in two years to discuss the future of Gibraltar. As in the past, no representatives from Gibraltar were included in the talks, which failed to end the continuing stalemate. In a speech before a UN committee in October, Gibraltar's chief minister, Joe Bossano, accused the British government of neglecting the colony's interests and emphasized Gibraltar's desire to seek economic independence and full sovereignty.

Caribbean and Bermuda. On November 14 Puerto Ricans voted by a slim margin of 48% to 46% to retain the island's commonwealth status with the U.S. rather than apply for statehood. The option of seeking full independence received less than 5% of the vote. Gov. Pedro Rosselló, who was elected in 1992 on a pro-statehood platform, agreed to abide by the results, while the opposition leader, Miguel Agosto, vowed to seek expanded links with the U.S.

Politicians and businessmen in Puerto Rico were preoccupied throughout most of the year by the threatened withdrawal by the U.S. government of Section 936 tax-code privileges, which allowed profits made in the territory by U.S. companies to remain tax free if they were reinvested in Puerto Rico. About 100,000 Puerto Ricans were directly dependent on employment generated by Section 936 companies. Congress eventually moderated the proposals, leaving existing profits in banks untaxed but imposing low tax rates on future profits.

The Cayman Islands became an unofficial transshipment centre for Cuban refugees during the year with the arrival of over 150 Cubans seeking passage to the U.S. Local residents protested the proposed construction of a "tent city" for the refugees. Since 1989 more than 250 Cubans had arrived in the Caymans en route to the U.S.

The ruling United Bermuda Party (UBP), led by Sir John Swan, was returned to power in Bermuda's general election in October, winning 22 of the 40 seats in the island's House of Assembly. It was the UBP's eighth successive election victory. The U.S. naval base in Bermuda, worth $20 million a year in revenue for the island's economy, won a reprieve in September when a clause in the U.S. defense-spending bill, which would have withdrawn funding for the base, was struck out after lobbying by the Bermuda government.

The right-wing Guadeloupe Objective Party, headed by Lucette Michaux-Chevry, succeeded in obtaining an absolute majority (22 of 41 seats) in Guadeloupe's regional council election in January, following annulment of the March 1992 election. The rerun was ordered by the French Council of State after it was found that a dissident group had incorrectly filed its electoral list.

In the Netherlands Antilles public protests erupted in St. Maarten in March because of dissatisfaction over the way the local council was running the island's affairs, particularly the utility services. The protesters called for the councillors' resignation and the holding of new elections. In November, Curaçao chose not to follow the example set by Aruba and voted overwhelmingly to remain a part of the Netherlands Antilles group. A week later Prime Minister Maria Liberia-Peters resigned and was replaced by Susanne Romer.

Former chief minister John Osborne vowed in February to "kick the British out of Montserrat" following his acquittal on corruption and conspiracy charges. He claimed he

Gov. Pedro Rosselló leads a demonstration in support of Puerto Rican statehood. In a three-choice plebiscite held on November 14, the island's voters chose to maintain Puerto Rico's commonwealth status, narrowly rejecting statehood and overwhelmingly opposing independence.
ALEX QUESADA—MATRIX

had been "framed" by the British colonial administration. Montserrat obtained a new governor in May, when Frank Savage succeeded the retiring David Taylor.

Pacific. It was a bad year for incumbent political leaders in U.S. territories. One-term governor Larry Guerrero of the Northern Marianas lost his reelection bid in November 1993. He was defeated by his predecessor in office, Froilan C. Tenorio. Guerrero followed in the path of Peter Tali Coleman, American Samoa's governor for 11 of the previous 15 years, who was defeated at the polls in November 1992. Coleman was succeeded by Sen. A.P. Lutali, who had previously served as governor (1985–89). Lutali accused Coleman of continuing to hire and promote staff after the election and of making advance payments for services to political appointees. Within months Lutali had addressed the territory's financial crisis by dismissing 20% of all government workers, most of them Coleman appointees hired on a temporary basis or on contract.

Pres. Ngiratkel Etpison of Palau (Belau) also lost reelection, to former vice president Kuniwo Nakamura. At the same time, 14 of Palau's 16 states voted for a constitutional change that opened the way for the controversial antinuclear constitution to be amended by simple majority and, as a consequence, for Palau to negotiate with the U.S. on a Compact of Free Association. In seven previous plebiscites 62–73% of voters had supported change, just short of the 75% previously required by the constitution.

In March, Frank Lui, a former Cabinet minister and a member of the Niue legislature since 1970, was named to succeed Young Vivian as prime minister. Vivian had held the post since the death of Sir Robert Rex, Niue's long-serving premier, in December 1992. Lui announced that his government would try to persuade Niueans to return home. About 12,000 Niueans lived in New Zealand, compared with some 2,400 living on Niue. In October the Cook Islands served as host for the South Pacific Festival of Arts. However, the festival, and especially the $NZ 11.6 million cultural centre built for it, gave the government a deficit of $NZ 6 million, its largest in 20 years.

The economy of French Polynesia was adversely affected by France's decision to join the international moratorium on nuclear testing; some 10,000 jobs and 20% of the territory's revenue were directly related to the testing program. The French government agreed to provide financial assistance to ease the loss. In December 1992 the Court of Appeal in Paris had upheld minor corruption charges against Gaston Flosse, a prominent local politician and former minister in the French government, and Jean Juventin, president of the Territorial Assembly. In March 1993, Flosse was elected to the French National Assembly as one of the territory's two representatives.

In New Caledonia, progress was reviewed on the implementation of the Matignon accords, under which a major development program would be followed by a referendum on the territory's political future in 1998. To some extent the process was soured by a controversy over the purchase by the Kanak-controlled Northern Province of major tourist assets in the south, the chief area of European settlement.

East Asia. The standoff between the U.K. and China over Gov. Chris Patten's proposals for expanding democracy dominated political life in British-run Hong Kong in 1993. Patten had proposed widening the franchise in the 1995 elections for the Legislative Council's 60 seats, only 20 of which were to be directly elected. The councillors' terms were supposed to last until 1999, two years after the 1997 return of sovereignty to China. Beijing (Peking) steadfastly denounced the proposals, insisting that they ran counter to the 1984 Sino-British Joint Declaration, the post-1997 Basic Law for the territory, and an earlier exchange of letters on electoral arrangements. Officials refused to hold talks with the British unless the proposals were dropped, and they threatened to set up a parallel political structure to prepare for the transition.

Dependent States[1]

Australia
- Christmas Island
- Cocos (Keeling) Islands
- Norfolk Island

Denmark
- Faeroe Islands
- Greenland

France
- French Guiana
- French Polynesia
- Guadeloupe
- Martinique
- Mayotte
- New Caledonia
- Réunion
- Saint Pierre and Miquelon
- Wallis and Futuna

Netherlands, The
- Aruba
- Netherlands Antilles

New Zealand
- Cook Islands
- Niue
- Tokelau

Norway
- Jan Mayen
- Svalbard

Portugal
- Macau

United Kingdom
- Anguilla
- Bermuda
- British Virgin Islands
- Cayman Islands
- Falkland Islands
- Gibraltar
- Guernsey
- Hong Kong
- Isle of Man
- Jersey
- Montserrat
- Pitcairn Island
- Saint Helena
- Turks and Caicos Islands

United States
- American Samoa
- Guam
- Northern Marianas
- Palau
- Puerto Rico
- Virgin Islands (of the U.S.)

[1]Excludes territories (1) to which Antarctic Treaty is applicable in whole or in part, (2) without permanent civilian population, (3) without internationally recognized civilian government (Western Sahara, Gaza Strip), or (4) representing unadjudicated unilateral or multilateral territorial claims.

In late March the Hong Kong government officially gazetted, or published, the proposals as a bill, setting the stage for a potential debate and vote in the Legislative Council. Shortly afterward China agreed to hold talks, but the negotiations dragged on for round after round with no visible progress. Public statements on both sides became more acrimonious. In October, Patten revealed that the British side had offered concessions that would greatly reduce the eligible electorate for the 40 non-directly elected seats, but China maintained its position. In December, Patten made good on earlier promises and introduced legislation on electoral reform. Beijing immediately broke off talks and declared an end to cooperation with the U.K.

Despite the political tension, the territory's economy continued to grow at a robust rate of 5%. The stock market became feverish in October, breaking records on a daily basis after the U.S. investment house Morgan Stanley gave it a highly bullish rating owing to China's growth prospects, and foreign money flooded in. In neighbouring Macau, which was due to be returned to China in 1999, boomtown-style development continued as gambling tycoon Stanley Ho gained Beijing's approval for a $1.4 billion land-reclamation project, set to expand Macau's mainland territory by 20%.

(BARRIE MACDONALD; DAVID RENWICK; MELINDA C. SHEPHERD; BERTON WOODWARD)

This article updates the *Macropædia* articles HONG KONG; PACIFIC ISLANDS; The WEST INDIES.

Polar Regions

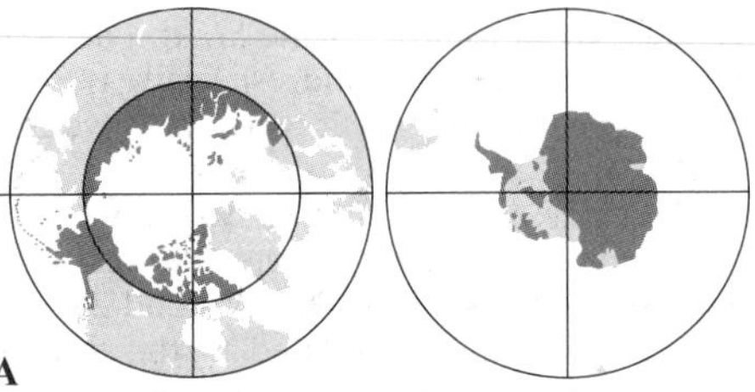

ANTARCTICA

Some 4,000 scientists and other personnel from two dozen nations continued to do research aimed at understanding the Antarctic and its involvement in global environmental change. They and some 6,500 tourists and adventurers were the only human visitors to the region, which comprises 9% of the Earth's land area and 8% of its oceans.

The 40 Antarctic Treaty nations met in Italy in November 1992—the latest of numerous consultative meetings held since the treaty entered into force in 1961. Delegates adopted recommendations about strengthening plans for specially protected areas, increasing Antarctic global change research, and increasing environmental monitoring and international data management. By October 1993 most of the treaty adherents, including all 26 consultative parties, had signed a comprehensive Protocol on Environmental Protection, drafted in Madrid in 1991. One nation, Spain, had ratified the protocol, but several nations were not expected to ratify until 1994. The U.S. Senate approved ratification in October 1992, and implementing legislation was still to be adopted. The protocol strengthened environmental protection measures and banned mining in Antarctica.

A U.S. court decision in January applied the National Environmental Policy Act (NEPA) to federal activities in Antarctica. NEPA had earlier applied only domestically, while Executive Order 12114 covered the environmental aspects of U.S. activities overseas. The Department of Justice decided "not to challenge the court's precise holding" but said that "the Administration does not embrace language in the opinion which may be interpreted to extend beyond this"; overseas federal activities in places other than Antarctica were still considered covered by the executive order, not NEPA.

Specialists from Argentina and The Netherlands removed the remaining fuel and lubricants from the wrecked Argentine ship *Bahía Paraíso*. The ship had struck a rock in January 1989 and sunk a kilometre and a half from Palmer Station, a U.S. research facility, resulting in Antarctica's largest oil spill and causing considerable animal and plant mortality. The complex oil-removal project, which involved, among other operations, 167 dives, extracted 148,390 litres (39,200 gal) from the ship's tanks and engines. The hulk, no longer considered a significant environmental threat, was expected to be left where it was. The copious biota that live and breed around Palmer Station and the wreck site had been studied intensively over the past quarter century, and the U.S. National Science Foundation in 1992 declared the area a long-term ecological research site, one of only 18 worldwide. Scientists who examined the area two years after the wreck found some effects remaining from the initial spillage of fuel, but said the volatility of the fluid, the amount spilled (640,000 litres—170,000 gal), and the dynamic weather and current conditions tended to minimize long-term contamination.

Among the most widely reported scientific findings from Antarctica was the current status of the ozone hole. In October 1993 several research stations in Antarctica reported the lowest stratospheric ozone levels ever measured anywhere above Earth. Chlorine from chlorofluorocarbons (CFCs), man-made compounds, was considered the major cause of stratospheric ozone depletion, although a laboratory experiment in 1993 indicated that bromine (also from industrial sources) might be responsible for up to 30% of the Antarctic ozone loss. A natural cause of the ozone hole—chlorine from volcanoes, particularly Mt. Erebus in Antarctica—had been suggested, but most scientists denied that volcanic chlorine could be a cause, because it combines with other elements in the lower atmosphere. Sulfur dioxide injected into the stratosphere by the 1991 eruption of Mt. Pinatubo in the Philippines, however, may have increased the chemical effectiveness in destroying ozone of chlorine and bromine already present, reducing ozone levels worldwide.

The ozone hole allows harmfully high levels of ultraviolet rays (UV) from the Sun to reach the Earth's surface. Ocean biologists working in Antarctica estimated that the increased UV reduces the productivity of marine phytoplankton in the marginal ice zone by about seven million tons of carbon a year, or about 2% of the total. Phytoplankton are tiny plants at the base of the Antarctic Ocean food chain. Scientists did not yet know if the populations of krill and other Antarctic sea life had been affected by the reduced phytoplankton.

U.S. researchers at the geographic South Pole announced in June the discovery of evidence of cosmic structures that formed just one million years after the universe began. Using two specially designed radio telescopes and taking advantage of the extremely dry and cold—and therefore clear—air over the Antarctic interior, they detected small temperature fluctuations in microwave radiation left over after the Big Bang.

On Vega Island, near the Antarctic Peninsula, Argentine and U.S. paleontologists discovered bird fossils that shed light on how birds were evolving 65 million–70 million years ago. The fossils suggested a creature with the body of a shore bird and the head of a duck. The bird lived at a key time in avian evolution, when primitive birds were being replaced by modern, toothless types. The discovery figured in one of the hottest debates in paleontology: the cause of the mass extinctions at the end of the Cretaceous. "You can't find this great horizon of death in Antarctica," one geologist said. "The rock record across the Antarctic Cretaceous-Tertiary boundary is among the best in the world—it's incredibly fossiliferous—but we don't see an abrupt extinction of life at that time." The bird and other recent fossil finds indicated that the polar regions had a much more important role in evolution than was generally thought.

The worldwide search for hard clues to climatic warming produced interesting recent results in and near Antarctica, although most were too localized for extrapolation to the global situation. British scientists reported that South Georgia's smaller land glaciers had been receding since the 1930s, and its larger valley and tidewater glaciers since the 1970s; the climate in this area had been warming since the 1950s. The Wordie Ice Shelf, on the west coast of the Antarctic Peninsula, had been retreating steadily since the mid-1960s and had had a big breakout in 1988–89; higher mean annual temperatures in the area were the probable cause. New Zealand scientists reported a dramatic increase since 1980 in the number of Adélie penguins in the Ross Sea region, probably a result of a recent warming of the Ross Sea climate. A Russian scientist suggested that monthly changes in the thickness and area of Antarctic sea ice accounted for a possible 3° C (5.4° F) increase in planetary mean air temperature. A U.S.-led team analyzed the works of many investigators to come up with a new estimate of Antarctica's "mass balance"—the difference between its receipt of freshwater (as snow and ice) and discharge (as iceberg calving and melting); they found a negative mass balance, or net loss, of 469 trillion tons per year. The new estimate departed from earlier calculations that indicated Antarctica was in mass balance. The net discharge might solve the mystery of an unattributed rise in the global sea level of 0.45 mm (0.02 in) per year.

Global questions aside, one of Antarctica's glacial recessions left a poignant postscript to a 1940–41 U.S. expedition that occupied Stonington Island just off the west coast of the Antarctic Peninsula. Then, as reported in the March 1993 *National Geographic,* a glacier bridged the small strait between the island and the shore, giving the expedition's Curtis-Wright Condor biplane the only route from the ship to a skiway behind the station. Called East Base and not occupied since 1948, the station had the oldest U.S. structures in Antarctica, and the Antarctic Treaty nations in 1989 declared it a historic site. When crews returned to make a small museum in one of the buildings, the glacial ramp—so critical to the 1940 expedition—was gone, replaced by open water and an ice cliff. (GUY G. GUTHRIDGE)

This article updates the *Macropædia* article ANTARCTICA.

GALEN ROWELL—MOUNTAIN LIGHT

Compacted trash is stacked at McMurdo Sound in preparation for shipment out of Antarctica. A 1991 protocol designed to strengthen environmental protection of the continent was still in the process of being ratified by Antarctic Treaty nations in 1993.

ARCTIC REGIONS

The United Nations proclaimed 1993 the International Year of the World's Indigenous Peoples. The declaration was a call to raise the profile of indigenous issues throughout the world, especially those concerned with human rights, the environment, economic development, education, and health. In keeping with the theme "a New Partnership," the indigenous aboriginal peoples of the Arctic made considerable progress in their efforts to participate in worldwide environmental and sustainable development activities. In September ministers representing the governments of Canada, Denmark, Finland, Iceland, Norway, Russia, Sweden, and the United States met in Greenland under the auspices of the Arctic Environmental Protection Strategy (AEPS) and issued the Nuuk Declaration on Environment and Development in the Arctic. The delegates reaffirmed their commitment to protecting and preserving the Arctic environment and fully recognized both the special relationship of the indigenous peoples to the Arctic and their unique contribution to the protection of the Arctic environment. The ministers also formally recognized the special role of indigenous peoples in environmental management and development in the Arctic, the significance of their knowledge and traditional practices, and the ways in which that knowledge could be shared with scientists.

In October U.S. Pres. Bill Clinton sent greetings to scientists and Inuit (Eskimo) leaders attending an international symposium in Reykjavík, Iceland, on the ecological effects of Arctic airborne contaminants. Clinton stated that the meeting represented an important step toward the sound environmental management of the Arctic since the adoption of AEPS two years earlier. He pointed out that with AEPS and the help of the indigenous Arctic peoples, sustainable economic development and environmental protection in the Arctic could be achieved.

While the state of Alaska was trying to cope with diminishing revenues from Prudhoe Bay—over 85% of the state's budget comes from oil production—a promising new find in Cook Inlet was announced by the Atlantic Richfield Co. (ARCO). The Sunfish discovery was estimated to hold as much as 750 million bbl of oil, making it the third largest usable oil field in Alaska.

In February Robert Anderson, the founder of ARCO, announced in Anchorage, Alaska, that he wanted to build a pipeline to take natural gas from the Canadian Arctic to southern Alaska and to markets on the Pacific Rim. The Mackenzie Porcupine Pipeline Co. plan called for a 1,200-km (750-mi) pipeline that would take gas from fields in the Mackenzie Delta to the Kenai Peninsula, south of Anchorage. The $12 billion project was similar to one submitted in the early 1980s by the Yukon Pacific Corp., which proposed a natural gas pipeline along the same route as the trans-Alaska pipeline to take gas from Prudhoe Bay to Valdez. The two projects targeted the Pacific Rim countries, where demand for electricity had far outstripped supply. The timing of the Mackenzie project was crucial—to start gas flowing by 1998, at least five years earlier than the Prudhoe

Inuit residents of Baffin Island prepare to start a trip. In May 1993 Prime Minister Brian Mulroney signed the agreement to create Nunavut (meaning "our land"), which would be carved out of the Northwest Territories, with about one-fifth of the area owned by the Inuit.
MIKE BEEDELL

Bay project. Rejecting proposals to develop the £7 billion Windy Craggy copper mine, the British Columbia government instead converted 930,000 ha (2.3 million ac) into the Tatshenshini and Alsek Wilderness Park. The announcement included plans to link the new park with adjoining parks in Alaska and the Yukon to create a 8.9 million-ha (22 million-ac) United Nations World Heritage Site.

In October it was reported that the Canadian government was considering a policy that would allow traditional food—caribou, seal, and whale blubber—to be used instead of cash for child-support and alimony payments in the Northwest Territories, where more than 20,000 Canadian Inuit live outside the cash economy. In the same month, *Alaska* magazine reported that the courts had granted the Indian communities of Ninilchik, Eklutna, and Knik the right to their own native-only "educational" subsistence fisheries, using scoops, stick fences, and nets. The permits would allow tribal elders to pass on to younger members the traditional methods of harvesting, preserving, and sharing fish.

The journal *Nature* published research findings that the tundra on Alaska's North Slope had recently begun releasing carbon dioxide (CO_2) into the Earth's atmosphere instead of storing it as in the past. Opinions differed on whether this was an alarming human-induced threat or a cyclic event and on what it could mean to the Arctic environment. The *New York Times* reported progress in cleaning up Arctic air, but the ground and water still needed work. Over the past decade, Arctic haze—mostly from Western European and Russian industrial smokestacks—had dropped by about 50%. The likely reason was that these areas had reduced the levels of sulfur dioxide emissions by switching from mostly coal and oil to cleaner-burning natural gas. In May at the Conservation of Arctic Flora and Fauna meeting in Fairbanks, Alaska, delegates were warned that surface oil pollution, heavy metals, and pesticides could result in a poisoning of the food chain in the circumpolar Arctic regions. Arctic policy makers and researchers attending a national workshop in Anchorage learned that levels of polychlorinated biphenyls (PCBs), potentially cancer-causing materials once common in electrical transformers, were as high in parts of Alaska as in the cities of the lower 48 states. They also considered evidence that the U.S.S.R. had dumped radioactive waste in the North Pacific for 25 years, starting in 1966. The U.S. Congress spent $10 million in 1993 to study sea life for signs of such contamination. International scientists meeting in June at Woods Hole, Mass., however, found no evidence of danger from the dumping. The *New York Times* reported in September that Western scientists had examined a sunken Russian submarine and had found that it had been torn apart by an explosion and had possibly leaked plutonium from its nuclear torpedoes. Because currents around the vessel were much weaker than previously believed, it was concluded that any radioactivity would remain on the seafloor rather than being swept toward the rich North Atlantic fisheries. In March Greenpeace reported that the former Soviet navy had used the Arctic Ocean as a giant nuclear scrapyard, dumping waste with more than double the radioactivity released in the Chernobyl disaster. The White Book Report, prepared at the request of Russian Pres. Boris Yeltsin, stated that the waste included 18 nuclear reactors from ships and submarines and more than 13,000 containers of solid radioactive waste.

In May, Yukon's 14 First Nations signed a historic land-claims agreement with the federal government. The Umbrella Final Agreement stipulated that some 8,000 beneficiaries would divide among themselves $280 million and 41,400 sq km (16,000 sq mi), or 8.6%, of the Yukon landmass. The agreement established a joint-management system for wildlife, land use, and other matters. The First Nations were granted responsibility for the areas of education, justice, environmental protection, child welfare, land-use planning, and zoning. The settlement also provided for Indian self-government, including a provision for First Nations to eventually raise revenue through taxation of its membership. In the same month, the *Whitehorse Star* reported that the Yukon would assume full responsibility for onshore oil and gas development in the North Yukon within 18 months. Both the Council for Yukon Indians and the Inuvialuit in the western Northwest Territories objected to the terms of the agreement, which they felt conflicted with their own respective land-claims agreements.

Canadian Prime Minister Brian Mulroney signed the Nunavut Agreement at Iqaluit in May, setting in motion the final steps for the creation of Nunavut, meaning "our land" in the Inuit language. The agreement gave the 17,500 Inuit residents outright ownership of an area of some 350,000 sq km (135,100 sq mi), one-fifth of the new territory. The agreement would also provide the Inuit with Can$1,140,000,000 over 14 years; rights to hunt, fish, and trap; and a form of self-government when the territory was created in 1999.

In August it was announced that private U.S. investors would pay some 1,000 Greenlanders $800,000 plus other benefits not to fish salmon for two years.

(KENNETH DE LA BARRE)

This article updates the *Macropædia* article The ARCTIC.

Major Revisions from the 1994 *Macropædia*

This section of the *Britannica Book of the Year* consists of articles or parts of articles reprinted from the *Macropædia*. The articles appearing here have been selected from among those recently revised or rewritten and have been chosen for their general interest or their timeliness.

The article INFORMATION PROCESSING AND INFORMATION SYSTEMS, which is reprinted in its entirety, has been extensively revised for the 1994 printing. The history of Cambodia, from the article SOUTHEAST ASIA, has been rewritten for 1994. The section on the history of Vietnam, beginning with the World War II period and independence and also from the article SOUTHEAST ASIA, has been extensively revised.

Subscribers desiring update sheets to put in their encyclopædia to indicate that an article has been revised or added and owners of older sets wishing information about the exact articles being replaced by the reprints should address their requests to Editorial Yearbooks, Encyclopædia Britannica, Inc., 310 South Michigan Avenue, Chicago, IL 60604. There is no charge for the article update sheets, but you must tell us the copyright year of your set of *Encyclopædia Britannica*.

Information Processing and Information Systems

In popular usage, the term information refers to facts and opinions provided and received during the course of daily life: one obtains information directly from other living beings, from mass media, from electronic data banks, and from all sorts of observable phenomena in the surrounding environment. A person using such facts and opinions generates more information, some of which is communicated to others during discourse, by instructions, in letters and documents, and through other media. Information organized according to some logical relationships is referred to as a body of knowledge, to be acquired by systematic exposure or study. Application of knowledge (or skills) yields expertise, and additional analytical or experiential insights are said to constitute instances of wisdom. Use of the term information is not restricted exclusively to its communication via natural language. Information is also registered and communicated through art and by facial expressions and gestures or by such other physical responses as shivering. Moreover, every living entity is endowed with information in the form of a genetic code. These information phenomena permeate the physical and mental world, and their variety is such that it has defied so far all attempts at a unified definition of information.

Interest in information phenomena has increased dramatically in the 20th century, and today they are the objects of study in a number of disciplines, including philosophy, physics, biology, linguistics, information and computer science, electronic and communications engineering, management science, and the social sciences. On the commercial side, the information service industry has become one of the newer industries worldwide. Almost all other industries—manufacturing and service—are increasingly concerned with information and its handling. The different, though often overlapping, viewpoints and phenomena of these fields lead to different (and sometimes conflicting) concepts and "definitions" of information.

This article touches on such concepts, particularly as they relate to information processing and information systems. In treating the basic elements of information processing, it distinguishes between information in analog and digital form, and it describes their acquisition, recording, organization, retrieval, display, and dissemination. In treating information systems, the article discusses system analysis and design and provides a descriptive taxonomy of the main system types. Some attention is also given to the social impact of information systems and to the field of information science.

General considerations

BASIC CONCEPTS

Interest in how information is communicated and how its carriers convey meaning has occupied, since the time of pre-Socratic philosophers, the field of inquiry called semiotics, the study of signs and sign phenomena. Signs are the irreducible elements of communication and the carriers of meaning. The American philosopher, mathematician, and physicist Charles S. Peirce is credited with having pointed out the three dimensions of signs, which are concerned with, respectively, the body or medium of the sign, the object that the sign designates, and the interpretant or interpretation of the sign. Peirce recognized that the fundamental relations of information are essentially triadic; in contrast, all relations of the physical sciences are re-

Signs and their dimensions

ducible to dyadic (binary) relations. Another American philosopher, Charles W. Morris, designated these three sign dimensions syntactic, semantic, and pragmatic, the names by which they are known today.

Information processes are executed by information processors. For a given information processor, whether physical or biological, a token is an object, devoid of meaning, that the processor recognizes as being totally different from other tokens. A group of such unique tokens recognized by a processor constitutes its basic "alphabet"; for example, the dot, dash, and space constitute the basic token alphabet of a Morse-code processor. Objects that carry meaning are represented by patterns of tokens called symbols. The latter combine to form symbolic expressions

A. Newell and H.A. Simon, *Human Problem Solving*, p. 20, © 1972, reprinted by permission of Prentice-Hall, Inc., Englewood Cliffs, N.J.

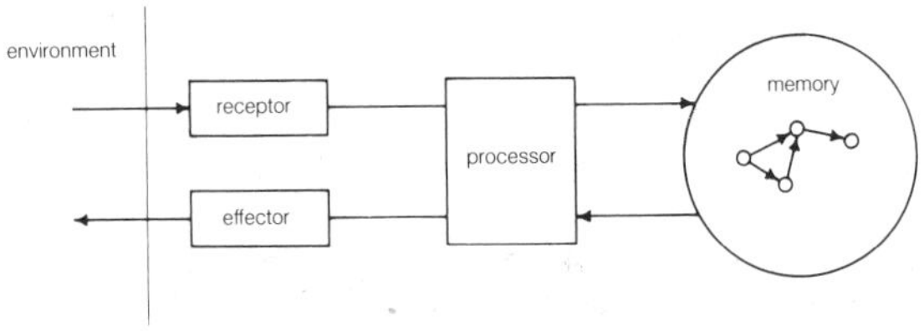

Figure 1: Structure of an information system.

that constitute inputs to or outputs from information processes and are stored in the processor memory.

Information processors are components of an information system, which is a class of constructs. An abstract model of an information system features four basic elements: processor, memory, receptor, and effector (Figure 1). The processor has several functions: (1) to carry out elementary information processes on symbolic expressions, (2) to store temporarily in the processor's short-term memory the input and output expressions on which these processes operate and which they generate, (3) to schedule execution of these processes, and (4) to change this sequence of operations in accordance with the contents of the short-term memory. The memory stores symbolic expressions, including those that represent composite information processes, called programs. The two other components, the receptor and the effector, are input and output mechanisms whose functions are, respectively, to receive symbolic expressions or stimuli from the external environment for manipulation by the processor and to emit the processed structures back to the environment.

The power of this abstract model of an information-processing system is provided by the ability of its component processors to carry out a small number of elementary information processes: reading; comparing; creating, modifying, and naming; copying; storing; and writing. The model, which is representative of a broad variety of such systems, has been found useful to explicate man-made information systems implemented on sequential information processors.

The cognitive sciences

Because it has been recognized that in nature information processes are not strictly sequential, increasing attention has been focused since 1980 on the study of the human brain as an information processor of the parallel type. The cognitive sciences, the interdisciplinary field that focuses on the study of the human mind, have contributed to the development of neurocomputers, a new class of parallel, distributed-information processors that mimic the functioning of the human brain, including its capabilities for self-organization and learning. So-called neural networks, which are mathematical models inspired by the neural circuit network of the human brain, are increasingly finding applications in areas such as pattern recognition, control of industrial processes, and finance, as well as in many research disciplines.

Table 1: Labour Distribution (%) in the United States, 1880–2000

	1880	1920	1955	1975	2000 (est.)
Agriculture and extractive	50	28	14	4	2
Manufacturing, commerce, industry	36	53	37	29	22
Information, knowledge, education	2	9	29	50	66
Other services	12	10	20	17	10

Source: Graham T.T. Molitor, "The Coming of the Information Society," *Communications Tomorrow*.

INFORMATION AS A RESOURCE AND COMMODITY

In the late 20th century, information has acquired two major utilitarian connotations. On the one hand, it is considered an economic resource, somewhat on par with other resources such as labour, material, and capital. This view stems from evidence that the possession, manipulation, and use of information can increase the cost-effectiveness of many physical and cognitive processes. The rise in information-processing activities in industrial manufacturing as well as in human problem solving has been remarkable. Analysis of one of the three traditional divisions of the economy, the service sector, shows a sharp increase in information-intensive activities since the beginning of the 20th century. By 1975 these activities accounted for half of the labour force of the United States (see Table 1), giving rise to the so-called information society.

Information as an expansive resource

As an individual and societal resource, information has some interesting characteristics that separate it from the traditional notions of economic resources. Unlike other resources, information is expansive, with limits apparently imposed only by time and human cognitive capabilities. Its expansiveness is attributable to the following: (1) it is naturally diffusive; (2) it reproduces rather than being consumed through use; and (3) it can be shared only, not exchanged in transactions. At the same time, information is compressible, both syntactically and semantically. Coupled with its ability to be substituted for other economic resources, its transportability at very high speeds, and its ability to impart advantages to the holder of information, these characteristics are at the base of such societal industries as research, education, publishing, marketing, and even politics. Societal concern with the husbanding of information resources has extended from the traditional domain of libraries and archives to encompass organizational, institutional, and governmental information under the umbrella of information resource management.

Importance of the information service sector

The second perception of information is that it is an economic commodity, which helps to stimulate the worldwide growth of a new segment of national economies—the information service sector. Taking advantage of the properties of information and building on the perception of its individual and societal utility and value, this sector provides a broad range of information products and services. By 1992 the market share of the U.S. information service sector had grown to about $25 billion (see Table 2). This was equivalent to about one-seventh of the country's computer market, which, in turn, represented roughly 40 percent of the global market in computers in that year. However, the probable convergence of computers and television (which constitutes a market share 100 times larger than computers) and its impact on information services, entertainment, and education are likely to restructure the respective market shares of the information industry before the onset of the 21st century.

Elements of information processing

Humans receive information with their senses: sounds through hearing; images and text through sight; shape, temperature, and affection through touch; and odours through smell. To interpret the signals received from the senses, humans have developed and learned complex systems of languages consisting of "alphabets" of symbols and stimuli and the associated rules of usage. This has enabled them to recognize the objects they see, understand the messages they read or hear, and comprehend the signs received through the tactile and olfactory senses.

The carriers of information-conveying signs received by the senses are energy phenomena—audio waves, light waves, and chemical and electrochemical stimuli. In engineering parlance, humans are receptors of analog signals; and, by a somewhat loose convention, the messages conveyed via these carriers are called analog-form information, or simply analog information. Until the development of the digital computer, cognitive information was stored

Table 2: U.S. Information Services Market
(in billions of dollars)

	1989	1990	1991	1992*	1993*	1994*
On-line transaction processing	2.590	2.753	2.927	3.483	4.120	4.379
Alarm monitoring/telemetry	2.176	2.502	2.827	3.166	3.544	3.969
Telemessaging services	1.025	1.096	1.172	1.279	1.369	1.482
Voice messaging	0.157	0.220	0.282	0.367	0.489	0.666
Electronic messaging	0.464	0.580	0.737	0.958	1.274	1.707
Database services	8.587	9.675	10.916	12.336	13.962	15.829
Residential data services	0.235	0.272	0.319	0.373	0.434	0.505
Voice information services	0.726	1.048	1.342	1.609	1.879	2.113
Enhanced facsimile	0.020	0.045	0.059	0.078	0.104	0.135
Electronic data exchange	0.097	0.160	0.264	0.435	0.696	1.114
Value-added network services	0.724	0.790	0.861	0.935	1.018	1.104
Business video services	0.066	0.078	0.092	0.112	0.128	0.143
Total	16.867	19.219	21.798	25.131	29.017	33.146

*Projected as of 1991.
Source: Reprinted from *Data Communications,* Sept. 1991. Copyright 9/91 McGraw-Hill, Inc. All rights reserved.

and processed only in analog form, basically through the technologies of printing, photography, and telephony.

Although humans are adept at processing information stored in their memories, analog information stored external to the mind is not processed easily. Modern information technology greatly facilitates the manipulation of externally stored information as a result of its representation as digital signals—*i.e.,* as the presence or absence of energy (electricity, light, or magnetism). Information represented digitally in two-state, or binary, form is often referred to as digital information. Modern information systems are characterized by extensive metamorphoses of analog and digital information. With respect to information storage and communication, the transition from analog information to digital is so pervasive that the end of the 20th century will likely witness a historic transformation of the manner in which humans create, access, and use information.

ACQUISITION AND RECORDING OF INFORMATION IN ANALOG FORM

The principal categories of information sources useful in modern information systems are text, video, and voice. One of the first ways in which prehistoric humans communicated was by sound; sounds represented concepts such as pleasure, anger, and fear, as well as objects of the surrounding environment, including food and tools. Sounds assumed their meaning by convention—namely, by the use to which they were consistently put. Combining parts of sound allowed representation of more complex concepts, gradually leading to the development of speech and eventually to spoken "natural" languages.

Development of writing systems

For information to be communicated broadly, it needs to be stored external to human memory; accumulation of human experience, knowledge, and learning would be severely limited without such storage, making necessary the development of writing systems.

Civilization can be traced to the time when humans began to associate abstract shapes with concepts and with the sounds of speech that represented them. Early recorded representations were those of visually perceived objects and events, as, for example, the animals and activities depicted in Paleolithic cave drawings. The evolution of writing systems proceeded through the early development of pictographic languages, in which a symbol would represent an entire concept. Such symbols would go through many metamorphoses of shape in which the resemblance between each symbol and the object it stood for gradually disappeared, but its semantic meaning would become more precise. As the conceptual world of humans became larger, the symbols, called ideographs, grew in number. Modern Chinese, a present-day result of this evolutionary direction of a pictographic writing system, has upward of 50,000 ideographs.

At some point in the evolution of written languages, the method of representation shifted from the pictographic to the phonetic: speech sounds began to be represented by an alphabet of graphic symbols. Combinations of a relatively small set of such symbols could stand for more complex concepts as words, phrases, and sentences. The invention of the written phonetic alphabet is thought to have taken place during the 2nd millennium BC. The pragmatic advantages of alphabetic writing systems over the pictographic became apparent twice in the present millennium: after the invention of the movable-type printing press in the 15th century and again with the development of information processing by electronic means since the mid-1940s.

Recording media and techniques

From the time early humans learned to represent concepts symbolically, they used whatever materials were readily available in nature for recording. The Sumerian cuneiform, a wedge-shaped writing system, was impressed by a stylus into soft clay tablets, which were subsequently hardened by drying in the sun or the oven. The earliest Chinese writing, dating to the 2nd millennium BC, is preserved on animal bone and shell, while early writing in India was done on palm leaves and birch bark. Applications of technology yielded other materials for writing. The Chinese had recorded their pictographs on silk, using brushes made from animal hair, long before they invented paper. The Egyptians first wrote on cotton, but they began using papyrus sheets and rolls made from the fibrous lining of the papyrus plant during the 4th millennium BC. The reed brush and a palette of ink were the implements with which they wrote hieroglyphic script. Writing on parchment, a material which was superior to papyrus and was made from the prepared skins of animals, became commonplace about 200 BC, some 300 years after its first recorded use, and the quill pen replaced the reed brush. By the 4th century AD, parchment came to be the principal writing material in Europe.

Paper was invented in China at the beginning of the 2nd century AD, and for some 600 years its use was confined to East Asia. In AD 751 Arab and Chinese armies clashed at the Battle of Talas, near Samarkand; among the Chinese taken captive were some papermakers from whom the Arabs learned the techniques. From the 7th century on, paper became the dominant writing material of the Islāmic world. Papermaking finally reached Spain and Sicily in the 12th century, and it took another three centuries before it was practiced in Germany.

With the invention of printing from movable type, typesetting became the standard method of creating copy. Typesetting was an entirely manual operation until the adoption of a typewriter-like keyboard in the 19th century. In fact, it was the typewriter that mechanized the process of recording original text. Although the typewriter was invented during the early 18th century in England, the first practical version, constructed by the American inventor Christopher Latham Sholes, did not appear until 1867. The mechanical typewriter finally found wide use after World War I. Today its electronic variant, the computer video terminal, is used pervasively to record original text.

Development of photography

Recording of original nontextual (image) information was a manual process until the development of photography during the early decades of the 19th century; drawing and carving were the principal early means of recording graphics. Other techniques were developed alongside printing—for example, etching in stone and metal. The invention of film and the photographic process added a new dimension to information acquisition: for the first time, complex visual images of the real world could be captured accurately. Photography provided a method of storing information in less space and more accurately than was previously possible with narrative information.

During the 20th century, versatile electromagnetic media have opened up new possibilities for capturing original analog information. Magnetic audio tape is used to capture speech and music, and magnetic videotape provides a low-cost medium for recording analog voice and video signals directly and simultaneously. Magnetic technology has other uses in the direct recording of analog information, including alphanumerics. Magnetic characters, bar codes, and special marks are printed on checks, labels, and forms for subsequent sensing by magnetic or optical readers and conversion to digital form. Banks, educational institutions, and the retail industry rely heavily on this technology. Nonetheless, paper and film continue to be the dominant media for direct storage of textual and visual information in analog form.

ACQUISITION AND RECORDING OF INFORMATION IN DIGITAL FORM

The versatility of modern information systems stems from their ability to represent information electronically as digital signals and to manipulate it automatically at exceedingly high speeds. Information is stored in binary devices, which are the basic components of digital technology. Because these devices exist only in one of two states, information is represented in them either as the absence or the presence of energy (electric pulse). The two states of binary devices are conveniently designated by the binary digits, or bits, zero (0) and one (1).

Coding systems

In this manner, alphabetic symbols of natural-language writing systems can be represented digitally as combinations of zeros (no pulse) and ones (pulse). Tables of equivalences of alphanumeric characters and strings of binary digits are called coding systems, the counterpart of writing systems. A combination of three binary digits can represent up to eight such characters; one comprising four digits, up to 16 characters; and so on. The choice of a particular coding system depends on the size of the character set to be represented. The widely used systems are the American Standard Code for Information Interchange (ASCII), a seven- or eight-bit code representing the English alphabet, numerals, and certain special characters of the standard computer keyboard; and the corresponding eight-bit Extended Binary Coded Decimal Interchange Code (EBCDIC), used for computers produced by IBM (International Business Machines Corp.) and most compatible systems. The digital representation of a character by eight bits is called a byte.

The seven-bit ASCII code is capable of representing up to 128 alphanumeric and special characters—sufficient to accommodate the writing systems of many phonetic scripts, including Latin and Cyrillic. Some alphabetic scripts require more than seven bits; for example, the Arabic alphabet, also used in the Urdu and Persian languages, has 28 consonantal characters (as well as a number of vowels and diacritical marks), but each of these may have four shapes, depending on its position in the word.

For digital representation of nonalphabetic writing systems, even the eight-bit code accommodating 256 characters is inadequate. Some writing systems that use Chinese characters, for example, have more than 50,000 ideographs (the minimal standard font for the Hanzi system in Chinese and the kanji system in Japanese has about 7,000 ideographs). Digital representation of such scripts can be accomplished in three ways. One approach is to develop a phonetic character set; the Chinese Pinyin, the Korean Hankul, and the Japanese hiragana phonetic schemes all have alphabetic sets similar in number to the Latin alphabet. As the use of phonetic alphabets in Oriental cultures is not yet widespread, they may be converted to ideographic by means of a dictionary lookup (see Figure 2). A second technique is to decompose ideographs into a small number of elementary signs called strokes, the sum of which constitutes a shape-oriented, nonphonetic alphabet. The third approach is to use more than eight bits to encode the large numbers of ideographs; for instance, two bytes can represent uniquely more than 65,000 ideographs. Because the eight-bit ASCII code is inadequate for a number of writing systems, either because they are nonalphabetic or because their phonetic scripts possess large numbers of diacritical marks, the computer industry in 1991 began formulating a new international coding standard based on 16 bits.

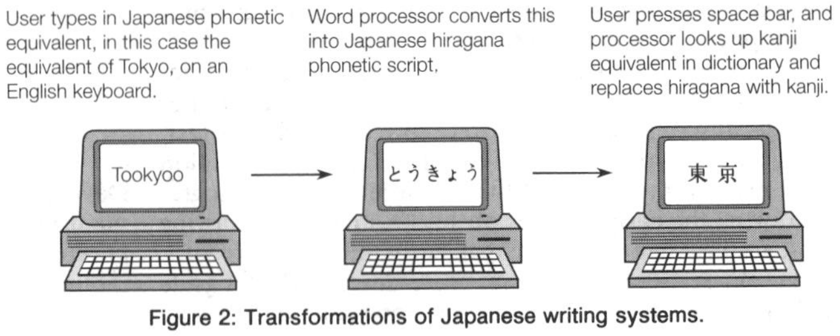

User types in Japanese phonetic equivalent, in this case the equivalent of Tokyo, on an English keyboard.
Word processor converts this into Japanese hiragana phonetic script.
User presses space bar, and processor looks up kanji equivalent in dictionary and replaces hiragana with kanji.
Tookyoo
とうきょう
東京

Figure 2: Transformations of Japanese writing systems.

Recording media. Punched cards and perforated paper tape were once widely used to store data in binary form. Today they have been supplanted by media based on electromagnetic and electro-optic technologies except in a few special applications.

Present-day storage media are of two types: random- and serial-, or sequential-, access. In random-access media (such as primary memory) the time required to access a given piece of data is independent of its location, while in serial-access media the access time depends on the data's location and the position of the read-write head. The typical serial-access medium is magnetic tape. The storage density of magnetic tape has increased considerably over the years, mainly by increases in the number of tracks packed across the width of the tape.

While magnetic tape remains a popular choice in applications requiring low-cost auxiliary storage and data exchange, new tape variants have begun entering the market of the 1990s. Video recording tape has been adapted for digital storage, and digital audio tape (DAT) surpasses all tape storage devices in offering the highest areal data densities. DAT technology uses a helical-scan recording method in which both the tape and the recording head move simultaneously, allowing extremely high recording densities. A four-millimetre DAT tape cassette has a capacity of up to eight billion bytes (eight gigabytes). The capacity of this tape is expected to increase by an order of magnitude well before the year 2000.

Magnetic disks

Another type of magnetic storage medium, the magnetic disk, provides rapid, random access to data. This device, developed in 1962, consists of either an aluminum or plastic platen coated with a metallic material. Information is recorded on a disk by turning the charge of the read-write head on and off, which produces magnetic "dots" representing binary digits in circular tracks. A block of data on a given track can be accessed without having to pass over a large portion of its contents sequentially, as in the case of tape. Data-retrieval time is thus reduced dramatically. Hard disk drives built into personal computers and workstations have storage capacities of up to several gigabytes. Large computers using disk cartridges can provide virtually unlimited mass storage.

During the 1970s the floppy disk—a small, flexible disk—was introduced for use in personal computers and other microcomputer systems. Compared with the storage capacity of the conventional hard disk, that of such a "soft" diskette is low—under three million characters. This medium is used primarily for loading and backing up personal computers.

Optical discs

An entirely different kind of recording and storage medium, the optical disc, became available during the early 1980s. The optical disc makes use of laser technology: digital data are recorded by burning a series of microscopic holes, or pits, with a laser beam into thin metallic film on the surface of a $4\frac{3}{4}$-inch (12-centimetre) plastic disc. In this way, information from magnetic tape is encoded on a master disc; subsequently, the master is replicated by a process called stamping. In the read mode, low-intensity laser light is reflected off the disc surface and is "read" by light-sensitive diodes. The radiant energy received by the diodes varies according to the presence of the pits, and this input is digitized by the diode circuits. The digital signals are then converted to analog information on a video screen or in printout form.

Since the introduction of this technology, three main types of optical storage media have become available: (1) rewritable, (2) write once, read many (WORM), and (3) compact disc, read-only memory (CD-ROM). Rewritable discs are functionally equivalent to magnetic disks, although the former are slower. WORM discs are used as an archival storage medium to enter data once and retrieve it many times. CD-ROM discs are the preferred medium for electronic distribution of digital libraries and software. To raise storage capacity, optical discs are arranged into "jukeboxes" holding as many as 10 million pages of text or more than one terabyte (one trillion bytes) of image data. The high storage capacities and random access of the magneto-optical, rewritable discs are particularly suited for storing multimedia information, in which text, image, and sound are combined.

Recording techniques. Digitally stored information is commonly referred to as data, and its analog counterpart is called source data. Vast quantities of nondocument analog data are collected, digitized, and compressed automatically by means of appropriate instruments in fields such as astronomy, environmental monitoring, scientific experimentation and modeling, and national security. The capture of information generated by humankind, in the form of packages of symbols called documents, is accomplished by manual and, increasingly, automatic techniques. Data are entered manually by striking the keys of a keyboard, touching a computer screen, or writing by hand on a digital tablet or its recent variant, the so-called pen computer. Manual data entry, a slow and error-prone process, is facilitated to a degree by special computer programs that include editing software, with which to insert formatting commands, verify spelling, and make text changes, and document-formatting software, with which to arrange and rearrange text and graphics flexibly on the output page.

It is estimated that 5 percent of all documents in the United States exist in digitized form and that two-thirds of the paper documents cannot be digitized by keyboard transcription because they contain drawings or still images and because such transcription would be highly uneconomic. Such documents are digitized economically by a process called document imaging (see Figure 3).

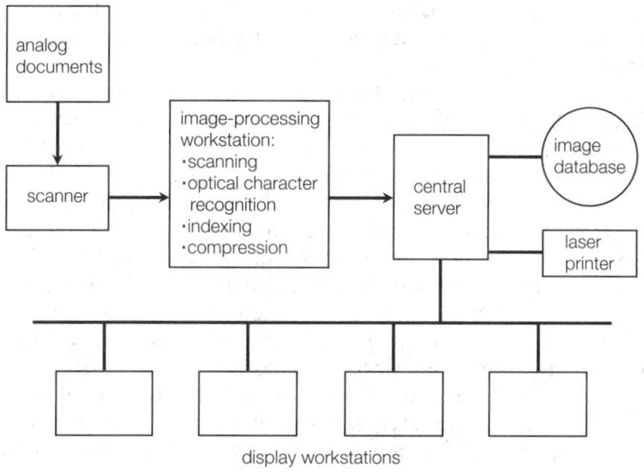

Figure 3: Document imaging.

Document imaging utilizes digital scanners to generate a digital representation of a document page. An image scanner divides the page into minute picture areas called pixels and produces an array of binary digits, each representing the brightness of a pixel. The resulting stream of bits is enhanced and compressed (to as little as 10 percent of the original volume) by a device called an image controller and is stored on a magnetic or optical medium. A large storage capacity is required, because it takes about 45,000 bytes to store a typical compressed text page of 2,500 characters and as much as 1,000,000 bytes to store a page containing an image. Aside from document imaging applications, digital scanning is used for transmission of documents via facsimile, in satellite photography, and in other applications.

An image scanner digitizes an entire document page for storage and display as an image and does not recognize characters and words of text. The stored material therefore cannot be linguistically manipulated by text processing and other software techniques. When such manipulation is desired, a software program performs the optical character recognition (OCR) function by converting each optically scanned character into an electric signal and comparing it with the internally stored representation of an alphabet of characters, so as to select from it the one that matches the scanned character most closely or to reject it as an unidentifiable token. The more sophisticated of present-day OCR programs distinguish shapes, sizes, and pitch of symbols—including handwriting—and learn from experience. A universal optical character recognition machine is not available, however, for even a single alphabet.

Optical character recognition

Still photographs can be digitized by scanning or transferred from film to a compact digital disc holding more than 100 images. A recent development, the digital camera, makes it possible to bypass the film/paper step completely by capturing the image into the camera's random-access memory or a special diskette and then transferring it to a personal computer. Since both technologies produce a graphics file, in either case the image is editable by means of suitable software.

The digital recording of sound is important, because speech is the most frequently used natural carrier of communicable information. Direct capture of sound into personal computers is accomplished by means of a digital signal processor (DSP) chip, a special-purpose device built into the computer to perform array-processing operations. Conversion of analog audio signals to digital recordings is a commonplace process that has been used for years by the telecommunications and entertainment industries. Although the resulting digital sound track can be edited, automatic speech recognition—analogous to the recognition of characters and words in text by means of optical character recognition—is still under development. When perfected, voice recognition is certain to have a tremendous impact on the way humans communicate with recorded information, with computers, and among themselves.

By the beginning of the 1990s, the technology to record (or convert), store in digital form, and edit all visually and aurally perceived signals—text, graphics, still images, animation, motion video, and sound—had thus become available and affordable. These capabilities have opened a way for a new kind of multimedia document that employs print, video, and sound to generate more powerful and colourful messages, communicate them securely at electronic speeds, and allow them to be modified almost at will. The traditional business letter, newspaper, journal, and book will no longer be the same.

INVENTORY OF RECORDED INFORMATION

The development of recording media and techniques enabled society to begin building a store of human knowledge. The idea of collecting and organizing written records is thought to have originated in Sumer about 5,000 years ago; Egyptian writing was introduced soon after. Early collections of Sumerian and Egyptian writings, recorded in cuneiform on clay tablets and in hieroglyphic script on papyrus, contained information about legal and economic transactions. In these and other early document collections (*e.g.*, those of China produced during the Shang dynasty in the 2nd millennium BC and Buddhist collections in India dating to the 5th century BC), it is difficult to separate the concepts of the archive and the library.

Development of document collections

From the Middle East the concept of document collections penetrated the Greco-Roman world. Roman kings institutionalized the population and property census as early as the 6th century BC. The great Library of Alexandria, established in the 3rd century BC, is best known as a large collection of papyri containing inventories of property, taxes, and other payments by citizens to their rulers and to each other. It is, in short, the ancient equivalent of today's administrative information systems.

The scholarly splendour of the Islāmic world from the 8th to 13th century AD can in large part be attributed to the maintenance of public and private book libraries. The Bayt al-Ḥikmah ("House of Wisdom"), founded in AD 830 in Baghdad, contained a public library with a large collection of materials on a wide range of subjects, and the 10th-century library of Caliph al-Ḥakam in Cordova, Spain, boasted more than 400,000 books.

The late but rapid development of European libraries from the 16th century on followed the invention of printing from movable type, which spurred the growth of the printing and publishing industries. Since the beginning of the 17th century, literature has become the principal medium for disseminating knowledge. The phrase primary literature is used to designate original information in various printed formats: newspapers, monographs, conference proceedings, learned and trade journals, reports, patents, bulletins, and newsletters. The scholarly journal, the classic medium of scientific communication, first appeared in 1665. Three hundred years later the number of periodical titles published in the world was estimated at more than 60,000, reflecting not only growth in the number of practitioners of science and expansion of its body of knowledge through specialization but also a maturing of the system of rewards that encourages scientists to publish.

Primary literature

The sheer quantity of printed information has for some time prevented any individual from fully absorbing even a minuscule fraction of it. Such devices as tables of contents, summaries, and indexes of various types, which aid in identifying and locating relevant information in primary literature, have been in use since the 16th century and led to the development of what is termed secondary literature during the 19th century. The purpose of secondary literature is to "filter" the primary information sources, usually by subject area, and provide the indicators to this literature in the form of reviews, abstracts, and indexes. Over the past 100 years there has evolved a system of disciplinary, national, and international abstracting and indexing services that acts as a gateway to several attributes of primary literature: authors, subjects, publishers, dates (and languages) of publication, and citations. The professional activity associated with these access-facilitating tools is called documentation.

Secondary literature

The quantity of printed materials also makes it impossible, as well as undesirable, for any institution to acquire and house more than a small portion of it. The husbanding of recorded information has become a matter of public policy, as many countries have established national libraries and archives to direct the orderly acquisition of analog-form documents and records. Since these institutions alone are not able to keep up with the output of such documents and records, new forms of cooperative planning and sharing recorded materials are evolving—namely, public and private, national and regional library networks and consortia.

The emergence of digital technology in the mid-20th century has affected humankind's inventory of recorded information dramatically. During the early 1960s computers were used to digitize text for the first time; the purpose was to reduce the cost and time required to publish two American abstracting journals, the *Index Medicus* of the National Library of Medicine and the *Scientific and Technical Aerospace Reports* of the National Aeronautics and Space Administration (NASA). By the late 1960s such bodies of digitized alphanumeric information, known as bibliographic and numeric databases, constituted a new type of information resource. This resource is husbanded outside the traditional repositories of information (libraries and archives) by database "vendors." Advances in computer storage, telecommunications, software for computer sharing, and automated techniques of text indexing and searching fueled the development of an on-line database service industry. Meanwhile, electronic applications to bibliographic control in libraries and archives have led to the development of computerized catalogs and of union catalogs in library networks. They also have resulted in the introduction of comprehensive automation programs in these institutions.

Bibliographic and numeric databases

The explosive growth of communications networks after 1990, particularly in the scholarly world, has accelerated the establishment of the "virtual library." At the leading edge of this development is public-domain information. Residing in thousands of databases distributed worldwide, a growing portion of this vast resource is now accessible almost instantaneously via the Internet, the web of computer networks linking the global communities of researchers and, increasingly, nonacademic organizations. Internet resources of electronic information include selected library catalogs, collected works of the literature, some abstracting journals, full-text electronic journals, encyclopaedias, scientific data from numerous disciplines, software archives, demographic registers, daily news summaries, environmental reports, and prices in commodity markets, as well as hundreds of thousands of electronic-mail and bulletin-board messages.

The vast inventory of recorded information can be useful only if it is systematically organized and if mechanisms exist for locating in it items relevant to human needs. The main approaches for achieving such organization are reviewed in the following section, as are the tools used to retrieve desired information.

ORGANIZATION AND RETRIEVAL OF INFORMATION

In any collection, physical objects are related by order. The ordering may be random or according to some characteristic called a key. Such characteristics may be intrinsic properties of the objects (*e.g.*, size, weight, shape, or colour), or they may be assigned from some agreed-upon set, such as object class or date of purchase. The values of the key are arranged in a sorting sequence that is dependent on the type of key involved: alphanumeric key values are usually sorted in alphabetic sequence, while other types may be sorted on the basis of similarity in class, such as books on a particular subject or flora of the same genus.

In most cases, order is imposed on a set of information objects for two reasons: to create their inventory and to facilitate locating specific objects in the set. There also exist other, secondary objectives for selecting a particular ordering, as, for example, conservation of space or economy of effort in fetching objects. Unless the objects in a collection are replicated, any ordering scheme is one-dimensional and unable to meet all the functions of ordering with equal effectiveness. The main approach for overcoming some of the limitations of one-dimensional ordering of recorded information relies on extended description of its content and, for analog-form information, of some features of the physical items. This approach employs various tools of content analysis that subsequently facilitate accessing and searching recorded information.

Description and content analysis of analog-form records. The collections of libraries and archives, the primary repositories of analog-form information, constitute one-dimensional ordering of physical materials in print (documents), in image form (maps and photographs), or in audio-video format (recordings and videotapes). To break away from the confines of one-dimensional ordering, librarianship has developed an extensive set of attributes in terms of which it describes each item in the collection. The rules for assigning these attributes are called cataloging rules. Descriptive cataloging is the extraction of bibliographic elements (author names, title, publisher, date of publication, etc.) from each item; the assignment of subject categories or headings to such items is termed subject cataloging.

Descriptive and subject cataloging

Conceptually, the library catalog is a table or matrix in which each row describes a discrete physical item and each column provides values of the assigned key. When such a catalog is represented digitally in a computer, any attribute can serve as the ordering key. By sorting the catalog on different keys, it is possible to produce a variety of indexes as well as subject bibliographies. More importantly, any of the attributes of a computerized catalog becomes a search key (access point) to the collection, surpassing the utility of the traditional card catalog.

The most useful access key to analog-form items is subject. The extensive lists of subject headings of library classification schemes provide, however, only a gross access

Indexing and abstracting

tool to the content of the items. A technique called indexing provides a refinement over library subject headings. It consists of extracting from the item or assigning to it subject and other "descriptors"—words or phrases denoting significant concepts (topics, names) that occur in or characterize the content of the record. Indexing frequently accompanies abstracting, a technique for condensing the full text of a document into a short summary that contains its main ideas (but invariably incurs an information loss and often introduces a bias). Computer-printed, indexed abstracting journals provide a means of keeping users informed of primary information sources.

Description and content analysis of digital-form information. The description of an electronic document generally follows the principles of bibliographic cataloging if the document is part of a database that is expected to be accessed directly and individually. When the database is an element of a universe of globally distributed database servers that are searchable in parallel, the matter of document naming is considerably more challenging, because several complexities are introduced. The document description must include the name of the database server—*i.e.,* its physical location. Because database servers may delete particular documents, the description must also contain a pointer to the document's logical address (the generating organization). In contrast to their usefulness in the descriptive cataloging of analog documents, physical attributes such as format and size are highly variable in the milieu of electronic documents and therefore are meaningless in a universal document-naming scheme. On the other hand, the data type of the document (text, sound, etc.) is critical to its transmission and use. Perhaps the most challenging design is the "living document"—a constantly changing pastiche consisting of sections electronically copied from different documents, interspersed with original narrative or graphics or voice comments contributed by persons in distant locations, whose different versions reside on different servers. Efforts are under way to standardize the naming of documents in the universe of electronic networks.

Machine indexing

The subject analysis of electronic text is accomplished by means of machine indexing, using one of two approaches: the assignment of subject descriptors from an unlimited vocabulary (free indexing) or their assignment from a list of authorized descriptors (controlled indexing). A collection of authorized descriptors is called an authority list or, if it also displays various relationships among descriptors such as hierarchy or synonymy, a thesaurus. The result of the indexing process is a computer file known as an inverted index, which is an alphabetic listing of descriptors and the addresses of their occurrence in the document body.

Full-text indexing, the use of every character string (word of a natural language) in the text as an index term, is an extreme case of free-text indexing: each word in the document (except function words such as articles and prepositions) becomes an access point to it. Used earlier for the generation of concordances in literary analysis and other computer applications in the humanities, full-text indexing placed great demands on computer storage because the resulting index is at least as large as the body of the text. With decreasing cost of mass storage, automatic full-text indexing capability has been incorporated routinely into state-of-the-art information-management software.

Text indexing may be supplemented by other syntactic techniques, so as to increase its precision or robustness. One such method, the Standard Generalized Markup Language (SGML), takes advantage of standard text markers used by editors to pinpoint the location and other characteristics of document elements (paragraphs and tables, for example). In indexing spatial data such as maps and astronomical images, the textual index specifies the search areas, each of which is further described by a set of coordinates defining a rectangle or irregular polygon. These digital spatial document attributes are then used to retrieve and display a specific point or a selected region of the document. There are other specialized techniques that may be employed to augment the indexing of specific document types, such as encyclopaedias, electronic mail, catalogs, bulletin boards, tables, and maps.

Semantic content analysis

The analysis of digitally recorded natural-language information from the semantic viewpoint is a matter of considerable complexity, and it lies at the foundation of such incipient applications as automatic question answering from a database or retrieval by means of unrestricted natural-language queries. The general approach has been that of computational linguistics: to derive representations of the syntactic and semantic relations among the linguistic elements of sentences and larger parts of the document. Syntactic relations are described by parsing (decomposing) the grammar of sentences (Figure 4). For semantic representation, three related formalisms dominate. In a so-called semantic network, conceptual entities such as objects, actions, or events are represented as a graph of linked nodes (Figure 5). "Frames" represent, in a similar graph network, physical or abstract attributes of objects and in a sense define the objects. In "scripts," events and actions rather than objects are defined in terms of their attributes.

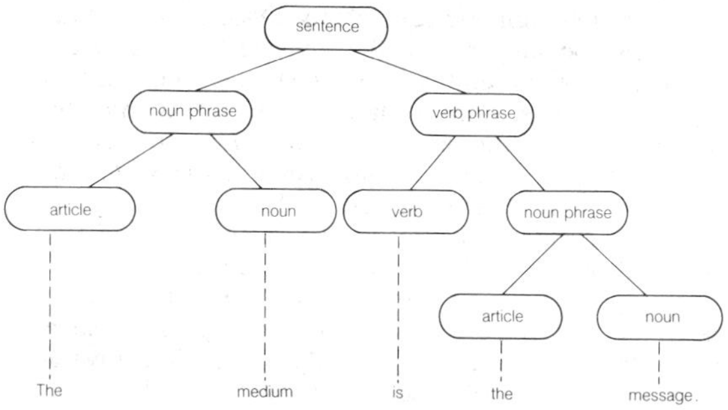

Figure 4: A parsing graph.

Indexing and linguistic analyses of text generate a relatively gross measure of the semantic relationship, or subject similarity, of documents in a given collection. Subject similarity is, however, a pragmatic phenomenon that varies with the observer and the circumstances of an observation (purpose, time, and so forth). A technique experimented with briefly in the mid-1960s, which assigned to each document one or more "roles" (functions) and one or more "links" (pointers to other documents having the same or a similar role), showed potential for a pragmatic measure of similarity; its use, however, was too unwieldy for the computing environment of the day. Some 20 years later, a similar technique became popular under the name "hypertext." In this technique, documents that a person or a group of persons consider related (by concept, sequence, hierarchy, experience, motive, or other characteristics) are connected via "hyperlinks," mimicking the way humans associate ideas. Objects so linked need not be only text; speech and music, graphics and images, and animation and video can all be interlinked into a "hypermedia" database. The objects are stored with their hyperlinks, and a user can easily navigate the network of associations by clicking with a mouse on a series of entries on a computer screen. Another technique that elicits semantic relationships from a body of text is SGML.

Image analysis

The content analysis of images is accomplished by two primary methods: image processing and pattern recognition. Image processing is a set of computational techniques

C.S. Shapiro, "Natural Language Processing," from A. Ralston and E.D. Reilly, Jr. (eds.), *Encyclopedia of Computer Science and Engineering*, Van Nostrand Reinhold, 1983

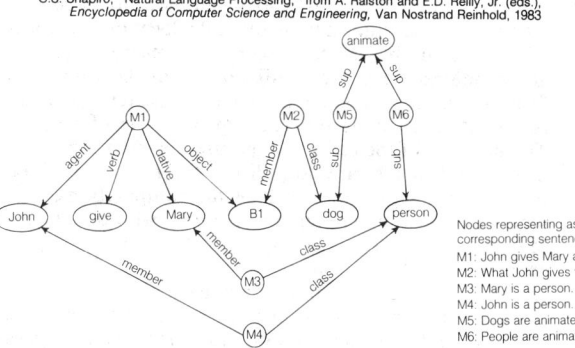

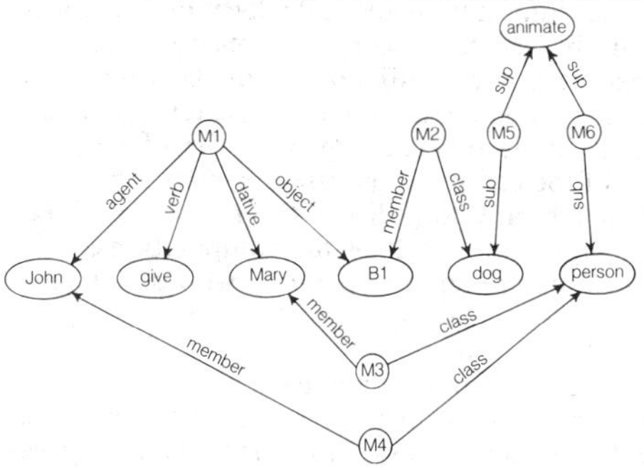

Figure 5: A semantic network representation.

for analyzing, enhancing, compressing, and reconstructing images. Pattern recognition is an information-reduction process: the assignment of visual or logical patterns to classes based on the features of these patterns and their relationships. The stages in pattern recognition involve measurement of the object to identify distinguishing attributes, extraction of features for the defining attributes, and assignment of the object to a class based on these features. Both image processing and pattern recognition have extensive applications in various areas, including astronomy, medicine, industrial robotics, and remote sensing by satellites.

Speech analysis

The immediate objective of content analysis of digital speech is the conversion of discrete sound elements into their alphanumeric equivalents. Once so represented, speech can be subjected to the same techniques of content analysis as natural-language text—*i.e.,* indexing and linguistic analysis. Converting speech elements into their alphanumeric counterparts is an intriguing problem because the "shape" of speech sounds embodies a wide range of many acoustic characteristics and because the linguistic elements of speech are not clearly distinguishable from one another. The technique used in speech processing is to classify the spectral representations of sound and to match the resulting digital spectrographs against prestored "templates" so as to identify the alphanumeric equivalent of the sound. (The obverse of this technique, the digital-to-analog conversion of such templates into sound, is a relatively straightforward approach to generating synthetic speech.)

Speech processing is complex as well as expensive in terms of storage capacity and computational requirements. State-of-the-art speech recognition systems can identify limited vocabularies and parts of distinctly spoken speech and can be programmed to recognize tonal idiosyncracies of individual speakers. When more robust and reliable techniques become available and the process is made computationally tractable (as is expected with parallel computers), humans will be able to interact with computers via spoken commands and queries on a routine basis. In many situations this may make the keyboard obsolete as a data-entry device.

Storage structures for digital-form information. Digital information is stored in complex patterns that make it feasible to address and operate on even the smallest element of symbolic expression, as well as on larger strings such as words or sentences and on images and sound.

From the viewpoint of digital information storage, it is useful to distinguish between "structured" data, such as inventories of objects that can be represented by short symbol strings and numbers, and "unstructured" data, such as the natural-language text of documents or pictorial images. The principal objective of all storage structures is to facilitate the processing of data elements based on their relationships; the structures thus vary with the type of relationship they represent. The choice of a particular storage structure is governed by the relevance of the relationships it allows to be represented to the information-processing requirements of the task or system at hand.

In information systems whose store consists of unstructured databases of natural-language records, the objective is to retrieve records (or portions thereof) based on the presence in the records of words or short phrases that constitute the query. Since there exists an index as a separate file that provides information about the locations of words and phrases in the database records, the relationships that are of interest (*e.g.,* word adjacency) can be calculated from the index. Consequently, the database text itself can be stored as a simple ordered sequential file of records. The majority of the computations use the index, and they access the text file only to pull out the records or those portions that satisfy the result of the computations. The sequential file structure remains popular, with document-retrieval software intended for use with personal computers and CD-ROM databases.

File structures

When relationships among data elements need to be represented as part of the records so as to make more efficient the desired operations on these records, two types of "chained" structures are commonly used: hierarchical and network. In the hierarchical file structure, records are arranged in a scheme resembling a family tree, with records related to one another from top to bottom. In the network file structure, records are arranged in groupings known as sets; these can be connected in any number of ways, giving rise to considerable flexibility. In both hierarchical and network structures, the relationships are shown by means of "pointers" (*i.e.,* identifiers such as addresses or keys) that become part of the records.

Another type of database storage structure, the relational structure, has become increasingly popular since the late 1970s. Its major advantage over the hierarchical and network structures is the ability to handle unanticipated data relationships without pointers. Relational storage structures are two-dimensional tables consisting of rows and columns, much like the conceptual library catalog mentioned above. The elegance of the relational model lies in its conceptual simplicity, the availability of theoretical underpinnings (relational algebra), and the ability of its associated software to handle data relationships without the use of pointers. The relational model was initially used for databases containing highly structured information. In the 1990s it has largely replaced the hierarchical and network models, and it has also become the model of choice for large-scale information-management applications, both textual and multimedia.

The feasibility of storing large volumes of full text on an economic medium (the digital optical disc) has renewed interest in the study of storage structures that permit more powerful retrieval and processing techniques to operate on cognitive entities other than words, to facilitate more extensive semantic content and context analysis, and to organize text conceptually into logical units rather than those dictated by printing conventions.

Query languages. The uses of databases are manifold. They provide a means of retrieving records or parts of records and performing various calculations before displaying the results. The interface by which such manipulations are specified is called the query language. Whereas early query languages were originally so complex that interacting with electronic databases could be done only by specially trained individuals, recent interfaces are more user-friendly, allowing casual users to access database information.

Types of query modes

The main types of popular query modes are the "menu," the"fill-in-the-blank" technique, and the structured query. Particularly suited for novices, the menu requires a person to choose from several alternatives displayed on the video terminal screen. The fill-in-the-blank technique is one in which the user is prompted to enter key words as search statements. The structured query approach is effective with relational databases. It has a formal, powerful syntax that is in fact a programming language, and it is able to accommodate logical operators. One implementation of this approach, the Structured Query Language (SQL), has the form

select [field Fa, Fb, . . . , Fn]
from [database Da, Db, . . . , Dn]
where [field Fa = abc] *and* [field Fb = def].

Structured query languages support database searching and other operations by using commands such as "find," "delete," "print," "sum," and so forth. The sentencelike structure of an SQL query resembles natural language except that its syntax is limited and fixed. Instead of using an SQL statement, it is possible to represent queries in tabular form. The technique, referred to as query-by-example (or QBE), displays an empty tabular form and expects the searcher to enter the search specifications into appropriate columns. The program then constructs an SQL-type query from the table and executes it.

The most flexible query language is of course natural language. The use of natural-language sentences in a constrained form to search databases is allowed by some commercial database management software. These programs parse the syntax of the query; recognize its action words and their synonyms; identify the names of files, records, and fields; and perform the logical operations required. Experimental systems that accept such natural-language queries in spoken voice have been developed; however, the ability to employ unrestricted natural language to query unstructured information will require further advances in machine understanding of natural language, particularly in techniques of representing the semantic and pragmatic context of ideas. The prospect of an intelligent conversation between humans and a large store of digitally encoded knowledge is not imminent.

Information searching and retrieval. State-of-the-art approaches to retrieving information employ two generic techniques: (1) matching words in the query against the database index (key-word searching) and (2) traversing the database with the aid of hypertext or hypermedia links.

Key-word searches

Key-word searches can be made either more general or more narrow in scope by means of logical operators (*e.g.*, disjunction and conjunction). Because of the semantic ambiguities involved in free-text indexing, however, the precision of the key-word retrieval technique—that is, the percentage of relevant documents correctly retrieved from a collection—is far from ideal, and various modifications have been introduced to improve it. In one such enhancement, the search output is sorted by degree of relevance, based on a statistical match between the key words in the query and in the document; in another, the program automatically generates a new query using one or more documents considered relevant by the user. Key-word searching has been the dominant approach to text retrieval since the early 1960s; hypertext has so far been largely confined to personal or corporate information-retrieval applications.

The exponential growth of the use of computer networks in the 1990s presages significant changes in systems and techniques of information retrieval. In a wide-area information service, a number of which began operating at the beginning of the 1990s on the Internet computer network, a user's personal computer or terminal (called a client) can search simultaneously a number of databases maintained on heterogeneous computers (called servers). The latter are located at different geographic sites, and their databases contain different data types and often use incompatible data formats. The simultaneous, distributed search is possible because clients and servers agree on a standard document addressing scheme and adopt a common communications protocol that accommodates all the data types and formats used by the servers. Communication with other wide-area services using different protocols is accomplished by routing through so-called gateways capable of protocol translation. The architecture of a typical networked information system is illustrated in Figure 6. Several representative clients are shown: a "dumb" terminal (*i.e.*, one with no internal processor), a personal computer (PC), and Macintosh (trademark; Mac), X Windows (trademark), and NeXT (trademark) machines. They have access to data on the servers sharing a common protocol as well as to data provided by services that require protocol conversion via the gateways. Network news is such a wide-area service, containing hundreds of news groups on a variety of subjects, by which users can read and post messages.

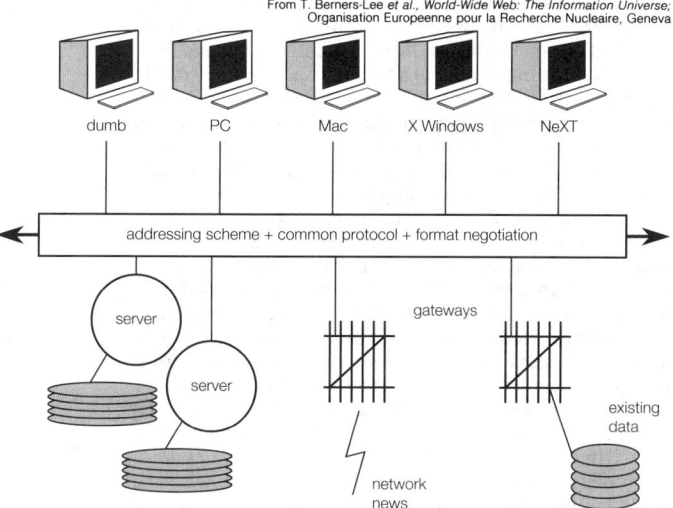

From T. Berners-Lee *et al.*, *World-Wide Web: The Information Universe;* Organisation Europeenne pour la Recherche Nucleaire, Geneva

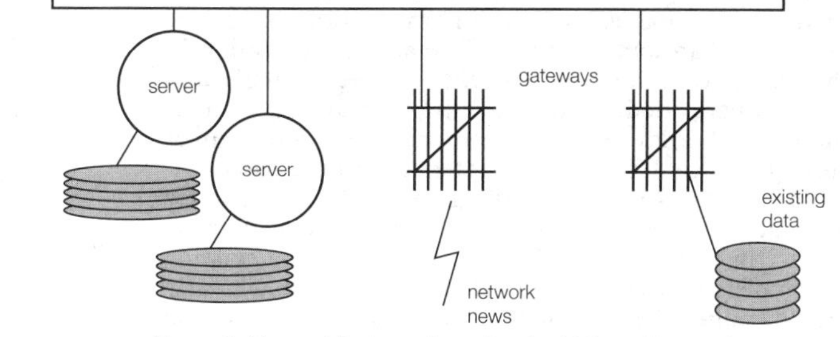

Figure 6: The architecture of a networked information system.

Evolving information-retrieval techniques, exemplified by an experimental interface to the NASA space shuttle reference manual, combine natural language, hyperlinks, and key-word searching. Other techniques, seeking higher levels of retrieval precision and effectiveness, are studied by researchers involved with artificial intelligence and neural networks. The next major milestone may be a computer program that traverses the seamless information universe of wide-area electronic networks and continuously filters its contents through profiles of organizational and personal interest: the information robot of the 21st century.

INFORMATION DISPLAY

For humans to perceive and understand information, it must be presented as print and image on paper; as print and image on film or on a video terminal; as sound via radio or telephony; as print, sound, and video in motion pictures, on television broadcasts, or at lectures and conferences; or in face-to-face encounters. Except for live encounters and audio information, such displays emanate increasingly from digitally stored data, with the output media being video, print, and sound.

Video. Possibly the most widely used video display device, at least in the industrialized world, is the television set. Designed primarily for video and sound, its image resolution is inadequate for alphanumeric data except in relatively small amounts. Use of the television set in text-oriented information systems has been limited to menu-oriented applications such as videotex, in which information is selected from hierarchically arranged menus (with the aid of a numeric keyboard attachment) and displayed in fixed frames. The television, computer, and communications technologies are, however, converging in a high-resolution digital television set capable of receiving alphanumeric, video, and audio signals.

Computer video terminals

The computer video terminal is today's ubiquitous interface that transforms computer-stored data into analog form for human viewing. The two basic apparatuses used are the cathode-ray tube (CRT) and the more recent flat-panel display. In CRT displays an electron gun emits beams of electrons on a phosphorus-coated surface; the beams are deflected, forming visible patterns representative of data. Flat-panel displays use one of four different media for visual representation of data: liquid crystal, light-emitting diodes, plasma panels, and electroluminescence. Advanced video display systems enable the user to scroll, page, zoom (change the scale of the details of the display image for enhancement), divide the screen into multiple colours and windows (viewing areas), and in some cases even activate commands by touching the screen instead of using the keyboard. The information capacity of the terminal screen depends on its resolution, which ranges from low (character-addressable) to high (bit-addressable). High resolution is indispensable for the display of graphic and video data in state-of-the-art workstations, such as those used in engineering or information systems design.

Print. Modern society continues to be dominated by printed information. The convenience and portability of print on paper make it difficult to imagine the paperless world that some have predicted. The generation of paper print has changed considerably, however. Although manual typesetting is still practiced for artwork, in special situations, and in some developing countries, electronic means of composing pages for subsequent reproduction by photoduplication and other methods has become commonplace.

Since the 1960s, volume publishing has become an automated process using large computers and high-speed printers to transfer digitally stored data on paper. The appearance of microcomputer-based publishing systems has proved to be another significant advance. Economical enough to allow even small organizations to become in-house publishers, these so-called desktop publishing systems are able to format text and graphics interactively on a high-resolution video screen with the aid of page-description command languages. Once a page has been

Desktop publishing systems

formatted, the entire image is transferred to an electronic printing or photocomposition device.

Printers. Computer printers are commonly divided into two general classes according to the way they produce images on paper: impact and nonimpact. In the first type, images are formed by the print mechanism making contact with the paper through an ink-coated ribbon. The mechanism consists either of print hammers shaped like characters or of a print head containing a row of pins that produce a pattern of dots in the form of characters or other images.

Most nonimpact printers form images from a matrix of dots, but they employ different techniques for transferring images to paper. The most popular type, the laser printer, uses a beam of laser light and a system of optical components to etch images on a photoconductor drum from which they are carried via electrostatic photocopying to paper. Light-emitting diode (LED) printers resemble laser printers in operation but direct light from energized diodes rather than a laser onto a photoconductive surface. Ion-deposition printers make use of technology similar to that of photocopiers for producing electrostatic images. Another type of nonimpact printer, the ink-jet printer, sprays electrically charged drops of ink onto the print surface.

Microfilm and microfiche. Alphanumeric and image information can be transferred from digital computer storage directly to film. Reel microfilm and microfiche (a flat sheet of film containing multiple microimages reduced from the original) were popular methods of document storage and reproduction for several decades. During the 1990s they have been largely replaced by optical disc technology (see above *Recording media*).

Speech synthesis

Voice. In synthetic speech generation, digitally prestored sound elements are converted to analog sound signals and combined to form words and sentences. Digital-to-analog converters are available as inexpensive boards for microcomputers or as software for larger machines. Human speech is the most effective natural form of communication, and so applications of this technology are becoming increasingly popular in situations where there are numerous requests for specific information (*e.g.*, time, travel, and entertainment), where there is a need for repetitive instruction, in electronic voice mail (the counterpart of electronic text mail), and in toys.

DISSEMINATION OF INFORMATION

The process of recording information by handwriting was obviously laborious and required the dedication of the likes of Egyptian scribes or monks in monasteries around the world. It was only after mechanical means of reproducing writing were invented that information records could be duplicated more efficiently and economically.

The first practical method of reproducing writing mechanically was block printing; it was developed in China during the T'ang dynasty (618–907). Ideographic text and illustrations were engraved in wooden blocks, inked, and copied on paper. Used to produce books as well as cards, charms, and calendars, block printing spread to Korea and Japan but apparently not to the Islāmic or European Christian civilizations. European woodcuts and metal engravings date only to the 14th century.

Printing from movable type was also invented in China (in the mid-11th century AD). There and in the bookmaking industry of Korea, where the method was applied more extensively during the 15th century, the ideographic type was made initially of baked clay and wood and later of metal. The large number of typefaces required for pictographic text composition continued to handicap printing in the Orient until the present time.

The invention of character-oriented printing from movable type (1440–50) is attributed to the German printer Johannes Gutenberg. Within 30 years of his invention, the movable-type printing press was in use throughout Europe. Character-type pieces were metallic and apparently cast from metallic molds; paper and vellum (calfskin parchment) were used to carry the impressions. Gutenberg's technique of assembling individual letters by hand was employed until 1886, when the German-born American printer Ottmar Mergenthaler developed the Linotype, a keyboard-driven device that cast lines of type automatically. Typesetting speed was further enhanced by the Monotype technique, in which a perforated paper ribbon, punched from a keyboard, was used to operate a type-casting machine. Mechanical methods of typesetting prevailed until the 1960s. Since that time they have been largely supplanted by the electronic and optical printing techniques described in the previous section.

Reproduction of graphics

Unlike the use of movable type for printing text, early graphics were reproduced from wood relief engravings in which the nonprinting portions of the image were cut away. Musical scores, on the other hand, were reproduced from etched stone plates. At the end of the 18th century the German printer Aloys Senefelder developed lithography, a planographic technique of transferring images from a specially prepared surface of stone. In offset lithography the image is transferred from zinc or aluminum plates instead of stone, and in photoengraving such plates are superimposed with film and then etched.

The first successful photographic process, the daguerreotype, was developed during the 1830s. The invention of photography, aside from providing a new medium for capturing still images and later video in analog form, was significant for two other reasons. First, recorded information (textual and graphic) could be easily reproduced from film and, second, the image could be enlarged or reduced. Document reproduction from film to film has been relatively unimportant, because both printing and photocopying (see below) are cheaper. The ability to reduce images, however, has led to the development of the microform, the most economical method of disseminating analog-form information.

Another technique of considerable commercial importance for the duplication of paper-based information is photocopying, or dry photography. Printing is most economical when large numbers of copies are required, but photocopying provides a fast and efficient means of duplicating records in small quantities for personal or local use. Of the several technologies that are in use, the most popular process, xerography, is based on electrostatics.

Distribution of digital information by electronic publishing

While the volume of information issued in the form of printed matter continues unabated, the electronic publishing industry has begun to disseminate information in digital form. The digital optical disc (see above *Recording media*) is developing as an increasingly popular means of issuing large bodies of archival information—for example, legislation, court and hospital records, encyclopaedias and other reference works, referral databases, and libraries of computer software. Full-text databases, each containing digital page images of the complete text of some 400 periodicals stored on CD-ROM, entered the market in 1990. The optical disc provides the mass production technology for publication in machine-readable form. It offers the prospect of having large libraries of information available in virtually every school and at many professional workstations.

The coupling of computers and digital telecommunications is also changing the modes of information dissemination. High-speed digital satellite communications facilitate electronic printing at remote sites; for example, the world's major newspapers and magazines transmit electronic page copies to different geographic locations for local printing and distribution. Updates of catalogs, computer software, and archival databases are distributed via electronic mail, a method of rapidly forwarding and storing bodies of digital information between remote computers.

Indeed, a large-scale transformation is taking place in modes of formal as well as informal communication. For more than three centuries, formal communication in the scientific community has relied on the scholarly and professional periodical, widely distributed to tens of thousands of libraries and to tens of millions of individual subscribers. In 1992 a major international publisher announced that its journals would gradually be available for computer storage in digital form; and in that same year the State University of New York at Buffalo began building a completely electronic, paperless library. The scholarly article, rather than the journal, is likely to become the basic unit of formal communication in scientific disciplines; digital copies of such an article will be transmitted electronically to subscribers or, more likely, on demand to individuals and organizations who learn of its existence through referral databases and new types of alerting information services. The Internet already offers instantaneous public access to vast resources of noncommercial information stored in computers around the world.

Similarly, the traditional modes of informal communications—various types of face-to-face encounters such as meetings, conferences, seminars, workshops, and classroom lectures—are being supplemented and in some cases replaced by electronic mail, electronic bulletin boards (a technique of broadcasting newsworthy textual and multimedia messages between computer users), and electronic teleconferencing and distributed problem-solving (a method of linking remote persons in real time by voice-and-image communication and special software called "groupware"). These technologies are forging virtual societal networks—communities of geographically dispersed individuals who have common professional or social interests.

Information systems

The primary vehicles for the purposeful, orchestrated processing of information are information systems—constructs that collect, organize, store, process, and display information in all its forms (raw data, interpreted data, knowledge, and expertise) and formats (text, video, and voice). In principle, any record-keeping system—*e.g.,* an address book or a train schedule—may be regarded as an information system. What sets modern information systems apart is their electronic dimension, which permits extremely fast, automated manipulation of digitally stored data and their transformation from and to analog representation.

IMPACT OF INFORMATION TECHNOLOGY

Electronic information systems are a phenomenon of the second half of the 20th century. Their evolution is closely tied with advances in two basic technologies: integrated circuits and digital communications.

Integrated circuits are silicon chips containing transistors that store and process information. Advances in the design of these chips, which were first developed in 1958, are responsible for an exponential increase in the cost performance of computer components. For more than two decades the capacity of the basic integrated circuit, the dynamic random-access memory (DRAM) chip, has doubled consistently in intervals of less than two years: from 1,000 transistors (1 kilobit) per chip in 1970 to 1,000,000 (1 megabit) in 1987, 16 megabits in 1993, and 1,000,000,000 (1 gigabit) predicted for the year 2000. A gigabit chip has the capacity of 125,000,000 bytes, approximately equivalent to 14,500 pages, or more than 12 volumes, of *Encyclopædia Britannica.*

Capacity of integrated circuits

The speed of microprocessor chips, measured in millions of instructions per second (MIPS), is also increasing near-exponentially: from 10 MIPS in 1985 to 100 MIPS in 1993, with 1,000 MIPS predicted for 1995. By the year 2000 a single chip may process 64 billion instructions per second. If in a particular computing environment in 1993 a chip supported 10 simultaneous users, in the year 2000 such a chip could theoretically support several thousand users.

Full exploitation of these developments for the realm of information systems requires comparable advances in software disciplines. Their major contribution has been to open the use of computer technology to persons other than computer professionals. Interactive applications in the office and home have been made possible by the development of easy-to-use software products for the creation, maintenance, manipulation, and querying of files and records. The database has become a central organizing framework for many information systems, taking advantage of the concept of data independence, which allows data sharing among diverse applications. Database management system (DBMS) software today incorporates high-level programming facilities that do not require one to specify in detail how the data should be processed. The programming discipline as a whole, however, progresses in an evolutionary manner. Whereas semiconductor field advances are measured by orders of magnitude, the writing and understanding of large suites of software that characterize complex information systems progress more slowly. The complexity of the data processes that comprise very large information systems has so far eluded major breakthroughs, and the cost-effectiveness of the software development sector improves only gradually.

The utility of computers is vastly augmented by their ability to communicate with one another, so as to share data and its processing. Local-area networks (LANs) permit the sharing of data, programs, printers, and electronic mail within offices and buildings. In wide-area networks, such as the Internet, which connect thousands of computers around the globe, computer-to-computer communication uses a variety of media as transmission lines—electric-wire audio circuits, coaxial cables, radio and microwaves (as in satellite communication), and, most recently, optical fibres. The latter are replacing coaxial cable in the Integrated Services Digital Network (ISDN), which is capable of carrying digital information in the form of voice, text, and video simultaneously. To communicate with another machine, a computer requires data circuit-terminating equipment, or DCE, which connects it to the transmission line. When an analog line such as a dial-up telephone line is used, the DCE is called a modem (for modulator/demodulator); it also provides the translation of the digital signal to analog and vice versa. By using data compression, the relatively inexpensive high-speed modems currently in use can transmit data at speeds of more than 100 kilobits per second. When digital lines are used, the DCE allows substantially higher speeds; for instance, the U.S. scholarly network NSFNET, set up by the National Science Foundation, transmits information at 45 million bits per second. The National Research and Education Network, proposed by the U.S. government in 1991, is designed to send data at speeds in the gigabit-per-second range, comfortably moving gigantic volumes of text, video, and sound across a web of digital highways.

Speed of data transmission

Computer networks are complex entities. Each network operates according to a set of procedures called the network protocol. The proliferation of incompatible protocols during the early 1990s has been brought under relative control by the Open Systems Interconnection (OSI) reference Model formulated by the International Organization for Standardization. To the extent that individual protocols conform to the OSI recommendations, computer networks can now be interconnected efficiently through gateways.

Computer networking facilitates the current trend toward distributed information systems. At the corporate level, the central database may be distributed over a number of computer systems in different locations, yet its querying and updating are carried out simultaneously against the composite database. An individual searching for public-access information can traverse disparate computer networks to peruse hundreds of autonomous databases and within seconds or minutes download a copy of the desired document into a personal workstation.

The future of information systems may be gleaned from several areas of current research. As all information carriers (text, video, and sound) can be converted to digital form and manipulated by increasingly sophisticated techniques, the ranges of media, functions, and capabilities of information systems are constantly expanding. Evolving techniques of natural-language processing and understanding, knowledge representation, and neural process modeling have begun to join the more traditional repertoire of methods of content analysis and manipulation. The use of these techniques opens the possibility of eliciting new knowledge from existing data, such as the discovery of a previously unknown medical syndrome or of a causal relationship in a disease. Computer visualization, a new field that has grown expansively since the early 1990s, deals with the conversion of masses of data emanating from instruments, databases, or computer simulations into visual displays—the most efficient method of human information reception, analysis, and exchange. Related to computer visualization is the research area of virtual reality or virtual worlds, which denotes the generation of synthetic environments through the use of three-dimensional displays and interaction devices. A number of research directions in this area are particularly relevant to future information systems: knowledge-based world modeling; the development of physical analogues for abstract quantitative and organizational data; and search and retrieval in large virtual worlds. The cumulative effect of these new research areas is a gradual transformation of the role of information systems from that of data processing to that of cognition aiding.

Present-day computers are remarkably versatile machines capable of assisting humans in nearly every problem-solving task that involves symbol manipulations. Television, on the other hand, has penetrated societies throughout the world as a noninteractive display device for combined video and audio signals. The impending convergence of three digital technologies—namely, the computer, very-high-definition television (V-HDTV), and ISDN data communications—is all but inevitable. In such a system, a large-screen multimedia display monitor, containing a 64-megabit primary memory and a billion-byte hard disk for data storage and playback, would serve as a computer and, over ISDN fibre links, an interactive television receiver.

ANALYSIS AND DESIGN OF INFORMATION SYSTEMS

The building of information systems falls within the domain of engineering. As is true with other engineering disciplines, the nature and tools of information systems engineering are evolving owing to both technological developments and better perceptions of societal needs for information services. Early information systems were designed to be operated by information professionals, and they frequently did not attain their stated social purpose. Modern information systems are increasingly used by persons who have little or no previous hands-on experience with information technology but who possess a much better perception about what this technology should accomplish in their professional and personal environments. A correct understanding of the requirements, preferences, and "information styles" of these end users is crucial to the design and success of today's information systems.

The methodology involved in building an information system consists of a set of iterative activities that are cumulatively referred to as the system's life cycle (Figure 7). The principal objective of the systems analysis phase is the specification of what the system is required to do. In the systems design phase such specifications are converted to a hierarchy of increasingly detailed charts that define the data required and decompose the processes to be carried out on data to a level at which they can be expressed as instructions of a computer program. The systems development phase consists of writing and testing computer software and of developing data input and output forms and conventions. Systems implementation is the installation of a physical system and the activities it entails, such as the training of operators and users. Systems maintenance refers to the further evolution of the functions and structure of a system that results from changing requirements and technologies, experience with the system's use, and fine-tuning of its performance.

Methodology of constructing information systems

L.C. Teague, Jr., and C.W. Pidgeon, *Structured Analysis Methods for Computer Information Systems*, © SRA, 1985

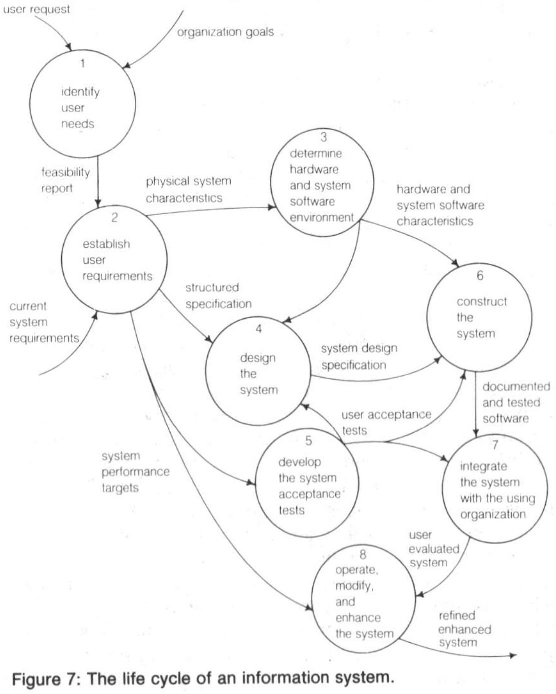

Figure 7: The life cycle of an information system.

Many information systems are implemented with generic, "off-the-shelf" software rather than with custom-built programs; versatile database management software and its nonprocedural programming languages fit the needs of small and large systems alike. The development of large systems that cannot use off-the-shelf software is an expensive, time-consuming, and complex undertaking. Prototyping, an interactive session in which users confirm a system's proposed functions and features early in the design stage, is a practice intended to raise the probability of success of such an undertaking. Some of the tools of computer-aided software engineering available to the systems analyst and designer verify the logic of systems design, automatically generate a program code from low-level specifications, and automatically produce software and system specifications. The eventual goal of information systems engineering is to develop software "factories" that use natural language and artificial intelligence techniques as part of an integrated set of tools to support the analysis and design of large information systems.

CATEGORIES OF INFORMATION SYSTEMS

A taxonomy of information systems is not easily developed, because of their diversity and continuing evolution in structure and function. Earlier distinctions—manual versus automated, interactive versus off-line, real-time versus batch-processing—are no longer appropriate. A more frequently made distinction is in terms of application: use in business offices, factories, hospitals, and so on. In the functional approach taken in this article, information systems may be divided into two categories: organizational systems and public information utilities. Information systems in formal organizations may be further distinguished according to their main purpose: support of managerial and administrative functions or support of operations and services. The former serve internal functions of the organizations, while the latter support the purposes for which these organizations exist.

Management-oriented information systems. The most important functions that top executives perform include setting policies, planning, and preparing budgets. At the strategic level, these decision-making functions are supported by executive information systems. The objective of these systems is to gather, analyze, and integrate internal (corporate) and external (public) data into dynamic profiles of key corporate indicators. Depending on the nature of the organization's business, such indicators may relate to the status of high-priority programs, health of the economy, inventory and cash levels, performance of financial markets, relevant efforts of competitors, utilization of manpower, legislative events, and so forth. The indicators are displayed as text, tables, graphics, or time series, and optional access is provided to more detailed data. The data emanate not only from within the organization's production and administrative departments but also from external information sources, such as public databases (Figure 8). Present-day efforts, drawing on research in neural computers and networks, are to enhance executive information systems with adaptive and self-organizing abilities by means of learning from the executives' changing information needs and uses.

Executive systems

In military organizations, the approximate equivalent of executive information systems is command-and-control systems. Their purpose is to maintain control over some

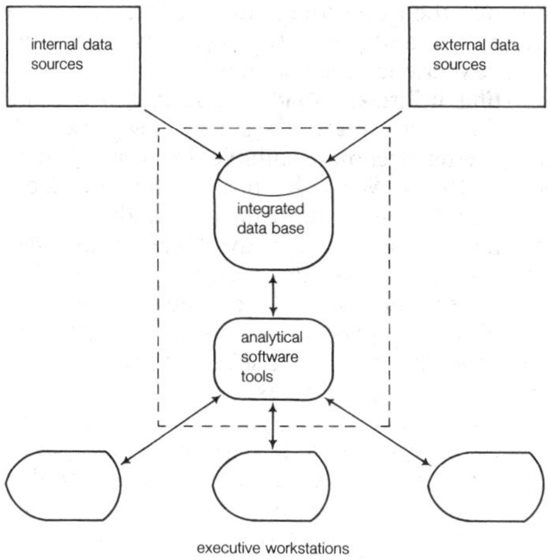

Figure 8: Structure of a typical executive information system.

Command-and-control systems

domain and, if needed, initiate corrective action. Their key characteristic is the real-time nature of the monitoring and decision-making functions. A command-and-control system typically assumes that the environment exercises pressure on the domain of interest (say, a naval force); the system then monitors the environment (collects intelligence data), analyzes the data, compares it with the desired state of the domain, and suggests actions to be taken. Systems of this kind are used at both strategic and tactical levels.

Both executive and military command-and-control systems make use of computational aids for data classification, modeling, and simulation. These capabilities are characteristic of a decision-support system (DSS), a composite of computer techniques for supporting executive decision making in relatively unstructured problem situations. Decision-support software falls into one of two categories: decision-aid programs, in which the decision maker assigns weighted values to every factor in the decision, and decision-modeling programs, in which the user explores different strategies to arrive at the desired outcome.

Administration-oriented information systems. Administrative functions in formal organizations have as their objective the husbanding and optimization of corporate resources—namely, employees and their activities, inventories of materials and equipment, facilities, and finances. Administrative information systems support this objective. Commonly called management information systems (MIS), they focus primarily on resource administration and provide top management with reports of aggregate data. Executive information systems may be viewed as an evolution of administrative information systems in the direction of strategic tracking, modeling, and decision making.

Typically, administrative information systems consist of a number of modules, each supporting a particular function. The modules share a common database whose contents may, however, be distributed over a number of machines and locations. Financial information systems have evolved from the initial applications of punched cards before World War II to integrated accounting and finance systems that cover general accounting, accounts receivable and payable, payroll, purchasing, inventory control, and financial statements such as balance sheets. Functionally close to payroll systems are personnel information systems, which support the administration of the organization's human resources. Job and salary histories, inventory of skills, performance reviews, and other types of personnel data are combined in the database to assist personnel administration, explore potential effects of reorganization or new salary scales (or changes in benefits), and match job requirements with skills. Project management information systems concentrate on resource allocation and task completion of organized activities; they usually incorporate such scheduling methods as the critical path method (CPM) or program evaluation and review technique (PERT).

Financial and personnel information systems

Since the advent of microcomputers, information processing in organizations has become heavily supported by office automation tools. These involve six basic applications: text processing, database, spreadsheet, graphics, communications, and networking. Administrative systems in smaller organizations are usually built as extensions of office automation tools; in large organizations these tools form an interface to custom software. The current trend in office automation is toward integrating the first five applications into a software utility, either delivered to each microprocessor workstation from a "server" on the corporate computer network or integrated into other applications software.

Administrative information systems abound in organizations in both the private and public sectors throughout the industrialized world. In the retail industry, point-of-sale terminals are linked into distributed administrative information systems that contain financial and inventory modules at the department, store, geographic area, and corporate chain levels, with modeling facilities that help to determine marketing strategies and optimize profits. Administrative information systems are indispensable to government; the agencies of virtually all U.S. municipalities with more than 10,000 inhabitants use such systems. The systems are generally centred around a generic database management system and are increasingly supported by software modules and programs that permit data modeling—*i.e.,* they acquire management orientation.

Service-oriented information systems. Such information systems provide support for the operations or services that organizations perform for society. The systems are vertically oriented to specific sectors and industries (*e.g.,* manufacturing, financial services, publishing, education, health, and entertainment). Rather than addressing management and administrative functions, they support activities and processes that are the reason for an organization's existence—in most cases, some kind of manufacturing activity or the rendering of services. Systems of this kind vary greatly, but they tend to fall into three main types: manufacturing, transaction, and expert systems.

The conceptual goal of modern factories is computer-integrated manufacturing (CIM). The phrase denotes data-driven automation that affects all components of the manufacturing enterprise: design and development engineering, manufacturing, marketing and sales, and field support and service. Computer-aided design (CAD) systems were first applied in the electronics industry. Today they feature three-dimensional modeling techniques for drafting and manipulating solid objects on the screen and for deriving specifications for programs to drive numerical-control machines. Once a product is designed, its production process can be outlined using computer-aided process planning (CAPP) systems that help to select sequences of operations and machining conditions. Models of the manufacturing system can be simulated by computers before they are built. The basic manufacturing functions—machining, forming, joining, assembly, and inspection—are supported by computer-aided manufacturing (CAM) systems and automated materials-handling systems. Inventory control systems seek to maintain an optimal stock of parts and materials by tracking inventory movement, forecasting requirements, and initiating procurement orders.

Computer-integrated manufacturing

The technological sophistication of manufacturing information systems is impressive, and it increasingly includes applications of robotics, computer vision, and expert systems (see COMPUTER SCIENCE: *Artificial intelligence*). The core of the CIM concept is an integrated database that supports the manufacturing enterprise and is linked with other administrative databases.

In nonmanufacturing service organizations the prevalent type of information system supports transaction processing. Transactions are sets of discrete inputs, submitted by users at unpredictable intervals, which call for database searching, analysis, and modification. The processor evaluates the request and executes it immediately. Portions of the processing function may be carried out at the intelligent terminal that originated the request so as to distribute the computational load. Response time (the elapsed time between the end of a request and the beginning of the reply) is an important characteristic of this type of real-time teleprocessing system. Large transaction-processing systems often incorporate private telecommunications networks.

Tele-processing transaction systems

Teleprocessing transaction systems constitute the foundation of service industries such as banking, insurance, securities, transportation, and libraries. They are replacing the trading floor of the world's major stock exchanges, linking the latter via on-line telecommunications into a global financial market. Again, the core of a transaction system is its integrated database. The focus of the system is the recipient of services rather than the system operator. Because of this, a local travel agent is able to plan the complete itinerary of a traveler—including reservations for airlines, hotels, rental cars, cultural and sports performances, and even restaurants, on any continent—and to tailor these to the traveler's schedule and budget.

A relatively new category of service-oriented information systems is the expert system, so called because its database stores a description of decision-making skills of human experts in some narrow domain of performance, such as medical image interpretation, taxation, brickwork design, configuration of computer system hardware, troubleshooting malfunctioning equipment, or beer brewing. The motivation for constructing expert systems is the desire to replicate the scarce, unstructured, and perhaps poorly documented empirical knowledge of specialists so that it can be readily used by others.

Components of expert systems

Expert systems have three components: (1) a software interface through which the user formulates queries by which the expert system solicits further information from the user and by which it explains to the user the reasoning process employed to arrive at an answer, (2) a database (called the knowledge base) consisting of axioms (facts) and rules for making inferences from these facts, and (3) a computer program (dubbed the inference engine) that executes the inference-making process.

The knowledge base is a linked structure of rules that the human expert applies, often intuitively, in problem solving. The process of acquiring such knowledge typically has three phases: a functional analysis of the environment, users, and tasks performed by the expert; identification of concepts of the domain of expertise and their classification according to various relationships; and an interview, by either human or automated techniques, of the expert (or experts) in action. The results of these steps are translated into so-called production rules (of the form "IF condition *x* exists, THEN action *y* follows") and stored in the knowledge base. Chains of production rules form the basis for the automated deductive capabilities of expert systems and for their ability to explain their actions to users.

Expert systems are a commercial variety of a class of computer programs called knowledge-based systems. Knowledge in expert systems is highly unstructured (*i.e.,* the problem-solving process of the domain is not manifest), and it is stated explicitly in relationships or deductively inferred from the chaining of propositions. Since every condition that may be encountered must be described by a rule, rule-based expert systems cannot handle unanticipated events (but can evolve with usage) and remain limited to narrow problem domains.

Another variant of expert systems, one that does not possess this limitation, employs a knowledge base that consists of structured descriptions of real-world problem situations and of decisions actually made by human experts. In medicine, for example, the patient record contains descriptions of personal data, physical and laboratory examinations, clinical diagnoses, proposed treatments, and the outcomes of such treatments. Given a large database of such records in a medical specialty, a physician may query the database as to decisions and events that appear analogous to those involving the present patient, so as to display the collective, real-world experience bearing on the situation. In contrast to rule-based expert systems, which are (ideally) intended to replace a human expert with a machine, knowledge bases containing descriptions of actual problem events may be used only as decision-aiding tools. They are attractive, however, because their development is usually a by-product of organizational information systems and because their usefulness (to practice, research, continuing education, and so forth) increases with the volume of expert experience they acquire.

Public information utilities. Aside from the proliferation of organizational information systems, new types of teleprocessing systems became available for use by the public during the 1970s. With the proliferation of electronic databases, the then-new industry of "database vendors" began to make these resources available via on-line database search systems. Today this industry operates for public access and uses hundreds of document databases, some of them in full text; corporate and industry data and news; stock quotations; diverse statistics and time series; and catalogs of products and services.

On-line database search systems

Recent services of public information utilities include transaction-processing systems: brokerage services to place on-line stock, bond, and options orders; home banking to pay bills and transfer funds; travel planning and reservations; and on-line catalog shopping. Some of these services combine on-line information retrieval (from, say, merchandise catalogs) and transaction processing (placing orders). Many include such functions as electronic mail and teleconferencing.

IMPACT OF COMPUTER-BASED INFORMATION SYSTEMS ON SOCIETY

Preoccupation with information and knowledge as an individual, organizational, and societal resource is stronger today than at any other time in history. The volume of books printed in 16th-century Europe is estimated to have doubled approximately every seven years. Interestingly, the same growth rate has been calculated for global scientific and technical literature in the 20th century and for business documents in the United States in the 1980s. If these estimates are reasonably correct, the growth of recorded information is a historical phenomenon, not peculiar to modern times. The present, however, has several new dimensions relative to the information resource: modern information systems collect and generate information automatically; they provide rapid, high-resolution access to the corpora of information; and they manipulate information with previously unattainable versatility and efficiency.

The proliferation of automatic data-logging devices in scientific laboratories, hospitals, transportation, and many other areas has created a huge body of primary data for subsequent analysis. Machines even generate new information: original musical scores are now produced by computers, as are graphics and video materials. Electronic professional workstations can be programmed to carry out any of a variety of functions. Some of those that handle word processing not only automatically look for spelling and punctuation errors but check grammar, diction, and style as well; they are able to suggest alternative word usage and rephrase sentences to improve their readability. Machines produce modified versions of recorded information and translate documents into other languages.

Modern information systems also bring new efficiency to the organization, retrieval, and dissemination of recorded information. The control of the world's information store has been truly revolutionized, revealing its diversity in hitherto unattainable detail. Information services provide mechanisms to locate documents nearly instantaneously and to copy and move many of them electronically. New digital storage technologies make it economical for some to obtain for personal possession those collections equivalent to the holdings of entire libraries and archives. Alternately, access to information resources on electronic networks permits the accumulation of highly individualized personal or corporate collections in analog or digital form or a combination of both.

As the imprint of technology expands, some of the fundamental concepts of the field, which often took centuries to evolve, are strained. For instance, information technology forces an extension of the traditional concept of the document as a fixed, printed object to include bodies of multimedia information. Because of their digital form, these objects are easy to manipulate; they are split into parts, recombined with others, reformatted from one medium to another, annotated in real time by people or machines, and readied for display in many different formats on various devices. Control of these "living" documents, which mimic human association and processing of ideas and are expected to become one of the most common units of the digital information universe, is but one of the challenges for the emerging virtual library of humankind.

Automatic information manipulation

An equally significant new dimension of modern information systems lies in their ability to manipulate information automatically. This capability is the result of representing symbolic information in digital form. Computer-based information systems are able to perform calculations, analyses, classifications, and correlations at levels of complexity and efficiency far exceeding human capabilities. They can simulate the performance of logical and mathematical models of physical processes and situations under diverse conditions. Information systems also have begun to mimic human cognitive processes: deductive inference in expert systems, contextual analysis in natural-language processing, and analogical and intuitive reasoning in information retrieval. Powerful information-transforming technologies now available or under development—data/text to graphics, speech to printed text, one natural language to another—broaden the availability of information and enhance human problem-solving capabilities. Computer visualization is dramatically altering methods of data interpretation by scientists; geographic information systems help drivers of the latest automobiles navigate cities; and interactive applications of networked multimedia computers may, for some, replace newspapers, compete with commercial broadcast television, and give new dimensions to the future of education and training at all levels of society.

Information systems applications are motivated by a desire to augment the mental information-processing functions of humans or to find adequate substitutes for them. Their effects have already been felt prominently in three domains: the economy, the governance of society, and the milieu of individual existence.

Effects on the economy. Information systems are a major tool for improving the cost-effectiveness of societal investments. In the realm of the economy, they may be expected to lead to higher productivity, particularly in the industrial and service sectors—in the former through automation of manufacturing and related processes, in the latter through computer-aided decision making, problem solving, administration, and support of clerical functions. Awareness that possession of information is tantamount to a competitive edge is stimulating the gathering of technical and economic intelligence at the corporate and national levels. Similarly, concern is mounting over the safeguarding and husbanding of proprietary and strategic information within the confines of organizations as well as within national borders. Computer crime, a phrase denoting illegal and surreptitious attempts to invade data banks in order to steal or modify records, or to release over computer networks software (called a virus) that corrupts data and programs, has grown at an alarming rate since the development of computer communications. In worst-case scenarios, computer crime is capable of causing large-scale chaos in financial, military, transportation, municipal, and other systems and services, with attendant economic consequences.

Changes in the distribution of labour

The growing number of information-processing applications is altering the distribution of labour in national economies. The deployment of information systems has resulted in the dislocation of labour and has already had an appreciable effect on unemployment in the United States. That country's economic recession during the early 1990s saw thousands of middle-management jobs relinquished, most permanently. The growth of computer-based information systems encourages a change in the traditional hierarchical structure of management (see below). As heavy automation is reverting production facilities from the labour-intensive nations to industrialized countries, the competitive potential of some of these nations is also likely to suffer an economic setback, at least in the short run. Singapore, a city-state of some three million people, has become very prosperous as giant foreign electronic firms located their manufacturing facilities there. It is bracing against such an economic setback by seeking to become the world's most intensive user and provider of electronic information systems for public services, international commerce and banking, and communications.

Effects on governance and management. For much of the history of humankind, formal organizations have been better equipped than the citizenry to take advantage of information: their record-keeping practices were more mature and efficient, they possessed better facilities and skills to collect and interpret information; and—with computational aids—they are now able to profit from the powerful analytical tools provided by information technology. Possession of information is not, however, tantamount to higher-quality governance or management, particularly if such possession is unilateral. As the number of recent political and financial scandals in various countries documents, it also entails possibilities of error and misuse.

It is the democratization of information, a characteristic of the last decades of the 20th century, that portends a beneficial impact on the quality of human governance and management. The public information and communication utilities that propagate this trend not only render the concerned citizen's access to information more equitable, they also help to forge informal societal networks that counterbalance the power of formal organizations and increasingly focus their style of management on consulting with the well-informed and on conveying greater concern. The concept of the "electronic town hall," an issue debated in the U.S. presidential elections of 1992, encapsulates the ideal of participatory democracy.

An environment that encourages the use of information technology and systems fosters what might be termed high information maturity on the part of the populace, a prerequisite of participatory democracy. Equitable access to information by all citizenry—rich and poor, privileged and disadvantaged—is one of the poignant societal issues facing humankind in the 21st century.

Computer-based information systems also impact the structure and management styles of corporations. The matrix organization, a structure in which departments and employees communicate directly with other organizational units, is an increasingly popular alternative to the hierarchical structure. Loose organizational decentralization imitates the observed principle of nature and of social organization suggesting that a unit size of roughly 150 persons communicates optimally and requires minimal managerial overhead. As business expansion and mergers extend the authoritative reach of large corporations and as the use of standard techniques of electronic document interchange forges flexible networks of firms in most industrial domains, leadership by consensus replaces authoritarian management. Information sharing and communication are the principal factors bringing about these changes, and information systems constitute the foundation that makes such sharing and communication effective.

Effects on the individual. An overt impact of modern information systems concerns the individual's standard and style of living. Information systems affect the scope and quality of health care, make social services more equitable, enhance personal comfort, provide a greater measure of safety and mobility, and extend the variety of leisure forms at one's disposal. More subtly but equally important, they also affect the content and style of an individual's work and in so doing perturb the social and legal practices and conventions to which one is accustomed. New kinds of information products and media necessitate a redefinition of the legal conventions regulating the ownership of products of the human intellect.

Concern over privacy and security

Moreover, massive data-collecting systems bring into sharp focus the elusive borderline between the common good and personal privacy, calling for the need to safeguard stored data against accidental or illegal access, disclosure, or misuse.

Individuals cannot ignore the impact of automation and information-processing systems on their skills and jobs. Information technology makes obsolete, in part or in entirety, many human functions: first mechanical and repetitive tasks were affected; now clerical and paraprofessional tasks are being automated; and eventually highly skilled and some professional functions will be made unnecessary. Individuals performing these functions face the probability of shorter periods of employment and the need to adapt or change their skills. As technologies, including information technology, grow more sophisticated, their learning curves stretch or the required skills become narrower; continuing training and education are likely to become a way of life for both employee and employer. Unlike the slow, gradual evolution of human labour in past generations, present-day changes are occurring rapidly and with little warning. Unless society members anticipate these effects and prepare to cope with them mentally and in practice, job dislocations and forced geographic relocations may prove traumatic for employees and their families.

The perhaps more fundamental issue of paramount long-term significance for society has to do with the well-being of the human spirit in an increasingly knowledge-intensive environment. In such an environment, knowledge is the principal and perhaps most valuable currency. The growing volume and the rate of obsolescence of knowledge compel the individual to live in the continuous presence of, and frequent interaction with, information resources and systems. Effective use of these resources and systems may be a modern definition of literacy, while the absence of such a skill may very well result in intellectual and possibly economic poverty and inequity. There is a real danger that humans, unwilling or incapable or not given access to information, may be relegated to an existence that falls short of the human potential.

(VLADIMIR SLAMECKA)

Southeast Asia

Cambodia

HISTORY

The importance of Cambodia's contributions to mainland Southeast Asia is out of proportion to its present reduced territory and limited political power. Between the 11th and the 13th century, the Khmer (Cambodian) state included much of the Indochinese Peninsula and incorporated large parts of present-day southern Vietnam, Laos, and eastern Thailand. The cultural influence of Cambodia on other countries, particularly Laos and Thailand, has been enormous.

Early history. It is not known for certain how long people have lived in what is now Cambodia, where they came from, or what languages they spoke before writing was introduced (using a Sanskrit-style alphabet) about the 3rd century AD. Dates based on carbon-14 measurements have established that people able to make pottery inhabited Cambodia as early as 4000 BC. These and subsequent finds have suggested that these early people, like Cambodians today, were of slight to medium build, constructed their houses on wooden piles, consumed a considerable quantity of fish, and raised pigs and water buffalo.

Whether the early inhabitants of Cambodia came originally or primarily from the north, west, or south is still being debated, as are theories about waves of different peoples moving through the region in prehistoric times. The notion of distinct Asian "races" that was popular until the 1950s has been discredited, and subsequent archaeological finds have suggested that prehistoric mainland Southeast Asia, including Cambodia, had a comparatively sophisticated culture. Some scholars even have attributed the first cultivation of rice and the first casting of bronze to the region.

Indian influences

Funan and Chenla. Indian influences were the most important of Cambodia's early history. They coincided with the first centuries AD, when Chinese and Indian pilgrims and traders stopped along the coasts of present-day Cambodia and Vietnam and exchanged silks and metals for spices, aromatic wood, ivory, and gold. Written sources from about this period are almost entirely in Chinese. A kingdom or group of kingdoms known to Chinese writers as "Funan" flourished in southern Cambodia at this time. Over a period of 300 years between the 3rd and 6th centuries AD, its rulers offered gifts from time to time to Chinese emperors. Chinese writers testified to the extent of Indian influence in the kingdom and cited a local story, dating from the 6th century, that traced its origins to an Indian Brahman named Kaundinya "who changed its institutions to follow Indian models." One early innovation was probably the introduction of large-scale irrigation, which allowed people to raise three or more crops of rice per year in some districts and brought unpromising areas under cultivation. Another was the worship of the Hindu god Śiva (Shiva), who was conceptualized as a tutelary ancestor or spirit of the soil and often was represented by a stone lingam, or phallus. A third was the relatively peaceful coexistence of Hinduism and Buddhism, which characterized Cambodia for more than a thousand years.

The most important legacy of Funan, though it may have been exaggerated by Chinese writers, was a relatively centralized state apparatus, culminating in a theoretically absolute ruler. The ruler presided over the agricultural workforce and commanded agricultural surpluses and off-season labour to sustain his lifestyle, support a priestly caste, and build fortresses, palaces, and temples. In a general way, these social arrangements characterized much of the medieval world, but it would be imprecise to use a term like "feudalism" to characterize Funan and its successor states. Instead, it is probably more fruitful to seek links between ancient and present-day Cambodia than between ancient Cambodia and countries far to the west about which the Khmer would have known nothing.

The appearance of Sanskrit inscriptions in the 6th century—the earliest known Khmer inscription dates from the early 7th century—has made it possible to use indigenous sources to supplement Chinese ones, but they all fail to clarify the confusing political developments that occurred in the Cambodian region between the decline of Funan in the 6th century and the founding of a centralized state in northwestern Cambodia about three centuries later. It has been common practice for modern writers to use "Chenla," the contemporary Chinese term for the region, when referring to Cambodia during this time. Chinese sources suggest that there were at least two kingdoms, known as "Water Chenla" and "Land Chenla," in Cambodia that vied for recognition from China in this period. Whereas the geographic centre for both Funan and Water Chenla lay in the Mekong delta south and east of Phnom Penh and extended into present-day Vietnam, the heartland of Land Chenla appears to have been farther up the Mekong, with an important cult site called Wat Phu located in present-day southern Laos. It seems likely that Water Chenla looked outward and welcomed foreign trade, while Land Chenla was more inward-looking and based its economy on intensive agriculture. Surviving inscriptions in Sanskrit and Khmer testify to a multitude of small kingdoms on Cambodian soil in the 7th, 8th, and 9th centuries. Remarkable sculptures and architectural remains also have survived from this period, displaying a mixture of Indian influence and local inspiration. The appearance of local styles reflected, in part, declining Indian commercial interest in the region beginning in the 7th century.

The Khmer state (Angkor). *Foundation of the kingdom.* In 790 a young Cambodian prince, claiming to be descended from the rulers of Funan, was consecrated in eastern Cambodia under the title Jayavarman II. Part of the ceremony involved breaking ties with "Java," which probably was not a reference to the island of Java but

Jayavarman II

to the kingdom of Śrīvijaya on the island of Sumatra. Over the next 10 years, Jayavarman extended his power northward into the Mekong River valley until, in 802, he was reconsecrated as a chakravartin (the ancient Indian conception of world ruler) in northwestern Cambodia. The capital seems to have been located in the Kulên Hills north of the present-day provincial capital of Siĕmréab (Siem Reap), where he died in 835. Despite the high status accorded him by subsequent Angkorean kings, Jayavarman II seems to have left no inscriptions of his own, and the monuments that can be dated to his reign were small and hastily built.

Jayavarman's real accomplishment was less tangible and longer-lasting, for he seems to have welded what came to be called Kambuja-desa into a confident, self-aware kingdom that superseded and came to control a range of smaller states. He was Cambodia's first nationally oriented king. Whether smaller states were forced into subservience or volunteered it is uncertain, but, despite the grandeur and apparent continuity of the Angkorean temples that were built over the next four centuries, Jayavarman II's successors were often powerless or were constrained by outside forces. Revolts and usurpations were frequent, as were foreign invasions. Rulers were subject to claims by family members, priests, generals, and bureaucrats. Some kings, especially usurpers, had more freedom of action than others. Those who ruled in periods of peace were also in a better position to undertake building programs and public works. Like their counterparts in medieval Europe, Cambodian kings were far removed from ordinary people. The king was perceived primarily in religious terms, and he assured the fertility of the soil and the well-being of the kingdom through the rituals he performed that were thought to obtain such guarantees. In exchange for his protection, the people were technically enslaved and liable for military service and corvée duty, although they actually spent most of their time growing crops to feed their families.

Toward the end of the 9th century, soon after Jayavarman II's death, the Cambodian capital shifted to the northern shores of the Tonle Sap, near present-day Phumĭ Rôluŏs. A king named Indravarman I (ruled 877–*c.* 890) constructed a large reservoir and several temples there, including a pyramidical structure called the Bakong—the first Cambodian temple to be built primarily of stone rather than brick. This so-called "temple mountain" became the model for many larger royal temples at Angkor. These served as monuments to the greatness of their patrons and, subsequently, as their tombs.

Yaśovarman I

Angkorean civilization. Indravarman's son and successor, Yaśovarman I (*c.* 890–*c.* 910), moved the capital again, this time closer to Siĕmréab. This was the foundation of Angkor—a name derived from the Sanskrit word *nagara,* meaning "city"—which has become one of the world's most celebrated archaeological sites, as well as the popular name for Cambodia's medieval civilization. The city that Yaśovarman founded, Yaśodharapura, retained that name and remained Cambodia's capital until it was abandoned in the 15th century. His temple mountain, now called Bakheng (literally, "Mighty Ancestor"), was built on a natural hill that overlooked a teeming city, the more distant rice-growing plain, and the Tonle Sap. The mountain occupied the centre of the city, just as Mount Meru, the mythical home in India of Hindu gods, was said to stand at the centre of the universe. Yaśovarman built a large reservoir nearby. The city wall of Yaśodharapura measured 2.5 miles (4 kilometres) on each side. For such an ambitious building program, the king needed to command a large labour pool. Other evidence suggests that his reign was characterized by tolerance toward a variety of Buddhist and Hindu sects that occasionally blended into local cults honouring ancestral spirits and spirits of the soil. Indeed, for all the apparent absolutism of its kings, a consistent feature of Angkorean civilization, unmatched in medieval Europe, was religious toleration.

After several decades of warfare, dislocations, and disorder—Yaśodharapura itself was abandoned for nearly 30 years—Rajendravarman II (ruled 944–968) restored the capital and set in motion a period of peace and prosperity that lasted nearly a century. During the reign of his successor, Jayavarman V (968–*c.* 1000), the rose-coloured sandstone shrine of Banteai Srei—arguably the loveliest temple at Angkor—was built on the outskirts of the capital under the patronage of a wealthy priestly family, one of whom had been Jayavarman's teacher. In Yaśodharapura itself, Jayavarman V began work on the imposing temple mountain now called Ta Keo, which was completed under his successor, Suryavarman I (ruled *c.* 1004–*c.*1050). Suryavarman I, an innovative and demanding monarch, was a usurper with links to princely families in what is now northeastern Thailand. His rise to power involved the subjugation of many areas that had become semi-independent under his predecessors and resembled that of Jayavarman II two centuries earlier. Suryavarman extended the Khmer empire westward into present-day Thailand, where he constructed the large mountaintop temple known as Preah Vihear. During his reign, the number of cities ruled from Yaśodharapura jumped from roughly 20 to nearly 50, and foreign trade increased, along with tighter bureaucratic control. His successor consolidated these gains, put down a dangerous rebellion, and was responsible for the temple mountain known today as the Baphuon.

The closing years of the 11th century were ones of turmoil and fragmentation. At different times, two and even three "absolute monarchs" contended, simultaneously, for the title of chakravartin. At the end of the century, however, a new dynasty—which was to last for more than a century—began to rule at Angkor. Its most powerful monarch took the name of Suryavarman II (ruled 1113–*c.* 1150), although he probably was not descended from the earlier king of that name. Like his namesake predecessor, Suryavarman II was a formidable military campaigner. He avenged earlier attacks on Angkor by armies launched from the kingdom of Champa, in what is now south-central Vietnam, and led expeditions into northern and southern Thailand. A campaign against Vietnam, which recently had declared its independence from China, was less successful, although earlier in his reign Suryavarman had renewed diplomatic relations with China.

Angkor Wat

Suryavarman's major accomplishment, from a 20th-century perspective, was his temple complex of Angkor Wat, still the largest religious structure in the world and one of the most beautiful. The temple, which eventually became his tomb and probably was an astronomical observatory as well, was dedicated to the Hindu god Vishnu. Its bas-reliefs, running for nearly a half mile inside its third enclosure, depict events in the well-known Indian epics the *Mahābhārata* and *Rāmāyaṇa*—confirming that these texts were widely known at Angkor—as well as Suryavarman himself holding court. The elegance of these carvings, the hundreds of graceful statues of angelic dancers (*apsaras*) that adorn the temple, and its reflection in the moats that surround it continue to give Angkor Wat an awe-inspiring air; in the 12th century, when its towers were gilded and its moats properly maintained, it must have been even more breathtaking.

Jayavarman VII. Suryavarman II's successor, Yaśovarman II, also reached into earlier history for his royal name, tracing his lineage to the Rôluŏs period. During his reign, several temples begun under Suryavarman were completed. Yaśovarman was overthrown by one of his officials after returning from a military campaign in Thailand. In the aftermath of the coup, a Cambodian prince, later to rule under the name of Jayavarman VII (1181–*c.* 1220), hurried home from Champa—it is uncertain from his inscriptions why he was there—to vie for the Cambodian throne. He arrived too late, and for the next 10 years he bided his time as the usurper lost control and Angkor was invaded and occupied by the Chams. In 1177, heading an army of his own, the prince attacked Angkor and defeated the Cham forces. The battles are vividly depicted in the bas-reliefs of his temple mountain, the Bayon. To forestall further Cham attacks, Jayavarman annexed the Cham capital, and Angkor controlled Champa until Jayavarman's death.

When his campaign against the Chams was over, the future monarch worked to bring Cambodia under his control. An inscription referred to the kingdom as being "shaded by many parasols," a metaphor for a multiplicity of rulers. In 1191, presumably when the process was complete, Jayavarman finally settled in Angkor. He soon embarked on a program of building and public works that was more extensive and grandiose than any in Angkorean history. According to his inscriptions, hundreds of thousands of people were involved in these projects.

Numerous temples, statues, stone bridges, and inscriptions in the Angkor region and elsewhere in Cambodia testify to the vigour of Jayavarman VII's long reign. He rebuilt and refortified the city. He was a fervent Buddhist of the Mahāyāna (Greater Vehicle) school, but, like most other Cambodian kings, he also tolerated and patronized Hinduism and local ancestor cults; several larger-than-life-size statues of the monarch depict him in meditation.

The Bayon

His extraordinary temple, the Bayon, with its multiple towers, each bearing faces of divinities turned in the cardinal directions, is perhaps the most intriguing of the monuments at Angkor. Like Yaśovarman I's Bakheng, the Bayon stood at the centre of the royal city—which had shifted since Yaśovarman's time—and symbolized Mount Meru. Many Hindu gods and the Buddha are depicted in the statuary of the temple, while the bas-reliefs depict scenes of ordinary life, providing a picture of 12th-century Cambodians at work, rest, and play that fails to emerge from the religiously oriented inscriptions or from carvings at other temples. The clothing, tools, houses, and oxcarts in the bas-reliefs closely resemble those in the Cambodian countryside today.

The decline of Angkor. After Jayavarman's death about 1220, few monuments were erected at Angkor, and fewer inscriptions were incised. Little by little, the Khmer empire began to contract. Jayavarman's campaigns neutralized Champa as a threat to Angkor, but, by the early 13th century, vigorous new kingdoms in what is now northern Thailand—centring on the city of Sukhothai—became powerful enough to throw off Angkorean domination, as did some Tai principalities in the south. In the mid-13th century, Tai armies even raided Angkor. For most of the century, however, Angkor remained a glittering, crowded, and wealthy city. It impressed a Chinese visitor, Chou Ta-kuan, who arrived there in 1296. Chou's account is the longest and most detailed description that has survived of the Khmer capital, supplementing the bas-reliefs of the Bayon. He left a picture of a bustling city in which the king still went forth in great pomp and ceremony.

Chou also observed monks of the Theravāda school of Buddhism at Angkor. This more orthodox and austere school flourished in kingdoms to the west of Cambodia and contrasted sharply with the lavish and elitist rituals associated with Hinduism and Mahāyāna Buddhism. When Chou visited Angkor, Theravāda Buddhism was still one religion among many. Soon afterward, however, it began to benefit from royal patronage, and the conversion of the majority of the population probably followed the conversion of members of the elite. Those disadvantaged by the change included the high-ranking priestly families who had built and maintained the temples and had supported the labourers at Angkor.

Some historians have considered the mass conversion to Theravāda Buddhism as having been responsible for the abandonment of Angkor, which certainly accompanied the conversion in the 14th and 15th centuries. That argument has been undermined by the fact that Theravāda Buddhists from Thailand profited from and even accelerated the collapse by their repeated military attacks, in which hundreds and perhaps thousands of Cambodians were led to captivity in Thailand.

Recorded Tai attacks on Angkor occurred in 1369, 1389, and 1431, after which the Khmer capital was definitely abandoned. There undoubtedly were other attacks as well.

Ayutthaya

In 1351 a Tai kingdom whose court modeled itself culturally on Angkor was founded at Ayutthaya (Ayudhya, or Siam), not far from modern Bangkok. The Tai capital remained at Ayutthaya for the next 400 years. It is tempting to imagine a transfusion of elite culture from Angkor to the more prosperous, more secure Tai court in the 14th and 15th centuries. It is also likely that the Khmer who remained at Angkor were drawn southward to the vicinity of Phnom Penh (said to have been founded in the mid-15th century) by the region's commercial possibilities. In any case, the smaller, outward-looking Khmer kingdom that replaced Angkor in the south earned its wealth primarily from trade rather than from intensive rice cultivation and the mobilization of labour for public works.

Tai and Vietnamese hegemony. In the century and a half that followed the abandonment of Angkor, what is known of Khmer history is a confusing mixture of uncertain dates, mythical figures, and complex dynastic rivalries. Cambodian chronicles for this period, composed several centuries afterward, are impossible to verify against inscriptions or other primary sources. Between the mid-14th and the end of the 16th century, all that is known for certain is that Angkor was abandoned, that the Tai court of Ayutthaya absorbed some of its culture and prestige, and that the political centre of Cambodia shifted to the south. Relations between the Tai and the Khmer remained uneasy.

In the late 16th century, a period of Tai weakness following wars with Myanmar (Burma) coincided with a time of Cambodian prosperity; and a Khmer monarch, Chan I (ruled 1516–66), reoccupied the Angkor area briefly, restoring some of the temples, adding some bas-reliefs to those at Angkor Wat, and leaving several new inscriptions. When the Tai recovered their strength in the 1590s, however, they invaded Cambodia in force and sacked the Khmer capital at Lovek, north of Phnom Penh, ushering in a period of Cambodian weakness vis-à-vis its neighbours that has endured to the present day.

Cambodian history from the beginning of the 17th century until the establishment of the French protectorate in 1863 is, indeed, a sorry record of weak kings being undermined by members of their families and forced to seek the protection of their stronger neighbours, Siam (Thailand) and Vietnam. Between 1603 and 1848, 22 monarchs occupied the Cambodian throne. The details of this unstable, humiliating period are perhaps less important than the record that is available of the manner in which Cambodia slowly fell under the suzerainty of its two neighbours. When a Cambodian monarch in the 1620s foolishly declared "independence" from Ayutthaya, for example, he sought assistance from the Nguyen overlords of southern Vietnam. In exchange, he was encouraged to marry a Nguyen princess and also to permit Vietnamese settlers to move into land near present-day Ho Chi Minh City (Saigon), which until then had been under his control. Over the next 200 years, Cambodian kings sought Tai or Vietnamese protection against their rivals in the royal family and against the foreign power temporarily out of favour. The costs in lost territory and diminished autonomy were considerable, but the monarchs had little bargaining power and no freedom to maneuver.

That Cambodia survived at all can be attributed to the fact that in the 18th century the Tai and the Vietnamese had other preoccupations. In the 1750s and '60s, Tai energies were taken up by wars with Myanmar, whose armies sacked and destroyed Ayutthaya in 1767. Soon afterward, the Nguyen rulers of southern Vietnam were engaged in a prolonged campaign to regain power from the usurping Tay Son rebels. Fighting spilled over from Vietnam into Cambodia, and the royal family fled to Thailand. By the end of the century a powerful Tai dynasty had established the kingdom of Siam and had installed itself in its new capital in Bangkok, and at the beginning of the 19th century the Nguyen founded a dynasty that governed all of Vietnam. A confrontation between the two powers in Cambodia was inevitable. In 1794, in exchange for placing a refugee Cambodian prince, Eng, on the Cambodian throne, the Siamese appropriated two Cambodian provinces, Bătdâmbâng (Battambang) and Siĕmréab (Siem Reap)—the latter including the abandoned ruins of Angkor. These provinces remained in Siamese hands until 1907. When Eng died after a short reign, he was replaced by his young son, who ruled as Chan II with Thai protection.

Loss of territory

Chan II's reign confirmed Cambodia's dual vassalage to Thailand and Vietnam. With three rebellious younger brothers and demanding patrons at the Siamese court, he sought assistance from Vietnam; the Siamese supported his brothers, who took refuge in Bangkok. The uneasy calm that ensued, with Chan acknowledging Siamese and Vietnamese suzerainty, ended with Chan's death in 1835. Vietnamese pressure was strong enough to ensure that a powerless princess named Mei was then enthroned, while the Vietnamese controlled most of the country. Not until 1841, when Chan's brother Duong (Duang; ruled 1848–60) returned from exile in Bangkok supported by Siamese troops, were the Cambodians able to exercise a small degree of independence. Fighting between the Siamese and Vietnamese continued in Cambodia for several years. Duong was crowned only after Vietnamese troops agreed to leave the country. Cambodia again became a Siamese protectorate. Duong tried hard to revitalize the kingdom's institutions, but his resources were desperately limited, and his reign was marred by several rebellions. When he died, he was succeeded by his son, Norodom, but conditions were too unstable in the kingdom for Norodom to be crowned.

French rule. *The protectorate.* French control over Cambodia was an offshoot of French involvement in the neighbouring provinces of Vietnam. Their decision to advance into Cambodia came only when they feared that British and Siamese expansion might threaten their access to the largely unmapped Mekong River, which they assumed (incorrectly) would provide them with access to central China. In 1863 French naval officers from Vietnam persuaded Norodom to sign a treaty that gave France control of Cambodia's foreign affairs. The effect of the treaty was to weaken Siamese protection. A French admiral participated in Norodom's coronation, with Siamese acquiescence, in 1864.

For the next 15 years or so, French protection was not especially demanding, and Norodom benefited from French military help in putting down a series of rebellions. By the late 1870s, however, French officials in Cambodia were pressing for greater control over internal affairs. Shocked by what they regarded as the ineptitude and barbarity of Norodom's court and anxious to turn a profit in Cambodia, they sought to introduce fiscal and judicial reforms. In doing this, the French knew that Norodom's half brother, Si Votha (Sisowath), who had ambitions for the throne, would cooperate with them. Norodom, however, resisted the reforms, which he correctly perceived as infringements on his power. Exasperated by his intransigence, the French in 1884 forced him at gunpoint to sign a document that virtually transformed Cambodia into a colony. Soon thereafter, provincial officials, feeling threatened, raised guerrilla armies to confront the French.

Anti-French rebellion

The rebellion, which lasted until mid-1886, was the only anti-French movement in the kingdom until after World War II. The French succeeded in suppressing it after agreeing to some concessions to the king, but Norodom's apparent victory was hollow. What the French had been unable to achieve by the convention of 1884, they proceeded to gain through piecemeal action. As Norodom's health declined and as senior Cambodian officials came to see their interests increasingly linked with French power, the way was opened for greater French control. In 1897 the French representative in Phnom Penh assumed executive authority, reducing the king's power to a minimum. Norodom died, embittered and overtaken by events, in 1904.

The first 40 years of the French protectorate—whatever French motives may have been—had guaranteed the survival of the Cambodian state and had saved the kingdom from being divided between its two powerful neighbours. Norodom's successor, Sisowath (ruled 1904–27), was more cooperative with the French and presided benignly over the partial modernization of the kingdom. The northwestern provinces of Bătdâmbâng and Siĕmréab were returned to Cambodia by the Siamese in 1907. By the time Sisowath died 20 years later, hundreds of miles of paved roads had been built, and thousands of acres of rubber plantations had been established by the French. Resistance to their rule, in sharp contrast to what was happening in neighbouring Vietnam, was almost nonexistent.

Sisowath's eldest son, Monivong, who reigned until 1941, was even more of a figurehead than his father had been. During the 1930s, a railway opened between Phnom Penh and the Siamese (Thai) border, while the first Cambodian-language newspaper, *Nagara Vatta* ("Angkor Wat"), affiliated with the Buddhist Institute in Phnom Penh, conveyed a mildly nationalist message to its readers.

World War II and the First Indochina War. When Monivong died in 1941, Japanese forces already had occupied the component states of the Indochinese Peninsula, while leaving the French in nominal control. In these difficult circumstances, the French governor-general, Jean Decoux, placed Monivong's grandson, Prince Norodom Sihanouk, on the Cambodian throne. Decoux was guided by the expectation that Sihanouk, then only 18 years old, could be easily controlled. In the long run, the French underestimated Sihanouk's political skills, but for the remainder of World War II he was a pliable instrument in their hands.

The effect of the Japanese occupation on Cambodia was less profound than it was elsewhere in Southeast Asia, but the overthrow of the French administration by the Japanese in March 1945, when the war was nearing its end, provided Cambodians with opportunities for political development. Pressed by the Japanese to do so, Sihanouk declared his country's independence, and for several months the government was led by Son Ngoc Thanh, a former editor of *Nagara Vatta,* who had been forced into exile in Japan in 1942.

Early postwar period

In October 1945, after the war was over, the French returned to Indochina, arrested Son Ngoc Thanh, and reestablished their control. Cambodia soon became an "autonomous state within the French Union," with its own constitution and a handful of political parties, but real power continued to rest in French hands. Between 1945 and the achievement of complete independence in 1953, however, several significant political developments occurred. The most important was the confrontation between Sihanouk and his advisers and the leaders of the pro-independence Democratic Party, which dominated the National Assembly. Cambodia was poorly prepared for parliamentary democracy, and the French were unwilling to give the National Assembly genuine power. The Democrats, for their part, suffered from internal dissension. The death in 1947 of their leader, Prince Yuthevong, was a severe blow, exacerbated by the assassination of Yuthevong's heir apparent, Ieu Koeuss, in early 1950. Outside Parliament, Son Ngoc Thanh, released from exile in France in 1951, formed a dissident movement, the Khmer Serei ("Free Khmer"), that opposed both Sihanouk and the French.

In June 1952 Sihanouk assumed control of the government. Many Cambodian students in France, among them Saloth Sar (who would become the future communist dictator Pol Pot), objected to Sihanouk's move, but inside Cambodia the king remained extremely popular. His self-styled "Royal Crusade" (a tour of several countries to elicit their support) wrested political independence from the French, anxious to compromise in any case, at the end of 1953. Sihanouk's success discredited the communist-dominated guerrilla movement in Cambodia—associated with the Viet Minh of Vietnam—and Son Ngoc Thanh's anticommunist Khmer Serei.

Independence. At the Geneva Conference convened in 1954 to reach a political settlement to the First Indochina War, Sihanouk's government was recognized as the sole legitimate authority within Cambodia. This decision prevented the Viet Minh from gaining any regional power in Cambodia, as they did in Laos.

While they recognized Sihanouk's role in gaining Cambodia's independence, Democrats and communists alike opposed his increasing authoritarianism. Unable to govern unopposed, Sihanouk abdicated the throne in March 1955 in favour of his father, Norodom Suramarit, and formed a mass political movement, the Sangkum Reastr Niyum ("People's Socialist Community"), whose members were forbidden to belong to other political parties. The effect of the move was to draw thousands of people away from the Democrats, who had expected to win the national elections scheduled for later in the year. When the elections took place, amid widely reported abuses by Sihanouk's police, the Sangkum won every seat in the National Assembly. From then until he was overthrown in 1970, Sihanouk was the central figure in Cambodian politics, sometimes as prime minister and—after his father's death in 1960, when no new monarch was named—as head of state. Overt political life was strictly controlled by the prince, his colleagues, and the police. Cambodian communists, a marginal group of fewer than a thousand members, operated clandestinely and enjoyed little success. In 1963 Saloth Sar, a schoolteacher who also was secretary of the party, fled Phnom Penh and took refuge in the forests along the Vietnamese border; from there he built the organization that later would be known as the Khmer Rouge.

Origin of the Khmer Rouge

Until the mid-1960s, when opposition to his rule intensified, Sihanouk was widely revered in Cambodia. He saw Thailand and what was then South Vietnam as the greatest threats to Cambodia's survival. These two countries were allied with the United States, which the prince distrusted. At the same time, Sihanouk feared the eventual success of the Vietnamese communists in their war against South Vietnam and the United States and was worried by the prospect of a unified Vietnam under communist control. To gain some freedom to maneuver, he proclaimed a policy of neutrality in international affairs. Convinced, however, of American involvement in two South Vietnamese-backed plots against the Cambodian state in 1959 and encouraged in his anti-Americanism by the French president Charles de Gaulle, whom he idolized, Sihanouk broke off relations with the United States in 1965. Soon afterward, he concluded secret agreements with the Vietnamese communists, who were allowed to station troops on Cambodian territory in outlying districts as long as they did not interfere with Cambodian civilians. The secret agreement protected Sihanouk's army from attacks by the Vietnamese but compromised his neutralist policies. After 1965, when the war in Vietnam intensified, he also edged toward an alliance with China.

Cambodia's internal politics after 1965 developed in a complex fashion. Elections in 1966, the first since 1951 not to be stage-managed by the prince, brought in a majority of National Assembly members who owed little or nothing to Sihanouk himself. Although the prince was still a revered figure among the rural populace, he became increasingly unpopular with the educated elite. Conservatives resented his break with the United States and his seemingly procommunist foreign policy, while Cambodian radicals opposed his internal policies, which were economically conservative and intolerant of dissent. A rebellion in Bătdâmbâng province in 1967, manipulated by local communists, convinced the prince that the greatest threat to his regime came from the radical sector, and without hesitation he began using severe measures—including imprisonment without trial, assassinations, and the burning of villages—to impose his will.

By 1969 Sihanouk's grip on Cambodian politics had loosened, and conflict between his army and communist guerrillas, especially in the northeast, had increased. Some anticommunist ministers led by Prince Sirik Matak and General Lon Nol plotted to depose Sihanouk, whose credibility with radicals had evaporated following his renewal of diplomatic relations with the United States. Sihanouk's elaborate policy of juggling major powers against each other had failed. Matak and Lon Nol worked closely with anticommunists in South Vietnam, including Son Ngoc Thanh, whose Khmer Serei movement had gained recruits among the Khmer-speaking minority in Vietnam.

Civil war. In March 1970, while the prince was visiting the Soviet Union, the National Assembly voted to remove him from office as chief of state. Confused and hurt, Sihanouk traveled on to Peking and accepted Chinese advice to resist the coup by taking charge of a united front government-in-exile. This government was to be allied with China and North Vietnam and was to use the Cambodian communist forces led by Saloth Sar, which only a few days before had been fighting against Sihanouk's army.

Lon Nol's government

In Phnom Penh, Lon Nol's new government was initially popular, particularly for his quixotic pledge to rid Cambodia of Vietnamese communist troops. In fact, the confrontation dragged Cambodia fully into the Vietnam conflict. In May 1970 an American and South Vietnamese task force invaded eastern Cambodia, but communist forces already had retreated to the west. Two offensives launched by Lon Nol—named for the semimythical Cambodian kingdom of Chenla—were smashed by the Vietnamese, and thereafter he assumed a defensive stance. North Vietnamese support for the communists diminished in 1973, following the cease-fire agreement reached in Paris with the Americans. The Cambodian communists, however, refused to adhere to the agreements, and in 1973 they were subjected to a massive American aerial bombardment—this occurring despite the fact that the United States and Cambodia were not at war and that no American troops were endangered by Cambodia. The bombing slowed communist attacks on Phnom Penh and wreaked havoc in the heavily populated countryside around the capital. The civil war lasted for two more years, but already by the end of 1973 the Lon Nol government controlled only Phnom Penh, the northwest, and a handful of provincial towns.

In the meantime, Sihanouk declined in importance. By the end of 1973 the Cambodian communists controlled every aspect of the resistance, although they still claimed Sihanouk as a figurehead. Lon Nol's isolated regime in Phnom Penh continued to receive large quantities of American aid, increasing opportunities for corruption.

In April 1975 the Lon Nol government collapsed. Communist forces entered Phnom Penh and immediately ordered its inhabitants to abandon the city and take up life in rural areas. Phnom Penh and other cities and towns throughout the country were emptied in less than a week. Thousands of city dwellers died on the forced marches, but in subsequent years conditions worsened.

Democratic Kampuchea. Over the next six months, following the directives of a still-concealed Communist Party of Kampuchea, Cambodia experienced the most rapid and radical social transformation in its history. Money, markets, and private property were abolished. Schools, hospitals, shops, offices, and monasteries were closed. Nothing was published, no one could travel without permission, and everyone was ordered to wear peasant work clothes. As in Mao Zedong's China, the poorest peasants were favoured at everyone else's expense—an irony that probably escaped the largely bourgeois leaders of the communist movement themselves. A handful of these men and women controlled everything in the country, but they remained in hiding and explained few of their decisions. Instead, they urged everyone to "build and defend" the country. In April 1976 Sihanouk resigned as head of state, soon after a new constitution had renamed the country Democratic Kampuchea. An unknown figure named Pol Pot became prime minister, and more than a year passed before observers outside the country were able to identify him as Saloth Sar.

Khmer Rouge policies

In 1976–77 the new regime, following the lead of Maoist China, sought to achieve the total collectivization of Cambodia, mobilizing its population into an unpaid labour force and seeking to double the average prerevolutionary yields of rice immediately and on a national scale. The human costs of this ill-conceived experiment were enormous. Conservative estimates are that between April 1975 and early 1979, when the regime was overthrown, at least one million Cambodians—about 15 percent of the total population—died from overwork, starvation, disease, or execution. Parallels have been drawn between these events and the fate of European Jews in World War II, Mao's Great Leap Forward in China in the late 1950s, and Josef Stalin's collectivization of Ukrainian agriculture in the Soviet Union in the 1930s. The Soviet and Chinese experiments, rather than the European Holocaust, appear to have been used as models by the Khmer Rouge, although the proportion of the population killed in Cambodia was greater than it had been in China or the Soviet Union. The number of deaths stemmed from the literalism with which plans were carried out, the cruelty of the inexperienced communist cadres, and—as far as executions were concerned—the suspicions of the leadership that the failure of their experiment could be traced to "traitors" in the pay of foreign powers. The Communist Party's interrogation centre in Phnom Penh was the site of more than 20,000 such executions. Those tortured and put to death included many who had served the party faithfully for years—victims of the extreme paranoia of Pol Pot and his colleagues.

Vietnamese intervention. The Khmer Rouge initially had been trained by the Vietnamese, but since the early 1970s they had been resentful and suspicious of Vietnam and Vietnamese intentions. Scattered skirmishes between the two sides in 1975 had escalated into open warfare by the end of 1977. Despite continuing infusions of Chinese aid, the Cambodians were no match for the Vietnamese forces. In December 1978 a large Vietnamese army moved into Cambodia, brushing aside the Democratic Kampuchean forces. Within two weeks the government had fled Phnom Penh for Thailand, and the Vietnamese had installed a puppet regime—the People's Republic of Kampuchea—consisting largely of Cambodian communists who had deserted Pol Pot in 1977–78.

Over the next decade, under the relatively benign tutelage of the Vietnamese, Cambodia struggled back to its feet. Private property was restored, schools and Buddhist practices were reintroduced, cities were repopulated, and, with freedom of movement, trade flourished. At the same time, at least 500,000 Cambodians, some one-fifth of them associated with the communists, fled to Thailand in the aftermath of Democratic Kampuchea's fall and because of the hardship, uncertainty, and disorder that accompanied the installation of the new regime. Of these, perhaps 200,000 people, including most of the surviving members of Cambodia's educated elite, sought refuge in other countries, while the rest came under the control of three resistance groups camped along the Thai-Cambodian border: Norodom Sihanouk and his followers, the Khmer Rouge, and the noncommunists under the leadership of Son Sann (a former prime minister). These groups were supported financially by foreign powers anxious to oppose Vietnam. Thousands of Cambodians continued to enter Thailand in the 1980s, and by the end of the decade those in refugee camps were thought to exceed 300,000.

In 1982 an uneasy alliance was reached among the three groups opposing the Vietnamese-backed regime in Phnom Penh, and a government-in-exile was established with Sihanouk as president and Son Sann as prime minister. This government, despite United Nations recognition, received little support from Cambodians inside the country and was largely ineffectual. The member groups of the coalition continued independently to resist the Phnom Penh regime, with the larger and better-equipped forces of the Khmer Rouge being the most effective.

Sihanouk's government-in-exile

Cambodia since 1990. The political stalemate that developed among the four groups vying for power was broken in the late 1980s, when international political pressure, an economic boycott of Cambodia led by the United States, and a reduction in aid from the Soviet Union contributed to Vietnam's decision to withdraw its forces from Cambodia (completed in 1989). Freed from Vietnamese tutelage, the Phnom Penh government took two initiatives that increased its popularity and were impossible to rescind: it legalized the ownership of real estate and officially encouraged the practice of Buddhism. The withdrawal of the Vietnamese also allowed the resistance factions to seek through negotiation the political objectives that they had been unable to obtain by military action against the Phnom Penh government; they were encouraged in this endeavour by their foreign patrons.

These negotiations, which had been conducted for some time and which had intensified after 1989, led in 1991 to two significant results. The first was the creation of a largely ceremonial coalition government—the Supreme National Council (SNC)—that contained representatives of all four factions. Although the SNC was recognized by the United Nations, effective control in most of Cambodia remained in the hands of the Phnom Penh regime. The second and more important result was the conclusion of a peace agreement among the factions that also provided for a popularly elected government. The UN Security Council, with the backing of the factions, endorsed this treaty and agreed to establish in the country a peacekeeping operation consisting of both soldiers and civil servants, which would monitor progress toward conducting elections, temporarily run several government ministries, and safeguard human rights. The operation, inaugurated in January 1992, has been difficult to implement, notably because of the lack of cooperation by the Khmer Rouge. By many measures, however, it has been considered a success, especially given the animosity among the factions that had produced an almost constant state of civil war, the battered condition of Cambodia's economic infrastructure, and such unacceptable alternatives for most Cambodians as the return of the communists to power or the prospect of the country being divided among its neighbours.

(DAVID P. CHANDLER)

Vietnam

HISTORY

World War II and independence. For five years during World War II, Indochina was a French-administered possession of Japan. On Sept. 22, 1940, Jean Decoux, the French governor-general appointed by the Vichy government after the fall of France, concluded an agreement with the Japanese that permitted the stationing of 30,000 Japanese troops in Indochina and the use of all major Vietnamese airports by the Japanese military. The agreement made Indochina the most important staging area for all Japanese military operations in Southeast Asia. The French administration cooperated with the Japanese occupation forces and was ousted only toward the end of the war (in March 1945), when the Japanese began to fear that the French forces might turn against them as defeat approached. After the French had been disarmed, Bao Dai, the last French-appointed emperor of Vietnam, was allowed to proclaim the independence of his country and to appoint a Vietnamese national government at Hue, but all real power remained in the hands of the Japanese military commanders.

Japanese ouster of the French

Meanwhile, in May 1941, at Ho Chi Minh's urging, the Communist Party formed a broad nationalist alliance under its leadership called the League for the Independence of Vietnam, which subsequently became known as the Viet Minh. After a short period in jail, Ho was released by the Chinese and began to cooperate with Allied forces by providing information on Japanese troop movements in Indochina. At the same time, he sought recognition of the Viet Minh as the legitimate representative of Vietnamese nationalist aspirations. When the Japanese surrendered in August 1945, the communist-led Viet Minh ordered a general uprising, and, with no one organized to oppose them, they were able to seize power in Hanoi. Bao Dai, the Vietnamese emperor, abdicated a few days later and declared his fealty to the newly proclaimed Democratic Republic of Vietnam.

Clearly the Communist Party had gained the upper hand in its struggle to outmaneuver its disorganized rivals, such as the noncommunist VNQDD. The French, however, were determined to restore their own colonial presence in Indochina and, with the aid of British occupation forces, seized control of Cochinchina. Thus, at the beginning of 1946, there were two Vietnams: a communist north and a noncommunist south.

(JOSEPH BUTTINGER/WILLIAM J. DUIKER)

The First Indochina War. Negotiations between the French and Ho Chi Minh led to an agreement in March 1946 that appeared to promise a peaceful solution. Under the agreement France would recognize the Viet Minh government and give Vietnam the status of a free state within the French Union. French troops were to remain in Vietnam, but they would be withdrawn progressively over five years. For a period in early 1946 the French cooperated with Ho Chi Minh as he consolidated the Viet Minh's dominance over other nationalist groups, in particular those politicians who were backed by the Chinese Nationalist Party.

Despite tactical cooperation between the French and the Viet Minh, their policies were irreconcilable: the French aimed to reestablish colonial rule, while Hanoi wanted total independence. French intentions were revealed in the decision of Georges-Thierry d'Argenlieu, the high commissioner for Indochina, to proclaim Cochinchina an autonomous republic in June 1946. Further negotiations did not resolve the basic differences between the French and the Viet Minh. In late November 1946 French naval vessels bombarded Haiphong, causing several thousand civilian casualties; the subsequent Viet Minh attempt to overwhelm French troops in Hanoi in December generally is considered to be the beginning of the First Indochina War.

Outbreak of war

Initially confident of victory, the French long ignored the real political cause of the war—the desire of the Vietnamese people, including their anticommunist leaders, to achieve unity and independence for their country. French efforts to deal with this problem were devious and ineffective. The French reunited Cochinchina with the rest of Vietnam in 1949, proclaiming the Associated State of Vietnam, and appointed the former emperor Bao Dai as chief of state. Most nationalists, however, denounced these maneuvers, and leadership in the struggle for independence from the French remained with the Viet Minh.

Meanwhile, the Viet Minh waged an increasingly successful guerrilla war, aided after 1949 by the new communist government of China. The United States, fearful of the spread of communism in Asia, sent large amounts of aid to the French. But the French were shaken by the fall of their garrison at Dien Bien Phu in May 1954 and agreed to negotiate an end to the war at an international conference in Geneva.

The two Vietnams (1954–65). The agreements concluded in Geneva in April–July 1954 (collectively called the Geneva Accords), which were signed by French and Viet Minh representatives, provided for a cease-fire and for a temporary division of the country into two military zones at latitude 17° N. All Viet Minh forces were to withdraw north of that line, and all French and Associated State of Vietnam troops were to remain south of it; permission was granted for refugees to move from one zone to the other within a given time limit. An international commission was established, composed of Canadian, Polish, and Indian members under an Indian chairman, to supervise the execution of the agreement.

This agreement left the Democratic Republic of Vietnam in control of only the northern half of the country. The last of the Geneva Accords—called the Final Declaration—provided for elections, supervised by the commission, to be held throughout Vietnam in July 1956 in order to unify the country. Viet Minh leaders appeared certain to win these elections, and the United States and South Vietnam would not approve or sign the Final Declaration; elections were never held.

The two Vietnams now began to reconstruct their war-ravaged country. With assistance from the Soviet Union and China, the Hanoi government in the north embarked on an ambitious program of socialist industrialization; they also began to collectivize agriculture in earnest in 1958. In the south a new government appointed by Bao Dai began to build a new country. Ngo Dinh Diem, a Roman Catholic, was named prime minister and succeeded with American support in stabilizing the anticommunist regime in Saigon. He eliminated pro-French elements in the military and abolished the local autonomy of several religious-political groups. Then, in a government-controlled referendum in October 1955, Diem removed Bao Dai as chief of state and made himself president of the Republic of Vietnam.

Rule of Diem

Diem's early success in consolidating power did not result in concrete political and economic achievements. Plans for land reform were sabotaged by entrenched interests. With the financial backing of the United States, the regime's chief energies were directed toward building up the military and a variety of intelligence and security forces to counter the still-influential Viet Minh. Totalitarian methods were directed against all who were regarded as opponents, and the favouritism shown to Roman Catholics alienated the majority Buddhist population. Loyalty to the president and his family was made a paramount duty, and Diem's brother, Ngo Dinh Nhu, founded an elitist party to clandestinely spy on officials, army officers, and prominent local citizens. Diem also refused to participate in the all-Vietnamese elections described in the Final Declaration. With support from the north, communist-led forces—popularly called the Viet Cong—launched an insurgency movement to seize power and reunify the country. The insurrection appeared close to succeeding, when Diem's army overthrew him in November 1963. Diem and his brother Nhu were killed in the coup.

The Second Indochina War. The government that seized power after Diem's ouster, however, was no more effective than its predecessor. A period of political instability followed, until the military firmly seized control in June 1965 under Nguyen Cao Ky. The militant Buddhists who had helped overthrow Diem strongly opposed Ky's government, but he was able to break their resistance. Civil liberties were restricted, political opponents—denounced as neutralists or pro-communists—were imprisoned, and political parties were allowed to operate only if they did not openly criticize government policy. The character of the regime remained largely unchanged after the presidential elections in September 1967, which led to the election of General Nguyen Van Thieu as president.

No less evident than the oppressive nature of the Saigon regime was its inability to cope with the Viet Cong. Aided by a steady infiltration of weapons and advisers from the north, the fighting strength of the insurgent movement grew from about 30,000 men in 1963 to about 150,000 in 1965 when, in the opinion of many American intelligence analysts, the survival of the Saigon regime was seriously threatened. In addition, the political opposition in the south to Saigon became much more organized. The National Front for the Liberation of the South, popularly called the National Liberation Front (NLF), had been organized in late 1960; within four years it had a huge following.

Growing American involvement in the war. Until 1960 the United States had supported the Saigon regime and its army only with military equipment, financial aid, and, as permitted by the Geneva Accords, 700 advisers for training the army. The number of advisers had increased to 17,000 by the end of 1963, and they were joined by an increasing number of American helicopter pilots. All this assistance, however, proved insufficient to halt the advance of the Viet Cong, and in February 1965 U.S. President Lyndon B. Johnson ordered the bombing of North Vietnam, hoping to prevent further infiltration of arms and troops into the south. Four weeks after the bombing began, the United States started sending troops into the south. By July the number of U.S. troops had reached 75,000; it continued to climb until it stood at more than 500,000 early in 1968. Fighting beside the Americans were some 600,000 regular South Vietnamese troops and regional and self-defense forces, as well as smaller contingents from South Korea, Thailand, Australia, and New Zealand.

Buildup of U.S. troops

Three years of intensive bombing of the north and fighting in the south, however, did not weaken the will and strength of the Viet Cong and their allies from the north. Infiltration of personnel and supplies down the famous Ho Chi Minh Trail continued at an escalated level, and regular troops from the north—now estimated at more than 100,000—played a growing role in the war. The continuing strength of the insurgent forces became evident in the so-called Tet Offensive of February 1968, during which the Viet Cong and North Vietnamese attacked more than 100 cities and military bases, holding on to some for several weeks. After that, a growing conviction in the U.S. government that continuing the war at the current levels was no longer politically acceptable led President Johnson to order a restriction of the bombing in the north. This decision opened the way for U.S. negotiations with Hanoi, which began in Paris in May 1968. After the bombing was halted over the entire north in November 1968, the Paris talks were enlarged to include representatives of the NLF and the Saigon regime.

The war continued under a new American president, Richard M. Nixon. Nixon began to withdraw U.S. troops gradually, but public opposition to the war escalated after he ordered attacks on the Ho Chi Minh Trail in Laos and Viet Cong sanctuaries inside Cambodia. In the meantime, the peace talks went on in Paris. (JOSEPH BUTTINGER/ MILTON EDGEWORTH OSBORNE/WILLIAM J. DUIKER)

Withdrawal of American troops. Finally, in January 1973 a peace treaty was signed by the United States and all three Vietnamese parties. It provided for the complete withdrawal of U.S. troops within 60 days and created a political process for the peaceful resolution of the conflict in the south. Nothing was said, however, about the presence of more than 100,000 North Vietnamese troops in South Vietnam. Signing the Paris Agreement did not bring an end to the fighting in Vietnam. The Saigon regime made a determined effort to eliminate the communist forces remaining in the south, while northern leaders continued to strengthen their own forces in preparation for a possible future confrontation. By late 1974, Hanoi had decided that victory could be achieved only through armed struggle, and early the next year North Vietnamese troops launched a major offensive against the south. Saigon's forces retreated in panic and disorder, and President Thieu ordered the abandonment of several northern provinces. Thieu's effort to stabilize the situation was too late, however, and on April 30, 1975, the communists entered Saigon in triumph. The Second Indochina War was finally at an end.

The Socialist Republic of Vietnam. Following the communist victory, Vietnam remained theoretically divided until July 2, 1976, when the Socialist Republic of Vietnam was officially proclaimed, with its capital at Hanoi. Vietnam at peace faced formidable problems. In the south alone, millions of people had been made homeless by the war, and more than one-seventh of the population had been killed or wounded; the costs in the north were probably as high or higher. Plans to reconstruct the country called for the expansion of industry in the north and of agriculture in the south. Within two years of the communist victory, however, it became clear that Vietnam would face major difficulties in realizing its goals.

Reunification of the country

Hanoi had been at war for more than a generation—indeed, Ho Chi Minh had died in 1969—and the bureaucracy was poorly trained to deal with the problems of peacetime economic recovery. The government encountered considerable resistance to its policies, particularly in the huge metropolis of Saigon (renamed Ho Chi Minh City in 1976), where members of the commercial sector—many of whom were ethnic Chinese—sought to avoid cooperating in the new socialist economic measures and resisted assignment to "new economic zones" in the countryside. During the late 1970s, the country also suffered major floods and drought that severely reduced food production. When the regime suddenly announced a program calling for the socialization of industry and agriculture in the south in early 1978, hundreds of thousands (mainly ethnic Chinese) fled the country on foot or by boat.

These internal difficulties were compounded by problems in foreign affairs. Perhaps unrealistically, the regime decided to pursue plans to form a close alliance with new revolutionary governments in neighbouring Laos and Cambodia (Kampuchea). Such plans risked incurring not only the hostility of the United States but also that of China, which had its own interests in those countries. As Sino-Vietnamese relations soured, Hanoi turned to Moscow and signed a treaty of friendship and cooperation with the Soviet Union. In the meantime, relations with the revolutionary Democratic Kampuchea (Khmer Rouge) government in Cambodia rapidly deteriorated when it refused Hanoi's offer of a close relationship among the three countries of the Indochinese Peninsula. Savage border fighting culminated in a Vietnamese invasion of Cambodia in December 1978. The Khmer Rouge were dislodged from power, and a pro-Vietnamese government was installed in Phnom Penh.

Khmer Rouge forces now took refuge in isolated areas of the country and began a guerrilla war of resistance against the new government, the latter backed by some 200,000 Vietnamese troops. In the meantime, China launched a brief but fierce punitive invasion along the Sino-Vietnamese border in early 1979 in response to Vietnamese actions in Cambodia. In less than three weeks, the Chinese destroyed major Vietnamese towns and inflicted heavy damage in the frontier zone, but they also suffered heavy casualties from the Vietnamese defenders.

Vietnam was now nearly isolated in the world. Apart from the protégé regime in Phnom Penh and the government of Laos, which also was heavily dependent on Vietnamese aid for its survival, the country was at odds with the remainder of its regional neighbours. The member states of the Association of Southeast Asian Nations opposed the Vietnamese occupation of Cambodia and joined with China in supporting guerrilla resistance forces represented by the Khmer Rouge and various noncommunist Cambodian groups. An economic trade embargo with Vietnam was imposed by the United States and most other Western countries. Only the Soviet Union and its allies in eastern Europe stood by Vietnam.

Under such severe external pressure, Vietnam suffered continuing economic difficulties. The cost of stationing troops in Cambodia and of maintaining a strong defensive position along the Chinese border was especially heavy. To make matters worse, the regime encountered continuing problems in integrating the southern provinces into a socialist economy. In the early 1980s the government announced a number of reforms to encourage efforts to build up the economy. Then, with the death of veteran party chief Le Duan in 1986 (Le Duan had succeeded Ho Chi Minh as party chief in 1960), the party launched a major program patterned after the Soviet Union's strategy of perestroika (restructuring). Vietnam also offered a number of concessions to bring about a peace settlement in Cambodia.

Vietnam's economic difficulties

The results of these changes have been inconclusive. New party leaders have announced their willingness to abandon doctrinaire Marxist-Leninist ideology in order to achieve rapid economic growth, but they have been unwilling to share power with noncommunist elements; a new constitution enacted in 1992, however, was seen as a step toward loosening party control of the government. In the meantime, a final peace settlement in Cambodia has remained elusive. Since the breakup of the Soviet Union in the early 1990s, Hanoi has improved relations with China, but its full acceptance into the family of nations has yet to be realized.

(MILTON EDGEWORTH OSBORNE/WILLIAM J. DUIKER)

Bibliography: Recent Books

The following list encompasses some 100 recent books in English that have been judged significant contributions to learning and understanding in their respective fields. Each citation includes a few lines of commentary to indicate the general tenor of the work. The citations are organized by broad subject area, using the 10 parts of the *Propædia* as an outline.

Matter and Energy

Steven Weinberg, *Dreams of a Final Theory* (1992), a challenging argument in favour of the Superconducting Super Collider and an explanation of its potential contribution to high-energy physics and to progress toward a single unified theory that would explain why nature is the way it is.

Gianfranco Vidali, *Superconductivity: The Next Revolution?* (1993), a clearly set-forth history of superconductivity, explaining its relation to quantum mechanics and discussing future applications.

William H. Brock, *The Norton History of Chemistry* (1993), an indispensable historical summary arranged by major schools of thought that discusses the texts and theories they have inspired.

Gary Taubes, *Bad Science: The Short Life and Weird Times of Cold Fusion* (1993), a lively account of a notorious scientific debacle, making the point that "Nature cannot be fooled."

John Gribbin, *In the Beginning: After COBE and Before the Big Bang* (1993), a history of the universe supporting the notion that it is a living organism and exploring the question, What is life?

Harry Y. McSween, Jr., *Stardust to Planets: A Geological Tour of the Solar System* (1993), a sprightly anecdotal introduction to planetary geology that tours Earth's "cosmic neighborhood," describing not only the planets (including the Earth) but also asteroids, comets, and the Moon and its "stony blanket."

The Earth

G. Brent Dalrymple, *The Age of the Earth* (1991), an authoritative history of methods employed to determine the age of the Earth, such as the study of rocks—including Moon rocks—analysis of meteorites, and radiometric techniques.

James Hamilton-Paterson, *The Great Deep: The Sea and Its Thresholds* (1992), a lyrically written appreciation of the sea and its profound importance to humankind, with meditations on everything from marine biology to seasickness.

Life on Earth

Peter Ward, *On Methuselah's Trail: Living Fossils and the Great Extinction* (1992), a fascinating and readable history of the evolution of prehistoric life-forms along with descriptions of the few "living fossils" that have survived and provided such remarkable insight into the "great extinction."

Howard Ensign Evans, *Pioneer Naturalists: The Discovery and Naming of North American Plants and Animals* (1993), lively profiles of 19th- and early 20th-century naturalists (arranged alphabetically) who discovered and classified the heretofore unknown flora and fauna of the American wilderness.

Andrew Kimbrell, *The Human Body Shop* (1993), a sobering look at the "bioindustrial age" and the ethical, technological, and philosophical dilemmas the world community will confront with the mining of DNA and other human and animal biochemicals.

Robin Marantz Henig, *A Dancing Matrix: Voyages Along the Viral Frontier* (1993), an unusual approach to viral research that analyzes how and why new viruses come into existence and that suggests that the age-old equilibrium between viruses and their human hosts is being upset by such social dislocations as economic depression, war, and overpopulation.

Donald Griffin, *Animal Minds* (1992), a scholarly, clearly written study of animal cognition providing convincing evidence that it is not sentimental anthropomorphism to assert that animals think and plan.

Sue Hubbell, *Broadsides from the Other Orders: A Book of Bugs* (1993), a chatty, entertaining, and informative study by a librarian turned beekeeper that provides an introduction to numerous insects and also to the entomologists who study them.

Tom Harris, *Death in the Marsh* (1991), a gripping and ominous description of the hunt for selenium, a toxic killer of wildlife, that exposes careless (and worse) water-management practices.

Richard Douthwaite, *The Growth Illusion: How Economic Growth Has Enriched the Few, Impoverished the Many, and Endangered the Planet* (1993), a sombre warning against continued heedless exploitation of the planet and its people, urging renewed attention to quality rather than unbridled growth.

W. Edward Stead and Jean Garner Stead, *Management for a Small Planet* (1992), a straightforward and commonsense argument for neutralizing the conflict between uncontrolled economic growth and "ecological sustainability," using business-management techniques in a pragmatic approach to conservation.

Garrett Hardin, *Living Within Limits: Ecology, Economics, and Population Taboos* (1993), a vivid, hard-hitting prescription for slowing the rate of overpopulation and the exhaustion of Earth's resources that it causes, with remedies suggested that may shock some and give nightmares to others.

James Howard Kunstler, *The Geography of Nowhere: The Rise and Decline of America's Man-Made Landscape* (1993), a gloomy but far from hopeless picture of present-day America's loss of community, character, and natural beauty because people see "their landscape as [an] exploitable commodity rather than [a] social resource."

Human Life

Christopher Stringer and Clive Gamble, *In Search of the Neanderthals* (1993), a challenging, well-reasoned argument that the Neanderthals were an evolutionary "dead end," not in the direct line of descent to modern humans.

Frank Ryan, *The Forgotten Plague: How the Battle Against TB Was Won—and Lost* (1993), a history of medicine's centuries-old effort to defeat tuberculosis, giving long-overdue recognition to the many scientists and physicians whose research brought victory within reach—until multi-drug-resistant bacteria and the AIDS virus returned this scourge to dangerous prominence.

Peter D. Kramer, *Listening to Prozac* (1993), a thought-provoking look at the ethical issues raised by psychopharmacology: do antidepressant drugs banish grief and "divine discontent" and foster "seamless" personalities?

Timothy Ferris, *The Mind's Sky: Human Intelligence in a Cosmic Context* (1992), a metaphysical study of the "galaxy of intelligences" in each mind that reveals the mind's interrelationship with the universe.

Mihaly Csikszentmihalyi, *The Evolving Self: A Psychology for the Third Millennium* (1993), a persuasive argument that understanding the human evolutionary past frees the self and enables it to give order and purpose to life.

George P. Fletcher, *Loyalty: An Essay on the Morality of Relationships* (1993), a wide-ranging discussion of the phenomenon that foresees a change in the nature of the commitment loyalty mandates, from a cerebral obligation to a more emotional bond.

Donald A. Norman, *Things That Make Us Smart* (1993), a clarion call for the kind of human-centred technology that would produce machines responsive to the way the human mind works rather than insistent on the mind's conforming to the machine.

C. John Sommerville, *The Discovery of Childhood in Puritan England* (1992), a readable and informative study of the beginnings of the concept of child development and of the child as a unique and special being, traced through Puritan emphasis on the family.

Human Society

Tim D. White, *Prehistoric Cannibalism at Mancos 5MTUMR-2346* (1992), an engrossing example of anthropology and prehistoric archaeology using meticulously amassed evidence to point, in this instance, to cannibalistic practices among the Anasazi of southwestern Colorado in the 12th century AD.

Michael Carrithers, *Why Humans Have Cultures: Explaining Anthropology and Social Diversity* (1993), an appreciation of the diversity, creativity, and flexibility of the interactive human intelligence that underlies cultures and an exploration of some fundamental issues in anthropology today.

Halim Barakat, *The Arab World: Society, Culture, and State* (1993), a comprehensive portrait of Arab society, its inner dynamics, and its complexity and a contribution to deeper understanding of Arabs and the Arab world.

Margaret Hindle Hazen and Robert M. Hazen, *Keepers of the Flame: The Role of Fire in American Culture, 1775–1925* (1992), a novel approach to America's urban and industrial past, using fire in its benign (the candle), malignant (great urban conflagrations), and romantic (the reappearance of the fireplace in domestic architecture) aspects as the point of entry into social history.

R. Howard Bloch, *Medieval Misogyny and the Invention of Western Romantic Love* (1991), a scholarly history of gender and the relation between men and women as influenced by and portrayed in courtly love literature.

William Rathje and Cullen Murphy, *Rubbish: The Archaeology of Garbage* (1992), an informative study of the interaction between material culture and human behaviour as revealed in a detailed account of the Garbage Project.

Sumiko Iwao, *The Japanese Woman: Traditional Image and Changing Reality* (1993), an informed and clearly written explanation of the modern Japanese woman and the conflicts her traditions inflict on her, designed to emphasize the surprisingly numerous parallels with her Western sisters.

Jerry Z. Muller, *Adam Smith in His Time and Ours* (1993), an imaginative and incisive reassessment, based on close reading, that places Smith's relevance for contemporary policy primarily in his mode of thought.

Bill Orr, *The Global Economy in the Nineties: A User's Guide* (1992), a dictionary-style handbook on many aspects of global economics; for example, world markets, output and trade, and governments' fiscal-management tools.

Alexander Rosenberg, *Economics—Mathematical Politics or Science of Diminishing Returns?* (1992), an academic's view of the weakness of economics: its inability to predict outcomes any more accurately today than it did 200 years ago.

Jacqueline Jones, *The Dispossessed: America's Underclasses from the Civil War to the Present* (1992), a sweeping economic and social history of the poor—rural and urban, Northern and Southern—whose thesis is that "poverty abides no line drawn by color or culture."

Barry Eichengreen, *Golden Fetters: The Gold Standard and the Great Depression, 1919–1939* (1992), a coherent history of economic policy and an explanation of how regulation of international monetary affairs through the gold standard contributed to the 1930s Depression.

Paul Bairoch, *Economics and World History: Myths and Paradoxes* (1993), a work taking the stand that periods of economic growth in the past have coincided with protectionist policies rather than with free trade.

Ravi Batra, *The Myth of Free Trade: A Plan for America's Economic Revival* (1993), a promotion of the notion of "competitive protectionism" that encourages divestiture, government subsidies for research and development, and the dissolution of corporate giants.

Patrick Low, *Trading Free: The GATT and U.S. Trade Policy* (1993), a penetrating examination of changing U.S. attitudes toward the world trading system and their effect on the accountability of government in policy matters.

Andrew Bard Schmookler, *The Illusion of Choice: How the Market Economy Shapes Our Destiny* (1993), a warning against the continued complacency and unbridled materialism that is seen as a threat, rivaling war, to the survival of civilization.

Rex Martin, *A System of Rights* (1993), an illuminating treatise on the meaning, importance, and philosophy of rights of all kinds, making clear, for example, the very significant difference between rights and entitlements.

Bernard Schwartz, *Main Currents in American Legal Thought* (1993), a magisterial but eminently readable history of legal philosophy and thought in America from the nation's colonial origins to the present, portraying the humanistic aspects of the law and presenting analyses and sketches of many of the nation's great legal minds.

John T. Bruer, *Schools for Thought: A Science of Learning in the Classroom* (1993), an eloquent plea for effective teaching, which, in turn, demands understanding of human cognition and respect for the importance of knowing "why."

Seymour Papert, *The Children's Machine: Rethinking the School in the Age of the Computer* (1993), an interesting if oversimplified attempt to give computer technology for children a positive spin by pointing out the affinity for electronics even elementary schoolers seem to have; the author asserts that the computer can actually advance literacy and education for children and suggests ways to accomplish this.

Art

Rudolph Binion, *Love Beyond Death: The Anatomy of a Myth in the Arts* (1993), a revealing analysis and history of 19th-century fascination with the love-death "marriage," including such themes as faithfulness beyond the grave and vampires and extending to the heavy-metal music of the present.

Armando Petrucci, *Public Lettering: Script, Power, and Culture* (1993), an original approach to an aspect of civic history, comparing the inscriptions on Roman public buildings and monuments with the lack of inscriptions on medieval walls and the welter of 20th-century urban graffiti.

John Dizikes, *Opera in America: A Cultural History* (1993), a well-written, detailed, and carefully researched account of how opera crossed the Atlantic and combined indigenous (the Broadway musical) with European traditions; the work includes theatres, performers, and productions of everything from horse opera to grand opera, 1735 to the present.

Gérard Herzhaft, *Encyclopedia of the Blues* (1993), scholarly coverage of major and minor blues artists and their works with a history of trends, regional variations, instruments, and producers; the work contains a discography and bibliography as well.

Spiro Kostof, *The City Assembled: The Elements of Urban Form Through History* (1992), a thought-provoking and literate examination of what settlement patterns have had in common through the ages and in all places and how cities, composed of walled edges, streets, public areas, churches, and suburbs, have been planned (or evolve) and ultimately decay.

Marilyn Oliver Hapgood, *Wallpaper and the Artist: From Dürer to Warhol* (1992), a copiously illustrated, in-depth examination of 400 years of wallpaper as an art form that holds the mirror up to life in homes ranging from grand to modest.

Technology

Neil Postman, *Technopoly: The Surrender of Culture to Technology* (1992), a cogent argument, using a comprehensive history of inventions beginning with the wheel, that technology, though it has brought many benefits to humankind, has always had a degrading effect on culture and aesthetics and now is eroding the human capacity for original thinking.

Richard Gillespie, *Manufacturing Knowledge: A History of the Hawthorne Experiments* (1993), the story of a pioneering social science study, undertaken at Western Electric's Hawthorne Works in Cicero, Ill., between 1924 and 1933, that analyzed such topics as worker productivity, job satisfaction, and workplace organization.

Jamie Cassels, *The Uncertain Promise of Law: Lessons from Bhopal* (1993), a dramatic use of the world's most devastating single industrial catastrophe as a metaphor for the inadequacy of a legal system that cannot provide justice for victims, raising harrowing questions about the fate of future victims of dangerous technologies.

Stephen Doheny-Farina, *Rhetoric, Innovation, Technology: Case Studies of Technical Communication in Technology Transfers* (1992), a description of the many intermediate steps required for moving a technological innovation from the laboratory to the market, in which the author asserts that rhetoric plays a vital role and should be included in the education of technical communicators.

Vernon W. Ruttan (ed.), *Why Food Aid?* (1993), a collection of essays contributed by economists and experts on agriculture and food aid, dealing with farm technology, food distribution, and famine in less developed countries and analyzing current policy and the direction reform might take.

Donald Broadbent (ed.), *Simulation of Human Intelligence* (1993), eight essays by scientists from various disciplines exploring the progress toward a better understanding of human cognition and the phenomenon of language and asking whether computers can ever simulate human thinking.

Daniel Crevier, *AI: The Tumultuous History of the Search for Artificial Intelligence* (1993), a informative account—part business history, part intellectual history—describing the scramble to create systems that can capture the human decision-making process and including mention of the rival technology of artificial neural networks.

Francis Hamit, *Virtual Reality and the Exploration of Cyberspace* (1993), a resource guide for and an explanation of virtual reality and its social, political, and business implications, with software for accessing DIASPAR, the network that explores the educational aspects of virtual reality.

Jim Bradbury, *The Medieval Siege* (1992), an engrossing and detailed history of the siege, its tactics, and its technology, from the end of the 5th century to the mid-16th century, describing its influence on the structure of cities and of society.

Henry S.F. Cooper, *The Evening Star: Venus Observed* (1993), a well-constructed account of planetary exploration based on the Magellan space probe, tracking its pioneering voyage to Venus and its close-ups of that planet in 1980, which provided earthlings with their first detailed pictures of this evening star.

Religion

Graham Hancock, *The Sign and the Seal* (1993), a gripping tale of the author's search for the lost Ark of the Covenant that reads like detective fiction although it supplies considerable history, primarily concerning the Israelites and the Ethiopians.

Burton L. Mack, *The Lost Gospel: The Book of Q and Christian Origins* (1993), the authoritative culmination of painstaking work by generations of scholars to reconstruct the Gospel of Thomas, which records the sayings of Jesus rather than giving a narrative of his life, death, and resurrection and which supplies a vivid portrait of his world and times.

Bernard McGinn, *The Presence of God: A History of Western Christian Mysticism* (1991), a scholarly study of the historical roots of Western mysticism, establishing its debt to the mysticism of the ancient world and tracing its origins among the Latin Christians of the 4th century.

John L. Esposito, *The Islamic Threat: Myth or Reality?* (1992), an important effort to explain the many faces of Islam and its one billion adherents in 45 countries by providing an informative historical background and an analysis of contemporary attitudes and politics.

Bernard Lewis, *Islam and the West* (1993), a historical survey of Islamic-European encounters in war and peace, commerce and culture, followed by an account of Western perceptions (and misapprehensions) of Islam based on those encounters.

The History of Mankind

Lawrence Guy Straus, *Iberia Before the Iberians: The Stone Age Prehistory of Cantabrian Spain* (1992), a specialized but clearly written effort to redress the balance of information on Stone Age art in France by examining the region north of the Bay of Biscay and supplying convincing evidence of a rich yet overlooked prehistoric culture.

John Wilkes, *The Illyrians* (1992), an authoritative study of the peoples, called Illyrians by the Greeks and the Romans and the probable ancestors of today's Albanians, who were living in the northwestern Balkans from about the 4th century BC.

Gay Robins, *Women in Ancient Egypt* (1993), a path-breaking study, based on both social history and the surviving art and documents, of this seldom-examined aspect of Egyptian life, which includes material about women of the lower classes.

Roger Bagnall, *Egypt in Late Antiquity* (1993), a magisterial history of the period from the late 3rd to the 5th century AD, when Egypt was under Roman rule but occupied by the Greeks and becoming Christianized.

Fatima Mernissi, *The Forgotten Queens of Islam* (1993), a fascinating history of 15 women who became rulers of Islam (the political entity) over the past 15 centuries and whose long-hidden stories reveal some surprising facts about the world of Muslim women.

Walter A. McDougall, *Let the Sea Make a Noise . . . a History of the North Pacific from Magellan to MacArthur* (1993), an ambitious and idiosyncratic but enthralling epic history of one-sixth of the Earth, the nations that lie along its shores, and their diverse cultures, meticulously researched and crammed with brilliant insights.

Alain Peyrefitte, *The Immobile Empire: The First Great Collision of East and West—the Astonishing History of Britain's Grand, Ill-Fated Expedition to Open China to Western Trade, 1792–94* (1992; originally published in French, 1989), an authoritative history of the opening of China, drawn from the unpublished and little-known diary of the only Englishman on the expedition to learn Chinese, the 12-year-old son of one of the British diplomats.

Richard Bowring and Peter Kornicki (eds.), *The Cambridge Encyclopedia of Japan* (1993), a complete, carefully researched, and beautifully produced volume arranged by topic (*e.g.,* geography, history, language and literature, religion, arts, politics), ideal for either the browser or the researcher.

James F. Searing, *West African Slavery and Atlantic Commerce: The Senegal River Valley, 1700–1860* (1993), a detailed and scholarly account, based on both oral traditions and European sources, of the effect of 18th-century slave commerce on the Senegal River valley societies.

William L. Fash, *Scribes, Warriors, and Kings: The City of Copán and the Ancient Maya* (1991), a synthesis of recent archaeological and linguistic advances that makes a persuasive argument for the study of early Mayan peasants and craftspeople as well as their elite rulers.

Tatiana Proskouriakoff, *Maya History* (1993), the posthumous work of a distinguished scholar in which written and archaeological records from primary Mayan sites in Yucatán, Belize, El Salvador, Guatemala, and Honduras are used as the basis for new historical data and insights, adding to what is known about this civilization.

Ted Morgan, *Wilderness at Dawn: The Settling of the North American Continent* (1993), a broad chronological panorama from 15,000 years ago to 1800 that focuses on the common people—red, yellow, white, and brown—and what they contributed to life in North America.

Anthony Reid, *Southeast Asia in the Age of Commerce: 1450–1680,* vol. 2, *Expansion and Crisis* (1993), a clear and engrossing account of the changes that defined the Age of Commerce, such as the spice trade, and the global boom that isolated Asia for the next 300 years by precipitating an economic crisis.

Stefan Kanfer, *The Last Empire: De Beers, Diamonds, and the World* (1993), an absorbing chronicle of the De Beers cartel from its beginnings as a farmstead to its development into the global gold and diamond giant that became South Africa's unsavoury shadow government.

Margaret T. Bixler, *Winds of Freedom: The Story of the Navajo Code Talkers of World War II* (1992), the dramatic story of forgotten heroes of the Pacific campaign in World War II, a group of Navajo soldiers who employed their native language as a code that proved to be indecipherable and who thus helped to shorten the U.S. war against the Japanese.

Harold G. Moore and Joseph L. Galloway, *We Were Soldiers Once—and Young: Ia Drang: The Battle That Changed the War in Viet Nam* (1992), the devastating events of a savage battle recounted by General Moore in unflinchingly comprehensive detail.

George Black and Robin Munro, *Black Hands of Beijing: Lives of Defiance in China's Democracy Movement* (1993), an informative and chilling account of three of the democracy movement's chief architects and conspirators before, during, and after Tiananmen Square and about whom little is known in the West.

Jeremy Harding, *The Fate of Africa: Trial by Fire* (1993), a readable and up-to-date account of the conditions in six African nations, in which the author, a journalist who is familiar with the continent, offers his impressions based on interviews and travel through Angola, Namibia, South Africa, Mozambique, Western Sahara, and Eritrea.

Kwame Anthony Appiah, *In My Father's House: Africa in the Philosophy of Culture* (1992), a profound, provocative philosophical meditation on African intellectual and political life pointing out the necessity for reciprocal and interdisciplinary understanding and exchange among Old, New, and Third Worlds.

The Branches of Knowledge

Jerry P. King, *The Art of Mathematics* (1992), an academic mathematician's chatty and informal effort to lower the resistance to his discipline by nonmathematicians as he offers a glimpse of the power and beauty of mathematics.

Annemarie Schimmel, *The Mystery of Numbers* (1993), an engrossing historical biography of numbers 1–22 (with a selection of other numbers as well), including number magic, number science, and number symbolism and dealing with most of the societies that developed symbols to express quantity.

Roger Lewin, *Complexity: Life at the Edge of Chaos* (1992), a chatty, simply expressed narrative description of the arcane principles of complexity and chaos and of the search for rules that would provide "a grand unification" of the life sciences.

Nina Hall (ed.), *Exploring Chaos: A Guide to the New Science of Disorder* (1991), a collection of articles on the new directions of mathematics—fractals and chaos theory—with lucid insights by well-known mathematicians and physicists that clarify the relationship between orderliness and randomness, subjects that are currently the focus of scholarly attention.

Nina Siu-Ngan Lam and Lee DeCola, *Fractals in Geography* (1993), a clear and intelligible explanation of the latest in physics and mathematics as applied to physical and human geography, written with both the layperson and the specialist in mind.

David Darling, *Equations of Eternity: Speculations on Consciousness, Meaning, and the Mathematical Rules That Orchestrate the Cosmos* (1993), philosophical and metaphysical reflections on human participation in the creation of the reality they observe.

Jo Ann Shroyer, *Quarks, Critters, and Chaos: What Science Terms Really Mean* (1993), a lexicon offering brief, clear definitions of the newest theories and developments in major scientific fields and including among its 100 entries explanations of the Gaia hypothesis, virtual reality, and cold fusion.

Paul Hoyningen-Heune, *Reconstructing Scientific Revolutions* (1993; originally published in German, 1989), a recapitulation of Thomas Kuhn's influential philosophy of science (1962), bringing it up to date with developments in the theory of knowledge and historiography.

Lawrence M. Krauss, *Fear of Physics: A Guide for the Perplexed* (1993), a reassuringly simple description of physics, which, the author maintains, is a "human, creative, intellectual activity, like art and music," with a glance at some of the cosmic questions physicists ask and try to answer.

David Lindley, *The End of Physics* (1993), an elegant speculation on the future of physics if a Unified Theory were to turn out to be unattainable, which concludes that if only the unanswerable questions remained, mythology would be the sole satisfactory response.

John Dupré, *The Disorder of Things: Metaphysical Foundations of the Disunity of Science* (1993), an ingenious use of biology as an example of the disorder, complexity, and pluralism of science in contrast to the principle of unity (whose advocates Dupré characterizes as "reductionist determinists").

John A. Moore, *Science as a Way of Knowing: The Foundations of Modern Biology* (1993), an original discussion of the biological limits that affect all ecosystems and that are revealing the "deficit spending" of the Earth's resources.

Arthur Zajonc, *Catching the Light: The Entwined History of Light and Mind* (1993), an intriguing approach to one of life's essentials, exploring its history and its poetic and scientific aspects.

Francis Haskell, *History and Its Images: Art and the Interpretation of the Past* (1993), a masterly and original synthesis of visual art with narrative history pointing out how they illuminate and explain each other.

Paul F. Gehl, *A Moral Art: Grammar, Society, and Culture in Trecento Florence* (1993), a readable scholarly account of the interaction of grammar, literacy, and culture in medieval Florence, its effect on all aspects of life, from mercantile to religious, and its culmination in the intellectual flowering of the Renaissance.

Mortimer J. Adler, *The Four Dimensions of Philosophy: Metaphysical, Moral, Objective, Categorical* (1993), a lucid overview of the principles and procedures of philosophy from antiquity to the present. (JEAN S. GOTTLIEB)

CONTRIBUTORS

Allaby, Michael. Writer and Lecturer. Author of *Ecology Facts; A Guide to Gaia.*
ENVIRONMENT *(in part)*
Allan, J.A. Professor of Geography, School of Oriental and African Studies, University of London.
WORLD AFFAIRS: *Libya*
Amedeo, Michael. Writer, Encyclopædia Britannica Educational Corp.; Freelance Entertainment Writer, *Chicago Sun-Times.*
BIOGRAPHIES *(in part)*
Anderson, D.F. Director, Department of Economic Affairs, International Iron & Steel Institute, Brussels. Author of *Steel Demand Forecasting* and others.
INDUSTRIAL REVIEW: *Iron and Steel*
Archibald, John J. Retired Feature Writer, *St. Louis* (Mo.) *Post-Dispatch;* Adjunct Professor, Washington University, St. Louis; Member of Professional Bowlers Association Hall of Fame.
SPORTS AND GAMES: *Bowling (in part)*
Armour, Ian D. Freelance Researcher and Writer. Coauthor of *Imperial Germany 1890–1918.*
WORLD AFFAIRS: *Bosnia and Herzegovina:* Special Report
Arnold, Guy. Freelance Writer. Author of *Modern Nigeria; Aid in Africa;* and others.
WORLD AFFAIRS: *Botswana; Burundi; Cape Verde; Chad; Comoros; Djibouti; Equatorial Guinea; Gambia, The; Ghana; Guinea-Bissau; Lesotho; Liberia; Madagascar; Maldives; Mauritius; Nigeria; Rwanda; São Tomé and Príncipe; Seychelles; Sierra Leone; Swaziland*
Arnold, Mavis. Freelance Journalist, Dublin.
WORLD AFFAIRS: *Ireland*
Arrington, Leonard J. Formerly Church Historian, Church of Jesus Christ of Latter-day Saints.
RELIGION: *Church of Jesus Christ of Latter-day Saints*
Balaban, Avraham. Professor of Modern Hebrew Literature, University of Florida, Gainesville. Author of *Between God and Beast: An Examination of Amos Oz's Prose.*
LITERATURE: *Hebrew*
Baptist, Ines T. Freelance Writer.
WORLD AFFAIRS: *Belize*
Barford, Michael F. Editor and Director, *Tabacosmos,* London.
INDUSTRIAL REVIEW: *Tobacco*
Barrett, David B. Hon. Research Adviser, United Bible Societies; Church Missionary Society, Church of England.
RELIGION: *World Religious Statistics*
Barrett, John C.A. Headmaster, The Leys School, Cambridge, England; Secretary, British Committee, World Methodist Council. Author of *Family Worship in Theory and Practice.*
RELIGION: *Methodist Churches*
Bass, Howard. Journalist and Broadcaster; Ice Hockey Correspondent, *Daily Telegraph,* London; Skiing and Skating Correspondent, *Daily Mail,* London. Author of 16 books on winter sports.
BIOGRAPHIES *(in part);* SPORTS AND GAMES: *Ice Hockey (in part); Ice Skating; Skiing*
Belaski, Ann. Copy Editor, Encyclopædia Britannica, Inc.
BIOGRAPHIES *(in part)*
Bernstein, Ellen. Editor, Encyclopædia Britannica Yearbooks.
BIOGRAPHIES *(in part)*
Bickelhaupt, David L. Professor Emeritus, Faculty of Finance, College of Business, Ohio State University, Columbus.
INDUSTRIAL REVIEW: *Insurance*
Bird, Thomas E. Director, Council for the Study of Ethics and Public Policy, Queens College, City University of New York.
LITERATURE: *Yiddish*
Bisman, Ronald W. North Island Editor, *New Zealand Harness Racing Weekly.* Author of *Cardigan Bay; Salute to Trotting.*
SPORTS AND GAMES: *Horse Racing (in part)*
Boddy, William C. Founder and Editor, *Motor Sport.* Full Member, Guild of Motoring Writers.
SPORTS AND GAMES: *Automobile Racing (in part)*
Boden, Edward. Publications Adviser, British Veterinary Association; formerly Editor, *Veterinary Record.*
HEALTH AND DISEASE: *Veterinary Medicine*
Booth, John Nicholls. Lecturer and Writer. Author of *The Quest for Preaching Power.*
RELIGION: *Unitarian (Universalist) Churches*
Boothroyd, Andrew T. University Lecturer and Fellow of Oriel College, Oxford Department of Physics, Clarendon Laboratory, University of Oxford, England.
PHYSICS
Boswall, Jeffery. Senior Lecturer in Biological Imaging, University of Derby, England.
LIFE SCIENCES: *Ornithology*
Box, Ben. Editor, Trade and Travel Publications *(South American Handbook* and others).
WORLD AFFAIRS: *Bolivia; Haiti; Panama; Peru; Venezuela*
Boye, Roger. Former Coin Columnist, *Chicago Tribune.*
PHILATELY AND NUMISMATICS: *Coins and Paper Money*
Boylan, Patrick J. Professor and Head, Department of Arts Policy and Management, City University, London. Author of *Museums 2000: Politics, People, Professionals and Profit* and others.
MUSEUMS *(in part)*
Bradsher, Henry S. Foreign Affairs Writer.
WORLD AFFAIRS: *Philippines*
Braidwood, Robert J. Professor Emeritus of Old World Prehistory, Oriental Institute and Department of Anthropology, University of Chicago. Author of *Prehistoric Men.*
ARCHAEOLOGY: *Eastern Hemisphere*
Brazee, Rutlage J. Geophysical Consultant.
EARTH SCIENCES: *Geophysics*
Brecher, Kenneth. Professor of Astronomy and Physics, Boston University. Coauthor and coeditor of *Astronomy of the Ancients.*
ASTRONOMY; ASTRONOMY: Sidebar
Brokopp, John G. Specialist in publicity, public relations, and writing about horse racing.
SPORTS AND GAMES: *Horse Racing (in part)*
Brooks, Tony. Retired Secretary-General, International Table Tennis Federation.
SPORTS AND GAMES: *Table Tennis*
Brown, Bess. Senior Research Analyst, Radio Free Europe/Radio Liberty.
WORLD AFFAIRS: *Kazakhstan; Kyrgyzstan; Tajikistan; Turkmenistan; Uzbekistan*
Brown, Heidi C.D. Technical Information Officer, British Glass Manufacturers Confederation, Sheffield, England.
INDUSTRIAL REVIEW: *Glass*
Brown, Maggie. Media Editor, The Independent Newspapers, London.
PUBLISHING: *Magazines (in part); Newspapers (in part)*
Brown-Humes, Christopher. Stockholm Correspondent, *Financial Times.*
WORLD AFFAIRS: *Sweden*
Burdin, Joel L. Coordinator of Educational Administration, Frostburg (Md.) State University.
EDUCATION *(in part)*
Burks, Ardath W. Emeritus Professor of Asian Studies, Rutgers University.
WORLD AFFAIRS: *Japan*
Butler, Frank. Former Sports Editor, *News of the World,* London. Author of *The Good, The Bad and The Ugly: A Story of Boxing.*
SPORTS AND GAMES: *Boxing*
Buttinger, Joseph. Freelance Writer. Author of *Vietnam: A Dragon Embattled.*
Macropædia: SOUTHEAST ASIA *(in part)*
Cafferty, Bernard. Associate Editor, *British Chess Magazine;* Chess Columnist, *The Sunday Times,* London.
SPORTS AND GAMES: *Chess*
Cameron, Sarah. Freelance Writer and Editor, Trade and Travel Publications.
WORLD AFFAIRS: *Costa Rica; Cuba; Dominican Republic; El Salvador; Guatemala; Honduras; Nicaragua*
Campbell, Robert. Architect and Architecture Critic. Author of *Cityscapes of Boston;* Coauthor of *American Architecture of the 1980s.*
ARCHITECTURE
Cantrell, Scott. Classical Music Editor, *Kansas City* (Mo.) *Star.*
MUSIC: *Classical*
Carter, Robert W. Journalist, London.
SPORTS AND GAMES: *Horse Racing (in part)*
Chandler, David P. Associate Professor of History, Monash University, Clayton, Australia. Author of *The Tragedy of Cambodian History.*
Macropædia: SOUTHEAST ASIA *(in part)*
Chapman, Kenneth F. Former Editor, *Stamp Collecting* and *Philatelic Magazine.*
PHILATELY AND NUMISMATICS: *Stamps*
Chappell, Duncan. Director, Australian Institute of Criminology.
CRIME, LAW ENFORCEMENT, AND PENOLOGY: *Crime; Law Enforcement*
Chapple, Abby. Writer and Consultant, Consumer Communications, Annapolis, Md.
INDUSTRIAL REVIEW: *Furniture*
Cheuse, Alan. Writing Faculty, English Department, George Mason University, Fairfax, Va.; Book Commentator, National Public Radio. Author of *The Light Possessed* and others.
LITERATURE: *English (in part)*
Clapham, Christopher S. Professor of Politics and International Relations, University of Lancaster, England. Author of *Transformation and Continuity in Revolutionary Ethiopia.*
WORLD AFFAIRS: *Eritrea; Ethiopia*
Clark, Janet H. Research Manager, Sedgwick Noble Lowndes. Author of *Europe's Labour Costs Crisis.*
ECONOMIC AFFAIRS: Special Report
Clarke, Judith L. Lecturer, Department of Journalism, Baptist College, Hong Kong.
WORLD AFFAIRS: *Cambodia; Vietnam*
Clarke, R.O. Lecturer and Consultant on Industrial Relations, London.
LABOUR-MANAGEMENT RELATIONS
Clough, Huw. Freelance Writer on Iberia and Latin America; Multimedia Editor.
WORLD AFFAIRS: *Chile; Colombia; Ecuador; Mexico*
Cogle, T.C.J. Consultant, *Electrical Review,* London.
INDUSTRIAL REVIEW: *Electrical*
Collins, Cheryl L. Freelance Writer.
BIOGRAPHIES *(in part)*
Cook, Kevin G. Global Publications Officer, International Organization of Consumers Unions, Santiago, Chile.
CONSUMER AFFAIRS *(in part)*
Cooper, Mary H. Staff Writer, *The CQ Researcher, Congressional Quarterly.* Author of *The Business of Drugs.*
LABOUR-MANAGEMENT RELATIONS: Special Report
Cooper, Melanie Anne. Senior Editorial Assistant, *Newsweek* magazine.
WORLD AFFAIRS: *United States:* Developments in the States in 1993
Costin, Stanley H. British Correspondent,

Nykytekstiili, Finland, and *Textilia,* The Netherlands.
FASHION AND DRESS *(in part)*
Coveney, Michael. Theatre Critic, *The Observer.* Author of *Maggie Smith: A Bright Particular Star* and others.
THEATRE *(in part)*
Craine, Anthony G. Copy Editor, Encyclopædia Britannica, Inc.
BIOGRAPHIES *(in part)*
Crampton, Richard J. Fellow, St. Edmund Hall, Oxford, England; formerly Professor of East European History, University of Kent at Canterbury. Author of *Bulgaria 1878–1918: A History* and others.
WORLD AFFAIRS: *Bulgaria*
Crowley, Edward. U.K. Editor, *Maritime Monitor,* Piraeus, Greece; Technical Journalist; Director, Technical Writing Services.
INDUSTRIAL REVIEW: *Shipbuilding;* TRANSPORTATION *(in part)*
Cunningham, Susan M. Economic and Political Analyst; Freelance Writer. Author of *Latin America Since 1945* (in preparation).
WORLD AFFAIRS: *Argentina; Brazil; Latin-American Affairs*
Curwen, Peter J. Reader in Business Policy, Sheffield Business School, England. Author of *The U.K. Publishing Industry* and others.
PUBLISHING: *Books (in part)*
Cviic, K.F. East European Specialist, Royal Institute of International Affairs, London.
WORLD AFFAIRS: *Bosnia and Herzegovina; Croatia; Macedonia; Slovenia; Yugoslavia*
Czerwinski, Edward J. Professor Emeritus of Slavic and Comparative Literature, State University of New York at Stony Brook. Author of *Contemporary Polish Theater and Drama (1956–1984);* Area Editor, *Theater Companies of the World.*
LITERATURE: *Eastern European (in part); Russian (in part)*
Davis, Donald A. Editor, *Drug & Cosmetic Industry* and *Cosmetic Insider's Report.*
INDUSTRIAL REVIEW: *Pharmaceuticals*
Deam, John B. Retired Technical Director, AMT—The Association for Manufacturing Technology, McLean, Va.
INDUSTRIAL REVIEW: *Machinery and Machine Tools*
de la Barre, Kenneth. Director, Katimavik, Montreal.
WORLD AFFAIRS: *Arctic Regions*
Deletant, Dennis J. Senior Lecturer in Romanian Studies, University of London. Author of *Studies in Romanian History; Colloquial Romanian.*
WORLD AFFAIRS: *Romania*
Denselow, Robin. Rock Music Critic, *The Guardian,* London; Current Affairs Reporter, BBC Television. Author of *When the Music's Over: The Politics of Pop.*
MUSIC: *Popular*
de Puy, Norman R. Minister, American Baptist Churches; Editor and Publisher, *Cabbages and Kings* newsletter.
RELIGION: *Baptist Churches*
Dicks, Geoffrey R. U.K. Economist, NatWest Markets. Author of *Sources of World Financial and Banking Information.*
INDUSTRIAL REVIEW: *Introduction*
Dirnbacher, Elfriede. Austrian Civil Servant.
WORLD AFFAIRS: *Austria*
Dixon, Bernard. Science Writer; Consultant. European Editor, *Bio/Technology;* Editor, *Medical Science Research.* Author of *Health and the Human Body* and others.
HEALTH AND DISEASE: *Mental Health; Overview (in part)*
Dooling, Dave. Consultant and Writer, D^2 Associates, Huntsville, Ala.
SPACE EXPLORATION
Dormer, Albert G. Bridge Correspondent, *The Times,* London. Coauthor of *Complete Book of Bridge* and others.
SPORTS AND GAMES: *Contract Bridge*
Dorris, Thomas Hartley. Communications Director, Life and Peace Institute, Uppsala, Sweden.
RELIGION: *Lutheran Communion*
Duiker, William J. Professor of East Asian History, Pennsylvania State University, University Park. Author of *The Communist Road to Power in Vietnam.*
Macropædia: SOUTHEAST ASIA *(in part)*
Earp, John H. Director, Halcrow Fox and Associates, Bristol, England.
TRANSPORTATION *(in part)*
Ehringer, Gavin Forbes. Rodeo Columnist, *Western Horseman,* Colorado Springs, Colo.
SPORTS AND GAMES: *Rodeo*
Eisenhammer, John. Chief Correspondent on Germany, *The Independent,* London.
WORLD AFFAIRS: *Germany*
Ellis, Roger. Editor, *Mining Journal.*
MINING
Emerson, Warren K. Writer and Photographer.
SPORTS AND GAMES: *Badminton*
Engels, Jan R. Retired Director, Centre Paul Hymans.
WORLD AFFAIRS: *Belgium*
Esposito, John L. Professor of Religion and International Affairs and Director of the Center for Muslim-Christian Understanding, Georgetown University. Author of *Islam: The Straight Path.*
WORLD AFFAIRS: *Middle Eastern Affairs:* Special Report
Farr, D.M.L. Professor Emeritus of History, Carleton University, Ottawa.
WORLD AFFAIRS: *Canada*
Fendell, Robert J. Newspaper Writer on automotive topics. Author of *How to Make Your Car Last* and others.
SPORTS AND GAMES: *Automobile Racing (in part)*
Finkelstein, Ellen. Product Coordinator, Encyclopædia Britannica, Inc.
BIOGRAPHIES *(in part);* HEALTH AND DISEASE: Sidebar; POPULATION AND POPULATION MOVEMENTS: Sidebar
Fisher, Lester E. Veterinarian and President of L.E.F. Co., Chicago.
BOTANICAL GARDENS AND ZOOS: Special Report
Flagg, Gordon. Senior Editor, *American Libraries* magazine.
LIBRARIES *(in part)*
Follett, Christopher. Denmark Correspondent, *The Times,* London; Danish Correspondent, Radio Sweden; Newscaster, Radio Denmark; Freelance Correspondent, Reuters. Author of *Fodspor paa Cypern.*
WORLD AFFAIRS: *Denmark*
Fornes, Andréa. Tokyo Correspondent, *Folha de São Paulo.*
BIOGRAPHIES *(in part)*
Fossli, Karen L. Oslo Correspondent, *Financial Times.*
WORLD AFFAIRS: *Norway*
Friday, Elbert W., Jr. Assistant Administrator for Weather Services, National Oceanic and Atmospheric Administration.
EARTH SCIENCES: *Meteorology*
Fridovich, Irwin. James B. Duke Professor of Biochemistry, Duke University Medical Center, Durham, N.C.
LIFE SCIENCES: *Molecular Biology (in part)*
Fridovich-Keil, Judith L. Assistant Professor, Department of Genetics and Molecular Medicine, Emory University School of Medicine, Atlanta, Ga.
LIFE SCIENCES: *Molecular Biology (in part)*
Friskin, Sydney E. Hockey Correspondent, *The Times,* London.
SPORTS AND GAMES: *Billiard Games (in part); Field Hockey*
Frost, David. Rugby Union Writer, *The Guardian,* London.
SPORTS AND GAMES: *Football (in part)*
Fuller, Elizabeth. Senior Research Analyst, Radio Free Europe/Radio Liberty Research Institute.
WORLD AFFAIRS: *Armenia; Azerbaijan; Georgia*
Gaddum, Anthony H. Chairman, H. T. Gaddum and Company Ltd., Silk Merchants, Macclesfield, Cheshire, England; Deputy Vice President, International Silk Association.
INDUSTRIAL REVIEW: *Textiles (in part)*
Ganado, Albert. Lawyer, Malta.
WORLD AFFAIRS: *Malta*
Ganguly, Dilip. Senior Correspondent, The Associated Press (USA), South Asia Bureau, New Delhi, India.
WORLD AFFAIRS: *Afghanistan; Bangladesh; Bhutan; Myanmar (Burma); Nepal; Pakistan; Sri Lanka*
Gibbons, Anne R. Freelance Writer.
LIFE SCIENCES: *Entomology*
Gibbons, J. Whitfield. Professor of Zoology, University of Georgia's Savannah River Ecology Laboratory, Aiken, S.C.
LIFE SCIENCES: *Zoology*
Gill, Martin J. Editor, *World Fishing Magazine.*
AGRICULTURE AND FOOD SUPPLIES: *Fisheries*
Girnius, Saulius A. Senior Research Analyst, Radio Free Europe/Radio Liberty Research Institute.
WORLD AFFAIRS: *Latvia; Lithuania*
Goldblatt, Howard C. Professor of Chinese, University of Colorado, Boulder. Author of *Chinese Literature for the 1980s* and others.
LITERATURE: *Chinese*
Goldsmith, Arthur. Editor-at-Large, *Popular Photography,* New York City.
PHOTOGRAPHY
Gottfried, Martin. Drama Critic, New York City. Author of *All His Jazz: The Life and Death of Bob Fosse; More Broadway Musicals.*
THEATRE *(in part)*
Gottlieb, Jean S. Freelance Editor.
BIBLIOGRAPHY
Greeman, Adrian Lee. Editor, *Construction Today.*
ENGINEERING PROJECTS: *Bridges*
Green, Anthony L. Senior Copy Editor, Encyclopædia Britannica, Inc.
BIOGRAPHIES *(in part)*
Greskovic, Robert J. Dance Reviewer, *Arts & Entertainment Monthly;* Freelance Writer.
DANCE *(in part)*
Griffiths, A.R.G. Senior Lecturer in History, Flinders University of South Australia. Author of *Contemporary Australia.*
BIOGRAPHIES *(in part);* WORLD AFFAIRS: *Australia; Nauru; Papua New Guinea*
Grossman, Joel W. Archaeologist.
ARCHAEOLOGY: *Western Hemisphere*
Grumet, Robert S. Anthropologist, New Hope, Pa.
ANTHROPOLOGY
Guthridge, Guy G. Manager, Polar Information Program, U.S. National Science Foundation.
WORLD AFFAIRS: *Antarctica*
Hands, David. Rugby Correspondent, *The Times,* London.
BIOGRAPHIES *(in part)*
Hannen, Mark. Competitions Officer, English Basket Ball Association.
SPORTS AND GAMES: *Basketball (in part)*
Harakas, Stanley S. Archbishop Iakovos Professor of Orthodox Theology, Holy Cross Greek Orthodox School of Theology, Brookline, Mass. Author of *Living the Faith: The "Praxis" of Eastern Orthodox Ethics.*
RELIGION: *The Orthodox Church; Oriental Orthodox Church*
Haub, Carl V. Demographer, Population Reference Bureau, Washington, D.C.
POPULATIONS AND POPULATION MOVEMENTS: *Demography*
Havard-Williams, P. Professor of Library and Information Studies, University of Botswana. Emeritus Professor, Loughborough University, Leicestershire, England.

LIBRARIES *(in part)*
Hawkland, William D. Chancellor Emeritus of Law and Boyd Professor, Louisiana State University.
LAW: *Court Decisions*
Hebblethwaite, Peter. Vatican Affairs Writer, *National Catholic Reporter,* Kansas City, Mo.
RELIGION: *Roman Catholic Church*
Hébert, Pierre. Professor *titulaire,* University of Sherbrooke, Que.
LITERATURE: *French (in part)*
Hemenway, Caroline. Freelance Writer and Editor.
NOBEL PRIZES *(in part)*
Hendershott, Myrl C. Professor of Oceanography, Scripps Institution of Oceanography, La Jolla, Calif.
EARTH SCIENCES: *Oceanography*
Hennelly, James. Researcher, Encyclopædia Britannica, Inc.
BIOGRAPHIES *(in part)*
Henschel, Milton. President, Watch Tower Bible and Tract Society.
RELIGION: *Jehovah's Witnesses*
Hoeksema, Klaas J. Staff Member, Institute for Polytechnics, Amsterdam.
WORLD AFFAIRS: *Netherlands, The; Suriname*
Hollobaugh, Jeff. Managing Editor, *Track and Field News.*
SPORTS AND GAMES: *Track and Field Sports*
Hope, Thomas W. Chairman, Hope Reports, Inc., Rochester, N.Y.
MOTION PICTURES *(in part)*
Hunnings, Neville March. Editorial Director, European Law Centre, Sweet & Maxwell, London. Editor, *Common Market Law Reports.*
LAW: *International Law*
IEIS. International Economic Information Services, London.
ECONOMIC AFFAIRS: *World Economy; Stock Exchanges (in part)*
Ingham, Kenneth. Emeritus Professor of History, University of Bristol, England. Author of *Politics in Modern Africa: The Uneven Tribal Dimension* and others.
WORLD AFFAIRS: *Angola; Kenya; Malawi; Mozambique; Sudan, The; Tanzania; Uganda; Zaire; Zambia; Zimbabwe*
Ingram, Derek. Editor, Gemini News Service, London. Author of *Commonwealth for a Colour-Blind World; The Imperfect Commonwealth.*
WORLD AFFAIRS: *Commonwealth of Nations*
Jackson, Martin. Consultant Editor, *Broadcast* magazine, London.
TELEVISION AND RADIO *(in part)*
Jardine, Adrian. Company Director. Member, Guild of Yachting Writers.
SPORTS AND GAMES: *Sailing*
Jaspert, W. Pincus. Technical and Editorial Consultant. International Editor, *American Printer* and *World-Wide Printer.* Author of *State of the Art* (4th ed.) and others.
INDUSTRIAL REVIEW: *Printing*
Jessell, Harry A. Executive Editor, *Broadcasting and Cable* magazine, Washington, D.C.
TELEVISION AND RADIO *(in part)*
Joffé, George. Journalist and Writer on North African and Middle Eastern Affairs.
WORLD AFFAIRS: *Algeria; Morocco; Tunisia*
Johnsson, William G. Editor, *Adventist Review.* Author of *Behold His Glory* and others.
RELIGION: *Seventh-day Adventist Church*
Jones, D.A.N. Novelist and Critic. Author of *Parade in Pairs; Never Had It So Good.*
LITERATURE: *Introduction; United Kingdom*
Jones, W. Glyn. Professor of European Literature, University of East Anglia, Norwich, England.
LITERATURE: *Danish*
Joseph, Lou. Freelance Science Writer, Chicago.
HEALTH AND DISEASE: *Dentistry*
Jotischky, Helma. Principal Research Officer, Paint Research Association, London.
INDUSTRIAL REVIEW: *Paints and Varnishes*
Juban, Yann. Jurist. International Wine and Vine Office, Paris.
INDUSTRIAL REVIEW: *Beverages (in part)*
Katz, William A. Professor, School of Information Science and Policy, State University of New York, Albany.
PUBLISHING: *Magazines (in part)*
Kelleher, John A. New Zealand Journalist. Formerly Editor, *The Dominion* and *Dominion Sunday Times,* Wellington, New Zealand.
WORLD AFFAIRS: *New Zealand*
Kellman, Jerold L. President, Gabriel House, Inc.
BIOGRAPHIES *(in part)*
Kellner, Peter. Political Commentator, BBC Television. Author of *The Civil Servants: An Inquiry into Britain's Ruling Class* and others.
BIOGRAPHIES *(in part);* WORLD AFFAIRS: *United Kingdom*
Kennedy, Richard M. Agricultural Economist, Agriculture and Trade Analysis Division of the Economic Research Service, U.S. Department of Agriculture.
AGRICULTURE AND FOOD SUPPLIES *(in part)*
Kilian, Michael D. Washington Columnist, *Chicago Tribune.* Author of *Flying Can Be Fun; Heavy Losses.*
SPORTS AND GAMES: *Aerial Sports*
Kimche, Jon. Formerly Editor, *New Middle East; Afro-Asian Affairs,* London. Author of *Palestine or Israel* and others.
WORLD AFFAIRS: *Israel*
Kind, Joshua B. Professor of Art History, Northern Illinois University, De Kalb. Author of *Rouault; Geometry as Abstract Art* and others.
MUSEUMS *(in part)*
Kirk, Margaret. United Kingdom Press Officer, Salvation Army.
RELIGION: *Salvation Army*
Kloos, Jean Clark Cameron. Consultant, Timber Research and Development Association.
INDUSTRIAL REVIEW: *Wood Products*
Knox, Richard A. Managing Editor, *Power Technology International* and *Power Generation Technology.*
INDUSTRIAL REVIEW: *Nuclear Industry*
Kolankiewicz, George. Lecturer in Sociology, University of Essex, England; Research Coordinator, Research Programme on East-West Studies, U.K. Economic and Social Research Council. Coauthor of *Social Groups in Polish Society* and others.
WORLD AFFAIRS: *Poland*
Kroll, Thomas E. Lecturer, Roosevelt University and Northwestern University; President, Thomas Kroll Associates. Author of *Introduction to Telecommunications.*
INDUSTRIAL REVIEW: *Microelectronics; Telecommunications*
Kushnick, Louis. Senior Lecturer, Department of American Studies, University of Manchester, England.
POPULATIONS AND POPULATION MOVEMENTS: *International Migration;* RACE AND ETHNIC RELATIONS
Lamb, Kevin M. Special Projects Writer, *Dayton* (Ohio) *Daily News.* Author of *Quarterbacks, Nickelbacks & Other Loose Change.*
BIOGRAPHIES *(in part);* SPORTS AND GAMES: *Football (in part)*
Laqueur, Walter. Chairman, International Research Council, Center for Strategic & International Studies, Washington, D.C. Author of *Europe in Our Time.*
WORLD AFFAIRS: *Introduction*
Larsson, Gerd. Japan Correspondent, *Dagens Industri.*
BIOGRAPHIES *(in part)*
Laskey, Elizabeth. Senior Copy Editor, Encyclopædia Britannica, Inc.
BIOGRAPHIES *(in part)*
Lawler, Nancy Ellen. Professor of Economics, Oakton Community College, Des Plaines, Ill. Author of *Soldiers of Misfortune* and others.
WORLD AFFAIRS: *Benin; Burkina Faso; Cameroon; Central African Republic; Congo; Côte d'Ivoire; Gabon; Guinea; Mali; Mauritania; Niger; Senegal; Togo*
Legassick, Martin. Senior Lecturer, History Department, University of the Western Cape, South Africa.
WORLD AFFAIRS: *Namibia; South Africa*
Legum, Colin. Associate Editor (1947–81), *The Observer;* Consultant Editor, *Africa Contemporary Record;* Editor, *Third World Reports,* London.
BIOGRAPHIES *(in part);* WORLD AFFAIRS: *African Affairs*
Lennox-Kerr, Peter. Editor, *High Performance Textiles* and *OE Report;* European Editor, *Textile World.* Author of *World Fibres Book.*
INDUSTRIAL REVIEW: *Textiles (in part)*
Levine, Beth S. Freelance Writer. Author of *Playgroups: A Complete Guide for Parents.*
PUBLISHING: *Books (in part)*
Levine, Lisbeth. Section Editor and Former Fashion Editor, *Chicago Sun-Times.*
FASHION AND DRESS *(in part); Fashion and Dress:* Sidebar
Levine, Steven I. Scholar in Residence, Asian-Pacific Studies Institute, Duke University, Durham, N.C. Author of *Anvil of Victory: The Communist Revolution in Manchuria* and others.
WORLD AFFAIRS: *China; Taiwan*
Litsky, Frank. Sportswriter, *New York Times.*
SPORTS AND GAMES: *Ice Hockey (in part)*
Litweiler, John. Jazz Critic; Contributor to *Down Beat, Chicago Tribune,* and other publications. Author of *Ornette Coleman: A Harmolodic Life.*
BIOGRAPHIES *(in part);* MUSIC: *Jazz*
Logan, Robert G. Sportswriter, *Daily Herald,* Arlington Heights, Ill. Author of *Cubs Win!* and others.
SPORTS AND GAMES: *Basketball (in part)*
Longmore, Andrew. Freelance Sportswriter, *The Times,* London; formerly Assistant Editor, *The Cricketer.*
BIOGRAPHIES *(in part);* SPORTS AND GAMES: *Cricket*
Luling, Virginia R. Social Anthropologist.
WORLD AFFAIRS: *Somalia*
McBride, Gail W. Freelance Medical Writer and Editor; formerly Medical News Editor, *Journal of the American Medical Association.*
HEALTH AND DISEASE: *Overview (in part)*
McCauley, Martin. Senior Lecturer in Politics, School of Slavonic and East European Studies, University of London.
WORLD AFFAIRS: *Commonwealth of Independent States*
Macdonald, Barrie. Professor of History, Massey University, Palmerston North, N.Z.
WORLD AFFAIRS: *Dependent States (in part); Fiji; Kiribati; Marshall Islands; Micronesia, Federated States of; Oceanian Affairs; Solomon Islands; Tonga; Tuvalu; Vanuatu; Western Samoa*
McGregor, Alan. Freelance Contributor, *The Times,* London; *The Lancet,* London; Swiss Radio International, Bern; CBS Radio, New York.
WORLD AFFAIRS: *Switzerland*
McLachlan, Keith S. Professor, School of Oriental and African Studies, University of London.
WORLD AFFAIRS: *Iran*
Mallett, H.M.F. Editor, *Wool Record Weekly Market Report,* Bradford, England.
INDUSTRIAL REVIEW: *Textiles (in part)*
Mango, Andrew. Foreign Affairs Analyst.
WORLD AFFAIRS: *Turkey*
Marples, David L. Associate Professor of History, University of Alberta, Canada. Author of *Ukraine Under Perestroika.*
WORLD AFFAIRS: *Belarus; Ukraine*
Martin, Marvin. Freelance Writer.
BIOGRAPHIES *(in part);* CONSUMER AFFAIRS: Sidebar; SOCIAL SECURITY AND WELFARE SERVICES: Sidebar; WORLD AFFAIRS: *Canada:* Sidebar; *United States:* Sidebar
Marty, Martin E. Fairfax M. Cone Distinguished Service Professor of the History of

Modern Christianity, University of Chicago.
RELIGION: Special Report
Mateja, James L. Auto Editor, Columnist, and Financial Reporter, *Chicago Tribune.* Author of *Used Cars: Finding the Best Buy.*
INDUSTRIAL REVIEW: *Automobiles (in part)*
Mathews, John H. Copy Editor, Encyclopædia Britannica, Inc.
BIOGRAPHIES *(in part)*
Matthíasson, Björn. Economist, Ministry of Finance, Iceland.
WORLD AFFAIRS: *Iceland*
Maunder, Michael. Head of Conservation Unit, Living Collections Department, Royal Botanic Gardens, Kew, England.
BOTANICAL GARDENS AND ZOOS *(in part)*
Mazie, David M. Staff Writer, *Reader's Digest;* Freelance Writer.
SOCIAL SECURITY AND WELFARE SERVICES *(in part)*
Mazze, Edward Mark. Dean, The Belk College of Business Administration, The University of North Carolina at Charlotte.
CONSUMER AFFAIRS *(in part);* INDUSTRIAL REVIEW: *Advertising*
Mermel, T.W. Consultant; formerly Chairman, Committee on World Register of Dams, International Commission on Large Dams.
ENGINEERING PROJECTS: *Dams; Dams table*
Michael, Tom. Writer, Encyclopædia Britannica, Inc.
BIOGRAPHIES *(in part)*
Millikin, Sandra. Architectural Historian.
ART EXHIBITIONS AND ART SALES: *Art Exhibitions;* ART EXHIBITIONS AND ART SALES: Sidebar
Modiano, Mario. Athens Correspondent (1952–90), *The Times,* London.
WORLD AFFAIRS: *Greece*
Moragne, Edward Paul. Index Supervisor, Encyclopædia Britannica, Inc.
BIOGRAPHIES *(in part)*
Morris, Jacqui M. Editor, *Oryx* magazine.
ENVIRONMENT *(in part)*
Morrison, Donald. Assistant Managing Editor, *Entertainment Weekly* magazine.
PUBLISHING: *Newspapers (in part);* WORLD AFFAIRS: *United States*
Nagy, Joseph L. Senior Editor, *Asiaweek* magazine, Hong Kong.
WORLD AFFAIRS: *Korea, Democratic People's Republic of; Korea, Republic of*
Naylor, Ernest. Lloyd Roberts Professor of Marine Zoology, University College of North Wales.
LIFE SCIENCES: *Marine Biology*
Netschert, Bruce C. Retired Vice President, National Economic Research Associates, Inc., Washington, D.C.
ENERGY
Neusner, Noam. Reporter, *Tampa Tribune.* Coauthor of *To Grow in Wisdom: An Anthology of Abraham J. Heschel.*
RELIGION: *Judaism*
Newby, Donald J. Bowls Correspondent, *Daily Telegraph,* London; formerly Editor, *World Bowls.* Author of various bowls publications.
SPORTS AND GAMES: *Lawn Bowls*
Niesz, Dale E. Director, Center for Ceramic Research, Rutgers University.
INDUSTRIAL REVIEW: *Ceramics*
Norman, Geraldine. Art Market Correspondent, *The Independent,* London. Author of *Nineteenth Century Painters and Painting;* Coauthor of *The Fake's Progress.*
ART EXHIBITIONS AND ART SALES: *Art Sales*
Nugent, Ann. Editor, *Dance Now;* Dance Critic, *The Stage.* Author of *Swan Lake: Stories of the Ballets.*
DANCE *(in part)*
Oberman, Bonnie. Writer and Editor.
NOBEL PRIZES *(in part)*
O'Donoghue, Michael. Lecturer in Gemmology, London Guildhall University.
INDUSTRIAL REVIEW: *Gemstones*
O'Dwyer, Thomas. Foreign Editor, *Jerusalem Post;* Writer on East Mediterranean and Middle East affairs.
WORLD AFFAIRS: *Cyprus*
Okano, Kazunori. Associate Editor, *Britannica International Yearbook,* Tokyo.
INDUSTRIAL REVIEW: *Automobiles (in part)*
Olney, P.J.S. Director, Federation of Zoos of Great Britain and Ireland. Editor, *International Zoo Yearbook.*
BOTANICAL GARDENS AND ZOOS *(in part)*
Olson, Kay Melchisedech. Executive Editor, *Flower & Garden* magazine, Kansas City, Mo.
GARDENING *(in part)*
Osborne, Keith. Editor, *British Rowing Almanack* (since 1960). Author of *Boat Racing in Britain, 1715–1975.*
SPORTS AND GAMES: *Rowing*
Osborne, Milton Edgeworth. Head, Asia-Pacific Branch, Office of National Assessments, Canberra, Australia. Author of *Southeast Asia: An Illustrated Introductory History.*
Macropædia: SOUTHEAST ASIA *(in part)*
Osterbind, Carter C. Associate, Gerontology Center, and Professor Emeritus of Economics, University of Florida.
INDUSTRIAL REVIEW: *Building and Construction*
Palmer, John. European Editor, *The Guardian,* Brussels.
WORLD AFFAIRS: *European Affairs (in part)*
Parker, Sandy. Publisher of weekly newsletter on fur industry; Copublisher, *Fur World.*
INDUSTRIAL REVIEW: *Furs*
Parming, Tönu. President, Estonian Publishing Co. Ltd., Toronto. Author of *A Case Study of a Soviet Republic: The Estonian SSR.*
WORLD AFFAIRS: *Estonia*
Pasco, Adam Gerhold. Editor, *BBC Gardeners' World* magazine; formerly Editor, *Garden News, Garden Answers,* and *Greenhouse* magazines.
GARDENING *(in part)*
Paul, Charles Robert, Jr. Consultant, U.S. Olympic Committee, Colorado Springs, Colo.
SPORTS AND GAMES: *Gymnastics; Weight Lifting*
Penfold, Robin C. Freelance Writer on industrial topics.
INDUSTRIAL REVIEW: *Plastics*
Perlinska, Agnieszka. Ph.D. Candidate in Department of Comparative Literature, New York University.
LITERATURE: *Eastern European (in part); Russian (in part)*
Pertile, Lino. Professor of Italian, University of Edinburgh, Scotland.
LITERATURE: *Italian*
Petherick, Karin. Reader in Swedish, University of London.
LITERATURE: *Swedish*
Pfeffer, Irving. Attorney. Author of *The Financing of Small Business.*
ECONOMIC AFFAIRS: *Stock Exchanges (in part)*
Pinfold, Geoffrey M. Director, NCL Stewart Scott Ltd., London. Author of *Reinforced Concrete Chimneys and Towers.*
ENGINEERING PROJECTS: *Buildings*
Poirié, François. Writer and Critic. Author of *La Passade légendaire; Ils dansent.*
LITERATURE: *French (in part)*
Polonsky, Naomi Bernards. Writer, Encyclopædia Britannica, Inc.
BIOGRAPHIES *(in part)*
Prasad, H.Y. Sharada. Formerly Information Adviser to the Prime Minister of India.
WORLD AFFAIRS: *India*
Prince, Greg W. Senior Editor, *Beverage World.*
INDUSTRIAL REVIEW: *Beverages (in part)*
Ranger, Robin. Senior Associate, National Institute for Public Policy, Washington, D.C.; Research Associate, CDISS, Lancaster University, U.K.
MILITARY AFFAIRS
Rapp, Susan. Associate Science Editor, *Compton's Encyclopedia.*
BIOGRAPHIES *(in part)*
Raymond, Judith E. Research Officer, Research and Documentation Branch, ISSA.
SOCIAL SECURITY AND WELFARE SERVICES *(in part)*
Rebelo, L.S. Reader Emeritus, Department of Portuguese Studies, King's College, University of London.
LITERATURE: *Portuguese (in part)*
Reed, Arthur. Senior Editor, Europe, *Air Transport World.* Author of *Britain's Aircraft Industry;* Coauthor of *RAE Farnborough.*
TRANSPORTATION *(in part)*
Reid, J.H. Professor of Contemporary German Studies, University of Nottingham, England. Author of *Writing Without Taboos: The New East German Literature* and others.
LITERATURE: *German*
Reid, Philip D. Louise C. Harrington Professor of Biological Sciences, Smith College, Northampton, Mass.
LIFE SCIENCES: *Botany*
Renwick, David. Freelance Journalist.
WORLD AFFAIRS: *Antigua and Barbuda; Bahamas, The; Barbados; Dependent States (in part); Dominica; Grenada; Guyana; Jamaica; Saint Kitts and Nevis; Saint Lucia; Saint Vincent and the Grenadines; Trinidad and Tobago*
Reynolds, Frank E. Professor of the History of Religions and Buddhist Studies, Divinity School, University of Chicago; Director, Institute for the Advanced Study of Religion.
RELIGION: *Buddhism (in part)*
Roberts, John. Tennis Correspondent, *The Independent,* London. Author of *The Team That Wouldn't Die.*
SPORTS AND GAMES: *Tennis*
Robinson, David. Film Critic and Historian, London. Author of *A History of World Cinema; Chaplin: His Life and Art.*
MOTION PICTURES *(in part)*
Roby, Anne. Freelance Writer and Editor.
WORLD AFFAIRS: *Andorra; Luxembourg; Monaco*
Rollin, Jack. Association Football Columnist, *Sunday Telegraph,* London. Editor, *Rothmans Football Yearbook.* Author of *World Cup 1930–1990* and others.
BIOGRAPHIES *(in part);* SPORTS AND GAMES: *Football (in part)*
Rutherford, Andrew. Reader, Faculty of Law, University of Southampton, England. Author of *Criminal Justice and the Pursuit of Decency* and others.
CRIME, LAW ENFORCEMENT, AND PENOLOGY: *Prisons and Penology*
Saeki, Shoichi. Professor Emeritus, Tokyo University. Author of *Japanese Autobiographies.*
LITERATURE: *Japanese*
Salisbury, Jonathan M. Publisher, *World Toy News,* U.K.
INDUSTRIAL REVIEW: *Games and Toys*
Saludo, Ricardo L. Senior Editor, *Asiaweek* magazine, Hong Kong.
WORLD AFFAIRS: *Indonesia; Malaysia*
Sanders, Alan J.K. Lecturer in Mongolian Studies, School of Oriental and African Studies, University of London. Author of *Mongolia: Politics, Economics and Society.*
WORLD AFFAIRS: *Mongolia*
Sarahete, Yrjö. General Secretary, Fédération Internationale des Quilleurs, Helsinki.
SPORTS AND GAMES: *Bowling (in part)*
Sarmiento, Sergio. Editor in Chief, Encyclopædia Britannica Publishers, Inc. (Latin America).
SPORTS AND GAMES: *Baseball (in part); Football (in part)*
Sauvage, Christian. Editor in Chief, Agence Presse Hachette; Chief of Political Service, *Journal du Dimanche.* Author of *Les Giscardiens.*
WORLD AFFAIRS: *France*
Scherer, Allan D. Director, United States Polo Association; Editor, *Polo Newsletter.*
SPORTS AND GAMES: *Polo*
Schneider, Johanna. Assistant Editor, *Amateur Wrestling News.*
SPORTS AND GAMES: *Wrestling*
Schoenfield, Albert. Member, U.S. Swimming

Olympic International Committee (1989–92). Formerly Publisher, *Swimming World*. Honouree, International Swimming Hall of Fame.
SPORTS AND GAMES: *Swimming*
Schöpflin, George. Lecturer in East European Political Institutions, London School of Economics and School of Slavonic and East European Studies, University of London.
WORLD AFFAIRS: *Czech Republic; European Affairs (in part); Hungary; Slovakia*
Schorr, Daniel. Senior News Analyst, National Public Radio. Author of *Clearing the Air; Don't Get Sick in America.*
Commentary: THE NEW WORLD DISORDER
Seddon, Stephen S. Index Editor, Encyclopædia Britannica, Inc.
BIOGRAPHIES *(in part)*
Shackleford, Peter. Chief of Environment, Planning, and Finance, World Tourism Organization, Madrid.
INDUSTRIAL REVIEW: *Tourism*
Shelley, Andrew. Events Manager, Squash Rackets Association, England.
SPORTS AND GAMES: *Squash Rackets*
Shepherd, Melinda C. Associate Editor, Encyclopædia Britannica Yearbooks.
WORLD AFFAIRS: *Dependent States (in part); Political Parties*
Sherry, Paul H. President, United Church of Christ, Cleveland, Ohio.
RELIGION: *United Church of Christ*
Slamecka, Vladimir. Emeritus Professor of Information and Computer Science, Georgia Institute of Technology, Atlanta. Coauthor of *National Information Systems.*
Macropædia: INFORMATION PROCESSING AND INFORMATION SYSTEMS
Smith, Donald. Editor, *Rubber World* magazine, Akron, Ohio.
INDUSTRIAL REVIEW: *Rubber*
Smith, Gregory O. Dean of Academic Affairs, American University of Rome.
WORLD AFFAIRS: *San Marino; Vatican City State*
Smith, Reuben W. Professor of History, University of the Pacific, Stockton, Calif.
RELIGION: *Islam*
Socor, Vladimir. Senior Research Analyst, Radio Free Europe/Radio Liberty Research Institute.
WORLD AFFAIRS: *Moldova*
Sorkin, Beverly E. Copy Editor, Encyclopædia Britannica, Inc.
BIOGRAPHIES *(in part)*
Spangenberg, N. Earl. Professor, College of Natural Resources, University of Wisconsin, Stevens Point. Editor, *HYDATA—News and Views.*
EARTH SCIENCES: *Hydrology*
Sparks, Karen M. Senior Editor, Encyclopædia Britannica Yearbooks.
WORLD AFFAIRS: *Liechtenstein*
Stephens, Sarah. Executive Secretary for Cooperation and Witness, World Alliance of Reformed Churches.
RELIGION: *Reformed, Presbyterian, and Congregational Churches*
Stern, Irwin. Senior Lecturer in Portuguese, Columbia University, New York City.
LITERATURE: *Portuguese (in part)*
Stewart, Ian. Professor of Mathematics, University of Warwick, England. Author of *Does God Play Dice?; Game, Set, and Math.*
MATHEMATICS
Støverud, Torbjørn. Honorary Research Fellow, University College, London.
LITERATURE: *Norwegian*
Sullivan, Christine. Freelance Writer.
BIOGRAPHIES *(in part)*
Sullivan, H. Patrick. Dean Emeritus of the College and Professor of Religion, Vassar College, Poughkeepsie, N.Y.
RELIGION: *Hinduism*
Summerhill, Edward M. Part-Time Staff Member, Reuters; Freelance Writer, Finnish News Agency.
WORLD AFFAIRS: *Finland*
Sumner, David E. Author of *The Episcopal Church's History: 1945–1985.* Columnist; Contributor to Episcopal Church periodicals.
RELIGION: *Anglican Communion*
Suzuki, Toshihiko. Senior Editor, Dobunshoin International, Tokyo.
SPORTS AND GAMES: *Baseball (in part)*
Swan, Russ. Editor, *World Highways,* Nottingham, England.
ENGINEERING PROJECTS: *Roads*
Swift, Richard N. Professor Emeritus of Politics, New York University, New York City.
WORLD AFFAIRS: *United Nations*
Synan, Vinson. Chairman, North American Renewal Service Committee. Author of *The Holiness-Pentecostal Movement.*
RELIGION: *Pentecostal Churches*
Taishoff, Lawrence B. Chairman, *Broadcasting and Cable* magazine, Washington, D.C.; Adviser, Cahners Consumer/Entertainment Publishing Division.
TELEVISION AND RADIO *(in part)*
Takayama, Hideko. Reporter, *Newsweek* magazine, Tokyo Bureau.
BIOGRAPHIES *(in part)*
Tateishi, Kay K. Freelance Writer and Translator, Tokyo.
BIOGRAPHIES *(in part)*
Taylor, Thomas F. General Secretary of Friends World Committee for Consultation.
RELIGION: *Religious Society of Friends*
Thomas, Robert Murray. Emeritus Professor of Education and Head, Program in International Education, University of California at Santa Barbara. Author of *International Comparative Education* and others.
EDUCATION *(in part)*
Turner, Darrell J. Writer on Religion; Former Editor and Writer, Religious News Service.
RELIGION: *Introduction*
UNHCR. The Office of the United Nations High Commissioner for Refugees.
POPULATIONS AND POPULATION MOVEMENTS: *Refugees*
Utt, Roger L. Editor, *Puerta del Sol,* Madrid; formerly Assistant Professor of Spanish, Department of Romance Languages and Literatures, University of Chicago.
LITERATURE: *Spanish (in part)*
Venzke, Bruce H. Associate Editor, *Pool & Billiard Magazine.* Member, Statistics and Records Committee, Billiard Congress of America; President, Billiard Congress of Wisconsin.
SPORTS AND GAMES: *Billiard Games (in part)*
Verdi, Robert William. Sports Columnist, *Chicago Tribune.*
SPORTS AND GAMES: *Baseball (in part)*
Wallenfeldt, Jeff. Copy Editor, Encyclopædia Britannica, Inc.
BIOGRAPHIES *(in part)*
Wallis, Shani. Independent Technical Journalist, London.
ENGINEERING PROJECTS: *Tunnels*
Walters, Jonathan S. Assistant Professor of Religion, Whitman College, Walla Walla, Wash.
RELIGION: *Buddhism (in part)*
Wanninger, Richard S. Director of Communications, United States Volleyball Association.
SPORTS AND GAMES: *Volleyball*
Warner, Edward S. Editor, *Telecom Data Networks* magazine, Telecom Publishing Group.
INFORMATION PROCESSING AND INFORMATION SYSTEMS *(in part)*
Warren, J. Robert. Executive Editor, *Chemical Business.*
INDUSTRIAL REVIEW: *Chemicals*
Way, Diane Lois. Historical Researcher.
BIOGRAPHIES *(in part)*
Weinthal, John R. Writer on the auto industry.
INDUSTRIAL REVIEW: *Automobiles (in part)*
Westberg, M. Victor. Manager, Committees on Publication, The First Church of Christ, Scientist, Boston.
RELIGION: *Church of Christ, Scientist*
Weston, Michele. Managing Editor, American Power Boat Association.
SPORTS AND GAMES: *Motorboating*
Whelan, John. Editor, *New Arabia,* London.
WORLD AFFAIRS: *Bahrain; Egypt; Iraq; Jordan; Kuwait; Lebanon; Middle Eastern and North African Affairs; Oman; Qatar; Saudi Arabia; Syria; United Arab Emirates; Yemen*
Whitney, Barbara. Copy Supervisor, Encyclopædia Britannica, Inc.
ARCHAEOLOGY: Sidebar; BIOGRAPHIES *(in part);* TELEVISION: Sidebar
Wilkinson, John R. Sportswriter, Coventry Newspapers Ltd., U.K.
SPORTS AND GAMES: *Cycling*
Williams, Michael. Golf Correspondent, *Daily Telegraph,* London.
SPORTS AND GAMES: *Golf*
Williams, Raymond Leslie. Professor of Spanish, University of Colorado, Boulder.
LITERATURE: *Spanish (in part)*
Willis, Clifford L. Director of News and Information, Office of Communication, Christian Church (Disciples of Christ).
RELIGION: *Christian Church (Disciples of Christ)*
Wilson, Derek. Former Staff String Correspondent, BBC, Rome.
WORLD AFFAIRS: *Italy*
Wilson, Michael. Freelance Aviation Writer and Consultant; Managing Editor, *Testimony.*
INDUSTRIAL REVIEW: *Aerospace*
Woodrow, Robert. Assistant Managing Editor, *Asiaweek* magazine, Hong Kong.
WORLD AFFAIRS: *Laos; Thailand*
Woods, Elizabeth. Writer. Author of *If Only Things Were Different (I): A Model for a Sustainable Society* and others.
LITERATURE: *English (in part)*
Woods, Michael. Science Editor, *Toledo* (Ohio) *Blade.*
CHEMISTRY
Woodward, Berton. Assistant Managing Editor, *Asiaweek* magazine, Hong Kong.
WORLD AFFAIRS: *Brunei; Dependent States (in part); Singapore; Southeast Asian Affairs*
Woollen, Anthony. Editor (1959–79), *Food Manufacture,* London. Editor, *Food Industries Manual* (20th ed.).
AGRICULTURE AND FOOD SUPPLIES: *Food Processing*
Wooller, Michael. Economist and Researcher on Iberia and South America.
WORLD AFFAIRS: *Paraguay; Portugal; Spain; Uruguay*
Wyllie, Peter John. Division of Geological and Planetary Sciences, California Institute of Technology.
EARTH SCIENCES: *Geology and Geochemistry*
Yamadori, Yuji. Director, Research and International Affairs, Japan Information Processing Development Center.
INFORMATION PROCESSING AND INFORMATION SYSTEMS *(in part)*
Young, M. Norvel. Chancellor Emeritus, Pepperdine University, Malibu, Calif. Author of *Preachers of Today.*
RELIGION: *Churches of Christ*
Zanga, Louis. Analyst, Radio Free Europe/Radio Liberty Research Institute.
WORLD AFFAIRS: *Albania*

1994
Britannica
World Data

Encyclopædia Britannica, Inc.
Chicago
Auckland/London/Madrid/Manila/Paris/Rome
Seoul/Sydney/Tokyo/Toronto

CONTENTS

INTRODUCTION

Britannica World Data provides a statistical portrait of some 220 countries and dependencies of the world, at a level appropriate to the size and importance of each. It contains 195 country statements (the "Nations of the World" section), ranging in length from one to four pages, and permits, in the 24 major thematic tables (the "Comparative National Statistics" section), simultaneous comparisons among all of these larger countries and 25 additional smaller dependent states.

Updated annually, *Britannica World Data* can be consulted as a separate work of reference developing a particular body of subject matter, but it is particularly intended as direct, structured support for many of Britannica's other reference works—encyclopaedias, yearbooks, atlases—at a level of detail that their editorial style or design do not permit.

Like the textual, graphic, or cartographic modes of expression of these other products, statistics possess their own inherent editorial virtues and weaknesses. Two principal goals in the creation of *Britannica World Data* were up-to-dateness and comparability, each possible to maximize separately, but not always possible to combine. If, for example, research on some subject is completed during a particular year (x), figures may be available for 100 countries for the preceding year ($x - 1$), for 140 countries for the year before that ($x - 2$), and for 180 countries for the year before that ($x - 3$).

Which year should be the basis of a thematic compilation for 220 countries so as to give the best combination of up-to-dateness and comparability? And, should $x - 1$ be adopted for the thematic table, ought up-to-dateness in the country table (for which year x is already available) be sacrificed for agreement with the thematic table? In general, the editors have opted for maximum up-to-dateness in the country statistical boxes and maximum comparability in the thematic tables, so as to take the best advantage of recent information.

Comparability, however, also resides in the meaning of the numbers compiled, which may differ greatly from country to country. The headnotes to the thematic tables explain many of these definitional problems; the Glossary serves the same purpose for the country statistical pages. Published data do not always provide the researcher or editor with a neat, unambiguous choice between a datum compiled on two different bases (say, railroad track length, or route length), one of which is wanted and the other not. More often a choice must be made among a variety of official, private, and external intergovernmental (UN, FAO, IMF) sources, each reporting its best data but each representing a set of problems: (1) of methodological variance from international conventions; (2) of analytical completeness (data for a single year may, successively, be projected [based on 10 months' data], preliminary [for 12 months], final, revised or adjusted, etc.); (3) of time frame, or accounting interval (data may represent a full Gregorian calendar year [preferred], a fiscal year, an Islamic or other national or religious year, a multiyear period or average [when a one-year statement would contain unrepresentative results]); (4) of continuity with previous data; and the like. Finally, published data on a particular subject may be complete and final but impossible to summarize in a simple manner. The education system of a single country may include, for example, public and private sectors; local, state, or national systems; varying grades, tracks, or forms within a single system; or opportunities for double-counting or fractional counting of a student, teacher, or institution. When no recent official data exist, the tables may show unofficial estimates, a range (of published opinion), analogous data, or no data at all. For certain subjects, especially population, the editors have prepared their own estimates.

The entrance of more than a score of newly independent countries onto the world stage since 1990 has displaced a number of smaller dependent states for which pages had been provided in past editions of *Britannica World Data*. These new countries, by virtue of their population, economic importance, and independent status, must, naturally, be assigned coverage commensurate with their importance, but, their present status being only recently acquired, most have not yet been assimilated by the information systems of international organizations like the UN. Thus, certain information provided must remain in the form published by the country itself, rather than the more-familiar international statistical presentations available for older states.

The published basis of the information compiled is the statistical collections of Encyclopædia Britannica, Inc., some of the principal elements of which are enumerated in the Bibliography. The information contained in those works is supplemented by unpublished data received in correspondence from the countries concerned. Usual holdings for a country with a well-developed statistical program may include any of the following kinds of documents: the national statistical abstract; the constitution; the most recent censuses of population; periodic or occasional reports on vital statistics, social indicators, agriculture, mining, labour, manufacturing, domestic and foreign trade, finance and banking, transportation, and communications.

The great majority of the social, economic, and financial data contained in this work should not be interpreted in isolation. Interpretive text of long perspective, such as that of the *Encyclopædia Britannica* itself; political, geographic, and topical maps, such as those in the *Britannica Atlas;* and recent analysis of political events and economic trends, such as that contained in the articles of the *Book of the Year,* will all help to supply balance, physical framework, and analytic focus that numbers alone cannot provide. By the same token, study of those sources will be made more concrete by use of *Britannica World Data* to supply up-to-date geographic, demographic, and economic data to illuminate the methodology of those works.

GLOSSARY

A number of terms that are used to classify and report data in the "Nations of the World" section require some explanation.

Those italicized terms that are used regularly in the country compilations to introduce specific categories of information (*e.g., birth rate, budget*) appear in this glossary in italic boldface type, followed by a description of the precise kind of information being offered and how it has been edited and presented.

All other terms are printed here in roman boldface type. Many terms have quite specific meanings in statistical reporting, and they are so defined here. Other terms have less specific application as they are used by different countries or organizations. Data in the country compilations based on definitions markedly different from those below will usually be footnoted.

Terms that appear in small capitals in certain definitions are themselves defined at their respective alphabetical locations.

Terms whose definitions are marked by an asterisk (*) refer to data supplied only in the larger two- to four-page country compilations.

access to services, a group of measures indicating a population's level of access to public services, including electrical power, treated public drinking water, sewage removal, and fire protection.*

activity rate, *see* participation/activity rates.

age breakdown, the distribution of a given population by age, usually reported here as percentages of total population in 15-year age brackets. When substantial numbers of persons do not know, or state, their exact age, distributions may not total 100.0%.

area, the total surface area of a country or its administrative subdivisions, including both land and inland (nontidal) water area. Land area is usually calculated from "mean low water" on a "plane table," or flat, basis.

area and population, a tabulation usually including the first-order administrative subdivisions of the country (such as the states of the United States), with capital (headquarters, or administrative seat), area, and population. When these subdivisions are especially numerous or, occasionally, nonexistent, a regional, electoral, census, or other nonadministrative scheme of subdivisions has been substituted.

associated state, *see* (free) association; *see* state.

atheist, in statements of religious affiliation, one who professes active opposition to religion; "nonreligious" refers to those professing only no religion, nonbelief, or doubt.

balance of payments, a financial statement for a country for a given period showing the balance among: (1) transactions in goods, services, and income between that country and the rest of the world, (2) changes in ownership or valuation of that country's monetary gold, SPECIAL DRAWING RIGHTS, and claims on and liabilities to the rest of the world, and (3) unrequited transfers and counterpart entries needed (in an accounting sense) to balance transactions and changes among any of the foregoing types of exchange that are not mutually offsetting. The United Nations *System of National Accounts* (SNA) provides a framework for international comparability in classifying such transactions, but detail of local law as to what constitutes a transaction, the basis of its valuation, and the size of a transaction visible to fiscal authorities all result in differences in the meaning of a particular national statement.*

balance of trade, the net value of all international goods trade of a country, usually excluding reexports (goods received only for transshipment), and the percentage that this net represents of total trade.

Balance of trade refers only to the "visible" international trade of goods as recorded by customs authorities and is thus a segment of a country's BALANCE OF PAYMENTS, which takes all visible and invisible trade with other countries into account. (Invisible trade refers to imports and exports of money, financial instruments, and services such as transport, tourism, and insurance.) A country has a favourable balance of trade when the value of exports exceeds that of imports.

barrel (bbl), a unit of liquid measure. The barrel conventionally used for reporting crude petroleum and petroleum products is equal to 42 U.S. gallons, or 159 litres. The number of barrels of crude petroleum per metric ton, ranging typically from 6.45 to 8.13, depends upon the specific gravity of the petroleum. The world average is roughly 7.33 barrels per ton.

birth rate, the number of live births annually per 1,000 of midyear population. Birth rates for individual countries may be compared with the estimated world annual average of 26.4 births per 1,000 population between 1990 and 1995.

budget, the annual receipts and expenditures— of a central government for its activities only; does not include state, provincial, or local governments or semipublic (parastatal, quasi-nongovernmental) corporations unless other-

Abbreviations

Measurements

cu m	cubic metre(s)
kg	kilogram(s)
km	kilometre(s)
kW	kilowatt(s)
kW-hr	kilowatt-hour(s)
metric ton-km	metric ton-kilometre(s)
mi	mile(s)
passenger-km	passenger-kilometre(s)
passenger-mi	passenger-mile(s)
short ton-mi	short ton-mile(s)
sq km	square kilometre(s)
sq m	square metre(s)
sq mi	square mile(s)
troy oz	troy ounce(s)
yr	year(s)

Political Units and International Organizations

CACM	Central American Common Market
Caricom	Caribbean Community and Common Market
CFA	Communauté Financière Africaine
CFP	Comptoirs Françaises du Pacifique
CIS	Commonwealth of Independent States
CUSA	Customs Union of Southern Africa
E.Ger.	East Germany
EEC	European Economic Community
FAO	United Nations Food and Agriculture Organization
IMF	International Monetary Fund
OECS	Organization of Eastern Caribbean States
U.A.E.	United Arab Emirates
U.K.	United Kingdom
U.S.	United States
U.S.S.R.	Union of Soviet Socialist Republics
W.Ger.	West Germany

Months

Jan.	January	Oct.	October
Feb.	February	Nov.	November
Aug.	August	Dec.	December
Sept.	September		

Miscellaneous

AIDS	Acquired Immune Deficiency Syndrome
avg.	average
c.i.f.	cost, insurance, and freight
commun.	communications
CPI	consumer price index
est.	estimate(d)
excl.	excluding
f.o.b.	free on board
GDP	gross domestic product
GNP	gross national product
govt.	government
incl.	including
mo.	month(s)
n.a.	not available (in text)
n.e.s.	not elsewhere specified
NMP	net material product
no.	number
pl.	plural
pos.	position
pub. admin.	public administration
PVC	Polyvinyl Chloride
SDR	Special Drawing Right
SITC	Standard International Trade Classification
svcs.	services
teacher tr.	teacher training
transp.	transportation
voc.	vocational
$	dollar (of any currency area)
£	pound (of any currency area)
...	not available (in tables)
—	none, less than half the smallest unit shown, or not applicable (in tables)

wise specified. Figures for budgets are limited to ordinary (recurrent) receipts and expenditures, wherever possible, and exclude capital expenditures—*i.e.,* funds for development and other special projects originating as foreign-aid grants or loans.

When both a recurrent and a capital budget exist for a single country, the former is the budget funded entirely from national resources (taxes, duties, excises, etc.) that would recur (be generated by economic activity) every year. It funds the most basic governmental services, those least able to suffer interruption. The capital budget is usually funded by external aid and may change its size considerably from year to year.

capital, usually, the actual seat of government and administration of a state. When more than one capital exists, each is identified by kind; when interim arrangements exist during the creation or movement of a national capital, the de facto situation is described.

Anomalous cases are annotated, such as those in which (1) the de jure designation under the country's laws differs from actual local practice (*e.g.,* Benin's designation of one capital in constitutional law, but another in actual practice), (2) international recognition does not validate a country's claim (as with the proclamation by Israel of a capital on territory not fully recognized as part of Israel), or (3) both a state and a capital have been proclaimed on territory recognized as part of another state (as with the Turkish Republic of Northern Cyprus).

capital budget, *see* budget.

causes of death, as defined by the World Health Organization, "the disease or injury which initiated the train of morbid events leading directly to death, or the circumstances of accident or violence which produced the fatal injury." This principle, the "underlying cause of death," is the basis of the medical judgment as to cause; the statistical classification system according to which these causes are grouped and named is the *International List of Causes of Death,* the latest revision of which is the Tenth. Reporting is usually in terms of events per 100,000 population. When data on actual causes of death are unavailable, information on morbidity, or illness rate, usually given as reported cases per 100,000 of infectious diseases (notifiable to WHO as a matter of international agreement), may be substituted.

chief of state/head of government, paramount national governmental officer(s) exercising the highest executive and/or ceremonial roles of a country's government. In general usage, the chief of state is the formal head of a national state. The primary responsibilities of the chief of state may range from the purely ceremonial—convening legislatures and greeting foreign officials—to the exercise of complete national executive authority. The head of government, when this function exists separately, is the officer nominally charged (by the constitution) with the majority of actual executive powers, though they may not in practice be exercised, especially in military or single-party regimes in which effective power may reside entirely outside the executive governmental machinery provided by the constitution. A prime minister, for example, usually understood to be the head of government, may in practice exercise only cabinet-level authority.

In communist countries an official identified as the chief of state may be the chairman of the policy-making organ, and the official given as the head of government the chairman of the nominal administrative/executive organ.

c.i.f. (trade valuation): *see* imports.

colony, an area annexed to, or controlled by, an independent state but not an integral part of it; a non-self-governing territory. A colony has a charter and may have a degree of self-government. A crown colony is a colony originally chartered by the British government.

commonwealth (U.K. and U.S.), a self-governing political entity that has regard to the common weal, or good; usually associated with the United Kingdom or United States. Examples include the Commonwealth of Nations (composed of independent states [from 1931 onward]), Puerto Rico since 1952, and the Northern Marianas since 1979.

communications, collectively, the means available for the public transmission of information within a country. Data are provided for daily newspapers, their number and total circulation, and the per capita rate of circulation implied by that total; for radio, television, and telephone receivers, total numbers and rates of availability are supplied. Telephone receiver data refer to the number of sets (stations) having access to the public switched network. Data for a few countries refer to the number of "main lines" through which subscribers' equipment is connected to the network.

constant prices, an adjustment to the members of a financial time series to eliminate the effect of inflation year by year. It consists of referring all data in the series to a single year so that "real" change may be seen.

constitutional monarchy, *see* monarchy.

consumer price index (CPI), also known as the retail price index, or the cost-of-living index, a series of index numbers assigned to the price of a selected "basket," or assortment, of basic consumer goods and services in a country or region to measure changes over time in prices paid by a typical household for those goods and services. Items included in the CPI are ordinarily determined by governmental surveys of typical household expenditures and are assigned weights relative to their proportion of those expenditures. Index values are period averages unless otherwise noted.

coprincipality, *see* monarchy.

current prices, the valuation of a financial aggregate as of the year reported.

daily per capita caloric intake (supply), the calories equivalent to the known average daily supply of foodstuffs for human consumption in a given country divided by the population of the country (and the proportion of that supply provided, respectively, by vegetable and animal sources). The daily per capita caloric intake of a country may be compared with the corresponding recommended minimum daily requirement. The latter is calculated by the Food and Agriculture Organization of the United Nations from the age and sex distributions, average body weights, and environmental temperatures in a given region to determine the calories needed to sustain a person there at normal levels of activity and health. The daily per capita caloric requirement ranges from 2,200 to 2,500.

de facto population, for a given area, the population composed of those actually present at a particular time, including temporary residents and visitors (such as immigrants not yet granted permanent status, "guest" or expatriate workers, refugees, or tourists), but excluding legal residents temporarily absent.

de jure population, for a given area, the population composed only of those legally resident at a particular time, excluding temporary residents and visitors (such as "guest" or expatriate workers, refugees, or tourists), but including legal residents temporarily absent.

deadweight tonnage, the maximum weight of cargo, fuel, fresh water, stores, and persons that may safely be carried by a ship. It is customarily measured in long tons of 2,240 pounds each, equivalent to 1.016 metric tons. Deadweight tonnage is the difference between the tonnage of a fully loaded ship and the fully unloaded tonnage of that ship.

See also gross ton.

death rate, the number of deaths annually per 1,000 of midyear population. Death rates for individual countries may be compared with the estimated world annual average of 9.2 deaths per 1,000 population between 1990 and 1995.

density (of population), usually, the DE FACTO POPULATION of a country divided by its total area. Special adjustment is made for large areas of inland water or other uninhabitable areas—*e.g.,* excluding the ice cap of Greenland.

department, a first-order civil administrative subdivision. The *overseas department* (France) is an overseas subdivision of the French Republic, almost equivalent to a department of metropolitan France, with elected representation in the French Parliament.

Dependent states[1]

Australia
- Christmas Island
- Cocos (Keeling) Islands
- Norfolk Island

Denmark
- Faeroe Islands
- Greenland

France
- French Guiana
- French Polynesia
- Guadeloupe
- Martinique
- Mayotte
- New Caledonia
- Réunion
- Saint Pierre and Miquelon
- Wallis and Futuna

Netherlands, The
- Aruba
- Netherlands Antilles

New Zealand
- Cook Islands
- Niue
- Tokelau

Norway
- Jan Mayen
- Svalbard

Portugal
- Macau

United Kingdom
- Anguilla
- Bermuda
- British Virgin Islands
- Cayman Islands
- Falkland Islands
- Gibraltar
- Guernsey
- Hong Kong
- Isle of Man
- Jersey
- Montserrat
- Pitcairn Island
- Saint Helena and Dependencies
- Turks and Caicos Islands

United States
- American Samoa
- Guam
- Northern Mariana Islands
- Palau
- Puerto Rico
- Virgin Islands (of the U.S.)

[1]Excludes territories (1) to which Antarctic Treaty is applicable in whole or in part, (2) without permanent civilian population, (3) without internationally recognized civilian government (Western Sahara, Gaza Strip), or (4) representing unadjudicated unilateral or multilateral territorial claims.

dependent state, constitutionally or statutorily organized political entity outside of and under the jurisdiction of an independent state (or a federal element of such a state) but not formally annexed to it (*see* Table).

direct taxes, taxes levied directly on firms and individuals, such as taxes on income, profits, and capital gains. The *immediate* incidence, or burden, of direct taxes is on the firms and individuals thus taxed; direct taxes on firms may, however, be passed on to consumers and other economic units in the form of higher prices for goods and services, blurring the distinction between direct and indirect taxation.

distribution of income/wealth, the portion of personal income or wealth accruing to households or individuals constituting each respective decile (tenth) or quintile (fifth) of a country's households or individuals.*

divorce rate, the number of legal, civilly recognized divorces annually per 1,000 population.

doubling time, the number of complete years required for a country to double its population at its current rate of natural increase.

earnings index, a series of index numbers comparing average wages in a collective industrial sample for a country or region with the same industries at a previous period to measure changes over time in those wages. It is most commonly reported for wages paid on a daily, weekly, or monthly basis; annual figures represent averages of these shorter periods. The scope of the earnings index varies from country to country; the index is often limited to earnings in manufacturing industries. The index for each country applies to all wage earners in a designated group and ordinarily takes into account basic wages (overtime is normally distinguished), bonuses, cost-of-living allowances, and contributions toward social security. Some countries include payments in kind. Contributions toward social security by employers are usually excluded, as are social security benefits received by wage earners.

economically active population, *see* population economically active.

education, tabulation of the principal elements of a country's educational establishment, classified as far as possible according to the country's own system of primary, secondary, and higher levels (the usual age limits for these levels being identified in parentheses), with total number of schools (physical facilities) and of teachers and students (whether full- or part-time). The student-teacher ratio is calculated whenever available data permit.

educational attainment, the distribution of the population age 25 and over with completed educations by the highest level of formal education attained or completed; it must sometimes be reported, however, for age groups still in school or for the economically active only.

emirate, empire, *see* monarchy.

enterprise, a legal entity formed to conduct a business, which it may do from more than one establishment (place of business or service point).

ethnic/linguistic composition, ethnic, racial, or linguistic composition of a national population, reported here according to the most reliable breakdown available, whether published in official sources (such as a census) or in external analysis (when the subject is not addressed in national sources).

exchange rate, the value of one currency compared with another, or with a standardized unit of account such as the SPECIAL DRAWING RIGHT, or as mandated by local statute when one currency is "tied" by a par value to another. Rates given usually refer to free market values when the currency itself is traded.

exports, material goods legally leaving a country (or customs area) and subject to customs regulations. The total value and distribution by percentage of the major items (in preference to groups of goods) exported are given, together with the distribution of trade among major trading partners (usually single countries or trading blocs). Valuation of goods exported is free on board (f.o.b.) unless otherwise specified. The value of goods exported and imported f.o.b. is calculated from the cost of production and excludes the cost of transport.

external debt, public and publicly guaranteed debt with a maturity of more than one year owed to nonnationals of a country and repayable in foreign currency, goods, or services. The debt may be an obligation of a national or subnational governmental body (or an agency of either), of an autonomous public body, or of a private debtor that is guaranteed by a public entity. The debt is usually either outstanding (contracted) or disbursed (drawn).

external territory (Australia), *see* territory.

federal, consisting of first-order political subdivisions that are prior to and independent of the central government in certain functions.

federal republic, *see* republic.

federation, union of coequal, preexisting political entities that retain some degree of autonomy and (usually) right of secession within the union.

fertility rate, *see* total fertility rate.

financial aggregates, tabulation of seven-year time series, providing principal measures of the financial condition of a country, including: (1) the exchange rate of the national currency against the U.S. dollar, the pound sterling, and the International Monetary Fund's SPECIAL DRAWING RIGHT (SDR), (2) the amount and kind of international reserves (holdings of SDRs, gold, and foreign currencies) and reserve position of the country in the IMF, and (3) principal economic rates and prices (central bank discount rate, government bond yields, and industrial stock [share] prices). For BALANCE OF PAYMENTS, the origin in terms of component balance of trade items and balance of invisibles (net) is given.*

fish catch, the live-weight equivalent of the aquatic animals (including fish, crustaceans, mollusks, etc., but excluding whales, seals, and other aquatic mammals) caught in freshwater or marine areas by national fleets and landed in domestic or foreign harbours for commercial, industrial, or subsistence purposes.

f.o.b. (trade valuation): *see* exports.

food, *see* daily per capita caloric intake.

form of government/political status, the structure of a country's administration provided for in normal constitutional operation—whether or not suspended by extralegal military or civil action, although such de facto administrations are identified—together with the number of members (elected, appointed, and ex officio) for each legislative house, named according to its English rendering. Dependent states (*see* Table) are classified according to the status of their political association with the administering country.

(free) association, late stage in the process by which U.K. and U.S. dependencies achieve independence; it usually implies a relation between a largely self-governing dependency and its administering power that is capable of termination in full independence at the instance of the dependent state, though always in consultation with the administering power.

global social product, *see* material product.

gross domestic product (GDP), the total value of the final goods and services produced by residents and nonresidents within a given country during a given year. The GDP excludes the value of net income earned abroad, which is included in the GROSS NATIONAL PRODUCT. Unless otherwise noted, the value is given in current prices of the year indicated.

gross national product (GNP), the total value of final goods and services produced both from within a given country *and* from external (foreign) transactions in a given year. Unless otherwise noted, the value is given in current prices of the year indicated. GNP is equal to GROSS DOMESTIC PRODUCT adjusted by net factor income from abroad, which is the income residents receive from abroad for factor services (labour, investment, and interest) less similar payments made to nonresidents who contribute to the domestic economy.

gross ton, volumetric unit of measure (equaling 100 cubic feet [2.83 cu m]) of the permanently enclosed volume of a ship, above and below decks available for cargo, stores, or passenger accommodation. Net, or register, tonnage exempts certain nonrevenue spaces—such as those devoted to machinery, bunkers, crew accommodations, and ballast—from the gross tonnage. *See also* deadweight tonnage.

head of government, *see* chief of state/head of government.

health, a group of measures including number of accredited physicians currently practicing or employed and their ratio to the total population; total hospital beds and their ratio; and INFANT MORTALITY RATE.

household, economically autonomous individual or group of individuals living in a single dwelling unit. A family household is one composed principally of individuals related by blood or marriage.

household income and expenditure, data for average size of a HOUSEHOLD (by number of individuals) and median household income. Sources of income and expenditures for major items of consumption are given as percentages.

In general, household income is the amount of funds, usually measured in monetary units, received by the members (generally those 14 years old and over) of a household in a given time period. The income can be derived from (1) wages or salaries, (2) nonfarm or farm SELF-EMPLOYMENT, (3) transfer payments, such as pensions, public assistance, unemployment benefits, etc., and (4) other income, including interest and dividends, rent, royalties, etc. The income of a household is expressed as a gross amount before deductions for taxes. Data on expenditure refer to consumption of personal or household goods and services; they normally exclude savings, taxes, and insurance; practice with regard to inclusion of credit purchases differs markedly.

immigration, usually, the number and origin of those immigrants admitted to a nation in a legal status that would eventually permit the granting of the right to settle permanently or to acquire citizenship.*

imports, material goods legally entering a country (or customs area) and subject to customs regulations; excludes financial movements. The total value and distribution by percentage of the major items (in preference to groups of goods) imported are given, together with the direction of trade among major trading partners (usually single countries), trading blocs (such as the European Economic Community), or customs areas (such as Belgium-Luxembourg). The value of goods imported is given free on board (f.o.b.) unless otherwise specified; f.o.b. is defined above under EXPORTS.

The principal alternate basis for valuation of goods in international trade is that of cost, insurance, and freight (c.i.f.); its use is restricted to imports, as it comprises the principal charges needed to bring the goods to the customs house in the country of destination. Because it inflates the value of imports relative to exports, more countries have, latterly, been estimating imports on an f.o.b. basis as well.

incorporated territory (U.S.), *see* territory.

independent, of a state, autonomous and controlling both its internal and external affairs. Its date usually refers to the date from which the country was in effective control of these affairs within its present boundaries, rather than the date independence was proclaimed or the date recognized as a de jure act by the former administering power.

indirect taxes, taxes levied on sales or transfers of selected intermediate goods and services, including excises, value-added taxes, and tariffs, that are ordinarily passed on to the ultimate consumers of the goods and services. Figures given for individual countries are limited to indirect taxes levied by their respective central governments unless otherwise specified.

infant mortality rate, the number of children per 1,000 live births who die before their first birthday. Total infant mortality includes neonatal mortality, which is deaths of children within one month of birth.

invisibles (invisible trade), *see* balance of trade.

kingdom, *see* monarchy.

labour force, portion of the POPULATION ECONOMICALLY ACTIVE (PEA) comprising those most fully employed or attached to the labour market (the unemployed are considered to be "attached" in that they usually represent persons previously employed seeking to be reemployed), particularly as viewed from a short-term perspective. It normally includes those who are self-employed, employed by others (whether full-time, part-time, seasonally, or on some other less than full-time basis), and, as noted above, the unemployed (both those previously employed and those seeking work for the first time). In the "gross domestic product and labour force" table, the majority of the labour data provided refer to population economically active, since PEA represents the longer-term view of working population and, thus, subsumes more of the marginal workers who are often missed by shorter-term surveys.

land use, distribution by classes of vegetational cover or economic use of the land area only (excluding inland water, for example, but not marshland), reported as percentages.

leisure, the principal monetary expenditures, uses, or reported preferences in the use of the individual's free time for recreation, rest, or self-improvement.*

life expectancy, the number of years a person born within a particular population group (age cohort) would be expected to live, based on actuarial calculations.

literacy, the ability to read and write a language with some degree of competence; the precise degree constituting the basis of a particular national statement is usually defined by the national census and is often tested by the census enumerator. Elsewhere, particularly where much adult literacy may be the result of literacy campaigns rather than passage through a formal educational system, definition and testing of literacy may be better standardized.

major cities, usually the five largest cities proper whose population is at least one-tenth that of the primate (largest) city; fewer will be listed if the size disparity is very great or there are fewer urban localities in the country. For multipage tables, 10 or more will be listed without regard for the size of the primate city.* All populations will refer to the most specific administrative or demographically defined city proper, unless a municipality or METROPOLITAN AREA is specified.

manufacturing, mining, and construction enterprises/retail sales and service enterprises, a detailed tabulation of the principal industries in these sectors, showing for each industry the number of enterprises and employees, wages in that industry as a percentage of the general average wage, and the value of that industry's output in terms of value added or turnover.*

marriage rate, the number of legal, civilly recognized marriages annually per 1,000 population.

material (or social) product, in the national accounting systems of the socialist countries, the aggregate (sometimes "global") value of all "productive" economic activity, generally omitting personal (nonpublic) services, financial activities, and the like that in conventional Western national accounts would contribute to the GROSS DOMESTIC PRODUCT, a more comprehensive measure that includes not only material output but also every identifiable service element of a national economy. Socialist countries that are members of the International Monetary Fund have begun, however, to report gross domestic, and national, product according to the *System of National Accounts* that forms the basis of international standardization of national accounts.

material well-being, a group of measures indicating the percentage of households or dwellings possessing certain goods or appliances, including automobiles, telephones, television receivers, refrigerators, air conditioners, and washing machines.*

merchant marine, the privately or publicly owned ships registered with the maritime authority of a nation (limited to those in Lloyd's of London statistical reporting of 100 or more GROSS TONS) that are employed in commerce, whether or not owned or operated by nationals of the country.

metropolitan area, a city and the region of dense, predominantly urban, settlement around the city; the population of the whole usually has strong economic and cultural affinities with the central city.

military expenditure, the apparent value of all identifiable military expenditure by the central government on hardware, personnel, pensions, research and development, etc., reported here both as a percentage of the GNP, with a comparison to the world average, and as a per capita value in U.S. dollars.

military personnel, *see* total active duty personnel.

mobility, the rate at which individuals or households change dwellings, usually measured between censuses and including international as well as domestic migration.*

monarchy, a government in which the CHIEF OF STATE holds office, usually hereditarily and for life, but sometimes electively for a term. The state may be a coprincipality, emirate, empire, kingdom, principality, sheikhdom, or sultanate. The powers of the monarch may range from absolute (*i.e.,* the monarch both reigns and rules) through various degrees of limitation of authority to nominal, as in a constitutional monarchy, in which the titular monarch reigns but others, as elected officials, effectively rule.

monetary unit, currency of issue, or that in official use in a given country; name, spelling, and abbreviation in English according to International Monetary Fund recommendations or local practice; name of the lesser, usually decimal, monetary unit constituting the main currency; and valuation in U.S. dollars and U.K. pounds sterling, usually according to market or commercial rates.

See also exchange rate.

natural increase, also called natural growth, or the balance of births and deaths, the excess of births over deaths in a population; the rate of natural increase is the difference between the BIRTH RATE and the DEATH RATE of a given population. Natural increase is added to the balance of migration to calculate the total growth of that population.

net material product, *see* material product.

nonreligious, *see* atheist.

official language(s), that (or those) prescribed for actual day-to-day conduct and publication of a country's official business. Other languages may have local protection, may be permitted in legal action (such as a trial), or may be "national languages," for the protection of which special provisions have been made, but these are not deemed official.

official name, the local official form(s), short or long, of a country's legal name(s) taken from the country's constitution or from other official documents. The English-language form is usually the protocol form in use by the country, the U.S. Department of State, and the United Nations.

official religion, generally, any religion prescribed or given special status or protection by the constitution or legal system of a country. Identification as such is not confined to constitutional documents utilizing the term explicitly.

organized territory (U.S.), *see* territory.

overseas department (France), *see* department.

overseas territory (France), *see* territory.

parliamentary state, *see* state.

part of a realm, a dependent Dutch political entity with some degree of self-government and having a special status above that of a colony (*e.g.,* the prerogative of rejecting for local application any law enacted by The Netherlands).

participation/activity rates, measures defining differential rates of economic activity within a population. Participation rate refers to the percentage of those employed or economically active who possess a particular characteristic (sex, age, etc.); activity rate refers to the fraction of the total population who *are* economically active.

passenger-miles, or **passenger-kilometres,** aggregate measure of passenger carriage by a specified means of transportation, equal to the number of passengers carried multiplied by the number of miles (or kilometres) each is transported. Figures given for countries are often calculated from ticket sales and ordinarily exclude passengers carried free of charge.

people's republic, *see* republic.

place of birth/national origin, if the former, numbers of native- and foreign-born population of a country by actual place of birth; if the latter, any of several classifications, including those based on origin of passport at original admission to country, on cultural heritage of family name, on self-designated (often multiple) origin of (some) ancestors, and on other systems for assigning national origin.*

political status, *see* form of government/political status.

population, the number of persons present within a country or other civil entity at the date of a census of population, survey, cumulation of a civil register, or other enumeration. Unless otherwise specified, populations given are DE FACTO, referring to those actually present, rather than DE JURE, those legally resident but not necessarily present on the referent date. If a time series, noncensus year, or per capita ratio referring to a country's total population is cited, it will usually refer to midyear of the calendar year indicated. Populations for cities will usually refer to the city proper—*i.e.,* the legally bounded corporate entity, or the most compact, contiguous, demographically urban portion of the entity defined by the local authorities. Occasionally it has been necessary to provide city figures for METROPOLITAN AREAS when the relevant civil entity at the core of a major agglomeration had an unrepresentatively small population.

population economically active, the total number of persons (above a set age for economic labour, usually 10–15 years) in all employment statuses—self-employed, wage- or salary-earning, part-time, seasonal, unemployed, etc. The International Labour Organisation defines the economically active as "all persons of either sex who furnish the supply of labour for the production of economic goods and services." National practices vary as regards the treatment of such groups as armed forces, inmates of institutions, persons seeking their first job, seasonal workers and persons engaged in part-time economic activities. In some countries, all or part of these groups may be included among the economically active, while in other countries the same groups may be treated as inactive. In general, however, the data on economically active population do not include students, women occupied solely in domestic duties, retired persons, persons living entirely on their own means, and persons wholly dependent upon others.

See also labour force.

population projection, the expected population in the years 2000 and 2010, embodying the country's own projections wherever possible. Estimates of the future size of a population are usually based on assumed levels of fertility, mortality, and migration. Projections in the tables, unless otherwise specified, are medium (*i.e.,* most likely) variants, whether based on external estimates by the United Nations, World Bank, or U.S. Department of Commerce or on those of the country itself.

price and earnings indexes, tabulation comparing the change in the CONSUMER PRICE INDEX over a period of seven years with the change in the general labour force's EARNINGS INDEX for the same period.

principality, *see* monarchy.

production, the physical quantity or monetary value of the output of an industry, usually tabulated here as the most important items or groups of items (depending on the available detail) of primary (extractive) and secondary (manufactured) production. When a single consistent measure of value, such as VALUE ADDED, can be obtained, this is given, ranked by value; otherwise, and more usually, quantity of production is given.

public debt, the current outstanding debt of all periods of maturity for which the central government and its organs are obligated. Publicly guaranteed private debt is excluded. For countries that report debt under the World Bank Debtor Reporting System (DRS), figures for outstanding, long-term EXTERNAL DEBT are given.

quality of working life, a group of measures including weekly hours of work (including overtime); rates per 100,000 for job-connected injury, illness, and mortality; coverage of labour force by insurance for injury, permanent disability, and death; workdays lost to labour strikes and stoppages; and commuting patterns (length of journey to work in minutes and usual method of transportation).*

railroads, mode of transportation by self-driven or locomotive-drawn cars over fixed rails. Length-of-track figures include all mainline and spurline running track but exclude switching sidings and yard track. Route length, when given, does not compound multiple running tracks laid on the same trackbed.

recurrent budget, *see* budget.

religious affiliation, distribution of nominal religionists, whether practicing or not, as a percentage of total population. This usually assigns to children the religion of their parents.

republic, a state with elected leaders and a centralized presidential form of government, local subdivisions being subordinate to the national government. A *federal republic* (as distinguished from a unitary republic) is a republic in which power is divided between the central government and the constituent subnational administrative divisions (*e.g.,* states, provinces, or cantons) in whom the central government itself is held to originate, the division of power being defined in a written constitution and jurisdictional disputes usually being settled in a court; sovereignty usually rests with the authority that has the power to amend the constitution. A *unitary republic* (as distinguished from a federal republic) is a republic in which power originates in a central authority and is not derived from constituent subdivisions. A *people's republic,* in the dialectics of Communism, is the first stage of development toward a communist state, the second stage being a *socialist republic.* An *Islamic republic* is structured around social, ethical, and religious precepts central to the Islamic faith.

retail price index, *see* consumer price index.

retail sales and service enterprises, *see* manufacturing, mining, and construction enterprises/retail sales and service enterprises.

roundwood, wood obtained from removals from forests, felled or harvested (with or without bark), in all forms.

rural, *see* urban-rural.

self-employment, work in which income derives from direct employment in one's own business, trade, or profession, as opposed to work in which salary or wages are earned from an employer.

self-governing, of a state, in control of its internal affairs in degrees ranging from control of most internal affairs (though perhaps not of public order or of internal security) to complete control of all internal affairs (*i.e.,* the state is autonomous) but having no control of external affairs or defense. In this work the term self-governing refers to the final stage in the successive stages of increasing self-government that generally precede independence.

service/trade enterprises, *see* manufacturing, mining, and construction enterprises/retail sales and service enterprises.

sex distribution, ratios, calculated as percentages, of male and female population to total population.

sheikhdom, *see* monarchy.

social deviance, a group of measures, usually reported as rates per 100,000, for principal categories of socially deviant behaviour, including specified crimes, alcoholism, drug abuse, and suicide.*

social participation, a group of measures indicative of the degree of social engagement displayed by a particular population, including rates of participation in such activities as elections, voluntary work or memberships, trade unions, and religion.*

social security, public programs designed to protect individuals and families from loss of income owing to unemployment, old age, sickness or disability, or death and to provide other services such as medical care, health and welfare programs, or income maintenance.

socialist republic, *see* republic.

sources of income, *see* household income and expenditure.

Special Drawing Right (SDR), a unit of account utilized by the International Monetary Fund (IMF) to denominate monetary reserves available under a quota system to IMF members to maintain the value of their national currency unit in international transactions.*

state, in international law, a political entity possessing the attributes of: territory, permanent civilian population, government, and the capacity to conduct relations with other states. Though the term is sometimes limited in meaning to fully independent and internationally recognized states, the more general sense of an entity possessing a *preponderance* of these characteristics is intended here. It is, thus, also a first-order civil administrative subdivision, especially of a federated union. An *associated state* is an autonomous state in free association with another that conducts its external affairs and defense. A *parliamentary state* is an independent state of the Commonwealth that is governed by a parliament and that may recognize the British monarch as its titular head.

structure of gross domestic product and labour force, tabulation of the principal elements of the national economy, according to standard industrial categories, together with the corresponding distribution of the labour force (when possible POPULATION ECONOMICALLY ACTIVE) that generates the GROSS DOMESTIC PRODUCT.

sultanate, *see* monarchy.

territory, a noncategorized political dependency; a first-order administrative subdivision; a dependent political entity with some degree of self-government, but with fewer rights and less autonomy than a colony because there is no charter. An *external territory* (Australia) is a territory situated outside the area of the country. An *organized territory* (U.S.) is a territory for which a system of laws and a settled government have been provided by an act of the United States Congress. An *overseas territory* (France) is an overseas subdivision of the French Republic with elected representation in the French Parliament, having individual statutes, laws, and internal organization adapted to local conditions. An *unincorporated territory* (U.S.) is a dependency of the United States with limited self-government, whose inhabitants can claim the fundamental but not all of the procedural rights (*e.g.,* trial by jury) guaranteed by the United States Constitution.

ton-miles, or **ton-kilometres,** aggregate measure of freight hauled by a specified means of transportation, equal to tons of freight multiplied by the miles (or kilometres) each ton is transported. Figures are compiled from waybills (nationally) and ordinarily exclude mail, specie, passengers' baggage, the fuel and stores of the conveyance, and goods carried free.

total active duty personnel, full-time active duty military personnel (excluding militias and part-time, informal, or other paramilitary elements), with their distribution by percentages among the major services.

total fertility rate, the sum of the current age-specific birth rates for each of the child-bearing years (usually 15–49). It is the probable number of births, given present fertility data, that would occur during the lifetime of each woman should she live to the end of her child-bearing years.

tourism, service industry comprising activities connected with domestic and international travel for pleasure or recreation; confined here to international travel and reported as expenditures in U.S.$ by tourists of all nationalities visiting a particular country and, conversely, the estimated expenditures of that country's nationals in all countries of destination.

transfer payments, *see* household income and expenditure.

transport, all mechanical methods of moving persons or goods. Data reported for national establishments include: for railroads, length of track and volume of traffic for passengers and cargo (but excluding mail, etc.); for roads, length of network and numbers of passenger cars and of commercial vehicles (*i.e.,* trucks and buses); for merchant marine, the number of vessels of more than 100 gross tons and their total deadweight tonnage; for air transport, traffic data for passengers and cargo and the number of airports with scheduled flights.

unincorporated territory (U.S.), *see* territory.

unitary republic, *see* republic.

urban-rural, social characteristic of local or national populations, defined by predominant economic activities, "urban" referring to a group of largely nonagricultural pursuits, "rural" to agriculturally oriented employment patterns. The distinction is usually based on the country's own definition of urban, which may depend only upon the size (population) of a place or upon factors like employment, administrative status, density of housing, etc.

value added, also called value added by manufacture, the gross output value of a firm or industry minus the cost of inputs—raw materials, supplies, and payments to other firms—required to produce it. Value added is the portion of the sales value or gross output value that is actually created by the firm or industry. Value added generally includes labour costs, administrative costs, and operating profits.

The Nations of the World

Afghanistan

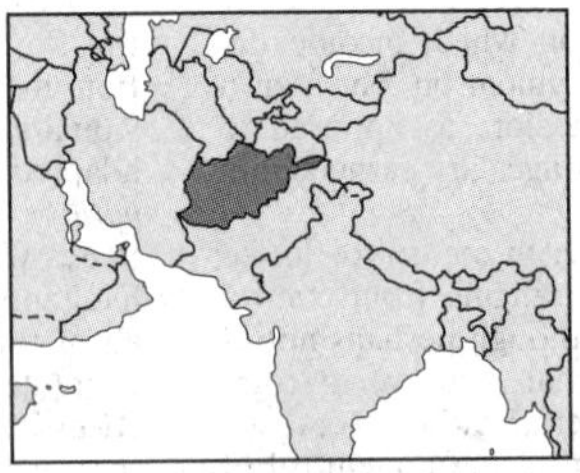

Official name: Islamic State of Afghanistan (Pashto and Dari [Persian] long-form names, n.a.).
Form of government[1]: Islamic state with an interim parliament[2] (250).
Chief of state: President.
Head of government: Prime Minister.
Capital: Kabul.
Official languages: Pashto; Dari (Persian).
Official religion: Islam.
Monetary unit: 1 afghani (Af) = 100 puls (puli); valuation (Oct. 4, 1993) 1 U.S.$ = Af 1,520; 1 £ = Af 2,304.

Area and population

Regions	area sq mi	area sq km	population 1988 estimate
Eastern	28,664	74,240	2,050,400
North-central	20,461	52,994	2,584,400
North-east	29,911	77,468	1,478,400
North-west	50,581	131,005	2,157,100
South-central	32,963	85,375	1,215,700
South-east	12,546	32,494	4,252,000
Western	76,699	198,649	1,666,400
TOTAL	251,825	652,225	15,404,400

Demography

Population (1993): 20,269,000.
Density (1993): persons per sq mi 80.5, persons per sq km 31.1.
Urban-rural (1990): urban 18.2%; rural 81.8%.
Sex distribution (1990): male 51.42%; female 48.58%.
Age breakdown (1990): under 15, 42.0%; 15–29, 27.3%; 30–44, 15.8%; 45–59, 10.1%; 60–74, 4.2%; 75 and over, 0.6%.
Population projection: (2000) 26,767,000; (2010) 33,539,000.
Doubling time: 24 years.
Ethnic composition (1983): Pashtun 52.3%; Tadzhik 20.3%; Uzbek 8.7%; Hazāra 8.7%; Chahar Aimak 2.9%; Turkmen 2.0%; Baluchi 1.0%; other 4.1%.
Religious affiliation (1989): Sunnī Muslim 74%; Shīʿī Muslim 25%; other 1%.
Major cities (1988): Kabul 1,424,400; Kandahār (Qandahār) 225,500; Herāt 177,300; Mazār-e Sharīf 130,600.

Vital statistics

Birth rate per 1,000 population (1993): 51 (world avg. 26.4).
Death rate per 1,000 population (1993): 22 (world avg. 9.2).
Natural increase rate per 1,000 population (1993): 29 (world avg. 17.2).
Total fertility rate (avg. births per childbearing woman; 1993): 6.7.
Life expectancy at birth (1993): male 44.0 years; female 43.0 years.
Major causes of death per 100,000 population: n.a.; however, in 1982, injuries and poisoning, infectious and parasitic diseases, and diseases of the respiratory system were the leading causes of death reported in hospitals.

National economy

Budget (1987–88). Revenue: Af 79,800,000,000 (1984–85; tax revenue 45.4%, nontax revenue 54.6%). Expenditures: Af 105,800,000,000 (1981–82; governmental ministries 50.0%, developmental budget 31.9%, foreign-debt service 13.9%, surplus 1.6%).
Public debt (external, outstanding; 1989): U.S.$4,964,000,000.
Production (metric tons except as noted). Agriculture, forestry, fishing (1992): wheat 1,650,000, grapes 330,000, corn (maize) 300,000, rice 300,000, potatoes 224,000, barley 150,000; livestock (number of live animals) 13,500,000 sheep, 2,150,000 goats, 1,650,000 cattle, 1,300,000 asses, 350,000 horses, 265,000 camels, 7,000,000 chickens; roundwood (1991) 6,759,000 cu m; fish catch (1991) 1,500. Mining and quarrying (1991): salt 12,000; copper 5,000; gypsum 3,000; barite 2,000. Manufacturing (by production value in Af '000,000,000; 1987–88): pharmaceutical products 462.5; food products 203.0; industrial chemicals (including fertilizers) 123.4; cement 104.0; textiles 15.6; salt 15.4. Construction (Af '000,000; 1985): 1,094. Energy production (consumption): electricity (kW-hr; 1991) 1,015,000,000 (1,015,000,000); coal (metric tons; 1991) 135,000 (135,000); petroleum products (metric tons; 1991) 3,000 (558,000); natural gas (cu m; 1991) 2,356,000,000 (1,421,000,000).
Household size. Average household size (1979)[3] 6.2.
Tourism: receipts (1988) U.S.$1,000,000; expenditures (1987) U.S.$1,000,000.
Population economically active (1989–90)[3]: total 6,009,000; activity rate of total population 38.0% (participation rates [1985]: ages 10–59, 43.1%; female 7.9%; unemployed 3.0%).

Price index (1985 = 100)

	1986	1987	1988	1989	1990	1991	1992 (March)
Consumer price index	96.8	115.7	138.7	242.9	344.7	540.0	805.3

Gross national product (1988): U.S.$3,100,000,000 (U.S.$220 per capita).

Structure of gross domestic product and labour force

	1989–90		1981–82	
	in value Af '000,000[4]	% of total value	labour force	% of labour force
Agriculture	65,600	52.6	2,194,770	57.3
Manufacturing, mining, and public utilities	35,600	28.5	466,860	12.2
Construction	7,200	5.8	48,880	1.3
Transp. and commun.	4,400	3.5	65,650	1.7
Trade	9,900	7.9	126,100	3.3
Public administration }			79,260	2.1
Public services }	2,000	1.6	204,940	5.3
Other }			642,360	16.8
TOTAL	124,700	100.0[5]	3,828,820	100.0

Land use (1991): forested 2.9%; meadows and pastures 46.0%; agricultural and under permanent cultivation 12.4%; other 38.7%.

Foreign trade

Balance of trade (current prices)

	1985	1986	1987	1988	1989	1990
Af '000,000	−23,863	−33,826	−17,917	−19,642	−24,217	−27,000
% of total	29.4%	37.8%	25.7%	33.0%	50.4%	53.2%

Imports (1990): U.S.$1,416,200,000 (1989–90; machinery 37.7%, basic manufactures 18.3%, minerals and fuels 10.9%). *Major import sources:* U.S.S.R. 56.3%; Japan 9.4%; Singapore 5.6%; India 2.9%; South Korea 2.2%.
Exports (1990): U.S.$794,400,000 (dried fruits and nuts 42.7%, carpets and rugs 16.5%, wool and hides 7.7%, cotton 1.1%). *Major export destinations:* U.S.S.R. 72.4%; Western Europe 11.0%; India 3.1%.

Transport and communications

Transport. Railroads (1988): length 10 km. Roads (1988): total length 19,200 km (paved 47%). Vehicles (1990): passenger cars 31,000; trucks and buses 25,000. Merchant marine: none. Air transport (1991): passenger-km 205,000,000; metric ton-km cargo 27,000,000; airports (1993) with scheduled flights 1.
Communications. Daily newspapers (1989): total number 16; total circulation 108,400[6]; circulation per 1,000 population 7.36[6]. Radio (1992): 1,500,000 receivers (1 per 12 persons). Television (1992): 100,000 receivers (1 per 181 persons). Telephones (1984): 31,200 (1 per 443 persons).

Education and health

Education (1988–89)

	schools	teachers	students	student/ teacher ratio
Primary	553	16,756	586,014	35.0
Secondary	819	5,715	271,000	47.4
Voc., teacher tr.	33	556	8,537	15.4
Higher	5	198	1,491	7.5

Educational attainment (1980). Percentage of population age 25 and over having: no formal schooling 88.5%; some primary education 6.8%; complete primary 0.3%; some secondary 1.2%; postsecondary 3.2%. *Literacy* (1990): percentage of total population age 15 and over literate 29.4%; males 44.1%; females 13.9%.
Health: physicians (1987) 2,957 (1 per 4,797 persons); hospital beds (1981–82) 6,875 (1 per 2,054 persons); infant mortality rate (1993) 161.
Food (1984–86): daily per capita caloric intake 2,290 (vegetable products 90%, animal products 10%); 91% of FAO recommended minimum requirement.

Military

Total active duty personnel (1993): no identifiable military units appear to represent the central government). *Military expenditure as percentage of GNP* (1984): 9.1% (world 5.6%); per capita expenditure U.S.$24.

[1]Central government in Kabul unites a number of Sunnī mujahedin guerrilla groups, who, following traditional deliberative and legislative models, have established a state, a parliament, and a constitution (through September 1993), though none is fully established in all of Afghanistan. [2]Consisting of a nonelective body (named by the previous *Shura*, or constituent assembly), having the purpose of establishing a constitution and restoring civilian government. [3]Based on settled population only. [4]At prices of 1978–79. [5]Detail does not add to total given because of rounding. [6]Circulation for 13 dailies only.

Albania

Official name: Republika e Shqipërisë (Republic of Albania).
Form of government: unitary multiparty republic with one legislative house (People's Assembly [140])[1].
Chief of state: President.
Head of government: Prime Minister.
Capital: Tiranë.
Official language: Albanian.
Official religion: none.
Monetary unit: 1 lek = 100 qindars; valuation (Oct. 4, 1993) 1 U.S.$ = 109.20 leks; 1 £ = 165.44 leks.

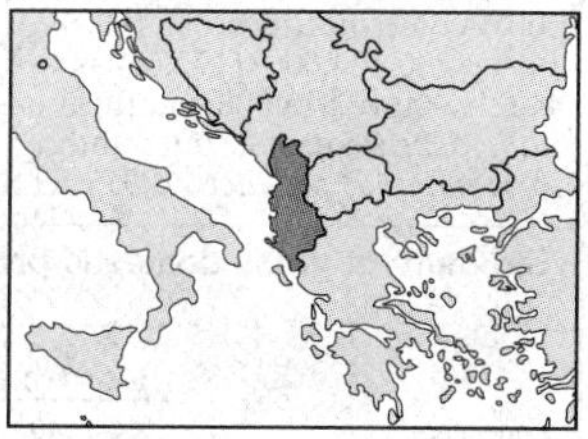

Area and population

Provinces	Capitals	area sq mi	area sq km	population 1990 estimate
Berat	Berat	396	1,027	180,489
Dibër	Peshkopi	605	1,568	153,775
Durrës	Durrës	327	848	251,029
Elbasan	Elbasan	572	1,481	248,676
Fier	Fier	454	1,175	251,115
Gjirokastër	Gjirokastër	439	1,137	67,392
Gramsh	Gramsh	268	695	44,791
Kolonjë	Ersekë	311	805	25,291
Korçë	Korçë	842	2,181	218,219
Krujë	Krujë	234	607	109,876
Kukës	Kukës	514	1,330	104,731
Lezhë	Lezhë	185	479	63,505
Librazhd	Librazhd	391	1,013	73,871
Lushnjë	Lushnjë	275	712	137,830
Mat	Burrel	397	1,028	78,754
Mirditë	Rrëshen	335	867	51,701
Përmet	Përmet	359	929	40,419
Pogradec	Pogradec	280	725	73,333
Pukë	Pukë	399	1,034	50,286
Sarandë	Sarandë	424	1,097	89,456
Shkodër	Shkodër	976	2,528	241,549
Skrapar	Çorovoda	299	775	47,605
Tepelenë	Tepelenë	315	817	51,022
Tiranë	Tiranë	478	1,238	374,483
Tropojë	Bajram	403	1,043	45,965
Vlorë	Vlorë	621	1,609	180,725
TOTAL		11,100[2]	28,748	3,255,891[2]

Demography

Population (1993): 3,422,000.
Density (1993): persons per sq mi 308.3, persons per sq km 119.0.
Urban-rural (1990): urban 36.1%; rural 63.9%.
Sex distribution (1990): male 51.40%; female 48.60%.
Age breakdown (1989): under 15, 33.0%; 15–29, 28.9%; 30–44, 18.5%; 45–59, 11.7%; 60–74, 5.9%; 75 and over, 2.0%.
Population projection: (2000) 3,862,000; (2010) 4,592,000.
Doubling time: 37 years.
Ethnic composition (1989): Albanian 98.0%; Greek 1.8%; Macedonian 0.1%; other 0.1%.
Religious affiliation (1992): a significant portion of the population are nonreligious; believers identify themselves as: Muslim 65%; Orthodox 20%; Roman Catholic 13%; other 2%.
Major cities (1990): Tiranë 243,000; Durrës 85,400; Elbasan 83,300; Shkodër 81,800; Vlorë 73,800.

Vital statistics

Birth rate per 1,000 population (1990): 25.2 (world avg. 27.1).
Death rate per 1,000 population (1990): 5.6 (world avg. 9.8).
Natural increase rate per 1,000 population (1990): 19.6 (world avg. 17.3).
Total fertility rate (avg. births per childbearing woman; 1991): 2.9.
Marriage rate per 1,000 population (1990): 8.9.
Divorce rate per 1,000 population (1990): 0.8.
Life expectancy at birth (1989–90): male 69.3 years; female 75.4 years.
Major causes of death per 100,000 population: n.a.; however, in 1983 the leading causes of death were cardiovascular diseases, diseases of the respiratory system, malignant neoplasms (cancers), and injuries.

National economy

Budget (1990). Revenue: 8,292,000,000 leks (surplus from state enterprises 73.1%, social insurance 11.7%, other 15.2%). Expenditures: 10,869,000,000 leks (economy 55.2%, social and cultural services 27.5%, defense 9.1%, administration 1.5%).
Public debt (1991): U.S.$350,000,000.
Tourism (1990): number of tourist arrivals 30,000; receipts from visitors, n.a.
Production (metric tons except as noted). Agriculture, forestry, fishing (1991): wheat 300,000, vegetables and melons 248,000, sugar beets 205,000, corn (maize) 180,000, potatoes 65,000, grapes 52,000, barley 26,000, sorghum 25,000, olives 18,000, oats 18,000, sunflower seeds 14,000, tobacco 12,000; livestock (number of live animals) 1,600,000 sheep, 1,000,000 goats, 650,000 cattle, 170,000 pigs, 100,000 horses, 76,000 mules and asses; roundwood 2,556,000 cu m; fish catch (1990) 11,961. Mining and quarrying (1991): ferronickel ore 1,273,000; chromite ore 612,000; copper 565,500; salt 52,000. Manufacturing (1990)[3]: crude oil 1,067,000; cement 644,000; bread 378,000; distillate fuel oils 374,000; flour 352,000; phosphate fertilizers 141,000; bitumen grit 95,000; urea 90,000; sulfuric acid 68,000; rolled steel 64,000; caustic soda 32,000; refractory bricks 25,000; soda ash 23,000; soaps and detergents 21,000; spare parts 481,000,000 leks; machinery and equipment 368,000,000 leks; footwear 5,990,000 pairs; heavy cloth 8,000,000 metres; beer 187,000 hectolitres; cigarettes 4,947,000 units; radio receivers 26,000 units; television receivers 18,000 units. Construction (1990): 12,428 units. Energy production (consumption): electricity (kW-hr; 1990) 3,718,000,000 (3,513,000,000); coal (metric tons; 1990) 1,059,000 (1,059,000); crude petroleum (barrels; 1990) 7,821,000 (7,821,000); petroleum products (metric tons; 1990) 1,200,000 (1,200,000); natural gas (cu m; 1990) 696,000,000 (397,000,000).
Gross national product (1991): U.S.$7,233,000,000 (U.S.$2,150 per capita).

Structure of net material product and labour force

	1990 value '000,000 leks	1990 % of total value	1990 labour force	1990 % of labour force
Agriculture	4,705	35.9	674,000	47.0
Manufacturing, mining, public utilities	5,486	41.8	338,000	23.6
Construction	845	6.4	97,000	6.8
Transp. and commun.	435	3.3	29,000	2.0
Trade	1,333	10.1	26,000	1.8
Pub. admin., defense; Services; Other	318	2.5	269,000	18.8
TOTAL	13,122	100.0	1,433,000	100.0

Population economically active (1989): total 1,599,766; activity rate of total population 50.3% (participation rates: ages 15–64, 90.2%; female 87.6%; unemployed [1992] as much as 50.0%).

Price and earnings indexes (1985 = 100)

	1985	1986	1987	1988	1989	1990
Consumer price index	...	...	...	...	...	...
Annual earnings index	100.0	100.9	101.3	101.9	102.8	106.5

Household income and expenditure. Average household size (1989) 4.7; income per household 14,505 leks (U.S.$ value, n.a.); sources of income: wages 80.2%, social insurance 13.0%; expenditure: n.a.
Land use (1990): forested 38.2%; meadows and pastures 14.7%; agricultural and under permanent cultivation 25.8%; other 21.3%.

Foreign trade

Balance of trade (current prices)

	1985	1986	1987	1988	1989	1990
'000,000 leks	−420	−175	−160	−668	−763	−1,522
% of total	9.1%	3.4%	3.1%	11.6%	11.2%	25.1%

Imports (1990): 3,795,000,000 leks (machinery and transport equipment 30.9%; fuels, minerals, and metals 24.5%; organic raw materials 15.7%; food 10.1%; chemical products 9.3%; consumer goods 8.4%). *Major import sources:* Italy 9.8%; West Germany 8.8%; East Germany 8.7%; Czechoslovakia 8.6%; Bulgaria 6.3%; China 6.2%; Austria 6.0%; Greece 5.5%; Yugoslavia 5.2%; Romania 4.8%; Poland 4.4%; Hungary 3.8%; France 2.6%.
Exports (1990): 2,273,000,000 leks (fuels, minerals, and metals 46.8%; food 22.1%; raw materials of plant and animal origin 15.4%; consumer goods 11.8%). *Major export destinations:* Czechoslovakia 14.8%; Italy 9.0%; Bulgaria 8.3%; Yugoslavia 6.9%; Hungary 5.7%; West Germany 5.3%; China 4.9%; Romania 4.7%; Poland 4.7%; Austria 4.7%; Greece 2.9%; Japan 2.1%.

Transport and communications

Transport. Railroads (1990): length 720 km; passenger-km 779,200,000; metric ton-km cargo 584,000,000. Roads (1990): total length 7,450 km (paved 38%). Vehicles (1991): passenger cars 16,000; trucks and buses 32,900. Merchant marine (1990): vessels (100 gross tons and over) 24; total deadweight tonnage 80,954. Air transport: passengers, n.a.; cargo, n.a.; airports (1993) with scheduled flights 1.
Communications. Daily newspapers (1990): total number 2; total circulation 135,000; circulation per 1,000 population 42. Radio (1991): 525,000 receivers (1 per 6.3 persons). Television (1989): 324,905[4] receivers (1 per 9.8 persons). Telephones (1990): 52,600 (1 per 62 persons).

Education and health

Education (1990)

	schools	teachers	students	student/teacher ratio
Primary (age 6–13)	1,726	28,798	557,000	19.3
Secondary (age 14–17)	47	2,318	68,000	29.3
Voc., teacher tr.	466	7,390	138,000	18.7
Higher	8	1,806	27,000	15.0

Educational attainment (1979). Percentage of population age 25 and over having: primary education 74.7%; secondary 20.9%; higher 4.4%. *Literacy* (1989)[5]: 91.8%; males 95.4%; females 88.0%.
Health (1990): physicians 5,566 (1 per 585 persons); hospital beds 19,000 (1 per 173 persons); infant mortality rate per 1,000 live births (1990) 28.3.
Food (1988–90): daily per capita caloric intake 2,585 (vegetable products 84%, animal products 16%); 97% of FAO recommended minimum requirement.

Military

Total active duty personnel (1992): 40,000 (army 67.5%, navy 5.0%, air force 27.5%). *Military expenditure as percentage of GNP* (1989): 4.1% (world 4.9%); per capita expenditure U.S.$50.

[1]A transitional constitution was adopted on April 29, 1991. [2]Detail does not add to total given because of rounding. [3]State sector only. [4]Families that had a television receiver. [5]Population age 10 years and older.

Algeria

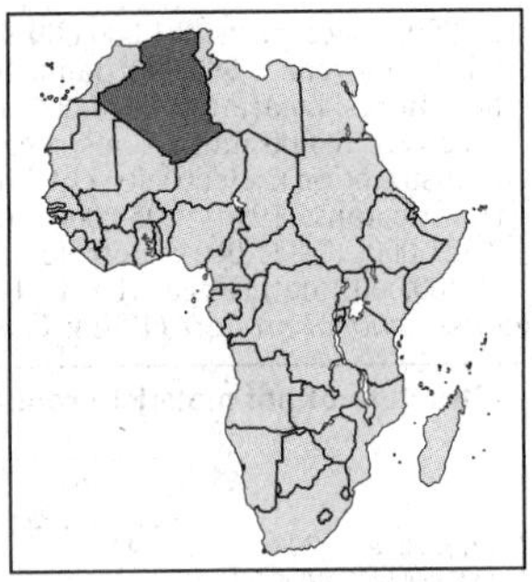

Official name: al-Jumhūrīyah al-Jazā'irīyah ad-Dīmuqrāṭīyah ash-Sha'bīyah (Arabic) (Democratic and Popular Republic of Algeria).
Form of government: military-dominated extraconstitutional administration with one interim legislative body (National Consultative Council [60]).
Chief of state: President assisted by High State Council.
Head of government: Prime Minister.
Capital: Algiers.
Official language: Arabic.
Official religion: Islam.
Monetary unit: 1 Algerian dinar (DA) = 100 centimes; valuation (Oct. 4, 1993) 1 U.S.$ = DA 19.20; 1 £ = DA 29.09.

Population (1987 census)

Wilāyat	population	Wilāyat	population
Adrar	217,678	Médéa	652,863
Aïn Defla	537,256	Mila	511,605
Aïn Temouchent	274,990	Mostaganem	505,932
Alger	1,690,191	M'Sila	604,693
Annaba	455,888	Naâma	113,700
Batna	752,617	Oran	932,473
el-Bayadh	153,254	Ouargla	284,454
Béchar	185,346	el-Oued	376,909
Bejaïa	700,952	Oum el-Bouaghi	403,936
Biskra	430,202	Relizane	544,877
Blida	702,188	Saïda	235,494
Bordj Bou Arreridj	424,828	Sétif	1,000,694
Bouira	526,900	Sidi bel-Abbès	446,277
Boumerdes	650,975	Skikda	622,510
ech-Chleff	684,192	Souk Ahras	296,077
Constantine	664,303	Tamanrasset	95,822
Djelfa	494,494	et-Tarf	275,315
Ghardaïa	216,140	Tébessa	410,233
Guelma	353,309	Tiaret	575,794
Illizi	18,930	Tindouf	16,428
Jijel	472,312	Tipaza	620,151
Khenchela	246,541	Tissemsilt	228,120
Laghouat	212,388	Tizi Ouzou	936,948
Mascara	566,901	Tlemcen	714,862
		TOTAL	23,038,942[1]

Demography

Area: 919,595 sq mi, 2,381,741 sq km.
Population (1993): 27,029,000[2].
Density (1993): persons per sq mi 29.4, persons per sq km 11.3.
Urban-rural (1990): urban 51.7%; rural 48.3%.
Sex distribution (1990): male 49.86%; female 50.14%.
Age breakdown (1990): under 15, 43.7%; 15–29, 28.7%; 30–44, 14.2%; 45–59, 8.1%; 60–74, 4.1%; 75 and over, 1.2%.
Population projection: (2000) 32,401,000; (2010) 40,062,000.
Doubling time: 28 years.
Ethnic composition (1983): Arab 82.6%; Berber 17.0%; other 0.4%.
Religious affiliation (1990): Muslim 99.9%, of which Sunnī 99.5%, Ibāḍīyah 0.4%; Roman Catholic 0.1%.
Major cities (1987): Algiers 1,507,241; Oran 609,823; Constantine 440,842; Annaba 222,518; Batna 181,601.

Vital statistics

Birth rate per 1,000 population (1991): 32.0 (world avg. 26.4); legitimacy rate, n.a.; marriage, however, is nearly universal.
Death rate per 1,000 population (1991): 7.0 (world avg. 9.2).
Natural increase rate per 1,000 population (1991): 25.0 (world avg. 17.2).
Total fertility rate (avg. births per childbearing woman; 1991): 4.9.
Marriage rate per 1,000 population (1990): 5.9.
Divorce rate per 1,000 population (1985): 2.1.
Life expectancy at birth (1990–95): male 65.0 years; female 67.3 years.
Notified cases of infectious diseases per 100,000 population (1988): hepatitis 13.4; dysentery 8.6; typhoid fever 8.3; meningitis 6.7.

National economy

Budget (1993). Revenue: DA 335,600,000,000 (hydrocarbons 57.5%, business taxes 9.8%, customs duties 8.9%). Expenditures: DA 503,900,000,000 (public investments 21.6%, nationalized industries 16.6%, welfare 8.3%, defense 5.9%, education 2.9%).
Tourism (1990): receipts from visitors U.S.$64,000,000; expenditures by nationals abroad U.S.$149,000,000.
Production (metric tons except as noted). Agriculture, forestry, fishing (1991): barley 1,751,000, wheat 1,741,000, potatoes 1,000,000, tomatoes 500,000, grapes 260,000, dates 215,000, oranges 190,000, olives 130,000; livestock (number of live animals) 13,350,000 sheep, 3,800,000 goats, 1,443,000 cattle; roundwood 2,221,000 cu m; fish catch (1990) 91,093. Mining and quarrying (1990): iron ore 2,941,000; phosphate rock 1,128,000; mercury 637,000 kilograms. Manufacturing (1990): cement 6,337,000; flour and semolina 2,588,000; bricks 1,679,000; pig iron 1,037,000; crude steel 767,000; edible oils 338,000; sugar 209,000; trucks 4,291 units. Construction: n.a. Energy production (consumption): electricity (kW-hr; 1990) 15,994,000,000 (15,934,000,000); coal (metric tons; 1990) 10,000 (1,210,000); crude petroleum (barrels; 1991) 290,124,000 (172,650,000[3]); petroleum products (metric tons; 1990) 41,058,000 (6,813,000); natural gas (cu m; 1991) 43,321,000,000 (19,034,000[3]).
Public debt (external, outstanding; December 1992): U.S.$26,160,000,000.
Gross national product (1991): U.S.$52,239,000,000 (U.S.$2,020 per capita).

Structure of gross domestic product and labour force

	1989		1990	
	in value U.S.$'000,000[4]	% of total value	labour force	% of labour force
Agriculture	3,240	7.1	907,490	15.9
Mining	8,532	18.7	55,000[5]	1.0[5]
Manufacturing	5,377	11.8	646,390	11.3
Public utilities	994	2.2	651,370	11.4
Construction	8,900	19.5		
Transp. and commun.	3,087	6.7	252,230	4.4
Trade	8,129	17.8	444,970	7.8
Finance, real estate	...	...	...	...
Pub. admin., defense	6,655	14.5	1,318,370	23.1
Other	779	1.7	1,435,180[6]	25.1[6]
TOTAL	45,693	100.0	5,711,000	100.0

Population economically active (1990): total 5,711,000; activity rate of population 22.8% (1987; participation rates: ages 15–64, 44.3%; female 9.2%; unemployed [1993] officially *c.* 20.0%, unofficially *c.* 40.0%).

Price and earnings indexes (1985 = 100)

	1986	1987	1988	1989	1990	1991	1992[7]
Consumer price index	112.4	120.7	127.9	139.8	163.0	200.3	242.0
Earnings index	...	...	...	...	...	...	...

Household income and expenditure. Average household size (1987) 6.9; income per household: n.a.; sources of income: n.a.; expenditure (1979–80): food and beverages 55.7%, clothing and footwear 9.1%, transportation and communications 6.7%, household furnishings 6.4%, housing and energy 5.4%.
Land use (1990): forested 2.0%; meadows and pastures 13.1%; agricultural and under permanent cultivation 3.2%; other (mostly desert) 81.7%.

Foreign trade[8]

Balance of trade (current prices)

	1986	1987	1988	1989	1990	1991
DA '000,000	−8,459	+7,583	+1,994	+1,865	+27,374	+59,299
% of total	10.8%	10.0%	2.2%	1.3%	13.6%	15.0%

Imports (1990): DA 87,018,000,000 (electrical and nonelectrical machinery 30.4%, food and beverages 19.4%, transportation equipment 13.5%). *Major import sources* (1991): France 26.3%; Italy 13.4%; Germany 8.9%; U.S. 8.8%; Spain 7.8%.
Exports (1990): DA 114,392,000,000 (petroleum and natural gas 96.9%, pig iron and crude steel 0.5%, wines 0.2%). *Major export destinations* (1991): Italy 21.7%; U.S. 16.8%; France 15.1%; Germany 8.3%; Spain 7.6%.

Transport and communications

Transport. Railroads (1990): route length 2,668 mi, 4,293 km; passenger-km 2,991,000,000; metric ton-km cargo 2,690,000,000. Roads (1991): total length 90,000 km (paved 70%). Vehicles (1991): passenger cars 760,000; trucks and buses 510,000. Merchant marine (1992): vessels (100 gross tons and over) 149; total deadweight tonnage 1,093,363. Air transport (1991)[9]: passenger-km 3,092,000,000; metric ton-km cargo 24,347,000; airports (1993) 25.
Communications. Daily newspapers (1992): total number 9; total circulation 1,412,000[10]; circulation per 1,000 population 54[10]. Radio (1992): 3,500,000 receivers (1 per 7.5 persons). Television (1992): 2,000,000 receivers (1 per 13 persons). Telephones (1990): 1,103,403 (1 per 23 persons).

Education and health

Education (1991–92)

	schools	teachers	students	student/ teacher ratio
Primary (age 6–11)	13,560	156,937	4,317,018	27.5
Secondary (age 12–18)	3,288	127,754	2,171,452	17.0
Voc., teacher tr.	147	6,343	127,963	20.2
Higher[11]	...	20,562	258,995	12.6

Educational attainment (1989). Percentage of economically active population age 16 and over having: no formal schooling 38.2%; Qur'anic education 0.9%; primary education 20.8%; secondary education 11.1%; vocational 19.7%; higher 9.3%. *Literacy* (1990): total population age 15 and over literate 8,090,000 (57.4%); males literate 4,840,000 (69.8%); females literate 3,250,000 (45.5%).
Health: physicians (1990) 23,550 (1 per 1,062 persons); hospital beds (1988) 60,514 (1 per 393 persons); infant mortality rate per 1,000 live births (1991) 57.0.
Food (1988–90): daily per capita caloric intake 2,944 (vegetable products 89%, animal products 11%); 123% of FAO recommended minimum requirement.

Military

Total active duty personnel (1992): 139,000 (army 86.3%, navy 5.0%, air force 8.7%). *Military expenditure as percentage of GNP* (1989): 5.1% (world 4.9%); per capita expenditure U.S.$94.

[1]De facto population. [2]Excludes *c.* 2,500,000 Algerians in France. [3]1990. [4]At factor cost. [5]Crude petroleum and natural gas only. [6]Includes 1,141,278 unemployed, of whom 862,117 were not previously employed. [7]March. [8]Imports c.i.f., exports f.o.b. [9]Air Algérie. [10]For seven newspapers only. [11]1989–90.

Andorra

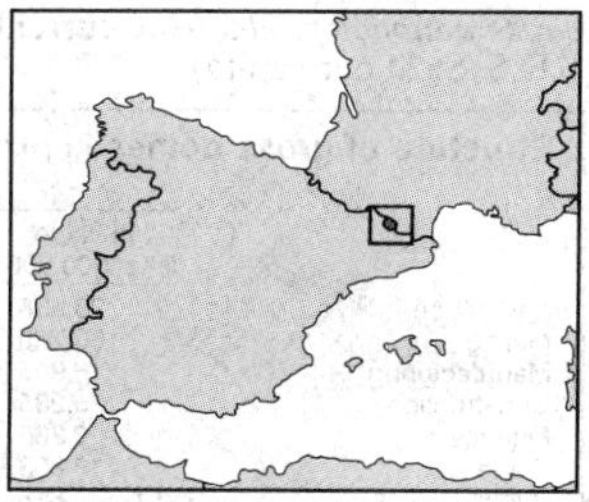

Official name: Principat (Co-Principat) or Senyoriu (Co-Senyoriu) d'Andorra; les Valls d'Andorra (Principality [or Co-Principality] of Andorra; the Valleys of Andorra).
Form of government: parliamentary coprincipality[1] with one legislative house (General Council of the Valleys [28]).
Chiefs of state: President of France; Bishop of Urgel, Spain.
Head of government: Chief executive.
Capital: Andorra la Vella.
Official language: Catalan.
Official religion: Roman Catholicism.
Monetary unit: There is no local currency of issue; the French franc and Spanish peseta are both in circulation. 1 franc (F) = 100 centimes; 1 peseta (Pta) = 100 céntimos.
Valuation (Oct. 4, 1993)
1 U.S.$ = F 5.67, 1 £ = F 8.58;
1 U.S.$ = Ptas 130.86,
1 £ = Ptas 198.25.

Area and population

		area		population
Parishes	**Capitals**	sq mi	sq km	1993[2] estimate
Andorra la Vella	Andorra la Vella	49[3]	127[3]	22,387
Canillo	Canillo }	74	191	2,193
Encamp	Encamp }			9,654
La Massana	La Massana	25	65	5,302
Les Escaldes-Engordany	—	[3]	[3]	13,177
Ordino	Ordino	33	85	1,652
Sant Julià de Lòria	Sant Julià de Lòria	[3]	[3]	7,234
TOTAL		181	468	61,599

Demography

Population (1993): 61,900.
Density (1993): persons per sq mi 342.0, persons per sq km 132.3.
Urban-rural (1990): urban 62.5%; rural 37.5%.
Sex distribution (1993): male 53.14%; female 46.86%.
Age breakdown (1993): under 15, 16.3%; 15–29, 27.7%; 30–44, 27.2%; 45–59, 15.1%; 60–74, 9.9%; 75 and over, 3.8%.
Population projection: (2000) 66,000; (2010) 71,000.
Doubling time: 82 years.
Ethnic composition (by nationality; 1993): Spanish 46.4%; Andorran 28.3%; Portuguese 11.1%; French 7.6%; British 1.8%; German 0.5%; other 4.3%.
Religious affiliation (1991): Roman Catholic 90.0%; other 10.0%.
Major cities (1993): Andorra la Vella 22,387; Les Escaldes 13,177; Encamp 9,654.

Vital statistics

Birth rate per 1,000 population (1992): 12.1 (world avg. 26.4).
Death rate per 1,000 population (1992): 3.6 (world avg. 9.2).
Natural increase rate per 1,000 population (1992): 8.5 (world avg. 17.2).
Total fertility rate (avg. births per childbearing woman; 1991): 1.3.
Marriage rate per 1,000 population (1992): 2.2.
Divorce rate per 1,000 population: n.a.
Life expectancy at birth (1990): male 74.0 years; female 81.0 years.
Major causes of death per 100,000 population: n.a.; however, health problems are those of a developed country—cardiovascular disease, hypertension, malignant neoplasms (cancers).

National economy

Budget (1990). Revenue: Ptas 12,470,000,000 (excise taxes on imported consumer goods and gasoline 87.4%). Expenditures: Ptas 21,370,000,000 (development expenditures 55.9%, of which public services 49.1%; current expenditures 41.1%, of which education and culture 10.6%, tourism and exports 6.1%).
Production (value of recorded exported products in Ptas '000 except as noted). Agriculture (1990): cattle 214,600, sheep and goats 11,200, horses and mules 5,800, tobacco 2,100, milk 1,600, sugar 1,200, natural honey 600. Quarrying (1990): marble 32,000. Manufacturing (1990): wearing apparel for men and boys 1,269,000; mineral water 435,700; electrical machinery and apparatus for industry 145,400; sports clothing 142,100; plastic products 61,400; scrap paper and pasteboard 43,300. Construction (1984): 90 buildings totaling 83,834 sq m were authorized for construction. Energy production (consumption): electricity (kW-hr; 1989) 140,000,000 ([1990] 278,300,000[4]); coal, none (n.a.); crude petroleum, none (n.a.); petroleum products (metric tons; 1986) none (95,349); natural gas, none (n.a.).
Population economically active (1989): total 24,734; activity rate of total population 55.1% (participation rates: ages 15–64, 74.3%; female 45.6%; unemployed, none).

Price and earnings indexes (1985 = 100)[5]

	1987	1988	1989	1990	1991	1992	1993[6]
Consumer price index	114.5	120.0	128.2	136.8	144.9	153.4	159.9
Earnings index	...	...	...	...	...	...	...

Gross national product (at current market prices; 1990): U.S.$1,062,000,000 (U.S.$20,160 per capita)[7].

Structure of labour force

	1989	
	labour force	% of labour force
Agriculture	291	1.2
Mining	...	...
Manufacturing	2,719	11.0
Construction	2,914	11.8
Public utilities	...	...
Transportation and communications	...	...
Trade	5,984	24.2
Restaurants, hotels	4,698	18.9
Finance, real estate, insurance	1,331	5.4
Pub. admin., defense	2,553	10.3
Other	4,127	16.7
Unknown	117	0.5
TOTAL	24,734	100.0

Land use (1991): forested 22.0%; meadows and pastures 56.0%; agricultural and under permanent cultivation 2.0%; other 20.0%.
Household income and expenditure. Average household size: n.a.; income per household: n.a.; sources of income: n.a.; expenditure: n.a.
Public debt: n.a.
Tourism: receipts from tourist arrivals, n.a.; expenditures by nationals abroad, n.a.; number of tourist arrivals (1988) approximately 12,000,000 annually, most of whom do not stay overnight; number of hotel rooms (1987) 35,000.

Foreign trade

Balance of trade (current prices)

	1985	1986	1987	1988	1989	1990
Ptas '000,000	...	−71,871	−73,200	−78,988	−89,007	−117,280
% of total	...	96.9%	93.8%	93.4%	94.2%	95.5%

Imports (1990): Ptas 120,023,000,000 (electrical and electronic equipment 11.9%, transport equipment 9.8%, wearing apparel 6.7%, nonelectrical machinery and equipment 5.0%, perfumes and cosmetics 4.8%, alcoholic beverages 4.6%, tobacco products 4.3%). *Major import sources:* France 36.7%; Spain 32.6%; Germany 7.0%; Japan 6.2%; Italy 3.2%.
Exports (1990): Ptas 2,743,000,000 (wearing apparel 52.1%, mineral water 15.9%, live cattle 7.8%, electrical and electronic equipment 7.3%, paper and paper products 2.9%). *Major export destinations:* France 64.1%; Spain 29.1%; Germany 3.5%; Portugal 1.4%.

Transport and communications

Transport. Railroads: none; however, both French and Spanish railways stop near the border. Roads (1991): total length 167 mi, 269 km (paved 74%). Vehicles (1990): passenger cars 34,168; trucks and buses 4,033. Merchant marine: vessels (100 gross tons and over) none. Airports (1993) with scheduled flights: none.
Communications. Daily newspapers (1992): total number 1; circulation 3,000; circulation per 1,000 population 50. Radio (1992): total number of receivers 10,000 (1 per 6.0 persons). Television (1990): total number of receivers 7,000 (1 per 7.5 persons). Telephones (1990): 20,750 (1 per 2.5 persons).

Education and health

Education (1990–91)

	schools	teachers	students	student/ teacher ratio
Primary (age 6–11)	...	...	...	...
Lower secondary (age 11–14)	12	...	2,303	...
Voc., teacher tr.	6	...	1,455	...
Higher	...	...	802[8, 9]	...

Educational attainment (mid-1980s). Percentage of population age 15 and over having: no formal schooling 5.5%; primary education 47.3%; secondary education 21.6%; postsecondary education 24.9%; unknown 0.7%. *Literacy* (1987): total population literate (virtually 100%).
Health (1990): physicians 105 (1 per 502 persons); hospital beds 121 (1 per 435 persons); infant mortality rate per 1,000 live births (1991–92 avg.) 6.4.
Food (1988–90)[10]: daily per capita caloric intake 3,533 (vegetable products 64%, animal products 36%); 142% of FAO recommended minimum requirement.

Military

Total active duty personnel (1990): none. France and Spain are responsible for Andorra's external security; a 100-person police force maintains domestic security.

[1]First constitution of country went into effect May 1993. [2]January 1. [3]Andorra la Vella includes Les Escaldes-Engordany and Sant Julià de Lòria. [4]Much electricity is imported from Spain. [5]In Spanish pesetas. [6]June. [7]Trade, tourism (including winter-season sports, fairs, and festivals), and the banking system (of some importance as a tax haven for foreign financial investment and transactions) are the primary sources of GNP. [8]Students attending universities in other countries. [9]1988–89. [10]Composite values derived from Spanish and French food data.

Angola

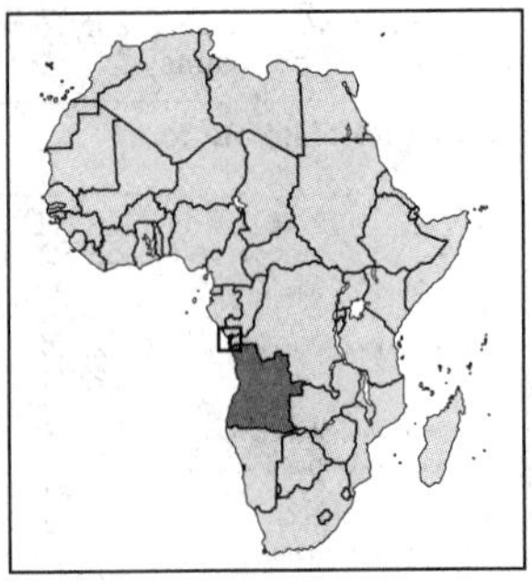

Official name: República de Angola (Republic of Angola).
Form of government: multiparty republic with one legislative house (National Assembly [220[1]]).
Head of state and government: President.
Capital: Luanda.
Official language: Portuguese.
Official religion: none.
Monetary unit: 1 New kwanza[2] (NKz) = 100 lwei; valuation (Oct. 4, 1993) 1 U.S.$ = NKz 4,000; 1 £ = NKz 6,080.

Area and population

Provinces	Capitals	area sq mi	area sq km	population 1993 estimate[3]
Bengo	Caxito	12,112	31,371	173,000
Benguela	Benguela	12,273	31,788	672,000
Bié	Kuito	27,148	70,314	1,184,000
Cabinda	Cabinda	2,807	7,270	174,000
Cunene	N'Giva	34,495	89,342	238,000
Huambo	Huambo	13,233	34,274	1,604,000
Huíla	Lubango	28,958	75,002	906,000
Kuando Kubango	Menongue	76,853	199,049	135,000
Kuanza Norte	N'Dalatando	9,340	24,190	394,000
Kuanza Sul	Sumbe	21,490	55,660	668,000
Luanda	Luanda	934	2,418	1,807,000
Lunda Norte	Lucapa	39,685	102,783	301,000
Lunda Sul	Saurimo	17,625	45,649	157,000
Malanje	Malanje	37,684	97,602	933,000
Moxico	Lwena	86,110	223,023	334,000
Namibe	Namibe	22,447	58,137	125,000
Uíge	Uíge	22,663	58,698	892,000
Zaire	M'Banza Kongo	15,494	40,130	219,000
TOTAL		481,354[4]	1,246,700	10,916,000

Demography

Population (1993): 10,916,000.
Density (1993): persons per sq mi 22.7, persons per sq km 8.8.
Urban-rural (1990): urban 28.3%; rural 71.7%.
Sex distribution (1991): male 48.80%; female 51.20%.
Age breakdown (1993): under 15, 45.0%; 15–29, 25.6%; 30–44, 15.1%; 45–59, 8.8%; 60 and over, 5.5%.
Population projection: (2000) 13,400,000; (2010) 18,082,000.
Doubling time: 25 years.
Ethnic composition (1983): Ovimbundu 37.2%; Mbundu 21.6%; Kongo 13.2%; Luimbe-Nganguela 5.4%; Nyaneka-Humbe 5.4%; Chokwe 4.2%; Luvale (Luena) 3.4%; Luchazi 2.4%; Ambo (Ovambo) 2.4%; Lunda 1.2%; Mbunda 1.2%; Portuguese 0.5%; mestizo 0.5%; other 0.4%.
Religious affiliation (1980): Christian 90.0%, of which Roman Catholic 68.7%, Protestant 19.8%; traditional beliefs 9.5%; other 0.5%.
Major cities: Luanda (1988) 1,134,000; Huambo (1983) 203,000; Benguela (1983) 155,000; Lobito (1983) 150,000; Lubango (1984) 105,000.

Vital statistics

Birth rate per 1,000 population (1990–95): 46.6 (world avg. 26.4).
Death rate per 1,000 population (1990–95): 18.6 (world avg. 9.2).
Natural increase rate per 1,000 population (1990–95): 28.0 (world avg. 17.2).
Total fertility rate (avg. births per childbearing woman; 1990–95): 6.3.
Marriage rate per 1,000 population (1972): 4.5.
Divorce rate per 1,000 population: n.a.
Life expectancy at birth (1990–95): male 44.9 years; female 48.1 years.
Major causes of death per 100,000 population (1973): accidents, poisoning, and violence 89.0; infectious and parasitic diseases 73.2; diseases of the respiratory system 24.6; diseases of the circulatory system 19.2; malignant neoplasms (cancers) 6.5.

National economy

Budget (1991). Revenue: NKz 186,383,000,000 (1989; tax revenue 82.8%, of which petroleum taxes 53.1%, income and property taxes 11.6%, domestic production taxes 9.5%, import duties 6.3%; nontax revenue 17.2%). Expenditures: NKz 275,468,000,000 (defense and internal security 36.9%; administration 23.9%; education 17.5%; health 7.5%; energy 3.6%; other 10.6%).
Public debt (external, outstanding; 1988): U.S.$1,356,000,000[5].
Tourism: receipts from visitors, n.a.; expenditures by nationals abroad, n.a.
Production (metric tons except as noted). Agriculture, forestry, fishing (1992): cassava 1,885,000, corn (maize) 369,000, sugarcane 320,000, bananas 280,000, sweet potatoes 170,000, millet 75,000, palm oil 40,000, dry beans 36,000, peanuts (groundnuts) 18,000, coffee 5,000; livestock (number of live animals) 3,200,000 cattle, 1,550,000 goats, 810,000 pigs, 250,000 sheep, 6,000,000 chickens; roundwood (1991) 6,593,000 cu m; fish catch (1991) 75,062. Mining and quarrying (1992): diamonds 900,000 carats. Manufacturing (1990): fresh meat 91,000[6]; bread 45,000; corn flour 35,000; wheat flour 22,000; laundry soap 7,556; sugar 3,190[7]; pasta 3,190[7]; leather shoes 132,000 pairs[7]; beer 410,000 hectolitres; soft drinks 69,050 hectolitres[7]; matches 6,357,000 boxes[7]. Construction (value in NKz '000,000; 1986); residential 608; nonresidential 1,977. Energy production (consumption): electricity (kW-hr; 1990) 1,840,000,000 (1,840,000,000); coal, none (none); crude petroleum (barrels; 1991) 180,205,000 ([1990] 11,506,000); petroleum products (metric tons; 1990) 1,311,000 (349,000); natural gas (cu m; 1990) 166,576,000 (166,576,000).

Gross national product (at current market prices; 1989): U.S.$6,010,000,000 (U.S. $620 per capita).

Structure of gross domestic product and labour force

	1991		1987	
	in value NKz '000,000[8]	% of total value	labour force	% of labour force
Agriculture	28,558	10.3	2,741,000	71.4
Mining	160,750	58.2	384,000	10.0
Manufacturing	6,935	2.5		
Construction	5,235	1.9		
Finance	2,360	0.9		
Trade	16,803	6.1		
Public utilities	818	0.3		
Transportation and communications	6,255	2.3		
Pub. admin., defense / Services	48,391	17.5	714,000	18.6
Other	...	...		
TOTAL	276,105	100.0	3,839,000	100.0

Population economically active (1987): total 3,839,000; activity rate of total population 41.9% (participation rates [1985]: ages 15–64, 71.8%; female 39.7%; unemployed, n.a.).
Price and earnings indexes: n.a.
Household income and expenditure. Average household size (1980) 4.8; annual income per household: n.a.; sources of income: n.a.; expenditure: n.a.
Land use (1991): forested 41.7%; meadows and pastures 23.3%; agricultural and under permanent cultivation 2.7%; other 32.3%.

Foreign trade

Balance of trade (current prices)

	1986	1987	1988	1989	1990	1991
U.S.$'000,000	+206	+953	+1,081	+1,191	+1,276	+2,080
% of total	8.6%	26.6%	28.1%	25.1%	25.1%	43.6%

Imports (1991): U.S.$1,347,000,000 (current consumption goods 50.2%, capital goods 20.2%, intermediate consumption goods 18.9%, transport equipment 6.8%). *Major import sources:* Portugal 29.8%; United States 10.5%; France 9.7%; Japan 7.8%; Brazil 7.3%.
Exports (1991): U.S.$3,427,000,000 (mineral fuels 89.8%, diamonds 5.5%). *Major export destinations:* United States 56.6%; Germany 5.6%; Brazil 4.9%; The Netherlands 4.2%; United Kingdom 3.4%; Belgium-Luxembourg 3.3%.

Transport and communications

Transport. Railroads (1988): route length 1,739 mi, 2,798 km; passenger-mi 203,000,000, passenger-km 326,000,000; short ton-mi cargo 1,178,000,000, metric ton-km cargo 1,720,000,000. Roads (1990): total length 45,118 mi, 72,611 km (paved 11%). Vehicles (1991): passenger cars 120,000; trucks and buses 40,000. Merchant marine (1992): vessels (100 gross tons and over) 113; total deadweight tonnage 123,479. Air transport (1985)[9]: passenger-mi 606,000,000, passenger-km 975,000,000; short ton-mi cargo 23,200,000, metric ton-km cargo 33,900,000; airports (1993) with scheduled flights 16.
Communications. Daily newspapers (1992): total number 4; total circulation 84,500[10]; circulation per 1,000 population 7.7[10]. Radio (1992): total number of receivers 450,000 (1 per 24 persons). Television (1992): total number of receivers 50,500 (1 per 210 persons). Telephones (1991): 78,000 (1 per 132 persons).

Education and health

Education (1989–90)

	schools	teachers	students	student/ teacher ratio
Primary (age 7–10)	6,308[11]	32,157[12]	1,041,126	...
Secondary (age 11–16)	5,276[11]	5,138	155,257	...
Voc., teacher tr.	...	539[13]	15,899	...
Higher	1[11]	383	6,048	15.8

Educational attainment: n.a. *Literacy* (1990): percentage of population age 15 and over literate 41.7%; males literate 55.6%; females literate 28.5%.
Health (1990): physicians 662 (1 per 15,136 persons); hospital beds 11,857 (1 per 845 persons); infant mortality rate per 1,000 live births (1990–95) 127.0.
Food (1985): daily per capita caloric intake 1,969 ([1979–81] vegetable products 92%, animal products 8%); (1984) 84% of FAO recommended minimum requirement.

Military

Total active duty personnel (1993): 45,000 (army 77.8%, navy 8.9%, air force 13.3%). *Military expenditure as percentage of GNP* (1984): 14.3% (world 5.7%); per capita expenditure U.S.$119.

[1]Excludes 3 seats for Angolans abroad not filled at October 1992 elections. [2]Black market value of the New kwanza in September 1993 was about 50,000 NKz = 1 U.S.$. [3]Unified national estimates and projections based on sample surveys, partial censuses, and analysis of provincial vital statistics. [4]Detail does not add to total given because of rounding. [5]Includes external long-term debt not guaranteed by the government. [6]1988. [7]1989. [8]At official prices of 1980. [9]TAAG Airline only. [10]Circulation for three newspapers only. [11]1985–86. [12]Includes preprimary. [13]1984–85.

Antigua and Barbuda

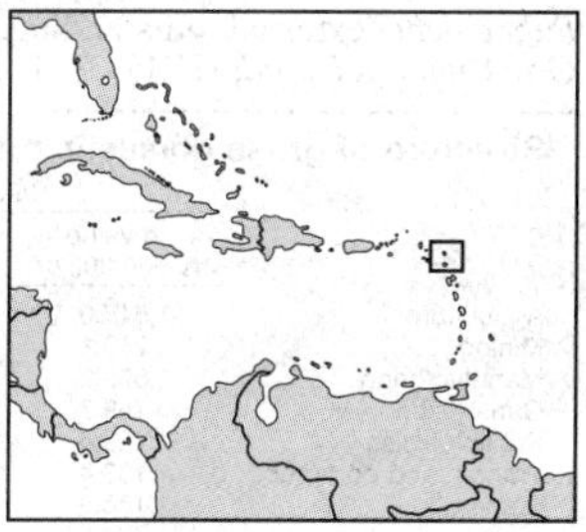

Official name: Antigua and Barbuda.
Form of government: constitutional monarchy with two legislative houses (Senate [17]; House of Representatives [17]).
Chief of state: British Monarch represented by Governor-General.
Head of government: Prime Minister.
Capital: Saint John's.
Official language: English.
Official religion: none.
Monetary unit: 1 East Caribbean dollar (EC$) = 100 cents; valuation (Oct. 4, 1993) 1 U.S.$ = EC$2.70; 1 £ = EC$4.10.

Area and population

	area		population
	sq mi	sq km	1991 census
Parishes[1]			
Saint George	10.2	26.4	...
Saint John's	26.2	67.9	...
Saint Mary	25.1	65.0	...
Saint Paul	17.7	45.8	...
Saint Peter	12.8	33.2	...
Saint Phillip	16.0	41.4	...
Islands[1]			
Barbuda	62.0	160.6	1,400
Redonda	0.5	1.3	2
TOTAL	170.5	441.6	65,962

Demography

Population (1993): 66,000.
Density (1993): persons per sq mi 387.1, persons per sq km 149.5.
Urban-rural (1991): urban 31.0%; rural 69.0%.
Sex distribution (1985): male 48.00%; female 52.00%.
Age breakdown (1985): under 15, 37.2%; 15–29, 30.8%; 30–44, 12.8%; 45–59, 11.5%; 60–74, 6.4%; 75 and over, 1.3%.
Population projection: (2000) 66,000; (2010) 66,000.
Doubling time: 58 years.
Ethnic composition (1988): black 89.0%; mixed 10.0%; other (mostly British, Portuguese, and Lebanese) 1.0%.
Religious affiliation (1980): Anglican 44.5%; other Protestant (largely Moravian, Methodist, and Seventh-day Adventist) 41.6%; Roman Catholic 10.2%; Rastafarian 0.7%; other 3.0%.
Major cities (1986): Saint John's 36,000; Codrington 1,200[3].

Vital statistics

Birth rate per 1,000 population (1991): 18.0 (world avg. 26.4); (1988) legitimate 23.4%; illegitimate 76.6%.
Death rate per 1,000 population (1991): 6.0 (world avg. 9.2).
Natural increase rate per 1,000 population (1991): 12.0 (world avg. 17.2).
Total fertility rate (avg. births per childbearing woman; 1991): 1.9.
Marriage rate per 1,000 population (1988): 4.9.
Divorce rate per 1,000 population (1988): 0.2.
Life expectancy at birth (1991): male 70.0 years; female 74.0 years.
Major causes of death per 100,000 population (1988): diseases of the circulatory system 237.5; malignant neoplasms (cancers) 44.5; diseases of the respiratory system 44.5; endocrine and metabolic disorders 25.4; ill-defined conditions 68.6.

National economy

Budget (1991). Revenue: EC$240,700,000 (current revenue 94.8%, of which consumption taxes 26.4%, import duties 17.6%, taxes on goods and services 16.5%, nontax revenue 14.5%; grants 3.4%; development revenue 1.8%). Expenditures: EC$281,700,000 (current expenditures 87.0%; development expenditures 13.0%).
Production (metric tons except as noted). Agriculture, forestry, fishing (1988): sugarcane 4,000[4], mangoes 1,000[4], melons 672, limes 249, eggplant 248, pumpkins 233, sweet potatoes 219, "Antiguan Black" pineapples 126, ginger 98, sea island cotton lint 36; livestock (number of live animals; 1991): 16,000 cattle, 13,000 sheep; roundwood, n.a.; fish catch (1990) 2,200 (of which spiny lobster 200). Mining and quarrying: crushed stone for local use. Manufacturing (1988): rum 4,000 hectolitres; wine and vodka 2,000 hectolitres; other manufactures include bedding, paints, and furniture. Construction (1988): gross value of building applications EC$221,800,000. Energy production (consumption): electricity (kW-hr; 1990) 95,000,000 (95,000,000); coal, none (none); crude petroleum, none (none); petroleum products (metric tons; 1990) negligible (98,000); natural gas, none (none).
Population economically active (1985): total 32,254; activity rate of total population 42.6% (participation rates: over age 16 [1983] 56.2%; female 40.1%; unemployed, n.a.[5]).

Price and earnings indexes (1987 = 100)

	1985	1986	1987	1988	1989	1990	1991
Consumer price index	94.6	96.5	100.0	103.4	108.9	117.3	119.7
Weekly earnings index[6]	...	...	100.0	110.0	122.1	122.1	122.1

Household income and expenditure. Average household size (1984) 3.5; income per household: n.a.; sources of income: n.a.; expenditure (1974)[7]: food and nonalcoholic beverages 42.9%, housing 23.3%, transportation 10.0%, clothing and footwear 7.5%, energy 5.5%, alcoholic beverages and tobacco 3.6%, other 7.2%.
Gross national product (at current market prices; 1992): U.S.$394,000,000 (U.S.$4,870 per capita).

Structure of gross domestic product and labour force

	1990[8]		1982	
	in value EC$'000,000	% of total value	labour force[9]	% of labour force[9]
Agriculture, fishing	37.3	4.1	2,090	9.0
Quarrying	17.6	1.9	60	0.3
Manufacturing	30.2	3.3	1,718	7.4
Construction	101.0	11.0	2,577	11.1
Public utilities	32.8	3.6	340	1.5
Transportation and communications	168.2	18.3	2,575	11.1
Trade, restaurants, and hotels	235.4	25.6	5,201	22.4
Finance, real estate	131.0	14.2	778	3.3
Pub. admin., defense	165.4	18.0	7,883	33.9
Services	58.9	6.4		
Other	–58.3[10]	–6.3[10]	—	—
TOTAL	919.4[11]	100.0[11]	23,222	100.0

Land use (1991): forested 11.0%; meadows and pastures 9.0%; agricultural and under permanent cultivation 18.0%; other 62.0%.
Public debt (external, outstanding; end of 1991): U.S.$260,000,000.
Tourism (1991): receipts from visitors U.S.$314,000,000; expenditures by nationals abroad U.S.$18,000,000.

Foreign trade[12]

Balance of trade (current prices)

	1986	1987	1988	1989	1990	1991
U.S.$'000,000	–187.9	–205.0	–203.2	–226.5	–252.4	–281.4
% of total	82.8%	85.6%	82.0%	82.2%	82.4%	82.6%

Imports (1990): U.S.$279,400,000 (manufactures 64.4%, nonfuel primary products 34.7%). *Major import sources* (1989)[13]: United States 27.0%; United Kingdom 16.0%; Canada 4.0%; OECS 3.0%; Italy 3.0%.
Exports (1990): U.S.$27,000,000 (manufactures 69.3%, nonfuel primary products 30.7%). *Major export destinations* (1989)[13]: United States 41.0%; United Kingdom 19.0%; Germany 19.0%.

Transport and communications

Transport. Railroads[14]. Roads (1990): total length 724 mi, 1,165 km (paved 33%). Vehicles (1991): passenger cars 13,650; trucks and buses 3,550. Merchant marine (1992): vessels (100 gross tons and over) 292; total deadweight tonnage 997,381. Air transport (1991): passenger-mi 121,000,000, passenger-km 195,000,000; short ton-mi cargo 137,000, metric ton-km cargo 200,000; airports (1993) with scheduled flights 2.
Communications. Daily newspapers: none[15]. Radio (1992): total number of receivers 75,000 (1 per 0.9 persons). Television (1992): total number of receivers 28,000 (1 per 2.3 persons). Telephones (1990): 15,980[16] (1 per 4.0 persons).

Education and health

Education (1991–92)

	schools	teachers	students	student/ teacher ratio
Primary (age 5–10)	43	549	10,770	19.6
Secondary (age 11–16)	12	353	4,373	12.5
Higher	1	45	590	13.1

Educational attainment: n.a. *Literacy* (1985): total population age 15 and over literate 45,000 (90.0%).
Health (1987): physicians (1988) 48 (1 per 1,333 persons); hospital beds 373 (1 per 207 persons); infant mortality rate per 1,000 live births (1992) 20.0.
Food (1988–90): daily per capita caloric intake 2,307 (vegetable products 64%, animal products 36%); 98% of FAO recommended minimum requirement.

Military

Total active duty personnel (1990): an almost 100-member defense force is part of the Eastern Caribbean regional security system. *Military expenditure as percentage of central government current expenditure* (1990–91): 1.4%[17].

[1]Community councils on Antigua and the local government council on Barbuda are the organs of local government. [2]Uninhabited. [3]1982. [4]1992. [5]Labour shortage of mid-1980s has eased. In 1990 and 1991 unemployment increased, particularly in the depressed construction sector. [6]Construction only. [7]Weights of consumer price index components. [8]At factor cost. [9]Wage earners and self-employed only. [10]Less imputed bank service charges. [11]Detail does not add to total given because of rounding. [12]Exports f.o.b.; imports c.i.f. [13]Estimated percentages. [14]48 mi (77 km) of privately owned track are mostly nonoperative. [15]Three weekly newspapers and one twice-weekly newspaper had a total circulation of 12,200 in 1990. [16]Number of lines. [17]May not agree with military expenditure as percentage of GNP because of different bases used.

Argentina

Official name: República Argentina (Argentine Republic).
Form of government: federal republic with two legislative houses (Senate [48]; Chamber of Deputies [257]).
Head of state and government: President.
Capital: Buenos Aires.
Official language: Spanish.
Official religion: Roman Catholicism.
Monetary unit: 1 peso (pl. pesos)[1] (Ps) = 100 centavos; valuation (Oct. 4, 1993) 1 U.S.$ = Ps 1.00; 1 £ = Ps 1.52.

Area and population

Provinces	Capitals	area sq mi	area sq km	population 1991 census[2]
Buenos Aires	La Plata	118,754	307,571	12,538,007
Catamarca	Catamarca	39,615	102,602	264,940
Chaco	Resistencia	38,469	99,633	799,302
Chubut	Rawson	86,752	224,686	356,445
Córdoba	Córdoba	63,831	165,321	2,764,176
Corrientes	Corrientes	34,054	88,199	780,778
Entre Ríos	Paraná	30,418	78,781	1,021,042
Formosa	Formosa	27,825	72,066	363,035
Jujuy	San Salvador de Jujuy	20,548	53,219	513,213
La Pampa	Santa Rosa	55,382	143,440	260,041
La Rioja	La Rioja	34,626	89,680	220,910
Mendoza	Mendoza	57,462	148,827	1,400,142
Misiones	Posadas	11,506	29,801	787,514
Neuquén	Neuquén	36,324	94,078	385,606
Río Negro	Viedma	78,384	203,013	506,314
Salta	Salta	60,034	155,488	863,688
San Juan	San Juan	34,614	89,651	526,263
San Luis	San Luis	29,633	76,748	286,379
Santa Cruz	Río Gallegos	94,187	243,943	159,726
Santa Fe	Santa Fe	51,354	133,007	2,782,809
Santiago del Estero	Santiago del Estero	52,645	136,351	670,388
Tierra del Fuego[3]	Ushuaia	8,329	21,571	69,450
Tucumán	San Miguel de Tucumán	8,697	22,524	1,142,321
Other federal entity				
Distrito Federal	Buenos Aires	77	200	2,960,976
TOTAL		1,073,518[4]	2,780,400	32,423,465

Demography

Population (1993): 33,507,000.
Density (1993): persons per sq mi 31.2, persons per sq km 12.0.
Urban-rural (1990): urban 86.2%; rural 13.8%.
Sex distribution (1991): male 48.90%; female 51.10%.
Age breakdown (1990): under 15, 29.9%; 15–29, 23.2%; 30–44, 19.5%; 45–59, 14.2%; 60–74, 9.9%; 75 and over, 3.3%.
Population projection: (2000) 36,492,000; (2010) 40,718,000.
Doubling time: 63 years.
Ethnic composition (1986): European 85%; mestizo, Amerindian, and other 15%.
Religious affiliation (1990): Roman Catholic 91.6%; other 8.4%.
Major cities (1991): Buenos Aires 2,960,976 (Greater Buenos Aires 12,582,321); Córdoba 1,179,067; Rosario 1,078,374[5]; La Plata 542,567.

Vital statistics

Birth rate per 1,000 population (1992): 20.0 (world avg. 26.4); (1982) legitimate 67.5%; illegitimate 29.8%; unknown 2.7%.
Death rate per 1,000 population (1992): 9.0 (world avg. 9.2).
Natural increase rate per 1,000 population (1992): 11.0 (world avg. 17.2).
Total fertility rate (avg. births per childbearing woman; 1992): 2.8.
Marriage rate per 1,000 population (1983): 6.0.
Life expectancy at birth (1992): male 67.0 years; female 74.0 years.
Major causes of death per 100,000 population (1988): circulatory diseases 347.8; cancers 142.2; accidents 54.3; respiratory diseases 47.6.

National economy

Budget (1989). Revenue: Ps 319,400,000[1] (social-security taxes 33.0%, export duties 19.0%, excise taxes 7.8%, general sales tax 6.6%, property tax 4.7%, import duties 3.9%, income taxes 2.0%). Expenditures: Ps 305,600,000[1] (social security 35.3%, economic services 16.0%, education 9.9%, defense 9.9%, transportation and communications 8.8%, debt service 7.4%).
Land use (1991): forested 21.6%; meadows and pastures 51.9%; agricultural and under permanent cultivation 9.9%; other 16.6%.
Production (metric tons except as noted). Agriculture, forestry, fishing (1992): sugarcane 18,500,000, soybeans 11,315,000, corn (maize) 10,699,000, wheat 9,400,000, sunflower seeds 3,800,000, sorghum 2,766,000, potatoes 2,650,000, grapes 1,821,000, tomatoes 725,000; livestock (number of live animals) 50,020,000 cattle, 23,711,000 sheep; roundwood (1991) 10,819,000 cu m; fish catch (1991) 640,636. Mining and quarrying (1991): silver 2,250,780 troy oz; gold 48,231 troy oz. Manufacturing (by value of production in U.S.$'000; 1988): textiles 2,884,000; motor vehicles 2,620,000; metal products 2,348,000; iron and steel 2,151,000; industrial chemicals 2,095,000; electrical machinery 1,485,000; beverages 1,459,000. Construction (authorized; 1984): 10,606,800 sq m. Energy production (consumption): electricity (kW-hr; 1991) 54,048,000,000 (54,923,000,000); coal (metric tons; 1991) 292,000 (1,317,000); crude petroleum (barrels; 1991) 181,077,000 (174,242,000); petroleum products (metric tons; 1991) 21,171,000 (17,911,000); natural gas (cu m; 1991) 30,776,824,000 (33,402,325,000).
Public debt (external, outstanding; 1991): U.S.$45,388,000,000.
Gross national product (1992): U.S.$200,206,000,000 (U.S.$6,050 per capita).

Structure of gross domestic product and labour force

	1990 in value A'000,000[1,6]	1990 % of total value	1980 labour force	1980 % of labour force
Agriculture	1,518.0	16.7	1,200,992	12.0
Mining	259.1	2.9	47,171	0.5
Manufacturing	1,878.2	20.7	1,985,995	19.9
Construction	169.7	1.9	1,003,175	10.1
Public utilities	489.4	5.4	103,256	1.0
Transp. and commun.	1,103.4	12.2	460,476	4.6
Trade	1,176.9	13.0	1,702,080	17.0
Finance	760.5	8.4	395,704	4.0
Pub. admin., defense; Services	1,708.1	18.8	2,399,039	24.0
Other	...	...	691,302	6.9
TOTAL	9,063.4[4]	100.0	9,989,190	100.0

Population economically active (1990): total 12,305,346; activity rate of total population 38.1% (participation rates: ages 15–64, 59.6%; female 28.2%; unemployed [1989] 7.3%).

Price and earnings indexes (1985 = 100)

	1986	1987	1988	1989	1990	1991	1992
Consumer price index	210.3	468.7	1,948	62,162	1,495,000	4,062,000	5,073,000
Hourly earnings index[7]	206.9	423.3	...	...	...	...	...

Household size and expenditure. Average household size (1991) 3.2; expenditure (1985–86): food 38.2%, transportation 11.6%, housing 9.3%, energy 9.0%, clothing and footwear 8.0%, health 7.9%, recreation and culture 7.5%, education 2.6%, other 5.9%.
Tourism (1991): receipts U.S.$2,336,000,000; expenditures U.S.$1,739,000,000.

Foreign trade[8]

Balance of trade (current prices)

	1986	1987	1988	1989	1990	1991
U.S.$'000,000	+2,446	+1,000	+4,051	+5,706	+8,627	+4,572
% of total	21.7%	8.5%	29.3%	42.5%	53.7%	23.6%

Imports (1991): U.S.$5,265,000,000 (machinery and transport equipment 34.4%, chemical products 22.1%, manufactured products 24.4%, petroleum and petroleum products 13.5%, food products and live animals 4.6%). *Major import sources:* U.S. 22.9%; Brazil 17.7%; Germany 8.8%; Italy 4.5%; Japan 4.5%; Chile 4.1%; Bolivia 3.7%.
Exports (1991): U.S.$9,169,000,000 (food products and live animals 39.1%, petroleum and petroleum products 21.2%, manufactured products 16.3%, vegetable and animal oils 10.6%, machinery and transport equipment 6.0%, chemical products 5.3%). *Major export destinations:* Brazil 11.8%; The Netherlands 11.4%; U.S. 10.3%; Germany 5.8%; Italy 5.2%; Spain 3.9%; Japan 3.7%; Chile 3.6%.

Transport and communications

Transport. Railroads (1989): route length (1988) 34,115 km; passenger-km 10,651,000,000; metric ton-km cargo 8,453,000,000. Roads (1986): total length 131,338 mi, 211,369 km (paved 27%). Vehicles (1990): passenger cars 4,283,700; commercial vehicles and buses 1,500,800. Merchant marine (1992): vessels (100 gross tons and over) 423; total deadweight tonnage 1,173,105. Air transport (1992)[9]: passenger-km 8,988,845,000; metric ton-km cargo 160,575,000; airports (1993) 49.
Communications. Daily newspapers (1990): total number 159; total circulation 4,000,000; circulation per 1,000 population 124. Radio (1992): 21,582,456 receivers (1 per 1.5 persons). Television (1992): 7,165,000 receivers (1 per 4.6 persons). Telephones (1990): 4,622,360 (1 per 7.0 persons).

Education and health

Education (1988–89)

	schools	teachers	students	student/teacher ratio
Primary (age 6–12)	21,207	259,579	4,998,973	19.3
Secondary (age 13–17)[10]	7,224	262,000	1,862,000	7.1
Higher	1,540[11]	70,000	959,000	13.7

Educational attainment (1980). Percentage of population age 25 and over having: no formal schooling 6.0%; less than primary education 32.0%; primary 34.6%; secondary 20.5%; higher 6.9%. *Literacy* (1990): percentage of total population age 15 and over literate 95.3%; males literate 95.5%; females literate 95.1%.
Health: physicians (1988) 96,000 (1 per 326 persons); hospital beds (1987) 150,000 (1 per 205 persons); infant mortality rate (1992) 34.0.
Food (1988–90): daily per capita caloric intake 3,068 (vegetable products 69%; animal products 31%); 131% of FAO recommended minimum requirement.

Military

Total active duty personnel (1993): 70,800 (army 57.0%, navy 30.4%, air force 12.6%). *Military expenditure as percentage of GNP* (1989): 3.4% (world 4.9%); per capita expenditure: U.S.$58.

[1]On Jan. 1, 1992, the austral was replaced by the peso at a ratio of 10,000:1. [2]Preliminary. [3]Area of Tierra del Fuego (province since 1991) excludes claims to British-held islands in the South Atlantic Ocean. [4]Detail does not add to total given because of rounding. [5]*Municipio.* [6]At 1970 prices. [7]Skilled workers in manufacturing only. [8]Import figures are f.o.b. in balance of trade and c.i.f. in commodities and trading partners. [9]Aerolineas Argentina only. [10]Secondary includes vocational and teacher training. [11]1987.

Armenia

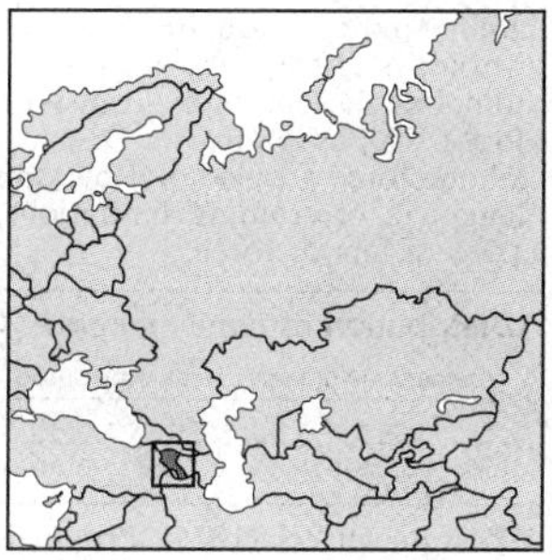

Official name: Hayastani Hanrapetut'yun (Republic of Armenia).
Form of government: unitary multiparty republic with a single legislative body (Supreme Council [185]).
Head of state: President.
Head of government: Prime Minister.
Capital: Yerevan.
Official language: Armenian.
Official religion: none.
Monetary unit[1]: 1 ruble = 100 kopecks; valuation (Oct. 4, 1993) free rate, 1 U.S.$ = 1,165 rubles; 1 £ = 1,765 rubles.

Area and population

Administrative subdivisions	Capitals	area sq mi	area sq km	population 1987 estimate
Cities[2]				
Gyumri	—	...	...	228,400
Kirovakan	—	...	...	169,400
Yerevan	—	...	...	1,184,500
Rural districts				
Abovyani	Abovyan	313	810	108,200
Akhuryani	Akhuryan	223	577	39,500
Amasiayi	Amasia	235	609	19,300
Anii	Maralik	166	429	19,700
Aparani	Aparan	228	591	19,900
Aragatsi	Tsaghkahovit	148	382	14,100
Ararati	Vedi	540	1,399	85,100
Artashati	Artashat	200	517	95,500
Art'iki	Art'ik	187	484	44,800
Ashtaraki	Ashtarak	267	692	36,400
Azizbekovi	Azizbekov	453	1,172	17,000
Baghramyani	Baghramyan	175	453	16,100
Ejmiadzini	Ejmiadzin	141	366	121,000
Ghap'ani	Ghap'an	529	1,371	61,500
Ghukasyani	Ghukasyan	211	547	9,800
Gorisi	Goris	290	752	38,000
Gugark'i	Gugark'	297	770	31,000
Hoktemberyani	Hoktemberyan	163	423	109,900
Hrazdani	Hrazdan	366	948	78,600
Ijevani	Ijevan	516	1,336	46,600
Kalininoyi	Kalinino	266	690	39,100
Kamoyi	Kamo	269	697	56,400
Krasnoselski	Krasnoselsk	269	697	27,900
Martunu	Martuni	458	1,185	67,900
Masisi	Masis	70	182	64,400
Meghru	Meghri	256	664	15,100
Nairii	Yeghvard	133	344	47,200
Noyemberyani	Noyemberyan	208	538	29,700
Sevani	Sevan	152	393	42,700
Shamshadini	Berd	318	824	34,200
Sisiani	Sisian	664	1,719	34,600
Spitaki	Spitak	212	549	46,300
Step'anavani	Step'anavan	246	637	36,500
T'alini	T'alin	421	1,091	35,100
T'umanyani	Alaverdi	433	1,121	58,200
Vardenisi	Vardenis	444	1,151	60,200
Yeghegnadzori	Yeghegnadzor	438	1,134	35,400
TOTAL		11,506[2]	29,800[3]	3,411,900[3]

Demography

Population (1993): 3,550,000.
Density (1993): persons per sq mi 308.9, persons per sq km 119.1.
Urban-rural (1991): urban 69.5%; rural 30.5%.
Sex distribution (1992): male 49.50%; female 50.50%.
Age breakdown (1990): under 15, 30.3%; 15–29, 25.7%; 30–44, 20.8%; 45–59, 13.6%; 60–69, 6.4%; 70 and over, 3.2%.
Population projection: (2000) 4,004,000; (2010) 4,755,000.
Doubling time: 47 years.
Ethnic composition (1989): Armenian 93.3%; Azerbaijani 2.6%; other 4.1%.
Religious affiliation: believers are predominantly Armenian Apostolic.
Major cities (1991): Yerevan 1,283,000; Gyumri 163,000[4]; Kirovakan 76,000[4].

Vital statistics

Birth rate per 1,000 population (1992): 21.6 (world avg. 26.4); (1989) legitimate 92.1%; illegitimate 7.9%.
Death rate per 1,000 population (1992): 6.5 (world avg. 9.2).
Natural increase rate per 1,000 population (1992): 15.1 (world avg. 17.2).
Total fertility rate (avg. births per childbearing woman; 1989): 2.6.
Marriage rate per 1,000 population (1989): 8.0.
Divorce rate per 1,000 population (1989): 1.2.
Life expectancy at birth (1990): male 67.4 years; female 73.3 years.
Major causes of death per 100,000 population (1990): circulatory diseases 305.9; cancers 98.3; accidents and violence 55.6; respiratory diseases 50.3.

National economy

Budget (1992). Revenue: 9,556,000,000 rubles (tax revenue 97.4%, of which value-added tax 49.2%, income tax 34.0%, excise taxes 10.5%; nontax revenue 2.6%). Expenditures: 10,746,000,000 rubles (education 29.9%; national economy 23.7%; health 18.3%; police 5.3%; defense 2.3%).
Production (metric tons except as noted). Agriculture, forestry, fishing (1992): vegetables (except potatoes) 472,000, potatoes 343,000, milk 300,000, wheat 160,000, grapes 160,000, meat 95,000, wool 2,000, tobacco 1,000; livestock (number of live animals) 1,000,000 sheep, 501,000 cattle, 9,000,000 poultry; roundwood (1991) 44,100 cu m; fish catch 4,480. Manufacturing (1992): cement 1,500,000; caustic soda 14,900; synthetic plastic 7,300; paper 4,400; chemical fibres 4,100; cotton fabrics 17,600,000 sq m; silk fabrics 9,300,000 sq m; wool fabrics 3,600,000 sq m; watches 2,200,000 pieces; car tires 900,000 units; metal-cutting equipment 7,100 units; automobiles 6,800 units; construction materials 800,000 cu m; leather shoes 11,300,000 pairs. Construction (1991): 1,910,000 cu m. Energy production (consumption): electricity (kW-hr; 1991) 9,500,000,000 (1990; 12,076,000,000); coal (metric tons; 1990) 50,000 (570,000); petroleum products (metric tons; 1990) 292,000 (4,346,000); natural gas (cu m; 1990) 170,000,000 (4,882,000,000).
Gross national product (1991): U.S.$7,349,000,000 (U.S.$2,150 per capita)[5].

Structure of gross domestic product and labour force

	1991		1990	
	in value '000,000 rubles	% of total value	labour force	% of labour force
Agriculture	3,946	32.0	117,300	5.7
Manufacturing, mining }	5,280	42.8	397,900	19.4
Public utilities }			55,300	2.7
Construction	1,700	13.8	161,600	7.9
Transp. and commun.	274	2.2	88,000	4.3
Trade	689	5.6	88,100	4.3
Finance	—	—	17,800	1.0
Pub. admin., defense	—	—	7,900	0.4
Services	—	—	413,300	20.2
Other	441	3.6	697,200[6]	34.1[6]
TOTAL	12,330	100.0	2,044,400	100.0

Land use (1988): forest 14.4%; pasture 35.2%; agriculture 21.6%; other 28.8%.
Population economically active (1991): total 1,900,000; activity rate of total population 55.5% (participation rates [1989]: ages 16–59 [male], 16–54 [female] 79.9%; female [1990] 49.4%; unemployed [1990] 3.6%).

Price and earnings indexes (1985 = 100)

	1985	1986	1987	1988	1989	1990	1991
Consumer price index	100.0	102.0	103.0	103.0	104.0	112.0	252.2
Monthly earnings index	100.0	102.3	105.9	109.2	121.9	133.7	...

Household income and expenditure. Average household size (1989) 4.7; income per household (1990) 11,100 rubles; sources of income (1990): salaries and wages 74.8%, social benefits 8.0%, agricultural income 4.9%, other 12.3%; expenditure (1990) 8,100 rubles: food 47.3%, clothing 17.4%, taxes 8.1%, services 7.1%, household furnishings 6.6%, other 13.5%.

Foreign trade

Balance of trade (current prices)

	1985	1986	1987	1988	1989	1990
'000,000 rubles	+20	+374	−135	−1,110	−1,207	−1,039
% of total	0.2%	3.5%	1.6%	12.8%	14.1%	12.7%

Imports (1990): 4,662,000,000 rubles (light-industrial products 25.0%, machine-building and metalworking machinery 20.9%, food 16.2%, chemical products 7.9%, agricultural imports 6.2%, energy products [except electricity] 6.1%). *Major import sources:* Russia 30.0%; Ukraine 18.7%; Belarus 7.2%.
Exports (1990): 3,523,000,000 rubles (light-industrial products 42.6%, machine-building and metalworking machinery 23.5%, food industry 11.7%, chemical products 6.0%). *Major export destinations:* Russia 60.9%; Ukraine 12.2%; Kazakhstan 11.1%; Uzbekistan 4.1%; Turkmenistan 3.3%.

Transport and communications

Transport. Railroads (1991): length 823 km; (1990) passenger-km 316,000,000; metric ton-km cargo 4,884,000,000. Roads (1991): total length 7,700 km (paved 99%). Vehicles (1988): passenger cars 230,100; trucks and buses, n.a. Air transport (1990): passenger km 5,556,900,000; metric ton-km cargo 49,000,000; airports (1993) 2.
Communications. Daily newspapers (1991): total number 82; total circulation 1,678,000; circulation per 1,000 population 469. Radio (1992): 621,000 receivers (1 per 5.5 persons). Television (1992): 702,000 receivers (1 per 4.9 persons). Telephones (1991): 650,000 (1 per 5.3 persons).

Education and health

Education (1991–92)

	schools	teachers	students	student/teacher ratio
Primary (age 6–13) }	1,374	54,000	592,000	11.0
Secondary (age 14–17) }				
Voc., teacher tr.	69	...	40,600	...
Higher	14	...	66,100	...

Educational attainment (1989). Percentage of population age 25 and over having: primary education or no formal schooling 7.4%; some secondary 18.6%; completed secondary and some postsecondary 57.7%; higher 13.8%.
Health (1990): physicians 14,519 (1 per 246 persons); hospital beds 30,482 (1 per 117 persons); infant mortality rate per 1,000 live births (1991) 17.9.

Military

Total active duty personnel (1993)[7]: *c.* 20,000 (army 100%). *Military expenditure as percentage of GNP*[8]: n.a.; per capita expenditure (1991): U.S.$43.

[1]The Armenian dram was introduced Nov. 22, 1993, to replace the Russian ruble, at a rate of 200 Russian rubles to 1 dram. [2]18 additional cities of republic jurisdiction exist. [3]Totals include 1,556 sq km (601 sq mi) and 86,700 persons not distributed by administrative subdivision. [4]1989; reduced in population by evacuation following Dec. 7, 1988, earthquake. [5]Ruble-area GNP and exchange-rate data are very speculative. [6]Includes self-employed and unemployed. [7]Total mobilization for war with Azerbaijan is not available; however, total reserve strength is 300,000. [8]Provisional; the estimated cost of the war with Azerbaijan is U.S.$15,000,000–18,000,000 a day.

Australia

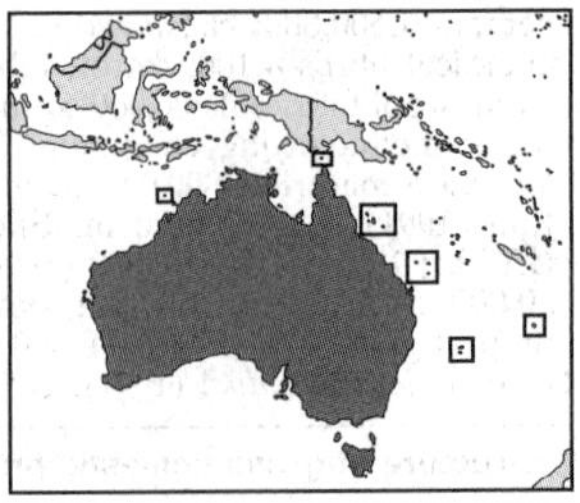

Official name: Commonwealth of Australia.
Form of government: federal parliamentary state (formally a constitutional monarchy) with two legislative houses (Senate [76]; House of Representatives [148]).
Chief of state: British Monarch represented by Governor-General.
Head of government: Prime Minister.
Capital: Canberra.
Official language: English.
Official religion: none.
Monetary unit: 1 Australian dollar ($A) = 100 cents; valuation (Oct. 4, 1993) 1 U.S.$ = $A 1.55; 1 £ = $A 2.35.

Area and population

States	Capitals	area sq mi	area sq km	population 1993[1] estimate
New South Wales	Sydney	309,500	801,600	5,999,900
Queensland	Brisbane	666,900	1,727,200	3,095,000
South Australia	Adelaide	379,900	984,000	1,460,100
Tasmania	Hobart	26,200	67,800	471,500
Victoria	Melbourne	87,900	227,600	4,461,400
Western Australia	Perth	975,100	2,525,500	1,672,500
Territories				
Australian Capital Territory	Canberra	900	2,400	298,300
Northern Territory	Darwin	519,800	1,346,200	168,300
TOTAL		2,966,200	7,682,300	17,627,000

Demography

Population (1993): 17,729,000.
Density (1993): persons per sq mi 6.0, persons per sq km 2.3.
Urban-rural (1986): urban 85.4%; rural 14.6%.
Sex distribution (1993): male 49.82%; female 50.18%.
Age breakdown (1992): under 15, 21.7%; 15–29, 23.7%; 30–44, 23.5%; 45–59, 15.5%; 60–74, 11.0%; 75 and over, 4.6%.
Population projection: (2000) 19,550,000; (2010) 21,952,000.
Doubling time: 87 years.
Ethnic composition (1986): white 95.2%; aboriginal 1.5%; Asian 1.3%; other 2.0%.
Religious affiliation (1986): Christian 73.0%, of which Roman Catholic 26.1%, Anglican Church of Australia 23.9%, other Protestant 17.4% (Uniting Church and Methodist 7.6%, Presbyterian 3.6%), Orthodox 2.7%; Muslim 0.7%; Buddhist 0.5%; Jewish 0.4%; no religion 12.7%; other 12.7%.
Major cities (1991): Sydney 3,538,900; Melbourne 3,022,200; Brisbane 1,334,700; Perth 1,143,300; Adelaide 1,023,600; Newcastle 427,703; Canberra 278,900; Wollongong 236,000; Hobart 181,800; Gold Coast 157,800.
Place of birth (1991): 77.3% native-born; 22.7% foreign-born, of which Europe 13.9% (United Kingdom 7.1%[2], Italy 1.5%, Yugoslavia 1.0%, Greece 0.8%, East and West Germany 0.7%, other Europe 1.9%), Asia and Middle East 4.8%, New Zealand 1.7%, Africa and the Americas 1.5%, other 0.8%.
Mobility (1988). Population age 15 and over living in the same residence as in 1987: 84.1%; different residence, same state 14.4%; different state or territory 1.5%.
Households (1991–92). Total number of households 5,852,518. Average household size 3.0; (1986) 1 person 19.5%, 2–3 persons 47.1%, 4–5 persons 28.2%, 6 or more persons 5.2%. Family households (1992): 4,298,710 (74.5%); nonfamily 1,553,808 (26.5%).
Immigration (1991): permanent immigrants admitted 116,650, from United Kingdom and Ireland 16.2%, Hong Kong 12.4%, Vietnam 9.2%, New Zealand 5.7%, Philippines 5.5%, India 5.0%, Malaysia 3.8%, China 2.9%, Lebanon 2.0%. Refugee arrivals: 7,095.

Vital statistics

Birth rate per 1,000 population (1992): 15.1 (world avg. 26.4); (1991) legitimate 77.0%; illegitimate 23.0%.
Death rate per 1,000 population (1992): 7.1 (world avg. 9.2).
Natural increase rate per 1,000 population (1992): 8.0 (world avg. 17.2).
Total fertility rate (avg. births per childbearing woman; 1992): 1.89.
Marriage rate per 1,000 population (1992): 6.6.
Divorce rate per 1,000 population (1992): 2.6.
Life expectancy at birth (1991): male 74.4 years; female 80.3 years.
Major causes of death per 100,000 population (1990): diseases of the circulatory system 318.0; cancers 180.0; diseases of the respiratory system 53.0; accidents, poisoning, and violence 46.0; diseases of the digestive system 24.0; endocrine, nutritional, and metabolic diseases 19.0.

Social indicators

Educational attainment (1992). Percentage of population age 15 to 69 having: no formal schooling 0.3%; incomplete secondary education 56.1%, of which completed secondary 14.8%[3]; postsecondary, technical, or other certificate/diploma 34.0%; university 9.6%.
Quality of working life (1991–92). Average workweek: 40.1 hours (17% overtime). Annual rate per 100,000 workers for: injury or accident, n.a.; industrial illness, n.a.; death, n.a. Proportion of employed persons insured for damages or income loss resulting from: injury 100%; permanent disability 100%; death 100%. Average days lost to labour stoppages per 1,000 workdays (1990): 0.5. Means of transportation to work (1986): private automobile 69.4%; public transportation 10.1%; motorcycle and bicycle 3.2%; foot 6.6%; other 10.7%. Discouraged job seekers among persons not in the labour force (considered by employers to be too young or too old, having language or training limitations, or no vacancies in line of work; 1991): 1.5% of labour force.

Distribution of family income (1990[4])

percentage of family income by decile

1	2	3	4	5	6	7	8	9	10 (highest)
1.4%	3.1%	4.2%	5.5%	6.9%	8.6%	10.6%	13.3%	17.2%	29.2%

Access to services (1976). Proportion of dwellings having access to: electricity 99.5%; bathroom 96.0%; flush toilet 92.2%; kitchen 97.9%; public sewer 73.4%.
Social participation. Eligible voters participating in last national election (1993): 95.3%; voting is compulsory. Population age 16 and over participating in voluntary work: n.a. Trade union membership in total workforce (1992): 39.6%. Practicing religious population in total affiliated population: n.a.
Social deviance (1988–89). Offense rate per 100,000 population for: murder and attempted murder 4.2; sexual assault 53.3; assault 401.9; auto theft 760.4; burglary and housebreaking 1,969.4; fraud and forgery 760.4. Incidence per 100,000 in general population of: alcoholism, n.a.; drug offenses (1985) 388.2; suicide (1989) 13.1.
Material well-being (1983). Households possessing: automobile 86.0%; telephone 85.0%; refrigerator 99.6%; air conditioner 32.3%; washing machine 91.7%; hot water 98.7%; central heating 3.9%; swimming pool 10.1%.

National economy

Gross national product (1992): U.S.$299,937,000,000 (U.S.$17,070 per capita).

Structure of gross domestic product and labour force

	1991–92 in value $A '000,000	% of total value	labour force	% of labour force
Agriculture	11,083	3.2	409,000	4.8
Mining	16,928	4.9	91,200	1.1
Manufacturing	50,424	14.7	1,111,600	13.0
Construction	27,343	8.0	518,200	6.0
Public utilities	12,627	3.7	107,600	1.3
Transportation and communications	28,427	8.3	521,700	6.1
Trade	48,696	14.2	1,596,500	18.5
Finance	77,093	22.5	884,800	10.4
Pub. admin., defense	15,049	4.4	353,200	4.1
Services	63,697	18.7	2,076,700	24.2
Other	−9,287[5]	−2.6[5]	902,400[6]	10.5[6]
TOTAL	342,080	100.0	8,572,900	100.0

Budget (1993–94). Revenue: $A 99,100,000,000 (1991–92; income tax 68.9%, of which individual 51.1%, corporate 17.8%; excise duties and sales tax 23.5%). Expenditures: $A 115,100,000,000 (1991–92; social security and welfare 34.2%; transfers to state governments 25.2%; transfers to the nonbudget sector 9.1%; interest on public debt 5.6%).
Public debt (1992): $A 68,722,000,000.
Tourism (1991): receipts from visitors U.S.$4,183,000,000; expenditures by nationals abroad U.S.$3,940,000,000.

Manufacturing, mining, and construction enterprises (1990–91)[7]

	no. of estab-lishments	no. of employees	Avg. annual wages[8] as a % of all wages	annual turnover ($A '000,000)
Manufacturing				
Food, beverages, and tobacco	3,972	169,100	92.3	34,974
Basic metal products	809	66,800	126.8	21,446
Machinery and equipment	5,717	121,900	103.7	16,334
Transport equipment	2,018	894,000	105.9	15,597
Chemical, petroleum, and coal products	1,131	52,000	127.4	23,485
Paper, printing, and publishing	4,694	104,300	111.1	14,793
Fabricated metal products	6,628	97,700	93.6	12,341
Miscellaneous manufacturing	3,755	60,800	94.5	8,541
Wood, wood products, and furniture	6,725	75,900	80.7	7,829
Nonmetallic mineral products	1,687	39,800	112.2	7,516
Clothing and footwear	2,557	55,600	74.8	4,969
Textiles	960	28,400	90.9	4,049
Mining[9]				
Coal, oil, and gas	261	35,266	155.1	13,243
Metallic minerals	353	34,308	198.0	11,090
Nonmetallic minerals	699	8,799	116.0	2,240
Construction	98,100	395,000[10]	104.0[11]	46,756[10]

Production (gross value in $A '000 except as noted). Agriculture, forestry, fishing (1991–92): livestock slaughtered 5,546,300 (cattle 3,658,800, poultry 787,000, pigs 638,500, sheep and lambs 462,000); wool 2,979,400, wheat 1,948,600, cotton 882,100, barley 641,200, sugarcane 602,000, grapes 410,400, potatoes 384,900, bananas 278,700, apples 251,200, oranges 193,800, rice 183,100, oats 177,900, sorghum 168,900, tomatoes 164,200, pears 112,600, tobacco 74,900, carrots 69,900, onions 59,700, peaches 44,900, cauliflower 41,800, pineapples 37,900, corn (maize) 37,300; livestock (number of live animals) 148,203,000 sheep, 23,880,000 cattle, 2,792,000 pigs, 62,364,000 poultry; roundwood (1991) 19,315,000 cu m; fish catch (1991) 227,300 metric tons. Mining and quarrying (metric tons [tons of contained metal]; 1991–92): iron ore 114,781,000; bauxite 39,983,000; zinc 1,021,000; lead 569,000; copper 339,-

000; tin 6,218; gold 241,141 kg; diamonds 35,000,000 carats. Manufacturing (metric tons except as noted; 1992–93): pig iron 6,445,000; cement 6,225,000; iron and steel slabs 2,246,000; beef and veal 1,837,300; sulfuric acid 868,000; lamb and mutton 648,800; pork 336,700; textile floor coverings 42,618,000 sq m; woven cotton cloth 41,410,000 sq m; woven woolen cloth 8,343,000 sq m; beer 18,050,000 hectolitres; electric motors 2,796,000 units; motor vehicles 291,000 units; colour television receivers 154,000 units. Construction (buildings completed, by value in $A '000; 1992–93): new dwellings 13,193,700; alterations and additions to dwellings 2,145,500; nonresidential 10,163,700.

Retail and service enterprises (1991–92)

	no. of establishments	no. of employees	total wages and salaries ($A '000,000)	annual turnover ($A '000,000)
Retail				
Motor vehicle dealers, gasoline and tire dealers	37,305	220,661	2,572[12]	44,954
Food stores	53,166	406,299	2,461[12]	40,811
Department and general stores	459	87,148	1,175[12]	9,880
Clothing, fabrics, and furniture stores	21,688	91,138	965[12]	8,495
Household appliances and hardware stores	14,268	75,355	629	12,012
Services[13]				
Real estate agents	5,741	42,196	835	2,201
Architectural services	4,534	17,717	354	1,030
Surveying services	1,104	6,872	116	309
Engineering and technical services	5,190	28,326	682	1,716
Legal services	6,459	55,363	500	3,069
Accounting services	6,048	49,479	503	2,334
Computing services	3,691	24,067	585	1,628
Advertising services	2,390	16,048	423	4,675
Debt collecting and credit reporting services	234	2,658	52	142
Pest control services	565	2,902	44	135
Cleaning services	4,181	44,322	330	622
Security/protection and business services	1,087	25,483	365	839

Energy production (consumption): electricity (kW-hr; 1991) 156,883,000,000 (156,883,000,000); coal (metric tons; 1991) 214,030,000 (98,881,000); crude petroleum (barrels; 1991) 199,768,000 (195,393,000); petroleum products (metric tons; 1991) 30,543,000 (31,713,000); natural gas (cu m; 1991) 21,545,-000,000 (16,804,000).

Population economically active (1991–92): total 8,572,900; activity rate of total population 47.9% (participation rates: ages 15–64, 63.0%; female 41.7%; unemployed 11.3%).

Price and earnings indexes (1985 = 100)

	1987	1988	1989	1990	1991	1992	1993[14]
Consumer price index	118.3	126.9	136.5	146.4	151.1	153.1	155.1
Weekly earnings index	113.4	121.2	131.0	142.2	149.4	155.3	157.7

Household income and expenditure (1991–92). Average household size 3.0; average annual income per household $A 53,800 (U.S.$41,157); sources of income: wages and salaries 62.3%, transfer payments 16.8%, self-employment 6.3%, other 14.6%; expenditure (1991–92): food and beverages 19.0%, housing 18.1%, transportation and communications 15.3%, recreation and education 9.4%, health 7.6%, household durable goods 6.4%, clothing and footwear 5.6%, energy 2.2%, other 16.4%.

Financial aggregates

	1987	1988	1989	1990	1991	1992	1993[15]
Exchange rate, $A 1.00 per:							
U.S. dollar	0.70	0.78	0.79	0.78	0.78	0.69	0.65
£	0.43	0.44	0.48	0.44	0.44	0.45	0.46
SDR	0.51	0.64	0.60	0.54	0.53	0.50	0.45
International reserves (U.S.$)							
Total (excl. gold; '000,000)	8,744	13,598	13,780	16,264	16,534	11,208	11,402
SDRs ('000,000)	389	334	307	311	290	96	88
Reserve pos. in IMF ('000,000)	268	275	322	349	351	420	412
Foreign exchange ('000,000)	8,107	12,989	13,150	15,605	15,894	10,536	10,730
Gold ('000,000 fine troy oz)	7.93	7.93	7.93	7.93	7.93	7.93	7.90
% world reserves	0.8	0.8	0.8	0.8	0.8	0.9	0.9
Interest and prices							
Central bank discount (%)	14.95	13.20	17.23	15.24	11.0	6.25	6.08[14]
Govt. bond yield (%)	13.17	12.18	15.14	13.46	9.94	7.00	6.23[14]
Industrial share prices (1985 = 100)	193.4	164.6	176.6	167.0	168.4	162.2	177.2[14]
Balance of payments (U.S.$'000,000)							
Balance of visible trade	+264	−696	−3,446	+366	+3,510	+1,573	+409[14]
Imports, f.o.b.	26,749	33,892	40,329	38,966	38,500	40,819	20,010[14]
Exports, f.o.b.	27,014	33,196	36,883	39,332	42,010	42,392	20,419[14]
Balance of invisibles	−7,582	−9,401	−13,885	−15,093	−13,362	−12,250	−5,120[14]
Balance of payments, current account	−7,318	−10,097	−17,331	−14,724	−9,852	−10,677	−4,711[14]

Land use (1990): meadows and pastures 54.6%; agricultural and under permanent cultivation 6.4%; other 39.0%[16].

Foreign trade

Balance of trade (current prices)

	1987	1988	1989	1990	1991	1992
$A '000,000	−726	−258	−4,100	1,194	4,141	2,898
% of total	1.0%	3.0%	4.1%	1.2%	4.0%	2.6%

Imports (1991–92): $A 50,983,000,000 (machinery 28.8%, of which office machines and automatic data-processing equipment 7.1%; basic manufactures 15.5%, of which textile yarn and fabrics 4.0%, paper and paper products 2.6%, nonferrous metals 0.7%; transport equipment 14.3%, of which road motor vehicles 9.4%; chemicals and related products 10.9%; mineral fuels and lubricants 5.4%; food and live animals 4.0%; crude materials [inedible] excluding fuels 2.5%; beverages and tobacco 0.8%). *Major import sources:* U.S. 23.0%; Japan 18.2%; U.K. 6.1%; Germany 5.9%; New Zealand 4.7%; Taiwan 3.9%; China 3.9%; France 2.6%; Italy 2.4%; South Korea 2.4%.

Exports (1991–92): $A 55,075,000,000 (crude materials excluding fuels 24.7%, of which metalliferous ores and metal scrap 13.8%, textile fibres and their waste 8.4%; mineral fuels and lubricants 19.7%, of which coal, coke, and briquettes 12.6%, petroleum, petroleum products, and natural gas 7.1%; food and live animals 17.6%, of which meat 6.2%, cereals 4.3%; machinery and transport equipment 9.1%; chemicals 3.1%). *Major export destinations:* Japan 26.5%; U.S. 9.5%; South Korea 6.1%; Singapore 5.8%; New Zealand 5.1%; Taiwan 4.6%; Hong Kong 3.8%; U.K. 3.5%; Indonesia 3.0%.

Trade by commodity group (1991–92)

	imports		exports	
SITC Group	$A '000,000	%	$A '000,000	%
00 Food and live animals	2,058	4.0	9,707	17.6
01 Beverages and tobacco	392	0.8	366	0.7
02 Crude materials, excluding fuels	1,281	2.5	13,619	24.7
03 Mineral fuels, lubricants, and related materials	2,731	5.4	10,871	19.7
04 Animal and vegetable oils, fat, and waxes	150	0.3	136	0.2
05 Chemicals and related products, n.e.s.	5,575	10.9	1,661	3.1
06 Basic manufactures	7,884	15.5	6,762	12.3
07 Machinery and transport equipment	21,994	43.1	5,027	9.1
08 Miscellaneous manufactured articles	7,768	15.2	1,617	2.9
09 Goods not classified by kind	1,150	2.3	5,309	9.7
TOTAL	50,983	100.0	55,075	100.0

Direction of trade (1990–91)

	imports		exports	
	$A '000,000	%	$A '000,000	%
Africa	115	0.2	491	0.9
Asia	19,498	39.9	31,273	59.6
Japan	8,854	18.1	14,443	27.5
South America	447	0.9	332	0.6
North and Central America	12,689	25.9	6,681	12.7
United States	11,478	23.5	5,790	11.0
Europe	12,938	26.4	8,396	16.0
EEC	10,678	21.8	6,340	12.1
U.S.S.R.	52	0.1	377	0.7
Other Europe	2,208	4.5	1,679	3.2
Oceania	2,859	5.8	3,780	7.2
New Zealand	2,150	4.4	2,566	4.9
Other	373	0.8	1,502	2.9
TOTAL	48,919	100.0[17]	52,455	100.0[17]

Transport and communications

Transport. Railroads (1991)[18]: route length 23,174 mi, 37,295 km; passenger-mi 1,359,051,000[19], passenger-km 2,187,120,000[19]; short ton-mi cargo 36,-414,000,000, metric ton-km cargo 53,163,000,000. Roads (1990): total length 503,474 mi, 810,264 km (paved 36%). Vehicles (1992): passenger cars 7,913,200; trucks and buses 2,041,300. Merchant marine (1992): vessels (100 gross tons and over) 695; total deadweight tonnage 3,857,271. Air transport (1990–91): passenger-mi 25,649,600,000, passenger-km 41,279,000; short ton-mi cargo 1,765,800,000, metric ton-km cargo 2,578,029,000; airports (1991) with scheduled flights 428.

Communications. Daily newspapers (1988): total number 71; total circulation 6,689,000; circulation per 1,000 population 405. Radio (1992): 20,000,000 receivers (1 per 0.9 persons). Television (1992): 8,000,000 receivers (1 per 2.2 persons). Telephones (1992)[20]: 8,046,029 (1 per 2.2 persons).

Education and health

Education (1992)

	schools	teachers	students	student/ teacher ratio
Primary (age 6–12)	9,957	97,955	1,804,370	18.4
Secondary (age 13–17)		104,110	1,294,596	12.4
Vocational[21]	234[22]	52,587[22]	985,942	...
Higher[23]	95	25,916	420,640	16.2

Literacy (1980): percentage of total population age 15 and over literate 99.5%.

Health (1992): physicians (1986) 36,610 (1 per 438 persons); hospital beds (1990) 86,036 (1 per 199 persons); infant mortality rate per 1,000 live births 7.0.

Food (1988–90): daily per capita caloric intake 3,302 (vegetable products 63%, animal products 37%); 124% of FAO recommended minimum requirement.

Military

Total active duty personnel (1992): 63,200 (army 45.2%, navy 24.2%, air force 30.6%). *Military expenditure as percentage of GNP:* 2.3% (world 5.0%); per capita expenditure U.S.$385.

[1]March 31. [2]Includes both Northern Ireland and Republic of Ireland. [3]Completed highest level of secondary school available. [4]December. [5]Less imputed bank service charges. [6]Mostly unemployed. [7]Excludes operations of single-establishment enterprises employing fewer than four persons. [8]Excludes the drawings of working proprietors. [9]1989–90. [10]1988–89. [11]1985. [12]1985–86. [13]1987–88. [14]Second quarter. [15]July. [16]Urban areas, state forests and mining leases, unoccupied land (mainly desert). [17]Detail does not add to total given because of rounding. [18]Government railways only. [19]1978–79. [20]Lines only. [21]Includes special education. [22]1986. [23]1989.

Austria

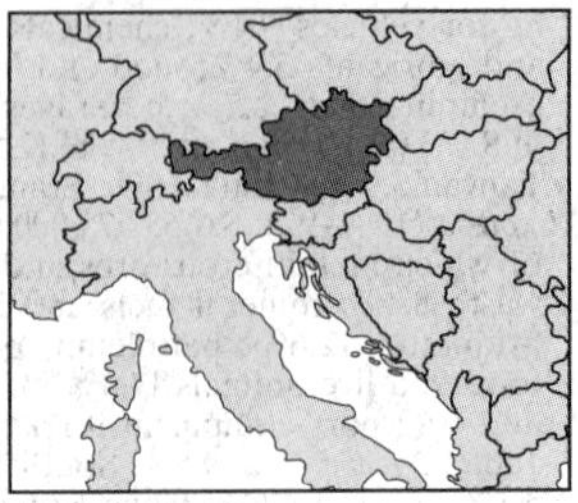

Official name: Republik Österreich (Republic of Austria).
Form of government: federal multiparty republic with two legislative houses (Federal Council [63]; National Council [183]).
Chief of state: President.
Head of government: Chancellor.
Capital: Vienna.
Official language: German.
Official religion: none.
Monetary unit: 1 Austrian Schilling (S) = 100 Groschen; valuation (Oct. 4, 1993) 1 U.S.$ = S 11.42; 1 £ = S 17.31.

Area and population

		area		population
States	Capitals	sq mi	sq km	1991 census
Burgenland	Eisenstadt	1,531	3,965	270,880
Kärnten	Klagenfurt	3,681	9,533	547,798
Niederösterreich	Sankt Pölten	7,403	19,174	1,473,813
Oberösterreich	Linz	4,626	11,980	1,333,480
Salzburg	Salzburg	2,762	7,154	482,365
Steiermark	Graz	6,327	16,388	1,184,720
Tirol	Innsbruck	4,883	12,648	631,410
Vorarlberg	Bregenz	1,004	2,601	331,472
Wien (Vienna)	—	160	415	1,539,848
TOTAL		32,378[1]	83,859[1]	7,795,786

Demography

Population (1993): 7,938,000.
Density (1993): persons per sq mi 245.2, persons per sq km 94.7.
Urban-rural (1991): urban 64.5%; rural 35.5%.
Sex distribution (1991): male 48.15%; female 51.85%.
Age breakdown (1991): under 15, 17.4%; 15–29, 23.7%; 30–44, 21.6%; 45–59, 17.2%; 60–74, 13.4%; 75 and over, 6.7%.
Population projection: (2000) 8,119,000; (2010) 8,232,000.
Doubling time: not applicable; population is stable.
Ethnic composition (national origin; 1991): Austrian 93.4%; citizens of former Yugoslavia 2.5%; Turkish 1.5%; German 0.7%; other 1.9%.
Religious affiliation (1991): Roman Catholic 78.3%; nonreligious and atheist 8.3%; Reformed-Lutheran tradition 54.9%; Muslim 2.1%; Jewish 0.1%; other (mostly Christian) 2.8%; unknown 3.5%.
Major cities (1991): Vienna 1,539,848; Graz 237,810; Linz 203,044; Salzburg 143,978; Innsbruck 118,112.

Vital statistics

Birth rate per 1,000 population (1992): 12.0 (world avg. 26.4); (1991) legitimate 75.2%; illegitimate 24.8%.
Death rate per 1,000 population (1992): 10.5 (world avg. 9.2).
Natural increase rate per 1,000 population (1992): 1.5 (world avg. 17.2).
Total fertility rate (avg. births per childbearing woman; 1991): 1.5.
Marriage rate per 1,000 population (1991): 5.6.
Divorce rate per 1,000 population (1991): 2.1.
Life expectancy at birth (1991): male 72.6 years; female 79.2 years.
Major causes of death per 100,000 population (1991): diseases of the circulatory system 562.3, of which ischemic heart diseases 216.6, cerebrovascular disease 143.6; malignant neoplasms (cancers) 246.8.

National economy

Budget (1991). Revenue: S 679,380,000,000 (tax revenue 90.4%, of which social-security contributions 36.2%, value-added tax 16.8%, individual income tax 15.9%; nontax revenue 8.9%). Expenditures: S 754,430,000,000 (social security and welfare 45.1%; health 12.9%; education 9.4%; general public services 5.4%; defense 2.4%).
National debt (end of year 1991): S 945,610,000,000.
Production (metric tons except as noted). Agriculture, forestry, fishing (1991): silage 4,252,000, sugar beets 2,522,000, corn (maize) 1,571,000, barley 1,427,000, wheat 1,375,000, potatoes 790,000, grapes 420,000, rye 350,000, apples 277,000, turnips 173,000, rapeseed 128,000; livestock (number of live animals) 3,688,000 pigs, 2,584,000 cattle, 13,139,000 chickens; roundwood 16,759,000 cu m; fish catch (1990) 4,800. Mining and quarrying (1992): iron ore 1,632,000, magnesite 978,000[2], high-grade graphite 19,700[2], zinc ore 14,900. Manufacturing (value added in S '000,000,000; 1989): electrical machinery and apparatus 39.1, nonelectrical machinery and apparatus 32.6; fabricated metal products 26.2; iron and steel 25.3; food products 23.7; transport equipment 16.5; cement, bricks, and tile 15.8. Construction (completed; 1991): residential 3,981,000 sq m; nonresidential, n.a. Energy production (consumption): electricity (kW-hr; 1992) 51,072,000,000 ([1990] 49,951,000,000); coal (metric tons; 1992) 1,644,000 ([1990] 6,282,000); crude petroleum (barrels; 1992) 8,328,000 ([1990] 56,925,000); petroleum products (metric tons; 1990) 7,900,000 (9,869,000); natural gas (cu m; 1992) 1,433,000,000 ([1990] 5,858,000,000).
Land use (1990): forested 39.0%; meadows and pastures 24.1%; agricultural and under permanent cultivation 18.2%; other 18.7%.
Tourism (1991): receipts from visitors U.S.$13,956,000,000; expenditures by nationals abroad U.S.$7,449,000,000.
Population economically active (1991): total 3,596,100; activity rate of total population 46.0% (participation rates: ages 15–64, 67.9%; female 41.0%; unemployed 6.2%[3]).

Price and earnings indexes (1985 = 100)

	1987	1988	1989	1990	1991	1992	1993[4]
Consumer price index	103.1	105.1	107.8	111.3	115.0	119.7	123.8
Monthly earnings index	107.8	111.8	116.7	125.1	131.6	138.0	...

Gross national product (at current market prices; 1991): U.S.$157,528,000,000 (U.S.$20,380 per capita).

Structure of gross domestic product and labour force

	1991			
	in value S '000,000	% of total value	labour force	% of labour force
Agriculture	53,000	2.8	258,600	7.2
Mining	502,270	26.2	12,200	0.3
Manufacturing			966,400	26.9
Construction	140,320	7.3	312,200	8.7
Public utilities	52,350	2.7	40,400	1.1
Transportation and communications	119,240	6.2	228,200	6.3
Trade, restaurants	315,240	16.5	688,300	19.1
Finance, real estate	321,540	16.8	236,300	6.6
Pub. admin., defense	269,180	14.1	813,400	22.6
Services	77,320	4.0		
Other	64,300[5]	3.4[5]	40,200	1.0
TOTAL	1,914,750[1]	100.0	3,596,100[1]	100.0[1]

Household income and expenditure. Average household size (1991) 2.6; net income per household[6] (1991) S 262,080 (U.S.$21,930); sources of income (1990): wages and salaries 55.5%, transfer payments 24.4%, other 20.1%; expenditure (1990): food and beverages 18.3%, transportation 16.5%, housing 13.6%, cafe and hotel expenditures 10.8%, clothing and footwear 9.5%.

Foreign trade[7]

Balance of trade (current prices)

	1987	1988	1989	1990	1991	1992
S '000,000	−51,520	−47,910	−62,180	−65,190	−86,300	−81,000
% of total	7.0%	5.9%	6.8%	6.5%	8.3%	7.7%

Imports (1991): S 591,900,000,000 (machinery and transport equipment 39.1%, of which passenger cars 7.6%, electrical machinery and apparatus 6.6%; chemicals and related products 9.7%; clothing 4.8%; food products 4.5%). *Major import sources:* Germany 41.5%; Italy 8.8%; Japan 4.8%; France 4.4%; Switzerland 4.2%; United States 3.9%.
Exports (1991): S 479,000,000,000 (machinery and transport equipment 38.3%, of which electrical machinery and apparatus 7.0%, general industrial machinery 6.3%, machines for special industries 5.9%; chemicals and related products 8.9%; paper and paper products 6.2%). *Major export destinations:* Germany 39.0%; Italy 9.4%; Switzerland 6.4%; France 4.4%; United Kingdom 3.6%; Hungary 3.0%.

Transport and communications

Transport. Railroads (1992): length (1991) 4,136 mi, 6,657 km; passenger-mi 5,864,000,000[8], passenger-km 9,437,000,000[8]; short ton-mi cargo 8,362,000,000[8], metric ton-km cargo 12,208,000,000[8]. Roads (1991): total length 77,700 mi, 125,000 km (paved 100%). Vehicles (1991): passenger cars 3,100,014; trucks and buses 268,577. Merchant marine (1992): vessels (100 gross tons and over) 26; total deadweight tonnage 208,504. Air transport (1992)[9]: passenger-mi 2,990,000,000, passenger-km 4,812,000,000; short ton-mi cargo 70,200,000, metric ton-km cargo 102,500,000; airports (1993) with scheduled flights 6.
Communications. Daily newspapers (1991): total number 23; total circulation 4,372,210; circulation per 1,000 population 559. Radio (1992): total receivers 4,700,000 (1 per 1.7 persons). Television (1992): total receivers 2,706,000 (1 per 2.9 persons). Telephones (1991): 4,732,000 (1 per 1.7 persons).

Education and health

Education (1991–92)

	schools	teachers	students	student/ teacher ratio
Primary (age 6–10)	3,389	29,929	380,883	12.7
Secondary (age 11–18)	1,509	52,028	414,875	8.0
Voc., teacher tr.	1,318	24,412	323,308	13.2
Higher	92	13,944	211,484	15.2

Educational attainment (1991). Percentage of population age 25 and over having: compulsory education (through lower secondary) 38.2%; terminal vocational at secondary level 45.2%; nonterminal general secondary or vocational 10.5%; higher 6.1%. *Literacy:* virtually 100%.
Health (1992): physicians 24,049 (1 per 327 persons); hospital beds 74,871 (1 per 105 persons); infant mortality rate per 1,000 live births 7.4.
Food (1988–90): daily per capita caloric intake 3,486 (vegetable products 64%, animal products 36%); 133% of FAO recommended minimum requirement.

Military

Total active duty personnel (1992): 52,000 (army 88.5%; navy, none; air force 11.5%). *Military expenditure as percentage of GNP* (1989): 1.1% (world 4.9%); per capita expenditure U.S.$184.

[1]Detail does not add to total given because of rounding. [2]1991. [3]Average of April 1, 1992–March 31, 1993. [4]June. [5]Value-added tax plus import duties (S 179,780,000,000) less imputed bank service charges (S 115,480,000,000). [6]Two-person households without children only. [7]Import figures are f.o.b. in balance of trade and c.i.f. in commodities and trading partners. [8]Federal railways only. [9]Austrian Airlines and Lauda Air.

Azerbaijan

Official name: Azärbayjan Respublikasi (Azerbaijani Republic).
Form of government: federal multiparty republic with a single legislative body (National Council [50]).
Head of state: President.
Head of government: Prime Minister.
Capital: Baku (Azerbaijani: Baky).
Official language: Azerbaijani.
Official religion: none.
Monetary unit: 1 manat = 100 gopik; valuation (Oct. 4, 1993) free rate, 1 U.S.$ = 116.50 manat; 1 £ = 176.50 manat. The manat was introduced Aug. 15, 1992, at a 10 to 1 ratio with the Russian ruble and circulated parallel with it; on June 20, 1993, the manat became the sole legal tender.

Area and population

		area		population
		sq mi	sq km	1991 estimate
Republics	**Capitals**			
Nagorno Karabakh	Stepanakert	1,700	4,400	193,300
Nakhichevan	Nakhichevan	2,100	5,500	305,700
Regions under republican jurisdiction	—	29,600	76,700	4,924,300
Cities				
Baku (City Soviet)	—	...	...	1,713,300
TOTAL		33,400	86,600	7,136,600

Demography

Population (1993): 7,398,000.
Density (1993): persons per sq mi 220.2, persons per sq km 85.0.
Urban-rural (1991): urban 53.7%; rural 46.3%.
Sex distribution (1992): male 49.31%; female 50.69%.
Age breakdown (1989): under 15, 32.8%; 15–29, 29.7%; 30–44, 16.8%; 45–59, 12.8%; 60–74, 5.7%; 75 and over, 2.2%.
Population projection: (2000) 8,324,000; (2010) 9,445,000.
Doubling time: 33 years.
Ethnic composition (1989): Azerbaijani 82.7%; Russian 5.7%; Armenian 5.6%; Lezgin 2.4%; Avar 0.6%; Ukrainian 0.5%; Tatar 0.4%; other 2.1%.
Religious affiliation (1991): Shīʿī Muslim 70%; Sunnī Muslim 30%.
Major cities (1991): Baku 1,080,500; Gyandzha (formerly Kirovabad) 282,200; Sumgait 236,200; Mingechaur 90,900; Nakhichevan 61,700.

Vital statistics

Birth rate per 1,000 population (1992): 27.0 (world avg. 26.4); (1989) legitimate 97.5%; illegitimate 2.5%.
Death rate per 1,000 population (1992): 6.3 (world avg. 9.2).
Natural increase rate per 1,000 population (1992): 20.7 (world avg. 17.2).
Total fertility rate (avg. births per childbearing woman; 1989): 2.8.
Marriage rate per 1,000 population (1989): 6.7.
Divorce rate per 1,000 population (1989): 1.7.
Life expectancy at birth (1990): male 66.9 years; female 74.8 years.
Major causes of death per 100,000 population (1989): diseases of the circulatory system 292.4; diseases of the respiratory system 88.9; malignant neoplasms (cancers) 72.1; accidents, poisoning, and violence 42.1; infectious and parasitic diseases 42.1; diseases of the digestive system 25.6; diseases of the nervous system 9.7; endocrine and metabolic disorders 8.6.

National economy

Budget (1991). Revenue: 10,336,200,000 rubles (tax revenue 57.7%, of which turnover tax 38.6%, enterprise profits tax 12.6%, individual income tax 5.8%; nontax revenue 42.3%). Expenditures: 9,630,500,000 rubles (social welfare and culture 57.4%, of which pensions 19.2%, education 18.6%, health 8.2%; national economy 42.1%).
Public debt (external, outstanding): n.a.
Production (metric tons except as noted). Agriculture, forestry, fishing (1992): fruit (except grapes) 1,580,000, cereals 1,305,000, grapes 1,100,000, wheat 900,000, vegetables (except potatoes) 880,000, cotton 480,000, potatoes 170,000, tobacco 63,000, tea 7,000; livestock (number of live animals) 5,102,000 sheep and goats, 1,800,000 cattle, 100,000 pigs, 35,000 horses; roundwood 86,700 cu m; fish catch 39,700. Mining and quarrying (1989): iron ore 718,200. Manufacturing (1992): iron rails 1,600,000; steel 573,000; sulfuric acid 552,000; rolled iron 459,000; steel pipes 411,000; mineral fertilizers 188,000; caustic soda 171,000; synthetic rubber 84,500; bicycles 312,000 units; refrigerators 7,400 units; pesticides 6,700 units; leather footwear 10,300,000 pairs; canned foods 628,000,000 cans; cotton fabrics 95,300,000 sq m; silk fabrics 30,100,000 sq m; woolen fabrics 9,200,000 sq m; cinder blocks 129,000,000 pieces; roofing tiles 78,400,000 pieces; reinforced concrete 1,200,000 cu m. Construction (1991): 2,600,000 sq m. Energy production (consumption): electricity (kW-hr; 1991) 23,300,000,000 (n.a.); coal, n.a. (n.a.); crude petroleum (barrels; 1991) 86,100,000 (n.a.); petroleum products (metric tons; 1991) 15,192,900 (7,079,100); natural gas (cu m; 1991) 11,655,000,000 (n.a.).
Tourism: receipts from visitors, n.a.; expenditures by nationals abroad, n.a.
Land use: n.a.
Gross national product (at current market prices; 1992): U.S.$6,290,000,000 (U.S.$870 per capita)[1].

Structure of net material product and labour force

	1992		1990	
	in value '000,000 rubles	% of total value	labour force	% of labour force
Agriculture	50,712	33.5	1,047,000	32.3
Mining, Manufacturing, Public utilities	73,242	48.3		
Construction	14,842	9.8		
Transportation and communications	3,948	2.6	2,195,000	67.7
Trade	1,317	0.9		
Finance	—	—		
Pub. admin., defense	—	—		
Services	—	—		
Other	7,519	4.9		
TOTAL	151,580	100.0	3,242,000	100.0

Population economically active (1991): total 2,901,000; activity rate of total population 39.8% (participation rates: ages 16–59 [male], 16–54 [female] 72.5%; female [1989] 42.6%; unemployed [1991] 3.7%).

Price and earnings indexes (1985 = 100)

	1985	1986	1987	1988	1989	1990	1991
Consumer price index	100.0	...	...	...	...	...	...
Monthly earnings index	100.0	99.0	101.2	104.9	109.8	119.6	195.1

Household income and expenditure. Average household size (1989) 4.8; income per household: n.a.; sources of income: n.a.; expenditure: n.a.

Foreign trade

Balance of trade (current prices)

	1987	1988	1989	1990	1991
'000,000 rubles	1,209	1,110	1,933	678	1,190
% of total	...	...	...	...	5.1%

Imports (1991): 11,009,800,000 rubles (food products 26.0%; machinery and equipment 18.2%; nonferrous metals 11.8%; textiles 11.0%; oil and gas 8.2%; ferrous metals 8.2%; chemicals and petrochemicals 5.8%; agricultural products 4.4%; timber, pulp, and paper 3.3%; building materials 1.4%). *Major import sources:* former Soviet republics 80.3%, of which Russia 56.1%, Ukraine 28.3%, Kazakhstan 5.3%, Belarus 2.8%, Estonia 1.4%; other countries 19.7%.
Exports (1991): 12,199,500,000 rubles (food products 31.9%; textiles 18.6%; machinery and equipment 17.7%; oil and gas 11.9%; chemicals and petrochemicals 9.5%; nonferrous metals 3.1%; ferrous metals 2.3%; agricultural products 2.3%; building materials 0.3%). *Major export destinations:* former Soviet republics 93.9%, of which Russia 59.7%, Ukraine 13.1%, Turkmenistan 4.5%, Kazakhstan 4.1%, Uzbekistan 2.6%, Baltic republics 2.1%; other countries 6.1%.

Transport and communications

Transport. Railroads (1991): length 1,299 mi, 2,090 km; passenger-mi 3,025,400,000, passenger-km 4,868,900,000; cargo traffic, n.a. Roads (1991): total length 22,800 mi, 36,700 km (paved 87%). Vehicles (1988): passenger cars 235,600; trucks and buses, n.a. Merchant marine: vessels (100 gross tons and over) n.a.; total deadweight tonnage, n.a. Air transport (1990): passenger-mi 3,025,400,000, passenger-km 4,868,900,000; cargo traffic, n.a.; airports (1993) with scheduled flights 1.
Communications. Daily newspapers (1990): total number 168; total circulation 520,000,000; circulation per 1,000 population 73. Radio (1992): total number of receivers 1,174,000 (1 per 6.1 persons). Television (1992): total number of receivers 1,522,000 (1 per 4.8 persons). Telephones (1991): 710,000 (1 per 10 persons).

Education and health

Education (1991–92)

	schools	teachers	students	student/ teacher ratio
Primary (age 6–13), Secondary (age 14–17)	4,332	139,000	1,375,000	9.9
Voc., teacher tr.	77	...	60,100	...
Higher	18	...	108,000	...

Educational attainment (1989). Percentage of population age 25 and over having: primary education or no formal schooling 12.2%; some secondary 19.2%; completed secondary and some postsecondary 58.1%; higher 10.5%.
Literacy: n.a.
Health (1990): physicians 28,000 (1 per 255 persons); hospital beds 72,700 (1 per 98 persons); infant mortality rate per 1,000 live births 25.3.
Food: daily per capita caloric intake, n.a.

Military

Total active duty personnel (1993): 5,000[2] (army 96.3%, navy[3], air force 3.7%). *Military expenditure as percentage of GNP* (1991): *c.* 12.5% (world *c.* 5.4%); per capita expenditure (1992) U.S.$26.

[1]Ruble-area GNP and exchange-rate data are very speculative. [2]Total mobilization data for war with Armenia is not available; however, total reserve strength is 560,000. [3]Azerbaijan shares a portion of the Caspian Flotilla.

Bahamas, The

Official name: The Commonwealth of The Bahamas.
Form of government: constitutional monarchy with two legislative houses (Senate [16]; House of Assembly [49]).
Chief of state: British Monarch represented by Governor-General.
Head of government: Prime Minister.
Capital: Nassau.
Official language: English.
Official religion: none.
Monetary unit: 1 Bahamian dollar (B$) = 100 cents; valuation (Oct. 4, 1993) 1 Bahamian dollar = U.S.$1.00 = £1.52.

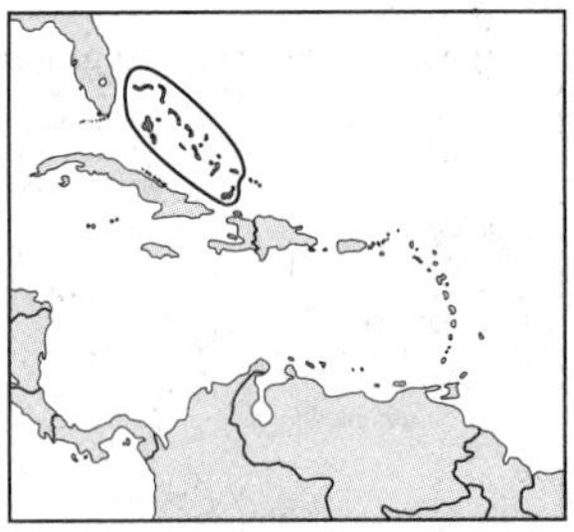

Area and population

Islands and Island Groups[2]	area[1] sq mi	area[1] sq km	population 1990 census
Abaco, Great and Little	649	1,681	10,034
Acklins	192	497	405
Andros	2,300	5,957	8,180
Berry Islands	12	31	628
Bimini Islands	9	23	1,639
Cat Island	150	388	1,698
Crooked and Long Cay	93	241	412
Eleuthera	187	484	7,993
Exuma, Great, and Exuma Cays	112	290	3,556
Grand Bahama	530	1,373	40,898
Harbour Island	3	8	1,219
Inagua, Great and Little	599	1,551	985
Long Island	230	596	2,954
Mayaguana	110	285	312
New Providence	80	207	172,196
Ragged Island	14	36	89
Rum Cay	30	78	53
San Salvador	63	163	465
Spanish Wells	10	26	1,372
Other uninhabited cays and rocks	9	23	—
TOTAL	5,382	13,939[3]	255,095[4]

Demography

Population (1993): 266,000.
Density (1993): persons per sq mi 49.4, persons per sq km 19.1.
Urban-rural (1990): urban 64.3%; rural 35.7%.
Sex distribution (1990): male 49.00%; female 51.00%.
Age breakdown (1985): under 15, 38.0%; 15–29, 27.9%; 30–44, 17.9%; 45–59, 10.5%; 60–74, 4.8%; 75 and over, 0.9%.
Population projection: (2000) 295,000; (2010) 334,000.
Doubling time: 48 years.
Ethnic composition (1988): black 80.0%; mixed 10.0%; white 10.0%.
Religious affiliation (1980): non-Anglican Protestant 55.2%, of which Baptist 32.1%, Methodist 6.1%, Church of God (Anderson Ind.) 5.7%; Anglican 20.1%; Roman Catholic 18.8%; other 5.9%.
Major cities (1990): Nassau 172,196[5]; Freeport/Lucaya 26,574; Marsh Harbour 3,611; Bailey Town 1,490; Dunmore Town (Harbour Island) 1,219.

Vital statistics

Birth rate per 1,000 population (1991): 19.7 (world avg. 26.4); (1990) legitimate 42.8%, illegitimate 57.2%.
Death rate per 1,000 population (1991): 5.1 (world avg. 9.2).
Natural increase rate per 1,000 population (1991): 14.6 (world avg. 17.2).
Total fertility rate (avg. births per childbearing woman; 1991): 2.1.
Marriage rate per 1,000 population (1990): 8.6.
Divorce rate per 1,000 population (1990): 1.7.
Life expectancy at birth (1991): male 68.3 years; female 75.3 years.
Major causes of death per 100,000 population (1990): diseases of the circulatory system 126.3, of which ischemic heart diseases 77.3; malignant neoplasms (cancers) 80.4; endocrine and metabolic disorders 72.2; diseases of the respiratory system 52.2.

National economy

Budget (1992). Revenue: B$520,315,000 (import taxes 50.1%, stamp taxes 13.1%, departure taxes 9.3%, fines and forfeits 6.7%, business and professional licenses 5.2%). Expenditures: B$571,340,000 (education 20.9%, health 14.5%, general administration 11.2%, interest on public debt 10.9%, public order 10.1%, transportation 8.2%, defense 3.4%).
National debt (March 1993): U.S.$1,351,000,000.
Production (value of production in B$'000 except as noted). Agriculture, forestry, fishing (1992): crayfish 20,000, other marine products (mostly snappers, groupers, conchs) 39,400, fruits and vegetables 22,800[6], poultry products 18,400[6]; roundwood 115,000 cu m[7]. Mining and quarrying (1991): salt 9,400; aragonite 3,600. Manufacturing (1992): pharmaceuticals 107,200; rum 19,600. Construction (gross value of buildings started in B$'000,000; 1992–93)[8]: residential 109; nonresidential 41. Energy production (consumption): electricity (kW-hr; 1990) 950,000,000 (950,000,000); coal, none (none); crude petroleum, none (none); petroleum products (metric tons; 1990) negligible (435,000); natural gas, none (none).
Tourism: receipts from visitors (1992) U.S.$1,185,000,000; expenditures by nationals abroad (1991) U.S.$205,000,000.
Gross national product (1992): U.S.$3,165,000,000 (U.S.$11,990 per capita).

Structure of gross domestic product and labour force

	1986 in value B$'000,000	1986 % of total value	1989 labour force	1989 % of labour force
Agriculture, fishing	90	4.5	4,970	3.9
Mining	} 206	} 10.3	360	0.3
Manufacturing			4,210	3.3
Public utilities			1,570	1.2
Construction	61	3.1	9,880	7.8
Transp. and commun.	219	10.9	8,880	7.0
Trade, restaurants	524	26.2	36,300	28.5
Finance, real estate	245	12.2	8,580	6.7
Pub. admin., defense	342	17.1	} 35,750	} 28.1
Services	315	15.7		
Other	—	—	16,900[9]	13.3[9]
TOTAL	2,003[3, 10]	100.0	127,400	100.0[3]

Population economically active (1989): total 127,400; activity rate of total population 51.2% (participation rates: ages 15–64 [1980] 70.5%; female 47.3%; unemployed [1992] 14.8%).

Price and earnings indexes (1985 = 100)

	1987	1988	1989	1990	1991	1992	1993
Consumer price index[11]	111.7	116.4	122.7	128.4	137.5	145.5	150.3[12]
Earnings index	...	...	...	...	...	...	...

Household income and expenditure. Average household size (1992) 3.7; income per household (1992) B$25,000 (U.S.$25,000); sources of income: n.a.; expenditure (1988)[13]: food and beverages 19.8%, housing 19.2%, transportation and communications 18.9%, household furnishings 10.2%, education 7.8%.
Land use (1991): forested 32.4%; meadows and pastures 0.2%; agricultural and under permanent cultivation 1.0%; other 66.4%.

Foreign trade[14]

Balance of trade (current prices)

	1986	1987	1988	1989	1990	1991
B$'000,000	−588	−309	−99	−534	−327	−211
% of total	9.8%	5.4%	2.4%	9.4%	5.9%	6.2%

Imports (1990): B$2,920,000,000 (crude petroleum for storage only 52.2%, distillate fuels 4.9%, gasoline 2.0%, road motor vehicles 1.9%, meat 1.4%). *Major import sources:* Saudi Arabia 36.9%; United States 35.6%; United Kingdom 3.7%; Nigeria 3.1%; Iraq 2.8%.
Exports (1990)[15]: B$2,593,000,000 (crude petroleum 58.8%, chemicals [mostly pharmaceuticals] 17.5%, residual fuel oils 12.9%, crayfish 1.7%, rum 1.1%). *Major export destinations:* United States 76.5%; Puerto Rico 17.3%; Belgium 1.0%; Canada 0.9%; United Kingdom 0.8%.

Transport and communications

Transport. Railroads: none. Roads (1990): total length of paved roads 2,094 mi, 3,370 km. Vehicles (1991): passenger cars 70,000; trucks and buses 15,000. Merchant marine (1992): vessels (100 gross tons and over) 1,061; total deadweight tonnage 33,081,652. Air transport (1991): passenger-mi 215,000,000, passenger-km 346,000,000; short ton-mi cargo 205,000, metric ton-km cargo 300,000; airports (1993) with scheduled flights 24.
Communications. Daily newspapers (1991): total number 3; total circulation 35,000; circulation per 1,000 population 135. Radio (1992): total receivers 200,000 (1 per 1.3 persons). Television (1992): total receivers 60,000 (1 per 4.5 persons). Telephones (1991): 144,570 (1 per 1.8 persons).

Education and health

Education (1990–91)

	schools	teachers	students	student/ teacher ratio
Primary (age 5–10)	100[16]	...	27,264[16]	...
Secondary (age 11–17)	37[16]	...	23,616[16]	...
Higher[17]	1	300	2,200	7.3

Educational attainment: n.a. *Literacy* (1986): total population age 15 and over literate 139,000 (95.0%).
Health (1992): physicians 357 (1 per 714 persons); hospital beds 1,020 (1 per 250 persons); infant mortality rate per 1,000 live births (1991) 23.8.
Food (1988–90): daily per capita caloric intake 2,777 (vegetable products 66%, animal products 34%); 115% of FAO recommended minimum requirement.

Military

Total active duty personnel (1992): 850 (all paramilitary coast guard). *Military expenditure as percentage of GNP:* n.a.

[1]Land area only of individual islands or island groups. [2]Family (Out) Islands (all islands other than New Providence) are administered by commissioners assigned by the central government. Extent of commissioner districts varies from part of an island to island groups. [3]Detail does not add to total given because of rounding. [4]Includes seven people not accounted for by island. [5]Population cited is for New Providence Island. [6]1990. [7]1991. [8]New Providence and Grand Bahama islands only. [9]Includes 1,990 not adequately defined and 14,910 unemployed. [10]GDP of 1990 equaled U.S.$2,810,000,000 (tourism accounted for 47% of the GDP). [11]New Providence Island only. [12]June. [13]Domestic purchases by resident households only; data for expenditures in restaurants and hotels are not available. [14]Imports c.i.f.; exports f.o.b. [15]*Exports* (1991): B$1,590,000,000 (chemicals [mostly pharmaceuticals] 48.4%, crude petroleum and petroleum products 35.3%, hormones 4.1%, crayfish 2.8%). [16]Data exclude 86 combined primary/secondary schools with 10,739 students. [17]1991–92; College of The Bahamas only.

Bahrain

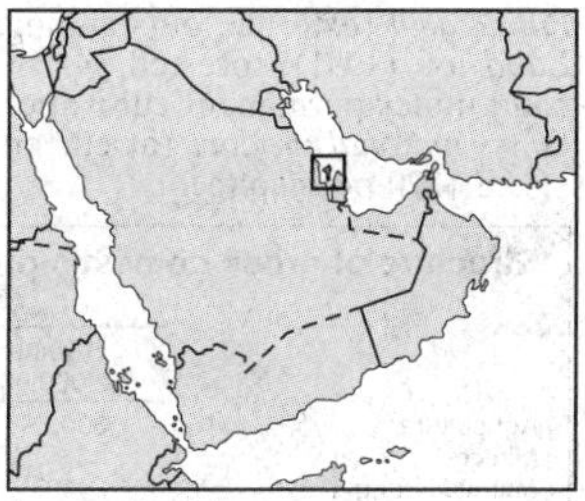

Official name: Dawlat al-Baḥrayn (State of Bahrain).
Form of government: monarchy (emirate) with an advisory Consultative Council (30).
Chief of state: Emir.
Head of government: Prime Minister.
Capital: Manama.
Official language: Arabic.
Official religion: Islam.
Monetary unit: 1 Bahrain dinar (BD) = 1,000 fils; valuation (Oct. 4, 1993) 1 BD = U.S.$2.70 = £1.75.

Area and population

Regions	area sq mi	area sq km	population 1981 census
al-Gharbīyah (Western)	60.2	156.1	14,503
al-Ḥadd	2.4	6.2	7,111
Jidd (Judd) Ḥafṣ	8.4	21.8	33,693
al-Manāmah	10.0	25.8	121,986
al-Muḥarraq	6.3	16.4	61,853
ar-Rifā'	112.6	291.6	28,150
ash-Shamālīyah (Northern)	14.3	37.0	22,117
Sitrah	11.1	28.8	22,993
al-Wusṭā (Central)	13.6	35.3	16,776
Towns with special status			
Ḥammād	5.1	13.1	...
Madīnat 'Īsā	4.8	12.4	21,275
Islands			
Ḥawār and other	19.5	50.6	341
TOTAL	268.4[1,2]	695.3[1,2]	350,798[3]

Demography

Population (1993): 486,000[3].
Density (1993): persons per sq mi 1,810.3, persons per sq km 699.0.
Urban-rural (1990): urban 83.0%; rural 17.0%.
Sex distribution (1993): male 57.14%; female 42.86%.
Age breakdown (1993): under 15, 36.2%; 15–29, 22.0%; 30–44, 26.2%; 45–59, 11.2%; 60–74, 3.8%; 75 and over, 0.6%.
Population projection: (2000) 654,000; (2010) 825,000.
Doubling time: 29 years.
Ethnic composition (1981): Bahraini Arab 68.0%; Persian, Indian, and Pakistani 24.7%; other Arab 4.1%; European 2.5%; other 0.7%.
Religious affiliation (1981): Muslim 85.0% (Shīʿī 60.0% and Sunnī 40.0%); Christian 7.3%; other 7.7%.
Major cities (1988): al-Manāmah 151,500; al-Muḥarraq 78,000; Jidd Ḥafṣ 48,000; ar-Rifā' 45,530[4]; Madīnat 'Īsā 39,783[4].

Vital statistics

Birth rate per 1,000 population (1991): 27.9 (world avg. 26.4); legitimate 100%.
Death rate per 1,000 population (1991): 3.7 (world avg. 9.2).
Natural increase rate per 1,000 population (1991): 24.2 (world avg. 17.2).
Total fertility rate (avg. births per childbearing woman; 1990): 3.9.
Marriage rate per 1,000 population (1991): 6.8.
Divorce rate per 1,000 population (1991): 1.3.
Life expectancy at birth (1991): male 71.0 years; female 76.0 years.
Major causes of death per 100,000 population (1991): diseases of the circulatory system 100.4; malignant neoplasms (cancers) 34.1; diseases of the respiratory system 29.7; accidents and violence 28.5; endocrine, nutritional, and metabolic diseases 17.4; congenital anomalies 13.8; diseases of the genitourinary system 13.4; diseases of the digestive system 10.7.

National economy

Budget (1991). Revenue: BD 511,800,000 (petroleum company dividends and oil field receipts 59.8%, non-oil revenue including grants and loans 40.2%). Expenditures: BD 534,300,000 (1990; public utilities 15.2%, defense 13.5%, education 10.1%, health 8.0%, transfer and loan repayments 7.0%, roads 5.0%).
Public debt (external, outstanding; 1989)[5]: U.S$1,240,000,000.
Population economically active (1991): total 226,448; activity rate of total population 44.6% (participation rates: ages 15–64, 66.1%; female 17.5%; unemployed 6.3%).

Price and earnings indexes (1985 = 100)

	1986	1987	1988	1989	1990	1991	1992
Consumer price index	97.7	96.0	96.3	97.7	98.6	99.4	99.4
Earnings index	...	...	...	...	...	...	...

Production (metric tons except as noted). Agriculture, forestry, fishing (1992): fruit (excluding melons) 23,000, cow's milk 19,000, dates 18,000, tomatoes 4,000, hen's eggs 2,950, onions 1,000, cucumbers 1,000; livestock (number of live animals) 17,000 goats, 15,000 cattle, 9,000 sheep 1,000 camels, 1,000,000 chickens; fish catch (1991) 7,553. Manufacturing (barrels; 1991): gas oil 28,072,000; fuel oil 23,571,000; naphtha 12,193,000; kerosene 9,319,000; jet fuel 8,586,000; gasoline 8,032,000; heavy lubricant distillate 2,613,000; petroleum bitumen 722,000; other manufactures include methanol, ammonia, aluminum metal and forms, plastics, and paper products. Construction (permits issued; 1991): residential 5,931; nonresidential 718. Energy production (consumption): electricity (kW-hr; 1991) 3,360,000,000 (3,276,000,000); coal, none (n.a.); crude petroleum (barrels; 1991) 15,373,000 (93,510,000); petroleum products (metric tons; 1991) 10,527,000 (831,000); natural gas (cu m; 1991) 6,321,000,000 (6,321,000,000).
Gross national product (at current market prices; 1991): U.S.$6,910,000,000 (U.S.$6,310 per capita).

Structure of gross domestic product and labour force

	1991 value in BD '000,000	% of total value	labour force	% of labour force
Agriculture	14.7	0.9	5,108	2.3
Mining	296.4	18.6	3,638	1.6
Manufacturing	264.1	16.5	26,618	11.8
Construction	91.7	5.7	26,738	11.6
Public utilities	24.3	1.5	2,898	1.3
Transp. and commun.	192.8	12.1	13,789	6.1
Trade	168.6	10.6	29,961	13.2
Finance	274.2	17.2	17,256	7.6
Pub. admin., defense	322.9	20.2	83,944	37.1
Services	81.2	5.1		
Other	−133.1	−8.3	16,498	7.3
TOTAL	1,597.8	100.0[2]	226,448	100.0[2]

Households. Average household size (1986) 6.5; income per household: n.a.; sources of income: n.a.; expenditure (1984): food and tobacco 33.3%, housing 21.2%, household durable goods 9.8%, transportation and communications 8.5%, recreation 6.4%, clothing and footwear 5.9%, education 2.7%, health 2.3%, energy and water 2.2%.
Land use (1991): meadows and pastures 5.9%; agricultural and under permanent cultivation 2.9%; built-on and wasteland (mostly sand plains and salt marshes) 91.2%.
Tourism (1991): receipts from visitors U.S.$162,000,000; expenditures by nationals abroad U.S.$98,000,000.

Foreign trade[6]

Balance of trade (current prices)

	1987	1988	1989	1990	1991	1992
BD '000,000	−5.7	+28.2	+3.1	+156.7	−73.1	−119.0
% of total	0.3%	1.6%	1.4%	5.9%	2.7%	4.4%

Imports (1991): BD 1,547,300,000 (nonpetroleum products 58.3%, crude petroleum products 41.7%). *Major import sources* (1989): Saudi Arabia 49.5%; Japan 10.4%; United States 7.8%; United Kingdom 7.6%; Italy 6.6%; Australia 3.5%; West Germany 3.3%; The Netherlands 1.9%; France 1.4%; India 1.0%; South Korea 0.9%.
Exports (1991): BD 1,320,900,000 (petroleum products 77.6%, aluminum products 11.3%). *Major export destinations* (1989): United States 25.7%; United Arab Emirates 19.3%; Japan 11.9%; India 10.8%; Canada 9.9%; Singapore 6.1%; Saudi Arabia 2.9%; Réunion 1.3%; Djibouti 1.2%.

Transport and communications

Transport. Railroads: none. Roads (1991): total length 1,660 mi, 2,671 km (paved 75%). Vehicles (1991): passenger cars 101,845; trucks and buses 28,866. Merchant marine (1992): vessels (100 gross tons and over) 87; total deadweight tonnage 192,487. Air transport (1992)[7]: passenger-mi 1,194,000,000, passenger-km 1,922,000,000; short ton-mi cargo 47,688,000, metric ton-km cargo 69,622,000; airports (1993) with scheduled flights 1.
Communications. Daily newspapers (1989): total number 3; total circulation 58,500; circulation per 1,000 population 116. Radio (1991): total number of receivers 250,000 (1 per 2.1 persons). Television (1991): total number of receivers 185,952 (1 per 2.8 persons). Telephones (1991): 162,126 (1 per 3.1 persons).

Education and health

Education (1987–88)

	schools	teachers	students	student/ teacher ratio
Primary (age 6–11)	131	3,673	60,519	16.5
Secondary (age 12–17)	35	1,563	33,148	21.2
Voc., teacher tr.	9	707	7,478	10.6
Higher	4	539	5,529	10.3

Educational attainment (1981). Percentage of population age 10 and over having: no formal education 27.2%; knowledge of reading and writing 26.3%; primary education 24.9%; secondary 13.3%; higher 8.3%. *Literacy* (1991): percentage of population age 15 and over literate 69.7%; males literate 76.5%; females literate 58.6%.
Health (1991): physicians 542 (1 per 953 persons); hospital beds 1,187 (1 per 435 persons); infant mortality rate per 1,000 live births (1991) 17.0.
Food: n.a.

Military

Total active duty personnel (1993): 7,150 (army 83.9%, navy 7.0%, air force 9.1%). *Military expenditure as percentage of GNP* (1989): 6.5% (world 4.9%); per capita expenditure U.S.$389.

[1]Total area includes numerous small uninhabited islands and dependencies of Bahrain. [2]Detail does not add to total given because of rounding. [3]The 1991 census, conducted in December, recorded a total population of 508,037. [4]1987. [5]Includes long-term private debt not guaranteed by the government. [6]Import figures are f.o.b. in balance of trade and c.i.f. for commodities and trading partners. [7]One-fourth apportionment of international flights of Gulf Air (jointly administered by the governments of Bahrain, Oman, Qatar, and the United Arab Emirates).

Bangladesh

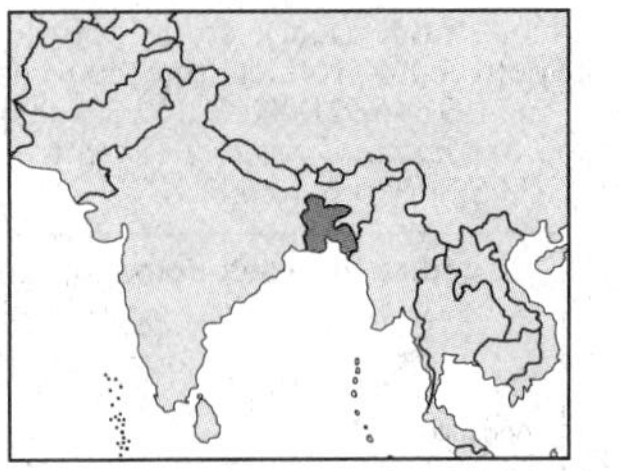

Official name: Gana Prajātantrī Bangladesh (People's Republic of Bangladesh).
Form of government: unitary multiparty republic with one legislative house (Parliament [330[1]]).
Chief of state: President.
Head of government: Prime Minister.
Capital: Dhākā.
Official language: Bengali.
Official religion: Islam.
Monetary unit: 1 Bangladesh taka (Tk) = 100 paisa; valuation (Oct. 4, 1993) 1 U.S.$ = Tk 39.49; 1 £ = Tk 59.83.

Area and population

		area		population
Divisions[2]	Administrative centres	sq mi	sq km	1991 census[3]
Chittagong	Chittagong	18,153	47,016	27,096,904
Dhākā	Dhākā	12,038	31,178	32,270,994
Khulna	Khulna	13,800	35,742	19,966,590
Rājshāhi	Rājshāhi	13,304	34,457	25,431,655
TOTAL		57,295	148,393	104,766,143

Demography

Population (1993): 115,075,000.
Density (1993): persons per sq mi 2,008.5, persons per sq km 775.5.
Urban-rural (1989): urban 24.4%; rural 75.6%.
Sex distribution (1991): male 51.47%; female 48.53%.
Age breakdown (1991): under 15, 43.6%; 15–49, 45.0%; 50–64, 7.7%; 65 and over, 3.7%.
Population projection: (2000) 132,401,000; (2010) 161,774,000.
Doubling time: 32 years.
Ethnic composition (1983): Bengali 97.7%; tribal (Chakmā, Gāro, Khāsi, Santāl, etc.) 1.0%; other 1.3%.
Religious affiliation (1991): Muslim 86.8%; Hindu 11.9%; other 1.3%.
Major cities (1991)[4]: Dhākā 6,105,160; Chittagong 2,040,663; Khulna 877,388; Rājshāhi 517,136; Mymensingh 185,517[5].

Vital statistics

Birth rate per 1,000 population (1991): 31.6 (world avg. 26.4).
Death rate per 1,000 population (1991): 11.0 (world avg. 9.2).
Natural increase rate per 1,000 population (1991): 20.6 (world avg. 17.2).
Total fertility rate (avg. births per childbearing woman; 1991): 4.9.
Marriage rate per 1,000 population (1991): 11.0.
Divorce rate per 1,000 population (1981): 3.6.
Life expectancy at birth (1991): male 56.5 years; female 55.6 years.
Major causes of death (1990; percentage of recorded deaths): typhoid fever 19.8%; old age 14.8%; tetanus 10.1%; tuberculosis and other respiratory diseases 8.7%; diarrhea 6.4%; suicide, accidents, and poisoning 5.1%; high blood pressure and heart diseases 5.0%.

National economy

Budget (1991–92). Revenue: Tk 91,001,000,000 (customs duties 30.7%, sales tax 17.3%, excise duties 14.9%, dividends and profits from public enterprises 11.0%, business tax 10.2%, income taxes 3.8%). Expenditures: Tk 80,833,000,000 (transfer payments 36.2%, employee compensation 33.6%, goods and services 27.8%, capital formation 2.4%).
Production (metric tons except as noted). Agriculture, forestry, fishing (1992): paddy rice 27,400,000, sugarcane 7,446,000, wheat 1,065,000, jute 898,000, bananas 630,000, pulses 506,000, oilseeds 378,000[6], condiments and spices 322,000[6], jackfruit 254,000[6], mangoes 183,000, pineapples 160,000, tea 45,000; livestock (number of live animals) 23,700,000 cattle, 18,000,000 goats, 820,000 buffalo, 700,000 sheep, 62,000,000 chickens, 12,000,000 ducks; roundwood (1991) 31,757,000 cu m; fish catch (1991) 892,700. Mining and quarrying (1989–90): marine salt 217,000; industrial limestone 30,000. Manufacturing (1991–92): chemical fertilizers 1,772,268; jute manufactures 407,100; sugar 195,418; iron and steel 70,594; food products 50,526; newsprint 48,528; paper 41,297; glass sheet 1,328,000 sq m; cotton yarn 327,000 bales; matches 12,794,000 gross boxes. Construction: n.a. Energy production (consumption): electricity (kW-hr; 1990) 8,057,000,000 (8,057,000,000); coal (metric tons; 1990) none (558,000); crude petroleum (barrels; 1990) 142,000 (8,690,000); petroleum products (metric tons; 1990) 777,000 (1,849,000); natural gas (cu m; 1990) 4,392,000,000 (4,392,000,000).
Household income. Average household size (1991) 5.3; average annual income per household (1985–86) Tk 30,933 (U.S.$1,035); sources of income (1985–86): self-employment 50.8%, wages and salaries 26.1%, transfer payments 0.5%, other 22.6%; expenditure (1985–86): food and drink 63.3%, housing and rent 8.8%, fuel and light 8.4%, clothing and footwear 5.9%, other 13.6%.
Population economically active (1989): total 50,700,000; activity rate of total population 46.9% (participation rates: over age 10, 71.6%; female 41.4%; unemployed 1.2%[7]).

Price and earnings indexes (1985 = 100)

	1986	1987	1988	1989	1990	1991	1992
Consumer price index	111.0	121.6	133.0	146.3	158.1	169.5	176.8
Daily earnings index[8]	125.8	148.4	158.1	164.5	180.6	...	...

Public debt (external, outstanding; 1991): U.S.$12,103,000,000.
Land use (1991): forested 14.5%; meadows and pastures 4.6%; agricultural and under permanent cultivation 70.2%; other 10.7%.
Gross national product (at current market prices; 1992): U.S.$24,805,000,000 (U.S.$220 per capita).

Structure of gross domestic product and labour force

	1990–91		1989	
	in value Tk '000,000	% of total value	labour force	% of labour force
Agriculture	300,596	36.0	32,573,000	64.2
Mining	72,913 (Mining and Manufacturing)	8.7 (Mining and Manufacturing)	89,000	0.2
Manufacturing			6,977,000	13.8
Construction	47,261	5.7	662,000	1.3
Public utilities	11,201	1.3	17,000	—
Transp. and commun.	97,697	11.7	1,278,000	2.5
Trade	68,279	8.2	4,130,000	8.1
Finance	16,299	2.0	238,000	0.5
Public admin., defense	38,191	4.6	4,736,000 (Public admin., defense and Services and other)	9.3 (Public admin., defense and Services and other)
Services and other	181,955	21.8		
TOTAL	834,392	100.0	50,700,000	100.0[9]

Tourism (1991): receipts from visitors U.S.$9,000,000; expenditures by nationals abroad U.S.$83,000,000.

Foreign trade

Balance of trade (current prices)

	1987	1988	1989	1990	1991	1992
Tk '000,000	−47,948	−39,386	−63,910	−55,550	−48,564	−55,276
% of total	46.6%	32.5%	43.1%	32.4%	28.2%	25.3%

Imports (1991–92): Tk 132,110,000,000 (textile yarn, fabrics, and made-up articles 19.8%; machinery and transport equipment 8.8%; petroleum and petroleum products 8.4%; chemicals 4.8%; iron and steel 2.8%; dairy products and eggs 1.9%). *Major import sources* (1990–91): Japan 10.5%; South Korea 9.4%; United States 7.0%; Hong Kong 6.8%; Singapore 6.6%; India 6.3%; China 5.8%; Yemen 3.9%.
Exports (1991–92): Tk 72,630,000,000 (ready-made garments 54.6%; jute manufactures 15.2%; fish and prawns 8.6%; hides, skins, and leather 7.3%; raw jute 5.5%; tea 2.6%). *Major export destinations* (1990–91): United States 28.9%; West Germany 9.6%; United Kingdom 7.7%; Italy 5.5%; Belgium 4.5%; Singapore 3.8%; Japan 3.4%; The Netherlands 3.2%.

Transport and communications

Transport. Railroads (1990–91): route length 1,706 mi, 2,746 km; passenger-mi 2,850,000,000, passenger-km 4,587,000,000; short ton-mi cargo 446,000,000, metric ton-km cargo 651,000,000. Roads (1990): total length 120,100 mi, 193,283 km (paved 4%). Vehicles (1991): passenger cars 67,000; trucks and buses 63,000. Merchant marine (1992): vessels (100 gross tons and over) 301; total deadweight tonnage 566,775. Air transport (1990–91)[10]: passenger-mi 1,407,000,000, passenger-km 2,264,000,000; short ton-mi cargo 68,000,000, metric ton-km cargo 100,000,000; airports with scheduled flights (1993) 7.
Communications. Daily newspapers (1990): total number 55; total circulation 1,212,000; circulation per 1,000 population 11. Radio (1992): 4,500,000 receivers (1 per 25 persons). Television (1992): 350,000 receivers (1 per 316 persons). Telephones (1990): 205,500 (1 per 519 persons).

Education and health

Education (1990–91)

	schools	teachers	students	student/ teacher ratio
Primary (age 6–10)	48,146	202,847	13,035,000	64.3
Secondary (age 11–17)	9,731	110,313	3,662,000	33.2
Voc., teacher tr.	153	1,440	27,891	19.4
Higher	997	23,332	767,385	32.9

Educational attainment (1981). Percentage of population age 25 and over having: no formal schooling 70.4%; primary education 24.1%; secondary 4.2%; postsecondary 1.3%. *Literacy* (1991): total population age 15 and over literate 34.8%; males literate 45.2%; females literate 23.7%.
Health (1991): physicians 21,004 (1 per 5,264 persons); hospital beds 34,353 (1 per 3,218 persons); infant mortality rate 111.0.
Food (1988–90): daily per capita caloric intake 2,037 (vegetable products 97%, animal products 3%); 88% of FAO recommended minimum requirement.

Military

Total active duty personnel (1993): 107,000 (army 86.9%, navy 7.0%, air force 6.1%). *Military expenditure as percentage of GNP* (1989): 1.6% (world 4.9%); per capita expenditure U.S.$3.

[1]Includes 30 seats reserved for women. [2]Geographic reorganization at the district level took place in 1984; each division is now divided into the following number of new districts: Chittagong 15, Dhākā 17, Khulna 16, and Rājshāhi 16. [3]Unadjusted results. [4]Metropolitan population. [5]Municipal population. [6]1989–90. [7]Excluding underemployment. [8]Skilled wage earnings in manufacturing. [9]Detail does not add to total given because of rounding. [10]Bangladesh Biman only.

Barbados

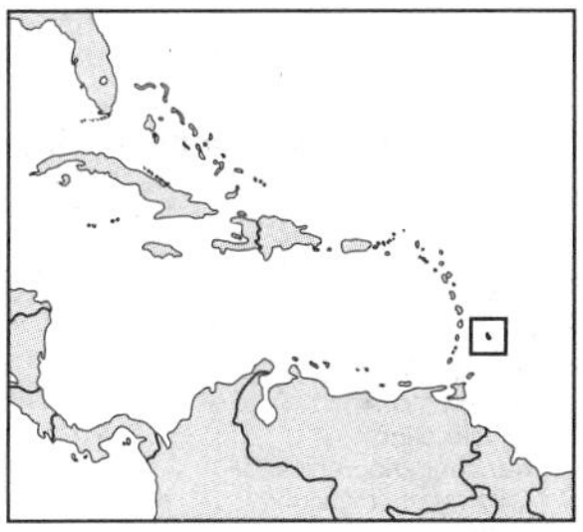

Official name: Barbados.
Form of government: constitutional monarchy with two legislative houses (Senate [21]; House of Assembly [28]).
Chief of state: British Monarch represented by Governor-General.
Head of government: Prime Minister.
Capital: Bridgetown.
Official language: English.
Official religion: none.
Monetary unit: 1 Barbados dollar (BDS$) = 100 cents; valuation (Oct. 4, 1993) 1 U.S.$ = BDS$2.01; 1 £ = BDS$3.06.

Area and population

	area		population
Parishes[1]	sq mi	sq km	1990 census
Christ Church	22	57	44,993
St. Andrew	14	36	6,426
St. George	17	44	18,390
St. James	12	31	20,827
St. John	13	34	10,206
St. Joseph	10	26	7,619
St. Lucy	14	36	9,454
St. Michael[2]	15	39	97,517
St. Peter	13	34	10,388
St. Philip	23	60	19,755
St. Thomas	13	34	11,508
TOTAL	166	430[3]	257,083

Demography

Population (1993): 260,000.
Density (1993): persons per sq mi 1,564, persons per sq km 603.8.
Urban-rural (1990): urban 37.9%; rural 62.1%.
Sex distribution (1992): male 47.80%; female 52.20%.
Age breakdown (1990): under 15, 24.1%; 15–29, 27.0%; 30–44, 22.1%; 45–59, 11.4%; 60 and over, 15.4%.
Population projection: (2000) 265,000; (2010) 274,000.
Doubling time: 77 years.
Ethnic composition (1988): black 80.0%; mixed 16.0%; white 4.0%.
Religious affiliation (1980): Anglican 39.7%; other Protestant 25.6%, of which Pentecostal 7.6%, Methodist 7.1%; nonreligious 17.5%; Roman Catholic 4.4%; not stated 2.7%; other 10.1%.
Major cities (1990): Bridgetown 6,070 (urban area 97,517); no other bounded localities exist.

Vital statistics

Birth rate per 1,000 population (1992): 16.2 (world avg. 26.4); (1979) legitimate 26.9%; illegitimate 73.1%.
Death rate per 1,000 population (1992): 9.1 (world avg. 9.2).
Natural increase rate per 1,000 population (1992): 7.1 (world avg. 17.2).
Total fertility rate (avg. births per childbearing woman; 1991): 1.8.
Marriage rate per 1,000 population (1989): 7.3.
Divorce rate per 1,000 population (1989): 1.6.
Life expectancy at birth (1990–95): male 72.9 years; female 77.9 years.
Major causes of death per 100,000 population (1988): diseases of the circulatory system 338.9, of which cerebrovascular disease 103.9, ischemic heart diseases 89.5; malignant neoplasms (cancers) 160.7; endocrine and metabolic disorders 79.8.

National economy

Budget (1992–93). Revenue: BDS$986,900,000[4] (tax revenue 93.6%, of which goods and services taxes 34.2%, personal income and company taxes 27.3%, import duties 7.3%; nontax revenue 6.4%). Expenditures: BDS$1,024,300,000 (current expenditure 91.4%, of which general public services 44.8%, economic services 20.0%, education 14.3%, health 11.6%; development expenditure 8.6%).
Production (metric tons except as noted). Agriculture, forestry, fishing (1992): raw sugar 55,000, sweet potatoes 2,419, yams 1,566, carrots 1,045, onions 745, cucumbers 489, tomatoes 440; livestock (number of live animals) 56,000 sheep, 45,000 pigs, 34,000 goats, 21,000 cattle; roundwood, n.a.; fish catch (1991) 2,697. Manufacturing (value added in BDS$'000; 1992): food, beverages, and tobacco (mostly sugar, molasses, rum, beer, and cigarettes) 101,200; paper products, printing, and publishing 28,800; metal products and assembly-type goods (mostly electronic components) 25,200; textiles and wearing apparel 12,200. Construction (value added in BDS$; 1992): 101,400,000. Energy production (consumption): electricity (kW-hr; 1992) 537,000,000 ([1990] 468,000,000); coal, none (none); crude petroleum (barrels; 1991) 454,000 ([1990] 2,091,000); petroleum products (metric tons; 1990) 267,000 (266,000); natural gas (cu m; 1992) 22,000,000 ([1990] 29,000,000).
Population economically active (1992): total 124,800; activity rate of total population 48.2% (participation rates: ages 15 and over, 66.2%; female 59.6%; unemployed 23.0%).

Price and earnings indexes (1985 = 100)

	1986	1987	1988	1989	1990	1991	1992
Consumer price index	101.3	104.7	109.8	116.6	120.2	127.7	135.4
Hourly earnings index	104.2	106.0	113.8	116.9	122.7	...	...

Household income and expenditure. Average household size (1980) 3.7; income per household (1988) BDS$13,455 (U.S.$6,690); sources of income: n.a.; expenditure (1978–79): food 43.2%, housing 13.1%, household operations 9.6%, alcohol and tobacco 8.4%, fuel and light 6.2%, clothing and footwear 5.1%, transportation 4.6%, other 9.8%.
Gross national product (at current market prices; 1991): U.S.$1,711,000,000 (U.S.$6,630 per capita).

Structure of gross domestic product and labour force

	1992		1991	
	in value BDS$'000,000	% of total value	labour force	% of labour force
Agriculture, fishing	164.2	5.2	5,700	4.7
Mining	17.0[5]	0.5[5]	...	...
Manufacturing	203.2	6.4	10,300	8.4
Construction	101.4	3.2	8,300	6.8
Public utilities	100.6[5]	3.2[5]	1,600	1.3
Transportation and communications	248.6	7.9	4,700	3.8
Trade, restaurants	816.2	25.8	16,100	13.1
Finance, real estate	453.1	14.3	4,000	3.3
Pub. admin., defense	480.4	15.2	41,800	34.2
Services	107.7	3.4		
Other	474.1[6]	15.0[6]	29,800[7]	24.4[7]
TOTAL	3,165.9[3]	100.0[3]	122,300	100.0

Public debt (1991): U.S.$948,000,000.
Tourism (1991): receipts from visitors U.S.$453,000,000; expenditures by nationals abroad U.S.$44,000,000.
Land use (1991): forested, negligible; meadows and pastures 9.3%; agricultural and under permanent cultivation 76.7%; other 14.0%.

Foreign trade[8]

Balance of trade (current prices)

	1987	1988	1989	1990	1991	1992
BDS$'000,000	−631.2	−703.9	−856.7	−858.8	−984.6	−568.8
% of total	50.4%	49.8%	53.4%	50.5%	53.6%	42.6%

Imports (1991): BDS$1,396,140,000 (retained imports 87.8%, of which machinery 16.7%, food and beverages 16.1%, construction materials 6.4%, chemicals 5.4%, fuels 4.8%; reexported imports 12.2%). *Major import sources:* United States 33.4%; United Kingdom 11.3%; Trinidad and Tobago 11.2%; Canada 6.2%; Netherlands Antilles 6.0%; Japan 5.1%.
Exports (1991): BDS$411,553,000 (domestic exports 58.7%, of which sugar 13.1%, chemicals 10.0%, electrical components 8.3%, clothing 4.3%, molasses 1.3%; reexports 41.3%, of which mineral fuels 28.3%). *Major export destinations:* United States 12.8%; United Kingdom 12.5%; Trinidad and Tobago 8.8%; Venezuela 7.8%; France 6.1%; Jamaica 5.9%.

Transport and communications

Transport. Railroads: none. Roads (1989): total length 977 mi, 1,573 km (paved 95%). Vehicles (1991): passenger cars 39,406; trucks and buses 9,318[9]. Merchant marine (1992): vessels (100 gross tons and over) 37; total deadweight tonnage 84,000. Air transport (1992): passenger arrivals 584,900, passenger departures 590,300; cargo unloaded 7,261 metric tons, cargo loaded 4,594 metric tons; airports (1993) with scheduled flights 1.
Communications. Daily newspapers (1992): total number 2; total circulation 41,008; circulation per 1,000 population 158. Radio (1992): total number of receivers 200,000 (1 per 1.3 persons). Television (1992): total number of receivers 69,350 (1 per 3.7 persons). Telephones (1990): 117,525 (1 per 2.2 persons).

Education and health

Education (1989–90)

	schools	teachers	students	student/ teacher ratio
Primary (age 3–11)[10]	104	1,602	29,539	18.4
Secondary (age 12–16)	33	1,406	21,259	15.1
Vocational[11]	8	79	996	12.6
Higher[12]	1	153	1,314	8.6

Educational attainment (1980). Percentage of population age 25 and over having: no formal schooling 0.8%; primary education 63.5%; secondary 32.3%; higher 3.3%. *Literacy* (1985): total population age 15 and over literate[13] 180,000 (98.0%).
Health: physicians (1986) 243 (1 per 1,042 persons); hospital beds (1987) 2,111 (1 per 121 persons); infant mortality rate per 1,000 live births (1992) 9.1.
Food (1988–90): daily per capita caloric intake 3,217 (vegetable products 73%, animal products 27%); 133% of FAO recommended minimum requirement.

Military

Total active duty personnel (1989): 154 (paramilitary marine and coast guard components only). *Military expenditure as percentage of GNP* (1988): 0.7% (world 5.0%); per capita expenditure U.S.$41.

[1]Parishes and city of Bridgetown have no local administrative function. [2]Includes city of Bridgetown. [3]Detail does not add to total given because of rounding. [4]Current revenue only. [5]Mining excludes natural gas; Public utilities includes natural gas. [6]Net indirect taxes. [7]Includes 20,900 unemployed persons. [8]Import figures are f.o.b. in balance of trade and c.i.f. in commodities and trading partners. [9]Includes taxis. [10]Includes preprimary. [11]1987–88. [12]University of the West Indies, Cave Hill campus. [13]National literacy standard based solely on school attendance. Functional literacy may be appreciably lower.

Belarus

Official name: Respublika Belarus (Republic of Belarus).
Form of government: unitary multiparty republic with a single legislative body (Supreme Council [360[1]]).
Head of state: Chairman of the Supreme Soviet.
Head of government: Prime Minister.
Capital: Minsk.
Official language: Belorussian.
Official religion: none.
Monetary unit[2]: Belarusian rubel (plural rubli) valuation (Oct. 4, 1993) free rate, 1 U.S.$ = 2,330 rubli; 1 £ = 3,530 rubli.

Area and population

		area		population
				1991[3]
Provinces	**Capitals**	sq mi	sq km	estimate
Brest	Brest	12,500	32,300	1,483,700
Homel (Gomel)	Homel	15,600	40,400	1,628,400
Hrodno (Grodno)	Hrodno	9,700	25,000	1,188,700
Mahilyoŭ (Mogilyov)	Mahilyoŭ	11,200	29,000	1,269,400
Minsk (Mensk)	Minsk	15,700	40,800	3,256,000
Vitebsk	Vitebsk	15,500	40,100	1,434,200
TOTAL		80,200	207,600	10,260,400

Demography

Population (1993): 10,353,000.
Density (1993): persons per sq mi 129.1, persons per sq km 49.7.
Urban-rural (1992): urban 67.6%; rural 32.4%.
Sex distribution (1992): male 47.00%; female 53.00%.
Age breakdown (1989): under 15, 23.0%; 15–29, 22.4%; 30–44, 20.6%; 45–59, 18.0%; 60–74, 11.5%; 75 and over, 4.5%.
Population projection: (2000) 10,509,000; (2010) 10,895,000.
Doubling time: not applicable; doubling time exceeds 100 years.
Ethnic composition (1989): Belorussian 77.9%; Russian 13.2%; Polish 4.1%; Ukrainian 2.9%; Jew 1.1%; other 0.8%.
Religious affiliation: believers are predominantly Belorussian Orthodox; there is a Roman Catholic minority.
Major cities (1991): Minsk 1,633,600; Homel 503,300; Vitebsk 369,200; Mahilyoŭ 363,000; Hrodno 284,800.

Vital Statistics

Birth rate per 1,000 population (1992): 12.9 (world avg. 26.4); (1990) legitimate 91.0%; illegitimate 9.0%.
Death rate per 1,000 population (1992): 11.2 (world avg. 9.2).
Natural increase rate per 1,000 population (1992): 1.7 (world avg. 17.2).
Total fertility rate (avg. births per childbearing woman; 1989): 2.0.
Marriage rate per 1,000 population (1989): 9.6
Divorce rate per 1,000 population (1989): 3.4.
Life expectancy at birth (1990): male 66.3 years; female 75.6 years.
Major causes of death per 100,000 population (1989): diseases of the circulatory system 563.7; malignant neoplasms (cancers) 167.6; accidents and violence 96.5; diseases of the respiratory system 79.8; diseases of the digestive system 21.3; diseases of the nervous system 7.8; infectious and parasitic diseases 7.5; endocrine and metabolic disorders 5.8.

National economy

Budget (1993). Revenue: 1,096,150,000,000 rubli (tax revenue 98.1%, of which individual income tax 30.4%, value-added tax 28.9%, excise tax 16.4%, other taxes 22.4%; nontax revenue 1.9%). Expenditures: 1,350,770,000,000 rubli (national economy 62.5%; education 15.6%; administration and defense 9.4%; health 7.5%; welfare and culture 5.0%).
Production (metric tons except as noted). Agriculture, forestry fishing (1992): potatoes 8,000,000, grain 5,940,000, sugar beets 1,350,000, other vegetables 850,000, wheat 400,000, fruit 280,000; livestock (number of live animals) 6,600,000 cattle, 4,700,000 pigs, 400,000 sheep and goats, 214,000 horses, 52,000,000 poultry; roundwood 6,700,000 cu m; fish catch 15,500. Mining and quarrying (1992): dolomite 8,400,000; potash 3,900,000; salt 360,000. Manufacturing (1991): fertilizers 5,200,000; cement 2,400,000; crude steel 1,100,000; synthetic plastics 717,000; synthetic fibres 443,000; paper 166,000; cinderblocks 2,200,000,000 units; roofing tiles 456,000,000 units; television receivers 1,103,000 units; cameras 965,000 units; radio receivers 932,000 units; bicycles 815,000 units; refrigerators 743,000 units; motorcycles 214,000 units; tractors 95,500 units; metal-cutting lathes 16,200 units; reinforced concrete 7,100,000 sq m. Construction (1991): 5,395,000 sq m. Energy production (consumption): electricity (kW-hr; 1991) 38,700,000,000 (51,744,000,000); coal (1991) none (1,500,000); crude petroleum (barrels; 1992) 14,344,000 (143,440,000); petroleum products, n.a. (n.a.); natural gas (cu m; 1991) 210,000,000 (15,400,000,000).
Population economically active (1992): 4,887,000; activity rate of total population 47.3% (participation rate [1989]: ages 16–59 [male], 16–54 [female] 91.4%; female [1991] 53.3%; unemployed [1992] 7.5%).

Price and earnings indexes (1985 = 100)

	1986	1987	1988	1989	1990	1991
Consumer price index	102.4	103.5	104.2	105.8	110.7	214.9
Monthly earnings index	103.9	109.4	119.5	131.3	...	...

Gross national product (at current market prices; 1992): U.S.$30,200,000,000 (U.S.$2,920 per capita).

Structure of net material product and labour force

	1992			
	in value '000,000 rubles	% of total value	labour force	% of labour force
Agriculture	8,200	29.3	981,000	20.1
Mining, Manufacturing, Public utilities	12,300	44.0	1,432,000	29.3
Construction	3,300	11.8	382,000	7.8
Transportation and commununications	1,400	5.1	331,000	6.8
Trade	1,600	5.5	327,000	6.7
Finance	—	—	...	...
Public administration, defense	—	—	171,600	3.5
Services	—	—	853,000	17.5
Other	1,200	4.3	409,400	8.3
TOTAL	28,000	100.0	4,887,000	100.0

Public debt (external, outstanding; 1992): 2,019,000,000 Russian rubles.
Tourism: receipts from visitors, n.a.; expenditures by nationals abroad, n.a.
Land use (1991): forested 32.7%; meadows and pastures 15.0%; agricultural and under permanent cultivation 43.5%; other 8.8%.
Household income and expenditure. Average household size (1989) 3.2; income per household (1991) 8,000 rubles; sources of income (1989): wages and salaries 71.6%, pensions and stipends 20.4%, other 8.0%; expenditure (1989): consumer goods 30.6%, food 29.0%, housing 2.7%, taxes 2.7%, other 35.0%.

Foreign trade

Balance of trade (current prices)

	1987	1988	1989	1990	1991	1992
'000,000,000 rubles	+1.2	+2.1	+1.0	−0.8	−1.8	−3.7
% of total	3.3%	5.6%	2.5%	2.1%	2.3%	4.7%

Imports (1992): 417,080,000,000 rubles[4] (machine building and metalworking machinery 35.2%, chemical and petrochemical products 9.7%, petroleum products 9.0%, consumer products 5.8%, food products 4.8%). *Major import sources:* Russia 66.9%; Ukraine 20.4%; Kazakhstan 3.6%; Uzbekistan 1.8%; Moldova 1.5%.
Exports (1992): 379,666,000,000 rubles[4] (machine building and metalworking machinery 50.0%, chemical and petrochemical products 17.3%, consumer products 8.6%, food products 5.8%, paper products 2.7%). *Major export destinations:* Russia 56.8%; Ukraine 22.8%; Kazakhstan 5.1%; Uzbekistan 3.4%; Moldova 2.4%.

Transport and communications

Transport. Railroads (1990): length 3,472 mi, 5,587 km; (1989) passenger-mi 10,268,000,000, passenger-km 16,525,000,000; (1989) short ton-mi cargo 57,034,000, metric ton-km cargo 81,734,000,000. Roads (1990): total length 29,900 mi, 48,100 km (paved 94%). Vehicles (1988): passenger cars 498,700; trucks and buses, n.a. Merchant marine: vessels (100 gross tons and over) n.a.; total deadweight tonnage, n.a. Air transport (1989): passenger-mi 3,575,000,000, passenger-km 5,754,000,000; short ton-mi cargo 34,000,000, metric ton-km cargo 49,000,000; airports (1993) with scheduled flights 1.
Communications. Daily newspapers (1989): total number 220; total circulation 2,674,000; circulation per 1,000 population 260. Radio (1992): total number of receivers 8,755,000 (1 per 1.2 persons). Television (1992): total number of receivers 3,538,000 (1 per 2.9 persons). Telephones (1991): 1,791,400 (1 per 5.8 persons).

Education and health

Education (1989–90)

	schools	teachers	students	student/ teacher ratio
Primary (age 6–13), Secondary (age 14–17)	5,187	123,000	1,489,000	12.1
Voc., teacher tr.	148	...	139,000	...
Higher	33	...	184,600	...

Educational attainment (1989). Percentage of population age 25 and over having: primary education or no formal schooling 23.0%; some secondary 16.8%; completed secondary and some postsecondary 49.4%; higher 10.8%.
Literacy: total population age 15 and over literate, n.a.; males literate, n.a.; females literate, n.a.
Health (1990): physicians 41,400 (1 per 248 persons); hospital beds 135,100 (1 per 76 persons); infant mortality rate (1992) per 1,000 live births 12.1.
Food: daily per capita caloric intake, n.a.

Military

Total active duty personnel (1993): 102,600[5] (army 86%, air force 14%). *Military expenditure as percentage of GNP* (1992): 3.1%; per capita expenditure U.S.$90.

[1]Includes 88 nonelective seats. [2]Belarusian rubel introduced May 25, 1992, at a rate of 1 rubel to 10 Russian rubles and circulated parallel with the Russian ruble; on Aug. 15, 1993, Belarusian rubel became sole legal tender at a fixed rate of 2 Belarusian rubli to 1 Russian ruble; on October 14 the fixed rate was changed to 3 rubli per Russian ruble. The Belarusian rubel is unofficially known as the zaichik. [3]January 1. [4]Trade figures are denominated in Russian rubles. [5]To be reduced to 90,000 upon formation of a National Armed Forces.

Belgium

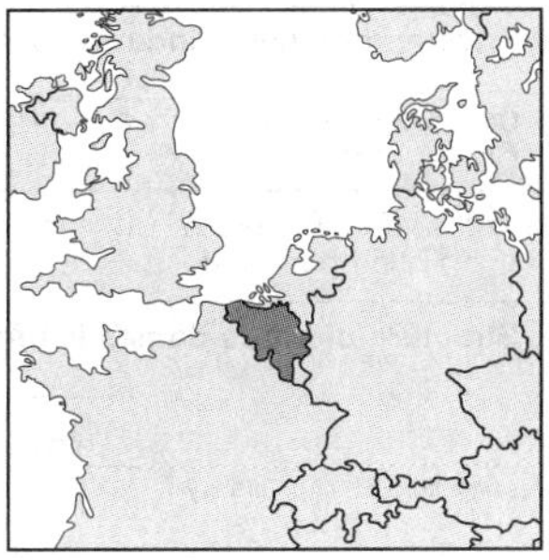

Official name: Koninkrijk België (Dutch); Royaume de Belgique (French) (Kingdom of Belgium).
Form of government: federal constitutional monarchy with two legislative houses (Senate [185[1]]; House of Representatives [212]).
Chief of state: Monarch.
Head of government: Prime Minister.
Capital: Brussels.
Official languages: Dutch; French; German.
Official religion: none.
Monetary unit: 1 Belgian franc (BF) = 100 centimes; valuation (Oct. 4, 1993) 1 U.S.$ = BF 35.15; 1 £ = BF 53.25.

Area and population

Regions[2] Provinces	Capitals	area sq mi	area sq km	population 1991 census
Brussels	—	62	162	954,045
Flanders	—	5,217[3]	13,511	5,768,925
Antwerp	Antwerp	1,107	2,867	1,605,167
Brabant[4]	—	813	2,106	970,701
East Flanders	Ghent	1,151	2,982	1,335,793
Limburg	Hasselt	935	2,422	750,435
West Flanders	Brugge	1,210	3,134	1,106,829
Wallonia	—	6,504[3]	16,845	3,255,711
Brabant[5]	—	421	1,091	321,144
Hainaut	Mons	1,461	3,786	1,278,791
Liège	Liège	1,491	3,862	999,646
Luxembourg	Arlon	1,714	4,440	232,813
Namur	Namur	1,416	3,666	423,317
TOTAL		11,783	30,518	9,978,681

Demography

Population (1993): 10,072,000.
Density (1993): persons per sq mi 854.5, persons per sq km 329.9.
Urban-rural (1991): urban 96.6%; rural 3.4%.
Sex distribution (1991): male 48.86%; female 51.14%.
Age breakdown (1991): under 15, 18.1%; 15–29, 21.8%; 30–44, 22.5%; 45–59, 16.9%; 60–74, 14.1%; 75 and over, 6.6%.
Population projection: (2000) 10,313,000; (2010) 10,668,000.
Doubling time: not applicable; doubling time exceeds 100 years.
Nationality (1991): Belgian 91.0%; Italian 2.4%; Moroccan 1.4%; French 0.9%; Turkish 0.8%; Dutch 0.6%; other 2.9%.
Religious affiliation (1980): Roman Catholic 90.0%; Muslim 1.1%; Protestant 0.4%; nonreligious and atheist 7.5%; other 1.0%.
Major cities (1992[6]): Brussels 136,424[7] (951,217[8]); Antwerp 465,783; Ghent 230,232; Charleroi 206,903; Liège 196,303.

Vital statistics

Birth rate per 1,000 population (1992): 11.5 (world avg. 26.4); (1987) legitimate 90.8%; illegitimate 9.2%.
Death rate per 1,000 population (1992): 10.6 (world avg. 9.2).
Natural increase rate per 1,000 population (1992): 0.9 (world avg. 17.2).
Total fertility rate (avg. births per childbearing woman; 1990–95): 1.6.
Marriage rate per 1,000 population (1991): 6.1.
Divorce rate per 1,000 population (1990): 2.0.
Life expectancy at birth (1988–90): male 72.4 years; female 79.1 years.
Major causes of death per 100,000 population (1987): diseases of the circulatory system 457.2, of which cerebrovascular disease 105.8; malignant neoplasms (cancers) 272.4.

National economy

Budget (1991). Revenue: BF 1,898,066,000,000 (direct taxes 38.3%; value-added, stamp, and similar duties 9.9%; customs and excise duties 7.9%). Expenditures: BF 2,322,005,000,000 (public debt 26.6%; government departments 24.9%; pension 10.3%; defense 4.4%).
Public debt (1990): U.S.$233,179,000,000.
Production (metric tons except as noted). Agriculture, forestry, fishing (1992)[9]: sugar beets 6,200,000, potatoes 1,800,000, wheat 1,480,000, barley 551,000, apples 502,000, tomatoes 320,000, corn (maize) 86,000, oats 52,000; livestock (number of live animals) 6,565,000 pigs, 3,313,000 cattle, 140,000 sheep, 20,000 horses; roundwood (1991) 5,082,000 cu m; fish catch (1991) 40,226, of which European plaice (flounder) 17,954, common sole 5,658, Atlantic cod 3,504. Mining and quarrying (1990): quartz 223,000; barite 35,000; marble 481 cu m. Manufacturing (value added in BF '000,000; 1988): metal products and machinery 325,048; food, beverages, and tobacco 205,912; chemicals and chemical products 179,349; pig iron, steel, and nonferrous metals 105,524; paper, printing, and publishing 77,767; furniture and fixtures 61,960; textiles 56,784; building materials 53,918; clothing and footwear 24,298. Construction (1990): residential 31,754,800 cu m; nonresidential 52,061,700 cu m. Energy production (consumption): electricity (kW-hr; 1990) 70,215,000,000 (66,491,-000,000); coal (metric tons; 1990) 2,357,000 (16,911,000); crude petroleum (barrels; 1990) none (184,657,000); petroleum products (metric tons; 1990) 23,671,000 (16,522,000); natural gas (cu m; 1990) 14,142,000 (12,111,500,000).
Household income and expenditure. Avg. household size (1981) 2.7; sources of income (1992): wages 49.6%, transfer payments 20.7%, property income 18.8%, self-employment 10.9%; expenditure (1990): food 22.0%, housing 16.1%, transp. 13.5%, health 11.5%, durable goods 9.4%, clothing 7.8%.

Gross national product (1991): U.S.$192,370,000,000 (U.S.$19,300 per capita).

Structure of gross domestic product and labour force

	1991 in value BF '000,000	1991 % of total value	1990 labour force	1990 % of labour force
Agriculture	130,800	1.9	100,000	2.4
Mining	17,200	0.2	8,100	0.2
Manufacturing	1,462,600	21.3	782,300	18.7
Construction	409,300	6.0	235,700	5.6
Public utilities	203,800	3.0	30,000	0.7
Transp. and commun.	562,900	8.2	257,100	6.2
Trade	1,439,800	20.9	634,400	15.2
Finance	1,168,800	17.0	327,600	7.8
Pub. admin., defense	867,700	12.6	1,389,000	33.2
Services	808,500	11.8		
Other	−194,400[10]	−2.8[10]	415,100[11]	9.9[11]
TOTAL	6,877,000	100.0[3]	4,179,200[3]	100.0[3]

Population economically active (1990): total 4,179,200; activity rate of total population 41.9% (participation rates: ages 15–64, n.a.; female 41.6%; unemployed 8.7%).

Price and earnings indexes (1985 = 100)

	1986	1987	1988	1989	1990	1991	1992
Consumer price index	101.3	102.9	104.1	107.3	111.0	114.6	117.3
Hourly earnings index	102.8	104.8	105.6	111.6	116.4	122.3	127.7

Land use (1990)[9]: forested 21.3%; meadows and pastures 20.4%; agricultural and under permanent cultivation 25.0%; other 33.3%.
Tourism (1991): receipts from visitors U.S.$3,468,000,000; expenditures by nationals abroad U.S.$5,543,000,000.

Foreign trade[9]

Balance of trade (current prices)

	1987	1988	1989	1990	1991	1992
BF '000,000	+124,300	+96,400	+177,300	+61,200	+21,700	+65,200
% of total	2.0%	1.4%	2.3%	0.8%	0.3%	0.8%

Imports (1991): BF 4,119,587,000,000 (machinery and transport equipment 26.0%, of which road vehicles and parts 9.9%; chemicals and chemical products 11.5%; mineral fuels and lubricants 8.4%, of which petroleum and petroleum products 6.0%; food and live animals 8.4%; nonindustrial [gem] diamonds 6.1%). *Major import sources:* Germany 23.5%; The Netherlands 17.2%; France 15.8%; U.K. 8.4%; U.S. 4.8%.
Exports (1991): BF 4,024,039,000,000 (machinery and transport equipment 27.0%, of which passenger cars 15.5%; chemicals 14.1%, of which plastics 5.1%; food and live animals 9.2%; iron and steel 7.2%; nonindustrial [gem] diamonds 6.4%; textiles 5.3%; petroleum and petroleum products 3.6%). *Major export destinations:* Germany 23.7%; The Netherlands 17.6%; France 16.1%; U.K. 8.6%; U.S. 4.9%; Italy 4.6%.

Transport and communications

Transport. Railroads (1991): route length 2,162 mi, 3,479 km; passenger-mi 4,207,000,000, passenger-km 6,770,000,000; short ton-mi cargo 5,584,000,000, metric ton-km cargo 8,153,000,000. Roads (1990[6]): total length 85,672 mi, 137,876 km (paved 97%). Vehicles (1991): passenger cars 3,970,317; trucks and buses 596,452. Merchant marine (1992): vessels (100 gross tons and over) 232; total deadweight tonnage 218,506. Air transport (1991): passenger-mi 3,866,822,000, passenger-km 6,223,059,000; short ton-mi cargo 332,766,000, metric ton-km cargo 485,830,000; airports (1993) with scheduled flights 3.
Communications. Daily newspapers (1991): total number 76; total circulation 3,609,000[12]; circulation per 1,000 population 361[12]. Radio (1991): 4,520,590 receivers (1 per 2.2 persons). Television (1992): 4,200,000 receivers (1 per 2.4 persons). Telephones (1990): 5,428,900 (1 per 1.8 persons).

Education and health

Education (1990–91)

	schools	teachers[13]	students	student/ teacher ratio
Primary (age 6–12)	4,584	71,064[14]	744,882	...
Secondary (age 12–18)	2,055	114,628	793,599	...
Voc., teacher tr.	397	14,548	137,175	...
Higher	21	10,517	111,845	...

Educational attainment (1977). Percentage of population age 25 and over having: less than secondary education 64.4%; lower secondary 16.0%; upper secondary 10.0%; vocational 3.7%; teacher's college 2.1%; university 3.8%. *Literacy* (1991): virtually 100% literate.
Health: physicians (1990) 33,442 (1 per 298 persons); hospital beds (1989) 96,-693 (1 per 103 persons); infant mortality rate per 1,000 live births (1992) 8.9.
Food (1988–90): daily per capita caloric intake 3,925 (vegetable products 60%, animal products 40%); 149% of FAO recommended minimum requirement.

Military

Total active duty personnel (1992): 80,700 (army 73.1%, navy 5.5%, air force 21.4%). *Military expenditure as percentage of GNP* (1989): 2.5% (world 4.9%); per capita expenditure U.S.$392.

[1]Includes one ex officio member from the royal family. [2]May 8, 1993, the legislature approved constitutional establishment of federal regions. [3]Detail does not add to total given because of rounding. [4]Composed of Brabant districts Hal-Vilvorde and Louvaine. [5]Composed of Brabant district Nivelles. [6]January 1. [7]1991. [8]Région Bruxelloise. [9]Includes Luxembourg. [10]Includes imputed bank service charges. [11]Includes 364,700 unemployed and 50,400 persons working abroad. [12]For 40 newspapers only. [13]1987–88. [14]Includes preschool teachers.

Belize

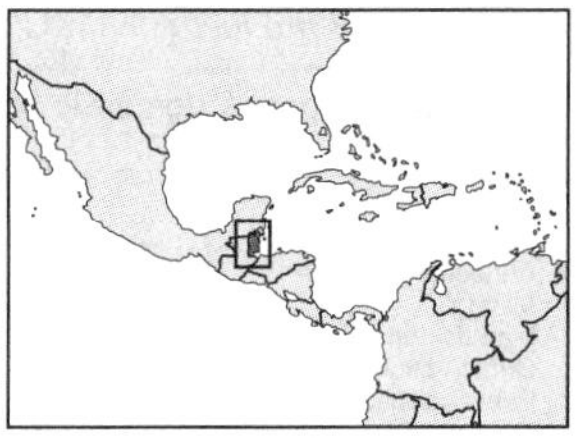

Official name: Belize.
Form of government: constitutional monarchy with two legislative houses (Senate [8[1]]; House of Representatives [29[2]]).
Chief of state: British Monarch represented by Governor-General.
Head of government: Prime Minister.
Capital: Belmopan.
Official language: English.
Official religion: none.
Monetary unit: 1 Belize dollar (BZ$) = 100 cents; valuation (Oct. 4, 1993) 1 U.S.$ = BZ$2.00[3]; 1 £ = BZ$3.04.

Area and population

		area		population
Districts	Capitals	sq mi	sq km	1992 estimate
Belize	Belize City	1,663	4,307	58,504
Cayo	San Ignacio	2,006	5,196	39,346
Corozal	Corozal	718	1,860	30,617
Orange Walk	Orange Walk	1,790	4,636	32,867
Stann Creek	Dangriga	986	2,554	18,829
Toledo	Punta Gorda	1,704	4,413	18,837
TOTAL		8,867	22,965[4]	199,000

Demography

Population (1993): 204,000.
Density (1993): persons per sq mi 23.0, persons per sq km 8.9.
Urban-rural (1992): urban 46.6%; rural 53.4%.
Sex distribution (1992): male 50.75%; female 49.25%.
Age breakdown (1992): under 15, 43.9%; 15–29, 27.9%; 30–44, 14.9%; 45–59, 7.2%; 60–74, 4.5%; 75 and over, 1.6%.
Population projection: (2000) 236,000; (2010) 276,000.
Doubling time: 21 years.
Ethnic composition (1991): mestizo (Spanish-Indian) 43.6%; Creole (predominantly black) 29.8%; Mayan Indian 11.0%; Garifuna (black-Carib Indian) 6.7%; white 3.9%; East Indian 3.5%; other or not stated 1.5%.
Religious affiliation (1991): Roman Catholic 57.7%; Protestant 28.5%, of which Anglican 6.9%, Pentecostal 6.3%, Methodist 4.2%, Seventh-day Adventist 4.1%, Mennonite 4.0%; other Christian 2.3%; Hindu 2.5%; nonreligious/other 9.0%.
Major cities (1992): Belize City 45,158; Orange Walk 11,728; San Ignacio/Santa Elena 9,533; Corozal 7,104; Belmopan 3,687.

Vital statistics

Birth rate per 1,000 population (1991): 38.0 (world avg. 26.4); legitimate 42.5%; illegitimate 57.5%.
Death rate per 1,000 population (1991): 5.0 (world avg. 9.2).
Natural increase rate per 1,000 population (1991): 33.0 (world avg. 17.2).
Total fertility rate (avg. births per childbearing woman; 1991): 4.6.
Marriage rate per 1,000 population (1991): 5.4.
Divorce rate per 1,000 population (1991): 0.5.
Life expectancy at birth (1991): male 67.0 years; female 72.0 years.
Major causes of death per 100,000 population (1990): accidents 92.6; ischemic heart diseases 84.7; diseases of the respiratory system 57.1; malignant neoplasms (cancers) 52.4; cerebrovascular disease 47.6; diabetes mellitus 37.0.

National economy

Budget (1992–93). Revenue: BZ$270,100,000 (current revenue 87.1%, of which taxes on international trade 42.4%, taxes on income and profits 18.2%, nontax revenue 15.9%; grants 10.3%; development revenue 2.6%). Expenditures: BZ$326,700,000 (current expenditures 51.7%; development expenditures 48.3%).
Production (metric tons except as noted). Agriculture, forestry, fishing (1992): sugarcane 1,122,000, oranges 98,300, grapefruits 43,300, bananas 29,400, corn (maize) 25,500, rice 6,600, coconuts (1991) 3,000, red kidney beans 2,500, cocoa 143, honey 62; livestock (number of live animals; 1991) 51,000 cattle, 26,000 pigs, 1,000,000 chickens; roundwood (1991) 188,000 cu m; fish catch (1990) 1,512, of which lobsters 615, freshwater and marine fish 421, shrimp 331, conchs 141. Mining and quarrying (1990): limestone 310,000; sand and gravel 206,000. Manufacturing (1992): sugar 102,100; molasses 30,400; flour 11,700; fertilizer (1991) 10,400; orange concentrate 81,800 hectolitres; beer 36,000 hectolitres; grapefruit concentrate 28,400 hectolitres; cigarettes (1991) 100,000,000 units; garments (mostly jeans, overalls, and shirts) 2,902,000 units. Construction (publicly financed buildings under construction; 1991): residential 180 units; nonresidential, n.a. Energy production (consumption): electricity (kW-hr; 1991–92) 124,800,000 (106,600,000); coal, none (none); crude petroleum, none (none); petroleum products (metric tons; 1990) none (83,000); natural gas, none (none).
Household income and expenditure. Average household size (1990) 4.9; median annual income per employed person (1991) BZ$6,150[5] (U.S.$3,075); sources of income: n.a.; expenditure (1980): food and beverages 51.5%, clothing and footwear 11.1%, household furnishings 10.1%, transportation and communications 6.5%, energy and water 6.0%, health care 3.4%, housing 2.3%, other 9.1%.
Population economically active (1991): total *c.* 65,000; activity rate of total population *c.* 34.0% (participation rates: over age 14, *c.* 63.0%; female [1983–84] 32.5%; unemployed 19.6%).

Price and earnings indexes (1985 = 100)

	1987	1988	1989	1990	1991	1992	1993[6]
Consumer price index	102.8	106.1	108.3	111.6	117.8	121.1	122.3
Earnings index	...	...	...	...	...	...	...

Gross national product (at current market prices; 1991): U.S.$389,000,000 (U.S.$2,050 per capita).

Structure of gross domestic product and labour force

	1992		1991	
	in value BZ$'000[7]	% of total value	labour force[8]	% of labour force
Agriculture, fishing, forestry	125,092	20.1	18,256	17.6
Mining	5,456	0.9	326	0.3
Manufacturing	96,152	15.5	5,951	5.7
Construction	46,260	7.4	4,059	3.9
Public utilities	13,792	2.2	721	0.7
Transportation and communications	85,793	13.8	2,925	2.8
Trade, restaurants	110,005	17.7	10,013	9.7
Finance, real estate, insurance	61,623	9.9	1,771	1.7
Pub. admin., defense	53,842	8.7	5,352	5.2
Services	45,070	7.3	5,967	5.8
Other	−21,521[9]	−3.5[9]	48,226	46.6
TOTAL	621,564	100.0	103,567	100.0

Public debt (external, outstanding; December 1992): U.S.$141,200,000.
Land use (1990): forested 44.4%; meadows and pastures 2.1%; agricultural and under permanent cultivation 2.5%; other 51.0%.
Tourism (1991): receipts from visitors U.S.$95,000,000; expenditures by nationals abroad U.S.$8,000,000.

Foreign trade[10]

Balance of trade (current prices)

	1987	1988	1989	1990	1991	1992
BZ$'000,000	−54.2	−96.6	−143.1	−126.0	−203.9	−213.6
% of total	11.6%	17.2%	22.3%	19.6%	28.8%	27.5%

Imports (1991): BZ$501,500,000 (machinery and transport 23.1%; manufactured goods 17.5%; mineral fuels 15.7%). *Major import sources*[11]: United States 54.0%; United Kingdom 13.0%; Mexico 9.0%; Japan 4.0%; The Netherlands 3.0%.
Exports (1991)[12]: BZ$239,300,000 (domestic exports 79.7%, of which sugar 34.8%, garments 14.7%, orange concentrate 6.7%, bananas 6.1%, lobster 5.2%; reexports 20.3%). *Major export destinations*[11]: United States 40.0%; United Kingdom 29.0%; Mexico 10.0%; Canada 6.0%; Jamaica 5.0%.

Transport and communications

Transport. Railroads: none. Roads (1990): total length 1,600 mi, 2,575 km (paved 13%). Vehicles (1991): passenger cars 12,075; trucks and buses 2,800. Merchant marine (1991): vessels (100 gross tons and over) 32; total deadweight tonnage 45,706. Air transport (1991)[13]: passenger arrivals 165,858, passenger departures 166,972; cargo loaded 304 metric tons, cargo unloaded 1,705 metric tons. Airports (1993) with scheduled flights 8.
Communications. Daily newspapers: none[14]. Radio (1992): total number of receivers 100,000 (1 per 2.0 persons). Television (1992): total number of receivers, 27,048 (1 per 7.4 persons). Telephones (1991–92): 21,276[15] (1 per 9.2 persons).

Education and health

Education (1990–91)

	schools	teachers	students	student/ teacher ratio
Primary (age 5–14)[16]	237	1,782	17,146	26.5
Secondary (age 14–18)	29	564	7,904	14.0
Voc., teacher tr. } Higher	8	...	1,726	...

Educational attainment (1991). Percentage of population age 25 and over having: no formal schooling 13.0%; primary education 64.3%; secondary 15.0%; higher (not university) 3.6%; university 3.0%; other/unknown 1.1%.
Literacy (1991): total population age 15 and over literate 99,000 (93%).
Health (1991): physicians 96 (1 per 2,021 persons); hospital beds 585 (1 per 332 persons); infant mortality rate per 1,000 live births 35.0.
Food (1988–90): daily per capita caloric intake 2,575 (vegetable products 70%, animal products 30%); 114% of FAO recommended minimum requirement.

Military

Total active duty personnel (1992): 665 (army 90.2%, maritime wing 7.5%, air wing 2.3%); British troops (1993) 1,400. *Military expenditure as percentage of GNP* (1989): 3.0% (world 4.9%); per capita expenditure U.S.$54.

[1]Excludes president of the Senate, who may be elected by the Senate from outside its appointive membership. [2]Excludes speaker of the House of Representatives, who may be elected by the House from outside its elected membership. [3]The Belize dollar is officially pegged to the U.S. dollar. [4]Detail does not add to total given because of rounding. [5]Estimated figure for 36,346 employees. [6]March. [7]At factor cost. [8]Data based on total population over age 14. [9]Less imputed bank service charges. [10]Import figures are f.o.b. in balance of trade and c.i.f. in commodities and trading partners. [11]Estimated data. [12]*Exports* (1992): BZ$278,500,000 (domestic exports 82.2%, of which sugar 27.0%, orange concentrate 14.8%, garments 11.7%, bananas 7.4%, grapefruit concentrate 4.7%; reexports 17.8%). [13]Belize international airport only. [14]Four weekly newspapers had a total circulation in 1992 of 24,200. [15]Number of lines. [16]1992–93.

Benin

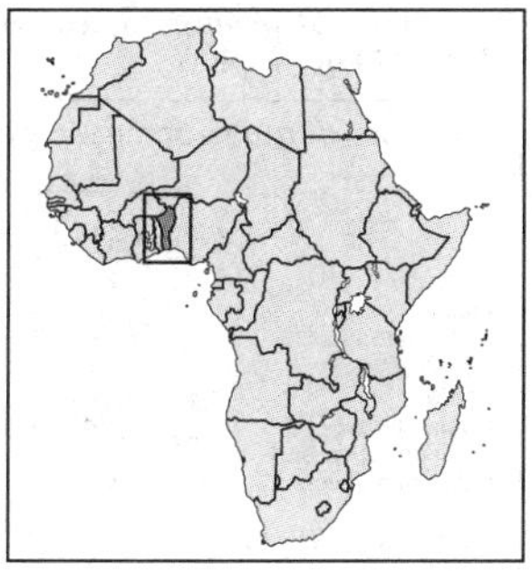

Official name: République du Bénin (Republic of Benin).
Form of government: multiparty republic with one legislative house (National Assembly [64]).
Head of state and government: President.
Capital[1]: Porto-Novo.
Official language: French.
Official religion: none.
Monetary unit: 1 CFA franc (CFAF) = 100 centimes; valuation (Oct. 4, 1993) 1 U.S.$ = CFAF 283.25; 1 £ = CFAF 429.12.

Area and population

Provinces	Capitals	area sq mi	area sq km	population 1987 estimate
Atacora	Natitingou	12,050	31,200	622,000
Atlantique	Cotonou	1,250	3,200	909,000
Borgou	Parakou	19,700	51,000	630,000
Mono	Lokossa	1,500	3,880	610,000
Ouémé	Porto-Novo	1,800	4,700	806,000
Zou	Abomey	7,200	18,700	731,000
TOTAL		43,500	112,680	4,308,000[2]

Demography

Population (1993): 5,091,000.
Density (1993): persons per sq mi 117.0, persons per sq km 45.2.
Urban-rural (1985): urban 26.5%; rural 73.5%.
Sex distribution (1990): male 49.37%; female 50.63%.
Age breakdown (1990): under 15, 46.6%; 15–29, 25.7%; 30–44, 14.7%; 45–59, 8.4%; 60–74, 3.8%; 75 and over, 0.8%.
Population projection: (2000) 6,269,000; (2010) 8,357,000.
Doubling time: 21 years.
Ethnic composition (1979): Fon 39.2%; Yoruba (Nago) 11.9%; Adja 11.0%; Bariba 8.5%; Somba (Otomary) 6.5%; Fulani (Peul) 5.6%; Djougou 3.0%; Dendi 2.1%; other 3.7%.
Religious affiliation (1991): traditional beliefs 62.0%; Christian 23.3%, of which Roman Catholic 21.0%, Protestant 2.3%; Muslim 12.0%; other 2.7%.
Major cities (1985): Cotonou 402,290; Porto-Novo 163,260; Parakou 66,000[3]; Abomey 54,000[3]; Kandi 53,000[3].

Vital statistics

Birth rate per 1,000 population (1991): 49.0 (world avg. 26.4).
Death rate per 1,000 population (1991): 16.0 (world avg. 9.2).
Natural increase rate per 1,000 population (1991): 33.0 (world avg. 17.2).
Total fertility rate (avg. births per childbearing woman; 1991): 7.0.
Marriage rate per 1,000 population (1980–85): 12.8.
Divorce rate per 1,000 population (1980–85): 0.8.
Life expectancy at birth (1991): male 49.0 years; female 52.0 years.
Major causes of death per 100,000 population (1986): n.a.; however, of the 184,310 reported cases of infectious diseases (notifiable to the World Health Organization): 82.0% were malaria, 4.2% dysentery, 4.0% measles, 2.6% pneumonia, 2.2% chicken pox, 1.4% mumps, 1.3% schistosomiasis.

National economy

Budget (1992). Revenue: CFAF 99,300,000,000 (current receipts 69.8%, of which fiscal receipts and customs duties 58.9%, other current receipts 10.9%; aid 15.2%; loans 15.0%). Expenditures: CFAF 136,600,000,000 (1991; general administration 39.1%, of which personnel costs 27.9%, material costs 11.1%; internal-debt service 22.6%; public-investment program 22.2%; external public-debt service 9.3%; social security 4.7%; highway fund 1.1%; other expenses 1.0%).
Production (metric tons except as noted). Agriculture, forestry, fishing (1992): yams 1,177,000, cassava 932,000, corn (maize) 399,000, seed cotton 170,000, sorghum 104,000, tomatoes 71,000, peanuts (groundnuts) 70,000, dry beans 50,000, sweet potatoes 28,000, millet 25,000, coconuts 20,000, bananas 13,000, mangoes 12,000, oranges 12,000, paddy rice 9,000, palm kernels 9,000, karité (a butter from the nut of the shea tree) 7,000[4], pineapples 3,000, coffee beans 1,000, cacao beans 900[5], tobacco 322[4]; livestock (number of live animals) 1,120,000 goats, 1,000,000 cattle, 920,000 sheep, 750,000 pigs, 25,000,000 chickens; roundwood (1991) 5,203,000 cu m; fish catch (1991) 41,000. Mining and quarrying (1990): marine salt 100, limestone is mined for use in cement. Manufacturing (1990): cement 275,000; meat 64,000; sugar 52,000[6]; cotton fibre 37,456[6, 7]; palm oil and palm kernel oil 13,140. Construction: n.a. Energy production (consumption): electricity (kW-hr; 1990) 5,000,000 (200,000,000); coal, none (none); crude petroleum (barrels; 1992) 1,423,500 (negligible); petroleum products (metric tons; 1990) none (136,000); natural gas, none (none).
Tourism (1991): receipts from visitors U.S.$29,000,000; expenditures by nationals abroad U.S.$10,000,000.
Population economically active (1990): total 2,180,000; activity rate of total population 47.1% (participation rates [1986]: ages 15–64, 60.2%; female 35.6%; unemployed, n.a.).

Price and earnings indexes (1985 = 100)

	1985	1986	1987	1988	1989	1990	1991
Consumer price index[8]	...	...	...	...	...	...	...
Hourly earnings index[9]	100.0	100.0	100.0	100.0	100.0	100.0	100.0

Land use (1991): forested 30.9%; meadows and pastures 4.0%; agricultural and under permanent cultivation 16.9%; other 48.2%.
Gross national product (at current market prices; 1992): U.S.$2,061,000,000 (U.S.$410 per capita).

Structure of gross domestic product and labour force

	1989 in value U.S.$'000,000	1989 % of total value	1979 labour force	1979 % of labour force
Agriculture	688	40.0	673,732	61.1
Mining and manufacturing	104	6.1	84,475	7.7
Public utilities	17	1.0	2,509	0.2
Construction	100	5.8	13,329	1.2
Trade and finance	335	19.5	234,130	21.2
Transportation and communications	315	18.3	23,535	2.1
Pub. admin., defense	143	8.3	71,713	6.5
Other	17	1.0		
TOTAL	1,719	100.0	1,103,423	100.0

Household income and expenditure. Average household size (1979) 5.4; income per household (1983) U.S.$240; sources of income: self-employment 73.7%, wages and salaries 26.3%; expenditure: n.a.
Public debt (external, outstanding; 1991): U.S.$1,291,000,000.

Foreign trade[10]

Balance of trade (current prices)

	1984	1985	1986	1987	1988	1989
CFAF '000,000	−81,830	−100.47	−98.23	−61.23	−80.84	−59.00
% of total	46.2%	42.9%	55.5%	13.3%	14.5%	40.7%

Imports (1991): U.S.$605,800,000 (1987; manufactured goods 38.5%, of which cotton yarn and fabric 10.5%, chemical products 5.6%; food products 23.5%, of which cereals 17.1%; machinery and transport equipment 13.5%, of which transport equipment 5.0%, nonelectrical equipment 4.9%, electrical equipment 3.6%; beverages and tobacco 7.6%). *Major import sources* (1989): India 23.4%; France 15.9%; The Netherlands 5.0%; Côte d'Ivoire 4.6%; Thailand 4.6%; United States 3.7%; West Germany 3.4%; Italy 3.2%; Taiwan 2.9%; Korea 2.7%.
Exports (1991): U.S.$350,300,000 (1987; cotton 55.6%; energy 27.5%; food products 4.3%, of which cocoa beans 0.9%, coffee 0.7%; palm kernel oil and palm oil 3.8%; manufactured goods 1.7%). *Major export destinations* (1989): Portugal 15.2%; Italy 9.9%; Thailand 9.6%; Taiwan 9.0%; United States 7.4%; Niger 6.2%; France 6.1%.

Transport and communications

Transport. Railroads (1993): length 359 mi, 578 km; passenger-mi 39,397,000[11], passenger-km 63,400,000[11]; short ton-mi cargo 111,313,000[11], metric ton-km cargo 162,500,000[11]. Roads (1990): total length 5,241 mi, 8,435 km (paved 12.3%). Vehicles (1991): passenger cars 25,000; trucks and buses 13,000. Merchant marine (1992): vessels (100 gross tons and over) 12; total deadweight tonnage 210. Air transport (1990)[12]: passenger-mi 144,363,000, passenger-km 232,329,000; short ton-mi cargo 26,971,000, metric ton-km cargo 39,374,000; airports (1993) with scheduled flights 1.
Communications. Daily newspapers (1990): total number 1; total circulation 12,000; circulation per 1,000 population 2.6. Radio (1992): total number of receivers 350,000 (1 per 14 persons). Television (1992): total number of receivers 20,000 (1 per 246 persons). Telephones (1988): 16,195 (1 per 279 persons).

Education and health

Education (1990)

	schools	teachers	students	student/ teacher ratio
Primary	2,808	13,180	457,140	34.7
Secondary	151[13]	2,493	72,256	29.0
Voc., teacher tr.[13]	13	687	6,879	10.0
Higher	13[13]	956	10,873	11.4

Educational attainment (1979). Percentage of population age 25 and over having: no formal schooling 89.2%; primary education 8.3%; some secondary 1.4%; secondary 0.8%; postsecondary 0.3%. *Literacy* (1990): total percentage of population age 15 and over literate 23.4%; males literate 31.7%; females literate 15.6%.
Health: physicians (1986) 363 (1 per 11,306 persons); hospital beds (1982) 4,902 (1 per 749 persons); infant mortality rate per 1,000 live births (1991) 119.0.
Food (1988–90): daily per capita caloric intake 2,383 (vegetable products 96%, animal products 4%); 104% of FAO recommended minimum requirement.

Military

Total active duty personnel (1993): 4,300 (army 88.4%, navy 3.5%, air force 8.1%). *Military expenditure as percentage of GNP* (1989): 2.0% (world 4.9%); per capita expenditure U.S.$7.

[1]Porto-Novo, the official capital established under the constitution, is the seat of the legislature, but the president and most government ministers reside in Cotonou. [2]1992 census total was 4,855,349. [3]1982. [4]1989–90. [5]1988–89. [6]1986. [7]Export figures. [8]No consumer price index is published, but inflation was estimated by the World Bank at an annual average of 8.0% during 1980–88. [9]January. [10]Figures do not include unaccountable reexports of black-market goods, which originate mainly in Nigeria and amounted to an estimated 90% of Benin's actual exports in 1981. [11]1991. [12]Air Afrique only. [13]1987–88.

Bhutan

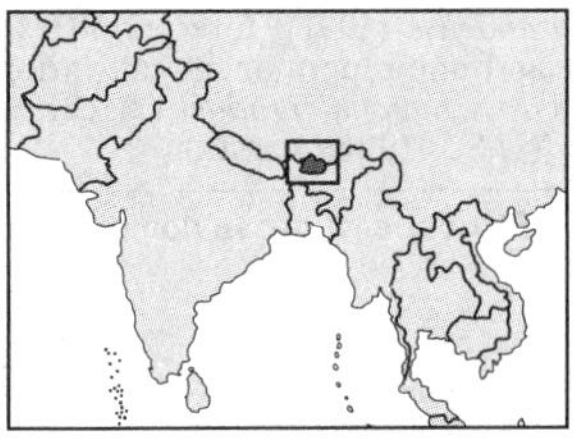

Official name: Druk-Yul (Kingdom of Bhutan).
Form of government: constitutional[1] monarchy with one legislative house (National Assembly [150[2]]).
Head of state and government: Monarch (*druk gyalpo*).
Capital: Thimphu.
Official language: Dzongkha (a Tibetan dialect).
Official religion: Mahāyāna Buddhism.
Monetary unit: 1 ngultrum[3] (Nu) = 100 chetrum; valuation (Oct. 4, 1993) 1 U.S.$ = Nu 31.15; 1 £ = Nu 47.19.

Area and population[4]

Districts	Capitals	area sq mi	area sq km	population[5] 1985 estimate
Bumthang	Jakar	1,150	2,990	23,900
Chirang	Damphu	310	800	108,800
Chhukha	Chhukha	...	...	...
Dagana	Dagana	540	1,400	28,400
Gaylegphug	Gaylegphug	1,020	2,640	111,300
Ha	Ha	830	2,140	16,700
Lhuntshi	Lhuntshi	1,120	2,910	39,600
Mongar	Mongar	710	1,830	73,200
Paro	Paro	580	1,500	45,600
Pema Gatsel	Pema Gatsel	150	380	37,100
Punakha	Punakha	2,330	6,040	33,600
Samchi	Samchi	830	2,140	172,100
Samdrup Jongkhar	Samdrup Jongkhar	900	2,340	73,100
Shemgang	Shemgang	980	2,540	44,500
Tashigang	Tashigang	1,640	4,260	177,700
Thimphu	Thimphu	630	1,620	58,700
Tongsa	Tongsa	570	1,470	26,000
Wangdi Phodrang	Wangdi Phodrang	1,160	3,000	47,200
TOTAL		18,150[6, 7]	47,000[6, 7]	1,285,300[8]

Demography[4]

Population (1993): 1,546,000.
Density (1993): persons per sq mi 85.2, persons per sq km 32.9.
Urban-rural (1985): urban 13.1%; rural 86.9%.
Sex distribution (1988): male 50.97%; female 49.03%.
Age breakdown (1988): under 15, 40.3%; 15–29, 26.4%; 30–44, 16.5%; 45–59, 10.5%; 60–74, 5.2%; 75 and over, 1.1%.
Population projection: (2000) 1,812,000; (2010) 2,266,000.
Doubling time: 32 years.
Ethnic composition (1983): Bhutiā (Ngalops) 62.5%; Nepalese (Gurung) 17.7%; Sharchops 13.2%; other 6.6%.
Religious affiliation (1980): Buddhist 69.6%; Hindu 24.6%; Muslim 5.0%; other 0.8%.
Major cities (1985): Thimphu 20,000; Phuntsholing 10,000[9].

Vital statistics[4]

Birth rate per 1,000 population (1991): 39.0 (world avg. 26.4); legitimate, n.a.; illegitimate, n.a.
Death rate per 1,000 population (1991): 19.0 (world avg. 9.2).
Natural increase rate per 1,000 population (1991): 20.0 (world avg. 17.2).
Total fertility rate (avg. births per childbearing woman; 1991): 5.9.
Marital status of population 15 years and over (1985): married 71.2%; single 19.7%; widowed 7.5%; divorced 1.6%.
Divorce rate per 1,000 population: n.a.
Life expectancy at birth (1991): male 50.0 years; female 48.7 years.
Major causes of death per 100,000 population (1987): n.a.; however, major health problems include diarrhea and dysentery, respiratory tract infections, parasitic worms, skin infections, malaria, and nutritional deficiencies.

National economy

Budget (1992–93). Revenue: Nu 2,919,000,000 (internal revenue 47.3%, grants from UN and other international agencies 33.1%, grants from government of India 19.6%). Expenditures: Nu 2,813,000,000 (capital expenditures 55.2%, current expenditures 44.8%).
Public debt (external, outstanding; 1991): U.S.$86,300,000.
Production (metric tons except as noted). Agriculture, forestry, fishing (1992): oranges 67,000, rice 43,000, corn (maize) 40,000, potatoes 34,000, sugarcane 12,000, green peppers and chilies 8,000, millet 7,000, wheat 5,000, apples 5,000, barley 4,000, pulses 2,000; livestock (number of live animals) 422,000 cattle, 74,000 pigs, 52,000 sheep, 40,000 goats; roundwood (1991) 1,560,000 cu m; fish catch (1991) 1,000. Mining and quarrying (1989): limestone 100,000; dolomite 50,000; gypsum 10,000. Manufacturing (value in Nu; 1980–81): distillery products 47,000,000; cement 36,000,000; chemical products 19,000,000; processed food 14,000,000; forest products 3,000,000. Construction (number of buildings completed; 1977–78): residential 10; nonresidential (guest house) 1. Energy production (consumption): electricity (kW-hr; 1990) 1,564,000,000 (172,000,000); coal (metric tons; 1990) 2,000 (18,000); crude petroleum, none (n.a.); petroleum products (metric tons; 1990) none (26,000); natural gas, none (n.a.).
Household income and expenditure. Average household size (1980) 5.4[4]; income per household: n.a.; sources of income: n.a.; expenditure (1979): food 72.3%, clothing 21.2%, energy 3.7%, household durable goods 0.7%, personal effects and other 2.1%.

Gross national product (at current market prices; 1992)[4]: U.S.$255,000,000 (U.S.$170 per capita).

Structure of gross domestic product and labour force

	1991 in value Nu '000,000	1991 % of total value	1984 labour force	1984 % of labour force
Agriculture	2,326.4	42.7	580,000[10]	87.2
Mining	53.8	1.0		
Manufacturing	467.7	8.6		
Construction	456.5	8.4		
Trade	416.4	7.6	6,000[10]	0.9
Public utilities	404.5	7.4		
Transportation and communications	375.7	6.9		
Finance	426.1	7.8		
Pub. admin., defense	601.6	11.0	23,000[10]	3.4
Services			56,000[10]	8.5[11]
Other	−78.7[12]	−1.4[12]	...	...
TOTAL	5,450.0	100.0	664,000	100.0

Population economically active (1984)[4]: total 664,000; activity rate of total population 52.7% (participation rates: ages 15–64, 94.8; female 55.0; unemployed 6.5).

Price and earnings indexes (1985 = 100)

	1985	1986	1987	1988	1989	1990	1991
Consumer price index	100.0	110.0	115.3	127.5	139.0	154.1	172.3
Earnings index	...	...	...	...	...	...	...

Land use (1991): forested 54.5%; meadows and pastures 5.8%; agricultural and under permanent cultivation 2.8%; other 36.9%.
Tourism (1990): receipts from visitors U.S.$2,000,000; expenditures by nationals abroad, n.a.

Foreign trade[13]

Balance of trade (current prices)

	1986–87	1987–88	1988–89	1989–90	1990–91	1991–92
Nu '000,000	−858.3	−482.7	−833.3	−545.4	−606.9	−687.9
% of total	50.1%	25.3%	28.6%	18.2%	17.9%	17.4%

Imports (1989)[14]: Nu 1,214,810,000 (petroleum products 8.5%, rice 5.8%, motor vehicles and parts 5.7%, machinery parts 2.9%, iron and steel products 2.9%, fabrics 2.3%). *Major import source* (1991–92): India 84.6%.
Exports (1989)[14]: Nu 985,930,000 (electricity 28.4%, minerals 18.5%, timber and wood manufactures 17.4%, cement 13.7%, fruit and vegetables 10.7%, alcoholic beverages 1.9%). *Major export destination* (1991–92): India 90.2%.

Transport and communications

Transport. Railroads: none. Roads (1990): total length 1,600 mi, 2,500 km (paved 72%). Vehicles (1988): passenger cars 2,590; trucks and buses 1,367. Merchant marine: none. Air transport (1986): passenger-mi 2,722,000, passenger-km 4,381,000; metric ton-km cargo, n.a.; airports (1993) with scheduled flights 1.
Communications. Daily newspapers: none[15]. Radio (1992): total number of receivers 28,000 (1 per 54 persons). Television (1983): total number of receivers 200 (1 per 6,180 persons). Telephones (1989): 2,105 (1 per 669 persons).

Education and health[4]

Education (1990)

	schools	teachers	students	student/ teacher ratio
Primary (age 7–11)	156	1,757	52,029	29.6
Secondary (age 12–16)	31	662	15,984	24.1
Voc., teacher tr.	8	149	1,822	12.2
Higher	2	57	519	9.1

Educational attainment: n.a. *Literacy* (1977): total population age 15 and over literate 124,000 (18.0%); males literate 98,000 (31.0%); females literate 26,000 (9.0%).
Health (1989): physicians 157 (1 per 8,969 persons); hospital beds 944 (1 per 1,492 persons); infant mortality rate per 1,000 live births (1991) 121.0.
Food (1975–77): daily per capita caloric intake 2,058 (vegetable products 98%, animal products 2%); 89% of FAO recommended minimum requirement.

Military

Total active duty personnel (1992): about 5,500 (army 100%).

[1]There is no formal constitution, but a form of constitutional monarchy is in place. [2]Includes 50 nonelective seats. [3]Indian currency is also accepted legal tender; the ngultrum is at par with the Indian rupee. [4]The population data used in this compilation, which is based on the now repudiated 1980 census, should be viewed with extreme care, as the actual 1992 population could range from 850,000 to 1,600,000. [5]Rural only. [6]2,700 sq mi (7,000 sq km) are not included in the district area totals. [7]Includes Chhukha area. [8]Includes urban population; includes Chhukha population. [9]1982. [10]Derived value. [11]Includes 6.5% with no occupation. [12]Imputed bank service charges. [13]Import figures are c.i.f. in balance of trade, commodities, and trading partners. [14]Trade data with India only. [15]A weekly newspaper is published from Thimphu in Dzongkha, Nepalese, and English, circulation (1989) 10,500.

Bolivia

Official name: República de Bolivia (Republic of Bolivia).
Form of government: unitary multiparty republic with two legislative houses (Chamber of Senators [27]; Chamber of Deputies [130]).
Head of state and government: President.
Capitals: La Paz (administrative); Sucre (judicial).
Official languages: Spanish, Aymara, Quechua.
Official religion: Roman Catholicism.
Monetary unit: 1 boliviano (Bs) = 100 centavos; valuation (Oct. 4, 1993) 1 U.S.$ = Bs 4.33; 1 £ = Bs 6.56.

Area and population

Departments	Capitals	area sq mi	area sq km	population 1992 census[1]
Beni	Trinidad	82,458	213,564	251,390
Chuquisaca	Sucre	19,893	51,524	451,722
Cochabamba	Cochabamba	21,479	55,631	1,093,625
La Paz	La Paz	51,732	133,985	1,883,122
Oruro	Oruro	20,690	53,588	338,893
Pando	Cobija	24,644	63,827	37,785
Potosí	Potosí	45,644	118,218	645,817
Santa Cruz	Santa Cruz	143,098	370,621	1,351,191
Tarija	Tarija	14,526	37,623	290,851
TOTAL		424,164	1,098,581	6,344,396

Demography

Population (1993): 7,715,000[2].
Density (1993): persons per sq mi 18.2, persons per sq km 7.0.
Urban-rural (1992): urban 57.7%; rural 42.3%.
Sex distribution (1992): male 49.25%; female 50.75%.
Age breakdown (1988): under 15, 41.1%; 15–29, 25.9%; 30–44, 17.0%; 45–59, 9.5%; 60–74, 4.7%; 75 and over, 1.3%; unknown 0.5%.
Population projection: (2000) 9,668,000; (2010) 12,700,000.
Doubling time: 24 years.
Ethnic composition (1982): mestizo 31.2%; Quechua 25.4%; Aymara 16.9%; white 14.5%; other 12.0%.
Religious affiliation (1980): Roman Catholic 92.5%; Bahāʾī 2.6%; other 4.9%.
Major cities (1992): La Paz 711,036; Santa Cruz 694,616; El Alto 404,367; Cochabamba 404,102; Oruro 183,194; Sucre 130,952; Potosí 112,291.

Vital statistics

Birth rate per 1,000 population (1988): 42.8 (world avg. 27.1).
Death rate per 1,000 population (1988): 14.1 (world avg. 9.8).
Natural increase rate per 1,000 population (1988): 28.7 (world avg. 17.3).
Total fertility rate (avg. births per childbearing woman; 1987): 6.1.
Marriage rate per 1,000 population (1980): 4.8.
Divorce rate per 1,000 population: n.a.
Life expectancy at birth (1987): male 51.0 years; female 55.0 years.
Major causes of death per 100,000 population: n.a.; however, major health problems include diseases of the respiratory system, gastrointestinal infections, measles, diphtheria, malaria, and tetanus.

National economy

Budget (1991). Revenue: Bs 2,841,700,000 (taxes on goods and services 34.0%, income of government enterprises 32.0%, social-security contributions 8.6%, property taxes 7.9%, taxes on international trade 6.0%, income taxes 5.1%). Expenditures: Bs 3,221,400,000 (education 18.7%, social security 18.6%, defense 13.1%, transportation and communications 12.8%, public services 11.6%, public order and safety 7.7%, health 3.3%).
Public debt (external, outstanding; 1991): U.S.$3,523,000,000.
Production (metric tons except as noted). Agriculture, forestry, fishing (1991): sugarcane 4,180,000, potatoes 855,000, bananas and plantains 573,000, corn (maize) 510,000, cassava 499,000, soybeans 384,000, rice 257,000, oranges and tangerines 127,000, wheat 103,000; livestock (number of live animals) 12,300,000 sheep, 5,600,000 cattle, 2,450,000 goats, 2,340,000 pigs, 630,000 asses, 320,000 horses; roundwood 1,632,000 cu m; fish catch (1990) 7,424. Mining and quarrying (metric tons of pure metal; 1992): zinc 66,678; lead 9,064; tin 7,681; antimony 3,272; silver 132,000 kg; gold 973 kg. Manufacturing (value added in Bs; 1989)[3]: food products 19,650,000; beverages 19,340,000; printing and publishing 3,770,000; wood products 3,160,000; nonferrous metals 2,760,000; textiles 2,740,000; drugs and medicines 2,710,000. Construction (1985)[4]: residential dwellings 226. Energy production (consumption): electricity (kW-hr; 1990) 1,955,000,000 (1,961,000,000); coal, none (none); crude petroleum (barrels; 1990) 7,093,000 (7,384,000); petroleum products (metric tons; 1990) 1,016,000 (999,000); natural gas (cu m; 1990) 3,033,000,000 (745,000,000).
Population economically active (1990): total 2,275,847; activity rate of total population 31.1% (participation rates: ages 15–64, 54.5%; female 23.8%; unemployed 19.0%).

Price and earnings indexes (1985 = 100)

	1985	1986	1987	1988	1989	1990	1991
Consumer price index	100.0	376.3	431.2	500.1	575.2	674.7	819.4
Monthly earnings index[5]	100.0	172.0	255.8	366.9	432.8	525.4	612.2

Gross national product (at current market prices; 1991): U.S.$4,799,000,000 (U.S.$650 per capita).

Structure of gross domestic product and labour force

	1991 in value Bs '000,000[6]	1991 % of total value	1988 labour force[7]	1988 % of labour force[7]
Agriculture	26,911	21.3	868,800	42.3
Mining	19,308	15.3	64,200	3.1
Manufacturing	17,333	13.7	179,700	8.7
Construction	3,364	2.7	110,000	5.4
Public utilities	1,241	1.0	18,900	0.9
Transportation and communications	10,771	8.5	108,300	5.3
Trade	16,457	13.0	259,500	32.6
Finance	14,951	11.8	32,600	1.6
Pub. admin., defense; Services	15,626	12.4	375,100	18.3
Other	379[8]	0.3[8]	36,200	1.8
TOTAL	126,341	100.0	2,053,300	100.0

Household income and expenditure. Average household size (1992): 3.8; average annual income per household: n.a.; sources of income: n.a.; expenditure (1979): food 41.4%, housing 12.5%, transportation and communications 12.5%, clothing and footwear 9.7%, household durable goods 8.9%, health 4.5%, recreation 3.1%, education 1.2%.
Tourism (1991): receipts from visitors U.S.$90,000,000; expenditures by nationals abroad U.S.$63,000,000.
Land use (1990): forested 51.3%; meadows and pastures 24.5%; agricultural and under permanent cultivation 2.1%; other 22.1%.

Foreign trade[9]

Balance of trade (current prices)

	1986	1987	1988	1989	1990	1991
U.S.$'000,000	−36.9	−85.4	+99.2	+301.8	+326.6	+59.0
% of total	3.2%	7.0%	9.0%	22.5%	21.4%	3.6%

Imports (1992): U.S.$543,100,000 (raw materials 47.4%, of which raw materials for industry 36.9%; capital goods 31.0%, of which capital goods for industry 19.2%, transport equipment 10.1%; consumer goods 21.0%, of which nondurable consumer goods 10.9%, durable consumer goods 10.1%). *Major import sources:* United States 26.0%; Brazil 14.3%; Japan 12.3%; Argentina 11.2%; Germany 8.4%; Chile 6.4%; Peru 2.2%.
Exports (1992): U.S.$340,100,000 (zinc 22.3%; natural gas 22.2%; tin 13.3%; soybeans 7.1%; silver 7.0%; timber 6.1%; sugar 4.1%; gold 3.6%; hides and skins 1.5%). *Major export destinations:* Argentina 25.3%; United Kingdom 17.2%; United States 13.3%; Belgium 12.0%; Peru 8.3%; Germany 5.9%; France 3.2%; Chile 2.2%.

Transport and communications

Transport. Railroads (1992): route length 2,264 mi, 3,643 km; passenger-mi 244,000,000, passenger-km 393,000,000; short ton-mi cargo 414,500,000, metric ton-km cargo 605,200,000. Roads (1988): total length 25,875 mi, 41,642 km (paved 4%). Vehicles (1991): passenger cars 265,000; trucks and buses 60,000. Merchant marine (1992): vessels (100 gross tons and over) 1; total deadweight tonnage 15,765. Air transport (1991): passenger-mi 740,000,000, passenger-km 1,192,000,000; short ton-mi cargo 25,755,000, metric ton-km cargo 37,601,000; airports (1993) with scheduled flights 19.
Communications. Daily newspapers (1990): total number 17; total circulation 400,000; circulation per 1,000 population 55. Radio (1992): total number of receivers 4,000,000 (1 per 1.9 persons). Television (1991): total number of receivers 610,000 (1 per 12 persons). Telephones (1989): 194,180 (1 per 37 persons).

Education and health

Education (1990–91)

	schools[10]	teachers	students	student/teacher ratio
Primary (age 6–13)	9,758	51,763	1,278,775	24.7
Secondary (age 14–17); Voc., teacher tr.	724; 47	12,434	219,232	17.6
Higher[10]	10	3,555	97,153	27.3

Educational attainment (1988). Percentage of population age 25 and over having: no formal schooling 25.6%; some primary 23.2%; primary education 23.5%; some secondary 7.0%; secondary 13.5%; some higher 2.6%; higher 3.6%; not specified 1.0%. *Literacy* (1990): total population age 15 and over literate 77.5%; males literate 84.7%; females literate 70.7%.
Health: physicians (1987) 3,174 (1 per 2,124 persons); hospital beds (1990) 6,190 (1 per 1,183 persons); infant mortality rate per 1,000 live births (1988) 102.0.
Food (1988–90): daily per capita caloric intake 2,013 (vegetable products 83%, animal products 17%); 84% of FAO recommended minimum requirement.

Military

Total active duty personnel (1992): 31,500 (army 73.0%, navy 14.3%, air force 12.7%). *Military expenditure as percentage of GNP* (1989): 4.3% (world 4.9%); per capita expenditure U.S.$26.

[1]Preliminary data; not adjusted for underenumeration. [2]Estimate is based on projections of the 1976 census results. [3]Establishments with 20 or more employees. [4]National government sponsored only. [5]Private sector earnings in La Paz. [6]In 1980 prices. [7]Population 10 years and over. [8]Net import duties. [9]Import figures are f.o.b. in balance of trade and c.i.f. for commodities and trading partners. [10]1986–87.

Bosnia and Herzegovina[1]

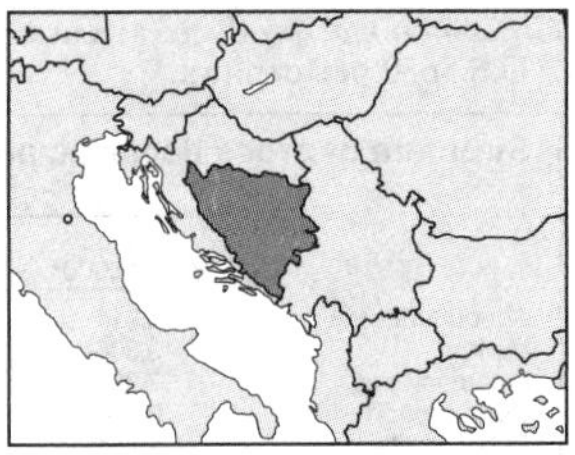

Official name: Republika Bosna i Hercegovina (Republic of Bosnia and Herzegovina).
Form of government: unitary multiparty republic with bicameral legislature (National Assembly [240[2]]).
Chief of state: President of collective presidency.
Head of government: Prime Minister.
Capital: Sarajevo.
Official language: Serbo-Croatian.
Official religion: none.
Monetary unit: [3].

Area and population (1991 census)

Districts	area sq km[4]	population	Districts	area sq km[4]	population
Banja Luka	1,232	195,139	Livno	994	39,526
Banovići	176	26,507	Ljubinje	326	4,162
Bihać	689	70,896	Ljubuški	289	27,182
Bijeljina	734	96,796	Lopare	429	32,400
Bileća	633	13,269	Lukavac	350	56,830
Bosanska Dubica	499	31,577	Maglaj	384	43,294
Bosanska Gradiška	762	60,062	Modriča	297	35,413
Bosanska Krupa	780	58,212	Mostar	1,300	126,067
Bosanski Brod	234	33,962	Mrkonjič Grad	679	27,379
Bosanski Novi	554	41,541	Neum	230	4,268
Bosanski Petrovac	853	15,552	Nevesinje	923	14,421
Bosanski Šamac	219	32,835	Odžak	205	30,651
Bosansko Grahovo	780	8,303	Olovo	408	16,901
Bratunac	793	33,575	Orašje	166	28,201
Brčko	493	87,332	Posušje	372	16,659
Breza	83	17,266	Prijedor	834	112,470
Bugojno	366	46,843	Prnjavor	631	46,894
Busovača	145	18,883	Prozor	477	19,601
Čajniće	275	8,919	Pucarevo	232	30,624
Čapljina	249	27,852	Rogatica	664	21,812
Çazin	381	63,406	Rudo	344	11,572
Çelinac	365	18,666	Sanski Most	984	60,119
Čitluk	181	14,709	Sarajevo	2,049	525,980
Derventa	516	56,328	Šekovići	195	9,639
Doboj	684	102,546	Šipovo	470	15,553
Donji Vakuf	338	24,232	Skender Vakuf	360	19,416
Foča	1,270	40,513	Sokolac	723	14,833
Fojnica	308	16,227	Srbac	447	21,660
Gacko	736	10,844	Srebrenica	527	37,211
Glamoč	1,096	12,421	Srebrenik	249	40,769
Goražde	383	37,505	Stolac	541	18,845
Gornji Vakuf	402	25,130	Tešanj	223	48,390
Graćanica	387	59,050	Teslič	846	59,632
Gradačac	405	56,378	Titov Drvar	950	17,079
Grude	218	15,976	Tomislavgrad	967	29,261
Han Pijesak	342	6,346	Travnik	563	70,402
Jablanica	289	12,664	Trebinje	1,205	30,879
Jajce	398	44,903	Tuzla	307	131,861
Kakanj	462	55,857	Ugljevik	199	25,641
Kalesija	272	41,795	Vareš	356	22,114
Kalinovik	732	4,657	Velika Kladuša	304	52,921
Kiseljak	165	24,081	Višegrad	448	21,202
Kladanj	325	16,028	Visoko	242	46,130
Ključ	850	37,233	Vitez	156	27,728
Konjic	1,101	43,636	Vlasenica	532	33,817
Kotor Varoš	574	36,670	Zavidovići	540	57,153
Kreševo	149	6,699	Zenica	500	145,577
Kupres	622	10,728	Žepče	210	22,840
Laktaši	387	29,910	Živinice	281	54,653
Lištica	388	26,437	Zvornik	500	81,111
			TOTAL	51,129[5]	4,365,639

Demography

Population (1993): 4,422,000.
Density (1993): persons per sq mi 224.0, persons per sq km 86.5.
Urban-rural (1981): urban 36.2%; rural 63.8%.
Sex distribution (1981): male 49.73%; female 50.27%.
Age breakdown (1981): under 15, 27.5%; 15–29, 29.0%; 30–44, 19.2%; 45–59, 15.8%; 60–74, 6.3%; 75 and over, 1.9%.
Population projection: (2000) 4,601,000; (2010) 4,871,000.
Doubling time: 90 years.
Ethnic composition (1991): Muslim 49.2%; Serb 31.3%; Croat 17.3%.
Religious affiliation (1992): Muslim 40%; Serbian Orthodox 31%; Roman Catholic 15%; Protestant 4%; other 10%.
Major cities (1991): Sarajevo 415,631; Banja Luka 142,634; Zenica 96,238.

Vital statistics

Birth rate per 1,000 population (1990): 14.1 (world avg. 27.1).
Death rate per 1,000 population (1990): 6.4 (world avg. 9.8).
Natural increase rate per 1,000 population (1990): 7.7 (world avg. 17.3).
Total fertility rate (avg. births per childbearing woman): n.a.
Life expectancy at birth (1980–82): male 68.0 years; female 73.0 years.
Major causes of death per 100,000 population (1989): circulatory diseases 344.1; malignant neoplasms (cancers) 122.6; accidents, violence, and poisoning 47.1; respiratory diseases 29.0; digestive system diseases 29.2.

National economy

Budget. Revenue: n.a. Expenditures: n.a.
Tourism (1991): total tourist nights 2,360,000.
Production (metric tons except as noted). Agriculture, forestry, fishing (1991): corn (maize) 763,000, wheat 413,000, potatoes 358,000; livestock (head) 1,317,000 sheep, 853,000 cattle, 617,000 pigs, 10,607,000 poultry; roundwood (1990) 5,379,000 cu m; fish catch (1990) 3,606. Mining (1990): iron ore 6,756,000; bauxite 1,702,000; lead-zinc ore 608,000. Manufacturing (1990): crude steel 1,421,000; pig iron 1,284,000; alumina 735,000. Construction (residential units constructed; 1990): 26,568. Energy production (consumption): electricity (kW-hr; 1990) 14,632,000,000 (12,557,000,000); coal (metric tons; 1990) 17,926,000 (n.a.); petroleum products (metric tons; 1990) 2,320,000 (n.a.).
Gross national product (1990): U.S.$10,667,000,000 (U.S.$2,454 per capita).

Structure of gross material product and labour force

	1989		1990	
	in value Din '000,000	% of total value	labour force[6]	% of labour force[6]
Agriculture	2,963	10.9	39,053	3.8
Manufacturing, mining	15,589	57.6	496,190	48.3
Construction	1,918	7.1	74,861	7.3
Public utilities	403	1.5	22,345	2.2
Transp. and commun.	1,600	5.9	68,798	6.7
Trade	3,777	13.9	130,914	12.8
Finance	} 834	} 3.1	38,686	3.8
Pub. admin., defense			} 155,411	} 15.1
Services				
Other				
TOTAL	27,084	100.0	1,026,258	100.0

Population economically active (1991): total 992,000; activity rate of total population 22.7% (participation rates: ages 15–64, n.a.; female [1990] 37.7%).

Price and earnings indexes (1985 = 100)

	1984	1985	1986	1987	1988	1989	1990[7]
Consumer price index	58	100	188	400	1,188	16,169	109,000
Monthly earnings index[8]	99	100	106	99	86	109	87

Land use (1990): forest 47.9%; pasture 31.0%; agricultural 15.5%; other 5.6%.
Household income and expenditure. Average household size (1991) 3.4; income per household (1990) Din 72,850 (U.S.$6,437); sources of income (1990): wages 53.2%, transfers 18.2%, self-employment 12.0%, other 16.6%; expenditure (1988): food 41.3%, clothing 8.3%, fuel and lighting 7.8%, housing 7.8%, transportation 6.0%, beverages and tobacco 5.7%, household durable goods 4.1%, education and entertainment 3.5%, health care 3.4%.

Foreign trade

Balance of trade (current prices)

	1985	1986	1987	1988	1989	1990
Din '000,000	–4	2	15	77	962	2,141
% of total	4.5%	1.2%	6.2%	9.2%	7.4%	4.8%

Imports (1990): Din 21,130,000,000 (mineral fuels 31.6%; raw materials and semifinished goods 26.8%; basic manufactures 17.5%; consumer goods 13.3%, of which food and tobacco 3.6%). *Major import sources:* n.a.
Exports (1990): Din 23,271,000,000 (machinery 20.8%; chemicals 9.4%; clothing 9.2%; furniture 5.0%). *Major export destinations:* n.a.

Transport and communications

Transport. Railroads (1990): length 646 mi, 1,039 km; passengers transported 11,197,000; cargo transported 35,054,000 tons. Roads (1991): total length 13,153 mi, 21,168 km (paved 54%). Vehicles (1990): passenger cars 438,080; trucks and buses 50,578. Airports (1993) with scheduled flights 1.
Communications. Daily newspapers (1990): total number 3; circulation 161,000; circulation per 1,000 population 37. Radio (1989): number of receivers 904,000 (1 per 4.8 persons). Television (1989): number of receivers 844,000 (1 per 5.1 persons). Telephones (1990): 727,316 (1 per 6.0 persons).

Education and health

Education (1990–91)

	schools	teachers	students	student/ teacher ratio
Primary (age 7–14)	2,205	23,369	539,875	23.1
Secondary (age 15–18)	238	9,030	172,063	19.1
Higher	44	2,802	37,541	13.4

Educational attainment (1981). Percentage of population age 15 and over having: less than full primary education 49.5%; primary 24.2%; secondary 21.7%; postsecondary and higher 4.3%. *Literacy* (1981): total population age 10 and over literate 2,962,400 (85.5%); males 96.5%; females 76.6%.
Health (1990): physicians (1989) 6,929 (1 per 624 persons); hospital beds 19,858 (1 per 219 persons); infant mortality rate per 1,000 live births 15.2.

Military

Total active duty personnel (1993)[9]: 60,000 (army 100%). *Military expenditure as percentage of GNP:* n.a.

[1]Data given refer to conditions prior to outbreak of civil war and subsequent de facto partition of Bosnia and Herzegovina. [2]159 seats occupied as of August 1993. [3]No national currency of issue exists. The principal currency in de facto use is the Yugoslav new dinar (Din), for which no exchange rate is offered, owing to persistent inflation since the late 1980s and to the current state of belligerency, in which extreme inflation, demonetization of transactions, barter, and use of external hard currencies prevent a simple characterization of the situation at year-end. [4]One sq km is equal to approximately 0.3861 sq mi. [5]Detail adds to 554 sq km more than total given; the reason for the discrepancy is unknown. [6]Excludes 28,000 workers in the private sector. [7]On Jan. 1, 1990, the new dinar, equal to 10,000 old dinars, was introduced. [8]Based on worker real net personal income. [9]Excludes two armed militias, 80,000 personnel in the Army of the Serbian Republic of Bosnia and Herzegovina and 30,000 personnel of the Croat Defense Council; and the 9,500-member UN protection force stationed in Bosnia and Herzegovina.

Botswana

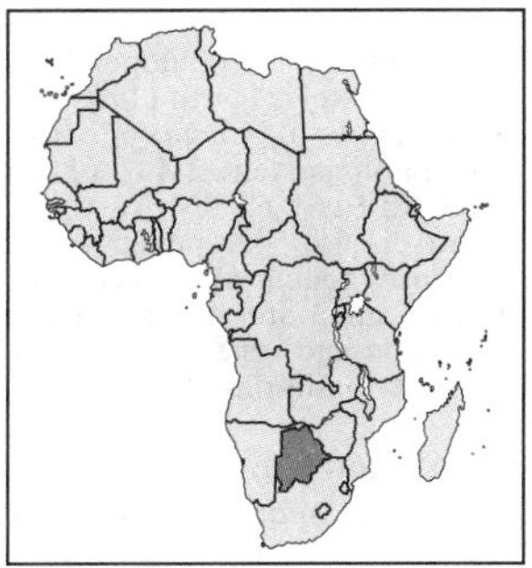

Official name: Republic of Botswana.
Form of government: multiparty republic with one legislative body[1] (National Assembly [40[2]]).
Head of state and government: President.
Capital: Gaborone.
Official language: English[3].
Official religion: none.
Monetary unit: 1 pula (P) = 100 thebe; valuation (Oct. 4, 1993) 1 U.S.\$ = P 2.54; 1 £ = P 3.84.

Area and population

Districts	Capitals	area sq mi	area sq km	population 1991 census[4]
Barolong	...	425	1,100	18,365
Central	Serowe	57,039[5]	147,730[5]	284,264
Ghanzi	Ghanzi	45,525	117,910	24,695
Kgalagadi	Tsabong	41,290	106,940	30,873
Kgatleng	Mochudi	3,073	7,960	57,168
Kweneng	Molepolole	13,857	35,890	169,835
North East	Masunga	1,977	5,120	43,361
North West				
Chobe	Kasane	8,031	20,800	14,186
Ngamiland	Maun	42,135	109,130	94,322
Ngwaketse	Kanye	10,568	27,370	129,474
Serowe/Palapye	...	5	5	111,300
South East	Ramotswa	687[5]	1,780[5]	31,101
Towns[6]				
Francistown	—	31	79	65,026
Gaborone	—	37	97	133,791
Jwaneng	—	39	100	11,199
Lobatse	—	12	30	25,992
Orapa	—	4	10	8,853
Palapye	—	8	21	17,131
Selebi-Pikwe	—	19	50	39,769
Sowa		...	...	2,220
Tlokweng	—	10	26	12,366
TOTAL		224,607	581,730	1,325,291

Demography

Population (1993): 1,406,000.
Density (1993): persons per sq mi 6.3, persons per sq km 2.4.
Urban-rural (1991): urban 24.1%; rural 75.9%.
Sex distribution (1990): male 47.70%; female 52.30%.
Age breakdown (1990): under 15, 46.1%; 15–29, 27.5%; 30–44, 14.1%; 45–59, 7.0%; 60–74, 4.0%; 75 and over, 1.3%.
Population projection: (2000) 1,782,000; (2010) 2,500,000.
Doubling time: 20 years.
Ethnic composition (1983): Tswana 75.5%; Shona 12.4%; San (Bushman) 3.4%; Khoikhoin (Hottentot) 2.5%; Ndebele 1.3%; other 4.9%.
Religious affiliation (1980): traditional beliefs 49.2%; Protestant 29.0%; African Christian 11.8%; Roman Catholic 9.4%; other 0.6%.
Major cities (1991): Gaborone 133,791; Francistown 65,026; Selebi-Pikwe 39,769; Molepolole 36,928; Kanye 31,341.

Vital statistics

Birth rate per 1,000 population (1990–95): 33.2 (world avg. 26.4); (1986) legitimate 28.8%[7]; illegitimate 71.2%[7].
Death rate per 1,000 population (1990–95): 5.7 (world avg. 9.2).
Natural increase rate per 1,000 population (1990–95): 27.5 (world avg. 17.2).
Total fertility rate (avg. births per childbearing woman; 1990–95): 4.3.
Marriage rate per 1,000 population (1986): 1.5.
Life expectancy at birth (1989): male 52.7 years; female 59.3 years.
Major causes of death (as percentage of total registered deaths; 1986): diseases of the circulatory system 17.3%; infectious and parasitic diseases 16.6%; malignant neoplasms (cancers) 13.4%; diseases of the respiratory system 12.2%; endocrine, nutritional, and metabolic diseases 6.1%.

National economy

Budget (1992–93). Revenue: P 4,160,600,000 (mineral royalties 44.7%, customs and excise taxes 24.4%, nontax revenue 19.2%, other [nonmineral] income taxes 8.9%). Expenditures: P 4,051,400,000 (recurrent expenditure 51.1%, development expenditure 34.9%, net lending 13.0%).
Population economically active (1984–85): total 367,949; activity rate of total population 37.0% (participation rates: ages 15–64, 72.7%; female 54.6%; unemployed [1986] 19.2%).

Price and earnings indexes (1985 = 100)

	1986	1987	1988	1989	1990	1991	1992
Consumer price index	110.0	120.8	130.9	146.0	162.7	181.8	211.2
Earnings index[8]	114.3	125.0	133.9	148.2	164.3	...	...

Production (metric tons except as noted). Agriculture, forestry, fishing (1992): vegetables and melons 16,000, cereals 15,000 (of which sorghum 11,000, corn [maize] 3,000, millet 1,000), pulses 12,000, fruits 11,000, roots and tubers 8,000, seed cotton 3,000, cottonseed 1,000, peanuts (groundnuts) 1,000; livestock (number of live animals) 2,500,000 cattle, 2,090,000 goats, 325,000 sheep, 153,000 mules and asses, 25,000[9] horses; roundwood (1991) 1,440,000 cu m; fish catch (1991) 1,900. Mining and quarrying (1992): diamonds 16,000,000 carats; copper 19,079; nickel 17,272; cobalt 208. Manufacturing (value added in P '000,000; 1986–87): food products 161.9; textiles 46.0; chemicals 20.8; wood products 10.3; paper and paper products 5.5. Construction (1985): residential 70,200 sq m; nonresidential 80,700 sq m. Energy production (consumption): electricity (kW-hr; 1991) 929,000,000 (929,000,000); coal (metric tons; 1991) 850,000 (n.a.); crude petroleum, none (n.a.).
Public debt (external, outstanding; 1991): U.S.\$535,900,000.
Tourism (1990): receipts U.S.\$65,000,000; expenditures U.S.\$39,000,000.
Gross national product (1992): U.S.\$3,802,000,000 (U.S.\$2,800 per capita).

Structure of gross domestic product and labour force

	1990–91 in value P '000,000	1990–91 % of total value	1990 labour force[10]	1990 % of labour force
Agriculture	361.3	5.2	6,500	3.3
Mining	2,873.0	41.6	7,800[11]	3.9
Manufacturing	276.9	4.0	23,300	11.7
Construction	393.4	5.7	29,300	14.8
Public utilities	160.9	2.3	2,100	1.1
Transp. and commun.	175.6	2.5	8,100	4.1
Trade	983.0	14.2	35,700	18.0
Finance and business services	354.8	5.1	13,200	6.6
Pub. admin., defense	1,284.2	18.6		
Services	166.0	2.4	72,500	36.5
Other	−117.5	−1.7		
TOTAL	6,911.6	100.0[12]	198,500	100.0

Household income and expenditure (1985–86). Average household size 5.0; average annual income per household P 3,910 (U.S.\$2,080); sources of income: wages and salaries 59.9%, transfers 30.8%, self-employment 9.3%; expenditure: food, beverages, and tobacco 39.4%, household durable goods 14.0%, rent and services 13.3%, transportation 13.1%, clothing 5.6%, health 2.3%.
Land use (1991): forested 19.2%; meadows and pastures 58.2%; agricultural and under permanent cultivation 2.5%; other 20.1%.

Foreign trade[13]

Balance of trade (current prices)

	1987	1988	1989	1990	1991	1992
P '000,000	1,445.8	831.2	1,174.9	231.1	492.1	518.2
% of total	35.1%	18.4%	18.6%	3.6%	5.0%	5.5%

Imports (1992): P 3,958,000,000 (1990; transport equipment 19.2%; machinery and electrical goods 18.5%; food, beverages, and tobacco 14.1%; chemical and rubber products 8.5%; metal and metal products 8.4%; textiles and footwear 8.4%; mineral fuels 6.4%; wood and paper 4.3%). *Major import sources* (1988): Customs Union of Southern Africa 77.4%; European countries 10.2%, of which U.K. 6.1%; U.S. 2.3%.
Exports (1992): P 3,638,000,000 (diamonds 78.8%; copper-nickel matte 5.9%; beef products 5.4%). *Major export destinations* (1988): European countries 85.9%, of which U.K. 1.1%; African countries 13.5%; U.S. 0.3%.

Transport and communications

Transport. Railroads (1992): length 551 mi, 887 km; passenger-km 257,000,000[14]; metric ton-km cargo 852,000[15]. Roads (1991): total length 11,933 mi, 19,204 km (paved 13%). Vehicles (1989): passenger cars 17,000; trucks and buses 28,000. Merchant marine: none. Air transport (1991)[16]: passenger-km 71,818,000; metric ton-km cargo 642,000; airports (1993) 6.
Communications. Daily newspapers (1991): total number 1; total circulation 40,000; circulation per 1,000 population 3.1. Radio (1992): total receivers 1,100,000 (1 per 1.2 persons). Television (1992): total receivers 13,800 (1 per 98 persons). Telephones (1990): 47,917 (1 per 26 persons).

Education and health

Education (1991)

	schools	teachers	students	student/ teacher ratio
Primary (age 6–13)	654	9,708	308,840	31.8
Secondary (age 14–18)	169	3,743	68,137	18.2
Voc., teacher tr.	40	759	7,057	9.3
Higher	1	370	3,352	9.1

Educational attainment (1981). Percentage of population age 25 and over having: no formal schooling 54.7%; some primary education 31.0%; complete primary 9.4%; some secondary 3.1%; complete secondary 1.3%; postsecondary 0.5%. *Literacy* (1990): total population over age 15 literate 486,500 (73.6%); males literate (83.7%); females literate (65.1%).
Health (1990): physicians 240 (1 per 5,417 persons); hospital beds 3,212 (1 per 395 persons); infant mortality rate (1988) 37.0.
Food (1988–90): daily per capita caloric intake 2,260 (vegetable products 86%, animal products 14%); 97% of FAO recommended minimum requirement.

Military

Total active duty personnel (1993): 6,100 (army 98.4%, navy, none [landlocked], air force 1.6%). *Military expenditure as percentage of GNP* (1989): 2.8% (world 4.9%); per capita expenditure U.S.\$52.

[1]In addition, the House of Chiefs, a 15-member body consisting of chiefs, subchiefs, and associated members, serves in an advisory capacity to the government. [2]Including four specially elected members and two nonelective seats. [3]Tswana is the national language. [4]Preliminary. [5]Areas for Central district and South East district include the area for Serowe/Palapye. [6]Areas are included with respective district totals; population figures are not included with district totals. [7]Registered births only. [8]Excludes government sector. [9]1989. [10]Formal sector only. [11]13,516 Tswana were employed in South African mines in 1990. [12]Detail does not add to total given because of rounding. [13]Import figures are f.o.b. in balance of trade and c.i.f. in commodities and trading partners. [14]1986–87. [15]1991. [16]Air Botswana only.

Brazil

Official name: República Federativa do Brasil (Federative Republic of Brazil).
Form of government: multiparty federal republic with 2 legislative houses (Senate [81]; Chamber of Deputies [503]).
Chief of state and government: President.
Capital: Brasília.
Official language: Portuguese.
Official religion: none.
Monetary unit: 1 cruzeiro real[1] = 100 centavos; valuation (Oct. 4, 1993) 1 U.S.$ = 128.47 cruzeiros reais; 1 £ = 194.64 cruzeiros reais.

Area and population

States	Capitals	area sq mi	area sq km	population 1991 census[2]
Acre	Rio Branco	59,343	153,698	417,437
Alagoas	Maceió	11,238	29,107	2,512,515
Amapá	Macapá	54,965	142,359	289,050
Amazonas	Manaus	605,390	1,567,954	2,088,682
Bahia	Salvador	218,912	566,979	11,801,810
Ceará	Fortaleza	56,253	145,694	6,353,346
Espírito Santo	Vitória	17,658	45,733	2,598,231
Goiás	Goiânia	131,339	340,166	4,024,547
Maranhão	São Luís	127,242	329,556	4,922,339
Mato Grosso	Cuiabá	348,040	901,421	2,020,581
Mato Grosso do Sul	Campo Grande	138,021	357,472	1,778,494
Minas Gerais	Belo Horizonte	226,497	586,624	15,746,200
Pará	Belém	481,405	1,246,833	5,084,726
Paraíba	João Pessoa	20,833	53,958	3,200,620
Paraná	Curitiba	76,959	199,324	8,415,659
Pernambuco	Recife	39,005	101,023	7,109,626
Piauí	Teresina	97,017	251,273	2,581,054
Rio de Janeiro	Rio de Janeiro	16,855	43,653	12,584,108
Rio Grande do Norte	Natal	20,528	53,167	2,413,618
Rio Grande do Sul	Pôrto Alegre	108,369	280,674	9,127,611
Rondônia	Pôrto Velho	92,039	238,379	1,130,400
Roraima	Boa Vista	86,880	225,017	215,790
Santa Catarina	Florianópolis	36,803	95,318	4,536,433
São Paulo	São Paulo	95,852	248,256	31,192,918
Sergipe	Aracaju	8,441	21,863	1,492,400
Tocantins	Palmas	107,075	277,322	920,133
Federal District				
Distrito Federal	Brasília	2,237	5,794	1,596,174
Disputed areas[3]		1,306	3,382	—
TOTAL		3,286,500[4, 5]	8,511,996[4, 5]	146,154,502[6]

Demography

Population (1993): 156,493,000.
Density (1993): persons per sq mi 47.6, persons per sq km 18.4.
Urban-rural (1991): urban 75.5%; rural 24.5%.
Sex distribution (1991): male 49.37%; female 50.63%.
Age breakdown (1990): under 15, 34.7%; 15–29, 28.3%; 30–44, 19.4%; 45–59, 10.5%; 60–74, 5.6%; 75 and over, 1.5%.
Population projection: (2000) 172,777,000; (2010) 194,002,000.
Doubling time: 38 years.
Ethnic composition (1980): Brazilian white 53.0%, of which Portuguese 15.0%, Italian 11.0%, Spanish 10.0%, German 3.0%; mulatto 22.0%; mestizo 12.0%; black 11.0%; Japanese 0.8%; Amerindian 0.1%; other 1.1%.
Religious affiliation (1980): Roman Catholic 87.8%[7], of which Spiritist Catholic 15.7%[8], Evangelical Catholic 9.0%[9]; Protestant (mostly Assemblies of God, other Pentecostal, and Baptist) 6.1%[10]; Afro-American Spiritist 2.0%[11]; Spiritist 1.7%[12]; nonreligious 1.0%; atheist 0.4%; Buddhist 0.3%; Jewish 0.2%; other 0.5%.
Major cities (1991): São Paulo 9,393,753 (metropolitan area 15,199,423); Rio de Janeiro 5,473,909 (9,600,528); Salvador 2,070,296 (2,472,131); Brasília 1,598,418; Belo Horizonte 1,529,560 (3,461,905); Recife 1,296,995 (2,859,469); Pôrto Alegre 1,237,223 (3,015,960); Manaus 1,005,634 (1,164,372); Goiânia 912,136 (1,268,303).

Other principal cities (1991)

	population		population		population
Aracaju	401,676	Juiz de Fora	377,538	São Bernardo do Campo	550,030
Avaré	555,433	Londriva	355,062	São Jose dos Campos	385,879
Campinas	748,076	Nova Iguaçu	562,062	Sorocaba	348,952
Campo Grande	516,403	Olinda	341,049	Sumaré	557,544
Fiera de Santana	340,034	Osasco	566,949	Teresina	556,073
Guarulhos	544,698	Ribeirão Prêto	416,186	Venda Nova	481,470
João Pessoa	497,306	Santo André	518,272		
		Santos	415,554		

Place of birth/national origin: n.a.
Mobility: n.a.
Families (1989). Average family size 3.9; 1–2 persons 25.8%, 3 persons 20.8%, 4 persons 21.3%, 5–6 persons 22.5%, 7 or more persons 9.6%.
Immigration (1982–84): permanent immigrants admitted 7,673, from Portugal 28.4%, Uruguay 8.7%, Argentina 8.2%.

Vital statistics

Birth rate per 1,000 population (1990–95): 26.1 (world avg. 26.4).
Death rate per 1,000 population (1990–95): 7.5 (world avg. 9.2).
Natural increase rate per 1,000 population (1990–95): 18.6 (world avg. 17.2).
Total fertility rate (avg. births per childbearing woman; 1991): 3.1.
Marriage rate per 1,000 population (1989): 5.7.
Divorce rate per 1,000 population (1989): 0.5.
Life expectancy at birth (1990–95): male 63.5 years; female 69.1 years.
Major causes of death per 100,000 population (1987)[13]: diseases of the circulatory system 211.0, of which cerebrovascular disease 71.5, ischemic heart diseases 62.6, diseases of pulmonary circulation and other forms of heart disease 50.6; malignant neoplasms (cancers) 73.3; diseases of the respiratory system 61.6; accidents 51.2; infectious and parasitic diseases 47.1; birth trauma and other conditions originating in the perinatal period 44.5; homicide and other violence 40.9; diseases of the digestive system 30.2; ill-defined conditions 152.9.

Social indicators

Educational attainment (1989). Percentage of population age 10 and over having: no formal schooling or less than one year of primary education 18.7%; incomplete primary 56.9%; complete primary 6.9%; incomplete secondary 11.9%; complete secondary or higher 5.5%; unknown 0.1%.

Distribution of income (1988)[14, 15]

percentage of national income by decile

1	2	3	4	5	6	7	8	9	10 (highest)
0.7	1.7	2.2	3.4	3.9	5.0	6.8	9.9	15.9	50.5

Quality of working life. Average workweek (1986): 79.9% of the labour force works 40 or more hours per week. Annual estimated rate per 100,000 insured urban workers (1987) for: injury or accident 4,030; industrial illness, n.a.; death 22. Proportion of labour force participating in national social insurance system (1988): 48.1%. Proportion of formally employed population receiving minimum wage (1993): 25.0%.
Access to services. Proportion of households having access to: electricity (1989) 86.9%, of which urban households having access 97.2%, rural households having access 53.2%; safe public (piped) water supply (1986) 69.9%, of which urban households having access 88.7%, rural households having access 11.6%; public sewage collection (1986) 58.5%, of which urban households having access 75.2%, rural households having access 6.5%.
Social participation. Eligible voters participating in last (October 1990) national election: *c.* 64%; although voting is mandatory, about 15% of the electorate did not vote and about 25% of those who did spoiled their ballots or cast blank votes. Trade union membership in total workforce: n.a. Practicing Roman Catholic population in total affiliated Roman Catholic population (1990): 25%.
Social deviance. The incidence of crime is not accurately reported. Crimes resulting in imprisonment (1989): 150,460, of which murder 7.0%; assault 10.8%; theft, burglary, and housebreaking 26.5%; robbery and extortion 11.5%; narcotics trafficking 6.1%; narcotics usage 5.6%. Suicide (1988): 4,700.
Leisure. Favourite leisure activities include: playing soccer, rehearsing all year in neighbourhood samba groups for celebrations of Carnival, and competing in water sports, volleyball, and basketball.
Material well-being (1989). Households possessing: radio receiver 83.4% (urban 85.9%, rural 75.0%); television receiver 72.6% (urban 83.3%, rural 37.6%); refrigerator 63.1%[16] (urban 75.4%, rural 25.1%).

National economy

Gross national product (at current market prices; 1992): U.S.$426,159,000,000 (U.S.$2,770 per capita).

Structure of gross domestic product and labour force

	1991 in value Cr$'000,000,000[1, 17]	1991 % of total value	1990 labour force[14]	1990 % of labour force
Agriculture	15,771	10.8	14,180,519	22.0
Mining	2,472	1.7	860,453 (Mining and Public utilities)	1.3 (Mining and Public utilities)
Public utilities	5,309	3.6		
Manufacturing	36,621	25.0	9,410.712	14.6
Construction	10,332	7.1	3,823,154	5.9
Transportation and communications	8,017	5.5	2,439,920	3.8
Trade	10,442[18]	7.1[18]	7,975,670[18]	12.4[18]
Finance, real estate	34,943	23.8	1,715,598[19]	2.7[19]
Pub. admin., defense	14,454	9.9	21,694,473[20] (Pub. admin., defense and Services)	33.6[20] (Pub. admin., defense and Services)
Services	19,902[20]	13.6[20]		
Other	−11,719[21]	−8.0[21]	2,367,482[22]	3.7[22]
TOTAL	146,544	100.0[4]	64,467,981	100.0

Budget (1991). Revenue: Cr$52,810,000,000,000[1] (current receipts 62.5%, of which social contributions 31.7% [including social security 17.0%], taxes 23.7% [including income taxes 11.9%]; development receipts 37.5%). Expenditures: Cr$52,810,000,000,000[1] (current expenditures 55.6%, of which transfers to parastatal[23] organizations 19.2%; development expenditures 44.4%, of which amortization of domestic debt 24.7%).
Public debt (external, outstanding; 1991): U.S.$87,477,000,000.
Production ('000 metric tons except as noted; 1992). Agriculture, forestry, fishing: sugarcane 270,672, corn (maize) 30,619, cassava 22,652, oranges 19,640, soybeans 19,161, rice 9,961, bananas 5,650, wheat 2,839, dry beans 2,804, potatoes 2,434, tomatoes 2,124, seed cotton 1,876, papayas 1,400, coffee 1,298, cottonseed 1,125, coconuts 878, pineapples 800, grapes 741, apples 611, tobacco leaves 583, cacao 343, cashews 97, palm oil 80; livestock (number of live animals) 153,000,000 cattle, 33,050,000 pigs, 19,500,000 sheep, 6,200,000 horses; roundwood (1991) 264,621,000 cu m; fish catch (1991) 800, of which freshwater fishes 207. Mining and quarrying: iron ore 150,000; bauxite 10,800; manganese 2,100; kaolin (clay) 850; zinc (metal content) 161[24]; copper (metal content) 37[24]; tin (metal content) 30; gold 2,450,000 troy oz; diamonds 1,500,000 carats[24]. Manufacturing (value added in U.S.$'000,000; 1988): food products 11,007; nonelectrical machinery 10,195; electrical machinery 8,823; iron and steel 8,126; textiles 7,443; transport equipment 7,257;

pharmaceuticals, cosmetics, and soaps 7,158; industrial chemicals 7,078; refined petroleum 6,910; fabricated metal products 4,631; nonmetallic mineral products 3,872; paper and paper products 3,617; wearing apparel (excluding footwear) 3,160; plastics 3,049. Construction (authorized[25]; 1987): residential 20,090,000 sq m; nonresidential 8,180,000 sq m.

Manufacturing enterprises (1985)

	no. of enterprises	number of labourers	wages of labourers as a % of avg. of all mfg. wages	value added in producer's prices (in U.S.$'000,000)
Chemical products (incl. refined petroleum, excl. pharmaceuticals)	5,066	287,742	191.7	11,668
Fabricated metals, iron and steel, and nonferrous metals	18,964	565,036	117.1	8,229
Food products	43,034	733,199	68.4	8,149
Nonelectrical machinery	11,088	552,163	146.5	6,337
Electrical machinery	4,573	315,767	138.5	5,392
Transport equipment	4,184	341,621	154.8	4,313
Textiles	5,570	351,360	75.1	4,185
Clothing and footwear	23,200	655,234	49.6	3,466
Nonmetallic mineral products	28,974	365,643	65.7	2,866
Paper and paper products	2,107	132,948	120.7	1,977
Plastics	2,975	146,151	85.1	1,505
Rubber products	1,421	71,656	136.3	1,248
Publishing and printing	9,053	164,523	100.1	1,208
Pharmaceuticals	930	49,048	173.7	1,110
Wood and wood products (excl. furniture)	17,129	218,059	48.4	1,091
Furniture	13,759	186,467	...	965
Beverages	2,798	77,167	...	835

Population economically active (1990)[14]: total 64,467,981; activity rate of total population 43.8% (participation rates: ages 15–59, 68.5%; female 35.5%; unemployed [March 1993] 15.8%[26]).

Price and earnings indexes (1988 = 100)

	1988	1989	1990	1991	1992	1993
Consumer price index	100.0	1,387	42,100	227,900	2,527,000	34,454,000[27]
Monthly earnings index[28]	100.0	1,502	31,400	...	...	...

Tourism (1991): receipts from visitors U.S.$1,559,000,000; expenditures by nationals abroad U.S.$1,224,000,000.

Retail trade enterprises (1985)

	no. of enterprises	total no. of employees	annual wage as a % of all trade wages	annual value of sales in U.S.$'000,000
General merchandise stores (including food products)	16,690	370,813	83.4	11,566
Vehicles, new and used; parts	38,900	268,989	123.9	10,473
Gas stations	21,751	169,831	100.0	8,831
Food, beverages, and tobacco	275,593	682,211	64.1	7,581
Clothing, footwear, and apparel	129,228	564,120	77.5	6,861
Hardware, appliances, and construction materials	48,166	268,817	90.4	5,548
Domestic goods, equipment, kitchenware, and antiques	28,830	194,214	102.5	4,119
Pharmaceutical and cosmetic products	43,929	185,901	82.5	3,115
Agricultural and industrial equipment and machinery	9,451	73,809	141.2	2,799
Books, magazines, newspapers	13,636	56,167	82.3	661

Family income and expenditure. Average family size (1987) 4.2; income per household of families having income (1986[14, 29]) 21,802 (old) cruzados[1] (U.S.$2,922); sources of income: n.a.; expenditure: n.a.

Financial aggregates[30]

	1988	1989	1990	1991	1992	1993[31]
Exchange rate, cruzeiros reais[1] per:						
U.S. dollar	.001	.011	.177	1.07	12.39	54.34
£	.002	.018	.341	2.00	18.73	81.98
SDR	.001	.015	.252	1.53	17.03	76.27
International reserves (U.S.$)						
Total (excl. gold; '000,000)	6,972	7,535	7,441	8,033	22,521	23,097
SDRs ('000,000)	—	—	8	9	1	11
Reserve pos. in IMF ('000,000)	—	—	—	—	—	—
Foreign exchange ('000,000)	6,971	7,535	7,430	8,020	22,520	23,082
Gold ('000,000 fine troy oz)	2.73	2.98	4.57	2.02	2.23	2.29
% world reserves	0.29	0.32	0.49	0.21	0.24	0.25
Interest and prices						
Central bank discount (%)	2,282	38,341	1,083	2,494	1,489	2,675
Govt. bond yield (%)	...	...	...	...	...	...
Industrial share prices	...	...	...	...	...	...
Balance of payments (U.S.$'000,000)						
Balance of visible trade	+19,168	+16,112	+10,747	+10,604	+15,610	...
Imports, f.o.b.	14,605	18,263	20,661	21,017	20,540	...
Exports, f.o.b.	33,773	34,375	31,408	31,621	36,150	...
Balance of invisibles	−15,146	−15,067	−14,537	−10,994	−9,010	...
Balance of payments, current account	+4,159	+1,025	−3,790	−390	+6,600	...

Energy production (consumption): electricity (kW-hr; 1991) 234,366,000,000 (261,161,000,000); coal (metric tons; 1991) 5,124,000 (16,811,000); crude petroleum (barrels; 1992) 228,593,000 (413,229,000[24]); petroleum products (metric tons; 1991) 47,538,000 (49,949,000); natural gas (cu m; 1992) 3,757,-000,000 (3,604,000,000[24]); carburant alcohol (hectolitres; 1991) 120,270,000 (n.a.).

Land use (1991): forested 58.0%; meadows and pastures 21.9%; agricultural and under permanent cultivation 7.3%; other 12.8%.

Foreign trade

Balance of trade (current prices)

	1987	1988	1989	1990	1991	1992
U.S.$'000,000	+11,173	+19,168	+16,112	+10,747	+10,604	+15,610
% of total	27.1%	39.6%	30.6%	20.6%	20.1%	27.5%

Imports (1991): U.S.$21,017,000,000 (crude petroleum 16.0%, nonelectrical machinery and apparatus 14.9%, electrical machinery and apparatus 8.8%, organic chemical products 6.8%, food 6.1%). *Major import sources:* United States 23.7%; Germany 9.0%; Argentina 7.7%; Saudi Arabia 6.4%; Japan 5.8%; Iran 4.4%; Italy 3.8%; France 2.9%; Venezuela 2.5%; Canada 2.4%.

Exports (1991): U.S.$31,621,000,000 (nonelectrical machinery and equipment 8.2%, iron ore 8.2%, transport equipment 6.8%, iron and steel fabricated products 6.1%, coffee beans 4.4%, soya products 4.3%, footwear 3.9%, electrical and electronic equipment 3.2%, crude aluminum 3.1%, orange juice 2.8%). *Major export destinations:* United States 19.9%; Japan 8.1%; The Netherlands 6.8%; Germany 6.6%; Argentina 4.7%; Italy 4.3%; Belgium-Luxembourg 3.4%; United Kingdom 3.3%; France 2.7%; South Korea 2.5%.

Transport and communications

Transport. Railroads: route length (1991) 19,885 mi, 32,002 km; (1990) passenger-mi 8,431,000,000, passenger-km 13,569,000,000; (1990) short ton-mi cargo 82,267,000,000, metric ton-km cargo 120,108,000,000. Roads (1990): total length 1,037,780 mi, 1,670,148 km (paved 10%). Vehicles (1990): passenger cars 12,127,562; trucks and buses 935,783. Merchant marine (1992): vessels (100 gross tons and over) 635; total deadweight tonnage 9,348,339. Air transport (1992)[32]: passenger-mi 17,538,000,000, passenger-km 28,225,-000,000; short ton-mi cargo 881,000,000, metric ton-km cargo 1,286,000,000; airports (1993) with scheduled flights 110.

Communications. Daily newspapers (1992): total number 205; total circulation 7,815,400[33]; circulation per 1,000 population 51[33]. Radio (1992): total number of receivers 60,000,000 (1 per 2.6 persons). Television (1992): total number of receivers 30,000,000 (1 per 5.1 persons). Telephones (1990): 14,125,396 (1 per 10 persons).

Education and health

Education (1990)

	schools	teachers	students	student/teacher ratio
Primary (age 7–14)	208,934	1,260,501	28,943,619	23.0
Secondary (age 15–18)	10,160	243,246	3,498,777	14.4
Higher	918	145,585	1,540,080	10.6

Literacy (1989)[34]: total population age 15 and over literate 76,052,856 (81.2%); males literate 37,022,807 (81.8%); females literate 39,030,049 (80.6%).

Health (1988): physicians 169,500 (1 per 848 persons); hospital beds 532,000 (1 per 270 persons); infant mortality rate per 1,000 live births (1991) 68.0.

Food (1988–90): daily per capita caloric intake 2,730 (vegetable products 84%, animal products 16%); 114% of FAO recommended minimum requirement.

Military

Total active duty personnel (1993): 296,700 (army 66.1%, navy 16.8%, air force 17.1%). *Military expenditure as percentage of GNP* (1988): 1.3% (world 5.1%); per capita expenditure U.S.$40.

[1]The cruzeiro real replaced the cruzeiro (Cr$) at a rate of 1,000 cruzeiros to 1 cruzeiro real on Aug. 2, 1993. Previously, the cruzeiro replaced the new cruzado (NCz$) at a rate of 1 to 1 on March 16, 1990, and the new cruzado replaced the (old) cruzado (Cz$) at a rate of 1,000 (old) to 1 new on Jan. 15, 1989. [2]Preliminary figures. [3]Area in dispute between Ceará and Piauí. [4]Detail does not add to total given because of rounding. [5]Land area excluding inland water is 3,265,076 sq mi (8,456,-508 sq km). [6]Revised preliminary census figure equals 146,917,459. [7]76% in 1990. [8]Spiritist Catholics actively and regularly practice medium religions; a large majority of Roman Catholics defer to Spiritist dogma and participate in organized Spiritism occasionally. [9]Evangelical Catholics are officially regarded as Roman Catholic but are affiliated to Protestant churches. [10]11% in 1990. [11]Non-Christian followers of Afro-Brazilian syncretistic religions ("low spiritism"). [12]Non-Christian followers of Kardecism ("high spiritism"). [13]Projected rates based on about 73% of total deaths. [14]Excludes rural economically active population of Acre, Amapá, Amazonas, Pará, Rondônia, and Roraima states. [15]As of 1992, 33,000,000 Brazilians lived in extreme poverty (more than half of whom lived in the nine states of the northeast). [16]1985. [17]At factor cost. [18]Excludes restaurants and hotels. [19]Includes classifications not adequately defined. [20]Includes restaurants and hotels. [21]Less imputed bank service charges. [22]Unemployed. [23]Formally, a nongovernmental organization created by the state. [24]1991. [25]Urban construction only for 74 cities. [26]São Paulo only. [27]Average of June and July. [28]Minimum wage. [29]Prices of September 1985. [30]End-of-period figures. [31]June. [32]Transbrasil, VARIG, Cruzeiro do Sul, and VASP airlines only. [33]184 newspapers only. [34]By official estimate; functional literacy, however, may be as low as 42% of total population over age 15.

Brunei

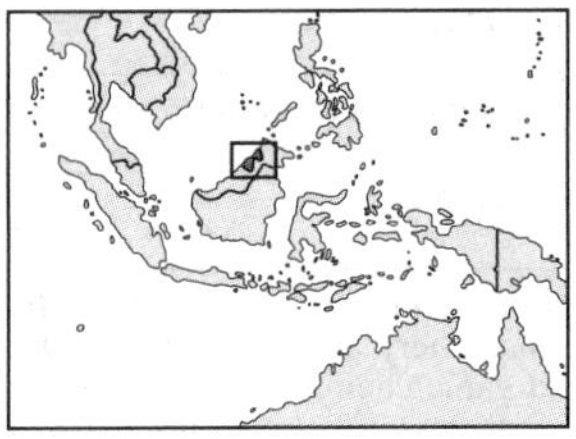

Official name: Negara Brunei Darussalam (State of Brunei, Abode of Peace).
Form of government: monarchy (sultanate)[1].
Head of state and government: Sultan.
Capital: Bandar Seri Begawan.
Official language: Malay[2].
Official religion: Islam.
Monetary unit: 1 Brunei dollar (B$) = 100 cents; valuation (Oct. 4, 1993) 1 U.S.$ = B$1.58; 1 £ = B$2.40.

Area and population

		area		population
Districts	Capitals	sq mi	sq km	1991 census
Belait	Kuala Belait	1,052	2,724	53,087
Brunei and Muara	Bandar Seri Begawan	220	571	170,357
Temburong	Bangar	504	1,304	7,695
Tutong	Tutong	450	1,166	29,724
TOTAL		2,226	5,765	260,863

Demography

Population (1993): 275,000.
Density (1993): persons per sq mi 123.5, persons per sq km 47.7.
Urban-rural (1993): urban 90.0%; rural 10.0%.
Sex distribution (1990): male 51.62%; female 48.38%.
Age breakdown (1990): under 15, 35.8%; 15–29, 30.8%; 30–44, 21.3%; 45–59, 8.1%; 60–69, 2.5%; 70 and over, 1.5%.
Population projection: (2000) 334,000; (2010) 432,000.
Doubling time: 27 years.
Ethnic composition (1990): Malay 68.9%; Chinese 17.7%; other indigenous 5.3%; Indian and other 8.1%.
Religious affiliation (1986): Muslim 66.5%; Buddhist 11.8%; Christian 8.9%; other religions 3.7%; nonreligious 9.1%.
Major cities (1981): Bandar Seri Begawan 52,300[3]; Seria 23,511; Kuala Belait 19,281; Tutong 6,161.

Vital statistics

Birth rate per 1,000 population (1991): 29.0 (world avg. 26.4); (1982) legitimate 99.6%; illegitimate 0.4%.
Death rate per 1,000 population (1991): 3.0 (world avg. 9.2).
Natural increase rate per 1,000 population (1991): 26.0 (world avg. 17.2).
Total fertility rate (avg. births per childbearing woman; 1991): 3.7.
Marriage rate per 1,000 population (1990): 6.3.
Divorce rate per 1,000 population (1987): 0.8.
Life expectancy at birth (1989): male 72.6 years; female 76.4 years.
Major causes of death per 100,000 population (1990): cardiovascular disease 65.2; malignant neoplasms (cancers) 36.7; respiratory diseases 14.8; conditions originating from perinatal period 13.7; motor vehicle accidents 13.7.

National economy

Budget (1990). Revenue: B$2,796,430,000 (indirect taxes 57.6%, government property 32.8%[4], commercial receipts 6.3%). Expenditures: B$2,790,490,000 (current expenditure 67.0%, development expenditure 16.6%).
Public debt (external, outstanding): none.
Tourism (1990): receipts from visitors U.S.$35,000,000; expenditures by nationals abroad, n.a.
Production (metric tons except as noted). Agriculture, forestry, fishing (1992): vegetables and melons 8,000, fruits (excluding melons) 5,000, eggs 3,000, rice 1,000, cassava 1,000, pineapples 1,000; livestock (number of live animals) 14,000 pigs, 10,000 buffalo, 1,000 cattle, 2,000,000 chickens; roundwood (1991) 295,000 cu m; fish catch (1991) 1,652. Mining and quarrying (1991): other than petroleum and natural gas (see below), none except sand and gravel for construction. Manufacturing (1989): gasoline 133,000; diesel oils 88,000; jet fuels 21,000; kerosene 12,000; naphtha 5,000. Construction (number of buildings completed; 1984): residential 195; nonresidential 5. Energy production (consumption): electricity (kW-hr; 1991) 1,242,000,000 (1,242,000,000); coal, none (none); crude petroleum (barrels; 1991) 53,178,000 (15,000); petroleum products (metric tons; 1991) 767,000 (652,000); natural gas (cu m; 1991) 8,699,000,000 (2,133,000,000).
Population economically active (1986): total 86,395; activity rate of total population 37.8% (participation rates: ages 15–64, 60.4%; female 30.7%; unemployed 6.1%).

Price and earnings indexes (1985 = 100)

	1983	1984	1985	1986	1987	1988	1989
Consumer price index	94.8	97.7	100.0	101.8	103.1	104.3	105.7
Monthly earnings index[5]	108.0	99.1	100.0	87.9	...	...	...

Household income and expenditure. Average household size (1986) 5.8; income per household: n.a.; sources of income: n.a.; expenditure (1977): food 45.1%, transportation and communications 17.2%, recreation, education, and cultural services 8.9%, household furnishings 8.3%, clothing and footwear 6.1%, rent and utilities 5.0%.
Gross national product (at current market prices; 1990)[6]: U.S.$3,943,000,000 (U.S.$15,650 per capita).

Structure of gross domestic product and labour force

	1990		1986	
	in value B$'000,000	% of total value	labour force	% of labour force
Agriculture	158.6	2.1	3,059	3.5
Mining, Manufacturing	3,128.3	41.6	6,006	7.0
Construction	214.8	2.8	9,424	10.9
Public utilities	30.0	0.4	2,042	2.4
Transportation and communications	555.8	7.4	6,883	8.0
Trade	790.0	10.5	8,022	9.3
Finance	407.2	5.4	4,330	5.0
Services	2,384.1	31.7	38,557	44.6
Other	−141.5	−1.9	8,072[7]	9.3[7]
TOTAL	7,527.3	100.0	86,395	100.0

Land use (1991): forested 40.8%; meadows and pastures 1.1%; agricultural and under permanent cultivation 1.3%; other 56.8%.

Foreign trade

Balance of trade (current prices)

	1984	1985	1986	1987	1988	1989
B$'000,000	+5,482	+5,184	+2,540	+2,655	+2,012	+1,334
% of total	67.3%	65.8%	46.7%	49.6%	40.9%	22.0%

Imports (1989): B$1,722,800,000 (1988; machinery and transport equipment 32.8%, manufactured goods 23.7%, food and live animals 16.5%, miscellaneous manufactured articles 11.7%, chemicals 6.6%, beverages and tobacco 4.6%, crude materials 1.1%, mineral fuels 0.9%). *Major import sources* (1988): ASEAN 43.4%, of which Singapore 36.3%, Malaysia 4.9%; EEC 40.3%; United States 6.8%; Japan 5.9%.
Exports (1989): B$3,693,500,000 (crude petroleum 46.9%, natural gas 44.6%, petroleum products 4.9%, other 3.6%). *Major export destinations* (1988): Japan 51.9%; South Korea 15.0%; ASEAN 14.5%, of which Thailand 7.7%, Singapore 5.1%; EEC 13.8%.

Transport and communications

Transport. Railroads (1993)[8]: length 12 mi, 19 km. Roads (1990): total length 1,397 mi, 2,248 km (paved 49%). Vehicles (1991): passenger cars 115,495; trucks and buses 13,019. Merchant marine (1992): vessels (100 gross tons and over) 51; total deadweight tonnage 349,718. Marine transport (1989): cargo loaded 13,196,000 metric tons, cargo unloaded 1,272,000 metric tons. Air transport (1992): passenger-mi 687,000,000, passenger-km 1,105,000,000; short ton-mi cargo 23,746,000, metric ton-km cargo 34,669,000; airports (1993) with scheduled flights 1.
Communications. Daily newspapers (1990): total number 1; total circulation 10,000; circulation per 1,000 population 38. Radio (1992): total number of receivers 100,000 (1 per 2.7 persons). Television (1992): total number of receivers 67,000 (1 per 4.0 persons). Telephones (1991): 53,314 (1 per 4.9 persons).

Education and health

Education (1989–90)

	schools	teachers	students	student/ teacher ratio
Primary (age 5–11)	162	2,912	49,611	17.0
Secondary (age 12–20)	19	1,713	19,761	11.5
Voc., teacher tr.	6	326	1,565	4.8
Higher	2	214	1,110	5.2

Educational attainment (1981). Percentage of population age 25 and over having: no formal schooling 32.1%; primary education 28.3%; secondary 30.1%; postsecondary and higher 9.4%. *Literacy* (1986): total population age 15 and over literate 121,281 (85.1%); males literate 67,714 (90.9%); females literate 53,567 (78.7%).
Health (1990): physicians 171 (1 per 1,473 persons); hospital beds 893 (1 per 281 persons); infant mortality rate per 1,000 live births (1991) 11.0.
Food (1988–90): daily per capita caloric intake 2,854 (vegetable products 80%, animal products 20%); 128% of FAO recommended minimum requirement.

Military

Total active duty personnel (1993): 4,400[9] (army 77.3%, navy 15.9%, air force 6.8%). *Military expenditure as percentage of GNP* (1983): 5.8% (world 6.1%); per capita expenditure U.S.$1,200.

[1]A nonelective 21-member body advises the sultan on legislative matters. [2]All official documents that must be published by law in Malay are, however, also required to be issued in an official English version as well. [3]1988 metropolitan area population estimate. [4]In 1983 more than 98% of state revenue was derived from exports of oil and gas. [5]Nonagricultural sectors only. [6]GDP data. [7]Mostly unemployed. [8]Privately owned. [9]All services form part of the army.

Bulgaria

Official name: Republika Bŭlgaria (Republic of Bulgaria).
Form of government: unitary multiparty republic with one legislative body (Parliament [240]).
Chief of state: President.
Head of government: Chairman of the Council of Ministers (Premier).
Capital: Sofia.
Official language: Bulgarian.
Official religion[1]: none.
Monetary unit: 1 lev (leva) = 100 stotinki; valuation (Oct. 4, 1993) 1 U.S.$ = 26.14 leva; 1 £ = 39.60 leva.

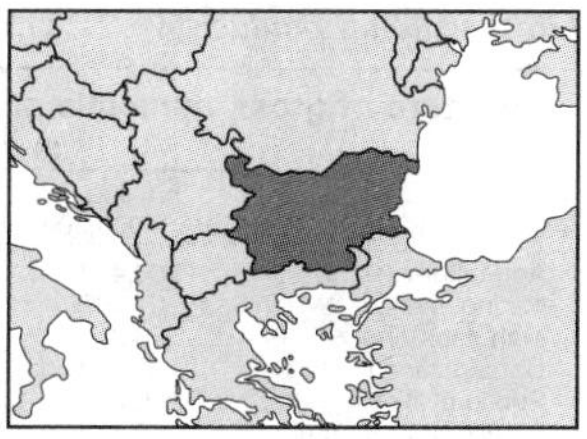

Area and population

Regions	Capitals	area sq mi	area sq km	population 1992 census
Burgas	Burgas	5,659	14,657	850,918
Khaskovo	Khaskovo	5,364	13,892	907,002
Lovech	Lovech	5,849	15,150	1,015,937
Montana (Mikhaylovgrad)	Mikhaylovgrad	4,095	10,607	630,493
Plovdiv	Plovdiv	5,262	13,628	1,218,593
Ruse (Razgrad)	Ruse	4,186	10,842	767,624
Sofiya	Sofia (Sofiya)	7,328	18,978	984,997
Varna	Varna	4,606	11,929	914,620
City Commune				
Sofiya	Sofia (Sofiya)	506	1,311	1,182,540
TOTAL		42,855	110,994	8,472,724

Demography

Population (1993): 8,465,000.
Density (1993): persons per sq mi 197.7, persons per sq km 76.3.
Urban-rural (1993): urban 67.1%; rural 32.9%.
Sex distribution (1993): male 49.14%; female 50.86%.
Age breakdown (1992): under 15, 19.8%; 15–29, 20.9%; 30–44, 21.3%; 45–59, 18.5%; 60–74, 14.8%; 75 and over, 4.7%.
Population projection: (2000) 8,383,000; (2010) 8,267,000.
Doubling time: not applicable; population is declining.
Ethnic composition (1992): Bulgarian 85.8%; Turkish 9.7%; Gypsy 3.4%; other 1.1%.
Religious affiliation (1992)[2]: Eastern Orthodox 87.0%; Muslim 12.7%; other 0.3%.
Major cities (1991): Sofia 1,140,795; Plovdiv 379,112; Varna 316,231; Burgas 211,579; Ruse 190,229.

Vital statistics

Birth rate per 1,000 population (1992): 10.5 (world avg. 26.4); (1990) legitimate 88.0%; illegitimate 12.0%.
Death rate per 1,000 population (1992): 12.7 (world avg. 9.2).
Natural increase rate per 1,000 population (1992): −2.2 (world avg. 17.2).
Total fertility rate (avg. births per childbearing woman; 1991): 1.9.
Marriage rate per 1,000 population (1991): 5.3.
Divorce rate per 1,000 population (1991): 12.3.
Life expectancy at birth (1989–91): male 68.0 years; female 74.7 years.
Major causes of death per 100,000 population (1991): diseases of the circulatory system 719.9; malignant neoplasms (cancers) 173.1; diseases of the respiratory system 92.1; accidents, poisoning, and violence 63.3; diseases of the digestive system 36.6; endocrine and metabolic disorders 17.3.

National economy

Budget (1991). Revenue: 62,967,000,000 leva (national economy 69.1%, taxes 29.9%). Expenditures: 70,476,500,000 leva (social security 28.2%, education and health 18.8%, economy 11.8%, administration and other 34.1%).
Public debt (external, outstanding; 1991): U.S.$11,923,000,000.
Tourism (1992): receipts from visitors U.S.$91,000,000.
Production (metric tons except as noted). Agriculture, forestry, fishing (1992): wheat 3,438,000, corn (maize) 1,854,000, barley 1,192,000, grapes 761,000, sunflower seeds 592,000, potatoes 568,000, tomatoes 439,000, apples 217,000; livestock (number of live animals; 1993) 4,814,000 sheep, 2,680,000 pigs, 974,000 cattle; roundwood 4,232,000 cu m; fish catch 27,000. Mining and quarrying (1992): iron ore 239,000; manganese 6,900. Manufacturing (1992): cement 2,090,000; crude steel 1,552,000; pig iron 853,000; fertilizers 690,900; paper 126,700; cotton fabrics 87,900,000 sq m; beer 4,658,000 hectolitres; wine 1,646,000 hectolitres; wearing apparel 11,711,000 pieces; refrigerators 105,400 units; television sets 60,600 units. Construction (1992): residential 1,386,000 sq m. Energy production (consumption): electricity (kW-hr; 1991) 35,587,000,000 (42,000,000,000); coal (metric tons; 1992) 30,340,000 (31,-110,000); crude petroleum (barrels; 1992) 389,000 (60,100,000[3]); petroleum products (metric tons; 1990) 6,177,000 (4,967,000); natural gas (cu m; 1992) 7,543,000 (5,263,000,000).
Household income and expenditure (1992). Average household size (1992) 2.8; income per household (1992) 34,347 leva (U.S.$1,467); sources of income (1992): wages and salaries 58.3%, transfer payments 27.3%, self-employment in agriculture 3.8%; expenditure (1992): food 38.0%, clothing 9.3%, transportation 8.5%, household durable goods 5.0%, housing 4.0%, education and culture 3.8%, health care 2.1%.
Gross national product (1992): U.S.$15,963,000,000[4] (U.S.$1,884 per capita).

Structure of gross domestic product and labour force

	1992 in value '000,000 leva[5]	% of total value[5]	labour force	% of labour force
Agriculture	20,200	10.4	324,150	13.1
Manufacturing, mining	90,800	46.6	948,530	38.3
Construction			156,223	6.3
Transp. and commun.	84,000	43.0	211,269	8.5
Trade			157,588	6.3
Public utilities, housing			47,737	1.9
Pub. admin., defense			630,778	25.4
Services			...	...
Other			2,784	0.2
TOTAL	195,000	100.0	2,479,059	100.0

Population economically active (1992): total 3,689,893; activity rate of total population 43.5% (participation rates: ages 16–59 [male], 16–54 [female] 55.6%; female 47.3%; unemployed 15.6%).

Price and earnings indexes (1985 = 100)

	1986	1987	1988	1989	1990	1991	1992
Consumer price index	103.5	103.6	104.1	106.7	132.1	579.2	1,039.1
Monthly earnings index	105.2	109.7	118.0	128.0	168.7	426.2	...

Land use (1990): forested 35.0%; meadows and pastures 18.1%; agricultural and under permanent cultivation 37.6%; other 9.3%.

Foreign trade

Balance of trade (current prices)

	1987	1988	1989	1990	1991	1992
'000,000 leva	−265.3	+489.4	+877.1	+244.6	+12,235.9	+1,049.1
% of total	1.0%	1.7%	3.3%	1.2%	11.9%	0.6%

Imports (1992): 80,595,700,000 leva (1991; machinery and equipment 38.9%; fuels, mineral raw materials, and metals 15.8%; chemical products and rubber 5.1%; consumer goods 4.4%). *Major import sources:* C.I.S. 28.6%; Germany 12.8%; Greece 5.9%; Italy 5.3%; Ukraine 5.1%.
Exports (1992): 81,644,800,000 leva (1991; machinery and equipment 30.6%; consumer goods 22.3%; food and beverages 15.3%; chemicals and rubber 10.9%; fuels, minerals, and metals 10.5%). *Major export destinations:* C.I.S. 24.9%; Germany 9.9%; Turkey 5.7%; Italy 5.2%; Poland 2.3%; United States 1.6%.

Transport and communications

Transport. Railroads (1992): track length 4,076 mi, 6,560 km; passenger-mi 3,351,000,000, passenger-km 5,393,000,000; short ton-mi cargo 5,314,000,000, metric ton-km cargo 7,758,000,000. Roads (1992): length 22,943 mi, 36,922 km (paved 92%). Vehicles (1990): cars 1,300,000; trucks and buses 200,000. Merchant marine (1992): vessels (100 gross tons and over) 222; deadweight tonnage 1,962,345. Air transport (1992): passenger-mi 1,863,000,000, passenger-km 2,999,000,000; short ton-mi cargo 29,000,000, metric ton-km cargo 43,000,000; airports (1993) with scheduled flights 3[6].
Communications. Daily newspapers (1988): total number 17; total circulation 2,396,000; circulation per 1,000 population 267. Radio (1993): 2,917,000 receivers (1 per 2.9 persons). Television (1992): 3,127,000 receivers (1 per 2.7 persons). Telephones (1993): 2,838,800 (1 per 3.0 persons).

Education and health

Education (1992–93)

	schools	teachers	students	student/ teacher ratio
Primary (age 6–14) / Secondary (age 15–17)	3,403	72,393	1,027,457	14.2
Voc., teacher tr.	512	18,760	224,246	11.9
Higher	87	21,976	192,270	8.7

Educational attainment (1983). Percentage of employed population having: postsecondary vocational certificate 15.6%; 4-year college 7.5%. *Literacy* (1980): total population age 15 and over literate 95.5%.
Health (1992): physicians 27,117 (1 per 312 persons); hospital beds 87,010 (1 per 97 persons); infant mortality rate per 1,000 live births 15.9.
Food (1987–89): daily per capita caloric intake 3,695 (vegetable products 75%, animal products 25%); 148% of FAO recommended minimum requirement.

Military

Total active duty personnel (1992): 107,000 (army 70.1%, navy 9.3%, air force 20.6%). *Military expenditure as percentage of GNP* (1991): 7.0% (world 5.0%); per capita expenditure U.S.$199.

[1]Bulgaria has no official religion; the 1991 constitution, however, refers to Eastern Orthodoxy as being the "traditional" religion. [2]Census data reflect the traditional religious identity of Bulgaria but apparently disregard the nonreligious, who may exceed half the adult population. [3]1990. [4]External estimates vary widely. [5]Data are based on estimates. [6]International only; the number of domestic airports is not available.

Burkina Faso

Official name: Burkina Faso (Burkina Faso).
Form of government: multiparty republic with one legislative house (National Assembly [107])[1].
Chief of state: President.
Head of government: Prime Minister.
Capital: Ouagadougou.
Official language: French.
Official religion: none.
Monetary unit: 1 CFA franc (CFAF) = 100 centimes; valuation (Oct. 4, 1993) 1 U.S.$ = CFAF 283.25; 1 £ = CFAF 429.12.

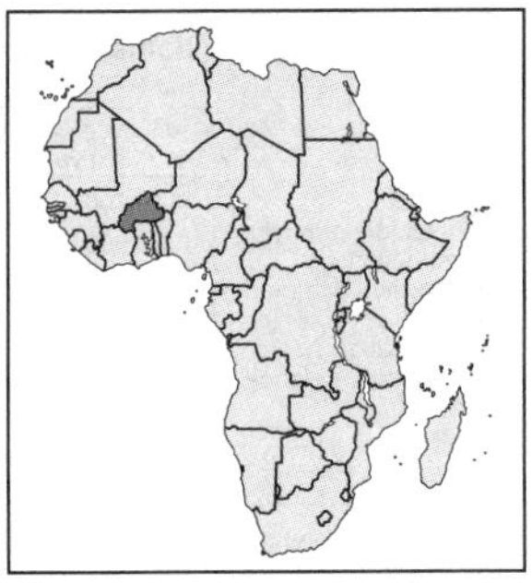

Area and population		area		population
				1985
Provinces	Capitals	sq mi	sq km	census
Bam	Kongoussi	1,551	4,017	162,575
Bazéga	Kombissiri	2,051	5,313	303,941
Bougouriba	Diébougou	2,736	7,087	220,895
Boulgou	Tenkodogo	3,488	9,033	402,236
Boulkiemde	Koudougou	1,598	4,138	365,223
Comoé	Banfora	7,102	18,393	249,967
Ganzourgou	Zorgho	1,578	4,087	195,652
Gnagna	Bogandé	3,320	8,600	229,152
Gourma	Fada N'Gourma	10,275	26,613	294,235
Houet	Bobo-Dioulasso	6,438	16,672	581,722
Kadiogo	Ouagadougou	451	1,169	459,826
Kénédougou	Orodara	3,207	8,307	139,973
Kossi	Nouna	5,088	13,177	332,960
Kouritenga	Koupéla	628	1,627	198,486
Mouhoun	Dédougou	4,032	10,442	288,735
Nahouri	Pô	1,484	3,843	105,509
Namentenga	Boulsa	2,994	7,755	198,890
Oubritenga	Ziniaré	1,812	4,693	304,265
Oudalan	Gorom Gorom	3,879	10,046	106,194
Passoré	Yako	1,575	4,078	223,830
Poni	Gaoua	4,000	10,361	235,480
Sanguie	Réo	1,994	5,165	217,277
Sanmatenga	Kaya	3,557	9,213	367,724
Sèno	Dori	5,202	13,473	228,905
Sissili	Léo	5,303	13,736	244,919
Soum	Djibo	5,154	13,350	186,812
Sourou	Tougan	3,663	9,487	268,108
Tapoa	Diapaga	5,707	14,780	158,859
Yatenga	Ouahigouya	4,746	12,292	536,578
Zoundwéogo	Manga	1,333	3,453	155,777
TOTAL		105,946	274,400	7,964,705

Demography

Population (1993): 9,780,000.
Density (1993): persons per sq mi 92.3, persons per sq km 35.6.
Urban-rural (1988): urban 8.6%; rural 91.4%.
Sex distribution (1990): male 48.10%; female 51.90%.
Age breakdown (1990): under 15, 49.1%; 15–29, 23.6%; 30–44, 13.3%; 45–59, 8.3%; 60–74, 4.5%; 75 and over, 1.2%.
Population projection: (2000) 11,884,000; (2010) 15,549,000.
Doubling time: 23 years.
Ethnic composition (1983): Mossi 47.9%; Mande 8.8%; Fulani 8.3%; Lobi 6.9%; Bobo 6.8%; Senufo 5.3%; Grosi 5.1%; Gurma 4.8%; Tuareg 3.3%; other 2.8%.
Religious affiliation (1980): traditional beliefs 44.8%; Muslim 43.0%; Christian 12.2%, of which Roman Catholic 9.8%, Protestant 2.4%.
Major cities (1985): Ouagadougou 441,514; Bobo-Dioulasso 228,668; Koudougou 51,926; Ouahigouya 38,902; Banfora 35,319.

Vital statistics

Birth rate per 1,000 population (1990–95): 47.0 (world avg. 26.4).
Death rate per 1,000 population (1990–95): 17.1 (world avg. 9.2).
Natural increase rate per 1,000 population (1990–95): 29.9 (world avg. 17.2).
Total fertility rate (avg. births per childbearing woman; 1990–95): 6.5.
Life expectancy at birth (1990–95): male 47.6 years; female 50.9 years.
Major causes of morbidity (percentage of reported cases of infectious disease; 1984): measles 39.6%; malaria 12.4%; tetanus 5.7%; diarrheal diseases 5.3%.

National economy

Budget (1991). Revenue: CFAF 154,420,000,000 (1990; import duties 32.4%; sales taxes 26.7%; personal income taxes 11.1%; administrative fees 2.3%). Expenditures: CFAF 176,862,000,000 (1990; education 19.4%; defense 16.9%; debt service 16.6%; health 7.2%; agriculture 5.1%).
Production (metric tons except as noted). Agriculture, forestry, fishing (1992): sorghum 1,179,000, millet 785,000, sugarcane 340,000, corn (maize) 310,000, seed cotton 250,000, pulses 120,000, peanuts (groundnuts) 110,000, rice 49,000, sweet potatoes 24,000, sesame 8,000, cassava 5,000; livestock (number of live animals) 6,860,000 goats, 5,350,000 sheep, 4,096,000 cattle, 18,000,000 chickens; roundwood (1991) 8,995,000 cu m; fish catch (1991) 7,012. Mining and quarrying (1988): manganese 15,000; phosphates 3,000; gold 3,049 kg[2]. Manufacturing (1990): wheat flour 23,000; soap 14,500; cotton yarn 300; bicycle and motorcycle tires 3,483,000 units; motorcycles and bicycles 63,000 units; footwear 470,000 pairs; beer 350,000 hectolitres; soft drinks 108,000 hectolitres. Construction (value added in CFAF; 1987): 2,800,000,000. Energy production (consumption): electricity (kW-hr; 1991) 157,000,000 (157,000,000); crude petroleum, none (n.a.); petroleum products (metric tons; 1991) none (182,000).

Gross national product (1992): U.S.$2,863,000,000 (U.S.$300 per capita).

Structure of gross domestic product and labour force	1987		1985	
	in value CFAF '000,000	% of total value	labour force	% of labour force
Agriculture	200,479	45.8	3,739,000	92.3
Mining	89	0.1		
Manufacturing	63,216	14.5	113,000	2.8
Construction	2,800	0.6		
Public utilities	6,645	1.5		
Transp. and commun.	19,349	4.4		
Finance	18,862	4.3		
Trade	53,801	12.3	199,000	4.9
Pub. admin., defense	65,226	14.9		
Services	...	...		
Other	6,865	1.6	...	...
TOTAL	437,332	100.0	4,051,000	100.0

Tourism: receipts (1991) U.S.$8,000,000; expenditures U.S.$34,000,000.
Public debt (external, outstanding; 1991): U.S.$871,000,000.
Population economically active: total (1985) 4,051,000; activity rate 51.0% (participation rates: over age 15, 83.0%; female 49.1%; unemployed 0.9%).

Price and earnings indexes (1985 = 100)	1986	1987	1988	1989	1990	1991
Consumer price index	97.4	94.8	98.6	98.8	97.8	102.5[3]
Hourly earnings index[4]	100.0	100.0	114.0	114.6	114.6	114.6

Household income and expenditure. Average household size (1985) 6.2; average annual income per household CFAF 303,000 (U.S.$640); sources of income: n.a.; expenditure (1985)[5]: food 38.7%; transportation 18.6%; electricity and fuel 13.7%; beverages 9.0%; health 5.2%; housing 5.1%.
Land use (1991): forested 23.9%; meadows and pastures 36.5%; agricultural and under permanent cultivation 13.0%; other 26.6%.

Foreign trade

Balance of trade (current prices)	1985	1986	1987	1988	1989	1990
CFAF '000,000	−82.91	−80.25	−55.23	−63.31	−91.40	−78.70
% of total	57.1%	58.3%	37.2%	43.0%	39.9%	32.2%

Imports (1990): CFAF 145,833,000,000 (manufactured goods 26.6%; machinery and transport equipment 24.1%, of which road transport equipment 8.6%, electrical machinery 6.2%; chemicals 14.3%; petroleum products 11.2%; cereals 6.4%; dairy products 3.3%; raw materials 2.1%; beverages and tobacco 2.0%). *Major import sources:* France 30.5%; Côte d'Ivoire 29.9%; Italy 4.7%; Japan 4.0%; Germany 3.3%; The Netherlands 3.1%.
Exports (1990): CFAF 41,282,000,000 (raw cotton 56.7%; manufactured goods 23.2%; hides and skins 7.4%; live animals 6.6%). *Major export destinations:* France 29.5%; Taiwan 12.9%; Portugal 8.2%; Italy 7.6%; Japan 5.7%; Tunisia 5.0%.

Transport and communications

Transport. Railroads (1984)[6]: route length[7] 308 mi, 495 km; passenger-km 679,790,000; metric ton-km cargo 469,675,000. Roads (1991): total length 8,161 mi, 13,134 km (paved 12%[8]). Vehicles (1990): passenger cars 12,000; trucks and buses 13,000. Merchant marine: none. Air transport (1989): passenger-km 254,000,000; metric ton-mi cargo 18,000,000; airports (1993) 2.
Communications. Daily newspapers (1992): total number 3; total circulation 17,000; circulation per 1,000 population 1.8. Radio (1992): 200,000 receivers (1 per 47 persons). Television (1992): 45,500 receivers (1 per 209 persons). Telephones (1988): 15,000 (1 per 569 persons).

Education and health

Education (1989–90)	schools	teachers	students	student/ teacher ratio
Primary	2,362	8,572	472,979	55.2
Secondary	113[9]	1,700[9]	82,931	33.7[9]
Vocational	18[8]	341	8,055	23.6
Higher	1[8]	205	5,675	27.7

Educational attainment. Percentage of population age 10 and over having: no formal schooling 86.1%; some primary 7.3%; general secondary 2.2%; specialized secondary and postsecondary 3.8%; other 0.6%. *Literacy* (1990): percentage of total population age 15 and over literate 18.2%; males 27.9%; females 8.9%.
Health: physicians (1988) 280 (1 per 29,914 persons); hospital beds (1984) 5,580 (1 per 1,359 persons); infant mortality rate (1990–95) 127.0.
Food (1988–90): daily per capita caloric intake 2,219 (vegetable products 96%, animal products 4%); 94% of FAO recommended minimum requirement.

Military

Total active duty personnel (1993): 7,200 (army 97.2%, navy, none, air force 2.8%). *Military expenditure as percentage of GNP* (1988): 2.7% (world 5.0%); per capita expenditure U.S.$7.

[1]Ruling political party defeated a fragmented opposition (26 other political parties) at multiparty legislative elections of May 1992. [2]Officially marketed gold only; does not include substantial illegal production. [3]Third quarter. [4]January 1; index refers to the *S.M.I.G.* (*salaire minimum interprofessionnel guaranti*), a form of minimum professional wage. [5]Weights of consumer price index components; Ouagadougou only. [6]Passenger-km and metric ton-km cargo figures are based on traffic between Abidjan, Côte d'Ivoire, and Ouagadougou. [7]1989. [8]1986. [9]1987–88.

Burundi

Official name: Republika y'u Burundi (Rundi); République du Burundi (French) (Republic of Burundi).
Form of government: unitary multiparty republic[1] with one legislative house (National Assembly [81]).
Head of state and government: President assisted by Prime Minister.
Capital: Bujumbura.
Official languages: Rundi; French.
Official religion: none.
Monetary unit: 1 Burundi franc (FBu) = 100 centimes; valuation (Oct. 4, 1993) 1 U.S.$ = FBu 244.49; 1 £ = FBu 370.40.

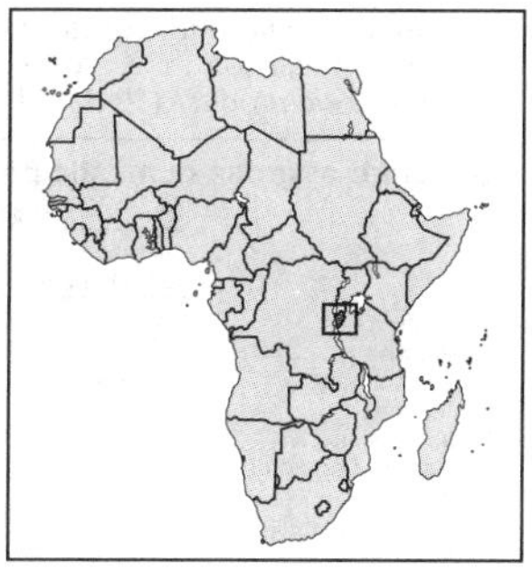

Area and population

Provinces	Capitals	area sq mi	area sq km	population 1990 census
Bubanza	Bubanza	420	1,089	222,953
Bujumbura	Bujumbura	509	1,319	608,931
Bururi	Bururi	952	2,465	385,490
Cankuzo	Cankuzo	759	1,965	142,707
Cibitoke	Cibitoke	631	1,636	279,843
Gitega	Gitega	764	1,979	565,174
Karuzi	Karuzi	563	1,457	287,905
Kayanza	Kayanza	476	1,233	443,116
Kirundo	Kirundo	658	1,703	401,103
Makamba	Makamba	757	1,960	223,799
Muramvya	Muramvya	593	1,535	441,653
Muyinga	Muyinga	709	1,836	373,382
Ngozi	Ngozi	569	1,474	482,246
Rutana	Rutana	756	1,959	195,834
Ruyigi	Ruyigi	903	2,339	238,567
TOTAL LAND AREA		10,019	25,949	
INLAND WATER		721	1,867	
TOTAL		10,740	27,816	5,292,793[2]

Demography

Population (1993): 5,665,000.
Density (1992)[3]: persons per sq mi 565.4, persons per sq km 218.3.
Urban-rural (1990): urban 6.3%; rural 93.7%.
Sex distribution (1990): male 48.63%; female 51.37%.
Age breakdown (1990): under 15, 46.4%; 15–29, 25.3%; 30–44, 15.4%; 45–59, 7.0%; 60–74, 4.0%; 75 and over, 1.7%; not determined 0.2%.
Population projection: (2000) 6,674,000; (2010) 8,437,000.
Doubling time: 22 years.
Ethnic composition (1983): Rundi 97.4%, of which Hutu 81.9%, Tutsi 13.5%; Twa Pygmy 1.0%; other 1.6%.
Religious affiliation (1990): Roman Catholic 65.1%; nonreligious 18.6%; Protestant 13.8%; Muslim 1.6%; traditional beliefs 0.3%; other 0.6%.
Major cities (1990): Bujumbura 236,334; Gitega 20,708; Bururi 15,816; Ngozi 14,511; Cibitoke 8,280.

Vital statistics

Birth rate per 1,000 population (1991): 47.0 (world avg. 26.4).
Death rate per 1,000 population (1991): 15.0 (world avg. 9.2).
Natural increase rate per 1,000 population (1991): 32.0 (world avg. 17.2).
Total fertility rate (avg. births per childbearing woman; 1991): 6.9.
Marriage rate per 1,000 population: n.a.
Divorce rate per 1,000 population: n.a.
Life expectancy at birth (1991): male 50.0 years; female 54.0 years.
Major causes of death (percentage of reported deaths from infectious diseases, 1990)[4]: diarrheal diseases 32.4%; malaria 25.2%; AIDS 17.6%; measles 13.4%; pulmonary tuberculosis 5.6%.

National economy

Budget (1992). Revenue: FBu 40,123,600,000 (customs duties 25.2%, excise duties 15.7%, income tax 13.9%, property tax 9.3%, administrative receipts 4.1%). Expenditures: FBu 41,333,600,000 (goods and services 53.8%, subsidies and transfers 19.9%, public debt 13.4%).
Public debt (external, outstanding; 1991): U.S.$898,000,000.
Tourism (1990): receipts from visitors U.S.$4,000,000; expenditures by nationals abroad U.S.$16,000,000.
Production (metric tons except as noted). Agriculture, forestry, fishing (1991): bananas 1,585,000, sweet potatoes 680,000, cassava 583,600, dry beans 338,300, corn (maize) 171,800, yams and taros 145,400, pumpkins 67,500, sorghum 65,200, potatoes 45,500, rice 40,200, coffee 34,200, palm kernels 14,500, peanuts (groundnuts) 13,900, millet 13,400, wheat 8,800, sugarcane 8,100; livestock (number of live animals) 930,000 goats, 435,000 cattle, 365,000 sheep, 4,000,000 chickens; roundwood 4,343,000 cu m; fish catch (1990) 17,395. Mining and quarrying (1990): peat 11,984; kaolin clay 5,281; lime 188; gold 289 troy oz. Manufacturing (1992): beer 1,161,551 hectolitres; carbonated beverages 159,914 hectolitres; cigarettes 452,390,000 units; blankets 196,212 units; footwear 450,567 pairs. Construction: n.a. Energy production (consumption): electricity (kW-hr; 1992) 99,600,000 (142,500,000); coal, none (n.a.); crude petroleum, none (n.a.); petroleum products (metric tons; 1991) none (72,000); natural gas, none (n.a.); peat (metric tons; 1991) 10,000 (10,000).
Land use (1990): forested 2.6%; meadows and pastures 35.6%; agricultural and under permanent cultivation 52.2%; other 9.6%.

Gross national product (at current market prices; 1991): U.S.$1,210,000,000 (U.S.$210 per capita).

Structure of gross domestic product and labour force

	1991 in value FBu '000,000[5]	1991 % of total value	1979 labour force	1979 % of labour force
Agriculture	105,535.5	48.5	2,246,200	93.1
Mining	2,217.5	1.0	1,400	0.1
Public utilities			1,700	0.1
Manufacturing	26,160.5	12.0	36,700	1.5
Construction	8,922.5	4.1	14,700	0.6
Transportation and communications	6,650.8	3.1	6,400	0.2
Trade	19,770.6	9.1	20,900	0.9
Finance	...	...	1,300	0.1
Pub. admin., defense	24,084.6	11.1	5,700	0.2
Services	3,844.4	1.8	75,000	3.1
Other	20,362.4	9.3	3,100	0.1
TOTAL	217,548.8	100.0	2,413,100	100.0

Population economically active (1991): total 2,779,777; activity rate of total population 52.9% (participation rates: ages 15–64, 91.4%; female 52.6%; unemployed, n.a.).

Price and earnings indexes (1985 = 100)

	1986	1987	1988	1989	1990	1991	1992[6]
Consumer price index	101.8	109.3	114.0	127.3	136.3	148.5	157.2
Monthly earnings index[7]	100.5	101.8	...	...	...	...	...

Household income and expenditure. Average household size (1990) 4.6; income per household: n.a.; sources of income: n.a.; expenditure[8]: food 59.6%, clothing and footwear 11.1%, furniture and household goods 6.0%, energy and water 5.8%, housing 4.4%, other 13.1%.

Foreign trade[9]

Balance of trade (current prices)

	1986	1987	1988	1989	1990	1991
FBu '000,000	−864	−12,273	−7,136	−13,719	−26,583	−28,144
% of total	2.2%	37.0%	16.6%	35.8%	51.0%	45.8%

Imports (1991): FBu 44,786,500,000 (machinery and transport equipment 34.9%, food and food products 11.6%, mineral oil 11.0%, construction materials 6.0%). *Major import sources:* Belgium-Luxembourg 14.5%; Iran 11.0%; France 9.8%; Japan 8.4%; Germany 8.2%; China 5.9%; Italy 3.6%.
Exports (1991): FBu 16,642,900,000 (coffee 81.0%, tea 9.1%, animal hides and skins 2.6%, cotton fabric 1.5%). *Major export destinations* (1990): Germany 13.7%; United States 11.7%; France 9.6%; United Kingdom 7.3%; Finland 6.2%; Zaire 3.2%; Kenya 2.2%.

Transport and communications

Transport. Railroads: none. Roads (1991): total length 3,893 mi, 6,265 km (paved 16%). Vehicles (1991): passenger cars 13,696; trucks and other vehicles 14,027. Merchant marine (1979): vessels (100 gross tons and over) 1; total gross tonnage 385. Air transport (1991)[10]: passenger arrivals 34,907, departures 34,375; cargo loaded 1,780 short tons (1,615 metric tons), unloaded 4,151 short tons (3,766 metric tons); airports (1993) with scheduled flights 1.
Communications. Daily newspapers (1992): total number 1; total circulation 20,000; circulation per 1,000 population 3.5. Radio (1992): total number of receivers 500,000 (1 per 11 persons). Television (1992): total number of receivers 4,500 (1 per 1,257 persons). Telephones (1991): 10,857 (1 per 506 persons).

Education and health

Education (1990–91)

	schools	teachers	students	student/ teacher ratio
Primary (age 6–11)	1,342	9,465	633,153	66.9
Secondary (age 12–18)	113	2,026	44,207	21.8
Higher	8	436	3,884	8.9

Educational attainment: n.a. *Literacy* (1990): percentage of total population age 7 and over literate 3,934,806 (74.3%); males literate 1,897,284 (73.7%); females literate 2,037,522 (74.9%).
Health (1990): physicians 168 (1 per 31,777 persons); hospital beds 10,370 (1 per 515 persons); infant mortality rate per 1,000 live births 111.0.
Food (1988–90): daily per capita caloric intake 1,948 (vegetable products 98%, animal products 2%); 84% of FAO recommended minimum requirement.

Military

Total active duty personnel (1991): 5,700 (army 96.5%, navy 0.9%, air force 2.6%). *Military expenditure as percentage of GNP* (1989): 2.6% (world 4.9%); per capita expenditure U.S.$5.

[1]A multiparty political system was approved by constitutional amendment of March 1992; presidential elections were held on June 1, 1993, and legislative elections on June 29, 1993. [2]Detail does not add to total given because of rounding. [3]Based on land area. [4]Data shown is for five provinces only. [5]Estimate. [6]November. [7]Nonagricultural employees in Bujumbura only; includes family allowances. [8]Weights of consumer price index components. [9]Import figures are f.o.b. in balance of trade and c.i.f. in commodities and trading partners. [10]Figures for Bujumbura airport only.

Cambodia

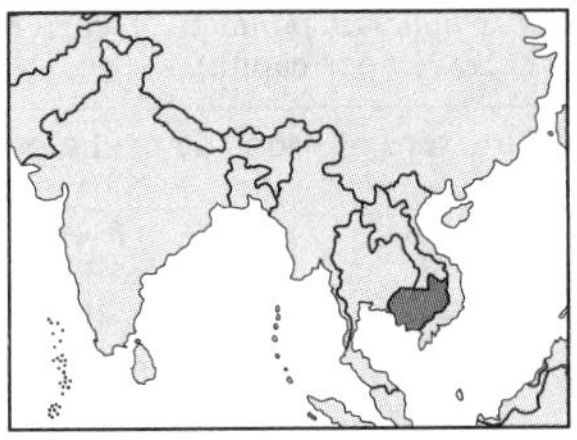

Official name: Preah Reach Ana Pak Kampuchea (Kingdom of Cambodia)[1].
Form of government: constitutional monarchy with one legislative house (National Assembly [120]).
Chief of state: King.
Head of government: Prime Minister.
Capital: Phnom Penh.
Official language: Khmer.
Official religion: Buddhism.
Monetary unit: 1 riel = 100 sen; valuation (Oct. 4, 1993) 1 U.S.$ = 3,500 riels; 1 £ = 5,320 riels.

Area and population

		area		population
Provinces	Capitals	sq mi	sq km	1987 estimate
Bântéay Méanchey	...	[2]	[2]	[2]
Bătdâmbâng	Bătdâmbâng	7,353[2]	19,044[2]	837,000[2]
Kâmpóng Cham	Kâmpóng Cham	4,053	10,498	1,244,000
Kâmpóng Chhnăng	Kâmpóng Chhnăng	2,131	5,520	257,000
Kâmpóng Saôm	Kâmpóng Saôm	27	69	61,000
Kâmpóng Spoe	Kâmpóng Spoe	2,709	7,016	396,000
Kâmpóng Thum	Kâmpóng Thum	4,730	12,251	441,000
Kâmpôt	Kâmpôt	3,808	9,862	412,000
Kândal	...	1,472	3,813	838,000
Kaôh Kŏng	Krŏng Kaôh Kŏng	4,301	11,140	30,000
Krâchéh	Krâchéh	4,283	11,094	182,000
Môndól Kiri	Senmonorom	5,517	14,288	18,000
Ŏtdâr Méanchey	...	[3]	[3]	[3]
Phnom Penh	Phnom Penh	18	46	564,000
Poŭthĭsăt	Poŭthĭsăt	4,900	12,692	204,000
Preăh Vihéar	Phnum Tbéng Meanchey	5,541	14,350	80,000
Prey Vêng	Prey Vêng	1,885	4,883	782,000
Rôtânôkiri	Lumphăt	4,163	10,782	52,000
Siĕmréab	Siĕmréab	4,207[3]	10,897[3]	555,000[3]
Stŏeng Trêng	Stŏeng Trêng	4,328	11,209	46,000
Svay Riĕng	Svay Riĕng	1,145	2,966	340,000
Takêv	Takêv	1,474	3,818	618,000
TOTAL LAND AREA		68,045	176,238	
INLAND WATER		2,192	5,678	
TOTAL		70,238[4]	181,916	7,957,000

Demography

Population (1993): 9,287,000.
Density (1993)[5]: persons per sq mi 136.5, persons per sq km 52.7.
Urban-rural (1990): urban 12.0%; rural 88.0%.
Sex distribution (1990): male 50%; female 50%.
Age breakdown (1990): under 15, 34.9%; 15–29, 29.6%; 30–44, 21.0%; 45–59, 9.6%; 60–74, 4.3%; 75 and over, 0.6%.
Population projection: (2000) 10,942,000; (2010) 13,402,000.
Doubling time: 28 years.
Ethnic composition (1979): Khmer 94.1%; Chinese 3.1%; Cham 2.3%; other (Thai, Lao, Kola, and Vietnamese) 0.5%. Estimates of Vietnamese in the early 1990s ranged from 120,000 to as many as 3,000,000.
Religious affiliation (1980): Buddhist 88.4%; Muslim 2.4%; other 9.2%.
Major cities (1987): Phnom Penh 800,000[6]; Bătdâmbâng 45,000; Kâmpóng Cham 33,000; Pursat 16,000; Kâmpóng Chhnăng 15,000.

Vital statistics

Birth rate per 1,000 population (1993): 40 (world avg. 26.4); legitimate, n.a.; illegitimate, n.a.
Death rate per 1,000 population (1993): 15 (world avg. 9.2).
Natural increase rate per 1,000 population (1993): 25 (world avg. 17.2).
Total fertility rate (avg. births per childbearing woman; 1993): 4.6.
Marriage rate per 1,000 population: n.a.
Divorce rate per 1,000 population: n.a.
Life expectancy at birth (1993): male 49 years; female 52 years.
Major causes of death per 100,000 population (registered deaths only; 1966): tuberculosis of the respiratory system 154; all accidents other than vehicle accidents 111; malaria 55; pneumonia 51.

National economy

Budget (1990). Revenue: international assistance 40.0%; state enterprises 25.0%; taxes 25.0%, of which import duties 17.5%, commerce 7.0%; other national sources 10.0%. Expenditures: n.a.
Public debt (external, outstanding; 1988): U.S.$704,000,000[7].
Production (metric tons except as noted). Agriculture, forestry, fishing (1992): rice 2,254,000, sugarcane 240,000, bananas 122,000, roots and tubers 117,000 (of which cassava 64,000, sweet potatoes 37,000), corn (maize) 50,000, dry beans 47,000, rubber 35,000, soybeans 18,000; livestock (number of live animals) 2,274,000 cattle, 1,729,000 pigs, 794,000 buffalo, 12,000,000 poultry; roundwood (1991) 6,387,000 cu m (the Khmer Rouge market additional quantities to Thai logging companies in areas they control); fish catch (1991) 110,100. Mining and quarrying (1993): legal mining is confined to fertilizers, salt, and construction materials; smuggling of gemstones from Khmer Rouge-controlled areas is believed extensive. Manufacturing (value of production in '000,000 riels; 1988): cigarettes 1,064.5; food 116.9; chemical products (including rubber) 83.5; light industries (including textiles) 63.2; mechanical equipment and parts 46.8; building materials 4.5. Construction: n.a. Energy production (consumption): electricity (kW-hr; 1991) 70,000,000 (70,000,000); coal, none (n.a.); crude petroleum, none (n.a.); petroleum products (metric tons; 1991) none (151,000); natural gas, none (n.a.).

Household income and expenditure. Average household size (1980) 5.6; income per household: n.a.; sources of income: n.a.; expenditure: n.a.
Gross domestic product (1991): U.S.$930,000,000 (U.S.$130 per capita).

Structure of gross domestic product and labour force

	1966		1989	
	in value '000,000 riels	% of total value	labour force	% of labour force
Agriculture	13,100	40.9	2,632,000	70.4
Mining and manufacturing	3,300	10.3		
Construction	1,700	5.3		
Public utilities	400	1.3		
Transp. and commun.	700	2.2	1,104,000	29.6
Trade	7,300	22.8		
Public admin., defense	3,900	12.2		
Services	1,600	5.0		
TOTAL	32,000	100.0	3,736,000	100.0

Population economically active (1992): total 3,964,000; activity rate of total population 43.1% (participation rates: ages 16–60, 91.2%; female 55.7%; unemployed, n.a.).

Price and earnings indexes (1970 = 100)

	1967	1968	1969	1970	1971	1972	1973
Consumer price index	79.5	84.1	89.4	100.0	172.0	215.2	556.1
Earnings index	...	...	...	...	...	...	...

Land use (1991): forested 75.8%; meadows and pastures 3.3%; agricultural and under permanent cultivation 17.4%; other 3.5%.
Tourism (1989): total number of tourist arrivals 3,272.

Foreign trade

Balance of trade (current prices)

	1983	1984	1985	1986	1987	1988
U.S.$'000,000	−96	−98	−105	...	...	−115
% of total	88.2%	87.1%	80.9%	...	...	64.2%

Imports (1988): U.S.$147,000,000 (1985; machinery and transport equipment 36.9%, of which transport equipment 10.9%; petroleum and petroleum products 30.2%; woven cotton fabrics 3.6%; synthetic fabrics 2.5%; cotton yarn 2.3%; basic manufactures 1.5%; chemicals 1.2%). *Major import sources* (1985): U.S.S.R. 93.5%; Japan 1.5%; France 1.1%; Australia 1.1%; United Kingdom 0.6%.
Exports (1988): U.S.$32,000,000 (1985; rubber 82.9%; basic manufactures 5.1%; miscellaneous manufactured articles 3.0%). *Major export destinations* (1985): U.S.S.R. 88.2%; United States 2.9%; Japan 2.9%.

Transport and communications

Transport. Railroads (1988): length 403 mi, 649 km; passenger-mi 33,554,000[8], passenger-km 54,000,000[8]; short ton-mi cargo 6,850,000[8], metric ton-km cargo 10,000,000[8]. Roads (1989): total length 9,200 mi, 14,800 km (paved 18%). Vehicles (1988): passenger cars 4,000; trucks and buses 7,100. Merchant marine (1992): vessels (100 gross tons and over) 3; total deadweight tonnage 3,839. Air transport (1977): passenger-mi 26,098,800, passenger-km 42,000,000; short ton-mi cargo 274,000, metric ton-km cargo 400,000; airports (1993) with scheduled flights 6.
Communications. Daily newspapers (1991): total number 1; total circulation 25,000; circulation per 1,000 population 2.8. Radio (1992): 800,000 receivers (1 per 11 persons). Television (1992): 70,000 receivers (1 per 128 persons). Telephones (1991): 2,900[9] (1 per 3,300 persons).

Education and health

Education (1992–93)

	schools	teachers	students	student/ teacher ratio
Primary (age 6–10)	4,539	42,405	1,465,958	35.6
Secondary (age 11–16)	440	19,540	239,363	12.2
Voc., teacher tr.	65	2,618	15,537	5.9
Higher	9	268	22,182	82.8

Educational attainment: n.a. *Literacy* (1987): total population age 15 and over literate 3,778,042 (74.3%); males literate 2,001,084 (85.0%); females literate 1,776,958 (65.0%).
Health (1988): physicians 303 (1 per 27,000 persons); hospital beds 12,953[10] (1 per 632[10] persons); infant mortality rate per 1,000 live births (1989) 131.
Food (1986–88): daily per capita caloric intake 2,174 (vegetable products 95%, animal products 5%); 81% of FAO recommended minimum requirement.

Military

Total active duty personnel (1993): 102,000[11] (army 49.0%, navy 1.0%, air force 1.0%, provincial 49.0%). Armed Khmer Rouge guerrillas may number 10,000–12,000. About 22,000 UNTAC[1] troops were withdrawn after civilian government was reestablished in 1993. *Military expenditure as percentage of GNP:* n.a.; per capita expenditure, n.a.

[1]The United Nations Transitional Authority in Cambodia (UNTAC) assumed administrative responsibility for Cambodia in March 1992. Cambodian sovereignty, however, was retained by a Supreme National Council (SNC) until UN-supervised elections were held May 23–29, 1993. The Kingdom of Cambodia was proclaimed from Sept. 24, 1993. [2]Bântéay Méanchey included in Bătdâmbâng. [3]Ŏtdâr Méanchey included in Siĕmréab. [4]Detail does not add to total given because of rounding. [5]Based on land area. [6]1989. [7]Includes long-term debt not guaranteed by the government. [8]1981. [9]Number of telephone lines. [10]Public hospitals only. [11]Figures include provincial, and exclude paramilitary, forces.

Cameroon

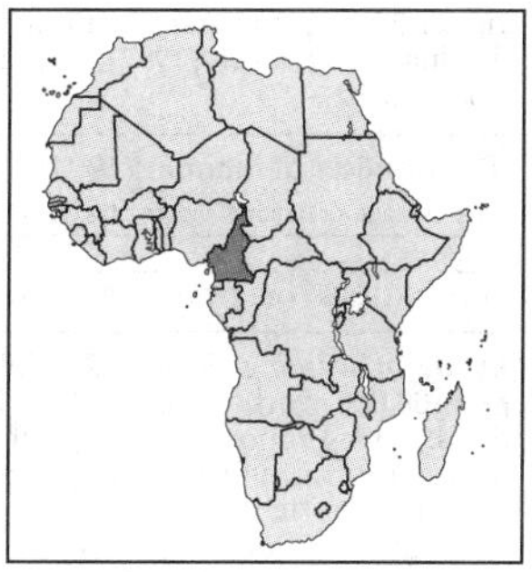

Official name: République du Cameroun (French); Republic of Cameroon (English).
Form of government: unitary multiparty republic with one legislative house (National Assembly [180]).
Chief of state: President.
Head of government: Prime Minister.
Capital: Yaoundé.
Official languages: French; English.
Official religion: none.
Monetary unit: 1 CFA franc (CFAF) = 100 centimes; valuation (Oct. 4, 1993) 1 U.S.$ = CFAF 283.25; 1 £ = CFAF 429.12.

Area and population

Provinces	Capitals	area sq mi	area sq km	population 1987 census
Adamoua	Ngaoundéré	24,591	63,691	495,200
Centre	Yaoundé	26,613	68,926	1,651,600
Est	Bertoua	42,089	109,011	517,200
Extrême-Nord	Maroua	13,223	34,246	1,855,700
Littoral	Douala	7,814	20,239	1,354,800
Nord	Garoua	25,319	65,576	832,200
Nord-Ouest	Bamenda	6,877	17,810	1,237,400
Ouest	Bafoussam	5,356	13,872	1,339,800
Sud	Ebolowa	18,189	47,110	373,800
Sud-Ouest	Buea	9,448	24,471	838,000
LAND AREA		179,519	464,952	
INLAND WATER		4,051	10,492	
TOTAL		183,569[1]	475,442[1]	10,495,700

Demography

Population (1993): 13,103,000.
Density (1993)[2]: persons per sq mi 73.2, persons per sq km 28.3.
Urban-rural (1990): urban 41.2%; rural 58.8%.
Sex distribution (1991): male 49.88%; female 50.12%.
Age breakdown (1991): under 15, 46.4%; 15–29, 24.4%; 30–44, 15.1%; 45–59, 8.6%; 60 and over, 5.5%.
Population projection: (2000) 16,701,000; (2010) 23,665,000.
Doubling time: 21 years.
Ethnic composition (1983): Fang 19.6%; Bamileke and Bamum 18.5%; Duala, Luanda, and Basa 14.7%; Fulani 9.6%; Tikar 7.4%; Mandara 5.7%; Maka 4.9%; Chamba 2.4%; Mbum 1.3%; Hausa 1.2%; French 0.2%; other 14.5%.
Religious affiliation (1990): Roman Catholic 34.7%; animist 26.0%; Muslim 21.8%; Protestant 17.5%.
Major cities (1987): Douala 810,000; Yaoundé 649,000; Garoua 142,000; Maroua 123,000; Bafoussam 113,000.

Vital statistics

Birth rate per 1,000 population (1990–95): 47.3 (world avg. 26.4).
Death rate per 1,000 population (1990–95): 13.3 (world avg. 9.2).
Natural increase rate per 1,000 population (1990–95): 34.0 (world avg. 17.2).
Total fertility rate (avg. births per childbearing woman; 1990–95): 6.9.
Life expectancy at birth (1990–95): male 53.5 years; female 56.5 years.
Major causes of death per 100,000 population: n.a.; however, major health problems include measles, malaria, tuberculosis of respiratory system, anemias, meningitis, and intestinal obstruction and hernia.

National economy

Budget (1991–92). Revenue: CFAF 545,000,000,000 (direct taxes 36.0%; customs duties 28.3%; petroleum royalties 22.0%). Expenditures: CFAF 545,000,000,000 (current expenditure 69.4%, of which education 13.0%, defense 8.8%, administration 4.6%, health 4.5%, finance 3.1%).
Public debt (external, outstanding; 1991): U.S.$5,027,000,000.
Gross national product (at current market prices; 1992): U.S.$10,036,000,000 (U.S.$820 per capita).

Structure of gross domestic product and labour force

	1989		1985	
	in value CFAF '000,000	% of total value	labour force	% of labour force
Agriculture	740	24.0	2,900,871	74.0
Mining	428	13.9	1,793	0.1
Manufacturing	406	13.2	174,498	4.5
Construction	168	5.5	66,684	1.7
Public utilities	36	1.2	3,522	0.1
Transp. and commun.	196	6.4	51,688	1.3
Trade	369	12.0	154,014	3.9
Finance	402	13.1	8,009	0.2
Public admin., defense	300	9.8	292,922	7.5
Services	65	2.1		
Other	...	...	263,634	6.7
TOTAL	3,076[3]	100.0[3]	3,917,635	100.0

Household income and expenditure. Average household size (1980) 5.2; average annual income per household (1983)[4] U.S.$420; sources of income: n.a.; expenditure (1983)[4]: food 33.6%, clothing and footwear 16.3%, housing 14.6%, transportation and communications 10.5%, recreation 5.1%, health 5.0%.
Tourism: receipts from visitors (1991) U.S.$15,000,000; expenditures by nationals abroad (1990) U.S.$283,000,000.

Population economically active (1987): total 4,269,000; activity rate of total population 39.4% (participation rates [1985]: ages 15–69, 66.3%; female 38.5%; unemployed, n.a.).

Price and earnings indexes (1985 = 100)

	1983	1984	1985	1986	1987	1988	1989
Consumer price index	88.7	98.7	100.0	107.7	114.2	124.0	124.0
Earnings index	...	...	...	...	...	...	...

Production (metric tons except as noted). Agriculture, forestry, fishing (1992): sugarcane 1,400,000, cassava 1,230,000, plantains 860,000, bananas 520,000, vegetables and melons 459,000, corn (maize) 380,000, sweet potatoes 160,000, palm oil 107,000, peanuts (groundnuts) 100,000, cacao 94,000, rice 90,000, yams 80,000, millet 55,000, palm kernels 53,000; livestock (number of live animals) 4,730,000 cattle, 3,560,000 goats, 3,560,000 sheep, 1,380,000 pigs; roundwood (1990) 14,216,000 cu m; fish catch (1990) 77,664. Mining and quarrying (1990): marble 200,000; pozzolana 130,000; aluminum 93,284; limestone 57,000; tin ore and concentrate 4. Manufacturing (1988): cement 586,000; palm oil 98,000; wheat flour 49,000; soap 23,400; footwear 1,733,000 pairs; sawn wood 568,000 cu m; beer 5,622,000 hectolitres; soft drinks 1,172,000 hectolitres. Construction (1983): residential 230,400 sq m; nonresidential 51,100 sq m. Energy production (consumption): electricity (kW-hr; 1990) 2,705,000,000 (2,705,000,000); coal (metric tons; 1990) 1,000 (1,000); crude petroleum (barrels; 1990) 61,098,000 (14,374,000); petroleum products (metric tons; 1990) 1,813,000 (1,760,000); natural gas, none (n.a.).
Land use (1991): forested 52.5%; meadows and pastures 17.8%; agricultural and under permanent cultivation 15.1%; other 14.6%.

Foreign trade[5]

Balance of trade (current prices)

	1985	1986	1987	1988	1989	1990
CFAF '000,000,000	−140.8	−265.1	−228.3	−68.8	+40.3	+141.5
% of total	17.9%	32.8%	32.1%	11.1%	5.2%	14.8%

Imports (1987): CFAF 526,186,000,000 (machinery and transport equipment 35.6%, of which road-transport equipment and parts 12.3%; motor-vehicle tires 5.5%; iron and steel 4.6%; flour products 3.4%; chemical products 3.2%; nonmetallic minerals 2.8%; paper and paper products 2.6%; plastic products 2.5%). *Major import sources* (1990): France 32.9%; Germany 10.6%; Japan 5.7%; Belgium-Luxembourg 5.5%; Italy 5.2%; United States 4.7%; The Netherlands 3.4%; Guinea 3.3%; United Kingdom 3.0%.
Exports (1990): CFAF 570,000,000,000 (crude petroleum 54.2%; cocoa 10.5%; coffee 10.0%; sawn wood and logs 7.9%; cotton 5.8%). *Major export destinations:* France 32.7%; United States 14.9%; The Netherlands 14.4%; Italy 7.8%; Germany 4.2%; Spain 4.2%; Korea 3.3%; China 1.9%; Equatorial Guinea 1.9%.

Transport and communications

Transport. Railroads (1989–90): route length 686 mi, 1,104 km; passenger-mi 284,000,000, passenger-km 457,000,000; short ton-mi cargo 514,000,000, metric ton-km cargo 751,000,000. Roads (1989): total length 29,950 mi, 48,200 km (paved 7%). Vehicles (1991): passenger cars 94,000; trucks and buses 82,000. Merchant marine (1992): vessels (100 gross tons and over) 47; total deadweight tonnage 39,797. Air transport (1987): passenger-mi 349,000,000, passenger-km 561,000,000; short ton-mi cargo 25,000,000, metric ton-km cargo 37,000,000; airports (1993) with scheduled flights 5.
Communications. Daily newspapers (1992): 1; total circulation 66,000; circulation per 1,000 population 5.2. Radio (1992): total number of receivers 2,000,000 (1 per 6.3 persons). Television (1992): total number of receivers 15,000 (1 per 844 persons). Telephones (1988): 60,770 (1 per 185 persons).

Education and health

Education (1989–90)

	schools	teachers	students	student/teacher ratio
Primary (age 6–14)	6,549	37,804	1,946,301	51.4
Secondary (age 15–24)	388[6]	11,400	366,528	32.2
Voc., teacher tr.	220[6]	6,267	90,633	14.5
Higher	5[6]	924[7]	24,651[7]	26.7[7]

Educational attainment (1976). Percentage of population age 15 and over having: no schooling 51.1%; primary education 41.7%; some postprimary 0.2%; secondary 5.7%; some postsecondary 0.3%; higher 0.2%; other 0.8%.
Literacy (1990): percentage of total population age 15 and over literate 54.1%; males literate 66.3%; females literate 42.6%.
Health: physicians (1986) 833 (1 per 12,540 persons); hospital beds (1984–85) 26,832 (1 per 377 persons); infant mortality rate (1990–95) 86.0.
Food (1988–90): daily per capita caloric intake 2,208 (vegetable products 93%, animal products 7%); 95% of FAO recommended minimum requirement.

Military

Total active duty personnel (1993): 8,100 (army 81.5%, navy 14.8%, air force 3.7%). *Military expenditure as percentage of GNP* (1989): 1.3% (world 4.9%); per capita expenditure U.S.$14.

[1]Detail does not add to total given because of rounding. [2]Based on land area. [3]Detail does not add to total given by source. [4]Capital city only. [5]Import figures are f.o.b. in balance of trade and c.i.f. for commodities and trading partners. [6]1986–87. [7]1988–89.

Canada

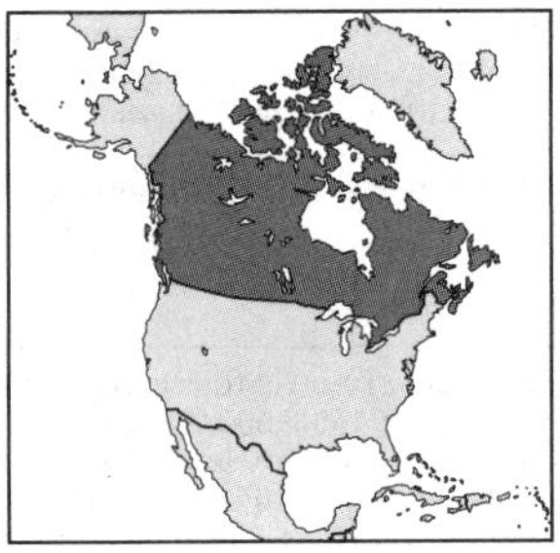

Official name: Canada.
Form of government: federal multiparty parliamentary state with two legislative houses (Senate [104]; House of Commons [295]).
Chief of state: Queen of Canada (British Monarch).
Representative of chief of state: Governor-General.
Head of government: Prime Minister.
Capital: Ottawa.
Official languages: English; French.
Official religion: none.
Monetary unit: 1 Canadian dollar (Can$) = 100 cents; valuation (Oct. 4, 1993) 1 U.S.$ = Can$1.34; 1 £ = Can$2.03.

Area and population

Provinces	Capitals	area sq mi	area sq km	population 1992 estimate
Alberta	Edmonton	255,287	661,190	2,628,000
British Columbia	Victoria	365,948	947,800	3,446,000
Manitoba	Winnipeg	250,947	649,950	1,112,000
New Brunswick	Fredericton	28,355	73,440	749,000
Newfoundland	St. John's	156,649	405,720	581,000
Nova Scotia	Halifax	21,425	55,490	921,000
Ontario	Toronto	412,581	1,068,580	10,593,000
Prince Edward Island	Charlottetown	2,185	5,660	130,000
Quebec	Quebec	594,860	1,540,680	7,143,000
Saskatchewan	Regina	251,866	652,330	1,004,000
Territories				
Northwest Territories	Yellowknife	1,322,910	3,426,320	62,000
Yukon Territory	Whitehorse	186,661	483,450	30,000
TOTAL		3,849,674	9,970,610	28,398,000[1]

Demography

Population (1993): 28,149,000.
Density (1993)[2]: persons per sq mi 7.3, persons per sq km 2.8.
Urban-rural (1991): urban 76.6%; rural 23.4%.
Sex distribution (1991): male 49.28%; female 50.72%.
Age breakdown (1991): under 15, 20.9%; 15–29, 22.7%; 30–44, 25.1%; 45–59, 15.3%; 60–74, 11.3%; 75 and over, 4.7%.
Population projection: (2000) 31,214,000; (2010) 36,182,000.
Doubling time: 87 years.
Ethnic origin (1986): British 34.4%; French 25.7%; German 3.6%; Italian 2.8%; Ukrainian 1.7%; Amerindian and Inuktitut (Eskimo) 1.5%; Chinese 1.4%; Dutch 1.4%; multiple origin and other 27.5%[3].
Religious affiliation (1991): Roman Catholic 45.2%; Protestant 36.2%; Eastern Orthodox 1.5%; nonreligious 12.4%; other 4.7%.
Major metropolitan areas (1991): Toronto 3,893,046; Montreal 3,127,242; Vancouver 1,602,502; Ottawa-Hull 920,857; Edmonton 839,924; Calgary 754,033; Winnipeg 652,354; Quebec 645,550; Hamilton 599,760; London 381,522.

Other metropolitan areas (1991)

	population		population		population
Chicoutimi-Jonquière	160,928	Regina	191,692	Sherbrooke	139,194
Halifax	320,501	St. Catharines–Niagara	364,552	Sudbury	157,613
Kitchener	356,421	St. John's	171,859	Trois Rivières	136,303
Oshawa	240,104	Saskatoon	210,023	Victoria	287,897
				Windsor	262,075

Place of birth (1986): 84.2% native-born; 15.8% foreign-born, of which United Kingdom 3.2%, other European 6.6%, Asian countries 3.2%, other 2.8%.
Mobility (1986). Population living in the same residence as in 1981: 56.3%; different residence, same municipality 24.2%; same province, different municipality 13.5%; different province 4.0%; different country 2.0%.
Households (1991). Total number of households 10,018,267. Average household size 2.7; (1985) 1 person 22.9%, 2 persons 31.4%, 3 persons 17.4%, 4 persons 17.6%, 5 persons 7.3%, 6 or more persons 3.4%. Family households: 7,356,168 (73.4%), nonfamily 2,662,099 (26.6%, of which 1 person 22.9%).
Immigration (1991): permanent immigrants admitted 230,781, from Asia 53.0%, Europe 20.2%, Central and South America 16.1%, Africa 7.2%, United States 2.3%, other 1.2%; refugee arrivals 18,374.

Vital statistics

Birth rate per 1,000 population (1990): 15.2 (world avg. 26.4); (1985) legitimate 83.8%; illegitimate 16.2%.
Death rate per 1,000 population (1990): 7.2 (world avg. 9.2).
Natural increase rate per 1,000 population (1990): 8.0 (world avg. 17.2).
Total fertility rate (avg. births per childbearing woman; 1991): 1.8.
Marriage rate per 1,000 population (1991): 7.0.
Divorce rate per 1,000 population (1991): 2.9.
Life expectancy at birth (1991): male 74.0 years; female 80.6 years.
Major causes of death per 100,000 population (1990): diseases of the circulatory system 282.5; malignant neoplasms (cancers) 197.2; diseases of the respiratory system 61.2; accidents and violence 49.1.

Social indicators

Educational attainment (1986). Percentage of population age 25 and over having: no formal schooling, negligible; less than complete primary education or complete primary 20.6%; secondary 35.0%; postsecondary vocational 25.1%; university without degree 8.3%; completed university 11.0%; graduates by level (1987): 4-year higher degree 101,960, master's 15,790, doctorate 2,385.

Distribution of income (1991)

percentage of national income by quintile

1	2	3	4	5 (highest)
5.3%	13.6%	19.7%	25.9%	35.5%

Quality of working life (1992). Average workweek: 38.3 hours. Annual rate per 100,000 workers for (1990): injury, accident, or industrial illness 7,543; death 5.1[4]. Proportion of labour force insured for damages or income loss resulting from: injury 99%; permanent disability 99%; death 99%. Average days lost to labour stoppages per 1,000 employee-workdays (1992): 0.4. Average duration of journey to work (1983): 23 minutes[5] (17.3% public transportation, 72.8% automobile, 9.9% other). Rate per 1,000 workers of discouraged (unemployed no longer seeking work; 1983): 10.5.
Access to services (1988). Proportion of households having access to: electricity 100.0%; public water supply 99.8%; public sewage collection 99.3%; public fire protection (1978) 90.4%.
Social participation. Eligible voters participating in last national election (October 1993): 69.7%. Population over 18 years of age participating in voluntary work (1987): 27.0%. Union membership in total workforce (1992): 29.7%. Practicing religious population in total affiliated population (1991): 87.6%.
Social deviance (1991). Offense rate per 100,000 population for: violent crime 1,085, of which assault 8.8, sexual assault 111.0, homicide 2.8; property crime 6,316, of which auto theft 510, burglary and housebreaking 1,589. Incidence per 100,000 in general population of: alcoholism 2,285; drug and substance abuse 258; suicide (1990) 11.5.
Leisure (1992). Favourite leisure activities (hours weekly): television 15.3; social time 12.7; reading 3.5; sports and entertainment 0.9.
Material well-being (1988). Households possessing: automobile 88.3%, of which two or more 25.1%; telephone 98.5%[6]; radio 99.1%[6]; television receiver 99.0%[6]; refrigerator 99.6%; central air conditioner 24.6%[7]; automatic washing machine 77.0%; cable television 69.0%; videocassette recorder 58.8%[7]; microwave oven 63.4%[7].

National economy

Gross national product (1992): U.S.$565,738,000,000 (U.S.$20,600 per capita).

Structure of gross domestic product and labour force

	1992 in value Can$'000,000[8]	% of total value	labour force	% of labour force
Agriculture	15,180	2.2	432,000	3.1
Mining	20,070	3.9	257,000	1.9
Manufacturing	88,107	17.9	1,788,000	12.9
Construction	29,034	6.6	681,000	4.9
Public utilities	16,179	4.1	922,000	6.6
Transportation and communications	42,910	8.5		
Trade	60,167	11.5	2,155,000	15.5
Finance	83,944	15.8	763,000	5.5
Pub. admin., defense	34,042	6.5	834,000	6.0
Services	114,006	23.0	4,408,000	31.8
Other	—	—	1,641,000[9]	11.8[9]
TOTAL	503,638[1, 10]	100.0	13,881,000	100.0

Budget (1992–93). Revenue: Can$140,981,000,000 (income taxes 54.3%, sales tax 21.0%, import duties 2.6%). Expenditures: Can$170,019,000,000 (public debt interest 23.3%, defense 7.0%, health 4.5%, education 2.6%, foreign assistance 2.2%).
National debt (1990–91): Can$443,278,000,000.
Tourism (1991): receipts from visitors U.S.$5,537,000,000; expenditures by nationals abroad U.S.$10,526,000,000.

Manufacturing, mining, and construction enterprises (1989)

	no. of estab-lishments	no. of employees	hourly wages as a % of avg. of all wages[11]	annual value added (Can$'000,000)
Manufacturing				
Transport equipment	1,537	215,000	119.4	17,630
Food and beverages	3,659	229,000	90.3	17,270
Chemicals and related products	1,622	102,000	114.8	13,350
Paper and related products	728	119,000	125.3	11,730
Primary metals	547	107,000	127.1	9,550
Machinery	4,599	164,000	101.3	9,100
Electrical and electronics products	1,383	129,000	105.0	8,870
Printing, publishing, and related products	5,207	141,000	105.4	8,490
Metal fabricating	3,919	147,000	96.5	7,930
Wood	2,697	113,000	93.8	5,980
Rubber and plastic	1,544	92,000	91.8	4,960
Clothing	2,898	122,000	56.5	4,010
Nonmetallic mineral products	1,444	43,000	...	3,600
Textiles	1,305	76,000	82.3	3,660
Furniture and fixtures	2,445	69,000	73.5	2,620
Petroleum and coal products	181	18,000	...	1,940
Tobacco products industries	19	5,000	90.5	1,080
Mining[12]	1,340	118,000	149.3	25,910
Construction[12]	...	800,000	112.3	28,182

Production (metric tons except as noted). Agriculture, forestry, fishing (1992): wheat 29,870,000, barley 10,919,000, corn (maize) 4,531,000, rapeseed 3,689,000, potatoes 3,529,000, oats 2,823,000, vegetables 1,869,000 (of which tomatoes 469,000, carrots 290,000, cabbage 148,000, onions 138,000), soybeans 1,387,000, sugar beets 776,000, apples 521,000, hops 480,000, lentils 344,000, linseed 334,000, rye 265,000; livestock (number of live animals) 13,002,000 cattle, 10,395,000 pigs, 914,000 sheep, 118,000,000 chickens;

roundwood (1991) 178,049,000 cu m; pelts (1990) 2,580,809 units; fish catch (1991) 1,529,779. Mining and quarrying (1992): iron ore 32,722,000; zinc 1,193,607; copper 744,687; lead 318,515; nickel 189,051; molybdenum 9,602; uranium 9,057; silver 1,147; gold 5,048,200 troy oz. Manufacturing (value in Can$'000,000; 1991): transportation equipment 49,355; food and beverages 43,633; chemical products 22,186; paper products 21,466; electrical products 17,820; petroleum and coal products 16,857; metal products 16,060; printing and publishing 12,411; rubber and plastic products 7,986; clothing 5,945; textiles 5,509; furniture 3,808; tobacco products 2,077; leather products 996. Construction (value of building permits; 1992): residential Can$17,161,000,000; nonresidential Can$9,834,000,000.

Service enterprises (1988)

	no. of enter-prises	no. of employees[13]	weekly wages as a % of all wages	annual sales (Can$'000,000)
Retail trade				
Motor vehicle dealers	...	79,800	...	35,917
Food stores	...	213,400	...	35,187
Service stations	...	63,700	...	14,612
Department stores	...	[14]	...	13,271
Clothing stores	...	50,200	...	7,486
Pharmacies	...	52,400	...	7,459
Furniture and appliance stores	...	62,100	...	4,447
Automotive stores	...	31,500	...	3,767
General merchandise	...	231,700[14]	...	3,109
Sporting goods	...	...	...	2,669
General stores	...	[14]	...	2,415
Hardware stores	...	17,300	...	1,824
Shoe stores	...	18,400	...	1,599
Jewelry stores	...	14,000	...	1,215
Variety stores	...	45,100	...	1,057

Energy production (consumption): electricity (kW-hr; 1991) 507,913,000,000 (489,485,000,000); coal (metric tons; 1991) 71,135,000 (50,622,000); crude petroleum (barrels; 1991) 566,983,000 (486,754,000); petroleum products (metric tons; 1991) 85,482,000 (74,397,000); natural gas (cu m; 1991) 111,172,000,000 (64,834,000,000).

Population economically active (1992): total 13,881,000; activity rate of total population 50.0% (participation rates: ages 15–64, 75.2%; female 45.2%; unemployed 11.8%).

Price and earnings indexes (1985 = 100)

	1986	1987	1988	1989	1990	1991	1992
Consumer price index	104.2	108.7	113.1	118.7	124.4	131.4	133.4
Hourly earnings index[15]	103.1	105.8	110.7	116.8	123.4	130.2	133.5

Household income and expenditure (1990). Average household size 2.8; average annual income per family Can$51,646 (U.S.$44,263); sources of income (1989): wages and salaries 65.4%, transfer payments 14.1%, self-employment 7.2%, other 13.3%; expenditure: housing 21.3%[16], transportation and communications 17.6%, food 16.2%, household durable goods 14.8%, clothing 5.5%, recreation 5.0%, health 1.8%, education 0.9%.

Financial aggregates

	1987	1988	1989	1990	1991	1992	1993[17]
Exchange rate, Can$ per:							
U.S. dollar	1.33	1.23	1.18	1.17	1.14	1.21	1.32
£	2.18	2.19	1.94	2.08	2.03	2.14	2.01
SDR	1.84	1.60	1.52	1.65	1.65	1.75	1.89
International reserves (U.S.$)							
Total (excl. gold; '000,000)	7,277	15,391	16,055	17,845	16,252	11,431	10,729
SDRs ('000,000)	399	1,369	1,377	1,526	1,582	1,039	1,092
Reserve pos. in IMF ('000,000)	661	505	528	517	592	1,011	1,005
Foreign exchange ('000,000)	6,218	13,517	14,150	15,802	14,079	9,382	8,633
Gold ('000,000 fine troy oz)	18.52	17.14	16.10	14.76	12.96	9.94	7.08
% world reserves	2.12	1.81	1.71	1.56	1.38	1.07	0.77
Interest and prices							
Central bank discount (%)	8.66	11.17	12.47	11.78	8.00	7.00	5.00
Govt. bond yield (%)	9.95	10.22	9.92	10.85	9.76	8.77	7.54
Industrial share prices (1985 = 100)	131.5	121.8	140.1	126.1	127.9	125.5	152.5[18]
Balance of payments (U.S.$'000,000)							
Balance of visible trade, of which:	8,960	8,157	5,986	8,785	5,162	8,183	...
Imports, f.o.b.	−89,092	−107,274	−116,985	−119,928	−121,696	−125,120	...
Exports, f.o.b.	98,052	115,432	122,971	128,713	126,858	133,303	...
Balance of invisibles	−17,714	−20,721	−25,721	−30,957	−30,505	31,195	...
Balance of payments, current account	−8,754	−12,564	−19,735	−22,172	−25,343	−23,012	...

Land use (1991): forested 39.0%; meadows and pastures 3.1%; agricultural and under permanent cultivation 5.0%; built-on, wasteland, and other 52.9%.

Foreign trade

Balance of trade (current prices)

	1987	1988	1989	1990	1991	1992
Can$'000,000,000	9.0	8.2	6.0	8.8	5.2	8.2
% of total	4.8%	3.7%	2.5%	3.5%	2.1%	3.2%

Imports (1992): Can$147,588,000,000 (1991; road motor vehicles 19.5%; chemicals 6.7%; food, feed, beverages, and tobacco 6.2%; crude petroleum 3.3%; iron and steel 1.9%; nonferrous metals 1.3%). *Major import sources* (1991): United States 63.5%; Japan 6.9%; United Kingdom 3.5%; Germany 2.8%; France 1.8%; South Korea 1.6%; Taiwan 1.5%; Italy 1.4%; Mexico 1.3%; Norway 1.2%.

Exports (1992): Can$156,567,000,000 (1991; road motor vehicles 21.0%; crude materials 12.1%; mineral fuels 10.8%, of which crude petroleum 4.2%, natural gas 2.9%; food 7.6%, of which wheat 2.6%; newsprint 4.0%; lumber 3.6%; wood pulp 3.4%; industrial machinery 2.5%; aluminum 2.1%; office equipment 1.9%; refined petroleum products 1.8%). *Major export destinations* (1991): United States 75.6%; Japan 5.0%; United Kingdom 2.1%; Germany 1.7%; South Korea 1.3%; France 1.3%; Italy 1.2%; Norway 1.0%; Mexico 1.0%; China 0.8%; Hong Kong 0.7%.

Trade by commodities (1991)

	imports		exports	
SITC Group	U.S.$'000,000	%	U.S.$'000,000	%
00 Food and live animals	6,647.2	5.6	9,587.1	7.6
01 Beverages and tobacco	615.2	0.5	857.4	0.7
02 Crude materials, excluding fuels	3,675.2	3.1	15,306.4	12.1
03 Mineral fuels, lubricants, and related materials	5,776.5	4.9	13,653.7	10.8
04 Animal and vegetable oils, fats, and waxes	...	...	...	...
05 Chemicals and related products, n.e.s.	7,905.8	6.7	6,605.6	5.2
06 Basic manufactures	14,910.0	12.6	20,652.3	16.3
07 Machinery and transport equipment	60,177.7	51.0	47,383.2	37.4
08 Miscellaneous manufactured articles	14,071.1	11.9	4,682.7	3.7
09 Goods not classified by kind	4,197.9	3.6	7,822.2	6.2
TOTAL	118,088.4[1]	100.0[1]	126,762.1[1]	100.0

Direction of trade (1992)

	imports		exports	
	Can$'000,000	%	Can$'000,000	%
Africa	1,164	0.8	899	0.6
Asia	23,073	15.0	17,241	10.7
Americas	101,364	66.1	128,786	79.8
United States	95,843	62.5	125,536	77.8
Mexico	2,668	1.7	741	0.4
South America	1,617	1.0	1,637	1.0
Europe	18,091[1]	11.8	13,678	8.5
EEC	14,380	9.4	11,259	7.0
U.S.S.R.	263	0.2	1,285	0.8
Other Europe	3,447	2.2	1,134	0.7
Oceania	1,016	0.7	807	0.5
TOTAL	153,299[19]	100.0[19]	161,297[20]	100.0[20]

Transport and communications

Transport. Railroads (1990): length 53,985 mi, 86,880 km; passenger-mi 724,500,000, passenger-km 1,166,000,000; short ton-mi cargo 163,978,000,000, metric ton-km cargo 239,404,000,000. Roads (1991): total length 527,794 mi, 849,404 km (paved 35%). Vehicles (1991): passenger cars 13,061,084; trucks and buses 3,744,012. Merchant marine (1992): vessels (100 gross tons and over) 1,185; total deadweight tonnage 2,896,830. Air transport (1991): passenger-mi 35,960,000,000, passenger-km 57,873,000,000; short ton-mi cargo 918,600,000, metric ton-km cargo 1,391,200,000; airports (1992) with scheduled flights 106.

Communications. Daily newspapers (1991): total number 106; total circulation 5,815,000; circulation per 1,000 population 207. Radio (1992): total number of receivers 22,600,000 (1 per 1.2 persons). Television (1992): total number of receivers 17,400,000 (1 per 1.7 persons). Telephones (1987): 20,126,490 (1 per 1.3 persons).

Education and health

Education (1990–91)

	schools	teachers	students	student/ teacher ratio
Primary (age 6–14)	12,200	154,698	2,371,558	15.3
Secondary (age 14–18)	...	164,125	2,292,735	14.0
Postsecondary and higher	270	61,682	1,359,208	22.0

Literacy (1986): total population age 15 and over literate 18,745,000 (96.6%); males literate (1975) 8,003,000 (95.6%); females literate (1975) 8,182,000 (95.7%).

Health (1989): physicians 58,470 (1 per 449 persons); hospital beds 183,775 (1 per 143 persons); infant mortality rate per 1,000 live births (1990) 6.8.

Food (1988–90): daily per capita caloric intake 3,242 (vegetable products 68%, animal products 32%); 122% of FAO recommended minimum requirement.

Military

Total active duty personnel (1993): 78,100 (army 25.6%, navy 16.0%, air force 26.4%, not identified by service 32.0%). *Military expenditure as percentage of GNP* (1989): 2.0% (world 4.9%); per capita expenditure U.S.$413.

[1]Detail does not add to total given because of rounding. [2]Based on land area of 3,558,096 sq mi (9,215,430 sq km). [3]Includes 4.6% who are of both French and British origin. [4]1987. [5]Urban areas. [6]1990. [7]1989. [8]At prices of 1986. [9]Unemployed. [10]GDP at current values in 1992 is Can$688,541,000,000. [11]1986. [12]1988. [13]1984. [14]Department and General stores included with General merchandise. [15]Manufacturing only. [16]Includes energy and utilities. [17]September. [18]August. [19]Total for imports includes Can$8,591,000,000 (5.6% of total imports; mostly special transactions) not distributable by region. [20]Detail does not add to total given because of discrepancies in estimates.

Cape Verde

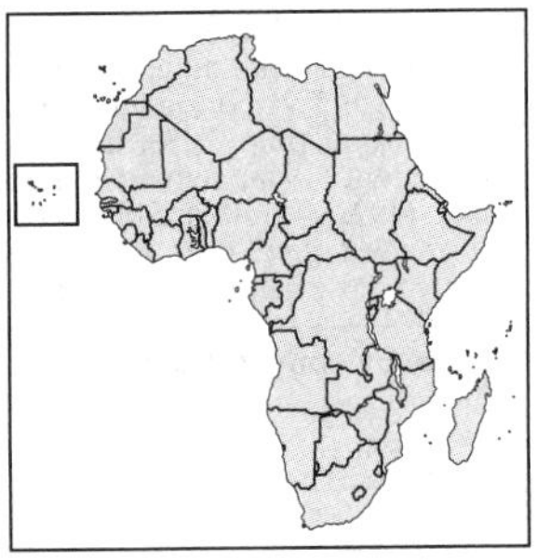

Official name: República de Cabo Verde (Republic of Cape Verde).
Form of government: multiparty[1] republic with one legislative house (National People's Assembly [79]).
Chief of state: President.
Head of government: Prime Minister.
Capital: Praia.
Official language: Portuguese.
Official religion: none.
Monetary unit: 1 escudo (C.V.Esc) = 100 centavos; valuation (Oct. 4, 1993) 1 U.S.$ = C.V.Esc 73.66; 1 £ = C.V.Esc 111.60.

Area and population

Island Groups Islands/Counties[2] Counties	Capitals	area sq mi	area sq km	population 1990 census[3]
Leeward Islands		696[4]	1,803	217,237
Brava	Nova Sintra	26	67	6,980
Fogo	São Filipe	184	476	33,860
Maio	Porto Inglês	104	269	4,964
Santiago		383	991	171,433
Praia	Praia	153	396	82,874
Santa Catarina	Assomada	94	243	37,274
Santa Cruz	Pedra Badejo	58	149	26,732
Tarrafal	Tarrafal	78	203	24,553
Windward Islands		861[4]	2,230	119,561
Boa Vista	Sal Rei	239	620	3,457
Sal	Santa Maria	83	216	7,998
Santo Antão		300	779	43,272
Paúl	Pombas	21	54	7,926
Porto Novo	Porto Novo	215	558	14,838
Ribeira Grande	Ponta do Sol	64	167	20,508
São Nicolau	Ribeira Brava	150	388	13,577
São Vicente	Mindelo	88	227	51,257
TOTAL		1,557	4,033	336,798

Demography

Population (1993): 350,000.
Density (1993): persons per sq mi 224.9, persons per sq km 86.8.
Urban-rural (1990): urban 29.7%; rural 70.3%.
Sex distribution (1990): male 48.00%; female 52.00%.
Age breakdown (1990): under 15, 44.8%; 15–29, 30.8%; 30–44, 10.2%; 45–59, 7.5%; 60 and over, 6.7%.
Population projection: (2000) 383,000; (2010) 436,000.
Doubling time: 19 years.
Ethnic composition (1986): mixed 71%; black 28%; white 1%.
Religious affiliation (1991): Roman Catholic 93.2%; Protestant and other 6.8%.
Major cities (1990): Praia 61,707; Mindelo 47,080; São Filipe 5,616.

Vital statistics

Birth rate per 1,000 population (1992): 48.0 (world avg. 26.4); (1975) legitimate 55.2%; illegitimate 44.8%.
Death rate per 1,000 population (1992): 10.0 (world avg. 9.2).
Natural increase rate per 1,000 population (1992): 38.0 (world avg. 17.2).
Total fertility rate (avg. births per childbearing woman; 1990–95): 5.3.
Marriage rate per 1,000 population (1988): 3.2.
Divorce rate per 1,000 population: n.a.
Life expectancy at birth (1992): male 60.0 years; female 64.0 years.
Major causes of death per 100,000 population (1987): enteritis and other diarrheal diseases 97.4; heart disease 77.9; malignant neoplasms (cancers) 47.9; pneumonia 46.4; accidents, poisoning, and violence 44.0.

National economy

Budget. Revenue (1987): C.V.Esc 3,428,939,000 (indirect taxes 38.2%, of which import duties 15.4%; direct taxes 21.2%, of which taxes from industry 7.2%; receipts from petroleum 3.1%). Expenditures (1986): C.V.Esc 2,798,000,000 (current expenditure 90.8%, of which salaries 43.6%, transfer payments 26.8%; capital expenditure 9.2%).
Public debt (external, outstanding; 1991): U.S.$147,000,000.
Tourism: n.a.
Land use (1991): forested 0.2%; meadows and pastures 6.2%; agricultural and under permanent cultivation 9.7%; other 83.9%.
Production (metric tons except as noted). Agriculture, forestry, fishing (1992): sugarcane 18,000, fruits (except melons) 12,000, vegetables (including melons) 11,000, coconuts 10,000, bananas 6,000, sweet potatoes 3,000, potatoes 3,000, cassava 2,000, dates 2,000; livestock (number of live animals) 110,000 goats, 86,000 pigs, 19,000 cattle; roundwood, n.a.; fish catch (1991) 8,490. Mining and quarrying (1990): salt 3,500. Manufacturing (C.V.Esc; 1987): cigars 232,253,000; flour 176,677,000; cocoa powder 94,439,000[5]; canned fish 78,401,000; bread 35,530,000[5]; alcoholic beverages 25,972,000; soft drinks 7,419,000 litres. Construction (1982): residential C.V.Esc 365,800,000; nonresidential C.V.Esc 1,700,000. Energy production (consumption): electricity (kW-hr; 1990) 36,000,000 (36,000,000); coal, none (none); crude petroleum, none (none); petroleum products (metric tons; 1990) none (27,000); natural gas, none (none).
Gross national product (at current market prices; 1992): U.S.$331,000,000 (U.S.$850 per capita).

Structure of gross domestic product and labour force

	1986 in value C.V.Esc '000,000	1986 % of total value	1980 labour force	1980 % of labour force
Agriculture	2,730.7	10.3	22,144	33.2
Manufacturing	2,279.9	8.6	1,871	2.8
Public utilities	377.7	1.4	336	0.5
Mining	135.7	0.5	535	0.8
Construction	4,124.5	15.6	18,873	28.3
Transportation and communications	3,489.0	13.2	3,411	5.1
Pub. admin., defense	4,388.9	16.6	2,128	3.2
Trade	5,625.4	21.3	3,930	5.9
Finance	1,723.3	6.5	226	0.4
Services	446.1	1.7		
Other	1,110.5	4.2	13,156	19.8
TOTAL	26,431.6[4]	100.0[4]	66,610	100.0

Population economically active (1980): total 66,610; activity rate of total population 22.5% (participation rates: ages 15–64, 42.9%; female 30.5%; unemployed, n.a.).

Price and earnings indexes (1985 = 100)

	1986	1987	1988	1989	1990	1991
Consumer price index	110.5	115.5	120.3	125.0	139.0	152.0
Earnings index	...	...	...	...	...	...

Household income and expenditure. Average household size (1980) 4.3; income per household: n.a.; sources of income: n.a.; expenditure (1986)[6]: food 63.4%, clothing and footwear 9.2%, beverages and tobacco 6.7%, other 20.7%.

Foreign trade

Balance of trade (current prices)

	1984	1985	1986	1987	1988	1989
C.V.Esc '000,000	−6,799	−7,081	−8,240	−6,714	−7,416	−8,179
% of total	94.1%	87.1%	92.1%	85.6%	93.8%	88.6%

Imports (1988): C.V.Esc 7,652,000,000 (foodstuffs and beverages 27.2%, machinery and apparatus 16.0%, transport equipment 12.4%, nonmetallic mineral products 11.5%, metal products 8.5%). *Major import sources:* Portugal 33.7%; The Netherlands 10.8%; Japan 5.8%; West Germany 5.2%; Brazil 5.0%; Sweden 4.9%.
Exports (1988): C.V.Esc 236,000,000 (bananas 36.7%, frozen tuna 30.5%, spiny lobster 9.4%, canned tuna 3.1%, refined sugar 3.0%). *Major export destinations:* Portugal 41.5%; Spain 30.3%; France 7.3%; The Netherlands 4.8%; Italy 4.3%.

Transport and communications

Transport. Railroads: none. Roads (1987): total length 3,489 mi, 5,615 km (paved 29%). Vehicles (1991): passenger cars 10,000; trucks and buses 5,000. Merchant marine (1992): vessels (100 gross tons and over) 42; total deadweight tonnage 30,921. Air transport (1987): passenger-mi 76,403,000, passenger-km 122,959,000; (1985) short ton-mi cargo 1,606,000, metric ton-km cargo 2,345,000; airports (1993) with scheduled flights 7.
Communications. Daily newspapers: none. Radio (1992): total number of receivers 50,000 (1 per 6.9 persons). Television (1987): total number of receivers 5,000 (1 per 65 persons). Telephones (1988): 7,840 (1 per 42 persons).

Education and health

Education (1989–90)

	schools	teachers	students	student/ teacher ratio
Primary (age 7–12)	367	2,028	67,761	33.4
Secondary (age 13–17)	16[7]	238	7,114	29.9
Voc., teacher tr.	3[7]	56[8]	752	...
Higher	...	...	...	...

Educational attainment (1980). Percentage of population age 25 and over having: no formal schooling or incomplete primary education 84.2%; complete primary 12.4%; secondary 1.7%; higher 0.5%; unknown 1.2%. *Literacy* (1985): total population age 15 and over literate 73,500 (47.4%); males literate 42,500 (61.4%); females literate 31,000 (38.6%).
Health (1987): physicians 77 (1 per 4,208 persons); hospital beds 625 (1 per 550 persons); infant mortality rate per 1,000 live births (1992) 61.0.
Food (1988–90): daily per capita caloric intake 2,778 (vegetable products 88%, animal products 12%); 118% of FAO recommended minimum requirement.

Military

Total active duty personnel (1992): 1,300 (army 76.9%, navy 15.4%, air force 7.7%). *Military expenditure as percentage of GNP* (1981): 12.1% (world 5.5%); per capita expenditure U.S.$43.

[1]Constitution revised Sept. 28, 1990, to adopt a multiparty system; first multiparty elections took place on Jan. 13, 1991. [2]Island/county areas are coterminous except Santiago and Santo Antão islands. [3]Preliminary results. [4]Detail does not add to total given because of rounding. [5]1986. [6]Praia only. [7]1986–87. [8]Vocational teachers only.

Central African Republic

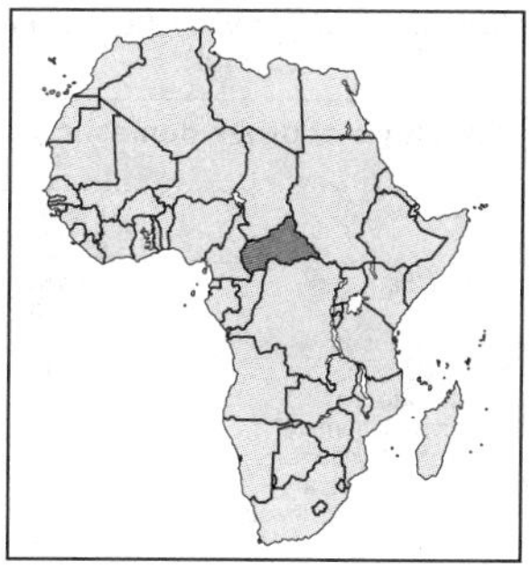

Official name: République Centrafricaine (Central African Republic).
Form of government: republic with a bicameral Congress that meets as two chambers, an upper (Economic and Regional Council[1]) and a lower (National Assembly [85]).
Chief of state: President.
Head of government: Prime Minister.
Capital: Bangui.
Official languages: French; Sango.
Official religion: none.
Monetary unit: 1 CFA franc (CFAF) = 100 centimes; valuation (Oct. 4, 1993) 1 U.S.$ = CFAF 283.25; 1 £ = CFAF 429.12.

Area and population

		area		population
Prefectures	Capitals	sq mi	sq km	1988 census
Bamingui-Bangoran	Ndélé	22,471	58,200	28,643
Basse-Kotto	Mobaye	6,797	17,604	194,750
Haut-Mbomou	Obo	21,440	55,530	27,113
Haute-Kotto	Bria	33,456	86,650	58,838
Kemo	Sibut	6,642	17,204	82,884
Lobaye	Mbaïki	7,427	19,235	169,554
Mambere-Kadei	Berbérati	11,661	30,203	230,364
Mbomou	Bangassou	23,610	61,150	119,252
Nana-Gribizi	Kaga-Bandoro	7,721	19,996	95,497
Nana-Mambere	Bouar	10,270	26,600	191,970
Ombella-Mpoko	Boali	12,292	31,835	180,857
Ouaka	Bambari	19,266	49,900	208,332
Ouham	Bossangoa	19,402	50,250	262,950
Ouham-Pendé	Bozoum	12,394	32,100	287,653
Sangha-Mbaere	Nola	7,495	19,412	65,961
Vakaga	Birao	17,954	46,500	32,118
Autonomous commune				
Bangui	Bangui	26	67	451,690
TOTAL		240,324	622,436	2,688,426

Demography

Population (1993): 2,998,000.
Density (1993): persons per sq mi 12.5, persons per sq km 4.8.
Urban-rural (1990): urban 46.7%; rural 53.3%.
Sex distribution (1988): male 49.14%; female 50.86%.
Age breakdown (1988): under 15, 43.2%; 15–29, 27.5%; 30–44, 15.0%; 45–59, 9.2%; 60–74, 4.1%; 75 and over, 0.8%; unknown 0.2%.
Population projection: (2000) 3,528,000; (2010) 4,449,000.
Doubling time: 24 years.
Ethnic composition (1983): Banda 28.6%; Baya (Gbaya) 24.5%; Ngbandi 10.6%; Azande 9.8%; Sara 6.9%; Mbaka 4.3%; Mbum 4.1%; Kare 2.4%; French 0.1%; other 8.7%.
Religious affiliation (1985): Protestant 40.0%; Roman Catholic 28.0%; traditional 24.0%; Muslim 8.0%.
Major cities (1988)[2]: Bangui 451,690; Bambari 52,092; Bouar 49,166; Berbérati 45,432; Bossangoa 41,877.

Vital statistics

Birth rate per 1,000 population (1990–95): 45.1 (world avg. 26.4); legitimate, n.a.; illegitimate, n.a.
Death rate per 1,000 population (1990–95): 16.3 (world avg. 9.2).
Natural increase rate per 1,000 population (1990–95): 28.8 (world avg. 17.2).
Total fertility rate (avg. births per childbearing woman; 1988): 6.1.
Marriage rate per 1,000 population: n.a.
Divorce rate per 1,000 population: n.a.
Life expectancy at birth (1990–95): male 48.0 years; female 53.0 years.
Morbidity (as percentage of reported cases of illness; 1984): malaria 13.3%; dysentery, enteritis, and other intestinal diseases 12.5%; respiratory diseases 9.9%, of which pneumonia 2.7%.

National economy

Budget (1993). Revenue: CFAF 60,200,000,000 (1991; fiscal receipts 87.3%; nonfiscal receipts 12.7%). Expenditures: CFAF 74,400,000,000 (current expenditure 60.0%; capital expenditure 40.0%, of which grants from abroad 31.9%).
Public debt (external, outstanding; 1991): U.S.$802,000,000.
Production (metric tons except as noted). Agriculture, forestry, fishing (1992): cassava 606,000, yams 220,000, bananas 94,000, plantains 68,000, corn (maize) 50,000, peanuts (groundnuts) 43,000, seed cotton 30,000, cottonseed 18,000, oranges 16,000, pulses 15,000, coffee 14,000, cotton lint 12,000, sorghum 10,000, rice 7,000; livestock (number of live animals) 2,700,000 cattle, 1,300,000 goats, 460,000 pigs, 3,000,000 chickens; roundwood (1991) 3,444,000 cu m; fish catch (1991) 13,500. Mining and quarrying (1992): diamonds 405,000 carats[3]. Manufacturing (value of production in CFAF '000,000; 1989): food, beverages, and tobacco 15,456; wood products 9,156; textiles, wearing apparel, and leather products 8,343; chemical products 3,555; metal products 2,199. Construction (1990)[4]: residential 14,700 sq m; nonresidential 11,200 sq m. Energy production (consumption): electricity (kW-hr; 1991) 96,000,000 (96,000,000); coal, none (none); crude petroleum, none (none); petroleum products (metric tons; 1991) none (68,000); natural gas, none (none).
Land use (1991): forested 57.4%; meadows and pastures 4.8%; agricultural and under permanent cultivation 3.2%; other 34.6%.
Gross national product (at current market prices; 1992): U.S.$1,296,000,000 (U.S.$410 per capita).

Structure of gross domestic product and labour force

	1991		1988	
	in value CFAF '000,000[5]	% of total value	labour force	% of labour force
Agriculture	127,710	41.6	1,113,900	80.4
Mining	9,020	2.9	15,400	1.1
Manufacturing	27,060	8.8	22,400	1.6
Construction	5,120	1.7	7,000	0.5
Public utilities	1,140	0.4	1,500	0.1
Transp. and commun.			1,500	0.1
Trade	116,070	37.8	118,000	8.5
Finance, real estate			1,500	0.1
Pub. admin., defense			91,700	6.6
Other	21,160[6]	6.8[6]	14,100	1.0
TOTAL	307,280	100.0	1,387,000	100.0

Tourism (1990): receipts U.S.$9,000,000; expenditures U.S.$41,000,000.
Population economically active (1992): total 1,450,000; activity rate of total population 45.7% (participation rates [1985]: ages 15–64, 81.6%; female 47.0%; unemployed, n.a.).

Price and earnings indexes (1985 = 100)

	1986	1987	1988	1989	1990	1991	1992
Consumer price index[7]	102.2	95.1	91.3	92.0	91.9	89.4	88.4[8]
Earnings index	...	...	...	...	...	...	...

Household income and expenditure. Average household size (1988) 4.7; average annual income per household CFAF 91,985 (U.S.$435); sources of income: n.a.; expenditure (1991)[9]: food 70.5%, clothing 8.5%, other manufactured products 7.6%, energy 7.3%, services (including transportation and communications, recreation, and health) 6.1%.

Foreign trade

Balance of trade (current prices)

	1986	1987	1988	1989	1990	1991
CFAF '000,000	−57,089	−17,174	−18,346	−6,009	−10,917	−11,328
% of total	55.4%	18.0%	22.5%	6.3%	17.9%	17.8%

Imports (1991): CFAF 44,772,000,000 (food products 18.7%; transportation equipment 13.3%; chemical products 12.5%; energy products 8.7%). *Major import sources:* Europe 61.7%, of which France 45.2%; Africa 24.7%; Asia 10.0%.
Exports (1991): CFAF 30,753,000,000 (diamonds 51.1%; cotton 18.9%; wood 13.4%; coffee 4.7%; tobacco 1.9%; gold 1.3%). *Major export destinations* (1990): Belgium-Luxembourg 65.9%; France 22.8%; Switzerland 5.0%; Germany 1.2%.

Transport and communications

Transport. Railroads: none. Roads (1991): total length 14,750 mi, 23,738 km (paved 2%). Vehicles (1991): passenger cars 8,221; trucks and buses 8,541. Merchant marine: vessels (100 gross tons and over) none. Air transport (1990)[10]: passenger-mi 144,362,000, passenger-km 232,329,000; short ton-mi cargo 12,119,000, metric ton-km cargo 17,694,000; airports (1993) with scheduled flights 1[11].
Communications. Daily newspapers (1990): total number 1; total circulation 2,000; circulation per 1,000 population 0.7. Radio (1992): 550,000 receivers (1 per 5.3 persons). Television (1992): 7,500 receivers (1 per 391 persons). Telephones (1991): 4,100[12] (1 per 716 persons).

Education and health

Education (1991)

	schools	teachers	students	student/teacher ratio
Primary (age 6–11)	930	4,004	308,409	90.4
Secondary (age 12–18) / Vocational	46	845	46,989	41.1[13]
Higher[14]	1	134	3,514[13]	18.9

Educational attainment (1975). Percentage of population age 15 and over having: no formal schooling 73.5%; primary education 22.8%; lower secondary 3.0%; upper secondary 0.6%; higher 0.1%. *Literacy* (1988): total population age 15 and over literate 33.6%; males literate 48.0%; females literate 20.3%.
Health: physicians (1990) 170 (1 per 16,447 persons); hospital beds (1991) 4,120 (1 per 695 persons); infant mortality rate per 1,000 live births (1991) 219.0.
Food (1988–90): daily per capita caloric intake 1,846 (vegetable products 88%, animal products 12%); 82% of FAO recommended minimum requirement.

Military

Total active duty personnel (1993): 3,800 (army 92.1%; navy, none; air force 7.9%). *Military expenditure as percentage of GNP* (1992): 2.2% (world [1989] 4.9%); per capita expenditure U.S.$8.

[1]Number of seats not available. [2]Population of Bangui is census figure; other figures are estimates. [3]A similar amount is believed to be smuggled out of the country annually. [4]Bangui only. [5]At constant prices of 1984. [6]Import duties plus value-added taxes. [7]Indigenous households in Bangui only. [8]Average of third quarter. [9]Weights of consumer price index components. [10]Total traffic of Air Afrique, an airline shared by 10 West African countries. [11]International air service only. [12]Number of subscribers. [13]1990. [14]University of Bangui only.

Chad

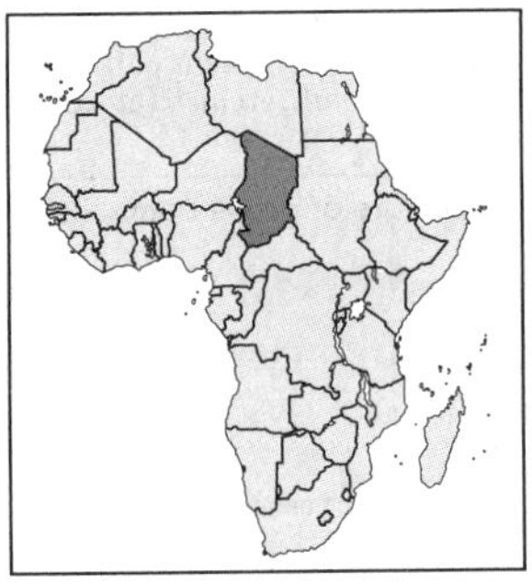

Official name: Jumhūrīyah Tshad (Arabic); République du Tchad (French) (Republic of Chad).
Form of government: transitional regime with one legislative house (Higher Transitional Council [57])[1].
Chief of state: President.
Head of government: Prime Minister.
Capital: N'Djamena.
Official languages: Arabic; French.
Official religion: none.
Monetary unit: 1 CFA franc (CFAF) = 100 centimes; valuation (Oct. 4, 1993) 1 U.S.$ = CFAF 283.25; 1 £ = CFAF 429.12.

Area and population

		area		population
Préfectures	Capitals	sq mi	sq km	1992 estimate
Batha	Ati	34,285	88,800	470,900
Biltine	Biltine	18,090	46,850	238,400
Borkou-Ennedi-Tibesti	Faya Largeau	231,795	600,350	119,200
Chari-Baguirmi	N'Djamena	32,010	82,910	924,000
Guéra	Mongo	22,760	58,950	280,200
Kanem	Mao	44,215	114,520	268,200
Lac	Bol	8,620	22,320	178,800
Logone Occidental	Moundou	3,357	8,695	399,400
Logone Oriental	Doba	10,825	28,035	417,300
Mayo-Kebbi	Bongor	11,625	30,105	941,900
Moyen-Chari	Sarh	17,445	45,180	709,400
Ouaddaï	Abéché	29,436	76,240	465,000
Salamat	Am Timan	24,325	63,000	143,000
Tandjilé	Laï	6,965	18,045	405,300
TOTAL		495,755[2]	1,284,000	5,961,000

Demography

Population (1993): 6,118,000.
Density (1993): persons per sq mi 12.3, persons per sq km 4.8.
Urban-rural (1990): urban 32.0%; rural 68.0%.
Sex distribution (1990): male 49.31%; female 50.69%.
Age breakdown (1990): under 15, 42.8%; 15–29, 26.0%; 30–44, 15.9%; 45–59, 9.6%; 60–74, 4.8%; 75 and over, 0.9%.
Population projection: (2000) 7,337,000; (2010) 9,491,000.
Doubling time: 28 years.
Ethnic composition (1983): Sara, Bagirmi, and Kreish 30.5%; Sudanic Arab 26.1%; Teda (Tubu) 7.3%; Mbum 6.5%; Masalit, Maba, and Mimi 6.3%; Tama 6.3%; Mubi 4.2%; Kanuri 2.3%; Hausa 2.3%; Masa 2.3%; Kotoko 2.1%; other 3.8%.
Religious affiliation (1989): Muslim 40.4%; Christian 33.0%; traditional beliefs 26.6%.
Major cities (1992): N'Djamena 687,800; Sarh 129,600; Moundou 117,500; Abéché 95,800; Koumra 48,700.

Vital statistics

Birth rate per 1,000 population (1990–95): 43.3 (world avg. 26.4); legitimate, n.a.; illegitimate, n.a.
Death rate per 1,000 population (1990–95): 17.9 (world avg. 9.2).
Natural increase rate per 1,000 population (1990–95): 25.4 (world avg. 17.2).
Total fertility rate (avg. births per childbearing woman; 1990): 6.0.
Marriage rate per 1,000 population: n.a.
Divorce rate per 1,000 population: n.a.
Life expectancy at birth (1990–95): male 45.9 years; female 49.1 years.
Major causes of death per 100,000 population: n.a.; however, major diseases include malaria, sleeping sickness, leprosy, venereal diseases, and tuberculosis.

National economy

Budget (1993)[3]. Revenue: CFAF 34,900,000,000 (1990; goods and services tax 33.2%, customs duties 28.8%, income tax 28.0%). Expenditures: CFAF 46,700,000,000 (1990; administrative 65.0%, defense 23.9%).
Public debt (external, outstanding; 1991): U.S.$546,900,000.
Tourism (1991): receipts from visitors U.S.$10,000,000; expenditures by nationals abroad U.S.$32,000,000.
Production (metric tons except as noted). Agriculture, forestry, fishing (1992): sugarcane 400,000, cassava 330,000, millet 295,000, yams 240,000, seed cotton 185,000, peanuts (groundnuts) 147,000, corn (maize) 91,000, pulses 60,000, rice 52,000, sweet potatoes 46,000, dates 32,000, mangoes 32,000, potatoes 18,000, onions 14,000, sesame seeds 14,000; livestock (number of live animals) 4,507,000 cattle, 3,012,000 goats, 2,043,000 sheep, 570,000 camels, 4,000,000 chickens; roundwood (1991) 4,141,000 cu m; fish catch (1991) 60,000. Mining and quarrying: clay, natron, tungsten, bauxite, and gold. Manufacturing (1988): beef and veal 53,000; refined sugar 27,000; salted, dried, or smoked fish 19,000[4]; goat meat 8,000; cattle hides 7,500; sheepskins and goatskins 3,318; mutton and lamb 1,000; wheat flour 1,000[5]; woven cotton fabrics 13,075,000 metres[5]; beer 117,000 hectolitres[6]; cigarettes 14,200,000 packets. Construction: n.a. Energy production (consumption): electricity (kW-hr; 1991) 85,000,000 (85,000,000); coal, none (n.a.); crude petroleum, none (n.a.); petroleum products (metric tons; 1991) none (82,000); natural gas, none (n.a.).
Household income and expenditure (1980). Average household size 3.9; average annual income per household CFAF 96,806 (U.S.$458); sources of income: n.a.; expenditure (1983)[7]: food 45.3%, health 11.9%, energy 5.8%, clothing 3.3%.

Gross domestic product (at current market prices; 1992): U.S.$1,255,000,000 (U.S.$210 per capita).

Structure of gross domestic product and labour force

	1989		1987	
	in value U.S.$'000,000	% of total value	labour force	% of labour force
Agriculture	418	41.3	1,439,000	77.4
Mining	3	0.3		
Manufacturing	157	15.5		
Construction	12	1.2	117,000	6.3
Public utilities	7	0.7		
Transportation and communications	22	2.2		
Trade and finance	298	29.5		
Pub. admin., defense	86	8.5	303,000	16.3
Services	8	0.8		
Other			...	...
TOTAL	1,011	100.0	1,859,000	100.0

Population economically active (1992): total 1,993,000; activity rate of total population 34.1% (participation rates [1987]: over age 10, 51.2%; female 21.6%; unemployed, n.a.).

Price and earnings indexes (1985 = 100)

	1986	1987	1988	1989	1990	1991	1992
Consumer price index	87.0	84.6	95.4	89.8	90.3	94.0	90.2
Earnings index	...	...	...	...	...	...	...

Land use (1991): forested 10.0%; meadows and pastures 35.7%; agricultural and under permanent cultivation 2.6%; other 51.7%.

Foreign trade

Balance of trade (current prices)

	1986	1987	1988	1989	1990	1991
CFAF '000,000	−20,253	−17,400	−7,470	−6,060	+364	−7,268
% of total	29.2%	20.9%	8.0%	5.8%	0.3%	6.2%

Imports (1991): CFAF 80,811,000,000 (1983; petroleum products 16.8%; cereal products 16.8%; pharmaceutical products and chemicals 11.5%; machinery and transport equipment 8.5%, of which transport equipment 7.3%; electrical equipment 5.7%; textiles 2.9%; raw and refined sugar 2.3%). *Major import sources* (1989): France 36.2%; United States 20.4%; Cameroon 18.4%; Italy 5.6%; West Germany 3.7%.
Exports (1991): CFAF 55,587,000,000 (1983; raw cotton 91.1%; live cattle and frozen bovine meat 1.8%; hides and skins 0.4%). *Major export destinations* (1989): Portugal 21.0%; West Germany 16.9%; Japan 13.3%; France 9.9%; Spain 8.4%.

Transport and communications

Transport. Railroads: none. Roads (1983): total length 24,855 mi, 40,000 km (paved 1%). Vehicles (1991): passenger cars 8,500; trucks and buses 6,500. Merchant marine: vessels (100 gross tons and over) none. Air transport (1990): passenger-mi 144,044,000, passenger-km 232,329,000; short ton-mi cargo 12,119,000, metric ton-km cargo 17,694,000; airports (1993) with scheduled flights 1.
Communications. Daily newspapers (1990): total number 1; total circulation 2,000; circulation per 1,000 population 0.3. Radio (1992): total number of receivers 1,260,000 (1 per 4.7 persons). Television (1987): total number of receivers 5,000 (1 per 1,050 persons). Telephones (1988): 9,856 (1 per 555 persons).

Education and health

Education (1989–90)

	schools	teachers	students	student/ teacher ratio
Primary (age 6–12)	1,868	7,327	492,231	67.2
Secondary (age 13–19)	66[8]	1,422	54,751	38.5
Voc., teacher tr.	25[4]	285[8]	3,819	15.1[8]
Higher	4[9]	59	2,969	50.3

Educational attainment: n.a. *Literacy* (1990): percentage of total population age 15 and over literate 29.8%; males literate 42.2%; females literate 17.9%.
Health: physicians (1980) 94 (1 per 47,640 persons); hospital beds (1978) 3,553 (1 per 1,190 persons); infant mortality rate per 1,000 live births (1990–95) 122.
Food (1987–89): daily per capita caloric intake 1,791 (vegetable products 92%, animal products 8%); 75% of FAO recommended minimum requirement.

Military

Total active duty personnel (1993): 25,200 (army 99.2%, navy, none, air force 0.8%). *Military expenditure as percentage of GNP* (1989): 5.6% (world 4.9%); per capita expenditure U.S.$8.

[1]The military regime that overthrew the constitutional government in December 1990 adopted a 30-month national charter (transitional constitution) in February 1991. A new 12-month transitional charter was adopted in April 1993 by a broadly representative National Council. The Council also elected a 57-member interim legislature, the Higher Transitional Council. [2]Detail does not add to total given because of rounding. [3]In addition to the current revenues and expenditures shown, there is an investment budget of CFAF 81,954,000,000, which is financed 57.9% by international grants, 42.1% by loans. [4]1987. [5]1983. [6]1986. [7]Capital city only. [8]1988–89. [9]1989.

Chile

Official name: República de Chile (Republic of Chile).
Form of government: multiparty republic with two legislative houses (Senate [47[1]]; Chamber of Deputies [120]).
Head of state and government: President.
Capital: Santiago[2].
Official language: Spanish.
Official religion: none.
Monetary unit: 1 peso (Ch$) = 100 centavos; valuation (Oct. 4, 1993) 1 U.S.$ = Ch$407.95; 1 £ = Ch$618.05.

Area and population[3]

Regions	Capitals	area sq mi	area sq km	population 1992 census[4]
Aisén del General Carlos Ibáñez del Campo	Coihaique	42,095	109,025	82,071
Antofagasta	Antofagasta	48,820	126,444	407,409
Araucanía	Temuco	12,300	31,858	774,959
Atacama	Copiapó	29,179	75,573	230,786
Bío-Bío	Concepción	14,258	36,929	1,729,920
Coquimbo	La Serena	15,697	40,656	502,460
Libertador General Bernardo O'Higgins	Rancagua	6,319	16,365	688,385
Los Lagos	Puerto Montt	25,868	66,997	953,330
Magallanes y la Antártica Chilena	Punta Arenas	50,979	132,034	142,932
Maule	Talca	11,700	30,302	834,053
Santiago, Región Metropolitana de	Santiago	5,926	15,349	5,170,293
Tarapacá	Iquique	22,663	58,698	341,112
Valparaíso	Valparaíso	6,331	16,396	1,373,967
TOTAL		292,135	756,626	13,231,677

Demography

Population (1993): 13,542,000.
Density (1993): persons per sq mi 46.4, persons per sq km 17.9.
Urban-rural (1992): urban 85.1%; rural 14.9%.
Sex distribution (1992): male 49.13%; female 50.87%.
Age breakdown (1992): under 15, 30.6%; 15–29, 27.0%; 30–44, 21.2%; 45–59, 12.2%; 60–74, 6.8%; 75 and over, 2.2%.
Population projection: (2000) 14,977,000; (2010) 16,850,000.
Doubling time: 41 years.
Ethnic composition (1983): mestizo 91.6%; Indian (mostly Araucanian) 6.8%; others (mainly European) 1.6%.
Religious affiliation (1982): Roman Catholic 80.7%; Protestant 6.1%; Jewish 0.2%; atheist and nonreligious 12.8%; other 0.2%.
Major cities (1992): Greater Santiago 5,180,757; Concepción 330,448; Viña del Mar 302,765; Valparaíso 276,737; Talcahuano 246,566.

Vital statistics

Birth rate per 1,000 population (1990): 23.3 (world avg. 27.1); legitimate 65.7%; illegitimate 34.3%.
Death rate per 1,000 population (1990): 6.0 (world avg. 9.8).
Natural increase rate per 1,000 population (1990): 17.3 (world avg. 17.3).
Total fertility rate (avg. births per childbearing woman; 1990): 2.6.
Marriage rate per 1,000 population (1990): 7.5.
Divorce rate per 1,000 population (1987): 0.4.
Life expectancy at birth (1990–95): male 68.5 years; female 75.6 years.
Major causes of death per 100,000 population (1990): diseases of the circulatory system 163.7; malignant neoplasms (cancers) 107.5; diseases of the respiratory system 73.1; accidents and adverse effects 72.8.

National economy

Budget (1991). Revenue: Ch$3,728,142,000,000 (income from taxes 63.0%, nontax revenue 37.0%). Expenditures: Ch$3,332,559,000,000 (social security and welfare 22.2%, current transfers 18.0%, remunerations 16.7%, public-debt service 14.4%, goods and services 9.5%, real investment 9.3%).
Public debt (external, outstanding; 1991): U.S.$10,024,000,000.
Production (metric tons except as noted). Agriculture, forestry, fishing (1992): sugar beets 2,978,000, wheat 1,557,000, potatoes 1,023,000, corn (maize) 911,000, oats 183,000, rice 134,000, rapeseed 62,000; livestock (number of live animals) 6,650,000 sheep, 3,300,000 cattle, 1,701,000 pigs; roundwood (1991) 18,817,000 cu m; fish catch (1991) 6,166,000. Mining (1992): iron 6,621,000; copper 1,917,800; manganese 49,857; zinc 29,730; molybdenum 14,840; silver 1,028,560 kg; gold 33,774 kg. Manufacturing (1991): cement 2,250,800; cellulose 798,000; refined sugar 353,300[5]; newsprint 172,900; noodles 55,200; carbonated drinks 7,197,000 hectolitres; tires 1,824,900 units; pressed-fibre panels 9,082,900 sq m; flat glass 5,730,300 sq m. Construction (1991)[6]: residential 5,212,547 sq m; nonresidential 2,429,714 sq m. Energy production (consumption): electricity (kW-hr; 1992) 22,146,000,000 ([1990] 18,372,000,000); coal (metric tons; 1991) 2,579,000 ([1990] 3,720,000); crude petroleum (barrels; 1990) 6,320,000 (44,676,000); petroleum products (metric tons; 1990) 6,105,000 (6,448,000); natural gas (cu m; 1991) 4,067,200,000 (4,067,200,000).
Land use (1991): forested 11.8%; meadows and pastures 18.1%; agricultural and under permanent cultivation 5.8%; other 64.3%.
Gross national product (1991): U.S.$28,897,000,000 (U.S.$2,160 per capita).

Structure of gross domestic product and labour force

	1991 in value Ch$'000,000[7]	1991 % of total value	1992 labour force	1992 % of labour force
Agriculture	44,500	8.7	828,970	17.1
Mining	37,000	7.3	92,220	1.9
Manufacturing	104,500	20.5	776,210	16.0
Construction	29,600	5.8	331,150	6.8
Public utilities	12,800	2.5	25,200	0.5
Transp. and commun.	37,400	7.4	326,710	6.7
Trade	94,200	18.5	817,810	16.9
Finance			229,320	4.7
Pub. admin., defense; Services[8] (Finance, Pub. admin., defense, Services, Other combined)	149,100	29.3	1,198,140	24.7
Other			227,374[9]	4.7[9]
TOTAL	509,100	100.0	4,853,104	100.0

Population economically active (1991): total 4,794,100; activity rate of total population 36.6% (participation rates: ages 15–64, 56.7%; female 34.5%; unemployed 5.3%).

Price and earnings indexes (1985 = 100)

	1986	1987	1988	1989	1990	1991	1992
Consumer price index	119.5	143.2	164.3	192.2	242.0	295.0	341.0
Monthly earnings index	122.5	146.1	178.6	212.7	287.9	349.0	421.0

Household income and expenditure. Average household size (1992) 4.1; average annual income per family (household; 1985)[10] Ch$440,738 at June prices (U.S.$2,840); sources of income (1976): wages and salaries 40.8%, transfer payments 8.0%, self-employment and other 51.2%; expenditure (1989): food 27.9%, clothing 22.5%, housing 15.2%, transportation 6.4%.
Tourism (1991): receipts U.S.$700,000,000; expenditures U.S.$409,000,000.

Foreign trade[11]

Balance of trade (current prices)

	1987	1988	1989	1990	1991	1992
U.S.$'000,000	+1,979	+2,219	+1,578	+1,273	+1,575	+749
% of total	21.5%	18.7%	10.8%	8.3%	9.7%	3.9%

Imports (1991): U.S.$7,685,800,000 (intermediate goods 57.8%; capital goods 23.9%; consumer goods 14.8%). *Major import sources:* U.S. 20.6%; Brazil 9.1%; Japan 8.4%; Argentina 7.2%; Germany 6.5%; France 3.1%; Nigeria 2.6%; Venezuela 2.6%.
Exports (1991): U.S.$9,048,400,000 (mining 48.5%; industrial products 36.6%, of which paper and paper products 4.9%, chemical and petroleum products 3.9%; fruits and vegetables 11.0%). *Major export destinations:* Japan 18.2%; U.S. 17.6%; Germany 7.8%; Brazil 4.9%; U.K. 4.5%; Taiwan 4.4%; France 4.3%; The Netherlands 4.0%.

Transport and communications

Transport. Railroads (1990): route length 2,778 mi, 4,470 km; passenger-km 1,076,000,000; metric ton-km cargo 1,572,000,000. Roads (1990): total length 49,457 mi, 79,593 km (paved 14%). Vehicles (1991): passenger cars 792,950; trucks and buses 412,462. Merchant marine (1992): vessels (100 gross tons and over) 392; total deadweight tonnage 854,850. Air transport (1990): passenger-km 2,980,000,000; metric ton-km cargo 689,844,000; airports (1993) with scheduled flights 16.
Communications. Daily newspapers (1990): total number 34; total circulation 890,800[12]; circulation per 1,000 population 68[12]. Radio (1992): 4,250,000 receivers (1 per 3.1 persons). Television (1992): 2,000,000 receivers (1 per 6.7 persons). Telephones (1990): 1,161,000 (1 per 13 persons).

Education and health

Education (1989)

	schools	teachers	students	student/ teacher ratio
Primary (age 6–13)	8,101	55,268	1,987,758	36.0
Secondary (age 14–17)	1,694[13]	...	607,709	...
Vocational	1,262[13]	...	134,301	...
Higher[13]	201	15,131[14]	233,148	...

Educational attainment (1982). Percentage of population age 25 and over having: no formal schooling 9.4%; primary education 56.6%; secondary 26.9%; higher 7.1%. *Literacy* (1990): total population age 15 and over literate 93.4%; males 93.5%; females 93.2%.
Health (1991): physicians 14,664 (1 per 895 persons); hospital beds 43,269 (1 per 303 persons); infant mortality rate per 1,000 live births (1990) 16.0.
Food (1988–90): daily per capita caloric intake 2,484 (vegetable products 82%, animal products 18%); 102% of FAO recommended minimum requirement.

Military

Total active duty personnel (1992): 91,800 (army 58.8%, navy 27.2%, air force 14.0%). *Military expenditure as percentage of GNP* (1989): 3.4% (world 4.9%); per capita expenditure U.S.$61.

[1]Includes 9 nonelective seats; legislative elections were to be held in December 1993. [2]Legislative bodies meet in Valparaíso. [3]Excludes the 480,000-sq mi (1,250,000-sq km) section of Antarctica claimed by Chile (and administered as part of Magallanes y la Antártica Chilena region) and "inland" (actually tidal) water areas. The 1992 census population of Chilean-claimed Antarctica was 126. [4]Preliminary figures not adjusted for undercount; 1993 midyear based on precensus demographic analysis. [5]1989. [6]Construction approved and already begun only. [7]In constant prices of 1977. [8]Services includes restaurants and hotels. [9]Includes an estimated 226,694 unemployed persons. [10]Greater Santiago area. [11]Import figures are f.o.b. in balance of trade and c.i.f. for commodities and trading partners. [12]Circulation for 32 newspapers only. [13]1988. [14]1984.

China

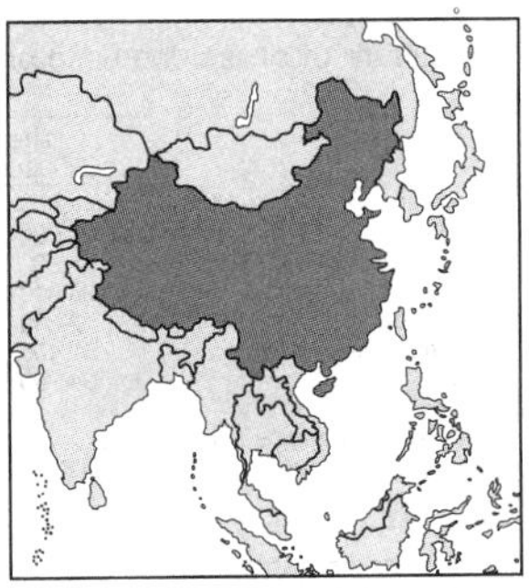

Official name: Chung-hua Jen-min Kung-ho-kuo (People's Republic of China).
Form of government: single-party people's republic with one legislative house (National People's Congress [2,978]).
Chief of state: President.
Head of government: Premier.
Capital: Peking (Beijing).
Official language: Mandarin Chinese.
Official religion: none.
Monetary unit: 1 Renminbi (yuan) (Y) = 10 jiao = 100 fen; valuation (Oct. 4, 1993) 1 U.S.$ = Y 5.78; 1 £ = Y 8.76.

Area and population[1, 2]

		area		population
Provinces	Capitals	sq mi	sq km	1992[3] estimate
Anhwei (Anhui)	Ho-fei (Hefei)	54,000	139,900	57,610,000
Chekiang (Zhejiang)	Hang-chou (Hangzhou)	39,300	101,800	42,020,000
Fukien (Fujian)	Fu-chou (Fuzhou)	47,500	123,100	30,790,000
Hainan (Hainan)	Hai-k'ou (Haikou)	13,200	34,300	6,740,000
Heilungkiang (Heilongjiang)	Harbin	179,000	463,600	35,750,000
Honan (Henan)	Cheng-chou (Zhengzhou)	64,500	167,000	87,630,000
Hopeh (Hebei)	Shih-chia-chuang (Shijiazhuang)	78,200	202,700	62,200,000
Hunan (Hunan)	Ch'ang-sha (Changsha)	81,300	210,500	62,090,000
Hupeh (Hubei)	Wu-han (Wuhan)	72,400	187,500	55,120,000
Kansu (Gansu)	Lan-chou (Lanzhou)	141,500	366,500	22,850,000
Kiangsi (Jiangxi)	Nan-ch'ang (Nanchang)	63,600	164,800	38,650,000
Kiangsu (Jiangsu)	Nanking (Nanjing)	39,600	102,600	68,440,000
Kirin (Jilin)	Ch'ang-ch'un (Changchun)	72,200	187,000	25,090,000
Kwangtung (Guangdong)	Canton (Guangzhou)	76,100	197,100	64,390,000
Kweichow (Guizhou)	Kuei-yang (Guiyang)	67,200	174,000	33,150,000
Liaoning (Liaoning)	Shen-yang (Shenyang)	58,300	151,000	39,900,000
Shansi (Shanxi)	T'ai-yüan (Taiyuan)	60,700	157,100	29,420,000
Shantung (Shandong)	Chi-nan (Jinan)	59,200	153,300	85,700,000
Shensi (Shaanxi)	Sian (Xi'an)	75,600	195,800	33,630,000
Szechwan (Sichuan)	Ch'eng-tu (Chengdu)	219,700	569,000	108,970,000
Tsinghai (Qinghai)	Hsi-ning (Xining)	278,400	721,000	4,540,000
Yunnan (Yunnan)	K'un-ming (Kunming)	168,400	436,200	37,820,000
Autonomous regions				
Inner Mongolia (Nei Monggol)	Hu-ho-hao-t'e (Hohhot)	454,600	1,177,500	21,840,000
Kwangsi Chuang (Guangxi Zhuang)	Nan-ning (Nanning)	85,100	220,400	43,240,000
Ningsia Hui (Ningxia Hui)	Yin-ch'uan (Yinchuan)	25,600	66,400	4,800,000
Sinkiang Uighur (Xinjiang Uygur)	Wu-lu-mu-c'hi (Urumqi)	635,900	1,646,900	15,550,000
Tibet (Xizang)	Lhasa	471,700	1,221,600	2,260,000
Municipalities				
Peking (Beijing)	—	6,500	16,800	10,940,000
Shanghai (Shanghai)	—	2,400	6,200	13,400,000
Tientsin (Tianjin)	—	4,400	11,300	9,090,000
TOTAL		3,696,100[4]	9,572,900[4]	1,158,230,000[5]

Demography

Population (1993): 1,179,467,000.
Density (1993): persons per sq mi 319.1, persons per sq km 123.2.
Urban-rural (1991): urban 26.4%; rural 73.6%.
Sex distribution (1991): male 51.34%; female 48.66%.
Age breakdown (1990): under 15, 27.7%; 15–29, 31.0%; 30–44, 20.7%; 45–59, 12.0%; 60–74, 6.9%; 75 and over, 1.7%.
Population projection: (2000) 1,286,709,000; (2010) 1,381,726,000.
Doubling time: 60 years.
Ethnic composition (1990): Han (Chinese) 91.96%; Chuang 1.37%; Manchu 0.87%; Hui 0.76%; Miao 0.65%; Uighur 0.64%; Yi 0.58%; Tuchia 0.50%; Mongolian 0.42%; Tibetan 0.41%; Puyi 0.23%; Tung 0.22%; Yao 0.18%; Korean 0.17%; Pai 0.14%; Hani 0.11%; Kazakh 0.10%; Tai 0.09%; Li 0.09%; other 0.51%.
Religious affiliation (1980): nonreligious 59.2%; Chinese folk-religionist 20.1%; atheist 12.0%; Buddhist 6.0%; Muslim 2.4%; Christian 0.2%; other 0.1%.
Major cities (1990): Shanghai 7,496,509; Peking 5,769,607; Tientsin 4,574,689; Shen-yang 3,603,712; Wu-han 3,284,229; Canton 2,914,281; Harbin 2,443,398; Chungking (Chongqing) 2,266,772; Nanking 2,090,204; Sian 1,959,044; Ta-lien (Dalian) 1,723,302; Ch'eng-tu 1,713,255; Ch'ang-ch'un 1,679,270; T'ai-yüan 1,533,884; Tsinan 1,480,915; Ch'ing-tao (Qingdao) 1,459,195; An-shan (Anshan) 1,203,986; Fu-shun 1,202,388; Lan-chou 1,194,640; Cheng-chou 1,159,679; Tzu-po (Zibo) 1,138,074; K'un-ming 1,127,411.
Households (1991). Average rural household size 4.7; urban household size 3.4. Family households (1990): 277,390,000 (99.4%); collective 1,671,000 (0.6%).

Vital statistics

Birth rate per 1,000 population (1992): 18.2 (world avg. 26.4).
Death rate per 1,000 population (1992): 6.6 (world avg. 9.2).
Natural increase rate per 1,000 population (1992): 11.6 (world avg. 17.2).
Total fertility rate (avg. births per childbearing woman; 1991): 2.3.
Marriage rate per 1,000 population (1991): 8.3.
Divorce rate per 1,000 population (1991): 0.7.
Life expectancy at birth (1990): male 68.6 years; female 71.8 years.
Major causes of death per 100,000 population (percentage distribution; 1991)[6]: malignant neoplasms (cancers) 22.4%; diseases of the circulatory system 21.1%; diseases of the respiratory system 15.2%; diseases of the heart 14.9%; injuries and poisoning 7.1%; digestive diseases 4.1%.

Social indicators

Educational attainment (1982). Percentage of population age 25 and over having: no schooling and incomplete primary 44.5%; completed primary 32.7%; completed junior secondary 16.1%; completed senior secondary 5.6%; postsecondary 1.1%.

Distribution of urban household income (1991)

avg. per capita income by quintile (avg. Y 1,713)

first quintile	second quintile	third quintile	fourth quintile	fifth quintile
Y 1,123	Y 1,439	Y 1,671	Y 1,951	Y 2,620

Quality of working life (1991). Average workweek: 48 hours. Annual rate per 100,000 workers for: injury or accident, n.a.; industrial illness, n.a.; death, n.a. Funds for pensions and social welfare relief (1991): Y 55,440,000,000. Average days lost to labour stoppages per 1,000 workdays: n.a. Average duration of journey to work: n.a. Method of transport: n.a. Rate per 1,000 workers of discouraged (unemployed no longer seeking work): n.a.
Access to services. Proportion of communes having access to electricity (1979) 87.1%. Percentage of urban population with: safe public water supply (1991) 90.6%; public sewage collection, n.a.; public fire protection, n.a.
Social participation. Eligible voters participating in last national election: n.a. Population participating in voluntary work: n.a. Trade union membership in total labour force (1988): 18.9%. Practicing religious population in total affiliated population: n.a.
Social deviance. Annual reported arrest rate per 100,000 population (1986) for: property violation 20.7; infringing personal rights 7.2; disruption of social administration 3.3; endangering public security[7] 1.0.
Leisure. Favourite leisure activities: n.a.
Material well-being (1991). Urban families possessing (number per family): wristwatches 2.7; bicycles 1.9; televisions 1.1; sewing machines 0.7; radios 0.4. Rural families possessing (number per family): wristwatches 1.8; bicycles 1.2; sewing machines 0.6; televisions 0.5.; radios 0.3.

National economy

Gross national product (at current market prices; 1991): U.S.$424,012,000,000 (U.S.$370 per capita).

Structure of gross national product and labour force

	1991			
	in value Y '000,000,000	% of total value	labour force ('000)[8]	% of labour force
Agriculture	528.86	26.6	350,160	60.0
Mining	...	...	1,000	0.2
Manufacturing	808.71	40.7	99,470	17.0
Construction	106.00	5.3	25,210	4.3
Public utilities	...	...	...	...
Transp. and commun.	120.30	6.1	15,150	2.6
Trade	88.72	4.5	31,000	5.3
Finance	...	...	2,340	0.4
Pub. admin.	...	...	11,360	2.0
Services	332.87	16.8	28,810	4.9
Other	...	...	19,100	3.3
TOTAL	1,985.46	100.0	583,600	100.0

Budget (1991). Revenue: Y 361,090,000,000 (taxes 82.8%; funds collected for energy and transport projects 5.2%). Expenditures: Y 381,360,000,000 (capital construction 19.4%; culture, education, and public health 18.6%; government administration 9.9%; subsidies 9.8%; defense 8.7%).
Public debt (external, outstanding; 1991): U.S.$50,502,000,000.
Tourism: receipts from visitors (1992) U.S.$3,950,000,000; expenditures by nationals abroad (1991) U.S.$417,000,000.

Retail and service enterprises (1991)

	no. of enter-prises	no. of employees	annual wage as a % of all wages	annual gross output value (Y '000,000)
Retail trade	9,241,000	21,987,000	...	...
Grocery stores	166,000	1,175,000	...	...
Department stores	160,000	1,882,000	...	...
Other food shops	117,000	786,000	...	...
Agricultural supplies stores	95,000	460,000	...	...
Electrical appliances stores	80,000	790,000	...	...
Household supplies stores	67,000	354,000	...	...
Grain and oil shops	66,000	685,000	...	...
Textile stores	38,000	259,000	...	...
Drugstores	28,000	217,000	...	...
Bookstores	27,000	134,000	...	...
Coal stores	15,000	176,000	...	...
Service trade	1,766,000	4,263,000	...	...
Repair shops	730,000	1,084,000	...	...
Barbershops	478,000	732,000	...	...
Hotels	181,000	1,368,000	...	...
Photo studios	95,000	215,000	...	...

Production (metric tons except as noted). Agriculture, forestry, fishing (1991): grains—rice 187,450,000, wheat 95,003,000, corn (maize) 93,350,000, sorghum 5,615,000, millet 4,501,000, barley 3,000,000; oilseeds—rapeseed 7,436,000, peanuts (groundnuts) 6,060,000, sunflower seeds 1,250,000; fruits and nuts—watermelons 6,280,000, oranges 5,385,000, apples 4,816,000, cantaloupes 3,135,000, walnuts 153,000; other—sweet potatoes 107,190,000, sugarcane 73,103,000, potatoes 35,533,000, seed cotton 16,989,000, sugar beets 16,237,000, soybeans 9,807,000, cabbage 8,103,000, tomatoes

5,690,000, cucumbers 4,148,000, tobacco leaves 3,121,000, eggplant 2,383,-000, tea 566,000; livestock (number of live animals) 363,975,000 pigs, 112,820,000 sheep, 97,378,000 goats, 81,407,000 cattle, 21,635,000 water buffalo, 11,198,000 asses, 10,174,000 horses, 2,077,000,000 chickens, 369,000,000 ducks; roundwood (1990) 277,015,000 cu m; fish catch (1990) 12,095,363. Mining and quarrying (1991): metal concentrates—copper 560,000, zinc 550,000, lead 300,000, tungsten 30,000, tin 26,000; metal ores—iron ore 170,-000,000, bauxite 2,500,000, manganese ore 1,600,000[9], silver 125,000[9], gold 90,000[9]; nonmetals—salt 25,530,000, gypsum 8,300,000, phosphates 4,100,-000[9], barite 1,750,000, fluorite 1,700,000, talc 1,600,000, graphite 200,000[9], asbestos 150,000. Manufacturing (1992): cement 304,000,000; rolled steel 65,340,000; chemical fertilizer 20,990,000; paper and paperboard 15,900,-000; sulfuric acid 13,960,000; sugar 8,155,000; cotton yarn 4.900,000; cotton fabrics 18,500,000,000 m; cigarettes 32,880,000 cases; colour television sets 13,140,000 units; household washing machines 7,127,000 units; household refrigerators 4,753,000 units; motor vehicles 1,082,000 units. Construction (1991): residential 940,020,000 sq m; nonresidential 251,050,000 sq m. Distribution of industrial production (percentage of total value of output by sector; 1978 [1991]): state-operated enterprises 80.6% (52.9%); collectives 19.2% (35.7%); privately operated enterprises 0.2% (11.4%). Retail sales (percentage of total sales by sector; 1978 [1991]): state-operated enterprises 90.5% (40.2%); collectives 7.4% (30.0%); privately operated enterprises 2.1% (29.8%).

Manufacturing and mining enterprises (1991)

	no. of enterprises	no. of employees[10]	annual wages as a % of avg. of all wages[11]	annual gross output value (Y '000,000)
Manufacturing				
Machinery, transport equipment, and basic manufactures,	105,451	18,010,000	96.7	540,490
of which,				
Industrial equipment	6,616	9,630,000	...	39,240
Transport equipment	11,203	2,290,000	...	97,575
Electronic goods	4,919	1,720,000	...	76,469
Measuring equipment	3,508	660,000	...	13,671
Textiles,	24,596	7,560,000	95.5	253,327
of which,				
Cotton	9,353	...	...	137,460
Foodstuffs,	39,319	4,670,000	87.5	147,335
of which,				
Grains and edible oils	12,104	...	...	37,751
Processed meat	...	...	...	...
Tobacco manufactures	329	...	...	54,745
Chemicals,	42,226	6,990,000	92.1	316,052
of which,				
Organic chemicals	6,775	...	...	49,121
Plastics	14,554	1,020,000	...	43,923
Building materials,	52,179	4,010,000	93.0	105,540
of which,				
Brick, tile, other	...	...	...	...
Cement (all forms)	5,374	856,000[12]	...	37,052
Secondary forest products (including paper and stationery)	30,909	2,410,000	96.1	63,607
Primary forest products	1,055	1,130,000	114.3	10,092
Mining				
Nonferrous and ferrous metals	3,982	1,000,000	107.6	16,121
Crude petroleum	35	770,000	...	51,495
Coal	9,682	5,550,000	119.8	51,886

Energy production (consumption): electricity (kW-hr; 1990) 618,000,000,000 (619,460,000,000); coal (metric tons; 1990) 1,080,000,000 (1,064,500,000); crude petroleum (barrels; 1990) 1,010,892,000 (800,515,000); petroleum products (metric tons; 1990) 85,877,000 (85,109,000); natural gas (cu m; 1990) 15,258,000,000 (15,258,000,000).

Financial aggregates[13]

	1987	1988	1989	1990	1991	1992	April 1993[14]
Exchange rate, Y per:							
U.S. dollar	3.72	3.72	4.72	5.22	5.43	5.75	5.71
£	6.96	6.73	7.58	10.06	10.16	8.70	8.99
SDR	5.28	5.01	6.21	7.43	7.77	7.91	8.13
International reserves (U.S.$)							
Total (excl. gold; '000,000)	16,305	18,541	17,960	29,586	43,674	20,620	20,816
SDRs ('000,000)	640	586	540	562	577	419	441
Reserve pos. in IMF ('000,000)	429	407	398	430	433	758	733
Foreign exchange	15,236	17,548	17,022	28,594	42,664	19,443	19,642
Gold ('000,000 fine troy oz)	12.7	12.7	12.7	12.7	12.7	12.7	12.7
% world reserves	1.3	1.3	1.4	1.4	1.4	1.4	1.4
Interest and prices							
Central bank discount (%)	...	...	...	...	...	...	...
Govt. bond yield (%)	...	...	...	...	...	...	...
Industrial share prices	...	...	...	...	...	...	...
Balance of payments (U.S.$'000,000)							
Balance of visible trade,	−1,661	−5,315	−5,620	+9,165	+8,743	...	...
of which:							
Imports, f.o.b.	−36,395	−46,369	−48,840	−42,354	−50,176	...	...
Exports, f.o.b.	34,734	41,054	43,220	51,519	58,919	...	...
Balance of invisibles	1,961	1,513	1,303	2,833	5,022	...	...
Balance of payments, current account	300	−3,802	−4,317	+11,998	+13,765	...	...

Household income and expenditure. Average household size (1991) 4.3; rural household 4.7, urban household 3.4. Average annual income per household Y 5,156; rural household Y 4,917, urban household Y 5,825. Sources of income: rural household (1991)—income from household businesses 83.1%, income from the collective 9.3%, rural new economic associations 0.3%, other 7.3%; urban household (1991)—wages 75.7%, business income 23.4%, other 0.9%. Expenditure (1991): rural household—food 56.8%, personal effects 11.6%, housing 11.1%, clothing 8.2%, fuel 4.3%, cultural activities 3.2%; urban household—food 53.8%, clothing 13.7%, personal effects 9.6%, cultural activities 6.0%, fuel 3.7%, medicines 2.2%, transportation 1.2%, rent 0.7%.
Population economically active (1987): total 584,569,200; activity rate of total population 54.7% (participation rates: over age 15, 76.8%; female 49.7%; unemployed 2.0%[15]). Urban work force by sector of employment, 1978 (1991): state-run enterprises 74,500,000 (106,640,000); collectives 20,000,000 (36,280,-000); self-employment or privately run enterprises 150,000 (9,755,000).

Price and earnings indexes (1985 = 100)

	1984	1985	1986	1987	1988	1989	1990
Consumer price index	89.4	100.0	107.0	116.4	140.5	163.4	165.5
Annual earnings index[16]	84.8	100.0	115.8	127.1	152.2	168.6	186.4

Land use (1990): forested 13.6%; meadows and pastures 42.9%; agricultural and under permanent cultivation 10.4%; other 33.1%.

Foreign trade[17]

Balance of trade (current prices)

	1987	1988	1989	1990	1991	1992
Y '000,000	−990	−11,810	−6,600	+62,570	+69,470	+57,730
% of total	0.3%	3.2%	1.7%	12.0%	10.2%	7.0%

Imports (1991): U.S.$63,719,000,000 (machinery and transport equipment 30.8%; products of textile industries, rubber and metal products 16.5%; chemical and related products 14.6%; inedible raw materials 7.9%; food and live animals 4.4%; mineral fuels and lubricants 3.3%). *Major import sources:* Hong Kong 27.4%; Japan 15.7%; United States 12.6%; Taiwan 5.7%; Germany 4.8%; U.S.S.R. 3.3%; Canada 2.6%; France 2.5%; Australia 2.4%; Italy 2.3%; Indonesia 2.2%.
Exports (1991): U.S.$71,910,000,000 (products of textile industries, rubber and metal products 20.1%; food and live animals 10.0%; machinery and transport equipment 9.9%; mineral fuels and lubricants 6.7%; chemicals and allied products 5.3%; inedible raw materials 4.8%). *Major export destinations:* Hong Kong 44.7%; Japan 14.3%; United States 8.6%; Germany 3.3%; South Korea 3.0%; Singapore 2.8%; U.S.S.R. 2.5%; The Netherlands 1.5%; Italy 1.3%; Thailand 1.2%; France 1.0%.

Transport and communications

Transport. Railroads (1991): length 42,261 mi, 68,013 km; (1992) passenger-mi 195,700,000,000, passenger-km 315,000,000,000; short ton-mi cargo 795,-900,000,000, metric ton-km cargo 1,162,000,000,000. Roads (1991): total length 646,931 mi, 1,041,136 km (paved 87%). Vehicles (1991): passenger cars 1,852,400; trucks and buses 4,208,800. Merchant marine (1992): vessels (100 gross tons and over) 2,390; total deadweight tonnage 20,657,996. Air transport (1992): passenger-mi 24,800,000,000, passenger-km 39,900,000,000; short ton-mi cargo 925,000,000, metric ton-km cargo 1,350,000,000; airports (1993) with scheduled flights 86.
Communications. Daily newspapers (1988): total number 78; total circulation 39,597,000[18]; circulation per 1,000 population 37[18]. Radio (1990): total number of receivers 209,500,000 (1 per 5.4 persons). Television (1990): total number of receivers 35,000,000 (1 per 32.4 persons). Telephones (1990): 12,735,400 (1 per 89 persons).

Education and health

Education (1991)

	schools	teachers	students	student/teacher ratio
Primary (age 7–13)	893,623	6,301,000	143,735,000	22.8
Secondary (age 13–17)	85,851	3,090,000	46,835,000	15.2
Secondary specialized	13,497	467,000	5,433,000	11.6
Higher	1,075	391,000	2,044,000	5.2

Literacy (1990): total population age 15 and over literate 636,112,000 (77.7%); males literate 364,687,000 (87.0%); females literate 271,425,000 (68.0%).
Health (1992): physicians 1,808,000 (1 per 648 persons); hospital beds 2,744,-000 (1 per 427 persons); infant mortality rate per 1,000 live births (1991) 33.0.
Food (1988–90): daily per capita caloric intake 2,641 (vegetable products 89%, animal products 11%); 112% of FAO recommended minimum requirement.

Military

Total active duty personnel (1992): 3,030,000 (army 75.9%, navy 8.6%, air force 15.5%). *Military expenditure as percentage of GNP* (1989): 3.7% (world 4.9%); per capita expenditure U.S.$20.

[1]Names of the provinces, autonomous regions, and municipalities are stated in conventional form, followed by Pinyin transliteration; names of capitals are stated in conventional form or Wade-Giles transliteration, followed by Pinyin transliteration. [2]Data for Taiwan, Quemoy, and Matsu are excluded. [3]January 1. [4]Includes 4,600 sq mi (11,900 sq km) not shown separately. [5]Total includes servicemen not assigned to any political division. [6]Based on urban sample population. [7]Excludes arrests for anti-Communist activities. [8]Social labour force. [9]1989. [10]In state-owned and collective-owned industries only. [11]1979. [12]1984. [13]Exchange rates and international reserves are end-of-year figures. [14]End-of-month figures for exchange rates and international reserves. [15]Rate of waiting for employment in cities and towns. [16]Average annual wage in industrial establishments in urban areas. [17]Imports and exports f.o.b. [18]Circulation data based on 58 dailies.

Colombia

Official name: República de Colombia (Republic of Colombia).
Form of government: unitary, multiparty republic with two legislative houses (Senate [102[1]]; House of Representatives [161]).
Head of state and government: President.
Capital: Santafé de Bogotá, D.C.
Official language: Spanish.
Official religion: none.
Monetary unit: 1 peso (Col$) = 100 centavos; valuation (Oct. 4, 1993) 1 U.S.$ = Col$804.95; 1 £ = Col$1,220.

Area and population

		area		population
Departments	**Capitals**	sq mi	sq km	1993 estimate
Amazonas	Leticia	42,342	109,665	54,939
Antioquia	Medellín	24,561	63,612	4,535,438
Arauca	Arauca	9,196	23,818	98,005
Atlántico	Barranquilla	1,308	3,388	1,741,279
Bolívar	Cartagena	10,030	25,978	1,479,043
Boyacá	Tunja	8,953	23,189	1,286,756
Caldas	Manizales	3,046	7,888	915,302
Caquetá	Florencia	34,349	88,965	317,122
Casanare	Yopal	17,236	44,640	181,609
Cauca	Popayán	11,316	29,308	946,577
Cesar	Valledupar	8,844	22,905	816,955
Chocó	Quibdó	17,965	46,530	357,201
Córdoba	Montería	9,660	25,020	1,132,425
Cundinamarca	Santafé de Bogotá, D.C.	8,735	22,623	1,689,516
Guainía	Puerto Inírida	27,891	72,238	13,194
Guaviare	Guaviare	16,342	42,327	66,676
Huila	Neiva	7,680	19,890	791,883
La Guajira	Riohacha	8,049	20,848	355,325
Magdalena	Santa Marta	8,953	23,188	994,838
Meta	Villavicencio	33,064	85,635	578,997
Nariño	Pasto	12,845	33,268	1,177,965
Norte de Santander	Cúcuta	8,362	21,658	1,022,816
Putumayo	Mocoa	9,608	24,885	229,798
Quindío	Armenia	712	1,845	418,333
Risaralda	Pereira	1,598	4,140	749,214
San Andrés y Providencia	San Andrés	17	44	42,409
Santander	Bucaramanga	11,790	30,537	1,665,069
Sucre	Sincelejo	4,215	10,917	620,059
Tolima	Ibagué	9,097	23,562	1,203,037
Valle	Cali	8,548	22,140	3,388,133
Vaupés	Mitú	25,200	65,268	35,798
Vichada	Puerto Carreño	38,703	100,242	19,471
Capital District				
Santafé de Bogotá, D.C.		613	1,587	5,025,989
TOTAL		440,831[2]	1,141,748	33,951,171

Demography

Population (1993): 33,951,000.
Density (1993): persons per sq mi 77.0, persons per sq km 29.7.
Urban-rural (1985): urban 67.2%; rural 32.8%.
Sex distribution (1992): male 49.60%; female 50.40%.
Age breakdown (1992): under 15, 34.4%; 15–29, 29.8%; 30–44, 20.0%; 45–59, 9.5%; 60–74, 4.9%; 75 and over, 1.4%.
Population projection: (2000) 37,822,000; (2010) 42,959,000.
Doubling time: 36 years.
Ethnic composition (1985): mestizo 58.0%; white 20.0%; mulatto 14.0%; black 4.0%; mixed black-Indian 3.0%; Amerindian 1.0%.
Religious affiliation (1992): Roman Catholic 92.7%; other 7.3%.
Major cities (1993): Santafé de Bogotá, D.C., 5,025,989; Cali 1,655,699; Medellín 1,594,967; Barranquilla 1,033,951; Cartagena 707,092.

Vital statistics

Birth rate per 1,000 population (1983–88): 27.9 (world avg. 27.1).
Death rate per 1,000 population (1983–88): 7.4 (world avg. 9.8).
Natural increase rate per 1,000 population (1983–88): 20.5 (world avg. 17.3).
Total fertility rate (avg. births per childbearing woman; 1981–86): 3.4.
Life expectancy at birth (1990–95): male 66.4 years; female 72.3 years.
Major causes of death per 100,000 population (1990)[3]: homicide with firearms 101.0; malignant neoplasms (cancers) 82.6; ischemic heart disease 70.4; accidents 49.0; infectious and parasitic diseases 25.5.

National economy

Budget (1991). Revenue: Col$4,459,837,000,000 (indirect taxes 38.6%, direct taxes 27.7%, credit resources 9.8%). Expenditures: Col$3,518,923,000,000 (finance and public credit 31.8%, education 16.6%, defense 9.8%, public works and transportation 6.2%, health 5.3%, police 5.1%).
Public debt (external, outstanding; 1991): U.S.$14,503,000,000.
Tourism (1991): receipts U.S.$410,000,000; expenditures U.S.$593,000,000.
Production (metric tons except as noted). Agriculture (1992): sugarcane 28,930,000, plantains 2,745,000, potatoes 2,131,000, bananas 1,900,000, rice 1,735,000, corn (maize) 1,056,000, coffee (green) 1,050,000, sorghum 752,000; livestock (number of live animals) 24,772,000 cattle, 3,708,000[4] vicuña, 2,644,000 pigs, 2,553,000 sheep; roundwood (1991) 19,702,000 cu m; fish catch (1991) 108,708. Mining and quarrying (1992): iron ore 657,210; gold 1,065,290 troy oz; silver 268,774 troy oz; emeralds (1990) U.S.$116,700,000[5]. Manufacturing (value added in Col$'000,000; 1989): processed food 490,322; beverages 373,927; textiles 310,239; chemical products 205,208; machinery and electrical apparatus 164,743; basic steel 142,791; metal products 137,920; transport equipment 126,916. Construction (1991)[6]: residential 6,598,079 sq m; nonresidential 1,952,344 sq m. Energy production (consumption): electricity (kW-hr; 1990) 36,000,000,000 (36,000,000,000); coal (metric tons; 1990) 19,000,000 (5,300,000); crude petroleum (barrels; 1990) 156,946,000 (96,168,000); petroleum products (metric tons; 1990) 10,645,000 (7,835,000); natural gas (cu m; 1990) 5,656,773,000 (5,656,773,000).
Gross national product (1992): U.S.$43,092,000,000 (U.S.$1,290 per capita).

Structure of gross domestic product and labour force

	1991		1980	
	in value Col$'000,000	% of total value	labour force	% of labour force
Agriculture	4,594,905	17.4	2,412,413	28.5
Mining	1,984,242	7.5	49,740	0.6
Manufacturing	5,189,473	19.7	1,136,735	13.4
Construction	1,223,596	4.6	242,191	2.9
Public utilities	803,883	3.0	44,233	0.5
Transp. and commun.	2,395,160	9.1	352,623	4.2
Trade	2,899,869	11.0	1,261,633	14.9
Finance }			278,210	3.2
Pub. admin., defense }	7,302,204	27.7 }	1,998,460	23.6
Services }				
Other }			690,762[7]	8.2[7]
TOTAL	26,393,332	100.0	8,467,000	100.0

Population economically active (1985): total 9,558,000; activity rate 34.3% (participation rates: over age 12, 49.4%; female 32.8%; unemployed 4.3%).

Price and earnings indexes (1985 = 100)

	1986	1987	1988	1989	1990	1991	1992
Consumer price index	118.9	146.6	187.8	236.3	305.1	397.9	505.5
Monthly earnings index[8]	104.0	103.6	103.1	105.0	...	...	...

Household income and expenditure. Avg. household size (1985) 4.7; sources of income (1988): wages 46.7%, self-employment 37.7%, transfer payments 8.5%; expenditure (1989): food 34.3%, transportation 15.6%, housing 8.2%, health care 6.6%, household durable goods 6.3%, clothing 6.0%.
Land use (1991): forested 48.1%; pastures 39.0%; agricultural 5.2%; other 7.7%.

Foreign trade[9]

Balance of trade (current prices)

	1987	1988	1989	1990	1991	1992
U.S.$'000,000	+735.0	+505.4	+729.9	+1,621.0	+2,720.1	+920.1
% of total	8.6%	5.3%	6.8%	13.6%	23.2%	7.1%

Imports (1991)[10]: U.S.$4,909,397,000 (machinery 25.3%, chemicals 11.0%, transport equipment 7.4%, steel products 6.9%, crude petroleum 6.0%, plastic products 3.9%). *Major import sources:* U.S. 37.7%; Japan 9.6%; Germany 9.5%; Venezuela 5.1%; Brazil 3.6%; France 3.6%; Switzerland 2.8%.
Exports (1991)[10]: U.S.$7,265,702,000 (petroleum and petroleum products 28.8%, coffee 18.4%, textile apparel 7.7%, fruits 6.1%, flowers 3.9%, iron and steel 2.4%). *Major export destinations:* U.S. 40.5%; Germany 11.0%; Venezuela 3.4%; France 3.1%; The Netherlands 3.0%; Peru 2.8%.

Transport and communications

Transport. Railroads (1991): route length (1987) 3,236 km; passenger-km 79,231,000; metric ton-km cargo 298,277,000. Roads (1989): total length 129,117 km (paved 8%). Vehicles (1989): cars 936,000; trucks and buses 364,000. Merchant marine (1992): vessels (100 gross tons and over) 101; deadweight tonnage 403,047. Air transport (1991): passenger-km 4,501,528,000; metric ton-km cargo 945,453,000; airports (1993) 64.
Communications. Daily newspapers (1992): 31; circulation 1,440,700; circulation per 1,000 population 23. Radio (1992): 34,487,000 receivers (1 per 1.0 persons). Television (1992): 5,500,000 receivers (1 per 6.1 persons). Telephones (1990): 2,909,243 (1 per 11 persons).

Education and health

Education (1991)

	schools	teachers	students	student/ teacher ratio
Primary (6–10)	41,044	143,193	4,310,970	30.1
Secondary (11–16)[11]	6,134[12]	119,742	2,377,947	19.9
Higher	235[13]	51,725[14]	474,787[14]	9.2[14]

Educational attainment (1985). Percentage of population age 25 and over having: no schooling 15.3%; primary education 50.1%; secondary 25.4%; higher 6.8%; not stated 2.4%. *Literacy* (1990): population age 15 and over literate 86.7%; males literate 87.5%; females literate 85.9%.
Health: physicians (1989) 29,353 (1 per 1,061 persons); hospital beds (1987) 45,761 (1 per 673 persons); infant mortality rate (1990–95) 37.0.
Food (1988–90): daily per capita caloric intake 2,453 (vegetable products 84%, animal products 16%); 106% of FAO recommended minimum requirement.

Military

Total active duty personnel (1993): 140,000 (army 85.7%, navy 9.3%, air force 5.0%). *Military expenditure as percentage of GNP* (1989): 2.1% (world 4.9%); per capita expenditure U.S.$24.

[1]Includes 2 nonelective seats for Amerindian communities. [2]Detail does not add to total given because of rounding. [3]Estimates based on about 75% of total deaths. [4]1991. [5]Value of foreign sales. [6]Construction permits issued for 11 urban centres. [7]Includes unemployed. [8]Real wages in the industrial sector. [9]Import figures are f.o.b. in balance of trade and c.i.f. in commodities and trading partners. [10]Estimate. [11]Secondary includes vocational and teacher training. [12]1988. [13]1987. [14]1989.

Comoros[1]

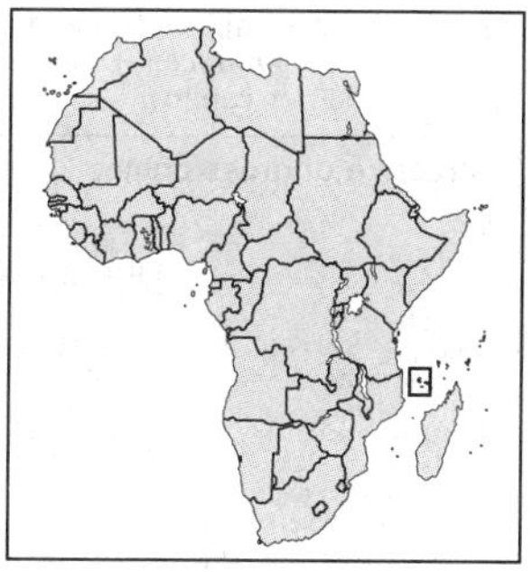

Official name: Jumhūrīyat al-Qumur al-Ittiḥādīyah al-Islāmīyah (Arabic); République Fédérale Islamique des Comores (French) (Federal Islamic Republic of the Comoros).
Form of government: federal Islamic republic with one legislative house (Federal Assembly [42])[2].
Chief of state: President.
Head of government: Prime Minister.
Capital: Moroni.
Official languages: Arabic; French.
Official religion: Islam.
Monetary unit: 1 Comorian franc (CF) = 100 centimes; valuation (Oct. 4, 1993) 1 U.S.$ = CF 283.25; 1 £ = CF 429.12.

Area and population

		area		population
Governorates/Islands[3]	Capitals	sq mi	sq km	1991 estimate
Mohéli (Mwali)	Fomboni	112	290	25,200
Grande Comore (Njazidja)	Moroni	443	1,148	255,800
Anjouan (Nzwani)	Mutsamudu	164	424	197,900
TOTAL		719	1,862	478,900

Demography

Population (1993): 516,000.
Density (1993): persons per sq mi 717.7, persons per sq km 277.1.
Urban-rural (1990): urban 27.8%; rural 72.2%.
Sex distribution (1990)[4]: male 50.64%; female 49.36%.
Age breakdown (1990)[4]: under 15, 48.3%; 15–29, 26.3%; 30–44, 13.8%; 45–59, 7.7%; 60–74, 3.3%; 75 and over, 0.6%.
Population projection: (2000) 661,000; (2010) 912,000.
Doubling time: 20 years.
Ethnic composition (1980): Comorian (a mixture of Bantu, Arab, and Malagasy peoples) 96.9%; Makua (a Bantu people from East Africa) 1.6%; French 0.4%; other 1.1%.
Religious affiliation (1990): Sunnī Muslim 99.4%; Roman Catholic 0.6%.
Major cities (1988): Moroni 22,000; Mutsamudu 14,000; Domoni 7,147[5]; Fomboni 7,000; Ouani 6,936[5].

Vital statistics

Birth rate per 1,000 population (1991): 47.5 (world avg. 26.4).
Death rate per 1,000 population (1991): 13.0 (world avg. 9.2).
Natural increase rate per 1,000 population (1991): 34.5 (world avg. 17.2).
Total fertility rate (avg. births per childbearing woman; 1991): 7.0.
Marriage rate per 1,000 population: n.a.
Divorce rate per 1,000 population: n.a.
Life expectancy at birth (1991): male 50.3 years; female 53.8 years.
Major causes of death per 100,000 population: n.a.; however, major diseases include malaria (afflicts 80% of the adult population), tuberculosis, leprosy, and kwashiorkor (a nutritional deficiency disease).

National economy

Budget (1992). Revenue: CF 25,061,000,000 (grants 45.0%; tax revenue 40.2%; loans 8.7%; nontax revenue 4.8%). Expenditures: CF 25,061,000,000 (current expenditures 64.9%, of which interest on the debt 2.7%; development expenditures 35.1%, of which debt amortization 7.0%).
Production (metric tons except as noted). Agriculture, forestry, fishing (1992): bananas 54,300, coconuts 50,000[4], cassava 46,840, pulses 7,000[4], copra 5,000[4], corn (maize) 3,590, rice 3,060, cloves 474[6], vanilla 236[6], ylang-ylang 45[6], other export crops grown in small quantities include coffee, cinnamon, and tuberoses; livestock (number of live animals) 126,000 goats[4], 47,000 cattle[4], 14,000 sheep[4]; roundwood, n.a.; fish catch (1991) 6,455[4], of which tuna 3,205[4]. Mining and quarrying (1991): sand, gravel, and crushed stone from coral mining for local construction. Manufacturing: products include processed vanilla and ylang-ylang, cement, handicrafts, soaps, soft drinks, woodwork, and clothing. Construction: n.a. Energy production (consumption): electricity (kW-hr; 1992) 27,200,000 (16,000,000[7]); coal, none (none); crude petroleum, none (none); petroleum products (metric tons; 1990) none (22,000); natural gas, none (none).
Population economically active (1985): total 117,216; activity rate of total population 29.6% (participation rates: ages 15–64, 53.1%; female 26.2%; unemployed, n.a.).

Price and earnings indexes (1985 = 100)

	1984	1985	1986	1987	1988	1989	1990
Consumer price index[8]	93.7	100.0	106.8	111.1	114.0	117.6	122.3
Earnings index	...	...	...	...	...	...	...

Tourism (1992): receipts from visitors U.S.$11,000,000; expenditures by nationals abroad U.S.$7,000,000.
Public debt (external, outstanding; 1991): U.S.$161,400,000.
Household income and expenditure. Average household size (1985) 5.6; income per household: n.a.; sources of income: n.a.; expenditure (1983)[9]: food and beverages 56.0%, energy 14.4%, clothing and footwear 10.0%, transportation and communications 6.6%, health care 5.0%, recreation 3.0%, tobacco 3.0%, other 2.0%.

Gross national product (at current market prices; 1992): U.S.$260,000,000 (U.S.$510 per capita).

Structure of gross domestic product and labour force

	1992		1980	
	in value CF '000,000	% of total value	labour force	% of labour force
Agriculture, fishing	27,396	39.6	53,063	53.3
Mining	...	...	62	0.1
Manufacturing	3,010	4.4	3,946	4.0
Construction	4,104	5.9	3,267	3.3
Public utilities	1,088	1.6	129	0.1
Transportation and communications	2,960	4.3	2,118	2.1
Trade, restaurants, hotels	18,164	26.3	1,873	1.9
Finance, insurance }	10,564	15.3	237	0.2
Public admin., defense }			2,435	2.5
Services	1,843	2.7	4,646	4.7
Other	—	—	27,687[10]	27.8[10]
TOTAL	69,129	100.0[11]	99,463	100.0

Land use (1991)[4]: forested 15.7%; meadows and pastures 6.7%; agricultural and under permanent cultivation 44.9%; other 32.7%.

Foreign trade[12]

Balance of trade (current prices)

	1987	1988	1989	1990	1991	1992
CF '000,000	−12,075	−9,249	−7,767	−9,157	−9,371	−12,292
% of total	63.4%	42.0%	40.1%	48.4%	40.0%	51.2%

Imports (1992): CF 18,139,000,000 (rice 11.9%, vehicles 10.7%, petroleum products 10.5%, meat and fish 6.5%, cement 4.8%, milk products 4.1%, unspecified commodities 40.9%). *Major import sources*[13]: France 52.0%; Italy 20.0%; Bahrain 4.0%; Singapore 4.0%; Japan 3.0%.
Exports (1992): CF 5,847,000,000 (vanilla 70.4%, ylang-ylang 19.5%, cloves 1.8%). *Major export destinations:* United States 47.4%; France 41.2%; Germany 5.3%.

Transport and communications

Transport. Railroads: none. Roads (1989)[4, 14]: total length 376 mi, 605 km. Vehicles (1989)[4]: passenger cars, 1,000; trucks and buses, 4,000. Merchant marine (1992): vessels (100 gross tons and over) 6; total deadweight tonnage 3,579. Air transport (1990): passenger-mi 1,900,000, passenger-km 3,000,000; short ton-mi cargo, n.a., metric ton-mi cargo, n.a.; airports (1993) with scheduled flights 4.
Communications. Daily newspapers: none[15]. Radio (1992): total number of receivers 50,000 (1 per 10 persons). Television (1990): total number of receivers 200 (1 per 2,310 persons). Telephones (1992): 3,851[16] (1 per 132 persons).

Education and health

Education (1989–90)

	schools	teachers	students	student/ teacher ratio
Primary (age 6–11)[17]	257	1,777	64,737	36.4
Secondary (age 12–18)	...	557	14,472	26.0
Higher	...	32	248	7.8

Educational attainment (1980). Percentage of population age 25 and over having: no formal schooling 56.7%; Qur'anic school education 8.3%; primary 3.6%; secondary 2.0%; higher 0.2%; not specified 29.2%. *Literacy* (1990): total population age 15 and over literate, about 125,000 (slightly more than 50%).
Health: physicians (1990) 42 (1 per 11,100 persons); hospital beds (1982) 813 (1 per 437 persons); infant mortality rate per 1,000 live births (1991) 87.0.
Food (1988–90)[4]: daily per capita caloric intake 1,760 (vegetable products 95%, animal products 5%); 75% of FAO recommended minimum requirement.

Military

Total active duty personnel (1990): 700–800 (army 100%). *Military expenditure as percentage of GNP* (1987): 1.9% (world 5.4%); per capita expenditure U.S.$7.

[1]Excludes Mayotte, a *collectivité territoriale* ("territorial collectivity") of France, unless otherwise indicated. [2]New constitution approved by referendum on June 7, 1992. [3]Island names in French and Comorian Swahili, respectively. [4]Includes Mayotte. [5]1980. [6]Exported production only. [7]1990. [8]GDP price deflator. [9]Weights of consumer price index components. [10]Not adequately defined. [11]Detail does not add to total given because of rounding. [12]Imports c.i.f.; exports f.o.b. [13]Estimated figures for 1991. [14]Paved roads only. [15]Weekly newspapers (1992): 1; total circulation 1,500. [16]Number of lines. [17]1987–88.

Congo

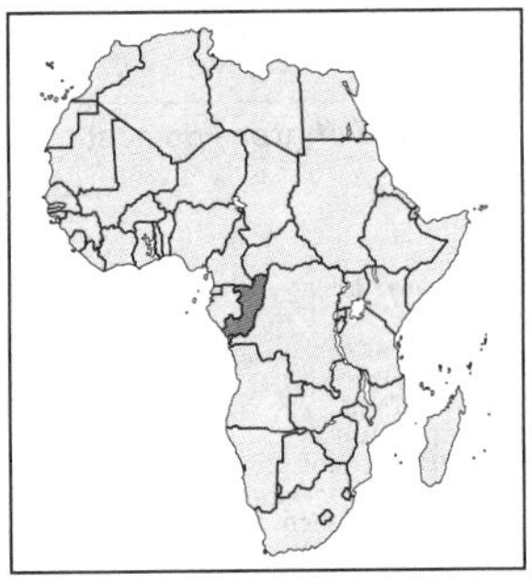

Official name: République du Congo (Republic of the Congo).
Form of government: multiparty republic with two legislative houses (Senate [60]; National Assembly [125]).
Chief of state: President.
Head of government: Prime Minister.
Capital: Brazzaville.
Official language: French.
Official religion: none.
Monetary unit: 1 CFA franc (CFAF) = 100 centimes; valuation (Oct. 4, 1993) 1 U.S.$ = CFAF 283.25; 1 £ = CFAF 429.12.

Area and population

		area		population
Regions	**Capitals**	sq mi	sq km	1992 estimate
Bouenza	Madingou	4,733	12,258	177,357
Cuvette	Owando	28,900	74,850	151,839
Kouilou	Pointe-Noire	5,270	13,650	89,296
Lékoumou	Sibiti	8,089	20,950	74,420
Likouala	Impfondo	25,500	66,044	70,675
Niari	Loubomo	10,007[1]	25,918[1]	120,077
Plateaux	Djambala	14,826	38,400	119,722
Pool	Kinkala	13,110	33,955	182,671
Sangha	Ouesso	21,542[2]	55,795[2]	35,961
Communes				
Brazzaville	—	39	100	937,579
Loubomo	—	7	18	83,605
Mossendjo	—	2[1]	5[1]	16,405
Nkayi	—	3	8	42,465
Ouesso	—	2[2]	5[2]	16,171
Pointe-Noire	—	17	44	576,206
TOTAL		132,047	342,000	2,694,449

Demography

Population (1993): 2,775,000.
Density (1993): persons per sq mi 21.0, persons per sq km 8.1.
Urban-rural (1990): urban 45.7%; rural 54.3%.
Sex distribution (1990): male 49.27%; female 50.73%.
Age breakdown (1990): under 15, 46.1%; 15–29, 25.8%; 30–44, 14.4%; 45–59, 8.5%; 60–74, 4.2%; 75 and over, 1.0%.
Population projection: (2000) 3,379,000; (2010) 4,396,000.
Doubling time: 23 years.
Ethnic composition (1983): Kongo 51.5%; Teke 17.3%; Mboshi 11.5%; Mbete 4.8%; Punu 3.0%; Sango 2.7%; Maka 1.8%; Pygmy 1.5%; other 5.9%.
Religious affiliation (1980): Roman Catholic 53.9%; Protestant 24.9%; African Christian 14.2%; traditional beliefs 4.8%; other 2.2%.
Major cities (1992): Brazzaville 937,579; Pointe-Noire 576,206; Loubomo 83,605; Nkayi 42,465; Mossendjo 16,405.

Vital statistics

Birth rate per 1,000 population (1990–95): 44.7 (world avg. 26.4); legitimate, n.a.; illegitimate, n.a.
Death rate per 1,000 population (1990–95): 14.7 (world avg. 9.2).
Natural increase rate per 1,000 population (1990–95): 30.0 (world avg. 17.2).
Total fertility rate (avg. births per childbearing woman; 1990–95): 6.3.
Marriage rate per 1,000 population: n.a.
Divorce rate per 1,000 population: n.a.
Life expectancy at birth (1990–95): male 52.1 years; female 57.3 years.
Morbidity (reported cases of infectious disease per 100,000 population; 1988): diarrhea 1,144; malaria 874; gonorrhea 160; schistosomiasis 133; hookworm 69.5.

National economy

Budget (1990). Revenue: CFAF 209,400,000,000 (petroleum revenue 58.6%; nonpetroleum receipts 40.9%; aid 0.5%). Expenditures: CFAF 268,800,000,000 (current expenditure 81.5%, of which salaries 29.6%, interest 29.6%, transfers, subsidies, goods, and services 22.4%; restructuring expenditure 7.9%; capital expenditure 7.3%; net lending 3.3%).
Tourism (1991): receipts from visitors U.S.$7,000,000; expenditures by nationals abroad U.S.$93,000,000.
Production (metric tons except as noted). Agriculture, forestry, fishing (1992): cassava 790,000, sugarcane 450,000, plantains 85,000, bananas 42,000, peanuts (groundnuts) 28,000, corn (maize) 26,000, avocados 24,000, palm oil 17,500, yams 13,000, pineapples 12,000, cacao beans 2,000, coffee 1,000; livestock (number of live animals) 275,000 goats, 110,000 sheep, 69,000 cattle; roundwood (1991) 3,760,000 cu m; fish catch (1991) 45,577. Mining and quarrying (1989): zinc concentrate 2,300; lead 1,400; gold 160 kg. Manufacturing (1989): cement 58,000; raw sugar 36,000[3]; wheat flour 16,000[4]; jet fuel 12,000; soap 1,500[4]; cigarettes 1,000; mineral water 28,948,000 hectolitres[4]; beer 744,000 hectolitres[4]; soft drinks 178,000 hectolitres[4]; veneer sheets 52,000 cu m; footwear 14,670 pairs. Construction: n.a. Energy production (consumption): electricity (kW-hr; 1991) 482,000,000 (587,000,000); coal (metric tons; 1991) none (1); crude petroleum (barrels; 1991) 54,983,000 (3,972,000); petroleum products (metric tons; 1991) 581,000 (557,000); natural gas (cu m; 1991) 2,127,000 (2,127,000).
Land use (1991): forested 62.2%; meadows and pastures 29.3%; agricultural and under permanent cultivation 0.5%; other 8.0%.

Public debt (external, outstanding; 1991): U.S.$3,989,000,000.
Gross national product (at current market prices; 1992): U.S.$2,502,000,000 (U.S.$1,030 per capita).

Structure of gross domestic product and labour force

	1989		1984	
	in value CFAF '000,000[5]	% of total value	labour force	% of labour force
Agriculture	106,900	13.8	291,365	51.7
Mining	216,200	28.0	7,324	1.3
Manufacturing	48,400	6.2	38,080	6.8
Construction	13,900	1.8	23,621	4.2
Public utilities	14,000	1.8	2,641	0.5
Trade	111,300	14.4	65,775	11.7
Transportation and communications	70,100	9.1	27,807	4.9
Finance			2,866	0.5
Pub. admin., defense } Services }	192,700	24.9	83,629	14.9
Other			19,826	3.5
TOTAL	773,500	100.0	562,934	100.0

Population economically active (1992): total 886,000; activity rate of total population 37.4% (participation rates [1984]: ages 15–64, 54.0%; female 45.6%; unemployed 2.3%[6]).

Price and earnings indexes (1985 = 100)

	1986	1987	1988	1989	1990	1991	1992
Consumer price index	102.4	104.0	109.0	113.1	113.4	117.5	120.0
Earnings index	...	...	...	...	...	...	...

Household income and expenditure. Average household size (1984) 5.2; income per household: n.a.; sources of income: n.a.; expenditure: n.a.

Foreign trade[7]

Balance of trade (current prices)

	1986	1987	1988	1989	1990	1991
CFAF '000,000,000	+64.8	+26.0	+87.2	+155.0	+105.4	+61.7
% of total	16.2%	9.1%	23.5%	36.3%	14.9%	10.9%

Imports (1990): U.S.$704,000,000 (1988; machinery and transport equipment 33.2%, of which machinery 22.4%, transport equipment 10.8%; food, beverages, and tobacco 21.3%; chemicals and chemical products 12.5%; metal manufactures 7.6%; basic manufactures 3.4%). *Major import sources:* France 48.1%; Cameroon 6.4%; Italy 6.1%; West Germany 4.2%; Zaire 4.1%; The Netherlands 3.9%.
Exports (1990): U.S.$1,085,000,000 (1988; petroleum and petroleum products 76.7%; wood and wood products 15.6%; diamonds 2.1%; iron and steel 0.1%). *Major export destinations:* United States 42.9%; France 16.1%; Belgium-Luxembourg 8.3%; Italy 7.8%; The Netherlands 7.2%; Spain 6.2%.

Transport and communications

Transport. Railroads (1990): length 494 mi, 795 km; passenger-mi 340,000,000, passenger-km 547,000,000; short ton-mi cargo 273,000,000, metric ton-km cargo 399,000,000. Roads (1991): total length 7,920 mi, 12,745 km (paved 10%). Vehicles (1991): passenger cars 27,000; trucks and buses 15,430. Merchant marine (1992): vessels (100 gross tons and over) 22; total deadweight tonnage 10,840. Air transport: n.a.; airports (1993) with scheduled flights 14.
Communications. Daily newspapers (1990): total number 5; total circulation 17,000; circulation per 1,000 population 7.0. Radio (1992): total number of receivers 250,000 (1 per 10.8 persons). Television (1992): total number of receivers 8,500 (1 per 317 persons). Telephones (1987): 19,239 (1 per 111 persons).

Education and health

Education (1990)

	schools	teachers	students	student/ teacher ratio
Primary (age 6–13)	1,655	7,626	502,918	65.9
Secondary (age 14–18)	238[8]	4,774[8]	172,026	34.7[8]
Voc., teacher tr.	60[8]	1,928	11,311	5.9
Higher	12[8]	1,112	10,671	9.6

Educational attainment (1984). Percentage of population age 25 and over having: no formal schooling 58.7%; some primary education 21.4%; secondary education 16.9%; postsecondary 3.0%. *Literacy* (1990): total population age 15 and over literate 56.6%; males literate 70.0%; females literate 43.9%.
Health (1989): physicians 567 (1 per 3,873 persons); hospital beds 4,817 (1 per 456 persons); infant mortality rate per 1,000 live births (1990–95) 65.
Food (1988–90): daily per capita caloric intake 2,295 (vegetable products 93%, animal products 7%); 103% of FAO recommended minimum requirement.

Military

Total active duty personnel (1993): 10,800 (army 92.6%, navy 2.7%, air force 4.7%). *Military expenditure as percentage of GNP* (1992): 3.8% (world [1989] 4.9%); per capita expenditure U.S.$47.

[1]Mossendjo is included with Niari. [2]Ouesso is included with Sangha. [3]1993. [4]1988. [5]At constant prices of 1978. [6]Previously employed only. [7]Import figures f.o.b. in balance of trade and trading partners, c.i.f. in commodities. [8]1989.

Costa Rica

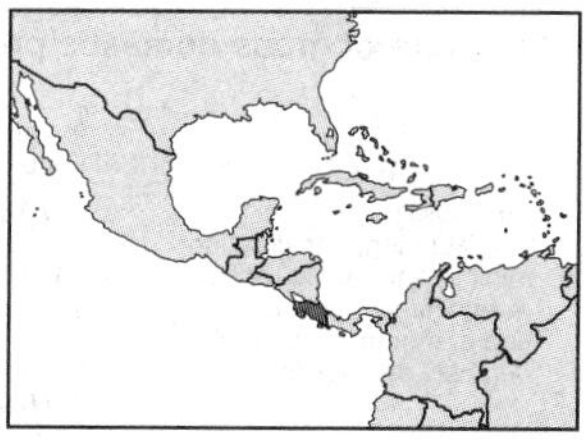

Official name: República de Costa Rica (Republic of Costa Rica).
Form of government: unitary multiparty republic with one legislative house (Legislative Assembly [57]).
Head of state and government: President.
Capital: San José.
Official language: Spanish.
Official religion: Roman Catholicism.
Monetary unit: 1 Costa Rican colón (₡) = 100 céntimos; valuation (Oct. 4, 1993) 1 U.S.$ = ₡144.73; 1 £ = ₡219.26.

Area and population

Provinces	Capitals	area sq mi	area sq km	population 1992[1] estimate
Alajuela	Alajuela	3,766	9,753	551,870
Cartago	Cartago	1,207	3,125	348,560
Guanacaste	Liberia	3,915	10,141	247,679
Heredia	Heredia	1,026	2,657	248,897
Limón	Limón	3,548	9,188	226,264
Puntarenas	Puntarenas	4,354	11,277	346,154
San José	San José	1,915	4,959	1,129,639
TOTAL		19,730[2]	51,100	3,099,063

Demography

Population (1993): 3,199,000.
Density (1993): persons per sq mi 162.2, persons per sq km 62.6.
Urban-rural (1991): urban 44.3%; rural 55.7%.
Sex distribution (1992): male 50.52%; female 49.48%.
Age breakdown (1991): under 15, 35.9%; 15–29, 28.1%; 30–44, 19.8%; 45–59, 9.7%; 60–74, 5.1%; 75 and over, 1.4%.
Population projection: (2000) 3,711,000; (2010) 4,366,000.
Doubling time: 31 years.
Ethnic composition (1990): white 85.0%; mestizo 8.0%; black/mulatto 3.0%; East Asian (mostly Chinese) 3.0%; other 1.0%.
Religious affiliation (1991): Roman Catholic 81.3%; other (mostly Protestant and nonreligious) 18.7%.
Major cities (1992): San José 302,574[3] (metropolitan area 1,040,000[4]); Desamparados 54,668[5]; Limón 50,939[6]; Alajuela 45,442; Puntarenas 38,274.

Vital statistics

Birth rate per 1,000 population (1991): 26.5 (world avg. 26.4); (1984) legitimate 62.8%; illegitimate 37.2%.
Death rate per 1,000 population (1991): 3.8 (world avg. 9.2).
Natural increase rate per 1,000 population (1991): 22.7 (world avg. 17.2).
Total fertility rate (avg. births per childbearing woman; 1991): 3.0.
Marriage rate per 1,000 population (1990): 7.6.
Divorce rate per 1,000 population (1990): 1.1.
Life expectancy at birth (1990–95): male 72.9 years; female 77.6 years.
Major causes of death per 100,000 population (1989): diseases of the circulatory system 110.1; malignant neoplasms (cancers) 81.2; diseases of the respiratory system 37.8; accidents, poisoning, and violence 22.1; diseases of the digestive system 20.3.

National economy

Budget (1991). Revenue: ₡162,520,000,000 (tax revenue 86.0%, of which social-security contributions by employers 20.0%, customs duties 14.6%, general sales taxes 12.9%, excises 12.9%; nontax revenue 14.0%). Expenditures: ₡171,100,000,000 (health 32.0%; education 19.1%; social security 12.5%; economic affairs and services 8.6%; public order and security 6.3%; defense, n.a.).
Public debt (external, outstanding; 1991): U.S.$3,316,000,000.
Gross national product (at current market prices; 1992): U.S.$6,299,000,000 (U.S.$2,010 per capita).

Structure of gross domestic product and labour force

	1991 in value ₡'000,000	% of total value	labour force	% of labour force
Agriculture, forestry, fishing	120,553	17.9	264,804	24.8
Mining }	127,421	18.9	1,531	0.1
Manufacturing }			201,964	19.0
Construction	17,871	2.7	69,197	6.5
Public utilities	24,000	3.6	11,735	1.1
Transp. and commun.	36,622	5.4	46,023	4.3
Trade, restaurants	134,881	20.0	165,621	15.5
Finance, real estate	78,119	11.6	38,514	3.6
Public administration	91,166	13.5 }	247,110	23.2
Services	42,312	6.3 }		
Other	—	—	19,202	1.8
TOTAL	672,945	100.0[2]	1,065,701	100.0[2]

Production (metric tons except as noted). Agriculture, forestry, fishing (1992): sugarcane 2,840,000, bananas 1,633,000, rice 209,000, coffee 168,000, pineapples 154,000, oranges 134,000, plantains 86,000, palm oil 75,000, corn (maize) 40,000, dry beans 36,000, other products include other tropical fruits, cut flowers, and ornamental plants grown for export; livestock (number of live animals) 1,741,000 cattle, 224,000 pigs, 4,000,000 chickens; roundwood 4,201,000 cu m; fish catch (1990) 21,133, of which shrimps 9,297. Mining and quarrying (1990): limestone 1,600,000, gold 14,800 troy oz. Manufacturing (value added in ₡'000,000; 1990): food products 26,153; alcoholic and nonalcoholic beverages 11,210; paper and paper products 3,940; plastic products 3,154; cement, cement products, bricks, and tiles 3,125; petroleum products 3,065; paints, varnishes, and soaps and other toiletries 2,986. Construction (completed; 1989): 1,914,000 sq m. Energy production (consumption): electricity (kW-hr; 1991) 3,876,000,000 ([1990] 3,772,000,000); coal, none (none); crude petroleum (barrels; 1990) none (3,057,000); petroleum products (metric tons; 1990) 372,000 (904,000); natural gas, none (none).
Population economically active (1991): total 1,065,701; activity rate of total population 37.1% (participation rates: ages 15–69, 58.7%; female 29.9%; unemployed [1992] 5.5%).

Price and earnings indexes (1985 = 100)

	1987	1988	1989	1990	1991	1992	1993[7]
Consumer price index	130.7	157.9	184.9	219.0	281.9	343.3	377.2
Monthly earnings index[8]	160.6	188.5	224.7	266.7	311.4	...	...

Tourism (1991): receipts from visitors U.S.$331,000,000; expenditures by nationals abroad U.S.$149,000,000.
Family income and expenditure. Average household size (1991) 4.5; (1983) income per urban family ₡181,416 (U.S.$4,415), income per rural family ₡98,328 (U.S.$2,393); sources of income: n.a.; expenditure (1980–85): food and beverages 33.0%, household furnishings 9.0%, housing 8.0%, clothing and footwear 8.0%, education 8.0%, transportation 8.0%, other 26.0%.
Land use (1991): forested 32.1%; meadows and pastures 45.6%; agricultural and under permanent cultivation 10.4%; other 11.9%.

Foreign trade[9]

Balance of trade (current prices)

	1987	1988	1989	1990	1991	1992
U.S.$'000,000	−90.7	−28.3	−136.4	−349.2	−97.5	−386.4
% of total	3.8%	1.1%	4.6%	10.8%	3.0%	9.5%

Imports (1991): U.S.$1,852,700,000 (basic manufactures for industry 38.0%; nondurable consumer goods 16.3%; capital goods for industry 15.1%; refined petroleum and derivatives 9.9%). *Major import sources:* United States 43.2%; Venezuela 6.6%; Japan 6.0%; Mexico 4.7%; Guatemala 4.4%.
Exports (1991)[10]: U.S.$1,590,300,000 (nontraditional exports 53.0%, of which garments 26.4%; bananas 25.1%; coffee 16.6%; beef 1.6%). *Major export destinations:* United States 43.8%; Germany 11.0%; Belgium-Luxembourg 4.8%; Italy 4.6%; Guatemala 3.7%.

Transport and communications

Transport. Railroads: route length (1991) 435 mi, 700 km; (1990) passenger-mi 26,500,000, passenger-km 42,600,000; (1987) short ton-mi cargo 102,700,000, metric ton-km cargo 150,000,000. Roads (1991): total length 22,081 mi, 35,536 km (paved 16%). Vehicles (1991): passenger cars 168,814; trucks and buses 95,066. Merchant marine (1992): vessels (100 gross tons and over) 24; total deadweight tonnage 8,368. Air transport (1992)[11]: passenger-mi 787,000,000, passenger-km 1,267,000,000; short-ton mi cargo 25,527,000, metric ton-km cargo 37,269,000; airports (1993) with scheduled flights 13.
Communications. Daily newspapers (1991): total number 4; total circulation 314,000; circulation per 1,000 population 102. Radio (1992): total number of receivers 255,000 (1 per 12 persons). Television (1992): total number of receivers 340,000 (1 per 9.2 persons). Telephones (1990): 398,300 (1 per 7.0 persons).

Education and health

Education (1990)

	schools	teachers	students	student/ teacher ratio
Primary (age 7–12)	3,268	13,651	435,205	31.9
Secondary (age 13–17)	179	5,808	125,738	21.6
Vocational	77	2,076	28,593	13.8
Higher[12]	4	6,451	57,789	9.0

Educational attainment (1984). Percentage of economically active population age 25 and over having: no formal schooling 8.3%; incomplete primary education 28.6%; complete primary 26.3%; secondary 22.6%; postsecondary and higher 14.2%. *Literacy* (1990): total population age 15 and over literate 1,798,000 (92.8%); males literate 913,000 (92.6%); females literate 885,000 (93.1%).
Health (1991): physicians 3,123 (1 per 981 persons); hospital beds 6,935 (1 per 442 persons); infant mortality rate per 1,000 live births 13.8.
Food (1988–90): daily per capita caloric intake 2,711 (vegetable products 83%, animal products 17%); 121% of FAO recommended minimum requirement.

Military

Military expenditure as percentage of GNP (1989): 0.4% (world 4.9%); per capita expenditure U.S.$7. The army was officially abolished in 1948. Paramilitary and police forces had 7,500 members in 1992.

[1]January 1. [2]Detail does not add to total given because of rounding. [3]Population of San José canton. [4]1990. [5]Within San José metropolitan area. [6]1991. [7]June. [8]July wages only, for nonagricultural employees. [9]Import figures are f.o.b. in balance of trade and c.i.f. for commodities and trading partners. [10]*Exports* (1990): U.S.$1,457,400,000 (nontraditional exports 54.1%, of which nontraditional manufactures [including garments, electronic components, fish products, and jewelry] 43.5%; nontraditional agricultural products [mostly tropical fruits, ornamental plants, and cut flowers] 10.6%). [11]Lacsa (Costa Rican Airlines). [12]Universities only.

Côte d'Ivoire

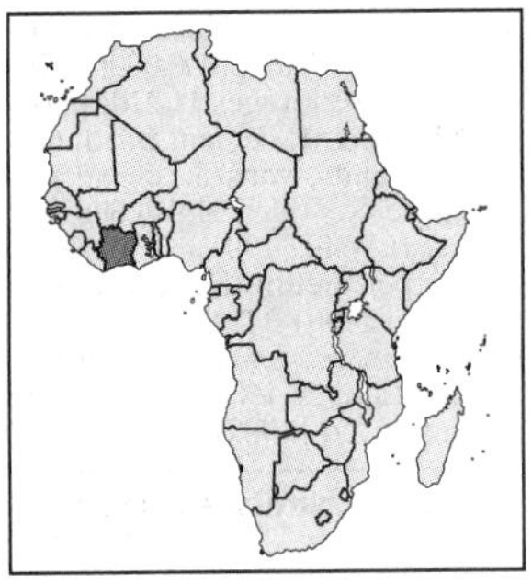

Official name: République de Côte d'Ivoire (Republic of Côte d'Ivoire [Ivory Coast][1]).
Form of government: multiparty republic with one legislative house (National Assembly [175]).
Chief of state: President.
Head of government: Prime Minister.
Capital: Abidjan (de facto; legislative).
Capital designate: Yamoussoukro (de jure; administrative).
Official language: French.
Official religion: none.
Monetary unit: 1 CFA franc (CFAF) = 100 centimes; valuation (Oct. 4, 1993) 1 U.S.$ = CFAF 283.25; 1 £ = CFAF 429.12.

Area and population (1988 census)

Department	area sq km[2]	population	Department	area sq km[2]	population
Abengourou	5,200	214,162	Guiglo	11,220	169,660
Abidjan	8,550	2,492,513	Issia	3,590	194,974
Aboisso	6,250	225,882	Katiola	9,420	131,221
Adzopé	5,230	237,265	Korhogo	12,500	387,947
Agboville	3,850	203,730	Lakota	2,730	115,948
Agnibilekrou	1,700	84,404	Man	4,990	286,860
Bangolo	2,060	80,374	Mankono	10,660	123,723
Béoumi	2,820	91,062	M'bahiakro	5,460	102,774
Biankouma	4,950	99,431	Odiénné	20,600	169,433
Bondoukou	10,040	175,632	Oumé	2,400	140,166
Bongouanou	5,570	225,432	Sakassou	1,880	59,494
Bouaflé	3,980	163,917	San-Pédro	6,900	168,174
Bouaké	4,700	453,074	Sassandra	5,190	107,616
Bouna	21,470	134,459	Séguéla	11,240	121,120
Boundiali	7,895	127,231	Sinfra	1,690	120,301
Dabakala	9,670	82,094	Soubré	8,270	309,307
Daloa	5,450	361,472	Tabou	5,440	59,708
Danané	4,600	222,045	Tanda	6,490	203,129
Daoukro	3,610	86,425	Tiassalé	3,370	132,626
Dimbokro	4,920	141,934	Tingréla	2,200	55,251
Divo	7,920	389,530	Touba	8,720	109,155
Duékoué	2,930	101,451	Toumodi	2,780	80,909
Ferkessedougou	17,728	172,850	Vavoua	6,160	169,454
Gagnoa	4,500	275,765	Yamoussoukro	6,160	284,613
Grand-Lahou	2,280	52,645	Zuénoula	2,830	114,440
			TOTAL	320,763	10,812,782

Demography

Population (1993): 13,459,000.
Density (1993): persons per sq mi 108.7, persons per sq km 42.0.
Urban-rural (1990): urban 40.4%; rural 59.6%.
Sex distribution (1990): male 50.93%; female 49.07%.
Age breakdown (1990): under 15, 48.2%; 15–29, 24.7%; 30–44, 12.0%; 45–59, 8.5%; 60 and over, 6.6%.
Population projection: (2000) 17,600,000; (2010) 25,503,000.
Ethnic composition (1975): Akan 41.4%; Kru 16.7%; Voltaic 15.7%; Malinke 14.9%; Southern Mande 10.2%; other 1.1%.
Religious affiliation (1988): Muslim 38.0%; Christian 27.5%; animist 17.0%; atheist 13.4%; other 4.1%.
Major cities (1988): Abidjan 2,168,000[3]; Bouaké 332,999; Daloa 122,933; Yamoussoukro 110,013; Gagnoa 85,094.

Vital statistics

Birth rate per 1,000 population (1990–95): 50.0 (world avg. 26.4).
Death rate per 1,000 population (1990–95): 13.2 (world avg. 9.2).
Natural increase rate per 1,000 population (1990–95): 36.8 (world avg. 17.2).
Total fertility rate (avg. births per childbearing woman; 1991): 7.4.
Life expectancy at birth (1990–95): male 52.8 years; female 56.2 years.
Major causes of death per 100,000 population: n.a.; however, the major infectious diseases include malaria, dysentery, yaws, pneumonia, leprosy.

National economy

Budget (1993). Revenue: CFAF 583,800,000,000 (current revenues 83.5%, of which taxes and duties 80.5%; loans 10.4%; returns on investments 4.8%; grants 1.3%). Expenditures: CFAF 583,800,000,000 (current expenses 75.8%; investments 24.2%).
Public debt (external, outstanding; 1991): U.S.$10,424,000,000.
Tourism (1991): receipts U.S.$46,000,000; expenditures U.S.$222,000,000.
Production (metric tons except as noted). Agriculture, forestry, fishing (1992): yams 2,450,000, sugarcane 1,600,000, cassava 1,350,000, plantains 1,170,000, cacao beans 700,000, rice 700,000, corn (maize) 425,000, coconuts 270,000, coffee 240,000; livestock (number of live animals) 1,200,000 sheep, 1,183,000 cattle, 919,000 goats; roundwood (1991) 13,061,000 cu m; fish catch (1991) 85,182. Mining and quarrying (1991): diamonds 280,000 carats. Manufacturing (1986): cement 770,000; beer 1,300,000 hectolitres; carbonated beverages 495,000 hectolitres; synthetic fibres 5,000,000 metres. Construction (in CFAF; 1984): 62,000,000,000. Energy production (consumption): electricity (kW-hr; 1992) 2,311,018,000 (1,946,170,000); coal, none (n.a.); crude petroleum (barrels; 1990) 2,301,000 (17,305,000); petroleum products (metric tons; 1990) 1,426,000 (1,426,000).
Land use (1991): forested 22.3%; meadows and pastures 40.9%; agricultural and under permanent cultivation 11.6%; other 25.2%.
Gross national product (1992): U.S.$8,939,000,000 (U.S.$700 per capita).

Structure of gross domestic product and labour force

	1992		1985	
	in value CFAF '000,000,000	% of total value	labour force	% of labour force
Agriculture	770.6	28.7	2,452,000	60.5
Manufacturing, construction, mining, and public utilities	453.8	16.9	409,000	10.1
Trade, finance, transp. and commun., pub. admin., defense, and services	1,074.0	40.0	1,192,000	29.4
Other	386.6	14.4	—	—
TOTAL	2,685.0	100.0	4,053,000	100.0

Population economically active (1992): total 4,826,000; activity rate 37.4% (participation rates [1985]: ages 15–64, 71.4%; female 34.7%).

Price and earnings indexes (1985 = 100)

	1986	1987	1988	1989	1990	1991	1992
Consumer price index	106.8	114.3	122.3	123.5	122.5	124.5	128.9
Hourly earnings index[4]	100.0	100.0	100.0	100.0	100.0	100.0	...

Household income and expenditure. Average household size (1988) 5.4; average annual income per household (1980) CFAF 500,000; sources of income: self-employment 49.9%, wages 44.9%, transfers and other resources 5.2%; expenditure (1992)[5]: food 48.0%, clothing 10.1%, energy and water 8.5%, housing 7.8%, transportation 6.8%.

Foreign trade

Balance of trade (current prices)

	1987	1988	1989	1990	1991	1992
U.S.$'000,000	+1,118.3	+1,078.1	+1,067.4	+1,417.0	...	+657.0
% of total	23.4%	24.1%	23.5%	29.4%	...	11.5%

Imports (1992): CFAF 601,629,000,000 (crude and refined petroleum 22.5%; machinery and transport equipment 21.2%; food and food products 16.6%; pharmaceuticals 5.7%; plastics 3.3%; paper and paper products 2.9%; chemicals 2.6%; iron 2.5%). *Major import sources:* France 34.2%; Nigeria 18.7%; Japan 4.2%; Germany 3.9%; The Netherlands 3.9%.
Exports (1992): CFAF 757,992,000,000 (food products 53.1%, of which cocoa beans and products 33.8%, coffee and coffee products 7.3%, fish products 3.4%; petroleum products 11.2%; wood and wood products 9.7%; cotton and cotton cloth 5.2%). *Major export destinations:* France 15.0%; The Netherlands 11.5%; Germany 5.8%; Italy 5.6%; Burkina Faso 5.3%; Mali 4.5%; Nigeria 4.3%; Belgium-Luxembourg 4.3%; United States 4.2%.

Transport and communications

Transport. Railroads (1992): route length 660 km; passenger-km 1,021,000,000[6]; metric ton-km cargo 578,000,000[6]. Roads (1992): total length 42,250 mi, 68,000 km (paved 8%). Vehicles (1991): passenger cars 170,000; trucks and buses 92,000. Merchant marine (1992): vessels (100 gross tons and over) 51; total deadweight tonnage 98,618. Air transport (1990): passenger-km 316,756,000; metric ton-km cargo 47,012,000; airports (1993) 7.
Communications. Daily newspapers (1990): total number 1; total circulation 90,000; circulation per 1,000 population 8. Radio (1992): 1,500,000 receivers (1 per 8.6 persons). Television (1992): 810,000 receivers (1 per 16 persons). Telephones (1991): 87,300 (1 per 143 persons).

Education and health

Education (1992)

	schools	teachers	students	student/ teacher ratio
Primary (age 7–12)	6,844	39,237	1,447,785	36.9
Secondary (age 13–19)[7]	147	9,263	289,510	31.3
Voc., teacher tr.	15	1,947[8]	3,094	...
Higher	1[9]	1,204[10]	19,660[3]	...

Educational attainment (1975). Percentage of population age 6 and over having: no formal schooling 75.3%; primary education 17.3%; secondary 5.1%; higher 0.5%. *Literacy* (1990): percentage of population age 15 and over literate 53.8%; males literate 66.9%; females literate 40.2%.
Health (1982): physicians 502 (1 per 17,847 persons); hospital beds 10,062 (1 per 891 persons); infant mortality rate per 1,000 live births (1990–95) 87.
Food (1988–90): daily per capita caloric intake 2,568 (vegetable products 94%, animal products 6%); 111% of FAO recommended minimum requirement.

Military

Total active duty personnel (1993): 7,100 (army 77.5%, navy 9.8%, air force 12.7%). *Military expenditure as percentage of GNP* (1992): 0.8% (world avg. [1989] 4.9%); per capita expenditure U.S.$6.1.

[1]From 1986, Côte d'Ivoire has requested that the French version of the country's name be utilized as the official protocol version in all languages. [2]One sq km is equal to approximately 0.3861 sq mi. [3]1990. [4]January 1; index refers to the S.M.I.G. (*salaire minimum interprofessionel garanti*), a form of minimum professional wage. [5]Weights of consumer price index components for a worker's family living in the capital city. [6]1987; traffic includes Burkina Faso. [7]Data do not include 208 private schools with 107,096 students. [8]1991. [9]1980. [10]1982.

Croatia

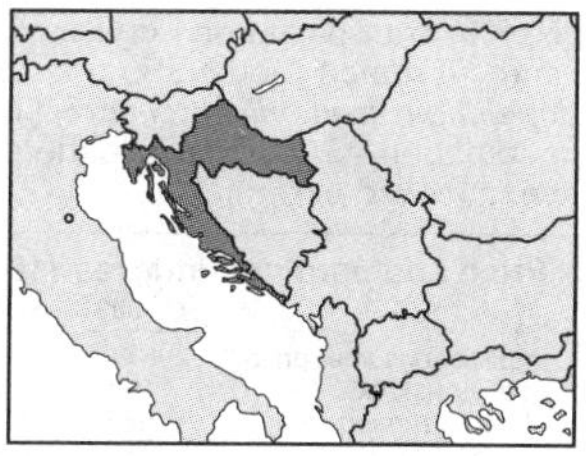

Official name: Republika Hrvatska (Republic of Croatia).
Form of government: multiparty republic with a two-chambered legislature (Chamber of Districts [68]; Chamber of Deputies [138]).
Head of state: President.
Head of government: Prime Minister.
Capital: Zagreb.
Official language: Croatian.
Official religion: none.
Monetary unit: Croatian dinar (HrD)[1] = 100 lipa; valuation (Oct. 4, 1993) 1 U.S.$ = HrD 7,181; 1 £ = HrD 10,879.

Area and population (1991 census)

Districts	population	Districts	population	Districts	population
Beli Manastir	54,265	Kaštela	32,286	Požega	71,745
Benkovac	33,378	Klanjec	10,917	Pregrada	16,939
Biograd na moru	17,661	Knin	42,954	Pula	85,326
Bjelovar	66,039	Koprivnica	61,052	Rab	9,205
Brač	13,824	Korčula	19,651	Rijeka	206,229
Buje	23,877	Kostajnica	14,851	Rovinj	19,727
Buzet	7,439	Krapina	26,382	Senj	9,205
Čabar	5,169	Križevci	39,248	Šibenik	85,002
Čakovec	119,866	Krk	16,402	Sinj	60,210
Čazma	15,263	Kutina	39,520	Sisak	84,348
Cres-Lošinj	11,796	Labin	25,983	Slavonski Brod	114,249
Crikvenica	19,154	Lastovo	1,228	Slunj	18,962
Đakovo	52,954	Ludbreg	21,848	Solin	27,402
Daruvar	30,092	Makarska	21,041	Split	207,147
Delnice	17,848	Metković	22,818	Sveti Ivan	
Donja Stubica	30,760	Našice	40,829	Zelina	17,152
Donji Lapac	8,054	Nova Gradiška	60,749	Titova Korenica	11,393
Donji Miholjac	20,365	Novi Marof	29,254	Trogir	22,168
Drniš	24,169	Novska	24,696	Valpovo	33,108
Dubrovnik	71,419	Obrovac	11,557	Varaždin	94,373
Duga Resa	30,485	Ogulin	29,095	Vinkovci	98,445
Đurđevac	40,901	Omiš	25,784	Virovitica	46,661
Dvor	14,555	Opatija	29,799	Vis	4,354
Garešnica	18,442	Orahovica	15,631	Vojnić	8,236
Glina	23,040	Osijek	165,253	Vrbovec	28,074
Gospić	29,049	Otočac	24,992	Vrbovsko	7,528
Gračac	10,434	Ozalj	14,787	Vrginmost	16,599
Grubišno Polje	14,206	Pag	7,969	Vrgorac	7,497
Hvar	11,459	Pakrac	27,589	Vukovar	84,189
Imotski	39,052	Pazin	19,006	Zabok	36,309
Ivanec	41,680	Petrinja	35,565	Zadar	136,572
Ivanić-Grad	25,592	Ploče	13,008	Zagreb	953,607
Jastrebarsko	32,422	Podravska Slatina	31,227	Zlatar	31,291
Karlovac	81,319	Poreč	22,988	Županja	49,026
				TOTAL	4,785,336

Demography

Population (1993): 4,821,000.
Density (1993): persons per sq mi 220.9, persons per sq km 85.3.
Urban-rural (1991): urban 50.8%; rural 49.2%.
Sex distribution (1991): male 48.46%; female 51.54%.
Age breakdown (1991): under 15, 19.4%; 15–29, 20.7%; 30–44, 22.7%; 45–59, 18.3%; 60–74, 12.9%; 75 and over, 4.5%; not stated 1.5%.
Population projection: (2000) 4,933,000; (2010) 5,098,000.
Doubling time: not applicable; population is stable.
Ethnic composition (1991): Croat 78.1%; Serb 12.2%; Bosnian 0.9%; Magyar 0.5%; Slovene 0.5%; other 7.8%.
Religious affiliation (1991): Roman Catholic 76.5%; Eastern Orthodox 11.1%; Muslim 1.2%; other 11.2%[3].
Major cities (1991): Zagreb 706,770; Split 189,388; Rijeka 167,964; Osijek 104,761; Zadar 76,343.

Vital statistics

Birth rate per 1,000 population (1991): 10.8 (world avg. 26.4); legitimate 93.0%; illegitimate 7.0%.
Death rate per 1,000 population (1991): 11.4 (world avg. 9.2).
Natural increase rate per 1,000 population (1991): 0.6 (world avg. 17.2).
Total fertility rate (avg. births per childbearing woman; 1991): 1.7.
Marriage rate per 1,000 population (1991): 4.5.
Divorce rate per 1,000 population (1991): 1.0.
Life expectancy at birth (1980–82): male 67.0 years; female 74.0 years.
Major causes of death per 100,000 population (1991): diseases of the circulatory system 571.8; malignant neoplasms (cancers) 226.1; accidents, violence, and poisoning 91.8; diseases of the digestive system 53.2.

National economy

Budget. Revenue: n.a. Expenditures: n.a.
Production (metric tons except as noted). Agriculture, forestry, fishing (1992): corn (maize) 1,538,000, wheat 658,000, sugar beets 525,000, potatoes 480,000, grapes 380,000, barley 107,000, plums 62,000; livestock (number of live animals) 1,182,000 pigs, 590,000 cattle, 539,000 sheep, 13,142,000 poultry; roundwood 3,096,000 cu m; fish catch 25,022, of which freshwater 6,246. Mining and quarrying (1991): lime 261,000; bauxite 112,000. Manufacturing (1991): ammonia 347,000; crude steel 214,000; pig iron 69,000; detergents 65,079; cotton fibre 12,448. Construction (1991): residential 1,772,000 sq m; nonresidential 1,702,000 sq m. Energy production (consumption): electricity (kW-hr; 1991) 8,830,000,000 (11,902,000,000); coal (metric tons; 1991) 146,000 (n.a.); crude petroleum (barrels; 1991) 14,116,000 (n.a.); petroleum products (metric tons; 1991) 1,814,758 (n.a.); natural gas (cu m; 1991) 1,839,000,000 (n.a.).
Gross national product (1990): U.S.$20,900,000,000 (U.S.$4,399 per capita).

Structure of gross domestic product and labour force

	1991			
	in value Din '000,000	% of total value	labour force[4]	% of labour force[4]
Agriculture	28,381	11.5	61,721	4.0
Mining / Manufacturing	90,618	37.0	490,145	31.7
Construction	20,532	8.4	98,757	6.4
Public utilities	2,825	1.2	28,377	1.8
Transp. and commun.	24,831	10.1	110,247	7.1
Trade	64,614	26.4	203,233	13.1
Finance			55,397	3.6
Pub. admin., defense / Services / Other (Finance, Pub. admin., defense, Services, Other)	13,378	5.4		
Pub. admin., defense / Services / Other			500,390	32.3
TOTAL	245,179	100.0	1,548,267	100.0

Population economically active (1991): total 1,568,000; activity rate of total population 32.9% (participation rates: ages 15–64, 57.1%; female 45.2%).

Price and earnings indexes (1985 = 100)

	1985	1986	1987	1988	1989	1990[5]	1991
Consumer price index	100	193	430	1,270	16,500	114,000	256,000
Annual earnings index[6]	100	109	100	93	114	95	71

Household income and expenditure. Average household size (1991) 2.9; income per household (1990) Din 165,813 (U.S.$14,650); sources (1990): self-employment 40.8%, wages 40.2%, transfers 12.1%, other 6.9%; expenditure (1988): food 34.2%, transportation 9.3%, clothing 8.6%, housing 8.3%, energy 7.6%, drink and tobacco 5.1%, durable goods 4.5%, health care 4.3%.
Land use (1991): forest 36.5%; pasture 36.0%; agricultural 23.5%; other 4.0%.

Foreign trade

Balance of trade (current prices)

	1986	1987	1988	1989	1990	1991
Din '000,000	−32	−31	−155	−3,774	−16,692	−6,296
% of total	16.0%	7.9%	10.2%	18.1%	20.2%	7.8%

Imports (1991): Din 43,359,000,000 (machinery 22.2%, mineral fuels 16.5%, consumer goods 14.5%, chemicals 13.5%, food 10.0%). *Major import sources:* Germany 21.9%; Italy 16.0%; U.S.S.R. 6.1%; Czechoslovakia 5.0%; Austria 4.6%.
Exports (1991): Din 37,063,000,000 (consumer goods 29.9%, machinery 22.8%, basic manufactures 14.8%, chemicals 11.8%, mineral fuels 6.5%). *Major export destinations:* Germany 28.5%; Italy 22.1%; U.S.S.R. 7.6%; The Netherlands 3.5%; Austria 2.9%.

Transport and communications

Transport. Railroads (1992): length 1,676 mi, 2,698 km; passenger-mi 934,000,000, passenger-km 1,503,000,000; short ton-mi cargo 2,477,000,000, metric ton-km cargo 3,617,000,000. Roads (1992): total length 16,739 mi, 26,938 km (paved 81%). Vehicles (1992): passenger cars 735,650; trucks and buses 72,043. Merchant marine (1992): fishing vessels 315. Airports (1993) with scheduled flights 4.
Communications. Daily newspapers (1990): 9; total circulation 715,000; circulation per 1,000 population 150. Radio (1990): 1,345,000 receivers (1 per 3.5 persons). Television (1990): 1,546,000 receivers (1 per 3.1 persons). Telephones (1992): 1,138,000 (1 per 4.2 persons).

Education and health

Education (1990–91)[7]

	schools	teachers	students	student/ teacher ratio
Primary (age 7–14)	2,074	23,988	434,901	18.1
Secondary (age 15–18)	220	12,201	188,305	15.4
Voc., teacher tr.	3	122	1,839	15.1
Higher	54	6,303	66,881	10.6

Educational attainment (1991). Percentage of population age 15 and over having: no schooling or unknown 10.1%; less than full primary education 21.2%; primary 23.4%; secondary 35.9%; postsecondary and higher 9.4%.
Literacy (1991): total population age 10 and over literate 3,734,000 (97.0%); males 98.8%; females 95.3%.
Health (1991): physicians 8,948 (1 per 535 persons); hospital beds 31,206 (1 per 153 persons); infant mortality rate per 1,000 live births 11.1.

Military

Total active duty personnel (1993): 103,300 (army 92.0%, navy 3.9%, air force and air defense 4.1%). *Military expenditure as percentage of GNP:* n.a.

[1]Also called the kuna from June 1993. [2]One sq km is equal to approximately 0.3861 sq mi. [3]Includes a significant minority of adherents of the Croatian Old Catholic Church, as well as small communities of Protestant Christians and Jews. [4]Excludes 58,000 workers in the private sector. [5]On Jan. 1, 1990, the new dinar, equal to 10,000 old dinars (Din), was introduced. [6]Based on worker real net personal income. [7]Data exclude private (combined) primary and secondary schools.

Cuba

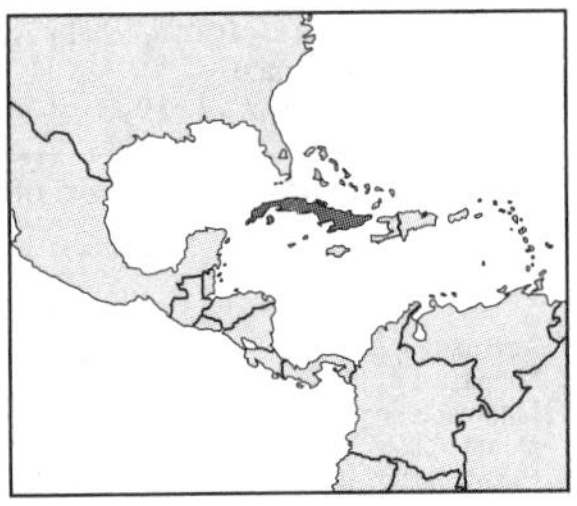

Official name: República de Cuba (Republic of Cuba).
Form of government: unitary socialist republic with one legislative house (National Assembly of the People's Power [589]).
Head of state and government: President.
Capital: Havana.
Official language: Spanish.
Official religion: none.
Monetary unit: 1 Cuban peso (CUP) = 100 centavos; valuation (Oct. 4, 1993) 1 U.S.$ = 0.75 CUP; 1 £ = 1.14 CUP.

Area and population

		area		population
Provinces	**Capitals**	sq mi	sq km	1989[1] estimate
Camagüey	Camagüey	6,174	15,990	732,056
Ciego de Avila	Ciego de Avila	2,668	6,910	358,059
Cienfuegos	Cienfuegos	1,613	4,178	358,589
Ciudad de la Habana[2]	—	281	727	2,077,938
Granma	Bayamo	3,232	8,372	781,331
Guantánamo	Guantánamo	2,388	6,186	491,422
Holguín	Holguín	3,591	9,301	982,722
La Habana[3]	Havana	2,213	5,731	636,889
Las Tunas	Las Tunas	2,544	6,589	485,136
Matanzas	Matanzas	4,625	11,978	602,996
Pinar del Río	Pinar del Río	4,218	10,925	684,725
Sancti Spíritus	Sancti Spíritus	2,604	6,744	424,243
Santiago de Cuba	Santiago de Cuba	2,382	6,170	980,002
Villa Clara	Santa Clara	3,345	8,662	801,456
Special municipality				
Isla de la Juventud	Nueva Gerona	926	2,398	71,097
TOTAL		42,804	110,861	10,468,661

Demography

Population (1993): 10,892,000.
Density (1993): persons per sq mi 254.5, persons per sq km 98.2.
Urban-rural (1990): urban 72.8%; rural 27.2%.
Sex distribution (1990): male 50.35%; female 49.65%.
Age breakdown (1989): under 15, 23.3%; 15–29, 31.7%; 30–44, 19.5%; 45–59, 13.7%; 60 and over, 11.8%.
Population projection: (2000) 11,502,000; (2010) 12,181,000.
Doubling time: 63 years.
Ethnic composition (1981): white 66.0%; mixed 21.9%; black 12.0%.
Religious affiliation (1980): nonreligious 48.7%; Roman Catholic 39.6%; atheist 6.4%; Protestant 3.3%; Afro-Cuban syncretist 1.6%; other 0.4%.
Major cities (1989[1]): Havana 2,077,938; Santiago de Cuba 397,024; Camagüey 278,958; Holguín 222,794; Guantánamo 197,868.

Vital statistics

Birth rate per 1,000 population (1991): 18.0 (world avg. 26.4).
Death rate per 1,000 population (1991): 7.0 (world avg. 9.2).
Natural increase rate per 1,000 population (1991): 11.0 (world avg. 17.2).
Total fertility rate (avg. births per childbearing woman; 1991): 1.9.
Marriage rate per 1,000 population (1991): 15.0.
Divorce rate per 1,000 population (1991): 4.1.
Life expectancy at birth (1991): male 73.0 years; female 78.0 years.
Major causes of death per 100,000 population (1989): diseases of the circulatory system 251.8; malignant neoplasms (cancers) 125.2; accidents, violence, and suicide 69.4; diseases of the respiratory system 34.0; diabetes mellitus 20.6.

National economy

Budget (1990). Revenue: CUP 12,463,200,000. Expenditures: CUP 14,448,400,000 (capital investment 37.7%; education and public health 20.4%; social, cultural, and scientific activities 17.3%; defense, internal security 9.5%; housing, community services 6.0%).
Production (metric tons except as noted). Agriculture, forestry, fishing (1992): sugarcane 58,000,000, oranges and tangerines 584,000, grapefruit 315,000, bananas and plantains 315,000, rice 308,000, cassava 290,000, tomatoes 258,000, potatoes 245,000, sweet potatoes 240,000, tobacco leaves 44,000; livestock (number of live animals) 4,700,000 cattle, 1,850,000 pigs, 27,000,000 chickens; roundwood (1991) 3,140,000 cu m; fish catch (1991) 165,236. Mining and quarrying (1990): chromite 51,000; nickel (metal content of ores) 46,509[4]. Manufacturing (in CUP '000,000; 1989): processed food (excluding fish and refined sugar) 1,843; refined sugar 1,610; nonelectrical machinery 709; fuels 655; beverages and tobacco products 521; chemicals and chemical products 445; construction materials 440; textiles (excluding ready-made clothing) 287. Construction (gross value of construction in CUP '000,000; 1989): residential 227; nonresidential 872. Energy production (consumption): electricity (kW-hr; 1991) 16,255,000,000 (16,255,000,000); coal (metric tons; 1991) none (200,000); crude petroleum (barrels; 1991) 5,159,000 (49,722,000); petroleum products (metric tons; 1991) 6,719,000 (10,451,000); natural gas (cu m; 1991) 30,753,000 (30,753,000).
Household income and expenditure. Average household size (1990) 3.7; average annual income per household (1982) CUP 3,680 (U.S.$4,330); sources of income (1982): wages and salaries 57.3%, bonuses and other payments 42.7%; personal consumption (1989) food 26.7%, other retail purchases 60.5%, transportation services 5.4%, energy 2.7%, value of self-produced and consumed food 1.5%, household repairs 1.3%, other 1.9%.
Population economically active (1988): total 4,570,236; activity rate of total population 43.7% (participation rates: over age 15, 56.9%; female 36.1%; unemployed 6.0%).

Price and earnings indexes (1985 = 100)

	1983	1984	1985	1986	1987	1988	1989
Implicit consumer price deflator index	94.9	98.0	100.0	101.4	102.8	103.1	...
Monthly earnings index[5]	95.9	99.0	100.0	100.1	98.1	99.6	100.0

Public debt (hard currency to the West; 1989): U.S.$6,800,000,000.
Tourism: receipts from visitors (1992) U.S.$382,000,000; expenditures by nationals abroad (1990) U.S.$48,000,000.
Gross national product (at current market prices; 1991): U.S.$17,000,000,000 (U.S.$1,580 per capita).

Structure of global social product and labour force

	1989			
	in value CUP '000,000	% of total value	labour force[5]	% of labour force
Agriculture	4,273	15.9	721,100	20.4
Mining[6]	1,039	3.9		
Manufacturing	10,617	39.4	767,500	21.8
Public utilities	733	2.7		
Construction	2,510	9.3	344,300	9.8
Transp. and commun.	2,151	8.0	235,900	6.7
Finance, insurance	—	—	21,700	0.6
Trade	5,401	20.1	395,300	11.2
Public administration	—	—	151,700	4.3
Services	—	—	835,700	23.7
Other	191	0.7	53,400	1.5
TOTAL	26,915	100.0	3,526,600	100.0

Land use (1991): forested 25.2%; meadows and pastures 27.0%; agricultural and under permanent cultivation 30.3%; other 17.5%.

Foreign trade[7]

Balance of trade (current prices)

	1984	1985	1986	1987	1988	1989
CUP '000,000	−1,751	−2,043	−2,275	−2,181	−2,062	−2,732
% of total	13.8%	14.6%	17.6%	16.8%	15.7%	20.2%

Imports (1989): CUP 8,124,200,000 (mineral fuels and lubricants 32.4%, machinery and transport equipment 31.2%, food and live animals 11.4%, basic manufactures 10.3%, chemicals 6.5%, inedible crude materials 3.8%). *Major import sources:* U.S.S.R. 68.0%; East Germany 4.4%; China 3.1%; Czechoslovakia 2.7%; Spain 2.3%; Argentina 2.2%.
Exports (1989): CUP 5,392,000,000 (sugar 73.2%, minerals and concentrates 9.2%, citrus and other agricultural products 3.9%, fish products 2.4%, raw tobacco and tobacco products 1.6%). *Major export destinations:* U.S.S.R. 59.9%; East Germany 5.3%; China 4.0%; Bulgaria 3.3%; Czechoslovakia 2.5%.

Transport and communications

Transport. Railroads (1991): length 3,033 mi, 4,881 km; passenger-km 3,025,000,000; metric ton-km cargo 1,368,000,000. Roads (1986): total length 28,928 mi, 46,555 km (paved 27%). Vehicles (1988): passenger cars 241,300; trucks and buses 208,400. Merchant marine (1992): vessels (100 gross tons and over) 393; total deadweight tonnage 924,591. Air transport (1991): passenger-km 3,070,000,000; metric ton-km cargo 34,794,000; airports with scheduled flights (1993) 10.
Communications. Daily newspapers (1990): total number 17; total circulation 1,315,000; circulation per 1,000 population 124. Radio (1992): 2,140,000 receivers (1 per 5.1 persons). Television (1992): 2,500,000 receivers (1 per 4.3 persons). Telephones (1991): 611,124 (1 per 18 persons).

Education and health

Education (1989–90)

	schools	teachers	students	student/ teacher ratio
Primary (age 6–11)	9,417	71,887	885,500	12.3
Secondary (age 12–17)	2,175	108,560	1,073,100	9.9
Voc., teacher tr.	618	30,252	312,000	10.3
Higher	35	24,499	242,400	9.9

Educational attainment (1981). Percentage of population age 25 and over having: no formal schooling or some primary education 39.6%; completed primary 26.6%; secondary 29.6%; higher 4.2%. *Literacy* (1985): total population age 15 and over literate 7,200,000 (96.0%).
Health (1989): physicians 34,752 (1 per 303 persons); hospital beds 74,407 (1 per 141 persons); infant mortality rate per 1,000 live births (1990) 10.7.
Food (1988–90): daily per capita caloric intake 3,129 (vegetable products 78%, animal products 22%); 135% of FAO recommended minimum requirement.

Military

Total active duty personnel (1993): 173,500 (army 83.6%, navy 7.8%, air force 8.6%). *Military expenditure as percentage of GNP* (1989): 3.9% (world 4.9%); per capita expenditure: U.S.$131.

[1]January 1. [2]Province coextensive with the city of Havana. [3]Province bordering the city of Havana on the east, south, and west. [4]Includes cobalt. [5]State sector only; excludes military and unemployed. [6]Mining includes metallurgy and refined petroleum products. [7]Imports c.i.f.; exports f.o.b.

Cyprus

Island of Cyprus

Area: 3,572 sq mi, 9,251 sq km.
Population (1993): 764,000[1].

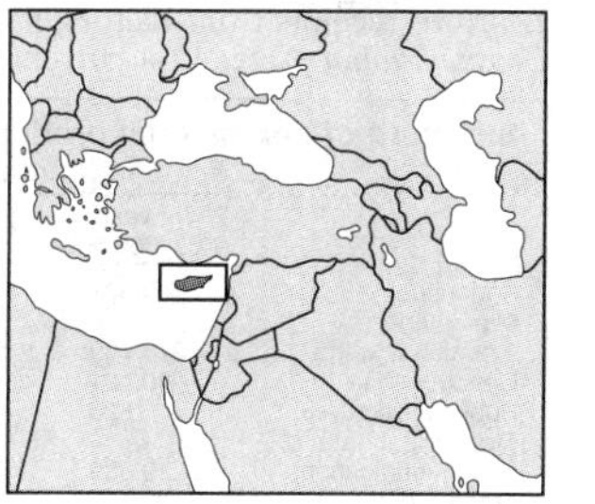

Two de facto states currently exist on the island of Cyprus: the Republic of Cyprus (ROC), predominantly Greek in character, occupying the southern two-thirds of the island, which is the original and still the internationally recognized de jure government of the whole island; and the Turkish Republic of Northern Cyprus (TRNC), proclaimed unilaterally Nov. 15, 1983, on territory originally secured for the Turkish Cypriot population by the July 20, 1974, intervention of Turkey. Only Turkey recognizes the TRNC, and the two ethnic communities have failed to reestablish a single state. Provision of separate data below does not imply recognition of either state's claims but is necessitated by the continuing lack of unified data.

Republic of Cyprus

Official name: Kipriakí Dimokratía (Greek); Kıbrıs Cumhuriyeti (Turkish) (Republic of Cyprus).
Form of government: unitary multiparty republic with a unicameral legislature (House of Representatives [80[2]]).
Head of state and government: President.
Capital: Nicosia.
Official languages: Greek; Turkish.
Monetary unit: 1 Cyprus pound (£C) = 100 cents; valuation (Oct. 4, 1993) 1 £C = U.S.$2.04 = £1.33.

Area and population

Districts	Capitals	area sq mi	area sq km	population[3] 1990[4] estimate
Famagusta	Famagusta	...	...	28,700
Larnaca	Larnaca	433	1,121	94,400
Limassol	Limassol	538	1,393	166,900
Nicosia	Nicosia	...	...	230,800
Paphos	Paphos	539	1,396	47,700
TOTAL		2,276[5]	5,896[5]	568,500

Demography

Population (1993): 586,000[3].
Urban-rural (1990): urban 68.5%; rural 31.5%.
Age breakdown (1990): under 15, 25.8%; 15–29, 23.7%; 30–44, 22.0%; 45–59, 14.6%; 60–74, 9.8%; 75 and over, 4.1%.
Ethnic composition: Greek Cypriot *c.* 95%; other *c.* 5%.
Religious affiliation (1990): Cypriot Orthodox 82.0%; Maronite 1.5%; other 16.5%.
Major urban areas (1991): Nicosia 166,500; Limassol 129,700.

Vital statistics

Birth rate per 1,000 population (1991): 18.6 (world avg. 26.4).
Death rate per 1,000 population (1991): 8.8 (world avg. 9.2).
Natural increase rate per 1,000 population (1991): 9.8 (world avg. 17.2).
Life expectancy at birth (1987–91): male 74.1 years; female 78.6 years.

National economy

Budget (1991). Revenue: £C 725,000,000 (income taxes 18.1%, import duties 15.6%, excises 11.2%). Expenditures: £C 843,000,000 (current expenditures 89.2%, development expenditures 10.8%).
Tourism: receipts (1992) U.S.$1,377,000,000; expenditures (1991) U.S.$200,000,000.
Household expenditure (1990): food, beverages, and expenditures in restaurants 29.2%, transportation and communications 15.8%.
Gross national product (1991): U.S.$6,135,000,000 (U.S.$8,640 per capita).

Structure of gross domestic product and labour force

	1992 in value £C '000,000	% of total value	labour force	% of labour force
Agriculture	181.2	6.0	35,000	12.2
Mining	7.7	0.3	700	0.2
Manufacturing	411.9	13.7	49,000	17.2
Construction	308.0	10.2	24,000	8.4
Public utilities	60.9	2.0	1,400	0.5
Transp. and commun.	254.8	8.5	15,900	5.6
Trade	641.5	21.3	64,500	22.6
Finance, insurance	470.2	15.6	18,200	6.4
Pub. admin., defense	367.0	12.2	56,300	19.7
Services	186.4	6.2		
Other	122.2	4.0	20,600[6]	7.2[6]
TOTAL	3,011.8	100.0	285,600	100.0

Production. Agriculture (value of production in £C '000,000; 1990): potatoes 30.8, milk 23.3, pork 17.6, sheep and goat meat 17.4, citrus fruits 16.1, grapes 15.9, poultry 15.8, barley 11.1. Manufacturing (value added in £C '000,000; 1990): wearing apparel 53.9; food 46.2; beverages 33.5; cement, bricks, and tiles 31.6. Energy production: electricity (kW-hr; 1991) 2,077,000,000.

Foreign trade[7]

Imports (1992): £C 1,490,800,000 (consumer goods 25.6%; transport equipment 15.7%; capital goods 11.3%; mineral fuels 8.5%). *Major import sources:* U.K. 11.3%; Japan 10.5%; Italy 9.7%; Germany 9.0%; U.S. 8.4%.
Exports (1992): £C 453,400,000 (domestic exports 50.9%, of which clothing 14.2%, potatoes 4.8%; reexports 49.1%). *Major export destinations:* U.K. 19.2%; Lebanon 12.1%; Greece 8.3%; Egypt 6.5%; ships' stores 10.3%.

Transport and communications

Transport. Roads (1991): total length 10,211 km (paved 53%). Vehicles (1991): cars 189,701; trucks and buses 84,024. Merchant marine (1992): vessels 1,416; deadweight tonnage 36,198,083. Air transport (1992)[8]: passenger-km 2,095,000,000; metric ton-km cargo 33,046,000; airports (1993) 1.
Communications. Daily newspapers (1991): 10; total circulation 86,000; circulation per 1,000 population 150. Television (1992): 234,000 receivers (1 per 2.5 persons). Telephones (1991): 348,810 (1 per 1.6 persons).

Education and health

Education (1990–91)

	schools	teachers	students	student/teacher ratio
Primary (age 5–12)	383	3,034	62,962	20.8
Secondary (age 12–18) / Vocational	108	3,735	44,614	11.9
Higher	26[9]	481[9]	6,554	12.2[9]

Educational attainment (1989). Percentage of population age 20 and over having: no formal schooling 6%; higher education 14%. *Literacy* (1989): population age 15 and over literate 95%; male 98%; female 92%.
Health (1990): physicians 1,208 (1 per 476 persons); hospital beds 3,423 (1 per 168 persons); infant mortality rate per 1,000 live births (1991) 9.8.

Turkish Republic of Northern Cyprus

Official name: Kuzey Kıbrıs Türk Cumhuriyeti (Turkish) (Turkish Republic of Northern Cyprus).
Capital: Lefkoşa (Nicosia).
Official language: Turkish.
Monetary unit: 1 Turkish lira (LT) = 100 kurush; valuation (Oct. 4, 1993) 1 U.S.$ = LT 12,073; 1 £ = LT 18,291.

Area and population

Districts	Administrative centres	area sq mi	area sq km	population[1] 1989 estimate
Lefkoşa (Nicosia)	Lefkoşa	...	...	78,772
Gazimağusa (Famagusta)	Gazimağusa	...	...	64,190
Girne (Kyrenia)	Girne	247	640	26,310
TOTAL		1,295	3,355	169,272

Population (1993): 178,000 (Lefkoşa 39,496[10]; Gazimağusa 20,516[10]).
Ethnic composition (1985): Turkish 98.7%; other 1.3%.

Structure of gross domestic product and labour force

	1991 in value LT '000,000,000	% of total value	labour force	% of labour force
Agriculture	207	9.1	19,094	26.1
Mining and manufacturing	279	12.3	6,845	9.3
Construction	133	5.9	7,518	10.3
Public utilities	35	1.5	1,202	1.6
Transp. and commun.	214	9.4	5,728	7.8
Trade	462	20.4	6,942	9.5
Finance, real estate	152	6.7	2,016	2.8
Pub. admin.	442	19.5	15,979	21.8
Services	144	6.4	6,776	9.3
Other	199[11]	8.8[11]	1,079[12]	1.5[12]
TOTAL	2,267	100.0	73,179	100.0

Budget (1991)[13]. Revenue: LT 713,000,000,000 (local taxes 51.2%, loans 23.9%, foreign aid 13.4%). Expenditures: LT 713,000,000,000 (current expenditure 84.6%, development expenditure 10.3%, defense 5.1%).
Imports (1991): U.S.$301,100,000 (machinery and transport equipment 21.4%, food 14.4%). *Major import sources:* Turkey 47.5%; U.K. 15.2%.
Exports (1991): U.S.$52,500,000 (citrus fruits 42.8%). *Major export destinations:* U.K. 67.4%; Turkey 13.9%.

Education (1991–92)

	schools	teachers	students	student/teacher ratio
Primary (age 7–12)	155	849	19,400	22.9
Secondary (age 13–18)	28	963	16,719	17.4
Vocational	10	254	2,761	10.9
Higher	4	201[9]	6,145	26.1[9]

Health (1989): physicians 250 (1 per 677 persons); hospital beds 1,042 (1 per 162 persons); infant mortality rate per 1,000 live births (1987–89 avg.) 6.3.

[1]Includes "settlers" from Turkey in the TRNC; excludes 30,000 Turkish military in the TRNC, 4,200 British military in the Sovereign Base Areas in the ROC, and 1,500 UN peacekeeping forces. [2]Twenty-four seats reserved for Turkish Cypriots are not occupied. [3]Population excludes British and UN military forces. [4]January 1. [5]Area includes 73 sq mi (256 sq km) of British military Sovereign Base Areas and *c.* 107 sq mi (*c.* 278 sq km) of the UN Buffer Zone. [6]Includes 5,200 unemployed. [7]Imports c.i.f.; exports f.o.b. [8]Cyprus Airways. [9]1989–90. [10]1989. [11]Customs duties. [12]Unemployed. [13]Eleven months only.

Czech Republic

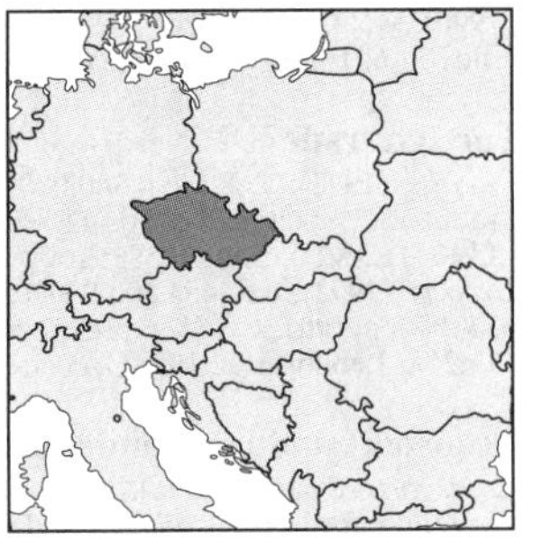

Official name: Česká Republika.
Form of government: unitary multiparty republic with two legislative houses (Senate [81[1]]; Chamber of Deputies [200]).
Chief of state: President.
Head of government: Prime Minister.
Capital: Prague.
Official language: Czech.
Official religion: none.
Monetary unit[2]: 1 Czech koruna (Kc) = 100 halura; valuation (Oct. 4, 1993) 1 U.S.$ = 28.75 Kc; 1 £ = 43.56 Kc.

Area and population

		area		population
		sq mi	sq km	1991 census
Regions	**Capitals**			
Jižní Čechy	České Budějovice	4,380	11,345	697,334
Jižní Morava	Brno	5,802	15,028	2,048,867
Severní Čechy	Ustí nad Labem	3,019	7,819	1,173,681
Severní Morava	Ostrava	4,273	11,067	1,961,508
Střední Čechy	Prague	4,245	10,994	1,112,374
Východní Čechy	Hradec Králové	4,340	11,240	1,232,646
Zapadní Čechy	Plzeň	4,199	10,875	860,311
Capital city				
Prague	—	192	496	1,212,010
TOTAL		30,450	78,864	10,298,731

Demography

Population (1993): 10,339,000.
Density (1993): persons per sq mi 339.5, persons per sq km 131.1.
Urban-rural: n.a.
Sex distribution (1991): male 48.60%; female 51.40%.
Age breakdown (1991): under 15, 21.2%; 15–29, 21.7%; 30–44, 22.8%; 45–59, 16.6%; 60–74, 12.5%; 75 and over, 5.2%.
Population projection: (2000) 10,456,000; (2010) 10,544,000.
Doubling time: not applicable; population growth is negligible.
Ethnic composition (1991): Czech 81.3%; Moravian 13.2%; Slovak 3.0%; Polish 0.6%; German 0.5%; Silesian 0.4%; Gypsy 0.3%; Hungarian 0.2%; Ukrainian 0.1%; other 0.4%.
Religious affiliation (1991): nonreligious and atheist 39.7%; Roman Catholic 39.2%; Protestant 4.1%, of which Czechoslovak Brethren Reformed 1.9%, Czechoslovak Hussite 1.7%, Silesian Evangelical 0.5%; Eastern Orthodox 0.2%; Greek Catholic 0.1%; other 16.7%.
Major cities (1991): Prague 1,212,010; Brno 387,986; Ostrava 327,553; Plzeň 173,129; Olomouc 105,690.

Vital statistics

Birth rate per 1,000 population (1992): 11.8 (world avg. 26.4); (1990) legitimate 91.8%; illegitimate 8.2%.
Death rate per 1,000 population (1992): 11.7 (world avg. 9.2).
Natural increase rate per 1,000 population (1992): 0.1 (world avg. 17.2).
Total fertility rate (avg. births per childbearing woman; 1990): 1.9.
Marriage rate per 1,000 population (1992): 7.2.
Divorce rate per 1,000 population (1992): 2.8.
Life expectancy at birth (1991): male 67.7 years; female 74.8 years.
Major causes of death per 100,000 population (1990): diseases of the circulatory system 698.6; malignant neoplasms (cancers) 274.4; accidents, poisoning, and violence 87.3; diseases of the respiratory system 52.3; diseases of the digestive system 48.5; endocrine and metabolic disorders 22.5.

National economy

Budget (1991). Revenue: Kčs 251,187,000,000[2] (receipts from enterprises 68.7%; taxes 20.1%). Expenditures: Kčs 259,582,000,000[2] (education, health, social welfare, and culture 48.1%; national economy 9.1%; defense 2.8%).
Public debt (external, outstanding; 1992): Kčs 6,923,000,000[2].
Production (metric tons except as noted). Agriculture, forestry, fishing (1991): cereals 7,845,000 (of which wheat 4,081,000, barley 2,833,000, corn [maize] 150,000, rye 353,000), sugar beets 4,013,000, potatoes 2,043,000; livestock (number of live animals; 1992) 4,491,000 pigs, 2,508,000 cattle (of which 940,000 dairy cows), 254,000 sheep, 30,834,000 poultry; roundwood 10,751,000 cu m; fish catch, n.a. Mining and quarrying (1991): iron ore 111,000; lead 17,835. Manufacturing (1991): crude steel 7,964,000; rolled steel 6,201,000; cement 5,619,000; flour 774,000; plastic and resins 540,000; phosphate fertilizers 46,341; cotton fabrics 345,905,000 m; beer 17,191,340 hectolitres; other alcoholic beverages 809,340 hectolitres; motor vehicles 172,748 units. Construction (1991): residential 2,212,000 sq m. Energy production (consumption): electricity (kW-hr; 1991) 60,646,000,000 (58,118,000,000); coal (1991) 78,359,000 (n.a.); crude petroleum (barrels; 1991) 500,000 (n.a.); petroleum products, n.a. (n.a.); natural gas, n.a. (n.a.).
Population economically active (1993[3]): total 5,270,433; activity rate of total population 50.9% (participation rates: ages 15–64 [1991] 77.9%; female 47.6%; unemployed 3.0%).

Price and earnings indexes (1985 = 100)

	1985	1986	1987	1988	1989	1990	1991
Consumer price index[4]	100.0	100.5	100.5	101.0	102.6	112.3	171.7
Annual earnings index	100.0	101.6	103.7	106.2	110.0	113.0	130.1

Tourism: receipts from visitors, n.a.; expenditures by nationals abroad, n.a.
Gross national product (at current market prices): n.a.

Structure of net material product and labour force

	1990		1991	
	in value Kčs '000,000[2]	% of total value	labour force	% of labour force
Agriculture	40,801	9.4	627,904	11.6
Mining and manufacturing	273,709	63.0	2,020,963	37.3
Construction	49,191	11.3	411,898	7.6
Public utilities	826	0.2	—	—
Transportation and communications	19,089	4.4	365,975	6.8
Trade	36,569	8.4	551,119	10.2
Finance	—	—	5	5
Pub. admin., defense	} 14,511	} 3.3	238,049	4.4
Services			1,005,054[5]	18.5[5]
Other			200,140	3.7
TOTAL	434,696	100.0	5,421,102	100.0[6]

Land use (1991): forested 33.3%; meadows and pastures 11.0%; agricultural and under permanent cultivation 43.4%; other 12.3%.
Household income and expenditure. Average household size (1991) 2.5; income per household (1989) Kčs 86,643[2,7] (U.S.$5,757); sources of income (1989): wages and salaries 71.9%, transfer payments 10.9%, other 17.2%; expenditure (1989): food and beverages 29.5%, clothing and footwear 9.9%, fuel and lighting 9.9%, household durable goods 5.3%, other 45.4%.

Foreign trade

Balance of trade (current prices)

	1986	1987	1988	1989	1990	1991
U.S.$'000,000	...	...	...	+454.6	−252.3	+339.7
% of total	...	...	...	5.7%	2.6%	3.0%

Imports (1991): U.S.$12,527,000,000 (chemicals, manufactured goods, and machinery 65.3%; fuels and lubricants 21.1%; food, beverages, and live animals 7.2%; raw materials including vegetable and animal products 6.4%). *Major import sources:* developed market economies 62.6%; economies in transition 31.3%; developing market economies 5.5%.
Exports (1991): U.S.$11,644,000,000 (chemicals, manufactured goods, and machinery 80.7%, of which machinery and transport equipment 22.8%; raw materials, fuels and lubricants, and animal and vegetable products 10.7%; food, beverages, and live animals 8.5%). *Major export destinations:* developed market economies 63.7%, of which European Community 43.3%; economies in transition 24.6%; developing market economies 10.6%.

Transport and communications

Transport. Railroads (1992): length (1991) 5,874 mi, 9,453 km; passengers transported (1990) 274,047,000; short ton-mi cargo 20,974,000,000, metric ton-km cargo 30,622,000,000. Roads (1991): total length 34,730 mi, 55,892 km (paved, n.a.). Vehicles (1991): passenger cars 2,435,645; trucks and buses 232,703. Merchant marine: n.a. Air transport: n.a.; airports (1993) with scheduled flights 4.
Communications. Daily newspapers (1990): total number 17; total circulation 3,788,000; circulation per 1,000 population 368. Radio (1991): total number of receivers 2,956,000 (1 per 3.5 persons). Television (1991): total number of receivers 3,246,000 (1 per 3.2 persons). Telephones (1991): 3,126,266 (1 per 3.3 persons).

Education and health

Education (1991–92)

	schools	teachers	students	student/teacher ratio
Primary (age 6–14)	4,065	64,072	1,166,000	18.2
Secondary (age 15–18)	258	7,050	113,450	16.1
Voc., teacher tr.	507	12,798	191,298	14.9
Higher	23	12,762	111,990	8.8

Educational attainment (1991). Percentage of adult population having: incomplete primary education 0.3%; primary and incomplete secondary 33.1%; complete secondary 58.3%; higher 7.2%; unknown 1.1%. *Literacy* (1990): total population age 15 and over literate 8,170,442 (100%); males literate 3,914,080 (100%); females literate 4,256,362 (100%).
Health (1991): physicians 32,285 (1 per 319 persons); hospital beds 105,382 (1 per 98 persons); infant mortality rate per 1,000 live births (1992) 9.9.
Food (1990): daily per capita caloric intake 3,303 (vegetable products 57%, animal products 43%); 134% of FAO recommended minimum requirement.

Military

Total active duty personnel (1993): 106,500 (army 66.6%, air force 33.4%). *Military expenditure as percentage of GNP:* n.a. Per capita expenditure: U.S.$77.

[1]Seats not yet occupied as of June 1993. [2]The Czech koruna was introduced Feb. 8, 1993, at par with the former Czechoslovak koruna (Kčs), which it replaced. For settlement of obligations existing prior to February 8 between the Czech and Slovak republics, an interim currency, the clearing koruna (XCS) was introduced. [3]January 31. [4]Cost-of-living index; wage earners only. [5]Services includes Finance. [6]Detail does not add to total given because of rounding. [7]Worker's household.

Denmark

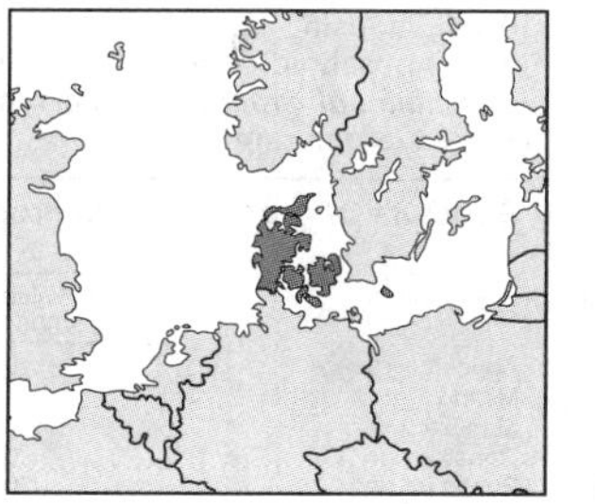

Official name: Kongeriget Danmark (Kingdom of Denmark).
Form of government: parliamentary state and constitutional monarchy with one legislative house (Folketing [179]).
Chief of state: Danish Monarch.
Head of government: Prime Minister.
Capital: Copenhagen.
Official language: Danish.
Official religion: Evangelical Lutheran.
Monetary unit: 1 Danish krone (Dkr; plural kroner) = 100 øre; valuation (Oct. 4, 1993) 1 U.S.$ = Dkr 6.57; 1 £ = Dkr 9.96.

Area and population[1]

		area		population
Counties	Capitals	sq mi	sq km	1993[2] estimate
Århus	Århus	1,761	4,561	609,890
Bornholm	Rønne	227	588	45,224
Frederiksborg	Hillerød	520	1,347	346,108
Fyn	Odense	1,346	3,486	465,239
København	—	203	526	603,883
Nordjylland	Ålborg	2,383	6,173	486,993
Ribe	Ribe	1,209	3,131	220,721
Ringkøbing	Ringkøbing	1,874	4,853	268,990
Roskilde	Roskilde	344	891	221,401
Sønderjylland	Åbenrå	1,520	3,938	251,306
Storstrøm	Nykøbing Falster	1,312	3,398	257,097
Vejle	Vejle	1,157	2,997	334,282
Vestsjælland	Sorø	1,152	2,984	286,290
Viborg	Viborg	1,592	4,122	229,888
Communes				
Copenhagen (København)	—	34	88	466,129
Frederiksberg	—	3	9	87,173
TOTAL		16,639[3]	43,094[3]	5,180,614

Demography

Population (1993): 5,187,000.
Density (1993): persons per sq mi 311.8, persons per sq km 120.4.
Urban-rural (1992): urban 84.9%; rural 15.1%.
Sex distribution (1993): male 49.31%; female 50.69%.
Age breakdown (1993): under 15, 17.0%; 15–29, 22.1%; 30–44, 21.7%; 45–59, 19.0%; 60–74, 13.2%; 75 and over, 7.0%.
Population projection: (2000) 5,245,000; (2010) 5,252,000.
Doubling time: not applicable; population is stable.
Ethnic composition (1993): Danish 96.5%; Asian 1.5%, of which Turkish 0.6%; other Scandinavian 0.5%; British 0.2%; German 0.2%; other 1.1%.
Religious affiliation (1992): Evangelical Lutheran 88.2%; other Christian 1.6%; Muslim 1.3%; other/nonreligious 8.9%.
Major cities (1992): Greater Copenhagen 1,339,395; Århus 204,139; Odense 140,886; Ålborg 114,970; Frederiksberg 87,173[4, 5].

Vital statistics

Birth rate per 1,000 population (1992): 13.1 (world avg. 26.4); legitimate 53.5%; illegitimate 46.5%.
Death rate per 1,000 population (1992): 11.8 (world avg. 9.2).
Natural increase rate per 1,000 population (1992): 1.3 (world avg. 17.2).
Total fertility rate (avg. births per childbearing woman; 1991): 1.7.
Marriage rate per 1,000 population (1991): 6.0.
Divorce rate per 1,000 population (1991): 2.5.
Life expectancy at birth (1990–91): male 72.2 years; female 77.7 years.
Major causes of death per 100,000 population (1991): malignant neoplasms (cancers) 289.8; ischemic heart disease 284.6; cerebrovascular disease 107.8.

National economy

Budget (1992). Revenue: Dkr 338,605,000,000 (indirect taxes 41.0%, direct taxes 39.8%, current transfers 7.1%). Expenditures: Dkr 368,508,000,000 (current expenditure 97.0%, development expenditure 3.0%).
National debt (end of year; 1992): Dkr 575,328,000,000.
Tourism (1992): receipts from visitors U.S.$3,784,000,000; expenditures by nationals abroad U.S.$3,779,000,000.
Population economically active (1991[6]): total 2,910,059; activity rate of total population 56.4% (participation rates: ages 16–66, 79.8%; female 46.4%; unemployed [April 1992–March 1993] 11.5%).

Price and earnings indexes (1985 = 100)

	1987	1988	1989	1990	1991	1992	1993[7]
Consumer price index	107.8	112.7	118.1	121.2	124.1	126.7	128.5
Hourly earnings index	115.9	123.2	128.1	133.1	138.3	142.3	...

Household income and expenditure. Average household size (1993) 2.2; income per household (1988) Dkr 199,354 (U.S.$29,613); principal sources of income (1988)[8]: wages and salaries 48.2%, self-employment 33.6%, transfers 18.2%; expenditure (1990): housing 21.6%, food, beverages, and tobacco 20.9%, transportation and communications 16.4%, recreation and education 10.5%, household furnishings 6.3%.
Production (in Dkr '000,000 except as noted). Agriculture, forestry, fishing (value added; 1992): pork 17,299, milk 11,739, beef 4,422, wheat 3,550, barley 2,585, flowers and plants 2,583, furs 1,022, poultry 1,144; roundwood 2,300,000 cu m; fish catch 1,816,000 metric tons. Mining and quarrying (1991): sand and gravel 27,800,000 cu m; chalk and limestone 4,100,000 cu m. Manufacturing (value added; 1991): nonelectrical machinery and apparatus 19,626; food other than meat 18,527; metal products 12,218; paints, soaps, and pharmaceuticals 10,147; processed meat 9,658; electrical machinery and apparatus 7,639; industrial chemicals 7,151. Construction (completed; 1992): residential 1,449,000 sq m; nonresidential 4,195,000 sq m. Energy production (consumption): electricity (kW-hr; 1992) 30,360,000,000 ([1991] 29,594,000,000); coal (metric tons; 1991) none (13,568,000); crude petroleum (barrels; 1991) 53,769,000 ([1990] 55,749,000); petroleum products (metric tons; 1990) 7,570,000 (7,823,000); natural gas (cu m; 1991) 3,745,000,000 (1,988,000,000).
Gross national product (at current market prices; 1991): U.S.$121,695,000,000 (U.S.$23,660 per capita).

Structure of gross domestic product and labour force

	1992		1990	
	in value Dkr '000,000[9]	% of total value	labour force	% of labour force
Agriculture, fishing	26,393	3.5	155,856	5.4
Mining	6,377	0.9	2,467	0.1
Manufacturing	141,850	19.0	579,065	19.9
Construction	41,834	5.6	201,461	6.9
Public utilities	14,327	1.9	20,349	0.7
Transp. and commun.	67,522	9.1	197,642	6.8
Trade, restaurants	107,424	14.4	428,685	14.7
Finance, real estate	148,497	19.9	256,824	8.8
Pub. admin., defense	166,360	22.3	1,018,504	35.0
Services	45,965	6.2		
Other	−20,810[10]	−2.8[10]	51,575[11]	1.8[11]
TOTAL	745,739	100.0	2,912,428	100.0[3]

Land use (1990): forested 11.6%; meadows and pastures 5.1%; agricultural and under permanent cultivation 60.7%; other 22.6%.

Foreign trade[12]

Balance of trade (current prices)

	1987	1988	1989	1990	1991	1992
Dkr '000,000	+8,891	+19,061	+18,764	+26,404	+32,060	+44,642
% of total	2.6%	5.4%	4.8%	6.5%	7.5%	10.3%

Imports (1992): Dkr 203,003,000,000 (intermediate goods for industries 44.6%, machinery 10.5%, food products 8.8%, transport equipment 6.7%). *Major import sources:* Germany 23.0%; Sweden 10.8%; United Kingdom 8.2%; United States 5.7%; France 5.6%; The Netherlands 5.5%.
Exports (1992): Dkr 238,718,000,000 (nonelectrical and electrical machinery 23.3%, chemical products 10.0%, fresh or frozen swine meat 6.6%, textiles and clothing 4.8%, furniture 4.3%). *Major export destinations:* Germany 23.6%; Sweden 10.5%; United Kingdom 10.1%; Norway 5.8%; France 5.7%; United States 4.9%.

Transport and communications

Transport. Railroads (1991): length 1,763 mi, 2,838 km; passenger-mi 2,981,000,000, passenger-km 4,797,000,000; short ton-mi cargo 1,273,000,000, metric ton-km cargo 1,858,000,000. Roads (1991): total length 44,125 mi, 71,012 km (paved 100%). Vehicles (1992): passenger cars 1,604,638; trucks and buses 315,511. Merchant marine (1992): vessels (100 gross tons and over) 456; total deadweight tonnage 7,569,069. Air transport (1991)[13]: passenger-mi 2,480,000,000, passenger-km 3,991,000,000; short ton-mi cargo 79,904,000, metric ton-km cargo 116,658,000; airports (1993) with scheduled flights 11.
Communications. Daily newspapers (1992): total number 42; total circulation 1,710,000; circulation per 1,000 population 332. Radio (1992): 2,235,000 receivers (1 per 2.3 persons). Television (1992): 2,500,000 receivers (1 per 2.1 persons). Telephones (1990): 5,000,000 (1 per 1.0 persons).

Education and health

Education (1991–92)

	schools	teachers	students	student/teacher ratio
Primary/lower secondary (age 7–15)	2,127	59,800	613,329	10.3
Upper secondary (age 16–18)	154	7,500	74,000	9.9
Vocational	204	...	149,000	...
Higher[14]	94	...	126,221	...

Educational attainment (1990). Percentage of population age 25–69 having: primary education 3.0%; completed lower secondary 23.4%; completed upper secondary or vocational 48.0%; advanced vocational 5.0%; undergraduate 7.4%; graduate 3.9%; unknown 9.3%. *Literacy:* virtually 100%.
Health: physicians (1990) 14,277 (1 per 360 persons); hospital beds (1991) 28,072 (1 per 184 persons); infant mortality rate per 1,000 live births (1992) 6.5.
Food (1988–90): daily per capita caloric intake 3,639 (vegetable products 54%, animal products 46%); 135% of FAO recommended minimum requirement.

Military

Total active duty personnel (1992): 29,200 (army 59.2%, navy 16.8%, air force 24.0%). *Military expenditure as percentage of GNP* (1989): 2.2% (world 4.9%); per capita expenditure U.S.$426.

[1]Excludes the Faeroe Islands and Greenland. [2]January 1. [3]Detail does not add to total given because of rounding. [4]1993. [5]Within Greater Copenhagen. [6]November. [7]June. [8]Excludes interest and dividends. [9]At factor cost. [10]Imputed bank service charges less other producers. [11]Includes 41,334 activities not adequately defined. [12]Import figures are f.o.b. in balance of trade and c.i.f. in commodities and trading partners. [13]Danish share of Scandinavian Airlines System; scheduled air service only. [14]1990–91.

Djibouti

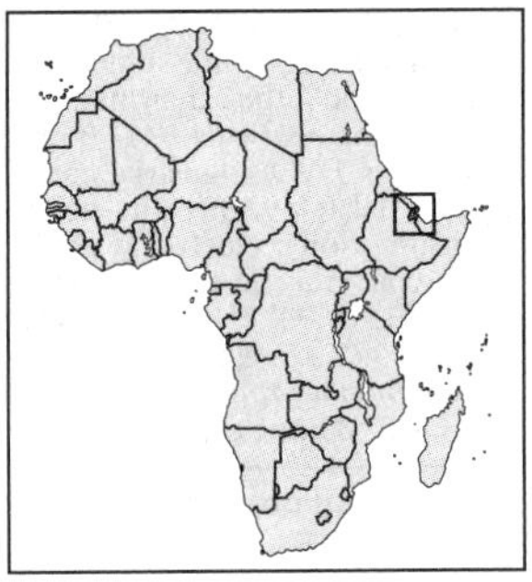

Official name: Jumhūrīyah Jībūtī (Arabic); République de Djibouti (French) (Republic of Djibouti).
Form of government: multiparty republic with one legislative house (National Assembly [65]).
Head of state and government: President.
Capital: Djibouti.
Official languages: Arabic; French.
Official religion: none.
Monetary unit: 1 Djibouti franc (DF) = 100 centimes; valuation (Oct. 4, 1993) 1 U.S.$ = DF 178.17; 1 £ = DF 270.82.

Area and population

		area[1]		population
Districts	Capitals	sq mi	sq km	1982 estimate
ʿAlī Sabīḥ (Ali-Sabieh)	ʿAlī Sabīḥ	925	2,400	15,000
Dikhil	Dikhil	2,775	7,200	30,000
Djibouti	Djibouti	225	600	200,000
Obock	Obock	2,200	5,700	15,000
Tadjoura (Tadjourah)	Tadjoura	2,825	7,300	30,000
TOTAL		8,950	23,200	335,000[2]

Demography

Population (1993): 565,000[3].
Density (1993): persons per sq mi 63.1, persons per sq km 24.4.
Urban-rural (1990): urban 80.7%; rural 19.3%.
Sex distribution (1990): male 50.37%; female 49.63%.
Age breakdown (1990): under 15, 45.2%; 15–29, 24.9%; 30–44, 16.1%; 45–59, 9.0%; 60 and over, 4.8%.
Population projection: (2000) 706,000; (2010) 949,000.
Doubling time: 24 years.
Ethnic composition (1983): Somali 61.7%, of which Issa 33.4%, Gadaboursi 15.0%, Issaq 13.3%; Afar 20.0%; Arab (mostly Yemeni) 6.0%; European 4.0%; other (refugees) 8.3%.
Religious affiliation (1988): Sunnī Muslim 96%; Christian 4%, of which Roman Catholic 2%, Protestant 1%, Orthodox 1%.
Major city and towns (1989): Djibouti 450,000[4]; ʿAlī Sabīḥ 4,000; Tadjoura 3,500; Dikhil 3,000.

Vital statistics

Birth rate per 1,000 population (1990–95): 45.8 (world avg. 26.4).
Death rate per 1,000 population (1990–95): 16.4 (world avg. 9.2).
Natural increase rate per 1,000 population (1990–95): 29.4 (world avg. 17.2).
Total fertility rate (avg. births per childbearing woman; 1990): 6.6.
Marriage rate per 1,000 population (1982): 6.7.
Divorce rate per 1,000 population (1982): 1.9.
Life expectancy at birth (1990–95): male 47.4 years; female 50.7 years.
Major causes of death (percentage of total deaths; 1984)[5]: diarrhea and acute dehydration 16.0%; malnutrition 16.0%; poisoning 11.0%; tuberculosis 6.0%; acute respiratory disease 6.0%; malaria 6.0%; anemia 6.0%; heart disease 2.0%; kidney disease 1.0%; other ailments 19.0%; no diagnosis 11.0%.

National economy

Budget (1993). Revenue: DF 29,011,000,000 (1990; current receipts 80.2%, of which indirect and direct taxes 72.9%, nontax revenue 7.3%; external development receipts 19.8%). Expenditures: DF 28,990,000,000 (defense 17.5%; education 9.4%; health 7.2%; debt service 5.2%; agriculture 1.6%; commerce 0.4%; industry 0.2%).
Public debt (external, outstanding; 1991): U.S.$175,500,000.
Tourism: receipts from visitors (1990) U.S.$6,000,000; expenditures by nationals abroad, n.a.
Production (metric tons except as noted). Agriculture, forestry, fishing (1992): vegetables and melons 22,000, of which tomatoes 1,000, eggplant (1985–86) 66; livestock (number of live animals) 506,000 goats, 450,000 sheep, 180,000 cattle, 61,000 camels, 8,000 asses; fish catch (1991) 380. Mining and quarrying: mineral production limited to locally used construction materials and evaporated salt. Manufacturing (1988): detail, n.a.; main items produced include furniture, nonalcoholic beverages, meat and hides, light electromechanical goods, and mineral water. Construction (1989): 53,900 sq m. Energy production (consumption): electricity (kW-hr; 1991) 178,000,000 (178,000,000); coal, none (n.a.); crude petroleum, none (n.a.); petroleum products (metric tons; 1991) none (117,000); natural gas, none (n.a.).
Population economically active (1988): total 230,000; activity rate of total population 44.9% (participation rates: over age 10, 67.0%; female 40.0%; unemployed [1987] *c.* 40–50%).

Price and earnings indexes (1985 = 100)

	1983	1984	1985	1986	1987	1988	1989
Consumer price index[6]	...	116.6	100.0	116.4	121.3	129.0	132.9
Earnings index[7]	...	...	...	...	...	...	...

Household income and expenditure. Average household size[8] (1985) 7.2; income per household: n.a.; sources of income (1976): wages and salaries 51.6%, self-employment 36.0%, transfer payments 10.5%, other 1.9%; expenditure (expatriate households; 1984): food 50.3%, energy 13.1%, recreation 10.4%, housing 6.4%, clothing 1.7%, personal effects 1.4%, health care 1.0%, household goods 0.3%, other 15.4%.
Gross national product (at current market prices; 1986): U.S.$216,600,000[9] (U.S.$475 per capita).

Structure of gross national product and labour force

	1989		1988	
	in value U.S.$'000,000	% of total value	labour force	% of labour force
Agriculture	10	2.9	176,000	76.6
Mining	—	—		
Manufacturing	17	4.9	21,000	9.0
Construction	20	5.8		
Public utilities	20	5.8		
Transportation and communications	46	13.4		
Trade, Finance	116	33.7	33,000	14.4
Pub. admin., defense	104	30.2		
Services	11	3.3		
TOTAL	344	100.0	230,000	100.0

Land use (1991): forested 0.3%; meadows and pastures 9.1%; agricultural and under permanent cultivation[10]; built-on, wasteland, and other 90.6%.

Foreign trade[11]

Balance of trade (current prices)

	1986	1987	1988	1989	1990	1991
DF '000,000	−29,847	−31,511	−31,655	−30,497	−33,763	−35,020
% of total	80.4%	88.0%	79.4%	77.5%	79.3%	85.0%

Imports (1991): DF 38,103,000,000 (food, beverages, and tobacco 32.7%; textiles and footwear 11.7%; fossil fuels 9.2%; machinery and electrical machinery 8.5%; transport equipment 7.1%; chemical products 6.2%; base metals and base metal products 6.2%). *Major import sources:* France 26.1%; Ethiopia 8.3%; Japan 7.2%; Italy 6.5%; Saudi Arabia 5.0%; United States 3.7%.
Exports (1991): DF 3,083,000,000 (unspecified special transactions 71.7%; live animals [including camels] 15.5%; food and food products 12.8%). *Major export destinations:* France 57.1%; Yemen 16.0%; Saudi Arabia 5.5%; Somalia 4.1%; Italy 3.2%.

Transport and communications

Transport. Railroads (1989): length 66 mi, 106 km; passenger-mi 182,000,000, passenger-km 293,000,000; short ton-mile cargo 81,700,000[12], metric ton-km cargo 119,300,000[12]. Roads (1991): total length 1,789 mi, 2,897 km (paved 13%). Vehicles (1991): passenger cars 13,000; trucks and buses 2,500. Merchant marine (1992): vessels (100 gross tons and over) 10; total deadweight tonnage 4,090. Air transport (1989)[13]: passenger arrivals 64,000, passenger departures 66,000; cargo loaded 1,100 metric tons, cargo unloaded 7,100 metric tons; airports (1993) with scheduled flights 3.
Communications. Weekly newspapers (1990): total number 1; total circulation 4,000; circulation per 1,000 population 7.6. Radio (1992): total number of receivers 30,000 (1 per 19 persons). Television (1992): total number of receivers 17,000 (1 per 33 persons). Telephones (1990): 5,666 subscribers (1 per 98 persons).

Education and health

Education (1991)

	schools	teachers	students	student/ teacher ratio
Primary (age 6–11)	69	737	31,926	43.3
Secondary (age 12–18), Voc., teacher tr.	26	329[14]	9,363	...
Higher	1	13	108	8.3

Educational attainment: n.a. *Literacy* (1987): percentage of population age 20 and over literate 33.7%.
Health (1989): physicians 97 (1 per 5,258 persons); hospital beds[15] 1,383 (1 per 369 persons); infant mortality rate per 1,000 live births (1990–95) 112.
Food: n.a.

Military

Total active duty personnel (1993): 3,300[16] (army 90.9%, navy 3.0%, air force 6.1%). *Military expenditure as percentage of GNP* (1984): 9.0% (world 5.6%); per capita expenditure U.S.$67.

[1]Original figures are those given in sq km; sq mi equivalent is rounded to appropriate level of generality. [2]Including 45,000 not distributed by district. [3]Excludes about 130,000 Somali refugees. [4]Not including 20,000 people categorized as transients. [5]Infants and children to age 10, district of Djibouti only. [6]European expatriate community only. [7]Minimum monthly wage remained constant between 1980 and 1986. [8]City of Djibouti only. [9]Estimate based on per capita GNP. [10]In 1988–89 only 1,005 acres (407 hectares) of land were cultivated. [11]The value of imports includes merchandise destined for Ethiopia and northern Somalia; that of exports excludes reexports coming from those areas. In 1980 the value of reexports from Ethiopia and northern Somalia was approximately five times greater than the value of domestic exports. Import figures are c.i.f. [12]Based on total weight of Ethiopian exports and imports transported to and from the port of Djibouti. [13]Djibouti International Airport only. [14]Public schools only. [15]Public health only. [16]Excludes 4,000 French troops.

Dominica

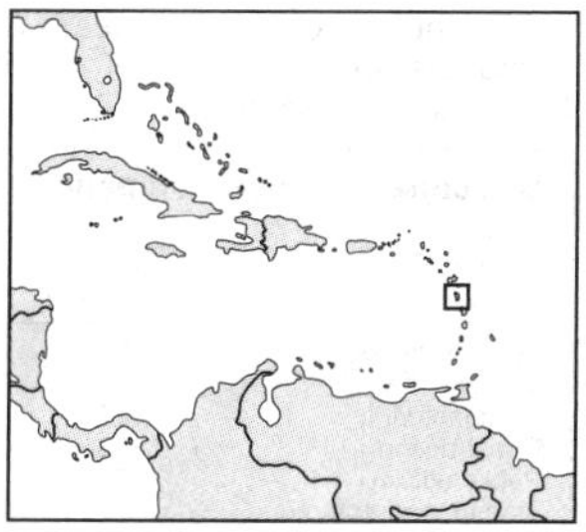

Official name: Commonwealth of Dominica.
Form of government: multiparty republic with one legislative house (House of Assembly [31][1]).
Chief of state: President.
Head of government: Prime Minister.
Capital: Roseau.
Official language: English.
Official religion: none.
Monetary unit: 1 East Caribbean dollar (EC$) = 100 cents; valuation (Oct. 4, 1993) 1 U.S.$ = EC$2.70; 1 £ = EC$4.10.

Area and population

	area		population
Parishes[2]	sq mi	sq km	1991 census
St. Andrew	69	179	11,106
St. David	49	127	6,977
St. George	21	54	20,365
St. John	23	60	4,990
St. Joseph	46	119	6,183
St. Luke	4	10	1,552
St. Mark	4	10	1,943
St. Patrick	32	83	8,929
St. Paul	26	67	7,495
St. Peter	11	29	1,643
TOTAL	290[3, 4]	750[3, 4]	71,183[5]

Demography

Population (1993): 73,900.
Density (1993): persons per sq mi 254.8, persons per sq km 98.5.
Urban-rural: n.a.
Sex distribution (1991): male 50.04%; female 49.96%.
Age breakdown (1989): under 15, 35.1%; 15–29, 28.1%; 30–44, 14.5%; 45–59, 9.5%; 60 and over, 11.7%; unknown, 1.1%.
Population projection: (2000) 82,000; (2010) 96,000.
Doubling time: 56 years.
Ethnic composition (1981): black 91.2%; mixed race 6.0%; Amerindian 1.5%; white 0.5%; not stated 0.6%; other 0.2%.
Religious affiliation (1991): Roman Catholic 67.4%; other 32.6%.
Major towns (1991): Roseau 15,853; Portsmouth 3,621; Marigot 2,919; Atkinson 2,518; Mahaut 2,372.

Vital statistics

Birth rate per 1,000 population (1990): 19.9 (world avg. 27.1).
Death rate per 1,000 population (1990): 7.4 (world avg. 9.8).
Natural increase rate per 1,000 population (1990): 12.5 (world avg. 17.3).
Total fertility rate (avg. births per childbearing woman; 1991): 2.7.
Marriage rate per 1,000 population (1990): 3.2.
Divorce rate per 1,000 population: n.a.
Life expectancy at birth (1991): male 73.0 years; female 79.0 years.
Major causes of death per 100,000 population (1990): diseases of the circulatory system 273.5, of which ischemic heart diseases 120.8, hypertensive disease 88.8; malignant neoplasms (cancers) 116.6; endocrine, metabolic, and nutritional disorders 51.4; diseases of the respiratory system 43.0; infectious and parasitic diseases 37.5.

National economy

Budget (1993–94). Revenue: EC$208,700,000 (current revenue 73.3%, external grants 13.5%, external loans 11.7%). Expenditures: EC$250,800,000 (current expenditures 59.1%, development expenditures 33.9%, debt repayment 4.4%).
Public debt (external, outstanding; 1991): U.S.$86,600,000.
Tourism: receipts from visitors (1991) U.S.$28,100,000; expenditures by nationals abroad (1990) U.S.$4,000,000.
Gross national product (at current market prices; 1992): U.S.$181,000,000 (U.S.$2,510 per capita).

Structure of gross domestic product and labour force

	1991		1989	
	in value EC$'000,000[6]	% of total value	labour force	% of labour force
Agriculture	101.6	25.5	7,900	25.8
Mining	3.8	1.0	3,400	11.1
Manufacturing	27.4	6.9		
Construction	29.1	7.3	2,800	9.2
Public utilities	12.9	3.2	300	1.0
Transportation and communications	64.8	16.3	1,600	5.2
Trade, hotels, restaurants	52.6	13.2	3,700	12.1
Finance, real estate, insurance	58.5	14.7	800	2.6
Pub. admin., defense	72.5	18.2	5,800	19.0
Services	4.2	1.1		
Other	–29.5[7]	–7.4[7]	4,300[8]	14.1[8]
TOTAL	397.9	100.0	30,600	100.0[4]

Population economically active (1989): total 30,600; activity rate of total population 37.5% (participation rates: ages 15–64, 62.3%; female 41.8%; unemployed [1992] 15.0%).

Price and earnings indexes (1985 = 100)

	1986	1987	1988	1989	1990	1991	1992
Consumer price index	103.0	108.0	110.4	117.3	121.6	128.8	135.6
Earnings index	...	...	...	...	...	...	...

Household income and expenditure. Average household size (1981) 4.3; income per household: n.a.; expenditure (1984)[9]: food and nonalcoholic beverages 43.1%, housing and utilities 16.1%, clothing and footwear 6.5%, alcoholic beverages and tobacco 2.0%, other 32.3%.
Production. Agriculture, forestry, fishing (value of production in EC$'000; 1991): bananas 39,600, root crops 32,800 (of which yams 9,800, dasheens 9,200, tanias 6,400, cassava 4,300), coconuts 4,600, plantains 3,700, grapefruit 3,500, oranges 3,300, cinnamon 2,400; livestock (number of live animals) 10,000 goats, 9,000 cattle, 8,000 sheep; roundwood, n.a.; fish catch (1991) 590 metric tons. Mining and quarrying (1990): pumice and volcanic ash 100,000 metric tons. Manufacturing (1990): coconut-based soaps 9,586 metric tons[10]; pasta products 156 metric tons; edible coconut oil 2,904 hectolitres; rum (1987) 2,614 hectolitres; bottled spring water 323,000 cases; other products include garments, furniture, and footwear. Construction (value of starts; 1990): U.S.$29,800,000. Energy production (consumption): electricity (kW-hr; 1990) 36,900,000 (30,700,000); coal, none (none); crude petroleum, none (none); petroleum products (metric tons; 1990) none (19,000); natural gas, none (none).
Land use (1991): forested 41.0%; meadows and pastures 3.0%; agricultural and under permanent cultivation 23.0%; other 33.0%.

Foreign trade[11]

Balance of trade (current prices)

	1986	1987	1988	1989	1990	1991
EC$'000,000	–33.5	–49.6	–86.3	–164.7	–167.4	–163.0
% of total	12.5%	16.1%	22.3%	39.7%	35.6%	36.0%

Imports (1991): EC$308,100,000 ([12]machinery and transport equipment 26.1%; basic manufactures 24.5%; food 17.3%; chemicals and chemical products 11.1%). *Major import sources*[13]: United States 33.0%; United Kingdom 25.0%; France 5.0%; St. Lucia 4.0%; Italy 4.0%; Japan 4.0%.
Exports (1991): EC$145,100,000 (bananas 55.8%, coconut-based laundry and toilet soaps 20.5%). *Major export destinations*[13]: United Kingdom 57.0%; Jamaica 9.0%; United States 7.0%; Italy 4.0%; Malaysia 4.0%.

Transport and communications

Transport. Railroads: none. Roads (1988): total length 470 mi, 756 km (paved, n.a.). Vehicles (1991): passenger cars 4,696; trucks and buses 4,616. Merchant marine (1992): vessels (100 gross tons and over) 7; total deadweight tonnage 3,153. Air transport (1991): passenger arrivals 43,312, passenger departures, n.a.; cargo unloaded 259 metric tons, cargo loaded 415 metric tons; airports (1993) with scheduled flights 2.
Communications. Daily newspapers: none[14]. Radio (1992): 45,000 receivers (1 per 1.6 persons). Television (1992): 5,200 receivers (1 per 14 persons). Telephones (1991): 12,404 (1 per 5.8 persons).

Education and health

Education (1990–91)

	schools	teachers	students	student/teacher ratio
Primary	65	626	14,427	23.0
Secondary	13	199	4,374	22.0
Higher	2	38[15]	388	9.5[15]

Educational attainment (1981). Percentage of population age 25 and over having: no formal schooling 6.6%; primary education 80.6%; secondary 11.1%; higher 1.7%. *Literacy* (1986): total population age 15 and over literate, *c.* 49,000 (94.4%).
Health (1990): physicians 37 (1 per 1,947 persons); hospital beds 292 (1 per 247 persons); infant mortality rate per 1,000 live births 18.4.
Food (1988–90): daily per capita caloric intake 2,911 (vegetable products 79%, animal products 21%); 120% of FAO recommended minimum requirement.

Military

Total active duty personnel (1990): none[16].

[1]Includes 10 nonelective seats. Nine of the 10 nonelective seats are potentially elective according to the constitution. [2]Dominica is divided into 10 parishes for statistical purposes only. Local government is based on city, town, or village councils. [3]Includes inland water area. [4]Detail does not add to total given because of rounding. [5]Preliminary figure; excludes institutionalized population. [6]At factor cost. [7]Less imputed service charges. [8]Activities not specified. [9]Weights of consumer price index components. [10]Coconut-based soap products were the main contributor to total value added of manufacturing sector in 1990. [11]Imports c.i.f.; exports f.o.b. [12]Based on 1990 imports totaling EC$318,400,000. [13]Estimated data. [14]Weekly newspapers (1991): total number 2; total circulation 5,050; circulation per 1,000 population 14. [15]1989–90. [16]300-member police force includes a coast guard unit.

Dominican Republic

Official name: República Dominicana (Dominican Republic).
Form of government: multiparty republic with two legislative houses (Senate [30]; Chamber of Deputies [120]).
Head of state and government: President.
Capital: Santo Domingo.
Official language: Spanish.
Official religion: none[1].
Monetary unit: 1 Dominican peso (RD$) = 100 centavos; valuation (Oct. 4, 1993) 1 U.S.$ = RD$12.91; 1 £ = RD$19.55.

Area and population

Provinces	Capitals	area sq mi	area sq km	population 1990 estimate
Azua	Azua	938	2,430	195,420
Bahoruco (Baoruco)	Neiba	531	1,376	87,376
Barahona	Barahona	976	2,528	152,405
Dajabón	Dajabón	344	890	64,123
Duarte	San Francisco de Macorís	499	1,292	261,725
El Seíbo	El Seíbo	641	1,659	97,590
Espaillat	Moca	386	1,000	182,248
Hato Mayor	Hato Mayor	514	1,330	77,823
Independencia	Jimaní	719	1,861	43,077
La Altagracia	Higüey	1,191	3,084	111,241
La Estrelleta	Elías Piña	690	1,788	72,651
La Romana	La Romana	209	541	169,223
La Vega	La Vega	916	2,373	303,047
María Trinidad Sánchez	Nagua	506	1,310	125,148
Monseñor Nouel	Bonao	388	1,004	124,794
Monte Cristi	Monte Cristi	768	1,989	92,678
Monte Plata	Monte Plata	841	2,179	174,799
Pedernales	Pedernales	373	967	18,896
Peravia	Baní	626	1,622	186,810
Puerto Plata	Puerto Plata	726	1,881	229,738
Salcedo	Salcedo	206	533	110,216
Samaná	Samaná	382	989	73,002
San Cristóbal	San Cristóbal	604	1,564	320,921
San Juan	San Juan	1,375	3,561	266,628
San Pedro de Macorís	San Pedro de Macorís	450	1,166	197,862
Sánchez Ramírez	Cotuí	453	1,174	140,635
Santiago	Santiago de los Caballeros	1,205	3,122	704,835
Santiago Rodríguez	Sabaneta	394	1,020	61,570
Santo Domingo[2]	—	570	1,477	2,411,895
Valverde	Mao	220	570	111,470
TOTAL		18,704[3]	48,443[3]	7,169,846

Demography

Population (1993): 7,634,000.
Density (1993): persons per sq mi 408.1, persons per sq km 157.6.
Urban-rural (1990): urban 60.4%; rural 39.6%.
Sex distribution (1990): male 50.82%; female 49.18%.
Age breakdown (1990): under 15, 37.9%; 15–29, 29.9%; 30–44, 17.6%; 45–59, 9.1%; 60–74, 4.4%; 75 and over, 1.1%.
Population projection: (2000) 8,621,000; (2010) 9,903,000.
Doubling time: 35 years.
Ethnic composition (1990): mixed 70%; white 15%; black 15%.
Religious affiliation (1990): Roman Catholic 90.8%; other 9.2%.
Major urban centres (1989): Santo Domingo 2,200,000; Santiago de los Caballeros 467,000; La Vega 189,000; San Pedro de Macorís 137,000.

Vital statistics

Birth rate per 1,000 population (1991): 27.0 (world avg. 26.4).
Death rate per 1,000 population (1991): 7.0 (world avg. 9.2).
Natural increase rate per 1,000 population (1991): 20.0 (world avg. 17.2).
Total fertility rate (avg. births per childbearing woman; 1991): 3.1.
Marriage rate per 1,000 population (1987): 2.3.
Divorce rate per 1,000 population (1987): 0.8.
Life expectancy at birth (1991): male 65.0 years; female 69.0 years.
Major causes of death per 100,000 population (1985): diseases of the circulatory system 100.3; infectious and parasitic diseases 51.4; diseases of the respiratory system 35.4; accidents, poisoning, and violence 33.7.

National economy

Budget (1992–93). Revenue: RD$18,137,000,000 (tax revenue 88.9%, of which import duties 37.1%, taxes on goods and services 36.0%, income taxes 15.1%; nontax revenue 5.8%; grants and loans 2.8%). Expenditures: RD$16,857,000,000 (development expenditure 60.5%; current expenditure 39.5%).
Public debt (external, outstanding; 1991): U.S.$3,471,000,000.
Tourism: receipts from visitors (1992) U.S.$970,000,000; expenditures by nationals abroad (1991) U.S.$154,000,000.
Production (metric tons except as noted). Agriculture, forestry, fishing (value of production in RD$'000,000; 1991): rice 3,105, beef 2,593, sugarcane 2,306, coffee 1,958, chicken meat 1,666, milk 1,252, plantains 1,143, eggs 688, beans 588, tobacco 554, bananas 474, coconuts 473, tomatoes 452, cacao beans 384, fish 89; roundwood 982,000 cu m. Mining: ferronickel (1991) 75,800; gold (1992) 122,600 troy oz. Manufacturing (1991)[4]: cement 1,231,000; refined sugar 86,000; beer 1,462,000 hectolitres; rum 382,000 hectolitres; cigarettes 202,200,000 20-unit packs. Construction (value of authorized construction in RD$'000,000; 1987): residential 352; nonresidential 253. Energy production (consumption): electricity (kW-hr; 1992) 4,626,000,000 (2,897,000,000); coal, none (none); crude petroleum (barrels; 1990) none (10,262,000); petroleum products (metric tons; 1990) 1,258,000 (1,735,000); natural gas, none (none).
Gross national product (1992): U.S.$7,613,000,000 (U.S.$1,040 per capita).

Structure of gross domestic product and labour force

	1992 in value RD$'000,000[5]	1992 % of total value	1981 labour force	1981 % of labour force
Agriculture	554	14.9	420,463	22.0
Mining	91	2.4	4,743	0.2
Manufacturing	627	16.8	224,437	11.7
Construction	306	8.2	80,850	4.3
Public utilities	74	2.0	13,891	0.7
Transp. and commun.	377	10.1	40,470	2.1
Trade	531	14.3	192,181	10.0
Finance, real estate	455	12.2	22,369	1.2
Pub. admin., defense	366	9.8	363,125	18.9
Services	346	9.3		
Other	—	—	552,859[6]	28.9
TOTAL	3,727	100.0	1,915,388	100.0

Population economically active (1981): total 1,915,388; activity rate of total population 33.9% (participation rates: ages 15–64, 53.6%; female 28.9%; unemployed [1992] 30.0%).

Price and earnings indexes (1985 = 100)

	1987	1988	1989	1990	1991	1992	1993
Consumer price index	127.2	183.7	267.1	425.9	655.3	685.5	711.2[7]
Monthly earnings index[8]	133.2	200.0	258.8	345.9	...	...	...

Household income and expenditure. Average household size (1981) 5.1; average income: n.a.; sources of income: n.a.; expenditure (1980–85): food and beverages 46.0%, housing 10.0%, household goods 8.0%.
Land use (1990): forested 12.7%; meadows and pastures 43.2%; agricultural and under permanent cultivation 29.9%; other 14.2%.

Foreign trade[9]

Balance of trade (current prices)

	1987	1988	1989	1990	1991	1992
U.S.$'000,000	−880	−718	−1,039	−1,058	−1,071	−1,591
% of total	38.2%	28.8%	36.0%	41.9%	44.8%	58.5%

Imports (1991): U.S.$1,729,000,000 (crude petroleum and petroleum products 25.3%, agricultural products 19.3%, forest products 3.0%). *Major import sources:* U.S. 45.5%; Venezuela 12.4%; Mexico 6.5%; Japan 5.2%.
Exports (1991): U.S.$658,000,000[10] (ferronickel 33.5%, raw sugar 20.1%, coffee 6.6%, gold alloy 6.0%, cacao 4.8%). *Major export destinations:* U.S. 56.0%; The Netherlands 15.1%; Puerto Rico 7.7%; Japan 3.6%; Belgium 3.1%.

Transport and communications

Transport. Railroads (1991)[11]: length 994 mi, 1,600 km. Roads (1989): total length 17,000 km (paved 17%). Vehicles (1991): passenger cars 139,069; trucks and buses 102,969. Merchant marine (1992): vessels (100 gross tons and over) 28; total deadweight tonnage 10,369. Air transport (1991): passenger-km 1,350,000,000; metric ton-km cargo 70,200,000; airports (1993) 5.
Communications. Daily newspapers (1990): total number 12; total circulation 230,000; circulation per 1,000 population 31. Radio (1992): 1,150,000 receivers (1 per 6.5 persons). Television (1992): 728,000 receivers (1 per 10 persons). Telephones (1988): 292,733 (1 per 24 persons).

Education and health

Education (1989–90)

	schools	teachers	students	student/teacher ratio
Primary (age 7–14)[12]	4,854	21,850	1,032,055	47.2
Secondary (age 15–18)[13]	...	9,963	426,962	42.9
Teacher tr.[13]	...	108	3,602	...
Higher[14]	7	4,984	70,134	14.1

Educational attainment (1981). Percentage of population age 25 and over having: no formal schooling 48.0%; incomplete primary education 31.7%; complete primary 4.0%; secondary 14.0%; higher 2.3%. *Literacy* (1990): total population age 15 and over literate, *c.* 3,710,000 (83.3%); males literate, *c.* 1,922,000 (84.8%); females literate, *c.* 1,788,000 (81.8%).
Health: physicians (1988) 7,332 (1 per 934 persons); hospital beds (1987) 13,169 (1 per 508 persons); infant mortality rate (1991) 60.0.
Food (1988–90): daily per capita caloric intake 2,310 (vegetable products 87%, animal products 13%); 102% of FAO recommended minimum.

Military

Total active duty personnel (1992): 22,200 (army 67.6%, navy 13.5%, air force 18.9%). *Military expenditure as percentage of GNP* (1989): 0.8% (world 4.9%); per capita expenditure U.S.$7.

[1]Roman Catholicism is the state religion per concordat with Vatican City. [2]National district. [3]Total includes 63 sq mi (163 sq km) of offshore islands not shown separately. [4]Excludes free-zone sector for reexport (mostly ready-made garments) employing (1992) 174,000; 1992 value added of free-zone sector equaled RD$3,800,000,000. [5]At prices of 1970. [6]Not adequately defined (421,628) and those seeking work for first time (131,231). [7]March. [8]Minimum wage. [9]Excludes free zones. [10]1991 reexports of free zones were estimated to equal U.S.$998,000,000. [11]Most track serves the sugar industry only, except for 65 mi (104 km) for public transport. [12]Public schools only. [13]1986–87. [14]1991–92; universities only.

Ecuador

Official name: República del Ecuador (Republic of Ecuador).
Form of government: unitary multiparty republic with one legislative house (National Congress [78]).
Head of state and government: President.
Capital: Quito.
Official language: Spanish.
Official religion: none.
Monetary unit: 1 Sucre (S/.) = 100 centavos; valuation (Oct. 4, 1993) 1 U.S.$ = S/. 1,933; 1 £ = S/. 2,929.

Area and population

Regions / Provinces	Capitals	area sq mi	area sq km	population 1990 census
Amazonica				
Morona-Santiago	Macas	13,100	33,930	84,216
Napo	Tena	9,918	25,690	103,387
Pastaza	Puyo	11,496	29,774	41,811
Sucumbíos	Nueva Loja	7,076	18,327	76,952
Zamora-Chinchipe	Zamora	8,923	23,111	66,167
Costa				
El Oro	Machala	2,259	5,850	412,572
Esmeraldas	Esmeraldas	5,884	15,239	306,628
Guayas	Guayaquil	7,916	20,503	2,515,146
Los Ríos	Babahoyo	2,770	7,175	527,559
Manabí	Portoviejo	7,289	18,879	1,031,927
Insular				
Galápagos	Puerto Baquerizo Moreno	3,093	8,010	9,785
Sierra				
Azuay	Cuenca	3,137	8,125	506,090
Bolívar	Guaranda	1,521	3,940	155,088
Cañar	Azogues	1,205	3,122	189,347
Carchi	Tulcán	1,392	3,605	141,482
Chimborazo	Riobamba	2,536	6,569	364,682
Cotopaxi	Latacunga	2,344	6,072	276,324
Imbabura	Ibarra	1,760	4,559	265,499
Loja	Loja	4,257	11,026	384,698
Pichincha	Quito	4,987	12,915	1,756,228
Tungurahua	Ambato	1,288	3,335	361,980
TOTAL		105,037[1]	272,045[2]	9,648,189[3]

Demography

Population (1993): 10,985,000.
Density (1993): persons per sq mi 104.6, persons per sq km 40.4.
Urban-rural (1990): urban 55.4%; rural 44.6%.
Sex distribution (1990): male 49.71%; female 50.29%.
Age breakdown (1990): under 15, 38.8%; 15–29, 28.5%; 30–44, 17.3%; 45–59, 9.0% 60–74, 4.7%, 75 and over, 1.7%.
Population projection: (2000) 12,712,000; (2010) 15,062,000.
Doubling time: 27 years.
Ethnic composition (1989): Amerindian 40.0%; mestizo 40.0%; white 15.0%; black 5.0%.
Religious affiliation (1990): Roman Catholic 92.1%; other 7.9%.
Major cities (1990): Guayaquil 1,508,844; Quito 1,100,847; Cuenca 194,981; Machala 144,197; Portoviejo 132,937.

Vital statistics

Birth rate per 1,000 population: (1990) 32.9[4] (world avg. 27.1); (1982) legitimate 67.9%; illegitimate 32.1%.
Death rate per 1,000 population (1990): 7.4[4] (world avg. 9.8).
Natural increase rate per 1,000 population (1990): 25.5[4] (world avg. 17.3).
Total fertility rate (avg. births per childbearing woman; 1990): 4.1.
Marriage rate per 1,000 population (1989): 6.0[4, 5].
Divorce rate per 1,000 population (1989): 0.5[4, 5].
Life expectancy at birth (1985–90): male 63.4 years; female 67.6 years.
Major causes of death per 100,000 population (1990): circulatory diseases 138.5; accidents, poisoning, and violence 116.7; respiratory diseases 84.0; neoplasms (cancers) 79.3; infectious and parasitic diseases 76.0.

National economy

Budget (1991). Revenue: S/. 1,820,147,000,000 (income from petroleum 46.5%, production and sales tax 24.3%, import duties 11.3%, income taxes 6.8%). Expenditures: S/. 1,955,328,000,000 (debt service 32.7%, public services 22.2%, education 18.3%, health 5.6%, transport and communications 4.8%).
Production (metric tons except as noted). Agriculture, forestry, fishing (1992): sugarcane 6,500,000, bananas 3,600,000, rice 981,000, plantains 930,000, corn (maize) 500,000, potatoes 375,000, soybeans 158,000, cacao 78,000; livestock (number of live animals) 4,665,000 cattle, 2,434,000 pigs, 1,511,000 sheep, 59,000,000 chickens; roundwood (1991) 7,762,000 cu m; fish catch (1991) 383,600. Mining and quarrying (1990): limestone 5,000,000; gold 344,000 troy oz. Manufacturing (value added in S/. '000,000; 1989): food products 129,457, of which beverages (including liquors) 18,750; chemical products 50,739; textiles 48,163; metal products 29,916. Construction (in S/.; 1991)[6]: residential 71,656,531,000; nonresidential 52,566,151,000. Energy production (consumption): electricity (kW-hr; 1990) 6,327,000,000 (6,327,000,000); crude petroleum (barrels; 1990) 106,494,000 (42,473,000); petroleum products (metric tons; 1990) 6,022,000 (4,713,000); natural gas (cu m; 1990) 99,998,000 (99,998,000).
Tourism (1991): receipts U.S.$189,000,000; expenditures U.S.$177,000,000.
Public debt (external, outstanding; 1991): U.S.$9,952,000,000.

Gross national product (1992): U.S.$11,790,000,000 (U.S.$1,070 per capita).

Structure of gross domestic product and labour force

	1991 in value S/. '000,000[7]	1991 % of total value	1990 labour force	1990 % of labour force
Agriculture	33,096	17.6	1,035,712	30.8
Mining	22,559	12.0	20,870	0.6
Manufacturing	28,494	15.2	370,338	11.0
Construction	5,232	2.8	196,716	5.9
Public utilities	3,088	1.6	12,660	0.4
Transp. and commun.	16,356	8.7	131,084	3.9
Trade	28,431	15.1	476,730	14.2
Finance	20,613	11.0	81,357	2.4
Pub. admin., defense / Services	27,996	14.9	838,129	24.9
Other	2,168	1.2	196,171[8]	5.8[8]
TOTAL	188,033	100.0[1]	3,359,767	100.0[1]

Population economically active (1990): total 3,359,767; activity rate of total population 34.8% (participation rates: ages 8 and over, 44.0%; female 26.4%; unemployed 1.3%).

Price and earnings indexes (1985 = 100)

	1986	1987	1988	1989	1990	1991	1992
Consumer price index	123.0	159.3	252.1	442.8	657.6	978.0	1,512.1
Hourly earnings index[9]	141.2	170.6	258.8	376.5	...	470.6	...

Household income and expenditure. Average household size (1990) 4.1; average annual income per household (1982) S/. 28,747 (U.S.$956); sources of income (1989): self-employment 74.9%, wages 17.4%, transfer payments 4.5%, interest, dividends, and rent 3.2%; expenditure (1989): food and tobacco 37.7%, clothing 12.1%, transportation and communications 11.7%, household furnishings 8.8%, housing and utilities 5.1%, health care 4.1%.
Land use (1991): forested 38.3%; meadows and pastures 18.7%; agricultural and under permanent cultivation 9.9%; other 33.1%.

Foreign trade[10]

Balance of trade (current prices)

	1987	1988	1989	1990	1991	1992
U.S.$'000,000	+232.2	+674.8	+719.7	+1,077.7	+736.0	+1,031.9
% of total	6.1%	18.2%	18.0%	24.7%	14.1%	20.7%

Imports (1991): U.S.$2,398,584,000 (industrial raw materials 41.2%, industrial capital goods 22.1%, transport equipment 14.0%, consumer goods 10.6%, agricultural raw materials 4.8%). *Major import sources:* United States 31.3%; Latin American Integration Association 21.8%; EEC 21.6%; Japan 9.7%.
Exports (1991): U.S.$2,851,415,000 (crude petroleum 37.1%, bananas 25.1%, shrimp 17.2%, petroleum products 3.3%, coffee 3.0%, cocoa 1.9%). *Major export destinations:* United States 48.5%; EEC 16.9%; Latin American Integration Association 12.6%; Andean Group 7.1%; Japan 2.2%.

Transport and communications

Transport. Railroads (1990): route length (1992) 965 km; passenger-km 82,000,000; metric ton-km cargo 5,000,000. Roads (1988): total length 37,636 km (paved 17%). Vehicles (1990): passenger cars 165,600; trucks and buses 207,300. Merchant marine (1992): vessels (100 gross tons and over) 154; deadweight tonnage 504,127. Air transport (1991): passenger-km 1,201,000,000; metric ton-km cargo 68,000,000; airports (1993) 14.
Communications. Daily newspapers (1990): total number 25; total circulation 920,000; circulation per 1,000 population 87. Radio (1992): 3,000,000 receivers (1 per 3.5 persons). Television (1992): 900,000 receivers (1 per 12 persons). Telephones (1990): 539,559 (1 per 19 persons).

Education and health

Education (1989–90)

	schools[11]	teachers	students	student/teacher ratio
Primary (age 4–12)	16,146	60,608	1,843,819	30.4
Secondary (age 12–18)[12, 13]	2,207	36,730	504,481	13.7
Vocational[13]		16,838	260,850	15.5
Higher	21	12,856	206,541	16.1

Educational attainment (1990). Percentage of population age 25 and over having: no formal schooling 17.0%; primary 43.7%; secondary 22.6%; post-secondary 12.7%; not stated 4.0%. *Literacy* (1990): total population age 15 and over literate 5,217,543 (88.3%); males 2,616,192 (90.5%); females 2,601,351 (86.2%).
Health (1990): physicians 9,785 (1 per 1,039 persons); hospital beds 17,004 (1 per 598 persons); infant mortality rate per 1,000 live births 51.7.
Food (1988–90): daily per capita caloric intake 2,399 (vegetable products 85%, animal products 15%); 105% of FAO minimum requirement.

Military

Total active duty personnel (1992): 58,000 (army 86.2%, navy 7.8%, air force 6.0%). *Military expenditure as percentage of GNP* (1989): 1.7% (world 4.9%); per capita expenditure U.S.$16.

[1]Detail does not add to total given because of rounding. [2]Includes 2,289 sq km (884 sq mi) not assigned to any region. [3]Total includes 70,621 persons not shown separately. [4]Excluding nomadic Indian tribes. [5]Based on incomplete registration. [6]Authorized construction in Cuenca, Guayaquil, and Quito only. [7]At constant 1975 prices. [8]Includes unemployed persons not previously employed. [9]General minimum wage. [10]Import figures are f.o.b. in balance of trade and c.i.f. for commodities and trading partners. [11]1986–87. [12]Includes teacher training. [13]1987–88.

Egypt

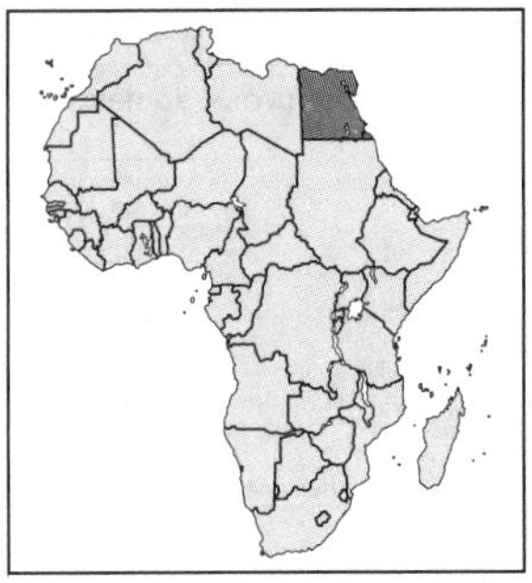

Official name: Jumhūrīyah Miṣr al-ʿArabīyah (Arab Republic of Egypt).
Form of government: republic with one legislative house (People's Assembly [454[1]]).
Chief of state: President.
Head of government: Prime Minister.
Capital: Cairo.
Official language: Arabic.
Official religion: Islam.
Monetary unit: 1 Egyptian pound (LE) = 100 piastres; valuation (Oct. 4, 1993) 1 U.S.$ = LE 3.32; 1 £ = LE 5.03.

Area and population

Regions / Governorates	Capitals	area sq mi	area sq km	population 1991 estimate
Frontier				
al-Baḥr al-Aḥmar	al-Ghurdaqah	78,643	203,685	112,000
Maṭrūḥ	Marsā Maṭrūḥ	81,897	212,112	193,000
Janūb Sīnāʾ	aṭ-Ṭūr	12,796	33,140	41,000
Shamāl Sīnāʾ	al-ʿArish	10,646	27,574	223,000
al-Wādī al-Jadīd	al-Kharijah	145,369	376,505	130,000
Lower Egypt				
al-Buḥayrah	Damanhūr	3,911	10,130	3,730,000
ad-Daqahlīyah	al-Manṣūrah	1,340	3,471	3,939,000
Dumyāṭ	Dumyāṭ	227	589	836,000
al-Gharbīyah	Ṭanṭā	750	1,942	3,240,000
al-Ismāʿīlīyah (Ismailia)	—	557	1,442	632,000
Kafr ash-Shaykh	Kafr ash-Shaykh	1,327	3,437	2,054,000
al-Minūfīyah	Shibīn al-Kawm	592	1,532	2,532,000
al-Qalyūbīyah	Banhā	387	1,001	2,880,000
ash-Sharqīyah	az-Zaqāzīq	1,614	4,180	3,899,000
Upper Egypt				
Aswān	Aswān	262	679	925,000
Asyūṭ	Asyūṭ	600	1,553	2,532,000
Banī Suwayf	Banī Suwayf	510	1,322	1,656,000
al-Fayyūm	al-Fayyūm	705	1,827	1,805,000
al-Jīzah	al-Jīzah	32,878	85,153	4,182,000
al-Minyā	al-Minyā	873	2,262	3,003,000
Qinā	Qinā	715	1,851	2,598,000
Sawhāj	Sawhāj	597	1,547	2,763,000
Urban				
Būr Saʿīd (Port Said)	—	28	72	449,000
al-Iskandarīyah (Alexandria)	—	1,034	2,679	3,295,000
al-Qāhirah (Cairo)	—	83	214	6,663,000
as-Suways (Suez)	—	6,888	17,840	376,000
TOTAL		385,229	997,739	54,688,000

Demography

Population (1993): 57,109,000.
Density (1993): persons per sq mi 148.2, persons per sq km 57.2.
Urban-rural (1986): urban 43.9%; rural 56.1%.
Sex distribution (1991): male 51.21%; female 48.79%.
Age breakdown (1986): under 15, 41.8%; 15–29, 26.1%; 30–44, 16.2%; 45–59, 10.4%; 60–74, 4.7%; 75 and over, 0.8%.
Population projection: (2000) 65,556,000; (2010) 77,251,000.
Doubling time: 30 years.
Ethnic composition (1983): Egyptian 99.8%; other 0.2%.
Religious affiliation (1990): Sunnī Muslim *c.* 90%; Christian *c.* 10%[2].
Major cities (1991): Cairo 6,663,000; Alexandria 3,295,000; al-Jīzah 2,156,000[3]; Shubrā al-Khaymah 811,000[3]; al-Maḥallah al-Kubrā 385,300[4].

Vital statistics

Birth rate per 1,000 population (1991): 30.8 (world avg. 26.4).
Death rate per 1,000 population (1991): 7.5 (world avg. 9.2).
Natural increase rate per 1,000 population (1991): 23.3 (world avg. 17.2).
Total fertility rate (avg. births per childbearing woman; 1987): 5.4.
Life expectancy at birth (1989): male 59.0 years; female 60.0 years.
Major causes of death per 100,000 population (1987): diseases of the circulatory system 314.4; diseases of the respiratory system 140.7; infectious and parasitic diseases 98.9; malignant neoplasms (cancers) 22.0.

National economy

Budget (1992–93). Revenue: LE 53,389,000,000 (general taxes 48.8%, of which sales taxes 13.9%, customs duties 10.1%; oil revenue 8.1%; Suez Canal fees 5.8%). Expenditures: LE 62,533,000,000 (debt servicing 31.4%; wages and salaries 16.0%; defense 7.4%; pensions and benefits 5.4%).
Public debt (external, outstanding; 1991): U.S.$36,028,000,000.
Tourism (1991): receipts U.S.$2,029,000,000; expenditures U.S.$225,000,000.
Production (metric tons except as noted). Agriculture, forestry, fishing (1992): sugarcane 11,624,000, corn (maize) 5,226,000, tomatoes 4,694,000, wheat 4,618,000, rice 3,908,000, oranges 1,690,000, sorghum 736,000, cotton (lint) 324,000; livestock (number of live animals; 1991) 4,697,000 goats, 4,270,000 sheep, 3,537,000 cattle, 2,527,000 buffalo, 35,465,000 chickens, 10,380,000 pigeons; roundwood (1991) 2,300,000 cu m; fish catch (1991) 298,013. Mining and quarrying (1990–91): clay 10,775,000; iron ore 2,144,000; phosphate rock 1,865,000; salt 1,125,000. Manufacturing (1991–92): cement 17,300,000; nitrate fertilizers 5,524,000; reinforcing iron 1,460,000; phosphate fertilizers 1,345,000; sugar 1,050,000; soap 365,000; cotton yarn 324,000; refrigerators 395,000 units; automobiles 7,700 units. Construction (1990–91): urban residential units 160,613. Energy production (consumption): electricity (kW-hr; 1991) 40,460,000,000 (40,460,000,000); coal (metric tons; 1991) n.a. (1,207,000); crude petroleum (barrels; 1991) 334,110,000 (178,000,000); petroleum products (metric tons; 1991) 24,199,000 (17,737,000); natural gas (cu m; 1991) 7,765,000,000 (7,765,000,000).
Gross national product (1992): U.S.$34,527,000,000 (U.S.$630 per capita).

Structure of gross domestic product and labour force

	1991–92 in value LE '000,000	1991–92 % of total value	1989 labour force	1989 % of labour force
Agriculture	11,622	19.7	6,335,200	39.5
Mining	1,908	3.2	43,300	0.3
Manufacturing	10,325	17.5	1,958,700	12.2
Construction	3,609	6.1	990,200	6.2
Public utilities	929[5]	1.6[5]	99,900	0.6
Transp. and commun.	4,781	8.1	780,200	4.9
Trade	11,745	19.9	1,340,000	8.4
Finance	3,831	6.5	255,300	1.6
Pub. admin., defense	5,702	9.6	3,115,500	19.4
Services	4,655	7.9		
Other	—	—	1,107,900[6]	6.9[6]
TOTAL	59,107	100.0[7]	16,033,600[8]	100.0

Population economically active (1991–92): total 15,268,000; activity rate of total population 27.3% (participation rates: ages 15–64, 47.6%; female [1986] 14.6%; unemployed 9.0%).

Price and earnings indexes (1985 = 100)

	1986	1987	1988	1989	1990	1991	1992
Consumer price index	123.9	148.3	174.4	211.5	247.0	295.9	336.1
Annual earnings index	108.8	114.7	...	...	...	...	...

Household income and expenditure. Average household size (1986) 4.9; sources of income: n.a.; expenditure (1986–87)[9]: food, beverages, and tobacco 55.7%, clothing 10.9%, housing 10.5%, furniture 5.0%.
Land use (1990): pasture 0.6%; agricultural 2.6%; other 96.8%.

Foreign trade

Balance of trade (current prices)

	1987	1988	1989	1990	1991	1992
LE '000,000	−7,117.0	−10,684.8	−9,228.1	−15,389.3	−10,932.2	−14,719.1
% of total	54.1%	57.2%	45.6%	52.5%	31.7%	42.0%

Imports (1991–92): U.S.$10,039,500,000 (machinery and transport equipment 23.5%; foodstuffs 19.0%; chemical products 11.1%; base metals 6.7%). *Major import sources:* European Economic Community 33.2%; U.S. 16.7%; other western European countries 12.2%; eastern Europe 5.3%; Australia 3.0%.
Exports (1991–92): U.S.$3,636,400,000 (petroleum and petroleum products 45.4%; cotton yarn, textiles, and fabrics 15.5%; engineering and metallurgical goods 9.6%). *Major export destinations:* European Economic Community 36.4%; Arab League 13.3%; eastern Europe 12.1%; U.S. 10.0%.

Transport and communications

Transport. Railroads (1990–91): length 5,489 mi, 8,831 km; passenger-km 43,185,000,000; metric ton-km cargo 3,162,000,000. Roads (1990): total length 30,326 mi, 48,804 km (paved 77%). Vehicles (1989): passenger cars 826,915; trucks and buses 550,649. Merchant marine (1992): vessels (100 gross tons and over) 444; total deadweight tonnage 1,685,245. Inland water (1992): Suez Canal, number of transits 16,629; metric ton cargo 369,800,000. Air transport (1992)[10]: passenger-km 6,322,727,000; metric ton-km cargo 109,227,000; airports (1993) with scheduled flights 10.
Communications. Daily newspapers (1990): total number 17; total circulation 3,307,100[11]; circulation per 1,000 population 62[11]. Radio (1991): 14,000,000 receivers (1 per 3.9 persons). Television (1991): 3,750,000 receivers (1 per 15 persons). Telephones (1991): 2,500,000 (1 per 22 persons).

Education and health

Education (1989–90)

	schools	teachers	students	student/teacher ratio
Primary (age 6–11)[12]	14,767	241,119	6,155,100	25.5
Secondary (age 12–17)[12]	6,558	155,941[13]	3,867,760[14]	...
Voc., teacher tr.	519[14]	72,237	1,015,809	14.1
Higher[15]	12	33,106[16]	656,179	...

Educational attainment (1986). Percentage of population age 15 and over having: no formal education 70.6%, of which literate 14.7%; primary and secondary 25.3%; higher 4.1%. *Literacy* (1990): total population age 15 and over literate 15,470,000 (48.4%); males 62.9%; females 33.8%.
Health: physicians (1990) 31,312 (1 per 1,698 persons); hospital beds (1991) 108,425 (1 per 504 persons); infant mortality rate (1989) 39.8.
Food (1988–90): daily per capita caloric intake 3,310 (vegetable products 92%, animal products 8%); 132% of FAO recommended minimum requirement.

Military

Total active duty personnel (1993): 430,000 (army 72.0%, navy 4.7%, air force [including air defense] 23.3%). *Military expenditure as percentage of GNP* (1989): 5.0% (world 4.9%); per capita expenditure U.S.$67.

[1]Includes 10 nonelective seats. [2]According to the 1986 census, the Christian population of Egypt was 5.9% of the total; this figure is considered by many authorities to understate the Christian population by as much as 60%. [3]1990. [4]1986. [5]Includes housing. [6]Unemployed and those seeking work for the first time. [7]Detail does not add to total given because of rounding. [8]Total includes 7,400 persons not classifiable by sector. [9]Weight of consumer price components; urban households only. [10]Egypt Air only. [11]Based on 12 dailies only. [12]Data exclude 1,399 primary and 1,290 secondary schools in the al-Azhar education system. [13]1987–88. [14]1983. [15]1988–89; universities only. [16]Excludes al-Azhar University.

El Salvador

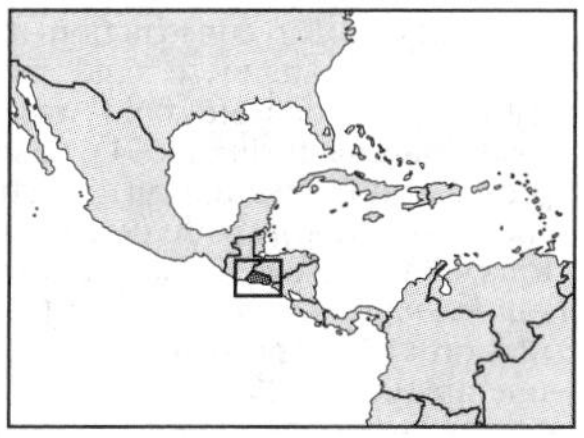

Official name: República de El Salvador (Republic of El Salvador).
Form of government: republic with one legislative house (Legislative Assembly [84]).
Chief of state and government: President.
Capital: San Salvador.
Official language: Spanish.
Official religion: none[1].
Monetary unit: 1 colón (₡) = 100 centavos; valuation (Oct. 4, 1993) 1 U.S.$ = ₡8.64; 1 £ = ₡13.08.

Area and population

Departments	Capitals	area sq mi	area sq km	population 1992 census[2]
Ahuachapán	Ahuachapán	479	1,240	260,563
Cabañas	Sensuntepeque	426	1,104	136,293
Chalatenango	Chalatenango	779	2,017	180,627
Cuscatlán	Cojutepeque	292	756	167,290
La Libertad	Nueva San Salvador	638	1,653	522,071
La Paz	Zacatecoluca	473	1,224	246,147
La Unión	La Unión	801	2,074	251,143
Morazán	San Francisco (Gotera)	559	1,447	166,772
San Miguel	San Miguel	802	2,077	380,442
San Salvador	San Salvador	342	886	1,477,766
San Vicente	San Vicente	457	1,184	135,471
Santa Ana	Santa Ana	781	2,023	451,620
Sonsonate	Sonsonate	473	1,226	354,641
Usulután	Usulután	822	2,130	317,079
TOTAL		8,124	21,041	5,047,925

Demography

Population (1993): 5,517,000[3].
Density (1993): persons per sq mi 679.7, persons per sq km 262.4.
Urban-rural (1991): urban 44.4%; rural 55.6%.
Sex distribution (1992): male 48.00%; female 52.00%.
Age breakdown (1990): under 15, 43.5%; 15–29, 28.0%; 30–44, 13.6%; 45–59, 9.0%; 60–74, 4.7%; 75 and over, 1.2%.
Population projection: (2000) 6,425,000; (2010) 7,772,000.
Doubling time: 26 years.
Ethnic composition (1988): mestizo (white and Indian) 89.0%; Indian 10.0%; white 1.0%.
Religious affiliation (1991): Roman Catholic 93.6%; other (mostly fundamentalist Protestant, Mormon, or Jehovah's Witness) 6.4%.
Major cities (1992): San Salvador 422,570 (metropolitan area 1,522,126); Santa Ana 202,337; San Miguel 182,817; Mejicanos (1989) 117,568; Nueva San Salvador 116,575.

Vital statistics

Birth rate per 1,000 population (1991): 34.0 (world avg. 26.4); (1988) legitimate 32.0%; illegitimate 68.0%.
Death rate per 1,000 population (1991): 7.0 (world avg. 9.2).
Natural increase rate per 1,000 population (1991): 27.0 (world avg. 17.2).
Total fertility rate (avg. births per childbearing woman; 1991): 4.1.
Marriage rate per 1,000 population (1989): 4.1.
Divorce rate per 1,000 population (1989): 0.4.
Life expectancy at birth (1991): male 63.0 years; female 68.0 years.
Major causes of death per 100,000 population (1990)[4]: diseases of the circulatory system 120.1; violence 73.3; accidents 63.3; infectious and parasitic diseases 52.4; diseases of the respiratory system 49.1; ill-defined conditions 92.8.

National economy

Budget (1991). Revenue: ₡5,783,000,000 (indirect taxes 48.9%, of which stamp duties 22.6%, import duties 11.1%, consumption taxes 9.8%; development income 24.6%; direct taxes 21.2%, of which income taxes 16.6%). Expenditures: ₡5,763,000,000 (current expenditure 81.4%; development expenditure 14.3%; debt amortization 4.3%).
Public debt (external, outstanding; 1991): U.S.$2,069,000,000.
Production (value added in ₡'000,000 except as noted). Agriculture, forestry, fishing (1992): coffee 1,323, sugarcane 444, aviculture 363, fish catch 233, beans 216, *maicillo* (variety of millet) 208, rice 95, forest products 87, corn (maize) 82, tobacco 60, bananas (1991) 63,000 metric tons; livestock (number of live animals) 1,243,000 cattle, 320,000 pigs, 5,000,000 chickens. Mining and quarrying (1990): limestone 1,700,000 metric tons. Manufacturing (1992): food products 3,807; beverages 1,458; textiles 651; petroleum products 619; chemical products 564; nonmetallic mineral products 532; clothing and footwear 477; tobacco products 456. Construction (1992): private residential 694; private nonresidential 271; total public 619. Energy production (consumption): electricity (kW-hr; 1991–92) 2,125,000,000 (2,016,000,000); coal, none (none); crude petroleum (barrels; 1990) none (4,918,000); petroleum products (metric tons; 1990) 620,000 (711,000); natural gas, none (none).
Household income and expenditure. Average household size (1978) 5.1; income per household: n.a.; sources of income: n.a.; expenditure (1976–77)[5]: food and beverages 42.8%, housing 11.7%, education and recreation 8.7%, household furnishings 8.5%.
Population economically active (1991)[6]: total 962,801; activity rate of total population 40.6% (participation rates: ages 15–64, 64.8%; female 45.1%; unemployed 7.5%).

Price and earnings indexes (1986 = 100)

	1987	1988	1989	1990	1991	1992	1993[7]
Consumer price index	124.9	149.6	176.0	218.2	249.6	277.6	329.7
Annual earnings index[8]	100.0	113.3	113.3	136.0[9]	...	...	...

Gross national product (at current market prices; 1991): U.S.$5,697,000,000 (U.S.$1,000 per capita).

Structure of gross domestic product and labour force

	1992 in value ₡'000,000	1992 % of total value	1991 labour force[6]	1991 % of labour force[6]
Agriculture	5,244	9.6	100,451	10.4
Mining	99	0.2	863	0.1
Manufacturing	10,300	18.9	212,843	22.1
Construction	1,584	2.9	53,292	5.5
Public utilities	1,269	2.3	7,270	0.8
Transportation and communications	2,634	4.8	50,596	5.3
Trade	19,253	35.3	237,196	24.6
Finance, real estate	4,442	8.2	27,633	2.9
Public admin., defense	4,007	7.4	250,322	26.0
Services	5,666	10.4		
Other	—	—	22,335	2.3
TOTAL	54,498	100.0	962,801	100.0

Tourism (1991): receipts U.S.$60,000,000; expenditures U.S.$157,000,000.
Land use (1990): forested 5.0%; meadows and pastures 29.4%; agricultural and under permanent cultivation 35.4%; other 30.2%.

Foreign trade[10]

Balance of trade (current prices)

	1986	1987	1988	1989	1990	1991
₡'000,000	−899	−2,016	−1,991	−3,717	−5,170	−6,560
% of total	10.6%	25.4%	24.6%	40.0%	36.9%	41.0%

Imports (1991): ₡11,276,000,000 (chemical products 15.1%, of which drugs and medicines 4.2%; mineral fuels 12.5%, of which crude petroleum 9.0%; food 9.3%; transport equipment 9.1%; nonelectrical machinery and equipment 8.1%). *Major import sources:* United States 39.6%; Guatemala 11.7%; Mexico 8.4%; Venezuela 6.1%; Japan 4.9%.
Exports (1991): ₡4,716,000,000 (coffee 37.8%; raw sugar 5.5%; pharmaceuticals 3.7%; shrimps 3.5%; cardboard boxes 3.2%). *Major export destinations:* United States 33.4%; Guatemala 18.4%; Germany 12.9%; Costa Rica 7.5%; The Netherlands 4.7%.

Transport and communications

Transport. Railroads (1991): route length 374 mi, 602 km; passenger-mi 4,881,000, passenger-km 7,855,000; short ton-mi cargo 25,029,000, metric ton-km cargo 36,541,000. Roads (1990): total length 7,764 mi, 12,495 km (paved 14%). Vehicles (1991): passenger cars 80,000; trucks and buses 80,000. Merchant marine (1992): vessels (100 gross tons and over) 15; total deadweight tonnage, n.a. Air transport (1990)[11]: passenger-mi 662,000,000, passenger-km 1,066,000,000; short ton-mi cargo 3,182,000, metric ton-km cargo 4,645,000; airports (1993) with scheduled flights 1.
Communications. Daily newspapers (1991): total number 6; total circulation 255,100; circulation per 1,000 population 48. Radio (1992): total number of receivers 1,935,000 (1 per 2.8 persons). Television (1992): total number of receivers 500,700 (1 per 11 persons). Telephones (1990): 249,938 (1 per 21 persons).

Education and health

Education (1989)

	schools	teachers	students	student/ teacher ratio
Primary (age 7–15)	4,160	25,318	1,016,181	40.1
Secondary (age 16–18)	468	...	28,370	28.2[12]
Vocational			66,708	...
Higher[13, 14]	6	2,637	53,277	20.2

Educational attainment (1980). Percentage of population over age 10 having: no formal schooling 30.1%; primary education 60.7%; secondary 6.9%; higher 2.3%. *Literacy* (1990): total population age 15 and over literate, *c.* 2,127,000 (73.0%); males literate, *c.* 1,048,000 (76.2%); females literate, *c.* 1,079,000 (70.0%).
Health: physicians (1991) 4,080 (1 per 1,322 persons); hospital beds (1989) 5,343 (1 per 973 persons); infant mortality rate per 1,000 live births (1991) 47.0.
Food (1984–86): daily per capita caloric intake 2,152 (1979–81; vegetable products 88%, animal products 12%); 94% of FAO recommended minimum requirement.

Military

Total active duty personnel (1992): 49,700 (army 80.5%, navy 2.6%, air force 4.8%, paramilitary 12.1%). *Military expenditure as percentage of GNP* (1989): 4.0% (world 4.9%); per capita expenditure U.S.$48.

[1]Roman Catholicism, although not official, enjoys special recognition in the constitution. [2]Preliminary figure not adjusted for underenumeration. [3]UN estimate. [4]Projected rates based on about 75% of total deaths. [5]Based on middle-income urban families. [6]Urban areas only. [7]June. [8]Miminum wages in manufacturing and services in San Salvador department. [9]April. [10]Imports c.i.f., exports f.o.b. [11]TACA International Airlines. [12]1988. [13]1991. [14]Universities only.

Equatorial Guinea

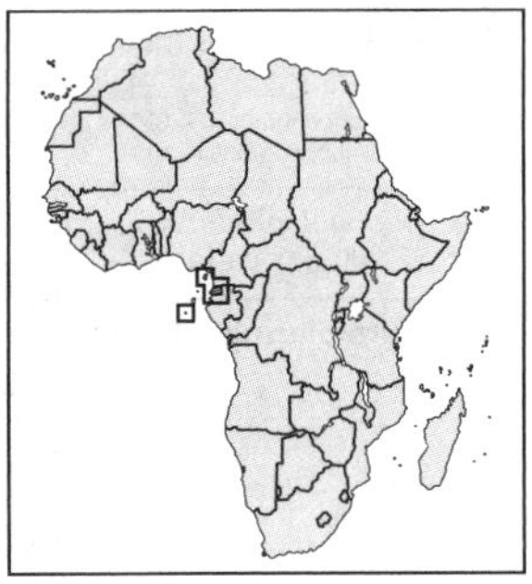

Official name: República de Guinea Ecuatorial (Republic of Equatorial Guinea).
Form of government[1]: transitional government with one legislative house (House of Representatives of the People [41[2]]).
Chief of state: President.
Head of government: Prime Minister.
Capital: Malabo.
Official language: Spanish.
Official religion: none.
Monetary unit[3]: 1 CFA franc (CFAF) = 100 centimes; valuation (Oct. 4, 1993) 1 U.S.$ = CFAF 283.25; 1 £ = CFAF 429.12.

Area and population

Regions / Provinces	area sq mi	area sq km	population 1987 estimate
Insular	785[4]	2,034	70,280
Annobón	7	17	2,360
Bioko Norte	300	776	56,600
Bioko Sur	479	1,241	11,320
Continental	10,045[4]	26,017	259,950
Centro-Sur	3,834	9,931	55,970
Kie-Ntem	1,522	3,943	74,050
Litoral	2,573	6,665	75,640
Wele-Nzas	2,115	5,478	54,290
TOTAL	10,831[4]	28,051	330,230

Demography

Population (1993): 377,000.
Density (1993): persons per sq mi 34.8, persons per sq km 13.4.
Urban-rural (1991): urban 37.0%; rural 63.0%.
Sex distribution (1991): male 48.54%; female 51.46%.
Age breakdown (1990): under 15, 42.6%; 15–29, 26.4%; 30–44, 14.2%; 45–59, 10.5%; 60–74, 5.3%; 75 and over, 1.0%.
Population projection: (2000) 448,000; (2010) 573,000.
Doubling time: 26 years.
Ethnic composition (1983): Fang 82.9%; Bubi 9.6%; Ndowe 3.8%; Annobonés 1.5%; Bujeba 1.4%; other 0.8%.
Religious affiliation (1980): Christian (mostly Roman Catholic) 88.8%; traditional beliefs 4.6%; atheist 1.4%; Muslim 0.5%; other 0.2%; none 4.5%.
Major cities (1983): Malabo 30,418; Bata 24,308; Ela-Nguema 6,179; Campo Yaunde 5,199; Los Angeles 4,079.

Vital statistics

Birth rate per 1,000 population (1992): 42.0 (world avg. 26.4); legitimate, n.a.; illegitimate, n.a.
Death rate per 1,000 population (1992): 15.0 (world avg. 9.2).
Natural increase rate per 1,000 population (1992): 27.0 (world avg. 17.2).
Total fertility rate (avg. births per childbearing woman; 1992): 5.4.
Marriage rate per 1,000 population: n.a.
Divorce rate per 1,000 population: n.a.
Life expectancy at birth (1992): male 49.0 years; female 53.0 years.
Major causes of death per 100,000 population: n.a.; however, major diseases include malaria (affecting about 60% of the population), cholera, leprosy, trypanosomiasis (sleeping sickness), and waterborne (especially gastrointestinal) diseases.

National economy

Budget (1990). Revenue: CFAF 7,520,000,000 (fiscal receipts 68.4%; other receipts 31.6%). Expenditures: CFAF 8,105,000,000 (current expenditure 85.9%, of which interest 28.6%, salaries 26.1%; capital expenditure 14.1%).
Public debt (external, outstanding; 1991): U.S.$210,000,000.
Gross national product (at current market prices; 1992): U.S.$144,000,000 (U.S.$330 per capita).

Structure of gross domestic product and labour force

	1989 in value CFAF '000,000	1989 % of total value	1983 labour force	1983 % of labour force
Agriculture, forestry	22,991	53.6	59,390	57.9
Manufacturing, mining	545	1.3	1,616	1.6
Construction	2,402	5.6	1,929	1.9
Public utilities	1,277	3.0	224	0.2
Transportation and communications	823	1.9	1,752	1.7
Trade	3,594	8.4	3,059	3.0
Finance	...	...	409	0.4
Pub. admin., defense	7,367	17.2	8,377	8.2
Services } Other	3,924	9.1		
			25,809	25.2
TOTAL	42,923	100.0[4]	102,565	100.0[4]

Production (metric tons except as noted). Agriculture, forestry, fishing (1992): roots and tubers 82,000 (of which cassava 47,000, sweet potatoes 35,000), bananas 17,000, coconuts 8,000, coffee 7,000, cacao beans 5,000, palm oil 5,000, palm kernels 3,000; livestock (number of live animals) 36,000 sheep, 8,000 goats, 5,000 pigs, 5,000 cattle; roundwood (1991) 607,000 cu m; fish catch (1991) 3,500. Mining and quarrying: details, n.a.; however, in addition to quarrying for construction materials, unexploited deposits of iron ore, lead, zinc, manganese, and molybdenum are present; the new offshore Alba gas-condensate field was ready for commercial production in late 1993. Manufacturing (1991): veneer sheets 10,000. Construction: n.a. Energy production (consumption): electricity (kW-hr; 1990) 18,000,000 (18,000,000); coal, none (n.a.); crude petroleum[5], none (n.a.); petroleum products (metric tons; 1990) none (37,000); natural gas, none (n.a.).
Population economically active (1989): total 144,000; activity rate of total population 41.7% (participation rates [1983]: ages 15–64, 66.7%; female 35.7%; unemployed 24.2%).

Price and earnings indexes (1985 = 100)

	1985	1986	1987	1988	1989	1990	1991
Consumer price index	100.0	82.0	72.0	73.0	78.0	78.0	76.0
Earnings index	...	...	...	...	...	...	...

Household income and expenditure. Average household size (1980) 4.5; income per household: n.a.; sources of income: n.a.; expenditure: n.a.
Tourism: tourism is a government priority but remains undeveloped.
Land use (1991): forested 46.2%; meadows and pastures 3.7%; agricultural and under permanent cultivation 8.2%; built-on, wasteland, and other 41.9%.

Foreign trade

Balance of trade (current prices)

	1985	1986	1987	1988	1989	1990
CFAF '000,000	−3,819	−6,822	−3,426	−2,949	−4,083	−8,522
% of total	15.5%	22.2%	12.8%	9.5%	12.1%	29.7%

Imports (1990): U.S.$68,300,000 (1989; food, beverages, and tobacco 26.4%; machinery and transport equipment 20.8%; fuels and lubricants 18.9%; chemicals 5.7%; other 28.2%). *Major import sources* (1985): Spain 30.2%; France 23.6%; Italy 14.6%; The Netherlands 4.8%; West Germany 4.1%; Belgium-Luxembourg 3.0%; China 2.4%; United States 1.9%; Japan 1.7%; Norway 1.5%; United Kingdom 1.1%; Switzerland 0.9%.
Exports (1990 est.): U.S.$37,000,000 (1989; food and live animals 57.0%, of which cocoa 42.4%; fuels and lubricants 19.5%; wood 19.4%; manufactured goods 2.8%). *Major export destinations* (1985): The Netherlands 37.6%; Spain 31.5%; West Germany 16.4%; Italy 5.0%; France 2.2%; Switzerland 1.4%; Portugal 1.3%; Belgium-Luxembourg 0.7%; Greece 0.3%.

Transport and communications

Transport. Railroads: none. Roads (1989): total length 1,667 mi, 2,682 km (paved 19%). Vehicles (1991): passenger cars 5,500; trucks and buses 3,500. Merchant marine (1992): vessels (100 gross tons and over) 3; total deadweight tonnage 6,699. Air transport (1985): passenger-mi 4,000,000, passenger-km 7,000,000; short ton-mi cargo 700,000, metric ton-km cargo 1,000,000; airports (1993) with scheduled flights 1.
Communications. Daily newspapers (1990): total number 2; total circulation 2,000; circulation per 1,000 population 6.0. Radio (1992): total number of receivers 100,000 (1 per 3.7 persons). Television (1992): total number of receivers 2,500 (1 per 147 persons). Telephones (1987): 2,000 (1 per 163 persons).

Education and health

Education (1987–88)

	schools	teachers	students	student/teacher ratio
Primary (age 6–11)	703	1,065	61,009	57.3
Secondary (age 12–17)	9	319	9,226	28.9
Voc., teacher tr.[6]	...	...	...	...
Higher	5	133	1,542	11.6

Educational attainment (1983). Percentage of population age 15 and over having: no schooling 35.4%; some primary education 46.6%; primary 13.0%; secondary 2.3%; postsecondary 1.1%; not specified 1.6%. *Literacy* (1983): percentage of total population age 15 and over literate 62.2%; males literate 77.8%; females literate 48.6%.
Health: physicians (1987) 90 (1 per 3,622 persons); hospital beds (1982) 3,200 (1 per 89 persons); infant mortality rate per 1,000 live births (1990–95) 117.
Food (latest): daily per capita caloric intake 2,230; 68% of FAO recommended minimum requirement.

Military

Total active duty personnel (1993): 1,300 (army 84.6%, navy 7.7%, air force 7.7%). *Military expenditure as percentage of GNP* (1981): 1.8% (world 5.8%); per capita expenditure U.S.$9.

[1]A new constitution establishing a multiparty system was approved in a national referendum on Nov. 17, 1991. Legislative elections were scheduled for Nov. 21, 1993. [2]Forty-one unopposed candidates elected July 10, 1988. Number of seats in legislative house per constitution is to range between a minimum of 45 and a maximum of 60. [3]As of Jan. 1, 1985, Equatorial Guinea became a member of the franc zone, substituting the CFA franc for the previous monetary unit, the ekwele (EK, plural bipkwele), effectively devaluing the latter by 82%. [4]Detail does not add to total given because of rounding. [5]Equatorial Guinea's offshore prospective oil-lease areas total about 13,450 sq km. [6]Efforts are being undertaken to provide the training necessary to qualify nondegree teachers for service. Also, teacher-training schools are to be expanded in order to increase the number of primary-school teachers.

Eritrea

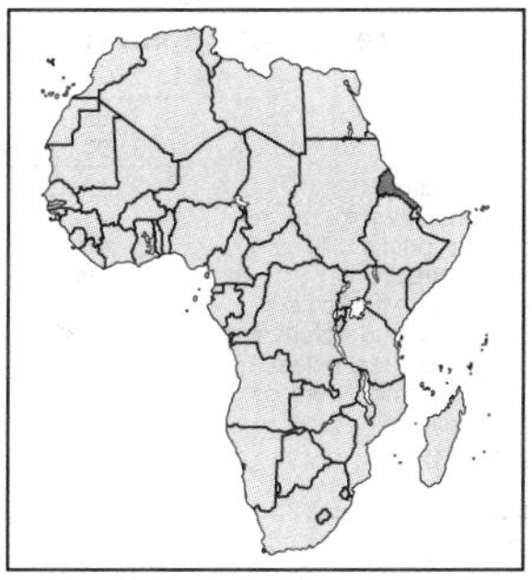

Official name: Eritrea.
Form of government: transitional regime[1] with one legislative house (National Assembly [60][2]).
Head of state and government: President assisted by State Council.
Capital: Asmara.
Official language: none.
Official religion: none.
Monetary unit: Ethiopian birr (Br) = 100 cents; valuation (Oct. 4, 1993) 1 U.S.$ = Br 5.00; 1 £ = Br 7.60.

Area and population

Provinces	Capitals	area[3] sq mi	area[3] sq km	population 1993 estimate
Akele Guzai	Adi Qayeh	3,200	8,400	...
Asmara	Asmara (Asmera)	100	200	...
Barka	Agordat (Akordat)	10,700	27,800	...
Dankalia	Asseb (Aseb)	9,400	24,300	...
Gash and Setit	Barentu	7,200	18,600	...
Hamasien	...	1,000	2,700	...
Sahel	Nakfa	6,300	16,400	...
Semhar	Massawa (Mitsiwa)	2,400	6,300	...
Senhit	Keren	2,300	5,900	...
Seraye	Mendefera	2,600	6,800	...
TOTAL		45,300[4]	117,400	3,670,000

Demography

Population (1993): 3,670,000.
Density (1993): persons per sq mi 81.0, persons per sq km 31.3.
Urban-rural (1989): urban 15.4%; rural 84.6%.
Sex distribution (1989): male 49.92%; female 50.08%.
Age breakdown (1993): under 15, 46.0%; 15–29, 23.1%; 30–44, 16.0%; 45–59, 8.9%; 60–74, 4.4%; 75 and over, 1.6%.
Population projection: (2000) 4,218,000; (2010) 5,690,000.
Doubling time: c. 15 years.
Linguistic composition (1976): Tigrinya 47.9%; Tigré 31.0%; Afar 4.2%; Beja 3.9%; Agew 3.1%; Saho 3.0%; Kunama 2.7%; Nara 2.1%; Amharic 1.7%; other 0.4%.
Religious affiliation (1993): believers are *c.* 50% Christian and *c.* 50% Muslim; there are also a few animists.
Major cities (1989): Asmara 342,706; Asseb 39,569; Keren 32,110; Massawa 19,404; Mendefera 14,833.

Vital statistics

Birth rate per 1,000 population (1981): 40.1–45.0 (world avg. 27.8).
Death rate per 1,000 population (1981): 15.0–17.0 (world avg. 10.4).
Natural increase rate per 1,000 population (1981): 25.1–28.0 (world avg. 17.4).
Total fertility rate (avg. births per childbearing woman): n.a.
Marriage rate per 1,000 population: n.a.
Divorce rate per 1,000 population: n.a.
Life expectancy at birth (1974): 46.1–51.0 years.
Major causes of death per 100,000 population: n.a.; morbidity (principal causes of illness) arises mainly in malaria and other infectious diseases, parasitic infections, malnutrition, diarrheal diseases, and dysenteries.

National economy

Budget: n.a.
Public debt: n.a.
Tourism (1984): 3 hotels totaling 87 rooms.
Production (metric tons except as noted). Agriculture, forestry, fishing: statistical detail, n.a. Sorghum is Eritrea's main crop; millet, oats, barley, teff, corn (maize), pulses, wheat, and oilseeds are also produced in significant quantities; livestock (1982–83) includes *c.* 2,300,000 goats, 880,000 cattle, 770,000 sheep, and *c.* 780,000 chickens; Red Sea fisheries landed *c.* 2,000 tons annually in the early 1990s, including lobster, prawns, sardines, sharks, anchovies, groupers, and snappers. Mining and quarrying: detail, n.a.; salt and sand and aggregate for construction are the principal minerals exploited; deposits of copper, zinc, mica, gold, iron, manganese, nickel, and lead exist but remain unexploited. Manufacturing (value added in Br '000; 1983–84): petroleum products 120,513; beverages 60,868, of which beer 54,275; food products 53,480; textiles 23,699, of which spinning and weaving 14,404, knitting products 5,816, rope and twine 3,479; chemical products 9,641; plastic products 9,423; tobacco products 6,262; nonmetallic mineral products 5,057; footwear 4,249; metal products 3,830; glass and glass products 3,258. Construction: reconstruction, after some 30 years of civil war, is a principal concern of the government. Energy production: energy resources include hydroelectricity, fossil fuels, geothermal power, coal, biogas, solar power, and wind; commercial electricity production for 1986–87 was 148,664,000 kW-hr.
Persons economically active: n.a.

Price and earnings indexes (1985 = 100)

	1986	1987	1988	1989	1990	1991	1992
Consumer price index[5]	90.2	88.0	94.2	101.6	106.8	145.0	160.3
Earnings index	...	...	...	...	...	...	...

Gross national product (at current market prices; 1993): *c.* U.S.$393,415,000 (U.S.$115 per capita).

Manufacturing value added and employment (current prices)

	1983–84 in value '000 birr	% of total value	labour force	% of labour force
Apparel	4,275	1.4	796	5.2
Chemical products	9,641	3.1	531	3.4
Food and beverages	114,348	36.5	3,267	21.3
Metal products	3,830	1.2	611	4.0
Nonmetallic products	5,057	1.6	511	3.3
Petroleum products	120,513	38.4	1,070	7.0
Plastic products	9,423	3.0	813	5.3
Textiles	23,699	7.5	6,341	41.4
Other	22,818	7.3	1,370	8.9
TOTAL	313,604	100.0	15,310	100.0[4]

Household income and expenditure. Average household size (1984) 4.5; average annual income per household: n.a.; sources of income: n.a.; expenditure: n.a.
Land use (1984): forested *c.* 5%; rough grazing and scrub *c.* 40%; agricultural and under permanent cultivation *c.* 5%; built-on, wasteland, and other *c.* 50%.

Foreign trade

Balance of trade (current prices): n.a.
Imports: n.a. *Major import sources:* n.a.
Exports: n.a. *Major export destinations:* n.a.

Transport and communications

Transport. Railroads (1993): none; a 190-mi (306-km) rail line formerly connected Massawa and Agordat, but it was dismantled during the war. Roads (1987–88)[6]: total length 559 mi, 899 km (paved 63%). Vehicles: n.a. Merchant marine: vessels (100 gross tons and over) n.a. Air transport (1987–88)[7]: passenger arrivals 57,694, passenger departures 62,240; short ton cargo handled 25,907, metric ton cargo handled 28,557; airports (1993) with scheduled flights 2.
Communications. Daily newspapers: none; (1992) 1 biweekly newspaper published; circulation *c.* 26,000; circulation per 1,000 population 7.8. Radio (1993): the government operates a station in Asmara. Television (1993): the government operates a station in Asmara. Telephones (1987–88)[6]: 12,375 (1 per 27 persons).

Education and health

Education (1985–86)

	schools	teachers	students	student/ teacher ratio
Primary (age 7–12)	280	3,032	196,587[8, 9]	...
Secondary (age 13–18)	18	604	...	...
Voc., teacher tr.	5[10]	...	...	...
Higher	1[9]	...	1,632[11]	...

Literacy (1993): total population literate *c.* 20%.
Health (1986–87): physicians 78 (1 per 36,000 persons); hospital beds 2,449 (1 per 1,100 persons); infant mortality rate per 1,000 live births (1993) 135.
Food: n.a.

Military

Total active duty personnel (1993): estimated strength of Eritrean armed forces (predominantly former guerrillas) is some 70,000 to 80,000.

[1]Transitional regime (independent May 24, 1993) to govern for up to four years pending the drafting of a constitution and holding of multiparty elections. [2]Excludes members of the central committee of the Eritrean People's Liberation Front, who are ex officio members of the Assembly. [3]Approximate figures. [4]Detail does not add to total given because of rounding. [5]Ethiopian CPI; no separate data available as yet. [6]City of Asmara only. [7]Asmara airport only. [8]Includes Secondary. [9]1987–88. [10]1975. [11]1986–87.

Estonia

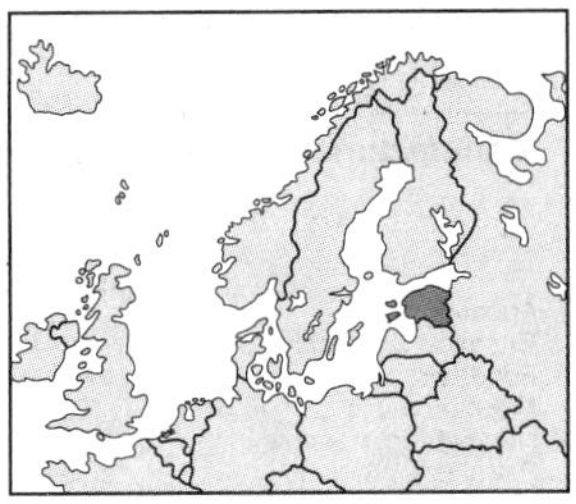

Official name: Eesti Vabariik (Republic of Estonia).
Form of government: unitary multiparty republic with a single legislative body (Parliament [101]).
Chief of state: President.
Head of government: Prime Minister.
Capital: Tallinn.
Official language: Estonian.
Official religion: none.
Monetary unit: 1 kroon[1] (EEK) = 100 senti; valuation (Oct. 4, 1993) 1 U.S.$ = EEK 12.93; 1 £ = EEK 19.58.

Area and population

		area		population
		sq mi	sq km	1992 estimate
Cities	**Capitals**			
Kohtla-Järve	—	[2]	[2]	74,081[3]
Narva	—	39	101	86,850[3]
Pärnu	—	14	35	57,060[3]
Sillamäe	—	4	10	21,130
Tallinn	—	71	183	492,434[3]
Tartu	—	15	39	113,410
Districts				
Harju	Keila	1,601	4,147	107,150
Hiiumaa	Kärdla	395	1,023	11,660
Ida-Viru	Jõhvi	1,258[2]	3,258[2]	38,673
Järva (Paide)	Paide	1,013	2,624	43,759
Jõgeva	Jõgeva	1,005	2,604	42,603
Lääne (Haapsalu)	Haapsalu	933	2,417	33,870
Lääne-Viru (Rakvere)	Rakvere	1,332	3,451	79,308
Pärnu	Pärnu	1,842	4,771	43,006
Põlva	Põlva	836	2,164	36,076
Rapla	Rapla	1,135	2,939	39,916
Saare (Kingissepa)	Kuressaare	1,126	2,917	40,548
Tartu	Tartu	1,186	3,071	49,287
Valga	Valga	789	2,044	41,050
Viljandi	Viljandi	1,381	3,578	64,879
Võru	Võru	890	2,305	45,221
TOTAL		17,462[4]	45,226[4]	1,561,971

Demography

Population (1993): 1,536,000.
Density (1993): persons per sq mi 88.0, persons per sq km 34.0.
Urban-rural (1992): urban 71.3%; rural 28.7%.
Sex distribution (1992): male 46.80%; female 53.20%.
Age breakdown (1991): under 15, 22.2%; 15–29, 21.0%; 30–44, 21.9%; 45–59, 17.6%; 60–74, 12.3%; 75 and over, 5.0%.
Population projection: (2000) 1,576,000; (2010) 1,625,000.
Ethnic composition (1989): Estonian 61.5%; Russian 30.3%; Ukrainian 3.1%; Belorussian 1.8%; Finnish 1.1%; other 2.2%.
Religious affiliation: believers are predominantly Evangelical Lutheran, with Orthodox and Baptist minorities.
Major cities (1992): Tallinn 471,608; Tartu 113,410; Narva 82,927; Pärnu 52,596; Kohtla-Järve 28,310.

Vital statistics

Birth rate per 1,000 population (1991): 12.3 (world avg. 26.4); legitimate 68.9%; illegitimate 31.1%.
Death rate per 1,000 population (1991): 12.6 (world avg. 9.2).
Natural increase rate per 1,000 population (1991): −0.3 (world avg. 17.2).
Total fertility rate (avg. births per childbearing woman; 1991): 1.8.
Marriage rate per 1,000 population (1991): 6.5.
Divorce rate per 1,000 population (1991): 3.7.
Life expectancy at birth (1990): male 64.7 years; female 74.9 years.
Major causes of death per 100,000 population (1990): diseases of the circulatory system, 746.7, of which ischemic heart diseases 465.9, cerebrovascular disease 233.4; malignant neoplasms (cancers) 194.2; accidents 90.4; suicide 26.8.

National economy

Budget (1991). Revenue: 5,843,600,000 rubles (income taxes on enterprises 23.5%, sales taxes 21.1%, excise duties 12.6%). Expenditures: 5,152,600,000 rubles (national economy 28.6%, education 16.9%, social security 13.4%, health 9.8%).
Public debt (external, outstanding; December 1991): none[5].
Tourism (1991): tourist arrivals 237,944.
Production (metric tons except as noted). Agriculture, forestry, fishing (1991): potatoes 648,000[6], barley 623,000, rye 127,000, vegetables 120,500, oats 107,000, fruits and berries 23,100; livestock (number of live animals) 799,000 pigs, 708,000 cattle, 143,000 sheep and goats; roundwood 1,653,000 cu m; fish catch 317,400. Mining and quarrying (1991): oil shale 19,600,000, peat 195,000. Manufacturing (value of production in '000,000 of rubles; 1991): food, beverages, and tobacco 4,501; textiles, clothing, and footwear 4,383; nonelectrical machinery and fabricated metal products 2,149; wood products, paper products, and publishing 1,743. Construction (completed; 1991): 329,000 sq m. Energy production (consumption): electricity (kW-hr; 1991) 14,627,000,000 (9,856,000,000); oil shale (metric tons; 1991) 19,600,000 (23,351,000); coal and coke (metric tons; 1991) none (377,000); crude petroleum, none (n.a.); natural gas (cu m; 1991) none (1,521,000,000).
Gross national product (1991): U.S.$6,088,000,000 (U.S.$3,830 per capita).

Structure of gross domestic product and labour force

	1991			
	in value '000,000 rubles	% of total value	labour force[7]	% of labour force
Agriculture	2,112	15.4	100,900	12.8
Manufacturing, mining, and public utilities	7,098	51.9	257,000	32.5
Construction	683	5.0	78,000	9.9
Trade, restaurants	766	5.6	69,000	8.7
Transp. and commun.	636	4.6	67,500	8.6
Finance, real estate }			4,000	0.5
Pub. admin., defense, services }	2,388	17.5	198,500	25.1
Other }			15,100	1.9
TOTAL	13,683	100.0	790,000	100.0

Population economically active (1989): total 856,000; activity rate of total population 54.7% (participation rates: ages 15–64, 79.7%; female 50.0%; unemployed [mid-1993] 6.0%).

Price and earnings indexes (1985 = 100)

	1986	1987	1988	1989	1990	1991	1992[8]
Consumer price index	107.2	110.8	115.4	121.7	144.2	435.6	5,100
Monthly earnings index	102.7	106.5	115.9	125.5	158.2	299.2	...

Household income and expenditure. Average household size (1989) 3.1; average annual income per household: n.a.; sources of income (1991): wages and salaries 78,2%, other 21.8%; expenditure (1991): food 45.0%, alcohol 4.2%, other 50.8%.
Land use (1989): forested 42.6%; meadows and pastures, n.a.; agricultural and under permanent cultivation 32.5%; other 24.9%.

Foreign trade

Balance of trade (current prices)

	1988	1989	1990	1991
'000,000 rubles	−700	−700	−793	+648
% of total	10.4%	10.1%	13.1%	6.8%

Imports (1991): 4,454,500,000 rubles (textiles and clothing 19.0%, machinery and parts 14.0%, mineral products 12.0%, vegetables 10.1%). *Major import sources:* former Soviet Union 84.8%, of which Russia 45.9%, Ukraine 7.9%, Lithuania 6.3%, Latvia 5.1%; United States 3.5%.
Exports (1991): 5,102,300,000 rubles (textiles and clothing 26.4%, machinery and parts 11.6%, chemicals and chemical products 11.0%, live animals and animal products 10.0%). *Major export destinations:* former Soviet Union 94.7%, of which Russia 56.5%, Ukraine 12.9%, Latvia 7.7%, Belarus 4.1%; Finland 2.3%.

Transport and communications

Transport. Railroads (1991): length 638 mi, 1,026 km; passenger-mi 791,000,000, passenger-km 1,273,000,000; (1990) short ton-mi cargo 4,779,000,000, metric ton-km cargo 6,977,000,000. Roads (1991): total length 9,203 mi, 14,811 km (paved 52%). Vehicles (1991): passenger cars 261,086; trucks and buses 85,585. Merchant marine (1992): vessels (1,000 gross tons and over) 234; total deadweight tonnage 680,367. Air transport (1991): passenger-mi 650,000,000, passenger-km 1,046,000,000; short ton-mi cargo 4,100,000, metric ton-km cargo 6,000,000; airports (1993) with scheduled flights 1.
Communications. Daily newspapers: total number (1992) 6; total circulation 425,000[9]; circulation per 1,000 population 272[9]. Radio (1989): total number of receivers 926,000 (1 per 1.7 persons). Television (1992): total number of receivers 600,000 (1 per 2.6 persons). Telephones (1991): 341,000 (1 per 4.6 persons).

Education and health

Education (1991–92)

	schools	teachers	students	student/ teacher ratio
Primary } Secondary }	690	17,952[10]	223,700	12.7[10]
Vocational	...	...	23,100[11]	...
Higher	10	3,168[11]	25,643	8.2[11]

Educational attainment (1989). Percentage of persons age 25 and over having: no formal schooling 2.2%; primary education 39.7%; secondary 45.1%; higher 13.7%. *Literacy* (1989): 99.7%.
Health (1991): physicians 6,005 (1 per 262 persons); hospital beds 18,096 (1 per 87 persons); infant mortality rate per 1,000 live births (1990) 12.4.
Food: daily per capita caloric intake, n.a.

Military

Total active duty personnel (1993): 2,500. *Military expenditure as a percentage of GNP:* n.a. About 5,000 Russian military personnel remained in Estonia as of September 1993.

[1]Kroon reintroduced June 20, 1992, replacing the ruble of the former Soviet Union, a nonconvertible currency for which no meaningful exchange rate can be offered. [2]Ida-Viru includes Kohtla-Järve. [3]Includes nearby town(s) administratively subordinate to the city government. [4]Total includes 597 sq mi (1,545 sq km) not distributed by administrative subdivision, largely the Estonian portion of Lake Peipus. [5]No agreement has been reached on Estonia's share of the former Soviet Union's total external debt. [6]1992. [7]Employed persons only. [8]September; estimated figure. [9]Three newspapers only. [10]1989–90. [11]1990–91.

Ethiopia

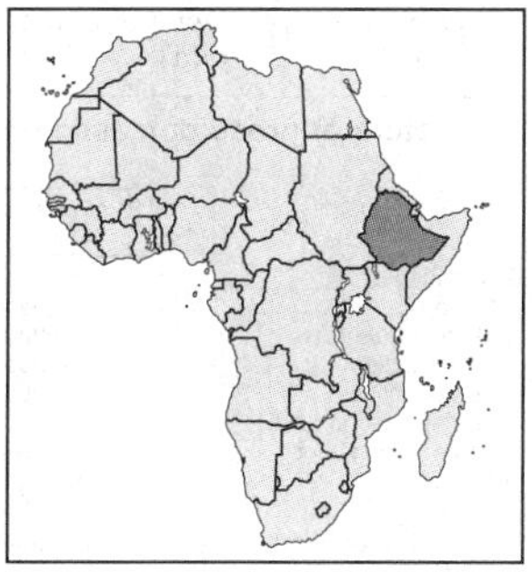

Official name: Ītyop'iya (Ethiopia).
Form of government[1]: transitional regime with one legislative house (Council of Representatives [87]).
Chief of state and government: President assisted by Prime Minister.
Capital: Addis Ababa.
Official Language: Amharic.
Official religion: none.
Monetary unit: 1 birr (Br) = 100 cents; valuation (Oct. 4, 1993) 1 U.S.$ = Br 5.00; 1 £ = Br 7.60.

Area and population

Regions	Capitals	area sq mi	area sq km	population 1993 estimate
Addis Ababa	...	2,003	5,188	2,657,559
Arsi	Asela	9,155	23,710	2,157,227
Asosa	...	8,906	23,067	570,910
Bale	Goba	25,996	67,330	1,063,382
Borena	...	36,301	94,018	723,746
Eastern Gojam	...	5,381	13,936	1,699,460
Eastern Harerge	...	34,981	90,600	2,774,346
Eastern Shewa	...	4,924	12,754	1,026,180
Gambela	...	10,064	26,065	195,023
Ilubabor	Mefa	12,905	35,059	3,117,220
Kefa	Jima	15,476	40,083	1,148,596
Metekel	...	11,768	30,481	416,380
Northern Gonder	...	23,946	62,020	2,038,164
Northern Omo	...	11,553	29,923	3,046,859
Northern Shewa	...	10,436	27,030	2,570,128
Northern Welo	...	11,906	30,835	1,621,520
Sidamo	Awasa	8,009	20,742	2,980,044
Southern Gonder	...	6,594	17,079	1,867,766
Southern Omo	...	8,494	22,000	269,197
Southern Shewa	...	6,486	16,799	3,235,768
Southern Welo	...	7,993	20,702	2,675,995
Welega	Nekemte	16,460	42,632	2,673,652
Western Gojam	...	6,675	17,289	2,210,466
Western Harerge	...	12,814	33,188	1,482,628
Western Shewa	...	8,964	23,218	2,934,434
Autonomous regions				
Aseb[2]	...	17,786	46,065	246,373
Dire Dawa	...	11,291	29,244	521,691
Ogaden	...	69,239	179,327	906,632
Tigray	Mekele	20,656	53,498	2,999,948
TOTAL		437,794[3]	1,133,882	51,831,290

Demography

Population (1993): 51,831,000.
Density (1993): persons per sq mi 118.4, persons per sq km 45.7.
Urban-rural (1993): urban 12.3%; rural 87.7%.
Sex distribution (1993): male 50.27%; female 49.73%.
Age breakdown (1993): under 15, 46.5%; 15–29, 22.8%; 30–44, 15.6%; 45–59, 8.9%; 60–74, 4.5%; 75 and over, 1.7%.
Population projection: (2000) 64,032,000; (2010) 86,019,000.
Ethnolinguistic composition (1983)[4]: Amhara 37.7%; Galla (Oromo) 35.3%; Tigrinya 8.6%; Gurage 3.3%; Ometo (Omotic) 2.7%; Sidamo 2.4%.
Religious affiliation (1980)[4]: Ethiopian Orthodox 52.5%; Muslim 31.4%; traditional beliefs 11.4%; other Christian 4.5%; other 0.2%.
Major cities (1988): Addis Ababa 1,673,060; Dire Dawa 117,734; Gonder 95,000; Nazret 90,975.

Vital statistics[4]

Birth rate per 1,000 population (1990–95): 48.4 (world avg. 26.4).
Death rate per 1,000 population (1990–95): 18.3 (world avg. 9.2).
Natural increase rate per 1,000 population (1990–95): 30.1 (world avg. 17.2).
Total fertility rate (avg. births per childbearing woman; 1990–95): 6.8.
Life expectancy at birth (1990–95): male 45.4 years; female 48.7 years.
Major causes of death (1987–88)[5]: infectious and parasitic diseases 33.1%; respiratory diseases 15.7%; digestive system diseases 10.7%.

National economy[4]

Budget (1989–90). Revenue: Br 3,093,000,000 (taxes 73.0%, of which income and profit tax 31.5%, excise tax 15.2%, import duties 13.8%, export duties 1.8%; nontax revenue 27.0%). Expenditures: Br 4,976,000,000 (general services 48.5%; economic development 21.3%, of which agriculture 5.3%; social services 12.7%, of which education 7.9%, public health 2.6%).
Tourism: receipts (1991) U.S.$20,000,000; expenditures (1990) U.S.$10,000,000.
Production (metric tons except as noted). Agriculture, forestry, fishing (1992): corn (maize) 1,650,000, sugarcane 1,620,000, sorghum 1,100,000, barley 1,000,000, wheat 900,000, pulses 815,000, potatoes 388,000, millet 280,000, yams 262,000, coffee 216,000, seed cotton 40,000; livestock (number of live animals) 31,000,000 cattle, 23,200,000 sheep, 18,100,000 goats, 8,580,000 horses, mules, and asses, 1,000,000 camels; roundwood (1991) 43,686,000 cu m; fish catch (1991) 4,500. Mining and quarrying (1991): cement 290,000; salt 94,000; limestone 85,000; gold 61,000 troy oz; platinum 42 troy oz. Manufacturing (gross value in Br '000[6]; 1989–90): food and beverages 750,000; textiles 403,000; leather and shoes 233,000; cigarettes 100,000; chemicals 97,000. Construction (authorized; 1987–88)[7]: residential 260,251 sq m; nonresidential 63,346 sq m, of which commercial 16,994 sq m. Energy production (consumption): electricity (kW-hr; 1991) 973,000,000 (973,000,000); coal, none (n.a.); crude petroleum (barrels; 1991) n.a. (5,278,000); petroleum products (metric tons; 1991) 656,000 (820,000); natural gas, n.a. (n.a.).
Land use (1991): forested 24.5%; meadows and pastures 40.7%; agricultural and under permanent cultivation 12.7%; other 22.1%.
Gross national product (1992): U.S.$5,958,000,000 (U.S.$110 per capita).

Structure of gross domestic product and labour force

	1989–90 in value Br '000,000	1989–90 % of total value	1988 labour force	1988 % of labour force
Agriculture	4,699.6	41.1	14,639,000	75.7
Mining	21.7	0.2		
Manufacturing	1,265.4	11.1	1,837,000	9.5
Construction	415.5	3.6		
Public utilities	171.2	1.5		
Transp. and commun.	826.1	7.2		
Trade	1,098.3	9.6		
Finance	407.9	3.6	2,862,000	14.8
Pub. admin., defense	1,436.7	12.5		
Services	853.9	7.5		
Other	239.9	2.1		
TOTAL	11,436.2	100.0	19,338,000	100.0

Public debt (external, outstanding; 1991): U.S.$3,301,000,000.
Population economically active (1988): total 19,338,000; activity rate of total population 43.3% (participation rates: age 10 and over, 63.5%; female 37.8%; unemployed [1990] 44.2%).

Price and earnings indexes (1985 = 100)

	1986	1987	1988	1989	1990	1991	1992
Consumer price index	90.2	88.0	94.2	101.6	106.8	145.0	160.3
Earnings index	...	...	...	...	...	...	...

Household income and expenditure. Average household size (1984) 4.5; income per household (1981–82) Br 1,728 (U.S.$835); sources of income: (1981–82): self-employment 79.5%, wages and salaries 0.2%, other 20.3%; expenditure (1988): food 66.7%, fuel and power 15.9%, clothing and footwear 6.8%, health care 3.1%, education 2.5%, household goods 2.1%.

Foreign trade[4]

Balance of trade (current prices)

	1987	1988	1989	1990	1991	1992
Br '000,000	−1,124.7	−1,081.2	−747.6	−1,271.6	−433.1	−1,360.5
% of total	43.3%	60.8%	29.1%	50.8%	55.5%	60.3%

Imports (1989–90): Br 1,831,000,000 (machinery [including aircraft] 16.7%, petroleum and petroleum products 12.3%, metal and metal wares 11.5%, road transport equipment 10.4%, food and beverages 7.2%). *Major import sources* (1991): U.S. 20.8%; former U.S.S.R. 16.3%; Italy 8.9%; Germany 8.4%; Japan 5.5%.
Exports (1989–90): Br 736,817,000 (coffee 55.0%, hides 18.1%, pulses 4.8%, petroleum products 3.6%). *Major export destinations* (1991): Germany 15.3%; Japan 14.5%; Yemen 13.9%; former U.S.S.R. 7.8%; U.K. 7.7%.

Transport and communications[4]

Transport. Railroads (1989)[8]: length 782 km; passenger-km 297,000,000; metric ton-km cargo 128,000,000. Roads (1991): total length 27,972 km (paved 15%). Vehicles (1991): passenger cars 37,799; trucks and buses 15,539. Merchant marine (1992): vessels (100 gross tons and over) 27; total deadweight tonnage 84,326. Air transport (1989): passenger-km 1,607,940,000; metric ton-km cargo 167,940,000; airports (1993) 25.
Communications. Daily newspapers (1992): 3; circulation 81,000; circulation per 1,000 population 1.6. Radio (1992): 3,300,000 receivers (1 per 15.3 persons). Television (1992): 100,000 receivers (1 per 505 persons). Telephones (1991): 168,728 (1 per 316 persons).

Education and health

Education (1988)

	schools	teachers	students	student/ teacher ratio
Primary (age 7–12)	8,584	65,993	2,855,846	43.3
Secondary (age 13–18)	1,209[9]	21,220	874,000	41.2
Voc., teacher tr.	...	763	8,243	10.8
Higher	11[10]	1,699	31,204	18.4

Educational attainment: n.a. *Literacy* (1980)[11]: total population age 15 and over literate 1,000,000 (4.8%); males (9.3%); females (0.5%).
Health (1986–87): physicians 1,241 (1 per 36,660 persons); hospital beds 11,745 (1 per 3,873 persons); infant mortality rate (1990–95) 122.0.
Food (1988–90): daily per capita caloric intake 1,699 (1979–81; vegetable products 93%, animal products 7%); (1984) 72% of FAO recommended minimum.

Military

Total active duty personnel (1993): following the independence of Eritrea in May 1993, the estimated strength of Ethiopian armed forces was some 100,000. *Military expenditure as percentage of GNP* (1989): 12.8% (world 4.9%); per capita expenditure U.S.$15.

[1]The central government was overthrown in May 1991, and a transitional government was formed in July 1991. Eritrean independence was recognized on May 24, 1993. [2]Estimates adjusted to exclude the Eritrean portion of Aseb area. [3]Detail does not add to total given because of rounding. [4]Includes Eritrea. [5]Percentage of illnesses in a sample population of hospital outpatients. [6]At constant prices of 1978–79. [7]Addis Ababa only. [8]Includes 62 mi (100 km) of the Chemin de Fer Djibouti-Ethiopien (CDE) in Djibouti; excludes 190 mi (306 km) of Northern Ethiopia Railway, not in use since 1978. [9]1985–86. [10]1983–84. [11]Adult illiteracy was 37% in 1987.

Fiji

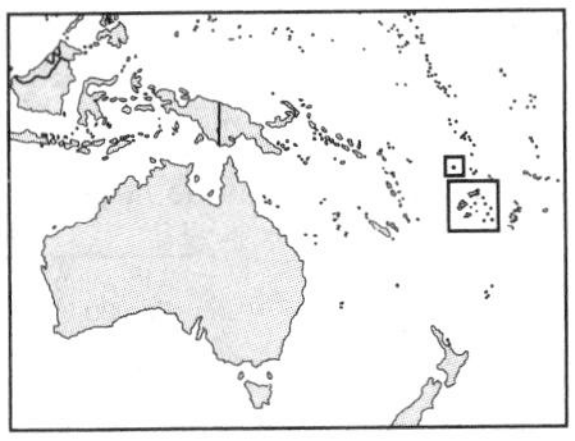

Official name: Sovereign Democratic Republic of Fiji.
Form of government: republic with two legislative houses (Senate [34[1]]; House of Representatives [70]).
Chief of state: President.
Head of government: Prime Minister.
Capital: Suva.
Official language: English.
Official religion: none.
Monetary unit: 1 Fiji dollar (F$) = 100 cents; valuation (Oct. 4, 1993) 1 U.S.$ = F$1.54; 1 £ = F$2.34.

Area and population

Divisions / Provinces	Capitals	area sq mi	area sq km	population 1986 census
Central	Suva			
Naitasiri	—	643	1,666	100,227
Namosi	—	220	570	4,836
Rewa	—	105	272	97,442
Serua	—	320	830	13,356
Tailevu	—	369	955	44,249
Eastern	Levuka			
Kadavu	—	185	478	9,805
Lau	—	188	487	14,203
Lomaiviti	—	159	411	16,066
Rotuma	—	18	46	2,688
Northern	Labasa			
Bua	—	532	1,379	13,986
Cakaudrove	—	1,087	2,816	40,433
Macuata	—	774	2,004	74,735
Western	Lautoka			
Ba	—	1,017	2,634	197,633
Nadroga-Navosa	—	921	2,385	54,431
Ra	—	518	1,341	31,285
TOTAL	—	7,056	18,274	715,375

Demography

Population (1993): 762,000.
Density (1993): persons per sq mi 108.0, persons per sq km 41.7.
Urban-rural (1987): urban 38.7%; rural 61.3%.
Sex distribution (1989): male 50.65%; female 49.35%.
Age breakdown (1989): under 15, 37.9%; 15–29, 28.6%; 30–44, 18.3%; 45–59, 9.9%; 60–74, 4.0%; 75 and over, 1.3%.
Population projection: (2000) 830,000; (2010) 923,000.
Doubling time: 32 years.
Ethnic composition (1992): Fijian 49.7%; Indian 45.3%[2]; other 5.0%.
Religious affiliation (1986): Christian 52.9%; Hindu 38.1%; Muslim 7.8%; Sikh 0.7%; other 0.5%.
Major cities (1986): Suva 69,665; Lautoka 28,728; Lami 8,601; Nadi 7,679; Ba 6,518.

Vital statistics

Birth rate per 1,000 population (1992): 24.8 (world avg. 26.4); (1978) legitimate 82.7%; illegitimate 17.3%.
Death rate per 1,000 population (1992): 5.1 (world avg. 9.2).
Natural increase rate per 1,000 population (1992): 19.7 (world avg. 17.2).
Total fertility rate (avg. births per childbearing woman; 1988): 3.1.
Marriage rate per 1,000 population (1987): 8.4.
Divorce rate per 1,000 population (1979): 0.7.
Life expectancy at birth (1987): male 61.0 years; female 65.0 years.
Major causes of death per 100,000 population (1987): diseases of the circulatory system 153.4; malignant neoplasms (cancers) 35.5; accidents, poisoning, and violence 32.2; diseases of the respiratory system 31.7; diabetes mellitus 27.3; infectious and parasitic diseases 18.2; birth trauma 16.5.

National economy

Budget (1992). Revenue: F$550,588,000 (income taxes, estate taxes, and gift duties 44.7%; customs duties and port dues 36.1%; fees, royalties, and sales 9.1%). Expenditures: F$600,616,000 (departmental expenditure 75.1%; public-debt charges 20.6%; pensions and gratuities 4.3%).
Production (metric tons except as noted). Agriculture, forestry, fishing (1992): sugarcane 3,533,000, paddy rice 29,038, copra 16,048, ginger 6,500; livestock (number of live animals) 160,000 cattle, 124,000 goats, 15,000 pigs; roundwood 413,329 cu m; fish catch (1991) 31,089. Mining and quarrying (1992): gold 3,701 kg; silver 1,258 kg. Manufacturing (1992): refined sugar 426,000; cement 84,400; flour 27,766; stock feed 24,601; coconut oil 9,234; soap 6,891; beer 173,400 hectolitres; paint 25,650 hectolitres. Construction (1991): residential 49,000 sq m; nonresidential 37,000 sq m. Energy production (consumption): electricity (kW-hr; 1990) 435,000,000 (435,000,000); coal (metric tons; 1990) none (14,000); crude petroleum, none (n.a.); petroleum products (metric tons; 1990) none (219,000); natural gas, none (n.a.).
Population economically active (1986): total 241,160; activity rate of total population 33.7% (participation rates: ages 15–64, 56.0%; female 21.2%; unemployed [1990] 6.4%).

Price and earnings indexes (1985 = 100)

	1986	1987	1988	1989	1990	1991	1992
Consumer price index	101.8	107.6	120.2	127.7	138.1	147.1	154.3
Daily earnings index	100.0	105.3	108.0	105.3	...	...	...

Gross national product (at current market prices; 1992): U.S.$1,550,000,000 (U.S.$2,070 per capita).

Structure of gross domestic product and labour force

	1992		1986	
	in value F$'000[3]	% of total value	labour force	% of labour force
Agriculture	186,871	21.1	106,305	44.1
Mining	1,644	0.2	1,345	0.5
Manufacturing	102,930	11.6	18,106	7.5
Construction	56,305	6.4	11,786	4.9
Public utilities	12,009	1.4	2,154	0.9
Transportation and communications	126,868	14.3	13,151	5.4
Trade	167,791	19.0	26,010	10.8
Finance	116,027	13.1	6,016	2.5
Pub. admin., defense; Services	148,566	16.8	36,619	15.2
Other	−34,099[4]	−3.9[4]	19,668[5]	8.2[5]
TOTAL	884,912	100.0	241,160	100.0

Public debt (external, outstanding; 1991): U.S.$267,900,000.
Household income and expenditure. Average household size (1986) 5.7; income per household (1980) F$2,837 (U.S.$3,546); sources of income (1973): wages and salaries 81.5%, self-employment 9.1%, other 9.4%; expenditure (1988): food 31.3%, housing and energy 11.9%, transportation and communications 11.3%, clothing and footwear 10.2%, household durable goods 7.8%.
Tourism (1991): receipts from visitors U.S.$211,000,000; expenditures by nationals abroad U.S.$45,000,000.
Land use (1991): forested 64.9%; agricultural and under permanent cultivation 13.2%; meadows and pastures 3.3%; other 18.6%.

Foreign trade

Balance of trade (current prices)

	1987	1988	1989	1990	1991	1992
F$'000,000	−131.4	−61.76	−253.87	−251.32	−279.57	−275.53
% of total	16.4%	5.6%	18.7%	14.1%	20.1%	20.9%

Imports (1992): F$938,448,000 (durable manufactures 24.9%; machinery and transport equipment 24.7%; food, beverages, and tobacco 15.4%; mineral fuels 14.2%; miscellaneous manufactured consumer articles 9.5%; chemicals 8.4%). *Major import sources:* Australia 32.2%; New Zealand 16.9%; Japan 10.3%; United States 8.8%; Singapore 6.4%; United Kingdom 3.2%; Hong Kong 3.0%; Taiwan 2.6%.
Exports (1992)[6]: F$541,745,000 (sugar 40.9%; gold 11.2%; fish 7.2%; timber 5.8%; molasses 2.4%; coconut oil 1.1%). *Major export destinations*[7]: United Kingdom 30.5%; Australia 17.5%; United States 12.7%; New Zealand 5.3%; Japan 5.2%; Canada 2.7%; Hong Kong 0.9%; Singapore 0.3%.

Transport and communications

Transport. Railroads (1990)[8]: length 370 mi, 595 km. Roads (1991): total length 2,996 mi, 4,821 km (paved 13%). Vehicles (1991): passenger cars 42,012; trucks and buses 29,225. Merchant marine (1992): vessels (100 gross tons and over) 64; total deadweight tonnage 60,444. Air transport (1990)[9]: passenger-mi 548,000,000, passenger-km 882,000,000; short ton-mi cargo 17,356,000, metric ton-km cargo 25,339,000; airports (1993) with scheduled flights 19.
Communications. Daily newspapers (1988): total number 2; total circulation 40,000; circulation per 1,000 population 56. Radio (1992): total number of receivers 450,000 (1 per 1.7 persons). Television (1990): total number of receivers 10,000 (1 per 73 persons). Telephones (1990): 72,584 (1 per 10 persons).

Education and health

Education (1990)

	schools	teachers	students	student/teacher ratio
Primary (age 5–15)	672[10]	4,272	143,553	33.6
Secondary (age 16–19)	140[10]	2,684	52,536	19.6
Voc., teacher tr.	44[10]	369	3,290	8.9
Higher	5[11]	320[10]	2,211[10]	6.9[10]

Educational attainment (1986). Percentage of population age 25 and over having: no formal schooling 28.3%; primary only 19.1%; some secondary 44.1%; secondary 4.1%; postsecondary 3.3%; other 1.1%. *Literacy* (1986): total population age 15 and over literate 87.0%; males literate 90.0%; females literate 84.0%.
Health (1990): physicians 300 (1 per 2,438 persons); hospital beds 1,747 (1 per 413 persons); infant mortality rate per 1,000 live births (1989) 17.1.
Food (1988–90): daily per capita caloric intake 2,769 (vegetable products 85%, animal products 15%); 121% of FAO recommended minimum requirement.

Military

Total active duty personnel (1992): 5,000 (army 94.0%, navy 6.0%, air force, none). *Military expenditure as percentage of GNP* (1989): 2.2% (world 4.9%); per capita expenditure U.S.$35.

[1]All seats are appointed. [2]The emigration of Indian population after the coup in 1987 has resulted in the reemergence of a Fijian majority. [3]Constant 1977 prices. [4]Less imputed bank service charges. [5]Not stated and unemployed. [6]Excludes reexports, valued at F$111,536,000. [7]Based on exports of local products only. [8]Owned by the Fiji Sugar Corporation. [9]Air Pacific only. [10]1986. [11]1983.

Finland

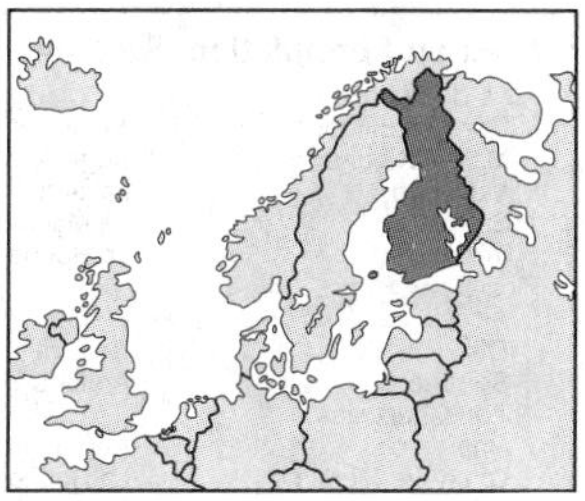

Official name: Suomen Tasavalta (Finnish); Republiken Finland (Swedish) (Republic of Finland).
Form of government: multiparty republic with one legislative house (Parliament [200]).
Chief of state: President.
Head of government: Prime Minister.
Capital: Helsinki.
Official languages: Finnish; Swedish.
Official religion: none[1].
Monetary unit: 1 markka (Fmk) = 100 penniä; valuation (Oct. 4, 1993) 1 U.S.$ = Fmk 5.82; 1 £ = Fmk 8.82.

Area and population

Provinces	Capitals	land area sq mi	land area sq km	population 1993[2] estimate
Häme	Hämeenlinna	6,309	16,341	688,355
Keski-Suomi	Jyväskylä	6,275	16,251	255,879
Kuopio	Kuopio	6,375	16,510	258,712
Kymi	Kouvola	4,163	10,783	335,093
Lappi	Rovaniemi	35,930	93,057	202,434
Mikkeli	Mikkeli	6,302	16,321	207,875
Oulu	Oulu	21,957	56,868	445,632
Pohjois-Karjala	Joensuu	6,866	17,782	177,803
Turku ja Pori	Turku	8,818	22,839	731,792
Uusimaa	Helsinki	3,822	9,898	1,277,801
Vaasa	Vaasa	10,200	26,418	448,363
Autonomous Province				
Åland (Ahvenanmaa)	Mariehamn (Maarianhamina)	590	1,527	25,008
TOTAL LAND AREA		117,604[3]	304,593[3]	
INLAND WATER		12,954	33,551	
TOTAL		130,559[3]	338,145[3]	5,054,747

Demography

Population (1993): 5,058,000.
Density (1993)[4]: persons per sq mi 43.0, persons per sq km 16.6.
Urban-rural (1993): urban 62.5%; rural 37.5%.
Sex distribution (1992): male 48.58%; female 51.42%.
Age breakdown (1992): under 15, 19.2%; 15–29, 20.3%; 30–44, 24.2%; 45–59, 17.6%; 60–74, 13.0%; 75 and over, 5.7%.
Population projection: (2000) 5,101,000; (2010) 5,081,000.
Doubling time: not applicable; population is stable.
Linguistic composition (1992): Finnish 93.4%; Swedish 5.9%; other 0.7%.
Religious affiliation (1992): Evangelical Lutheran 87.3%; Finnish (Greek) Orthodox 1.1%; nonreligious 10.6%; other 1.0%.
Major cities (1993[2]): Helsinki 501,741 (metropolitan area 848,253); Espoo 178,899[5]; Tampere 175,202; Turku 160,320; Vantaa 159,462[5].

Vital statistics

Birth rate per 1,000 population (1991): 13.1 (world avg. 26.4); (1990) legitimate 74.8%; illegitimate 25.2%.
Death rate per 1,000 population (1991): 9.8 (world avg. 9.2).
Natural increase rate per 1,000 population (1991): 3.3 (world avg. 17.2).
Total fertility rate (avg. births per childbearing woman; 1991): 1.8.
Marriage rate per 1,000 population (1991): 4.7.
Divorce rate per 1,000 population (1990): 2.6.
Life expectancy at birth (1989): male 70.8 years; female 78.9 years.
Major causes of death per 100,000 population (1990): ischemic heart diseases 282.4; malignant neoplasms (cancers) 202.2; cerebrovascular disease 120.5; diseases of the respiratory system 75.1; accidents 56.6.

National economy

Budget (1992). Revenue: Fmk 170,175,000,000 (tax revenue 70.0%, of which sales taxes 27.6%, income and property taxes 20.6%, excise duties 11.4%; loans 17.1%). Expenditures: Fmk 170,173,000,000 (social security 22.8%; education 15.9%; health 8.6%; pensions 6.3%; transportation and communications 6.2%; agriculture 6.2%; defense 5.3%).
Tourism (1992): receipts from visitors U.S.$1,316,000,000; expenditures by nationals abroad U.S.$2,405,000,000.
Production (metric tons except as noted). Agriculture, forestry, fishing (1991): silage 4,642,000, barley 1,778,000, oats 1,155,000, sugar beets 1,043,000, potatoes 672,000, carrots 38,700, strawberries 9,200, cut flowers 76.4 hectares; livestock (number of live animals) 1,315,000 cattle, 1,290,000 pigs, 285,900 reindeer[6]; roundwood 34,091,000 cu m; fish catch (1990) 97,391. Mining and quarrying (1991): zinc concentrate 107,000; gold 70,700 troy oz. Manufacturing (value added in Fmk '000,000; 1990): nonelectrical machinery 12,770; wood pulp, paper, and paperboard 11,960; food products 9,870; printing and publishing 8,060; electrical machinery 7,000; fabricated metal products 6,710; transport equipment 5,380. Construction (completed; 1991): residential 18,650,000 cu m; nonresidential 28,290,000 cu m. Energy production (consumption): electricity (kW-hr; 1991) 55,068,000,000 (65,261,000,000[7]); coal (metric tons; 1990) none (6,227,000); crude petroleum (barrels; 1990) none (67,883,000); petroleum products (metric tons; 1990) 9,043,000 (8,627,000); natural gas (cu m; 1990) none (2,695,000,000).
Household income and expenditure. Average household size (1989) 2.3; income per household Fmk 153,600 (U.S.$35,794); sources of income: wages and salaries 65.4%, transfer payments 21.4%, self-employment 8.4%, other 4.8%; expenditure (1990): transportation and communications 18.4%, food 16.0%, housing 14.7%, recreation and education 10.7%.

Gross national product (at current market prices; 1991): U.S.$121,982,000,000 (U.S.$24,400 per capita).

Structure of gross domestic product and labour force

	1991 in value Fmk '000,000	% of total value	labour force	% of labour force
Agriculture, fishing	13,085	3.0	208,000	8.1
Forestry	10,559	2.4		
Mining	1,260	0.3	5,000	0.2
Manufacturing	85,044	19.3	512,000	20.0
Public utilities	11,648	2.7	28,000	1.1
Construction	37,995	8.6	217,000	8.5
Transp. and commun.	37,424	8.5	183,000	7.2
Trade, restaurants	47,584	10.8	379,000	14.8
Finance, real estate	89,166	20.3	206,000	8.0
Pub. admin., defense	90,423	20.5	787,000	30.8
Services	32,771	7.4		
Other	−16,596	−3.8	33,000	1.3
TOTAL	440,363	100.0	2,559,000[3]	100.0

Population economically active (1991): total 2,559,000; activity rate of total population 51.1% (participation rates: ages 15–64, 75.5%; female 47.0%; unemployed [March 1992–February 1993] 14.0%).

Price and earnings indexes (1985 = 100)

	1987	1988	1989	1990	1991	1992	1993[8]
Consumer price index	107.1	112.6	120.0	127.3	132.6	136.0	138.6
Annual earnings index	114.4	124.7	135.7	148.2	157.6	160.5	...

National debt (end of December 1991): Fmk 83,900,000,000.
Land use (1990): forested 76.2%; meadows and pastures 0.4%; agricultural and under permanent cultivation 8.0%; other 15.4%.

Foreign trade[9]

Balance of trade (current prices)

	1987	1988	1989	1990	1991	1992
Fmk '000,000	+4,845	+6,136	+2,928	+2,799	+9,141	+16,558
% of total	2.8%	3.5%	1.5%	1.4%	5.6%	8.3%

Imports (1992): Fmk 94,988,000,000 (raw materials 52.1%; consumer goods 21.9%; mineral fuels 10.3%). *Major import sources:* Germany 16.9%; Sweden 11.7%; United Kingdom 8.6%; Russia 7.1%; United States 6.1%; Japan 5.5%; France 4.6%.
Exports (1992): Fmk 107,471,000,000 (metal products and machinery 33.3%; paper, paper products, and publishing 30.3%; chemicals and chemical products 11.3%). *Major export destinations:* Germany 15.6%; Sweden 12.8%; United Kingdom 10.7%; France 6.7%; United States 5.9%; The Netherlands 5.2%; Italy 4.0%.

Transport and communications

Transport. Railroads: route length (1991) 3,646 mi, 5,867 km; passenger-mi 1,645,000,000, passenger-km 2,647,000,000; short ton-mi cargo 5,230,000,000, metric ton-km cargo 7,635,000,000. Roads (1992): total length 47,649 mi, 76,684 km (paved 61%). Vehicles (1991): passenger cars 1,922,541; trucks and buses 273,358. Merchant marine (1992): vessels (100 gross tons and over) 263; total deadweight tonnage 989,270. Air transport (1991)[10]: passenger-mi 6,116,000,000, passenger-km 9,842,000,000; short ton-mi cargo 95,539,000, metric ton-km cargo 139,484,000; airports (1993) 24.
Communications. Daily newspapers (1992): total number 60; total circulation 2,640,381; circulation per 1,000 population 524. Radio (1992): 4,950,000 receivers (1 per 1.0 person). Television (1992): 1,900,000 receivers (1 per 2.7 persons). Telephones (1990): 3,700,000 (1 per 1.3 persons).

Education and health

Education (1990–91)

	schools	teachers	students	student/ teacher ratio
Primary (age 7–15)[11]	4,845	42,601	583,676	13.7
Secondary (age 16–18)[12]	464	6,185	101,625	16.4
Voc. (incl. higher)	593	...	164,249	...
Higher	20	7,788	110,646	14.2

Educational attainment (1991). Percentage of population age 25 and over having: incomplete upper-secondary education 49.4%; complete upper-secondary or vocational 39.3%; some postsecondary 4.5%; undergraduate 2.2%; graduate 4.2%; postgraduate 0.4%. *Literacy:* virtually 100%.
Health (1990): physicians (1991) 12,357 (1 per 406 persons); hospital beds 62,424 (1 per 80 persons); infant mortality rate per 1,000 live births 5.9.
Food (1988–90): daily per capita caloric intake 3,066 (vegetable products 59%, animal products 41%); 113% of FAO recommended minimum requirement.

Military

Total active duty personnel (1992): 32,800 (army 83.2%, navy 7.6%, air force 9.2%). *Military expenditure as percentage of GNP* (1989): 1.6% (world 4.9%); per capita expenditure U.S.$360.

[1]The Evangelical Lutheran and Finnish (Greek) Orthodox churches have special recognition. [2]January 1. [3]Detail does not add to total given because of rounding. [4]Based on land area only. [5]Within metropolitan Helsinki. [6]Excluding calves. [7]1990. [8]February. [9]Import figures are f.o.b. in balance of trade and c.i.f. in commodities and trading partners. [10]Finnair only. [11]Includes lower-secondary. [12]Excludes lower-secondary.

France

Official name: République Française (French Republic).
Form of government: republic with two legislative houses (Parliament; Senate [321], National Assembly [577]).
Chief of state: President.
Head of government: Prime Minister.
Capital: Paris.
Official language: French.
Official religion: none.
Monetary unit: 1 franc (F) = 100 centimes; valuation (Oct. 4, 1993) 1 U.S.$ = F 5.67; 1 £ = F 8.58.

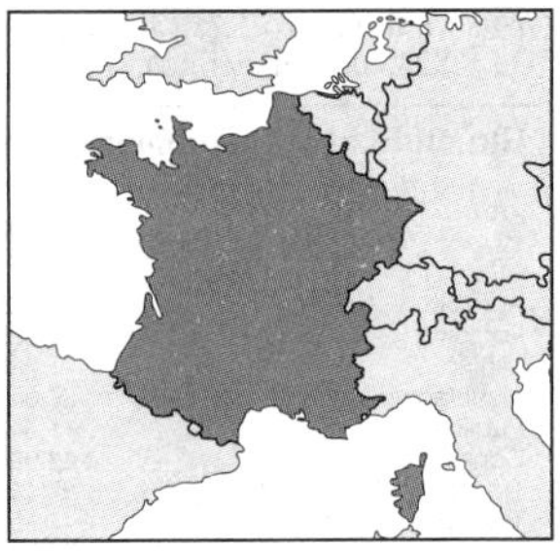

Area and population

		area		population
Regions Departments	Capitals	sq mi	sq km	1992 estimate
Alsace				
Bas-Rhin	Strasbourg	1,836	4,755	962,900
Haut-Rhin	Colmar	1,361	3,525	676,600
Aquitaine				
Dordogne	Périgueux	3,498	9,060	388,700
Gironde	Bordeaux	3,861	10,000	1,232,200
Landes	Mont-de-Marsan	3,569	9,243	314,100
Lot-et-Garonne	Agen	2,070	5,361	306,900
Pyrénées-Atlantiques	Pau	2,952	7,645	585,000
Auvergne				
Allier	Moulins	2,834	7,340	355,300
Cantal	Aurillac	2,211	5,726	157,900
Haute-Loire	Le Puy	1,922	4,977	206,300
Puy-de-Dôme	Clermont-Ferrand	3,077	7,970	597,700
Basse-Normandie				
Calvados	Caen	2,142	5,548	620,300
Manche	Saint-Lô	2,293	5,938	481,500
Orne	Alençon	2,356	6,103	296,600
Bretagne				
Côtes-d'Armor	Saint-Brieuc	2,656	6,878	538,400
Finistère	Quimper	2,600	6,733	839,700
Ille-et-Vilaine	Rennes	2,616	6,775	811,800
Morbihan	Vannes	2,634	6,823	626,000
Bourgogne				
Côte-d'Or	Dijon	3,383	8,763	499,100
Nièvre	Nevers	2,632	6,817	231,400
Saône-et-Loire	Mâcon	3,311	8,575	555,700
Yonne	Auxerre	2,868	7,427	326,000
Centre				
Cher	Bourges	2,793	7,235	323,000
Eure-et-Loir	Chartres	2,270	5,880	403,000
Indre	Châteauroux	2,622	6,791	237,300
Indre-et-Loire	Tours	2,366	6,127	536,000
Loiret	Orléans	2,616	6,775	591,700
Loir-et-Cher	Blois	2,449	6,343	309,200
Champagne-Ardenne				
Ardennes	Charleville-Mézières	2,019	5,229	294,700
Aube	Troyes	2,318	6,004	290,400
Haute-Marne	Chaumont	2,398	6,211	202,900
Marne	Châlons-sur-Marne	3,151	8,162	558,200
Corse				
Corse-du-Sud	Ajaccio	1,550	4,014	119,400
Haute-Corse	Bastia	1,802	4,666	131,900
Franche-Comté				
Doubs	Besançon	2,021	5,234	488,400
Haute-Saône	Vesoul	2,070	5,360	227,600
Jura	Lons-le-Saunier	1,930	4,999	252,400
Territoire de Belfort	Belfort	235	609	135,500
Haute-Normandie				
Eure	Évreux	2,332	6,040	524,800
Seine-Maritime	Rouen	2,424	6,278	1,228,200
Île-de-France				
Essonne	Évry	696	1,804	1,111,500
Hauts-de-Seine	Nanterre	68	176	1,400,500
Paris	Paris	40	105	2,158,300
Seine-et-Marne	Melun	2,284	5,915	1,124,000
Seine-Saint-Denis	Bobigny	91	236	1,399,600
Val-de-Marne	Créteil	95	245	1,227,100
Val-d'Oise	Pontoise	481	1,246	1,080,000
Yvelines	Versailles	882	2,284	1,335,000
Languedoc-Roussillon				
Aude	Carcassonne	2,370	6,139	303,000
Gard	Nîmes	2,260	5,853	598,700
Hérault	Montpellier	2,356	6,101	817,900
Lozère	Mende	1,995	5,167	72,200
Pyrénées-Orientales	Perpignan	1,589	4,116	371,400
Limousin				
Corrèze	Tulle	2,261	5,857	236,300
Creuse	Guéret	2,149	5,565	129,000
Haute-Vienne	Limoges	2,131	5,520	353,500
Lorraine				
Meurthe-et-Moselle	Nancy	2,024	5,241	709,700
Meuse	Bar-le-Duc	2,400	6,216	195,100
Moselle	Metz	2,400	6,216	1,010,000
Vosges	Épinal	2,268	5,874	383,800
Midi-Pyrénées				
Ariège	Foix	1,888	4,890	137,000
Aveyron	Rodez	3,373	8,736	268,000
Gers	Auch	2,416	6,257	175,400
Haute-Garonne	Toulouse	2,436	6,309	952,700
Haute-Pyrénées	Tarbes	1,724	4,464	224,600
Lot	Cahors	2,014	5,217	157,500
Tarn	Albi	2,223	5,758	341,800
Tarn-et-Garonne	Montauban	1,435	3,718	204,000
Nord-Pas-de-Calais				
Nord	Lille	2,217	5,742	2,532,900
Pas-de-Calais	Arras	2,576	6,671	1,436,400
Pays de la Loire				
Loire-Atlantique	Nantes	2,631	6,815	1,065,200
Maine-et Loire	Angers	2,767	7,166	711,800
Mayenne	Laval	1,998	5,175	279,300
Sarthe	Le Mans	2,396	6,206	515,700
Vendée	La Roche-sur-Yon	2,595	6,720	515,000
Picardie				
Aisne	Laon	2,845	7,369	535,200
Oise	Beauvais	2,263	5,860	743,100
Somme	Amiens	2,382	6,170	548,900
Poitou-Charentes				
Charente	Angoulême	2,300	5,956	341,600
Charente-Maritime	La Rochelle	2,650	6,864	531,400
Deux-Sèvres	Niort	2,316	5,999	345,800
Vienne	Poitiers	2,699	6,990	383,100
Provence–Alpes-Côte d'Azur				
Alpes-de-Haute-Provence	Digne	2,674	6,925	133,800
Alpes-Maritimes	Nice	1,660	4,299	997,700
Bouches-du-Rhône	Marseille	1,964	5,087	1,777,900
Hautes-Alpes	Gap	2,142	5,549	115,500
Var	Toulon	2,306	5,973	845,600
Vaucluse	Avignon	1,377	3,567	478,700
Rhône-Alpes				
Ain	Bourg-en-Bresse	2,225	5,762	485,100
Ardèche	Privas	2,135	5,529	279,000
Drôme	Valence	2,521	6,530	420,300
Haute-Savoie	Annecy	1,694	4,388	590,400
Isère	Grenoble	2,869	7,431	1,032,100
Loire	Saint-Étienne	1,846	4,781	747,500
Rhône	Lyon	1,254	3,249	1,526,700
Savoie	Chambéry	2,327	6,028	359,600
TOTAL		210,026	543,965	57,217,600

Demography

Population (1993): 57,690,000.
Density (1993): persons per sq mi 274.7, persons per sq km 106.1.
Urban-rural (1990): urban 74.3%; rural 25.7%.
Sex distribution (1991): male 48.69%; female 51.31%.
Age breakdown (1991): under 15, 20.1%; 15–29, 22.5%; 30–44, 22.7%; 45–59, 15.5%; 60–74, 12.6%; 75 and over, 6.6%.
Population projection: (2000) 59,965,000; (2010) 63,371,000.
Doubling time: not applicable; doubling time exceeds 100 years.
Ethnolinguistic composition (1982): French (mother tongue) 93.2%, of which fully or substantially bilingual in Occitan 2.7%, German (mostly Alsatian) 2.3%, Breton 1.0%, Catalan 0.4%; Arabic 2.6%; other 4.2%.
Religious affiliation (1980): Roman Catholic 76.4%; other Christian 3.7%; atheist 3.4%; Muslim 3.0%; other 13.5%.
Major cities (1990): Paris 2,152,423 (metropolitan area 9,060,257); Marseille 800,550 (1,231,082); Lyon 415,487 (1,262,223); Toulouse 358,688 (608,430); Nice 342,439 (475,507); Strasbourg 252,338 (338,483); Nantes 244,995 (492,-255); Bordeaux 210,336 (685,456); Montpellier 207,996 (236,788).
National origin (1990): French 93.6%, of which Martiniquais 0.2%, Guadeloupian 0.2%, Reunionese 0.2%; Portuguese 1.1%; Algerian 1.1%; Moroccan 1.0%; Italian 0.4%; Spanish 0.4%; Turkish 0.3%; other 2.1%.
Mobility (1990). Population living in same residence as in 1982: 51.4%; same region 89.0%; different region 8.8%; different country 2.2%.
Households (1990). Average household size 2.6; 1 person 27.1%, 2 persons 29.6%, 3 persons 17.7%, 4 persons 15.7%, 5 persons 6.7%, 6 persons or more 3.2%. Family households: 14,118,940 (72.1%); nonfamily 5,471,460 (27.9%, of which 1-person 24.6%).
Immigration (1991): permanent immigrants admitted 65,310 (Morocco 20.6%, Algeria 9.7%, Turkey 9.3%, Tunisia 5.1%, Portugal 1.4%, Yugoslavia 1.3%).

Vital statistics

Birth rate per 1,000 population (1992): 12.9 (world avg. 26.4); (1990) legitimate 69.9%; illegitimate 30.1%.
Death rate per 1,000 population (1992): 9.1 (world avg. 9.2).
Natural increase rate per 1,000 population (1992): 3.8 (world avg. 17.2).
Total fertility rate (avg. births per childbearing woman; 1991): 1.8.
Marriage rate per 1,000 population (1992): 4.7.
Divorce rate per 1,000 population (1990): 1.9.
Life expectancy at birth (1991): male 72.9 years; female 81.1 years.
Major causes of death per 100,000 population (1990): heart disease and other circulatory diseases 307.6; malignant neoplasms (cancers) 250.0; respiratory diseases 67.1; digestive tract diseases 47.7.

Social indicators

Educational attainment (1990). Percentage of population age 25 and over having: primary 22.1%; lower secondary 7.8%; higher secondary and vocational 29.4%; postsecondary 11.6%; undeclared attainment 29.1%.

Distribution of income (1984)

percentage of household income by quintile				
1	2	3	4	5 (highest)
7.1%	12.3%	17.1%	23.2%	40.3%

Quality of working life. Average workweek (1992): 39.1 hours. Annual rate per 100,000 workers (1991) for: injury or accident 5,383 (deaths 7.4); accidents in transit to work 338 (deaths 3.1); industrial illness 16.6[1]; death 4.8[1]. Proportion of labour force insured for damages or income loss resulting from: injury, permanent disability, or death, n.a. Average days lost to labour stoppages per 1,000 workers (1992): 21.0. Average length of journey to work (1990)[2]: 8.7 mi (14 km).
Social deviance. Offense rate per 100,000 population (1990) for: murder 4.4; rape 7.7[1]; other assault 86.5[3]; theft (including burglary and housebreak-

ing) 4,302.7[4]. Incidence per 100,000 in general population of: alcoholism (deaths related to alcoholism; 1985) 63.6; drug and substance abuse, n.a.; suicide (1988) 20.8.
Access to services (1990). Proportion of dwellings having: central heating 78.9%; piped water 99.7%; indoor plumbing 93.5%; natural gas (1982) 48.9%.
Social participation. Eligible voters participating in last (March 1993) national election: 78.0%. Population over 15 years of age participating in voluntary associations: 28.0%.
Leisure (1987–88). Participation rate for favourite leisure activities: watching television 82%; reading magazines 79%; listening to radio 75%; entertaining relatives 64%; visiting relatives 61%; attending fairs/expositions 56%.
Material well-being (1991). Households possessing: automobile 76.8%; television receiver 94.7%, of which colour 89.1%; videocassette recorder 37.1%; refrigerator 97.9%; washing machine 88.4%.

National economy

Gross national product (1992): U.S.$1,278,936,000 (U.S.$22,320 per capita).

Structure of gross domestic product and labour force

	1991[5]			
	in value F '000,000	% of total value	labour force	% of labour force
Agriculture	387,668	5.7	1,839,100	7.5
Mining / Manufacturing	1,255,989	18.4	4,022,900	16.5
Construction	355,635	5.3	1,599,100	6.5
Public utilities	150,962	2.2	162,600	0.7
Transp. and commun.	391,367	5.9	1,302,300	5.2
Trade	1,027,170	15.2	3,936,200	16.1
Finance	286,926	4.2	601,900	2.4
Pub. admin., defense	1,078,848	15.9	5,640,300	23.1
Services	1,570,464	23.3	3,190,100	13.1
Other	261,488[6]	3.9[6]	2,203,000[7]	8.9[7]
TOTAL	6,766,517	100.0	24,497,500	100.0

Budget (1992). Revenue: F 1,440,373,000,000 (value-added taxes 44.0%, direct contributions 38.1%, customs taxes 9.0%). Expenditure (1991): F 1,559,959,000,000 (current expenditures 80.9%, defense 13.0%, capital expenditure 6.1%).

Manufacturing enterprises (1991)

	no. of enter-prises	no. of employees	annual salaries as a % of avg. of all salaries	annual value added (F '000,000)
Food products	55,197	569,100	87	190,443
Electrical machinery	15,620	453,400	118	156,885
Transport equipment	4,293	543,500	108	154,115
Mechanical equipment	32,134	437,900	104	122,101
Iron and steel	27,847	453,000	96	119,642
Petroleum refineries	180	51,400	174	112,454
Printing, publishing	30,359	238,800	125	78,109
Textiles and wearing apparel	29,701	340,900	78	68,417
Rubber products	5,875	210,600	94	55,748
Industrial chemicals	1,442	120,000	128	51,734
Paper and paper products	1,916	104,000	102	34,773
Metal products	442	90,400	103	34,331
Glass products	1,536	54,400	104	17,246
Footwear	4,236	69,500	75	13,877

Production (metric tons except as noted). Agriculture, forestry, fishing (1992): wheat 32,600,000, sugar beets 31,334,000, corn (maize) 14,613,000, barley 10,474,000, grapes 8,514,000, potatoes 6,495,000, apples 2,324,000, sunflower seeds 2,158,000, rapeseed 1,862,000, tomatoes 760,000, oats 690,000, sorghum 577,000, cauliflower 572,000, peaches 520,000, pears 394,000, rye 207,000, soybeans 77,000; livestock (number of live animals) 20,928,000 cattle, 12,384,000 pigs, 10,597,000 sheep, 1,221,000 goats; roundwood (1991) 44,752,000 cu m; fish catch (1991) 812,793. Mining and quarrying (1992): iron ore 5,700,000; potash salts 1,200,000; zinc 16,500[8]; uranium 2,085[8]; gold 83,590 troy oz[8]. Manufacturing (1992): cement 21,600,000; crude steel 18,000,000; pig iron 14,412,000[9]; sulfuric acid 4,187,000[1]; aluminum 636,700; rubber products 521,800[9], of which tires 61,368,000 units[1]; automobiles 3,214,800 units[9]. Construction (dwelling units completed; 1992) 248,400.

Retail trade enterprises (1988)

	no. of enter-prises	no. of employees	weekly wages as a % of all wages	annual turnover (F '000,000)
Large food stores	3,955	356,006	...	470,805
Small food stores	89,024	232,533	...	115,766
butcher shops	43,353	131,099	...	60,835
Clothing stores	72,677	202,405	...	100,163
Pharmacies	21,356	117,955	...	82,089
Department stores	1,492	62,021	...	52,601
Furniture stores	7,757	54,435	...	47,427
Electrical and electronics stores	11,190	59,158	...	36,784
Publishing and paper	22,017	53,373	...	26,035
Gas, coal, and other energy products	3,418	14,855	...	19,426

Energy production (consumption)[10]: electricity (kW-hr; 1991) 454,702,000,000 (401,472,000,000); coal (metric tons; 1991) 12,498,000 (30,389,000); crude petroleum (barrels; 1991) 21,644,000 (550,473,000); petroleum products (metric tons; 1991) 70,380,000 (77,449,000); natural gas (cu m; 1991) 3,376,441,000 (38,701,000,000).
Household income and expenditure. Average household size (1991) 2.6; average annual income per household (1991) F 205,400 (U.S.$37,720). Sources of income (1990): wages and salaries 52.4%, social security 26.1%, self-employment 21.2%; expenditure (1992): housing 20.3%, food and tobacco 18.9%, transportation and communications 16.3%, health 10.0%, recreation 7.6%, clothing 6.2%.

Tourism (1991): receipts from visitors U.S.$21,300,000,000; expenditures by nationals abroad U.S.$12,338,000,000.
Population economically active (1992): total 24,832,000; activity rate of total population 54.7% (participation rates: ages 15–64, 65.5%[1]; female 43.3%; unemployed 9.2%).

Price and earnings indexes (1985 = 100)

	1986	1987	1988	1989	1990	1991	1992
Consumer price index	102.5	105.9	108.8	112.6	116.4	120.2	123.0
Hourly earnings index	104.5	109.4	112.8	118.1	119.9	125.0	129.5

Public debt (1991): F 1,800,600,000,000 (U.S.$319,136,000,000).

Financial aggregates

	1988	1989	1990	1991	1992	1993[11]
Exchange rate, F per:						
U.S. dollar	6.06	5.79	5.13	5.18	5.51	5.67
£	10.96	9.30	9.89	9.67	9.37	8.62
SDR	8.15	7.80	7.30	7.41	7.57	8.03
International reserves (U.S.$)						
Total (excl. gold; '000,000)	25,364	24,611	36,778	31,284	27,028	32,083[12]
SDRs ('000,000)	1,390	1,329	1,283	1,326	163	463
Reserve pos. in IMF ('000,000)	1,615	1,414	1,428	1,666	2,482	2,456
Foreign exchange	22,359	28,910	21,868	28,292	24,384	29,499[12]
Gold ('000,000 fine troy oz)	81.85	81.85	81.85	81.85	81.85	81.89
% world reserves	8.7	8.7	8.7	8.7	8.7	8.7
Interest and prices						
Central bank discount (%)	9.50	9.50	9.50	9.50	9.50	9.50
Govt. bond yield (%)	9.06	8.79	9.96	9.05	8.60	6.33
Industrial share prices (1985 = 100)	162.1	234.9	207.7	220.8	244.2	279.9
Balance of payments (U.S.$'000,000)						
Balance of visible trade	−8,537	−10,651	−13,667	−10,139	1,661	...
Imports, f.o.b.	168,726	181,412	220,339	217,233	223,561	...
Exports, f.o.b.	160,188	170,761	206,672	207,084	225,222	...
Balance of invisibles	3,742	5,031	−105	3,991	1,819	...
Balance of payments, current account	−4,795	−5,620	−13,772	−6,148	3,480	...

Land use (1991): forested 27.0%; meadows and pastures 20.3%; agricultural and under permanent cultivation 35.0%; other 17.7%.

Foreign trade

Balance of trade (current prices)

	1987	1988	1989	1990	1991	1992
F '000,000,000	−30.7	−32.8	−44.2	−51.3	−81.5	−31.1
% of total	1.7%	1.6%	1.9%	2.1%	3.2%	1.3%

Imports (1992): F 1,263,948,000,000 (machinery 24.5%; agricultural products 11.7%; transport equipment 11.0%; fuels 8.5%). *Major import sources:* Germany 18.7%; Italy 10.6%; Belgium-Luxembourg 8.6%; U.S. 8.4%; U.K. 7.7%; Spain 5.4%; The Netherlands 5.1%; Japan 4.1%.
Exports (1992): F 1,248,816,000,000 (machinery 27.2%; agricultural products 16.1%; transport equipment 13.8%, of which automobiles 6.8%). *Major export destinations:* Germany 17.3%; Italy 10.7%; U.K. 9.1%; Belgium-Luxembourg 9.0%; Spain 7.0%; U.S. 6.4%; The Netherlands 4.8%.

Transport and communications

Transport. Railroads (1992): route length 34,074 km; passenger-km 62,990,000,000; metric ton-km cargo 50,370,000,000. Roads (1991): total length 810,000 km (paved [1985] 92%). Vehicles (1991): passenger cars 23,810,000; trucks and buses 5,192,000. Merchant marine (1992): vessels (100 gross tons and over) 729; total deadweight tonnage 4,981,027. Air transport (1992): passenger-km 43,082,000,000; metric ton-km cargo 7,801,300,000; airports (1993) with scheduled flights 62.
Communications. Daily newspapers (1990): number 79; circulation 11,792,000; circulation per 1,000 population 210. Radio (1992): 49,000,000 receivers (1 per 1.2 persons). Television (1992): 29,300,000 receivers (1 per 1.9 persons). Telephones (1987)[13]: 33,357,900 (1 per 1.7 persons).

Education and health

Education (1990–91)

	schools	teachers	students[14]	student/ teacher ratio
Primary (age 6–10)	44,131	309,876	4,110,000	13.1
Secondary (age 11–18) / Voc., teacher tr.	11,325	413,304	5,552,000	13.1
Higher	1,062[15]	53,110	1,839,700	32.0

Literacy (1980): total population literate 41,112,000 (98.8%); males literate 19,933,000 (98.9%); females literate 21,179,000 (98.7%).
Health (1991): physicians 152,096 (1 per 374 persons); hospital beds (1990) 702,184 (1 per 81 persons); infant mortality rate 6.7[14].
Food (1988–90): daily per capita caloric intake 3,593 (vegetable products 61%, animal products 39%); 143% of FAO recommended minimum requirement.

Military

Total active duty personnel (1993): 411,600 (army 58.6%, navy 15.9%, air force 22.0%, other 3.5%). *Military expenditure as percentage of GNP* (1992): 2.7% (world [1989] 4.9%); per capita expenditure U.S.$610.

[1]1989. [2]Distance measured "as the bird flies." [3]Including rape. [4]1991. [5]Although sectoral breakdowns were unavailable, GDP for 1992 grew 1.25%. [6]Includes value-added taxes, customs duties, and imputed bank service charges. [7]Unemployed. [8]Metal content of ores. [9]1990. [10]All energy statistics include Monaco. [11]September, unless otherwise noted. [12]June. [13]Does not include public telephones. [14]1992. [15]1988–89.

Gabon

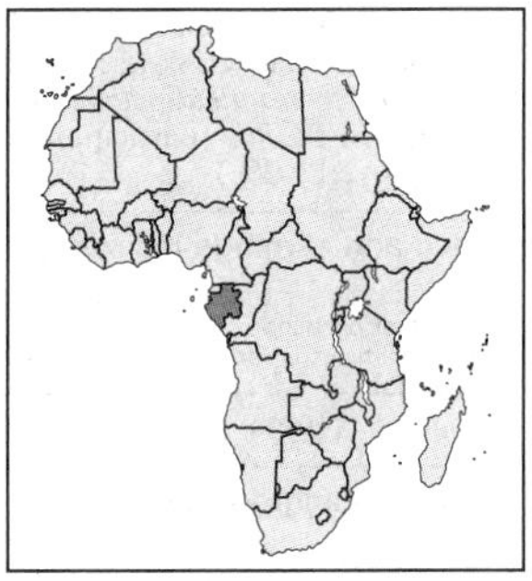

Official name: République Gabonaise (Gabonese Republic).
Form of government: unitary multiparty republic with one legislative house (National Assembly [120]).
Chief of state: President.
Head of government: Prime Minister.
Capital: Libreville.
Official language: French.
Official religion: none.
Monetary unit: 1 CFA franc (CFAF) = 100 centimes; valuation (Oct. 4, 1993) 1 U.S.$ = CFAF 283.25; 1 £ = CFAF 429.12.

Area and population

		area		population
Provinces	Capitals	sq mi	sq km	1978 estimate[1]
Estuaire	Libreville	8,008	20,740	359,000
Haut-Ogooué	Franceville	14,111	36,547	213,000
Moyen-Ogooué	Lambaréné	7,156	18,535	49,000
Ngounié	Mouila	14,575	37,750	118,000
Nyanga	Tchibanga	8,218	21,285	98,000
Ogooué-Ivindo	Makokou	17,790	46,075	53,000
Ogooué-Lolo	Koulamoutou	9,799	25,380	49,000
Ogooué-Maritime	Port-Gentil	8,838	22,890	194,000
Woleu-Ntem	Oyem	14,851	38,465	166,000
TOTAL		103,347[2]	267,667	1,300,000[2]

Demography

Population (1993)[1]: 1,280,000.
Density (1993)[1]: persons per sq mi 12.4, persons per sq km 4.8.
Urban-rural (1990): urban 45.7%; rural 54.3%.
Sex distribution (1990): male 49.23%; female 50.77%.
Age breakdown (1990): under 15, 32.5%; 15–29, 30.4%; 30–44, 15.3%; 45–59, 12.9%; 60–74, 7.3%; 75 and over, 1.6%.
Population projection[1]: (2000) 1,604,000; (2010) 2,052,000.
Doubling time: 26 years.
Ethnic composition (1983): Fang 35.5%; Mpongwe 15.1%; Mbete 14.2%; Punu 11.5%; other 23.7%.
Religious affiliation (1980): Christian 96.2%, of which Roman Catholic 65.2%, Protestant 18.8%, African indigenous 12.1%; traditional religion 2.9%; Muslim 0.8%; other 0.1%.
Major cities (1988): Libreville 352,000; Port-Gentil 164,000; Franceville 75,000.

Vital statistics

Birth rate per 1,000 population (1990–95): 43.4 (world avg. 26.4).
Death rate per 1,000 population (1990–95): 16.0 (world avg. 9.2).
Natural increase rate per 1,000 population (1990–95): 27.4 (world avg. 17.2).
Total fertility rate (avg. births per childbearing woman; 1990): 5.8.
Marriage rate per 1,000 population: n.a.
Divorce rate per 1,000 population: n.a.
Life expectancy at birth (1990–95): male 51.9 years; female 55.2 years.
Major causes of death per 100,000 population: n.a.; however, major diseases include malaria, measles, shigellosis (infection with dysentery), trypanosomiasis, and tuberculosis.

National economy

Budget (1993). Revenue: CFAF 398,500,000,000 (customs duties and other current revenues 46.0%; oil revenues 41.9%; loans and grants 12.1%). Expenditures: CFAF 398,500,000,000 (current expenditure 78.8%, of which running costs 58.7%, public debt 20.1%; capital expenditure 21.2%).
Public debt (external, outstanding; 1991): U.S.$2,935,000,000.
Tourism (1991): receipts from visitors U.S.$8,000,000; expenditures by nationals abroad U.S.$152,000,000.
Production (metric tons except as noted). Agriculture, forestry, fishing (1992): roots and tubers 447,000, cassava 260,000, plantains 245,000, sugarcane 160,000, corn (maize) 24,000, peanuts (groundnuts) 16,000, bananas 9,000, palm oil 5,000, cacao beans 2,000, coffee 2,000; livestock (number of live animals) 170,000 sheep, 164,000 pigs, 82,000 goats, 29,000 cattle, 2,000,000 chickens; roundwood (1991) 4,286,000 cu m; fish catch (1991) 22,000. Mining and quarrying (1991): manganese 1,600,000; uranium 710[3]. Manufacturing (1989): cement 117,000; flour 25,976; refined sugar 20,905; beer 460,200 hectolitres; soft drinks 297,200 hectolitres; cigarettes 17,800,000 packs[4]; textiles CFAF 2,420,000,000[4]. Construction: n.a. Energy production (consumption): electricity (kW-hr; 1991) 914,000,000 (914,000,000); crude petroleum (barrels; 1991) 132,903,000 (17,495,000); petroleum products (metric tons; 1991) 640,000 (438,000); natural gas (cu m; 1991) 305,931,000 (305,931,000); fuelwood (cu m; 1991) 2,653,000 (2,653,000).
Land use (1991): forested 77.5%; meadows and pastures 18.2%; agricultural and under permanent cultivation 1.8%; other 2.5%.
Population economically active (1992): total 534,000; activity rate of total population 43.2% (participation rates [1985]: ages 15–64, 68.2%; female 38.4%; unemployed, n.a.).

Price and earnings indexes (1985 = 100)

	1986	1987	1988	1989	1990	1991	1992
Consumer price index	102.3	104.6	109.7	103.2	111.1	118.7	100.8
Earnings index	...	...	...	...	...	...	...

Gross national product (at current market prices; 1992): U.S.$5,380,000,000 (U.S.$4,480 per capita).

Structure of gross domestic product and labour force

	1990		1988	
	in value CFAF '000,000	% of total value	labour force	% of labour force
Agriculture, forestry, fishing	123,200	11.4	326,400	69.0
Mining	518,400	47.8	61,900	13.1
Manufacturing	54,500	5.0		
Construction	67,800	6.2		
Public utilities	23,400	2.2		
Transportation and communications	88,100	8.1	84,700	17.9
Trade	131,100	12.1		
Finance; Pub. admin., defense; Services; Other, including taxes on imports	78,200[5]	7.2[5]		
TOTAL	1,084,600[2]	100.0	473,000	100.0

Household income and expenditure. Average household size (1980) 4.0; income per household: n.a.; sources of income (1983): private sector 73.4%, public sector 26.6%; expenditure (1983)[6]: food and tobacco 54.7%, clothing and footwear 17.5%, housing 13.0%, transportation and communications 6.3%.

Foreign trade

Balance of trade (current prices)

	1989	1990	1991	1992
CFAF '000,000	+279,000	+466,000	+397,000	+384,000
% of total	37.0%	52.6%	45.7%	45.5%

Imports (1992): CFAF 230,000,000,000 (1989; machinery and mechanical equipment 29.2%, food and agricultural products 14.6%, transport equipment 12.5%, manufactured products 12.1%, metal and metal products 11.2%, chemical products 5.4%, mining products 1.6%). *Major import sources:* France 50.0%; United States 9.0%; Japan 7.0%; other EEC 22.0%; Africa 5.0%.
Exports (1992): CFAF 614,000,000,000 (crude petroleum and petroleum products 80.0%, wood 9.0%, manganese ore and concentrate 7.0%, uranium ore and concentrate 2.0%). *Major export destinations* (1989): France 36.2%; United States 26.1%; The Netherlands 6.2%; Japan 3.3%; Côte d'Ivoire 2.9%; Italy 2.3%.

Transport and communications

Transport. Railroads (1993): length 414 mi, 668 km; passenger-mi 21,000,000[7], passenger-km 34,000,000[7]; short ton-mi cargo 126,000,000[7], metric ton-km cargo 184,000,000[7]. Roads (1987): total length 4,286 mi, 6,898 km (paved 11%). Vehicles (1991): passenger cars 23,000; trucks and buses 17,000. Merchant marine (1992): vessels (100 gross tons and over) 29; total deadweight tonnage 30,186. Air transport (1990)[8]: passenger-mi 276,679,000, passenger-km 445,273,000; short ton-mi cargo 17,863,000, metric ton-km cargo 26,079,000; airports (1993) with scheduled flights 17.
Communications. Daily newspapers (1990): total number 1; total circulation 20,000; circulation per 1,000 population 17. Radio (1992): total number of receivers 250,000 (1 per 5.0 persons). Television (1992): total number of receivers 40,000 (1 per 31 persons). Telephones (1991): 19,000 (1 per 64 persons).

Education and health

Education (1987)

	schools	teachers	students	student/ teacher ratio
Primary	992	4,229	195,049	46.1
Secondary	51[9]	1,512	32,922	21.8
Voc., teacher tr.	29[9]	759	15,352	20.2
Higher[10, 11]	1	363	2,896	8.0

Educational attainment: n.a. *Literacy* (1990): total population age 15 and over literate 60.7%; males literate 73.5%; females literate 48.5%.
Health (1984): physicians 565 (1 per 2,000 persons); hospital beds 10,980 (1 per 103 persons); infant mortality rate per 1,000 live births (1990–95) 94.0.
Food (1984–86): daily per capita caloric intake 2,700 (vegetable products 88%, animal products 12%); (1984) 104% of FAO recommended minimum requirement.

Military

Total active duty personnel (1993): 4,750 (army 68.4%, navy 10.5%, air force 21.1%), not including 500 French troops. *Military expenditure as percentage of GNP* (1989): 4.5% (world 4.9%); per capita expenditure U.S.$132.

[1]Population distribution is based on country estimate, which is substantially higher than estimates from external sources (such as the United Nations and the World Bank), which form the basis of the 1993 estimate. [2]Detail does not add to total given because of rounding. [3]1990. [4]1984. [5]Less imputed bank service charges. [6]Libreville only. [7]1987. [8]Air Gabon only. [9]1984–85. [10]Universities only. [11]1988.

Gambia, The

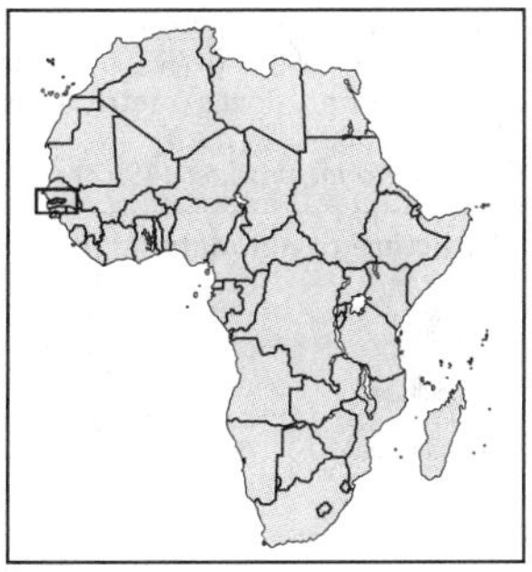

Official name: Republic of The Gambia.
Form of government: multiparty republic with one legislative house (House of Representatives [50[1]]).
Head of state and government: President.
Capital: Banjul.
Official language: English.
Official religion: none.
Monetary unit: 1 dalasi (D) = 100 butut; valuation (Oct. 4, 1993) 1 U.S.$ = D 9.33; 1 £ = D 14.14.

Area and population

Divisions	Capitals	area sq mi	area sq km	population 1983 census[2]
Kombo St. Mary[3, 4]	Kanifing	29	76	101,504
Lower River	Mansakonko	625	1,618	55,263
MacCarthy Island	Kuntaur/Georgetown	1,117	2,894	126,004
North Bank	Kerewan	871	2,256	112,225
Upper River	Basse	799	2,069	111,388
Western	Brikama	681	1,764	137,245
City				
Banjul[4]	—	5	12	44,188
TOTAL		4,127	10,689	687,817

Demography

Population (1993): 1,033,000.
Density (1993)[5]: persons per sq mi 284.8, persons per sq km 109.9.
Urban-rural (1988): urban 21.5%; rural 78.5%.
Sex distribution (1993): male 50.16%; female 49.84%.
Age breakdown (1990): under 15, 44.1%; 15–29, 24.8%; 30–44, 16.1%; 45–59, 10.1%; 60 and over, 4.9%.
Population projection: (2000) 1,227,000; (2010) 1,546,000.
Doubling time: 28 years.
Ethnic composition (1983): Malinke 40.4%; Fulani 18.7%; Wolof 14.6%; Dyola 10.3%; Soninke 8.2%; other 7.8%.
Religious affiliation (1983): Muslim 95.4%; Christian 3.7%; traditional beliefs and other 0.9%.
Major cities/urban areas (1986): Serekunda 102,600[3]; Banjul 44,188[4, 6] (Greater Banjul 145,692[4, 6]); Brikama 24,300; Bakau 23,600[3]; Farafenni 10,168[6].

Vital statistics

Birth rate per 1,000 population (1990–95): 44.9 (world avg. 26.4); legitimate, n.a.; illegitimate, n.a.
Death rate per 1,000 population (1990–95): 19.5 (world avg. 9.2).
Natural increase rate per 1,000 population (1990–95): 25.4 (world avg. 17.2).
Total fertility rate (avg. births per childbearing woman; 1990–95): 6.2.
Marriage rate per 1,000 population: n.a.
Divorce rate per 1,000 population: n.a.
Life expectancy at birth (1990–95): male 43.4 years; female 46.6 years.
Major causes of death per 100,000 population: n.a.; however, major infectious diseases include malaria, gastroenteritis and dysentery, pneumonia and bronchitis, measles, schistosomiasis, and whooping cough.

National economy

Budget (1991–92). Revenue: D 827,000,000 (tax revenue 71.5%, of which import duties and excises 62.4%, income taxes 9.0%; nontax revenue and grants 28.5%). Expenditures: D 704,400,000 (administrative expenses 31.1%; goods and services 23.4%; interest payments 21.2%; transportation and communications 11.2%; agriculture 5.8%; public services 4.6%; education and culture 3.5%).
Production (metric tons except as noted). Agriculture, forestry, fishing (1992): peanuts (groundnuts) 80,000, millet 65,000, corn (maize) 24,000, paddy rice 22,000, seed cotton 7,000, cassava 6,000, pulses (mostly beans) 4,000, palm oil 2,500, palm kernels 2,000; livestock (number of live animals) 400,000 cattle, 150,000 goats, 121,000 sheep; roundwood (1991) 940,000 cu m; fish catch (1991) 23,743, of which inland water 2,500, Atlantic Ocean 21,243. Mining and quarrying: sand and gravel are excavated for local use. Manufacturing (value of production in D '000; 1982): processed food, including peanut and palm-kernel oil 62,878; beverages 10,546; textiles 3,253; chemicals and related products 1,031; nonmetals 922; printing and publishing 358; leather 150. Construction: n.a. Energy production (consumption): electricity (kW-hr; 1990) 67,000,000 (67,000,000); coal, none (none); crude petroleum, none (none); petroleum products (metric tons; 1990) none (61,000); natural gas, none (none).
Population economically active (1983): total 325,623; activity rate of total population 47.3% (participation rates: ages 15–64 78.2%; female 46.3%; unemployed, n.a.).

Price and earnings indexes (1985 = 100)

	1986	1987	1988	1989	1990	1991	1992
Consumer price index	156.6	193.4	216.0	233.9	262.5	285.0	312.1
Daily earnings index[7]	104.6	90.2	...	...	...	...	...

Tourism: receipts from visitors (1991) U.S.$26,000,000; expenditures by nationals abroad (1990) U.S.$8,000,000.
Household income and expenditure. Average household size (1983) 8.3; income per household: n.a.; sources of income: n.a.; expenditure (1986)[8]: food and beverages 58.0%, clothing and footwear 17.5%, energy and water 5.4%, housing 5.1%, education, health, transportation and communications, recreation, and other 14.0%.
Public debt (external, outstanding; 1991): U.S.$307,300,000.
Gross national product (at current market prices; 1992): U.S.$362,000,000 (U.S.$390 per capita).

Structure of gross domestic product and labour force

	1991–92[9] in value D'000,000	1991–92[9] % of total value	1983 labour force	1983 % of labour force
Agriculture	113.6	23.3	239,940	73.7
Mining	—	—	66	0.0
Manufacturing	30.7	6.3	8,144	2.5
Construction	31.8	6.5	4,373	1.3
Public utilities	3.2	0.7	1,233	0.4
Transportation and communications	84.8	17.4	8,014	2.5
Trade	114.7	23.6	16,551	5.1
Finance	33.9	7.0	4,577	1.4
Public administration	57.7	11.8	8,295	2.5
Services	16.7	3.4	9,381	2.9
Other	—	—	25,049[10]	7.7[10]
TOTAL	487.1	100.0	325,623	100.0

Land use (1991): forested 15.0%; meadows and pastures 9.0%; agricultural and under permanent cultivation 18.0%; built-on area, wasteland, and other 58.0%.

Foreign trade[11]

Balance of trade (current prices)

	1986	1987	1988	1989	1990	1991
D '000,000	−497.0	−615.9	−530.7	−1,023.0	−1,252.4	−1,292.0
% of total	51.3%	52.3%	40.6%	72.1%	66.1%	63.9%

Imports (1990–91): D 1,759,374,000 (food 30.4%; basic manufactures 18.1%; machinery and transport equipment 14.7%; mineral fuels and lubricants 10.7%; chemicals and related products 6.8%). *Major import sources* (1990): United Kingdom 17.2%, China 13.9%; France 10.9%, Germany 8.5%; Hong Kong 8.5%; Belgium-Luxembourg 5.7%.
Exports (1990–91): D 332,189,000 (reexports 59.1%[12]; domestic exports 40.9%, of which peanuts 12.4%, fish and fish preparations 9.1%, peanut meal 1.9%). *Major export destinations* (1990): Belgium-Luxembourg 44.8%; New Zealand 35.4%; Guinea 4.0%; United Kingdom 3.0%; France 3.0%; Switzerland 2.4%.

Transport and communications

Transport. Railroads: none. Roads (1990): total length 1,483 mi, 2,386 km (paved 32%). Vehicles (1990): passenger cars 6,500; trucks and buses 1,500. Merchant marine (1992): vessels (100 gross tons and over) 11; total deadweight tonnage 2,029. Air transport (1990): passenger arrivals and departures 199,350; cargo 2,233 metric tons; airports (1993) with scheduled flights 1.
Communications. Daily newspapers (1991): total number 1; total circulation 1,000; circulation per 1,000 population 1.1. Radio (1992): total number of receivers 180,000 (1 per 5.2 persons). Television: none. Telephones (1991): 11,000 (1 per 80 persons).

Education and health

Education (1990–91)

	schools	teachers	students	student/ teacher ratio
Primary (age 8–14)	233	2,757	86,101	31.2
Secondary (age 15–21)	14	279	6,434	26.1
Secondary vocational	18	477	13,966	29.3
Postsecondary[13]	9	177	1,489	8.4

Educational attainment (1973). Percentage of population age 20 and over having: no formal schooling 90.8%; primary education 6.2%; secondary 2.6%; higher 0.4%. *Literacy* (1990): total population age 15 and over literate 27.2%; males literate 39.0%; females literate 16.0%.
Health (1990–91): physicians 61 (1 per 14,536 persons); hospital beds 601 (1 per 1,475 persons); infant mortality rate per 1,000 live births (1990–95) 132.
Food (1988–90): daily per capita caloric intake 2,290 (vegetable products 94%, animal products 6%); 96% of FAO recommended minimum requirement.

Military

Total active duty personnel (1992): 800. *Military expenditure as percentage of GNP* (1989): 0.7% (world 4.9%); per capita expenditure U.S.$1.

[1]Includes 5 indirectly elected chiefs and 9 nonelective seats; excludes the speaker of the House of Representatives, who may be elected from outside its membership. [2]Preliminary. [3]Kombo St. Mary includes the urban areas of Serekunda and Bakau. [4]Kombo St. Mary and Banjul city make up Greater Banjul. [5]Based on land area, which is 8,613 sq km (3,325 sq mi). [6]1983. [7]December; nonagricultural employees only. [8]Low-income population in Banjul and Kombo St. Mary only; weights of consumer price index components. [9]At factor cost in constant prices of 1976–77. [10]Not adequately defined. [11]Imports c.i.f.; exports f.o.b. [12]Mostly unofficial trade with Senegal. [13]1984–85.

Georgia

Official name: Sakartvelos Respublikis (Republic of Georgia).
Form of government: unitary multiparty republic with a single legislative body (Parliament [235]).
Head of state: Chairman of State Council (president).
Head of government: Prime Minister.
Capital: Tbilisi.
Official language: Georgian.
Official religion: none.
Monetary unit: (until April 5, 1993) 1 ruble = 100 kopecks; valuation (Oct. 4, 1993) free rate, U.S.$ = 1,165 rubles; 1 £ = 1,765 rubles. Georgian coupon[1] introduced April 5, 1993, at par with Russian ruble and circulated parallel with it; on August 20, the Georgian coupon became sole legal tender, floating against all currencies; valuation not available.

Area and population

Autonomous republics	Capitals	area sq mi	area sq km	population 1991[2] estimate
Abkhazia	Sukhumi	3,300	8,600	533,800
Adzharia	Batumi	1,200	3,000	381,500
Autonomous region				
South Ossetia[3]	Tskhinvali	1,500	3,900	} 4,548,900
Regions under republican jurisdiction	—	20,900	54,200	}
TOTAL		26,900	69,700	5,464,200

Demography

Population (1993): 5,493,000.
Density (1993): persons per sq mi 204.1, persons per sq km 78.8.
Urban-rural (1991): urban 55.8%; rural 44.2%.
Sex distribution (1991): male 47.6%; female 52.4%.
Age breakdown (1989): under 15, 24.8%; 15–29, 24.1%; 30–44, 19.2%; 45–59, 17.5%; 60–74, 10.8%; 75 and over, 3.6%.
Population projection: (2000) 5,569,000; (2010) 5,680,000.
Doubling time: 77 years.
Ethnic composition (1989): Georgian 70.1%; Armenian 8.1%; Russian 6.3%; Azerbaijani 5.7%; Ossetes 3.0%; Greek 1.9%; Abkhazian 1.8%; other 3.1%.
Religious affiliation: believers are predominantly Georgian Orthodox (65%); minorities include Muslims (11%), Russian Orthodox (10%), and Armenian Orthodox (8%).
Major cities (1991): Tbilisi 1,283,000; Kutaisi 238,200; Rustavi 161,900; Batumi 137,500; Sukhumi 120,000.

Vital statistics

Birth rate per 1,000 population (1990): 17.0 (world avg. 27.1); (1989) legitimate 82.3%; illegitimate 17.7%.
Death rate per 1,000 population (1990): 8.4 (world avg. 9.8).
Natural increase rate per 1,000 population (1990): 8.6 (world avg. 17.3).
Total fertility rate (avg. births per childbearing woman; 1989): 2.1.
Marriage rate per 1,000 population (1989): 7.2.
Divorce rate per 1,000 population (1989): 1.3.
Life expectancy at birth (1991): male 68.7 years; female 76.1 years.
Major causes of death per 100,000 population (1989): diseases of the circulatory system 553.2; diseases of the respiratory system 513.0; malignant neoplasms (cancers) 98.6; accidents, poisoning, and violence 58.2; diseases of the digestive system 32.1; infectious and parasitic diseases 13.5; endocrine and metabolic disorders 12.0; diseases of the nervous system 4.1.

National economy

Budget (1992). Revenue: 18,872,000,000 rubles (profit tax 37.6%, value-added tax 26.3%, individual income tax 10.5%, turnover tax 4.5%). Expenditures: 42,672,000,000 rubles (national economy 48.7%, social and cultural affairs 28.8%, government administration 15.3%, other 6.9%).
Production (metric tons except as noted). Agriculture, forestry, fishing (1992): fruit (other than grapes) 1,090,000, vegetables (other than potatoes) 880,000, grapes 550,000, milk 500,000, corn (maize) 210,000, potatoes 200,000, wheat 180,000, barley 59,000, sugarbeets 16,000, sunflower seeds 14,000, soybeans 6,000; livestock (number of live animals) 1,500,000 sheep, 1,100,000 cattle, 850,000 pigs, 20,000,000 poultry; roundwood, n.a.; fish catch (1990) 104,000. Mining and quarrying (1991): manganese ore 491,000. Manufacturing (1991): crude steel 961,700; rolled ferrous metals 818,100; rolled steel 817,900; cast iron 500,800; steel tubes 452,800; canned food 385,300; mineral fertilizers 134,500; meat and sausage 43,900; synthetic resins and plastics 26,400; synthetic fibres 20,000; soap 6,900; bricks 170,600,000 pieces; cement tiles 12,600,000 pieces; footwear 13,300,000 pairs; knitwear 24,300,000 units; colour television sets 39,200 units; machine tools 1,417 units; prefabricated concrete structures 1,451,000 cu m; ceramic tiles 348,300 cu m; silk fabrics 27,100,000 sq m; cotton fabrics 16,700,000 sq m; wool fabrics 6,100,000 sq m; carpets 500,000 sq m; grape wine 1,261,600 hectolitres; beer 600,100 hectolitres; cognac 146,000 hectolitres; vodka and liqueurs 77,400 hectolitres. Construction (1990): 1,313,000,000,000 rubles. Energy production (consumption): electricity (kW-hr; 1991) 13,376,000,000 (n.a.); coal (metric tons; 1991) 698,000 (n.a.); crude petroleum (barrels; 1992) 897,000 (n.a.); petroleum products (metric tons; 1991) 2,215,400 (n.a.); natural gas (cu m; 1991) 44,900,000 (n.a.).
Gross national product (1992): U.S.$4,670,000,000 (U.S.$850 per capita)[4].

Structure of net material product and labour force

	1992 in value '000,000 rubles	1992 % of total value	1991 labour force	1991 % of labour force
Agriculture	21,934	29.4	682,200	27.1
Mining	}		...	...
Manufacturing	} 25,407	34.1	487,700	19.4
Public utilities	}		110,100	4.4
Construction	5,813	7.8	224,800	9.0
Transportation and communications	15,288	20.5	103,500	4.1
Trade	1,720	2.3	227,000	9.0
Finance	—	—	12,000	0.5
Public administration, defense	—	—	48,100	1.9
Services	—	—	538,900	21.5
Other	4,393	5.9	79,700	3.1
TOTAL	74,555	100.0	2,514,000	100.0

Population economically active (1991): total 2,514,000; activity rate of total population 45.9% (participation rates [1990]: ages 16–59 [male], 16–54 [female] 91.1%; female [1989] 45.9%; unemployed [1989] 3.5%).

Price and earnings indexes (1985 = 100)

	1986	1987	1988	1989	1990	1991
Consumer price index	100.0	...	...	...	...	...
Monthly earnings index	101.8	105.7	111.4	126.4	144.4	206.6

Land use (1990): forested 0.4%; meadows and pastures 28.6%; agricultural and under permanent cultivation 1.2%; other 69.8%.
Household income and expenditure. Average household size (1989) 4.1; income per household: n.a.; sources of income (1988): wages and salaries 71.4%, pensions and stipends 10.8%, income from personal plots 7.3%, other 10.5%; expenditure (1988): food and beverages 38.3%, clothing and footwear 14.8%, social and cultural 9.2%, furniture and household utensils 5.9%, building materials 2.0%, utilities 0.3%.

Foreign trade

Balance of trade (current prices)

	1988	1989	1990	1991
'000,000 rubles	−592	−385	−855	−1,154
% of total	4.8%	3.1%	6.7%	8.6%

Imports (1991): 7,266,000,000 rubles (machinery and equipment 18.4%, light-industry products 16.5%, food 14.6%, oil and gas 9.6%, chemicals 9.6%, ferrous metals 4.1%, nonferrous metallurgical products 3.3%). *Major import sources:* former Soviet republics 89.6%; other countries 10.4%.
Exports (1991): 6,112,000,000 rubles (food 34.5%, light-industry products 19.3%, machinery and metalworking equipment 13.7%, ferrous metallurgy 5.8%, chemicals 3.5%, building materials 1.1%). *Major export destinations:* former Soviet republics 98.0%; other countries 2.0%.

Transport and communications

Transport. Railroads (1990): length 976 mi, 1,570 km; (1989) passenger-mi 10,600,000, passenger-km 17,000,000; cargo traffic, n.a. Roads (1989): length 21,000 mi, 33,900 km (paved 87%). Vehicles (1988): passenger cars 427,400; trucks and buses, n.a. Merchant marine: vessels (1,000 gross tons and over) 54; total deadweight tonnage 1,108,068. Air transport (1989): passenger-mi 3,290,500,000, passenger-km 5,295,600,000; short ton-mi cargo, n.a., metric ton-km cargo, n.a.; airports (1993) with scheduled flights 1.
Communications. Daily newspapers (1989): total number 147; total circulation 3,677,000; circulation per 1,000 population 671. Radio and television (1990): total number of receivers 3,760,000 (1 per 1.5 persons). Telephones (1991): 1,047,000 (1 per 5.2 persons).

Education and health

Education (1989–90)

	schools	teachers	students	student/ teacher ratio
Primary (age 6–13)	} 3,788	...	924,700	...
Secondary (age 14–17)	}			
Voc., teacher tr.	...	...	...	...
Higher	19	...	93,100	...

Educational attainment (1989). Percentage of population age 25 and over having: primary education or no formal schooling 12.3%; some secondary 15.2%; completed secondary and some postsecondary 57.4%; higher 15.1%.
Health (1990): physicians 32,100 (1 per 170 persons); hospital beds 60,000 (1 per 90 persons); infant mortality rate per 1,000 live births 15.9.
Food: daily per capita caloric intake, n.a.

Military

Total active duty personnel (1993): 13,000 (army, n.a., navy, n.a., air force, n.a.). *Military expenditure as percentage of GNP:* n.a.; per capita expenditure, n.a.

[1]Interim currency unit until its eventual replacement by a new national currency, the lari, when the economic situation has stabilized. [2]January 1. [3]In December 1990 the Supreme Soviet of the Republic of Georgia abolished the South Ossetian autonomous oblast. [4]Ruble-area GNP and exchange-rate data are very speculative.

Germany

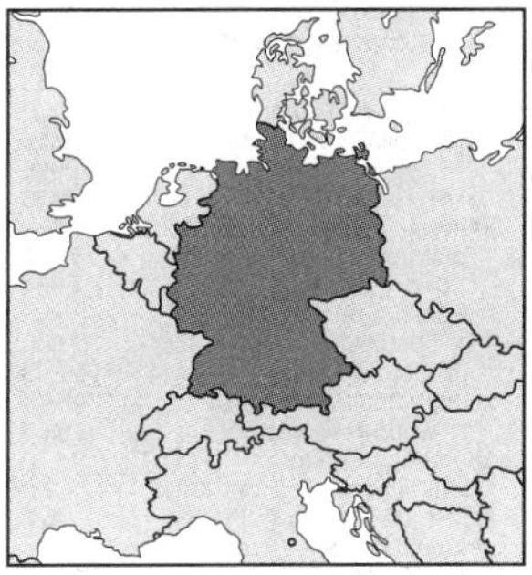

Official name: Bundesrepublik Deutschland (Federal Republic of Germany).
Form of government: federal multiparty republic with two legislative houses (Federal Council [69]; Federal Diet [662]).
Chief of state: President.
Head of government: Chancellor.
Seat of government: Bonn (Berlin is capital-designate).
Official language: German.
Official religion: none.
Monetary unit: 1 Deutsche Mark (DM) = 100 Pfennige; valuation (Oct. 4, 1993) 1 U.S.$ = DM 1.62; 1 £ = DM 2.46.

Area and population

States Administrative districts	Capitals	area sq mi	area sq km	population 1992 estimate
Baden-Württemberg	Stuttgart	13,804[1]	35,751[1]	10,001,900
Freiburg	Freiburg	3,613	9,357	2,012,900
Karlsruhe	Karlsruhe	2,671	6,919	2,577,300
Stuttgart	Stuttgart	4,076	10,558	3,751,200
Tübingen	Tübingen	3,443	8,918	1,660,500
Bayern	Munich	27,241	70,554[1]	11,596,000
Mittelfranken	Ansbach	2,798	7,246	1,621,500
Niederbayern	Landshut	3,989	10,331	1,093,000
Oberbayern	Munich	6,768	17,529	3,848,200
Oberfranken	Bayreuth	2,792	7,231	1,084,000
Oberpfalz	Regensburg	3,742	9,691	1,020,400
Schwaben	Augsburg	3,858	9,993	1,655,500
Unterfranken	Würzburg	3,294	8,532	1,273,400
Berlin	—	343	889	3,446,000
Brandenburg	Potsdam	11,219	29,053	2,542,700
Bremen	Bremen	156	404	683,700
Hamburg	Hamburg	292	755	1,668,800
Hessen	Wiesbaden	8,152[1]	21,114	5,837,400
Darmstadt	Darmstadt	2,875	7,445	3,596,100
Giessen	Giessen	2,078	5,381	1,016,100
Kassel	Kassel	3,200	8,288	1,225,200
Mecklenburg-Vorpommern	Schwerin	9,111	23,598	1,891,700
Niedersachsen	Hannover	18,287[1]	47,364[1]	7,475,800
Braunschweig	Braunschweig	3,126	8,097	1,655,400
Hannover	Hannover	3,493	9,048	2,081,700
Lüneburg	Lüneburg	5,891	15,260	1,512,400
Weser-Ems	Oldenburg	5,775	14,958	2,226,300
Nordrhein-Westfalen	Düsseldorf	13,155[1]	34,070	17,509,900
Arnsberg	Arnsberg	3,088	7,999	3,758,900
Detmold	Detmold	2,516	6,517	1,924,800
Düsseldorf	Düsseldorf	2,042	5,288	5,253,200
Köln	Köln	2,844	7,365	4,068,100
Münster	Münster	2,664	6,901	2,504,900
Rheinland-Pfalz	Mainz	7,664	19,846	3,821,300
Koblenz	Koblenz	3,125	8,093	1,422,600
Rheinhessen-Pfalz	Mainz	2,637	6,830	1,909,600
Trier	Trier	1,902	4,923	489,100
Saarland	Saarbrücken	992	2,570	1,076,900
Sachsen	Dresden	7,080	18,338	4,678,900
Sachsen-Anhalt	Magdeburg	7,893	20,443	2,823,300
Schleswig-Holstein	Kiel	6,074	15,731	2,648,500
Thüringen	Erfurt	6,275	16,251	2,572,100
TOTAL		137,735[1]	356,733[1]	80,274,900

Demography

Population (1993): 81,187,000.
Density (1993): persons per sq mi 589.4, persons per sq km 227.9.
Urban-rural (1990): urban 85.3%; rural 14.7%.
Population projection: (2000) 85,646,000; (2010) 92,444,000.
Major cities (1991): Berlin 3,437,900; Hamburg 1,660,700; Munich 1,236,500; Cologne 955,500; Frankfurt am Main 647,200; Essen 626,100; Dortmund 599,900; Stuttgart 583,700; Düsseldorf 576,700; Duisburg 536,700; Hannover 514,400; Leipzig 507,800.

Other principal cities (1991)

	population		population		population
Aachen	243,200	Heidelberg	138,000	Oberhausen	224,000
Augsburg	258,300	Heilbronn	116,200	Offenbach am	
Bergisch		Herne	178,400	Main	115,200
Gladbach	104,100	Hildesheim	105,400	Oldenburg	143,800
Bielefeld	320,000	Ingolstadt	106,400	Osnabrück	164,000
Bochum	397,400	Karlsruhe	276,500	Paderborn	122,700
Bonn	294,300	Kassel	194,800	Pforzheim	113,600
Bottrop	118,700	Kiel	246,600	Potsdam	139,500
Braunschweig	258,500	Koblenz	108,800	Recklingshausen	125,500
Bremerhaven	130,800	Krefeld	245,000	Regensburg	122,300
Chemnitz	291,400	Leverkusen	161,000	Remscheid	123,400
Cottbus	124,900	Lübeck	215,200	Reutlingen	104,300
Darmstadt	139,500	Ludwigshafen		Rostock	246,600
Dresden	488,000	am Rhein	163,700	Saarbrücken	191,500
Erfurt	207,200	Magdeburg	277,200	Salzgitter	144,800
Erlangen	102,600	Mainz	180,800	Schwerin	126,800
Freiburg		Mannheim	312,000	Siegen	109,800
im Breisgau	191,600	Moers	105,000	Solingen	165,600
Furth	104,400	Mönchenglad-		Ulm	111,000
Gelsenkirchen	293,400	bach	260,700	Wiesbaden	261,800
Gera	128,000	Mülheim		Witten	105,300
Göttingen	122,700	an der Ruhr	177,200	Wolfsburg	129,200
Hagen	214,100	Münster	261,400	Wuppertal	383,900
Halle an der Saale	307,200	Neuss	147,200	Würzburg	128,000
Hamm	180,100	Nürnberg	494,900	Zwickau	113,600

Sex distribution (1992): male 48.38%; female 51.62%.
Age breakdown (1992): under 15, 14.6%; 15–29, 21.3%; 30–44, 22.4%; 45–59, 19.9%; 60–74, 14.8%; 75 and over, 7.0%.
Doubling time: not applicable; doubling time exceeds 100 years.
Ethnic composition (by nationality; 1990): German 93.4%; Turkish 2.1%, of which Kurdish 0.5%; Yugoslav 0.8%; Italian 0.7%; Greek 0.4%; Polish 0.4%; Spanish 0.2%; other 2.1%.
Religious affiliation: (former West Germany; 1987) Roman Catholic 42.9%; Lutheran-Reformed and Lutheran traditions 41.6%; Muslim 2.7%; Reformed tradition 0.6%; Jewish 0.1%; other 12.9%; (former East Germany; 1990) Protestant 47.0%; Roman Catholic 7.0%; unaffiliated and other 46.0%.
Households (1990). Number of households 34,827,000; average household size 2.3; 1 person 33.7%, 2 persons 30.2%, 3 persons 17.5%, 4 persons 13.4%, 5 or more persons 5.2%.

Vital statistics

Birth rate per 1,000 population (1991): 10.4 (world avg. 26.4); legitimate 84.9%; illegitimate 15.1%.
Death rate per 1,000 population (1991): 11.4 (world avg. 9.2).
Natural increase rate per 1,000 population (1991): –1.0 (world avg. 17.2).
Total fertility rate (avg. births per childbearing woman; 1990)[2]: 1.5.
Marriage rate per 1,000 population (1990): 5.7.
Divorce rate per 1,000 population (1991): 1.7.
Life expectancy at birth: (former West Germany; 1988–90) male 72.6 years; female 79.0 years; (former East Germany; 1989): male 70.1 years; female 76.4 years.
Major causes of death per 100,000 population (1991): diseases of the circulatory system 543.1; malignant neoplasms (cancers) 258.3, of which stomach, colon, and rectum 57.6, bronchial, lung, and tracheal 42.7; diseases of the respiratory system 64.5, of which pneumonia 20.2, chronic bronchitis 18.2; chronic liver disease and cirrhosis 23.8.

Social indicators

Educational attainment (1989)[2]. Percentage of population age 25 and over having: less than full primary education 0.9%; primary and lower (junior) secondary 67.2%; primary and intermediate secondary 17.7%; vocational postsecondary and certification for higher education 14.2%, of which postsecondary vocational degree 6.6%, university graduates (all levels) 5.7%.
Quality of working life[2]. Average workweek (1992): 39.0 hours. Annual rate per 100,000 workers (1986) for: injuries or accidents at work 5,911; deaths, including commuting accidents, 8.0. Proportion of labour force insured for damages or income loss resulting from: injury, virtually 100%; permanent disability, virtually 100%; death, virtually 100%. Average days lost to labour stoppages per 1,000 workers (1992): 3.8.

Distribution of income (1984)[2]

percentage of household income by quintile

1	2	3	4	5 (highest)
6.8	12.7	17.8	24.0	38.7

Access to services[2]. Proportion of dwellings (1987) having: electricity, virtually 100%; piped water supply, virtually 100%; flush sewage disposal 98.3%; public fire protection, virtually 100%.
Social participation. Eligible voters participating in last (December 1990) national election 77.8%. Trade union membership in total workforce (1991): 29.4%. Practicing religious population (1991): 4% of Protestants and 21% of Catholics "regularly" attend religious services.
Social deviance (1990)[2]. Offense rate per 100,000 population for: murder and manslaughter 4; sexual abuse 59, of which child molestation 20, rape and forcible sexual assault 14; robbery 56; assault and battery 106; larceny 4,258. Incidence per 100,000 in general population (late 1970s) of: alcoholism 2,500 to 3,000; drug and substance abuse 650; suicide 19[4].
Material well-being (1992)[2]. Households possessing: automobile 81.4%; telephone 97.4%; colour television receiver 96.1%; refrigerator, virtually 100%; washing machine 94.4%; home freezer 70.1%.

Recreational and leisure activities

(Monthly household expenditures, 1992; median income)[2]

Activity	DM	percentage
Vacations	195	26.6
Expenditures for motor vehicles	95	12.9
Sporting and camping equipment and sporting events	94	12.8
Televisions, radios, and their fees	89	12.2
Books, newspapers, and magazines	55	7.5
Gardening and pets	46	6.3
Games and toys	36	4.9
Photographic and moviemaking equipment and film	19	2.6
Visits to theatre and cinema	17	2.3
Tools	7	1.0
Other activities	80	10.9
TOTAL	733	100.0

National economy

Budget (1992). Revenue: DM 1,483,293,000,000 (1990; taxes 54.9%, social-security contributions 39.3%). Expenditures: DM 1,610,907,000,000 (1990; current transfers 43.0%, consumption 41.1%, debt interest payments 5.9%).
Total national debt (1993[3]): DM 651,180,000,000.
Production (value of production in DM except as noted; 1991–92). Agriculture[2], forestry, fishing: cereal grains 5,572,000,000, fruits 2,757,000,000, flowers and ornamental plants 2,300,000,000, sugar beets 2,099,000,000, grapes for wine 2,049,000,000, potatoes 1,477,000,000, vegetables 1,411,000,000, nurseries 1,350,000,000, oilseed crops 1,277,000,000; livestock:

13,411,000,000 dairy cattle, 10,483,000,000 pigs, 8,026,000,000 beef cattle, 1,732,000,000 chicken eggs, 1,273,000,000 poultry; roundwood (1991) 44,874,000 cu m; fish catch (metric tons; 1991) 241,615. Mining and quarrying (metric tons; 1992): potash 37,300,000; iron ore 184,000; zinc 11,800; lead 1,600. Manufacturing (value added at factor cost in DM; 1992): capital equipment 288,667,000,000, of which machinery 70,805,000,000, electrical equipment 78,903,000,000, transport equipment 60,985,000,000; chemicals (including pharmaceuticals) 54,671,000,000; food and beverages 27,642,000,000; calculators and computers 23,008,000,000; plastics and other synthetic products 19,016,000,000; iron founding 14,447,000,000; furniture and other wood products 14,347,000,000; stone and ceramic products 12,525,000,000; printing and copy machines 12,345,000,000; textiles 9,578,000,000; precision instruments 9,102,000,000; paper and cardboard products 6,881,000,000; office equipment 6,398,000,000; clothing 5,417,000,000; musical instruments and toys 3,131,000,000; fine pottery and ceramic products 2,162,000,000. Construction (1991): residential 36,153,000 sq m; nonresidential 39,420,000 sq m.

Service enterprises (1991)

	no. of enter-prises	no. of employees	weekly wage as a % of all wages	annual turnover (DM '000,000)
Gas	151	37,000	...	42,228
Water	183	40,000	...	3,443
Electrical power	462	296,000	...	147,076
Transport				
air	133	57,390	...	20,270
buses	6,054	192,869	...	12,586
rail	1	416,199	...	14,697
shipping	1,449	9,076	...	...
Communications				
press	2,452	240,075	...	31,096
film[5]	615	3,000	...	836
Postal services	17,616[6]	652,573	...	68,346
Hotels and restaurants	135,141	652,251	...	60,257
Wholesale trade	36,605[6]	1,214,000	...	1,015,984
Retail trade	152,629	2,241,000	...	605,755

Energy production (consumption): electricity (kW-hr; 1991) 573,752,000,000 (575,052,000,000); hard coal (metric tons; 1991) 183,460,000 (189,091,000); lignite (metric tons; 1991) 385,350,000 (387,246,000); crude petroleum (barrels; 1991) 24,676,000 (665,478,000); petroleum products (metric tons; 1991) 86,864,000 (113,008,000); natural gas (cu m; 1991) 16,133,000,000 (68,817,000,000).

Manufacturing, mining, and construction enterprises (1991)

	no. of enter-prises	no. of tradesmen and professionals	wages as a % of avg. of all wages[7]	annual gross production value (DM '000,000)
Manufacturing	44,178	8,988,000	101.4	2,021,973
of which				
Road motor vehicles	2,158	980,000	112.1	290,861
Machinery (nonelectric)	6,302	1,381,000	105.5	227,783
Machinery and appliances (electric)	3,505	1,132,000	103.1	231,862
Chemical	1,382	722,000	127.7	207,637
Food and beverages	4,697	644,000	84.5	211,519
Petroleum and natural gas	60	8	160.5	8
Calculators, computers	2,431	381,000	92.4	68,812
Plastics	2,248	302,000	87.0	61,325
Iron and steel	126	230,000	105.6	52,188
Textiles	1,390	289,000	101.2	42,522
Wood and wood products	2,569	261,000	86.5	44,854
Mining and quarrying	101	287,000	107.1	39,485
Construction	19,373	1,338,000	83.8	179,773

Gross national product (at current market prices; 1992): U.S.$2,098,720,000,000 (U.S.$26,180 per capita).

Structure of gross domestic product and labour force

	1992			
	in value DM '000,000	% of total value	labour force	% of labour force
Agriculture	32,810	1.2	925,000	3.0
Public utilities, mining	74,600	2.7	451,000	1.5
Manufacturing	783,490	27.9	8,941,000	29.4
Construction	161,280	5.7	1,928,000	6.3
Transp. and commun.	150,880	5.4	1,666,000	5.5
Trade	232,870	8.3	3,985,000	13.1
Finance, real estate	356,310	12.7	940,000	3.1
Services	527,930	18.8	5,838,000	19.2
Pub. admin., defense	288,730	10.3	4,399,000	14.4
Other (productive)	70,290	2.5	1,377,000	4.5
Other (accounting)	127,600	4.5	—	—
TOTAL	2,806,790	100.0	30,450,000	100.0

Population economically active (1992): total 40,087,000; activity rate of total population 49.9% (participation rates: ages 15–64, 60.0%; female 42.0%; unemployed [1992] 6.6%).

Price and earnings indexes (1985 = 100)

	1987	1988	1989	1990	1991	1992	1993[9]
Consumer price index	100.1	101.4	104.2	107.0	110.7	116.5	119.7
Hourly earnings index	107.6	112.1	116.5	122.5	130.2	149.5	152.1

Household income and expenditure[2]. Average household size (1991) 2.3; average annual income per household (1992) DM 74,076 (U.S.$47,485); sources of take-home income (1992): wages 81.7%, self-employment 10.2%, transfer payments 8.1%; expenditure (1992): food 14.5%, rent 13.5%, household operations and maintenance 8.2%, entertainment and education 6.8%, transportation 5.7%, clothing and footwear 4.9%.

Land use (1991): forest 29.7%; pasture 15.3%; agriculture 33.8%; other 21.2%.

Financial aggregates[10]

	1987	1988	1989	1990	1991	1992	1993 (Sept.)
Exchange rate, DM per:							
U.S. dollar	1.5815	1.7803	1.6978	1.4940	1.5160	1.6140	1.6199
£	2.9598	3.2215	2.7258	2.8804	2.8360	2.4404	2.4472
SDR	2.2436	2.3957	2.2312	2.1255	2.1685	2.2193	2.2977
International reserves (U.S.$)							
Total (excl. gold; '000,000)	78,756	58,528	60,709	67,902	63,001	90,967	85,343
SDRs ('000,000)	1,964	1,857	1,804	1,880	1,917	841	968
Reserve pos. in IMF ('000,000)	3,900	3,346	3,043	3,056	3,567	4,239	4,139
Foreign exchange	72,893	53,324	55,862	62,967	57,517	85,877	80,236
Gold ('000,000 fine troy oz)	95.18	95.18	95.18	95.18	95.18	95.18	95.18
% world reserves	10.05	10.04	10.10	10.12	10.13	10.22[9]	...
Interest and prices							
Central bank discount (%)	2.5	3.5	6.0	6.0	8.0	8.3	7.3[11]
Govt. bond yield (%)	5.8	6.1	7.1	8.9	8.6	7.7	6.5[11]
Industrial share prices (1985 = 100)[12]	124.5	104.0	133.0	152.8	135.8	115.0	124.7[11]
Balance of payments (U.S.$'000,000,000)							
Balance of visible trade	+70.21	+79.78	+77.74	+71.70	+23.53	32.86	...
Imports, f.o.b.	208.28	228.85	247.22	319.61	354.49	374.03	...
Exports, f.o.b.	278.49	308.63	324.96	391.31	378.02	406.89	...
Balance of invisibles	−23.92	−29.13	−20.09	−25.44	−43.01	−58.43	...
Balance of payments, current account	+46.28	+50.65	+57.65	+46.27	−19.48	−25.56	...

Tourism (1991)[2]: receipts from visitors U.S.$10,947,000,000; expenditures by nationals abroad U.S.$31,650,000,000.

Foreign trade

Balance of trade (current prices)[2]

	1987	1988	1989	1990	1991	1992
DM '000,000,000	+127.88	+139.23	+147.85	+118.90	+15.31	+29.46
% of total	13.8%	13.9%	13.0%	9.9%	1.2%	2.7%

Imports (1992)[2]: DM 627,950,000,000 (machinery and transport equipment 34.6%, of which transport equipment 10.0%, electrical machinery other than office equipment 8.0%, office equipment 4.5%; chemicals and chemical products 8.6%, of which organic chemical products 2.0%, unfabricated plastics 1.7%; food and beverages 8.5%, of which fruits and vegetables 3.1%, meat and meat products 1.6%, milk and milk products 0.9%; mineral fuels 7.3%, of which crude petroleum and petroleum products 5.6%, natural gas 1.4%; clothing and wearing apparel 6.1%; thread, yarn, and finished spinning goods 3.0%; iron and steel 3.0%). *Major import sources:* France 12.1%; The Netherlands 9.6%; Italy 9.2%; Belgium-Luxembourg 7.1%; United Kingdom 6.9%; United States 6.7%; Japan 6.0%; Austria 4.4%; Switzerland 4.0%.

Exports (1992)[2]: DM 657,410,000,000 (machinery and transport equipment 49.6%, of which transport equipment 16.6%, electrical machinery other than office equipment 8.9%, office equipment 2.2%; chemicals and chemical products 12.6%, of which organic chemical products 2.6%, unfabricated plastics 2.2%, medical and pharmaceutical products 1.7%). *Major export destinations:* France 13.1%; Italy 9.4%; The Netherlands 8.4%; United Kingdom 7.8%; Belgium-Luxembourg 7.5%; United States 6.6%; Austria 6.0%; Switzerland 5.4%; Spain 4.2%; Japan 2.2%; Sweden 2.2%.

Transport and communications

Transport. Railroads (1991): length 56,813 mi, 91,432 km; passengers carried 1,530,000,000; passenger-mi 35,439,000,000, passenger-km 57,034,000,000; short ton-mi cargo 56,315,000,000, metric ton-km cargo 82,219,000,000. Roads (1989)[2]: total length 308,614 mi, 496,652 km (paved 99%). Vehicles (1991): passenger cars 32,007,000; trucks and buses 1,619,000. Merchant marine (1992): vessels (100 gross tons and over) 1,574; total deadweight tonnage 5,636,000. Air transport (1990): passengers carried 253,788,000; passenger-mi 71,030,000,000, passenger-km 114,312,000,000; short ton-mi cargo 3,020,000,000, metric ton-km cargo 4,410,000,000; airports (1993) with scheduled flights 40.

Communications. Daily newspapers (1991)[2]: total number 352; total circulation 25,427,000; circulation per 1,000 population 402. Radio (1992): 35,302,000 receivers (1 per 2.3 persons). Television (1992): 31,516,000[2, 13] receivers (1 per 2.5 persons). Telephones (1990): 43,636,000 (1 per 1.8 persons).

Education and health

Education (1991–92)

	schools	teachers	students	student/ teacher ratio
Primary (age 6–10) / Secondary (age 10–19)	42,315	611,338	9,142,565	14.9
Voc., teacher tr.[14]	8,110	116,343	2,557,881	22.0
Higher	318	171,025[2]	1,827,229	10.7[2]

Health (1992): physicians 251,877 (1 per 319 persons); dentists 56,342 (1 per 1,425 persons); hospital beds 665,565 (1 per 121 persons); infant mortality rate per 1,000 live births 6.8.

Food (1988–90): daily per capita caloric intake 3,522 (vegetable products 65%, animal products 35%); 132% of FAO recommended minimum requirement.

Military

Total active duty personnel (1993): 408,200 (army 70.3%, navy 7.6%, air force 22.1%). *Military expenditure as percentage of GNP* (1992): 1.6% (world 5.0%); per capita expenditure U.S.$416.

[1]Detail does not add to total given because of rounding. [2]Former West Germany only. [3]August. [4]1987. [5]1984. [6]1990. [7]1989. [8]Data withheld for reasons of confidentiality. [9]September. [10]End-of-period figures unless footnoted otherwise. [11]Through June. [12]Period averages. [13]Data include officially registered sets only. [14]1991.

Ghana

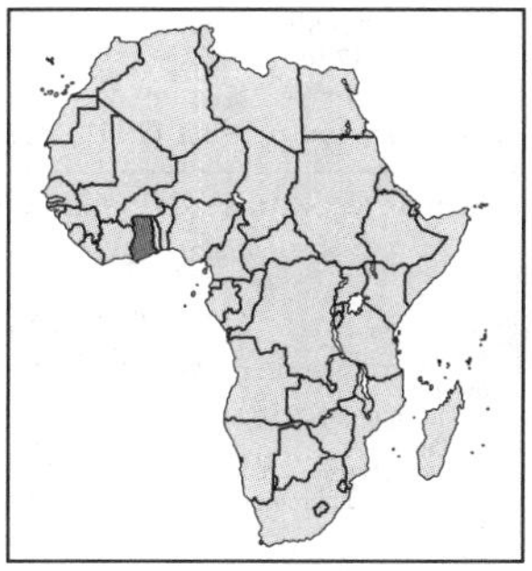

Official name: Republic of Ghana.
Form of government: unitary multiparty republic with one legislative house (House of Parliament [200])[1].
Head of state and government: President.
Capital: Accra.
Official language: English.
Official religion: none.
Monetary unit: 1 cedi (₵) = 100 pesewas; valuation (Oct. 4, 1993) 1 U.S.$ = ₵659.97; 1 £ = ₵999.85.

Area and population		area		population
				1988[2]
Regions	Capitals	sq mi	sq km	estimate
Ashanti	Kumasi	9,417	24,389	2,308,100
Brong-Ahafo	Sunyani	15,273	39,557	1,332,200
Central	Cape Coast	3,794	9,826	1,262,200
Eastern	Koforidua	7,461	19,323	1,855,800
Greater Accra	Accra	1,253	3,245	1,580,000
Northern	Tamale	27,175	70,384	1,285,900
Upper East	Bolgatanga	3,414	8,842	853,200
Upper West	Wa	7,134	18,476	483,600
Volta	Ho	7,942	20,570	1,338,200
Western	Sekondi-Takoradi	9,236	23,921	1,278,300
TOTAL		92,098[3]	238,533	13,577,500

Demography

Population (1993): 15,636,000.
Density (1993): persons per sq mi 169.8, persons per sq km 65.5.
Urban-rural (1990): urban 33.0%; rural 67.0%.
Sex distribution (1990): male 49.64%; female 50.36%.
Age breakdown (1990): under 15, 46.8%; 15–29, 26.2%; 30–44, 14.4%; 45–59, 8.0%; 60–74, 3.8%; 75 and over, 0.8%.
Population projection: (2000) 18,733,000; (2010) 24,253,000.
Doubling time: 23 years.
Ethnolinguistic composition (1983): Akan 52.4%; Mossi 15.8%; Ewe 11.9%; Ga-Adangme 7.8%; Gurma 3.3%; Yoruba 1.3%; other 7.5%.
Religious affiliation (1980): Christian 62.6%, of which Protestant 27.9%, Roman Catholic 18.7%, African indigenous 16.0%; traditional beliefs 21.4%; Muslim 15.7%, of which Aḥmadīyah 7.9%; other 0.3%.
Major cities (1988): Accra 949,100; Kumasi 385,200; Tamale 151,100; Tema 110,000; Sekondi-Takoradi 103,600.

Vital statistics

Birth rate per 1,000 population (1990–95): 43.2 (world avg. 26.4); legitimate, n.a.; illegitimate, n.a.
Death rate per 1,000 population (1990–95): 12.3 (world avg. 9.2).
Natural increase rate per 1,000 population (1990–95): 30.9 (world avg. 17.2).
Total fertility rate (avg. births per childbearing woman; 1990–95): 6.1.
Life expectancy at birth (1990–95): male 54.2 years; female 57.8 years.
Major causes of death per 100,000 population: n.a.; however, major infectious diseases include malaria, tuberculosis, leprosy, trypanosomiasis (sleeping sickness), and onchocerciasis (river blindness).

National economy

Budget (1993). Revenue: ₵667,400,000,000 (excise and value-added taxes 43.9%, of which petroleum tax 32.5%; import-export duties 25.6%; income and property taxes 11.5%; divestiture of government assets 8.2%). Expenditures: ₵652,100,000,000 (1990; current expenditures 79.1%, of which education 25.5%, debt service 10.7%, health 10.1%, social security and welfare 7.2%, defense 3.5%, transportation and communications 1.3%; capital expenditures 20.9%).
Production (metric tons except as noted). Agriculture, forestry, fishing (1992): roots and tubers 6,200,000 (of which cassava 4,000,000, taro 1,200,000, yams 1,000,000), bananas and plantains 1,204,000, cereals 970,000 (of which corn [maize] 580,000, sorghum 210,000, rice 100,000, millet 80,000), cacao 280,000, coconuts 220,000, green peppers 160,000, sugarcane 110,000, peanuts (groundnuts) 100,000, oranges 50,000, palm kernels 34,000, lemons and limes 30,000, pulses 20,000; livestock (number of live animals) 2,600,000 sheep, 2,500,000 goats, 1,400,000 cattle, 500,000 pigs, 11,000,000 chickens; roundwood (1991) 17,122,000 cu m; fish catch (1991) 364,959 (of which anchovies 74,668). Mining and quarrying (1991): bauxite 324,313; manganese ore 319,777; gold 26,310 kg; diamonds 687,736 carats. Manufacturing (1990): cement 678,600; kerosene, gasoline, and diesel fuel 526,100; wheat flour 108,422; soap 35,065; cocoa cake, cocoa butter, and cocoa liquor 23,208; margarine 3,560; iron rods 382; toothpaste 213; textiles 29,500,000 metres; soft drinks 3,350,000 hectolitres; beer 628,000 hectolitres; evaporated milk 208,000 hectolitres; ice cream 9,930 hectolitres; cigarettes 1,805,000,000 units. Construction (value added in ₵'000; 1988): 26,446,700. Energy production (consumption): electricity (kW-hr; 1991) 6,108,688,000 ([1990] 5,003,000,000); coal (metric tons; 1990) none (3,000); crude petroleum (barrels; 1990) none (7,433,000); petroleum products (metric tons; 1990) 503,000 (609,000); natural gas, none (n.a.).
Household income and expenditure. Average household size (1983) 4.9; average annual income per household (1978) ₵9,600 (U.S.$[4]); sources of income: n.a.; expenditure (1978): food and beverages 57.4%, clothing and footwear 14.3%, housing and energy 11.5%, transportation and communications 3.3%, health care 1.3%.

Gross national product (1991): U.S.$6,176,000,000 (U.S.$400 per capita).

Structure of gross domestic product and labour force	1990		1984	
	in value ₵'000,000	% of total value	labour force	% of labour force
Agriculture	972,323.8	47.9	3,310,967	59.4
Mining	35,824.2	1.8	26,828	0.5
Manufacturing	187,523.9	9.2	588,418	10.5
Construction	62,210.7	3.1	64,686	1.2
Public utilities	36,612.4	1.6	15,437	0.3
Transp. and commun.	89,417.2	4.4	122,806	2.2
Trade	385,808.8	19.0	792,147	14.2
Finance	78,421.2	3.9	27,475	0.5
Pub. admin., defense	172,012.8	8.5	97,548	1.7
Services	2,158.4	0.1	376,168	6.7
Other	9,372.9[5]	0.5[5]	157,624[6]	2.8[6]
TOTAL	2,031,686.3	100.0[3]	5,580,104	100.0

Tourism (1992): receipts from visitors U.S.$169,000,000; expenditures by nationals abroad U.S.$13,000,000[7].
Population economically active (1984): total 5,580,104; activity rate of total population 45.4% (participation rates: over age 15, 82.5%; female 51.2%; unemployed 2.8%).

Price and earnings indexes (1985 = 100)	1986	1987	1988	1989	1990	1991	1992
Consumer price index	124.6	174.2	228.8	286.5	393.2	464.1	510.8
Monthly earnings index	167.3	258.4	...	...	...	...	...

Public debt (external, outstanding; 1991): U.S.$2,958,000,000.
Land use (1991): forested 35.1%; meadows and pastures 22.0%; agricultural and under permanent cultivation 12.0%; other 30.9%.

Foreign trade

Balance of trade (current prices)	1984	1985	1986	1987	1988	1989
₵'000,000	+637.1	−4,070.0	+11,578.0	+7,594.0	+32,080	−49,087
% of total	1.6%	5.8%	8.1%	2.6%	8.5%	8.2%

Imports (1989): ₵346,218,000,000 (1987; machinery and transport equipment 28.1%; mineral fuels and lubricants 14.0%; chemicals 12.0%; food and live animals 5.2%; beverages and tobacco 0.4%). *Major import sources* (1987): United Kingdom 41.4%; Nigeria 13.2%; West Germany 11.5%; United States 11.1%; Japan 4.3%; France 3.8%.
Exports (1989): ₵274,784,000,000 (1986; food and live animals 60.4%, of which cocoa 53.9%; logs and sawn timber 17.9%; gold 15.5%; manganese ore 1.1%; industrial diamonds 0.7%). *Major export destinations* (1987): United Kingdom 27.0%; United States 18.6%; The Netherlands 13.5%; U.S.S.R. 9.2%; Japan 9.0%; West Germany 8.3%.

Transport and communications

Transport. Railroads (1990): route length 592 mi, 953 km; passenger-mi 172,400,000, passenger-km 277,500,000; short ton-mi cargo 86,920,000, metric ton-km cargo 126,900,000. Roads (1992): total length 22,800 mi, 36,700 km (paved 20%). Vehicles (1989): passenger cars 57,897; trucks and buses 30,125. Merchant marine (1992): vessels (100 gross tons and over) 155; total deadweight tonnage 130,977. Air transport (1990): passenger-mi 253,270,000, passenger-km 407,600,000; short ton-mi cargo 45,753,000, metric ton-km cargo 66,798,000; airports (1993) with scheduled flights 3.
Communications. Daily newspapers (1992): total number 3; total circulation 240,000; circulation per 1,000 population 23. Radio (1992): 3,593,920 receivers (1 per 4.2 persons). Television (1992): 250,000 receivers (1 per 60 persons). Telephones (1989): 77,105 (1 per 189 persons).

Education and health

Education (1989–90)	schools	teachers	students	student/ teacher ratio
Primary (6–12)	9,831	62,859	1,703,074	27.1
Secondary (13–20)[8]	5,415	45,429	793,388	17.5
Voc., teacher tr.[8]	58	2,317	30,221	13.0
Higher	3	700	9,274	13.2

Educational attainment (1984). Percentage of population age 25 and over having: no formal schooling 60.4%; primary education 7.1%; middle school 25.4%; secondary 3.5%; vocational and other postsecondary 2.9%; higher 0.6%. *Literacy* (1990): total population age 15 and over literate 4,960,000 (60.4%); males literate 2,835,000 (70.0%); females literate 2,125,000 (50.9%).
Health: physicians (1989) 628 (1 per 22,452 persons); hospital beds (1991) 18,477 (1 per 791 persons); infant mortality rate per 1,000 live births (1985–90) 90.
Food (1988–90): daily per capita caloric intake 2,144 (vegetable products 95%, animal products 5%); 93% of FAO minimum recommended requirement.

Military

Total active duty personnel (1993): 6,850 (army 73.0%, navy 12.4%, air force 14.6%). *Military expenditure as percentage of GNP* (1989): 0.6% (world 4.9%); per capita expenditure U.S.$2.

[1]Many opposition parties boycotted the December 1992 elections. [2]January 1. [3]Detail does not add to total given because of rounding. [4]Unofficial 1978 exchange rate (7.5 to 9.9 times the official rate) does not permit meaningful conversion into other currencies. [5]Import duties less imputed bank service charges. [6]Unemployed only. [7]1990. [8]1988–89.

Greece

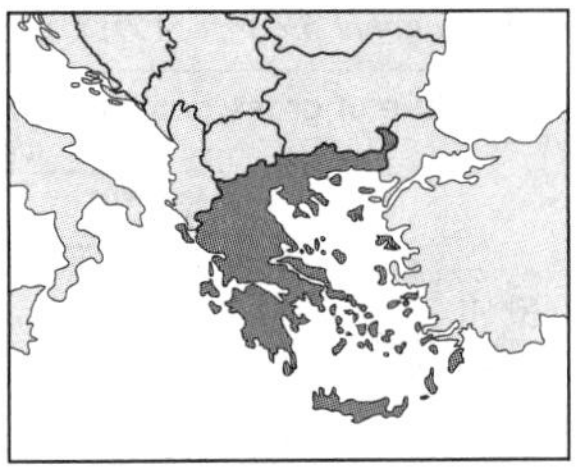

Official name: Ellinikí Dimokratía (Hellenic Republic).
Form of government: unitary multiparty republic with one legislative house (Greek Chamber of Deputies [300]).
Chief of state: President.
Head of government: Prime Minister.
Capital: Athens.
Official language: Greek.
Official religion: Eastern Orthodox.
Monetary unit: 1 drachma (Dr) = 100 lepta; valuation (Oct. 4, 1993) 1 U.S.$ = Dr 234.28; 1 £ = Dr 354.94.

Area and population

Regions		area sq mi	area sq km	population 1991 census
Anatolikí Makedhonía kai Thráki	(Eastern Macedonia and Thrace)	5,466	14,157	570,261
Attikí	(Attica)	1,470	3,808	3,522,769
Dhytikí Ellás	(Western Greece)	4,382	11,350	702,027
Dhytikí Makedhonía	(Western Macedonia)	3,649	9,451	292,751
Iónioi Nísoi	(Ionian Islands)	891	2,307	191,003
Ípiros	(Epirus)	3,553	9,203	339,210
Kedrikí Makedhonía	(Central Macedonia)	7,393	19,147	1,737,623
Kríti	(Crete)	3,218	8,336	536,980
Nótion Aiyaíon	(Southern Aegean)	2,041	5,286	257,522
Pelopónnisos	(Peloponnesos)	5,981	15,490	605,663
Stereá Ellás	(Central Greece)	6,004	15,549	578,876
Thessalía	(Thessaly)	5,420	14,037	731,230
Vóreion Aiyaíon	(Northern Aegean)	1,481	3,836	198,241
TOTAL		50,949	131,957	10,264,156

Demography

Population (1993): 10,310,000.
Density (1993): persons per sq mi 202.4, persons per sq km 78.1.
Urban-rural (1990): urban 62.5%; rural 37.5%.
Sex distribution (1991): male 49.00%; female 51.00%.
Age breakdown (1990): under 15, 19.3%; 15–29, 22.1%; 30–44, 20.1%; 45–59, 18.9%; 60–74, 13.5%; 75 and over, 6.1%.
Population projection: (2000) 10,493,000; (2010) 10,518,000.
Doubling time: not applicable; doubling time exceeds 100 years.
Ethnic composition (1983): Greek 95.5%; Macedonian 1.5%; Turkish 0.9%; Albanian 0.6%; other 1.5%.
Religious affiliation (1980): Christian 98.1%, of which Eastern Orthodox 97.6%, Roman Catholic 0.4%, Protestant 0.1%; Muslim 1.5%; other 0.4%.
Major cities (1991): Athens 748,110; Thessaloníki 377,951; Piraiévs 169,622; Pátrai 155,180; Peristérion 145,854.

Vital statistics

Birth rate per 1,000 population (1992): 10.1 (world avg. 26.4); legitimate 96.1%; illegitimate 3.9%.
Death rate per 1,000 population (1992): 9.5 (world avg. 9.2).
Natural increase rate per 1,000 population (1992): 0.6 (world avg. 17.2).
Total fertility rate (avg. births per childbearing woman; 1990–95): 1.5.
Marriage rate per 1,000 population (1991): 6.2.
Divorce rate per 1,000 population (1990): 0.6.
Life expectancy at birth (1990): male 74.6 years; female 79.8 years.
Major causes of death per 100,000 population (1991): malignant neoplasms (cancers) 196.5; cerebrovascular disease 184.5; diseases of pulmonary circulation and other forms of heart disease 164.8; ischemic heart disease 116.8.

National economy

Budget (1991). Revenue: Dr 5,962,851,000,000[1] (indirect and excise taxes 39.5%, direct taxes 16.9%, European Community 0.9%). Expenditures: Dr 6,071,220,000,000 (1989; health and social insurance 20.4%, defense 10.2%, education and culture 9.0%, police and other sectors 2.6%).
Public debt (1991): U.S.$15,380,000,000.
Tourism (1991): receipts from visitors U.S.$2,566,000,000; expenditures by nationals abroad U.S.$1,011,000,000.
Production (metric tons except as noted). Agriculture, forestry, fishing (1991): sugar beets 3,350,000, wheat 2,750,000, tomatoes 1,990,000, corn (maize) 1,700,000, grapes 1,300,000, potatoes 1,100,000, olives 1,050,000, oranges 703,000, barley 500,000, cotton 190,000, tobacco 178,000, onions 150,000, rice 127,000; livestock (number of live animals) 9,759,000 sheep, 5,918,000 goats, 1,143,000 pigs, 634,000 cattle, 145,000 asses, 27,000,000 chickens; roundwood 2,345,000 cu m; fish catch (1990) 128,867. Mining and quarrying (1991): bauxite 2,133,521; nickel ore 2,072,000; iron ore 474,700[2, 3]; zinc ore 57,500[3]; lead ore 44,030[3]; manganese 11,500[3, 4]. Manufacturing (value added in Dr; 1991): food, beverages, and tobacco 459,832,000,000; chemicals 327,896,000,000; textiles 210,042,000,000; paper and printing 161,741,000,000; transport equipment 148,072,000,000; clothing and footwear 104,690,000,000. Construction (authorized; 1990): residential 46,434,236 cu m; nonresidential 12,535,570 cu m. Energy production (consumption): electricity (kW-hr; 1990) 35,002,000,000 (35,713,000,000); coal (metric tons; 1990) 51,896,000 (53,119,000); crude petroleum (barrels; 1990) 5,549,000 (105,449,000); petroleum products (metric tons; 1990) 15,464,000 (13,165,000); natural gas (cu m; 1990) 101,278,000 (101,278,000).
Household income and expenditure. Average household size (1988) 3.1; income per household (1982) Dr 252,300 (U.S.$3,777); sources of income (1990): property and entrepreneurial income 43.0%, wages and salaries 39.5%, transfer payments 17.5%; expenditure (1990): food, beverages, and tobacco 37.9%, transportation 14.3%, housing 9.0%, clothing and footwear 8.7%, other 30.1%.
Gross national product (1991): U.S.$65,504,000,000 (U.S.$6,230 per capita).

Structure of gross domestic product and labour force

	1991 in value Dr '000,000	1991 % of total value	1990 labour force	1990 % of labour force
Agriculture	1,808,575	16.3	892,700	22.2
Mining	156,440	1.4	22,900	0.6
Manufacturing	1,866,587	16.8	746,800	18.7
Construction	731,018	6.6	259,700	6.5
Public utilities	290,270	2.6	38,200	1.0
Transp. and commun.	824,884	7.4	258,700	6.5
Trade	1,699,958[5]	15.3[5]	672,100	16.8
Finance	[5]	[5]	187,100	4.7
Pub. admin., defense	2,078,833	18.7	720,600	18.0
Services	879,254	7.9		
Other	772,972[6]	7.0[6]	201,000[7]	5.0[7]
TOTAL	11,108,791	100.0	3,999,800	100.0

Population economically active (1990): total 3,999,800; activity rate of total population 39.6% (participation rates: ages 15–64, 57.7%[2]; female 37.1%; unemployed 3.8%).

Price and earnings indexes (1985 = 100)

	1986	1987	1988	1989	1990	1991	1992
Consumer price index	123.0	143.2	162.5	184.9	222.6	265.9	308.0
Hourly earnings index	112.7	123.5	146.3	176.3	210.5	245.6	...

Land use (1990): forested 20.3%; meadows and pastures 40.8%; agricultural and under permanent cultivation 30.5%; other 8.4%.

Foreign trade

Balance of trade (current prices)

	1987	1988	1989	1990	1991	1992
Dr '000,000,000	−688.4	−861.4	−1,199.2	−1,613.3	−1,886.1	−2,113.5
% of total	28.1%	33.8%	30.8%	44.3%	37.3%	36.8%

Imports (1992): Dr 4,441,848,500,000 (machinery and transport equipment 34.1%, of which automobiles 8.7%; food, beverages, and tobacco 11.7%, of which meat products 1.4%, dairy products 1.2%, coffee 0.3%; chemical products 10.6%, of which medicinal and pharmaceutical products 0.5%; crude petroleum 7.4%). *Major import sources:* Germany 20.2%; Italy 14.2%; France 7.8%; The Netherlands 6.9%; Japan 6.4%; United Kingdom 5.5%; United States 3.6%; Belgium-Luxembourg 3.5%.
Exports (1992): Dr 1,816,406,800,000 (food, beverages, and tobacco 27.8%, of which tobacco 6.7%, olive oil 5.2%, olives 1.1%; clothing 21.5%; petroleum products 4.9%; textiles 3.5%; furs and raw skins 1.0%). *Major export destinations:* Germany 23.1%; Italy 18.0%; France 7.2%; United Kingdom 7.0%; United States 4.0%; Cyprus 3.4%.

Transport and communications

Transport. Railroads (1991): route length 1,570 mi, 2,527 km; passenger-mi 969,300,000, passenger-km 1,560,000,000; short ton-mi cargo 419,000,000, metric ton-km cargo 612,000,000. Roads (1990): total length 80,800 mi, 130,000 km (paved 79%). Vehicles (1991): passenger cars 1,790,939; trucks and buses 817,729. Merchant marine (1992): vessels (100 gross tons and over) 1,872; total deadweight tonnage 45,276,567. Air transport (1991): passenger-mi 3,848,367,000, passenger-km 6,193,359,000; short ton-mi cargo 78,226,000, metric ton-km cargo 114,208,000; airports (1993) with scheduled flights 34.
Communications. Daily newspapers (1990): total number 143; total circulation 1,130,100[8]; circulation per 1,000 population, n.a. Radio (1992): 4,085,492 receivers (1 per 2.5 persons). Television (1992): 2,300,000 receivers (1 per 4.5 persons). Telephones (1990): 4,698,810 (1 per 2.2 persons).

Education and health

Education (1992–93)

	schools	teachers	students	student/ teacher ratio
Primary (age 6–12)	7,634	37,549	745,666	19.9
Secondary (age 12–18)	2,988	45,794	700,488	15.3
Voc., teacher tr.	695	14,319	190,443	13.3
Higher	17	13,007[9]	187,644[9]	14.4[9]

Educational attainment (1981). Percentage of population age 25 and over having: no formal schooling (illiterate) 11.4%; some primary education 16.8%; completed primary 44.1%; lower secondary 6.0%; higher secondary 13.5%; some postsecondary 2.5%; a degree from institution of higher education 4.9%. *Literacy* (1990): total population age 15 and over literate 7,550,000 (93.2%); males literate 3,925,000 (97.6%); females literate 3,625,000 (89.1%).
Health: physicians (1989) 33,151 (1 per 303 persons); hospital beds (1990) 51,329 (1 per 199 persons); infant mortality rate per 1,000 live births (1992) 8.2.
Food (1988–90): daily per capita caloric intake 3,775 (vegetable products 75%, animal products 25%); 142% of FAO recommended minimum requirement.

Military

Total active duty personnel (1992): 159,300 (army 70.9%, navy 12.3%, air force 16.8%). *Military expenditure as percentage of GNP* (1989): 5.9% (world 4.9%); per capita expenditure U.S.$309.

[1]Includes Dr 2,358,154,000,000 of domestic borrowing. [2]1988. [3]Metal content of ore. [4]1987. [5]Trade includes Finance. [6]Income from ownership of buildings. [7]Includes 150,200 unemployed. [8]For 28 dailies only. [9]1988–89.

Grenada

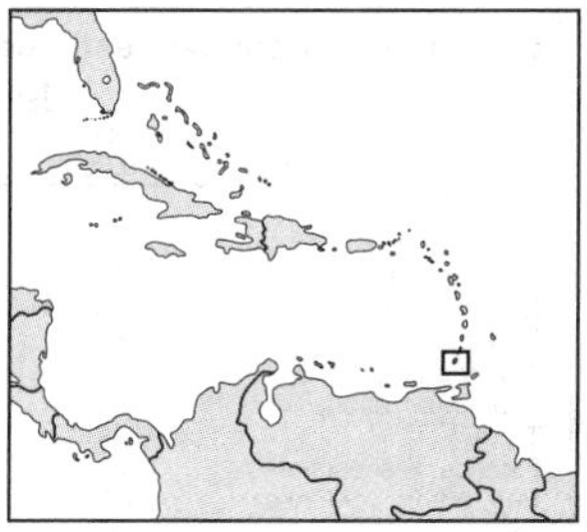

Official name: Grenada.
Form of government: constitutional monarchy with two legislative houses (Senate [13]; House of Representatives [15[1]]).
Chief of state: British Monarch represented by Governor-General.
Head of government: Prime Minister.
Capital: St. George's.
Official language: English.
Official religion: none.
Monetary unit: 1 East Caribbean dollar (EC$) = 100 cents; valuation (Oct. 4, 1993) 1 U.S.$ = EC$2.70; 1 £ = EC$4.10.

Area and population

Local Councils	Principal towns	area sq mi	area sq km	population 1991 census[2]
Carriacou	Hillsborough	10	26	4,595
Petite Martinique	...	3	8	720
St. Andrew	Grenville	38	99	23,531
St. David	...	17	44	10,703
St. George	...	25[3]	65[3]	24,719
St. John	Gouyave	14	35	8,547
St. Mark	Victoria	10	25	3,785
St. Patrick	Sauteurs	16	42	9,652
Town				
St. George's	—	[3]	[3]	4,439
TOTAL		133	344	90,691

Demography

Population (1993): 91,000.
Density (1993): persons per sq mi 684.2, persons per sq km 264.5.
Urban-rural (1991)[4]: urban 32.2%; rural 67.8%.
Sex distribution (1991): male 49.35%; female 50.65%.
Age breakdown (1988): under 15, 35.9%; 15–29, 28.5%; 30–44, 14.2%; 45–59, 8.5%; 60 and over, 11.3%; not stated, 1.6%.
Population projection: (2000) 92,000; (2010) 94,000.
Doubling time: 28 years.
Ethnic composition (1991): black 82.0%; mixed 13.0%; white 1.0%; other 4.0%.
Religious affiliation (1980): Roman Catholic 59.3%; Protestant 34.5%, of which Anglican 17.1%, Seventh-day Adventist 5.7%, Pentecostal 3.9%; other 6.2%.
Major localities (1991): St. George's 4,439; Gouyave 2,980[5]; Grenville 2,100[5]; Victoria 2,000[5].

Vital statistics

Birth rate per 1,000 population (1989): 33.0 (world avg. 27.1).
Death rate per 1,000 population (1989): 8.3 (world avg. 9.8).
Natural increase rate per 1,000 population (1989): 24.7 (world avg. 17.3).
Total fertility rate (avg. births per childbearing woman; 1991): 3.0.
Marriage rate per 1,000 population: n.a.
Divorce rate per 1,000 population: n.a.
Life expectancy at birth (1991): male 69.0 years; female 74.0 years.
Major causes of death per 100,000 population (1984): diseases of the circulatory system 290.3; malignant neoplasms (cancers) 90.5; endocrine and metabolic diseases 62.9; diseases of the respiratory system 54.1; accidents and violence 47.9; diseases of the digestive system 39.5.

National economy

Budget (1993). Revenue: EC$227,000,000 (current revenue 69.6%; development revenue 30.4%, of which foreign loans 14.1%, foreign grants 11.0%, special fund based on the sale of national assets 5.3%). Expenditures: EC$245,000,000 (current expenditures 72.2%; development expenditures 27.8%).
Public debt (external, outstanding; 1991): U.S.$95,800,000.
Tourism: receipts from visitors (1992) U.S.$41,900,000; expenditures by nationals abroad (1990) U.S.$7,000,000.
Gross national product (at current market prices; 1992): U.S.$210,000,000 (U.S.$2,310 per capita).

Structure of gross domestic product and labour force

	1991 in value EC$'000,000[6]	1991 % of total value	1988 labour force	1988 % of labour force
Agriculture	68.8	15.5	5,560	14.3
Quarrying	1.9	0.5	111	0.3
Manufacturing	24.3	5.5	2,835	7.3
Construction	48.1	10.8	3,531	9.1
Public utilities	14.3	3.2	389	1.0
Transportation and communications	66.2	14.9	1,696	4.4
Trade, restaurants	90.4	20.4	5,421	13.9
Finance, real estate	44.3	10.0	778	2.0
Pub. admin., defense	91.5	20.6	5,949	15.3
Services	12.9	2.9		
Other	−18.9[7]	−4.3[7]	12,650[8]	32.5[8]
TOTAL	443.8	100.0	38,920	100.0[9]

Production (metric tons except as noted). Agriculture, forestry, fishing (1992): bananas 10,000, coconuts 7,000, sugarcane 6,000, roots and tubers 4,000, nutmeg 2,235, cacao 2,200, mangoes 2,000, avocados 2,000, grapefruit 2,000[10], mace 160, other crops include soursop, sapodilla plums, cinnamon, cloves, and pimiento; livestock (number of live animals) 11,000 sheep, 11,000 goats, 7,000 pigs, 4,000 cattle; roundwood, n.a.; fish catch 1,990. Mining and quarrying: excavation of gravel for local use. Manufacturing (1990): wheat flour 8,000; beer 25,000 hectolitres; rum 2,000 hectolitres; cigarettes 22,000,000 units; clothing (1989) EC$3,800,000 in export sales; other products include edible coconut oil, paints, poultry feed, and aerated beverages. Construction: n.a. Energy production (consumption): electricity (kW-hr; 1990) 51,000,000 (51,000,000); coal, none (none); crude petroleum, none (none); petroleum products (metric tons; 1990) none (39,000); natural gas, none (none).
Household income and expenditure. Average household size (1991) 3.7; income per household (1988) EC$7,097 (U.S.$2,629); sources of income: n.a.; expenditure (1987): food 38.7%, housing 11.9%, transportation 9.1%, personal effects and medical care 8.6%, household furnishings 8.3%, household operations 5.4%.
Population economically active (1988): total 38,920; activity rate of total population 39.9% (participation rates: ages 15–65, 72.7%; female 48.6%; unemployed [1992] more than 30.0%).

Price and earnings indexes (1985 = 100)

	1986	1987	1988	1989	1990	1991	1992
Consumer price index	100.5	99.7	103.6	109.4	112.4	115.4	120.0[11]
Earnings index	...	...	...	...	...	...	...

Land use (1991): forested 9.0%; meadows and pastures 3.0%; agricultural and under permanent cultivation 35.0%; other 53.0%.

Foreign trade[12]

Balance of trade (current prices)

	1986	1987	1988	1989	1990	1991
U.S.$'000,000	−54.7	−56.7	−59.4	−70.7	−80.1	−97.2
% of total	48.7%	47.1%	47.5%	55.5%	60.4%	70.8%

Imports (1991): U.S.$117,200,000 (machinery and transport equipment 24.2%, food 23.9%, basic manufactures 20.2%, chemicals and chemical products 8.5%). *Major import sources:* United States 31.2%; Trinidad and Tobago 15.9%; United Kingdom 13.8%; Japan 7.0%; Canada 5.2%.
Exports (1991): U.S.$20,000,000 (bananas 20.0%, nutmeg 17.6%, cocoa beans 16.3%, fresh fruit 8.9%, mace 5.0%). *Major export destinations:* United Kingdom 22.7%; United States 14.2%; Canada 13.3%; Trinidad and Tobago 13.1%; Germany 10.9%.

Transport and communications

Transport. Railroads: none. Roads (1991): total length 700 mi, 1,127 km (paved 51%). Vehicles: n.a. Merchant marine (1992): vessels (100 gross tons and over) 3; total deadweight tonnage 484. Air transport (1991)[13]: passenger arrivals 101,694, passenger departures 104,695; cargo loaded 1,275 metric tons, cargo unloaded 457 metric tons; airports (1993) with scheduled flights 2.
Communications. Daily newspapers (1991): none[14]. Radio (1992): total number of receivers 80,000 (1 per 1.1 persons). Television (1992): total number of receivers 30,000 (1 per 3.0 persons). Telephones (1990): 10,930 (1 per 8.3 persons).

Education and health

Education (1991–92)

	schools	teachers	students	student/ teacher ratio
Primary (age 5–11)	57	763[15]	21,358	26.5[15]
Secondary (age 12–16)	18	331[15]	6,834	19.7[15]
Vocational	...	...	...	...
Higher	2	91	586	6.4

Educational attainment (1981). Percentage of population age 25 and over having: no formal schooling 2.2%; primary education 87.8%; secondary 8.5%; higher 1.5%. *Literacy* (1988): total population age 15 and over literate 49,000 (85.0%).
Health (1990): physicians 56 (1 per 1,617 persons); hospital beds 325 (1 per 279 persons); infant mortality rate per 1,000 live births (1991) 29.0.
Food (1988–90): daily per capita caloric intake 2,400 (vegetable products 77%, animal products 23%); 99% of FAO recommended minimum requirement.

Military

Total active duty personnel (1990):[16]. *Military expenditure as percentage of GNP:* n.a.; per capita expenditure, n.a.

[1]Excludes the speaker who may be elected from outside its elected membership. [2]Preliminary; excludes 434 institutionalized residents and 33 Grenadians in foreign service. [3]St. George local council includes St. George's town. [4]Urban defined as St. George's town and St. George local council. [5]1979. [6]Current prices at factor cost. [7]Less imputed bank service charges. [8]Includes 1,752 persons in activities not adequately defined and 10,898 unemployed. [9]Detail does not add to total given because of rounding. [10]1991. [11]Average of second and third quarters. [12]Imports c.i.f.; exports f.o.b. [13]Point Salines airport. [14]Weekly newspapers (1991): total number 4; total circulation 12,000. [15]1990–91. [16]The 632-member police force includes a paramilitary unit.

Guadeloupe

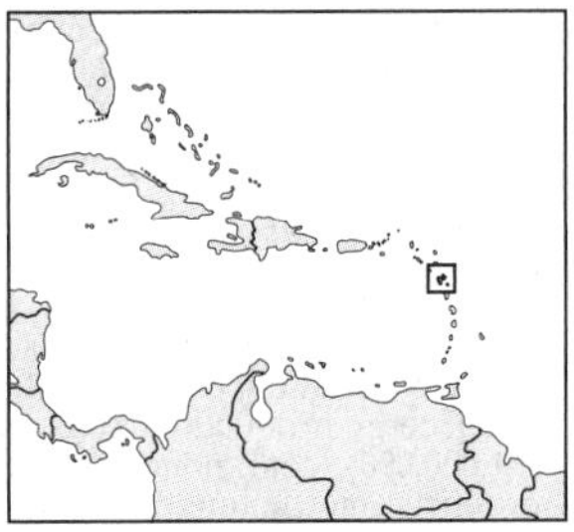

Official name: Département de la Guadeloupe (Department of Guadeloupe).
Political status: overseas department (France) with two legislative houses (General Council [42]; Regional Council [41]).
Chief of state: President of France.
Heads of government: Commissioner of the Republic (for France); President of the General Council (for Guadeloupe); President of the Regional Council (for Guadeloupe).
Capital: Basse-Terre.
Official language: French.
Official religion: none.
Monetary unit: 1 French franc (F) = 100 centimes; valuation (Oct. 4, 1993) 1 U.S.$ = F 5.67; 1 £ = F 8.58.

Area and population

		area		population
Arrondissements	Capitals	sq mi	sq km	1990 census
Basse-Terre[1]	Basse-Terre	332	861	151,979
Pointe-à-Pitre[2]	Pointe-à-Pitre	297	769	192,643
Saint-Martin–Saint-Barthélemy[3]	Marigot	29	75	33,556
TOTAL		687[4]	1,780[4]	378,178[5]

Demography

Population (1993): 418,000.
Density (1993): persons per sq mi 614.3, persons per sq km 237.1.
Urban-rural (1990): urban 48.4%; rural 51.6%.
Sex distribution (1991): male 48.88%; female 51.12%.
Age breakdown (1991): under 15, 24.8%; 15–29, 29.5%; 30–44, 21.4%; 45–59, 12.5%; 60–74, 8.3%; 75 and over, 3.5%.
Population projection: (2000) 473,000; (2010) 541,000.
Doubling time: 58 years.
Ethnic composition (1991): Creole (mulatto) 77.0%; black 10.0%; Guadeloupe mestizo (French–East Asian) 10.0%; white 2.0%; other 1.0%.
Religious affiliation (1991[6]): Roman Catholic 88.1%; other 11.9%.
Major communes (1990): Les Abymes 62,809; Saint-Martin 28,524; Pointe-à-Pitre 26,083 (141,000[7, 8]); Le Gosier 20,708; Basse-Terre 14,000 (53,000[7]).

Vital statistics

Birth rate per 1,000 population (1992): 17.7 (world avg. 26.4); legitimate 39.3%; illegitimate 60.7%.
Death rate per 1,000 population (1992): 5.6 (world avg. 9.2).
Natural increase rate per 1,000 population (1992): 12.1 (world avg. 17.2).
Total fertility rate (avg. births per childbearing woman; 1990–95): 2.2.
Marriage rate per 1,000 population (1992): 4.7.
Divorce rate per 1,000 population (1992): 1.1.
Life expectancy at birth (1991): male 70.0 years; female 77.0 years.
Major causes of death per 100,000 population (1988): diseases of the circulatory system 191.2; malignant neoplasms (cancers) 115.3; accidents and violence 73.7; diseases of the digestive system 39.5; diseases of the respiratory system 29.1.

National economy

Budget (1991). Revenue: F 1,964,000,000 (receipts from French central government and local administrative bodies 38.2%, new loans 21.5%, subsidies for investments 10.6%, taxes on motor fuels 7.4%). Expenditures: F 1,964,000,000 (capital investments and works 30.8%, health and social services 23.1%, debt amortization 7.4%).
Public debt (external, outstanding; 1988[9]): U.S.$41,000,000.
Tourism (1991): receipts from visitors U.S.$284,000,000; expenditures by nationals abroad, n.a.
Production (metric tons except as noted). Agriculture, forestry, fishing (1992): sugarcane 723,000, bananas 110,000, yams 10,000, sweet potatoes 7,000, plantains 7,000, melons 5,000, tomatoes 4,000, pineapples 4,000, lemons and limes 2,000, mangoes 2,000, eggplants 1,000, foliage and plants 60[10, 11], cut flowers 29[10, 11]; livestock (number of live animals) 68,000 cattle, 64,000 goats, 54,000 pigs; roundwood (1991) 17,000 cu m; fish catch (1991) 8,444. Mining and quarrying (1988): pozzolana 240,000. Manufacturing (1990): cement 291,144; rum 72,133 hectolitres; raw sugar 53,200[12]; other products include clothing, wooden furniture and posts, and metalware. Construction (buildings authorized; 1991): residential 225,761 sq m; nonresidential 217,761 sq m. Energy production (consumption): electricity (kW-hr; 1992) 901,000,000 (775,000,000); coal, none (none); crude petroleum, none (none); petroleum products (metric tons; 1990) none (336,000); natural gas, none (none).
Household income and expenditure. Average household size (1991) 3.4; income per household (1980) F 72,898 (U.S.$16,142); sources of income (1980): wages and salaries 76.8%, rent 4.0%, other 19.2%; expenditure (1984–85): food and beverages 29.8%, housing, household furnishings, and energy 26.3%, transportation and communications 13.3%, clothing and footwear 8.2%, other 22.4%.
Gross national product (at current market prices; 1987): U.S.$1,170,000,000 (U.S.$3,200 per capita).

Structure of gross domestic product and labour force

	1982		1986	
	in value F '000,000	% of total value	labour force	% of labour force
Agriculture	742	10.1	9,379	7.2
Mining and manufacturing	389	5.3	6,072	4.7
Construction	345	4.7	8,825	6.8
Public utilities	−50	−0.7	763	0.6
Transportation and communications	355	4.8	4,006	3.1
Trade	1,249	17.0	9,561	7.4
Finance, real estate	728	9.9	18,736	14.5
Pub. admin., defense	2,333	31.7	31,388	24.3
Services	1,105	15.0		
Other	162	2.2	40,641[13]	31.4[13]
TOTAL	7,358	100.0	129,371	100.0

Population economically active (1990): total 172,418; activity rate of total population 45.6% (participation rates: ages 15–64, 68.0%; female 45.5%; unemployed [1993] 22.2%).

Price and earnings indexes (1985 = 100)[14]

	1986	1987	1988	1989	1990	1991	1992[15]
Consumer price index	101.3	104.9	106.9	109.9	114.0	116.0	117.6
Monthly earnings index[16]	100.4	102.0	105.0	107.0	112.2	114.4	115.8

Land use (1991): forested 39.1%; meadows and pastures 13.6%; agricultural and under permanent cultivation 18.3%; other 29.0%.

Foreign trade

Balance of trade (current prices)

	1986	1987	1988	1989	1990	1991
F '000,000	−4,709	−5,665	−6,260	−6,995	−8,439	−8,209
% of total	75.9%	83.4%	77.5%	83.8%	86.3%	79.8%

Imports (1991): F 9,248,619,000 (consumer goods 29.3%; food and agriculture products 19.4%; machinery and equipment 18.8%; transport vehicles and parts 9.2%). *Major import sources:* France 60.2%; other EEC 13.7%; United States 8.4%; Japan 2.4%; Martinique 1.9%.
Exports (1991): F 831,311,000 (agricultural products 69.6%, of which bananas 35.5%, sugar 24.4%, consumer goods 14.7%; machinery and equipment 9.9%). *Major export destinations:* France 70.3%; Martinique 17.0%; French Guiana 2.4%; other EEC 0.9%.

Transport and communications

Transport. Railroads: none. Roads (1990): total length 1,286 mi, 2,069 km (paved [1986] 80%). Vehicles (1985): passenger cars 95,962; trucks and buses 28,134. Merchant marine (1992): vessels (100 gross tons and over) 20; deadweight tonnage 4,430. Air transport (1991)[17]: passenger arrivals 653,545, passenger departures 668,720; cargo loaded 7,434 metric tons, cargo unloaded 4,765 metric tons; airports (1993) with scheduled flights 6.
Communications. Daily newspapers (1991): total number 1; total circulation 25,000; circulation per 1,000 population 63. Radio (1992): total number of receivers 100,000 (1 per 4.1 persons). Television (1992): total number of receivers 150,000 (1 per 2.8 persons). Telephones (1992): 138,504 (1 per 3.0 persons).

Education and health

Education (1990–91)

	schools	teachers	students	student/teacher ratio
Primary (age 6–10)	222	2,064	38,531	18.7
Secondary (age 11–17) / Vocational	86	3,329	51,928	15.6
Higher[18]	1	...	6,517	...

Educational attainment (1982). Percentage of population age 25 and over having: no formal schooling 10.7%; primary education 54.6%; secondary 29.5%; higher 5.2%. *Literacy* (1982): total population age 15 and over literate 225,400 (90.1%); males literate 108,700 (89.7%); females literate 116,700 (90.5%).
Health (1990): physicians 555 (1 per 703 persons); hospital beds 3,278 (1 per 119 persons); infant mortality rate per 1,000 live births (1992) 10.4.
Food (1988–90): daily per capita caloric intake 2,777 (vegetable products 74%, animal products 26%); 115% of FAO recommended minimum requirement.

Military

Total active duty personnel (1992): 8,200 French troops[19].

[1]Comprises Basse-Terre 327 sq mi (848 sq km), pop. 149,943, and Îles des Saintes 5 sq mi (13 sq km), pop. 2,036. [2]Comprises Grande-Terre 228 sq mi (590 sq km), pop. 177,570; Marie-Galante 61 sq mi (158 sq km), pop. 13,463; La Désirade 8 sq mi (20 sq km), pop. 1,610; and the uninhabited Îles de la Petite-Terre. [3]Comprises the French part of Saint-Martin 20 sq mi (52 sq km), pop. 28,518; Saint-Barthélemy 8 sq mi (21 sq km), pop. 5,038; and the small, uninhabited island of Tintamarre. [4]Total area includes 29 sq mi (75 sq km) not allocated by arrondissement. [5]Preliminary; final 1990 census total was 386,987. [6]January 1. [7]Urban agglomeration. [8]Includes Les Abymes. [9]Includes external long-term private debt not guaranteed by the government. [10]1989. [11]Export only. [12]1991. [13]Unemployed. [14]Base and indexes are end of year unless footnoted. [15]End of March. [16]Based on minimum-level wage of public employees. [17]Pointe-à-Pitre airport only. [18]University of Antilles–French Guiana, Guadeloupe campus. [19]Includes Martinique and French Guiana.

Guatemala

Official name: República de Guatemala (Republic of Guatemala).
Form of government: republic with one legislative house (Congress of the Republic [116]).
Head of state and government: President.
Capital: Guatemala City.
Official language: Spanish.
Official religion: none.
Monetary unit: 1 Guatemalan quetzal (Q) = 100 centavos; valuation (Oct. 4, 1993) 1 U.S.$ = Q 5.83; 1 £ = Q 8.83.

Area and population

		area		population
Departments	Capitals	sq mi	sq km	1993 estimate[1]
Alta Verapaz	Cobán	3,354	8,686	630,109
Baja Verapaz	Salamá	1,206	3,124	194,696
Chimaltenango	Chimaltenango	764	1,979	364,239
Chiquimula	Chiquimula	917	2,376	262,799
El Progreso	Guastatoya (Progreso)	742	1,922	113,047
Escuintla	Escuintla	1,693	4,384	575,362
Guatemala	Guatemala City	821	2,126	2,131,354
Huehuetenango	Huehuetenango	2,857	7,400	764,864
Izabal	Puerto Barrios	3,490	9,038	347,863
Jalapa	Jalapa	797	2,063	201,024
Jutiapa	Jutiapa	1,243	3,219	370,033
Petén	Flores	13,843	35,854	280,726
Quetzaltenango	Quetzaltenango	753	1,951	589,906
Quiché	Santa Cruz del Quiché	3,235	8,378	612,169
Retalhuleu	Retalhuleu	717	1,856	253,494
Sacatepéquez	Antigua Guatemala	180	465	190,950
San Marcos	San Marcos	1,464	3,791	744,618
Santa Rosa	Cuilapa	1,141	2,955	279,417
Sololá	Sololá	410	1,061	257,705
Suchitepéquez	Mazatenango	969	2,510	382,071
Totonicapán	Totonicapán	410	1,061	315,061
Zacapa	Zacapa	1,039	2,690	167,907
TOTAL		42,042[2]	108,889	10,029,414

Demography

Population (1993)[1]: 9,713,000.
Density (1993): persons per sq mi 231.0, persons per sq km 89.2.
Urban-rural (1993): urban 38.4%; rural 61.6%.
Sex distribution (1990): male 50.52%; female 49.48%.
Age breakdown (1990): under 15, 45.4%; 15–29, 26.7%; 30–44, 14.6%; 45–59, 8.2%; 60–74, 4.1%; 75 and over, 1.0%.
Population projection: (2000) 11,809,000; (2010) 15,242,000.
Doubling time: 27 years.
Ethnic composition (1987): Amerindian 45%; Ladino (Hispanic/Amerindian) 45%; white 5%; black 2%; other mixed race and Chinese 3%.
Religious affiliation (1986): Roman Catholic *c.* 75%, of which Catholic/traditional syncretist *c.* 25%; Protestant (mostly fundamentalist) *c.* 25%.
Major cities (1993): Guatemala City 1,132,730; Mixco 390,441; Villa Nueva 144,123; Chinautla 57,402; Amatitlan 37,177.

Vital statistics

Birth rate per 1,000 population (1992): 34.0 (world avg. 26.4).
Death rate per 1,000 population (1992): 8.0 (world avg. 9.2).
Natural increase rate per 1,000 population (1992): 26.0 (world avg. 17.2).
Total fertility rate (avg. births per childbearing woman; 1992): 4.6.
Marriage rate per 1,000 population (1988): 5.4.
Divorce rate per 1,000 population (1988): 0.2.
Life expectancy at birth (1992): male 61.0 years; female 66.0 years.
Major causes of death per 100,000 population (1988): infectious and parasitic diseases 121.6; diseases of the respiratory system 110.8; perinatal causes 58.7; malnutrition 50.2; dehydration 18.5.

National economy

Budget (1992). Revenue: Q 5,524,000,000 (tax revenue 81.8%, of which taxes on goods and services 36.5%, customs duties 21.9%, income taxes 19.1%; nontax revenue 18.2%). Expenditures: Q 4,570,000,000 (1990; education 14.3%; defense 12.7%; transportation 8.2%; health 8.1%; agriculture 3.7%).
Tourism (1991): receipts from visitors U.S.$211,000,000; expenditures by nationals abroad U.S.$67,000,000.
Land use (1990): forested 34.6%; meadows and pastures 12.9%; agricultural and under permanent cultivation 17.4%; other 35.1%.
Production (metric tons except as noted). Agriculture, forestry, fishing (1991): sugarcane 9,797,000, corn (maize) 1,150,000, bananas 470,000, coffee 195,000, tomatoes 128,000, dry beans 110,000, seed cotton 110,000, sorghum 80,000, cottonseed 60,000, plantains 55,000; livestock (number of live animals) 1,695,000 cattle, 1,110,000 pigs, 675,000 sheep; roundwood 8,049,000 cu m; fish catch (1990) 6,894. Mining and quarrying (1990): iron ore 6,370; antimony ore 1,400. Manufacturing (value added in Q '000,000; 1989[3]): food products 138.0; beverages 66.2; clothing and footwear 47.6; textiles 43.2; metal products 30.2. Construction (value of buildings authorized in Q '000,000; 1991)[4]: residential 170.2; nonresidential 127.5. Energy production (consumption): electricity (kW-hr; 1990) 2,325,000,000 (2,325,000,000); crude petroleum (barrels; 1990) 1,262,000 (4,975,000); petroleum products (metric tons; 1990) 598,000 (962,000).
Gross national product (1991): U.S.$8,816,000,000 (U.S.$930 per capita).

Structure of gross domestic product and labour force

	1992		1990	
	in value Q '000,000[3]	% of total value	labour force	% of labour force
Agriculture	928.6	25.8	1,625,125	58.1
Mining	11.2	0.2	2,797	0.1
Manufacturing	537.1	14.9	380,408	13.6
Construction	74.1	2.0	114,682	4.1
Public utilities	101.1	2.5	8,391	0.3
Transp. and commun.	309.8	8.1	69,928	2.5
Trade	874.7	24.0	204,190	7.3
Finance, real estate	340.4	9.3		
Pub. admin., defense	267.2	7.1	335,654	12.0
Services	218.6	6.1		
Other	—	—	55,942[5]	2.0[5]
TOTAL	3,662.8	100.0	2,797,117	100.0

Public debt (external, outstanding; 1991): U.S.$2,103,000,000.
Population economically active (1990): total 2,797,117; activity rate of total population 31.4% (participation rates: ages 15–64, 46.5%; female [1989] 25.5%; unemployed 2.9%[6]).

Price and earnings indexes (1985 = 100)

	1986	1987	1988	1989	1990	1991	1992
Consumer price index	136.9	153.8	170.5	189.9	268.1	357.1	393.0
Annual earnings index[7]	117.0	144.2	193.1	229.0	263.5	333.6	427.2

Household income and expenditure. Average household size (1989) 5.4; income per household (1989) Q 4,306 (U.S.$1,529); sources of income: n.a.; expenditure (1981): food 64.4%, housing and energy 16.0%, transportation and communications 7.0%, household furnishings 5.0%, clothing 3.1%.

Foreign trade[8]

Balance of trade (current prices)

	1987	1988	1989	1990	1991	1992
U.S.$'000,000	−345.8	−391.5	−389.2	−207.4	−197.3	−1,190.8
% of total	14.9%	16.1%	14.9%	8.0%	7.5%	35.7%

Imports (1991): U.S.$1,851,300,000 (primary and intermediate materials for industry 39.5%, capital goods 19.0%, nondurable consumer goods 14.2%, petroleum 4.5%). *Major import sources:* United States 41.3%; Mexico 6.6%; Japan 6.6%; El Salvador 5.3%; Germany 4.7%; Venezuela 4.5%.
Exports (1991): U.S.$1,234,800,000 (coffee 22.7%, sugar 11.4%, bananas 6.5%, cardamon 3.5%, cotton 1.7%). *Major export destinations:* United States 37.0%; El Salvador 12.9%; Costa Rica 6.3%; Mexico 5.2%; Nicaragua 4.2%; Germany 3.8%.

Transport and communications

Transport. Railroads (1990)[9]: route length 570 mi, 917 km; passenger-km 10,099,000; metric ton-km cargo 42,700,000. Roads (1990): total length 8,297 mi, 13,352 km (paved 26%). Vehicles (1991): passenger cars 145,000; trucks and buses 105,000. Merchant marine (1992): vessels (100 gross tons and over) 8; total deadweight tonnage 353. Air transport (1991)[10]: passenger-km 230,000,000; metric ton-km cargo 9,200,000; airports (1993) 2.
Communications. Daily newspapers (1990): total number 5; total circulation 190,000; circulation per 1,000 population 21. Radio (1992): 400,000 receivers (1 per 24 persons). Television (1992): 475,000 receivers (1 per 20 persons). Telephones (1990): 250,000 (1 per 36 persons).

Education and health

Education (1990)

	schools	teachers	students	student/ teacher ratio
Primary (age 7–12)	9,265	36,850	1,270,144	34.5
Secondary (age 13–18) Voc., teacher tr.	1,877	19,817	291,171	14.7
Higher[11]	5	4,346	69,532	16.0

Educational attainment (1989). Percentage of population age 25 and over having: no formal schooling 50.0%; incomplete primary education 21.6%; complete primary 16.2%; secondary 9.2%; higher 3.0%. *Literacy* (1989): total population age 15 and over literate 2,809,000 (60.3%); males literate 1,544,000 (69.7%); females literate 1,265,000 (51.7%).
Health (1987): physicians 3,579 (1 per 2,356 persons); hospital beds 13,667 (1 per 602 persons); infant mortality rate per 1,000 live births (1989) 43.6.
Food (1988–90): daily per capita caloric intake 2,254 (vegetable products 94%, animal products 6%); 103% of FAO recommended minimum requirement.

Military

Total active duty personnel (1992): 44,600 (army 94.2%, navy 2.7%, air force 3.1%). *Military expenditure as percentage of GNP* (1989): 1.6% (world 4.9%); per capita expenditure U.S.$15.

[1]Population of departments and cities taken from official projections based on 1973–81 intercensal growth rates and subsequent vital (birth and death) rates; 1993 national population estimate based on demographic surveys taken in October 1986–August 1987 and April–July 1989. [2]Detail does not add to total given because of rounding. [3]At prices of 1958. [4]Private construction in Guatemala City metropolitan area only. [5]Persons in activities not adequately defined. [6]Officially unemployed; 63% of economically active population is estimated to be underemployed. [7]Based on employees entitled to social security. [8]Import figures are f.o.b. in balance of trade and c.i.f. for commodities and trading partners. [9]Guatemala Railways only. [10]Aviateca Airlines only. [11]1989.

Guinea

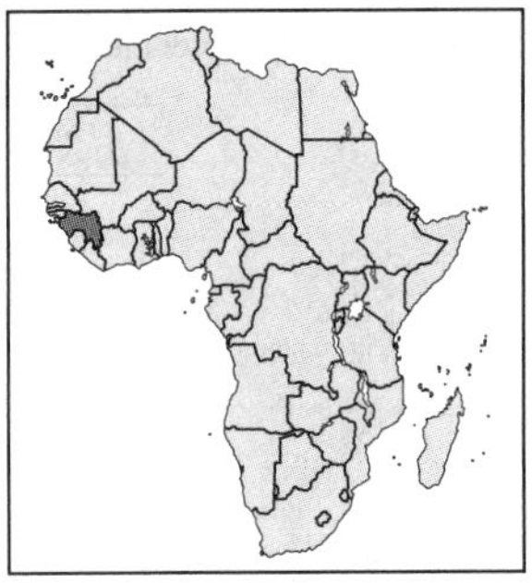

Official name: République de Guinée (Republic of Guinea).
Form of government: transitional government (composed of a 15-member Transitional Committee for National Recovery)[1].
Head of state and government: President (and Head of Transitional Committee for National Recovery)[1].
Capital: Conakry.
Official language: French.
Official religion: none.
Monetary unit: 1 Guinean franc (GF) = 100 cauris; valuation (Oct. 4, 1993) 1 U.S.$ = GF 806.39; 1 £ = GF 1,222.

Area and population

		area		population
				1983
Regions	Capitals	sq mi	sq km	census
Beyla	Beyla	6,738	17,452	161,347
Boffa	Boffa	1,932	5,003	141,719
Boké[2]	Boké	3,881	10,053	225,207
Conakry	Conakry	119	308	705,280
Coyah (Dubréka)	Coyah	2,153	5,576	134,190
Dabola	Dabola	2,317	6,000	97,986
Dalaba	Dalaba	1,313	3,400	132,802
Dinguiraye	Dinguiraye	4,247	11,000	133,502
Faranah[2]	Faranah	4,788	12,400	142,923
Forécariah	Forécariah	1,647	4,265	116,464
Fria	Fria	840	2,175	70,413
Gaoual	Gaoual	4,440	11,500	135,657
Guéckédou	Guéckédou	1,605	4,157	204,757
Kankan	Kankan	7,104	18,400	229,861
Kérouané	Kérouané	3,070	7,950	106,872
Kindia	Kindia	3,409	8,828	216,052
Kissidougou	Kissidougou	3,425	8,872	183,236
Koubia	Koubia	571	1,480	98,053
Koundara	Koundara	2,124	5,500	94,216
Kouroussa	Kouroussa	4,647	12,035	136,926
Labé	Labé	973	2,520	253,214
Lélouma	Lélouma	830	2,150	138,467
Lola	Lola	1,629	4,219	106,654
Macenta	Macenta	3,363	8,710	193,109
Mali	Mali	3,398	8,800	210,889
Mamou	Mamou	2,378	6,160	190,525
Mandiana	Mandiana	5,000	12,950	136,317
Nzérékoré	Nzérékoré	1,460	3,781	216,355
Pita	Pita	1,544	4,000	227,912
Siguiri	Siguiri	7,626	19,750	209,164
Télimélé	Télimélé	3,119	8,080	243,256
Tougué	Tougué	2,394	6,200	113,272
Yomou	Yomou	843	2,183	74,417
TOTAL		94,926[3]	245,857	5,781,014

Demography

Population (1993): 7,418,000.
Density (1993): persons per sq mi 78.1, persons per sq km 30.2.
Urban-rural (1990): urban 25.6%; rural 74.4%.
Sex distribution (1990): male 50.17%; female 49.83%.
Age breakdown (1990): under 15, 46.7%; 15–29, 25.9%; 30–44, 15.0%; 45–59, 8.0%; 60 and over, 4.4%.
Population projection: (2000) 8,879,000; (2010) 11,451,000.
Doubling time: 27 years.
Ethnic composition (1990): Fulani 40.3%; Malinke 25.8%; Susu 11.0%; Kissi 6.5%; Kpelle 4.8%; other 11.6%.
Religious affiliation (1988): Muslim 85.0%; traditional beliefs 5.0%; Christian 1.5%; other 8.5%.
Major cities (1983): Conakry 705,280; Kankan 88,760; Labé 65,439; Kindia 55,904.

Vital statistics

Birth rate per 1,000 population (1991): 47.0 (world avg. 26.4).
Death rate per 1,000 population (1991): 21.0 (world avg. 9.2).
Natural increase rate per 1,000 population (1991): 26.0 (world avg. 17.2).
Total fertility rate (avg. births per childbearing woman; 1990): 6.5.
Life expectancy at birth (1990–95): male 44.0 years; female 45.0 years.
Major causes of death per 100,000 population: n.a.; however, major diseases include malaria, venereal disease, tuberculosis, and measles.

National economy

Budget (1992). Revenue: GF 415,200,000,000 (mineral sector 46.3%; other 53.7%). Expenditures: GF 593,100,000,000 (capital spending 52.3%; current expenditure 47.7%, of which personnel 22.4%, services 14.7%).
Public debt (external, outstanding; 1991): U.S.$2,401,000,000.
Tourism: n.a.
Production (metric tons except as noted). Agriculture, forestry, fishing (1992): roots and tubers 885,000 (of which cassava 660,000, yams 100,000), rice 757,000, vegetables and melons 420,000, plantains 420,000, citrus fruit 230,000, sugarcane 225,000, bananas 170,000, corn (maize) 94,000, pineapples 85,000, peanuts (groundnuts) 78,000, pulses 60,000, palm kernels 40,000, coffee 30,000, coconuts 18,000, eggs 14,490; livestock (number of live animals) 1,800,000 cattle, 510,000 sheep, 460,000 goats, 33,000 pigs, 13,000,000 chickens; roundwood (1991) 3,988,000 cu m; fish catch (1991) 37,500. Mining and quarrying (1991): bauxite 17,800,000; alumina 640,000; diamonds 200,000 carats; gold 2,500 kg. Manufacturing (value of production in GF '000; 1985): corrugated and sheet iron 571,081; plastics 462,242; tobacco products 375,154; cement 326,138; printed matter 216,511; fruit juice 75,763; beer 69,934; matches 22,449. Construction: n.a. Energy production (consumption): electricity (kW-hr; 1991) 521,000,000 (521,000,000); coal, none (n.a.); crude petroleum, none (n.a.); petroleum products (metric tons; 1991) none (334,000); natural gas, none (n.a.).
Gross national product (at current market prices; 1992): U.S.$3,083,000,000 (U.S.$510 per capita).

Structure of gross domestic product and labour force

	1990		1983	
	in value GF '000,000,000	% of total value	labour force	% of labour force
Agriculture	551	27.8	1,423,615	78.2
Mining	474	23.9	12,241	0.7
Manufacturing	71	3.6	11,215	0.6
Construction	111	5.6	9,115	0.5
Public utilities	16	0.8	3,205	0.2
Transp. and commun.	71	3.6	29,496	1.6
Trade	434	21.9	37,309	2.0
Finance			3,556	0.2
Pub. admin., defense / Services	222	11.2	137,600	7.5
Other	32	1.6	155,679	8.5
TOTAL	1,982	100.0	1,823,031	100.0

Population economically active (1992): total 2,590,000; activity rate of total population 42.3% (participation rates [1983]: ages 15–64, 63.5%; female 39.4%; unemployed, n.a.).

Price index (1987 = 100)

	1988	1989	1990	1991	1992	1993[4]
Consumer price index	129.6	163.3	194.2	233.1	...	...

Household income and expenditure. Average household size (1983) 6.7; average annual income per capita (1984) GS 7,660 (U.S.$305); sources of income: n.a.; expenditure (1985): food 61.5%, health care 11.2%, clothing and footwear 7.9%, housing and energy 7.3%, transportation 5.1%.
Land use (1991): forested 59.1%; meadows and pastures 25.0%; agricultural and under permanent cultivation 3.0%; other 12.9%.

Foreign trade[5]

Balance of trade (current prices)

	1985	1986	1987	1988	1989	1990	1991
U.S.$'000,000	+111	+147	+120	+10	+146	+177	+33.2
% of total	11.0%	12.6%	9.6%	0.7%	10.6%	11.8%	2.7%

Imports (1990): U.S.$693,000,000 (1988; intermediate goods 33.7%, capital goods 13.1%, petroleum products 10.5%, food products 9.8%, consumer goods 9.7%). *Major import sources:* France 36.0%; U.S. 9.0%; Belgium-Luxembourg 9.0%; Germany 6.0%; Italy 5.0%.
Exports (1990): U.S.$788,000,000 (bauxite 56.9%, alumina 20.7%, diamonds 8.9%, gold 5.8%, coffee 4.5%, fish 1.8%). *Major export destinations:* U.S. 23.0%; France 14.0%; Germany 14.0%; Spain 13.0%; Ireland 9.0%.

Transport and communications

Transport. Railroads (1993): route length 411 mi, 662 km. Roads (1988): total length 17,600 mi, 28,400 km (paved 4%). Vehicles (1991): passenger cars 14,000; trucks and buses 13,000. Merchant marine (1992): vessels (100 gross tons and over) 23; total deadweight tonnage 1,749. Air transport (1986): passenger-mi 17,873,000, passenger-km 28,764,000; short ton-mi cargo 1,684,000, metric ton-km cargo 2,458,000; airports (1993) with scheduled flights 1.
Communications. Daily newspapers (1988): 1; total circulation 13,000; circulation per 1,000 population 2.0. Radio (1992): 130,000 receivers (1 per 56 persons). Television (1992): 65,000 receivers (1 per 111 persons). Telephones (1990): 19,602 (1 per 355 persons).

Education and health

Education (1990)

	schools	teachers	students	student/ teacher ratio
Primary (age 7–12)[6]	2,442	8,113	310,064	38.2
Secondary (age 13–18)	225[7]	4,846	75,674	15.6
Voc., teacher tr.	35[7]	1,130	10,268	9.1
Higher[7]	10	805[8]	6,245[8]	7.8[8]

Educational attainment: n.a. *Literacy* (1990): percentage of total population age 15 and over literate 24.0%; males 34.9%; females 13.4%.
Health (1988): physicians 672 (1 per 9,732 persons); hospital beds 3,382 (1 per 1,934 persons); infant mortality rate per 1,000 live births (1990–95) 134.
Food (1988–90): daily per capita caloric intake 2,242 (vegetable products 96%, animal products 4%); 97% of FAO recommended minimum requirement.

Military

Total active duty personnel (1993): 9,700 (army 87.6%, navy 4.1%, air force 8.3%). *Military expenditure as percentage of GNP* (1988): 1.2% (world 5.1%); per capita expenditure U.S.$4.

[1]Transitional government established January 1991 was to end with multiparty elections scheduled for December 1993. [2]The provinces of Boké and Faranah were abolished by presidential decree in January 1988. [3]Detail does not add to total given because of rounding. [4]Inflation, measured by the consumer price index, was 10.2% for the year ending March 31, 1993. [5]Imports c.i.f.; exports f.o.b. [6]1989. [7]1987–88. [8]Universities only.

Guinea-Bissau

Official name: Républica da Guiné-Bissau (Republic of Guinea-Bissau).
Form of government: transitional regime with one legislative house (National People's Assembly [150])[1].
Chief of state: President.
Head of government: Prime Minister.
Capital: Bissau.
Official language: Portuguese.
Official religion: none.
Monetary unit: 1 Guinea-Bissau peso (PG) = 100 centavos; valuation (Oct. 4, 1993) 1 U.S.$ = PG 4,964; 1 £ = PG 7,520.

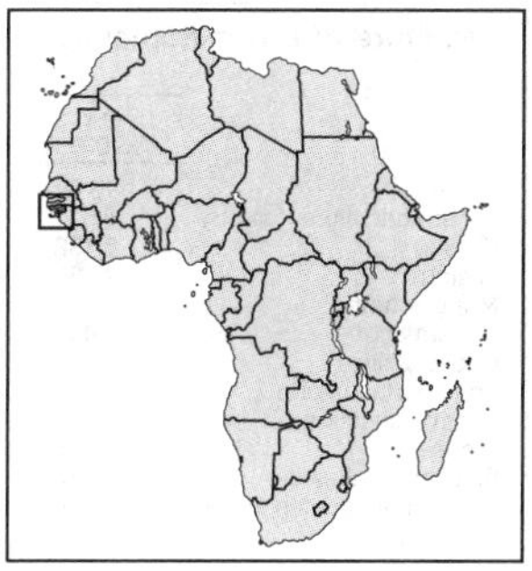

Area and population

Regions	Capitals	area sq mi	area sq km	population 1979 census[2]
Bafatá	Bafatá	2,309	5,981	115,656
Biombo[3]	Bissau	324	840	51,796
Bolama	Bolama	1,013	2,624	25,449
Cacheu	Cacheu	1,998	5,175	127,514
Gabú	Gabú	3,533	9,150	103,683
Oio	Farim	2,086	5,403	131,271
Quinara	Fulacunda	1,212	3,138	35,567
Tombali	Catió	1,443	3,736	55,088
Autonomous Sector				
Bissau[3]	—	30	78	107,281
TOTAL		13,948	36,125	753,305

Demography

Population (1993): 1,036,000.
Density (1993): persons per sq mi 74.3, persons per sq km 28.7.
Urban-rural (1990): urban 19.9%; rural 80.1%.
Sex distribution (1990): male 49.17%; female 50.83%.
Age breakdown (1990): under 15, 40.9%; 15–29, 24.9%; 30–44, 16.7%; 45–59, 10.9%; 60–74, 5.6%; 75 and over, 1.0%.
Population projection: (2000) 1,200,000; (2010) 1,480,000.
Doubling time: 29 years.
Ethnic composition (1979): Balante 27.2%; Fulani 22.9%; Malinke 12.2%; Mandyako 10.6%; Pepel 10.0%; other 17.1%.
Religious affiliation (1992): traditional beliefs 54%; Muslim 38%; Christian 8%.
Major cities (1979): Bissau 125,000[4]; Bafatá 13,429; Gabú 7,803; Mansôa 5,390; Catió 5,179.

Vital statistics

Birth rate per 1,000 population (1991): 42.0 (world avg. 26.4); legitimate, n.a.; illegitimate, n.a.
Death rate per 1,000 population (1991): 18.0 (world avg. 9.2).
Natural increase rate per 1,000 population (1991): 24.0 (world avg. 17.2).
Total fertility rate (avg. births per childbearing woman; 1990): 6.0.
Marriage rate per 1,000 population: n.a.
Divorce rate per 1,000 population: n.a.
Life expectancy at birth (1990–95): male 41.9 years; female 45.1 years.
Major causes of death per 100,000 population: n.a.; however, major diseases include tuberculosis of the respiratory system, whooping cough, typhoid fever, cholera, bacillary dysentery and amebiasis, malaria, pneumonia, and meningococcal infections.

National economy

Budget (1989). Revenue: PG 42,740,000,000 (1988; tax revenue 43.7%, of which excise tax 15.4%, export duties 14.1%; grants from abroad 38.5%; nontax revenue 17.8%). Expenditures (1989): PG 190,431,000,000 (capital expenditures 61.4%[5]; current expenditures 38.6%).
Public debt (external, outstanding; 1991): U.S.$573,700,000.
Production (metric tons except as noted). Agriculture, forestry, fishing (1992): rice 123,000, fruits 67,000, roots and tubers (sweet potatoes and cassava) 61,000, plantains 33,000, cashews 30,000, coconuts 25,000, millet 25,000, peanuts (groundnuts) 20,000, vegetables 20,000, corn (maize) 12,000, sorghum 10,000, palm kernels 8,000, sugarcane 6,000, copra 5,000, bananas 5,000, palm oil 5,000, seed cotton 1,000; livestock (number of live animals) 450,000 cattle, 300,000 pigs, 250,000 sheep, 250,000 goats, 1,000,000 chickens; roundwood (1991) 569,000 cu m; fish catch (1991) 5,000. Mining and quarrying: extraction of construction materials only. Manufacturing (in PG '000,000; 1982): beverages 143.7, of which beer 122.3, orangeade and lemonade 16.5; clothing 14.0[6]; peanut oil 7.0; palm oil 2.4. Construction (value added in Esc[7]; 1987): 520,000,000. Energy production (consumption): electricity (kW-hr; 1991) 41,000,000 (41,000,000); coal, none (none); crude petroleum, none (none); petroleum products (metric tons; 1991) none (67,000); natural gas, none (none).
Population economically active (1992): total 461,000; activity rate of total population 45.8% (participation rates: ages 15–64 [1979] 41.0%; female 3.6%; unemployed, n.a.).

Price and earnings indexes (1985 = 100)

	1983	1984	1985	1986	1987	1988	1989
Consumer price index	35.4	60.4	100.0	82.0	72.0	73.0	78.0
Annual earnings index	50.8	75.6	100.0	129.9	...	...	...

Gross national product (at current market prices; 1992): U.S.$214,400,000 (U.S.$210 per capita).

Structure of gross domestic product and labour force

	1989 in value U.S.$'000,000	1989 % of total value	1979 labour force	1979 % of labour force
Agriculture	99	45.4	153,069	71.9
Mining }	11	5.0	162	0.1
Manufacturing }			2,905	1.4
Construction	14	6.4	1,667	0.8
Public utilities	3	1.4	162	0.1
Transportation and communications	2	0.9	2,372	1.1
Trade }	60	27.5	5,085	2.4
Finance }			162	0.1
Pub. admin., defense	17	7.8 }	26,194	12.3
Services }	12	5.6 }		
Other }			21,232[8]	10.0[8]
TOTAL	218	100.0	213,010	100.0[9]

Tourism: n.a.
Land use (1991): forested 38.1%; meadows and pastures 38.4%; agricultural and under permanent cultivation 12.0%; other 11.5%.
Household income and expenditure. Average household size (1981) 4.1; income per household: n.a.; sources of income: n.a.; expenditure: n.a.

Foreign trade

Balance of trade (current prices)

	1983	1984	1985	1986	1987	1988
U.S.$'000,000	−49.8	−42.7	−51.4	−43.1	−29.3	−37.4
% of total	74.0%	55.1%	68.9%	69.2%	63.0%	54.0%

Imports (1991): U.S.$90,000,000 (1988; transport equipment 28.7%, building materials 17.9%, foodstuffs 8.6%, fuel and lubricants 8.6%, other 36.2%). *Major import sources* (1989): Italy 27.3%; Portugal 23.0%; Thailand 7.6%; The Netherlands 7.2%; France 4.3%; Senegal 4.2%; U.S.S.R. 3.0%.
Exports (1991): U.S.$23,000,000 (1988; cashews 52.8%, peanuts [groundnuts] 11.3%, frozen fish 3.1%). *Major export destinations* (1989): Portugal 34.4%; Spain 19.2%; France 18.1%; Japan 6.7%; The Netherlands 6.1%; Italy 6.0%; Belgium-Luxembourg 4.5%.

Transport and communications

Transport. Railroads: none. Roads (1989): total length 2,175 mi, 3,500 km (paved 15%). Vehicles (1991): passenger cars 3,300; trucks and buses 2,400. Merchant marine (1992): vessels (100 gross tons and over) 19; total deadweight tonnage 1,846. Air transport (1985): passenger-mi 6,000,000, passenger-km 9,000,000; short ton-mi cargo 700,000, metric ton-km cargo 1,000,000; airports (1993) with scheduled flights 2.
Communications. Daily newspapers (1990): total number 1; total circulation 6,000; circulation per 1,000 population 6. Radio (1992): total number of receivers 35,000 (1 per 29 persons). Television: n.a. Telephones (1991): 15,000 (1 per 67 persons).

Education and health

Education (1988)

	schools	teachers	students	student/ teacher ratio
Primary (age 7–13)	632[10]	3,065[10]	79,035	24.6[10]
Secondary (age 13–18)	12[11]	824[11]	5,505	7.8[11]
Voc., teacher tr.	4[10]	107	825	7.7

Educational attainment (1979). Percentage of population age 7 and over having: no formal schooling or knowledge of reading and writing 90.4%; primary education 7.9%; secondary 1.0%; technical 0.5%; higher 0.2%. *Literacy* (1990): total population age 15 and over literate 211,200 (36.5%); males literate 138,800 (50.2%); females literate 72,400 (24.0%).
Health (1986): physicians 274 (1 per 3,263 persons); hospital beds 2,430 (1 per 368 persons); infant mortality rate per 1,000 live births (1990–95) 140.
Food (1984–86): daily per capita caloric intake 2,278 (vegetable products 93%, animal products 7%); 84% of FAO recommended minimum requirement.

Military

Total active duty personnel (1993): 7,200 (army 94.4%, navy 4.2%, air force 1.4%). *Military expenditure as percentage of GNP* (1987): 2.4% (world 5.4%); per capita expenditure U.S.$4.

[1]Constitution was amended in June 1991, opposition parties were legalized in November 1991, and transitional government was to exist until March 1994. [2]Preliminary. [3]Biombo region excludes Bissau city. [4]1988. [5]In 1987 capital expenditures were divided: economic affairs 40%, of which agriculture, forestry, and fishing 20.1%; general public services 25.5%; health 5.4%; education 5.2%; defense 4.4%. [6]Production figure for first three quarters only. [7]Esc is the abbreviation for Portuguese escudo. [8]Not adequately defined. [9]Detail does not add to total given because of rounding. [10]1987. [11]1986.

Guyana

Official name: Co-operative Republic of Guyana.
Form of government: unitary multiparty republic with one legislative house (National Assembly [65[1]]).
Head of state and government: President.
Capital: Georgetown.
Official language: English.
Official religion: none.
Monetary unit: 1 Guyana dollar (G$) = 100 cents; valuation (Oct. 4, 1993) 1 U.S.$ = G$126.00; 1 £ = G$191.52.

Area and population

		area		population
Administrative Regions	Capitals	sq mi	sq km	1986 estimate
Region 1 (Barima/Waini)	Mabaruma	7,853	20,339	18,516
Region 2 (Pomeroon/Supenaam)	Anna Regina	2,392	6,195	41,966
Region 3 (Essequibo Islands/West Demerara)	Vreed-en-Hoop	1,450	3,755	102,760
Region 4 (Demerara/Mahaica)	Paradise	862	2,233	310,758
Region 5 (Mahaica/Berbice)	Fort Wellington	1,610	4,170	55,556
Region 6 (East Berbice/Corentyne)	New Amsterdam	13,998	36,255	148,967
Region 7 (Cuyuni/Mazaruni)	Bartica	18,229	47,213	17,941
Region 8 (Potaro/Siparuni)	Mahdia	7,742	20,052	5,672
Region 9 (Upper Takutu/Upper Essequibo)	Lethem	22,313	57,790	15,338
Region 10 (Upper Demerara/Berbice)	Linden	6,595	17,081	38,598
TOTAL		83,044[2]	215,083[2]	756,072[3]

Demography

Population (1993): 730,000.
Density (1993)[4]: persons per sq mi 9.6, persons per sq km 3.7.
Urban-rural (1992–93): urban 31.0%; rural 69.0%.
Sex distribution (1990): male 49.50%; female 50.50%.
Age breakdown (1990): under 15, 33.4%; 15–29, 33.2%; 30–44, 18.8%; 45–59, 8.7%; 60–74, 4.6%; 75 and over, 1.3%.
Population projection: (2000) 730,000; (2010) 730,000.
Doubling time: 44 years[5].
Ethnic composition (1992–93): East Indian 49.4%; black (African Negro and Bush Negro) 35.6%; mixed 7.1%; Amerindian 6.8%; Portuguese 0.7%; Chinese 0.4%.
Religious affiliation (1990): Christian 52.0%, of which Protestant 33.8% (including Anglican 17.0%), Roman Catholic 18.2%; Hindu 34.0%; Muslim 9.0%; other 5.0%.
Major cities (1985): Georgetown 195,000; Linden 30,000; New Amsterdam 20,000.

Vital statistics

Birth rate per 1,000 population (1991): 23.0 (world avg. 26.4).
Death rate per 1,000 population (1991): 7.0 (world avg. 9.2).
Natural increase rate per 1,000 population (1991): 16.0 (world avg. 17.2).
Total fertility rate (avg. births per childbearing woman; 1991): 2.7.
Marriage rate per 1,000 population: n.a.
Divorce rate per 1,000 population: n.a.
Life expectancy at birth (1991): male 61.0 years; female 68.0 years.
Major causes of death per 100,000 population (1984): diseases of the circulatory system 202.5, of which cerebrovascular disease 79.0; diseases of the digestive system 74.0; accidents and violence 56.5; diseases of the respiratory system 39.8; malignant neoplasms (cancers) 37.1.

National economy

Budget (1992–93). Revenue: G$19,880,000,000 (current revenue 96.4%, of which consumption taxes 25.9%, income taxes on companies 21.4%, import duties 10.2%, personal income taxes 9.0%; development revenue 3.6%). Expenditures: G$23,357,000,000 (current expenditure 78.5%, of which interest payments on debt 30.6%, personal emoluments 14.9%; development expenditure 21.5%).
Production (metric tons except as noted). Agriculture, forestry, fishing (1992): raw sugar 247,000, rice 168,300, coconuts 48,000, roots and tubers 32,000, plantains 23,000, bananas 20,000, oranges 15,000; livestock (number of live animals) 225,000 cattle, 130,000 sheep, 60,000 pigs; roundwood 189,000 cu m; fish catch 37,100, of which shrimps and prawns 4,700. Mining and quarrying (1992): bauxite 895,000; gold 79,600 troy oz; diamonds 21,900 carats[6]. Manufacturing (1992): flour 34,700; rum 218,200 hectolitres; beer and stout 142,900 hectolitres; cigarettes 318,000,000 units; refrigerators 6,464 units; pharmaceuticals 20,300,000 tablets; other products include cotton cloth and dyed and printed fabrics. Construction: n.a. Energy production (consumption): electricity (kW-hr; 1991) 219,000,000 (150,400,000[7]); coal, none (none); crude petroleum, none (none); petroleum products (metric tons; 1991) none (277,000); natural gas, none (none).
Tourism: receipts from visitors (1991) U.S.$30,000,000; expenditures by nationals abroad, n.a.
Household income and expenditure. Average household size (1980) 5.1; income per household: n.a.; sources of income: n.a.; expenditure (1970)[8]: food, beverages, and tobacco 42.5%, rent and water 21.4%, clothing and footwear 8.6%, education and recreation 6.4%, fuel and light 5.2%, other 15.9%.
Gross national product (at current market prices; 1992): U.S.$266,000,000 (U.S.$330 per capita).

Structure of gross domestic product and labour force

	1992		1980	
	in value G$'000,000[9]	% of total value	labour force	% of labour force
Sugar	11,469	28.4		
Other agriculture, forestry	5,620	13.9	50,316	20.4
Fishing	3,132	7.8		
Mining	4,736	11.7	9,669	3.9
Manufacturing	1,760[10]	4.4[10]	28,980	11.8
Construction	1,405	3.5	7,024	2.8
Public utilities	[10]	[10]	2,850	1.2
Transportation and communications	2,312	5.7	9,412	3.8
Trade	2,016	5.0	15,231	6.2
Finance, real estate	3,650	9.0	2,944	1.2
Pub. admin., defense	3,595	9.0	29,948	12.1
Services	664	1.6	29,295	11.9
Other	—	—	61,002[11]	24.7[11]
TOTAL	40,359	100.0	246,671	100.0

Public debt (external, outstanding; 1991): U.S.$1,554,000,000.
Population economically active (1987): total 270,074; activity rate of total population 35.7% (participation rates: ages 15–64, 60.4%; female 29.9%; unemployed [end of 1991] 13.5%).

Price and earnings indexes (1990 = 100)[12]

	1990	1991	1992	1993
Consumer price index	100.0	180.2	207.2	206.1[13]
Earnings index	...	...	...	...

Land use (1991): forested 83.2%; meadows and pastures 6.2%; agricultural and under permanent cultivation 2.5%; other 8.1%.

Foreign trade[14]

Balance of trade (current prices)

	1987	1988	1989	1990	1991	1992
G$'000,000	+6	+140	−889	−2,082	−4,596	−11,636
% of total	0.1%	3.2%	6.8%	9.3%	7.2%	13.9%

Imports (1991): G$34,274,900,000 (capital goods 40.6%; fuels and lubricants 21.9%; consumer goods 19.2%). *Major import sources*[15]: United States 34.0%; United Kingdom 14.0%; Trinidad and Tobago 12.0%; Japan 6.0%; Canada 5.0%.
Exports (1991): G$29,678,700,000 (domestic exports 95.7%, of which sugar 35.3%, bauxite 30.2%, gold 7.8%, rice 7.1%, shrimps 6.8%, timber 1.5%; re-exports 4.3%). *Major export destinations*[16]: United Kingdom 40.2%; United States 17.0%; Canada 10.8%; Caricom countries 6.0%; Japan 4.4%.

Transport and communications

Transport. Railroads[17]: length (1990) 55 mi, 88 km. Roads (1993): total length 4,474 mi, 7,200 km (paved 10%). Vehicles (1991): passenger cars 24,000; trucks and buses 9,000. Merchant marine (1992): vessels (100 gross tons and over) 82; total deadweight tonnage 13,509. Air transport (1991)[18]: passenger-mi 133,000,000, passenger-km 214,000,000; short ton-mi cargo 1,900,000, metric ton-km cargo 2,800,000; airports (1993) with scheduled flights 1[19].
Communications. Daily newspapers (1992): total number 1; total circulation 60,000; circulation per 1,000 population 80. Radio (1992): total number of receivers 310,000 (1 per 2.4 persons). Television (1992): total number of receivers 15,000 (1 per 50 persons). Telephones (1990): 16,003 (1 per 47 persons).

Education and health

Education (1989–90)

	schools	teachers	students	student/ teacher ratio
Primary (age 6–11)	423	4,010[20]	118,015[20]	...
Secondary (age 12–17)	93	...	72,096[20]	...
Voc., teacher tr.	8	176	5,388	30.6
Higher[21, 22]	1	370	2,391	6.5

Educational attainment (1980). Percentage of population age 25 and over having: no formal schooling 8.1%; primary education 72.8%; secondary 17.3%; higher 1.8%. *Literacy* (1990): total population age 15 and over literate, *c.* 490,000 (96.4%); males literate, *c.* 245,000 (97.5%); females literate, *c.* 245,000 (95.4%).
Health: physicians (1990) 286 (1 per 2,552 persons); hospital beds (1987) 2,204 (1 per 341 persons); infant mortality rate per 1,000 live births (1991) 51.0.
Food (1988–90): daily per capita caloric intake 2,495 (vegetable products 86%, animal products 14%); 110% of FAO recommended minimum requirement.

Military

Total active duty personnel (1993): 1,700[23] (army 88.2%, navy 5.9%, air force 5.9%). *Military expenditure as percentage of GNP* (1989): 2.7% (world 4.9%); per capita expenditure U.S.$8.

[1]Includes 12 indirectly elected seats. [2]Includes inland water area equaling *c.* 7,000 sq mi (*c.* 18,000 sq km). [3]Sample survey; estimated population based on 1992–93 sample survey adjusted for underenumeration was 730,000. [4]Based on land area only. [5]Net migration nearly equals natural-increase rate. [6]1991. [7]1990. [8]Weights of consumer price index components for Georgetown, New Amsterdam, and Linden only. [9]At factor cost. [10]Manufacturing includes Public utilities. [11]Represents "not stated." [12]Base and index are end-of-year. [13]March. [14]Imports c.i.f.; exports f.o.b. [15]Estimated figures. [16]Domestic exports only. [17]The two railways are privately owned and are used to transport minerals. [18]Scheduled traffic only. [19]International only; the number of domestic airports with scheduled air service is not available. [20]1988–89. [21]University of Guyana. [22]1991–92. [23]Excludes 3,000 paramilitary.

Haiti

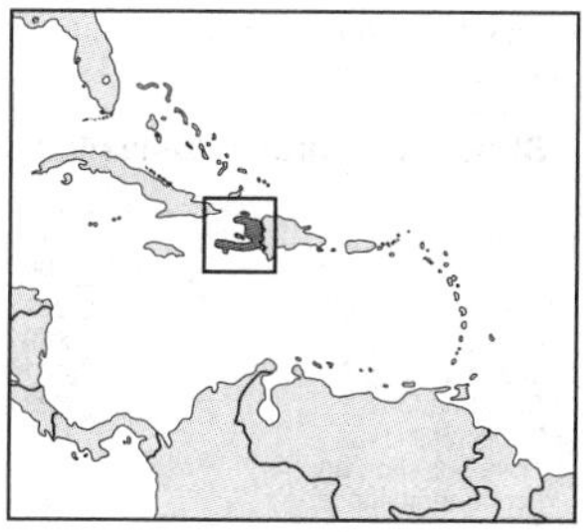

Official name: Repiblik Dayti (Haitian Creole); République d'Haïti (French) (Republic of Haiti).
Form of government: military-dominated extraconstitutional regime[1] with two legislative houses (Senate [27]; Chamber of Deputies [83]).
Chief of state: President[1, 2].
Head of government: Prime Minister.
Capital: Port-au-Prince.
Official languages: Haitian Creole; French.
Official religion: none[3].
Monetary unit: 1 gourde (G) = 100 centimes; valuation (Oct. 4, 1993) 1 U.S.$ = G 12.00; 1 £ = G 18.24.

Area and population

		area[4]		population
Departements	Capitals	sq mi	sq km	1992 estimate
Artibonite	Gonaïves	1,924	4,984	961,447
Centre	Hinche	1,419	3,675	467,514
Grande Anse	Jérémie	1,278	3,310	616,151
Nord	Cap-Haïtien	813	2,106	724,084
Nord-Est	Fort-Liberté	697	1,805	239,734
Nord-Ouest	Port-de-Paix	840	2,176	395,442
Ouest	Port-au-Prince	1,864	4,827	2,285,044
Sud	Les Cayes	1,079	2,794	630,007
Sud-Est	Jacmel	781	2,023	444,323
TOTAL		10,695	27,700	6,763,746

Demography

Population (1993): 6,902,000.
Density (1993): persons per sq mi 645.3, persons per sq km 249.2.
Urban-rural (1990): urban 30.3%; rural 69.7%.
Sex distribution (1990): male 49.03%; female 50.97%.
Age breakdown (1990): under 15, 40.2%; 15–29, 27.7%; 30–44, 16.3%; 45–59, 9.6%; 60–74, 4.9%; 75 and over, 1.3%.
Population projection: (2000) 8,003,000; (2010) 8,876,000.
Doubling time: 25 years.
Ethnic composition (1985): black 95.0%; mulatto 4.9%; white 0.1%.
Religious affiliation (1982): Roman Catholic 80.3%[5]; Protestant 15.8%, of which Baptist 9.7%, Pentecostal 3.6%; nonreligious 1.2%; other 2.7%.
Major cities (1992): Port-au-Prince 752,600 (metropolitan area 1,255,078); Carrefour 241,223[6]; Delmas 200,251[6]; Cap-Haïtien 92,122; Gonaïves 63,291.

Vital statistics

Birth rate per 1,000 population (1991): 43.0 (world avg. 26.4).
Death rate per 1,000 population (1991): 15.0 (world avg. 9.2).
Natural increase rate per 1,000 population (1991): 28.0 (world avg. 17.2).
Total fertility rate (avg. births per childbearing woman; 1991): 4.8.
Marriage rate per 1,000 population: n.a.
Divorce rate per 1,000 population: n.a.
Life expectancy at birth (1991): male 52.0 years; female 55.0 years.
Major causes of death per 100,000 population (1982)[7]: infectious and parasitic diseases 46.0; diseases of the circulatory system 11.9; diseases associated with malnutrition 8.5; diseases of the respiratory system 8.3; endocrine and metabolic disorders 8.0; ill-defined conditions 115.2.

National economy

Budget (1991–92). Revenue: G 992,900,000 (general sales taxes 17.9%; income taxes 15.3%; import duties 14.1%; excises 10.8%). Expenditures: G 1,838,800,000 (current expenditures 94.6%, of which extrabudgetary 38.6%; development expenditure 5.4%).
Tourism (1991–92): receipts from visitors U.S.$45,000,000; expenditures by nationals abroad U.S.$21,000,000.
Public debt (external, outstanding; 1991): U.S.$609,000,000.
Production (metric tons except as noted). Agriculture, forestry, fishing (1991): sugarcane 3,100,000, sweet potatoes 380,000, mangoes 280,000, plantains 280,000, bananas 220,000, corn (maize) 145,000, rice 120,000, sorghum 70,000, dry beans 55,000, coffee 37,000, oranges 29,000, sisal 10,000, cacao 5,000; livestock (number of live animals) 1,400,000 cattle, 1,200,000 goats, 930,000 pigs; roundwood 5,957,000 cu m; fish catch (1990) 7,500. Mining and quarrying (1990): limestone 287,000. Manufacturing (1991–92)[8]: cement 106,400; flour 11,600; essential oils (mostly amyris, neroli, and vetiver) 112; cigarettes 898,000,000 units; articles assembled for reexport (value of production in G '000,000) 632, of which garments 294, sports equipment and toys 100, electronic components 90, luggage and handbags 25. Construction: n.a. Energy production (consumption): electricity (kW-hr; 1991–92) 359,000,000 (212,000,000); coal, none (none); crude petroleum, none (none); petroleum products (metric tons; 1990) none (203,000); natural gas, none (none).
Population economically active (1990): total 2,679,140; activity rate of total population 41.1% (participation rates: ages 15–64, 64.8%; female 40.0%; unemployed [1989] unofficially 60.0%).

Price and earnings indexes (1985 = 100)

	1986	1987	1988	1989	1990	1991	1992
Consumer price index	103.3	91.5	95.2	101.8	123.7	142.8	162.4[9]
Annual earnings index	100.0	100.0	100.0	108.4	...	...	...

Household income and expenditure. Average household size (1982) 4.4; average annual income of wage earners (1984): urban (G 1,545 [U.S.$309]), rural (G 629 [U.S.$126]); expenditure (1976): food and beverages 77.9%[10], housing 8.3%, household furnishings 4.0%, clothing and footwear 3.2%.
Gross national product (1991): U.S.$2,471,000,000 (U.S.$370 per capita).

Structure of gross domestic product and labour force

	1991		1990	
	in value G '000,000[11]	% of total value	labour force	% of labour force
Agriculture	1,740	34.0	1,535,444	57.3
Mining	7	0.1	24,012	0.9
Manufacturing	669	13.1	151,387	5.6
Construction	319	6.2	28,001	1.0
Public utilities	50	1.0	2,577	0.1
Transp. and commun.	106	2.1	20,691	0.8
Trade, restaurants	838	16.4	352,970	13.2
Finance, real estate	316	6.2	5,057	0.2
Pub. admin., defense	726	14.2	155,347	5.8
Services	195	3.8		
Other	146[12]	2.9[12]	403,654[13]	15.1[13]
TOTAL	5,112	100.0	2,679,140	100.0

Land use (1990): forested 1.4%; meadows and pastures 18.0%; agricultural and under permanent cultivation 32.8%; other 47.8%.

Foreign trade[14, 15]

Balance of trade (current prices)

	1986–87	1987–88	1988–89	1989–90	1990–91	1991–92
U.S.$'000,000	−161.7	−160.4	−163.9	−168.5	−201.3	−202.4
% of total	27.3%	30.4%	35.4%	34.0%	33.6%	57.5%

Imports (1991–92): U.S.$277,100,000 (food and live animals 28.6%, mineral fuels 21.4%, basic manufactures 13.2%, chemicals and chemical products 8.0%). *Major import sources* (1989–90): United States 46.1%; Caribbean area 11.8%; France 7.4%; Japan 7.1%; Canada 6.6%.
Exports (1991–92)[16]: U.S.$74,700,000 (local manufactures—mostly processed foods, electrical equipment, textiles, and clothing—62.5%, coffee 12.4%, wood and sisal handicrafts 8.4%, essential oils 6.9%, sisal and twine 2.4%). *Major export destinations* (1989–90): United States 47.8%; France 10.7%; Italy 10.1%; Belgium 9.7%; Caribbean area 6.8%.

Transport and communications

Transport. Railroad (1990)[17]: route length 25 mi, 40 km. Roads (1988): total length 2,485 mi, 4,000 km (paved 15%). Vehicles (1991): passenger cars 33,000; trucks and buses 22,000. Merchant marine (1992): vessels (100 gross tons and over) 4; total deadweight tonnage 429. Air transport (1990)[18]: passenger arrivals 261,063, passenger departures 283,828; cargo unloaded 10,343 metric tons, cargo loaded 10,791 metric tons; airports (1993) with scheduled flights 2.
Communications. Daily newspapers (1991): total number 4; total circulation 44,500; circulation per 1,000 population 6.7. Radio (1992): total number of receivers 3,000,000 (1 per 2.3 persons). Television (1992): total number of receivers 25,000 (1 per 271 persons). Telephones (1990): 82,000 (1 per 79 persons).

Education and health

Education (1991–92)

	schools	teachers	students	student/ teacher ratio
Primary (age 6–12)	5,625[19]	26,208	1,148,400[20]	47.4[20]
Secondary (age 13–18) Voc., teacher tr.	...	9,470	184,968	19.5
Higher[21]	2	530	6,475	12.2

Educational attainment (1982). Percentage of population age 25 and over having: no formal schooling 76.9%; primary education 15.2%; secondary 7.2%; higher 0.7%. *Literacy* (1990): total population age 15 and over literate 2,096,900 (53.0%); males literate 1,128,000 (59.1%); females literate 968,000 (47.4%).
Health (1989): physicians 944 (1 per 6,083 persons); hospital beds 4,566 (1 per 1,258 persons); infant mortality rate per 1,000 live births (1991) 106.0.
Food (1988–90): daily per capita caloric intake 2,005 (vegetable products 89%, animal products 11%); 89% of FAO recommended minimum requirement.

Military

Total active duty personnel (1992): 7,400 (army 94.6%, navy 3.4%, air force 2.0%). *Military expenditure as percentage of GNP* (1989): 1.9% (world 4.9%); per capita expenditure U.S.$7.

[1]UN-brokered agreement of July 1993 to end military rule October 1993 with reinstatement of constitutionally elected president failed. [2]Office declared vacant June 1992. [3]Roman Catholicism has special recognition. [4]Estimated. [5]About 80% of all Roman Catholics also practice voodoo. [6]Within Port-au-Prince metropolitan area. [7]Public health facilities only. [8]Local production data for fiscal year ending September 30; reexport production data for fiscal year ending March 31. [9]Average of second and third quarters. [10]Excludes alcoholic beverages. [11]At prices of 1976. [12]Import duties. [13]Includes 63,975 not adequately defined and 339,679 officially unemployed. [14]Import figures c.i.f., export figures f.o.b. for fiscal year ending September 30. [15]The import and export value of preassembled and assembled U.S.-made components is excluded. Virtually all components used in the export assembly plants are imported. [16]Export value (1991–92) of assembled components equals U.S.$94,400,000 (garments constitute 72.2% of total, sports equipment and toys 12.1%, electronic components 8.1%). [17]The only railway is privately owned and used intermittently to haul sugarcane. [18]Port-au-Prince Airport only. [19]1988–89. [20]1989–90. [21]Port-au-Prince universities only.

Honduras

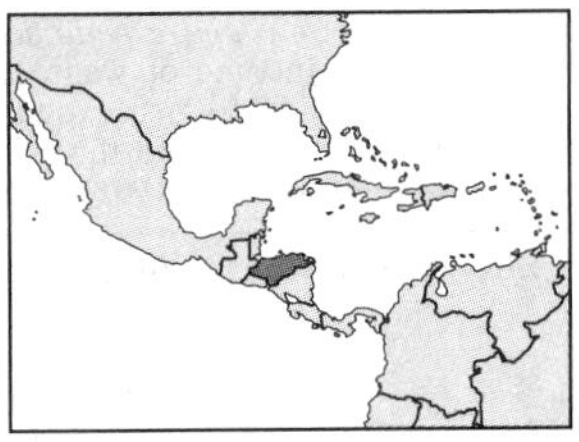

Official name: República de Honduras (Republic of Honduras).
Form of government: multiparty republic with one legislative house (Congress [128]).
Head of state and government: President.
Capital: Tegucigalpa[1].
Official language: Spanish.
Official religion: none.
Monetary unit: 1 Honduran lempira (L) = 100 centavos; valuation (Oct. 4, 1993) 1 U.S.$ = L 6.91; 1 £ = L 10.47.

Area and population

		area		population
				1991
Departments	Administrative centres	sq mi	sq km	estimate
Atlántida	La Ceiba	1,641	4,251	255,000
Choluteca	Choluteca	1,626	4,211	309,000
Colón	Trujillo	3,427	8,875	164,000
Comayagua	Comayagua	2,006	5,196	257,000
Copán	Santa Rosa de Copán	1,237	3,203	226,000
Cortés	San Pedro Sula	1,527	3,954	706,000
El Paraíso	Yuscarán	2,787	7,218	277,000
Francisco Morazán	Tegucigalpa	3,068	7,946	878,000
Gracias a Dios	Puerto Lempira	6,421	16,630	37,000
Intibucá	La Esperanza	1,186	3,072	130,000
Islas de la Bahía	Roatán	100	261	24,000
La Paz	La Paz	900	2,331	112,000
Lempira	Gracias	1,656	4,290	180,000
Ocotepeque	Nueva Ocotepeque	649	1,680	77,000
Olancho	Juticalpa	9,402	24,351	309,000
Santa Bárbara	Santa Bárbara	1,975	5,115	291,000
Valle	Nacaome	604	1,565	121,000
Yoro	Yoro	3,065	7,939	355,000
TOTAL		43,277	112,088	4,708,000

Demography

Population (1993): 5,148,000.
Density (1993): persons per sq mi 119.0, persons per sq km 45.9.
Urban-rural (1991): urban 41.1%; rural 58.9%.
Sex distribution (1990): male 50.07%; female 49.93%.
Age breakdown (1990): under 15, 44.6%; 15–29, 28.3%; 30–44, 14.4%; 45–59, 7.8%; 60–74, 3.9%; 75 and over, 1.0%.
Population projection: (2000) 6,260,000; (2010) 7,904,000.
Doubling time: 23 years.
Ethnic composition (1987): mestizo 89.9%; Amerindian 6.7%; black (including Black Carib) 2.1%; white 1.3%.
Religious affiliation (1986): Roman Catholic 85.0%; Protestant (mostly fundamentalist, Moravian, and Methodist) 10.0%; other 5.0%.
Major cities (1989): Tegucigalpa 608,100[2]; San Pedro Sula 300,400; La Ceiba 71,600; El Progreso 63,400; Choluteca 57,400.

Vital statistics

Birth rate per 1,000 population (1991): 39.0 (world avg. 26.4); legitimate, n.a.; illegitimate, n.a.
Death rate per 1,000 population (1991): 8.0 (world avg. 9.2).
Natural increase rate per 1,000 population (1991): 31.0 (world avg. 17.2).
Total fertility rate (avg. births per childbearing woman; 1991): 5.3.
Marriage rate per 1,000 population (1983): 4.9.
Divorce rate per 1,000 population (1983): 0.4.
Life expectancy at birth (1989): male 63.0 years; female 67.0 years.
Major causes of death per 100,000 population (1983): diseases of the circulatory system 48.4; infectious and parasitic diseases 46.6; accidents and violence 42.2; diseases of the respiratory system 26.3.

National economy

Budget (1991). Revenue: L 5,902,000,000 (current revenue 82.1%, of which taxes on production and consumption 17.2%, import duties 11.6%, income taxes 10.6%; capital revenue 17.9%). Expenditures: L 5,902,000,000 (current expenditure 63.8%; public-debt service 19.2%; capital expenditure 17.0%).
Public debt (external, outstanding; 1991): U.S.$2,866,000,000.
Production (metric tons except as noted). Agriculture, forestry, fishing (1992): sugarcane 3,004,000, bananas 1,086,000, corn (maize) 582,000, plantains 182,000, coffee 135,000, palm oil 78,000, sorghum 69,000, dry beans 46,000, rice 41,000; livestock (number of live animals) 2,351,000 cattle, 750,000 pigs; roundwood (1991) 6,288,000 cu m; fish catch (1991) 20,989. Mining and quarrying (1990): zinc concentrate 29,628; lead (metal content) 5,785. Manufacturing (1991): cement 693,000; raw sugar 385,000; wheat flour 217,000; beer 671,000 hectolitres; milk 507,000 hectolitres; cigarettes 2,528,000,000 units. Construction (value of private construction in L '000,000; 1992)[3]: residential 151.4; nonresidential 126.3. Energy production (consumption): electricity (kW-hr; 1990) 1,105,000,000 (1,268,000,000); coal, none (none); crude petroleum (barrels; 1990) none (1,942,000); petroleum products (metric tons; 1990) 245,000 (511,000); natural gas, none (none).
Household income and expenditure. Average household size (1988) 5.4; income per household: n.a.; sources of income (1985): wages and salaries 58.8%, transfer payments 1.8%, other 39.4%; expenditure (1986): food 44.4%, utilities and housing 22.4%, clothing and footwear 9.0%, household furnishings 8.3%, health care 7.0%, transportation and communications 3.0%, other 5.9%.

Gross national product (at current market prices; 1992): U.S.$2,980,000,000 (U.S.$550 per capita).

Structure of gross domestic product and labour force

	1991			
	in value L '000,000[4]	% of total value	labour force	% of labour force
Agriculture	3,262	22.8	702,900	46.1
Mining	269	1.9	4,100	0.3
Manufacturing	2,424	17.0	179,600	11.8
Construction	623	4.4	88,700	5.8
Public utilities	476	3.3	10,300	0.7
Transportation and communications	770	5.4	42,800	2.8
Trade	1,857	13.0	156,500	10.3
Finance, real estate	2,051	14.4	27,900	1.8
Public admin., defense	1,050	7.3 }	310,500	20.4
Services	1,507	10.5 }		
TOTAL	14,289	100.0	1,523,300	100.0

Population economically active (1991): total 1,523,300; activity rate of total population 37.6% (participation rates: over age 15, 80.1%; female 30.2%; unemployed [1990] 40.0%).

Price and earnings indexes (1985 = 100)

	1986	1987	1988	1989	1990	1991	1992
Consumer price index	104.4	106.9	111.8	122.8	151.4	202.8	220.6
Weekly earnings index[5]	100.0	100.0	100.0	100.0	100.0	...	...

Land use (1991): forested 28.4%; meadows and pastures 23.0%; agricultural and under permanent cultivation 16.5%; other 32.1%.
Tourism (1991): receipts from visitors U.S.$31,000,000; expenditures by nationals abroad U.S.$37,000,000.

Foreign trade[6]

Balance of trade (current prices)

	1986	1987	1988	1989	1990	1991
L '000,000	+124.7	−99.0	−47.3	+5.4	−29.8	+11.9
% of total	3.8%	2.8%	1.3%	0.1%	0.8%	0.7%

Imports (1991): U.S.$879,800,000 (machinery and transport equipment 25.9%, mineral fuels 18.8%, chemical products 15.8%, plastics and resins 7.8%, base-metal products 7.4%). *Major import sources:* United States 40.5%; Japan 9.0%; Mexico 7.3%; Venezuela 6.6%; The Netherlands 6.0%.
Exports (1991): U.S.$808,100,000 (bananas 42.3%, coffee 19.2%, shrimp and lobsters 12.8%, lead and zinc 4.7%, roundwood 2.0%). *Major export destinations:* United States 53.8%; Germany 8.7%; Belgium 7.0%; Japan 5.4%; Italy 3.6%.

Transport and communications

Transport. Railroads (1989): length (1990) 583 mi, 939 km; passenger-km 7,700,000; metric ton-km cargo 30,200,000. Roads (1990): total length 7,066 mi, 11,371 km (paved 21%). Vehicles (1990): passenger cars 88,982; trucks and buses 18,049. Merchant marine (1992): vessels (100 gross tons and over) 966; total deadweight tonnage 1,437,321. Air transport (1990): passenger-mi 321,000,000, passenger-km 516,000,000; short ton-mi cargo 2,000,000, metric ton-km cargo 3,000,000; airports (1993) with scheduled flights 9.
Communications. Daily newspapers (1990): total number 5; total circulation 199,000; circulation per 1,000 population 39. Radio (1992): total number of receivers 1,800,000 (1 per 2.8 persons). Television (1992): total number of receivers 160,000 (1 per 31 persons). Telephones (1991): 94,147 (1 per 46 persons).

Education and health

Education (1991)

	schools	teachers	students	student/teacher ratio
Primary (age 7–13)	7,487	25,854	923,902	35.7
Secondary (age 14–19)	540	8,517	132,953	15.6
Voc., teacher tr.	5[7]	581[7]	47,727	13.7[7]
Higher	5	2,740	34,333	12.5

Educational attainment (1988). Percentage of population age 10 and over having: no formal schooling 33.4%; primary education 50.1%; secondary education 13.4%; higher 3.1%. *Literacy* (1990): total population age 15 and over literate 2,082,000 (73.1%); males literate 1,078,000 (75.5%); females literate 1,004,000 (70.6%).
Health (1991): physicians (1990) 2,900 (1 per 1,586 persons); hospital beds 5,303 (1 per 818 persons); infant mortality rate per 1,000 live births 48.0.
Food (1988–90): daily per capita caloric intake 2,210 (vegetable products 89%, animal products 11%); 98% of FAO recommended minimum.

Military

Total active duty personnel (1992): 16,800 (army 83.3%, navy 6.0%, air force 10.7%). *Military expenditure as percentage of GNP* (1989): 3.2% (world 4.9%); per capita expenditure U.S.$33.

[1]Tegucigalpa and adjacent city of Comayagüela jointly form the capital according to the constitution. [2]Population cited is for Central District (Tegucigalpa and Comayagüela). [3]Tegucigalpa, San Pedro Sula, and 10 other urban centres. [4]At factor cost. [5]Official minimum wages in all sectors. Minimum wages were fixed from June 1981 to Jan. 1, 1990, when new minimum wages were introduced. [6]Import figures are f.o.b. in balance of trade and c.i.f. for commodities and trading partners. [7]1989.

Hong Kong

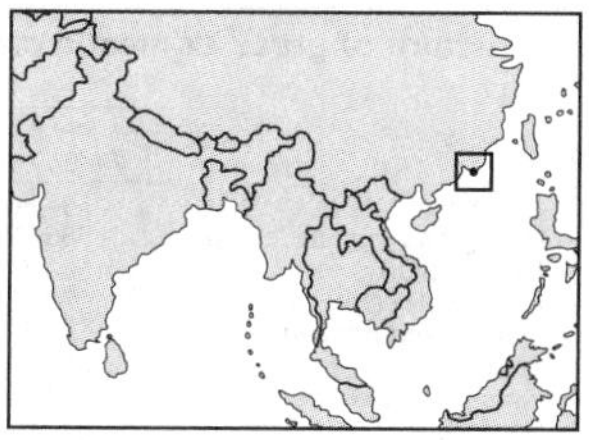

Official name: Hsiang Kang (Chinese); Hong Kong (English).
Political status: Crown Colony (United Kingdom)[1] with one legislative house (Legislative Council [60[2]]).
Chief of state: British Monarch.
Head of government: Governor.
Capital: none[3].
Official languages: Chinese; English.
Official religion: none.
Monetary unit: 1 Hong Kong dollar (HK$) = 100 cents; valuation (Oct. 4, 1993) 1 U.S.$ = HK$7.80; 1 £ = HK$11.86.

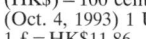

Area and population

Area	area[4] sq mi	area[4] sq km	population 1991 census
Hong Kong Island	30.8	79.9	1,214,253
Kowloon and New Kowloon	16.5	42.7	1,975,265
New Territories	368.0	953.1	2,321,661
Marine	—	—	11,102
TOTAL	415.3	1,075.7	5,609,951[5]

Demography

Population (1993): 5,858,000.
Density (1993): persons per sq mi 14,116.6, persons per sq km 5,450.7.
Urban-rural (1993): urban 100.0%.
Sex distribution (1992): male 50.93%; female 49.07%.
Age breakdown (1992)[6]: under 15, 20.5%; 15–29, 24.9%; 30–44, 27.8%; 45–59, 13.5%; 60–74, 10.1%; 75 and over, 3.2%.
Population projection: (2000) 6,198,000; (2010) 6,716,000.
Doubling time: 87 years.
Linguistic composition (1991)[7]: Chinese 96.8%, of which Cantonese 88.7%; English 2.2%; other 1.0%.
Religious affiliation (1992): predominantly Buddhist and Taoist; however, there are about 258,000 Protestants, 254,800 Roman Catholics, 50,000 Muslims, and 12,000 Hindus.
Major cities: no bounded localities exist within Hong Kong.

Vital statistics

Birth rate per 1,000 population (1992): 12.3 (world avg. 26.4); legitimate (1985) 94.5%; illegitimate 5.5%.
Death rate per 1,000 population (1992): 5.3 (world avg. 9.2).
Natural increase rate per 1,000 population (1992): 7.0 (world avg. 17.2).
Total fertility rate (avg. births per childbearing woman; 1990): 1.2.
Marriage rate per 1,000 population (1991): 7.3.
Divorce rate per 1,000 population (1991): 1.2.
Life expectancy at birth (1992): male 75.1 years; female 80.7 years.
Major causes of death per 100,000 population (1992): malignant neoplasms (cancers) 155.6; diseases of the circulatory system 153.0; diseases of the respiratory system 96.1; accidents and poisoning 28.8; diseases of the genitourinary system 21.1; diseases of the digestive system 21.1.

National economy

Budget (1992–93). Revenue: HK$135,646,000,000 (earnings and profit taxes 41.2%; indirect taxes 29.9%, of which entertainment and stamp duties 16.9%, duties 5.3%; capital revenue 10.0%). Expenditures: HK$127,298,000,000 (education 17.3%; transportation and public works 14.2%; general services support 12.9%; law and order 12.7%; housing 11.4%; health 10.8%; social welfare 6.3%; culture and recreation 5.1%).
Public debt: n.a.
Gross domestic product (at current market prices; 1992): U.S.$95,928,000,000 (U.S.$16,500 per capita).

Structure of gross domestic product and labour force

	1991 in value HK$'000,000	1991 % of total value	1991 labour force	1991 % of labour force
Agriculture	1,441	0.2	22,400	0.8
Mining	222	—	400	—
Manufacturing	94,491	14.7	729,000	26.0
Construction	32,106	5.0	230,000	8.2
Public utilities	13,463	2.1	18,200	0.7
Transp. and commun.	58,970	9.1	278,100	9.9
Trade	154,423	23.9	744,900	26.6
Finance, insurance, and real estate	205,032	31.8	231,400	8.3
Pub. admin., defense, and services	93,601	14.5	539,400	19.3
Other	–8,866[8]	–1.3[8]	5,000	0.2
TOTAL	644,883	100.0	2,798,800	100.0

Production (metric tons except as noted). Agriculture, forestry, fishing (1992): vegetables 95,000, fruits and nuts 2,730, milk 1,180, field crops 540, eggs 52,600,000 units; livestock (number of live animals; 1991) 313,420 pigs[9], 820 cattle, 13,082,000 chickens; roundwood (1990) 193,000 cu m; fish catch 228,480. Mining and quarrying (1990): clay and kaolin 16,587; feldspar 3,820. Manufacturing (value added in HK$; 1990): wearing apparel 18,924,000,000; textiles 14,051,000,000; electrical and electronic products 11,361,000,000; publishing and printed material 6,842,000,000; basic metals and fabricated metal products 6,336,000,000; plastic products 5,923,000,000. Construction (1992): residential 714,000 sq m; nonresidential 1,578,000 sq m. Energy production (consumption): electricity (kW-hr; 1990) 28,938,000,000 (27,141,000,000); coal (metric tons; 1990) none (8,932,000); petroleum products (metric tons; 1990) none (2,600,000); natural gas (cu m; 1990) none (385,800,000).
Population economically active (1992): total 2,768,000; activity rate of total population 47.6% (participation rates: over age 15, 61.9%; female 45.6%; unemployed 1.9%).

Price and earnings indexes (1985 = 100)

	1986	1987	1988	1989	1990	1991	1992
Consumer price index	102.9	108.6	116.6	128.4	140.8	157.3	171.9
Daily earnings index[10]	110.2	123.5	141.8	166.3	187.8	182.0	...

Household income and expenditure (1991). Average household size 3.4; monthly income per household HK$9,964 (U.S.$1,282); sources of income: n.a.; expenditure (1989–90): food 34.2%, housing 25.6%, transportation and vehicles 7.6%, clothing and footwear 7.5%, durable goods 3.8%.
Tourism (1992): receipts from visitors U.S.$6,136,000,000; expenditures by nationals abroad, n.a.
Land use (1992): forested 20.5%; agricultural and under permanent cultivation 6.1%; fishponds 1.5%; built-on, scrublands, and other 71.9%.

Foreign trade

Balance of trade (current prices)

	1987	1988	1989	1990	1991	1992
HK$'000,000	+86	–5,717	+7,728	–2,656	–13,096	–30,342
% of total	—	0.6%	0.7%	0.2%	0.1%	1.6%

Imports (1992): HK$955,295,000,000 (machinery and transport equipment 32.1%, of which electrical machinery 10.0%, telecommunications equipment 7.9%; textile yarn and fabrics 10.6%; apparel and accessories 8.4%; chemicals and related products 7.1%; photographic apparatus, watches, and clocks 4.8%; food and live animals 4.6%). *Major import sources:* China 37.1%; Japan 17.4%; Taiwan 9.1%; United States 7.4%; South Korea 4.6%; Singapore 4.1%; Germany 2.3%; United Kingdom 2.0%.
Exports (1992): HK$234,123,000,000[11] (clothing accessories and apparel 33.0%; office and automatic data processing machines 8.8%; electrical machinery 8.6%; watches and clocks 8.1%; textile fabrics 7.4%; telecommunications equipment 5.5%; metal products 3.0%; articles of artificial resins and plastics 2.0%; paper and paper products 1.2%). *Major export destinations:* United States 27.6%; China 26.5%; Germany 6.4%; United Kingdom 5.4%; Japan 4.7%; Singapore 4.4%; Taiwan 2.8%.

Transport and communications

Transport. Railroads (1992): route length 21 mi, 34 km; passenger-mi 1,939,000,000, passenger-km 3,120,000,000; short ton-mi cargo 41,000,000, metric ton-km cargo 60,000,000. Roads (1992): total length 969 mi, 1,559 km (paved 100%). Vehicles (1992): passenger cars 237,055; trucks and buses 155,836. Merchant marine (1992): vessels (100 gross tons and over) 387; total deadweight tonnage 11,688,605. Air transport (1992): passenger arrivals 8,451,000, passenger departures 8,636,000; airports (1993) with scheduled flights 1.
Communications. Daily newspapers (1992): total number 67; total circulation 2,930,000[12]; circulation per 1,000 population 505[12]. Radio (1992): total number of receivers 2,500,000 (1 per 2.3 persons). Television (1992): total number of receivers 1,749,000 (1 per 3.3 persons). Telephones (1992): 3,600,000 (1 per 1.6 persons).

Education and health

Education (1992–93)

	schools	teachers[13]	students	student/ teacher ratio[13]
Primary (age 6–11)	652	19,346	501,625	26.7
Secondary (age 12–18)	494	20,360	461,460	22.5
Vocational	34[14]	2,488[15]	50,782	18.5[15]
Higher	12	1,422[15]	68,694	32.4[15]

Educational attainment (1991). Percentage of population age 15 and over having: no formal schooling 12.8%; primary education 25.2%; secondary 45.8%; matriculation 4.9%; nondegree higher 5.4%; higher degree 5.9%.
Literacy (1985): total population age 15 and over literate 3,668,000 (88.1%); males literate 2,040,000 (94.7%); females literate 1,628,000 (80.9%).
Health (1992): physicians 6,818[16] (1 per 848 persons); hospital beds 26,385 (1 per 219 persons); infant mortality rate per 1,000 live births (1992) 5.0.
Food (1988–90): daily per capita caloric intake 2,860 (vegetable products 70%, animal products 30%); 125% of FAO recommended minimum requirement.

Military

Total active duty personnel (1991): 6,500[17] (army 87.7%; navy 7.7%; air force 4.6%). *Military expenditure as percentage of GNP* (1984): 0.6% (world 5.9%); per capita expenditure U.S.$39.

[1]On July 1, 1997, Hong Kong will revert to China as a Special Administrative Region in which the existing socioeconomic system would remain unchanged for a period of 50 years. [2]Includes 21 nonelective seats. [3]Victoria, for some time, had been regarded as the capital because it is the seat of the British administration of the Crown Colony. [4]Excludes the surface areas of reservoirs. [5]Includes 35,823 transients and 51,847 Vietnamese migrants not enumerated by area. [6]Excludes transients and Vietnamese refugees. [7]Excludes about 59,900 Vietnamese refugees, about 1% of the population. [8]Indirect taxes less subsidies. [9]Excludes local pigs not slaughtered in abattoirs. [10]In manufacturing. [11]Excludes reexports valued at HK$690,829,000,000. [12]Thirty-one newspapers only. [13]1991–92. [14]1989–90. [15]1987–88. [16]Registered personnel; all may not be present and working in the country. [17]British forces with a few locally enlisted personnel.

Hungary

Official name: Magyar Köztársaság (Republic of Hungary).
Form of government: unitary multiparty republic with one legislative house (National Assembly [394[1]]).
Chief of state: President.
Head of government: Prime Minister.
Capital: Budapest.
Official language: Hungarian.
Official religion: none.
Monetary unit: 1 forint (Ft) = 100 filler; valuation (Oct. 4, 1993) 1 U.S.$ = Ft 96.50; 1 £ = Ft 146.20.

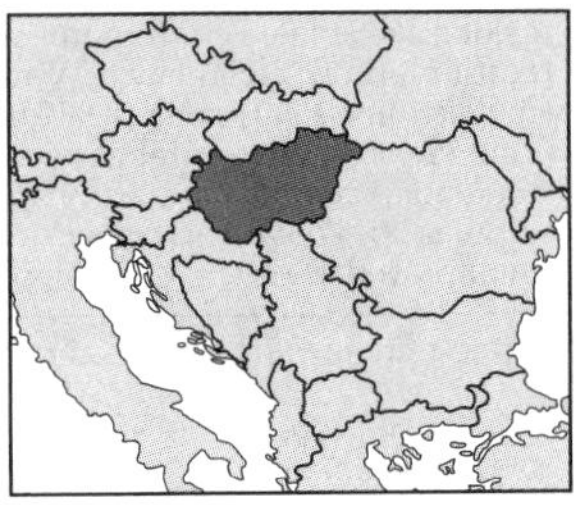

Area and population

Counties	Capitals	area sq mi	area sq km	population 1992[2] estimate
Bács-Kiskun	Kecskemét	3,229	8,362	542,000
Baranya	Pécs	1,732	4,487	418,000
Békés	Békéscsaba	2,175	5,632	407,000
Borsod-Abaúj-Zemplén	Miskolc	2,798	7,247	755,000
Csongrád	Szeged	1,646	4,263	438,000
Fejér	Székesfehérvár	1,688	4,373	423,000
Győr-Moson-Sopron	Győr	1,549	4,012	428,000
Hajdú-Bihar	Debrecen	2,398	6,211	549,000
Heves	Eger	1,404	3,637	333,000
Jász-Nagykun-Szolnok	Szolnok	2,165	5,607	422,000
Komárom-Esztergom	Tatabánya	869	2,251	313,000
Nógrád	Salgótarján	982	2,544	225,000
Pest	Budapest[3]	2,469	6,394	975,000
Somogy	Kaposvár	2,331	6,036	343,000
Szabolcs-Szatmár-Bereg	Nyíregyháza	2,293	5,938	567,000
Tolna	Szekszárd	1,430	3,704	252,000
Vas	Szombathely	1,288	3,337	275,000
Veszprém	Veszprém	1,810	4,689	378,000
Zala	Zalaegerszeg	1,461	3,784	304,000
Capital City				
Budapest[3]		203	525	1,992,000
TOTAL		35,920	93,033	10,337,000[4]

Demography

Population (1993): 10,296,000.
Density (1993): persons per sq mi 286.6, persons per sq km 110.6.
Urban-rural (1990): urban 61.9%; rural 38.1%.
Sex distribution (1992): male 47.99%; female 52.01%.
Age breakdown (1991): under 15, 19.9%; 15–29, 20.5%; 30–44, 22.6%; 45–59, 18.0%; 60–74, 13.6%; 75 and over, 5.4%.
Population projection: (2000) 10,094,000; (2010) 9,812,000. The population has declined at an average annual rate of 0.3% since 1980.
Ethnic composition (nationality; 1990): Magyar 97.8%; Gypsy 1.4%; German 0.3%; Croatian 0.1%; Romanian 0.1%; Slovak 0.1%.
Religious affiliation (1989): Christian 87.9%, of which Roman Catholic 64.1%, Protestant 23.3%, Orthodox 0.5%; Jewish 0.9%; atheist and nonreligious 11.2%.
Major cities (1992[2]): Budapest 1,992,343; Debrecen 214,712; Miskolc 191,623; Szeged 177,506; Pécs 169,486.

Vital statistics

Birth rate per 1,000 population (1992): 11.7 (world avg. 26.4); (1990) legitimate 86.9%; illegitimate 13.1%.
Death rate per 1,000 population (1992): 14.2 (world avg. 9.2).
Natural increase rate per 1,000 population (1992): −2.5 (world avg. 17.2).
Total fertility rate (avg. births per childbearing woman; 1991): 1.8.
Marriage rate per 1,000 population (1992): 5.5.
Divorce rate per 1,000 population (1991): 2.3.
Life expectancy at birth (1990): male 65.1 years; female 73.7 years.
Major causes of death per 100,000 population (1991): diseases of the circulatory system 733.0; malignant neoplasms (cancers) 303.6; accidents and self-inflicted injuries 119.8.

National economy

Budget (1991). Revenue: Ft 1,588,700,000,000 (payments by enterprises 31.0%, income tax 21.0%, turnover tax 18.0%). Expenditures: Ft 1,641,800,000,000 (1990; social security 26.8%, education 9.4%, health 6.2%, defense 5.6%).
Production (metric tons except as noted). Agriculture, forestry, fishing (1992): corn (maize) 4,301,000, wheat 3,444,000, sugar beets 2,974,000, barley 1,555,000[5], potatoes 925,000, apples 859,000[5], grapes 759,000[5], sunflower seeds 757,000, rye 281,000[5]; livestock (number of live animals) 5,364,000 pigs, 1,752,000 sheep, 1,159,000 cattle; roundwood (1991) 5,776,000 cu m; fish catch (1990) 38,888. Mining and quarrying (1991): limestone 6,572,000[6]; bauxite 2,036,710; manganese ore 54,383. Manufacturing (1992): cement 2,236,000; rolled steel 1,660,000; crude steel 1,559,000; pig iron 1,176,000; alumina 548,000; fertilizers 330,800[5]; cotton fabrics 102,903,000 sq m; leather footwear 18,725,000 pairs; buses 3,546 units; diesel motors 3,278 units. Construction (in Ft '000,000; 1990): residential 17,126[7]. Energy production (consumption): electricity (kW-hr; 1992) 31,396,000,000 (34,265,000,000); coal (metric tons; 1992) 15,836,000 (17,891,000[6]); crude petroleum (barrels; 1992) 13,380,000 (42,353,000[6]); petroleum products (metric tons; 1990) 6,931,000 (7,550,000); natural gas (cu m; 1992) 4,932,000,000 (10,446,000,000[6]).
Tourism (1991): receipts from visitors U.S.$1,002,300,000; expenditures by nationals abroad U.S.$442,800,000.
Public debt (external, outstanding; 1991): U.S.$19,221,000,000.
Gross national product (1991): U.S.$28,244,000,000 (U.S.$2,690 per capita).

Structure of gross domestic product and labour force

	1991 in value Ft '000,000	1991 % of total value	1992[2] labour force	1992[2] % of labour force
Agriculture	234,803	10.2	588,900	12.7
Mining and manufacturing	585,585	25.4	1,286,200[8]	27.7[8]
Construction	133,743	5.8	272,800	5.9
Public utilities	76,360	3.3	[8]	[8]
Transp. and commun.	192,371	8.4	372,900	8.0
Trade	284,910	12.4	564,200	12.1
Finance, real estate	179,937	7.8		
Services	343,059	14.9	1,156,800	24.9
Other	270,732[9]	11.8[9]	406,100[10]	8.7[10]
TOTAL	2,301,500	100.0	4,647,900	100.0

Population economically active (1992[2]): total 4,641,800; activity rate of total population 41.0% (participation rates: working age 81.1%[5]; female 46.3%; unemployed 8.7%).

Price and earnings indexes (1985 = 100)

	1986	1987	1988	1989	1990	1991	1992
Consumer price index	105.3	113.9	132.5	154.8	199.5	206.5	231.9
Monthly earnings index	107.4	117.0	129.9	152.0	182.1	...	...

Household income and expenditure. Average household size (1991) 2.8; income per household (1988) Ft 176,150 (U.S.$3,500); sources of income (1992): wages 46.1%, social income 22.4%, self-employment 11.9%; expenditure (1990): food and beverages 40.6%, transportation and communications 12.9%, housing 7.9%, clothing 7.9%, household durable goods 6.7%, culture and recreation 6.4%.
Land use (1990): forested 18.2%; meadows and pastures 12.7%; agricultural and under permanent cultivation 56.9%; other 12.2%.

Foreign trade[11]

Balance of trade (current prices)

	1985	1986	1987	1988	1989	1990
Ft '000,000,000	+22.6	−11.8	−5.0	+40.2	+56.2	+67.7
% of total	2.8%	1.4%	0.6%	4.1%	5.2%	5.9%

Imports (1992): Ft 878,500,000,000 (industrial consumer goods 22.2%, machinery and transport equipment 20.7%, fuels and electrical energy 14.6%, food and live animals 5.9%). *Major import sources* (1991): Germany 21.4%; U.S.S.R. 15.3%; Austria 13.3%; Italy 7.2%; Czechoslovakia 4.1%; Switzerland 3.4%; Japan 2.7%; The Netherlands 2.7%.
Exports (1992): Ft 844,000,000,000 (industrial consumer goods 26.2%, food and live animals 24.0%, machinery and transport equipment 12.0%, fuels and electrical energy 2.7%). *Major export destinations* (1991): Germany 21.4%; U.S.S.R. 15.3%; Austria 13.3%; Italy 7.6%; Yugoslavia 3.7%; U.S. 3.2%; France 2.9%.

Transport and communications

Transport. Railroads (1991): length 8,200 mi, 13,200 km; passenger-mi 6,591,000,000, passenger-km 10,607,000,000; short ton-mi cargo 8,177,000,000, metric ton-km cargo 11,938,000,000. Roads (1991): total length 18,591 mi, 29,919 km (paved 99%). Vehicles (1991): passenger cars 2,015,455; trucks and buses 225,220. Merchant marine (1992): vessels (100 gross tons and over) 15; total deadweight tonnage 93,204. Air transport (1991): passenger-mi 799,500, passenger-km 1,286,700; short ton-mi cargo 5,698,000, metric ton-km cargo 8,319,000; airports (1993) with scheduled flights 1.
Communications. Daily newspapers (1990): total number 29; total circulation 2,759,300; circulation per 1,000 population 266. Radio (1992): 6,000,000 (1 per 1.7 persons). Television (1992): 4,261,600 (1 per 2.4 persons). Telephones (1991): 1,989,800 (1 per 5.2 persons).

Education and health

Education (1991–92)

	schools	teachers	students	student/ teacher ratio
Primary (age 6–13)	3,641	95,300	1,129,300	11.8
Secondary (age 14–17)	780	24,017	309,400	12.9
Vocational	317	6,765	204,700	30.2
Higher	77	17,477	107,200	6.1

Educational attainment (1984). Percentage of population age 7 and over having: no formal schooling 1.3%; primary education 65.5%; secondary 27.1%; higher 6.1%. *Literacy* (1984): total population age 15 and over literate 8,269,850 (98.9%); males literate 3,934,250 (99.2%); females literate 4,335,600 (98.6%).
Health (1991): physicians 39,508 (1 per 262 persons); hospital beds 104,072 (1 per 100 persons); infant mortality rate per 1,000 live births (1992) 14.0.
Food (1988–90): daily per capita caloric intake 3,608 (vegetable products 63%; animal products 37%); 137% of FAO recommended minimum.

Military

Total active duty personnel (1992): 80,800 (army 78.6%, air force 21.4%). *Military expenditure as percentage of GNP* (1989): 6.3% (world 4.9%); per capita expenditure U.S.$391.

[1]Includes eight nonelective seats. [2]January 1. [3]Budapest has separate county status. The area and population of the city are excluded from the larger county (Pest), which it administers. [4]Detail does not add to total given because of rounding. [5]1991. [6]1990. [7]Includes hotel construction. [8]Mining and manufacturing includes Public utilities. [9]Other material activities and balance of taxes on products. [10]Unemployed. [11]Import figures are f.o.b. in balance of trade and c.i.f. for commodities and trading partners.

Iceland

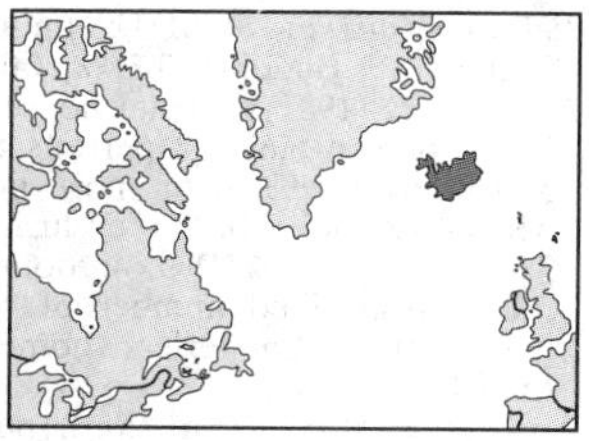

Official name: Lýdhveldidh Ísland (Republic of Iceland).
Form of government: unitary multiparty republic with one legislative house (Althing [63][1]).
Chief of state: President.
Head of government: Prime Minister.
Capital: Reykjavík.
Official language: Icelandic.
Official religion: Evangelical Lutheran.
Monetary unit: 1 króna (ISK) = 100 aurar; valuation (Oct. 4, 1993) 1 U.S.$ = ISK 69.25; 1 £ = ISK 104.92.

Area and population

Regions[2]	Administrative centres	area sq mi	area sq km	population 1992[3] estimate
Austurland	Egilsstadhir	8,491	21,991	13,058
Höfudhborgarsvædhi	Reykjavík	765[4]	1,982[4]	151,779
Nordhurland eystra	Akureyri	8,636	22,368	26,678
Nordhurland vestra	Saudhárkrókur	5,055	13,093	10,359
Sudhurland	Selfoss	9,735	25,214	20,671
Sudhurnes	Keflavík	[4]	[4]	15,487
Vestfirdhir	Ísafjördhur	3,657	9,470	9,685
Vesturland	Borgarnes	3,360	8,701	14,476
TOTAL		39,699	102,819	262,193

Demography

Population (1993): 264,000.
Density (1993)[5]: persons per sq mi 8.6, persons per sq km 3.4.
Urban-rural (1992): urban 91.2%; rural 8.8%.
Sex distribution (1992): male 50.15%; female 49.85%.
Age breakdown (1992): under 15, 24.7%; 15–29, 24.2%; 30–44, 22.5%; 45–59, 13.6%; 60–74, 10.3%; 75 and over, 4.7%.
Population projection: (2000) 279,000; (2010) 295,000.
Doubling time: 66 years.
Ethnic composition (1992)[6]: Icelandic 96.1%; Danish 0.9%; Swedish 0.5%; persons born in the United States 0.4%; German 0.3%; other 1.8%.
Religious affiliation (1991): Protestant 96.2%, of which Evangelical Lutheran 92.2%, other Lutheran 3.1%; Roman Catholic 1.0%; nonreligious 1.4%; other 1.4%.
Major cities (1992): Reykjavík 100,850 (urban area 151,130); Kópavogur 16,-832[7]; Hafnarfjördhur 16,107[7]; Akureyri 14,665; Keflavík 7,508.

Vital statistics

Birth rate per 1,000 population (1991): 17.6 (world avg. 26.4); legitimate 43.6%; illegitimate 56.4%.
Death rate per 1,000 population (1991): 7.0 (world avg. 9.2).
Natural increase rate per 1,000 population (1991): 10.6 (world avg. 17.2).
Total fertility rate (avg. births per childbearing woman; 1991): 2.2.
Marriage rate per 1,000 population (1991): 4.8.
Divorce rate per 1,000 population (1991): 2.1.
Life expectancy at birth (1990–91): male 75.1 years; female 80.8 years.
Major causes of death per 100,000 population (1991): diseases of the circulatory system 313.2, of which ischemic heart diseases 191.9, cerebrovascular disease 68.6; malignant neoplasms (cancers) 172.9; diseases of the respiratory system 77.5.

National economy

Budget (1992). Revenue: ISK 103,447,000,000 (sales tax 38.6%, income tax 19.3%, import duties 9.4%, taxes on alcohol and tobacco 6.2%). Expenditures: ISK 110,607,000,000 (health and welfare 46.4%, education 15.3%, general services 9.9%, communications 7.0%).
Production (metric tons except as noted). Agriculture, forestry, fishing (1992): potatoes 6,300, dried hay 2,087,000 cu m, silage 912,000 cu m; livestock (number of live animals) 487,300 sheep, 76,000 cattle, 75,200 horses; fish (value of catch in ISK '000,000; 1991): cod 21,810, redfish 6,040, haddock 4,770, shrimp 4,250. Mining and quarrying (1992): diatomite 20,000. Manufacturing (value added in ISK '000,000; 1989): food products 18,928; printing and publishing 4,200; fabricated metal products and machinery 4,167; wood furniture 1,964; nonmetallic mineral products 1,646. Construction (completed): residential (1991) 660,000 cu m; nonresidential (1990) 1,003,000 cu m. Energy production (consumption): electricity (kW-hr; 1991) 4,432,000,-000 (4,427,000,000); coal (metric tons; 1990) none (70,000); crude petroleum, none (none); petroleum products (metric tons; 1990) none (637,000); natural gas, none (none).
Land use (1990): forested 1.2%; meadows and pastures 22.7%; agricultural and under permanent cultivation 0.1%; other 76.0%.
Population economically active (March 1993): total 148,700; activity rate of total population 56.5% (participation rates: ages 16–74, 81.8%; female 46.6%; unemployed [April 1992–March 1993] 3.5%).

Price and earnings indexes (1985 = 100)

	1987	1988	1989	1990	1991	1992	1993[8]
Consumer price index	143.4	181.3	221.7	254.3	268.5	283.0	293.6
Hourly wages index	188.3	238.4	270.2	291.0	313.9	325.1	...

Tourism (1992): receipts from visitors U.S.$219,700,000; expenditures by nationals abroad U.S.$288,000,000.

Gross national product (at current market prices; 1991): U.S.$5,814,000,000 (U.S.$22,580 per capita).

Structure of gross national product and labour force

	1991 in value ISK '000,000[9]	1991 % of total value	1990 labour force[10]	1990 % of labour force
Agriculture	9,900	2.7	6,166	4.8
Fishing	34,600	9.4	7,087	5.6
Fish processing	18,400	5.0	7,659	6.0
Manufacturing	45,300	12.3	15,577	12.3
Construction	31,600	8.6	12,382	9.7
Public utilities	15,800	4.3	1,110	0.9
Transportation and communications	28,700	7.8	8,415	6.6
Trade	51,100	13.9	18,109	14.3
Finance, real estate	64,800	17.6	10,136	8.0
Pub. admin., defense	57,000	15.5	22,751	17.9
Services	23,600	6.4	15,373	12.1
Other	−12,900[11]	−3.5[11]	2,255[12]	1.8[12]
TOTAL	367,900[13]	100.0	127,020	100.0

Public debt (external, outstanding; end of 1992): U.S.$2,281,000,000.
Household income and expenditure. Average household size (1985) 2.9; average net income from employment for persons filing tax returns (1991) ISK 1,154,000 (U.S.$19,561); sources of income (1991)[14]: wages and salaries 74.4%, transfer payments 16.6%, self-employment 3.0%, other 6.0%; expenditure (1987): food and beverages 21.1%, transportation and communications 18.6%, housing 11.2%, household furnishings 11.1%, clothing and footwear 10.4%, expenditures in restaurants and hotels 8.5%, recreation 8.2%.

Foreign trade[15]

Balance of trade (current prices)

	1987	1988	1989	1990	1991	1992
ISK '000,000	−2,207	−576	+6,943	+4,540	−3,253	−392
% of total	2.0%	0.5%	4.5%	2.5%	1.7%	0.2%

Imports (1992): ISK 96,895,000,000 (consumer goods 21.7%; capital goods [except transport equipment] 18.4%; transport equipment 16.1%, of which ships 7.0%; food and beverages 8.6%; fuels and lubricants 8.2%). *Major import sources:* Norway 14.6%; Germany 12.4%; Denmark 8.8%; United Kingdom 8.5%; United States 8.3%; The Netherlands 7.5%; Sweden 6.8%.
Exports (1992): ISK 87,833,000,000 (marine products 79.6%, of which frozen cod fillets 18.2%, uncured salted fish 9.6%, frozen shrimp 8.1%, fresh whole fish chilled or on ice 8.0%; aluminum 9.2%; ferrosilicon 1.9%). *Major export destinations:* United Kingdom 25.1%; Germany 12.5%; United States 11.4%; France 9.9%; Japan 7.5%; Denmark 5.6%.

Transport and communications

Transport. Railroads: none. Roads (1992): total length 7,121 mi, 11,460 km (paved 20%). Vehicles (1991): passenger cars 120,862; trucks and buses 16,012. Merchant marine (1992): vessels (100 gross tons and over) 394; total deadweight tonnage 114,851. Air transport (1992)[16]: passenger-mi 1,143,-000,000, passenger-km 1,840,000,000; short ton-mi cargo 21,114,000, metric ton-km cargo 30,826,000; airports (1993) with scheduled flights 19.
Communications. Daily newspapers (1992): total number 6; total circulation 132,700; circulation per 1,000 population 508. Radio (1992): total number of receivers 155,000 (1 per 1.7 persons). Television (1992): total number of receivers 76,250 (1 per 3.4 persons). Telephones (1991): 135,559[17] (1 per 1.9 persons).

Education and health

Education (1991–92)

	schools	teachers	students	student/ teacher ratio
Primary (age 7–12)	...	...	25,809	...
Secondary (age 13–20)	...	...	29,985	...
Higher[18]	5	369[19]	5,450	14.0[19]

Educational attainment: n.a. *Literacy:* virtually 100%.
Health: physicians (1989) 715 (1 per 355 persons); hospital beds (1988) 4,307 (1 per 58 persons); infant mortality rate per 1,000 live births (1991) 5.5.
Food (1988–90): daily per capita caloric intake 3,473 (vegetable products 60%, animal products 40%); 131% of FAO recommended minimum requirement.

Military

Total active duty personnel (1992): 130 coast guard personnel; NATO-sponsored U.S.-manned Iceland Defense Force (1992): 3,000 (navy 60.0%, air force 40.0%). *Military expenditure as percentage of GNP* (1989): none (world average 4.9%).

[1]Meets as single chamber since dissolution of the Upper House in May 1991. [2]Regions have limited administrative authority. [3]December 1. [4]Höfudhborgarsvædhi includes Sudhurnes. [5]Population density calculated with reference to 29,800 sq mi (77,100 sq km) area free of glaciers, lava fields, and lakes. [6]By country of birth. [7]Within Reykjavík urban area. [8]June. [9]Data estimated from percentage distribution of sectors. [10]Man-years. [11]Net of imputed bank service charges and income not classified elsewhere. [12]Unemployed. [13]GDP (1991) equals ISK 382,900,000,000. [14]For persons filing tax returns. [15]Import figures are f.o.b. in balance of trade and c.i.f. in commodities and trading partners. [16]Icelandair only. [17]Number of subscribers. [18]1990–91. [19]Four institutions only.

India

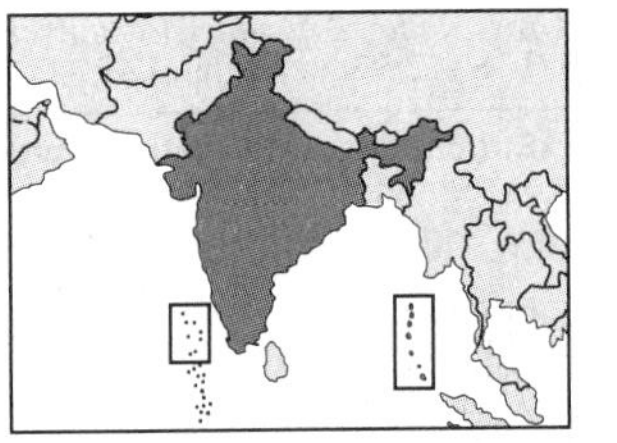

Official name: Bhārat (Hindī); Republic of India (English).
Form of government: multiparty federal republic with two legislative houses (Council of States [245][1], House of the People [545][2]).
Chief of state: President.
Head of government: Prime Minister.
Capital: New Delhi.
Official languages: Hindī; English.
Official religion: none.
Monetary unit: 1 Indian rupee (Re, plural Rs) = 100 paise; valuation (Oct. 4, 1993) 1 U.S.$ = Rs 31.15; 1 £ = Rs 47.19.

Area and population

States	Capitals	area sq mi	area sq km	population 1991 census
Andhra Pradesh	Hyderābād	106,204	275,068	66,508,008
Arunāchal Pradesh	Itānagar	32,333	83,743	864,558
Assam	Dispur	30,285	78,438	22,414,322
Bihār	Patna	67,134	173,877	86,374,465
Goa	Panaji	1,429	3,702	1,169,793
Gujarāt	Gāndhīnagar	75,685	196,024	41,309,582
Haryāna	Chandīgarh	17,070	44,212	16,463,648
Himāchal Pradesh	Shimla	21,495	55,673	5,170,877
Jammu and Kashmir	Srīnagar	38,830	100,569	7,718,700[3]
Karnātaka	Bangalore	74,051	191,791	44,977,201
Kerala	Trivandrum	15,005	38,863	29,098,518
Madhya Pradesh	Bhopāl	171,215	443,446	66,181,170
Mahārāshtra	Bombay	118,800	307,690	78,937,187
Manipur	Imphāl	8,621	22,327	1,837,149
Meghālaya	Shillong	8,660	22,429	1,774,778
Mizoram	Āīzawl	8,140	21,081	689,756
Nāgāland	Kohīma	6,401	16,579	1,209,546
Orissa	Bhubaneshwar	60,119	155,707	31,659,736
Punjab	Chandīgarh	19,445	50,362	20,281,969
Rājasthān	Jaipur	132,140	342,239	44,005,990
Sikkim	Gangtok	2,740	7,096	406,457
Tamil Nādu	Madras	50,216	130,058	55,858,946
Tripura	Agartala	4,049	10,486	2,757,205
Uttar Pradesh	Lucknow	113,673	294,411	139,112,287
West Bengal	Calcutta	34,267	88,752	68,077,965
Union Territories				
Andaman and Nicobar Islands	Port Blair	3,185	8,249	280,661
Chandīgarh	Chandīgarh	44	114	642,015
Dādra and Nagar Haveli	Silvassa	190	491	138,477
Damān and Diu	Damān	43	112	101,586
Delhi	Delhi	572	1,483	9,420,644
Lakshadweep	Kavaratti	12	32	51,707
Pondicherry	Pondicherry	190	492	807,785
TOTAL		1,222,243[4]	3,165,596[4]	846,302,688

Demography

Population (1993): 896,567,000.
Density (1993)[4]: persons per sq mi 733.5, persons per sq km 283.2.
Urban-rural (1991): urban 25.7%; rural 74.3%.
Sex distribution (1991): male 51.90%; female 48.10%.
Age breakdown (1990): under 15, 36.0%; 15–29, 27.7%; 30–44, 18.0%; 45–59, 11.2%; 60–74, 5.9%; 75 and over, 1.2%.
Population projection: (2000) 1,018,673,000; (2010) 1,189,396,000.
Doubling time: 33 years.
Linguistic composition (1981)[5]: Hindī (lingua franca) 45.00%; Hindī (including associated languages and dialects) 38.77%; Telugu 7.96%; Bengalī 7.56%; Marāṭhī 7.28%; Tamil 6.56%; Urdū 5.18%; Gujarātī 4.87%; Kannaḍa 3.95%; Malayālam 3.81%; Oṛiyā 3.36%; Punjābī 2.73%; English (lingua franca) 2.50%; Assamese 1.64%[6]; Bhīlī/Bhilodī 0.65%; Santhālī 0.62%; Kashmirī 0.47%; Goṇḍī 0.29%; Sindhī 0.29%; Konkaṇī 0.23%; Dogrī 0.22%; Tulu 0.20%; Kurukh 0.19%; Nepālī 0.18%; Khandeshī 0.17%; Manipurī 0.13%; other 2.69%.
Place of birth (foreign born; 1981): other Asia 7,875,399, of which Bangladesh 4,170,524, Pakistan 2,736,038, Nepal 501,292, Sri Lanka 211,514, Myanmar 134,783; Africa 42,726; Europe 13,046; United States and Canada 5,923.
Major cities (urban agglomerations; 1991): Greater Bombay 9,925,891 (12,596,243); Delhi 7,206,704 (8,419,084); Calcutta 4,399,819 (11,021,915); Madras 3,841,396 (5,421,985); Bangalore 3,302,296 (4,130,288); Hyderābād 3,145,939 (4,253,759); Ahmadābād 2,954,526 (3,312,216); Kānpur 1,879,420 (2,029,889); Nāgpur 1,624,752 (1,664,006); Lucknow 1,619,115 (1,669,204); Pune 1,566,651 (2,493,987); New Delhi[7] 301,297.

Other principal cities (1991)

	population		population		population
Āgra	891,790	Indore	1,091,674	Rājkot	612,458
Allahābād	806,486	Jabalpur	764,586	Rānchi	599,306
Amritsar	708,835	Jaipur	1,458,183	Sholāpur (Solāpur)	604,215
Aurangābād	573,272	Jalandhar (Jullundur)	509,510	Srīnagar	594,775[11]
Bareilly	590,661	Jodhpur	666,279	Sūrat	1,505,872
Bhopāl	1,062,771	Kalyān[9]	1,014,557	Thāne (Thāna)[9]	803,389
Chandīgarh	510,565	Kota	537,371	Trivandrum	699,872
Cochin (Kochi)	582,588	Ludhiāna	1,042,740	Vadodara (Baroda)	1,061,598
Coimbatore	816,321	Madurai	940,989	Vārānasi (Benares)	932,399
Farīdābād	617,717	Meerut	753,778	Vijayawāda	701,827
Guwāhāti	584,342	Mysore	606,755	Vishākhapatnam	752,037
Gwalior	690,765	Nāshik (Nāsik)	656,925		
Howrah (Hāora)[8]	950,435	Patna	917,243		
Hubli-Dhārwād	648,298	Pimpri-Chinchwad[10]	517,083		

Religious affiliation (1981)[12]: Hindu 82.64%; Muslim 11.35%; Christian 2.43%; Sikh 1.97%; Buddhist 0.71%; Jain 0.48%; Zoroastrian 0.01%; other 0.41%.
Households (1981)[12]. Total households 119,230,710. Average household size 5.6; 1 person 5.6%, 2 persons 8.3%, 3 persons 11.0%, 4 persons 14.6%, 5 persons 15.9%, 6 or more persons 44.6%. Average number of rooms per household 2.0; no exclusive room 0.6%, 1 room 44.7%, 2 rooms 28.6%, 3 rooms 12.2%, 4 rooms 6.3%, 5 rooms 2.7%, 6 or more rooms 3.1%, unspecified number of rooms 1.8%. Average number of persons per room 2.8. Shelterless (homeless) population estimated (1987) at more than 100,000,000.
Emigration (1987 estimation): persons living abroad 12,697,000 (accepting foreign citizenship 8,200,000), of which in Nepal (1980) 3,800,000 (2,388,000); Malaysia 1,170,000 (1,029,000); Middle Eastern countries 1,064,000 (102,000); Sri Lanka 1,028,000 (457,000); South Africa 850,000 (850,000); United Kingdom 789,000 (395,000); Mauritius 701,000 (700,000); United States 500,000 (287,000); Trinidad and Tobago 430,000 (430,000); Fiji 339,000 (339,000); Myanmar 330,000 (50,000); Canada 229,000 (129,000).

Vital statistics

Birth rate per 1,000 population (1991): 32.5 (world avg. 26.4).
Death rate per 1,000 population (1991): 11.4 (world avg. 9.2).
Natural increase rate per 1,000 population (1991): 21.1 (world avg. 17.2).
Total fertility rate (avg. births per childbearing woman; 1991): 3.8.
Marital status of male (female) population age 25 and over (1981): single 6.4% (1.1%); married 87.4% (79.4%); widowed 5.7% (18.8%); divorced or separated 0.5% (0.7%).
Life expectancy at birth (1991): male 57.7 years; female 58.7 years.
Major causes of death (rural areas only; 1990)[13]: senility 24.4%[14]; infectious and parasitic diseases 18.0%; diseases of the respiratory system 15.7%; diseases of the circulatory system 10.9%; accidents and injuries 6.9%; prematurity at birth 4.9%; diseases of the digestive system 3.7%; cancers 3.4%; anemias 3.2%; suicide 1.6%; diseases of the nervous system 1.3%; diabetes 0.7%.

Social indicators

Educational attainment (1981)[12]. Percentage of population age 25 and over having: no formal schooling (illiterate) 64.8%; no formal schooling (literate) 1.0%; some primary education 7.1%; completed primary 10.9%; some secondary 6.2%; completed secondary 7.1%; higher vocational 0.4%; completed undergraduate degree 2.5%.

Distribution of expenditure (1989–90)

percentage of household expenditure by quintile

1	2	3	4	5 (highest)
8.8%	12.5%	16.2%	21.3%	41.2%

Quality of working life. Average workweek (1989): 42 hours. Rate of fatal (nonfatal) injuries per 100,000 workers: industrial workers (1985) 15 (5,301); miners (1990) 32 (172); railway workers (1987–88) 17 (1,188). Employees covered under Employee's State Insurance Scheme (1989) 6,807,000; number of beneficiaries 26,411,000. Average days lost to labour stoppages per 1,000 workdays (1989): 20.
Access to services (1990). Proportion of villages having access to electricity 83.4%. Proportion of urban (rural) population having access to: safe water supply 84.0% (74.0%); safe sewage disposal 46.0% (2.0%).
Social participation. Eligible voters participating in last (May/June 1991) national election: 53%. Verified trade union membership in total workforce (1986): less than 5% (about 10,000,000 workers).
Social deviance (1984). Offense rate per 100,000 population for: murder 3.4; dacoity (gang robbery) 1.4; theft and housebreaking 43.7; rape 0.8. Rate of suicide per 100,000 population (1990): 6.9.
Availability of consumer durables. Local production in 1980 (1991): automobiles 31,000 (165,000); motorcycles 102,000 (431,000); black and white television receivers 369,000 (3,100,000); colour television receivers, none (880,000); refrigerators 278,000 (1,322,000); air conditioners 44,000 (80,000).

National economy

Gross national product (1991): U.S.$284,668,000,000 (U.S.$330 per capita).

Structure of gross domestic product and labour force

	1990–91[15] in value Rs '000,000,000	1990–91[15] % of total value	1981[12] labour force	1981[12] % of labour force
Agriculture	1,501	31.8	172,713,291	66.4
Mining	109	2.3	1,301,632	0.5
Manufacturing	878	18.6	26,554,517	10.2
Construction	271	5.7	3,864,104	1.5
Public utilities	103	2.2	989,490	0.3
Transp. and commun.	339	7.2	6,206,697	2.4
Trade, restaurants	588	12.4	12,638,204	4.9
Finance, real estate	390	8.2	1,822,229	0.7
Pub. admin., defense	269	5.7	18,514,810	7.1
Services	279	5.9		
Other	—	—	15,670,144[16]	6.0[16]
TOTAL	4,727	100.0	260,275,118	100.0

Budget (1992–93). Revenue: Rs 1,145,200,000,000 (tax revenue 60.8%, of which excise taxes 27.2%, customs duties 22.0%, corporation taxes 7.1%; nontax revenue 39.2%, of which economic services 21.1%, interest receipts 11.8%). Expenditures: Rs 1,284,000,000,000 (interest payments and debt servicing 24.9%; transportation 13.3%; grants to state governments 12.7%; defense 9.9%; agriculture 5.2%; communications 4.8%; social services 2.9%).
Production (in '000 metric tons except as noted). Agriculture, forestry, fishing (1991): sugarcane 240,290, rice 110,945, wheat 54,522, potatoes 15,254,

sorghum 10,800, mangoes 9,700, millet 9,000, corn (maize) 8,200, peanuts (groundnuts) 7,000, coconuts 6,550, bananas 6,400, cassava 5,600, chickpeas 5,196, rapeseed 5,152, seed cotton 5,106, dry beans 4,052, cottonseed 3,404, tomatoes 3,100, palm oil 2,800, soybeans 2,100, oranges 1,890, cotton lint 1,700, barley 1,642, jute 1,620, apples 1,020, sunflower seed 850, lentils 835, sesame seed 800, tea 730, chilies 609[17], tobacco 560, turmeric 340[17], cashews 305[18], ginger 154[17], black pepper 43[17]; livestock (number of live animals) 198,400,000 cattle, 112,000,000 goats, 77,000,000 water buffalo, 55,740,000 sheep; roundwood 279,801,000 cu m; fish catch (1990) 3,619, of which freshwater fish 1,371. Mining and quarrying (1991): limestone 71,000; iron ore (metal content) 36,300; bauxite 4,836; dolomite 2,458[19]; manganese 1,385; chromite 958; magnesite 547[19]; zinc (metal content) 98; copper (metal content) 61; gold 63,430 troy oz; diamonds 18,010 carats[19]. Manufacturing (1991–92): cement 51,660; steel ingots 14,194[19]; refined sugar 12,852; finished steel 11,118[19]; nitrogenous fertilizers 7,068[19]; paper and paperboard 2,527; jute manufactures 1,450; soda ash 1,404; aluminum 513; nylon and polyester yarns 261[19]; bicycles 7,128,000 units; diesel engines 1,795,000 units[19]; motorcycles and scooters 1,608,000 units; passenger cars and jeeps 192,000 units; passenger buses and trucks 155,000 units; cotton cloth 12,158,000,000 metres; drugs and pharmaceuticals Rs 9,000,000,000[20]; computer software Rs 8,008,000,000[21, 22]; gold jewelry Rs 7,390,000,000[22]; silk goods Rs 6,760,000,000[22]. Construction (value in Rs; 1984) residential 87,010,000,000; nonresidential 40,730,000,000.

Manufacturing enterprises (1987–88)[23]

	no. of factories	no. of persons engaged	avg. wages as a % of avg. of all wages	annual value added (Rs '000,000)[15]
Chemicals and chemical products,	6,578	555,000	148.6	37,368
of which paints, soaps, etc.	3,171	215,000	92.7	10,487
drugs and medicine	1,497	135,000	170.0	8,631
industrial chemicals	1,049	84,000	166.7	7,429
fertilizers and pesticides	515	78,000	207.7	6,805
Textiles (excl. clothing)	12,029	1,414,000	87.8	28,581
Iron and steel	5,147	564,000	131.0	22,202
Food products	18,333	1,025,000	56.7	21,721
Electrical machinery/apparatus,	4,241	376,000	149.1	21,715
of which radios and televisions	1,070	109,000	130.8	5,131
Nonelectrical machinery/apparatus	7,584	447,000	129.1	19,455
Transport equipment,	3,318	485,000	147.9	18,810
of which motor vehicles	1,463	173,000	171.4	9,879
Refined petroleum	96	18,000	243.7	12,488
Bricks, tiles, cement	7,595	350,000	67.0	9,286
Metal products	6,390	209,000	100.2	7,147
Rubber products	1,762	94,000	120.8	5,333
Printing and publishing	3,187	164,000	117.1	4,828
Tobacco products	7,483	390,000	29.5	4,419
Paper and paper products	1,909	135,000	100.0	3,807
Nonferrous metals	1,037	60,000	148.1	3,508
Plastic products	2,023	66,000	84.5	2,568

Energy production (consumption): electricity (kW-hr; 1991–92) 286,700,000,000 ([1990] 286,940,000,000); coal (metric tons; 1991–92) 229,000,000 ([1990] 218,939,000); crude petroleum (barrels; 1992) 211,800,000 ([1990] 379,980,000); petroleum products (metric tons; 1990) 39,456,000 (44,766,000); natural gas (cu m; 1992) 13,796,000,000 ([1990] 10,303,000,000).

Financial aggregates[24]

	1987	1988	1989	1990	1991	1992	1993[25]
Exchange rate, Rs per:							
U.S. dollar	12.88	14.95	17.03	18.07	25.83	26.20	31.38
£	24.10	27.05	27.35	34.84	48.33	39.61	48.91
SDR	18.27	20.12	22.39	25.71	36.95	36.02	44.82
International reserves (U.S.$)							
Total (excl. gold; '000,000)	6,454	4,899	3,859	1,521	3,627	5,757	6,879
SDRs ('000,000)	159	96	113	316	46	4	41
Reserve pos. in IMF ('000,000)	691	656	640	—	—	292	304
Foreign exchange ('000,000)	5,603	4,148	3,105	1,205	3,580	5,461	6,534
Gold ('000,000 fine troy oz)	10.449	10.449	10.449	10.692	11.282	11.348	11.390
% world reserves	1.1	1.1	1.1	1.1	1.2	1.2	1.2
Interest and prices							
Central bank discount (%)	10.0	10.0	10.0	10.0	12.0	12.0	...
Advance (prime) rate (%)	16.5	16.5	16.5	16.5	17.9	18.9	...
Industrial share prices (1985 = 100)[26]	111.9	115.0	173.8	241.3	325.1	596.7	...
Balance of payments (U.S.$'000,000)							
Balance of visible trade	−5,777	−6,581	−6,110	...	...	...	...
Imports, f.o.b.	17,661	20,091	22,254	...	...	...	...
Exports, f.o.b.	11,884	13,510	16,144	...	...	...	...
Balance of invisibles	+585	−567	−716	...	...	...	...
Balance of payments, current account	−5,192	−7,148	−6,826	...	...	...	...

Public debt (external, outstanding; 1991): U.S.$64,315,000,000.
Land use (1990): forested 22.4%; meadows and pastures 4.1%; agricultural and under permanent cultivation 56.9%; other 16.6%.
Population economically active (1981)[12]: total 260,275,118; activity rate of total population 39.1% (participation rates: over age 15, 60.7%; female 27.0%; unemployed[27] [March 1990] 13.1%).

Price and earnings indexes (1984 = 100)

	1987	1988	1989	1990	1991	1992	1993[28]
Consumer price index	124.9	136.6	145.1	158.1	180.0	201.1	206.2
Monthly earnings index[29]	...	162.0	179.5	...	...	...	...

Household income and expenditure. Average household size[30] (1981) 5.5; income per household: n.a.; sources of income (1984–85): salaries and wages 42.2%, self-employed 39.7%, interest 8.6%, profits and dividends 6.0%, rent 3.5%; expenditure (1989–90): food and beverages 49.2%, clothing and footwear 12.8%, transportation and communications 9.6%, housing 6.5%, household furnishings 5.3%, energy 4.6%.

Service enterprises (1980)

	no. of enterprises	no. of employees	annual value added (Rs '000,000)[31]
Wholesale and retail trade	6,046,200	10,228,700	477,060
Transportation, storage	429,800	1,551,200	236,490
Community and personal services	3,177,700	13,128,800	222,330
Construction	152,000	451,200	220,180
Finance and insurance	273,500	1,570,800	172,300
Real estate and business services	...	...	168,820
Electricity, gas, and steam	33,700	363,500	86,610
Communications	98,900	530,900	41,400
Restaurants and hotels	807,000	2,080,500	29,140

Tourism: receipts from visitors (1992) U.S.$1,540,000,000; expenditures by nationals abroad (1990) U.S.$425,000,000.

Foreign trade[32, 33]

Balance of trade (current prices)

	1986–87	1987–88	1988–89	1989–90	1990–91	1991–92
Rs '000,000	−53,990	−43,326	−49,417	−40,249	−61,163	+12,031
% of total	17.7%	12.1%	10.9%	6.8%	8.6%	1.4%

Imports (1991–92): Rs 478,130,000,000 (mineral fuels and lubricants 27.5%; machinery, transport equipment, and fabricated metals 21.7%; pearls and precious and semiprecious stones [mostly diamonds] 10.1%; fertilizers 4.7%; iron and steel 4.5%). *Major import sources* (1990–91): U.S. 12.1%; Germany 8.0%; Japan 7.5%; U.K. 6.7%; Saudi Arabia 6.7%; Belgium 6.3%; U.S.S.R. 5.9%; United Arab Emirates 4.4%.
Exports (1991–92): Rs 439,780,000,000 (cut and polished diamonds 14.0%; ready-made garments 12.3%; chemicals and chemical products 8.4%; cotton yarn, fabrics, and thread 7.3%; leather and leather manufactures 7.0%; iron ore 3.3%; fish products 3.1%; electronics 3.0%; tea 2.6%). *Major export destinations* (1990–91): U.S.S.R. 16.1%; U.S. 14.7%; Japan 9.3%; Germany 7.8%; U.K. 6.5%; Belgium 3.8%; Hong Kong 3.3%; Italy 3.1%.

Transport and communications

Transport. Railroads (1992): route length 38,662 mi, 62,220 km; passenger-mi 195,762,000,000, passenger-km 315,049,000,000; short ton-mi cargo 173,807,000,000, metric ton-km cargo 253,754,000,000. Roads (1990–91): total length 1,266,000 mi, 2,037,000 km (paved 49%). Vehicles (1991): passenger cars 2,490,805; trucks and buses 2,176,944. Merchant marine (1992): vessels (100 gross tons and over) 888; total deadweight tonnage 10,365,939. Air transport (1992)[34]: passenger-mi 10,336,000,000, passenger-km 16,634,000,000; short ton-mi cargo 294,302,000, metric ton-km cargo 429,674,000; airports (1993) with scheduled flights 95.
Communications. Daily newspapers (1989–90): total number 2,538; total circulation (1992) 16,800,000[35]; circulation per 1,000 population 19[35]. Radio (1992): 55,000,000 receivers (1 per 16 persons). Television (1992): 20,000,000 receivers (1 per 44 persons). Telephones (1990–91): 6,021,000 (1 per 141 persons).

Education and health

Education (1990–91)

	schools	teachers	students	student/ teacher ratio
Primary (age 6–10)	558,392	1,636,898	99,118,320	60.6
Secondary (age 11–17)	219,595	2,331,797	51,381,096	22.0
Higher	7,301	...	4,430,000	...

Literacy (1990): total population age 15 and over literate 261,200,000 (48.2%); males literate 173,200,000 (61.8%); females literate 88,000,000 (33.7%).
Health (1990): physicians 365,000 (1 per 2,337 persons); hospital beds (1991) 645,900 (1 per 1,323 persons); infant mortality rate 80.0[36].
Food (1988–90): daily per capita caloric intake 2,229 (vegetable products 93%, animal products 7%); 101% of FAO recommended minimum requirement.

Military

Total active duty personnel (1992): 1,265,000 (army 87.0%, navy 4.3%, air force 8.7%). *Military expenditure as percentage of GNP* (1989): 3.1% (world 4.9%); per capita expenditure U.S.$10.

[1]Council of States can have a maximum number of 250 members; a maximum of 12 of these members may be nominated by the president. [2]Includes 2 nonelective seats. [3]Census not conducted; population based on projection of 1989 official estimate. [4]Excludes 46,976 sq mi (121,667 sq km) of territory claimed by India as part of Jammu and Kashmir but occupied by Pakistan or China. [5]Mother tongue unless otherwise noted. [6]Percentage based on 1971 census. [7]Within Delhi urban agglomeration. [8]Within Calcutta urban agglomeration. [9]Within Greater Bombay urban agglomeration. [10]Within Pune urban agglomeration. [11]1981 census. [12]Excludes Assam. [13]Percentage breakdown based on 21,028 deaths recorded at 1,305 nationally dispersed primary-health-centre villages. [14]Deceased over age 60 with no apparent sickness. [15]At factor cost. [16]Not adequately defined. [17]1988–89. [18]1991–92. [19]1990–91. [20]Value of production. [21]1992–93. [22]Value of exports. [23]Establishments with 10 or more workers using electrical power or 20 or more workers not using electrical power. [24]End of period unless otherwise noted. [25]May. [26]Annual average. [27]Applicants registered at employment exchanges. [28]March. [29]Public sector only. [30]Excludes shelterless population. [31]1989–90. [32]Import figures are f.o.b. in balance of trade and c.i.f. in commodities and trading partners. [33]Fiscal year beginning April 1. [34]Air-India and Indian Airlines only. [35]123 principal dailies only. [36]Based on a sample registration scheme.

Indonesia

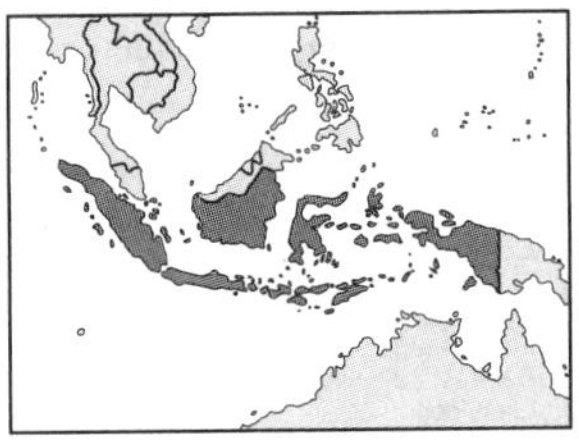

Official name: Republik Indonesia (Republic of Indonesia).
Form of government: unitary multiparty republic with two legislative houses (House of People's Representatives [500[1]]; People's Consultative Assembly [1,000[2]]).
Head of state and government: President.
Capital: Jakarta.
Official language: Bahasa Indonesia.
Official religion: monotheism.
Monetary unit: 1 Indonesian rupiah (Rp) = 100 sen; valuation (Oct. 4, 1993) 1 U.S.$ = Rp 2,088; 1 £ = Rp 3,163.

Area and population

		area		population
Metropolitan district	Capitals	sq mi	sq km	1990 census
Jakarta Raya	Jakarta	228	590	8,259,266
Provinces				
Bali	Denpasar	2,147	5,561	2,777,811
Bengkulu	Bengkulu	8,173	21,168	1,179,122
Irian Jaya	Jayapura	162,928	421,981	1,648,708
Jambi	Jambi	17,297	44,800	2,020,568
Jawa Barat	Bandung	17,877	46,300	35,384,352
Jawa Tengah	Semarang	13,207	34,206	28,520,643
Jawa Timur	Surabaya	18,502	47,921	32,503,991
Kalimantan Barat	Pontianak	56,664	146,760	3,229,153
Kalimantan Selatan	Banjarmasin	14,541	37,660	2,597,572
Kalimantan Tengah	Palangkaraya	58,919	152,600	1,396,486
Kalimantan Timur	Samarinda	78,162	202,440	1,876,663
Lampung	Tanjung Karang	12,860	33,307	6,017,573
Maluku	Ambon	28,767	74,505	1,857,790
Nusa Tenggara Barat	Mataram	7,790	20,177	3,369,649
Nusa Tenggara Timur	Kupang	18,485	47,876	3,268,644
Riau	Pakanbaru	36,510	94,561	3,303,976
Sulawesi Selatan	Ujung Pandang	28,101	72,781	6,981,646
Sulawesi Tengah	Palu	26,921	69,726	1,711,327
Sulawesi Tenggara	Kendari	10,690	27,686	1,349,619
Sulawesi Utara	Menado	7,345	19,023	2,478,119
Sumatera Barat	Padang	19,219	49,778	4,000,207
Sumatera Selatan	Palembang	40,034	103,688	6,313,074
Sumatera Utara	Medan	27,331	70,787	10,256,027
Timor Timur	Dili	5,743	14,874	747,750
Special autonomous districts				
Aceh	Banda Aceh	21,387	55,392	3,416,156
Yogyakarta	Yogyakarta	1,224	3,169	2,913,054
TOTAL		741,052	1,919,317	179,378,946

Demography

Population (1993): 188,216,000.
Density (1993): persons per sq mi 254.0, persons per sq km 98.1.
Urban-rural (1991): urban 31.4%; rural 68.6%.
Sex distribution (1990): male 49.88%; female 50.12%.
Age breakdown (1990): under 15, 36.5%; 15–29, 28.3%; 30–44, 18.1%; 45–59, 10.7%; 60–74, 5.3%; 75 and over, 1.1%.
Population projection: (2000) 211,351,000; (2010) 238,245,000.
Doubling time: 34 years.
Ethnolinguistic composition (1990): Javanese 39.4%; Sundanese 15.8%; Indonesian (Malay) 12.1%; Madurese 4.3%; Minang 2.4%; other 26.0%.
Religious affiliation (1990): Muslim 87.2%; Christian 9.6%, of which Roman Catholic 3.6%; Hindu 1.8%; Buddhist 1.0%; other 0.4%.
Major cities (1990): Jakarta 8,259,266; Surabaya 2,421,016; Bandung 2,026,893; Medan 1,685,972; Semarang 1,005,316.

Vital statistics

Birth rate per 1,000 population (1991): 32.2 (world avg. 26.4).
Death rate per 1,000 population (1991): 11.7 (world avg. 9.2).
Natural increase rate per 1,000 population (1991): 20.5 (world avg. 17.2).
Total fertility rate (avg. births per childbearing woman; 1991): 3.7.
Marriage rate per 1,000 population (1989–90): 7.9[3].
Divorce rate per 1,000 population (1989–90): 0.7[3].
Life expectancy at birth (1991): male 55.6 years; female 58.9 years.
Major causes of death: n.a.; however, major diseases include tuberculosis, malaria, dysentery, cholera, and plague.

National economy

Budget (1991–92). Revenue: Rp 50,555,000,000,000 (royalties from energy production 29.7%, aid for development 20.5%, value-added tax 16.3%, income tax 15.9%, nontax revenues 5.6%, import duties 5.1%). Expenditures: Rp 50,555,000,000,000 (development 39.6%, debt service 28.4%, civil service 15.3%, subsidies for autonomous regions 9.2%).
Public debt (external, outstanding; 1991): U.S.$48,003,000,000.
Tourism (1991): receipts U.S.$2,515,000,000; expenditures U.S.$949,000,000.
Production (metric tons except as noted). Agriculture, forestry, fishing (1992): rice 47,770,000, sugarcane 23,121,000, cassava 16,318,000, corn (maize) 7,987,000, palm oil 3,162,000, rubber 1,294,000, copra 1,135,000; livestock (number of live animals) 11,400,000 goats, 11,000,000 cattle, 5,900,000 sheep, 3,400,000 buffalo; roundwood (1991) 172,984,000 cu m; fish catch (1991) 3,186,000. Mining and quarrying (1992): nickel ore 2,510,000; copper ore[4] 906,657; bauxite 800,000; iron ore[4] 287,820; tin ore[4] 29,389; silver 100,690 kg. Manufacturing (1990): cement 15,972,000; fertilizer 6,991,000; paper 165,620[5]; cigarettes 13,941,870,000 units[5]. Energy production (consumption): electricity (kW-hr; 1990) 44,260,000,000 (44,260,000,000); coal (metric tons; 1990) 7,327,000 (3,499,000); crude petroleum (barrels; 1990) 531,993,000 (273,139,000); petroleum products (metric tons; 1990) 32,150,000 (24,641,000); natural gas (cu m; 1990) 40,453,000,000 (11,155,000,000).
Gross national product (1992): U.S.$121,467,000,000 (U.S.$660 per capita).

Structure of gross domestic product and labour force

	1991		1989	
	in value Rp '000,000,000	% of total value	labour force	% of labour force
Agriculture	44,218.4	19.5	41,097,381	54.0
Mining	30,901.4	13.6	...	...
Manufacturing	48,335.9	21.3	6,496,655	8.5
Construction	12,855.8	5.7	...	...
Public utilities	1,575.0	0.7	...	...
Transp. and commun.	13,467.3	5.9	...	...
Trade	37,726.2	16.6	10,777,639	14.2
Finance, real estate	16,008.6	7.0		
Pub. admin., defense	14,621.6	6.4	11,725,261	15.4
Services	7,452.6	3.3		
Other	...	...	5,991,820[6]	7.9[6]
TOTAL	227,162.8	100.0	76,088,756	100.0

Population economically active: total (1989) 76,088,756; activity rate 43.5% (participation rates: ages 15–64, 68.6%; female 39.9%; unemployed 2.9%).

Price and earnings indexes (1985 = 100)

	1986	1987	1988	1989	1990	1991	1992
Consumer price index	105.8	115.6	124.9	133.0	142.9	156.1	167.8
Monthly earnings index[7]	108.4	114.7	...	...	...	...	...

Household income and expenditure. Average household size (1990) 4.5; income per household: n.a.; sources of income (1976): wages 42.1%, self-employment 41.5%, transfer payments 2.5%; expenditure (1990): food 51.4%, housing and utilities 20.1%, clothing 5.5%, durable goods 2.9%.
Land use (1991): forested 60.3%; meadows and pastures 6.5%; agricultural and under permanent cultivation 12.3%; other 20.9%.

Foreign trade

Balance of trade (current prices)

	1987	1988	1989	1990	1991	1992
U.S.$'000,000	+5,625	+7,419	+7,229	+6,240	+6,075	+4,937
% of total	19.6%	23.5%	19.6%	13.8%	11.6%	9.2%

Imports (1991): U.S.$25,868,800,000 (machinery and transport equipment 45.0%, chemicals 13.3%, mineral fuels 9.0%, crude materials 8.3%). *Major import sources:* Japan 24.5%; U.S. 13.1%; Germany 8.0%.
Exports (1991): U.S.$29,142,000,000 (crude petroleum 19.5%, natural gas 14.3%, plywood 9.9%, garments 7.9%, preparation rubber 3.3%). *Major export destinations:* Japan 36.9%; U.S. 12.0%; Singapore 8.3%.

Transport and communications

Transport. Railroads (1991): route length 6,583 km; passenger-km 9,768,000,000; metric ton-km cargo 3,468,000,000. Roads (1989): length 266,326 km (paved 44%). Vehicles (1991): passenger cars 1,372,673; trucks and buses 1,533,152. Merchant marine (1992): vessels (100 gross tons and over) 2,014; deadweight tonnage 3,130,175. Air transport (1992): passenger-km 14,919,000,000; metric ton-km cargo 460,220,000; airports (1993) 117.
Communications. Daily newspapers (1990): total number 64; total circulation 3,010,000; circulation per 1,000 population 28. Radio (1992): 22,000,000 receivers (1 per 8.4 persons). Television (1992): 11,000,000 receivers (1 per 17 persons). Telephones (1989): 1,015,275 (1 per 172 persons).

Education and health

Education (1990–91)[8]

	schools	teachers	students	student/teacher ratio
Primary (age 7–12)	147,064	1,331,993	26,308,423	19.8
Secondary (age 13–18)	28,834	707,987	8,236,018	11.6
Voc., teacher tr.	3,823	108,536	1,352,009	12.5
Higher[9]	900	141,094	1,485,894	10.5

Educational attainment (1985). Percentage of population age 25 and over having: no schooling 30.3%; less than complete primary 32.2%; primary 22.8%; some secondary 6.4%; secondary 7.1%; higher 1.2%. *Literacy* (1987): total population age 15 and over literate 80,233,132 (77.6%); males literate 43,062,304 (85.6%); females literate 37,170,828 (70.0%).
Health: physicians (1989–90) 25,752 (1 per 6,861 persons); hospital beds (1990–91) 120,711 (1 per 1,490 persons); infant mortality rate per 1,000 live births (1991) 90.
Food (1988–90): daily per capita caloric intake 2,605 (vegetable products 97%, animal products 3%); 121% of FAO recommended minimum.

Military

Total active duty personnel (1992): 283,000 (army 76.0%, navy 15.5%, air force 8.5%). *Military expenditure as percentage of GNP* (1989): 1.7% (world 4.9%); per capita expenditure U.S.$9.

[1]Includes 100 nonelective seats reserved for the military. [2]Includes the 500 members of the House of People's Representatives plus 500 other delegates. [3]Muslim population only. [4]Concentrates. [5]1988. [6]Includes unemployed. [7]Based on daily average wages of agricultural estate workers. [8]Refers to schools under the Department of Education and Culture only. [9]1989–90.

Iran

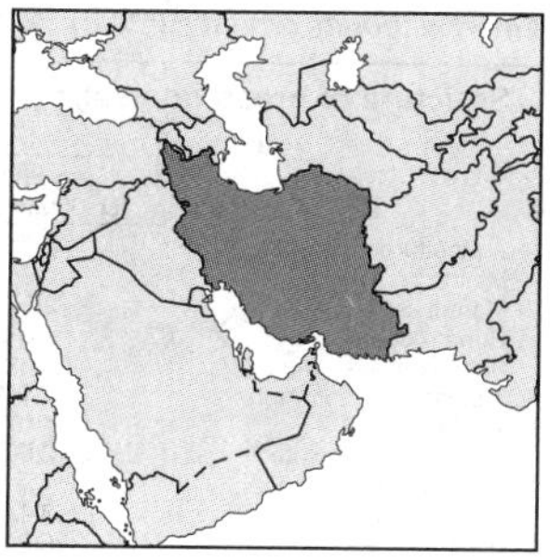

Official name: Jomhūrī-ye Eslamī-ye Irān (Islamic Republic of Iran).
Form of government: unitary Islamic republic with one legislative house (Islamic Consultative Assembly [270]).
Supreme leader: Rahbar (religious guide).
Head of state and government: President.
Capital: Tehrān.
Official language: Farsī (Persian).
Official religion: Islam.
Monetary unit: 1 rial (Rls); valuation (Oct. 4, 1993) 1 U.S.$ = Rls 1,587; 1 £ = Rls 2,404.

Area and population

Provinces	Capitals	area sq mi	area sq km	population 1986 census
Āzārbāyjān-e Gharbī	Orūmīyeh	14,517	37,599	1,971,677
Āzārbāyjān-e Sharqī	Tabrīz	25,421	65,842	4,114,084
Bākhtarān	Bākhtarān	9,121	23,622	1,462,965
Būshehr	Būshehr	9,792	25,360	612,183
Chahār Maḩāll va Bakhtīārī	Shahr Kord	5,722	14,820	631,179
Eşfahān	Eşfahān	40,852	105,805	3,294,916
Fārs	Shīrāz	48,505	125,627	3,193,769
Gīlān	Rasht	5,722	14,820	2,081,037
Hamadān	Hamadān	7,508	19,445	1,505,826
Hormozgān	Bandar ʿAbbās	25,243	65,379	762,206
Īlām	Īlām	7,369	19,086	382,091
Kermān	Kermān	71,690	185,675	1,622,958
Khorāsān	Mashhad	121,887	315,687	5,280,605
Khūzestān	Ahvāz	25,688	66,532	2,681,978
Kohkīlūyeh va Būyer Aḩmadī	Yāsūj	5,289	13,699	411,828
Kordestān	Sanandaj	10,756	27,858	1,078,415
Lorestān	Khorramābād	11,027	28,560	1,367,029
Markazī	Arāk	11,402	29,530	1,082,109
Māzandarān	Sarī	18,010	46,645	3,419,346
Semnān	Semnān	35,345	91,544	417,035
Sīstān va Balūchestān	Zāhedān	70,066	181,471	1,197,059
Tehrān	Tehrān	10,896	28,221	8,712,087
Yazd	Yazd	24,704	63,984	574,028
Zanjān	Zanjān	14,047	36,382	1,588,600
TOTAL LAND AREA		630,578[1]	1,633,189[1]	
INLAND WATER		1,880[2]	4,868[2]	
TOTAL		632,457[1]	1,638,057	49,445,010[3]

Demography

Population (1993): 60,768,000[4].
Density (1993): persons per sq mi 96.1, persons per sq km 37.1.
Urban-rural (1992): urban 57.0%; rural 43.0%.
Sex distribution (1990): male 50.78%; female 49.22%.
Age breakdown (1990): under 15, 45.9%; 15–29, 25.9%; 30–44, 14.6%; 45–59, 7.9%; 60–74, 4.6%; 75 and over, 1.1%.
Population projection: (2000) 71,253,000; (2010) 89,446,000.
Doubling time: 20 years.
Ethnic composition (1983): Persian 45.6%; Azerbaijani 16.8%; Kurdish 9.1%; Gīlakī 5.3%; Luri 4.3%; Māzandarānī 3.6%; Baluchi 2.3%; Arab 2.2%; Bakhtiari 1.7%; Turkmen 1.5%; Armenian 0.5%; other 7.1%.
Religious affiliation (1986): Muslim 98.6% (Shīʿī 90.8%, Sunnī 7.8%); Christian 0.7%; Bahāʾī 0.5%; Zoroastrian 0.1%; Jewish 0.1%.
Major cities (1986): Tehrān 6,042,584; Mashhad 1,463,508; Eşfahān 986,753; Tabriz 971,482; Shīrāz 848,289.

Vital statistics

Birth rate per 1,000 population (1991): 44.0 (world avg. 26.4).
Death rate per 1,000 population (1991): 9.0 (world avg. 9.2).
Natural increase rate per 1,000 population (1991): 35.0 (world avg. 17.2).
Total fertility rate (avg. births per childbearing woman; 1991): 6.2.
Marriage rate per 1,000 population (1989): 8.5.
Life expectancy at birth (1991): male 64.0 years; female 65.0 years.
Major causes of death per 100,000 population (1989)[5]: diseases of the circulatory system 249.2; accidents and violence 101.0; malignant neoplasms (cancers) 58.8; diseases of the respiratory system 48.9.

National economy

Budget (1991–92). Revenue: Rls 6,900,000,000 (oil and gas exports 51.0%, taxes 40.0%). Expenditures: Rls 8,200,000,000 (current expenditure 68.7%, development expenditure 31.3%).
Production (metric tons except as noted). Agriculture, forestry, fishing (1991): wheat 8,785,000[6], sugar beets 4,960,000[6], barley 3,196,000[6], rice 2,430,000[6], sugarcane 2,000,000, grapes 1,650,000, apples 1,350,000, oranges 1,270,000, dates 570,000, pistachios 170,000; livestock (head) 45,000,000 sheep, 6,900,000 cattle; roundwood 6,792,000 cu m; fish catch 277,444. Mining and quarrying (1991): iron ore (concentrate) 20,200,000; copper ore (concentrate) 8,800,000. Manufacturing (value added, in Rls '000,000; 1987–88): textiles (excl. wearing apparel) 232,000; bricks, tiles, and cement 225,600; tobacco products 161,900; food products 148,300; nonelectrical machinery 95,600; iron and steel 75,500. Construction (completed; 1988): residential 13,081,000 sq m; nonresidential 853,000 sq m. Energy production (consumption): electricity (kW-hr; 1991–92) 64,126,000,000 (49,175,000,000); coal (metric tons; 1990) 1,300,000 (1,700,000); crude petroleum (barrels; 1992) 1,251,000,000 ([1991] 310,500,000); petroleum products (metric tons; 1990) 34,560,000 (40,114,000); natural gas (cu m; 1991–92) 35,100,000,000 (32,200,000,000).

Public debt (external, outstanding; 1991): U.S.$2,736,000,000.
Gross national product (1991): U.S.$127,366,000,000 (U.S.$2,320 per capita).

Structure of gross domestic product and labour force

	1991–92 in value Rls '000,000,000[7]	1991–92 % of total value	1986 labour force	1986 % of labour force
Agriculture	11,341	24.2	3,208,613	25.0
Petroleum, natural gas	3,840	8.2 }	32,377	0.3
Other mining	224	0.5 }		
Manufacturing	7,260	15.5	1,460,132	11.4
Construction	1,798	3.8	1,207,459	9.4
Public utilities	601	1.3	91,064	0.7
Transp. and commun.	3,332	7.1	630,704	4.9
Trade, restaurants	8,636	18.5	875,919	6.8
Finance, real estate	5,411	11.6	114,302	0.9
Pub. admin., defense	3,627	7.8 }	3,050,943	23.7
Services	1,087	2.3 }		
Other	−380[8]	−0.8[8]	2,183,189[9]	17.0[9]
TOTAL	46,777	100.0	12,854,702	100.0[1]

Tourism (1991–92): receipts U.S.$57,000,000; expenditures U.S.$734,000,000.
Population economically active (1986): total 12,854,702; activity rate 26.0% (participation rates: ages 15–64, 46.8%; female 10.3%; unemployed [1992] 25–30%).

Price and earnings indexes (1987–88 = 100)

	1987–88	1988–89	1989–90	1990–91	1991–92
Consumer price index	100.0	128.9	151.3	164.9	197.3
Daily earnings index[10]	100.0	121.9	144.0	157.5	181.2

Household income and expenditure. Average household size (1986) 5.1; income per urban household (1988) Rls 1,339,970 (U.S.$19,536); sources of urban income (1988): wages 37.4%, self-employment 30.5%, other 32.1%; expenditure (1989–90): food and hotels 46.7%, housing and energy 23.5%.
Land use (1990): forested 11.0%; meadows and pastures 26.9%; agricultural and under permanent cultivation 9.2%; other 52.9%.

Foreign trade

Balance of trade (current prices)

	1986–87	1987–88	1988–89	1989–90	1990–91	1991–92
U.S.$'000,000	−4,656	−1,320	−810	−1,585	−1,758	−9,030
% of total	24.5%	5.2%	3.6%	5.7%	4.5%	19.7%

Imports (1991–92): U.S.$27,445,000,000 (motor vehicles and machinery 28.5%, iron and steel 15.0%, food and medicine 11.5%). *Major import sources* (1991)[11]: Germany 20.6%; Japan 12.6%; Italy 8.9%; U.A.E. 4.8%; U.K. 4.6%.
Exports (1991–92): U.S.$18,415,000,000 (crude petroleum 85.8%, carpets 6.1%, pistachios 1.6%, copper bars 1.0%, leather 0.4%). *Major export destinations* (1991)[12]: Japan 15.9%; Italy 9.4%; France 7.5%; The Netherlands 6.7%; Belgium-Luxembourg 6.3%; Brazil 6.0%.

Transport and communications

Transport. Railroads (1991): route length 2,838 mi, 4,567 km; (1989–90) passenger-km 4,752,000,000; metric ton-km cargo 7,963,000,000. Roads (1991): length 94,130 mi, 151,488 km (paved [1989] 34%). Vehicles (1991): passenger cars 1,600,000; trucks and buses 600,000. Merchant marine (1992): vessels (100 gross tons and over) 403; total deadweight tonnage 8,345,269. Air transport (1991)[13]: passenger-km 5,457,000,000; metric ton-km cargo 86,105,000; airports (1993) with scheduled flights 19.
Communications. Daily newspapers (1990): 21; circulation 1,500,000; circulation per 1,000 population 27. Radio (1992): 12,000,000 receivers (1 per 5.0 persons). Television (1992): 2,250,000 receivers (1 per 26 persons). Telephones (1990): 2,270,000 (1 per 25 persons).

Education and health

Education (1990–91)

	schools	teachers	students	student/ teacher ratio
Primary (age 7–11)	59,280	339,189	9,369,646	27.6
Secondary (age 12–18)	18,445[14]	197,630	4,822,087	24.4
Voc., teacher tr.	1,006[14]	18,643	262,745	14.1
Higher	44[15]	23,376	312,076	13.4

Educational attainment (1986). Percentage of population age 25 and over having: no formal schooling 12.8%; secondary education 38.0%; higher 7.8%.
Literacy (1990): total population age 15 and over literate 18,200,000 (54.0%); males literate 11,600,000 (64.5%); females literate 6,600,000 (43.3%).
Health (1991–92): physicians 22,000 (1 per 2,685 persons); hospital beds 85,810 (1 per 688 persons); infant mortality rate (1991) 66.0.
Food (1986–88): daily per capita caloric intake 3,317 (vegetable products 90%, animal products 10%); 130% of FAO recommended minimum requirement.

Military

Total active duty personnel (1992): 528,000 (revolutionary guard corps 32.2%, army 57.8%, navy 3.4%, air force 6.6%). *Military expenditure as percentage of GNP* (1989): 2.2%[16] (world 4.9%); per capita expenditure U.S.$158[16].

[1]Detail does not add to total given because of rounding. [2]Area of Lake Urmia. [3]1992 de jure census total is 58,110,227. [4]De facto estimate including refugees. [5]Projected rates based on about 21% of total deaths. [6]1991–92. [7]At factor cost. [8]Less imputed bank service charge. [9]Includes 1,818,740 unemployed. [10]Construction sector only. [11]Based on imports totaling U.S.$21,688,000,000. [12]Based on exports totaling U.S.$15,916,000,000. [13]Iran Air. [14]1989–90. [15]Universities only. [16]Defense costs are highly tentative; barter and countertrade agreements are excluded.

Iraq

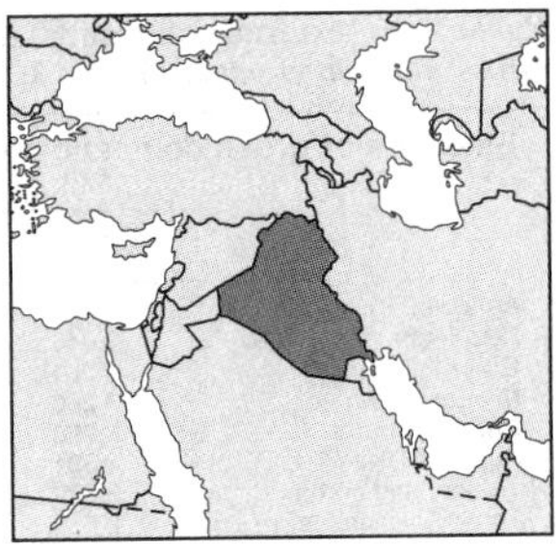

Official name: al-Jumhūrīyah al-ʿIrāqīyah (Republic of Iraq).
Form of government: unitary multiparty[1] republic with one legislative house (National Assembly [250]).
Head of state and government: President.
Capital: Baghdad.
Official language: Arabic[2].
Official religion: Islam.
Monetary unit: 1 Iraqi dinar (ID) = 20 dirhams = 1,000 fils; valuation (Oct. 4, 1993) 1 ID = U.S.$3.23[3]; 1 ID = £2.13.

Area and population

Governorates	Capitals	area[4] sq mi	area[4] sq km	population 1991 estimate
al-Anbār	ar-Ramādī	53,208	137,808	865,500
Bābil	al-Ḥillah	2,163	5,603	1,221,100
Baghdād	Baghdad	1,572	4,071	3,910,900
al-Baṣrah[4]	Basra	7,363	19,070	1,168,800
Dhī Qār	an-Nāṣirīyah	4,981	12,900	1,030,900
Diyālā	Baʿqūbah	6,828	17,685	1,037,600
Karbalāʾ	Karbalāʾ	1,944	5,034	567,600
Maysān	al-ʿAmārah	6,205	16,072	524,200
al-Muthannā	as-Samāwah	19,977	51,740	350,000
an-Najaf	an-Najaf	11,129	28,824	666,400
Nīnawā	Mosul	14,410	37,323	1,618,700
al-Qādisiyah	ad-Dīwānīyah	3,148	8,153	595,600
Ṣalāḥ ad-Dīn	Tikrīt	9,407	24,363	772,200
at-Taʾmīm	Kirkūk	3,737	9,679	605,900
Wāsiṭ	al-Kūt	6,623	17,153	605,700
Kurdish Autonomous Region[5]				
Dahūk	Dahūk	2,530	6,553	309,300
Irbīl	Irbīl	5,820	15,074	928,400
as-Sulaymānīyah	as-Sulaymānīyah	6,573	17,023	1,124,200
LAND AREA		167,618	434,128	
OTHER[6]		357	924	
TOTAL		167,975	435,052	17,903,000

Demography

Population (1993): 19,435,000.
Density (1993): persons per sq mi 115.7, persons per sq km 44.7.
Urban-rural (1991): urban 70.4%; rural 29.6%.
Sex distribution (1991): male 50.28%; female 49.72%.
Age breakdown (1991): under 15, 44.5%; 15–29, 28.9%; 30–44, 14.1%; 45–59, 7.3%; 60–74, 3.9%; 75 and over, 1.3%.
Population projection: (2000) 23,947,000; (2010) 30,834,000.
Doubling time: 18 years.
Ethnic composition (1983): Arab 77.1%; Kurd 19.0%; Turkmen 1.4%; Persian 0.8%; Assyrian 0.8%; other 0.9%.
Religious affiliation (1990): Shīʿī Muslim 61.5%; Sunnī Muslim 34.0%; Christian 3.7%, of which Eastern-rite Roman Catholic 2.5%, Nestorian 0.8%, Orthodox 0.4%; Yazīdī syncretist 0.8%.
Major cities (1985): Baghdad (1987) 3,844,608; Basra 616,700; Mosul 570,926; Irbīl 333,903; as-Sulaymānīyah 279,424.

Vital statistics

Birth rate per 1,000 population (1991): 46.0 (world avg. 26.4).
Death rate per 1,000 population (1991)[7]: 7.0 (world avg. 9.2).
Natural increase rate per 1,000 population (1991): 39.0 (world avg. 17.2).
Total fertility rate (avg. births per childbearing woman; 1991): 6.2.
Marriage rate per 1,000 population (1990): 8.1.
Life expectancy at birth (1991)[8]: male 46.0 years; female 57.0 years.
Major causes of death (1993). Deprivation of medical care (because of acute medical supply shortages) and malnutrition partly caused by Iraq's unwillingness to sell petroleum under strict UN supervision.

National economy

Budget (1992). Revenue: ID 13,935,000,000. Expenditures: ID 13,935,000,000. Details of the 1992 and 1993 proposed budgets were not released by the National Assembly. Special emphasis was to be placed on the reconstruction of the infrastructure.
Tourism (1989): receipts U.S.$59,000,000; expenditures, n.a.
Public debt (external, outstanding; April 1991): U.S.$109,000,000,000.
Production (metric tons except as noted). Agriculture, forestry, fishing (1992): wheat 600,000, dates 580,000, tomatoes 480,000, grapes 470,000, watermelons 450,000, barley 400,000, cucumbers 320,000, oranges 185,000, rice 150,000, corn (maize) 100,000; livestock (number of live animals) 9,000,000 sheep, 1,400,000 cattle; roundwood (1991) 155,000 cu m; fish catch (1991) 12,100. Mining and quarrying (1991): sulfur 430,000; phosphate rock 400,000; gypsum 190,000. Manufacturing (value added in ID '000,000; 1990): petroleum products and chemical products 668; nonmetal mineral products 152; food 114; textiles 91; paper products, printing, and publishing 78; beverages 56; footwear 56; electrical machinery 54; nonelectrical machinery 53; tobacco products 53. Construction (authorized; 1991): residential 4,558,000 sq m; nonresidential 410,000 sq m. Energy production (consumption): electricity (kW-hr; 1990) 29,478,000,000 (26,132,000,000); coal, none (none); crude petroleum (barrels; 1992) 99,300,000 ([1990] 137,700,000); petroleum products (metric tons; 1990) 17,430,000 (10,191,000); natural gas (cu m; 1991) 1,310,000,000 ([1990] 1,153,000,000).

Gross national product (1990): U.S.$73,000,000,000[9] (U.S.$4,110 per capita).

Structure of gross domestic product and labour force

	1990 in value ID '000,000[10]	1990 % of total value	1988 labour force	1988 % of labour force
Agriculture	5,119	20.3	477,264	11.6
Mining	2,981	11.8	60,701	1.5
Manufacturing	2,578	10.2	337,293	8.2
Construction	2,012	8.0	460,788	11.2
Public utilities	220	0.9	41,200	1.0
Transp. and commun.	2,119	8.4	266,233	6.4
Trade	4,071	16.1	281,877	6.8
Finance, real estate	2,669	10.6	41,532	1.0
Pub. admin., defense, and services	3,472	13.7	2,160,406	52.3
TOTAL	25,241	100.0	4,127,294	100.0

Population economically active (1988): total 4,127,294; activity rate of total population 24.7% (participation rates: ages 15–64, 45.3%; female 12.0%; unemployed, n.a.).

Price and earnings indexes (1988 = 100)

	1988	1989	1990	1991	1992[11]
Consumer price index	100.0	...	161.2	461.9	605.4
Earnings index	...	...	...	...	...

Household income and expenditure (1988). Average household size 8.9; sources of income: self-employment 33.9%, wages and salaries 23.9%, transfers 23.0%, rent 18.6%; expenditure: food and beverages 50.2%, housing and energy 19.9%, clothing and footwear 10.6%.
Land use (1991): forested 4.3%; meadows and pastures 9.1%; agricultural and under permanent cultivation 12.5%; built-on, wasteland, and other 74.1%.

Foreign trade[12, 13]

Balance of trade (current prices)

	1986	1987	1988	1989	1990	1991
U.S.$'000,000	−1,183	+1,599	+356	+2,477	+5,519	+13
% of total	6.2%	9.7%	1.9%	11.3%	36.3%	2.2%

Imports (1990): U.S.$4,834,000,000 (machinery and transport equipment 30.3%, food and live animals 27.9%, chemical and pharmaceutical products 8.8%). *Major import sources* (1991)[14]: Jordan 32.4%; Turkey 16.9%; Australia 9.9%; Egypt 8.5%; France 7.4%.
Exports (1990): U.S.$10,353,000,000 (1989; fuels and other energy 99.5%, food and agricultural raw materials 0.5%). *Major export destinations* (1991)[15]: Jordan 84.5%; Italy 5.4%.

Transport and communications

Transport. Railroads (1991): route length 1,484 mi, 2,389 km; passenger-mi 271,000,000, passenger-km 436,000,000; short ton-mi cargo 223,000,000, metric ton-km cargo 326,000,000. Roads (1989): total length 28,305 mi, 45,554 km (paved 84%). Vehicles (1991): passenger cars 744,252; trucks and buses 295,744. Merchant marine (1992): vessels (100 gross tons and over) 131; total deadweight tonnage 1,578,822. Air transport (1992): [16].
Communications. Daily newspapers (1990): total number 6; total circulation 650,000; circulation per 1,000 population 37. Radio (1992): 3,500,000 receivers (1 per 5.4 persons). Television (1992): 1,000,000 receivers (1 per 19 persons). Telephones (1990): 712,109 (1 per 25 persons).

Education and health

Education (1991–92)

	schools	teachers	students	student/teacher ratio
Primary (age 6–11)	8,875	127,578	3,316,036	26.0
Secondary (age 12–17)	2,746	43,937	1,084,715	24.7
Voc., teacher tr.	296	9,957	152,903	15.4
Higher	20	10,520	197,786	18.8

Educational attainment: n.a. *Literacy* (1990): total population age 15 and over literate 6,030,000 (59.7%); males literate 3,570,000 (69.8%); females literate 2,460,000 (49.3%).
Health (1991): physicians 9,366 (1 per 1,922 persons); hospital beds (1990) 31,227 (1 per 568 persons); infant mortality rate per 1,000 live births 80.0[8].
Food (1991)[8]: daily per capita caloric intake 2,300–2,400; 93–97% of FAO recommended minimum requirement.

Military

Total active duty personnel (1993): 382,000 (army 91.6%, navy 0.5%, air force 7.9%). *Military expenditure as percentage of GNP* (1990): 18.2% (world, n.a.); per capita expenditure U.S.$749.

[1]Multipartyism authorized by a September 1991 law. [2]Kurdish is official in the Kurdish Autonomous Region only. [3]Official pegged rate; black market rate was about 90 Iraqi dinars per U.S.$ in October 1993. [4]Includes territory ceded to Kuwait as of Jan. 15, 1993, per UN resolution of May 1992. Iraq continues to claim Kuwait per official announcement of Feb. 28, 1993. [5]De facto self-government as of May 1992 elections. [6]Territorial water at the mouth of the Shaṭṭ al-ʿArab. [7]Excludes war-related deaths. [8]Postwar estimate. [9]By mid-1992 the UN embargo was estimated to have reduced the GNP by at least 50%. [10]At factor cost. [11]February. [12]Imports c.i.f.; exports f.o.b. [13]UN-imposed trade sanctions began August 1990. [14]Based on estimated imports equaling U.S.$284,000,000. [15]Based on estimated exports equaling U.S.$297,000,000. [16]UN sanctions stopped international service from March 1991; lack of spare parts ended domestic service from June 1992.

Ireland

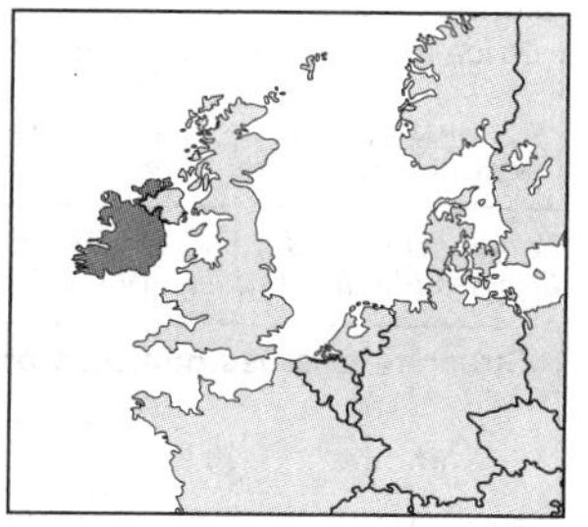

Official name: Éire (Irish); Ireland[1] (English).
Form of government: unitary multiparty republic with two legislative houses (Senate [60[2]]; House of Representatives [166]).
Chief of state: President.
Head of government: Prime Minister.
Capital: Dublin.
Official languages: Irish; English.
Official religion: [3].
Monetary unit: 1 Irish pound (£Ir) = 100 new pence; valuation (Oct. 4, 1993) 1 £Ir = U.S.$1.45 = £0.95.

Area and population

Provinces / Counties	area sq mi	area sq km	population 1991 census[4]
Connacht	6,611	17,122	422,909
Galway[5]	2,293	5,940	180,304
Leitrim	581	1,525	25,297
Mayo	2,084	5,398	110,696
Roscommon	951	2,463	51,876
Sligo	693	1,796	54,736
Leinster	7,580	19,633	1,860,037
Carlow	346	896	40,946
Dublin[5]	356	922	1,024,429
Kildare	654	1,694	122,516
Kilkenny	796	2,062	73,613
Laoighis	664	1,719	52,325
Longford	403	1,044	30,293
Louth	318	823	90,707
Meath	902	2,336	105,540
Offaly	771	1,998	58,448
Westmeath	681	1,763	61,882
Wexford	908	2,351	102,045
Wicklow	782	2,025	97,293
Munster	9,315	24,127	1,008,443
Clare	1,231	3,188	90,826
Cork[5]	2,880	7,460	409,814
Kerry	1,815	4,701	121,719
Limerick[5]	1,037	2,686	161,856
Tipperary North Riding	771	1,996	57,829
Tipperary South Riding	872	2,258	74,791
Waterford[5]	710	1,838	91,608
Ulster	3,093	8,012	232,012
Cavan	730	1,891	52,756
Donegal	1,865	4,830	127,994
Monaghan	498	1,291	51,262
TOTAL LAND AREA	26,600	68,895[6]	
INLAND WATER	537	1,390	
TOTAL	27,137	70,285	3,523,401

Demography

Population (1993): 3,516,000.
Density (1993): persons per sq mi 129.6, persons per sq km 50.0.
Urban-rural (1990): urban 57.1%; rural 42.9%.
Sex distribution (1991): male 49.74%; female 50.26%.
Age breakdown (1986): under 15, 28.9%; 15–29, 24.7%; 30–44, 18.8%; 45–59, 12.8%; 60–74, 10.7%; 75 and over, 4.1%.
Population projection: (2000) 3,492,000; (2010) 3,458,000.
Doubling time: not applicable; doubling time exceeds 100 years.
Place of birth (1986): native born 93.7%; England and Wales 3.6%; Northern Ireland 1.0%; United States 0.4%; Scotland 0.4%; other 0.9%.
Religious affiliation (1981): Roman Catholic 93.1%; Church of Ireland (Anglican) 2.8%; Presbyterian 0.4%; other 3.7%.
Major cities (1991)[7]: Dublin 477,675; Cork 127,024; Limerick 52,040; Galway 50,842; Waterford 40,345.

Vital statistics

Birth rate per 1,000 population (1992): 14.5 (world avg. 26.4); (1991) legitimate 83.4%; illegitimate 16.6%.
Death rate per 1,000 population (1992): 8.7 (world avg. 9.2).
Natural increase rate per 1,000 population (1992): 5.8 (world avg. 17.2).
Total fertility rate (avg. births per childbearing woman; 1990–95): 2.4.
Life expectancy at birth (1985–87): male 71.0 years; female 76.7 years.
Major causes of death per 100,000 population (1991): heart and circulatory diseases 407.4, of which ischemic heart disease 228.8; malignant neoplasms (cancers) 207.5; respiratory disease 75.4, of which pneumonia 58.7.

National economy

Budget (1993). Revenue: £Ir 9,958,000,000 (income taxes 35.9%, value-added tax 23.6%, excise taxes 19.4%). Expenditures: £Ir 10,480,000,000 (1991; debt service 25.9%, social welfare 19.9%, health 14.8%, education 13.3%).
Public debt (1991): U.S.$46,184,000,000.
Tourism (1991): receipts U.S.$1,511,000,000; expenditures U.S.$1,125,000,000.
Production (metric tons except as noted). Agriculture, forestry, fishing (1991): sugar beets 1,400,000, barley 1,281,000, wheat 703,000, potatoes 650,000, oats 100,000, milk 56,900,000 hectolitres; livestock (number of live animals) 9,099,000 sheep, 7,116,000 cattle, 1,069,000 pigs; roundwood 1,677,000 cu m; fish catch (1990) 230,500. Mining and quarrying (1991): gypsum 342,800; zinc ore 186,800[8]; lead ore 40,200[8]. Manufacturing (value added in £Ir; 1989): metals and engineering goods 3,373,800,000; food products 1,785,700,000; chemical products 1,354,100,000; nonmetallic mineral products 442,300,000; paper, printing, and publishing 412,100,000; textiles 188,200,000. Construction (1990): residential 2,741,000 sq m; nonresidential 3,146,000,000 sq m. Energy production (consumption): electricity (kW-hr; 1990) 14,515,000,000 (14,515,000,000); coal (metric tons; 1990) 35,000 (3,034,000); crude petroleum (barrels; 1990) none (13,308,000); petroleum products (metric tons; 1990) 1,456,000 (3,716,000); natural gas (cu m; 1991) 3,763,000,000 ([1990] 3,671,000,000).
Gross national product (1991): U.S.$37,738,000,000 (U.S.$10,780 per capita).

Structure of gross domestic product and labour force

	1990		1991	
	in value £Ir '000,000	% of total value	labour force	% of labour force
Agriculture	2,337	10.1	154,000	11.5
Mining			7,000	0.5
Manufacturing	8,530	37.0	224,000	16.8
Construction			78,000	5.8
Public utilities			14,000	1.1
Transp. and commun.	4,426	19.2	65,000	4.9
Trade			229,000[9]	17.2[9]
Pub. admin., defense	1,363	5.9	68,000	5.1
Services			286,000	21.4
Finance	6,396	27.8	[9]	[9]
Other			209,000[10]	15.7[10]
TOTAL	23,052	100.0	1,334,000	100.0

Population economically active (1991): total 1,334,000; activity rate of total population 37.9% (participation rates: ages 15–64, 59.2%[11]; female 30.5%[11]; unemployed 15.5%).

Price and earnings indexes (1985 = 100)

	1986	1987	1988	1989	1990	1991	1992
Consumer price index	103.8	107.1	109.4	113.8	117.6	121.4	125.1
Hourly earnings index	107.3	112.3	117.3	121.8	127.4	134.6	140.8

Household income and expenditure. Average household size (1983) 3.9; income per household: n.a.; sources of income (1987): wages and salaries 58.6%, self-employment 13.3%, interest and dividends 8.2%; expenditure (1990): food 28.9%, rent and household goods 14.0%, transportation 10.3%.
Land use (1990): forest 5.0%; pasture 68.1%; agricultural 13.7%; other 13.2%.

Foreign trade

Balance of trade (current prices)

	1987	1988	1989	1990	1991	1992
£Ir '000,000	2,004	2,574	2,880	2,458	2,784	4,062
% of total	10.3%	11.7%	11.0%	9.4%	10.2%	13.9%

Imports (1991): £Ir 12,853,400,000 (machinery and transport equipment 34.7%, chemicals 13.3%, food 9.6%, petroleum and petroleum products 5.9%, beverages and tobacco 1.4%). *Major import sources:* U.K. 37.5%; U.S. 15.0%; Germany 8.2%; Japan 5.0%; The Netherlands 4.4%; France 4.3%.
Exports (1991): £Ir 15,024,600,000 (machinery and transport equipment 29.4%, food 20.0%, chemical products 17.7%, beverages and tobacco 2.4%). *Major export destinations:* U.K. 26.7%; Germany 12.7%; France 9.5%; U.S. 8.7%.

Transport and communications

Transport. Railroads (1990): length 2,814 km; passenger-km 1,224,000,000; metric ton-km cargo 589,000,000. Roads (1991): length 92,303 km (paved 94%). Vehicles (1991): passenger cars 836,583; trucks and buses 152,719. Merchant marine (1992): vessels (100 gross tons and over) 189; total deadweight tonnage 208,573. Air transport (1990): passenger-km 3,804,000,000; metric ton-km cargo 431,618,000; airports (1993) 10.
Communications. Daily newspapers (1991): 7; total circulation 632,300; circulation per 1,000 population 179. Radio (1992): 2,000,000 (1 per 1.8 persons). Television (1992): 1,000,000 (1 per 3.5 persons). Telephones (1990): 916,207 (1 per 3.8 persons).

Education and health

Education (1990–91)

	schools	teachers	students	student/teacher ratio
Primary (age 6–11)	3,437	20,430[12]	543,979	...
Secondary (age 12–18)	478	11,550	213,047	18.4
Voc., teacher tr.	350	7,294	129,369	17.7
Higher	49	3,934[13]	64,098	16.0[13]

Educational attainment (1981). Percentage of population age 25 and over having: primary education 52.3%; secondary 23.3%; some postsecondary 16.5%; university or like institution 7.9%. *Literacy* (1987): virtually 100% literate.
Health (1991): physicians (1984) 5,180 (1 per 681 persons); hospital beds 13,806[14] (1 per 255 persons); infant mortality rate 9.1.
Food (1988–90): daily per capita caloric intake 3,952 (vegetable products 62%, animal products 38%); 157% of FAO recommended minimum requirement.

Military

Total active duty personnel (1991): 12,900 (army 86.8%, navy 7.0%, air force 6.2%). *Military expenditure as percentage of GNP* (1989): 1.6% (world 4.9%); per capita expenditure U.S.$128.

[1]As provided by the constitution; the 1948 Republic of Ireland Act provides precedent for this longer formulation of the official name but, per official sources, "has not changed the usage *Ireland* as the name of the state in the English language." [2]Includes 11 nonelective seats. [3]Although a 1973 amendment to the Irish constitution deleted sections that had given "special position" to the Roman Catholic church, much doctrinal language remains. [4]Preliminary. [5]Includes county borough(s). [6]Detail does not add to total given because of rounding. [7]County boroughs. [8]Metal content of ores. [9]Trade includes Finance. [10]Unemployed. [11]1988. [12]National schools only. [13]1988–89. [14]Acute-care public hospitals only.

Israel

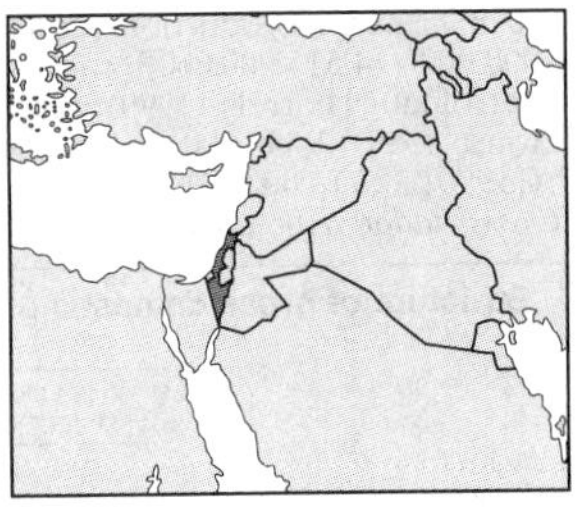

Official name: Medinat Yisra'el (Hebrew); Isrā'īl (Arabic) (State of Israel).
Form of government: multiparty republic with one legislative house (Knesset [120]).
Chief of state: President.
Head of government: Prime Minister.
Capital: Jerusalem is the proclaimed capital of Israel (from Jan. 23, 1950) and the actual seat of government, but recognition of its status as capital by the international community has largely been withheld pending final settlement of territorial and other issues through peace talks between Israel and the Arab parties concerned.
Official languages: Hebrew; Arabic.
Official religion: none.
Monetary unit: 1 New (Israeli) sheqel (NIS) = 100 agorot; valuation (Oct. 4, 1993) 1 U.S.$ = NIS 2.84; 1 £ = NIS 4.30.

Area and population

Districts	Capitals	area[1] sq mi	area[1] sq km	population 1992[2] estimate
Central (Ha Merkaz)	Ramla	479	1,242	1,078,100
Haifa (Ḥefa)	Haifa	330	854	680,700
Jerusalem (Yerushalayim)	Jerusalem	215	557	600,900
Northern (Ha Ẕafon)	Tiberias	1,347	3,490	855,600
Southern (Ha Darom)	Beersheba	5,555	14,387	617,800
Tel Aviv	Tel Aviv–Yafo	66	170	1,131,700
TOTAL		7,992	20,700	4,964,800[3, 4]

Demography

Population (1993): 5,451,000[3, 5].
Density (1993)[5, 6]: persons per sq mi 644.1, persons per sq km 248.7.
Urban-rural (1992): urban 90.4%; rural 9.6%.
Sex distribution (1991): male 49.70%; female 50.30%.
Age breakdown (1991): under 15, 30.7%; 15–29, 24.9%; 30–44, 20.4%; 45–59, 11.5%; 60–74, 8.7%; 75 and over, 3.8%.
Population projection: (2000) 6,250,000; (2010) 6,875,000.
Doubling time: 47 years.
Ethnic composition (1992): Jewish 81.9%; Arab and other 18.1%.
Religious affiliation (1992): Jewish 81.9%; Muslim (mostly Sunnī) 13.9%; Christian 2.5%; Druze and other 1.7%.
Major cities (1992): Jerusalem 544,200; Tel Aviv–Yafo 353,200; Haifa 251,000; Ḥolon 161,800; Petah Tiqwa 148,900; Bat Yam 146,400.

Vital statistics

Birth rate per 1,000 population (1992): 21.4 (world avg. 26.4); (1988)[7] legitimate 98.8%; illegitimate 1.2%.
Death rate per 1,000 population (1992): 6.6 (world avg. 9.2).
Natural increase rate per 1,000 population (1992): 14.8 (world avg. 17.2).
Total fertility rate (avg. births per childbearing woman; 1991): 2.9.
Marriage rate per 1,000 population (1991): 6.5.
Divorce rate per 1,000 population (1991): 1.3.
Life expectancy at birth (1991): male 74.9 years; female 78.4 years.
Major causes of death per 100,000 population (1989): diseases of the circulatory system 264.3; malignant neoplasms (cancers) 121.0; accidents 29.8; diseases of the respiratory system 42.9.

National economy

Budget (1992). Revenue: NIS 108,590,000,000 (income tax and property tax 21.5%, internal loans 20.6%, value-added tax 16.9%, external loans 15.8%). Expenditures: NIS 108,590,000,000 (debt 18.3%, defense 16.2%, interest on loans 13.0%, labour and social welfare 9.5%, education and culture 7.1%).
Production (metric tons except as noted). Agriculture, forestry, fishing (1992): fodder 1,391,000, grapefruit 378,000, tomatoes 328,000, wheat 180,000, potatoes 173,000, watermelons 110,200, seed cotton 34,000; livestock (number of live animals) 360,000 sheep, 349,000 cattle, 111,000 goats, 23,000,000 chickens; roundwood (1991) 113,000 cu m; fish catch (1991) 20,723. Mining and quarrying (1991): phosphate rock 2,267,000; potash 1,958,000; phosphoric acid 230,000; bromine 135,000; bromine compounds 125,000. Manufacturing (1991): cement 3,340,000; sulfuric acid 136,300; polyethylene 124,613; paper 97,221; cardboard 84,911; chlorine 36,105; ammonium sulfate 14,875; wine 11,952,000 litres. Construction (1991): residential 5,190,000 sq m; nonresidential 1,200,000 sq m. Energy production (consumption): electricity (kW-hr; 1991) 20,857,000 (19,265,000); coal (metric tons; 1991) none (4,049,000); crude petroleum (barrels; 1991) 82,000 (53,530,000); petroleum products (metric tons; 1990) 7,633,000 (7,590,000); natural gas (cu m; 1991) 27,000,000 (27,000,000).
Tourism (1991): receipts from visitors U.S.$1,306,000,000; expenditures by nationals abroad U.S.$1,783,000,000.
Land use (1990): forested 5.5%; meadows and pastures 7.2%; agricultural and under permanent cultivation 21.5%; other 65.8%.
Population economically active (1992)[8]: total 1,858,000; activity rate of total population 35.3% (participation rates: over age 15, 52.0%; female 42.5%; unemployed 11.2%).

Price and earnings indexes (1985 = 100)

	1986	1987	1988	1989	1990	1991	1992[9]
Consumer price index	148	178	206	248	291	346	385
Monthly earnings index	161	212	258	312	366	425	471

Public debt (1991): U.S.$81,938,000,000.
Gross national product (1991): U.S.$59,128,000,000 (U.S.$11,330 per capita).

Structure of gross domestic product and labour force

	1989		1992	
	in value NIS '000,000	% of total value	labour force	% of labour force
Agriculture	1,922	3.1	57,900	3.1
Manufacturing, mining	11,937	19.2	348,800	18.8
Construction	3,319	5.3	107,500	5.8
Public utilities	1,649	2.7	14,500	0.8
Transp. and commun.	5,582	9.0	104,000	5.6
Trade	7,174	11.6	229,200	12.3
Finance	14,344	23.1	172,300	9.2
Public and community services	2,545	4.1	483,300	26.0
Services }	13,625	21.9	121,900	6.5
Other }			218,600[10]	11.8[10]
TOTAL	62,097	100.0	1,858,000[8]	100.0[11]

Household income and expenditure (1991). Average household size 3.7; monthly income per household[12] NIS 4,777 (U.S.$2,096); sources of income (1989)[12]: salaries and wages 87.2%, allowances and assistance 10.5%, self-employment 2.2%; expenditure (1992): food, beverages, and tobacco 25.1%, housing 21.7%, household durable goods 6.7%, clothing 5.4%, transportation 4.3%, energy 4.2%.

Foreign trade

Balance of trade (current prices)

	1987	1988	1989	1990	1991	1992
U.S.$'000,000	−3,253.8	−2,841.8	−2,358.1	−3,504.0	−5,473.3	−6,135.0
% of total	16.6%	13.1%	10.0%	13.1%	19.6%	19.8%

Imports (1992): U.S.$18,813,600,000 (investment goods 17.2%; diamonds 16.3%; fuel and lubricants 9.1%; consumer goods 6.3%). *Major import sources:* U.S. 17.2%; Belgium 12.6%; Germany 11.9%; U.K. 8.0%; Switzerland 7.1%; Italy 7.0%; Japan 5.3%; France 4.4%.
Exports (1992): U.S.$13,082,300,000 (machinery 30.7%; worked diamonds 24.5%; chemicals 11.8%; textiles 7.3%; food, beverages, and tobacco 4.2%; rubber and plastic 3.4%). *Major export destinations:* U.S. 30.5%; U.K. 7.6%; Germany 5.8%; Japan 5.3%; Hong Kong 5.1%; Belgium 4.9%; France 4.3%; The Netherlands 4.2%; Italy 3.5%.

Transport and communications

Transport. Railroads (1990): route length 357 mi, 574 km; (1989–90) passenger-mi 94,858,000, passenger-km 152,660,000; short ton-mi cargo 710,700,000, metric ton-km cargo 1,037,600,000. Roads (1991): total length 8,266 mi, 13,300 km (paved 100%). Vehicles (1991): passenger cars 848,000; trucks and buses 165,000. Merchant marine (1992): vessels (100 gross tons and over) 58; total deadweight tonnage 723,418. Air transport (1990)[13]: passenger-mi 4,363,000,000, passenger-km 7,021,000,000; short ton-mi cargo 568,856,000, metric ton-km cargo 830,516,000; airports (1992) with scheduled flights 7.
Communications. Daily newspapers (1989): total number (1990) 22; total circulation 1,611,000; circulation per 1,000 population 350. Radio (1991): 2,250,000 receivers (1 per 2.2 persons). Television (1991): 1,200,000 receivers (1 per 4.1 persons). Telephones (1990): 2,425,000 (1 per 2.0 persons).

Education and health

Education (1991–92)

	schools	teachers	students	student/ teacher ratio
Primary (age 6–13)	1,712	43,461[14]	633,680	...
Secondary (age 14–17)	781	48,489	437,571	9.0
Vocational	381	...	121,601	...
Higher	7	6,017[15]	78,640	...

Educational attainment (1991). Percentage of population age 25 and over having: no formal schooling 6.7%; primary education 22.5%; secondary 39.6%; postsecondary, vocational, and higher 31.2%. *Literacy* (1983): total population age 15 and over literate 2,542,403 (91.8%); males literate 1,312,258 (95.0%); females literate 1,230,145 (88.7%).
Health (1992): physicians (1987) 11,895 (1 per 345 persons); hospital beds 29,527 (1 per 177 persons); infant mortality rate per 1,000 live births 9.3.
Food (1988–90): daily per capita caloric intake 3,220 (vegetable products 79%, animal products 21%); 125% of FAO recommended minimum.

Military

Total active duty personnel (1992): 176,000 (army 76.1%, navy 5.7%, air force 18.2%). *Military expenditure as percentage of GNP* (1989): 12.8% (world 4.9%); per capita expenditure U.S.$1,323.

[1]Excluding West Bank (2,270 sq mi [5,879 sq km]), Gaza Strip (146 sq mi [378 sq km]), Golan Heights (444 sq mi [1,150 sq km]), and East Jerusalem (27 sq mi [70 sq km]). [2]January 1. [3]Includes population of East Jerusalem and Golan Heights (27,200). [4]Excludes Israelis in Jewish localities (pop. 94,100) in the West Bank and Gaza Strip. [5]Includes Israelis in Jewish localities in the West Bank and Gaza Strip. [6]Includes area and population of East Jerusalem and Golan Heights. [7]Jewish population only. [8]Excludes armed forces; includes Israelis in occupied territories. [9]June. [10]Mostly unemployed. [11]Detail does not add to total given because of rounding. [12]Urban population only. [13]El Al only. [14]Teaching posts financed by Ministry of Education and Culture only. [15]1990–91.

Italy

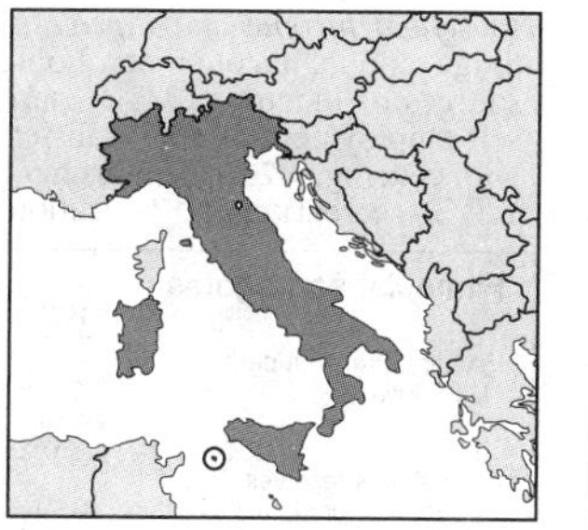

Official name: Repubblica Italiana (Italian Republic).
Form of government: republic with two legislative houses (Senate [325[1]]; Chamber of Deputies [630]).
Chief of state: President.
Head of government: Prime Minister.
Capital: Rome.
Official language: Italian.
Official religion: none.
Monetary unit: 1 lira (Lit, plural lire) = 100 centesimi; valuation (Oct. 4, 1993) 1 U.S.$ = Lit 1,589; 1 £ = Lit 2,407.

Area and population

Regions / Provinces	Capitals	area sq mi	area sq km	population 1991 census
Abruzzi	L'Aquila	4,168	10,794	1,249,388
Chieti	Chieti	999	2,587	379,689
L'Aquila	L'Aquila	1,944	5,034	301,296
Pescara	Pescara	473	1,225	291,115
Teramo	Teramo	752	1,948	277,288
Basilicata	Potenza	3,858	9,992	591,897
Matera	Matera	1,331	3,447	200,519
Potenza	Potenza	2,527	6,545	391,378
Calabria	Catanzaro	5,823	15,080	2,010,195
Catanzaro	Catanzaro	2,026	5,247	711,526
Cosenza	Cosenza	2,568	6,650	730,081
Reggio di Calabria	Reggio di Calabria	1,229	3,183	568,588
Campania	Naples	5,249	13,595	5,625,575
Avellino	Avellino	1,078	2,792	430,210
Benevento	Benevento	800	2,071	291,036
Caserta	Caserta	1,019	2,639	825,294
Napoli	Naples	452	1,171	3,023,366
Salerno	Salerno	1,900	4,922	1,055,669
Emilia-Romagna	Bologna	8,542	22,123	3,984,055
Bologna	Bologna	1,429	3,702	943,269
Ferrara	Ferrara	1,016	2,632	363,451
Forlì	Forlì	1,123	2,910	618,670
Modena	Modena	1,039	2,690	611,883
Parma	Parma	1,332	3,449	401,952
Piacenza	Piacenza	1,000	2,589	271,167
Ravenna	Ravenna	718	1,859	351,296
Reggio nell'Emilia	Reggio nell'Emilia	885	2,292	422,367
Friuli-Venezia Giulia	Trieste	3,029	7,845	1,216,398
Gorizia	Gorizia	180	467	139,315
Pordenone	Pordenone	878	2,273	279,784
Trieste	Trieste	82	212	267,118
Udine	Udine	1,889	4,893	530,181
Lazio	Rome	6,642	17,203	5,145,763
Frosinone	Frosinone	1,251	3,239	478,393
Latina	Latina	869	2,251	475,633
Rieti	Rieti	1,061	2,749	145,848
Roma	Rome	2,066	5,352	3,764,298
Viterbo	Viterbo	1,395	3,612	281,591
Liguria	Genoa	2,092	5,418	1,701,788
Genova	Genoa	709	1,836	961,276
Imperia	Imperia	446	1,155	218,616
La Spezia	La Spezia	341	882	230,835
Savona	Savona	596	1,545	291,061
Lombardia	Milan	9,211	23,857	8,940,594
Bergamo	Bergamo	1,066	2,760	943,584
Brescia	Brescia	1,846	4,782	1,062,416
Como	Como	798	2,067	799,050
Cremona	Cremona	684	1,771	328,279
Mantova	Mantova	903	2,339	371,472
Milano	Milan	1,066	2,762	3,957,547
Pavia	Pavia	1,145	2,965	496,924
Sondrio	Sondrio	1,240	3,212	174,781
Varese	Varese	463	1,199	806,541
Marche	Ancona	3,743	9,693	1,446,751
Ancona	Ancona	749	1,940	445,877
Ascoli Piceno	Ascoli Piceno	806	2,087	364,220
Macerata	Macerata	1,071	2,774	298,371
Pesaro e Urbino	Pesaro	1,117	2,892	338,283
Molise	Campobasso	1,713	4,438	320,916
Campobasso	Campobasso	1,123	2,909	230,380
Isernia	Isernia	590	1,529	90,536
Piemonte	Turin	9,807	25,399	4,338,262
Alessandria	Alessandria	1,375	3,560	441,225
Asti	Asti	583	1,511	209,348
Cuneo	Cuneo	2,665	6,903	552,722
Novara	Novara	1,388	3,594	505,399
Torino	Turin	2,637	6,830	2,254,622
Vercelli	Vercelli	1,159	3,001	374,946
Puglia	Bari	7,470	19,348	3,970,525
Bari	Bari	1,980	5,129	1,507,059
Brindisi	Brindisi	710	1,838	402,639
Foggia	Foggia	2,774	7,185	685,804
Lecce	Lecce	1,065	2,759	783,714
Taranto	Taranto	941	2,437	591,309
Sardegna	Cagliari	9,301	24,090	1,645,192
Cagliari	Cagliari	2,662	6,895	770,113
Nuoro	Nuoro	2,720	7,044	267,281
Oristano	Oristano	1,016	2,631	155,474
Sassari	Sassari	2,903	7,520	452,324
Sicilia (Sicily)	Palermo	9,926	25,709	4,989,871
Agrigento	Agrigento	1,175	3,042	472,800
Caltanissetta	Caltanissetta	822	2,128	273,978
Catania	Catania	1,371	3,552	1,036,480
Enna	Enna	989	2,562	185,008
Messina	Messina	1,254	3,248	690,882
Palermo	Palermo	1,927	4,992	1,233,359
Ragusa	Ragusa	623	1,614	281,779
Siracusa	Siracusa	814	2,109	397,328
Trapani	Trapani	951	2,462	418,257

Area and population (continued)

Regions / Provinces	Capitals	area sq mi	area sq km	population 1991 census
Toscana	Florence	8,877	22,992	3,599,085
Arezzo	Arezzo	1,248	3,232	315,874
Firenze	Florence	1,498	3,879	1,217,454
Grosseto	Grosseto	1,739	4,504	216,535
Livorno	Livorno	468	1,213	342,130
Lucca	Lucca	684	1,773	378,350
Massa-Carrara	Massa-Carrara	447	1,157	199,057
Pisa	Pisa	945	2,448	394,277
Pistoia	Pistoia	373	965	270,054
Siena	Siena	1,475	3,821	265,354
Trentino-Alto Adige	Bolzano	5,258	13,618	934,731
Bolzano-Bozen	Bolzano	2,857	7,400	478,617
Trento	Trento	2,401	6,218	456,114
Umbria	Perugia	3,265	8,456	822,972
Perugia	Perugia	2,446	6,334	598,181
Terni	Terni	819	2,122	224,791
Valle d'Aosta	Aosta	1,259	3,262	117,208
Veneto	Venice	7,090	18,364	4,452,667
Belluno	Belluno	1,420	3,678	211,140
Padova	Padova	827	2,142	846,711
Rovigo	Rovigo	691	1,789	246,784
Treviso	Treviso	956	2,477	745,991
Venezia	Venice	950	2,460	839,847
Verona	Verona	1,195	3,096	810,079
Vicenza	Vicenza	1,051	2,722	752,115
TOTAL		116,324	301,277	57,103,833

Demography

Population (1993): 57,235,000.
Density (1993): persons per sq mi 492.0, persons per sq km 190.0.
Urban-rural (1991): urban 67.1%; rural 32.9%.
Sex distribution (1991): male 48.61%; female 51.39%.
Age breakdown (1988): under 15, 17.8%; 15–29, 24.1%; 30–44, 20.1%; 45–59, 18.6%; 60–74, 13.5%; 75 and over, 5.9%.
Population projection: (2000) 57,274,000; (2010) 56,270,000.
Doubling time: not applicable; population stable.
Ethnolinguistic composition (1983): Italian 94.1%; Sardinian 2.7%; Rhaetian 1.3%; other 1.9%.
Religious affiliation (1980): Roman Catholic 83.2%; nonreligious 13.6%; atheist 2.6%; other 0.6%.
Major cities (1991): Rome 2,791,354; Milan 1,432,184; Naples 1,206,013; Turin 991,870; Palermo 734,238; Genoa 701,032; Bologna 411,803; Florence 408,403; Catania 364,176; Bari 353,032; Venice 317,837.
National origin (1980): Italian 98.8%; foreign-born 1.2%, of which Austrian 0.4%, French 0.2%, Slovene 0.2%, Albanian 0.1%, other 0.3%.
Mobility (1981). Population living in the same residence as in 1976: 92.4%.
Households. Average household size (1988) 2.9; composition of households: 1 person 19.2%, 2 persons 23.7%, 3 persons 23.0%, 4 persons 23.6%, 5 or more persons 10.5%. Family households (1983): 15,205,000 (85.3%); nonfamily 2,617,000 (14.7%), of which 1-person 13.0%.
Immigration (1989): immigrants admitted 81,201, from Europe 48.2%, of which West Germany 16.2%, Switzerland 7.8%; Africa 14.0%; Argentina 9.3%; Asia 9.2%; U.S. 5.4%.

Vital statistics

Birth rate per 1,000 population (1991): 9.8 (world avg. 26.4); (1990) legitimate 93.7%; illegitimate 6.3%.
Death rate per 1,000 population (1991): 9.6 (world avg. 9.2).
Natural increase rate per 1,000 population (1991): 0.2 (world avg. 17.2).
Total fertility rate (avg. births per childbearing woman; 1985–90): 1.4.
Marriage rate per 1,000 population (1990): 5.4.
Divorce rate per 1,000 population: (1990): 0.4.
Life expectancy at birth (1989): male 73.5 years; female 80.0 years.
Major causes of death per 100,000 population (1991): diseases of the circulatory system 420.8; malignant neoplasms (cancers) 276.0; accidents and violence 68.8; diseases of the respiratory system 59.2; diseases of the digestive system 49.9.

Social indicators

Educational attainment (1981). Percentage of population age 25 and over having: no formal schooling 19.3%[2]; primary education 47.4%; lower secondary 18.0%; upper secondary 11.2%; higher 4.1%.

Distribution of income (1986)
percentage of household income by quintile

1	2	3	4	5 (highest)
6.8	12.0	16.7	23.5	41.0

Quality of working life. Average workweek (1985): 36.6 hours. Annual rate per 100,000 workers (1988) for: injury or accident 3,697; industrial illness 405[3]; death 5.7. Percentage of labour force insured for damages or income loss (1992) resulting from: injury 100%; permanent disability 100%; death 100%. Number of working days lost to labour stoppages per 1,000 workers (1991): 862. Average duration of journey to work: n.a. Rate per 1,000 workers of discouraged (unemployed no longer seeking work; 1990): 1.1.
Material well-being. Rate per 1,000 of population possessing (1990): telephone 555; automobile 426; television 261 (colour 188[4]). Households possessing (1979): television 72%; refrigerator 91%; washing machine 88%.
Social participation. Eligible voters participating in last national election (1992): 67.0%. Population participating in voluntary work: n.a. Trade union membership in total workforce (1990): *c.* 28%. Practicing Roman Catholic population in total affiliated population which attended church weekly (early 1990s) 25.0%.
Social deviance (1992). Offense rate per 100,000 population for: murder 2.7; rape 2.2; assault 179.1; theft, including burglary and housebreaking 2,641.

Access to services (1981). Proportion of dwellings having access to: electricity 99.5%; safe water supply 98.7%; toilet facilities 98.5%; bath facilities 86.4%.
Leisure (1988). Favourite leisure activities (as percentage of household spending on culture): sporting events 19.0%; cinema 18.5%; theatre 13.7%.

National economy

Gross national product (1991): U.S.$1,072,198,000,000 (U.S.$18,580 per capita).

Structure of gross domestic product and labour force

	1991 in value (Lit '000,000,000)	% of total value	labour force	% of labour force
Agriculture	46,857	3.3	1,823,000	7.5
Mining	299,576	21.0	227,000	1.0
Manufacturing			4,731,000	19.5
Construction	84,071	5.9	1,957,000	8.1
Public utilities	74,362	5.2	...	...
Transp. and commun.	81,899	5.7	1,149,000	4.8
Trade	263,158	18.5	4,660,000	19.2
Finance	176,471	12.4	1,003,000	4.1
Pub. admin., defense	183,481	12.8	6,042,000	24.9
Services	194,398	13.6		
Other	23,069[5]	1.6[5]	2,653,000[6]	10.9[6]
TOTAL	1,427,342	100.0	24,245,000	100.0

Budget (1990). Revenue: Lit 404,048,000,000,000 (income taxes 37.7%, of which individual 30.9%, corporate 6.7%; value-added and excise taxes 30.0%; social-security taxes 29.5%; property taxes 1.4%). Expenditures: Lit 459,616,000,000,000 (1988; social security and welfare 39.7%; debt service 16.3%; health 11.8%; education and culture 9.7%; transportation 7.4%; defense 3.8%).
Public debt (1991): U.S.$1,141,100,000,000.
Tourism (1991): receipts U.S.$19,688,000,000; expenditures U.S.$13,300,000,000.

Manufacturing, mining, and construction enterprises (1987)

	no. of enterprises[7]	no. of employees[8]	hourly wages as a % of avg. of all wages[9]	annual value added (Lit '000,000,000)
Manufacturing				
Machinery (nonelectrical)	3,873	376,000	98.0	18,030
Industrial chemicals	1,082	212,000	119.7	15,600
Transport equipment	730	309,000	117.7	14,598
Electrical machinery	1,554	272,000	112.1	13,490
Textiles	3,279	230,000	84.4	10,961
Pottery, ceramics, and glass	2,180	166,000	...	9,558
Food products	1,640	150,000	92.2	8,120
Iron and steel	1,024	183,000	122.6	7,739
Metal products	2,620	172,000	86.7	7,198
Printing, publishing	985	85,000	103.2	5,592
Wearing apparel	2,423	170,000	75.0	5,397
Plastic products	1,328	79,000	84.4	4,613
Paper and paper products	672	60,000	102.2	3,709
Petroleum and gas	17	6,000	136.6	2,400
Mining and quarrying	348	21,000	...	3,206
Construction	326,000[10]	1,849,000	...	53,465

Production (metric tons except as noted). Agriculture, forestry, fishing (1992): sugar beets 14,960,000, grapes 10,538,000, wheat 9,037,000, corn (maize) 7,799,000, tomatoes 5,956,000, potatoes 2,736,000, olives 2,489,000, apples 2,469,000, barley 1,759,000, peaches 1,316,000, pears 1,189,000, soybeans 1,057,000; livestock (number of live animals; 1991) 11,575,000 sheep, 9,520,000 pigs, 8,647,000 cattle, 138,000,000 chickens; roundwood (1991) 8,393,000 cu m; fish catch 355,358. Mining and quarrying (1991): rock salt 3,503,891; feldspar 1,384,000; potash 428,868; barite 86,542; zinc 70,046; magnesium 35,565; lead 20,042. Manufacturing (1991): cement 40,321,569; crude steel 25,100,622; pig iron 11,561,849; plastics 3,124,507; sulfuric acid 2,964,997; caustic soda 1,045,292; textiles 496,195[11]; wine 61,680,000 hectolitres[4]; beer 11,502,571 hectolitres[12]; olive oil 7,527,000 hectolitres; 5,028,676 washing machines; 4,155,481 refrigerators; 2,653,952 motorized road vehicles, of which 1,631,943 automobiles, 775,884 motorcycles, scooters, and mopeds, 246,725 trucks and buses; 2,434,484 televisions, of which 2,433,067 colour. Construction (1990): residential 91,868,714 cu m; commercial, industrial, and other 105,754,412 cu m.

Service enterprises (1990)

	no. of enterprises[9]	no. of employees	hourly wage as a % of all wages	annual value added (Lit '000,000,000)
Public utilities	1,398	230,000[4]	...	53,292[4]
Transportation Communications	132,164	1,146,000	...	76,321
Finance	89,092	895,000	...	157,215
Wholesale and retail trade	1,495,702	4,537,000	...	244,344
Pub. admin., services	...	5,986,000	...	166,675

Energy production (consumption): electricity (kW-hr; 1991) 222,041,000,000 (257,123,000,000); coal (metric tons; 1991) 961,000 (19,706,000); crude petroleum (barrels; 1991) 29,516,000 (16,851,000,000); petroleum products (metric tons; 1991) 82,168,000 (89,581,000); natural gas (cu m; 1991) 16,851,000,000 (43,759,000,000).
Population economically active (1991): total 24,245,000; activity rate of total population 42.4% (participation rates: ages 14–64, 59.3%; female 37.1%; unemployed 10.9%).

Price and earnings indexes (1985 = 100)

	1986	1987	1988	1989	1990	1991	1992
Consumer price index	105.9	110.9	116.5	123.8	131.8	140.1	147.4
Earnings index	104.8	111.6	118.4	125.6	134.7	147.9	155.5

Household income and expenditure (1990). Average household size 2.8; average annual income per household (1984) Lit 19,692,000 (U.S.$11,208); sources of income (1988): salaries and wages 42.0%, property income and self-employment 37.6%, transfer payments 19.6%; expenditure (1991): food and beverages 20.2%, housing 15.4%, transportation and communications 12.1%, recreation and education 9.1%.

Financial aggregates

	1988	1989	1990	1991	1992	1993[13]
Exchange rate, Lit per:						
U.S. dollar	1,301.6	1,372.1	1,198.1	1,240.6	1,232.4	1,499.8
£	2,318.7	2,249.8	2,138.1	2,195.1	2,175.8	2,277.7
SDR	1,757.2	1,669.6	1,607.8	1,646.5	2,022.4	2,166.5
International reserves (U.S.$)						
Total (excl. gold; '000,000)	34,715	46,720	62,927	48,679	27,643	26,221[14]
SDRs ('000,000)	949	998	1,037	930	238	252[14]
Reserve pos. in IMF ('000,000)	1,266	1,444	1,714	2,255	2,439	2,462[14]
Foreign exchange ('000,000)	32,500	44,278	60,176	45,495	24,966	23,507[14]
Gold ('000,000 fine troy oz)	66.67	66.67	66.67	66.67	66.67	66.67[14]
% world reserves	7.1	7.1	7.1	7.1	7.1	7.3[14]
Interest and prices						
Central bank discount (%)	12.50	14.21	12.50	12.00	12.00	10.50[14]
Govt. bond yield (%)	10.16	10.72	11.51	10.10	10.33[13]	...
Industrial share prices (1985 = 100)	185.1	214.2	194.3	152.8	137.0	158.2[15]
Balance of payments (U.S.$'000,000)						
Balance of visible trade	−1,362	−2,167	724	−895	2,410	...
Imports, f.o.b.	−128,816	−142,285	−169,216	−169,701	−175,240	...
Exports, f.o.b.	128,048	140,118	169,940	168,806	177,650	...
Balance of invisibles	−3,619	−6,403	3,555	2,020	...	...
Balance of payments, current account	−6,190	−10,886	−14,222	−21,451	−25,422	...

Land use (1990): forested 22.4%; meadows and pastures 16.2%; agricultural and under permanent cultivation 39.4%; other 22.0%.

Foreign trade

Balance of trade (current prices)

	1987	1988	1989	1990	1991	1992
Lit '000,000,000	−6,533	−1,012	−3,358	+724	−1,913	2,229
% of total	2.2%	0.3%	0.8%	0.2%	0.4%	0.5%

Imports (1992): Lit 232,111,000,000,000 (1991; machinery and transport equipment 33.2%, of which transport equipment 13.6%, precision machinery 6.0%; chemicals and chemical products 14.8%; metal and semiprocessed metal 8.1%; food and live animals 7.1%; crude petroleum 5.9%; textiles 3.9%). *Major import sources* (1991): Germany 20.9%; France 14.2%; The Netherlands 5.7%; U.K. 5.7%; U.S. 5.6%; Switzerland 4.4%.
Exports (1992): Lit 219,436,000,000,000 (1991; machinery and transport equipment 41.9%, of which automobiles 4.9%, electrical machinery 4.8%, precision machinery 4.0%; chemicals and chemical products 9.9%; textiles 8.6%; wearing apparel 7.8%, of which shoes 3.0%; metal and processed metal 6.4%). *Major export destinations* (1991): Germany 21.0%; France 15.2%; U.S. 6.9%; U.K. 6.7%; Spain 5.1%.

Transport and communications

Transport. Railroads (1992): length 12,176 mi, 19,595 km; passenger-mi 30,050,000,000, passenger-km 48,361,000,000; short ton-mi cargo 15,091,000,000, metric ton-km cargo 22,033,000,000. Roads (1989): total length 188,838 mi, 303,906 km (paved 100%). Vehicles (1991): passenger cars 28,200,000; trucks and buses 2,521,000. Merchant marine (1992): vessels (100 gross tons and over) 1,636; total deadweight tonnage 10,940,065. Air transport (1991)[16]: passenger-mi 13,481,899,000, passenger-km 21,697,055,000; short ton-mi cargo 1,337,514,000, metric ton-km cargo 1,952,737,000; airports (1993) 32.
Communications. Daily newspapers (1991): total number 89; total circulation 7,295,400[17]; circulation per 1,000 population 128[17]. Radio (1991): 14,817,197 receivers (1 per 3.9 persons). Television (1991): 17,000,500 receivers (1 per 3.4 persons). Telephones (1990): 32,037,396 (1 per 1.8 persons).

Education and health

Education (1991–92)

	schools	teachers	students	student/teacher ratio
Primary (age 6–10)	22,491	186,397	2,985,398	16.0
Secondary (age 11–18)	9,932	109,999	2,154,711	19.6
Voc., teacher tr.	7,952	135,136	2,864,885	21.2
Higher[18]	82	54,991	1,334,821	24.3

Literacy (1990): total population age 15 and over literate 47,507,000 (97.1%); males literate 22,832,000 (97.8%); females literate 24,675,000 (96.4%).
Health (1991): physicians (1989) 249,704 (1 per 228 persons); hospital beds 373,062 (1 per 153 persons); infant mortality rate per 1,000 live births 8.3.
Food (1988–90): daily per capita caloric intake 3,498 (vegetable products 74%, animal products 26%); 139% of FAO recommended minimum requirement.

Military

Total active duty personnel (1992): 354,000 (army 64.9%, navy 13.6%, air force 21.5%). *Military expenditure as percentage of GNP* (1989): 2.4% (world 4.9%); per capita expenditure U.S.$360.

[1]Includes 10 nonelective seats. [2]More than two-thirds are age 55 and over. [3]1978. [4]1988. [5]Imputed bank charges less duties on imports. [6]Unemployed. [7]Enterprises with 20 or more persons engaged. [8]Total number of persons engaged. [9]1981. [10]All enterprises (1982). [11]1990. [12]1987. [13]June. [14]May. [15]April. [16]Alitalia only. [17]For 65 newspapers only. [18]1990–91.

Jamaica

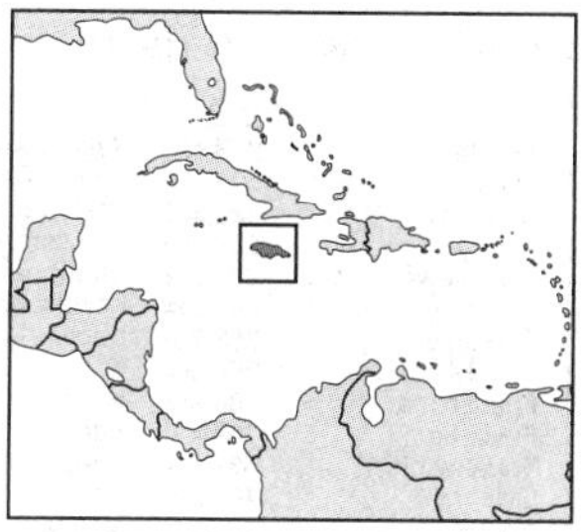

Official name: Jamaica.
Form of government: constitutional monarchy with two legislative houses (Senate [21]; House of Representatives [60]).
Chief of state: British Monarch represented by governor-general.
Head of government: Prime Minister.
Capital: Kingston.
Official language: English.
Official religion: none.
Monetary unit: 1 Jamaica dollar (J$) = 100 cents; valuation (Oct. 4, 1993) 1 U.S.$ = J$27.15; 1 £ = J$41.13.

Area and population

Parishes	Capitals	area sq mi	area sq km	population 1992[1] estimate
Clarendon	May Pen	462	1,196	219,400
Hanover	Lucea	174	450	66,000
Kingston	[2]	8	22	[3]
Manchester	Mandeville	321	830	167,900
Portland	Port Antonio	314	814	77,600
Saint Andrew	[2]	166	431	679,100[3]
Saint Ann	Saint Ann's Bay	468	1,213	151,700
Saint Catherine	Spanish Town	460	1,192	364,400
Saint Elizabeth	Black River	468	1,212	145,300
Saint James	Montego Bay	230	595	161,000
Saint Mary	Port Maria	236	611	113,000
Saint Thomas	Morant Bay	287	743	87,500
Trelawny	Falmouth	338	875	73,800
Westmoreland	Savanna-la-Mar	312	807	128,800
TOTAL		4,244	10,991	2,435,500

Demography

Population (1993): 2,472,000.
Density (1993): persons per sq mi 582.5, persons per sq km 224.9.
Urban-rural (1990): urban 52.3%; rural 47.7%.
Sex distribution (1992): male 50.14%; female 49.86%.
Age breakdown (1992): under 15, 32.5%; 15–29, 30.9%; 30–44, 17.3%; 45–59, 9.3%; 60 and over, 10.0%.
Population projection: (2000) 2,642,000; (2010) 2,907,000.
Doubling time: 38 years.
Ethnic composition (1982): black 74.7%; mixed black 12.8%; East Indian 1.3%; other 11.2%, of which not stated 9.5%.
Religious affiliation (1982): Protestant 55.9%, of which Church of God 18.4%, Baptist 10.0%, Anglican 7.1%, Seventh-day Adventist 6.9%, Pentecostal 5.2%; Roman Catholic 5.0%; nonreligious or atheist 17.7%; not stated 11.2%; other 10.2%, of which Rastafarian *c.* 5.0%.
Major cities (1991): Kingston 103,771[4] (metropolitan area 587,798); Spanish Town 92,383; Portmore 90,138; Montego Bay 83,446; May Pen 46,785.

Vital statistics

Birth rate per 1,000 population (1992): 23.9 (world avg. 26.4); (1987) legitimate 14.9%, illegitimate 85.1%.
Death rate per 1,000 population (1992): 5.4 (world avg. 9.2).
Natural increase rate per 1,000 population (1992): 18.5 (world avg. 17.2).
Total fertility rate (avg. births per childbearing woman; 1991): 2.7.
Marriage rate per 1,000 population (1991): 5.4.
Divorce rate per 1,000 population (1991): 0.5.
Life expectancy at birth (1990–95): male 71.4 years; female 75.8 years.
Major causes of death per 100,000 population (1985): diseases of the circulatory system 229.6; malignant neoplasms (cancers) 91.4; diseases of the respiratory system 36.8; endocrine and metabolic disorders 29.1.

National economy

Budget (1992–93). Revenue J$21,029,400,000 (tax revenue 89.3%, of which income taxes 37.1%, consumption taxes 27.7%, stamp duties 5.6%; nontax revenue 5.1%). Expenditures: J$26,871,100,000 (current expenditure 59.3%, of which debt interest 24.1%; development expenditure 40.7%).
Production (metric tons except as noted). Agriculture, forestry, fishing (1992): sugarcane 2,525,000, yams 214,400, vegetables 109,300, bananas 76,700, citrus fruits 47,600, plantains 39,500, legumes 11,300, coffee 10,000, cacao beans 6,194, pimientos 1,773; livestock (number of live animals; 1991) 440,000 goats, 300,000 cattle, 250,000 pigs; roundwood (1991) 180,000 cu m; fish catch (1990) 10,432. Mining and quarrying (1992): crude bauxite 4,131,800; alumina 2,917,000; gypsum 145,000. Manufacturing (1992): sugar 228,000; flour 144,300; poultry meat 35,000; beer and stout 804,200 hectolitres; rum 150,400 hectolitres; cigarettes 1,321,000,000 units. Construction (1991): residential units completed 3,793[5]; factory space completed 6,989 sq m[6]. Energy production (consumption): electricity (kW-hr; 1990) 2,730,000,000 (2,730,000,000); coal, none (none); crude petroleum (barrels; 1990) none (6,643,000); petroleum products (metric tons; 1990) 850,000 (1,405,000); natural gas, none (none).
Household income and expenditure. Average household size (1991) 4.2; average annual income per household (1988) J$8,356 (U.S.$1,525); sources of income (1989): wages and salaries 66.1%, self-employment 19.3%, transfers 14.6%; expenditure (1988)[7]: food and beverages 55.6%, housing 7.9%, fuel and other household supplies 7.4%, health care 7.0%, transportation 6.4%, clothing and footwear 5.1%, household furnishings 2.8%, other 7.8%.
Gross national product (at current market prices; 1991): U.S.$3,365,000,000 (U.S.$1,380 per capita).

Structure of gross domestic product and labour force

	1992 in value J$'000,000	1992 % of total value	1992 labour force	1992 % of labour force
Agriculture	5,777	7.9	247,300	23.0
Mining	6,845	9.4	5,800	0.5
Manufacturing	14,399	19.7	101,900	9.5
Construction	9,382	12.9	59,100	5.5
Public utilities	1,837	2.5	4,900	0.4
Transp. and commun.	5,582	7.7	36,300	3.4
Trade	18,194	24.9	172,100	16.0
Pub. admin., defense	4,408	6.0		
Finance, real estate	8,685	11.9	272,700	25.4
Services	3,297	4.5		
Other	−5,423[8]	−7.4[8]	175,000[9]	16.3[9]
TOTAL	72,983	100.0	1,074,900[10]	100.0

Population economically active (1992): total 1,074,900; activity rate of total population 44.0% (participation rates: ages 14–64, 71.6%[6]; female 47.0%; unemployed 15.7%).

Price and earnings indexes (1985 = 100)

	1986	1987	1988	1989	1990	1991	1992
Consumer price index	115.1	122.8	132.9	152.0	185.3	280.0	496.4
Earnings index	...	...	...	...	...	...	...

Public debt (external, outstanding; 1991): U.S.$3,751,000,000.
Tourism (1991): receipts from visitors U.S.$850,000,000; expenditures by nationals abroad U.S.$54,000,000.
Land use (1990): forested 17.1%; meadows and pastures 17.5%; agricultural and under permanent cultivation 24.8%; other 40.6%.

Foreign trade[11]

Balance of trade (current prices)

	1987	1988	1989	1990	1991	1992
U.S.$'000,000	−525	−601	−873	−785	−654	−636
% of total	27.0%	26.5%	30.4%	25.3%	22.2%	23.2%

Imports (1992): J$38,267,482,000 (raw materials 66.3%, of which fuels 17.3%; consumer goods 17.1%; capital goods 16.6%, of which machinery and apparatus 11.7%). *Major import sources* (1991): United States 52.6%; Venezuela 5.6%; United Kingdom 5.3%; Germany 4.6%; Japan 3.8%; Canada 3.6%; Mexico 3.4%.
Exports (1992): J$24,099,100,000 (alumina 44.7%; bauxite 8.4%; raw sugar 7.8%; bananas 3.8%; rum 1.7%; coffee 1.6%). *Major export destinations* (1991): United States 40.0%; United Kingdom 14.0%; Germany 10.2%; Canada 9.6%; Norway 6.5%; Ghana 2.4%.

Transport and communications

Transport. Railroads (1991): route length 129 mi, 208 km; passenger-mi 12,127,000[6], passenger-km 19,516,000[6]; short ton-mi cargo 1,700,000, metric ton-km cargo 2,482,000. Roads (1991): total length 10,212 mi, 16,435 km (paved 29%). Vehicles (1991): passenger cars 97,500; trucks and buses 18,000. Merchant marine (1992): vessels (100 gross tons and over) 12; total deadweight tonnage 16,207. Air transport (1992)[12]: passenger-mi 888,559,000, passenger-km 1,430,000,000; short ton-mi cargo 14,235,000, metric ton-km cargo 20,783,000; airports (1993) with scheduled flights 4.
Communications. Daily newspapers (1992): total number 3; total circulation 130,400; circulation per 1,000 population 53. Radio (1992): 1,500,000 receivers (1 per 1.6 persons). Television (1992): 484,000 receivers (1 per 5.1 persons). Telephones (1991): 192,100 (1 per 13 persons).

Education and health

Education (1991–92)[13]

	schools	teachers	students	student/ teacher ratio
Primary (age 6–11)[14]	788	9,948	389,005	39.1
Secondary (age 12–16)	126	8,213	150,986	18.4
Voc., teacher tr.	17	1,018	14,875	14.6
Higher	15[15]	1,047[16]	19,173[17]	17.9[16]

Educational attainment (1982). Percentage of population age 25 and over having: no formal schooling 3.2%; some primary education 79.8%; some secondary 15.0%; complete secondary and higher 2.0%. *Literacy* (1990): total population age 15 and over literate 1,630,000 (98.4%); males literate 800,000 (98.2%); females literate 830,000 (98.6%).
Health: physicians[18] (1992) 397 (1 per 6,159 persons); hospital beds (1991) 5,181 (1 per 457 persons); infant mortality rate per 1,000 live births (1989) 27.0.
Food (1988–90): daily per capita caloric intake 2,558 (vegetable products 83%, animal products 17%); 114% of FAO recommended minimum requirement.

Military

Total active duty personnel (1992): 3,320 (army 90.4%; coast guard 4.5%; air force 5.1%). *Military expenditure as percentage of GNP* (1989): 1.1% (world 4.9%); per capita expenditure U.S.$14.

[1]January 1. [2]The parishes of Kingston and Saint Andrew are jointly administered from the Half Way Tree section of Saint Andrew. [3]Kingston included with Saint Andrew. [4]City of Kingston is coextensive with Kingston parish. [5]80% public sector. [6]1990. [7]Weights of consumer price index components. [8]Less imputed service charges. [9]Includes 169,200 unemployed. [10]Detail does not add to total given because of rounding. [11]Import figures are c.i.f. [12]Air Jamaica only. [13]Public schools only. [14]Includes lower-secondary students at all-age schools. [15]1988–89. [16]1987–88. [17]1989–90. [18]Public health only.

Japan

Official name: Nihon (Japan).
Form of government: constitutional monarchy with a National Diet consisting of two legislative houses (House of Councillors [252]; House of Representatives [512]).
Chief of state: Emperor.
Head of government: Prime Minister.
Capital: Tokyo.
Official language: Japanese.
Official religion: none.
Monetary unit: 1 yen (¥) = 100 sen; valuation (Oct. 4, 1993) 1 U.S.$ = ¥105.78; 1 £ = ¥160.25.

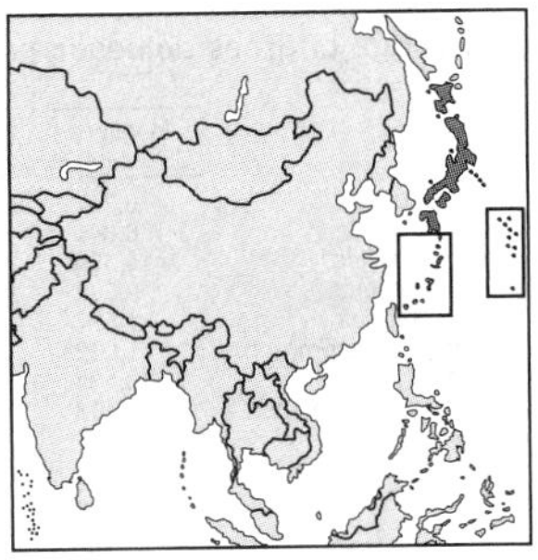

Area and population

Regions Prefectures	Capitals	area sq mi	area sq km	population 1992[1] estimate
Chūbu				
Aichi	Nagoya	1,984	5,139	6,766,000
Fukui	Fukui	1,619	4,192	824,000
Gifu	Gifu	4,091	10,596	2,080,000
Ishikawa	Kanazawa	1,621	4,198	1,169,000
Nagano	Nagano	5,245	13,585	2,165,000
Niigata	Niigata	4,857	12,579	2,475,000
Shizuoka	Shizuoka	3,001	7,773	3,701,000
Toyama	Toyama	1,642	4,252	1,120,000
Yamanashi	Kōfu	1,723	4,463	862,000
Chūgoku				
Hiroshima	Hiroshima	3,269	8,467	2,867,000
Okayama	Okayama	2,738	7,092	1,932,000
Shimane	Matsue	2,559[2]	6,629[2]	775,000
Tottori	Tottori	1,349[2]	3,494[2]	615,000
Yamaguchi	Yamaguchi	2,358	6,107	1,565,000
Hokkaidō				
Hokkaidō (Territory)	Sapporo	32,247	83,520	5,659,000
Kantō				
Chiba	Chiba	1,989	5,151	5,673,000
Gumma	Maebashi	2,454	6,356	1,983,000
Ibaraki	Mito	2,353	6,094	2,895,000
Kanagawa	Yokohama	928	2,403	8,104,000
Saitama	Urawa	1,467	3,799	6,561,000
Tochigi	Utsunomiya	2,476	6,414	1,957,000
Kinki				
Hyōgo	Kōbe	3,236	8,381	5,466,000
Mie	Tsu	2,231	5,778	1,811,000
Nara	Nara	1,425	3,692	1,401,000
Shiga	Ōtsu	1,551	4,016	1,246,000
Wakayama	Wakayama	1,824	4,725	1,078,000
Kyūshū				
Fukuoka	Fukuoka	1,916	4,963	4,852,000
Kagoshima	Kagoshima	3,539	9,167	1,787,000
Kumamoto	Kumamoto	2,860	7,408	1,845,000
Miyazaki	Miyazaki	2,986	7,735	1,167,000
Nagasaki	Nagasaki	1,588	4,113	1,552,000
Ōita	Ōita	2,447	6,338	1,233,000
Saga	Saga	942	2,440	878,000
Ryukyu				
Okinawa	Naha	871	2,255	1,238,000
Shikoku				
Ehime	Matsuyama	2,190	5,672	1,511,000
Kagawa	Takamatsu	727	1,883	1,024,000
Kōchi	Kōchi	2,744	7,107	817,000
Tokushima	Tokushima	1,601	4,146	830,000
Tohoku				
Akita	Akita	4,484[3]	11,613[3]	1,219,000
Aomori	Aomori	3,714[3]	9,619[3]	1,472,000
Fukushima	Fukushima	5,322	13,784	2,115,000
Iwate	Morioka	5,898	15,277	1,414,000
Miyagi	Sendai	2,815	7,292	2,277,000
Yamagata	Yamagata	3,601	9,327	1,255,000
Metropolis				
Tōkyō[4]	Tokyo	836	2,166	11,874,000
Urban prefectures				
Kyōto[5]	Kyōto	1,781	4,613	2,606,000
Ōsaka[5]	Ōsaka	722	1,869	8,735,000
TOTAL		145,883[6, 7]	377,835[6, 7]	124,452,000[7]

Demography

Population (1993): 124,670,000.
Density (1993): persons per sq mi 854.6, persons per sq km 330.0.
Urban-rural (1990): urban 77.4%; rural 22.6%.
Sex distribution (1993): male 49.08%; female 50.92%.
Age breakdown (1993): under 15, 16.9%; 15–29, 22.1%; 30–44, 21.1%; 45–59, 20.8%; 60–74, 13.8%; 75 and over, 5.3%.
Population projection: (2000) 126,894,000; (2010) 129,410,000.
Doubling time: not applicable; doubling time exceeds 100 years.
Composition by nationality (1991): Japanese 99.0%; Korean 0.6%; Chinese 0.1%; other 0.3%.
Place of birth (1991): 99.2% native-born; 0.8% foreign-born (mainly Korean).
Immigration (1990): permanent immigrants/registered aliens admitted 984,500, from North and South Korea 69.3%, Taiwan, Hong Kong, and China 14.0%, Philippines 4.0%, United States 3.5%, United Kingdom 0.9%, Malaysia 0.4%, Canada 0.4%, France 0.3%, West Germany 0.3%, Australia 0.3%, other 6.6%.
Major cities (1992[1]): Tokyo 8,129,377; Yokohama 3,298,897; Ōsaka 2,603,272; Nagoya 2,162,007; Sapporo 1,716,624; Kōbe 1,499,195; Kyōto 1,456,527; Fukuoka 1,261,658; Kawasaki 1,195,464; Hiroshima 1,096,919; Kita-Kyūshū 1,020,877.

Other principal cities (1991[1])

	population		population		population
Akashi	278,458	Kakogawa	246,357	Okayama	601,094
Akita	305,726	Kanazawa	445,522	Okazaki	315,633
Amagasaki	497,333	Kashiwa	312,690	Ōmiya	416,421
Aomori	287,354	Kasugai	270,927	Ōtsu	265,313
Asahikawa	361,736	Kawagoe	311,605	Sagamihara	551,762
Chiba	841,914	Kawaguchi	448,142	Sakai	808,084
Fujisawa	358,757	Kōchi	318,009	Sendai	941,794
Fukui	254,008	Koriyama	320,209	Shimonoseki	260,692
Fukushima	280,958	Koshigaya	291,399	Shizuoka	474,388
Fukuyama	369,401	Kumamoto	636,144	Suita	342,020
Funabashi	537,614	Kurashiki	416,703	Takamatsu	330,568
Gifu	409,928	Machida	355,843	Takatsuki	360,748
Hachiōji	481,548	Maebashi	288,410	Tokorozawa	311,654
Hakodate	306,465	Matsudo	461,438	Tokushima	264,503
Hamamatsu	557,881	Matsuyama	450,796	Toyama	323,015
Higashi-Ōsaka	516,333	Miyazaki	291,036	Toyohashi	346,741
Himeji	460,627	Morioka	281,870	Toyonaka	406,126
Hirakata	394,935	Nagano	350,673	Toyota	340,621
Hiratsuka	250,280	Nagasaki	442,373	Urawa	434,976
Ibaraki	254,915	Naha	302,357	Utsunomiya	432,633
Ichihara	267,004	Nara	353,726	Wakayama	396,171
Ichikawa	446,897	Neyagawa	257,810	Yamagata	250,620
Ichinomiya	264,990	Niigata	488,654	Yao	277,071
Iwaki	357,932	Nishinomiya	425,711	Yokkaichi	280,523
Kagoshima	537,775	Ōita	417,051	Yokosuka	435,846

Religious affiliation (1989): Shintō and related religions 39.5%; Buddhism 38.3%; Christian 3.9%; other 18.3%.
Households (1990). Total households 40,670,000; average household size 3.0; composition of households 1 person 23.1%, 2 persons 20.6%, 3 persons 18.1%, 4 persons 21.7%, 5 persons 9.3%, 6 or more persons 7.2%. Family households 31,204,000 (76.7%); nonfamily 9,466,000 (23.3%), of which 1 person 9,390,000 (23.1%).

Type of household (1988)

Total number of dwelling units: 37,413,000

	number of dwellings	percentage of total
by kind of dwelling		
exclusive entry (do not share bathroom or kitchen)	34,701,000	92.8
combined with nondwelling	2,712,000	7.3
detached house	23,311,000	62.3
apartment building	11,409,000	30.5
tenement (substandard or overcrowded building)	2,490,000	6.7
other	203,000	0.5
by legal tenure of householder		
owned	22,948,000	61.3
rented	14,015,000	37.5
other	450,000	1.2
by kind of amenities		
flush toilet	24,300,000	65.0
bathroom	34,126,000	91.2
by year of construction		
prior to 1945	2,701,000	7.3
1945–70	11,487,000	31.1
1971–80	13,543,000	36.8
1981–83	3,564,000	9.7
1984–88	5,556,000	15.1

Mobility (1980). Population living in same residence from birth 24.0%; different residence established prior to October 1975, 44.0%; different residence established after October 1975, 32.0%, of which: same prefecture 24.1%; different prefecture 7.7%.

Vital statistics

Birth rate per 1,000 population (1992): 9.9 (world avg. 26.4); (1985) legitimate 99.0%; illegitimate 1.0%.
Death rate per 1,000 population (1992): 6.9 (world avg. 9.2).
Natural increase rate per 1,000 population (1992): 3.0 (world avg. 17.2).
Total fertility rate (avg. births per childbearing woman; 1990): 1.5.
Marriage rate per 1,000 population (1991): 6.0[8]; median age at first marriage (1987) men 28.3 years, women 25.6 years.
Divorce rate per 1,000 population (1991)[8]: 1.4.
Life expectancy at birth (1991): male 76.1 years; female 82.1 years.
Major causes of death per 100,000 population (1991): malignant neoplasms (cancers) 180.5; heart diseases 136.3; cerebrovascular diseases 95.6; pneumonia and bronchitis 61.6; accidents and adverse effects 26.8; senility without mention of psychosis 18.7; suicide 16.0; nephritis, nephrotic syndrome, and nephrosis 13.7; cirrhosis of the liver 13.6; diabetes mellitus 7.8; hypertensive diseases 7.3.

Social indicators

Educational attainment (1990). Percentage of population age 25 years and over having: primary 34.3%; secondary education 44.5%; postsecondary 21.2%.

Distribution of income (1989)

percentage of average household income by quintile

1	2	3	4	5 (highest)
10.9	15.5	18.7	23.3	31.6

Quality of working life. Average workweek (1992): 44.4 hours. Annual rate of industrial deaths per 100,000 workers (1991): 1.0. Proportion of labour force insured for damages or income loss resulting from injury, permanent disability, and death (1991): 50.1%. Average man-days lost to labour stoppages per 1,000,000 workdays (1990): 8.9. Average duration of journey to work (1988)[9]: 26.8 minutes (1983; 26.7% private automobile, 67.4% public transportation, 5.5% taxi, 0.4% other). Rate per 1,000 workers of discouraged (unemployed no longer seeking work; 1987): 10.1.

Access to services (1989). Proportion of households having access to: gas supply 64.6%; safe public water supply 94.0%; public sewage collection 89.4%.

Social participation. Eligible voters participating in last national election (1993): 67.3%. Population 15 years and over participating in social service activities on a voluntary basis (1987): 25.2%. Trade union membership in total workforce (1991): 24.5%.

Social deviance (1990). Offense rate per 100,000 population for: homicide 1.0; rape 1.2; robbery 1.3; larceny and theft 1,169.5. Incidence in general population of: alcoholism, n.a.; drug and substance abuse, n.a. Rate of suicide per 100,000 population (1991): 16.0.

Leisure/use of personal time

Discretionary daily activities (1991)
(Population age 15 years and over)

	weekly average hrs./min.
Total discretionary daily time	5:56[7]
of which	
Hobbies and amusements	0:36
Sports	0:11
Learning (except schoolwork)	0:12
Social activities	0:05
Associations	0:29
Radio, television, newspapers, and magazines	2:23
Rest and relaxation	1:21
Other activities	0:21

Major leisure activities (1991)
(Population age 15 years and over)

	percentage of participation		
	male	female	total
Hobbies and amusements	93.0	90.8	91.9
Sports	84.2	72.1	78.0
Light exercises	30.8	34.1	32.0
Swimming	27.1	20.8	23.8
Bowling	33.0	23.1	27.9
Learning (except schoolwork)	36.3	37.0	36.7
Travel			
Domestic	72.7	68.3	70.4
Foreign	10.4	7.6	9.0

Material well-being (1992). Households possessing: automobile 78.6%; telephone, virtually 100%; colour television receiver 99.3%; refrigerator 98.9%; air conditioner 69.8%; washing machine 99.4%; vacuum cleaner 98.7%; videocassette recorder 71.5%; camera 86.8%; microwave oven 79.2%; compact disc player 45.0%.

National economy

Gross national product (at current market prices; 1992): U.S.$3,507,859,000,000 (U.S.$28,220 per capita).

Structure of gross domestic product and labour force

	1991		1992	
	in value ¥'000,000,000[10]	% of total value	labour force	% of labour force
Agriculture, fishing	9,511	2.3	4,110,000	6.2
Mining	1,106	0.3	60,000	0.1
Manufacturing	132,832	32.0	15,690,000	23.8
Construction	35,959	8.7	6,190,000	9.4
Public utilities	15,200	3.7	330,000	0.5
Transportation and communications	26,639	6.4	3,850,000	5.8
Trade	57,382	13.8	14,360,000	21.8
Finance	65,410	15.8	2,620,000	4.0
Pub. admin., defense	25,701	6.2	2,040,000	3.1
Services	66,873	16.1	14,810,000	22.5
Other	−21,417[11]	−5.2[11]	1,720,000[12]	2.6[12]
TOTAL	415,196[13]	100.0[7]	65,780,000	100.0[7]

Budget (1993). Revenue: ¥64,211,200,000,000 (income tax 42.0%; corporation tax 24.8%; value-added tax 8.5%; liquor and tobacco tax 4.8%; stamp duties 2.7%; customs duties 1.4%). Expenditures: ¥72,354,800,000,000 (transfers to local governments 21.6%; national debt 21.3%; social security 18.2%; public works 11.8%; culture, education, and science promotion 8.0%; national defense 6.4%; pensions 2.4%).

Public debt (1992): U.S.$1,393,600,000,000.

Population economically active (1992): total 65,780,000; activity rate of total population 52.9% (participation rates: age 15 and over 71.2%; female 40.7%; unemployed 2.2%).

Price and earnings indexes (1985 = 100)

	1987	1988	1989	1990	1991	1992	1993[14]
Consumer price index	100.7	101.4	103.7	106.9	110.4	112.3	114.1
Monthly earnings index	105.0	108.6	112.1	116.3	120.4	122.9	126.4

Household income and expenditure (1990)[15]. Average household size 3.7; average annual income per household ¥6,585,200 (U.S.$48,900); sources of income: wages and salaries 58.0%, transfer payments 19.4%, self-employment 11.6%, other 11.0%; expenditure (1991): food 19.3%, transportation 8.1%, reading and recreation 7.6%, clothing and footwear 5.7%, housing 4.2%, fuel, light, and water charges 4.1%, education 4.0%, furniture and household utensils 3.2%, medical care 2.0%.

Tourism (1991): receipts from visitors U.S.$3,435,000,000; expenditures by nationals abroad U.S.$23,983,000,000.

Land use (1991): forested 66.7%; meadows and pastures 1.7%; agricultural and under permanent cultivation 12.1%; other 19.5%.

Manufacturing and mining enterprises (1990)

	no. of establishments	avg. no. of persons engaged	annual wages as a % of avg. of all contract wages[16]	annual value added (¥'000,000,000)
Electrical machinery	36,116	1,944,000	95.4	20,123
Nonelectrical machinery	46,669	1,198,000	120.9	13,704
Transport equipment	15,539	943,000	126.6	12,582
Chemical products	5,352	401,000	143.9	11,211
Food, beverages, and tobacco	50,775	1,222,000	76.4	10,706
Fabricated metal products	51,871	847,000	98.7	8,056
Printing and publishing	29,646	555,000	124.2	6,368
Iron and steel	6,477	338,000	150.5	6,208
Ceramic, stone, and clay	20,753	459,000	100.0	5,096
Plastic products	20,077	435,000	91.7	3,959
Textiles	30,517	531,000	72.6	3,109
Paper and paper products	11,404	284,000	103.0	3,070
Apparel products	31,985	577,000	50.9	2,191
Nonferrous metal products	4,280	169,000	122.2	2,104
Precision instruments	7,191	245,000	101.2	1,971
Furniture and fixtures	17,094	231,000	82.6	1,757
Lumber and wood products	20,322	253,000	77.3	1,664
Rubber products	5,816	172,000	102.4	1,630
Petroleum and coal products	1,074	33,000	159.9	741
Leather products	5,796	79,000	72.1	475
Mining[16]	780	29,000	136.5	227

Energy production (consumption): electricity (kW-hr; 1991) 888,086,000,000 (888,086,000,000); coal (metric tons; 1991) 8,068,000 (117,938,000); crude petroleum (barrels; 1991) 1,525,000 (1,441,000,000); petroleum products (metric tons; 1991) 164,082,000, of which (by volume) diesel 33.2%, heavy fuel oil 25.0%, gasoline 19.9%, kerosene and jet fuel 12.1% (188,558,000); natural gas (cu m; 1991) 2,165,000,000 (55,151,000,000). Composition of energy supply by source (1990): crude oil and petroleum products 58.3%, coal 16.6%, natural gas 10.1%, nuclear power 9.4%, hydroelectric power 4.2%, other 1.4%. Domestic energy demand by end use (1990): mining and manufacturing 44.4%, residential and commercial 24.4%, transportation 23.1%, agriculture, forestry, and fisheries 3.7%, other 4.4%.

Financial aggregates

	1987	1988	1989	1990	1991	1992	1993[14]
Exchange rate[17], ¥ per:							
U.S. dollar	123.50	125.85	143.45	134.40	125.20	124.75	105.15
£	237.05	228.29	226.21	258.41	234.21	188.62	158.85
SDR	175.20	169.36	188.52	191.21	179.09	171.53	149.14
International reserves (U.S.$)							
Total (excl. gold; '000,000)	80,973	96,728	83,957	78,501	72,059	71,623	98,797
SDRs ('000,000)	2,463	2,936	2,447	3,042	2,579	1,094	1,526
Reserve pos. in IMF ('000,000)	2,853	3,278	3,518	5,971	7,722	8,641	8,555
Foreign exchange ('000,000)	75,657	90,514	77,992	69,487	61,758	61,888	88,716
Gold ('000,000 fine troy oz)	24.23	24.23	24.23	24.23	24.23	24.23	24.23
% world reserves	2.6	2.6	2.6	2.6	2.6	2.6	2.6
Interest and prices							
Central bank discount (%)[17]	2.50	2.50	4.25	6.00	4.50	3.25	1.75
Govt. bond yield (%)	4.21	4.27	5.05	7.36	6.53	4.94	3.69[18]
Industrial share prices (1985 = 100)	196.4	213.9	257.8	218.8	184.9	136.9	167.3[18]
Balance of payments (U.S.$'000,000,000)							
Balance of visible trade	96.4	95.0	76.9	63.6	103.1	132.4	...
Imports, f.o.b.	128.2	164.8	192.7	216.8	203.5	198.5	...
Exports, f.o.b.	224.6	259.8	269.6	280.4	306.6	330.9	...
Balance of invisibles	−5.7	−11.3	−15.6	−22.2	−17.7	−14.8	...
Balance of payments, current account	87.0	79.6	57.0	35.9	72.9	117.6	...

Retail and wholesale trade and services (1991)

	no. of establishments	avg. no. of employees	annual sales (¥'000,000,000)
Retail trade	1,519,186	6,936,000	140,634
Food and beverages	622,751	2,542,000	41,453
Grocery	68,913	643,000	16,404
Liquors	106,650	315,000	6,323
General merchandise	4,347	440,000	19,898
Department stores	2,004	427,000	19,574
Motor vehicles and bicycles	93,230	566,000	18,934
Apparel and accessories	240,989	809,000	14,844
Furniture and home furnishings	158,104	587,000	11,987
Gasoline service stations	72,807	385,000	11,234
Books and stationery	76,730	600,000	4,722
Wholesale trade	475,967	4,773,000	572,982
Machinery and equipment	111,046	1,286,000	130,512
General machinery except electrical	54,612	577,000	47,910
Motor vehicles and parts	17,318	222,000	32,019
General merchandise	705	51,000	98,548
Minerals and metals	22,657	264,000	61,300
Farm, livestock, and fishery products	43,331	416,000	60,273
Food and beverages	56,656	561,000	47,677
Textiles, apparel, and accessories	44,748	506,000	38,517
Building materials	63,885	444,000	35,698
Chemicals	18,140	179,000	24,457
Drugs and toilet goods	21,319	291,000	19,783
Medical services[19]	171,986	2,026,000	...
Educational services[19]	84,512	2,065,000	...

Production (metric tons except as noted). Agriculture, forestry, fishing (1992): rice 13,255,000, sugar beets 3,823,000, potatoes 3,650,000, cabbages 2,500,000, sugarcane 1,863,000, mandarin oranges 1,400,000, sweet potatoes 1,300,000, onions 1,300,000, apples 1,025,000, raw sugar 987,000, cucumbers 870,000, wheat 800,000, tomatoes 740,000, watermelons 730,000, carrots 640,000, eggplants 500,000, pears 452,000, barley 340,000, grapes 276,000, pumpkins 265,000, strawberries 219,000, soybeans 197,000, peaches 192,000, dry beans 140,000, tea 85,000, green beans 80,000, tobacco leaves 77,000, green peas 50,000, cow's milk 8,300,000, hen's eggs

2,586,000; livestock (number of live animals) 10,966,000 pigs, 4,980,000 cattle (of which 42% dairy cows), 35,000 goats, 29,000 sheep, 26,000 horses, 337,000,000 poultry; roundwood (1991) 28,272,000 cu m; fish catch (1991) 9,307,000, of which sardines 2,964,000, Alaska pollack 554,000, prawns and shrimp 522,000, Japanese scallops 368,000, Japanese anchovies 329,000, oysters 239,000, squid 219,000, crabs 78,000, river eels 39,000, carp 16,000. Mining and quarrying (1992): limestone 203,780,000; silica stone 19,319,000; dolomite 4,853,000; silica sand 3,864,000; pyrophyllite 771,000; pyrophyllite clay 284,000; zinc 134,510; lead 18,000; copper 12,047; tungsten 578; silver 178,300 kg; gold 8,890 kg. Manufacturing (1991): crude steel 109,649,000; semifinished steel 102,727,000; cement 89,564,000; hot-rolled steel products 87,982,000; pig iron 79,985,000; paper pulp 11,556,500; sulfuric acid 7,057,100; plastic products 5,516,800; compound fertilizers 2,803,100; spun yarn 939,100; synthetic fabrics 2,591,760,000 sq m; cotton fabrics 1,603,280,000 sq m; finished products (in number of units) 477,216,000 watches and clocks, 69,371,000 electronic desk calculators, 26,058,000 videocassette recorders, 18,164,000 telephones, 17,657,000 35-mm cameras, 13,438,000 colour television receivers, 9,753,100 passenger cars, 7,447,900 bicycles, 6,981,000 vacuum cleaners, 5,587,000 automatic washing machines, 5,212,000 electric refrigerators, 4,547,000 facsimile machines, 4,282,000 microwave ovens, 4,178,000 stereo recorders, 3,028,600 motorcycles, 2,654,700 photocopy machines, 1,456,800 typewriters. Construction (value in ¥ '000,000; 1991): residential 25,080,000; nonresidential 27,160,000.

Foreign trade[20]

Balance of trade (current prices)

	1987	1988	1989	1990	1991	1992
¥'000,000,000	+12,107	+11,903	+11,235	+10,398	+13,093	+15,922
% of total	22.2%	21.3%	17.4%	14.3%	18.3%	22.7%

Imports (1992): ¥29,527,000,000,000 (mineral fuels, lubricants, and related materials 22.6%, of which crude petroleum and petroleum products 15.6%; food, beverages, and tobacco 16.0%; machinery and transport equipment 14.1%, of which electrical equipment 5.5%, transport equipment 2.3%; chemicals and chemical products 7.4%). *Major import sources:* United States 22.4%; China 7.3%; Australia 5.3%; Indonesia 5.3%; South Korea 5.0%; Germany 4.6%; Saudi Arabia 4.4%; Taiwan 4.0%; Canada 3.3%; Malaysia 2.8%; Thailand 2.6%; France 2.3%.

Exports (1992): ¥43,011,000,000,000 (motor vehicles 17.8%; office machinery 7.5%; chemicals 5.6%, of which plastic materials 1.5%; scientific and optical equipment 4.0%; iron and steel products 3.9%; power-generating machinery 2.9%; textiles and allied products 2.5%; tape recorders 1.8%; metalworking machinery 1.1%; radio receivers 0.9%; television receivers 0.7%). *Major export destinations:* United States 28.2%; Taiwan 6.2%; Hong Kong 6.1%; Germany 6.0%; South Korea 5.2%; Singapore 3.8%; United Kingdom 3.6%; China 3.5%; Thailand 3.0%; Canada 2.1%; Australia 2.1%.

Trade by commodity group (1992)

	imports		exports	
SITC group	U.S.$'000,000	%	U.S.$'000,000	%
00 Food and live animals; 01 Beverages and tobacco	37,289	16.0	1,765	0.5
02 Crude materials, excluding fuels	23,326[21]	10.0[21]	2,116[21]	0.6[21]
03 Mineral fuels, lubricants, and related materials	52,739	22.6	1,720	0.5
04 Animal and vegetable oils, fats, and waxes	[21]	[21]	[21]	[21]
05 Chemicals and related products, n.e.s.	16,847	7.2	18,771	5.5
06 Basic manufactures	14,296	6.1	22,247	6.5
07 Machinery and transport equipment	32,801	14.1	172,186	50.7
08 Miscellaneous manufactured articles	34,615	14.8	85,309	25.1
09 Goods not classified by kind	21,108	9.1	35,536	10.5
TOTAL	233,021	100.0[7]	339,650	100.0[7]

Direction of trade (1992)

	imports		exports	
	U.S.$'000,000	%	U.S.$'000,000	%
Africa	3,518	1.5	6,407	1.9
Asia	105,076	45.1	132,268	38.9
South America	6,446	2.8	5,173	1.5
North America and Central America	62,261	26.7	113,747	33.4
United States	52,693	22.6	96,716	28.4
other North and Central Am.	9,568	4.1	17,031	5.0
Europe	40,808	17.5	73,736	21.7[7]
EEC	31,399	13.5	62,921	18.5
U.S.S.R.[22]	2,507	1.0	1,164	0.3
other Europe	6,902	3.0	9,651	2.8
Oceania	14,848	6.4	8,780	2.6
TOTAL	232,947[7]	100.0	339,991[7]	100.0

Transport and communications

Transport. Railroads (1991): length 23,690 mi, 38,125 km; rolling stock (1985) locomotives 3,177, passenger cars 46,192, freight cars 40,951; passengers carried 22,581,000,000; passenger-mi 242,976,000,000, passenger-km 391,032,000,000; short ton-mi cargo 18,732,000,000, metric ton-km cargo 27,348,000,000. Roads (1992): total length 691,488 mi, 1,112,844 km (paved 71%). Vehicles (1992): passenger cars 38,963,861; trucks 22,449,421; buses 248,624. Merchant marine (1992): vessels (100 gross tons and over) 10,091; total deadweight tonnage 37,815,779. Air transport (1991): passengers carried 68,688,000; passenger-mi 66,320,000,000, passenger-km 106,732,000,000; short ton-mi cargo 3,423,000,000, metric ton-km cargo 4,997,000,000; airports (1993) with scheduled flights 71. Shares of domestic passenger traffic by mode of transportation (1991): automobiles and light motor vehicles 54.8%; railway 25.2%; buses 9.6%; ships 0.2%; airplanes 0.1%.

Distribution of traffic (1991)

	cargo carried ('000,000 tons)	% of national total	passengers carried ('000,000)	% of national total
Road	6,261.0	90.5	48,974.0	54.8
Rail (intercity)	86.0	1.2	22,560.0	25.2
Urban transport	—	—	17,582.0	19.7
road	—	—	8,582.0	9.6
rail	—	—	9,000.0	10.1
Inland water	572.0	8.3	162.0	0.2
Air	0.9	0.0	69.0	0.1
TOTAL	6,919.9	100.0	89,347.0	100.0

Communications. Daily newspapers (1992): total number 121; total circulation 71,690,000; circulation per 1,000 population 577. Radio (1992): 97,000,000 receivers (1 per 1.3 persons). Television (1992): 100,000,000 receivers (1 per 1.2 persons). Telephones (1991): 55,888,000[23] (1 per 2.2 persons).

Other communications media (1991)

	titles		traffic ('000)
Print		**Electronic**	
Books (new)	42,345	Telegram	47,460
of which		Domestic	46,960
Social sciences	10,251	International	500
Fiction	8,833	Telex	17,200[24]
Engineering	3,601		
Arts	3,785		
Natural sciences	3,036		
History	2,627	**Post**	
Philosophy	2,010	Mail	23,815,000
Magazines/journals	3,918	Domestic	23,407,000
Weekly	107	International	408,000
Monthly	2,700	Parcels	413,300
		Domestic	408,000
Cinema		International	5,300
Feature films (greater than 1,600 m)	255[25]		

Radio and television broadcasting (1991): total radio stations 1,269, of which commercial 413; total television stations 36,250[26], of which commercial 18,900. Commercial broadcasters' broadcasting hours (by percentage of programs; 1990): reports—radio 13.8%, television 19.0%; education—radio 5.0%, television 11.9%; culture—radio 16.0%, television 24.4%; entertainment—radio 64.3%, television 42.6%. Advertisements (daily average; 1990): radio 168, television 290.

Education and health

Education (1992)

	schools	teachers	students	student/teacher ratio
Primary (age 6–11)	24,730	441,000	8,947,000	20.3
Secondary (age 12–17)	16,801	567,000	10,256,000	18.1
Higher	1,114	150,000	2,817,000	18.9

Literacy: total population age 15 and over literate, virtually 100%.

Health (1990): physicians 210,197 (1 per 588 persons); dentists 73,041 (1 per 1,691 persons); nurses 365,298[25] (1 per 336[25] persons); pharmacists 130,604 (1 per 946 persons); midwives 24,056[27] (1 per 5,082[27] persons); hospital beds (1991) 1,686,000 (1 per 74 persons), of which (1989) general 72.9%, mental 22.2%, tuberculosis 3.3%, other 1.6%; infant mortality rate per 1,000 live births (1991) 4.4.

Food (1988–90): daily per capita caloric intake 2,921 (vegetable products 79%, animal products 21%); 125% of FAO recommended minimum.

Military

Total active duty personnel (1993): 237,700 (army 63.1%, navy 18.1%, air force 18.8%). *Military expenditure as percentage of GNP* (1989): 1.0% (world 4.9%); per capita expenditure U.S.$231.

[1]October 1; preliminary. [2]Excludes Lake Naka (38 sq mi [98 sq km]), which is part of both Shimane and Tottori prefectures. [3]Excludes Lake Towada (23 sq mi [60 sq km]), which is part of both Akita and Aomori prefectures. [4]Part of Kantō geographical region. [5]Part of Kinki geographical region. [6]1987 survey; includes Lake Naka and Lake Towada. [7]Detail does not add to total given because of rounding. [8]Figures relate only to Japanese nationals in Japan. [9]Applies to passengers carried within metropolitan areas only. [10]At prices of 1985. [11]Import duties and statistical discrepancy less imputed bank service charge. [12]Mostly unemployed. [13]GDP in current values for 1991 is ¥450,795,000,000,000. [14]July. [15]Worker's household. [16]1988. [17]End of period. [18]August. [19]1985. [20]Import figures are f.o.b. in balance of trade and c.i.f. in commodities and trading partners. [21]Crude materials includes Animal and vegetable oils, fats, and waxes. [22]Data refer to U.S.S.R. as constituted prior to 1991. [23]Number of subscribers. [24]1990. [25]1989. [26]Includes satellite broadcasting. [27]1987.

Jordan

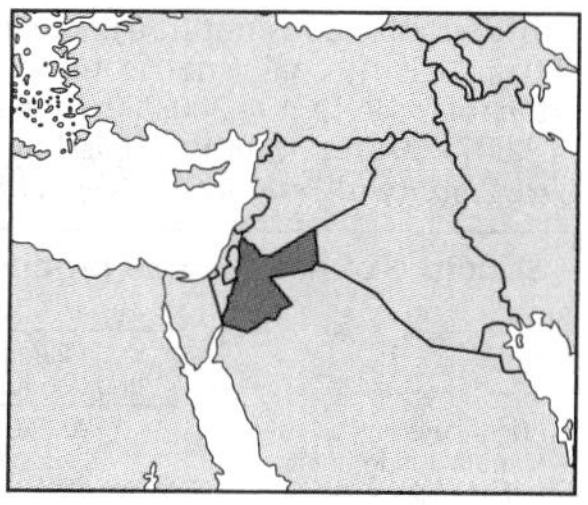

Official name: al-Mamlakah al-Urdunnīyah al-Hāshimīyah (al-Urdun) (Hashemite Kingdom of Jordan).
Form of government: constitutional monarchy[1] with a National Assembly comprising two legislative houses (Senate [40 appointed by king]; House of Deputies [80]).
Chief of state: King.
Head of government: Prime Minister (on king's authority).
Capital: Amman.
Official language: Arabic.
Official religion: Islam.
Monetary unit: 1 Jordan dinar (JD) = 1,000 fils; valuation (Oct. 4, 1993) JD 1.00 = U.S.$1.45 = £0.96.

Area and population

		area		population
Governorates	Capitals	sq mi	sq km	1991[2] estimate
'Ammān	Amman	4,097	10,612	1,444,400
al-Balqā'	aṣ-Ṣalt	425	1,100	235,300
Irbid	Irbid	985	2,551	814,600
al-Karak	al-Karak	1,548	4,010	140,000
Ma'ān	Ma'ān	13,954	36,141	113,200
al-Mafraq	al-Mafraq	10,475	27,129	127,200
aṭ-Ṭafīlah	aṭ-Ṭafīlah	850	2,202	47,400
az-Zarqā'	az-Zarqā'	2,008	5,201	530,900
TOTAL		34,342	88,946	3,453,000

Demography

Population (1993): 3,764,000.
Density (1993): persons per sq mi 109.6, persons per sq km 42.3.
Urban-rural (1990): urban 68.0%; rural 32.0%.
Sex distribution (1990): male 51.46%; female 48.54%.
Age breakdown (1990): under 15, 43.6%; 15–29, 31.6%; 30–44, 12.0%; 45–59, 8.3%; 60–74, 3.4%; 75 and over, 1.1%.
Population projection: (2000) 4,790,000; (2010) 6,760,000.
Doubling time: 17 years.
Ethnic composition (1983): Arab 99.2%, of which Palestinian *c.* 50.0%; Circassian 0.5%; Armenian 0.1%; Turk 0.1%; Kurd 0.1%.
Religious affiliation (1980): Sunnī Muslim 93.0%; Christian 4.9%; other 2.1%.
Major cities (1989): Amman 936,300; az-Zarqā' 318,055; Irbid 167,785; ar-Ruṣayfah 72,580; aṣ-Ṣalt 47,585.

Vital statistics

Birth rate per 1,000 population (1991): 45.7 (world avg. 26.4).
Death rate per 1,000 population (1991): 4.7 (world avg. 9.2).
Natural increase rate per 1,000 population (1991): 41.0 (world avg. 17.2).
Total fertility rate (avg. births per childbearing woman; 1991): 7.1.
Marriage rate per 1,000 population (1990): 10.0.
Divorce rate per 1,000 population (1990): 1.5.
Life expectancy at birth (1991): male 70.0 years; female 73.0 years.
Major causes of death per 100,000 population: n.a.; however, major diseases include tuberculosis, typhoid, paratyphoid fevers, salmonella, hepatitis, and dysentery; nonvenereal syphilis is widespread in the southern desert region.

National economy

Budget (1992). Revenue: JD 1,163,000,000 (1991; direct and indirect taxes 77.8%, foreign grants and loans 22.2%). Expenditures: JD 1,270,000,000 (1988; administration 42.9%, defense and security 25.8%, economic development 15.2%, social welfare 13.2%, transportation and communications 2.8%).
Production (metric tons except as noted). Agriculture, forestry, fishing (1992): tomatoes 479,100, citrus fruit 125,500, olives 110,300, melons 86,500, barley 69,400, wheat 65,900, eggplants 49,200, cucumbers 33,900, cauliflower and cabbage 30,900, grapes 28,900, bananas 23,500; livestock (number of live animals) 2,000,000 sheep, 600,000 goats, 32,000 cattle, 18,000 camels, 55,000,000 chickens; roundwood (1991) 9,000 cu m; fish catch (1991) 22. Mining and quarrying (1992): phosphate ore 4,296,000; potash 1,260,000. Manufacturing (value of production in JD '000; 1989): petroleum refining 240,660; chemicals 207,199; food products 115,932; plastic and plastic products 40,947; paper and paper products 33,088; furniture and wood products 31,594; textiles 22,865; electrical machinery 18,541; clothing 12,285; transport equipment 2,587. Construction (1989)[3]: 1,816,630 sq m. Energy production (consumption): electricity (kW-hr; 1991) 3,723,000,000 (3,723,000,000); coal, none (n.a.); crude petroleum (barrels; 1991) 51,000 (17,526,000); petroleum products (metric tons; 1991) 2,222,000 (2,950,000); natural gas, none (n.a.).
Public debt (external, outstanding; 1991): U.S.$7,570,000,000.
Population economically active (1992): total 706,000; activity rate of total population 19.3% (participation rates: over age 15 [1986] 39.0%; female [1988] 10.9%; unemployed [1992] 15.0%).

Price and earnings indexes (1985 = 100)

	1986	1987	1988	1989	1990	1991	1992
Consumer price index	100.0	99.8	106.4	133.8	155.4	168.1	174.8
Daily earnings index	111.4	121.3	123.8	126.2	128.7	128.7	...

Tourism (1991): receipts from visitors U.S.$317,000,000; expenditures by nationals abroad U.S.$281,000,000.
Household income and expenditure. Average household size (1984) 6.9; income per household (1979) JD 1,820 (U.S.$6,055); sources of income: n.a.; expenditure (1986): food and beverages 37.8%; housing and energy 6.3%; transportation 5.8%; clothing and footwear 5.5%; household durable goods 4.8%; health care 4.0%; education 3.3%; other goods and services 32.5%.
Gross national product (at current market prices; 1992): U.S.$4,402,000,000 (U.S.$1,150 per capita).

Structure of gross domestic product and labour force

	1992		1990	
	in value JD '000,000	% of total value	labour force	% of labour force
Agriculture	204.0	7.3	38,266	7.3
Mining	116.1	4.2	53,468	10.2
Manufacturing	426.0	15.3		
Construction	152.4	5.5	51,895	9.9
Public utilities	70.9	2.5	6,815	1.3
Transportation and communications	428.0	15.4	44,557	8.5
Trade	269.9	9.7	52,944	10.1
Finance	518.7	18.6	16,774	3.2
Pub. admin., defense	550.0	19.9	259,478	49.5
Services	102.8	3.7		
Other	−61.4[4]	−2.2[4]		
TOTAL	2,782.4	100.0[5]	524,197	100.0

Land use (1991): forested 0.8%; meadows and pastures 8.9%; agricultural and under permanent cultivation 4.5%; wasteland (mostly desert), built-on, and other 85.8%.

Foreign trade

Balance of trade (current prices)[6]

	1987	1988	1989	1990	1991	1992
JD '000,000	−499	−639	−585	1,009	−994	−1,462
% of total	44.1%	45.6%	31.5%	41.7%	39.2%	46.8%

Imports (1992): JD 2,214,002,000 (food and live animals 18.8%, of which cereals 4.0%; mineral fuels 13.7%; machinery and appliances 12.4%; transport [mainly equipment and parts] 12.2%; iron and steel 6.0%; clothing and textiles 4.3%; plastics 2.8%). *Major import sources:* Iraq 13.3%; United States 11.1%; Germany 8.4%; Japan 6.0%; Italy 5.0%; United Kingdom 4.9%; Turkey 4.4%; France 3.5%.
Exports (1992): JD 633,755,000 (phosphate fertilizers 19.3%; potash 13.6%; fertilizers 11.4%; phamaceuticals 8.7%; fruits and vegetables 7.9%; soap and detergents 5.5%; cement 3.5%). *Major export destinations:* India 15.2%; Saudi Arabia 11.1%; Iraq 7.7%; Indonesia 4.6%; Turkey 2.4%; China 2.2%; South Korea 1.9%.

Transport and communications

Transport. Railroads (1991): route length 490 mi, 789 km; passengers carried (1988) 31,304; short ton-mi cargo 542,000,000, metric ton-km cargo 791,000,000. Roads (1990): total length 3,733 mi, 6,007 km (paved 100%). Vehicles (1991): passenger cars 172,075; trucks and buses 41,409. Merchant marine (1992): vessels (100 gross tons and over) 5; total deadweight tonnage 113,557. Air transport (1990): passenger-mi 1,729,000,000, passenger-km 2,782,000,000; short ton-mi cargo 173,754,000, metric ton-km cargo 253,676,000; airports (1993) with scheduled flights 2.
Communications. Daily newspapers (1990): total number 5; total circulation 230,000; circulation per 1,000 population 73. Radio (1991): 700,000 receivers (1 per 4.7 persons). Television (1991): 250,000 receivers (1 per 13 persons). Telephones (1991): 350,000 (1 per 9.4 persons).

Education and health

Education (1989–90)

	schools	teachers	students	student/ teacher ratio
Primary (age 6–14)	2,983	21,073	590,275	28.0
Secondary (age 15–17)	622	10,264[7]	357,754	11.5[7]
Voc., teacher tr.	30	2,135	26,525	12.4
Higher	55[7]	3,435	69,389	20.2

Educational attainment (1979). Percentage of population age 14 and over having: no formal schooling 47.9%; primary education 19.8%; secondary 26.4%; higher 5.9%. *Literacy* (1990): percentage of population age 15 and over literate 80.1%; males literate 89.3%; females literate 70.3%.
Health (1991): physicians 4,246 (1 per 813 persons); hospital beds (1990) 5,753 (1 per 571 persons); infant mortality rate per 1,000 live births 38.0.
Food (1984–86): daily per capita caloric intake 2,498 (vegetable products 89%, animal products 11%); 120% of FAO recommended minimum requirement.

Military

Total active duty personnel (1993): 100,600 (army 89.5%, navy 0.6%, air force 9.9%). *Military expenditure as percentage of GNP* (1989): 12.7% (world 4.9%); per capita expenditure U.S.$175.

[1]Political parties legalized July 1992; November 1993 legislative elections were multiparty. [2]January 1. [3]Private sector only. [4]Less imputed bank service charges. [5]Detail does not add to total given because of rounding. [6]Includes reexports. [7]1988–89.

Kazakhstan

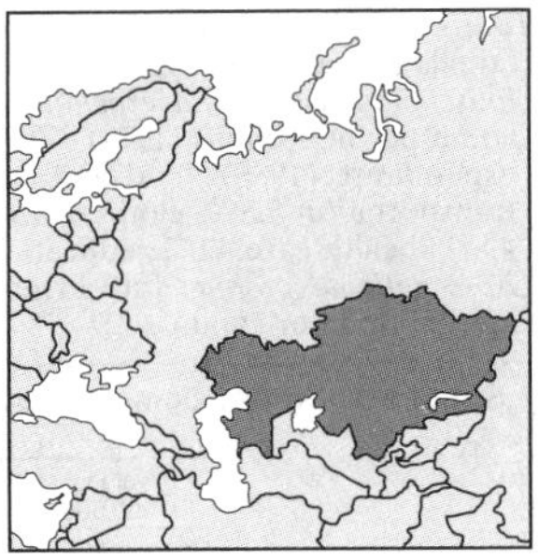

Official name: Qazaqstan Respublikasï (Republic of Kazakhstan).
Form of government[1]: unitary multiparty republic with a single legislative body (Parliament [360]).
Head of state: President.
Head of government: Prime Minister.
Capital: Almaty (formerly Alma-Ata).
Official language: Kazakh.
Official religion: none.
Monetary unit: 1 ruble = 100 kopecks; valuation (Oct. 4, 1993) free rate, 1 U.S.$ = 1,165 rubles; 1 £ = 1,765 rubles.

Area and population

		area		population
Provinces[2]	Capitals	sq mi	sq km	1991 estimate
Akmola	Akmola	35,600	92,100	885,400
Aktyubinsk	Aktyubinsk	115,300	298,700	752,900
Alma-Ata (Almaty)	Alma-Ata (Almaty)	40,600	105,100	2,153,700
Atyrau	Atyrau	43,800	113,500	447,100
Dzhambul	Auliye-Ata (Dzhambul)	55,700	144,200	1,056,400
Dzhezkazgan	Dzhezkazgan	121,000	313,400	496,200
East Kazakhstan	Ust-Kamenogorsk	37,600	97,300	949,000
Karaganda	Karaganda	45,500	117,900	1,339,900
Kokchetav	Kokchetav	30,200	78,100	669,400
Kustanay	Kustanay	44,200	114,500	1,074,400
Kzyl-Orda	Kzyl-Orda	88,100	228,100	664,900
Mangistau	Aktau	63,800	165,100	331,700
North Kazakhstan	Petropavlosk	17,100	44,300	610,400
Pavlodar	Pavlodar	49,200	127,500	956,900
Semipalatinsk	Semipalatinsk	69,300	179,600	841,900
South Kazakhstan	Chimkent	44,900	116,300	1,879,200
Taldy-Kurgan	Taldy-Kurgan	45,700	118,500	731,000
Turgay	Arkalyk	43,200	111,900	304,600
West Kazakhstan	Uralsk	58,400	151,200	648,000
TOTAL		1,049,200	2,717,300	16,793,100[3]

Demography

Population (1993): 17,186,000.
Density (1993): persons per sq mi 16.4, persons per sq km 6.3.
Urban-rural (1991): urban 57.4%; rural 42.6%.
Sex distribution (1992): male 48.52%; female 51.48%.
Age breakdown (1991): under 15, 31.4%; 15–29, 25.1%; 30–44, 21.3%; 45–59, 12.2%; 60–69, 6.1%; 70 and over, 3.9%.
Population projection: (2000) 18,261,000; (2010) 21,720,000.
Doubling time: 50 years.
Ethnic composition (1989): Kazakh 39.7%; Russian 37.8%; German 5.8%; Ukrainian 5.4%; Uzbek 2.0%; Tatar 2.0%; other 7.3%.
Religious affiliation: believers are predominantly Sunnī Muslims (Ḥanafīyah); there is a Christian minority (mainly Russian Orthodox and Baptist).
Major cities (1991): Alma-Ata (Almaty) 1,156,200; Karaganda 608,600; Chimkent 438,800; Semipalatinsk 344,700; Pavlodar 342,500.

Vital statistics

Birth rate per 1,000 population (1991): 21.0 (world avg. 26.4); (1991) legitimate 87.6%; illegitimate 12.4%.
Death rate per 1,000 population (1991): 8.0 (world avg. 9.2).
Natural increase rate per 1,000 population (1991): 13.0 (world avg. 17.2).
Total fertility rate (avg. births per childbearing woman; 1989): 2.8.
Marriage rate per 1,000 population (1991): 9.8.
Divorce rate per 1,000 population (1991): 2.9.
Life expectancy at birth (1991): male 63.8 years; female 73.1 years.
Major causes of death per 100,000 population (1991): diseases of the circulatory system 361.0; malignant neoplasms (cancers) 136.5; accidents, poisoning, and violence 107.3; diseases of the respiratory system 74.1; diseases of the digestive system (1989) 24.6; infectious and parasitic diseases 24.6; endocrine and metabolic disorders 6.3; diseases of the nervous system 6.1.

National economy

Budget (1993). Revenue: 1,031,300,000,000 rubles (current revenue 96.8%, of which taxes on goods and services 29.2%, income and capital-gains taxes 26.8%, taxes on international trade 9.3%, other tax revenue 26.2%, nontax revenue 5.3%; grants 2.9%; capital revenue 0.3%). Expenditures: 1,229,700,000,000 rubles (national economy 16.7%; education 16.2%; defense and public safety 11.4%; foreign economic activity 11.0%; health care 8.3%; social security 6.4%).
Public debt (external, outstanding): n.a.
Tourism: receipts from visitors, n.a.; expenditures by nationals abroad, n.a.
Production (metric tons except as noted). Agriculture, forestry, fishing (1992): seed cotton 250,000,000, grain 23,075,000, wheat 18,500,000, corn 13,274,000, millet 3,085,000, potatoes 2,200,000, vegetables (other than potatoes) 1,300,000, sugar beets 1,300,000, rye 700,000, oats 600,000, rice 500,000, sunflower seeds 115,000, fruit (other than grapes) 98,300, grapes 75,000; livestock (number of live animals) 34,555,700 sheep and goats, 9,592,400 cattle, 2,976,100 pigs, 1,666,400 horses, 145,100 camels; roundwood (1991) 1,974,000 cu m; fish catch, n.a. Mining and quarrying (1991): iron ore 21,993,000; chrome 3,616,000; manganese 131,500. Manufacturing (1991): steel 6,377,000; rolled ferrous metals 4,721,000; mineral fertilizers 1,516,000; textiles 249,100,000 sq m; carpets 2,048,000 sq m; shoes 34,100,000 pairs; bulldozers 11,280 units; metal-cutting machines 2,381 units; forge press machines 1,165 units; excavators 577 units. Construction (1991): residential 6,125,000 sq m. Energy production (consumption): electricity (kW-hr; 1991) 86,128,000,000 (118,805,000,000); coal (metric tons; 1991) 130,315,000 (n.a.); crude petroleum (barrels; 1991) 194,300,000 (n.a.); petroleum products (metric tons; 1991) 18,007,000 (n.a.); natural gas (cu m; 1991) 7,885,000,000 (n.a.).
Gross national product (1992): U.S.$28,499,000,000 (U.S.$1,680 per capita)[4].

Structure of net material product and labour force

	1991			
	in value '000,000 rubles	% of total value	labour force[5]	% of labour force[5]
Agriculture	20,246	33.9	1,207,000	17.9
Manufacturing, mining }	23,546	39.4	1,385,000	20.5
Public utilities }			260,000	3.9
Construction	5,401	9.0	674,000	10.0
Transp. and commun.	2,219	3.7	693,000	10.3
Trade	3,085	5.1	522,000	7.7
Finance	—	—	41,000	0.6
Public administration, defense	—	—	114,000	1.7
Services	—	—	1,845,000	27.4
Other	5,251	8.9	...	...
TOTAL	59,748	100.0	6,741,000	100.0

Population economically active (1991): total 7,484,000; activity rate of total population 43.5% (participation rates: ages 16–59 [male], 16–54 [female] 81.1%; female 60.0%; unemployed [1989] 2.2%).

Price and earnings indexes (1985 = 100)

	1986	1987	1988	1989	1990	1991	1992
Consumer price index	101.9	103.7	103.7	104.1	123.4	191.5	c. 1,731
Monthly earnings index	103.3	106.9	115.1	125.3	142.3	215.6	...

Land use (1989): forested 6.3%; meadows and pastures 68.7%; agricultural and under permanent cultivation 13.1%; other 11.9%.
Household income and expenditure. Average household size (1989) 4.0; income per household (1991) 5,290 rubles; sources of income: salaries and wages 75.0%, social benefits 16.7%, other 8.3%; expenditure: food 35.7%, consumer goods 32.3%, taxes 6.6%, housing 2.4%.

Foreign trade

Balance of trade (current prices)

	1990	1991	1992
U.S.$'000,000	−10,280	−3,160	−1,670
% of total	26.5%	13.4%	10.2%

Imports (1991): 19,780,000,000 rubles (raw materials and consumer goods 67.4%, machinery and equipment 32.6%). *Major import sources:* Cuba 19.7%; China 15.1%; United States 12.5%; Poland 4.3%.
Exports (1991): 15,486,000,000 rubles (1989; raw materials and consumer goods 99.0%, machinery and equipment 1.0%). *Major export destinations:* The Netherlands 8.3%; Belgium 5.5%; Greece 4.9%; China 4.7%.

Transport and communications

Transport. Railroads (1991): length 13,173 mi, 21,200 passenger-mi 12,100,000,000, passenger-km 19,400,000,000; short ton-mi cargo 256,300,000, metric ton-km cargo 374,200,000. Roads (1992): total length 102,464 mi, 164,900 km (paved 69%). Vehicles (1988): passenger cars 734,800; trucks and buses, n.a. Merchant marine: vessels (100 gross tons and over) n.a.; total deadweight tonnage, n.a. Air transport (1992): passenger-mi 7,800,000,000, passenger-km 12,600,000,000; short ton-mi cargo 48,000,000, metric ton-km cargo 70,000,000; airports (1993) with scheduled flights 6[6].
Communications. Newspapers (1989): total number 450; total circulation 6,700,000; circulation per 1,000 population 405. Radio (1992): total number of receivers 4,188,000 (1 per 4.1 persons). Television (1992): total number of receivers 4,795,000 (1 per 3.6 persons). Telephones (1992): 2,209,000 (1 per 7.8 persons).

Education and health

Education (1991–92)

	schools	teachers	students	student/ teacher ratio
Primary (age 7–13) } Secondary (age 14–17) }	8,841	262,600	3,226,400	12.3
Voc., teacher tr.	3,115	...	1,091,600	...
Higher	61	...	288,000	...

Educational attainment (1989). Percentage of population age 25 and over having: primary education or no formal schooling 16.2%; some secondary 19.8%; completed secondary and some postsecondary 54.1%; higher 9.9%.
Literacy: total population age 15 and over literate, n.a.; males literate, n.a.; females literate, n.a.
Health (1992): physicians[7] 67,600 (1 per 254 persons); hospital beds 230,400 (1 per 75 persons); infant mortality rate per 1,000 live births 27.4.
Food: daily per capita caloric intake, n.a.

Military

Total active duty personnel (1993): about 44,000 (army forces include air forces). *Military expenditure as percentage of GNP:* 3.6%; per capita expenditure U.S.$41.

[1]On Dec. 10, 1993, the Parliament voted to dissolve itself and called for elections to be held on March 7, 1993. [2]Local government was directly subordinated to the president in January 1992. [3]Detail does not add to total given because of rounding. [4]Ruble-area GNP and exchange-rate data are very speculative. [5]State sector only. [6]International only; the number of domestic airports is not available. [7]Data include dentists.

Kenya

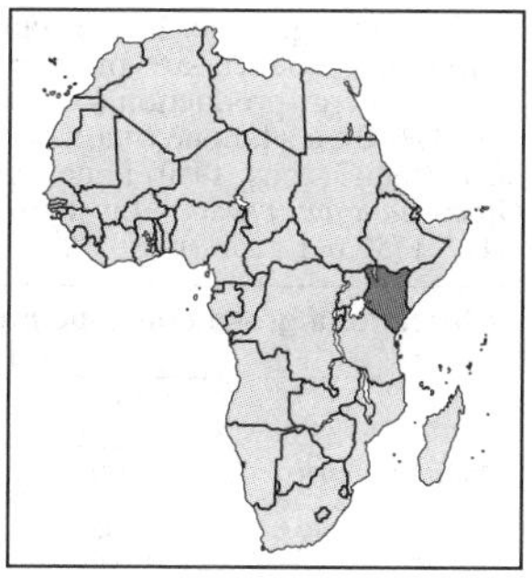

Official name: Jamhuri ya Kenya (Swahili); Republic of Kenya (English).
Form of government: unitary multiparty republic with one legislative house (National Assembly [202[1]]).
Head of state and government: President.
Capital: Nairobi.
Official languages: Swahili; English.
Official religion: none.
Monetary unit: 1 Kenya shilling (K Sh) = 100 cents; valuation (Oct. 4, 1993) 1 U.S.$ = K Sh 68.75; 1 £ = K Sh 104.15.

Area and population

		area		population
Provinces	Provincial headquarters	sq mi	sq km	1990 estimate
Central	Nyeri	5,087	13,176	3,691,700
Coast	Mombasa	32,279	83,603	2,150,400
Eastern	Embu	61,734	159,891	4,367,900
North Eastern	Garissa	48,997	126,902	640,600
Nyanza	Kisumu	6,240	16,162	4,322,700
Rift Valley	Nakuru	67,131	173,868	5,356,900
Western	Kakamega	3,228	8,360	2,836,700
Special area				
Nairobi	—	264	684	1,504,900
TOTAL		224,961[2]	582,646	24,871,800

Demography

Population (1993): 28,113,000.
Density (1993): persons per sq mi 125.0, persons per sq km 48.3.
Urban-rural (1991): urban 25.3%; rural 74.7%.
Sex distribution (1993): male 49.95%; female 50.05%.
Age breakdown (1993): under 15, 51.1%; 15–29, 26.6%; 30–44, 12.6%; 45–59, 6.4%; 60–74, 2.8%; 75 and over, 0.5%.
Population projection: (2000) 37,505,000; (2010) 50,726,000.
Doubling time: 19 years.
Ethnic composition (1979): Kenyan 98.8% (Kikuyu 20.9%, Luhya 13.8%, Luo 12.8%, Kamba 11.3%, Kalenjin 10.8%, other Kenyan 29.2%); other 1.2%.
Religious affiliation (1987): Christian 73.0%, of which Roman Catholic 27.0%, Protestant 19.0%, other Christian (mostly African Indigenous, Anglican, and Eastern Orthodox) 27.0%; traditional beliefs 19.0%; Muslim 6.0%; other 2.0%.
Major cities (1984): Nairobi 1,504,900[3]; Mombasa 425,600; Kisumu 167,100; Nakuru 101,700; Machakos 92,300[4].

Vital statistics

Birth rate per 1,000 population (1990–95): 47.0 (world avg. 26.4).
Death rate per 1,000 population (1990–95): 9.7 (world avg. 9.2).
Natural increase rate per 1,000 population (1990–95): 37.3 (world avg. 17.2).
Total fertility rate (avg. births per childbearing woman; 1990–95): 6.8.
Life expectancy at birth (1990–95): male 59.0 years; female 63.0 years.
Major causes of death per 100,000 population: n.a.; however, major infectious diseases include AIDS, malaria, gastroenteritis, venereal diseases, diarrhea and dysentery, trachoma, amebiasis, and schistosomiasis.

National economy

Budget (1991–92). Revenue: K Sh 66,066,000,000 (indirect taxes 49.5%, of which sales tax 29.1%, custom and excise duties 19.0%; direct taxes 24.0%; grants 15.5%; nontax revenue 8.6%). Expenditures: K Sh 70,650,000,000 (recurrent expenditure 69.1%; development expenditure 30.9%).
Production (metric tons except as noted). Agriculture, forestry, fishing (1992): sugarcane 4,430,000, corn (maize) 2,561,000, cassava 770,000, sweet potatoes 600,000, plantains 360,000, pineapple 270,000, pulses 258,000, potatoes 240,000, bananas 220,000, wheat 200,000, tea 188,000, sorghum 107,000, coffee 70,000, millet 55,000, coconuts 43,000, sisal 35,000, barley 34,000, tomatoes 32,000, seed cotton 28,000, cottonseed 19,000, cashew nuts 15,000, sunflower seeds 15,000, copra 7,000; livestock (number of live animals) 11,000,000 cattle, 7,500,000 goats, 6,000,000 sheep; roundwood (1991) 36,861,000 cu m; fish catch (1991) 198,637, of which freshwater fish 94.5%. Mining and quarrying (1991): soda ash 240,000; fluorite 77,400; salt 72,500; limestone 41,800; garnet 127 kg[5]. Manufacturing (1990): cement 1,512,000; sugar 414,000; wheat flour 172,000; beer 3,311,000 hectolitres; mineral water 1,713,000 hectolitres; alcoholic beverages 12,000 hectolitres; paint 9,300 hectolitres. Construction (1986): residential 136,000 sq m; nonresidential 180,000 sq m. Energy production (consumption): electricity (kW-hr; 1990) 3,044,000,000 (3,215,000,000); coal (metric tons; 1990) none (151,000); crude petroleum (barrels; 1990) none (15,899,000); petroleum products (metric tons; 1990) 2,088,000 (1,467,000).
Public debt (external, outstanding; 1991): U.S.$4,789,000,000.
Household income and expenditure. Average household size (1980) 6.2; average annual income per household: n.a.; sources of income: n.a.; expenditure (1980): food 46.5%, housing 10.0%, furniture and utensils 9.4%, transportation 8.4%, clothing and footwear 7.7%, energy 2.6%, health 2.2%, education 1.0%.
Population economically active (1985): total 8,389,000; activity rate of total population 40.7% (participation rates: ages 15–64, 76.2%; female 40.9%; unemployed, n.a.).

Price and earnings indexes (1985 = 100)

	1986	1987	1988	1989	1990	1991	1992
Consumer price index	103.9	111.9	124.4	140.5	162.4	194.6	252.1
Monthly earnings index[6]	57.9	64.5	68.3	97.2	...	...	...

Gross national product (at current market prices; 1992): U.S.$8,543,000,000 (U.S.$330 per capita).

Structure of gross domestic product and labour force

	1990			
	in value K Sh '000,000	% of total value	labour force[7]	% of labour force
Agriculture	48,829.0	24.3	269,700	19.1
Mining	487.8	0.2	4,200	0.3
Manufacturing	19,748.0	9.8	187,700	13.3
Construction	13,743.2	6.9	71,400	5.1
Public utilities	2,510.6	1.3	22,400	1.6
Transp. and commun.	11,963.4	6.0	74,200	5.3
Trade	18,952.6	9.5	114,000	8.1
Finance	27,722.8	13.8	65,200	4.6
Pub. admin., defense	26,465.0	13.2	600,200	42.6
Services	2,271.2	1.1		
Other	27,978.8[8]	13.9[8]	—	—
TOTAL	200,652.0[3]	100.0	1,409,000	100.0

Tourism (1991): receipts from visitors U.S.$424,000,000; expenditures by nationals abroad U.S.$24,000,000.
Land use (1991): forested 4.1%; meadows and pastures 66.9%; agricultural and under permanent cultivation 4.3%; other 24.7%.

Foreign trade[9]

Balance of trade (current prices)

	1986	1987	1988	1989	1990	1991
K Sh '000,000	−3,271	−9,063	−11,137	−18,131	−18,164	−11,890
% of total	7.7%	22.3%	22.6%	31.3%	27.7%	16.4%

Imports (1990): K Sh 51,024,100,000 (machinery and transport equipment 42.2%, crude petroleum 14.7%, manufactured goods 14.6%, chemicals 13.3%, food and live animals 6.1%). *Major import sources:* U.K. 18.5%; Japan 9.1%; U.S. 9.1%; West Germany 7.9%; France 5.8%; Italy 4.7%; The Netherlands 3.4%; India 1.8%.
Exports (1990): K Sh 24,397,600,000[10] (tea 25.9%, coffee [not roasted] 18.4%, petroleum products 12.4%, fruits and vegetables 12.2%, soda ash 2.0%). *Major export destinations:* U.K. 18.1%; West Germany 10.4%; The Netherlands 5.7%; Uganda 5.2%; U.S. 3.4%.

Transport and communications

Transport. Railroads (1990–91): route length 1,885 mi, 3,034 km; passenger-mi 451,400,000, passenger-km 726,500,000; short ton-mi cargo 1,315,200,000, metric ton-km cargo 1,920,200,000. Roads (1991): total length 38,881 mi, 62,573 km (paved 13%). Vehicles (1990): passenger cars 157,166; trucks and buses 172,023. Merchant marine (1992): vessels (100 gross tons and over) 29; total deadweight tonnage 11,649. Air transport (1992)[11]: passenger-mi 828,062,000, passenger-km 1,332,639,000; short ton-mi cargo 82,950,000, metric ton-km cargo 121,105,000; airports (1993) with scheduled flights 14.
Communications. Daily newspapers: total number (1992) 5; total circulation 328,000[12]; circulation per 1,000 population 12[12]. Radio (1992): 4,200,000 receivers (1 per 6.4 persons). Television (1992): 260,000 receivers (1 per 104 persons). Telephones (1990): 383,116 (1 per 66 persons).

Education and health

Education (1989–90)

	schools	teachers	students	student/ teacher ratio
Primary (age 5–11)	14,691	163,609	5,389,300	32.9
Secondary (age 12–17)	2,654	28,056	640,735	22.8
Voc., teacher tr.[13]	24	1,332[14]	15,456	13.4[14]
Higher	15	...	29,231	...

Educational attainment (1979). Percentage of population over age 25 having: no formal schooling 58.6%; primary education 32.2%; some secondary 7.9%; complete secondary and higher 1.3%. *Literacy* (1985): total population over age 15 literate 5,758,000 (59.2%); males literate 3,311,000 (69.6%); females literate 2,447,000 (49.2%).
Health (1989): physicians 3,266 (1 per 7,313 persons); hospital beds 32,534 (1 per 734 persons); infant mortality rate per 1,000 live births (1990–95): 63.0.
Food (1988–90): daily per capita caloric intake 2,064 (vegetable products 86%, animal products 14%); 89% of FAO recommended minimum requirement.

Military

Total active duty personnel (1993): 24,400 (army 84.0%, navy 5.7%, air force 10.3%). *Military expenditure as percentage of GNP* (1989): 2.7% (world 4.9%); per capita expenditure U.S.$9.

[1]Includes 14 nonelective seats. [2]Detail does not add to total given because of rounding. [3]1990. [4]1983. [5]1989. [6]Manufacturing employees only. [7]Employed persons only. [8]Indirect taxes less subsidies and imputed bank service charges. [9]Import figures are f.o.b. in balance of trade and c.i.f. in commodities and trading partners. [10]Includes K Sh 239,000,000 reexports. [11]Kenya Airways only. [12]Circulation for four newspapers only. [13]Teacher training only. [14]1987–88.

Kiribati

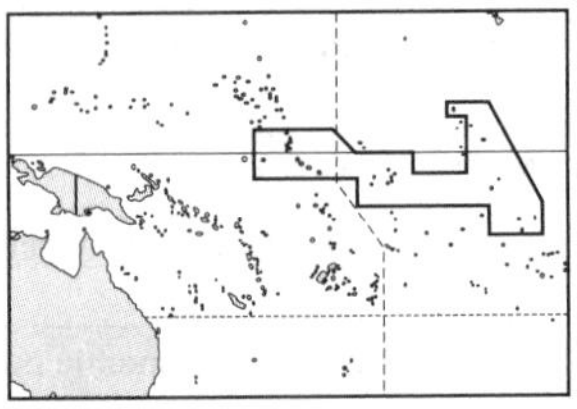

Official name: Republic of Kiribati.
Form of government: unitary republic with one legislature (House of Assembly [41[1]]).
Head of state and government: President.
Capital: Bairiki, on Tarawa Atoll.
Official language: English.
Official religion: none.
Monetary unit: 1 Australian Dollar ($A) = 100 cents; valuation (Oct. 4, 1993) 1 U.S.$ = $A 1.55; 1 £ = $A 2.35.

Area and population

Island Groups / Islands	Capitals	area[2] sq mi	area[2] sq km	population 1990 census
Gilberts Group	Bairiki Islet	110	286[3]	67,508
Abaiang	Tuarabu	7	18	5,233
Abemama	Kariatebike	11	27	3,218
Aranuka	Takaeang	5	12	1,002
Arorae	Roreti	3	9	1,440
Banaba	Anteeren	2	6	284
Beru	Taubukinberu	7	18	2,909
Butaritari	Butaritari	5	13	3,774
Kuria	Tabontebike	6	16	990
Maiana	Tebangetua	6	17	2,180
Makin	Makin	3	8	1,762
Marakei	Rawannawi	5	14	2,863
Nikunau	Rungata	7	19	1,994
Nonouti	Teuabu	8	20	2,814
Onotoa	Buariki	6	16	2,100
Tabiteuea North	Utiroa	10	26	3,201
Tabiteuea South	Buariki	5	12	1,331
Tamana	Bakaka	2	5	1,385
Tarawa North	Abaokoro	6	15	3,648
Tarawa South	Bairiki	6	16	25,380
Line Group	Kiritimati	192	496	4,782
Northern		167	432	—
Kiritimati (Christmas)	London	150	388	2,537
Tabuaeran (Fanning)	Paelau	13	34	1,309
Teraina (Washington)	Washington	4	10	936
Southern (Caroline, Flint, Malden, Starbuck, Vostok)		25	64	—
Phoenix Group (Birnie, Enderbury, Kanton [Canton], McKean, Manra [Sydney], Nikumaroro [Gardner], Orona [Hull], Rawaki [Phoenix])	Kanton	11	29	45
TOTAL		313	811	72,335

Demography

Population (1993): 76,900.
Density (1993)[4]: persons per sq mi 274.6, persons per sq km 105.9.
Urban-rural (1990): urban 34.8%; rural 65.2%.
Sex distribution (1990): male 49.45%; female 50.55%.
Age breakdown (1990): under 15, 40.3%; 15–29, 27.5%; 30–44, 17.3%; 45–59, 9.2%; 60–74, 4.8%; 75 and over, 0.9%.
Population projection: (2000) 87,700; (2010) 106,000.
Doubling time: 33 years.
Ethnic composition (1990): I-Kiribati 97.4%; mixed (part I-Kiribati and other) 1.5%; Tuvaluan 0.5%; European 0.2%; other 0.4%.
Religious affiliation (1990): Roman Catholic 53.4%; Kiribati Protestant (Congregational) 39.2%; Bahā'ī 2.4%; Seventh-day Adventist 1.9%; Mormon 1.6%; other 1.5%.
Major cities (1990): Urban Tarawa 25,154.

Vital statistics

Birth rate per 1,000 population (1992): 33.0 (world avg. 26.4); legitimate, n.a.; illegitimate, n.a.
Death rate per 1,000 population (1992): 12.0 (world avg. 9.2).
Natural increase rate per 1,000 population (1992): 21.0 (world avg. 17.2).
Total fertility rate (avg. births per childbearing woman; 1992): 3.9.
Marriage rate per 1,000 population (1988): 5.2.
Divorce rate per 1,000 population: n.a.
Life expectancy at birth (1992): male 52.0 years; female 56.0 years.
Major causes of death per 100,000 population (1990): infectious intestinal diseases 79.4; certain conditions originating in the perinatal period 38.2; pneumonia 26.5; cerebrovascular disease 23.5; tuberculosis 20.6; chronic liver disease and cirrhosis 20.6; meningitis 19.2.

National economy

Budget (1991). Revenue: $A 22,800,000 (1988; nontax revenue 46.0%, of which reserve fund drawdown 32.1%, fishing licenses 9.8%; tax revenue 28.4%, of which import duties 9.4%, income tax 4.9%; development revenue 25.6%). Expenditures: $A 22,800,000 (1988; education 16.1%; development 15.9%; health 13.0%; natural resources 7.3%; communications 7.0%; public works 6.6%).
Production (metric tons except as noted). Agriculture, forestry, fishing (1992): coconuts 65,000, roots and tubers 14,000 (of which taro 3,000), copra 8,000, vegetables and melons 5,000, bananas 4,000; livestock (number of live animals) 9,000 pigs, 191,000 chickens[5]; fish catch (1991) 30,000. Mining and quarrying: none. Manufacturing (1988): processed copra 14,406; other important products are processed fish, baked goods, clothing, and handicrafts. Energy production (consumption): electricity (kW-hr; 1990) 7,000,000 (7,000,000); coal, none (n.a.); crude petroleum, none (n.a.); petroleum products (metric tons; 1990) none (7,000); natural gas, none (n.a.).
Gross national product (at current market prices; 1991): U.S.$53,000,000 (U.S.$750 per capita).

Structure of gross domestic product and labour force

	1989 in value $A '000	1989 % of total value	1990 labour force	1990 % of labour force
Agriculture, fishing	10,939	24.5	23,137[6]	71.0[6]
Mining	—	—	—	—
Manufacturing	836	1.9	622	1.9
Construction	1,760	3.9	339	1.0
Public utilities	775	1.7	301	0.9
Transp. and commun.	6,344	14.2	921	2.8
Trade	6,050	13.5	1,341	4.1
Finance	3,410	7.6	441	1.4
Pub. admin., defense	11,276	25.2	2,123	6.5
Services	1,205	2.7	2,286	7.0
Other	2,120	4.8	1,099[7]	3.4[7]
TOTAL	44,715	100.0	32,610	100.0

Public debt (external, outstanding; 1989): U.S.$16,000,000.
Population economically active (1990): total 32,610; activity rate of total population 45.1% (participation rates: over age 15, 75.6%; female 46.4%; unemployed 2.8%).

Price and earnings indexes (1985 = 100)

	1986	1987	1988	1989	1990	1991	1992
Consumer price index	107.8	111.8	113.8	120.8	126.9	131.7	138.3
Earnings index	...	...	...	...	...	...	...

Household income and expenditure. Average household size (1990) 6.6; income per household: n.a.; sources of income (1978): wages 69.7%, self-employment 21.4%, transfer payments 6.0%, other 2.9%; expenditure (1982): food 50.0%, tobacco and alcohol 14.0%, clothing 8.0%, transportation 8.0%, housing, energy, and household operation 7.5%.
Tourism (1991): receipts from visitors U.S.$2,000,000; expenditures by nationals abroad, n.a.
Land use (1990): forested 2.8%; agricultural and under permanent cultivation 52.1%; other 45.1%.

Foreign trade

Balance of trade (current prices)

	1987	1988	1989	1990	1991	1992
$A '000	−22,274	−21,515	−22,161	−30,765	−29,529	−44,017
% of total	79.5%	61.7%	63.3%	80.7%	80.0%	77.2%

Imports (1992): $A 50,530,000 (machinery and transport equipment 47.3%; food 21.1%; manufactured goods 8.0%; mineral fuels 7.8%; beverages and tobacco 5.0%; chemicals 3.5%; crude materials 1.2%). *Major import sources:* Australia 38.4%; Japan 22.7%; Fiji 11.3%; New Zealand 5.4%; China 3.3%; United States 2.9%; Hong Kong 1.0%.
Exports (1992): $A 6,513,000 (domestic exports 86.7%, of which copra 66.8%, fish and fish preparations 11.3%; reexports 13.3%). *Major export destinations:* United States 12.3%; Australia 4.8%; Denmark 4.5%; Fiji 4.1%; New Zealand 1.6%; United Kingdom 0.9%.

Transport and communications

Transport. Roads (1991): total length 398 mi, 640 km (paved 5%). Vehicles (1982): passenger cars 307; trucks and buses 130. Merchant marine (1992): vessels (100 gross tons and over) 7; total deadweight tonnage 2,685. Air transport (1990): passenger-mi 5,331,000, passenger-km 8,579,000; short ton-mi cargo 514,000, metric ton-km cargo 750,000; airports (1993) with scheduled flights 18.
Communications. Daily newspapers: none. Radio (1992): total number of receivers 10,000 (1 per 7.5 persons). Television: none. Telephones (1988): 1,304 (1 per 54 persons).

Education and health

Education (1990)

	schools	teachers	students	student/teacher ratio
Primary (age 6–13)	104	514	14,709	28.6
Secondary (age 14–18)	9	172	2,713	15.8
Voc., teacher tr.	6	75	290	3.9
Higher[8]	—	—	—	—

Educational attainment (1990)[9]. Percentage of population age 15 and over having: no schooling 6.9%; primary 67.8%; secondary 24.5%; higher 0.6%; not stated 0.2%. *Literacy* (1985): total population age 15 and over literate 90%.
Health (1990): physicians 16 (1 per 4,483 persons); hospital beds 283 (1 per 253 persons); infant mortality rate per 1,000 live births (1991) 63.0.
Food (1988–90): daily per capita caloric intake 2,517 (vegetable products 89%, animal products 11%); 110% of FAO recommended minimum requirement.

[1]Includes two nonelective members. [2]Includes uninhabited islands. [3]Detail does not add to total given because of rounding. [4]Density based on inhabited island areas (280 sq mi, 726 sq km) only. [5]1982. [6]Includes 20,568 persons engaged in "village work" (subsistence agriculture or fishing). [7]Includes 900 unemployed. [8]54 students overseas. [9]For indigenous population.

Korea, North

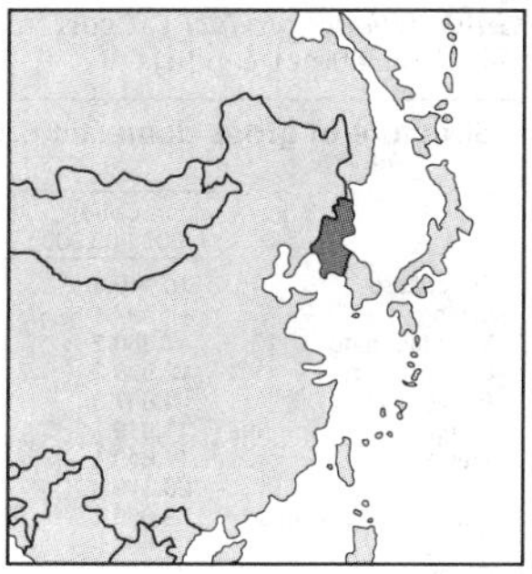

Official name: Chosŏn Minjujuŭi In'min Konghwaguk (Democratic People's Republic of Korea).
Form of government: unitary single-party republic with one legislative house (Supreme People's Assembly [687]).
Chief of state: President.
Head of government: Premier.
Capital: P'yŏngyang-si.
Official language: Korean.
Official religion: none.
Monetary unit: 1 won = 100 chŏn; valuation (Oct. 4, 1993) 1 U.S.$ = 2.13 won; 1 £ = 3.23 won.

Area and population

		area		population[1]
Provinces	Capitals	sq mi	sq km	1987 estimate
Chagang-do	Kanggye	6,551	16,968	1,156,000
Hamgyŏng-namdo	Hamhŭng	7,324	18,970	2,547,000
Hamgyŏng-pukto	Ch'ŏngjin	6,784	17,570	2,003,000
Hwanghae-namdo	Haeju	3,090	8,002	1,914,000
Hwanghae-pukto	Sariwŏn	3,092	8,007	1,409,000
Kangwŏn-do	Wŏnsan	4,306	11,152	1,227,000
P'yŏngan-namdo	P'yŏngsan	4,470	11,577	2,653,000
P'yŏngan-pukto	Sinŭiju	4,707[2]	12,191[2]	2,380,000
Yanggang-do	Hyesan	5,528	14,317	628,000
Special cities				
Kaesŏng-si	—	485	1,255	331,000
Namp'o-si	—	291	753	715,000
P'yŏngyang-si	—	772	2,000	2,355,000
Special district				
Hyangsan-chigu	—	[2]	[2]	28,000
TOTAL		47,400	122,762	19,346,000

Demography

Population (1993): 22,646,000.
Density (1993): persons per sq mi 477.8, persons per sq km 184.5.
Urban-rural (1990): urban 59.8%; rural 40.2%.
Sex distribution (1990): male 49.36%; female 50.64%.
Age breakdown (1990): under 15, 29.4%; 15–29, 33.8%; 30–44, 20.4%; 45–59, 10.6%; 60–74, 4.7%; 75 and over, 1.1%.
Population projection: (2000) 25,491,000; (2010) 28,491,000.
Doubling time: 37 years.
Ethnic composition (1989): Korean 99.8%; Chinese 0.2%.
Religious affiliation (1980): atheist or nonreligious 67.9%; traditional beliefs 15.6%; Ch'ŏndogyo 13.9%; Buddhist 1.7%; Christian 0.9%.
Major cities (1987): P'yŏngyang-si 2,355,000; Hamhŭng 701,000; Ch'ŏngjin 520,000; Namp'o 370,000; Sunch'ŏn 356,000.

Vital statistics

Birth rate per 1,000 population (1993): 23 (world avg. 26.4).
Death rate per 1,000 population (1993): 5 (world avg. 9.2).
Natural increase rate per 1,000 population (1993): 18 (world avg. 17.2).
Total fertility rate (avg. births per childbearing woman; 1993): 2.4.
Marriage rate per 1,000 population (1987): 9.3.
Divorce rate per 1,000 population (1987): 0.2.
Life expectancy at birth (1993): male 68 years; female 74 years.
Major causes of death per 100,000 population (1986): diseases of the circulatory system 224.9; malignant neoplasms (cancers) 69.0; diseases of the digestive system 51.6; diseases of the respiratory system 46.7; injuries and poisoning 38.2; infectious and parasitic diseases 19.4.

National economy

Budget (1992). Revenue: 39,500,900,000 won (1984; turnover tax 55.0%, payments by state enterprises 30.0%). Expenditures: 39,500,900,000 won (national economy 67.5%, social and cultural affairs 19.6%, defense 11.6%, administration 1.3%).
Public debt (external, outstanding; 1991): U.S.$7,000,000,000.
Tourism (1986): total number of tourist arrivals 85,000.
Population economically active (1987)[3]: total 12,517,000; activity rate of total population 61.7% (participation rates: ages 15–64, n.a.; female, n.a.; unemployed, n.a.).
Price and earnings indexes: n.a.
Production (metric tons except as noted). Agriculture, forestry, fishing (1992): rice 5,000,000, corn (maize) 4,400,000, potatoes 1,975,000, cabbages 850,000, sweet potatoes 500,000, soybeans 400,000, wheat 195,000, barley 145,000, pears 122,000, peaches 105,000, watermelons 104,000, tomatoes 70,000, cucumbers and gherkins 70,000, tobacco leaves 67,000, millet 60,000, oats 56,000; livestock (number of live animals) 3,300,000 pigs, 1,300,000 cattle, 390,000 sheep, 300,000 goats, 44,000,000 chickens; roundwood (1991) 4,737,000 cu m; fish catch (1991) 1,700,100. Mining and quarrying (1991): iron ore 10,000,000; magnesite (metal content) 1,600,000; phosphate rock 500,000; sulfur 240,000; zinc 200,000; lead (metal content) 80,000; fluorspar 41,000; graphite 35,000; copper 15,000; gold 5,000 kg; silver 50 kg. Manufacturing (1990): cement 16,300,000; crude steel 8,000,000; pig iron 6,500,000; coke 3,600,000; steel semimanufactures 3,200,000; chemical fertilizers 1,400,000; gasoline 945,000; meat 220,000; textile fabrics 210,000,000 m. Construction: n.a. Energy production (consumption): electricity (kW-hr; 1991) 53,500,000 (53,500,000); coal (metric tons; 1991) 67,000,000 (69,100,000); crude petroleum (barrels; 1991) none (20,588,000); petroleum products (metric tons; 1991) 2,945,000 (4,535,000); natural gas, none (n.a.).
Household income and expenditure. Average household size (1987) 4.8; average annual income per household (1980) 3,677 won (U.S.$4,275); sources of income: n.a.; expenditure (1984)[4]: food 46.5%, clothing 29.9%, furniture 3.8%, energy 3.3%, housing 0.6%.
Gross national product (1991): U.S.$23,300,000,000 (U.S.$1,100 per capita).

Structure of gross domestic product and labour force

	1982			
	in value '000,000 won	% of total value	labour force	% of labour force
Agriculture	...	...	3,726,000	44.1
Mining and manufacturing	...	...		
Construction	...	...	2,790,000	33.0
Public utilities	...	...		
Transportation and communications	...	...	418,000	4.9
Trade	...	...		
Finance	...	...		
Pub. admin., defense	...	...	1,521,000	18.0
Services	...	...		
Other	...	...		
TOTAL	11,800	100.0	8,455,000	100.0

Land use (1991): forested 74.5%; meadows and pastures 0.4%; agricultural and under permanent cultivation 16.7%; other 8.4%.

Foreign trade

Balance of trade (current prices)

	1986	1987	1988	1989	1990	1991
U.S.$'000,000	−180.5	−391.7	−315.2	−433.9	−420.5	−764.7
% of total	11.9%	20.0%	14.1%	21.0%	21.0%	35.6%

Imports (1990): U.S.$2,540,000,000 (crude petroleum, coal and coke, industrial machinery and transport equipment [including trucks], industrial chemicals, textile yarn and fabrics, and grain are among the major imports). *Major import sources* (1985): U.S.S.R. 36.1%; China 18.8%; Japan 13.2%; western European countries 4.0%; Hong Kong 3.5%.
Exports (1990): U.S.$1,720,000,000 (minerals [including lead, magnesite, zinc], metallurgical products [iron and steel, nonferrous metals], cement, agricultural products [including fish, grain, fruit and vegetables, tobacco], and manufactured goods [textile fabrics, clothing] are among the major exports). *Major export destinations* (1985): U.S.S.R. 43.6%; Japan 15.1%; China 13.4%; western European countries 4.3%; Australia 3.3%; Hong Kong 3.1%.

Transport and communications

Transport. Railroads (1989): length 3,122 mi, 5,024 km; (latest) passenger-mi 2,100,000,000, passenger-km 3,400,000,000; (latest) short ton-mi cargo 5,100,000,000, metric ton-km cargo 9,100,000,000. Roads (1988): total length 14,290 mi, 23,000 km (paved 2%). Vehicles (1988): passenger cars 248,000. Merchant marine (1992): vessels (100 gross tons and over) 100; total deadweight tonnage 951,222. Air transport (1979): passenger-mi 52,200,000, passenger-km 84,000,000; short ton-mi cargo 1,370,000, metric ton-km cargo 2,000,000; airports (1993) with scheduled flights 1.
Communications. Daily newspapers (1987): total number 16; total circulation 3,000,000[5]; circulation per 1,000 population 140[5]. Radio (1992): total number of receivers 4,700,000 (1 per 4.7 persons). Television (1991): total number of receivers 250,000 (1 per 87 persons). Telephones (1988): 30,000[6] (1 per 700 persons).

Education and health

Education (1987)

	schools[7]	teachers	students	student/ teacher ratio
Primary (age 6–9)	4,792	...	1,492,000	...
Secondary (age 10–15)			2,655,000	...
Voc., teacher tr.	473	...	220,000	...
Higher	281	9,244[8]	301,000	...

Educational attainment (1987–88). Percentage of population age 16 and over having attended or graduated from postsecondary-level school: 13.7%. *Literacy* (1984): 99%.
Health (1989): physicians 57,690 (1 per 370 persons); hospital beds 290,590 (1 per 74 persons); infant mortality rate per 1,000 live births (1993) 24.
Food (1987–89): daily per capita caloric intake 2,797 (vegetable products 92%, animal products 8%); 120% of FAO recommended minimum requirement.

Military

Total active duty personnel (1993): 1,127,000 (army 88.7%, navy 4.0%, air force 7.3%). *Military expenditure as percentage of GNP* (1991): 22.0% (world [1989] 4.9%); per capita expenditure (1989) U.S.$285.

[1]Civilian population only. [2]P'yŏngan-pukto includes special district of Hyangsan-chigu. [3]The Democratic People's Republic of Korea categorizes economically active as including students in higher education, retirees, and heads of households, as well as those in the civilian labour force. [4]Workers and clerical workers only. [5]Four dailies only. [6]Number of telephone lines. [7]1986. [8]1982.

Korea, South

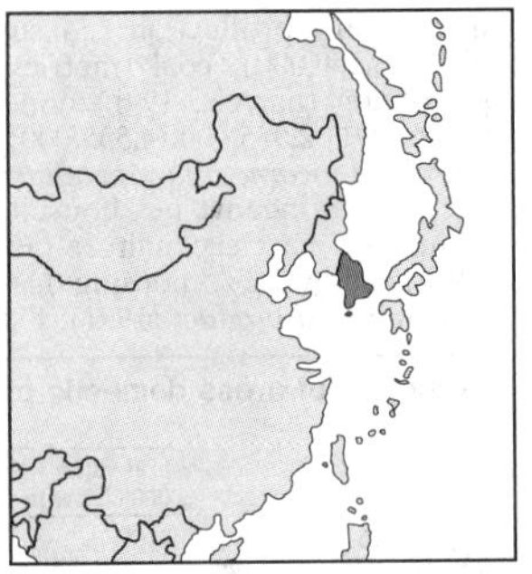

Official name: Taehan Min'guk (Republic of Korea).
Form of government: unitary multiparty republic with a National Assembly (299 members).
Chief of state: President.
Head of government: Prime Minister.
Capital: Seoul.
Official language: Korean.
Official religion: none.
Monetary unit: 1 won (W) = 100 chon; valuation (Oct. 4, 1993) 1 U.S.$ = W 814.40; 1 £ = W 1,234.

Area and population

		area		population
		sq mi	sq km	1990 census
Provinces	**Capitals**			
Cheju-do	Cheju	705	1,825	514,605
Chŏlla-namdo	Kwangju	4,561	11,812	2,507,439
Chŏlla-pukto	Chŏnju	3,109	8,053	2,069,960
Ch'ungch'ŏng-namdo	Taejŏn	3,211	8,317	2,013,926
Ch'ungch'ŏng-pukto	Ch'ŏngju	2,872	7,437	1,389,686
Kangwŏn-do	Ch'unch'ŏn'	6,524	16,898	1,580,430
Kyŏnggi-do	Suwŏn	4,158	10,769	6,155,632
Kyŏngsang-namdo	Masan	4,545	11,771	3,672,396
Kyŏngsang-pukto	Taegu	7,507	19,443	2,860,595
Special cities				
Inch'ŏn-si	Inch'ŏn	121	313	1,817,919
Kwangju-si	Kwangju	193	501	1,139,003
Pusan-si	Pusan	203	526	3,798,113
Sŏul-t'ŭkpyŏlsi	Seoul	234	605	10,612,577
Taegu-si	Taegu	176	456	2,229,040
Taejŏn-si	Taejŏn	207	537	1,049,578
TOTAL		38,326	99,263	43,410,899

Demography

Population (1993): 44,042,000.
Density (1993): persons per sq mi 1,149.1, persons per sq km 443.7.
Urban-rural (1990): urban 74.4%; rural 25.6%.
Sex distribution (1992): male 50.34%; female 49.66%.
Age breakdown (1992): under 15, 24.8%; 15–29, 29.3%; 30–44, 23.8%; 45–59, 14.0%; 60–74, 6.5%; 75 and over, 1.6%.
Population projection: (2000) 46,789,000; (2010) 49,683,000.
Doubling time: 77 years.
Ethnic composition (1990): Korean 99.9%; other 0.1%.
Religious affiliation (1991): religious[1] 54.0%, of which Buddhist 27.6%, Protestant 18.6%, Roman Catholic 5.7%, Confucian 1.0%, Wonbulgyo 0.3%, Ch'ondogyo 0.2%, other 0.6%; nonreligious 46.0%.
Major cities (1990): Seoul 10,612,577; Pusan 3,798,113; Taegu 2,229,040; Inch'ŏn 1,817,919; Kwangju 1,139,003.

Vital statistics

Birth rate per 1,000 population (1993): 15.0 (world avg. 26.4).
Death rate per 1,000 population (1993): 6.0 (world avg. 9.2).
Natural increase rate per 1,000 population (1993): 9.0 (world avg. 17.2).
Total fertility rate (avg. births per childbearing woman; 1993): 1.6.
Marriage rate per 1,000 population (1989): 7.3.
Divorce rate per 1,000 population (1989): 1.1.
Life expectancy at birth (1993): male 69.0 years; female 76.0 years.
Major causes of death per 100,000 population (1990): diseases of the circulatory system 133.1; malignant neoplasms (cancers) 89.6; accidents, poisoning, and violence 68.8; diseases of the digestive system 36.1; diseases of the respiratory system 13.8.

National economy

Budget (1992). Revenue: W 42,756,000,000,000 (taxes on goods and services 34.9%, income taxes 33.2%, nontax revenue 9.7%, customs duties 8.2%). Expenditures: W 40,364,000,000,000 (defense 22.1%, economic development 16.5%, education 16.2%, social security and welfare 9.8%).
Public debt (external, outstanding; 1991): U.S.$22,246,000,000.
Production (metric tons except as noted). Agriculture, forestry, fishing (1991): rice 7,478,000, cabbages 2,731,000, oranges 600,000, apples 542,000, dry onions 530,000, garlic 481,000, barley 340,000, soybeans 183,000; livestock (number of live animals) 4,528,000 pigs, 2,126,000 cattle, 74,000,000 chickens; roundwood 6,485,000 cu m; fish catch 2,983,200. Mining and quarrying (1992): iron ore 221,502; zinc concentrate 43,766; lead concentrate 27,255; tungsten ore 445. Manufacturing (1992): cement 43,270,000; pig iron 19,238,000; urea fertilizers 889,456; newsprint 602,196; caustic soda 506,953; synthetic fabrics 3,162,057,000 sq m; television receivers 16,173,000 units; passenger cars 1,293,698 units. Construction (1992): residential 69,437,000 sq m; nonresidential 67,410,000 sq m. Energy production (consumption): electricity (kW-hr; 1990) 118,738,000,000 (118,738,000,000); coal (metric tons; 1990) 17,217,000 (43,405,000); crude petroleum (barrels; 1990) none (306,321,000); petroleum products (metric tons; 1990) 36,325,000 (40,597,000); natural gas (cu m; 1990) none (3,243,000,000).
Household income and expenditure (1992)[2]. Average household size (1990) 3.8; income per household W 15,516,000 (U.S.$19,800); sources of income: wages 84.2%, other 15.8%; expenditure: food and beverages 28.4%, education and recreation 14.7%, clothing and footwear 8.2%, transportation and communications 8.2%, health care 5.5%, household durable goods 5.1%, energy 5.0%, housing 3.6%, other 21.3%.

Gross national product (at current market prices; 1991): U.S.$274,464,000,000 (U.S.$6,340 per capita).

Structure of gross domestic product and labour force

	1991			
	in value W '000,000,000[3]	% of total value	labour force	% of labour force
Agriculture	10,146.8	7.1	3,103,000	16.3
Mining	697.1	0.5	68,000	0.4
Manufacturing	47,966.2	33.6	4,936,000	26.0
Construction	12,938.2	9.1	1,543,000	8.1
Public utilities	4,887.3	3.4	67,000	0.4
Transp. and commun.	11,919.7	8.4	985,000	5.2
Trade	17,649.1	12.4	4,082,000	21.5
Finance	20,179.6	14.2	1,017,000	5.3
Pub. admin., defense	9,059.7	6.4	2,775,000	14.6
Services	7,404.5	5.2		
Other	−257.3[4]	−0.2[4]	436,000[5]	2.3[5]
TOTAL	142,590.9	100.0[6]	19,012,000	100.0[6]

Population economically active (1991): total 19,012,000; activity rate 43.9% (participation rates: ages 15 and over, 60.6%; female 40.3%; unemployed 2.3%).

Price and earnings indexes (1985 = 100)

	1986	1987	1988	1989	1990	1991	1992
Consumer price index	102.8	105.9	113.9	119.9	130.2	142.8	151.7
Monthly earnings index	109.0	121.7	145.8	182.6	219.3	256.3	...

Tourism (1991): receipts from visitors U.S.$3,426,000,000; expenditures by nationals abroad U.S.$3,784,000,000.
Land use (1990): forested 65.6%; meadows and pastureland 0.8%; agricultural and under permanent cultivation 21.4%; other 12.2%.

Foreign trade

Balance of trade (current prices)

	1987	1988	1989	1990	1991	1992
U.S.$'000,000	+6,940	+8,510	+2,875	−701	−3,968	−588
% of total	9.8%	10.6%	3.6%	0.8%	3.6%	0.4%

Imports (1992): U.S.$81,775,300,000 (machinery and transport equipment 35.4%, mineral fuels and lubricants 17.9%, manufactured goods 14.6%, inedible crude materials 10.2%, chemicals 9.4%). *Major import sources:* Japan 23.8%; United States 22.4%; Germany 4.6%; Saudi Arabia 4.6%; Australia 3.8%; Indonesia 2.8%; Singapore 2.2%; Malaysia 2.2%.
Exports (1992): U.S.$76,631,500,000 (machinery and transport equipment 42.5%, manufactured goods 24.1%, chemicals 5.8%, food and live animals 2.8%, mineral fuels 2.3%). *Major export destinations:* United States 23.6%; Japan 15.1%; Hong Kong 7.7%; Singapore 4.2%; Germany 3.8%; Taiwan 3.0%; Indonesia 2.5%; Panama 2.4%.

Transport and communications

Transport. Railroads (1991): length 4,092 mi, 6,586 km; passenger-km 33,468,000,000; metric ton-km cargo 14,496,000,000. Roads (1989): total length 34,659 mi, 55,778 km (paved 61%). Vehicles (1991): passenger cars 2,727,852; trucks and buses 1,519,964. Merchant marine (1992): vessels (100 gross tons and over) 2,138; total deadweight tonnage 11,724,942. Air transport (1991): passenger-km 19,957,000,000; metric ton-km cargo 2,664,000,000; airports (1993) with scheduled flights 12.
Communications. Daily newspapers (1991): total number 77; total circulation 13,000,000[7]; circulation per 1,000 population 309[7]. Radio (1992): 42,000,000 receivers (1 per 1.0 persons). Television (1992): 8,700,000 receivers (1 per 5.0 persons). Telephones (1990): 15,736,229 (1 per 2.7 persons).

Education and health

Education (1992)

	schools	teachers	students	student/ teacher ratio
Primary (age 6–13)	6,122	138,880	4,560,128	32.8
Secondary (age 14–19) / Vocational	4,274	191,672	4,461,857	23.3
Higher	592	46,524	1,588,246	34.1

Educational attainment (1990). Percentage of population age 6 and over having: primary education or less 33.7%, of which no formal schooling (1985) 14.3%; some secondary and secondary 52.1%; postsecondary 14.2%. *Literacy* (1990): total population age 15 and over literate 96.3%; males literate 99.1%; females literate 93.5%.
Health (1990): physicians 42,554 (1 per 1,007 persons); hospital beds 99,843 (1 per 429 persons); infant mortality rate per 1,000 live births (1993) 15.0.
Food (1988–90): daily per capita caloric intake 2,826 (vegetable products 87%, animal products 13%); 120% of FAO recommended minimum requirement.

Military

Total active duty personnel (1992): 633,000 (army 82.1%, navy 9.5%, air force 8.4%). *Military expenditure as percentage of GNP* (1989): 4.3% (world 4.9%); per capita expenditure: U.S.$214.

[1]Refers to persons who have received commandments, accepted baptism, or entered a faith and who participate in a religious function regularly or put the religious idea into practice. [2]Excludes farm households. [3]At 1985 constant prices. [4]Import duties less imputed bank service charges. [5]Unemployed. [6]Detail does not add to total given because of rounding. [7]Circulation for 1988.

Kuwait

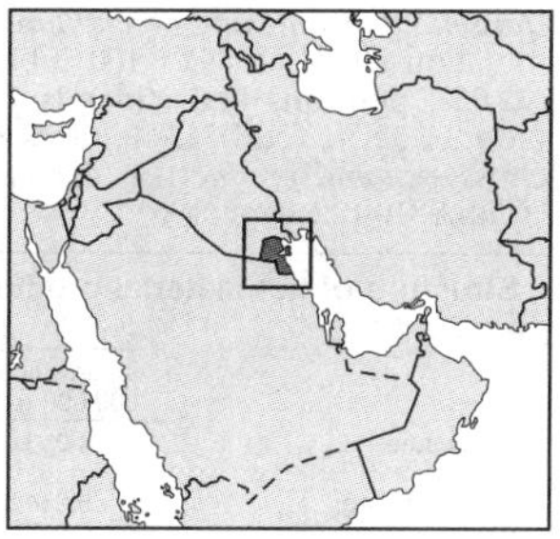

Official name: Dawlat al-Kuwayt (State of Kuwait).
Form of government: Constitutional monarchy with one legislative body (National Assembly [60[1]]).
Head of state and government: Emir, assisted by Prime Minister.
Capital: Kuwait City.
Official language: Arabic.
Official religion: Islam.
Monetary unit: 1 Kuwaiti dinar (KD) = 1,000 fils; valuation (Oct. 4, 1993) 1 KD = U.S.$3.33 = £2.22.

Area and population

		area[2]		population
Governorates[3]	Capitals	sq mi	sq km	1985 census
al-Aḥmadī	al-Aḥmadī	1,984	5,138	301,513
al-Farwānīyah	al-Farwānīyah	...	...	416,644
al-Jahrāʾ	al-Jahrāʾ	4,372	11,324	241,285
Capital	Kuwait City	38	98	241,356
Ḥawallī	Ḥawallī	138	358	496,503
Islands[4]	—	347	900	...
TOTAL		6,880[5]	17,818	1,697,301

Demography

Population (1993): 1,433,000.
Density (1993): persons per sq mi 208.3, persons per sq km 80.4.
Urban-rural (1990): urban 95.6%; rural 4.4%.
Sex distribution (1993): male 57.02%; female 42.98%.
Age breakdown (1990): under 15, 35.5%; 15–29, 24.6%; 30–44, 27.2%; 45–59, 10.3%; 60–74, 2.1%; 75 and over, 0.3%.
Population projection: (2000) 1,702,000; (2010) 2,177,000.
Doubling time (1992): 16 years.
Ethnic composition (by nationality; 1993): Kuwaiti 43.3%; non-Kuwaiti (including other Arab, South Asian, Palestinian, and Badoun [stateless immigrants]) 56.7%.
Religious affiliation (1986): Muslim 90.0%, of which Sunnī 63.0%, Shīʿah 27.0%; Christian 8.0%; Hindu 2.0%.
Major cities (1985): as-Sālimīyah 153,220; Ḥawallī 145,215; al-Jahrāʾ 111,165; al-Farwānīyah 68,665; Kuwait City 44,224.

Vital statistics

Birth rate per 1,000 population (1992): 24.5 (world avg. 26.4); legitimate, n.a.; illegitimate, n.a.
Death rate per 1,000 population (1992): 2.2 (world avg. 9.2).
Natural increase rate per 1,000 population (1992): 22.3 (world avg. 17.2).
Total fertility rate (avg. births per childbearing woman; 1989): 3.9.
Marriage rate per 1,000 population (1989): 5.4.
Divorce rate per 1,000 population (1989): 1.5.
Life expectancy at birth (1989): male 72.0 years; female 76.0 years.
Major causes of death per 100,000 population (1989): circulatory diseases 79.7; accidents, poisoning, and violence 28.8; malignant neoplasms (cancers) 28.1; congenital anomalies 16.0; respiratory diseases 13.4; endocrine, nutritional, and metabolic diseases 7.2; diseases of the nervous system 7.1; infectious and parasitic diseases 5.9; diseases of the digestive system 5.1.

National economy

Budget (1993–94). Revenue: KD 2,713,700,000 (oil revenue 89.2%). Expenditures: KD 3,937,000,000 (1991–92; defense 43.4%; electricity, water, and public utilities 7.6%; education 7.5%; administrative services 3.9%; health 3.1%; transportation and communications 1.2%).
Public debt (external, outstanding; 1989): U.S.$610,000,000[6].
Tourism (1990): receipts from visitors U.S.$80,000,000; expenditures by nationals abroad U.S.$2,315,000,000.
Gross national product (at current market prices; 1989): U.S.$33,089,000,000 (U.S.$16,150 per capita).

Structure of gross domestic product and labour force

	1992		1988	
	in value KD '000,000	% of total value	labour force	% of labour force
Agriculture	22.3	0.3	8,756	1.3
Mining (oil sector)	2,718.7	42.1	6,028	0.9
Manufacturing	932.6	14.5	50,160	7.2
Construction	127.3	2.0	107,404	15.4
Public utilities	−95.2	−1.5	6,908	1.0
Transportation and communications	128.0	2.0	36,938	5.3
Trade	488.7	7.6	79,882	11.4
Finance	178.3	2.8	22,132	3.2
Pub. admin., defense } Services	1,950.9	30.2	370,238	53.0
Other	—	—	10,472	1.5
TOTAL	6,451.6	100.0	698,918	100.0[5]

Production (metric tons except as noted). Agriculture, forestry, fishing (1992): onions 10,000, tomatoes 3,000, cucumbers and gherkins 1,000, eggplants 1,000, garlic 1,000; livestock (number of live animals) 297,000 sheep, 5,000 cattle, 1,000 goats, 1,000 camels, 1,000,000 chickens; fish catch (1991) 1,979. Mining and quarrying (1990): sulfur 202,377; lime 50,000. Manufacturing (1992): cement 533,500; ammonia (urea) 257,300; flour 104,900; bread 63,500; bran 34,100; concrete pipes 12,800; liquefied caustic soda 12,200; chlorine gas 10,800; biscuits 1,300; detergents 700; hydrochloric acid 1,427,900 gallons; concrete slabs 695,700 sq m; sodium hydrochloride 7,560 cu m. Construction (floor area approved for construction; 1989): residential 2,563,000 sq m; nonresidential 416,000 sq m. Energy production (consumption): electricity (kW-hr; 1992) 16,786,000,000 (14,110,000,000); coal, none (none); crude petroleum (barrels; 1991) 71,600,000 (53,400,000); petroleum products (metric tons; 1991) 5,255,000 (2,366,000); natural gas (cu m; 1991) 474,100,000 (474,100,000).
Population economically active (1990): total 722,495; activity rate of total population 37.2% (participation rates [1988]: ages 15–64, 56.1%; female 18.8%; unemployed 1.9%).

Price and earnings indexes (1985 = 100)

	1986	1987	1988	1989	1990[7]	1991	1992
Consumer price index	101.0	101.6	103.1	106.6	108.7	...	...
Earnings index	...	...	...	...	...	...	...

Household income and expenditure. Average household size (1986) 7.4; annual income per household (1973)[8] KD 4,246 (U.S.$12,907); sources of income: wages and salaries 53.8%, self-employment 20.8%, other 25.4%; expenditure (1986–87): food, beverages, and tobacco 28.1%, housing and energy 15.5%, transportation 13.7%, household appliances and services 11.2%, clothing and footwear 8.1%, education and recreation 5.2%, health 0.7%.
Land use (1991): forested 0.1%; meadows and pastures 7.6%; agricultural and under permanent cultivation 0.3%; other, built-up, and wasteland 92.0%.

Foreign trade

Balance of trade (current prices)

	1987	1988	1989	1990	1991	1992
KD '000,000	+774	+452	+1,529	+886	−1,105	−234
% of total	20.2%	26.4%	29.2%	27.9%	69.0%	5.6%

Imports (1989): KD 1,849,410,000 (machinery and transport equipment 29.5%, manufactured goods 22.1%, food and live animals 17.3%, miscellaneous manufactured articles 17.2%, chemical products 7.7%, fuels 1.0%). *Major import sources:* United States 14.6%; Japan 11.4%; West Germany 7.8%; United Kingdom 6.4%; Italy 5.7%; South Korea 3.9%; France 3.6%.
Exports (1989): KD 3,378,000,000 (crude petroleum and petroleum products 92.2%). *Major export destinations:* Japan 18.8%; The Netherlands 9.2%; United States 8.4%; Pakistan 5.9%; Singapore 4.6%; India 4.2%; Italy 4.1%; Denmark 3.5%; Taiwan 3.3%.

Transport and communications

Transport. Railroads: none. Roads (1990): total length 2,655 mi, 4,273 km (paved 100%). Vehicles (1992): passenger cars 579,841; trucks and buses 126,754. Merchant marine (1992): vessels (100 gross tons and over) 209; total deadweight tonnage 3,188,526. Air transport (1991): passenger-mi 1,185,994,000, passenger-km 1,908,264,000; short ton-mi cargo 197,624,000, metric ton-km cargo 288,526,000; airports (1993) with scheduled flights 1.
Communications. Daily newspapers (1992): total number 9; total circulation 655,000; circulation per 1,000 population 550. Radio (1992): total number of receivers 1,000,000 (1 per 1.1 persons). Television (1992): total number of receivers 800,000 (1 per 1.5 persons). Telephones (1988): 361,989 (1 per 5.4 persons).

Education and health

Education (1992–93)

	schools	teachers	students	student/ teacher ratio
Primary (age 6–9)	182	8,045	125,055	15.5
Secondary (age 10–17)	252	13,739	141,126	10.3
Voc., teacher tr.	35	527	2,725	5.2
Higher[9]	1	927	12,341	13.3

Educational attainment (1988). Percentage of population age 25 and over having: no formal schooling 44.8%; primary education 8.6%; some secondary 15.1%; complete secondary 15.1%; higher 16.4%. *Literacy* (1988): total population age 15 and over literate 961,880 (79.7%); males literate 574,739 (83.3%); females literate 387,141 (74.9%).
Health (1992): physicians 2,215 (1 per 515 persons); hospital beds 4,039[10] (1 per 347 persons); infant mortality rate per 1,000 live births (1989) 14.8.
Food (1987–89): daily per capita caloric intake 3,146 (vegetable products 75%, animal products 25%); 130% of FAO recommended minimum requirement.

Military

Total active duty personnel (1993): 13,700 (army [including central staff] 73.0%, navy 8.8%, air force 18.2%). *Military expenditure as percentage of GNP* (1989): 6.2% (world 4.9%); per capita expenditure U.S.$692.

[1]Including 10 nonelective members appointed by the emir. [2]Area of governorates reflects situation prior to Amiri Decree No. 156 of 1988, which established al-Farwānīyah governorate. [3]Governorates have no administrative function. [4]Bubian Island 333 sq mi (863 sq km) and Warba Island 14 sq mi (37 sq km). [5]Detail does not add to total given because of rounding. [6]Includes external long-term debt not guaranteed by the government. [7]May. [8]Kuwaiti households only. [9]1989–90. [10]Public hospitals only.

Kyrgyzstan

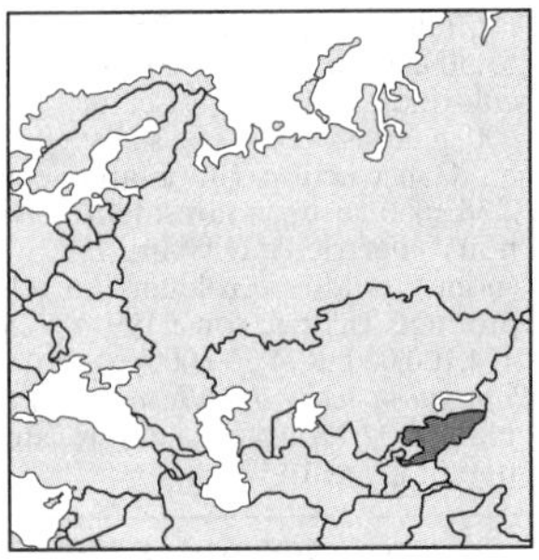

Official name: Kyrgyzstan Respublikasy (Republic of Kyrgyzstan).
Form of government: unitary multiparty republic with a single legislative body (Great Council [350]).
Head of state: President.
Head of government: Prime Minister.
Capital: Bishkek (formerly Frunze).
Official language: Kyrgyz.
Official religion: none.
Monetary unit: som (decimal unit, n.a.) valuation (Oct. 4, 1993) free rate, 1 U.S.$ = 5.83 som; 1 £ = 8.83 som.

Area and population

Provinces	Capitals	area sq mi	area sq km	population 1991 estimate
Chu	Kara-Balta	7,200	18,700	791,200
Dzhalal-Abad	Dzhalal-Abad	15,200	39,500	782,200
Issyk-Kul	Issyk-Kul	16,800	43,500	426,400
Naryn	Naryn	18,300	47,300	259,900
Osh	Osh	14,700	38,100	1,322,600
Talas	Talas	4,400	11,400	198,600
City of republic subordination				
Bishkek (Frunze)	—	...	...	641,400
TOTAL		76,600	198,500	4,422,200[1]

Demography

Population (1993): 4,526,000.
Density (1993): persons per sq mi 59.1, persons per sq km 22.8.
Urban-rural (1992): urban 37.9%; rural 62.1%.
Sex distribution (1991): male 49.10%; female 50.90%.
Age breakdown (1989): under 15, 37.5%; 15–29, 27.0%; 30–44, 16.3%; 45–59, 10.9%; 60–74, 6.2%; 75 and over, 2.1%.
Population projection: (2000) 4,921,000; (2010) 5,548,000.
Doubling time: 32 years.
Ethnic composition (1989): Kyrgyz 52.4%; Russian 21.5%; Uzbek 12.9%; Ukrainian 2.5%; German 2.4%; Tatar 1.6%; other 6.7%.
Religious affiliation: believers are predominantly Sunnī Muslim (Ḥanafīyah).
Major cities (1991): Bishkek (Frunze) 631,300; Osh 218,700; Dzhalal-Abad 74,200; Tokmak 71,200; Przhevalsk 64,300.

Vital statistics

Birth rate per 1,000 population (1991): 29.1 (world avg. 26.4); (1990) legitimate 87.0%; illegitimate 13.0%.
Death rate per 1,000 population (1991): 6.9 (world avg. 9.2).
Natural increase rate per 1,000 population (1991): 22.2 (world avg. 17.2).
Total fertility rate (avg. births per childbearing woman; 1990): 3.7.
Marriage rate per 1,000 population (1990): 9.9.
Divorce rate per 1,000 population (1990): 1.8.
Life expectancy at birth (1991): male 64.3 years; female 72.6 years.
Major causes of death per 100,000 population (1989): diseases of the circulatory system 284.2; diseases of the respiratory system 143.7; accidents, poisoning, and violence 86.0; malignant neoplasms (cancers) 73.2; infectious and parasitic diseases 31.4; diseases of the digestive system 28.7; diseases of the nervous system 7.9; endocrine and metabolic disorders 5.3.

National economy

Budget (1992). Revenue: 11,967,000,000 rubles[2] (tax revenue 95.4%, of which value-added tax 42.9%, excise duties 27.2%, enterprise profits tax 22.7%, individual income tax 1.8%; nontax revenue 4.6%, of which highway fees 1.7%, privatization fees 0.8%). Expenditures: 17,053,000,000 rubles[2] (social welfare and culture 55.9%, of which education 24.8%, social security 15.8%, health 13.4%; national economy 19.2%; interest obligations 12.9%; law enforcement 3.6%).
Production (metric tons except as noted). Agriculture, forestry, fishing (1992): grain 1,417,000, vegetables (other than potatoes) 385,000, potatoes 325,000, fruit (other than grapes) 126,000, seed cotton 55,000, grapes 26,000; livestock (number of live animals) 9,500,000 sheep and goats, 1,200,000 cattle, 315,000 horses, 300,000 pigs; roundwood (1990) 6,000 cu m; fish catch 1,000. Mining and quarrying (1992): detail not available; however, antimony, gold, and mercury are mined. Manufacturing (1991): cement 1,300,000; milk 1,132,000; meat 222,800; wool 36,600; eggs 650,000,000 units. Construction (1991): residential 1,232,000 sq m. Energy production (consumption): electricity (kW-hr; 1992) 12,140,000,000 (9,760,000,000); coal (metric tons; 1992) 2,250,000 (4,300,000); crude petroleum (barrels; 1992) 896,500 (896,500); petroleum products (metric tons; 1992) none (1,550,000); natural gas (cu m; 1992) 68,000,000 (1,947,000,000).
Land use: forested, n.a.; meadows and pastures, n.a.; agricultural and under permanent cultivation, n.a.; other, n.a.
Population economically active (1991): total 1,754,000; activity rate of total population 42.8% (participation rates [1990]: ages 16–59 [male], 16–54 [female] 80.0%; female 49.5%; unemployed [1989] 2.6%).

Price and earnings indexes (1985 = 100)

	1985	1986	1987	1988	1989
Consumer price index	100.0	101.0	102.0	102.0	104.0
Monthly earnings index	100.0	102.3	105.4	112.9	121.4

Household income and expenditure (1990). Average household size 4.7; income per household (1989) 6,100 rubles[2]; sources of income: wages and salaries 72.0%, pensions and stipends 7.5%, other 20.5%; expenditure: consumer goods 33.5%, food 32.9%, taxes 8.2%, alcohol 2.8%, housing 2.0%.
Gross national product (at current market prices; 1992): U.S.$3,653,000,000 (U.S.$810 per capita)[3].

Structure of net material product and labour force

	1991 in value '000,000 rubles[2]	1991 % of total value	1990 labour force[4]	1990 % of labour force[4]
Agriculture	4,058.0	36.4	227,100	18.8
Mining, Manufacturing, Public utilities	5,054.0	45.3	284,400	22.6
Construction	864.0	7.7	128,100	10.2
Transportation and communications	307.0	2.8	92,200	7.3
Trade	—	—	106,000	8.5
Finance	—	—	7,000	0.1
Public administration, defense	—	—	...	...
Services	869.0	7.8	384,500	30.6
Other	—	—	23,600	1.9
TOTAL	11,152.0	100.0	1,252,900	100.0

Tourism: receipts from visitors, n.a.; expenditures by nationals abroad, n.a.
Public debt (external, outstanding): n.a.

Foreign trade

Balance of trade (current prices)

	1987	1988	1989	1990	1991
'000,000 rubles	−458	−435	−813	−417	−958
% of total	9.9%	7.9%	13.8%	7.9%	8.2%

Imports (1991): 5,373,000,000 rubles[2] (light-industrial products 23.0%, machinery and equipment 22.0%, chemicals 10.5%, oil and gas 10.1%, food 8.1%, ferrous metals 5.4%, nonferrous metals 5.2%, pulp and paper 3.3%, building materials 1.5%). *Major import sources:* former Soviet republics.
Exports (1991): 6,331,000,000 rubles[2] (machinery and equipment 33.2%, light-industrial products 30.0%, food 18.0%, nonferrous metals 7.8%, electricity 3.0%, agricultural products 2.8%). *Major export destinations:* former Soviet republics.

Transport and communications

Transport. Railroads (1990): length 490 mi, 789 km; passengers 1,364,000; short ton cargo 113,100. Roads (1990): total length 11,900 mi, 19,100 km (paved 86%). Vehicles (1988): passenger cars 173,800; trucks and buses, n.a. Merchant marine: vessels (100 gross tons and over) n.a.; total deadweight tonnage, n.a. Air transport (1990): passenger-mi 2,304,200,000, passenger-km 3,708,300,000; short ton-mi cargo, n.a.; metric ton-km cargo, n.a.; airports (1992) with scheduled flights 1.
Communications. Daily newspapers (1990): total number 128; total circulation 1,622,000; circulation per 1,000 population 367. Radio (1991): 825,000 receivers (1 per 18.5 persons). Television (1991): 875,000 receivers (1 per 19.6 persons). Telephones (1991): 342,000 (1 per 7.7 persons).

Education and health

Education (1991–92)

	schools	teachers	students	student/teacher ratio
Primary (age 6–13)	1,796	76,000	949,000	12.5
Secondary (age 14–17)	1,334			
Voc., teacher tr.	48	...	42,700	...
Higher	12	...	58,000	...

Educational attainment (1989). Percentage of population age 19 and over having: primary education 4.7%; some secondary 20.9%; completed secondary 44.4%; some postsecondary 19.3%; higher 10.7%. *Literacy:* total population age 15 and over literate, n.a.; males literate, n.a.; females literate, n.a.
Health (1992): physicians[5] 16,400 (1 per 271 persons); hospital beds 54,100 (1 per 82 persons); infant mortality rate per 1,000 live births 29.7.
Food: daily per capita caloric intake, n.a.

Military

Total active duty personnel (1993): 12,000 (army 100%). *Military expenditure as percentage of GNP* (1992): 1.2% (world 5.0%); per capita expenditure U.S.$10.

[1]Detail does not add to total given because of rounding. [2]The value of the ruble during 1989–92 ranged from an official 1.61 rubles to more than 300 rubles per 1 U.S.$. [3]Ruble-area GNP and exchange-rate data are very speculative. [4]State sector only. [5]Data include dentists.

Laos

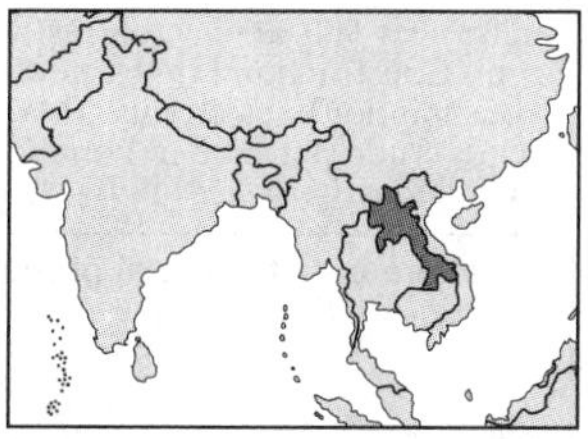

Official name: Sathalanalat Paxathipatai Paxaxôn Lao (Lao People's Democratic Republic).
Form of government: unitary single-party people's republic with one legislative house (National Assembly[1] [79]).
Chief of state: President.
Head of government: Prime Minister.
Capital: Vientiane.
Official language: Lao.
Official religion: none.
Monetary unit: 1 kip (KN) = 100 at; valuation (Oct. 4, 1993) 1 U.S.$ = KN 720.00; 1 £ = KN 1,094.

Area and population

		area		population
Provinces	Capitals	sq mi	sq km	1990 estimate
Attapu	Attapu	3,985	10,320	80,000
Bokeo	Houayxay	1,919	4,970	64,000
Bolikhamxay	Pakxan	6,359	16,470	145,000
Champasak	Pakxé	5,952	15,415	469,000
Houaphan	Xam Nua	6,371	16,500	243,000
Khammouan	Thakhek	6,299	16,315	249,000
Louang Namtha	Louang Namtha	3,600	9,325	114,000
Louangphrabang	Louangphrabang	6,515	16,875	339,000
Oudomxay	Xay	8,182	21,190	291,000
Phôngsali	Phôngsali	6,282	16,270	142,000
Saravan	Saravan	4,010	10,385	211,000
Savannakhét	Savannakhét	8,525	22,080	640,000
Vientiane	Vientiane	7,718	19,990	312,000
Xaignabouri	Xaignabouri	4,554	11,795	182,000
Xékong	Thong	2,959	7,665	58,000
Xiangkhoang	Phônsavan	6,685	17,315	189,000
Municipalities				
Vientiane	—	1,514	3,920	442,000
TOTAL		91,429	236,800	4,170,000

Demography

Population (1993): 4,533,000.
Density (1993): persons per sq mi 49.6, persons per sq km 19.1.
Urban-rural (1993): urban 19.0%; rural 81.0%.
Sex distribution (1990): male 50.25%; female 49.75%.
Age breakdown (1990): under 15, 43.7%; 15–29, 26.0%; 30–44, 16.2%; 45–59, 9.2%; 60–74, 4.2%; 75 and over, 0.7%.
Population projection: (2000) 5,435,000; (2010) 6,710,000.
Doubling time: 24 years.
Ethnic composition (1983): Lao-Lum (Lao) 67.0%; Lao-Theung (Mon-Khmer) 16.5%; Lao-Tai (Tai) 7.8%; Lao-Soung (Miao [Hmong] and Man [Yao]) 5.2%; other 3.5%.
Religious affiliation (1980): Buddhist 57.8%; tribal religionist 33.6%; Christian 1.8%, of which Roman Catholic 0.8%, Protestant 0.2%; Muslim 1.0%; atheist 1.0%; Chinese folk-religionist 0.9%; none 3.8%; other 0.1%.
Major cities (1985): Vientiane 178,203; Savannakhét 96,652; Louangphrabang 68,399; Pakxé 47,323.

Vital statistics

Birth rate per 1,000 population (1993): 44.0 (world avg. 26.4).
Death rate per 1,000 population (1993): 15.0 (world avg. 9.2).
Natural increase rate per 1,000 population (1993): 29.0 (world avg. 17.2).
Total fertility rate (avg. births per childbearing woman; 1993): 6.5.
Marriage rate per 1,000 population: n.a.
Divorce rate per 1,000 population: n.a.
Life expectancy at birth (1993): male 50.0 years; female 53.0 years.
Major causes of death per 100,000 population (incomplete, 1990): malaria 7.6; pneumonia 3.0; meningitis 1.5; diarrhea 1.2; tuberculosis 0.8.

National economy

Budget (1991). Revenue: KN 79,022,000,000 (1990; taxes 76.0%, nontax revenue 24.0%). Expenditures: KN 147,895,000,000 (current expenditure 55.4%, capital expenditure 44.6%).
Public debt (external, outstanding; 1991): U.S.$1,096,000,000.
Tourism (1991): total number of tourist arrivals 20,614.
Population economically active (1989): total 1,888,000; activity rate of total population 49.0% (participation rates [1985]: ages 15–64, 84.2%; female 45.3%; unemployed, n.a.).

Price and earnings indexes (1985 = 100)

	1982	1983	1984	1985	1986[2]
Consumer price index	30.1	39.6	60.5	100.0	136.2
Earnings index	...	...	...	...	...

Production (metric tons except as noted). Agriculture, forestry, fishing (1991): rice 1,400,000, sweet potatoes 220,000, sugarcane 97,000, cassava 66,000, corn (maize) 60,000, onions 42,000, potatoes 33,000, pineapples 32,000, melons 32,000, oranges 22,000, bananas 18,000; livestock (number of live animals) 1,390,000 pigs, 1,100,000 water buffalo, 865,000 cattle, 143,000 goats, 45,000 horses, 8,000,000 chickens; roundwood 4,340,000 cu m; fish catch (1990) 20,000. Mining and quarrying (1990): gypsum 90,000; rock salt 8,000; tin (metal content) 500; gemstones (mainly sapphires) 30,000 carats. Manufacturing (1990): domestic animal feed 2,500; washing powder 2,000; plastic products 282; nails 114; textiles 368,800 metres; clothing 863,500 pieces; cigarettes 30,000,000 packets; plywood 1,000,000 sheets; ceramic articles 41,300 units; beer and soft drinks 75,500 hectolitres; fish sauce 1,200 hectolitres. Construction: n.a. Energy production (consumption): electricity (kW-hr; 1991) 828,000,000 (192,000,000); coal (metric tons; 1981) 1,000 (1,000); crude petroleum, n.a. (n.a.); petroleum products (metric tons; 1990) none (74,000); natural gas, n.a. (n.a.).
Gross national product (at current market prices; 1991): U.S.$965,000,000 (U.S.$230 per capita).

Structure of gross domestic product and labour force

	1991		1989	
	in value KN '000,000	% of total value	labour force	% of labour force
Agriculture	386,503	53.3	1,359,000	72.0
Manufacturing	97,723	13.5		
Mining	995	0.1		
Construction	27,029	3.7		
Public utilities	12,451	1.7		
Transportation and communications	40,521	5.6	529,000	28.0
Trade	56,838	7.8		
Finance	21,489	3.0		
Pub. admin., defense	45,709	6.3		
Services / Other	35,717	4.9		
TOTAL	724,975	100.0[3]	1,888,000	100.0

Household income and expenditure. Average household size (1985) 6.0; average annual income per household KN 3,710 (U.S.$371); sources of income: n.a.; expenditure: n.a.
Land use (1990): forested 53.6%; meadows and pastures 3.4%; agricultural and under permanent cultivation 3.8%; other 39.2%.

Foreign trade[4]

Balance of trade (current prices)

	1986	1987	1988	1989	1990	1991
U.S.$'000,000	−131.0	−154.0	−125.0	−162.0	−127.8	−131.7
% of total	54.4%	55.4%	49.8%	58.7%	46.4%	45.8%

Imports (1989): U.S.$219,000,000 (major imports include cereals, other food products, petroleum products, agricultural and general machinery, and transport equipment). *Major import sources:* Thailand 55.1%; Japan 22.0%; China 4.0%; Hong Kong 0.5%.
Exports (1989): U.S.$57,000,000 (wood 33.3%, electricity 23.8%, coffee 14.3%, tin 3.2%). *Major export destinations:* Thailand 37.4%; China 11.6%; Japan 7.3%; Hong Kong 0.6%.

Transport and communications

Transport. Railroads: none. Roads (1991): total length 8,757 mi, 14,093 km (paved 24%). Vehicles (1991): passenger cars 21,269; trucks and buses 14,790. Merchant marine (1992): vessels (100 gross tons and over) 1; total deadweight tonnage 1,469. Air transport (1986): passenger-mi 11,000,000, passenger-km 18,000,000; short ton-mi cargo 1,370,000, metric ton-km cargo 2,000,000; airports (1993) with scheduled flights 13.
Communications. Daily newspapers (1990): total number 3; total circulation 14,000; circulation per 1,000 population 3.0. Radio (1992): total number of receivers 425,000 (1 per 10 persons). Television (1992): total number of receivers 32,000 (1 per 138 persons). Telephones (1990): 7,100 (1 per 596 persons).

Education and health

Education (1989–90)

	schools	teachers	students	student/ teacher ratio
Primary (age 6–10)	6,435	19,970	563,734	28.2
Secondary (age 11–16)	750	10,048	125,636	12.5
Voc., teacher tr.	139[5]	1,672	12,262	7.3
Higher	9	698	4,730	6.8

Educational attainment (1985). Percentage of population age 6 and over having: no schooling 49.3%; primary 41.2%; secondary 9.1%; higher 0.4%.
Literacy (1985): total population age 15 and over literate 83.9%; males literate 92.0%; females literate 75.8%.
Health (1990): physicians 1,173 (1 per 3,555 persons); hospital beds 10,364 (1 per 402 persons); infant mortality rate per 1,000 live births (1993) 96.
Food (1984–86): daily per capita caloric intake 2,190 (vegetable products 90%, animal products 10%); 101% of FAO recommended minimum requirement.

Military

Total active duty personnel (1992): 37,000 (army 89.2%, navy 1.4%, air force 9.4%). *Military expenditure as percent of GNP* (1984): 10.5% (world 5.7%); per capita expenditure U.S.$16.

[1]Formerly known as the Supreme People's Assembly. [2]January–June. [3]Detail does not add to total given because of rounding. [4]Import figures are c.i.f. in balance of trade and commodities. [5]1988–89.

Latvia

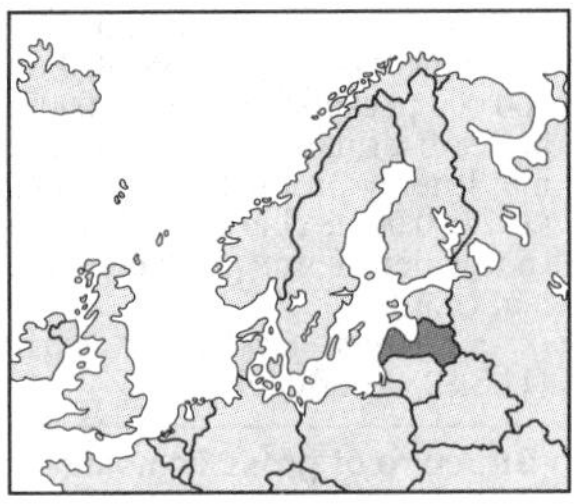

Official name: Latvijas Republika (Republic of Latvia).
Form of government: unitary multiparty republic with a single legislative body (Supreme Council [100]).
Chief of state: President.
Head of government: Prime Minister.
Capital: Rīga.
Official language: Latvian.
Official religion: none.
Monetary unit: 1 lats[1] (plural lati) = 10 santimi.

Area and population

		area		population
Cities of republic jurisdiction	**Capitals**	sq mi	sq km	1992[2] estimate
Daugavpils	—	28	72	127,279
Jelgava	—	23	60	73,917
Jūrmala	—	39	100	60,901
Liepāja	—	23	60	113,815
Rēzekne	—	7	17	43,073
Rīga	—	114	295	897,078
Ventspils	—	18	46	50,435
Rural districts				
Aizkraukle	Aizkraukle	988	2,558	45,093
Alūksne	Alūksne	867	2,246	28,631
Balvi	Balvi	920	2,384	33,576
Bauska	Bauska	727	1,884	55,612
Cēsis	Cēsis	1,182	3,062	63,820
Daugavpils	Daugavpils	975	2,526	46,329
Dobele	Dobele	649	1,680	44,749
Gulbene	Gulbene	724	1,876	30,243
Jēkabpils	Jēkabpils	1,158	2,998	61,435
Jelgava	Jelgava	623	1,613	39,137
Krāslava	Krāslava	883	2,288	41,019
Kuldīga	Kuldīga	966	2,503	41,361
Liepāja	Liepāja	1,386	3,589	54,475
Limbaži	Limbaži	1,005	2,602	41,436
Ludza	Ludza	991	2,566	41,747
Madona	Madona	1,293	3,348	49,953
Ogre	Ogre	701	1,816	66,040
Preiļi	Preiļi	788	2,042	45,342
Rēzekne	Rēzekne	1,025	2,654	42,899
Rīga	Rīga	1,194	3,094	152,070
Saldus	Saldus	824	2,134	40,235
Talsi	Talsi	1,061	2,748	50,603
Tukums	Tukums	949	2,457	59,069
Valka	Valka	944	2,444	37,119
Valmiera	Valmiera	918	2,377	63,067
Ventspils	Ventspils	954	2,471	15,400
TOTAL		24,946[3]	64,610	2,656,958

Demography

Population (1993): 2,596,000.
Density (1993): persons per sq mi 104.1, persons per sq km 40.2.
Urban-rural (1992[2]): urban 69.5%; rural 30.5%.
Sex distribution (1992[2]): male 46.56%; female 53.44%.
Age breakdown (1992[2]): under 15, 21.4%; 15–29, 20.7%; 30–44, 21.4%; 45–59, 18.3%; 60–74, 13.1%; 75 and over, 5.1%.
Population projection: (2000) 2,647,000; (2010) 2,704,000.
Ethnic composition (1992): Latvian 52.5%; Russian 34.0%; Belorussian 4.4%; Ukrainian 3.4%; Polish 2.2%; Lithuanian 1.3%; Jewish 0.6%; other 1.6%.
Religious affiliation: believers are predominantly Evangelical Lutheran, Russian Orthodox, or Roman Catholic.
Major cities (1992[2]): Rīga 897,078; Daugavpils 127,279; Liepāja 113,815; Jelgava 73,917; Jūrmala 60,901.

Vital statistics

Birth rate per 1,000 population (1992): 12.0 (world avg. 26.4); (1991) legitimate 81.6%; illegitimate 18.4%.
Death rate per 1,000 population (1992): 13.5 (world avg. 9.2).
Natural increase rate per 1,000 population (1992): −1.5 (world avg. 17.2).
Total fertility rate (avg. births per childbearing woman; 1989–90): 2.0.
Marriage rate per 1,000 population (1991): 8.4.
Divorce rate per 1,000 population (1991): 4.2.
Life expectancy at birth (1991): male 63.7 years; female 74.5 years.
Major causes of death per 100,000 population (1990): diseases of the circulatory system 756.5; malignant neoplasms (cancers) 204.9; accidents, poisoning, and violence 138.9; diseases of the respiratory system 49.6.

National economy

Budget (1993). Revenue: 81,143,000,000 Latvian rubles (social-security taxes 43.6%; value-added taxes 14.9%; profit tax 10.7%; income tax 7.8%; customs duties 6.7%). Expenditures: 80,724,000,000 Latvian rubles (1991; economic affairs 46.8%; social affairs 28.6%, of which education and science 11.1%, social security 11.1%, health 6.1%).
Production (metric tons except as noted). Agriculture, forestry, fishing (1991): potatoes 944,000, corn (maize) 785,000, barley 762,000, sugar beets 378,000, vegetables 209,000, wheat 186,000, fruits and berries 100,000; livestock (number of live animals) 1,383,000 cattle, 1,247,000 pigs, 531,000 dairy cows, 190,000 sheep, 10,395,000 poultry; roundwood 1,421,000 cu m; fish catch 369,900. Mining and quarrying (1990): peat 253,000; gypsum 105,000. Manufacturing (1991): steel 800,000; cement 720,000; processed milk 609,600; processed meats 269,100; paper 107,000; plastics 29,000; telephones 2,019,000 units; diesel engines 162,000 units; buses 15,800 units; rail passenger cars 500 units; beer 900,000 hectolitres; vodka 220,000 hectolitres; textiles 90,700,000 sq m. Construction (1991): new residential 432,000 sq m. Energy production (consumption): electricity (kW-hr; 1991) 5,600,000,000 (n.a.); coal, none (n.a.); crude petroleum, none (n.a.); natural gas, none (n.a.).
Gross national product (1991): U.S.$9,193,000,000 (U.S.$3,410 per capita).

Structure of net material product and labour force

	1992		1991	
	in value '000,000 Latvian rubles	% of total value	labour force	% of labour force
Agriculture	45,221	24.8	83,000	5.7
Manufacturing and mining	70,029	38.5	351,400	24.0
Construction	13,049	7.2	82,200	5.6
Utilities	11,530	6.3	...	...
Transportation and communications			103,700	7.1
Trade			119,600	8.2
Finance	42,173	23.2		
Pub. admin., defense			194,000	13.3
Services				
Other			528,000[4]	36.1[4]
TOTAL	182,002	100.0	1,461,900	100.0

Population economically active (1991): total 1,461,900; activity rate of total population 54.8% (participation rates: ages 16–59/55[5, 6], 93.4%; female, n.a.; unemployed 4.4%).

Price and earnings indexes (1985 = 100)

	1985	1986	1987	1988	1989	1990	1991
Consumer price index	100.0	105.4	110.0	114.0	119.3	131.8	358.9
Monthly earnings index	100.0	102.8	106.6	115.9	127.6	148.5	286.6

Household income and expenditure. Average household size (1989) 3.1; average annual income per household: n.a.; sources of income (1991): wages and salaries 63.2%, pensions and transfers 16.6%, self-employment 5.3%, other 14.9%; expenditure (1991): food and alcohol 45.2%, consumer goods 34.8%, rent and social services 7.1%.
Land use (1990): forested 31.2%; meadows and pastures 28.1%; agricultural and permanent cultivation 28.6%; other 12.1%.

Foreign trade

Balance of trade (current prices)

	1988	1989	1990	1991
'000,000 rubles	−700	−617	−784	+1,396
% of total	6.7%	5.4%	6.5%	10.0%

Imports (1991): 6,309,000,000 rubles (textiles 22.0%, chemical products 14.4%, machinery and equipment 13.7%, food and agricultural products 13.6%, fuels 8.8%). *Major import sources:* Russia 44.5%; Lithuania 10.1%; Ukraine 8.7%; Belarus 5.9%; Estonia 5.2%; Kazakhstan 4.4%.
Exports (1991): 7,705,000,000 rubles (machinery and equipment 24.8%, food and agricultural products 21.7%, textiles 12.9%, chemical products 8.2%, forestry products 5.4%). *Major export destinations:* Russia 54.2%; Ukraine 12.0%; Belarus 6.9%; Lithuania 5.4%; Kazakhstan 3.8%; Estonia 3.2%.

Transport and communications

Transport. Railroads (1991): length 2,397 km; passenger-km 3,929,000,000; metric-km cargo 16,700,000,000. Roads (1991): total length 60,224 km (paved 55%). Vehicles (1991): passenger cars 328,436; trucks and buses 70,545. Merchant marine (1992): cargo vessels 261; total deadweight tonnage 1,436,899. Air transport (1991): passenger-km 2,999,000,000; metric ton-km cargo 22,000,000[6]; airports (1993) 1.
Communications. Total newspapers (1991): total number 188; total circulation 3,676,000; circulation per 1,000 population 1,377. Radio (1991): 1,396,000 receivers (1 per 1.9 persons). Television (1991): 1,126,000 receivers (1 per 2.4 persons). Telephones (1991): 746,000 (1 per 3.6 persons).

Education and health

Education (1991–92)

	schools	teachers	students	student/ teacher ratio
Primary / Secondary	943	33,712[7]	330,468	9.8
Voc., teacher tr.[8]	57	...	36,100	...
Higher	14	...	46,279	...

Educational attainment (1989). Percentage of persons age 15 and over having: primary or less 18.7%; incomplete secondary 23.4%; complete secondary 46.4%; some higher 11.5%. *Literacy:* approximately 98%.
Health (1991): physicians 12,203 (1 per 218.7 persons); hospital beds 36,106 (1 per 73.9 persons); infant mortality rate per 1,000 live births (1992) 17.4.

Military

Total active duty personnel (1992): 2,550. *Military expenditure:* n.a. Until 1991, the U.S.S.R. was responsible for Latvia's external security; about 40,000 of its troops remained in Latvia at year-end 1992.

[1]The lats (pre-World War II Latvian currency), reintroduced in parallel with the Latvian ruble (LR; at 200 LR per lats) on March 5, 1993, became the sole official currency Oct. 18, 1993. From May 7, 1993, LR circulated in parallel at par with the Soviet ruble, serving temporarily as the sole legal tender until introduction of the lats on March 5, 1993. [2]January 1. [3]Detail does not add to total given because of rounding. [4]Includes 313,600 employed outside the state sector, 65,000 unemployed, and 149,300 not allocated by sector. [5]Males retire at age 59, females at 55. [6]1990. [7]Includes part-time teachers. [8]1990–91.

Lebanon

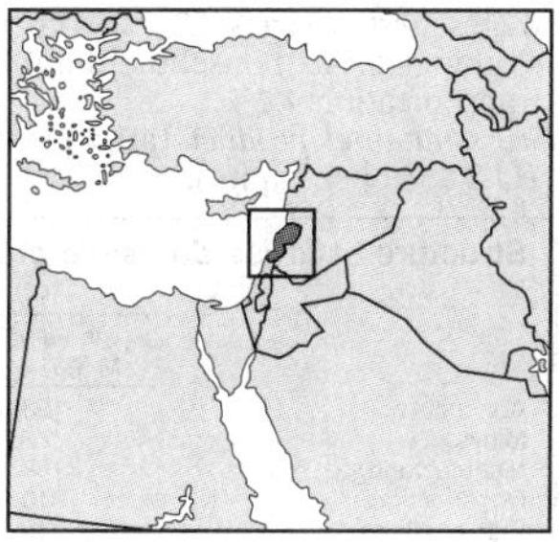

Official name: al-Jumhūrīyah al-Lubnānīyah (Republic of Lebanon).
Form of government: unitary multiparty republic with one legislative house (National Assembly [128])[1].
Chief of state: President.
Head of government: Prime Minister.
Capital: Beirut.
Official language: Arabic.
Official religion: none.
Monetary unit: 1 Lebanese pound (LL) = 100 piastres; valuation (Oct. 4, 1993) 1 U.S.$ = LL 1,711; 1 £ = LL 2,593.

Area and population

		area		population
Governorates	**Capitals**	sq mi	sq km	1970 estimate
Bayrūt	Beirut (Bayrūt)	7	18	474,870
al-Biqā'	Zaḥlah	1,653	4,280	203,520
Jabal Lubnān	B'abdā	753	1,950	833,055
al-Janūb	Sidon (Ṣaydā)	772	2,001	249,945
ash-Shamāl	Tripoli (Ṭarābulus)	765	1,981	364,935
TOTAL		3,950	10,230	2,126,325

Demography

Population (1993): 2,909,000.
Density (1993): persons per sq mi 736.5, persons per sq km 284.4.
Urban-rural (1990): urban 83.7%; rural 16.3%.
Sex distribution (1990): male 48.58%; female 51.42%.
Age breakdown (1990): under 15, 35.4%; 15–29, 30.5%; 30–44, 15.3%; 45–59, 9.9%; 60–74, 6.6%; 75 and over, 2.3%.
Population projection: (2000) 3,312,000; (2010) 3,777,000.
Doubling time: during the 1970–75 prewar period the average growth rate was 2.6%; however, the dislocation of the population by the civil war between 1976 and 1991 rendered both the absolute size and principal components of population change (births, deaths, migration) highly problematic.
Ethnic composition (1993): Lebanese, *c.* 80%; Palestinian 12%; Armenian 5%; Syrian, Kurd, and other 3%.
Religious affiliation: no official data exist subsequent to the 1932 census, when Christians (predominantly Maronite Roman Catholic) were a slight majority; it is thought that Muslims today constitute the majority, but by what margin is highly uncertain. Unofficial and CIA estimates (1984/1986) indicated that the main religious groups were distributed as follows: Shīʿī Muslim 32/41%; Maronite Christian 24.5/16%; Sunnī Muslim 21/27%; Druze 7/7%; Greek Orthodox 6.5/5%; Greek Catholic 4/3%; Armenian Christian 4%/n.a.; other 1/1%.
Major cities (1990): Beirut 1,500,000; Tripoli 160,000; Zaḥlah 45,000; Sidon (Ṣaydā) 38,000; Tyre 14,000.

Vital statistics

Birth rate per 1,000 population (1990–95): 29.6 (world avg. 26.4).
Death rate per 1,000 population (1990–95): 7.7 (world avg. 9.2).
Natural increase rate per 1,000 population (1990–95): 21.9 (world avg. 17.2).
Total fertility rate (avg. births per childbearing woman; 1990–95): 3.4.
Life expectancy at birth (1990–95): male 61.5 years; female 69.0 years.
Major causes of death: normally, cardiovascular and gastrointestinal diseases, including typhoid fever and dysentery; but violence and acts of war were also among the principal causes of mortality between 1975 and 1991.

National economy

Budget (1994). Revenue: LL 2,195,795,000,000 (almost entirely taxation, direct and indirect). Expenditures: LL 4,206,705,000,000 (debt service 35%, government salaries 32%, defense 22%, education 10%).
Production (metric tons except as noted). Agriculture, forestry, fishing (1992): grapes 290,000, potatoes 250,000, oranges 245,000, tomatoes 200,000, apples 190,000, cucumbers 150,000, lemons and limes 80,000, onions 60,000; opium poppies and marijuana were important cash crops in the late 1980s and early 1990s but were reportedly eradicated in 1993; livestock (number of live animals) 465,000 goats, 230,000 sheep, 72,000 cattle, 20,000,000 chickens; roundwood (1991) 481,000 cu m; fish catch (1991) 1,800. Mining and quarrying (1991): lime 10,000; salt 3,000; gypsum 2,000. Manufacturing (1990): cement 900,000; paper 37,000; cardboard 35,000; cigarettes 1,800,000,000 units; petroleum refining, dairying, curing of leather, meat cutting, and milling of flour are also significant. Construction (1987): 4,938,000 sq m. Energy production (consumption): electricity (kW-hr; 1991) 4,750,000,000 (4,790,000,000); coal, n.a. (none); crude petroleum (barrels; 1991) none (3,780,000); petroleum products (metric tons; 1991) 519,000 (2,579,000); natural gas, none (n.a.).
Household income and expenditure. Average household size (1987) 5.0; average annual income per household (1985) LL 120,000 (U.S.$6,630; in constant prices, about 75% of 1966 income levels); sources of income (1974): wages and salaries 27.9%, transfers 3.0%, other 69.1%; expenditure (1966)[2]: food 42.8%, housing 16.8%, clothing 8.6%, health care 7.2%.
Tourism (1980): number of tourist arrivals 135,548[3].
Population economically active (1986): total 693,812; activity rate of total population 25.1% (participation rates: over age 15, 39.9%; female 21.7%; unemployed [1991] reported by the national trade union at 30% but perhaps as low as 7–8% according to a 1987 study of 60,000 households).

Consumer price index (1985 = 100)

	1981	1982	1983	1984	1985	1986	1987
Consumer price index	40.6	48.7	51.9	61.0	100.0	204.6	1,030.6

Public debt (external, outstanding; 1991): U.S.$576,900,000.
Gross domestic product (at current market prices; 1992): estimated at U.S.$3,-500,000,000–4,000,000,000 (U.S.$1,250–1,425 per capita).

Structure of gross domestic product and labour force

	1990		1986	
	in value LL '000,000[4]	% of total value	labour force	% of labour force
Agriculture	205,005	9.8	132,211	19.1
Mining	—	—	694	0.1
Manufacturing	293,168	14.1	123,647	17.8
Construction	76,906	3.7	43,357	6.2
Public utilities	121,988	5.8	6,668	1.0
Transp. and commun.	87,488	4.2	48,242	7.0
Trade	659,752	31.7	114,706	16.5
Finance	179,220	8.6	24,224	3.5
Real estate and business services	207,588	10.0	200,063	28.8
Pub. admin., defense	251,199	12.1		
TOTAL	2,082,314	100.0	693,812	100.0

Land use (1991): forested 7.8%; meadows and pastures 1.0%; agricultural and under permanent cultivation 29.9%; wasteland and other areas 61.3%.

Foreign trade

Balance of trade (current prices)

	1987	1988	1989	1990	1991	1992
U.S.$'000,000	−293	−716	−874	−1,419	−2,983	−6,182
% of total	56.7%	58.6%	64.9%	67.8%	75.2%	76.7%

Imports (1987): LL 402,027,000,000 (1982; consumer goods 40.0%, machinery and transport equipment 35.0%, petroleum products 20.0%). *Major import sources:* Italy 10.7%; Turkey 8.5%; France 8.1%; West Germany 5.9%.
Exports (1987): LL 132,716,000,000 (1985; jewelry 10.2%, clothing 5.2%, pharmaceutical products 4.9%, metal products 4.8%). *Major export destinations:* Saudi Arabia 8.7%; Switz. 7.6%; Jordan 6.0%; Kuwait 5.4%; U.S. 5.2%.

Transport and communications

Transport. Railroads (1982)[5]: length (1986) 417 km; passenger-km 8,570,000; metric ton-km cargo 42,010,000. Roads (1987): total length 7,370 km (paved 85%). Vehicles (1985): passenger cars 300,000; trucks and buses 49,560. Merchant marine (1992): vessels (100 gross tons and over) 163; total deadweight tonnage 438,165. Air transport (1992)[6]: passenger-km 1,285,197,000; metric ton-km cargo 37,192,000; airports (1993) with scheduled flights 1.
Communications. Daily newspapers (1986): total number 39; total circulation 572,734[7]; circulation per 1,000 population 211.6[7]. Radio (1992): 2,150,000 receivers (1 per 1.3 persons). Television (1991): 838,037 receivers (1 per 3.3 persons). Telephones (1993): 351,000 (1 per 8.3 persons).

Education and health

Education (1984–85)

	schools	teachers	students[8]	student/ teacher ratio
Primary (age 5–9)	2,130	22,810[9]	399,029	...
Secondary (age 10–16)	1,405[9]	21,344[9]	279,849	...
Voc., teacher tr.	181[9]	3,506	30,407	10.6
Higher	18[9]	7,460	70,510	9.5

Educational attainment (1970). Percentage of population age 25 and over having: no formal schooling 45.6%, of which, ability to read and write 35.6%; incomplete primary education 28.5%; complete primary 10.8%; incomplete secondary 7.1%; complete secondary 4.9%; higher 3.1%. *Literacy* (1990): total population age 15 and over literate, *c.* 1,538,800 (80.1%); males literate, *c.* 798,100 (87.8%); females literate, *c.* 739,100 (73.1%).
Health: physicians (1986) 3,509 (1 per 771 persons); hospital beds (1982) 11,-400 (1 per 263 persons); infant mortality rate per 1,000 live births (1990) 44.0.
Food (1979–81): daily per capita caloric intake 2,995 (vegetable products 84%, animal products 16%); 120% of FAO recommended minimum requirement.

Military

Total active duty personnel (1993): Lebanese national armed forces 41,300 (army 96.9%, navy 1.2%, air force 1.9%). External regular military forces include: UN peacekeeping force in Lebanon 5,400; Syrian army 30,000. Most civilian militias were progressively disbanded after the civil war ended in 1991. According to external analysts, however, the following factions were still active in 1993, though on a much reduced scale[10]: Palestine Liberation Organization (all factions) 11,500; Shīʿī Muslim (pro-Iran Hezbollah [Party of God]) 3,000; Maronite Christian (Lebanese Forces [Phalange]) 3,000; Shīʿī Muslim (pro-Syrian Amal) 2,000; Druze (Progressive Socialist Party) a few hundred. *Military expenditure as percentage of GDP* (1990): 4.2% (world, n.a.); per capita expenditure: U.S.$52.

[1]The current legislature was elected between August and October 1992; one-half of its membership is Christian and one-half Muslim/Druze. [2]Weights based on consumer price index components. For capital city only. [3]Approximately one-fourth the annual prewar rates of the early 1970s. [4]The domestic economy reportedly became increasingly "dollarized" as more transactions were quoted or paid in dollars during the late 1980s and early '90s. By 1993, however, the pound had once again stabilized against the dollar. [5]Apart from a 14-mi (23-km) section delivering oil from the Zahrani refinery to a thermal power station serving Beirut, no passenger or general cargo track is currently in use. [6]MEA-Airliban international flights only. [7]For 20 newspapers only. [8]1986–87. [9]1981–82. [10]Active personnel.

Lesotho

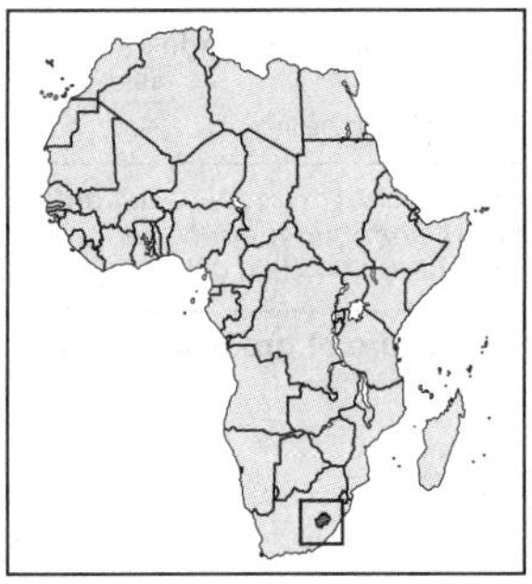

Official name: Lesotho (Sotho); Kingdom of Lesotho (English).
Form of government: multiparty republic[1] with 2 legislative houses (National Assembly [65]; Senate [[2]]).
Chief of state: King.
Head of government: Prime Minister.
Capital: Maseru.
Official languages: Sotho; English.
Official religion: Christianity.
Monetary unit: 1 loti (plural maloti [M]) = 100 lisente; valuation (Oct. 4, 1993) 1 U.S.$ = M 3.45; 1 £ = M 5.23.

Area and population

		area		population
				1987
Districts	Capitals	sq mi	sq km	estimate
Berea	Teyateyaneng	858	2,222	199,600
Butha-Buthe	Butha-Buthe	682	1,767	103,000
Leribe	Hlotse	1,092	2,828	264,600
Mafeteng	Mafeteng	818	2,119	200,600
Maseru	Maseru	1,652	4,279	319,100
Mohale's Hoek	Mohale's Hoek	1,363	3,530	168,600
Mokhotlong	Mokhotlong	1,573	4,075	76,600
Qacha's Nek	Qacha's Nek	907	2,349	65,600
Quthing	Quthing	1,126	2,916	113,200
Thaba-Tseka	Thaba-Tseka	1,649	4,270	106,800
TOTAL		11,720	30,355	1,617,700

Demography

Population (1993): 1,903,000.
Density (1993): persons per sq mi 162.4, persons per sq km 62.7.
Urban-rural (1988): urban 18.9%; rural 81.1%.
Sex distribution (1987): male 48.15%; female 51.85%.
Age breakdown (1987): under 15, 40.7%; 15–29, 25.2%; 30–44, 16.6%; 45–59, 10.7%; 60–74, 5.5%; 75 and over, 1.3%.
Population projection: (2000) 2,282,000; (2010) 2,958,000.
Doubling time: 24 years.
Ethnic composition (1983): Sotho 99.7%; other 0.3%.
Religious affiliation (1980): Roman Catholic 43.5%; Protestant (mostly Lesotho Evangelical) 29.8%; Anglican 11.5%; other Christian 8.0%; traditional beliefs 6.2%; other 1.0%.
Major urban centres (1986): Maseru 109,382; Maputsoe 20,000; Teyateyaneng 14,251; Mafeteng 12,667; Hlotse 9,595.

Vital statistics

Birth rate per 1,000 population (1990–95): 40.2 (world avg. 26.4); legitimate, n.a.; illegitimate, n.a.
Death rate per 1,000 population (1990–95): 11.0 (world avg. 9.2).
Natural increase rate per 1,000 population (1990–95): 29.2 (world avg. 17.2).
Total fertility rate (avg. births per childbearing woman; 1990–95): 5.8.
Marriage rate per 1,000 population: n.a.
Divorce rate per 1,000 population: n.a.
Life expectancy at birth (1990–95): male 54.0 years; female 63.0 years.
Major causes of death per 100,000 population: n.a.; however, major diseases include malaria, typhoid fever, and infectious and parasitic diseases.

National economy

Budget (1991–92). Revenue: M 1,116,200,000 (tax revenue 74.7%, of which customs receipts 46.2%, sales tax 11.0%, income tax 8.0%, company tax 6.2%; grants and other nontax revenue 25.3%). Expenditures: M 1,075,000,000 (recurrent expenditure 63.2%, of which personal emoluments 30.3%, interest payments 6.9%, subsidies and transfers 6.5%, other goods and services 19.6%; capital expenditure 36.8%).
Production (metric tons except as noted). Agriculture, forestry, fishing (1992): corn (maize) 61,000, fruit 18,000, sorghum 10,000, roots and tubers 8,000, peas 4,000, beans 3,000; livestock (number of live animals) 1,460,000 sheep, 1,060,000 goats, 536,000 cattle, 129,000 asses, 122,000 horses, 75,000 pigs, 1,000,000 chickens; roundwood (1991) 631,000 cu m; fish catch (1991) 15. Mining and quarrying (1988): sand and gravel 50,000 cu m. Manufacturing (total value added; 1990): M 180,800,000, of which food and beverages 47.2%, textiles, apparel, and leather 39.8%, chemical products 2.1%, printing and publishing 2.0%, iron and steel products 1.6%, furniture and fixtures 1.2%. Construction (total value added; 1990): M 259,700. Energy production (consumption): electricity (kW-hr; 1988) 1,000,000 (n.a.); coal, none (n.a.); petroleum, none (n.a.); natural gas, none (n.a.).
Public debt (external, outstanding; 1991): U.S.$405,900,000.
Tourism (1991): receipts from visitors U.S.$18,000,000; expenditures by nationals abroad U.S.$11,000,000.
Population economically active (1985–86): total 716,270; activity rate of total population 45.7% (participation rates: ages 15–64, 79.8%; female 45.5%; unemployed [1988] 23%).

Price and earnings indexes (1985 = 100)

	1985	1986	1987	1988	1989	1990	1991
Consumer price index	100.1	118.0	131.9	147.0	168.6	188.2	221.5
Earnings index	...	...	...	...	...	...	...

Household income and expenditure. Average household size (1986) 4.8; average annual income per household (1986–87) M 2,832 (U.S.$1,297); sources of income (1986–87): transfer payments 44.7%, self-employment 27.8%, wages and salaries 22.4%, other 5.1%; expenditure (1989): food 48.0%, clothing 16.4%, household durable goods 11.9%, housing and energy 10.1%, transportation 4.7%.
Gross national product (at current market prices; 1991): U.S.$1,053,000,000 (U.S.$580 per capita).

Structure of gross domestic product and labour force

	1991		1985–86	
	in value M '000,000	% of total value	labour force	% of labour force
Agriculture	193.8	11.8	474,171	66.2
Mining	3.7	0.2	6,446	0.9
Manufacturing	198.2	12.1	19,339	2.7
Construction	310.5	18.9	31,516	4.4
Public utilities	19.3	1.2	1,433	0.2
Transp. and commun.	53.7	3.3	5,014	0.7
Trade	127.2	7.7	22,204	3.1
Finance	89.1	5.4	3,581	0.5
Pub. admin., defense	259.1	15.8	17,907	2.5
Services	139.3	8.5	126,780	17.7
Other	249.7[3]	15.2[3]	7,879	1.1
TOTAL	1,643.8[4]	100.0[4]	716,270[5]	100.0[5]

Land use (1991): meadows and pastures 65.9%; agricultural and under permanent cultivation 11.2%; other 22.9%.

Foreign trade[6]

Balance of trade (current prices)

	1986	1987	1988	1989	1990	1991
M '000,000	−834.6	−830.5	−1,106.3	−1,072.1	−1,517.0	−1,992.9
% of total	87.8%	81.4%	79.2%	75.8%	83.2%	84.3%

Imports (1991): M 2,259,690,000 (1985; manufactured goods [excluding chemicals, machinery, and transport equipment] 44.1%, of which clothing 9.3%, footwear 4.2%, blankets and traveling rugs 3.8%; food and live animals 18.2%, of which cereals [all forms] 6.1%, sugar [all forms] 2.3%; machinery and transport equipment 15.5%, of which trucks and vans 2.0%; petroleum products 7.3%). *Major import sources:* Customs Union of Southern Africa 94.1%; Asia 3.4%; Europe 1.4%, of which European Economic Community 1.3%; the Americas 0.3%.
Exports (1991): M 186,165,000 (manufactured goods 83.1%, of which machinery and transport equipment 2.8%; food and live animals 11.6%, of which preserved vegetables 4.3%, cornmeal 1.6%, wheat flour 1.2%; crude materials 3.7%, of which mohair 2.4%, wool 1.1%; chemicals 1.6%). *Major export destinations:* Customs Union of Southern Africa 42.1%; Europe 30.0%, of which European Economic Community 27.9%; the Americas 25.4%; Asia 0.4%.

Transport and communications

Transport. Railroads (1991): length 1.6 mi, 2.6 km. Roads (1988): total length 2,930 mi, 4,715 km (paved 12%). Vehicles (1986): passenger cars 6,363; trucks and buses 15,379. Merchant marine: vessels (100 gross tons and over) none. Air transport (1992)[7]: passenger-mi 4,767,000, passenger-km 7,671,000; ton-mi cargo 21,200, metric ton-km cargo 31,000; airports (1993) with scheduled flights 1.
Communications. Daily newspapers (1991): total number 5; total circulation 24,000; circulation per 1,000 population 13. Radio (1992): total number of receivers 420,000 (1 per 4.4 persons). Television (1992): total number of receivers 50,000 (1 per 37 persons). Telephones (1988): 28,583 (1 per 56 persons).

Education and health

Education (1991–92)

	schools	teachers	students	student/ teacher ratio
Primary (age 6–12)	1,198	6,685	361,144	54.0
Secondary (age 13–17)	179	2,407	46,572	19.3
Voc., teacher tr.	10	227	2,167	9.5
Higher	1	204	1,421	7.0

Educational attainment (1986–87). Percentage of population age 10 and over having: no formal education 22.9%; primary 52.8%; secondary 23.2%; higher 0.6%. *Literacy* (1985): total population age 15 and over literate 655,400 (73.6%); males literate 273,800 (62.4%); females literate 381,600 (84.5%).
Health (1987): physicians 103 (1 per 15,728 persons); hospital beds 2,409 (1 per 672 persons); infant mortality rate per 1,000 live births (1990–95) 89.
Food (1988–90): daily per capita caloric intake 2,121 (vegetable products 93%, animal products 7%); 93% of FAO recommended minimum requirement.

Military

Total active duty personnel (1992): 2,000[8]. *Military expenditure as percentage of GNP* (1987): 2.2% (world 5.4%); per capita expenditure U.S.$10.

[1]New constitution, effective April 1993, ended seven years of military rule. [2]Composed of chiefs and eight nominated members; total number not known. [3]Indirect taxes less imputed bank service charges. [4]Detail does not add to total given because of rounding. [5]Approximately 110,000 to 120,000 persons (45% of Lesotho's adult male labour force) were employed in South Africa in 1987. [6]Import figures are f.o.b. in balance of trade and c.i.f. in commodities and trading partners. [7]Lesotho Airways only. [8]Royal Lesotho Defence Force.

Liberia

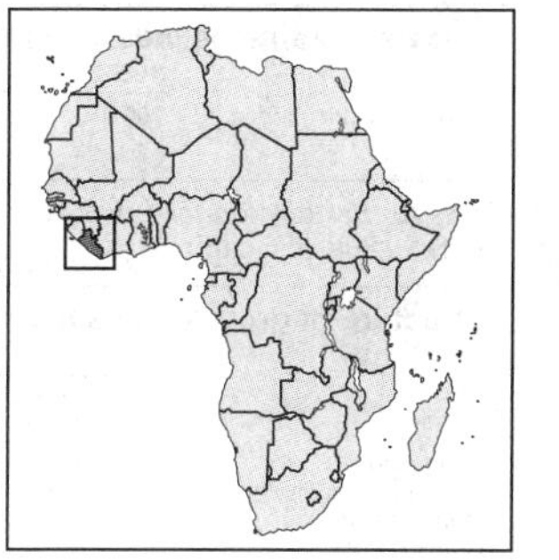

Official name: Republic of Liberia.
Form of government: transitional (UN-brokered) regime with one interim legislative house (Transitional Legislative Assembly [35])[1].
Head of state and government: President.
Capital: Monrovia.
Official language: English.
Official religion: none.
Monetary unit: 1 Liberian dollar (L$) = 100 cents; valuation (Oct. 4, 1993) 1 U.S.$ = L$1.00; 1 £ = L$1.52.

Area and population

Counties	Capitals	area sq mi	area sq km	population 1986 estimate
Bomi	Tubmanburg	755	1,955	67,300
Bong	Gbarnga	3,127	8,099	268,100
Grand Bassa	Buchanan	3,382	8,759	166,900
Grand Cape Mount	Robertsport	2,250	5,827	83,900
Grand Gedeh	Zwedru	6,575	17,029	109,000
Grand Kru[2]	Barclayville	[3]	[3]	[3]
Lofa	Voinjama	7,475	19,360	261,000
Margibi[4]	Kakata	1,260	3,263	104,000
Maryland	Harper	2,066[3]	5,351[3]	137,700[3]
Montserrado	Bensonville	1,058	2,740	582,400
Nimba	Sanniquellie	4,650	12,043	325,700
Rivercess	Rivercess City	1,693	4,385	39,900
Sinoe	Greenville	3,959	10,254	65,400
TOTAL		38,250	99,067[5]	2,221,300[6]

Demography

Population (1993): 2,844,000[7].
Density (1993): persons per sq mi 74.4, persons per sq km 28.7.
Urban-rural (1990): urban 45.9%; rural 54.1%.
Sex distribution (1990): male 50.60%; female 49.40%.
Age breakdown (1984): under 15, 43.2%; 15–29, 28.2%; 30–44, 14.7%; 45–59, 7.7%; 60–74, 4.4%; 75 and over, 1.8%.
Population projection: (2000) 3,565,000; (2010) 4,829,000.
Doubling time: 22 years.
Ethnic composition (1984): Kpelle 19.4%; Bassa 13.8%; Grebo 9.0%; Gio 7.8%; Kru 7.3%; Mano 7.1%; other 35.6%.
Religious affiliation (1984): Christian 67.7%; Muslim 13.8%[8]; traditional beliefs and other 18.5%.
Major cities (1974): Monrovia 421,058[9]; Buchanan 23,999; Congo Town 21,495; Yekepa 14,189; Tubmanburg 14,089.

Vital statistics

Birth rate per 1,000 population (1990–95): 46.7 (world avg. 26.4).
Death rate per 1,000 population (1990–95): 14.1 (world avg. 9.2).
Natural increase rate per 1,000 population (1990–95): 32.6 (world avg. 17.2).
Total fertility rate (avg. births per childbearing woman; 1990–95): 6.7.
Marriage rate per 1,000 population: n.a.
Divorce rate per 1,000 population: n.a.
Life expectancy at birth (1990–95): male 54.0 years; female 57.0 years.
Major causes of death per 100,000 population (1985)[10]: complications during pregnancy 632.6[9]; malaria 79.8; pneumonia 64.2; anemia 50.2; malnutrition 23.4; measles 12.7.

National economy

Budget (1993). Revenue: L$249,825,000 (1989; income and profits taxes 33.9%; import duties and consular fees 29.6%; excise tax 12.7%; property taxes 1.9%). Expenditures: L$273,930,000 (1988; current expenditure 91.1%, of which wages and salaries 34.1%, interest on public debt 13.1%, goods and services 7.8%, subsidies and grants 5.1%; development expenditure 8.9%).
Tourism: receipts from visitors (1986) U.S.$6,000,000; expenditures by nationals abroad, n.a.
Population economically active (1984): total 704,321; activity rate 33.5% (participation rates: ages 15–64, 56.3%; female 41.0%; unemployed 12.5%).

Price and earnings indexes (1985 = 100)

	1984	1985	1986	1987	1988	1989	1990[11]
Consumer price index	100.6	100.0	103.6	108.8	119.3	130.6	139.4
Earnings index	...	...	...	...	...	...	...

Production (metric tons except as noted). Agriculture, forestry, fishing (1992): cassava 300,000, sugarcane 225,000, rice 110,000, bananas 80,000, plantains 33,000, natural rubber 22,000, sweet potatoes 18,000, yams 15,000, oranges 7,000, pineapples 7,000, cacao beans 1,000; livestock (number of live animals) 220,000 sheep, 220,000 goats, 120,000 pigs, 38,000 cattle, 4,000,000 chickens; roundwood (1991) 6,134,000 cu m; fish catch (1991) 9,620. Mining and quarrying (1989): iron ore 7,007,000; diamonds 350,000 carats[12]; gold 23,600 troy oz. Manufacturing (1986): cement 96,350; palm oil 35,000; cigarettes 91,235,200 units; soft drinks 115,092 hectolitres; beer 105,547 hectolitres. Construction: n.a. Energy production (consumption): electricity (kW-hr; 1991) 450,000,000 (450,000,000); coal, none (n.a.); crude petroleum, none (n.a.); petroleum products (metric tons; 1991) none (90,000); natural gas, none (n.a.).
Public debt (external, outstanding; 1991): U.S.$1,127,000,000.

Household income and expenditure. Average household size (1983) 4.3; income per household: n.a.; sources of income: n.a.; expenditure (1963)[13]: food 34.4%, rent 14.9%, clothing and footwear 13.8%, household goods and services 6.1%, beverages and tobacco 5.7%, fuel and light 5.0%.
Gross national product (1988): U.S.$975,200,000 (U.S.$400 per capita).

Structure of gross domestic product and labour force

	1989 in value L$'000,000	1989 % of total value	1984 labour force	1984 % of labour force
Agriculture	410.7	34.4	481,177	68.3
Mining	122.3	10.2	17,500	2.5
Manufacturing	81.6	6.8	10,699	1.5
Construction	26.3	2.2	4,072	0.6
Public utilities	19.0	1.6	2,878	0.4
Transp. and commun.	79.1	6.6	13,986	2.0
Trade	63.3	5.3	46,850	6.6
Finance	141.8	11.9	2,117	0.3
Pub. admin., defense	139.4	11.7	61,168	8.7
Services	35.5	3.0		
Other	74.8[14]	6.3[14]	63,874[15]	9.1[15]
TOTAL	1,193.6[5]	100.0	704,321	100.0

Land use (1991): forested 17.8%; meadows and pastures 58.9%; agricultural and under permanent cultivation 3.9%; other 19.4%.

Foreign trade

Balance of trade (current prices)

	1983	1984	1985	1986	1987	1988
L$'000,000	+73.8	+137.6	+189.4	+184.1	+115.9	+160.6
% of total	9.4%	17.1%	27.8%	29.1%	17.9%	25.4%

Imports (1989): L$346,218,000 (1988; machinery and transport equipment 31.1%, petroleum and petroleum products 22.7%, basic manufactures 16.4%, food and live animals 16.4%, chemicals 5.8%). *Major import sources* (1986): United States 32.2%; West Germany 9.7%; Japan 8.4%; United Kingdom 7.6%; The Netherlands 6.3%; Spain 2.5%; Belgium-Luxembourg 2.5%.
Exports (1989): L$249,784,000 (1988; iron ore 55.1%, rubber 28.0%, logs and timber 8.4%, diamonds 2.1%, gold 1.8%, coffee 1.5%). *Major export destinations* (1986): West Germany 32.2%; United States 19.3%; Italy 15.7%; France 8.8%; Belgium-Luxembourg 5.8%; The Netherlands 4.4%; Spain 4.1%.

Transport and communications

Transport. Railroads (1990)[16]: route length 304 mi, 490 km; short ton-mi cargo 1,746,000,000[12, 17], metric ton-km cargo 2,549,000,000[12, 17]. Roads (1987): total length 5,011 mi, 8,064 km (paved 9%). Vehicles (1991): passenger cars 8,000; trucks and buses 4,000. Merchant marine (1992): vessels (100 gross tons and over) 1,672; total deadweight tonnage 97,373,965. Air transport (1980): passenger-mi 10,600,000, passenger-km 17,000,000; short ton-mi cargo 68,000, metric ton-km cargo 100,000; airports (1993) 1.
Communications. Daily newspapers (1990): total number 8; total circulation 35,000; circulation per 1,000 population 13.6. Radio (1992): 600,000 receivers (1 per 4.6 persons). Television (1992): 45,000 receivers (1 per 61 persons). Telephones (1988): 8,736 (1 per 278 persons).

Education and health

Education (1980)

	schools	teachers	students	student/ teacher ratio
Primary (age 6–12)	1,651	9,099	227,431	25.0
Secondary (age 13–18)	419	1,129	51,666	45.8
Voc., teacher tr.	6	63	2,322	36.9
Higher	3	472[18]	5,095[18]	10.8[18]

Educational attainment (1974). Percentage of population age 25 and over having: no grade completed 87.1%; some primary education 4.8%; complete primary 1.5%; some secondary 5.1%; higher 1.5%. *Literacy* (1990): total population age 15 and over literate 547,800 (39.5%); males literate 350,200 (49.8%); females literate 197,600 (28.8%).
Health: physicians (1983) 221 (1 per 9,324 persons); hospital beds (1981) 3,000 (1 per 653 persons); infant mortality rate (1985–90) 87.0.
Food (1988–90): daily per capita caloric intake 2,259 (vegetable products 96%, animal products 4%); 98% of FAO recommended minimum requirement.

Military

Total active duty personnel (1993): as a result of the civil war, the Armed Forces of Liberia (AFL) has ceased to exist. *Military expenditure as percentage of GNP* (1987): 3.8% (world 5.4%); per capita expenditure U.S.$17.

[1]Transitional government to be in place from August 1993 to February 1994. [2]New county created from Kru Coast and Sasstown territories and part of Maryland county. [3]Figures for Grand Kru included in Maryland. [4]New county created from Marshall and Gibi territories. [5]Detail does not add to total given because of rounding. [6]Includes 10,000 persons not accounted for. [7]Includes Liberian refugees residing in surrounding countries, estimated to number from 600,000 to more than 1,000,000. [8]Some external sources estimate the Muslim population to exceed 30%. [9]1984. [10]Hospital inpatient morbidity rates. [11]July 1. [12]1988. [13]Monrovia only. [14]Import duties less imputed bank service charges. [15]Includes 34,991 unemployed. [16]For iron-ore transport only. [17]Lamco and Bong Mining Company railroads only. [18]1987.

Libya

Official name: al-Jamāhīrīyah al-ʿArabīyah al-Lībīyah ash-Shaʿbīyah al-Ishtirākīyah (Socialist People's Libyan Arab Jamahiriya).
Form of government: socialist state with one policy-making body (General People's Congress [750]).
Chief of state: Muʿammar al-Qadhdhāfī (de facto)[1]; Secretary of General People's Congress (de jure).
Head of government: Secretary of the General People's Committee (prime minister).
Capital: Tripoli[2].
Official language: Arabic.
Official religion: Islam.
Monetary unit: 1 Libyan dinar (LD) = 1,000 dirhams; valuation (Oct. 4, 1993) 1 Libyan dinar = U.S.$3.45 = £2.22.

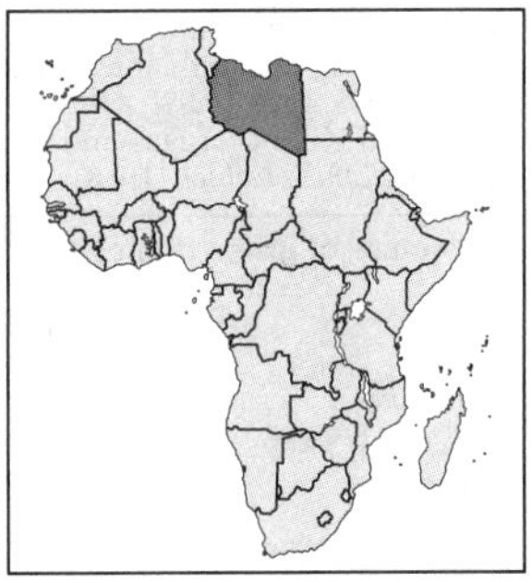

Area and population

Baladīyāt	Capitals	area sq mi	area sq km	population 1988 estimate
Banghāzī	Banghāzī	5,800	15,000	512,200
al-Jabal al-Akhḍar	al-Bayḍā'	14,300	37,000	308,300
al-Jabal al-Gharbī	Gharyān	33,600	87,000	204,300
Khalīj Surt	Surt	145,200	376,000	382,100
al-Kufrah	al-Kufrah	186,900	484,000	23,800
Margib	al-Khums	11,200	29,000	408,900
Marzūq	Marzūq	135,100	350,000	45,200
Nikāt al-Khums	Zuwārah	39,000	101,000	196,000
Sabhā	Sabhā	31,700	82,000	121,700
Ṭarābulus	Tripoli (Ṭarābulus)	1,200	3,000	1,083,100
Ṭubruq	Ṭubruq	32,400	84,000	110,900
Wādī al-Ḥa'iṭ	Awbārī	40,500	105,000	49,600
az-Zāwiyah	az-Zāwiyah	1,500	4,000	326,500
TOTAL		678,400	1,757,000	3,772,600

Demography

Population (1993): 4,573,000.
Density (1993): persons per sq mi 6.7, persons per sq km 2.6.
Urban-rural (1990): urban 82.4%; rural 17.6%.
Sex distribution (1990): male 52.41%; female 47.59%.
Age breakdown (1990): under 15, 45.8%; 15–29, 25.6%; 30–44, 15.6%; 45–59, 8.8%; 60–74, 3.5%; 75 and over, 0.6%.
Population projection: (2000) 5,559,000; (2010) 6,990,000.
Doubling time: 21 years.
Ethnic composition (1984): Libyan Arab and Berber 89.0%; other 11.0%.
Religious affiliation (1992): Sunnī Muslim 97.0%; other 3.0%.
Major cities (1988): Tripoli 591,100; Banghāzī 446,250; Miṣrātah 121,700; az-Zāwiyah 89,338.

Vital statistics

Birth rate per 1,000 population (1990–95): 41.9 (world avg. 26.4).
Death rate per 1,000 population (1990–95): 8.1 (world avg. 9.2).
Natural increase rate per 1,000 population (1990–95): 33.8 (world avg. 17.2).
Total fertility rate (avg. births per childbearing woman; 1990–95): 6.4.
Marriage rate per 1,000 population (1988): 4.5[3].
Divorce rate per 1,000 population (1988): 0.6[3].
Life expectancy at birth (1990–95): male 61.6 years; female 65.0 years.
Major causes of death per 100,000 population: n.a.; however, the major causes of death during the 1980s were pneumonia, dysentery and diarrhea, cardiovascular disease, accidents, and malignant neoplasms (cancers).

National economy

Budget (1990–91). Revenue: LD 2,640,000,000 (current revenue 55.7%, of which oil revenues 31.0%, income taxes 24.0%, customs duties 17.0%, stamp duties 4.2%; capital revenue 44.3%). Expenditures: LD 2,640,000,000 (current expenditures 55.7%, of which allocations to municipal people's committees 39.4%, education and scientific research 4.3%, health 2.7%; capital expenditures 44.3%, of which agriculture and land reclamation 13.6%, industry 5.3%).
Public debt (long-term debt; 1991): U.S.$3,500,000,000.
Production (metric tons except as noted). Agriculture, forestry, fishing (1992): watermelons 215,000, tomatoes 175,000, wheat 150,000, potatoes 150,000, barley 145,000, oranges 98,000, onions 86,000, dates 76,000, olives 72,000, almonds 34,500; livestock (number of live animals) 5,600,000 sheep, 1,250,000 goats, 155,000 camels, 135,000 cattle, 58,000,000 chickens; roundwood (1991) 645,000 cu m; fish catch (1991) 7,833. Mining and quarrying (1991): lime 260,000; gypsum 180,000; salt 12,000. Manufacturing (1990): cement 2,700,000; gasoline 2,100,000; naphtha 2,080,000; jet fuel 1,540,000; meat 118,000. Construction (gross value in LD; 1982): residential 127,051,000; nonresidential 200,877,000. Energy production (consumption): electricity (kW-hr; 1991) 19,500,000,000 (19,500,000,000); coal (metric tons; 1991) none (5,000); crude petroleum (barrels; 1991) 526,400,000 (110,000,000); petroleum products (metric tons; 1991) 12,967,000 (7,300,000); natural gas (cu m; 1991) 10,170,000,000 (8,360,000,000).
Population economically active (1987): total 1,005,000; activity rate of total population 25.0% (participation rates: ages 10 and over, 37.6%; female 6.9%; unemployed, n.a.).

Price and earnings indexes (1980 = 100)

	1980	1981	1982	1983	1984	1985	1986
Consumer price index	100.0	...	137.6	152.2	165.8	...	...
Earnings index	...	...	...	...	...	...	...

Gross domestic product (at current market prices; 1990): U.S.$28,900,000,000 (U.S.$6,800 per capita).

Structure of gross domestic product and labour force

	1989 in value LD '000,000	% of total value	labour force	% of labour force
Agriculture	395.5	5.5	191,600	19.2
Mining and quarrying	2,008.0	27.8	23,700	2.4
Manufacturing	560.5	7.8	92,200	9.3
Construction	920.0	12.7	156,300	15.7
Public utilities	152.5	2.1	28,500	2.9
Transportation and communications	440.0	6.1	78,500	7.9
Trade	490.5	6.8	52,800	5.3
Finance, insurance	622.0	8.6	15,000	1.5
Pub. admin., defense	1,543.5	21.4	308,000	31.0
Services	91.0	1.2	48,300	4.8
TOTAL	7,223.5	100.0	994,900	100.0

Household income and expenditure. Average household size (1980) 5.1; income per household: n.a.; sources of income: n.a.; expenditure (1977): food 37.2%, housing and energy 32.2%, transportation 9.4%, education and recreation 8.5%, clothing 6.9%, health care 3.3%.
Land use (1991): forested 0.4%; meadows and pastures 7.6%; agricultural and under permanent cultivation 1.2%; desert and built-up areas 90.8%.
Tourism (1990): receipts from visitors U.S.$6,000,000; expenditures by nationals abroad U.S.$424,000,000.

Foreign trade

Balance of trade (current prices)[4]

	1987	1988	1989	1990	1991	1992
U.S.$'000,000	+3,708	+2,633	+4,244	+5,212	+4,763	+4,447
% of total	29.9%	23.5%	32.5%	31.9%	28.8%	29.6%

Imports (1989): U.S.$5,497,000,000 (foodstuffs 42.3%, agricultural goods 18.5%, medical goods 12.4%, capital goods 12.4%). *Major import sources:* Italy 21.2%; West Germany 12.2%; United Kingdom 6.8%; France 6.2%.
Exports (1989): U.S.$7,750,000,000 (crude petroleum 96.8%). *Major export destinations:* Italy 57.8%; West Germany 26.6%; Spain 13.8%; France 8.3%; United Kingdom 3.0%.

Transport and communications

Transport. Railroads: none. Roads (1987): total length 11,992 mi, 19,300 km (paved 56%). Vehicles (1991): passenger cars 450,000; trucks and buses 330,000. Merchant marine (1992): vessels (100 gross tons and over) 150; total deadweight tonnage 1,223,589. Air transport (1992)[5]: passenger-mi 693,230,000, passenger-km 1,115,616,000; short ton-mi cargo 2,610,000, metric ton-km cargo 3,810,000; airports (1993) with scheduled flights 12.
Communications. Daily newspapers (1990): total number 1; circulation 40,000; circulation per 1,000 population 9.5. Radio (1992): total number of receivers 1,000,000 (1 per 4.4 persons). Television (1992): total number of receivers 500,000 (1 per 8.9 persons). Telephones (1988): 500,000 (1 per 8.0 persons).

Education and health

Education (1988–89)

	schools	teachers	students	student/ teacher ratio
Primary (age 6–12)	2,744[6]	77,424	1,193,637	15.4
Secondary (age 13–18)	1,555[6]	30,524[7]	389,530[8]	12.2[7]
Voc., teacher tr.	195[6]	3,051[7]	97,117	10.0[7]
Higher	10	...	47,300	...

Educational attainment (1973). Percentage of population age 25 and over having: no formal schooling (illiterate) 72.7%; incomplete primary education 18.8%; complete primary 3.5%; secondary 4.0%; higher 1.0%. *Literacy* (1990): percentage of total population age 15 and over literate 63.8%; males literate 75.4%; females literate 50.4%.
Health: physicians (1984) 5,272 (1 per 690 persons); hospital beds (1982) 16,051 (1 per 207 persons); infant mortality rate per 1,000 live births (1985–90) 82.0.
Food (1988–90): daily per capita caloric intake 3,293 (vegetable products 86%, animal products 14%); 140% of FAO recommended minimum requirement.

Military

Total active duty personnel (1993): 70,000 (army 57.2%, navy 11.4%, air force 31.4%). *Military expenditure as percentage of GNP* (1989): 14.9% (world 4.9%); per capita expenditure U.S.$808.

[1]No formal titled office exists. [2]Policy-making body (General People's Congress) meets in Surt. [3]Registered events; incomplete to some degree. [4]Dollar values based on IMF Direction of Trade Statistics (DOTS), which are compiled from available reports of trading partners (not the subject country's reports) and may, thus, be substantially incomplete. [5]Libyan Arab Airlines. [6]1982–83. [7]1984–85. [8]1987–88.

Liechtenstein

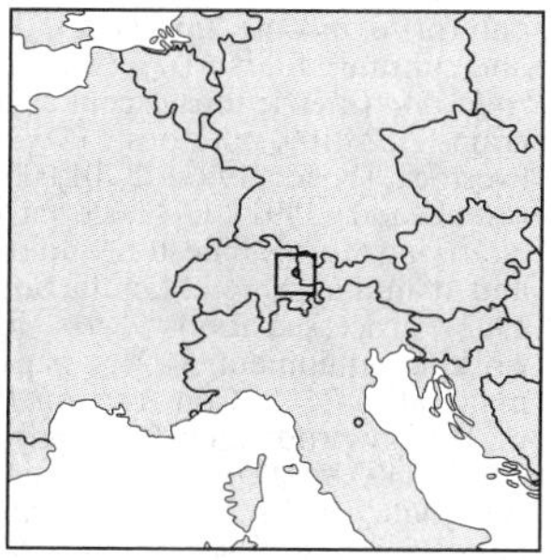

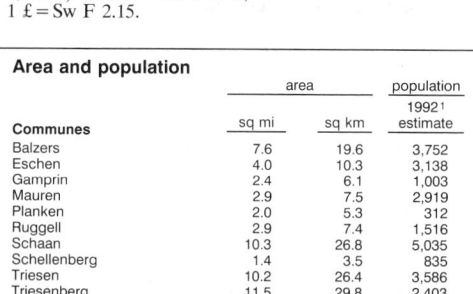

Official name: Fürstentum Liechtenstein (Principality of Liechtenstein).
Form of government: constitutional monarchy with one legislative house (Diet [25]).
Chief of state: Prince.
Head of government: Head of the Government.
Capital: Vaduz.
Official language: German.
Official religion: none.
Monetary unit: 1 Swiss franc (Sw F) = 100 centimes; valuation (Oct. 4, 1993) 1 U.S.$ = Sw F 1.42; 1 £ = Sw F 2.15.

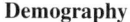

Area and population

Communes	area sq mi	area sq km	population 1992[1] estimate
Balzers	7.6	19.6	3,752
Eschen	4.0	10.3	3,138
Gamprin	2.4	6.1	1,003
Mauren	2.9	7.5	2,919
Planken	2.0	5.3	312
Ruggell	2.9	7.4	1,516
Schaan	10.3	26.8	5,035
Schellenberg	1.4	3.5	835
Triesen	10.2	26.4	3,586
Triesenberg	11.5	29.8	2,403
Vaduz	6.7	17.3	4,887
TOTAL	61.8[2]	160.0	29,386

Demography

Population (1993): 30,100.
Density (1993): persons per sq mi 487.1, persons per sq km 188.1.
Urban-rural: n.a.
Sex distribution (1992): male 48.92%; female 51.08%.
Age breakdown (1992): under 15, 19.4%; 15–29, 24.8%; 30–44, 25.4%; 45–59, 16.8%; 60–74, 9.5%; 75 and over, 4.1%.
Population projection: (2000) 33,300; (2010) 38,500.
Doubling time: 89 years.
National composition (1992): Liechtensteiner 62.5%; Swiss 15.6%; Austrian 7.6%; German 3.7%; other 10.6%.
Religious affiliation (1992): Roman Catholic 86.3%; Protestant 7.9%; other 5.8%.
Major cities (1990): Schaan 4,930; Vaduz 4,874.

Vital statistics

Birth rate per 1,000 population (1991): 14.2 (world avg. 26.4); legitimate 92.3%; illegitimate 7.7%.
Death rate per 1,000 population (1991): 6.4 (world avg. 9.2).
Natural increase rate per 1,000 population (1991): 7.8 (world avg. 17.2).
Total fertility rate: n.a.
Marriage rate per 1,000 population (1991): 6.3.
Divorce rate per 1,000 population (1991): 1.2.
Life expectancy at birth (1991): male 69.5 years; female 73.6 years.
Major causes of death per 100,000 population (1991): diseases of the circulatory system 277.9, of which heart disease 178.0 (including ischemic heart disease 102.7); malignant neoplasms (cancers) 154.1; diseases of the respiratory system 41.1; accidents, poisoning, and acts of violence 30.8 (including suicide 6.8).

National economy

Budget (1991). Revenue: Sw F 439,394,370 (taxes and interest 67.6%; post, telephone, and telegraph 15.7%; other revenue sources include real estate capital-gains taxes and death and estate taxes). Expenditures: Sw F 436,001,034 (financial affairs 40.9%; education 15.0%; post, telephone, and telegraph 12.4%; social affairs 11.6%).
Public debt: none.
Tourism (1992): 143,003 tourist arrivals; receipts from visitors, n.a.; expenditures by nationals abroad, n.a.
Population economically active (1991[3]): total 14,698; activity rate of total population 50.0% (participation rates: ages 15–64, 70.8%; female 37.8%; unemployed 0.1%).

Price and earnings indexes (December 1982 = 100)

	1986	1987	1988	1989	1990	1991	1992
Consumer price index[4]	108.2	109.7	111.8	115.4	121.6	128.7	133.7
Earnings index	...	...	...	...	...	...	...

Household income and expenditure. Average household size (1980) 3.0; income per household: n.a.; sources of earned income (1987): wages and salaries 92.9%, self-employment 7.1%; expenditure (1990)[5]: rent 20.9%, food 17.7%, transportation 11.0%, education and self-improvement 9.7%, clothing 7.0%, health 4.7%.
Production (metric tons except as noted). Agriculture, forestry, fishing (1991): silo corn (maize) 27,880[6], milk 13,146, potatoes 1,040[6], wheat 460[6], barley 416[6]; livestock (number of live animals) 6,204 cattle, 3,543 pigs, 2,689 sheep; commercial timber 10,333 cu m. Mining and quarrying: n.a. Manufacturing (1991): whipped cream 1,252; yogurt 77; cheese 6; wine 789.8 hectolitres; small-scale precision manufacturing includes optical lenses, electron microscopes, electronic equipment, and high-vacuum pumps; metal manufacturing, construction machinery, and ceramics are also important. Construction (1991): residential 256,930 cu m; nonresidential 271,094 cu m. Energy production (consumption): electricity (kW-hr; 1991) 153,777,000 (224,944,000); coal (metric tons; 1991) none (35); petroleum products (metric tons; 1991) none (56,505); natural gas (cu m; 1991) none (15,755,000).
Gross national product (at current market prices; 1991): *c.* U.S.$978,000,000 (U.S.$33,510 per capita).

Structure of gross domestic product and labour force

	1988 in value Sw F '000	1988 % of total value	1991 labour force	1991 % of labour force
Agriculture	...	...	346	2.4
Mining	...	...	57	0.4
Manufacturing	...	...	4,811	32.7
Construction	...	...	1,217	8.3
Public utilities	...	...	182	1.2
Transportation and communications	...	...	454	3.1
Trade	...	...	1,666	11.3
Finance, insurance, real estate	...	...	1,052	7.2
Pub. admin., defense	...	...	609	4.1
Services	...	...	4,195	28.5
Other	...	...	109[7]	0.7[7]
TOTAL	1,700,000	100.0	14,698	100.0[2]

Land use (latest): forested 34.8%; meadows and pastures 15.7%; agricultural and under permanent cultivation 24.3%; other 25.2%.

Foreign trade

Balance of trade (current prices)

	1986	1987	1988	1989	1990	1991
Sw F '000,000	+761.6	+737.6	+745.2	+742.8	+757.1	+822.8
% of total	44.4%	42.0%	37.3%	29.8%	27.8%	31.4%

Imports (1991): Sw F 898,280,000 (machinery and transport equipment 29.2%; limestone, cement, and other building materials 13.7%; metal products 10.8%; unrefined and semifabricated metal 6.1%; chemical products 6.0%; food, beverages, and tobacco 2.2%, of which fruits and vegetables 0.2%; wood and cork 1.1%). *Major import sources:* n.a.
Exports (1991): Sw F 1,721,100,000 (machinery and transport equipment 47.3%; metal products 18.0%; other finished goods 13.8%; chemical products 8.1%; limestone, cement, and other building materials 6.9%). *Major export destinations:* European Economic Community countries 45.4%; Switzerland 14.8%; other European Free Trade Association countries 5.5%.

Transport and communications

Transport. Railroads (1990): length 11.5 mi, 18.5 km; passenger and cargo traffic, n.a. Roads (1989): total length 201 mi, 323 km. Vehicles (1991): passenger cars 17,328; trucks and buses 1,748. Merchant marine: none. Air transport: none.
Communications. Daily newspapers (1991): total number 2; total circulation 17,195; circulation per 1,000 population 589. Radio (1991): total number of receivers 10,558 (1 per 2.8 persons). Television (1991): total number of receivers 10,099 (1 per 2.9 persons). Telephones (1991): 17,499 (1 per 1.7 persons).

Education and health

Education (1990–91)

	schools	teachers	students	student/ teacher ratio
Primary (age 7–12)	14	115	1,892	16.4
Secondary (age 13–19)	8	80	1,092	13.6
Vocational[8]	1	74[9]	147	...

Educational attainment (1980). Percentage of population age 25 and over having: no formal schooling 0.2%; primary and lower secondary education 47.6%; higher secondary and vocational 41.0%; some postsecondary 6.6%; university 4.6%. *Literacy:* virtually 100%.
Health: physicians (1991) 29 (1 per 1,007 persons); hospital beds (1985) 100 (1 per 269 persons); infant mortality rate per 1,000 live births (1985–89) 7.0.
Food (1987–89)[10]: daily per capita caloric intake 3,530 (vegetable products 62%, animal products 38%); 133% of FAO recommended minimum requirement.

Military

Total active duty personnel: none. *Military expenditure as percentage of GNP:* none.

[1]January 1. [2]Detail does not add to total given because of rounding. [3]December 31. [4]The index is for Switzerland, which is united with Liechtenstein in a customs and monetary union. [5]Household expenditures are taken from a 1986 Swiss sample survey; a similarity of consumption patterns is assumed. [6]1987. [7]Includes 80 unclassifiable and 29 unemployed persons. [8]1988–89. [9]Includes part-time teachers. [10]Figures are derived from statistics for Switzerland and Austria.

Lithuania

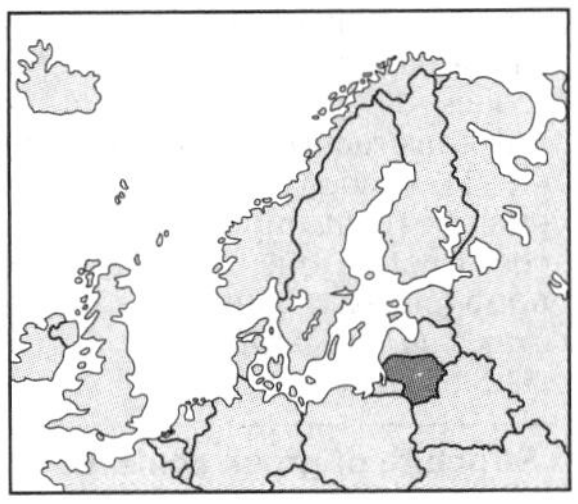

Official name: Lietuvos Respublika (Republic of Lithuania).
Form of government: unitary multiparty republic with a single legislative body, the Seimas (141).
Head of state: President[1].
Head of government: Prime Minister.
Capital: Vilnius.
Official language: Lithuanian.
Official religion: none.
Monetary unit[2]: 1 litas = 100 centai; valuation (Oct. 4, 1993) 1 U.S.$ = 4.23 litai; 1 £ = 6.41 litai.

Area and population

		area		population
Cities of republic jurisdiction		sq mi	sq km	1989 estimate
Alytus	—	1	3	73,100
Birštonas	—	5	12	4,100
Druskininkai	—	8	22	22,500
Kaunas	—	46	120	422,600
Klaipėda	—	27	71	204,000
Marijampolė	—	8	20	50,500
Neringa	—	35	90	2,500
Palanga	—	27	69	19,400
Panevėžys	—	12	30	126,500
Šiauliai	—	27	69	145,000
Vilnius	—	110	286	582,400
Regions	**Capitals**			
Akmenė	Naujoji Akmenė	407	1,055	37,800
Alytus	Alytus	545	1,411	32,700
Anykščiai	Anykščiai	681	1,765	38,300
Biržai	Biržai	570	1,476	38,600
Ignalina	Ignalina	581	1,505	59,000
Jonava	Jonava	364	944	54,000
Joniškis	Joniškis	445	1,152	32,900
Jurbarkas	Jurbarkas	582	1,507	40,200
Kaišiadorys	Kaišiadorys	451	1,169	40,200
Kaunas	Kaunas	588	1,522	85,500
Kėdainiai	Kėdainiai	647	1,677	69,400
Kelmė	Kelmė	660	1,710	42,900
Klaipėda	Gargždai	527	1,366	45,000
Kretinga	Kretinga	385	997	44,100
Kupiškis	Kupiškis	417	1,080	25,900
Lazdijai	Lazdijai	595	1,542	33,400
Marijampolė	Marijampolė	599	1,551	49,200
Mažeikiai	Mažeikiai	390	1,009	61,200
Molėtai	Molėtai	528	1,368	27,300
Pakruojis	Pakruojis	508	1,316	30,700
Panevėžys	Panevėžys	849	2,199	41,900
Pasvalys	Pasvalys	498	1,289	36,800
Plungė	Plungė	653	1,691	53,900
Prienai	Prienai	443	1,148	39,500
Radviliškis	Radviliškis	631	1,635	54,800
Raseiniai	Raseiniai	607	1,573	46,100
Rokiškis	Rokiškis	697	1,806	47,800
Šakiai	Šakiai	623	1,613	41,600
Šalčininkai	Šalčininkai	578	1,498	41,500
Šiauliai	Šiauliai	701	1,815	49,900
Šilalė	Šilalė	459	1,188	31,700
Šilutė	Šilutė	866	2,243	69,000
Širvintos	Širvintos	350	906	21,500
Skuodas	Skuodas	352	911	26,600
Švenčionys	Švenčionys	653	1,692	37,800
Tauragė	Tauragė	455	1,179	52,600
Telšiai	Telšiai	556	1,439	59,200
Trakai	Trakai	640	1,657	81,700
Ukmergė	Ukmergė	539	1,395	52,500
Utena	Utena	475	1,229	52,300
Varėna	Varėna	933	2,416	38,500
Vilkaviškis	Vilkaviškis	497	1,286	52,200
Vilnius	Vilnius	855	2,215	93,800
Zarasai	Zarasai	515	1,334	25,900
TOTAL		25,213[3]	65,301[3]	3,690,000

Demography

Population (1993): 3,798,000.
Density (1993): persons per sq mi 150.6, persons per sq km 58.2.
Urban-rural (1993): urban 68.5%; rural 31.5%.
Sex distribution (1993): male 47.33%; female 52.67%.
Age breakdown (1991): under 15, 22.6%; 15–29, 22.8%; 30–44, 20.9%; 45–59, 17.4%; 60–74, 11.5%; 75 and over, 4.8%.
Population projection: (2000) 3,946,000; (2010) 4,120,000.
Ethnic composition (1992): Lithuanian 79.6%; Russian 9.4%; Polish 7.0%; Belorussian 1.7%; other 2.3%.
Religious affiliation (1990): Roman Catholic, about 80%; Russian Orthodox, Old Believer, Evangelical Lutheran, and nonreligious minorities.
Major cities (1993): Vilnius 590,100; Kaunas 429,000; Klaipėda 206,400.

Vital statistics

Birth rate per 1,000 population (1992): 14.3 (world avg. 26.4).
Death rate per 1,000 population (1992): 11.0 (world avg. 9.2).
Natural increase rate per 1,000 population (1992): 3.3 (world avg. 17.2).
Life expectancy at birth (1991): male 65.3 years; female 76.1 years.
Major causes of death per 100,000 population (1992): circulatory diseases 594; cancers 196; accidents 139; respiratory diseases 41.

National economy

Budget (1992). Revenue: 53,722,300,000 rubles (social-security contributions 38.3%; taxes on goods and services 29.6%; individual income tax 13.4%; enterprise income tax 7.6%). Expenditures: 53,152,000,000 rubles (social and cultural affairs 67.7%; national economy 32.3%).
Production (metric tons except as noted). Agriculture, forestry, fishing (1992): grains 2,225,100, potatoes 1,079,200, sugar beets 621,500, vegetables 259,800; livestock (head; 1993) 1,701,000 cattle, 1,359,800 pigs, 8,258,900 poultry; roundwood (1991) 1,443,000 cu m; fish catch (1991) 317,000. Mining and quarrying (1986): limestone, dolomite, and clay are quarried for construction and manufacturing. Manufacturing (value of production, '000,000 rubles; 1992): processed foods 95,914; light industry 56,142; machinery and metal-working equipment 54,266; paper and pulp products 19,428; construction materials 17,411. Construction (1992): residential construction 872,000 sq m. Energy production (consumption): electricity (kW-hr; 1992) 18,707,000,000 (13,403,800,000); coal (terajoule; 1992) none (17,445); crude petroleum (terajoule; 1992) 2,724 (137); petroleum products (terajoule; 1992) none (106,317); natural gas (cu m; 1992) 4,093,000,000 (1,322,000,000).
Gross national product (1991): U.S.$10,220,000,000 (U.S.$2,710 per capita).

Structure of gross national product and labour force

	1991		1992	
	in value '000,000 rubles	% of total value	labour force[3]	% of labour force[4]
Agriculture, forestry	8,100.2	21.2	343,200	18.6
Manufacturing, mining	18,198.6	47.7	535,300	29.0
Construction	1,861.3	4.9	169,400	9.2
Transp. and commun.	2,014.3	5.3	124,000	6.7
Trade	3,634.5	9.5	227,400	12.3
Finance, pub. admin., defense }	5,309.7	13.9	40,000	2.2
Services, public utilities }			344,700	18.6
Other	−932.0	−2.5	64,400	3.5
TOTAL	38,186.6	100.0	1,848,400	100.0[5]

Population economically active (1992): total 2,126,400; activity rate of total population 56.5% (participation rates: ages 16–60/55[6], 88.2%; female 48.4%; unemployed 20.7%).

Price and earnings indexes (1985 = 100)

	1986	1987	1988	1989	1990	1991	1992
Consumer price index[7]	...	...	...	...	100.0	316.0	3,546.0
Monthly earnings index	102.6	107.4	117.4	128.4	149.2	387.9	2,995.3

Household income and expenditure (1992). Avg. household size (1989) 3.2; sources of income: wages 66.4%, pensions and grants 18.7%, self-employment in agriculture 9.7%, other 5.2%; expenditures: food 50.3%, nonfood goods 23.2%, taxes 9.6%, services 8.4%, agricultural expenses 4.2%.
Land use (1990): forest 28%; pasture 17%; agricultural 35%; other 20%.

Foreign trade

Imports (1992): 77,142,800,000 rubles (from Commonwealth of Independent States [CIS]: petroleum and gas 48.9%, machinery 13.3%, chemicals 9.8%, light industry 6.0%, coal 4.6%). *Major import sources:* CIS-member countries 78.8%, of which Russia 57.7%, Ukraine 7.7%, Belarus 5.8%; Germany 4.7%.
Exports (1992): 107,754,400,000 rubles (to CIS: machinery 29.2%, light industry 20.9%, food products 13.5%). *Major export destinations:* CIS countries 65.4%, of which Russia 31.8%, Ukraine 14.5%; Germany 4.6%.

Transport and communications

Transport. Railroads (1992): length 2,996 km; passenger-km 2,740,000,000; metric ton-km cargo 11,337,000,000. Roads (1991): total length 44,500 km (paved 80%). Vehicles (1992): passenger cars 565,320; trucks and buses 92,056. Merchant marine (1992): vessels (100 gross tons and over) 52; total deadweight tonnage 373,911. Air transport (1992): passenger-km 917,000,000; metric ton-km cargo 5,253,000; airports (1993) 1.
Communications. Daily newspapers (1983): 12; circulation (1990) all newspapers 5,780,000; circulation per 1,000 population 1,547. Radio (1992): 1,420,000 receivers (1 per 2.7 persons). Television (1992): 1,400,000 receivers (1 per 2.7 persons). Telephones (1992): 886,300 (1 per 4.3 persons).

Education and health

Education (1992–93)

	schools	teachers	students	student/ teacher ratio
Primary and secondary	2,219	43,900	512,400	11.7
Voc., teacher tr.	104	4,638	42,000	9.1
Higher	17	9,003[7]	55,000	7.3[8]

Educational attainment (1979). Percentage of persons having: incomplete primary 12.5%; complete primary 31.7%; incomplete secondary 23.1%; complete secondary 25.0%; higher 7.7%. *Literacy:* n.a.
Health (1992): physicians 13,764 (1 per 274 persons); hospital beds 44,500 (1 per 85 persons); infant mortality rate 16.5.

Military

Total active duty personnel (1993): 9,800 (army 94.9%, navy 2.5%, air force 2.6%). Russia withdrew its last soldiers in August 1993.

[1]The constitution adopted by referendum on Oct. 25, 1992, provided for a presidential form of government. [2]The talonas was introduced on May 1, 1992, to circulate in parallel, and valued at par, with the Russian ruble. Lithuania left the ruble area on Oct. 1, 1992, when the talonas was made the sole legal tender and was allowed to float. On June 25, 1993, the talonas was replaced by the litas at a fixed conversion rate of 100 talonai per 1 litas. The litas was established as the sole official currency as of July 20, 1993. [3]Total includes 12 sq mi (30 sq km) not distributed by administrative subdivision. [4]State sector only. [5]Detail does not add to total given because of rounding. [6]Males retire at age 60, females at 55. [7]1990 = 100. [8]1987–88.

Luxembourg

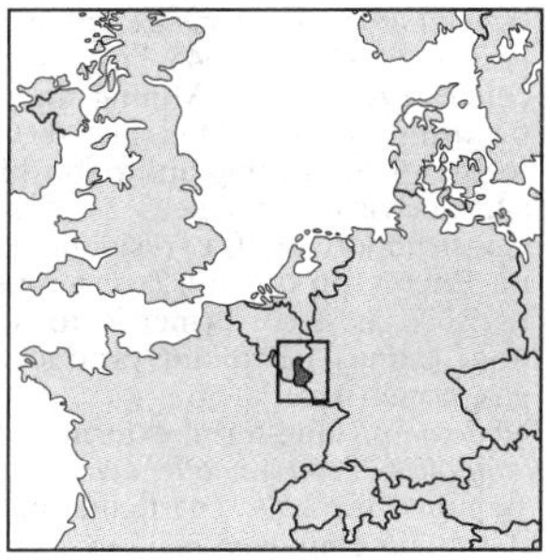

Official name: Groussherzogtum Lëtzebuerg (Luxemburgian); Grand-Duché de Luxembourg (French); Grossherzogtum Luxemburg (German) (Grand Duchy of Luxembourg).
Form of government: constitutional monarchy with two legislative houses (Council of State [21]; Chamber of Deputies [60]).
Chief of state: Grand Duke.
Head of government: Prime Minister.
Capital: Luxembourg.
Official language: none. Luxemburgian (national); French (used for most official purposes); German (lingua franca).
Official religion: none.
Monetary unit: 1 Luxembourg franc (Lux F) = 100 centimes; valuation (Oct. 4, 1993) 1 U.S.$ = Lux F 35.15; 1 £ = Lux F 53.25.

Area and population	area		population
Districts / Cantons	sq mi	sq km	1991 census
Diekirch	447	1,157	56,896
Clervaux	128	332	10,263
Diekirch	92	239	23,258
Redange	103	267	11,073
Vianden	21	54	2,720
Wiltz	102	265	9,582
Grevenmacher	203	525	42,837
Echternach	72	186	11,726
Grevenmacher	82	211	18,113
Remich	49	128	12,998
Luxembourg	349	904	284,329
Capellen	77	199	31,817
Esch	94	243	116,389
Luxembourg (Ville et Campagne)	92	238	116,988
Mersch	86	224	19,135
TOTAL	999	2,586	384,062

Demography

Population (1993): 392,000.
Density (1993): persons per sq mi 392.4, persons per sq km 151.6.
Urban-rural (1991): urban 85.9%; rural 14.1%.
Sex distribution (1992): male 49.08%; female 50.92%.
Age breakdown (1989): under 15, 17.1%; 15–29, 22.3%; 30–44, 23.3%; 45–59, 18.5%; 60–74, 12.8%; 75 and over, 6.0%.
Population projection: (2000) 403,000; (2010) 412,000.
Doubling time: not applicable; population stable.
Ethnic composition (nationality; 1992): Luxemburger 70.6%; Portuguese 10.4%; Italian 5.1%; French 3.4%; Belgian 2.5%; German 2.3%; other 5.7%.
Religious affiliation (1989): Roman Catholic 94.6%; Protestant 1.1%; other 4.3%.
Major cities (1991): Luxembourg 75,377; Esch-sur-Alzette 24,012; Dudelange 14,677; Differdange 8,489; Schifflange 6,859.

Vital statistics

Birth rate per 1,000 population (1991): 12.9 (world avg. 26.4); legitimate 87.8%; illegitimate 12.2%.
Death rate per 1,000 population (1991): 9.7 (world avg. 9.2).
Natural increase rate per 1,000 population (1991): 3.2 (world avg. 17.2).
Total fertility rate (avg. births per childbearing woman; 1991): 1.6.
Marriage rate per 1,000 population (1991): 6.7.
Divorce rate per 1,000 population (1991): 2.0.
Life expectancy at birth (1985–87): male 70.6 years; female 77.9 years.
Major causes of death per 100,000 population (1991): circulatory diseases 437.6, of which cerebrovascular disease 177.2, ischemic heart disease and myocardial infarction 123.5; malignant neoplasms (cancers) 248.8; accidents and suicide 72.6, of which suicide 19.9.

National economy

Budget (1993). Revenue: Lux F 124,604,800,000 (income and excise taxes 56.5%, customs taxes 15.4%). Expenditures: Lux F 126,236,600,000 (social security 20.6%, education 12.9%, transportation 9.2%, administration 8.0%, defense 2.7%, debt service 1.8%).
Public debt (1990): U.S.$348,000,000.
Production (metric tons except as noted). Agriculture, forestry, fishing (1991): barley 65,000, wheat 39,500, potatoes 19,200, oats 17,200, wine grapes 8,600; livestock (number of live animals; 1991) 219,544 cattle, 66,592 pigs; roundwood (1989) 326,715 cu m. Mining and quarrying (1987): metal ores, none; sand and gravel 956,810; gypsum 420,000; crushed stone 344,841. Manufacturing (1991): steel ingots and castings 3,363,000; pig iron 2,463,000; milk 262,300; meat products 25,300; wine 151,100 hectolitres. Construction (1990): residential and semiresidential 490,958 sq m; nonresidential 171,530 sq m. Energy production (consumption): electricity (kW-hr; 1990) 1,374,000,000 (5,242,000,000); coal (metric tons; 1990) none (197,000); crude petroleum, none (n.a.); petroleum products (metric tons; 1990) none (1,462,000); natural gas (cu m; 1990) none (461,286,000).

Gross national product (at current market prices; 1991): U.S.$11,761,000,000 (U.S.$31,080 per capita).

Structure of gross domestic product and labour force

	1991			
	in value Lux F '000,000	% of total value	labour force	% of labour force
Agriculture	4,477	1.4	5,631	3.4
Mining	997	0.3	34	0.1
Manufacturing	77,303	24.3	29,711	18.0
Construction	23,905	7.5	15,347	9.3
Public utilities	5,264	1.6	1,876	1.1
Transp. and commun.	22,139	6.9	11,319	6.9
Trade	52,285	16.4	32,462	19.7
Finance	44,236	13.9	21,137	12.8
Pub. admin., defense	46,800	14.7	44,756	27.2
Services	48,656	15.3		
Other	−7,258[1]	−2.3[1]	2,441	1.5
TOTAL	318,804	100.0	164,713[2]	100.0

Population economically active (1991): total 164,713; activity rate of total population 42.8% (participation rates: ages 15–64, 61.6%; female 35.9%; unemployed 1.5%).

Price and earnings indexes (1985 = 100)

	1986	1987	1988	1989	1990	1991	1992
Consumer price index	100.3	100.2	101.7	105.1	109.0	112.4	115.9
Hourly earnings index	106.0	106.5	108.9	114.7	118.4	...	...

Household income and expenditure. Average household size (1991) 2.6; income per household (1982) Lux F 751,800 (U.S.$16,455); sources of income (1987): wages and salaries 88.6%, self-employment 9.1%, transfer payments 2.3%; expenditure (1990): transportation and communications 17.9%, food and beverages 14.2%, housing 14.1%, household goods and furniture 10.3%, health 7.6%, clothing and footwear 6.4%.
Tourism (1989): receipts from visitors U.S.$286,000,000.
Land use (1988): forested 34.3%; meadows and pastures 27.3%; agricultural and under permanent cultivation 21.5%; other 16.9%.

Foreign trade

Balance of trade (current prices)

	1986	1987	1988	1989	1990	1991
Lux F '000,000	−13,390	−24,530	−20,549	−31,200	−40,200	−62,800
% of total	3.9%	7.0%	5.2%	6.8%	8.7%	13.4%

Imports (1991): Lux F 277,110,000,000 (metal products, machinery, and transport equipment 48.7%, of which transport equipment 14.2%; mineral products 11.9%; chemical products 7.8%; food and beverages 4.5%). *Major import sources:* Belgium 39.2%; Germany 30.0%; France 11.9%; The Netherlands 4.1%; Italy 2.1%; U.S. 2.0%.
Exports (1991): Lux F 214,353,000,000 (metal products, machinery, and transport equipment 56.9%, of which transport equipment 7.5%; plastic materials and rubber manufactures 12.6%; textile yarn, fabrics, and related products 6.0%; chemical products 5.0%; food, beverages, and tobacco 3.6%). *Major export destinations:* Germany 29.6%; France 17.3%; Belgium 17.1%; The Netherlands 5.1%; U.K. 5.1%; Italy 4.4%; U.S. 3.3%.

Transport and communications

Transport. Railroads (1991): route length 168 mi, 271 km; passenger-mi 175,000,000, passenger-km 282,000,000; short ton-mi cargo 488,000,000, metric ton-km cargo 713,000,000. Roads (1991): total length 3,163 mi, 5,091 km (paved 99%). Vehicles (1992): passenger cars 200,739; trucks and buses 20,367. Merchant marine (1992): vessels (100 gross tons and over) 54; total deadweight tonnage 2,603,611. Air transport (1990): passenger arrivals 484,278, departures 489,000; short ton-mi cargo 606,902,000[3], metric ton-km cargo 886,062,000[3]; airports (1993) with scheduled flights 1.
Communications. Daily newspapers (1992): total number 5; total circulation 149,000; circulation per 1,000 population 382. Radio (1992): 230,000 receivers (1 per 1.7 persons). Television (1992): 100,500 receivers (1 per 3.9 persons). Telephones (1991): 191,760 (1 per 2.0 persons).

Education and health

Education (1990–91)

	schools	teachers	students	student/teacher ratio
Primary (age 6–11)[4]	...	1,740	26,612	15.3
Secondary (age 12–18)	...	1,922	7,594	...
Voc., teacher tr.	...		11,430	...
Higher	...		4,957	...

Educational attainment: n.a. *Literacy* (1990): virtually 100% literate.
Health (1991): physicians 780 (1 per 496 persons); hospital beds 4,438 (1 per 87 persons); infant mortality rate per 1,000 live births 9.2.
Food (1988–90): daily per capita caloric intake 3,925 (vegetable products 60%, animal products 40%); 149% of FAO recommended minimum.

Military

Total active duty personnel (1992): 800 (army 100.0%). *Military expenditure as percentage of GNP* (1988): 1.0% (world 5.0%); per capita expenditure U.S.$235.

[1]Imputed bank service charges. [2]Detail does not add to total given because of rounding. [3]1987. [4]Public schools only.

Macau

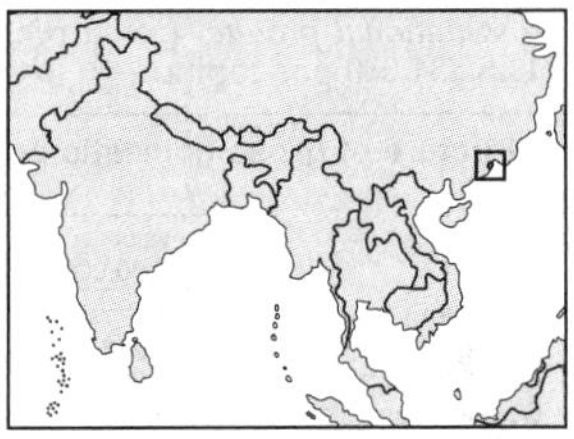

Official name: Ao-men (Chinese); Macau (Portuguese).
Political status: special territory[1] (Portugal) with one legislative house (Legislative Assembly [23[2]]).
Head of state and government: Governor.
Capital: Macau.
Official languages[1]: Chinese (Cantonese); Portuguese.
Official religion: Roman Catholicism.
Monetary unit: 1 pataca[3] (MOP) = 100 avos; valuation (Oct. 4, 1993) 1 U.S.$ = MOP 7.93; 1 £ = MOP 12.02.

Area and population

		area		population
Districts	Capital	sq mi	sq km	1991 census
Parishes				
Islands		4.4	11.3	10,148
Nossa Senhora Carmo (Taipa)	—	1.6	4.1	7,037
São Francisco Xavier (Coloane)	—	2.8	7.2	3,111
Macau	Macau	2.6[4]	6.7	326,460
Nossa Senhora Fátima	—	1.0	2.7	120,445
Santo António	—	0.4	1.1	103,712
São Lázaro	—	0.2	0.6	30,813
São Lourenço	—	0.4	0.9	43,746
Sé	—	0.5	1.4	27,744
Marine Area	—	—	—	2,856
TOTAL		6.9[4]	18.0	339,464

Demography

Population (1993): 378,000.
Density (1993): persons per sq mi 54,783, persons per sq km 21,000.
Urban-rural (1991): urban, virtually 100%[5].
Sex distribution (1991): male 48.49%; female 51.51%.
Age breakdown (1991): under 15, 24.6%; 15–29, 26.9%; 30–44, 29.4%; 45–59, 9.5%; 60–74, 7.3%; 75 and over, 2.3%.
Population projection: (2000) 493,000; (2010) 713,000.
Doubling time: 58 years.
Nationality (1991): Chinese 68.2%; Portuguese 27.9%; English 1.8%; other 2.1%.
Religious affiliation (1981): Buddhist 45.1%; Christian 8.7%, of which Roman Catholic 7.4%, Protestant 1.3%; nonreligious 45.8%; other 0.4%.
Major city (1991): Macau 326,460.

Vital statistics

Birth rate per 1,000 population (1991): 19.5 (world avg. 26.4); legitimate, n.a.; illegitimate, n.a.
Death rate per 1,000 population (1991): 3.8 (world avg. 9.2).
Natural increase rate per 1,000 population (1991): 15.7 (world avg. 17.2).
Total fertility rate (avg. births per childbearing woman; 1988): 1.5.
Marriage rate per 1,000 population (1991): 5.7.
Divorce rate per 1,000 population (1991): 0.5.
Life expectancy at birth (1988): male 75.1 years; female 80.3 years.
Major causes of death per 100,000 population (1991): diseases of the circulatory system 140.9; malignant neoplasms (cancers) 76.1; diseases of the respiratory system 52.6; accidents, poisoning, and violence 27.2; diseases of the digestive system 18.4; diseases of the genitourinary system 11.3; obstetric and perinatal disorders 8.5; infectious and parasitic diseases 7.9; endocrine and metabolic disorders 5.7.

National economy

Budget (1991). Revenue: 5,777,667,000 patacas (recurrent receipts 78.9%, autonomous agency receipts 13.9%, capital receipts 5.5%). Expenditures: 5,777,667,000 patacas (recurrent payments 56.7%, capital payments 29.4%, autonomous agency expenditures 13.9%).
Tourism (1991): number of tourist arrivals 6,080,268.
Land use (1992): built-on area, wasteland, and other 100.0%.
Gross domestic product (at current market prices; 1991): U.S.$4,158,000,000 (U.S.$11,880 per capita).

Structure of labour force

	1990	
	labour force	% of labour force
Agriculture	...	...
Mining	...	...
Manufacturing	72,050	32.6
Construction	19,330	8.7
Public utilities	2,538	1.1
Transportation and communications	10,349	4.7
Trade	47,708	21.6
Finance	7,550	3.4
Public administration	...	...
Services	...	...
Other	61,701	27.9
TOTAL	221,226	100.0

Production (metric tons except as noted). Agriculture, forestry, fishing (1991): grapes 3,000, eggs 645; livestock (number of live animals) 1,000 pigs; fish catch (1990) 2,530. Mining and quarrying (1982): granite 656,920. Manufacturing (value added in '000,000 patacas; 1990): wearing apparel 1,852; textiles 736; printing and publishing 73; leather products 68; metal products 64; electrical appliances 57; furniture and fixtures 40; food products 40. Construction (1991): residential 885,536 sq m; nonresidential 374,514 sq m. Energy production (consumption): electricity (kW-hr; 1990) 790,000,000 (879,000,000); coal (metric tons) none (none); crude petroleum (barrels) none (none); petroleum products (metric tons; 1990) none (335,000); natural gas, none (n.a.).
Public debt (long-term, external; 1988): U.S.$190,000,000.
Population economically active (1990): total 221,226; activity rate of total population 64.9% (participation rates [1981]: over age 10, 61.5%; female 37.1%; unemployed 3.9%).

Price and earnings indexes (1985 = 100)

	1985	1986	1987	1988	1989	1990	1991
Consumer price index[6]	100.0	102.0	106.7	115.1	125.1	135.1	147.9
Earnings index	...	...	...	...	...	...	...

Household income and expenditure. Average household size (1980) 4.8; income per household: n.a.; sources of income: n.a.; expenditure (1982–83): food 42.0%, housing 22.8%, education, health, and other services 8.1%, clothing and footwear 7.3%, transportation 4.9%, energy 4.9%, household durable goods 2.9%.

Foreign trade[7]

Balance of trade (current prices)

	1986	1987	1988	1989	1990	1991
'000,000 patacas	+1,312	+2,216.4	+1,632.0	+1,314.7	+1,295.1	−1,506.4
% of total	8.2%	10.9%	7.2%	5.2%	5.0%	5.3%

Imports (1991): 14,832,422,000 patacas (raw materials 52.9%, capital goods 16.3%, foodstuffs 8.8%, fuels and lubricants 4.4%). *Major import sources:* Hong Kong 34.8%; China 21.5%; Japan 17.4%; European Economic Community 8.1%; Taiwan 6.1%; United States 4.6%.
Exports (1991): 13,326,068,000 patacas (textiles and garments 69.5%, toys 5.8%, hides and skins 2.5%, radio and television equipment 2.4%, machinery and mechanical appliances 2.4%). *Major export destinations:* European Economic Community 38.2%; United States 31.7%; Hong Kong 13.1%; China 8.4%; Japan 1.6%; Australia 0.8%.

Transport and communications

Transport. Railroads: none. Roads (1988): total length 60 mi, 97 km (paved 100%). Vehicles (1991): passenger cars 27,223; trucks and buses 5,560. Merchant marine (1990): vessels 6; total gross tonnage 3,512. Air transport: none.
Communications. Daily newspapers (1990): total number 8; total circulation 240,000; circulation per 1,000 population 704. Radio (1991): total number of receivers 250,000 (1 per 1.9 persons). Television (1991): total number of receivers 70,000 (1 per 6.8 persons). Telephones (1991): 113,281 (1 per 3.1 persons).

Education and health

Education (1990–91)

	schools	teachers	students	student/ teacher ratio
Primary (age 6–11)	69	1,088	34,972	32.1
Secondary (age 12–18)	21	913	17,601	19.3
Teacher tr.	2	30	388	12.9
Higher	9	478	7,037	14.7

Educational attainment (1981). Percentage of economically active population age 10 and over having: no formal schooling 13.8%; primary education 22.6%; some secondary 27.2%; complete secondary 20.5%; some post-secondary 13.0%; higher 2.9%. *Literacy* (1981): total population age 10 and over literate 127,359 (61.3%); males literate 80,102 (76.4%); females literate 47,257 (46.2%).
Health (1991): physicians 311 (1 per 1,137 persons); hospital beds 1,155 (1 per 306 persons); infant mortality rate per 1,000 live births 7.5.
Food (1988–90): daily per capita caloric intake 2,294 (vegetable products 76%, animal products 24%); 100% of FAO recommended minimum requirement.

Military

Total active duty personnel (1990): the Portuguese garrison has been replaced by a paramilitary force of 1,800 men drawn from the Chinese residents only.

[1]An Organic Law (constitution), effective May 10, 1990, made Chinese co-official (with Portuguese) and changed the territory's status to special territory. [2]Enlarged to 23 seats by 1990 Organic Law from previous 17 seats. [3]The pataca free-floats with the Hong Kong dollar and has a parity of 1.03 patacas = HK$1.00. [4]Detail does not add to total given because of rounding. [5]0.8% of Macau's population live on sampans and other vessels. [6]Excluding rent. [7]Import figures are c.i.f.

Macedonia

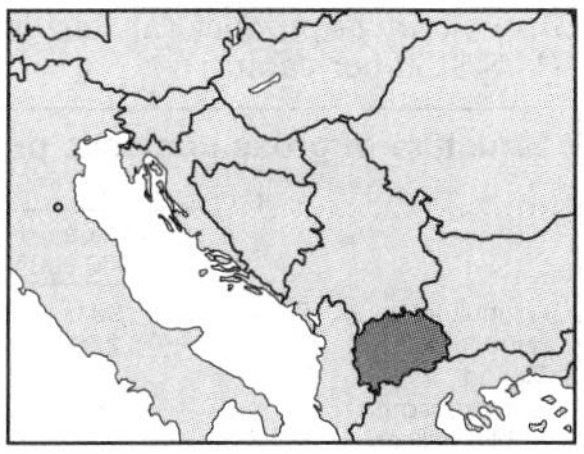

Official name[1]: Republika Makedonija (Republic of Macedonia).
Form of government: unitary multiparty republic with a unicameral legislature (Assembly [120]).
Head of state: President.
Head of government: Prime Minister.
Capital: Skopje.
Official language: Macedonian.
Official religion: none.
Monetary unit[2]: denar; valuation (Oct. 4, 1993) 1 U.S.$ = denar 27.00; 1 £ = denar 41.04.

Area and population (1991 census)

Districts	area sq km[3]	population	Districts	area sq km[3]	population
Berovo	806	20,395	Negotino	734	23,246
Bitolj	1,798	122,173	Ohrid	1,069	65,531
Brod	924	11,671	Prilep	1,675	98,327
Debar	274	26,266	Probištip	326	16,556
Delčevo	589	25,531	Radoviš	735	30,975
Demir Hisar	443	12,078	Resen	739	23,203
Gevgelija	757	35,055	Şkopje	1,818	563,301
Gostivar	1,341	116,107	Štip	815	51,947
Kavadarci	1,132	41,852	Struga	507	62,950
Kičevo	854	55,157	Strumica	952	94,517
Kočani	570	50,122	Sveti Nikole	649	21,569
Kratovo	376	11,329	Tetovo	1,080	180,654
Kriva Palanka	720	25,601	Titov Veles	1,536	67,535
Kruševo	239	12,620	Valandovo	331	12,264
Kumanovo	1,212	135,529	Vinica	432	19,903
			TOTAL	25,713[4]	2,033,964

Demography

Population (1993): 2,063,000.
Density (1993): persons per sq mi 207.8, persons per sq km 80.2.
Urban-rural (1981): urban 53.9%; rural 46.1%.
Sex distribution (1981): male 50.71%; female 49.29%.
Age breakdown (1981): under 15, 29.1%; 15–29, 27.1%; 30–44, 19.6%; 45–59, 14.8%; 60–74, 7.1%; 75 and over, 2.3%.
Population projection: (2000) 2,157,000; (2010) 2,298,000.
Doubling time: 70 years.
Ethnic composition (1991): Macedonian 64.6%; Albanian 21.0%; Turkish 4.8%; Romanian 2.7%; Serb 2.2%; other 4.7%.
Religious affiliation (1991): most believers are Christians, predominantly of the Eastern Orthodox Church; other Christians include members of the Macedonian Orthodox Church and the Roman Catholic Church; there is also a substantial Islamic and a small Jewish community.
Major cities (1991)[5]: Skopje 563,301 (408,143[6]); Tetovo 180,654 (46,523[6]); Kumanovo 135,529 (60,842[6]); Bitolj (Bitola) 122,173 (78,507[6]).

Vital statistics

Birth rate per 1,000 population (1990): 16.9 (world avg. 27.1).
Death rate per 1,000 population (1990): 7.0 (world avg. 9.8).
Natural increase rate per 1,000 population (1990): 9.9 (world avg. 17.3).
Total fertility rate (avg. births per childbearing woman): n.a.
Marriage rate per 1,000 population (1989): 7.9.
Divorce rate per 1,000 population (1989): 0.5.
Life expectancy at birth (1980–82): male 68.0 years; female 72.0 years.
Major causes of death per 100,000 population (1989): diseases of the circulatory system 346.2; malignant neoplasms (cancers) 102.4; diseases of the respiratory system 49.8; accidents, violence, and poisoning 34.5; diseases of the digestive system 18.2.

National economy

Budget. Revenue: n.a. Expenditures: n.a.
External debt: U.S.$850,000,000.
Production (metric tons except as noted). Agriculture, forestry, fishing (1992): wheat 200,000, grapes 191,000, corn (maize) 95,000, potatoes 66,000, plums 19,000; livestock (number of live animals) 2,250,000 sheep, 282,000 cattle, 171,000 pigs, 5,000,000 poultry; roundwood (1990) 1,063,000 cu m; fish catch (1990) 1,572 (all freshwater). Mining and quarrying (1990): copper ore 3,706,000; lead-zinc ore 1,357,000; kaolin and dolomite 467,000; gypsum 54,000; lime 47,000; iron ore 44,000; refined silver 15,000; sand and gravel 194,000 cu m. Manufacturing (1990): rolled zinc products 6,907,000; hot rolled iron slabs 619,000; steel plates 507,000; crude steel 247,000; fermented tobacco 26,481; hydrochloric acid 24,000; refined lead 22,000; soap and detergents 21,000; refined zinc 17,000; cotton yarn 15,000; household ceramics 8,872; husked rice 8,715; fancy candies 7,392; aluminum ingots 5,500; zinc alloys 5,000; woolen yarn 5,000; chocolate products 2,903; glues 2,700; cosmetics 2,225; knitted underwear 2,075; knitted outerwear 2,034; cheese 1,149; rubber goods 348; cocoa powder 41; cotton fabric 40,000,000 sq m; ready-made underwear 30,000,000 sq m; ready-made outerwear 20,000,000 sq m; woolen fabric 9,000,000 sq m; silk fabric 5,900,000 sq m; upper shoe leather 2,259,000 sq m; domestic animal fur 851,000 sq m; carpets 555,000 sq m; leather outerwear 446,000 sq m; wine 634,000 hectolitres; brandy 39,000 hectolitres; leather footwear 6,638,000 pairs; silver and gold jewelry 994 kg; refrigerators 156,000 units; toys 85,000 units; buses 953 units. Construction (residential units constructed; 1990): 10,189. Energy production (consumption): electricity (kW-hr; 1990) 5,755,000,000 (5,369,000,000); coal (metric tons; 1990) 6,635,000 (n.a.); crude petroleum, none (n.a.); petroleum products (metric tons; 1990) 1,472,500 (n.a.); natural gas, none (n.a.).

Gross national product (1992): U.S.$3,715,000,000 (U.S.$1,812 per capita).

Structure of gross domestic product and labour force

	1989		1990	
	in value Din '000,000	% of total value	labour force	% of labour force
Agriculture	2,105	16.8	42,184	8.3
Mining and manufacturing	6,979	55.6	213,169	42.0
Construction	709	5.7	47,637	9.4
Public utilities	166	1.3	10,476	2.1
Transp. and commun.	543	4.3	26,249	5.2
Trade	1,807	14.4	63,593	12.5
Finance			14,422	2.8
Public admin., defense	240	1.9		
Services			89,597	17.7
Other				
TOTAL	12,549	100.0	507,327[7]	100.0[7]

Population economically active (1992): total 695,000; activity rate of total population 33.9% (participation rates: ages 15–64, n.a.; female [1990] 37.7%; unemployed [1992] 24.8%).

Price and earnings indexes (1990 = 100)

	1990	1991	1992
Consumer price index	100	115	2,035
Annual earnings index[8]	100	100	1,065

Land use (1990): forested 37.4%; meadows and pastures 25.9%; agricultural and under permanent cultivation 15.6%; other 21.1%.
Tourism (1991): total tourist nights 2,766,000.
Household income and expenditure. Average household size (1991) 3.9; income per household (1990) Din 75,556 (U.S.$6,676); sources of income (1990): wages and salaries 57.7%, self-employment 17.1%, transfer payments 16.2%, other 9.0%; expenditure (1988): food 37.5%, clothing and footwear 7.8%, fuel and lighting 7.8%, transportation and communications 6.5%, housing 5.7%, drink and tobacco 4.9%, household durable goods 4.2%, education and entertainment 3.3%, health care 3.0%.

Foreign trade

Balance of trade (current prices)

	1991	1992
U.S.$'000,000	−225	+15
% of total	6.1%	1.0%

Imports (1990): Din 12,601,000,000 (raw materials and semifinished goods 33.2%; consumer goods 28.4%, of which food, beverages, and tobacco 14.8%, clothing and footwear 4.9%, medicine and pharmaceuticals 0.6%; mineral fuels 19.1%; basic manufactures 10.7%; machinery 6.7%, of which electrical motors 1.0%; transport equipment 0.5%). *Major import sources:* n.a.
Exports (1990): Din 6,555,000,000 (clothing and footwear 20.7%; machinery and transport equipment 14.2%, of which transport equipment 1.3%; chemicals 4.6%; food 3.6%; textiles 2.2%; medicine and pharmaceuticals 0.8%; furniture 0.5%). *Major export destinations:* n.a.

Transport and communications

Transport. Railroads (1990): length 693 km; passengers transported 4,406,000; cargo transported 6,377,000 tons. Roads (1991): total length 10,591 km (paved 48%). Vehicles (1990): passenger cars 230,993; trucks and buses 22,594. Merchant marine: n.a. Air transport: n.a.; airports (1993) 1.
Communications. Daily newspapers (1990): total number 2; total circulation 52,000; circulation per 1,000 population 26. Radio (1989): 449,000 receivers (1 per 4.5 persons). Television (1989): 385,000 receivers (1 per 5.2 persons). Telephones (1990): 356,837 (1 per 5.7 persons).

Education and health

Education (1990–91)

	schools	teachers	students	student/teacher ratio
Primary (age 7–14)	1,063	12,987	268,963	20.7
Secondary (age 15–18)	90	4,200	74,886	17.8
Higher	27	2,101	26,413	12.6

Educational attainment (1981). Percentage of population age 15 and over having: less than full primary education 45.3%; primary 28.1%; secondary 21.2%; postsecondary and higher 5.1%; unknown 0.3%. *Literacy* (1981): total population age 10 and over literate 1,365,000 (89.1%); males literate 729,000 (94.2%); females literate 636,000 (83.8%).
Health (1990): physicians (1989) 4,331 (1 per 464 persons); hospital beds 11,804 (1 per 171 persons); infant mortality rate per 1,000 live births 35.3.

Military

Total active duty personnel (1993): 10,400 (army 100%). *Military expenditure as percentage of GNP:* n.a.; per capita expenditure, n.a.

[1]Member of the United Nations under the name Former Yugoslav Republic of Macedonia. [2]Macedonia, as part of Yugoslavia, utilized the Yugoslav (old) dinar (Din) until Jan. 1, 1990, when it was replaced by the Yugoslav (new) dinar (Din) at a rate of 10,000 old for 1 new. Macedonia left the Yugoslav currency area in September 1991, utilizing a local coupon alone until May 1992, when a transitional local currency, the denar, was introduced. The denar (valued initially at denar 255 = 1 U.S.$) was established at par with the Yugoslav (new) dinar but circulated in parallel with the coupon until May 1993, when a differently defined denar was introduced, replacing both the transitional denar and the coupon. [3]One sq km is equal to approximately 0.3861 sq mi. [4]Total includes 280 sq km of inland water not distributed by district. [5]Populations refer to municipal areas, not cities proper. [6]City proper, 1981 census. [7]Excludes 15,000 workers in the private sector. [8]Based on worker real net personal income.

Madagascar

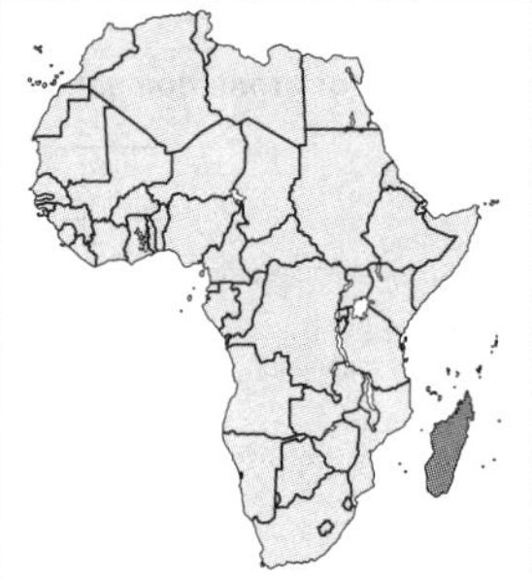

Official name: Repoblikan'i Madagasikara (Malagasy); République de Madagascar (French) (Republic of Madagascar).
Form of government: unitary multiparty republic with one legislative house[1] (138).
Chief of state: President.
Head of government: Prime Minister.
Capital: Antananarivo.
Official languages: Malagasy; French.
Official religion: none.
Monetary unit: 1 Malagasy franc (FMG) = 100 centimes; valuation (Oct. 4, 1993) 1 U.S.$ = FMG 1,824; 1 £ = FMG 2,764.

Area and population

		area		population
Provinces	Capitals	sq mi	sq km	1990 estimate[2]
Antananarivo	Antananarivo	22,503	58,283	3,998,000
Antsirañana	Antsirañana	16,620	43,046	750,000
Fianarantsoa	Fianarantsoa	39,526	102,373	2,539,000
Mahajanga	Mahajanga	57,924	150,023	1,314,000
Toamasina	Toamasina	27,765	71,911	1,663,000
Toliara	Toliara	62,319	161,405	1,740,000
TOTAL		226,658	587,041	12,004,000

Demography

Population (1993): 13,255,000.
Density (1993): persons per sq mi 58.5, persons per sq km 22.6.
Urban-rural (1990): urban 21.9%; rural 78.1%.
Sex distribution (1990): male 49.97%; female 50.03%.
Age breakdown (1990): under 15, 45.6%; 15–29, 26.7%; 30–44, 15.0%; 45–59, 7.7%; 60–69, 3.3%; 70 and over, 1.7%.
Population projection: (2000) 16,579,000; (2010) 22,431,000.
Doubling time: 22 years.
Ethnic composition (1983): Malagasy 98.9%, of which Merina 26.6%, Betsimisaraka 14.9%, Betsileo 11.7%, Tsimihety 7.4%, Sakalava 6.4%, Antandroy 5.3%; Comorian 0.3%; Indian and Pakistani 0.2%; French 0.2%; Chinese 0.1%; other 0.3%.
Religious affiliation (1980): Christian 51.0%, of which Roman Catholic 26.0%, Protestant 22.8%; traditional beliefs 47.0%; Muslim 1.7%; other 0.3%.
Major cities (1990): Antananarivo 802,400; Toamasina 145,400; Fianarantsoa 124,500; Mahajanga 122,000.

Vital statistics

Birth rate per 1,000 population (1990–95): 44.9 (world avg. 26.4); legitimate, n.a.; illegitimate, n.a.
Death rate per 1,000 population (1990–95): 12.6 (world avg. 9.2).
Natural increase rate per 1,000 population (1990–95): 32.3 (world avg. 17.2).
Total fertility rate (avg. births per childbearing woman; 1993): 6.1.
Marriage rate per 1,000 population: n.a.
Divorce rate per 1,000 population: n.a.
Life expectancy at birth (1990–95): male 54.0 years; female 57.0 years.
Major causes of death per 100,000 population: n.a.; however, major causes of death include communicable diseases and respiratory diseases.

National economy

Budget (1993). Revenue: FMG 1,470,548,000,000 (1987; taxes 80.2%, of which import duties 14.9%, excises 14.8%, income tax 12.5%; other receipts 19.8%). Expenditures: FMG 2,457,749,000,000 (1987; current expenditure 77.3%, of which education 12.3%, defense 7.5%, health 4.2%, agriculture 1.8%, public works 0.7%).
Public debt (external, outstanding; 1991): U.S.$3,381,000,000.
Tourism (1991): receipts from visitors U.S.$26,000,000; expenditures by nationals abroad U.S.$32,000,000.
Production (metric tons except as noted). Agriculture, forestry, fishing (1992): rice 2,450,000, cassava 2,320,000, sugarcane 1,900,000, sweet potatoes 440,000, potatoes 276,000, bananas 220,000, mangoes 170,000, corn (maize) 165,000, taro 100,000, oranges 85,000, coconuts 85,000, coffee 85,000, pineapples 50,000, beans 37,000, peanuts (groundnuts) 34,000, seed cotton 27,000; livestock (number of live animals) 10,276,000 cattle, 1,493,000 pigs, 1,311,000 goats, 770,000 sheep, 23,000,000 chickens; roundwood (1991) 8,335,000 cu m; fish catch (1991) 101,020. Mining and quarrying (1992): chromite concentrate 150,000; salt 30,000[3]; graphite 17,500; mica 1,950; gold 2,894 troy oz[4]. Manufacturing (1990): raw sugar 111,000; cement 20,000; soap 14,900; palm oil 3,800; paint 2,400; cigarettes 1,955; beer 298,000 hectolitres. Construction (1986)[5]: residential 19,700 sq m; nonresidential 5,700 sq m. Energy production (consumption): electricity (kW-hr; 1991) 569,000,000 (569,000,000); coal (metric tons; 1991) none (13,000); crude petroleum (barrels; 1991) none (1,356,000); petroleum products (metric tons; 1991) 170,000 (326,000); natural gas, none (n.a.).
Household income and expenditure. Average household size (1980) 4.7; average annual income per household: n.a.; sources of income (1975)[6]: wages and salaries 58.8%, self-employment 14.1%, other 27.1%; expenditure (1983)[7]: food 60.4%, fuel and light 9.1%, clothing and footwear 8.6%, household goods and utensils 2.4%.

Gross national product (at current market prices; 1992): U.S.$2,844,000,000 (U.S.$230 per capita).

Structure of gross domestic product and labour force

	1987			
	in value U.S.$'000,000[8]	% of total value	labour force	% of labour force
Agriculture	981	42.0	3,651,000	77.9
Manufacturing	276	11.8	462,000	9.9
Mining	6	0.3		
Construction	88	3.8		
Public utilities	26	1.1		
Transportation and communications	188	8.0	574,000	12.2
Trade	299	12.8		
Finance; Services	183	7.8		
Pub. admin., defense	289	12.4		
TOTAL	2,336	100.0	4,687,000	100.0

Population economically active (1987): total 4,687,000; activity rate of total population 44.3% (participation rates [1985]: ages 15–64, 74.9%; female 44.2%; unemployed [1982] 0.6%).

Price and earnings indexes (1985 = 100)

	1986	1987	1988	1989	1990	1991	1992
Consumer price index	114.5	131.7	167.0	182.1	203.5	221.0	253.1
Earnings index	...	...	...	...	...	...	...

Land use (1991): forested 26.4%; meadows and pastures 58.5%; agricultural and under permanent cultivation 5.3%; other 9.8%.

Foreign trade

Balance of trade

	1986	1987	1988	1989	1990	1991
FMG '000,000,000	+14.8	+85.9	−39.9	+50.8	−244.5	−93.0
% of total	3.6%	13.8%	4.9%	5.3%	21.0%	7.7%

Imports (1991): FMG 796,700,000,000 (1989; machinery 13.6%; vehicles and parts 10.4%; electrical equipment 7.3%; rice 7.2%; crude petroleum 5.5%; pharmaceutical products 3.2%; fats, waxes, and oils 2.5%). *Major import sources:* France 27.7%; Japan 4.8%; Iran 4.5%; Bahrain 4.4%; Germany 4.1%; Italy 2.9%; United States 2.8%.
Exports (1991): FMG 559,070,000,000 (1989; coffee 25.2%; vanilla 13.4%; cloves and clove oil 10.2%; sugar 7.8%; shrimps 7.5%). *Major export destinations:* France 27.4%; United States 12.4%; Japan 9.5%; Germany 8.5%; Italy 7.0%; Réunion 5.1%; Singapore 4.7%; United Kingdom 3.5%.

Transport and communications

Transport. Railroads (1990): route length 655 mi, 1,054 km; passenger-mi 121,750,000, passenger-km 195,938,000; short ton-mi cargo 144,040,000, metric ton-km cargo 210,295,000. Roads (1989): total length 33,700 mi, 54,200 km (paved 10%). Vehicles (1991): passenger cars 46,359; trucks and buses 33,296. Merchant marine (1992): vessels (100 gross tons and over) 85; total deadweight tonnage 82,077. Air transport (1991): passenger-mi 151,910,000, passenger-km 244,476,000; short ton-mi cargo 52,515,000[3], metric ton-km cargo 76,670,000[3]; airports (1993) with scheduled flights 50.
Communications. Daily newspapers (1990): total number 5; total circulation 53,000[9]; circulation per 1,000 population 4[9]. Radio (1992): total number of receivers 1,500,000 (1 per 8.8 persons). Television (1992): total number of receivers 130,000 (1 per 99 persons). Telephones (1990): 60,005 (1 per 203 persons).

Education and health

Education (1989–90)

	schools	teachers	students	student/ teacher ratio
Primary (age 6–13)	13,555	37,932	1,512,322	39.9
Secondary (14–18)	1,142[10]	14,382	331,238	23.0
Voc., teacher tr.	61[11]	1,630	17,674	10.8
Higher	5[10]	960	37,046	38.6

Educational attainment: n.a. *Literacy* (1990): percentage of total population age 15 and over literate 80.2%; males literate 87.7%; females literate 72.9%.
Health: physicians (1985) 1,189 (1 per 8,610 persons); hospital beds (1982) 20,800 (1 per 442 persons); infant mortality rate per 1,000 live births (1990–95) 110.
Food (1988–90): daily per capita caloric intake 2,156 (vegetable products 89%, animal products 11%); 95% of FAO recommended minimum requirement.

Military

Total active duty personnel (1993): 21,000 (army 95.2%, navy 2.4%, air force 2.4%). *Military expenditure as percentage of GNP* (1989): 1.5% (world 4.9%); per capita expenditure U.S.$3.

[1]Legislature dissolved November 1991. Presidential election held Feb. 10, 1993; legislative election held June 1993 (legislative house not yet named). [2]Based on official 1985 projections. [3]1990. [4]1988. [5]Capital city only. [6]Malagasy households only. [7]Weights of consumer price index components in Antananarivo only; housing not included. [8]At factor cost. [9]For four newspapers only. [10]1988–89. [11]1987–88.

Malaŵi

Official name: Republic of Malaŵi.
Form of government: multiparty[1] republic with one legislative house (National Assembly [146[2]]).
Head of state and government: President[3].
Capital: Lilongwe[4].
Official language: English[5].
Official religion: none.
Monetary unit: 1 Malaŵi kwacha (MK) = 100 tambala; valuation (Oct. 4, 1993) 1 U.S.$ = MK 4.35; 1 £ = MK 6.60.

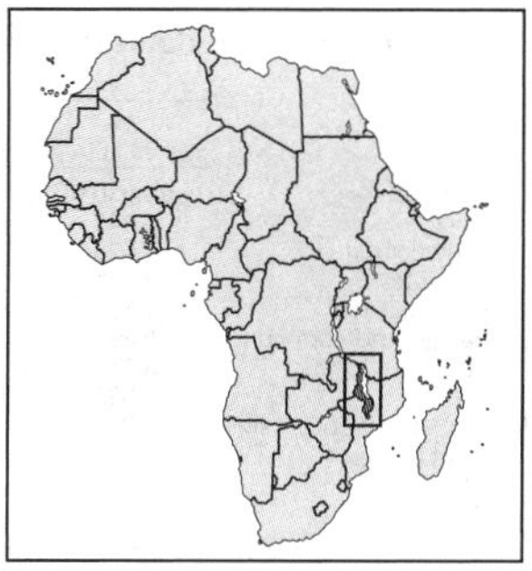

Area and population

Regions / Districts	Capitals	area sq mi	area sq km	population 1987 census
Central	Lilongwe	13,742	35,592	3,110,986
Dedza	Dedza	1,399	3,624	411,787
Dowa	Dowa	1,174	3,041	322,432
Kasungu	Kasungu	3,042	7,878	323,453
Lilongwe	Lilongwe	2,378	6,159	976,627
Mchinji	Mchinji	1,296	3,356	249,843
Nkhotakota	Nkhotakota	1,644	4,259	158,044
Ntcheu	Ntcheu	1,322	3,424	358,767
Ntchisi	Ntchisi	639	1,655	120,860
Salima	Salima	848	2,196	189,173
Northern	Mzuzu	10,398	26,931	911,787
Chitipa	Chitipa	1,353	3,504	96,794
Karonga	Karonga	1,141	2,955	148,014
Mzimba	Mzimba	4,027	10,430	433,696
Nkhata Bay	Nkhata Bay	1,579	4,090	138,381
Rumphi	Rumphi	2,298	5,952	94,902
Southern	Blantyre	12,260	31,753	3,965,734
Blantyre	Blantyre	777	2,012	589,525
Chikwawa	Chikwawa	1,836	4,755	316,733
Chiradzulu	Chiradzulu	296	767	210,912
Machinga	Machinga	2,303	5,964	515,265
Mangochi	Mangochi	2,422	6,272	496,578
Mulanje	Mulanje	1,332	3,450	638,062
Mwanza	Mwanza	886	2,295	121,513
Nsanje	Nsanje	750	1,942	204,374
Thyolo	Thyolo	662	1,715	431,157
Zomba	Zomba	996	2,580	441,615
TOTAL LAND AREA		36,400	94,276[6]	
INLAND WATER		9,347	24,208	
TOTAL		45,747	118,484	7,988,507

Demography

Population (1993): 10,581,000[7].
Density (1993)[8]: persons per sq mi 290.7, persons per sq km 112.2.
Urban-rural (1987): urban 10.7%; rural 89.3%.
Sex distribution (1987): male 48.40%; female 51.60%.
Age breakdown (1987): under 15, 46.0%; 15–29, 25.4%; 30–44, 14.5%; 45–59, 8.1%; 60 and over, 6.0%.
Population projection: (2000) 12,612,000; (2010) 16,455,000.
Doubling time: 20 years.
Ethnic composition (1983): Maravi (including Nyanja, Chewa, Tonga, and Tumbuka) 58.3%; Lomwe 18.4%; Yao 13.2%; Ngoni 6.7%; other 3.4%.
Religious affiliation (1980): Christian 64.5%, of which Protestant 33.7%, Roman Catholic 27.6%; traditional beliefs 19.0%; Muslim 16.2%; other 0.3%.
Major cities (1987): Blantyre 333,120; Lilongwe 223,318; Mzuzu 44,217.

Vital statistics

Birth rate per 1,000 population (1987): 41.2 (world avg. 27.1).
Death rate per 1,000 population (1987): 14.1 (world avg. 9.8).
Natural increase rate per 1,000 population (1987): 27.1 (world avg. 17.3).
Total fertility rate (avg. births per childbearing woman; 1990–95): 7.6.
Marriage rate per 1,000 population (1977): 7.8.
Divorce rate per 1,000 population (1977): 1.4.
Life expectancy at birth (1990–95): male 48.4 years; female 49.7 years.
Major causes of death per 100,000 population (1986)[9]: infectious and parasitic diseases 711, of which malaria 270, diarrheal diseases 148, measles 128; malnutrition 267; diseases of the respiratory system 265.

National economy

Budget (1992–93). Revenue: MK 1,291,200,000 (recurrent revenue 84.6%, of which income tax 32.7%, surtax 29.6%). Expenditures: MK 1,478,100,000 (administrative 42.1%; debt service 25.9%; wages and salaries 18.5%).
Public debt (external, outstanding; 1991): U.S.$1,528,000,000.
Production (metric tons except as noted). Agriculture (1992) sugarcane 1,950,000, corn (maize) 657,000, potatoes 330,000, plantains 140,000, tobacco 139,000, cassava 129,000, bananas 85,000, dry beans 78,000, tea 28,000, peanuts (groundnuts) 23,000, sorghum 4,000; livestock (number of live animals; 1992) 967,000 cattle, 887,000 goats, 238,000 pigs, 195,000 sheep; roundwood (1991) 8,515,000 cu m; fish catch (1991) 63,726. Mining and quarrying (1991): limestone 184,000; cement 69,000. Manufacturing (value added in MK '000; 1986): chemicals 30,805; textiles 19,630; food products 11,988; beverages 11,988; tobacco 9,480; printing and publishing 9,250. Construction (value in MK; 1990): 26,950,000[10]. Energy production (consumption): electricity (kW-hr; 1990) 587,000,000 (587,000,000); coal (metric tons; 1990) none (19,000); petroleum products (metric tons; 1990) none (145,000).
Land use (1991): forested 37.4%; meadows and pastures 19.5%; agricultural and under permanent cultivation 18.0%; other 25.1%.
Gross national product (1992): U.S.$1,905,000,000 (U.S.$210 per capita).

Structure of gross domestic product and labour force

	1992 in value MK '000,000[11]	1992 % of total value	1987 labour force	1987 % of labour force
Agriculture	275.0	28.3	2,699,900	81.8
Mining	...	...	1,662	0.1
Manufacturing	142.3	14.6	95,594	2.9
Construction	43.0	4.4	52,101	1.6
Public utilities	26.2	2.7	6,808	0.2
Transp. and commun.	59.6	6.1	16,726	0.5
Trade	129.5	13.3	103,203	3.1
Finance	115.8	11.9	7,142	0.2
Public administration	154.8	15.9 }	137,142	4.2
Services	44.9	4.6 }		
Other	−19.0[12]	−1.9[12]	179,920[13]	5.4[13]
TOTAL	972.1	100.0[6]	3,300,198	100.0

Population economically active (1987): total 3,300,198; activity rate 41.7% (participation rates: ages 15–64, 84.6%; female 51.5%; unemployed 5.4%).

Price and earnings indexes (1985 = 100)

	1986	1987	1988	1989	1990	1991	1992
Consumer price index	114.0	142.7	191.1	214.9	240.3	270.7	333.2
Monthly earnings index	109.4	129.9	145.8	169.7	...	...	...

Household income and expenditure (1979–80). Average household size (1987) 4.3; income per household MK 1,934 (U.S.$2,419); sources of income: wages 83.3%, household enterprise 6.0%; expenditure (1985)[14]: food 32.9%, transportation 17.6%, housing 13.3%, clothing and footwear 10.7%.
Tourism (1990): receipts U.S.$8,000,000; expenditures U.S.$13,000,000.

Foreign trade[15]

Balance of trade (current prices)

	1987	1988	1989	1990	1991	1992
MK '000,000	+222.7	+139.4	−96.1	+180.1	+140.9	−103.4
% of total	22.1%	10.1%	6.1%	8.7%	5.6%	3.4%

Imports (1991): MK 1,975,799,000 (1989; basic manufactures 40.6%, machinery and equipment 14.9%, transport equipment 14.3%, consumer goods 11.1%, building and construction materials 5.7%). *Major import sources* (1989): South Africa 36.8%; U.K. 17.1%; W.Ger. 6.3%; Japan 6.3%.
Exports (1991): MK 1,299,330,000 (tobacco 75.6%, tea 8.0%, sugar 6.1%, cotton 2.6%). *Major export destinations* (1989): U.K. 21.0%; U.S. 12.8%; W.Ger. 10.5%; South Africa 9.7%.

Transport and communications

Transport. Railroads (1991): route length 495 mi, 797 km; passenger-km 91,680,000; metric ton-km cargo 59,147,000. Roads (1989): total length 7,590 mi, 12,215 km (paved 22%). Vehicles (1989): passenger cars 16,118; trucks and buses 17,394. Merchant marine (1991): vessels (100 gross tons and over) 1; total deadweight tonnage 300. Air transport (1990)[16]: passenger-km 79,000,000; metric ton-km cargo 14,273,000; airports (1993) 4.
Communications. Daily newspapers (1992): total number 1; total circulation 20,000; circulation per 1,000 population 2.0. Radio (1992): total number of receivers 1,060,000 (1 per 9.7 persons). Television (1992): total number of receivers, n.a. Telephones (1991): 54,000 (1 per 183 persons).

Education and health

Education (1989–90)

	schools	teachers	students	student/ teacher ratio
Primary (age 6–13)	2,624	20,580	1,325,453	64.4
Secondary (age 14–18)	94	1,096	29,326	26.8
Teacher tr., voc.	13	250	3,679	14.7
Higher	4	235	2,685	11.4

Educational attainment (1987). Percentage of population age 5 and over having: no formal education 54.9%; primary education 41.7%; secondary and higher 3.4%. *Literacy* (1987): total population age 5 and over literate 2,746,143 (41.6%); males literate 1,665,559 (52.4%); females literate 1,080,584 (31.6%).
Health (1987): physicians (1984) 262 (1 per 27,094 persons); hospital beds 12,617 (1 per 627 persons); infant mortality rate per 1,000 live births 159.0.
Food (1988–90): daily per capita caloric intake 2,049 (vegetable products 97%, animal products 3%); 88% of FAO recommended minimum requirement.

Military

Total active duty personnel (1993): 10,400 (army 96.2%, marines 1.9%, air force 1.9%). *Military expenditure as percentage of GNP* (1989): 2.3% (world 4.9%); per capita expenditure U.S.$4.

[1]A referendum June 14, 1993, approved a multiparty system of government; legislative elections were due to take place in December 1993. [2]Excludes 5 seats (of 141 elective) left vacant at the June 1992 elections (candidates were disqualified before the election) and includes 10 nonelective seats appointed by the president. [3]Acting president of Presidential Council from Oct. 13, 1993. [4]Some government offices (including parliament) remain in the former capital, Zomba. [5]Chewa is the national language. [6]Detail does not add to total given because of rounding. [7]Includes Mozambican refugees, estimated to number about 1,100,000 in 1993. [8]Based on land area. [9]Estimates based on reported inpatient deaths in hospitals, constituting an estimated 8% of total deaths. [10]Cities of Blantyre, Lilongwe, and Mzuzu only. [11]At constant prices of 1978. [12]Less imputed bank service charges. [13]Includes 179,263 unemployed persons. [14]Weights of consumer price index components, cities of Blantyre and Lilongwe only. [15]Import figures are f.o.b. in balance of trade and c.i.f. in commodities and trading partners. Reexports included in balance of trade, excluded from commodities and trading partners. [16]Air Malaŵi only.

Malaysia

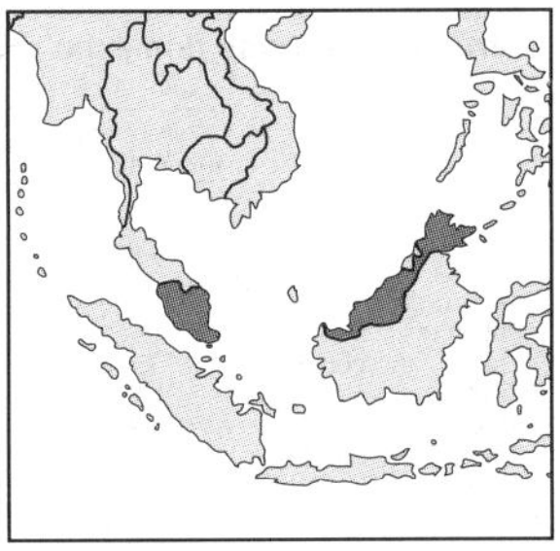

Official name: Malaysia.
Form of government: federal constitutional monarchy with two legislative houses (Senate [69[1]]; House of Representatives [180]).
Chief of state: Yang di-Pertuan Agong (Paramount Ruler).
Head of government: Prime Minister.
Capital: Kuala Lumpur.
Official language: Malay.
Official religion: Islam.
Monetary unit: 1 ringgit, or Malaysian dollar (M$) = 100 cents; valuation (Oct. 4, 1993) 1 U.S.$ = M$2.55; 1 £ = M$3.87.

Area and population

Regions / States	Capitals	area sq mi	area sq km	population 1991 census[2]
East Malaysia				
Sabah	Kota Kinabalu	28,425	73,620	1,736,902
Sarawak	Kuching	48,050	124,449	1,648,217
West Malaysia				
Johor	Johor Baharu	7,331	18,986	2,074,297
Kedah	Alor Setar	3,639	9,426	1,304,800
Kelantan	Kota Baharu	5,769	14,943	1,181,680
Melaka	Melaka	637	1,650	504,502
Negeri Sembilan	Seremban	2,565	6,643	691,150
Pahang	Kuantan	13,886	35,965	1,036,724
Perak	Ipoh	8,110	21,005	1,880,016
Perlis	Kangar	307	795	184,070
Pulau Pinang	George Town	398	1,031	1,065,075
Selangor	Shah Alam	3,072	7,956	2,289,236
Terengganu	Kuala Terengganu	5,002	12,955	770,931
Federal Territories				
Kuala Lumpur	—	94	243	1,145,075
Labuan	—	35	91	54,307
TOTAL LAND AREA		127,320	329,758	
INLAND WATER		264	684	
TOTAL		127,584	330,442	17,566,982

Demography

Population (1993): 19,077,000.
Density (1993): persons per sq mi 149.5, persons per sq km 57.7.
Urban-rural (1993): urban 43.0%; rural 57.0%.
Sex distribution (1991): male 50.44%; female 49.56%.
Age breakdown (1990): under 15, 36.8%; 15–29, 28.6%; 30–44, 18.7%; 45–59, 9.8%; 60 and over, 6.1%.
Population projection: (2000) 22,140,000; (2010) 25,986,000.
Doubling time: 32 years.
Ethnic composition (1990): Malay and other indigenous (Orang Asli, or Bumiputera) 61.7%; Chinese 29.7%; Indian 8.1%; other nonindigenous 0.5%.
Religious affiliation (1980): Muslim 52.9%; Buddhist 17.3%; Chinese folk-religionist 11.6%; Hindu 7.0%; Christian 6.4%; other 4.8%.
Major cities (1980): Kuala Lumpur 1,209,800[3]; Ipoh 293,849; George Town 248,241; Johor Baharu 246,395; Petaling Jaya 207,805.

Vital statistics

Birth rate per 1,000 population (1991): 27.0 (world avg. 26.4).
Death rate per 1,000 population (1991): 5.0 (world avg. 9.2).
Natural increase rate per 1,000 population (1991): 22.0 (world avg. 17.2).
Total fertility rate (avg. births per childbearing woman; 1993): 3.6.
Marriage rate per 1,000 population (1979): 1.7.
Divorce rate per 1,000 population (1979): 0.02.
Life expectancy at birth (1993): male 69.0 years; female 73.0 years.
Major causes of death per 100,000 population (1989): diseases of the circulatory system 63.1; accidents, homicide, and other violence 36.0; infectious and parasitic diseases 33.1; malignant neoplasms (cancers) 31.9; obstetric and perinatal causes 22.6; senility and ill-defined conditions 149.3.

National economy

Budget (1993). Revenue: M$39,119,000,000 (income tax 37.9%, nontax revenue 24.3%, import duties 12.8%, sales taxes 9.3%). Expenditures: M$32,290,000,000 (social services 32.5%, security 15.7%, administration 10.7%, economic services 7.8%).
Production (metric tons except as noted). Agriculture, forestry, fishing (1991): palm oil 6,145,000, rice 1,550,000, rubber 1,250,000, bananas 509,000, cacao beans 225,000, pineapples 225,000; livestock (number of live animals) 2,400,000 pigs, 658,000 cattle, 315,000 goats, 200,000 sheep, 190,000 buffalo, 148,000,000 chickens; roundwood 49,327,000 cu m; fish catch (1990) 604,128. Mining and quarrying (1991): iron ore 354,869; bauxite 347,418; copper concentrates 98,313; tin concentrates 20,518. Manufacturing (1990): cement 5,881,000; poultry feed 1,165,805; fertilizer 921,111; refined sugar 800,913; standard rubber 800,739; iron and steel bars 785,142; processed latex 255,947; plywood 1,197,385 cu m; radio receivers 37,019,000 units; television receivers 2,168,817 units; passenger cars 130,908 units. Construction (completed; 1986)[4]: residential 8,809,100 sq m; nonresidential 959,900 sq m. Energy production (consumption): electricity (kW-hr; 1990) 24,723,000,000 (24,666,000,000); coal (metric tons; 1990) 120,000 (1,860,000); crude petroleum (barrels; 1990) 229,444,000 (68,922,000); petroleum products (metric tons; 1990) 8,924,000 (13,452,000); natural gas (cu m; 1990) 12,756,000,000 (3,402,000,000).
Gross national product (1991): U.S.$45,787,000,000 (U.S.$2,490 per capita).

Structure of gross domestic product and labour force

	1991 in value M$'000,000[5]	% of total value	labour force	% of labour force
Agriculture	14,836	17.3	1,834,800	25.3
Mining	8,043	9.3	39,400	0.5
Manufacturing	24,628	28.7	1,374,100	18.9
Construction	3,271	3.8	455,900	6.3
Public utilities	1,687	1.9	...	...
Transp. and commun.	5,999	7.0	297,000	4.1
Trade	9,717	11.3	...	...
Finance	8,535	9.9	240,300	3.3
Pub. admin., defense	8,905	10.4	853,900	11.8
Services	1,781	2.1	1,753,500[6]	24.2[6]
Other	−1,479[7]	−1.7[7]	409,000	5.6
TOTAL	85,923	100.0	7,257,900	100.0

Public debt (external, outstanding; 1991): U.S.$16,447,000,000.
Tourism (1991): receipts from visitors U.S.$1,530,000,000; expenditures by nationals abroad U.S.$1,503,000,000.
Population economically active (1990): total 7,046,500; activity rate 39.7% (participation rates: ages 15–64, 66.5%; female 35.5%; unemployed 6.0%).

Price index (1985 = 100)

	1986	1987	1988	1989	1990	1991	1992
Consumer price index	100.7	101.6	103.6	106.5	109.3	114.1	119.5

Household income and expenditure. Average household size (1980) 5.2; annual income per household (1987) M$12,890 (U.S.$5,120); sources of income: n.a.; expenditure (1983): food 28.7%, transportation 20.9%, recreation and education 11.0%, housing 10.2%, household durable goods 7.7%, clothing and footwear 4.3%, health 2.5%.
Land use (1990): forested 58.8%; meadows and pastures 0.1%; agricultural and under permanent cultivation 14.9%; other 26.2%.

Foreign trade[8]

Balance of trade (current prices)

	1987	1988	1989	1990	1991	1992
M$'000,000	+11,864	+16,048	+12,725	+7,947	+3,165	+11,446
% of total	17.1%	17.0%	10.3%	5.3%	1.7%	5.9%

Imports (1991): M$100,831,000,000 (machinery and transport equipment 53.9%; manufactured goods 15.9%; chemicals 7.7%; food 5.5%; mineral fuels 4.2%; inedible crude materials 2.8%). *Major import sources* (1990): Japan 24.1%; U.S. 16.8%; Singapore 15.0%; U.K. 5.5%; Taiwan 5.5%; W.Ger. 4.3%; Australia 3.7%.
Exports (1991): M$94,497,000,000 (machinery and transport equipment 41.2%; mineral fuels 15.7%; inedible crude materials 11.8%; basic manufactures 7.8%; animal and vegetable oils 6.6%; food, beverages, and tobacco 4.0%). *Major export destinations* (1990): Singapore 22.8%; U.S. 16.9%; Japan 15.8%; South Korea 4.6%; U.K. 3.9%; W.Ger. 3.9%; Thailand 3.5%.

Transport and communications

Transport. Railroads (1991): track length 1,381 mi, 2,222 km; passenger-km 1,752,000,000[9]; metric ton-km cargo 1,272,000,000[9]. Roads (1989): total length 32,623 mi, 52,501 km (paved 68%). Vehicles (1991): passenger cars 2,000,000; trucks and buses 400,000. Merchant marine (1992): vessels (100 gross tons and over) 552; total deadweight tonnage 2,916,315. Air transport (1992): passenger-km 14,929,000,000; metric ton-km cargo 740,124,000; airports (1993) with scheduled flights 39.
Communications. Daily newspapers (1990): total number 45; circulation 2,500,000; circulation per 1,000 population 140. Radio (1992): 3,500,000 receivers (1 per 5.2 persons). Television (1992): 2,000,000 receivers (1 per 9.1 persons). Telephones (1990): 2,022,581 (1 per 8.8 persons).

Education and health

Education (1990)

	schools	teachers	students	student/ teacher ratio
Primary (age 7–12)	6,828	120,025	2,447,206	20.4
Secondary (age 13–19)	1,261	69,493	1,335,377	19.2
Voc., teacher tr.	81	3,902	39,187	10.0
Higher	44	10,103	117,267	11.6

Educational attainment (1980). Percentage of population age 25 and over having: no formal schooling 36.6%; primary education 42.1%; secondary 19.4%; higher 1.9%. *Literacy* (1990 est.): total population age 15 and over literate 78.4%; males literate 86.5%; females literate 70.4%.
Health (1989): physicians 6,577 (1 per 2,638 persons); hospital beds 38,003 (1 per 457 persons); infant mortality rate per 1,000 live births (1991) 13.0.
Food (1988–90): daily per capita caloric intake 2,671 (vegetable products 85%, animal products 15%); 120% of FAO recommended minimum.

Military

Total active duty personnel (1992): 127,500 (army 82.4%, navy 8.2%, air force 9.4%). *Military expenditure as percentage of GNP* (1989): 2.9% (world 4.9%); per capita expenditure U.S.$60.

[1]Includes 43 appointees of the paramount ruler; some of the remaining 26 elected seats were unoccupied in 1993. [2]Preliminary results. [3]1989. [4]Results of the Central Bank Survey of four major towns: Kuala Lumpur, Shah Alam, Kelang, and Seberang Prai. [5]At constant prices of 1978. [6]Includes data for Public utilities and Trade. [7]Net bank service charges. [8]Import figures are f.o.b. in balance of trade. [9]Peninsular Malaysia and Singapore.

Maldives

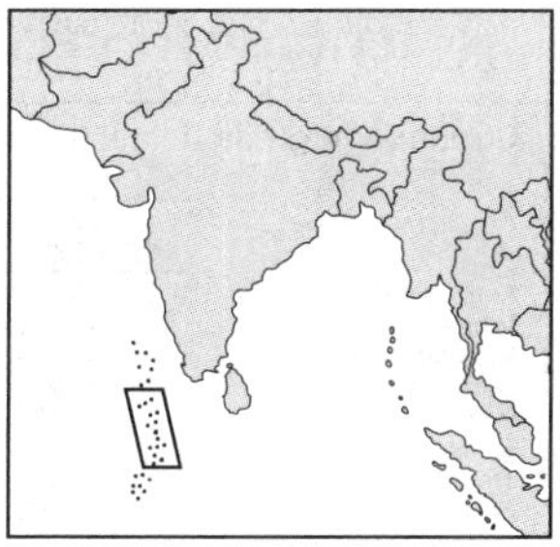

Official name: Divehi Jumhuriyya (Republic of Maldives).
Form of government: republic with one legislative house (People's Council [48[1]]).
Head of state and government: President.
Capital: Male'.
Official language: Divehi.
Official religion: Islam.
Monetary unit: 1 Maldivian Rufiyaa (Rf) = 100 laari; valuation (Oct. 4, 1993) 1 U.S.$ = Rf 11.89; 1 £ = Rf 18.01.

Area and population[2]

		area		population
				1990
Administrative atolls	Capitals	sq mi	sq km	census
North Thiladhunmathi (Haa-Alifu)	Dhidhdhoo	...	...	12,031
South Thiladhunmathi (Haa-Dhaalu)	Nolhivaranfaru	...	...	12,890
North Miladhunmadulu (Shaviyani)	Farukolhu-funadhoo	...	...	9,022
South Miladhunmadulu (Noonu)	Manadhoo	...	...	8,437
North Maalhosmadulu (Raa)	Ugoofaaru	...	...	11,303
South Maalhosmadulu (Baa)	Eydhafushi	...	...	7,716
Faadhippolhu (Lhaviyani)	Naifaru	...	...	7,224
Male' (Kaafu)	Thulusdhoo	...	...	6,726
Ari Atoll Uthuru Gofi (Alifu)	Rasdhoo	...	...	3,998
Ari Atoll Dhekunu Gofi (Alifu)	Mahibadhoo	...	...	5,029
Felidhu Atoll (Vaavu)	Felidhoo	...	...	1,579
Mulakatholhu (Meemu)	Muli	...	...	4,186
North Nilandhe Atoll (Faafu)	Magoodhoo	...	...	2,614
South Nilandhe Atoll (Dhaalu)	Kudahuvadhoo	...	...	4,199
Kolhumadulu (Thaa)	Veymandoo	...	...	8,189
Hadhdhunmathi (Laamu)	Hithadhoo	...	...	9,101
North Huvadhu Atoll (Gaafu-Alifu)	Viligili	...	...	7,295
South Huvadhu Atoll (Gaafu-Dhaalu)	Thinadhoo	...	...	10,417
Foammulah (Gnyaviyani)	Foahmulah	...	...	6,160
Addu Atoll (Seenu)	Hithadhoo	...	...	15,177
Male'		...	...	55,130
TOTAL		115	298	213,215[3]

Demography

Population (1993): 237,000.
Density (1993): persons per sq mi 2,060.9, persons per sq km 795.3.
Urban-rural (1993): urban 30.0%; rural 70.0%.
Sex distribution (1990): male 51.28%; female 48.72%.
Age breakdown (1990): under 15, 46.9%; 15–29, 26.7%; 30–44, 12.3%; 45–59, 9.0%; 60–74, 4.0%; 75 and over, 0.8%; not stated, 0.3%.
Population projection: (2000) 286,000; (2010) 369,000.
Doubling time: 23 years.
Ethnic composition: the majority is principally of Sinhalese and Dravidian extraction; Arab, African, and Negrito influences are also present.
Religious affiliation: virtually 100% Sunnī Muslim.
Major cities (1990): Male' 55,130.

Vital statistics

Birth rate per 1,000 population (1993): 38.0 (world avg. 26.4); legitimate, n.a.; illegitimate, n.a.
Death rate per 1,000 population (1993): 8.0 (world avg. 9.2).
Natural increase rate per 1,000 population (1993): 30.0 (world avg. 17.2).
Total fertility rate (avg. births per childbearing woman; 1993): 6.1.
Marriage rate per 1,000 population (1990): 10.6.
Divorce rate per 1,000 population (1990): 7.9.
Life expectancy at birth (1993): male 65.0 years; female 62.0 years.
Major causes of death per 100,000 population (1988): rheumatic fever 106.0; ischemic heart diseases 65.0; bronchitis, emphysema, and asthma 61.0; tetanus 23.5; tuberculosis 13.0; accidents and suicide 10.0.

National economy

Budget (1992). Revenue: Rf 1,021,000,000 (1990; nontax revenue 34.8%, import duties 25.5%, foreign grants 18.2%, tourism tax 15.3%). Expenditures: Rf 1,512,400,000 (economic development 23.9%, atoll development 21.6%, education 14.7%, public order and safety 7.7%, health 7.3%).
Public debt (external, outstanding; 1991): U.S.$77,200,000.
Production (metric tons except as noted). Agriculture, forestry, fishing (1992): vegetables and melons 20,000, coconuts 13,000, fruits (excluding melons) 10,000, roots and tubers (including cassava, sweet potatoes, and yams) 9,000, copra 2,000; fish catch (1991) 80,713. Mining and quarrying: coral for construction materials. Manufacturing: details, n.a.; however, major industries include boat building and repairing, coir yarn and mat weaving, coconut and fish processing, lacquerwork, garment manufacturing, and handicrafts. Construction: n.a. Energy production (consumption): electricity (kW-hr; 1991) 28,000,000 (28,000,000); coal, none (n.a.); petroleum products (metric tons; 1991) none (31,000); natural gas, none (n.a.).
Tourism (1991): receipts from visitors U.S.$87,000,000; expenditures by nationals abroad U.S.$18,000,000.
Household income and expenditure. Average household size (1990) 7.1; income per household: n.a.; sources of income: n.a.; expenditure (1981)[4]: food and beverages 61.8%, housing equipment 17.0%, clothing 8.0%, recreation and education 5.9%, transportation 2.6%, health 2.5%, rent 1.6%.
Gross national product (at current market prices; 1992): U.S.$114,000,000 (U.S.$500 per capita).

Structure of gross domestic product and labour force

	1991		1990	
	in value Rf '000[5]	% of total value	labour force	% of labour force
Agriculture[6]	248,410	23.7	14,117	25.0
Mining	19,800	1.9	496	0.9
Manufacturing }	61,190	5.8	8,441	15.0
Public utilities }			445	0.8
Construction	91,090	8.7	3,151	5.6
Transportation and communications	61,310	5.8	5,321	9.4
Trade	183,070	17.5	8,884	15.7
Finance	43,520	4.2	1,058	1.9
Public administration, defense	85,380	8.1 }	11,848	21.0
Services	254,320	24.3 }		
Other	...	...	2,674	4.7
TOTAL	1,048,090	100.0	56,435	100.0

Population economically active (1990): total 56,435; activity rate of total population 26.5% (participation rates: ages 15–64, 50.2%; female 19.9%; unemployed 0.9%).
Land use (1991): forested 3.3%; meadows and pastures 3.3%; agricultural and under permanent cultivation 10.0%; built-on, wasteland, and other 83.4%.

Foreign trade[7]

Balance of trade (current prices)

	1986	1987	1988	1989	1990	1991
U.S.$'000,000	−33,459	−47,932	−54,977	−50,963	−65,114	−83,500
% of total	40.5%	43.8%	40.7%	36.3%	38.5%	43.7%

Imports (1990): Rf 1,315,406,000 (food, beverages, and tobacco 28.9%; basic manufactures 24.5%; machinery and transport equipment 21.7%; mineral fuels 15.8%; chemicals 4.8%). *Major import sources:* Japan 6.5%; West Germany 5.1%; Sri Lanka 4.8%; Thailand 4.2%; United Kingdom 4.1%.
Exports (1990): Rf 502,717,000 (apparel and clothing 27.6%; frozen skipjack tuna 26.3%; canned fish 25.2%; dried skipjack tuna 10.7%). *Major export destinations:* United States 24.4%; United Kingdom 18.5%; Thailand 18.1%; Sri Lanka 13.0%; Japan 8.5%; Singapore 4.9%.

Transport and communications

Transport. Railroads: none. Roads: total length, n.a. Vehicles (1990): passenger cars 623; trucks and buses 813. Merchant marine (1992): vessels (100 gross tons and over) 44; total deadweight tonnage 78,994. Air transport (1990): passenger arrivals 217,953, passenger departures 217,841; cargo loaded 2,263 metric tons, cargo unloaded 7,711 metric tons; airports (1993) with scheduled flights 1.
Communications. Daily newspapers (1990): total number 2; total circulation 2,000; circulation per 1,000 population 7. Radio (1992): total number of receivers 25,000 (1 per 9.2 persons). Television (1992): total number of receivers 4,750 (1 per 48 persons). Telephones (1990): 6,241 (1 per 35 persons).

Education and health

Education (1986)

	schools	teachers	students	student/ teacher ratio
Primary (age 6–11)	243	1,138	41,812	36.7
Secondary (age 11–18)	9	291	3,581	12.3
Voc., teacher tr.	10	52	462	8.9
Higher	—	—	—	—

Educational attainment (1990). Percentage of population age 15 and over having: no standard passed 25.6%; primary standard 37.2%; middle standard 25.9%; secondary standard 6.3%; preuniversity 3.4%; higher 0.4%; not stated 1.2%. *Literacy* (1985): total population age 15 and over literate 90,189 (90.4%); males literate 47,412 (90.6%); females literate 42,777 (90.1%).
Health (1990): physicians 40 (1 per 5,377 persons); hospital beds[8] 167 (1 per 1,288 persons); infant mortality rate per 1,000 live births (1993) 53.
Food (1984–86): daily per capita caloric intake 2,033 (vegetable products 91%, animal products 9%); 92% of FAO recommended minimum requirement.

Military

Total active duty personnel: Maldives maintains a single security force numbering about 700–1,000; it performs both army and police functions.

[1]Includes 8 nonelective seats. [2]Maldives is divided into 20 administrative districts corresponding to atoll groups; arrangement shown here is from north to south; total area excludes 34,634 sq mi (89,702 sq km) of tidal waters. [3]Includes 4,792 people in resort and industrial islands. [4]Weights of consumer price index components. [5]At 1985 prices. [6]Primarily fishing. [7]Import figures are f.o.b. in balance of trade and c.i.f. for commodities and trading partners. [8]In government establishments only.

Mali

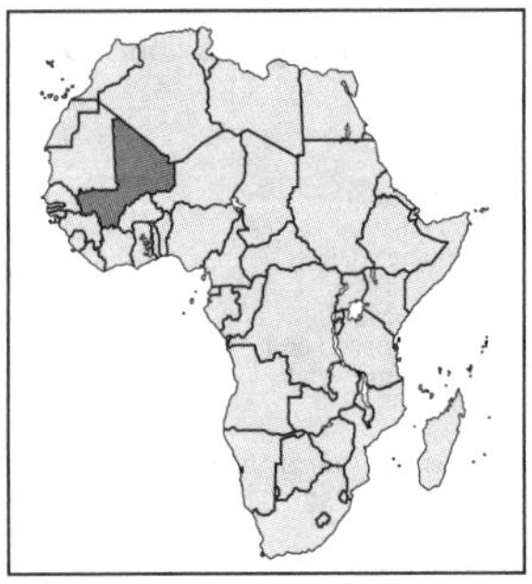

Official name: République du Mali (Republic of Mali).
Form of government: multiparty[1] republic with one legislative house (National Assembly [116]).
Chief of state: President.
Head of government: Prime Minister.
Capital: Bamako.
Official language: French.
Official religion: none.
Monetary unit: 1 CFA franc (CFAF) = 100 centimes; valuation (Oct. 4, 1993) 1 U.S.$ = CFAF 283.25; 1 £ = CFAF 429.12.

Area and population

Regions	Capitals	area sq mi	area sq km	population 1993 estimate
Gao	Gao	124,326	322,002	395,000
Kayes	Kayes	46,233	119,743	1,196,000
Koulikoro	Koulikoro	37,007	95,848	1,395,000
Mopti	Mopti	30,508	79,017	1,377,000
Ségou	Ségou	25,028	64,821	1,515,000
Sikasso	Sikasso	27,135	70,280	1,461,000
Tombouctou	Timbuktu (Tombouctou)	191,743[2]	496,611[2]	452,000
District				
Bamako	Bamako	97	252	856,000
TOTAL		482,077	1,248,574	8,646,000[3]

Demography

Population (1993): 8,646,000.
Density (1993): persons per sq mi 17.9, persons per sq km 6.9.
Urban-rural (1993): urban 25.5%; rural 74.5%.
Sex distribution (1993): male 48.85%; female 51.15%.
Age breakdown (1991): under 15, 48.3%; 15–29, 22.5%; 30–44, 14.3%; 45–59, 8.8%; 60–74, 4.9%; 75 and over, 1.2%.
Population projection: (2000) 9,980,000; (2010) 12,252,000.
Doubling time: 23 years.
Ethnic composition (1983): Bambara 31.9%; Fulani 13.9%; Senufo 12.0%; Soninke 8.8%; Tuareg 7.3%; Songhai 7.2%; Malinke 6.6%; Dogon 4.0%; Dyula 2.9%; Bobo 2.4%; Arab 1.2%; other 1.8%.
Religious affiliation (1983): Muslim 90%; traditional beliefs 9%; Christian 1%.
Major cities (1987): Bamako 646,163; Ségou 88,877; Mopti 73,979; Sikasso 73,050; Gao 54,874.

Vital statistics

Birth rate per 1,000 population (1992): 52.0 (world avg. 26.4); legitimate, n.a.; illegitimate, n.a.
Death rate per 1,000 population (1992): 21.0 (world avg. 9.2).
Natural increase rate per 1,000 population (1992): 31.0 (world avg. 17.2).
Total fertility rate (avg. births per childbearing woman; 1992): 7.3.
Marriage rate per 1,000 population (1990)[4]: 0.4.
Divorce rate per 1,000 population: n.a.
Life expectancy at birth (1992): male 43.0 years; female 47.0 years.
Major causes of death per 100,000 population: n.a.; morbidity ([notified cases of illness] by cause as a percentage of all reported infectious disease; 1985): malaria 62.1%; measles 10.3%; amebiasis 10.3%; syphilis and gonococcal infections 6.0%; influenza 4.9%; other principal causes in 1989 included polio and conditions originating in the perinatal period.

National economy

Budget (1992). Revenue: CFAF 214,800,000,000 (fiscal receipts 52.2%, nonfiscal receipts 12.5%). Expenditures: CFAF 222,500,000,000 (capital expenditure 45.8%, current expenditure 45.3%).
Public debt (external, outstanding; 1991): U.S.$2,392,000,000.
Tourism (1991): receipts from visitors U.S.$12,000,000; expenditures by nationals abroad U.S.$60,000,000.
Population economically active (1987): total 2,722,000; activity rate of total population 31.9% (participation rates: over age 10, 48.3%; female 15.3%; unemployed 1.3%[5]).

Price and earnings indexes (1985 = 100)

	1985	1986	1987	1988	1989	1990	1991
Consumer price index[6]	100.0	96.3	88.5	92.7	93.7	94.6	97.3
Hourly earnings index[7]	100.0	134.7	134.7	134.7	134.7	134.7	172.2

Production (metric tons except as noted). Agriculture, forestry, fishing (1992): millet 794,000, sorghum 706,000, rice 405,000, seed cotton 299,000, corn (maize) 165,000, peanuts (groundnuts) 165,000, cassava 73,000, sweet potatoes 55,000; livestock (number of live animals) 13,316,000 goats and sheep, 5,373,000 cattle, 600,000 asses, 250,000 camels, 85,000 horses, 75,000 pigs; roundwood (1991) 5,768,000 cu m; fish catch (1991) 60,031. Mining and quarrying (1991): limestone 25,000[8]; phosphate 8,000; gold 5,352 kg. Manufacturing (1991): cotton fibre 46,396; sugar 29,040; cement 10,953; soft drinks 64,750 hectolitres; beer 37,754 hectolitres; shoes 127,000 pairs; cigarettes 141,757 cartons. Construction: n.a. Energy production (consumption): electricity (kW-hr; 1991) 241,941,000 (1990; 214,000,000); coal, none (n.a.); crude petroleum, none (n.a.); petroleum products (metric tons; 1990) none (134,000); natural gas, none (n.a.).

Gross national product (at current market prices; 1991): U.S.$2,412,000,000 (U.S.$280 per capita).

Structure of gross domestic product and labour force

	1991 in value CFAF '000,000	1991 % of total value	1987 labour force	1987 % of labour force
Agriculture	320,169	45.6	2,243,000	82.4
Mining	10,326	1.5	68,000	2.5
Manufacturing	48,260	6.8		
Construction	27,920	4.0		
Public utilities	9,432	1.3		
Transp. and commun.	30,974	4.4	411,000	15.1
Trade	109,131	15.5		
Finance	8,202	1.2		
Pub. admin., defense / Services	105,185	15.0		
Other	33,026[9]	4.7[9]	...	...
TOTAL	702,625	100.0	2,722,000	100.0

Household income and expenditure. Average household size (1987) 5.6; average annual income per household: n.a.; sources of income: n.a.; expenditure: n.a.
Land use (1991): forested 5.7%; meadows and pastures 24.6%; agricultural and under permanent cultivation 1.7%; other 68.0%.

Foreign trade[10]

Balance of trade (current prices)

	1984	1985	1986	1987	1988	1989
CFAF '000,000,000	−71.5	−131.7	−100.5	−70.2	−79.0	−70.1
% of total	28.6%	45.4%	41.4%	31.0%	33.0%	28.6%

Imports (1990): CFAF 187,735,000,000 (machinery, appliances, and transport equipment 29.3%; food products 12.7%; chemicals 9.2%; petroleum products 9.1%). *Major import sources:* France 27.2%; Côte d'Ivoire 18.8%; Senegal 5.8%; Germany 5.6%; The Netherlands 4.8%; U.S.S.R. 4.8%; Belgium-Luxembourg 4.0%; Italy 3.3%; Saudi Arabia 3.0%; United Kingdom 2.7%; Guinea 2.6%; Hong Kong 2.4%; Spain 1.9%; United States 1.7%.
Exports (1990): CFAF 101,920,000,000 (raw cotton and cotton products 44.9%; live animals 24.0%; gold and diamonds 12.5%). *Major export destinations:* U.S.S.R. 12.5%; Algeria 11.6%; Taiwan 10.5%; Belgium-Luxembourg 9.1%; France 7.1%; China 5.2%; Canada 4.9%; Germany 4.4%; Morocco 4.4%.

Transport and communications

Transport. Railroads (1990): route length (1988) 401 mi, 646 km; passenger-mi 304,155,000, passenger-km 489,491,000; short ton-mi cargo 187,176,000, metric ton-km cargo 273,273,000. Roads (1987): total length 11,185 mi, 18,000 km (paved 8%). Vehicles (1991): passenger cars 22,000; trucks and buses 9,000. Merchant marine: vessels (100 gross tons and over) none. Air transport (1983): passenger-mi 68,000,000, passenger-km 110,000,000; short ton-mi cargo 411,000, metric ton-km cargo 600,000; airports (1993) with scheduled flights 1.
Communications. Daily newspapers (1992): total number 1; total circulation 40,000; circulation per 1,000 population 4.7. Radio (1992): total number of receivers 150,000 (1 per 56 persons). Television (1992): total number of receivers 10,000 (1 per 846 persons). Telephones (1990): 11,165 (1 per 730 persons).

Education and health

Education (1990–91)

	schools	teachers	students	student/teacher ratio
Primary (age 6–14)	1,342	7,706	353,694	45.9
Secondary (age 15–17)[11]	307	3,061	60,518	19.8
Higher	7	675	5,536[12]	...

Educational attainment (1976). Percentage of adult population age 25 and over having: no formal schooling 95.4%; primary education 3.8%; secondary 0.6%; postsecondary and higher 0.2%. *Literacy* (1990): percentage of total population age 15 and over literate 32.0%; males literate 40.8%; females literate 23.9%.
Health (1983): physicians 349 (1 per 20,602 persons); hospital beds 4,215 (1 per 1,706 persons); infant mortality rate per 1,000 live births (1992) 110.
Food (1988–90): daily per capita caloric intake 2,259 (vegetable products 91%, animal products 9%); 96% of FAO recommended minimum requirement.

Military

Total active duty personnel (1992): 7,350 (army 93.9%, navy 0.7%, air force 5.4%). *Military expenditure as percentage of GNP* (1989): 2.0% (world 4.9%); per capita expenditure U.S.$5.

[1]Multiparty legislative elections of February–March 1992 were boycotted by most opposition parties. [2]Area for Tombouctou region is estimated as a residue between total reported area and the remainder of the regions. [3]Detail does not add to total given because of rounding. [4]Bamako only. [5]Urban areas only; estimated. [6]General price index. [7]Minimum hourly wages of industrial workers. [8]1987. [9]Less imputed bank service charges. [10]Imports c.i.f. [11]Excludes vocational. [12]1986–87.

Malta

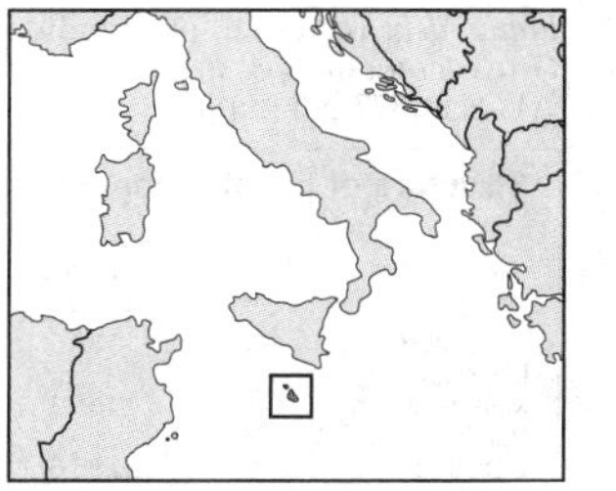

Official name: Repubblika ta' Malta (Maltese); Republic of Malta (English).
Form of government: unitary multiparty republic with one legislative house (House of Representatives [65]).
Chief of state: President.
Head of government: Prime Minister.
Capital: Valletta.
Official languages: Maltese; English.
Official religion: Roman Catholicism.
Monetary unit: 1 Maltese lira (Lm) = 100 cents = 1,000 mils; valuation[1] (Oct. 4, 1993) 1 Lm = U.S.$2.63 = £1.75.

Area and population

Census regions[2]	area sq mi	area sq km	population 1992 estimate[3]
Gozo and Comino	27	70	26,507
Inner Harbour	6	15	101,977
Northern	30	78	34,367
Outer Harbour	12	32	104,169
South Eastern	20	53	45,669
Western	27	69	46,854
TOTAL	122	316[4]	359,543

Demography

Population (1993): 363,000.
Density (1993): persons per sq mi 2,975.4, persons per sq km 1,148.7.
Urban-rural (1985): urban 85.3%; rural 14.7%.
Sex distribution (1992[3]): male 49.42%; female 50.58%.
Age breakdown (1992[3]): under 15, 23.0%; 15–29, 21.4%; 30–44, 24.1%; 45–59, 16.6%; 60–74, 11.0%; 75 and over, 3.9%.
Population projection: (2000) 379,000; (2010) 399,000.
Doubling time: 102 years.
Ethnic composition (by nationality; 1980): Maltese 95.7%; British 2.1%; other 2.2%.
Religious affiliation (1990): Roman Catholic 98.9%; other 1.1%.
Major cities (1992[3]): Birkirkara 21,437; Qormi 19,525; Hamrun 13,694; Sliema 13,546; Valletta 9,183.

Vital statistics

Birth rate per 1,000 population (1991): 14.8 (world avg. 26.4); legitimate 96.0%; illegitimate 4.0%.
Death rate per 1,000 population (1991): 8.0 (world avg. 9.2).
Natural increase rate per 1,000 population (1991): 6.8 (world avg. 17.2).
Total fertility rate (avg. births per childbearing woman; 1990): 2.0.
Marriage rate per 1,000 population (1991): 7.1.
Divorce rate per 1,000 population: n.a.
Life expectancy at birth (1991): male 73.6 years; female 78.3 years.
Major causes of death per 100,000 population (1991): diseases of the circulatory system 400.0; malignant neoplasms (cancers) 168.5; diseases of the respiratory system 56.5; endocrine, nutritional, and metabolic diseases of the blood and blood-forming organs 44.2; diseases of the digestive system 28.6; accidents, poisonings, and violence 26.7.

National economy

Budget (1993). Revenue: Lm 385,115,000 (1992; customs and excise taxes 23.6%, national insurance and Central Bank contributions 20.6%, income tax 19.2%, Central Bank profits 5.1%). Expenditures: Lm 364,972,000 (1992; national insurance benefits 41.1%, education 12.3%, health 9.8%, debt service 4.7%).
Public debt (1990): U.S.$565,407,000.
Production (wholesale value in Lm except where noted). Agriculture, forestry, fishing (1991): vegetables 5,119,473 (of which tomatoes 790,380, melons 662,023, carrots 376,803, cauliflower 360,376, onions 219,405), fruits 1,004,481 (of which peaches 277,821, strawberries 179,373), potatoes 679,511; livestock (number of live animals; 1992) 107,000 pigs, 23,000 cattle, 6,000 sheep, 5,000 goats, 1,000,000 chickens; fish catch (metric tons; 1991) 713. Quarrying (1989): 1,334,000. Manufacturing (value of sales in Lm; 1991): machinery and transport equipment 233,882,000, of which transport equipment 23,822,000; food and beverages 76,257,000; textiles and wearing apparel 75,628,000; printing and publishing 28,802,000; chemicals 24,462,000; tobacco products 13,509,000. Construction (1990): 37,962,000. Energy production (consumption): electricity (kW-hr; 1990) 1,100,000,000 (1,100,000,000); coal (metric tons; 1990) none (300,000); crude petroleum, none (n.a.); petroleum products (metric tons; 1990) none (320,000); natural gas, none (n.a.).
Population economically active (1992): total 136,482; activity rate of total population 37.8% (participation rates: ages 15–64 [1985] 45.9%; female 26.0%; unemployed 3.9%).

Price and earnings indexes (1987 = 100)

	1986	1987	1988	1989	1990	1991	1992
Consumer price index	99.5	100.0	101.1	101.8	104.8	107.5	112.0
Annual earnings index	...	100.0	103.8	106.9	108.6	117.8	121.4

Household income and expenditure. Average household size (1985) 3.3; average annual income per household (1982) Lm 4,736 (U.S.$11,399); sources of income (1990): wages and salaries 47.7%, professional and unincorporated enterprises 16.6%, rents, dividends, and interest 13.2%; expenditure (1990): food and beverages 29.0%, transportation and communications 16.6%, household furnishings and operations 7.6%, clothing and footwear 7.4%, recreation, entertainment, and education 7.4%, housing 5.5%, health 3.6%, tobacco 3.6%.
Tourism (1991): receipts from visitors U.S.$574,000,000; expenditures by nationals abroad U.S.$140,000,000.
Gross national product (1991): U.S.$2,598,000,000 (U.S.$6,850 per capita).

Structure of gross domestic product and labour force

	1991 in value Lm '000	1991 % of total value	1992 labour force	1992 % of labour force
Agriculture	23,439	3.3	2,926	2.1
Manufacturing	188,129	26.5	34,455	25.2
Mining	26,511	3.7		
Construction			5,790	4.2
Public utilities	5	5	5	5
Transportation and communications	41,845	5.9	10,992	8.0
Trade	101,374	14.3	13,833	10.1
Finance	101,926[6]	14.3[6]	3,566	2.6
Pub. admin., defense	162,396[5]	22.8[5]	39,158[5]	28.7[5]
Services	65,129	9.2	15,411	11.3
Other	...	...	10,351[7]	7.6[7]
TOTAL	710,749	100.0	136,482	100.0[4]

Land use (1991): agricultural and under permanent cultivation 40.6%; other (infertile clay soil with underlying limestone) 59.4%.

Foreign trade[8]

Balance of trade (current prices)

	1987	1988	1989	1990	1991	1992
Lm '000,000	−184.3	−168.1	−169.0	−172.8	−214.5	−182.9
% of total	30.6%	26.3%	22.3%	18.3%	21.1%	15.7%

Imports (1991): Lm 683,164,000 (machinery and transport equipment 47.0%, semimanufactured goods 18.2%, food and live animals 9.0%, chemicals and chemical products 6.9%, mineral fuels 5.0%, nonfuel materials 1.8%, beverages and tobacco 1.1%). *Major import sources:* Italy 35.9%; U.K. 14.8%; Germany 11.2%; France 4.8%; U.S. 4.1%.
Exports (1991): Lm 405,409,000 (machinery and transport equipment 29.4%, clothing and footwear 13.2%, reexports 8.3%, semimanufactured goods 7.2%, food and live animals 1.7%, beverages and tobacco 1.5%). *Major export destinations:* Italy 38.1%; Germany 17.1%; U.K. 5.9%; Libya 4.5%; U.S. 3.8%; The Netherlands 1.6%.

Transport and communications

Transport. Railroads: none. Roads (1992): total length 988 mi, 1,588 km (paved 92%). Vehicles (1992): passenger cars 120,320; trucks and buses 27,978. Merchant marine (1992): vessels (100 gross tons and over) 889; total deadweight tonnage 17,073,207. Air transport (1991): passenger-mi 630,197,000, passenger-km 1,014,205,000; short ton-mi cargo 3,840,000, metric ton-km cargo 5,607,000; airports (1993) with scheduled flights 1.
Communications. Daily newspapers (1992): total number 3; total circulation 68,000; circulation per 1,000 population 192. Radio (1993): 90,000 receivers (1 per 4.0 persons). Television (1993): 146,107 receivers (1 per 2.5 persons). Telephones (1991): 191,876 (1 per 1.9 persons).

Education and health

Education (1990–91)

	schools	teachers	students	student/teacher ratio
Primary (age 5–10)	194	1,455	36,899	25.4
Secondary (age 11–17)	43	1,594	25,891	16.2
Voc., teacher tr.	31	710	6,653	9.4
Higher[9]	1	244	2,511	10.3

Educational attainment (1967). Percentage of economically active population having: no formal schooling 10.8%; primary education 60.4%; lower secondary 3.4%; upper secondary 17.6%; technical secondary 3.9%; postsecondary and higher 3.9%. *Literacy* (1985): total population age 15 and over literate 250,419 (96.0%); males literate 121,899 (96.2%); females literate 128,520 (95.9%).
Health (1991): physicians 805 (1 per 444 persons); hospital beds 3,326 (1 per 107 persons); infant mortality rate per 1,000 live births 9.6.
Food (1988–90): daily per capita caloric intake 3,169 (vegetable products 72%, animal products 28%); 128% of FAO recommended minimum requirement.

Military

Total active duty personnel (1993): 1,650 (army 100%). *Military expenditure as percentage of GNP* (1989): 1.1% (world 4.9%); per capita expenditure U.S.$62.

[1]The Maltese lira is tied to the currencies of several principal trading partners. [2]Although Gozo is administered separately, the island of Malta has no first-order administrative subdivisions; data are reported according to census regions. [3]January 1. [4]Detail does not add to total given because of rounding. [5]Pub. admin., defense includes Public utilities. [6]Finance includes income from property. [7]Includes 5,332 unemployed. [8]Import figures are f.o.b. in balance of trade and c.i.f. for commodities and trading partners. [9]1989–90.

Marshall Islands

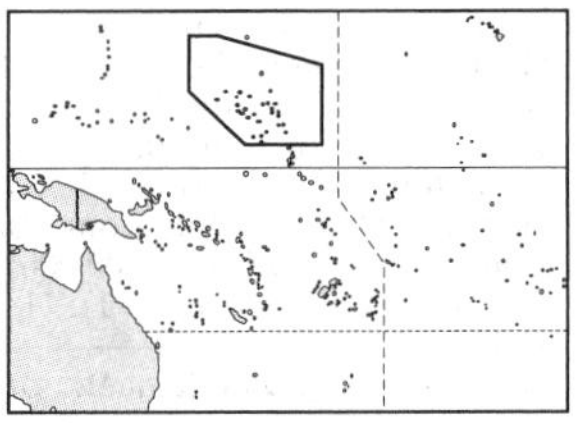

Official name: Majōl (Marshallese); Republic of the Marshall Islands (English).
Form of government: unitary republic with two legislative houses (Council of Iroij [12][1]; Nitijela [33]).
Head of state and government: President.
Capital: Majuro.
Official languages: Marshallese (Kajin-Majōl); English.
Official religion: none.
Monetary unit: 1 U.S. dollar (U.S.$) = 100 cents; valuation (Oct. 4, 1993) 1 £ = U.S.$1.52.

Area and population

Election districts	area sq mi	area sq km	population 1988 census
Ailinglaplap	5.67	14.69	1,715
Ailuk	2.07	5.36	488
Arno	5.00	12.95	1,656
Aur	2.17	5.62	438
Bikini	2.32	6.00	10
Ebon	2.22	5.75	741
Enewetak and Ujelang	2.93	7.59	715
Jabat	0.22	0.57	112
Jaluit	4.38	11.34	1,709
Kili	0.36	0.93	602
Kwajalein	6.33	16.39	9,311
Lae	0.56	1.45	319
Lib	0.36	0.93	115
Likiep	3.97	10.28	482
Majuro	3.75	9.71	19,664
Maloelap	3.79	9.82	796
Mejit	0.72	1.86	445
Mili	6.15	15.93	854
Namorik	1.07	2.77	814
Namu	2.42	6.27	801
Rongelap	3.07	7.95	0
Ujae	0.72	1.86	448
Utrik	0.94	2.43	409
Wotho	1.67	4.32	90
Wotje	3.16	8.18	646
Other atolls	4.05	10.49	0
TOTAL	70.07	181.48[2]	43,380

Demography

Population (1993): 52,000.
Density (1993): persons per sq mi 742.1, persons per sq km 286.5.
Urban-rural (1988): urban 64.5%; rural 35.5%.
Sex distribution (1992): male 51.05%; female 48.95%.
Age breakdown (1992): under 15, 50.5%; 15–29, 25.2%; 30–44, 14.4%; 45–59, 5.9%; 60–74, 3.2%; 75 and over, 0.8%.
Population projection: (2000) 66,700; (2010) 87,300.
Doubling time: 18 years.
Ethnic composition (1988): Marshallese 96.9%; other Pacific islanders 1.7%; Filipino 0.5%; all other 0.9%.
Religious affiliation (1973): Protestant 90.1%; Roman Catholic 8.5%; other 1.4%.
Major cities (1988): Dalap-Uliga-Darrit 14,649; Ebeye 8,324.

Vital statistics

Birth rate per 1,000 population (1991): 47.0 (world avg. 26.4).
Death rate per 1,000 population (1991): 8.0 (world avg. 9.2).
Natural increase rate per 1,000 population (1991): 39.0 (world avg. 17.2).
Total fertility rate (avg. births per childbearing woman; 1991): 7.1.
Marriage rate per 1,000 population: n.a.
Divorce rate per 1,000 population: n.a.
Life expectancy at birth (1989): male 60.0 years; female 63.0 years.
Major causes of death per 100,000 population (1988–91)[3]: circulatory diseases 87.6; infectious and parasitic diseases 74.4; respiratory diseases 62.8; accidents, injuries, and violence 37.5; digestive diseases 37.5; malignant neoplasms (cancers) 27.6.

National economy

Budget (1990–91). Revenue: U.S.$34,704,774 (U.S. government grants 35.3%, income tax 21.4%, import tax 17.0%, fishing rights 5.3%, fuel taxes 1.5%). Expenditures: U.S.$44,128,786 (health services 18.9%, education 17.5%, public works and social programs 12.5%, transportation and communications 4.4%, internal security 3.4%).
Production (metric tons except as noted). Agriculture, forestry, fishing (1991): copra 5,545, fruits 1,809 (of which pandanus 836, breadfruit 645, bananas 264, papaya 64), tubers 1,500 (of which taro 1,300, sweet potatoes 182), vegetables 136 (of which cabbage 36, pumpkins 36); livestock consists mostly of swine and poultry; roundwood, n.a.; fish catch (1989) 12,193[4]. Mining and quarrying: quarrying of sand and aggregate for local construction only. Manufacturing: n.a.; however, coconut oil and processed (mostly frozen) fish are the most important products; the manufacture of handicrafts and personal items (clothing, mats, boats, etc.) by individuals is also important. Construction: n.a. Energy production (consumption): electricity (kW-hr; 1991) 45,759,000 (45,759,000); coal, none (n.a.); gasoline, oil, and lubricants (barrels; 1988)[5] n.a. (84,588); natural gas, none (n.a.).
Public debt (external, outstanding): n.a.
Gross domestic product (at current market prices; 1991): U.S.$75,694,000 (U.S.$1,577 per capita).

Structure of private (nongovernmental) gross sales and labour force

	1981 in value U.S.$'000	1981 % of total value	1988 labour force	1988 % of labour force
Agriculture	32.5	0.1	2,150	18.7
Mining	...	...	2	—
Manufacturing	155.3	0.5	945	8.2
Public utilities	—	—	82	0.7
Construction	2,235.6	7.5	1,076	9.4
Transportation and communications	1,682.7	5.6	537	4.7
Trade, restaurants, hotels	25,150.6	83.8	1,394	12.1
Finance, insurance, real estate	510.5	1.7	833	7.3
Public administration	—	—	3,035	26.4
Services	235.9	0.8		
Other	—	—	1,434[6]	12.5[6]
TOTAL	30,003.1	100.0	11,488	100.0

Land use (1989)[7]: forested 22.5%; meadows and pastures 13.5%; agricultural and under permanent cultivation 33.1%; other 30.9%.
Household income and expenditure. Average household size (1988) 8.7; income per household (1979) U.S.$3,366; sources of income: n.a.; expenditure (latest): food 57.7%, housing 15.6%, clothing 12.0%, personal effects and other 14.7%.
Population economically active (1988): total 11,488; activity rate of total population 26.5% (participation rates: over age 14, 54.1%; female 30.1%; unemployed 12.5%).

Price and earnings indexes (1985 = 100)

	1985	1986	1987	1988	1989	1990	1991
Consumer price index	100.0	108.5	105.1	109.0	111.6	112.3	116.1
Earnings index	...	...	...	...	...	...	...

Tourism (1986): receipts from visitors U.S.$366,832; expenditures by nationals abroad, n.a.

Foreign trade

Balance of trade (current prices)

	1986	1987	1988	1989	1990	1991
U.S.$'000,000	−29.4	−31.6	−31.7	−41.9	−53.9	−53.5
% of total	92.7%	89.2%	88.3%	89.4%	94.0%	90.3%

Imports (1991): U.S.$56,442,000 (food and live animals 24.3%, machinery and transport equipment 16.2%, mineral fuels and lubricants 11.1%, beverages and tobacco 9.9%, manufactured goods 9.7%). *Major import sources:* United States 58.5%; Guam 16.3%; Japan 9.6%; Australia 1.6%.
Exports (1991): U.S.$2,890,000 (crude coconut oil 48.3%, frozen fish 27.0%, live animals 17.9%, trochus shells 6.1%). *Major export destinations* (1983): United States 79.4%; other 20.6%.

Transport and communications

Transport. Railroads: none. Roads: n.a. Vehicles (1991): passenger cars 1,332; trucks and buses 75. Merchant marine (1992): vessels (100 gross tons and over) 35; total deadweight tonnage 4,182,356. Air transport: n.a.; airports (1993) with scheduled flights 24.
Communications. Daily newspapers (1991): there are no dailies, only weeklies, of which there are two with a total circulation of over 10,000. Radio (1990): total number of receivers, n.a.; but there are two radio stations. Television (1990): total number of receivers, n.a.; but there are two television stations. Telephones (1988): 800 (1 per 53 persons).

Education and health

Education (1991–92)

	schools	teachers	students	student/ teacher ratio
Primary (age 6–14)	102	515	12,248	23.8
Secondary (age 15–18)	8[8]	137	2,215	16.2
Voc., teacher tr.	...	...	...	...
Higher	...	...	...	...

Educational attainment (1988). Percentage of population age 25 and over having: no grade completed 5.1%; elementary education 43.2%; secondary 39.7%; higher 11.4%; not stated 0.6%. *Literacy* (latest): total population age 15 and over literate 19,377 (91.2%); males literate 9,993 (92.4%); females literate 9,384 (90.0%).
Health (1985): physicians 17 (1 per 2,217 persons); hospital beds 54 (1 per 698 persons); infant mortality rate per 1,000 live births (1991) 53.0.
Food: daily per capita caloric intake, n.a.

Military

Under the 1984 Compact of Free Association, the United States provides for the defense of the Republic of the Marshall Islands.

[1]Council of Iroij is an advisory body only. [2]Detail does not add to total given because of rounding. [3]Registered deaths only. [4]Total for foreign vessels only, including 6,762 metric tons caught by Japanese vessels. [5]Imports only. [6]Includes 1,432 unemployed. [7]Data are for the former Trust Territory of the Pacific Islands. [8]1986–87.

Martinique

Official name: Département de la Martinique (Department of Martinique).
Political status: overseas department (France) with two legislative houses (General Council [45]; Regional Council [41]).
Chief of state: President of France.
Heads of government: Commissioner of the Republic (for France); President of the General Council (for Martinique); President of the Regional Council (for Martinique).
Capital: Fort-de-France.
Official language: French.
Official religion: none.
Monetary unit: 1 French franc (F) = 100 centimes; valuation (Oct. 4, 1993) 1 U.S.$ = F 5.67; 1 £ = F 8.58.

Area and population

		area		population
Arrondissements	**Capitals**	sq mi	sq km	1990 census
Fort-de-France	Fort-de-France	147	381	187,275
Le Marin	Le Marin	158	409	93,411
La Trinité	La Trinité	131	338	78,893
TOTAL		436	1,128	359,579

Demography

Population (1993): 377,000.
Density (1993): persons per sq mi 864.7, persons per sq km 334.2.
Urban-rural (1990): urban 80.5%; rural 19.5%.
Sex distribution (1990): male 48.36%; female 51.64%.
Age breakdown (1990): under 15, 23.1%; 15–29, 28.9%; 30–44, 20.5%; 45–59, 13.5%; 60–74, 9.7%; 75 and over, 4.3%.
Population projection: (2000) 415,000; (2010) 458,000.
Doubling time: 62 years.
Ethnic composition (1983): mulatto 93.7%; French (metropolitan and Martinique white) 2.6%; East Indian 1.7%; other 2.0%.
Religious affiliation (1991): Roman Catholic 88.6%; other (mostly Seventh-day Adventist, Jehovah's Witness, syncretist, and nonreligious) 11.4%.
Major urban areas (1990): Fort-de-France 100,072; Le Lamentin 30,026; Schoelcher 19,825; Sainte-Marie 19,683; Le Robert 17,675.

Vital statistics

Birth rate per 1,000 population (1992): 17.1 (world avg. 26.4); legitimate 34.6%; illegitimate 65.4%.
Death rate per 1,000 population (1992): 5.9 (world avg. 9.2).
Natural increase rate per 1,000 population (1992): 11.2 (world avg. 17.2).
Total fertility rate (avg. births per childbearing woman; 1990–95): 2.0.
Marriage rate per 1,000 population (1992): 4.5.
Divorce rate per 1,000 population (1992): 1.0.
Life expectancy at birth (1989): male 71.0 years; female 77.0 years.
Major causes of death per 100,000 population (1988): diseases of the circulatory system 210.4; malignant neoplasms (cancers) 127.9; accidents, poisoning, and violence 40.3; diseases of the digestive system 34.0; endocrine and metabolic disorders 28.4.

National economy

Budget (1991). Revenue: F 1,755,000,000 (general receipts from French central government and local administrative bodies 49.2%, tax receipts 29.2%, new loans 11.6%, public-works subsidies 6.0%). Expenditures: F 1,755,000,000 (health and social assistance 35.0%, improvements to public works and property 34.0%, other administrative services 16.2%, debt amortization 3.3%).
Public debt (external, outstanding; 1987)[1]: U.S.$30,000,000.
Production (metric tons except as noted). Agriculture, forestry, fishing (1992): bananas 255,000, sugarcane 98,443, pineapples 16,182, plantains 10,000, yams 9,000, cucumbers 4,000, sweet potatoes 3,000, tomatoes 3,000, melons 1,768[2], avocados 1,000, limes 862[3], flowers and foliage 139[2], pimientos 170[2, 3]; livestock (number of live animals) 63,000 sheep, 49,000 pigs, 35,000 cattle; roundwood (1991) 12,000 cu m; fish catch (1991) 3,587. Mining and quarrying (1988): pumice 132,000; sand and gravel for local construction. Manufacturing (1992): cement 262,417; processed pineapples 9,613; sugar 6,547; rum 75,411 hectolitres; other products include clothing, fabricated metals, and yawls and sails. Construction (buildings authorized; 1992): residential, n.a.; nonresidential 213,888 sq m. Energy production (consumption): electricity (kW-hr; 1992) 761,375,000 (425,111,000); coal, none (none); crude petroleum (barrels; 1992) none (5,409,000); petroleum products (metric tons; 1992) 493,180 (493,180); natural gas, none (none).
Household income and expenditure. Average household size (1990) 3.3; income per household (1979) F 70,009 (U.S.$17,415); sources of income (1979): wages and salaries 74.2%, rent 4.8%, other 21.0%; expenditure (1993): food and beverages 32.1%, transportation and communications 20.7%, housing and energy 10.6%, household durable goods 9.4%, clothing and footwear 8.0%, education and recreation 5.4%, health care 5.2%, other 8.6%.
Tourism (1991): receipts from visitors U.S.$255,000,000; expenditures by nationals abroad, n.a.

Gross national product (at current market prices; 1987): U.S.$1,429,000,000 (U.S.$4,100 per capita).

Structure of gross domestic product and labour force

	1982		1986	
	in value F '000,000	% of total value	labour force	% of labour force
Agriculture, fishing	720	8.1	10,364	7.1
Mining, manufacturing	552	6.2	5,769	4.0
Construction	324	3.6	6,894	4.7
Public utilities	96	1.1	1,303	0.9
Transportation and communications	390	4.4	5,870	4.0
Trade, restaurants, hotels	1,541	17.4	12,399	8.5
Finance, real estate, insurance	630	7.1	19,296	13.2
Pub. admin., defense, services	4,267	48.1	32,894	22.6
Other	354	4.0	51,135[4]	35.0[4]
TOTAL	8,874	100.0	145,924	100.0

Population economically active (1990): total 164,870; activity rate of total population 44.5% (participation rates: ages 15–64 [1986] 67.4%; female 47.5%; unemployed 32.1%).

Price and earnings indexes (1985 = 100)[5]

	1986	1987	1988	1989	1990	1991	1992
Consumer price index	102.6	106.3	108.8	112.4	116.8	118.3	126.6
Monthly earnings index[6]	100.9	103.0	106.1	108.9	111.3	114.2	121.5

Land use (1991): forested 44.3%; meadows and pastures 17.9%; agricultural and under permanent cultivation 18.9%; other 18.9%.

Foreign trade[7]

Balance of trade (current prices)

	1987	1988	1989	1990	1991	1992
F '000,000	−5,544	−6,551	−6,732	−7,970	−7,934	−7,982
% of total	70.4%	73.7%	73.5%	72.7%	78.4%	75.6%

Imports (1992): F 9,266,944,000 (1991; food products 19.3%, machinery 14.9%, chemical products 11.0%, transport equipment 10.7%, mineral fuels 7.8%, metal manufactures 7.5%). *Major import sources:* France 60.5%; United States 3.0%; Venezuela 1.2%; Guadeloupe 1.0%; other Caribbean 1.7%.
Exports (1992): F 1,284,786,000 (1991; bananas 38.9%, refined petroleum 20.6%, rum 10.1%, melons 2.4%, fertilizer 1.2%). *Major export destinations:* France 61.9%; Guadeloupe 29.8%; French Guiana 4.0%.

Transport and communications

Transport. Railroads: none. Roads (1989): total length 1,050 mi, 1,690 km (paved [1988] 75%). Vehicles (1985): passenger cars 135,269; trucks and buses 7,328. Merchant marine (1992): vessels (100 gross tons and over) 6; total deadweight tonnage 1,121. Air transport (1992): passenger arrivals 666,108, passenger departures 662,724; cargo unloaded 6,917 metric tons, cargo loaded 6,167 metric tons; airports (1993) with scheduled flights 1.
Communications. Daily newspapers (1990): total number 1; total circulation 30,000; circulation per 1,000 population 82. Radio (1992): total number of receivers 60,000 (1 per 6.2 persons). Television (1992): total number of receivers 65,000 (1 per 5.7 persons). Telephones (1990): 158,723 (1 per 2.3 persons).

Education and health

Education (1988–89)

	schools	teachers	students	student/ teacher ratio
Primary (age 6–11)	210	2,004	32,986	16.4
Secondary (age 12–18) } Vocational }	75[8]	2,745[8]	31,234 } 8,035 }	16.5[8]
Higher	1	40[8]	2,743	30[8]

Educational attainment (1982). Percentage of population age 25 and over having: no formal schooling 9.8%; primary education 62.7%; secondary 21.2%; higher 6.3%. *Literacy* (1982): total population age 15 and over literate 206,807 (92.5%); males literate 97,538 (91.8%); females literate 109,269 (93.2%).
Health (1990): physicians 623 (1 per 580 persons); hospital beds 3,571 (1 per 101 persons); infant mortality rate per 1,000 live births 7.1.
Food (1988–90): daily per capita caloric intake 2,768 (vegetable products 75%, animal products 25%); 114% of FAO recommended minimum requirement.

Military

Total active duty personnel (1992): 8,200 French troops[9].

[1]Includes external long-term private debt not guaranteed by the government. [2]Production for export only. [3]1990. [4]Unemployed. [5]All figures are end-of-year unless otherwise footnoted. [6]Based on minimum-level wage of public employees. [7]Imports c.i.f.; exports f.o.b. [8]1986–87. [9]Includes troops stationed in Guadeloupe and French Guiana.

Mauritania

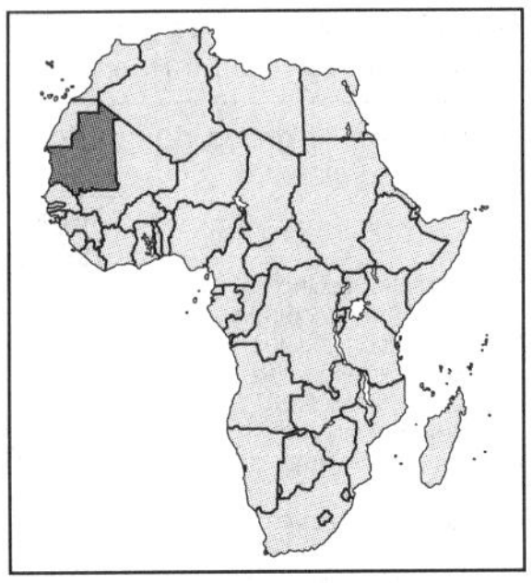

Official name: al-Jumhūrīyah al-Islāmīyah al-Mūrītānīyah (Arabic) (Islamic Republic of Mauritania).
Form of government: republic with two legislative houses (Senate [56]; National Assembly [79]).
Head of state and government: President.
Capital: Nouakchott.
Official languages: Arabic[1].
Official religion: Islam.
Monetary unit: 1 Mauritanian Ouguiya (UM) = 5 khoums; valuation (Oct. 4, 1993) 1 U.S.$ = UM 112.98; 1 £ = UM 171.17.

Area and population

		area		population
Regions	**Capitals**	sq mi	sq km	1988 census
el-'Açâba	Kiffa	13,900	36,000	167,123
Adrar	Atar	83,100	215,300	61,043
Brakna	Aleg	14,000	37,100	192,157
Dakhlet Nouadhibou	Nouadhibou	11,600	30,000	63,030
Gorgol	Kaédi	5,400	14,000	184,359
Guidimaka	Sélibaby	4,000	10,000	116,436
Hodh ech-Chargui	Néma	64,000	166,000	212,203
Hodh el-Gharbi	'Ayoûn el-'Atroûs	22,000	57,000	159,296
Inchiri	Akjoujt	19,000	49,000	14,613
Tagant	Tidjikdja	36,000	93,000	64,908
Tiris Zemmour	Fdérik	98,600	255,300	33,147
Trarza	Rosso	26,000	67,000	202,596
District				
Nouakchott	Nouakchott	400	1,000	393,325
TOTAL		398,000	1,030,700	1,864,236

Demography

Population (1993): 2,171,000.
Density (1993): persons per sq mi 5.5, persons per sq km 2.1.
Urban-rural (1988): urban 39.1%; rural 60.9%.
Sex distribution (1990): male 49.41%; female 50.59%.
Age breakdown (1990): under 15, 44.6%; 15–29, 25.8%; 30–44, 15.5%; 45–59, 9.1%; 60–74, 4.2%; 75 and over, 0.7%.
Population projection: (2000) 2,665,000; (2010) 3,572,000.
Doubling time: 22 years.
Ethnic composition (1993): Moor 70.0% (of which about 40% "black" Moor [Haratin, or African Sudanic] and about 30% "white" Moor [Bidan, or Arab-Berber]); other black African 30.0% (including [1983] Wolof 6.8%, Tukulor 5.3%, Soninke 2.8%, Fulani 1.1%, other 2.5%).
Religious affiliation (1980): Muslim 99.4%; Christian 0.4%; other 0.2%.
Major cities (1988): Nouakchott 393,325; Nouadhibou 59,198; Kaédi 30,515; Kiffa 29,292; Rosso 27,783.

Vital statistics

Birth rate per 1,000 population (1991): 49.6 (world avg. 26.4); legitimate, n.a.; illegitimate, n.a.
Death rate per 1,000 population (1991): 17.5 (world avg. 9.2).
Natural increase rate per 1,000 population (1991): 32.1 (world avg. 17.2).
Total fertility rate (avg. births per childbearing woman; 1991): 7.2.
Marriage rate per 1,000 population: n.a.
Divorce rate per 1,000 population: n.a.
Life expectancy at birth (1991): male 44.0 years; female 50.0 years.
Morbidity (notified cases of infectious disease per 100,000 population; 1984): enteritis and diarrhea 10,566; conjunctivitis 7,080; malaria 2,897; scarlet fever 2,476; measles 714.0; chicken pox 306.4.

National economy

Budget (1993). Revenue: UM 32,000,000,000 (1991; tax revenue 75.3%, of which import and export duties 30.2%, value-added tax 26.5%, excise tax 18.6%). Expenditures: UM 32,200,000,000 (1991; administrative expenses 35.8%; defense 12.1%; interest on debt 7.8%).
Tourism (1988): receipts from visitors U.S.$14,000,000; expenditures by nationals abroad U.S.$27,000,000.
Land use (1991): forested 4.2%; meadows and pastures 38.3%; agricultural and under permanent cultivation 0.2%; desert 57.3%.
Production (metric tons except as noted). Agriculture, forestry, fishing (1992): sorghum 50,000, pulses 19,000, rice 18,000, dates 12,000, vegetables (including melons) 11,000, roots and tubers 6,000 (of which sweet potatoes 3,000, yams 3,000), millet 3,000, corn (maize) 2,000; livestock (number of live animals) 5,400,000 sheep, 3,600,000 goats, 1,400,000 cattle, 990,000 camels, 154,000 asses, 18,000 horses, 4,000,000 chickens; roundwood (1991) 13,000 cu m; fish catch (1991) 90,000. Mining and quarrying (1990): iron ore (gross weight) 11,550,000; gypsum 3,600. Manufacturing (1990): cow's milk 97,000; meat 44,000, of which fresh beef and veal 17,000, fresh mutton and lamb 6,000, goat meat 5,000; hides and skins 4,720; cheese 1,841; butter 680. Construction (1984): 42,478 sq m. Energy production (consumption): electricity (kW-hr; 1990) 140,000,000 (140,000,000); coal (metric tons; 1990) none (6,000); crude petroleum (barrels; 1990) none (6,250,000); petroleum products (metric tons; 1990) 730,000 (796,000); natural gas, none (n.a.).
Household income and expenditure. Average household size (1980) 5.0; income per household: n.a.; sources of income: n.a.; expenditure (1988): food and beverages 77.2%, housing 13.7%, clothing and footwear 5.8%, health 1.0%, education 0.8%.
Gross national product (at current market prices; 1992): U.S.$1,083,000,000 (U.S.$520 per capita).

Structure of gross domestic product and labour force

	1989		1987	
	in value UM '000,000	% of total value	labour force	% of labour force
Agriculture	24,709	29.8	380,800	66.0
Mining	7,696	9.3	57,700	10.0
Manufacturing	8,240	9.9		
Public utilities / Construction	5,264	6.3		
Transportation and communications	3,846	4.6	138,500	24.0
Trade and finance	9,665	11.8		
Services	4,683	5.6		
Pub. admin., defense	11,034	13.3		
Other (indirect taxes net of subsidies)	7,818	9.4	—	—
TOTAL	82,955	100.0	577,000	100.0

Population economically active (1990): total 678,000; activity rate of total population 33.5% (participation rates: over age 10, 49.7%; female 22.1%; unemployed [1988] 50.0%).

Price and earnings indexes (1985 = 100)

	1986	1987	1988	1989	1990	1991	1992
Consumer price index	107.4	116.2	117.7	133.0	141.7	149.7	164.9
Earnings index	...	...	...	...	...	...	...

Public debt (external, outstanding; 1991): U.S.$1,912,000,000.

Foreign trade

Balance of trade (current prices)

	1985	1986	1987	1988	1989	1990
UM '000,000	+10,110	+9,404	+3,395	+4,576	+8,277	+3,838
% of total	21.3%	17.7%	5.7%	6.4%	12.4%	5.8%

Imports (1990): UM 31,286,000,000 (1988; machinery and transport equipment 51.0%, food 30.6%, consumer goods 9.0%, crude petroleum and petroleum products 7.0%). *Major import sources:* France 45.7%; Belgium 9.8%; West Germany 9.1%; United States 7.4%; Spain 7.3%; Algeria 6.0%; China 5.9%; The Netherlands 4.1%; Japan 2.8%; Thailand 1.9%.
Exports (1990): UM 35,124,000,000 (1989; fish 58.6%, iron ore 31.3%). *Major export destinations:* Japan 21.2%; Italy 14.2%; U.S.S.R. 11.9%; France 11.0%; Belgium 10.8%; Spain 8.6%; United Kingdom 5.0%; Côte d'Ivoire 3.6%; United States 3.1%; Greece 2.0%.

Transport and communications

Transport. Railroads (1990): route length 428 mi, 689 km; passenger-mi 4,350,000[2], passenger-km 7,000,000[2]; short ton-mi cargo 5,393,000,000, metric ton-km cargo 7,873,000,000. Roads (1989): total length 4,696 mi, 7,558 km (paved 23%). Vehicles (1991): passenger cars 10,000; trucks and buses 5,000. Merchant marine (1992): vessels (100 gross tons and over) 126; total deadweight tonnage 23,875. Air transport (1990)[3]: passenger-mi 144,363,000, passenger-km 232,329,000; short ton-mi cargo 26,971,000, metric ton-km cargo 39,374,000; airports (1993) with scheduled flights 10.
Communications. Daily newspapers (1990): total number 1; total circulation, n.a. Radio (1992): total number of receivers 300,000 (1 per 7.0 persons). Television (1992): total number of receivers 1,100 (1 per 1,916 persons). Telephones (1989)[4]: 4,581 (1 per 431 persons).

Education and health

Education (1990)

	schools	teachers	students	student/ teacher ratio
Primary (age 6–11)	1,214	3,497	155,116	44.4
Secondary (age 12–17)	44[5]	1,995	35,758	17.9
Voc., teacher tr.	6[5]	178	1,567	8.8
Higher	7	270	5,810	21.5

Educational attainment: n.a. *Literacy* (1990): percentage of total population age 15 and over literate 34.0%; males literate 47.1%; females literate 21.4%.
Health: physicians (1990) 151 (1 per 13,167 persons); hospital beds (1988) 1,556 (1 per 1,217 persons); infant mortality rate per 1,000 live births (1991) 94.
Food (1988–90): daily per capita caloric intake 2,447 (vegetable products 81%, animal products 19%); 106% of FAO recommended minimum requirement.

Military

Total active duty personnel (1993): 15,600 (army 96.2%, navy 2.6%, air force 1.2%). *Military expenditure as percentage of GNP* (1992): 3.1% (world 4.9%); per capita expenditure U.S.$17.

[1]The 1991 constitution names Arabic as the official language and the following as national languages: Arabic, Fulani, Soninke, and Wolof. [2]1984. [3]Air Afrique traffic only. [4]Number of subscribers. [5]1986.

Mauritius

Official name: Republic of Mauritius.
Form of government: republic with one legislative house (Legislative Assembly [70[1]]).
Chief of state: President.
Head of government: Prime Minister.
Capital: Port Louis.
Official language: English.
Official religion: none.
Monetary unit: 1 Mauritian rupee (Mau Re; plural Mau Rs) = 100 cents; valuation (Oct. 4, 1993) 1 U.S.$ = Mau Rs 17.64; 1 £ = Mau Rs 26.73.

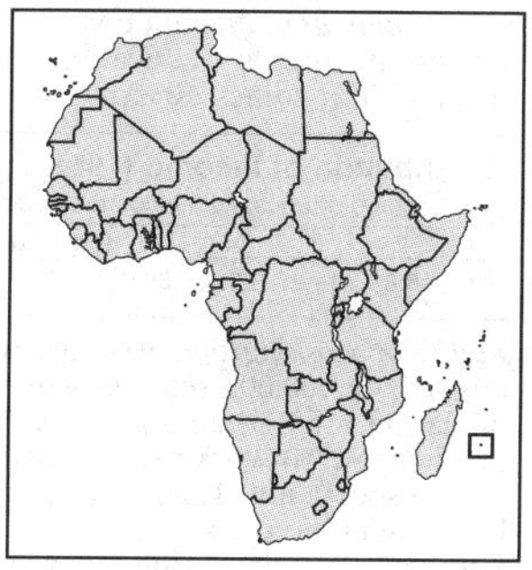

Area and population

Islands Districts/Dependencies	area sq mi	 sq km	population 1991[2] estimate
Mauritius	720	1,865	1,054,546
Black River	100	259	41,819
Flacq	115	298	119,721
Grand Port	100	260	102,308
Moka	89	231	67,594
Pamplemousses	69	179	100,896
Plaines Wilhems	78	203	324,172
Port Louis	17	43	142,645
Rivière du Rempart	57	148	90,974
Savanne	95	245	64,417
Mauritian dependencies			
Agalega[3] Cargados Carajos Shoals (Saint Brandon)[3]	27	71	500
Rodrigues[4]	40	104	37,782
TOTAL	788[5]	2,040[5]	1,092,828

Demography

Population (1993)[6]: 1,103,000.
Density (1993): persons per sq mi 1,399.7, persons per sq km 540.7.
Urban-rural (1991)[7]: urban 40.7%; rural 59.3%.
Sex distribution (1991): male 49.80%; female 50.20%.
Age breakdown (1990)[7]: under 15, 29.6%; 15–29, 29.0%; 30–44, 22.0%; 45–59, 11.3%; 60–74, 6.5%; 75 and over, 1.6%.
Population projection[6]: (2000) 1,191,000; (2010) 1,329,000.
Doubling time: 50 years.
Ethnic composition (1988): Indo-Pakistani 68.0%; Creole (mixed Caucasian, Indo-Pakistani, and African) 25.0%; Chinese 3.0%; white 3.0%; other 1.0%.
Religious affiliation (1983)[7]: Hindu 52.5%; Roman Catholic 25.7%; Muslim 12.9%; Protestant 4.4%; Buddhist 0.4%; other 4.1%.
Major cities (1991): Port Louis 142,645; Beau Bassin–Rose Hill 95,711; Curepipe 66,790; Quatre Bornes 66,572; Vacoas-Phoenix 57,227.

Vital statistics

Birth rate per 1,000 population (1991): 20.7 (world avg. 26.4); (1985) legitimate 72.8%; illegitimate 27.2%.
Death rate per 1,000 population (1991): 6.6 (world avg. 9.2).
Natural increase rate per 1,000 population (1991): 14.1 (world avg. 17.2).
Total fertility rate (avg. births per childbearing woman; 1990)[7]: 2.2.
Marriage rate per 1,000 population (1990)[7]: 10.6.
Divorce rate per 1,000 population (1990)[7]: 0.5.
Life expectancy at birth (1988–90)[7]: male 65.0 years; female 73.0 years.
Major causes of death per 100,000 population (1991)[7]: diseases of the circulatory system 286.9; diseases of the respiratory system 64.5; malignant neoplasms (cancers) 54.6; homicide, suicide, and accidents 49.4.

National economy

Budget (1992–93). Revenue: Mau Rs 11,555,000,000 (tax revenue 87.6%, of which import and stamp duties 39.8%, income tax 14.1%, sales tax 9.0%). Expenditures: Mau Rs 10,710,000,000 (social services 34.9%, of which education, art, and culture 13.7%, social security 11.1%, health 8.3%; public-debt service 30.1%).
Tourism (1991): receipts from visitors U.S.$262,000,000; expenditures by nationals abroad U.S.$110,000,000.
Public debt (external, outstanding; 1991): U.S.$794,000,000.
Gross national product (at current market prices; 1992): U.S.$3,011,000,000 (U.S.$2,740 per capita).

Structure of gross domestic product and labour force

	1992 in value Mau Rs '000,000[8]	 % of total value	 labour force[9, 10]	 % of labour force[9, 10]
Agriculture	4,125	10.4	44,300	15.7
Mining	50	0.1	200	0.1
Manufacturing	9,135	23.0	109,300	38.7
Construction	2,900	7.3	10,600	3.8
Public utilities	905	2.3	3,400	1.2
Transportation and communications	4,810	12.1	13,600	4.8
Trade	6,815	17.2	19,000	6.7
Finance	4,820	12.2	...	...
Pub. admin., defense	3,875	9.8	68,400	24.2
Services	2,145	5.4		
Other	...	...	13,600	4.8
TOTAL	39,700[5]	100.0[5]	282,400	100.0

Production (metric tons except as noted). Agriculture, forestry, fishing (1991): sugarcane 5,621,000, green tea 30,635, potatoes 16,000, tomatoes 9,390, bananas 6,470, black tea 6,000, cabbages 4,000, onions 3,000, corn (maize) 2,115, pineapples 1,480, peanuts (groundnuts) 1,340, tobacco 876; livestock (number of live animals; 1992) 95,000 goats, 34,000 cattle, 10,000 pigs, 7,000 sheep; roundwood 17,000 cu m; fish catch 19,611. Mining and quarrying (1990): sand 800,000, salt 3,000. Manufacturing (1990): raw sugar 624,302; molasses 168,023; manufactured tea 5,751; clothing 97,624,000 pieces[11]; beer and stout 281,243 hectolitres. Construction (1990): residential 887,230 sq m; nonresidential 227,340 sq m. Energy production (consumption): electricity (kW-hr; 1991) 613,600,000 (621,900,000); coal (metric tons; 1990) none (75,000); crude petroleum, none (none); petroleum products (metric tons; 1990) none (286,000); natural gas, none (none).
Population economically active (1991)[7]: total 462,600; activity rate of total population 44.5% (participation rates: ages 15–64, 68.0%; female 34.9%; unemployed 10.6%).

Price and earnings indexes (1985 = 100)

	1986	1987	1988	1989	1990	1991	1992
Consumer price index	101.6	102.2	111.5	125.6	142.6	152.6	159.6
Monthly earnings index[10]	106.3	112.8	143.3	169.8	179.4	207.7	230.7

Household income and expenditure. Average household size (1990) 4.5[7]; income per household (1979) Mau Rs 15,540 (U.S.$2,430); sources of income (1989): salaries and wages 51.7%, entrepreneurial income 37.1%, transfer payments 11.2%; expenditure (1980–81)[12]: food, beverages, and tobacco 50.4%, clothing and footwear 10.5%, housing 10.4%, transportation 10.0%, energy 6.4%, health care 3.0%, other 9.3%.
Land use (1991): forested 28.1%; meadows and pastures 3.4%; agricultural and under permanent cultivation 52.2%; other 16.3%.

Foreign trade[13]

Balance of trade (current prices)

	1986	1987	1988	1989	1990	1991
U.S.$'000,000	+58.2	−16.2	−167.8	−211.1	−280.0	−222.6
% of total	4.5%	0.9%	7.7%	9.6%	10.6%	8.4%

Imports (1991–92): Mau Rs 25,716,000,000 (manufactured goods classified chiefly by material 35.3%, machinery and transport equipment 24.9%, food 10.9%, mineral fuels and lubricants 7.6%, chemicals 7.1%, inedible crude materials excluding fuels 3.4%, animal and vegetable oils and fats 1.1%). *Major import sources:* France 13.9%; South Africa 12.4%; Japan 7.1%; United Kingdom 7.0%; Germany 4.8%; India 4.8%; Hong Kong 4.3%; Taiwan 4.2%.
Exports (1991–92): Mau Rs 19,416,000,000 (clothing and textiles 52.8%, sugar 28.1%, diamonds and synthetic stones 2.0%, fish and fish preparations 1.7%). *Major export destinations:* United Kingdom 36.3%; France 20.3%; United States 12.2%; Germany 10.2%; Italy 4.9%.

Transport and communications

Transport. Railroads: none. Roads (1991): total length 1,138 mi, 1,831 km (paved 93%). Vehicles (1991): passenger cars 30,882; buses 2,021. Merchant marine (1992): vessels (100 gross tons and over) 35; total deadweight tonnage 152,197. Air transport (1992)[14]: passenger-mi 1,716,582,000, passenger-km 2,762,576,000; short ton-mi cargo 59,017,000, metric ton-km cargo 86,163,000; airports (1993) with scheduled flights 1.
Communications. Daily newspapers (1992): total number 7; total circulation 92,000; circulation per 1,000 population 84. Radio (1992): 250,000 receivers (1 per 4.6 persons). Television (1992): 138,111 receivers (1 per 7.9 persons). Telephones (1991): 85,597 (1 per 13 persons).

Education and health

Education (1991)

	schools	teachers[15]	students	student/ teacher ratio[15]
Primary (age 5–12)	279	6,507	129,154	21.1
Secondary (age 12–20)	125	3,728	79,327	21.0
Voc., teacher tr.	7	69[16]	587	...
Higher	2	382[17]	2,199	5.7[17]

Educational attainment (1983). Percentage of population age 25 and over having: no formal education 24.2%; incomplete primary 28.1%; primary 23.2%; incomplete secondary 13.1%; secondary 7.7%; higher 3.6%; other 0.1%. *Literacy* (1983)[7]: total population age 15 and over literate 501,262 (81.8%); males literate 267,835 (89.0%); females literate 233,427 (74.8%).
Health (1991): physicians 1,090 (1 per 996 persons); hospital beds 3,094 (1 per 351 persons); infant mortality rate per 1,000 live births 23.0.
Food (1988–90): daily per capita caloric intake 2,897 (vegetable products 87%, animal products 13%); 128% of FAO recommended minimum requirement.

Military

Total active duty personnel: none; however, a special 1,300-person paramilitary force ensures internal security. *Military expenditure as percentage of GNP* (1989): 0.9% (world 4.9%); per capita expenditure U.S.$4.

[1]Includes 8 nonelective seats. [2]January 1. [3]Administered directly from Port Louis. [4]Administered by resident commissioner assisted by local council. [5]Detail does not add to total given because of rounding. [6]Based on 1990 census figures. [7]Island of Mauritius only. [8]At factor cost. [9]Employed persons in establishments employing 10 or more persons. [10]March. [11]1988. [12]Current weights of CPI components; Island of Mauritius only. [13]Import figures are f.o.b. in balance of trade and c.i.f. for commodities and trading partners. [14]Air Mauritius only. [15]1990. [16]1982. [17]1989.

Mexico

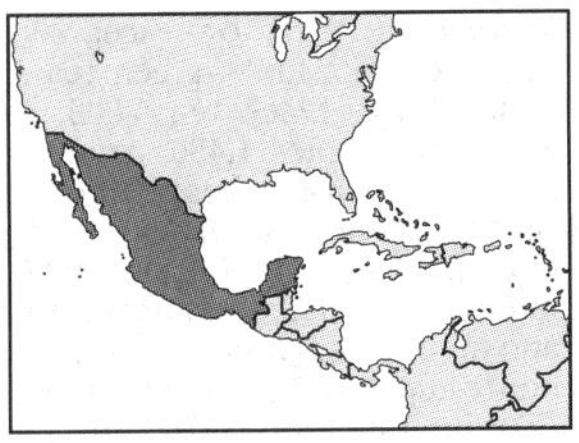

Official name: Estados Unidos Mexicanos (United Mexican States).
Form of government: federal republic with two legislative houses (Senate [64]; Chamber of Deputies [500]).
Chief of state and head of government: President.
Capital: Mexico City.
Official language: Spanish.
Official religion: none.
Monetary unit: 1 new peso[1] (Mex$) = 100 centavos; valuation (Oct. 4, 1993) 1 U.S.$ = Mex$3.12; 1 £ = Mex$4.73.

Area and population

		area		population
				1990
States	Capitals	sq mi	sq km	census
Aguascalientes	Aguascalientes	2,112	5,471	719,659
Baja California Norte	Mexicali	26,997	69,921	1,660,855
Baja California Sur	La Paz	28,369	73,475	317,764
Campeche	Campeche	19,619	50,812	535,185
Chiapas	Tuxtla Gutiérrez	28,653	74,211	3,210,496
Chihuahua	Chihuahua	94,571	244,938	2,441,873
Coahuila	Saltillo	57,908	149,982	1,972,340
Colima	Colima	2,004	5,191	428,510
Durango	Durango	47,560	123,181	1,349,378
Guanajuato	Guanajuato	11,773	30,491	3,982,593
Guerrero	Chilpancingo	24,819	64,281	2,620,637
Hidalgo	Pachuca	8,036	20,813	1,888,366
Jalisco	Guadalajara	31,211	80,836	5,302,689
México	Toluca	8,245	21,355	9,815,795
Michoacán	Morelia	23,138	59,928	3,548,199
Morelos	Cuernavaca	1,911	4,950	1,195,059
Nayarit	Tepic	10,417	26,979	824,643
Nuevo León	Monterrey	25,067	64,924	3,098,736
Oaxaca	Oaxaca	36,275	93,952	3,019,560
Puebla	Puebla	13,090	33,902	4,126,101
Querétaro	Querétaro	4,420	11,449	1,051,235
Quintana Roo	Chetumal	19,387	50,212	493,277
San Luis Potosí	San Luis Potosí	24,351	63,068	2,003,187
Sinaloa	Culiacán	22,521	58,328	2,204,054
Sonora	Hermosillo	70,291	182,052	1,823,606
Tabasco	Villahermosa	9,756	25,267	1,501,744
Tamaulipas	Ciudad Victoria	30,650	79,384	2,249,581
Tlaxcala	Tlaxcala	1,551	4,016	761,277
Veracruz	Jalapa (Xalapa)	27,683	71,699	6,228,239
Yucatán	Mérida	14,827	38,402	1,362,940
Zacatecas	Zacatecas	28,283	73,252	1,276,323
Federal District				
Distrito Federal	—	571	1,479	8,235,744
TOTAL		756,066	1,958,201	81,249,645

Demography

Population (1993): 89,955,000.
Density (1993): persons per sq mi 119.0, persons per sq km 45.9.
Urban-rural (1990): urban 71.3%; rural 28.7%.
Sex distribution (1990): male 49.10%; female 50.90%.
Age breakdown (1990): under 15, 38.3%; 15–29, 29.4%; 30–44, 16.6%; 45–59, 8.9%; 60–74, 4.5%; 75 and over, 1.7%; unspecified 0.6%.
Population projection: (2000) 102,555,000; (2010) 118,455,000.
Doubling time: 27 years.
Ethnic composition (1990): mestizo 60.0%; Amerindian 30.0%; Caucasian 9.0%; other 1.0%.
Religious affiliation (1990): Roman Catholic 89.7%; Protestant (including Evangelical) 4.9%; Jewish 0.1%; other 2.1%; none 3.2%.
Major cities (1990): Mexico City 9,815,795; Guadalajara 1,650,042; Ciudad Netzahualcóyotl 1,255,456; Monterrey 1,068,996; Puebla 1,007,170; Juarez 789,522; León 758,279; Tijuana 698,752; Mérida 523,422; Chihuahua 516,153.
Place of birth (1990): 93.1% native-born; 6.9% foreign-born and unknown.
Mobility (1980). Population living in the same state as in 1970: 89.1%; different state 10.9%.
Households. Total households (1992) 17,152,000; distribution by size (1980): 1 person 5.4%, 2 persons 10.2%, 3 persons 12.4%, 4 persons 14.3%, 5 persons 13.5%, 6 persons 11.7%, 7 or more persons 32.5%. Family households (1983): 13,996,700 (94.6%); nonfamily 798,900 (5.4%).
Immigration (1987): permanent immigrants admitted 72,649.
Emigration (1991): legal immigrants into the United States 946,200.

Vital statistics

Birth rate per 1,000 population (1990): 31.2 (world avg. 27.1); (1983) legitimate 72.5%; illegitimate 27.5%.
Death rate per 1,000 population (1990): 5.0 (world avg. 9.8).
Natural increase rate per 1,000 population (1990): 26.2 (world avg. 17.3).
Total fertility rate (avg. births per childbearing woman; 1990): 3.7.
Marriage rate per 1,000 population (1991): 7.6.
Divorce rate per 1,000 population (1991): 0.6.
Life expectancy at birth (1990): male 66.5 years; female 73.1 years.
Major causes of death per 100,000 population (1991): diseases of the circulatory system 99.0; accidents 68.8; endocrine and metabolic disorders 53.5; malignant neoplasms (cancers) 50.3; diseases of the respiratory system 47.1; diseases of the digestive system 39.7; infectious and parasitic diseases 34.9.

Social indicators

Access to services (1992). Proportion of dwellings having: electricity 89.3%; piped water supply 81.0%; drained sewage 66.1%.
Educational attainment (1990). Percentage of population age 15 and over having: no primary education 13.4%; some primary 22.8%; completed primary 19.3%; some secondary 42.5%; other 2.0%.

Distribution of income (1983)

percentage of household income by quintile

1	2	3	4	5 (highest)
4.0	8.8	14.2	22.4	50.6

Quality of working life. Average workweek (1991): 45.5[2] hours. Annual rate (1986) per 100,000 insured workers for: temporary disability 9,077; indemnification for permanent injury 281; death 23. Labour stoppages (1988): 68, involving 4,750 workers. Average duration of journey to work: n.a. Method of transport: n.a. Rate per 1,000 workers of discouraged (unemployed no longer seeking work): n.a.
Social participation. Eligible voters participating in last national election (1988): *c.* 50%. Population participating in voluntary work: n.a. Trade union membership in total workforce: n.a. Practicing religious population in total affiliated population: national average of weekly attendance (1993) 11%; (1970) weekly 10% of urban dwellers, 25% of rural dwellers; yearly 55% of urban dwellers, 73% of rural dwellers.
Social deviance (1991). Criminal cases tried by local authorities per 100,000 population for: murder 60.3; rape 22.4; other assault 301.0; theft 703.8. Incidence per 100,000 in general population of: alcoholism, n.a.; drug and substance abuse, n.a.[3]; suicide 1.54[4].
Leisure (1985). Favourite leisure activities (average daily paid attendance): cinema 582,416; sporting events 31,518; live theatre 16,400; museums and archaeological sites 12,169; bullfights 3,049.
Material well-being (1985). Households possessing: radio 96%; television 73%; washing machine 33%; automobile 29%; telephone 27%; refrigerator 23%.

National economy

Gross national product (1992): U.S.$295,090,000,000 (U.S.$3,470 per capita).

Structure of gross domestic product and labour force

	1991			
	in value Mex$'000,000,000[1]	% of total value	labour force	% of labour force
Agriculture	76,127.0	8.9	8,189,759	26.2
Mining	19,796.6	2.3	217,692	0.7
Manufacturing	189,399.8	22.2	4,805,943	15.4
Construction	33,366.0	3.9	1,871,577	6.0
Public utilities	12,317.3	1.5	151,172	0.5
Transportation and communications	71,947.8	8.4	1,141,444	3.7
Trade	228,004.1	26.7	6,149,629	19.7
Finance	98,610.6	11.6	1,294,884	4.1
Pub. admin., defense } Services }	133,492.1	15.7	6,526,569	20.9
Other	−10,278.2[5]	−1.2[5]	880,379[6]	2.8[6]
TOTAL	852,783.1	100.0	31,229,048	100.0

Budget (1991). Revenue: Mex$147,703,000,000,000[1] (income taxes 29.2%, value-added taxes 22.7%, petroleum revenues 21.0%, import duties 6.6%). Expenditures: Mex$148,404,000,000,000[1] (interest on public debt 29.2%, revenue sharing with state governments 18.0%, wages and salaries 18.0%, transfers 13.8%).
Tourism (1992): receipts from visitors U.S.$6,641,000,000; expenditures by nationals abroad U.S.$3,964,700,000.

Manufacturing, mining, and construction enterprises (1988)

	no. of enter-prises	no. of employees ('000)	yearly wages as a % of avg. of all wages[7]	value added (Mex$'000,000[1])
Manufacturing	138,835	2,640.5	166.2	20,950,900
Metal products	26,414	759.3	...	6,605,300
Chemicals	4,948	354.9	...	4,228,000
Food, beverages, and tobacco	50,454	543.7	130.0	3,378,700
Textiles and apparel	16,621	423.3	122.8	2,414,800
Iron and steel	871	100.4	...	1,332,400
Nonmetallic mineral products	14,343	150.9	...	1,177,700
Paper and printing	7,762	141.4	...	1,127,900
Wood and wood products	15,951	135.4	...	497,000
Nonelectrical machinery and transport equipment	[8]	[8]	...	[8]
Electrical machinery	[8]	[8]	...	[8]
Other manufactures	1,471	31.1	...	189,200
Mining	2,073	153.0	198.2	1,643,800
Construction	5,308	342.4	131.8	1,414,800

Production (metric tons except as noted). Agriculture, forestry, fishing (1992): sugarcane 35,332,000, corn (maize) 13,630,000, sorghum 5,287,000, wheat 3,583,000, oranges 2,329,000, bananas 1,685,000, mangoes 1,182,000, dry beans 858,000, lemons 765,000, avocados 699,000, soybeans 626,000, cantaloupes 621,000, apples 542,000, barley 485,000, grapes 457,000, rice 280,000, pineapples 277,000, strawberries 85,000, cottonseed 57,000, walnuts 22,000; livestock (number of live animals) 32,417,000 cattle, 13,840,000 pigs, 10,644,000 goats, 6,750,000 turkeys, 6,184,000 sheep, 6,180,000 horses, 3,194,000 mules, 3,189,000 asses, 282,000,000 chickens; roundwood (1991) 23,617,000 cu m; fish catch 1,125,756, of which sardines 323,832. Mining and quarrying (metal content of ores; 1992): iron ore 5,154,043; zinc 289,119; copper 279,042; lead 178,840; manganese 137,746; silver 2,317; gold 10.40; (nonmetals; 1992) salt 7,395,152; gypsum 2,960,126; sulfur 1,484,497; barite 443,782; fluorite 209,210. Manufacturing (gross value of production in Mex$'000; 1991): machinery and equipment 64,992,052; food, beverages, and tobacco products 44,891,619; chemical products 40,241,144; metal products 21,950,164; mineral products 11,769,531; paper and paper products 8,366,246; textiles 8,223,393. Construction (gross value of new construction, in Mex$'000,000[1]; 1985): residential 154,835; nonresidential 168,096.

Trade and service enterprises (1985)

	no. of establish-ments	no. of employees	yearly wage as a % of avg. of all wages[7]	annual income (Mex$'000,000[1])
Trade	618,059	1,780,700	...	14,348,200
Wholesale	30,264	329,100	...	5,205,700
Retail	587,795	1,451,600	...	9,142,500
Boutiques (excluding food products)	223,601	600,200	...	3,022,900
Food and tobacco speciality stores	339,736	588,500	...	2,050,800
Automobile, tire, and auto parts dealers	16,768	104,400	...	1,737,600
Small supermarkets and grocery stores	4,512	96,400	...	1,227,300
Gasoline stations	2,395	23,900	...	708,700
Other	783	38,200	...	395,200
Services	341,436	1,401,500	85.2	3,476,900
Professional services	21,040	193,000	77.9	645,700
Food and beverage services	109,108	341,400	...	620,600
Transp. and travel agencies	3,058	41,000	133.4	353,400
Lodging	7,819	111,500	...	283,900
Automotive repair	55,850	148,500	...	209,800
Educational services (private)	8,227	124,200	134.3	166,000
Medical and social assistance	38,606	101,000	206.4	151,700
Amusement services (cinemas and theatres)	2,915	29,500	148.9	144,500
Recreation	8,323	41,000	...	139,500
Other repair	36,031	64,200	...	86,500
Commercial and professional organizations	3,209	41,900	77.9	67,400
Other	47,250	164,300	49.9	607,900

Energy production (consumption): electricity (kW-hr; 1992) 131,501,000,000 (1991; 126,375,000,000); coal (metric tons; 1991) 10,500,000 (10,700,000); crude petroleum (barrels; 1992) 975,000,000 (1991; 471,147,000); petroleum products (metric tons; 1991) 74,020,000 (79,708,000); natural gas (cu m; 1991) 41,956,000,000 (44,784,000,000).

Population economically active (1991): total 31,229,048; activity rate of total population 37.5% (participation rates: ages 15–64, 59.9%; female 31.2%; unemployed 2.2%).

Price and earnings indexes (1985 = 100)

	1986	1987	1988	1989	1990	1991	1992
Consumer price index	186.2	431.7	924.6	1,109.6	1,405.4	1,723.8	1,991.2
Monthly earnings index	175.7	411.5	873.0	1,166.8	1,522.6	1,965.7	...

Household income and expenditure. Average household size (1992) 4.8; income per household (1989) Mex$3,461[1] (U.S.$1,384); sources of income (1983): wages and salaries 52.4%, property and entrepreneurship 23.6%, transfer payments 5.6%, other 18.4%; expenditure (1990): food, beverages, and tobacco 35.7%, housing (includes household furnishings) 22.7%, transportation and communications 10.9%, clothing and footwear 7.5%, recreation and entertainment 5.0%, health and medical services 4.0%.

Financial aggregates[9]

	1987	1988	1989	1990	1991	1992	1993 (8 mo.)
Exchange rate, Mex$ per:							
U.S. dollar	1,378.2	2,273.1	2,461.5	2,812.6	3,018.4	3,094.9	3,123.6
£	2,258.7	4,049.3	4,036.1	5,020.0	5,114.2	5,464.0	4,675.4
SDR	1,782.1	3,054.9	3,470.7	4,190.3	4,392.9	4,283.7	4,337.5
International reserves (U.S.$)							
Total (excl. gold; '000,000)	12,464	5,279	6,329	9,863	17,726	18,942	24,233[10]
SDRs ('000,000)	706	394	383	417	586	548	377
Reserve pos. in IMF ('000,000)	—	—	—	—	—	—	—
Foreign exchange	11,758	4,885	5,946	9,446	17,140	18,394	23,847[10]
Gold ('000,000 fine troy oz)	2.54	2.56	1.03	0.92	0.92	0.69	0.55[10]
% world reserves	0.27	0.27	0.11	0.10	0.10	0.07	0.06[10]
Interest and prices							
Treasury bill rate	103.07	61.95	45.01	34.76	19.28	15.62	13.85
Balance of payments (U.S.$'000,000)							
Balance of visible trade,	+8,433	+1,752	−645	−4,433	−11,063	−20,677	...
of which:							
Imports, f.o.b.	−12,222	−18,905	−23,410	−31,271	−38,184	−48,193	...
Exports, f.o.b.	20,655	20,657	22,765	26,838	27,121	27,516	...
Balance of invisibles	+12,401	−691	−4,603	−16,153	−24,346	−43,488	...
Balance of payments, current account	+3,968	−2,443	−3,958	−7,117	−13,283	−22,811	...

Public debt (external, outstanding; 1992): U.S.$76,087,100,000.

Land use (1990): forested 22.0%; meadows and pastures 39.0%; agricultural and under permanent cultivation 13.0%; other 26.0%.

Foreign trade

Balance of trade (current prices)

	1987	1988	1989	1990	1991	1992
Mex$'000,000,000	+11,794.1	+4,635.0	−863.8	−7,494.0	−27,746	−57,138
% of total	25.6%	5.2%	6.0%	4.7%	14.4%	25.1%

Imports (1991): U.S.$38,184,000,000 (metallic products, machinery, and equipment 52.9%; chemical products 8.9%; food, beverages, and tobacco 6.8%; iron and steel 5.7%; textiles and clothing 3.7%). *Major import sources:* U.S. 65.6%; Germany 6.1%; Japan 4.7%; France 2.5%; Brazil 2.1%; Canada 1.8%; Italy 1.6%; Spain 1.5%.

Exports (1991): U.S.$31,254,000,000 (metallic products, machinery, and equipment 28.0%, of which automobile 11.6%, machinery and electrical 5.6%; crude petroleum 26.1%; chemical products 6.3%; processed food and beverages 3.9%). *Major export destinations:* U.S. 58.7%; Japan 4.0%; Spain 3.7%; Canada 3.6%; France 1.9%; Germany 1.7%; U.K. 1.0%; Brazil 0.6%.

Trade by commodity group (1990)

SITC group	imports U.S.$'000,000	imports %	exports U.S.$'000,000	exports %
00 Food and live animals	3,653	13.0	2,762	10.3
01 Beverages and tobacco	163	0.6	304	1.1
02 Crude materials, excluding fuels	1,853	6.6	1,112	4.2
03 Mineral fuels, lubricants, and related materials	1,163	4.2	9,876	37.0
04 Animal and vegetable oils, fats, and waxes	368	1.3	—	—
05 Chemicals and related products, n.e.s.	3,150	11.2	1,820	6.8
06 Basic manufactures	4,166	14.8	3,095	11.6
07 Machinery and transport equipment	10,144	36.1	6,650	24.9
08 Miscellaneous manufactured articles	2,998	10.7	1,070	4.0
09 Goods not classified by kind	405	1.5	—	—
TOTAL[11]	28,063	100.0	26,714[12]	100.0[12]

Direction of trade (1992)

	imports U.S.$'000,000	imports %	exports U.S.$'000,000	exports %
Western Hemisphere	43,433	74.2	36,905	86.4
United States	40,598	69.3	32,624	76.4
Latin America and the Caribbean	2,222	3.8	2,074	4.8
Canada	613	1.1	2,207	5.2
Europe	8,305	14.2	3,557	8.3
EEC	7,305	12.5	3,340	7.8
EFTA	907	1.6	159	0.4
U.S.S.R.	22	—	24	—
Other Europe	71	0.1	34	0.1
Asia	6,438	11.0	1,924	4.5
Japan	3,805	6.5	1,130	2.6
Africa	121	0.2	55	0.2
Other	248	0.4	250	0.6
TOTAL	58,545	100.0	42,700[12]	100.0

Transport and communications

Transport. Railroads (1992): route length 16,363 mi, 26,334 km; passenger-mi 2,765,000,000, passenger-km 4,450,000,000; short ton-mi cargo 23,562,000,000, metric ton-km cargo 34,400,000,000. Roads (1992): total length 151,309 mi, 243,509 km (paved 35%[13]). Vehicles (1991): passenger cars 7,400,000; trucks and buses 3,300,000. Merchant marine (1992): vessels (100 gross tons and over) 635; total deadweight tonnage 1,495,311. Air transport (1991)[14]: passenger-mi 10,839,100,000, passenger-km 17,443,800,000; short ton-mi cargo 1,182,031,000, metric ton-km cargo 1,725,742,000; airports (1993) 54.

Communications. Daily newspapers (1986): total number 392; total circulation 11,256,000; circulation per 1,000 population 142. Radio (1992): 16,325,000 receivers (1 per 5.4 persons). Television (1991): 12,350,000 receivers (1 per 6.7 persons). Telephones (1992): 11,128,000 (1 per 7.6 persons).

Education and health

Education (1992–93)

	schools	teachers	students	student/teacher ratio
Primary (age 6–12)	86,636	481,466	14,500,000	30.1
Secondary (age 12–18)	25,131	352,865	5,980,000	16.9
Voc., teacher tr.	6,571	77,347	1,076,700	13.9
Higher	1,832	128,212	1,256,100	9.8

Literacy (1990): total population age 15 and over literate 43,354,067 (87.4%); males literate 21,575,645 (90.2%); females literate 21,778,422 (84.8%).

Health (1991): physicians 97,506 (1 per 885 persons); hospital beds 63,103 (1 per 1,367 persons); infant mortality rate per 1,000 live births (1988) 46.6.

Food (1988–90): daily per capita caloric intake 3,062 (vegetable products 82%, animal products 18%); 131% of FAO recommended minimum requirement.

Military

Total active duty personnel (1993): 175,000 (army 74.3%, navy 21.1%, air force 4.6%). *Military expenditure as percentage of GNP* (1989): 0.5% (world 4.9%); per capita expenditure U.S.$11.

[1]1 new peso = 1,000 (old) pesos; the (old) peso will be withdrawn by 1995. [2]Manufacturing only. [3]Through 1982, cannabis remained the most abused drug. [4]1987. [5]Imputed bank service charge. [6]Includes 694,965 unemployed. [7]1984. [8]Included in Metal products. [9]Exchange rates and treasury bill rates are expressed in period averages; international reserves are expressed in end-of-period rates. [10]End of May. [11]Totals include adjustments of unspecified nature. [12]Detail does not add to total given because of rounding. [13]1989. [14]All scheduled traffic of Mexicana and AeroMexico airlines.

Micronesia, Federated States of

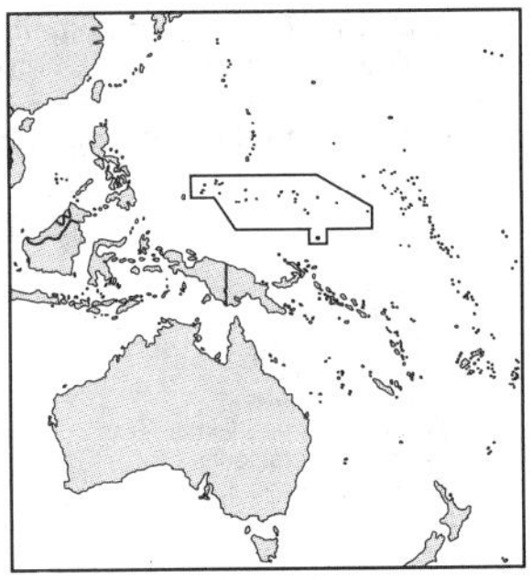

Official name: Federated States of Micronesia.
Political status: federal republic in free association with the United States with one legislative house (National Congress [14])[1].
Head of state and government: President.
Capital: Palikir.
Official language: none.
Official religion: none.
Monetary unit: 1 U.S. dollar (U.S.$) = 100 cents; valuation (Oct. 4, 1993) 1 £ = U.S.$1.52.

Area and population

States / Major Islands	area sq mi	area sq km	population 1990 estimate
Chuuk (Truk)	49.1	127.2	53,700
Wenn (Moen) Islands	7.0	18.1	14,218[2]
Kosrae	42.3	109.6	7,200
Kosrae Island	42.3	109.6	7,200
Pohnpei	133.3	345.2	33,100
Pohnpei Island	129.0	334.1	30,000
Yap	45.9	118.9	13,900
Yap Island	38.7	100.2	6,951[2]
TOTAL	270.8[3]	701.4[3]	107,900

Demography

Population (1993): 103,000.
Density (1993): persons per sq mi 380.4, persons per sq km 146.8.
Urban-rural (1980): urban 19.4%; rural 80.6%.
Sex distribution (1990): male 50.73%; female 49.27%.
Age breakdown (1980): under 15, 46.4%; 15–29, 26.8%; 30–44, 12.6%; 45–59, 8.5%; 60–74, 4.5%; 75 and over, 1.2%.
Population projection: (2000) 110,000; (2010) 120,000.
Doubling time: 23 years.
Ethnic composition (1980): Trukese 41.1%; Pohnpeian 25.9%; Mortlockese 8.3%; Kosraean 7.4%; Yapese 6.0%; Ulithian, or Woleaian, 4.0%; Pingelapese, or Mokilese, 1.2%; Western Trukese 1.0%; Palauan 0.4%; Filipino 0.2%; other 4.5%.
Religious affiliation: Christianity is the predominant religious tradition, with the Kosraeans, Pohnpeians, and Trukese being mostly Protestant and the Yapese mostly Roman Catholic.
Major cities (1980): Wenn (Moen) 10,351; Tol 6,705; Kolonia 5,549.

Vital statistics

Birth rate per 1,000 population (1985–89): 37.9[4] (world avg. 27.1); legitimate, n.a.; illegitimate, n.a.
Death rate per 1,000 population (1985–89): 8.0[4] (world avg. 9.8).
Natural increase rate per 1,000 population (1985–89): 29.9[4] (world avg. 17.3).
Total fertility rate (avg. births per childbearing woman; 1985–89): 5.6.
Marriage rate per 1,000 population: n.a.
Divorce rate per 1,000 population: n.a.
Life expectancy at birth (1985)[5]: male 64.0 years; female 68.1 years.
Major causes of death per 100,000 population (1985)[5]: diseases of the cerebrovascular system 85.7; major infectious diseases 39.6, of which intestinal diseases 14.3, septicemia 8.9; pneumonia, influenza, and tuberculosis 29.7; malignant and benign neoplasms (cancers) 23.1; homicide, suicide, and accidents 22.0.

National economy

Budget (1990). Revenue: U.S.$161,988,000 (external grants 73.2%; tax revenue 8.5%; fishing rights fees 7.8%). Expenditures: U.S.$127,779,000 (current expenditures 79.4%, of which education 18.2%, health 11.8%, public works 10.2%, transportation 2.7%, public safety 2.6%; capital expenditure 20.6%).
Public debt (external, outstanding): n.a.
Tourism (1990): number of visitors 23,171.
Production (metric tons except as noted). Agriculture, forestry, fishing: n.a.; however, Micronesia's major crops include coconuts (which provide annually more than 4,000 tons of copra), breadfruit, cassava, sweet potatoes, and a variety of tropical fruits (including bananas); livestock comprises mostly pigs and poultry; fish catch (1990) 3,640, of which skipjack tuna 600. Mining and quarrying: quarrying of sand and aggregate for local construction only. Manufacturing: n.a.; however, copra and coconut oil[6] are the most important products; the manufacture of handicrafts and personal items (clothing, mats, boats, etc.) by individuals is also important. Construction: n.a. Energy production (consumption): electricity (kW-hr; 1990) 40,000,000 (40,000,000); coal, none (n.a.); crude petroleum, none (n.a.); petroleum products[7] (metric tons; 1988) none (52,000); natural gas, none (n.a.).
Household income and expenditure. Average household size (1988–89) 8.5; annual income per household (1989) U.S.$3,435; sources of income: wages and salaries 67.2%, self-employment 18.0%, operating surplus 14.8%; expenditure (1985): food and beverages 73.5%.
Land use (1984)[7]: forested 22.5%; meadows and pastures 13.5%; agricultural and under permanent cultivation 33.5%; other 30.5%.

Gross national product (at current market prices; 1989): U.S.$157,400,000 (U.S.$1,595 per capita).

Structure of gross domestic product and labour force

	1983 in value U.S.$'000,000	1983 % of total value	1990 labour force	1990 % of labour force
Agriculture and fishing	44.9	42.2	12,700	41.6
Trade	12.7	11.9	[8]	[8]
Public administration	31.5	29.6	6,300	20.7
Manufacturing			1,600	5.2
Construction			1,900	6.2
Transportation, communications, and public utilities	17.4	16.3	...	...
Finance			...	...
Services			3,700[8]	12.1[8]
Other			4,400[9]	14.4[9]
TOTAL	106.5	100.0	30,500[3]	100.0[3]

Population economically active (1990): total 30,500; activity rate of total population 60.6% (participation rates: ages 15–64, 60.6%; female 46.9%; unemployed 13.5%).
Price and earnings indexes: n.a.

Foreign trade

Balance of trade (current prices)

	1984	1985	1986	1987	1988	1989
U.S.$'000,000	−35.1	−37.5	−41.9	−41.2	−65.4	−65.6
% of total	90.1%	89.9%	90.2%	96.9%	93.4%	82.2%

Imports (1989): U.S.$72,724,800 (food, beverages, and tobacco 34.0%; manufactured goods 26.2%; machinery and transport equipment 16.1%; mineral fuels 9.9%; chemicals 4.5%). *Major import sources:* United States 37.7%; Guam 27.7%; Japan 23.6%; Australia 3.0%.
Exports (1989): U.S.$7,065,200 (1988; copra 25.6%; manufactured goods 12.8%; animal and vegetable oils 2.2%). *Major export destinations* (1988): Japan 58.2%; South Pacific Region 32.7%; United States 0.6%.

Transport and communications

Transport. Railroads: none. Roads (1990): total length 140 mi, 226 km (paved 17%). Vehicles: passenger cars, trucks, and buses, n.a. Merchant marine (1992): vessels (100 gross tons and over) 17; deadweight tonnage 6,863. Air transport: n.a.; airports (1993) with scheduled flights 4.
Communications. Daily newspapers: there are no private newspapers. Radio (1992): total number of receivers 70,000 (1 per 1.5 persons). Television (1992): total number of receivers 7,000 (1 per 15 persons). Telephones (1986): 1,556 (1 per 61 persons).

Education and health

Education (1987–88)

	schools	teachers	students	student/teacher ratio
Elementary (age 6–12)	177	1,051[10]	25,139	22.2[10]
Secondary (age 13–18)	16	314[10]	5,385	13.2[10]
College[11]	1	...	[12]	...

Educational attainment (1980). Percentage of population age 25 and over having: no formal schooling 24.8%; some primary education 38.2%; primary 11.7%; some secondary 7.7%; secondary 9.6%; higher 8.0%. *Literacy* (1980): total population age 15 and over literate 30,074 (76.7%); males literate 13,710 (67.0%); females literate 16,364 (87.2%).
Health (1989): physicians 32 (1 per 3,084 persons); hospital beds 319 (1 per 309 persons); infant mortality rate per 1,000 live births (1985–89) 52.2.
Food: daily per capita caloric intake, n.a.

Military

External security is provided by the United States.

[1]On Nov. 3, 1986, the United States unilaterally terminated the UN trusteeship it held over the Federated States of Micronesia (FSM), thus formally initiating their free-association political status. On Dec. 22, 1990, the United Nations Security Council joined the Trusteeship Council, which had endorsed the termination of the trusteeship in May 1986. [2]1985. [3]Detail does not add to total given because of rounding. [4]Discrepancy among birth, death, and natural increase rates due to the use of weighted averages of values calculated separately for each state. [5]Registered deaths only. [6]In 1985 FSM exported 2,503 metric tons of coconut oil to the United States. [7]Includes all areas formerly constituting the U.S. Trust Territory of the Pacific Islands. [8]Services includes Trade. [9]Includes 4,100 unemployed. [10]1983–84. [11]In 1985, 1,200 students were enrolled in colleges and universities in the United States. [12]In 1989, fewer than 300 students were enrolled in the College of Micronesia.

Moldova

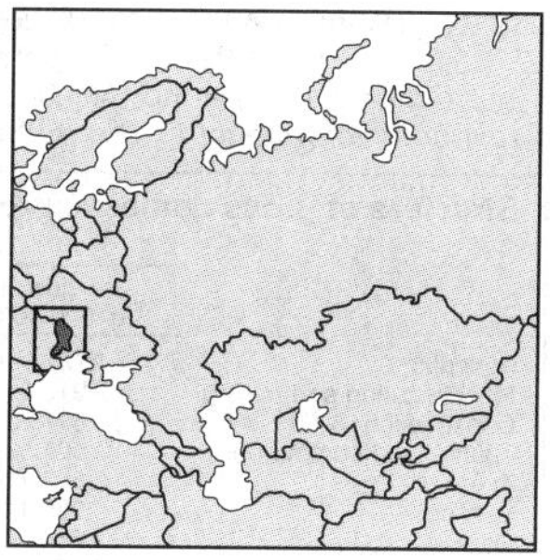

Official name: Republica Moldova (Republic of Moldova).
Form of government: unitary multiparty republic with a single legislative body (Parliament [380[1]]).
Head of state: President.
Head of government: Prime Minister.
Capital: Chişinău.
Official language: Romanian.
Official religion: none.
Monetary unit: (until Nov. 30, 1993) 1 ruble = 100 kopecks; valuation (Oct. 4, 1993) free rate, 1 U.S.$ = 1,165 rubles; 1 £ = 1,765 rubles. Moldovan coupon[2] introduced Sept. 22, 1993, and circulated parallel with the Russian ruble; on Nov. 30, 1993, a new national currency, the leu, was introduced at a 1,000 to 1 ratio with the Moldovan coupon and circulates parallel with it. Valuation as of Nov. 30, 1993: 1 U.S.$ = 3.85 lei; 1 £ = 5.71.

Area

Administrative subdivisions

Cities	area sq km[3]	Rural districts	area sq km[3]	Rural districts	area sq km[3]
Bălţi	...	Anenii Noi	830	Hânceşti	
Cahul	...	Basarabeasca	660	(Kotovsk)	1,350
Chişinău	160	Brinceni	810	Ialoveni	...
Dubăsari	...	Cahul	800	Leova	720
Orhei	...	Cainari	...	Nisporeni	760
Râbniţa	...	Călăraş	760	Ocniţa	660
Soroca	...	Camenca	820	Orhei	1,100
Tighina (Bendery)	...	Cantemir	860	Râbniţa	850
Tiraspol	...	Căuşeni	1,120	Rezina	670
Ungheni	...	Ciadâr-Lunga	720	Rişcani	1,000
		Cimişlia	1,170	Sângerei	...
		Comrat	840	Slobozia	960
		Criuleni	850	Şoldăneşti	...
		Donduşeni	890	Soroca	870
		Drochia	780	Ştefan-Vodă	
		Dubăsari	670	(Suvorovo)	1,030
		Edineţ	860	Străşeni	760
		Făleşti	1,070	Taraclia	...
		Floreşti	830	Teleneşti	860
		Glodeni	760	Ungheni	1,070
		Grigoriopol	820	Vulcăneşti	930
				TOTAL	33,700[4]

Demography

Population (1993): 4,362,000.
Density (1993): persons per sq mi 335.5, persons per sq km 129.4.
Urban-rural (1992): urban 47.1%; rural 52.9%.
Sex distribution (1992): male 47.08%; female 52.92%.
Age breakdown (1989): under 15, 27.9%; 15–29, 22.9%; 30–44, 21.0%; 45–59, 15.6%; 60–74, 9.7%; 75 and over, 2.9%.
Population projection: (2000) 4,399,000; (2010) 4,453,000.
Doubling time: not applicable; doubling time exceeds 100 years.
Ethnic composition (1989): Moldovan 64.5%; Ukrainian 13.8%; Russian 13.0%; Gagauz 3.5%; Jewish 2.0%; Bulgarian 1.5%; other 1.7%.
Religious affiliation: believers are predominantly Moldovan Orthodox.
Major cities (1991): Chişinău 753,500; Tiraspol 186,000; Bălţi 164,900; Tighina (Bendery) 141,500; Râbniţa 62,900.

Vital statistics

Birth rate per 1,000 population (1992): 16.5 (world avg. 26.4); (1989) legitimate 89.6%; illegitimate 10.4%.
Death rate per 1,000 population (1992): 10.5 (world avg. 9.2).
Natural increase rate per 1,000 population (1992): 6.0 (world avg. 17.2).
Total fertility rate (avg. births per childbearing woman; 1989): 2.5.
Marriage rate per 1,000 population (1990): 9.4.
Divorce rate per 1,000 population (1990): 3.0.
Life expectancy at birth (1990): male 65.0 years; female 71.8 years.
Major causes of death per 100,000 population (1989): diseases of the circulatory system 452.2; malignant neoplasms (cancers) 131.6; accidents and violence 105.3; diseases of the digestive system 85.4; diseases of the respiratory system 64.2; infectious and parasitic diseases 12.4; endocrine and metabolic disorders 8.3; diseases of the nervous system 8.2.

National economy

Budget (1991). Revenue: 6,403,100,000 rubles (tax revenue 86.3%, of which turnover tax 44.2%, enterprise profits tax 26.8%, individual income tax 7.8%, sales tax 7.1%; nontax revenue 13.7%, of which remainder from previous budget 2.7%, various fees 1.5%, revaluation of inventory 1.4%). Expenditures: 6,401,400,000 rubles (social welfare and culture 50.9%, of which education 21.4%, social security 15.3%, health 12.2%, culture and art 2.0%; national economy 38.2%; transfers to union budget 3.4%; government administration 1.7%).
Production (metric tons except as noted). Agriculture, forestry, fishing (1992): sugar beets 2,200,000, fruit (except grapes) 1,370,000, vegetables (except potatoes) 1,300,000, grain 1,106,000, grapes 720,000, potatoes 300,000; livestock (number of live animals) 1,404,000 pigs, 1,189,000 sheep, 1,021,000 cattle, 23,000,000 poultry; roundwood (1991) 125,000 cu m; fish catch (1991) 5,200. Manufacturing ('000,000 rubles; 1991): food 3,244; machinery 2,435; textiles 2,400; building materials 397; wood products 389; chemicals 272; ferrous metals 110. Construction (1990): 433,400,000 rubles. Energy production (consumption): electricity (kW-hr; 1990) 15,690,000,000 (20,161,000,000); coal (metric tons; 1990) none (4,576,000); crude petroleum (barrels; 1990) none (51,625,000); petroleum products (metric tons; 1990) none (4,919,000); natural gas (cu m; 1990) none (4,004,000,000).
Gross national product (1992): U.S.$5,493,600,000 (U.S.$1,260 per capita)[5].

Structure of net material product and labour force

	1991			
	in value '000,000 rubles	% of total value	labour force	% of labour force
Agriculture	7,836	41.8	739,000	35.7
Mining Manufacturing Public utilities }	7,048	37.6	424,000	20.5
Construction	1,296	6.9	153,000	7.4
Transp. and commun.	711	3.8	67,000	3.2
Trade	1,757	9.4	137,000	6.6
Finance	—	— }	519,000	25.1
Pub. admin., defense	—	—		
Services	—	—		
Other	105	0.5	31,000[6]	1.5[6]
TOTAL	18,753	100.0	2,070,000	100.0

Population economically active (1991): total 2,070,000; activity rate of total population 47.4% (participation rates [1989]: ages 16–59 [male], 16–54 [female] 86.3%; female 50.0%; unemployed 4.2%).
Land use (1986): forested 37.6%; meadows and pastures 8.8%; agricultural and under permanent cultivation 53.6%.
Household income and expenditure. Average household size (1989) 3.4; income per household (1990) 4,000 rubles; sources of income (1990): salaries and wages 69.1%, pensions and stipends 12.2%, income from sale of agricultural products 6.7%, financial receipts 4.3%, other 7.7%; expenditure (1990): food and consumer goods 73.4%, services 6.7%, other 19.9%.

Foreign trade

Balance of trade (current prices)

	1987	1988	1989	1990
'000,000 rubles	−287.2	−1,023	−1,155	−284.7
% of total	2.6%	9.2%	9.6%	2.3%

Imports (1990): 6,461,400,000 rubles (machinery and equipment 28.8%, textiles 20.2%, chemicals 11.3%, energy products 8.6%, food products 7.1%). *Major import sources:* Russia 38.7%; Ukraine 17.2%; Belarus 8.6%; Uzbekistan 5.3%; Lithuania 2.7%.
Exports (1990): 6,176,700,000 rubles (food products 44.2%, textiles 19.6%, machinery and equipment 16.9%, agricultural exports 7.3%, chemical products 3.4%). *Major export destinations:* Russia 61.6%; Ukraine 14.1%; Belarus 7.2%; Uzbekistan 3.4%; Kazakhstan 2.9%.

Transport and communications

Transport. Railroads (1991): length 1,150 km; passenger-km 8,875,000,000; metric ton-km cargo 15,007,000,000. Roads (1991): total length 10,300 km (paved 94%). Vehicles (1988): passenger cars 177,100; Air transport (1990): passenger-km 2,352,000,000; metric ton-km cargo 19,000,000; airports (1993) with scheduled flights 1.
Communications. Daily newspapers (1990): total number 240; total circulation 309,000,000; circulation per 1,000 population 71. Radio (1991): 1,421,000 receivers (1 per 3.1 persons). Television (1991): 1,264,000 receivers (1 per 3.4 persons). Telephones (1991): 494,890 (1 per 8.8 persons).

Education and health

Education (1991–92)

	schools	teachers	students	student/ teacher ratio
Primary (age 7–13) Secondary (age 14–17) }	1,654	53,000	725,000	13.7
Voc., teacher tr.	53	...	47,200	...
Higher	11	...	52,200	...

Educational attainment (1989). Percentage of population age 15 and over having: no formal schooling or some primary education 24.5%; some secondary 20.4%; secondary or some postsecondary 46.4%; higher 8.7%.
Health (1991): physicians 17,400 (1 per 251 persons); hospital beds 56,400 (1 per 77 persons); infant mortality rate per 1,000 live births (1992) 19.8.

Military

Total active duty personnel (1993): 8,400 (army 76.6%, air force 23.4%). *Military expenditure as percentage of GDP* (1992): 18.4% (world, *c.* 5.0%); per capita expenditure U.S.$51.

[1]Total seats at 1990 elections, including 10 left vacant at those elections and, subsequently, those vacated by withdrawal of more than 100 representatives from constituencies in the unilaterally proclaimed Gagauz and Transdniester republics. [2]Introduced to permit eventual replacement of the ruble by new national currency, the leu. [3]One sq km is equal to approximately 0.3861 sq mi. [4]Total includes 3,190 sq km (1,230 sq mi) not distributable by administrative subdivision. [5]Ruble-area GNP and exchange-rate data are very speculative. [6]Data include film, media, forestry, and computer services.

Mongolia

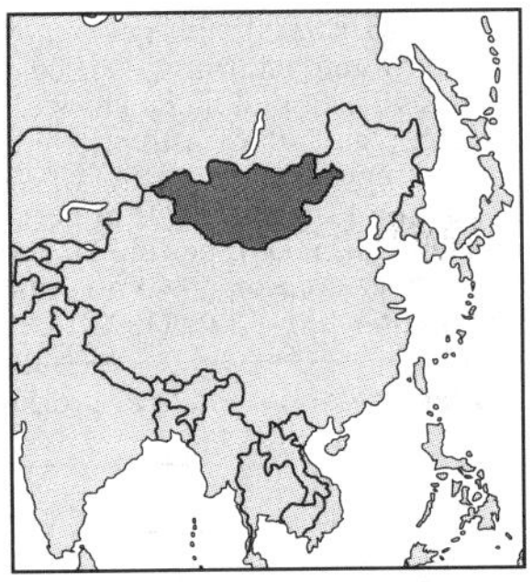

Official name: Mongol Uls (Mongolia).
Form of government: unitary multiparty republic with one legislative house (State Great Hural [76]).
Chief of state: President.
Head of government: Prime Minister.
Capital: Ulaanbaatar (Ulan Bator).
Official language: Khalkha Mongolian.
Official religion: none.
Monetary unit: 1 tugrik (Tug) = 100 möngö; valuation (Oct. 4, 1993) 1 U.S.$ = Tug 397.10; 1 £ = Tug 601.60.

Area and population

		area		population
		sq mi	sq km	1991 estimate
Provinces	**Capitals**			
Arhangay	Tsetserleg	21,000	55,000	89,200
Bayan-Ölgiy	Ölgiy	18,000	46,000	99,300
Bayanhongor	Bayanhongor	45,000	116,000	78,700
Bulgan	Bulgan	19,000	49,000	56,700
Dornod	Choybalsan	47,700	123,500	82,600
Dornogovĭ	Saynshand	43,000	111,000	58,600
Dundgovĭ	Mandalgovi	30,000	78,000	51,900
Dzavhan	Uliastay	32,000	82,000	93,600
Govĭ-Altay	Altay	55,000	142,000	65,100
Hentiy	Öndörhaan	32,000	82,000	76,700
Hovd	Hovd	29,000	76,000	81,100
Hövsgöl	Mörön	39,000	101,000	106,900
Ömnögovĭ	Dalandzadgad	64,000	165,000	43,500
Övörhangay	Arvayheer	24,000	63,000	100,400
Selenge	Sühbaatar	16,000	42,000	92,000
Sühbaatar	Baruun-Urt	32,000	82,000	53,500
Töv	Dzüünmod	31,000	81,000	105,900
Uvs	Ulaangom	27,000	69,000	91,800
Autonomous municipalities				
Darhan	—	100	200	88,600
Erdenet	—	300	800	58,200
Ulaanbaatar	—	800	2,000	575,000
TOTAL		604,800[1]	1,566,500	2,149,300

Demography

Population (1993): 2,256,000.
Density (1993): persons per sq mi 3.7, persons per sq km 1.4.
Urban-rural (1990): urban 58.0%; rural 42.0%.
Sex distribution (1991): male 49.89%; female 51.11%.
Age breakdown (1989): under 15, 41.9%; 15–29, 29.2%; 30–44, 14.6%; 45–59, 8.5%; 60 and over, 5.8%.
Population projection: (2000) 2,635,000; (2010) 3,290,000.
Doubling time: 28 years.
Ethnic composition (1989): Khalkha Mongol 78.8%; Kazakh 5.9%; Dörbed Mongol 2.7%; Bayad 1.9%; Buryat Mongol 1.7%; Dariganga Mongol 1.4%; other 7.6%.
Religious affiliation: although formal freedom of worship exists, all traditional forms of religious practice (lamaistic Buddhism, shamanism, Islam, and others) have been greatly reduced during the 20th century; reliable data on the current situation do not exist.
Major cities (1991): Ulaanbaatar (Ulan Bator) 536,600; Darhan 80,100; Erdenet 48,500; Choybalsan 38,600; Ölgiy 29,400.

Vital statistics

Birth rate per 1,000 population (1991): 33.0 (world avg. 26.4); legitimate, n.a.; illegitimate, n.a.
Death rate per 1,000 population (1991): 8.0 (world avg. 9.2).
Natural increase rate per 1,000 population (1991): 25.0 (world avg. 17.2).
Total fertility rate (avg. births per childbearing woman; 1993): 4.6.
Marriage rate per 1,000 population (1989): 7.8.
Divorce rate per 1,000 population (1989): 0.5.
Life expectancy at birth (1993): male 63 years; female 65 years.
Major causes of death per 100,000 population: n.a.; however, in the 1980s, major causes of mortality included diseases of the respiratory system, diseases of the cardiovascular system, malignant neoplasms (cancers), diseases of the digestive system, and injuries, accidents, and poisoning.

National economy

Budget (1991). Revenue: Tug 9,013,700,000 (taxes 89.5%, of which deductions from profits 28.9%, turnover tax 24.2%, windfall gains 23.1%; nontax revenue 10.5%, of which social insurance contributions 9.6%). Expenditures: Tug 11,050,400,000 (1990; economy 47.2%; social and cultural services 40.5%; defense 8.0%; administration and other 4.3%).
Public debt (external; 1991): U.S.$16,800,000,000.
Tourism (1990): number of international arrivals 147,200.
Production (metric tons except as noted). Agriculture, forestry, fishing (1992): cereals 492,000 (of which wheat 460,000), potatoes 76,000, vegetables 20,000; livestock (number of live animals) 15,040,000 sheep, 5,200,000 goats, 2,900,000 cattle, 2,300,000 horses, 564,000 camels, 188,000 pigs; roundwood (1991) 2,390,000 cu m; fish catch (1991) 100. Mining and quarrying (1991): copper 90,300; molybdenum 1,130; silver 15,500 kg; gold 800 kg. Manufacturing (value added by manufacturing, Tug '000,000; 1990): food products 691.1; textiles 429.8; leather and hides 302.6; construction materials 153.5; clothing and apparel 140.2; wood products 131.0; chemicals 127.3; printing and publishing 44.4; glass and ceramics 12.2. Construction (1991): residential 112,000 sq m; nonresidential, n.a. Energy production (consumption): electricity (kW-hr; 1991) 3,500,000,000 (3,650,000,000); coal (metric tons; 1991) 7,775,000 (7,175,000); crude petroleum, none (n.a.); petroleum products (metric tons; 1991) none (666,000); natural gas, none (n.a.).
Gross national product (1990): U.S.$240,700,000 (U.S.$112 per capita).

Structure of gross domestic product and labour force

	1989		1990	
	in value Tug '000,000	% of total value	labour force	% of labour force
Agriculture	1,722.9	16.1	191,500	27.6
Manufacturing and mining	2,919.8	27.2	123,400	17.8
Construction	617.2	5.8	44,600	6.4
Transp. and commun.	903.8	8.4	55,000	7.9
Trade	2,327.4	21.7	49,200	7.1
Services[2]	1,285.4	12.0	185,000	26.6
Other	954.4[3]	8.9[3]	45,700[4]	6.6[4]
TOTAL	10,730.9	100.0[1]	694,400	100.0

Population economically active (1990): total 694,400; activity rate of total population 32.3% (participation rates: ages 15–64 [1985] 82.2%; female [1987] 52.4%; unemployed 6.6%).

Price and earnings indexes (1985 = 100)

	1985	1986	1987	1988	1989	1990	1991[5]
Consumer price index	100.0	99.0	99.0	99.0	99.0	213.5	254.6
Monthly earnings index	100.0	100.4	101.0	101.3	102.9	103.2	...

Household income and expenditure. Average family size (1989) 4.8; income per household (1992)[6] Tug 5,500 (U.S.$140); sources of income (1990): wages and salaries 74.4%[7], transfer payments 13.5%, self-employment 3.3%, other 8.8%; expenditure (1990): products 82.1%, services 17.9%.
Land use (1991): forested 8.9%; meadows and pastures 79.5%; agricultural and under permanent cultivation 0.9%; other 10.7%.

Foreign trade

Balance of trade (current prices)[8]

	1986	1987	1988	1989	1990	1991
U.S.$'000,000	−587	−542	−629	−744	−314	−80
% of total	28.4%	24.9%	27.5%	31.8%	26.1%	10.3%

Imports (1990): Tug 2,751,100,000 (machinery and transport equipment 31.1%; fuels, minerals, and metals 27.2%; consumer goods 21.6%; food products 8.8%; chemical products and rubber 5.3%). *Major import sources:* U.S.S.R. 71.5%; Germany 4.1%; Czechoslovakia 3.7%; China 2.4%; Hungary 2.2%.
Exports (1990): Tug 1,967,400,000 (minerals and metals 48.1%; raw materials and food products 27.3%; consumer goods 20.1%; construction materials 3.9%). *Major export destinations:* U.S.S.R. 78.3%; Czechoslovakia 4.5%; Bulgaria 2.5%; Hungary 2.1%.

Transport and communications

Transport. Railroads (1990): length (1991) 1,445 mi, 2,325 km; passenger-km 524,100,000; metric ton-km cargo 5,087,800,000. Roads (1988): total length 30,600 mi, 49,200 km (paved 2%). Vehicles (1989): passenger cars 5,660; trucks and buses 29,794. Merchant marine: vessels (100 gross tons and over) none. Air transport (1991): passenger-km 408,100,000; metric ton-km cargo 3,800,000; airports (1993) with scheduled flights 1.
Communications. Daily newspapers (1990): total number 2; total circulation 222,000; circulation per 1,000 population 106. Radio (1992): total number of receivers 275,000 (1 per 7.8 persons). Television (1992): total number of receivers 120,000 (1 per 18 persons). Telephones (1991): 68,480 (1 per 31 persons).

Education and health

Education (1990–91)

	schools	teachers	students	student/teacher ratio
Primary and secondary (age 8–18)	634	20,600	440,900	21.4
Vocational	75	2,500	47,600	19.0
Higher	9	1,465	13,829	9.4

Educational attainment (1989). Percentage of population age 10 and over having: primary education 33.7%; some secondary 31.9%; complete secondary 16.9%; vocational secondary 9.4%; some higher and complete higher 8.1%.
Literacy (1989): total population age 10 and over literate 97.9%.
Health (1991): physicians 6,318 (1 per 340 persons); hospital beds 26,350 (1 per 83 persons); infant mortality rate per 1,000 live births 64.0.
Food (1988–90): daily per capita caloric intake 2,361[9] (vegetable products 61%, animal products 39%); 97% of FAO recommended minimum requirement.

Military

Total active duty personnel (1993): 21,250 (army 94.1%; navy, none; air force 5.9%). *Military expenditure as percentage of GDP* (1992): 1.8%; per capita expenditure (1989) U.S.$122.

[1]Detail does not add to total given because of rounding. [2]Services includes finance, public administration, and defense. [3]Other includes depreciation of fixed capital. [4]Unemployed. [5]April. [6]Urban households. [7]Includes income from agricultural cooperatives. [8]Trade in convertible currencies. [9]FAO estimate; alternate 1988–90 data reported by World Bank: 2,578 calories. According to Mongolian sources, November 1992 consumption was 1,875 calories (urban) and 2,092 (rural).

Morocco

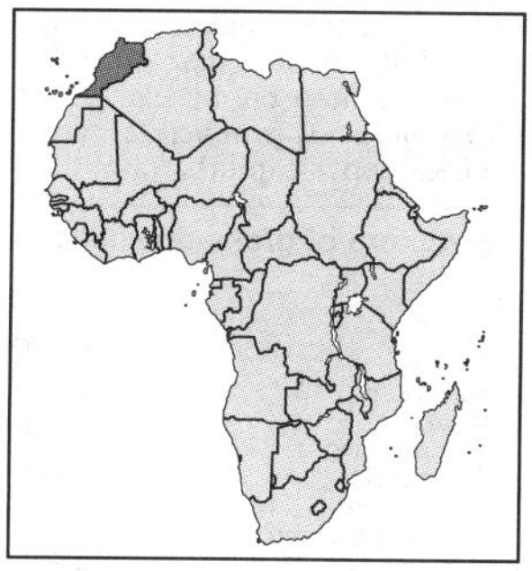

Official name: al-Mamlakah al-Maghribīyah (Kingdom of Morocco).
Form of government: constitutional monarchy with one legislative house (Chamber of Representatives [333]).
Chief of state: King.
Head of government: King assisted by Prime Minister.
Capital: Rabat.
Official language: Arabic.
Official religion: Islam.
Monetary unit: 1 Moroccan dirham (DH) = 100 Moroccan francs; valuation (Oct. 4, 1993) 1 U.S.$ = DH 9.04; 1 £ = DH 13.70.

Area and population (1992 est.)

Provinces[1]	area sq km[2]	population	Provinces[1]	area sq km[2]	population
Agadir	5,910	807,000	Safi	7,285	848,000
Azilal	10,050	419,000	Settat	9,750	790,000
Ben Slimane	2,760	204,000	Sidi Kacem	4,060	602,000
Béni Mellal	7,075	936,000	Tan-Tan	17,295	55,000
Boulemane	14,395	156,000	Tangier	1,195	566,000
Chaouen			Taounate	5,585	603,000
(Chefchaouen)	4,350	363,000	Taroudannt	16,460	658,000
Essaouira	6,335	428,000	Tata	25,925	107,000
Fès	5,400	1,029,000	Taza	15,020	715,000
Figuig	55,990	108,000	Tétouan	6,025	864,000
Guelmim	28,750	168,000	Tiznit	6,960	381,000
al-Hoceima	3,550	371,000			
Ifrane	3,310	116,000	**Prefectures**		
el-Jadida	6,000	928,000	Ain Chok–		
el-Kelaa des Srarhna	10,070	684,000	Hay Hassani		452,000
Kénitra	4,745	920,000	Ain Sebaa–		
Khémisset	8,305	473,000	Hay Mohammadi		587,000
Khénifra	12,320	442,000	Ben Msik–	1,615	984,000
Khouribga	4,250	547,000	Sidi Othmane		
Marrakech	14,755	1,525,000	Casablanca-Anfa		1,069,000
Meknès	3,995	753,000	Mohammadia-		
Nador	6,130	796,000	Znata		219,000
Ouarzazate	41,550	649,000	Rabat		690,000
Oujda	20,700	974,000	Salé	1,275	656,000
er-Rachidia	59,585	503,000	Skhirate-Temara		199,000
			TOTAL	458,730	25,344,000

Demography

Population (1993): 26,494,000.
Density (1993): persons per sq mi 149.6, persons per sq km 57.8.
Urban-rural (1992): urban 49.5%; rural 50.5%.
Sex distribution (1990): male 50.15%; female 49.85%.
Age breakdown (1990): under 15, 40.5%; 15–29, 28.3%; 30–44, 16.8%; 45–59, 8.4%; 60–74, 4.8%; 75 and over, 1.2%.
Population projection: (2000) 30,947,000; (2010) 36,810,000.
Doubling time: 29 years.
Ethnic composition (1986): Arab 70%; Berber 30%; other, less than 1%.
Religious affiliation (1982): Muslim (mostly Sunnī) 98.7%; Christian 1.1%.
Major cities (1982): Casablanca 2,139,204; Rabat 518,616; Fès 448,823.

Vital statistics

Birth rate per 1,000 population (1990–95): 32.6 (world avg. 26.4).
Death rate per 1,000 population (1990–95): 8.3 (world avg. 9.2).
Natural increase rate per 1,000 population (1990–95): 24.3 (world avg. 17.2).
Total fertility rate (avg. births per childbearing woman; 1990): 4.7.
Life expectancy at birth (1990–95): male 61.6 years; female 65.0 years.
Major causes of death (1989)[3]: childhood diseases 22.9%; circulatory diseases 15.4%; accidents 7.3%; infectious and parasitic diseases 6.3%; cancers 5.6%.

National economy

Budget (1992). Revenue: DH 73,427,000,000 (indirect taxes 21.8%; extraordinary revenue 21.4%; customs duties 19.8%; stamp duties 4.0%). Expenditures: DH 73,317,000,000 (current expenditure 81.5%, of which debt payments 30.6%; investment expenditure 18.5%).
Public debt (external, outstanding; 1991): U.S.$20,132,000,000.
Land use (1991): forested 20.3%; meadows 46.8%; agricultural 21.1%; built-on, wasteland, and other 11.8%.
Tourism (1991): receipts from visitors U.S.$1,052,000,000; expenditures by nationals abroad U.S.$190,000,000.
Production (metric tons except as noted). Agriculture, forestry, fishing (1992): sugar beets 2,754,000, wheat 1,562,000, barley 1,081,000, sugarcane 994,000, tomatoes 900,000, potatoes 900,000; livestock (number of live animals) 17,000,000 sheep, 5,500,000 goats, 3,300,000 cattle, 42,000,000 chickens; roundwood (1991) 2,549,000 cu m; fish catch (1991) 592,881. Mining and quarrying (value of production in DH '000,000; 1991): phosphate rock 4,424.3; lead 260.5; copper 196.0; zinc 145.3; mineral water 136.4; fluorspar 66.0; barite 62.8; iron ore 22.2. Manufacturing (1990): cement 5,381,000; refined sugar 746,000; wine 44,000; passenger automobiles and commercial vehicles 16,000 units. Construction (value added in DH; 1989): 9,217,000. Energy production (consumption): electricity (kW-hr; 1991) 9,834,000,000 (10,475,000,000); coal (metric tons; 1991) 555,000 (1,760,000); crude petroleum (barrels; 1991) 96,200 (44,700,000); petroleum products (metric tons; 1991) 4,631,000 (5,374,000); natural gas (cu m; 1991) 34,633,000 (34,633,000).
Gross national product (1992): U.S.$27,047,000,000 (U.S.$1,030 per capita).

Structure of gross domestic product and labour force

	1991		1982	
	in value DH '000,000	% of total value	labour force	% of labour force
Agriculture	41,800	18.0	2,351,629	39.2
Mining	5,033	2.2	63,360	1.1
Manufacturing	40,376	17.4	930,615	15.5
Construction	12,267	5.3	437,464	7.3
Public utilities	14,393	6.2	22,465	0.4
Transp. and commun.	14,800	6.4	140,981	2.3
Trade	48,626	20.9	498,130	8.3
Finance	...	...		
Pub. admin., defense	29,000	12.5	532,803	8.9
Services	26,385	11.3	474,109	7.9
Other			547,704[4]	9.1[4]
TOTAL	232,680	100.0[5]	5,999,260	100.0

Population economically active (1990)[6]: total 3,895,126; activity rate 32.5% (participation rates: over age 15, 49.6%; female 26.1%; unemployed [1993] 16.0%).

Price index (1985 = 100)

	1986	1987	1988	1989	1990	1991	1992
Consumer price index	108.7	111.7	114.3	117.9	126.0	136.1	142.8
Earnings index[7]	100.0	100.0	109.9	120.9	152.7	...	...

Household income and expenditure. Average household size (1982) 5.8; expenditure (1972–73)[8]: food 54.0%, clothing 8.5%, housing 7.0%, transportation 6.9%.

Foreign trade[9]

Balance of trade (current prices)

	1986	1987	1988	1989	1990	1991
DH '000,000	–9,390	–8,707	–5,853	–14,130	–16,755	–13,327
% of total	17.5%	15.7%	9.0%	20.0%	19.3%	15.1%

Imports (1991): DH 59,720,000,000 (capital goods 26.9%; crude oil 14.3%; consumer goods 11.6%; food, beverages, and tobacco 8.4%). *Major import sources:* France 24.2%; Spain 8.3%; Italy 7.0%; Germany 5.9%.
Exports (1991): DH 37,283,000,000 (food 27.9%; consumer goods 26.0%; minerals 11.0%). *Major export destinations:* France 31.8%; Spain 8.8%; India 7.0%.

Transport and communications

Transport. Railroads (1990): route length 1,893 km; passenger-km 2,237,000,000; metric ton-km cargo 5,107,000,000. Roads (1991): total length 59,474 km (paved 50%). Vehicles (1991): passenger cars 719,216; trucks and buses 287,649. Merchant marine (1992): vessels (100 gross tons and over) 492; total deadweight tonnage 586,221. Air transport (1989): passenger-km 2,700,000,000; metric ton-km cargo 35,016,000; airports (1993) with scheduled flights 16.
Communications. Daily newspapers (1989): total number 11; total circulation 360,000[10]; circulation per 1,000 population 15[10]. Radio (1992): 4,500,000 receivers (1 per 5.8 persons). Television (1992): 1,210,000 receivers (1 per 21.7 persons). Telephones (1991): 560,789 (1 per 46 persons).

Education and health

Education (1990–91)

	schools	teachers	students	student/ teacher ratio
Primary (age 7–12)	4,052	87,839	2,483,691	28.3
Secondary (age 13–17)[11]	1,080	69,915	1,121,193	16.0
Vocational[12]	562	5,359	68,802	12.8
Higher	35	7,713	225,001	29.2

Educational attainment (1982). Percentage of population age 25 and over having: no formal education 47.8%; some primary education 47.8%; some secondary 3.8%; higher 0.6%. *Literacy* (1990): total population over age 15 literate 49.5%; males 61.3%; females literate 38.0%.
Health (1990): physicians 5,665 (1 per 4,415 persons); hospital beds 26,066[13] (1 per 959 persons); infant mortality rate (1990–95) 68.0.
Food (1988–90): daily per capita caloric intake 3,031 (vegetable products 94%, animal products 6%); 125% of FAO recommended minimum requirement.

Military

Total active duty personnel (1993): 195,500 (army 89.5%, navy 3.6%, air force 6.9%). *Military expenditure as percentage of GNP* (1989): 5.5% (world 4.9%); per capita expenditure U.S.$48.

[1]Provincial capitals have same name as province. [2]One sq km is approximately equal to 0.3861 sq mi. [3]Registered deaths of urban population only. [4]Unemployed, not previously employed only. [5]Detail does not add to total given because of rounding. [6]Urban labour force only, representing the total urban employed and unemployed. [7]Based on minimum hourly wage of workers 18 years of age and older; values reflect adjustments made to the minimum wage during the year. [8]Weights of consumer price index components. [9]Import figures are f.o.b. in balance of trade. [10]For 8 newspapers only. [11]Public institutions only. [12]Excludes teacher training. [13]Public only.

Mozambique

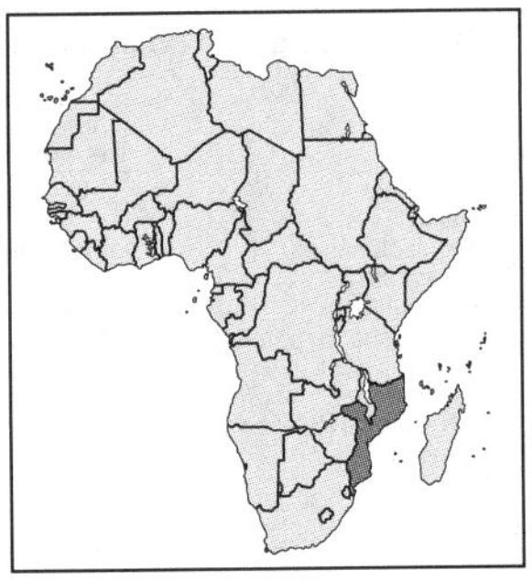

Official name: República de Moçambique (Republic of Mozambique).
Form of government: unitary republic[1] with a single legislative house (Assembly of the Republic [249]).
Chief of state and head of government: President.
Capital: Maputo.
Official language: Portuguese.
Official religion: none.
Monetary unit: 1 metical (Mt.; plural meticais) = 100 centavos; valuation (Oct. 4, 1993) 1 U.S.$ = Mt. 4,415; 1 £ = Mt. 6,689.

Area and population

		area		population
Provinces	Capitals	sq mi	sq km	1991 estimate
Cabo Delgado	Pemba	31,902	82,625	1,202,221
Gaza	Xai-Xai	29,231	75,709	1,401,485
Inhambane	Inhambane	26,492	68,615	1,156,958
Manica	Chimoio	23,807	61,661	609,512
Maputo	Maputo	9,944	25,756	840,757
Nampula	Nampula	31,508	81,606	2,841,416
Niassa	Lichinga	49,828	129,055	686,650
Sofala	Beira	26,262	68,018	1,427,493
Tete	Tete	38,890	100,724	734,561
Zambézia	Quelimane	40,544	105,008	2,619,281
City				
Maputo	—	232	602	931,591
TOTAL LAND AREA		308,642[2]	799,379	
INLAND WATER		5,019	13,000	
TOTAL		313,661	812,379	14,451,925[3]

Demography

Population (1993)[3]: 15,243,000.
Density (1993)[4]: persons per sq mi 49.4, persons per sq km 19.1.
Urban-rural (1980): urban 13.2%; rural 86.8%.
Sex distribution (1990)[5]: male 49.32%; female 50.68%.
Age breakdown (1990)[5]: under 15, 44.0%; 15–29, 26.2%; 30–44, 15.4%; 45–59, 9.2%; 60–74, 4.4%; 75 and over, 0.8%.
Population projection: (2000) 18,350,000; (2010) 23,604,000.
Doubling time: 26 years.
Ethnolinguistic composition (1983): Makua 47.3%; Tsonga 23.3%; Malawi 12.0%; Shona 11.3%; Yao 3.8%; Swahili 0.8%; Makonde 0.6%; Portuguese 0.2%; other 0.7%.
Religious affiliation (1980): traditional beliefs 47.8%; Christian 38.9%, of which Roman Catholic 31.4%; Muslim 13.0%; other 0.3%.
Major cities (1991): Maputo 931,591; Beira 298,847; Nampula 250,473.

Vital statistics

Birth rate per 1,000 population (1990–95): 44.0 (world avg. 26.4).
Death rate per 1,000 population (1990–95): 17.0 (world avg. 9.2).
Natural increase rate per 1,000 population (1990–95): 27.0 (world avg. 17.2).
Total fertility rate (avg. births per childbearing woman; 1990–95): 6.2.
Marriage rate per 1,000 population (1974): 0.7.
Divorce rate per 1,000 population (1973): 0.01.
Life expectancy at birth (1990–95): male 46.9 years; female 50.2 years.
Major infectious diseases (certified cases per 100,000 population; 1980): measles 227.4; pulmonary tuberculosis 55.9; viral hepatitis 19.2; leprosy 13.8; cholera 4.6; tetanus 4.5.

National economy

Budget (1991). Revenue: Mt. 447,000,000,000 (sales tax 39.6%, customs taxes 24.4%, individual income tax 17.7%). Expenditures: Mt. 958,000,000,000 (defense and security 18.6%, wages and salaries 10.5%).
Production (metric tons except as noted). Agriculture, forestry, fishing (1992): cassava 3,239,000, sugarcane 320,000, coconuts 300,000, corn (maize) 133,000, peanuts (groundnuts) 80,000, bananas 80,000, sorghum 66,000; livestock (number of live animals) 1,250,000 cattle, 385,000 goats, 170,000 pigs, 118,000 sheep, 22,000,000 chickens; roundwood (1991) 16,065,000 cu m; fish catch (1991) 34,000. Mining and quarrying (1992): marine salt 46,900[6]; bauxite 8,000; copper 133[6, 7]; garnet 2,250 kg; gemstones 15,000 carats. Manufacturing (1990): cement 76,767; wheat flour 49,368; raw sugar 33,141; soap 8,843; cotton threads 4,676; beer 352,900 hectolitres; cigarettes 414,000,000 units; poplin 3,664,000 sq m. Construction (1974): residential 247,000 sq m; nonresidential 121,000 sq m. Energy production (consumption): electricity (kW-hr; 1991) 490,000,000 (815,000,000); coal (metric tons; 1991) 42,000 (62,000); crude petroleum (1991) none (none[8]); petroleum products (metric tons; 1991) none[8] (268,000); natural gas, none (none).
Population economically active (1980): total 5,671,290; activity rate of total population 48.6% (participation rates: over age 15, 87.3%; female 52.4%; unemployed 1.7%).

Price and earnings indexes (1985 = 100)

	1985	1986	1987	1988	1989	1990	1991
Consumer price index	100.0	138.7	365.2	548.2	778.9	1,145.0	1,526.0
Earnings index	...	...	...	...	...	...	...

Public debt (external, outstanding; 1991): U.S.$4,039,000,000.
Household income and expenditure. Average household size (1980) 4.2; income per household: n.a.; sources of income: n.a.; expenditure: n.a.
Gross national product (at current market prices; 1992): U.S.$994,320,000 (U.S.$60 per capita).

Structure of gross domestic product and labour force

	1990		1980	
	in value Mt. '000,000	% of total value	labour force	% of labour force
Agriculture	637,000	37.3	4,754,831	83.8
Mining	390,000[9]	22.9[9]	73,425	1.3
Manufacturing			273,369	4.8
Construction	225,000	13.2	42,121	0.7
Public utilities	...	...	10	10
Transportation and communications	162,400	9.5	77,025	1.4
Trade and finance	292,200	17.1	112,244	2.0
Pub. admin., defense			243,449[10]	4.3[10]
Services				
Other			94,826[11]	1.7[11]
TOTAL	1,706,700[2]	100.0	5,671,290	100.0

Tourism: n.a.
Land use (1991): forested 18.0%; meadows and pastures 56.1%; agricultural and under permanent cultivation 4.0%; other 21.9%.

Foreign trade[12]

Balance of trade (current prices)

	1986	1987	1988	1989	1990	1991
U.S.$'000,000	−464	−528	−612	−670	−648	−737
% of total	74.6%	73.1%	74.8%	76.1%	71.8%	69.5%

Imports (1989): U.S.$775,000,000 (foodstuffs 22.1%, capital equipment 18.8%, machinery and spare parts 13.3%, crude petroleum and derivatives 7.5%). *Major import sources:* South Africa 23.2%; U.S.S.R. 9.8%; United States 7.1%; Portugal 6.8%; Italy 6.0%.
Exports (1990): U.S.$126,400,000 (shrimps 34.3%, cashew nuts 11.3%, cotton 6.9%, sugar 6.3%, timber 1.3%). *Major export destinations:* Spain 17.9%; United States 11.6%; Japan 10.4%; Portugal 5.6%.

Transport and communications

Transport. Railroads (1990): route length (1991) 1,857 mi, 2,988 km; passenger-mi 49,020,000, passenger-km 78,900,000; short ton-mi cargo 288,600,000, metric ton-km cargo 421,400,000. Roads (1991): total length 16,955 mi, 27,287 km (paved 17%). Vehicles (1991): passenger cars 88,000; trucks and buses 24,000. Merchant marine (1992): vessels (100 gross tons and over) 107; total deadweight tonnage 31,645. Air transport (1992): passenger-mi 252,900,000, passenger-km 407,000,000; short ton-mi cargo 7,057,000, metric ton-km cargo 10,303,000; airports (1993) with scheduled flights 7.
Communications. Daily newspapers (1992): total number 2; total circulation 49,000; circulation per 1,000 population 3.3. Radio (1992): total number of receivers 500,000 (1 per 30 persons). Television (1992): total number of receivers 35,000 (1 per 424 persons). Telephones (1991): 69,477 (1 per 211 persons).

Education and health

Education (1988)

	schools	teachers	students	student/teacher ratio
Primary (age 5–9)[13]	3,647	21,410	1,199,669	56.0
Secondary (age 10–16)[14]	207	3,422	107,080	31.3
Voc., teacher tr.	32	968	10,604	10.9
Higher	2	457	2,562	5.6

Educational attainment (1980). Percentage of population age 25 and over having: no formal schooling 80.7%; primary education 18.2%; secondary 0.9%; higher 0.2%. *Literacy* (1990): percentage of total population age 15 and over literate 32.9%; males literate 45.1%; females literate 21.3%.
Health (1988): physicians 342 (1 per 43,536 persons); hospital beds 12,129 (1 per 1,227 persons); infant mortality rate per 1,000 live births (1990–95) 130.0.
Food (1988–90): daily per capita caloric intake 1,805 (vegetable products 97%, animal products 3%); 77% of FAO recommended minimum requirement.

Military

Total active duty personnel (1993): 50,000[15] (army 90.0%, navy 2.0%, air force 8.0%). *Military expenditure as percentage of GNP* (1989): 9.7% (world 4.9%); per capita expenditure U.S.$8.

[1]Mozambique adopted a new multiparty constitution, which became effective on Nov. 30, 1990; multiparty elections have been postponed until 1995. [2]Detail does not add to total given because of rounding. [3]Excludes refugees in nearby countries, estimated at about 1.3 million. [4]Density is based on land area. [5]Includes refugees in nearby countries. [6]1990. [7]Metal content only. [8]Internal disorder and a lack of foreign exchange have brought importation of crude petroleum and the production of refined petroleum products practically to a halt. [9]Includes fishing industry. [10]Services includes Public utilities. [11]Unemployed. [12]Import figures are c.i.f. [13]Includes initiation classes in which pupils learn Portuguese. [14]Includes the two stages of secondary education and the upper-level primary stage. [15]Excludes an estimated 5,900 to 7,500 United Nations forces.

Myanmar (Burma)

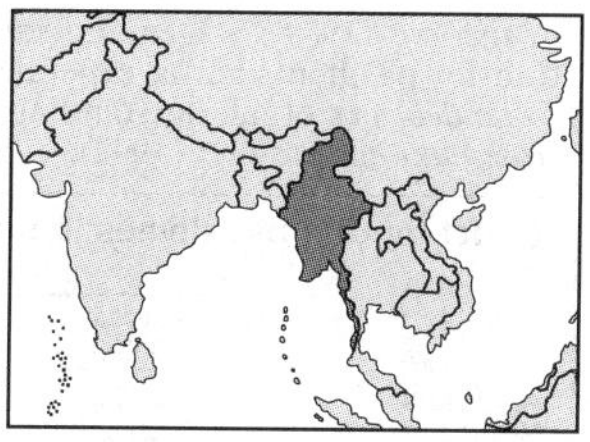

Official name: Pyidaungzu Myanma Naingngandaw (Union of Myanmar).
Form of government: military regime[1].
Head of state and government: Chairman of the State Law and Order Restoration Council.
Capital: Yangôn (Rangoon).
Official language: Burmese.
Official religion: none.
Monetary unit: 1 Myanmar kyat (K) = 100 pyas; valuation (Oct. 4, 1993) 1 U.S.$ = K 6.25; 1 £ = K 9.48.

Area and population

Divisions	Capitals	area sq mi	area sq km	population 1983 census
Irrawaddy (Ayeyarwady)	Bassein (Pathein)	13,567	35,138	4,994,061
Magwe (Magway)	Magwe (Magway)	17,305	44,820	3,243,166
Mandalay	Mandalay	14,295	37,024	4,577,762
Pegu (Bago)	Pegu (Bago)	15,214	39,404	3,799,791
Sagaing	Sagaing	36,535	94,625	3,862,172
Tenasserim (Tanintharyi)	Tavoy (Dawei)	16,735	43,343	917,247
Yangôn	Yangôn (Rangoon)	3,927	10,171	3,965,916
States				
Chin	Hakha	13,907	36,019	368,949
Kachin	Myitkyinā	34,379	89,041	904,794
Karen	Pa-an (Hpa-an)	11,731	30,383	1,055,359
Kayah	Loi-kaw	4,530	11,733	168,429
Mon	Moulmein (Mawlamyine)	4,748	12,297	1,680,157
Rakhine (Arakan)	Sittwe (Akyab)	14,200	36,778	2,045,559
Shan	Taunggyi	60,155	155,801	3,716,841
TOTAL		261,228	676,577	35,307,913[2]

Demography

Population (1993): 44,613,000.
Density (1993): persons per sq mi 170.8, persons per sq km 65.9.
Urban-rural (1993): urban 25.0%; rural 75.0%.
Sex distribution (1988): male 49.57%; female 50.43%.
Age breakdown (1988): under 15, 36.8%; 15–29, 29.5%; 30–44, 17.1%; 45–59, 10.3%; 60 and over, 6.3%.
Population projection: (2000) 51,567,000; (2010) 61,631,000.
Doubling time: 33 years.
Ethnic composition (1983): Burman 69.0%; Shan 8.5%; Karen 6.2%; Rakhine 4.5%; Mon 2.4%; Chin 2.2%; Kachin 1.4%; other 5.8%.
Religious affiliation (1983): Buddhist 89.4%; Christian 4.9%; Muslim 3.8%; tribal religions 1.1%; Hindu 0.5%; other 0.3%.
Major cities (1983): Yangôn (Rangoon) 2,513,023; Mandalay 532,949; Moulmein (Mawlamyine) 219,961; Pegu (Bago) 150,528; Bassein (Pathein) 144,096.

Vital statistics

Birth rate per 1,000 population (1993): 32.0 (world avg. 26.4).
Death rate per 1,000 population (1993): 11.0 (world avg. 9.2).
Natural increase rate per 1,000 population (1993): 21.0 (world avg. 17.2).
Total fertility rate (avg. births per childbearing woman; 1993): 4.1.
Marriage rate per 1,000 population: n.a.
Divorce rate per 1,000 population: n.a.
Life expectancy at birth (1993): male 56.0 years; female 60.0 years.
Major causes of death per 100,000 population (1978): pneumonia 16.1; heart diseases 10.5; enteritis and other diarrheal diseases 10.0; tuberculosis 9.4; malignant neoplasms (cancers) 6.5; cerebrovascular disease 4.1; malaria 3.5.

National economy

Budget (1990–91). Revenue: K 8,929,000,000 (revenue from taxes 50.4%, receipts from state economic enterprises 49.6%). Expenditures: K 14,235,000,000 (current expenditures 78.8%, capital expenditures 21.2%).
Tourism (1991): receipts from visitors U.S.$13,000,000; expenditures by nationals abroad U.S.$1,000,000.
Production (metric tons except as noted). Agriculture, forestry, fishing (1992): rice 13,771,000, sugarcane 2,400,000, pulses 642,000, peanuts (groundnuts) 466,000, plantains 245,000, corn (maize) 241,000, onions 190,000, sesame seeds 183,000, millet 167,000, potatoes 154,000, seed cotton 68,000, tobacco leaves 53,000, jute 23,000; livestock (number of live animals) 9,470,000 cattle, 2,514,000 pigs, 2,099,000 buffalo, 1,360,000 sheep and goats, 4,000,000 ducks, 25,000,000 chickens; roundwood (1991) 23,585,000 cu m; fish catch (1991) 769,236. Mining and quarrying (1990–91): copper concentrates 31,500; gypsum 30,536; refined lead 2,750; tin concentrates 676; refined silver 190,000 troy oz. Manufacturing (value of production in '000,000 kyats; 1987–88): food and beverages 23,549.8; clothing and wearing apparel 1,606.6; industrial raw materials 1,468.9; construction materials 1,120.9; transport vehicles 719.0; personal goods 327.8. Construction (units; 1987–88)[3]: residential 1,193; nonresidential 1,483. Energy production (consumption): electricity (kW-hr; 1990) 2,601,000,000 (2,601,000,000); coal (metric tons; 1990) 78,000 (118,000); crude petroleum (barrels; 1990) 6,376,000 (6,376,000); petroleum products (metric tons; 1990) 566,000 (567,000); natural gas (cu m; 1990) 1,075,000,000 (1,075,000,000).
Household income and expenditure. Average household size (1983) 5.2; average annual income per household: n.a.; sources of income: n.a.; expenditure (1978)[4]: food and beverages 64.4%, clothing and footwear 8.0%, fuel and lighting 7.8%, household rent and repairs 3.8%, tobacco 3.7%, other 12.3%.
Gross national product (at current market prices; 1989–90): U.S.$16,330,000,000 (U.S.$400 per capita).

Structure of gross domestic product and labour force

	1991–92 in value K '000,000	1991–92 % of total value	1989–90 labour force	1989–90 % of labour force
Agriculture	84,509	56.6	10,614,000	67.6
Mining	952	0.6	78,000	0.5
Manufacturing	12,095	8.1	1,137,000	7.2
Construction	2,350	1.6	174,000	1.1
Public utilities	464	0.3	17,000	0.1
Transp. and commun.	4,178	2.8	385,000	2.5
Trade	34,093	22.9	1,405,000	8.9
Finance	273	0.2	956,000	6.1
Public admin., services	5,675	3.8		
Other	4,667	3.1	935,000	6.0
TOTAL	149,256	100.0	15,701,000	100.0

Public debt (external, outstanding; 1991): U.S.$4,557,000,000.
Population economically active (1989–90): total 15,701,000; activity rate of total population 38.2% (participation rates: ages 15–64 [1983] 64.2%; female [1987–88] 35.3%; unemployed [1987–88] 4.3%).

Price and earnings indexes (1985 = 100)

	1986	1987	1988	1989	1990	1991	1992
Consumer price index	109.3	136.4	158.3	201.3	236.8	313.2	381.9
Monthly earnings index[5]	101.7	113.5	199.2	277.6	...	...	...

Land use (1991): forested 49.3%; meadows and pastures 0.5%; agricultural and under permanent cultivation 15.3%; other 34.9%.

Foreign trade[6]

Balance of trade (current prices)

	1987	1988	1989	1990	1991	1992
K '000,000	−173.5	−346.8	+274.9	+485.0	−1,055.4	−338.1
% of total	5.6%	14.2%	10.6%	13.5%	16.7%	4.9%

Imports (1991–92): K 3,870,000,000 (1989–90; machinery and equipment 51.4%, industrial raw materials 31.4%, consumer goods 17.1%). *Major import sources* (1990–91): Singapore 19.7%; Japan 18.3%; China 17.0%; Malaysia 5.2%; Australia 4.0%; United States 3.2%; Thailand 2.6%.
Exports (1991–92): K 2,584,000,000 (1989–90; agricultural products 31.5%, forest products 23.8%, minerals and gems 8.7%, animal and marine products 4.5%). *Major export destinations* (1990–91): Singapore 13.2%; Thailand 11.1%; Japan 8.1%; China 7.4%; Hong Kong 6.5%; South Korea 4.0%; Sri Lanka 3.6%.

Transport and communications

Transport. Railroads (1990–91): route length 1,949 mi, 3,137 km; passenger-mi 2,781,000,000, passenger-km 4,476,000,000; short ton-mi cargo 395,000,000, metric ton-km cargo 576,000,000. Roads (1988): total length 14,579 mi, 23,463 km (paved 38%). Vehicles (1991): passenger cars 35,000; trucks and buses 35,000. Merchant marine (1992): vessels (100 gross tons and over) 144; total deadweight tonnage 1,354,005. Air transport (1990–91): passenger-mi 137,700,000, passenger-km 221,600,000; short ton-mi cargo 5,649,000, metric ton-km cargo 8,248,000; airports (1993) with scheduled flights 20.
Communications. Daily newspapers (1990): total number 2; total circulation 200,000; circulation per 1,000 population 5. Radio (1992): total receivers 3,200,000 (1 per 14 persons). Television (1992): total receivers 1,000,000 (1 per 44 persons). Telephones (1988): 80,568 (1 per 501 persons).

Education and health

Education (1991–92)

	schools	teachers	students	student/teacher ratio
Primary (age 5–9)	36,499	198,909	5,759,700	29.0
Secondary (age 10–15)	2,920	67,503	1,316,600	19.5
Voc., teacher tr.	103	2,158	26,600	12.3
Higher	36	6,416	260,200	40.6

Educational attainment (1983). Percentage of population age 25 and over having: no formal schooling 55.8%; primary education 39.4%; secondary 4.6%; religious 0.1%; postsecondary 0.1%. *Literacy* (1983): total population age 15 and over literate 16,472,494 (78.5%); males literate 8,816,031 (85.8%); females literate 7,656,463 (71.6%).
Health (1990–91): physicians 12,427 (1 per 3,389 persons); hospital beds 26,294 (1 per 1,602 persons); infant mortality rate per 1,000 live births (1993) 80.
Food (1988–90): daily per capita caloric intake 2,454 (vegetable products 96%, animal products 4%); 114% of FAO recommended minimum requirement.

Military

Total active duty personnel (1993): 286,000 (army 92.7%, navy 4.2%, air force 3.1%). *Military expenditure as percentage of GNP* (1989): 3.7% (world 4.9%); per capita expenditure U.S.$15.

[1]Multiparty elections were held on May 27, 1990, for seats in a 492-seat National Assembly; although the opposition party, the National League for Democracy, won a majority of the seats, the military government has refused to hand over power. [2]Includes 7,710 persons not distributed by area. [3]Construction Corporation activity only. [4]Based on 24 rural townships. [5]Wages in manufacturing. [6]Import figures are f.o.b. in balance of trade and c.i.f. in commodities and trading partners.

Namibia[1]

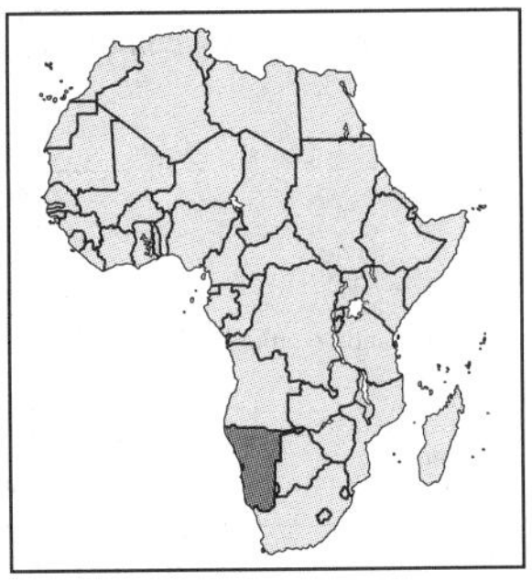

Official name: Republic of Namibia.
Political status: unitary multiparty republic with two legislative houses (National Assembly [72[2]]; National Council [26]).
Head of state and government: President.
Capital: Windhoek.
Official language: English.
Official religion: none.
Monetary unit[3]: 1 Namibian dollar (Nam$) = 100 cents; valuation (Oct. 4, 1993) 1 U.S.$ = Nam$3.45; 1 £ = Nam$5.22.

Area and population[4]

Regions	Capitals	area sq mi	area sq km	population 1992 estimate
Caprivi	—	7,541	19,532	92,000
Erongo[4]	—	24,168	62,595	75,500
Hardap	—	42,428	109,888	80,000
Karas	—	62,288	161,324	73,000
Khomas	—	14,210	36,804	161,000
Kunene	—	55,697	144,254	58,500
Ohangwena	—	4,086	10,582	178,000
Okavango	—	16,763	43,417	136,000
Omaheke	—	32,715	84,731	55,600
Omusati	—	5,265	13,637	158,000
Oshana	—	2,042	5,290	159,000
Oshikoto	—	10,273	26,607	176,000
Otjozondjupa	—	40,667	105,327	85,000
Other		2	6	1,000
TOTAL		318,146[5]	823,994	1,488,600

Demography

Population (1993): 1,537,000.
Density (1993): persons per sq mi 4.8, persons per sq km 1.9.
Urban-rural (1991): urban 32.8%; rural 67.2%.
Sex distribution (1991): male 49.78%; female 50.22%.
Age breakdown (1990): under 15, 45.7%; 15–29, 25.5%; 30–44, 15.0%; 45–59, 8.6%; 60–74, 4.3%; 75 and over, 0.9%.
Population projection: (2000) 1,906,000; (2010) 2,533,000.
Doubling time: 23 years.
Ethnic composition (1989): Ovambo 49.8%; Kavango 9.3%; Herero 7.5%; Damara 7.5%; white 6.4%; Nama 4.8%; other 14.7%.
Religious affiliation (1981): Lutheran 51.2%; Roman Catholic 19.8%; Dutch Reformed 6.1%; Anglican 5.0%; other 17.9%.
Major cities (1988): Windhoek 114,500; Swakopmund 15,500; Rundu 15,000; Rehoboth 15,000; Keetmanshoop 14,000.

Vital statistics

Birth rate per 1,000 population (1990–95): 41.6 (world avg. 26.4).
Death rate per 1,000 population (1990–95): 10.6 (world avg. 9.2).
Natural increase rate per 1,000 population (1990–95): 31.0 (world avg. 17.2).
Total fertility rate (avg. births per childbearing woman; 1990–95): 5.7.
Life expectancy at birth (1990–95): male 57.5 years; female 60.0 years.
Major causes of death per 100,000 population: n.a.; however, major diseases include malaria, tuberculosis, and trypanosomiasis (sleeping sickness).

National economy

Budget (1992–93). Revenue: R 2,997,000,000 (1991–92; customs and excise taxes 42.8%, of which general sales tax 13.9%; individual income taxes 10.7%; mining taxes 4.4%; nontax revenues 3.7%). Expenditures: R 3,545,000,000 (education 19.6%; national defense 4.9%; finance 4.7%; health and welfare 3.8%).
Tourism (1991): receipts U.S.$6,100,000; expenditures, n.a.
Production (metric tons except as noted). Agriculture, forestry, fishing (1992): roots and tubers 220,000, fruits 35,000, vegetables and melons 30,000, corn (maize) 13,000, millet 12,000, pulses 7,000, sorghum 4,000, wool 1,200, karakul pelts 770,627 units[6]; livestock (number of live animals) 3,000,000 sheep, 2,100,000 cattle, 1,972,000 goats; fish catch (1991) 204,517. Mining and quarrying (1992): diamonds 1,548,000 carats, mostly gem quality; zinc 68,300; copper 37,500; lead 31,700; uranium 1,973; silver 2,848,000 troy oz; gold 64,288 troy oz. Manufacturing (1991): n.a.; products include cut gems (primarily diamonds), fur products (karakul), processed foods (fish, meats, and dairy products), textiles, carved wood products, refined metals (copper and lead). Construction (value of buildings completed in R '000,000; 1990): residential 44.6; nonresidential 92.4. Energy production (consumption): electricity (kW-hr; 1992) 1,714,000,000 (1,714,000,000); coal, none (n.a.); crude petroleum, none (n.a.).
Population economically active: total (1988) *c.* 230,000; activity rate of total population, *c.* 18% (participation rates [1984]: ages 15–64, *c.* 56%; female 20.4%; unemployed [1988] *c.* 20%).

Price and earnings indexes (1985 = 100)[7]

	1984	1985	1986	1987	1988	1989	1990
Consumer price index	89.3	100.0	113.4	127.7	144.1	165.9	185.7
Earnings index	...	...	...	...	...	...	...

Household income and expenditure. Average household size (1981) 4.8; average annual income per household (1980) R 3,223 (U.S.$4,143); sources of income (1989): wages and salaries 70.0%, income from property 24.4%, transfer payments 5.2%; expenditure: n.a.
Public debt (external, outstanding; 1989): U.S.$1,880,000,000.
Gross national product (1992): U.S.$2,496,000,000 (U.S.$1,630 per capita).

Structure of gross domestic product and labour force

	1990 in value R '000,000	1990 % of total value	1988 labour force[8, 9]	1988 % of labour force[8, 9]
Agriculture	750.0	15.4	36,071	19.5
Mining	1,050.0	21.6	10,062	5.5
Manufacturing	303.0	6.2	9,442	5.1
Construction	113.0	2.3	12,657	6.8
Public utilities	96.0	2.0	1,273	0.7
Transportation and communications	318.0	6.5	7,880	4.3
Trade	605.0	12.4	29,394	15.9
Finance	365.0	7.5	4,327	2.3
Services	98.0	2.0	25,167	13.6
Public administration and defense	1,019.0	20.9	48,520	26.3
Other	151.0	3.1	...	...
TOTAL	4,868.0	100.0[5]	184,793	100.0

Land use (1991): forested 22.0%; meadows and pastures 46.2%; agricultural and under permanent cultivation 0.8%; other 31.0%.

Foreign trade

Balance of trade (current prices)

	1986	1987	1988	1989	1990	1991
R '000,000	+511.7	+97.0	+179.5	+332.0	...	−174.6
% of total	14.8%	2.8%	4.4%	6.6%	...	2.6%

Imports (1991): R 3,410,600,000 (1988; chemical and petroleum products 21.5%; food and agricultural products 17.1%; machinery and transport equipment 6.6%; other 46.2%). *Major import source:* South Africa 75–100%.
Exports (1991): R 3,236,000,000 (minerals 75.9%, of which diamonds 30.5%; agricultural products 11.0%, of which cattle 5.8%, karakul pelts 0.9%). *Major export destinations* (1986): United States 25%; South Africa 19%; Japan 15%.

Transport and communications

Transport. Railroads: length (1991) 1,480 mi, 2,382 km; passenger-km 565,000,000; metric ton-km 1,678,000,000. Roads (1992): total length 26,024 mi, 41,882 km (paved 11%). Number of registered motor vehicles (1991): 122,331. Merchant marine (1992): vessels (100 gross tons and over) 30; total deadweight tonnage 5,874. Air transport (1990)[10]: passenger-km 561,565,000; metric ton-km cargo 3,309,000; airports (1992) with scheduled flights 11.
Communications. Daily newspapers (1993): total number 5; total circulation 49,500; circulation per 1,000 population 32. Radio (1990): 240,000 receivers (1 per 5.6 persons). Television (1992): 27,000 receivers (1 per 55 persons). Telephones (1992): 89,722 (1 per 17 persons).

Education and health

Education (1990)

	schools	teachers	students	student/teacher ratio
Primary (age 6–12)	1,134[11]	...	313,528	...
Secondary (age 13–19)	...	2,534	74,331	29.3
Voc., teacher tr.	9[12]	140[11]	1,666[11]	11.9[11]
Higher	...	213[13]	2,507[13]	11.8[13]

Educational attainment (1977). Percentage of labour force having: no formal schooling 59.8%; primary education 33.2%; secondary 5.0%; higher 2.0%.
Literacy (1985): total population age 15 and over literate 474,000 (72.5%); males literate 239,000 (74.2%); females literate 235,000 (70.8%).
Health: physicians (1992) 324 (1 per 4,594 persons); hospital beds (1988) 7,540 (1 per 166 persons); infant mortality rate per 1,000 live births (1990–95) 97.
Food (1979–81): daily per capita caloric intake 2,197 (vegetable products 77%, animal products 23%); 96% of FAO recommended minimum requirement.

Military

Total active duty personnel (1993): 8,100 (army 98.8%, navy 1.2%). *Military expenditure as percentage of GNP* (1984): 7.7% (world 5.9%); per capita expenditure U.S.$113.

[1]On March 21, 1990, Namibia achieved independence, its constitution (approved Feb. 9, 1990) became effective, the 72-member Constituent Assembly (elected Nov. 7–11, 1989) became the National Assembly, and a president (elected Feb. 6, 1990, by the Constituent Assembly) was sworn in. [2]Seventy-two elected and up to six appointed members. [3]As of June 1992, the Namibian dollar circulates at par and concurrently with the South African rand (R). [4]Excludes from Erongo Region the 434 sq mi (1,124 sq km) district of Walvis Bay (1992 pop. estimate, 23,000) that is jointly administered with South Africa from November 1992. [5]Detail does not add to total given because of rounding. [6]1987. [7]Windhoek only. [8]Employed persons only. [9]Formal sector only. [10]Namib Air only. [11]1989. [12]1988. [13]1991.

Nepal

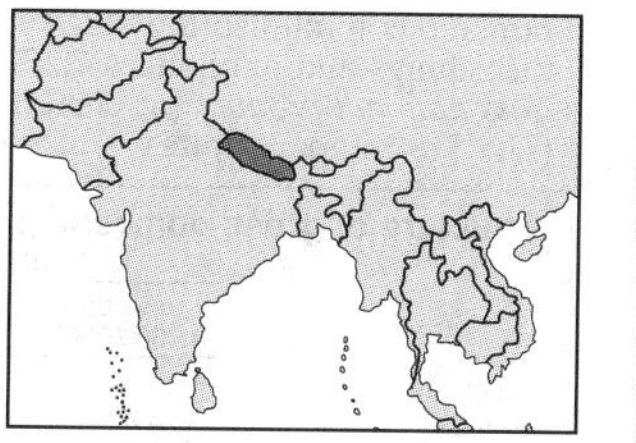

Official name: Nepāl Adhirājya (Kingdom of Nepal).
Form of government: constitutional monarchy with two legislative houses (National Council [60[1]]; House of Representatives [205]).
Chief of state: King.
Head of government: Prime Minister.
Capital: Kāthmāndu.
Official language: Nepālī.
Official religion: Hinduism.
Monetary unit: 1 Nepalese rupee (NRs) = 100 paisa (pice); valuation (Oct. 4, 1993) 1 U.S.$ = NRs 46.09; 1 £ = NRs 69.83.

Area and population

Development regions Zones	Capitals	area sq mi	area sq km	population 1991 census
Eastern	Dhankūtā	10,987	28,456	4,448,374
Koshī		3,733	9,669	1,730,932
Mechī		3,165	8,196	1,119,422
Sāgarmāthā		4,089	10,591	1,598,020
Central	Kāthmāndu	10,583	27,410	6,174,237
Bāgmatī		3,640	9,428	2,246,868
Janakpur		3,733	9,669	2,058,735
Nārāyanī		3,210	8,313	1,868,634
Western	Pokharā	11,351	29,398	3,751,922
Dhawalāgiri		3,146	8,148	491,727
Gandakī		4,740	12,275	1,262,694
Lumbinī		3,465	8,975	1,997,501
Mid-western	Surkhet	16,362	42,378	2,406,095
Bherī		4,071	10,545	1,101,653
Karnālī		8,244	21,351	261,246
Rāptī		4,047	10,482	1,043,196
Far-western	Dipāyal	7,544	19,539	1,681,453
Mahākālī		2,698	6,989	664,800
Setī		4,846	12,550	1,016,653
TOTAL		56,827	147,181	18,462,081

Demography

Population (1993): 19,264,000.
Density (1993): persons per sq mi 339.0, persons per sq km 130.9.
Urban-rural (1991): urban 9.6%; rural 90.4%.
Sex distribution (1991): male 51.63%; female 48.37%.
Age breakdown (1991): under 15, 42.3%; 15–29, 25.7%; 30–44, 16.7%; 45–59, 9.7%; 60–74, 4.7%; 75 and over, 0.9%.
Population projection: (2000) 20,847,000; (2010) 23,062,000.
Doubling time: 28 years.
Ethnic composition (1991): Nepalese 53.2%; Bihārī (including Maithilī and Bhojpurī) 18.4%; Tharu 4.8%; Tamang 4.7%; Newār 3.4%; Magar 2.2%; Abadhi 1.7%; other 11.6%.
Religious affiliation (1991): Hindu 86.2%; Buddhist 7.8%; Muslim 3.8%; Christian 0.2%; Jain 0.1%; other 1.9%.
Major cities (municipalities; 1991): Kāthmāndu 419,073; Birātnagar 130,129; Lalitpur 117,203; Pokharā 95,311; Birganj 68,764.

Vital statistics

Birth rate per 1,000 population (1993): 38.0 (world avg. 26.4).
Death rate per 1,000 population (1993): 13.0 (world avg. 9.2).
Natural increase rate per 1,000 population (1993): 25.0 (world avg. 17.2).
Total fertility rate (avg. births per childbearing woman; 1993): 5.4.
Marriage rate per 1,000 population: n.a.
Divorce rate per 1,000 population: n.a.
Life expectancy at birth (1993): male 54.0 years; female 53.0 years.
Major causes of death per 100,000 population: n.a.; however, the leading causes of mortality are infectious and parasitic diseases, diseases of the respiratory system, diseases of the nervous system, diseases of the circulatory system, and injuries and poisoning.

National economy

Budget (1992–93). Revenue: NRs 31,975,600,000 (1990–91; import duties 23.9%, foreign grants 20.3%, general sales tax 14.6%, excise taxes 10.0%, administrative fees and charges 9.1%, income taxes 7.9%, property taxes 4.3%). Expenditures: NRs 33,595,000,000 (1990–91; transportation and communications 12.6%, education 10.9%, agriculture 9.6%, interest payments 8.3%, general public services 8.0%, housing 6.8%, defense 5.9%, health 4.7%).
Tourism (1991): receipts from visitors U.S.$126,000,000; expenditures by nationals abroad U.S.$38,000,000.
Land use (1990): forested 18.1%; meadows and pastures 14.6%; agricultural and under permanent cultivation 19.4%; other 47.9%.
Production (metric tons except as noted). Agriculture, forestry, fishing (1991): rice 3,600,000, corn (maize) 1,235,000, sugarcane 1,106,000, wheat 836,000, potatoes 738,000, pulses 279,000, millet 220,000, barley 28,000, jute 16,000, tobacco 7,000; livestock (number of live animals) 6,350,000 cattle, 5,355,000 goats, 3,101,000 buffalo, 925,000 sheep, 575,000 pigs; roundwood 18,704,000 cu m; fish catch (1990) 14,546. Mining and quarrying (1990): limestone 295,000; magnesite 25,000; talc 1,798; garnet 20,000 kg. Manufacturing (1990–91): cement 182,000; sugar 41,400; soap 21,400; jute goods 15,000; tea 1,400; cigarettes 6,137,000,000 units[2]; shoes 710,000 pairs[2]. Construction: n.a. Energy production (consumption): electricity (kW-hr; 1990) 739,000,000 (771,000,000); coal (metric tons; 1990) none (35,000); petroleum products (metric tons; 1990) none (174,000); natural gas, none (none).
Gross national product (at current market prices; 1991): U.S.$3,453,000,000 (U.S.$180 per capita).

Structure of gross domestic product and labour force

	1991–92 in value[3] NRs '000,000	1991–92 % of total value	1991 labour force	1991 % of labour force
Agriculture	71,946	55.4	...	80.5
Mining	148	0.1	...	...
Manufacturing	8,026	6.2	...	1.7
Construction	9,298	7.2	...	0.8
Public utilities	968	0.7	...	0.1
Transportation and communications	5,760	4.4	...	0.6
Trade	7,567	5.8	...	3.3
Finance	9,196	7.1	...	0.3
Services	8,576	6.6	...	10.7
Other	8,490[4]	6.5[4]	...	2.0
TOTAL	129,975	100.0	...	100.0

Population economically active (1986): total 7,760,155; activity rate of total population 45.5% (participation rates: ages 15–64, 82.5%; female 34.7%; unemployed [1980] 5.5%).

Price and earnings indexes (1985 = 100)

	1986	1987	1988	1989	1990	1991	1992
Consumer price index	119.0	131.8	143.6	156.3	169.2	195.5	229.1
Earnings index	...	...	...	...	...	...	...

Public debt (external, outstanding; 1991): U.S.$1,705,000,000.
Household income and expenditure (1984–85). Average household size (1991) 5.6; income per household NRs 14,796 (U.S.$853); sources of income: self-employment 63.4%, wages and salaries 25.1%, rent 7.5%, other 4.0%; expenditure: food and beverages 61.2%, housing 17.3%, clothing 11.7%, health care 3.7%, education and recreation 2.9%, transportation and communications 1.2%, other 2.0%.

Foreign trade[5]

Balance of trade (current prices)

	1987	1988	1989	1990	1991	1992
NRs '000,000	−7,659.6	−10,780	−10,796	−13,037	−17,059	−16,255
% of total	52.8%	54.6%	56.2%	51.4%	46.5%	33.7%

Imports (1990–91): NRs 24,197,900,000 (basic manufactured goods 26.0%; machinery and transport equipment 25.1%; chemicals 12.5%; mineral fuels and lubricants 9.4%; food and live animals, chiefly for food 8.6%; crude materials except fuels 8.5%). *Major import sources:* India 32.1%; Singapore 14.0%; Japan 12.9%; New Zealand 5.0%; China 4.6%; France 3.0%.
Exports (1990–91): NRs 7,603,700,000 (basic manufactures 57.3%; food and live animals, chiefly for food 14.7%; crude materials except fuels 4.3%; animal and vegetable oils 2.4%). *Major export destinations:* West Germany 35.9%; India 22.4%; United States 18.4%; Switzerland 6.5%; Belgium 2.3%; United Kingdom 2.2%.

Transport and communications

Transport. Railroads (1990–91): route length 33 mi, 53 km; passengers carried 1,068,000; freight handled 14,554 metric tons. Roads (1991): total length 4,599 mi, 7,401 km (paved 41%). Vehicles (1990–91): passenger cars 4,949; trucks and buses 3,363. Merchant marine: none. Air transport (1991): passenger-mi 439,000,000, passenger-km 706,000,000; short ton-mi cargo 7,500,000, metric ton-km cargo 11,000,000; airports (1993) with scheduled flights 6.
Communications. Daily newspapers (1990): total number 28; total circulation 150,000; circulation per 1,000 population 7.9. Radio (1992): 600,000 receivers (1 per 33 persons). Television (1990): 35,100 receivers (1 per 539 persons). Telephones (1989): 44,514 (1 per 415 persons).

Education and health

Education (1991)

	schools	teachers	students	student/ teacher ratio
Primary (age 6–10)	18,694	74,495	2,884,275	38.7
Secondary (age 11–15) / Vocational	6,124	24,632	773,808	31.4
Higher	3	4,694[6]	154,528	21.8[6]

Educational attainment (1981). Percentage of population age 25 and over having: no formal schooling 41.2%; primary education 29.4%; secondary 22.7%; higher 6.8%. *Literacy* (1991): total population age 15 and over literate 4,255,000 (37.7%); males literate 2,975,000 (51.7%); females literate 1,280,000 (23.3%).
Health (1990–91): physicians 1,196 (1 per 16,007 persons); hospital beds 4,768 (1 per 4,015 persons); infant mortality rate per 1,000 live births (1991) 98.
Food (1988–90): daily per capita caloric intake 2,205 (vegetable products 94%, animal products 6%); 100% of FAO recommended minimum requirement.

Military

Total active duty personnel (1992): 35,000 (army 99.4%, air force 0.6%). *Military expenditure as percentage of GNP* (1989): 1.2% (world 4.9%); per capita expenditure U.S.$2.

[1]Includes 10 members nominated by the king. [2]1989–90. [3]Preliminary. [4]Includes indirect taxes. [5]Import figures are f.o.b. in balance of trade and c.i.f. for commodities and trading partners. [6]1989.

Netherlands, The

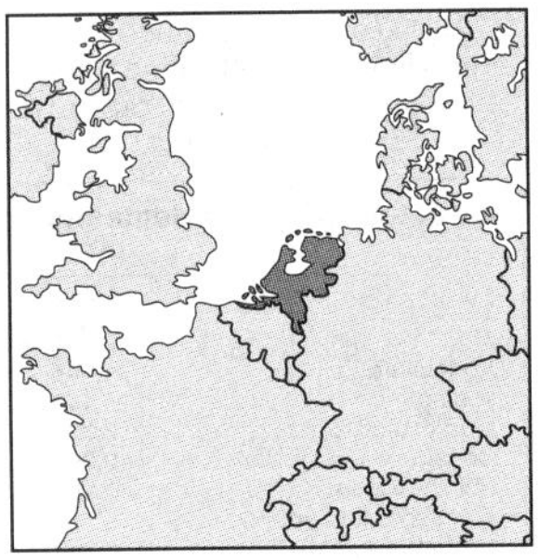

Official name: Koninkrijk der Nederlanden (Kingdom of The Netherlands).
Form of government: constitutional monarchy with a parliament (States General) comprising two legislative houses (First Chamber [75]; Second Chamber [150]).
Chief of state: Monarch.
Head of government: Prime Minister.
Seat of government: The Hague.
Capital: Amsterdam.
Official language: Dutch.
Official religion: none.
Monetary unit: 1 Netherlands guilder (f.) = 100 cents; valuation (Oct. 4, 1993) 1 U.S.$ = f. 1.82; 1 £ = f. 2.76.

Area and population

		area		population
Provinces	Capitals	sq mi	sq km	1992[1] estimate
Drenthe	Assen	1,025	2,654	445,600
Flevoland	Lelystad	549	1,422	232,800
Friesland	Leeuwarden	1,295	3,353	601,800
Gelderland	Arnhem	1,935	5,011	1,828,800
Groningen	Groningen	906	2,346	555,200
Limburg	Maastricht	838	2,170	1,115,500
Noord-Brabant	's-Hertogenbosch	1,910	4,946	2,225,300
Noord-Holland	Haarlem	1,029	2,665	2,421,700
Overijssel	Zwolle	1,289	3,339	1,032,400
Utrecht	Utrecht	514	1,331	1,037,300
Zeeland	Middelburg	692	1,792	359,200
Zuid-Holland	The Hague	1,123	2,908	3,271,500
TOTAL LAND AREA		13,103[2]	33,937	
INLAND WATER		3,060	7,926	
TOTAL		16,163	41,863	15,129,200[3]

Demography

Population (1993): 15,302,000.
Density (1992)[4] : persons per sq mi 1,167.8, persons per sq km 450.9.
Urban-rural (1992[1]): urban 89.0%; rural 11.0%.
Sex distribution (1992[1]): male 49.44%; female 50.56%.
Age breakdown (1992[1]): under 15, 18.3%; 15–29, 23.6%; 30–44, 23.8%; 45–59, 16.8%; 60–74, 12.0%; 75 and over, 5.5%.
Population projection: (2000) 16,052,000; (2010) 16,722,000.
Doubling time: not applicable; vital rates and net migration in near balance.
Ethnic composition (by nationality; 1991[1]): Netherlander 95.3%; Turkish 1.4%; Moroccan 1.1%; German 0.3%; other 1.9%.
Religious affiliation (1991): Roman Catholic 34.0%; Dutch Reformed Church 17.0%; Calvinist 8.0%; Muslim 3.1%; other 0.9%; no religion 37.0%.
Major cities (1992[1]): Amsterdam 713,407; Rotterdam 589,707; The Hague 445,287; Utrecht 232,705; Eindhoven 193,966.

Vital statistics

Birth rate per 1,000 population (1991): 13.2 (world avg. 26.4); legitimate 88.0%; illegitimate 12.0%.
Death rate per 1,000 population (1991): 8.6 (world avg. 9.2).
Natural increase rate per 1,000 population (1991): 4.6 (world avg. 17.2).
Total fertility rate (avg. births per childbearing woman; 1991): 1.6.
Marriage rate per 1,000 population (1991): 6.3.
Divorce rate per 1,000 population (1991): 1.9.
Life expectancy at birth (1991): male 74.0 years; female 80.2 years.
Major causes of death per 100,000 population (1991): malignant neoplasms (cancers) 249.9, of which lung cancer 56.1; ischemic heart diseases 145.4; cerebrovascular diseases 84.4; accidents, poisoning, and violence 36.3.

National economy

Budget (1990). Revenue: f. 175,165,000,000 (income and corporate taxes 43.7%, value-added taxes 21.2%, excise and import taxes 6.9%, natural-gas royalties 3.0%). Expenditures: f. 201,403,000,000 (social security and public health 22.6%, education and culture 16.7%, debt service 11.4%, defense 7.2%, transportation 5.9%).
Public debt (1993[5]): U.S.$195,935,000,000.
Tourism (1991): receipts from visitors U.S.$4,078,000,000; expenditures by nationals abroad U.S.$7,886,000,000.
Production (metric tons except as noted). Agriculture, forestry, fishing (1992): sugar beets 8,251,200, potatoes 7,595,300, wheat 1,016,800, onions 573,300; livestock (number of live animals) 14,161,000 pigs, 4,920,000 cattle, 1,954,000 sheep; roundwood (1990) 1,411,000 cu m; fish catch (1989) 421,613. Manufacturing (value added in f. '000,000; 1990): foodstuffs 7,900; electrical machinery 7,131; chemicals and chemical products 7,046; machinery and transport equipment 4,782; publishing and printing 3,992. Construction (buildings completed by value in f. '000; 1990): residential 10,805,000; nonresidential 15,009,000. Energy production (consumption): electricity (kW-hr; 1991) 74,252,000,000 (83,406,000,000); coal (metric tons; 1991) none (12,231,000,000); crude petroleum (barrels; 1991) 22,327,000 (354,683,000); petroleum products (metric tons; 1991) 55,426,000 (28,114,000); natural gas (cu m; 1991) 89,958,000,000 (49,850,000,000).
Household income and expenditure (1991). Average household size 2.4; income per household f. 55,300 (U.S.$29,600); sources of income (1990): wages 49.5%, transfer payments 29.0%, self-employment 21.5%; expenditure: rent 18.5%, food, beverages, and tobacco 15.4%, medical care 12.7%, transportation and communications 12.7%, education and recreation 10.5%, household furnishings and appliances 7.2%, clothing and footwear 6.9%, other 16.1%.
Gross national product (at current market prices; 1991): U.S.$278,839,000,000 (U.S.$18,560 per capita).

Structure of gross domestic product and labour force

	1991		1990	
	in value f. '000,000	% of total value	labour force	% of labour force
Agriculture	21,264	4.3	289,000	4.2
Mining	18,796	3.8	11,000	0.2
Manufacturing	101,979	20.6	1,185,000	17.2
Construction	28,926	5.8	409,000	6.0
Public utilities	9,295	1.9	41,000	0.6
Transp. and commun.	34,606	7.0	382,000	5.6
Trade	78,881	16.0	1,104,000	16.1
Finance	[6]	[6]	646,000	9.4
Pub. admin., defense	[6]	[6]	2,229,000	32.4
Services	220,600[6]	44.6[6]		
Other	−19,935[7]	−4.0[7]	574,000[8]	8.4[8]
TOTAL	494,410[2]	100.0	6,872,000[2]	100.0[2]

Population economically active (1991): total 7,133,000; activity rate of total population 47.3% (participation rates: ages 15–64, 69.6%; female 39.7%; unemployed 8.6%).

Price and earnings indexes (1985 = 100)

	1987	1988	1989	1990	1991	1992	1993[5]
Consumer price index	99.4	100.1	101.2	103.7	107.7	111.7	113.5
Hourly earnings index	103.0	104.3	105.7	108.8	112.7	112.7	...

Land use (1991): forested 8.8%; meadows and pastures 31.8%; agricultural and under permanent cultivation 26.8%; other 32.6%.

Foreign trade

Balance of trade (current prices)

	1987	1988	1989	1990	1991	1992
f. '000,000	13,201	17,647	19,277	22,345	26,131	22,225
% of total	3.6%	4.5%	4.4%	4.9%	5.6%	4.7%

Imports (1991): f. 234,609,000,000 (machinery and transport equipment 32.8%, of which transport equipment 9.5%; foodstuffs, beverages, and tobacco 12.0%; chemicals and chemical products 10.7%; mineral fuels 9.8%; metals and metal products 7.4%; textiles 7.2%; raw materials, oils, and fats 5.3%). *Major import sources:* Germany 26.4%; Belgium-Luxembourg 14.6%; U.K. 8.9%; U.S. 8.0%; France 7.8%.
Exports (1991): f. 248,809,000,000 (machinery and transport equipment 24.7%, of which transport equipment 6.0%; foodstuffs, beverages, and tobacco 20.6%; chemicals and chemical products 16.9%; mineral fuels 10.4%; metals and metal products 6.9%; textiles 4.9%). *Major export destinations:* Germany 30.9%; Belgium-Luxembourg 15.0%; France 11.2%; U.K. 9.8%; Italy 6.7%.

Transport and communications

Transport. Railroads (1992): length 2,780 km[9]; passenger-km 12,792,000,000; metric ton-km cargo 3,072,000,000[9]. Roads (1992): total length 118,214 km (paved 89%). Vehicles (1992): passenger cars 5,658,000; trucks and buses 797,000. Merchant marine (1992): vessels (100 gross tons and over) 1,076; total deadweight tonnage 4,190,997. Air transport (1990): passenger-km 28,356,000,000; metric ton-km cargo 2,207,800,000; airports (1993) 5.
Communications. Daily newspapers (1990): total number 45; total circulation 4,944,000; circulation per 1,000 population 332. Radio (1991): total number of receivers 12,146,299 (1 per 1.2 persons). Television (1991): total number of receivers 5,000,000 (1 per 3.0 persons). Telephones (1986): 9,080,000 (1 per 1.6 persons).

Education and health

Education (1991–92)

	schools	teachers[10]	students	student/ teacher ratio[10]
Primary (age 6–12)	9,436	99,031	1,518,000	15.7
Secondary (age 12–18)	1,189	89,370	673,000	7.7
Voc., teacher tr.	943	18,613	505,000	28.0
Higher	318	30,952[11]	378,000	10.2

Educational attainment (1985). Percentage of population[12] ages 25–64 having: primary education 16.7%; secondary 61.8%; higher 20.0%; other 1.5%.
Literacy (1990): virtually 100% literate.
Health (1991): physicians 37,481 (1 per 400 persons); hospital beds 88,361 (1 per 170 persons); infant mortality rate per 1,000 live births 6.5.
Food (1988–90): daily per capita caloric intake 3,078 (vegetable products 68%, animal products 32%); 114% of FAO recommended minimum requirement.

Military

Total active duty personnel (1993): 74,600 (army 58.0%, navy 19.9%, air force 17.2%, other[13] 4.9%). *Military expenditure as percentage of GNP* (1992): 2.6% (world 5.0%); per capita expenditure U.S.$524.

[1]January 1. [2]Detail does not add to total given because of rounding. [3]Includes 2,100 persons having no fixed municipality of residence. [4]Based on land area only. [5]June. [6]Services includes Finance and Pub. admin., defense. [7]Imputed bank service charge. [8]Includes 516,000 unemployed persons. [9]1991. [10]1990–91. [11]1985–86. [12]Economically active population (4,612,000) only. [13]Includes 3,900 military police.

New Zealand

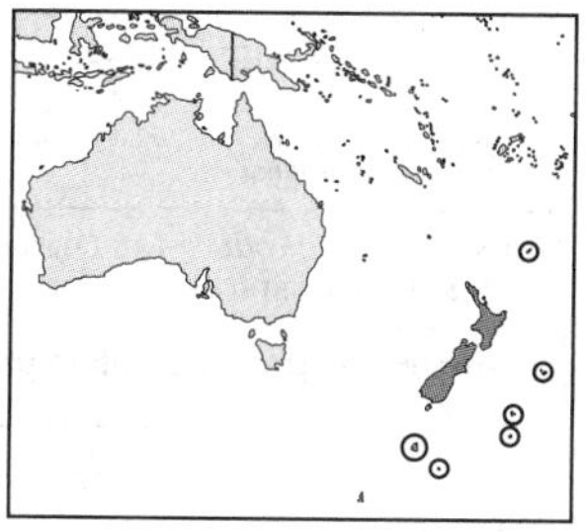

Official name: New Zealand (English); Aotearoa (Maori).
Form of government: constitutional monarchy with one legislative house (House of Representatives [99]).
Chief of state: British Monarch, represented by Governor-General.
Head of government: Prime Minister.
Capital: Wellington.
Official languages: English; Maori.
Official religion: none.
Monetary unit: 1 New Zealand dollar ($NZ) = 100 cents; valuation (Oct. 4, 1993) 1 U.S.$ = $NZ 1.82; 1 £ = $NZ 2.76.

Area and population

Islands / Regional Councils	area sq mi	area sq km	population 1992 estimate[1]
North Island	44,702	115,777	2,574,300
Auckland	...	...	966,300
Bay of Plenty	...	...	210,500
Gisborne[2]	...	...	44,300
Hawkes Bay	...	...	139,400
Manawatu-Wanganui	...	...	228,800
Northland	...	...	132,300
Taranaki	...	...	107,200
Waikato	...	...	341,200
Wellington	...	...	404,300
South Island	58,384	151,215	879,700
Canterbury	...	...	442,200
Nelson-Marlborough[2, 3]	...	...	114,400
Otago	...	...	185,600
Southland	...	...	102,500
West Coast	...	...	35,000
Remainder[4, 5]	...	...	900
Offshore islands[6]	322	854	...
Stewart Island[7]	674	1,746	...
Chatham Islands[8]	372	963	...
TOTAL	104,454	270,534	3,454,900

Demography

Population (1993): 3,520,000.
Density (1993): persons per sq mi 33.7, persons per sq km 13.0.
Urban-rural (1991): urban 75.9%; rural 24.1%.
Sex distribution (1992): male 49.27%; female 50.73%.
Age breakdown (1992): under 15, 23.0%; 15–29, 24.2%; 30–44, 22.5%; 45–59, 14.6%; 60–74, 11.0%; 75 and over, 4.7%.
Population projection: (2000) 3,802,000; (2010) 4,128,000.
Doubling time: 75 years.
Ethnic composition (1991): New Zealand European 73.8%; New Zealand Maori 9.6%; Pacific Island Polynesian 3.6%; multiethnic 4.5%; other 8.5%.
Religious affiliation (1991): Anglican 21.4%; Presbyterian 16.0%; Roman Catholic 14.8%; Methodist 4.1%; nonreligious 19.7%; other 24.0%.
Major cities (1992): Auckland 316,900; Christchurch 293,700; Manukau 229,-800; North Shore 153,300; Wellington 150,100.

Vital statistics

Birth rate per 1,000 population (1992): 17.2 (world avg. 26.4); legitimate 63.3%; illegitimate 36.7%.
Death rate per 1,000 population (1992): 7.9 (world avg. 9.2).
Natural increase rate per 1,000 population (1992): 9.3 (world avg. 17.2).
Total fertility rate (avg. births per childbearing woman; 1992): 2.1.
Marriage rate per 1,000 population (1991): 6.7.
Divorce rate per 1,000 population (1989): 0.3.
Life expectancy at birth (1991): male 72.0 years; female 77.9 years.
Major causes of death per 100,000 population (1990): diseases of the circulatory system 319.7, of which ischemic heart disease 201.3; malignant neoplasms (cancers) 199.1; diseases of the respiratory system 77.2; accidents 40.4; diseases of the digestive system 16.6; diabetes mellitus 13.3.

National economy

Budget (1991–92): $NZ 27,552,000,000 (income tax 56.1%, goods and services tax 21.2%, interest and profits 10.1%, excise duties 6.6%). Expenditures: $NZ 29,468,000,000 (social services 36.3%, education 16.0%, health 13.1%, administration 9.9%).
Public debt (year ending June 30, 1992): $NZ 26,378,000,000.
Tourism (1991): receipts U.S.$1,021,000,000; expenditures U.S.$1,408,000,000.
Production (metric tons except as noted). Agriculture, forestry, fishing (1992): barley 382,000, corn (maize) 183,400, wheat 180,700, peas 65,100, oats 57,200; livestock (number of live animals) 52,568,000 sheep, 8,144,000 cattle, 533,000 goats, 411,000 pigs; roundwood (1991) 13,987,000 cu m; fish catch (1991) 609,031. Mining and quarrying (1991): limestone 3,108,653; iron ore and sand concentrate 2,264,849; serpentine 13,647; silver 11,371 kg; gold 6,758 kg. Manufacturing (1991–92): wood pulp 1,343,300; chemical fertilizers 994,000[9]; cement 599,000; beer 362,656,000 litres[9]; carbonated soft drinks 179,378,000 litres; footwear 4,022,000 pairs[9]. Construction ($NZ '000; 1992–93): residential 2,284,800; nonresidential 1,088,500. Energy production (consumption; 1990): electricity (kW-hr; 1992) 31,905,000,000 (30,158,000,000); coal (metric tons; 1991) 2,080,000 (2,015,000); crude petroleum (barrels; 1992) 13,959,000 (32,743,000); petroleum products (metric tons; 1992) 3,292,000 (4,260,000); natural gas (cu m; 1992) 6,877,100,000 (4,605,900,000).
Gross national product (1992): U.S.$41,840,000,000 (U.S.$12,000 per capita).

Structure of gross domestic product and labour force

	1990–91 in value $NZ '000,000	1990–91 % of total value	1992 labour force	1992 % of labour force
Agriculture	5,380	7.4	152,900	9.4
Mining	1,042	1.4	3,500	0.2
Manufacturing	12,790	17.5	239,400	14.8
Construction	3,097	4.2	78,200	4.8
Public utilities	2,081	2.8	12,200	0.8
Transp. and commun.	5,926	8.0	87,800	5.4
Trade	11,943	16.4	312,200	19.3
Finance	17,020	23.2	154,800	9.6
Pub. admin., defense	8,613	11.7 }	415,600	25.7
Services	2,379	3.2 }		
Other	3,068[10]	4.2[10]	163,600[11]	10.1[11]
TOTAL	73,339	100.0	1,620,200	100.0[12]

Population economically active (1992[1]): total 1,641,300; activity rate 48.1% (participation rates: over age 15, 63.8%; female 43.4%; unemployed 11.1%).

Price and earnings indexes (1985 = 100)

	1986	1987	1988	1989	1990	1991	1992
Consumer price index	113.2	131.0	139.4	147.3	156.3	160.4	162.1
Weekly earnings index	116.4	125.7	141.6	147.3	153.7	157.6	162.1

Household income and expenditure. Average household size (1991) 2.9; annual income per household (1989–90) $NZ 39,800 (U.S.$23,760); sources of income (1987–88): wages and salaries 68.7%, transfer payments 14.1%, self-employment 8.1%; expenditure (1989–90): housing 22.7%, transportation 18.3%, food 16.6%, household durable goods 13.6%, clothing 4.6%.
Land use (1991): forested 25.5%; meadows and pastures 51.2%; agricultural and under permanent cultivation 3.1%; other 20.2%.

Foreign trade

Balance of trade (current prices)

	1987	1988	1989	1990	1991	1992
$NZ '000,000	+927.9	+3,215.0	+1,380.6	+1,349.1	+3,359.6	+2,451.0
% of total	4.0%	13.6%	4.8%	4.4%	11.2%	7.2%

Imports (1992–93): $NZ 15,980,000,000 (machinery 24.8%; minerals, chemicals, and plastics 23.1%; transport equipment 13.5%; basic manufactures 8.1%; food and live animals 6.9%; metals and metal products 6.0%; textiles, clothing, and footwear 6.0%). *Major import sources:* Australia 21.7%; U.S. 18.5%; Japan 17.4%; U.K. 6.2%.
Exports (1992–93): $NZ 17,334,000,000 (food and live animals 48.1%; basic manufactures 24.1%; minerals, chemicals, and plastics 9.4%; metals and metal products 6.6%). *Major export destinations:* Australia 21.7%; Japan 16.1%; U.S. 13.0%; U.K. 7.0%; South Korea 4.9%; Germany 2.8%.

Transport and communications

Transport. Railroads (1990): length 2,627 mi, 4,227 km; passenger-km (1984) 458,160,000; short ton-mi cargo (1988–89) 1,837,000,000, metric ton-km cargo 2,682,000,000. Roads (1992): total length 58,605 mi, 94,315 km (paved 73%). Vehicles (1991): passenger cars 1,551,350; trucks and buses 800,518. Merchant marine (1992): vessels (100 gross tons and over) 139; total deadweight tonnage 279,805. Air transport (1990): passenger-mi 6,591,000,000, passenger-km 10,608,000,000; short ton-mi cargo 227,000,000, metric ton-km cargo 332,000,000; airports (1993) 36.
Communications. Daily newspapers (1990): total number 35; total circulation 1,100,000; circulation per 1,000 population 322. Radio (1991): 3,100,000 receivers (1 per 1.1 persons). Television (1991): 1,100,000 receivers (1 per 3.1 persons). Telephones (1988): 2,403,000 (1 per 1.4 persons).

Education and health

Education (1991)

	schools	teachers	students	student/ teacher ratio
Primary (age 5–12)[14]	2,491	22,186	418,698	18.9
Secondary (age 13–17)	337	15,586	230,210	14.8
Voc., teacher tr.	29	4,498[15]	77,142	...
Higher[16]	7	3,761[15]	87,973	...

Educational attainment (1991). Percentage of population age 25 and over having: primary and some secondary education 54.9%; secondary 31.1%; higher 6.9%; not specified 6.1%. *Literacy:* virtually 100.0%.
Health (1989): physicians 9,453 (1 per 359 persons); hospital beds 29,352 (1 per 114 persons); infant mortality rate per 1,000 live births (1991): 8.3.
Food (1988–90): daily per capita caloric intake 3,461 (vegetable products 59%, animal products 41%); 131% of FAO recommended minimum requirement.

Military

Total active duty personnel (1993): 10,800 (army 44.3%, air force 34.4%, navy 21.3%). *Military expenditure as percentage of GNP* (1989): 2.9% (world 5.0%); per capita expenditure U.S.$347.

[1]Provisional; March 5. [2]Reorganized as a unitary authority that is administered by a district council with regional powers. [3]Reorganized as three separate unitary authorities: Nelson city, Tasman district, and Marlborough district. [4]Includes the population of Kermadec Islands and persons on oil rigs. [5]Includes the population of Chatham Islands county and Campbell Island. [6]Excludes islands in Regional Councils. [7]Part of Southland Regional Council. [8]Chatham Islands county remains outside any Regional Council. [9]1990–91. [10]Includes import duties less imputed bank service charges. [11]Includes 162,300 unemployed. [12]Detail does not add to total given because of rounding. [13]Third quarter. [14]Includes 67 composite schools that provide both primary and secondary education. [15]1990. [16]Universities only.

Nicaragua

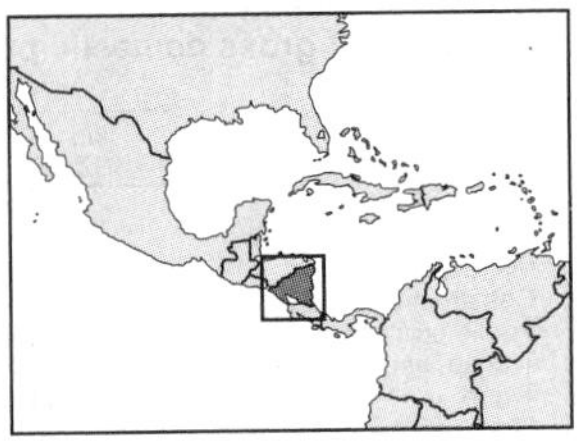

Official name: República de Nicaragua (Republic of Nicaragua).
Form of government: unitary multiparty republic with one legislative house (National Assembly [92[1]]).
Head of state and government: President.
Capital: Managua.
Official language: Spanish.
Official religion: none.
Monetary unit: 1 córdoba oro (C$)[2] = 100 centavos; valuation (Oct. 4, 1993) 1 U.S.$ = C$6.17; 1 £ = C$9.35.

Area and population

		area[3]		population
Departments	Capitals	sq mi	sq km	1991 estimate
Boaco	Boaco	1,639	4,244	121,561
Carazo	Jinotepe	405	1,050	154,989
Chinandega	Chinandega	1,902	4,926	335,596
Chontales	Juigalpa	2,463	6,378	141,676
Estelí	Estelí	902	2,335	171,215
Granada	Granada	359	929	154,912
Jinotega	Jinotega	3,766	9,755	178,195
León	León	1,972	5,107	350,275
Madriz	Somoto	619	1,602	98,737
Managua	Managua	1,418	3,672	1,108,720
Masaya	Masaya	228	590	211,123
Matagalpa	Matagalpa	3,291	8,523	350,627
Nueva Segovia	Ocotal	1,206	3,123	124,659
Río San Juan	San Carlos	2,885	7,473	44,576
Rivas	Rivas	832	2,155	138,676
Zelaya	Bluefields	22,999	59,566	313,694
TOTAL LAND AREA		46,884[4]	121,428	
INLAND WATER		3,997	10,351	
TOTAL		50,880[4]	131,779	3,999,231

Demography

Population (1993): 4,265,000.
Density (1993)[5]: persons per sq mi 91.0, persons per sq km 35.2.
Urban-rural (1991): urban 61.0%; rural 39.0%.
Sex distribution (1991): male 50.14%; female 49.86%.
Age breakdown (1991): under 15, 45.6%; 15–29, 27.5%; 30–44, 15.2%; 45–59, 7.3%; 60–74, 3.6%; 75 and over, 0.8%.
Population projection: (2000) 5,261,000; (2010) 6,824,000.
Doubling time: 23 years.
Ethnic composition (1985): mestizo (Spanish/Indian) 77.0%; white 10.0%; black 9.0%; Amerindian 4.0%.
Religious affiliation (1990): Roman Catholic 90.7%; other (mostly Baptist, Moravian, and Pentecostal) 9.3%.
Major cities (1985): Managua 682,111; León 100,982; Granada 88,636; Masaya 74,946; Chinandega 67,792.

Vital statistics

Birth rate per 1,000 population (1991): 37.0 (world avg. 26.4).
Death rate per 1,000 population (1991): 7.0 (world avg. 9.2).
Natural increase rate per 1,000 population (1991): 30.0 (world avg. 17.2).
Total fertility rate (avg. births per childbearing woman; 1991): 4.7.
Marriage rate per 1,000 population (1988): 2.1.
Divorce rate per 1,000 population (1990): 0.2.
Life expectancy at birth (1990–95): male 64.8 years; female 68.5 years.
Major causes of death per 100,000 population (1990)[6]: infectious and parasitic diseases 162.7; diseases of the circulatory system 120.7, of which cerebrovascular disease 40.2; diseases of the respiratory system 74.2; accidents 46.2; malignant neoplasms (cancers) 46.0.

National economy

Budget (1991). Revenue: C$1,447,000,000 (tax revenue 91.0%, of which import duties 18.4%, gasoline taxes 14.4%, property taxes 14.2%, beer taxes 5.9%; nontax revenue 5.0%). Expenditures: C$1,848,000,000 (current expenditure 89.7%; development expenditure 10.3%).
Production (metric tons except as noted). Agriculture, forestry, fishing (1992): sugarcane 2,563,000, corn (maize) 231,000, rice 158,000, bananas 135,000, dry beans 79,000, sorghum 74,000, cassava 71,000, oranges 68,000, seed cotton 67,000, plantains 64,000, coffee 45,000, sesame seed 10,000; livestock (number of live animals) 1,680,000 cattle, 709,000 pigs; roundwood (1990) 4,077,000 cu m; fish catch 5,709, of which crustaceans (1990) 1,803. Mining and quarrying (1991): gold 32,700 troy oz. Manufacturing (value of production in C$'000,000; 1991[7]): processed foods 450; beverages 437; chemicals and chemical products 307; tobacco products 253; cement, bricks, and tile 165; metal products 152. Construction (completed; 1991): 569 cu m. Energy production (consumption): electricity (kW-hr; 1990) 1,038,000,000 (1,238,000,000); coal, none (none); crude petroleum (barrels; 1990) none (3,592,000); petroleum products (metric tons; 1990) 460,000 (628,000); natural gas, none (none).
Household income and expenditure. Average household size (1980) 6.9; income per household: n.a.; sources of income: n.a.; expenditure: n.a.
Tourism (1991): receipts from visitors U.S.$17,000,000; expenditures by nationals abroad U.S.$28,000,000.
Population economically active (1991): total 1,386,300; activity rate of total population 34.7% (participation rates: over age 15, 62.0%; female 33.2%; unemployed [1993] 40.0%).

Price and earnings indexes (1988 = 100)

	1988	1989	1990	1991	1992
Consumer price index	100.0	4,809	364,772	1,824,000	2,004,000
Monthly earnings index	...	...	...	...	...

Gross national product (at current market prices; 1991): U.S.$1,897,000,000 (U.S.$340 per capita).

Structure of gross domestic product and labour force

	1991			
	in value C$'000,000,000,000[8]	% of total value	labour force	% of labour force
Agriculture	10,193	30.8	415,400	30.0
Mining	237	0.7	9,000	0.6
Manufacturing	5,582	16.8	188,200	13.6
Construction	1,144	3.5	30,200	2.2
Public utilities	423	1.3	10,300	0.7
Transportation and communications	1,379	4.2	42,600	3.1
Trade	7,877	23.8	195,500	14.1
Finance, real estate	1,985	6.0	24,700	1.8
Pub. admin., defense	2,884	8.7	98,100	7.1
Services	1,441	4.3	183,900	13.3
Other	—	—	188,400[9]	13.6[9]
TOTAL	33,144[4]	100.0[4]	1,386,300	100.0[4]

Public debt (external, outstanding; 1991): U.S.$8,703,000,000.
Land use (1991): forested 27.5%; meadows and pastures 45.9%; agricultural and under permanent cultivation 10.7%; other 15.9%.

Foreign trade

Balance of trade (current prices)

	1986	1987	1988	1989	1990	1991
U.S.$'000,000	−609.6	−622.7	−270.4	−234.9	−343.5	−395.8
% of total	55.2%	50.9%	33.1%	29.0%	34.8%	35.3%

Imports (1990): U.S.$664,700,000 (nondurable consumer goods 23.2%, petroleum products 16.4%, capital goods for transport 14.6%, capital goods for industry 11.9%). *Major import sources* (1991): United States 21.3%; former U.S.S.R. 10.2%; Cuba 8.0%; Costa Rica 7.8%; Guatemala 7.3%; Venezuela 7.1%.
Exports (1990): U.S.$321,200,000[10] (coffee 21.0%, meat 20.0%, cotton 11.4%, sugar 10.8%, bananas 7.2%). *Major export destinations* (1991): United States 16.4%; Germany 14.4%; Japan 11.0%; Canada 11.0%; Italy 7.8%.

Transport and communications

Transport. Railroads (1991): route length 186 mi, 300 km; (1989) passenger-mi 15,800,000, passenger-km 25,400,000; short ton-mi cargo 46,600,000, metric ton-km cargo 68,000,000. Roads (1988): total length 9,319 mi, 14,997 km (paved 10%). Vehicles (1991): passenger cars 35,000; trucks and buses 35,000. Merchant marine (1992): vessels (100 gross tons and over) 25; total deadweight tonnage 1,295. Air transport (1990)[11]: passenger-mi 68,800,000, passenger-km 110,700,000; short ton-mi cargo 2,451,000, metric ton-km cargo 3,579,000; airports (1993) with scheduled flights 3.
Communications. Daily newspapers (1991): total number 3; total circulation 113,000; circulation per 1,000 population 28. Radio (1992): 880,000 receivers (1 per 4.7 persons). Television (1992): 210,000 receivers (1 per 20 persons). Telephones (1990): 47,000 (1 per 82 persons).

Education and health

Education (1991)

	schools	teachers	students	student/ teacher ratio
Primary (age 7–12)[12]	4,535	20,141	674,045	33.5
Secondary (age 13–18) / Voc., teacher tr.	427	4,188[13]	179,998	41.5[13]
Higher	10	3,469	34,846	10.0

Educational attainment: n.a. *Literacy* (1986): total population age 15 and over literate 74.0%.
Health (1991): physicians 2,125 (1 per 1,882 persons); hospital beds 4,974 (1 per 804 persons); infant mortality rate per 1,000 live births 60.0.
Food (1984–86): daily per capita caloric intake 2,472 (vegetable products, n.a., animal products, n.a.); 110% of FAO recommended minimum requirement.

Military

Total active duty personnel (1992): 14,700 (army 88.4%, navy 3.4%, air force 8.2%). *Military expenditure as percentage of central government expenditure* (1991): 16.0%.

[1]Includes two unsuccessful 1990 presidential candidates meeting special conditions. [2]The córdoba oro (gold cordoba), introduced in August 1990, circulated simultaneously with the new córdoba until April 30, 1991, when the new córdoba ceased to be legal tender; on April 30, 1 córdoba oro equaled 5,000,000 new córdobas. The new córdoba had been introduced in February 1988 at the rate of 1 new córdoba to 1,000 (old) córdobas. [3]Lakes and lagoons are excluded from the areas of departments. [4]Detail does not add to total given because of rounding. [5]Based on land area. [6]Projected rates based on about 50% of total deaths. [7]At prices of May 1989 new córdobas; establishments employing 60 or more persons only. [8]At current prices in new córdobas. [9]Unemployed persons previously employed. [10]Estimated exports (1991): U.S.$266,000,000 (cotton 16.5%, coffee 13.9%, bananas 10.2%, fish 6.6%, gold 2.8%). [11]Aeronica only. [12]Includes preprimary. [13]1990.

Niger

Official name: République du Niger (Republic of Niger).
Form of government: unitary multiparty republic[1] with one legislative body (High Council of the Republic [83]).
Chief of state: President.
Head of government: Prime Minister.
Capital: Niamey.
Official language: French.
Official religion: none.
Monetary unit: 1 CFA franc (CFAF) = 100 centimes; valuation (Oct. 4, 1993) 1 U.S.$ = CFAF 283.25; 1 £ = CFAF 429.12.

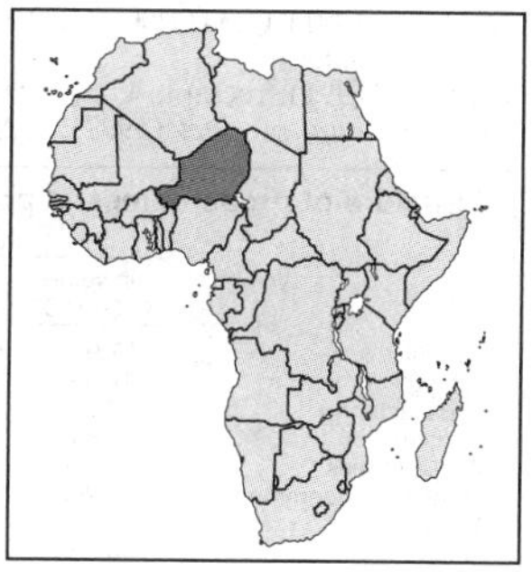

Area and population

Departments	Capitals	area[2] sq mi	area[2] sq km	population 1988 census[3]
Agadez	Agadez	244,869	634,209	205,232
Diffa	Diffa	54,138	140,216	187,230
Dosso	Dosso	11,970	31,002	1,018,058
Maradi	Maradi	14,896	38,581	1,386,549
Tahoua	Tahoua	41,188	106,677	1,306,948
Tillabéry	Tillabéry	34,863	90,293	1,715,118
Zinder	Zinder	56,151	145,430	1,409,417
TOTAL		458,075	1,186,408	7,228,552

Demography

Population (1993): 8,516,000.
Density (1993): persons per sq mi 18.6, persons per sq km 7.2.
Urban-rural (1988): urban 15.3%; rural 84.7%.
Sex distribution (1988): male 49.53%; female 50.47%.
Age breakdown (1988): under 15, 48.7%; 15–29, 24.8%; 30–44, 14.6%; 45–59, 6.8%; 60–74, 3.6%; 75 and over, 1.5%.
Population projection: (2000) 10,775,000; (2010) 14,988,000.
Doubling time: 22 years.
Ethnic composition (1988): Hausa 52.8%; Zerma-Songhai 21.0%; Tuareg 10.6%; Fulani 9.8%; Kanuri-Nanga 4.5%; Teda 0.5%; Arab 0.3%; Gurma 0.3%; other 0.2%.
Religious affiliation (1988): Muslim, primarily Sunnī, 98.6%; other, mostly traditional beliefs, 1.4%.
Major cities (1988): Niamey 392,169; Zinder 119,838; Maradi 109,386; Tahoua 49,941; Agadez 49,361.

Vital statistics

Birth rate per 1,000 population (1990–95): 51.3 (world avg. 26.4).
Death rate per 1,000 population (1990–95): 18.7 (world avg. 9.2).
Natural increase rate per 1,000 population (1990–95): 32.6 (world avg. 17.2).
Total fertility rate (avg. births per childbearing woman; 1990): 7.1.
Marriage rate per 1,000 population: n.a.
Divorce rate per 1,000 population: n.a.
Life expectancy at birth (1990–95): male 44.9 years; female 48.1 years.
Major causes of death (1989): n.a.; however, among selected major causes registered at medical facilities are measles, diarrhea, meningitis, malaria, pneumonia, tetanus, viral hepatitis, and poliomyelitis.

National economy

Budget (1992). Revenue: CFAF 188,400,000,000 (current revenues 44.3%, foreign loans 31.2%, external aid and gifts 24.5%). Expenditures: CFAF 188,400,000,000 (current expenditures 45.0%, capital expenditures 38.0%, amortization of public debt 17.0%).
Public debt (external, outstanding; 1991): U.S.$1,278,000,000.
Tourism (1991): receipts from visitors U.S.$16,000,000; expenditures by nationals abroad U.S.$40,000,000.
Gross national product (at current market prices; 1992): U.S.$2,537,000,000 (U.S.$310 per capita).

Structure of gross domestic product and labour force

	1991 in value CFAF '000,000	1991 % of total value	1988 labour force	1988 % of labour force
Agriculture	245,995	37.5	1,764,049	78.0
Mining	34,516	5.3	5,295	0.2
Manufacturing	43,921	6.7	65,803	2.9
Construction	15,085	2.3	13,742	0.6
Public utilities	15,341	2.3	1,778	0.1
Transportation and communications	26,727	4.1	14,764	0.6
Trade and finance	117,083	17.8	210,354	9.3
Pub. admin., defense; Services	143,557	21.9	123,262	5.4
Other	14,500	2.1	63,147	2.9
TOTAL	656,725	100.0	2,262,194	100.0

Production (metric tons except as noted). Agriculture, forestry, fishing (1992): millet 1,784,000, pulses 608,000, sorghum 393,000, roots and tubers 253,000, vegetables and melons 251,000, onions 170,000, sugarcane 140,000, rice 70,000, peanuts (groundnuts) 40,000, wheat 7,000, corn (maize) 3,000, seed cotton 2,000, tobacco leaf 1,000; livestock (number of live animals) 5,400,000 goats, 3,400,000 sheep, 1,800,000 cattle, 450,000 asses, 363,000 camels, 82,000 horses; roundwood (1991) 5,116,000 cu m; fish catch (1991) 3,150. Mining and quarrying (1991): uranium 2,777. Manufacturing (1989): cement 15,900; soap 9,200; meat 8,700; beer 118,000 hectolitres; beverages 80,300 hectolitres; cotton textiles 20,000,000 sq m. Construction (value added in CFAF; 1989): 26,748,000,000. Energy production (consumption): electricity (kW-hr; 1991) 168,000,000 (356,000,000); coal (metric tons; 1991) 157,000 (157,000); crude petroleum, none (n.a.); petroleum products (metric tons; 1991) none (194,000); natural gas, none (n.a.).
Population economically active (1992): total 4,130,000; activity rate of total population 50.0% (participation rates [1988]: over age 10, 53.5%; female 20.7%; unemployed, n.a.).

Price and earnings indexes (1985 = 100)

	1986	1987	1988	1989	1990	1991	1992
Consumer price index	96.8	90.3	89.0	86.5	85.8	79.1	75.6
Hourly earnings index[4]	100.0	100.0	100.0	100.0	100.0	100.0	100.0

Household income and expenditure. Average household size (1988) 6.4; income per household: n.a.; sources of income (1977): self-employment 59.5%, family 30.1%, salary or wages 4.8%, employer 0.7%; expenditure (1983): food and beverages 50.5%, household expenses 19.1%, clothing 7.3%.
Land use (1991): forested 1.5%; meadows and pastures 7.0%; agricultural and under permanent cultivation 2.8%; other 88.7%.

Foreign trade[5]

Balance of trade (current prices)

	1985	1986	1987	1988	1989	1990
CFAF '000,000	−46,300	−11,400	−12,000	−20,900	−20,900	−5,000
% of total	17.1%	4.7%	5.2%	8.6%	8.4%	2.8%

Imports (1989): CFAF 134,800,000,000 (raw materials and machinery 42.5%, consumer goods 36.6%, cereals 12.2%, petroleum products 6.0%). *Major import sources:* France 32.1%; Côte d'Ivoire 10.7%; West Germany 4.9%; Japan 4.5%; Italy 4.0%; Nigeria 3.5%; The Netherlands 3.5%.
Exports (1989): CFAF 113,900,000,000 (uranium 71.5%, live animals 10.5%, cowpeas 5.2%). *Major export destinations:* France 64.9%; Nigeria 11.4%; Spain 8.4%; Canada 2.6%; Côte d'Ivoire 0.8%.

Transport and communications

Transport. Railroads (1992): none[6]. Roads (1990): total length 6,996 mi, 11,258 km (paved 29%). Vehicles (1991): passenger cars 18,000; trucks and buses 18,000. Air transport (1990)[7]: passenger-mi 144,363,000, passenger-km 232,329,000; short ton-mi cargo 26,971,000, metric ton-km cargo 39,374,000; airports (1993) with scheduled flights 1.
Communications. Daily newspapers (1991): total number 1; total circulation 5,000; circulation per 1,000 population 0.6. Radio (1992): total number of receivers 400,000 (1 per 21 persons). Television (1992): total number of receivers 25,000 (1 per 331 persons). Telephones (1988): 12,760 (1 per 572 persons).

Education and health

Education (1989)

	schools	teachers	students	student/ teacher ratio
Primary (age 7–12)	2,097	7,915	317,840	40.1
Secondary (age 13–19)	105	2,443	63,379	25.9
Voc., teacher tr.	7	226	2,437	10.8
Higher[8]	3	341[9]	4,506	11.1[9]

Educational attainment (1988). Percentage of population age 25 and over having: no formal schooling 85.0%; Koranic education 11.2%; primary education 2.5%; secondary 1.1%; higher 0.2%. *Literacy* (1988): percentage of total population age 15 and over literate 10.8%; males literate 16.7%; females literate 5.4%.
Health: physicians (1989) 140 (1 per 52,900 persons); hospital beds (1979) 3,261 (1 per 1,633 persons); infant mortality rate per 1,000 live births (1990–95) 124.0.
Food (1988–90): daily per capita caloric intake 2,239 (vegetable products 95%, animal products 5%); 95% of FAO recommended minimum requirement.

Military

Total active duty personnel (1993): 5,300 (army 98.1%, air force 1.9%). *Military expenditure as percentage of GNP* (1992): 1.0% (world [1989] 4.9%); per capita expenditure U.S.$3.

[1]Transitional government ended April 1993. [2]The departmental areas and total shown are obsolete. The total area, according to recent official estimates, is 497,000 sq mi (1,287,000 sq km); but subtotals distributing this total among the departments remain unpublished. [3]De jure. [4]Guaranteed minimum wage for professionals. [5]Import figures are c.i.f. in balance of trade, commodities, and trading partners. [6]Niger is a cofounder of the Common Benin-Niger Organization for Railroads and Transport, currently maintaining rail operations only in Benin but having the purpose of extending rail services from the sea at Cotonou, Benin, to Dosso and, ultimately, Niamey, Niger; in the interim, freight transported between the two countries is carried by truck. [7]Air Afrique. [8]1988. [9]Université de Niamey and École Nationale d'Administration du Niger only.

Nigeria

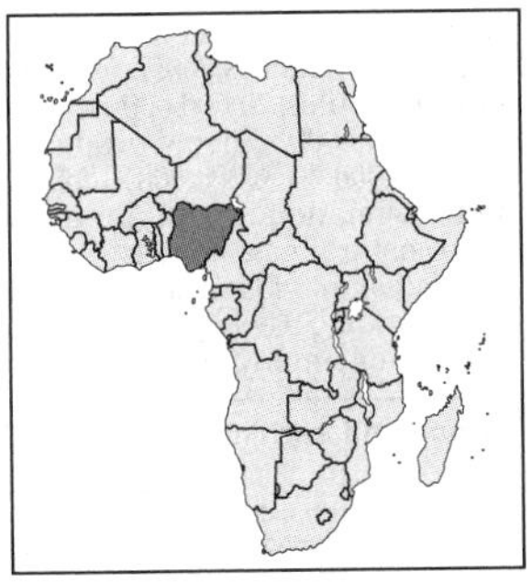

Official name: Federal Republic of Nigeria.
Form of government: military regime[1].
Head of state and government: military leader.
Capital: Abuja (Federal Capital Territory)[2].
Official language: English.
Official religion: none.
Monetary unit: 1 Nigerian naira (₦) = 100 kobo; valuation (Oct. 4, 1993) 1 U.S.$ = ₦29.78; 1 £ = ₦45.12.

Area and population		area		population
		sq mi	sq km	1991 census
States	**Capitals**			
Abia	Umuahia	10,516[3]	27,237[3]	2,297,978
Adamawa	Yola	35,286[4]	91,390[4]	2,124,049
Akwa Ibom	Uyo	[3]	[3]	2,359,736
Anambra	Awka	6,824	17,675	2,767,903
Bauchi	Bauchi	24,944	64,605	4,294,413
Benue	Makurdi	17,442[5]	45,174[5]	2,780,398
Borno	Maiduguri	44,942[6]	116,400[6]	2,596,589
Cross River	Calabar	[3]	[3]	1,865,604
Delta	Asaba	13,707[7]	35,500[7]	2,570,181
Edo	Benin City	[7]	[7]	2,159,848
Enugu	Enugu	[3]	[3]	3,161,295
Imo	Owerri	4,575	11,850	2,485,499
Jigawa	Dutse	16,712[8]	43,285[8]	2,829,929
Kaduna	Kaduna	27,122[9]	70,245[9]	3,969,252
Kano	Kano	[8]	[8]	5,632,040
Katsina	Katsina	[9]	[9]	3,878,344
Kebbi	Birnin Kebbi	39,589[10]	102,535[10]	2,062,226
Kogi	Lokoja	[5]	[5]	2,099,046
Kwara	Ilorin	25,818	66,869	1,566,469
Lagos	Ikeja	1,292	3,345	5,685,781
Niger	Minna	25,111	65,037	2,482,367
Ogun	Abeokuta	6,472	16,762	2,338,570
Ondo	Akure	8,092	20,959	3,884,485
Osun	Oshogbo	14,558[11]	37,705[11]	2,203,016
Oyo	Ibadan	[11]	[11]	3,488,789
Plateau	Jos	22,405	58,030	3,283,704
Rivers	Port Harcourt	8,436	21,850	3,983,857
Sokoto	Sokoto	[10]	[10]	4,392,391
Taraba	Jalingo	[4]	[4]	1,480,590
Yobe	Damaturu	[6]	[6]	1,411,481
Federal Capital Territory				
Abuja	Abuja	2,824	7,315	378,671
TOTAL		356,669[12]	923,768	88,514,501

Demography

Population (1993): 91,549,000.
Density (1993): persons per sq mi 256.8, persons per sq km 99.1.
Urban-rural (1990): urban 35.2%; rural 64.8%.
Sex distribution (1990): male 49.53%; female 50.47%.
Age breakdown (1990): under 15, 47.4%; 15–29, 26.0%; 30–44, 14.4%; 45–59, 8.0%; 60–74, 3.5%; 75 and over, 0.7%.
Population projection: (2000) 105,885,000; (2010) 130,344,000.
Doubling time: 22 years.
Ethnic composition (1983): Hausa 21.3%; Yoruba 21.3%; Igbo (Ibo) 18.0%; Fulani 11.2%; Ibibio 5.6%; Kanuri 4.2%; Edo 3.4%; Tiv 2.2%; Ijaw 1.8%; Bura 1.7%; Nupe 1.2%; other 8.1%.
Religious affiliation (1980): Christian 49.0%, of which Protestant 26.3%, Roman Catholic 12.1%, African indigenous 10.6%; Muslim 45.0%; other 6.0%.
Major cities (1992): Lagos 1,347,000; Ibadan 1,295,000; Kano 699,900; Ogbomosho 660,600; Oshogbo 441,600; Ilorin 430,600.

Vital statistics

Birth rate per 1,000 population (1990–95): 46.5 (world avg. 26.4).
Death rate per 1,000 population (1990–95): 14.0 (world avg. 9.2).
Natural increase rate per 1,000 population (1990–95): 32.5 (world avg. 17.2).
Total fertility rate (avg. births per childbearing woman; 1990–95): 6.6.
Life expectancy at birth (1990–95): male 50.8 years; female 54.3 years.
Major causes of death per 100,000 population: n.a.

National economy

Budget (1993). Revenue: ₦83,500,000,000 (1992; petroleum royalties and rents 62.0%; petroleum profit tax 12.8%; import duties 11.6%; company income tax 3.9%). Expenditures: ₦53,700,000,000 (1992; recurrent expenditure 64.3%, of which debt service 53.7%, defense 2.9%, education 2.8%, police 2.5%, health 1.4%; capital expenditure 35.7%).
Production (metric tons except as noted). Agriculture, forestry, fishing (1992): cassava 20,000,000, yams 20,000,000, sorghum 4,100,000, rice 3,453,000, millet 3,200,000, corn (maize) 1,700,000, sugarcane 1,400,000, plantains 1,350,000, peanuts (groundnuts) 1,214,000; livestock (number of live animals) 24,000,000 goats, 15,700,000 cattle, 13,500,000 sheep; roundwood (1991) 111,059,000 cu m; fish catch (1991) 266,562. Mining and quarrying (1991): limestone 1,435,405; marble 52,379. Manufacturing (value added in U.S.$'000,000; 1990): food and beverages 703; textiles 373; chemical products 165; metal products 160; machinery and transport equipment 159; paper products 62; rubber and plastic products 61. Construction (dwellings completed; 1982): 31,038. Energy production (consumption): electricity (kW-hr; 1991) 9,955,000,000 (9,955,000,000); coal (metric tons; 1991) 90,000 (55,000); crude petroleum (barrels; 1991) 71,034,000 (87,960,000); petroleum products (metric tons; 1991) 11,341,000 (11,510,000); natural gas (cu m; 1991) 4,345,000,000 (4,345,000,000).
Tourism (1991): receipts U.S.$39,000,000; expenditures U.S.$839,000,000.
Gross national product (1992): U.S.$32,603,000,000 (U.S.$320 per capita).

Structure of gross domestic product and labour force	1991		1986	
	in value ₦'000,000	% of total value	labour force	% of labour force
Agriculture	37,000	39.2	13,259,000	43.1
Mining	12,000	12.7	6,800	0.1
Manufacturing	7,800	8.3	1,263,700	4.1
Construction	1,800	1.9	545,600	1.8
Public utilities	500	0.5	130,400	0.4
Transp. and commun.	3,200	3.4	1,111,900	3.6
Trade	12,400	13.1	7,417,400	24.1
Finance	8,500	9.0	120,100	0.4
Pub. admin., defense	8,400	8.9	4,902,100	15.9
Services	2,800	3.0		
Other	...	...	2,008,500[13]	6.5[13]
TOTAL	94,400	100.0	30,765,500	100.0

Public debt (external, outstanding; 1991): U.S.$33,245,000,000.
Population economically active (1986): total 30,765,500; activity rate 31.1% (participation rates: ages 15–64, 58.8%; female 33.3%; unemployed 4.1%).

Price and earnings indexes (1985 = 100)	1986	1987	1988	1989	1990	1991	1992
Consumer price index	105.7	117.7	181.8	273.5	293.7	331.9	479.8
Earnings index	...	...	...	...	...	...	...

Household income and expenditure. Avg. household size (1983) 5.0; annual income per household (1981) ₦2,300 (U.S.$3,745)[14]; sources of income (1979): self-employment 49.4%, wages 36.2%, interest 5.4%, rent 4.7%, transfer payments 4.3%; expenditures (1979): food 53.0%, fuel and light 11.4%, clothing 6.0%, transportation 4.7%, household goods 3.8%, other 21.1%.
Land use (1991): forested 12.7%; pastures 43.9%; agricultural 35.5%; other 7.9%.

Foreign trade

Balance of trade (current prices)	1987	1988	1989	1990	1991	1992
₦'000,000	+15,401	+8,283	+29,730	+68,587	+40,696	+76,298
% of total	35.2%	14.2%	34.5%	45.4%	20.2%	22.8%

Imports (1992): ₦143,151,200,000 (machinery and transport equipment 43.2%; manufactured goods [mostly iron and steel products, textiles, and paper products] 27.8%; chemicals 16.0%; food 8.8%; mineral fuels 0.4%). *Major import sources* (1991): Germany 13.8%; U.K. 13.6%; U.S. 11.8%; France 8.9%.
Exports (1992): ₦205,613,100,000 (crude petroleum 97.9%; cocoa beans 0.6%; rubber 0.4%; fertilizer 0.2%; other exports include cocoa products, textiles, and cashew nuts). *Major export destinations* (1991): U.S. 40.7%; Spain 12.6%; Germany 8.6%; The Netherlands 5.0%; France 5.0%; Italy 4.0%.

Transport and communications

Transport. Railroads (1987): length 3,505 km; passenger-km 3,808,277,000; metric ton-km cargo 1,743,000,000. Roads (1984): total length 124,000 km (paved 48%). Vehicles (1990): passenger cars 785,000; trucks and buses 625,000. Merchant marine (1992): vessels (100 gross tons and over) 271; total deadweight tonnage 733,329. Air transport (1991): passenger-km 1,064,300,000; metric ton-km cargo 22,700,000; airports (1992) 14.
Communications. Daily newspapers (1990): total number 24; total circulation 1,553,000[15]; circulation per 1,000 population 18[15]. Radio (1992): 10,000,000 receivers (1 per 9.0 persons). Television (1991): 4,100,000 receivers (1 per 30 persons). Telephones (1988): 722,070 (1 per 115 persons).

Education and health

Education (1990–91)	schools	teachers	students	student/ teacher ratio
Primary (age 6–12)	35,446	353,600	13,776,854	38.9
Secondary (age 12–17)	5,594[15]	141,491	3,123,277	22.1
Voc., teacher tr.	376[16]	15,738[17]	391,583[17]	24.9[17]
Higher[17]	...	19,601	307,207	15.7

Literacy (1990): total population age 15 and over literate 29,538,200 (50.7%); males literate 17,792,300 (62.3%); females literate 11,745,000 (39.5%).
Health (1986): physicians 16,003 (1 per 6,573 persons); hospital beds 90,668 (1 per 1,160 persons); infant mortality rate (1990–95) 96.0.
Food (1988–90): daily per capita caloric intake 2,200 (vegetable products 97%, animal products 3%); 93% of FAO recommended minimum requirement.

Military

Total active duty personnel (1993): 78,800 (army 78.7%, navy 9.3%, air force 12.0%). *Military expenditure as percentage of GNP* (1989): 0.5% (world 4.9%).

[1]Civilian government (in place since Aug. 26, 1993) was overthrown by a military coup in November 1993. [2]The transfer of the capital from Lagos to Abuja in the Federal Capital Territory that was to have been completed in 1992 has not occurred, due to internal turmoil. [3]Abia includes Akwa Ibom, Cross River, and Enugu. [4]Adamawa includes Taraba. [5]Benue includes Kogi. [6]Borno includes Yobe. [7]Delta includes Edo. [8]Jigawa includes Kano. [9]Kaduna includes Katsina. [10]Kebbi includes Sokoto. [11]Osun includes Oyo. [12]Detail does not add to total given because of rounding. [13]Includes 1,263,600 unemployed persons. [14]Urban households only. [15]For 15 newspapers only. [16]1987–88. [17]1988–89.

Norway

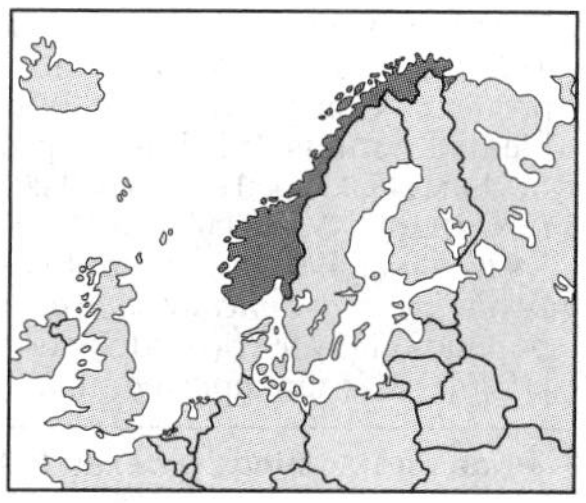

Official name: Kongeriket Norge (Kingdom of Norway).
Form of government: constitutional monarchy with one legislative house (Parliament [165]).
Chief of state: King.
Head of government: Prime Minister.
Capital: Oslo.
Official language: Norwegian.
Official religion: Evangelical Lutheran.
Monetary unit: 1 Norwegian krone (NKr) = 100 øre; valuation (Oct. 4, 1993) 1 U.S.$ = NKr 7.10; 1 £ = NKr 10.76.

Area and population

Counties	Capitals	area[1] sq mi	sq km	population 1992[2] estimate
Akershus	—	1,898	4,917	424,895
Aust-Agder	Arendal	3,557	9,212	98,429
Buskerud	Drammen	5,763	14,927	226,390
Finnmark	Vadsø	18,779	48,637	76,002
Hedmark	Hamar	10,575	27,388	187,330
Hordaland	Bergen	6,036	15,634	416,753
Møre og Romsdal	Molde	5,832	15,104	239,357
Nordland	Bodø	14,798	38,327	240,349
Nord-Trøndelag	Steinkjer	8,673	22,463	127,450
Oppland	Lillehammer	9,753	25,260	182,583
Oslo	Oslo	175	454	473,344
Østfold	Moss	1,615	4,183	238,618
Rogaland	Stavanger	3,529	9,141	346,574
Sogn og Fjordane	Leikanger	7,195	18,634	107,203
Sør-Trøndelag	Trondheim	7,271	18,831	253,695
Telemark	Skien	5,913	15,315	163,407
Troms	Tromsø	10,021	25,954	148,738
Vest-Agder	Kristiansand	2,811	7,281	147,158
Vestfold	Tønsberg	856	2,216	200,956
TOTAL		125,050	323,878	4,299,231[3]

Demography

Population (1993): 4,308,000.
Density (1993): persons per sq mi 34.4, persons per sq km 13.3.
Urban-rural (1990): urban 75.0%; rural 25.0%.
Sex distribution (1992): male 49.45%; female 50.55%.
Age breakdown (1992): under 15, 19.0%; 15–29, 22.7%; 30–44, 21.9%; 45–59, 15.6%; 60–74, 13.6%; 75 and over, 7.2%.
Population projection: (2000) 4,426,000; (2010) 4,550,000.
Doubling time: not applicable; doubling time exceeds 100 years.
Ethnic composition (by country of citizenship; 1992): Norway 96.5%; Denmark 0.4%; Sweden 0.3%; United Kingdom 0.3%; Pakistan 0.3%; United States 0.2%; Vietnam 0.2%; other 1.8%.
Religious affiliation (1980): Lutheran 87.9%; nonreligious 3.2%; other 8.9%.
Major cities (1993)[4]: Oslo 473,344; Bergen 218,105; Trondheim 140,718; Stavanger 101,463; Baerum 92,739.

Vital statistics

Birth rate per 1,000 population (1992): 14.0 (world avg. 26.4); (1991) legitimate 59.1%; illegitimate 40.9%.
Death rate per 1,000 population (1992): 10.5 (world avg. 9.2).
Natural increase rate per 1,000 population (1992): 3.5 (world avg. 17.2).
Total fertility rate (avg. births per childbearing woman; 1991): 1.9.
Marriage rate per 1,000 population (1991): 4.6.
Divorce rate per 1,000 population (1991): 2.4.
Life expectancy at birth (1991): male 74.0 years; female 80.1 years.
Major causes of death per 100,000 population (1991): ischemic heart disease 254.1; malignant neoplasms (cancers) 231.8; cerebrovascular disease 124.7.

National economy

Budget (1993). Revenue: NKr 307,172,000,000 (social-security taxes 24.9%, value-added taxes 23.4%, taxes on interest and dividends 12.6%, taxes on petroleum income and activity 3.3%, ordinary income tax 2.4%). Expenditures: NKr 331,938,000,000 (social security and welfare 24.6%, health 8.3%, debt service 6.5%).
Public debt (1990): U.S.$23,430,000,000.
Land use (1990): forested 27.1%; meadows and pastures 0.4%; agricultural and under permanent cultivation 2.8%; built-up and other 69.7%.
Tourism (1991): receipts from visitors U.S.$1,574,000,000; expenditures by nationals abroad U.S.$3,207,000,000.
Production (metric tons except as noted). Agriculture, forestry, fishing (1992): barley 663,000, oats 568,000, potatoes 415,000, wheat 246,000; livestock (number of live animals) 1,083,100 sheep[5], 981,300 cattle, 763,700 pigs; roundwood (1991) 10,987,000 cu m; fish catch 2,389,665, of which capelin 807,500, herring 220,000, cod 215,220, mackerel 207,781. Mining and quarrying (1991)[6]: iron ore 2,028,000, zinc 17,520[7], copper 17,400, lead 3,000[7]. Manufacturing (value added in NKr '000,000; 1991): machinery and equipment 28,441, of which transport equipment 6,494, electrical equipment 5,159; food products 17,368; paper and paper products 13,369; chemical products 10,691; wood and wood products 4,770. Construction (1992): residential 1,747,000 sq m; nonresidential 1,711,000 sq m. Energy production (consumption): electricity (kW-hr; 1990) 121,601,000,000 (105,651,000,000); coal (metric tons; 1990) 311,000 (779,000); crude petroleum (barrels; 1990) 622,051,000 (99,218,000); petroleum products (metric tons; 1990) 13,069,000 (7,761,000); natural gas (cu m; 1990) 19,883,000,000 (1,746,000,000).

Gross national product (1991): U.S.$102,885,000,000 (U.S.$24,160 per capita).

Structure of gross domestic product and labour force

	1991 in value NKr '000,000	% of total value	labour force	% of labour force
Agriculture	20,052	2.9	116,000	5.5
Mining	3,908	0.6	21,000	1.0
Crude petroleum and natural gas	99,664	14.5	...	...
Manufacturing	92,591	13.5	294,000	13.8
Construction	24,705	3.6	130,000	6.1
Public utilities	26,386	3.8	21,000	1.0
Transp. and commun.	61,738	9.0	162,000	7.6
Trade	75,315[8]	11.0[8]	354,000	16.7
Finance	61,709	9.0	153,000	7.2
Pub. admin., defense	111,910	16.3		
Services	67,231	9.8	869,000[9]	40.9[9]
Other	41,479	6.0		
TOTAL	686,686[10]	100.0	2,126,000[10]	100.0[10]

Population economically active (1992): total 2,130,000; activity rate of total population 49.5% (participation rates: ages 16–64, 76.3%; female 44.2%; unemployed 5.9%).

Price and earnings indexes (1985 = 100)

	1986	1987	1988	1989	1990	1991	1992
Consumer price index	107.2	116.5	124.3	130.0	135.4	140.0	143.3
Hourly earnings index	110.0	128.0	135.0	141.0	149.6	157.2	162.3

Household income and expenditure. Average household size (1990) 2.4; consumption expenditure per household (1990) NKr 165,400 (U.S.$26,400); sources of income (1990): wages and salaries 59.4%, social security 23.3%, self-employment and property income 17.3%; expenditure (1990): housing 18.9%, food 18.4%, transportation 12.6%, clothing and footwear 7.6%, household furniture and equipment 6.8%, beverages and tobacco 6.7%.

Foreign trade

Balance of trade (current prices)

	1987	1988	1989	1990	1991	1992
NKr '000,000	−3,645	−2,976	+27,248	+48,231	+59,565	+61,730
% of total	1.2%	1.0%	7.9%	12.9%	15.9%	16.4%

Imports (1992): NKr 161,931,000,000 (machinery and transport equipment 37.8%, of which road vehicles 6.1%, ships 4.0%; metals and metal products 9.6%, of which iron and steel 4.5%; food products 4.4%, of which fruits and vegetables 1.6%; petroleum products 3.3%, of which crude petroleum 0.6%). *Major import sources:* Sweden 15.4%; Germany 14.4%; U.K. 9.3%; Denmark 7.5%.
Exports (1992): NKr 218,374,000,000 (fuels and fuel products 44.5%, of which crude petroleum 37.9%, natural gas 6.6%; machinery and transport equipment 14.8%; metals and metal products 10.7%, of which aluminum 4.4%; food products 7.6%, of which fish 6.6%). *Major export destinations:* U.K. 24.2%; Germany 13.2%; Sweden 9.4%; The Netherlands 7.1%.

Transport and communications

Transport. Railroads (1991): route length 4,027 km; passenger-km 2,201,000,000; metric ton-km cargo 2,548,000,000. Roads (1993): total length 89,737 km (1991; paved 70%). Vehicles (1992): passenger cars 1,619,438; trucks and buses 390,272. Merchant marine (1992): vessels (100 gross tons and over) 2,499; total deadweight tonnage 38,298,755. Air transport (1991): passenger-km 7,105,603,000; metric ton-km cargo 783,058,000; airports (1993) 47.
Communications. Daily newspapers (1992): total number 59; total circulation 2,119,000; circulation per 1,000 population 495. Radio (1992): 3,300,000 receivers (1 per 1.3 persons). Television (1992): 1,500,000 receivers (1 per 2.9 persons). Telephones (1991)[11]: 2,198,243 (1 per 1.9 persons).

Education and health

Education (1991–92)

	schools	teachers[12]	students	student/ teacher ratio[12]
Primary (age 7–12)	3,389	33,961	467,502	14.0
Secondary (age 13–18) and vocational	831	20,647	243,558	11.5
Higher	211	7,556	148,865	18.3

Educational attainment (1991). Percentage of population age 16 and over having: lower secondary education 42.9%; higher secondary 41.4%; higher 15.7%. *Literacy* (1991): virtually 100% literate.
Health (1991): physicians (1993) 14,084 (1 per 305 persons); hospital beds 24,004 (1 per 177 persons); infant mortality rate per 1,000 live births 6.4.
Food (1988–90): daily per capita caloric intake 3,221 (vegetable products 65%, animal products 35%); 120% of FAO recommended minimum requirement.

Military

Total active duty personnel (1992): 32,700 (army 48.6%, navy 22.3%, air force 29.1%). *Military expenditure as percentage of GNP* (1989): 3.3% (world avg. 4.9%); per capita expenditure U.S.$691.

[1]Excludes Svalbard and Jan Mayen, (24,360 sq mi [63,080 sq km]). [2]January 1. [3]Includes the Norwegian population of Svalbard and Jan Mayen, registered as residents in municipalities on the mainland. [4]Population of municipalities. [5]One year and over. [6]Metal content of ore. [7]1990. [8]Includes hotels. [9]Includes 116,000 unemployed. [10]Detail does not add to total given because of rounding. [11]Main lines only. [12]1990–91.

Oman

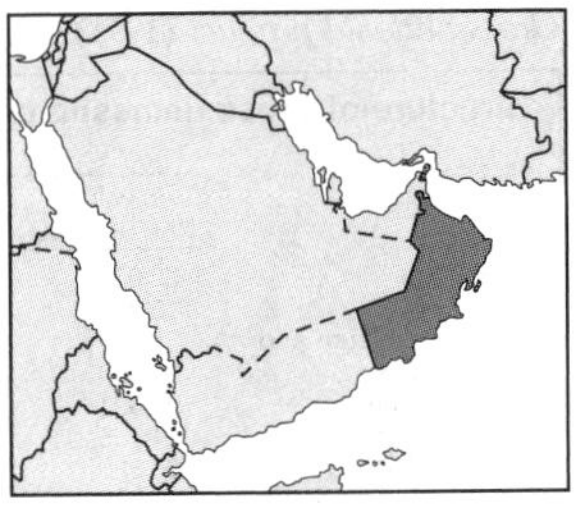

Official name: Salṭanat ʿUmān (Sultanate of Oman).
Form of government: monarchy[1].
Head of state and government: Sultan.
Capital: Muscat.
Official language: Arabic.
Official religion: Islam.
Monetary unit: 1 rial Omani (RO) = 1,000 baizas; valuation (Oct. 4, 1993) 1 RO = U.S.$2.63 = £1.72.

Area and population

		area[2]		population[3]
		sq mi	sq km	1990 estimate
Regions[4]	**Centres[5]**			
al-Bāṭinah	ar-Rustāq; Ṣuḥār	5,320	13,770	416,200
ad-Dākhilīyah	Nizwā; Samā'il	29,770	77,110	197,400
al-Janūbīyah	Salālah	45,370	117,510	146,900
Masqaṭ	Muscat (Masqaṭ)	1,420	3,670	410,000
Musandam	Khaṣab	590	1,530	21,400
ash-Sharqīyah	Ibrā; Ṣūr	16,190	41,920	206,500
aẓ-Ẓāhirah	al-Buraymī; 'Ibri	19,490	50,490	131,600
TOTAL		118,150	306,000	1,530,000

Demography

Population (1993): 1,698,000.
Density (1993): persons per sq mi 14.4, persons per sq km 5.5.
Urban-rural (1990): urban 11.0%; rural 89.0%.
Sex distribution (1990): male 52.95%; female 47.05%.
Age breakdown (1990): under 15, 46.7%; 15–29, 23.6%; 30–44, 17.2%; 45–59, 8.3%; 60–74, 3.5%; 75 and over, 0.7%.
Population projection: (2000) 2,165,000; (2010) 3,063,000.
Doubling time: 20 years.
Ethnic composition (1990): Omani Arab 73.5%; Pakistani (mostly Baluchi) 21.0%; other 5.5%.
Religious affiliation (1984): Muslim 86%; Hindu 13%; other 1%.
Major cities (1990): Muscat 85,000[6]; Nizwā 62,880; Samā'il 44,721; Salālah 10,000[6].

Vital statistics

Birth rate per 1,000 population (1990–95): 40.5 (world avg. 26.4).
Death rate per 1,000 population (1990–95): 4.9 (world avg. 9.2).
Natural increase rate per 1,000 population (1990–95): 35.6 (world avg. 17.2).
Total fertility rate (avg. births per childbearing woman; 1990–95): 6.7.
Marriage rate per 1,000 population: n.a.
Divorce rate per 1,000 population: n.a.
Life expectancy at birth (1990–95): male 67.7 years; female 71.8 years.
Morbidity (reported cases of illness per 100,000 population; 1989): influenza 6,823; malaria 1,235; chicken pox 1,156; mumps 1,048; amebic dysentery 376; measles 294; bacillary dysentery 206; infectious hepatitis 96; tuberculosis 33; brucellosis 15.

National economy

Budget (1993). Revenue: RO 1,698,500,000 (oil revenue 76.7%; other 23.3%). Expenditures: RO 2,138,500,000 (recurrent budget 67.2%, of which civil ministries 38.1%, defense 29.5%, education 9.1%, general public services 5.3%, fuel and energy 5.3%, health 4.6%; capital development projects 32.8%).
Public debt (external, outstanding; 1991): U.S.$2,270,000,000.
Gross national product (at current market prices; 1990): U.S.$9,503,000,000 (U.S.$6,327 per capita).

Structure of gross domestic product and labour force

	1990			
	in value RO '000,000	% of total value	labour force	% of labour force
Agriculture	126.9	3.1	146,400	27.7
Mining	2,068.0	50.6	2,800	0.5
Manufacturing	151.1	3.7	32,800	6.2
Construction	124.7	3.1	104,800	19.8
Public utilities	51.2	1.3	4,100	0.8
Transportation and communications	132.2	3.2	14,500	2.7
Trade	467.1	11.4	87,500	16.5
Finance	293.3	7.2	9,400	1.8
Pub. admin., defense	656.7	16.1	81,000	15.3
Services	83.7	2.0	45,800	8.7
Other	−70.9[7]	−1.7[7]	—	—
TOTAL	4,084.0	100.0	529,100	100.0

Tourism: receipts from visitors (1991) U.S.$63,000,000; expenditures by nationals abroad (1990) U.S.$47,000,000.
Household income and expenditure. Average household size (1986) 3.7; income per household: n.a.; sources of income: n.a.; food expenditure (1978): meat and eggs 20.6%, cereals 15.2%, fruits and nuts 12.4%, vegetables 11.9%, dairy products 10.3%, other foods 29.6%.
Production (metric tons except as noted). Agriculture, forestry, fishing (1992): vegetables and melons 163,000 (of which watermelons 30,000), dates 130,000, bananas 25,000, mangoes 10,000, onions 9,000, potatoes 5,000, papayas 3,000, tobacco leaf 2,000, wheat 1,000; livestock (number of live animals) 730,000 goats, 145,000 sheep, 140,000 cattle, 92,000 camels, 3,000,000 chickens; fish catch (1991) 117,780. Mining and quarrying (1990): copper 15,200; silver 2,500 kg; gold 20 kg. Manufacturing (value added in RO '000; 1990): textiles and apparel 13,957; metal products 2,303; machinery and equipment 1,797; chemical products 840; food products and beverages 715; wood products 439; paper products 282; other major products include refined petroleum products. Construction (1989): number of residential permits 3,408; nonresidential permits 353. Energy production (consumption): electricity (kW-hr; 1991) 5,548,000,000 (5,548,000,000); coal, none (none); crude petroleum (barrels; 1991) 249,420,000 (25,153,000); petroleum products (metric tons; 1991) 3,426,000 (1,496,000); natural gas (cu m; 1991) 2,673,200,000 (2,673,200,000).
Population economically active (1990)[8]: total 680,850; activity rate of total population 39.9% (participation rates: ages 15–64 [1986] 60.9%; female [1986] 7.5%; unemployed, n.a.).

Price and earnings indexes (1985 = 100)

	1985	1986	1987	1988	1989	1990	1991[9]
Consumer price index[10]	100.0	107.1	109.8	111.6	113.2	114.7	118.4
Earnings index	...	...	...	...	...	...	...

Land use (1991): meadows and pastures 4.7%; agricultural and under permanent cultivation 0.3%; other (mostly desert and developed area) 95.0%.

Foreign trade

Balance of trade (current prices)

	1986	1987	1988	1989	1990	1991
RO '000,000	+142.3	+694.2	+501.1	+789.1	+1,197.5	+776.6
% of total	8.0%	35.7%	24.9%	33.1%	39.4%	26.2%

Imports (1991): U.S.$3,193,972,000 (machinery and transport equipment 41.9%, of which road motor vehicles 11.8%, civil-engineering and construction machinery 6.4%; basic manufactured goods 17.5%, of which iron and steel 5.6%; food and live animals 13.8%; miscellaneous manufactured articles 7.8%; chemicals 5.9%; beverages and tobacco 4.0%). *Major import sources:* United Arab Emirates 25.3%; Japan 20.5%; United Kingdom 10.0%; United States 7.6%; West Germany 5.2%.
Exports (1991): U.S.$1,759,564,000 (petroleum 86.1%; road motor vehicles 4.5%; nonferrous metals [copper and aluminum] 0.9%). *Major export destinations* (1989): Japan 37.2%; South Korea 26.7%; Taiwan 8.6%; Singapore 3.9%; United Kingdom 3.4%; China 3.2%; United States 3.1%.

Transport and communications

Transport. Railroads: none. Roads (1991): total length 17,053 mi, 27,438 km (paved 18%). Vehicles (1991): automobiles 173,939, trucks and buses 88,123. Merchant marine (1992): vessels (100 gross tons and over) 26; total deadweight tonnage 11,727. Air transport (1992)[11]: passenger-mi 1,194,400,000, passenger-km 1,922,100,000; short ton-mi cargo 47,780,000, metric ton-km cargo 69,756,000; airports (1993) with scheduled flights 6.
Communications. Daily newspapers (1991): total number 4; total circulation 61,500; circulation per 1,000 population 39. Radio (1992): total number of receivers 900,000 (1 per 1.8 persons). Television (1992): total number of receivers 1,500,000 (1 per 1.1 persons). Telephones (1991): 262,560 (1 per 6.1 persons).

Education and health

Education (1989–90)

	schools	teachers	students	student/ teacher ratio
Primary (age 6–14)	671	12,344	304,207	24.6
Secondary (age 15–17)	128	2,219	36,617	16.5
Voc., teacher tr.	25	728	5,596	7.7
Higher	5	482	3,925	8.1

Educational attainment: n.a. *Literacy* (1990): total population age 6 and over literate 41%; males literate 58%; females literate 24%.
Health (1990): physicians 1,393 (1 per 1,078 persons); hospital beds 3,952 (1 per 380 persons); infant mortality rate per 1,000 live births (1990–95) 30.
Food: daily per capita caloric intake, n.a.

Military

Total active duty personnel (1993): 36,700 (army 81.0%[12], navy 9.5%, air force 9.5%); foreign troops 3,700. *Military expenditure as percentage of GNP* (1989): 20.3% (world 4.9%); per capita expenditure U.S.$1,085.

[1]The sultan is assisted by an appointed 60-member advisory council consisting of 59 governorate representatives and the sultan's representative, who leads the body. [2]Approximate; no comprehensive survey of surface area has ever been carried out in Oman. [3]The first census of Oman was scheduled for late 1993; figures given represent official 1990 estimates of the Omani government. [4]Regions are divided into 59 wilāyat (provinces). [5]Centres of the regions are not administrative capitals. [6]1982. [7]Net imputed bank service charges. [8]Non-Omani workers constitute approximately 55–60% of the labour force. [9]Average of first two quarters. [10]Applies to food and beverages in the capital area only. [11]One-fourth apportionment of international flights of Gulf Air. [12]Including personnel of Royal Household units not formally part of army table of organization.

Pakistan

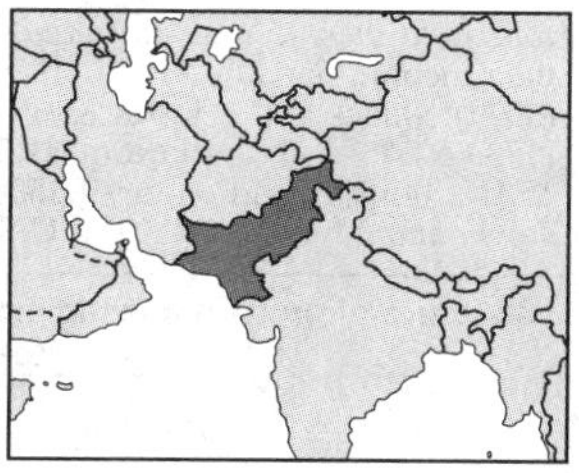

Official name: Islām-ī Jamhūrīya-e Pākistān (Islamic Republic of Pakistan).
Form of government: multiparty, federal Islamic republic with two legislative houses (Senate [87]; National Assembly [217]).
Chief of state: President.
Chief of government: Prime Minister.
Capital: Islāmābād.
Official language: Urdū.
Official religion: Islam.
Monetary unit: 1 Pakistan Rupee (PRs) = 100 paisa; valuation (Oct. 4, 1993) 1 U.S.$ = PRs 29.60; 1 £ = PRs 44.85.

Area and population

Provinces	Capitals	area[1] sq mi	area[1] sq km	population 1983 estimate[2]
Balochistān	Quetta	134,051	347,190	4,611,000
North-West Frontier	Peshāwar	28,773	74,521	11,658,000
Punjab	Lahore	79,284	205,344	50,460,000
Sindh	Karāchi	54,407	140,914	20,312,000
Federally Administered Tribal Areas	...	10,509	27,220	2,329,000
Federal Capital Area				
Islāmābād	...	350	906	359,000
TOTAL		307,374	796,095	89,729,000

Demography

Population (1993): 127,962,000[2].
Density (1993): persons per sq mi 376.7, persons per sq km 145.4.
Urban-rural (1993): urban 32.0%; rural 68.0%.
Sex distribution (1991): male 52.50%; female 47.50%.
Age breakdown (1988): under 15, 46.3%; 15–29, 24.6%; 30–44, 14.0%; 45–59, 9.0%; 60–74, 4.8%; 75 and over, 1.3%.
Population projection: (2000) 154,794,000; (2010) 197,672,000.
Doubling time: 24 years.
Linguistic composition (1981): Punjābī 48.2%; Pashto 13.1%; Sindhī 11.8%; Saraiki 9.8%; Urdū 7.6%; other 9.5%.
Religious affiliation (1981): Muslim 96.7%; Christian 1.6%; Hindu 1.5%; other 0.2%.
Major cities (1981): Karāchi 5,208,132; Lahore 2,952,689; Faisalābād 1,104,209; Rāwalpindi 794,843; Islāmābād 204,364.

Vital statistics

Birth rate per 1,000 population (1993): 40.0 (world avg. 26.4).
Death rate per 1,000 population (1993): 11.0 (world avg. 9.2).
Natural increase rate per 1,000 population (1993): 29.0 (world avg. 17.2).
Total fertility rate (avg. births per childbearing woman; 1993): 6.1.
Marriage rate per 1,000 population (1975–80): 10.7.
Divorce rate per 1,000 population (1975–80): 0.3.
Life expectancy at birth (1991): male 59.3 years; female 60.7 years.
Major causes of death (percentage of total deaths; 1987): malaria 18.2%; childhood diseases 12.1%; diseases of digestive system 9.8%; diseases of respiratory system 9.2%; infection of intestinal tract 7.7%.

National economy

Budget (1992–93). Revenue: PRs 261,000,000,000 (customs duties 27.3%, non-tax receipts 25.8%, excise taxes 16.9%, income taxes 12.6%). Expenditures: PRs 218,815,000,000 (public-debt service 42.6%, defense 37.5%, grants to local authorities 4.2%, subsidies 2.3%, education and health 1.9%).
Production (metric tons except as noted). Agriculture, forestry, fishing (1991–92): sugarcane 35,656,000, wheat 14,643,000, rice 3,243,000, corn (maize) 1,203,000, gram 511,000, jowar 228,000, cotton 12,867,000 bales; livestock (number of live animals; 1991) 36,673,000 goats, 30,160,000 sheep, 17,785,000 cattle, 15,031,000 buffalo, 1,005,000 camels, 193,000,000 poultry; roundwood (1991) 27,174,000 cu m; fish catch (1990) 479,036. Mining and quarrying (1991–92): limestone 8,528,000; rock salt 833,000; gypsum 471,000; silica sand 132,000; chromite 28,000. Manufacturing (1991–92): cement 8,300,000; chemical fertilizers 2,795,000, of which urea 1,898,000; refined sugar 2,322,000; cotton yarn 1,171,000; chemicals 372,000; vegetable products 319,000; jute textiles 100,900; paper and paperboard 63,000; cotton textiles 308,000,000 sq m; cigarettes 29,670,000,000 units; motor-vehicle tires 798,000 units; bicycles 478,000 units. Construction (value in PRs; 1984): residential 8,490,000,000; nonresidential 14,579,000,000. Energy production (consumption): electricity (kW-hr; 1990) 43,899,000,000 (43,899,000,000); coal (metric tons; 1990) 2,751,000 (3,616,000); crude petroleum (barrels; 1990) 19,485,000 (46,920,000); petroleum products (metric tons; 1990) 5,733,000 (10,116,000); natural gas (cu m; 1990) 12,264,000,000 (12,264,000,000).
Public debt (external, outstanding; 1991): U.S.$17,632,000,000.
Household income and expenditure (1988). Average household size 6.3; income per household PRs 25,572 (U.S.$1,420); sources of income: self-employment 56.0%, wages and salaries 22.0%, other 22.0%; expenditure: food 47.0%, housing 12.0%, clothing and footwear 8.0%, other 33.0%.
Gross national product (at current market prices; 1991): U.S.$46,725,000,000 (U.S.$400 per capita).

Structure of gross domestic product and labour force

	1991–92 in value PRs '000,000	% of total value	labour force	% of labour force
Agriculture	268,103	22.3	14,643,000	44.6
Mining	7,302	0.6	51,000	0.2
Manufacturing	185,546	15.4	3,873,000	11.8
Construction	46,199	3.8	2,095,000	6.4
Public utilities	34,034	2.8	259,000	0.8
Transportation and communications	94,161	7.8	1,652,000	5.0
Trade	177,335	14.8	4,102,000	12.5
Finance	77,222	6.4	280,000	0.8
Pub. admin., defense	84,818	7.1	4,160,000	12.7
Services	80,111	6.7		
Other	147,515	12.3	1,699,000[3]	5.2[3]
TOTAL	1,202,346	100.0	32,814,000	100.0

Population economically active (1991–92): total 32,814,000; activity rate of total population 28.0% (participation rates: ages 15–64, 50.8%; female 14.2%; unemployed 5.1%).

Price and earnings indexes (1985 = 100)

	1986	1987	1988	1989	1990	1991	1992
Consumer price index	103.5	108.4	117.9	127.2	138.7	155.0	169.8
Monthly earnings index	105.3	...	...	...	...	...	...

Tourism (1991): receipts from visitors U.S.$163,000,000; expenditures by nationals abroad U.S.$555,000,000.
Land use (1990): forested 4.6%; meadows and pastures 6.5%; agricultural and under permanent cultivation 26.9%; built-on, wasteland, and other 62.0%.

Foreign trade[4]

Balance of trade (current prices)

	1987	1988	1989	1990	1991	1992
PRs '000,000	–19,938	–27,036	–37,093	–24,896	–28,537	–31,283
% of total	12.1%	14.2%	16.1%	9.3%	8.4%	7.9%

Imports (1991–92): PRs 229,889,400,000 (petroleum products 15.0%, specialized machinery 14.0%, road vehicles 5.3%, vegetable oil and fats 4.4%, organic chemicals 4.0%, power-generating machinery 3.9%, wheat 3.7%, iron and steel manufactures 3.5%). *Major import sources:* Japan 14.3%; U.S. 10.5%; Germany 7.9%; U.K. 5.5%; Saudi Arabia 5.2%; France 4.7%; China 4.3%; Malaysia 4.2%; Italy 4.1%.
Exports (1991–92): PRs 171,727,700,000 (textile fabrics 48.7%, ready-made garments 19.7%, cotton 8.4%, rice 6.0%, leather and leather goods 3.6%, fresh fish 1.7%, professional instruments 1.3%). *Major export destinations:* U.S. 12.8%; Japan 8.3%; Hong Kong 7.3%; Germany 7.1%; U.K. 6.6%; Dubai 4.4%; Saudi Arabia 4.3%; France 3.9%.

Transport and communications

Transport. Railroads (1991–92): route length 5,453 mi, 8,775 km; passenger-mi 11,285,000,000, passenger-km 18,161,000,000; short ton-mi cargo 4,085,000,000, metric ton-km cargo 5,964,000,000. Roads (1990–91): total length 87,040 mi, 140,077 km (paved 46%). Vehicles (1991): passenger cars 721,150; trucks and buses 200,160. Merchant marine (1992): vessels (100 gross tons and over) 73; total deadweight tonnage 513,823. Air transport (1991): passenger-km 9,062,000,000; metric ton-km cargo 373,793,000; airports (1993) with scheduled flights 35.
Communications. Daily newspapers (1990): total number 237; total circulation 1,817,000; circulation per 1,000 population 15. Radio (1992): total number of receivers 10,000,000 (1 per 13 persons). Television (1992): total number of receivers 2,080,000 (1 per 63 persons). Telephones (1990–91): 1,188,000 (1 per 105 persons).

Education and health

Education (1990–91)

	schools	teachers	students	student/ teacher ratio
Primary (age 5–9)	127,575	218,300	8,856,000	40.6
Secondary (age 10–14)	13,604	184,200	3,397,000	18.4
Voc., teacher tr.	930	8,722	108,000	12.4
Higher	733	26,050	658,900	25.3

Educational attainment (1981). Percentage of population age 25 and over having: no formal schooling 78.9%; some primary education 8.7%; some secondary 10.5%; postsecondary 1.9%. *Literacy* (1981): total population age 15 and over literate 11,938,790 (25.6%); males literate 8,709,162 (36.0%); females literate 3,229,628 (15.2%).
Health (1990): physicians 51,883 (1 per 2,364 persons); hospital beds 71,897 (1 per 1,706 persons); infant mortality rate per 1,000 live births (1991) 91.
Food (1988–90): daily per capita caloric intake 2,280 (vegetable products 87%, animal products 13%); 99% of FAO recommended minimum requirement.

Military

Total active duty personnel (1992): 580,000 (army 88.8%, navy 3.4%, air force 7.8%). *Military expenditure as percentage of GNP* (1989): 6.8% (world 4.9%); per capita expenditure U.S.$21.

[1]Excludes the 32,323-sq mi (83,716-sq km) Pakistani-occupied part of Jammu and Kashmir. [2]1983 provincial estimates exclude and 1993 estimate includes Afghan refugees and residents of Pakistani-occupied Jammu and Kashmir. [3]Includes unemployed. [4]Import figures are f.o.b. in balance of trade and c.i.f. for commodities and trading partners.

Panama

Official name: República de Panamá (Republic of Panama).
Form of government: multiparty republic with one legislative house (Legislative Assembly [68]).
Head of state and government: President assisted by Vice Presidents.
Capital: Panama City.
Official language: Spanish.
Official religion: none.
Monetary unit: 1 balboa (B) = 100 cents; valuation (Oct. 4, 1993) 1 U.S.$ = B 1.00; 1 £ = B 1.52.

Area and population

		area		population
Provinces	**Capitals**	sq mi	sq km	1992 estimate
Bocas del Toro	Bocas del Toro	3,376	8,745	88,385
Chiriquí	David	3,341	8,653	396,842
Coclé	Penonomé	1,902	4,927	177,070
Colón	Colón	1,888	4,890	222,577[1]
Darién[2]	La Palma	6,437	16,671	45,020
Herrera	Chitré	904	2,341	108,714
Los Santos	Las Tablas	1,470	3,806	82,810
Panamá	Panama City	4,590	11,887	1,168,492
Veraguas	Santiago	4,339	11,239	224,676
Special territory				
Comarca de San Blas	El Porvenir	910	2,357	[1]
TOTAL		29,157	75,517[3]	2,514,586

Demography

Population (1993): 2,563,000.
Density (1993): persons per sq mi 87.9, persons per sq km 33.9.
Urban-rural (1990): urban 53.7%; rural 46.3%.
Sex distribution (1990): male 50.61%; female 49.39%.
Age breakdown (1990): under 15, 34.8%; 15–29, 29.2%; 30–44, 18.2%; 45–59, 10.3%; 60–74, 5.5%; 75 and over, 2.0%.
Population projection: (2000) 2,893,000; (2010) 3,324,000.
Doubling time: 34 years.
Ethnic composition (1987): mestizo 60.0%; black and mulatto 20.0%; white 10.0%; Amerindian 8.0%; Asian 2.0%.
Religious affiliation (1985): Roman Catholic 84.0%; Protestant 4.8%; Muslim 4.5%; Bahā'ī 1.1%; Hindu 0.3%; other 5.3%.
Major cities (1990): Panama City 413,505; San Miguelito 243,025[4]; David 65,763[5]; Colón 54,654; Barú 46,093[5].

Vital statistics

Birth rate per 1,000 population (1991): 25.5 (world avg. 26.4); (1985) legitimate 28.1%; illegitimate 71.9%.
Death rate per 1,000 population (1991): 5.2 (world avg. 9.2).
Natural increase rate per 1,000 population (1991): 20.3 (world avg. 17.2).
Total fertility rate (avg. births per childbearing woman; 1991): 2.9.
Marriage rate per 1,000 population (1991): 4.5.
Divorce rate per 1,000 population (1991): 0.6.
Life expectancy at birth (1991): male 70.6 years; female 74.7 years.
Major causes of death per 100,000 population (1990): diseases of the circulatory system 111.4, of which ischemic heart diseases 45.3, cerebrovascular disease 39.9; malignant neoplasms (cancers) 57.8; accidents 30.2; homicide and violence 20.8; infectious and parasitic diseases 20.0.

National economy

Budget (1993). Revenue: B 1,834,935,000 (current revenue 77.5%, of which indirect taxes 25.5%, direct taxes 21.1%, income from state enterprises 13.5%; development revenue 22.5%, of which loans 15.5%). Expenditures: B 1,834,935,000 (current transfers 18.4%; development expenditure 18.2%; internal debt payments 12.5%; education 11.2%; external debt payments 10.6%; health 6.9%).
Production (metric tons except as noted). Agriculture, forestry, fishing (1991): sugarcane 1,272,000, bananas 1,170,000, rice 180,000, corn (maize) 94,000, plantains 74,000, tomatoes 31,000, oranges 29,000, coffee 11,000, tobacco 2,000; livestock (number of live animals) 1,399,000 cattle, 256,000 pigs; roundwood 1,872,000 cu m; fish catch (value of production in B '000): shrimps 28,600, fish 8,500, lobster 5,700. Mining and quarrying (1990): limestone 393,000; gold 2,700 troy oz. Manufacturing (value added in B '000; 1990): food products 121,000; beverages 54,100; paints, soaps, and pharmaceuticals 31,600; tobacco products 26,400; wearing apparel 25,900; paper and paper products 23,700. Construction (value of construction in B '000; 1991): residential 86,000; nonresidential 43,500. Energy production (consumption): electricity (kW-hr; 1991) 2,790,000,000 (2,186,000,000); coal (metric tons; 1990) none (35,000); crude petroleum (barrels; 1990) none (8,722,000); petroleum products (metric tons; 1990) 1,121,000 (740,000); natural gas (cu m; 1990) none (60,428,000).
Population economically active (1991): total 858,509[6]; activity rate of total population 34.8% (participation rates: ages 15 and over, 57.4%; female [1989] 33.2%; unemployed [1992] 14.0%).

Price and earnings indexes (1985 = 100)

	1987	1988	1989	1990	1991	1992	1993[7]
Consumer price index	100.9	101.3	101.4	102.2	103.5	105.4	105.7
Weekly earnings index[8]	102.8	103.4	100.7	...	97.6	...	...

Household income and expenditure. Average household size (1990) 4.4; median income per household (1980) B 2,950 (U.S.$2,950); sources of income (1979): wages and salaries 85.3%, transfers 9.2%, other 5.5%; expenditure (1983–84)[9]: food and beverages 34.9%, transportation and communications 15.1%, housing and energy 12.6%, education and recreation 11.7%.
Gross national product (1991): U.S.$5,254,000,000 (U.S.$2,180 per capita).

Structure of gross domestic product and labour force

	1992		1991	
	in value B '000,000[10]	% of total value	labour force[6]	% of labour force[6]
Agriculture	236.7	10.8	196,252	22.9
Mining	4.3	0.2	782	0.1
Manufacturing	202.8	9.2	81,119	9.4
Construction	117.5	5.3	33,775	3.9
Public utilities	86.2	3.9	9,466	1.1
Transp. and commun.	549.2[11]	25.0[11]	54,205	6.3
Trade	259.1	11.8	167,347	19.5
Finance, real estate	322.2	14.7	34,471	4.0
Pub. admin.	285.8	13.0	226,836	26.4
Services	189.0	8.6		
Other	−54.1[12]	−2.5[12]	54,256[13]	6.3[13]
TOTAL	2,198.7	100.0	858,509	100.0[3]

Public debt (external, outstanding; 1991): U.S.$3,939,000,000.
Tourism (1991): receipts from visitors U.S.$196,000,000; expenditures by nationals abroad U.S.$108,000,000.
Land use (1990): forested 43.4%; meadows and pastures 20.5%; agricultural and under permanent cultivation 8.6%; other 27.5%.

Foreign trade[14, 15]

Balance of trade (current prices)

	1987	1988	1989	1990	1991	1992
B '000,000	−727.4	−275.3	−452.8	−893.9	−1,071.4	−1,329.1
% of total	45.4%	25.7%	35.3%	50.1%	54.2%	57.0%

Imports (1991): B 1,695,000,000 (mineral fuels 15.2%, machinery and apparatus 13.8%, chemicals and chemical products 12.0%, transport equipment 11.9%). *Major import sources:* U.S. 35.3%; Colón Free Zone 16.7%; Japan 6.8%; Ecuador 6.2%; Costa Rica 2.8%.
Exports (1991): B 452,100,000 (bananas 43.5%, shrimps 11.1%, raw sugar 5.4%, clothing 4.4%, coffee 2.9%). *Major export destinations:* U.S. 29.4%; Germany 25.6%; Italy 8.6%; Costa Rica 5.9%; Belgium-Luxembourg 4.7%.

Transport and communications

Transport. Railroads (1992): route length 362 mi, 583 km; (1989) passenger-mi 375,000, passenger-km 600,000; (1989) short ton-mi cargo 1,850,000, metric ton-km cargo 2,700,000. Roads (1992): total length 6,216 mi, 10,004 km (paved 32%). Vehicles: passenger cars (1990) 150,903; trucks and buses 72,744. Merchant marine (1992): vessels (100 gross tons and over) 5,217; total deadweight tonnage 79,255,644. Panama Canal traffic (1992): oceangoing transits 12,636; cargo 159,615,000 metric tons. Air transport (1991): passenger-mi 169,000,000, passenger-km 272,000,000; short ton-mi cargo 1,645,000, metric ton-km cargo 2,400,000; airports (1993) with scheduled flights 8.
Communications. Daily newspapers (1990): total number 8; total circulation 170,000; circulation per 1,000 population 70. Radio (1992): 450,000 receivers (1 per 5.6 persons). Television (1992): 204,539 receivers (1 per 12 persons). Telephones (1991): 273,335 (1 per 9.0 persons).

Education and health

Education (1991)

	schools	teachers	students	student/teacher ratio
Primary (age 6–11)	2,683	13,598	349,858	25.7
Secondary (age 12–17) / Voc., teacher tr.	345	9,929	198,138	20.0
Higher	9	3,390	58,625	17.3

Educational attainment (1990). Percentage of population age 25 and over having: no formal schooling 12.3%; incomplete primary education 21.2%; complete primary education 22.9%; secondary 30.4%; higher 13.2%. *Literacy* (1990): total population age 15 and over literate 1,385,000 (88.1%); males literate 705,000 (88.1%); females literate 680,000 (88.2%).
Health (1991): physicians 2,831 (1 per 871 persons); hospital beds 7,407 (1 per 333 persons); infant mortality rate per 1,000 live births 21.3.
Food (1988–90): daily per capita caloric intake 2,269 (vegetable products 80%, animal products 20%); 98% of FAO recommended minimum requirement.

Military

Total active duty personnel (1992): 11,700 (national police force 94.0%, national maritime service 3.0%, national air service 3.0%). U.S. forces in former Canal Zone 10,500. *Military expenditure as percentage of GNP* (1989): 3.4% (world 4.9%); per capita expenditure U.S.$59.

[1]Colón includes Comarca de San Blas. [2]Includes Comarca Emberá created in 1983 for dispersed Amerindians. [3]Detail does not add to total given because of rounding. [4]Population of urban district. [5]Population of the cabecera, the seat, or "head" of the municipality. [6]Excludes nonresidents in former Canal Zone and indigenous areas and institutional households. [7]May. [8]Panama City metropolitan area only. [9]Panama City only. [10]At prices of 1970. [11]Includes trans-Panamanian oil pipeline, commission of Panama Canal, and all activities of Colón Free Zone. [12]Net of imputed bank service charges and import fees. [13]Includes 610 not adequately defined and 53,646 unemployed without previous employment. [14]Import figures are f.o.b. in balance of trade and c.i.f. in commodities and trading partners. [15]Excludes Colón Free Zone (1991 imports f.o.b. B 3,681,000,000; 1991 reexports f.o.b. B 3,960,000,000).

Papua New Guinea

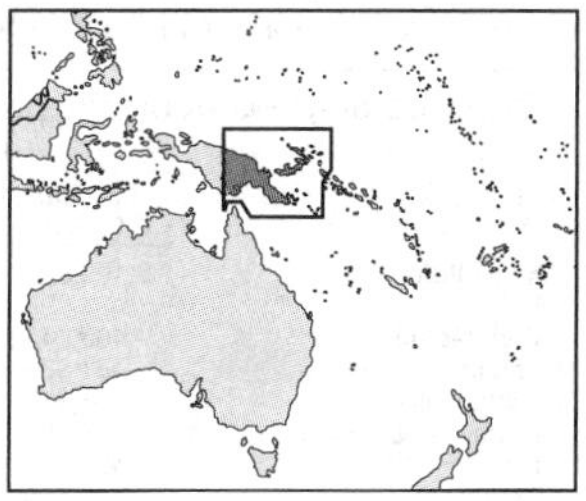

Official name: Independent State of Papua New Guinea.
Form of government: constitutional monarchy with one legislative house (National Parliament [109]).
Chief of state: British Monarch represented by Governor-General.
Head of government: Prime Minister.
Capital: Port Moresby.
Official language: English[1].
Official religion: none.
Monetary unit: 1 Papua New Guinea kina (K) = 100 toea; valuation (Oct. 4, 1993) 1 U.S.$ = K 0.99; 1 £ = K 1.50.

Area and population

		area		population
Provinces	Administrative centres	sq mi	sq km	1990 census[2]
Central	Port Moresby (Central)	11,400	29,500	140,584
Eastern Highlands	Goroka	4,300	11,200	299,619
East New Britain	Rabaul	6,000	15,500	184,408
East Sepik	Wewak	16,550	42,800	248,308
Enga	Wabag	4,950	12,800	238,357
Gulf	Kerema	13,300	34,500	68,060
Madang	Madang	11,200	29,000	270,299
Manus	Lorengau	800	2,100	32,830
Milne Bay	Alotau (Samarai)	5,400	14,000	157,288
Morobe	Lae	13,300	34,500	363,535
National Capital District	Port Moresby	100	240	193,242
New Ireland	Kavieng	3,700	9,600	87,194
North Solomons (Bougainville)	Arawa (Buka)	3,600	9,300	159,500[3]
Oro (Northern)	Popondetta	8,800	22,800	96,762
Sandaun (West Sepik)	Vanimo	14,000	36,300	135,185
Simbu (Chimbu)	Kundiawa	2,350	6,100	183,801
Southern Highlands	Mendi	9,200	23,800	302,724
Western	Daru	38,350	99,300	108,705
Western Highlands	Mount Hagen	3,300	8,500	291,090
West New Britain	Kimbe	8,100	21,000	127,547
TOTAL		178,704[4]	462,840	3,689,038[5]

Demography

Population (1993): 3,918,000.
Density (1993): persons per sq mi 21.9, persons per sq km 8.5.
Urban-rural (1990)[2]: urban 15.2%; rural 84.8%.
Sex distribution (1990)[2]: male 52.09%; female 47.91%.
Age breakdown (1990): under 15, 40.4%; 15–29, 28.8%; 30–44, 16.9%; 45–59, 9.3%; 60–74, 4.3%; 75 and over, 0.3%.
Population projection: (2000) 4,568,000; (2010) 5,511,000.
Doubling time: 32 years.
Ethnic composition (1983): New Guinea Papuan 84.0%; New Guinea Melanesian 15.0%; other 1.0%.
Religious affiliation (1980): Protestant 58.4%; Roman Catholic 32.8%; Anglican 5.4%; traditional beliefs 2.5%; Bahā'ī 0.6%; other 0.3%.
Major cities (1990)[2]: Port Moresby 193,242; Lae 80,655; Madang 27,057; Wewak 23,224; Goroka 17,855.

Vital statistics

Birth rate per 1,000 population (1993): 33.0 (world avg. 26.4); legitimate, n.a.; illegitimate, n.a.
Death rate per 1,000 population (1993): 11.0 (world avg. 9.2).
Natural increase rate per 1,000 population (1993): 22.0 (world avg. 17.2).
Total fertility rate (avg. births per childbearing woman; 1993): 4.8.
Marriage rate per 1,000 population: n.a.
Life expectancy at birth (1993): male 55.0 years; female 57.0 years.
Major causes of death per 100,000 population (1984): pneumonia 27.6; conditions originating from perinatal period 10.9; malaria 9.3; diarrheal diseases 9.0; meningitis 7.7; tuberculosis 6.7.

National economy

Budget (1992). Revenue: K 1,194,500,000 (personal income tax 19.8%, foreign grants 19.3%, import duties 18.0%, company tax 15.3%, nontax revenue 15.0%, excise duties 8.0%). Expenditures: K 1,245,300,000 (administrative 41.1%, transfers to provincial governments 25.0%, capital works 10.0%, interest payments 8.8%).
Public debt (external, outstanding; 1991): U.S.$1,601,000,000.
Production (metric tons except as noted). Agriculture, forestry, fishing (1992): bananas 1,250,000, coconuts 780,000, sweet potatoes 475,000, sugarcane 450,000, yams 220,000, taro 217,000, palm oil 206,000, cassava 113,000, copra 110,000, palm kernels 57,000, coffee 47,000, cacao 34,000, pineapples 13,000, tea 9,000; livestock (number of live animals) 1,010,000 pigs, 105,000 cattle, 3,000,000 chickens; roundwood (1991) 8,188,000 cu m; fish catch (1991) 25,330. Mining and quarrying (1990): copper 196,500; silver 101,400 kg; gold 32,800 kg. Manufacturing (value added, in K; 1985): food, beverages, and tobacco 162,558,000; metals, metal products, machinery, and equipment 47,493,000; wood and wood products 29,807,000. Construction (value in K; 1986)[6]: residential K 19,369,000; nonresidential K 55,675,000. Energy production (consumption): electricity (kW-hr; 1990) 1,790,000,000 (1,790,000,000); coal (metric tons; 1990) none (1,000); crude petroleum (barrels) none (n.a.); petroleum products (metric tons; 1990) none (743,000); natural gas, none (n.a.).
Gross national product (1992): U.S.$3,853,000,000 (U.S.$950 per capita).

Structure of gross domestic product and labour force

	1991		1980	
	in value K '000,000	% of total value	labour force[7]	% of labour force[7]
Agriculture	936.5	26.0	564,500	77.0
Mining	612.9	17.0	4,300	0.6
Manufacturing	345.1	9.6	14,000	1.9
Construction	224.0	6.2	21,600	2.9
Public utilities	59.2	1.6	2,800	0.4
Transp. and commun.	243.0	6.7	17,400	2.4
Trade	358.5	9.9	25,100	3.4
Finance	147.6	4.1	4,500	0.6
Pub. admin., defense / Services	678.7	18.8	77,100	10.5
Other	...	...	1,500	0.2
TOTAL	3,605.5	100.0[4]	732,800	100.0[4]

Tourism: receipts from visitors (1991) U.S.$47,000,000; expenditures by nationals abroad (1990) U.S.$42,000,000.
Land use (1991): forested 84.4%; agricultural and under permanent cultivation 0.9%; meadows and pastures 0.2%; other 14.5%.
Population economically active (1980)[7]: total 732,800; activity rate 24.6% (participation rates: over age 10, 35.2%; female 39.8%; unemployed 12.8%[8]).

Price and earnings indexes (1985 = 100)

	1986	1987	1988	1989	1990	1991	1992
Consumer price index	105.5	109.0	114.9	120.9	128.4	137.3	143.3
Weekly earnings index[9]	104.5	109.5	112.8	118.6	122.4	129.9	135.8

Household income and expenditure. Average household size (1980) 4.6; income per household (1975–76) K 2,771 (U.S.$3,483); sources of income (1970): wages and salaries 57.3%, transfer payments 1.1%, self-employment and other 41.6%; expenditure (1987)[10]: food and beverages 40.9%, transportation and communications 13.0%, housing 12.5%, clothing and footwear 6.2%, heating and lighting 4.9%, services and other 22.5%.

Foreign trade[11]

Balance of trade (current prices)

	1987	1988	1989	1990	1991	1992
K '000,000	+174.4	+214.7	−47.2	+38.5	−52.7	+475.2
% of total	8.3%	9.4%	2.1%	1.8%	2.0%	15.7%

Imports (1992): K 1,275,000,000 (1989; machinery and transport equipment 41.6%; basic manufactures 20.1%; food and live animals 15.1%; chemicals 6.3%; mineral fuels, lubricants, and related materials 5.1%). *Major import sources* (1990): Australia 50.6%; Japan 14.4%; U.S. 10.4%; Singapore 9.2%; New Zealand 3.6%; U.K. 2.5%; China 2.3%.
Exports (1992): K 1,730,600,000 (gold 43.1%; copper ore and concentrates 18.1%; timber 8.1%; palm oil and copra 4.4%; coffee 3.9%; cocoa beans 2.0%). *Major export destinations* (1990): Japan 29.7%; Australia 27.9%; W.Ger. 17.1%; South Korea 10.5%; U.K. 4.6%; U.S. 2.6%.

Transport and communications

Transport. Railroads: none. Roads (1986): total length 12,263 mi, 19,736 km (paved 6%). Vehicles (1988): passenger cars 17,532; trucks and buses 29,021. Merchant marine (1992): vessels (100 gross tons and over) 87; total deadweight tonnage 40,855. Air transport (1991): passenger-mi 227,000,000, passenger-km 365,000,000; short ton-mi cargo 8,200,000, metric ton-km cargo 12,000,000; airports (1993) with scheduled flights 101.
Communications. Daily newspapers (1990): total number 2; total circulation 49,000; circulation per 1,000 population 13. Radio (1992): 235,000 receivers (1 per 16 persons). Television (1992): 10,000 receivers (1 per 383 persons). Telephones (1990): 63,200 (1 per 59 persons).

Education and health

Education (1989)

	schools	teachers	students	student/ teacher ratio
Primary (age 7–12)	2,692	13,171	417,818	31.7
Secondary (age 13–16)	122[12]	2,306	57,676	25.0
Voc., teacher tr.	112[12]	751	9,331	12.4
Higher[12]	2	902	6,397	7.1

Educational attainment (1990). Percentage of population age 25 and over having: no formal schooling 82.6%; some primary education 8.2%; completed primary 5.0%; some secondary 4.2%. *Literacy* (1990): total population age 15 and over literate 52.0%; males literate 64.9%; females literate 37.8%.
Health (1989): physicians 361 (1 per 9,953 persons); hospital beds 15,335 (1 per 234 persons); infant mortality rate (1993) 53.0.
Food: daily per capita caloric intake (1987) 2,145 (1980–82; vegetable products 90%, animal products 10%); (1984) 82% of FAO minimum.

Military

Total active duty personnel (1993): 3,800 (army 84.2%, navy 13.2%, air force 2.6%). *Military expenditure as percentage of GNP* (1989): 1.4% (world 4.9%); per capita expenditure U.S.$13.

[1]The national languages are English, Tok Pisin, and Motu. [2]Preliminary results; excludes North Solomons and five census divisions. [3]Estimate. [4]Detail does not add to total given because of rounding. [5]Includes non-citizens. [6]Completed new buildings. [7]Citizens of Papua New Guinea over age 10 involved in "money-raising activities" only. [8]1977; in six urban centres. [9]Minimum wage of urban labourers. [10]Weights of retail price index components. [11]Import figures are f.o.b. in balance of trade and c.i.f. for commodities and trading partners. [12]1986.

Paraguay

Official name: República del Paraguay[1] (Republic of Paraguay).
Form of government: multiparty republic with two legislative houses (Senate [45]; Chamber of Deputies [80]).
Head of state and government: President.
Capital: Asunción.
Official languages: Spanish; Guaraní.
Official religion: none[2].
Monetary unit: 1 Paraguayan Guaraní (₲) = 100 céntimos; valuation (Oct. 4, 1993) 1 U.S.$ = ₲1,772; 1 £ = ₲2,685.

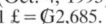

Area and population		area		population
Regions Departments	Capitals	sq mi	sq km	1992 census
Occidental		95,338	246,925	97,208
Alto Paraguay	Fuerte Olimpo	31,795	82,349	11,816
Boquerón	Filadelfia	35,393	91,669	26,292
Presidente Hayes	Pozo Colorado	28,150	72,907	59,100
Oriental		61,710	159,827	4,026,342
Alto Paraná	Ciudad del Este	5,751	14,895	403,858
Amambay	Pedro Juan Caballero	4,994	12,933	97,158
Asunción[3]	—	45	117	502,426
Caaguazú	Coronel Oviedo	4,430	11,474	383,319
Caazapá	Caazapá	3,666	9,496	128,550
Canindiyú	Salto del Guairá	5,663	14,667	96,826
Central	Asunción	952	2,465	864,540
Concepción	Concepción	6,970	18,051	166,946
Cordillera	Caacupé	1,910	4,948	206,097
Guairá	Villarrica	1,485	3,846	162,244
Itapúa	Encarnación	6,380	16,525	375,748
Misiones	San Juan Bautista	3,690	9,556	88,624
Ñeembucú	Pilar	4,690	12,147	69,884
Paraguarí	Paraguarí	3,361	8,705	203,012
San Pedro	San Pedro	7,723	20,002	277,110
TOTAL		157,048	406,752	4,123,550[4]

Demography

Population (1993): 4,613,000[4].
Density (1993): persons per sq mi 29.4, persons per sq km 11.3.
Urban-rural (1992): urban 50.5%; rural 49.5%.
Sex distribution (1992): male 50.19%; female 49.81%.
Age breakdown (1992): under 15, 40.1%; 15–29, 27.6%; 30–44, 18.7%; 45–59, 8.3%; 60–74, 4.2%; 75 and over, 1.1%.
Population projection: (2000) 5,464,000; (2010) 6,926,000.
Doubling time: 26 years.
Ethnic composition (1980): mestizo (Spanish-Guaraní) 90.8%; Amerindian 3.0%; German 1.7%; other 4.5%.
Religious affiliation (1980): Roman Catholic 96.0%; Protestant 2.1%; other 1.9%.
Major cities (1992): Asunción 502,426; Ciudad del Este 133,893; San Lorenzo 133,311; Lambaré 99,681; Fernando de la Mora 95,287.

Vital statistics

Birth rate per 1,000 population (1991): 33.6 (world avg. 26.4); (1985) legitimate 68.7%[5]; illegitimate 31.3%[5].
Death rate per 1,000 population (1991): 6.4 (world avg. 9.2).
Natural increase rate per 1,000 population (1991): 27.2 (world avg. 17.2).
Total fertility rate (avg. births per childbearing woman; 1991): 4.4.
Marriage rate per 1,000 population (1990): 1.8[5].
Divorce rate per 1,000 population: n.a.
Life expectancy at birth (1991): male 65.0 years; female 69.4 years.
Major causes of death per 100,000 population (1986): diseases of the circulatory system 157.5; infectious and parasitic diseases 60.7; malignant neoplasms (cancers) 48.3; diseases of the respiratory system 43.4.

National economy

Budget (1992). Revenue: ₲1,274,550,000,000 (taxes on goods and services 38.7%, income on fixed assets 14.0%, customs duties 12.4%, income tax 7.1%, pension funds 5.6%, sales tax 4.1%, real estate taxes 1.8%). Expenditures: ₲1,429,959,000,000 (education 15.7%, public works 11.5%, defense 11.1%, housing 8.2%, interior 7.4%, public health 6.8%).
Public debt (external, outstanding; 1991): U.S.$1,799,000,000.
Production (metric tons except as noted). Agriculture, forestry, fishing (1992): cassava 3,300,000, sugarcane 2,788,000, soybeans 1,315,000, seed cotton 670,000, corn (maize) 466,000, oranges 355,000, lint cotton 215,000, bananas 140,000, sweet potatoes 86,000; livestock (number of live animals) 7,800,000 cattle, 2,600,000 pigs, 18,000,000 chickens; roundwood (1991) 8,466,000 cu m; fish catch (1991) 13,000. Mining and quarrying (1990): limestone 600,000; kaolin 74,000; gypsum 4,500. Manufacturing (value of production in ₲'000,000; 1990): woven cotton fabric 207,600; processed meat 162,593; naphtha 76,813; gasoline 74,624; beer 70,054; soft drinks 68,197; cement 43,494; sugar 41,787; wheat flour 25,162. Construction (1985): residential 60,800 sq m; nonresidential 163,200 sq m. Energy production (consumption): electricity (kW-hr; 1990) 2,434,000,000 (1,837,000,000); coal, none (none); crude petroleum (barrels; 1990) none (2,555,000); petroleum products (metric tons; 1990) 342,000 (537,000); natural gas, none (none).
Tourism (1991): receipts from visitors U.S.$145,000,000; expenditures by nationals abroad U.S.$122,000,000.

Gross national product (1991): U.S.$5,374,000,000 (U.S.$1,210 per capita).

Structure of gross domestic product and labour force	1991		1982	
	in value ₲'000,000	% of total value	labour force	% of labour force
Agriculture	2,199,327	26.6	445,518	42.9
Mining	30,092	0.4	1,406	0.1
Manufacturing	1,405,345	17.0	124,658	12.0
Construction	451,879	5.5	69,900	6.7
Public utilities	235,850	2.8	2,605	0.3
Transp. and commun.	326,024	3.9	30,524	2.9
Trade	2,487,440	30.0	85,961	8.3
Finance	158,585	1.9	18,019	1.7
Pub. admin., defense Services	986,230	11.9	174,228	16.8
Other			86,444	8.3
TOTAL	8,280,772	100.0	1,039,258[6]	100.0

Population economically active (1982): total 1,039,258; activity rate 51.5% (participation rates: ages 15–64, 57.5%; female 19.7%; unemployed [1989] 9.2%).

Price and earnings indexes (1985 = 100)	1986	1987	1988	1989	1990	1991	1992
Consumer price index	131.7	160.5	124.1	248.7	343.7	427.1	491.7
Earnings index	...	...	...	...	...	...	...

Household income and expenditure. Average household size (1992) 4.7; sources of income (1987): wages and salaries 39.4%, transfer payments 2.5%, other 58.1%; expenditure (1980): food 48.7%, housing 16.4%, clothing 9.7%, household durable goods 6.2%, transportation and communications 4.5%.
Land use (1991): forested 33.3%; meadows and pastures 53.9%; agricultural and under permanent cultivation 5.6%; other 7.2%.

Foreign trade

Balance of trade (current prices)	1985	1986	1987	1988	1989	1990
₲'000,000	−75,892	−150,210	−115,975	+28,520	+376,875	−234,684
% of total	28.2%	44.9%	21.8%	4.5%	22.5%	10.9%

Imports (1992): U.S.$1,237,148,000 (machinery and transport equipment 21.7%, of which transport equipment 8.3%; fuels and lubricants 11.7%; tobacco and beverages 9.0%; chemicals and pharmaceuticals 6.8%; iron products 3.8%). *Major import sources:* Brazil 21.3%; Argentina 16.2%; United States 13.7%; Japan 11.4%; United Kingdom 4.5%; Germany 4.1%; Italy 2.1%.
Exports (1992): U.S.$656,555,000 (cotton fibres 31.9%; soybean flour 20.9%; oilseed cakes 8.3%; timber 8.1%; processed meat 7.2%; vegetable oil 6.4%, of which tung oil 0.9%; hides and skins 5.7%; perfume oils 2.2%; tobacco 1.0%). *Major export destinations:* Brazil 26.1%; The Netherlands 21.2%; Argentina 9.8%; United States 5.2%; Italy 3.4%; Germany 3.1%; France 2.1%.

Transport and communications

Transport. Railroads (1988): route length 274 mi, 441 km; passenger-mi 13,573,000, passenger-km 21,843,000; short ton-mi cargo 13,580,000, metric ton-km cargo 19,826,000. Roads (1988): total length 15,957 mi, 25,681 km (paved 9%). Vehicles (1990): passenger cars 117,067; buses 3,375. Merchant marine (1992): vessels (100 gross tons and over) 38; total deadweight tonnage 38,513. Air transport (1990): passenger-mi 355,019,000, passenger-km 571,349,000; short ton-mi cargo 2,427,000, metric ton-km cargo 3,543,000; airports (1993) with scheduled flights 1.
Communications. Daily newspapers (1992): total number 6; total circulation 123,000[7]; circulation per 1,000 population 27[7]. Radio (1992): 775,000 receivers (1 per 5.8 persons). Television (1992): 350,000 receivers (1 per 13 persons). Telephones (1990): 128,394 (1 per 33 persons).

Education and health

Education (1990–91)	schools	teachers	students	student/ teacher ratio
Primary (age 7–12)	4,602	27,490	687,331	25.0
Secondary (age 13–18)[8]	1	9,444[9]	153,206	17.4[9]
Higher	2	2,694[10]	32,884	...

Educational attainment (1982). Percentage of population age 25 and over having: no formal schooling 13.6%; primary education 64.7%; secondary 15.5%; higher 3.4%; not stated 2.8%. *Literacy* (1990): percentage of total population age 15 and over literate 90.1%; males literate 92.1%; females literate 88.1%.
Health (1991): physicians 2,992 (1 per 1,470 persons); hospital beds 5,388 (1 per 816 persons); infant mortality rate per 1,000 live births (1990–95) 39.0.
Food (1988–90): daily per capita caloric intake 2,684 (vegetable products 82%, animal products 18%); 116% of FAO recommended minimum requirement.

Military

Total active duty personnel (1992): 16,500 (army 75.7%, navy 18.2%, air force 6.1%). *Military expenditure as percentage of GNP* (1989): 1.4% (world 4.9%); per capita expenditure U.S.$13.

[1]Guaraní form not available. [2]Roman Catholicism, although not official, enjoys special recognition in the 1992 constitution. [3]Asunción is the capital city, not a department. [4]Preliminary 1992 census figure is not adjusted for undercount. The 1993 population figure is adjusted for estimated undercount. [5]Civil Registry records only. [6]Detail does not add to total given because of rounding. [7]For four newspapers only. [8]Includes vocational education and teacher training. [9]1988. [10]1985.

Peru

Official name: República del Perú (Spanish) (Republic of Peru).
Form of government[1]: unitary multiparty republic with one legislative house (Congress [80][2]).
Head of state and government: President.
Capital: Lima.
Official languages: Spanish; Quechua.
Official religion: Roman Catholicism.
Monetary unit[3]: 1 nuevo sol = 100 céntimos; valuation (Oct. 4, 1993) 1 U.S.$ = 2.10 nuevos soles; 1 £ = 3.19 nuevos soles.

Area and population

Regions	Capitals	area sq mi	area sq km	population 1993 census
Andres Avelino Cáceres	...	40,707	105,430	1,909,799
Arequipa	...	24,458	63,345	924,745
Chavín	...	15,686	40,627	940,481
Grau	...	15,661	40,562	1,594,922
Inca	...	66,696	172,741	1,456,122
José Carlos Mariátegui	...	40,081	103,809	1,399,508
La Libertad	...	9,873	25,570	1,279,472
Loreto	...	142,414	368,852	673,329
Los Libertadores-Wari	...	34,340	88,939	1,434,554
Nor Oriental del Marañón	...	33,486	86,728	2,540,432
Ucayali	...	39,541	102,411	307,813
Departments				
Lima	...	13,437	34,802	6,483,901
San Martín	...	19,789	51,253	545,154
Constitutional Province				
Callao	Callao	57	147	638,234
TOTAL		496,225[4]	1,285,216	22,128,466

Demography

Population (1993): 22,916,000.
Density (1993): persons per sq mi 46.2, persons per sq km 17.8.
Urban-rural (1993): urban 71.8%; rural 28.2%.
Sex distribution (1993): male 50.32%; female 49.68%.
Age breakdown (1991): under 15, 37.2%; 15–29, 29.1%; 30–44, 17.7%; 45–59, 10.0%; 60–74, 4.9%; 75 and over, 1.1%.
Population projection: (2000) 26,276,000; (2010) 31,047,000.
Doubling time: 28 years.
Ethnic composition (1981): Quechua 47.1%; mestizo 32.0%; white 12.0%; Aymara 5.4%; other Amerindian 1.7%; other 1.8%.
Religious affiliation (1989): Roman Catholic 92.5%; Protestant 5.5%.
Major cities (1990): Lima 6,115,700; Arequipa 621,700; Callao 572,300; Trujillo 532,000; Chiclayo 419,600.

Vital statistics

Birth rate per 1,000 population (1990–95): 29.0 (world avg. 26.4); (1977) legitimate 57.8%; illegitimate 42.2%.
Death rate per 1,000 population (1990–95): 7.6 (world avg. 9.2).
Natural increase rate per 1,000 population (1990–95): 21.4 (world avg. 17.2).
Total fertility rate (avg. births per childbearing woman; 1990–95): 3.6.
Marriage rate per 1,000 population (1982): 6.0[5].
Life expectancy at birth (1990–95): male 62.7 years; female 66.6 years.
Major causes of death per 100,000 population (1989): diseases of the circulatory system 115.3; respiratory diseases 100.2; infectious diseases 84.5; malignant neoplasms 72.9; accidents, poisoning, and violence 53.6.

National economy

Budget (1992). Revenue: 5,651,680,000 nuevos soles (taxes on goods and services 58.8%; income taxes 13.3%; import duties 10.1%; nontax revenue 7.6%). Expenditures: 7,526,990,000 nuevos soles (current expenditure 72.7%, of which transfer payments 32.4%, wages and salaries 13.9%; capital expenditure 14.9%; public debt amortization 12.4%).
Production (metric tons except as noted). Agriculture, forestry, fishing (1992): sugarcane 7,000,000, potatoes 989,000, rice 827,000, plantains 677,000, corn (maize) 510,000, cassava 405,000, seed cotton 108,000, coffee 85,000; livestock (number of live animals) 12,079,000 sheep, 3,961,000 cattle, 2,417,000 pigs, 62,000,000 chickens; roundwood (1991) 7,912,000 cu m; fish catch (1991) 6,944,172. Mining and quarrying (1992): iron ore 1,849,000; zinc 603,000; copper 369,000; lead 194,000; silver 1,572. Manufacturing (value in '000,000 nuevos soles[6]; 1992): processed foods 163.6; base metal products 157.0; beverages and tobacco 63.6; textiles 58.2; industrial chemicals 46.9; apparel 33.2; wood products 32.6. Construction (value in '000,000 nuevos soles[6]; 1992): residential 22.4; nonresidential 14.6. Energy production (consumption): electricity (kW-hr; 1991) 14,828,000,000 (14,828,000,000); coal (metric tons; 1991) 140,000 (140,000); crude petroleum (barrels; 1991) 45,249,000 (50,627,000); petroleum products (metric tons; 1991) 6,545,000 (5,198,000); natural gas (cu m; 1991) 520,000,000 (520,000,000).
Household income and expenditure. Average household size (1986) 5.2; income per household (1987) I/. 175,180[3] (U.S.$3,742); sources of income (1987): business income 59.3%, wages 35.7%, transfers 5.0%; expenditure (1989): food 31.5%, household durables 11.3%, recreation and education 11.2%, clothing and footwear 10.7%, transportation 6.8%, health 4.5%, other 24.0%.
Gross national product (1992): U.S.$21,249,000,000 (U.S.$950 per capita).

Structure of gross domestic product and labour force

	1992 in value[6] S/. '000,000	1992 % of total value	1990 labour force	1990 % of labour force
Agriculture	437.7	13.2	2,605,000	34.0
Mining	354.6	10.7	183,900	2.4
Manufacturing	713.4	21.5	804,500	10.5
Construction	218.4	6.6	283,500	3.7
Public utilities	...	...	23,000	0.3
Transp. and commun.	...	...	337,100	4.4
Trade	411.5	12.4	1,195,200	15.6
Finance	...	...	183,900	2.4
Services	1,180.2[7]	35.6[7]	2,045,700[8]	26.7[8]
TOTAL	3,315.8	100.0	7,661,800	100.0

Population economically active (1990): total 7,661,800; activity rate of total population 34.3% (participation rates: over age 15, 56.4%; female [1985–86] 38.3%; unemployed 8.3%).

Price and earnings indexes (1985 = 100)

	1986	1987	1988	1989	1990[9]	1991[9]	1992[9]
Consumer price index	178	331	2,536	88,733	6,727	34,274	59,476
Monthly earnings index[10]	200	379	1,406	39,141	2,130	15,041	24,774

Land use (1991): forest 53.2%; pasture 21.2%; agricultural 2.9%; other 22.7%.
Public debt (external, outstanding; 1991): U.S.$15,080,000,000.
Tourism (1991): receipts U.S.$277,000,000; expenditures U.S.$881,000,000.

Foreign trade

Balance of trade (current prices)

	1987	1988	1989	1990	1991	1992
U.S.$'000,000	−307.8	+127.9	+1,523.9	+585.3	−165.0	−566.7
% of total	5.5%	2.4%	27.6%	9.8%	2.4%	7.5%

Imports (1992): U.S.$4,051,000,000 (raw and intermediate materials 44.0%, machinery and transport equipment 27.6%, consumer goods 20.8%). *Major import sources:* U.S. 27.2%; Colombia 8.1%; Japan 7.7%; Argentina 6.2%; Brazil 5.2%; Germany 4.6%; Venezuela 3.4%.
Exports (1992): U.S.$3,484,000,000 (copper 23.1%, fish flour 12.6%, zinc 9.6%, gold 6.2%, petroleum and derivatives 5.6%, lead 4.6%, silver 2.2%). *Major export destinations:* U.S. 21.4%; Japan 9.8%; China 7.0%; U.K. 6.3%; Italy 6.0%; Brazil 4.7%; Germany 4.1%; Venezuela 3.1%.

Transport and communications

Transport. Railroads (1991): route length 2,157 mi, 3,472 km; passenger-km 319,772,000; metric ton-km cargo 826,848,000. Roads (1992): total length 43,460 mi, 69,942 km (paved 11%). Vehicles (1992): passenger cars 402,351; trucks and buses 257,884. Merchant marine (1992): vessels (100 gross tons and over) 623; total deadweight tonnage 615,582. Air transport (1991): passenger-km 1,759,000,000; metric ton-km cargo 25,000,000; airports (1993) 25.
Communications. Daily newspapers (1990): total number 66; total circulation 1,700,000; circulation per 1,000 population 79. Radio (1992): 4,400,000 receivers (1 per 5.1 persons). Television (1992): 2,000,000 receivers (1 per 11 persons). Telephones (1991): 799,000 (1 per 28 persons).

Education and health

Education (1991)

	schools[11]	teachers	students	student/ teacher ratio
Primary (age 6–11)	28,860	138,455	4,053,801	29.3
Secondary (age 12–16)	6,462	96,969	1,996,181	20.6
Voc., teacher tr.	1,524	11,289	312,669	27.7
Higher	493	44,361	751,234	16.9

Educational attainment (1981). Percentage of population age 25 and over having: no formal schooling 20.1%; less than primary education 33.2%; primary 21.1%; secondary 20.8%; higher 4.8%. *Literacy* (1991): total population age 15 and over literate 89.3%; males 95.9%; females 82.6%.
Health (1990): physicians (1989) 21,856 (1 per 997 persons); hospital beds 35,715 (1 per 625 persons); infant mortality rate per 1,000 live births (1990–95) 75.8.
Food (1988–90): daily per capita caloric intake 2,037 (vegetable products 86%, animal products 14%); 87% of FAO recommended minimum requirement.

Military

Total active duty personnel (1993): 115,000 (army 65.2%, navy 21.7%, air force 13.1%). *Military expenditure as percentage of GNP* (1987): 4.9% (world 5.4%); per capita expenditure U.S.$106.

[1]On April 5, 1992, the president of Peru dissolved the legislature, suspended the constitution, and took control of the government. A referendum held on Oct. 31, 1993, approved a new constitution. [2]Interim legislative body elected November 1992. [3]A new currency, the nuevo sol, was introduced in January 1991, replacing the inti (abbrev.: I/.) at the rate of one million intis for one nuevo sol. It was in effect from July 1, 1991, when new bills and coins became available. [4]Detail does not add to total given because of rounding. [5]Excludes Indian jungle population; based on incomplete information. [6]At 1979 prices. [7]Includes finance, public administration, and other. [8]Includes public administration and other. [9]1985 = 0.1. [10]Estimate for Lima metropolitan area only. [11]1990.

Philippines

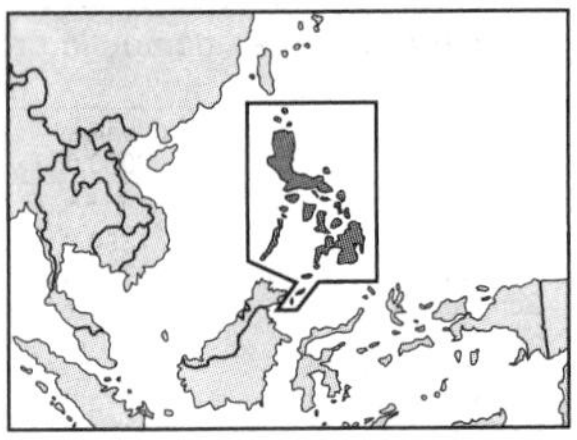

Official name: Republika ng Pilipinas (Pilipino); Republic of the Philippines (English).
Form of government: unitary republic with two legislative houses (Senate [24]; House of Representatives [201[1]]).
Chief of state and head of government: President.
Capital: Manila.
Official languages: Pilipino; English.
Official religion: none.
Monetary unit: 1 Philippine peso (₱) = 100 centavos; valuation (Oct. 4, 1993) 1 U.S.$ = ₱ 27.57; 1 £ = ₱ 41.78.

Area and population

	area		population
Regions	sq mi	sq km	1990 census[2]
Bicol	6,808	17,633	3,910,000
Cagayan Valley	10,362	26,838	2,341,000
Central Luzon	7,039	18,231	6,199,000
Central Mindanao	5,549	14,373	1,814,000
Central Visayas	5,773	14,951	4,593,000
Eastern Visayas	8,275	21,432	3,055,000
Ilocos	4,958	12,840	3,551,000
National Capital	246	636	7,929,000
Northern Mindanao	10,937	28,328	3,510,000
Southern Mindanao	12,237	31,693	4,457,000
Southern Tagalog	18,117	46,924	8,266,000
Western Mindanao	6,194	16,042	2,461,000
Western Visayas	7,808	20,223	5,392,000
Autonomous Regions			
Cordillera	7,063	18,294	1,146,000
Muslim Mindanao	4,493	11,638	2,056,000
TOTAL	115,860[3]	300,076	60,685,000[3]

Demography

Population (1993): 64,954,000.
Density (1993): persons per sq mi 560.9, persons per sq km 216.5.
Urban-rural (1993): urban 43.0%; rural 57.0%.
Sex distribution (1990): male 50.23%; female 49.77%.
Age breakdown (1990): under 15, 38.6%; 15–29, 28.6%; 30–44, 18.1%; 45–59, 9.3%; 60–74, 4.4%; 75 and over, 1.0%.
Population projection: (2000) 74,555,000; (2010) 86,682,000.
Doubling time: 30 years.
Ethnic composition (by mother tongue of households; 1980): Tagalog 29.7%; Cebuano 24.2%; Ilocano 10.3%; Hiligaynon Ilongo 9.2%; Bicol 5.6%; Samar-Leyte 4.0%; Pampango 2.8%; Pangasinan 1.8%; other 12.5%[3].
Religious affiliation (1980): Roman Catholic 84.1%; Aglipayan (Philippine Independent Church) 6.2%; Muslim 4.3%; Protestant 3.9%; other 1.5%.
Major cities (1990): Manila 1,876,194; Quezon City 1,587,140; Caloocan 615,726; Cebu 610,000; Makati 465,896.

Vital statistics

Birth rate per 1,000 population (1993): 30.0 (world avg. 26.4); (1982) legitimate 93.9%; illegitimate 6.1%.
Death rate per 1,000 population (1993): 7.0 (world avg. 9.2).
Natural increase rate per 1,000 population (1993): 23.0 (world avg. 17.2).
Total fertility rate (avg. births per childbearing woman; 1993): 3.9.
Marriage rate per 1,000 population (1990): 6.9.
Life expectancy at birth (1993): male 63.0 years; female 67.0 years.
Major causes of death per 100,000 population (1989): pneumonia 77.0; heart diseases 74.6; vascular diseases 56.1; tuberculosis 43.8; malignant neoplasms (cancers) 36.5; accidents 19.6; diarrhea 13.5; measles 11.2.

National economy

Budget (1991). Revenue: ₱ 206,381,000,000 (taxes on goods and services 37.2%; income taxes 26.5%; customs duties 25.4%; nontax revenues 10.6%). Expenditures: ₱ 254,384,000,000 (debt service 29.7%; education 15.5%; power, water, transport, and communications 10.5%; defense 10.2%; general public services 10.2%; agriculture 8.5%; health 4.0%).
Tourism (1991): receipts from visitors U.S.$1,281,000,000; expenditures by nationals abroad U.S.$61,000,000.
Production (metric tons except as noted). Agriculture, forestry, fishing (1992): sugarcane 27,300,000, rice 9,185,000, coconuts 8,465,000, corn (maize) 4,570,000, bananas 3,900,000, centrifugal sugar 2,081,000, copra 1,670,000, cassava 1,320,000, pineapples 1,170,000, sweet potatoes 670,000; livestock (number of live animals) 8,032,000 pigs, 2,569,000 buffalo, 2,449,000 goats, 1,656,000 cattle, 63,000,000 chickens; roundwood (1991) 38,738,000 cu m; fish catch (1991) 2,311,797. Mining and quarrying (value in ₱ '000,000; 1991): gold 7,924; copper concentrate 7,543; sand and gravel 2,257; salt 2,178; coal 1,378; nickel ore 660. Manufacturing (gross value added in ₱ '000,000; 1991): food products 125,188; petroleum and coal products 35,991; industrial chemicals 25,133; footwear and wearing apparel 20,506; beverages 14,696; electrical machinery 12,106; textiles 10,384. Construction (authorized; 1989): residential 5,212,000 sq m; nonresidential 4,264,000 sq m. Energy production (consumption): electricity (kW-hr; 1991) 22,484,000,000 (22,484,000,000); coal (metric tons; 1991) 1,265,000 (2,577,000); crude petroleum (barrels; 1991) 1,202,000 (80,142,000); petroleum products (metric tons; 1991) 9,491,000 (10,903,000).
Public debt (external, outstanding; 1991): U.S.$24,530,000,000.

Gross national product (1992): U.S.$49,344,000,000 (U.S.$770 per capita).

Structure of gross domestic product and labour force

	1991			
	in value ₱ '000,000	% of total value	labour force	% of labour force
Agriculture	261,700	21.1	10,403,000	41.2
Mining	17,500	1.4	150,000	0.6
Manufacturing	316,200	25.5	2,391,000	9.5
Construction	62,100	5.0	1,046,000	4.1
Public utilities	30,600	2.5	99,000	0.4
Transp. and commun.	73,900	6.0	1,143,000	4.5
Trade	171,700	13.9	3,172,000	12.6
Finance	48,500	3.9	451,000	1.8
Services } Other	256,400	20.7	4,116,000	16.3
			2,276,000[5]	9.0[5]
TOTAL	1,238,700[3]	100.0	25,246,000[3]	100.0

Population economically active (1991): total 25,246,000; activity rate 40.2% (participation rates: ages 15–64, 64.5%; female 36.3%; unemployed 9.0%).

Price index (1985 = 100)

	1986	1987	1988	1989	1990	1991	1992
Consumer price index	100.8	104.6	113.7	127.6	145.7	172.9	188.3

Household income and expenditure (1990). Average household size 5.3; income per family ₱ 79,091 (U.S.$3,253); sources of income: wages and self-employment 96.8%, pensions, social security, and related benefits 3.2%; expenditure: food, beverages, and tobacco 59.4%, household furnishings and operations 13.0%, transportation 4.5%, fuel and power 3.9%, clothing 3.6%.
Land use (1991): forested 34.0%; meadows and pastures 4.3%; agricultural and under permanent cultivation 26.8%; other 34.9%.

Foreign trade[6]

Balance of trade (current prices)

	1987	1988	1989	1990	1991	1992
₱ '000,000	−22,368	−24,023	−57,713	−86,604	−89,465	−121,250
% of total	8.8%	7.5%	14.6%	17.0%	15.6%	19.6%

Imports (1991): U.S.$12,857,000,000 (machinery and transport equipment 25.2%, mineral fuels and lubricants 14.9%, basic manufactures 14.3%, chemicals 11.2%, food and live animals 6.9%, inedible crude materials 5.2%). *Major import sources:* United States 20.1%; Japan 19.5%; Taiwan 6.8%; Canada 6.8%; Saudi Arabia 5.3%; South Korea 5.1%; Hong Kong 4.9%; Germany 3.9%; Singapore 3.8%; Australia 3.2%.
Exports (1991): U.S.$8,839,000,000 (food and live animals 13.9%, machinery and transport equipment 13.9%, basic manufactures 8.0%, inedible crude materials 5.5%, animal and vegetable oils and fats 3.5%, chemicals 3.4%). *Major export destinations:* United States 34.7%; Japan 19.9%; Germany 5.7%; Hong Kong 4.4%; United Kingdom 4.2%; The Netherlands 3.8%; Singapore 2.6%; South Korea 2.6%; Thailand 2.5%.

Transport and communications

Transport. Railroads (1991): route length 658 mi, 1,059 km; passenger-mi 113,200,000, passenger-km 182,100,000; short ton-mi cargo 6,400,000, metric ton-km cargo 9,400,000. Roads (1991): total length 99,813 mi, 160,633 km (paved 14%). Vehicles (1991): passenger cars 456,606; trucks and buses 848,633. Merchant marine (1992): vessels (100 gross tons and over) 1,499; total deadweight tonnage 13,807,113. Air transport[7] (1992): passenger-mi 8,010,000,000, passenger-km 12,891,000,000; short ton-mi cargo 213,667,000, metric ton-km cargo 311,948,000; airports (1993) with scheduled flights 21.
Communications. Daily newspapers (1990): total number (1988) 47; circulation 3,400,000; circulation per 1,000 population 54. Radio (1992): 4,000,000 receivers (1 per 15.9 persons). Television (1992): 7,000,000 receivers (1 per 9.1 persons). Telephones (1991): 1,097,390 (1 per 57 persons).

Education and health

Education (1990–91)

	schools	teachers	students	student/teacher ratio
Primary (age 7–12)	34,081	311,013	10,427,077	33.5
Secondary (age 13–16)	5,550	122,688	4,033,597	32.9
Voc., teacher tr.	1,262	13,265	361,736	27.3
Higher	809	56,880	1,347,750	23.7

Educational attainment (1980). Percentage of population age 25 and over having: no grade completed 11.7%; elementary education 53.8%; secondary 18.8%; college 15.2%; not stated 0.5%. *Literacy* (1980): total population age 15 and over literate 25,139,700 (88.7%); males literate 12,772,200 (89.9%); females literate 12,367,500 (87.5%).
Health (1989): physicians 57,270 (1 per 1,062 persons); hospital beds 89,280 (1 per 683 persons); infant mortality rate per 1,000 live births (1993) 40.
Food (1988–90): daily per capita caloric intake 2,341 (vegetable products 89%, animal products 11%); 104% of FAO recommended minimum requirement.

Military

Total active duty personnel (1992): 106,500 (army 63.8%, navy 21.6%, air force 14.6%). *Military expenditure as percentage of GNP* (1989): 2.2% (world 4.9%); per capita expenditure U.S.$16.

[1]Excludes 50 nonelective seats allotted to sectoral interests, of which only a small number have been filled. [2]Preliminary results. [3]Detail does not add to total given because of rounding. [4]Manufacturing establishments with 10 or more workers. [5]Mostly unemployed. [6]Import figures are f.o.b. in balance of trade and c.i.f. for commodities and trading partners. [7]Philippines Airlines only.

Poland

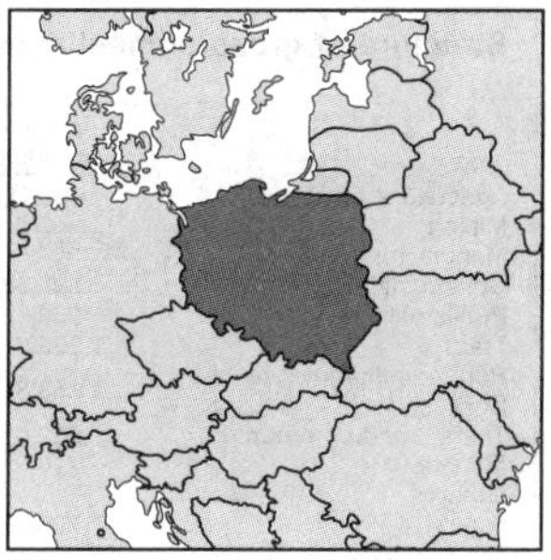

Official name: Rzeczpospolita Polska (Republic of Poland).
Form of government: unitary multiparty republic with two legislative houses (Senate [100]; Diet [460]).
Chief of state: President.
Head of government: Prime Minister.
Capital: Warsaw.
Official language: Polish.
Official religion: none.
Monetary unit: 1 złoty (Zł) = 100 groszy; valuation (Oct. 4, 1993) 1 U.S.$ = Zł 19,657; 1 £ = Zł 29,780.

Area and population

		area		population
Provinces	Capitals	sq mi	sq km	1992[1] estimate
Biała Podlaska	Biała Podlaska	2,065	5,348	306,200
Białystok	Białystok	3,882	10,055	695,200
Bielsko-Biała	Bielsko-Biała	1,430	3,704	906,700
Bydgoszcz	Bydgoszcz	3,996	10,349	1,116,000
Chełm	Chełm	1,493	3,866	248,100
Ciechanów	Ciechanów	2,456	6,362	429,800
Częstochowa	Częstochowa	2,387	6,182	777,000
Elbląg	Elbląg	2,356	6,103	481,000
Gdańsk	Gdańsk	2,855	7,394	1,438,900
Gorzów	Gorzów Wielkopolski	3,276	8,484	502,800
Jelenia Góra	Jelenia Góra	1,690	4,378	518,600
Kalisz	Kalisz	2,514	6,512	713,500
Katowice	Katowice	2,568	6,650	4,006,600
Kielce	Kielce	3,556	9,211	1,127,300
Konin	Konin	1,984	5,139	470,700
Koszalin	Koszalin	3,270	8,470	511,100
Kraków	Kraków	1,256	3,254	1,234,500
Krosno	Krosno	2,202	5,702	497,900
Legnica	Legnica	1,559	4,037	518,500
Leszno	Leszno	1,604	4,154	389,400
Łódź	Łódź	588	1,523	1,136,600
Łomża	Łomża	2,581	6,684	348,200
Lublin	Lublin	2,622	6,792	1,019,600
Nowy Sącz	Nowy Sącz	2,153	5,576	703,300
Olsztyn	Olsztyn	4,759	12,327	757,200
Opole	Opole	3,295	8,535	1,021,200
Ostrołęka	Ostrołęka	2,509	6,498	398,800
Piła	Piła	3,168	8,205	483,500
Piotrków	Piotrków Trybunalski	2,419	6,266	643,000
Płock	Płock	1,976	5,117	517,800
Poznań	Poznań	3,147	8,151	1,339,400
Przemyśl	Przemyśl	1,713	4,437	408,300
Radom	Radom	2,816	7,294	753,200
Rzeszów	Rzeszów	1,698	4,397	728,800
Siedlce	Siedlce	3,281	8,499	653,600
Sieradz	Sieradz	1,880	4,869	408,600
Skierniewice	Skierniewice	1,529	3,960	420,700
Słupsk	Słupsk	2,878	7,453	416,800
Suwałki	Suwałki	4,050	10,490	474,100
Szczecin	Szczecin	3,854	9,981	975,900
Tarnobrzeg	Tarnobrzeg	2,426	6,283	601,700
Tarnów	Tarnów	1,603	4,151	674,600
Toruń	Toruń	2,065	5,348	660,600
Wałbrzych	Wałbrzych	1,609	4,168	740,500
Warszawa	Warszawa	1,463	3,788	2,419,600
Włocławek	Włocławek	1,700	4,402	430,100
Wrocław	Wrocław	2,427	6,287	1,130,700
Zamość	Zamość	2,695	6,980	490,500
Zielona Góra	Zielona Góra	3,424	8,868	662,500
TOTAL		120,727	312,683	38,309,200

Demography

Population (1993): 38,521,000.
Density (1993): persons per sq mi 319.1, persons per sq km 123.2.
Urban-rural (1993): urban 62.1%; rural 37.9%.
Sex distribution (1992): male 48.83%; female 51.17%.
Age breakdown (1991): under 15, 24.6%; 15–29, 21.1%; 30–44, 24.3%; 45–59, 14.8%; 60–74, 11.3%; 75 and over, 3.9%.
Population projection: (2000) 39,547,000; (2010) 41,089,000.
Ethnic composition (1990): Polish 98.7%; Ukrainian 0.6%; other 0.7%.
Religious affiliation (1992): Roman Catholic 93.5%; Orthodox 1.5%.
Major cities (1992): Warsaw 1,653,300; Łódź 844,900; Kraków 751,300.

Vital statistics

Birth rate per 1,000 population (1992): 13.4 (world avg. 26.4); (1985) legitimate 95.0%; illegitimate 5.0%.
Death rate per 1,000 population (1992): 10.3 (world avg. 9.2).
Natural increase rate per 1,000 population (1992): 3.1 (world avg. 17.2).
Total fertility rate (avg. births per childbearing woman; 1991): 2.1.
Marriage rate per 1,000 population (1992): 5.7.
Divorce rate per 1,000 population (1992): 0.8.
Life expectancy at birth (1991): male 66.1 years; female 75.3 years.
Major causes of death per 100,000 population (1991): diseases of the circulatory system 542.5; malignant neoplasms (cancers) 193.4.

National economy

Budget (1992). Revenue: Zł 312,800,000,000,000 (1991; turnover tax 29.0%, income tax 25.5%). Expenditures: Zł 381,900,000,000,000 (1991; social benefits and programs 20.5%, interest on debts 18.9%).
Public debt (external, outstanding; 1991): U.S.$44,057,000,000.
Tourism (1990): receipts U.S.$266,000,000; expenditures U.S.$220,000,000.
Gross national product (1992): U.S.$75,193,000,000 (U.S.$1,960 per capita).

Structure of gross domestic product and labour force

	1991			
	in value Zł '000,000,000	% of total value	labour force	% of labour force
Agriculture	56,495.2	6.9	4,961,200	30.1
Mining and manufacturing	331,358.5	40.2	4,403,500	26.7
Public utilities	18,928.9	2.3	...	...
Construction	84,349.4	10.2	1,090,900	6.6
Transp. and commun.	46,167.3	5.6	895,500	5.4
Trade	107,713.7	13.1	1,459,000	8.9
Finance }	162,559.7	19.7	...	...
Public administration }			...	...
Services }			424,900	2.6
Other	16,757.2[2]	2.0[2]	3,241,500	19.7
TOTAL	824,329.9	100.0	16,476,500	100.0

Production (metric tons except as noted). Agriculture (value added in Zł '000,000; 1992): potatoes 23,400,000, sugar beets 11,100,000, wheat 7,400,000, rye 4,000,000; livestock (number of live animals; 1992) 22,100,000 pigs, 8,200,000 cattle; roundwood (1991) 17,182,000 cu m; fish catch (1991) 457,389. Mining and quarrying (1991): electrolytic copper 378,000; zinc 126,000; lead 50,800; aluminum 45,800. Manufacturing (value of production in Zł '000,000,000; 1991): machinery and transport equipment 5,909.0; chemicals 1,731.3; food 964.2. Construction (1991): 86,433 units, of which residential 44,519. Energy production (consumption): electricity ('000,000 kW-hr; 1990) 136,337 (135,297); coal ('000 metric tons; 1990) 215,000 (188,800); crude petroleum (barrels; 1990) 1,187,000 (94,457,000); petroleum products ('000 metric tons; 1990) 10,183 (11,863); natural gas ('000,000 cu m; 1990) 2,508 (9,546).
Population economically active (1992): total 17,529,000; activity rate of total population 45.6% (participation rates: ages 18–64 [male], 18–59 [female] 79.5%; female [18–59] 48.2%; unemployed 13.7%).

Price and earnings indexes (1985 = 100)

	1986	1987	1988	1989	1990	1991	1992
Consumer price index	117.7	147.4	236.1	828.9	5,684.3	9,680.2	13,812.9
Monthly earnings index	121.1	147.0	270.4	1,035.7	4,817.7	7,696.9	...

Household income and expenditure. Avg. household size (1991) 3.6; avg. annual income (1991) Zł 40,521,000 (U.S.$3,830); sources of income: wages 34.0%, transfer payments 20.7%, self-employment 4.3%, other 41.0%; expenditure (1991): food 47.9%, clothing 9.5%, recreation 7.1%, housing 9.9%.
Land use (1992): forest 28.0%; meadow 12.9%; agric. 46.8%; other 12.3%.

Foreign trade

Balance of trade (current prices)

	1987	1988	1989	1990	1991	1992
Zł '000,000,000	+361	+740	+4,612	+51,935	−6,543	+69,791
% of total	5.9%	6.6%	13.4%	25.1%	2.0%	18.6%

Imports (1992): Zł 164,259,300,000,000 (1991; machinery and transport equipment 37.6%, fuel and power 18.8%, chemicals 12.6%, food 10.4%, consumer goods 6.1%). *Major import sources* (1991): Germany 26.5%; U.S.S.R. 14.1%; Austria 6.3%; The Netherlands 4.9%; Italy 4.5%.
Exports (1992): Zł 157,715,900,000,000 (1991; machinery and transport equipment 22.4%, iron and steel products 15.9%, chemicals 11.6%, fuel and power 10.7%, food 10.0%, light-industrial products 6.1%). *Major export destinations* (1991): Germany 29.4%; U.S.S.R. 11.0%; U.K. 7.1%; The Netherlands 5.2%; Czechoslovakia 4.6%; Austria 4.5%.

Transport and communications

Transport. Railroads (1991): length 25,848 km; passenger-km 40,115,000,000; metric ton-km cargo 65,146,000,000. Roads (1991): total length 363,116 km (paved 62%). Vehicles (1991): passenger cars 5,261,000; trucks and buses 1,137,000. Merchant marine (1992): vessels (100 gross tons and over) 644; total deadweight tonnage 4,314,308. Air transport (1991): passenger-km 3,589,000,000; metric ton-km cargo 45,000,000; airports (1993) 12.
Communications. Daily newspapers (1991): 68; circulation 5,258,000; circulation per 1,000 population 136. Radio (1991): 10,400,000 (1 per 3.7 persons). Television (1991): 10,000,000 (1 per 3.8 persons). Telephones (1992): 5,480,000 (1 per 7.0 persons).

Education and health

Education (1991–92)

	schools	teachers	students	student/ teacher ratio
Primary (age 7–14)	18,578	321,500	5,302,700	16.5
Secondary (age 15–18)	1,565	26,600	548,800	20.6
Voc., teacher tr.	8,826	89,500	1,728,000	19.3
Higher	117	63,200	423,500	6.7

Educational attainment (1988). Percentage of population age 15 and over having: no formal schooling or less than full primary education 6.4%; primary 38.8%; secondary 48.3%; higher 6.5%. *Literacy* (1988): 98.7%.
Health (1992): physicians 82,925 (1 per 464 persons); hospital beds 326,361 (1 per 118 persons); infant mortality rate per 1,000 live births 14.2.
Food (1988–90): daily per capita caloric intake 3,426 (vegetable products 66%, animal products 34%); 131% of FAO recommended minimum.

Military

Total active duty personnel (1992): 296,500 (army 65.5%, navy 6.5%, air force 28.0%). *Military expenditure as percentage of GNP* (1989): 8.9% (world 4.9%); per capita expenditure U.S.$408.

[1]January 1. [2]Other material activities.

Portugal

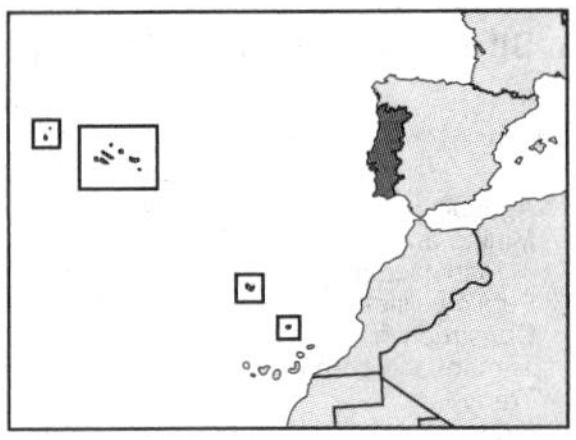

Official name: República Portuguesa (Portuguese Republic).
Form of government: parliamentary state with one legislative house (Assembly of the Republic [230]).
Chief of state: President.
Head of government: Prime Minister.
Capital: Lisbon.
Official language: Portuguese.
Official religion: none.
Monetary unit: 1 escudo (Esc) = 100 centavos; valuation (Oct. 4, 1993) 1 U.S.$ = Esc 167.26; 1 £ = Esc 253.40.

Area and population

Continental Portugal Districts	Capitals	area sq mi	area sq km	population 1991 census
Aveiro	Aveiro	1,084	2,808	656,000
Beja	Beja	3,948	10,225	167,900
Braga	Braga	1,032	2,673	746,100
Bragança	Bragança	2,551	6,608	158,300
Castelo Branco	Castelo Branco	2,577	6,675	214,700
Çoimbra	Çoimbra	1,524	3,947	427,600
Évora	Évora	2,854	7,393	173,500
Faro	Faro	1,915	4,960	340,100
Guarda	Guarda	2,131	5,518	187,800
Leiria	Leiria	1,357	3,515	427,800
Lisboa	Lisbon (Lisboa)	1,066	2,761	2,063,800
Portalegre	Portalegre	2,342	6,065	134,300
Porto	Porto	925	2,395	1,622,300
Santarém	Santarém	2,605	6,747	442,700
Setúbal	Setúbal	1,955	5,064	713,700
Viana do Castelo	Viana do Castelo	871	2,255	248,700
Vila Real	Vila Real	1,671	4,328	237,100
Viseu	Viseu	1,933	5,007	401,000
Azores (Açores) Autonomous Region[1]	Ponta Delgada	868	2,247	236,700
Madeira Autonomous Region	Funchal	306	794	253,000
TOTAL		35,672[2]	92,389[2]	9,853,000[3]

Demography

Population (1993): 9,823,000.
Density (1993): persons per sq mi 275.4, persons per sq km 106.3.
Urban-rural (1990): urban 33.6%; rural 66.4%.
Sex distribution (1992[4]): male 48.26%; female 51.74%.
Age breakdown (1987): under 15, 22.7%; 15–29, 24.6%; 30–44, 18.8%; 45–59, 16.5%; 60–74, 12.6%; 75 and over, 4.8%.
Population projection: (2000) 9,735,000; (2010) 9,610,000.
Nationality (1989): Portuguese 99.0%; Cape Verdean 0.3%; Brazilian 0.1%; Spanish 0.1%; British 0.1%; American 0.1%; other 0.3%.
Religious affiliation (1981): Christian 96.0%, of which Roman Catholic 94.5%, Protestant 0.6%, other Christian (mostly Apostolic Catholic and Jehovah's Witness) 0.9%; nonreligious 3.8%; Jewish 0.1%; Muslim 0.1%.
Major cities (1988[4]): Lisbon 830,500; Porto 350,000; Amadora 95,518.

Vital statistics

Birth rate per 1,000 population (1992): 12.0 (world avg. 26.4); (1990) legitimate 85.5%; illegitimate 14.5%.
Death rate per 1,000 population (1992): 13.5 (world avg. 9.2).
Natural increase rate per 1,000 population (1992): −1.5 (world avg. 17.2).
Total fertility rate (avg. births per childbearing woman; 1990–95): 1.5.
Marriage rate per 1,000 population (1990): 7.3.
Divorce rate per 1,000 population (1990): 0.9.
Life expectancy at birth (1990–95): male 71.1 years; female 78.1 years.
Major causes of death per 100,000 population (1991): circulatory diseases 470.9, of which cerebrovascular diseases 254.3, ischemic heart disease 96.7; malignant neoplasms (cancers) 185.0; respiratory diseases 72.8.

National economy

Budget (1992). Revenue: Esc 3,132,600,000,000 (indirect taxes 55.1%, direct taxes 37.2%). Expenditures: Esc 3,362,900,000,000 (1988; education 12.4%, health 9.8%, defense 6.6%, administration 5.3%, public works 2.8%).
Public debt (1992): U.S.$39,922,000,000.
Tourism (1991): receipts from visitors U.S.$3,700,000,000; expenditures by nationals abroad U.S.$1,027,000,000.
Production (metric tons except as noted). Agriculture, forestry, fishing (1992): grapes 1,450,000, potatoes 1,293,000, tomatoes 700,000, corn (maize) 616,000, wheat 301,000, olives 221,000, cork 180,000[5], rice 155,000, oats 45,000; livestock (number of live animals) 5,847,000 sheep, 2,580,000 pigs, 1,370,000 cattle; roundwood (1991) 11,181,000 cu m; fish catch (1991) 325,349. Mining and quarrying (1992): copper pyrites 608,616; kaolin 95,900; zinc 22,154; tungsten 1,864. Manufacturing (value of production in Esc '000,000; 1989): cotton and synthetic fibres 222,717; refined petroleum 148,274; clothing 138,659; motor vehicles 113,924; knitted fabrics 105,339; dairy products 90,282; iron and steel 70,919; cement 57,720; alcoholic beverages 47,489. Construction (1990): residential 4,197,912 sq m; nonresidential 2,045,167 sq m. Energy production (consumption): electricity (kW-hr; 1991) 28,871,000,000 (29,963,000,000); coal (metric tons; 1991) 270,000 (4,381,000); crude petroleum (barrels; 1991) none (70,229,000); petroleum products (metric tons; 1991) 8,769,000 (9,834,000); natural gas, none (n.a.).
Gross national product (1992): U.S.$75,565,000,000 (U.S.$7,670 per capita).

Structure of gross domestic product and labour force

	1990 in value Esc '000,000	1990 % of total value	1992 labour force	1992 % of labour force
Agriculture	490,787	6.3	530,600	11.3
Mining } Manufacturing	2,275,815	29.2	22,900 1,126,100	0.5 23.8
Construction	585,382	7.5	386,000	8.1
Public utilities	250,629	3.2	34,900	0.7
Trade	1,352,031	17.4	935,600	19.8
Pub. admin., defense } Services	1,653,845	21.2	1,290,900	27.2
Transp. and commun.	462,412	5.9	224,800	4.7
Finance	720,037	9.2	143,100	3.0
Other	...	...	42,400[6]	0.9[6]
TOTAL	7,790,937[3]	100.0[3]	4,737,200[3]	100.0

Population economically active (1992): total 4,737,200; activity rate of total population 48.2% (participation rates: ages 15–64, 68.2%; female 44.3%; unemployed 4.1%).

Price and earnings indexes (1985 = 100)

	1986	1987	1988	1989	1990	1991	1992
Consumer price index	111.8	122.2	133.9	150.8	170.9	190.3	207.3
Daily earnings index	117.4	133.5	152.5	176.4	184.4	209.5	...

Household income and expenditure. Average household size (1981) 3.8; income per household: n.a.; sources of income (1992): wages and salaries 41.1%, property and entrepreneurial income 37.0%, transfer payments 21.9%; expenditure (1986): food 34.7%, transportation and communications 15.4%, clothing and footwear 10.3%, cafes and hotels 9.7%, housing 5.0%, health 4.5%, recreation 4.3%, other 16.1%.
Land use (1991): forested 32.3%; meadows and pastures 9.1%; agricultural and under permanent cultivation 34.5%; other 24.1%.

Foreign trade

Balance of trade (current prices)

	1987	1988	1989	1990	1991	1992
Esc '000,000	−457,800	−580,000	−705,000	−918,600	−1,067,800	−1,144.6
% of total	15.2%	16.0%	15.2%	16.4%	18.5%	18.8%

Imports (1992): Esc 4,048,797,000,000 (machinery and transport equipment 35.6%, of which road vehicles and parts 23.3%; chemicals and chemical products 8.9%; textiles 6.4%; office machines 2.1%). *Major import sources:* Spain 16.6%; Germany 15.0%; France 12.8%; Italy 10.2%; U.K. 7.2%; The Netherlands 6.9%.
Exports (1992): Esc 2,453,041,000,000 (textiles and wearing apparel 29.4%; machinery and transport equipment 19.9%, of which electrical equipment 5.6%; footwear 8.8%; cork and wood products 4.4%; chemicals and chemical products 4.2%). *Major export destinations:* Germany 19.2%; Spain 14.7%; France 14.2%; U.K. 10.1%.

Transport and communications

Transport. Railroads (1991): route length 2,066 mi, 3,325 km; passenger-km 5,693,000,000; metric ton-km cargo 1,783,000,000. Roads (1989): total length 43,605 mi, 70,176 km (paved 86%). Vehicles (1990): passenger cars 3,208,286; trucks and buses 189,822[7]. Merchant marine (1992): vessels (100 gross tons and over) 332; total deadweight tonnage 1,129,382. Air transport (1991): passenger-km 7,024,948,000; metric ton-km cargo 162,740,000; airports (1993) 13.
Communications. Daily newspapers (1991): total number 30; total circulation 525,000[8]; circulation per 1,000 population 50[8]. Radio (1992): 2,475,000 receivers (1 per 4.0 persons). Television (1992): 1,789,703 receivers (1 per 5.5 persons). Telephones (1991): 3,565,300 (1 per 2.8 persons).

Education and health

Education (1992–93)

	schools	teachers	students	student/ teacher ratio
Primary (age 5–11)	11,771	71,788	925,936	12.9
Secondary (age 12–19)	1,368	64,479[9]	815,491	...
Vocational	220	[9]	84,932	...
Higher[10]	250	30,998	214,403	6.9

Educational attainment (1981). Percentage of population age 25 and over having: no formal schooling 4.4%; primary education 76.2%; secondary 19.0%; postsecondary 0.1%; higher 0.3%. *Literacy* (1990): total population age 15 and over literate 6,769,270 (86.8%); males literate 3,208,634 (86.7%); females literate 3,560,636 (86.9%).
Health (1991): physicians 28,310 (1 per 348 persons); hospital beds 44,585 (1 per 221 persons); infant mortality rate per 1,000 live births (1991) 10.8.
Food (1988–90): daily per capita caloric intake 3,342 (vegetable products 76%, animal products 24%); 136% of FAO recommended minimum requirement.

Military

Total active duty personnel (1993): 50,700 (army 53.7%, navy 24.6%, air force 21.7%). *Military expenditure as percentage of GNP* (1989): 3.3% (world 4.9%); per capita expenditure U.S.$141.

[1]Comprises three districts not shown separately. [2]Includes 156 sq mi (404 sq km) of inland water. [3]Detail does not add to total given because of rounding. [4]January 1. [5]1991. [6]Newly unemployed only. [7]1987. [8]For 24 newspapers only. [9]Secondary includes Vocational. [10]Includes teacher colleges.

Puerto Rico

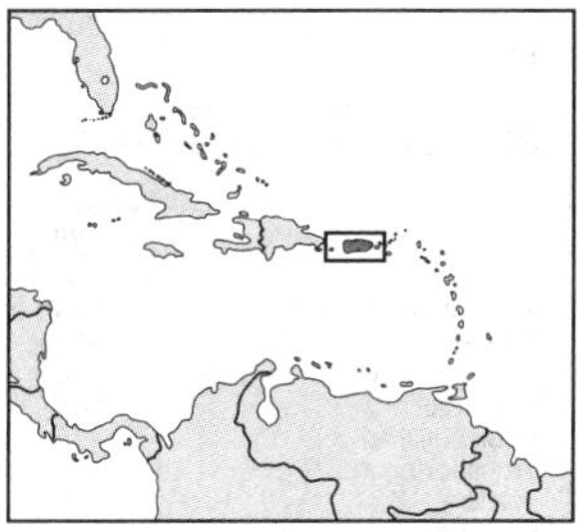

Official name: Estado Libre Asociado de Puerto Rico; Commonwealth of Puerto Rico.
Political status: self-governing commonwealth in association with the United States, having two legislative houses (Senate [29[1]]; House of Representatives [53][1]).
Chief of state: President of the United States.
Head of government: Governor.
Capital: San Juan.
Official languages: Spanish; English.
Official religion: none.
Monetary unit: 1 U.S. dollar (U.S.$) = 100 cents; valuation (Oct. 4, 1993) 1 £ = U.S.$1.52.

Population (1990 census)

Municipio	population	Municipio	population	Municipio	population
Adjuntas	19,451	Fajardo	36,882	Naguabo	22,620
Aguada	35,911	Florida	8,689	Naranjito	27,914
Aguadilla	59,335	Guánica	19,984	Orocovis	21,158
Agunas Buenas	25,424	Guayama	41,588	Patillas	19,633
Aibonito	24,971	Guayanilla	21,581	Peñuelas	22,515
Añasco	25,234	Guaynabo	92,886	Ponce	187,749
Arecibo	93,385	Gurabo	28,737	Quebradillas	21,425
Arroyo	18,910	Hatillo	32,703	Rincón	12,213
Barceloneta	20,947	Hormigueros	15,212	Río Grande	45,648
Barranquitas	25,605	Humacao	55,203	Sabana Grande	22,843
Bayamón	220,262	Isabela	39,147	Salinas	28,335
Cabo Rojo	38,521	Jayuya	15,527	San Germán	34,962
Caguas	133,447	Juana Díaz	45,198	San Juan	437,745
Camuy	28,917	Juncos	30,612	San Lorenzo	35,163
Canóvanas	36,816	Lajas	23,271	San Sebastián	38,799
Carolina	177,806	Lares	29,015	Santa Isabel	19,318
Cataño	34,587	Las Marías	9,306	Toa Alta	44,101
Cayey	46,553	Las Piedras	27,896	Toa Baja	89,454
Ceiba	17,145	Loíza	29,307	Trujillo Alto	61,120
Ciales	18,084	Luquillo	18,100	Utuado	34,980
Cidra	35,601	Manatí	38,692	Vega Alta	34,559
Coamo	33,837	Maricao	6,206	Vega Baja	55,997
Comerío	20,265	Maunabo	12,347	Vieques	8,602
Corozal	33,095	Mayagüez	100,371	Villalba	23,559
Culebra	1,542	Moca	32,926	Yabucoa	36,483
Dorado	30,759	Morovis	25,288	Yauco	42,058
				TOTAL	3,522,037

Demography

Area: 3,515 sq mi, 9,104 sq km.
Population (1993): 3,612,000.
Density (1993): persons per sq mi 1,027.5, persons per sq km 396.7.
Urban-rural (1990): urban 71.2%; rural 28.8%.
Sex distribution (1990): male 48.43%; female 51.57%.
Age breakdown (1990): under 15, 27.2%; 15–29, 25.1%; 30–44, 20.4%; 45–59, 14.1%; 60–74, 9.2%; 75 and over, 4.0%.
Population projection: (2000) 3,832,000; (2010) 4,169,000.
Doubling time: 61 years.
Ethnic composition (1980): white 80.0%; black 20.0%.
Religious affiliation (1984): Roman Catholic 85.3%; Protestant 4.7%; other 10.0%.
Major cities (1990): San Juan 426,832; Ponce 159,151; Caguas 92,429; Mayagüez 83,010; Arecibo 49,545.

Vital statistics

Birth rate per 1,000 population (1991): 18.2 (world avg. 26.4); (1990) legitimate 63.2%; illegitimate 36.8%.
Death rate per 1,000 population (1991): 7.4 (world avg. 9.2).
Natural increase rate per 1,000 population (1991): 10.8 (world avg. 17.2).
Total fertility rate (avg. births per childbearing woman; 1991): 2.2.
Marriage rate per 1,000 population (1990): 9.4.
Divorce rate per 1,000 population (1990): 3.9.
Life expectancy at birth (1988–90): male 70.2 years; female 78.5 years.
Major causes of death per 100,000 population (1990): heart disease 169.7; malignant neoplasms (cancers) 116.4; diabetes mellitus 47.5; cerebrovascular disease 34.0; pneumonia 33.7.

National economy

Budget (1992). Revenue: U.S.$5,857,000,000 (income taxes 36.2%, excise taxes 15.4%, service charges 5.5%, property taxes 1.1%, other receipts 41.8%). Expenditures: U.S.$5,607,000,000 (education 30.3%, public safety and protection 11.4%, welfare 10.8%, health 10.7%, debt service 6.2%).
Public debt (outstanding; 1992): U.S.$13,840,200,000.
Tourism: receipts from visitors (1992) U.S.$1,511,300,000; expenditures by nationals abroad (1990) U.S.$647,000,000.
Production (in U.S.$'000,000 except as noted). Agriculture, forestry, fishing (gross farm income; 1992): milk 201.3, poultry 88.6, vegetables 87.5, coffee 64.2, pork 55.1, beef 48.7, fruit 40.8, eggs 24.3, sugar 15.4; livestock (number of live animals; 1991) 599,000 cattle, 209,000 pigs; roundwood, n.a.; fish catch (1990) 2,062 metric tons. Mining (value of production; 1989): stone 47. Manufacturing (value added in U.S.$'000,000; 1992): chemicals, pharmaceuticals, and allied products 6,554; machinery and metal products 2,598; food products 1,689; clothing 496; printing and publishing 153; stone, clay, and glass products 152. Construction (authorized; 1985): residential 1,798,000 sq m; nonresidential 41,000 sq m. Energy production (consumption): electricity (kW-hr; 1990) 15,328,000,000 (15,328,000,000); coal (metric tons; 1990) none (200,000); crude petroleum (barrels; 1990) none (45,808,000); petroleum products (metric tons; 1990) 5,210,000 (7,045,000); natural gas, none (none).
Gross national product (1992): U.S.$23,620,000,000 (U.S.$6,626 per capita).

Structure of gross domestic product and labour force

	1992			
	in value U.S.$'000,000	% of total value	labour force	% of labour force
Agriculture	461.5	1.4	34,000	2.9
Manufacturing	13,154.9	38.7	164,000	14.0
Mining }	788.7	2.3	...	...
Construction }			55,000	4.7
Public utilities }	2,840.7	8.4	16,000	1.4
Transp. and commun. }			38,000	3.3
Trade	5,008.2	14.7	193,000	16.5
Finance, real estate	4,458.0	13.1	32,000	2.7
Pub. admin., defense	3,737.8	11.0 }	443,000	37.9
Services	3,547.0	10.5 }		
Other	−27.7[2]	−0.1[2]	193,000[3]	16.5[3]
TOTAL	33,969.1[4]	100.0	1,170,000[4]	100.0[4]

Population economically active (1992): total 1,170,000; activity rate 32.7% (participation rates: ages 16–64, 46.1%; female 37.1%[5]; unemployed 16.5%).

Price and earnings indexes (1985 = 100)

	1986	1987	1988	1989	1990	1991	1992
Consumer price index	99.2	100.7	104.0	107.7	112.0	117.8	120.3
Hourly earnings index[6]	102.3	104.6	107.1	111.1	116.4	121.2	...

Household income and expenditure. Average family size (1990) 3.3; income per family (1992) U.S.$22,896; sources of income (1992): wages and salaries 53.7%, transfers 29.3%, self-employment 7.3%, rent 5.2%, other 4.5%; expenditure (1992): food and beverages 22.7%, housing and energy 13.1%, transportation 12.3%, household furnishings 11.7%, health care 11.6%, recreation 8.6%, clothing 8.4%, education 3.4%, other 8.2%.
Land use (1990): forested 20.0%; meadows and pastures 37.7%; agricultural and under permanent cultivation 14.3%; other 28.0%.

Foreign trade

Balance of trade (current prices)

	1987	1988	1989	1990	1991	1992
U.S.$'000,000	+1,354	+1,327	+2,312	+3,584	+5,419	+5,857
% of total	5.9%	5.3%	7.6%	10.2%	14.6%	16.2%

Imports (1992): U.S.$15,194,500,000 (chemicals [all forms] 22.3%; food 13.1%; electrical machinery 9.6%; petroleum and petroleum products 6.9%; nonelectrical machinery 6.6%; transport equipment 6.0%; wood, paper, and printed products 5.5%). *Major import sources* (1990): U.S. 68.7%; Venezuela 4.4%; Japan 3.2%; Dominican Republic 2.0%; The Bahamas 1.8%; U.K. 1.0%.
Exports (1992): U.S.$21,051,200,000 (chemicals and chemical products 43.5%; food 14.3%; computers 11.9%; electrical machinery 8.4%). *Major export destinations* (1990): U.S. 86.9%; Dominican Republic 2.0%; U.S. Virgin Islands 1.4%; U.K. 0.8%; The Netherlands 0.7%.

Transport and communications

Transport. Railroads (1988)[7]: length 59 mi, 96 km. Roads (1986): total length 5,810 mi, 9,351 km (paved 87%). Vehicles (1989–90): passenger cars 1,315,587; trucks 205,565. Merchant marine: n.a. Air transport (1990–91): passenger arrivals 4,245,137, passenger departures 4,262,164; cargo loaded and unloaded 222,172 metric tons[8]; airports (1993) with scheduled flights 8.
Communications. Daily newspapers (1992): total number 4; total circulation 473,000; circulation per 1,000 population 132. Radio (1992): 2,000,000 receivers (1 per 1.8 persons). Television (1992): 830,000 receivers (1 per 4.3 persons). Telephones (1990): 1,062,086 (1 per 3.3 persons).

Education and health

Education (1985–86)

	schools	teachers	students	student/ teacher ratio
Primary (age 5–12)	1,542	18,359	427,582	23.3
Secondary (age 13–18)	395	13,612	334,661	24.6
Voc., teacher tr.	52	...	149,191	...
Higher	45	9,045	156,818	17.3

Educational attainment (1990). Percentage of population age 25 and over having: primary education 26.8%; some secondary 23.5%; complete secondary 21.0%; higher 28.7%. *Literacy* (1990): total population age 18 and over literate 2,122,860 (89.7%); males literate 1,001,878 (89.6%); females literate 1,120,982 (89.7%).
Health (1988): physicians 9,422 (1 per 349 persons); hospital beds 13,609 (1 per 254 persons); infant mortality rate per 1,000 live births (1991) 13.0.
Food: daily per capita caloric intake, n.a.

Military

Total active duty personnel (1992): 3,518 U.S. personnel.

[1]Includes (1992; each house) two special at-large seats above usual legally mandated membership of body that were created under a constitutional provision to limit majority party's control of either house to two-thirds. [2]Statistical discrepancy. [3]Unemployed. [4]Detail does not add to total given because of rounding. [5]1990. [6]Manufacturing sector only. [7]Privately owned railway for sugarcane transport only. [8]Handled by the Luis Muñoz Marín International Airport only.

Qatar

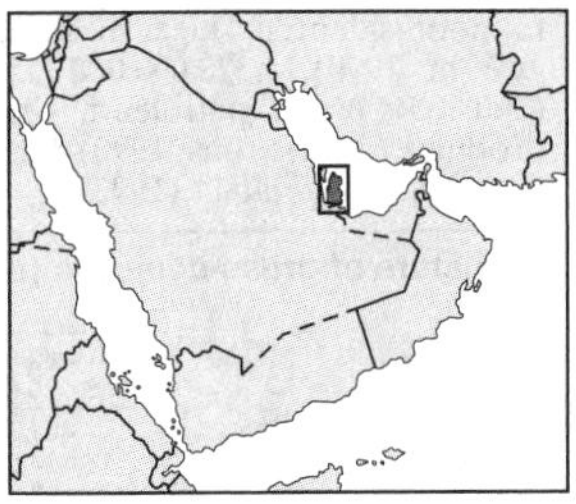

Official name: Dawlat Qaṭar (State of Qatar).
Form of government: monarchy (emirate)[1]; Islamic law is the basis of legislation in the state.
Head of state and government: Emir.
Capital: Doha.
Official language: Arabic.
Official religion: Islam.
Monetary unit: 1 riyal (QR) = 100 dirhams; valuation (Oct. 4, 1993) 1 U.S.$ = QR 3.61; 1 £ = QR 5.47.

Area and population		area		population
				1991[2]
Municipalities	Capitals	sq mi	sq km	estimate
ad-Dawḥah (Doha)	—	51	132	296,821
al-Ghuwayrīyah	al-Ghuwayrīyah	241	622	2,223
Jarayān al-Bāṭinah	Jarayān al-Bāṭinah	1,434	3,715	3,721
al-Jumaylīyah	al-Jumaylīyah	990	2,565	9,856
al-Khawr	al-Khawr	385	996	12,286
ar-Rayyān	ar-Rayyān	343	889	125,665
ash-Shamāl	Madinat ash-Shamāl	348	901	5,984
Umm Ṣalāl	Umm Ṣalāl Muḥammad	190	493	15,246
al-Wakrah	al-Wakrah	430	1,114	32,352
TOTAL		4,412	11,427	504,154

Demography

Population (1993): 521,000.
Density (1993): persons per sq mi 118.1, persons per sq km 45.6.
Urban-rural (1990): urban 89.5%; rural 10.5%.
Sex distribution (1986): male 67.15%; female 32.85%.
Age breakdown (1991): under 15, 27.8%; 15–29, 29.4%; 30–44, 32.3%; 45–59, 8.6%; 60–74, 1.5%; 75 and over, 0.4%.
Population projection: (2000) 659,000; (2010) 831,000.
Doubling time: 39 years.
Ethnic composition (1983): South Asian 34%; Qatari 20%; other Arab 25%; Iranian 16%; other 5%.
Religious affiliation (1980): Muslim (mostly Sunnī) 92.4%; Christian 5.9%; Hindu 1.1%; Bahāʾī 0.2%; other 0.4%.
Major cities (1987): Doha 236,131; ar-Rayyān 99,939; al-Wakrah 25,747; Umm Saʿīd 12,111.

Vital statistics

Birth rate per 1,000 population (1991): 19.4 (world avg. 26.4); legitimate, n.a.; illegitimate, n.a.
Death rate per 1,000 population (1991): 1.8 (world avg. 9.2).
Natural increase rate per 1,000 population (1991): 17.6 (world avg. 17.2).
Total fertility rate (avg. births per childbearing woman; 1990): 5.7.
Marriage rate per 1,000 population (1991): 3.0.
Divorce rate per 1,000 population (1991): 0.8.
Life expectancy at birth (1986): male 65.2 years; female 67.6 years.
Major causes of death per 100,000 population (1991): diseases of the circulatory system 56.9; injuries and poisoning 31.9; neoplasms (including benign neoplasms) 16.1; certain conditions originating in the perinatal period 11.3; diseases of the respiratory system 10.1; endocrine, metabolic, and nutritional diseases and immunity disorders 6.0; diseases of the digestive system 5.0; signs, symptoms, and ill-defined conditions 9.7.

National economy

Budget (1991–92). Revenue: QR 8,438,000,000 (1989–90; crude oil 85.0%). Expenditures: QR 11,706,000,000 (wages and salaries 36.8%; state capital development projects 17.9%, of which electricity and water 7.0%, housing and public buildings 6.7%, social and health services 1.9%, education 0.5%).
Production (metric tons except as noted). Agriculture, forestry, fishing (value of production in QR '000; 1991): forage 97,316, milk and dairy products 95,712, vegetables and other crops (except cereals) 77,271, beef 36,031, poultry meat 29,868, fruits and dates 23,629, eggs 14,257, cereals 2,713; livestock (number of live animals; 1991) 132,000 sheep, 80,000 goats, 23,000 camels, 10,000 cattle; roundwood, n.a.; fish catch (1991) 5,417. Mining and quarrying (1991): limestone 850,000; sulfur 53,000; gypsum, sand and gravel, and clay are also produced. Manufacturing (value added in QR '000; 1990): chemicals and petroleum products 2,442,119; paper and paper products 62,486; food, beverages, and tobacco 44,535; fabricated metal products and machinery 30,554; furniture and wood products 24,319; clothing and textiles 19,212. Construction (1986): residential 391,400 sq m; nonresidential 167,600 sq m. Energy production (consumption): electricity (kW-hr; 1991) 4,624,000,000 (4,624,000,000); coal, none (n.a.); crude petroleum (barrels; 1991) 137,970,000 (n.a.); petroleum products (metric tons; 1991) 2,359,000 (559,800); natural gas (cu m; 1991) 8,212,000,000 (5,853,000,000).
Tourism (1991): receipts and expenditures, n.a.; total number of tourists staying in hotels 142,652.
Population economically active (1988): total 292,568; activity rate of total population 53.7% (participation rates: ages 15–64, 80.8%; female 11.2%; unemployed [1986] 0.5%).

Price and earnings indexes (1985 = 100)	1985	1986	1987	1988	1989	1990	1991
Consumer price index	100.0	101.6	104.3	109.1	112.7	116.1	120.2
Earnings index	...	...	...	...	...	...	...

Gross national product (at current market prices; 1991): U.S.$6,968,000,000 (U.S.$15,870 per capita).

Structure of gross domestic product and labour force	1991		1988	
	in value QR '000,000	% of total value	labour force	% of labour force
Agriculture	215	0.9	4,544	1.6
Oil sector	8,250	34.0	7,657	2.6
Manufacturing	3,120	12.8	10,627	3.6
Construction	950	3.9	64,213	21.9
Public utilities	415	1.7	3,672	1.3
Transportation	697	2.9	11,877	4.1
Trade	1,528	6.3	34,246	11.7
Finance	2,610	10.7	6,172	2.1
Pub. admin., defense / Services / Other	6,504	26.8	149,560	51.1
TOTAL	24,289	100.0	292,568	100.0

Household income and expenditure. Average household size (1986) 6.4; income per household: n.a.; sources of income (1988): wages and salaries 80.8%, rents and royalties 10.6%, self-employment 5.6%, other 3.0%; expenditure (1988): housing 26.6%, food 24.5%, transportation 13.0%, recreation and personal effects 11.1%, clothing 9.1%, education 4.3%, energy and water 1.9%, health 1.0%.
Public debt (external, outstanding; 1989): U.S.$1,100,000,000.
Land use (1990): meadows and pastures 5.3%; agricultural and under permanent cultivation 0.5%; built-up, desert, and other 94.2%.

Foreign trade

Balance of trade (current prices)	1986	1987	1988	1989	1990	1991
QR '000,000	+2,730	+3,224	+2,253	+4,827	+7,992	+5,206
% of total	25.4%	28.7%	19.8%	33.9%	39.3%	31.2%

Imports (1991): QR 6,261,200,000 (machinery and transport equipment 42.4%; manufactured goods 19.0%; food and live animals 15.2%; chemicals and chemical products 6.2%; beverages and tobacco 1.2%). *Major import sources:* Japan 13.6%; United Kingdom 11.8%; United States 11.6%; Germany 8.5%; Italy 5.6%; France 5.2%; United Arab Emirates 4.3%; Saudi Arabia 4.1%; Australia 3.5%.
Exports (1991): QR 11,308,000,000 (crude petroleum, petroleum products, and liquefied gas 86.9%; non-oil exports 13.1%). *Major export destinations* (1989): Japan 54.4%; Thailand 5.0%; Singapore 4.0%; South Korea 3.6%; United Arab Emirates 3.4%; Italy 2.7%; India 2.7%; Saudi Arabia 2.5%.

Transport and communications

Transport. Railroads: none. Roads (1988): total length 671 mi, 1,080 km (paved 63%). Vehicles (1991): passenger cars 117,966; trucks and buses 55,234. Merchant marine (1992): vessels (100 gross tons and over) 65; total deadweight tonnage 635,580. Air transport (1991)[4]: passenger-mi 1,042,000,000, passenger-km 1,676,000,000; short ton-mi cargo 35,100,000, metric ton-km cargo 51,245,000; airports (1993) with scheduled flights 1.
Communications. Daily newspapers (1991): total number 4; total circulation 80,000[5]; circulation per 1,000 population 217[5]. Radio (1991): total number of receivers 250,000 (1 per 1.8 persons). Television (1990): total number of receivers 160,000 (1 per 2.8 persons). Telephones (1991): 145,736 (1 per 3.5 persons).

Education and health

Education (1990–91)[6]	schools	teachers	students	student/ teacher ratio
Primary (age 6–11)	155	2,843	53,050	18.7
Secondary (age 12–17)	34	1,015	9,669	9.5
Vocational	3	102	877	8.6
Higher[7]	1	561	6,548	11.7

Educational attainment (1986). Percentage of population age 25 and over having: no formal education 53.3%, of which illiterates 24.3%; primary 9.8%; preparatory (lower secondary) 10.1%; secondary 13.3%; postsecondary 13.3%; other 0.2%. *Literacy* (1986): total population age 15 and over literate 201,733 (75.7%); males literate 149,980 (76.8%); females literate 51,753 (72.5%).
Health (1991): physicians 764 (1 per 660 persons); hospital beds 1,098 (1 per 459 persons); infant mortality rate per 1,000 live births (1990) 31.0.
Food: daily per capita caloric intake, n.a.

Military

Total active duty personnel (1992): 7,500 (army 80.0%, navy 9.3%, air force 10.7%). *Military expenditure as percentage of GNP* (1985): 46.9% (world 5.7%); per capita expenditure U.S.$6,700.

[1]Provisional constitution of 1970 provided limited constitutional forms but has not been fully implemented. [2]Midyear estimate. [3]Unemployed. [4]One-fourth apportionment of international flights of Gulf Air. [5]1990. [6]Public schools only; available detail for private schools (1990–91) included 13,805 primary students, 1,280 secondary students, and 1,124 teachers. [7]1991–92.

Réunion

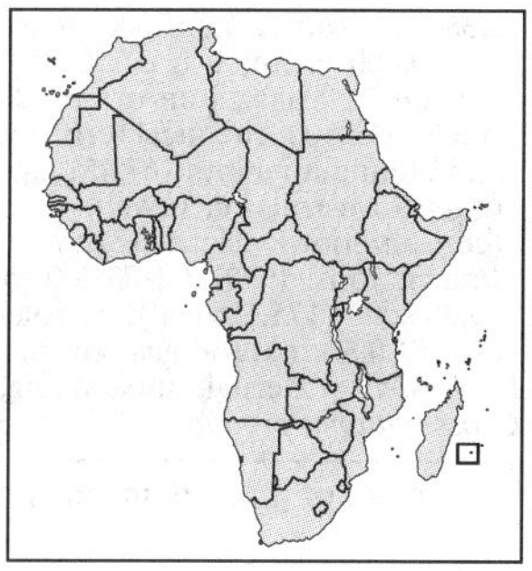

Official name: Département de la Réunion (Department of Reunion).
Political status: overseas department (France) with two legislative houses (General Council [47]; Regional Council [45]).
Chief of state: President of France.
Heads of government: Commissioner of the Republic (for France); President of General Council (for Réunion); President of Regional Council (for Réunion).
Capital: Saint-Denis.
Official language: French.
Official religion: none.
Monetary unit: 1 French franc (F) = 100 centimes; valuation (Oct. 4, 1993) 1 U.S.$ = F 5.67; 1 £ = F 8.58.

Area and population

		area		population
				1990
Arrondissements	**Capitals**	sq mi	sq km	census
Saint-Benoît	Saint-Benoît	284	736	85,132
Saint-Denis	Saint-Denis	164	423	207,158
Saint-Paul	Saint-Paul	180	467	113,071
Saint-Pierre	Saint-Pierre	339	878	192,462
TOTAL		970[1, 2]	2,512[1, 2]	597,823

Demography

Population (1993): 634,000.
Density (1993): persons per sq mi 653.6, persons per sq km 252.4.
Urban-rural (1990): urban 73.4%; rural 26.6%.
Sex distribution (1990): male 49.22%; female 50.78%.
Age breakdown (1990): under 15, 31.3%; 15–29, 29.5%; 30–44, 19.6%; 45–59, 11.5%; 60–74, 6.2%; 75 and over, 1.9%.
Population projection: (2000) 718,000; (2010) 857,000.
Doubling time: 40 years.
Ethnic composition (1983): mixed race 63.5%; East Indian 28.2%; Chinese 2.2%; white 1.9%; East African 1.1%; other 3.1%.
Religious affiliation (1990): Roman Catholic 89.6%; Muslim 2.0%; other 8.4%.
Major cities (1990): Saint-Denis 100,926; Le Port 29,190; Le Tampon 27,300; Saint-André 25,237; Saint-Pierre 23,899.

Vital statistics

Birth rate per 1,000 population (1991): 23.2 (world avg. 26.4); legitimate 46.0%; illegitimate 54.0%.
Death rate per 1,000 population (1991): 5.5 (world avg. 9.2).
Natural increase rate per 1,000 population (1991): 17.7 (world avg. 17.2).
Total fertility rate (avg. births per childbearing woman; 1991): 2.6.
Marriage rate per 1,000 population (1990): 6.4.
Divorce rate per 1,000 population (1990): 1.3.
Life expectancy at birth (1991): male 69.0 years; female 78.3 years.
Major causes of death per 100,000 population (1988): diseases of the circulatory system 180.0; malignant neoplasms (cancers) 88.9; accidents and violence 69.0; diseases of the digestive system 58.9; diseases of the respiratory system 41.4.

National economy

Budget (1992). Revenue: F 4,237,000,000 (receipts from the French central government and local administrative bodies 50.1%, new loans 15.6%). Expenditures: F 4,237,000,000 (current expenditures 63.0%, development expenditures 37.0%).
Public debt (external, outstanding; 1989)[3]: U.S.$63,000,000.
Tourism (1991): receipts U.S.$135,000,000; expenditures, n.a.
Gross national product (at current market prices; 1989): U.S.$1,853,000,000 (U.S.$3,140 per capita).

Structure of gross domestic product and labour force

	1989[4]		1990	
	in value F '000,000	% of total value	labour force	% of labour force
Agriculture	1,940	7.5	11,256	4.8
Manufacturing	840	3.2	10,087	4.3
Construction	2,580	9.9	16,519	7.1
Public utilities	450	1.7	1,316	0.6
Transportation and communications	970	3.7	7,309	3.1
Trade, restaurants	5,280	20.3	17,689	7.6
Finance, real estate, insurance	700	2.7	27,630	11.8
Pub. admin., defense	3,740	14.4 }	54,382	23.3
Services	9,500	36.6 }		
Other	—	—	87,378[5]	37.4[5]
TOTAL	26,000	100.0	233,566	100.0

Production (metric tons except as noted). Agriculture, forestry, fishing (1991): sugarcane 1,973,000[6], pe-tsai (Chinese cabbage) and black nightshade 8,059[7], bananas 7,000, pineapples 6,750, onions 5,203[7], eggplant 3,000, pimento 380, ginger 95, vanilla 93[6], tobacco 22[6], geranium essence 16[6]; livestock (number of live animals) 87,000 pigs, 31,000 goats, 19,000 cattle; roundwood 36,000 cu m; fish (value of catch in F '000,000; 1992) lobster 43, other 47. Mining and quarrying: gravel and sand for local use. Manufacturing (value added in F '000,000; 1990): alcoholic and nonalcoholic beverages (mostly rum) 172; construction materials (mostly cement) 162; printing and publishing 145; fabricated metals 144; sugar, molasses, and related products 124. Construction (value of public construction; 1988): residential F 258,200,000; nonresidential F 1,587,000,000. Energy production (consumption): electricity (kW-hr; 1992) 1,090,000,000 (921,000,000); coal, none (none); crude petroleum, none (none); petroleum products (metric tons; 1990) none (299,000); natural gas, none (none).
Population economically active (1990): total 233,566; activity rate of total population 39.1% (participation rates: ages 15–64, 60.3%; female 41.1%; unemployed [1992] 35.0%).

Price and earnings indexes (December 1985 = 100)[8]

	1987	1988	1989	1990	1991	1992	1993[9]
Consumer price index	104.8	106.4	111.6	116.1	119.6	122.9	130.3
Monthly earnings index[10]	102.0	105.0	108.0	110.6	112.2	116.3	118.3

Household income and expenditure. Average household size (1990) 3.8; income per household (1987) F 90,000 (U.S.$14,970); sources of income (1987): wages and salaries and self-employment 67.5%, transfer payments 29.7%, other 2.8%; expenditure (1986–87): transportation and communications 24.9%, food and beverages 22.4%, housing 11.8%, recreation and education 10.1%, clothing and footwear 7.9%, household furnishings 6.0%, other 16.9%.
Land use (1990): forested 35.2%; meadows and pastures 4.8%; agricultural and under permanent cultivation 20.8%; other 39.2%.

Foreign trade

Balance of trade (current prices)

	1987	1988	1989	1990	1991	1992
F '000,000	−7,865	−8,781	−10,067	−10,747	−11,975	−11,542
% of total	81.6%	80.6%	83.1%	84.1%	87.6%	83.9%

Imports (1992): F 12,650,000,000 (food and agricultural products 19.9%, electrical and nonelectrical machinery 16.3%, transport equipment 14.1%, chemical products 9.0%, base metals and fabricated-metal products 6.4%). *Major import sources:* France 69.5%; other EEC countries 11.5%; Bahrain 4.3%; Indian Ocean countries 4.2%.
Exports (1992): F 1,108,000,000 (food products [mostly sugar] 80.0%, electrical and nonelectrical machinery 6.8%, transport equipment 4.5%). *Major export destinations:* France 76.5%; other EEC countries 7.8%; Indian Ocean countries 9.0%; Japan 4.8%.

Transport and communications

Transport. Railroads (1984): route length 384 mi[11], 614 km[11]; traffic, n.a. Roads (1989): total length 1,690 mi, 2,719 km (paved, n.a.). Vehicles (1991): passenger cars 150,000; trucks and buses 50,000. Merchant marine (1992): vessels (100 gross tons and over) 7; total deadweight tonnage 33,476. Air transport (1991): passenger arrivals 405,586, passenger departures 405,278; cargo unloaded 11,470 metric tons, cargo loaded 3,019 metric tons; airports (1993) with scheduled flights 1.
Communications. Daily newspapers (1990): total number 3; total circulation 65,000; circulation per 1,000 population 108. Radio (1992): total number of receivers 150,000 (1 per 4.2 persons). Television (1992): total number of receivers 90,500 (1 per 6.9 persons). Telephones (1992): 180,088 (1 per 3.4 persons).

Education and health

Education (1991–92)

	schools	teachers	students	student/ teacher ratio
Primary (age 6–10)	360	...	72,744[2]	...
Secondary (age 11–17) } Voc., teacher tr. }	95	...	87,834[12]	...
Higher[13]	1	183	6,300	34.4

Educational attainment (1986–87). Percentage of population age 25 and over having: no formal schooling 18.8%; primary education 44.3%; lower secondary 21.6%; upper secondary 11.0%; higher 4.3%. *Literacy* (1986–87): total population age 15 and over literate 298,965 (78.2%); males literate 141,006 (75.9%); females literate 157,959 (80.3%).
Health (1991): physicians (1992) 1,034 (1 per 597 persons); hospital beds 2,933 (1 per 210 persons); infant mortality rate per 1,000 live births 7.3.
Food (1988–90): daily per capita caloric intake 3,082 (vegetable products 81%, animal products 19%); 136% of FAO recommended minimum requirement.

Military

Total active duty personnel (1992): 3,400 French troops[14].

[1]Includes 3 sq mi (8 sq km) not distributed by arrondissement. [2]Indian Ocean islets administered by France from Réunion are excluded from total. Areas of these islets, which have no permanent population, are: Îles Glorieuses 1.7 sq mi (4.3 sq km), Île Juan de Nova 1.9 sq mi (4.8 sq km), Île Tromelin 0.3 sq mi (0.8 sq km), Bassas da India 0.1 sq mi (0.2 sq km), Île Europa 7.8 sq mi (20.2 sq km). [3]Includes long-term private debt not guaranteed by the government. [4]At factor cost. [5]Includes 86,118 unemployed. [6]1992. [7]1990. [8]Indexes refer to December. [9]March. [10]Based on minimum-level wage of public employees. [11]For sugar industry only. [12]1992–93. [13]University only. [14]Includes troops stationed on Mayotte.

Romania

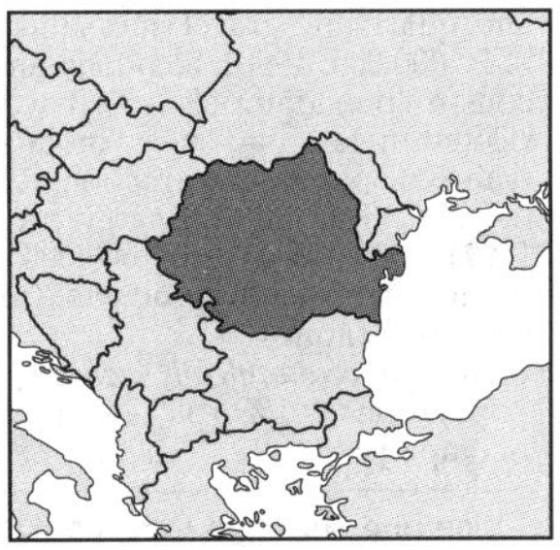

Official name: România (Romania).
Form of government: unitary republic with two legislative houses (Senate [143]; Assembly of Deputies [341[1]]).
Chief of state: President.
Head of government: Prime Minister.
Capital: Bucharest.
Official language: Romanian.
Official religion: none.
Monetary unit: 1 Romanian leu (plural lei) = 100 bani; valuation (Oct. 4, 1993) 1 U.S.$ = 940.50 lei; 1 £ = 1,425 lei.

Area and population

		area		population
Counties	**Capitals**	sq mi	sq km	1992[2] census
Alba	Alba Iulia	2,406	6,231	414,200
Arad	Arad	2,954	7,652	487,400
Arges	Pitești	2,626	6,801	680,600
Bacău	Bacău	2,551	6,606	736,100
Bihor	Oradea	2,909	7,535	634,100
Bistrița-Năsăud	Bistrița	2,048	5,305	327,200
Botoșani	Botoșani	1,917	4,965	458,900
Brăila	Brăila	1,824	4,724	392,100
Brașov	Brașov	2,066	5,351	642,500
Buzău	Buzău	2,344	6,072	516,300
Călărași	Călărași	1,959	5,074	338,800
Caraș-Severin	Reșița	3,283	8,503	375,800
Cluj	Cluj-Napoca	2,568	6,650	735,100
Constanța	Constanța	2,724	7,055	748,000
Covasna	Sfântu Gheorghe	1,431	3,705	232,600
Dâmbovița	Târgoviște	1,559	4,036	559,900
Dolj	Craiova	2,862	7,413	761,100
Galați	Galați	1,708	4,425	639,900
Giurgiu	Giurgiu	1,356	3,511	313,100
Gorj	Târgu Jiu	2,178	5,641	400,100
Harghita	Miercurea-Ciuc	2,552	6,610	347,700
Hunedoara	Deva	2,709	7,016	548,000
Ialomița	Slobozia	1,718	4,449	304,000
Iași	Iași	2,112	5,469	806,800
Maramureș	Baia Mare	2,400	6,215	538,500
Mehedinți	Drobeta-Turnu Severin	1,892	4,900	332,100
Mureș	Târgu Mureș	2,585	6,696	607,300
Neamț	Piatra Neamț	2,274	5,890	577,600
Olt	Slatina	2,126	5,507	521,000
Prahova	Ploiești	1,812	4,694	873,200
Sălaj	Zalău	1,486	3,850	266,300
Satu Mare	Satu Mare	1,701	4,405	400,100
Sibiu	Sibiu	2,093	5,422	452,800
Suceava	Suceava	3,303	8,555	700,800
Teleorman	Alexandria	2,224	5,760	482,300
Timiș	Timișoara	3,356	8,692	700,300
Tulcea	Tulcea	3,255	8,430	270,200
Vâlcea	Râmnicu Vâlcea	2,203	5,705	436,300
Vaslui	Vaslui	2,045	5,297	457,800
Vrancea	Focșani	1,878	4,863	392,600
Muncipality				
Bucharest	Bucharest	703	1,820	2,351,000
TOTAL		91,699[3]	237,500	22,760,500

Demography

Population (1993): 22,789,000.
Density (1993): persons per sq mi 248.5, persons per sq km 95.6.
Urban-rural (1992): urban 54.4%; rural 45.6%.
Sex distribution (1992): male 49.13%; female 50.87%.
Age breakdown (1989): under 15, 23.9%; 15–29, 22.4%; 30–44, 20.8%; 45–59, 17.6%; 60–74, 11.3%; 75 and over, 4.0%.
Population projection: (2000) 23,272,000; (2010) 23,980,000.
Ethnic composition (1992): Romanian 89.4%; Hungarian 7.1%; Gypsy 1.8%; German 0.5%; Ukrainian 0.3%; other 0.9%.
Religious affiliation (1992): Romanian Orthodox 86.8%; Roman Catholic 5.0%; Greek Orthodox 3.5%; Pentacostal 1.0%; Muslim 0.2%; other 3.5%.
Major cities (1992): Bucharest 2,064,474; Constanța 350,476; Iași 342,994; Timișoara 334,278; Cluj-Napoca 328,008.

Vital statistics

Birth rate per 1,000 population (1991): 11.9 (world avg. 26.4).
Death rate per 1,000 population (1991): 10.9 (world avg. 9.2).
Natural increase rate per 1,000 population (1991): 1.0 (world avg. 17.2).
Total fertility rate (avg. births per childbearing woman; 1989): 2.2.
Marriage rate per 1,000 population (1991): 7.9.
Divorce rate per 1,000 population (1990): 1.4.
Life expectancy at birth (1987–89): male 66.5 years; female 72.4 years.
Major causes of death per 100,000 population (1990): circulatory disease 635.6; cancer 140.3.

National economy

Budget (1991). Revenue: 787,940,000,000 lei (income tax 35.2%, of which corporate 13.3%; social security 28.9%; value-added taxes 23.2%; customs duties 3.1%). Expenditures: 779,980,000,000 lei (social security and welfare 26.5%; defense 10.3%; education 10.0%; health 9.2%).
Tourism (1991): receipts U.S.$103,000,000; expenditures U.S.$114,000,000.
Production (metric tons except as noted). Agriculture (1991): corn (maize) 10,493,000, wheat 5,442,000, sugar beets 4,687,000, potatoes 1,900,000, grapes 849,000, cabbages 780,000, oats 258,000, dry onions 180,000, soybeans 179,000; livestock (number of live animals) 14,062,000 sheep, 12,003,000 pigs, 5,381,000 cattle, 1,005,000 goats, 121,000,000 chickens; roundwood (1991) 14,769,000 cu m; fish catch (1990) 127,659. Mining and quarrying (1990): bauxite 3,000,000; iron ore 600,000; lead 30,000. Manufacturing (1991): raw steel 7,115,500; chemical fertilizers 1,091,626; sulfuric acid 745,400; aluminum and aluminum alloys 167,451; synthetic rubber 54,583; television sets 389,227 units. Construction (1989): residential 5,409,000 sq m. Energy production (consumption): electricity (kW-hr; 1990) 64,161,100,000 (73,782,000,000); coal (metric tons; 1990) 38,183,200 (51,700,000); crude petroleum (barrels; 1990) 59,095,000 (175,685,000); petroleum products (metric tons; 1990) 21,705,000 (12,951,000); natural gas (cu m; 1990) 28,335,600,000 (30,832,500,000).
Public debt (external, outstanding; 1991): U.S.$334,000,000.
Gross national product (1991): U.S.$31,079,000,000 (U.S.$1,620 per capita).

Structure of gross domestic product and labour force

	1990		1991	
	in value '000,000 lei	% of total value	labour force	% of labour force
Agriculture	151,900	18.0	3,133,100	29.1
Mining, manufacturing, and public utilities	407,000	48.2	3,817,400	35.4
Construction	47,900	5.7	462,700	4.3
Transp. and commun.	56,500	6.7	680,900	6.3
Trade	59,300	7.0	871,900	8.1
Finance	13,400	1.6		
Pub. admin.	67,300	8.0	1,663,700	15.4
Services	13,100	1.5		
Other	27,600	3.3	156,100	1.4
TOTAL	844,000	100.0	10,785,800	100.0

Population economically active (1991): total 10,785,800; activity rate 46.9% (participation rates [1990]: ages 15–64, 68.9%; female 42.6%; unemployed, n.a.).

Price and earnings indexes (1985 = 100)

	1986	1987	1988	1989	1990	1991	1992
Consumer price index	102.2	103.3	106.2	107.0	111.5	306.0	854.1
Annual earnings index	101.4	102.0	104.6	108.7	120.2	265.2	720.9

Household income and expenditure. Average household size (1992) 3.1; income per household (1989) 73,500 lei (U.S.$4,940); sources of income (1982): wages 62.6%; expenditure (1989): food 51.1%, housing 16.4%, clothing 15.7%.
Land use (1990): forest 27.8%; pasture 20.5%; agricultural 43.6%; other 8.1%.

Foreign trade[4]

Balance of trade (current prices)

	1986	1987	1988	1989	1990	1991
U.S.$'000,000	+1,679	+2,179	+3,750	+2,050	−3,244	−1,182
% of total	9.4%	11.6%	19.7%	10.8%	21.7%	12.5%

Imports (1990): 209,912,000,000 lei (raw materials 47.6%, machinery 23.7%, chemicals 6.4%). *Major import sources:* U.S.S.R. 23.6%; Germany 11.4%; Saudi Arabia 8.3%; Iran 5.9%; U.S. 4.6%; Poland 4.3%.
Exports (1990): 135,191,000,000 lei (raw materials and mineral fuels 33.7%, machinery and transport equipment 30.8%, manufactured goods 21.2%, chemicals 6.5%). *Major export destinations:* U.S.S.R. 25.2%; Germany 10.2%; Italy 8.8%; U.S. 5.8%; France 3.4%; Czechoslovakia 3.2%; Turkey 2.8%.

Transport and communications

Transport. Railroads (1992): length[5] 6,887 mi, 11,083 km; passenger-km 24,276,000,000; metric ton-km cargo 27,780,000,000. Roads (1992): length 95,099 mi, 153,014 km (paved 51%). Vehicles (1992): cars 1,397,118; trucks and buses 332,273. Merchant marine (1992): vessels (100 gross tons and over) 439; total deadweight tonnage 4,845,539. Air transport (1991): passenger-km 3,842,000,000; metric ton-km cargo 78,000,000; airports (1993) 16.
Communications. Daily newspapers (1990): total number 65; total circulation 1,245,000; circulation per 1,000 population 54. Radios (1990): 2,982,852 (1 per 7.8 persons). Televisions (1990): 3,675,140 (1 per 6.3 persons). Telephones (1990): 3,022,934 subscribers (1 per 7.7 persons).

Education and health

Education (1991–92)

	schools	teachers	students	student/teacher ratio
Primary (age 6–13)	13,985	159,199	2,639,279	16.6
Secondary (age 14–17)	1,209	55,013	778,420	14.2
Voc., teacher tr.	1,101	6,619	430,210	65.0
Higher	48	17,615	215,226	12.2

Educational attainment (1992). Percentage of population age 12 and over having: no schooling 4.6%; primary education 54.9%; secondary 35.1%; postsecondary 5.4%. *Literacy* (1983): 95.8%.
Health (1991): physicians 41,813 (1 per 549 persons); hospital beds 215,796 (1 per 106 persons); infant mortality rate per 1,000 live births (1991) 22.7.
Food (1988–90): daily per capita caloric intake 3,081 (vegetable products 78%, animal products 22%); 116% of FAO recommended minimum requirement.

Military

Total active duty personnel (1992): 200,000 (army 80.5%, navy 9.5%, air force 10.0%). *Military expenditure as percentage of GNP* (1989): 6.1% (world 4.9%); per capita expenditure U.S.$299.

[1]Includes 13 nonelective seats. [2]Preliminary results of Jan. 7, 1992, census. [3]Detail does not add to total given because of rounding. [4]Import figures are f.o.b. in balance of trade and c.i.f. for commodities and trading partners. [5]1991.

Russia

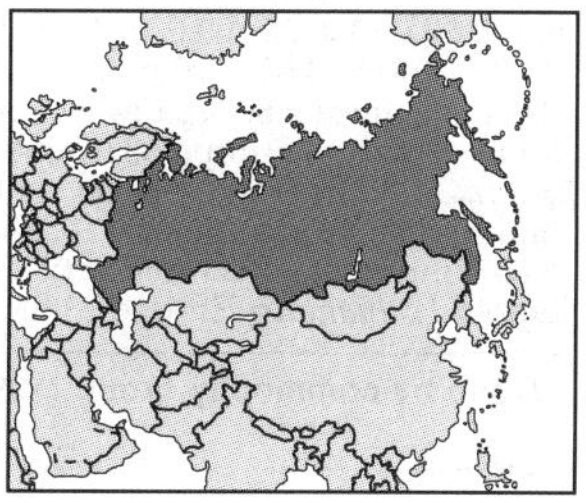

Official name: Rossiyskaya Federatsiya (Russian Federation).
Form of government: federal multiparty republic with a bicameral legislative body (Federal Assembly comprising a Federation Council [178] and a State Duma [450])[1].
Head of state: President.
Head of government: Prime Minister.
Capital: Moscow.
Official language: Russian.
Official religion: none.
Monetary unit: 1 ruble = 100 kopecks; valuation (Oct. 4, 1993) free rate, 1 U.S.$ = 1,165 rubles; 1 £ = 1,765 rubles.

Area and population

Federal Republics / Other entities	Capitals	area sq mi	area sq km	population 1992 estimate
Adygea	Maykop	2,900	7,600	442,000
Bashkortostan	Ufa	55,400	143,600	4,008,000
Buryatia	Ulan-Ude	135,600	351,300	1,059,000
Chechenia[2, 3]	...	[4]	[4]	[4]
Chuvashia	Cheboksary	7,100	18,300	1,353,000
Dagestan	Makhachkala	19,400	50,300	1,890,000
Gorno-Altay	Gorno-Altaisk	35,700	92,600	198,000
Ingushetia[2, 3]	Grozny	7,400[4]	19,300[4]	1,308,000[4]
Kabardino-Balkaria	Nalchik	4,800	12,500	784,000
Kalmykia (Khalmg Tangch)	Elista	29,400	76,100	327,000
Karachay-Cherkessia	Cherkessk	5,400	14,100	431,000
Karelia	Petrozavodsk	66,600	172,400	800,000
Khakassia	Abakan	23,900	61,900	581,000
Komi	Syktyvkar	160,600	415,900	1,255,000
Mari El	Ioshkar-Ola	9,000	23,200	762,000
Mordvinia	Saransk	10,100	26,200	964,000
North Ossetia	Vladikavkaz	3,100	8,000	695,000
Russia	Moscow	4,709,800[5]	12,198,300	125,115,000
Regions (Oblasts)				
Amur[6]	Blagoveshchensk	140,400	363,700	1,075,000
Arkhangelsk	Arkhangelsk	226,800	587,400	1,571,000
Astrakhan	Astrakhan	17,000	44,100	1,010,000
Belgorod	Belgorod	10,500	27,100	1,408,000
Bryansk	Bryansk	13,500	34,900	1,464,000
Chelyabinsk	Chelyabinsk	33,900	87,900	3,638,000
Chita	Chita	166,600	431,500	1,391,000
Irkutsk	Irkutsk	296,500	767,900	2,872,000
Ivanovo	Ivanovo	9,200	23,900	1,312,000
Kaliningrad[6]	Kaliningrad	5,800	15,100	894,000
Kaluga	Kaluga	11,500	29,900	1,081,000
Kamchatka	Petropavlovsk-Kamchatsky	182,400	472,300	472,000
Kemerovo	Kemerovo	36,900	95,500	3,181,000
Kirov	Kirov	46,600	120,800	1,700,000
Kostroma	Kostroma	23,200	60,100	812,000
Kurgan	Kurgan	27,400	71,000	1,115,000
Kursk	Kursk	11,500	29,800	1,335,000
Leningrad	St. Petersburg	33,200[7]	85,900[7]	1,673,000
Lipetsk	Lipetsk	9,300	24,100	1,234,000
Magadan	Magadan	178,100	461,400	363,000
Moskva (Moscow)	Moscow	18,100[8]	47,000[8]	6,707,000
Murmansk	Murmansk	55,900	144,900	1,148,000
Nizhny Novgorod	Nizhny Novgorod	28,900	74,800	3,704,000
Novgorod	Novgorod	21,400	55,300	752,000
Novosibirsk	Novosibirsk	68,800	178,200	2,803,000
Omsk	Omsk	53,900	139,700	2,170,000
Orenburg	Orenburg	47,900	124,000	2,204,000
Oryol (Orel)	Oryol	9,500	24,700	903,000
Penza	Penza	16,700	43,200	1,514,000
Perm	Perm	62,000	160,600	3,109,000
Pskov	Pskov	21,400	55,300	841,000
Rostov	Rostov-na-Donu	38,900	100,800	4,363,000
Ryazan	Ryazan	15,300	39,600	1,344,000
Sakhalin	Yuzhno-Sakhalinsk	33,600	87,100	719,000
Samara	Samara	20,700	53,600	3,296,000
Saratov	Saratov	38,700	100,200	2,711,000
Smolensk	Smolensk	19,200	49,800	1,163,000
Sverdlovsk[6]	Yekaterinburg	75,200	194,800	4,719,000
Tambov	Tambov	13,200	34,300	1,310,000
Tomsk	Tomsk	122,400	316,900	1,012,000
Tula	Tula	9,900	25,700	1,844,000
Tver	Tver	32,500	84,100	1,668,000
Tyumen	Tyumen	554,100	1,435,200	3,137,000
Ulyanovsk (Simbirsk)	Simbirsk	14,400	37,300	1,444,000
Vladimir	Vladimir	11,200	29,000	1,656,000
Volgograd	Volgograd	44,000	113,900	2,643,000
Vologda[6]	Vologda	56,300	145,700	1,362,000
Voronezh	Voronezh	20,200	52,400	2,475,000
Yaroslavl	Yaroslavl	14,100	36,400	1,472,000
Autonomous Region				
Yevreyskaya (Jewish)	Birobidzhan	13,900	36,000	221,000
Territories (Krays)				
Altay	Barnaul	65,300	169,100	2,666,000
Khabarovsk	Khabarovsk	304,500	788,600	1,634,000
Krasnodar	Krasnodar	29,300	76,000	4,797,000
Krasnoyarsk	Krasnoyarsk	903,400	2,339,700	3,051,000
Primorye (Maritime)[6]	Vladivostok	64,100	165,900	2,309,000
Stavropol	Stavropol	25,700	66,500	2,536,000
Autonomous cities				
Moscow	—	[8]	[8]	8,957,000
St. Petersburg[6]	—	[7]	[7]	5,004,000
Autonomous districts (Okrugs)[9]				
Aga-Buryat	*Aginskoye*	*7,300*	*19,000*	*79,000*
Chukchi (Chukotka)	Anadyr	284,800	737,700	146,000
Evenk	*Tyra*	*296,400*	*767,600*	*25,000*
Khanty-Mansi	*Khanty-Mansiysk*	*202,000*	*523,100*	*1,305,000*
Komi-Permyak	*Kudymkar*	*12,700*	*32,900*	*160,000*
Koryak	*Palana*	*116,400*	*301,500*	*39,000*
Nenets	*Naryan-Mar*	*68,100*	*176,400*	*54,000*
Taymyr	*Dudinka*	*332,900*	*862,100*	*53,000*
Ust-Orda Buryat	*Ust-Ordynsky*	*8,600*	*22,400*	*140,000*
Yamalo-Nenets	*Salekhard*	*289,700*	*750,300*	*479,000*
Sakha (Yakutia)	Yakutsk	1,198,200	3,103,200	1,093,000
Tatarstan[3]	Kazan	26,300	68,000	3,696,000
Tuva (Tyva)	Kyzyl-Orda	65,800	170,500	306,000
Udmurtia	Izhevsk	16,300	42,100	1,637,000
TOTAL		6,592,800	17,075,400	148,704,000

Demography

Population (1993): 148,000,000.
Density (1993): persons per sq mi 22.4, persons per sq km 8.7.
Urban-rural (1992): urban 73.7%; rural 26.3%.
Sex distribution (1992): male 47.00%; female 53.00%.
Age breakdown (1992): under 15, 22.6%; 15–29, 20.6%; 30–44, 24.3%; 45–59, 15.9%; 60–69, 10.1%; 70 and over, 6.4%.
Population projection: (2000) 146,239,000; (2010) 143,477,000.
Doubling time: not applicable; doubling time exceeds 100 years.
Ethnic composition (1989): Russian 81.5%; Tatar 3.8%; Ukrainian 3.0%; Chuvash 1.2%; Bashkir 0.9%; Belorussian 0.8%; Mordovian 0.7%; Chechen 0.6%; German 0.6%; other 6.9%.
Religious affiliation: believers are predominantly Russian Orthodox; there are Catholic, Protestant, Muslim, Old Believer, and Jewish minorities.
Major cities (1992): Moscow 8,747,000; St. Petersburg 4,437,000; Novosibirsk 1,442,000; Nizhny Novgorod 1,441,000; Yekaterinburg 1,371,000; Samara 1,239,000; Omsk 1,169,000; Chelyabinsk 1,143,000; Kazan 1,104,000; Perm 1,099,000; Ufa 1,097,000.

Other principal cities (1992)

	population		population		population
Astrakhan	512,000	Krasnoyarsk	925,000	Simbirsk	656,000
Barnaul	606,000	Naberezhnye Chelny	514,000	Tolyattigrad	666,000
Irkutsk	639,000	Novokuznetsk	600,000	Tula	541,000
Izhevsk	651,000	Orenburg	557,000	Vladivostok	648,000
Kemerovo	521,000	Penza	552,000	Volgograd	1,006,000
Khabarovsk	615,000	Rostov-na-Donu	1,027,000	Voronezh	902,000
Krasnodar	635,000	Saratov	909,000	Yaroslavl	637,000

Mobility (1989). Population living in the same residence as in 1988: 78.8%; different residence, same oblast 11.5%; different republic 9.7%.
Emigration (1990): 103,609.
Households (1989). Total family households 40,246,000; average household size 3.2; 2 persons 34.2%; 3 persons 28.0%; 4 persons 25.2%; 5 persons or more 12.6%. Population in family households: 128,787,000 (87.0%), nonfamily population 19,254,000 (13.0%).

Vital statistics

Birth rate per 1,000 population (1991): 12.1 (world avg. 26.4); (1990) legitimate 85.4%; illegitimate 14.6%.
Death rate per 1,000 population (1991): 11.4 (world avg. 9.2).
Natural increase rate per 1,000 population (1991): 0.7 (world avg. 17.2).
Total fertility rate (avg. births per childbearing woman; 1991): 1.7.
Marriage rate per 1,000 population (1991): 8.6.
Divorce rate per 1,000 population (1991): 4.0.
Life expectancy at birth (1991): male 63.5 years; female 74.3 years.
Major causes of death per 100,000 population (1991): circulatory diseases 620.0; malignant neoplasms (cancers) 198.0; accidents, poisoning, and violence 142.0, of which suicide 26.5, murder 15.2; respiratory diseases 57.0; digestive diseases 27.5[10]; infectious and parasitic diseases 12.6[10].

Social indicators

Educational attainment (1989). Percentage of population age 15 and over having: primary or no formal education 19.4%; some secondary 21.0%; secondary and some postsecondary 48.3%; higher and postgraduate 11.3%.
Quality of working life (1990). Average workweek: 40 hours. Annual rate per 100,000 workers of: injury or accident 569; industrial illness 5.3; death 11.2. Proportion of labour force insured for damages or income loss resulting from: injury 100%; permanent disability 100%; death 100%. Average days lost to labour stoppages per 1,000 workdays (1990): 2.9.
Access to services (1990). Proportion of dwellings having access to: electricity, virtually 100%; safe public water supply 94%; public sewage collection 92%; central heating 92%; bathroom 87%; gas 72%; hot water 79%.
Social participation. Eligible voters participating in last national election: 96%. Population participating in voluntary work: n.a. Trade union membership in total workforce (1989): 100%. Practicing religious population in total affiliated population: n.a.
Social deviance. Offense rate per 100,000 population (1992) for: murder 10.9; rape 9.5; serious bodily injury 40.9; burglary and housebreaking 76.7; larceny-theft 566.9. Incidence per 100,000 in general population (1992) of: alcoholism 1,727.5; substance abuse 25.1; suicide 26.5.
Material well-being (1992). Goods possessed per 100 households: automobile 19; radio receiver 102; television receiver 118; refrigerator 92; camera 28; motorcycle 24; bicycle 69; tape recorder 54.

National economy

Budget (1992). Revenue: 3,285,000,000 rubles (foreign activity 30.2%; value-added tax 29.6%; enterprise profits tax 15.3%; royalty on oil 4.7%; royalty on gas 4.7%; individual income tax 3.5%; excise taxes 3.5%). Expenditures: 3,111,600,000 rubles (social welfare and culture 28.1%, of which social benefits 8.2%; debt services 27.2%, of which foreign debt 17.4%; defense 13.2%; national economy 13.1%; subsidies 6.2%).

Gross national product (1991): U.S.$479,546,000 (U.S.$3,220 per capita).

Structure of gross domestic product and labour force

	1991			
	in value '000,000 rubles	% of total value	labour force	% of labour force
Agriculture	100,200	16.0	9,970,000	13.5
Mining, Manufacturing, Public utilities	228,100	36.4	20,117,000	27.3
Construction	57,300	9.1	10,778,000	14.6
Transp. and commun.	43,100	6.9	5,750,000	7.8
Trade	162,900 (Trade, Finance, Services, Pub. admin., defense)	26.0 (Trade, Finance, Services, Pub. admin., defense)	5,626,000	7.6
Finance, Services			14,653,000	19.9
Pub. admin., defense			2,479,000	3.3
Other	34,700	5.6	4,436,000	6.0
TOTAL	626,300	100.0	73,809,000	100.0

Public debt (external, outstanding; 1993)[11]: U.S.$72,500,000,000.
Tourism: receipts from visitors, n.a.; expenditures by nationals abroad, n.a.
Production (metric tons except as noted). Agriculture, forestry, fishing (1991): corn (maize) 151,000,000, wheat 38,899,000, potatoes 34,330,000, hay 29,300,000, sugar beets 24,280,000, barley 22,100,000, fodder crops 11,600,000, rye 10,600,000, oats 10,400,000, vegetables (other than potatoes) 10,400,000, sunflower seeds 2,900,000, peas 2,100,000, millet 1,000,000, rice 773,000, buckwheat 688,000; livestock (number of live animals; 1992): 54,700,000 cattle, 52,200,000 sheep, 35,400,000 pigs, 3,100,000 goats, 2,600,000 horses; roundwood 65,800,000 cu m; fish catch 6,966,000. Mining and quarrying (1991): iron ore 97,300,000. Manufacturing (1991): cement 77,500,000; crude steel 77,100,000; rolled steel 55,100,000; pig iron 48,900,000; mineral fertilizers 15,042,000; sulfuric acid 11,600,000; cellulose 6,400,000; paper 4,765,000; synthetic resins and plastics 2,963,000; cardboard 2,619,000; caustic soda 2,042,000; detergents 695,000; synthetic fibres 528,500; soap 411,000; cotton fabrics 5,295,000,000 sq m; silk fabrics 947,000,000 sq m; linen fabrics 497,000,000 sq m; wool fabrics 386,000,000 sq m; carpets 44,200,000 sq m; ceramic tiles 24,000,000 sq m; leather 10,860,000 sq m; tableware 532,000,000 pieces; knitted garments 19,000,000 pieces; fur hats 8,900,000 pieces; cigarettes 144,000,000,000 units; watches 61,600,000 units; tires 44,800,000 units; washing machines 5,541,000 units; vacuum cleaners 4,707,000 units; television receivers 4,439,000 units; bicycles 3,866,000 units; refrigerators 3,710,000 units; tape recorders 3,623,000 units; cameras 1,905,000 units; sewing machines 1,583,000 units; passenger cars 1,030,000 units; motorcycles 714,000 units; video recorders 319,000 units; machine tools 12,600 units; robots 900 units; furniture 5,779,000,000 rubles[12]; agricultural machinery 2,143,000,000 rubles[12]; chemical equipment 675,000,000 rubles[12]; oil equipment 192,000,000 rubles[12]; forge press machines 60,000,000 rubles[12]; pharmaceuticals 2,522,000 rubles[12]; leather footwear 336,400,000 pairs; beer 27,830,000 hectolitres; vodka and liquors 14,250,000 hectolitres; champagne 7,100,000 hectolitres; grape wine 7,050,000 hectolitres; brandy 630,000 hectolitres. Construction (1991): residential 49,400,000 sq m.

Manufacturing, mining, and construction enterprises (1991)

	no. of enter-prises	no. of employees	monthly wages as a % of avg. of all wages[12]	value added ('000,000 rubles)
Manufacturing				
Machinery and metal products	5,429	9,970,000	98.2	3,105
Fuel and energy	1,486	1,378,000	133.3	1,652
Metallurgy	428	1,274,000	124.3	6,321
Chemicals, petrochemicals, pulp, and paper	4,796	2,840,000	94.1	4,977
Light industry	4,725	2,145,000	80.0	...
Food	6,056	1,533,000	100.1	1,041
Other industries[12]	2,729	3,018,000	...	...
Building materials	2,217	7,018,000	108.2	962

Energy production (consumption): electricity (kW-hr; 1991) 1,068,000,000 ([1990] 1,068,200,000); coal (metric tons; 1991) 353,300,000 (395,000,000); crude petroleum (barrels; 1991) 3,313,000,000 (3,700,000,000); petroleum products, n.a. (n.a.); natural gas (cu m; 1991) 643,000,000,000 (643,000,000,000); peat (metric tons; 1991) 4,700,000 (5,200,000); oil shale (metric tons; 1991) 4,200,000 (4,600,000).
Energy production by source (1991): thermal 73.1%, hydroelectric 15.7%, nuclear and other 11.2%.
Population economically active (1991): total 73,809,000; activity rate of total population 49.6% (participation rates [1989]: ages 16–59 [male], 16–54 [female] 89.6%; female 52.4%; unemployed 9.0%).

Price and earnings indexes (1985 = 100)

	1985	1986	1987	1988	1989	1990	1991
Consumer price index	100.0	...	...	...	...	...	...
Monthly earnings index	100.0	103.2	107.3	116.8	128.4	147.4	263.2

Land use (1991): forested *c.* 45.6%; meadows and pastures 5.1%; agricultural and under permanent cultivation 7.7%; other 41.6%.
Household income and expenditure. Average household size (1989) 3.2; income per household: n.a.; sources of income (1991): wages and salaries 81.0%, pensions and stipends 12.5%, other 6.5%; expenditure (1991): food and nonalcoholic beverages 33.9%, clothing and footwear 20.8%, taxes and other financial payments 9.5%, furniture and household appliances 7.3%, culture 4.0%, alcoholic beverages 3.0%, housing 1.3%.

Foreign trade

Balance of trade: n.a.
Imports (1991): 25,800,000,000 rubles (machinery and transport equipment 33.2%, food 24.6%, misc. manufactured articles 16.7%, fuels and lubricants 8.9%, chemicals 8.4%, raw materials excl. fuels 4.9%, textiles 3.3%). *Major import sources:* Europe 63.0%; Americas 17.0%; Asia 17.0%.
Exports (1991): 29,500,000,000 rubles (fuels and lubricants 62.7%, machinery and transport equipment 10.2%, textiles 8.8%, raw materials excl. fuels 5.8%, misc. manufactured articles 3.8%, chemicals 6.5%, food 2.2%). *Major export destinations:* Europe 73.0%; Asia 20.5%; Americas 4.2%; Africa 2.2%.

Trade by commodity group (1991)

	imports		exports	
SITC group	'000,000 rubles	%	'000,000 rubles	%
00 Food and live animals	6,300	24.6	700	2.2
02 Raw materials, excl. fuels	1,300	4.9	1,700	5.8
03 Mineral fuels, lubricants	2,300	8.9	18,500	62.7
05 Chemicals	2,200	8.4	1,900	6.5
65 Textile yarn, fabrics	800	3.3	2,600	8.8
07 Machinery and transport equipment	8,600	33.2	3,000	10.2
08 Misc. manufactured articles	4,300	16.7	1,100	3.8
09 Goods, n.e.s.	...	...	...	...
TOTAL	25,800	100.0	29,500	100.0

Direction of trade (1990)

	imports		exports	
	'000,000 rubles	%	'000,000 rubles	%
Former Soviet republics	22,600	47.3	29,100	70.0
Other countries	25,200	52.7	12,500	30.0
TOTAL	47,800	100.0	41,600	100.0

Transport and communications

Transport. Railroads (1992): length 158,100 km; passenger-km 254,700,000,000; metric ton-km cargo 2,326,000,000. Roads (1992): total length 893,000 km (paved 74%). Vehicles (1992): passenger cars 9,661,000; trucks and buses 465,000. Merchant marine: vessels (100 gross tons and over) n.a.; total deadweight tonnage, n.a. Air transport (1992): passenger-km 150,400,000,000; metric ton-km cargo 2,400,000; airports (1993) 58.

Distribution of traffic (1991)

	cargo carried ('000,000 tons)	% of national total	passengers carried ('000,000)	% of national total
Intercity transport			30,173	61.5
Road	2,731	47.1	27,302	55.7
Rail	1,956	33.7	2,696	5.4
Sea and river	618	10.7	89	0.2
Air	2	...	86	0.2
Pipeline	496	8.5	—	—
Urban transport			18,858	38.5
Road	—	—	526	1.1
Rail	—	—	18,332	37.4
TOTAL	5,803	100.0	49,031	100.0

Communications. Daily newspapers (1990): total number 4,808; total circulation 166,000,000; circulation per 1,000 population 112. Radio (1992): 48,800,000 receivers (1 per 3 persons). Television (1992): 54,200,000 receivers (1 per 2.7 persons). Telephones (1992): 24,353,000 (1 per 6.1 persons).

Education and health

Education (1991–92)

	schools	teachers	students	student/teacher ratio
Primary (age 6–13), Secondary (age 14–17)	69,900	1,516,000	20,936,000	13.8
Voc., teacher tr.	2,605	...	2,201,900	...
Higher	519	...	1,668,000	...

Literacy: population age 15 and over literate, n.a.; males, n.a.; females, n.a.
Health (1992): physicians 657,600 (1 per 226 persons); hospital beds 1,998,000 (1 per 74 persons); infant mortality rate per 1,000 live births (1991) 17.8.
Food (1992): daily per capita caloric intake 2,100 (vegetable products, n.a., animal products, n.a.); 82% of FAO recommended minimum.

Military

Total active duty personnel (1992): 2,720,000 (Commonwealth of Independent States [CIS] centrally controlled 12.7%, Russian general purpose [army] 64.6%, navy 11.7%, air force 11.0%). *Military expenditure as percentage of GNP* (1991): 5.1% (world 5.0%); per capita expenditure U.S.$353.

[1]The president of the Russian Federation dissolved the former Congress of People's Deputies on Sept. 22, 1993; a new constitution, approved by referendum Dec. 11–12, 1993, created a new legislative body, the Federal Assembly, elections to which were held at the same time. Neither house had met by year-end. [2]The former Chechen-Ingush republic was split into two separate republics June 4, 1992; although both are formally recognized by the Russian Federation, details on final status within the federation remain undetermined. [3]Republic is not signatory to the March 31, 1992, treaty establishing the Russian Federation. [4]Ingushetia's area and population include Chechenia. [5]Detail does not add to total given because of rounding. [6]Entity has formally proclaimed itself a republic; final status remains undetermined. [7]Leningrad region includes area of autonomous city of St. Petersburg. [8]Moskva region includes area of autonomous city of Moscow. [9]With the exception of the Chukchi autonomous district (identified in Roman type), which has formally separated from Magadan region, all autonomous districts are administratively part of another national administrative subdivision, within which their area and population are included. [10]1989. [11]Total as of March 31, 1993; Russia has also assumed responsibility for the governmental and commercial debts of the former U.S.S.R., estimated to constitute a further U.S.$88,000,000,000. [12]1990.

Rwanda

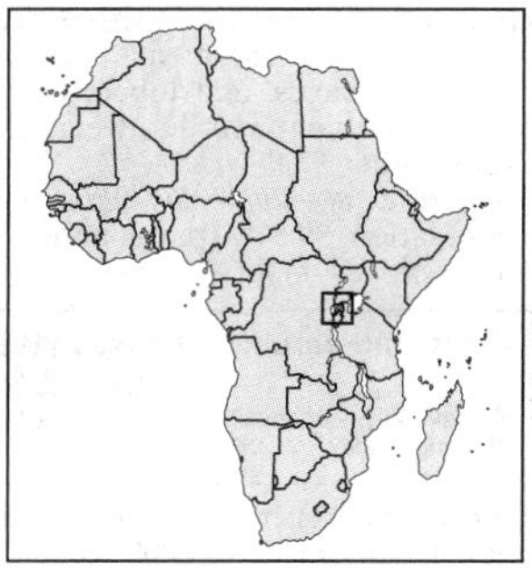

Official name: Repubulika y'u Rwanda (Rwanda); République Rwandaise (French) (Republic of Rwanda).
Form of government: transitional regime with one legislative house (Transitional National Assembly [70])[1].
Chief of state: President[1].
Head of government: Prime Minister[1].
Capital: Kigali.
Official languages: Rwanda; French.
Official religion: none.
Monetary unit: 1 Rwanda franc (RF); valuation (Oct. 4, 1993) 1 U.S.$ = RF 143.89; 1 £ = RF 218.00.

Area and population

		area		population
				1991
Prefectures	Capitals	sq mi	sq km	census
Butare	Butare	709	1,837	766,839
Byumba	Byumba	1,838	4,761	783,350
Cyangugu	Cyangugu	712	1,845	515,129
Gikongoro	Gikongoro	794	2,057	464,585
Gisenyi	Gisenyi	791	2,050	734,697
Gitarama	Gitarama	845	2,189	851,516
Kibungo	Kibungo	1,562	4,046	655,368
Kibuye	Kibuye	658	1,705	470,747
Kigali	Kigali (city)	1,159	3,002	918,869
Kigali (city)	—	45	116	237,782
Ruhengeri	Ruhengeri	642	1,663	766,112
TOTAL		9,757[2]	25,271	7,164,994[3]

Demography

Population (1993): 7,584,000.
Density (1993): persons per sq mi 777.3, persons per sq km 300.1.
Urban-rural (1991): urban 5.4%; rural 94.6%.
Sex distribution (1991): male 48.67%; female 51.33%.
Age breakdown (1990): under 15, 49.0%; 15–29, 26.1%; 30–44, 13.5%; 45–59, 7.5%; 60–74, 3.3%; 75 and over, 0.6%.
Population projection: (2000) 9,377,000; (2010) 12,698,000.
Doubling time: 21 years.
Ethnic composition (1983): Hutu 90%; Tutsi 9%; Twa 1%.
Religious affiliation (1988): Roman Catholic 65%; traditional beliefs 17%; Protestant 9%; Muslim 9%.
Major cities (1991): Kigali 237,782[3]; Ruhengeri 29,578[4]; Butare 28,645[4]; Gisenyi 21,918[4].

Vital statistics

Birth rate per 1,000 population (1990–95): 52.1 (world avg. 26.4); (1978) legitimate 94.9%; illegitimate 5.1%.
Death rate per 1,000 population (1990–95): 18.2 (world avg. 9.2).
Natural increase rate per 1,000 population (1990–95): 33.9 (world avg. 17.2).
Total fertility rate (avg. births per childbearing woman; 1990–95): 8.5.
Marriage rate per 1,000 population (1984)[5]: 2.5.
Divorce rate per 1,000 population: n.a.
Life expectancy at birth (1990–95): male 44.8 years; female 47.3 years.
Major causes of death per 100,000 population (1984)[6]: complications of pregnancy, childbirth, and birth injury 192.4; infectious and parasitic diseases (including malaria, typhoid, trypanosomiasis [sleeping sickness], pneumonia, tuberculosis, bacillary dysentery and amebiasis, diphtheria, meningococcal infection, and poliomyelitis) 11.8; diseases of the digestive system 10.3; diseases of the nervous system 10.1; accidents, poisoning, and violence 5.2.

National economy

Budget (1991). Revenue: RF 23,217,100,000 (import and export duties 29.7%, taxes on goods and services 22.6%, income tax 13.3%, property taxes 1.9%). Expenditures: RF 39,033,200,000 (defense 33.8%, economy and finance 28.3%, education 17.1%, foreign affairs and cooperation 4.2%, health 3.3%, infrastructure 3.2%, justice 2.8%).
Public debt (external, outstanding; 1991): U.S.$780,000,000.
Production (metric tons except as noted). Agriculture, forestry, fishing (1992): plantains 2,900,000, roots and tubers 1,530,000 (of which sweet potatoes 770,000, cassava 400,000, potatoes 280,000), cereals 301,000 (of which sorghum 175,000, corn [maize] 100,000), coffee 35,000, tea 14,000, tobacco 4,000; livestock (number of live animals) 1,100,000 goats, 610,000 cattle, 395,000 sheep, 142,000 pigs; roundwood (1991) 5,620,000 cu m; fish catch (1991) 3,551. Mining and quarrying (1990): cassiterite (tin ore) 1,048; wolframite (tungsten ore) 289; gold (1991) 22,505 troy oz. Manufacturing (1991): cement 57,000; lye soap 9,000; sugar 2,969[7]; beer 915,000 hectolitres; soft drinks 101,000 hectolitres; footwear 24,000 pairs; blankets 406,876 units[7]; matches 70,942,000 boxes[7]. Construction (1981): residential 59,600 sq m; nonresidential 34,400 sq m. Energy production (consumption): electricity (kW-hr; 1991) 179,000,000 (186,000,000); coal, none (n.a.); petroleum products (metric tons; 1991) none (132,000); natural gas (cu m; 1991) 128,135 (128,135).
Tourism (1990): receipts from visitors U.S.$10,000,000; expenditures by nationals abroad U.S.$23,000,000.
Land use (1991): forested 22.3%; meadows and pastures 18.6%; agricultural and under permanent cultivation 47.0%; other 12.1%.
Population economically active (1989): total 3,143,056; activity rate of total population (1987) 49.9% (participation rates: ages 14–74, 46.3%; female 53.5%; unemployed, n.a.).

Price and earnings indexes (1985 = 100)

	1986	1987	1988	1989	1990	1991	1992
Consumer price index	98.9	103.0	106.0	107.1	111.6	133.5	146.2
Earnings index	...	...	...	...	...	...	...

Gross national product (at current market prices; 1992): U.S.$1,818,000,000 (U.S.$250 per capita).

Structure of gross domestic product and labour force

	1989			
	in value RF '000,000	% of total value	labour force	% of labour force
Agriculture	75,690	39.8	2,832,557	90.1
Mining	790	0.4	4,691	0.2
Manufacturing	24,930	13.1	45,089	1.4
Construction	12,880	6.8	38,237	1.2
Public utilities	950	0.5	2,562	0.1
Transportation and communications	12,930	6.8	7,333	0.2
Trade	24,400	12.8	80,026	2.6
Finance	16,050	8.4	3,128	0.1
Pub. admin., defense } Services }	15,760	8.3	120,019	3.8
Other	5,840	3.1	9,414	0.3
TOTAL	190,220	100.0	3,143,056	100.0

Household income and expenditure. Average household size (1991) 4.7; average annual income per household (1983) RF 122,870 (U.S.$1,300); sources of income (1977): self-employment (profits, interest, etc.) 71.0%, salaries and wages 16.5%, transfers 9.5%; expenditure (1982)[8]: food 44.2%, housing 13.2%, clothing and footwear 11.4%, transportation 10.3%, household equipment 8.4%.

Foreign trade[9]

Balance of trade (current prices)

	1987	1988	1989	1990	1991	1992
RF '000,000	−10,562	−11,403	−10,918	−6,834	−15,181	−17,729
% of total	37.1%	40.7%	41.7%	27.0%	39.6%	49.9%

Imports (1991): RF 38,474,500,000 (machinery and transport equipment 14.5%, of which machinery 11.1%, transport equipment 3.4%; mineral fuels and lubricants 12.8%; food, beverages, and tobacco 11.4%; construction materials 3.9%). *Major import sources:* Belgium-Luxembourg 17.1%; Kenya 13.4%; France 6.8%; Germany 6.0%; Italy 2.8%; The Netherlands 2.7%; United Kingdom 2.1%; United States 1.0%; Zaire 0.7%.
Exports (1991): RF 11,971,200,000 (coffee 60.2%; tea 23.4%). *Major export destinations:* Germany 21.3%; The Netherlands 18.8%; Belgium-Luxembourg 11.8%; United Kingdom 6.4%; United States 5.8%; Italy 1.7%.

Transport and communications

Transport. Railroads: none. Roads (1990): total length 8,185 mi, 13,173 km (paved 9%). Vehicles: passenger cars (1991) 10,217; trucks and buses (1990) 2,048. Merchant marine: none. Air transport (1991): passenger arrivals 29,000, passenger departures 30,000; metric ton cargo loaded 2,674, metric ton cargo unloaded 4,794; airports (1993) with scheduled flights 3.
Communications. Daily newspapers (1992): total number, none; total circulation per 1,000 population, n.a. Radio (1992): total number of receivers 630,000 (1 per 12 persons). Television: none. Telephones (1991): 15,092 (1 per 480 persons).

Education and health

Education (1989–90)

	schools	teachers	students	student/ teacher ratio
Primary (age 7–15)	1,671	18,524	1,058,529	57.1
Secondary (age 16–19)	...	4,022[10]	65,323	...
Higher	3[11]	646	3,389	5.2

Educational attainment (1978). Percentage of population age 25 and over having: no formal schooling 76.9%; some primary education 16.8%; complete primary education 4.0%; some secondary and complete secondary education 2.0%; some postsecondary vocational and higher education 0.3%. *Literacy* (1990): percentage of total population age 15 and over literate 50.2%; males literate 63.9%; females literate 37.1%.
Health (1984): physicians 177[12] (1 per 33,170 persons); hospital beds 9,046 (1 per 649 persons); infant mortality rate per 1,000 live births (1990–95) 110.0.
Food (1988–90): daily per capita caloric intake 1,913 (vegetable products 97%, animal products 3%); 82% of FAO recommended minimum requirement.

Military

Total active duty personnel (1993): 5,200 (army 96.2%, navy, none, air force 3.8%). *Military expenditure as percentage of GNP* (1988): 1.6% (world 5.0%); per capita expenditure U.S.$5.

[1]A formal agreement of Aug. 4, 1993 (joining the mostly single-party Rwandan government and opposition parties in a new united transitional government), had not been implemented as of November 1993. [2]Detail does not add to total given because of rounding. [3]De facto figure (present resident population plus visitors). [4]Resident population only. [5]Excludes marriages not registered in court. [6]In hospitals only. [7]1990. [8]Weights of consumer price index components. [9]Imports f.o.b. in balance of trade and c.i.f. in commodities and trading partners. [10]Includes vocational and teacher training. [11]1985. [12]Excludes foreign physicians.

Saint Kitts and Nevis

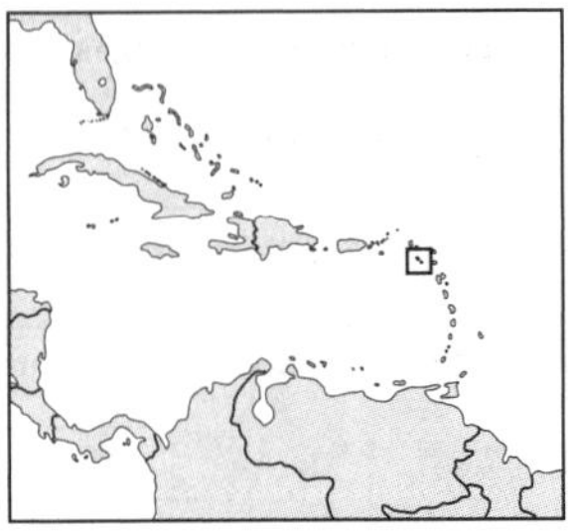

Official name: Federation of Saint Kitts and Nevis[1].
Form of government: constitutional monarchy with one legislative house (National Assembly [15[2]]).
Chief of state: British Monarch represented by Governor-General.
Head of government: Prime Minister.
Capital: Basseterre.
Official language: English.
Official religion: none.
Monetary unit: 1 Eastern Caribbean dollar (EC$) = 100 cents; valuation (Oct. 4, 1993) 1 U.S.$ = EC$2.70; 1 £ = EC$4.10.

Area and population

		area		population
Islands[3]	Capitals	sq mi	sq km	1991 census[4]
Nevis[5]	Charlestown	36.0	93.2	9,130
St. Kitts	Basseterre	68.0	176.2	32,696
TOTAL		104.0	269.4	41,826

Demography

Population (1993): 41,800.
Density (1993): persons per sq mi 401.9, persons per sq km 155.2.
Urban-rural (1990): urban 48.9%; rural 51.1%.
Sex distribution (1990): male 51.56%; female 48.44%.
Age breakdown (1990): under 15, 32.5%; 15–29, 25.6%; 30–44, 18.9%; 45–59, 10.1%; 60–74, 8.9%; 75 and over, 4.0%.
Population projection: (2000) 42,000; (2010) 42,000.
Doubling time: 58 years.
Ethnic composition (1988): black 86.0%; mixed 11.0%; white 2.0%; Indo-Pakistani 1.0%.
Religious affiliation (1985): Protestant 76.4%, of which Anglican 36.2%, Methodist 32.3%, Roman Catholic 10.7%; other 12.9%.
Major towns (1990): Basseterre 15,000; Charlestown 1,200.

Vital statistics

Birth rate per 1,000 population (1990): 23.0 (world avg. 27.1); (1983) legitimate 19.2%; illegitimate 80.8%.
Death rate per 1,000 population (1990): 10.8 (world avg. 9.8).
Natural increase rate per 1,000 population (1990): 12.2 (world avg. 17.3).
Total fertility rate (avg. births per childbearing woman; 1991): 2.6.
Marriage rate per 1,000 population: n.a.
Divorce rate per 1,000 population: n.a.
Life expectancy at birth (1991): male 64.0 years; female 71.0 years.
Major causes of death per 100,000 population (1985): diseases of the circulatory system 443.2, of which cerebrovascular disease 220.5, diseases of pulmonary circulation and other heart disease 122.7; malignant neoplasms (cancers) 95.5; diseases of the respiratory system 81.8; infectious and parasitic diseases 50.0; ill-defined conditions 102.3.

National economy

Budget (1991). Revenue: EC$93,400,000 (tax revenue 73.0%, of which income taxes 20.0%, import duties 19.5%, consumption taxes 17.5%; nontax revenue 25.2%; development revenue 1.5%). Expenditures: EC$103,900,000 (current expenditure 91.0%; development expenditure 9.0%).
Production (metric tons except as noted). Agriculture, forestry, fishing (1991): sugarcane 219,100, coconuts 2,000, potatoes 308[6], mangoes 272[6]; livestock (number of live animals) 15,000 sheep, 10,000 goats, 5,000 cattle; roundwood, n.a.; fish catch 1,750. Mining and quarrying: excavation of sand for local use. Manufacturing (1990): raw sugar 20,400[7]; molasses 5,600; aerated beverages 54,500 hectolitres; alcoholic beverages 26,500 hectolitres; other manufactures include garments, electronic components, plastics, and ethanol. Construction: n.a. Energy production (consumption): electricity (kW-hr; 1990) 37,000,000 (37,000,000); coal, none (none); crude petroleum, none (none); petroleum products (metric tons; 1990) none (21,000); natural gas, none (none).
Public debt (external, outstanding; end of 1991): U.S.$36,800,000.
Gross national product (at current market prices; 1992): U.S.$182,100,000 (U.S.$4,670 per capita).

Structure of gross domestic product and labour force

	1991		1984	
	in value EC$'000,000[8]	% of total value	labour force[9]	% of labour force[9]
Agriculture	28.1	7.1	4,380	29.6
Mining	2.7	0.7	—	—
Manufacturing	50.7	12.8	2,170	14.7
Construction	53.3	13.5	400	2.7
Public utilities	5.0	1.3	1,030	7.0
Transportation and communications	61.9	15.6	450	3.0
Trade, restaurants	88.8	22.4	940	6.3
Finance, real estate	43.7	11.0	280	1.9
Pub. admin., defense	70.8	17.9 }	4,700	31.7
Services	13.1	3.3 }		
Other	−22.0[10]	−5.6[10]	460	3.1
TOTAL	396.1	100.0	14,810	100.0

Household income and expenditure. Average household size (1980) 3.7; income per household: n.a.; sources of income: n.a.; expenditure (1978)[11]: food, beverages, and tobacco 55.6%, household furnishings 9.4%, housing 7.6%, clothing and footwear 7.5%, fuel and light 6.6%, transportation 4.3%, other 9.0%.
Population economically active (1980): total 17,125; activity rate of total population 39.5% (participation rates: ages 15–64, 69.5%; female 41.0%; unemployed[12]).

Price and earnings indexes (1985 = 100)

	1986	1987	1988	1989	1990	1991	1992
Consumer price index	100.0	101.0	101.2	106.3	110.8	115.5	118.8
Earnings index	...	...	...	...	...	...	...

Tourism (1991): receipts from visitors U.S.$74,000,000; expenditures by nationals abroad U.S.$4,000,000.
Land use (1990): forested 17.0%; meadows and pastures 3.0%; agricultural and under permanent cultivation 39.0%; other 41.0%.

Foreign trade[13]

Balance of trade (current prices)

	1986	1987	1988	1989	1990	1991
EC$'000,000	−76.1	−108.4	−141.7	−153.6	−212.2	−206.4
% of total	34.2%	40.3%	47.4%	46.4%	61.5%	64.3%

Imports (1990): EC$299,000,000 ([14]food and live animals 15.6%, nonelectrical machinery 13.1%, road vehicles 7.1%, metal manufactures 6.8%, refined petroleum 4.8%). *Major import sources* (1989): United States 41.3%; Caricom countries 15.6%, of which Trinidad and Tobago 7.4%; United Kingdom 14.0%.
Exports (1990): EC$74,700,000 (sugar and molasses 34.0%, garments 20.0%, other goods [including sea island cotton, coconut oil, electronic goods, and transport equipment] 46.0%). *Major export destinations* (1989): United States 54.6%; United Kingdom 26.1%; Caricom countries 8.9%, of which Trinidad and Tobago 4.1%.

Transport and communications

Transport. Railroads (1990)[15]: length 22 mi, 36 km. Roads (1992): total length 186 mi, 300 km (paved 42%). Vehicles (1990): passenger cars 4,000; trucks and buses, n.a. Merchant marine (1992): vessels (100 gross tons and over) 1; total deadweight tonnage 550. Air transport: passenger arrivals (1990) 116,180; passenger departures, n.a.; cargo handled, n.a.; airports (1993) with scheduled flights 2.
Communications (1992). Daily newspapers[16]: none. Radio: total number of receivers 25,000 (1 per 1.7 persons). Television: total number of receivers 9,500 (1 per 4.4 persons). Telephones (1990): 9,600[17] (1 per 4.4 persons).

Education and health

Education (1991–92)

	schools	teachers	students	student/teacher ratio
Primary (age 5–12)	31	342	6,978	20.4
Secondary (age 13–17)	7	298	4,645	15.6
Voc., teacher tr.	2	35	189	5.4
Higher	1	3	36	12.0

Educational attainment (1980). Percentage of population age 25 and over having: no formal schooling 1.1%; primary education 29.6%; secondary 67.2%; higher 2.1%. *Literacy* (1991): 98.0%.
Health (1990): physicians 28 (1 per 1,498 persons); hospital beds 268 (1 per 156 persons); infant mortality rate per 1,000 live births 22.0.
Food (1988–90): daily per capita caloric intake 2,435 (vegetable products 76%, animal products 24%); 101% of FAO recommended minimum requirement.

Military

Total active duty personnel (1990): the 340-member police force includes a paramilitary unit.

[1]Saint Christopher and Nevis and Federation of Saint Christopher and Nevis are both officially acceptable, variant, short- and long-form names of the country. [2]Includes four nonelective seats. [3]Parish subdivisions of both islands are for statistical purposes only. [4]Preliminary. [5]Nevis has full internal self-government. The Nevis legislature is subordinate to the National Assembly only with regard to external affairs and defense. [6]1990. [7]1992. [8]At factor cost. [9]Employed persons only. [10]Less imputed bank service charges. [11]Weights of consumer price index components. [12]Official data not available. Unemployment rates were thought to be low in 1990 and 1991 because of labour shortages in construction and the sugar industry. [13]Import figures are f.o.b. in balance of trade and c.i.f. for commodities and trading partners. [14]Commodity percentages are for 1988 based on imports equaling EC$251,500,000. [15]Light railway serving the sugar industry on Saint Kitts. [16]Total circulation of one weekly newspaper and one twice-weekly newspaper is 9,000. [17]Number of subscribers.

Saint Lucia

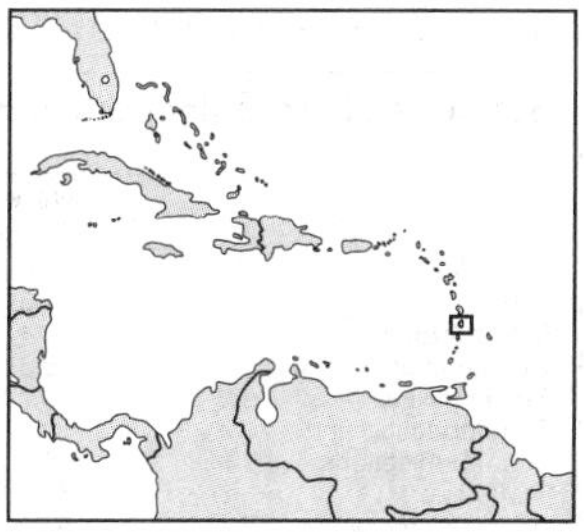

Official name: Saint Lucia.
Form of government: constitutional monarchy with two legislative houses (Senate [11]; House of Assembly [17]).
Chief of state: British Monarch represented by Governor-General.
Head of government: Prime Minister.
Capital: Castries.
Official language: English.
Official religion: none.
Monetary unit: 1 Eastern Caribbean Dollar (EC$) = 100 cents; valuation (Oct. 4, 1993) 1 U.S.$ = EC$2.70; 1 £ = EC$4.10.

Area and population

		area		population
				1991
Administrative regions	Capitals	sq mi	sq km	census
Anse-la-Raye	Anse-la-Raye	22	57	6,834
Babonneau	Babonneau	17	44	8,285
Castries	Castries	28	73	45,768
Dennery	Dennery	26	67	11,168
Gros Islet	Gros Islet	22	57	11,446
Micoud	Micoud	30	78	15,088
Soufrière	Soufrière	27	70	14,088
Vieux Fort	Vieux Fort	36	93	20,631
TOTAL		238[1]	617[1]	133,308

Demography

Population (1993): 136,000.
Density (1993): persons per sq mi 571.4, persons per sq km 220.4.
Urban-rural (1990): urban 46.4%; rural 53.6%.
Sex distribution (1991): male 48.49%; female 51.51%.
Age breakdown (1991): under 15, 36.8%; 15–29, 29.4%; 30–44, 16.3%; 45–59, 8.7%; 60–74, 6.3%; 75 and over, 2.5%.
Population projection: (2000) 143,000; (2010) 155,000.
Doubling time: 35 years.
Ethnic composition (1985): black 87.0%; mixed 9.1%; East Indian 2.6%; white 1.3%.
Religious affiliation (1991): Roman Catholic 79.0%; Protestant 15.5%, of which Seventh-day Adventist 6.5%, Pentecostal 3.0%; other 5.5%.
Major city (1991): Castries 11,147.

Vital statistics

Birth rate per 1,000 population (1992): 26.5 (world avg. 26.4); (1990) legitimate 10.0%; illegitimate 90.0%.
Death rate per 1,000 population (1992): 6.4 (world avg. 9.2).
Natural increase rate per 1,000 population (1992): 20.1 (world avg. 17.2).
Total fertility rate (avg. births per childbearing woman; 1991): 3.1.
Marriage rate per 1,000 population (1989): 2.7.
Divorce rate per 1,000 population (1989): 0.3.
Life expectancy at birth (1990): male 68.6 years; female 74.4 years.
Major causes of death per 100,000 population (1990): diseases of the circulatory system 209.5, of which ischemic heart diseases 109.7, hypertensive disease 58.8, cerebrovascular disease 35.0; malignant neoplasms (cancers) 48.3; diseases of the respiratory system 33.7; ill-defined conditions 81.3.

National economy

Budget (1991–92). Revenue: EC$303,100,000 (consumption duties on imported goods 26.9%, income taxes 25.8%, import duties 18.9%, taxes on domestic goods and services 9.0%). Expenditures: EC$298,400,000 (current expenditures 75.0%, development expenditures and net lending 25.0%).
Public debt (external, outstanding; 1991): U.S.$69,900,000.
Tourism: receipts from visitors (1991) U.S.$173,000,000; expenditures by nationals abroad U.S.$17,000,000.
Production. Agriculture, forestry, fishing (export value in EC$'000 except as noted; 1990): 184,100[2], copra 2,600[3], breadfruit 642, pepper 599, mangoes 498, cacao beans 338, plantains 248, ginger 82; livestock (number of live animals; 1992) 16,000 sheep, 12,000 cattle, 12,000 pigs, 12,000 goats; roundwood, n.a.; fish catch 910[3] metric tons. Mining and quarrying: excavation of sand for local construction and pumice. Manufacturing (value of production in EC$'000; 1990): alcoholic beverages and tobacco 26,113, of which rum 6,306; paper products and cardboard boxes 16,362[4]; garments 14,309; refined coconut oil 9,097; raw coconut oil 7,034; copra 5,810; other manufactures include electronic components. Construction (buildings approved; 1990): residential 70,000 sq m; nonresidential 18,300 sq m. Energy production (consumption): electricity (kW-hr; 1990) 126,900,000 (111,800,000); coal, none (none); crude petroleum, none (none); petroleum products (metric tons; 1990) none (53,000); natural gas, none (none).
Household income and expenditure. Average household size (1991) 4.0; income per household: n.a.; sources of income: n.a.; expenditure (1982)[5]: food 46.8%, housing 13.5%, clothing and footwear 6.5%, transportation and communications 6.3%, household furnishings 5.8%, fuel and light 4.5%, recreation and education 3.2%, beverages and tobacco 2.8%, health care 2.3%, other 8.3%.
Population economically active (1980): total 42,200; activity rate of total population 37.2% (participation rates: ages 15–64, 69.9%; female 39.1%; unemployed [1990] 13.0%).

Price and earnings indexes (1988 = 100)

	1987	1988	1989	1990	1991	1992	1993
Consumer price index	99.2	100.0	104.1	109.0	115.2	121.0	120.8[6]
Earnings index[7]	...	100.0	103.0	106.1	109.3	...	...

Gross national product (at current market prices; 1992): U.S.$454,000,000 (U.S.$2,910 per capita).

Structure of gross domestic product and labour force

	1990[8]		1985	
	in value EC$'000,000	% of total value	labour force	% of labour force
Agriculture	115.8	13.8	...	33.9
Mining	6.1	0.7	...	0.2
Manufacturing	67.4	8.0	...	10.4
Construction	50.5	6.0	...	3.2
Public utilities	26.7	3.2	...	1.4
Transportation and communications	141.6	16.8	...	4.5
Trade, restaurants	202.4	24.1	...	18.5
Finance, real estate	112.8	13.4	...	2.6
Pub. admin., defense	123.0	14.6	...	25.3
Services	29.7	3.5		
Other	−34.6[9]	−4.1[9]	—	—
TOTAL	841.4	100.0	...	100.0

Land use (1991): forested 13.0%; meadows and pastures 5.0%; agricultural and under permanent cultivation 30.0%; other 52.0%.

Foreign trade[10]

Balance of trade (current prices)

	1986	1987	1988	1989	1990	1991
EC$'000,000	−194.0	−268.9	−275.1	−436.8	−388.7	−500.7
% of total	30.2%	38.5%	35.0%	41.9%	36.1%	45.8%

Imports (1990): EC$732,400,000 (machinery and transport equipment 21.4%, of which road vehicles 6.7%, electrical machinery and appliances 4.7%; food and live animals 19.4%, of which meat and meat preparations 5.5%; crude petroleum and petroleum products 6.7%; paper and paperboard 5.8%). *Major import sources:* United States 34.2%; Caricom countries 17.9%, of which Trinidad and Tobago 9.4%; United Kingdom 14.2%; Japan 6.2%; Canada 3.0%.
Exports (1990): EC$343,700,000 (bananas 58.1%; clothing 15.3%; paper and paperboard 4.8%; beer and ale 3.7%; refined coconut oil 2.5%). *Major export destinations:* United Kingdom 53.1%; United States 23.4%.

Transport and communications

Transport. Railroads: none. Roads (1990): total length 500 mi, 805 km (paved 56%). Vehicles (1991): passenger cars 7,000; trucks and buses 4,000. Merchant marine (1992): vessels (100 gross tons and over) 7; total deadweight tonnage 2,070. Air transport (1990): passenger arrivals 223,467, passenger departures 226,630; cargo unloaded 1,480 metric tons, cargo loaded 2,766 metric tons; airports (1993) with scheduled flights 2.
Communications. Daily newspapers: none[11]. Radio (1992): total number of receivers 90,000 (1 per 1.5 persons). Television (1992): total number of receivers 25,000 (1 per 5.4 persons). Telephones (1990): 13,751[12] (1 per 11 persons).

Education and health

Education (1989–90)

	schools	teachers	students	student/teacher ratio
Primary (age 5–11)	83	1,112	32,636	29.3
Secondary (age 12–16)	13	376	6,771	18.0
Voc., teacher tr. / Higher	1	...	763	...

Educational attainment (1980). Percentage of population age 25 and over having: no formal schooling 17.5%; primary education 74.4%; secondary 6.8%; higher 1.3%. *Literacy* (1990): about 80%.
Health (1990): physicians 60 (1 per 2,521 persons); hospital beds 534 (1 per 283 persons); infant mortality rate per 1,000 live births (1992) 18.5.
Food (1988–90): daily per capita caloric intake 2,424 (vegetable products 75%, animal products 25%); 100% of FAO recommended minimum requirement.

Military

Total active duty personnel (1990):[13].

[1]Total includes the uninhabited 30 sq mi (78 sq km) Central Forest Reserve. [2]1992. [3]1991. [4]Export production only. [5]Castries administrative region only. [6]May. [7]Public sector only. [8]At factor cost. [9]Less imputed bank service charges. [10]Imports c.i.f.; exports f.o.b. [11]Three newspapers published once or twice a week have a total circulation (1990) of 18,000. [12]Number of subscribers. [13]The 300-member police force includes a specially trained paramilitary unit.

Saint Vincent and the Grenadines

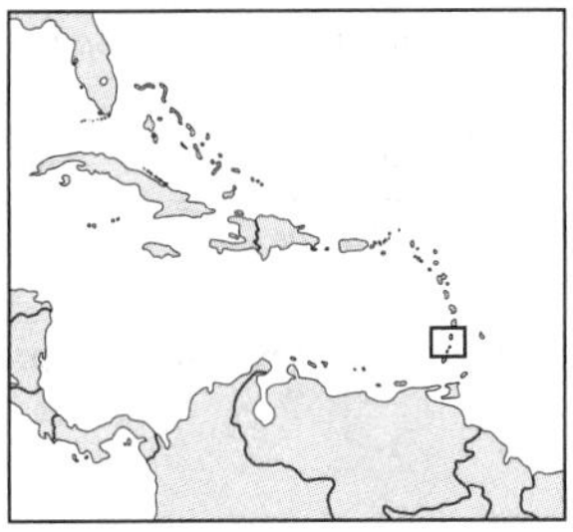

Official name: Saint Vincent and the Grenadines.
Form of government: constitutional monarchy with one legislative house (House of Assembly [21][1]).
Chief of state: British Monarch represented by Governor-General.
Head of government: Prime Minister.
Capital: Kingstown.
Official language: English.
Official religion: none.
Monetary unit: 1 Eastern Caribbean Dollar (EC$) = 100 cents; valuation (Oct. 4, 1993) 1 U.S.$ = EC$2.70; 1 £ = EC$4.10.

Area and population

	area		population
Constituencies[2]	sq mi	sq km	1991 census
Island of Saint Vincent[3]			
Barrouallie	14.2	36.8	5,199
Bridgetown	7.2	18.6	7,532
Calliaqua	11.8	30.6	20,290
Chateaubelair	30.9	80.0	6,045
Colonarie	13.4	34.7	7,890
Georgetown	22.2	57.5	7,303
Kingstown (city)	1.9	4.9	15,466
Kingstown (suburbs)	6.4	16.6	10,757
Layou	11.1	28.7	5,993
Marriaqua	9.4	24.3	8,864
Sandy Bay	5.3	13.7	2,793
Saint Vincent Grenadines			
Northern Grenadines[4]	9.0	23.3	5,514
Southern Grenadines[4]	7.5	19.4	2,853
TOTAL	150.3	389.3[5]	106,499

Demography

Population (1993): 109,000.
Density (1993): persons per sq mi 725.2, persons per sq km 280.0.
Urban-rural (1991)[6]: urban 24.6%; rural 75.4%.
Sex distribution (1991): male 49.92%; female 50.08%.
Age breakdown (1985): under 15, 37.4%; 15–29, 32.7%; 30–44, 14.9%; 45–59, 7.5%; 60–74, 5.6%; 75 and over, 1.9%.
Population projection: (2000) 116,000; (2010) 127,000.
Doubling time: 39 years.
Ethnic composition (1986): black 65.5%; mulatto 19.0%; East Indian 5.5%; white (mostly Portuguese) 3.5%; Amerindian/black 2.0%; other 4.5%.
Religious affiliation (1980): Protestant 80.5%, of which Anglican 41.6%, Methodist 20.9%, Baptist 5.9%, Seventh-day Adventist 4.4%; Roman Catholic 11.6%; other 7.9%.
Major city (1991): Kingstown 15,466.

Vital statistics

Birth rate per 1,000 population (1991): 24.3 (world avg. 26.4); legitimate, n.a.; illegitimate, n.a.
Death rate per 1,000 population (1991): 6.1 (world avg. 9.2).
Natural increase rate per 1,000 population (1991): 18.2 (world avg. 17.2).
Total fertility rate (avg. births per childbearing woman; 1991): 2.6.
Marriage rate per 1,000 population (1991): 4.2.
Divorce rate per 1,000 population (1991): 0.8.
Life expectancy at birth (1991): male 68.0 years; female 72.0 years.
Major causes of death per 100,000 population (1991): diseases of the circulatory system 189.4, of which hypertensive disease 90.0, diseases of pulmonary circulation and other forms of heart disease 55.3; malignant neoplasms (cancers) 107.8; endocrine and metabolic disorders 49.7.

National economy

Budget (1991). Revenue: EC$176,200,000 (income taxes 24.7%, consumption taxes on imported goods 23.7%, nontax revenue 16.1%, import duties 13.2%, foreign grants 9.3%). Expenditures: EC$184,100,000 (current expenditure 76.0%, development expenditure 24.0%).
Public debt (external, outstanding; December 1992): U.S.$67,600,000.
Land use (1990): forested 36.0%; meadows and pastures 5.0%; agricultural and under permanent cultivation 28.0%; other 31.0%.
Tourism: receipts from visitors (1992) U.S.$52,700,000; expenditures by nationals abroad (1991) U.S.$7,000,000.
Production (metric tons except as noted). Agriculture, forestry, fishing (1991): bananas 82,400[7], coconuts 20,000, eddoes and dasheens[8] 5,000, sweet potatoes 2,500, mangoes 2,000, plantains 1,500, lemons and limes 1,000, ginger 859, arrowroot starch 63, soursops, guavas, and papaws are other important fruits; livestock (number of live animals) 15,000 sheep, 9,000 pigs, 8,000 cattle; roundwood, n.a.; fish catch (1990) 8,370, of which squids and octopuses 4,393. Mining and quarrying: sand and gravel for local use. Manufacturing (value added in EC$'000; 1988): beverages and tobacco products 9,686; food products 9,499; textiles, clothing, and footwear 3,872; metal products and electrical machinery 2,510. Construction (gross floor area planned; 1991): 110,600 sq m. Energy production (consumption): electricity (kW-hr; 1991) 53,000,000 (49,000,000); coal, none (none); crude petroleum, none (none); petroleum products (metric tons; 1990) none (26,000); natural gas, none (none).

Gross national product (1991): U.S.$187,000,000 (U.S.$1,730 per capita).

Structure of gross domestic product and labour force

	1991[9]		1980	
	in value EC$'000,000	% of total value	labour force	% of labour force
Agriculture	85.8	17.8	8,928	25.7
Mining	1.3	0.3	108	0.3
Manufacturing	43.4	9.0	1,781	5.1
Construction	45.8	9.5	3,549	10.2
Public utilities	23.7	4.9	402	1.2
Transportation and communications	105.6	22.0	1,882	5.4
Trade	68.5	14.3	2,566	7.4
Finance, real estate	54.9	11.4	351	1.0
Pub. admin., defense	73.2	15.2	7,579	21.8
Services	8.5	1.8		
Other	−30.0[10]	−6.2[10]	7,593[11]	21.9[11]
TOTAL	480.7	100.0	34,739	100.0

Population economically active (1991): total 42,030; activity rate of total population 39.5% (participation rates: over age 15 [1980] 60.9%; female [1980] 36.1%; unemployed [1992] 19.0%).

Price and earnings indexes (1985 = 100)

	1986	1987	1988	1989	1990	1991	1992
Consumer price index	101.0	104.4	104.6	107.6	115.8	122.2	126.0
Annual earnings index	107.0	...	...	...	...	...	...

Household income and expenditure. Average household size (1991) 3.9; income per household (1988) EC$4,579 (U.S.$1,696); sources of income: n.a.; expenditure (1975–76): food and beverages 59.8%, clothing 7.7%, household furnishings 6.6%, housing 6.3%, energy 6.2%, other 13.4%.

Foreign trade[12]

Balance of trade (current prices)

	1986	1987	1988	1989	1990	1991
EC$'000,000	−63.2	−125.1	−99.9	−142.5	−144.0	−162.3
% of total	15.5%	30.7%	17.8%	26.1%	24.4%	27.7%

Imports (1990): EC$367,400,000 (basic manufactures 23.9%; food products 21.7%; machinery and transport equipment 21.7%). *Major import sources:* United States 36.0%; United Kingdom 17.7%; Trinidad and Tobago 12.5%; Barbados 4.1%; Canada 3.9%.
Exports (1990)[13]: EC$223,300,000 (domestic exports 94.0%, of which bananas 53.9%, flour 8.7%, varieties of taro roots 4.3%; reexports 6.0%). *Major export destinations:* United Kingdom 54.0%; Trinidad and Tobago 12.1%; United States 10.4%; Saint Lucia 6.2%.

Transport and communications

Transport. Railroads: none. Roads (1991): total length 586 mi, 943 km (paved 16%). Vehicles (1991): passenger cars 5,350; trucks and buses 2,814. Merchant marine (1992): vessels (100 gross tons and over) 881; total deadweight tonnage 7,044,189. Air transport (1991): passenger arrivals 107,109, passenger departures 114,732; airports (1993) with scheduled flights 5.
Communications. Daily newspapers: none[14]. Radio (1992): total number of receivers 55,000 (1 per 2.0 persons). Television (1992): total number of receivers 17,700 (1 per 6.1 persons). Telephones (1990): 16,837 (1 per 6.4 persons).

Education and health

Education (1991–92)

	schools	teachers	students	student/ teacher ratio
Primary (age 5–11)	60	1,215	24,134	19.9
Secondary (age 12–18)	21	408	7,124	17.5
Voc., teacher tr.	2	...	337	...

Educational attainment (1980). Percentage of population age 25 and over having: no formal schooling 2.4%; primary education 88.0%; secondary 8.2%; higher 1.4%. *Literacy* (1983): total population age 15 and over literate 54,000 (85.0%).
Health: physicians (1992) 40 (1 per 2,690 persons); hospital beds (1987) 404 (1 per 258 persons); infant mortality rate per 1,000 live births (1989–91 avg.) 20.3.
Food (1988–90): daily per capita caloric intake 2,460 (vegetable products 85%, animal products 15%); 102% of FAO recommended minimum requirement.

Military

Total active duty personnel (1987): 570-member police force includes 80-member paramilitary unit. *Military expenditure as percentage of central government expenditure* (1989–90): 5.6%[15].

[1]Includes 6 nonelective seats. [2]For statistical purposes and the election of legislative representatives. [3]For local administration, the island of Saint Vincent is divided into five parishes; population by parish is not available. [4]Both a constituency and a parish. [5]Detail does not add to total given because of rounding. [6]Urban defined as Kingstown and suburbs. [7]1992. [8]Varieties of taro roots. [9]At factor cost. [10]Less imputed bank service charges. [11]Not adequately defined. [12]Imports c.i.f.; exports f.o.b. [13]*Exports* (1991): EC$212,000,000 (bananas 42.8%, flour 10.0%, rice 1.9%). [14]Weekly newspapers: 2. [15]May not agree with military expenditure as percentage of GNP because of different bases used.

San Marino

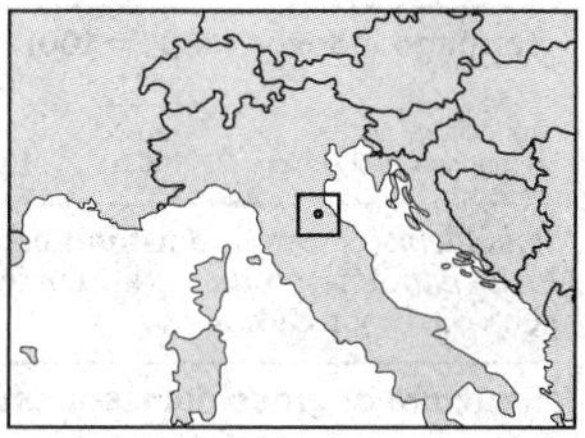

Official name: Serenissima Repubblica di San Marino (Most Serene Republic of San Marino).
Form of government: unitary multiparty republic with one legislative house (Great and General Council [60]).
Head of state and government: Captains-Regent (2).
Capital: San Marino.
Official language: Italian.
Official religion: none.
Monetary unit: 1 Italian lira (Lit; plural lire) = 100 centesimi; valuation (Oct. 4, 1993) 1 U.S.$ = Lit 1,589; 1 £ = Lit 2,407.

Area and population

		area		population
Castles	Capitals	sq mi	sq km	1993[1] estimate
Acquaviva	Acquaviva	1.88	4.86	1,217
Borgo Maggiore	Borgo	3.48	9.01	5,026
Chiesanuova	Chiesanuova	2.11	5.46	787
Città	San Marino	2.74	7.09	4,335
Domagnano	Domagnano	2.56	6.62	2,100
Faetano	Faetano	2.99	7.75	765
Fiorentino	Fiorentino	2.53	6.56	1,662
Montegiardino	Montegiardino	1.28	3.31	647
Serravalle/Dogano	Serravalle	4.07	10.53	7,537
TOTAL		23.63[2]	61.19	24,076

Demography

Population (1993): 24,100.
Density (1993): persons per sq mi 1,019.9, persons per sq km 393.8.
Urban-rural (1993[1]): urban 89.8%; rural 10.2%.
Sex distribution (1993[1]): male 49.74%; female 50.26%.
Age breakdown (1993[1]): under 15, 15.3%; 15–29, 24.2%; 30–44, 23.5%; 45–59, 17.8%; 60–74, 13.6%; 75 and over, 5.6%.
Population projection: (2000) 26,000; (2010) 30,000.
Doubling time: not applicable; natural population growth is negligible, averaging only 0.3% during 1988–92.
Ethnic composition (1993[3]): Sammarinesi 79.6%; Italian 17.5%; other 2.9%.
Religious affiliation (1980): Roman Catholic 95.2%; no religion 3.0%; other 1.8%.
Major cities (1993[1]): Serravalle/Dogano 4,695; San Marino 2,397; Borgo Maggiore 2,306; Murata 1,416; Domagnano 1,021.

Vital statistics

Birth rate per 1,000 population (1988–92): 10.4 (world avg. 26.4); (1985) legitimate 95.2%; illegitimate 4.8%.
Death rate per 1,000 population (1988–92): 7.2 (world avg. 9.2).
Natural increase rate per 1,000 population (1998–92): 3.2 (world avg. 17.2).
Total fertility rate (avg. births per childbearing woman; 1984): 1.3.
Marriage rate per 1,000 population (1988–92): 5.8.
Divorce rate per 1,000 population (1988–92): 0.8.
Life expectancy at birth (1980–85): male 70.7 years; female 76.2 years.
Major causes of death per 100,000 population (1988–92): diseases of the circulatory system 347.6; malignant neoplasms (cancers) 233.8; accidents, violence, and suicide 42.3; diseases of the respiratory system 19.8.

National economy

Budget (1991). Revenue: Lit 379,337,000,000 (mainly receipts from postage stamp sales, tourism, and customs duties [collected by Italy and paid as a subsidy]). Expenditures: Lit 379,337,000,000 ([4]finance and economic planning 31.0%, internal affairs 11.3%, health and social security 9.0%, education and culture 7.1%, public works 6.3%).
Public debt: n.a.
Tourism: number of tourist arrivals (1992) 3,208,290; receipts from visitors (1983) U.S.$56,454,000; expenditures by nationals abroad, n.a.
Gross national product (at current market prices; 1987): U.S.$188,000,000 (U.S.$8,590 per capita).

Structure of labour force (1993[1])

	labour force	% of labour force
Agriculture	296	2.1
Manufacturing	4,591	32.5
Construction and public utilities	1,106	7.8
Transportation and communications	285	2.0
Trade	2,402	17.0
Finance and insurance	339	2.4
Services	1,116	7.9
Public administration and defense	3,475	24.6
Other	503[5]	3.6[5]
TOTAL	14,113	100.0[2]

Production (metric tons except as noted). Agriculture, forestry, fishing[4]: wheat *c.* 4,400, grapes *c.* 700, barley *c.* 500; livestock (number of live animals; 1992) 1,038 cattle, 830 pigs, 100 sheep. Manufacturing (1992): processed meats 396,443 kg, of which beef 210,729 kg, pork 104,244 kg, veal 17,999 kg; cheese 90,048 kg; butter 16,516 kg; yogurt 7,763 kg; milk 974,233 litres; other major products include textiles, cement, paper, leather, bricks, pottery, tiles, postage stamps, gold and silver jewelry, paints, synthetic rubber, and furniture. Construction (new units completed; 1992): residential 131; nonresidential 60. Energy production (consumption): all electrical power is imported via electrical grid from Italy (consumption, n.a.); coal, none (n.a.); crude petroleum, none (n.a.); petroleum products, none (n.a.); natural gas, none (n.a.).
Population economically active (1993[1]): total 14,113; activity rate of total population 58.6% (participation rates: ages 15–64 [1992] 72.9%; female 40.8%; unemployed 3.6%).

Price and earnings indexes (1985 = 100)

	1987	1988	1989	1990	1991	1992	1993[6]
Consumer price index	114.6	120.7	127.4	135.9	146.4	154.0	159.7
Earnings index	...	...	...	...	...	...	...

Household income and expenditure. Total number of households (1993[1]) 8,707; average household size 2.8; income per household: n.a.; sources of income: n.a.; expenditure (1985)[7]: food, beverages, and tobacco 30.4%, transportation and communications 14.5%, housing, fuel, and electrical energy 9.7%, clothing and footwear 8.8%, recreation, entertainment, education, and culture 8.1%, furniture, appliances, and goods and services for the home 7.5%, health and sanitary services 5.1%, other goods and services 15.9%.
Land use (1985): agricultural and under permanent cultivation 74%; meadows and pastures 22%; forested, built-on, wasteland, and other 4%.

Foreign trade

Balance of trade: n.a. San Marino and Italy form a single customs area; separate figures for San Marino are not available.
Imports (1992): manufactured goods of all kinds, oil, and gold. *Major import source:* Italy.
Exports (1992): wine, wheat, woolen goods, furniture, wood, ceramics, building stone, dairy products, meat, and postage stamps. *Major export destination:* Italy.

Transport and communications

Transport. Railroads: none (nearest rail terminal is at Rimini, Italy, 17 mi [27 km] northeast). Roads (1987): total length 147 mi, 237 km. Vehicles (1993[3]): passenger cars 21,769; trucks and buses 3,559. Merchant marine: vessels (100 gross tons and over) none. Air transport: airports with scheduled flights, none; there is, however, a heliport that provides passenger and cargo service between San Marino and Rimini, Italy, during the summer months.
Communications. Daily newspapers (1992): 6; circulation per 1,000 population, n.a. Radio (1991): total number of receivers 12,535 (1 per 1.9 persons). Television (1990): total number of receivers 8,000 (1 per 2.9 persons). Telephones (1988): 15,700 (1 per 1.5 persons).

Education and health

Education (1991–92)

	schools	teachers	students	student/ teacher ratio
Primary (age 6–10)	14	218	1,200	5.5
Secondary (age 11–18)	3	129	841	6.5
Voc., teacher tr.	...	...	317	...
Higher	...	...	...	...

Educational attainment (1993). Percentage of the adult labour force having: basic literacy or primary education 25.6%; secondary 39.7%; some post-secondary 29.0%; higher degree 5.7%. *Literacy* (1986): total population age 15 and over literate 18,135 (98.0%); males literate 8,957 (98.2%); females literate 9,178 (97.7%).
Health (1987): physicians 60 (1 per 375 persons); hospital beds 149 (1 per 151 persons); infant mortality rate per 1,000 live births (1988–92) 12.2.
Food (1988–90)[8]: daily per capita caloric intake 3,498 (vegetable products 74%, animal products 26%); 139% of FAO recommended minimum requirement.

Military

Total active duty personnel (1992): none[9]. *Military expenditure as percentage of national budget* (1987): 0.9% (world 5.4%); per capita expenditure (1987) U.S.$82.

[1]January 1. [2]Detail does not add to total given because of rounding. [3]April 1. [4]Early 1980s. [5]Unemployed. [6]May. [7]Weighting coefficients for component expenditures are those of the 1985 official Italian consumer price index. [8]Figures are for Italy. [9]Defense is provided by a public security force of about 50; all fit males ages 16–55 constitute a militia.

São Tomé and Príncipe

Official name: República democrática de São Tomé e Príncipe (Democratic Republic of São Tomé and Príncipe).
Form of government: multiparty[1] republic with one legislative house (National People's Assembly [55]).
Chief of state: President.
Head of government: Prime Minister.
Capital: São Tomé.
Official language: Portuguese.
Official religion: none.
Monetary unit: 1 dobra (Db) = 100 cêntimos; valuation (Oct. 4, 1993) 1 U.S.$ = Db 238.26; 1 £ = Db 360.96.

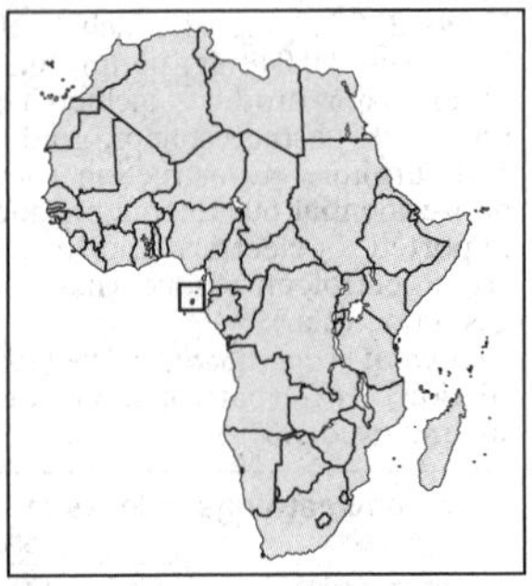

Area and population

Islands Districts	Capitals	area sq mi	area sq km	population 1991 census[2]
Príncipe		55	142	5,639
Paguê	Santo António	55	142	5,639
São Tomé		332	859	114,507
Aqua Grande	São Tomé	7	17	43,420
Cantagalo	Santana	46	119	11,421
Caué	São João Angolares	103	267	5,541
Lemba	Neves	88	229	9,448
Lobata	Guadalupe	41	105	13,101
Mé-Zóchi	Trindade	47	122	31,576
TOTAL		386	1,001	120,146

Demography

Population (1993): 125,000.
Density (1993): persons per sq mi 323.8, persons per sq km 124.9.
Urban-rural (1988): urban 40.5%; rural 59.5%.
Sex distribution (1991): male 49.42%; female 50.58%.
Age breakdown (1989): under 15, 38.1%; 15–29, 22.0%; 30–44, 16.9%; 45–59, 11.9%; 60 and over, 7.6%; not stated, 3.5%.
Population projection: (2000) 146,000; (2010) 182,000.
Doubling time: 23 years.
Ethnolinguistic composition: mestiços, angolares (descendants of Angolan slaves), forros (descendants of freed slaves), serviçais (alien contract labourers), tongas (children of serviçais) speak Portuguese; non-Portuguese-speaking Europeans speak French and Spanish.
Religious affiliation (1991): Roman Catholic, about 80.8%; remainder mostly Protestant, predominantly Seventh-day Adventist and an indigenous Evangelical Church.
Major cities (1991): São Tomé 43,420; Trindade 11,388[3]; Santana 6,190[3]; Neves 5,919[3]; Santo Amaro 5,878[3].

Vital statistics

Birth rate per 1,000 population (1992): 38.0 (world avg. 26.4); (1977) legitimate 9.8%; illegitimate 90.2%.
Death rate per 1,000 population (1992): 8.0 (world avg. 9.2).
Natural increase rate per 1,000 population (1992): 30.0 (world avg. 17.2).
Total fertility rate (avg. births per childbearing woman; 1992): 5.2.
Marriage rate per 1,000 population: n.a.
Divorce rate per 1,000 population: n.a.
Life expectancy at birth (1992): male 64.0 years; female 68.0 years.
Major causes of death per 100,000 population (1987): malaria 160.6; direct obstetric causes 76.7; pneumonia 74.0; influenza 61.5; anemias 47.3; hypertensive disease 32.1.

National economy

Budget (1988). Revenue: Db 975,000,000 (indirect taxes 44.4%; income from property 16.0%; nondurable goods 11.3%; direct taxes 10.2%). Expenditures: Db 1,115,000,000 (current expenditure 82.4%, of which wages and salaries 45.5%; capital expenditure 17.6%).
Tourism (1990): receipts from visitors U.S.$1,000,000; expenditures by nationals abroad U.S.$2,000,000.
Production (metric tons except as noted). Agriculture, forestry, fishing (1992): coconuts 42,000, cassava 5,000, fruits (other than melons) 5,000, cacao 3,000, copra 3,000, bananas 3,000, palmetto 3,000[4], vegetables and melons 3,000, cereals 1,000, taro 742[5], palm kernel 250; livestock (number of live animals) 4,000 goats, 4,000 cattle, 3,000 pigs, 2,000 sheep; roundwood (1991) 9,000 cu m; fish catch (1991) 2,996, principally marine fish and shellfish. Mining and quarrying: some quarrying to support local construction industry. Manufacturing (1987): bread 2,459; soap 604; coconut oil 330; ice 191[6]; palm oil 177; limes 22[6]; corn (maize) flour 18[6]; sawn wood 3,272 cu m; beer 28,540 hectolitres; bottled water 13,750 hectolitres; soft drinks 10,460 hectolitres; other products include clothing, bricks, and clay products. Construction (1972): buildings authorized 44 (5,561 sq m, of which residential 3,698, mixed residential-commercial 1,361, commercial 502). Energy production (consumption): electricity (kW-hr; 1990) 15,000,000 (15,000,000); coal, none (n.a.); crude petroleum, none (n.a.); petroleum products (metric tons; 1990) none (22,000); natural gas, none (n.a.).
Household income and expenditure. Average household size (1981): 4.0; income per household: n.a.; sources of income: n.a.; expenditure: n.a.
Population economically active (1987): total 20,912; activity rate of total population 18.5% (participation rates [1981]: ages 15–64, 61.1%; female 32.4%; unemployed 30.7%[5]).

Earnings indexes (1981 = 100)

	1981	1982	1983	1984	1985	1986
Agricultural sector	100.0	93.6	98.5	103.0	97.2	96.3
Nonagricultural sectors	100.0	101.4	100.7	107.7	107.7	123.8

Public debt (external, outstanding; 1991): U.S.$147,100,000.
Gross national product (at current market prices; 1991): U.S.$42,000,000 (U.S.$350 per capita).

Structure of gross domestic product and labour force

	1989 in value Db '000,000	1989 % of total value	1987 labour force	1987 % of labour force
Agriculture	927.7	24.6	8,448	40.4
Mining	4.0	0.1 }		
Manufacturing	363.8	9.7 }	1,129[7]	5.4[7]
Public utilities	93.2	2.5 }		
Construction	332.9	8.8	742	3.5
Transportation and communications	454.7	12.1	455	2.2
Trade	376.5	10.0	[7]	[7]
Finance	45.9	1.2	[7]	[7]
Pub. admin., defense	1,165.0	31.0 }	3,708	17.7
Services	...	... }		
Other	...	...	6,430[8]	30.7[8]
TOTAL	3,763.7	100.0	20,912	100.0[9]

Land use (1991): meadows and pastures 1.0%; agricultural and under permanent cultivation 38.6%; forest, built-on, wasteland, and other 60.4%.

Foreign trade[10]

Balance of trade (current prices)

	1984	1985	1986	1987	1988	1989
Db '000,000	−732.1	−765.2	−252.6	−268.4	−127.4	−726
% of total	40.4%	54.8%	26.9%	25.8%	8.3%	35.0%

Imports (1988): Db 1,733,000,000 (food and other agricultural products 35.2%, capital goods 30.5%, intermediate goods 27.8%, mineral fuels and lubricants 6.5%). *Major import sources* (1987): Portugal 33.7%; East Germany 12.1%; Spain 11.3%; Angola 8.8%; West Germany 8.4%; France 6.5%; The Netherlands 5.4%; Norway 4.2%; Belgium-Luxembourg 3.5%.
Exports (1988): Db 927,000,000 (cocoa 95.4%, copra 4.0%, coconuts 0.3%, pulses 0.3%). *Major export destinations:* West Germany 52.3%; East Germany 20.2%; The Netherlands 12.7%.

Transport and communications

Transport. Railroads: none. Roads (1988): total length 236 mi, 380 km (paved 66%). Vehicles (1975): passenger cars 1,774; trucks and buses 265. Merchant marine (1992): vessels (100 gross tons and over) 4; total deadweight tonnage 2,277. Air transport (1985): passenger-mi 3,800,000, passenger-km 6,100,000; short ton-mi cargo 70,000, short ton-km cargo 100,000; airports (1993) with scheduled flights 2.
Communications. Daily newspapers: none; 2 government weeklies (circulation, n.a.). Radio (1992): total number of receivers 31,000 (1 per 4.0 persons). Television: none. Telephones (1988): 2,800 (1 per 42 persons).

Education and health

Education (1989)

	schools	teachers	students	student/ teacher ratio
Primary (age 6–13)	64	559	19,822	35.5
Secondary (age 14–18)	11[11]	318	7,446	23.4
Voc., teacher tr.	2[11]	18[12]	289	...
Higher	...	...	700[13]	...

Educational attainment (1981). Percentage of population age 25 and over having: no formal schooling 56.6%; incomplete primary education 18.0%; primary 19.2%; incomplete secondary 4.6%; complete secondary 1.3%; postsecondary 0.3%. *Literacy* (1981): total population age 15 and over literate 28,114 (54.2%); males literate 17,689 (70.2%); females literate 10,425 (39.1%).
Health (1987): physicians 40 (1 per 2,819 persons); hospital beds (1983) 640 (1 per 158 persons); infant mortality rate per 1,000 live births (1992) 58.
Food (1988–90): daily per capita caloric intake 2,153 (vegetable products 95%, animal products 5%); 92% of FAO recommended minimum requirement.

Military

Total active duty personnel (1992): a gendarmerie of about 900 men was to be established in the early 1990s. *Military expenditure as percentage of GNP* (1980): 1.6% (world 5.4%); per capita expenditure U.S.$6.

[1]Multiparty system effective as of January 1991 elections. [2]Preliminary. [3]1981. [4]1988. [5]1987. [6]1983. [7]Manufacturing includes Trade and Finance. [8]Unemployed. [9]Detail does not add to total given because of rounding. [10]Import figures are c.i.f. [11]1984–85. [12]Vocational teachers only. [13]Students abroad, 1982–83.

Saudi Arabia

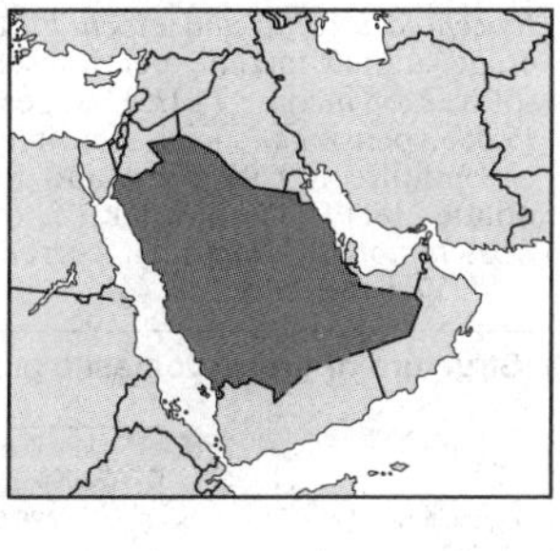

Official name: al-Mamlakah al-ʿArabīyah as-Saʿūdīyah (Kingdom of Saudi Arabia).
Form of government: monarchy.
Head of state and government: King.
Capital: Riyadh.
Official language: Arabic.
Official religion: Islam.
Monetary unit: 1 Saudi riyal (SRls) = 100 halalah; valuation (Oct. 4, 1993) 1 U.S.$ = SRls 3.76; 1 £ = SRls 5.69.

Area and population

Geographic Regions / Administrative Regions[2]	Capitals	area sq mi	area sq km	population 1985 estimate
al-Gharbīyah (Western)	—	...	...	3,043,189
al-Bāḥah	al-Bāḥah	...	...	...
al-Madīnah	Medina (al-Madīnah)	...	...	...
Makkah	Mecca (Makkah)	...	...	...
al-Janūbīyah (Southern)	—	...	...	625,017
ʿAsīr	Abha	...	...	...
Jīzān	Jīzān	...	...	...
Najrān	Najrān	...	...	...
ash-Shamālīyah (Northern)	—	...	...	679,476
al-Ḥudūd ash-Shamālīyah (Northern Borders)	ʿArʿar	...	...	...
al-Jawf	Sakākah	...	...	...
Tabūk	Tabūk	...	...	...
ash-Sharqīyah (Eastern)	—	...	...	3,030,765
ash-Sharqīyah (Eastern)	ad-Dammām	...	...	...
al-Wūsṭā (Central)	—	...	...	3,632,092
Ḥāʾil	Ḥāʾil	...	...	...
al-Qaṣīm	Buraydah	...	...	...
ar-Riyāḍ	Riyadh (ar-Riyāḍ)	...	...	...
TOTAL		865,000	2,240,000	11,010,539[1]

Demography

Population (1993): 17,419,000.
Density (1993): persons per sq mi 20.1, persons per sq km 7.8.
Urban-rural (1990): urban 77.3%; rural 22.7%.
Sex distribution (1990): male 55.82%; female 44.18%.
Age breakdown (1990): under 15, 42.9%; 15–29, 24.6%; 30–44, 19.6%; 45–59, 8.3%; 60–74, 3.9%; 75 and over, 0.7%.
Population projection: (2000) 22,621,000; (2010) 32,095,000.
Doubling time: 23 years.
Ethnic composition (1983): Saudi 82.0%; Yemeni 9.6%; other Arab 3.4%; other 5.0%.
Religious affiliation (1980): Muslim (mostly Sunnī) 98.8%; Christian 0.8%; other 0.4%.
Major cities (1980): Riyadh (ar-Riyāḍ) 1,308,000[3]; Jiddah 1,500,000[4]; Mecca (Makkah) 550,000; aṭ-Ṭāʾif 300,000.

Vital statistics

Birth rate per 1,000 population (1990–95): 35.8 (world avg. 26.4).
Death rate per 1,000 population (1990–95): 4.9 (world avg. 9.2).
Natural increase rate per 1,000 population (1990–95): 30.9 (world avg. 17.2).
Total fertility rate (avg. births per childbearing woman; 1990–95): 6.7.
Marriage rate per 1,000 population: n.a.
Divorce rate per 1,000 population: n.a.
Life expectancy at birth (1990–95): male 67.8 years; female 70.9 years.
Major causes of death per 100,000 population: n.a.; however, principal infectious diseases include malaria, diarrheal diseases, cholera, trachoma, cerebrospinal meningitis, yellow fever, typhoid, tuberculosis, and lung infections. Parasitic infections, motor vehicle accidents, and metabolic disorders are also significant.

National economy

Budget (1993). Revenue: SRls 169,150,000,000 (1990; oil revenues 72.8%). Expenditures: SRls 196,950,000,000 (defense and security 30.3%, education 17.3%, health and social development 7.2%, transportation and communications 4.6%, economic resource development 4.5%).
Public debt (external, outstanding; 1989): U.S.$1,187,000,000.
Production (metric tons except as noted). Agriculture, forestry, fishing (1992): wheat 4,100,000, dates 545,000, tomatoes 480,000, watermelons 450,000, barley 410,000, grapes 105,000, cucumbers and gherkins 93,000, pumpkins, squash, and gourds 79,000, eggplants 72,000, potatoes 50,000, carrots 19,000, onions 15,000; livestock (number of live animals) 6,008,000 sheep, 3,350,000 goats, 419,000 camels, 216,000 cattle, 102,000 asses, 83,000,000 chickens; fish catch (1991) 43,251. Mining and quarrying (1991): gypsum 375,000; gold 4,300 kg. Manufacturing (1991): cement 11,371,280; steel 1,850,000; fuel oils 161,700,000 barrels; diesel oil 147,439,000 barrels; gasoline and naphtha 128,594,000 barrels; jet fuel 48,642,000 barrels; asphalt and related products 22,501,000 barrels. Construction (1991): residential 16,077,677 sq m; nonresidential 2,204,894 sq m. Energy production (consumption): electricity (kW-hr; 1991) 47,710,000,000 (47,710,000,000); coal, n.a. (n.a.); crude petroleum (barrels; 1991) 2,965,000,000 (539,000,000); petroleum products (metric tons; 1991) 88,131,000 (39,304,000); natural gas (cu m; 1991) 31,822,000,000 (31,822,000,000).
Tourism: receipts from visitors (1989) U.S.$2,050,000,000; expenditures by nationals abroad (1988) U.S.$2,000,000,000.
Pilgrims to Mecca from abroad (1989): 774,560.
Land use (1991): forested 0.6%; meadows and pastures 39.5%; agricultural and under permanent cultivation 1.1%; built-on, waste, and other 58.8%.
Population economically active (1988): total 5,368,804; activity rate of total population 36.3% (participation rates: ages 15–64, 59.1%; female 3.5%).

Price and earnings indexes (1985 = 100)

	1986	1987	1988	1989	1990	1991	1992[3]
Consumer price index	96.8	95.2	96.2	97.1	99.1	103.6	103.2
Earnings index	...	...	...	...	...	...	...

Gross national product (1992): U.S.$126,320,000,000 (U.S.$7,940 per capita).

Structure of gross domestic product and labour force

	1990 in value SRls '000,000	% of total value	labour force	% of labour force
Agriculture	22,200	6.4	569,200	9.9
Mining	1,700	0.5	3,500	0.1
Oil sector	122,300	35.0	46,800	0.8
Manufacturing	33,100	9.5	374,900	6.5
Construction	31,800	9.1	944,100	16.4
Public utilities	−800	−0.2	126,900	2.2
Transp. and commun.	21,700	6.2	262,300	4.5
Trade	28,200	8.1	898,300	15.6
Finance	23,000	6.6	99,000	1.7
Pub. admin., defense	56,200	16.1	624,800	10.8
Services and other	9,900	2.8	1,822,000	31.6
TOTAL	349,300	100.0[5]	5,771,800	100.0[5]

Household income and expenditure. Average household size (1986) 6.6; income per household: n.a.; sources of income: n.a.; expenditure (1988)[6]: food 37%, housing 21%, transportation and communications 15%, clothing 8%, household furnishings 7%, education and entertainment 2%.

Foreign trade[7]

Balance of trade (current prices)

	1986	1987	1988	1989	1990	1991
SRls '000,000,000	+8.6	+16.5	+15.1	+32.3	+82.1	+77.2
% of total	6.1%	10.5%	9.0%	17.9%	32.8%	27.5%

Imports (1991): SRls 108,881,300,000 (transport equipment 21.0%, machinery and appliances 19.4%, metals and metal articles 9.1%, textiles and clothing 8.4%, chemicals 7.4%, live animals and animal products 5.2%). *Major import sources:* U.S. 20.2%; Japan 13.7%; U.K. 11.3%; Germany 7.8%; Switzerland 4.9%; Italy 4.6%; France 4.0%; South Korea 3.0%; Taiwan 2.0%; The Netherlands 1.9%; Belgium 1.9%.
Exports (1991): SRls 178,974,100,000 (crude petroleum 78.1%, refined petroleum products 13.2%, other 8.7%). *Major export destinations:* U.S. 22.9%; Japan 16.0%; The Netherlands 6.0%; South Korea 5.6%; Singapore 5.1%; France 4.6%; Italy 4.3%; Bahrain 3.3%; Brazil 2.8%; Taiwan 2.8%; India 2.3%.

Transport and communications

Transport. Railroads (1989–90): route length (1991) 864 mi, 1,390 km; passenger-mi 93,800,000, passenger-km 151,000,000; short ton-mi cargo 487,700,000, metric ton-km cargo 712,000,000. Roads (1992): total length 79,350 mi, 127,698 km (paved 31%). Vehicles (1991): passenger cars 2,762,132; trucks and buses 2,286,541. Merchant marine (1992): vessels (100 gross tons and over) 301; total deadweight tonnage 1,381,651. Air transport (1992)[8]: passenger-mi 10,913,600,000, passenger-km 17,563,300,000; short ton-mi cargo 465,180,000, metric ton-km cargo 679,159,000; airports (1993) with scheduled flights 24.
Communications. Daily newspapers (1989): total number 10; total circulation 664,300; circulation per 1,000 population 49. Radio (1992): 5,000,000 receivers (1 per 3.1 persons). Television (1992): 4,500,000 receivers (1 per 3.0 persons). Telephones (1991): 1,466,311 (1 per 10.0 persons).

Education and health

Education (1990–91)

	schools	teachers	students	student/teacher ratio
Primary (age 6–12)	9,097	120,453	1,876,916	15.6
Secondary (age 13–18)	4,643	63,399	859,642	13.6
Voc., teacher tr.	190	3,193	31,490	9.9
Higher	72	12,224	147,079	12.0

Educational attainment (1986). Percentage of population age 25 and over having: no formal schooling 31.8%; primary, secondary, or higher education 68.2%. *Literacy* (1990): percentage of population age 15 and over literate 62.4%; males literate 73.1%; females literate 48.1%.
Health (1991): physicians 25,543 (1 per 523 persons); hospital beds 40,923 (1 per 359 persons); infant mortality rate per 1,000 live births 69.0.
Food (1988–90): daily per capita caloric intake 2,929 (vegetable products 84%, animal products 16%); 121% of FAO recommended minimum requirement.

Military

Total active duty personnel (1993): 101,000 (army 71.3%, navy 10.9%, air force 17.8%). *Military expenditure as percentage of GNP* (1989): 16.0% (world 4.9%); per capita expenditure U.S.$897.

[1]Preliminary 1992 census total 16,927,294; detail, n.a. [2]13 administrative regions created September 1993. [3]1981 estimate. [4]1983 estimate. [5]Detail does not add to total given because of rounding. [6]Urban middle-income households only. [7]Import figures are f.o.b. in balance of trade and c.i.f. in commodities and trading partners. [8]Domestic and international operation of Saudi Arabian Airlines.

Senegal

Official name: République du Sénégal (Republic of Senegal).
Form of government: multiparty republic with one legislative house (National Assembly [120]).
Chief of state: President.
Head of government: Prime Minister.
Capital: Dakar.
Official language: French.
Official religion: none.
Monetary unit: 1 CFA franc (CFAF) = 100 centimes; valuation (Oct. 4, 1993) 1 U.S.$ = CFAF 283.25; 1 £ = CFAF 429.12.

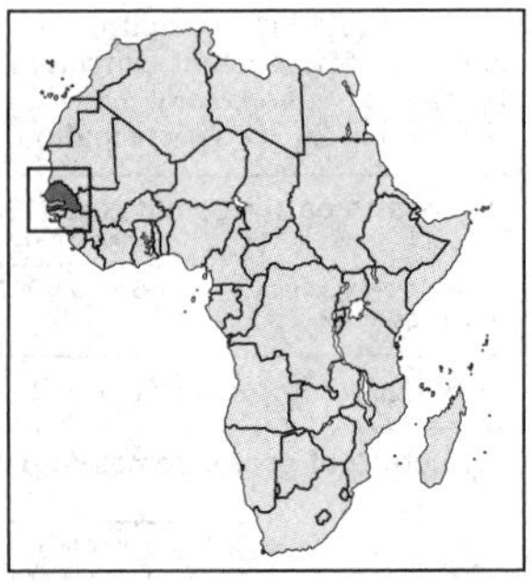

Area and population

		area		population
Regions	Capitals	sq mi	sq km	1988 census
Dakar	Dakar	212	550	1,571,614
Diourbel	Diourbel	1,683	4,359	620,197
Fatick	Fatick	3,064	7,935	507,651
Kaolack	Kaolack	6,181	16,010	805,859
Kolda	Kolda	8,112	21,011	593,199
Louga	Louga	11,270	29,188	507,572
Saint-Louis	Saint-Louis	17,034	44,117	656,941
Tambacounda	Tambacounda	23,012	59,602	383,572
Thiès	Thiès	2,549	6,601	937,412
Ziguinchor	Ziguinchor	2,834	7,339	398,067
TOTAL		75,951	196,712	6,982,084

Demography

Population (1993): 7,899,000.
Density (1993): persons per sq mi 104.0, persons per sq km 40.2.
Urban-rural (1988): urban 38.6%; rural 61.4%.
Sex distribution (1988): male 48.65%; female 51.35%.
Age breakdown (1988): under 15, 47.5%; 15–29, 26.1%; 30–44, 13.6%; 45–59, 7.8%; 60 and over, 5.0%.
Population projection: (2000) 9,519,000; (2010) 12,424,000.
Doubling time: 23 years.
Ethnic composition (1988): Wolof 43.5%; Fulani- (Peul-) Tukulor 24.1%; Serer 14.9%; Diola 5.3%; Malinke 4.3%; other 7.9%.
Religious affiliation (1988): Sunnī Muslim 94.0%; Christian, predominantly Roman Catholic, 4.9%; traditional beliefs and other 1.1%.
Major cities (1992): Dakar 1,729,823; Thiès 201,350; Kaolack 179,894; Ziguinchor 148,831; Saint-Louis 125,717.

Vital statistics

Birth rate per 1,000 population (1991): 44.0 (world avg. 26.4).
Death rate per 1,000 population (1991): 13.0 (world avg. 9.2).
Natural increase rate per 1,000 population (1991): 31.0 (world avg. 17.2).
Total fertility rate (avg. births per childbearing woman; 1991): 6.2.
Marriage rate per 1,000 population: n.a.
Divorce rate per 1,000 population: n.a.
Life expectancy at birth (1991): male 54.0 years; female 56.0 years.
Major causes of death (percentage of officially confirmed deaths from infectious diseases only; 1988): malaria 44.8%; tetanus 17.8%; meningitis 15.3%; tuberculosis of respiratory system 10.4%.

National economy

Budget (1993). Revenue: CFAF 479,600,000,000 (1990; current revenue 86.0%, of which import duties 28.0%, personal and corporate income taxes 17.0%, value-added taxes 16.9%, personal property taxes 3.1%; aid, grants, and subsidies 13.9%). Expenditures: CFAF 539,100,000,000 (1990; debt service 22.4%; public services 16.0%; agriculture 13.9%; education 11.0%; defense 6.1%; transportation and communications 4.9%; public order and security 4.5%; industry 3.2%; health 2.3%).
Public debt (external, outstanding; 1991): U.S.$2,838,000,000.
Production (metric tons except as noted). Agriculture, forestry, fishing (1992): sugarcane 837,000, peanuts (groundnuts) 578,000, millet 446,000, paddy rice 177,000, sorghum 117,000, corn (maize) 115,000, seed cotton 51,000; livestock (number of live animals) 3,600,000 sheep, 2,800,000 cattle, 2,400,000 goats, 310,000 pigs; roundwood (1991) 5,098,000 cu m; fish catch (1991) 319,693. Mining and quarrying (1992): calcium phosphate 2,283,500; cement 603,100; aluminum phosphate 119,300[1]. Manufacturing (1988): peanut oil 202,200; wheat flour 103,600; sugar 82,000[2]; fresh fish 72,400[3]; nitrogenous fertilizers 68,000; soap 32,900; cotton fibres 19,200; canned fish 18,000[3]; carbonated beverages 238,000 hectolitres; beer 170,000 hectolitres; footwear 561,400 pairs. Construction (authorized; 1989)[4]: residential 273,100 sq m; nonresidential 45,600 sq m. Energy production (consumption): electricity (kW-hr; 1991) 756,000,000 (756,000,000); coal, none (n.a.); crude petroleum (barrels; 1991) none (5,912,000); petroleum products (metric tons; 1991) 700,000 (756,000); natural gas, none (n.a.).
Population economically active (1992): total 3,288,000; activity rate of total population 42.5% (participation rates [1988]: over age 10, 46.2%; female 26.0%; unemployed 12.0%).

Price and earnings indexes (1985 = 100)

	1986	1987	1988	1989	1990	1991	1992
Consumer price index	106.4	101.8	99.9	100.4	100.7	98.9	98.8
Hourly earnings index[5]	100.0	100.0	100.0	104.7	109.5	109.5	109.5

Household income and expenditure[6]. Average household size (1988) 8.8; average annual income per household (1975) CFAF 1,105,800 (U.S.$5,160); sources of income (1975): wages and salaries 51.6%, remittances and gifts 17.5%, pensions, social security, and related benefits 12.5%, other 18.4%; expenditure (1979): food and tobacco 57.5%, housing, maintenance, and utilities 18.4%, clothing 11.9%, transport 5.4%, other 6.8%.
Gross national product (at current market prices; 1992): U.S.$6,110,000,000 (U.S.$780 per capita).

Structure of gross domestic product and labour force

	1990		1982	
	in value CFAF '000,000,000	% of total value	labour force[7]	% of labour force
Agriculture	326.5	20.5	10,654	9.1
Mining			1,918	1.6
Manufacturing	248.0	15.6	30,736	26.4
Public utilities			3,221	2.8
Construction	46.2	2.9	8,402	7.2
Transp. and commun.	150.5	9.5	24,789	21.2
Trade	388.6	24.5	14,648	12.6
Finance			7,921	6.8
Services	428.7	27.0	14,339	12.3
Pub. admin., defense				
Other	...	...	...	...
TOTAL	1,588.5	100.0	116,628	100.0

Tourism (1991): receipts from visitors U.S.$171,000,000; expenditures by nationals abroad U.S.$103,000,000.
Land use (1991): forested 54.6%; meadows and pastures 16.1%; agricultural and under permanent cultivation 12.2%; other 17.1%.

Foreign trade

Balance of trade (current prices)

	1985	1986	1987	1988	1989	1990
CFAF '000,000,000	−100.1	−93.0	−130.3	−169.6	−168.4	−105.8
% of total	21.4%	18.7%	28.8%	35.5%	27.6%	20.8%

Imports (1992): CFAF 390,200,000,000 (1990; machinery and transportation equipment 21.3%, petroleum products 16.0%, wheat and wheat products 11.1%, rice 5.7%, dairy products 2.9%, pharmaceutical products 2.8%, paper and paper products 2.4%). *Major import sources* (1990): France 32.9%; Nigeria 7.5%; Italy 6.5%; United States 5.3%; Côte d'Ivoire 4.5%; Spain 4.2%; West Germany 3.6%; Japan 3.6%; The Netherlands 3.1%; Thailand 2.9%; Gabon 2.7%; Pakistan 2.3%.
Exports (1992): CFAF 221,600,000,000 (1990; peanut oil 16.6%, petroleum products 12.4%, canned fish 11.5%, fresh fish 11.1%, phosphates 9.3%, shellfish 8.4%). *Major export destinations* (1990): France 34.9%; India 10.6%; Mali 7.1%; Italy 7.0%; The Netherlands 5.3%; Spain 2.9%; Côte d'Ivoire 2.8%; Cameroon 2.5%; Japan 2.0%; Philippines 1.8%.

Transport and communications

Transport. Railroads (1993): length 562 mi, 904 km; (1987–88) passenger-mi 24,882,000, passenger-km 40,043,468; short ton-mi cargo 276,213,000, metric ton-km cargo 403,289,000. Roads (1988): total length 8,772 mi, 14,117 km (paved 27%). Vehicles (1991): passenger cars 97,000; trucks and buses 40,000. Merchant marine (1992): vessels (100 gross tons and over) 183; total deadweight tonnage 27,473. Air transport (1990)[8]: passenger-mi 144,276,000, passenger-km 232,329,000; short ton-mi cargo 26,971,000, metric ton-km cargo 39,374,000; airports (1993) with scheduled flights 9.
Communications. Daily newspapers (1990): total number 1; total circulation 45,000; circulation per 1,000 population 6.2. Radio (1992): total number of receivers 850,000 (1 per 9.0 persons). Television (1992): total number of receivers 61,000 (1 per 126 persons). Telephones (1991): 50,000 (1 per 150 persons).

Education and health

Education (1990–91)

	schools	teachers	students	student/ teacher ratio
Primary (age 6–12)	2,458	13,394	708,299	52.9
Secondary (age 13–18)	321	4,791[3]	173,490	34.8[3]
Vocational	13	259[3]	6,435	24.6[3]
Higher	18	770[1]	18,862	19.3[1]

Educational attainment (1988). Percentage of population age 6–34 having: no formal schooling 62.6%; primary education 25.7%; secondary 8.4%; higher 0.8%; other 2.5%. *Literacy* (1988): percentage of total population age 15 and over literate 28.6%; males literate 38.8%; females literate 19.4%.
Health (1988): physicians 407 (1 per 17,072 persons); hospital beds 6,127 (1 per 1,134 persons); infant mortality rate per 1,000 live births (1991) 86.0.
Food (1988–90): daily per capita caloric intake 2,322 (vegetable products 91%, animal products 9%); 98% of FAO recommended minimum requirement.

Military

Total active duty personnel (1993): 9,700 (army 87.6%, navy 7.2%, air force 5.2%). *Military expenditure as percentage of GNP* (1992): 2.1% (world [1989] 4.9%); per capita expenditure U.S.$16.

[1]1988. [2]1990. [3]1989. [4]Capital region only. [5]January 1; index refers to the *S.M.I.G.* (*salaire minimum interprofessionnel garanti*), a form of minimum professional wage. [6]Traditional African households in Dakar. [7]Wage earners, excluding armed forces only. [8]Air Afrique only.

Seychelles

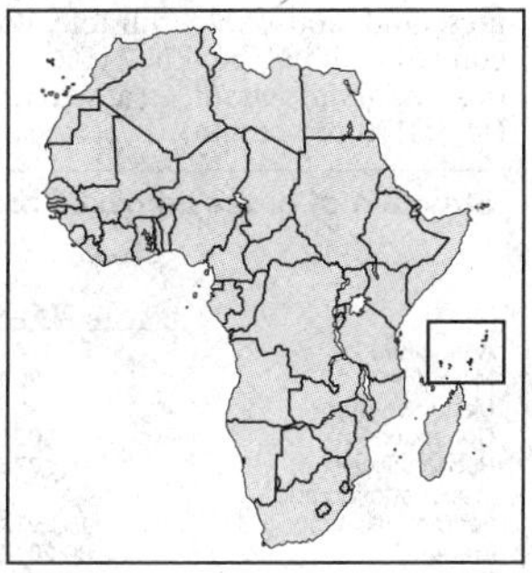

Official name: Repiblik Sesel (Creole); Republic of Seychelles (English); République des Seychelles (French).
Form of government: multiparty republic with one legislative house (National Assembly [43]).
Head of state and government: President.
Capital: Victoria.
Official languages[1]: none.
Official religion: none.
Monetary unit: 1 Seychelles rupee (SR) = 100 cents; valuation (Oct. 4, 1993) 1 U.S.$ = SR 5.06; 1 £ = SR 7.67.

Area and population

Island Groups	Capital	area sq mi	area sq km	population 1987 census
Central (Granitic) group				
La Digue and satellites	—	6	15	1,926
Mahé and satellites	Victoria	61	158	61,183
Praslin and satellites	—	16	42	5,002
Silhouette	—	8	20	191
Other islands	—	2	4	0
Outer (Coralline) islands	—	83	214	296
TOTAL		176	455[2]	68,598

Demography

Population (1993): 71,300.
Density (1993): persons per sq mi 405.1, persons per sq km 156.7.
Urban-rural (1990): urban 59.3%; rural 40.7%.
Sex distribution (1989): male 49.96%; female 50.04%.
Age breakdown (1989): under 15, 35.1%; 15–29, 31.5%; 30–44, 15.3%; 45–59, 9.2%; 60–74, 6.5%; 75 and over, 2.4%.
Population projection: (2000) 75,000; (2010) 80,500.
Doubling time: 46 years.
Ethnic composition (1983): Seychellois Creole (mixture of Asian, African, and European) 89.1%; Indian 4.7%; Malagasy 3.1%; Chinese 1.6%; English 1.5%.
Religious affiliation (1987): Roman Catholic 88.6%; other Christian (mostly Anglican) 8.5%; Hindu 0.4%; other 2.5%.
Major city (1987): Victoria 24,325.

Vital statistics

Birth rate per 1,000 population (1992): 22.6 (world avg. 26.4); (1989) legitimate 27.2%; illegitimate 72.8%.
Death rate per 1,000 population (1992): 7.4 (world avg. 9.2).
Natural increase rate per 1,000 population (1992): 15.2 (world avg. 17.2).
Total fertility rate (avg. births per childbearing woman; 1990): 2.8.
Marriage rate per 1,000 population (1984): 6.0.
Divorce rate per 1,000 population (1985): 0.7.
Life expectancy at birth (1991): male 65.0 years; female 75.0 years.
Major causes of death per 100,000 population (1985–89): diseases of the circulatory system 263.5, of which cerebrovascular disease 57.4; malignant neoplasms (cancers) 116.9; diseases of the respiratory system 77.1, of which pneumonia 49.0; accidents and adverse effects 44.4; infectious and parasitic diseases 42.9; diseases of the digestive system 40.5.

National economy

Budget (1993). Revenue: SR 1,186,100,000 (customs taxes and duties 47.9%, business taxes 11.8%, transfers from Social Security Fund 10.5%, dividends and interest 6.4%, administrative fees 6.4%, grants 5.3%). Expenditures: SR 1,335,600,000 (debt service 15.0%, capital projects 15.0%, education 10.8%, social security 7.3%, health 7.1%, tourism and transport 5.6%, defense 5.0%).
Tourism (1992): receipts from visitors SR 599,500,000; expenditures by nationals abroad U.S.$12,200,000[3].
Land use (1989): forested 18.5%; agricultural and under permanent cultivation 22.2%; built-on, wasteland, and other 59.3%.
Gross national product (at current market prices; 1992): U.S.$376,000,000 (U.S.$5,450 per capita).

Structure of gross domestic product and labour force

	1991 in value SR '000,000	% of total value	labour force[4]	% of labour force
Agriculture	95.0	4.8	2,181	9.1
Mining, manufacturing, and construction	336.6	17.0	4,279	17.9
Tourism	364.3	18.4	4,418	18.4
Transportation and communications	455.4	23.0	3,842	16.0
Finance	158.4	8.0		
Public admin., defense	265.3	13.4	9,238	38.6
Other	304.9	15.4		
TOTAL	1,980.1[2]	100.0	23,958	100.0

Production (metric tons except as noted). Agriculture, forestry, fishing (1992): coconuts 7,000, bananas 2,000, copra 1,000, cinnamon 333, tea 224; livestock (number of live animals) 19,000 pigs, 5,000 goats, 2,000 cattle, 185,200[5] chickens; fish catch (1991) 5,746, of which (1989) jack 36.9%, snapper 20.8%, mackerel 6.7%, kawakawa 5.3%. Mining and quarrying (1985): guano 4,500. Manufacturing (1992): canned tuna 5,283; beer and stout 69,980 hectolitres; soft drinks 61,330 hectolitres; cigarettes 62,000,000 units. Energy production (consumption): electricity (kW-hr; 1992) 108,000,000 (108,000,000); coal, none (n.a.); crude petroleum, none (n.a.); petroleum products (metric tons; 1990) none (54,000); natural gas, none (n.a.).
Population economically active (1992): total 24,392; activity rate of total population 34.4% (participation rates [1989]: ages 15–64, 74.3%; female 42.5%; unemployed [1987] 6.3%).

Price and earnings indexes (1985 = 100)

	1986	1987	1988	1989	1990	1991	1992
Consumer price index	103.0	102.9	104.7	106.4	110.6	112.7	116.4
Earnings index	...	...	...	...	...	...	...

Public debt (external, outstanding; 1991): U.S.$154,000,000.
Household income and expenditure. Average household size (1987) 4.5; average annual income per household (1978) SR 18,480 (U.S.$2,658); sources of income: wages and salaries 77.2%, self-employment 3.8%, transfer payments 3.2%; expenditure (1983–84): food and beverages 53.9%, housing 13.6%, energy and water 9.1%, household and personal goods 6.6%, transportation 6.4%, clothing and footwear 4.2%, recreation 1.4%.

Foreign trade

Balance of trade (current prices)

	1987	1988	1989	1990	1991	1992
SR '000,000	−511.6	−546.4	−627.8	−692.3	−660.0	−760.8
% of total	67.3%	61.7%	63.9%	53.4%	56.7%	63.0%

Imports (1992): SR 984,280,000 (manufactured goods 30.8%, of which metal manufactures 4.1%, paper products 2.6%; machinery and transport equipment 20.7%, of which vehicles 4.1%, electrical machinery and parts 3.7%, communications equipment 2.6%; food and live animals 18.5%, of which cereals 4.8%, vegetables and fruits 3.4%, dairy products 3.1%; mineral fuels, lubricants, and related materials 17.0%, of which petroleum products 16.8%; chemicals 7.5%; beverages and tobacco 2.6%; other 2.9%). *Major import sources:* Singapore 16.2%; Bahrain 15.9%; South Africa 14.4%; United Kingdom 13.0%; Japan 4.8%; France 4.5%; Italy 3.6%; United States 2.5%; The Netherlands 2.4%.
Exports (1992): SR 223,454,000[6] (petroleum products 53.3%[7]; canned tuna 29.8%; other fish 8.1%; cinnamon bark 0.9%; food, beverages, tobacco, and chemicals 0.8%[7]; copra 0.3%). *Major export destinations*[8]: France 42.7%; United Kingdom 21.1%; Réunion 11.4%.

Transport and communications

Transport. Railroads: none. Roads (1992): total length 198 mi, 319 km (paved 66%). Vehicles (1991): passenger cars 4,700; trucks and buses 1,600. Merchant marine (1992): vessels (100 gross tons and over) 9; total deadweight tonnage 3,337. Air transport (1992): passenger arrivals 107,000, passenger departures 107,000; metric ton cargo unloaded 2,869, metric ton cargo loaded 916; airports (1993) with scheduled flights 1.
Communications. Daily newspapers (1990): total number 1; total circulation 3,200; circulation per 1,000 population 47. Radio (1992): total number of receivers 30,000 (1 per 2.4 persons). Television (1992): total number of receivers 8,200 (1 per 8.7 persons). Telephones (1992): 10,068[9] (1 per 7.0 persons).

Education and health

Education (1993)

	schools	teachers	students	student/ teacher ratio
Primary (age 6–15)	25[10]	685	12,851	18.8
Secondary (age 16–18)	4[5]	553	7,337	13.3
Voc., teacher tr.	1[5]	190	1,682	8.9

Educational attainment (1987). Percentage of population age 12 and over having: no formal schooling 7.8%; primary education 51.5%; some secondary 12.2%; complete secondary 13.4%; vocational 9.9%; postsecondary 3.1%; unspecified 2.1%. *Literacy* (1987): total population age 15 and over literate 37,984 (84.2%); males literate 18,427 (82.9%); females literate 19,557 (85.7%).
Health (1992): physicians 61 (1 per 1,164 persons); hospital beds 413 (1 per 172 persons); infant mortality rate per 1,000 live births 11.9.
Food (1988–90): daily per capita caloric intake 2,356 (vegetable products 85%, animal products 15%); 101% of FAO recommended minimum requirement.

Military

Total active duty personnel (1991): 1,300 (army 76.9%, navy 15.4%, air force 7.7%). *Military expenditure as percentage of GNP* (1989): 4.2% (world 4.9%); per capita expenditure U.S.$206[11].

[1]Creole, English, and French are all national languages per 1993 constitution. [2]Detail does not add to total given because of rounding. [3]1991. [4]Excludes self-employed and domestic workers. [5]1986. [6]Includes SR 120,889,000 of reexports. [7]Items reexported. [8]Domestic export only. [9]Number of lines. [10]1988. [11]At prices of 1987.

Sierra Leone

Official name: Republic of Sierra Leone.
Form of government: military regime[1].
Head of state and government: Chairman, Supreme Council of State.
Capital: Freetown.
Official language: English.
Official religion: none.
Monetary unit: 1 leone (Le) = 100 cents; valuation (Oct. 4, 1993) 1 U.S.$ = Le 546.01; 1 £ = Le 827.20.

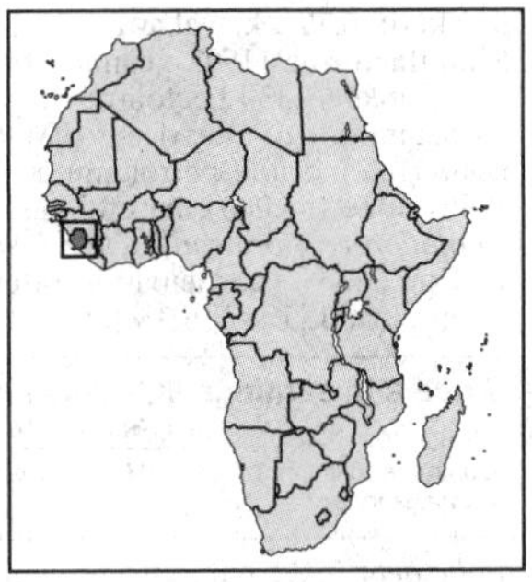

Area and population

Provinces / Districts	Capitals	area sq mi	area sq km	population 1985 census[2]
Eastern Province	Kenema	6,005	15,553	960,551
Kailahun	Kailahun	1,490	3,859	233,839
Kenema	Kenema	2,337	6,053	337,055
Kono	Sefadu	2,178	5,641	389,657
Northern Province	Makeni	13,875	35,936	1,262,226
Bombali	Makeni	3,083	7,985	315,914
Kambia	Kambia	1,200	3,108	186,231
Koinaduga	Kabala	4,680	12,121	183,286
Port Loko	Port Loko	2,208	5,719	329,344
Tonkolili	Magburaka	2,704	7,003	247,451
Southern Province	Bo	7,604	19,694	740,510
Bo	Bo	2,015	5,219	268,671
Bonthe (incl. Sherbro)	Bonthe	1,339	3,468	105,007
Moyamba	Moyamba	2,665	6,902	250,514
Pujehun	Pujehun	1,585	4,105	116,318
Western Area[3]	Freetown	215	557	554,243
TOTAL		27,699	71,740	3,517,530

Demography

Population (1993): 4,491,000.
Density (1993): persons per sq mi 162.1, persons per sq km 62.6.
Urban-rural (1990): urban 32.2%; rural 67.8%.
Sex distribution (1990): male 49.12%; female 50.88%.
Age breakdown (1985): under 15, 41.4%; 15–29, 26.1%; 30–44, 17.1%; 45–59, 10.3%; 60–74, 4.5%; 75 and over, 0.6%.
Population projection: (2000) 5,437,000; (2010) 7,172,000.
Doubling time: 26 years.
Ethnic composition (1983): Mende 34.6%; Temne 31.7%; Limba 8.4%; Kono 5.2%; Bullom-Sherbro 3.7%; Fulani 3.7%; Kuranko 3.5%; Yalunka 3.5%; Kissi 2.3%; other 3.4%.
Religious affiliation (1980): traditional beliefs 51.5%; Sunnī Muslim 39.4%; Protestant 4.7%; Roman Catholic 2.2%; Anglican 1.2%; other 1.0%.
Major cities (1985): Freetown 469,776; Koidu–New Sembehun 80,000; Bo 26,000; Kenema 13,000; Makeni 12,000.

Vital statistics

Birth rate per 1,000 population (1990–95): 48.1 (world avg. 26.4); legitimate, n.a.; illegitimate, n.a.
Death rate per 1,000 population (1990–95): 21.6 (world avg. 9.2).
Natural increase rate per 1,000 population (1990–95): 26.5 (world avg. 17.2).
Total fertility rate (avg. births per childbearing woman; 1990–95): 6.5.
Marriage rate per 1,000 population: n.a.
Divorce rate per 1,000 population: n.a.
Life expectancy at birth (1990–95): male 41.4 years; female 44.6 years.
Major causes of death per 100,000 population: n.a.; however, the major diseases are malaria, tuberculosis, leprosy, whooping cough, measles, tetanus, and diarrhea.

National economy

Budget (1990–91). Revenue: Le 18,499,000,000 (taxes 91.5%, grants 6.8%, nontax revenue 1.7%). Expenditures: Le 22,662,000,000 (recurrent expenditure 82.8%, development expenditure 17.2%).
Public debt (external, outstanding; 1991): U.S.$642,000,000.
Tourism (1990): receipts from visitors U.S.$19,000,000; expenditures by nationals abroad U.S.$7,000,000.
Production (metric tons except as noted). Agriculture, forestry, fishing (1992): rice 420,000, cassava 91,000, sugarcane 70,000, palm oil 60,000, pulses 40,000, palm kernels 35,000, plantains 31,000, coffee 25,000, cacao beans 24,000, millet 24,000, tomatoes 23,000, sorghum 22,000, peanuts (groundnuts) 20,000, sweet potatoes 11,000, corn (maize) 11,000; livestock (number of live animals) 333,000 cattle, 275,000 sheep, 152,000 goats, 50,000 pigs, 6,000,000 chickens; roundwood (1991) 3,146,000 cu m; fish catch (1991) 50,000. Mining and quarrying (1992): bauxite 1,365,000; rutile (a titanium ore) 148,990; diamonds 344,082 carats; gold 2,981 oz. Manufacturing (1990): salt 17,369[4]; nails 197[5]; beer and stout 59,590 hectolitres; mineral water 6,010 hectolitres[5]; paint 2,000 litres; cigarettes 1,159,000,000 units[5]. Construction (value added in Le; 1988): 500,000,000. Energy production (consumption): electricity (kW-hr; 1990) 224,000,000 (224,000,000); coal, none (n.a.); crude petroleum (barrels; 1990) none (2,089,000); petroleum products (metric tons; 1990) 259,000 (213,000); natural gas, none (n.a.).
Household income and expenditure. Average household size (1983) 4.7; average annual income per household (1984): U.S.$320; sources of income (1984): self-employment 61.6%, wages and salaries 27.9%, other 10.5%; expenditure (1986): food, beverages, and tobacco 67.7%, housing 14.1%, transportation and communications 8.2%, clothing and footwear 2.8%, furniture, furnishings, and household durable goods 2.2%, recreation, entertainment, and education 1.4%, health 1.1%.
Gross national product (at current market prices; 1992): U.S.$740,000,000 (U.S.$170 per capita).

Structure of gross domestic product and labour force

	1990–91 in value Le '000,000	1990–91 % of total value	1988 labour force[6]	1988 % of labour force[6]
Agriculture	52,494.4	35.3	7,262	10.4
Mining	14,132.8	9.5	5,845	8.3
Manufacturing	12,999.8	8.8	8,616	12.3
Construction	1,869.5	1.3	7,259	10.3
Public utilities	77.5	0.1	2,713	3.9
Transportation and communications	13,292.2	8.9	7,718	11.0
Trade	30,201.9	20.3	5,058	7.2
Finance	18,503.9	12.4		
Pub. admin., defense	4,524.9	3.0	25,714	36.6
Services	555.1	0.4		
Other	...	...	...	...
TOTAL	148,652.0	100.0	70,185	100.0

Population economically active (1985): total 1,352,000; activity rate of total population 36.9% (participation rates: ages 15–64, 62.9%; female 33.7%; unemployed [registered; 1986] 9.0%).

Price index (1985 = 100)

	1986	1987	1988	1989	1990	1991	1992
Consumer price index	180.9	504.1	676.9	1,088.5	2,296.2	4,654.0	7,702.4

Land use (1991): forested 28.6%; meadows and pastures 30.8%; agricultural and under permanent cultivation 8.9%; other 31.7%.

Foreign trade

Balance of trade (current prices)

	1987	1988	1989	1990	1991	1992
Le '000,000	+752.8	−1,260.3	−1,327.9	+1,475.9	+3,903.8	+14,449.7
% of total	8.8%	15.9%	7.4%	3.6%	4.6%	10.9%

Imports (1992): Le 65,176,599,000 (food and live animals 34.3%; machinery and transport equipment 18.9%; basic manufactured goods 14.1%; chemicals 10.9%; minerals, fuels, and lubricants 10.4%). *Major import sources* (1990): Nigeria 29.0%; United Kingdom 14.4%; Germany 10.1%; United States 8.2%; The Netherlands 5.6%.
Exports (1992): Le 74,872,411,000 (rutile 43.9%; bauxite 25.9%; diamonds 20.5%; coffee 1.8%; cocoa 1.4%). *Major export destinations* (1990): Belgium-Luxembourg 25.1%; United States 13.1%; Germany 8.9%; The Netherlands 8.3%; United Kingdom 7.3%.

Transport and communications

Transport. Railroads (1990): length 52 mi, 84 km. Roads (1989): total length 4,660 mi, 7,500 km (paved 20%). Vehicles (1991): passenger cars 35,870; trucks and buses 11,789. Merchant marine (1992): vessels (100 gross tons and over) 62; total deadweight tonnage 18,384. Air transport (1985)[7]: passenger-mi 68,290,000, passenger-km 109,903,000; short ton-mi cargo 1,400,000, metric ton-km cargo 2,044,000; airports (1993) with scheduled flights 1.
Communications. Daily newspapers (1991): total number 1; total circulation 10,000; circulation per 1,000 population 2.3. Radio (1992): 900,000 receivers (1 per 4.9 persons). Television (1992): 25,000 receivers (1 per 175 persons). Telephones (1990): 26,550 (1 per 160 persons).

Education and health

Education (1989–90)

	schools	teachers	students	student/ teacher ratio
Primary (age 5–11)	1,795	10,850	367,426	33.9
Secondary (age 12–18)	232[8]	5,544	97,049	17.5
Voc., teacher tr.[9]	16	475	6,086	12.8
Higher	2	600	4,752	7.9

Educational attainment (1974). Percentage of population age 5 and over having: no formal schooling 81.3%; primary education 12.1%; secondary 5.9%; higher 0.7%. *Literacy* (1990): total population age 15 and over literate 478,300 (20.7%); males literate (30.7%); females literate (11.3%).
Health: physicians (1988) 300 (1 per 13,150 persons); hospital beds 4,025 (1 per 980 persons); infant mortality rate per 1,000 live births (1985–90) 154.
Food (1988–90): daily per capita caloric intake 1,899 (vegetable products 96%, animal products 4%); 83% of FAO recommended minimum requirement.

Military

Total active duty personnel (1993): 6,150 (army 97.6%, navy 2.4%, air force, none). *Military expenditure as percentage of GNP* (1988): 0.7% (world 5.0%); per capita expenditure U.S.$1.

[1]Constitutional government overthrown April 1992; legislature dissolved May 1992. [2]Preliminary figures exclude adjustment for underenumeration; adjusted total is 3,700,000. [3]Not officially a province; the administration of the Western Area is split among Greater Freetown (the city and its suburbs) and other administrative bodies. [4]1988. [5]1989. [6]Registered employment only. [7]International flights only. [8]1988–89. [9]1985–86.

Singapore

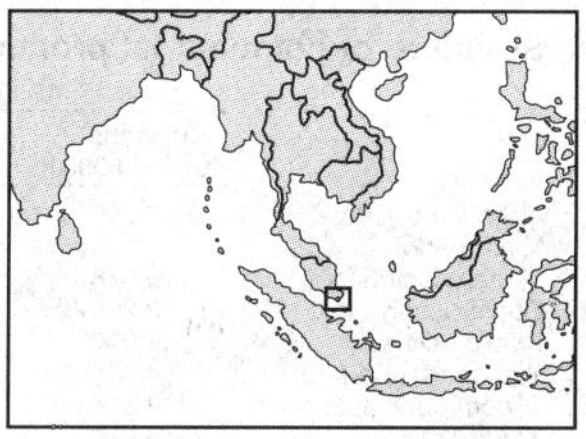

Official name: Hsin-chia-p'o Kung-ho-kuo (Mandarin Chinese); Republik Singapura (Malay); Singapore Kudiyarasu (Tamil); Republic of Singapore (English).
Form of government: unitary multiparty republic with one legislative house (Parliament [87][1]).
Chief of state: President.
Head of government: Prime Minister.
Capital: Singapore.
Official languages: Chinese; Malay; Tamil; English.
Official religion: none.
Monetary unit: 1 Singapore dollar (S$) = 100 cents; valuation (Oct. 4, 1993) 1 U.S.$ = S$1.58; 1 £ = S$2.40.

Population (1990 census)

Census division[2]	population	Census division[2]	population	Census division[2]	population
Alexandra	27,245	Henderson	18,445	Nee Soon East	58,651
Aljunied	51,669	Hong Kah Central	48,379	Nee Soon South	49,771
Ang Mo Kio	35,814	Hong Kah North	33,265	Pasir Panjang	35,824
Ayer Rajah	44,977	Hong Kah South	37,900	Paya Lebar	41,903
Bedok	22,032	Hougang	36,774	Potong Pasir	32,992
Boon Lay	39,249	Jalan Besar	28,298	Punggol	68,270
Boon Teck	22,652	Jalan Kayu	34,907	Queenstown	19,676
Braddell Heights	47,738	Joo Chiat	35,777	Radin Mas	35,730
Brickworks	10,593	Jurong	74,696	Sembawang	28,039
Bukit Batok	44,918	Kaki Bukit	32,782	Serangoon Gardens	44,702
Bukit Gombak	46,149	Kallang	34,178	Siglap	36,022
Bukit Merah	18,666	Kampong Chai Chee	33,928	Tampines East	41,474
Bukit Panjang	95,827	Kampong Glam	29,481	Tampines North	73,634
Bukit Timah	47,056	Kampong Kembangan	33,510	Tampines West	38,833
Buona Vista	23,873	Kampong Ubi	40,682	Tanah Merah	32,314
Cairnhill	48,445	Kebun Baru	36,878	Tanglin	43,544
Changi	50,003	Kim Keat	28,538	Tanjong Pagar	29,217
Changkat	41,995	Kim Seng	23,683	Teck Ghee	26,622
Cheng San	27,821	Kolam Ayer	22,420	Telok Blangah	29,157
Chong Boon	32,174	Kreta Ayer	29,631	Thomson	71,345
Chong Pang	38,613	Kuo Chuan	26,968	Tiong Bahru	27,468
Chua Chu Kang	43,465	Leng Kee	28,886	Toa Payoh	22,811
Clementi	37,635	Macpherson	23,764	Ulu Pandan	42,923
Eunos	52,976	Marine Parade	31,003	West Coast	46,052
Fengshan	27,285	Moulmein	33,872	Whampoa	18,285
Geylang Serai	36,800	Mountbatten	23,891	Yio Chu Kang	28,589
Geylang West	34,560	Nee Soon Central	47,032	Yuhua	32,733
				TOTAL	3,016,379

Demography

Area: 247 sq mi, 639 sq km.
Population (1993): 2,876,000[3].
Density (1993): persons per sq mi 11,643.7, persons per sq km 4,500.8.
Urban-rural: urban 100.0%.
Sex distribution (1992): male 50.52%; female 49.48%.
Age breakdown (1992): under 15, 23.1%; 15–29, 25.6%; 30–44, 28.5%; 45–59, 13.4%; 60 and over, 9.4%.
Population projection: (2000) 3,315,000; (2010) 4,061,000.
Doubling time: 56 years.
Ethnic composition (1992): Chinese 77.6%; Malay 14.2%; Indian[4] 7.1%; other 1.1%.
Religious affiliation (1991): Buddhist, Taoist, and other traditional beliefs 53.9%; Muslim 15.4%; Christian 12.6%; Hindu 3.6%; nonreligious 14.5%.
Major cities: Singapore has no separately defined cities within its borders.

Vital statistics

Birth rate per 1,000 population (1992): 17.1 (world avg. 26.4).
Death rate per 1,000 population (1992): 4.7 (world avg. 9.2).
Natural increase rate per 1,000 population (1992): 12.4 (world avg. 17.2).
Total fertility rate (avg. births per childbearing woman; 1992): 1.7.
Marriage rate per 1,000 population (1991): 9.0.
Divorce rate per 1,000 population (1991): 1.6.
Life expectancy at birth (1990): male 72.3 years; female 77.5 years.
Major causes of death per 100,000 population (1991): malignant neoplasms (cancers) 121.5; cardiovascular diseases 107.1; diseases of the respiratory system 77.8; cerebrovascular diseases 60.2; accidents, poisoning, and violence 15.4.

National economy

Budget (1992–93). Revenue: S$18,577,800,000 (tax revenue 68.8%, development fund account 17.9%, nontax revenue 7.3%, sinking fund account 6.0%). Expenditures: S$16,641,600,000 (administration 28.0%, government development 16.0%, debt servicing 14.6%, manpower 14.2%, grants 10.6%).
Public debt (external, outstanding; 1990): U.S.$3,481,000,000.
Production (metric tons except as noted). Agriculture, forestry, fishing (1991): vegetables 4,597, fruits 280; livestock (number of live animals) 1,000,000 ducks, 4,000,000 chickens; fish catch (1992) 9,198. Mining and quarrying (value added in S$; 1991): granite 114,100,000. Manufacturing (value added in S$; 1991): electronic products and components 7,813,400,000; petroleum refining and petroleum products 1,988,000,000; transport equipment 1,705,600,000; paints, pharmaceuticals, and chemical products 1,457,500,000; nonelectrical machinery 1,413,900,000; fabricated metal products 1,382,100,000; industrial chemicals and gases 1,078,100,000. Construction (1991): residential 2,597,200 sq m; nonresidential 1,991,600 sq m. Energy production (consumption): electricity (kW-hr; 1990) 15,617,600,000 (14,194,300,000); crude petroleum (barrels; 1990) none (299,511,000); petroleum products (metric tons; 1990) 34,396,000 (10,490,000).
Household income and expenditure. Average household size (1984) 3.9; income per household S$20,800 (U.S.$9,700); sources of income (1977–78): wages 75.4%, self-employment 18.7%, transfer payments 2.0%, other 3.9%; expenditure (1990): food 18.7%, recreation and education 15.3%, transportation and communications 13.7%, rent and utilities 9.2%, furniture and household equipment 8.9%, clothing and footwear 7.4%, health 4.4%.
Gross national product (1991): U.S.$39,249,000,000 (U.S.$12,890 per capita).

Structure of gross domestic product and labour force

	1992			
	in value S$'000,000[5]	% of total value	labour force[6]	% of labour force[6]
Agriculture	161.7	0.3	5,000	0.3
Quarrying	76.0	0.1	500	—
Manufacturing	17,868.2	27.7	434,100	27.5
Construction	4,340.6	6.7	103,200	6.5
Public utilities	1,353.5	2.1	8,000	0.5
Transp. and commun.	9,562.0	14.9	158,400	10.1
Trade	11,033.9	17.1	356,000	22.6
Finance	16,624.9	25.8	171,400	10.9
Services	6,596.5	10.3	339,400	21.5
Other	−3,201.4[7]	−5.0[7]	...	...
TOTAL	64,415.9	100.0	1,576,200[8]	100.0[8]

Population economically active (1991): total 1,554,316; activity rate of total population 56.3% (participation rates: ages 15 and over, 73.2%; female 39.8%; unemployed 1.7%).

Price and earnings indexes (1985 = 100)

	1986	1987	1988	1989	1990	1991	1992
Consumer price index	98.6	99.1	100.6	103.0	106.6	110.2	112.7
Monthly earnings index	100.8	104.0	112.6	123.6	135.1	147.6	...

Land use (1990): forested 4.9%; agricultural 1.6%; other 93.5%.
Tourism (1991): receipts from visitors U.S.$5,020,000,000; expenditures by nationals abroad U.S.$2,019,000,000.

Foreign trade[9]

Balance of trade (current prices)

	1987	1988	1989	1990	1991	1992
S$'000,000	−4,265	−4,159	−4,143	−8,559	−5,770	−7,490
% of total	3.4%	2.6%	2.3%	4.3%	2.7%	3.5%

Imports (1992): S$117,529,700,000 (crude petroleum 8.8%, office machines 7.8%, telecommunications apparatus 6.2%, petroleum products 4.0%, electric power machinery 3.2%). *Major import sources:* Japan 21.1%; United States 16.5%; Malaysia 14.7%; Saudi Arabia 5.1%; Taiwan 4.0%; Thailand 3.7%; Germany 3.3%; China 3.1%.
Exports (1992): S$103,351,000,000 (office machines 20.4%, petroleum products 10.7%, telecommunications apparatus 9.4%, clothing 2.9%, optical instruments 2.3%). *Major export destinations:* United States 21.1%; Malaysia 12.5%; Hong Kong 7.8%; Japan 7.6%; Thailand 6.2%; Germany 4.2%.

Transport and communications

Transport. Railroads (1992): length 26 km. Roads (1991): total length 2,924 km (paved 97%). Vehicles (1992): passenger cars 302,824; trucks and buses 128,993. Merchant marine (1992): vessels (100 gross tons and over) 946; total deadweight tonnage 14,929,172. Air transport (1992): passenger-km 37,105,000,000; metric ton-km cargo 2,306,204,000; airports (1993) 1.
Communications. Daily newspapers (1991): total number 8; total circulation 877,523; circulation per 1,000 population 318. Radio (1992): 800,000 receivers (1 per 3.5 persons). Television (1992): 550,000 receivers (1 per 5.1 persons). Telephones (1988): 1,271,000 (1 per 2.1 persons).

Education and health

Education (1991)

	schools	teachers	students	student/ teacher ratio
Primary (age 6–11)	202	9,843	260,286	26.4
Secondary (age 12–18)	186	9,200	185,713	20.2
Voc., teacher tr.	23	1,586	28,871	18.2
Higher	6	4,959	60,373	12.2

Educational attainment (1980). Percentage of population age 25 and over having: no schooling or incomplete primary 43.7%; primary education 38.3%; secondary 14.6%; postsecondary 3.4%. *Literacy* (1990): total population age 10 and over literate 90.7%; males literate 95.7%; females literate 85.6%.
Health (1991): physicians 3,648 (1 per 757 persons); hospital beds 9,801 (1 per 282 persons); infant mortality rate per 1,000 live births (1992) 5.0.
Food (1988–90): daily per capita caloric intake 3,121 (vegetable products 76%, animal products 24%); 136% of FAO recommended minimum requirement.

Military

Total active duty personnel (1993): 55,500 (army 81.1%, navy 8.1%, air force 10.8%). *Military expenditure as percentage of GNP* (1989): 5.1% (world 4.9%); per capita expenditure U.S.$557.

[1]Includes six nonelected members. [2]The census divisions have no administrative function. [3]De jure population. [4]Includes Sri Lankan. [5]At prices of 1985. [6]Employed only. [7]Imputed bank service charges. [8]Detail does not add to total given because of rounding. [9]Import figures are f.o.b. in balance of trade and c.i.f. for commodities and trading partners.

Slovakia

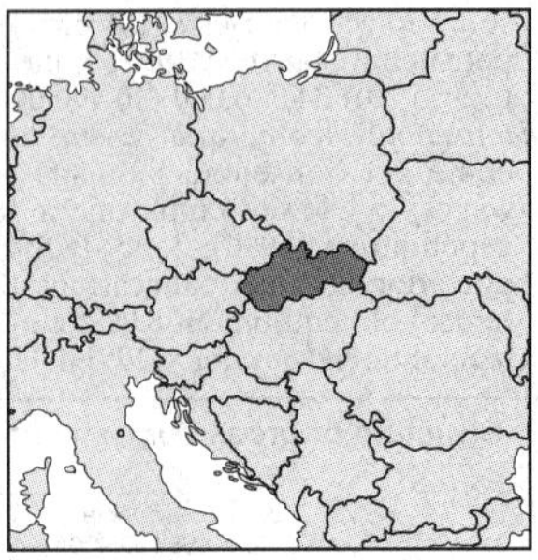

Official name: Slovenská Republika (Slovak Republic).
Form of government: unitary multiparty republic with one legislative house (National Council [150]).
Chief of state: President.
Head of government: Prime Minister.
Capital: Bratislava.
Official language: Slovak.
Official religion: none.
Monetary unit: 1 Slovak koruna[1] (Sk) = 100 halura; valuation (Oct. 4, 1993) 1 U.S.$ = 31.79 Sk; 1 £ = 48.16 Sk.

Area and population

		area		population
Regions	**Capitals**	sq mi	sq km	1991 census
Stredné Slovensko	Banská Bystrica	6,943	17,982	1,609,806
Východné Slovensko	Košice	6,253	16,194	1,505,495
Zapadné Slovensko	Bratislava	5,595	14,492	1,712,181
Capital city				
Bratislava	—	142	368	445,089
TOTAL		18,933	49,036	5,268,935

Demography

Population (1993): 5,329,000.
Density (1993): persons per sq mi 281.5, persons per sq km 108.7.
Urban-rural (1991): urban 56.8%; rural 43.2%.
Sex distribution (1992): male 48.83%; female 51.17%.
Age breakdown (1991): under 15, 25.0%; 15–29, 22.7%; 30–44, 22.8%; 45–59, 14.6%; 60–74, 10.7%; 75 and over, 4.2%.
Population projection: (2000) 5,513,000; (2010) 5,777,000.
Doubling time: not applicable; population growth is negligible.
Ethnic composition (1991): Slovak 85.7%; Hungarian 10.8%; Gypsy 1.4%; Czech 1.0%; Ruthenian 0.3%; Ukrainian 0.3%; German 0.1%; Moravian 0.1%; other 0.3%.
Religious affiliation (1991): Roman Catholic 60.3%; nonreligious and atheist 9.7%; Protestant 7.9%, of which Slovak Evangelical 6.2%, Reformed Christian 1.6%; Greek Catholic 3.4%; Eastern Orthodox 0.7%; other 18.0%.
Major cities (1991): Bratislava 441,453; Košice 234,840; Nitra 89,888; Prešov 87,788; Banská Bystrica 85,007.

Vital statistics

Birth rate per 1,000 population (1992): 14.4 (world avg. 26.4); (1990) legitimate 92.8%; illegitimate 7.2%.
Death rate per 1,000 population (1992): 10.2 (world avg. 9.2).
Natural increase rate per 1,000 population (1992): 4.2 (world avg. 17.2).
Total fertility rate (avg. births per childbearing woman; 1991): 2.0.
Marriage rate per 1,000 population (1992): 6.4.
Divorce rate per 1,000 population (1992): 1.6.
Life expectancy at birth (1991): male 66.9 years; female 75.2 years.
Major causes of death per 100,000 population (1990): diseases of the circulatory system 594.8; malignant neoplasms (cancers) 195.4; diseases of the respiratory system 75.1; accidents, poisoning, and violence 74.4; diseases of the digestive system 54.3; endocrine and metabolic disorders 14.9.

National economy

Budget (1991). Revenue: Kčs 125,078,000,000[1] (receipts from enterprises 79.4%; taxes 13.1%). Expenditures: Kčs 133,430,000,000[1] (education, health, social welfare, and culture 62.2%; national economy 17.5%; defense 2.6%).
Public debt (external, outstanding): n.a.
Production (metric tons except as noted). Agriculture, forestry, fishing (1991): cereals 4,004,000 (of which wheat 2,124,000, barley 960,000, corn [maize] 712,000, rye 131,000), sugar beets 1,502,000, potatoes 670,000; livestock (number of live animals) 2,428,000 pigs, 1,396,000 cattle (of which 501,000 dairy cows), 531,000 sheep, 13,000 horses, 13,866,000 poultry; roundwood 4,399,000 cu m; fish catch, n.a. Mining and quarrying (1991): iron ore 1,627,000; copper 25,273; zinc 811. Manufacturing (1991): crude steel 4,107,000; rolled steel 3,066,000; cement 2,680,000; plastic and resins 404,000; flour 333,000; phosphate fertilizers 121,988; cotton fabrics 62,335,000 m; beer 3,387,360 hectolitres; other alcoholic beverages 624,840 hectolitres; refrigerators and freezers 514,745 units; motor vehicles 3,806 units. Construction (1991): residential 1,147,000 sq m. Energy production (consumption): electricity (kW-hr; 1991) 22,732,000,000 (27,069,000,000); coal (metric tons; 1991) 4,148,000 (n.a.); crude petroleum (barrels; 1991) 529,000 (n.a.); petroleum products, n.a. (n.a.); natural gas, n.a. (n.a.).
Population economically active (1993): total 2,548,733; activity rate of total population 47.9% (participation rates [1991]: ages 15–64, 76.0%; female 50.1%; unemployed 12.5%[3]).

Price and earnings indexes (1985 = 100)

	1986	1987	1988	1989	1990	1991	1992
Consumer price index[4]	100.6	100.8	101.1	102.5	113.3	176.9	194.6
Annual earnings index	101.9	103.9	107.3	110.1	114.9	132.1	...

Gross national product (at current market prices; 1992): U.S.$10,229,000,000 (U.S.$1,930 per capita).

Structure of net material product and labour force

	1990		1991	
	in value Kčs '000,000[1]	% of total value	labour force	% of labour force
Agriculture	17,089	9.2	364,762	13.9
Mining and manufacturing	115,578	62.2	867,256	33.1
Construction	22,298	12.0	242,701	9.3
Public utilities	1,077	0.6	—	—
Transportation and communications	8,384	4.5	164,945	6.3
Trade	16,556	8.9	245,629	9.4
Finance	—	—	[2]	[2]
Pub. admin., defense	} 4,858	} 2.6	99,398	3.8
Services			498,253[2]	19.0[2]
Other			134,991	5.2
TOTAL	185,840	100.0	2,617,935	100.0

Land use (1991): forested 40.6%; meadows and pastures 16.5%; agricultural and under permanent cultivation 33.4%; other 9.5%.
Household income and expenditure. Average household size (1991) 2.9; income per household (1991) Kčs 105,227[1,5] (U.S.$3,595[5]); sources of income (1991): wages and salaries 59.1%, transfer payments 21.6%, other 19.3%; expenditure (1989): food and beverages 31.9%, clothing and footwear 11.8%, fuel and light 6.6%, household durable goods 4.4%, other 45.3%.
Tourism (1992): tourist arrivals 5,900.

Foreign trade

Balance of trade (current prices)

	1991	1992
Kčs '000,000[1]	−14,064	−2,103
% of total	6.7%	1.1%

Imports (1992): Kčs 100,697,000,000[1] (1991; petroleum and petroleum products 35.3%; machinery and transport equipment 23.9%; raw materials 12.7%; chemical products 8.8%; semimanufactured products 7.8%). *Major import sources* (1991): former U.S.S.R. 42.8%; Germany 14.0%; Austria 8.3%; Poland 3.6%; Hungary 3.0%.
Exports (1992): Kčs 98,594,000,000[1] (1991; semimanufactured products 36.2%; machinery and transport equipment 22.5%; manufactured goods 15.7%; chemical products 12.2%; food, beverages, and tobacco 7.7%). *Major export destinations* (1991): former U.S.S.R. 24.6%; Germany 19.8%; Poland 8.0%; Austria 5.9%; Italy 5.1%.

Transport and communications

Transport. Railroads (1991): length 2,275 mi, 3,661 km; passengers transported (1990) 405,800,000; short ton-mi cargo 11,818,000,000, metric ton-km cargo 17,254,000,000. Roads (1991): total length 11,101 mi, 17,866 km (paved, n.a.). Vehicles (1991): passenger cars 906,129; trucks and buses 109,106. Merchant marine: n.a. Air transport: n.a.; airports (1993) with scheduled flights 4.
Communications. Daily newspapers (1990): total number 12; total circulation 1,291,000; circulation per 1,000 population 246. Radio (1991): total number of receivers 1,094,000 (1 per 4.8 persons). Television (1991): total number of receivers 1,309,000 (1 per 4.0 persons). Telephones (1991): 1,305,443 (1 per 4.0 persons).

Education and health

Education (1991–92)	schools	teachers	students	student/ teacher ratio
Primary (age 6–14)	2,415	37,812	716,416	18.9
Secondary (age 15–18)	147	3,875	59,347	15.3
Voc., teacher tr.	204	6,343	99,751	15.7
Higher	13	7,873	61,272	7.8

Educational attainment (1991). Percentage of adult population having: incomplete primary education 0.5%; primary and incomplete secondary 30.6%; complete secondary 58.6%; higher 9.4%; unknown 0.9%. *Literacy* (1990): total population age 15 and over literate 3,980,202 (100%); males literate 1,916,410 (100%); females literate 2,063,792 (100%).
Health (1991): physicians 16,101 (1 per 328 persons); hospital beds 47,901 (1 per 110 persons); infant mortality rate per 1,000 live births 13.2.
Food (1990): daily per capita caloric intake 3,335 (vegetable products 63%, animal products 37%); 135% of FAO recommended minimum requirement.

Military

Total active duty personnel (1993): 47,000 (army 70.2%, air force 29.8%). *Military expenditure as percentage of GNP:* n.a.; per capita expenditure U.S.$54.

[1]The Slovak koruna was introduced Feb. 8, 1993, at par with the former Czechoslovak koruna (Kčs), which it replaced. For settlement of obligations existing prior to February 8 between the Czech and Slovak republics, an interim currency, the clearing koruna (XCS) was introduced. [2]Services includes Finance. [3]Estimate. [4]Cost of living index; wage earners only. [5]Worker's household.

Slovenia

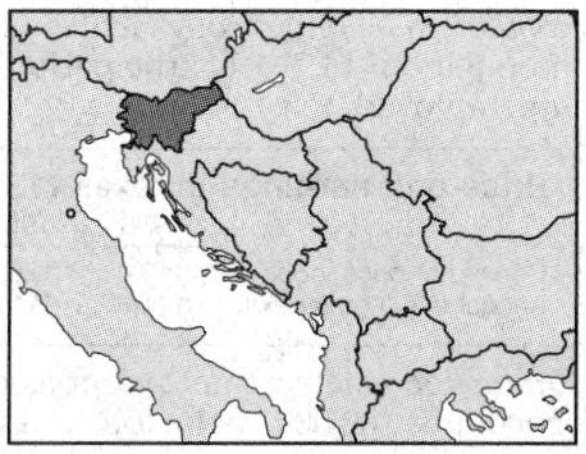

Official name: Republika Slovenija (Republic of Slovenia).
Form of government: multiparty republic with two legislative houses (State Council [40]; State Assembly [90]).
Head of state: President.
Head of government: Prime Minister.
Capital: Ljubljana.
Official language: Slovene.
Official religion: none.
Monetary unit: 1 Slovene tolar (SIT) = 100 stotin; valuation (Oct. 4, 1993) 1 Yugoslav dinar (Din) = 1.11 tolars; 1 U.S.$ = 115.48 tolarji; 1 £ = 174.95 tolarji.

Area and population (1991 census)

Districts	area sq km[1]	population	Districts	area sq km[1]	population
Ajdovščina	352	22,830	Metlika	108	8,197
Brežice	268	24,700	Mozirje	508	16,533
Celje	230	66,443	Murska Sobota	692	63,716
Çerknica	483	15,197	Nova Gorica	605	58,860
Črnomelj	486	18,301	Novo Mesto	759	59,171
Domžale	240	44,404	Ormož	212	17,656
Dravograd	105	8,582	Pesnica	169	18,137
Gornja Radgona	210	21,334	Piran	45	16,761
Grosuplje	421	28,282	Postojna	492	20,072
Hrastnik	58	11,096	Ptuj	645	68,846
Idrija	425	17,221	Radlje ob Dravi	346	17,026
Ilirska Bistrica	480	14,687	Radovljica	641	34,578
Izola	28	13,806	Ravne na Koroškem	304	27,499
Jesenice	375	32,108	Ribnica	256	12,733
Kamnik	289	28,927	Ruše	209	15,654
Kočevje	766	18,479	Šentjur pri Celju	240	19,317
Koper	273	45,218	Sevnica	293	18,784
Kranj	453	72,814	Şežana	698	23,838
Krško	345	28,615	Škofja Loka	512	38,622
Lasko	250	19,012	Slovenj Gradec	286	21,135
Lenart	204	17,144	Slovenska Bistrica	369	32,541
Lendava	256	26,120	Şlovenske Konjice	222	22,206
Litija	328	18,986	Šmarje pri Jelšah	400	31,807
Ljubljana-Bežigrad	46	58,243	Tolmin	939	20,999
Ljubljana-Center	5	28,921	Trbovlje	58	19,372
Ljubljana-Moste Polje	152	72,235	Trebnje	308	17,731
Ljubljana-Šiška	156	83,310	Tržič	155	15,095
Ljubljana-Vič Rudnik	543	80,582	Velenje	182	42,688
Ljutomer	179	18,817	Vrhnika	169	19,458
Logatec	173	9,827	Zagorje ob Savi	147	16,825
Maribor	359	153,053	Žalec	349	39,688
			TOTAL	20,256	1,974,839

Demography

Population (1993): 1,997,000.
Density (1993): persons per sq mi 255.3, persons per sq km 98.6.
Urban-rural (1991): urban 48.9%; rural 51.1%.
Sex distribution (1992): male 48.52%; female 51.48%.
Age breakdown (1992): under 15, 20.0%; 15–29, 22.4%; 30–44, 23.7%; 45–59, 17.4%; 60–74, 11.9%; 75 and over, 4.6%.
Population projection: (2000) 2,068,000; (2010) 2,173,000.
Doubling time: not applicable; doubling time exceeds 100 years.
Ethnic composition (1991): Slovene 87.8%; Croat 2.8%; Serb 2.4%; Bosnian 1.4%; Magyar 0.4%; other 5.2%.
Religious affiliation (1991): most believers are Christians and are predominantly adherents of the Roman Catholic Church; other Christians are members of the Slovene Old Catholic Church, a few Protestant denominations, and the Eastern Orthodox Church; there are also small Muslim and Jewish communities.
Major cities (1991): Ljubljana 276,133; Maribor 108,122; Celje 41,279; Kranj 37,318; Velenje 27,665.

Vital statistics

Birth rate per 1,000 population (1991): 10.8 (world avg. 26.4); legitimate 73.6%; illegitimate 26.4%.
Death rate per 1,000 population (1991): 9.7 (world avg. 9.2).
Natural increase rate per 1,000 population (1991): 1.1 (world avg. 17.2).
Total fertility rate (avg. births per childbearing woman; 1991): 1.4.
Marriage rate per 1,000 population (1991): 4.1.
Divorce rate per 1,000 population (1991): 0.9.
Life expectancy at birth (1989–90): male 69.4 years; female 77.3 years.
Major causes of death per 100,000 population (1991): circulatory diseases 447.6; cancers 214.9; accidents 92.6; digestive diseases 44.0; respiratory diseases 37.7; endocrine and metabolic disorders 19.1.

National economy

Budget (1992). Revenue: Din 437,072,000,000. Expenditures: n.a.
Tourism (1990): receipts U.S.$852,000,000; expenditures, n.a.
Production (metric tons except as noted). Agriculture, forestry, fishing (1992): potatoes 368,000, grapes 213,000, corn (maize) 207,000, wheat 200,000, sugar beets 97,000, plums 9,000; livestock (number of live animals) 529,000 pigs, 484,000 cattle, 28,000 sheep, 12,000,000 poultry; roundwood (1991) 2,098,000 cu m; fish catch (1991) 5,012, of which freshwater 805. Mining and quarrying (1991): lead-zinc ore 162,000; bauxite 48,000; mercury 9. Manufacturing (1991): cement 973,000; crude steel 287,000; aluminum ingots 90,164; soap and detergents 48,438; cotton yarn 14,821; leather footwear 9,124,000 pairs; refrigerators 744,000 units; bicycles 218,000 units; telephones 160,000 units; passenger cars 82,536 units. Construction (1991): residential 147,806 sq m; nonresidential 17,547 sq m. Energy production (consumption): electricity (kW-hr; 1991) 12,668,000,000 (n.a.); coal (metric tons; 1991) 5,158,000 (n.a.); crude petroleum (barrels; 1991) 17,584 (n.a.); petroleum products (metric tons; 1991) 126,000 (n.a.); natural gas (cu m; 1991) 19,271,000 (n.a.).
Gross national product (1991): U.S.$14,157,000,000 (U.S.$7,150 per capita).

Structure of gross material product and labour force

	1991			
	in value Din '000,000	% of total value	labour force	% of labour force
Agriculture	27,968	7.9	120,495	12.7
Mining Manufacturing	188,915	53.3	301,122	31.8
Construction	30,978	8.7	40,643	4.3
Public utilities	3,717	1.0	12,911	1.4
Transp. and commun.	20,502	5.8	46,578	4.9
Trade	54,237	15.3	104,391	11.0
Finance	12,664	3.5	48,750	5.2
Pub. admin., defense			25,024	2.7
Services	15,513	4.5	174,706	18.5
Other			71,146[2]	7.5[2]
TOTAL	354,494	100.0	945,766[3]	100.0[3]

Population economically active (1991): total 945,766; activity rate of total population 47.8% (participation rates: ages 10–64, 63.2%; female 46.7%; unemployed 7.1%).

Price and earnings indexes (1985 = 100)

	1985	1986	1987	1988	1989	1990	1991
Consumer price index	100	196	455	1,370	18,900	123,000	264,000
Earnings index[4]	100	114	108	96	113	79	...

Land use (1990): forest 50.3%; pasture 32.2%; agricultural 12.0%; other 5.5%.
Household income and expenditure. Average household size (1991) 2.8; income per household (1990) Din 161,589 (U.S.$14,277); sources of income (1990): wages 59.4%, transfers 17.5%, self-employment 14.5%, other 8.6%; expenditure (1988): food 27.6%, transportation 12.8%, housing 9.5%, clothing 8.9%, energy 6.6%, education and entertainment 5.9%, household durable goods 5.4%, drink and tobacco 4.7%, health care 4.2%.

Foreign trade

Balance of trade (current prices)

	1986	1987	1988	1989	1990	1991
Din '000,000	−5.7	+5.0	+99.0	+638.0	−6,336.0	−2,339.0
% of total	3.0%	1.2%	6.3%	3.6%	6.4%	1.1%

Imports (1991): SIT 104,497,000,000 (machinery and transport equipment 34.6%; basic manufactures 18.9%; chemicals 15.7%; consumer goods 13.2%, of which food 5.7%; mineral fuels 8.7%). *Major import sources:* Germany 24.6%; Italy 16.0%; France 12.1%; Austria 9.6%; U.S. 3.6%.
Exports (1991): SIT 102,158,000,000 (machinery and transport equipment 38.1%; basic manufactures 28.1%; consumer goods 21.2%, of which food 4.6%; chemicals 8.3%; raw materials except fuels 2.9%). *Major export destinations:* Germany 26.5%; Italy 18.9%; France 11.5%; former U.S.S.R. 7.9%; Austria 5.8%; U.S. 4.3%.

Transport and communications

Transport. Railroads (1991): length 746 mi, 1,201 km; passenger-mi 505,000,000, passenger-km 814,000,000; short ton-mi cargo 2,223,000,000, metric ton-km cargo 3,246,000,000. Roads (1991): total length 9,045 mi, 14,553 km (paved 72%). Vehicles (1991): passenger cars 594,289; trucks and buses 35,627. Merchant marine (1990): fishing vessels 42. Air transport (1991): passenger-mi 359,000,000, passenger-km 577,000,000; short ton-mi cargo 832,900,000, metric ton-km cargo 1,216,000; airports (1993) 1.
Communications. Daily newspapers (1990): total number 3; total circulation 220,000; circulation per 1,000 population 112. Radio (1989): 687,000 receivers (1 per 2.9 persons). Television (1989): 528,500 receivers (1 per 3.7 persons). Telephones (1991): 769,000 (1 per 2.6 persons).

Education[5] and health

Education (1991–92)

	schools	teachers	students	student/ teacher ratio
Primary (age 7–14)	850	14,873	225,640	15.2
Secondary (age 15–18)	243	8,931	101,670	11.4
Voc., teacher tr.	78	986	4,847	4.9
Higher	28	2,575	36,504	14.2

Educational attainment (1991). Percentage of population age 15 and over having: less than full primary education 13.7%; primary 27.9%; secondary 45.6%; postsecondary and higher 12.8%. *Literacy* (1981): total population age 10 and over literate 1,584,500 (99.2%); males 99.3%; females 99.1%.
Health (1991): physicians (1989) 4,071 (1 per 481 persons); hospital beds 11,816 (1 per 167 persons); infant mortality rate per 1,000 live births 8.4.

Military

Total active duty personnel (1993): 15,000 (army 100%). *Military expenditure as percentage of GNP:* n.a.; per capita expenditure (1992) U.S.$171.

[1]One sq km is equal to approximately 0.3861 sq mi. [2]Mostly unemployed. [3]Excludes 33,154 (3.5%) workers in the private sector. [4]Based on worker real net personal income. [5]Includes adult education.

Solomon Islands

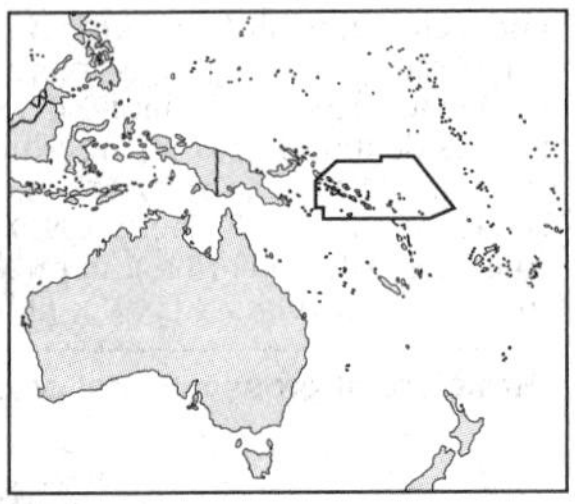

Official name: Solomon Islands.
Form of government: constitutional monarchy with one legislative house (National Parliament [47]).
Chief of state: British Monarch represented by Governor-General.
Head of government: Prime Minister.
Capital: Honiara.
Official language: English.
Official religion: none.
Monetary unit: 1 Solomon Islands dollar (SI$) = 100 cents; valuation (Oct. 4, 1993) 1 U.S.$ = SI$3.22; 1 £ = SI$4.87.

Area and population

		area		population
Provinces	Capitals	sq mi	sq km	1991 estimate
Central Islands	Tulagi	497	1,286	20,914
Guadalcanal	Honiara	2,060	5,336	60,692
Isabel	Buala	1,597	4,136	16,526
Makira	Kira Kira	1,231	3,188	25,307
Malaita	Auki	1,631	4,225	86,710
Temotu	Santa Cruz	334	865	16,500
Western	Gizo	3,595	9,312	64,732
Capital Territory				
Honiara	—	8	22	36,919
TOTAL		10,954[1]	28,370	328,300

Demography

Population (1993): 349,000.
Density (1993): persons per sq mi 31.9, persons per sq km 12.3.
Urban-rural (1986): urban 15.7%; rural 84.3%.
Sex distribution (1991): male 51.73%; female 48.27%.
Age breakdown (1991): under 15, 46.4%; 15–29, 27.2%; 30–44, 14.5%; 45–59, 7.8%; 60–74, 3.5%; 75 and over, 0.6%.
Population projection: (2000) 433,000; (2010) 569,000.
Doubling time: 21 years.
Ethnic composition (1986): Melanesian 94.2%; Polynesian 3.7%; other Pacific Islander 1.4%; European 0.4%; Asian 0.2%; other 0.1%.
Religious affiliation (1986): Christian 96.7%, of which Protestant 77.5%, Roman Catholic 19.2%; Baha'i 0.4%; traditional beliefs 0.2%; other and no religion 2.7%.
Major cities (1986)[2]: Honiara 35,288[3]; Gizo 3,727; Auki 3,262; Kira Kira 2,585; Buala 1,913.

Vital statistics

Birth rate per 1,000 population (1993): 37.0 (world avg. 26.4).
Death rate per 1,000 population (1993): 4.0 (world avg. 9.2).
Natural increase rate per 1,000 population (1993): 33.0 (world avg. 17.2).
Total fertility rate (avg. births per childbearing woman; 1993): 5.4.
Marriage rate per 1,000 population: n.a.
Divorce rate per 1,000 population: n.a.
Life expectancy at birth (1993): male 69.0 years; female 73.0 years.
Major causes of death per 100,000 population: n.a.; however, major diseases include malaria, tuberculosis, and leprosy[4].

National economy

Budget (1992). Revenue: SI$228,400,000 (1991; taxes on foreign trade 46.8%, income taxes 29.2%, nontax revenue 14.3%, foreign grants 9.7%). Expenditures: SI$255,900,000 (1991; administrative 33.2%, interest payments 12.6%, capital expenditure 10.7%).
Tourism (1991): receipts from visitors U.S.$5,000,000; expenditures by nationals abroad U.S.$13,000,000.
Land use (1991): forested 91.5%; meadows and pastures 1.4%; agricultural and under permanent cultivation 2.0%; other 5.1%.
Gross national product (at current market prices; 1992): U.S.$238,000,000 (U.S.$710 per capita).

Structure of gross domestic product and labour force

	1991		1992	
	in value SI$'000[5]	% of total value	labour force[6]	% of labour force
Agriculture	75,900	31.2	6,355	23.7
Mining	...	...		
Manufacturing	16,100	6.6	2,040	7.6
Construction			1,109	4.1
Public utilities	19,700	8.1	386	1.4
Transportation and communications			1,418	5.3
Trade	31,300	12.9	3,201	11.9
Finance			1,195	4.5
Pub. admin., defense	55,700	22.9	4,273	15.9
Services			6,865	25.6
Other	44,300	18.2	...	...
TOTAL	243,000	100.0[1]	26,842	100.0

Household income and expenditure. Average household size (1986) 6.4; average annual income per household (1983) SI$1,010[7] (U.S.$1,160); sources of income (1983): wages and salaries 74.1%, self-employment, remittances, gifts, and other assistance 25.9%; expenditure (1990)[8]: food 51.1%, drinks and tobacco 13.7%, housing 8.8%, transportation 8.4%, clothing 3.9%.

Population economically active (1986): total 39,210[6]; activity rate of total population 13.7% (participation rates: ages 15–60, 98.6%; female 25.4%; unemployed, n.a.).

Price and earnings indexes (1985 = 100)

	1986	1987	1988	1989	1990	1991	1992
Consumer price index	113.6	126.1	147.2	169.1	183.9	211.6	234.3
Annual earnings index[6]	111.6	121.3	194.2	248.8	216.9	262.8	304.8

Production (metric tons except as noted). Agriculture, forestry, fishing (1992): coconuts 160,000, palm oil and kernels 32,700, copra 30,000, cacao beans 5,000; livestock (number of live animals) 54,000 pigs, 13,000 cattle; roundwood 640,000 cu m; fish catch 39,900. Mining and quarrying (1992): gold 1,061 troy oz. Manufacturing (1992): processed fish 36,788; sawn timber 18,400 cu m; other major industries include beer brewing, soap and tobacco manufacturing, garment manufacturing, weaving, wood carving, fibreglass products, boatbuilding, and leatherworking. Construction (gross value in SI$ in Honiara; 1992): residential 3,699,000; nonresidential 4,012,000. Energy production (consumption): electricity (kW-hr; 1990) 30,000,000 (30,000,000); coal, none (n.a.); petroleum products (metric tons; 1990) none (53,000); natural gas, none (n.a.).
Public debt (external, outstanding; 1991): U.S.$99,300,000.

Foreign trade

Balance of trade (current prices)

	1987	1988	1989	1990	1991	1992
SI$'000	−6,646	−32,710	−45,920	−18,340	−73,100	−9,300
% of total	2.5%	8.7%	11.7%	5.0%	13.9%	1.5%

Imports (1991): SI$142,300,000 (machinery and transport equipment 32.5%, manufactured goods 22.8%, mineral fuels and lubricants 20.6%, food 14.9%). *Major import sources* (1990): Australia 35.3%; Japan 16.3%; Singapore 14.4%; other Asian countries 11.3%; New Zealand 9.3%; United Kingdom 1.5%.
Exports (1991): SI$226,500,000 (fish products 47.0%, timber products 23.6%, palm oil products 7.8%, cacao beans 5.9%, copra 5.4%). *Major export destinations* (1990): Japan 39.2%; United Kingdom 23.4%; other Asian countries 14.2%; Australia 4.6%; The Netherlands 1.4%.

Transport and communications

Transport. Railroads: none. Roads (1987)[9]: total length 1,300 mi, 2,100 km (paved 8%). Vehicles (1986): passenger cars 1,350; trucks and buses 2,026. Merchant marine (1992): vessels (100 gross tons and over) 33; total deadweight tonnage 4,985. Air transport (1992): passenger-mi 117,100,000, passenger-km 188,400,000; short ton-mi cargo 25,000[10], metric ton-km cargo 37,000[10]; airports (1993) with scheduled flights 22.
Communications. Daily newspapers[11]: none. Radio (1992): total number of receivers 38,000 (1 per 8.9 persons). Television: none. Telephones (1989): 7,000 (1 per 44 persons).

Education and health

Education (1991)

	schools	teachers	students	student/ teacher ratio
Primary (age 7–12)	520	2,388	60,259	25.2
Secondary (age 13–18) / Voc., teacher tr.	23	364	6,363	17.5
Higher	—	—	—	—

Educational attainment (1986)[12]. Percentage of population age 25 and over having: no schooling 44.4%; primary education 46.2%; secondary 6.8%; higher 2.6%. *Literacy* (1976): total population age 15 and over literate 55,500 (54.1%); males 33,600 (62.4%); females 21,900 (44.9%).
Health: physicians (1988) 31 (1 per 9,852 persons); hospital beds (1986) 1,479 (1 per 193 persons); infant mortality rate per 1,000 live births (1991) 39.0.
Food (1988–90): daily per capita caloric intake 2,278 (vegetable products 90%, animal products 10%); 100% of FAO recommended minimum requirement.

Military

Total active duty personnel: no military forces are maintained, but a police force of 475 provides internal security.

[1]Detail does not add to total given because of rounding. [2]Ward populations. [3]1990. [4]Reported cases of these diseases in 1986 were: malaria 72,108, tuberculosis 337, and leprosy 260. [5]At 1984 factor cost. [6]Population employed in the monetary sector only. [7]Public-service earnings. [8]Retail price index components. [9]Includes 500 mi (800 km) of privately maintained roads mainly for plantation use. [10]1984. [11]In 1988 there were three weekly newspapers with a combined circulation of 10,000. [12]Indigenous population only.

Somalia[1]

Official name: Soomaaliya (Somali)(Somalia).
Form of government: interim UN-imposed regime.
Head of state and government: Special Envoy assisted by military command of UN-administered operation in Somalia (for United Nations); no effective local government (for Somalia).
Capital: Mogadishu.
Official languages: Somali; Arabic.
Official religion: Islam.
Monetary unit: 1 Somali shilling (So.Sh.) = 100 cents; valuation (Oct. 4, 1993) 1 U.S.$ = So.Sh. 2,601; 1 £ = So.Sh. 3,940.

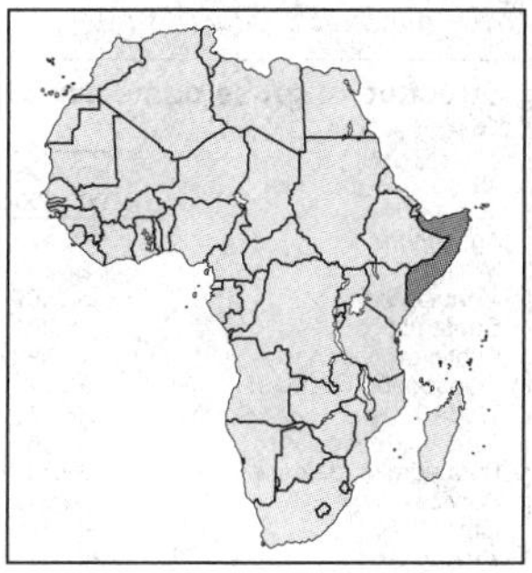

Area and population

Regions	Capitals	area sq mi	area sq km	population 1980 estimate
Bakool	Xuddur	10,000	27,000	148,700
Banaadir	Mogadishu (Muqdisho)	400	1,000	520,100
Bari	Boosaaso	27,000	70,000	222,300
Bay	Baydhabo	15,000	39,000	451,000
Galguduud	Dhuusamarreeb	17,000	43,000	255,900
Gedo	Garbahaarrey	12,000	32,000	235,000
Hiiraan	Beledweyne	13,000	34,000	219,300
Jubbada Dhexe	Bu'aale	9,000	23,000	147,800
Jubbada Hoose	Kismaayo	24,000	61,000	272,400
Mudug	Gaalkacyo	27,000	70,000	311,200
Nugaal	Garoowe	19,000	50,000	112,200
Sanaag	Ceerigaabo	21,000	54,000	216,500
Shabeellaha Dhexe	Jawhar	8,000	22,000	352,000
Shabeellaha Hoose	Marka	10,000	25,000	570,700
Togdheer	Burao	16,000	41,000	383,900
Woqooyi Galbeed	Hargeysa	17,000	45,000	655,000
TOTAL		246,000[2]	637,000	5,074,000

Demography[3]

Population (1993): 8,050,000.
Density (1993): persons per sq mi 32.7, persons per sq km 12.6.
Urban-rural (1990): urban 36.4%; rural 63.6%.
Sex distribution (1990): male 47.70%; female 52.30%.
Age breakdown (1990): under 15, 47.0%; 15–29, 23.4%; 30–44, 16.6%; 45–59, 8.6%; 60–74, 3.7%; 75 and over, 0.7%.
Population projection: (2000) 9,736,000; (2010) 13,114,000.
Doubling time: 22 years.
Ethnic composition (1983): Somali 98.3%; Arab 1.2%; Bantu 0.4%; other 0.1%.
Religious affiliation (1980): Sunnī Muslim 99.8%; Christian 0.1%; other 0.1%.
Major cities (1981): Mogadishu 500,000; Hargeysa 70,000; Kismaayo 70,000; Berbera 65,000; Marka 60,000.

Vital statistics[3]

Birth rate per 1,000 population (1990–95): 50.2 (world avg. 26.4); legitimate, n.a.; illegitimate, n.a.
Death rate per 1,000 population (1990–95): 18.5 (world avg. 9.2).
Natural increase rate per 1,000 population (1990–95): 31.7 (world avg. 17.2).
Total fertility rate (avg. births per childbearing woman; 1990–95): 7.0.
Marriage rate per 1,000 population: n.a.
Divorce rate per 1,000 population: n.a.
Life expectancy at birth (1990–95): male 45.4 years; female 48.6 years.
Major causes of death per 100,000 population: n.a.; however, major diseases include leprosy, malaria, tetanus, and tuberculosis.

National economy

Budget (1991). Revenue: So.Sh. 151,453,000,000 (domestic revenue sources, principally indirect taxes and import duties 60.4%; external grants and transfers 39.6%). Expenditures: So.Sh. 141,141,000,000 (general services 46.9%; economic and social services 31.2%; debt service 7.0%).
Tourism: receipts from visitors (1986) U.S.$8,000,000; expenditures by nationals abroad (1983) U.S.$13,000,000.
Production (metric tons except as noted). Agriculture, forestry, fishing (1992): corn (maize) 101,000, sorghum 92,000, bananas 55,000, sugarcane 50,000, roots and tubers 33,000, vegetables 26,000, sesame seed 10,000, beans 9,000, dates 8,000, rice 8,000, seed cotton 2,000, peanuts (groundnuts) 1,000; livestock (number of live animals) 6,000,000 goats, 4,000,000 sheep, 4,000,000 camels, 1,000,000 cattle; roundwood (1991) 7,326,000 cu m; fish catch (1991) 16,100. Mining and quarrying (1990): salt 30,000. Manufacturing (value added in So.Sh. '000,000; 1988): food 794; cigarettes and matches 562; hides and skins 420; paper and printing 328; plastics 320; chemicals 202; beverages 144. Construction (value added in So.Sh.; 1991): 51,100,000,000. Energy production (consumption): electricity (kW-hr; 1991) 110,000,000 (110,000,000); coal, none (n.a.); crude petroleum (barrels; 1991) n.a. (806,000); petroleum products (metric tons; 1991) none (59,000); natural gas, none (n.a.).
Household income and expenditure. Average household size (1980) 4.9; income per household: n.a.; sources of income: n.a.; expenditure (1983)[4]: food and tobacco 62.3%, housing 15.3%, clothing 5.6%, energy 4.3%, other 12.5%.
Public debt (external, outstanding; 1991): U.S.$1,929,000,000.
Gross national product (at current market prices; 1990): U.S.$946,000,000 (U.S.$150 per capita).

Structure of gross domestic product and labour force

	1991 in value So.Sh. '000,000	1991 % of total value	1987 labour force	1987 % of labour force
Agriculture	867,500	64.5	1,893,000	71.8
Mining	2,700	0.2	251,000	9.5
Manufacturing	59,200	4.4		
Construction	51,100	3.8		
Public utilities	9,400	0.7		
Transportation and communications	80,700	6.0	493,000	18.7
Trade	125,000	9.3		
Finance	45,700	3.4		
Pub. admin., defense	80,700	6.0		
Services	30,900	2.3		
Other	−8,100	−0.6		
TOTAL	1,344,900[2]	100.0	2,637,000	100.0

Population economically active (1987): total 2,637,000; activity rate of total population 42.3% (participation rates: over age 10, 63.1%; female 48.7%; unemployed, n.a.).

Price and earnings indexes (1985 = 100)

	1983	1984	1985	1986	1987	1988	1989[5]
Consumer price index	38.0	72.6	100.0	135.8	174.0	316.6	707.1
Earnings index	...	...	...	...	...	...	...

Land use (1991): forested 14.4%; meadows and pastures 68.5%; agricultural and under permanent cultivation 1.7%; other 15.4%.

Foreign trade[6]

Balance of trade (current prices)

	1986	1987	1988	1989	1990	1991
U.S.$'000,000	−317	−262	−224	−252	−328	−336
% of total	63.8%	59.1%	65.9%	60.3%	62.1%	58.3%

Imports (1991): U.S.$456,000,000 (1988; petroleum 33.1%, agricultural inputs [including fertilizers, pesticides, and seeds] 20.9%, food 10.5%, machinery and transport equipment 9.7%, manufactured raw materials 5.8%, construction materials 2.7%). *Major import sources* (1990): Italy 30.8%; The Netherlands 8.8%; Bahrain 6.0%; United Kingdom 5.9%; Djibouti 5.9%; China 4.9%; Germany 4.7%; Thailand 4.6%.
Exports (1991): U.S.$120,000,000 (live animals 56.7%, bananas 26.7%). *Major export destinations* (1990): Italy 28.7%; Saudi Arabia 23.4%; Yemen 19.1%; United Arab Emirates 10.7%.

Transport and communications

Transport. Railroads: none. Roads (1988): total length 13,845 mi, 22,281 km (paved 14%). Vehicles (1991): passenger cars 10,500; trucks and buses 12,000. Merchant marine (1992): vessels (100 gross tons and over) 28; total deadweight tonnage 18,496. Air transport (1989): passenger-mi 154,000,000, passenger-km 248,000,000; short ton-mi cargo 5,000,000, metric ton-km cargo 8,000,000; airports (1993) with scheduled flights, n.a.
Communications. Daily newspapers (1992): total number 1; total circulation, n.a. Radio (1992): total number of receivers 400,000 (1 per 20 persons). Television (1987): total number of receivers 3,000 (1 per 2,270 persons). Telephones (1989): 9,000 (1 per 809 persons).

Education and health

Education (1986–87)

	schools	teachers	students	student/teacher ratio
Primary (age 6–14)	1,125	8,208	171,830	20.9
Secondary (age 15–18)	82	2,109	42,764	20.3
Voc., teacher tr.	21	498	4,809	9.7
Higher	1	262[7]	1,692	...

Educational attainment: n.a. *Literacy* (1990): percentage of total population age 15 and over literate 24.1%; males literate 42.7%; females literate 14.0%.
Health: physicians (1987) 323 (1 per 19,071 persons); hospital beds (1985) 5,536 (1 per 1,053 persons); infant mortality rate per 1,000 live births (1990–95) 122.
Food (1988–90): daily per capita caloric intake 1,874 (vegetable products 69%, animal products 31%); 81% of FAO recommended minimum requirement.

Military

Total active duty personnel (1993)[8]: following the 1991 revolution, no national armed forces had yet been formed. *Military expenditure as percentage of GNP* (1986): 3.2% (world 5.5%); per capita expenditure U.S.$6.

[1]Proclamation of a "Somaliland Republic" by the Somali National Congress May 18, 1991, on territory corresponding to the former British Somaliland (which unified with the former Italian Trust Territory of Somalia to form Somalia in 1960) has received no international recognition. This entity would represent about a quarter of Somalia's territory and a quarter to a third of its population; a new president was elected in May 1993. [2]Detail does not add to total given because of rounding. [3]Population size, structure, and vital rates are as assessed by the United Nations in 1990, prior to the outbreak of civil war in 1991. Data do not account for subsequent emigration of up to 1,000,000 refugees to surrounding countries (December 1992; principally Ethiopia 400,000, Kenya 320,000, Djibouti 85,000), massive internal refugee displacements, or estimated excess mortality of over 300,000 from starvation, violence, and disease since 1991. Total de facto population may have been as low as 4,500,000 in late 1992. [4]Capital city only. [5]Third quarter. [6]Imports are c.i.f. [7]1980–81. [8]As of May 1993 there were an estimated 30,800 UN-sponsored military and civilian personnel in Somalia.

South Africa[1]

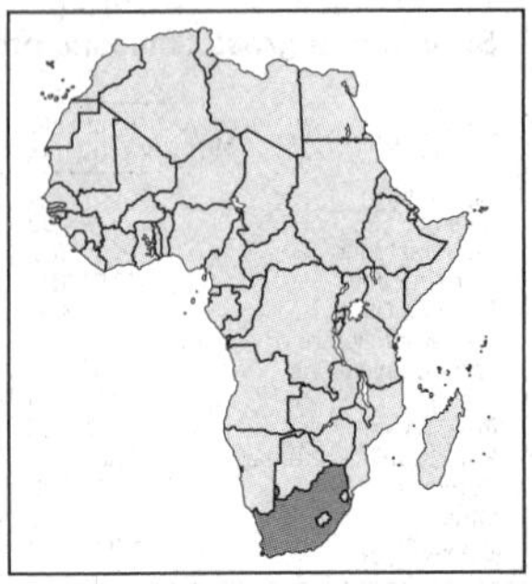

Official name: Republiek van Suid-Afrika (Afrikaans); Republic of South Africa (English).
Form of government: multiparty republic[2].
Head of state and government: State President[3].
Capitals: Pretoria (executive); Bloemfontein (judicial); Cape Town (legislative).
Official languages: Afrikaans; English.
Official religion: none.
Monetary unit: 1 rand (R) = 100 cents; valuation (Oct. 4, 1993) 1 U.S.$ = R 3.45; 1 £ = R 5.23.

Area and population[4]

Provinces	Capitals	area sq mi	area sq km	population 1991 census
Cape[5]	Cape Town	247,638	641,379	6,471,000
Natal	Pietermaritzburg	21,344	55,281	2,606,000
Orange Free State	Bloemfontein	49,165	127,338	2,093,000
Transvaal	Pretoria	87,658	227,034	10,419,000
Self-governing territories				
Gazankulu	Giyani	2,535	6,565	608,000
KaNgwane	Louieville	1,476	3,823	498,000
KwaNdebele	KwaMhlangu	1,253	3,244	516,000
KwaZulu	Ulundi	13,928	36,074	5,220,000
Lebowa	Lebowakgomo	8,430	21,833	2,279,000
Qwaqwa	Phuthaditjhaba	253	655	453,000
TOTAL		433,680	1,123,226	31,163,000

Demography

Population (1993): 33,071,000 (40,786,000[6]).
Density (1993): persons per sq mi 76.3 (86.0[6]), persons per sq km 29.4 (33.2[6]).
Urban-rural (1990)[6]: urban 59.5%; rural 40.5%.
Sex distribution (1990)[6]: male 49.73%; female 50.27%.
Age breakdown (1990)[6]: under 15, 38.8%; 15–29, 27.2%; 30–44, 17.9%; 45–59, 10.1%; 60–74, 4.7%; 75 and over, 1.3%.
Population projection[6]: (2000) 48,425,000; (2010) 62,241,000.
Doubling time[6]: 27 years.
Ethnic composition (1991)[6]: black 75.6%, of which Zulu 27.4%, Xhosa 12.4%, northern Sotho 10.9%, southern Sotho 8.5%, Tswana 6.0%, Tsonga *c.* 5.0%, Swazi *c.* 4.0%; white 13.2%; Coloured 8.6%, of which Cape Malay 1.0%; Asian 2.6%.
Religious affiliation (1991): Christian 67.9%, of which black independent churches 22.2%, Afrikaans Reformed 12.2%, Roman Catholic 7.8%, Methodist 6.2%, Anglican 4.0%, Lutheran 2.5%; Hindu 1.3%; Muslim 1.1%; not specified 28.1%; other 1.6%.
Major cities (1991)[7]: Johannesburg 1,907,229; Cape Town 1,869,144; Durban 1,106,971; Pretoria 1,025,790; Port Elizabeth 825,799.

Vital statistics

Birth rate per 1,000 population (1991)[6]: 34.0 (world avg. 26.4).
Death rate per 1,000 population (1991)[6]: 8.0 (world avg. 9.2).
Natural increase rate per 1,000 population (1991)[6]: 26.0 (world avg. 17.2).
Total fertility rate (avg. births per childbearing woman; 1991)[6]: 4.4.
Life expectancy at birth (1991)[6]: male 61.0 years; female 67.0 years.
Major causes of death per 100,000 population (1991): accidents and violence 106.1; diseases of the circulatory system 100.7; malignant neoplasms (cancers) 58.4; infectious and parasitic diseases 46.5; diseases of the respiratory system 45.7; ill-defined conditions 116.9.

National economy

Budget (1992–93). Revenue: R 84,749,000,000 (individual income taxes 41.6%, sales taxes 22.1%, company income taxes [excluding gold mining] 15.2%, fuel levy 9.1%). Expenditures: R 118,097,000,000 (education 20.7%, economic services 15.6%, interest on debt 14.8%, health 10.7%, defense 9.1%).
National debt (end of year, 1992): U.S.$45,364,000,000.
Production (in R '000,000 except as noted). Agriculture, forestry, fishing (in value of production; 1991–92): poultry and eggs 4,236, beef 2,856, corn (maize) 1,537, temperate fruits 1,373, wheat 1,308, hay 1,237, sugarcane 1,141, milk 1,098, sheep and goat meat 884, grapes 750, citrus fruits 679, tobacco 507; roundwood (1991) 19,679,000 cu m[6]; fish catch (1991) 498,884 metric tons[6]. Mining and quarrying (in value of sales; 1992): gold 18,775; coal 9,345; platinum-group metals 2,164; iron ore 1,139; copper 1,025; manganese 600; lime and limestone 495; chrome 411[8]; diamonds 10,156,000 carats. Manufacturing (in value added; 1990): food and beverages 7,810; chemicals 6,614; iron and steel 6,013; transport equipment 5,148; metal products 4,376; paper and paper products 4,234; petroleum products 2,858; electrical apparatus 2,394; textiles 2,040. Construction (buildings completed in value of construction; 1991): residential 2,979; nonresidential 3,763. Energy production (consumption)[6, 9]: electricity (kW-hr; 1991) 169,645,000,000 (163,963,000,000); coal (metric tons; 1991) 176,174,000 (133,527,000); crude petroleum (barrels; 1991) none (115,814,000); petroleum products (metric tons; 1991) 13,770,000 (10,548,000); natural gas, none (none).
Household income and expenditure. Average household size (1983) 4.5; average annual income per household (1980) R 8,829 (U.S.$11,349); sources of income (1990): wages and salaries 75.9%, interest, dividends, rent, etc., 19.8%, transfers 4.3%; expenditure (1990): food 34.2%, transportation 15.1%, household goods 10.7%, clothing and footwear 7.5%.

Gross national product (1992)[6]: U.S.$106,108,000,000 (U.S.$2,670 per capita).

Structure of gross domestic product and labour force

	1991 in value R '000,000[10]	% of total value	labour force	% of labour force
Agriculture	12,495	4.7	1,004,986	9.8
Mining	27,695	10.4	679,981	6.7
Manufacturing	66,567	24.9	1,260,324	12.3
Construction	8,201	3.1	460,111	4.5
Public utilities	11,892	4.5	88,018	0.9
Transp. and commun.	22,249	8.3	437,385	4.3
Trade	36,173	13.5	1,218,145	11.9
Finance, real estate	39,683	14.8	444,598	4.4
Pub. admin., defense	39,549	14.8	2,339,345	22.9
Services	4,645	1.7		
Other	−1,772[11]	−0.7[11]	2,282,410	22.3
TOTAL	267,377	100.0	10,215,303[12]	100.0

Population economically active (1991): total 10,215,303[12]; activity rate of total population 38.9% (participation rates: ages 20–64 [1985] 68.3%; female 41.0%; unemployed [unofficial estimate in mid-1993] 48.0%[6].

Price and earnings indexes (1985 = 100)

	1987	1988	1989	1990	1991	1992	1993[13]
Consumer price index	136.7	155.4	178.2	203.8	235.0	267.7	294.1
Monthly earnings index[14]	134.1	154.8	180.4	205.0	227.5	...	...

Tourism (1991): receipts U.S.$1,046,000,000; expenditures U.S.$1,047,000,000.
Land use (1991)[6]: forest 3.7%; pasture 66.6%; agriculture 10.8%; other 18.9%.

Foreign trade

Balance of trade (current prices)

	1987	1988	1989	1990	1991	1992
R '000,000	+15,167	+9,643	+13,888	+16,861	+18,476	+16,157
% of total	20.9%	10.9%	13.5%	16.0%	16.0%	13.5%

Imports (1991): R 48,339,000,000 (machinery and apparatus 14.9%, transport equipment 14.1%, chemicals and chemical products 11.2%, textiles and clothing 5.2%). *Major import sources:* Germany 16.7%; U.S. 12.4%; U.K. 10.6%; Japan 9.7%; not specified 19.5%.
Exports (1991): R 66,815,000,000 (gold 29.4%, base metals and metal products 14.4%, mineral fuels [mostly coal] 11.6%, precious stones [mostly diamonds] 10.1%). *Major export destinations:* Italy 8.4%; Germany 6.6%; Japan 6.3%; U.S. 6.1%; U.K. 5.8%; not specified 44.9%.

Transport and communications

Transport. Railroads (1991)[15]: route length 21,617 km; passenger-km 1,205,400,000[16, 17]; metric ton-km cargo 93,019,000,000[17]. Roads (1991): length 188,392 km (paved 30%). Vehicles (1991): passenger cars 3,461,395; trucks and buses 1,863,354. Merchant marine (1992): vessels 219; total deadweight tonnage 282,533. Air transport (1992)[18]: passenger-km 9,511,000,000; metric ton-km cargo 263,487,000; airports (1993) 36[6].
Communications. Daily newspapers (1992): total number 19; total circulation 1,311,926; circulation per 1,000 population 41. Radio (1992)[6]: 10,000,000 receivers (1 per 3.9 persons). Television (1992)[6]: 3,445,000 receivers (1 per 11 persons). Telephones (1991): 5,208,086 (1 per 6.1 persons).

Education and health

Education (1992)

	schools	teachers	students	student/teacher ratio
Primary/Secondary	20,648	322,493	8,374,564	26.0
Voc., teacher tr.	197	14,876	147,009	9.9
Tertiary vocational	12	6,865	113,870	16.6
University	17	31,863	318,944	10.0

Educational attainment (1990)[6]. Percentage of all-age population group (black, white, Coloured, Asian) having: no formal schooling (34.4%, 7.8%, 15.5%, 11.4%); primary education (45.2%, 10.3%, 32.6%, 21.8%); secondary (19.8%, 56.4%, 48.9%, 60.3%); technical/teacher training (0.5%, 10.1%, 2.3%, 2.5%); undergraduate (0.06%, 6.7%, 0.3%, 1.7%); graduate (0.05%, 8.7%, 0.4%, 2.3%). *Literacy* (1980): total population age 15 and over literate 76.4%; males literate 77.8%; females literate 75.1%.
Health (1991): physicians (1992) 25,375 (1 per 1,271 persons); hospital beds 141,977 (1 per 221 persons); infant mortality rate 51.0[6].
Food (1988–90)[6]: daily per capita caloric intake 3,133 (vegetable products 87%, animal products 13%); 128% of FAO recommended minimum.

Military

Total active duty personnel (1993): 67,500 (army 69.6%, navy 6.7%, air force 14.8%, intraservice medical service 8.9%). *Military expenditure as percentage of GNP* (1989): 4.4% (world 4.9%); per capita expenditure U.S.$125.

[1]Data exclude the South African-recognized republics of Transkei, Bophuthatswana, Venda, and Ciskei (TBVC states) unless otherwise footnoted; reincorporation of these states into South Africa was under negotiation in December 1993. [2]Government was in transition between September 1993 and April 1994. New interim constitution was adopted on Dec. 22, 1993. [3]Transitional Executive Council met for first time in December 1993; it was to act as a check on the State President. [4]TBVC states had an area of 39,610 sq mi (102,589 sq km) in 1986 and a population of 7,715,000 in 1993. [5]Includes area of Walvis Bay, to be jointly administered with Namibia until Feb. 28, 1994. [6]Includes TBVC states. [7]Population of metropolitan areas. [8]1991. [9]Includes Botswana, Lesotho, Namibia, and Swaziland. [10]At factor cost. [11]Net of imputed bank service charges and other producers. [12]Based on preliminary unadjusted census. [13]June. [14]Manufacturing only. [15]South African Railways. [16]Excludes suburban traffic. [17]1990–91. [18]SAA only.

Spain

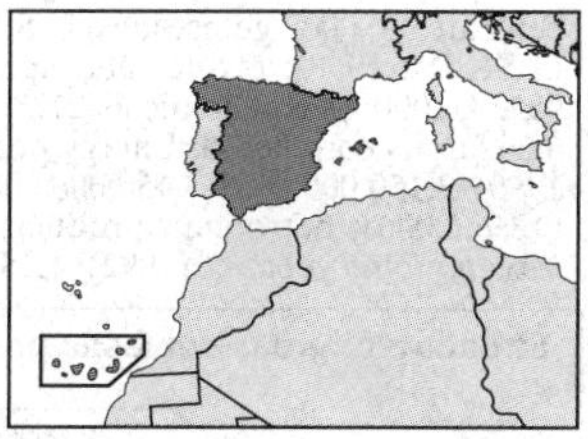

Official name: Reino de España (Kingdom of Spain).
Form of government: constitutional monarchy with two legislative houses (Senate [251[1]]; Congress of Deputies [350]).
Chief of state: King.
Head of government: Prime Minister.
Capital: Madrid.
Official language: Spanish.
Official religion: none.
Monetary unit: 1 peseta (Pta) = 100 céntimos; valuation (Oct. 4, 1993) 1 U.S.$ = Ptas 130.86; 1 £ = Ptas 198.25.

Area and population

Autonomous communities	Capitals	area sq mi	area sq km	population 1992 estimate
Andalucía	Seville	33,694	87,268	6,983,734
Aragón	Zaragoza	18,398	47,650	1,207,338
Asturias	Oviedo	4,079	10,565	1,118,610
Baleares (Balearic Islands)	Palma de Mallorca	1,936	5,014	685,686
Canarias (Canary Islands)	Santa Cruz de Tenerife	2,796	7,242	1,501,651
Cantabria	Santander	2,042	5,289	526,400
Castilla-La Mancha	Toledo	30,591	79,230	1,716,665
Castilla y León	Valladolid	36,368	94,193	2,618,228
Cataluña	Barcelona	12,328	31,930	6,018,154
Extremadura	Mérida	16,063	41,602	1,131,195
Galicia	Santiago de Compostela	11,365	29,434	2,792,802
La Rioja	Logroño	1,944	5,034	260,282
Madrid	Madrid	3,087	7,995	4,910,199
Murcia	Murcia	4,370	11,317	1,038,126
Navarra	Pamplona	4,023	10,421	521,670
País Vasco (Basque Country)	Vitoria (Gasteiz)	2,803	7,261	2,129,523
Valencia	Valencia	8,998	23,305	3,797,671
TOTAL SPAIN		194,885	504,750	38,957,934
Enclaves in Northern Morocco				
Ceuta	—	7.1	18.5	70,746
Melilla	—	5.4	14.0	56,403
Other enclaves (*plazas de soberanía*)	—	0.26	0.66	...
TOTAL		194,897.79[2]	504,783.16	39,085,083

Demography

Population (1993): 39,141,000[3].
Density (1993): persons per sq mi 200.8, persons per sq km 77.5.
Urban-rural (1990): urban 78.4%; rural 21.6%.
Sex distribution (1993): male 49.09%; female 50.91%.
Age breakdown (1993): under 15, 17.9%; 15–29, 25.0%; 30–44, 20.9%; 45–59, 16.5%; 60–69, 10.2%; 70 and over, 9.5%.
Population projection: (2000) 39,879,000; (2010) 40,317,000.
Doubling time: not applicable; doubling time exceeds 100 years.
Ethnolinguistic composition (1989): Spanish 72.3%; Catalan 16.3%; Galician 8.1%; Basque 2.3%; other 1.0%.
Religious affiliation (1980): Roman Catholic 97.0%; Protestant 0.4%; nonreligious and atheist 2.6%.
Major cities (1991)[4]: Madrid 2,909,792; Barcelona 1,623,542; Valencia 752,909; Seville 659,126; Zaragoza 586,219.

Vital statistics

Birth rate per 1,000 population (1991): 9.9 (world avg. 26.4); (1988) legitimate 92.0%; illegitimate 8.0%.
Death rate per 1,000 population (1991): 8.7 (world avg. 9.2).
Natural increase rate per 1,000 population (1991): 1.2 (world avg. 17.2).
Total fertility rate (avg. births per childbearing woman; 1990–95): 1.7.
Marriage rate per 1,000 population (1991): 5.4.
Life expectancy at birth (1990–95): male 74.4 years; female 80.3 years.
Major causes of death per 100,000 population (1990): circulatory diseases 441.8; malignant neoplasms (cancers) 259.4; respiratory diseases 105.4.

National economy

Budget (1993[5]). Revenue: Ptas 13,405,000,000,000 (direct taxes 48.6%; indirect taxes 39.4%, of which value-added tax on products 11.8%; other taxes on production 12.0%). Expenditures: Ptas 14,828,000,000,000 (current transfers between public administrations 53.0%; wages and salaries 16.9%).
Tourism (1991): receipts from visitors U.S.$19,004,000,000; expenditures by nationals abroad U.S.$4,530,000,000.
Production (metric tons except as noted). Agriculture, forestry, fishing (1992): sugar beets 7,475,000, barley 5,995,000, grapes 5,676,000, potatoes 5,271,000, wheat 4,464,000, oranges 2,724,000, tomatoes 2,616,000, corn (maize) 2,609,000, onions 995,000; livestock (number of live animals) 24,625,000 sheep, 17,240,000 pigs, 4,924,000 cattle, 3,000,000 goats; roundwood (1991) 17,272,000 cu m; fish catch (1991) 1,350,000. Mining and quarrying (metal content in metric tons; 1991): iron ore 3,564,000; zinc 261,200; lead 46,000. Manufacturing (value added, in Ptas '000,000; 1990): machinery and transport equipment 2,175,761; food products 1,564,469; chemical products 921,075; paper products 662,993; wood and cork products 379,452; clothing and footwear 338,083; textiles 306,572. Construction (1991): dwellings 281,059. Energy production (consumption): electricity (kW-hr; 1991) 155,704,000,000 (155,025,000,000); coal (metric tons; 1991) 33,562,000 (47,659,000); crude petroleum (barrels; 1991) 8,333,000 (412,509,000); petroleum products (metric tons; 1991) 48,062,000 (39,326,000); natural gas (cu m; 1991) 2,353,538,000 (11,067,741,000).
Gross national product (1992): U.S.$547,942,000,000 (U.S.$14,030 per capita).

Structure of gross domestic product and labour force

	1992 in value Ptas '000,000	% of total value	labour force	% of labour force
Agriculture	2,072,500	3.5	1,445,800	9.5
Mining			74,100	0.5
Manufacturing	13,666,800	23.2	3,022,400	20.0
Public utilities			81,200	0.5
Construction	5,056,700	8.6	1,537,900	10.1
Transp. and commun.	...	...	783,200	5.2
Trade			2,905,000	19.2
Finance			817,500	5.4
Services	34,195,000	58.1	3,467,300	22.9
Pub. admin., defense				
Other	3,861,100[6]	6.6[6]	1,020,300[7]	6.7[7]
TOTAL	58,851,900[2]	100.0	15,154,800[2]	100.0

Public debt (1992[8]): Ptas 23,582,000,000,000 (U.S.$205,700,000,000).
Population economically active (1992): total 15,154,800; activity rate of total population 38.8% (participation rates: ages 16–64, 60.0%; female 43.1%; unemployed 14.9%).

Price and earnings indexes (1985 = 100)

	1986	1987	1988	1989	1990	1991	1992
Consumer price index	108.8	114.5	120.0	128.2	136.8	144.9	153.4
Monthly earnings index	110.1	119.7	129.1	136.3	148.2	160.3	172.6

Household income and expenditure. Average household size (1991) 3.4; income per household (1991) Ptas 2,408,000 (U.S.$23,200); sources of income (1988): wages and salaries 47.8%, profits and self-employment 32.1%, social security 15.5%; expenditure (1991): food 25.4%, housing 19.3%, transportation 12.8%, clothing and footwear 9.8%, household goods and services 6.4%.
Land use (1991): forested 31.8%; meadows and pastures 20.6%; agricultural and under permanent cultivation 40.2%; other 7.4%.

Foreign trade

Balance of trade (current prices)

	1987	1988	1989	1990	1991	1992
Ptas '000,000	–1,493.0	–1,954.7	–2,722.0	–2,765.4	–2,724.3	–3,022.5
% of total	15.1%	17.2%	20.6%	19.7%	19.6%	18.6%

Imports (1992): Ptas 10,205,009,000,000 (machinery 12.4%; agricultural products 10.1%; energy products 9.8%, of which crude petroleum 9.6%; transportation equipment 9.7%). *Major import sources:* Germany 16.4%; France 15.9%; Italy 9.8%; U.K. 7.3%; Japan 4.7%.
Exports (1992): Ptas 6,605,660,000,000 (transport equipment 21.4%; agricultural products 13.6%; machinery 8.4%). *Major export destinations:* France 20.2%; Germany 15.7%; Italy 10.9%; U.K. 7.7%.

Transport and communications

Transport. Railroads (1991): route length 12,563 km; passenger-km 15,228,000,000; metric ton-km cargo 10,668,000,000. Roads (1991): length 331,961 km (paved 99%). Vehicles (1991): cars 12,537,099; trucks and buses 2,615,033. Merchant marine (1992): vessels 2,190; deadweight tonnage 5,077,275. Air transport (1992): passenger-km 27,240,000,000; metric ton-km cargo 620,844,000; airports (1993) with scheduled flights 24.
Communications. Daily newspapers (1992): total number 81; total circulation 1,760,483[9]; circulation per 1,000 population 45[9]. Radio (1992): 12,000,000 receivers (1 per 3.3 persons). Television (1992): 17,000,000 receivers (1 per 2.3 persons). Telephones (1987): 15,476,776 (1 per 2.5 persons).

Education and health

Education (1992–93)

	schools	teachers	students	student/teacher ratio
Primary (age 6–11)	38,512[10]	267,725[10]	4,474,775	...
Secondary (age 12–18)	23,107	170,144	2,558,717	15.0
Vocational[11]	2,668	63,236	1,234,045	19.5
Higher	1,415	67,166[11]	1,261,012	18.8

Educational attainment (1986). Percentage of population age 25 and over having: no formal schooling 5.2%; less than primary education 40.3%; primary 29.9%; incomplete secondary 8.9%; completed secondary 8.7%; higher 7.0%.
Literacy (1991): total population age 10 and over literate 33,338,300 (85.4%); males literate 16,458,400 (85.1%); females literate 16,879,900 (84.3%).
Health (1991): physicians 153,306 (1 per 257 persons); hospital beds 168,514 (1 per 234 persons); infant mortality rate (1990) 7.7.
Food (1988–90): daily per capita caloric intake 3,472 (vegetable products 68%, animal products 32%); 141% of FAO recommended minimum requirement.

Military

Total active duty personnel (1993): 200,700 (army 69.2%, navy 15.9%, air force 14.9%). *Military expenditure as percentage of GNP* (1989): 2.1% (world 4.9%); per capita expenditure U.S.$200.

[1]At the June 1993 elections, 204 seats were directly elected and 47 indirectly elected by the parliaments of the autonomous communities. [2]Detail does not add to total given because of rounding. [3]Estimate based on 1981 census. [4]For *municipios*, which may contain rural population. [5]Preliminary. [6]Import taxes and value-added tax on products. [7]Includes 624,100 unemployed persons not previously employed. [8]December. [9]For 36 newspapers only. [10]Includes preschool. [11]1988–89.

Sri Lanka

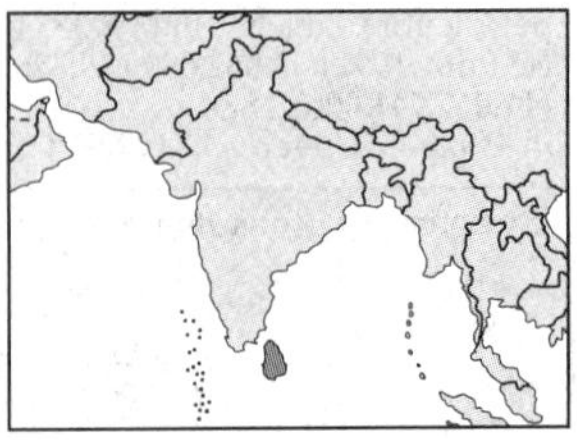

Official name: Sri Lankā Prajathanthrika Samajavadi Janarajaya (Sinhala); Ilangai Jananayaka Socialisa Kudiarasu (Tamil) (Democratic Socialist Republic of Sri Lanka).
Form of government: unitary multiparty republic with one legislative house (Parliament [225]).
Head of state and government: President.
Capitals: Colombo (administrative) and Sri Jayewardenepura Kotte (legislative).
Official languages: Sinhala; Tamil.
Official religion: none.
Monetary unit: 1 Sri Lanka rupee (SL Rs) = 100 cents; valuation (Oct. 4, 1993) 1 U.S.$ = SL Rs 48.56; 1 £ = SL Rs 73.57.

Area and population

		area		population
Districts	Capitals	sq mi	sq km	1991 estimate
Amparai	Amparai	1,705	4,415	482,000
Anuradhapura	Anuradhapura	2,772	7,179	716,000
Badulla	Badulla	1,104	2,861	718,000
Batticaloa	Batticaloa	1,102	2,854	417,000
Colombo	Colombo	270	699	1,965,000
Galle	Galle	638	1,652	946,000
Gampaha	Gampaha	536	1,387	1,532,000
Hambantota	Hambantota	1,007	2,609	517,000
Jaffna	Jaffna	396	1,025	871,000
Kalutara	Kalutara	617	1,598	945,000
Kandy	Kandy	749	1,940	1,258,000
Kegalle	Kegalle	654	1,693	751,000
Kilinochchi	Kilinochchi	494	1,279	101,000
Kurunegala	Kurunegala	1,859	4,816	1,428,000
Mannar	Mannar	771	1,996	132,000
Matale	Matale	770	1,993	421,000
Matara	Matara	495	1,283	776,000
Monaragala	Monaragala	2,177	5,639	351,000
Mullaitivu	Mullaitivu	1,010	2,617	92,000
Nuwara Eliya	Nuwara Eliya	672	1,741	541,000
Polonnaruwa	Polonnaruwa	1,271	3,293	319,000
Puttalam	Puttalam	1,186	3,072	598,000
Ratnapura	Ratnapura	1,264	3,275	941,000
Trincomalee	Trincomalee	1,053	2,727	315,000
Vavuniya	Vavuniya	759	1,967	114,000
TOTAL		25,332	65,610	17,247,000

Demography

Population (1993): 17,616,000.
Density (1993): persons per sq mi 695.4, persons per sq km 268.5.
Urban-rural (1993): urban 22.0%; rural 78.0%.
Sex distribution (1991): male 50.98%; female 49.02%.
Age breakdown (1991): under 15, 35.2%; 15–24, 21.1%; 25–44, 26.5%; 45–59, 10.6%; 60–69, 4.0%; 70 and over, 2.6%.
Population projection: (2000) 19,098,000; (2010) 21,159,000.
Doubling time: 46 years.
Ethnic composition (1981): Sinhalese 74.0%; Tamil 18.2%; Sri Lankan Moor 7.1%; other 0.7%.
Religious affiliation (1981): Buddhist 69.3%; Hindu 15.5%; Muslim 7.6%; Christian 7.5%; other 0.1%.
Major cities (1990): Colombo 615,000; Dehiwala–Mount Lavinia 196,000; Moratuwa 170,000; Jaffna 129,000; Sri Jayewardenepura Kotte 109,000.

Vital statistics

Birth rate per 1,000 population (1991): 21.2 (world avg. 26.4); (1982) legitimate 94.6%; illegitimate 5.4%.
Death rate per 1,000 population (1991): 5.8 (world avg. 9.2).
Natural increase rate per 1,000 population (1991): 15.4 (world avg. 17.2).
Total fertility rate (avg. births per childbearing woman; 1993): 2.5.
Marriage rate per 1,000 population (1989): 8.4.
Divorce rate per 1,000 population (1988): 0.2.
Life expectancy at birth (1993): male 70.0 years; female 74.0 years.
Major causes of death per 100,000 population (1986): diseases of the circulatory system 101.9; violence and poisoning 77.8; diseases of the nervous system 45.3; respiratory diseases 36.1; infectious and parasitic diseases 32.2.

National economy

Budget (1991). Revenue: SL Rs 74,640,000,000 (sales and turnover tax 29.7%, import duties 24.5%, excise taxes 14.3%, income taxes 10.5%, nontax revenue 10.0%). Expenditures: SL Rs 135,190,000,000 (public-debt service 16.6%, transfer payments 16.2%, administration 12.7%, defense 8.7%, transport 5.2%, education 4.7%, power 3.9%, food and cooperatives 3.8%).
Public debt (external, outstanding; 1991): U.S.$5,653,000,000.
Tourism (1991): receipts U.S.$156,000,000; expenditures U.S.$92,000,000.
Production (metric tons except as noted). Agriculture, forestry, fishing (1992): rice 2,250,000, coconuts 1,750,000, sugarcane 890,000, cassava 302,000, tea 179,000, copra 130,000, rubber 105,000, sweet potatoes 60,000; livestock (number of live animals) 1,568,000 cattle, 896,000 buffalo, 502,000 goats; roundwood (1991) 9,096,000 cu m; fish catch (1991) 198,063. Mining and quarrying (1990): quartz stone 1,300,000; limestone 642,000; titanium concentrate 80,000; gemstones U.S.$14,000,000. Manufacturing (value added, in SL Rs; 1990): textiles and apparel 27,930,000,000; food and tobacco 21,955,000,000; petrochemicals 21,215,000,000. Construction (1990): residential, 6,262 units completed. Energy production (consumption): electricity (kW-hr; 1990) 3,150,000,000 (3,150,000,000); crude petroleum (barrels; 1990) none (12,732,000); petroleum products (metric tons; 1990) 1,684,000 (1,264,000).
Gross national product (1992): U.S.$9,400,000,000 (U.S.$540 per capita).

Structure of gross domestic product and labour force

	1991		1990	
	in value SL Rs '000,000	% of total value	labour force	% of labour force
Agriculture	82,359	22.3	2,851,056	40.9
Mining	4,190	1.1	161,351	2.3
Manufacturing	62,734	17.0	868,500	12.5
Construction	26,164	7.1	183,398	2.6
Public utilities	6,500	1.8	13,409	0.2
Transp. and commun.	35,293	9.5	246,781	3.5
Trade	75,579	20.4	510,451	7.3
Finance	19,315	5.2	49,467	0.7
Pub. admin., defense	26,634	7.2	980,266	14.1
Services	11,261	3.0		
Other	19,865	5.4	1,104,109[1]	15.9[1]
TOTAL	369,894	100.0	6,968,788	100.0

Population economically active: total (1990) 6,968,788; activity rate 43.2% (participation rates: ages 15 and over, 61.5%; female 37.3%; unemployed 14.4%).

Price and earnings indexes (1985 = 100)

	1986	1987	1988	1989	1990	1991	1992
Consumer price index	108.0	116.3	132.6	147.9	179.7	201.6	224.6
Average wage index[2]	105.4	110.7	138.4	159.4	189.1	211.3	242.9

Household income and expenditure (1990). Average household size (1981) 5.2; income per household SL Rs 86,200 (U.S.$2,200); sources of income: wages 50.3%, property income and self-employment 41.5%, transfers 8.2%; expenditure: food and beverages 59.1%, transportation 15.4%, clothing 6.4%, household furnishings 5.1%, housing and energy 4.6%.
Land use (1991): forested 32.5%; meadows and pastures 6.8%; agricultural and under permanent cultivation 29.4%; other 31.3%.

Foreign trade

Balance of trade (current prices)

	1987	1988	1989	1990	1991	1992
SL Rs '000,000	−13,146	−17,058	−15,135	−17,485	−29,612	−27,128
% of total	13.8%	15.4%	11.9%	9.9%	14.9%	11.0%

Imports (1991): SL Rs 100,738,000,000 (machinery and transport equipment 26.5%, basic manufactures 24.0%, food and live animals 20.3%, mineral fuels 13.9%). *Major import sources:* Japan 11.6%; India 7.1%; U.S. 5.7%; U.K. 5.4%; Iran 4.7%; China 3.3%; Pakistan 2.4%; Australia 1.2%.
Exports (1991): SL Rs 67,792,000,000 (basic manufactures 50.9%, food and live animals 34.5%, crude materials excluding fuels 6.1%, machines and transport equipment 3.9%). *Major export destinations:* U.S. 28.4%; Germany 7.6%; U.K. 6.4%; Japan 5.2%; Canada 1.6%; Pakistan 1.6%; Australia 1.1%; India 0.6%.

Transport and communications

Transport. Railroads (1991): route length 1,423 km; passenger-km 2,625,000,000; metric ton-km cargo 151,200,000. Roads (1990): total length 25,952 km (paved 81%). Vehicles (1991): passenger cars 180,135; trucks and buses 146,799. Merchant marine (1992): vessels (100 gross tons and over) 66; total deadweight tonnage 472,625. Air transport (1992): passenger-km 4,165,000,000; metric ton-km cargo 109,859,000; airports (1993) 1.
Communications. Daily newspapers (1990): total number 18; total circulation 550,000; circulation per 1,000 population 32. Radio (1992): 2,200,000 receivers (1 per 7.9 persons). Television (1992): 700,000 receivers (1 per 25 persons). Telephones (1990): 166,000 (1 per 102 persons).

Education and health

Education (1991)

	schools	teachers	students	student/ teacher ratio
Primary[3] (age 5–10)	9,527	67,019	2,081,104	31.1
Secondary (age 11–17)	9,041	106,792	2,105,959	19.7
Voc., teacher tr.	23	437	8,908	20.4
Higher	8	1,937	31,447	16.2

Educational attainment (1981). Percentage of population age 25 and over having: no schooling 15.5%; less than complete primary education 12.1%; complete primary 52.3%; postprimary 14.7%; secondary 3.0%; higher 1.1%; unspecified 1.3%. *Literacy* (1986): percentage of population age 15 and over literate 84.3%; males literate 88.3%; females literate 80.1%.
Health: physicians (1991) 2,962 (1 per 5,823 persons); hospital beds (1990) 47,738 (1 per 356 persons); infant mortality rate per 1,000 live births (1993) 24.
Food (1988–90): daily per capita caloric intake 2,246 (vegetable products 95%, animal products 5%); 101% of FAO recommended minimum.

Military

Total active duty personnel (1993): 110,800 (army 81.2%, navy 9.1%, air force 9.7%). *Military expenditure as percentage of GNP* (1989): 3.2% (world 4.9%); per capita expenditure U.S.$13.

[1]Includes unemployed. [2]Agricultural minimum rates. [3]Public schools only.

Sudan, The

Official name: Jumhūrīyat as-Sūdān (Republic of the Sudan).
Form of government: Islamic military regime with one transitional legislative house (Transitional National Assembly [302][1]).
Head of state and government: President.
Capitals: Khartoum (executive); Omdurman (legislative).
Official language: Arabic.
Official religion: [2].
Monetary unit: 1 Sudanese dinar (Dsd)[3]; valuation (Oct. 4, 1993) 1 U.S.$ = Dsd 12.90; 1 £ = Dsd 19.56.

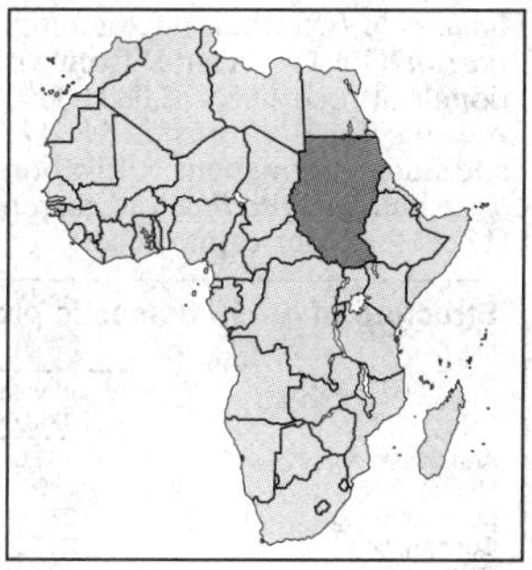

Area and population

		area		population
States	Capitals	sq mi	sq km	1983 census
A'ālī an-Nīl (Upper Nile)	Malakāl	92,198	238,792	1,599,605
Baḥr al-Ghazāl (Bahr el-Ghazal)	Wāw	77,566	200,894	2,265,510
Dārfūr (Darfur)	al-Fāshir	196,404	508,684	3,093,699
al-Istiwā'īyah (Equatoria)	Juba	76,436	197,969	1,406,181
al-Kharṭūm (Khartoum)	Khartoum	10,875	28,165	1,802,299
Kurdufān (Kordofan)	al-Ubayyiḍ	146,817	380,255	3,093,294
ash-Shamālīyah (Northern)	ad-Dāmir	183,800	476,040	1,083,024
ash-Sharqīyah (Eastern)	Kassalā	128,987	334,074	2,208,209
al-Wusṭā (Central)	Wad Madanī	53,675	139,017	4,012,543
TOTAL		966,757[4]	2,503,890	20,564,364[5]

Demography

Population (1993): 25,000,000.
Density (1993): persons per sq mi 25.9, persons per sq km 10.0.
Urban-rural (1990): urban 22.0%; rural 78.0%.
Sex distribution (1990): male 50.23%; female 49.77%.
Age breakdown (1990): under 15, 45.2%; 15–29, 26.1%; 30–44, 15.4%; 45–59, 8.7%; 60–74, 3.9%; 75 and over, 0.7%.
Population projection: (2000) 30,513,000; (2010) 43,045,000.
Doubling time: 23 years.
Ethnic composition (1983): Sudanese Arab 49.1%; Dinka 11.5%; Nuba 8.1%; Beja 6.4%; Nuer 4.9%; Azande 2.7%; Bari 2.5%; Fur 2.1%; Shilluk 1.7%; Lotuko 1.5%; other 9.5%.
Religious affiliation (1992): Sunnī Muslim 74.7%; traditional beliefs 17.1%; Christian 8.2%, of which Roman Catholic 7.0%.
Major cities (1983): Omdurman 526,287[6]; Khartoum 476,218[6]; Khartoum North 341,146[6]; Port Sudan (1990) *c.* 215,000[7]; Wad Madanī (1987) *c.* 145,000.

Vital statistics

Birth rate per 1,000 population (1991): 44.0 (world avg. 26.4).
Death rate per 1,000 population (1991): 13.0 (world avg. 9.2).
Natural increase rate per 1,000 population (1991): 31.0 (world avg. 17.2).
Total fertility rate (avg. births per childbearing woman; 1991): 6.2.
Marriage rate per 1,000 population: n.a.
Divorce rate per 1,000 population: n.a
Life expectancy at birth (1991): male 52.0 years; female 54.0 years.
Major causes of death per 100,000 population: n.a.

National economy

Budget (1993–94). Revenue: Dsd 1,553,100,000 (direct taxes 38.6%; indirect taxes 35.4%; loans and grants 26.0%). Expenditures: Dsd 2,337,000,000 (current expenditures 69.6%, of which social and welfare expenditure 7.5%; development expenditures 30.4%).
Tourism (1991): receipts from visitors U.S.$8,000,000; expenditures by nationals abroad U.S.$12,000,000.
Public debt (external, outstanding; 1991): U.S.$9,221,000,000.
Population economically active (1983)[8]: total 6,342,981; activity rate of total population 35.1% (participation rates: ages 15–64, 57.4%; female 29.1%; unemployed, n.a.).

Price and earnings indexes (1985 = 100)

	1986	1987	1988	1989	1990	1991	1992
Consumer price index	124.5	150.7	247.1	412.0	680.4	1,521	3,311
Earnings index	...	...	...	...	...	...	...

Production (metric tons except as noted). Agriculture, forestry, fishing (1992): sugarcane 4,600,000, sorghum 3,700,000, wheat 895,000, peanuts (groundnuts) 454,000, millet 424,000, sesame seeds 330,000, seed cotton 261,000, cottonseed 170,000, yams 129,000, cotton lint 87,000, gum arabic 30,200[9]; livestock (number of live animals; 1991–92) 67,000,000 cattle, 21,600,000 sheep, 18,700,000 goats, 2,800,000 camels; roundwood 23,449,000 cu m; fish catch (1990) 38,848. Mining and quarrying (1991): salt 75,000; chromite concentrate 10,000; gypsum 7,000. Manufacturing (1989): wheat flour 733,900; refined sugar 356,200; cement 166,500[9]; plastics 12,195[10]; yarn 9,700[10]; perfumes 2,500[10]; textiles 58,600,000 metres[10]; cigarettes 1,300,000,000 units; tires and tubes 256,300 units. Construction: n.a. Energy production (consumption): electricity (kW-hr; 1990) 1,327,000,000 (1,327,000,000); coal, none (none); crude petroleum (barrels; 1990) none (7,440,000); petroleum products (metric tons; 1990) 836,000 (1,036,000); natural gas, none (none).
Gross national product (1990): U.S.$10,107,000,000 (U.S.$400 per capita).

Structure of gross domestic product and labour force

	1988–89		1983	
	in value LSd '000,000	% of total value	labour force[8]	% of labour force[8]
Agriculture	26,450	36.0	4,028,705	63.5
Mining }	6,030	8.2	6,534	0.1
Manufacturing }			266,693	4.2
Construction	3,330	4.5	139,282	2.2
Public utilities	1,320	1.8	43,728	0.7
Transportation and communications	...	...	215,474	3.4
Trade and finance	...	...	314,676	5.0
Pub. admin., defense	8,630	11.7 }	550,409	8.7
Services	27,800	37.8 }		
Other	...	...	777,480[11]	12.2[11]
TOTAL	73,560	100.0	6,342,981	100.0

Household income and expenditure. Average household size (1980) 5.3; income per household: n.a.[12]; sources of income: n.a.; expenditure (1983): food and beverages 63.6%, housing 11.5%, household goods 5.5%, clothing and footwear 5.3%, health care 4.1%, energy 3.8%.
Land use (1991): forested 18.8%; meadows and pastures 46.3%; agricultural and under permanent cultivation 5.4%; desert and other 29.5%.

Foreign trade[13]

Balance of trade (current prices)

	1986	1987	1988	1989	1990	1991
LSd '000,000	−1,569	−1,116	−2,482	−2,991	−3,009	−5,760
% of total	48.5%	27.2%	35.1%	33.1%	39.3%	59.7%

Imports (1989): LSd 6,014,000,000 (basic manufactures 23.1%, machinery 17.1%, transport equipment 13.3%, chemicals and medicines 7.6%, wheat and wheat flour 5.4%, coffee and tea 4.2%). *Major import sources* (1991)[14]: Saudi Arabia 13.5%; United Kingdom 10.3%; Italy 8.5%; Germany 7.8%; China 7.6%; United States 7.2%; Japan 4.1%.
Exports (1989): LSd 3,023,000,000 (cotton 44.6%, sesame seeds 11.0%, gum arabic 10.4%, sorghum 9.8%, livestock 6.4%, hides and skins 3.8%). *Major export destinations* (1991)[15]: Thailand 17.3%; former U.S.S.R. 10.9%; Saudi Arabia 10.0%; Italy 9.5%; Germany 8.8%; Japan 7.8%; France 5.1%.

Transport and communications

Transport. Railroads (1991): route length (1990) 3,029 mi, 4,874 km; passenger-mi 311,000,000, passenger-km 501,000,000; short ton-mi cargo 442,000,000, metric ton-km cargo 646,000,000. Roads (1990): total length *c.* 14,000 mi, *c.* 22,500 km (paved 9%). Vehicles (1991): passenger cars 116,000; trucks and buses 57,000. Merchant marine (1992): vessels (100 gross tons and over) 16; total deadweight tonnage 62,244. Air transport (1992)[16]: passenger-mi 317,608,000, passenger-km 511,142,000; short ton-mi cargo 23,708,000, metric ton-km cargo 34,613,000; airports (1993) with scheduled flights 13.
Communications. Daily newspapers (1990): total number 3[17]; total circulation, n.a. Radio (1992): 6,000,000 receivers (1 per 4.1 persons). Television (1992): 250,000 receivers (1 per 99 persons). Telephones (1991): 73,000 (1 per 334 persons).

Education and health

Education (1991–92)

	schools	teachers	students	student/ teacher ratio
Primary (age 7–12)	8,501	64,227	2,079,649	32.4
Secondary (age 13–18)	2,578	20,024	446,898	22.3
Voc., teacher tr.	67	1,648	26,953	16.4
Higher	24	1,943	54,345	28.0

Educational attainment: n.a. *Literacy* (1990): total population age 15 and over literate 3,750,000 (27.1%); males 2,940,000 (42.7%); females 810,000 (11.7%).
Health (1986): physicians 2,405[18] (1 per 9,439 persons); hospital beds 18,571 (1 per 1,222 persons); infant mortality rate (1991) 85.
Food (1988–90): daily per capita caloric intake 2,043 (vegetable products 83%, animal products 17%); 87% of FAO recommended minimum.

Military

Total active duty personnel (1993): 72,800[19] (army 93.4%, navy 2.5%, air force 4.1%). *Military expenditure as percentage of GNP* (1989): 2.2% (world 4.9%); per capita expenditure U.S.$12.

[1]Appointed interim legislature. Total number of seats includes seats assigned to southern Sudan (area at war with central government). [2]Islam was being imposed in 1993. [3]A new currency, the Sudanese dinar (introduced May 1992 at a value equal to 10 Sudanese pounds [LSd]), is gradually replacing the Sudanese pound. [4]Detail does not add to total given because of rounding. [5]Preliminary 1993 census figure was 25,000,000. [6]Khartoum urban agglomeration: 1990 est. (including Omdurman and Khartoum North) 1,950,000; 1993 est. (including Omdurman, Khartoum North, squatters, and displaced persons from southern Sudan) *c.* 3,500,000. [7]Excluding about 300,000 refugees from Eritrea. [8]Excludes nomads, the homeless, and institutionalized persons. [9]1990. [10]1986–87. [11]Includes 592,759 unemployed not previously employed. [12]Average annual income of paid worker (1992) U.S.$216. [13]Imports c.i.f.; exports f.o.b. [14]Based on estimated imports of LSd 7,704,000,000. [15]Based on estimated exports of LSd 1,944,000,000. [16]Sudan Airways only. [17]Government-controlled dailies. Press censorship imposed since military coup of 1989. [18]Government-employed only. [19]Excludes 30,000–50,000 members of the Islamic paramilitary group.

Suriname

Official name: Republiek Suriname (Republic of Suriname).
Form of government: multiparty republic with one legislative house (National Assembly [51]).
Head of state and government: President.
Capital: Paramaribo.
Official language: Dutch.
Official religion: none.
Monetary unit: 1 Suriname guilder (Sf) = 100 cents; valuation (Oct. 4, 1993) 1 U.S.$ = Sf 1.79[1]; 1 £ = Sf 3.03[1].

Area and population

Districts[2]	Capitals	area sq mi	area sq km	population 1980 census
Brokopondo	Brokopondo	2,843	7,364	6,621
Commewijne	Nieuw Amsterdam	908	2,353	20,063
Coronie	Totness	1,507	3,902	2,777
Marowijne	Albina	1,786	4,627	16,125
Nickerie	Nieuw Nickerie	2,067	5,353	32,690
Para	Onverwacht	2,082	5,393	12,827
Saramacca	Groningen	1,404	3,636	10,808
Sipaliwini	...	50,412	130,566	23,226
Wanica	Lelydorp	171	443	60,725
Town district				
Paramaribo	Paramaribo	71	183	167,798
TOTAL		63,251[3]	163,820[3]	355,240[4]

Demography

Population (1993): 405,000.
Density (1993): persons per sq mi 6.4, persons per sq km 2.5.
Urban-rural (1988): urban 65.2%; rural 34.8%.
Sex distribution (1990): male 49.53%; female 50.47%.
Age breakdown (1991): under 15, 33.9%; 15–29, 32.8%; 30–44, 17.4%; 45–59, 9.8%; 60–74, 4.9%; 75 and over, 1.2%.
Population projection: (2000) 410,000; (2010) 416,000.
Doubling time: 41 years.
Ethnic composition (1983): Indo-Pakistani 37.0%; Suriname Creole 31.3%; Javanese 14.2%; Bush Negro 8.5%; Amerindian 3.1%; Chinese 2.8%; Dutch 1.4%; other 1.7%.
Religious affiliation (1983): Hindu 26.0%; Roman Catholic 21.6%; Muslim 18.6%; Protestant (mostly Moravian) 18.0%; other 15.8%.
Major cities (1980): Paramaribo 192,109[5]; Nieuw Nickerie 6,078; Meerzorg 5,355; Marienburg 3,633.

Vital statistics

Birth rate per 1,000 population (1988): 23.2 (world avg. 27.1); legitimate, n.a.; illegitimate, n.a.
Death rate per 1,000 population (1988): 6.1 (world avg. 9.8).
Natural increase rate per 1,000 population (1988): 17.1 (world avg. 17.3).
Total fertility rate (avg. births per childbearing woman; 1990–95): 2.6.
Marriage rate per 1,000 population (1985): 6.1.
Divorce rate per 1,000 population (1985): 1.5.
Life expectancy at birth (1985–90): male 67.1 years; female 72.1 years.
Major causes of death per 100,000 population (1987)[6]: diseases of the circulatory system 178.6, of which ischemic heart disease 60.7, diseases of pulmonary circulation and other forms of heart disease 47.2; homicide, suicide, and other violence 68.5; malignant neoplasms (cancers) 57.2; diseases of the respiratory system 33.7; ill-defined conditions 67.6.

National economy

Budget (1991). Revenue: Sf 989,300,000 (direct taxes 45.3%; indirect taxes 32.6%; bauxite levy 20.3%; aid 1.3%). Expenditures: Sf 1,615,400,000 (current expenditures 98.4%, of which general public services 42.8%, transfers 16.7%, debt service 10.3%; capital expenditures 1.6%).
Production (metric tons except as noted). Agriculture, forestry, fishing (1992): rice 190,000, bananas 49,000, sugarcane 45,000, coconuts 13,000, oranges 11,000, plantains 9,000, cucumbers 4,000, cassava 3,000, tomatoes 3,000, palm oil 1,600; livestock (number of live animals) 95,000 cattle, 31,000 pigs; roundwood (1991) 140,000 cu m; fish catch (1991) 4,100. Mining and quarrying (1991): bauxite 3,136,000; gold 707 troy oz[7]. Manufacturing (1991): alumina 1,510,000; aluminum 30,700; cement 24,128; palm oil 1,069; sugar 307[7]; plywood 5,608 cu m; shoes 110,274 pairs; soft drinks 265,300 hectolitres; beer 122,180 hectolitres; cigarettes 337,000,000 units. Construction (value of buildings authorized; 1985): residential Sf 46,500,000; nonresidential Sf 8,100,000. Energy production (consumption): electricity (kW-hr; 1991) 1,400,000,000 (1,400,000,000); hard coal (metric tons; 1991) none (n.a.); crude petroleum (barrels; 1991) 1,451,000 (1,153,000); petroleum products (metric tons; 1991) none (464,000); natural gas, none (none).
Population economically active (1990)[8]: total 99,010; activity rate of total population 24.6% (participation rates: ages 15–64, 59.2%; female 41.3%; unemployed 15.5%).

Price and earnings indexes (1985 = 100)

	1984	1985	1986	1987	1988	1989	1990
Consumer price index[9]	90.1	100.0	117.9	180.7	195.4	196.9	239.7
Earnings index	...	...	...	...	...	...	...

Public debt (external, outstanding; 1986): U.S.$69,600,000.
Tourism (1991): receipts from visitors U.S.$11,000,000; expenditures by nationals abroad U.S.$12,000,000.
Land use (1991): forested 95.2%; meadows and pastures 0.1%; agricultural and under permanent cultivation 0.4%; other 4.3%.
Gross national product (at current market prices; 1992): U.S.$1,727,000,000 (U.S.$3,690 per capita).

Structure of gross domestic product and labour force

	1991		1990[8]	
	in value Sf '000,000[10]	% of total value	labour force	% of labour force
Agriculture, forestry	362.0	12.0	2,890	2.9
Mining	89.0	2.9	2,380	2.4
Manufacturing	277.0	9.2	8,840	8.9
Construction	260.0	8.6	3,910	3.9
Public utilities	160.0	5.3	...	...
Transportation and communications	209.0	6.9	5,270	5.3
Trade	523.0	17.3	13,770	13.9
Finance, real estate	676.0	22.3	2,550	2.6
Pub. admin., defense	677.0	22.4	36,720	37.1
Services	36.0	1.2		
Other	−246.0[11]	−8.1[11]	22,680[12]	22.9[12]
TOTAL	3,025.0[13]	100.0	99,010	100.0[13]

Household income and expenditure. Average household size (1980) 3.9; income per household: n.a.; sources of income (1975): wages and salaries 74.6%, transfer payments 3.2%, other 22.2%; expenditure (1968–69)[9]: food and beverages 40.0%, household furnishings 12.3%, clothing and footwear 11.0%, transportation and communications 9.5%, recreation and education 8.4%, energy 6.9%, housing 4.4%, other 7.5%.

Foreign trade

Balance of trade (current prices)

	1985	1986	1987	1988	1989	1990
Sf '000,000	+54.1	−5.0	+17.3	+103.6	+268.3	+93.1
% of total	4.8%	0.6%	1.6%	14.3%	16.1%	5.8%

Imports (1990): Sf 842,500,000 (semimanufactured goods 41.0%, machinery and transport equipment 19.1%, fuels and lubricants 15.6%). *Major import sources:* United States 40.9%; The Netherlands 23.5%; Trinidad and Tobago 9.2%; Netherlands Antilles 5.2%; Brazil 4.3%.
Exports (1990): Sf 843,600,000 (alumina 73.9%, aluminum 8.2%, shrimps 7.6%, rice 5.4%, bananas 2.2%, wood and wood products 0.2%). *Major export destinations:* Norway 35.6%; The Netherlands 28.8%; United States 11.4%; Japan 6.8%; Brazil 4.8%; France 4.7%.

Transport and communications

Transport. Railroads (1991): length 187 mi, 301 km; passengers, not applicable; cargo, n.a. Roads (1990): total length 5,688 mi, 9,153 km (paved 29%). Vehicles (1990): passenger cars 36,755; trucks and buses 14,473. Merchant marine (1992): vessels (100 gross tons and over) 24; total deadweight tonnage 15,721. Air transport (1988)[14]: passenger-mi 344,729,000, passenger-km 554,759,000; short ton-mi cargo 15,735,000, metric ton-km cargo 22,973,000; airports (1993) with scheduled flights 3.
Communications. Daily newspapers (1991): total number 1; total circulation 18,000; circulation per 1,000 population 43. Radio (1992): total number of receivers 247,741 (1 per 1.6 persons). Television (1992): total number of receivers 43,000 (1 per 9.4 persons). Telephones (1991): 54,000 (1 per 7.5 persons).

Education and health

Education (1991–92)

	schools	teachers	students	student/ teacher ratio
Primary (age 6–11)	301	2,918	63,083	21.6
Secondary (age 12–18)	89	1,684	26,708	15.8
Voc., teacher tr.[15]	64	1,283	15,996	12.5
Higher[16]	1	...	2,164	...

Educational attainment: n.a. *Literacy* (1990): total population age 15 and over literate 262,700 (94.9%); males literate 128,700 (95.1%); females literate 134,000 (94.7%).
Health: physicians (1990) 299 (1 per 1,348 persons); hospital beds (1989) 1,901 (1 per 212 persons); infant mortality rate per 1,000 live births (1986) 26.5.
Food (1988–90): daily per capita caloric intake 2,436 (vegetable products 86%, animal products 14%); 108% of FAO recommended minimum requirement.

Military

Total active duty personnel (1993): 1,800[17] (army 77.8%, navy 13.3%, air force 8.9%). *Military expenditure as percentage of GNP* (1989): 3.0% (world 4.9%); per capita expenditure U.S.$100.

[1]Official rate; multiple rate system used by Suriname is not accepted by the IMF. [2]Districts reorganized in 1985. [3]Area excludes 6,809 sq mi (17,635 sq km) of territory disputed with Guyana. [4]Detail does not add to total given because of computational discrepancies. [5]1988. [6]Based on 71.6% of total deaths. [7]1990. [8]Districts of Wanica and Paramaribo only. [9]For Paramaribo and environs. [10]At factor costs. [11]Imputed bank service charges. [12]Includes 15,360 unemployed. [13]Detail does not add to total given because of rounding. [14]SLM (Suriname Airways) only. [15]1984–85. [16]1989–90. [17]All services are part of the army.

Swaziland

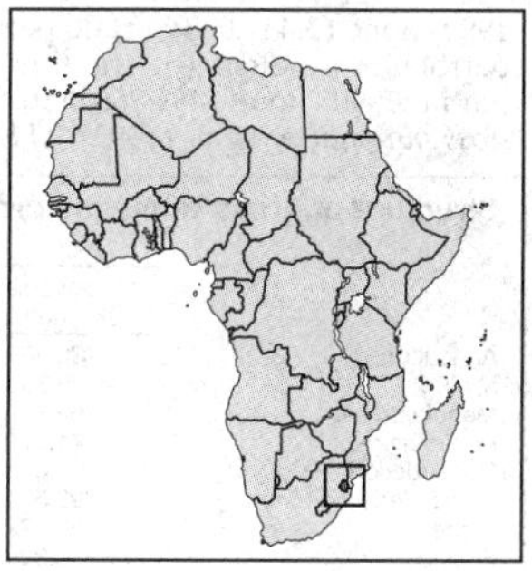

Official name: Umbuso weSwatini (Swazi); Kingdom of Swaziland (English).
Form of government[1]: monarchy with two legislative houses (Senate [30[2]]. House of Assembly [65[2]]).
Head of state and government: King, assisted by Prime Minister.
Capitals: Mbabane (administrative); Lobamba (royal and legislative).
Official languages: Swazi; English.
Official religion: none.
Monetary unit: 1 lilangeni[3] (plural emalangeni [E]) = 100 cents; valuation (Oct. 4, 1993) 1 U.S.$ = E 3.45; 1 £ = E 5.23.

Area and population

		area		population
Districts	Capitals	sq mi	sq km	1986 census[4]
Hhohho	Mbabane	1,378	3,569	178,936
Lubombo	Siteki	2,296	5,947	153,958
Manzini	Manzini	1,571	4,068	192,596
Shiselweni	Nhlangano	1,459	3,780	155,569
TOTAL		6,704	17,364	681,059

Demography

Population (1993): 814,000.
Density (1993): persons per sq mi 127.6, persons per sq km 49.3.
Urban-rural (1989): urban 31.7%; rural 68.3%.
Sex distribution (1986): male 47.22%; female 52.78%.
Age breakdown (1986): under 15, 47.3%; 15–29, 26.6%; 30–44, 13.4%; 45–59, 7.4%; 60–74, 3.4%; 75 and over, 1.3%; unknown, 0.6%.
Population projection: (2000) 984,000; (2010) 1,270,000.
Doubling time: 20 years.
Ethnic composition (1983): Swazi 84.3%; Zulu 9.9%; Tsonga 2.5%; Indian 0.8%; Pakistani 0.8%; Portuguese 0.2%; other 1.5%.
Religious affiliation (1980): Christian 77.0%, of which Protestant 37.3%, Roman Catholic 10.8%; African indigenous 28.9%; traditional beliefs 20.9%; other 2.1%.
Major cities (1986): Manzini 52,000; Mbabane 38,290; Nhlangano 4,107; Piggs Peak 3,223; Siteki 2,271.

Vital statistics

Birth rate per 1,000 population (1990–95): 46.7 (world avg. 26.4); legitimate, n.a.; illegitimate, n.a.
Death rate per 1,000 population (1990–95): 11.1 (world avg. 9.2).
Natural increase rate per 1,000 population (1990–95): 35.6 (world avg. 17.2).
Total fertility rate (avg. births per childbearing woman; 1990–95): 6.5.
Marriage rate per 1,000 population: n.a.
Divorce rate per 1,000 population: n.a.
Life expectancy at birth (1990–95): male 56.2 years; female 59.8 years.
Major causes of death (1985)[5]: respiratory diseases 11.3%; infectious intestinal diseases 10.4%; circulatory diseases 7.5%; tuberculosis 7.1%; malnutrition 6.5%; accidents and injuries 6.0%; perinatal conditions 5.6%.

National economy

Budget (1992–93). Revenue: E 910,100,000 (receipts from Customs Union of Southern Africa 52.0%; tax on income and profits 35.9%; sales tax 11.5%; foreign-aid grants 5.1%; property income 4.9%; fees, services, and fines 1.2%). Expenditures: E 1,010,200,000 (recurrent expenditure 68.1%, of which education 18.1%, general administration 17.6%, economic services 9.4%, justice and police 6.1%, health 5.9%, defense 5.1%, public-debt payments 2.7%).
Land use (1991): forested 6.0%; meadows and pastures 68.9%; agricultural and under permanent cultivation 12.2%; other 12.9%.
Tourism (1991): receipts from visitors U.S.$26,000,000; expenditures by nationals abroad U.S.$20,000,000.
Gross national product (at current market prices; 1992): U.S.$927,000,000 (U.S.$1,080 per capita).

Structure of gross domestic product and labour force

	1991		1986	
	in value E '000	% of total value	labour force	% of labour force
Agriculture	299,300	13.4	30,197	18.8
Mining	24,400	1.1	5,245	3.3
Manufacturing	603,700	27.1	14,742	9.2
Construction	53,200	2.4	7,661	4.8
Public utilities	36,800	1.7	1,315	0.8
Transp. and commun.	105,800	4.7	7,526	4.7
Trade	193,100	8.7	12,348	7.7
Finance	225,100	10.1	1,931	1.2
Pub. admin., defense	301,900	13.5	32,309	20.1
Services	42,500	1.9		
Other	342,200[6]	15.4[6]	47,081[7]	29.4[7]
TOTAL	2,228,000	100.0	160,355	100.0

Population economically active (1986): total 160,355; activity rate of total population 23.5% (participation rates: ages 15 and over, 44.1%; female 34.2%; unemployed 27.0%).

Price and earnings indexes (1985 = 100)

	1986	1987	1988	1989	1990	1991	1992
Consumer price index	113.7	129.0	144.9	157.9	178.1	198.1	216.5
Earnings index[8]	112.1	121.5	120.0	...	...	...	...

Public debt (external, outstanding; 1991): U.S.$254,400,000.
Production (metric tons except as noted). Agriculture, forestry, fishing (1992): sugarcane 3,600,000, corn (maize) 54,000, grapefruit 52,000, seed cotton 28,000, lint cotton 10,000, roots and tubers 10,000 (of which potatoes 6,000, sweet potatoes 4,000), pulses 4,000; livestock (number of live animals) 753,000 cattle, 406,000 goats, 31,000 pigs, 23,000 sheep, 1,000,000 chickens; roundwood (1991) 2,223,000 cu m; fish catch (1991) 105. Mining and quarrying (1992): asbestos 46,000; diamonds 15,553 carats. Manufacturing (value added in E; 1987): food and beverages 119,550,000, of which sugarcane milling 66,650,000, beverage processing 31,770,000; paper and paper products 71,650,000; textiles and garments 16,510,000; wood and wood products 9,270,000; machinery and equipment 7,700,000; nonmetallic mineral products 6,330,000. Construction (value in E; 1991)[9]: residential 27,800,000; nonresidential 48,000,000. Energy production (consumption): electricity (kW-hr; 1990) 150,000,000 (1986; 650,000,000); coal (metric tons; 1992) 100,220 (1989; 28,454); crude petroleum, n.a. (n.a.); petroleum products, n.a. (n.a.); natural gas, n.a. (n.a.).
Household income and expenditure. Average household size (1986) 5.3; annual income per household (1985) E 332 (U.S.$151); sources of income (1985): wages and salaries 44.4%, self-employment 22.2%, transfers 12.2%, other 21.2%; expenditure (1985): food and beverages 33.5%, rent and fuel 13.4%, household durable goods 12.8%, transportation and communications 8.8%, clothing and footwear 6.0%, recreation 3.3%.

Foreign trade[10]

Balance of trade (current prices)

	1986	1987	1988	1989	1990	1991
E '000,000	−40.6	−110.2	−57.3	−56.7	−100.6	−109.7
% of total	3.0%	6.8%	2.8%	2.1%	3.3%	3.4%

Imports (1991): E 1,713,936,000 (machinery and transport equipment 23.9%; minerals, fuels, and lubricants 15.9%; manufactured items 15.4%; foodstuffs 14.3%). *Major import sources* (1989–90): South Africa 91.3%; Switzerland 1.5%; United Kingdom 0.9%; Japan 0.9%; West Germany 0.8%.
Exports (1991): E 1,319,811,000 (sugar 33.5%; wood and wood products 11.5%; canned fruits 3.8%; asbestos 2.2%). *Major export destinations* (1989): South Africa 44.7%; Canada 7.3%; United States 4.3%; United Kingdom 3.4%; Mozambique 3.2%.

Transport and communications

Transport. Railroads (1992): length 326 mi, 525 km; passengers, n.a.; short ton-mi cargo 73,300,000[11], metric ton-km cargo 107,000,000[11]. Roads (1990): total length 1,740 mi, 2,801 km (paved 26%). Vehicles (1991): passenger cars 25,333; trucks and buses 8,603. Merchant marine: none; landlocked state. Air transport (1992)[12]: passenger-mi 25,608,000, passenger-km 41,212,000; short ton-mi cargo 101,000, metric ton-km cargo 147,000; airports (1993) with scheduled flights 1.
Communications. Daily newspapers (1992): total number 2; total circulation 21,000; circulation per 1,000 population 24. Radio (1992): total number of receivers 65,000 (1 per 13 persons). Television (1992): total number of receivers 12,500 (1 per 66 persons). Telephones (1991): 19,546 (1 per 40 persons).

Education and health

Education (1991)

	schools	teachers	students	student/ teacher ratio
Primary (age 6–13)	523	5,015	183,738	36.6
Secondary (age 14–18)	153	2,149	50,676	23.6
Voc., teacher tr.	8	280	772	2.8
Higher	1	146	1,705	11.7

Educational attainment (1986). Percentage of population age 25 and over having: no formal schooling 42.1%; some primary education 23.9%; complete primary 10.5%; some secondary 19.2%; complete secondary and higher 4.3%. *Literacy* (1986): total population age 15 and over literate 240,171 (67.0%); males literate 112,578 (69.0%); females literate 127,593 (65.0%).
Health (1984): physicians 80 (1 per 7,971 persons); hospital beds 1,608 (1 per 396 persons); infant mortality rate per 1,000 live births (1990–95) 107.0.
Food (1988–90): daily per capita caloric intake 2,634 (vegetable products 91%, animal products 9%); 114% of FAO recommended minimum requirement.

Military

Total active duty personnel (1983): 2,657. *Military expenditure as percentage of GNP* (1989): 1.7% (world 4.9%); per capita expenditure U.S.$13.

[1]The government announced on Oct. 9, 1992, that a new constitution would be forthcoming; nonparty legislative elections took place on Sept. 25, 1993, and Oct. 11, 1993. [2]Includes 10 nonelective seats. [3]The lilangeni is at par with the South African rand. [4]Preliminary. [5]Percentage of deaths of known cause at government, mission, and private hospitals. [6]Includes indirect taxes less imputed bank service charges and subsidies. [7]Includes 43,925 unemployed. [8]Manufacturing sector only. [9]Urban areas under the jurisdiction of the Manzini and Mbabane town councils only. [10]Import figures are f.o.b. in balance of trade and c.i.f. in commodities and trading partners. [11]1984. [12]Royal Swazi National Airways only; international flights only.

Sweden

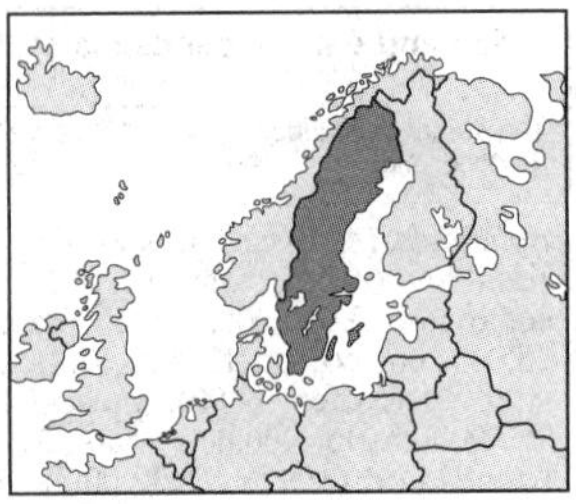

Official name: Konungariket Sverige (Kingdom of Sweden).
Form of government: constitutional monarchy and parliamentary state with one legislative house (Parliament [349]).
Chief of state: King.
Head of government: Prime Minister.
Capital: Stockholm.
Official language: Swedish.
Official religion: Church of Sweden (Lutheran).
Monetary unit: 1 Swedish krona (SKr) = 100 ore; valuation (Oct. 4, 1993) 1 U.S.$ = SKr 8.07; 1 £ = SKr 12.23.

Area and population

Counties	Capitals	area sq mi	area sq km	population 1993[1] estimate
Älvsborg	Vänersborg	4,400	11,395	445,921
Blekinge	Karlskrona	1,136	2,941	151,266
Gävleborg	Gävle	7,024	18,191	289,190
Göteborg och Bohus	Göteborg	1,985	5,141	747,849
Gotland	Visby	1,212	3,140	57,578
Halland	Halmstad	2,106	5,454	261,172
Jämtland	Östersund	19,090	49,443	135,910
Jönköping	Jönköping	3,839	9,944	309,867
Kalmar	Kalmar	4,313	11,170	241,912
Kopparberg	Falun	10,886	28,194	290,245
Kristianstad	Kristianstad	2,350	6,087	292,993
Kronoberg	Växjö	3,266	8,458	178,961
Malmöhus	Malmö	1,907	4,938	793,696
Norrbotten	Luleå	38,191	98,913	266,089
Örebro	Örebro	3,289	8,519	274,325
Östergötland	Linköping	4,078	10,562	408,268
Skaraborg	Mariestad	3,065	7,937	278,860
Södermanland	Nyköping	2,340	6,060	257,858
Stockholm	Stockholm	2,505	6,488	1,669,840
Uppsala	Uppsala	2,698	6,989	278,610
Värmland	Karlstad	6,789	17,584	284,691
Västerbotten	Umeå	21,390	55,401	255,987
Västernorrland	Härnösand	8,370	21,678	260,829
Västmanland	Västerås	2,433	6,302	260,096
TOTAL LAND AREA		158,661[2]	410,929	
INLAND WATER		15,071	39,035	
TOTAL		173,732	449,964	8,692,013

Demography

Population (1993): 8,727,000.
Density (1993)[3]: persons per sq mi 55.0, persons per sq km 21.2.
Urban-rural (1991[1]): urban 83.4%; rural 16.6%.
Sex distribution (1993[1]): male 49.41%; female 50.59%.
Age breakdown (1993[1]): under 15, 18.5%; 15–29, 20.3%; 30–44, 20.5%; 45–59, 18.3%; 60–74, 14.3%; 75 and over, 8.1%.
Population projection: (2000) 8,960,000; (2010) 9,179,000.
Ethnic composition (1993[1]): Swedish 90.4%; Finnish 2.4%; other 7.2%.
Religious affiliation (1992[1]): Church of Sweden 88.2% (nominally; about 30% nonpracticing); Roman Catholic 1.7%; Pentecostal 1.1%; other 9.0%.
Major cities (1993[1]): Stockholm 684,576; Göteborg 433,811; Malmö 236,684; Uppsala 174,554; Linköping 126,377.

Vital statistics

Birth rate per 1,000 population (1992): 14.1 (world avg. 26.4); (1990) legitimate 53.0%; illegitimate 47.0%.
Death rate per 1,000 population (1992): 10.9 (world avg. 9.2).
Natural increase rate per 1,000 population (1992): 3.2 (world avg. 17.2).
Total fertility rate (avg. births per childbearing woman; 1991): 2.1.
Marriage rate per 1,000 population (1992): 4.2.
Divorce rate per 1,000 population (1992): 2.5.
Life expectancy at birth (1987–91): male 74.6 years; female 80.3 years.
Major causes of death per 100,000 population (1989): heart disease 416.8; malignant neoplasms (cancers) 234.8; cerebrovascular disease 114.1.

National economy

Budget (1992–93). Revenue: SKr 397,724,000,000 (value-added and excise taxes 46.5%, social-security contributions 17.9%, nontax revenue 12.6%, income and capital gains taxes 10.8%, property taxes 5.1%). Expenditures: SKr 478,483,000,000 (health and social affairs 27.1%, interest on national debt 14.3%, education and culture 11.4%, defense 7.8%).
Public debt (1993): U.S.$100,950,000,000.
Tourism (1991): receipts from visitors U.S.$2,726,000,000; expenditures by nationals abroad U.S.$6,104,000,000.
Production (metric tons except as noted). Agriculture, forestry, fishing (1992): sugar beets 2,000,000, wheat 1,410,000, barley 1,260,000, potatoes 1,260,000, oats 810,000; livestock (number of live animals) 2,017,890 pigs, 1,706,778 cattle, 418,783 sheep; roundwood (1991) 50,200,000 cu m; fish catch (1991) 227,989, of which Baltic herring 95,231. Mining and quarrying (1992): iron ore 12,588,000[4]; copper 339,000; zinc 311,000; lead 144,000. Manufacturing (value added, in SKr '000,000; 1990): machinery and transport equipment 141,238; paper and paper products 52,047; food and beverages 30,517; wood and wood products 22,148; textiles and wearing apparel 5,731. Construction (1991): 66,886 dwellings completed. Energy production (consumption): electricity (kW-hr; 1990) 146,535,000,000 (144,647,000,000); coal (metric tons; 1990) none (3,451,000); crude petroleum (barrels; 1990) 22,000 (122,500,000); petroleum products (metric tons; 1990) 15,780,000 (12,824,000); natural gas (cu m; 1990) none (492,760,000).
Gross national product (1992): U.S.$233,190,000,000 (U.S.$26,800 per capita).

Structure of gross domestic product and labour force

	1991		1992	
	in value SKr '000,000	% of total value	labour force	% of labour force
Agriculture	33,366	2.7	140,000	3.2
Mining	3,333	0.3	11,000	0.3
Manufacturing	262,319	20.9	794,000	17.9
Public utilities	41,370	3.3	36,000	0.8
Construction	94,034	7.5	271,000	6.1
Transp. and commun.	93,584	7.4	300,000	6.8
Trade	136,573	10.9	601,000	13.6
Finance	285,320	22.7	383,000	8.7
Pub. admin., defense / Services	360,304	28.7	1,651,000	37.3
Other	−54,968[5]	−4.4[5]	241,000[6]	5.3[6]
TOTAL	1,255,235	100.0	4,428,000	100.0

Population economically active (1992): total 4,428,000; activity rate of total population 51.0% (participation rates [1990]: ages 16–64, 84.8%; female 48.0%; unemployed [1992] 5.3%).

Price and earnings indexes (1985 = 100)

	1986	1987	1988	1989	1990	1991	1992
Consumer price index	104.2	108.6	114.9	122.3	135.1	147.8	151.1
Hourly earnings index	106.1	115.2	124.3	136.6	149.4	156.5	163.7

Household income and expenditure. Average household size (1990) 2.1; median income per household SKr 119,000 (U.S.$18,400); sources of income (1990): wages and salaries 63.0%, transfer payments 23.5%, self-employment 13.5%; expenditure (1990): housing and energy 25.7%, food 21.9%, transportation 18.1%, education and recreation 9.4%.
Land use (1991): forested 68.1%; meadows and pastures 1.3%; agricultural and under permanent cultivation 6.8%; other 23.8%.

Foreign trade

Balance of trade (current prices)

	1987	1988	1989	1990	1991	1992
SKr '000,000	29,827	31,208	23,098	23,272	38,343	42,894
% of total	5.6%	5.4%	3.6%	3.5%	6.1%	7.0%

Imports (1992): SKr 289,720,000,000 (machinery and transport equipment 36.0%, of which transport equipment 10.0%, electrical machinery 9.7%; chemicals 10.6%; food 7.0%; clothing 6.2%). *Major import sources:* Germany 18.5%; U.S. 8.8%; U.K. 8.6%; Denmark 7.8%; Norway 6.9%; Finland 6.2%.
Exports (1992): SKr 326,010,000,000 (machinery and transport equipment 42.7%, of which transport equipment 15.0%, electrical machinery 9.7%; paper products 11.1%; chemicals 9.2%; wood and wood pulp 6.2%; iron and steel products 5.7%). *Major export destinations:* Germany 15.0%; U.K. 9.7%; Norway 8.4%; U.S. 8.2%; Denmark 7.2%; Finland 5.8%.

Transport and communications

Transport. Railroads (1991): length 6,960 mi[7], 11,202 km[7]; passenger-mi 3,388,000,000, passenger-km 5,453,000,000; short ton-mi cargo 15,219,000,000, metric ton-km cargo 22,219,000,000. Roads (1989): total length 83,060 mi, 133,673 km (paved 71%). Vehicles (1992): passenger cars 3,588,600; trucks and buses 329,200. Merchant marine (1992): vessels (100 gross tons and over) 664; total deadweight tonnage 3,327,699. Air transport (1991): passenger-mi 4,115,000,000, passenger-km 6,622,000,000; short ton-mi cargo 117,807,000, metric ton-km cargo 171,995,000; airports (1993) 42.
Communications. Daily newspapers (1991): total number 176; total circulation 4,831,000; circulation per 1,000 population 561. Radio (1991): 7,271,556 receivers (1 per 1.2 persons). Television (1991): 3,750,000 receivers (1 per 2.3 persons). Telephones (1983): 7,410,000 (1 per 1.1 persons).

Education and health

Education (1992–93)

	schools	teachers	students	student/teacher ratio
Primary (age 7–12)	4,745	93,950	887,323	9.4
Secondary (age 13–18)	600	29,585	306,165	10.4
Higher[8]	...	27,523[9]	272,718	9.9

Educational attainment (1990). Percentage of population age 16–64 having: primary education 37.1%; lower secondary education 29.4%; higher secondary 12.2%; some postsecondary 21.3%. *Literacy* (1988): virtually 100%.
Health: physicians (1990) 21,800 (1 per 395 persons); hospital beds (1990) 48,894 (1 per 175 persons); infant mortality rate per 1,000 live births (1991) 6.2.
Food (1988–90): daily per capita caloric intake 2,978 (vegetable products 63%, animal products 37%); 111% of FAO requirement.

Military

Total active duty personnel (1992): 60,500 (army 71.9%, navy 15.7%, air force 12.4%). *Military expenditure as percentage of GNP* (1989): 2.6% (world 4.9%); per capita expenditure U.S.$574.

[1]January 1. [2]Detail does not add to total given because of rounding. [3]Density based on land area only. [4]Metal content of ore. [5]Includes statistical discrepancies less imputed bank service charges. [6]Includes 233,000 unemployed. [7]1990. [8]1989–90. [9]Includes graduate assistants.

Switzerland

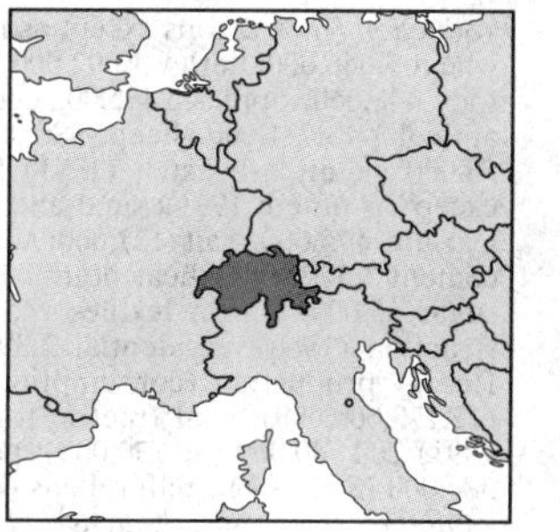

Official name: Confédération Suisse (French); Schweizerische Eidgenossenschaft (German); Confederazione Svizzera (Italian) (Swiss Confederation).
Form of government: federal state with two legislative houses (Council of States [46]; National Council [200]).
Head of state and government: President.
Capitals: Bern (administrative); Lausanne (judicial).
Official languages: French; German; Italian.
Official religion: none.
Monetary unit: 1 Swiss Franc (Sw F) = 100 centimes; valuation (Oct. 4, 1993) 1 U.S.$ = Sw F 1.42; 1 £ = Sw F 2.15.

Area and population

Cantons	Capitals	area sq mi	area sq km	population 1992[1] estimate
Aargau	Aarau	542	1,404	504,547
Appenzell Ausser-Rhoden[2]	Herisau	94	243	52,346
Appenzell Inner-Rhoden[2]	Appenzell	67	173	13,714
Basel-Landschaft[2]	Liestal	165	428	231,063
Basel-Stadt[2]	Basel	14	37	193,512
Bern	Bern	2,336	6,051	952,595
Fribourg	Fribourg	645	1,671	211,606
Genève	Geneva	109	282	378,849
Glarus	Glarus	265	685	38,114
Graubünden	Chur	2,743	7,105	173,028
Jura	Delémont	323	836	66,408
Luzern	Luzern	576	1,493	324,044
Neuchâtel	Neuchâtel	310	803	162,458
Nidwalden[2]	Stans	107	276	33,285
Obwalden[2]	Sarnen	189	491	29,478
Sankt Gallen	Sankt Gallen	782	2,026	426,689
Schaffhausen	Schaffhausen	115	298	72,454
Schwyz	Schwyz	351	908	112,986
Solothurn	Solothurn	305	791	230,068
Thurgau	Frauenfeld	383	991	210,237
Ticino	Bellinzona	1,086	2,812	290,001
Uri	Altdorf	416	1,077	33,979
Valais	Sion	2,017	5,224	253,882
Vaud	Lausanne	1,240	3,211	592,970
Zug	Zug	92	239	86,357
Zürich	Zürich	668	1,729	1,159,080
TOTAL		15,940	41,284	6,833,750[3]

Demography

Population (1993): 6,996,000.
Density (1993): persons per sq mi 438.9, persons per sq km 169.5.
Urban-rural (1991): urban 59.7%; rural 40.3%.
Sex distribution (1992): male 48.90%; female 51.10%.
Age breakdown (1990): under 15, 16.8%; 15–29, 22.8%; 30–44, 23.2%; 45–59, 18.0%; 60–74, 12.5%; 75 and over, 6.7%.
Population projection: (2000) 7,446,000; (2010) 7,660,000.
Linguistic composition (1990): German 63.6%; French 19.2%; Italian 7.6%; Yugoslav languages 2.5%; Spanish 1.7%; Romansch 0.6%; other 4.8%.
Religious affiliation (1990): Roman Catholic 46.1%; Protestant 40.0%; Muslim 1.5%; Jewish 0.3%; nonreligious/unknown 8.9%; other 3.2%.
Major cities (1991): Zürich 341,276 (841,052[4]); Basel 171,036 (360,350[4]); Geneva 167,167 (394,783[4]); Bern 134,629 (299,466[4]); Lausanne 123,159.

Vital statistics

Birth rate per 1,000 population (1992): 12.6 (world avg. 26.4); (1991) legitimate 93.5%; illegitimate 6.5%.
Death rate per 1,000 population (1992): 9.1 (world avg. 9.2).
Natural increase rate per 1,000 population (1992): 3.5 (world avg. 17.2).
Total fertility rate (avg. births per childbearing woman; 1991): 1.6.
Marriage rate per 1,000 population (1992): 6.5.
Life expectancy at birth (1990–91): male 74.1 years; female 80.9 years.
Major causes of death per 100,000 population (1991): heart disease 271.6, of which ischemic 150.9, other 120.7; malignant neoplasms (cancers) 244.0.

National economy

Budget (1991)[5]. Revenue: Sw F 33,490,000,000 (turnover taxes 29.9%, direct federal taxes 20.5%, motor fuel fees 9.6%). Expenditures: Sw F 35,501,000,000 (welfare 22.8%, defense 17.5%, transportation 15.3%).
National debt (end of year 1991): SwF 45,487,000,000.
Tourism (1992): receipts from visitors U.S.$9,324,000,000; expenditures by nationals abroad U.S.$7,261,000,000.
Production (metric tons except as noted). Agriculture, forestry, fishing (1991): milk 3,850,000, sugar beets 897,000, potatoes 725,000, wheat 574,000, barley 357,000, apples 190,000, grapes 178,000; livestock (number of live animals) 1,829,000 cattle, 1,723,000 pigs; roundwood 4,070,000 cu m; fish catch (1990) 4,176. Mining (1991): salt 400,000. Manufacturing (value added in U.S.$'000,000; 1990): nonelectrical machinery 7,544; food products 5,832; electrical goods and electronics 5,713; industrial chemicals 4,800; printing and publishing 4,222; metal products 3,944. Construction (in Sw F '000,000; 1991): residential 21,413; nonresidential 35,464. Energy production (consumption): electricity (kW-hr; 1990) 55,846,000,000 (53,738,000,000); coal (metric tons; 1990) none (332,000); crude petroleum (barrels; 1990) none (21,983,000); petroleum products (metric tons; 1990) 2,890,000 (11,257,000); natural gas (cu m; 1990) 3,600,000 (1,945,000,000).
Gross national product (1991): U.S.$225,890,000,000 (U.S.$33,510 per capita).

Structure of gross domestic product and labour force

	1990		1992	
	in value Sw F '000,000	% of total value	labour force	% of labour force
Agriculture	9,664	3.1	194,800	5.4
Manufacturing } Mining }	76,722	24.4	858,000	24.0
Mining } Public utilities }			25,300	0.7
Public utilities	6,011	1.9		
Construction	26,224	8.4	329,300	9.2
Transp. and commun.	18,556	5.9	218,400	6.1
Trade	56,531	18.0	735,600	20.6
Finance, insurance[6]	67,158	21.4	452,100	12.7
Pub. admin., defense } Services }	63,037	20.1		
Pub. admin., defense			136,800	3.8
Services			620,000	17.4
Other	−9,913[7]	−3.2[7]	2,500	0.1
TOTAL	313,990	100.0	3,572,800[8]	100.0[8]

Population economically active (1991): total 3,595,400; activity rate of total population 52.3% (participation rates: age 15 and over [1988] 62.9%; female 38.3%; unemployed [May 1992–April 1993] 3.8%).

Price and earnings indexes (1985 = 100)

	1987	1988	1989	1990	1991	1992	1993[9]
Consumer price index	102.2	104.1	107.4	113.2	119.8	124.7	128.9
Hourly earnings index	106.0	109.8	113.9	120.6	128.9	135.1	...

Household income and expenditure. Average household size (1990) 2.5; average income per household (1982) Sw F 61,000 (U.S.$30,045); sources of income (1990): wages 64.9%, transfer payments 14.5%, other 20.6%; expenditure (1991): food 19.9%, housing 15.3%, health and personal effects 12.6%, transportation and communications 11.8%.
Land use (1990): forested 26.4%; meadows and pastures 40.5%; agricultural and under permanent cultivation 10.4%; other 22.7%.

Foreign trade[10]

Balance of trade (current prices)

	1987	1988	1989	1990	1991	1992
Sw F '000,000	−6,950	−7,519	−9,998	−7,397	−6,144	+268
% of total	4.9%	4.8%	5.6%	4.0%	3.4%	0.2%

Imports (1992): Sw F 92,330,000,000 (machinery and electronics 19.7%; chemical products 12.4%; vehicles 10.7%; clothing and footwear 9.5%). *Major import sources:* Germany 33.4%; France 10.8%; Italy 10.0%; U.S. 6.4%; U.K. 5.8%; Japan 4.3%.
Exports (1992): Sw F 92,142,000,000 (machinery and electronics 27.6%; chemical products 23.1%; precision instruments, watches, and jewelry 20.6%). *Major export destinations:* Germany 23.4%; France 9.5%; Italy 8.7%; U.S. 8.5%; U.K. 6.6%; Japan 3.7%.

Transport and communications

Transport. Railroads[11]: length (1990) 3,126 mi, 5,031 km; passenger-km (1991) 12,384,000,000; metric ton-km cargo (1991) 8,112,000,000. Roads (1991): total length 44,183 mi, 71,106 km. Vehicles (1991): passenger cars 3,085,372; trucks and buses 291,457. Merchant marine (1992): vessels (100 gross tons and over) 24; total deadweight tonnage 602,084. Air transport (1992)[12]: passenger-km 16,154,000,000; metric ton-km cargo 1,063,000,000; airports (1993) with scheduled flights 6.
Communications. Daily newspapers (1991): total number 103; total circulation 2,851,832; circulation per 1,000 population 415. Radio (1992): 2,685,000 receivers (1 per 2.6 persons). Television (1992): 2,200,000 receivers (1 per 3.2 persons). Telephones (1990): 6,152,834 (1 per 1.1 persons).

Education and health

Education (1991–92)

	schools	teachers	students	student/teacher ratio
Primary (age 7–12)	...	...	414,129	...
Secondary (age 13–19)	...	...	393,047	...
Voc., teacher tr.	...	...	207,410	...
Higher	...	...	143,192	...

Educational attainment (1988). Percentage of resident Swiss (resident alien) population age 30 and over having completed: lower secondary education or less 33.9% (45.2%); upper secondary 47.5% (31.2%); higher 18.6% (23.6%).
Literacy: virtually 100.0%.
Health (1990): physicians *c.* 22,000 (1 per 311 persons); hospital beds 55,071 (1 per 124 persons); infant mortality rate (1992) 6.8.
Food (1988–90): daily per capita caloric intake 3,508 (vegetable products 61%, animal products 39%); 130% of FAO recommended minimum.

Military

Total active duty personnel (1992): 1,600[13]. *Military expenditure as percentage of GNP* (1989): 2.1% (world 4.9%); per capita expenditure U.S.$566.

[1]January 1. [2]Demicanton; functions as a full canton. [3]Includes 1,190,991 resident aliens. [4]Population of urban agglomeration. [5]Confederation-level only. [6]Includes consulting services. [7]Imputed bank charges less import duties. [8]Labour force includes 948,700 foreign workers. [9]May. [10]Import figures are f.o.b. in balance of trade and c.i.f. in commodities and trading partners. [11]Swiss Federal Railways. [12]Swissair only. [13]Excludes 565,000 army reservists and 60,000 air corps reservists.

Syria

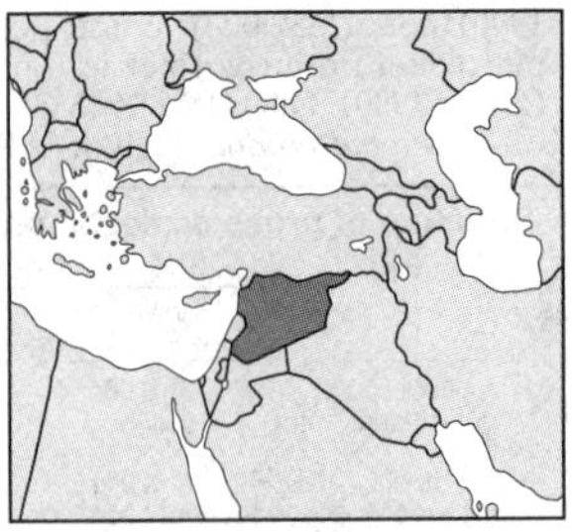

Official name: al-Jumhūrīyah al-ʿArabīyah as-Sūrīyah (Syrian Arab Republic).
Form of government: unitary multiparty[1] republic with one legislative house (People's Council [250]).
Head of state and government: President.
Capital: Damascus.
Official language: Arabic.
Official religion: none[2].
Monetary unit: 1 Syrian pound (LS) = 100 piastres; valuation (nonessential [imports] rate; Oct. 4, 1993) 1 U.S.$ = LS 21.50; 1 £ = LS 32.68.

Area and population		area		population
				1992
Governorates	Capitals	sq mi	sq km	estimate
Darʿā	Darʿā	1,440	3,730	568,000
Dayr az-Zawr	Dayr az-Zawr	12,765	33,060	565,000
Dimashq	Damascus	6,962	18,032	1,373,000
Ḥalab	Aleppo	7,143	18,500	2,677,000
Ḥamāh	Ḥamāh	3,430	8,883	1,046,000
al-Ḥasakah	al-Ḥasakah	9,009	23,334	965,000
Ḥimṣ	Homs	16,302	42,223	1,209,000
Idlib	Idlib	2,354	6,097	870,000
al-Lādhiqīyah	Latakia	887	2,297	783,000
al-Qunayṭirah	al-Qunayṭirah	719[3]	1,861[3]	41,000
ar-Raqqah	ar-Raqqah	7,574	19,616	485,000
as-Suwaydāʾ	as-Suwaydāʾ	2,143	5,550	281,000
Ṭarṭūs	Ṭarṭūs	730	1,892	644,000
Municipality				
Damascus	—	41	105	1,451,000
TOTAL		71,498[3]	185,180[3]	12,958,000

Demography

Population (1993): 13,398,000.
Density (1993): persons per sq mi 187.4, persons per sq km 72.4.
Urban-rural (1990): urban 50.4%; rural 49.6%.
Sex distribution (1990): male 51.08%; female 48.92%.
Age breakdown (1990): under 15, 49.3%; 15–29, 22.4%; 30–44, 14.3%; 45–59, 7.5%; 60–74, 5.0%; 75 and over, 1.5%.
Population projection: (2000) 16,925,000; (2010) 22,991,000.
Doubling time: 19 years.
Ethnic composition (1981): Arab 88.8%; Kurdish 6.3%; other 4.9%.
Religious affiliation (1980): Muslim (mostly Sunnī) 89.6%; Christian 8.9%; other 1.5%.
Major cities (1992): Damascus 1,451,000; Aleppo 1,445,000; Homs 518,000; Latakia 284,000; Ḥamāh 254,000.

Vital statistics

Birth rate per 1,000 population (1990–95): 42.5 (world avg. 26.4).
Death rate per 1,000 population (1990–95): 5.7 (world avg. 9.2).
Natural increase rate per 1,000 population (1990–95): 36.8 (world avg. 17.2).
Total fertility rate (avg. births per childbearing woman; 1990–95): 6.3.
Marriage rate per 1,000 population (1988)[4]: 7.5.
Divorce rate per 1,000 population (1988)[4]: 0.7.
Life expectancy at birth (1990–95): male 65.2 years; female 69.2 years.
Major causes of death per 100,000 population (1981): diseases of the circulatory system 60.7; accidents and adverse effects 18.3; infectious and parasitic diseases 15.1.

National economy

Budget (1992). Revenue: LS 93,043,000,000 (taxes and duties 38.0%, foreign revenues 21.0%). Expenditures: LS 93,043,000,000 (defense 26.3%, administration 17.5%, education 12.2%, agriculture 10.1%, health 3.1%).
Tourism (1991): receipts from visitors U.S.$300,000,000; expenditures by nationals abroad U.S.$210,000,000.
Land use (1991): steppe and pasture 42.1%; cultivable 30.6%; forested 4.0%; other 23.3%.
Gross national product (1990): U.S.$12,404,000,000 (U.S.$1,020 per capita).

Structure of gross domestic product and labour force	1990		1991	
	in value LS '000,000	% of total value	labour force	% of labour force
Agriculture	76,261	27.7	916,952	26.3
Mining	39,608	14.4	6,651	0.2
Manufacturing	16,366	5.9	456,162	13.1
Construction	9,828	3.6	340,779	9.8
Public utilities	−199	−0.1	8,422	0.2
Transportation and communications	25,382	9.2	166,965	4.8
Trade	68,244	24.8	378,250	10.9
Finance	9,719	3.5	24,651	0.7
Pub. admin.	27,528	10.0 }	951,104	27.3
Services	4,512	1.6 }		
Other productive activities	103	0.1	...	...
Other	−2,274[5]	−0.8[5]	235,432[6]	6.8[6]
TOTAL	275,078	100.0[7]	3,485,368	100.0[7]

Production (metric tons except as noted). Agriculture, forestry, fishing (1992): wheat 3,046,000, barley 1,092,000, seed cotton 689,000, grapes 533,000, tomatoes 448,000, apples 248,000, eggplants 127,000; livestock (number of live animals) 15,781,000 sheep, 986,000 goats, 765,000 cattle; roundwood (1991) 58,000 cu m; fish catch (1991) 5,500. Mining and quarrying (metric tons except as noted; 1991): sand and gravel 8,000,000; phosphate rock 1,359,000; gypsum 175,000; salt 127,000; marble 18,000 cu m. Manufacturing (1990): cement 3,500,000; wheat flour 1,171,000; nitrogenous fertilizers 108,000; raw sugar 65,000; cotton textiles 24,000; soap 15,000; rugs 945,000 sq m. Construction (1988): residential 2,390,000 sq m; nonresidential 339,000 sq m. Energy production (consumption): electricity (kW-hr; 1991) 12,179,000,000 (12,179,000,000); coal (metric tons) none (n.a.); crude petroleum (barrels; 1991) 202,740,000 (86,130,000); petroleum products (metric tons; 1991) 11,384,000 (8,929,000); natural gas (cu m; 1991) 294,710,000 (294,710,000).
Population economically active (1991): total 3,845,368; activity rate of total population 27.8% (participation rates: ages 15–64 [1986] 46.7%; female 10.2%; unemployed 6.1%).

Price and earnings indexes (1985 = 100)	1986	1987	1988	1989	1990	1991	1992
Consumer price index	136.0	216.9	292.0	325.4	388.4	418.1	457.9
Annual earnings index[8]	132.7	...	...	...	...	...	...

Public debt (external, outstanding; 1991): U.S.$14,932,000,000.
Average household size (1986): 5.7; income per household: n.a.; sources of income: n.a.; expenditure (1970)[9]: food 48.8%, housing 17.7%, clothing and footwear 9.1%, household durable goods 5.1%, fuel and light 4.6%, transportation and communications 3.8%, education and recreation 3.1%.

Foreign trade

Balance of trade (current prices)	1986	1987	1988	1989	1990	1991
LS '000,000	−4,626	−10,418	−7,879	+12,140	+22,661	+12,873
% of total	30.8%	25.5%	20.7%	21.9%	31.4%	18.8%

Imports (1991): LS 27,740,000,000 (1989; food, beverages, and tobacco 21.1%; machinery and equipment 17.6%; chemicals and chemical products 16.8%; basic metals industries 11.9%; textiles 8.1%). *Major import sources:* France 12.6%; Germany 9.6%; United States 8.4%; Turkey 7.6%; Italy 6.9%; China 4.4%; U.S.S.R. 3.7%; Belgium-Luxembourg 3.4%; Japan 3.2%.
Exports (1991): LS 40,613,000,000 (1989; crude petroleum and petroleum products 39.2%; textiles, wearing apparel, and leather 29.3%; chemicals and chemical products 11.8%; food, beverages, and tobacco 6.0%). *Major export destinations:* U.S.S.R. 44.3%; France 10.7%; Italy 9.9%; Germany 8.6%; Saudi Arabia 5.8%; Lebanon 4.3%; United Kingdom 2.3%; Iran 1.6%.

Transport and communications

Transport. Railroads (1991): route length 1,766 km; passenger-km 1,600,000,000; metric ton-km cargo 1,350,000,000. Roads (1990): total length 29,732 km (paved 78%). Vehicles (1991): passenger cars 119,040; trucks and buses 135,416. Merchant marine (1992): vessels (100 gross tons and over) 94; total deadweight tonnage 210,369. Air transport (1991): passenger-km 1,157,000,000; metric ton-km cargo 14,414,000; airports (1993) with scheduled flights 5.
Communications. Daily newspapers (1990): total number 9; total circulation 236,400; circulation per 1,000 population 19.5. Radio (1992): 2,850,000 receivers (1 per 4.5 persons). Television (1992): 700,000 receivers (1 per 18.5 persons). Telephones (1991): 707,728 (1 per 17.7 persons).

Education and health

Education (1990–91)	schools	teachers	students	student/ teacher ratio
Primary (age 6–11)	9,683	97,811	2,452,086	25.1
Secondary (age 12–18)	2,077[10]	43,184	847,783	19.6
Voc., teacher tr.	238[10]	8,806	66,476	7.5
Higher	44[10]	4,605[11]	175,317	...

Educational attainment (1984). Percentage of population age 10 and over having: no schooling 32.0%; knowledge of reading and writing 28.4%; primary education 31.3%; secondary 4.9%; certificate 2.0%; higher 1.9%.
Literacy (1990): percentage of population age 15 and over literate 64.5%; males literate 78.3%; females literate 50.8%.
Health (1990): physicians 11,682 (1 per 1,037 persons); hospital beds 13,603 (1 per 891 persons); infant mortality rate per 1,000 live births (1990–95) 39.0.
Food (1988–90): daily per capita caloric intake 3,122 (vegetable products 88%, animal products 12%); 126% of FAO recommended minimum requirement.

Military

Total active duty personnel (1993): 408,000 (army 73.5%, navy 2.0%, air force 24.5%). *Military expenditure as percentage of GNP* (1989): 11.6% (world 4.9%); per capita expenditure U.S.$186.

[1]Parties ideologically compatible with the Baʿth Party. [2]Islam is required to be the religion of the head of state and is the basis of the legal system. [3]Includes territory in the Golan Heights recognized internationally as part of Syria (located between the 1949 Israel-Syria Armistice line [west] and the 1974 UN Disengagement of Forces zone [east]) that has been occupied by Israel since 1967. Israel's unilateral annexation of this territory in December 1981 has received no international recognition. [4]Syrian Arabs only. [5]Includes imputed bank service charge and statistical discrepancy. [6]Unemployed, previously employed, and never previously employed. [7]Detail does not add to total given because of rounding. [8]Public sector only. [9]Weights of consumer price index components for Damascus only. [10]1989–90. [11]1986–87; university-level institutions only.

Taiwan

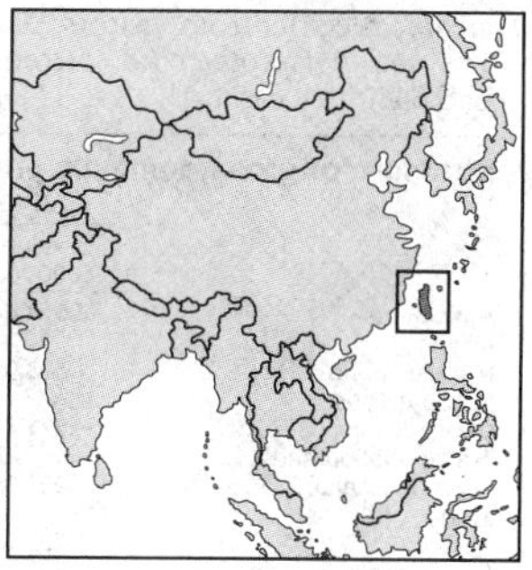

Official name: Chung-hua Min-kuo (Republic of China).
Form of government: multiparty republic with a National Assembly (384[1]) and Legislative Yuan (161).
Chief of state: President.
Head of government: Premier.
Capital: Taipei.
Official language: Mandarin Chinese.
Official religion: none.
Monetary unit: 1 New Taiwan dollar (NT$) = 100 cents; valuation (Oct. 4, 1993) 1 U.S.$ = NT$26.91; 1 £ = NT$40.78.

Area and population[2]

Counties	Capitals	area sq mi	area sq km	population 1992[3] estimate
Chang-hua	Chang-hua	415	1,074	1,267,475
Chia-i	Chia-i	734	1,902	558,121
Hsin-chu	Hsin-chu	551	1,428	388,184
Hua-lien	Hua-lien	1,787	4,629	356,124
I-lan	I-lan	825	2,137	458,456
Kao-hsiung	Feng-shan	1,078	2,793	1,152,501
Miao-li	Miao-li	703	1,820	553,399
Nan-t'ou	Nan-t'ou	1,585	4,106	542,124
P'eng-hu	Ma-kung	49	127	94,929
P'ing-tung	P'ing-tung	1,072	2,776	902,457
T'ai-chung	Feng-yuan	792	2,051	1,332,836
T'ai-nan	Hsin-ying	778	2,016	1,051,314
T'ai-pei	Pan-ch'iao	792	2,052	3,182,959
T'ai-tung	T'ai-tung	1,357	3,515	254,776
T'ao-yüan	T'ao-yüan	471	1,221	1,427,805
Yün-lin	Tou-liu	498	1,291	753,224
Municipalities				
Chia-i	—	23	60	258,464
Chi-lung	—	51	133	360,495
Hsin-chu	—	40	104	333,104
Kao-hsiung	—	59	154	1,405,652
T'ai-chung	—	63	163	802,355
T'ai-nan	—	68	176	696,808
Taipei	—	105	272	2,679,629
TOTAL		13,900[4]	36,000	20,813,191

Demography

Population (1993)[5]: 20,926,000.
Density (1993)[5]: persons per sq mi 1,499.2, persons per sq km 578.9.
Urban-rural (1991)[6]: urban 74.7%; rural 25.3%.
Sex distribution (1993[3])[6]: male 51.58%; female 48.42%.
Age breakdown (1991)[6]: under 15, 26.3%; 15–29, 27.6%; 30–44, 23.8%; 45–59, 12.2%; 60–74, 8.2%; 75 and over, 1.9%.
Population projection: (2000) 22,548,000; (2010) 25,085,000.
Doubling time: 67 years.
Ethnic composition (1986): Taiwanese 84.0%; mainland Chinese 14.0%; aborigine 2.0%.
Religious affiliation (1980): Chinese folk-religionist 48.5%; Buddhist 43.0%; Christian 7.4%; Muslim 0.5%; other 0.6%.
Major cities (1993[3])[6]: Taipei 2,679,629; Kao-hsiung 1,405,652; T'ai-chung 802,355; T'ai-nan 696,808; Chi-lung 360,495.

Vital statistics

Birth rate per 1,000 population (1992): 15.5 (world avg. 26.4); (1991)[6] legitimate 97.6%; illegitimate 2.4%.
Death rate per 1,000 population (1992): 5.3 (world avg. 9.2).
Natural increase rate per 1,000 population (1992): 10.2 (world avg. 17.2).
Total fertility rate (avg. births per childbearing woman; 1991)[6]: 1.7.
Marriage rate per 1,000 population (1992): 8.2.
Divorce rate per 1,000 population (1992): 1.4.
Life expectancy at birth (1991): male 71.8 years; female 77.2 years.
Major causes of death per 100,000 population (1991)[6]: malignant neoplasms 96.0; cerebrovascular diseases 69.1; accidents and suicide 66.7; heart disease 58.8; diabetes 20.6; liver diseases 17.6; pneumonia 12.9.

National economy

Budget (1991)[7]. Revenue: NT$1,438,686,000,000 (income taxes 13.5%, surplus of public enterprises 6.6%, commodity tax 6.0%, customs duties 5.5%). Expenditures: NT$1,416,625,000,000 (administration and defense 26.9%, economic development 22.7%, education 20.7%).
Production (metric tons except as noted). Agriculture, forestry, fishing (1991): sugarcane 4,536,231, rice 1,818,732, citrus fruits 544,251, corn (maize) 321,322, pineapples 241,477, sweet potatoes 224,272, bananas 196,663; livestock (number of live animals) 10,089,137 pigs, 175,765 goats and sheep, 134,238 cattle; timber 74,190 cu m; fish catch 1,316,651. Mining and quarrying (1990): silver 3,926 kg. Manufacturing (1992): cement 21,463,718; steel ingots 3,286,094; paperboard 2,950,366; fertilizers 1,951,249; synthetic fibre 1,832,076; polyvinyl chloride plastics 1,042,564; electronic calculators 16,153,034 units; microcomputer systems 3,265,437 units; sewing machines 3,208,430 units; colour televisions 1,738,975 units. Construction (1992): total residential and nonresidential 36,914,000 sq m. Energy production (consumption): electricity (kW-hr; 1992) 93,888,000,000 (58,040,966,000[8]); coal (metric tons; 1990) 472,050 (3,202,000[9]); crude petroleum (barrels; 1986) 704,700 (n.a.); natural gas (cu m; 1990) 1,128,877,000 (n.a.).
Gross national product (1992): U.S.$210,453,000,000 (U.S.$10,196 per capita).

Structure of gross domestic product and labour force[6]

	1992 in value NT$'000,000	% of total value	labour force[10]	% of labour force[10]
Agriculture	185,076	3.6	1,065,000	12.2
Mining	26,468	0.5	18,000	0.2
Manufacturing	1,712,332	33.0	2,587,000	29.5
Construction	266,813	5.2	779,000	8.9
Public utilities	149,588	2.9	37,000	0.4
Transp. and commun.	331,967	6.4	450,000	5.1
Trade	839,061	16.1	1,771,000	20.2
Finance	1,009,529	19.4	420,000	4.8
Pub. admin., defense	589,518	11.3	1,505,000	17.2
Services	339,714	6.5		
Other	−252,798[11]	−4.9[11]	132,000[12]	1.5[12]
TOTAL	5,197,268	100.0	8,764,000	100.0

Public debt (foreign; 1991): U.S.$3,859,000,000.
Tourism (1991): receipts from visitors U.S.$2,018,000,000.
Population economically active (1990): total 10,236,324; activity rate 50.5% (participation rates: age 15–64, 72.5%; female 38.5%; unemployed 1.7%).

Price and earnings indexes (1985 = 100)[6]

	1986	1987	1988	1989	1990	1991	1992[13]
Consumer price index	100.7	101.2	102.5	107.0	111.5	115.5	123.4
Monthly earnings index[14]	110.1	121.0	134.2	153.8	176.1	195.7	...

Household income and expenditure (1991). Average household size 3.9; income per household (1990) NT$627,511 (U.S.$23,147[15]); sources of income (1990): wages 60.5%, self-employment, transfer payments 5.9%, other 13.3%; expenditure: food 29.3%, rent, fuel, and power 23.8%, education 16.8%, transportation 13.6%, health care 5.1%, clothing 4.7%, other 6.7%.
Land use (1980): forested 55.0%; agricultural 25.2%; other 19.8%.

Foreign trade

Balance of trade (current prices)

	1987	1988	1989	1990	1991	1992
NT$'000,000	592,545	306,852	359,832	330,980	350,013	231,668
% of total	21.0%	9.7%	11.5%	10.1%	9.4%	6.0%

Imports (1992): NT$1,816,294,000,000 (electronic machinery 17.5%, nonelectrical machinery 13.5%, chemicals 9.9%, road motor vehicles 8.4%, iron and steel 6.9%, crude petroleum 4.2%). *Major import sources:* Japan 30.2%; U.S. 21.9%; Germany 5.4%; Korea 3.2%; Australia 2.9%; Hong Kong 2.5%.
Exports (1992): NT$2,047,962,000,000 (nonelectrical machinery 19.6%, electronic machinery 16.9%, plastic articles 5.9%, transportation equipment 5.2%, synthetic fibres 5.0%, footwear 4.6%, knitted articles 4.3%, iron and steel products 4.0%). *Major export destinations:* U.S. 28.9%; Hong Kong 18.9%; Japan 10.9%; Germany 4.4%; Singapore 3.1%.

Transport and communications

Transport. Railroads (1992): track length 4,600 km; passenger-km 9,348,788,000; metric ton-km cargo 2,062,657,000. Roads (1991): total length 19,490 km (paved 86%). Vehicles (1992): passenger cars 3,033,651; trucks and buses 751,627. Merchant marine (1992): vessels (100 gross tons and over) 649; total deadweight tonnage 9,241,283. Air transport (1992): passenger-km 33,645,361,000; metric ton-km cargo 4,275,144,000; airports (1993) 12.
Communications. Daily newspapers (1988): total number 93; total circulation 4,000,000; circulation per 1,000 population 202. Radio (1992): 8,620,000 receivers (1 per 2.4 persons). Television (1992): 7,000,000 receivers (1 per 3.0 persons). Telephones (1991): 9,254,000 (1 per 2.2 persons).

Education and health

Education (1991–92)

	schools	teachers	students	student/ teacher ratio
Primary (age 6–12)	2,495	84,304	2,293,444	27.2
Secondary (age 13–18)	883	69,206	1,394,463	20.2
Vocational	212	18,000	475,852	26.4
Higher	123	29,444	612,376	20.8

Educational attainment (1991). Percentage of population age 25 and over having: no formal schooling 2.0%; less than complete primary education 7.1%; primary 30.8%; incomplete secondary 21.5%; secondary 24.4%; some college 8.0%; higher 6.2%. *Literacy* (1991): population age 15 and over literate 14,063,682 (92.8%); males 7,589,475 (96.8%); females 6,474,207 (88.2%).
Health (1991): physicians 23,629 (1 per 868 persons); hospital beds 92,785 (1 per 221 persons); infant mortality rate per 1,000 live births 5.1.
Food: daily per capita caloric intake (1990) 3,020 (1988; vegetable products 77%, animal products 23%); 118% of FAO recommended minimum.

Military

Total active duty personnel (1991): 360,000 (army 72.2%, navy 8.3%, air force 19.5%). *Military expenditure as percentage of GNP* (1989): 5.4% (world 4.9%); per capita expenditure U.S.$397.

[1]Occupied seats as of mid-1992. [2]Excludes Quemoy and Matsu groups (Kinma area) of occupied Fukien province. Areas of Quemoy islands and Matsu islands equal 58 sq mi (150 sq km) and 11 sq mi (28 sq km), respectively; beginning-of-year 1991 population estimates equal 42,754 and 5,585, respectively. [3]End of May. [4]Detail does not add to total given because of rounding. [5]Includes Quemoy and Matsu groups. [6]For Taiwan area only, excluding Quemoy and Matsu groups. [7]General government. [8]By industry only. [9]1986. [10]Civilian employed persons only. [11]Import duties less imputed bank service charge. [12]Unemployed. [13]October. [14]In manufacturing. [15]Based on the average exchange rate.

Tajikistan

Official name: Jumhurii Tojikistan (Republic of Tajikistan).
Form of government: parliamentary republic with one legislative house (Supreme Soviet [230]).
Chief of state: Speaker of the Supreme Soviet (de facto President).
Head of government: Chairman of the Council of Ministers (Prime Minister).
Capital: Dushanbe.
Official language: Tajik (Tojik).
Official religion: none.
Monetary unit: 1 Russian ruble = 100 kopecks; valuation (Oct. 4, 1993) free rate, 1 U.S.$ = 1,165 rubles; 1 £ = 1,765 rubles.

Area and population

		area		population
				1991
Autonomous republic	**Capitals**	sq mi	sq km	estimate
Badakhshan	Khorog	24,600	63,700	167,100
Provinces				
Khudzhand	Khudzhand	10,100	26,100	1,635,900
Kulyab	Kulyab	4,600	12,000	668,100
Kurgan-Tyube	Kurgan-Tyube	4,900	12,600	1,113,500
Regions under republican jurisdiction	—	11,000	28,400	1,181,800
City				
Dushanbe	—	100	300	591,900
TOTAL		55,300	143,100	5,358,300

Demography

Population (1993): 5,705,000.
Density (1993): persons per sq mi 103.3, persons per sq km 39.9.
Urban-rural (1992): urban 30.9%; rural 69.1%.
Sex distribution (1992): male 49.60%; female 50.40%.
Age breakdown (1989): under 15, 42.9%; 15–29, 28.1%; 30–44, 13.8%; 45–59, 9.0%; 60–74, 4.6%; 75 and over, 1.6%.
Population projection: (2000) 6,766,000; (2010) 8,632,000.
Doubling time: 21 years.
Ethnic composition (1989): Tajik 62.3%; Uzbek 23.5%; Russian 7.6%; Tatar 1.4%; Kyrgyz 1.3%; Ukrainian 0.8%; German 0.6%; other 2.5%.
Religious affiliation (1990): believers are predominantly Sunnī Muslim (Ḥanafīyah).
Major cities (1989): Dushanbe 582,400; Khudzhand (formerly Leninabad) 164,500; Kulyab 79,300; Kurgan-Tyube 58,400; Ura-Tyube 47,700.

Vital statistics

Birth rate per 1,000 population (1992): 38.9 (world avg. 26.4); (1989) legitimate 93.0%; illegitimate 7.0%.
Death rate per 1,000 population (1992): 6.1 (world avg. 9.2).
Natural increase rate per 1,000 population (1992): 32.8 (world avg. 17.2).
Total fertility rate (avg. births per childbearing woman; 1989): 5.1.
Marriage rate per 1,000 population (1989): 9.2.
Divorce rate per 1,000 population (1989): 1.5.
Life expectancy at birth (1991): male 66.8 years; female 71.9 years.
Major causes of death per 100,000 population (1989): diseases of the circulatory system 197.5; diseases of the respiratory system 138.8; infectious and parasitic diseases 81.2; malignant neoplasms (cancers) 51.9; violence, poisoning, and accidents 48.4; diseases of the digestive system 23.0; diseases of the nervous system 8.9; endocrine and metabolic disorders 6.9.

National economy

Production (metric tons except as noted). Agriculture, forestry, fishing (1992): seed cotton 819,000, vegetables (except potatoes) 628,000, potatoes 181,000, fruit (except grapes) 171,000, wheat 141,000, grapes 121,000, corn 60,000, barley 47,000, rice 24,000; livestock (number of live animals) 3,400,000 sheep and goats, 1,400,000 cattle, 100,000 pigs; roundwood, n.a.; fish catch, 39,000. Mining and quarrying: detail not available; however, antimony, mercury, and molybdenum are mined. Manufacturing (1991): cement 1,000,000; cotton yarn 102,000; vegetable oil 93,200; mineral fertilizers 84,100; canned food 284,000,000 units; bricks 263,000,000 units; refrigerators 145,000 units; leather footwear 9,000,000 pairs; woven cotton fabrics 102,000,000 sq m; reinforced concrete 800,000 cu m. Construction (1991): residential 1,224,000 sq m. Energy production (consumption): electricity (kW-hr; 1991) 17,500,000,000 (n.a.); coal (metric tons; 1991) 313,000 (n.a.); crude petroleum (barrels; 1991) 733,000 (n.a.); petroleum products, n.a. (n.a.); natural gas (cu m; 1991) 93,000,000 (n.a.).
Population economically active (1992): total 2,575,000; activity rate of total population 46.2% (participation rates: ages 16–59 [male], 16–54 [female] 80.5%; female [1990] 39.0%; unemployed [1990] 2.0%).

Price and earnings indexes (1985 = 100)

	1986	1987	1988	1989	1990
Consumer price index	...	...	...	...	...
Monthly earnings index	102.7	105.1	112.2	119.2	131.1

Tourism: receipts from visitors, n.a.; expenditures by nationals abroad, n.a.
Gross national product (at current market prices; 1992): U.S.$2,536,700,000 (U.S.$480 per capita)[1].

Structure of gross domestic product and labour force

	1990			
	in value '000,000 rubles	% of total value	labour force[2]	% of labour force[2]
Agriculture	2,014.6	38.3	831,000	42.9
Mining, Manufacturing, Public utilities	1,503.0	28.5	260,700	13.5
Construction	771.7	14.7	160,800	8.3
Transportation and communications	221.0	4.2	64,700	3.3
Trade	—	—	145,400	7.5
Finance	750.7	14.3	—	—
Public administration, defense	—	—	38,800	2.0
Services	—	—	436,900	22.5
Other	—	—	—	—
TOTAL	5,261.0	100.0	1,938,300	100.0

Budget (1991). Revenue: 5,457,000,000 rubles (union transfers 46.6%, turnover tax 17.5%, enterprise profits tax 11.1%, individual income tax 6.1%, sales tax 4.0%, duties and local taxes 3.1%). Expenditures: 5,020,000,000 rubles (social welfare and culture 62.5%, national economy 26.2%).
Public debt (external, outstanding): n.a.
Land use: n.a.
Household income and expenditure. Average household size (1989) 6.1; income per household: n.a.; sources of income: n.a.; expenditure: n.a.

Foreign trade

Balance of trade (current prices)

	1991
'000,000 rubles	512.0
% of total	6.3%

Imports (1991): 3,815,600,000 rubles (no breakdown available). *Major import sources:* former Soviet republics 90.8%; other 9.2%.
Exports (1991): 4,327,600,000 rubles (no breakdown available). *Major export destinations:* former Soviet republics 91.2%; other 8.8%.

Transport and communications

Transport. Railroads (1990): length 553.6 mi, 891.0 km; passenger-mi 6,094,400,000, passenger-km 9,808,000,000; short ton-mi cargo 7,617,000,000, metric ton-km cargo 11,121,000,000. Roads (1990): total length 8,324,000 mi, 13,396,000 km (paved 93%). Vehicles (1988): passenger cars 209,100; trucks and buses, n.a. Merchant marine: vessels (100 gross tons and over) n.a.; total deadweight tonnage, n.a. Air transport (1989): passenger-mi 3,214,600,000, passenger-km 5,173,400,000; short ton-mi cargo 22,124,000, metric ton-km cargo 32,300,000; airports (1992) with scheduled flights 1.
Communications. Daily newspapers (1990): total number 74; total circulation 1,598,000; circulation per 1,000 population 298.2. Radio (1992): total number of receivers 854,000 (1 per 6.7 persons). Television (1992): total number of receivers 860,000 (1 per 6.6 persons). Telephones (1992): 303,000 (1 per 18.8 persons).

Education and health

Education (1991–92)

	schools	teachers	students	student/ teacher ratio
Primary (age 6–13), Secondary (age 14–17)	3,179	99,000	1,310,000	13.2
Voc., teacher tr.	...	...	...	...
Higher	13	...	69,300	...

Educational attainment (1989). Percentage of population age 25 and over having: primary education or no formal schooling 16.3%; some secondary 21.1%; completed secondary and some postsecondary 55.1%; higher 7.5%.
Literacy: n.a.
Health (1990): physicians 14,500 (1 per 362 persons); hospital beds 56,500 (1 per 93 persons); infant mortality rate per 1,000 live births 40.6.
Food: daily per capita caloric intake, n.a.

Military

Total active duty personnel (1993): 6,000 (army 100%). *Military expenditure as percentage of GNP* (1992): 2.8% (world 5.0%); per capita expenditure U.S.$35.

[1]Ruble-area GNP and exchange-rate data are highly speculative. [2]State sector.

Tanzania

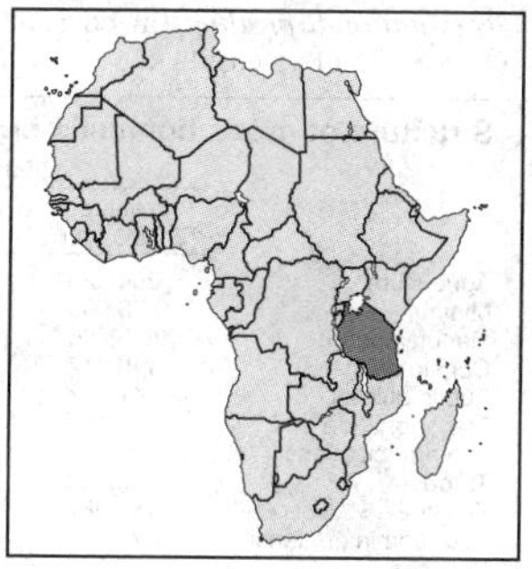

Official name: Jamhuri ya Muungano wa Tanzania (Swahili); United Republic of Tanzania (English).
Form of government: unitary[1] multiparty[2] republic with one legislative house (National Assembly [255[3]]).
Head of state and government: President.
Seat of government: Dar es Salaam[4] (Capital designate, Dodoma).
Official languages: Swahili; English.
Official religion: none.
Monetary unit: 1 Tanzanian shilling (T Sh) = 100 cents; valuation (Oct. 4, 1993) 1 U.S.$ = T Sh 445.74; 1 £ = T Sh 675.30.

Area and population

		area		population
Regions	Capitals	sq mi	sq km	1988 census
Arusha	Arusha	31,778	82,306	1,351,675
Coast	Dar es Salaam	12,512	32,407	638,015
Dar es Salaam	—	538	1,393	1,360,850
Dodoma	Dodoma	15,950	41,311	1,237,819
Iringa	Iringa	21,955	56,864	1,208,914
Kagera	Bukoba	10,961	28,388	1,326,183
Kigoma	Kigoma	14,300	37,037	854,817
Kilimanjaro	Moshi	5,139	13,309	1,108,699
Lindi	Lindi	25,501	66,046	646,550
Mara	Musoma	7,555	19,566	970,942
Mbeya	Mbeya	23,301	60,350	1,476,199
Morogoro	Morogoro	27,336	70,799	1,222,737
Mtwara	Mtwara	6,451	16,707	889,494
Mwanza	Mwanza	7,564	19,592	1,878,271
Pemba North	Wete	222	574	137,399
Pemba South	Chake Chake	128	332	127,640
Rukwa	Sumbawanga	26,500	68,635	694,974
Ruvuma	Songea	24,517	63,498	783,327
Shinyanga	Shinyanga	19,607	50,781	1,772,549
Singida	Singida	19,051	49,341	791,814
Tabora	Tabora	29,402	76,151	1,036,293
Tanga	Tanga	10,351	26,808	1,283,636
Zanzibar North	Mkokotoni	182	470	97,028
Zanzibar South and Central	Koani	330	854	70,184
Zanzibar West	Zanzibar	89	230	208,327
TOTAL LAND AREA		341,217[5]	883,749	
INLAND WATER		22,800	59,050	
TOTAL		364,017	942,799	23,174,336

Demography

Population (1993): 26,542,000.
Density (1993)[6]: persons per sq mi 77.8, persons per sq km 30.0.
Urban-rural (1990): urban 32.8%; rural 67.2%.
Sex distribution (1990): male 49.44%; female 50.56%.
Age breakdown (1990): under 15, 49.1%; 15–29, 25.6%; 30–44, 13.9%; 45–59, 7.6%; 60–74, 3.2%; 75 and over, 0.6%.
Population projection: (2000) 32,292,000; (2010) 42,732,000.
Doubling time: 21 years.
Ethnolinguistic composition (1983): Nyamwezi and Sukuma 21.1%; Swahili 8.8%; Hehet and Bena 6.9%; Makonde 5.9%; Haya 5.9%; other 51.4%.
Religious affiliation (1984): Christian 34%; Muslim 33%; traditional beliefs and other 33%.
Major cities (1988): Dar es Salaam 1,360,850; Mwanza 223,013; Dodoma 203,833; Tanga 187,634; Zanzibar 157,634.

Vital statistics

Birth rate per 1,000 population (1991): 49.5 (world avg. 26.4).
Death rate per 1,000 population (1991): 15.2 (world avg. 9.2).
Natural increase rate per 1,000 population (1991): 34.3 (world avg. 17.2).
Total fertility rate (avg. births per childbearing woman; 1991): 7.0.
Life expectancy at birth (1991): male 50.0 years; female 55.0 years.
Major causes of death per 100,000 population: n.a.; however, the major diseases include malaria, bilharziasis, tuberculosis, and sleeping sickness.

National economy

Budget (1991–92). Revenue: T Sh 215,162,000,000[7] (1986–87; sales tax 46.4%, income tax 21.2%, customs and excise tax 11.7%). Expenditures: T Sh 227,973,000,000 (1986–87; public administration 25.5%, defense 20.1%, economic services 16.4%, education 6.4%, health 3.7%).
Public debt (external, outstanding; 1991): U.S.$5,786,000,000.
Tourism (1991): receipts from visitors U.S.$95,000,000; expenditures by nationals abroad (1990) U.S.$19,000,000.
Production (metric tons except as noted). Agriculture (1992): cassava 7,111,000, corn (maize) 2,226,000, sugarcane 1,410,000, bananas 794,000, plantains 794,000, sorghum 587,000, rice 392,000, coconuts 365,000, millet 263,000, sweet potatoes 257,000, seed cotton 218,000, potatoes 200,000, dry beans 195,000, mangoes 185,000, cottonseed 142,000; livestock (number of live animals) 13,217,000 cattle, 9,073,000 goats, 3,706,000 sheep, 330,000 pigs, 25,000,000 chickens; roundwood (1991) 35,545,000 cu m; fish catch (1991) 400,300. Mining and quarrying (1992): salt 77,000; gold 3.2; diamonds 67,250 carats. Manufacturing (1989): cement 460,000; fresh meat and poultry 231,000; sugar 110,000; hides and skins 33,000; wheat flour 21,000; soap 19,800; cotton textiles 46,000,000 sq m. Construction: n.a. Energy production (consumption): electricity (kW-hr; 1991) 901,000,000 (901,000,000); coal (metric tons; 1991) 75,000 (75,000); crude petroleum (barrels; 1991) none (4,075,000); petroleum products (metric tons; 1991) 544,000 (640,000).
Gross national product (1992): U.S.$2,848,000,000 (U.S.$110 per capita).

Structure of gross domestic product and labour force

	1990		1988	
	in value T Sh '000,000	% of total value	labour force	% of labour force
Agriculture	233,804	47.2	9,861,000	82.0
Mining	4,815	1.0		
Manufacturing	20,436	4.1		
Construction	12,650	2.6	560,000	4.7
Public utilities	5,088	1.0		
Transp. and commun.	36,242	7.3		
Trade	57,717	11.6		
Finance	24,123	4.9	1,612,000	13.4
Pub. admin., defense; Services	31,968	6.4		
Other	69,020	13.9	...	...
TOTAL	495,863	100.0	12,033,000	100.0[5]

Population economically active (1988): total 12,033,000; activity rate of total population 47.4% (participation rates: over age 10, 74.3%; female 45.2%).

Price index (1985 = 100)

	1986	1987	1988	1989	1990	1991	1992
Consumer price index	132.4	172.1	225.8	284.1	340.1	415.9	507.7

Household income and expenditure. Avg. household size (1988) 5.2; income per household: n.a.; sources of income: n.a.; expenditure (1981): food 54.3%, clothing 10.8%, housing 8.6%, energy 6.6%, transportation 6.4%.
Land use (1991): forested 46.1%; meadows and pastures 39.5%; agricultural and under permanent cultivation 3.8%; other 10.6%.

Foreign trade

Balance of trade (current prices)

	1986	1987	1988	1989	1990	1991
T Sh '000,000	−14,716	−31,917	−41,690	−73,326	−88,440	−139,035
% of total	39.5%	46.3%	43.5%	41.6%	35.3%	46.8%

Imports (1991): T Sh 218,021,000,000 (1988; machinery and transport equipment 45.6%, basic manufactures 16.3%, fuel 10.2%, chemicals 8.8%, metals 5.5%, food 5.4%). *Major import sources* (1988): U.K. 16.2%; West Germany 10.5%; Japan 10.5%; Italy 8.5%; Sweden 3.8%; The Netherlands 3.5%; Denmark 3.4%; U.S. 3.2%; Yugoslavia 1.1%.
Exports (1991): T Sh 78,986,000,000 (1988; coffee 25.9%, cotton 23.6%, sisal 1.4%). *Major export destinations* (1988): West Germany 22.6%; U.K. 16.6%; The Netherlands 6.9%; Singapore 5.9%; Italy 5.2%; Japan 4.8%; Finland 3.1%; Portugal 3.1%; U.S. 2.8%; France 2.5%.

Transport and communications

Transport. Railroads (1990): length 3,569 km; passenger-km 3,420,000,000[8]; metric ton-km cargo 1,248,000,000[8]. Roads (1989): length 82,114 km (paved 4.2%). Vehicles (1990): passenger cars 45,000; trucks and buses 55,000. Merchant marine (1992): vessels (100 gross tons and over) 43; deadweight tonnage 48,465. Air transport (1992)[9]: passenger-km 174,372,000; metric ton-km 2,120,000; airports (1993) with scheduled flights 12.
Communications. Daily newspapers: total number (1989) 2; total circulation 180,000; circulation per 1,000 population 7.6. Radio (1992): 4,000,000 receivers (1 per 6.5 persons). Television (1992): 80,000 receivers (1 per 323 persons). Telephones (1990): 140,131 (1 per 174 persons).

Education and health

Education (1989)

	schools	teachers	students	student/ teacher ratio
Primary (age 7–13)[10]	10,431	98,392	3,258,601	33.1
Secondary (age 14–19)	288[11]	7,863	145,748	18.5
Voc., teacher tr.	63[11]	1,015	13,263	13.1
Higher	4	1,206	5,254	4.4

Educational attainment (1978). Percentage of population age 10 and over having: no schooling 48.6%; some primary education 40.7%; completed primary 8.7%; secondary and higher 1.9%. *Literacy* (1978): percentage of total population age 15 and over literate 46.3%; males literate 62.2%; females literate 31.4%; estimated total literacy in 1987: 94.0%.
Health (1984): physicians 1,065 (1 per 19,775 persons); hospital beds 22,800 (1 per 924 persons); infant mortality rate per 1,000 live births (1991) 105.
Food (1988–90): daily per capita caloric intake 2,195 (vegetable products 94%, animal products 6%); 95% of FAO recommended minimum requirement.

Military

Total active duty personnel (1993): 49,500 (army 90.9%, navy 2.0%, air force 7.1%). *Military expenditure as percentage of GNP* (1989): 4.1% (world 4.9%); per capita expenditure U.S.$5.

[1]Federal governmental structures exist in the Zanzibar constitution and House of Representatives, and in 1993 legislation authorizing a similar house in Tanganyika. [2]Multiparty system became official May 1992; multiparty elections began locally in 1993 and were scheduled to continue at various levels until completed in 1995. [3]Includes 180 directly elected, 35 indirectly elected, 15 presidential nominees, and 25 ex officio members. [4]Government in process of being transferred from Dar es Salaam to Dodoma; legislative branch meets in Dodoma. [5]Detail does not add to total given because of rounding. [6]Based on land area. [7]Includes foreign grants and loans. [8]1989. [9]Air Tanzania only. [10]Excludes Zanzibar and Pemba. [11]1986–87.

Thailand

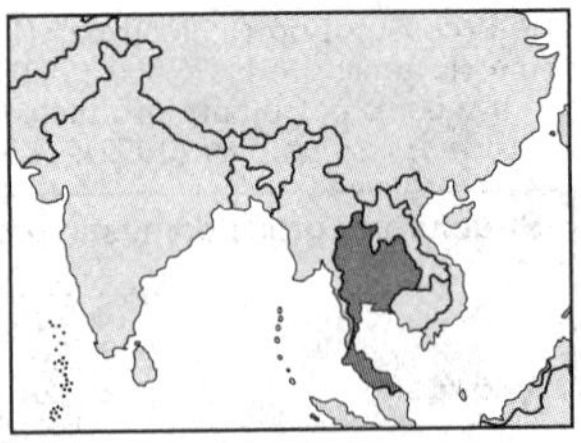

Official name: Muang Thai, or Prathet Thai (Kingdom of Thailand).
Form of government: constitutional monarchy with two legislative houses (Senate [270]; House of Representatives [360]).
Chief of state: King.
Head of government: Prime Minister[1].
Capital: Bangkok.
Official language: Thai.
Official religion: Buddhism.
Monetary unit: 1 Thai baht (B) = 100 stangs; valuation (Oct. 4, 1993) 1 U.S.$ = B 24.93; 1 £ = B 37.78.

Area and population

	area		population
Regions[2]	sq mi	sq km	1992 estimate[3]
Bangkok Metropolis	2,995	7,758	8,661,228
Central	6,407	16,594	2,822,518
Eastern	14,094	36,503	3,738,670
Northeastern	65,195	168,854	20,059,015
Northern	65,500	169,644	11,682,315
Southern	27,303	70,715	7,401,746
Western	16,621	43,047	3,423,473
TOTAL	198,115	513,115	57,788,965

Demography

Population (1993): 57,829,000[4].
Density (1993): persons per sq mi 291.9, persons per sq km 112.7.
Urban-rural (1992): urban 17.7%; rural 82.3%.
Sex distribution (1992): male 50.21%; female 49.79%.
Age breakdown (1990): under 20, 44.3%; 20–39, 34.2%; 40–59, 15.4%; 60–69, 3.9%; 70 and over, 2.2%.
Population projection: (2000) 65,534,000; (2010) 76,656,000.
Doubling time: 50 years.
Ethnic composition (1983): Thai 79.5%, of which Siamese 52.6%, Lao 26.9%; Chinese 12.1%; Malay 3.7%; Khmer 2.7%; other 2.0%.
Religious affiliation (1989): Buddhist 94.3%; Muslim 4.0%; Christian 0.5%; other 1.2%.
Major cities (1991)[3]: Bangkok 5,620,591; Nonthaburi 264,201; Nakhon Ratchasima 202,503; Chiang Mai 161,541; Khon Kaen 131,478.

Vital statistics

Birth rate per 1,000 population (1993): 20.0 (world avg. 26.4).
Death rate per 1,000 population (1993): 6.0 (world avg. 9.2).
Natural increase rate per 1,000 population (1993): 14.0 (world avg. 17.2).
Total fertility rate (avg. births per childbearing woman; 1993): 2.2.
Marriage rate per 1,000 population (1991): 7.3.
Divorce rate per 1,000 population (1991): 0.8.
Life expectancy at birth (1993): male 66.0 years; female 71.0 years.
Major causes of death per 100,000 population (1990)[5]: diseases of the heart 153.6; accidents and poisoning 125.5; malignant neoplasms (cancers) 117.7; suicide, homicide, and other injury 45.8; cardiovascular diseases 44.9; liver and pancreatic diseases 39.9; pneumonia and other lung diseases 31.3.

National economy

Budget (1991–92). Revenue: B 488,600,000,000 (1990–91; taxes 89.7%, state enterprises 4.6%, sale of property and services 3.6%). Expenditures: B 426,800,000,000 (1990–91; economic services 22.1%, education 19.1%, defense 16.3%, debt service 15.1%, public utilities and health 13.5%, internal security 5.0%, general administration 3.8%).
Production (metric tons except as noted). Agriculture, forestry, fishing (1992): sugarcane 46,805,000, cassava 21,130,000, rice 18,500,000, corn (maize) 3,610,000, bananas 1,630,000, rubber 1,400,000, coconuts 1,353,000, soybeans 480,000, dry beans 322,000, cabbages 194,000, sorghum 140,000; livestock (number of live animals) 6,820,000 cattle, 5,100,000 pigs, 4,793,000 buffalo, 136,000,000 chickens; roundwood (1991) 37,940,000 cu m; fish catch (1991) 3,065,170. Mining and quarrying (1992): limestone 25,272,000; gypsum 7,111,000; zinc ore 407,000; marble 86,995; fluorite 51,597; lead ore 27,946; tin concentrates 11,484. Manufacturing (1991): cement 19,210,000; refined sugar 3,994,828; chemical fertilizer 458,103; synthetic fibre 225,017[6]; jute products 152,263[6]; motorcycles 600,119 units. Construction (1990): residential 16,343,000 sq m; nonresidential 13,449,000 sq m. Energy production (consumption): electricity (kW-hr; 1990) 46,175,000,000 (46,796,000,000); coal (metric tons; 1990) 12,421,000 (12,639,000); crude petroleum (barrels; 1990) 8,650,000 (81,164,000); petroleum products (metric tons; 1990) 12,614,000 (19,588,000); natural gas (cu m; 1990) 5,498,000,000 (5,498,000,000).
Land use (1991): forested 27.4%; meadows and pastures 1.6%; agricultural and under permanent cultivation 45.3%; other 25.7%.
Tourism (1991): receipts from visitors U.S.$3,923,000,000; expenditures by nationals abroad U.S.$1,266,000,000.
Population economically active (1990): total 31,749,600; activity rate of total population 58.2% (participation rates: over age 13, 77.2%; female 46.9%; unemployed 4.9%).

Price and earnings indexes (1985 = 100)

	1986	1987	1988	1989	1990	1991	1992
Consumer price index	101.8	104.4	108.4	114.2	121.0	127.9	133.1
Earnings index	...	...	...	...	...	...	...

Gross national product (at current market prices; 1992): U.S.$101,432,000,000 (U.S.$1,750 per capita).

Structure of gross domestic product and labour force

	1990		1991	
	in value B '000,000	% of total value	labour force[7]	% of labour force
Agriculture	254,523	12.4	13,988,100	45.4
Mining	73,500	3.6	81,900	0.3
Manufacturing	535,396	26.1	4,090,400	13.3
Construction	146,817	7.2	1,865,800	6.1
Public utilities	47,367	2.3	142,700	0.4
Transportation and communications	138,752	6.8	900,200	2.9
Trade	312,738	15.2	3,698,100	12.0
Finance	188,882	9.2		
Pub. admin., defense	74,603	3.6	3,348,000	10.9
Services	278,630	13.6		
Other	...	...	2,690,200[8]	8.7[8]
TOTAL	2,051,208	100.0	30,805,400	100.0

Public debt (external, outstanding; 1991): U.S.$13,292,000,000.
Household income and expenditure (1990). Average household size 4.1; average annual income per household B 67,452 (U.S.$2,636); sources of income: wages and salaries 35.8%, self-employment 34.2%, transfer payments 5.8%, other 24.2%; expenditure: food, tobacco, and beverages 38.4%, housing 23.8%, transportation and communications 13.3%, clothing 6.1%, medical and personal care 5.5%, education and recreation 3.6%, other 9.3%.

Foreign trade[9]

Balance of trade (current prices)

	1987	1988	1989	1990	1991	1992
B '000,000	−1,900	−59,529	−71,417	−172,323	−139,742	−107,887
% of total	0.3%	6.9%	6.5%	12.7%	8.8%	6.1%

Imports (1991): B 959,408,000,000 (electrical power equipment and machinery 33.5%, mineral fuels and lubricants 9.2%, iron and steel 7.8%, chemicals 7.8%, transport equipment 6.3%, precious stones 5.6%). *Major import sources:* Japan 29.4%; United States 10.6%; Singapore 8.0%; Germany 5.6%; Taiwan 4.8%; South Korea 4.2%; Malaysia 3.2%; China 3.0%; United Kingdom 2.3%.
Exports (1991): B 723,112,000,000 (electrical power equipment and machinery 22.9%, textiles and apparel 13.1%, fish and fish preparations 10.3%, precious stones 5.3%, cereals 4.8%, rubber and rubber articles 4.4%, footwear 3.3%). *Major export destinations:* United States 21.3%; Japan 18.1%; Singapore 8.1%; Germany 5.2%; Hong Kong 4.7%; The Netherlands 4.4%; United Kingdom 3.6%; France 2.5%; Malaysia 2.4%.

Transport and communications

Transport. Railroads (1991)[10]: route length 2,399 mi, 3,861 km; passenger-mi 7,965,000,000, passenger-km 12,820,000,000; short ton-mi cargo 2,305,128,000, metric ton-km cargo 3,365,431,000. Roads (1990): total length 44,844 mi, 72,170 km (paved 55%). Vehicles (1991): passenger cars 735,326; trucks and buses 1,903,220. Merchant marine (1992): vessels (100 gross tons and over) 351; total deadweight tonnage 1,194,470. Air transport (1992): passenger-mi 12,737,000,000, passenger-km 20,498,000,000; short ton-mi cargo 634,495,000, metric ton-km cargo 926,347,000; airports (1993) with scheduled flights 26.
Communications. Daily newspapers (1990): total number 34; total circulation 4,000,000; circulation per 1,000 population 72. Radio (1992): 10,000,000 receivers (1 per 5.7 persons). Television (1992): 3,300,000 receivers (1 per 17 persons). Telephones (1991): 1,553,160 receivers (1 per 36 persons).

Education and health

Education (1989)

	schools	teachers	students	student/ teacher ratio
Primary (age 7–12)	32,858	365,246	6,496,758	17.8
Secondary (age 13–18)	1,437[11]	107,033	1,836,610	17.2
Voc., teacher tr.	1,528[11]	23,525	381,139	16.2
Higher	43	52,317	952,012	18.2

Educational attainment (1980). Percentage of population age 25 and over having: no formal schooling 20.5%; primary education 67.3%; secondary 9.3%; postsecondary 2.9%. *Literacy* (1985): total population age 15 and over literate 28,451,390 (88.8%); males literate 14,877,240 (93.2%); females literate 13,574,150 (84.5%).
Health (1990): physicians 12,520 (1 per 4,377 persons); hospital beds 90,740 (1 per 604 persons); infant mortality rate per 1,000 live births (1991) 25.0.
Food (1988–90): daily per capita caloric intake 2,280 (vegetable products 91%, animal products 9%); 103% of FAO recommended minimum requirement.

Military

Total active duty personnel (1992): 283,000 (army 67.1%, navy 17.7%, air force 15.2%). *Military expenditure as percentage of GNP* (1989): 2.7% (world 4.9%); per capita expenditure U.S.$34.

[1]The new constitution requires that future prime ministers be elected members of Parliament. [2]Actual local administration is based on 73 provinces. [3]Based on registration records. [4]Based on preliminary 1990 census results, which are lower than the 1990 registration records estimate. [5]Imputed rates calculated from registered deaths. [6]1990. [7]May; economically active persons 13 years and over. [8]Mostly unemployed. [9]Import figures are f.o.b. in balance of trade and c.i.f. for commodities and trading partners. [10]Traffic data refer to fiscal year ending September 30. [11]1980.

Togo

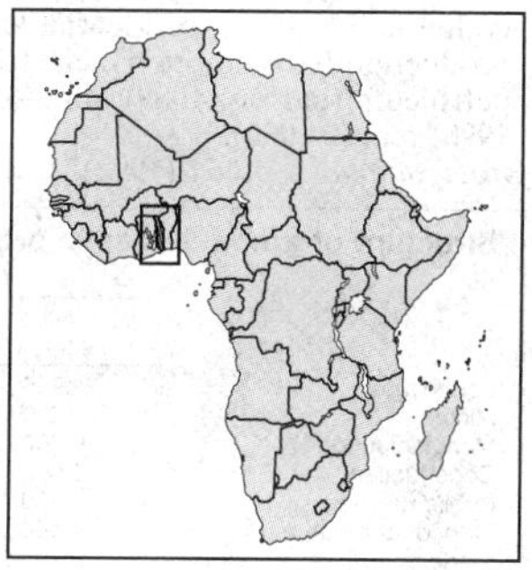

Official name: République Togolaise (Republic of Togo).
Form of government: militarily controlled regime with one interim legislative body (High Council of the Republic [79])[1].
Chief of state: President.
Head of government: Prime Minister.
Capital: Lomé.
Official language: French.
Official religion: none.
Monetary unit: 1 CFA franc (CFAF) = 100 centimes; valuation (Oct. 4, 1993) 1 U.S.$ = CFAF 283.25; 1 £ = CFAF 429.12.

Area and population

Regions / Prefectures	Capitals	area sq mi	area sq km	population 1981 census
Centrale	Sokodé			273,138
Sotouboua	Sotouboua	2,892	7,491	131,637
Tchamba	Tchamba	1,214	3,143	44,810
Tchaoudjo	Sokodé	984	2,549	96,691
De la Kara	Kara			426,651
Assoli	Bafilo	362	938	32,425
Bassar	Bassar	2,444	6,330	118,934
Binah	Pagouda	180	465	50,081
Doufelgou	Niamtougou	432	1,120	59,331
Kéran	Kandé	419	1,085	44,844
Kozah	Kara	653	1,692	121,036
Des Plateaux	Atakpamé			650,393
Amou	Amlamé	773	2,003	78,125
Haho	Notsé	1,406	3,641	110,768
Kloto	Kpalimé	1,072	2,777	186,778
Ogou	Atakpamé	2,349	6,083	165,143
Wawa	Badou	954	2,471	109,579
Des Savanes	Dapaong			329,144
Oti	Sansanné-Mango	1,453	3,762	77,803
Tône	Dapaong	1,869	4,840	251,341
Maritime	Lomé			1,040,241
Golfe	Lomé	133	345	447,806
Lacs	Aného	275	713	137,855
Vo	Vogan	290	750	150,575
Yoto	Tabligbo	483	1,250	100,682
Zio	Tsévié	1,288	3,337	203,323
TOTAL		21,925	56,785	2,719,567

Demography

Population (1993): 3,810,000.
Density (1993): persons per sq mi 173.8, persons per sq km 67.1.
Urban-rural (1990): urban 25.7%; rural 74.3%.
Sex distribution (1990): male 49.45%; female 50.55%.
Age breakdown (1990): under 15, 45.3%; 15–29, 26.0%; 30–44, 15.0%; 45–59, 8.7%; 60 and over, 5.0%.
Population projection: (2000) 4,668,000; (2010) 6,238,000.
Doubling time: 20 years.
Ethnic composition (1981): Ewe-Adja 43.1%; Tem-Kabre 26.7%; Gurma 16.1%; Kebu-Akposo 3.8%; Ana-Ife (Yoruba) 3.2%; non-African 0.3%; other 6.8%.
Religious affiliation (1981): traditional beliefs 58.9%; Roman Catholic 21.5%; Muslim 12.1%; Protestant 6.8%; other 0.7%.
Major cities (1983): Lomé 366,476; Sokodé 48,098[2]; Kpalimé 27,669[2].

Vital statistics

Birth rate per 1,000 population (1991): 49.0 (world avg. 26.4).
Death rate per 1,000 population (1991): 13.0 (world avg. 9.2).
Natural increase rate per 1,000 population (1991): 36.0 (world avg. 17.2).
Total fertility rate (avg. births per childbearing woman; 1991): 7.1.
Marriage rate per 1,000 population (1979): 2.3.
Life expectancy at birth (1991): male 54.0 years; female 58.0 years.
Morbidity (reported cases of illness per 100,000 population; 1978): infectious and parasitic diseases 26,926; diseases of the respiratory system 9,296; diseases of the digestive system 8,007; accidents, poisoning, and trauma 7,172.

National economy

Budget (1992). Revenue: CFAF 95,800,000,000 (tax revenue 82.6%, nontax revenue 17.4%). Expenditures: CFAF 95,800,000,000 (1990; general public services 25.4%, education 23.1%, defense 14.9%, debt service 14.1%, economic services 7.4%, health 5.2%).
Production (metric tons except as noted). Agriculture, forestry, fishing (1992): cassava 480,000, yams 393,000, corn (maize) 239,000, sorghum 109,000, millet 82,000, cottonseed 55,000, rice 26,000, pulses 24,000, peanuts (groundnuts) 22,000, bananas 16,000, coconuts 14,000, palm oil 14,000, coffee 13,000, oranges 12,000, tomatoes 9,000, cacao beans 7,000; livestock (number of live animals) 2,000,000 goats, 1,500,000 sheep, 800,000 pigs, 320,000 cattle, 6,000,000 chickens; roundwood (1991) 1,234,000 cu m; fish catch (1991) 12,524. Mining and quarrying (1991): phosphate rock 2,965,000; salt 600,000[3]; marble 6,500[4]. Manufacturing (1987): cement 388,000[5]; wheat flour 58,000; beer 452,000 hectolitres; soft drinks 142,000 hectolitres[6]; footwear 29,000 pairs[7]. Construction (value added in CFAF; 1987): 14,200,000,000. Energy production (consumption): electricity (kW-hr; 1991) 60,000,000 (350,000,000); crude petroleum, none (n.a.); petroleum products (metric tons; 1991) none (171,000).
Gross national product (1992): U.S.$1,517,000,000 (U.S.$390 per capita).

Structure of gross domestic product and labour force

	1989 in value U.S.$'000,000	1989 % of total value	1988 labour force	1988 % of labour force
Agriculture	425	35.1	935,000	70.1
Mining	91	7.5	145,000 (Mining–Public utilities)	10.9 (Mining–Public utilities)
Manufacturing	86	7.2		
Construction	44	3.6		
Public utilities	49	4.0		
Transp. and commun.	82	6.8	254,000 (Transp.–Services)	19.0 (Transp.–Services)
Trade, Finance	274	22.6		
Pub. admin., defense	118	9.7		
Services	43	3.5		
TOTAL	1,212	100.0	1,334,000	100.0

Population economically active: total (1992) 1,501,000; activity rate of total population 39.9% (participation rates [1985]: ages 15–64, 69.5%; female 37.5%; unemployed [1980] 2.3%).

Price and earnings indexes (1985 = 100)

	1985	1986	1987	1988	1989	1990	1991
Consumer price index	100.0	104.1	104.2	104.0	103.2	104.2	104.7
Hourly earning index[8]	100.0	100.0	105.5	105.5	105.5	105.5	105.5

Household income and expenditure. Average household size (1980) 5.6; average annual income per household CFAF 102,000 (U.S.$452); sources of income: n.a.; expenditure (1970): food and beverages 60.9%, housing 9.9%, transportation 8.2%, clothing 7.7%, household durable goods 3.9%.
Public debt (external, outstanding; 1991): U.S.$1,143,000,000.
Tourism (1991): receipts from visitors U.S.$50,000,000; expenditures by nationals abroad U.S.$48,000,000.
Land use (1991): forested 29.3%; meadows and pastures 32.9%; agricultural and under permanent cultivation 12.4%; other 25.4%.

Foreign trade[9]

Balance of trade (current prices)

	1986	1987	1988	1989	1990	1991
CFAF '000,000,000	−29.7	−36.2	−52.5	−51.1	−63.1	−36.2
% of total	13.2%	19.8%	26.7%	24.6%	30.2%	20.2%

Imports (1991): CFAF 125,222,000,000 (1989; machinery and transport equipment 25.0%, food products 18.5%, cotton yarn and fabrics 11.3%, chemicals 9.8%, refined petroleum products 6.1%). *Major import sources* (1989): France 29.6%; The Netherlands 11.8%; W.Ger. 7.6%; U.S. 5.7%; Japan 4.2%; U.K. 4.2%; Italy 3.0%.
Exports (1991): CFAF 71,433,000,000 (1989; calcium phosphates 53.2%, cotton [ginned] 15.8%, coffee 9.0%, cocoa beans 5.0%, machinery and transport equipment 1.2%). *Major export destinations* (1989): Canada 12.5%; France 8.7%; Spain 7.7%; Italy 7.5%; The Netherlands 6.3%; U.K. 5.5%; Poland 4.4%; Portugal 3.7%; Benin 2.9%.

Transport and communications

Transport. Railroads (1992): length 326 mi, 525 km; passenger-km 109,000,000[10]; metric ton-km cargo 11,000,000[10]. Roads (1990): total length 7,545 km (paved 24%). Vehicles (1991): passenger cars 26,000; trucks and buses 16,000. Merchant marine (1992): vessels (100 gross tons and over) 8; total deadweight tonnage 20,633. Air transport (1990)[11]: passenger-km 232,329,000; metric ton-km cargo 39,374,000; airports (1993) with scheduled flights 1.
Communications. Daily newspapers (1990): total number 2; total circulation 10,000[12]; circulation per 1,000 population 2.9[12]. Radio (1992): 700,000 receivers (1 per 5.3 persons). Television (1992): 23,000 receivers (1 per 161 persons). Telephones (1991): 21,460 (1 per 170 persons).

Education and health

Education (1990)

	schools	teachers	students	student/teacher ratio
Primary (age 6–11)	2,471	10,739	597,503	55.6
Secondary (age 12–18)	314	4,182	120,572	28.8
Vocational	18[13]	371	7,132	19.2
Higher[14]	1[13]	324	7,732	23.9

Educational attainment (1981). Percentage of population age 15 and over having: no formal schooling 76.5%; primary education 13.5%; secondary 8.7%; higher 1.3%. *Literacy* (1990): total population age 15 and over literate 821,600 (43.0%); males 56.0%; females 31.0%.
Health: physicians (1985) 230 (1 per 12,992 persons); hospital beds (1982) 3,655 (1 per 752 persons); infant mortality rate (1991) 110.0.
Food (1988–90): daily per capita caloric intake 2,269 (vegetable products 95%, animal products 5%); 99% of FAO recommended minimum requirement.

Military

Total active duty personnel (1993): 5,250 (army 91.3%, navy 3.8%, air force 4.9%). *Military expenditure as percentage of GNP* (1991): 3.1% (world [1989] 4.9%); per capita expenditure U.S.$12.

[1]Three transitional governments from mid-1991 were followed by a "crisis government" in January 1993. New constitution approved by referendum in September 1992 but still not in effect by November 1993. Five major opposition groups boycotted the August 1993 presidential elections. [2]1981. [3]1982. [4]1990. [5]1991. [6]1988. [7]Excludes rubber. [8]January 1 figures. [9]Import figures are f.o.b. in balance of trade and c.i.f. for commodities and trading partners. [10]1986. [11]Air Afrique only. [12]For one daily only. [13]1987. [14]Universities only.

Tonga

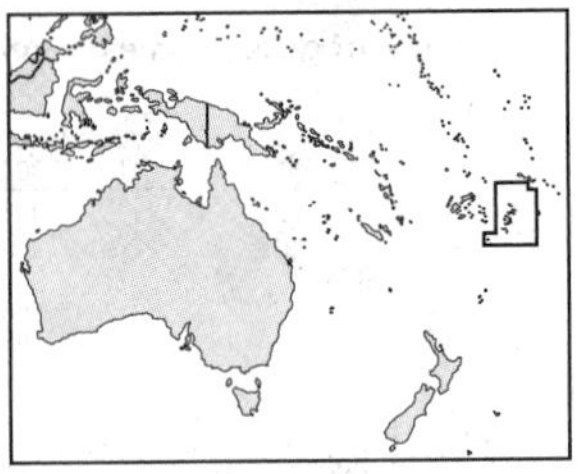

Official name: Pule'anga Fakatu'i 'o Tonga (Tongan); Kingdom of Tonga (English).
Form of government: constitutional monarchy with one legislative house (Legislative Assembly [30][1]).
Head of state and government: King assisted by Privy Council.
Capital: Nuku'alofa.
Official languages: Tongan; English.
Official religion: none.
Monetary unit: 1 pa'anga[2] (T$) = 100 seniti; valuation (Oct. 4, 1993) 1 U.S.$ = T$1.56; 1 £ = T$2.35.

Area and population

Divisions / Districts	Capitals	area sq mi	area sq km	population 1986 census
'Eua	'Ohonua	33.7	87.4	4,393
'Eua Fo'ou		...	...	1,995
'Eua Motu'a		...	...	2,398
Ha'apai	Pangai	42.5	110.0	8,979
Foa		...	...	1,409
Ha'ano		...	...	892
Lulunga		...	...	1,588
Mu'omu'a		...	...	897
Pangai		...	...	2,840
'Uiha		...	...	1,353
Niuas	Hihifo	27.7	71.7	2,379
Niua Fo'ou		...	...	763
Niua Toputapu		...	...	1,616
Tongatapu	Nuku'alofa	100.6	260.5	63,614
Kolofo'ou		...	...	15,782
Kolomotu'a		...	...	13,117
Kolovai		...	...	4,023
Lapaha		...	...	6,992
Nukunuku		...	...	5,790
Tatakamotonga		...	...	6,778
Vaini		...	...	11,132
Vava'u	Neiafu	46.0	119.2	15,170
Hahake		...	...	2,292
Hihifo		...	...	2,095
Leimatu'a		...	...	2,875
Motu		...	...	1,387
Neiafu		...	...	5,273
Pangaimotu		...	...	1,248
TOTAL LAND AREA		289.5[3]	749.9[3]	
INLAND WATER		11.4	29.6	
TOTAL		300.9	779.5	94,535

Demography

Population (1993): 99,100.
Density (1993)[4]: persons per sq mi 342.3, persons per sq km 132.2.
Urban-rural (1986): urban 30.7%; rural 69.3%.
Sex distribution (1986): male 50.30%; female 49.70%.
Age breakdown (1986): under 15, 40.6%; 15–29, 29.0%; 30–44, 13.8%; 45–59, 10.2%; 60–74, 5.0%; 75 and over, 1.4%.
Population projection: (2000) 103,000; (2010) 105,000.
Doubling time: 29 years.
Ethnic composition (1986): Tongan 95.5%; part Tongan 2.8%; other 1.7%.
Religious affiliation (1986): Free Wesleyan 43.0%; Roman Catholic 16.0%; Mormon 12.1%; Free Church of Tonga 11.0%; Church of Tonga 7.3%; other 10.6%.
Major cities (1984): Nuku'alofa (1986) 21,383; Mu'a 4,047; Neiafu 3,948; Haveluloto 3,136; Pangai-Hihifo 2,179.

Vital statistics

Birth rate per 1,000 population (1991): 30.7 (world avg. 26.4).
Death rate per 1,000 population (1991): 6.4 (world avg. 9.2).
Natural increase rate per 1,000 population (1991) 24.3 (world avg. 17.2).
Total fertility rate (avg. births per childbearing woman; 1988): 4.0.
Marriage rate per 1,000 population (1990): 7.3.
Divorce rate per 1,000 population (1985): 0.6.
Life expectancy at birth (1980–85): male 61.0 years; female 64.8 years.
Major causes of death per 100,000 population (1988)[5]: diseases of the circulatory system 112.2; malignant neoplasms 59.8; diseases of the respiratory system 37.7; infectious diseases 30.4; injuries and poisoning 18.9.

National economy

Budget (1993–94). Revenue: T$51,640,000 (foreign-trade taxes 50.5%, government services revenue 16.8%, direct taxes 11.0%, interest and rent 10.2%, indirect taxes 9.7%). Expenditures: T$51,620,000 (general administration 17.1%, education 16.9%, health 12.1%, law and order 11.6%, public works and communications 11.4%, public debt 8.5%, agriculture 5.1%).
Tourism (1991): receipts from visitors U.S.$10,000,000; expenditures by nationals abroad U.S.$2,000,000.
Production (metric tons except as noted). Agriculture, forestry, fishing (1992): yams 33,000, taro 27,000, coconuts 25,000, cassava 15,000, vegetables (including melons) 15,000, sweet potatoes 14,000, fruits (excluding melons) 13,000, copra 2,000; livestock (number of live animals) 97,000 pigs, 16,000 goats, 10,000 cattle, 4,000 horses; roundwood (1991) 5,000 cu m; fish catch (1991) 1,889. Mining and quarrying (1982): coral 150,000; sand 25,000. Manufacturing (output in T$; 1991): food products and beverages 7,281,000; chemical products 2,297,000; furniture 1,511,000; metal products 1,198,000; publishing and printing 1,068,000; wearing apparel 970,000. Construction (value in T$; 1984): residential 9,552,300; nonresidential 11,377,100. Energy production (consumption): electricity (kW-hr; 1990) 22,000,000 (22,000,000); petroleum (barrels; 1989) none (154,000); petroleum products (metric tons; 1990) n.a. (24,000).
Gross national product (1992): U.S.$136,000,000 (U.S.$1,350 per capita).

Structure of gross domestic product and labour force

	1988–89 in value T$'000[6]	1988–89 % of total value	1986 labour force	1986 % of labour force
Agriculture	24,200	33.7	10,429	42.9
Mining	600	0.8	27	0.1
Manufacturing	6,500	9.1	622	2.6
Construction	4,000	5.6	1,741	7.2
Public utilities	800	1.1	326	1.3
Transp. and commun.	4,400	6.1	1,176	4.8
Trade	6,900	9.6	1,612	6.6
Finance	2,900	4.0	465	1.9
Pub. admin., defense; Services	12,500	17.4	5,492	22.6
Other	9,000[7]	12.5[7]	2,434	10.0
TOTAL	71,800	100.0[8]	24,324	100.0

Public debt (external, outstanding; 1991): U.S.$50,200,000.
Population economically active (1986): total 24,324; activity rate 25.8% (participation rates: ages 15–64, 44.7%; female 21.5%; unemployed 9.1%).

Price and earnings indexes (1985 = 100)

	1986	1987	1988	1989	1990	1991	1992
Consumer price index	121.7	127.4	140.0	145.8	159.9	176.8	190.9
Quarterly earnings index[9]	112.0	101.7	130.9	176.2	175.0	200.0	...

Household income and expenditure. Average household size (1986) 6.3; income per household: n.a.; sources of income: n.a.; expenditure (1984)[10]: food 49.3%, household operations 13.3%, housing 10.5%, tobacco and beverages 7.0%, transportation 5.8%, clothing and footwear 5.6%.
Land use (1991): forested 11.1%; meadows and pastures 5.6%; agricultural and under permanent cultivation 66.7%; other 16.6%.

Foreign trade

Balance of trade (current prices)

	1987	1988	1989	1990	1991	1992
T$'000,000	–58.0	–50.3	–54.0	–49.8	–42.1	–53.9
% of total	74.4%	70.9%	73.5%	62.1%	47.4%	63.9%

Imports (1992): T$84,280,000 (food and live animals 25.4%, basic manufactures 20.4%, machinery and transport equipment 19.3%, mineral fuels 13.0%, chemicals 6.2%). *Major import sources:* New Zealand 29.7%; Australia 23.9%; Japan 12.5%; Fiji 11.9%; U.S. 8.5%.
Exports (1992): T$17,250,000 (squash 50.3%, vanilla beans 12.1%, fish 8.9%, root crops 3.9%, coconut products 3.2%). *Major export destinations:* Japan 51.6%; U.S. 21.6%; Australia 11.1%; New Zealand 10.0%; Fiji 2.0%.

Transport and communications

Transport. Railroads: none. Roads (1992): total length 386 km (paved 76%). Vehicles (1990): passenger cars 1,009, commercial vehicles 2,430. Merchant marine (1992): vessels (100 gross tons and over) 15; total deadweight tonnage 13,740. Air transport (1990): passenger-km 5,897,000; metric ton-km cargo 12,000; airports (1993) with scheduled flights 4.
Communications. Daily newspapers (1990): 1; total circulation 7,000; circulation per 1,000 population 74. Radio (1992): 66,000 receivers (1 per 1.5 persons). Television: n.a.[11]. Telephones (1990): 5,212 (1 per 18 persons).

Education and health

Education (1990)

	schools	teachers	students	student/teacher ratio
Primary (age 6–11)	115	689	16,522	24.0
Secondary (age 12–18)	57[12]	767	13,877	18.1
Voc., teacher tr.	9	65	872	13.4
Higher	1[13]	17[14]	705[14]	41.5[14]

Educational attainment (1976). Percentage of population age 25 and over having: no formal schooling 0.4%; incomplete primary education 37.3%; complete primary 12.4%; lower secondary 45.6%; secondary 0.1%; postsecondary 0.1%; higher 0.6%; special education 2.4%; other 1.1%. *Literacy* (1976): total population age 15 and over literate 46,456 (92.8%); males 23,372 (92.9%); females 23,084 (92.8%).
Health (1989): physicians 45 (1 per 2,130 persons); hospital beds 307 (1 per 312 persons); infant mortality rate per 1,000 live births (1988) 49.0.
Food (1988–90): daily per capita caloric intake 2,967 (vegetable products 81%, animal products 19%); 130% of FAO recommended minimum requirement.

Military

Total active duty personnel (1991): Tonga has a national police (defense) force of about 300. *Military expenditure as percentage of GNP* (1989): 4.9% (world 4.9%); per capita expenditure U.S.$21.

[1]Includes 21 nonelective seats. [2]The pa'anga is now linked to an international basket of currencies rather than to the Australian dollar. [3]Total includes 39.0 sq mi (101.1 sq km) of uninhabited islands. [4]Density is based on land area. [5]Excludes deaths from nonintestinal infectious diseases. [6]At constant 1981–82 prices. [7]Includes indirect taxes less subsidies. [8]Detail does not add to total given because of rounding. [9]In manufacturing. [10]Current weight of consumer price index components. [11]Tonga has no authorized television service, but a "pirate" station began transmitting in mid-1984. [12]1987. [13]1986. [14]1985.

Trinidad and Tobago

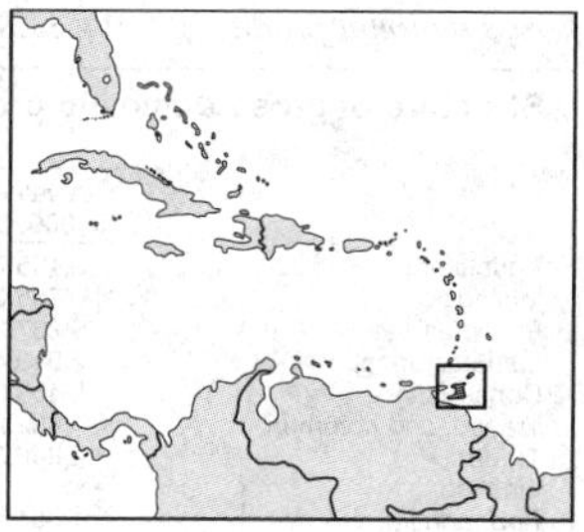

Official name: Republic of Trinidad and Tobago.
Form of government: multiparty republic with two legislative houses (Senate [31]; House of Representatives [36[1]]).
Chief of state: President.
Head of government: Prime Minister.
Capital: Port of Spain.
Official language: English.
Official religion: none.
Monetary unit: 1 Trinidad and Tobago dollar (TT$) = 100 cents; valuation (Oct. 4, 1993) 1 U.S.$ = TT$5.48; 1 £ = TT$8.30.

Area and population

Counties	Capitals	area sq mi	area sq km	population 1990 census[2]
Caroni	Chaguanas	191.0	494.7	120,508
Nariva/Mayaro	Rio Claro	349.0	903.9	36,781
St. Andrew/St. David	Sangre Grande	360.0	932.4	62,944
St. George	...	354.0	916.9	445,620
St. Patrick	Siparia	252.0	652.7	120,129
Victoria	Princes Town	315.0	815.9	210,833
Unitary State				
Tobago	Scarborough	116.0	300.4	50,282
Cities				
Port of Spain	—	4.0	10.4	50,878
San Fernando	—	3.0	7.8	30,092
Boroughs				
Chaguanas		23.0	59.6	56,601
Arima	—	4.0	10.4	29,695
Point Fortin	—	9.0	23.3	20,025
TOTAL		1,980.1[3]	5,128.4	1,234,388

Demography

Population (1993): 1,249,000.
Density (1993): persons per sq mi 630.8, persons per sq km 243.5.
Urban-rural (1990): urban 69.1%; rural 30.9%.
Sex distribution (1991): male 53.33%; female 46.67%.
Age breakdown (1991): under 15, 30.5%; 15–29, 26.4%; 30–44, 22.1%; 45–59, 12.6%; 60 and over, 8.4%.
Population projection: (2000) 1,304,000; (2010) 1,386,000.
Doubling time: 60 years.
Ethnic composition (1986): black 43.0%; East Indian 36.0%; mixed 16.0%; white 2.0%; Chinese 1.0%; other 2.0%.
Religious affiliation (1990): Christian 70.0%, of which Roman Catholic 36.0%, Anglican 13.0%; Hindu 23.0%; Muslim 6.0%; other 1.0%.
Major cities (1990): Chaguanas 56,601; Port of Spain 50,878; San Fernando 30,092; Arima 29,695; Point Fortin 20,025; Scarborough 3,000.

Vital statistics

Birth rate per 1,000 population (1991): 18.1 (world avg. 26.4).
Death rate per 1,000 population (1991): 6.6 (world avg. 9.2).
Natural increase rate per 1,000 population (1991): 11.5 (world avg. 17.2).
Total fertility rate (avg. births per childbearing woman; 1991): 2.8.
Marriage rate per 1,000 population (1991): 5.7.
Divorce rate per 1,000 population (1991): 1.1.
Life expectancy at birth (1990–95): male 69.7 years; female 74.7 years.
Major causes of death per 100,000 population (1991): diseases of the circulatory system 260.0, of which ischemic heart diseases 113.5, cerebrovascular disease 75.9; malignant neoplasms (cancers) 83.4; diabetes mellitus 83.3.

National economy

Budget (1992): Revenue: TT$6,176,000,000 (individual income taxes 19.7%, petroleum-sector corporate taxes 15.5%, value-added taxes 15.3%, import duties 9.2%, nontax revenues 7.9%). Expenditures: TT$6,943,400,000 (current expenditures 92.0%, development expenditures 8.0%).
Tourism (1991): receipts from visitors U.S.$101,000,000; expenditures by nationals abroad U.S.$111,000,000.
Production (metric tons except as noted). Agriculture, forestry, fishing (1991): sugarcane 1,292,000[4], coconuts 40,000, rice 19,950, oranges 8,000, bananas 6,000, grapefruit 4,000, corn (maize) 3,000, cocoa 1,140[4], coffee 706[4]; livestock (number of live animals) 60,000 cattle, 52,000 goats, 50,000 pigs; roundwood 72,000 cu m; fish catch 3,300[5]. Mining and quarrying (1992): natural asphalt 18,800. Manufacturing (1992): anhydrous ammonia and urea (nitrogenous fertilizers) 2,362,200; steel billets 552,800; cement 482,000; methanol 481,700; steel wire rods 446,100; raw sugar 110,400; beer and stout 395,000 hectolitres; rum 164,200 proof hectolitres. Construction (authorized; 1991): residential 207,400 sq m; nonresidential 32,700 sq m. Energy production (consumption): electricity (kW-hr; 1991) 3,636,000,000 (3,105,000,000[5]); coal, none (none); crude petroleum (barrels; 1992) 49,550,000 (33,989,000[5]); petroleum products (metric tons; 1991) 5,359,000 (976,000[5]); natural gas (cu m; 1992) 7,335,300,000 (5,306,900,000).
Land use (1990): forested 42.9%; meadows and pastures 2.1%; agricultural and under permanent cultivation 23.4%; other 31.6%.
Public debt (external, outstanding; 1991): U.S.$1,817,000,000.
Gross national product (at current market prices; 1991): U.S.$4,525,000,000 (U.S.$3,620 per capita).

Structure of gross domestic product and labour force

	1992 in value TT$'000,000	1992 % of total value	1991 labour force	1991 % of labour force
Agriculture[6]	585	2.5	51,100	10.4
Petroleum[7], natural gas, quarrying	5,283	22.8	23,000	4.7
Manufacturing[8]	2,072	9.0	53,300	10.8
Construction	1,935	8.4	74,500	15.1
Public utilities	371	1.6	9,200	1.9
Transp. and commun.	2,029	8.8	29,600	6.0
Trade	3,530	15.3	82,800	16.8
Finance, real estate	2,766	12.0	32,400	6.6
Pub. admin., defense	2,757	11.9	134,900	27.4
Services	1,516	6.6		
Other	285[9]	1.2[9]	1,200	0.2
TOTAL	23,129	100.0[3]	492,200[3]	100.0[3]

Population economically active (1991): total 492,200; activity rate of total population 39.8% (participation rates: ages 15–64, 64.4%; female 36.0%; unemployed [1992] 19.7%).

Price and earnings indexes (1985 = 100)

	1987	1988	1989	1990	1991	1992	1993
Consumer price index	119.3	128.5	143.2	159.0	165.1	175.8	191.6[10]
Weekly earnings index	106.2	108.0	108.9	115.2	115.3	118.6[11]	...

Household income and expenditure. Average household size (1990) 4.1; income per household (1988) TT$17,083 (U.S.$4,444); sources of income: n.a.; expenditure (1981–82): food and beverages 27.7%, housing 22.7%, clothing and footwear 15.5%, transportation 13.2%, household furnishings 8.8%, other 12.1%.

Foreign trade[12]

Balance of trade (current prices)

	1987	1988	1989	1990	1991	1992
TT$'000,000	+877	+1,114	+1,517	+3,480	+1,352	+1,862
% of total	9.1%	11.4%	12.7%	24.5%	8.7%	13.3%

Imports (1991): TT$7,085,000,000 (nondurable consumer goods 19.4%, of which food 11.5%; capital goods 16.8%; mineral fuels and lubricants 14.7%; chemical products [mostly medicines and plastics] 12.6%). *Major import sources* (1992): United States 41.4%; EEC 15.7%, of which United Kingdom 7.8%; Venezuela 9.7%; Japan 6.8%; Canada 5.1%.
Exports (1991): TT$8,437,000,000 (petroleum products 33.1%; crude petroleum 30.7%; ammonia 9.2%; iron and steel bar rods 5.6%; urea 3.4%; methanol 3.1%; sugar 1.6%). *Major export destinations* (1992): United States 47.0%; Caricom 13.8%, of which Barbados 3.4%, Guyana 2.3%; EEC 5.4%.

Transport and communications

Transport. Railroads: none. Roads (1987): total length 4,906 mi, 7,895 km (paved 46%). Vehicles (1991): passenger cars 150,196; trucks and buses 60,006. Merchant marine (1992): vessels (100 gross tons and over) 53; total deadweight tonnage 17,533. Air transport (1991): passenger-mi 1,944,000,000, passenger-km 3,129,000,000; short ton-mi cargo 10,100,000, metric ton-km cargo 14,800,000; airports (1993) with scheduled flights 2.
Communications. Daily newspapers (1992): total number 4; total circulation 174,852; circulation per 1,000 population 138. Radio (1992): 700,000 receivers (1 per 1.8 persons). Television (1992): 250,000 receivers (1 per 5.1 persons). Telephones (1991): 226,012 (1 per 5.5 persons).

Education and health

Education (1990–91)

	schools	teachers	students	student/teacher ratio
Primary (age 5–11)	476	7,473	193,922	25.9
Secondary (age 12–16)	100[13]	4,856	96,599	19.9
Vocational	...	...	731	...
Higher[14]	1	471	4,541	9.6

Educational attainment (1980). Percentage of population age 25 and over having: no formal schooling 7.1%; primary education 66.5%; secondary 21.7%; higher 2.7%; other 2.0%. *Literacy* (1985): total population age 15 and over literate 751,600 (96.1%).
Health (1990): physicians 802 (1 per 1,543 persons); hospital beds[15] 3,894 (1 per 318 persons); infant mortality rate per 1,000 live births (1991) 18.0.
Food (1988–90): daily per capita caloric intake 2,770 (vegetable products 85%, animal products 15%); 114% of FAO recommended minimum requirement.

Military

Total active duty personnel (1992): 2,650 (army 100.0%). *Military expenditure as percentage of GNP* (1989): 1.6% (world 4.9%); per capita expenditure U.S.$48.

[1]Excludes speaker, who may be elected from outside the House of Representatives. [2]Preliminary data. [3]Detail does not add to total given because of rounding. [4]1992. [5]1990. [6]Includes sugar industry. [7]Includes refined petroleum. [8]Excludes refined petroleum and sugar industries. [9]Net of value-added taxes less imputed bank service charges. [10]May. [11]August. [12]Exports f.o.b.; imports c.i.f. [13]1988–89. [14]1991–92; University of the West Indies, St. Augustine campus. [15]Includes nursing homes.

Tunisia

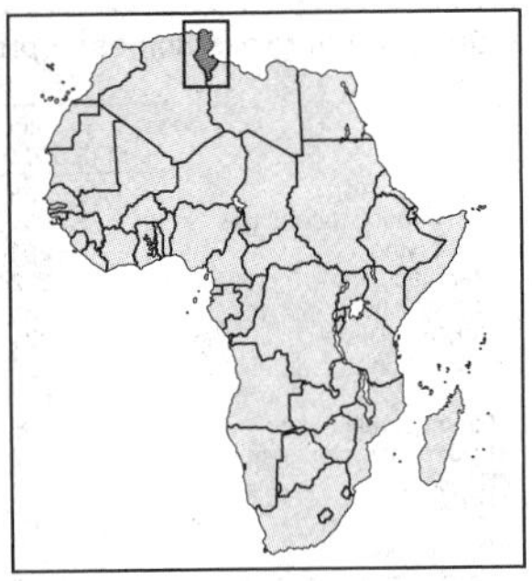

Official name: al-Jumhūrīyah at-Tūnisīyah (Republic of Tunisia).
Form of government: multiparty republic with one legislative house (Chamber of Deputies [141]).
Chief of state: President.
Head of government: Prime Minister.
Capital: Tunis.
Official language: Arabic.
Official religion: Islam.
Monetary unit: 1 dinar (D) = 1,000 millimes; valuation (Oct. 4, 1993) D 1.00 = U.S.$0.99 = £0.65.

Area and population

		area		population
Governorates	**Capitals**	sq mi	sq km	1991[1] estimate
al-Ariānah	al-Ariānah	602	1,558	548,700
Bājah	Bājah	1,374	3,558	301,500
Banzart	Bizerte (Banzart)	1,423	3,685	452,400
Bin ʿArūs	Bin ʿArūs	294	761	316,200
Jundūbah	Jundūbah	1,198	3,102	407,400
al-Kāf	al-Kāf	1,917	4,965	272,300
Madanīn	Madanīn	3,316	8,588	357,800
al-Mahdīyah	al-Mahdīyah	1,145	2,966	318,200
al-Munastīr	al-Munastīr	393	1,019	333,900
Nābul	Nābul	1,076	2,788	538,300
Qābis	Qābis	2,770	7,175	282,000
Qafṣah	Qafṣah	3,471	8,990	283,400
al-Qaṣrayn	al-Qaṣrayn	3,114	8,066	362,600
al-Qayrawān	al-Qayrawān	2,591	6,712	497,800
Qibilī	Qibilī	8,527	22,084	117,800
Ṣafāqis	Ṣafāqis	2,913	7,545	677,600
Sīdī Bū Zayd	Sīdī Bū Zayd	2,700	6,994	345,100
Siliānah	Siliānah	1,788	4,631	246,200
Sūsah	Sūsah	1,012	2,621	398,700
Tatāuīn	Tatāuīn	15,015	38,889	121,000
Tawzar	Tawzar	1,822	4,719	78,100
Tūnis	Tunis (Tūnis)	134	346	833,600
Zaghwān	Zaghwān	1,069	2,768	131,300
TOTAL		63,378[2]	164,150[2]	8,222,000[3]

Demography

Population (1993): 8,530,000.
Density (1993): persons per sq mi 134.5, persons per sq km 52.0.
Urban-rural (1985): urban 53.0%; rural 47.0%.
Sex distribution (1991): male 50.69%; female 49.31%.
Age breakdown (1991): under 15, 36.6%; 15–29, 28.9%; 30–44, 16.9%; 45–59, 10.1%; 60–74, 5.9%; 75 and over, 1.6%.
Population projection: (2000) 9,670,000; (2010) 11,161,000.
Doubling time: 28 years.
Ethnic composition (1983): Arab 98.2%; Berber 1.2%; French 0.2%; Italian 0.1%; other 0.3%.
Religious affiliation (1980): Sunnī Muslim 99.4%; Christian 0.3%; Jewish 0.1%; other 0.2%.
Major cities (commune; 1989): Tunis 620,149; Ṣafāqis 221,770; Aryānah 131,403; Ettadhamen 111,793; Sūsah 101,071.

Vital statistics

Birth rate per 1,000 population (1991): 25.0 (world avg. 26.4); (1974) legitimate 99.8%; illegitimate 0.2%.
Death rate per 1,000 population (1991): 6.3 (world avg. 9.2).
Natural increase rate per 1,000 population (1991): 18.7 (world avg. 17.2).
Total fertility rate (avg. births per childbearing woman; 1990–95): 3.4.
Marriage rate per 1,000 population (1991): 7.2.
Divorce rate per 1,000 population (1991): 1.5.
Life expectancy at birth (1990–95): male 66.4 years; female 68.7 years.
Major causes of death per 100,000 population: n.a.; however, of approximately 9,000 deaths[4] for which a cause was reported in 1988, complications of pregnancy and childbirth 25.0%; diseases of the circulatory system 20.7%; infectious and parasitic diseases 19.7%; accidents and poisoning 10.9%.

National economy

Budget (1991). Revenue: D 2,966,524,000 (indirect taxes 60.8%, direct taxes 17.0%, investment 12.5%). Expenditures: D 3,015,401,000 (finance 29.5%, education 21.8%, national economy 9.8%, interior affairs 9.7%, health 8.0%, defense 5.8%, agriculture 3.6%).
Public debt (external, outstanding; 1991): U.S.$7,369,000,000.
Land use (1990): forested 4.2%; meadows and pastures 21.6%; agricultural and under permanent cultivation 29.5%; other 44.7%.
Production (metric tons except as noted). Agriculture, forestry, fishing (1991): wheat 1,786,000, barley 721,000, tomatoes 590,000, olives 330,000, watermelons 248,000, potatoes 220,000, sugar beets 210,000, oranges 117,000, grapes 90,000, dates 75,000, alfalfa 70,000[5]; livestock (number of live animals) 6,290,000 sheep, 1,313,000 goats, 631,000 cattle; roundwood (1990) 3,249,000 cu m; fish catch (1990) 92,129. Mining and quarrying (1991): phosphate rock 6,707,000[6]; iron ore 280,000; zinc 4,900. Manufacturing (1991): cement 4,195,000; phosphoric acid 912,500; flour 566,400; crude steel 192,000[7]. Construction (1982): residential building authorized 2,679,000 sq m. Energy production (consumption): electricity (kW-hr; 1990) 5,536,000,000 (5,506,000,000); coal (metric tons; 1990) none (15,000); crude petroleum (barrels; 1990) 34,893,000 (9,065,000); petroleum products (metric tons; 1990) 1,658,000 (3,005,000); natural gas (cu m; 1990) 303,900,000 (2,925,900,000).

Gross national product (1991): U.S.$12,417,000,000 (U.S.$1,450 per capita).

Structure of gross domestic product and labour force

	1991		1989	
	in value D '000,000	% of total value	labour force	% of labour force
Agriculture	2,135.2	17.8	543,100	23.0
Mining	765.8	6.4	36,600	1.6
Public utilities	237.2	2.0		
Manufacturing	2,049.4	17.1	422,300	17.9
Construction	459.8	3.9	295,200	12.5
Transp. and commun.	832.2	7.0		
Trade	2,840.3	23.7	349,000	14.8
Finance				
Pub. admin., defense	1,591.4	13.3	465,400	19.7
Services				
Other	1,058.1[8]	8.8[8]	249,000[9]	10.5[9]
TOTAL	11,970.4[3]	100.0	2,360,600	100.0

Population economically active (1989): total 2,360,000, activity rate of total population 28.8% (participation rates: ages 15–64, 42.2%; female 20.9%; unemployed 13.4%).

Price and earnings indexes (1985 = 100)

	1986	1987	1988	1989	1990	1991	1992
Consumer price index	105.8	113.4	120.6	129.5	138.3	149.7	157.8
Monthly earnings index	...	...	...	...	...	...	...

Household income and expenditure. Average household size (1989) 6.1; income per household: n.a.; sources of income: n.a.; expenditure (1985): food and beverages 39.0%, household durable goods 11.2%, housing 10.7%, transportation 9.0%, recreation 7.1%, clothing and footwear 6.0%, energy 5.1%, health care 3.0%, education 1.8%, other 7.1%.
Tourism (1990): receipts from visitors U.S.$953,000,000; expenditures by nationals abroad U.S.$179,000,000.

Foreign trade

Balance of trade (current prices)

	1987	1988	1989	1990	1991	1992
D '000,000	−569.9	−898.9	−1,089.8	−1,439.7	−1,037.5	−1,726.1
% of total	13.9%	17.9%	16.3%	18.9%	13.1%	24.2%

Imports (1992): D 5,689,000,000 (textiles 10.9%, chemical products 2.8%, iron and steel products 2.7%, clothing and accessories 2.6%, olive oil 2.4%, pharmaceutical products 2.2%). *Major import sources:* France 25.4%; Italy 18.1%; Germany 14.0%; U.S. 5.0%; Belgium 4.7%; Spain 3.1%; Japan 2.3%.
Exports (1992): D 3,567,000,000 (clothing and accessories 30.0%, petroleum and petroleum products 13.3%, phosphoric acid 4.0%, olive oil 3.9%, phosphates 3.4%, chemical products 3.3%). *Major export destinations:* France 27.1%; Italy 17.1%; Germany 17.0%; Belgium 6.9%; Libya 4.4%; Spain 2.7%; The Netherlands 2.6%.

Transport and communications

Transport. Railroads (1991): route length 1,343 mi, 2,162 km; passenger-mi 634,000,000, passenger-km 1,020,000,000; short ton-mi cargo 1,242,000,000, metric ton-km cargo 1,813,000,000. Roads (1989): total length 18,133 mi, 29,183 km (paved 60%). Vehicles (1989): passenger cars 321,101; trucks and buses 208,596. Merchant marine (1992): vessels (100 gross tons and over) 77; total deadweight tonnage 443,290. Air transport (1991): passenger-mi 875,000,000, passenger-km 1,408,000,000; short ton-mi cargo 12,200,000, metric ton-km cargo 17,800,000; airports (1993) 5.
Communications. Daily newspapers (1992): total number 6; total circulation 230,000[10]; circulation per 1,000 population 28[10]. Radio (1992): 1,700,000 receivers (1 per 4.9 persons). Television (1992): 650,000 receivers (1 per 13 persons). Telephones (1992): 337,063 (1 per 24 persons).

Education and health

Education (1991–92)

	schools	teachers	students	student/ teacher ratio
Primary (age 6–11)	3,940	51,948	1,426,215	27.5
Secondary (age 12–18)	599	25,445	589,674	23.2
Voc., teacher tr.[11, 12]	...	237	3,839	16.2
Higher	...	3,901[13]	76,097	14.0[13]

Educational attainment (1989). Percentage of population age 25 and over having: no formal schooling 54.9%; primary 26.9%; secondary 14.3%; higher 3.4%; unspecified 0.5%. *Literacy* (1990): total population age 15 and over literate 65.3%; males literate 74.2%; females literate 56.3%.
Health (1989): physicians 4,313 (1 per 1,834 persons); hospital beds (1991) 16,116 (1 per 510 persons); infant mortality rate (1990–95) 44.0.
Food (1988–90): daily per capita caloric intake 3,122 (vegetable products 91%, animal products 9%); 131% of FAO recommended minimum requirement.

Military

Total active duty personnel (1992): 35,000 (army 77.1%, navy 12.9%, air force 10.0%). *Military expenditure as percentage of GNP* (1989): 2.8% (world 4.9%); per capita expenditure U.S.$34.

[1]January. [2]Total includes 3,714 sq mi (9,620 sq km) of territory in the southwest part of Tunisia that is not distributed by governorate. [3]Detail does not add to total given because of rounding. [4]Recorded deaths from urban areas only, including complete figures for Tunis. [5]1988. [6]1990. [7]1989. [8]Indirect taxes less subsidies. [9]Includes 218,300 unemployed. [10]Circulation for four dailies only. [11]1987–88. [12]Teacher training only. [13]1988–89.

Turkey

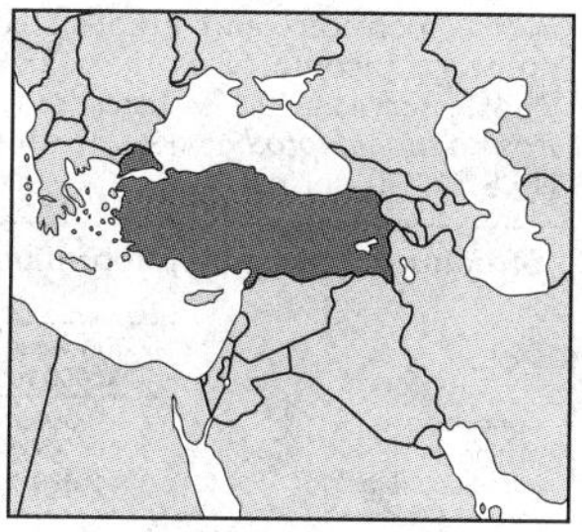

Official name: Türkiye Cumhuriyeti (Republic of Turkey).
Form of government: multiparty republic with one legislative house (Turkish Grand National Assembly [450]).
Chief of state: President.
Head of government: Prime Minister.
Capital: Ankara.
Official language: Turkish.
Official religion: none.
Monetary unit: 1 Turkish lira (LT) = 100 kurush; valuation (Oct. 4, 1993) 1 U.S.$ = LT 12,073; 1 £ = LT 18,291.

Area and population

Geographic regions[1]	area sq mi	area sq km	population 1990 census
Akdeniz kıyısı (Mediterranean Coast)	22,933	59,395	5,443,867
Batı Anadolu (West Anatolia)	29,742	77,031	3,864,661
Doğu Anadolu (East Anatolia)	68,074	180,180	6,867,415
Güneydoğu Anadolu (Southeast Anatolia)	15,347	35,880	2,699,776
İç Anadolu (Central Anatolia)	91,254	236,347	13,096,179
Karadeniz kıyısı (Black Sea Coast)	31,388	81,295	6,827,304
Marmara ve Ege kıyıları (Marmara and Aegean coasts)	33,035	85,560	11,698,384
Trakya (Thrace)	9,175	23,764	5,975,449
TOTAL	300,948	779,452	56,473,035

Demography

Population (1993): 59,869,000.
Density (1993): persons per sq mi 198.9, persons per sq km 76.8.
Urban-rural (1990): urban 61.3%; rural 38.7%.
Sex distribution (1990): male 51.20%; female 48.80%.
Age breakdown (1990): under 15, 35.6%; 15–29, 28.8%; 30–44, 17.9%; 45–59, 10.7%; 60–74, 5.5%; 75 and over, 1.5%.
Population projection: (2000) 69,694,000; (2010) 78,524,000.
Doubling time: 32 years.
Ethnic composition (1983): Turkish 85.7%; Kurdish 10.6%; Arab 1.6%; Circassian 0.3%; Turkmen 0.3%; Georgian 0.2%; other 1.3%.
Religious affiliation (1986): Sunnī Muslim *c.* 90.0%; Alevi (nonorthodox Shīʿi sect) *c.* 9.6%; Christian *c.* 0.4%, of which Eastern Orthodox *c.* 0.2%.
Major cities (1990): Istanbul 6,620,241; Ankara 2,559,471; İzmir 1,757,414; Adana 916,150; Bursa 834,576; Gaziantep 603,434; Konya 513,346.

Vital statistics

Birth rate per 1,000 population (1991): 28.0 (world avg. 26.4).
Death rate per 1,000 population (1991): 6.0 (world avg. 9.2).
Natural increase rate per 1,000 population (1991): 22.0 (world avg. 17.2).
Total fertility rate (avg. births per childbearing woman; 1991): 3.4.
Marriage rate per 1,000 population (1989): 7.9.
Divorce rate per 1,000 population (1989): 0.5.
Life expectancy at birth (1991): male 68.0 years; female 72.0 years.
Major causes of death per 100,000 population: n.a.; however, of the 150,475 deaths (approximately 30% of total deaths[2]) for which a cause was reported in 1989, diseases of the circulatory system represented 41.2%; malignant neoplasms (cancers) 10.1%; accidental death 3.3%; pneumonia 3.1%.

National economy

Budget (1992). Revenue: LT 179,449,000,000,000 (direct taxes 39.9%; indirect taxes 39.2%; nontax revenue 17.8%). Expenditures: LT 223,055,000,000,000 (current expenditures 50.7%; development expenditures 49.3%, of which interest payments 18.1%, investment expenditures 14.4%).
Public debt (external, outstanding; December 1992): U.S.$42,046,000,000.
Tourism (1992): receipts from visitors U.S.$3,639,000,000; expenditures by nationals abroad U.S.$776,000,000.
Production (in '000 metric tons except as noted). Agriculture, forestry, fishing (1991): wheat 20,400, sugar beets 15,097, barley 7,800, potatoes 4,600, grapes 3,500, corn (maize) 2,100, apples 1,900, cottonseed 984, sunflower seeds 800, oranges 770, olives 720, lentils 700, cotton (lint) 616, hazelnuts 320, tobacco 243, sultana raisins 130; livestock (number of live animals) 40,553,000 sheep, 11,377,000 cattle; roundwood 15,764,000 cu m; fish catch (1990) 382,170. Mining (1990)[3]: coal 1,923; crude petroleum 1,773; boron minerals 573; chrome 219. Manufacturing (1989)[3]: refined petroleum 6,371; spinning and weaving of textiles 4,921; food products 4,445; iron and steel 3,727; industrial chemicals 2,680; paints, soaps, and pharmaceuticals 2,273. Construction (completed; 1991): residential 46,377,000 sq m; nonresidential 16,165,000 sq m. Energy production (consumption): electricity (kW-hr; 1991) 60,219,000,000 ([1990] 56,813,000,000); coal (metric tons; 1991) 42,947,000 ([1990] 52,227,000); crude petroleum (barrels; 1990) 20,764,000 (171,595,000); petroleum products (metric tons; 1990) 20,370,000 (19,870,000); natural gas (cu m; 1990) 181,952,000 (3,065,322,000).
Household income and expenditure (1987). Average household size 4.8; income per household LT 3,680,500 (U.S.$4,294); sources of income: self-employment 51.4%, wages and salaries 24.1%, rent and interest 13.7%, transfers 10.8%; expenditure: food and beverages 33.1%, housing 14.7%, clothing 12.3%, household furnishings 11.5%.
Gross national product (at current market prices; 1991): U.S.$103,888,000,000 (U.S.$1,820 per capita).

Structure of gross domestic product and labour force

	1991 in value LT '000,000'000[4]	% of total value	labour force	% of labour force
Agriculture	99,376	17.4	9,667,524	45.9
Mining	10,860	1.9	144,215	0.7
Manufacturing	111,236	19.5	3,154,902	15.0
Construction	37,387	6.6	1,064,437	5.1
Public utilities	14,334	2.5	15,624	0.1
Transportation and communications	84,115	14.7	851,120	4.0
Trade	100,152	17.5	2,312,387	11.0
Finance, real estate	42,076	7.4	446,322	2.1
Pub. admin., defense	58,879	10.3 }	2,797,667	13.3
Services	12,281	2.2 }		
Other	—	—	590,795[5]	2.8[5]
TOTAL	570,696	100.0	21,044,993	100.0

Population economically active (1991): total 21,044,993; activity rate of total population 37.5% (participation rates: ages 15–64, 59.6%; female 31.1%; unemployed [1992] 11.8%).

Price and earnings indexes (1985 = 100)

	1986	1987	1988	1989	1990	1991	1992
Consumer price index	135	187	328	535	858	1,424	2,422
Daily earnings index[6]	132	206	344	766	1,430	3,487	6,062

Land use (1990): forested 26.2%; meadows and pastures 11.0%; agricultural and under permanent cultivation 36.3%; other 26.5%.

Foreign trade[7]

Balance of trade (current prices)

	1986	1987	1988	1989	1990	1991
U.S.$'000,000	−2,960	−3,204	−1,900	−3,316	−8,140	−6,349
% of total	16.5%	13.6%	7.5%	12.5%	23.9%	18.9%

Imports (1992): U.S.$22,871,000,000 (nonelectrical machinery 19.2%; crude petroleum 12.5%; transport equipment 10.6%; iron and steel 10.1%; electrical and electronic equipment 8.4%). *Major import sources:* Germany 16.4%; United States 11.4%; Italy 8.4%; Saudi Arabia 7.3%; France 5.9%; former U.S.S.R. 5.4%; United Kingdom 5.2%; Japan 4.9%.
Exports (1992): U.S.$14,715,000,000 (textiles 36.1%, of which clothing 24.9%; agricultural products 15.4%; iron and steel 14.3%; manufactured agricultural products 8.4%). *Major export destinations:* Germany 25.5%; Italy 13.0%; United States 5.9%; France 5.5%; United Kingdom 5.4%; former U.S.S.R. 4.7%.

Transport and communications

Transport. Railroads (1992): route length (1991) 5,238 mi, 8,429 km; passenger-mi 3,892,000,000, passenger-km 6,264,000,000; short ton-mi cargo 5,648,000,000, metric ton-km cargo 8,246,000,000. Roads (1991): total length 228,421 mi, 367,608 km (paved [1988] 14%). Vehicles (1991): passenger cars 1,864,344; trucks and buses 756,905. Merchant marine (1992): vessels (100 gross tons and over) 880; total deadweight tonnage 7,114,289. Air transport (1992)[8]: passenger-mi 3,491,000,000, passenger-km 5,619,000,000; short ton-mi cargo 80,063,000, metric ton-km cargo 116,890,000; airports (1993) with scheduled flights 24.
Communications. Daily newspapers (1991)[9]: total number 31; total circulation 4,054,000; circulation per 1,000 population 71. Radio (1992): total number of receivers 7,100,000 (1 per 8.3 persons). Television (1992): total number of receivers 10,530,000 (1 per 5.6 persons). Telephones (1991): 8,199,568 (1 per 7.1 persons).

Education and health

Education (1990–91)

	schools	teachers	students	student/teacher ratio
Primary (age 6–10)	51,055	225,852	6,861,711	30.4
Secondary (age 11–16)	7,185[10]	109,136	2,897,655	26.6
Voc., teacher tr.	2,542[10]	50,265	910,487	18.1
Higher	387[10]	34,469	749,921	21.8

Educational attainment (1985). Percentage of population age 25 and over having: no formal schooling 40.1%; primary education 44.4%; secondary 11.6%; higher 3.9%. *Literacy* (1990): total population age 15 and over literate 29,400,000 (80.7%); males literate 16,800,000 (89.7%); females literate 12,600,000 (71.1%).
Health (1990): physicians 50,639 (1 per 1,108 persons); hospital beds 120,738 (1 per 465 persons); infant mortality rate per 1,000 live births (1991) 54.0.
Food (1988–90): daily per capita caloric intake 3,196 (vegetable products 92%, animal products 8%); 127% of FAO recommended minimum requirement.

Military

Total active duty personnel (1992): 560,300 (army 80.3%, navy 9.3%, air force 10.4%). *Military expenditure as percentage of GNP* (1989): 4.1% (world 4.9%); per capita expenditure U.S.$57.

[1]Administratively divided into 73 provinces. [2]Province and district centres only. [3]Value added in LT '000,000,000. [4]At factor cost. [5]Unemployed persons not previously employed. [6]Private sector only. [7]Imports are f.o.b. in balance of trade and c.i.f. in commodities and trading partners. [8]Turkish Airlines only. [9]Principal daily newspapers in Istanbul, Ankara, and five other large cities. [10]1989–90.

Turkmenistan

Official name: Türkmenistan Jumhuriyäti (Republic of Turkmenistan).
Form of government: republic with a single legislative body (Majlis[1] [50]).
Head of state and government: President.
Capital: Ashgabat.
Official language: Turkmen.
Official religion: none.
Monetary unit (until Oct. 31, 1993): 1 ruble = 100 kopecks; valuation (Oct. 4, 1993) free rate, 1 U.S.$ = 1,165 rubles; 1 £ = 1,765 rubles. The manat was introduced Sept. 1, 1993, at a 1,000 to 1 ratio with the Russian ruble and circulated parallel with it; on Nov. 1, 1993, the manat became the sole legal tender at par with the U.S. dollar.

Area and population

		area		population
Provinces	Capitals	sq mi	sq km	1991 estimate
Balkan	Nebit-Dag	90,300	233,900	925,500
Chärjew	Chardzhou	36,200	93,800	774,700
Mary	Mary	33,500	86,800	859,500
Dashhowuz	Tashauz	28,400	73,600	738,000
City				
Ashgabat	—	...	...	416,400
TOTAL		188,500[2]	488,100	3,714,100

Demography

Population (1993): 4,294,000.
Density (1993): persons per sq mi 22.8, persons per sq km 8.8.
Urban-rural (1992): urban 45.1%; rural 54.9%.
Sex distribution (1989): male 49.30%; female 50.70%.
Age breakdown (1989): under 15, 40.5%; 15–29, 28.8%; 30–44, 15.5%; 45–59, 9.1%; 60–74, 4.7%; 75 and over, 1.4%.
Population projection: (2000) 4,904,000; (2010) 5,927,000.
Doubling time: 27 years.
Ethnic composition (1989): Turkmen 72.0%; Russian 9.5%; Uzbek 9.0%; Kazakh 2.5%; Tatar 1.1%; other 5.9%.
Religious affiliation: believers are predominantly Sunnī Muslim (Ṣūfī).
Major cities (1991): Ashgabat 416,400; Chärjew 166,400; Dashhowuz 117,000; Mary 94,900; Nebit-Dag 89,100.

Vital statistics

Birth rate per 1,000 population (1992): 33.6 (world avg. 26.4); (1989) legitimate 96.5%; illegitimate 3.5%.
Death rate per 1,000 population (1992): 7.3 (world avg. 9.2).
Natural increase rate per 1,000 population (1992): 26.3 (world avg. 17.2).
Total fertility rate (avg. births per childbearing woman; 1989): 4.3.
Marriage rate per 1,000 population (1989): 9.8.
Divorce rate per 1,000 population (1989): 1.4.
Life expectancy at birth (1990): male 62.9 years; female 69.7 years.
Major causes of death per 100,000 population (1989): diseases of the circulatory system 275.3; diseases of the respiratory system 160.6; infectious and parasitic diseases 79.3; malignant neoplasms (cancers) 65.1; accidents, poisoning, and violence 62.4; diseases of the digestive system 32.2; diseases of the nervous system 9.1; endocrine and metabolic disorders 8.0.

National economy

Budget (1991). Revenue: 6,489,000,000 rubles (nontax revenue 69.6%, of which corporation profit transfer 23.9%, union transfers 21.7%; tax revenue 30.4%, of which turnover tax 10.3%, company profit tax 8.0%, individual income tax 5.4%, sales tax 4.8%). Expenditures: 5,597,000,000 rubles (social and cultural affairs 56.9%, of which social security 26.7%, education and science 19.7%, health 9.4%; national economy 39.0%; government administration 2.7%).
Public debt (external, outstanding): n.a.
Production (metric tons except as noted). Agriculture, forestry, fishing (1992): seed cotton 1,290,000, vegetables 360,000, grain 320,000, fruit 228,000; livestock (number of live animals) 5,600,000 sheep and goats, 1,400,000 cattle, 300,000 pigs, 8,000,000 poultry; roundwood (1990) 4,000,000 cu m; fish catch 20,949. Mining and quarrying (1989): sulfur 5,547,000; sodium sulphate 261,000. Manufacturing (1991): light industry 2,028, of which textiles 1,745; fuel 989; food 700; building materials 285; electricity 250; machinery and metalworking equipment 246; chemicals and petroleum products 192; paper products 64; pharmaceuticals 12; printing 8. Construction (1992): 20,754,000 sq m. Energy production (consumption): electricity (kW-hr; 1991) 17,171,400,000 (8,337,000,000); coal: n.a. (n.a.); crude petroleum (barrels; 1989) 42,601,960 (n.a.); petroleum products (metric tons; 1991) 7,131,800,000 (2,024,300,000); natural gas (cu m; 1991) 84,300,000,000 (9,500,000,000).
Land use (1986): forested 35.4%; meadows and pastures 62.3%; agricultural and under permanent cultivation 2.3%.
Household income and expenditure. Average household size (1989) 5.6; income per household: n.a.; sources of income (1991): wages and salaries 61.9%, pensions and grants 26.0%, income from agriculture sales 9.4%, nonwage income of workers 2.7%; expenditure (1991): food and clothing 79.4%, services 10.1%, taxes and other payments 10.5%.
Gross national product (at current market prices; 1992): U.S.$4,898,390,000 (U.S.$1,270 per capita)[3].

Structure of net material product and labour force

	1991			
	in value '000,000 rubles	% of total value	labour force	% of labour force
Agriculture	6,389.7	46.4	674,800	42.6
Mining, Manufacturing, Public utilities	2,699.1	19.6	168,000	10.6
Construction	3,126.1	22.7	151,300	9.5
Transportation and communications	578.4	4.2	63,500	4.0
Trade	—	—	90,000	5.7
Finance	—	—	...	...
Public administration, defense	—	—	...	...
Services	—	—	410,400	25.9
Other	977.7	7.1	27,400	1.7
TOTAL	13,771.0	100.0	1,585,400	100.0

Population economically active (1991): total: 1,585,400; activity rate of total population 42.7% (participation rates [1989]: ages 16–59 [male], 16–54 [female] 84.2%; female [1990] 52.2%; unemployed [1991] 20–25%).

Price and earnings indexes (1985 = 100)

	1985	1986	1987	1988	1989	1990	1991
Consumer price index	100.0	101.0	102.0	107.0	112.4	125.0	195.2
Monthly earnings index	100.0	101.0	103.8	109.0	115.7	127.5	196.1

Tourism: n.a.

Foreign trade

Balance of trade (current prices)

	1987	1988	1989	1990	1991
'000,000 rubles	−477	−284	−676	−971	+898
% of total	8.9%	5.1%	11.3%	15.5%	6.1%

Imports (1991): 5,938,000,000 rubles (detail, n.a.). *Major import sources:* former Soviet republics 91.8%; foreign countries 8.2%.
Exports (1991): 7,836,000,000 rubles (detail, n.a.). *Major export destinations:* former Soviet republics.

Transport and communications

Transport. Railroads (1990): length 1,317 mi, 2,120 km; passengers 9,000,000; short ton cargo 37,600,000, metric ton-km cargo 34,100,000. Roads (1990): total length 8,300 mi, 13,400 km (paved 86%). Vehicles (1988): passenger cars 170,600; trucks and buses, n.a. Merchant marine: vessels (100 gross tons and over) n.a.; total deadweight tonnage, n.a. Air transport (1989): passenger-mi 2,021,000,000, passenger-km 3,253,000,000; short ton-mi cargo 222,000,000, metric ton-km cargo 324,200,000; airports (1993) with scheduled flights 1.
Communications. Daily newspapers (1989): total number 66; total circulation 1,141,000; circulation per 1,000 population 307. Radio (1991): 823,000 receivers (1 per 5.2 persons). Televisions (1991): 705,000 receivers (1 per 6.1 persons). Telephones (1991): 279,000 (1 per 14 persons).

Education and health

Education (1991–92)

	schools	teachers	students	student/teacher ratio
Primary (age 6–13), Secondary (age 14–17)	1,791	60,000	842,000	14.1
Voc., teacher tr.	41	...	33,700	...
Higher	9	...	41,700	...

Educational attainment (1989). Percentage of population age 25 and over having: primary education or no formal schooling 13.6%; some secondary 21.3%; completed secondary and some postsecondary 56.8%; higher 8.3%.
Literacy: n.a.
Health (1990): physicians 13,200 (1 per 274 persons); hospital beds 42,000 (1 per 86 persons); infant mortality rate per 1,000 live births 47.0.
Food: daily per capita caloric intake, n.a.

Military

Total active duty personnel (1993): CIS joint control 28,000 (100% army).
Military expenditure as a percentage of GNP (1992): 8.8% (world 5.0%); per capita expenditure U.S.$112.

[1]Constitution of May 18, 1992, provided for transitional status of former Supreme Soviet as Majlis (from May 19) until a permanent representative body, the People's Council (Khalk Maslakhaty), could be constituted. [2]Detail does not add to total given because of rounding. [3]Ruble-area GNP and exchange-rate data are very speculative.

Tuvalu

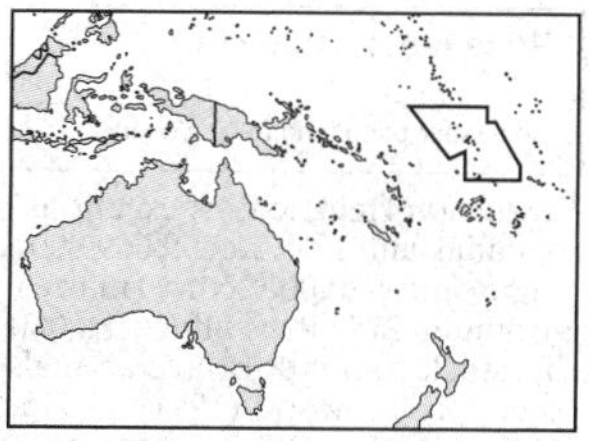

Official name: Tuvalu.
Form of government: constitutional monarchy with one legislative house (Parliament [12]).
Chief of state: British Monarch, represented by Governor-General.
Head of government: Prime Minister.
Capital: Fongafale, on Funafuti atoll.
Official language: none.
Official religion: none.
Monetary unit[1]: 1 Tuvalu Dollar = 1 Australian Dollar ($T = $A) = 100 Tuvalu and Australian cents; valuation (Oct. 4, 1993) 1 U.S.$ = $A 1.55; 1 £ = $A 2.35.

Area and population

	area		population
Islands[2]	sq mi	sq km	1985 census
Funafuti	0.91	2.36	2,810
Nanumaga	1.00	2.59	672
Nanumea	1.38	3.57	879
Niulakita	0.16	0.41	74
Niutao	0.82	2.12	904
Nui	1.27	3.29	604
Nukufetau	1.18	3.06	694
Nukulaelae	0.64	1.66	315
Vaitupu	1.89	4.90	1,231
TOTAL	9.25	23.96	8,229[3, 4]

Demography

Population (1993): 9,500.
Density (1993): persons per sq mi 1,027.0, persons per sq km 396.5.
Urban-rural (1991): urban 43.0%; rural 57.0%.
Sex distribution (1991): male 46.00%; female 54.00%.
Age breakdown (1991): under 15, 34.7%; 15–64, 59.4%; 65 and over, 5.9%.
Population projection: (2000) 11,000; (2010) 14,000.
Doubling time: 35 years.
Ethnic composition (1979): Tuvaluan (Polynesian) 91.2%; mixed (Polynesian/Micronesian/other) 7.2%; European 1.0%; other 0.6%.
Religious affiliation (1979): Church of Tuvalu (Congregational) 96.9%; Seventh-day Adventist 1.4%; Bahā'ī 1.0%; Roman Catholic 0.2%; other 0.5%.
Major locality (1990): Fongafale, on Funafuti atoll, 3,432.

Vital statistics

Birth rate per 1,000 population (1990): 30.0 (world avg. 27.1); (1989) legitimate 82.2%; illegitimate 17.8%.
Death rate per 1,000 population (1990): 10.0 (world avg. 9.8).
Natural increase rate per 1,000 population (1990): 20.0 (world avg. 17.3).
Total fertility rate (avg. births per childbearing woman; 1990): 3.1.
Marriage rate per 1,000 population: n.a.
Divorce rate per 1,000 population: n.a.
Life expectancy at birth (1990): male 60.0 years; female 63.0 years.
Major causes of death per 100,000 population (1985): diseases of the digestive system 170.0; diseases of the circulatory system 150.0; diseases of the respiratory system 120.0; diseases of the nervous system 120.0; malignant neoplasms (cancers) 70.0; infectious and parasitic diseases 40.0; endocrine and metabolic disorders 20.0; ill-defined conditions 430.0; in 1992 the leading causes of death included liver diseases, meningitis, tuberculosis, and still and perinatal deaths; other health problems included acute respiratory infections, diarrhea, filariasis, conjunctivitis, fish poisoning, diabetes, rheumatism, and hypertension.

National economy

Budget (1990). Recurrent revenue: $A 5,301,000 (local sources [including fisheries licenses, import duties, sales tax, and income and company taxes] 77.4%; Tuvalu Trust Fund[5] 22.6%). Expenditures: $A 10,826,000[6] (1987; capital [development] expenditures 68.9%, of which marine transport 20.7%, education 13.0%, fisheries 5.6%, health 3.1%; current expenditures 31.1%).
Gross domestic product (at current market prices; 1990): U.S.$8,750,000 (U.S.$967 per capita).

Structure of gross domestic product and labour force

	1990		1991	
	in value $A	% of total value	labour force	% of labour force
Agriculture, fishing, forestry	2,699,000	24.1	4,020	68.0
Mining	302,000	2.7	—	—
Manufacturing[7]	358,000	3.2	60	1.0
Construction	1,635,000	14.6	240	4.0
Public utilities	235,000	2.1	—	—
Transportation and communications	403,000	3.6	60	1.0
Trade, hotels, and restaurants	1,669,000	14.9	240	4.0
Finance	997,000	8.9	—	—
Pub. admin., defense / Services	2,901,000	25.9	1,290	22.0
TOTAL	11,199,000	100.0	5,910	100.0

Production (metric tons except as noted). Agriculture[8], forestry, fishing (1992): coconuts 3,000, fruits 1,000, hens' eggs 16[9], other agricultural products include breadfruit, pulaka (taro), bananas, pandanus fruit, sweet potatoes, and pawpaws; livestock (number of live animals) 12,000 pigs[10]; forestry, n.a.; fish catch (1991) 1,460, of which tuna 71.2%. Mining and quarrying: n.a.[11]. Manufacturing (1984): copra 840 metric tons; handicrafts and baked goods are also important. Construction: n.a.; however, the main areas of construction activity are roadworks, coastal protection, government facilities, and water-related infrastructure projects. Energy production (consumption): electricity (kW-hr; 1991) 1,188,000 (1,188,000); coal, none (none); crude petroleum, none (n.a.); petroleum products, none (n.a.); natural gas, none (none).
Public debt: n.a.
Tourism (1991): number of visitors 976; receipts from visitors $A 169,700[12]; hotel occupancy 95%[12].
Population economically active (1991): total 5,910; activity rate of total population 65.3% (participation rates: ages 15–64, 85.5%; female [1979] 51.3%; unemployed [1979] 4.0%).

Price and earnings indexes (1986 = 100)

	1986	1987	1988	1989	1990	1991
Consumer price index	100.0	111.0	113.3	116.3	123.2	130.0
Earnings index[13]	100.0	102.5	105.0	110.0	112.5	...

Household income and expenditure. Average household size (1979) 6.4; average annual income per household $A 2,575; sources of income: agriculture and other 61.2%, cash economy only 17.9%, agriculture only 14.9%, other 6.0%; expenditure (1992)[14]: food 45.5%, housing and household operations 11.5%, transportation 10.5%, alcohol and tobacco 10.5%, clothing 7.5%, other 14.5%.
Land use (1983): agricultural and under permanent cultivation 75%[15]; other 25%.

Foreign trade

Balance of trade (current prices)

	1984	1985	1986	1987	1988	1989
$A '000	−3,637	−3,969	−4,076	−4,946	−6,780	−5,158
% of total	85.4%	92.7%	99.9%	99.9%	99.7%	99.5%

Imports (1989): $A 5,170,000 (food 29.3%, manufactured goods 28.2%, petroleum and petroleum products 12.8%, machinery and transport equipment 12.2%, chemicals 7.1%, beverages and tobacco 3.9%). *Major import sources* (1986): Australia 40.6%; New Zealand 10.9%; United Kingdom 5.1%; Japan 3.0%; United States 1.0%.
Exports (1990): $A 30,400 (1989; clothing and footwear 29.5%, copra 21.5%, fruits and vegetables 8.0%). *Major export destinations:* n.a.

Transport and communications

Transport. Railroads: none. Roads (1985): total length 5 mi, 8 km (paved, none). Vehicles[16]: passenger cars, n.a.; trucks and buses, n.a. Merchant marine (1992): vessels (100 gross tons and over) 6; total deadweight tonnage 16,005. Air transport (1977): passenger arrivals (Funafuti) 1,443; cargo, n.a.; airports (1993) with scheduled flights 1.
Communications. Daily newspapers: none. Radio (1992): total number of receivers 4,000 (1 per 2.4 persons). Television: none. Telephones (1991): 230 (1 per 55 persons).

Education and health

Education (1987)

	schools	teachers	students	student/teacher ratio
Primary (age 5–11)	11	64	1,364	21.3
Secondary (age 12–18)	1	15[17]	243	...
Vocational[17]	8	16	354	22.1
Higher	—	—	—	—

Educational attainment (1979). Percentage of population age 25 and over having: no formal schooling 0.4%; primary education 93.0%; secondary 6.1%; higher 0.5%. *Literacy* (1990): total population literate in Tuvaluan 8,593 (95.0%); literacy in English estimated at 45.0%.
Health (1990): physicians 4 (1 per 2,261 persons); hospital beds 30 (1 per 302 persons); infant mortality rate per 1,000 live births 78.6.
Food: daily per capita caloric intake, n.a.

Military

Total active duty personnel (1987): there is a police force numbering 32.

[1]The value of the Tuvalu Dollar is pegged to the value of the Australian Dollar, which is also legal currency in Tuvalu. [2]Local government councils have been established on all islands except Niulakita. [3]Total includes 46 persons unaccounted for in island populations. [4]De facto population; about 1,500 Tuvaluans live abroad, mainly in Nauru or on foreign fishing vessels. [5]The Tuvalu Trust Fund was capitalized in 1987 with $A 27.7 million to replace recurrent grant aid from the United Kingdom; the Fund was valued at $A 36 million in late 1991. [6]Figure includes $A 5,200,000 of capital expenditures, paid for, primarily, by foreign-aid contributions that are not part of recurrent revenue. [7]Including cottage industry. [8]Because of poor soil quality, only limited subsistence agriculture is possible on the islands. [9]1989. [10]Other livestock include goats. [11]Research into the mineral potential of Tuvalu's maritime exclusive economic zone (289,500 sq mi [750,000 sq km] of the Pacific Ocean) is currently being conducted by the South Pacific Geo-Science Commission. [12]1990. [13]Average minimum wage. [14]Weights of consumer price index components. [15]Capable of supporting coconut palms, pandanus, and breadfruit. [16]There are several cars, tractors, trailers, and light trucks on Funafuti; a few motorcycles are in use on most islands. [17]1982–83.

Uganda

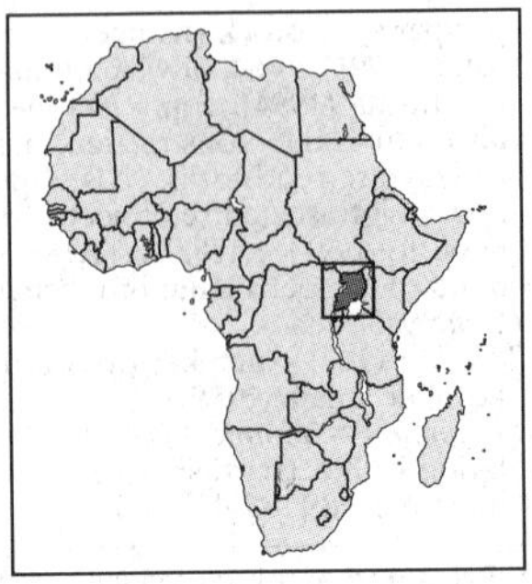

Official name: Republic of Uganda.
Form of government: transitional military regime with one interim legislative body (National Resistance Council [278[1]])[2].
Head of state and government: President assisted by Prime Minister.
Capital: Kampala.
Official languages: English; Swahili.
Official religion: none.
Monetary unit: 1 Uganda shilling (U Sh) = 100 cents; valuation (Oct. 4, 1993) 1 U.S.$ = U Sh 1,171; 1 £ = U Sh 1,774.

Area and population

Regions Districts	Capitals	area sq mi	area sq km	population 1991 census[3]
Central				
Kalangala	...	...	...	16,400
Kampala	Kampala	70	180	773,500
Kiboga	...	...	...	140,800
Luwero	Luwero	3,550	9,200	449,200
Masaka	Kasawa Bukoto	6,310	16,330	831,300
Mpigi	Mpigi	2,400	6,220	915,400
Mubende	Bageza	3,980	10,310	497,500
Mukono	Kawuga Mukono	5,500	14,240	816,200
Rakai	Byakabanda	1,920	4,970	382,000
Eastern				
Iganga	Bulamogi	5,060	13,110	944,000
Jinja	Jinja	280	730	284,900
Kamuli	Namwendwa	1,680	4,350	480,700
Kapchorwa	Kaptanya	670	1,740	116,300
Kumi	Kumi	1,100	2,860	237,000
Mbale	Bunkoko	980	2,550	706,600
Pallisa	...	...	...	355,000
Soroti	Soroti	3,880	10,060	430,900
Tororo	Sukulu	1,780	4,550	554,000
Northern				
Apac	Apac	2,510	6,490	460,700
Arua	Olaki	3,020	7,830	624,600
Gulu	Bungatira	4,530	11,740	338,700
Kitgum	Labongo	8,230	16,140	350,300
Kotido	Kotido	5,100	13,210	190,700
Lira	Lira	2,800	7,250	498,300
Moroto	Katikekile	5,450	14,110	171,500
Moyo	Moyo	1,930	5,010	178,500
Nebbi	Nebbi	1,120	2,890	315,900
Western				
Bundibugyo	Busaru	900	2,340	116,000
Bushenyi	Bumbaire	2,080	5,400	734,800
Hoima	Hoima	3,820	9,900	197,800
Kabale	Rubale	960	2,490	412,800
Kabarole	Karambe	3,230	8,360	741,400
Kasese	Rukoki	1,240	3,200	343,000
Kibaale	...	...	...	219,300
Kisoro	...	...	...	184,900
Masindi	Nyangeya	3,720	9,640	253,500
Mbarara	Kakika	4,190	10,840	929,600
Rukungiri	Kagunga	1,060	2,750	388,000
TOTAL LAND AREA		76,080	197,040	
INLAND WATER[4]		16,990	44,000	
TOTAL		93,070[5]	241,040[5]	16,582,700[5]

Demography

Population (1993): 17,741,000.
Density (1993)[6]: persons per sq mi 233.2, persons per sq km 90.0.
Urban-rural (1991): urban 11.3%; rural 88.7%.
Sex distribution (1991): male 49.00%; female 51.00%.
Age breakdown (1985): under 15, 48.5%; 15–29, 25.8%; 30–44, 14.1%; 45–59, 7.4%; 60–74, 3.6%; 75 and over, 0.6%.
Population projection: (2000) 21,168,000; (2010) 27,244,000.
Doubling time: 19 years.
Ethnic composition (1983): Ganda 17.8%; Teso 8.9%; Nkole 8.2%; Soga 8.2%; Gisu 7.2%; Chiga 6.8%; Lango 6.0%; Rwanda 5.8%; other 31.1%.
Religious affiliation (1980): Roman Catholic 49.6%; Protestant 28.7%; Muslim 6.6%; other 15.1%.
Major cities (1991): Kampala 773,000; Jinja 61,000; Mbale 54,000.

Vital statistics

Birth rate per 1,000 population (1990–95): 51.5 (world avg. 26.4).
Death rate per 1,000 population (1990–95): 14.1 (world avg. 9.2).
Natural increase rate per 1,000 population (1990–95): 37.4 (world avg. 17.2).
Total fertility rate (avg. births per childbearing woman; 1990–95): 7.3.
Life expectancy at birth (1990–95): male 51.4 years; female 54.7 years.
Major causes of death per 100,000 population: n.a.

National economy

Budget (1991–92). Revenue: U Sh 182,340,000,000 (1990–91; sales and excise taxes 36.6%; customs duties 35.7%, of which export tax on coffee 9.5%; income taxes 9.5%). Expenditures: U Sh 410,310,000,000 (1990–91; current expenditures 79.2%, of which security 51.7%, education 16.5%, public services 16.2%, health 5.5%; capital expenditures 20.8%).
Tourism: receipts from visitors (1991) U.S.$15,000,000; expenditures by nationals abroad U.S.$18,000,000.
Population economically active (1991): total 8,363,000; activity rate of total population 49.9% (participation rates: ages 15–64, 78.9%[7]; female 41.6%[8]).

Price index (1985 = 100)

	1986	1987	1988	1989	1990	1991	1992
Consumer price index	261.0	783.0	2,519.0	3,743.0	4,983.0	6,382.0	9,728.0

Production (metric tons except as noted). Agriculture, forestry, fishing (1992): bananas and plantains 8,669,000, cassava 3,780,000, sweet potatoes 1,752,000, sugarcane 920,000, corn (maize) 595,000, millet 593,000, dry beans 402,000, sorghum 375,000, coffee 180,000, peanuts (groundnuts) 138,000, tea 9,000; livestock (number of live animals) 5,100,000 cattle, 3,350,000 goats, 1,980,000 sheep; roundwood (1991) 15,715,000 cu m; fish catch (1991) 254,900. Mining and quarrying (1991): tungsten (wolfram) 98.3; tin ore 72.2; gold 24,832 troy oz. Manufacturing (1990): soap 30,600; sugar 28,900; animal feed 15,000; cement 14,960; metal products 1,300; footwear 319,000 pairs; fabrics 8,200,000 sq m; 1,289,700,000 cigarettes; beer 194,000 hectolitres. Construction: n.a. Energy production (consumption): electricity (kW-hr; 1991) 783,000,000 (671,000,000); petroleum products (metric tons; 1991) none (296,000).
Gross national product (1992): U.S.$2,968,000,000 (U.S.$170 per capita).

Structure of gross domestic product and labour force

	1990 in value U Sh '000,000	1990 % of total value	1987 labour force	1987 % of labour force
Agriculture	363,273	35.4	6,240,000	82.6
Manufacturing and mining	69,891	6.8		
Construction	73,860	7.2	385,000	5.1
Public utilities	9,538	0.9		
Transp. and commun.	102,342	10.0		
Trade	220,557	21.5		
Finance	53,520	5.2	929,000	12.3
Pub. admin., defense	100,737	9.8		
Services	33,364	3.2		
TOTAL	1,027,082	100.0	7,554,000	100.0

Household size. Average household size (1983) 4.8; income per household: n.a.; expenditure (1989–90)[9]: food 57.1%, rent, education, and health 15.7%, fuel and lighting 7.3%, transportation 5.9%, clothing 5.5%.
Land use (1991): forested 27.6%; meadows and pastures 9.0%; agricultural and under permanent cultivation 33.8%; other 29.6%.
Public debt (external, outstanding; 1991): U.S.$2,325,000,000.

Foreign trade

Balance of trade (current prices)

	1987	1988	1989	1990	1991	1992
U Sh '000,000	−19,051	−55,716	−23,471	−48,013	+23,012	−363,753
% of total	41.0%	48.9%	17.4%	27.1%	8.5%	53.3%

Imports (1991): U Sh 137,250,000,000 (1984; sugar 16.0%, motor vehicles 10.8%, clothing and fabrics 9.6%, construction materials 8.0%, food 5.4%). *Major import sources:* Kenya 23.3%; U.K. 15.0%; Japan 9.3%; Germany 6.9%.
Exports (1991): U Sh 146,661,000,000 (1990; unroasted coffee 79.6%, cotton 3.3%, tea 1.2%). *Major export destinations:* The Netherlands 21.5%; France 16.2%; U.S. 11.9%; Spain 11.1%; Germany 10.9%; Italy 7.9%.

Transport and communications

Transport. Railroads (1990): route length 1,240 km; passenger-km 109,000,000; metric ton-km cargo 103,000,000. Roads (1986): total length 28,332 km (paved 22%). Vehicles (1990): passenger cars 35,492; trucks and buses 14,902. Merchant marine (1992): vessels (100 gross tons and over) 2; total deadweight tonnage 8,600[10]. Air transport (1990)[11]: passenger-km 67,000,000; metric ton-km cargo 3,000,000; airports (1992) 1.
Communications. Daily newspapers (1990): total number 6; total circulation 63,800; circulation per 1,000 population 3.7. Radio (1992): 3,500,000 receivers (1 per 4.9 persons). Television (1992): 115,000 receivers (1 per 150 persons). Telephones (1991): 59,424 (1 per 287 persons).

Education and health

Education (1989)

	schools	teachers	students	student/ teacher ratio
Primary (age 5–11)	7,905	75,561	2,633,764	34.8
Secondary (age 12–15)	774	13,356	240,334	18.0
Voc., teacher tr.	136	2,081	23,179	11.1
Higher	9	934[12]	5,778	8.8[12]

Educational attainment (1969). Percentage of population age 25 and over having: no formal schooling or less than one full year 58.2%; primary education 33.9%; lower secondary 5.0%; upper secondary 2.5%; higher 0.4%.
Literacy (1990): population age 15 and over literate 4,586,000 (48.3%); males literate 2,900,000 (62.2%); females literate 1,686,000 (34.9%).
Health: physicians (1984) 700 (1 per 20,300 persons); hospital beds (1989) 20,136 (1 per 817 persons); infant mortality rate (1990–95) 94.0.
Food (1988–90): daily per capita caloric intake 2,178 (vegetable products 94%, animal products 6%); 93% of FAO recommended minimum requirement.

Military

Total active duty personnel (1993): 60,000 (army 99.4%, navy 0.3%, air force 0.3%). *Military expenditure as percentage of GNP* (1988): 1.5% (world 5.0%); per capita U.S.$4.

[1]Includes 68 nonelective seats. [2]Constitution of 1967 suspended July 1985. [3]Preliminary. [4]Includes swamps. [5]Detail does not add to total given because of rounding. [6]Based on land area. [7]1985. [8]1987. [9]Kampala and Entebbe only. [10]1988. [11]Uganda Airlines only. [12]1984.

Ukraine

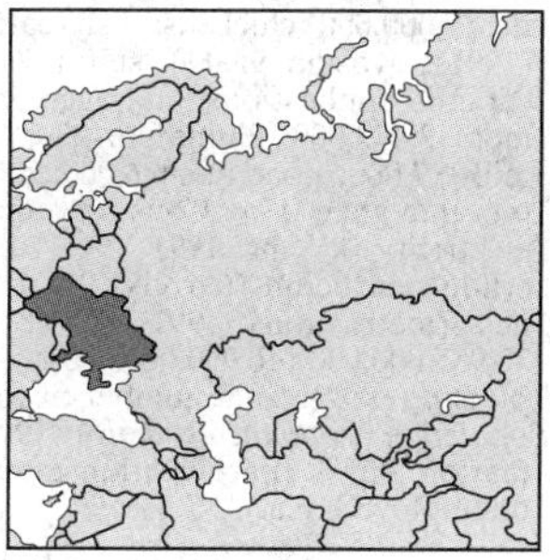

Official name: Ukrayina (Ukraine).
Form of government: unitary multiparty republic with a single legislative body (Supreme Council [450]).
Head of state: President.
Head of government: Prime Minister.
Capital: Kiev (Kyyiv).
Official language: Ukrainian.
Official religion: none.
Monetary unit: karbovanets[1] (no minor unit); valuation (Oct. 4, 1993) free rate, 1 U.S.$ = 16,827 karbovantsy; 1 £ = 25,493 karbovantsy.

Area and population

		area		population
Autonomous republic	Capitals	sq mi	sq km	1991 estimate
Crimea (Krym)	Simferopol	10,400	27,000	2,596,000
Provinces				
Cherkasy	Cherkasy	8,100	20,900	1,531,800
Chernihiv	Chernihiv	12,300	31,900	1,398,000
Chernivtsi	Chernivtsi	3,100	8,100	940,500
Dnipropetrovsk	Dnipropetrovsk	12,300	31,900	3,918,600
Donetsk	Donetsk	10,200	26,500	5,352,600
Ivano-Frankivsk	Ivano-Frankivsk	5,400	13,900	1,451,500
Kharkiv	Kharkiv	12,100	31,400	3,188,600
Kherson	Kherson	11,000	28,500	1,270,000
Khmelnytsky	Khmelnytsky	8,000	20,600	1,521,500
Kirovohrad	Kirovohrad	9,500	24,600	1,247,500
Kyyiv (Kiev)	Kiev	11,200	28,900	4,588,900
Luhansk	Luhansk	10,300	26,700	2,877,400
Lviv	Lviv	8,400	21,800	2,771,300
Mykolayiv	Mykolayiv	9,500	24,600	1,350,800
Odessa	Odessa	12,900	33,300	2,634,500
Poltava	Poltava	11,100	28,800	1,762,800
Rivne	Rivne	7,800	20,100	1,181,600
Sumy	Sumy	9,200	23,800	1,430,700
Ternopil	Ternopil	5,300	13,800	1,177,100
Vinnytsya	Vinnytsya	10,200	26,500	1,908,400
Volyn	Volodymyr-Volynsky	7,800	20,200	1,072,700
Zakarpatska	Uzhhorod	4,900	12,800	1,271,600
Zaporizhzhya	Zaporizhzhya	10,500	27,200	2,108,500
Zhytomyr	Zhytomyr	11,600	29,900	1,503,700
TOTAL		233,100	603,700	52,056,600

Demography

Population (1993): 52,344,000.
Density (1993): persons per sq mi 224.6, persons per sq km 86.7.
Urban-rural (1992): urban 67.8%; rural 32.2%.
Sex distribution (1992): male 46.43%; female 53.57%.
Age breakdown (1991): under 15, 21.5%; 15–29, 21.0%; 30–44, 20.6%; 45–59, 18.5%; 60–69, 10.7%; 70 and over, 7.7%.
Population projection: (2000) 53,362,000; (2010) 54,851,000.
Ethnic composition (1989): Ukrainian 72.7%; Russian 22.1%; Jewish 0.9%; Belorussian 0.9%; Moldovan 0.6%; Bulgarian 0.5%; Polish 0.4%; other 1.9%.
Religious affiliation: believers are predominantly Ukrainian Orthodox; there is a Ukrainian Catholic minority.
Major cities (1992): Kiev 2,651,300; Kharkiv 1,622,000; Dnipropetrovsk 1,190,000; Donetsk 1,121,000; Odessa 1,096,000.

Vital statistics

Birth rate per 1,000 population (1991): 12.1 (world avg. 26.4); legitimate 88.1%; illegitimate 11.9%.
Death rate per 1,000 population (1991): 12.9 (world avg. 9.2).
Natural increase rate per 1,000 population (1991): −0.8 (world avg. 17.2).
Total fertility rate (avg. births per childbearing woman; 1991): 1.8.
Marriage rate per 1,000 population (1991): 9.5.
Divorce rate per 1,000 population (1991): 3.9.
Life expectancy at birth (1991): male 66.0 years; female 75.0 years.
Major causes of death per 100,000 population (1991): circulatory diseases 671.7; cancers 202.2; accidents 117.3; respiratory diseases 74.5; diseases of the digestive system (1989) 30.1; infectious diseases (1989) 11.6.

National economy

Budget (1993). Revenue: 8,121,300,000,000 karbovantsy (tax revenue 87.6%, of which value-added tax 24.5%, corporate tax 16.6%, foreign trade tax 12.4%; nontax revenue 12.4%). Expenditures: 9,094,600,000,000 karbovantsy (current expenditure 92.4%, of which social safety net 20.3%, national economy 14.6%, education 13.6%, health care 11.4%, capital expenditure 7.6%).
Production (metric tons except as noted). Agriculture, forestry, fishing (1992): sugar beets 28,600,000, potatoes 20,400,000, wheat 19,500,000, corn (maize) 2,800,000, sunflower seeds 2,100,000, grapes 655,000; livestock (number of live animals) 7,900,000 cattle, 2,700,000 pigs, 2,300,000 sheep and goats; roundwood 8,900,000 cu m; fish catch 1,300,000. Mining and quarrying (1992): iron ore 75,700,000; manganese 5,800,000. Manufacturing (1991): synthetic fibres 191,400,000; crude steel 45,000,000; pig iron 36,600,000; cement 21,700,000; steel pipes 7,000,000; sugar 3,500,000; computers 1,746,300,000 rubles[2]; agricultural machinery 946,200,000 rubles[2]; coal equipment 847,000,000 rubles[2]; metal-cutting equipment 560,200,000 rubles[2]; automated machinery 482,600,000 rubles[2]; chemical equipment 302,100,000 rubles[2]; leather goods 281,900,000 rubles[2]; forge press machines 237,100,000 rubles[2]; optical instruments 168,000,000 rubles[2]; textile machinery 18,600,000 rubles[2]. Construction (1991): residential 14,454,000 sq m. Energy production (consumption): electricity (kW-hr; 1992) 252,600,000,000 (n.a.); coal (metric tons; 1992) 133,600,000 (n.a.); crude petroleum (barrels; 1991) 35,900,000 (n.a.); natural gas (cu m; 1992) 20,900,000,000 (n.a.).
Gross national product (at current market prices; 1992): U.S.$86,817,000,000 (U.S.$1,670 per capita)[3].

Structure of net material product and labour force

	1991			
	in value '000,000 rubles	% of total value	labour value	% of labour force
Agriculture	60,400	28.7	6,675,000	27.3
Mining / Manufacturing	90,800	43.1	6,913,000	28.3
Public utilities			857,000	3.5
Construction	29,100	13.8	1,639,000	6.7
Transp. and commun.	9,400	4.5	1,699,000	7.0
Trade	12,000	5.7	1,699,000	7.0
Finance	—	—	133,000	0.5
Pub. admin., defense	—	—	325,000	1.3
Services	—	—	3,650,000	14.9
Other	8,900	4.2	857,900	3.5
TOTAL	210,600	100.0	24,447,900	100.0

Population economically active (1991): total 24,447,900; activity rate of total population 47.0% (participation rates [1989]: ages 16–59 [male], 16–54 [female] 88.4%; female 54.5%; unemployed 3.1%).

Price and earnings indexes (1985 = 100)

	1986	1987	1988	1989	1990	1991	1992
Consumer price index	104.0	107.0	116.0	130.0	152.0	250.6	c. 3,622
Monthly earnings index	103.9	106.8	116.8	129.2	149.7	220.9	c. 3,100

Land use (1991): forested 15.9%; meadows and pastures 10.7%; agricultural and under permanent cultivation 53.9%; other 19.5%.
Household income and expenditure (1991). Average household size (1990) 3.2; income per household 13,400 karbovantsy[1]; sources of income: wages 51.8%, pensions 20.4%, financial receipts 11.7%, sales of agricultural products 7.2%, other 8.9%; expenditure: food and nonalcoholic beverages 39.2%, consumer goods 32.2% (of which furniture and household appliances 6.8%), entertainment and culture 6.3%, alcoholic beverages 2.1%, housing 1.7%.

Foreign trade

Balance of trade (current prices)

	1987	1988	1989	1990	1991	1992
'000,000,000 rubles	−6.2	−2.9	−6.5	−8.1	−12.1	−188.0
% of total	6.6%	3.0%	6.3%	8.1%	10.6%	4.3%

Imports (1992): 2,255,000,000,000 rubles (1990; machinery 34.8%, textiles 18.0%, chemicals 10.6%, food 7.4%, oil and gas 7.3%, ferrous metals 5.0%). *Major import sources:* Western countries 69.0%, of which Spain 12.3%, Britain 10.9%, Germany 10.6%, Italy 4.1%; former Soviet republics 31.0%.
Exports (1992): 2,067,000,000,000 rubles (1990; machinery 39.2%, ferrous metals 16.6%, food 14.7%, chemicals 8.5%, textiles 5.0%). *Major export destinations:* Western countries 51.0%; former Soviet republics 49.0%.

Transport and communications

Transport. Railroads (1991): length 22,799 km; passenger-km 76,000,000,000; metric ton-km cargo 474,000,000,000. Roads (1991): total length 167,800 km (paved 94%). Vehicles (1988): passenger cars 2,920,000. Air transport (1990): passenger-km 16,100,000,000; metric ton-km cargo 125,000,000; airports (1992) 20.
Communications (1991). Daily newspapers: total number 1,891; total circulation 26,804,000; circulation per 1,000 population 52. Radio: total number of receivers 14,520,000 (1 per 4.1 persons). Television: total number of receivers 17,024,000 (1 per 3.0 persons). Telephones: 6,908,000 (1 per 7.5 persons).

Education and health

Education (1991–92)

	schools	teachers	students	student/teacher ratio
Primary (age 6–13) / Secondary (age 14–17)	21,904	543,000	7,102,000	13.1
Voc., teacher tr.	754	...	739,200	...
Higher	156	...	876,200	...

Educational attainment (1989). Percentage of population age 15 and over having: some primary education 6.8%; completed primary 13.8%; some secondary 18.4%; completed secondary 31.1%; some postsecondary 19.5%; higher 10.4%. *Literacy:* n.a.
Health (1992): physicians 228,900 (1 per 228 persons); hospital beds 700,300 (1 per 75 persons); infant mortality rate per 1,000 live births (1991) 13.9.

Military

Total active duty personnel (1992): 230,000 (army 65.2%, air force and air defense 34.8%). The Black Sea Fleet of the former U.S.S.R. (headquarters: Sevastopol, Ukraine) remained to be divided with Russia and Georgia at year-end. Commonwealth of Independent States- (CIS-) controlled Strategic Nuclear Forces constituted a third military establishment during a two-year transition period.

[1]On Nov. 12, 1992, Ukraine replaced the Russian ruble with the karbovanets as the national currency. [2]1990. [3]Ruble-area GNP and exchange-rate data are very speculative.

United Arab Emirates

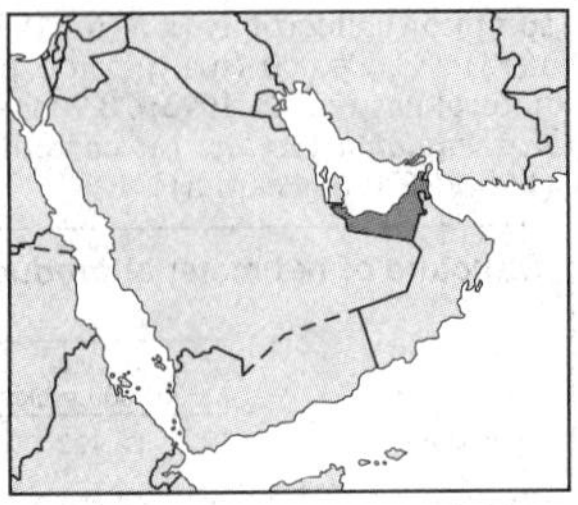

Official name: al-Imārāt al-ʿArabīyah al-Muttaḥidah (United Arab Emirates).
Form of government: federation of seven emirates with one appointive advisory body (Federal National Council [40[1]]).
Chief of state: President.
Head of government: Prime Minister.
Capital: Abu Dhabi.
Official language: Arabic.
Official religion: Islam.
Monetary unit: 1 U.A.E. dirham (Dh) = 100 fils; valuation (Oct. 4, 1993) 1 U.S.$ = Dh 3.69; 1 £ = Dh 5.57.

Area and population

		area		population
Emirates	Capitals	sq mi	sq km	1991 estimate
Abu Dhabi (Abū Ẓaby)	Abu Dhabi	28,210[2]	73,060[2]	798,000
ʿAjmān (Ajman)	ʿAjmān	100	260	76,000
Dubayy (Dubai)	Dubayy	1,510	3,900	501,000
Al-Fujayrah (Fujairah)	Al-Fujayrah	500	1,300	63,000
Ra's al-Khaymah (Ras al-Khaimah)	Ra's al-Khaymah	660	1,700	130,000
Ash-Shāriqah (Sharjah)	Ash-Shāriqah	1,000	2,600	314,000
Umm al-Qaywayn (Umm al-Qaiwain)	Umm al-Qaywayn	300	780	27,000
TOTAL		32,280	83,600	1,909,000

Demography

Population (1993): 1,986,000.
Density (1993): persons per sq mi 66.2, persons per sq km 25.6.
Urban-rural (1990): urban 77.8%; rural 22.2%.
Sex distribution (1990): male 67.40%; female 32.60%.
Age breakdown (1990): under 15, 30.6%; 15–29, 19.8%; 30–44, 33.8%; 45–59, 12.6%; 60–74, 2.6%; 75 and over, 0.6%.
Population projection: (2000) 2,281,000; (2010) 2,781,000.
Doubling time: 43 years.
Ethnic composition (1983): Arab 87.1%, of which Arab from United Arab Emirates 30.7%; Pakistani and Indian 9.1%; Persian 1.7%; Baluchi 0.8%; African 0.8%; British 0.2%; American 0.1%; other 0.2%.
Religious affiliation (1980): Muslim 94.9% (Sunnī 80%, Shīʿī 20%); Christian 3.8%; other 1.3%.
Major cities (1989): Dubayy 585,189; Abu Dhabi 363,432; al-ʿAyn 176,411; ash-Shāriqah 125,000[3]; Ra's al-Khaymah 42,000[3].

Vital statistics

Birth rate per 1,000 population (1990–95): 20.3 (world avg. 26.4); legitimate, n.a.; illegitimate, n.a.
Death rate per 1,000 population (1990–95): 3.9 (world avg. 9.2).
Natural increase rate per 1,000 population (1990–95): 16.4 (world avg. 17.2).
Total fertility rate (avg. births per childbearing woman; 1990): 4.3.
Marriage rate per 1,000 population (1990): 2.6.
Divorce rate per 1,000 population (1990): 0.9.
Life expectancy at birth (1990–95): male 69.8 years; female 74.1 years.
Major causes of death per 100,000 population (1989)[4]: accidents and poisoning 43.7; diseases of the circulatory system 34.3; malignant neoplasms (cancers) 13.7; respiratory diseases 8.1.

National economy

Budget (1992). Revenue: Dh 16,716,900,000 (domestic revenues 74.8%; other sources 25.2%). Expenditures: Dh 15,538,000,000 (current expenditures 95.4%, of which [1989] defense 43.9%, education 15.0%, public safety 13.5%, health 6.9%, economic services 4.3%; development expenditures 4.5%).
Gross national product (at current market prices; 1991): U.S.$32,813,000,000 (U.S.$19,870 per capita).

Structure of gross domestic product and labour force

	1992		1990	
	in value Dh '000,000	% of total value	labour force	% of labour force
Agriculture	2,450	1.9	43,100	6.3
Mining	53,584	41.5	10,000	1.5
Manufacturing	10,044	7.8	63,400	9.2
Construction	11,100	8.6	119,200	17.3
Public utilities	2,600	2.0	20,600	3.0
Transportation and communications	7,160	5.5	71,700	10.4
Trade	12,885	10.0	101,400	14.7
Finance, real estate	14,173	11.0	18,800	2.7
Pub. admin., defense	14,376	11.1 }	241,300	35.0
Services	3,536	2.7 }		
Other	−2,650[5]	−2.1[5]	—	—
TOTAL	129,258	100.0	689,500	100.0[6]

Public debt (external, outstanding; 1989): U.S.$9,300,000,000.
Production (metric tons except as noted). Agriculture, forestry, fishing (1992): dates 175,000, tomatoes 85,000, eggplants 60,000, cabbages 55,000, lemons and limes 24,000, pumpkins and squash 16,000, green peppers 13,000, cauliflowers 12,000, cucumbers 12,000, mangoes 10,000; livestock (number of live animals) 720,000 goats, 275,000 sheep, 122,000 camels, 55,000 cattle, 7,000,000 chickens; fish catch (1991) 92,300. Mining and quarrying (1991): gypsum 95,000; sulfur 74,000; lime 45,000; also marble, shale for ceramic applications, and aggregate for cement. Manufacturing (1991): cement 3,473,000; aluminum 239,000; mutton and lamb meat 22,000; goat's milk 17,000; goat meat 6,000; cow's milk 6,000; beef and veal 3,000; butter and ghee 174. Construction: n.a. Energy production (consumption): electricity (kW-hr; 1991) 13,790,000,000 (13,790,000,000); coal, none (n.a.); crude petroleum (barrels; 1991) 841,250,000 (63,800,000); petroleum products (metric tons; 1991) 13,511,000 (6,475,000); natural gas (cu m; 1991) 32,955,000,000 (16,990,000,000).
Tourism (1992): total number of tourist arrivals 50,000.
Population economically active (1992): total 733,500; activity rate of total population 36.9% (participation rates [1986]: ages 15–64, 76.7%; female 6.6%; unemployed, n.a.).

Price and earnings indexes (1985 = 100)

	1984	1985	1986	1987	1988	1989	1990
Consumer price index[7]	97.3	100.0	97.0	101.8	105.2	100.7	109.4
Earnings index	...	...	...	...	...	...	...

Household income and expenditure. Average household size (1986) 6.8; income per household: n.a.; sources of income: n.a.; expenditure: n.a.
Land use (1991): forested, virtually none; meadows and pastures 2.4%; agricultural and under permanent cultivation 0.5%; built-on, wasteland, and other 97.1%.

Foreign trade

Balance of trade (current prices)

	1987	1988	1989	1990	1991	1992
Dh '000,000	+25,928	+19,090	+27,420	...	+30,200	+21,800
% of total	33.9%	28.9%	28.1%	...	22.8%	14.6%

Imports (1989): Dh 35,080,000,000 (1987; machinery and transport equipment 30.5%, basic manufactures 16.8%, food and live animals 15.8%, chemicals 6.9%, mineral fuels 4.0%, crude minerals 1.8%). *Major import sources:* Japan 15.0%; United Kingdom 9.4%; United States 8.4%; West Germany 7.6%; Italy 4.7%; France 3.7%; Thailand 3.4%; Saudi Arabia 3.1%; China 2.9%; The Netherlands 2.5%; Australia 2.5%; Singapore 2.3%; Belgium-Luxembourg 1.2%; Switzerland 1.2%; Turkey 1.2%.
Exports (1989): Dh 62,500,000,000 (crude petroleum 65.6%, nonpetroleum exports and reexports 34.4%). *Major export destinations:* Japan 32.1%; Singapore 4.8%; India 4.4%; South Korea 4.3%; United States 3.9%; Oman 3.0%; Australia 2.4%; France 1.8%; Italy 1.7%; United Kingdom 1.4%; West Germany 1.2%; Brazil 1.1%; Bangladesh 0.8%; The Netherlands 0.6%; Belgium-Luxembourg 0.6%; Iran 0.4%; Iraq 0.3%.

Transport and communications

Transport. Railroads: none. Roads (1984): total length 2,709 mi, 4,360 km (paved [1981] 61%). Vehicles (1990): passenger cars 302,000; trucks and buses 157,000. Merchant marine (1992): vessels (100 gross tons and over) 276; total deadweight tonnage 1,491,728. Air transport (1991)[8]: passenger-mi 1,859,000,000, passenger-km 2,992,000,000; short ton-mi cargo 98,625,000, metric ton-km cargo 143,990,000; airports (1993) with scheduled flights 4.
Communications. Daily newspapers (1991): total number 9; total circulation 246,600[9]; circulation per 1,000 population 127[9]. Radio (1992): total number of receivers 420,000 (1 per 4.6 persons). Television (1992): total number of receivers 170,000 (1 per 11 persons). Telephones (1991): 777,179 (1 per 2.5 persons).

Education and health

Education (1990–91)

	schools	teachers	students	student/ teacher ratio
Primary (age 6–11) }	354[10]	12,526	228,980	18.3
Secondary (age 12–18) }		8,565 }	107,881 }	12.6
Vocational	9[11] }		766 }	
Higher[12]	1	494	8,496	17.2

Educational attainment (1975). Percentage of population age 25 and over having: no formal schooling 72.2%; primary education 5.2%; secondary 16.6%; higher 6.0%. *Literacy* (1986): total population age 15 and over literate 858,149 (73.0%); males literate 657,579 (74.5%); females literate 200,570 (68.4%).
Health (1991): physicians 3,090 (1 per 618 persons); hospital beds 6,540 (1 per 292 persons); infant mortality rate per 1,000 live births 12.
Food (1987–89): daily per capita caloric intake 3,295 (vegetable products 77%, animal products 23%); 136% of FAO recommended minimum requirement.

Military

Total active duty personnel (1993): 57,500 (army 92.2%, navy 3.5%, air force 4.3%). *Military expenditure as percentage of GNP* (1989): 5.3% (world 4.9%); per capita expenditure U.S.$695.

[1]All appointed seats. [2]Approximate, based on reported total and on reported partial areas for smaller emirates. [3]1980. [4]Registered; Abu Dhabi Emirate only. [5]Less imputed bank service charges and indirect taxes net of subsidies. [6]Detail does not add to total given because of rounding. [7]City of Abu Dhabi only. [8]Emirates (airline) and one-fourth apportionment of international flights of Gulf Air only. [9]Based on seven dailies only. [10]1987–88. [11]1985–86. [12]1988–89.

United Kingdom

Official name: United Kingdom of Great Britain and Northern Ireland.
Form of government: constitutional monarchy with two legislative houses (House of Lords [1,211]; House of Commons [651]).
Chief of state: Sovereign.
Head of government: Prime Minister.
Capital: London.
Official language: English.
Official religion: Churches of England and Scotland "established" (protected by the state, but not "official") in their respective countries; no established church in Northern Ireland or Wales.
Monetary unit: 1 pound sterling (£) = 100 new pence; valuation (Oct. 4, 1993) 1 £ = U.S.$1.52; 1 U.S.$ = £0.66.

Area and population

Countries	Capitals	area sq mi	area sq km	population 1991 estimate
England	London	50,363	130,439	48,068,400[1]
Counties				
Avon	Bristol	520	1,346	962,000
Bedfordshire	Bedford	477	1,235	534,200
Berkshire	Reading	486	1,259	752,500
Buckinghamshire	Aylesbury	727	1,883	640,200
Cambridgeshire	Cambridge	1,316	3,409	669,900
Cheshire	Chester	899	2,329	966,400
Cleveland	Middlesbrough	225	583	557,500
Cornwall[2]	Truro	1,376	3,564	475,200
Cumbria	Carlisle	2,629	6,810	489,700
Derbyshire	Matlock	1,016	2,631	939,700
Devon	Exeter	2,591	6,711	1,040,000
Dorset	Dorchester	1,025	2,654	662,900
Durham	Durham	941	2,436	604,300
East Sussex	Lewes	693	1,795	716,500
Essex	Chelmsford	1,418	3,672	1,548,800
Gloucestershire	Gloucester	1,020	2,643	538,700
Greater London[3]	London	610	1,579	6,803,100
Greater Manchester[3]	Manchester	497	1,287	2,561,600
Hampshire	Winchester	1,458	3,777	1,578,700
Hereford & Worcester	Worcester	1,516	3,927	686,000
Hertfordshire	Hertford	631	1,634	989,500
Humberside	Hull	1,356	3,512	874,500
Isle of Wight	Newport	147	381	126,600
Kent	Maidstone	1,441	3,731	1,538,800
Lancashire	Preston	1,183	3,064	1,408,300
Leicestershire	Leicester	986	2,553	890,800
Lincolnshire	Lincoln	2,284	5,915	592,600
Merseyside[3]	Liverpool	252	652	1,441,000
Norfolk	Norwich	2,073	5,368	759,400
North Yorkshire	Northallerton	3,208	8,309	720,800
Northamptonshire	Northhampton	914	2,367	587,100
Northumberland	Newcastle upon Tyne	1,943	5,032	307,100
Nottinghamshire	Nottingham	836	2,164	1,015,400
Oxfordshire	Oxford	1,007	2,608	579,600
Shropshire	Shrewsbury	1,347	3,490	412,600
Somerset	Taunton	1,332	3,451	469,400
South Yorkshire[3]	Barnsley	602	1,560	1,292,700
Staffordshire	Stafford	1,049	2,716	1,047,400
Suffolk	Ipswich	1,466	3,797	661,900
Surrey	Kingston upon Thames	648	1,679	1,035,500
Tyne and Wear[3]	Newcastle upon Tyne	208	540	1,125,500
Warwickshire	Warwick	765	1,981	489,900
West Midlands[3]	Birmingham	347	899	2,619,000
West Sussex	Chichester	768	1,989	713,600
West Yorkshire[3]	Wakefield	787	2,039	2,066,200
Wiltshire	Trowbridge	1,344	3,480	575,100
Northern Ireland[4]	Belfast	5,452	14,120	1,594,400
Scotland	Edinburgh	30,418	78,783	5,100,000
Regions				
Borders	Newton Saint Boswells	1,814	4,698	104,100
Central	Stirling	1,042	2,700	272,800
Dumfries and Galloway	Dumfries	2,481	6,425	147,800
Fife	Glenrothes	509	1,319	346,500
Grampian	Aberdeen	3,379	8,752	514,400
Highland	Inverness	10,092	26,137	204,200
Lothian	Edinburgh	683	1,770	750,500
Strathclyde	Glasgow	5,318	13,773	2,296,300
Tayside	Dundee	2,951	7,643	391,900
Island areas[5] (TOTAL)	—	2,149	5,566	71,500
Wales	Cardiff	8,019	20,768	2,886,400[1]
Counties				
Clwyd	Mold	937	2,427	413,800
Dyfed	Carmarthen	2,227	5,768	350,900
Gwent	Newport	531	1,376	446,900
Gwynedd	Caernarvon	1,494	3,869	240,100
Mid Glamorgan	Cardiff	393	1,018	541,600
Powys	Llandrindod Wells	1,960	5,077	118,700
South Glamorgan	Cardiff	161	416	405,900
West Glamorgan	Swansea	316	817	368,700
TOTAL		94,251	244,110	57,649,200

Demography

Population (1993): 58,080,000.
Density (1993): persons per sq mi 612.2, persons per sq km 237.9.
Urban-rural (1985): urban 91.5%; rural 8.5%.
Sex distribution (1991): male 48.82%; female 51.18%.
Age breakdown (1991): under 15, 19.2%; 15–29, 22.5%; 30–44, 21.0%; 45–59, 16.6%; 60–74, 13.7%; 75 and over, 7.0%.
Population projection: (2000) 59,520,000; (2010) 60,986,000.
Doubling time: not applicable; doubling time exceeds 100 years.
Ethnic composition (1991)[6]: white 94.2%; Asian Indian 1.4%; Pakistani 0.9%; West Indian 0.8%; African 0.3%; Chinese 0.3%; Bangladeshi 0.2%; Arab 0.1%; other and not stated 1.8%.
Religious affiliation (adults professing a current church membership; 1990): Christian 79.5%, of which Roman Catholic 21.4%, Anglican 20.2%, Presbyterian 14.2%, Methodist 5.3%, Baptist 2.6%; Muslim 10.9%; Sikh 4.3%; Hindu 1.5%; Jewish 1.2%; other 2.6%.
Major cities (1991): Greater London 6,803,100; Birmingham 994,500; Leeds 706,300; Glasgow 687,600; Sheffield 520,300; Liverpool 474,500; Bradford 468,700; Edinburgh 438,800; Manchester 432,600; Bristol 392,600.
Place of birth (1985): native-born 93.5% (50,720,000); foreign-born 5.9%, of which Ireland 1.0%, India 0.7%, Caribbean 0.5%, Pakistan 0.4%; not stated 0.6%.
Mobility (1981). Population living in the same residence as 1980: 90.9%; different residence, same country (of the U.K.) 8.2%; different residence, different country within the U.K. 0.4%; from outside the U.K. 0.5%.
Households (1990–91)[6, 7]. Average household size 2.5 (3.1); 1 person 26% (20%), 2 persons 34% (26%), 3 persons 17% (16%), 4 persons 16% (17%), 5 persons 6% (10%), 6 or more persons 2% (11%). Family households (1987): 17,836,500 (77.4%), nonfamily 5,208,500 (22.6%, of which 1-person 9.9%).
Immigration (annual average; 1987–91): permanent residents 242,300, from United States 11.2%, Australia 10.1%, Bangladesh, India, and Sri Lanka 5.5%, New Zealand 5.4%, Pakistan 4.1%, South Africa 3.3%.

Vital statistics

Birth rate per 1,000 population (1991): 13.8 (world avg. 26.4); legitimate 70.2%; illegitimate 29.8%.
Death rate per 1,000 population (1991): 11.2 (world avg. 9.2).
Natural increase rate per 1,000 population (1991): 2.6 (world avg. 17.2).
Total fertility rate (avg. births per childbearing woman; 1991): 1.8.
Marriage rate per 1,000 population (1991): 6.5.
Divorce rate per 1,000 population (1990): 3.0[6].
Life expectancy at birth (1991): male 73.2 years; female 78.6 years.
Major causes of death per 100,000 population (1991): diseases of the circulatory system 516.9, of which ischemic heart disease 296.9, cerebrovascular disease 135.9; malignant neoplasms (cancers) 281.0; diseases of the respiratory system 126.4, of which pneumonia 59.0; diseases of the digestive system 36.4; accidents and violence 35.7; diseases of the endocrine system 19.6, of which diabetes mellitus 15.0; diseases of the genitourinary system 13.1.

Social indicators

Educational attainment (1981). Percentage of population age 25 and over having: primary or secondary education only 89.7%; some postsecondary 4.8%; bachelor's or equivalent degree 4.9%; higher university degree 0.6%.

Distribution of disposable income (1990)

percentage of household income by quintile

1	2	3	4	5 (highest)
6.6	11.2	16.3	23.5	42.4

Quality of working life (1991). Average workweek (hours): male 42.2, female 37.4 (overtime [1986]; male 8.6%, female 2.1%). Annual rate per 100,000 workers for: injury or accident 752.6; industrial diseases 0.5[8]; death 1.5. Proportion of labour force (employed persons) insured for damages or income loss resulting from: injury 100%; permanent disability 100%; death 100%. Average days lost to labour stoppages per 1,000 employee workdays 1991: 0.2. Principal means of transport to work (1991; London only): public transportation 81%, private automobile 15%, motor or pedal cycle 2%, other 2%.
Access to services (1990)[6]. Proportion of households having access to: bath or shower 98%; toilet 99%; central heating 80%.
Social participation. Eligible voters participating in last national election: 76.3%. Population age 16 and over participating in voluntary work (1987)[6]: 22%. Trade union membership in total workforce (1990) 34.9%.
Social deviance (1991). Offense rate per 100,000 population for: theft and handling stolen goods 5,338.1; burglary 2,345.6; violence against the person 363.9; fraud and forgery 357.3; robbery 92.5; sexual offense 57.9. Incidence per 100,000 population of: registered drug addicts 36.5[9]; suicide 7.9.
Leisure (1990). Favourite leisure activities (hours weekly): watching television 23.5; listening to radio 10.1; reading 2.6[10]; cultural activities 1.5[10].
Material well-being (1991). Households possessing: automobile 67%, telephone 88%, television receiver 98% (colour 95%), refrigerator 95%, central heating 82%, washing machine 87%, videocassette recorder 68%.

National economy

Gross national product (1992): U.S.$1,024,025,000,000 (U.S.$17,770 per capita).

Structure of gross domestic product and labour force

	1992 in value £'000,000	% of total value	labour force	% of labour force
Agriculture	9,309	1.8	577,000	2.1
Mining	9,842	1.9	11	11
Manufacturing	114,698	22.2	4,985,000[11]	18.0[11]
Construction	32,002	6.2	1,515,000	5.5
Public utilities	13,717	2.7	414,000	1.5
Transp. and commun.	41,613	8.1	1,497,000	5.4
Trade	72,549	14.1	5,351,000	19.3
Finance	121,704	23.6	3,086,000	11.1
Pub. admin., defense	89,114	17.3		
Services	32,892	6.4	10,314,000[12]	37.1[12]
Other	−22,846[13]	−4.4[13]		
TOTAL	514,594	100.0[1]	27,739,000	100.0

Budget (1992–93). Revenue: £201,885,000,000 (income tax 36.4%, taxes on expenditures 18.5%, social-security contributions 17.4%). Expenditures: £235,630,000,000 (social-security benefits 29.7%, national health service 12.6%, defense 10.3%, debt interest 8.0%, education and science 3.4%).
Total national debt (March 1991): £190,209,000,000.

Financial aggregates

	1987	1988	1989	1990	1991	1992	1993[14]
Exchange rate:							
U.S. dollar per £	1.64	1.78	1.64	1.78	1.77	1.76	1.49
SDRs per £	1.32	1.34	1.22	1.36	1.31	1.10	1.06
International reserves (U.S.$)							
Total (excl. gold; '000,000,000)	41.72	44.10	34.77	35.85	41.89	36.64	37.06[15]
SDRs ('000,000,000)	1.38	1.32	1.14	1.25	1.31	0.54	0.41
Reserve pos. in IMF ('000,000,000)	1.78	1.67	1.64	1.68	1.85	2.01	1.96
Foreign exchange ('000,000,000)	38.56	41.12	31.99	32.93	38.73	34.09	34.77[15]
Gold ('000,000 fine troy oz)	19.01	19.00	18.99	18.97	18.89	18.61	18.45[15]
% world reserves	2.0	2.0	2.0	2.0	2.0	2.0	2.0[15]
Interest and prices							
Central bank discount (%)	...	...	...	...	...	...	...
Govt. bond yield (%) long term	9.48	9.36	9.58	11.08	9.92	9.15	8.39[15]
Industrial share prices (1985 = 100)	163.8	147.6	176.5	173.3	190.2	198.0	222.4[15]
Balance of payments (U.S.$'000,000)							
Balance of visible trade,	−17,962	−36,994	−39,157	−32,400	−17,990	−24,618	...
Imports, f.o.b.	148,247	180,527	190,898	214,693	201,081	212,058	...
Exports, f.o.b.	130,285	143,534	151,741	182,293	183,091	187,440	...
Balance of invisibles	10,363	8,205	3,570	3,010	6,768	3,904	...
Balance of payments, current account	−7,599	−28,789	−35,587	−29,390	−11,222	−20,714	...

Tourism (1991): receipts from visitors U.S.$12,873,000,000; expenditures by nationals abroad U.S.$17,648,000,000.

Manufacturing, mining, and construction enterprises (1990)

	no. of enterprises[16]	no. of employees	annual wages as a % of avg. of all wages[10]	annual value added (£'000,000)
Manufacturing				
Food, beverages, and tobacco	8,916	591,000	103.0	14,390
Transport equipment	4,233	533,000	...	13,622
Mechanical engineering	23,322	588,000	108.4	13,300
Electrical and data-processing equipment	9,644	566,000	96.8	12,750
Paper and paper products; printing and publishing	21,495	462,000	133.8	12,004
Chemical engineering	3,137	290,000	118.1	11,120
Rubber and plastic	4,785	234,000	118.1	5,026
Metal manufacturing	1,186	136,000	102.8	3,638
Timber and wood products	13,794	207,000	98.1	3,459
Clothing and footwear	11,207	298,000	85.6	3,448
Textiles	4,466	196,000	79.2	2,941
Mineral-oil processing	123	14,000	118.1	2,492
Mining				
Extraction of coal, mineral oil, and natural gas	...	113,000	118.1	9,781
Extraction of minerals other than fuels	793	19,100[16]	103.1	742.3[16]
Construction	185,854	1,163,000	...	20,681

Production (metric tons except as noted). Agriculture, forestry, fishing (1992): wheat 14,185,000, sugar beets 8,500,000, potatoes 7,882,000, barley 7,386,000, turnips and rutabagas 3,451,000[17, 18], corn (maize) 1,657,000[17, 19], rapeseed 1,166,000, cabbage 780,000, oats 523,000; livestock (number of live animals) 28,932,000 sheep, 11,623,000 cattle, 7,519,000 pigs; roundwood (1991) 6,409,000 cu m; fish catch (1991) 823,225. Mining (1991): limestone 91,999,000; iron 13,200; tin 2,300; lead 1,440. Manufacturing (total sales in £'000,000; 1991): motor vehicles and parts 18,508; aerospace equipment 11,532; electronic data-processing and telecommunications equipment 8,081; basic electrical equipment 3,504; mechanical lifting and handling equipment 4,422; constructional steelwork 2,531; boilers 2,308. Construction (value in £; 1991)[6]: residential 5,656,000,000; nonresidential 19,311,000,000, of which commercial 8,224,000,000, industrial 5,314,000,000.

Retail trade enterprises (1990)

	no. of enterprises	no. of employees	weekly wage as a % of all wages	annual turnover (£'000,000)[20]
Food and grocery, of which	65,800	857,000	...	46,404
large grocery	78	527,000	...	35,196
other grocery	21,287	109,000	...	4,400
meats	13,383	72,000	...	2,737
Household goods, of which	49,744	314,000	...	19,438
electrical and musical goods	12,286	94,000	...	6,996
furniture	12,419	61,000	...	4,816
Drink, confectionery, and tobacco, of which	48,349	290,000	...	12,713
tobacco and confectionery	42,891	243,000	...	9,885
Clothing and footwear, of which	31,621	307,000	...	12,172
women's, girls', and infants' wear	17,047	124,000	...	4,854
footwear	4,306	85,000	...	2,806
men's and boys' wear	3,994	40,000	...	2,115
Pharmaceuticals	7,941	85,000	...	4,431
Mail order	43	32,000	...	3,693

Energy production (consumption): electricity (kW-hr; 1990) 318,979,000,000 (330,922,000,000); coal (metric tons; 1990) 89,303,000 (100,249,000); crude petroleum (barrels; 1990) 656,722,000 (568,604,000); petroleum products (metric tons; 1990) 81,919,000 (79,470,000); natural gas (cu m; 1990) 53,895,000,000 (61,895,000,000).

Population economically active (1992): total 27,739,000; activity rate of total population 48.0% (participation rates: ages 15–64, 61.1%[16]; female 48.3%; unemployed 9.8%).

Price and earnings indexes (1985 = 100)

	1986	1987	1988	1989	1990	1991	1992
Consumer price index	103.4	107.7	113.0	121.8	133.4	141.2	146.4
Annual earnings index	107.9	116.3	126.4	137.9	151.3	163.4	173.6

Household income and expenditure (1991). Average household size 2.5[6]; average annual income per household (1989) £15,800 (U.S.$25,900); sources of income (1990): wages and salaries 60.7%, rent, dividends, and interest 13.5%, income from self-employment 13.4%, social-security benefits 12.3%; expenditure (1991): food and beverages 18.4%, transport and vehicles 17.0%, housing 14.0%, household goods 6.2%, clothing 5.7%, energy 3.9%.
Land use (1991): forested 10.0%; meadows and pastures 46.3%; agricultural and under permanent cultivation 27.3%; other 16.4%.

Foreign trade

Balance of trade (current prices)

	1987	1988	1989	1990	1991	1992
£'000,000	−17,926	−37,446	−39,157	−31,131	−17,990	−24,618
% of total	6.4%	11.5%	11.4%	7.8%	4.7%	6.2%

Imports (1992): £125,896,000,000 (machinery and transport equipment 37.6%, of which road vehicles 9.6%, data-processing equipment 6.6%; chemicals and chemical products 9.2%, of which organic chemicals 2.2%; food and live animals 9.0%, of which vegetables and fruits 2.6%, meat and meat preparations 1.6%; petroleum and petroleum products 4.2%; paper and paperboard 3.1%; textile yarn and fabrics 3.1%; nonferrous metals 2.1%; iron and steel products 2.0%). *Major import sources:* Germany 15.1%; U.S. 10.9%; France 9.7%; The Netherlands 7.9%; Japan 5.9%; Italy 5.4%; Belgium-Luxembourg 4.6%; Ireland 4.0%; Switzerland 3.1%; Norway 3.1%.
Exports (1992): £108,298,000,000 (machinery and transport equipment 40.8%, of which road vehicles 8.2%, data-processing equipment 6.1%, power-generating machinery and equipment 5.1%, machinery specialized for particular industries 3.7%; chemicals and chemical products 13.8%, of which organic chemicals 3.4%; petroleum and petroleum products 6.1%; iron and steel products 2.8%; professional, scientific, and controlling instruments 2.8%; nonmetallic mineral manufactures 2.7%). *Major export destinations:* Germany 13.9%; United States 11.2%; France 10.6%; The Netherlands 7.8%; Italy 5.7%; Ireland 5.3%; Belgium-Luxembourg 5.3%; Spain 4.1%; Sweden 2.2%; Japan 2.0%; Saudi Arabia 1.8%.

Transport and communications

Transport. Railroads (1992)[21]: length 23,518 mi[22], 37,849 km[22]; passenger-mi 19,919,000,000, passenger-km 32,057,000,000; short ton-mi cargo 10,512,000,000, metric ton-km cargo 15,347,000,000. Roads (1990)[6]: total length 222,472 mi, 358,034 km (paved 100%). Vehicles (1991)[6]: passenger cars 19,737,000; trucks and buses 2,773,000. Merchant marine (1992): vessels (100 gross tons and over) 1,631; total deadweight tonnage 4,355,063. Air transport (1991): passenger-mi 54,188,500,000, passenger-km 87,208,110,000; short ton-mi cargo 1,636,100,000[22], metric ton-km cargo 2,388,700,000[22]; airports (1993) with scheduled flights 53.
Communications. Daily newspapers (1990): total number 99; total circulation 22,253,500; circulation per 1,000 population 388. Radio (1990): 57,456,832 receivers (1 per 1.0 person). Television (1991): 19,546,000 licenses (1 per 2.9 persons). Telephones (1984): 29,517,991 receivers (1 per 1.9 persons).

Education and health

Education (1990–91)[23]

	schools	teachers	students	student/teacher ratio
Primary (age 5–10)	24,135	219,200	4,812,300	21.9
Secondary (age 11–19)	4,790	229,100	3,473,300	15.2
Voc., teacher tr.[24, 25]	724	93,000[26]	539,718	...
Higher[27]	48	49,377	370,254	7.5

Literacy (1990): total population literate, virtually 100%[28].
Health (1981): physicians 92,172 (1 per 611 persons); hospital beds (1987) 388,700 (1 per 146 persons); infant mortality rate (1991) 7.4.
Food (1988–90): daily per capita caloric intake 3,270 (vegetable products 66%, animal products 34%); 130% of FAO recommended minimum requirement.

Military

Total active duty personnel (1992): 293,500 (army 49.5%, navy 21.2%, air force 29.3%). *Military expenditure as percentage of GNP* (1989): 4.2% (world 4.9%); per capita expenditure U.S.$605.

[1]Detail does not add to total given because of rounding. [2]Includes separately administered Isles of Scilly (area 6 sq mi [16 sq km]; pop. 2,900). [3]Geographic entity only; since April 1, 1986, the administrative functions of the former metropolitan county councils have been dispersed among other local authorities. [4]Comprises 26 local government districts not shown separately. [5]Includes three separately administered island groups (Orkney 377 sq mi [976 sq km], pop. 19,600; Shetland 553 sq mi [1,432 sq km], pop. 22,500; Western Isles 1,119 sq mi [2,898 sq km], pop. 29,400). [6]Great Britain only. [7]Figures in parentheses are for Northern Ireland (1984). [8]1982. [9]England and Wales only. [10]1984. [11]Manufacturing includes Mining. [12]Includes 2,732,000 unemployed not distributed by sector. [13]Plus rent; less imputed bank service charges. [14]August. [15]June. [16]1988. [17]Primarily for fodder. [18]1987. [19]1991. [20]Includes value-added taxes. [21]British Rail only. [22]1990. [23]Public sector only. [24]Third level. [25]1987–88. [26]1984–85. [27]Universities only. [28]A survey in 1986–87, however, put the number of functional illiterates at 9–12% of the adult population.

United States

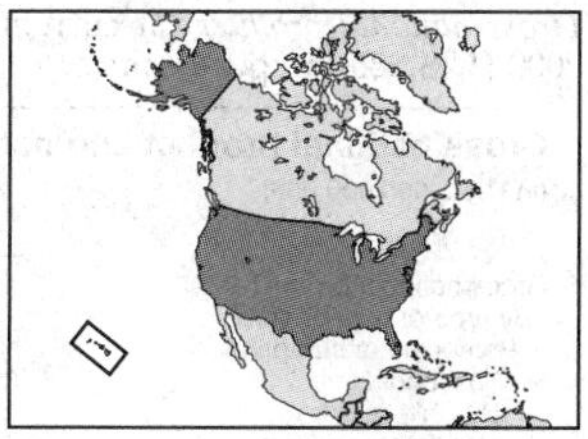

Official name: United States of America.
Form of government: federal republic with two legislative houses (Senate [100]; House of Representatives [435[1]]).
Head of state and government: President.
Capital: Washington, D.C.
Official language: English.
Official religion: none.
Monetary unit: 1 dollar (U.S.$) = 100 cents; valuation (Oct. 4, 1993) 1 U.S.$ = £0.66; 1 £ = U.S.$1.52.

Area and population

		area[2]		population
States	Capitals	sq mi	sq km	1993 estimate
Alabama	Montgomery	51,705	133,915	4,187,000
Alaska	Juneau	591,004	1,530,693	599,000
Arizona	Phoenix	114,000	295,259	3,936,000
Arkansas	Little Rock	53,187	137,754	2,424,000
California	Sacramento	158,706	411,407	31,211,000
Colorado	Denver	104,091	269,594	3,566,000
Connecticut	Hartford	5,018	12,997	3,277,000
Delaware	Dover	2,045	5,294	700,000
Florida	Tallahassee	58,664	151,939	13,679,000
Georgia	Atlanta	58,910	152,576	6,917,000
Hawaii	Honolulu	6,471	16,760	1,172,000
Idaho	Boise	83,564	216,430	1,099,000
Illinois	Springfield	57,871	149,885	11,697,000
Indiana	Indianapolis	36,413	94,309	5,713,000
Iowa	Des Moines	56,275	145,752	2,814,000
Kansas	Topeka	82,277	213,096	2,531,000
Kentucky	Frankfort	40,410	104,659	3,789,000
Louisiana	Baton Rouge	47,752	123,677	4,295,000
Maine	Augusta	33,265	86,156	1,239,000
Maryland	Annapolis	10,460	27,091	4,965,000
Massachusetts	Boston	8,284	21,455	6,012,000
Michigan	Lansing	97,102	251,493	9,476,000
Minnesota	St. Paul	86,614	224,329	4,517,000
Mississippi	Jackson	47,689	123,514	2,643,000
Missouri	Jefferson City	69,697	180,514	5,234,000
Montana	Helena	147,046	380,847	839,000
Nebraska	Lincoln	77,355	200,349	1,607,000
Nevada	Carson City	110,561	286,352	1,389,000
New Hampshire	Concord	9,279	24,032	1,125,000
New Jersey	Trenton	7,787	20,168	7,879,000
New Mexico	Santa Fe	121,593	314,924	1,616,000
New York	Albany	52,735	136,583	18,197,000
North Carolina	Raleigh	52,669	136,412	6,945,000
North Dakota	Bismarck	70,702	183,117	635,000
Ohio	Columbus	44,787	115,998	11,091,000
Oklahoma	Oklahoma City	69,956	181,185	3,231,000
Oregon	Salem	97,073	251,418	3,032,000
Pennsylvania	Harrisburg	46,043	119,251	12,048,000
Rhode Island	Providence	1,212	3,139	1,000,000
South Carolina	Columbia	31,113	80,582	3,643,000
South Dakota	Pierre	77,116	199,730	715,000
Tennessee	Nashville	42,144	109,152	5,099,000
Texas	Austin	266,807	691,027	18,031,000
Utah	Salt Lake City	84,899	219,887	1,860,000
Vermont	Montpelier	9,614	24,900	576,000
Virginia	Richmond	40,767	105,586	6,491,000
Washington	Olympia	68,139	176,479	5,255,000
West Virginia	Charleston	24,232	62,758	1,820,000
Wisconsin	Madison	66,215	171,496	5,038,000
Wyoming	Cheyenne	97,809	253,324	470,000
District				
Dist. of Columbia	—	69	179	578,000
TOTAL		3,679,192[3]	9,529,063	257,908,000[3]

Demography

Population (1993)[4]: 258,233,000.
Density (1993): persons per sq mi 70.2, persons per sq km 27.1.
Urban-rural (1990): urban 75.2%; rural 24.8%.
Sex distribution (1991): male 48.77%; female 51.23%.
Age breakdown (1991): under 15, 21.9%; 15–29, 22.7%; 30–44, 24.4%; 45–59, 14.3%; 60–74, 11.4%; 75 and over, 5.3%.
Population projection: (2000) 275,326,000; (2010) 298,620,000.
Doubling time: 99 years.
Population by race and Hispanic[5] origin (1990): non-Hispanic white 75.6%; non-Hispanic black 11.8%; Hispanic 9.0%; Asian and Pacific Islander 2.9%; American Indian and Eskimo 0.7%.
Religious affiliation (1990): Christian 86.5%, of which Protestant 52.7%, Roman Catholic 26.2%, other Christian 7.6%; Muslim 1.9%; Jewish 1.8%; nonreligious 7.5%; other 2.3%.
Mobility (1989–90). Population living in the same residence as in 1987: 82.0%; different residence, same county 11.0%; different county, same state 3.0%; different state 3.0%; moved from abroad 1.0%.
Households (1992). Total households 95,669,000 (married-couple families 52,457,000 [54.8%]). Average household size 2.6; 1 person 25.1%, 2 persons 32.1%, 3 persons 17.1%, 4 persons 15.4%, 5 or more persons 10.3%. Family households: 67,173,000 (70.2%); nonfamily 28,496,000 (29.8%), of which 1-person 24.0%.
Immigration (1991[6]): permanent immigrants admitted 1,827,167, from Mexico 51.8%, Philippines 3.5%, former U.S.S.R. 3.1%, Vietnam 3.0%, Haiti 2.6%, El Salvador 2.6%, India 2.5%, Dominican Republic 2.3%, China 1.8%, South Korea 1.5%, Guatemala 1.4%, Jamaica 1.3%, Pakistan 1.1%, Colombia 1.1%, Iran 1.1%. Refugee arrivals (1991[6]): 100,229.
Major cities (1990): New York 7,322,564; Los Angeles 3,485,398; Chicago 2,783,726; Houston 1,630,553; Philadelphia 1,585,577; San Diego 1,110,549; Detroit 1,027,974; Dallas 1,006,877; Phoenix 983,403; San Antonio 935,933.

Other principal cities (1990)

	population		population		population
Akron	223,019	Fort Worth	447,619	Oklahoma City	441,719
Albuquerque	384,736	Fresno	354,202	Omaha	335,795
Anaheim	266,406	Honolulu	365,272	Pittsburgh	369,879
Anchorage	226,338	Indianapolis	741,952	Portland (Ore.)	437,319
Arlington (Tex.)	261,721	Jacksonville	672,971	Riverside	226,505
Atlanta	394,017	Jersey City	228,537	Rochester (N.Y.)	231,636
Aurora (Colo.)	222,103	Kansas City (Mo.)	435,146	Sacramento	369,365
Austin	465,622	Las Vegas	258,295	St. Louis	396,685
Baltimore	736,014	Lexington (Ky.)	225,366	St. Paul	272,235
Baton Rouge	219,531	Long Beach	429,433	St. Petersburg	238,629
Birmingham	265,968	Louisville	269,063	San Francisco	723,959
Boston	574,283	Memphis	610,337	San Jose	782,248
Buffalo	328,123	Mesa	288,091	Santa Ana	293,742
Charlotte	395,934	Miami	358,548	Seattle	516,259
Cincinnati	364,040	Milwaukee	628,088	Tampa	280,015
Cleveland	505,616	Minneapolis	368,383	Toledo	332,943
Colorado Springs	281,140	Nashville	510,784	Tucson	405,390
Columbus	632,910	New Orleans	496,938	Tulsa	362,307
Corpus Christi	257,453	Newark	275,221	Virginia Beach	393,069
Denver	467,610	Norfolk	261,229	Washington, D.C.	606,900
El Paso	515,342	Oakland	372,242	Wichita	304,011

Place of birth (1990): native-born 227,078,000 (91.3%); foreign-born 21,632,000 (8.7%), of which Mexico 4,447,000, Germany (East and West) 1,163,000, Philippines 998,000, Canada 871,000, United Kingdom 765,000, Cuba 751,000, South Korea 663,000, Italy 640,000, Vietnam 556,000, China 543,000, India 463,000, Japan 422,000, Poland 397,000, U.S.S.R. 337,000, Portugal 219,000, Greece 189,000, other 8,208,000.

Vital statistics

Birth rate per 1,000 population (1993[7]): 15.7 (world avg. 26.4); (1990) legitimate 76.6%; illegitimate 23.4%.
Death rate per 1,000 population (1993[7]): 8.6 (world avg. 9.2).
Natural increase rate per 1,000 population (1993[7]): 7.1 (world avg. 17.2).
Total fertility rate (avg. births per childbearing woman; 1990): 2.1.
Marriage rate per 1,000 population (1993[7]): 9.1; median age at first marriage (1991): men 26.3 years, women 24.1 years.
Divorce rate per 1,000 population (1993[7]): 4.7.
Life expectancy at birth (1991): white male 73.0 years, black and other male 68.1 years; white female 79.7 years, black and other female 76.2 years.
Major causes of death per 100,000 population (12 months ending May 1993): cardiovascular diseases 350.0, of which ischemic heart disease 180.0, other forms of heart disease 76.2, cerebrovascular diseases 57.4, atherosclerosis 5.3, other cardiovascular diseases 10.5; malignant neoplasms (cancers) 195.3; diseases of the respiratory system 71.9, of which pneumonia 30.2; accidents and adverse effects 31.6, of which motor-vehicle accidents 14.1; diabetes mellitus 21.3; acquired immune deficiency syndrome (AIDS) 13.7; suicide 12.2; chronic liver disease and cirrhosis 9.1; homicide 8.5.
Morbidity rates of infectious diseases per 100,000 population (1991): gonorrhea 245.6; chicken pox 58.2; syphilis 50.9; salmonellosis 19.1; acquired immune deficiency syndrome (AIDS) 17.3; tuberculosis 10.4; hepatitis A (infectious) 9.6; shigellosis 9.3; hepatitis B (serum) 7.1; aseptic meningitis 5.7; measles (rubeola) 3.8.
Incidence of chronic health conditions per 1,000 population (1990): chronic sinusitus 129.3; arthritis 123.3; deformities or orthopedic impairments 115.6; hypertension 108.5; hearing impairment 93.2; hay fever 88.7; heart conditions 77.2; chronic bronchitis 50.3; asthma 41.2; hemorrhoids 37.8.

Social indicators

Educational attainment (1991). Percentage of population age 25 and over having: incomplete primary education 6.2%; primary 4.4%; incomplete secondary 11.0%; secondary 38.6%; some postsecondary 18.4%; 4-year higher degree and more 21.4%. Number of earned degrees (1991–92): bachelor's degree 1,105,000; master's degree 344,000; doctor's degree 39,800; first-professional degrees (in fields such as medicine, theology, and law) 74,900.

Distribution of income (1992)

percentage of national household income by quintile

1	2	3	4	5 (highest)
3.8	9.4	15.8	24.2	46.9

Quality of working life (1992). Average workweek: 34.4 hours (9.6% overtime[8]). Annual rate per 100,000 workers for (1991): injury or accident 1,700; death 9.9. Proportion of labour force insured for damages or income loss resulting from: injury, permanent disability, and death (1988) 56.6%. Average days per 1,000 workdays lost to labour stoppages (1992): 0.1. Average duration of journey to work (1979): 22.5 minutes (private automobile 85.7%, public transportation 5.9%, bicycle or motorcycle 1.3%, foot 3.9%, work at home 2.3%, other 0.9%). Rate per 1,000 workers of discouraged (unemployed no longer seeking work; 1991): 8.1.
Access to services (1987). Proportion of dwellings having access to: electricity virtually 100.0%; safe public water supply 98.6%; public sewage collection 99.2%; public fire protection, n.a.
Social participation. Eligible voters participating in last presidential election (1992): 54.0%. Population age 16 and over participating in voluntary work (1989): 20.4%. Trade union membership in total workforce (1991): 16.1%. Practicing religious population in total affiliated population (church attendance; 1987): once a week 47%; once in six months 67%; once a year 74%.

Social deviance (1992). Offense rate per 100,000 population for: murder 9.3; rape 42.8; robbery 263.6; aggravated assault 441.8; motor-vehicle theft 631.5; burglary and housebreaking 1,168.2; larceny-theft 3,103.0; drug-abuse violation 309.2[9]; drunkenness 260.1[9]. Drug and substance users (population age 26 and over; 1991): alcohol 52.5%; marijuana 3.3%; cocaine 0.8%; tranquilizers 0.5%; analgesics 0.5%; stimulants 0.2%; hallucinogens 0.1%; heroin, n.a. Rate per 100,000 population of suicide (1993): 12.2.

Crime rates per 100,000 population in metropolitan areas (1992)

		violent crime			
	total	murder	rape	robbery	assault
Atlanta	940.2	12.7	59.6	370.1	497.8
Baltimore	1,359.4	16.7	53.9	637.1	651.7
Boston	686.5	3.5	33.6	183.3	466.1
Chicago	...	14.6	...	577.4	653.7
Dallas	1,124.5	17.5	64.1	422.7	620.2
Detroit	980.8	16.5	66.6	366.1	531.6
Houston	1,012.0	17.6	57.6	399.2	537.3
Los Angeles	1,778.6	20.9	42.0	750.1	965.6
Miami	2,037.0	17.0	54.2	902.5	1,063.2
Minneapolis	478.0	4.3	53.5	180.4	239.8
New York	2,163.7	27.1	38.2	1,237.1	861.4
Philadelphia	673.1	11.0	33.6	329.6	298.9
Pittsburgh	409.7	4.3	29.3	179.1	197.0
St. Louis	1,003.4	15.7	173.2	276.5	537.9
San Francisco	1,085.9	11.0	38.2	578.1	458.5
Washington, D.C.	774.9	15.7	30.7	328.1	400.4

		property crime		
	total	burglary	larceny	auto theft
Atlanta	6,991.7	1,631.7	4,488.9	871.1
Baltimore	6,022.9	1,358.0	3,824.3	840.6
Boston	4,040.5	982.7	2,321.6	736.2
Chicago	5,357.0	1,129.1	3,384.3	843.6
Dallas	7,327.2	1,686.0	4,584.1	1,057.1
Detroit	5,506.3	1,065.5	3,397.0	1,043.7
Houston	5,935.7	1,480.2	3,124.8	1,330.7
Los Angeles	5,629.0	1,400.3	2,779.3	1,449.5
Miami	10,299.5	2,348.6	6,172.4	1,778.4
Minneapolis	5,108.3	1,051.5	3,576.0	480.8
New York	6,326.8	1,403.0	3,202.2	1,721.4
Philadelphia	3,769.0	784.3	2,225.2	759.5
Pittsburgh	2,872.1	612.7	1,623.0	636.5
St. Louis	4,904.6	1,194.3	3,105.6	604.7
San Francisco	5,960.1	1,107.0	3,821.4	1,031.6
Washington, D.C.	4,796.6	837.2	3,286.3	673.1

Leisure (1976). Favourite leisure activities (weekly hours): watching television 9.6; social time 7.6; reading 3.7; cultural activities 1.5.
Material well-being (1992). Occupied dwellings with householder possessing: automobile 84.9%[10]; telephone 93.9%; radio receiver 99.0%; television receiver 98.3%; air conditioner 69.9%[11]; washing machine 76.3%[11]; videocassette recorder 72.5%; cable television 60.2%.
Recreational expenditures (1991): U.S.$258,700,000,000[12] (television and radio receivers 21.7%; nondurable toys and sports equipment 11.0%; sports supplies 10.2%; magazines and newspapers 7.8%; golfing, bowling, and other participatory activities 7.3%; books and maps 6.0%; spectator amusements 4.0%, of which spectator sports 1.5%, theatre and opera 1.4%, movies 1.1%; flowers, seeds, and potted plants 3.6%).

National economy

Budget (1994). Revenue: U.S.$1,241,300,000,000 (individual income tax 44.2%, social-insurance taxes and contributions 37.4%, corporation income tax 9.7%, other 8.7%). Expenditures: U.S.$1,500,100,000,000 (social security and medicare 31.2%, defense 18.4%, income security 14.2%, interest on debt 13.8%, health 7.6%, other 14.8%).
Total national debt (1993): U.S.$4,351,100,000,000.

Manufacturing, mining, and construction enterprises (1993)

	no. of enterprises[13]	no. of employees	hourly wage as a % of all wages	value added (U.S.$'000,000)[9]
Manufacturing				
Chemical and related products	12,109	1,078,200	137.4	154,793
Transportation equipment	10,500	1,698,500	146.1	151,979
Food and related products	20,624	1,733,100	96.6	145,336
Machinery, except electrical	52,135	1,882,100	118.1	124,235
Electric and electronic machinery	15,962	1,503,100	104.4	106,669
Instruments and related products	10,326	875,600	113.6	82,536
Fabricated metal products	36,105	1,306,900	108.3	76,670
Paper and related products	6,342	683,100	124.4	58,281
Rubber and plastic products	14,515	889,700	97.9	50,295
Primary metals	6,771	673,500	129.8	46,605
Apparel and related products	22,872	975,700	65.6	33,432
Stone, clay, and glass products	16,166	523,300	110.2	31,839
Lumber and wood	33,982	698,800	89.8	26,995
Textile-mill products	6,412	666,900	82.7	26,925
Tobacco products	138	46,200	161.4	24,484
Petroleum and coal products	2,254	158,100	170.2	24,024
Furniture and fixtures	11,613	481,000	86.6	20,669
Leather and leather products	2,193	116,400	70.7	4,293
Miscellaneous manufacturing industries	16,544	362,400	86.4	19,999
Mining				
Oil and gas extraction	22,910	352,600	130.5	80,049[13]
Coal mining	3,905	95,900	158.7	17,068[13]
Nonmetallic, except fuels	5,775	104,300	118.7	9,233[13]
Metal mining	1,027	48,000	140.4	4,610[13]
Construction				
Special trade contractors	342,000	3,019,900	136.7	117,480[13]
Heavy construction contractors	36,600	779,800	132.5	44,940[13]
General contractors and operative builders	157,600	1,117,400	126.1	33,802[13]

Gross national product (at current market prices; 1992): U.S.$5,905,700,000,000 (U.S.$23,150 per capita).

Gross national product and national income
(in U.S.$'000,000,000)

	1988	1989	1990	1991	1992
Gross national product	4,873.7	5,200.8	5,465.1	5,677.5	6,038.6
By type of expenditure					
Personal consumption expenditures	3,238.2	3,450.1	3,657.3	3,887.7	4,139.9
Durable goods	457.5	474.6	480.3	446.1	497.3
Nondurable goods	1,060.0	1,130.1	1,193.7	1,251.5	1,300.9
Services	1,720.7	1,845.5	1,983.3	2,190.1	2,341.6
Gross private domestic investment	747.1	771.2	741.0	721.1	796.5
Fixed investment	720.8	742.9	746.1	731.3	789.1
Changes in business inventories	26.2	28.3	−5.0	−10.2	7.3
Net exports of goods and services	−74.1	−46.1	−31.2	−21.8	−29.6
Exports	552.0	626.2	672.8	598.2	640.5
Imports	626.1	672.3	704.0	620.0	670.1
Government purchases of goods and services	962.5	1,025.6	1,098.1	1,090.5	1,131.8
Federal	380.3	400.1	424.0	447.3	448.8
State and local	582.3	625.6	674.1	643.2	313.8
By major type of product					
Goods output	1,935.1	2,072.7	2,143.3	2,182.5	2,312.8
Durable goods	860.2	906.6	928.0	888.4	977.9
Nondurable goods	1,074.9	1,166.0	1,215.2	1,294.1	1,334.9
Services	2,488.6	2,671.2	2,864.2	3,030.3	3,221.1
Structures	450.0	456.9	457.4	464.7	504.6
National income (incl. capital consumption adjustment)	3,984.9	4,223.3	4,418.4	4,544.2	4,836.6
By type of income					
Compensation of employees	2,905.1	3,079.0	3,244.2	3,390.8	3,582.0
Proprietors' income	354.2	379.3	402.5	368.0	414.3
Rental income of persons	16.3	8.2	6.9	−10.4	−8.9
Corporate profits	311.6	275.2	298.3	346.3	407.2
Net interest	371.8	324.0	466.7	449.5	442.0
By industry division (excl. capital consumption adjustment)					
Agriculture, forestry, fishing	94.7	101.0	103.4	90.9	100.9
Mining and construction	248.3	261.5	267.3	246.8	251.3
Manufacturing	782.2	803.8	806.5	841.0	895.3
Durable	453.7	465.6	461.5	464.2	501.7
Nondurable	328.6	338.2	345.0	376.8	393.6
Transportation	131.2	136.6	144.0	140.8	151.0
Communications	87.4	87.4	92.8	95.3	103.7
Public utilities	86.8	90.2	92.0	99.0	101.5
Wholesale and retail trade	569.5	607.5	638.8	669.3	700.3
Finance, insurance, real estate	562.0	613.8	647.5	685.0	748.9
Services	799.9	883.0	963.4	1,002.5	1,085.8
Government and government enterprise	566.9	41.7	648.4	699.5	734.5
Other	33.5	37.6	41.7	17.4	7.3

Structure of gross domestic product and labour force

	1989		1992	
	in value U.S.$'000,000,000	% of total value	labour force[14]	% of labour force[14]
Agriculture	113	2.2	3,653,000	2.8
Mining	80	1.5	720,000	0.6
Manufacturing	966	18.7	21,620,000	16.8
Construction	248	4.8	8,118,000	6.3
Public utilities	156	3.0	1,665,000	1.3
Transp. and commun.	306	5.9	7,018,000	5.4
Trade	825	16.0	26,431,000	20.6
Finance	897	17.4	13,359,000	10.4
Public administration, defense	619	12.0	44,939,000	35.0
Services	971	18.8		
Other	−18[15]	−0.3[15]	1,018,000[16]	0.8[16]
TOTAL	5,163	100.0	128,540,000[3]	100.0

Business activity (1989): number of businesses 19,561,000 (sole proprietorships 73.1%, active corporations 18.5%, active partnerships 8.4%), of which services 8,328,000, wholesaling and retailing 3,624,000; business receipts $11,598,000,000,000 (active corporations 90.0%, sole proprietorships 6.0%, active partnerships 4.0%), of which wholesaling and retailing $3,419,000,000,000, services $1,068,000,000,000; net profit $536,000,000,000 (active corporations 72.6%, sole proprietorships 24.8%, partnerships 2.6%), of which services $112,000,000,000, wholesaling and retailing $53,000,000,000. New business concerns and business failures (1992): total number of new incorporations 667,341; total failures 96,750, of which commercial service 26,795, retail trade 18,989; failure rate per 10,000 concerns 110; current liabilities of failed concerns $93,755,600,000, of which retail trade $11,771,900,000, manufacturing and mining $9,697,600,000; average liability $1,031,900. Business expenditures for new plant and equipment (1991): total $528,390,000,000, of which trade, services, and communications $246,320,000,000, manufacturing businesses $182,810,000,000 (nondurable goods 57.5%, durable goods 42.5%), public utilities $66,570,000,000, transportation $22,660,000,000, mining $10,020,000,000.
Production. Agriculture, forestry, fishing (value of production/catch in U.S.$'000,000 except as noted; 1991): corn (maize) 18,036, soybeans 11,078, hay 9,801, wheat 5,801, cotton lint 4,927, tobacco 2,968, potatoes 2,095, tomatoes 1,797, apples 1,778, grapes 1,732, oranges 1,679, peanuts (groundnuts) 1,392, sorghum 1,347, rice 1,166, sugar beets 1,067, barley 1,007, sugarcane 874, lettuce 810, strawberries 634, onions 581, almonds 540, dry edible beans 524, cottonseed 494, sweet corn 493, peaches 393, grapefruit 383, pecans 310, carrots 309, sunflowers 305, lemons 295, oats 289, walnuts 280, pears 274, broccoli 242, cranberries 207, celery 206; livestock (number of live animals; 1992) 99,559,000 cattle, 57,684,000 pigs, 10,750,000 sheep, 5,450,000 horses, 1,437,000,000 chickens; roundwood 495,800,000 cu m; fish and shellfish catch

3,308, of which fish 1,680 (including salmon 360, Alaska pollack 242), shellfish 1,628 (including shrimp 513, crabs 415). Mining and quarrying (value of production in U.S.$'000,000; 1991): crude petroleum (1990) 53,772, natural gas 30,300, bituminous coal and lignite 21,598, stone 5,382, copper 3,931, gold 3,386, portland cement 3,343, sand and gravel 3,196, iron ore 1,674, clays 1,505, phosphate rock 1,109, lime 891, salt 836. Manufacturing (metric tons except as noted; 1992): crude steel 84,322,000; paper and paperboard 75,243,000; wood pulp 59,277,000; pig iron 47,377,000; sulfuric acid 40,278,000; coke 21,237,000; phosphoric acid 11,502,000; newsprint 6,424,000; cheese 2,943,000; aerospace vehicles (sales) U.S.$121,852,000,000; machine tools (new orders for metal-cutting-type tools) U.S.$1,756,350,000; cotton fabric 3,846,000,000 sq m; carpets and rugs 1,134,300,000 sq m; footwear 167,803,000 pairs; motor-vehicle tires 230,250,000 units; major household appliances 44,306,000 units, of which 7,760,000 refrigerators, 8,390,000 microwave ovens, 6,514,000 washing machines, 4,719,000 clothes driers; radio receivers 21,552,000 units; television receivers 21,304,000 units; new passenger cars (factory sales) 5,684,000 units; new trucks and buses (factory sales) 4,042,000 units. Construction (completed; 1992): private U.S.$275,060,000,000, of which residential U.S.$187,820,000,000, nonresidential U.S.$87,240,000,000; public U.S.$51,875,000,000, of which residential U.S.$4,151,000,000, nonresidential U.S.$47,724,000,000.

Retail and wholesale trade and services (1992)

	no. of establishments	no. of employees	hourly wage as a % of all wages	annual sales or receipts (U.S.$'000,000)
Retail trade[17]	1,529,700	19,527,000	67.2	1,962,400
Automotive dealers	83,800	1,233,000	102.2	398,100
Food stores	186,100	3,174,000	71.5	384,000
General merchandise group stores	36,600	2,384,000	68.1	247,400
Eating and drinking places	402,600	6,813,000	50.0[18]	201,900
Gasoline service stations	104,800	627,000	61.7	133,000
Furniture, home furnishings, equipment stores	108,100	799,000	87.6	105,800
Apparel and accessory stores	150,200	1,129,000	64.6	105,000
Building materials, hardware, garden supply, and mobile home dealers	71,900	783,000	80.0	103,000
Drugstores and proprietary stores	50,000	603,000	72.4	77,300
Liquor stores	30,800	116,000	...	25,600
Wholesale trade[19]	466,700	6,073,000	108.2	1,828,000
Durable goods	292,800	3,474,000	111.4	904,500
Machinery, equipment, and supplies	114,400	753,000	111.3	170,100
Motor vehicles, automotive equipment	43,000	451,000	98.7	167,700
Professional and commercial equipment	...	749,000	131.8	130,700
Electrical goods	35,300	464,000	115.1	119,900
Metals and minerals, except petroleum	11,100	131,000	112.0	73,800
Lumber and other construction materials	19,100	222,000	104.7	67,700
Hardware, plumbing, heating equipment and supplies	23,100	268,000	106.3	47,800
Furniture and home furnishings	14,500	140,000	97.9	33,000
Miscellaneous durable goods	...	296,000	86.6	93,800
Nondurable goods	173,900	2,599,000	104.0	923,500
Groceries and related products	42,100	868,000	105.0	274,800
Petroleum and petroleum products	16,700	176,000	100.1	125,800
Farm-products raw materials	12,600	116,000	77.3	109,100
Apparel and accessories	16,900	211,000	100.1	73,400
Paper and paper products	16,800	237,000	109.3	51,000
Drugs, drug proprietaries, and druggists' sundries	4,900	198,000	124.1	64,300
Beer, wine, and distilled alcoholic beverages	5,800	150,000	122.1	56,500
Chemicals and allied products	12,700	140,000	124.8	37,400
Miscellaneous nondurable goods	45,300	503,000	88.6	131,100
Services[17, 20]	2,059,300	29,345,000	99.1	1,201,500
Health	436,700	8,583,000	108.1	261,300
Business, except computer services	251,800	4,864,000	84.2	190,700
Computer and data-processing services	40,500	833,000	150.7	91,300
Legal services	142,400	923,000	143.0	88,700
Automotive repair, services, garages	156,600	880,000	86.8	73,300
Management and public relations	39,800	667,000	127.3	64,800
Engineering services	33,100	595,000	157.6	59,700
Hotels and motels	39,200	1,607,000	68.2	58,300
Personal services	186,100	1,073,000	70.7	54,600
Amusement and recreation	75,200	1,352,000	71.1	46,700
Motion pictures	35,400	410,000	111.3	41,100

Energy production (consumption): electricity (kW-hr; 1992) 2,797,000,000,000 (2,757,000,000,000); coal (metric tons; 1992) 907,400,000 (809,700,000); crude petroleum (barrels; 1992) 2,617,000,000 (4,895,000,000); petroleum products (metric tons; 1991) 758,400,000 (828,600,000); natural gas (cu m; 1992) 503,332,000,000 (558,946,000,000). Domestic production of energy by source (1992): coal 32.4%, natural gas (dry) 27.4%, crude petroleum 22.7%, nuclear power 9.9%, hydroelectric power 3.8%, natural-gas-plant liquids 3.5%, other 0.3%.

Energy consumption by source (1992): petroleum and petroleum products 40.7%, natural gas 24.7%, coal 22.9%, nuclear energy 8.0%, hydroelectric power 3.4%, other 0.3%; by end use: industrial 37.2%, residential and commercial 35.5%, transportation 27.3%.

Household income and expenditure. Average household size (1992) 2.6; average (mean) annual income per household (1992) U.S.$39,020, of which average white household U.S.$40,780, average Hispanic[5] household U.S.$29,602, average black household U.S.$25,409; sources of income (1989): wages and salaries 64.4%, transfer payments 12.3%, self-employment 7.9%, other 15.4%; expenditure (1989): housing 15.9%, health care 15.3%, transportation and communications 14.5%, food and nonalcoholic beverages 10.7%, recreation 7.7%, clothing and footwear 6.6%, expenditures in restaurants and hotels 6.0%, other 23.3%.

Selected household characteristics (1992). Total number of households 96,391,000, of which (by race) white 85.2%, black 11.6%, other 3.2%; in central cities 31.4%, in suburbs 46.3%, outside metropolitan areas 22.3%; (by tenure) owned 62,220,000 (64.5%), rented 32,499,000 (33.7%); family households[21] 67,173,000, of which married couple 78.1%, female head with children under age 18, 10.5%, female head without children under 18, 6.9%, other 4.5%; nonfamily households 28,496,000, of which female living alone 50.4%, male living alone 33.7%, other 15.9%.

Financial aggregates

	1987	1988	1989	1990	1991	1992	1993[22]
Exchange rate, U.S.$ per:							
£[23]	1.64	1.78	1.64	1.78	1.77	1.76	1.52
SDR[23]	1.29	1.34	1.28	1.36	1.37	1.41	1.42
International reserves (U.S.$)[24]							
Total (excl. gold; '000,000,000)	34.72	36.74	63.55	72.26	66.66	60.27	64.78
SDRs ('000,000,000)	10.28	9.64	9.95	10.99	11.24	8.50	9.20
Reserve pos. in IMF ('000,000,000)	11.35	9.75	9.05	9.08	9.49	11.76	12.10
Foreign exchange ('000,000,000)	13.09	17.36	44.55	52.19	45.93	40.01	43.47
Gold ('000,000 fine troy oz)	262.38	261.87	261.93	261.91	261.91	261.84	261.87
% world reserves	27.69	27.62	27.78	27.84	27.86	28.13	28.57
Interest and prices							
Central bank discount (%)[24]	6.0	6.5	7.0	6.5	3.5	3.0	3.0
Govt. bond yield (%)[23]	7.67	8.24	8.56	8.25	6.81	5.31	4.17
Industrial share prices[23] (1985 = 100)	159.2	147.6	178.2	188.1	214.6	236.1	249.0
Balance of payments ($'000,000,000)							
Balance of visible trade	−159.49	−126.97	−115.71	−108.84	−73.44	−96.14	...
Imports, f.o.b.	−409.77	−447.31	−477.38	−497.55	−489.40	−536.28	...
Exports, f.o.b.	250.28	320.34	361.67	388.71	415.96	440.14	...
Balance of invisibles	−0.71	0.60	14.51	18.38	69.75	29.84	...
Balance of payments, current account	−160.20	−126.37	−101.20	−90.46	−3.69	−66.30	...

Population economically active (1992): total 128,548,000[14]; activity rate of total population 50.4% (participation rates: ages 15–64, 74.9%; female 45.1%; unemployed [September 1992–August 1993] 7.1%).

Price and earnings indexes (1985 = 100)

	1987	1988	1989	1990	1991	1992	1993[25]
Consumer price index	105.7	109.9	115.2	121.4	126.6	130.4	134.2
Hourly earnings index[26]	103.9	106.7	110.0	113.6	117.3	120.1	123.0

Average employee earnings

	average hourly earnings in U.S.$		average weekly earnings in U.S.$	
	July 1992	July 1993	July 1992	July 1993
Manufacturing				
Durable goods	12.03	12.29	495.84	511.26
Lumber and wood products	9.46	9.64	384.08	391.38
Furniture and fixtures	9.00	9.28	357.30	368.42
Stone, clay, and glass products	11.68	11.90	498.74	511.70
Primary metal industries	13.77	14.07	593.49	613.45
Fabricated metal products	11.39	11.65	470.41	482.31
Machinery, except electrical	12.49	12.76	520.83	543.58
Electrical and electronic equipment	11.05	11.25	448.63	462.38
Transportation equipment	15.12	15.57	621.43	650.83
Instruments and related products	11.93	12.26	481.97	497.76
Miscellaneous manufacturing	9.11	9.37	358.01	364.49
Nondurable goods	10.73	11.02	430.27	444.11
Food and kindred products	10.18	10.47	409.24	425.08
Tobacco manufactures	18.38	18.62	700.28	670.32
Textile mill products	8.60	8.88	350.88	363.19
Apparel and other textile products	6.94	7.02	256.78	259.74
Paper and allied products	13.13	13.50	568.53	583.20
Printing and publishing	11.76	11.91	443.35	453.77
Chemicals and allied products	14.49	14.82	618.72	637.26
Petroleum and coal products	17.70	18.43	768.18	812.76
Rubber and miscellaneous plastics products	10.39	10.61	427.03	436.07
Leather and leather products	7.28	7.55	280.28	288.41
Nonmanufacturing				
Metal mining	15.37	15.10	657.84	649.30
Coal mining	17.12	17.18	700.21	731.87
Oil and gas extraction	14.01	14.08	606.63	613.89
Nonmetallic minerals, except fuels	12.29	12.78	566.57	604.49
Construction	14.05	14.35	546.55	566.83
Transportation and public utilities	13.43	13.65	526.46	546.00
Wholesale trade	11.38	11.71	434.72	448.49
Retail trade	7.10	7.24	208.03	214.30
Finance, insurance, and real estate	10.73	11.24	381.99	400.14
Hotels, motels, and tourist courts	7.28	7.38	227.14	233.95
Health services	11.39	11.76	374.73	386.90
Legal services	14.98	15.22	521.30	528.13
Miscellaneous services	15.45	15.62	576.29	573.25

Tourism (1992): receipts from visitors U.S.$55,300,000,000; expenditures by nationals abroad U.S.$44,300,000,000; number of foreign visitors (1991) 14,734,000 (6,119,000 from Europe, 4,017,000 from Asia, 1,270,000 from Central America and the Caribbean, 1,272,000 from South America); number of

nationals traveling abroad[27] (1991) 14,521,000 (6,317,000 to Europe and the Mediterranean, 5,155,000 to Latin America[28]).
Land use (1991): forested 31.3%; meadows and pastures 26.1%; agricultural and under permanent cultivation 20.5%; other 22.1%.

Foreign trade

Balance of trade (current prices)

	1986	1987	1988	1989	1990	1991	1992
U.S.$'000,000,000	−138.3	−152.1	−118.5	−109.4	−101.7	−99.2	−84.5
% of total	23.3%	23.0%	15.5%	13.1%	11.4%	9.8%	8.6%

Imports (1992): U.S.$532,665,000,000 (machinery and transport equipment 43.4%, of which motor vehicles and parts 13.4%; basic and miscellaneous manufactures 29.2%; mineral fuels and lubricants 10.3%; chemicals and related products 5.2%; food and live animals 4.3%). *Major import sources:* Canada 18.5%; Japan 18.1%; Mexico 6.6%; Germany 5.4%; China 4.8%; Taiwan 4.6%; U.K. 3.8%; South Korea 3.1%; France 2.8%; Italy 2.3%; Singapore 2.1%; Saudi Arabia 1.9%; Hong Kong 1.8%.
Exports (1992): U.S.$448,164,000,000 (machinery and transport 44.8%, of which motor vehicles and parts 7.2%; basic and miscellaneous manufactures 18.8%; chemicals and related products 9.8%; food and live animals 7.3%; inedible crude materials 5.7%). *Major export destinations:* Canada 20.2%; Japan 10.7%; Mexico 9.1%; U.K. 5.1%; Germany 4.7%; Taiwan 3.4%; South Korea 3.3%; France 3.3%; The Netherlands 3.1%; Belgium-Luxembourg 2.2%.

Trade by commodity group (1992)

	imports		exports	
SITC Group	U.S.$'000,000	%	U.S.$'000,000	%
00 Food and live animals	22,646	4.2	32,864	7.3
01 Beverages and tobacco	5,380	1.0	7,064	1.6
02 Crude materials, excluding fuels	13,968	2.6	25,367	5.7
03 Mineral fuels, lubricants, and related materials	54,694	10.3	11,122	2.5
04 Animal and vegetable oils, fat, and waxes	1,074	0.2	1,447	0.3
05 Chemicals and related products, n.e.s.	27,684	5.2	43,956	9.8
06 Basic manufactures	60,371	11.3	36,302	8.1
07 Machinery and transport equipment	231,336	43.4	200,934	44.8
08 Miscellaneous manufactured articles	95,009	17.8	48,001	10.7
09 Goods not classified by kind	20,503	3.8	41,107	9.2
TOTAL	532,665	100.0[3]	448,164	100.0

Direction of trade (1992)

	imports		exports	
	U.S.$'000,000	%	U.S.$'000,000	%
Africa	15,116	2.7	9,881	2.2
South Africa	1,795	0.3	2,425	0.5
Other	13,321	2.4	7,456	1.7
Americas	173,150	31.3	165,895	37.0[3]
Canada	101,292	18.3	90,156	20.2
Caribbean countries and Central America	10,206	1.8	11,751	2.6
Mexico	35,886	6.5	40,598	9.1
South America	25,766	4.7	23,390	5.2
Asia	243,176	44.0	141,994	31.7[3]
Japan	99,481	18.0	47,764	10.7
Other Asia	143,695	26.0	94,230	21.1
Europe	114,495	20.7	116,150	26.0
EC	95,926	17.3	100,121	22.4
Other Western Europe	15,907	2.9	10,090	2.3
Former U.S.S.R.	921	0.2	3,730	0.8
Eastern Europe	1,741	0.3	2,209	0.5
Oceania	5,530	1.0	10,642	2.4
Australia	3,971	0.7	8,913	2.0
Other Oceania	1,559	0.3	1,729	0.4
Other	1,149	0.2	2,838	0.6
TOTAL	552,616	100.0[3]	447,400	100.0[3]

Transport and communications

Transport. Railroads (1991): length 140,000 mi, 225,000 km; passenger-mi 13,697,000,000, passenger-km 22,043,000,000; short ton-mi cargo 1,078,018,000,000, metric ton-km cargo 1,573,880,000,000. Roads (1991): total length 3,888,460 mi, 6,257,882 km (paved 59%). Vehicles (1991): passenger cars 142,955,623; trucks and buses 45,416,312. Merchant marine (1992): vessels (100 gross tons and over) 5,710; total deadweight tonnage 25,646,378. Air transport (1992): passenger-mi 493,928,000,000, passenger-km 794,901,000,000; short ton-mi cargo 15,330,000,000, metric ton-km cargo 22,381,000,000; localities (1993) with scheduled flights 834[29]. Certified route passenger/cargo air carriers (1991) 69; operating revenue (U.S.$'000,000; 1991) 74,942, of which domestic 56,119, international 18,823; operating expenses 76,669, of which domestic 56,596, international 20,073.

Intercity passenger and freight traffic by mode of transportation (1991)

	cargo traffic ('000,000,000 ton-mi)	% of nat'l total	passenger traffic ('000,000,000 passenger-mi)	% of nat'l total
Rail	1,078	37.4	14	0.7
Road	758	26.3	1,647	81.9
Inland water	462	16.0	—	—
Air	10	0.3	351	17.4
Petroleum pipeline	578	20.0	—	—
TOTAL	2,886	100.0	2,012	100.0

Communications. Daily newspapers (1991): total number 1,586; total circulation 60,700,000; circulation per 1,000 population 240. Radio (1992): total number of receivers 520,000,000 (1 per 0.5 persons). Television (1992): total number of receivers 215,000,000 (1 per 1.2 persons). Telephones (1991; access lines): 130,110,173 (1 per 1.9 persons).

Other communications media (1992)

	titles		titles
Print			
Books (new)	44,528	Home economics	90
of which		Industrial arts	106
Agriculture	486	Journalism and communications	90
Art	1,224	Labour and industrial relations	70
Biography	1,831	Law	273
Business	1,250	Library and information sciences	118
Education	1,071	Literature and language	158
Fiction	4,710	Mathematics and science	238
General works	1,920	Medicine	182
History	2,097	Philosophy and religion	130
Home economics	739	Physical education and recreation	151
Juvenile	4,811	Political science	136
Language	549	Psychology	138
Law	949	Sociology and anthropology	149
Literature	2,057	Zoology	94
Medicine	2,993		
Music	312	**Cinema**[9]	
Philosophy, psychology	1,657	Feature films	424
Poetry, drama	830		traffic
Religion	2,296	**Cellular telephones**	
Science	2,489	Number of subscribers	8,900,000
Sociology, economics	6,836		(pieces of mail)
Sports, recreation	977	**Post**[9]	
Technology	2,031	Mail	165,851,000,000
Travel	383	Domestic	165,058,000,000
Periodicals[10]	3,731	International	793,000,000
of which			
Agriculture	153		
Business and economics	262		
Chemistry and physics	170		
Children's periodicals	78		
Education	203		
Engineering	265		
Fine and applied arts	145		
General interest	181		
History	151		

Education and health

Education (1990–91)

	schools	teachers	students	student/teacher ratio
Primary (age 6–13)	101,050	1,387,625	26,305,999	19.0
Secondary and vocational (age 14–17)		967,142	14,206,244	14.7
Higher, including teacher-training colleges	3,406	825,700	8,175,012	9.9

Literacy: studies in the late 1980s indicated that adult "functional" literacy may not exceed 85%.
Health (1990): doctors of medicine 615,400[30] (1 per 406 persons), of which office-based practice 359,900 (including specialties in internal medicine 16.1%, general and family practice 16.0%, pediatrics 7.4%, obstetrics and gynecology 7.1%, general surgery 6.8%, psychiatry 5.6%, anesthesiology 4.9%, orthopedics 3.9%, ophthalmology 3.6%); doctors of osteopathy 30,900; nurses (1991) 1,758,500 (1 per 144 persons); dentists (1992) 155,058 (1 per 1,647 persons); hospital beds (1991) 1,196,800 (1 per 211 persons), of which nonfederal 92.0% (community hospitals 77.2%, psychiatric 12.5%, long-term general and special 2.1%), federal 8.0%; infant mortality rate per 1,000 live births (1992) 8.5.
Food (1988–90): daily per capita caloric intake 3,642 (vegetable products 70%, animal products 30%); 138% of FAO recommended minimum requirement. Per capita consumption of major food groups (pounds annually; 1991): dairy products 564.7; grains 184.3; sweeteners 140.2; potatoes 130.5; red meat 112.0; fresh vegetables 106.0; fresh fruits 90.6; poultry products 87.4; fats and oils 63.6; fish and shellfish 14.8.

Military

Total active duty personnel (1993): 1,729,700 (army 33.9%, navy 29.5%, air force 26.0%, marines 10.6%). *Military expenditure as percentage of GNP* (1989): 5.8% (world 4.9%); per capita expenditure U.S.$1,222. *Military aid* (1992): total $4,060,000,000 (Middle East 77.8%, of which Israel 44.3%, Egypt 32.1%; Europe 16.5%, of which Turkey 12.4%; Latin America 3.0%).

[1]Excludes 5 nonvoting delegates. [2]Total area excluding U.S. share of Great Lakes is 3,618,770 sq mi (9,372,571 sq km). [3]Detail does not add to total given because of rounding. [4]Includes military personnel residing overseas. [5]Persons of Hispanic origin may be of any race. [6]Fiscal year ending September 30. [7]Year ending June 30. [8]Excludes construction and mining. [9]1991. [10]1988. [11]1990. [12]Constant 1987 dollars. [13]1987. [14]Excludes military personnel overseas. [15]Statistical discrepancy. [16]Includes unemployed persons not previously employed. [17]Number of establishments for 1990. [18]Excludes tips. [19]Number of establishments for 1987. [20]Annual receipts for 1991. [21]March. [22]September. [23]Annual average. [24]End of year. [25]June. [26]Manufacturing sector only. [27]Excludes Canada and Mexico. [28]Includes Central and South America. [29]Includes 292 localities in Alaska. [30]547,300 professionally active.

Uruguay

Official name: República Oriental del Uruguay (Oriental Republic of Uruguay).
Form of government: republic with two legislative houses (Senate [31][1]; Chamber of Representatives [99]).
Head of state and government: President.
Capital: Montevideo.
Official language: Spanish.
Official religion: none.
Monetary unit: 1 peso uruguayo (NUr$) = 1,000 new pesos; valuation (Oct. 4, 1993) 1 U.S.$ = NUr$4.17; 1 £ = NUr$6.32.

Area and population

Departments	Capitals	area sq mi	area sq km	population 1985 census
Artigas	Artigas	4,605	11,928	69,145
Canelones	Canelones	1,751	4,536	364,248
Cerro Largo	Melo	5,270	13,648	78,416
Colonia	Colonia del Sacramento	2,358	6,106	112,717
Durazno	Durazno	4,495	11,643	55,077
Flores	Trinidad	1,986	5,144	24,739
Florida	Florida	4,022	10,417	66,474
Lavalleja	Minas	3,867	10,016	61,466
Maldonado	Maldonado	1,851	4,793	94,314
Montevideo	Montevideo	205	530	1,311,976
Paysandú	Paysandú	5,375	13,922	103,763
Río Negro	Fray Bentos	3,584	9,282	48,644
Rivera	Rivera	3,618	9,370	89,475
Rocha	Rocha	4,074	10,551	66,601
Salto	Salto	5,468	14,163	108,487
San José	San José de Mayo	1,927	4,992	89,893
Soriano	Mercedes	3,478	9,008	79,439
Tacuarembó	Tacuarembó	5,961	15,438	83,498
Treinta y Tres	Treinta y Tres	3,679	9,529	46,869
TOTAL LAND AREA		67,574	175,016	
INLAND WATER		463	1,199	
TOTAL		68,037	176,215	2,955,241

Demography

Population (1993): 3,149,000.
Density (1993)[2]: persons per sq mi 46.6, persons per sq km 18.0.
Urban-rural (1990): urban 85.5%; rural 14.5%.
Sex distribution (1990): male 48.74%; female 51.26%.
Age breakdown (1990): under 15, 25.8%; 15–29, 23.0%; 30–44, 18.9%; 45–59, 15.8%; 60–74, 11.9%; 75 and over, 4.6%.
Population projection: (2000) 3,274,000; (2010) 3,453,000.
Doubling time: 83 years.
Ethnic composition (1990): white (mostly Spanish, Italian, or mixed Spanish-Italian) 86.0%; mestizo 8.0%; mulatto or black 6.0%.
Religious affiliation (1988): Roman Catholic 66.0%; Protestant 2.0%; Jewish 0.8%; nonreligious and atheist 31.2%.
Major cities (1985): Montevideo 1,311,976; Salto 80,823; Paysandú 76,191; Las Piedras 58,288; Rivera 57,316.

Vital statistics

Birth rate per 1,000 population (1990): 18.3 (world avg. 27.1); (1983) legitimate 73.8%; illegitimate 26.2%.
Death rate per 1,000 population (1990): 9.9 (world avg. 9.8).
Natural increase rate per 1,000 population (1990): 8.4 (world avg. 17.3).
Total fertility rate (avg. births per childbearing woman; 1990): 2.3.
Marriage rate per 1,000 population (1988): 7.0.
Divorce rate per 1,000 population (1988): 2.1.
Life expectancy at birth (1990): male 69.1 years; female 76.7 years.
Major causes of death per 100,000 population (1990): diseases of the circulatory system 378.4; malignant neoplasms (cancers) 222.8; respiratory diseases 76.3; accidents 47.0; diseases of the digestive system 39.1.

National economy

Budget (1992). Revenue: NUr$6,771,250,000,000 (direct taxes 78.7%, receipts from foreign trade 9.9%). Expenditures: NUr$6,654,107,000,000 (social security and welfare 57.9%, general public services 15.9%, capital investments 9.1%, interest on public debt 7.7%, subsidies 5.9%).
Public debt (external, outstanding; 1991): U.S.$2,843,000,000.
Tourism (1991): receipts U.S.$333,000,000; expenditures U.S.$100,000,000.
Production (metric tons except as noted). Agriculture, forestry, fishing (1992): rice 622,000, sugarcane 430,000, barley 214,000, sugar beets 160,000, corn (maize) 82,000, wheat 73,000; livestock (number of live animals) 25,702,000 sheep, 9,508,000 cattle, 475,000 horses; roundwood (1991) 3,829,000 cu m; fish catch (1991) 143,710. Mining and quarrying (1990): hydraulic cement 500,000; gypsum 145,000. Manufacturing (value added in NUr$'000,000; 1987): food products (excluding beverages) 73,085; textiles 47,375; petroleum products 47,053; chemicals and chemical products 40,322; beverages 33,906; transport equipment 32,641; tobacco products 19,829; leather products 17,540; paper and paper products 15,729. Construction (approvals; 1988): residential 277,425 sq m; nonresidential 31,380 sq m. Energy production (consumption): electricity (kW-hr; 1990) 7,372,000,000 (6,042,000,000); coal, none (none); crude petroleum (barrels; 1990) none (8,796,000); petroleum products (metric tons; 1990) 1,084,000 (1,164,000); natural gas, none (n.a.).
Gross national product (1991): U.S.$8,895,000,000 (U.S.$2,860 per capita).

Structure of gross domestic product and labour force

	1991 in value NUr$'000,000	1991 % of total value	1985 labour force	1985 % of labour force
Agriculture	1,870,210	9.8	170,183	14.5
Mining	34,632	0.2	1,771	0.1
Manufacturing	4,812,491	25.1	214,945	18.3
Construction	726,369	3.8	64,385	5.4
Public utilities	535,656	2.8	17,377	1.5
Transp. and commun.	1,219,852	6.4	59,289	5.0
Trade	2,391,110	12.5	139,242	11.9
Finance	2,406,887	12.6	42,688	3.6
Pub. admin., defense	1,683,800	8.8 }	369,260	31.4
Services	4,525,850	23.6 }		
Other	−1,071,389[3]	−5.6[3]	97,668[4]	8.3[4]
TOTAL	19,135,468	100.0	1,176,808	100.0

Population economically active (1990): total 1,241,900[5]; activity rate 40.1% (participation rates: ages 20 and over, 55.9%; female 31.8%; unemployed [1988] 8.3%).

Price and earnings indexes (1985 = 100)

	1986	1987	1988	1989	1990	1991	1992
Consumer price index	176.4	288.5	467.9	844.4	1,794	3,624	6,105
Monthly earnings index[6]	186.7	319.8	524.8	946.1	1,844	3,909	6,706

Household income and expenditure. Avg. household size (1985) 3.3; avg. annual income per household (1985) NUr$266,261 (U.S.$2,625); sources of income[5]: wages 53.5%, self-employment 17.0%, transfer payments and other 29.5%; expenditure (1982–83)[7]: food 39.9%, housing 17.6%, transportation and communications 10.4%, health care 9.3%, clothing 7.0%, durable goods 6.3%, recreation 3.1%, education 1.3%, personal effects and other 5.1%.
Land use (1991): forested 3.8%; meadows and pastures 77.3%; agricultural and under permanent cultivation 7.5%; other 11.4%.

Foreign trade[8]

Balance of trade (current prices)

	1987	1988	1989	1990	1991	1992
U.S.$'000,000	+99.6	+300.3	+478.8	+435.4	+44.9	−248.9
% of total	4.4%	12.0%	17.6%	14.8%	1.4%	6.8%

Imports (1992): U.S.$2,058,193,000 (machinery and appliances 20.2%; transport equipment 15.8%; chemical products 12.6%; mineral products 11.9%; synthetic plastics, resins, and rubber 6.9%; base metals and products 5.4%; textile products 5.1%). *Major import sources* (1991): Brazil 22.8%; Argentina 17.4%; United States 12.1%; Germany 4.9%; France 3.2%.
Exports (1992): U.S.$1,702,501,000 (textiles and textile products 27.1%; live animals and live-animal products 22.5%; hides and skins 12.2%; vegetable products 10.6%; mineral products 5.0%; food, beverages, and tobacco 4.5%). *Major export destinations* (1991): Brazil 24.0%; Argentina 11.2%; United States 10.2%; Germany 8.6%; Italy 3.9%.

Transport and communications

Transport. Railroads[9]: route length (1992) 3,002 km; passenger-km (1987) 140,600,000; metric ton-km cargo (1990) 204,000,000. Roads (1985): length 52,000 km (paved 23%). Vehicles (1990): passenger cars 379,600; trucks and buses 49,900. Merchant marine (1992): vessels (100 gross tons and over) 93; deadweight tonnage 172,520. Air transport (1990): passenger-km 471,000,000; metric ton-km cargo 2,600,000; airports (1993) 7.
Communications. Daily newspapers (1990): total number 30; total circulation 720,000; circulation per 1,000 population 233. Radio (1992): total receivers 1,800,000 (1 per 1.7 persons). Television (1991): total receivers 700,000 (1 per 4.4 persons). Telephones (1990): 579,159 (1 per 5.4 persons).

Education and health

Education (1989)

	schools	teachers	students	student/teacher ratio
Primary (age 6–11)	2,735	19,391	359,455	18.5
Secondary (age 12–17)	293	13,571[10, 11]	196,851	...
Vocational	95[11]	...	56,084	...
Higher	2	5,925[11]	63,777	10.5[11]

Educational attainment (1985). Percentage of population age 25 and over having: no formal schooling 7.5%; less than primary education 26.6%; primary 31.2%; secondary 19.9%; higher 14.8%. *Literacy* (1985): population age 15 and over literate 95.0%; males 975,200 (94.5%); females 1,074,300 (95.4%).
Health (1990): physicians 9,061 (1 per 341 persons); hospital beds (1983) 23,400 (1 per 127 persons); infant mortality rate per 1,000 live births (1991) 20.0.
Food (1988–90): daily per capita caloric intake 2,668 (vegetable products 65%, animal products 35%); 100% of FAO recommended minimum requirement.

Military

Total active duty personnel (1992): 24,700 (army 69.6%, navy 18.2%, air force 12.2%). *Military expenditure as percentage of GNP* (1988): 2.2% (world 5.0%); per capita expenditure U.S.$55.

[1]Includes the vice president, who serves as ex officio presiding officer. [2]Based on land area. [3]Includes indirect taxes less subsidies. [4]Includes unemployed not previously employed. [5]From urban areas only. [6]Salaried employees only. [7]Weights of consumer price index components in Montevideo. [8]Import figures are f.o.b. in balance of trade and c.i.f. for commodities and trading partners. [9]Passenger service ceased in 1988. [10]Public only. [11]1988.

Uzbekistan

Official name: Ozbekistan Jumhuriyäti (Republic of Uzbekistan).
Form of government: multiparty republic with a single legislative body (Supreme Soviet [500]).
Head of state: President.
Head of government: Prime Minister.
Capital: Tashkent (Toshkent).
Official language: Uzbek.
Official religion: none.
Monetary unit[1]: 1 Russian ruble = 100 kopecks; valuation (Oct. 4, 1993) free rate, 1 U.S.$ = 1,165 rubles; 1 £ = 1,765 rubles.

Area and population

Autonomous Republic	Administrative centres	area sq mi	area sq km	population 1992 estimate
Karakalpakstan	Nukus	63,700	164,900	1,311,000
Provinces				
Andizhan (Andijan)	Andizhan	1,600	4,200	1,839,000
Bukhara	Bukhara	54,900	142,100	1,232,000
Dzhizak (Djizak)	Dzhizak	7,900	20,500	806,000
Fergana	Fergana	2,700	7,100	2,282,000
Kashka Darya	Karshi	11,000	28,400	1,756,000
Khorezm	Urgench	2,400	6,300	1,100,000
Namangan	Namangan	3,100	7,900	1,604,000
Samarkand	Samarkand	9,500	24,500	2,265,000
Surkhan Darya	Termez	8,000	20,800	1,385,000
Syr Darya	Gulistan	2,000	5,100	587,000
Tashkent (Toshkent)	Tashkent	6,000	15,600	4,331,000
TOTAL		172,700[2]	447,400	20,498,000

Demography

Population (1993): 21,179,000.
Density (1993): persons per sq mi 122.6, persons per sq km 47.3.
Urban-rural (1992): urban 40.0%; rural 60.0%.
Sex distribution (1992): male 49.40%; female 50.60%.
Age breakdown (1989): under 15, 40.8%; 15–29, 28.4%; 30–44, 15.0%; 45–59, 9.3%; 60–74, 4.7%; 75 and over, 1.8%.
Population projection: (2000) 22,812,000; (2010) 25,367,000.
Doubling time: 25 years.
Ethnic composition (1989): Uzbek 71.4%; Russian 8.3%; Tajik 4.7%; Kazakh 4.1%; Tatar 2.4%; Kara-Kalpak 2.1%; Crimean Tatar 1.0%; Korean 0.9%; Kyrgyz 0.9%; Ukrainian 0.8%; Turkmen 0.6%; other 2.8%.
Religious affiliation (1990): believers are predominantly Sunnī Muslim (Ḥanafīyah).
Major cities (1992): Tashkent 2,119,900; Samarkand 372,000; Namangan 333,000; Andizhan 302,000; Bukhara 235,000.

Vital statistics

Birth rate per 1,000 population (1991): 34.5 (world avg. 26.4); (1989) legitimate 95.8%; illegitimate 4.2%.
Death rate per 1,000 population (1991): 6.2 (world avg. 9.2).
Natural increase rate per 1,000 population (1991): 28.3 (world avg. 17.2).
Total fertility rate (avg. births per childbearing woman; 1989): 4.0.
Marriage rate per 1,000 population (1991): 12.9.
Divorce rate per 1,000 population (1991): 1.6.
Life expectancy at birth (1990): male 66.2 years; female 72.6 years.
Major causes of death per 100,000 population (1989): diseases of the circulatory system 251.3; diseases of the respiratory system 119.3; accidents, poisoning, and violence 60.1; malignant neoplasms (cancers) 55.9; infectious and parasitic diseases 44.5; diseases of the digestive system 27.1; diseases of the nervous system 9.1; endocrine and metabolic disorders 6.5.

National economy

Budget (1992). Revenue: 74,700,000,000 rubles (price differential tax 36.1%, turnover tax 26.2%, excise tax 12.7%, corporate income tax 12.7%, individual income tax 5.5%). Expenditures: 86,200,000,000 rubles (social and cultural affairs 27.3%, subsidies 24.7%, national economy 18.9%).
Tourism: n.a.
Land use (1989): forested 4.2%; meadows and pastures 52.5%; agricultural and under permanent cultivation 10.1%; other 33.2%.
Production (metric tons except as noted). Agriculture, forestry, fishing (1992): seed cotton 4,000,000, vegetables (except potatoes) 3,750,000, milk 2,860,000, fruit (except grapes) and berries 960,000, wheat 900,000, watermelons 560,000, rice 530,000, grapes 460,000, corn (maize) 445,000, potatoes 335,000, barley 300,000, rye 10,000; livestock (number of live animals; 1991) 10,100,000 sheep and goats (of which 900,000 goats), 5,100,000 cattle, 900,000 pigs, 108,000 horses; roundwood (1990) 15,000 cu m; fish catch (1991) 27,400. Mining and quarrying: detail not available; however, gold, copper, lead, and molybdenum are mined. Manufacturing (1991): cement 6,191,000; sulfuric acid 2,392,600; mineral fertilizers 1,660,000; cotton fibre 1,531,500; steel 860,400; pig iron 761,000; meat 477,800; detergents 211,500; plastics and resins 142,000; synthetic fibre 49,300; cardboard 41,500; wool 25,300; paper 20,200; jute 12,300; bricks 2,088,000 units; eggs 1,327,000 units; tractors 21,100 units; cotton cloth 391,700,000 m; carpets and rugs 5,750,000 cu m; footwear 45,400,000 pairs. Construction (1991): residential 9,363,000,000 sq m. Energy production (consumption): electricity (kW-hr; 1992) 57,400,000,000 (54,800,000,000); coal (metric tons; 1992) 6,200,000 (10,400,000); crude petroleum (barrels; 1992) 20,663,000 (61,865,000); petroleum products, n.a. (n.a.); natural gas (cu m; 1992) 41,600,000,000 (37,800,000,000).
Gross national product (at current market prices; 1992): U.S.$18,398,000,000 (U.S.$860 per capita).

Structure of net material product and labour force

	1991 in value '000,000 rubles	% of total value	labour force[3]	% of labour force[3]
Agriculture	19,879.0	43.2	1,977,000	29.1
Mining / Manufacturing / Public utilities	15,246.2	33.2	1,200,000	17.6
Construction	4,905.7	10.7	714,000	10.5
Transp. and commun.	1,930.5	4.2	251,000	3.7
Trade	4,001.7	8.7	462,000	6.8
Finance	—	—	...	...
Pub. admin., defense	—	—	...	...
Services	—	—	2,067,000	30.4
Other	—	—	129,000	1.9
TOTAL	45,963.1	100.0	6,800,000	100.0

Public debt (external, outstanding; 1991): U.S.$2,000,000,000.
Population economically active (1992): total 8,322,700; activity rate of total population 39.2% (participation rates [1989]: ages 16–59 [male], 16–54 [female] 78.2%; female 43.8%; unemployed [1990] 3.9%).

Price and earnings indexes (1985 = 100)

	1985	1986	1987	1988	1989	1990	1991
Consumer price index	100.0	...	...	...	...	126.6	117.2
Earnings index	...	...	...	...	...	...	...

Household income and expenditure (1992). Average household size (1989) 5.5; income per household 2,343 rubles; sources of income: wages and salaries 61.8%, subsidies, grants, and nonwage income 22.8%, other 15.4%; expenditure: food and consumer goods 72.4%, other 27.6%.

Foreign trade

Balance of trade (current prices)

	1987	1988	1989	1990
'000,000,000 rubles	−3.9	−1.2	−3.5	−3.7
% of total	20.8%	8.5%	17.0%	18.4%

Imports (1991): 20,200,000,000 rubles (foodstuffs and agricultural commodities 47.2%; consumer goods 43.5%; raw materials and processed industrial goods 4.9%; machinery and transport equipment 4.3%). *Major import sources:* mostly former Soviet republics.
Exports (1991): 19,600,000,000 rubles (raw materials and processed industrial goods 64.0%, of which cotton 33.6%; chemical products, fertilizers, and rubber 14.0%; fuel, mineral raw materials, and metals 4.5%; foodstuffs and agricultural commodities 4.4%; machinery and transport equipment 2.5%). *Major export destinations:* mostly former Soviet republics.

Transport and communications

Transport. Railroads (1991): length 4,225 mi, 6,800 km; passenger-mi 3,231,000,000, passenger-km 5,200,000,000; short ton-mi cargo 48,357,000,000, metric ton-km cargo 70,600,000,000. Roads (1990): total length 55,431 mi, 89,207 km (paved 83%). Vehicles (1988): passenger cars 790,800; trucks and buses, n.a. Merchant marine: vessels (100 gross tons and over) n.a.; total deadweight tonnage, n.a. Air transport (1991): passenger-mi 6,524,000,000, passenger-km 10,500,000,000; short ton-mi cargo 60,754,000,000; metric ton-km cargo 88,700,000,000; airports (1993) with scheduled flights 1.
Communications. Daily newspapers (1990): total number 279; total circulation 5,158,400; circulation per 1,000 population 249.1. Radio (1991): total number of receivers 3,677,000 (1 per 5.6 persons). Television (1991): total number of receivers 3,308,000 (1 per 6.3 persons). Telephones (1991): 1,458,000 (1 per 14.3 persons).

Education and health

Education (1991–92)

	schools	teachers	students	student/ teacher ratio
Primary (age 6–13) / Secondary (age 14–17)	8,557	384,000	4,721,400	12.3
Voc., teacher tr.	243	...	254,400	...
Higher	52	...	337,400	...

Educational attainment (1989). Percentage of population age 25 and over having: primary education or no formal schooling 13.3%; some secondary 19.8%; completed secondary and some postsecondary 57.7%; higher 9.2%.
Literacy: n.a.
Health (1992): physicians 71,100 (1 per 300 persons); hospital beds 257,000 (1 per 83 persons); infant mortality rate per 1,000 live births 35.5.
Food: daily per capita caloric intake, n.a.

Military

Total active duty personnel (1993): 38,000 (army 99.0%, air force 1.0%. *Military expenditure as percentage of GNP* (1992): 0.2%; per capita expenditure U.S.$10.

[1]The monetary systems of Uzbekistan and Russia were unified on Sept. 17, 1993. [2]Detail does not add to total given because of rounding. [3]State sector only.

Vanuatu

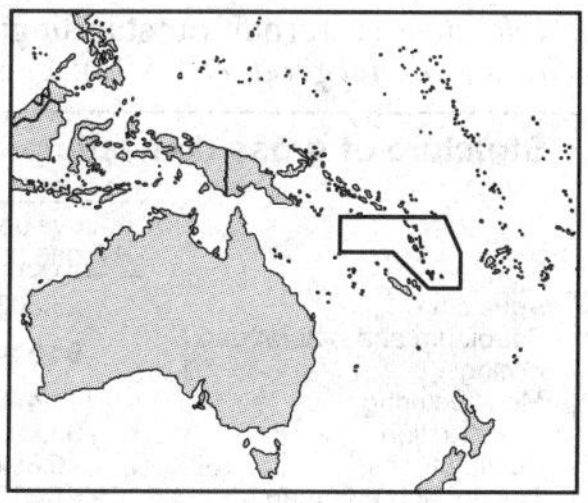

Official name: Ripablik blong Vanuatu (Bislama); République de Vanuatu (French); Republic of Vanuatu (English).
Form of government: republic with a single legislative house (Parliament [46]).
Chief of state: President.
Head of government: Prime Minister.
Capital: Vila.
Official languages: Bislama; French; English.
Official religion: none.
Monetary unit: vatu (VT); valuation (Oct. 4, 1993) 1 U.S.$ = VT 123.03; 1 £ = VT 186.39.

Area and population

		area		population
Local Government Regions	Capitals	sq mi	sq km	1989 census
Ambae/Maéwo	Longana	270	699	10,958
Ambrym	Eas	257	666	7,191
Banks/Torres	Sola	341	882	5,985
Éfaté	Vila	356	923	30,868
Épi	Ringdove	172	446	3,628
Malekula	Lakatoro	793	2,053	19,298
Paama	Liro	23	60	1,696
Pentecost	Loltong	193	499	11,341
Santo/Malo	Luganville	1,640	4,248	25,581
Shepherd	Morua	33	86	3,975
Taféa	Isangel	629	1,628	22,423
TOTAL		4,707	12,190	142,944

Demography

Population (1993): 160,000.
Density (1993): persons per sq mi 34.0, persons per sq km 13.1.
Urban-rural (1989): urban 18.4%[1]; rural 81.6%.
Sex distribution (1989): male 51.60%; female 48.40%.
Age breakdown (1989)[2]: under 15, 45.5%; 15–29, 26.6%; 30–44, 15.2%; 45–59, 8.4%; 60–74, 3.7%; 75 and over, 0.6%.
Population projection: (2000) 189,000; (2010) 231,000.
Doubling time: 23 years.
Ethnic composition (1989): Ni-Vanuatu 98.0%; other 2.0%.
Religious affiliation (1989): Christian 77.2%, of which Presbyterian 35.8%, Roman Catholic 14.5%, Anglican 14.0%, Seventh-day Adventist 8.2%; Custom 4.6%; nonreligious 1.7%; unknown 4.0%; other 12.5%.
Major towns (1989): Vila (Port-Vila) 19,400; Luganville (Santo) 6,900; Port Olry 884[3]; Isangel 752[3].

Vital statistics

Birth rate per 1,000 population (1991): 36.0 (world avg. 26.4).
Death rate per 1,000 population (1991): 5.0 (world avg. 9.2).
Natural increase rate per 1,000 population (1991): 31.0 (world avg. 17.2).
Total fertility rate (avg. births per childbearing woman; 1991): 6.2.
Marriage rate per 1,000 population (1985): *c.* 7.4.
Divorce rate per 1,000 population (1985): less than 0.7.
Life expectancy at birth (1985): male 61.1 years; female 59.3 years.
Major causes of death per 100,000 population (1985)[4]: infectious and parasitic diseases 69.3; diseases of the respiratory system 60.5; diseases of the circulatory system 37.6; accidents and violence 23.6; malignant neoplasms (cancers) 22.9; ill-defined conditions 117.3.

National economy

Budget (1989). Revenue: VT 4,154,700,000 (taxes on international trade 58.6%; taxes on goods and services 22.7%; nontax revenue 16.8%). Expenditures: VT 7,287,200,000 (manufacturing, mining, and construction 21.4%; public services 13.7%; education 12.6%; transportation and communications 10.5%; agriculture 6.7%; health 6.6%).
Tourism (1991): receipts from visitors U.S.$30,000,000; expenditures by nationals abroad U.S.$1,000,000.
Land use (1991): forested 1.3%; meadows and pastures 2.1%; agricultural 11.8%; limestone, volcanic rock, and other 84.8%.
Production (metric tons except as noted). Agriculture, forestry, fishing (1992): coconuts 300,000, roots and tubers 51,000, copra 27,000, bananas 12,000, vegetables and melons 9,000, cacao beans 2,000, corn (maize) 1,000; livestock (number of live animals) 131,000 cattle, 60,000 pigs, 11,000 goats; roundwood (1991) 63,000 cu m; fish catch (1991) 3,200. Mining and quarrying (1985): small quantities of coral-reef limestone, crushed stone, sand, and gravel. Manufacturing (value added in '000 VT; 1984): food, beverages, and tobacco 358,000; wood products 96,000; fabricated metal products 60,000; paper products, including printing and publishing, 48,800; nonmetallic mineral products 24,600; handicrafts 14,600; textiles, clothing, and leather 12,900. Construction (approvals in Vila and Luganville; 1992): residential 20,386 sq m; nonresidential 19,876 sq m. Energy production (consumption): electricity (kW-hr; 1992) 28,681,000 (28,681,000); coal, none (none); crude petroleum, none (none); petroleum products (metric tons; 1990) none (22,000); natural gas, none (none).
Population economically active (1989): total 66,957; activity rate of total population 47.0% (participation rates: ages 15–64, 85.0%; female 46.3%; unemployed 0.5%).

Price and earnings indexes (1985 = 100)

	1986	1987	1988	1989	1990	1991	1992
Consumer price index	103.9	118.3	132.2	142.7	151.1	160.6	168.1
Earnings index	...	...	...	...	...	...	...

Public debt (external, outstanding; 1991): U.S.$38,100,000.
Gross national product (at current market prices; 1992): U.S.$188,000,000 (U.S.$1,210 per capita).

Structure of gross domestic product and labour force

	1990		1989	
	in value VT '000,000	% of total value	labour force	% of labour force
Agriculture	3,582	20.0	40,889	61.1
Mining	...	...	1	—
Manufacturing	1,050	5.9	891	1.3
Construction	1,033	5.8	1,302	1.9
Public utilities	339	1.9	109	0.2
Transportation and communications	1,517	8.5	1,030	1.5
Trade	5,772	32.2	2,712	4.0
Finance	1,743	9.7	646	1.0
Pub. admin., defense	1,985	11.1	7,891	11.8
Services	1,278	7.1		
Other	−400[5]	−2.2[5]	11,486	17.2
TOTAL	17,899	100.0	66,957	100.0

Household income and expenditure (1985)[1]. Average household size (1989) 5.1; income per household U.S.$11,299; sources of income: wages and salaries 59.0%, self-employment 33.7%; expenditure (1987)[6]: food and beverages 45.5%, clothing and footwear 14.1%, housing 10.2%, transportation 9.8%.

Foreign trade[7]

Balance of trade (current prices)

	1987	1988	1989	1990	1991	1992
VT '000,000	−5,508	−5,000	−5,319	−8,566	−7,364	−6,689
% of total	58.6%	54.8%	50.9%	66.0%	67.0%	56.8%

Imports (1992): VT 9,228,000,000 (machinery and transport equipment 27.5%; food and live animals 17.4%; basic manufactures 14.9%; mineral fuels 9.0%; chemical products 6.6%; beverages and tobacco 4.1%). *Major import sources:* Australia 38.7%; New Zealand 10.0%; Japan 9.1%; France 7.9%; New Caledonia 6.3%; Fiji 5.2%; Hong Kong 3.5%; Singapore 2.8%.
Exports (1992): VT 2,539,000,000 (domestic exports 74.5%, of which copra 32.8%, beef and veal 13.3%, seashells 8.0%, cacao beans and preparations 6.5%, timber 3.5%; reexports 25.5%). *Major export destinations*[8]: Japan 19.9%; Australia 10.9%; New Caledonia 5.9%; South Korea 5.6%.

Transport and communications

Transport. Railroads: none. Roads (1984): total length 660 mi, 1,062 km (paved 24%). Vehicles (1990): passenger cars 4,200; trucks and buses 2,800. Merchant marine (1992): vessels (100 gross tons and over) 280; total deadweight tonnage 3,259,594. Air transport (1990): domestic passenger arrivals 96,009, international passenger arrivals 44,547; international cargo unloaded 536 metric tons, international cargo loaded (1987) 133 metric tons; airports (1993) with scheduled flights 28.
Communications. Daily newspapers: none. Radio (1992): total number of receivers 20,000 (1 per 7.8 persons). Television (1987): total number of receivers 1,000 (1 per 136 persons). Telephones (1986): 3,240 (1 per 40 persons).

Education and health

Education (1991)

	schools	teachers	students	student/ teacher ratio
Primary (age 6–11)[9]	267	869	24,952	28.7
Secondary (age 11–18)	21[10]	208	3,799	18.3
Voc., teacher tr.	...	...	261	...
Higher	1	...	124	...

Educational attainment (1989). Percentage of population age 6 and over having: no formal schooling or less than one year 22.3%; some primary education 52.6%; lower-level secondary 18.3%; upper-level secondary and higher 4.8%; not stated 2.0%. *Literacy* (1979): total population age 15 and over literate 32,120 (52.9%); males 18,550 (57.3%); females 13,570 (47.8%).
Health (1990): physicians 20 (1 per 7,345 persons); hospital beds 364 (1 per 404 persons); infant mortality rate per 1,000 live births (1991) 36.0.
Food (1988–90): daily per capita caloric intake 2,736 (vegetable products 81%, animal products 19%); 120% of FAO recommended minimum requirement.

Military

Total active duty personnel: Vanuatu has a paramilitary force of about 300.

[1]Vila and Luganville only. [2]For indigenous population only. [3]1979. [4]Deaths reported to the Ministry of Health only. [5]Imputed bank service charges. [6]Weights of consumer price index components. [7]Imports c.i.f.; exports f.o.b. [8]Destination of domestic exports only. [9]Excludes independent private schools. [10]1986.

Venezuela

Official name: República de Venezuela (Republic of Venezuela).
Form of government: federal multiparty republic with two legislative houses (Senate [49[1]]; Chamber of Deputies [201]).
Head of state and government: President.
Capital: Caracas.
Official language: Spanish.
Official religion: none.
Monetary unit: 1 bolívar (B, plural Bs) = 100 céntimos; valuation[2] (Oct. 4, 1993) 1 U.S.$ = Bs 97.39; 1 £ = Bs 147.54.

Area and population		area		population
				1990
States	**Capitals**	sq mi	sq km	census
Anzoátegui	Barcelona	16,700	43,300	924,074
Apure	San Fernando de Apure	29,500	76,500	305,132
Aragua	Maracay	2,700	7,014	1,194,982
Barinas	Barinas	13,600	35,200	456,246
Bolívar	Ciudad Bolívar	91,900	238,000	968,695
Carabobo	Valencia	1,795	4,650	1,558,608
Cojedes	San Carlos	5,700	14,800	196,526
Delta Amacuro	Tucupita	15,500	40,200	91,085
Falcón	Coro	9,600	24,800	632,513
Guárico	San Juan de Los Morros	25,091	64,986	525,737
Lara	Barquisimeto	7,600	19,800	1,270,196
Mérida	Mérida	4,400	11,300	615,503
Miranda	Los Teques	3,070	7,950	2,026,229
Monagas	Maturín	11,200	28,900	503,176
Nueva Esparta	La Asunción	440	1,150	280,777
Portuguesa	Guanare	5,900	15,200	625,576
Sucre	Cumaná	4,600	11,800	722,707
Táchira	San Cristóbal	4,300	11,100	859,861
Trujillo	Trujillo	2,900	7,400	520,292
Yaracuy	San Felipe	2,700	7,100	411,980
Zulia	Maracaibo	24,400	63,100	2,387,208
Other federal entities				
Amazonas	Puerto Ayacucho	67,900	175,750	60,207
Dependencias Federales	—	50	120	2,245
Distrito Federal	Caracas	745	1,930	2,265,874
TOTAL		352,144[3]	912,050	19,405,429

Demography

Population (1993): 20,662,000.
Density (1993): persons per sq mi 58.7, persons per sq km 22.7.
Urban-rural (1990): urban 84.0%; rural 16.0%.
Sex distribution (1990): male 49.74%; female 50.26%.
Age breakdown (1990): under 15, 38.3%; 15–29, 28.1%; 30–44, 18.6%; 45–59, 9.3%; 60–74, 4.5%; 75 and over, 1.2%.
Population projection: (2000) 24,072,000; (2010) 29,157,000.
Doubling time: 28 years.
Ethnic composition (1981): mestizo 69%; white 20%; black 9%; Indian 2%.
Religious affiliation (1987): Roman Catholic 91.7%; other 8.3%.
Major cities (1990): Caracas 1,290,087; Maracaibo 1,206,726; Valencia 955,005; Barquisimeto 723,587; Maracay 538,616.

Vital statistics

Birth rate per 1,000 population (1991): 30.4 (world avg. 26.4); (1974) legitimate 47.0%; illegitimate 53.0%.
Death rate per 1,000 population (1991): 4.5 (world avg. 9.2).
Natural increase rate per 1,000 population (1991): 25.9 (world avg. 17.2).
Total fertility rate (avg. births per childbearing woman; 1990): 3.6.
Marriage rate per 1,000 population (1990): 5.5.
Divorce rate per 1,000 population (1989): 1.2.
Life expectancy at birth (1990): male 67.0 years; female 73.3 years.
Major causes of death per 100,000 population (1990): heart diseases 75.3; malignant neoplasms (cancers) 49.3; accidents 38.1; perinatal problems 32.4; cerebrovascular diseases 27.8; pneumonia 15.1.

National economy

Budget (1991). Revenue: Bs 726,340,000,000 (oil revenues 56.2%, tax revenues 23.0%, nontax revenues 20.8%). Expenditures: Bs 715,354,000,000 (operating expenses 85.7%, public-debt service 14.3%).
Tourism (1991): receipts U.S.$365,000,000; expenditures U.S.$1,011,000,000.
Production (metric tons except as noted). Agriculture, forestry, fishing (1992): sugarcane 6,700,000, bananas 1,215,000, corn (maize) 904,000, rice 595,000, sorghum 528,000, plantains 510,000, cassava 382,000, coffee 72,000, cacao 14,000; livestock (number of live animals) 14,192,000 cattle; roundwood (1991) 1,290,000 cu m; fish catch (1991) 352,835. Mining and quarrying (1991): iron ore 19,959,000; bauxite 2,100,000; aluminum ore 605,000; gold 80,400 troy oz. Manufacturing (value added in Bs '000; 1990): base metals 60,320,000; food products 56,737,000; chemicals 51,838,000; beverages 27,350,000; metal products 15,770,000; textiles 13,658,000; paper and paper products 12,982,000; tobacco 12,826,000; electrical machinery 11,506,000. Construction (in Bs; 1990): residential 14,092,000,000; nonresidential 87,917,000,000. Energy production (consumption): electricity (kW-hr; 1990) 61,000,000,000 (61,000,000,000); coal (metric tons; 1990) 1,864,000 (200,000); crude petroleum (barrels; 1990) 770,567,000 (336,074,000); petroleum products (metric tons; 1990) 48,145,000 (16,448,000); natural gas (cu m; 1990) 17,711,000,000 (17,711,000,000).

Public debt (external, outstanding; 1991): U.S.$25,189,000,000.
Gross national product (1991): U.S.$52,775,000,000 (U.S.$2,610 per capita).

Structure of gross domestic product and labour force	1991			
	in value Bs '000,000[4]	% of total value	labour force	% of labour force
Agriculture	26,303	5.0	851,187	11.5
Petroleum and natural gas / Mining	94,344	17.9	78,357	1.1
Manufacturing	115,476	21.9	1,176,449	16.0
Construction	30,826	5.8	668,802	9.1
Public utilities	8,854	1.7	71,202	1.0
Transp. and commun.	27,215	5.2	440,789	6.0
Trade	70,931	13.4	1,557,965	21.1
Finance	69,283	13.1	440,447	6.0
Pub. admin., defense	47,313	9.0	2,073,023	28.1
Services	33,639	6.4		
Other	3,743	0.7	17,449	0.2
TOTAL	527,927	100.0[3]	7,375,670	100.0[3]

Population economically active (1990): total 7,173,317; activity rate 36.1% (participation rates: over age 15, 59.1%; female 31.5%; unemployed 9.9%).

Price and earnings indexes (1985 = 100)	1986	1987	1988	1989	1990	1991	1992
Consumer price index	111.5	142.9	185.0	340.9	480.1	644.3	846.8
Monthly earnings index[5]	105.4	115.6	139.3	207.8	309.5	...	...

Household income and expenditure. Average household size (1990) 5.1; average annual income per household (1981) Bs 42,492 (U.S.$9,899); sources of income: n.a.; expenditure (1990): food 37.1%, rent and utilities 9.4%, clothing 8.3%, transportation and communications 5.1%, education and recreation 4.9%, household furnishings and maintenance 2.8%.
Land use (1991): forested 33.9%; meadows and pastures 20.1%; agricultural and under permanent cultivation 4.4%; other 41.6%.

Foreign trade

Balance of trade (current prices)	1987	1988	1989	1990	1991	1992
Bs '000,000	+7,510	−65,434	+232,261	+529,115	+286,500	+154,700
% of total	3.2%	18.2%	33.5%	46.7%	20.1%	9.3%

Imports (1990): U.S.$6,607,792,000 (machinery and transport equipment 33.3%, chemicals 14.3%, basic metal manufactures 9.9%, vegetable products 5.8%, mineral products 5.3%, paper products 4.2%). *Major import sources:* U.S. 45.4%; W.Ger. 9.9%; Italy 4.8%; Brazil 3.9%; Japan 3.8%; France 3.5%; U.K. 3.0%.
Exports (1990): U.S.$18,044,254,000 (crude petroleum and petroleum products 79.7%, iron ore 1.8%). *Major export destinations:* U.S. 47.3%; Puerto Rico 4.2%; The Netherlands 3.9%; W.Ger. 3.7%; Japan 2.8%; Canada 2.6%.

Transport and communications

Transport. Railroads (1991): route length 226 mi, 363 km; passenger-km 60,000,000; metric ton-km cargo 48,000,000. Roads (1990): total length 48,174 mi, 77,529 km (paved 34%). Vehicles (1991): passenger cars 1,590,000; trucks and buses 319,000. Merchant marine (1992): vessels (100 gross tons and over) 271; total deadweight tonnage 1,355,419. Air transport (1991): passenger-km 5,939,000,000; metric ton-km cargo 132,000,000; airports (1993) with scheduled flights 31.
Communications. Daily newspapers (1990): total number 54; total circulation 2,800,000; circulation per 1,000 population 142. Radio (1992): 8,100,000 receivers (1 per 2.5 persons). Television (1992): 3,700,000 receivers (1 per 5.5 persons). Telephones (1990): 1,793,731 (1 per 11.0 persons).

Education and health

Education (1990–91)	schools	teachers	students	student/ teacher ratio
Primary (age 7–12)	15,445	199,104	4,052,947	20.4
Secondary (age 13–17)[6]	1,517	30,844	281,419	9.1
Higher	99	46,137	550,030	11.9

Educational attainment (1990). Percentage of population age 10 and over having: no formal schooling 9.5%; primary education 45.7%; secondary 35.9%; higher 8.9%. *Literacy* (1990): total population age 15 and over literate 13,371,743 (92.2%); males 6,742,992 (93.5%); females 6,628,751 (91.1%).
Health (1990): physicians (1989) 32,616 (1 per 576 persons); hospital beds 52,010 (1 per 370 persons); infant mortality rate per 1,000 live births 25.9.
Food (1988–90): daily per capita caloric intake 2,443 (vegetable products 84%, animal products 16%); 99% of FAO recommended minimum.

Military

Total active duty personnel (1992): 75,000 (army 76.0%, navy 14.7%, air force 9.3%). *Military expenditure as percentage of GNP* (1989): 1.0% (world 4.9%); per capita expenditure U.S.$22.

[1]In addition, three former presidents hold lifetime membership. [2]Venezuela's three-tiered system of official exchange rates was replaced on March 14, 1989, by a unified market-determined exchange rate. The free-market rate governs as a luxury-goods rate. [3]Detail does not add to total given because of rounding. [4]At 1984 prices. [5]Blue-collar workers. [6]Includes vocational and teacher training.

Vietnam

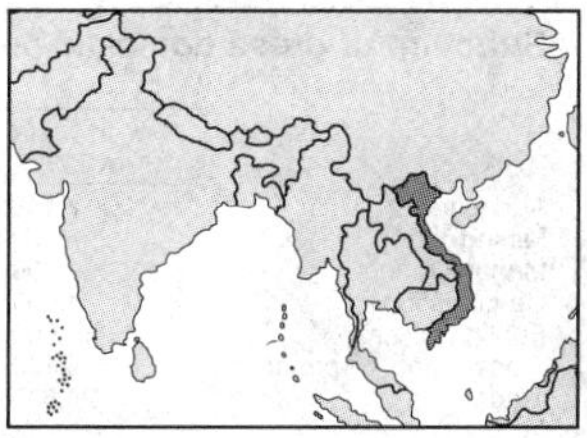

Official name: Cong Hoa Xa Hoi Chu Nghia Viet Nam (Socialist Republic of Vietnam).
Form of government: socialist republic with one legislative house (National Assembly [395]).
Chief of state: President.
Head of government: Prime Minister.
Capital: Hanoi.
Official language: Vietnamese.
Official religion: none.
Monetary unit: 1 dong (D) = 10 hao = 100 xu; valuation (Oct. 4, 1993) 1 U.S.$ = D 10,672; 1 £ = D 16,168.

Area and population

Regions Provinces	Capitals	area sq mi	 sq km	population 1991 estimate
Dong bang song Cuu Long		15,280	39,575[1]	14,882,600
An Giang	Long Xuyen	1,322	3,424	1,849,700
Ben Tre	Ben Tre	868	2,247	1,264,300
Can Tho	Can Tho	2,379[2]	6,161[2]	1,695,000
Dong Thap	Cao Lamh	1,265	3,276	1,401,600
Kien Giang	Rach Gia	2,410	6,243	1,266,000
Long An	Tan An	1,675	4,338	1,177,100
Minh Hai	Bac Lieu	2,969	7,689	1,642,600
Soc Trang	...	[2]	[2]	1,123,900
Tien Giang	My Tho	903	2,339	1,557,400
Tra Vinh	...	1,489	3,857	901,100
Vinh Long	...			1,003,900
Dong bang song Hong		4,813	12,466[1]	13,275,600
Ha Tay	...	827	2,143	2,130,000
Hai Hung	Hai Duong	985	2,552	2,554,500
Haiphong (MUNICIPALITY)	—	581	1,504	1,516,900
Hanoi (CAPITAL)	—	361	934	2,095,000
Nam Ha	...	1,471	3,810	2,473,700
Ninh Binh	...			800,100
Thai Binh	Thai Binh	588	1,524	1,705,400
Dong Nam Bo		9,067[1]	23,484[1]	8,194,200
Ba Ria-Vung Tau	...	754	1,954	532,100
Dong Nai	Bien Hoa	2,266	5,868	1,742,400
Ho Chi Minh City (MUNICIPALITY)	—	807	2,090	4,075,700
Song Be	Thu Dau Mot	3,686	9,546	1,017,000
Tay Ninh	Ho Chi Minh City	1,555	4,027	827,000
Duyen hai mien trung		17,693	45,824[1]	6,995,600[1]
Binh Dinh	Quy Nhon	2,346	6,076	1,295,000
Binh Thuan	...	4,410[3]	11,422[3]	823,600
Khanh Hoa	Nha Trang	2,030	5,258	871,700
Ninh Thuan	...	[3]	[3]	412,000
Phu Yen	Tuy Hoa	2,017	5,223	670,500
Quang Nam-Da Nang	Da Nang	4,629	11,988	1,832,300
Quang Ngai	Quang Ngai	2,261	5,856	1,090,400
Khu Bon cu		19,760	51,178	9,054,200
Ha Tinh	...	2,338	6,055	1,234,500
Nghe An	...	6,321	16,371	2,561,900
Quang Binh	Dong Hoi	3,082	7,983	693,200
Quang Tri	Dong Ha	1,773	4,592	490,800
Thanh Hoa	Thanh Hoa	4,312	11,168	3,152,900
Thua Thien-Hue	Hue	1,934	5,009	920,900
Mien nui va trung du		39,745	102,938[1]	11,542,800
Bac Thai	Thai Nguyen	2,511	6,503	1,082,600
Cao Bang	Cao Bang	3,261	8,445	591,500
Ha Bac	Bac Giang	1,782	4,615	2,172,900
Ha Giang	...	2,240	5,802	489,900
Hoa Binh	...	1,781	4,613	722,900
Lai Chau	Lai Chau	6,618	17,140	467,600
Lang Son	Lang Son	3,153	8,167	643,600
Lao Cai	...	3,106	8,045	491,500
Quang Ninh	Hai Duong	2,293	5,939	848,200
Son La	Son La	5,487	14,210	726,800
Tuyen Quang	...	3,023	7,830	597,200
Vinh Phu	Viet Tri	1,862	4,823	2,097,700
Yen Bai	...	2,628	6,807	610,400
Tay Nguyen		21,455[1]	55,569	2,688,900
Dac Lac	Buon Me Thoat	7,645	19,800	1,072,300
Gia Lai	...	5,899	15,278	773,800
Kon Tum	...	3,984	10,318	149,800
Lam Dong	Da Lat	3,929	10,173	693,000
TOTAL		127,813	331,033	67,678,700[4]

Demography

Population (1993): 70,902,000.
Density (1993): persons per sq mi 554.7; persons per sq km 214.2.
Urban-rural (1989): urban 20.1%; rural 79.9%.
Sex distribution (1991): male 49.07%; female 50.93%.
Age breakdown (1989): under 15, 39.0%; 15–29, 28.7%; 30–44, 16.0%; 45–59, 9.1%; 60–74, 5.6%; 75 and over, 1.6%.
Population projection: (2000) 81,516,000; (2010) 97,097,000.
Ethnic composition (1989): Vietnamese 87.1%; Tho (Tay) 1.8%; Chinese (Hoa) 1.5%; Tai 1.5%; Khmer 1.4%; Muong 1.4%; Nung 1.1%; other 4.2%.
Religious affiliation (1980): Buddhist 55.3%; Roman Catholic 7.0%.
Major cities (1992): Ho Chi Minh City 4,075,700; Hanoi 2,095,000.

Vital statistics

Birth rate per 1,000 population (1993): 29.0 (world avg. 26.4).
Death rate per 1,000 population (1993): 8.0 (world avg. 9.2).
Natural increase rate per 1,000 population (1993): 21.0 (world avg. 17.2).
Total fertility rate (avg. births per childbearing woman; 1993): 3.8.
Life expectancy at birth (1993): male 62 years; female 67 years.
Morbidity (cases of reportable infectious disease per 100,000 population; 1990): malaria 2,564; trachoma 241; diarrhea 183.

National economy

Budget (1990). Revenue: D 6,490,000,000,000 (transfers from state enterprises 49.9%, foreign sources 18.0%, taxes 15.0%). Expenditures: D 8,090,000,000,000 (current expenditures 65.7%, capital expenditures 23.0%).
Public debt (external, outstanding; 1989): U.S.$15,072,000,000.
Gross national product (1990): U.S.$15,200,000,000 (U.S.$230 per capita).

Structure of net material product and labour force

	1991 in value D '000,000,000	 % of total value	 labour force	 % of labour force
Agriculture, forestry, fishing	23,563.3	51.7	22,608,600	72.7
Mining, manufacturing	10,370.7	22.8	3,400,000	10.9
Construction	2,014.9	4.4	821,200	2.6
Transp. and commun.	878.4	1.9	537,000	1.7
Trade	8,148.3	18.0	1,724,100	5.5
Finance	—	—	106,500	0.3
Pub. admin.	—	—	1,194,000	3.8
Services	—	—		
Other	575.3	1.2	699,600	2.3
TOTAL	45,550.9	100.0	31,091,000	100.0[1]

Tourism (1989): receipts from visitors U.S.$59,000,000.
Production (metric tons except as noted). Agriculture, forestry, fishing (1992): rice 21,500,000, sugarcane 5,900,000, cassava 3,000,000, sweet potatoes 2,110,000, bananas 1,265,000, coconuts 1,050,000, corn (maize) 660,000; livestock (number of live animals) 12,140,000 pigs, 3,135,000 cattle, 2,867,000 buffalo, 110,000,000 poultry; roundwood (1991) 29,525,000 cu m; fish catch (1991) 877,000. Mining and quarrying (1991): phosphate rock 274,000; gold 1,300 kg. Manufacturing (1991): cement 3,177,000; fertilizers 434,000; sugar 344,000; steel 130,000; paper 103,000; textiles 277,000,000 sq m; bricks 3,566,500,000 units[5]; bicycles 108,000 units[5]. Energy production (consumption): electricity (kW-hr; 1991) 8,550,000,000 (8,550,000,000); coal (metric tons; 1991) 5,000,000 (4,050,000); crude petroleum (barrels; 1991) 13,670,000 (293,200); petroleum products (metric tons; 1991) 38,000 (2,588,000).
Population economically active (1989): total 30,521,019; activity rate 47.4% (participation rates: ages 15–64, 79.9%; female 51.7%; unemployed 5.8%).
Household income and expenditure. Average household size (1989) 4.8; income per household (1990)[6] D 577,008 (U.S.$93); expenditure (1990): food 62.4%, clothing 5.0%, household goods 4.6%, education 2.9%, housing 2.5%.
Land use (1991): forest 28.7%; pasture 1.1%; agricultural 19.6%; other 50.6%.

Foreign trade

Balance of trade (current prices)

	1986	1987	1988	1989	1990	1991
U.S.$'000,000	−1,366	−1,601	−1,719	−620	−348	−224
% of total	46.4%	48.4%	45.3%	13.7%	6.7%	5.4%

Imports (1991): U.S.$2,194,000,000 (machinery and transp. equip. 26.0%, fuels and lubricants 22.9%, general manufactures 22.0%, chemicals 16.3%). *Major import sources* (1985): U.S.S.R. 69.2%; Japan 8.2%; Singapore 7.0%.
Exports (1991): U.S.$1,970,000,000 (fuels and lubricants 35.6%, food and live animals 34.3%, raw materials 13.5%). *Major export destinations* (1985): U.S.S.R. 51.1%; Hong Kong 13.8%; Japan 9.1%; Singapore 8.6%.

Transport and communications

Transport. Railroads (1990): length (1991) 3,220 km; passenger-km 1,913,000,000; metric ton-km cargo 847,000,000. Roads (1991): total length 88,000 km (paved 11%[7]). Vehicles (1976): passenger cars 100,000; trucks and buses 200,000. Merchant marine (1992): vessels (100 gross tons and over) 230; total deadweight tonnage 872,752. Air transport (1990): passenger-km 87,000,000; metric ton-km cargo 1,000,000; airports (1993) with scheduled flights 12.
Communications. Daily newspapers (1990): 4; total circulation 525,000[8]; circulation per 1,000 population 7.9[8]. Radio (1991): 7,000,000 receivers (1 per 9.7 persons). Television (1992): 2,500,000 receivers (1 per 27 persons). Telephones (1989): 123,000 (1 per 526 persons).

Education and health

Education (1990–91)

	schools	teachers	students	student/ teacher ratio
Primary and secondary (age 7–18)	16,516	434,800	11,882,500	27.3
Vocational	268	10,400	135,400	13.0
Higher	106	21,900	129,600	5.9

Educational attainment (1989). Percentage of population 25 and over having: no formal education (illiterate) 16.6%; some primary 46.6%; complete primary 23.5%; secondary 6.5%; postsecondary and higher 6.8%. *Literacy* (1991): persons 15 and over literate 88.0%; males 93.0%; females 84.0%.
Health: physicians (1990) 23,300 (1 per 2,843 persons); hospital beds (1989) 217,600 (1 per 298 persons); infant mortality rate (1991) 48.
Food (1991): daily per capita caloric intake 1,943 (1984–86; vegetable products 94%, animal products 6%); 89% of FAO recommended minimum.

Military

Total active duty personnel (1993): 857,000 (army 81.7%, navy 4.9%, air force 13.4%). *Military expenditure as percentage of GNP* (1986): 19.4% (world 5.5%); per capita expenditure U.S.$44.

[1]Detail does not add to total given because of rounding. [2]Can Tho includes Soc Trang. [3]Binh Thuan includes Ninh Thuan. [4]Total includes 1,044,800 persons in special enumeration groups not distributed in province and region estimates. [5]1990. [6]Wage workers and government officials only. [7]1988. [8]For three newspapers only.

Western Samoa

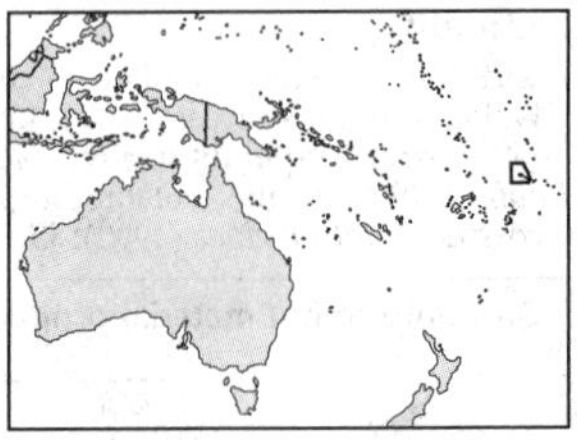

Official name: Malo Sa'oloto Tuto'atasi o Samoa i Sisifo (Samoan); Independent State of Western Samoa (English).
Form of government: constitutional monarchy[1] with one legislative house (Legislative Assembly [48][2]).
Chief of state: Head of State.
Head of government: Prime Minister.
Capital: Apia.
Official languages: Samoan; English.
Official religion: none.
Monetary unit: 1 tala (WS$, plural tala) = 100 sene; valuation (Oct. 4, 1993) 1 U.S.$ = WS$2.55; 1 £ = WS$3.87.

Area and population

Islands / Political Districts	area sq mi	area sq km	population 1986 census
Savaii	659	1,707	44,930
Fa'aseleleaga			...
Gaga'emauga			...
Gaga'ifomauga			...
Palauli			...
Satupa'itea			...
Vaisigano			...
Upolu	432	1,119	112,228
A'ana			...
Aiga-i-le-Tai			...
Atua			...
Tuamasaga			...
Vaa-o-Fonoti			...
TOTAL	1,093[3]	2,831[3]	157,158[4]

Demography

Population (1993): 163,000.
Density (1993): persons per sq mi 149.1, persons per sq km 57.6.
Urban-rural (1993): urban 23.0%; rural 77.0%.
Sex distribution (1986): male 52.96%; female 47.04%.
Age breakdown (1986): under 15, 41.2%; 15–29, 30.8%; 30–44, 13.3%; 45–59, 9.1%; 60–74, 4.4%; 75 and over, 1.2%.
Population projection: (2000) 174,000; (2010) 192,000.
Doubling time: 25 years.
Ethnic composition (1982): Samoan (Polynesian) *c.* 88%; Euronesian *c.* 10%; European *c.* 2%.
Religious affiliation (1986): Congregational 47.2%; Roman Catholic 22.3%; Methodist 15.1%; Mormon 8.6%; other 6.8%.
Major city (1981): Apia 33,170.

Vital statistics

Birth rate per 1,000 population (1991): 34.0 (world avg. 26.4); (1978) legitimate 43.5%; illegitimate 56.5%.
Death rate per 1,000 population (1991): 6.0 (world avg. 9.2).
Natural increase rate per 1,000 population (1991): 28.0 (world avg. 17.2).
Total fertility rate (avg. births per childbearing woman; 1991): 4.5.
Marriage rate per 1,000 population (1989)[5]: 5.3.
Divorce rate per 1,000 population (1989)[5]: 0.2.
Life expectancy at birth (1991): male 64.0 years; female 69.0 years.
Major causes of death per 100,000 population (1985)[5]: diseases of the circulatory system 42.0; malignant neoplasms (cancers) 18.2; diseases of the respiratory system 13.2; infectious and parasitic diseases 8.8; diabetes mellitus 5.6.

National economy

Budget (1990). Revenue: WS$121,100,000 (tax revenue 74.6%, of which taxes on international trade 43.2%, income tax 17.4%, taxes on goods and services 13.5%; nontax revenue 25.5%, of which rents, royalties, and interest 6.9%). Expenditures: WS$158,700,000 (development expenditure 59.2%; current expenditure 40.8%).
Public debt (external, outstanding; 1991): U.S.$112,900,000.
Production (metric tons except as noted). Agriculture, forestry, fishing (1992): coconuts 95,000, taro 37,000, bananas 18,000, copra 10,000, papayas 9,000, pineapples 6,000, mangoes 5,000, avocados 2,000, cow's milk 2,000; livestock (number of live animals) 1,000,000 goats, 270,000 pigs, 31,000 cattle; roundwood (1991) 131,000 cu m; fish catch (1991) 565. Mining and quarrying: n.a. Manufacturing (in WS$'000; 1990): beer 8,708, cigarettes 6,551, coconut cream 5,576, sawn wood 3,662, coconut oil 3,442, corned meat 2,905, soap 1,487, paints 1,457. Construction (permits issued in WS$; 1990): residential 4,421,000; commercial, industrial, and other 12,874,000. Energy production (consumption): electricity (kW-hr; 1990) 50,000,000 (50,000,000); coal, none (n.a.); crude petroleum, none (n.a.); petroleum products (metric tons; 1990) none (41,000).
Household income and expenditure. Average household size (1981) 5.1; income per household (1972) WS$1,518 (U.S.$2,200); sources of income (1972): wages 49.4%, self-employment 22.8%, remittances, gifts, and other assistance 18.0%, land rent 8.7%, other 1.1%; expenditure (1987)[6]: food 58.8%, transportation 9.0%, housing and furnishings 5.1%, fuel and light 5.0%, clothing 4.2%, other goods and services 1.9%, other 16.0%.
Gross national product (at current market prices; 1992): U.S.$153,000,000 (U.S.$940 per capita).

Structure of gross domestic product and labour force

	1989 in value WS$'000	1989 % of total value	1986 labour force	1986 % of labour force
Agriculture	117,100	47.1	29,023	63.6
Mining	...	... }	1,587	3.5
Manufacturing	31,600	12.7 }		
Construction	4,600	1.9	62	0.1
Public utilities	11,000	4.4	855	1.9
Transp. and commun.	5,200	2.1	1,491	3.3
Trade	25,600	10.3	1,710	3.7
Finance	...	...	842	1.8
Pub. admin., defense, government services	31,000	12.5	9,436	20.7
Other services }	22,300	9.0		
Other }			629	1.4
TOTAL	248,400	100.0	45,635	100.0

Population economically active (1991): total 45,819; activity rate of total population 28.7% (participation rates: ages 15–64 [1981] 48.6%; female [1986] 18.8%).

Price and earnings indexes (1985 = 100)

	1986	1987	1988	1989	1990	1991	1992
Consumer price index	107.2	110.6	120.0	127.7	147.2	145.2	157.6
Earnings index	...	...	...	...	...	...	...

Tourism (1991): receipts from visitors U.S.$18,000,000; expenditures by nationals abroad U.S.$2,000,000.
Land use (1991): forested 47.3%; meadows and pastures 0.4%; agricultural and under permanent cultivation 43.1%; other 9.2%.

Foreign trade[7]

Balance of trade (current prices)

	1987	1988	1989	1990	1991	1992
WS$'000	−94,240	−111,729	−109,249	−137,300	−196,994	−238,965
% of total	65.4%	64.0%	65.4%	77.0%	83.9%	89.3%

Imports (1992): WS$278,392,000 (1983; food 21.3%, machinery 21.0%, petroleum products 18.4%, miscellaneous manufactured articles 7.4%, chemicals 5.9%, animal oils and fats 0.5%). *Major import sources* (1991): New Zealand 38.3%; Australia 22.0%; United States 10.3%; Japan 9.5%; Fiji 6.5%; Germany 1.9%; American Samoa 1.9%.
Exports (1992): WS$14,349,000 (1991; taro 37.5%, coconut cream 28.8%, automotive wiring harnesses 15.3%, beer 4.6%, cigarettes 3.8%). *Major export destinations* (1991): New Zealand 49.1%; Australia 23.0%; American Samoa 13.8%; United States 7.1%.

Transport and communications

Transport. Railroads: none. Roads (1987): total length[8] 1,296 mi, 2,085 km (paved 19%). Vehicles (1989): passenger cars 2,514; trucks and buses 3,048. Merchant marine (1992): vessels (100 gross tons and over) 7; total deadweight tonnage 6,501. Air transport: passengers, n.a.; cargo, n.a.; airports (1993) with scheduled flights 2.
Communications. Daily newspapers: none. Radio (1992): 75,000 receivers (1 per 2.1 persons). Television (1987): 6,000 receivers (1 per 26 persons). Telephones (1988): 5,455 (1 per 29 persons).

Education and health

Education (1986–87)

	schools	teachers	students	student/ teacher ratio
Primary (age 5–11)	164[9]	1,511[10]	40,755	27.0
Secondary (age 12–18)	38[11]	492	11,395	23.2
Voc., teacher tr.	4[9]	37	228	6.2
Higher[9]	6	25	271	10.8

Educational attainment (1981). Percentage of population age 25 and over having: some primary education 16.5%; complete primary 24.5%; some secondary 52.1%; complete secondary 3.1%; higher 2.0%; unknown 1.8%.
Literacy (1981): virtually 100%.
Health: physicians (1990) 44 (1 per 3,584 persons); hospital beds (1989) 644 (1 per 255 persons); infant mortality rate per 1,000 live births (1991) 47.0.
Food (1988–90): daily per capita caloric intake 2,695 (vegetable products 81%, animal products 19%); 118% of FAO recommended minimum requirement.

Military

No military forces are maintained; New Zealand is responsible for defense.

[1]According to the constitution, the current Head of State, paramount chief HH Malietoa Tanumafili II, will hold office for life. Upon his death, the monarchy will functionally cease, and future Heads of State will be elected by the Legislative Assembly. [2]Includes the Head of State as an ex officio member. [3]Total includes 2 sq mi (5 sq km) of uninhabited islands. [4]The provisional total for the 1991 census is 159,862. [5]Registered only. [6]Consumer price index components. [7]Import figures are f.o.b. in balance of trade and c.i.f. in commodities and trading partners. [8]Total length includes 733 mi (1,180 km) of plantation roads. [9]1983. [10]Includes some secondary teachers. [11]1982.

Yemen

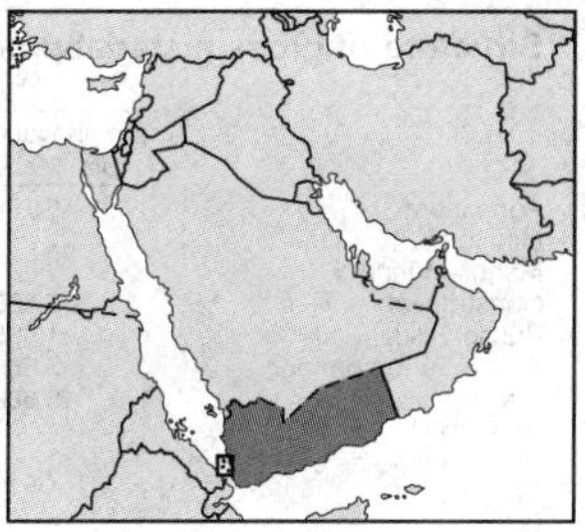

Official name: al-Jumhūrīyah al-Yamanīyah (Republic of Yemen).
Form of government: multiparty republic[1] with one legislative house (Council of Representatives [301]).
Head of state: President assisted by Presidential Council.
Head of government: Prime Minister assisted by Council of Ministers.
Capital: Ṣan'ā'.
Official language: Arabic.
Official religion: Islam.
Monetary unit: 1 Yemen rial (YRls) = 100 fils; 1 Yemeni dinar (YD) = 1,000 fils; valuation (Oct. 4, 1993) 1 U.S.$ = YRls 16.50 = YD 0.46; 1 £ = YRls 25.08 = YD 0.70.

The Republic of Yemen was formed on May 22, 1990, by the union of the former Yemen Arab Republic (North Yemen) and People's Democratic Republic of Yemen (South Yemen).

Area and population

Governorates	Capitals	area sq mi	area sq km	population 1986 estimate[2]
North Yemen				
al-Bayḍā'	al-Bayḍā'	4,310	11,170	295,439
Dhamār	Dhamār	3,430	8,870	698,823
Ḥajjah	Ḥajjah	3,700	9,590	720,000
al-Ḥudaydah	al-Ḥudaydah	5,240	13,580	1,052,086
Ibb	Ibb	2,480	6,430	1,254,128
al-Jawf	al-Jawf	...	...	42,762
al-Maḥwīt	al-Maḥwīt	830	2,160	260,836
Ma'rib	Ma'rib	15,400	39,890	95,326
Ṣa'dah	Ṣa'dah	4,950	12,810	323,124
Ṣan'ā'	Ṣan'ā'	7,840	20,310	1,664,518
Ta'izz	Ta'izz	4,020	10,420	1,419,708
South Yemen				
Abyān	Zinjibār	8,297	21,489	279,241
'Adan	Aden	2,695	6,980	326,919
Ḥaḍramawt	al-Mukallā	59,991	155,376	537,095
Laḥij	Laḥij	4,928	12,766	458,385
al-Mahrah	al-Ghayḍah	25,618	66,350	44,225
Shabwah	'Atāq	28,536	73,908	192,324
TOTAL		182,278[3, 4]	472,099[3]	9,664,939

Demography

Population (1993): 12,459,000.
Density (1993)[5]: persons per sq mi 60.7, persons per sq km 23.4.
Urban-rural (1990): urban 21.4%; rural 78.6%.
Sex distribution (1990): male 49.32%; female 50.68%.
Age breakdown (1990): under 15, 52.5%; 15–29, 21.9%; 30–44, 13.0%; 45–59, 7.7%; 60–74, 3.6%; 75 and over, 1.3%.
Population projection: (2000) 14,878,000; (2010) 19,173,000.
Doubling time: 20 years.
Ethnic composition (1986): predominantly Arab.
Religious affiliation (1980): Muslim 99.9%, of which Sunnī 53.0%, Shī'ī 46.9%; other 0.1%.
Major cities (1986): Ṣan'ā' 427,150; Aden 318,000[6]; Ta'izz 178,043; al-Ḥudaydah 155,110; al-Mukallā 59,100[6].

Vital statistics

Birth rate per 1,000 population (1991): 51.3 (world avg. 26.4).
Death rate per 1,000 population (1991): 16.2 (world avg. 9.2).
Natural increase rate per 1,000 population (1991): 35.1 (world avg. 17.2).
Total fertility rate (avg. births per childbearing woman; 1991): 7.4.
Marriage rate per 1,000 population: n.a.
Life expectancy at birth (1991): male 49.0 years; female 51.0 years.
Major causes of death per 100,000 population: n.a.; however, major diseases include malaria, tuberculosis, leprosy, and intestinal infections.

National economy

Budget (1992). Revenue: YRls 32,008,000,000 (1990; tax revenue 59.8%, property income 30.4%). Expenditures: YRls 53,637,000,000 (defense 21.9%, education 14.3%, general public services 6.3%, health 3.5%).
Public debt (external, outstanding; 1991): U.S.$5,207,000.
Production (metric tons except as noted). Agriculture, forestry, fishing (1992): sorghum 459,000, tomatoes 172,000, watermelons 170,000, potatoes 165,000, wheat 152,000, grapes 145,000, onions 70,000, millet 66,000, bananas 55,000, papayas 50,000; livestock (number of live animals) 3,850,000 sheep, 3,470,000 goats, 1,190,000 cattle, 690,000 asses, 185,000 camels, 3,000 horses, 24,000,000 chickens; roundwood (1991) 324,000 cu m; fish catch (1991) 85,261. Mining and quarrying (1991): salt 225,000; gypsum 75,000. Manufacturing (1988)[7]: flour 23,700; wheat bran 10,500; canned tomatoes 1,265; cotton lint 800; foam rubber 715; soft drinks 49,000,000 bottles; beer 5,200,000 litres; textiles 2,600,000 metres; cigarettes 1,166,000,000 units. Construction: n.a. Energy production (consumption): electricity (kW-hr; 1990) 1,740,000 (1,740,000); coal, none (n.a.); crude petroleum (barrels; 1990) 68,148,000 (31,691,000); petroleum products (metric tons; 1990) 4,026,000 (2,722,000).
Gross national product (at current market prices; 1991): U.S.$6,746,000,000 (U.S.$540 per capita).

Population economically active (1986): total 2,043,237; activity rate of total population 19.6% (participation rates: 15–64, 41.2%; female 12.1%; unemployed [1993] *c.* 40%).

Structure of gross domestic product and labour force

	1990 in value YD '000,000	1990 % of total value	1986 labour force	1986 % of labour force
Agriculture	16,101	20.9	1,151,348	56.3
Mining	7,030	9.1	11,771	0.6
Manufacturing	6,586	8.5	94,913	4.6
Public utilities	1,400	1.8	160,952	7.9
Construction	3,394	4.4	32,852	1.6
Transp. and commun.	6,015	7.8	107,611	5.3
Trade	9,590	12.4	248,979	12.2
Finance	4,929	6.4	8,757	0.4
Pub. admin., defense	18,201	23.6	226,054	11.1
Services	667	0.9	...	...
Other	3,246[8]	4.2[8]	...	...
TOTAL	77,159	100.0	2,043,237	100.0

Household income and expenditure. Average household size (1986) 5.6; income per household: n.a.; sources of income: n.a.; expenditure: n.a.

Price index (1985 = 100)[9]

	1985	1986	1987	1988	1989	1990
Consumer price index	100.0	121.1	140.3	155.2	178.8	240.0

Tourism: receipts from visitors (1992) U.S.$47,000,000; expenditures by nationals abroad (1989) U.S.$81,000,000.
Land use (1991): forested 7.7%; meadows and pastures 30.4%; agricultural and under permanent cultivation 2.8%; other 59.1%.

Foreign trade

Balance of trade (current prices)[10]

	1982	1983	1984	1985	1986	1987
YRls '000,000	−8,235	−9,439	−8,449	−7,782	−8,466	−13,460
% of total	78.4%	83.1%	79.0%	77.2%	78.4%	90.4%

Imports (1987)[10]: U.S.$1,370,700,000 (food and live animals 31.6%, basic manufactured goods 28.6%, machinery and transport equipment 21.9%, chemical products 9.3%, raw materials 5.8%, beverages and tobacco 2.4%). *Major import sources:* Japan 12.0%; United States 10.8%; The Netherlands 10.0%; West Germany 7.1%; France 6.3%; Italy 5.3%; Saudi Arabia 5.3%.
Exports (1987)[10]: U.S.$69,000,000 (coffee 16.6%, cigarettes 15.6%, biscuits 13.6%, leather 12.5%, grapes 8.6%, sesame seeds 4.2%). *Major export destinations:* Saudi Arabia 53.6%; South Yemen 24.0%; Italy 8.2%; Japan 4.0%.

Transport and communications

Transport. Railroads: none. Roads (1988): total length 39,200 km (paved 5.7%). Vehicles (1992): passenger cars 165,438; trucks and buses 219,105. Merchant marine (1992): vessels (100 gross tons and over) 40; deadweight tonnage 13,653. Air transport (1990): passenger-km 1,032,248,000; metric ton-km cargo 11,661,000; airports (1993) with scheduled flights 12.
Communications. Daily newspapers (1990)[10]: total number 2; total circulation 120,000; circulation per 1,000 population 10. Radio (1991): 325,000 receivers (1 per 36 persons). Television (1991): 300,000 receivers (1 per 39 persons). Telephones (1988): 70,000 (1 per 157 persons).

Education and health

Education (1990–91)[10]

	schools	teachers	students	student/ teacher ratio
Primary (age 7–12)	7,313[11]	35,350	1,291,372	36.5
Secondary (age 13–18)	942[12]	12,106	394,578	32.6
Voc., teacher tr.	73[12]	1,247	26,119	20.9
Higher[11]	1	470	23,457	49.9

Educational attainment (1986)[10]. Percentage of population age 10 and over having: no formal schooling 74.2%; reading and writing ability 19.8%; primary education 4.0%; secondary education 0.6%; higher 0.6%; not specified 0.8%. *Literacy* (1990): percentage of total population age 15 and over literate 38.5%; males literate 53.3%; females literate 26.3%.
Health (1986): physicians 1,886 (1 per 5,531 persons); hospital beds 10,485 (1 per 995 persons); infant mortality rate per 1,000 live births (1991) 121.0.
Food (1986–88): daily per capita caloric intake 2,284 (vegetable products 90%, animal products 10%); 94% of FAO recommended minimum requirement.

Military

Total active duty personnel (1992): 64,500 (army 93.0%, navy 2.3%, air force 4.4%). *Military expenditure as percentage of GNP* (1991): 15.7% (world 5.0%); per capita expenditure U.S.$89.

[1]A general election on April 27, 1993, effectively terminated the transitional administration. [2]Based on North Yemen's 1986 census results and South Yemen's 1986 estimates. [3]Former North Yemeni territorial claims with regard to alignment of the long-undemarcated eastern boundary with Saudi Arabia (which increased Yemen's claimed total area to 205,356 sq mi [531,869 sq km]) were under negotiation with Saudi Arabia in 1993. [4]Detail does not add to total given because of rounding. [5]Based on the higher total area estimate of 205,356 sq mi (531,869 sq km). [6]1984. [7]Democratic Republic of Yemen only. [8]Import duties less imputed bank service charges. [9]Urban areas only. [10]Yemen Arab Republic only. [11]1988–89. [12]1985–86.

Yugoslavia

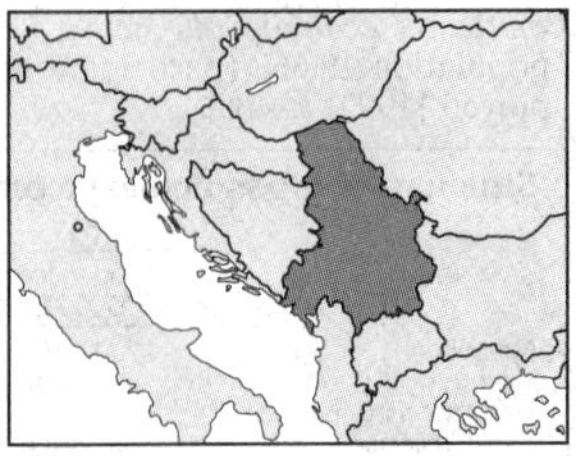

Official name: Savezna Republika Jugoslavija (Federal Republic of Yugoslavia).
Form of government: federal multiparty republic with two legislative houses (Chamber of Republics [40]; Chamber of Citizens [138]).
Chief of state: Federal President.
Head of government: Prime Minister.
Capital: Belgrade.
Official language: Serbo-Croatian.
Official religion: none.
Monetary unit: 1 Yugoslav new dinar (Din) = 100 paras; valuation (Oct. 4, 1993) 1 U.S.$ = Din 104.24; 1 £ = Din 157.92.

Area and population

		area		population
				1991
Republics	Capitals	sq mi	sq km	census
Montenegro	Podgorica	5,333	13,812	615,267
Serbia	Belgrade	21,609	55,968	5,824,211
Autonomous provinces[1]				
Kosovo and Metohia	Priština	4,203	10,887	1,954,747
Vojvodina	Novi Sad	8,304	21,506	2,012,605
TOTAL		39,449	102,173	10,406,830

Demography

Population (1993): 10,560,568.
Density (1993): persons per sq mi 267.7, persons per sq km 103.4.
Urban-rural (1991): urban 52.0%; rural 48.0%.
Sex distribution (1991): male 49.6%; female 50.4%.
Age breakdown (1991): under 15, 22.8%; 15–29, 21.6%; 30–44, 21.7%; 45–59, 17.1%; 60–74, 12.2%; 75 and over, 3.5%; unknown, 1.1%.
Population projection: (2000) 11,114,000; (2010) 11,440,000.
Doubling time: not applicable; doubling time exceeds 100 years.
Ethnic composition (1991): Serb 62.3%; Albanian 16.6%; Montenegrin 5.0%; Yugoslav 3.3%; Hungarian 3.3%; Muslim 3.1%; Croat 1.1%; other 5.3%.
Religious affiliation (1991): most believers are affiliated with the Serbian Orthodox Church; there are also Muslim, Roman Catholic, and Protestant minorities.
Major cities (1991): Belgrade 1,136,786; Novi Sad 178,896; Niš 175,555; Kragujevac 146,607; Subotica 100,219.

Vital statistics

Birth rate per 1,000 population (1991): 14.1 (world avg. 26.4).
Death rate per 1,000 population (1991): 9.2 (world avg. 9.2).
Natural increase rate per 1,000 population (1991): 4.9 (world avg. 17.2).
Total fertility rate (avg. births per childbearing woman): n.a.
Marriage rate per 1,000 population (1991): 5.6.
Divorce rate per 1,000 population (1991): 0.7.
Life expectancy at birth (1980–82)[2]: male 68.2 years; female 73.2 years.
Major causes of death per 100,000 population (1991): diseases of the circulatory system 548.1; malignant neoplasms (cancers) 162.1; accidents, violence, and poisoning 58.7; diseases of the respiratory system 49.6; diseases of the digestive system (1989) 26.3.

National economy

Budget (1991–92). Revenue: Din 132,000,000,000 (financed largely by the National Bank and foreign reserves). Expenditures: Din 132,000,000,000 (subsidies to enterprises 50%, defense 42%, administration 8%).
Land use (1990): forested 29.5%; meadows and pastures 20.7%; agricultural and under permanent cultivation 35.7%; other 14.1%.
Production (metric tons except as noted). Agriculture, forestry, fishing (1992): corn (maize) 4,511,000, wheat 1,920,000, potatoes 711,000, grapes 384,000, plums 379,000; livestock (number of live animals) 3,844,000 pigs, 2,715,000 sheep, 1,975,000 cattle, 26,039,000 poultry; roundwood (1991) 2,028,000 cu m; fish catch (1991) 36,511. Mining and quarrying (1992): copper ore 25,758,000; lead-zinc ore 1,237,000; bauxite 900,000; lime 565,000; magnesite 185,000; aluminum and ingots 75,792; salt 47,000; antimony ore 19,715; asbestos ore 12,000; refined silver 70,000 kg. Manufacturing (1992): wheat flour 1,130,000; crude steel 725,000; sulfuric acid 293,000; nitric acid 163,000; canned fruit 123,000; electrolytic copper 115,000; welded pipes 64,000; rolled copper 29,000; polyvinyl chloride powder 24,000; linoleum flooring 24,000; refined lead 23,000; rolled aluminum 23,000; canned meat 23,000; cotton yarn 18,035; medicines 16,082; zinc 14,000; knitted clothing 6,768; household ceramics 2,638; woolen fabrics 25,476,000 sq m; parquet flooring 995,000 cu m; liquor 37,329,000 hectolitres; hosiery 46,000,000 pairs; leather footwear 16,043,000 pairs; high-voltage bulbs 21,000,000 units; furniture 1,562,000 units; kitchen ranges 278,000 units; refrigerators 85,075 units; bicycles 65,000 units; television receivers 51,000 units; gasoline engines 49,000 units; telephones 29,000 units; automobiles 26,000 units; tractors 14,000 units; automobile tires 4,435 units; trucks 4,200 units; radios 689 units; railway-goods cars 118 units. Construction (residential units constructed; 1991): 20,831. Energy production (consumption): electricity (kW-hr; 1991) 36,488,000,000 (39,453,000,000); coal (metric tons; 1992) 40,105,000 (40,410,000); crude petroleum (barrels; 1991) 8,539,000,000 (8,063,000); petroleum products (metric tons; 1991) 2,159,000 (3,077,000); natural gas (cu m; 1991) 846,000,000 (749,000).
Gross national product (1990)[2]: U.S.$31,867,000,000 (U.S.$3,093 per capita).

Structure of gross material product and labour force

	1991			
	in value Din '000,000	% of total value	labour force[3]	% of labour force[3]
Agriculture	10,738	13.9	115,000	5.0
Mining / Manufacturing	30,538	39.6	992,000	43.4
Construction	5,638	7.3	185,000	8.1
Public utilities	1,085	1.4	51,000	2.2
Transp. and commun.	5,559	7.2	162,000	7.1
Trade	15,683	20.3	240,000	10.5
Finance	7,814	10.3	86,000	3.7
Pub. admin., defense / Services / Other			453,000	20.0
TOTAL	77,055,000	100.0	2,284,000	100.0

Tourism (1992): total tourist nights 12,220,000.
Population economically active (1992): total 3,076,142; activity rate of total population 29.6% (participation rates: ages 15–64, n.a.; female [1992] 45.3%; unemployed 24.3%).

Price and earnings indexes (1985 = 100)

	1985	1986	1987	1988	1989	1990[4]	1991
Consumer price index	100	190	419	1,232	16,511	112,780	245,000
Monthly earnings index[5]	100	205	436	1,180	19,893	103,567	...

Household income and expenditure. Average household size (1991) 3.5; income per household (1990) Din 88,569 (U.S.$7,826); sources of income (1991): wages and salaries 50.1%, transfer payments 18.9%, self-employment 11.4%, other 16.5%; expenditure (1991): food 36.2%, fuel and light 9.2%, clothing and footwear 8.1%, transportation and communications 7.7%, housing 6.8%, beverages and tobacco 6.1%, health care 4.1%, education and entertainment 4.0%, household durable goods 3.3%.

Foreign trade

Balance of trade (current prices)

	1985	1986	1987	1988	1989	1990
Din '000,000	−12	−10	−8	−27	−1,375	−21,587
% of total	5.4%	3.1%	1.3%	1.2%	4.5%	17.4%

Imports (1991): Din 104,591,000,000 (machinery and transport equipment 22.7%, of which road vehicles 6.8%; mineral fuels and lubricants 19.0%; chemicals 13.7%; manufactured goods 10.4%, of which textiles 3.2%; food and live animals 8.4%, of which beverages 0.8%). *Major import sources:* Germany 20.2%; former U.S.S.R. 12.6%; Italy 10.6%; U.S. 4.1%; Austria 3.9%.
Exports (1991): Din 89,707,000,000 (manufactured goods 49.9%, of which clothing 14.2%, iron and steel 5.4%, textile products 4.3%; machinery and transport equipment 19.6%; food and live animals 11.8%, of which fruits and vegetables 3.7%; chemicals 9.1%). *Major export destinations:* Germany 23.1%; former U.S.S.R. 17.8%; Italy 14.0%; U.S. 4.4%; Romania 4.3%.

Transport and communications

Transport. Railroads (1991): length 2,453 mi, 3,947 km; passengers transported[2] 50,954,000; cargo transported[2] 49,599,000 tons. Roads (1991): total length 28,595 mi, 46,019 km (paved 59%). Vehicles (1991): passenger cars 1,406,000; trucks and buses 132,100. Merchant marine (1992): fishing vessels 12. Air transport: n.a.; airports (1993) with scheduled flights 5.
Communications. Daily newspapers (1990)[2]: total number 12; total circulation 1,006,000; circulation per 1,000 population 98. Radio (1989): 182,780 receivers (1 per 5.8 persons). Television (1989): 1,642,522 receivers (1 per 6.4 persons). Telephones (1991): 2,028,000 (1 per 5.1 persons).

Education and health

Education (1991–92)

	schools	teachers	students	student/ teacher ratio
Primary (age 7–14)	4,442	51,393	936,469	18.2
Secondary (age 15–18)	538	24,977	347,916	13.9
Higher	145	11,629[6]	132,814[6]	11.4

Educational attainment (1981)[2]. Percentage of population age 15 and over having: less than full primary education 44.6%; primary 24.4%; secondary 24.7%; postsecondary and higher 5.7%. *Literacy* (1981)[2]: total population age 10 and over literate 7,411,500 (89.2%); males literate 4,236,900 (95.4%; females literate 3,174,600 (83.2%).
Health (1991): physicians 25,873 (1 per 402 persons); hospital beds 60,301 (1 per 175 persons); infant mortality rate per 1,000 live births 20.9.
Food (1990)[2]: daily per capita caloric intake 3,545 (1988–90; vegetable products 93%, animal products 7%); 140% of FAO recommended minimum requirement.

Military

Total active duty personnel (1992): 135,000 (army 74.1%, air force 21.5%, navy 4.4%). *Military expenditure as percentage of government expenditure:* 42%.

[1]The autonomous provinces are administratively part of the Republic of Serbia. [2]Data refer to Yugoslavia as constituted prior to 1991. [3]Excludes 66,000 workers in the private sector. [4]On Jan. 1, 1990, the new dinar, equal to 10,000 old dinars, was introduced. [5]Based on worker nominal net personal income. [6]Number of teachers and students is reduced because of a boycott of Serbian schools by Albanians.

Zaire

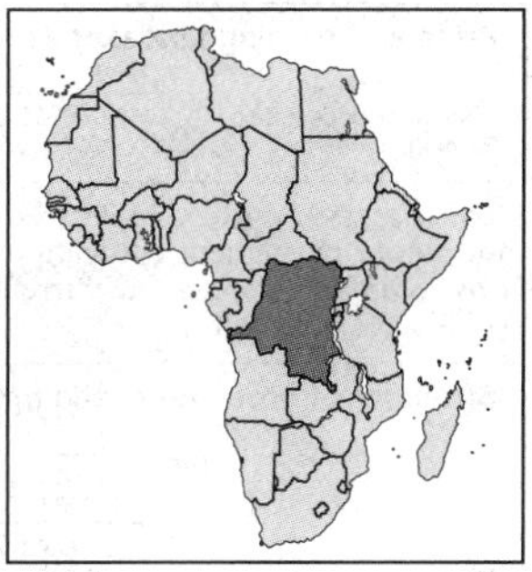

Official name: République du Zaïre (Republic of Zaire).
Form of government: Unitary republic[1].
Chief of state: President[1].
Head of government: Prime Minister[1].
Capital: Kinshasa.
Official language: French.
Official religion: none.
Monetary unit: 1 zaïre (Z) = 100 makuta (singular likuta) = 10,000 sengi; valuation (Oct. 4, 1993) 1 U.S.$ = Z 8,751,200; 1 £ = Z 13,258,000.

Area and population

		area		population
Regions	Capitals	sq mi	sq km	1991 estimate
Bandundu	Bandundu	114,154	295,658	4,617,000
Bas-Zaïre	Matadi	20,880	54,078	2,485,000
Equateur	Mbandaka	155,712	403,292	4,312,000
Haute-Zaïre	Kisangani	194,302	503,239	5,073,000
Kasai-Occidental	Kananga	60,605	156,967	2,982,000
Kasai-Oriental	Mbuji-Mayi	64,949	168,216	3,338,000
Kinshasa	—	3,848	9,965	3,804,000
Maniema	Kindu	50,916[2]	131,871[2]	[3]
Nord-Kivu	Goma	23,188[2]	60,057[2]	6,728,000[3]
Shaba	Lubumbashi	191,845	496,877	5,207,000
Sud-Kivu	Bukavu	25,048[2]	64,875[2]	[3]
TOTAL		905,446[4]	2,345,095	38,543,000[4]

Demography

Population (1993): 42,473,000.
Density (1993): persons per sq mi 46.9, persons per sq km 18.1.
Urban-rural (1985): urban 44.2%; rural 55.8%.
Sex distribution (1984): male 49.18%; female 50.82%.
Age breakdown (1985): under 15, 45.2%; 15–29, 26.0%; 30–44, 15.5%; 45–59, 8.7%; 60–74, 3.9%; 75 and over, 0.7%.
Population projection: (2000) 52,644,000; (2010) 70,841,000.
Doubling time: 22 years.
Ethnic composition (1983): Luba 18.0%; Kongo 16.1%; Mongo 13.5%; Rwanda 10.3%; Azande 6.1%; Bangi and Ngale 5.8%; Rundi 3.8%; Teke 2.7%; Boa 2.3%; Chokwe 1.8%; Lugbara 1.6%; Banda 1.4%; other 16.6%.
Religious affiliation (1980): Roman Catholic 48.4%; Protestant 29.0%; indigenous Christian 17.1%; traditional beliefs 3.4%; Muslim 1.4%; other 0.7%.
Major cities (1991): Kinshasa 3,804,000; Lubumbashi 739,082; Mbuji-Mayi 613,027; Kisangani 373,397; Kananga 371,862.

Vital statistics

Birth rate per 1,000 population (1990–95): 45.3 (world avg. 26.4).
Death rate per 1,000 population (1990–95): 13.0 (world avg. 9.2).
Natural increase rate per 1,000 population (1990–95): 32.3 (world avg. 17.2).
Total fertility rate (avg. births per childbearing woman; 1990–95): 6.1.
Marriage rate per 1,000 population (1977)[5]: 0.07.
Divorce rate per 1,000 population (1977): 0.02.
Life expectancy at birth (1990–95): male 52.3 years; female 55.7 years.
Major causes of death per 100,000 population (1977)[6]: measles 9.6; meningitis 1.1; influenza 0.4; whooping cough 0.3.

National economy

Budget (1992–93). Revenue: Z 3,513,084,000,000,000,000[7] (1991; revenue from mining 30.4%, external trade taxes 26.8%, income tax 18.6%, petroleum tax 15.8%, other revenue 8.4%). Expenditures: Z 4,525,450,000,000,000,000[7] (1991; service of external and internal debt 28.4%, capital expenditure 20.5%, administration 20.0%).
Tourism (1990): receipts from visitors U.S.$7,000,000; expenditures by nationals abroad U.S.$16,000,000.
Production (metric tons except as noted). Agriculture, forestry, fishing (1992): cassava 18,300,000, plantains 1,830,000, sugarcane 1,150,000, corn (maize) 920,000, peanuts (groundnuts) 440,000, bananas 405,000, sweet potatoes 380,000, rice 365,000, yams 310,000, mangoes 212,000, papayas 210,000, oranges 156,000, pineapples 145,000, dry beans 123,000, coffee 98,000, seed cotton 77,000, palm kernels 76,000, dry peas 63,000, avocados 47,000, carrots 47,000, tomatoes 41,000, onions 31,000, cabbage 29,000, natural rubber 11,000; livestock (number of live animals) 3,080,000 goats, 1,650,000 cattle, 920,000 sheep, 840,000 pigs, 21,000,000 chickens; roundwood (1991) 40,079,000 cu m; fish catch (1991) 160,000. Mining and quarrying (1992): copper 144,000; zinc 45,000; cobalt 6,600; cassiterite 2,176[8]; wolframite 16[8]; gold 4,500 kg[9]; diamonds 15,000,000 carats. Manufacturing (1988): cement 460,000[11]; palm oil 182,000[8]; sulfuric acid 152,000; corn flour 89,685[11]; sugar 71,000[9]; soap 47,109; animal feedstuff 20,000; explosives 19,500; plastics 7,586[11]; iron and steel products 5,875; paint 2,458; medicine 45[11]; printed fabrics 44,370,000 sq m; cigarettes 5,236,000,000 units; tires 102,000 units; bicycles 5,830 units; automobiles 2,038 units; beer 4,590,000 hectolitres; carbonated beverages 1,923,000 hectolitres; leather shoes 2,954,000 pairs. Construction (1985): residential 20,000 sq m; nonresidential 39,000 sq m. Energy production (consumption): electricity (kW-hr; 1991) 6,168,000 (5,972,000); coal (metric tons; 1991) 128,000 (174,000); crude petroleum (barrels; 1991) 10,043,000 (2,712,000); petroleum products (metric tons; 1991) 340,000 (986,000); natural gas, none (n.a.).
Household income and expenditure. Average household size (1982) 6.0; average annual income per household Z 1,200 (U.S.$209); sources of income: n.a.; expenditure (1985): food 61.7%, housing and energy 11.5%, clothing and footwear 9.7%, transportation 5.9%, furniture and utensils 4.9%, medical care 2.6%, recreation and education 2.0%.
Gross national product (1991): U.S.$8,123,000,000 (U.S.$220 per capita).

Structure of gross domestic product and labour force

	1988		1987	
	in value Z '000,000	% of total value	labour force	% of labour force
Agriculture	162,672.4[12]	26.1[12]	8,413,000	67.4
Mining	131,413.9	21.1	} 1,847,000	} 14.8
Manufacturing	9,977.0	1.6		
Construction	12,558.3[13]	2.0[13]		
Public utilities	24,166.2	3.9		
Transp. and commun.	3,378.0	0.5		
Trade	108,300.1	17.4	} 2,222,000	} 17.8
Finance, Pub. admin., defense, Services	139,478.2	22.4		
Other	30,877.4[14]	5.0[14]		
TOTAL	622,821.5	100.0	12,482,000	100.0

Public debt (external, outstanding; 1991): U.S.$9,151,000,000.
Population economically active (1987): total 12,482,000; activity rate 38.4% (participation rates: over age 10, 57.4%; female 40.8%; unemployed, n.a.).

Price and earnings indexes (1985 = 100)

	1986	1987	1988	1989	1990	1991	1992
Consumer price index	144.4	258.0	510.5	1,041.7	1,888.4	42,575	1,800,597
Annual earnings index	...	...	...	...	...	...	...

Land use (1991): forested 76.7%; meadows and pastures 6.6%; agricultural and under permanent cultivation 3.5%; other 13.2%.

Foreign trade

Balance of trade (current prices)

	1986	1987	1988	1989	1990	1991
Z '000,000	+13,228	+36,258	+86,582	+198,966	+168,029	+3,385,300
% of total	11.3%	19.8%	26.0%	26.3%	13.3%	15.1%

Imports (1990): Z 1,106,500,000,000 (1987; machinery and transport equipment 45.5%, of which mining equipment 32.0%, transport equipment 7.8%; food, beverages, and tobacco 14.6%; energy 13.8%; consumer goods 7.4%; minerals 5.4%; chemical products 4.4%; textiles and clothing 3.7%). *Major import sources:* Belgium-Luxembourg 25.4%; France 11.3%; China 10.6%; Germany 10.0%; U.S. 9.8%; Japan 2.7%.
Exports (1990): Z 1,537,200,000,000 (copper 47.6%; diamonds 11.4%; crude petroleum 10.8%; coffee 5.7%). *Major export destinations:* Belgium-Luxembourg 54.4%; U.S. 12.5%; France 6.9%; Germany 6.2%; Italy 4.1%; Japan 1.7%.

Transport and communications

Transport. Railroads (1989)[15]: length 3,275 mi, 5,270 km; passenger-mi 162,000,000, passenger-km 260,000,000; short ton-mi cargo 1,186,000,000, metric ton-km cargo 1,732,000,000. Roads (1989): total length 91,000 mi, 146,500 km (paved 12%). Vehicles (1985): passenger cars 24,253; trucks and buses 60,528. Merchant marine (1992): vessels (100 gross tons and over) 27; total deadweight tonnage 30,692. Air transport (1991)[16]: passenger-mi 89,627,000, passenger-km 144,242,000; short ton-mi cargo 14,415,000, metric ton-km cargo 21,046,000; airports (1993) with scheduled flights 24.
Communications. Daily newspapers (1988): total number 7; total circulation 45,000; circulation per 1,000 population 1.4. Radio (1992): 3,400,000 receivers (1 per 12 persons). Television (1992): 22,000 receivers (1 per 1,870 persons). Telephones (1988): 32,116 (1 per 1,144 persons).

Education and health

Education (1987–88)

	schools	teachers	students	student/ teacher ratio
Primary (age 6–11)	10,817	113,468[17]	4,356,516	36.6[17]
Secondary (age 12–17)	4,276[18]	49,153[18]	507,944	21.7[18]
Voc., teacher tr.	[18]	[18]	558,407	[18]
Higher	...	3,506	52,800	15.1

Educational attainment: n.a. *Literacy* (1984): percentage of total population age 15 and over literate 38.2%; males literate 57.4%; females literate 20.4%.
Health (1985): physicians 1,318 (1 per 23,193 persons); hospital beds 64,071 (1 per 476 persons); infant mortality rate per 1,000 live births (1985–90) 83.
Food (1988–90): daily per capita caloric intake 2,130 (vegetable products 97%, animal products 3%); 96% of FAO recommended minimum requirement.

Military

Total active duty personnel (1993): 28,100 (army 89.0%, navy 4.6%, air force 6.4%). *Military expenditure as percentage of GNP* (1988): 2.6% (world 5.0%); per capita expenditure U.S.$7.

[1]Military-dominated regime as of October 1992; transitional government, after several failed attempts, still pending as of November 1993. [2]Estimate. [3]Nord-Kivu includes Manlema and Sud-Kivu. [4]Detail does not add to total given because of rounding. [5]Registered marriages only. [6]Infectious diseases only. [7]Zaire is experiencing hyperinflation. [8]1990. [9]1991. [10]1989. [11]1987. [12]Includes Z 103,323,500,000 in the subsistence sector. [13]Includes Z 12,083,100,000 in the subsistence sector. [14]Import taxes and duties less imputed bank service charge. [15]Traffic statistics are for services operated by the Zaire National Railways (SNCZ), which controls more than 90% of the country's total rail facility. [16]Air Zaire only. [17]1986–87. [18]Secondary includes Voc., teacher tr.

Zambia

Official name: Republic of Zambia.
Form of government: multiparty republic with one legislative house (National Assembly [151[1]]).
Head of state and government: President.
Capital: Lusaka.
Official language: English.
Official religion: none.
Monetary unit: 1 Zambian kwacha (K) = 100 ngwee; valuation (Oct. 4, 1993) 1 U.S.$ = K 350.66; 1 £ = K 531.25.

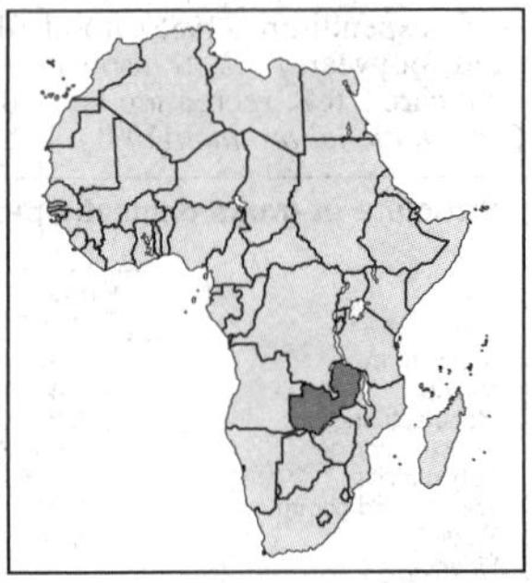

Area and population

		area		population
				1990
Provinces	**Capitals**	sq mi	sq km	census
Central	Kabwe	36,446	94,395	725,611
Copperbelt	Ndola	12,096	31,328	1,579,542
Eastern	Chipata	26,682	69,106	973,818
Luapula	Mansa	19,524	50,567	526,705
Lusaka	Lusaka	8,454	21,896	1,207,980
Northern	Kasama	57,076	147,826	867,795
North-Western	Solwezi	48,582	125,827	383,146
Southern	Livingstone	32,928	85,283	946,353
Western	Mongu	48,798	126,386	607,497
TOTAL		290,586	752,614	7,818,447

Demography

Population (1993): 8,504,000.
Density (1993): persons per sq mi 29.3, persons per sq km 11.3.
Urban-rural (1990): urban 42.0%; rural 58.0%.
Sex distribution (1990): male 49.16%; female 50.84%.
Age breakdown (1986): under 15, 47.0%; 15–29, 25.8%; 30–44, 14.6%; 45–59, 8.3%; 60 and over, 4.3%.
Population projection: (2000) 10,559,000; (2010) 14,386,000.
Doubling time: 19 years.
Ethnolinguistic composition (1980): Bemba peoples 36.2%; Maravi (Nyanja) peoples 17.6%; Tonga peoples 15.1%; North-Western peoples 10.1%; Barotze peoples 8.2%; Mambwe peoples 4.6%; Tumbuka peoples 4.6%; other 3.6%.
Religious affiliation (1980): Christian 72.0%, of which Protestant 34.2%, Roman Catholic 26.2%, African Christian 8.3%; traditional beliefs 27.0%; Muslim 0.3%; other 0.7%.
Major cities (1990): Lusaka 982,362; Ndola 376,311; Kitwe 348,571; Mufulira 175,025.

Vital statistics

Birth rate per 1,000 population (1990–95): 50.3 (world avg. 26.4); legitimate, n.a.; however, marriage is both early and universal, suggesting that legitimate births are a relatively high proportion of all births.
Death rate per 1,000 population (1990–95): 12.4 (world avg. 9.2).
Natural increase rate per 1,000 population (1990–95): 37.9 (world avg. 17.2).
Total fertility rate (avg. births per childbearing woman; 1990–95): 7.2.
Marriage rate per 1,000 population: n.a.
Divorce rate per 1,000 population: n.a.
Life expectancy at birth (1990–95): male 54.4 years; female 56.5 years.
Major causes of death per 100,000 population: n.a.; almost two-thirds of the reported illnesses are related to nutritional deficiencies and infectious and parasitic diseases.

National economy

Budget (1993). Revenue: K 231,900,000,000 (1992; customs duties and excise taxes 62.6%, income tax 24.8%, mineral revenue 5.4%). Expenditures: K 231,900,000,000 (1989; economic services 35.0%, education 10.9%, health 7.2%, community services 2.4%).
Production (metric tons except as noted). Agriculture, forestry, fishing (1992): corn (maize) 464,000, sugarcane 1,150,000, fruits and vegetables 347,000 (of which onions 25,000, tomatoes 25,000, oranges 4,000), cassava 270,000, seed cotton 69,000, wheat 62,000, millet 48,000, sweet potatoes 25,000, soybeans 25,000, peanuts (groundnuts) 21,000, sorghum 15,000, sunflower seeds 6,000, tobacco 5,000; livestock (number of live animals) 3,095,000 cattle, 560,000 goats, 290,000 pigs, 63,000 sheep, 19,000,000 chickens; roundwood (1991) 13,719,000 cu m; fish catch (1991) 65,945. Mining and quarrying (1992): copper 386,763; zinc 6,339; cobalt 4,741; lead 2,673; gold 4,352 troy oz. Manufacturing (1990): cement 432,000; sulfuric acid 276,000[2]; raw sugar 147,000; cigarettes 1,500,000,000 units. Construction (value in K; 1985): buildings 151,100,000; other construction 43,200,000. Energy production (consumption): electricity (kW-hr; 1991) 7,775,000,000 (6,295,000,000); coal (metric tons; 1991) 380,000 (375,000); crude petroleum (barrels; 1991) none (3,960,000); petroleum products (metric tons; 1991) 499,000 (437,000); natural gas, none (n.a.).
Household income and expenditure. Average household size (1981) 5.8; average annual income per household (1981) K 1,041 (U.S.$908); sources of income (1981): wages and salaries 94.0%, other 6.0%; expenditure (1977): food 37.7%, housing 11.0%, clothing 8.3%, transportation 4.3%, education 2.1%, health 1.0%.
Population economically active (1990): total 2,716,000; activity rate of total population 34.9% (participation rates: ages 15–64, 60.1%[3]; female 28.2%[3]; unemployed 17.4%[4]).

Price and earnings indexes (1985 = 100)

	1986	1987	1988	1989	1990	1991	1992
Consumer price index	154.0	224.3	346.9	793.5	1,674.4	3,224.9	9,588.5
Earnings index	...	...	...	...	...	...	...

Land use (1991): forested 38.7%; meadows and pastures 40.4%; agricultural and under permanent cultivation 7.1%; other 13.8%.
Gross national product (at current market prices; 1992): U.S.$2,487,000,000 (U.S.$290 per capita).

Structure of gross domestic product and labour force

	1990			
	in value K '000,000	% of total value	labour force	% of labour force
Agriculture	20,630.8	18.2	1,872,000	68.9
Mining	10,216.7	9.0	56,800	2.1
Manufacturing	36,106.6	31.8	50,900	1.9
Construction	4,418.8	3.9	29,100	1.1
Public utilities	594.2	0.5	8,900	0.3
Transportation and communications	5,501.2	4.8	25,600	0.9
Trade	13,726.9	12.1	30,700	1.1
Finance	8,083.5	7.1	24,200	0.9
Public admin., defense	6,698.4	5.9	111,600	4.1
Services	352.6	0.3		
Other	7,011.2[5]	6.2[5]	506,100	18.6
TOTAL	113,340.9	100.0[6]	2,716,000[6]	100.0[6]

Public debt (external, outstanding; 1991): U.S.$4,954,000,000.
Tourism (1991): receipts from visitors U.S.$35,000,000; expenditures by nationals abroad U.S.$91,000,000.

Foreign trade

Balance of trade (current prices)

	1986	1987	1988	1989	1990	1991
K '000,000	−1,373.3	+1,431.1	+2,888.1	+7,753.2	+7,787.0	−2,139
% of total	18.2%	10.2%	17.3%	26.6%	11.0%	2.2%

Imports (1990): K 27,307,900,000 (1988; machinery and transport equipment 38.3%; basic manufactures 19.8%; chemicals 16.9%; mineral fuels, lubricants, and electricity 12.3%; food 3.8%). *Major import sources:* South Africa 16.9%; United Kingdom 12.2%; Germany 11.6%; United States 10.2%; Japan 6.7%.
Exports (1990): K 33,802,600,000 (1988; copper 85.2%; cobalt 6.1%; zinc 1.6%; tobacco 0.3%; lead 0.2%). *Major export destinations* (1988): United States 10.3%; Japan 3.5%; United Kingdom 2.5%; West Germany 1.5%; South Africa 0.7%.

Transport and communications

Transport. Railroads (1989–90): length 1,345 mi, 2,164 km; passenger-mi 166,-690,000, passenger-km 268,262,000; short ton-mi cargo 855,200,000, metric ton-km cargo 1,248,500,000. Roads (1991): total length 23,214 mi, 37,359 km (paved 18%). Vehicles (1982): passenger cars 105,783; trucks and buses 94,780. Merchant marine: vessels (100 gross tons and over) none. Air transport (1991): passenger-mi 407,091,000, passenger-km 655,151,000; short ton-mi cargo 14,857,000, metric ton-km cargo 21,691,000; airports (1993) with scheduled flights 8.
Communications. Daily newspapers (1989): total number 2; total circulation 179,000; circulation per 1,000 population 24. Radio (1992): total number of receivers 1,660,380 (1 per 5.0 persons). Television (1992): total number of receivers 200,000 (1 per 41 persons). Telephones (1991): 104,518 (1 per 78 persons).

Education and health

Education (1989)

	schools	teachers	students	student/ teacher ratio
Primary (age 7–13)	3,489	32,348[2]	1,446,847	44.1[2]
Secondary (age 14–18)	480	5,786[2]	161,349[2]	27.9[2]
Voc., teacher tr.	26	846	8,218	9.7
Higher	2	320	6,247	19.5

Educational attainment (1980). Percentage of population age 25 and over having: no formal schooling 54.7%; some primary education 34.4%; some secondary 10.5%; higher 0.4%. *Literacy* (1990): population age 15 and over literate 3,131,000 (72.8%); males literate 1,676,000 (80.8%); females literate 1,455,000 (65.3%).
Health: physicians (1984) 798 (1 per 8,437 persons); hospital beds (1989) 22,461 (1 per 349 persons); infant mortality rate per 1,000 live births (1990–95) 72.0.
Food (1988–90): daily per capita caloric intake 2,016 (vegetable products 95%, animal products 5%); 87% of FAO recommended minimum requirement.

Military

Total active duty personnel (1993): 21,600 (army 92.6%, navy, none, air force 7.4%). *Military expenditure as percentage of GNP* (1989): 1.4% (world 4.9%); per capita expenditure U.S.$8.

[1]President may appoint a maximum of 8 additional members. [2]1988. [3]1985. [4]1987. [5]Import duties less imputed bank service charges. [6]Detail does not add to total given because of rounding.

Zimbabwe

Official name: Republic of Zimbabwe.
Form of government: multiparty republic with one legislative house (House of Assembly [150[1]]).
Head of state and government: President.
Capital: Harare.
Official language: English.
Official religion: none.
Monetary unit: 1 Zimbabwe dollar (Z$) = 100 cents; valuation (Oct. 4, 1993) 1 U.S.$ = Z$6.52; 1 £ = Z$9.87.

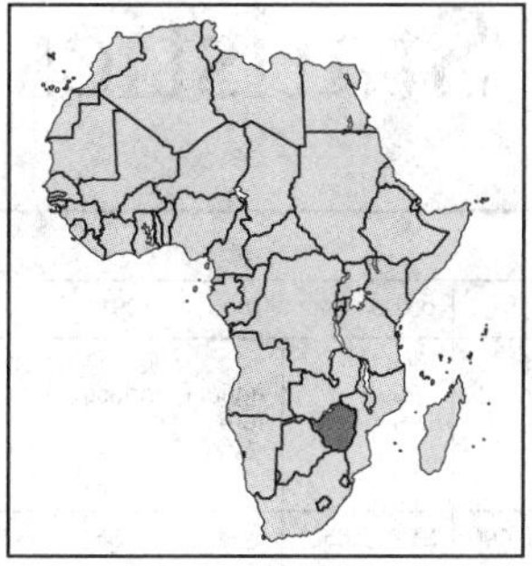

Area and population

		area		population
				1992
Provinces	**Capitals**	sq mi	sq km	census[2]
Bulawayo	—	185	479	620,936
Harare	—	337	872	1,478,810
Manicaland	Mutare	14,077	36,459	1,537,676
Mashonaland Central	Bindura	10,945	28,347	857,318
Mashonaland East	Marondera	12,444	32,230	1,033,336
Mashonaland West	Chinhoyi	22,178	57,441	1,116,928
Masvingo	Masvingo	21,840	56,566	1,221,845
Matabeleland North	...	28,967	75,025	640,957
Matabeleland South	Gwanda	20,916	54,172	591,747
Midlands	Gweru	18,983	49,166	1,302,214
TOTAL		150,872	390,757	10,401,767

Demography

Population (1993): 10,687,000.
Density (1993): persons per sq mi 70.8, persons per sq km 27.3.
Urban-rural (1988): urban 26.4%; rural 73.6%.
Sex distribution (1992): male 48.80%; female 51.20%.
Age breakdown (1990): under 15, 45.5%; 15–29, 28.3%; 30–44, 15.1%; 45–59, 7.2%; 60–74, 3.1%; 75 and over, 0.8%.
Population projection: (2000) 12,608,000; (2010) 15,561,000.
Doubling time: 23 years.
Ethnolinguistic composition (1982): African 97.6%, of which Shona-speaking Bantu 70.8%, Ndebele-speaking Bantu 15.8%; European 2.0%; Asian 0.1%; other 0.3%.
Religious affiliation (1980): Christian 44.8%, of which Protestant (including Anglican) 17.5%, African indigenous 13.6%, Roman Catholic 11.7%; animist 40.4%; other 14.8%.
Major cities (1992): Harare 1,184,169; Bulawayo 620,936; Chitungwiza 274,035; Mutare 131,808; Gweru 124,735.

Vital statistics

Birth rate per 1,000 population (1990–95): 39.9 (world avg. 26.4).
Death rate per 1,000 population (1990–95): 8.9 (world avg. 9.2).
Natural increase rate per 1,000 population (1990–95): 31.0 (world avg. 17.2).
Total fertility rate (avg. births per childbearing woman; 1991): 4.8.
Marriage rate per 1,000 population: n.a.
Divorce rate per 1,000 population: n.a.
Life expectancy at birth (1987): male 57.9 years; female 61.4 years.
Major causes of death per 100,000 population: n.a.; major causes of death include malnutrition, measles, pneumonia, malaria, and diarrheal diseases.

National economy

Budget (1993–94). Revenue: Z$13,300,000,000 (income tax 45.6%; customs duties 16.2%; sales tax 15.3%; revenue from investments and property 6.5%; international grants 5.3%; excise tax 3.8%). Expenditures: Z$14,684,870,000 (recurrent expenditures 78.7%, of which goods and services 48.7%, transfer payments 29.9%).
Population economically active (1986–87): total 3,260,000; activity rate of total population 38.3% (participation rates: over age 15, 76.5%; female 36.6%; unemployed 7.2%[3]).

Price and earnings indexes (1985 = 100)

	1986	1987	1988	1989	1990	1991	1992
Consumer price index	114.3	128.6	138.1	155.9	183.0	227.5	332.7
Monthly earnings index	125.8	139.5	134.3	173.9	...	...	...

Production (metric tons except as noted). Agriculture, forestry, fishing (1992): corn (maize) 362,000, sugarcane 300,000, tobacco leaves 202,000, vegetables (including melons) 132,000, wheat 81,000, soybeans 51,000, cottonseed 47,000, peanuts (groundnuts) 34,000, sorghum 29,000; livestock (number of live animals) 4,700,000 cattle, 2,570,000 goats, 580,000 sheep, 290,000 pigs, 13,000,000 chickens; roundwood (1991) 7,925,000 cu m; fish catch (1991) 22,155 metric tons. Mining and quarrying (value of production in Z$; 1991): gold 753,600,000; nickel 354,000,000; asbestos 195,000,000; coal 176,900,000; copper 103,000,000; chrome 71,700,000. Manufacturing (value in Z$; 1986–87): foodstuffs 1,295,600,000; chemicals and petroleum products 994,400,000; beverages and tobacco 666,800,000; textiles, canvas, and yarns 595,100,000; clothing and footwear 364,400,000; paper, printing, and publishing 293,400,000; transport equipment 175,700,000; nonmetallic mineral products 174,700,000; wood and furniture 161,000,000; metal and metal products 108,300,000; other manufactured goods 52,000,000. Construction (Z$; 1991): commercial 560,979,000; residential 520,084,000; industrial 186,560,000. Energy production (consumption): electricity (kW-hr; 1990) 9,559,000,000 (10,433,000,000); coal (metric tons; 1990) 4,958,000 (4,968,000); crude petroleum, none (none); petroleum products (metric tons; 1990) none (563,000); natural gas, none (none).
Public debt (external, outstanding; 1991): U.S.$2,604,000,000.
Household income and expenditure. Average household size (1992) 4.8; income per household Z$1,689 (U.S.$2,628); sources of income: n.a.; expenditure (1987): food, beverages, and tobacco 30.1%, household durable goods 11.1%, clothing, footwear, and textiles 10.3%, energy 7.3%, housing 6.5%, transportation 6.1%, education 6.0%, health service 3.8%, recreation 0.6%.
Gross national product (1991): U.S.$6,220,000,000 (U.S.$650 per capita).

Structure of gross domestic product and labour force

	1991			
	in value Z$'000,000	% of total value	labour force[4]	% of labour force[4]
Agriculture	3,709	19.5	239,400	20.2
Mining	1,175	6.2	51,100	4.3
Manufacturing	4,849	25.5	206,500	17.4
Construction	368	1.9	83,600	7.0
Public utilities	567	3.0	8,900	0.8
Transp. and commun.	1,243	6.5	56,600	4.8
Trade	1,898	10.0	101,500	8.5
Finance	1,133	6.0	18,400	1.5
Pub. admin., defense	1,230	6.5	94,100	7.9
Services	2,352	12.4	239,400	20.2
Other	479[5]	2.5[5]	87,800	7.4
TOTAL	19,003	100.0	1,187,300	100.0

Land use (1991): forested 49.3%; meadows and pastures 12.5%; agricultural and under permanent cultivation 7.3%; other 30.9%.
Tourism (1990): receipts from visitors U.S.$47,000,000.

Foreign trade

Balance of trade (current prices)

	1986	1987	1988	1989	1990	1991
Z$'000,000	529.9	629.7	896.5	...	–296.8	–1,867.4
% of total	13.9%	15.3%	17.8%	...	3.4%	14.4%

Imports (1991): Z$7,397,200,000 (1990; machinery and transport equipment 37.3%, of which transport equipment 11.6%; fuels 15.6%, of which petroleum products 12.2%; chemicals 15.5%; manufactured goods 14.4%, of which bars, rods, and sections 1.9%, paper and paperboard 1.3%). *Major import sources:* South Africa 19.9%; United Kingdom 11.5%; United States 11.4%; Germany 7.3%; Japan 4.6%; Botswana 3.5%; France 2.1%; Switzerland 2.0%; The Netherlands 1.9%.
Exports (1991): Z$5,529,800,000 (1990; domestic exports 85.4%, of which tobacco 17.0%; gold sales 13.8%; ferroalloys 9.0%; corn [maize] 6.1%; nickel metal 5.8%; cotton 4.9%; asbestos 4.1%; sugar 2.9%; copper 1.6%). *Major export destinations*[6]: Germany 10.1%; United Kingdom 9.3%; South Africa 7.6%; United States 5.6%; Botswana 5.0%; Japan 4.7%; Malaŵi 4.1%; Italy 3.9%; The Netherlands 3.7%; Mozambique 3.1%; Zambia 3.0%.

Transport and communications

Transport. Railroads (1991): route length 1,714 mi, 2,759 km; passenger-mi 355,057,000, passenger-km 571,410,000; short ton-mi cargo 3,695,000, metric ton-km cargo 5,394,000. Roads (1989): total length 52,964 mi, 85,237 km (paved 19%). Vehicles (1990): passenger cars 178,000; trucks and buses 82,000. Merchant marine: none. Air transport (1990): passenger-mi 491,000,000, passenger-km 791,000,000; short ton-mi cargo 14,907,000, metric ton-km cargo 21,764,000; airports (1993) with scheduled flights 6.
Communications. Daily newspapers (1992): total number 2; total circulation 208,032; circulation per 1,000 population 21. Radio (1992): 522,000 receivers (1 per 19 persons). Television (1992): 137,090 receivers (1 per 72 persons). Telephones (1990): 300,955 (1 per 32 persons).

Education and health

Education (1992)

	schools	teachers	students	student/ teacher ratio
Primary (age 7–13)	4,567	60,834	2,306,809	37.9
Secondary (age 14–19)	1,518	23,233	657,344	28.3
Voc., teacher tr.	25	1,479	27,431	18.5
Higher[7]	28	2,414	39,406	16.3

Educational attainment (1986–87). Percentage of employed population age 15 and over having: no formal schooling 24.5%; primary 42.9%; secondary and tertiary 31.7%. *Literacy* (1985): total population age 15 and over literate 3,413,000 (76.0%); males literate 1,846,000 (81.5%); females literate 1,567,000 (66.8%).
Health: physicians (1987) 1,243 (1 per 6,951 persons); hospital beds (1985) 19,913 (1 per 411 persons); infant mortality rate per 1,000 live births (1989) 67.
Food (1988–90): daily per capita caloric intake 2,256 (vegetable products 93%, animal products 7%); 94% of FAO recommended minimum requirement.

Military

Total active duty personnel (1993): 48,200 (army 97.5%, air force 2.5%). *Military expenditure as percentage of GNP* (1989): 6.3% (world 4.9%); per capita expenditure U.S.$38.

[1]Includes 30 nonelective seats. [2]Preliminary results. [3]Does not take into consideration seasonal unemployment of communal workers. [4]Wage-earning workers only. [5]Less imputed bank service charges. [6]Excludes gold sales and reexports. [7]Includes postsecondary vocational and teacher training at the higher level.

Comparative National Statistics

World and regional summaries

region/bloc	area and population, 1993						gross national product, 1991						labour force, 1990		
	area		population			population projection, 2010	total ('000,000 U.S.$)	% agricul- ture	% industry	% ser- vices	growth rate, 1980–91	GNP per capita (U.S.$)	total ('000)	% male	% female
	square miles	square kilometres	total	per sq mi	per sq km										
World	52,497,790	135,968,570	5,511,947,000	105.0	40.5	7,035,950,000	21,878,650	6	35	59	3.1	4,100	2,363,545	63.9	36.1
Africa	11,724,900	30,367,210	669,752,000	57.1	22.1	1,045,885,000	411,170	19	36	45	1.9	650	242,784	65.6	34.4
Central Africa	2,553,070	6,612,400	80,165,000	31.4	12.1	133,731,000	35,100	23	35	42	2.5	470	26,428	64.7	35.3
East Africa	2,471,320	6,400,640	210,457,000	85.2	32.9	343,460,000	48,190	30	22	48	2.6	240	85,082	58.8	41.2
North Africa	3,287,810	8,515,370	148,948,000	45.3	17.5	217,445,000	157,620	16	39	45	1.1	1,100	40,016	84.6	15.4
Southern Africa	1,034,470	2,679,260	46,446,000	44.9	17.3	71,502,000	98,260	5	44	51	3.4	2,230	14,532	64.3	35.7
West Africa	2,378,230	6,159,540	183,736,000	77.3	29.8	279,747,000	72,000	37	28	35	1.3	410	76,726	63.8	36.2
Americas	16,297,790	42,211,120	750,885,000	46.1	17.8	932,298,000	7,342,340	3	30	66	2.9	10,080	293,723	66.5	33.5
Anglo-America[3]	8,368,970	21,675,560	286,505,000	34.2	13.2	334,938,000	6,256,950	2	29	69	3.1	22,340	135,438	58.7	41.3
Canada	3,849,670	9,970,610	28,149,000	7.3	2.8	36,182,000	568,770	2	33	65	3.1	20,810	13,360	60.2	39.8
United States	3,679,190	9,529,060	258,733,000	70.2	27.1	298,620,000	5,686,040	2	29	69	3.1	22,500	122,005	58.6	41.4
Latin America	7,928,820	20,535,560	464,380,000	58.6	22.6	597,360,000	1,085,390	10	36	53	1.6	2,420	158,285	73.1	26.9
Caribbean	90,650	234,750	35,046,000	386.6	149.3	42,106,000	69,450	9	39	52	−0.1	2,420	13,813	66.9	33.1
Central America	202,080	523,390	30,609,000	151.5	58.5	45,708,000	31,230	19	21	60	1.3	1,080	9,520	78.5	21.5
Mexico	756,070	1,958,200	89,955,000	119.0	45.9	118,455,000	252,380	9	30	61	1.5	2,920	30,487	72.9	27.1
South America	6,880,020	17,819,220	308,770,000	44.9	17.3	391,091,000	732,330	11	39	50	1.9	2,450	104,465	73.6	26.4
Andean Group	2,110,520	5,466,280	109,718,000	52.0	20.1	144,612,000	177,470	10	40	50	1.6	1,680	34,715	75.6	24.4
Brazil	3,286,500	8,512,000	156,493,000	47.6	18.4	194,002,000	447,320	10	39	51	2.5	2,950	55,026	72.6	27.4
Other South America	1,483,000	3,840,940	42,559,000	28.7	11.1	52,477,000	107,540	15	38	47	−0.1	2,590	14,724	72.4	27.6
Asia	12,323,160	31,916,760	3,335,672,000	270.7	104.5	4,265,013,000	5,736,340	9	40	51	4.8	1,780	1,436,522[4]	64.7[4]	35.3[4]
Eastern Asia	4,546,920	11,776,450	1,400,317,000	308.0	118.9	1,625,433,000	4,320,820	5	42	53	5.2	3,160	775,590	57.4	42.6
China	3,696,120	9,572,900	1,179,467,000	319.1	123.2	1,381,726,000	424,010	27	42	32	9.4	370	669,693	56.7	43.3
Japan	145,850	377,750	124,670,000	854.8	330.0	129,410,000	3,337,190	3	42	56	4.3	26,930	62,202	62.1	37.9
South Korea	38,330	99,270	44,042,000	1,149.0	443.7	49,683,000	274,460	8	45	47	10.0	6,340	18,664	66.2	33.8
Other Eastern Asia	666,620	1,726,530	52,138,000	78.2	30.2	64,614,000	285,160	4	37	59	7.2	5,640	25,031	58.8	41.2
South Asia	1,971,810	5,106,920	1,198,536,000	607.8	234.7	1,629,237,000	370,430	31	26	42	5.4	320	411,136	77.4	22.6
India	1,222,560	3,166,410	889,567,000	733.4	283.1	1,189,396,000	284,670	31	27	41	5.5	330	322,944	74.8	25.2
Pakistan	339,700	879,810	127,962,000	376.7	145.4	197,672,000	46,730	26	26	49	6.5	390	33,698	87.5	12.5
Other South Asia	409,550	1,060,700	174,007,000	424.9	164.0	242,169,000	39,020	37	19	43	3.8	240	54,494	86.2	13.8
Southeast Asia	1,735,230	4,494,240	462,562,000	266.6	102.9	610,902,000	375,540	19	38	43	5.0	850	189,297	63.0	37.0
ASEAN	1,185,080	3,069,370	333,227,000	281.2	108.6	432,062,000	335,640	15	40	45	5.5	1,050	132,060	65.6	34.4
Non-ASEAN	550,150	1,424,870	129,335,000	235.1	90.8	178,840,000	39,900	53	20	28	1.8	320	57,237	57.1	42.9
Southwest Asia	4,069,200	10,530,150	274,257,000	67.4	26.0	399,441,000	669,550	17	39	44	2.3	2,580	60,499[4]	76.2[4]	23.8[4]
Central Asia	1,542,250	3,994,400	53,612,000	34.8	13.4	73,366,000	88,910	38	46	16	2.8	1,730	[4]	[4]	[4]
Gulf Cooperation Council	1,024,580	2,653,650	23,561,000	23.0	8.9	41,682,000	190,470	5	55	41	0.1	8,970	6,511	91.7	8.3
Iran	632,460	1,638,060	60,768,000	96.1	37.1	89,446,000	127,370	21	21	58	2.5	2,210	15,253	82.0	18.0
Other Southwest Asia	869,910	2,253,040	136,316,000	156.7	60.5	194,947,000	262,800	17	33	50	4.0	2,030	38,735[4]	71.3[4]	28.7[4]
Europe	8,868,120	22,968,380	727,997,000	82.1	31.7	757,861,000	8,047,250	4	36	60	2.3	11,100	378,335[4]	57.7[4]	42.3[4]
Eastern Europe	7,437,080	19,261,960	345,963,000	46.5	18.0	351,924,000	925,620	16	49	35	1.7	2,670	208,749[4]	53.0[4]	47.0[4]
Russia	6,592,850	17,075,400	148,000,000	22.4	8.7	143,477,000	479,550	13	48	39	2.0	3,230	146,634[4]	52.0[4]	48.0[4]
Other Eastern Europe	844,230	2,186,560	197,963,000	234.5	90.5	208,447,000	446,070	19	50	31	1.4	2,260	62,115[4]	55.4[4]	44.6[4]
Western Europe	1,431,040	3,706,420	382,034,000	267.0	103.1	405,937,000	7,121,640	3	34	63	2.4	18,810	169,586	63.6	36.4
EFTA	517,360	1,339,960	33,291,000	64.3	24.8	34,997,000	833,030	4	35	61	2.3	25,360	15,917	58.1	41.9
European Community	912,470	2,363,270	347,935,000	381.3	147.2	370,028,000	6,277,520	3	34	63	2.4	18,200	153,330	64.1	35.9
France	210,030	543,970	57,690,000	274.7	106.1	63,371,000	1,167,750	3	29	68	2.3	20,470	25,404	60.1	39.9
Germany	137,740	356,730	81,187,000	589.4	227.6	92,444,000	1,820,900	2	39	59	2.3	22,770	38,981	60.7	39.3
Italy	136,330	301,300	57,235,000	492.0	190.0	56,270,000	1,072,200	3	33	64	2.4	18,780	23,339	68.1	31.9
Spain	194,900	504,780	39,141,000	200.8	77.5	40,317,000	486,610	5	35	60	3.2	12,470	14,456	75.5	24.5
United Kingdom	94,250	244,110	58,080,000	616.2	237.9	60,986,000	963,700	1	35	64	2.8	16,720	27,766	61.4	38.6
Other EC	159,220	412,380	54,602,000	342.9	132.4	56,640,000	766,360	5	30	65	2.2	14,140	23,384	66.5	33.5
Other Western Europe	1,210	3,190	808,000	666.7	253.4	912,000	11,090	4	20	76	3.9	14,040	339	68.1	31.9
Oceania	3,283,820	8,505,100	27,641,000	8.4	3.2	34,893,000	341,550	4	31	65	2.8	12,730	12,181	63.0	37.0
Australia	2,966,150	7,682,300	17,729,000	6.0	2.3	21,952,000	287,770	3	31	65	2.8	16,650	7,963	61.9	38.1
Pacific Ocean Islands	317,670	822,800	9,912,000	31.2	12.0	12,941,000	53,780	10	27	63	1.3	5,630	4,218	65.0	35.0

[1]Refers only to the long-term external public and publicly guaranteed debt of the 116 countries that report under the World Bank's Debtor Reporting System (DRS). [2]Continental and regional totals may

Africa

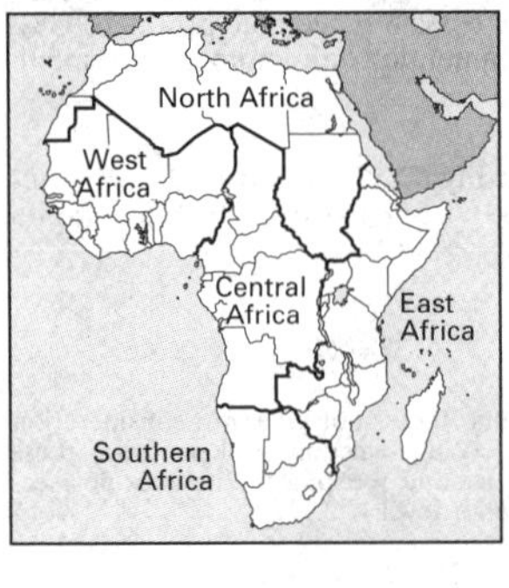

Americas

Asia

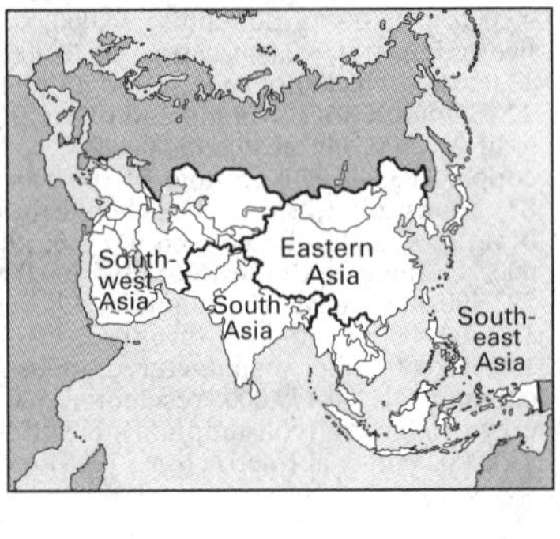

economic indicators							social indicators (latest)								region/bloc
pop. per 1,000 ha of arable land, 1991	electricity consump-tion (kW-hr per capita), 1991	trade ('000,000 U.S.$), 1992			debt ('000,000 U.S.$), 1991[1]		life expec-tancy (years)		health			food (% FAO recom-mended minimum), 1988–90	literacy (%)		
		imports (c.i.f.)	exports[2] (f.o.b.)	balance[2]	total	% of GNP	male	female	pop. per doctor	infant mor-tality per 1,000 births	pop. having safe water (%)		male	female	
3,950	2,227	3,846,100	3,687,000	−159,100	1,084,133	27.3	63.4	67.5	750	62.7	78	114	80.8	67.9	World
3,900	482	113,860	98,900	−14,960	231,550	85.3	53.1	56.4	4,170	91.7	49	100	56.4	36.8	Africa
3,440	168	6,940	6,100	−840	30,178	81.5	50.8	54.2	14,330	88.3	37	91	58.1	26.5	Central Africa
4,800	135	15,990	13,110	−2,880	37,599	90.5	50.6	54.1	13,020	104.1	35	85	52.5	40.2	East Africa
4,000	652	43,070	49,490	−3,580	99,094	83.9	59.8	61.8	1,900	63.2	67	122	61.7	35.0	North Africa
2,950	3,709	21,670	14,660	−7,010	1,196	21.9	59.4	65.3	1,630	56.2	46	124	77.1	74.9	Southern Africa
3,570	109	26,190	23,440	−2,750	63,483	91.6	50.0	53.3	7,570	102.0	55	95	49.8	28.5	West Africa
2,000	5,822	859,410	833,430	−25,980	329,378	31.0	67.7	73.8	560	35.9	88	123	90.6	88.8	Americas
1,210	12,843	681,650	657,080	−24,570	—	—	72.1	79.0	420	8.3	100	136	95.7	95.3	Anglo-America[3]
600	18,134	127,950	125,820	−2,130	—	—	73.3	80.0	450	6.8	100	122	95.6	95.7	Canada
1,360	12,281	552,620	529,980	−22,640	—	—	72.0	78.9	420	8.5	100	138	95.7	95.3	United States
3,380	1,452	177,760	176,350	−1,410	329,378	31.0	64.9	70.6	710	45.5	80	114	86.9	83.8	Latin America
7,350	1,464	18,650	17,200	−1,450	10,487	53.5	66.5	71.1	570	55.5	69	114	86.7	83.9	Caribbean
5,250	479	11,210	18,100	+6,890	23,123	72.2	64.5	68.9	1,500	43.7	64	103	77.1	69.6	Central America
3,730	1,440	61,300	58,420	−2,880	78,456	28.5	66.5	73.1	600	24.2	71	131	89.5	85.1	Mexico
3,010	1,551	86,600	79,040	−7,560	217,312	29.5	64.4	69.9	730	51.9	85	110	87.1	84.6	South America
5,720	1,297	41,730	37,320	−4,410	78,271	42.0	64.4	69.8	920	51.2	77	98	91.4	86.4	Andean Group
2,930	1,723	23,260	21,600	−1,160	87,477	21.6	63.5	69.1	850	57.0	97	114	81.8	80.6	Brazil
1,430	1,568	21,610	20,120	−1,490	51,564	35.5	67.6	73.5	370	32.0	62	126	95.1	94.4	Other South America
6,850	849[4]	1,004,110[4]	919,840[4]	−84,270[4]	354,783	22.7	63.3	66.0	1,020	63.8	77	109	77.6[4]	58.8[4]	Asia
13,350	1,362	595,390	549,830	−45,560	72,748	11.2	69.3	73.0	640	30.5	78	114	89.0	73.1	Eastern Asia
12,480	592	81,740	82,920	+1,180	50,502	13.6	68.6	71.8	650	33.0	74	112	87.0	68.0	China
30,280	7,161	232,950	209,030	−23,920	—	—	75.9	81.8	580	4.6	100	125	100.0	100.0	Japan
22,430	2,411	81,410	68,610	−12,800	22,246	7.9	69.0	76.0	1,010	15.0	100	120	99.1	93.5	South Korea
11,940	2,878	199,300	189,270	−10,030	—	—	70.1	75.6	530	19.3	97	121	97.3	92.0	Other Eastern Asia
5,540	322	42,780	37,330	−5,450	100,099	30.6	57.7	58.4	2,560	84.5	80	99	57.8	31.3	South Asia
5,190	360	23,640	20,050	−3,590	62,842	25.6	57.7	58.7	2,340	80.0	86	101	61.8	33.7	India
5,870	390	9,380	8,910	−470	17,632	38.4	59.3	60.7	2,360	91.0	56	99	36.0	15.2	Pakistan
8,100	83	9,760	8,370	−1,390	19,625	54.6	56.2	55.5	5,750	100.9	67	89	50.4	28.8	Other South Asia
7,350	393	207,920	180,890	−27,030	107,925	34.3	59.2	63.0	3,020	66.4	61	112	87.8	76.1	Southeast Asia
7,670	507	202,770	176,270	−26,500	102,272	34.9	59.5	63.1	2,930	67.5	70	114	88.0	76.2	ASEAN
6,620	92	5,150	4,620	−530	5,653	27.2	58.4	62.8	3,260	63.9	36	106	87.2	75.9	Non-ASEAN
2,600	1,376[4]	158,030[4]	146,690[4]	−11,340[4]	74,012[4]	27.2[4]	64.0	68.4	630	58.3	88	126	79.7[4]	60.7[4]	Southwest Asia
1,190	[4]	[4]	[4]	[4]	[4]	[4]	65.0	72.4	280	34.9	100	132	[4]	[4]	Central Asia
9,010	3,898	73,950	69,770	−4,180	2,270	24.0	66.0	69.1	650	60.3	92	123	72.9	50.2	Gulf Cooperation Council
4,090	949	23,200	21,110	−2,090	2,736	2.6	64.0	65.0	2,690	66.0	89	125	73.8	55.8	Iran
3,230	1,121	60,880[4]	55,810[4]	−5,070[4]	69,006[4]	44.3[4]	63.1	68.2	740	61.6	82	124	83.9[4]	64.7[4]	Other Southwest Asia
2,370	5,760[4]	1,865,930[4]	1,800,310[4]	−65,620[4]	166,253[4]	15.6[4]	69.3	77.0	300	12.1	98	134	98.7[4]	98.0[4]	Europe
1,530	5,147[4]	119,600[4]	112,660[4]	−6,940[4]	146,737[4]	14.7[4]	65.2	74.4	270	16.9	97	132	98.7[4]	98.0[4]	Eastern Europe
1,110	5,818[4]	47,990[4]	43,670[4]	−4,320[4]	54,436[4]	7.4[4]	63.5	74.3	230	17.8	100	132	99.0[4]	99.0[4]	Russia
2,140	3,572[4]	71,620[4]	68,990[4]	−2,630[4]	92,301[4]	35.3[4]	66.4	74.4	320	16.2	95	132	97.9[4]	95.7[4]	Other Eastern Europe
4,800	6,431	1,746,320	1,685,810	−60,510	19,516	28.8	73.0	79.4	330	7.5	100	135	98.8	97.9	Western Europe
4,090	13,216	218,470	212,010	−6,460	—	—	73.4	79.9	350	6.4	99	122	100.0	100.0	EFTA
4,870	5,794	1,524,100	1,470,350	−53,750	19,374	29.8	72.9	79.4	330	7.6	100	136	98.7	97.7	European Community
3,160	7,044	241,240	235,750	−5,490	—	—	73.0	81.1	380	6.7	100	143	98.9	98.7	France
6,920	7,199	407,950	367,650	−40,300	—	—	72.2	78.7	310	7.5	100	132	100.0	100.0	Germany
6,320	4,452	190,680	174,120	−16,560	—	—	73.5	80.0	230	8.3	100	139	97.8	96.4	Italy
2,560	3,972	98,620	96,220	−2,400	—	—	74.4	80.3	260	7.7	100	141	97.0	92.5	Spain
8,800	5,860	220,870	206,090	−14,780	—	—	72.7	78.3	610	7.4	100	130	100.0	100.0	United Kingdom
5,220	5,077	364,750	390,520	+25,770	19,374	29.8	72.4	78.6	360	8.5	98	136	97.3	95.6	Other EC
23,940	3,189	3,760	3,440	−320	142	5.4	73.0	78.2	540	7.3	100	131	98.3	98.1	Other Western Europe
570	7,071	58,050	50,800	−7,250	2,169	40.2	69.8	75.4	520	22.4	89	123	94.2	91.3	Oceania
370	9,045	43,830	39,250	−4,580	—	—	73.9	80.0	440	8.2	99	124	99.5	99.5	Australia
12,520	3,551	14,220	11,550	−2,670	2,169	40.2	62.7	66.9	780	36.8	69	122	83.2	73.7	Pacific Ocean Islands

contain undistributable detail. [3]Anglo-America includes Canada, the United States, Greenland, Bermuda, and St. Pierre and Miquelon. [4]Data for Russia refer to all 15 republics of the former U.S.S.R.

Europe

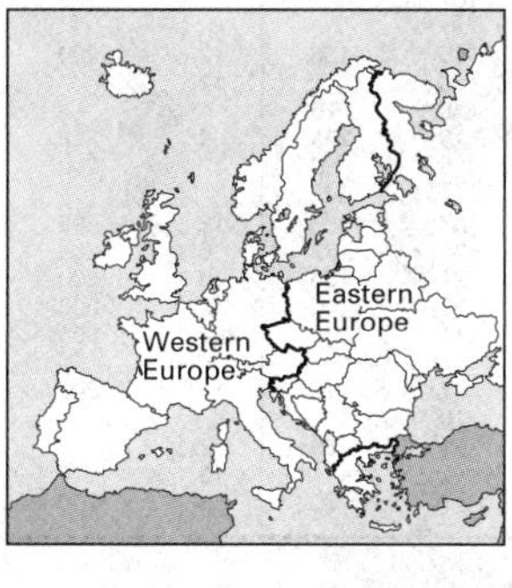

Eastern Europe

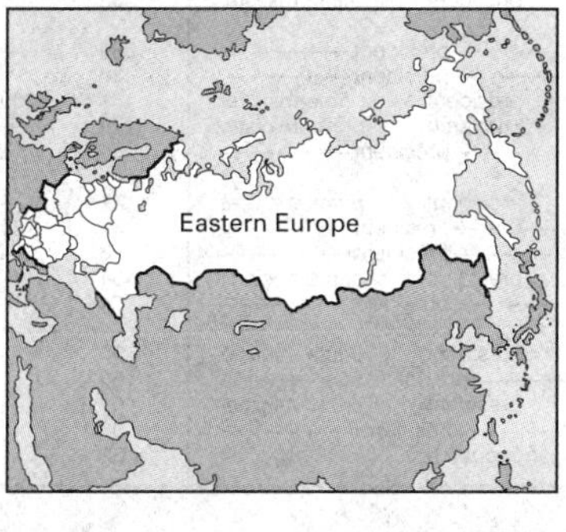

Oceania

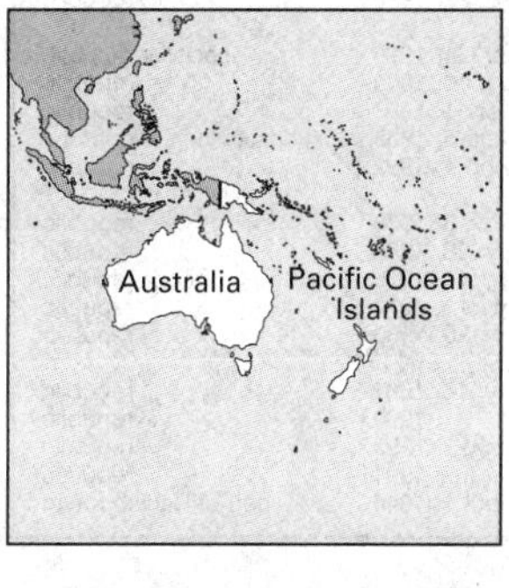

Government and international organizations

This table summarizes principal facts about the governments of the countries of the world, their branches and organs, the topmost layers of local government constituting each country's chief administrative subdivisions, and the participation of their central governments in the principal intergovernmental organizations of the world.

In this table "date of independence" may refer to a variety of circumstances. In the case of the newest countries, those that attained full independence after World War II, the date given is usually just what is implied by the heading—the date when the country, within its present borders, attained full sovereignty over both its internal and external affairs. In the case of longer established countries, the choice of a single date may be somewhat more complicated, and grounds for the use of several different dates often exist. The reader should refer to *Macropædia* and *Micropædia* articles on national histories and relevant historical acts. In cases of territorial annexation or dissolution, the date given here refers either to the final act of union of a state composed of smaller entities or to the final act of separation from a larger whole (*e.g.,* the separation of Bangladesh from Pakistan in 1971).

The date of the current, or last, constitution is in some ways a less complicated question, but governments sometimes do not, upon taking power, either adhere to existing constitutional forms or trouble to terminate the previous document and legitimize themselves by the installation of new constitutional forms. Often, however, the desire to legitimize extraconstitutional political activity by associating it with existing forms of long precedent leads to partial or incomplete modification, suspension, or abrogation of a constitution, so that the actual day-to-day conduct of government may be largely unrelated to the provisions of a constitution still theoretically in force. When a date in this column is given in italics, it refers to a document that has been suspended, abolished by extraconstitutional action, or modified extensively.

The characterizations adopted under "type of government" represent a compromise between the forms provided for by the national constitution and the more pragmatic language that a political scientist might adopt to describe these same systems. For an explanation of the application of these terms in the Britannica World Data, *see* the Glossary at page 541.

The positions denoted by the terms "chief of state" and "head of government" are usually those identified with those functions by the constitution. The duties of the chief of state may range from largely ceremonial responsibilities, with little or no authority over the day-to-day conduct of government, to complete executive authority as the effective head of government. In certain countries, an official of a political party or a revolutionary figure outside the constitutional structure may exercise the powers of both positions.

Membership in the legislative house(s) of each country as given here includes all elected or appointed members, as well as ex officio members (those who by virtue of some other office or title are members of the body), whether voting or nonvoting. The legislature of a country with a unicameral system is shown as the upper house in this table.

The number of administrative subdivisions for each country is listed down

Government and international organizations

country	date of independence[a]	date of current or last constitution[b]	type of government	executive branch[c]		legislative branch[d]		admin. subdivisions		seaward claims	
				chief of state	head of government	upper house (members)	lower house (members)	first-order (number)	second-order (number)	territorial (nautical miles)	fishing/economic (nautical miles)
Afghanistan	Aug. 19, 1919	Sept. 27, 1993[1]	republic	president	prime minister	250	—	...	...	—	—
Albania	Nov. 28, 1912	April 29, 1991[1]	republic	president	prime minister	140	—	27	*c.* 200	12	[2]
Algeria	July 5, 1962	*Feb. 23, 1989*	republic[4]	president HSC	prime minister	60[5]	—	48	1,508	12	12
American Samoa	—	July 1, 1967	territory (U.S.)	U.S. president	governor	18	21	3	15	12	200
Andorra	Dec. 6, 1288	May 4, 1993	parl. coprincipality	[7]	chief executive	28	—	7	...	—	—
Angola	Nov. 11, 1975	Aug. 27, 1992	republic	president		220	—	18	163	20	200
Antigua and Barbuda	Nov. 1, 1981	Nov. 1, 1981	constitutional monarchy	British monarch	prime minister	17	17	30	—	12[8]	200[8]
Argentina	July 9, 1816	July 9, 1853	federal republic	president		48	257	24	...	12	200
Armenia	Sept. 23, 1991	April 1978	republic	president	prime minister	260	—	37	...	—	—
Aruba	—	Jan. 1, 1986	overseas territory (Neth.)	Dutch monarch	[9]	21	—	...	...	12	200
Australia	Jan. 1, 1901	July 9, 1900	federal parl. state[11]	British monarch	prime minister	76	148	8	*c.* 900	12	200
Austria	Oct. 30, 1918	Oct. 1, 1920	federal republic	president	chancellor	63	183	9	99	—	—
Azerbaijan	Aug. 30, 1991	April 1978	republic	president	prime minister	50	—	2	64	...	...
Bahamas, The	July 10, 1973	July 10, 1973	constitutional monarchy	British monarch	prime minister	16	49	—	...	3	200
Bahrain	Aug. 15, 1971	June 1973	monarchy (emirate)	emir	prime minister	30[5]	—	1	—	3	[12]
Bangladesh	March 26, 1971	Dec. 16, 1972	republic	president	prime minister	330	—	4	64	12	200
Barbados	Nov. 30, 1966	Nov. 30, 1966	constitutional monarchy	British monarch	prime minister	21	28	—	—	12	200
Belarus	Aug. 25, 1991	April 1978	republic	chairman SS	prime minister	360	—	6	118[13]	—	—
Belgium	Oct. 4, 1830	May 5, 1993	fed. const. monarchy	monarch	prime minister	185	212	9	589	12	[12]
Belize	Sept. 21, 1981	Sept. 21, 1981	constitutional monarchy	British monarch	prime minister	8	29	6	...	12	200
Benin	Aug. 1, 1960	Dec. 2, 1990	republic	president		64	—	6	84	200	200
Bermuda	—	June 8, 1968	colony (U.K.)	British monarch	[14]	11	40	11	—	12	200
Bhutan	March 24, 1910	—	[15]	king		150	—	4	18	—	—
Bolivia	Aug. 6, 1825	Feb. 2, 1967	republic	president		27	130	9	111	—	—
Bosnia and Herzegovina	March 3, 1992	1990	republic[16]	president CP	prime minister	240[17]	—	100	...	...	...
Botswana	Sept. 30, 1966	Sept. 30, 1966	republic	president		15[5]	40	21	...	—	—
Brazil	Sept. 7, 1822	Oct. 5, 1988	federal republic	president		81	503	27	4,493	200	200
Brunei	Jan. 1, 1984	*Sept. 29, 1959*	monarchy (sultanate)	sultan		21[5]	—	4	—	12	200
Bulgaria	Oct. 5, 1908	July 12, 1991	republic	president	prime minister	240	—	9	273	12	200
Burkina Faso	Aug. 5, 1960	June 11, 1991[1]	republic	president	prime minister	107	—	30	250	—	—
Burundi	July 1, 1962	March 13, 1992[1]	republic	president[18]		81	—	15	113	—	—
Cambodia	Nov. 9, 1953	Sept. 24, 1993	constitutional monarchy	king	[19]	120	—	22	...	12	200
Cameroon	Jan. 1, 1960	June 2, 1972	republic	president	prime minister	180	—	10	49	50	[2]
Canada	July 1, 1867	April 17, 1982	federal parl. state[11]	Canadian GG[20]	prime minister	110[21]	295	12	...	12	200
Cape Verde	July 5, 1975	Sept. 28, 1990	republic	president	prime minister	79	—	14	31	12[8]	200[8]
Central African Republic	Aug. 13, 1960	Nov. 21, 1986	republic	president	prime minister	85	—	17	52	—	—
Chad	Aug. 11, 1960	April 6, 1993[1]	republic	president	prime minister	57	—	14	54	—	—
Chile	Sept. 18, 1810	March 11, 1981	republic	president		47	120	13	51	12	200
China	1523 BC	Dec. 4, 1982	people's republic	president	premier SC	2,978	—	30	338	12	[2]
Colombia	July 20, 1810	July 5, 1991	republic	president		102	161	33	1,011	12	200
Comoros	July 6, 1975	June 7, 1992	federal Islamic republic	president	prime minister	42	—	3	7	12	200
Congo	Aug. 15, 1960	March 15, 1992[22]	republic	president	prime minister	60	125	15	47	200	[2]
Costa Rica	Sept. 15, 1821	Nov. 9, 1949	republic	president		57	—	7	81	12	200
Côte d'Ivoire	Aug. 7, 1960	Oct. 31, 1960	republic	president	prime minister	175	—	10	49	12	200
Croatia	June 25, 1991	Dec. 22, 1990	republic	president	prime minister	68	138	101	...	...	...
Cuba	May 20, 1902	Feb. 24, 1976	socialist republic	president		589	—	15	168	12	200
Cyprus[23]	Aug. 16, 1960	Aug. 16, 1960	republic	president		80[17]	—	...	...	12	[2]
Czech Republic	Jan. 1, 1993	Jan. 1, 1993	republic	president	prime minister	81[24]	200	8	76	—	—
Denmark	*c.* 800	June 5, 1953	constitutional monarchy	monarch	prime minister	179	—	16	275	3	200
Djibouti	June 27, 1977	Sept. 4, 1992	republic	president		65	—	5	9	12	200
Dominica	Nov. 3, 1978	Nov. 3, 1978	republic	president	prime minister	31	—	37	—	12	200
Dominican Republic	Feb. 27, 1844	Nov. 28, 1966	republic	president		30	120	30	136	6	200
Ecuador	May 24, 1822	Aug. 10, 1979	republic	president		78	—	21	168	200	200
Egypt	Feb. 28, 1922	Sept. 11, 1971	republic	president	prime minister	454	—	26	...	12[25]	200[25]
El Salvador	Jan. 30, 1841	Dec. 20, 1983	republic	president		84	—	14	262	200	200
Equatorial Guinea	Oct. 12, 1968	Nov. 16, 1991[22]	republic[4]	president	prime minister	80	—	7	18	12	200
Eritrea	May 24, 1993	1993[26]	republic[4]	president SC		60[27]	—	10	...	...	...
Estonia	Aug. 20, 1991	July 3, 1992	republic	president	prime minister	101	—	21	59	...	...
Ethiopia	*c.* 1000 BC	July 1991[1]	republic	president[18]		87[28]	—	...	...	12	[2]
Faeroe Islands	—	April 1, 1948	part of Danish realm	Danish monarch	[29]	32	—	7	50	3	200

to the second level. A single country may, depending on its size, complexity, and historical antecedents, have as many as five levels of administrative subordination or it may have none at all. Each level of subordination may have several kinds of subdivisions.

Finally, in the second half of the table are listed the memberships each country maintains in the principal international intergovernmental organizations of the world. This part of the table may also be utilized to provide a complete membership list for each of these organizations as of Dec. 1, 1993.

Notes for the column headings

a. The date may also be either that of the organization of the present form of government or the inception of the present administrative structure (federation, confederation, union, etc.).
b. Constitutions whose dates are in italic type had been wholly or substantially suspended or abolished as of late 1993.
c. For abbreviations used in this column see the list on the facing page.
d. When a legislative body has been adjourned or otherwise suspended, figures in parentheses indicate the number of members in the legislative body as provided for in constitution or law.
e. Vatican City also a member.
f. States contributing funds to or receiving aid from UNICEF in 1993.
g. Palestine (Liberation Organization) also a member.

International organizations, conventions

ACP	African, Caribbean, and Pacific (Lomé IV) convention
ADB	Asian Development Bank
APEC	Asia-Pacific Economic Cooperation Council
CARICOM	Caribbean Community and Common Market
EC	The European Communities
ECOWAS	Economic Community of West African States
EEC	European Economic Community
FAO	Food and Agriculture Org.
GATT	General Agreement on Tariffs and Trade
GCC	Gulf Cooperation Council
I-ADB	Inter-American Development Bank
IAEA	International Atomic Energy Agency
IBRD	International Bank for Reconstruction and Development
ICAO	International Civil Aviation Org.
ICJ	International Court of Justice
IDA	International Development Assn.
IDB	Islamic Development Bank
IFC	International Finance Corporation
ILO	International Labour Org.
IMF	International Monetary Fund
IMO	International Maritime Org.
ITU	International Telecommunication Union
LAS	League of Arab States
OAS	Organization of American States
OAU	Organization of African Unity
OPEC	Organization of Petroleum Exporting Countries
SPC	South Pacific Commission
UNCTAD	United Nations Conference on Trade and Development
UNESCO	United Nations Educational Scientific and Cultural Org.
UNICEF	United Nations Children's Fund
UNIDO	United Nations Industrial Development Org.
UPU	Universal Postal Union
WHO	World Health Org.
WIPO	World Intellectual Property Org.
WMO	World Meteorological Org.

Abbreviations used in the executive-branch column

CM	Council of Ministers
CP	Collective Presidency
CTRN	Transitional Committee for National Recovery
FC	Federal Council
GG	Governor-General
GPC	General People's Committee
HSC	High State Council
PC	Presidential Council
PRC	Provisional Ruling Council
SC	State Council
SLORC	State Law and Order Restoration Council
SCS	Supreme Council of State
SS	Supreme Soviet

membership in international organizations																																					country
United Nations (date of admission)	UN organs★ and affiliated intergovernmental organizations																				Commonwealth of Nations	regional multipurpose						economic									
	UNCTAD★[e]	UNICEF★[f]	ICJ★	FAO	GATT	IAEA[e]	IBRD	ICAO	IDA	IFC	ILO	IMF	IMO	ITU[e]	UNESCO	UNIDO	UPU[e]	WHO	WIPO[e]	WMO		EC	GCC	LAS[g]	OAS	OAU	SPC	ACP	ADB	APEC	CARICOM	ECOWAS	EEC	I-ADB	IDB[g]	OPEC	
1946	●	●	●	●		●	●	●	●	●	●	●		●	●	●	●	●		●									●						●		Afghanistan
1955	●	●	●	●	●[3]	●	●	●	●	●	●	●	●	●	●	●	●	●	●	●																	Albania
1962	●	●	●	●	●[6]	●	●	●	●	●	●	●	●	●	●	●	●	●	●	●				●		●									●	●	Algeria
—																	●										●										American Samoa
1993																																					Andorra
1976	●	●	●	●	●[6]		●	●	●	●	●	●	●	●	●	●	●	●	●	●						●		●									Angola
1981	●	●	●	●	●		●	●		●	●	●	●	●	●		●[6]	●		●	●				●			●			●						Antigua and Barbuda
1945	●	●	●	●	●	●	●	●	●	●	●	●	●	●	●	●	●	●	●	●					●									●			Argentina
1992	●	●			●[3]		●	●			●	●		●	●	●	●	●		●																	Armenia
—															●[10]		●																				Aruba
1945	●	●	●	●	●	●	●	●	●	●	●	●	●	●	●	●	●	●	●	●	●						●		●	●							Australia
1955	●	●	●	●	●	●	●	●	●	●	●	●	●	●	●	●	●	●	●	●									●					●			Austria
1992	●	●					●	●			●	●		●	●		●[6]	●																			Azerbaijan
1973	●	●	●	●	●[6]		●	●		●	●	●	●	●	●	●	●	●	●	●	●				●			●			●			●			Bahamas, The
1971	●		●	●	●[6]		●	●		●	●	●	●	●	●	●	●	●		●			●	●											●		Bahrain
1974	●	●	●	●	●	●	●	●	●	●	●	●	●	●	●	●	●	●	●	●	●								●						●		Bangladesh
1966	●	●	●	●	●		●	●		●	●	●	●	●	●	●	●	●	●	●	●				●			●			●			●			Barbados
1945	●	●			●[3]	●	●				●	●		●	●	●	●	●	●	●																	Belarus
1945	●	●	●	●	●	●	●	●	●	●	●	●	●	●	●	●	●	●	●	●		●							●				●	●			Belgium
1981	●	●	●	●	●		●	●	●	●	●	●	●	●	●	●	●	●		●	●				●			●			●						Belize
1960	●	●	●	●	●		●	●	●	●	●	●	●	●	●	●	●	●	●	●						●		●				●			●		Benin
—																	●				●																Bermuda
1971	●	●	●	●			●	●	●			●		●	●	●	●	●											●								Bhutan
1945	●	●	●	●	●	●	●	●	●	●	●	●	●	●	●	●	●	●		●					●									●			Bolivia
1992													●			●	●[6]	●																			Bosnia and Herzegovina
1966	●	●	●	●	●		●	●	●	●	●	●		●	●	●	●	●		●	●					●		●									Botswana
1945	●	●	●	●	●	●	●	●	●	●	●	●	●	●	●	●	●	●	●	●					●									●			Brazil
1984	●	●	●		●[6]			●					●	●			●	●		●	●									●					●		Brunei
1955	●	●	●	●		●	●	●	●	●	●	●	●	●	●	●	●	●	●	●																	Bulgaria
1960	●	●	●	●	●		●	●	●	●	●	●		●	●	●	●	●	●	●						●		●				●			●		Burkina Faso
1962	●	●	●	●	●		●	●	●	●	●	●		●	●	●	●	●	●	●						●		●									Burundi
1955	●	●	●	●	●[6]	●	●	●	●		●	●	●	●	●		●	●		●									●								Cambodia
1960	●	●	●	●	●	●	●	●	●	●	●	●	●	●	●	●	●	●	●	●						●		●							●		Cameroon
1945	●	●	●	●	●	●	●	●	●	●	●	●	●	●	●	●	●	●	●	●	●				●				●	●				●			Canada
1975	●	●	●	●	●[6]		●	●	●	●	●	●	●	●	●	●	●	●		●						●		●				●					Cape Verde
1960	●	●	●	●	●		●	●	●	●	●	●		●	●	●	●	●	●	●						●		●									Central African Republic
1960	●	●	●	●	●		●	●	●		●	●		●	●	●	●	●	●	●						●		●							●		Chad
1945	●	●	●	●	●	●	●	●	●	●	●	●	●	●	●	●	●	●	●	●					●									●			Chile
1945	●	●	●	●		●	●	●	●	●	●	●	●	●	●	●	●	●	●	●										●							China
1945	●	●	●	●	●	●	●	●	●	●	●	●	●	●	●	●	●	●	●	●					●									●			Colombia
1975	●	●	●	●			●	●	●		●	●		●	●	●	●	●		●				●		●		●							●		Comoros
1960	●	●	●	●	●		●	●	●	●	●	●	●	●	●	●	●	●	●	●						●		●									Congo
1945	●	●	●	●	●	●	●	●	●	●	●	●	●	●	●	●	●	●	●	●					●									●			Costa Rica
1960	●	●	●	●	●	●	●	●	●	●	●	●	●	●	●	●	●	●	●	●						●		●				●					Côte d'Ivoire
1992								●			●	●	●	●	●	●	●	●	●	●																	Croatia
1945	●	●	●	●	●	●		●			●		●	●	●	●	●	●	●	●					●												Cuba
1960	●	●	●	●	●	●	●	●	●	●	●	●	●	●	●	●	●	●	●	●	●												●[10]				Cyprus[23]
1993		●			●							●	●		●	●		●																			Czech Republic
1945	●	●	●	●	●	●	●	●	●	●	●	●	●	●	●	●	●	●	●	●		●							●				●	●			Denmark
1977	●	●	●	●			●	●	●	●	●	●	●	●	●	●	●	●		●				●		●		●							●		Djibouti
1978	●	●	●	●	●		●		●	●	●	●	●		●	●	●	●		●	●				●			●			●						Dominica
1945	●	●	●	●	●	●	●	●	●	●	●	●	●	●	●	●	●	●		●					●			●			●[3]			●			Dominican Republic
1945	●	●	●	●		●	●	●	●	●	●	●	●	●	●	●	●	●	●	●					●									●			Ecuador
1945	●	●	●	●	●	●	●	●	●	●	●	●	●	●	●	●	●	●	●	●				●		●									●		Egypt
1945	●	●	●	●	●	●	●	●	●	●	●	●	●	●	●	●	●	●	●	●					●									●	●		El Salvador
1968	●	●	●	●	●[6]		●	●	●	●	●	●	●	●	●	●	●	●								●		●									Equatorial Guinea
1993													●					●						●[6]		●											Eritrea
1991	●			●	●[3]	●	●	●			●	●		●	●					●																	Estonia
1945	●	●	●	●		●	●	●	●	●	●	●	●	●	●	●	●	●		●						●		●									Ethiopia
—																	●																				Faeroe Islands

Government and international organizations (continued)

country	date of independence[a]	date of current or last constitution[b]	type of government	executive branch[c]: chief of state	executive branch[c]: head of government	legislative branch[d]: upper house (members)	legislative branch[d]: lower house (members)	admin. subdivisions: first-order (number)	admin. subdivisions: second-order (number)	seaward claims: territorial (nautical miles)	seaward claims: fishing/economic (nautical miles)
Fiji	Oct. 10, 1970	July 25, 1990	republic	president	prime minister	34	70	...	...	12[8]	200[8]
Finland	Dec. 6, 1917	July 17, 1919	republic	president	prime minister	200	—	12	460	4	12
France	August 843	Oct. 4, 1958	republic	president	prime minister	321	577	22	96	12	200
French Guiana	—	Feb. 28, 1983	overseas dept. (Fr.)	French president	[30]	19	31	2	21	12	200
French Polynesia	—	Sept. 6, 1984	overseas territory (Fr.)	French president	[31]	41	—	5	48	12	200
Gabon	Aug. 17, 1960	March 26, 1991	republic	president	prime minister	120	—	9	37	12	200
Gambia, The	Feb. 18, 1965	April 24, 1970	republic	——president——		50	—	7	35	12	200
Gaza Strip	—	—	Israeli military	—	area commander	—	—	3	—	—	—
Georgia	April 9, 1991	1921[32]	republic	chairman (parl.)	prime minister	(235)	—	3	65	...	...
Germany	May 5, 1955	May 23, 1949	federal republic	president	chancellor	69	662	16	26	[33]	200
Ghana	March 6, 1957	Jan. 7, 1993	republic	——president——		200	—	117	...	12	200
Gibraltar	—	May 23, 1969	colony (U.K.)	British monarch	governor	18	—	—	—	12	200
Greece	Feb. 3, 1830	June 11, 1975	republic	president	prime minister	300	—	13	52	6/10	[2]
Greenland	—	May 1, 1979	part of Danish realm	Danish monarch	[29]	27	—	3	18	3	200
Grenada	Feb. 7, 1974	Feb. 7, 1974	constitutional monarchy	British monarch	prime minister	13	15	9	...	12	200
Guadeloupe	—	Feb. 28, 1983	overseas dept. (Fr.)	French president	[30]	42	41	3	34	12	200
Guam	—	Aug. 1, 1950	territory (U.S.)	U.S. president	governor	21	—	19	—	12	200
Guatemala	Sept. 15, 1821	Jan. 14, 1986	republic	——president——		116	—	22	330	12	200
Guernsey	—	Jan. 1, 1949[34]	crown dependency (U.K.)	British monarch[34]	bailiff	60	—	1	2	12	200
Guinea	Oct. 2, 1958	Dec. 23, 1990[1]	republic	——president CTRN——		15[28]	—	31	175	12	200
Guinea-Bissau	Sept. 10, 1974	May 16, 1984	republic[4]	president	prime minister	150	—	9	37	12	200
Guyana	May 26, 1966	Oct. 6, 1980	cooperative republic	——president——		65	—	10	26	12	200
Haiti	Jan. 1, 1804	March 29, 1987	republic[36]	president[37]	prime minister	27	83	9	...	12	200
Honduras	Nov. 5, 1838	Jan. 20, 1982	republic	——president——		128	—	18	289	12	200
Hong Kong	—	[34]	crown colony (U.K.)	British monarch	governor	60	—	...	19	12	[2]
Hungary	Nov. 16, 1918	Oct. 18, 1989[1]	republic	president	prime minister	394	—	20	168	—	—
Iceland	June 17, 1944	June 17, 1944	republic	president	prime minister	63	—	...	201	12	200
India	Aug. 15, 1947	Jan. 26, 1950	federal republic	president	prime minister	245	545	32	474	12	200
Indonesia	Aug. 17, 1945	Aug. 17, 1945	republic	——president——		1,000	500	27	296	12[8]	200[8]
Iran	Oct. 7, 1906	Dec. 2–3, 1979	Islamic republic	——president[38]——		270	—	24	215	12	50[39]
Iraq	Oct. 3, 1932	Sept. 22, 1968[32]	republic	——president——		250	—	16[40]	96	12	[2]
Ireland	Dec. 6, 1921	Dec. 29, 1937	republic	president	prime minister	60	166	32	81	12	200
Isle of Man	—	1961[34]	crown dependency (U.K.)	British monarch[35]	chief minister	10	24	24	—	12[41]	200
Israel	May 14, 1948	June 1950[34]	republic	president	prime minister	120	—	6	15	12	[2]
Italy	March 17, 1861	Jan. 1, 1948	republic	president	prime minister	325	630	20	94	12	[2]
Jamaica	Aug. 6, 1962	Aug. 6, 1962	constitutional monarchy	British monarch	prime minister	21	60	13	—	12	200
Japan	c. 660 BC	May 3, 1947	constitutional monarchy	emperor	prime minister	252	511	47	3,260	12[42]	200
Jersey	—	Jan. 1, 1949[34]	crown dependency (U.K.)	British monarch[35]	bailiff	58	—	—	—	12	200
Jordan	May 25, 1946	Jan. 8, 1952	constitutional monarchy	——king[18]——		40	80	8	44	3	[2]
Kazakhstan	Dec. 16, 1991	Jan. 28, 1993	republic	president	prime minister	(360)	—	19	218	—	—
Kenya	Dec. 12, 1963	Dec. 12, 1963	republic	——president——		202	—	8	40	12	200
Kiribati	July 12, 1979	July 12, 1979	republic	——president——		41	—	24	—	12[8]	200[8]
Korea, North	Sept. 9, 1948	Dec. 27, 1972	socialist republic	president	premier	687	—	13	172	12	200
Korea, South	Aug. 15, 1948	Feb. 25, 1988	republic	president	prime minister	299	—	15	204	12[43]	12
Kuwait	June 19, 1961	Nov. 16, 1962	const. mon. (emirate)	——emir[18]——		60	—	—	—	12	[2]
Kyrgyzstan	Aug. 31, 1991	May 5, 1993	republic	president	prime minister	350	—	7	89	—	—
Laos	Oct. 23, 1953	Aug. 15, 1991	republic	president	prime minister	85	—	17	114	—	—
Latvia	Aug. 21, 1991	Nov. 7, 1922[34]	republic	president	prime minister	100	—	33	49	...	...
Lebanon	Nov. 26, 1941	Sept. 21, 1990	republic	president	prime minister	128	—	...	...	12	[2]
Lesotho	Oct. 4, 1966	April 2, 1993	constitutional monarchy	king	prime minister	...[5]	65	11	...	—	—
Liberia	July 26, 1847	July 25, 1993[44]	republic[4]	——president——		35[28]	—	...	...	200	[2]
Libya	Dec. 24, 1951	March 2, 1977	socialist state[45]	rev. leader	sec. GPC	750	—	14	c. 1,500	12[46]	[2]
Liechtenstein	July 12, 1806	Oct. 5, 1921	constitutional monarchy	prince	head of govt.	25	—	11	—	—	—
Lithuania	Sept. 6, 1991	Oct. 25, 1992[22]	republic	president	prime minister	141	—	55	81	...	...
Luxembourg	May 10, 1867	Oct. 17, 1868	constitutional monarchy	grand duke	prime minister	21[5]	60	3	12	—	—
Macau	—	May 10, 1990	special terr. (Port.)	——governor——		23	—	2	7	6	12
Macedonia	April 1992	Nov. 20, 1991	republic	president	prime minister	120	—	30	...	—	—
Madagascar	June 26, 1960	Aug. 19, 1992[22]	republic	president	prime minister	138	—	6	111	12	200
Malaŵi	July 6, 1964	July 6, 1966	republic	——acting president——		151	—	3	24	—	—
Malaysia	Aug. 31, 1957	Aug. 31, 1957	fed. const. monarchy	paramount ruler	prime minister	69	180	15	133	12	200
Maldives	July 26, 1965	Nov. 11, 1968	republic	——president——		48	—	20	202	8, 25	25
Mali	Sept. 22, 1960	Jan. 5, 1992	republic	president	prime minister	116	—	8	46	—	—
Malta	Sept. 21, 1964	Dec. 13, 1974	republic	president	prime minister	65	—	1	—	12	25
Marshall Islands	Dec. 22, 1990	May 1, 1979	republic	——president——		12[5]	33	26	—	12	200
Martinique	—	Feb. 28, 1983	overseas dept. (Fr.)	French president	[30]	45	41	3	34	12	200
Mauritania	Nov. 28, 1960	July 21, 1991	republic	——president——		56	79	13	50	12	200
Mauritius	March 12, 1968	March 12, 1992	republic	president	prime minister	70	—	11	105	12	200
Mayotte	—	Dec. 24, 1976	terr. collectivity (Fr.)	French president	[47]	17	—	17	—	12	200
Mexico	Sept. 16, 1810	Feb. 5, 1917	federal republic	——president——		64	500	32	2,378	12	200
Micronesia	Dec. 22, 1990	May 10, 1979	federal republic	——president——		14	—	4	...	12	200
Moldova	Aug. 27, 1991	April 1978	republic	president	prime minister	380[17]	—	...	40	—	—
Monaco	Feb. 2, 1861	Dec. 17, 1962	constitutional monarchy	prince	min. of state	18	—	—	—	12	[2]
Mongolia	March 13, 1921	Feb. 12, 1992	republic	president	prime minister	76	—	21	258	—	—
Morocco	March 2, 1956	Oct. 9, 1992	constitutional monarchy	——king[18]——		333	—	43[48]	...	12	200
Mozambique	June 25, 1975	Nov. 30, 1990	republic	——president——		249	—	11	143	12	200
Myanmar (Burma)	Jan. 4, 1948	*Jan. 4, 1974*	republic	——chairman SLORC——		(492)	—	14	314	12	200
Namibia	March 21, 1990	March 21, 1990	republic	——president——		26	72	13	—	12	200
Nauru	Jan. 31, 1968	Jan. 31, 1968	republic	——president——		18	—	—	—	12	200
Nepal	Nov. 13, 1769	Nov. 9, 1990	constitutional monarchy	king	prime minister	60	205	14	75	—	—
Netherlands, The	March 30, 1814	Feb. 17, 1983	constitutional monarchy	monarch	prime minister	75	150	12	646	12	200
Netherlands Antilles	—	Dec. 29, 1954	overseas territory (Neth.)	Dutch monarch	[9]	22	—	5	—	12	200
New Caledonia	—	[34]	overseas territory (Fr.)	French president	[50]	54	—	3	32	12	200
New Zealand	Sept. 26, 1907	June 30, 1852[34]	constitutional monarchy	British monarch	prime minister	99	—	12	74	12	200
Nicaragua	April 30, 1838	Jan. 9, 1987	republic	——president——		92	—	16	143	200	200
Niger	Aug. 3, 1960	Dec. 26, 1992[22]	republic	president	prime minister	83	—	7	36	—	—

membership in international organizations																																					country
United Nations (date of admission)	UN organs★ and affiliated intergovernmental organizations																				Commonwealth of Nations	regional multipurpose						economic									
	UNCTAD★[e]	UNICEF★[f]	ICJ★	FAO	GATT	IAEA[e]	IBRD	ICAO	IDA	IFC	ILO	IMF	IMO	ITU[e]	UNESCO	UNIDO	UPU[e]	WHO	WIPO[e]	WMO		EC	GCC	LAS[g]	OAS	OAU	SPC	ACP	ADB	APEC	CARICOM	ECOWAS	EEC	I-ADB	IDB[g]	OPEC	
1970	●	●	●	●	●[6]		●	●	●	●	●	●	●	●	●	●	●	●	●	●							●	●	●								Fiji
1955	●	●	●	●	●	●	●	●	●	●	●	●	●	●	●	●	●	●	●	●									●					●			Finland
1945	●	●	●	●	●	●	●	●	●	●	●	●	●	●	●	●	●	●	●	●		●					●		●				●	●			France
—																	●																				French Guiana
—																	●			●							●										French Polynesia
1960	●	●	●	●	●	●	●	●	●	●	●	●	●	●	●	●	●	●	●	●						●		●							●	●	Gabon
1965	●	●	●	●	●		●	●	●	●		●	●	●	●	●	●	●	●	●	●					●		●				●			●		Gambia, The
—																	●																				Gaza Strip
1992							●					●			●	●		●																			Georgia
1973	●	●	●	●	●	●	●	●	●	●	●	●	●	●	●	●	●	●	●	●		●							●				●	●			Germany
1957	●	●	●	●	●	●	●	●	●	●	●	●	●	●	●	●	●	●	●	●	●					●		●				●					Ghana
—																	●				●																Gibraltar
1945	●	●	●	●	●	●	●	●	●	●	●	●	●	●	●	●	●	●	●	●		●											●				Greece
—																	●																				Greenland
1974	●	●	●	●	●[6]		●	●	●	●	●	●		●	●	●	●	●			●				●			●			●						Grenada
—																	●																				Guadeloupe
—																	●										●										Guam
1945	●	●	●	●	●	●	●	●	●	●	●	●	●	●	●	●	●	●	●	●					●									●			Guatemala
—																	●				●																Guernsey
1958	●	●	●	●			●	●	●	●	●	●	●	●	●	●	●	●	●	●						●		●				●			●		Guinea
1974	●	●	●	●	●[6]		●	●	●	●	●	●	●	●	●	●	●	●	●	●						●		●				●			●		Guinea-Bissau
1966	●	●	●	●	●		●	●	●	●	●	●	●	●	●	●	●	●	●	●	●				●			●			●			●			Guyana
1945	●	●	●	●	●	●	●	●	●	●	●	●	●	●	●	●	●	●	●	●					●			●			●[3]			●			Haiti
1945	●	●	●	●			●	●	●	●	●	●	●	●	●	●	●	●	●	●					●									●			Honduras
—		●			●								●[10]				●			●	●								●	●							Hong Kong
1955	●	●	●	●	●	●	●	●	●	●	●	●	●	●	●	●	●	●	●	●																	Hungary
1946	●	●	●	●	●	●	●	●	●	●	●	●	●	●	●	●	●	●	●	●																	Iceland
1945	●	●	●	●	●	●	●	●	●	●	●	●	●	●	●	●	●	●	●	●	●								●								India
1950	●	●	●	●	●	●	●	●	●	●	●	●	●	●	●	●	●	●	●	●									●	●					●	●	Indonesia
1945	●	●	●	●		●	●	●	●	●	●	●	●	●	●	●	●	●	●	●																●	Iran
1945	●	●	●	●		●	●	●	●	●	●	●	●	●	●	●	●	●	●	●				●											●	●	Iraq
1955	●	●	●	●	●	●	●	●	●	●	●	●	●	●	●	●	●	●	●	●		●											●				Ireland
—																	●				●																Isle of Man
1949	●	●	●	●	●	●	●	●	●	●	●	●	●	●	●	●	●	●	●	●														●			Israel
1955	●	●	●	●	●	●	●	●	●	●	●	●	●	●	●	●	●	●	●	●		●							●				●	●			Italy
1962	●	●	●	●	●	●	●	●		●	●	●	●	●	●	●	●	●	●	●	●				●			●			●			●			Jamaica
1956	●	●	●	●	●	●	●	●	●	●	●	●	●	●	●	●	●	●	●	●									●	●				●			Japan
—																	●				●																Jersey
1955	●	●	●	●		●	●	●	●	●	●	●	●	●	●	●	●	●	●	●				●											●		Jordan
1992	●	●			●[3]		●	●				●			●		●	●																			Kazakhstan
1963	●	●	●	●	●	●	●	●	●	●	●	●	●	●	●	●	●	●	●	●	●					●		●									Kenya
—		●			●[6]		●	●	●	●		●		●	●		●	●			●						●	●	●								Kiribati
1991	●	●		●		●		●					●	●	●	●	●	●	●	●																	Korea, North
1991	●	●		●	●	●	●	●	●	●	●	●	●	●	●	●	●	●	●	●									●	●							Korea, South
1963	●	●	●	●	●	●	●	●	●	●	●	●	●	●	●	●	●	●	●	●			●	●											●	●	Kuwait
1992	●	●					●				●	●			●		●[6]	●																			Kyrgyzstan
1955	●	●	●	●			●	●	●	●	●	●		●	●	●	●	●		●									●								Laos
1991	●			●			●	●			●	●		●	●			●	●	●																	Latvia
1945	●	●	●	●		●	●	●	●	●	●	●	●	●	●	●	●	●	●	●				●											●		Lebanon
1966	●	●	●	●	●		●	●	●	●	●	●		●	●	●	●	●	●	●	●					●		●									Lesotho
1945	●	●	●	●		●	●	●	●	●	●	●	●	●	●	●	●	●	●	●						●		●				●					Liberia
1955	●	●	●	●		●	●	●	●	●	●	●	●	●	●	●	●	●	●	●				●		●									●	●	Libya
1990	●	●	●			●	●							●			●		●																		Liechtenstein
1991	●			●			●	●			●	●		●	●	●	●	●	●	●																	Lithuania
1945	●	●	●	●	●	●	●	●	●	●	●	●	●	●	●	●	●	●	●	●		●											●				Luxembourg
—				●	●								●[10]				●																				Macau
1993																																					Macedonia
1960	●	●	●	●	●	●	●	●	●	●	●	●	●	●	●	●	●	●	●	●						●		●									Madagascar
1964	●	●	●	●	●		●	●	●	●	●	●	●	●	●	●	●	●	●	●	●					●		●									Malaŵi
1957	●	●	●	●	●	●	●	●	●	●	●	●	●	●	●	●	●	●	●	●	●								●	●					●		Malaysia
1965	●	●	●	●	●		●	●	●	●		●	●	●	●	●	●	●		●	●								●						●		Maldives
1960	●	●	●	●	●	●	●	●	●	●	●	●		●	●	●	●	●	●	●						●		●				●			●		Mali
1964	●	●	●	●	●		●	●			●	●	●	●	●	●	●	●	●	●	●												●[10]				Malta
1991	●	●					●	●	●			●					●[6]	●									●		●								Marshall Islands
—																	●																				Martinique
1961	●	●	●	●	●		●	●	●	●	●	●	●	●	●	●	●	●	●	●				●		●		●				●			●		Mauritania
1968	●	●	●	●	●	●	●	●	●	●	●	●	●	●	●	●	●	●	●	●	●					●		●									Mauritius
—																	●																				Mayotte
1945	●	●	●	●	●	●	●	●	●	●	●	●	●	●	●	●	●	●	●	●					●					●[6]	●[3]			●			Mexico
1991	●	●						●									●[6]	●									●		●								Micronesia
1992	●				●[3]		●	●			●	●		●			●	●																			Moldova
1993	●	●				●		●					●	●	●		●	●	●																		Monaco
1961	●	●	●	●		●	●	●	●	●	●	●		●	●	●	●	●	●	●									●								Mongolia
1956	●	●	●	●	●	●	●	●	●	●	●	●	●	●	●	●	●	●	●	●				●											●		Morocco
1975	●	●	●	●	●		●	●	●	●	●	●	●	●	●	●	●	●		●						●		●									Mozambique
1948	●	●	●	●	●	●	●	●	●	●	●	●	●	●	●	●	●	●		●									●								Myanmar (Burma)
1990	●	●		●	●	●	●			●	●	●		●	●	●	●	●	●	●	●					●		●									Namibia
—								●						●			●				●[49]						●		●								Nauru
1955	●	●	●	●			●	●	●	●	●	●	●	●	●	●	●	●		●									●								Nepal
1945	●	●	●	●	●	●	●	●	●	●	●	●	●	●	●	●	●	●	●	●		●							●				●	●			Netherlands, The
—															●[10]		●			●																	Netherlands Antilles
—																	●			●							●										New Caledonia
1945	●	●	●	●	●	●	●	●	●	●	●	●	●	●	●	●	●	●	●	●	●						●			●							New Zealand
1945	●	●	●	●	●	●	●	●	●	●	●	●	●	●	●	●	●	●	●	●					●				●					●			Nicaragua
1960	●	●	●	●	●	●	●	●	●	●	●	●		●	●	●	●	●	●	●						●		●				●			●		Niger

Government and international organizations (continued)

country	date of independence[a]	date of current or last constitution[b]	type of government	executive branch[c]: chief of state	executive branch[c]: head of government	legislative branch[d]: upper house (members)	legislative branch[d]: lower house (members)	admin. subdivisions: first-order (number)	admin. subdivisions: second-order (number)	seaward claims: territorial (nautical miles)	seaward claims: fishing/economic (nautical miles)
Nigeria	Oct. 1, 1960	*Oct. 1, 1979*	federal republic	—chairman PRC—		(91)	(593)	31	589	30	200
Northern Mariana Is.	—	Jan. 9, 1978	commonwealth (U.S.)	U.S. president	governor	9	18	4	—	12	200
Norway	June 7, 1905	May 17, 1814	constitutional monarchy	king	prime minister	165	—	19	448	4	200
Oman	Dec. 20, 1951	—	monarchy (sultanate)	—sultan—		60[5]	—	59	—	12	200
Pakistan	Aug. 14, 1947	Aug. 14, 1973	federal Islamic republic	president	prime minister	87	217	5[51]	17[51]	12	200
Panama	Nov. 3, 1903	Oct. 11, 1972[32]	republic	—president[52]—		68	—	11	67	200	[2]
Papua New Guinea	Sept. 16, 1975	Sept. 16, 1975	constitutional monarchy	British monarch	prime minister	109	—	20	...	12[8]	200[8]
Paraguay	May 14, 1811	June 22, 1992	republic	—president—		45	80	18	217	—	—
Peru	July 28, 1821	Oct. 31, 1993[22]	republic	—president—		80[28]	—	14	187	200	200
Philippines	July 4, 1946	Feb. 11, 1987	republic	—president—		24	200[53]	15	75	[25]	200[8]
Poland	Nov. 10, 1918	Dec. 8, 1992[54]	republic	president	prime minister	100	460	49	2,459	12	[55]
Portugal	c. 1140	April 25, 1976	parliamentary state	president	prime minister	230	—	22	...	12	200
Puerto Rico	—	July 25, 1952	commonwealth (U.S.)	U.S. president	governor	29	53	78	...	12	200
Qatar	Sept. 3, 1971	July 1970[32]	monarchy	—emir—		35[5]	—	9	—	3	[56]
Réunion	—	Feb. 28, 1983	overseas dept. (Fr.)	French president	[30]	47	45	4	24	12	200
Romania	May 21, 1877	Dec. 13, 1991	republic	president	prime minister	143	341	41	260	12[25]	200[25]
Russia	Dec. 8, 1991	July 7, 1992[57]	federal republic	president	prime minister	178[58]	450[58]	89	1,857	...	...
Rwanda	July 1, 1962	June 10, 1991	republic[4]	president	prime minister	70	—	11	145	—	—
St. Kitts and Nevis	Sept. 19, 1983	Sept. 19, 1983	constitutional monarchy	British monarch	prime minister	15	—	1	—	12	200
St. Lucia	Feb. 22, 1979	Feb. 22, 1979	constitutional monarchy	British monarch	prime minister	11	17	8	—	12	200
St. Vincent	Oct. 27, 1979	Oct. 27, 1979	constitutional monarchy	British monarch	prime minister	21	—	7	—	12	200
San Marino	855	Oct. 8, 1600	republic	—captains-regent (2)—		60	—	9	—	—	—
São Tomé and Príncipe	July 12, 1975	Sept. 10, 1990	republic	president	prime minister	55	—	2	7	12[8]	200[8]
Saudi Arabia	Sept. 23, 1932	—	monarchy	—king—		62[5]	—	13	...	12	[2]
Senegal	Aug. 20, 1960	March 7, 1963	republic	president	prime minister	120	—	10	31	12[25]	200[25]
Seychelles	June 29, 1976	June 18, 1993	republic	—president—		43	—	...	...	12	200
Sierra Leone	April 27, 1961	*Oct. 1, 1991*	republic	—chairman SCS—		(127)	—	4	148	200	[2]
Singapore	Aug. 9, 1965	June 3, 1959[34]	republic	president	prime minister	87	—	—	—	3	...
Slovakia	Jan. 1, 1993	Jan. 1, 1993	republic	president	prime minister	150	—	4	38	—	—
Slovenia	June 25, 1991	Dec. 23, 1991	republic	president	prime minister	40	90	62	...	...	...
Solomon Islands	July 7, 1978	July 7, 1978	constitutional monarchy	British monarch	prime minister	47	—	8	...	12[8]	200[8]
Somalia	July 1, 1960	July 1, 1960	UN-imposed regime[59]	—[60]—		...	—	...	...	200	200
South Africa	May 31, 1910	Nov. 18, 1993[61]	republic[62]	—state president[62]—		[62]	—	[62]	[62]	12	200
Bophuthatswana	Dec. 6, 1977	Dec. 6, 1977	republic[64]	—president—		108	—	12	76	—	—
Ciskei	Dec. 4, 1981	*Dec. 4, 1981*	republic[64]	—chairman of military committee—		(87)	—	7	42	—	—
Transkei	Oct. 26, 1976	*Dec. 1963*	republic[64]	—head of military council—		(150)	—	9	28	—	—
Venda	Sept. 13, 1979	*Sept. 13, 1979*	republic[64]	—head of state—		(92)	—	4	28	—	—
Spain	1492	Dec. 29, 1978	constitutional monarchy	king	prime minister	251	350	17	50	12	200
Sri Lanka	Feb. 4, 1948	Sept. 7, 1978	republic	—president—		225	—	25	...	12	200
Sudan, The	Jan. 1, 1956	*Oct. 10, 1985*	Islamic military regime	—president—		302	—	9	66	12	[2]
Suriname	Nov. 25, 1975	Nov. 25, 1987	republic	—president—		51	—	10	—	12	200
Swaziland	Sept. 6, 1968	*Sept. 6, 1968*	monarchy	—king[18]—		30	65	4	40	—	—
Sweden	before 836	Jan. 1, 1975	constitutional monarchy	king	prime minister	349	—	24	286	12	[12]
Switzerland	Sept. 22, 1499	May 29, 1874	federal state	—president FC—		46	200	26	3,003	—	—
Syria	April 17, 1946	March 14, 1973	republic	—president—		250	—	14	59	35	[2]
Taiwan	Oct. 25, 1945	Dec. 25, 1947[34]	republic	president	premier	384[65]	161	3	21	24	200
Tajikistan	Sept. 9, 1991	April 1978	republic	de facto president	prime minister	80[28]	—	3	...	—	—
Tanzania	Dec. 9, 1961	April 25, 1977	republic	—president—		255	—	25	99	12	200
Thailand	1350	Dec. 9, 1991	constitutional monarchy	king	prime minister	270	360	73	711	12	200
Togo	April 27, 1960	Sept. 27, 1992[22]	republic[66]	president	prime minister	79[28]	—	5	21	30	200
Tonga	June 4, 1970	Nov. 4, 1875	constitutional monarchy	—monarch[67]—		30	—	5	23	12	200
Trinidad and Tobago	Aug. 31, 1962	July 27, 1976	republic	president	prime minister	31	36	12	...	12[8]	200[8]
Tunisia	March 20, 1956	June 1, 1959	republic	president	prime minister	141	—	23	246	12	[2]
Turkey	Oct. 29, 1923	Nov. 7, 1982	republic	president	prime minister	450	—	73	829	12[68]	[12]
Turkmenistan	Oct. 27, 1991	May 18, 1992	republic	—president—		50	—	5	...	—	—
Tuvalu	Oct. 1, 1978	Sept. 15, 1986	constitutional monarchy	British monarch	prime minister	12	—	8	—	12[8]	200[8]
Uganda	Oct. 9, 1962	*Sept. 8, 1967*	republic[4]	—president[18]—		278[28]	—	38	...	—	—
Ukraine	Aug. 24, 1991	April 1978	republic	president	prime minister	450	—	25	485	12	200
United Arab Emirates	Dec. 2, 1971	Dec. 2, 1971[32]	federation of emirates	president	prime minister	40[5]	—	7	—	...	[12]
United Kingdom	Oct. 14, 1066	[69]	constitutional monarchy	monarch	prime minister	1,211[5]	651	3[70]	86	12[41]	200
United States	July 4, 1776	March 4, 1789	federal republic	—president—		100	435	51	3,043[71]	12	200
Uruguay	Aug. 25, 1828	Feb. 15, 1967	republic	—president—		31	99	19	...	200	200
Uzbekistan	Aug. 31, 1991	Dec. 8, 1992	republic	president	prime minister	500	—	13	...	...	...
Vanuatu	July 30, 1980	July 30, 1980	republic	president	prime minister	46	—	11	...	12[8]	200[8]
Venezuela	July 5, 1811	Jan. 23, 1961	federal republic	—president—		52	201	24	202	12	200
Vietnam	Sept. 2, 1945	April 15, 1992	socialist republic	president	prime minister	395	—	53	467	12	200
Virgin Islands (U.S.)	—	July 22, 1954	territory (U.S.)	U.S. president	governor	15	—	2	—	12	200
West Bank	—	—	Israeli military	—	area commander	—	—	7	—	—	—
Western Sahara	—	—	annexture of Morocco	—	—	—	—	4	8	12	200
Western Samoa	Jan. 1, 1962	Oct. 28, 1960	[73]	head of state	prime minister	48	—	...	—	12	200
Yemen	December 1918	May 16, 1991	republic[4]	president PC	prime minister CM	301	—	17	...	12	200
Yugoslavia	Dec. 1, 1918	April 27, 1992	federal republic	federal president	prime minister	40	138	2	2	12	...
Zaire	June 30, 1960	Feb. 15, 1978[76]	republic[76]	president[76]	prime minister[76]	222[76]	—	11	41	12	200
Zambia	Oct. 24, 1964	Aug. 30, 1991	republic	—president—		151	—	9	57	—	—
Zimbabwe	April 18, 1980	April 18, 1980	republic	—president—		150	—	10	...	—	—

[1]Transitional constitution. [2]Territorial sea claim assumed to claim fishing/economic rights within the same zone. [3]Observer status. [4]Transitional government. [5]Body with limited or no legislative authority. [6]Full membership pending. [7]President of France and Bishop of Urgel, Spain. [8]Measured from claimed archipelagic baselines. [9]Executive responsibilities divided between (for The Netherlands) the governor and (locally) the prime minister. [10]Associate member. [11]Formally a constitutional monarchy. [12]Defined by equidistant line. [13]1990. [14]Executive responsibilities divided between (for the U.K.) the governor and (locally) the premier of the Cabinet. [15]Resembles a constitutional monarchy without a formal constitution. [16]Central government has ineffective control because of civil war. [17]Includes unoccupied seats. [18]Assisted by the prime minister. [19]First president assisted by second president. [20]Governor-general can exercise all the powers of the reigning monarch of the Commonwealth. Royal assent to the monarch is a matter of choice. [21]Temporarily increased from 104. [22]Date of referendum approving new constitution. [23]Republic of Cyprus only. [24]Seats not occupied as of mid-1993. [25]Zone defined by geographic coordinates. [26]Official proclamations organizing government. [27]Excludes the central committee of the Eritrean People's Liberation Front. [28]Interim legislature. [29]Executive responsibilities divided between (for Denmark) the high commissioner and (locally) the prime minister. [30]Executive responsibilities divided among (for France) the commissioner and (locally) the president of the General Council and the president of the Regional Council. [31]Executive responsibilities divided between (for France) the high commissioner and (locally) the president of the Council of Ministers. [32]Provisional constitution. [33]3 nautical miles in Baltic Sea, 16 nautical miles in North Sea. [34]Evolving body of constitutional law. [35]Represented by the lieutenant governor. [36]Military-dominated extraconstitutional regime. [37]Office vacant from June 1992 through November 1993. [38]Shares coexecutive authority with spiritual leader. [39]Sea of Oman only; median line boundaries in the Persian Gulf. [40]De facto administration. [41]Median line between the Isle of Man and the United Kingdom. [42]3 nautical miles in 5 straits. [43]3 nautical miles in

membership in international organizations																																					country
United Nations (date of admission)	UN organs★ and affiliated intergovernmental organizations																				Commonwealth of Nations	regional multipurpose						economic									
	UNCTAD★[e]	UNICEF★[f]	ICJ★	FAO	GATT	IAEA[e]	IBRD	ICAO	IDA	IFC	ILO	IMF	IMO	ITU[e]	UNESCO	UNIDO	UPU[e]	WHO	WIPO[e]	WMO		EC	GCC	LAS[g]	OAS	OAU	SPC	ACP	ADB	APEC	CARICOM	ECOWAS	EEC	I-ADB	IDB[g]	OPEC	
1960	●	●	●	●	●	●	●	●	●	●	●	●	●	●	●	●	●	●		●	●					●		●				●				●	Nigeria
—																	●										●										Northern Mariana Is.
1945	●	●	●	●	●	●	●	●	●	●	●	●	●	●	●	●	●	●	●	●									●					●			Norway
1971	●	●	●	●			●	●	●	●		●	●	●	●	●	●	●		●			●	●											●		Oman
1947	●	●	●	●	●	●	●	●	●	●	●	●	●	●	●	●	●	●	●	●	●								●						●		Pakistan
1945	●	●	●	●		●	●	●	●	●	●	●	●	●	●	●	●	●	●	●					●									●			Panama
1975	●	●	●	●	●[6]		●	●	●	●	●	●	●	●	●	●	●	●		●	●						●	●	●	●[6]							Papua New Guinea
1945	●	●	●	●		●	●	●	●	●	●	●		●	●	●	●	●	●	●					●									●			Paraguay
1945	●	●	●	●	●	●	●	●	●	●	●	●	●	●	●	●	●	●	●	●					●									●			Peru
1945	●	●	●	●	●	●	●	●	●	●	●	●	●	●	●	●	●	●	●	●									●	●							Philippines
1945	●	●	●	●	●	●	●	●	●	●	●	●	●	●	●	●	●	●	●	●																	Poland
1955	●	●	●	●	●	●	●	●		●	●	●	●	●	●	●	●	●	●	●		●											●	●			Portugal
—																	●	●[10]													●[3]						Puerto Rico
1971	●	●	●	●	●[6]	●	●	●			●	●	●	●	●	●	●	●	●	●			●	●											●	●	Qatar
—																	●																				Réunion
1955	●	●	●	●	●	●	●	●	●	●	●	●	●	●	●	●	●	●	●	●																	Romania
1991	●				●[3]	●	●	●	●		●	●	●	●	●	●	●	●	●	●																	Russia
1962	●	●	●	●	●		●	●	●	●	●	●		●	●	●	●	●	●	●						●		●									Rwanda
1983	●	●	●	●	●[6]		●		●			●			●	●	●	●			●				●			●			●						St. Kitts and Nevis
1979	●	●	●	●	●		●	●	●	●	●	●	●		●	●	●	●		●	●				●			●			●						St. Lucia
1980	●	●	●	●	●		●	●	●			●	●	●	●	●	●	●			●				●			●			●						St. Vincent
1992	●	●	●					●			●	●		●	●		●	●		●																	San Marino
1975	●	●	●	●	●[6]		●	●	●		●	●		●	●	●	●	●		●						●		●									São Tomé and Príncipe
1945	●	●	●	●		●	●	●	●	●	●	●	●	●	●	●	●	●	●	●			●	●											●	●	Saudi Arabia
1960	●	●	●	●	●	●	●	●	●	●	●	●	●	●	●	●	●	●	●	●						●		●				●			●		Senegal
1976	●	●	●	●	●[6]		●	●		●	●	●	●		●	●	●	●		●	●					●		●									Seychelles
1961	●	●	●	●	●	●	●	●	●	●	●	●	●	●	●	●	●	●	●	●	●					●		●				●			●		Sierra Leone
1965	●	●	●		●	●	●	●		●	●	●	●	●			●	●	●	●	●								●	●							Singapore
1993					●							●	●			●		●																			Slovakia
1992								●			●	●		●	●	●	●	●	●	●																	Slovenia
1978	●	●	●	●	●[6]		●	●	●	●	●	●	●	●			●	●		●	●						●	●	●								Solomon Islands
1960	●	●	●	●			●	●	●	●	●	●	●	●	●	●	●	●	●	●				●		●		●							●		Somalia
1945	●	●	●		●	●	●	●	●	●		●		●				●	●	[63]																	South Africa
—																																					Bophuthatswana
—																																					Ciskei
—																																					Transkei
—																																					Venda
1955	●	●	●	●	●	●	●	●	●	●	●	●	●	●	●	●	●	●	●	●		●							●				●	●			Spain
1955	●	●	●	●	●	●	●	●	●	●	●	●	●	●	●	●	●	●	●	●	●								●								Sri Lanka
1956	●	●	●	●		●	●	●	●	●	●	[63]	●	●	●	●	●	●	●	●				●		●		●							●		Sudan, The
1975	●	●	●	●	●		●	●			●	●	●	●	●	●	●	●	●	●					●			●			●[3]			●			Suriname
1968	●	●	●	●	●		●	●	●	●	●	●		●	●	●	●	●	●	●	●					●		●									Swaziland
1946	●	●	●	●	●	●	●	●	●	●	●	●	●	●	●	●	●	●	●	●									●					●			Sweden
—	●	●	●	●	●	●	●	●	●	●	●	●	●	●	●	●	●	●	●	●									●					●			Switzerland
1945	●	●	●	●		●	●	●	●	●	●	●	●	●	●	●	●	●		●				●											●		Syria
—					●[3]																								●	●							Taiwan
1992	●	●					●					●					●[6]	●																			Tajikistan
1961	●	●	●	●	●	●	●	●	●	●	●	●	●	●	●	●	●	●	●	●	●					●		●									Tanzania
1946	●	●	●	●	●	●	●	●	●	●	●	●	●	●	●	●	●	●	●	●									●	●							Thailand
1960	●	●	●	●	●		●	●	●	●	●	●	●	●	●	●	●	●	●	●						●		●				●					Togo
—	●	●		●	●[6]		●	●	●	●		●		●	●	●	●	●			●						●	●	●								Tonga
1962	●	●	●	●	●		●	●	●	●	●	●	●	●	●	●	●	●	●	●	●				●			●			●			●			Trinidad and Tobago
1956	●	●	●	●	●	●	●	●	●	●	●	●	●	●	●	●	●	●	●	●				●		●									●		Tunisia
1945	●	●	●	●	●	●	●	●	●	●	●	●	●	●	●	●	●	●	●	●									●				●[10]		●		Turkey
1992	●	●			●[3]		●					●					●[6]	●																			Turkmenistan
—		●			●[6]										●		●				●[49]						●	●	●								Tuvalu
1962	●	●	●	●	●	●	●	●	●	●	●	●		●	●	●	●	●	●	●	●					●		●							●		Uganda
1945	●	●			●[3]	●	●	●			●	●		●	●	●	●	●	●	●																	Ukraine
1971	●	●	●	●	●[6]	●	●	●	●	●	●	●	●	●	●	●	●	●	●	●			●	●											●	●	United Arab Emirates
1945	●	●	●	●	●	●	●	●	●	●	●	●	●	●	●[3]	●	●	●	●	●	●	●					●		●				●	●			United Kingdom
1945	●	●	●	●	●	●	●	●	●	●	●	●	●	●	●[3]	●	●	●	●	●					●		●		●	●				●			United States
1945	●	●	●	●	●	●	●	●	●	●	●	●	●	●	●	●	●	●	●	●					●									●			Uruguay
1992	●	●					●	●			●	●		●			●[6]	●		●																	Uzbekistan
1981	●	●	●	●			●	●	●	●		●	●	●		●	●	●		●	●						●	●	●								Vanuatu
1945	●	●	●	●	●	●	●	●		●	●	●	●	●	●	●	●	●	●	●					●						●[3]			●		●	Venezuela
1977	●	●	●	●		●	●	●	●	●	●	●	●	●	●	●	●	●	●	●									●								Vietnam
—																	●																				Virgin Islands (U.S.)
—																																					West Bank
—																										●[72]											Western Sahara
1976	●	●	●	●			●		●	●		●		●	●		●	●			●						●	●	●								Western Samoa
1947	●	●	●	●	●[6]		●	●	●	●	●	●	●	●	●	●	●	●	●	●				●											●		Yemen
[74]	●		●	●	●	●	●	●	●	●	●	●	●	●	●	●	●	[75]	●	●														●			Yugoslavia
1960	●	●	●	●	●	●	●	●	●	●	●	●	●	●	●	●	●	●	●	●						●		●									Zaire
1964	●	●	●	●	●	●	●	●	●	●	●	●		●	●	●	●	●	●	●	●					●		●									Zambia
1980	●	●	●	●	●	●	●	●	●	●	●	●		●	●	●	●	●	●	●	●					●		●									Zimbabwe

Korean Strait. [44]UN-brokered peace agreement. [45]Formally a *jamahiriya,* translated as "the masses of people." [46]Based on Gulf of Sidra closing line (32° 30′ N), in part. [47]Executive responsibilities divided between (for France) the high commissioner and (locally) the president of the General Council. [48]Excludes Western Sahara. [49]Special member. [50]Executive responsibilities divided between (for France) the high commissioner and (locally) the president of the Territorial Congress. [51]Excludes federally administered tribal areas and the Pakistani-occupied part of Jammu and Kashmir. [52]Assisted by vice presidents. [53]Elective seats only. [54]"Little constitution." [55]Defined by international treaties. [56]Limits of continental shelf or median line boundaries. [57]Date of presidential decree strengthening the role of the Security Council. [58]As of Dec. 12, 1993, elections. [59]Somaliland (the former colonially administered area of British Somaliland in northern Somalia) declared its unilateral independence from Somalia in May 1991. [60]Special Envoy assisted by the military command of the UN-administered operation in Somalia. [61]Date draft constitution approved. [62]Government in transition between September 1993 and April 1994. [63]Suspended membership. [64]Dissolution possible as of April 1994. [65]Occupied seats mid-1992. [66]Power struggle between government and opposition forces from late 1991 through late 1993. [67]Assisted by Privy Council. [68]Black Sea and Mediterranean Sea; 6 nautical miles in Aegean Sea. [69]Based on evolving body of statutes and common law. [70]England and Wales form a single administrative entity. [71]County governments. [72]Membership held by the Sahrawi Arab Democratic Republic. [73]Mixed political system approximating a constitutional monarchy. [74]Seat in the UN General Assembly was not recognized as of Sept. 15, 1992. [75]Debarred. [76]Power struggle between government and opposition forces from late 1992 through late 1993.

Area and population

This table provides the area and population for each of the countries of the world and for all but the smallest political dependencies having a permanent civilian population. The data represent the latest published and unpublished data for both the surveyed area of the countries and their populations, the latter both as of a single year (1993) to provide the best comparability and as of the most recent census to provide the fullest comparison of certain demographic measures that are not always available between successive national censuses. The 1993 midyear estimates represent a combination of national, United Nations (UN) or other international organizations, and *Encyclopædia Britannica* estimates so as to give the best fit to available published series, to take account of unpublished information received in correspondence, and to incorporate the results of very recent censuses for which published analyses are not yet available.

One principal point to bear in mind when studying these statistics is that all of them, whatever degree of precision may be implied by the exactness of the numbers, are estimates—all of varying, and some of suspect, accuracy—even when they *contain* a very full enumeration. The United States—which has a long tradition both of census taking and of the use of the most sophisticated analytical tools in processing the data—is unable to determine within 2.1% (the estimated 1990 undercount) its total population nationally. And that is an *average* underenumeration. In states and larger cities, where enumeration of particular populations, both legal and illegal, is most difficult, the accuracy of the enumerated count may be off as much as 4% at a state level and as much as 10% for a single city. The high accuracy attained by census operations in China may approach 0.25% of rigorously maintained civil population registers. Other national census operations not so based, however, are inherently less accurate. For example, Ethiopia's first-ever census in 1984 resulted in figures that were 30% or more above prevailing estimates; Nigeria's 1991 census corrected decades of miscounts and was well below prevailing estimates. An undercount of 2–8% is more typical, but even census operations offering results of 30% or more above or below prevailing estimates can still represent well-founded benchmarks from which future planning may proceed. The editors have tried to take account of the range of variation and accuracy in published data, but it is difficult to establish a value for many sources of inaccuracy unless some country or agency has made a conscientious effort to establish both the relative accuracy (precision) of its estimate and the absolute magnitude of the quantity it is trying to measure—for example, the number of people in Cambodia who died at the hands of the Khmer Rouge. If a figure of 1,000,000 is adopted, what is its accuracy: ± 1%, 10%, 50%? Are the original data documentary or evidentiary, complete or incomplete, analytically biased or unbiased, in good agreement with other published data?

Many similar problems exist and in endless variations: What is the extent of southern European immigration to western Europe in search of jobs? How many refugees from Afghanistan, Mozambique, or Ethiopia are there in surrounding countries? How many undocumented aliens are there in the United States? How many Palestinians are there in the Middle East (they are politically inconvenient to enumerate everywhere)? How many Amerindians exist (remain, preserving their original language and a mode of life unassimilated by the larger national culture) in the countries of South America? How many people have died or emigrated as a result of the civil violence in Central America?

Still, much information is accurate, well founded, and updated regularly.

Area and population

country	area			population (latest estimate)					population (latest census)				
	square miles	square kilometres	rank	total midyear 1993	rank	density per sq mi	density per sq km	% annual growth rate 1988–93	census year	total	male (%)	female (%)	urban (%)
Afghanistan	251,825	652,225	41	20,269,000	44	80.5	31.1	5.2	1979	13,051,358[1]	51.4	48.6	15.1
Albania	11,100	28,748	142	3,422,000	124	308.3	119.0	1.7	1989	3,182,417	51.5	48.5	35.7
Algeria	919,595	2,381,741	11	27,029,000	34	29.4	11.3	2.6	1987	23,038,942	49.9	50.1	49.7
American Samoa	77	199	204	52,800	206	685.7	265.3	3.8	1990	46,773	51.4	48.6	33.4
Andorra	181	468	192	61,900	203	342.0	132.3	4.5	1992[2]	61,599	53.1	46.9	66.2[3]
Angola	481,354	1,246,700	24	10,916,000	63	22.7	8.8	2.9	1970	5,673,046	52.1	47.9	14.2
Antigua and Barbuda	171	442	194	66,000	201	386.0	149.3	0.0	1991	65,962[4]	48.0[4]	52.0[4]	32.0[4]
Argentina	1,073,518	2,780,400	8	33,507,000	31	31.2	12.1	1.4	1991	32,608,687	49.0	51.0	86.2[5]
Armenia	11,500	29,800	141	3,550,000	121	308.7	119.1	1.6	1989	3,287,677	49.3	50.7	67.8
Aruba	75	193	205	69,500	200	926.7	360.1	2.8	1991	66,687	49.2	50.8	...
Australia	2,966,200	7,682,300	6	17,729,000	49	6.0	2.3	1.4	1991	16,849,496	49.6	50.4	85.4[6]
Austria	32,378	83,859	115	7,938,000	84	245.2	94.7	0.9	1991	7,795,786	48.2	51.8	64.5
Azerbaijan	33,400	86,600	113	7,398,000	90	221.5	85.4	1.2	1989	7,037,867	48.7	51.3	53.8
Bahamas, The	5,382	13,939	158	266,000	174	49.4	19.1	1.6	1990	255,095	49.0	51.0	64.3
Bahrain	268	695	186	486,000	163	1,813.4	699.3	1.5	1981	350,798	58.4	41.6	80.7
Bangladesh	57,295	148,383	93	115,075,000	9	2,008.5	755.5	2.0	1991	109,876,977	51.4	48.6	16.4[5]
Barbados	166	430	195	260,000	176	1,566.3	604.7	0.3	1990[7]	257,083	47.7	52.3	37.9[5]
Belarus	80,200	207,600	85	10,353,000	68	129.1	49.9	0.4	1989	10,199,709	46.9	53.1	65.5
Belgium	11,787	30,528	139	10,072,000	72	854.5	329.9	0.3	1991	9,978,681	48.9	51.1	96.6[3]
Belize	8,867	22,965	150	204,000	180	23.0	8.9	2.6	1991	184,340	50.8[8]	49.2[8]	46.6[8]
Benin	43,500	112,680	101	5,091,000	103	117.0	45.2	3.2	1992	4,855,349	49.4[5]	50.6[5]	37.7[5]
Bermuda	21	54	211	60,800	204	2,895.2	1,125.9	0.8	1991[7]	58,460	48.5	51.5	100.0
Bhutan	18,150	47,000	131	1,546,000	143	85.2	32.9	2.4	1980	1,165,000	51.4[9]	48.6[9]	3.9[9]
Bolivia	424,164	1,098,581	28	7,715,000	86	18.2	7.0	2.5	1992	6,344,396	49.3	50.7	57.7
Bosnia and Herzegovina	19,741	51,129	127	4,422,000	111	224.0	86.5	0.6	1991	4,365,639	49.7[11]	50.3[11]	36.2[11]
Botswana	224,607	581,730	47	1,406,000	147	6.3	2.4	3.4	1991	1,326,796	47.8[5]	52.2[5]	23.9
Brazil	3,286,500	8,511,996	5	156,493,000	5	47.6	18.4	1.7	1991	146,917,459	49.4	50.6	75.5
Brunei	2,226	5,765	167	275,000	173	123.5	47.7	3.0	1991	260,863	51.4[5]	48.6[5]	59.4[11]
Bulgaria	42,855	110,994	103	8,466,000	82	197.5	76.3	−1.2	1992	8,472,724	49.1	50.9	67.1
Burkina Faso	105,946	274,400	73	9,780,000	74	92.3	35.6	2.8	1985[7]	7,964,705	48.1	51.9	11.7
Burundi	10,740	27,816	145	5,665,000	96	527.5	203.7	2.3	1990[3]	5,292,793	48.7[5]	51.3[5]	5.5[5]
Cambodia	70,238	181,916	89	9,287,000	76	132.2	51.1	2.6	1981	6,684,000	46.3[9]	53.7[9]	10.3[9]
Cameroon	183,569	475,442	53	13,103,000	60	71.4	27.6	3.4	1987	10,516,232	49.0	51.0	38.3
Canada	3,849,674	9,970,610	2	28,149,000	32	7.3	2.8	1.5	1991	27,296,859	49.3	50.7	77.1[5]
Cape Verde	1,557	4,033	169	350,000	171	224.8	86.8	1.3	1990	336,798	48.0	52.0	44.8
Central African Republic	240,324	622,436	43	2,998,000	128	12.5	4.8	2.4	1988	2,688,426	49.1	50.9	46.7[5]
Chad	495,755	1,284,000	22	6,118,000	93	12.3	4.8	2.5	1975	4,029,917	47.7	52.3	16.0
Chile	292,135	756,626	38	13,542,000	56	46.4	17.9	1.6	1992	13,254,727	49.1	50.9	85.1[8]
China	3,696,100	9,572,900	3	1,179,467,000	1	319.1	123.2	1.4	1990	1,133,682,501	51.6	48.4	26.4
Colombia	440,831	1,141,748	26	33,951,000	30	77.0	29.7	1.6	1985	30,062,193	49.5	50.5	67.0[4]
Comoros	719	1,862	175	516,000	162	717.7	277.1	3.6	1980	335,150	49.9	50.1	23.2
Congo	132,047	342,000	63	2,775,000	132	21.0	8.1	5.4	1984[7]	1,909,248	48.7	51.3	52.0
Costa Rica	19,730	51,100	128	3,199,000	126	162.1	62.6	2.3	1984	2,416,809	50.0	50.0	43.9
Côte d'Ivoire	124,504	322,463	68	13,459,000	57	108.1	41.7	3.9	1988	10,812,782	50.9[5]	49.1[5]	39.1
Croatia	21,829	56,538	126	4,821,000	105	220.9	85.3	0.6	1991	4,784,265	48.5	51.5	50.8[11]
Cuba	42,804	110,861	104	10,892,000	64	254.5	98.2	0.9	1981	9,723,605	50.6	49.4	69.0
Cyprus	3,572	9,251	164	764,000	155	213.9	82.6	1.1	1982[7]	642,731	49.7	50.3	63.5
Czech Republic	30,450	78,864	116	10,332,000	69	339.3	131.0	0.1	1991	10,302,215	48.5	51.5	...
Denmark	16,639	43,094	133	5,187,000	101	311.7	120.4	0.2	1993[2]	5,180,614	49.3	50.7	84.9[8]
Djibouti	8,950	23,200	149	565,000	160	63.1	24.4	2.9	1960–61	81,200	...	...	80.7[5]
Dominica	290	750	184	73,900	197	254.8	98.5	0.4	1991	71,794	50.0	50.0	...
Dominican Republic	18,704	48,443	130	7,634,000	87	408.1	157.6	2.2	1981	5,647,977	50.1	49.9	52.0
Ecuador	105,037	272,045	74	10,985,000	62	104.6	40.4	2.5	1990	9,648,189	49.7	50.3	55.4
Egypt	385,229	997,739	30	57,109,000	21	148.2	57.2	2.5	1986	48,205,049	51.1	48.9	43.9
El Salvador	8,124	21,041	151	5,517,000	97	679.1	262.2	2.1	1992	5,047,925	49.0[5]	51.0[5]	44.4[3]

The sources of these data are censuses; national population registers (cumulated periodically); registration of migration, births, deaths, and so on; sample surveys to establish demographic conditions; and the like.

The statistics provided for area and population by country are ranked, and the population densities based on those values are also provided. The population densities, for purposes of comparison within this table, are calculated on the bases of the 1993 midyear population estimate as shown and of total area of the country. Elsewhere in individual country presentations the reader may find densities calculated on more specific population figures and more specialized area bases: land area for Finland (because of its many lakes) or ice-free area for Greenland (most of which is ice cap). The data in this section conclude with the estimated average annual growth rate for the country (including both natural growth and net migration) during the five-year period, 1988–93.

In the section containing census data, information supplied includes the census total (usually de facto, the population actually present, rather than de jure, the population legally resident, who might be anywhere); the male-female breakdown; the proportion that is urban (according to the country's own definition of the term "urban," which differs very much from country to country); and finally an analysis of the age structure of the population by 15-year age groups. This last analysis may be particularly useful in distinguishing the type of population being recorded—young, fast-growing nations show a high proportion of people under 30 (most countries in sub-Saharan Africa and the Middle East have nearly one-half of their population under 15 years), while other nations (for example Sweden, which suffered no age-group losses in World War II) exhibit quite uniform proportions.

Finally, a section is provided giving the population of each country at 10-year intervals from 1940 to 2010. The data for years past represent the best available analysis of the published data by the country itself, by the demographers of the United Nations, or by the editors of Britannica. The projections for 2000 and 2010 similarly represent the best fit of available data through the early 1990s with projected population structure and growth rates during the next two decades. The evidence of the last 20 years with respect to similar estimates published about 1970, however, shows how cloudy is the glass through which these numbers are read. In 1970 no respectable Western analyst would have imagined proposing that mainland China could achieve the degree of birth control that it apparently has since then (as evidenced by the results of 1982 and 1990 censuses); on the other hand, even the Chinese admit that their methods have been somewhat Draconian and that they have already seen some backlash in terms of higher birth rates among those who have so far postponed larger families. How much is "some" by 2000? Compound that problem with all the social, economic, political, and biological factors that can affect 220 countries' populations, and the difficulty facing the prospective compiler of such projections may be appreciated.

Specific data about the vital rates affecting the data in this table may be found in great detail in both the country statistical boxes in "The Nations of the World" section and in the *Vital statistics, marriage, family* table, beginning at page 786.

Percentages in this table for male and female population will always total 100.0, but percentages by age group may not, for reasons such as nonresponse on census forms, "don't know" responses (which are common in countries with poor birth registration systems), and the like.

age distribution (%)						population (by decade, '000s)								country
0–14	15–29	30–44	45–59	60–74	75 and over	1940	1950	1960	1970	1980	1990	2000 projection	2010 projection	
44.5	26.9	15.8	8.6	3.6	0.6	...	8,150	9,829	12,431	16,063	16,556	26,767	33,539	Afghanistan
33.0	28.9	18.5	11.7	5.9	1.9	1,088	1,215	1,607	2,136	2,671	3,256	3,862	4,592	Albania
43.9	28.0	13.9	8.4	4.2	1.6	7,688	8,956	10,800	14,330	18,666	25,012	32,401	40,062	Algeria
38.1	29.0	18.1	9.4	4.3	1.1	13	19	20	27	33	47	67	86	American Samoa
16.3	27.7	27.2	15.1	9.9	3.8	5	6	8	19	33	53	66	71	Andorra
41.7	23.2	17.0	7.4	3.8	1.0	3,738	4,131	4,816	5,588	7,722	10,020	13,400	18,082	Angola
37.2[4]	30.8[4]	12.8[4]	11.5[4]	6.4[4]	1.3[4]	34	45	55	66	66	66	66	66	Antigua and Barbuda
29.9[5]	23.2[5]	19.5[5]	14.2[5]	9.9[5]	3.3[5]	14,169	17,150	20,611	23,788	27,820	32,195	36,492	40,718	Argentina
30.3	25.7	20.8	13.6	6.4	3.2	1,320	1,354	1,867	2,520	3,067	3,335	4,004	4,755	Armenia
24.4	22.0	27.0	16.1	7.2	3.0	31	51	57	61	60	64	72	75	Aruba
22.1	24.2	23.4	15.0	11.1	4.4	7,079	8,219	10,315	12,552	14,741	17,065	19,550	21,952	Australia
17.4	23.7	21.6	17.2	13.4	6.7	6,684	6,935	7,048	7,447	7,549	7,718	8,119	8,232	Austria
32.8	29.7	16.8	12.8	5.7	2.2	3,274	2,896	3,895	5,172	6,165	7,134	8,002	8,951	Azerbaijan
32.2	30.8	19.7	10.6	5.0	1.8	70	79	113	169	210	255	295	334	Bahamas, The
32.9	34.5	20.0	8.8	3.1	0.7	90	127	162	215	342	484	582	734	Bahrain
41.4[5]	29.5[5]	15.5[5]	8.8[5]	3.9[5]	0.9[5]	41,259	45,482	54,699	68,171	88,792	108,362	132,401	161,774	Bangladesh
24.1[5]	27.0[5]	22.1[5]	11.4[5]	—15.4[5]—		179	209	232	235	249	257	265	274	Barbados
23.0	22.4	20.6	18.0	11.5	4.5	9,046	7,745	8,190	9,040	9,650	10,260	10,509	10,895	Belarus
18.2	21.8	22.5	16.9	14.1	6.6	8,301	8,639	9,153	9,690	9,859	9,967	10,313	10,668	Belgium
43.9[8]	27.9[8]	14.9[8]	7.2[8]	4.5[8]	1.6[8]	56	68	90	120	146	189	236	276	Belize
46.6[5]	25.7[5]	14.7[5]	8.4[5]	3.8[5]	0.8[5]	...	2,046	2,273	2,693	3,459	4,622	6,269	8,357	Benin
19.5	24.0	26.8	16.4	—13.3—		31	37	43	53	55	59	65	70	Bermuda
39.2[10]	26.5[10]	16.3[10]	10.9[10]	—7.1[10]—		500	726	853	1,045	1,165	1,442	1,812	2,266	Bhutan
41.4[5]	27.1[5]	16.3[5]	9.4[5]	4.8[5]	1.0[5]	2,508	2,765	3,405	4,265	5,581	7,171	9,038	11,087	Bolivia
27.5[11]	29.0[11]	19.2[11]	15.8[11]	6.3[11]	2.0[11]	...	2,662	3,240	3,703	4,107	4,347	4,601	4,871	Bosnia and Herzegovina
46.1[5]	27.5[5]	14.1[5]	7.2[5]	4.0[5]	1.3[5]	278	407	490	581	905	1,270	1,782	2,500	Botswana
34.7[5]	28.3[5]	19.4[5]	10.5[5]	5.6[5]	1.5[5]	41,525	52,901	71,539	93,139	121,286	149,042	172,777	194,002	Brazil
33.9[5]	27.2[5]	19.8[5]	12.1[5]	5.8[5]	1.2[5]	36	48	84	129	185	252	334	432	Brunei
20.2[3]	20.8[3]	21.4[3]	18.3[3]	14.4[3]	4.8[3]	6,344	7,251	7,867	8,490	8,862	8,991	8,383	8,267	Bulgaria
48.3	23.4	13.4	8.7	4.7	1.4	3,036	3,584	4,350	5,412	6,599	9,012	11,884	15,549	Burkina Faso
45.5[5]	27.0[5]	15.6[5]	7.1[5]	3.8[5]	0.9[5]	1,887	2,435	2,908	3,350	4,120	5,280	6,674	8,437	Burundi
44.2[9]	28.2[9]	14.7[9]	8.4[9]	4.0[9]	0.5[9]	3,400	4,346	5,433	6,938	6,400	8,592	10,942	13,402	Cambodia
46.4	24.5	14.6	8.7	4.1	1.6	...	4,467	5,297	6,610	8,653	11,833	16,701	23,665	Cameroon
20.9	22.7	25.1	15.3	11.3	4.7	11,693	13,737	17,909	21,324	24,067	26,929	31,215	36,182	Canada
43.8[5]	31.7[5]	11.0[5]	7.2[5]	4.7[5]	1.9[5]	181	148	199	272	296	337	383	436	Cape Verde
43.2	27.5	15.0	9.2	4.1	0.8	991	1,311	1,500	1,793	2,257	2,793	3,528	4,449	Central African Republic
40.6	28.3	17.2	9.5	—4.4—		2,351	2,658	3,064	3,652	4,477	5,678	7,337	9,491	Chad
30.6[8]	27.0[8]	21.2[8]	12.2[8]	6.8[8]	2.2[8]	5,063	6,091	7,585	9,368	11,104	12,916	14,977	16,850	Chile
27.7	31.0	20.7	12.1	6.9	1.7	530,000	556,613	667,070	818,316	981,242	1,133,683	1,286,709	1,381,726	China
36.1	31.2	17.2	9.5	4.6	1.4	9,097	11,268	15,321	20,884	26,906	32,300	37,822	42,959	Colombia
47.2	23.2	14.8	7.6	5.1	1.8	119	148	177	245	333	463	661	912	Comoros
44.7	27.2	13.3	9.1	4.6	0.7	...	815	960	1,182	1,631	2,264	3,379	4,396	Congo
37.9	31.5	15.8	9.2	4.4	1.2	619	862	1,236	1,731	2,246	2,994	3,711	4,366	Costa Rica
48.3[5]	24.6[5]	14.4[5]	8.5[5]	3.6[5]	0.7[5]	2,350	2,775	3,799	5,515	8,194	11,997	17,600	25,503	Côte d'Ivoire
19.4	20.7	22.7	18.3	12.9	4.5	...	3,851	4,140	4,411	4,588	4,770	4,933	5,098	Croatia
30.3	27.6	19.1	12.1	8.2	2.7	4,566	5,752	7,019	8,565	9,724	10,631	11,502	12,181	Cuba
25.0	26.6	20.1	13.8	—14.5—		413	494	573	615	627	740	824	917	Cyprus
21.0	21.8	22.6	16.8	12.7	5.1	...	8,925	9,539	9,830	10,292	10,298	10,449	10,536	Czech Republic
17.0	22.1	21.7	19.0	13.2	7.0	3,832	4,271	4,581	4,929	5,123	5,141	5,245	5,252	Denmark
45.2[5]	24.9[5]	16.1[5]	9.0[5]	—4.8[5]—		44	60	78	158	355	517	695	934	Djibouti
35.1[12]	28.1[12]	14.5[12]	9.5[12]	—11.7[12]—		45	51	60	70	75	72	82	96	Dominica
40.6	30.1	15.1	8.7	—5.5—		1,759	2,313	3,160	4,343	5,648	7,168	8,621	9,903	Dominican Republic
38.8	28.5	17.3	9.0	4.7	1.7	2,546	3,307	4,421	5,958	8,123	10,164	12,712	15,062	Ecuador
39.5	26.4	16.9	10.6	5.2	1.0	16,942	20,461	26,085	33,329	40,546	53,153	66,013	79,061	Egypt
44.4[5]	27.6[5]	13.4[5]	8.9[5]	4.6[5]	1.1[5]	1,550	1,931	2,527	3,534	4,525	5,172	6,425	7,772	El Salvador

Area and population (continued)

country	area			population (latest estimate)					population (latest census)				
	square miles	square kilo-metres	rank	total midyear 1993	rank	density per sq mi	density per sq km	% annual growth rate 1988–93	census year	total	male (%)	female (%)	urban (%)
Equatorial Guinea	10,831	28,051	144	377,000	169	34.8	13.4	2.5	1983	300,000	48.3	51.7	28.2
Eritrea	45,300	117,400	100	3,421,000	125	75.5	29.1	3.1	1984	2,614,699	49.8	50.2	14.4
Estonia	17,413	45,100	132	1,536,000	145	88.2	34.1	−0.4	1989	1,572,916	46.9	53.1	71.6
Ethiopia	437,794	1,133,882	27	52,078,000	23	119.0	45.9	3.3	1984	39,570,253	50.0	50.0	10.0
Faeroe Islands	540	1,399	177	46,800	208	86.7	33.5	−0.2	1993[2]	46,801	51.9	48.1	...
Fiji	7,056	18,274	155	762,000	156	108.0	41.7	1.2	1986	715,375	50.7	49.3	38.7
Finland	130,559	338,145	64	5,058,000	104	38.7	15.0	0.4	1990	4,998,478	48.5	51.5	79.7
France	210,026	543,965	48	57,690,000	19	274.7	106.1	0.6	1990	56,625,026	48.7	51.3	74.3[5]
French Guiana	33,399	86,504	114	128,000	187	3.8	1.5	4.3	1990	114,808	52.1	47.9	73.4[13]
French Polynesia	1,544	4,000	170	212,000	179	137.3	53.0	2.5	1988	188,814	52.1	47.9	55.0
Gabon	103,347	267,667	76	1,280,000	148	12.4	4.8	3.3	1960–61	448,564	47.1	52.9	45.7[5]
Gambia, The	4,127	10,689	162	1,033,000	153	250.3	96.6	4.1	1993	1,025,867	50.2	49.8	21.2[14]
Gaza Strip	140	363	198	712,000	158	5,085.7	1,961.4	4.3	1991[2]	642,700	50.3	49.7	...
Georgia	26,900	69,700	121	5,493,000	98	204.2	78.8	0.3	1989	5,443,359	47.2	52.8	55.7
Germany	137,735	356,733	62	81,187,000	12	589.4	227.6	0.8	1987[15]	61,077,042	48.0	52.0	85.3[5]
Ghana	92,098	238,533	81	15,636,000	53	169.8	65.6	2.6	1984	12,296,081	49.3	50.7	32.0
Gibraltar	2.2	5.8	215	29,100	213	13,227.3	5,017.2	−0.1	1991[16]	26,703	51.0	49.0	...
Greece	50,949	131,957	96	10,310,000	70	202.4	78.1	0.6	1991	10,264,156	49.0	51.0	62.5[5]
Greenland	840,000	2,175,600	14	55,700	205	0.1	0.0	0.3	1992[2]	55,385	53.6	46.4	84.5
Grenada	133	344	200	91,000	194	684.2	264.5	0.2	1991	91,158	49.4	50.6	32.2
Guadeloupe	687	1,780	176	419,000	164	609.9	235.4	2.2	1990	387,034	48.9	51.1	48.4
Guam	209	541	190	143,000	185	684.2	264.3	2.4	1990	133,152	53.3	46.7	38.2
Guatemala	42,042	108,889	105	9,713,000	75	231.0	89.2	2.8	1981[7]	6,043,559	49.8	50.2	34.3
Guernsey	30	78	209	63,500	202	2,116.7	814.1	1.2	1991[18]	58,867	48.1	51.9	...
Guinea	94,926	245,857	78	7,418,000	89	78.1	30.2	2.6	1983	5,781,014	48.6	51.4	26.0
Guinea-Bissau	13,948	36,125	137	1,038,000	152	74.3	28.7	2.1	1979	767,739	48.2	51.8	14.0
Guyana	83,044	215,083	84	755,000	157	9.1	3.5	0.0	1980	758,619	49.5	50.5	30.5[9]
Haiti	10,695	27,700	146	6,902,000	92	645.3	249.2	2.0	1982	5,053,792	48.5	51.5	20.6
Honduras	43,277	112,088	102	5,148,000	102	119.0	45.9	3.3	1988	4,376,839	49.6	50.4	43.7[5]
Hong Kong	415	1,075	179	5,932,000	94	14,294.8	5,519.3	1.1	1991[7]	5,674,114	51.1	48.9	93.1[6]
Hungary	35,920	93,033	110	10,296,000	71	286.6	110.7	−0.3	1990	10,375,323	48.1	51.9	61.8
Iceland	39,699	102,819	106	264,000	175	6.7	2.6	1.1	1992[2]	262,193	50.2	49.8	91.2
India	1,222,559	3,166,414	7	896,567,000	2	733.4	283.1	2.0	1991	846,302,688	51.9	48.1	25.7
Indonesia	741,052	1,919,317	16	188,216,000	4	254.0	98.1	1.8	1990	179,378,946	49.9	50.1	30.9
Iran	632,457	1,638,057	18	60,768,000	15	96.1	37.1	3.0	1992[7]	58,110,227	51.1[6]	48.9[6]	57.3
Iraq	167,975	435,052	58	19,435,000	45	115.7	44.7	3.1	1987	16,335,199	51.4	48.6	70.2
Ireland	27,137	70,285	120	3,516,000	123	129.6	50.0	−0.1	1991	3,523,401	49.7	50.3	57.1[5]
Isle of Man	221	572	189	71,500	198	323.5	125.0	1.4	1991[7]	69,788	48.3	51.7	51.1
Israel[19]	7,992	20,700	152	5,451,000	99	682.1	263.3	3.7	1983[7, 20]	4,037,620	49.8	50.2	86.9
Italy	116,333	301,302	71	57,235,000	20	492.0	190.0	0.1	1991	57,103,833	48.6	51.4	67.1
Jamaica	4,244	10,991	161	2,472,000	135	582.5	224.9	1.0	1991	2,366,067	48.9	51.1	47.8[13]
Japan	145,850	377,750	61	124,670,000	8	854.8	330.0	0.3	1990	123,611,167	49.1	50.9	77.4
Jersey	45	116	208	85,900	195	1,908.9	740.5	1.0	1991	84,082	48.6	51.4	...
Jordan[21]	34,342	88,946	112	3,764,000	118	109.6	42.3	5.0	1979	2,132,997	52.3	47.7	59.5
Kazakhstan	1,049,200	2,717,300	9	17,186,000	52	16.4	6.3	0.9	1989	16,536,511	48.5	51.5	57.2
Kenya	224,961	582,646	46	28,113,000	33	125.0	48.3	4.2	1979	15,327,061	49.7	50.3	15.1
Kiribati	313	811	181	76,900	196	245.7	94.8	2.3	1990	72,298	49.6	50.4	34.8
Korea, North	47,399	122,762	98	22,646,000	40	477.8	184.5	1.9	[22]	[22]	49.0[5]	51.0[5]	59.8[5]
Korea, South	38,330	99,274	108	44,042,000	25	1,149.0	443.6	0.9	1990[7]	43,410,899	50.2	49.8	74.4
Kuwait	6,880	17,818	156	1,433,000	146	208.3	80.4	−5.3	1985	1,697,301	56.9	43.1	100.0
Kyrgyzstan	76,600	198,500	86	4,526,000	109	59.1	22.8	1.3	1989	4,290,442	48.9	51.1	38.2
Laos	91,429	236,800	83	4,533,000	108	49.6	19.1	2.8	1985	3,584,803	49.0	51.0	15.9[4]
Latvia	24,900	64,500	124	2,596,000	133	104.3	40.2	−0.6	1989	2,680,029	46.6	53.4	71.1
Lebanon	3,950	10,230	163	2,909,000	129	736.5	284.4	1.4	1970	2,126,325	50.8	49.2	60.1
Lesotho	11,720	30,355	140	1,903,000	141	162.4	62.7	2.6	1986[7]	1,577,536	48.2	51.8	16.0
Liberia	38,250	99,067	109	2,844,000	131	74.4	28.7	3.3	1984	2,101,628	50.6	49.4	38.8
Libya	678,400	1,757,000	17	4,573,000	107	6.7	2.6	2.9	1984	3,637,488	53.6	46.4	64.5[4]
Liechtenstein	62	160	207	30,100	212	485.5	188.1	1.5	1980	25,215	49.6	50.4	...
Lithuania	25,213	65,301	123	3,753,000	119	148.9	57.5	0.4	1989	3,689,779	47.4	52.6	68.0
Luxembourg	999	2,586	172	392,000	166	392.4	151.6	1.0	1991	384,062	48.8[3]	51.2[3]	85.9[3]
Macau	6.9	18.0	214	378,000	167	54,782.6	21,000.0	4.0	1991	339,464	48.5	51.5	97.0
Macedonia	9,928	25,713	148	2,063,000	138	207.8	80.2	0.6	1991	2,033,964	50.7[11]	49.3[11]	53.9[11]
Madagascar	226,658	587,041	45	13,255,000	59	58.5	22.6	3.3	1974–75	7,603,790	50.0	50.0	16.3
Malawi	45,747	118,484	99	10,581,000	66	231.3	89.3	4.2	1987	7,988,507	48.4	51.6	10.7
Malaysia	127,584	330,442	65	19,077,000	47	149.5	57.7	2.4	1991	17,566,982	50.4	49.6	43.0[5]
Maldives	115	298	202	237,000	177	2,060.9	795.3	3.3	1990	213,215	51.3	48.7	25.9
Mali	482,077	1,248,574	23	8,646,000	78	17.9	6.9	2.0	1987	7,696,348	48.9	51.1	22.0
Malta	122	316	201	363,000	170	2,975.4	1,148.7	0.9	1985	345,418	49.2	50.8	85.3
Marshall Islands	70	181	206	52,100	207	744.3	287.8	4.1	1988	43,380	51.1	48.9	64.5
Martinique	436	1,128	178	377,000	168	864.7	334.2	1.4	1990	359,579	48.4	51.6	80.5
Mauritania	398,000	1,030,700	29	2,171,000	137	5.5	2.1	3.0	1988	1,864,236	49.5	50.5	39.1
Mauritius	788	2,040	174	1,103,000	150	1,399.7	540.7	1.1	1983	1,002,178	49.8	50.2	41.7[23]
Mayotte	144	374	197	104,000	191	722.2	278.1	5.6	1991	94,385	52.0	48.0	59.7[24]
Mexico	756,066	1,958,201	15	89,955,000	11	119.0	45.9	2.1	1990	81,249,645	49.1	50.9	71.3
Micronesia	271	701	185	103,000	192	380.1	146.9	1.3	1980	73,160	51.1	48.9	19.4
Moldova	13,000	33,700	138	4,362,000	112	335.5	129.4	0.2	1989	4,337,592	47.5	52.5	46.9
Monaco	0.75	1.95	216	30,500	211	40,666.7	15,641.0	0.9	1990	29,972	47.5	52.5	100.0
Mongolia	604,800	1,566,500	19	2,256,000	136	3.7	1.4	2.2	1989	2,043,100	48.9	51.1	57.1
Morocco	177,117	458,730	55	26,494,000	36	149.6	57.8	2.2	1982	20,419,555[25]	50.1	49.9	42.7
Mozambique	313,661	812,379	36	15,243,000	55	48.6	18.8	2.4	1980	12,130,000	48.7	51.3	13.2
Myanmar (Burma)	261,228	676,577	40	44,613,000	24	170.8	65.9	2.2	1983	35,313,905	49.6	50.4	24.0
Namibia	318,146	823,994	35	1,537,000	144	4.8	1.9	3.9	1991	1,401,711	48.6	51.4	32.8
Nauru	8.2	21.2	213	10,000	215	1,219.5	471.7	1.9	1983	8,042	...	...	...
Nepal	56,827	147,181	94	19,264,000	46	339.0	130.9	1.7	1991	18,462,081	49.9	50.1	9.6
Netherlands, The	16,033	41,526	134	15,302,000	54	954.4	368.5	0.7	1993[2]	15,239,182	49.4	50.6	89.0[26]

age distribution (%) 0–14	15–29	30–44	45–59	60–74	75 and over	population (by decade, '000s) 1940	1950	1960	1970	1980	1990	2000 projection	2010 projection	country
41.7	25.1	15.7	11.2	5.3	1.0	...	211	244	291	255	350	448	573	Equatorial Guinea
46.1	23.0	15.9	8.9	4.4	1.6	...	1,215	1,502	1,901	2,384	3,126	4,218	5,690	Eritrea
22.2	21.4	21.0	18.5	11.7	5.1	1,054	1,101	1,216	1,365	1,481	1,583	1,576	1,625	Estonia
46.6	22.7	15.6	8.9	4.5	1.7	...	18,358	22,689	28,722	36,056	47,618	64,032	86,019	Ethiopia
24.4	—59.0—			—16.6—		27	31	35	39	43	48	47	47	Faeroe Islands
38.2	29.5	17.8	9.6	3.8	0.8	218	289	394	520	634	732	830	923	Fiji
19.3	20.5	24.6	17.1	12.9	5.7	3,698	4,009	4,430	4,606	4,780	4,986	5,101	5,081	Finland
19.1	22.6	22.8	15.6	12.8	7.1	41,300	41,736	45,684	50,770	53,880	56,735	59,965	63,371	France
33.4	27.3	23.2	10.2	4.4	1.5	30	27	33	49	69	116	163	206	French Guiana
36.0	29.7	18.9	10.4	4.1	0.9	50	62	84	109	151	197	246	296	French Polynesia
33.0[5]	29.3[5]	15.8[5]	12.9[5]	7.3[5]	1.7[5]	442	469	486	504	806	1,159	1,604	2,052	Gabon
43.8[14]	26.5[14]	15.7[14]	7.3[14]	—5.7[14]—		193	232	357	458	632	917	1,227	1,546	Gambia, The
50.4	—39.1—		—10.5—			...	...	...	370	451	627	908	1,283	Gaza Strip
24.8	24.1	19.2	17.5	10.8	3.6	3,612	3,527	4,160	4,708	5,075	5,460	5,569	5,680	Georgia
14.6	24.0	20.1	20.6	13.6	7.2	57,400	68,373	72,673	77,772	78,289	79,433	85,646	92,444	Germany
45.0	26.4	14.6	8.1	4.1	1.8	3,636	5,297	6,958	8,789	11,222	14,470	18,733	24,253	Ghana
19.6	21.3	22.6	18.2	12.9	5.3	14	23	24	26	30	29	29	29	Gibraltar
18.4[3]	22.0[3]	20.5[3]	18.6[3]	14.0[3]	6.3[3]	7,319	7,566	8,327	8,793	9,643	10,089	10,493	10,518	Greece
26.7	26.9	25.1	14.5	—6.8—		19	23	33	41	50	56	57	59	Greenland
35.9[17]	28.5[17]	14.2[17]	8.5[17]	—11.3[17]—		71	76	90	95	89	91	92	94	Grenada
24.9	29.5	21.4	12.5	8.3	3.4	180	206	265	320	327	390	473	541	Guadeloupe
30.0	30.0	22.6	10.8	5.5	1.1	22	59	67	85	107	133	167	198	Guam
44.9	26.8	14.8	8.5	3.9	1.1	2,201	3,024	4,005	5,263	6,783	8,920	11,809	15,242	Guatemala
17.0	23.3	22.2	16.8	13.5	7.2	44	44	45	51	55	61	69	78	Guernsey
46.3[4]	26.1[4]	14.9[4]	8.4[4]	3.7[4]	0.6[4]	...	3,245	3,660	4,388	5,407	6,876	8,879	11,451	Guinea
44.3	25.5	15.1	8.2	4.7	2.2	341	411	520	653	787	973	1,200	1,480	Guinea-Bissau
40.8	30.5	14.0	8.8	4.4	1.2	344	423	560	702	759	754	755	755	Guyana
39.2	26.9	15.6	10.0	5.4	2.9	2,827	3,261	3,807	4,535	5,370	6,486	8,003	8,876	Haiti
44.6[5]	28.3[5]	14.4[5]	7.8[5]	3.9[5]	1.1[5]	1,146	1,390	1,873	2,553	3,316	4,681	6,260	7,904	Honduras
23.0	25.0	26.2	—25.8—			1,786	1,974	3,074	3,942	5,063	5,705	6,360	7,026	Hong Kong
21.3	19.4	22.5	17.9	13.4	5.6	9,280	9,338	9,984	10,353	10,693	10,365	10,094	9,812	Hungary
24.7	24.2	22.5	13.6	10.3	4.7	121	143	176	204	228	255	279	295	Iceland
36.0[5]	27.7[5]	18.0[5]	11.2[5]	5.9[5]	1.2[5]	317,000	357,561	442,344	554,911	688,856	846,191	1,018,673	1,189,396	India
36.6	28.3	18.1	10.6	5.2	1.1	70,500	75,449	92,701	119,467	146,449	178,302	211,351	238,245	Indonesia
45.5[6]	26.4[6]	13.6[6]	9.1[6]	4.2[6]	1.2[6]	14,000	16,913	21,554	28,359	38,783	55,928	71,253	89,446	Iran
45.2	27.2	14.2	7.0	3.7	1.4	3,745	5,180	6,847	9,356	13,043	17,751	23,947	30,834	Iraq
28.9[6]	24.7[6]	18.8[6]	12.8[6]	10.7[6]	4.1[6]	2,958	2,969	2,834	2,954	3,421	3,526	3,492	3,458	Ireland
17.3	20.7	20.4	17.0	15.3	9.2	52	55	49	52	64	69	77	86	Isle of Man
32.6	26.4	18.0	12.3	9.4	3.1	...	...	2,114	2,958	3,896	4,739	6,250	6,875	Israel[19]
21.4[11]	22.4[11]	20.0[11]	18.7[11]	12.7[11]	4.7[11]	43,840	46,769	50,223	53,565	56,235	57,003	57,274	56,270	Italy
38.4[13]	28.8[13]	13.8[13]	9.4[13]	6.9[13]	2.6[13]	1,212	1,403	1,629	1,891	2,133	2,403	2,642	2,907	Jamaica
18.2	21.7	22.2	20.1	12.6	4.8	73,075	83,200	93,419	103,720	116,807	123,478	126,894	129,410	Japan
15.5	24.9	23.9	17.0	11.9	6.8	51	57	63	71	76	84	92	101	Jersey
51.6	23.4	13.4	7.4	3.1	1.1	...	1,095	1,384	1,795	2,181	3,282	4,790	6,760	Jordan[21]
31.9	26.3	19.4	13.2	6.9	2.3	6,148	6,703	9,996	13,110	14,940	16,742	18,261	21,720	Kazakhstan
51.4	24.8	13.2	7.0	3.0	0.6	4,470	6,018	8,115	11,225	16,667	24,872	37,505	50,726	Kenya
40.3	27.5	17.3	9.2	4.8	0.9	29	33	41	49	57	72	88	106	Kiribati
28.6[5]	34.6[5]	19.8[5]	10.5[5]	5.2[5]	1.3[5]	...	9,740	10,568	14,388	17,999	21,412	25,491	28,491	Korea, North
25.7	30.4	22.9	13.4	6.1	1.5	...	21,147	25,142	32,976	38,124	42,869	46,789	49,683	Korea, South
36.8	28.3	24.1	8.6	1.8	0.4	...	145	292	748	1,358	2,125	1,702	2,177	Kuwait
37.5	27.0	16.3	10.9	6.2	2.1	1,528	1,740	2,173	2,965	3,631	4,395	4,922	5,548	Kyrgyzstan
44.2	25.2	14.4	9.9	4.9	1.4	1,075	1,949	2,382	2,962	3,292	4,170	5,435	6,710	Laos
21.4	21.7	20.3	19.2	12.0	5.3	1,886	1,949	2,129	2,374	2,544	2,684	2,647	2,704	Latvia
42.6	23.8	16.7	9.1	—7.7—		965	1,443	1,857	2,469	2,669	2,740	3,312	3,777	Lebanon
40.7	25.1	16.6	10.7	5.6	1.3	566	766	885	1,043	1,358	1,760	2,282	2,958	Lesotho
43.2	28.2	14.7	7.7	4.4	1.8	...	758	1,004	1,393	1,876	2,575	3,565	4,829	Liberia
46.4[4]	25.0[4]	16.2[4]	8.6[4]	3.3[4]	0.6[4]	900	1,029	1,349	1,982	3,054	4,206	5,559	6,990	Libya
23.0	26.5	24.1	14.1	9.2	3.1	11	14	16	21	26	29	33	39	Liechtenstein
22.6	23.8	20.0	17.9	10.9	4.8	2,925	2,567	2,779	3,148	3,439	3,737	3,829	3,985	Lithuania
17.1[12]	22.3[12]	23.3[12]	18.5[12]	12.8[12]	6.0[12]	296	296	314	339	364	382	403	412	Luxembourg
24.1	27.2	29.4	9.6	7.3	2.3	375	188	169	221	243	329	493	722	Macau
29.1[11]	27.1[11]	19.6[11]	14.8[11]	7.1[11]	2.2[11]	...	1,229	1,392	1,629	1,900	2,024	2,157	2,298	Macedonia
44.4	25.7	14.2	10.0	4.6	1.1	4,034	4,230	5,309	6,742	8,790	12,010	16,579	22,431	Madagascar
46.1	25.4	14.5	8.0	—6.0—		1,696	3,033	3,481	4,511	6,183	9,582	12,612	16,455	Malawi
38.1[5]	28.1[5]	18.4[5]	9.6[5]	4.5[5]	1.2[5]	...	6,187	7,908	10,466	13,764	17,756	22,140	25,986	Malaysia
46.9	26.7	12.3	9.0	4.0	0.8	81	82	106	128	155	216	286	369	Maldives
46.1	23.9	15.0	8.9	4.9	1.2	3,388	3,426	4,224	5,690	6,816	8,130	9,980	12,252	Mali
24.1	23.2	23.0	15.4	10.5	3.8	270	308	329	326	324	354	379	399	Malta
51.0	24.5	14.6	5.5	3.6	0.8	...	11	15	22	31	46	68	87	Marshall Islands
23.1	28.9	20.5	13.5	9.7	4.3	200	222	252	287	326	361	415	458	Martinique
44.1	26.6	15.0	8.1	4.7	1.4	666	781	970	1,245	1,483	1,988	2,665	3,572	Mauritania
32.6	31.7	17.8	10.9	5.7	1.3	428	479	662	824	957	1,075	1,191	1,329	Mauritius
47.0	27.4	15.0	6.5	3.0	1.2	16	17	25	35	52	89	150	250	Mayotte
38.3	29.4	16.6	8.9	4.5	1.7	19,815	25,828	34,993	48,934	67,046	84,486	102,555	118,455	Mexico
46.4	26.8	12.6	8.5	4.5	1.1	...	30	40	57	73	101	110	120	Micronesia
27.9	22.9	21.0	15.6	9.7	2.9	2,468	2,341	3,004	3,595	4,002	4,365	4,399	4,453	Moldova
12.3	16.7	21.2	20.4	17.9	10.8	20	22	23	24	27	30	32	32	Monaco
41.9	29.2	14.6	8.5	—5.8—		750	747	931	1,248	1,663	2,122	2,635	3,290	Mongolia
42.2	28.3	14.1	9.2	4.8	1.5	7,750	8,953	11,640	15,126	19,082	25,009	30,947	36,810	Morocco
44.4	26.7	15.9	8.7	3.6	0.7	...	6,458	7,584	9,390	12,103	14,161	18,350	23,604	Mozambique
40.7	27.7	15.0	10.5	—6.1—		...	17,832	21,746	27,102	33,821	41,825	51,567	61,631	Myanmar (Burma)
44.4[5]	25.8[5]	15.2[5]	8.6[5]	5.0[5]	1.0[5]	336	405	522	761	1,002	1,348	1,906	2,533	Namibia
...	...	...	...	...	...	3	4	5	7	8	9	11	13	Nauru
41.4[11]	25.5[11]	17.4[11]	10.0[11]	4.7[11]	1.0[11]	7,000	8,000	9,180	11,232	14,655	18,420	20,847	23,062	Nepal
18.3[26]	23.6[26]	23.8[26]	16.8[26]	12.0[26]	5.5[26]	8,834	10,027	11,417	12,958	14,150	14,952	16,052	16,722	Netherlands, The

Area and population (continued)

country	area			population (latest estimate)					population (latest census)				
	square miles	square kilo-metres	rank	total midyear 1993	rank	density per sq mi	density per sq km	% annual growth rate 1988–93	census year	total	male (%)	female (%)	urban (%)
Netherlands Antilles	308	800	182	192,000	181	623.4	240.0	0.2	1981	171,620	48.3	51.7	...
New Caledonia	7,172	18,576	154	180,000	182	25.1	9.7	2.2	1989	164,173	51.1	48.9	59.4
New Zealand	104,454	270,534	75	3,520,000	122	33.7	13.0	0.9	1991	3,434,950	49.3	50.7	75.9
Nicaragua	50,880	131,779	97	4,265,000	115	83.8	32.4	3.3	1971	1,877,952	48.3	51.7	48.0
Niger	497,000	1,287,000	20	8,516,000	80	17.1	6.6	3.2	1988[7]	7,228,552	49.5	50.5	15.3
Nigeria	356,669	923,768	32	91,549,000	10	256.7	99.1	2.1	1991	88,514,501	50.3	49.7	35.2[5]
Northern Mariana Islands	184	477	191	45,400	209	246.7	95.2	4.2	1990	43,345	52.6	47.4	28.0
Norway	125,050	323,878	67	4,308,000	113	34.5	13.3	0.5	1990	4,247,546	49.4	50.6	75.0[5]
Oman	118,150	306,000	70	1,698,000	142	14.4	5.5	4.0	[22]	[22]	53.0[5]	47.0[5]	10.6[5]
Pakistan	339,697	879,811	34	127,962,000	7	376.7	145.4	2.9	1981[27]	84,253,644	52.5	47.5	28.3
Panama	29,157	75,517	118	2,563,000	134	87.9	33.9	2.0	1990	2,329,329	50.6	49.4	53.7
Papua New Guinea	178,704	462,840	54	3,918,000	116	21.9	8.5	2.2	1990	3,529,538[28]	52.1[28]	47.9[28]	15.2[28]
Paraguay	157,048	406,752	59	4,613,000	106	29.4	11.3	2.7	1992	4,123,550	50.2	49.8	50.5
Peru	496,225	1,285,216	21	22,916,000	38	46.2	17.8	2.1	1981	17,005,210	49.7	50.3	64.9
Philippines	115,860	300,076	72	64,954,000	14	560.6	216.5	2.2	1990	60,684,887	50.3	49.7	48.6
Poland	120,727	312,683	69	38,512,000	29	319.1	123.2	0.3	1988	37,878,641	48.7	51.3	61.2
Portugal	35,672	92,389	111	9,823,000	73	275.4	106.3	−0.1	1981[7]	9,833,014	48.2	51.8	29.7
Puerto Rico	3,515	9,104	165	3,612,000	120	1,027.6	396.7	0.9	1990	3,522,037	48.4	51.6	71.2
Qatar	4,412	11,427	160	539,000	161	122.2	47.2	4.7	1986	369,079	67.2	32.8	88.0[4]
Réunion	970	2,512	173	634,000	159	653.6	252.4	1.8	1990	597,828	49.2	50.8	73.4
Romania	91,699	237,500	82	22,789,000	39	248.5	96.0	−0.2	1992	22,760,449	49.1	50.9	54.4
Russia	6,592,800	17,075,400	1	148,000,000	6	22.4	8.7	0.2	1989	147,400,537	46.9	53.1	73.6
Rwanda	10,169	26,338	147	7,584,000	88	745.8	287.9	3.1	1991	7,164,994	48.7	51.3	5.4
St. Kitts and Nevis	104	269	203	41,800	210	401.9	155.4	−0.2	1991	41,862	51.6[5]	48.4[5]	48.9[5]
St. Lucia	238	617	188	136,000	186	571.4	220.4	0.8	1991	133,308	48.5	51.5	46.4[5]
St. Vincent and the Grenadines	150	389	196	109,000	189	726.7	280.2	0.9	1991	106,499	49.9	50.1	24.6
San Marino	24	61	210	24,100	214	1,004.2	395.1	1.2	1976	19,149	50.4	49.6	90.0[5]
São Tomé and Príncipe	386	1,001	180	125,000	188	323.8	124.9	2.2	1991	120,146	49.4	50.6	40.5[17]
Saudi Arabia	865,000	2,240,000	13	17,419,000	51	20.1	7.8	3.9	1992	16,929,294	55.9	44.1	77.3[5]
Senegal	75,951	196,712	87	7,899,000	85	104.0	40.2	2.7	1988	6,928,405	48.7	51.3	38.6
Seychelles	176	455	193	71,300	199	405.1	156.7	0.7	1987	68,598	49.7	50.3	35.5
Sierra Leone	27,699	71,740	119	4,491,000	110	162.1	62.6	2.6	1985	3,517,530	49.6	50.4	31.8
Singapore	247	639	187	2,876,000	130	11,643.7	4,500.8	2.0	1990[7]	2,705,115	50.6	49.4	100.0
Slovakia	18,933	49,035	129	5,329,000	100	281.5	108.7	0.5	1991	5,268,935	48.9	51.1	...
Slovenia	7,821	20,256	153	1,997,000	139	255.3	98.6	0.5	1991	1,974,839	48.6[11]	51.4[11]	48.9[11]
Solomon Islands	10,954	28,370	143	349,000	172	31.9	12.3	2.7	1986	285,176	51.9	48.1	15.7
Somalia	246,000	637,000	42	8,050,000	83	32.7	12.6	2.7	1975	4,089,203	50.1	49.9	25.4
South Africa[29]	473,290	1,225,815	25	40,786,000	27	86.2	33.3	2.3	1991[30]	26,504,191	48.8	51.2	60.3
Bophuthatswana	16,988	44,000	—	2,564,000	—	150.9	58.3	2.6	1980	1,287,814	46.9[31]	53.1[31]	14.2[31]
Ciskei	2,996	7,760	—	897,000	—	299.4	115.6	2.6	1985	831,636	47.3	52.7	49.8
Transkei	16,855	43,653	—	3,664,000	—	217.4	83.9	2.6	1980	2,334,946	41.2[31]	58.8[31]	3.2[31]
Venda	2,771	7,176	—	590,000	—	212.9	82.2	2.6	1985	459,986	41.0[32]	59.0[32]	2.1[32]
Spain	194,898	504,783	51	39,141,000	28	200.8	77.5	0.2	1991	38,999,181	49.1	50.9	75.3
Sri Lanka	25,332	65,610	122	17,616,000	50	695.4	268.5	1.2	1981	14,848,364	50.8	49.2	21.5
Sudan, The	966,757	2,503,890	10	25,000,000	37	25.9	10.0	1.4	1983	21,623,907	50.8	49.2	20.5
Suriname	63,251	163,820	92	405,000	165	6.4	2.5	0.3	1980	354,860	49.5	50.5	44.8[9]
Swaziland	6,704	17,364	157	814,000	154	121.4	46.9	2.7	1986	681,059	47.2	52.8	22.8
Sweden	173,732	449,964	56	8,727,000	77	50.2	19.4	0.7	1992[2]	8,692,013	49.4	50.6	83.1[32]
Switzerland	15,943	41,293	135	6,966,000	91	438.8	169.4	0.7	1990[33]	6,873,687	49.3	50.7	59.7[3]
Syria	71,498	185,180	88	13,398,000	58	187.4	72.4	3.4	1981	9,052,628	51.1	48.9	47.1
Taiwan	13,969	36,179	136	20,926,000	42	1,498.0	578.4	1.1	1990[7]	20,393,628	52.1	47.9	74.5
Tajikistan	55,300	143,100	95	5,705,000	95	103.2	39.9	2.6	1989	5,108,576	49.7	50.3	32.6
Tanzania	364,017	942,799	31	26,542,000	35	72.9	28.2	2.8	1988	23,174,336	48.9	51.1	32.8[5]
Thailand	198,115	513,115	50	57,829,000	18	291.9	112.7	1.9	1990	54,532,300	49.6	50.4	18.7
Togo	21,925	56,785	125	3,810,000	117	173.8	67.1	2.9	1981	2,719,567	48.7	51.3	15.2
Tonga	301	780	183	99,100	193	329.2	127.1	0.7	1986[7]	94,649	50.3	49.7	30.7
Trinidad and Tobago	1,980	5,128	168	1,249,000	149	630.8	243.6	0.6	1990	1,234,388	50.1	49.9	69.1[5]
Tunisia	63,378	164,150	91	8,530,000	79	134.6	52.0	1.9	1984	6,975,450	50.8	49.2	52.8
Turkey	300,948	779,452	37	59,869,000	16	198.9	76.8	2.2	1990	56,473,035	50.4[24]	49.6[24]	45.9[24]
Turkmenistan	188,500	488,100	52	4,294,000	114	22.8	8.8	4.3	1989	3,533,925	49.3	50.7	45.4
Tuvalu	9.4	24.4	212	9,500	216	1,010.6	389.3	2.1	1985	8,229	47.4	52.6	...
Uganda	93,070	241,040	80	17,741,000	48	190.6	73.6	2.6	1991	16,671,705	49.1	50.9	11.3
Ukraine	233,100	603,700	44	52,344,000	22	224.6	86.7	0.3	1989	51,706,746	46.3	53.7	66.9
United Arab Emirates	30,000	77,700	117	1,986,000	140	66.2	25.6	3.1	1985	1,622,464	64.9	35.1	80.8[11]
United Kingdom	94,251	244,110	79	58,080,000	17	616.2	237.9	0.4	1991[7]	56,467,000	48.4	51.6	89.1[5]
United States	3,679,192	9,529,063	4	258,233,000	3	70.2	27.1	1.1	1990[34]	248,709,873	48.7	51.3	75.2
Uruguay	68,037	176,215	90	3,149,000	127	46.3	17.9	0.6	1985	2,955,241	48.7	51.3	86.2
Uzbekistan	172,700	447,400	57	21,901,000	41	126.8	49.0	2.2	1989	19,905,158	49.3	50.7	40.7
Vanuatu	4,707	12,190	159	160,000	184	34.0	13.1	2.8	1989	142,630	51.6	48.4	17.7
Venezuela	352,144	912,050	33	20,609,000	43	58.5	22.6	2.2	1990	19,405,429	49.7	50.3	84.0
Vietnam	127,246	329,566	66	70,902,000	13	557.2	215.1	2.2	1989	64,411,713	48.7	51.3	20.1
Virgin Islands (U.S.)	136	352	199	104,000	190	764.7	295.5	0.5	1990	101,809	48.3	51.7	37.2
West Bank	2,270	5,900	166	1,054,000	151	464.3	178.6	3.6	1991[2]	957,000	50.3	49.7	...
Western Sahara	97,344	252,120	77	213,000	178	2.2	0.8	2.5	1970	76,425	...	...	...
Western Samoa	1,093	2,831	171	163,000	183	149.1	57.6	0.6	1991	159,682	53.0[6]	47.0[6]	20.5[6]
Yemen	205,356	531,869	49	12,519,000	61	61.0	23.5	3.6	1986[35]	9,274,173[36]	47.3[11]	52.7[11]	10.2[11]
Yugoslavia	39,449	102,173	107	10,561,000	67	267.7	103.4	0.3	1991	10,337,504	49.7[11]	50.3[11]	46.8[11]
Zaire	905,446	2,345,095	12	42,473,000	26	46.9	18.1	3.3	1984	29,671,407	49.2	50.8	36.6[4]
Zambia	290,586	752,614	39	8,504,000	81	29.3	11.3	3.1	1990	7,818,447	49.2	50.8	42.0
Zimbabwe	150,872	390,757	60	10,687,000	65	70.8	27.3	3.2	1992	10,401,767	48.8	51.2	23.0[13]

[1]Settled population only. [2]Civil register; not a census. [3]1991 estimate. [4]1985 estimate. [5]1990 estimate. [6]1986 census. [7]Data are for de jure population. [8]1992 estimate. [9]1980 estimate. [10]1982 estimate. [11]1981 census. [12]1989 estimate. [13]1982 census. [14]1983 census. [15]Former West Germany only. [16]Excludes visitors, transients, and family members of British servicemen. [17]1988 estimate. [18]Data exclude Alderney (population 2,297) and Sark (population 604). [19]Excluding territory occupied after 1967. [20]Includes East Jerusalem and Israeli residents in the occupied

age distribution (%)						population (by decade, '000s)								country
0–14	15–29	30–44	45–59	60–74	75 and over	1940	1950	1960	1970	1980	1990	2000 projection	2010 projection	
30.0	29.9	19.5	11.3	6.7	2.6	77	112	136	163	171	190	194	198	Netherlands Antilles
32.6	28.6	19.8	12.1	5.4	1.6	53	59	79	110	140	170	204	238	New Caledonia
23.2	24.6	22.4	14.4	10.9	4.5	1,636	1,908	2,372	2,820	3,169	3,417	3,802	4,128	New Zealand
48.1	25.6	14.1	7.4	3.8	1.1	825	1,109	1,472	1,972	2,771	3,871	5,261	6,824	Nicaragua
48.7	24.8	14.6	6.8	3.6	1.5	1,700	2,291	2,913	4,016	5,565	7,735	10,618	14,333	Niger
47.4[5]	26.0[5]	14.4[5]	8.0[5]	3.5[5]	0.6[5]	...	33,320	42,366	56,346	69,875	86,015	105,885	130,344	Nigeria
23.8	33.5	30.7	9.1	2.3	0.5	48	6	9	10	17	44	50	58	Northern Mariana Islands
18.8	22.9	22.1	15.1	13.9	7.2	2,973	3,265	3,581	3,877	4,086	4,241	4,426	4,550	Norway
46.7[5]	23.6[5]	17.2[5]	8.3[5]	3.5[5]	0.7[5]	...	413	505	654	984	1,530	2,165	3,063	Oman
44.5	23.9	15.4	9.3	5.3	1.6	28,300	39,513	49,955	65,706	85,299	118,122	154,794	197,672	Pakistan
34.8	29.2	18.2	10.2	5.5	2.0	620	893	1,148	1,531	1,956	2,418	2,893	3,324	Panama
40.4[5]	28.6[5]	17.0[5]	9.3[5]	4.3[5]	0.3[5]	1,308	1,613	1,920	2,419	2,966	3,671	4,568	5,511	Papua New Guinea
40.4[5]	28.0[5]	18.1[5]	8.2[5]	4.3[5]	1.1[5]	1,111	1,351	1,778	2,290	3,147	4,277	5,464	6,926	Paraguay
41.2	27.9	15.6	9.3	4.4	1.6	6,784	7,632	9,931	13,193	17,295	21,550	26,276	31,047	Peru
39.6	28.7	17.3	9.2	4.2	1.1	16,459	20,988	27,561	36,850	48,286	60,921	74,555	86,682	Philippines
25.4	21.2	23.3	15.5	10.4	4.2	31,500	24,824	29,561	32,526	35,578	38,110	39,547	41,089	Poland
25.5	23.5	18.0	17.2	11.9	3.9	7,696	8,405	8,826	9,040	9,766	9,868	9,735	9,610	Portugal
27.2	25.1	20.4	14.1	9.2	4.0	1,878	2,218	2,360	2,721	3,204	3,528	3,832	4,169	Puerto Rico
27.8	29.3	32.3	8.6	1.6	0.4	...	47	59	151	229	484	659	831	Qatar
29.5	29.8	20.3	11.7	6.5	2.1	221	244	338	447	507	601	718	857	Réunion
23.9[12]	22.4[12]	20.8[12]	17.6[12]	11.3[12]	4.0[12]	15,907	16,311	18,407	20,799	22,201	23,201	23,272	23,980	Romania
23.1	22.0	21.9	17.6	11.2	4.2	110,098	105,018	119,906	130,392	138,914	148,292	146,239	143,477	Russia
45.6	28.6	12.4	8.4	3.9	0.9	1,910	2,120	2,742	3,728	5,113	6,925	9,377	12,698	Rwanda
32.5[5]	25.6[5]	18.9[5]	10.1[5]	8.9[5]	4.0[5]	43	49	51	46	43	42	42	42	St. Kitts and Nevis
36.8	29.4	16.3	8.7	6.3	2.5	70	79	86	101	122	132	143	155	St. Lucia
37.4[4]	32.7[4]	14.9[4]	7.5[4]	5.6[4]	1.9[4]	61	67	80	86	99	105	116	127	St. Vincent and the Grenadines
24.4	23.0	19.9	17.4	11.4	3.9	10	13	15	19	21	23	26	30	San Marino
46.3[11]	25.0[11]	11.6[11]	10.0[11]	5.3[11]	1.8[11]	60	60	64	74	94	117	146	182	São Tomé and Príncipe
42.9[5]	24.6[5]	19.9[5]	8.4[5]	3.4[5]	0.7[5]	...	3,201	4,075	5,745	10,399	15,557	22,621	32,095	Saudi Arabia
47.5	26.1	13.6	7.8	—5.0—		1,857	2,600	3,076	4,267	5,651	7,292	9,519	12,424	Senegal
33.6	30.3	15.3	10.7	7.1	2.9	32	34	42	54	64	70	75	81	Seychelles
43.9[4]	25.6[4]	15.7[4]	9.6[4]	4.5[4]	0.7[4]	1,700	1,809	2,165	2,692	3,336	4,151	5,437	7,172	Sierra Leone
23.2	27.3	27.7	12.7	6.9	2.2	751	1,022	1,639	2,075	2,282	2,705	3,315	4,061	Singapore
25.0	22.7	22.8	14.6	10.7	4.2	...	3,472	4,137	4,557	5,002	5,252	5,513	5,777	Slovakia
23.0[11]	24.2[11]	20.6[11]	17.9[11]	10.1[11]	4.0[11]	...	1,473	1,580	1,718	1,886	1,968	2,068	2,174	Slovenia
47.3	25.7	13.9	8.1	—4.9—		94	104	125	163	230	319	433	569	Solomon Islands
45.6	24.9	15.5	7.4	—5.4—		...	2,423	2,935	3,668	5,345	7,497	9,736	13,114	Somalia
32.1	29.4	20.7	10.5	5.7	1.6	10,353	12,458	15,925	22,460	29,799	37,909	48,425	62,241	South Africa[29]
52.6[31]	21.3[31]	10.4[31]	—13.6[31]—		2.1[31]	...	...	...	...	1,335	2,364	3,132	4,194	Bophuthatswana
44.9	26.2	15.0	6.9	5.5	1.5	...	...	...	...	682	827	1,096	1,468	Ciskei
43.7[31]	21.5[31]	13.3[31]	—20.3[31]—		1.2[31]	...	...	...	...	2,336	3,377	4,476	5,994	Transkei
43.3[31]	20.3[31]	12.4[31]	—22.7[31]—		1.3[31]	...	...	...	...	345	544	721	966	Venda
18.4[8]	25.1[8]	20.6[8]	—35.9[8]—			25,757	27,868	30,303	33,779	37,581	38,959	39,879	40,317	Spain
35.3	29.6	17.9	10.6	5.2	1.4	5,972	7,678	9,889	12,514	14,747	16,993	19,098	21,159	Sri Lanka
45.1[4]	26.1[4]	15.6[4]	8.7[4]	3.8[4]	0.7[4]	8,500	9,322	11,256	14,090	19,449	24,023	30,513	43,045	Sudan, The
39.3	29.5	13.8	10.0	4.5	2.8	193	215	247	292	355	403	410	417	Suriname
47.3	26.6	13.4	7.4	3.4	1.3	154	253	320	409	565	751	984	1,270	Swaziland
18.5	20.3	20.5	18.3	14.3	8.1	6,371	7,041	7,498	8,081	8,310	8,559	8,960	9,179	Sweden
16.8	22.8	23.2	18.0	12.5	6.7	4,234	4,715	5,429	6,270	6,362	6,851	7,446	7,660	Switzerland
48.5	25.8	12.5	8.3	3.7	1.2	2,597	3,495	4,561	6,305	8,704	12,116	16,925	22,991	Syria
27.1	27.8	23.1	12.3	7.9	1.8	5,987	7,619	10,668	14,583	17,705	20,279	22,548	25,085	Taiwan
42.9	28.1	13.8	9.0	4.6	1.6	1,525	1,532	2,083	2,942	3,968	5,303	6,766	8,632	Tajikistan
47.2[5]	26.7[5]	14.2[5]	7.8[5]	3.3[5]	0.7[5]	...	7,892	10,073	13,273	18,441	24,403	32,292	42,732	Tanzania
28.8	30.4	21.2	12.3	5.7	1.6	15,296	20,010	26,392	35,745	45,044	54,799	65,534	76,656	Thailand
49.8	24.8	13.1	6.8	3.3	2.0	834	1,201	1,465	1,954	2,614	3,493	4,668	6,238	Togo
40.6	29.0	13.8	10.1	5.0	1.4	37	50	65	80	92	97	103	105	Tonga
31.3[5]	26.9[5]	21.5[5]	12.2[5]	—8.1[5]—		503	668	828	941	1,082	1,227	1,304	1,386	Trinidad and Tobago
39.7	28.8	14.2	10.7	5.4	1.2	2,887	3,530	4,221	5,137	6,392	8,074	9,670	11,161	Tunisia
37.1[24]	26.3[24]	17.1[24]	12.6[24]	—6.9[24]—		17,723	20,809	27,509	35,321	44,438	56,098	69,694	78,524	Turkey
40.5	28.8	15.5	9.1	4.7	1.4	1,302	1,211	1,594	2,189	2,860	3,668	4,904	5,927	Turkmenistan
31.8[33]	31.7[33]	15.2[33]	13.2[33]	6.3[33]	1.7[33]	4	5	5	6	8	9	11	13	Tuvalu
48.3[5]	26.6[5]	13.9[5]	7.2[5]	3.4[5]	0.7[5]	4,233	5,969	7,551	9,806	12,779	16,447	21,168	27,244	Uganda
21.5	21.0	20.6	18.5	10.7	7.7	41,340	36,906	42,783	47,317	50,034	51,892	53,362	54,851	Ukraine
31.9[4]	24.9[4]	32.1[4]	8.7[4]	1.9[4]	0.5[4]	...	70	90	223	1,015	1,844	2,281	2,781	United Arab Emirates
19.1	21.9	21.2	16.7	14.1	7.0	48,226	50,290	52,372	55,632	56,329	57,411	59,520	60,986	United Kingdom
21.5	23.4	23.9	14.4	11.5	5.3	132,594	152,271	180,671	204,879	227,722	249,924	275,326	298,620	United States
26.6	22.8	18.3	16.5	11.4	4.3	1,974	2,194	2,531	2,824	2,914	3,094	3,274	3,453	Uruguay
40.8	28.4	15.0	9.3	4.7	1.8	6,551	6,314	8,559	11,973	15,977	20,515	25,449	31,539	Uzbekistan
45.5	26.6	15.2	8.4	3.7	0.6	43	52	65	86	115	148	189	231	Vanuatu
38.3	28.1	18.6	9.3	4.5	1.2	3,740	5,009	7,502	10,604	15,024	19,321	23,622	27,607	Venezuela
39.0	28.7	16.0	9.1	5.6	1.6	20,209	22,725	30,172	41,063	53,722	66,233	81,096	95,704	Vietnam
28.9	23.7	22.0	16.0	7.3	2.2	25	27	32	75	97	102	107	113	Virgin Islands (U.S.)
47.8	—40.2—		—12.0—			...	...	...	608	721	937	1,315	1,803	West Bank
42.9	27.2	16.3	7.4	4.4	1.8	...	14	32	76	155	199	250	316	Western Sahara
41.1[6]	30.9[6]	13.3[6]	9.1[6]	4.4[6]	1.2[6]	61	82	111	143	155	159	174	192	Western Samoa
45.7[11]	23.2[11]	15.1[11]	10.5[11]	4.7[11]	0.8[11]	...	4,529	5,538	6,276	7,936	11,282	15,859	21,797	Yemen
24.2[11]	23.8[11]	19.9[11]	19.4[11]	9.1[11]	3.2[11]	...	7,131	8,050	8,910	9,842	10,529	11,114	11,440	Yugoslavia
45.2[4]	25.9[4]	15.5[4]	8.7[4]	3.9[4]	0.7[4]	10,370	13,055	16,151	21,368	27,896	38,619	52,644	70,841	Zaire
48.4[5]	27.2[5]	13.7[5]	7.0[5]	3.1[5]	0.7[5]	1,484	2,440	3,141	4,189	5,634	7,783	10,559	14,386	Zambia
51.0[13]	26.3[13]	13.4[13]	6.5[13]	1.2[13]	1.6[13]	1,940	2,730	3,840	5,308	7,100	9,730	12,608	15,561	Zimbabwe

territories. [21]Excluding West Bank. [22]No census ever taken. [23]Island of Mauritius only. [24]1985 census. [25]Including 163,868 in Western Sahara. [26]1992 civil register. [27]Excludes Afghan refugees and residents of Pakistani-occupied Jammu and Kashmir. [28]Excludes North Solomons Province. [29]Includes black national states shown separately. [30]Excludes Bophuthatswana, Ciskei, Transkei, and Venda. [31]1970 census. [32]1980 census. [33]1979 census. [34]Excludes 515,000 armed forces overseas. [35]Former Yemen Arab Republic only. [36]Includes 1,168,199 nationals abroad.

Major cities and national capitals

The following table lists the principal cities or municipalities (those exceeding 100,000 in population [50,000 for Anglo-America]) of the countries of the world, together with figures for each national capital (indicated by a ★), regardless of size.

Most of the populations given refer to a so-called city proper, that is, a legally defined, incorporated, or chartered area defined by administrative boundaries and by national or state law. Some data, however, refer to the municipality, or commune, similar to the medieval city-state in that the city is governed together with its immediately adjoining, economically dependent areas, whether urban or rural in nature. Some countries define no other demographic or legal entities within such communes or municipalities, but many identify a centre, seat, head (*cabecera*), or locality that corresponds to the most densely populated, compact, contiguous core of the municipality. Because the amount of work involved in carefully defining these "centres" may be considerable, the necessary resources usually exist only at the time of a national census (generally 5 or 10 years apart). Between censuses, therefore, it may be possible only to track the growth of the municipality as a whole. Thus, in order to provide the most up-to-date data for cities in this table, figures referring to municipalities or communes may be given (identified by the abbreviation "MU"), even though the country itself may define a smaller, more closely knit city proper. Specific identification of municipalities is provided in this table *only* when the country also publishes data for a more narrowly defined city proper; it is *not* provided when the sole published figure is the municipality, whether or not this is the proper local administrative term for the entity.

Problems also exist in the identification of cities in terms of named legal entities. There is, for example, a single municipality (*commune*) named Brussel (Brussels) at the centre of the Brussels agglomeration in Belgium; the *commune* numbers only about 136,000 population, while the agglomeration, which is understood by most people to constitute the city, numbers nearly a million. Both are shown so as to apprise the reader of the existence of a problem.

For certain countries, more than one form of the name of the city is given, usually to permit recognition of recent place name changes or of forms of the place name likely to be encountered in press stories if the title of the city's entry in the *Encyclopædia Britannica* is spelled according to a different romanization or spelling policy. Chinese names, for example, are given first in their Wade-Giles spelling (the scholarly system used by Britannica) and then, parenthetically, in their Pinyin spelling, the official Chinese system now encountered in press reports, official documents, and maps.

Sources for this data were usually the national census and statistical abstracts of the countries concerned, supplemented by correspondence with most national statistical offices to solicit unpublished data.

Major cities and national capitals

country city	population
Afghanistan (1988 est.)	
Herāt	177,300
★ Kābul	1,424,400
Kandahār (Qandahār)	225,500
Mazār-e Sharīf	130,600
Albania (1990)	
★ Tiranë	243,000
Algeria (1987)	
★ Algiers	1,507,241
Annaba	222,518
Batna	181,601
Béchar	107,311
Bejaïa	114,534
Biskra	128,280
Blida (el-Boulaida)	127,284
ech-Cheliff	129,976
Constantine (Qacentina)	440,842
Mostaganem	114,037
Oran (Wahran)	609,823
Sétif	170,182
Sidi bel Abbès	152,778
Skikda	128,747
Tébessa	107,559
Tlemcen (Tilimsen)	107,632
American Samoa (1990)	
★ Pago Pago	3,519
Andorra (1990)	
★ Andorra la Vella	20,437
Angola (1990 est.)	
★ Luanda	1,544,400
Lubango	105,000[1]
Antigua and Barbuda (1986 est.)	
★ Saint John's	36,000
Argentina (1991; MU)	
Almirante Brown	449,105
Avellaneda	346,620
Bahía Blanca	271,467
Berazategui	243,690
★ Buenos Aires	2,960,976
Caseros	340,343[2]
Catamarca	110,489
Concordia	138,905
Córdoba	1,179,067
Corrientes	267,742
Esteban Echeverría	276,017
Florencio Varela	253,554
Formosa	165,700
General San Martín	407,506
General Sarmiento	646,891
Godoy Cruz	141,553[2]
La Matanza	1,121,164
La Plata	542,567
La Rioja	106,281
Lanús	466,755
Lomas de Zamora	572,769
Mar del Plata	414,696[2]
Mendoza	121,696
Merlo	390,031
Moreno	287,188
Morón	641,541
Paraná	277,338
Posadas	219,824
Quilmes	509,445
Resistencia	218,438[2]
Río Cuarto	217,717
Rosario	875,664[2]
Salta	373,857
San Fernando	144,761
San Isidro	299,022
San Juan	119,399
San Justo	946,715[2]
San Luis	121,146
San Miguel de Tucumán	473,014
San Salvador de Jujuy	124,950[2]
Santa Fe	442,214
Santiago del Estero	201,709
Tigre	256,005
Tres de Febrero	349,221
Vicente López	289,142
Villa Nueva (Guaymallén)	157,334[2]
Armenia (1991 est.)	
Kumayri (Leninakan)	120,000[3]
★ Yerevan	1,283,000
Aruba (1991)	
★ Oranjestad	20,046
Australia (1991)[4, 5]	
Adelaide	1,023,597
Brisbane	1,334,017
★ Canberra	278,904
Geelong	145,323
Gold Coast	157,859
Hobart	181,832
Melbourne	3,022,157
Newcastle	427,824
Perth	1,143,249
Sunshine Coast	126,142
Sydney	3,538,749
Townsville-Thuringowa (urban centre)	101,398
Wollongong	235,966
Austria (1991)	
Graz	237,810
Innsbruck	118,112
Linz	203,044
Salzburg	143,978
★ Vienna	1,539,848
Azerbaijan (1991 est.)	
★ Baku (Baky)	1,080,500
Gyandzha	282,200
Sumgait	236,200
Bahamas, The (1990)	
★ Nassau	172,196
Bahrain (1991)	
★ al-Manāmah	120,937
Bangladesh (1991)	
Barisāl	180,014
Brāhmanbāria	114,297
Chittagong	1,566,070
Comilla	164,509
★ Dhākā (Dacca)	3,637,892
Dinājpur	136,657
Gāzipur	100,690
Jamālpur	108,416
Jessore	176,398
Khulna	601,051
Mymensingh	198,662
Naogaon	109,156
Nārāyanganj	288,008
Narsinghdi	100,120
Nawābganj	131,260
Pābna	113,146
Rājshāhi	324,532
Rangpur	220,849
Saidpur	110,494
Sirājganj	100,003
Sylhet	114,284
Tangail	111,783
Tongi	165,099
Barbados (1990)	
★ Bridgetown	6,070
Belarus (1991 est.)	
Baranovichi	166,700
Bobruysk	223,000
Borisov	150,200
Brest	277,000
Gomel	503,300
Grodno	284,800
★ Minsk	1,633,600
Mogilyov	363,000
Mozyr	103,000
Orsha	125,300
Pinsk	123,800
Vitebsk	361,500
Belgium (1992 est.)	
Antwerp	465,783
Brugge (Bruges)	116,717
★ Brussels	136,424[6]
Agglomeration	951,217
Charleroi	206,903
Ghent	230,232
Liège (Luik)	196,303
Namur	104,304
Schaerbeek	102,702[6]
Belize (1992 est.)	
★ Belmopan	3,687
Benin (1985 est.)	
★ Cotonou (official)	402,290
★ Porto-Novo (de facto)	163,260
Bermuda (1991)	
★ Hamilton	1,100
Bhutan (1987 est.)	
★ Paro (administrative)	3,000[7]
★ Thimphu (official)	15,000
Bolivia (1992)	
Cochabamba	404,102
El Alto	404,367
★ La Paz (administrative)	711,036
Oruro	183,194
Potosí	112,291
Santa Cruz	694,616
★ Sucre (judicial)	130,952
Bosnia and Herzegovina (1991; MU)	
Banja Luka	195,139
Doboj	102,546
Mostar	126,067
Prijedor	112,470
★ Sarajevo	525,980
Tuzla	131,861
Zenica	145,577
Botswana (1991)	
★ Gaborone	133,468
Brazil (1980)	
Americana	121,794
Anápolis	160,520
Aracaju	287,934
Araçatuba	113,486
Barra Mansa	123,421
Bauru	178,861
Belém	758,117
Belo Horizonte	1,441,567
Blumenau	144,819
★ Brasília	411,305
Campina Grande	222,102
Campinas	566,627
Campo Grande	282,857
Campos	174,218
Canoas	213,999
Carapicuíba	185,763
Caruaru	137,636
Cascavel	100,351
Caxias do Sul	198,824
Contagem	111,697
Cuiabá	167,894
Curitiba	842,818
Diadema	228,594
Divinópolis	108,344
Duque de Caxias	306,243
Feira de Santana	227,004
Florianópolis	153,547
Fortaleza	647,917
Franca	143,620
Goiânia	702,858
Governador Valadares	173,699
Guarulhos	395,117
Imperatriz	111,818
Ipatinga	105,083
Itabuna	129,938
Jacareí	104,241
João Pessoa	290,247
Joinville	217,074
Juàzeiro do Norte	125,248
Juiz de Fora	299,432
Jundiaí	210,015
Lages	108,768
Limeira	137,812
Londrina	257,899
Maceió	375,771
Manaus	611,763
Marília	103,904
Maringá	158,047
Mauá	205,817
Mogi das Cruzes	122,265
Montes Claros	151,881
Mossoró	118,007
Natal	376,446
Nilópolis	103,033
Niterói	382,736
Nova Iguaçu	491,766
Novo Hamburgo	132,066
Olinda	266,751
Osasco	473,856
Passo Fundo	103,121
Pelotas	197,092
Petrópolis	150,249
Piracicaba	179,395
Ponta Grossa	171,111
Porto Alegre	1,114,867
Porto Velho	101,644
Presidente Prudente	127,623
Recife	1,183,391
Ribeirão Prêto	300,828
Rio Claro	103,174
Rio de Janeiro	5,090,700
Rio Grande	124,706
Salvador	1,491,642
Santa Maria	151,202
Santarém	102,181
Santo André	549,556
Santos	410,933
São Bernardo do Campo	381,097
São Caetano do Sul	163,030
São Carlos	109,167
São Gonçalo	221,591
São João de Meriti	210,574
São José do Rio Prêto	172,027
São José dos Campos	268,034
São Luís	182,258
São Paulo	7,032,547
São Vicente	192,770
Sorocaba	254,672
Taubaté	155,376
Teresina	339,042
Uberaba	180,228
Uberlândia	230,185
Vitória	165,090
Vitória da Conquista	125,516
Volta Redonda	177,772
Brunei (1991)	
★ Bandar Seri Begawan	21,484
Bulgaria (1992 est.)	
Burgas	211,597
Dobrich (Tolbukhin)	116,066
Pleven	137,466
Plovdiv	379,112
Ruse	190,229
Shumen	112,091
Sliven	114,596
★ Sofia	1,140,795
Stara Zagora	162,368
Varna	316,231
Burkina Faso (1985)	
Bobo Dioulasso	228,668
★ Ouagadougou	441,514
Burundi (1990)	
★ Bujumbura	235,440
Gitega	101,827
Cambodia (1989 est.)	
★ Phnom Penh	800,000
Cameroon (1987)	
Bafoussam	113,000
Bamenda	110,000

country city	population
Douala	810,000
Garoua	142,000
Maroua	123,000
Nkongsamba	112,000
★ Yaoundé	649,000
Canada (1991)	
Barrie	62,728
Beauport	69,158
Brampton	234,445
Brantford	81,997
Brossard	64,793
Burlington	129,575
Burnaby	158,858
Calgary	710,677
Cambridge	92,772
Charlesbourg	70,788
Chicoutimi	62,670
Dartmouth	67,798
Delta	88,978
East York	102,696
Edmonton	616,741
Etobicoke	309,993
Guelph	87,976
Halifax	114,455
Hamilton	318,499
Hull	60,707
Jonquiere	57,933
Kamloops	67,057
Kelowna	75,950
Kingston	56,597
Kitchener	168,282
Laval	314,398
Lethbridge	60,974
London	303,165
Longueuil	129,874
Markham	153,811
Mississauga	463,388
Moncton	57,010
Montreal	1,017,666
Montreal-Nord	85,516
Nanaimo	60,129
Niagara Falls	75,399
North Bay	55,405
North York	562,564
Oakville	114,670
Oshawa	129,344
★ Ottawa	313,987
Peterborough	68,371
Prince George	69,653
Quebec	167,517
Red Deer	58,134
Regina	179,178
Richmond	126,624
Saint Catharines	129,300
Saint-Hubert	74,027
Saint John	74,969
Saint John's	95,770
Saint-Laurent	72,402
Sainte-Foy	71,133
Sarnia-Clearwater	74,167
Saskatoon	186,058
Sault Sainte Marie	81,476
Scarborough	524,598
Sherbrooke	76,429
Sudbury	92,884
Surrey	245,173
Thunder Bay	113,746
Toronto	635,395
Vancouver	471,844
Verdun	61,307
Victoria	71,228
Waterloo	71,181
Windsor	191,435
Winnipeg	616,790
York	140,525
Cape Verde (1990)	
★ Praia	61,797
Central African Republic (1988)	
★ Bangui	451,690
Chad (1992 est.)	
Moundou	117,500
★ N'Djamena	687,800
Sarh	129,600
Chile (1992; MU)	
Antofagasta	226,749
Arica	169,217
Calama	120,602
Chillán	158,731
Concepción	330,448
Copiapó	100,946
Coquimbo	122,872
Curicó	103,919
Iquique	152,654
La Serena	120,336
Los Angeles	142,136
Osorno	128,709
Puente Alto	254,534
Puerto Montt	130,737
Punta Arenas	113,661
Quilpué	102,824
Rancagua	187,134
San Bernardo	188,580
★ Santiago (administrative)	4,385,481
Talca	171,467
Talcahuano	246,566
Temuco	240,880
Valdívia	122,436
★ Valparaíso (legislative)	276,736
Viña del Mar	302,765
China (1990 est.)[8]	
A-ch'eng (Acheng)	197,595
A-k'o-su (Aksu)	164,092
An-ch'ing (Anqing)	250,718
An-k'ang (Ankang)	142,170
An-shan (Anshan)	1,203,986
An-shun (Anshun)	174,142
An-ta (Anda)	136,446
An-yang (Anyang)	420,332
Canton (Guangzhou)	2,914,281
Chan-chiang (Zhanjiang)	400,997
Ch'ang-chi (Changji)	132,260
Chang-chia-k'ou (Zhangjiakou)	529,136
Ch'ang-chih (Changzhi)	317,144
Ch'ang-chou (Changzhou)	531,470
Chang-chou (Zhangzhou)	181,424
Ch'ang-ch'un (Changchun)	1,679,270
Ch'ang-sha (Changsha)	1,113,212
Ch'ang-shu (Changshu)	181,805
Ch'ang-te (Changde)	301,276
Chao-ch'ing (Zhaoqing)	194,784
Ch'ao-chou (Chaozhou)	313,469
Ch'ao-hsien (Chaoxian)	123,676
Chao-tung (Zhaodong)	179,976
Ch'ao-yang (Chaoyang)	222,394
Chen-chiang (Zhenjiang)	368,316
Cheng-chou (Zhengzhou)	1,159,679
Ch'eng-te (Chengde)	246,799
Ch'eng-tu (Chengdu)	1,713,255
Chi-an (Ji'an)	148,583
Chi-hsi (Jixi)	683,885
Chi-lin (Jilin)	1,036,858
Chi-nan (Jinan)	1,480,915
Chi-ning (Jining) (*Inner Mongolia*)	163,552
Chi-ning (Jining) (*Shantung*)	265,248
Ch'i-t'ai-ho (Qitaihe)	214,957
Ch'i-tung (Qidong)	126,872
Chia-hsing (Jiaxing)	211,526
Chia-mu-ssu (Jiamusi)	493,409
Chiang-men (Jiangmen)	230,587
Chiang-yin (Jiangyin)	213,659
Chiang-yu (Jiangyou)	175,753
Chiao-hsien (Jiaoxian)	153,364
Chiao-nan (Jiaonan)	121,397
Chiao-tso (Jiaozuo)	409,100
Ch'ien-chiang (Qianjiang)	205,504
Ch'ih-feng (Chifeng)	350,077
Chin-ch'ang (Jinchang)	105,287
Chin-ch'eng (Jincheng)	136,396
Chin-chou (Jinzhou)	569,518
Ch'in-chou (Qinzhou)	114,586
Chin-hsi (Jinxi)	357,052
Chin-hua (Jinhua)	144,280
Ch'in-huang-tao (Qinhuangdao)	364,972
Ch'ing-chou (Qingzhou)	128,258
Ch'ing-tao (Qingdao)	1,459,195
Ching-te-chen (Jingdezhen)	281,183
Ch'ing-yüan (Qingyuan)	164,641
Chiu-chiang (Jiujiang)	291,187
Chiu-t'ai (Jiutai)	180,130
Chou-k'ou (Zhoukou)	146,288
Chou-shan (Zhoushan)	156,317
Chu-ch'eng (Zhucheng)	102,134
Ch'ü-ching (Qujing)	178,669
Ch'u-chou (Quzhou)	112,373
Chu-chou (Zhuzhou)	409,924
Chu-hai (Zhuhai)	164,747
Ch'u-hsien (Chuxian)	125,341
Chu-ma-tien (Zhumadian)	123,232
Ch'üan-chou (Quanzhou)	185,154
Chung-shan (Zhongshan)	278,829
Chungking (Chongqing)	2,266,772
Feng-ch'eng (Fengcheng)	193,784
Fo-shan (Foshan)	303,160
Fu-chin (Fujin)	103,104
Fu-chou (Fuzhou) (*Fukien*)	874,809
Fu-chou (Fuzhou) (*Kiangsi*)	121,949
Fu-hsin (Fuxin)	635,473
Fu-ling (Fuling)	173,878
Fu-shun (Fushun)	1,202,388
Fu-yang (Fuyang)	179,572
Fu-yü (Fuyu)	192,981
Ha-mi (Hami)	161,315
Hai-ch'eng (Haicheng)	205,560
Hai-k'ou (Haikou)	280,153
Hai-la-erh (Hailar)	180,650
Hai-lun (Kailun)	133,565
Hai-ning (Haining)	100,478
Han-chung (Hanzhong)	169,930
Han-tan (Handan)	837,552
Hang-chou (Hangzhou)	1,099,660
Harbin	2,443,398
Heng-shui (Hengshui)	104,269
Heng-yang (Hengyang)	487,148
Ho-fei (Hefei)	733,278
Ho-kang (Hegang)	522,747
Ho-pi (Hebi)	212,976
Ho-tse (Heze)	189,293
Ho-yuan (Heyuan)	120,101
Hsi-ch'ang (Xichang)	134,419
Hsi-ning (Xining)	551,776
Hsia-men (Xiamen)	368,786
Hsiang-fan (Xiangfan)	410,407
Hsiang-t'an (Xiangtan)	441,968
Hsiao-kan (Xiaogan)	166,280
Hsiao-shan (Xiaoshan)	162,930
Hsien-ning (Xianning)	136,811
Hsien-t'ao (Xiantao)	222,884
Hsien-yang (Xianyang)	352,125
Hsin-hsiang (Xinxiang)	473,762
Hsin-t'ai (Xintai)	281,248
Hsin-yang (Xinyang)	192,509
Hsin-yu (Xinyu)	173,524
Hsing-ch'eng (Xingcheng)	102,384
Hsing-hua (Xinghua)	161,910
Hsing-t'ai (Xingtai)	302,789
Hsü-ch'ang (Xuchang)	208,815
Hsü-chou (Xuzhou)	805,695
Hsuan-ch'eng (Xuancheng)	112,673
Hu-chou (Huzhou)	218,071
Hu-ho-hao-t'e (Hohhot)	652,534
Hua-tien (Huadian)	175,873
Huai-an (Huai'an)	131,149
Huai-hua (Huaihua)	126,785
Huai-nan (Huainan)	703,934
Huai-pei (Huaibei)	366,549
Huai-yin (Huaiyin)	239,675
Huang-shan (Huangshan)	102,628
Huang-shih (Huangshi)	457,601
Hui-chou (Huizhou)	161,023
Hun-chiang (Hunjiang)	482,043
Hung-hu (Honghu)	190,772
I-ch'ang (Yichang)	371,601
I-cheng (Yizheng)	109,268
I-ch'un (Yichun)	795,789
I-ch'un (Yichun) (*Kiangsi*)	151,585
I-hsing (Yixing)	200,824
I-ning (Yining)	177,193
I-pin (Yibin)	241,019
I-yang (Yiyang)	185,818
Jen-ch'iu (Renqiu)	114,256
Jih-chao (Rizhao)	185,048
Jui-an (Rui'an)	156,468
K'ai-feng (Kaifeng)	507,763
K'ai-li (Kaili)	113,958
K'ai-yuan (Kaiyuan)	124,219
Kan-chou (Ganzhou)	220,129
Kashgar (Kashi)	174,570
Ko-chiu (Gejiu)	214,294
K'o-la-ma-i (Karamay)	197,602
K'u-erh-le (Korla)	159,344
Kuang-shui (Guangshui)	102,770
Kuang-yüan (Guangyuan)	182,241
Kuei-hsien (Guixian)	114,025
Kuei-lin (Guilin)	364,130
K'uei-t'un (Kuitun)	118,553
Kuei-yang (Guiyang)	1,018,619
K'un-ming (Kunming)	1,127,411
K'un-shan (Kunshan)	102,052
Kung-chu-ling (Gongzhuling)	226,569
Lai-chou (Laizhou)	198,664
Lai-wu (Laiwu)	246,833
Lai-yang (Laiyang)	137,080
Lan-chou (Lanzhou)	1,194,640
Lang-fang (Langfang)	148,105
Lao-ho-k'ou (Laohekou)	123,366
Le-shan (Leshan)	341,128
Lei-yang (Leiyang)	130,115
Leng-shui-chiang (Lengshuijiang)	137,994
Lhasa	106,885
Li-ling (Liling)	108,504
Li-yang (Liyang)	109,520
Liang-ch'eng (Liangcheng)	156,307
Liao-ch'eng (Liaocheng)	207,844
Liao-yang (Liaoyang)	492,559
Liao-yüan (Liaoyuan)	354,141
Lien-yüan (Lianyuan)	118,858
Lien-yün-kang (Lianyungang)	354,139
Lin-ch'ing (Linqing)	123,958
Lin-fen (Linfen)	187,309
Lin-ho (Linhe)	133,183
Lin-i (Linyi)	324,720
Liu-chou (Liuzhou)	609,320
Liu-p'an-shui (Liupanshui)	363,954
Lo-ho (Luohe)	126,438
Lo-yang (Luoyang)	759,752
Long-yen (Longyan)	134,481
Lou-ti (Loudi)	128,418
Lu-an (Lu'an)	144,248
Lu-chou (Luzhou)	262,892
Lung-ching (Longjing)	139,417
Lung-k'ou (Longkou)	148,362
Ma-an-shan (Ma'anshan)	305,421
Man-chou-li (Manzhouli)	120,023
Mao-ming (Maoming)	178,683
Mei-ho-k'ou (Meihekou)	209,038
Mei-hsien (Meixian)	132,156
Mi-shan (Mishan)	132,744
Mien-yang (Mianyang)	262,947
Mu-tan-chiang (Mudanjiang)	571,705
Nan-ch'ang (Nanchang)	1,086,124
Nan-ch'ung (Nanchong)	180,273
Nan-ning (Nanning)	721,877
Nan-p'ing (Nanping)	195,064
Nan-t'ung (Nantong)	343,341
Nan-yang (Nanyang)	243,303
Nanking (Nanjing)	2,090,204
Nei-chiang (Neijiang)	256,012
Ning-po (Ningbo)	552,540
O-ch'eng (Echeng)	190,123
Pai-ch'eng (Baicheng)	217,987
Pai-yin (Baiyin)	204,970
P'an-chih-hua (Panzhihua) (Tu-k'ou [Dukou])	415,466
P'an-shan (Panshan)	362,773
Pang-pu (Bengbu)	449,245
Pao-chi (Baoji)	337,765
Pao-ting (Baoding)	483,155
Pao-t'ou (Baotou)	983,508
Pei-an (Bei'an)	204,899
Pei-hai (Beihai)	112,673
Pei-p'iao (Beipiao)	194,301
★ Peking (Beijing)	5,769,607
Pen-hsi (Benxi)	768,778
Pin-chou (Binzhou)	133,555
P'ing-hsiang (Pingxiang)	425,579
P'ing-ting-shan (Pingdingshan)	410,775
P'ing-tu (Pingdu)	150,123
Po-chou (Bozhou)	106,346
P'u-ch'i (Puqi)	117,264
P'u-yang (Puyang)	175,988
San-men-hsia (Sanmenxia)	120,523
San-ming (Sanming)	160,691
San-ya (Sanya)	102,820
Sha-shih (Shashi)	281,352
Shan-t'ou (Shantou)	578,630
Shan-wei (Shanwei)	107,847
Shao-hsing (Shaoxing)	179,818
Shao-kuan (Shaoguan)	350,043
Shao-yang (Shaoyang)	247,227
Shang-chih (Shangzhi)	215,373
Shang-ch'iu (Shangqiu)	164,880
Shang-jao (Shangrao)	132,455
Shanghai	7,496,509
Shen-chen (Shenzhen)	350,727
Shen-yang (Shenyang)	3,603,712
Shih-chia-chuang (Shijiazhuang)	1,068,439
Shih-ho-tzu (Shihezi)	299,676
Shih-shou (Shishou)	104,571
Shih-tsui-shan (Shizuishan)	257,862
Shih-yen (Shiyan)	273,786
Shuang-ch'eng (Shuangcheng)	142,659
Shuang-ya-shan (Shuangyashan)	386,081
Sian (Xi'an)	1,959,044
Ssu-p'ing (Siping)	317,223
Su-ch'ien (Suqian)	105,021
Su-chou (Suzhou) (*Anhwei*)	151,862
Su-chou (Suzhou) (*Kiangsu*)	706,459
Sui-hua (Suihua)	227,881
Sui-ning (Suining)	146,086
Ta-an (Da'an)	138,963
Ta-ch'ing (Daqing)	657,297
Ta-hsien (Daxian)	188,101
Ta-li (Dali)	136,554
Ta-lien (Dalian)	1,723,302
Ta-t'ung (Datong)	798,319
T'ai-an (Tai'an)	350,696
T'ai-chou (Taizhou)	152,442
T'ai-yüan (Taiyuan)	1,533,884
Tan-chiang (Danjiang)	103,211
Tan-tung (Dandong)	523,699
Tan-yang (Danyang)	169,603
T'ang-shan (Tangshan)	1,044,194
T'ao-nan (Taonan)	150,168
Te-chou (Dezhou)	195,485
Te-yang (Deyang)	182,488
T'eng-hsien (Tengxian)	315,083
T'ieh-fa (Tiefa)	131,807
T'ieh-li (Tieli)	265,683
T'ieh-ling (Tieling)	254,842
T'ien-men (Tianmen)	186,332
T'ien-shui (Tianshui)	244,974
Tientsin (Tianjin)	4,574,689
Tsa-lan-t'un (Zalantun)	130,031
Ts'ang-chou (Cangzhou)	242,708
Tsao-chuang (Zaozhuang)	380,846
Tsao-yang (Zaoyang)	162,198
Tsitsihar (Qiqihar)	1,070,051
Tsun-i (Zunyi)	261,862
Tu-chiang-yen (Dujiangyan)	123,357
Tu-yun (Duyun)	132,971
Tun-hua (Dunhua)	235,100
T'ung-ch'uan (Tongchuan)	280,657
T'ung-hua (Tonghua)	324,600
Tung-kuan (Dongguan)	308,669
T'ung-liao (Tongliao)	255,129
T'ung-ling (Tongling)	228,017
Tung-t'ai (Dongtai)	192,247
Tung-ying (Dongying)	281,728
Tz'u-hsi (Cixi)	107,329
Tzu-hsing (Zixing)	110,048
Tzu-kung (Zigong)	393,184
Tzu-po (Zibo)	1,138,074
Wa-fang-tien (Wafangdian)	251,733
Wan-hsien (Wanxian)	156,823
Wei-fang (Weifang)	428,522
Wei-hai (Weihai)	128,888
Wei-nan (Weinan)	140,169
Wen-chou (Wenzhou)	401,871
Wen-teng (Wendeng)	133,910
Wu-chou (Wuzhou)	210,452
Wu-hai (Wuhai)	264,081
Wu-han (Wuhan)	3,284,229
Wu-hsi (Wuxi)	826,833
Wu-hu (Wuhu)	425,740
Wu-lan-hao-t'e (Ulanhot)	159,538
Wu-lu-mu-ch'i (Ürümqi)	1,046,898
Wu-wei (Wuwei)	133,101
Ya-k'o-she (Yakeshi)	377,869
Yang-chiang (Yangjiang)	215,196
Yang-chou (Yangzhou)	312,892
Yang-ch'üan (Yangquan)	362,268
Yen-an (Yan'an)	113,277
Yen-ch'eng (Yancheng)	296,831
Yen-chi (Yanji)	230,892
Yen-t'ai (Yantai)	452,127
Yin-ch'uan (Yinchuan)	356,652
Ying-k'ou (Yingkou)	421,589
Yü-lin (Yulin)	144,467
Yü-men (Yumen)	109,234
Yü-shu (Yushu)	131,861
Yü-tz'u (Yuci)	191,356
Yu-yao (Yuyao)	114,065
Yüan-chiang (Yuanjiang)	107,004
Yüeh-yang (Yueyang)	302,800
Yun-ch'eng (Yuncheng)	108,359
Yung-an (Yong'an)	111,762

Major cities and national capitals (continued)

country city	population
Colombia (1992 est.)	
Armenia	212,300
Barrancabermeja	137,406[9]
Barranquilla	1,018,800
Bello	208,439[9]
Bucaramanga	349,400
Buenaventura	174,397[9]
Cali	1,624,400
Cartagena	688,300
Cúcuta	450,300
Florencia	108,300
Floridablanca	137,975[9]
Ibagué	334,100
Itagüí	137,215[9]
Manizales	327,100
Medellín	1,581,400
Montería	265,800
Neiva	232,600
Palmira	185,224[9]
Pasto	303,400
Pereira	336,000
Popayán	203,800
Quibdó	119,000
Ríohacha	126,300
Santa Marta	286,500
★ Santafé de Bogotá, D.C.	4,921,300
Sincelejo	167,600
Soledad	169,681[9]
Tuluá	101,699[9]
Tunja	112,400
Valledupar	251,600
Villavicencio	233,000
Comoros (1988 est.)	
★ Moroni	22,000
Congo (1992 est.)	
★ Brazzaville	937,579
Pointe-Noire	576,206
Costa Rica (1992 est.)	
★ San José	302,574
Côte d'Ivoire (1984 est.)	
★ Abidjan	1,850,000
Bouaké	220,000
Yamoussoukro	120,000
Croatia (1991)	
Osijek	129,792
Rijeka	167,964
Split	200,459
★ Zagreb	867,865
Cuba (1990 est.)	
Bayamo	125,021
Camagüey	283,008
Cienfuegos	123,600
Guantánamo	200,381
★ Havana	2,096,054
Holguín	228,052
Las Tunas	119,400
Manzanillo	107,650
Matanzas	113,724
Pinar del Río	121,774
Santa Clara	194,354
Santiago de Cuba	405,354
Cyprus (1991 est.)[4]	
Limassol	129,700
★ Nicosia	166,500[10]
Czech Republic (1991)	
Brno	387,986
Liberec	101,934
Olomouc	105,690
Ostrava	327,553
Plzen	173,129
★ Prague	1,212,010
Denmark (1992 est.)	
Ålborg	114,970
Århus	204,139
★ Copenhagen	1,339,395[4]
Odense	140,886
Djibouti (1988 est.)	
★ Djibouti	290,000
Dominica (1991)	
★ Roseau	15,853
Dominican Republic (1989 est.)	
La Romana	136,000
La Vega	189,000
San Pedro de Macorís	137,000
Santiago de los Caballeros	467,000
★ Santo Domingo	2,200,000
Ecuador (1990)	
Ambato	124,166
Cuenca	194,981
Guayaquil	1,508,444
Machala	144,197
Manta	125,505
Portoviejo	132,937
★ Quito	1,100,847
Santo Domingo	114,422
Egypt (1991 est.)	
Alexandria	3,295,000
Aswān	215,000
Asyūṭ	313,000
Banhā	133,000
Banī Suwayf	174,000
Būr Saʿīd (Port Said)	449,000
★ Cairo	6,663,000
Damanhūr	216,000
al-Fayyūm	244,000
Hulwan (Helwan)	352,300[11]
al-Ismāʿīlīyah	247,000
al-Jīzah (Giza)	2,096,000
Kafr ad-Dawwar	221,000
Kafr ash-Shaykh	102,910[12]
al-Maḥallah al-Kubrā	400,000
al-Manṣūrah	362,000
al-Minyā	203,000
Qinā	137,000
Sawhāj	152,000
Shibīn al-Kawm	153,000
Shubrā al-Khaymah	812,000
as-Suways (Suez)	376,000
Ṭanṭā	372,000
al-Uqṣur (Luxor)	142,000
az-Zaqāzīq	279,000
El Salvador (1992; MU)	
Mejicanos	117,568[13]
Nueva San Salvador	116,575
San Miguel	182,817
★ San Salvador	422,570
Santa Ana	202,337
Soyapango	104,470[13]
Equatorial Guinea (1983)	
★ Malabo	31,630
Eritrea (1989 est.)	
★ Asmera	342,706
Estonia (1992 est.)	
★ Tallinn	471,608
Tartu	113,410
Ethiopia (1989 est.)	
★ Addis Ababa	1,732,080
Dire Dawa	121,887
Faeroe Islands (1993 est.)	
★ Tórshavn	16,091
Fiji (1986)	
★ Suva	69,665
Finland (1993 est.)	
Espoo	178,899
★ Helsinki	501,741
Oulu	103,540
Tampere	175,202
Turku	160,320
Vantaa	159,462
France (1990)	
Aix-en-Provence	126,854
Amiens	136,234
Angers	146,163
Besançon	119,194
Bordeaux	213,274
Boulogne-Billancourt	101,971
Brest	153,099
Caen	115,624
Clermont-Ferrand	140,167
Dijon	151,636
Grenoble	153,973
Le Havre	197,219
Le Mans	148,465
Lille	178,301
Limoges	136,407
Lyon	422,444
Marseille	807,726
Metz	123,920
Montpellier	210,866
Mulhouse	109,905
Nancy	102,410
Nantes	252,029
Nice	345,674
Nîmes	133,607
Orléans	107,965
★ Paris	2,175,200
Perpignan	108,049
Reims	185,164
Rennes	203,533
Rouen	105,470
Saint-Étienne	201,569
Strasbourg	255,937
Toulon	170,167
Toulouse	365,933
Tours	133,403
Villeurbanne	119,848
French Guiana (1990)	
★ Cayenne	41,659
French Polynesia (1988)	
★ Papeete	23,555
Gabon (1988 est.)	
★ Libreville	352,000
Port-Gentil	164,000
Gambia, The (1986 est.)	
★ Banjul	44,188[14]
Serekunda	102,600
Gaza Strip (1988 est.)	
Gaza (Ghazzah)	57,000
Georgia (1991 est.)	
Batumi	137,500
Kutaisi	238,200
Rustavi	161,900
Sukhumi	120,000
★ Tbilisi	1,279,000
Germany (1992 est.)	
Aachen	244,442
Augsburg	259,884
Bergisch Gladbach	104,470
Berlin	3,466,031
Bielefeld	322,132
Bochum	398,578
★ Bonn	296,244
Bottrop	118,758
Braunschweig	259,127
Bremen	552,746
Bremerhaven	130,938
Chemnitz	287,511
Cologne (Köln)	956,690
Cottbus	123,321
Darmstadt	140,040
Dortmund	601,007
Dresden	485,132
Duisburg	537,441
Düsseldorf	577,561
Erfurt	204,912
Erlangen	102,433
Essen	626,989
Frankfurt am Main	654,079
Freiburg im Breisgau	193,775
Fürth	105,297
Gelsenkirchen	293,839
Gera	126,521
Göttingen	124,331
Hagen	214,085
Halle	303,019
Hamburg	1,668,757
Hamm	180,323
Hannover	517,476
Heidelberg	139,392
Heilbronn	117,427
Herne	179,137
Hildesheim	105,674
Ingolstadt	107,375
Jena	100,967
Kaiserslautern	100,541
Karlsruhe	278,579
Kassel	196,828
Kiel	247,107
Koblenz	109,046
Krefeld	245,772
Leipzig	503,191
Leverkusen	161,147
Lübeck	215,999
Ludwigshafen	165,368
Magdeburg	275,238
Mainz	182,867
Mannheim	314,685
Moers	105,322
Mönchengladbach	262,581
Mülheim an der Ruhr	177,042
Munich (München)	1,229,052
Münster	264,181
Neuss	147,663
Nürnberg	497,496
Oberhausen	224,659
Offenbach am Main	115,790
Oldenburg	145,161
Osnabrück	165,143
Paderborn	125,730
Pforzheim	115,547
Potsdam	139,025
Recklingshausen	125,966
Regensburg	123,002
Remscheid	123,618
Reutlingen	105,835
Rostock	244,452
Saarbrücken	192,030
Salzgitter	115,381
Schwerin	125,959
Siegen	110,374
Solingen	165,924
Stuttgart	591,946
Ulm	112,173
Wiesbaden	264,022
Witten	105,242
Wolfsburg	128,995
Wuppertal	385,463
Würzburg	128,512
Zwickau	112,565
Ghana (1988 est.)	
★ Accra	949,113
Kumasi	385,192
Sekondi-Takoradi	103,653
Tamale	151,069
Tema	109,975
Gibraltar (1993 est.)	
★ Gibraltar	29,100[15]
Greece (1991)	
★ Athens	748,110
Iráklion	117,167
Kallithéa	110,738
Larissa	113,426
Pátrai (Patras)	155,180
Peristérion	145,854
Piraiévs (Piraeus)	169,622
Thessaloníki	377,951
Greenland (1993 est.)	
★ Nuuk (Godthåb)	12,653
Grenada (1991)	
★ Saint George's	4,439
Guadeloupe (1990)	
★ Basse-Terre	14,107
Guam (1990)	
★ Agana	1,139
Guatemala (1993 est.; MU)	
★ Guatemala City	1,132,730
Mixco	390,441
Villa Nueva	144,123
Guernsey (1991)	
★ St. Peter Port	16,648
Guinea (1983)	
★ Conakry	705,280
Guinea-Bissau (1988 est.)	
★ Bissau	125,000
Guyana (1986 est.)	
★ Georgetown	150,368
Haiti (1992 est.)	
Carrefour	241,223
Delmas	200,251
★ Port-au-Prince	752,600
Honduras (1990 est.; MU)	
San Pedro Sula	321,197
★ Tegucigalpa	608,100[16]
Hong Kong (1993 est.)	
Hong Kong	5,932,000[15]
Hungary (1992 est.)	
★ Budapest	2,015,955
Debrecen	216,137
Győr	130,293
Kecskemét	104,563
Miskolc	192,355
Nyíregyháza	114,955
Pécs	170,542
Szeged	177,679
Székesfehérvár	109,311
Iceland (1992 est.)	
★ Reykjavík	100,850
India (1991)	
Abohar	107,016
Ādoni	135,718
Agartala	157,636
Āgra	899,195
Ahmadābād	2,872,865
Ahmadnagar	181,015
Āizawl	154,343
Ajmer	401,930
Akola	327,946
Alandur	125,009
Alīgarh	479,978
Allahābād	806,447
Alleppey	174,606
Alwar	206,107
Ambāla	119,535
Ambattur	223,332
Amrāvati	433,746
Amritsar	709,456
Amroha	136,893
Anand	110,144
Anantapur	174,792
Āra (Arrah)	156,871
Āsānsol	261,836
Aurangābād	572,634
Āvadi	180,291
Baharampur	115,036
Bahraich	135,352
Bally	181,978
Bālurghāt	119,829
Bangalore	2,650,659
Bānkura	114,927
Barāhanagar	223,770
Bārāsat	107,365
Barddhamān (Burdwān)	244,789
Bareilly	583,473
Barrackpore	133,429
Basīrhāt	101,652
Bathinda (Bhatinda)	159,144
Beāwar	105,357
Belgaum	325,639
Bellary	245,758
Bhāgalpur	254,993
Bharatpur	148,506
Bharūch (Broach)	132,312
Bhātpāra	304,298
Bhāvnagar	400,636
Bhilainagar	389,601
Bhīlwāra	183,791
Bhīmavaram	125,495
Bhind	109,731
Bhiwandi	378,546
Bhiwāni	121,449
Bhopāl	1,063,662
Bhubaneshwar	411,542
Bhusāwal	144,804
Bīd (Bhīr)	112,351
Bīdar	107,542
Bihār Sharīf	200,976
Bijāpur	186,846
Bīkaner	415,355
Bilāspur	190,911
Bokāro	350,540
Bombay (Greater)	9,909,547
Brahmapur	210,585
Budaun	116,706
Bulandshahr	126,737
Burhānpur	172,809
Burnpur	174,704
Calcutta	4,388,262
Calicut (Kozhikode)	419,531
Chandannagar	122,351
Chandīgarh	502,992
Chandrapur	225,841
Chhapra	136,824
Chittoor	133,233
Cochin	564,038
Coimbatore	853,402
Cuddalore	143,774
Cuddapah	121,422
Cuttack	402,390
Darbhanga	218,274
Dāvangere	265,971
Dehra Dūn	270,028
Delhi	7,174,755
Dewās	163,699
Dhānbād	151,334
Dhūle (Dhūlia)	277,957
Dibrugarh	118,374
Dindigul	182,293
Durg	150,513
Durgāpur	415,986
Elūru	212,918
Erode	158,774
Etāwah	124,032
Faizābād	125,012
Farīdābād	613,828
Farrukhābād-cum-Fatehgarh	193,624
Fatehpur	117,203
Fīrozābād	215,089
Gadag-Betigeri	133,918
Gāndhīdhām	104,392
Gāndhīnagar	121,746
Gangānagar	161,377
Gaya	291,220
Ghāziābād	460,949
Gonda	106,078
Gondia	109,271
Gorakhpur	489,850
Gudivāda	101,635
Gulbarga	303,139
Guna	100,389

country city	population
Guntakal	107,560
Guntūr	471,020
Gurgaon	120,790
Guwāhāti (Gauhāti)	577,591
Gwalior	692,982
Hābra	100,142
Haldīa	100,109
Haldwāni-cum-Kāthgodam	102,744
Hālisahar	113,670
Hāpur	146,591
Haridwār (Hardwār)	148,882
Hāthras	113,653
Hindupur	104,635
Hisār (Hissār)	172,873
Hoshiārpur	122,528
Howrah (Hāora)	946,732
Hubli-Dhārwād	647,640
Hugli-Chunchura	142,388
Hyderābād	2,991,884
Ichalkaranji	214,835
Imphāl	196,268
Indore	1,086,673
Ingrāj Bāzār	139,018
Jabalpur	739,961
Jaipur	1,454,678
Jalandhar (Jullundur)	519,530
Jalgaon	241,603
Jālna	174,958
Jammu	206,135[11]
Jāmnagar	325,475
Jamshedpur	461,212
Jaunpur	136,287
Jhānsi	301,304
Jodhpur	648,621
Jūnāgadh	130,132
Kākināda	279,875
Kalyān	1,014,062
Kāmārhāti	266,625
Kānchipuram	145,028
Kānchrāpāra	100,059
Kānpur	1,958,282
Karīmnagar	148,349
Karnāl	173,742
Katihār	135,348
Khammam	127,812
Khandwa	145,111
Kharagpur	189,010
Kolhāpur	405,118
Kota	536,444
Krishnanagar	120,918
Kukatpalle	185,378
Kulti-Barākar	108,930
Kumbakonam	139,449
Kurnool	236,313
Lātūr	197,164
Lucknow	1,592,010
Ludhiāna	1,012,062
Machilīpatnam (Masulipatam)	159,007
Madras	3,795,028
Madurai	951,696
Mahbūbnagar	116,775
Mālegaon	342,431
Mālkājgiri	126,066
Mandya	119,970
Mangalore	272,819
Māngo	110,024
Mathura	226,850
Maunāth Bhanjan	136,447
Medinīpur (Midnāpore)	125,098
Meerut	752,078
Miraj	121,564
Mirzāpur-cum-Vindhyāchal	169,368
Modinagar	102,307
Moga	108,213
Morādābād	416,836
Morena	147,095
Munger (Monghyr)	150,042
Murwāra (Katni)	163,699
Muzaffarnagar	240,057
Muzaffarpur	240,450
Mysore	480,006
Nadiād	166,852
Nāgercoil	189,482
Nāgpur	1,622,225
Naihāti	132,032
Nānded	274,626
Nandyāl	120,171
Nāshik (Nāsik)	646,896
Navadwīp	125,247
Navsāri	125,980
Nellore	316,445
★ New Delhi	294,149
Neyveli	117,471
Nizāmābād	240,924
Noida	167,440
North Barrackpore	100,513
North Dum Dum	151,298
Ongole	100,544
Pālghāt	122,964
Pāli	136,797
Pallavaram	111,194
Pānihāti	275,359
Pānīpat	191,010
Parbhani	190,235
Pathānkot	142,862
Patiāla	253,341
Patna	916,980
Pīlībhīt	106,329
Pimpri-Chinchwad	515,962
Pondicherry	202,648
Porbandar	116,546
Proddatūr	133,860
Pune	1,559,558
Puri	124,835
Pūsa	122,086
Quilon	139,717
Qutubullapur	105,380
Rāe Bareli	130,101
Rāichūr	157,477
Rāiganj	151,454
Raipur	437,887
Rāj Nāndgaon	125,394
Rājahmundry	326,071
Rājapālaiyam	114,042
Rājkot	556,137
Rāmagundam	213,962
Rāmpur	242,752
Rānchi	598,498
Ratlām	183,370
Raurkela Steel Township	215,489
Rewa	128,918
Rishra	102,649
Rohtak	215,844
Sāgar	195,106
Sahāranpur	373,904
Salem	363,934
Sambalpur	130,766
Sambhal	150,012
Sāngli	193,181
Satna	156,321
Shāhjahānpur	237,663
Shāntipur	109,911
Shiliguri (Silīguri)	226,677
Shillong	130,691
Shimoga	178,882
Shivpuri	108,271
Sholāpur (Solapur)	603,870
Shrīrāmpur	137,087
Sīkar	148,235
Silchar	115,045
Sirsa	112,542
Sitāpur	120,595
Sonīpat	142,992
South Dum Dum	230,507
Srīnagar	586,038[11]
Sūrat	1,496,943
Surendranagar	105,973
Tāmbaram	106,590
Tellicherry	103,577
Tenāli	143,836
Thāne (Thāna)	796,620
Thanjāvūr	200,216
Tiruchchirāppalli	386,628
Tirunelveli	135,762
Tirupati	174,393
Tirupper (Tiruppūr)	235,076
Tiruvannāmalai	108,291
Tiruvottiyūr	167,851
Titāgarh	113,831
Tonk	100,020
Trivandrum	523,733
Tumkūr	138,598
Tuticorin	205,105
Udaipur	307,682
Ujjain	366,787
Ulhāsnagar	368,822
Uluberia	155,188
Unnāo	107,246
Uttarpāra-Kotrung	100,867
Vadodara (Baroda)	1,021,084
Vārānasi (Benares)	925,962
Vellore	172,467
Vijayawāda	701,351
Vishākhapatnam	750,024
Vizianagaram	159,461
Warangal	446,760
Wardha	102,974
Yamunanagar	144,250
Yavatmāl (Yeotmāl)	108,591
Indonesia (1990)	
Ambon	206,260
Balikpapan	309,492
Banda Aceh	143,409
Bandar Lampung	458,215
Bandung	2,026,893
Banjarmasin	443,738
Bengkulu	146,439
Binjai	127,222
Blitar	113,064
Bogor	271,711
Cilacap	113,893[17]
Cimahi	105,940[17]
Cirebon	245,307
Denpasar	261,263[17]
★ Jakarta	8,259,266
Jambi	301,359
Jayapura	149,618[17]
Jember	140,105[17]
Kediri	235,602
Madiun	165,999
Magelang	123,213
Malang	650,295
Manado	275,374
Mataram	141,387[17]
Medan	1,685,972
Padang	477,344
Palembang	1,084,483
Pangkal Pinang	108,411
Pasuruan	134,019
Pekalongan	227,535
Pekanbaru	341,328
Pematangsiantar	203,834
Pontianak	387,112
Probolinggo	131,291
Purwokerto	105,395[17]
Samarinda	335,016
Semarang	1,005,316
Sukabumi	119,981
Sumba	355,073[17]
Surabaya	2,421,016
Surakarta	504,176
Tanjung Balai	102,095
Tanjung Karang-Telukbetung	284,275[17]
Tasikmalaya	165,297[17]
Tebing Tinggi	116,767
Tegal	225,770
Ujung Pandang	913,196
Yogyakarta	412,392
Iran (1986)	
Ahvāz	579,826
Āmol	118,242
Arāk	265,349
Ardabīl	281,973
Bābol	115,320
Bākhtarān	560,514
Bandar 'Abbās	201,642
Bandar-e Būshehr	120,787
Borūjerd	183,879
Dezfūl	151,420
Eṣfahān (Isfahan)	986,753
Gorgān	139,430
Hamadān	272,499
Islāmshahr (Eslāmshahr)	215,129
Karaj	275,100
Kāshān	138,599
Kermān	257,284
Khomeynīshahr	104,647
Khorramābād	208,592
Khvoy	115,343
Malāyer	103,640
Marāgheh	100,679
Mashhad (Meshed)	1,463,508
Masjed-e Soleymān	104,787
Najafābād	129,058
Neyshābūr	109,285
Orūmīyeh	300,746
Qā'emshahr	109,288
Qazvīn	248,591
Qom	543,139
Rājaishahr	117,852
Rasht	290,897
Sabzevār	129,103
Sanandaj	204,537
Sārī	141,020
Shīrāz	848,289
Tabrīz	971,482
★ Tehrān	6,042,584
Yazd	230,483
Zāhedān	281,923
Zanjān	215,261
Iraq (1985 est.)	
al-'Amārah	131,758
★ Baghdad	3,841,268[18]
Ba'qūbah	114,516
Basra	616,700
al-Ḥillah	215,249
Irbīl	333,903
Karbalā'	184,574
Kirkūk	570,000[19]
Mosul	570,926
an-Najaf	242,603
an-Nāṣirīyah	138,842
ar-Ramādī	137,388
as-Sulaymānīyah	279,424
Ireland (1991)	
Cork	127,024
★ Dublin	477,675
Isle of Man (1991)	
★ Douglas	22,214
Israel (1992 est.)	
Bat Yam	146,400
Beersheba (Be'er Sheva')	128,400
Bene Beraq	121,200
Haifa (Ḥefa)	251,000
Ḥolon	161,800
★ Jerusalem (Yerushalayim, Al-Quds)	544,200
Netanya	139,700
Petaḥ Tiqwa	148,900
Ramat Gan	122,700
Rishon le-Ẕiyyon	145,600
Tel Aviv–Yafo	353,200
Italy (1991 est.; MU)	
Ancona	103,268
Bari	353,032
Bergamo	117,886
Bologna	411,803
Bolzano	100,380
Brescia	196,766
Cagliari	211,719
Catania	364,176
Catanzaro	103,802
Cosenza	104,483
Ferrara	140,600
Florence (Firenze)	408,403
Foggia	159,541
Forlì	109,755
Genoa (Genova)	701,032
La Spezia	103,008
Latina	103,630
Lecce	102,344
Livorno	171,265
Messina	274,846
Milan (Milano)	1,432,184
Modena	177,501
Monza	123,188
Naples (Napoli)	1,206,013
Novara	103,349
Padua (Padova)	218,186
Palermo	734,238
Parma	173,991
Perugia	150,576
Pescara	128,553
Piacenza	103,536
Pisa	101,500
Prato	166,688
Ravenna	136,724
Reggio di Calabria	178,496
Reggio nell'Emilia	131,880
Rimini	130,896
★ Rome (Roma)	2,791,354
Salerno	151,374
Sassari	120,011
Siracusa	125,444
Taranto	244,033
Terni	109,809
Torre del Greco	102,647
Trento	102,124
Trieste	231,047
Turin (Torino)	991,870
Venice (Venezia)	317,837
Verona	258,946
Vicenza	109,333
Jamaica (1991)	
★ Kingston	103,771
Japan (1992 est.)	
Abiko	122,232
Ageo	200,701
Aizuwakamatsu	119,123
Akashi	278,458
Akishima	106,939
Akita	305,726
Amagasaki	497,333
Anjō	146,770
Aomori	287,354
Asahikawa	361,736
Asaka	106,524
Ashikaga	167,696
Atsugi	203,775
Beppu	129,882
Chiba	841,914
Chigasaki	207,237
Chōfu	199,647
Daitō	127,130
Ebetsu	102,815
Ebina	109,483
Fuchu	213,554
Fuji	226,587
Fujieda	122,322
Fujinomiya	118,735
Fujisawa	358,757
Fukui	254,008
Fukuoka	1,261,658
Fukushima	280,958
Fukuyama	369,401
Funabashi	537,614
Gifu	409,928
Habikino	116,225
Hachinohe	241,086
Hachiōji	481,548
Hadano	160,146
Hakodate	306,465
Handa	102,976
Hamamatsu	557,881
Higashi-Kurume	113,375
Higashi-Murayama	136,343
Higashi-Ōsaka	516,333
Hikone	101,476
Himeji	460,627
Hino	167,436
Hirakata	394,935
Hiratsuka	250,280
Hirosaki	174,921
Hiroshima	1,096,919
Hitachi	202,380
Hōfu	118,833
Ibaraki	254,915
Ichihara	267,004
Ichikawa	446,897
Ichinomiya	264,990
Ikeda	104,268
Ikoma	102,325
Imabari	121,874
Iruma	141,093
Ise	103,448
Isesaki	118,679
Ishinomaki	121,550
Itami	186,650
Iwaki	357,932
Iwakuni	109,047
Iwatsuki	108,512
Izumi	147,514
Joetsu	130,503
Kadoma	142,317
Kagoshima	537,775
Kakamigahara	131,494
Kakogawa	246,357
Kamakura	173,492
Kanazawa	445,522
Kariya	123,800
Kashihara	117,366
Kashiwa	312,690
Kasugai	270,927
Kasukabe	193,900
Katsuta	112,650
Kawachi-Nagano	112,180
Kawagoe	311,605
Kawaguchi	448,142
Kawanishi	141,743
Kawasaki	1,195,464
Kiryū	124,556
Kisarazu	125,682
Kishiwada	188,997
Kita-Kyūshū	1,020,877
Kitami	108,206
Kobe	1,499,195
Kochi	318,009
Kodaira	168,698
Kofu	200,611
Koganei	107,716
Kokubunji	103,157
Komaki	131,837
Komatsu	106,546
Koriyama	320,209
Koshigaya	291,399
Kumagaya	155,118
Kumamoto	636,144
Kurashiki	416,703
Kure	213,474
Kurume	231,825
Kushiro	203,314
Kyōto	1,456,527
Machida	355,843
Maebashi	288,410
Matsubara	134,858
Matsudo	461,438
Matsue	144,262
Matsumoto	202,998
Matsuyama	450,796
Matsuzaka	119,575
Minakoyojō	130,436
Minō	124,251
Misato	132,317
Mishima	106,934
Mitaka	166,644
Mito	246,600
Miyazaki	291,036
Moriguchi	156,602
Morioka	281,870
Muroran	116,192
Musashino	138,452
Nagano	350,673
Nagaoka	187,635
Nagareyama	144,335
Nagasaki	442,373
Nagoya	2,162,007
Naha	302,357
Nara	353,726
Narashino	153,791
Neyagawa	257,810
Niigata	488,654
Niihama	128,996
Niiza	141,420
Nishinomiya	425,711
Nobeoka	128,894
Noda	117,155
Numazu	212,724
Obihiro	169,803
Odawara	196,011
Ōgaki	149,439
Ōita	417,051
Okayama	601,094
Okazaki	315,633
Okinawa	108,588
Ōme	132,238
Ōmiya	416,421
Ōmuta	147,994
Ōsaka	2,603,272
Ōta	142,949
Otaru	162,148
Ōtsu	265,313
Oyama	146,487
Saga	170,145

Major cities and national capitals (continued)

country city	population
Sagamihara	551,762
Sakai	808,084
Sakata	100,744
Sakura	152,826
Sapporo	1,716,624
Sasebo	245,017
Sayama	160,558
Sendai	941,794
Seto	127,329
Shimizu	474,388
Shimonoseki	260,692
Shizuoka	474,388
Sōka	210,410
Suita	342,020
Suzuka	178,008
Tachikawa	154,901
Takamatsu	330,568
Takaoka	175,413
Takarazuka	204,552
Takasaki	238,043
Takatsuki	360,748
Tama	148,148
Tokorozawa	311,654
Tokushima	264,503
Tokuyama	110,232
★ Tokyo	8,129,377
Tomakomai	164,484
Tondabayashi	115,579
Tottori	144,161
Toyama	323,015
Toyohashi	346,741
Toyokawa	113,527
Toyonaka	406,126
Toyota	340,621
Tsu	161,436
Tsuchiura	130,369
Tsukuba	149,944
Ube	175,505
Ueda	120,717
Uji	181,195
Urawa	434,976
Urayasu	120,789
Utsunomiya	432,633
Wakayama	396,171
Yachiyo	152,463
Yaizu	113,857
Yamagata	250,620
Yamaguchi	131,161
Yamato	201,200
Yao	277,071
Yatsushiro	107,807
Yokkaichi	280,523
Yokohama	3,298,897
Yokosuka	435,846
Yonago	132,167
Zama	116,000
Jersey (1991)	
★ St. Helier	28,123
Jordan (1990 est.)	
★ Amman	1,213,300
Irbid	314,680
as-Salṭ	162,850
az-Zarqā'	514,980
Kazakhstan (1991 est.)	
Aktyubinsk	266,600
★ Alma-Ata (Almaty)	1,156,200
Aqtau (Shevchenko)	169,000
Atyrau (Guryev)	156,700
Chimkent	438,800
Dzhambul	312,300
Dzhezkazgan	111,100
Ekibastuz	138,900
Karaganda	608,600
Kokchetav	143,300
Kustanay	233,900
Kzyl-Orda	158,200
Pavlodar	342,500
Petropavlovsk	248,300
Rudny	128,800
Semipalatinsk	344,700
Taldy-Kurgan	136,100
Temirtau	213,100
Tselinograd	286,000
Uralsk	214,000
Ust-Kamenogorsk	332,900
Kenya (1984 est.)	
Kisumu	167,100
Mombasa	425,600
★ Nairobi	1,504,900[20]
Nakuru	101,700
Kiribati (1990)	
★ Bairiki	2,226
Korea, North (1987 est.)	
Anju	186,000
Ch'ŏngjin	520,000
Haeju	195,000
Hamhŭng-Hungnam	701,000
Hŭich'ŏn	163,000
Kaesŏng	120,000
Kanggye	211,000
Kimch'aek (Songjin)	179,000
Kusŏng	177,000
Namp'o	370,000
★ P'yŏngyang	2,355,000
Sinp'o	158,000
Sinŭiju	289,000
Sunch'ŏn	356,000
Tanch'ŏn	284,000
Tŏkch'ŏn	217,000
Wŏnsan	274,000
Korea, South (1990)	
Andong	116,958
Ansan	252,418
Anyang	481,291
Ch'angwŏn	323,223
Cheju	232,643
Chinhae	120,212
Chinju	255,695
Ch'ŏnan	211,363
Ch'ŏngju	477,783
Chŏnju	517,059
Ch'unch'ŏn	174,224
Ch'ungju	128,425
Hanam	101,325
Inch'ŏn	1,817,919
Iri	203,382
Kangnŭng	152,678
Kimhae	106,206
Kumi	206,121
Kunp'o	100,059
Kunsan	218,205
Kuri	109,374
Kwangju	1,139,003
Kwangmyŏng	328,593
Kyŏngju	141,896
Masan	493,731
Mokp'o	243,064
P'ohang	317,768
Puch'ŏn	667,993
Pusan	3,798,113
★ Seoul (Sŏul)	10,612,577
Shihŭng	107,176
Sŏngnam	540,754
Sunch'ŏn	167,214
Suwŏn	644,805
Taegu	2,229,040
Taejŏn	1,049,578
Ŭijŏngbu	212,352
Ulsan	682,411
Wŏnju	162,415
Yŏsu	173,169
Kuwait (1985)	
Ḥawallī	145,215
★ Kuwait (al-Kuwayt)	44,224
as-Sālimīyah	153,220
Kyrgyzstan (1991 est.)	
★ Bishkek (Frunze)	641,400
Osh	238,200
Laos (1990 est.; MU)	
★ Vientiane	442,000
Latvia (1992 est.)	
Daugavpils	127,279
Liepāja	113,815
★ Rīga	897,078
Lebanon (1985 est.)	
★ Beirut (Bayrūt)	1,910,000[4, 20]
an-Nabaṭīyah	100,000
Sidon (Ṣaydā)	100,000
Tripoli (Ṭarābulus)	500,000
Zaḥlah	200,000
Lesotho (1986)	
★ Maseru	109,382[4]
Liberia (1984)	
★ Monrovia	421,058
Libya (1988 est.)	
Banghāzī	446,250
Misrātah	121,669
★ Tripoli (Ṭarābulus)	591,062
Liechtenstein (1992 est.)	
★ Vaduz	4,887
Lithuania (1993 est.)	
Kaunas	429,000
Klaipėda	206,400
Panevėžys	132,000
Šiauliai	147,800
★ Vilnius	590,100
Luxembourg (1991)	
★ Luxembourg	75,622
Macau (1991)	
★ Macau (Santo Nome de Deus)	326,460
Macedonia (1991; MU)	
Bitola	122,173
Giostivar	116,107
Kumanovo	135,529
★ Skopje (Skopije)	563,301
Tetovo	180,654
Madagascar (1990 est.)	
★ Antananarivo	802,390
Fianarantsoa	124,489
Mahajanga	121,967
Toamasina	145,431
Malaŵi (1987)	
Blantyre	333,120
★ Lilongwe (administrative)	223,318
★ Zomba (legislative)	43,250
Malaysia (1980)	
George Town (Pinang)	248,241
Ipoh	293,849
Johor Baharu	246,395
Kelang	192,080
Kota Baharu	167,872
★ Kuala Lumpur	565,329
Kuala Terengganu	180,296
Kuantan	131,547
Petaling Jaya	207,805
Port Kelang	192,080
Seremban	132,911
Taiping	146,002
Maldives (1990)	
★ Male	55,130
Mali (1992 est.)	
★ Bamako	745,787
Malta (1992 est.)	
★ Valletta	9,183
Marshall Is. (1988)	
★ Majuro	17,649
Martinique (1990)	
★ Fort-de-France	101,540
Mauritania (1988)	
★ Nouakchott	393,325
Mauritius (1991 est.)	
★ Port Louis	142,087
Mayotte (1985)	
★ Mamoudzou	7,325
Mexico (1990)	
Acapulco	515,374
Aguascalientes	440,425
Atizapán de Zaragoza (Ciudad López Mateos)	315,059
Campeche	150,518
Cancún	167,730
Celaya	214,856
Chihuahua	516,153
Ciudad Apodaca	103,364
Ciudad Madero	160,331
Ciudad Obregón	219,980
Ciudad Santa Catarina	162,707
Ciudad Victoria	194,996
Coatzacoalcos	198,817
Colima	106,967
Córdoba	130,695
Cuautla	110,242
Cuernavaca	279,187
Culiacán	415,046
Durango	348,036
Ensenada	169,426
Gómez Palacio	164,092
Guadalajara	1,650,042
Guadalupe	535,332
Hermosillo	406,417
Heroica Nogales	105,873
Irapuato	265,042
Juárez	789,522
La Paz	137,641
León	758,279
Los Mochis	162,659
Matamoros	266,055
Mazatlán	262,705
Mérida	523,422
Mexicali	438,377
★ Mexico City	9,815,795[21]
Minatitlán	142,060
Monclova	177,792
Monterrey	1,068,996
Morelia	428,486
Nezahualcóyotl	1,255,456
Nuevo Laredo	218,413
Oaxaca	212,818
Orizaba	114,216
Pachuca	174,013
Poza Rica	151,739
Puebla	1,007,170
Querétaro	385,503
Reynosa	265,663
Salamanca	123,190
Saltillo	420,947
San Luis Potosí	488,238
San Nicolás de los Garza	436,603
San Pedro Garza García	113,017
Soledad de Graciano Sanchez	123,943
Tampico	272,690
Tapachula	138,858
Tehuacán	139,450
Tepic	206,967
Tijuana	698,752
Tlaquepaque	328,031
Toluca	327,865
Tonala	151,190
Torreón	439,436
Tuxtla	289,626
Uruapan	187,623
Veracruz	438,821
Villahermosa	261,231
Xalapa (Jalapa) Enríquez	279,451
Zacatecas	100,051
Zamora de Hidalgo	109,751
Zapopan	668,323
Micronesia	
★ Palikir	—
Moldova (1991 est.)	
Bălți	164,900
★ Chișinău (Kishinyov)	676,700
Tighina (Bendery)	141,500
Tiraspol	186,000
Monaco (1990)	
★ Monaco	29,972[15]
Mongolia (1992 est.)	
★ Ulaanbaatar (Ulan Bator)	600,900
Morocco (1982)	
Agadir	110,479
Casablanca (Dar el-Beida)	2,139,204
Fès (Fez)	448,823
Kenitra	188,194
Khouribga	127,181
Marrakech	439,728
Meknès	319,783
Mohammedia	105,120
Oujda	260,082
★ Rabat	518,616
Safi	197,309
Salé	289,391
Tanger	266,346
Tétouan	199,615
Mozambique (1991 est.)	
Beira	298,847
Chimoio	108,818
★ Maputo (Lourenço Marques)	931,591
Matala	337,239
Nacala	125,208
Nampula	250,473
Quelimane	146,206
Tete	112,221
Myanmar (Burma) (1983)	
Bassein (Pathein)	144,096
Mandalay	532,949
Monywa	106,843
Moulmein (Mawlamyine)	219,961
Pegu (Bago)	150,528
Sittwe (Akyab)	107,621
Taunggye	108,231
★ Yangôn (Rangoon)	2,513,023
Namibia (1991)	
★ Windhoek	144,558
Nauru (1983)	
★ Yaren	559
Nepal (1991; MU)	
Birātnagar	130,129
★ Kāthmāndu	419,073
Lalitpur	117,203
Netherlands, The (1993 est.)	
Amersfoort	104,390
★ Amsterdam (capital)	713,407
Apeldoorn	148,745
Arnhem	132,928
Breda	126,709
Dordrecht	112,687
Eindhoven	195,267
Enschede	147,349
Groningen	170,038
Haarlem	149,315
Haarlemmermeer	102,781
Leiden	113,838
Maastricht	118,285
Nijmegen	146,993
Rotterdam	596,023
★ The Hague (seat of government)	444,661
Tilburg	162,398
Utrecht	234,170
Zaanstad	131,785
Zoetermeer	102,937
Netherlands Antilles (1985 est.)	
★ Willemstad	125,000[4]
New Caledonia (1989)	
★ Nouméa	65,110
New Zealand (1991)	
Auckland	315,925
Christchurch	292,537
Dunedin	116,524
Hamilton	101,276
Manukau	225,928
North Shore	151,330
Waitakere	136,600
★ Wellington	149,598
Nicaragua (1985 est.)	
León	100,982
★ Managua	682,111
Niger (1988)	
Maradi	112,965
★ Niamey	398,265
Zinder	120,892
Nigeria (1993 est.)[22]	
Aba	277,300
Abeokuta	396,500
★ Abuja (capital designate)	298,300[23]
Ado-Ekiti	333,400
Akure	150,500
Awka	103,100
Benin City	212,900
Bida	116,500
Calabar	161,700
Deba Habe	128,400
Ede	284,900
Effon-Alaiye	142,000
Enugu	293,200
Gombe	100,000
Gusau	146,600
Ibadan	1,328,000
Ife	275,400
Ijebu-Ode	145,100
Ikare	130,600
Ikerre	227,000
Ikire	114,400
Ikirun	168,400
Ikorodu	171,500
Ila	244,000
Ilawe-Ekiti	171,500
Ilesha	351,000
Ilobu	184,600
Ilorin	441,500
Inisa	111,100
Iseyin	202,000
Iwo	335,800
Jos	191,400
Kaduna	317,400
Kano	625,500
Katsina	191,600
Kumo	137,400
Lafia	113,600
★ Lagos	1,408,000
Maiduguri	296,300
Makurdi	114,200
Minna	127,000
Mushin	309,100
Offa	183,000
Ogbomosho	677,200
Oka	132,800
Ondo	157,300
Onitsha	345,000
Oshogbo	444,400
Owo	170,300
Oyo	237,900
Port Harcourt	380,300
Sapele	129,100
Shagamu	108,700
Shaki	161,500

country city	population
Shomolu	137,100
Sokoto	190,100
Warri	116,900
Zaria	351,800
Northern Mariana Is. (1990)	
★ Saipan	38,896
Norway (1993 est.; MU)	
Bergen	218,105
★ Oslo	473,344
Trondheim	140,718
Oman (1982 est.)	
★ Muscat	85,000
Pakistan (1981)	
Bahāwalpur	180,263
Chiniot	105,559
Dera Ghāzi Khān	102,007
Faisalābād (Lyallpur)	1,104,209
Gujrānwāla	658,753
Gujrāt	155,058
Hyderābād	751,529
★ Islamābād	204,364
Jhang	195,558
Jhelum	106,462
Karāchi	5,208,132
Kasūr	155,523
Lahore	2,952,689
Lahore Cantonment	237,000
Lārkāna	123,890
Mardān	147,977
Mīrpur Khās	124,371
Multān	730,070
Nawābshāh	102,139
Okāra	153,483
Peshāwar	566,248
Quetta	285,719
Rahīm Yār Khān	119,036
Rāwalpindi	794,843
Sāhiwāl	150,954
Sargodha	291,362
Sheikhūpura	141,168
Siālkot	302,009
Sukkur	190,551
Wāh Cantonment	122,335
Panama (1990)	
★ Panama City	411,549
San Miguelito	242,529
Papua New Guinea (1990)	
★ Port Moresby (National Capital District)	193,242
Paraguay (1992)	
★ Asunción	502,426
Ciudad del Este	133,893
San Lorenzo	133,311
Peru (1990 est.)	
Arequipa	621,700
Ayacucho	101,600
Callao	588,600
Chiclayo	419,600
Chimbote	296,600
Cuzco	275,000
Huancayo	207,600
Ica	152,300
Iquitos	269,500
Juliaca	134,700
★ Lima	421,570
Metro Lima-Callao	6,115,700
Piura	315,800
Pucallpa	153,000
Sullana	154,800
Tacna	150,200
Trujillo	532,000
Philippines (1990)	
Angeles	236,000
Bacolod	364,000
Bago	124,000
Baguio	183,000
Batangas	184,000
Butuan	228,000
Cabanatuan	173,000
Cadiz	120,000
Cagayan de Oro	340,000
Calbayog	113,000
Caloocan	746,000
Cebu	610,000
Cotabato	127,000
Dagupan	122,000
Davao	850,000
General Santos	250,000
Iligan	227,000
Iloilo	311,000
Lapu-Lapu	146,000
Las Piñas	286,000
Legaspi	121,000
Lipa	160,000
Lucena	151,000
Makati	452,000
Malabon	277,000
Mandaluyong	247,000
Mandaue	180,000
★ Manila	1,587,000
Metro Manila	7,832,000
Marikina	308,000
Muntilupa	278,000
Naga	115,000
Navotas	186,000
Olongapo	192,000
Ormoc	129,000
Pagadian	107,000
Parañaque	300,000
Pasay	354,000
Pasig	395,000
Quezon City	1,632,000
Roxas	103,000
San Carlos (*Negros Occidental*)	106,000
San Carlos (*Pangasinan*)	124,000
San Juan del Monte	127,000
San Pablo	161,000
Surigao	100,000
Tacloban	138,000
Tagig	267,000
Toledo	120,000
Valenzuela	340,000
Zamboanga	444,000
Poland (1992 est.)	
Białystok	273,300
Bielsko-Biała	184,400
Bydgoszcz	383,600
Bytom	232,200
Chorzów	131,500
Czestochowa	258,700
Dąbrowo Górnicza	139,200
Elbląg	126,900
Gdańsk	466,500
Gdynia	251,800
Gliwice	215,700
Gorzów Wielkopolski	125,200
Grudziadz	102,900
Jastrzębie-Zdrój	104,600
Kalisz	106,500
Katowice	366,900
Kielce	215,000
Koszalin	109,800
Kraków	751,300
Legnica	106,100
Łódź	844,900
Lublin	352,500
Olsztyn	164,800
Opole	128,900
Płock	125,300
Poznań	589,700
Radom	229,700
Ruda Śląska	171,600
Rybnik	144,800
Rzeszów	154,800
Słupsk	102,400
Sosnowiec	259,000
Szczecin	414,200
Tarnów	121,900
Toruń	202,000
Tychy	138,800
Wałbrzych	141,200
★ Warsaw (Warszawa)	1,653,300
Włocławek	122,800
Wodzisław Śląskie	112,200
Wrocław	643,600
Zabrze	205,800
Zielona Góra	114,900
Portugal (1991)	
★ Lisbon	677,790
Porto	350,000[24]
Puerto Rico (1990)	
Bayamón	202,103
Carolina	162,404
Ponce	159,151
★ San Juan	426,832
Qatar (1987 est.)	
★ Doha	236,131
Réunion (1990)	
★ Saint-Denis	122,875
Romania (1992)	
Arad	190,088
Bacău	204,495
Baia Mare	148,815
Botoşani	126,204
Brăila	234,706
Braşov	323,835
★ Bucharest	2,064,474
Buzău	148,247
Cluj-Napoca	328,008
Constanţa	350,476
Craiova	303,520
Drobeta-Turnu Severin	115,526
Focşani	101,296
Galaţi	325,788
Iaşi	342,994
Oradea	220,848
Piatra Neamţ	123,175
Piteşti	179,479
Ploieşti	252,073
Râmnicu Vâlcea	113,356
Satu Mare	131,859
Sibiu	169,696
Suceava	114,355
Timişoara	334,278
Tirgu Mureş	163,625
Russia (1992)	
Abakan	158,000
Achinsk	122,000
Almetyevsk	133,000
Angarsk	269,000
Anzhero-Sudzhensk	106,000
Arkhangelsk	414,000
Armavir	163,000
Arzamas	112,000
Astrakhan	512,000
Balakovo	203,000
Balashikha	138,000
Barnaul	606,000
Belgorod	314,000
Berezniki	197,000
Biysk	235,000
Blagoveshchensk	214,000
Bratsk	259,000
Bryansk	461,000
Cheboksary	442,000
Chelyabinsk	1,143,000
Cherepovets	317,000
Cherkessk	119,000
Chita	377,000
Dimitrovgrad	129,000
Dzerzhinsk	287,000
Elektrostal	153,000
Engels	183,000
Glazov	107,000
Grozny	388,000
Irkutsk	639,000
Ivanovo	480,000
Izhevsk	651,000
Kaliningrad	411,000
Kaliningrad (*Moscow oblast*)	162,000
Kaluga	347,000
Kamensk-Uralsky	209,000
Kamyshin	125,000
Kansk	110,000
Kazan	1,104,000
Kemerovo	521,000
Khabarovsk	615,000
Khimki	135,000
Kineshma	104,000
Kirov	493,000
Kiselyovsk	126,000
Kislovodsk	118,000
Kolomna	164,000
Kolpino	145,000
Komsomolsk-na-Amure	319,000
Kostroma	282,000
Kovrov	162,000
Krasnodar	635,000
Krasnoyarsk	925,000
Kurgan	365,000
Kursk	435,000
Kuznetsk	101,000
Leninsk-Kuznetsky	132,000
Lipetsk	464,000
Lyubertsy	164,000
Magadan	152,000
Magnitogorsk	441,000
Makhachkala	339,000
Maykop	155,000
Mezhdurechensk	108,000
Miass	170,000
Michurinsk	109,000
★ Moscow	8,747,000
Murmansk	468,000
Murom	127,000
Mytishchi	154,000
Naberezhnye Chelny (Brezhnev)	514,000
Nakhodka	166,000
Nalchik	242,000
Nevinnomyssk	125,000
Nikolo-Beryozovka (Neftekamsk)	113,000
Nizhnekamsk	199,000
Nizhnevartovsk	243,000
Nizhny Novgorod (Gorky)	1,441,000
Nizhny Tagil	437,000
Noginsk	122,000
Norilsk	165,000
Novgorod	235,000
Novocheboksarsk	121,000
Novocherkassk	188,000
Novokuybyshevsk	113,000
Novokuznetsk	600,000
Novomoskovsk (*Tula oblast*)	145,000
Novorossiysk	190,000
Novoshakhtinsk	107,000
Novosibirsk	1,442,000
Novotroitsk	107,000
Obninsk	105,000
Odintsovo	129,000
Oktyabrsky	107,000
Omsk	1,169,000
Orekhovo-Zuyevo	136,000
Orenburg	557,000
Orsk	273,000
Oryol	347,000
Penza	552,000
Perm	1,099,000
Pervouralsk	144,000
Petropavlovsk-Kamchatsky	273,000
Petrozavodsk	280,000
Podolsk	208,000
Prokopyevsk	272,000
Pskov	209,000
Pyatigorsk	132,000
Rostov-na-Donu	1,027,000
Rubtsovsk	172,000
Ryazan	529,000
Rybinsk (Andropov)	252,000
Saint Petersburg (Leningrad)	4,437,000
Salavat	152,000
Samara (Kuybyshev)	1,239,000
Saransk	322,000
Sarapul	111,000
Saratov	909,000
Serov	106,000
Serpukhov	141,000
Severodvinsk	250,000
Shakhty	228,000
Shchyolkovo	109,000
Simbirsk (Ulyanovsk)	656,000
Smolensk	352,000
Sochi	344,000
Solikamsk	110,000
Stary Oskol	184,000
Stavropol	332,000
Sterlitamak	254,000
Surgut	260,000
Syktyvkar	226,000
Syzran	175,000
Taganrog	293,000
Tambov	311,000
Tolyatti (Toliatti)	666,000
Tomsk	505,000
Tula	541,000
Tver (Kalinin)	456,000
Tyumen	496,000
Ufa	1,097,000
Ukhta	112,000
Ulan-Ude	366,000
Usolye-Sibirskoye	107,000
Ussuriysk	161,000
Ust-Ilimsk	114,000
Velikiye Luki	116,000
Vladikavkaz (Ordzhonikidze)	325,000
Vladimir	356,000
Vladivostok	648,000
Volgodonsk	182,000
Volgograd	1,006,000
Vologda	290,000
Volzhsky	281,000
Vorkuta	116,000
Voronezh	902,000
Votkinsk	105,000
Yakutsk	198,000
Yaroslavl	637,000
Yekaterinburg (Sverdlovsk)	1,371,000
Yelets	121,000
Yoshkar-Ola	249,000
Yuzhno-Sakhalinsk	165,000
Zagorsk	115,600
Zelenograd	170,000
Zhukovsky	101,000
Zlatoust	208,000
Rwanda (1991)	
★ Kigali	232,733
St. Kitts and Nevis (1990 est.)	
★ Basseterre	15,000
St. Lucia (1991)	
★ Castries	11,147
St. Vincent and The Grenadines (1991)	
★ Kingstown	15,466
San Marino (1992 est.)	
★ San Marino	2,397
São Tomé and Príncipe (1990 est.)	
★ São Tomé	43,420
Saudi Arabia (1980 est.)	
ad-Dammām	200,000
Jiddah	1,500,000[25]
Mecca (Makkah)	550,000
Medina (al-Madinah)	290,000
★ Riyadh (ar-Riyad)	1,308,000[19]
aṭ-Ṭā'if	300,000
Senegal (1992 est.)	
★ Dakar	1,729,823
Kaolack	179,894
St.-Louis	125,717
Thiès	201,350
Ziguinchor	148,831
Seychelles (1987)	
★ Victoria	24,325
Sierra Leone (1985)	
★ Freetown	469,776
Singapore (1992 est.)[15]	
★ Singapore	2,792,000
Slovakia (1991)	
★ Bratislava	441,453
Košice	234,840
Slovenia (1992 est.)	
★ Ljubljana	276,153
Maribor	108,122
Solomon Islands (1986)	
★ Honiara	30,499
Somalia (1985 est.)	
★ Mogadishu	700,000
South Africa (1985)	
★ Bloemfontein (judicial)	104,381
Boksburg	110,832
★ Cape Town (legislative)	776,617
Metro Cape Town	1,911,521
Durban	634,301
Metro Durban	982,075
Germiston	116,718
Johannesburg	632,369
Metro Johannesburg	1,609,408
Pietermaritzburg	133,809
Port Elizabeth	272,844
★ Pretoria (executive)	443,059
Metro Pretoria	822,925
Roodepoort	141,764
Soweto	864,000[24]
Bophuthatswana	
★ Mmabatho	...
Ciskei (1986 est.)	
★ Bisho	2,850
Mdantsane	242,823
Transkei (1984 est.)	
★ Umtata	80,000
Venda (1985)	
★ Thohoyandou	10,166
Spain (1991; MU)	
Albacete	128,718
Alcalá de Henares	159,355
Alcorcón	139,641
Algeciras	101,063
Alicante	261,255
Almería	153,288
Badajoz	121,924
Badalona	206,585
Baracaldo	104,883
Barcelona	1,623,542
Bilbao	368,710
Burgos	160,381
Cádiz	153,550
Cartagena	166,736
Castellón de la Plana	133,180
Córdoba	300,229
Coruña, La	245,459
Donostia (San Sebastián)	169,933
Elche	181,658
Fuenlabrada	144,723
Getafe	138,704
Gijón	259,054
Granada	254,034
Hospitalet de Llobregat	269,241
Huelva	141,041
Jaén	101,938
Jerez de la Frontera	182,939
La Laguna	109,485
Leganés	171,400

Major cities and national capitals (continued)

country / city	population
León	144,137
Lleida (Lérida)	111,880
Logroño	121,066
★ Madrid	2,909,792
Málaga	512,136
Mataró	101,501
Móstoles	192,018
Murcia	318,838
Ourense (Orense)	101,623
Oviedo	194,919
Palma (de Mallorca)	296,754
Palmas de Gran Canaria, Las (Is. Canarias)	342,030
Pamplona	179,251
Sabadell	184,460
Salamanca	162,544
Santa Coloma de Gramanet	132,173
Santa Cruz de Tenerife	189,317
Santander	189,069
Sevilla (Seville)	659,126
Tarragona	110,003
Terrassa	154,300
Valencia	752,909
Valladolid	328,365
Vigo	274,629
Vitoria (Gasteiz)	204,961
Zaragoza (Saragossa)	586,219
Sri Lanka (1990 est.)	
★ Colombo (administrative)	615,000
Dehiwala-Mount Lavinia	196,000
Jaffna	129,000
Kandy	104,000
Moratuwa	170,000
★ Sri Jayawardenepura Kotte (legislative and judicial)	109,000[26]
Sudan, The (1983)	
Juba	116,000[27]
★ Khartoum (executive)	476,218
Khartoum North	341,146
Nyala	111,693
★ Omdurman (legislative)	526,287
Port Sudan	206,727
al-Qaḍārif	116,876
al-Ubayyiḍ	140,024
Wad Madanī	141,065
Waw	116,000[27]
Suriname (1986 est.)	
★ Paramaribo	77,558
Swaziland (1986)	
★ Mbabane	38,290
Sweden (1993 est.; MU)	
Borås	102,840
Göteborg	433,811
Helsingborg	110,614
Jönköping	112,802
Linköping	126,377
Malmö	236,684
Norrköping	120,798
Örebro	123,188
★ Stockholm	684,576
Uppsala	174,554
Västerås	120,889
Switzerland (1992 est.)	
Basel (Bâle)	172,768
★ Bern (Berne)	134,393
Geneva (Genève)	167,697
Lausanne	123,149
Zürich	343,106
Syria (1992 est.)	
Aleppo (Ḥalab)	1,445,000
★ Damascus (Dimashq)	1,451,000
Dayr az-Zawr	125,000
Ḥamāh	229,000
al-Ḥasakah	106,000
Homs (Ḥims)	518,000
Latakia (al-Ladhiqiyah)	284,000
al-Qāmishlī	151,000
ar-Raqqah	130,000
Taiwan (1992 est.)	
Chang-hua	217,328
Chi-lung (Keelung)	355,894
Chia-i	258,468
Chung-ho	379,968
Chung-li	276,878
Feng-shan (Kao-hsiung-hsien)	293,522
Fêng-yüan	154,175
Hsin-chu	328,911
Hsin-chuang	308,293
Hsin-tien	233,277
Hua-lien	107,504
Kao-hsiung	1,396,425
Pan-ch'iao (T'ai-pei-hsien)	542,942
P'ing-tung	212,335
San-chu'ung	378,397
T'ai-chung	774,197
T'ai-nan	689,541
T'ai-tung	108,086
★ Taipei (T'ai-pei)	2,717,992
T'ao-yuan	246,056
Yung-ho	247,473
Tajikistan (1991 est.)	
★ Dushanbe	582,400
Khodzhent (Leninabad)	164,500
Tanzania (1988)	
★ Dar es Salaam	1,360,850
Mbeya	194,000[28]
Mwanza	252,000[28]
Tabora	214,000[28]
Tanga	187,634
Zanzibar	157,634
Thailand (1991 est.)	
★ Bangkok	5,620,591
Chiang Mai	161,541
Hat Yai	142,351
Khon Kaen	131,478
Nakhon Ratchasima	202,503
Nakhon Sawan	108,569
Nonthanburi	264,201
Togo (1983 est.)	
★ Lomé	366,476
Tonga (1986)	
★ Nuku'alofa	21,383
Trinidad and Tobago (1990)	
★ Port-of-Spain	50,878
Tunisia (1989)	
Aryānah	131,403
Ettadhamen	111,793
Ṣafāqis (Sfax)	221,770
Sūsah	101,071
★ Tunis	620,149
Turkey (1990)	
Adana	916,150
Adapazari	171,225
Adıyaman	100,045
★ Ankara	2,559,471
Antakya	123,871
Antalya	378,208
Aydın	107,011
Balıkesir	170,589
Batman	147,347
Bursa	834,576
Çorum	116,810
Denizli	204,118
Diyarbakır	381,144
Edirne	102,345
Elazığ	204,603
Erzurum	242,391
Eskişehir	413,082
Gaziantep	603,434
Gebze	159,116
İçel	422,357
İskenderun	154,807
Isparta	112,117
Istanbul	6,620,241
İzmir	1,757,414
İzmit	256,882
Kahramanmaraş	228,129
Karabük	105,373
Kayseri	421,362
Kırıkkale	185,431
Konya	513,346
Kütahya	130,944
Malatya	281,776
Manisa	158,928
Ordu	102,107
Osmaniye	122,307
Samsun	303,979
Sivas	221,512
Tarsus	187,508
Trabzon	143,941
Urfa (Şanlıurfa)	276,528
Uşak	105,270
Van	153,111
Zonguldak	116,725
Turkmenistan (1991 est.)	
★ Ashkhabad (Ashgabat)	412,200
Chardzhou	166,400
Tashauz	117,000
Tuvalu (1985 est.)	
★ Funafuti	2,810
Uganda (1991)	
★ Kampala	773,463
Ukraine (1991 est.)	
Berdyansk	135,000
Bila Tserkva (Belaya Tserkov)	204,000
Cherkasy (Cherkassy)	302,000
Chernihiv (Chernigov)	306,000
Chernivtsi (Chernovtsy)	259,000
Dniprodzerzhynsk (Dneprodzerzhinsk)	284,000
Dnipropetrovsk (Dnepropetrovsk)	1,189,000
Donetsk	1,121,000
Horlivka (Gorlovka)	337,000
Ivano-Frankivsk (Ivano-Frankovsk)	226,000
Kamyanets-Podilsky (Kamenets-Podolsky)	105,000
Kerch	178,000
Kharkiv (Kharkov)	1,623,000
Kherson	365,000
Khmelnytsky (Khmelnitsky)	245,000
★ Kiev (Kyyiv)	2,635,000
Kirovohrad	278,000
Komunarsk	126,000
Kostyantynivka (Konstantinovka)	108,000
Kramatorsk	201,000
Krasny Luch	113,000
Kremenchuk (Kremenchug)	241,000
Kryvy Rih (Krivoy Rog)	724,000
Luhansk (Voroshilovgrad)	504,000
Lutsk	210,000
Lviv (Lvov)	802,000
Lysychansk (Lisichansk)	126,000
Makiyivka (Makeyevka)	424,000
Mariupol (Zhdanov)	522,000
Melitopol	177,000
Mykolayiv (Nikolayev)	512,000
Nikopol	159,000
Odesa (Odessa)	1,101,000
Oleksandriya (Aleksandriya)	105,000
Pavlohrad	134,000
Poltava	320,000
Rivne (Rovno)	239,000
Sevastopol	366,000
Severodonetsk	133,000
Simferopol	353,000
Slovyansk (Slavyansk)	137,000
Stakhanov	113,000
Sumy	301,000
Ternopil (Ternopol)	218,000
Uzhhorod	123,000
Vinnytsya (Vinnitsa)	381,000
Yenakiyeve (Yenakiyevo)	120,000
Yevpatoriya	111,000
Zaporizhzhya (Zaporozhye)	897,000
Zhytomyr (Zhitomir)	298,000
United Arab Emirates (1989 est.)	
★ Abu Dhabi (Abū Ẓaby)	363,432
Al-'Ayn	176,441
Dubai (Dubayy)	585,189
Sharjah (ash-Shāriqah)	125,123[17]
United Kingdom (1981)	
Aberdeen	190,465
Belfast	354,400
Birmingham	1,024,118
Blackburn	110,254
Blackpool	149,012
Bolton	143,921
Bournemouth	148,382
Bradford	295,048
Brighton	137,985
Bristol	420,234
Cardiff	266,267
Coventry	322,573
Derby	220,681
Dudley	187,367
Dundee	174,345
Edinburgh	420,169
Glasgow	765,030
Gloucester	108,150
Huddersfield	148,544
Ipswich	131,131
Kingston upon Hull	325,485
Leeds	451,841
Leicester	328,835
Liverpool	544,861
★ London	6,677,928
Luton	164,743
Manchester	448,604
Middlesbrough	159,421
Newcastle upon Tyne	203,591
Newport	116,658
Northampton	155,694
Norwich	173,286
Nottingham	277,203
Oldbury/Smethwick	153,461
Oldham	107,830
Oxford	119,909
Peterborough	114,733
Plymouth	242,560
Poole	124,974
Portsmouth	177,905
Preston	168,405
Reading	198,341
Rotherham	123,312
St. Helens	114,822
Sheffield	477,257
Slough	106,822
Southampton	214,802
Southend-on-Sea	156,969
Stockport	136,792
Stoke-on-Trent	275,168
Sunderland	195,896
Sutton Coldfield	103,097
Swansea	175,172
Swindon	128,493
Walsall	178,852
West Bromwich	154,531
Wolverhampton	265,631
York	126,377
United States (1990)	
Abilene (*Texas*)	106,654
Akron (*Ohio*)	223,019
Alameda (*Calif.*)	76,459
Albany (*Ga.*)	78,122
Albany (*N.Y.*)	101,082
Albuquerque (*N.M.*)	384,736
Alexandria (*Va.*)	111,183
Alhambra (*Calif.*)	82,106
Allentown (*Pa.*)	105,090
Altoona (*Pa.*)	51,881
Amarillo (*Texas*)	157,615
Anaheim (*Calif.*)	266,406
Anchorage (*Alaska*)	226,338
Anderson (*Ind.*)	59,459
Ann Arbor (*Mich.*)	109,592
Antioch (*Calif.*)	62,195
Appleton (*Wis.*)	65,695
Arlington (*Texas*)	261,721
Arlington (*Va.*)	170,936
Arlington Heights (*Ill.*)	75,460
Arvada (*Colo.*)	89,235
Asheville (*N.C.*)	61,607
Atlanta (*Ga.*)	394,017
Aurora (*Colo.*)	222,103
Aurora (*Ill.*)	99,581
Austin (*Texas*)	465,622
Bakersfield (*Calif.*)	174,820
Baldwin Park (*Calif.*)	69,330
Baltimore (*Md.*)	736,014
Baton Rouge (*La.*)	219,531
Battle Creek (*Mich.*)	53,540
Bayonne (*N.J.*)	61,444
Baytown (*Texas*)	63,850
Beaumont (*Texas*)	114,323
Beaverton (*Ore.*)	53,310
Bellevue (*Wash.*)	86,874
Bellflower (*Calif.*)	61,815
Bellingham (*Wash.*)	52,179
Berkeley (*Calif.*)	102,724
Bethlehem (*Pa.*)	71,428
Billings (*Mont.*)	81,151
Binghamton (*N.Y.*)	53,008
Birmingham (*Ala.*)	265,968
Bloomington (*Ill.*)	51,972
Bloomington (*Ind.*)	60,633
Bloomington (*Minn.*)	86,335
Boca Raton (*Fla.*)	61,492
Boise City (*Idaho*)	125,738
Bossier City (*La.*)	52,721
Boston (*Mass.*)	574,283
Boulder (*Colo.*)	83,312
Bridgeport (*Conn.*)	141,686
Bristol (*Conn.*)	60,640
Brockton (*Mass.*)	92,788
Broken Arrow (*Okla.*)	58,043
Brooklyn Park (*Minn.*)	56,381
Brownsville (*Texas*)	98,962
Bryan (*Texas*)	55,002
Buena Park (*Calif.*)	68,784
Buffalo (*N.Y.*)	328,123
Burbank (*Calif.*)	93,643
Burnsville (*Minn.*)	51,288
Camarillo (*Calif.*)	52,303
Cambridge (*Mass.*)	95,802
Camden (*N.J.*)	87,492
Canton (*Ohio*)	84,161
Cape Coral (*Fla.*)	74,991
Carlsbad (*Calif.*)	63,126
Carrollton (*Texas*)	82,169
Carson (*Calif.*)	83,995
Cedar Rapids (*Iowa*)	108,751
Cerritos (*Calif.*)	53,240
Champaign (*Ill.*)	63,502
Chandler (*Ariz.*)	90,533
Charleston (*S.C.*)	80,414
Charleston (*W.V.*)	57,287
Charlotte (*N.C.*)	395,934
Chattanooga (*Tenn.*)	152,466
Chesapeake (*Va.*)	151,976
Cheyenne (*Wyo.*)	50,008
Chicago (*Ill.*)	2,783,726
Chicopee (*Mass.*)	56,632
Chino (*Calif.*)	59,682
Chula Vista (*Calif.*)	135,163
Cicero (*Ill.*)	67,436
Cincinnati (*Ohio*)	364,040
Clarksville (*Tenn.*)	75,494
Clearwater (*Fla.*)	98,784
Cleveland (*Ohio*)	505,616
Cleveland Heights (*Ohio*)	54,052
Clifton (*N.J.*)	71,742
Clovis (*Calif.*)	50,323
College Station (*Texas*)	52,456
Colorado Springs (*Colo.*)	281,140
Columbia (*Mo.*)	69,101
Columbia (*S.C.*)	98,052
Columbus (*Ga.*)	179,278
Columbus (*Ohio*)	632,910
Compton (*Calif.*)	90,454
Concord (*Calif.*)	111,348
Coon Rapids (*Minn.*)	52,978
Coral Springs (*Fla.*)	79,443
Corona (*Calif.*)	76,095
Corpus Christi (*Texas*)	257,453
Costa Mesa (*Calif.*)	96,357
Council Bluffs (*Iowa*)	54,315
Cranston (*R.I.*)	76,060
Dallas (*Texas*)	1,006,877
Daly City (*Calif.*)	92,311
Danbury (*Conn.*)	65,585
Danville (*Va.*)	53,056
Davenport (*Iowa*)	95,333
Dayton (*Ohio*)	182,044
Daytona Beach (*Fla.*)	61,921
Dearborn (*Mich.*)	89,286
Dearborn Heights (*Mich.*)	60,838
Decatur (*Ill.*)	83,885
Denton (*Texas*)	66,270
Denver (*Colo.*)	467,610
Des Moines (*Iowa*)	193,187
Des Plaines (*Ill.*)	53,223
Detroit (*Mich.*)	1,027,974
Diamond Bar (*Calif.*)	53,672
Dothan (*Ala.*)	53,589
Downey (*Calif.*)	91,444
Dubuque (*Iowa*)	57,546
Duluth (*Minn.*)	85,493
Durham (*N.C.*)	136,611
East Lansing (*Mich.*)	50,677
East Orange (*N.J.*)	73,552
East Providence (*R.I.*)	50,380
Eau Claire (*Wis.*)	56,856
Edmond (*Okla.*)	52,315
El Cajon (*Calif.*)	88,693
El Monte (*Calif.*)	106,209
El Paso (*Texas*)	515,342
Elgin (*Ill.*)	77,010
Elizabeth (*N.J.*)	110,002
Elyria (*Ohio*)	56,746
Encinitas (*Calif.*)	55,386
Erie (*Pa.*)	108,718
Escondido (*Calif.*)	108,635
Euclid (*Ohio*)	54,875
Eugene (*Ore.*)	112,669
Evanston (*Ill.*)	73,233
Evansville (*Ind.*)	126,272
Everett (*Wash.*)	69,961
Fairfield (*Calif.*)	77,211
Fall River (*Mass.*)	92,703
Fargo (*N.D.*)	74,111
Farmington Hills (*Mich.*)	74,652
Fayetteville (*N.C.*)	75,695
Flint (*Mich.*)	140,761
Florissant (*Mo.*)	51,206
Fontana (*Calif.*)	87,535
Fort Collins (*Colo.*)	87,758
Fort Lauderdale (*Fla.*)	149,377
Fort Smith (*Ark.*)	72,798
Fort Wayne (*Ind.*)	173,072
Fort Worth (*Texas*)	447,619
Fountain Valley (*Calif.*)	53,691
Fremont (*Calif.*)	173,339
Fresno (*Calif.*)	354,202
Fullerton (*Calif.*)	114,144

[1]1984 estimate. [2]City proper; 1980 census. [3]1989 census. [4]Population refers to widest officially defined agglomeration or metropolitan area. [5]Population of the statistical division containing the city. [6]1991 census. [7]1982 estimate. [8]Excludes the agricultural population of the named civil division. [9]1985 census. [10]Excludes population of Lefkoşa (Turkish-occupied Nicosia), estimated at 37,400 in 1985. [11]1986 estimate. [12]1986 census. [13]1989 estimate. [14]1983 census. [15]No separate areas within the state are distinguished administratively as cities. [16]Population includes Comayagüela.

country / city	population
Gainesville (*Fla.*)	84,770
Galveston (*Texas*)	59,070
Garden Grove (*Calif.*)	143,050
Garland (*Texas*)	180,650
Gary (*Ind.*)	116,646
Gastonia (*N.C.*)	54,732
Glendale (*Ariz.*)	148,134
Glendale (*Calif.*)	180,038
Grand Prairie (*Texas*)	99,616
Grand Rapids (*Mich.*)	189,126
Great Falls (*Mont.*)	55,097
Greeley (*Colo.*)	60,536
Green Bay (*Wis.*)	96,466
Greensboro (*N.C.*)	183,521
Greenville (*S.C.*)	58,282
Gresham (*Ore.*)	68,235
Hamilton (*Ohio*)	61,368
Hammond (*Ind.*)	84,236
Hampton (*Va.*)	133,793
Harrisburg (*Pa.*)	52,376
Hartford (*Conn.*)	139,739
Haverhill (*Mass.*)	51,418
Hawthorne (*Calif.*)	71,349
Hayward (*Calif.*)	111,498
Henderson (*Nev.*)	64,942
Hesperia (*Calif.*)	50,418
Hialeah (*Fla.*)	188,004
High Point (*N.C.*)	69,496
Hollywood (*Fla.*)	121,697
Honolulu (*Ha.*)	365,272
Houston (*Texas*)	1,630,553
Huntington (*W.V.*)	54,844
Huntington Beach (*Calif.*)	181,519
Huntington Park (*Calif.*)	56,065
Huntsville (*Ala.*)	159,789
Independence (*Mo.*)	112,301
Indianapolis (*Ind.*)	731,327
Inglewood (*Calif.*)	109,602
Iowa City (*Iowa*)	59,738
Irvine (*Calif.*)	110,330
Irving (*Texas*)	155,037
Jackson (*Miss.*)	196,637
Jacksonville (*Fla.*)	672,971
Janesville (*Wis.*)	52,133
Jersey City (*N.J.*)	228,537
Joliet (*Ill.*)	76,836
Kalamazoo (*Mich.*)	80,277
Kansas City (*Kan.*)	149,767
Kansas City (*Mo.*)	435,146
Kenner (*La.*)	72,033
Kenosha (*Wis.*)	80,352
Kettering (*Ohio*)	60,569
Killeen (*Texas*)	63,535
Knoxville (*Tenn.*)	165,121
La Crosse (*Wis.*)	51,003
La Habra (*Calif.*)	51,266
La Mesa (*Calif.*)	52,931
Lafayette (*La.*)	94,440
Lake Charles (*La.*)	70,580
Lakeland (*Fla.*)	70,576
Lakewood (*Calif.*)	73,557
Lakewood (*Colo.*)	126,481
Lakewood (*Ohio*)	59,718
Lancaster (*Calif.*)	97,291
Lancaster (*Pa.*)	55,551
Lansing (*Mich.*)	127,321
Laredo (*Texas*)	122,899
Largo (*Fla.*)	65,674
Las Cruces (*N.M.*)	62,126
Las Vegas (*Nev.*)	258,295
Lawrence (*Kan.*)	65,608
Lawrence (*Mass.*)	70,207
Lawton (*Okla.*)	80,561
Lexington (*Ky.*)	225,366
Lincoln (*Neb.*)	191,972
Little Rock (*Ark.*)	175,795
Livermore (*Calif.*)	56,741
Livonia (*Mich.*)	100,850
Lodi (*Calif.*)	51,874
Long Beach (*Calif.*)	429,433
Longmont (*Colo.*)	51,555
Longview (*Texas*)	70,311
Lorain (*Ohio*)	71,245
Los Angeles (*Calif.*)	3,485,398
Louisville (*Ky.*)	269,063
Lowell (*Mass.*)	103,439
Lubbock (*Texas*)	186,206
Lynchburg (*Va.*)	66,049
Lynn (*Mass.*)	81,245
Lynwood (*Calif.*)	61,945
McAllen (*Texas*)	84,021
Macon (*Ga.*)	106,612
Madison (*Wis.*)	191,262
Malden (*Mass.*)	53,884
Manchester (*N.H.*)	99,567
Medford (*Mass.*)	57,407
Melbourne (*Fla.*)	59,646
Memphis (*Tenn.*)	610,337
Merced (*Calif.*)	56,216
Meriden (*Conn.*)	59,479
Mesa (*Ariz.*)	288,091
Mesquite (*Texas*)	101,484
Miami (*Fla.*)	358,548
Miami Beach (*Fla.*)	92,639
Midland (*Texas*)	89,443
Midwest City (*Okla.*)	52,267
Milpitas (*Calif.*)	50,686
Milwaukee (*Wis.*)	628,088
Minneapolis (*Minn.*)	368,383
Mission Viejo (*Calif.*)	72,820
Mobile (*Ala.*)	196,278
Modesto (*Calif.*)	164,730
Monroe (*La.*)	54,909
Montebello (*Calif.*)	59,564
Monterey Park (*Calif.*)	60,738
Montgomery (*Ala.*)	187,106
Mount Prospect (*Ill.*)	53,170
Mount Vernon (*N.Y.*)	67,153
Mountain View (*Calif.*)	67,460
Muncie (*Ind.*)	71,035
Napa (*Calif.*)	61,842
Naperville (*Ill.*)	85,351
Nashua (*N.H.*)	79,662
Nashville (*Tenn.*)	488,374
National City (*Calif.*)	54,249
New Bedford (*Mass.*)	99,922
New Britain (*Conn.*)	75,491
New Haven (*Conn.*)	130,474
New Orleans (*La.*)	496,938
New Rochelle (*N.Y.*)	67,265
New York City (*N.Y.*)	7,322,564
Newark (*N.J.*)	275,221
Newport Beach (*Calif.*)	66,643
Newport News (*Va.*)	170,045
Newton (*Mass.*)	82,585
Niagara Falls (*N.Y.*)	61,840
Norfolk (*Va.*)	261,229
Norman (*Okla.*)	80,071
North Charleston (*S.C.*)	70,218
North Little Rock (*Ark.*)	61,741
Norwalk (*Calif.*)	94,279
Norwalk (*Conn.*)	78,331
Oak Lawn (*Ill.*)	56,182
Oak Park (*Ill.*)	53,648
Oakland (*Calif.*)	372,242
Oceanside (*Calif.*)	128,398
Odessa (*Texas*)	89,699
Ogden (*Utah*)	63,909
Oklahoma City (*Okla.*)	444,719
Olathe (*Kan.*)	63,352
Omaha (*Neb.*)	335,795
Ontario (*Calif.*)	133,179
Orange (*Calif.*)	110,658
Orem (*Utah*)	67,561
Orlando (*Fla.*)	164,693
Oshkosh (*Wis.*)	55,006
Overland Park (*Kan.*)	111,790
Owensboro (*Ky.*)	53,549
Oxnard (*Calif.*)	142,216
Palm Bay (*Fla.*)	62,632
Palmdale (*Calif.*)	68,842
Palo Alto (*Calif.*)	55,900
Pasadena (*Calif.*)	131,591
Pasadena (*Texas*)	119,363
Passaic (*N.J.*)	58,041
Paterson (*N.J.*)	140,891
Pawtucket (*R.I.*)	72,644
Pembroke Pines (*Fla.*)	65,452
Pensacola (*Fla.*)	58,165
Peoria (*Ariz.*)	50,618
Peoria (*Ill.*)	113,504
Philadelphia (*Pa.*)	1,585,577
Phoenix (*Ariz.*)	983,403
Pico Rivera (*Calif.*)	59,177
Pine Bluff (*Ark.*)	57,140
Pittsburgh (*Pa.*)	369,879
Plano (*Texas*)	128,713
Plantation (*Fla.*)	66,692
Pleasanton (*Calif.*)	50,553
Plymouth (*Minn.*)	50,889
Pomona (*Calif.*)	131,723
Pompano Beach (*Fla.*)	72,411
Pontiac (*Mich.*)	71,166
Port Arthur (*Texas*)	58,724
Port St. Lucie (*Fla.*)	55,866
Portland (*Maine*)	64,358
Portland (*Ore.*)	437,319
Portsmouth (*Va.*)	103,907
Providence (*R.I.*)	160,728
Provo (*Utah*)	86,835
Pueblo (*Colo.*)	98,640
Quincy (*Mass.*)	84,985
Racine (*Wis.*)	84,298
Raleigh (*N.C.*)	207,951
Rancho Cucamonga (*Calif.*)	101,409
Rapid City (*S.D.*)	54,523
Reading (*Pa.*)	78,380
Redding (*Calif.*)	66,462
Redlands (*Calif.*)	60,394
Redondo Beach (*Calif.*)	60,167
Redwood City (*Calif.*)	66,072
Reno (*Nev.*)	133,850
Rialto (*Calif.*)	72,388
Richardson (*Texas*)	74,840
Richmond (*Calif.*)	87,425
Richmond (*Va.*)	203,056
Riverside (*Calif.*)	226,505
Roanoke (*Va.*)	96,397
Rochester (*Minn.*)	70,745
Rochester (*N.Y.*)	231,636
Rochester Hills (*Mich.*)	61,766
Rockford (*Ill.*)	139,426
Rosemead (*Calif.*)	51,638
Roseville (*Mich.*)	51,412
Royal Oak (*Mich.*)	65,410
Sacramento (*Calif.*)	369,365
Saginaw (*Mich.*)	69,512
St. Charles (*Mo.*)	54,555
St. Clair Shores (*Mich.*)	68,107
St. Joseph (*Mo.*)	71,852
St. Louis (*Mo.*)	396,685
St. Paul (*Minn.*)	272,235
St. Petersburg (*Fla.*)	238,629
Salem (*Ore.*)	107,786
Salinas (*Calif.*)	108,777
Salt Lake City (*Utah*)	159,936
San Angelo (*Texas*)	84,474
San Antonio (*Texas*)	935,933
San Bernardino (*Calif.*)	164,164
San Buenaventura (Ventura) (*Calif.*)	92,575
San Diego (*Calif.*)	1,110,549
San Francisco (*Calif.*)	723,959
San Jose (*Calif.*)	782,248
San Leandro (*Calif.*)	68,223
San Mateo (*Calif.*)	85,486
Sandy (*Utah*)	75,058
Santa Ana (*Calif.*)	293,742
Santa Barbara (*Calif.*)	85,571
Santa Clara (*Calif.*)	93,613
Santa Clarita (*Calif.*)	110,642
Santa Fe (*N.M.*)	55,859
Santa Maria (*Calif.*)	61,284
Santa Monica (*Calif.*)	86,905
Santa Rosa (*Calif.*)	113,313
Santee (*Calif.*)	52,902
Sarasota (*Fla.*)	50,961
Savannah (*Ga.*)	137,560
Schaumburg (*Ill.*)	68,586
Schenectady (*N.Y.*)	65,566
Scottsdale (*Ariz.*)	130,069
Scranton (*Pa.*)	81,805
Seattle (*Wash.*)	516,259
Shreveport (*La.*)	198,525
Simi Valley (*Calif.*)	100,217
Sioux City (*Iowa*)	80,505
Sioux Falls (*S.D.*)	100,814
Skokie (*Ill.*)	59,432
Somerville (*Mass.*)	76,210
South Bend (*Ind.*)	105,511
South Gate (*Calif.*)	86,284
South San Francisco (*Calif.*)	54,312
Southfield (*Mich.*)	75,728
Sparks (*Nev.*)	53,367
Spokane (*Wash.*)	177,196
Springfield (*Ill.*)	105,227
Springfield (*Mass.*)	156,983
Springfield (*Mo.*)	140,494
Springfield (*Ohio*)	70,487
Stamford (*Conn.*)	108,056
Sterling Heights (*Mich.*)	117,810
Stockton (*Calif.*)	210,943
Suffolk (*Va.*)	52,141
Sunnyvale (*Calif.*)	117,229
Sunrise (*Fla.*)	64,407
Syracuse (*N.Y.*)	163,860
Tacoma (*Wash.*)	176,664
Tallahassee (*Fla.*)	124,773
Tampa (*Fla.*)	280,015
Taylor (*Mich.*)	70,811
Tempe (*Ariz.*)	141,865
Terre Haute (*Ind.*)	57,483
Thornton (*Colo.*)	55,031
Thousand Oaks (*Calif.*)	104,352
Toledo (*Ohio*)	332,943
Topeka (*Kan.*)	119,883
Torrance (*Calif.*)	133,107
Trenton (*N.J.*)	88,675
Troy (*Mich.*)	72,884
Troy (*N.Y.*)	54,269
Tucson (*Ariz.*)	405,390
Tulsa (*Okla.*)	367,302
Tuscaloosa (*Ala.*)	77,759
Tustin (*Calif.*)	50,689
Tyler (*Texas*)	75,450
Union City (*Calif.*)	53,762
Union City (*N.J.*)	58,012
Upland (*Calif.*)	63,374
Utica (*N.Y.*)	68,637
Vacaville (*Calif.*)	71,479
Vallejo (*Calif.*)	109,199
Victoria (*Texas*)	55,076
Vineland (*N.J.*)	54,780
Virginia Beach (*Va.*)	393,069
Visalia (*Calif.*)	75,636
Vista (*Calif.*)	71,872
Waco (*Texas*)	103,590
Walnut Creek (*Calif.*)	60,569
Waltham (*Mass.*)	57,878
Warren (*Mich.*)	144,864
Warren (*Ohio*)	50,793
Warwick (*R.I.*)	85,427
★ Washington, D.C.	606,900
Waterbury (*Conn.*)	108,961
Waterloo (*Iowa*)	66,467
Waukegan (*Ill.*)	69,392
Waukesha (*Wis.*)	56,958
West Allis (*Wis.*)	63,221
West Covina (*Calif.*)	96,086
West Haven (*Conn.*)	54,021
West Palm Beach (*Fla.*)	67,643
West Valley City (*Utah*)	86,976
Westland (*Mich.*)	84,724
Westminster (*Calif.*)	78,118
Westminster (*Colo.*)	74,625
Wheaton (*Ill.*)	51,464
Whittier (*Calif.*)	77,671
Wichita (*Kan.*)	304,011
Wichita Falls (*Texas*)	96,259
Wilmington (*Del.*)	71,529
Wilmington (*N.C.*)	55,530
Winston-Salem (*N.C.*)	143,485
Worcester (*Mass.*)	169,759
Wyoming (*Mich.*)	63,891
Yakima (*Wash.*)	54,827
Yonkers (*N.Y.*)	188,082
Yorba Linda (*Calif.*)	52,422
Youngstown (*Ohio*)	95,732
Yuma (*Ariz.*)	54,923
Uruguay (1985)	
★ Montevideo	1,251,647
Uzbekistan (1991 est.)	
Amalyk	116,400
Andizhan	298,300
Angren	132,600
Bukhara	249,600
Chirchik	158,400
Dzhizak	110,900
Fergana	226,500
Karshi	168,000
Kokand	175,000
Margilan	124,900
Namangan	319,200
Navoi	111,600
Nukus	179,600
Samarkand	370,500
★ Tashkent (Toshkent)	2,113,300
Urgench	130,400
Vanuatu (1989)	
★ Vila	19,311
Venezuela (1990)	
Acarigua	130,627
Barcelona	106,061
Barinas	152,853
Barquisimeto	602,622
Baruta	292,618[4]
Cabimas	197,613[4]
★ Caracas	1,824,892
Catia la Mar	136,250
Ciudad Bolívar	225,846
Ciudad Guayana (San Felix de Guayana)	536,506
Coro	124,616
Cumaná	212,492
Guacara	122,701
Guarenas	186,506
Los Teques	143,519
Maracaibo	1,207,513
Maracay	354,428
Maturín	207,382
Mérida	167,992
Petare	531,866
Pozuelos	106,155
San Cristóbal	220,697
Turmero	211,368
Valencia	903,076
Valera	111,114[4]
Vietnam (1989)	
Bien Hoa	190,086[29]
Cam Rahn	114,041
Can Tho	208,326
Da Nang	370,670
Haiphong	456,049
★ Hanoi	1,088,862
Ho Chi Minh City (Saigon)	3,169,135
Hong Gai	123,073
Hue	211,085
Long Xuyen	217,171
My Tho	101,496[29]
Nam Dinh	165,649
Nha Trang	213,687
Qui Nhon	160,091
Thai Nguyen	126,066
Thanh Hoa	103,981[29]
Viet Tri	116,140
Vinh	154,040[29]
Vung Tau	124,634
Virgin Islands (U.S.) (1990)	
★ Charlotte Amalie	12,331
West Bank (1987 est.)	
Nābulus	106,944
★ —	—
Western Sahara (1982)	
★ El Aaiún (Laayoune)	93,875
Western Samoa (1991)	
★ Apia	32,859
Yemen (1986)	
★ Aden (economic)	318,000[1]
Al-Hudaydah	155,110
★ Ṣan'ā' (political)	427,185
Ta'izz	178,430
Yugoslavia (1991)	
★ Belgrade (Beograd)	1,136,786
Kragujevac	146,607
Niš	175,555
Novi Sad	178,896
Priština	148,656[30]
Subotica	100,219
Zaire (1991 est.)	
Boma	246,207
Bukavu	209,566
Kananga	371,862
Kikwit	182,850
★ Kinshasa	3,804,000
Kisangani	373,397
Kolwezi	544,497
Likasi	279,839
Lubumbashi	739,082
Matadi	172,926
Mbandaka	165,623
Mbuji-Mayi	613,027
Zambia (1990)	
Chingola	167,954
Kabwe	166,519
Kitwe	338,207
Luanshya	146,275
★ Lusaka	982,362
Mufulira	152,944
Ndola	376,311
Zimbabwe (1987 est.)	
Bulawayo	495,317[31]
Chitungwiza	229,000
★ Harare	863,000

[17]1980 census. [18]1987 census. [19]1981 estimate. [20]1990 estimate. [21]Distrito Federal. [22]Projections based on a repudiated census taken in 1963. [23]Federal Capital Territory; 1992 estimate. [24]1988 estimate. [25]1983 estimate. [26]Population refers to Kotte only. [27]1980 estimate. [28]1985 estimate. [29]1979 census. [30]1981 census. [31]1982 census.

Language

This table presents estimated data on the principal language communities of the countries of the world. The countries, and the principal languages (occasionally, language families) represented in each, are listed alphabetically. A bullet (●) indicates those languages that are official in each country. The sum of the estimates equals the 1993 population of the country given in the "Area and population" table.

The estimates represent, so far as national data collection systems permit, the distribution of mother tongues (a mother tongue being the language spoken first and, usually, most fluently by an individual). Many countries do not collect any official data whatever on language use, and published estimates not based on census or survey data usually span a substantial range of uncertainty. The editors have adopted the best-founded distribution in the published literature (indicating uncertainty by the degree of rounding shown) but have also adjusted or interpolated using data not part of the base estimate(s).

A variety of approaches have been used to approximate mother-tongue distribution when census data were unavailable. Some countries collect data on ethnic or "national" groups only; for such countries ethnic distribution often had to be assumed to conform roughly to the distribution of language communities. This approach, however, should be viewed with caution, because a minority population is not always free to educate its children in its own language and because better economic opportunities often draw minority group members into the majority-language community. For some countries, a given individual may be visible in national statistics only as a passport-holder of a foreign country, however long he may remain resident. Such persons, often guest workers, have sometimes had to be assumed to be speakers of the principal language of their home country. For other countries, the language mosaic may be so complex, the language communities so minute in size, scholarly study so inadequate, or the census base so obsolete that it was possible only to assign percentages to entire groups, or families, of related languages, despite their mutual unintelligibility (Papuan and Melanesian languages in Papua New Guinea, for instance). For some countries in the Americas, so few speakers of any single indigenous language remain that it was necessary to combine these groups as *Amerindian* so as to give a fair impression of their aggregate size within their respective countries.

No systematic attempt has been made to account for populations that may legitimately be described as bilingual, unless the country itself collects data on that basis, as does Bolivia or the Comoros, for example. Where a nonindigenous official or excolonial language constitutes a lingua franca of the country, however, speakers of the language as a second tongue are shown in italics, even though very few may speak it as a mother tongue. No comprehensive effort has been made to distinguish between dialect communities *usually* classified as belonging to the same language, though such distinctions were possible for some countries—*e.g.,* between French and Occitan (the dialect of southern France) or among the various dialects of Chinese.

In giving the names of Bantu languages, grammatical particles specific to a language's autonym (name for itself) have been omitted (the form *Rwanda* is used here, for example, rather than *kinyaRwanda,* and *Tswana* instead of *seTswana*). Parenthetical alternatives are given for a number of languages that differ markedly from the name of the people speaking them (such as Kurukh, spoken by the Oraon tribes of India) or that may be combined with other groups sometimes distinguishable in national data but appearing here under the name of the largest member—*e.g.,* "Tamil (and other Indian languages)" combining data on South Asian Indian populations in Singapore. The term *creole* as used here refers to distinguishable dialectal communities related to a national, official, or former colonial language (such as the French creole that survives in Mauritius from the end of French rule in 1810).

Language

Major languages by country	Number of speakers
Afghanistan[1]	
Iranian languages	
● Dari (Persian)	10,460,000
Chahar Aimak	1,280,000
Hazāra	3,850,000
Kizilbash	200,000
Tajik	5,130,000
Nūristāni group	160,000
● Pashto	7,700,000
Turkic languages	
Turkmen	510,000
Uzbek	1,280,000
Other	160,000
Albania[1]	
● Albanian	3,352,000
Greek	63,000
Macedonian	5,000
Other	1,000
Algeria[1]	
● Arabic	22,320,000
Berber	4,580,000
French	*12,000,000*
Other	130,000
American Samoa	
● English	2,000
English (lingua franca)	*52,000*
● Samoan	48,000
Tongan	2,000
Other	2,000
Andorra[2]	
● Catalan (Andorran)	18,000
English	1,000
French	5,000
Portuguese	7,000
Spanish	29,000
Other	3,000
Angola[1]	
Ambo (Ovambo)	260,000
Chokwe	460,000
Herero	80,000
Kongo	1,440,000
Luchazi	260,000
Luimbe-Nganguela	590,000
Lunda	130,000
Luvale (Luena)	390,000
Mbunda	130,000
Mbundu	2,360,000
Nyaneka-Humbe	590,000
Ovimbundu	4,060,000
● Portuguese	*3,800,000*
Other	170,000
Antigua and Barbuda	
● English	...
English/English Creole	63,000
Other	1,000
Argentina	
Amerindian languages	370,000
Italian	590,000
● Spanish	32,150,000
Other	370,000
Armenia	
● Armenian	3,310,000
Azerbaijani	90,000
Other	140,000
Aruba	
● Dutch	4,000
English	6,000
Papiamento	53,000
Spanish	5,000
Other	1,000
Australia	
Aboriginal languages	46,000
Arabic/Lebanese	131,000
Chinese	161,000
Dutch	76,000
● English	15,311,000
French	64,000
German	135,000
Greek	328,000
Hungarian	37,000
Italian	498,000
Maltese	71,000
Polish	82,000
Russian	27,000
South Slavic languages	218,000
Spanish	87,000
Turkish	39,000
Vietnamese	73,000
Other	346,000
Austria[2]	
● German	7,470,000
Polish	18,000
Romanian	17,000
South Slavic languages	202,000
Turkish	121,000
Other	111,000
Azerbaijan	
Armenian	350,000
● Azerbaijani	6,090,000
Lezgian	160,000
Russian	560,000
Other	240,000
Bahamas, The	
● English	...
English/English Creole	210,000
French (Haitian) Creole	50,000
Bahrain[2]	
● Arabic	350,000
Other	140,000
Bangladesh[1]	
● Bengali	112,460,000
Chakmā	430,000
English	*3,000,000*
Gāro	100,000
Khāsī	90,000
Marma (Magh)	220,000
Mro	30,000
Santhālī	80,000
Tripuri	80,000
Urdū	210,000
Other	1,370,000
Barbados	
Bajan (English Creole)	234,000
● English	26,000
Belarus	
● Belorussian	6,800,000
Polish	60,000
Russian	3,310,000
Ukrainian	130,000
Other	110,000
Belgium[2, 3]	
Arabic	160,000
● Dutch	5,970,000
● French	3,290,000
● German	90,000
Italian	240,000
Spanish	50,000
Turkish	90,000
Other	170,000
Belize	
Black Carib (Garífuna)	14,000
● English	103,000
English Creole (lingua franca)	*150,000*
German	3,000
Mayan languages	20,000
Spanish	64,000
Spanish (lingua franca)	*120,000*
Benin[1]	
Adja	560,000
Bariba	430,000
Dendi	110,000
Djougou	150,000
Fon	2,000,000
● French	*790,000*
Fulani (Peul)	280,000
Houéda (Péda)	430,000
Somba (Otamary)	330,000
Yoruba (Nago)	610,000
Other	190,000
Bermuda	
● English	56,000
Other	4,000
Bhutan[1]	
Assamese	200,000
● Dzongkha (Bhutiā)	970,000
Nepālī (Gurung, Rai, and Limbū)	270,000
Other	100,000
Bolivia	
● Aymara	171,000
Guaraní	2,000
● Quechua	404,000
● Spanish	3,400,000
Spanish-Aymara	1,454,000
Spanish-Guaraní	25,000
Spanish-Quechua	1,906,000
Spanish-others	137,000
Other	218,000
Bosnia and Herzegovina	
● Serbo-Croatian	4,380,000
Other	40,000
Botswana[1]	
● English	...
Khoikhoin (Hottentot)	35,000
Ndebele	18,000
San (Bushmen)	49,000
Shona	174,000
Tswana	1,061,000
Other	68,000
Brazil[1]	
Amerindian languages	270,000
German	860,000
Italian	660,000
Japanese	750,000
● Portuguese	152,500,000
Other	1,460,000
Brunei	
Chinese	26,000
English	10,000
● Malay	125,000
Malay-Chinese	2,000
Malay-English	80,000
English-Chinese	6,000
Malay-Chinese-English	11,000
Other	15,000
Bulgaria[1]	
Armenian	20,000
● Bulgarian	7,060,000
French	*240,000*
Macedonian	210,000
Romany	290,000
Russian	20,000
Turkish	820,000
Other	50,000
Burkina Faso[1, 4]	
● French	*580,000*
Fulani	810,000
Hausa	10,000
Mande languages	
Busansi (Bisa)	190,000
Dyula	70,000
Marka (Soninke)	240,000
Samo	280,000
Songhai	150,000
Tamashek (Tuareg)	330,000
Voltaic (Gur) languages	
Bobo	670,000
Gurunsi (Grusi)	500,000
Gurma	470,000
Lobi	680,000
Mossi	4,690,000
Senufo	520,000
Other	70,000
Burundi[1]	
● French	*530,000*
● Rundi	5,520,000
Hutu	4,640,000
Tutsi	760,000
Twa	50,000
Other[5]	150,000
Cambodia[1]	
Cham	220,000
Chinese	290,000
● Khmer	8,230,000
Vietnamese	510,000
Other[6]	40,000
Cameroon[1]	
Chadic languages	
Buwal (Bura)	260,000
Hausa	160,000
Kotoko	140,000
Mandara (Wandala)	740,000
Masana (Masa)	510,000
● English	...
● French	*1,970,000*
Niger-Congo languages	
Adamawa-Eastern languages	
Chamba	310,000
Gbaya	160,000
Mbum	170,000
Benue-Congo languages	
Bamileke (Medumba)-Widikum (Mogha-mo)-Bamum (Mum)	2,430,000
Basa (Bassa)	140,000
Duala	1,430,000
Fang (Pangwe)-Beti-Bulu	2,570,000
Ibibio (Efik)	20,000
Jukun	90,000
Lundu	360,000
Maka	640,000
Tikar	970,000
Tiv	340,000
Wute	40,000
Kwa languages	
Igbo	70,000
West Atlantic languages	
Fulani	1,260,000
Saharan languages	
Kanuri	40,000

Major languages by country	Number of speakers
Semitic languages	
Arabic	130,000
Other	100,000
Canada	
● English	17,117,000
● French	6,756,000
English-French	225,000
English-other	417,000
French-other	48,000
English-French-other	31,000
Aboriginal (Amerindian and Eskimo [Inuktitut]) languages	203,000
Arabic	45,000
Chinese	296,000
Czech	25,000
Danish	23,000
Dutch	138,000
Filipino (Pilipino)	48,000
Finnish	28,000
German	487,000
Greek	124,000
Hungarian	76,000
Italian	507,000
Polish	138,000
Portuguese	172,000
Punjābī	70,000
Russian	28,000
Serbo-Croatian	45,000
Spanish	93,000
Ukrainian	231,000
Vietnamese	45,000
Yiddish	25,000
Other	341,000
Cape Verde	
Crioulo (Portuguese Creole)	350,000
● Portuguese	...
Central African Republic[1]	
Banda	860,000
Baya (Gbaya)	730,000
● French	*340,000*
Kare	70,000
Mbaka	130,000
Mbum	120,000
Ngbandi	320,000
Sango (lingua franca)	*750,000*
Sara	210,000
Zande (Azande)	290,000
Other	260,000
Chad[1]	
● Arabic	1,600,000
Dagu	140,000
● French	*800,000*
Hausa	140,000
Kanuri	140,000
Kotoko	130,000
Masa	140,000
Masalit, Maba, and Mimi	380,000
Mbum	400,000
Mubi	260,000
Sara, Bagirmi, and Kreish	1,870,000
Tama	380,000
Teda (Tubu)	450,000
Other	100,000
Chile[1]	
Araucanian (Mapuche)	600,000
Aymara	170,000
Rapa Nui	3,000
● Spanish	12,410,000
Other	500,000
China[1]	
Achang	30,000
Bulang (Blang)	90,000
Ch'iang (Qiang)	210,000
Chinese (Han)	1,084,580,000
Cantonese (Yüeh [Yue])	*54,000,000*
Hakka	*40,000,000*
Hsiang (Xiang)	*52,000,000*
Kan (Gan)	*26,000,000*
● Mandarin	*775,000,000*
Min	*44,000,000*
Wu	*92,000,000*
Chingpo (Jingpo)	120,000
Chuang (Zhuang)	16,120,000
Daghur (Daur)	130,000
Evenk (Ewenki)	30,000
Gelo	460,000
Hani (Woni)	1,300,000
Hui	8,950,000
Kazakh	1,160,000
Korean	2,000,000
Kyrgyz	150,000
Lahu	430,000
Li	1,160,000
Lisu	600,000
Manchu	10,220,000
Maonan	70,000
Miao	7,700,000
Mongol	5,000,000
Mulam	170,000
Nakhi (Naxi)	290,000
Nu	30,000
Pai (Bai)	1,660,000
Pumi	30,000
Puyi (Chung-chia)	2,650,000
Salar	90,000
She	660,000
Shui	360,000
Sibo (Xibe)	180,000
Tai (Dai)	1,070,000
Tajik	40,000
Tibetan	4,780,000
Tu	200,000
T'u-chia (Tujia)	5,940,000
Tung (Dong)	2,620,000
Tung-hsiang (Dongxiang)	390,000
Uighur	7,510,000
Wa (Va)	370,000
Yao	2,220,000
Yi	6,840,000
Other	930,000
Colombia[1]	
Amerindian languages	300,000
Arawakan	40,000
Cariban	20,000
Chibchan	150,000
Other	90,000
English Creole	50,000
● Spanish	34,760,000
Comoros	
● Arabic	...
Comorian	387,000
Comorian-French	67,000
Comorian-Malagasy	28,000
Comorian-Arabic	9,000
Comorian-Swahili	2,000
Comorian-French-other	20,000
● French	*30,000*
Other	2,000
Congo[1]	
Bubangi	30,000
● French	*810,000*
Kongo	1,430,000
Kota	30,000
Lingala (lingua franca)	...
Maka	50,000
Mbete	130,000
Mboshi	320,000
Monokutuba (lingua franca)	*1,700,000*
Punu	80,000
Sango	80,000
Teke	480,000
Other	140,000
Costa Rica	
Chibchan languages	10,000
Bribrí	6,000
Cabécar	4,000
Chinese	6,000
English Creole	64,000
● Spanish	3,119,000
Côte d'Ivoire[1]	
Akan (including Baule and Anyi)	5,570,000
● French	*4,700,000*
Kru (including Bete)	2,240,000
Malinke (including Dyula and Bambara)	2,000,000
Southern Mande (including Dan and Guro)	1,370,000
Voltaic ([Gur] including Senufo and Lobi)	2,120,000
Other	160,000
Croatia	
● Serbo-Croatian	4,630,000
Other	190,000
Cuba	
● Spanish	10,892,000
Cyprus[1]	
● Greek	560,000
● Turkish	180,000
Other	30,000
Czech Republic[1]	
Bulgarian	3,000
● Czech	8,400,000
German	48,000
Greek	3,000
Hungarian	21,000
Moravian	1,361,000
Polish	59,000
Romanian	1,000
Romany	34,000
Russian	4,000
Ruthenian	2,000
Silesian	44,000
Slovak	309,000
Ukrainian	7,000
Other	36,000
Denmark[2]	
● Danish	5,006,000
English	18,000
German	9,000
Iranian languages	8,000
Norwegian	10,000
South Slavic languages	11,000
Swedish	8,000
Turkish	34,000
Other	82,000
Djibouti[1]	
Afar	110,000
● Arabic	30,000
● French	*50,000*
Somali	350,000
Gadaboursi	80,000
Issa	190,000
Issaq	80,000
Other	70,000
Dominica	
● English	3,000
French Creole	52,000
French Creole-English	19,000
Dominican Republic	
French (Haitian) Creole	150,000
● Spanish	7,470,000
Ecuador	
Quechua (and other Indian languages)	770,000
● Spanish	10,220,000
Egypt[1]	
● Arabic	56,420,000
French	*260,000*
Other	690,000
El Salvador	
● Spanish	5,517,000
Equatorial Guinea[1]	
Bubi	55,000
Fang	271,000
French	...
● Spanish	...
Other[7]	50,000
Eritrea	
Cushitic languages	
Afar	150,000
Agew (Awngi)	110,000
Beja	130,000
Saho	100,000
Nilotic languages	
Kunama	90,000
Nara	70,000
Semitic languages	
Amharic	60,000
● Arabic	...
Tigré	1,060,000
● Tigrinya	1,640,000
Other	10,000
Estonia	
● Estonian	950,000
Russian	530,000
Other	50,000
Ethiopia[1]	
● Amharic	15,640,000
Gurage	2,440,000
Oromo (Galla)	16,150,000
Sidamo	1,670,000
Somali	2,110,000
Tigrinya	3,740,000
Other	8,880,000
Faeroe Islands	
● Danish	...
● Faeroese	47,000
Fiji[1]	
● English	*150,000*
Fijian	373,000
Hindī	352,000
Other	37,000
Finland	
● Finnish	4,722,000
● Swedish	298,000
Other	38,000
France	
Arabic[8]	1,460,000
English[8]	80,000
● French[8, 9, 10]	54,030,000
Basque	*80,000*
Breton	*570,000*
Catalan (Rousillonais)	*210,000*
Corsican	*170,000*
Dutch (Flemish)	*100,000*
German (Alsatian)	*1,310,000*
Occitan	*1,560,000*
Italian[8]	260,000
Polish[8]	50,000
Portuguese[8]	660,000
Spanish[8]	220,000
Turkish[8]	200,000
Other[8]	730,000
French Guiana	
Amerindian languages	4,000
English Creole	2,000
● French	...
French Creoles	116,000
Other	6,000
French Polynesia[11]	
Chinese	12,000
● French	171,000
Polynesian languages	193,000
Other	41,000
Gabon[1]	
Fang	450,000
● French	*430,000*
Kota	50,000
Mbete	180,000
Mpongwe (Onyènè)	190,000
Punu, Sira, Nzebi	220,000
Teke	20,000
Other	170,000
Gambia, The	
Dyola	100,000
● English	...
Fulani	180,000
Malinke	380,000
Soninke	80,000
Wolof	140,000
Other	70,000
Gaza Strip	
Arabic	712,000
Hebrew	4,000
Georgia	
Abkhaz	90,000
Armenian	380,000
Azerbaijani	310,000
● Georgian	3,930,000
Ossetian	130,000
Russian	490,000
Other	170,000
Germany[2]	
● German	75,830,000
Greek	320,000
Italian	560,000
Polish	300,000
Portuguese	90,000
South Slavic languages	670,000
Spanish	140,000
Turkish	1,710,000
Kurdish	*400,000*
Vietnamese	60,000
Other	1,500,000
Ghana[1]	
Akan	8,200,000
● English	...
Ewe	1,860,000
Ga-Adangme	1,210,000
Gurma	520,000
Hausa (lingua franca)	*9,400,000*
Mole-Dagbani (Mossi)	2,480,000
Other	1,370,000
Gibraltar[2]	
Arabic	2,000
● English	26,000
Spanish	...
Other	1,000
Greece[1]	
Albanian	60,000
● Greek	9,850,000
Macedonian	160,000
Turkish	90,000
Other	150,000
Greenland[2]	
● Danish	8,000
● Greenlandic	47,000
Grenada	
● English	...
English/English Creole	91,000
Guadeloupe	
French Creole/French	398,000
● French	...
Other	21,000
Guam	
● Chamorro	42,000
Chinese	2,000
Chuukese (Trukese)	2,000
● English	53,000
English (lingua franca)	*142,000*
Japanese	3,000
Korean	5,000
Palauan	2,000
Philippine languages	29,000
Other	5,000
Guatemala	
Black Carib (Garífuna)	20,000
Mayan languages	3,410,000
Cakchiquel	870,000
Kekchí	470,000
Mam	270,000
Quiché	980,000
● Spanish	6,290,000
Guernsey	
English	64,000
French	...
Guinea[1]	
● French	*630,000*
Mande languages	
Kpelle	340,000
Loma	170,000
Malinke	1,720,000
Susu	820,000
Yalunka	220,000
Other	510,000
West Atlantic languages	
Basari-Koniagi	90,000
Fulani (Peul)	2,870,000
Kissi	440,000
Other	230,000
Other	10,000
Guinea-Bissau	
Balante	151,000
Crioulo (Portuguese Creole)	44,000
Crioulo-Portuguese	23,000
Crioulo-other (except Portuguese)	310,000
Fulani	172,000
Malinke	71,000
Mandyako	51,000
Pepel	29,000
● Portuguese	—
Portuguese-other (except Crioulo)	84,000
Other	102,000
Guyana	
Amerindian languages	14,000
Arawakan	5,000
Cariban	9,000
● English	...
English Creoles	590,000
Other (includes Caribbean Hindī and English)	151,000
Haiti	
● French	60,000
French-Haitian (French) Creole	830,000
● Haitian (French) Creole	6,010,000
Honduras	
Black Carib (Garífuna)	106,000
English Creole	16,000
Miskito	15,000
● Spanish	5,009,000
Other	2,000
Hong Kong	
Chinese	
● Cantonese	5,260,000
Cantonese (lingua franca)	*5,680,000*
Chiu Chau	83,000
Fukien (Min)	113,000
Hakka	95,000
Putonghua (Mandarin)	66,000
Putonghua (lingua franca)	*1,070,000*
Sze Yap	24,000
● English	131,000
English (lingua franca)	*1,870,000*
Filipino (Pilipino)	6,000
Japanese	12,000
Other	143,000
Hungary[1]	
German	160,000
● Hungarian	9,950,000
Romanian	20,000
Romany	*410,000*
Slovak	110,000
South Slavic languages	30,000
Other	20,000

Language (continued)

Major languages by country	Number of speakers
Iceland[2]	
● Icelandic	248,000
Other	16,000
India	
Austro-Asiatic languages	
Ho	1,060,000
Khariā	260,000
Khāsī	830,000
Korkū	480,000
Muṇḍā	460,000
Mundari	990,000
Santālī	5,540,000
Savara (Sora)	310,000
Dravidian languages	
Goṇḍī	2,570,000
Kannaḍa	35,380,000
Khond	270,000
Koyā	320,000
Kui	670,000
Kurukh (Oraon)	1,660,000
Malayālam	34,150,000
Tamil	58,860,000
Telugu	71,350,000
Tulu	1,810,000
English	310,000
● English (lingua franca)	*29,000,000*
Indo-Iranian (Indo-Aryan) languages	
Assamese	14,670,000
Bengali	67,770,000
Bhīlī (Bhilodī)	5,860,000
Barel	*400,000*
Bhilalī	*400,000*
Dogrī	2,000,000
Gujarātī	43,670,000
Halabī	690,000
● Hindī	347,610,000
Anga (Angika)	*700,000*
Baghelkhaṇḍī	*400,000*
Bāgṛī	*1,700,000*
Banjārī	*800,000*
Bhojpurī	*23,500,000*
Bundelkhaṇḍī	*600,000*
Chhattīsgaṛhī	*11,000,000*
Garhwālī	*2,100,000*
Gojrī	*500,000*
Hāṛautī	*500,000*
Khorthā (Khottā)	*800,000*
Kumaunī	*2,000,000*
Lamanī (Banjārī)	*2,000,000*
Magahī (Magadhī)	*10,900,000*
Maithilī	*10,000,000*
Mālvī	*1,100,000*
Manḍealī	*400,000*
Mārwārī	*7,700,000*
Mewārī	*1,300,000*
Nagpurī	*500,000*
Nīmāḍī	*1,300,000*
Pahārī	*2,100,000*
Rājasthānī	*3,400,000*
Sadānī (Sadrī)	*1,300,000*
Surgujiā	*900,000*
Hindī (lingua franca)	*403,000,000*
Kashmirī	4,180,000
Khandeshī	1,560,000
Kiṣan	200,000
Konkanī	2,080,000
Marāṭhī	65,300,000
Nepali (Gorkhali)	1,650,000
Oṛiyā	30,110,000
Punjābī	24,460,000
Sindhī	2,560,000
Kachchī	*800,000*
Urdū	46,480,000
Sino-Tibetan languages	
Adi	160,000
Āo	140,000
Gāro	540,000
Lushai (Mizo)	510,000
Meithei (Manipurī)	1,190,000
Nissī	180,000
Tripuri	650,000
Other	15,100,000
Indonesia	
Balinese	3,120,000
Banjarese	3,290,000
Batak	4,180,000
Buginese	4,140,000
● Indonesian (Malay)	22,790,000
Javanese	74,210,000
Madurese	8,150,000
Minang	4,440,000
Sundanese	29,680,000
Other	34,200,000
Iran[1]	
Armenian	290,000
Iranian languages	
Bakhtyārī (Lurī)	1,020,000
Baluchi	1,390,000
● Farsī (Persian)	27,730,000
Farsī (lingua franca)	*50,300,000*
Gīlakī	3,210,000
Kurdish	5,550,000
Lurī	2,630,000
Māzandarānī	2,190,000
Other	1,320,000
Semitic languages	
Arabic	1,310,000
Other	150,000
Turkic languages	
Afshari	690,000
Azerbaijani	10,220,000
Qashqa'i	770,000
Shahsavani	360,000
Turkish (mostly Pishagchi, Bayat, and Qajar)	440,000
Turkmen	950,000
Other	120,000
Other	450,000
Iraq[1]	
● Arabic	14,990,000
Assyrian	160,000
Kurdish	3,690,000
Persian	160,000
Turkish	70,000
Turkmen	260,000
Other	110,000
Ireland	
● English	3,340,000
● Irish	180,000
Isle of Man	
● English	72,000
Israel	
● Arabic	1,002,000
English	65,000
French	45,000
German	36,000
● Hebrew	3,749,000
Hungarian	31,000
Romanian	85,000
Russian	94,000
Spanish	46,000
Yiddish	117,000
Other	182,000
Italy[1]	
Albanian	120,000
Catalan	30,000
French	300,000
German	300,000
Greek	40,000
● Italian	53,840,000
Rhaetian	730,000
Friulian	710,000
Ladin	20,000
Sardinian	1,520,000
Slovene	120,000
Other	230,000
Jamaica	
● English	660,000
English Creoles	1,730,000
Hindī and other Indian languages	50,000
Other	30,000
Japan[2]	
Ainu	25,000
Chinese	170,000
English	70,000
● Japanese	123,360,000
Korean	700,000
Philippine languages	60,000
Other	230,000
Jersey	
English	86,000
● French	...
Jersey Norman French	*6,000*
Jordan[1]	
● Arabic	3,730,000
Other	30,000
Kazakhstan	
German	540,000
● Kazakh	6,750,000
Russian	8,140,000
Tatar	240,000
Uighur	180,000
Ukrainian	340,000
Uzbek	330,000
Other	660,000
Kenya[1]	
Bantu languages	
Bajun (Rajun)	70,000
Basuba	110,000
Embu	330,000
Gusii (Kisii)	1,730,000
Kamba	3,170,000
Kikuyu	5,880,000
Kuria	160,000
Luhya	3,890,000
Mbere	110,000
Meru	1,540,000
Nyika (Mijikenda)	1,340,000
Pokomo	70,000
Swahili	10,000
● Swahili (lingua franca)	*18,000,000*
Taita	280,000
Cushitic languages	
Oromo languages	
Boran	130,000
Gabbra	60,000
Gurreh	150,000
Orma	60,000
Somali languages	
Degodia	170,000
Ogaden	50,000
Somali	290,000
English (lingua franca)	*2,200,000*
Nilotic languages	
Kalenjin	3,030,000
Luo	3,590,000
Masai	440,000
Sambur	130,000
Teso	240,000
Turkana	380,000
Semitic languages	
Arabic	70,000
Other	630,000
Kiribati[1]	
● English	...
Kiribati (Gilbertese)	76,000
Tuvaluan (Ellice)	400
Other	500
Korea, North[1]	
Chinese	40,000
● Korean	22,610,000
Korea, South[1]	
Chinese	40,000
● Korean	43,990,000
Kuwait	
● Arabic	1,460,000
Other	50,000
Kyrgyzstan	
● Kyrgyz	2,380,000
Russian	1,160,000
Uzbek	570,000
Other	410,000
Laos[1]	
● Lao-Lum (Lao)	3,040,000
Lao-Soung (Miao [Hmong] and Man [Yao])	240,000
Lao-Tai (Tai)	360,000
Lao-Theung (Mon-Khmer)	750,000
Other[12]	160,000
Latvia	
● Latvian	1,350,000
Russian	1,090,000
Other	150,000
Lebanon[1]	
● Arabic	2,710,000
Armenian	170,000
French	*700,000*
Other	30,000
Lesotho[1]	
● English	...
● Sotho	1,620,000
Zulu	290,000
Liberia[1]	
● English	*570,000*
Krio (English Creole)	*2,600,000*
Kwa (Kru) languages	
Bassa	394,000
Belle (Bellleh)	15,000
De (Dey)	10,000
Grebo	255,000
Krahn	108,000
Kru	208,000
Mande (Northern) languages	
Gbandi	80,000
Kpelle	552,000
Loma	161,000
Malinke (Mandingo)	145,000
Mende	22,000
Vai	102,000
Mande (Southern) languages	
Gio (Dan)	223,000
Mano	202,000
West Atlantic (Mel) languages	
Gola	113,000
Kissi	115,000
Other	140,000
Libya[1]	
● Arabic	4,390,000
Berber	140,000
Other[13]	50,000
Liechtenstein[2]	
● German	26,900
Italian	1,000
Other	2,000
Lithuania	
● Lithuanian	3,010,000
Polish	220,000
Russian	440,000
Other	80,000
Luxembourg[2]	
Belgian	9,000
French	13,000
German	9,000
Italian	21,000
Luxemburgian	289,000
Portuguese	32,000
Spanish	2,000
Other	17,000
Macau	
Chinese	
● Cantonese	330,000
Mandarin	4,000
Other Chinese languages	30,000
English	2,000
● Portuguese	10,000
Other	4,000
Macedonia	
Albanian	420,000
● Macedonian	1,440,000
Romany	40,000
Serbo-Croatian	70,000
Turkish	70,000
Other	20,000
Madagascar[1]	
● French	*1,400,000*
● Malagasy	13,120,000
Other	140,000
Malaŵi[1]	
Chewa (Maravi)	6,170,000
● English	*530,000*
Lomwe	1,940,000
Ngoni	710,000
Yao	1,400,000
Other	360,000
Malaysia	
Bajau	120,000
Chinese	1,100,000
Chinese-others	630,000
Dusan	200,000
● English	100,000
English-others	210,000
English (lingua franca)	*5,800,000*
Iban	450,000
Iban-others	70,000
● Malay	8,220,000
Malay-others	2,920,000
Tamil	740,000
Tamil-others	10,000
Other	4,290,000
Maldives	
● Divehi (Maldivian)	237,000
Mali[1]	
Afro-Asiatic languages	
Berber languages	
Tamashek (Tuareg)	650,000
Semitic languages	
Arabic (Maure)	140,000
● French	*700,000*
Niger-Congo languages	
Mande languages	
Bambara	2,810,000
Bobo Fing	10,000
Dyula	260,000
Malinke, Khasonke, and Wasulunka	590,000
Samo (Duun)	60,000
Soninke	770,000
Voltaic (Gur) languages	
Bwa (Bobo)	210,000
Dogon	350,000
Mossi	40,000
Senufo and Minianka	1,060,000
West Atlantic languages	
Fulani and Tukulor	1,230,000
Nilo-Saharan languages	
Songhai	630,000
Other	20,000
Malta[1]	
● English	8,000
● Maltese	346,000
Other	8,000
Marshall Islands[2]	
● English	...
● Marshallese	50,500
Other	1,600
Martinique	
French Creole/French	365,000
● French	...
Other	12,000
Mauritania[1]	
● Arabic	...
French	*120,000*
Fulani	20,000
Ḥassānīyah Arabic	1,770,000
Soninke	60,000
Tukulor	120,000
Wolof	150,000
Zenaga	20,000
Other	30,000
Mauritius	
Bhojpurī	217,000
● English	2,000
French	40,000
French Creole	612,000
Hindī	123,000
Marāṭhī	14,000
Tamil	39,000
Telugu	17,000
Urdū	26,000
Other	13,000
Mayotte[14]	
Mahorais (local dialect of Comorian Swahili)	91,000
Other Comorian Swahili dialects	40,000
Malagasy	35,000
● French	44,000
Other	7,000
Mexico	
Amerindian languages	7,100,000
Amuzgo	40,000
Aztec (Nahuatl)	1,610,000
Chatino	40,000
Chinantec	150,000
Chocho	20,000
Chol	170,000
Chontal	50,000
Cora	20,000
Cuicatec	20,000
Huastec	160,000
Huave	20,000
Huichol	30,000
Kanjobal	20,000
Mame	20,000
Mayo	50,000
Mazahua	180,000
Mazatec	220,000
Mixe	130,000
Mixtec	520,000
Otomí	380,000
Popoluca	40,000
Purepecha	130,000
Tarahumara	70,000
Tepehua	10,000
Tepehuan	20,000
Tlapanec	90,000
Tojolabal	50,000
Totonac	280,000
Triqsi	20,000
Tzeltal	360,000
Tzotzil	320,000
Yaqui	10,000
Yucatec (Mayan)	950,000
Zapotec	530,000
Zoque	60,000
Other	320,000
● Spanish	82,860,000
Spanish-Amerindian languages	*5,770,000*
Micronesia	
Chuukese (Trukese)	42,800
● English	500
Kosraean	7,500
Mortlockese	7,800
Palauan	400
Pohnpeian	24,400
Woleaian	3,800
Yapese	6,000
Other	9,700
Moldova	
Gagauz	140,000
● Romanian	2,700,000
Russian	1,010,000
Ukrainian	370,000
Other	130,000
Monaco[2]	
English	2,000
● French	12,000
Italian	5,000
Monegasque	5,000
Other	6,000

Major languages by country	Number of speakers
Mongolia[1]	
Bayad	44,000
Buryat	42,000
Dariganga	35,000
Dörbed	64,000
Dzakhchin	28,000
Kazakh	119,000
● Khalkha (Mongolian)	1,749,000
Ould	12,000
Torgut	12,000
Uryankhai	27,000
Other	125,000
Morocco[1]	
● Arabic	17,220,000
Berber	8,740,000
Other[6]	530,000
Mozambique	
Chopi	440,000
Chuabo	870,000
Koti	50,000
Lomwe	1,190,000
Makonde	290,000
Makua	4,230,000
Marendje	530,000
Mwani	70,000
Ngulu	10,000
Nsenga	40,000
Nyanja	510,000
Nyungwe	340,000
Phimbi	20,000
● Portuguese	190,000
Ronga	550,000
Sena	1,430,000
Shona	1,000,000
Swahili	10,000
Swazi	10,000
Tonga	290,000
Tsonga	1,890,000
Tswa	910,000
Yao	250,000
Zulu	10,000
Other	100,000
Myanmar (Burma)[1]	
● Burmese	30,770,000
Chin	970,000
Kachin (Chingpo)	610,000
Karen	2,770,000
Kayah	180,000
Mon	1,080,000
Rakhine (Arakanese)	2,010,000
Shan	3,780,000
Other	2,440,000
Namibia[1]	
Bergdama (Damara)	120,000
East Caprivian (mostly Lozi)	60,000
● English	*130,000*
Herero	120,000
Kavango (Okavango)	140,000
Nama	70,000
Ovambo (Ambo [Kwanyama])	760,000
San (Bushmen)	40,000
Other	220,000
Nauru	
Chinese	900
English	800
Kiribati (Gilbertese)	1,800
● Nauruan	5,800
Tuvaluan (Ellice)	800
Nepal	
Austro-Asiatic (Munda) languages	
Santālī	30,000
Indo-Aryan languages	
Bengali	20,000
Bhojpurī	1,340,000
Dhanwar	20,000
Hindī	170,000
Hindī (Awadhī dialect)	350,000
Maithilī	2,390,000
● Nepālī (Eastern Pahāṛī)	10,760,000
Rājbanśī	90,000
Tharu	980,000
Urdū	210,000
Tibeto-Burman languages	
Bhutiā (Sherpa)	120,000
Chepang	20,000
Gurung	230,000
Limbū	260,000
Magar	450,000
Newārī	700,000
Rai and Kirāntī	390,000
Tamāng	940,000
Thakali	10,000
Thami	10,000
Other	710,000
Netherlands, The[2]	
Arabic	144,000
● Dutch	14,656,000
Dutch and Frisian	*580,000*
Turkish	182,000
Other	320,000
Netherlands Antilles	
● Dutch	...
English	15,000
Papiamento	165,000
Other	12,000
New Caledonia[1]	
● French	60,000
Melanesian languages	83,000
Polynesian languages (mostly Wallisian)	21,000
Other	16,000
New Zealand	
● English	3,288,000
● Maori	113,000
Other	120,000
Nicaragua	
English Creole	42,000
Misumalpan languages	
Miskito	168,000
Sumo	10,000
● Spanish	4,041,000
Other	4,000
Niger[1]	
Arabic	20,000
● French	*1,300,000*
Fulani (Fulfulde)	880,000
Hausa	4,570,000
Hausa (lingua franca)	*6,000,000*
Kanuri	360,000
Songhai, Zerma, and Dendi	1,790,000
Tamashek (Tuareg)	790,000
Teda (Tubu)	50,000
Other	60,000
Nigeria[1]	
Arabic	300,000
Bura	1,400,000
Edo	3,100,000
● English (lingua franca)	*14,000,000*
English Creole (lingua franca)[15]	*32,000,000*
Fulani	10,300,000
Hausa	19,500,000
Hausa (lingua franca)	*46,000,000*
Ibibio	5,100,000
Igbo (Ibo)	16,500,000
Ijo (Ijaw)	1,600,000
Kanuri	3,800,000
Nupe	1,100,000
Tiv	2,100,000
Yoruba	19,500,000
Other	7,200,000
Northern Mariana Islands	
Carolinian	2,200
Chamorro	13,600
Chinese	3,200
Chuukese (Trukese)	1,100
● English	2,200
English (lingua franca)	*41,100*
Japanese	900
Korean	2,900
Palauan	1,600
Philippine languages	15,500
Other	2,300
Norway[2]	
Danish	18,000
English	23,000
● Norwegian	4,159,000
Swedish	12,000
Other	96,000
Oman	
● Arabic (Omani)	1,250,000
Baluchī	320,000
Farsi (Persian)	50,000
Swahili	30,000
Urdū	40,000
Other	20,000
Pakistan	
Baluchī	3,850,000
Brāhūī	1,540,000
English (lingua franca)	*15,000,000*
Pashto	16,810,000
Punjābī	
Punjābī	61,640,000
Hindko	3,110,000
Sindhī	
Sindhī	15,060,000
Siraikī	12,580,000
● Urdū	9,730,000
Other	3,650,000
Panama	
Amerindian languages	214,000
Bokotá	4,000
Chibchan	190,000
Cuna	52,000
Guaymí	136,000
Teribe	2,000
Chocó	19,000
Embera	16,000
Waunama	3,000
Chinese	8,000
English Creoles	345,000
● Spanish	1,994,000
Other[16]	3,000
Papua New Guinea[1]	
● English	*60,000*
Melanesian languages	780,000
Papuan languages	3,060,000
Tok Pisin (English Creole)	*2,600,000*
Other[17]	80,000
Paraguay	
German	40,000
● Guaraní	1,851,000
Guaraní-Spanish	2,243,000
Portuguese	146,000
● Spanish	299,000
Other	34,000
Peru	
Aymara	210,000
● Quechua	1,740,000
● Spanish	16,730,000
Spanish-Aymara	370,000
Spanish-Quechua	3,250,000
Spanish-others	320,000
Other	300,000
Philippines	
Aklanon	630,000
Bicol	4,520,000
Bolinao (Zambal)	280,000
Cebuano	15,840,000
Chavacano	340,000
Chinese	160,000
Davaweno	190,000
● English (lingua franca)	*34,000,000*
● Filipino (Pilipino; Tagalog)	15,470,000
Hamtikanon	540,000
Hiligaynon/Ilongo	6,490,000
Ibanag	380,000
Ifugao	200,000
Ilocano	7,230,000
Kankanai	240,000
Maguindanao	780,000
Manobo	200,000
Maranao	930,000
Masbate	480,000
Pampango	2,230,000
Pangasinan	1,460,000
Romblon	270,000
Samal	380,000
Samar-Leyte (Waray-Waray)	3,000,000
Subanon	220,000
Sulu-Moro (Tau Sug)	510,000
Other	1,980,000
Poland	
Belorussian	190,000
German	500,000
● Polish	37,600,000
Ukrainian	230,000
Portugal[2]	
● Portuguese	9,730,000
Other	100,000
Puerto Rico	
English	18,000
● Spanish	1,854,000
Spanish-English	1,693,000
Other	46,000
Qatar[2]	
● Arabic	220,000
Other[18]	320,000
Réunion	
● French	*190,000*
French Creole	580,000
Other[19]	60,000
Romania	
Bulgarian	9,000
German	119,000
Hebrew	9,000
Hungarian	1,623,000
● Romanian	20,378,000
Romany	410,000
Russian	39,000
Serbo-Croatian	34,000
Slovak	21,000
Tatar	25,000
Turkish	30,000
Ukrainian	66,000
Other	27,000
Russia	
Adyghian	120,000
Armenian	360,000
Avar	540,000
Azerbaijani	280,000
Bashkir	990,000
Belorussian	440,000
Buryat	360,000
Chechen	890,000
Chuvash	1,380,000
Dargin	350,000
Georgian	90,000
German	350,000
Ingush	210,000
Kabardinian	380,000
Kalmyk	160,000
Karachay	150,000
Kazakh	560,000
Komi	240,000
Komi-Permyak	110,000
Kumyk	270,000
Lak	100,000
Lezgian	240,000
Mari	530,000
Mordovinian	750,000
Ossetian	380,000
Romanian	120,000
Romany	130,000
● Russian	128,150,000
Tabasaran	90,000
Tatar	4,750,000
Tuvinian	200,000
Udmurt	510,000
Ukrainian	1,880,000
Uzbek	100,000
Yakut	360,000
Other	1,460,000
Rwanda	
● French	*520,000*
● Rwanda	7,580,000
St. Kitts and Nevis	
● English	...
English/English Creole	42,000
St. Lucia	
● English	27,000
English/French Creole	109,000
St. Vincent and the Grenadines	
● English	...
English/English Creole	108,000
Other	1,000
San Marino[1]	
● Italian	24,000
São Tomé and Príncipe	
Crioulo (Portuguese Creole)	125,000
● Portuguese	...
Saudi Arabia[1]	
● Arabic	16,550,000
Other	870,000
Senegal[1]	
Diola (Dyola)	430,000
● French	*390,000*
Fulani (Peul)-Tukulor	1,800,000
Malinke (Mandingo)	360,000
Serer	1,150,000
Wolof	3,390,000
Wolof (lingua franca)	*5,500,000*
Other	770,000
Seychelles	
English	2,000
French	1,000
● Seselwa (French Creole)	66,000
Other	3,000
Sierra Leone[1]	
● English	...
Krio (English Creole [lingua franca])	...
Mande languages	
Kono-Vai	230,000
Kuranko	160,000
Mende	1,550,000
Susu	60,000
Yalunka	160,000
West Atlantic languages	
Bullom-Sherbro	170,000
Fulani	170,000
Kissi	100,000
Limba	370,000
Temne	1,420,000
Other	80,000
Singapore[1]	
Chinese	2,232,000
● English	*1,076,000*
● Malay	408,000
● Mandarin Chinese	...
● Tamil (and other Indian languages)	204,000
Other	33,000
Slovakia[1]	
Bulgarian	1,000
Czech	54,000
German	6,000
Hungarian	573,000
Moravian	4,000
Polish	3,000
Romany	82,000
Russian	2,000
Ruthenian	17,000
Silesian	1,000
● Slovak	4,563,000
Ukrainian	14,000
Other	10,000
Slovenia	
Serbo-Croatian	140,000
● Slovene	1,820,000
Other	40,000
Solomon Islands[1]	
● English	...
Melanesian languages	299,000
Papuan languages	30,000
Polynesian languages	13,000
Other[20]	7,000
Somalia[1]	
● Arabic	...
English	...
● Somali	7,910,000
Other	140,000
South Africa[21]	
● Afrikaans	6,390,000
● English	3,540,000
Nguni	17,710,000
Ndebele	830,000
Swazi	950,000
Xhosa	7,110,000
Zulu	8,810,000
Sotho	10,000,000
North Sotho	3,550,000
South Sotho	2,740,000
Tswana (Western Sotho)	3,720,000
Tsonga	1,390,000
Venda	790,000
Other	970,000
Bophuthatswana[22]	
● Afrikaans	...
● English	...
Nguni	360,000
North Ndebele	70,000
South Ndebele	60,000
Swazi	40,000
Xhosa	120,000
Zulu	90,000
Sotho	1,980,000
North Sotho	160,000
South Sotho	100,000
● Tswana	1,710,000
Tsonga	170,000
Venda	20,000
Other	30,000
Ciskei[22]	
● English	...
● Xhosa	880,000
Other	20,000
Transkei[22]	
● English	...
● Xhosa	3,450,000
Other	210,000
Venda[22]	
● Afrikaans	...
● English	...
● Venda	530,000
Other	60,000
Spain[2]	
Basque (Euskera)	590,000
● Castilian Spanish	31,570,000
Catalan (Català)	5,130,000
English	100,000
Galician (Gallego)	1,570,000
Other	270,000
Sri Lanka	
English	10,000
English-Sinhalese	970,000
English-Sinhalese-Tamil	640,000
English-Tamil	200,000
● Sinhalese	10,630,000
Sinhalese-Tamil	1,650,000
● Tamil	3,460,000
Other	60,000
Sudan, The[1]	
● Arabic	12,340,000
Azande	680,000
Bari	620,000
Beja	1,600,000

Language (continued)

Major languages by country	Number of speakers
Dinka	2,890,000
Fur	520,000
Lotuko	370,000
Nubian	2,030,000
Nuer	1,230,000
Shilluk	430,000
Other	2,330,000
Suriname	
● Dutch	...
English	...
Sranantonga	160,000
Sranantonga-other	160,000
Other (mostly Hindī, Javanese, and Saramacca)	80,000
Swaziland[1]	
● English	...
● Swazi	730,000
Zulu	20,000
Other[23]	60,000
Sweden[2]	
Arabic	49,000
Danish	44,000
English	31,000
Finnish	216,000
German	45,000
Iranian languages	44,000
Norwegian	51,000
Polish	38,000
South Slavic languages	45,000
Spanish	53,000
● Swedish	7,905,000
Turkish	27,000
Other	178,000
Switzerland	
● French	1,345,000
● German	4,452,000
● Italian	533,000
Romansch	41,000
Other	625,000
Syria[1]	
● Arabic	11,900,000
Armenian	380,000
Kurdish	840,000
Other	280,000
Taiwan	
Austronesian languages	340,000
Ami	125,000
Atayal	80,000
Bunun	39,000
Paiwan	61,000
Puyuma	8,000
Rukai	8,000
Saisiyat	4,000
Tsou	6,000
Yami	4,000
Chinese	
Hakka	2,120,000
● Mandarin	2,760,000
Min (South Fukien)	15,690,000
Other	20,000
Tajikistan	
Russian	550,000
● Tajik	3,550,000
Uzbek	1,320,000
Other	280,000
Tanzania[1]	
Chaga (Chagga), Pare	1,300,000
● English	*800,000*
Gogo	1,040,000
Ha	910,000
Haya	1,560,000
Hehe	1,820,000
Iramba	760,000
Luguru	1,300,000
Luo	220,000
Makonde	1,560,000
Masai	260,000
Ngoni	350,000
Nyakyusa	1,430,000
Nyamwezi (Sukuma)	5,600,000
Shambala	1,130,000
● Swahili	2,340,000
Swahili (lingua franca)	*24,000,000*
Tatoga	200,000
Yao	650,000
Other	4,080,000
Thailand[1]	
Chinese	7,010,000
Karen	210,000
Malay	2,100,000
Mon-Khmer languages	
Khmer	730,000
Kuy	620,000
Other	200,000
Thai languages	
Lao	15,550,000
● Thai (Siamese)	30,400,000
Other	400,000
Other	600,000
Togo[1]	
● French	*650,000*
Chadic languages	
Hausa	10,000
Kwa languages	
Adja-Ewe group	
Adja	119,000
Ane (Mina)	216,000
Anlo	3,000
Ewe	884,000
Fon	38,000
Hwe	4,000
Kpessi	3,000
Peda-Hula (Pla)	15,000
Watyi (Ouatchi)	392,000
Ana-Ife group	
Ahlo	7,000
Ana (Ana-Ife)	95,000
Anyana	8,000
Nago	10,000
Yoruba	7,000
Kebu-Akposo group	
Adele	8,000
Akposo	102,000
Kebu	44,000
Voltaic (Gur) languages	
Kabre-Tem group	
Kabre	525,000
Kotokoli (Tem)	219,000
Namba (Lamba)	116,000
Naudemba (Losso)	156,000
para-Gurma group	
Basari	67,000
Chekossi (Akan)	45,000
Chamba	37,000
Dye (Gangam)	36,000
Gurma	129,000
Konkomba	54,000
Moba	205,000
Mossi	10,000
Tamberma	21,000
Yanga	11,000
West Atlantic (Mel) languages	
Fulani (Peul)	52,000
Other	161,000
Tonga	
● English	...
● Tongan	97,000
Other	2,000
Trinidad and Tobago	
● English	...
English Creole	1,249,000
French Creole	...
Hindī	...
Spanish	...
Tunisia	
● Arabic	5,970,000
Arabic-French	2,240,000
Arabic-French-English	270,000
Arabic-other	10,000
Other-no Arabic	20,000
Other	20,000
Turkey[1, 24]	
Arabic	820,000
Kurdish	3,720,000
● Turkish	55,050,000
Other	280,000
Turkmenistan	
Russian	470,000
● Turkmenian	2,850,000
Uzbek	340,000
Other	300,000
Tuvalu	
● English	...
Kiribati (Gilbertese)	700
Tuvaluan (Ellice)	8,800
Uganda[1]	
Bantu languages	
Ganda (Luganda)	3,150,000
Gisu	1,270,000
Gwere	510,000
Kiga (Chiga)	1,210,000
Konjo	240,000
Nkole	1,460,000
Nyoro	580,000
Rundi	550,000
Rwanda	1,030,000
Soga	1,460,000
Swahili (lingua franca)	*6,200,000*
Toro	570,000
Central Sudanic languages	
Lugbara	680,000
Madi	240,000
English	*180,000*
Nilotic languages	
Acholi	820,000
Alur	300,000
Karamojong	360,000
Kuman	180,000
Lango	1,070,000
Padhola	290,000
Teso	1,580,000
Other	170,000
Ukraine	
Belorussian	160,000
Bulgarian	170,000
Hungarian	160,000
Polish	30,000
Romanian	350,000
Russian	17,190,000
● Ukrainian	33,850,000
Other	450,000
United Arab Emirates[2]	
● Arabic	840,000
Other[18]	1,150,000
United Kingdom	
● English	56,380,000
Scots-Gaelic	80,000
Welsh	550,000
Other	940,000
United States	
Amharic	40,000
Arabic	400,000
Armenian	170,000
Bengali	40,000
Cajun	40,000
Chinese (including Formosan)	1,450,000
Czech	100,000
Danish	40,000
Dutch	160,000
● English	222,550,000
English (lingua franca)	*250,760,000*
Finnish	60,000
French	1,910,000
French Creole (mostly Haitian)	210,000
German	1,730,000
Greek	440,000
Gujarātī	110,000
Hebrew	160,000
Hindī (including Urdū)	370,000
Hungarian	170,000
Ilocano	50,000
Italian	1,470,000
Japanese	480,000
Korean	700,000
Kru (Gullah)	70,000
Lithuanian	60,000
Malayālam	40,000
Miao (Hmong)	90,000
Mon-Khmer (mostly Cambodian)	140,000
Navajo	170,000
Norwegian	90,000
Pennsylvania Dutch	90,000
Persian	230,000
Polish	810,000
Portuquese	480,000
Punjābī	60,000
Romanian	70,000
Russian	270,000
Samoan	40,000
Serbo-Croatian	130,000
Slovak	90,000
Spanish	19,430,000
Swedish	90,000
Syriac	40,000
Tagalog	940,000
Thai (including Laotian)	230,000
Turkish	50,000
Ukrainian	110,000
Vietnamese	570,000
Yiddish	240,000
Other	760,000
Uruguay	
● Spanish	3,040,000
Other	110,000
Uzbekistan	
Crimean Tatar	190,000
Karakalpak	420,000
Kazakh	800,000
Korean	110,000
Kyrgyz	150,000
Russian	2,300,000
Tajik	940,000
Tatar	390,000
Turkish	110,000
Turkmenian	120,000
Ukrainian	80,000
● Uzbek	15,100,000
Other	470,000
Vanuatu	
● Bislama (English Creole)	*130,000*
● English	...
● French	*50,000*
Melanesian languages	157,000
Other	3,000
Venezuela	
● Amerindian languages	210,000
Goajiro	80,000
Warrau (Warao)	30,000
Other	100,000
● Spanish	20,810,000
Other	470,000
Vietnam[1]	
Bahnar	150,000
Cham	110,000
Chinese (Hoa)	990,000
Hre	110,000
Jarai	270,000
Khmer	980,000
Ko'ho	100,000
Man (Mien, or Yao)	520,000
Miao (Meo, or Hmong)	610,000
Mnong	70,000
Muong	1,000,000
Nung	770,000
Rhadé	210,000
Roglai	80,000
San Chay (Cao Lan)	130,000
San Diu	110,000
Sedang	110,000
Stieng	60,000
Tai	1,140,000
Tho (Tay)	1,300,000
● Vietnamese	61,180,000
Other	480,000
Virgin Islands (U.S.)	
● English	85,000
French	3,000
Spanish	14,000
Other	3,000
West Bank	
Arabic	1,050,000
Hebrew	100,000
Western Sahara	
Arabic	213,000
Western Samoa	
● English	1,000
● Samoan	78,000
Samoan-English	85,000
Yemen[1]	
● Arabic	12,270,000
Other	250,000
Yugoslavia	
Albanian	1,440,000
Hungarian	400,000
Romanian	60,000
Romany	100,000
● Serbo-Croatian	8,150,000
Slovak	70,000
Vlach	140,000
Other	200,000
Zaire[1]	
Azande	2,590,000
Boa	990,000
Chokwe	7,800,000
● French	*3,300,000*
Kongo	6,820,000
Kongo (lingua franca)	*13,000,000*
Lingala (lingua franca)	*29,000,000*
Luba	7,640,000
Lugbara	680,000
Mongo	5,730,000
Ngala and Bangi	2,450,000
Rundi	1,640,000
Rwanda	4,360,000
Swahili (lingua franca)	*21,000,000*
Teke	1,160,000
Other	7,640,000
Zambia[25]	
Bemba group	3,090,000
Aushi (Ushi)	150,000
Bemba	2,120,000
Bisa	120,000
Lala	240,000
Lamba	200,000
Other	250,000
● English	*700,000*
Lozi (Barotse) group	700,000
Lozi (Barotse)	510,000
Luyi (Luyana)	130,000
Nkoya	50,000
Other	10,000
Mambwe group	390,000
Lungu	80,000
Mambwe	140,000
Mwanga (Winawanga)	160,000
Other	10,000
North-Western group	860,000
Chokwe	50,000
Kaonde	230,000
Luchazi	50,000
Lunda	220,000
Luvale (Luena)	170,000
Mbunda	130,000
Nyanja (Maravi) group	1,500,000
Chewa	450,000
Ngoni	170,000
Nsenga	390,000
Nyanja (Maravi)	440,000
Other	50,000
Tonga (Ila-Tonga) group	1,280,000
Ila	70,000
Lenje	150,000
Soli	60,000
Tonga	930,000
Other	70,000
Tumbuka group	390,000
Senga	70,000
Tumbuka	320,000
Other	310,000
Zimbabwe	
● English	230,000
Ndebele (Nguni)	1,640,000
Nyanja	230,000
Shona	7,300,000
Other	720,000

[1]Figures given represent ethnolinguistic groups. [2]Data refer to nationality (usually resident aliens holding foreign passports). [3]Data are partly based on place of residence. [4]Majority of population speak Moré (language of the Mossi); Dyula is language of commerce. [5]Swahili also spoken. [6]French also spoken. [7]Pidgin English and Portuguese Creole also spoken. [8]Based on "nationality" at 1982 census. [9]Includes naturalized citizens. [10]French is the universal language throughout France; traditional dialects and minority languages are retained regionally in the approximate numbers shown, however. [11]Data reflect multilingualism; total 1993 population is 212,000. [12]English and French also spoken. [13]English and Italian also spoken. [14]Data reflect ability to speak the language, not mother tongue; 1993 population estimate is 104,000. [15]Includes speakers of standard English. [16]English also spoken. [17]Hiri (Police Motu) also spoken. [18]Mostly Pakistanis, Indians, and Iranians. [19]Gujarātī and Chinese also spoken. [20]Solomon Islands Pidgin (English) is the lingua franca. [21]Includes the Black national states also shown separately. [22]Excludes adjustment for significant elements of change such as territorial transfers and migration. [23]Afrikaans and Portuguese also spoken. [24]Recent semiofficial projections for ethnic groups based on mother tongue data collected in the 1935 and 1965 censuses. Other current published estimates differ considerably, especially with respect to Kurdish speakers, who may number substantially higher. [25]Groups are officially defined geographic divisions; elements comprising them are named by language.

Religion

The following table presents statistics on religious affiliation for each of the countries of the world. An assessment was made for each country of the available data on distribution of religious communities within the total population; the best available figures, whether originating as census data, membership figures of the churches concerned, or estimates by external analysts in the absence of reliable local data, were applied as percentages to the estimated 1993 midyear population of the country to obtain the data shown below.

Several concepts govern the nature of the available data, each useful separately but none the basis of any standard of international practice in the collection of such data. The word "affiliation" was used above to describe the nature of the relationship joining the religious bodies named and the populations shown. This term implies some sort of formal, usually documentary, connection between the religion and the individual (a baptismal certificate, a child being assigned the religion of its parents on a census form, maintenance of one's name on the tax rolls of a state religion, etc.) but says nothing about the nature of the individual's personal religious practice, in that the individual may have lapsed, never been confirmed as an adult, joined another religion, or may have joined an organization that is formally atheist.

The user of these statistics should be careful to note that not only does the nature of the affiliation (with an organized religion) differ greatly from country to country, but the social context of religious practice does also. A country in which a single religion has long been predominant will often show more than 90% of its population to be *affiliated,* while in actual fact, no more than 10% may actually *practice* that religion on a regular basis. Such a situation often leads to undercounting of minority religions (where someone [head of household, communicant, child] is counted at all), blurring of distinctions seen to be significant elsewhere (a Hindu country may not distinguish Protestant [or even Christian] denominations; a Christian country may not distinguish among its Muslim or Buddhist citizens), or double-counting in countries where an individual may conscientiously practice more than one "religion" at a time.

Until 1989 communist countries had for long consciously attempted to ignore, suppress, or render invisible religious practice within their borders. Countries with large numbers of adherents of traditional, often animist, religions and belief systems usually have little or no formal methodology for defining the nature of local religious practice. On the other hand, countries with strong missionary traditions, or good census organizations, or few religious sensitivities may have very good, detailed, and meaningful data.

The most comprehensive work available is DAVID B. BARRETT (ed.), *World Christian Encyclopedia* (1982); it examines both the theoretical and practical problems of collecting and analyzing religious statistics, assembles a mine of national detail, and establishes a basis for further study.

Religion

Religious affiliation	1993 population
Afghanistan	
Sunnī Muslim	17,030,000
Shī'ī Muslim	3,040,000
other	200,000
Albania	
Muslim	2,220,000
Albanian Orthodox	680,000
Roman Catholic	440,000
other	70,000
Algeria	
Sunnī Muslim	26,890,000
other	140,000
American Samoa	
Congregational	30,000
Roman Catholic	11,000
other	12,000
Andorra	
Roman Catholic	56,000
other	6,000
Angola	
Roman Catholic	7,500,000
Protestant	2,160,000
traditional beliefs	1,040,000
other	220,000
Antigua and Barbuda	
Anglican	29,000
Protestant	27,000
Roman Catholic	7,000
other	2,000
Argentina	
Roman Catholic	30,710,000
other	2,800,000
Armenia	
Armenian Apostolic (Orthodox)	2,840,000
other (mostly Roman Catholic and Muslim)	710,000
Aruba	
Roman Catholic	62,000
other	8,000
Australia	
Roman Catholic	4,620,000
Anglican	4,230,000
Uniting Church and Methodist	1,340,000
Presbyterian	640,000
other Protestant	1,100,000
Orthodox	480,000
nonreligious	2,250,000
other	3,070,000
Austria	
Roman Catholic	6,700,000
Evangelical Lutheran	440,000
atheist and nonreligious	470,000
other	330,000
Azerbaijan	
Believers are predominantly Shī'ī Muslim; Sunnī Muslim (Ḥanafīyah) minority.	
Bahamas, The	
Protestant	147,000
Anglican	53,000
Roman Catholic	50,000
other	16,000
Bahrain	
Shī'ī Muslim	290,000
Sunnī Muslim	120,000
other	80,000
Bangladesh	
Muslim	99,710,000
Hindu	13,960,000
other	1,400,000
Barbados	
Anglican	103,000
Protestant	66,000
other	91,000
Belarus	
Belorussian Orthodox	8,700,000
Roman Catholic	1,535,000
Jewish	115,000
Belgium	
Roman Catholic	9,060,000
other	1,010,000
Belize	
Roman Catholic	127,000
Anglican	24,000
other	53,000
Benin	
traditional beliefs	3,160,000
Roman Catholic	1,070,000
Muslim	610,000
other	250,000
Bermuda	
Anglican	23,000
Methodist	10,000
Roman Catholic	8,000
other	20,000
Bhutan	
Buddhist	1,080,000
Hindu	380,000
other	90,000
Bolivia	
Roman Catholic	7,140,000
other	580,000
Bosnia and Herzegovina	
Sunnī Muslim	1,770,000
Serbian Orthodox	1,370,000
Roman Catholic	660,000
Protestant	180,000
other	440,000
Botswana	
traditional beliefs	690,000
Protestant	370,000
African Christian	170,000
Roman Catholic	130,000
other	50,000
Brazil	
Roman Catholic (including syncretic Afro-Catholic cults having Spiritist beliefs and rituals)	118,900,000
Evangelical Protestant	17,200,000
other	20,300,000
Brunei	
Muslim	183,000
other	93,000
Bulgaria	
Bulgarian Orthodox	7,410,000
Muslim	890,000
other	170,000
Burkina Faso	
traditional beliefs	4,380,000
Muslim	4,210,000
Christian[1]	1,190,000
Burundi	
Roman Catholic	3,690,000
nonreligious	1,060,000
other	920,000
Cambodia	
Buddhist	8,210,000
other	1,080,000
Cameroon	
Roman Catholic	4,550,000
traditional beliefs	3,400,000
Muslim	2,860,000
Protestant	2,290,000
Canada	
Roman Catholic	13,330,000
Protestant	8,260,000
Anglican	2,850,000
Eastern Orthodox	420,000
Jewish	350,000
Muslim	120,000
Sikh	80,000
Hindu	80,000
nonreligious	2,080,000
other	590,000
Cape Verde	
Roman Catholic	332,000
Protestant	18,000
Central African Republic	
Protestant	1,480,000
Roman Catholic	990,000
traditional beliefs	360,000
other	170,000
Chad	
Muslim	2,690,000
traditional beliefs	1,390,000
Roman Catholic	1,280,000
Protestant	710,000
other	50,000
Chile	
Roman Catholic	10,930,000
Protestant	830,000
other	1,780,000
China	
nonreligious	698,000,000
Chinese folk-religionist	237,000,000
atheist	142,000,000
Buddhist	71,000,000
Muslim	28,000,000
other	4,000,000
Colombia	
Roman Catholic	31,480,000
other	2,480,000
Comoros	
Sunnī Muslim	514,000
Christian	2,000
Congo	
Roman Catholic	1,500,000
Protestant	680,000
African Christian	390,000
other	210,000
Costa Rica	
Roman Catholic	2,600,000
other	600,000
Côte d'Ivoire	
Muslim	5,100,000
Roman Catholic	2,800,000
traditional beliefs	2,300,000
nonreligious	1,800,000
Protestant	900,000
other	600,000
Croatia	
Roman Catholic	3,690,000
Serbian Orthodox	540,000
Sunnī Muslim	60,000
other	540,000
Cuba	
Roman Catholic	4,310,000
nonreligious	5,300,000
atheist	700,000
other	580,000
Cyprus	
Greek Orthodox	550,000
Muslim (mostly Sunnī)	180,000
other (mostly Christian)	30,000
Czech Republic	
Roman Catholic	4,050,000
Evangelical Church of Czech Brethren	190,000
Czechoslovak Hussite	170,000
Silesian Evangelical	50,000
Eastern Orthodox	20,000
atheist and nonreligious	4,100,000
other	1,750,000
Denmark	
Evangelical Lutheran	4,576,000
other	611,000
Djibouti	
Sunnī Muslim	531,000
Christian[1]	34,000
Dominica	
Roman Catholic	57,000
other	17,000
Dominican Republic	
Roman Catholic	6,930,000
other	700,000
Ecuador	
Roman Catholic	10,210,000
other	780,000
Egypt	
Sunnī Muslim	51,400,000
Christian (mostly Coptic[2])	5,700,000
El Salvador	
Roman Catholic	5,160,000
other	350,000
Equatorial Guinea	
Roman Catholic	310,000
other	70,000
Eritrea	
Christian (mostly Ethiopian Orthodox)	1,700,000
Muslim	1,700,000
Estonia	
Believers are predominantly affiliated with the Evangelical Lutheran Church of Estonia; Russian Orthodox and Protestant minorities.	
Ethiopia	
Ethiopian Orthodox	26,260,000
Muslim (mostly Sunnī)	15,200,000
traditional beliefs	6,160,000
other	2,910,000
Faeroe Islands	
Evangelical Lutheran	35,000
other	12,000
Fiji	
Christian (mostly Methodist and Roman Catholic)	403,000
Hindu	291,000
Muslim	60,000
other	8,000

Religion (continued)

Religious affiliation	1993 population
Finland	
Evangelical Lutheran	4,417,000
other	641,000
France	
Roman Catholic	44,080,000
nonreligious	7,040,000
atheist	1,960,000
Muslim	1,730,000
Jewish	640,000
other	2,240,000
French Guiana	
Roman Catholic	96,000
other	32,000
French Polynesia	
Protestant	99,000
Roman Catholic	84,000
other	29,000
Gabon	
Roman Catholic	830,000
Protestant	240,000
African Christian	150,000
other	60,000
Gambia, The	
Muslim (mostly Sunnī)	985,000
other	48,000
Gaza Strip	
Muslim (mostly Sunnī)	703,000
other	9,000
Georgia	
Georgian Orthodox	3,570,000
Sunnī Muslim	600,000
Russian Orthodox	550,000
Armenian Apostolic (Orthodox)	440,000
other	330,000
Germany	
Evangelical Lutheran	32,650,000
Roman Catholic	28,690,000
Muslim	1,730,000
other (mostly nonreligious or unaffiliated)	18,120,000
Ghana	
Protestant	3,910,000
traditional beliefs	3,350,000
Roman Catholic	2,920,000
African Christian	2,500,000
Muslim	2,450,000
Anglican	330,000
other	180,000
Gibraltar	
Roman Catholic	22,000
other	7,000
Greece	
Greek Orthodox	10,060,000
Muslim	150,000
other	100,000
Greenland	
Evangelical Lutheran	55,000
other	1,000
Grenada	
Roman Catholic	54,000
Anglican	16,000
other	21,000
Guadeloupe	
Roman Catholic	380,000
other	40,000
Guam	
Roman Catholic	114,000
Protestant	22,000
other	8,000
Guatemala	
Roman Catholic	7,280,000
Protestant	2,430,000
Guernsey	
Anglican	41,000
other	23,000
Guinea	
Muslim	6,310,000
Christian	590,000
traditional beliefs	520,000
Guinea-Bissau	
traditional beliefs	670,000
Muslim	310,000
Christian	50,000
Guyana	
Hindu	280,000
Protestant	122,000
Anglican	108,000
Roman Catholic	86,000
Muslim	66,000
other	93,000
Haiti	
Roman Catholic	5,540,000
Baptist	670,000
Pentacostal	250,000
other	440,000
Honduras	
Roman Catholic	4,380,000
Protestant	510,000
other	260,000
Hong Kong	
Buddhist and Taoist	4,380,000
Roman Catholic	270,000
Protestant	220,000
other	1,060,000
Hungary	
Roman Catholic	6,600,000
Protestant	2,400,000
nonreligious and atheist	1,160,000
Jewish	90,000
other	50,000
Iceland	
Evangelical Lutheran	243,000
other	21,000
India[3]	
Hindu	719,000,000
Muslim	99,000,000
Sikh	17,000,000
Roman Catholic	10,000,000
Protestant	8,000,000
Buddhist	6,000,000
Jain	4,000,000
other	4,000,000
Indonesia	
Muslim	164,140,000
Protestant	11,370,000
Roman Catholic	6,740,000
Hindu	3,440,000
Buddhist	1,940,000
other	580,000
Iran	
Shīʿī Muslim	55,000,000
Sunnī Muslim	4,740,000
other	1,030,000
Iraq	
Shīʿī Muslim	12,150,000
Sunnī Muslim	6,710,000
other	580,000
Ireland	
Roman Catholic	3,272,000
other	244,000
Isle of Man	
Anglican	44,000
other	27,000
Israel	
Jewish[4]	4,240,000
Muslim (mostly Sunnī)	760,000
other	230,000
Italy	
Roman Catholic	47,560,000
nonreligious	7,780,000
atheist	1,490,000
other	410,000
Jamaica	
Protestant	1,230,000
Anglican	180,000
Roman Catholic	120,000
other	940,000
Japan	
Shintoist[5]	109,950,000
Buddhist[5]	97,090,000
Christian	1,470,000
other	10,600,000
Jersey	
Anglican	53,000
Roman Catholic	20,000
other	13,000
Jordan	
Sunnī Muslim	3,500,000
other	260,000
Kazakhstan	
Believers are predominantly Sunnī Muslim (Ḥanafīyah); Christian minorities (mainly Russian Orthodox and Baptist).	
Kenya	
Roman Catholic	7,420,000
Protestant	5,430,000
traditional beliefs	5,310,000
African Christian	4,950,000
Anglican	2,040,000
Muslim	1,690,000
other	1,290,000
Kiribati	
Roman Catholic	41,000
Congregational	30,000
other	8,000
Korea, North	
atheist and nonreligious	15,380,000
traditional beliefs	3,530,000
Ch'ŏndogyo	3,150,000
other	580,000
Korea, South	
Buddhist	15,990,000
Confucian	10,770,000
Protestant	10,280,000
Roman Catholic	2,270,000
Wonbulgyo	1,150,000
Ch'ŏndogyo	1,020,000
Taejong	500,000
other	2,070,000
Kuwait	
Kuwaiti nationals are predominantly Sunnī Muslim; Shīʿī Muslim minority.	
Kyrgyzstan	
Believers are predominantly Sunnī Muslim (Ḥanafīyah).	
Laos	
Buddhist	2,620,000
traditional beliefs	1,520,000
other	390,000
Latvia	
Believers are predominantly affiliated with the Latvian Evangelical Lutheran Church; Russian Orthodox, Roman Catholic, and Protestant minorities.	
Lebanon	
Shīʿī Muslim	1,050,000
Sunnī Muslim	680,000
Maronite Christian	580,000
Druze	200,000
Greek Orthodox	160,000
Greek Catholic	100,000
Armenian Christian	100,000
other	30,000
Lesotho	
Roman Catholic	830,000
Protestant	570,000
other	500,000
Liberia	
Christian	1,930,000
traditional beliefs	530,000
Muslim	390,000
Libya	
Sunnī Muslim	4,440,000
other	140,000
Liechtenstein	
Roman Catholic	26,000
other	4,000
Lithuania	
Roman Catholic	3,000,000
other (mostly Russian Orthodox, Old Believer, Evangelical Lutheran, and nonreligious)	750,000
Luxembourg	
Roman Catholic	369,000
other	23,000
Macau	
Buddhist	170,000
nonreligious	170,000
other	40,000
Macedonia	
Macedonian Orthodox	1,220,000
Sunnī Muslim	540,000
other	310,000
Madagascar	
Christian[1]	6,760,000
traditional beliefs	6,230,000
other	270,000
Malaŵi	
Christian[1]	6,820,000
traditional beliefs	2,010,000
Muslim	1,710,000
other	30,000
Malaysia	
Muslim	10,090,000
Buddhist	3,300,000
Chinese folk-religionist	2,210,000
Hindu	1,340,000
Christian	1,220,000
other	920,000
Maldives	
Sunnī Muslim	237,000
Mali	
Muslim	7,780,000
traditional beliefs	780,000
Christian	90,000
Malta	
Roman Catholic	363,000
other	4,000
Marshall Islands	
Believers are predominantly Protestant (mainly Congregational); Roman Catholic minority.	
Martinique	
Roman Catholic	330,000
other	40,000
Mauritania	
Sunnī Muslim	2,160,000
other	10,000
Mauritius	
Hindu	580,000
Roman Catholic	280,000
Muslim	140,000
Protestant	50,000
other	50,000
Mayotte	
Sunnī Muslim	101,000
Christian	3,000
Mexico	
Roman Catholic	80,680,000
Protestant and Evangelical Catholic	4,400,000
Jewish	70,000
nonreligious	2,910,000
other	1,900,000
Micronesia	
Believers are about equally Roman Catholic and Protestant (mainly Congregational).	
Moldova	
Russian (Moldovan) Orthodox	2,810,000
other (mostly nonreligious)	1,550,000
Monaco	
Roman Catholic	28,000
other	3,000
Mongolia	
atheist and nonreligious	1,480,000
traditional beliefs	700,000
other	80,000
Morocco	
Muslim (mostly Sunnī)	26,120,000
other	340,000
Mozambique	
traditional beliefs	7,290,000
Roman Catholic	4,790,000
Muslim	1,980,000
other	1,180,000
Myanmar (Burma)	
Buddhist	39,900,000
Christian	2,190,000
Muslim	1,710,000
traditional beliefs	510,000
Hindu	230,000
other	70,000
Namibia	
Lutheran	787,000
Roman Catholic	304,000
Dutch Reformed	94,000
Anglican	77,000
other	275,000
Nauru	
Congregational	5,500
other	4,500
Nepal	
Hindu	17,240,000
Buddhist	1,020,000
Muslim	510,000
other	490,000
Netherlands, The	
Roman Catholic	5,510,000
Dutch Reformed Church (NHK)	2,910,000
Reformed Churches	1,220,000
Muslim	420,000
nonreligious	4,900,000
other	340,000
Netherlands Antilles	
Roman Catholic	161,000
other	31,000
New Caledonia	
Roman Catholic	106,000
other	73,000
New Zealand	
Anglican	750,000
Presbyterian	560,000
Roman Catholic	520,000
Methodist	140,000
Baptist	70,000
Ratana	50,000
Mormon	50,000
nonreligious	690,000
other	680,000
Nicaragua	
Roman Catholic	3,870,000
other	400,000
Niger	
Sunnī Muslim	8,400,000
other	120,000
Nigeria	
Muslim	41,200,000
Protestant	24,080,000
Roman Catholic	11,080,000
African Christian	9,700,000
traditional beliefs	5,130,000
other	370,000
Northern Mariana Islands	
Roman Catholic	38,000
other	7,000
Norway	
Evangelical Lutheran (Church of Norway)	3,786,000
other	522,000
Oman	
Muslim	1,460,000
other	240,000

Religious affiliation	1993 population
Pakistan	
Muslim (mostly Sunnī)	123,870,000
Christian	2,000,000
Hindu	1,930,000
other	170,000
Panama	
Roman Catholic	2,150,000
other	410,000
Papua New Guinea	
Protestant	2,290,000
Roman Catholic	1,290,000
Anglican	210,000
other	130,000
Paraguay	
Roman Catholic	4,430,000
other	180,000
Peru	
Roman Catholic	21,090,000
other	1,820,000
Philippines	
Roman Catholic	54,630,000
Aglipayan	4,030,000
Muslim	2,790,000
Protestant	2,270,000
other	1,230,000
Poland	
Roman Catholic	36,520,000
Polish Orthodox	580,000
other	1,420,000
Portugal	
Roman Catholic	9,280,000
other	540,000
Puerto Rico	
Roman Catholic	3,080,000
other	530,000
Qatar	
Muslim (mostly Sunnī)	500,000
other	40,000
Réunion	
Roman Catholic	560,000
other	70,000
Romania	
Romanian Orthodox	19,790,000
Roman Catholic	1,140,000
other	1,860,000
Russia	
Believers are predominantly affiliated with the Russian Orthodox Church; Roman Catholic, Protestant, Muslim, Jewish, and Buddhist minorities.	
Rwanda	
Roman Catholic	4,930,000
traditional beliefs	1,900,000
Protestant	680,000
Muslim	80,000
St. Kitts and Nevis	
Anglican	14,000
Methodist	12,000
other	17,000
St. Lucia	
Roman Catholic	107,000
other	29,000
St. Vincent and the Grenadines	
Anglican	45,000
Methodist	23,000
Roman Catholic	13,000
other	28,000
San Marino	
Roman Catholic	23,000
other	1,000
São Tomé and Príncipe	
Roman Catholic	100,000
Protestant	30,000
Saudi Arabia	
Muslim (mostly Sunnī)	17,210,000
other	210,000
Senegal	
Sunnī Muslim	7,430,000
Christian	390,000
other	90,000
Seychelles	
Roman Catholic	63,000
other	8,000
Sierra Leone	
traditional beliefs	2,310,000
Sunnī Muslim	1,770,000
other	410,000
Singapore	
Buddhist and Taoist	1,550,000
Muslim	442,000
Protestant	225,000
Roman Catholic	139,000
Hindu	102,000
nonreligious	403,000
other	15,000
Slovakia	
Roman Catholic	3,220,000
Slovak Evangelical	330,000
atheist	520,000
other	1,260,000
Slovenia	
Roman Catholic	1,880,000
other	120,000
Solomon Islands	
Protestant	146,000
Anglican	118,000
Roman Catholic	67,000
other	17,000
Somalia	
Sunnī Muslim	8,030,000
other	20,000
South Africa[6]	
Christian	22,460,000
Protestant	11,190,000
Dutch (Afrikaans) Reformed Churches	4,040,000
Nederduitse Gereformeerde	3,560,000
Gereformeerde	180,000
Nederduitsch Hervormde	300,000
other Protestant	7,160,000
Methodist	2,060,000
Presbyterian	450,000
United Congregational	420,000
Lutheran	830,000
Apostolic Faith Mission of South Africa	440,000
New Apostolic Church	160,000
other Apostolic	460,000
Baptist	280,000
Pentecostal Protestant	80,000
African Protestant Church	40,000
Full Gospel	220,000
Pentecostal	20,000
Salvation Army	30,000
Seventh-day Adventist	100,000
Swiss	40,000
Assemblies of God	170,000
other	1,350,000
Roman Catholic	2,570,000
Anglican	1,320,000
Greek Orthodox	30,000
Black independent churches	7,330,000
Zion Christian Church	1,540,000
other	5,790,000
Mormon	10,000
Hindu	430,000
Muslim	370,000
Jewish	120,000
other beliefs	30,000
nonreligious	400,000
not stated	9,310,000
Bophuthatswana	
Christian	2,320,000
traditional beliefs	250,000
Ciskei	
Christian	650,000
traditional beliefs	250,000
Transkei	
Christian[1]	2,560,000
traditional beliefs	1,100,000
Venda	
traditional beliefs	460,000
Christian	130,000
Spain	
Roman Catholic	37,730,000
other	1,410,000
Sri Lanka	
Buddhist	12,210,000
Hindu	2,730,000
Muslim	1,330,000
Roman Catholic	1,210,000
other	140,000
Sudan, The	
Sunnī Muslim	18,250,000
traditional beliefs	4,180,000
Christian[1]	2,270,000
other	300,000
Suriname	
Hindu	111,000
Roman Catholic	92,000
Muslim	79,000
Protestant	76,000
other	46,000
Swaziland	
Christian[1]	630,000
traditional beliefs	170,000
other	20,000
Sweden	
Church of Sweden (Lutheran)	7,700,000
other	1,027,000
Switzerland	
Roman Catholic	3,330,000
Protestant	3,100,000
other	570,000
Syria	
Sunnī Muslim	9,910,000
Shīʿī Muslim	2,010,000
Christian[1]	1,210,000
other	270,000
Taiwan	
Chinese folk-religionist	10,150,000
Buddhist	9,000,000
Christian[1]	1,550,000
other	230,000
Tajikistan	
Sunnī Muslim	4,560,000
Shīʿī Muslim	1,140,000
Tanzania	
Muslim	9,000,000
Christian	9,000,000
traditional beliefs	9,000,000
Thailand	
Buddhist	54,570,000
Muslim	2,280,000
Christian	310,000
other	670,000
Togo	
traditional beliefs	2,240,000
Roman Catholic	820,000
Sunnī Muslim	460,000
Protestant	260,000
other	30,000
Tonga	
Free Wesleyan	43,000
Roman Catholic	16,000
other	44,000
Trinidad and Tobago	
Roman Catholic	450,000
Hindu	287,000
Anglican	221,000
Protestant	204,000
Muslim	75,000
other	12,000
Tunisia	
Sunnī Muslim	8,480,000
other	60,000
Turkey	
Muslim (mostly Sunnī)	59,390,000
other	480,000
Turkmenistan	
Muslim (mostly Sunnī)	3,650,000
Russian Orthodox	430,000
other	210,000
Tuvalu	
Congregational	9,200
other	300
Uganda	
Roman Catholic	8,800,000
Anglican	4,650,000
traditional beliefs	2,240,000
Muslim (mostly Sunnī)	1,170,000
other	880,000
Ukraine	
Believers are predominantly affiliated with the Ukrainian Orthodox Church; Ukrainian Autocephalous Orthodox and Ukrainian Catholic (Uniate) minorities.	
United Arab Emirates	
Sunnī Muslim	1,590,000
Shīʿī Muslim	320,000
other	80,000
United Kingdom	
Christian[1]	50,470,000
Church of England	32,990,000
Protestant	8,710,000
Roman Catholic	7,610,000
Eastern Orthodox	350,000
other Christian	810,000
Muslim	810,000
Hindu	410,000
Jewish	315,000
Sikh	230,000
nonreligious and atheist	5,520,000
other	325,000
United States[7]	
Christian[1]	223,240,000
Protestant	131,570,000
Roman Catholic	67,710,000
Anglican	4,470,000
Eastern Orthodox	750,000
other Christian	6,870,000
other Christian (denomination not stated)	11,880,000
Muslim	4,910,000
Jewish	4,620,000
Buddhist	590,000
Hindu	340,000
New-Religionist	150,000
Baha'i	50,000
nonreligious	19,320,000
agnostic	1,760,000
other (mostly not stated)	3,250,000
Uruguay	
Roman Catholic	2,080,000
other	1,070,000
Uzbekistan	
Believers are predominantly Sunnī Muslim (Ḥanafīyah).	
Vanuatu	
Presbyterian	57,000
Roman Catholic	23,000
Anglican	22,000
other	58,000
Venezuela	
Roman Catholic	18,940,000
other	1,670,000
Vietnam	
Buddhist	47,260,000
Roman Catholic	6,390,000
New-Religionist	
Cao Dai	2,500,000
Hoa Hao	1,500,000
other	13,260,000
Virgin Islands (U.S.)	
Protestant	48,000
Roman Catholic	35,000
other	21,000
West Bank	
Muslim (mostly Sunnī)	1,050,000
Jewish[8]	240,000
Christian and other	80,000
Western Sahara	
Sunnī Muslim	213,000
Western Samoa	
Congregational	77,000
Roman Catholic	35,000
other	51,000
Yemen	
Muslim	12,500,000
other	20,000
Yugoslavia	
Serbian Orthodox	6,860,000
Sunnī Muslim	2,010,000
Roman Catholic	420,000
Protestant	110,000
other	1,160,000
Zaire	
Roman Catholic	20,560,000
Protestant	12,320,000
African Christian	7,260,000
traditional beliefs	1,440,000
Muslim	590,000
other	300,000
Zambia	
Christian[1]	6,120,000
traditional beliefs	2,300,000
other	90,000
Zimbabwe	
Christian[1]	6,200,000
traditional beliefs	4,330,000
other	160,000

[1]Includes affiliated and nominal Christians. [2]Official 1986 census figure is 5.9 percent. [3]Excludes Assam. [4]Excludes Israelis in Jewish settlements in the West Bank and East Jerusalem. [5]Many Japanese practice both Shintoism and Buddhism. [6]Excludes black republics listed separately. [7]For additional denominational detail, *see* the article WORLD AFFAIRS (North America): *United States*. [8]Includes Israelis in Jewish settlements in the West Bank and East Jerusalem.

Vital statistics, marriage, family

This table provides some of the basic measures of the factors that influence the size, direction, and rates of population change within a country. The accuracy of these data depends on the effectiveness of each respective national system for registering vital and civil events (birth, death, marriage, etc.) and on the sophistication of the analysis that can be brought to bear upon the data so compiled.

Data on birth rates, for example, depend not only on the completeness of registration of births in a particular country but also on the conditions under which those data are collected: Do all births take place in a hospital? Are the births reported comparably in all parts of the country? Are the records of the births tabulated at a central location in a timely way with an effort to eliminate inconsistent reporting of birth events, perinatal mortality, etc.? Similar difficulties attach to death rates but with the added need to identify "cause of death." Even in a developed country such identifications are often left to nonmedical personnel, and in a developing country with, say, only one physician for every 10,000 population, there will be too few physicians to perform autopsies to assess accurately the cause of death after the fact and also too few to provide ongoing care at a level where records would permit inference about cause of death based on prior condition or diagnosis.

Calculating natural increase, which at its most basic is simply the difference between the birth and death rates, may be affected by the differing degrees of completeness of birth and death registration for a given country. The total fertility rate may be understood as the average number of children that would be borne per woman if all childbearing women lived to the end of their childbearing years and bore children at each age at the average rate for that age. Calculating a meaningful fertility rate requires analysis of changing age structure of the female population over time, changing mortality rates among mothers and their infants, and changing medical practice at births, each improvement of natural survivorship or medical support leading to greater numbers of live-born children and greater numbers of children who survive their first year (the basis for measurement of infant mortality, another basic indicator of demographic conditions and trends within a population).

As indicated above, data for causes of death are not only particularly difficult to obtain, since many countries are not well equipped to collect the data, but also difficult to assess, as their accuracy may be suspect and their meaning may be subject to varying interpretation. Take the case of a citizen of a less developed country who dies of what is clearly a lung infection: Was the death complicated by chronic malnutrition, itself complicated by a parasitic infestation, these last two together so weakening the subject that he died of an infection that he might have survived had his general health been better? Similarly, in a developed country: Someone may die from what is identified in an autopsy as a cerebrovascular accident, but if that accident occurred in a vascular system that was weakened by diabetes, what was the actual cause of death? Statistics on causes of death seek to identify the "underlying" cause (that which sets the final train of events leading to death in motion) but often must settle for the most proximate cause or symptom. Even this kind of analysis may be misleading for those charged with interpreting the data with a view to ordering health-care priorities for a particular country. The eight groups of causes of death utilized here include most, but not all, of the detailed

Vital statistics, marriage, family

country	vital rates						causes of death (rate per 100,000 population)								
	year	birth rate per 1,000 population	death rate per 1,000 population	infant mortality rate per 1,000 live births	rate of natural increase per 1,000 population	total fertility rate	year	infectious and parasitic diseases	malignant neoplasms (cancers)	endocrine and metabolic disorders	diseases of the nervous system	diseases of the circulatory system	diseases of the respiratory system	diseases of the digestive system	accidents, poisoning, and violence
Afghanistan	1991	43.7	20.0	164.0	23.7	6.3	...	...	...	...	...	...	...	...	...
Albania	1990	25.2	5.6	28.2[2]	19.6	2.9[2]	...	...	...	...	...	...	...	...	...
Algeria	1991	32.0	7.0	57.0	25.0	4.9	...	...	...	...	...	...	...	...	...
American Samoa	1990	39.3	5.1	13.5	34.2	5.2	1990	16.4[4]	46.8	16.4[5]	...	131.1[6]	65.6[7]	...	58.5
Andorra	1992	12.1	3.6	6.4[8]	8.7	1.3[2]	...	...	...	...	...	...	...	...	...
Angola	1990–95	46.6	18.6	127.0	28.0	6.3	...	...	...	...	...	...	...	...	...
Antigua and Barbuda	1991	18.0	6.0	20.0[9]	12.0	1.9	1988	14.0	44.5	25.4	7.6	237.5	44.5	15.2	5.1
Argentina	1991	20.0	9.0	31.0	11.0	2.7	1989	26.2	142.2	27.1	9.6	347.8	47.6	36.2	54.3
Armenia	1991	21.6	6.5	17.9	15.1	2.6[12]	1990	13.0[12]	98.3	14.2[12]	4.0[12]	305.9	50.3	21.7	55.6
Aruba	1991	17.2	6.4	9.6[12]	10.8	1.8[13]	1989	9.8	118.7	45.5	4.9	243.8	29.3	29.3	13.0
Australia	1992	15.1	7.1	8.2[14]	8.0	1.9[14]	1988	4.4	178.8	16.4	13.0	333.1	54.6	25.1	51.3
Austria	1992	12.0	10.5	7.4	1.5	1.5[2]	1991	3.3	246.8	26.6	15.0	562.3	49.9	52.8	69.0
Azerbaijan	1991	27.0	6.3	25.3	20.7	2.8[12]	1989	42.1	72.1	8.6	9.7	292.4	88.9	25.6	42.1
Bahamas, The	1990	19.6	5.3	28.4	14.3	2.1[2]	1990	18.0	80.4	72.2	11.0	126.3	52.2	29.0	40.8
Bahrain	1991	27.9	3.7	17.0	24.2	4.7[14]	1988	2.4	34.1	14.6	2.2	110.0	15.0	3.8	23.7
Bangladesh	1990	32.8	11.3	94.0	21.5	4.9[2]	...	...	...	...	...	...	...	...	...
Barbados	1992	16.2	9.1	9.1	7.1	1.8[2]	1988	19.8	160.7	79.8	15.2	338.9	47.9	36.6	44.0
Belarus	1991	12.9	11.2	12.1	1.7	2.0[12]	1990	7.1	171.8	7.1[15]	9.7	545.8	73.6	22.2	100.5
Belgium	1992	11.5	10.6	8.9	0.9	1.6[16]	1987	8.5	272.4	24.3	32.3	429.5	77.9	39.0	69.4
Belize	1991	38.0	5.0	35.0	33.0	4.6	1990	...	52.4	37.0[5]	...	164.0	57.1	32.8	92.6[17]
Benin	1991	49.0	16.0	119.0	33.0	7.0	...	...	...	...	...	...	...	...	...
Bermuda	1990	15.0	7.5	7.8	7.5	1.8[12]	1990	...	181.5	...	...	344.4	25.2	...	38.6
Bhutan	1991	39.0	19.0	128.2[14]	20.0	5.9	...	...	...	...	...	...	...	...	...
Bolivia	1988	42.8	14.1	102.0	28.7	6.1[18]	...	...	...	...	...	...	...	...	...
Bosnia and Herzegovina	1990	14.1	6.4	15.2	7.7	...	1989	9.9	122.6[19]	12.6	11.9	344.1	29.0	29.2	47.1
Botswana	1990–95	43.9	9.5	58.0	34.4	6.4	...	...	...	...	...	...	...	...	...
Brazil	1990–95	26.1	7.5	57.0	18.6	3.2	1987[21]	*47*	*73*	*19*	*9*	*211*	*62*	*30*	*92*
Brunei	1991	29.0	3.0	11.0	26.0	3.7	1986	5.3	27.0	...	...	80.0	23.4	...	39.8
Bulgaria	1992	10.5	12.7	15.9	−2.2	1.6	1991	6.0	172.7	21.3	6.0	764.5	67.5	34.0	57.9
Burkina Faso	1990–95	47.0	17.1	127.0	29.9	6.5	...	...	...	...	...	...	...	...	...
Burundi	1991	47.0	15.0	111.0	32.0	6.9	...	...	...	...	...	...	...	...	...
Cambodia	1989	41.8	16.9	131.0	24.9	4.6	...	...	...	...	...	...	...	...	...
Cameroon	1990–95	47.3	13.3	86.0	34.0	6.9	...	...	...	...	...	...	...	...	...
Canada	1991	15.2	7.2	6.8	8.0	1.7[3]	1990	4.8	197.2	23.5	18.3	282.5	61.2	26.3	49.1
Cape Verde	1992	48.0	10.0	61.0	38.0	5.3[16]	1980	153.7	43.8	20.6	16.5	135.8	72.3	27.7	30.1
Central African Republic	1990–95	45.1	16.3	95.0	28.8	6.2	...	...	...	...	...	...	...	...	...
Chad	1990–95	43.3	17.9	122.0	25.4	5.8	...	...	...	...	...	...	...	...	...
Chile	1990	23.3	6.0	16.0	17.3	2.6	1989	21.1	105.7	11.1	8.7	157.8	64.5	45.8	74.7
China	1992	18.2	6.6	33.0[2]	11.6	2.3[2]	1989[22]	23.0	113.1	7.0[15]	4.1	204.8	121.5	27.2	56.5
Colombia	1990–95	25.8	6.9	37.0	18.9	2.9	1990[21]	*26*	*83*	*17*	*10*	*193*	*53*	*23*	*159*
Comoros	1991	47.5	13.0	87.0	34.5	7.0	...	...	...	...	...	...	...	...	...
Congo	1990–95	46.1	13.2	65.0	32.9	6.3	...	...	...	...	...	...	...	...	...
Costa Rica	1990	27.4	3.8	15.3	23.6	3.0[2]	1989	11.9	81.2	15.6	7.7	110.1	37.8	20.3	22.1
Côte d'Ivoire	1990–95	50.0	13.2	87.0	36.8	7.4	...	...	...	...	...	...	...	...	...
Croatia	1991	10.8	11.4	11.1	−0.6	1.7[14]	1990	10.8	226.1[19]	14.9[15]	6.9	571.8	29.5	53.2	91.8
Cuba	1991	18.0	7.0	10.7[14]	11.0	1.9	1990	9.4	128.7	23.3	10.6	294.7	58.0	26.3	79.9
Cyprus	1991	18.6	8.8	9.8	9.8	2.4[3]	...	...	...	...	...	...	...	...	...
Czech Republic	1992	11.8	11.7	9.9	0.1	1.9[14]	1990	4.3	274.4[19]	22.5	10.2	698.6	52.3	48.5	87.3
Denmark	1991	12.5	11.6	7.3	0.9	1.7	1991	8.1	289.8	19.7	11.5	510.1	84.5	40.3	72.4
Djibouti	1990–95	45.8	16.4	112.0	29.4	6.6	...	...	...	...	...	...	...	...	...
Dominica	1990	22.3	7.1	18.4	15.2	2.7[2]	1990	37.5	116.6	51.4	9.7	273.5	43.0	20.8	18.0
Dominican Republic	1991	27.0	7.0	60.0	20.0	3.1	1985	51.4	27.4	12.3	8.6	100.3	35.4	22.3	33.7
Ecuador	1990	32.9	7.4	51.7	25.5	4.1	1990[25]	*76*	*79*	*20*	*14*	*139*	*84*	*41*	*103*
Egypt	1991	30.8	7.5	49.6[18]	23.3	5.4[18]	1987	98.9	22.0	9.1	13.6	314.4	140.7	45.8	39.1
El Salvador	1991	34.0	7.0	47.0	27.0	4.1	1990[21]	*52*	*43*	*17*	*12*	*120*	*49*	*38*	*137*

causes classified by the World Health Organization and would not, thus, aggregate to the country's crude death rate for the same year. Among the lesser causes excluded by the present classification are: benign neoplasms; nutritional disorders; anemias; mental disorders; kidney and genitourinary diseases not classifiable under the main groups; maternal deaths (for which data *are* provided, however, in the "Health services" table); diseases of the skin and musculoskeletal systems; congenital and perinatal conditions; and general senility and other ill-defined (ill-diagnosed) conditions, a kind of "other" category.

Expectation of life is probably the most accurate single measure of the quality of life in a given society. It summarizes in a single number all of the natural and social stresses that operate upon individuals in that society. The number may range from as few as 40 years of life in the least developed countries to as much as 80 years for women in the most developed nations. The lost potential in the years separating those two numbers is prodigious, regardless of how the loss arises—wars and civil violence, poor public health services, or poor individual health practice in matters of nutrition, exercise, stress management, and so on.

Data on marriages and marriage rates probably are less meaningful in terms of international comparisons than some of the measures mentioned above because the number, timing, and kinds of social relationships that substitute for marriage depend on many kinds of social variables—income, degree of social control, heterogeneity of the society (race, class, language communities), or level of development of civil administration (if one must travel for a day or more to obtain a legal civil ceremony, one may forgo it). Nevertheless, the data for a single country say specific things about local practice in terms of the age at which a man or woman typically marries, and the overall rate will at least define the number of legal civil marriages, though it cannot say anything about other, less formal arrangements (here the figure for the legitimacy rate for children in the next section may identify some of the societies in which economics or social constraints may operate to limit the number of marriages that are actually confirmed on civil registers). The available data usually include both first marriages and remarriages after annulment, divorce, widowhood, or the like.

The data for families provide information about the average size of a family unit (individuals related by blood or civil register) and the average number of children under a specified age (set here at 15 to provide a consistent measure of social minority internationally, though legal minority depends on the laws of each country). When well-defined family data are not collected as part of a country's national census or vital statistics surveys, data for households are substituted on the assumption that most households worldwide represent families in some conventional sense. In the older countries of Europe and North America, increasing numbers of households are composed of unrelated individuals (unmarried heterosexual couples, aged [or younger] groups sharing limited [often fixed] incomes for reasons of economy, or homosexual couples); such arrangements are not yet so common in the rest of the world that they represent great numbers overall. Very few census programs, even in developed countries, make adequate provision for distinguishing these households.

expectation of life at birth (latest year)		nuptiality, family, and family planning																country
		marriages			age at marriage (latest)						families (F), households (H) (latest)							
					groom (percent)			bride (percent)			families (households)		children		induced abortions		
male	female	year	total number	rate per 1,000 population	19 and under	20–29	30 and over	19 and under	20–29	30 and over	total ('000)	size	number under age 15	percent legitimate	number	ratio per 100 live births	
44.0	43.0	...	...	...	...	...	...	...	...	...	H 2,110	H 6.2	H 2.8[1]	...	...	...	Afghanistan
69.3	75.4	1989	27,655	8.6	1.2	78.2	20.6	20.0	74.9	5.1	F 675	F 4.7	F 1.6	...	...	...	Albania
65.0	67.3	1988	139,930	5.9	0.7[3]	67.1[3]	32.2[3]	29.8[3]	61.4[3]	8.8[3]	H 3,322	H 6.9	H 3.0	...	...	...	Algeria
69.0	74.0	1990	370	7.8	...	...	...	...	...	...	H 7	H 7.0	H 2.7	72.0	...	...	American Samoa
74.0	81.0	1992	135	2.2	...	...	...	...	...	...	...	...	...	...	...	...	Andorra
44.9	48.1	...	...	...	...	...	...	...	...	...	...	H 4.8	...	...	...	...	Angola
70.0	74.0	1988	382	4.9	1.0[10]	37.4[11]	61.6	3.7[10]	52.4[11]	43.9	H 15	H 4.2	H 1.9	23.4	...	...	Antigua and Barbuda
68.0	74.0	1983	177,010	6.0	5.6	71.5	22.9	26.0	58.6	15.4	H 7,104	H 3.9	H 1.2	67.5	...	...	Argentina
67.4	73.3	1989	27,257	7.8	2.7	77.0	20.3	34.0	54.2	11.8	H 559	H 4.7	H 1.8	92.1	26,141	34.7	Armenia
71.6	76.8	1991	515	7.6	...	...	...	...	...	...	H 15	H 4.0	...	63.2	...	...	Aruba
73.9	80.0	1990	116,959	6.8	1.3	59.0	39.7	6.2	64.9	28.9	F 4,140	F 3.1	F 0.5	80.0	...	...	Australia
72.6	79.2	1991	44,106	5.6	1.7	60.9	37.4	6.8	68.1	25.1	H 3,021	H 2.6	H 0.5	75.2	...	...	Austria
67.0	74.8	1989	71,874	10.4	1.2	80.4	18.4	24.8	63.9	11.3	H 1,381	H 4.8	H 1.7	97.5	42,134	23.2	Azerbaijan
68.8	76.3	1990	2,182	8.6	1.3	53.8	44.9	5.3	61.1	33.6	H 68	H 3.8	...	41.2	...	...	Bahamas, The
71.0	76.0	1990	2,942	5.8	1.8	69.8	28.4	26.2	59.9	13.9	H 67	H 6.5	H 2.2	...	...	...	Bahrain
56.4	55.4	1990	1,130,000	10.8	...	...	...	...	...	...	H 19,700	H 5.3	...	...	...	...	Bangladesh
72.9	77.9	1989	2,047	8.0	0.2	43.2	56.6	1.7	58.7	39.6	H 67	H 3.7	H 1.5	26.9	...	...	Barbados
66.3	75.6	1989	97,929	9.6	4.1	74.7	21.2	26.2	55.6	18.2	H 2,796	H 3.2	H 0.8	92.1	140,900	86.3	Belarus
72.4	79.1	1988	59,075	6.0	1.4	74.5	24.1	9.3	73.6	17.7	F 3,613	F 2.7	F 0.5	90.8	...	...	Belgium
67.0	72.0	1991	1,047	5.4	7.8	58.1	34.1	27.4	50.6	22.0	H 38	H 4.9	H 2.2	42.5	822	12.1	Belize
49.0	52.0	1980–85	...	12.8	...	...	...	...	...	...	...	H 5.4	...	...	...	...	Benin
73.0	79.0	1990	907	15.2	0.2	37.4	62.4	1.5	49.4	49.1	H 22	H 2.6	H 0.5	63.9	92	11.0	Bermuda
49.2	47.8	...	...	...	...	...	...	...	...	...	...	H 5.4	...	...	...	...	Bhutan
51.0	55.0	1980	26,990	4.8	8.3	75.1	16.6	26.1	55.4	18.5	H 1,050	H 4.4	H 1.8	80.9	...	...	Bolivia
68.0	73.0	1990	31,449	7.0	2.3[12]	76.0[12]	21.7[12]	28.5[12]	59.3[12]	12.2[12]	H 1,203	H 3.6	H 1.1[20]	...	...	...	Bosnia and Herzegovina
52.7	59.3	1986	1,638	1.5	—	33.0	67.0	5.0	69.2	25.8	H 125	H 5.7	H 2.0	28.8	17	0.1	Botswana
63.5	69.1	1989	827,928	5.7	8.0	73.1	18,9	34.7	54.3	11.0	F 31,888	F 4.2	...	...	...	...	Brazil
72.6	76.4	1986	1,673	7.4	5.6	72.5	21.9	12.5	58.9	28.6	H 23	H 5.8	H 2.5	99.6	...	...	Brunei
68.0	74.7	1991	48,820	5.3	5.9[14]	76.6[14]	17.5[14]	38.0[14]	51.8[14]	10.2[14]	F 2,627	F 3.3	F 0.7	88.0	144,644	137.5	Bulgaria
47.6	50.9	...	...	...	...	...	...	...	...	...	...	H 4.9	...	...	...	...	Burkina Faso
50.0	54.0	...	...	...	...	...	...	...	...	...	...	H 4.6	...	...	...	...	Burundi
46.5	49.4	...	...	...	...	...	...	...	...	...	...	H 5.6	...	...	...	...	Cambodia
53.5	56.5	...	...	...	...	...	...	...	...	...	...	H 5.2	...	...	...	...	Cameroon
73.3	80.0	1989	190,640	7.3	1.2	58.8	40.0	5.4	64.9	29.7	F 6,735	F 3.1	F 0.8	83.8	70,705	18.0	Canada
60.0	64.0	1988	1,040	3.2	2.3	62.4	35.3	17.0	61.1	21.9	F 59	F 5.1	...	55.2	...	...	Cape Verde
48.0	53.0	...	...	...	...	...	...	...	...	...	...	H 4.3	...	...	...	...	Central African Republic
45.9	49.1	...	...	...	...	...	...	...	...	...	...	H 3.9	...	...	...	...	Chad
68.5	75.6	1990	98,702	7.5	4.9	72.9	22.2	20.3	64.6	15.1	H 1,690	H 4.5	H 2.0	65.7	29	—	Chile
68.6	71.8	1991	9,509,849	8.3	...	...	...	...	...	...	H 278.6[23]	H 4.1	H 1.1	...	10,500,000	47.7	China
66.4	72.3	1980	102,448	3.8	6.4	69.6	24.0	31.5	56.5	12.0	F 4,772	F 5.4	F 2.5	75.2	...	...	Colombia
50.3	53.8	...	...	...	...	...	...	...	...	...	...	H 5.6	...	...	...	...	Comoros
52.1	57.3	...	...	...	...	...	...	...	...	...	H 326	H 4.7	H 2.0	...	...	...	Congo
72.9	77.6	1990	22,703	7.6	7.5	65.6	26.9	27.8	54.6	17.6	F 472	F 5.0	F 1.7	62.8	...	...	Costa Rica
52.8	56.2	...	...	...	...	...	...	...	...	...	...	H 4.5	...	...	...	...	Côte d'Ivoire
67.0	74.0	1991	21,550	4.5	1.2[12]	72.4[12]	26.4[12]	19.5[12]	64.8[12]	15.7[12]	H 1,544	H 3.1	H 0.6	...	...	...	Croatia
73.0	78.0	1989	85,535	8.1	8.3	57.0	34.7	24.3	49.9	25.8	F 2,002	H 4.2	H 1.6	...	151,146	81.7	Cuba
74.1	78.6	1989	5,597	8.1	0.8	70.5	28.7	17.8	66.0	16.2	H 160	H 3.5	H 1.1	99.6	...	...	Cyprus
67.7	74.8	1990	90,953	8.8	7.8	70.5	21.7	32.1	52.9	15.0	H 4,052	H 2.5	H 0.5	91.8	126,055	96.2	Czech Republic
72.2	77.7	1991	31,099	6.0	0.5	44.4	55.1	2.1	56.9	41.0	F 2,800	F 1.8	F 0.2	53.5	21,456	35.0	Denmark
47.4	50.7	...	...	...	...	...	...	...	...	...	...	H 5.6	...	96.8	...	...	Djibouti
73.0	79.0	1990	228	3.3	—	41.2	58.8	3.1	58.3	38.6	H 18	H 4.3	H 2.2	...	...	...	Dominica
65.0	69.0	1987	15,642	2.3	8.0[24]	63.0[24]	29.0[24]	29.7[24]	51.0[24]	19.3[24]	H 753	H 5.1	H 2.5	32.8	562	0.5	Dominican Republic
63.4	67.6	1989	62,996	6.0	12.2	64.5	23.3	33.7	52.2	14.1	...	H 4.1	...	67.9	...	...	Ecuador
59.0	60.0	1990	456,000	8.3	5.9[3]	61.8[3]	32.3[3]	40.4[3]	49.2[3]	10.4[3]	H 9,733	H 4.9	H 2.1	100.0	...	...	Egypt
63.0	68.0	1989	23,167	4.4	6.2	57.0	36.8	22.1	52.9	25.0	H 686	H 5.4	H 2.4	32.0	...	...	El Salvador

Vital statistics, marriage, family (continued)

country	vital rates						causes of death (rate per 100,000 population)								
	year	birth rate per 1,000 population	death rate per 1,000 population	infant mortality rate per 1,000 live births	rate of natural increase per 1,000 population	total fertility rate	year	infectious and parasitic diseases	malignant neoplasms (cancers)	endocrine and metabolic disorders	diseases of the nervous system	diseases of the circulatory system	diseases of the respiratory system	diseases of the digestive system	accidents, poisoning, and violence
Equatorial Guinea	1992	42.0	15.0	117.0[16]	27.0	5.4	...	...	...	...	...	...	...	...	...
Eritrea[26]	...	...	...	...	...	...	...	...	...	...	...	...	...	...	...
Estonia	1991	12.3	12.6	12.4[14]	−0.3	1.8	1990	8.1	194.2	5.0[5]	1.3[27]	746.7	24.6	11.0	124.8
Ethiopia[26]	1990–95	48.4	18.3	122.0	30.1	6.8	...	...	...	...	...	...	...	...	...
Faeroe Islands	1992	16.8	8.4	8.5[2]	8.4	2.7[14]	1991	6.3	187.8	16.9[5]	—	392.4	61.2	6.3	40.1
Fiji	1990	24.8	4.9	27.0[13]	19.9	3.1	1985	31.3	53.3	29.1[5]	2.7[15]	190.8	43.1	13.3	48.5
Finland	1991	13.1	9.8	5.9[14]	3.3	1.8	1991	7.8	192.0	12.6	18.4	484.5	68.8	37.5	92.8
France	1992	12.9	9.1	6.7	3.8	1.8[2]	1990	12.1	243.1	25.1	19.9	307.6	67.1	47.7	85.1
French Guiana	1990	31.5	5.2	15.8	26.3	3.7[2]	1984	55.2	62.7	10.1[5]	3.8[15]	152.9	25.1	33.8	104.0
French Polynesia	1990	27.4	4.6	10.4	22.8	3.9	1984	21.2	67.7	10.0	19.4	120.1	36.5	17.7	58.9
Gabon	1990–95	43.4	16.0	94.0	27.4	5.3	...	...	...	...	...	...	...	...	...
Gambia, The	1990–95	44.9	19.5	132.0	25.4	6.2	...	...	...	...	...	...	...	...	...
Gaza Strip	1991	43.0	6.0	41.0	37.0	6.9	...	...	...	...	...	...	...	...	...
Georgia	1990	17.0	8.4	15.9	8.6	2.1[12]	1989	13.5	98.6	12.0	4.1	553.2	51.4	32.1	58.2
Germany	1990	11.4	11.6	7.5[2]	−0.2	1.5[12, 29]	1990	7.6	258.5	29.0	15.8	583.4	71.7	52.6	57.9
Ghana	1990–95	43.2	12.3	81.0	30.9	6.1	...	...	...	...	...	...	...	...	...
Gibraltar	1991	20.2	9.1	5.7	11.1	2.8	1987	17.0	203.9	—	—	601.4	34.0	23.8	3.4
Greece	1990	10.1	9.2	9.7	0.9	1.8[12]	1990	6.0	192.6	10.6	6.6	486.5	51.3	22.0	44.0
Greenland	1991	21.4	7.9	27.7	13.5	2.4	1991	14.5	127.2	3.6[5]	5.4[27]	178.0	49.0	10.9	272.5
Grenada	1989	33.0	8.3	29.0[2]	24.7	3.0[2]	1984	13.5	90.5	62.9	11.4	290.3	54.1	39.5	47.9
Guadeloupe	1992	17.7	5.6	10.4	12.1	2.3[12]	1988	20.8	115.3	23.0	12.3	191.2	29.1	39.5	73.7
Guam	1988	27.4	3.8	9.9	23.6	3.1	1989	8.5	49.5	24.0[5]	...	139.3	35.6[3]	16.2	65.8
Guatemala	1992	34.0	8.0	43.6[12]	26.0	4.6	1984	211.5	29.8	29.6	9.0	57.2	145.7	21.7	52.0
Guernsey	1991	12.5	10.4	1.3[14]	2.1	1.6[12]	1990	8.4	314.3	11.8	15.1	430.3	112.6	30.3	20.2
Guinea	1991	47.0	21.0	134.0	26.0	6.5	...	...	...	...	...	...	...	...	...
Guinea-Bissau	1991	42.0	18.0	140.0	24.0	6.0	...	...	...	...	...	...	...	...	...
Guyana	1991	23.0	7.0	51.0	16.0	2.7	1984	19.3	37.1	33.3	11.6	202.5	39.8	74.0	56.5
Haiti	1991	43.0	15.0	106.0	28.0	4.8	...	...	...	...	...	...	...	...	...
Honduras	1991	39.0	8.0	48.0	31.0	5.3	1983	46.6	12.4	5.3	7.8	48.4	26.3	16.7	42.2
Hong Kong	1992	12.0	5.0	5.0	7.0	1.2[14]	1991	16.7	153.8	4.7[15]	4.0	140.8	81.5	21.3	32.2
Hungary	1992	11.7	14.2	14.8	−2.5	1.8[2]	1991	8.9	303.6	19.9	11.7	733.0	60.4	88.8	124.5
Iceland	1991	17.6	7.0	5.5	10.6	2.2	1991	5.0	172.9	8.9	16.3	313.2	77.5	17.4	46.9
India	1991	32.5	11.4	80.0[14]	21.1	3.8	...	...	...	...	...	...	...	...	...
Indonesia	1991	32.2	11.7	90.0	20.5	3.7	...	...	...	...	...	...	...	...	...
Iran	1991	44.0	9.0	66.0	35.0	6.2	...	...	...	...	...	...	...	...	...
Iraq	1991	46.0	7.0	80.0	39.0	6.2	...	...	...	...	...	...	...	...	...
Ireland	1991	15.7	9.0	9.1	6.7	2.4	1990	5.4	203.1	17.5	17.4	408.5	127.2	24.0	41.9
Isle of Man	1992	12.3	13.1	2.3	−0.8	1.8[12]	1992	18.4	299.9	7.1[5]	—	640.8	209.3	18.4	59.4
Israel	1992	21.4	6.6	9.3	14.8	2.9[2]	1989	11.3	121.0	23.9	8.9	264.3	42.9	17.4	43.7
Italy	1991	9.8	9.6	8.3	0.2	1.4[16]	1989	3.6	247.9	36.9	16.1	402.5	57.8	51.5	49.1
Jamaica	1992	23.9	5.4	27.0[12]	18.5	2.7[2]	1985	30.0	91.4	29.1	13.6	229.6	36.8	21.4	17.4
Japan	1991	9.9	6.7	4.6	3.2	1.5[14]	1991	10.1	181.7	9.7	5.3	247.4	83.2	31.2	45.8
Jersey	1991	12.5	9.9	6.0[12]	2.6	1.3[12]	...	...	...	...	...	...	...	...	...
Jordan	1991	45.7	4.7	38.0	41.0	7.1	...	...	...	...	...	...	...	...	...
Kazakhstan	1991	21.0	8.0	27.4	13.0	2.8[12]	1989	24.6	131.1	6.3	6.1	333.9	79.4	24.6	99.9
Kenya	1990–95	47.0	9.7	63.0	37.3	6.8	...	...	...	...	...	...	...	...	...
Kiribati	1992	33.0	12.0	63.0[2]	21.0	3.9	...	...	...	...	...	...	...	...	...
Korea, North	1993	23.0	5.0	24.0	18.0	2.4	1986	19.4	69.0	3.0[15]	6.5	224.9	46.7	51.6	38.2
Korea, South	1993	15.0	6.0	15.0	11.0	1.6	1990	12.8	89.8[19]	11.2[15]	4.9	133.1	17.7	36.1	68.8
Kuwait	1989	25.9	2.3	14.0	23.6	3.9	1987	6.7	25.5	6.9	1.3	73.6	16.5	4.9	31.4
Kyrgyzstan	1991	29.1	6.9	29.7	22.2	3.8[12]	1989	31.4	73.2	5.3	7.9	284.2	143.7	28.7	86.0
Laos	1993	44.0	15.0	96.0	29.0	6.5	...	...	...	...	...	...	...	...	...
Latvia	1991	13.0	13.1	15.6	−0.1	2.0[12]	1989	12.8	207.7	7.5	6.6	731.2	37.5	26.5	130.0
Lebanon	1990–95	29.6	7.7	40.0	21.9	3.4	...	...	...	...	...	...	...	...	...
Lesotho	1990–95	40.2	11.0	89.0	29.2	5.8	...	...	...	...	...	...	...	...	...
Liberia	1990–95	46.7	14.1	126.0	32.6	6.7	...	...	...	...	...	...	...	...	...
Libya	1988	46.0	7.0	82.0[32]	39.0	6.6	...	...	...	...	...	...	...	...	...
Liechtenstein	1991	14.3	6.4	—	7.9	...	1991	13.7	154.1	6.8[5]	...	273.9	30.8	10.3	30.8
Lithuania	1992	14.3	11.0	16.5	3.3	2.0[12]	1989	8.7	179.2	5.7	8.0	594.3	47.0	22.0	117.4
Luxembourg	1991	12.9	9.7	9.2	3.2	1.6	1991	3.1	247.3	17.6	19.6	437.7	60.2	41.1	72.6
Macau	1991	19.5	3.8	7.5	15.7	1.5[13]	1991	7.9	76.1	5.7	1.4	140.9	52.6	18.4	27.2
Macedonia	1990	16.9	7.0	35.3	9.9	...	1989	20.3	102.4[19]	13.3	5.1	346.2	49.8	18.2	34.5
Madagascar	1990–95	44.9	12.6	110.0	32.3	6.5	...	...	...	...	...	...	...	...	...
Malaŵi	1990–95	55.4	19.0	138.0	36.4	7.6	1986[35]	*711*	*27*	*25*	*60*	*50*	*265*	*34*	*78*
Malaysia	1991	27.0	5.0	13.0	22.0	3.6	1989[36]	*62*	*60*	*11*	*7*[15]	*117*	*14*	*11*	*67*
Maldives	1993	38.0	8.0	53.0	30.0	6.1	1988	31.3	—	—	—	170.1	66.2	—	9.9
Mali	1992	52.0	21.0	110.0	31.0	7.3	...	...	...	...	...	...	...	...	...
Malta	1991	14.8	8.0	9.6	6.8	1.9[32]	1991	4.2	167.6	41.9	13.1	401.4	56.7	28.8	26.5
Marshall Islands	1991	47.0	8.0	30.3	39.0	7.1	1985	35.5	32.7	38.2	27.3	70.9	109.1	13.6	49.1
Martinique	1992	17.0	5.9	6.2	11.1	1.9[12]	1988	21.3	127.9	28.3	10.7[24]	210.4	30.0	34.0	40.3
Mauritania	1991	49.6	17.5	94.0	32.1	7.2	...	...	...	...	...	...	...	...	...
Mauritius	1990	20.7	6.6	23.0[2]	14.1	2.2	1991	13.5	54.6	42.7	7.1	286.9	64.5	31.1	49.4
Mayotte	1991	43.7	6.0	38.0	37.7	6.8[12]	...	...	...	...	...	...	...	...	...
Mexico	1990	31.2	5.0	24.2	26.2	3.7	1990	48.8	48.7	39.9	7.4	99.1	52.3	39.3	69.5
Micronesia	1985–89	37.9	8.0	52.2	29.9	5.6	1984	20.4	27.1	6.8	4.5	53.2	47.5	5.7	23.8
Moldova	1991	16.5	10.5	19.8	6.0	2.5[12]	1989	12.4	131.6	8.3	8.2	452.2	64.2	85.4	105.3
Monaco	1988	22.9	18.5	9.0[12]	4.4	1.2[12]	...	...	...	...	...	...	...	...	...
Mongolia	1991	32.9	8.8	64.0[14]	24.1	4.7[14]	...	...	...	...	...	...	...	...	...
Morocco	1990–95	32.6	8.3	68.0	24.3	4.7	...	...	...	...	...	...	...	...	...
Mozambique	1990–95	44.0	17.0	130.0	27.0	6.2	...	...	...	...	...	...	...	...	...
Myanmar (Burma)	1993	32.0	11.0	80.0	21.0	4.1	...	...	...	...	...	...	...	...	...
Namibia	1990–95	41.6	10.6	97.0	31.0	5.7	...	...	...	...	...	...	...	...	...
Nauru	1989	21.0	5.0	41.0	16.0	2.5	1976–81[37]	33.0	38.0	24.0	13.0	89.0	16.0	53.0	116.0
Nepal	1991	39.0	15.0	98.0	24.0	5.6	...	...	...	...	...	...	...	...	...
Netherlands, The	1991	13.2	8.6	6.5	4.6	1.6	1991	6.0	249.9	30.3	18.4	365.6	71.2	31.5	36.3

expectation of life at birth (latest year)		nuptiality, family, and family planning															country
		marriages			age at marriage (latest)						families (F), households (H) (latest)						
		year	total number	rate per 1,000 population	groom (percent)			bride (percent)			families (households)		children		induced abortions		
male	female				19 and under	20–29	30 and over	19 and under	20–29	30 and over	total ('000)	size	number under age 15	percent legitimate	number	ratio per 100 live births	
49.0	53.0	...	...	...	...	...	...	...	...	...	...	H 4.5	...	...	...	...	Equatorial Guinea
...	...	...	...	...	...	...	...	...	...	...	...	...	...	...	...	...	Eritrea[26]
64.7	74.9	1990	11,774	8.0	7.1	61.1	31.8	23.2	50.1	26.7	H 427	H 3.1	H 0.8	68.9	21,404	95.9	Estonia
45.4	48.7	...	...	...	...	...	...	...	...	...	...	H 4.5	...	...	...	...	Ethiopia[26]
72.8	79.6	1990	203	4.3	1.0[18]	68.8[18]	30.2[18]	8.8[18]	70.7[18]	20.5[18]	F 14	F 3.0	F 0.9	57.5	26	3.3	Faeroe Islands
61.0	65.2	1987	6,039	8.4	6.6	68.7	24.7	31.0	55.8	13.2	F 97	F 6.0	F 2.5	82.7	...	...	Fiji
70.8	78.9	1989	25,043	5.0	1.3	61.1	37.6	5.0	68.0	27.0	F 1,163	H 2.5	F 0.9	74.8	12,658	20.0	Finland
73.0	81.1	1992	269,940	4.7	0.4[10]	61.7[10]	37.9[10]	3.3[10]	69.5[10]	27.2[10]	H 20,899	H 2.7	H 1.0	71.8	161,646	21.2	France
63.4	69.7	1990	465	4.1	...	...	...	...	...	...	H 33	H 3.4	H 1.2	20.3	388	16.8	French Guiana
66.1	71.3	1990	987	4.9	11.3[18, 28]	75.8[18, 28]	12.9[18, 28]	41.5[18, 28]	52.5[18, 28]	6.0[18, 28]	H 40	H 4.7	H 1.7	41.5	...	...	French Polynesia
51.9	55.2	...	...	...	...	...	...	...	...	...	H 136	H 4.0	...	...	...	...	Gabon
43.4	46.6	...	...	...	...	...	...	...	...	...	H 123	H 4.9	H 3.4	...	...	...	Gambia, The
65.0	67.0	...	...	...	...	...	...	...	...	...	...	...	...	...	...	...	Gaza Strip
68.7	76.1	1989	38,288	7.0	5.7	66.2	28.1	27.8	55.7	16.5	H 1,244	H 4.1	H 1.1	82.3	68,883	75.6	Georgia
72.2[29]	78.7[29]	1990	516,550	6.5	0.7[29]	57.8[29]	41.5[29]	4.4[29]	68.4[29]	27.2[29]	F 22,882[29]	F 2.7[29]	F 0.5[29]	89.5	149,196	16.9	Germany
54.2	57.8	...	...	...	...	...	...	...	...	...	H 2,355	H 4.9	H 2.2	...	...	...	Ghana
73.4	80.4	1991	229	8.2	...	...	...	...	...	...	H 8	H 3.2	H 0.7	97.1	...	...	Gibraltar
72.6	77.6	1990	59,125	5.9	1.7[3]	64.5[3]	33.8[3]	25.8[3]	58.6[3]	15.6[3]	H 2,990	H 3.3	H 0.7	97.9	180	0.2	Greece
60.7	68.4	1990	465	8.4	0.2	45.8	54.0	2.8	61.1	36.1	F 31	F 1.8	F 0.5	28.0	962	80.7	Greenland
69.0	74.0	...	...	...	...	...	...	...	...	...	H 24	H 3.7	H 2.2	...	...	...	Grenada
70.0	77.0	1992	1,880	4.7	0.6[3]	56.8[3]	42.6[3]	8.8[3]	67.5[3]	23.7[3]	H 112	H 3.4	H 0.9	40.0	561	8.7	Guadeloupe
69.5	75.6	1987	1,512	12.0	0.6	57.5	41.9	2.9	65.1	32.0	H 31	H 4.0	H 1.3	67.8	...	...	Guam
61.0	66.0	1988	46,155	5.4	15.9	55.7	28.4	41.5	38.0	20.5	H 1,102	H 5.5	H 2.7	34.8	...	...	Guatemala
...	...	1990	403	6.8	...	...	...	...	...	...	H 21	H 2.6	H 0.5	80.2	...	...	Guernsey
44.0	45.0	...	...	...	...	...	...	...	...	...	H 1,064	H 4.7	...	...	...	...	Guinea
41.9	45.1	...	...	...	...	...	...	...	...	...	H 124	H 4.1	H 2.8	11.3	...	...	Guinea-Bissau
61.0	68.0	...	...	...	...	...	...	...	...	...	H 150	H 5.1	H 2.1	...	...	...	Guyana
52.0	55.0	...	...	...	...	...	...	...	...	...	H 1,147	H 4.4	H 1.8	...	...	...	Haiti
63.0	67.0	1983	19,875	4.9	7.7	65.1	27.2	27.9	58.5	13.6	H 463	H 5.7	H 2.8	...	...	...	Honduras
75.1	80.7	1990	47,188	8.1	0.6[12]	50.6[12]	48.8[12]	3.3[12]	66.2[12]	30.5[12]	H 1,582	H 3.4	H 0.7	94.5	17,600	25.2	Hong Kong
65.1	73.7	1991	66,000	6.4	5.2	72.4	22.4	27.3	57.5	15.2	F 3,058	F 2.9	F 0.8	86.9	90,394	71.9	Hungary
75.1	80.8	1991	1,236	4.8	0.5	56.1	43.4	2.9	67.5	29.6	H 85	H 2.9	H 1.3	43.6	714	15.0	Iceland
57.7	58.7	...	...	...	...	...	...	...	...	...	H 97,093	H 5.5	H 2.4	...	596,345	2.4	India
55.6	58.9	1989–90[31]	1,210,570	7.8	...	...	...	...	...	...	H 39,695	H 4.5	H 1.8	...	...	...	Indonesia
64.0	65.0	1989	458,708	8.5	...	...	...	...	...	...	H 9,759	H 5.1	H 2.2	...	...	...	Iran
46.0	57.0	1990	143,518	8.1	...	...	...	...	...	...	H 1,873	H 8.9	H 4.1	...	...	...	Iraq
71.0	76.7	1991	16,859	4.8	1.1[12]	72.2[12]	26.7[12]	3.7[12]	80.6[12]	15.7[12]	H 726	H 3.9	H 1.3	83.4	...	...	Ireland
...	...	1992	451	6.5	1.6	53.7	44.7	5.5	61.9	32.6	...	...	...	74.5	...	...	Isle of Man
74.9	78.4	1990	30,683	6.5	3.4	74.0	22.6	22.5	66.8	10.7	H 1,291	H 3.7	H 1.2	98.8	15,918	15.8	Israel
73.5	80.0	1990	312,585	5.4	1.0[13]	69.9[13]	29.1[13]	10.0[13]	75.7[13]	14.3[13]	F 19,766	F 2.8	F 0.5	93.7	165,456	29.8	Italy
71.4	75.8	1991	13,254	5.4	...	...	...	...	...	...	H 509	H 4.3	H 2.0	14.9	...	...	Jamaica
75.9	81.8	1990	722,138	5.8	1.2[28]	61.8[28]	37.0[28]	3.4[28]	79.6[28]	17.0[28]	F 22,240	F 5.4	F 1.2	99.0	456,797	37.4	Japan
...	...	...	...	...	...	...	...	...	...	...	H 29	H 2.6	H 0.4	88.1	313	29.2	Jersey
70.0	73.0	1989	31,508	8.1	5.0	74.7	20.3	40.2	54.3	5.5	H 375	H 6.9	H 3.4	...	...	...	Jordan
63.8	73.1	1989	165,380	10.0	3.8	76.0	20.2	26.0	58.2	15.8	H 3,824	H 4.0	H 1.4	88.0	358,124	93.7	Kazakhstan
59.0	63.0	...	...	...	...	...	...	...	...	...	H 1,938	H 6.2	H 2.7	...	...	...	Kenya
52.0	56.0	1988	352	5.2	...	...	...	...	...	...	H 10	H 6.1	F 2.0	...	...	...	Kiribati
68.0	74.0	1987	188,007	9.3	...	...	...	...	...	...	H 4,054	H 4.8	H 1.7	...	...	...	Korea, North
69.0	76.0	1989	309,872	7.3	0.3	77.1	22.6	2.7	89.5	7.8	H 11,355	H 3.8	H 1.0	99.5	...	...	Korea, South
72.0	76.0	1989	11,051	5.4	3.2	69.5	27.3	31.2	57.3	11.5	H 246	H 7.4	H 1.6	...	...	...	Kuwait
64.2	72.6	1989	41,790	9.7	2.2	82.4	15.4	29.8	59.5	10.7	H 856	H 4.2	H 1.9	87.3	87,212	66.3	Kyrgyzstan
50.0	53.0	...	...	...	...	...	...	...	...	...	...	H 5.3	...	...	...	...	Laos
64.2	74.6	1989	24,496	9.1	6.5	63.5	30.0	22.7	51.8	25.5	H 732	H 3.1	H 0.8	83.1	48,957	125.8	Latvia
65.1	69.0	...	...	...	...	...	...	...	...	...	H 405	H 5.3	H 2.2	...	...	...	Lebanon
54.0	63.0	...	...	...	...	...	...	...	...	...	H 330	H 4.8	H 2.0	...	...	...	Lesotho
54.0	57.0	...	...	...	...	...	...	...	...	...	H 474	H 5.0	...	...	...	...	Liberia
59.1	62.5	...	...	...	...	...	...	...	...	...	F 383	F 5.4	F 2.9	...	...	...	Libya
66.1	72.9	1991	183	6.3	1.1[10]	54.1[33]	44.8[34]	2.2[10]	72.7[33]	25.1[34]	H 8	H 3.0	H 0.7	92.3	...	...	Liechtenstein
65.3	76.1	1990	36,310	9.8	7.4	70.0	22.6	24.2	56.5	19.3	H 1,000	H 3.2	H 0.8	93.3	27,504	48.4	Lithuania
70.6	77.9	1991	2,592	6.7	1.2	53.5	45.3	7.6	62.3	30.1	H 145	H 2.8	H 0.5	87.8	...	...	Luxembourg
75.1	80.3	1990	1,794	3.7	0.1	53.1	46.8	1.4	72.0	26.6	H 50	H 4.8	H 1.8	99.3	...	...	Macau
68.0	72.0	1990	15,973	7.5	4.2[12]	79.0[12]	16.8[12]	27.5[12]	64.3[12]	8.2[12]	H 435[20]	H 4.4[20]	H 1.3[20]	...	...	...	Macedonia
54.0	57.0	...	...	...	...	...	...	...	...	...	H 1,709	H 4.7	H 2.0	...	...	...	Madagascar
48.4	49.7	...	...	...	...	...	...	...	...	...	...	H 4.5	...	...	...	...	Malaŵi
69.0	73.0	...	...	...	...	...	...	...	...	...	H 3,580	H 4.9	...	...	...	...	Malaysia
65.0	62.0	...	...	...	...	...	...	...	...	...	H 23	H 6.1	H 2.7	...	...	...	Maldives
43.0	47.0	...	...	...	...	...	...	...	...	...	H 1,364	H 5.6	...	...	...	...	Mali
73.7	78.1	1990	2,498	7.0	2.6	77.1	20.3	11.6	76.9	11.5	H 76	H 3.6	H 1.2	98.2	...	...	Malta
59.6	62.6	...	...	...	...	...	...	...	...	...	H 5	H 8.7	...	...	...	...	Marshall Islands
71.0	77.0	1992	1,646	4.4	0.1[13]	46.8[13]	53.1[13]	3.3[13]	61.5[13]	35.2[13]	H 107	H 3.3	H 0.8	33.9	1,753	30.6	Martinique
44.0	50.0	...	...	...	...	...	...	...	...	...	H 246	H 5.0	...	...	...	...	Mauritania
65.0	73.0	1990	11,252	10.9	1.5	60.2	38.3	21.7	60.3	18.0	F 155	F 5.3	F 2.0	72.8	...	...	Mauritius
54.0	58.0	...	...	...	...	...	...	...	...	...	H 19	H 4.9	H 2.3	89.2	...	...	Mayotte
66.5	73.1	1986	578,895	7.3	16.6	65.6	17.8	38.5	50.5	11.0	H 16,203	H 5.0	H 1.9	72.5	...	...	Mexico
64.0	68.1	...	...	...	...	...	...	...	...	...	H 11	H 7.0	...	...	...	...	Micronesia
65.0	71.8	1989	39,928	9.4	3.9	76.3	19.8	31.6	52.5	15.9	H 1,144	H 3.4	H 1.1	89.6	90,860	110.5	Moldova
72.0	80.0	1987	...	7.5	...	...	...	...	...	...	H 14	H 2.2	H 0.3	96.8	...	...	Monaco
61.2	63.8	1989	16,100	7.8	...	...	...	...	...	...	F 428	F 4.8	...	...	...	...	Mongolia
61.6	65.0	...	...	...	...	...	...	...	...	...	H 2,819	H 5.8	H 2.5	...	...	...	Morocco
46.9	50.2	...	...	...	...	...	...	...	...	...	F 1,860	F 4.4	F 2.0	73.1	...	...	Mozambique
56.0	60.0	...	...	...	...	...	...	...	...	...	...	H 5.2	...	...	...	...	Myanmar (Burma)
57.5	60.0	...	...	...	...	...	...	...	...	...	...	H 4.8	...	...	...	...	Namibia
64.0	69.0	...	...	...	...	...	...	...	...	...	H 1	H 8.0	H 2.6	...	...	...	Nauru
55.4	52.6	...	...	...	...	...	...	...	...	...	H 3,345	H 5.5	H 2.3	...	...	...	Nepal
74.0	80.2	1990	95,649	6.4	0.5	60.3	39.2	3.1	70.2	26.7	H 6,185	H 2.4	H 0.4	88.0	17,300	9.7	Netherlands, The

Vital statistics, marriage, family (continued)

country	vital rates						causes of death (rate per 100,000 population)								
	year	birth rate per 1,000 population	death rate per 1,000 population	infant mortality rate per 1,000 live births	rate of natural increase per 1,000 population	total fertility rate	year	infectious and parasitic diseases	malignant neoplasms (cancers)	endocrine and metabolic disorders	diseases of the nervous system	diseases of the circulatory system	diseases of the respiratory system	diseases of the digestive system	accidents, poisoning, and violence
Netherlands Antilles	1991	18.3	5.8	6.3[12]	12.5	...	1987[38]	...	150.6	31.9	10.8	205.4	41.0	21.1	41.6
New Caledonia	1993	21.0	7.0	29.0	14.0	2.7	...	...	...	...	...	...	...	...	...
New Zealand	1992	17.2	7.9	8.3[2]	9.3	2.1	1989	4.7	198.4	17.4	14.3	353.2	87.9	22.9	59.6
Nicaragua	1991	37.0	7.0	60.0	30.0	4.7	1990[36]	*163*	*46*	*13*	*10*	*121*	*74*	*26*	*80*
Niger	1990–95	51.3	18.7	124.0	32.6	7.1	...	...	...	...	...	...	...	...	...
Nigeria	1990–95	46.5	14.0	96.0	32.5	6.6	...	...	...	...	...	...	...	...	...
Northern Mariana Islands	1987	45.6	5.5	4.1	40.1	...	1987	18.7	70.2[19]	23.4	14.0	135.7	70.2	9.4	145.1
Norway	1992	14.0	10.5	6.4[2]	3.5	1.9[2]	1990	7.3	232.3	15.1	18.6	509.7	108.8	31.8	63.3
Oman	1991	41.0	6.0	40.0	35.0	6.7	...	...	...	...	...	...	...	...	...
Pakistan	1993	40.0	11.0	91.0[2]	29.0	6.1	...	...	...	...	...	...	...	...	...
Panama	1991	26.0	5.0	21.0	21.0	2.8	1990	20.0	57.8	11.0[5]	1.9[27]	111.4	18.9	7.4	51.0
Papua New Guinea	1993	33.0	11.0	53.0	22.0	4.8	...	...	...	...	...	...	...	...	...
Paraguay	1990	34.1	6.5	39.0[16]	27.6	4.3[16]	1987[40]	51.5	48.4	20.6	9.5	156.0	41.4	23.1	40.0
Peru	1990	32.8	8.3	80.7	24.5	4.2	1989[41]	*85*	*73*	*19*	*11*	*115*	*100*	*36*	*67*
Philippines	1993	30.0	7.0	40.0	23.0	3.9	1984	179.8	30.2	13.4	...	100.6	...	...	16.8
Poland	1991	14.3	10.6	15.0	3.7	2.1	1991	7.6	188.5	16.8	8.3	542.5	38.5	31.3	80.3
Portugal	1990	11.8	10.4	11.0	1.4	1.7[16]	1991	8.4	185.0	37.7	9.6	470.9	72.8	50.2	70.8
Puerto Rico	1991	18.2	7.4	13.0	10.8	2.4[13]	1990	17.6	116.3	89.0	15.6	249.9	74.2	41.4	65.5
Qatar	1991	19.4	1.8	31.0[14]	17.6	5.7[14]	1991	4.4	16.1[19]	6.0[15]	4.2	56.9	10.1	5.0	31.9
Réunion	1991	23.2	5.5	8.3	17.7	2.6[14]	1988	12.3	88.4	23.5[15]	16.9	180.0	41.4	58.9	69.0
Romania	1991	11.9	10.9	22.7	1.0	2.2[12]	1991	8.3	143.0	11.5	8.2	658.2	91.3	51.8	72.8
Russia	1991	12.1	11.4	17.8	0.7	17.7	1989	12.6	187.4	6.5	6.9	598.0	58.2	27.5	125.8
Rwanda	1990–95	50.0	15.6	112.2	34.4	8.0	...	...	...	...	...	...	...	...	...
St. Kitts and Nevis	1990	23.0	10.8	22.2[12]	12.2	2.6[2]	1985	50.0	95.5	20.5[5]	11.4	443.2	81.8	25.0	29.5
St. Lucia	1990	23.2	5.6	17.7	17.6	3.1[2]	1990	27.8	48.3	25.8	6.6	209.5	33.7	28.4	36.4
St. Vincent and the Grenadines	1990	23.9	6.4	21.3[42]	17.5	2.6[2]	1990	20.8	89.6	36.8	22.6	244.5	37.7	17.9	48.1
San Marino	1988–92	10.4	7.2	12.2	3.2	...	1988–92[37]	0.9	233.8	2.6[5]	1.7[27]	347.6	19.8	11.2	42.8
São Tomé and Príncipe	1992	38.0	8.0	58.0	30.0	5.2	1987	240.7	19.6	5.3[5]	2.7[27]	143.5	86.5	15.2	14.3
Saudi Arabia	1991	36.6	6.3	69.0	30.3	6.7	...	...	...	...	...	...	...	...	...
Senegal	1991	44.0	13.0	86.0	31.0	6.2	...	...	...	...	...	...	...	...	...
Seychelles	1991	24.2	7.7	12.9	16.5	2.8	1985–89[37]	42.9	116.9	10.6	7.9	263.5	77.1	40.5	67.0
Sierra Leone	1990–95	48.1	21.6	143.0	26.5	6.5	...	...	...	...	...	...	...	...	...
Singapore	1992	17.1	4.7	5.0	12.4	1.7	1991	10.9	121.5	12.8	3.9	171.1	77.8	13.5	15.4
Slovakia	1991	14.9	10.4	13.2	4.5	2.1[14]	1990	2.5	195.4[19]	14.9	7.3	594.8	75.1	54.3	74.4
Slovenia	1990	12.1	9.9	8.9	2.2	...	1989	8.6	206.6[19]	11.2	7.3	426.2	73.9	58.8	94.9
Solomon Islands	1991	40.0	5.0	39.0	35.0	6.2	...	...	...	...	...	...	...	...	...
Somalia	1990–95	46.8	18.1	122.0	28.7	6.6	...	...	...	...	...	...	...	...	...
South Africa	1991	34.0	8.0	51.0	26.0	4.4	1988	68.3	70.2	24.8[15]	10.7	133.9	69.6	17.0	110.6
Bophuthatswana	1982	...	...	89.0	...	...	...	...	...	...	...	...	...	...	...
Ciskei	1982	...	...	89.0	...	...	...	...	...	...	...	...	...	...	...
Transkei	1982	...	...	89.0	...	...	...	...	...	...	...	...	...	...	...
Venda	1982	...	...	89.0	...	...	...	...	...	...	...	...	...	...	...
Spain	1991	9.9	8.7	7.7[14]	1.2	1.7[16]	1989	9.6	192.9	29.4	11.1	344.9	75.5	48.0	49.7
Sri Lanka	1991	21.2	5.8	24.0[43]	15.4	2.5[43]	1986	32.2	27.7	9.0	45.3	101.9	36.1	15.5	77.8
Sudan, The	1991	44.0	13.0	85.0	31.0	6.2	...	...	...	...	...	...	...	...	...
Suriname	1990–95	24.5	5.6	28.0	18.9	2.6	1987[44]	*35*	*57*	*42*	*10*	*179*	*34*	*25*	*69*
Swaziland	1990–95	46.7	11.1	107.0	35.6	6.5	...	...	...	...	...	...	...	...	...
Sweden	1992	14.1	10.9	5.6	3.2	2.1[2]	1989	7.2	235.1	19.7	12.3	554.4	80.9	36.2	60.9
Switzerland	1992	12.6	9.1	6.8	3.5	1.6[2]	1991	13.3	244.0	24.3[15]	16.4	403.5	60.9	26.9	78.6
Syria	1990–95	42.5	5.7	39.0	36.8	6.3	1981[21]	*22*	*12*	*7*	*13*	*86*	*19*	*8*	*27*
Taiwan	1991	15.6	5.2	5.1	10.4	1.7	1991	...	96.0	20.6[5]	...	140.1[43]	24.6[44]	17.6[45]	66.7[46]
Tajikistan	1991	38.9	6.1	40.6	32.8	5.1[12]	1989	81.2	51.9	6.9	8.9	197.5	138.8	23.0	48.4
Tanzania	1991	49.5	15.2	105.0	34.3	7.0	...	...	...	...	...	...	...	...	...
Thailand	1991	20.9	6.7	25.0	14.2	2.4	1990[45]	50.0	119.7	...	30.6	182.7	39.4	56.1	92.7
Togo	1991	49.0	13.0	110.0	36.0	7.1	...	...	...	...	...	...	...	...	...
Tonga	1991	30.7	6.4	49.0[13]	24.3	4.0[13]	1980	53.5	46.9	13.1	3.3	61.1	41.5	17.5	14.2
Trinidad and Tobago	1991	18.1	6.6	18.0	11.5	2.8	1991	22.5	83.4	83.3[5]	2.4[27]	260.0	31.1	13.7	51.4
Tunisia	1991	25.0	6.3	44.0[16]	18.7	3.4[16]	...	...	...	...	...	...	...	...	...
Turkey	1991	28.0	6.0	54.0	22.0	3.6	1988[46]	*39*	*83*	*9*	*3*[15]	*391*	*30*	*15*	*31*
Turkmenistan	1991	33.6	7.3	47.0	26.3	4.3[12]	1989	79.3	65.1	8.0	9.1	275.3	160.6	32.2	62.4
Tuvalu	1991	29.0	10.0	33.0	19.0	3.1	1985	40.0	70.0	20.0	120.0	150.0	120.0	170.0	...
Uganda	1990–95	51.5	14.1	94.0	37.4	7.3	...	...	...	...	...	...	...	...	...
Ukraine	1991	12.1	12.9	13.9	−0.8	1.9[14]	1990	11.6	196.3	6.7[15]	7.4	644.7	60.5	31.3	107.7
United Arab Emirates	1990–95	20.3	3.9	22.0	16.4	4.3	...	...	...	...	...	...	...	...	...
United Kingdom	1991	13.8	11.2	7.4	2.6	1.8	1991	4.8	281.0	19.6	22.6	516.9	126.4	36.4	35.7
United States	1992	15.9	8.5	8.5	7.4	2.0[2]	1992	25.3[47]	203.1	19.6[5]	0.3[27]	355.9	65.3[30]	15.6	55.0
Uruguay	1990	18.3	9.9	20.0[2]	8.4	2.3[16]	1990	16.0	222.8	25.5	16.2	378.4	76.3	39.1	61.7
Uzbekistan	1991	34.5	6.2	35.5	28.3	4.0[12]	1989	44.5	55.9	6.5	9.1	251.3	119.3	24.7	60.1
Vanuatu	1991	36.0	5.0	36.0	31.0	6.2	1985[48]	69.3	22.9	16.2	11.8	37.6	60.5	12.5	23.6
Venezuela	1990	29.9	4.7	25.9	25.2	3.6	1989	30.0	51.1	18.6	7.4	115.0	29.0	18.8	61.4
Vietnam	1993	29.0	8.0	37.0	21.0	3.8	1979	48.0	54.0	...	...	123.8	...	...	...
Virgin Islands (U.S.)	1988	22.0	5.0	13.1	17.0	2.6[12]	1989	10.8	78.9	36.5[5]	—	232.7	14.8[30]	12.8	56.2
West Bank	1991	36.0	6.0	40.0	30.0	4.8	...	...	...	...	...	...	...	...	...
Western Sahara	1991	48.0	23.0	177.0	25.0	7.3	...	...	...	...	...	...	...	...	...
Western Samoa	1991	34.0	6.0	47.0	28.0	4.5	...	...	...	...	...	...	...	...	...
Yemen	1991	51.3	16.2	121.0	35.1	7.4	...	...	...	...	...	...	...	...	...
Yugoslavia	1991	14.6	9.8	20.9	4.8	...	1989	12.7	148.3[19]	20.1	7.3	524.3	47.7	26.3	49.3
Zaire	1990–95	45.3	13.0	75.0	32.3	6.1	...	...	...	...	...	...	...	...	...
Zambia	1990–95	50.3	12.4	72.0	37.9	7.2	...	...	...	...	...	...	...	...	...
Zimbabwe	1990–95	39.9	8.9	55.0	31.0	5.3	...	...	...	...	...	...	...	...	...

[1]Excludes nomadic tribes. [2]1991. [3]1986. [4]Septicemia only. [5]Diabetes mellitus only. [6]Cerebrovascular disease and heart disease only. [7]Chronic obstructive pulmonary diseases, pneumonia, and influenza only. [8]1991–92 average. [9]1992. [10]Under 21 years of age. [11]21–29 years of age. [12]1989. [13]1988. [14]1990. [15]Includes nutritional disorders. [16]1990–95. [17]Accidents only. [18]1987. [19]Includes benign neoplasms. [20]1981. [21]Projected rates based on about 75 percent of total deaths. [22]Estimates based on selected urban and rural areas. [23]Millions of households. [24]1985. [25]Projected rates based on about 65 percent of total deaths. [26]Ethiopia includes Eritrea. [27]Meningitis only. [28]First marriages only. [29]Former West Germany only. [30]Bronchitis, pneumonia, influenza,

expectation of life at birth (latest year): male	female	nuptiality, family, and family planning — marriages: year	total number	rate per 1,000 population	age at marriage (latest) — groom (percent): 19 and under	20–29	30 and over	bride (percent): 19 and under	20–29	30 and over	families (F), households (H) (latest) — families (households):	total ('000)	size	children: number under age 15	percent legitimate	induced abortions: number	ratio per 100 live births	country
71.1	75.8	1991	1,220	6.4	...	...	...	...	...	...	H	41	H 3.7	H 2.1	51.6	...	...	Netherlands Antilles
66.5	71.8	1987	729	4.5	0.5	54.5	45.0	10.2	61.9	27.9		...	H 4.1	...	48.1	...	...	New Caledonia
72.0	77.9	1989	22,733	6.8	1.2	58.7	40.1	5.5	66.0	28.5	H	1,178	H 2.9	H 0.7	64.3	10,200	17.6	New Zealand
64.8	68.5	1988	7,530	2.1	18.1[10, 24]	—81.9[24, 39]—		48.2[10, 24]	—51.8[23, 39]—			...	H 6.9	...	...	...	...	Nicaragua
44.9	48.1	...	...	...	...	...	...	...	...	...	H	1,130	H 6.4	...	...	...	...	Niger
50.8	54.3	...	...	...	...	...	...	...	...	...	H	14,441	H 5.0	...	...	...	...	Nigeria
59.0	64.0	1987	685	31.2	2.5	50.2	47.3	5.7	70.4	23.9	H	7	H 4.6	H 1.5	53.9	...	...	Northern Mariana Islands
74.0	80.1	1990	21,926	5.2	0.7	56.2	43.1	3.7	68.9	27.4	F	1,981	F 2.1	F 0.4	59.1	15,551	25.5	Norway
65.0	68.0	...	...	...	...	...	...	...	...	...	H	350	H 3.7	...	...	...	...	Oman
59.3	60.7	...	...	...	...	...	...	...	...	...		...	H 6.3	...	...	...	...	Pakistan
72.0	76.0	1991	10,528	4.5	3.6[12]	55.0[12]	41.4[12]	15.6[12]	55.8[12]	28.6[12]	H	524	H 4.4	H 1.5	28.1	...	...	Panama
55.0	57.0	...	...	...	...	...	...	...	...	...	H	674	H 4.6	...	...	...	...	Papua New Guinea
65.1	69.5	1987	17,741	4.5	3.8	64.4	31.8	34.0	46.5	19.5	H	579	H 5.2	...	68.7	...	...	Paraguay
61.5	65.3	1982	109,200	6.0	5.5	60.4	34.1	25.9	51.4	22.6	H	3,099	H 5.2	...	57.8	...	...	Peru
63.0	67.0	1988	393,514	6.7	8.3	69.7	22.0	26.0	61.0	13.0	F	9,566	F 5.7	F 2.4	93.9	...	...	Philippines
66.1	75.3	1990	255,369	6.7	4.9	76.1	19.0	22.0	64.6	13.4	F	9,435	F 3.6	F 0.9	95.0	59,417	10.9	Poland
70.6	77.6	1990	71,654	7.3	4.2	75.2	20.6	19.0	67.3	13.7	H	2,954	H 3.8	H 0.8	85.5	...	...	Portugal
70.2	78.5	1989	31,642	8.9	11.4	57.3	31.3	23.7	52.3	24.0	F	563	F 4.1	F 1.8	63.2	...	...	Puerto Rico
65.2	67.6	1990	1,370	2.8	4.8	71.6	23.6	32.9	58.6	8.5	H	61	H 6.4	...	...	...	...	Qatar
69.0	78.3	1990	3,831	6.4	1.2	65.2	33.6	12.5	66.8	20.7	H	158	H 3.8	H 1.1	47.3	4,302	31.7	Réunion
66.5	72.4	1989	177,943	7.7	4.6	72.7	22.7	29.9	55.8	14.3	H	7,115	H 3.1	...	...	992,265	315.3	Romania
63.5	74.3	1989	1,384,307	9.4	5.8	66.9	27.3	27.4	49.0	23.6	H	40,426	H 3.2	H 0.8	86.5	4,242,028	196.3	Russia
48.8	52.2	1982	14,313	2.6	...	...	...	...	...	...	H	894	H 5.2	...	94.9	...	...	Rwanda
64.0	71.0	...	...	...	...	...	...	...	...	...	H	12	H 3.7	H 1.4	19.2	...	...	St. Kitts and Nevis
68.6	74.4	1989	395	2.7	0.8	34.4	64.8	3.5	45.1	51.4	H	25	H 4.6	H 2.0	10.0	...	...	St. Lucia
68.0	72.0	1990	503	4.7	0.5[3]	41.6[3]	57.9[3]	6.4[3]	59.5[3]	34.1[3]	H	20	H 4.8	H 2.0	...	...	...	St. Vincent and the Grenadines
70.7	76.2	1989	169	7.4	0.6	75.1	24.3	5.3	85.3	9.5	F	8	F 2.8	F 0.5	95.2	...	...	San Marino
64.0	68.0	...	...	...	...	...	...	...	...	...		...	...	...	9.8	...	...	São Tomé and Príncipe
65.0	68.0	...	...	...	...	...	...	...	...	...	H	1,513	H 6.6	...	...	...	...	Saudi Arabia
54.0	56.0	...	...	...	...	...	...	...	...	...	H	1,167	H 4.8	...	...	...	...	Senegal
65.0	75.0	1987	622	9.4	1.0	54.2	44.8	6.4	65.1	28.5	H	13	H 4.8	H 1.9	27.2	9	0.5	Seychelles
41.4	44.6	...	...	...	...	...	...	...	...	...	H	749	H 4.7	...	...	...	...	Sierra Leone
70.3	75.8	1988	24,853	9.4	0.4	66.5	33.1	5.1	79.1	15.8	H	510	H 3.9	H 1.3	...	21,226	48.7	Singapore
66.9	75.2	1990	40,435	7.7	7.0	78.2	14.8	32.8	57.7	9.5	H	1,832	H 2.9	H 0.7	92.8	56,176	69.9	Slovakia
67.0	75.0	1990	9,131	4.7	0.7[12]	75.3[12]	24.0[12]	13.2[12]	73.3[12]	13.5[12]	H	642	H 3.1	H 0.7[21]	...	...	...	Slovenia
59.9	61.4	...	...	...	...	...	...	...	...	...	F	41	F 5.6	F 2.3	...	...	...	Solomon Islands
45.4	48.6	...	...	...	...	...	...	...	...	...		...	H 4.9	...	...	...	...	Somalia
61.0	67.0	...	...	...	...	...	...	...	...	...		...	H 4.5	...	75.9	...	...	South Africa
—57.0—		...	...	...	...	...	...	...	...	...		...	...	...	...	...	...	Bophuthatswana
—57.0—		...	...	...	...	...	...	...	...	...	H	144	H 6.2	...	...	...	...	Ciskei
—57.0—		...	...	...	...	...	...	...	...	...		...	...	...	...	...	...	Transkei
—57.0—		...	...	...	...	...	...	...	...	...	H	70	H 5.4	...	...	...	...	Venda
74.4	80.3	1989	215,840	5.6	2.6[13]	76.4[13]	21.0[13]	11.6[13]	77.0[13]	11.4[13]	F	10,665	F 3.5	...	92.0	...	...	Spain
70.0	74.0	1989	141,533	8.4	0.5[24]	71.1[24]	28.4[24]	16.9[24]	73.0[24]	10.1[24]	H	2,721	H 5.2	H 1.9	94.6	...	...	Sri Lanka
52.0	54.0	...	...	...	...	...	...	...	...	...	H	3,471	H 5.3	...	...	...	...	Sudan, The
67.1	72.1	1988	2,200	5.5	...	...	...	...	...	...		...	H 3.9	...	...	...	...	Suriname
56.2	59.8	...	...	...	...	...	...	...	...	...	H	112	H 5.0	...	...	1,145	...	Swaziland
74.6	80.3	1990	40,477	4.7	0.4	46.8	52.8	2.2	60.2	37.6	H	3,670	H 2.2	H 0.5	53.0	37,489	30.2	Sweden
74.1	80.9	1990	46,603	6.8	0.2	53.3	46.5	2.4	67.9	29.7	H	2,500	H 2.5	...	93.5	...	...	Switzerland
65.2	69.2	1988	101,946	7.5	...	...	...	...	...	...	F	1,151	H 6.2	F 2.4	...	...	...	Syria
71.8	77.2	1990	143,886	7.1	1.5	62.3	36.2	6.0	77.7	16.3	H	5,093	H 4.0	H 1.0	97.6	...	...	Taiwan
66.8	71.9	1989	47,616	9.2	2.1	86.8	11.1	39.0	54.3	6.7	H	799	H 6.1	H 2.7	93.0	54,494	27.2	Tajikistan
50.0	55.0	...	...	...	...	...	...	...	...	...	H	3,435	H 5.1	H 2.3	...	...	...	Tanzania
64.4	68.5	1991	406,326	7.3	...	...	...	...	...	...	H	10,418	H 5.3	H 1.9	...	...	...	Thailand
54.0	58.0	...	...	...	...	...	...	...	...	...	H	479	H 5.6	...	...	...	...	Togo
61.0	64.8	1990	710	7.3	...	...	...	...	...	...	F	15	F 6.1	F 2.7	80.6	...	...	Tonga
69.7	74.7	1991	7,009	5.7	5.9	61.0	33.1	25.5	52.6	21.9	H	301	H 4.1	H 1.3	...	9	—	Trinidad and Tobago
66.4	68.7	1990	55,300	6.9	0.4[12]	63.6[12]	36.0[12]	21.5[12]	66.8[12]	11.7[12]	H	1,313	H 5.5	...	99.8	23,300	10.9	Tunisia
68.0	72.0	1989	450,763	7.9	8.5[13]	75.9[13]	15.6[13]	36.1[13]	56.5[13]	7.4[13]	H	9,730	H 5.2	H 2.0	...	...	...	Turkey
62.9	69.7	1989	34,890	9.8	3.0	87.4	9.6	16.1	77.1	6.8	H	598	H 5.6	H 2.4	96.5	39,068	31.3	Turkmenistan
61.0	63.0	...	...	...	...	...	...	...	...	...	H	1	H 6.4	H 2.2	82.2	...	...	Tuvalu
51.4	54.7	...	...	...	...	...	...	...	...	...	H	2,766	H 4.8	...	...	...	...	Uganda
65.6	74.9	1989	489,330	9.5	5.5	70.2	24.3	32.9	46.7	20.4	H	14,507	H 3.2	H 0.8	89.2	1,080,000	145.2	Ukraine
69.8	74.1	...	...	...	...	...	...	...	...	...	H	247	H 6.8	...	...	...	...	United Arab Emirates
72.7	78.3	1989	392,042	6.8	2.1	60.5	37.4	7.6	64.6	27.8	H	21,672	H 2.7	H 1.7	72.1	184,092	23.1	United Kingdom
72.0	78.9	1992	2,362,000	9.2	4.5[13]	54.1[13]	41.4[13]	11.8[13]	55.7[13]	32.5[13]	F	63,558	F 2.6	F 1.0	76.6	1,354,000	35.5	United States
68.9	75.3	1987	21,812	7.2	7.2	63.3	29.5	24.7	54.2	21.1	H	863	H 3.3	H 0.9	73.8	...	...	Uruguay
66.1	72.4	1989	200,681	10.0	2.3	87.4	10.3	37.9	55.2	6.9	H	3,415	H 5.5	H 2.4	95.8	226,276	33.8	Uzbekistan
61.1	59.3	...	...	...	...	...	...	...	...	...	H	28	H 5.1	H 2.2	...	...	...	Vanuatu
67.0	73.3	1989	111,970	5.8	11.6	62.9	25.5	31.5	52.3	16.2	H	2,707	H 5.3	H 2.2	47.0	...	...	Venezuela
62.0	67.0	...	...	...	...	...	...	...	...	...	H	12,958[49]	H 4.8[49]	H 1.9[49]	...	...	...	Vietnam
66.7	70.7	1987	1,906	18.0	4.5	50.9	44.6	1.0	38.4	60.6	H	32	H 3.1	H 1.0	38.4	...	...	Virgin Islands (U.S.)
67.0	69.0	...	...	...	...	...	...	...	...	...		...	...	...	...	...	...	West Bank
39.0	41.0	...	...	...	...	...	...	...	...	...		...	...	...	...	...	...	Western Sahara
64.0	69.0	1989	833	5.3	0.5	52.7	46.8	8.6	61.3	30.1	F	20	F 7.8	F 3.8	43.5	...	...	Western Samoa
49.0	51.0	...	...	...	...	...	...	...	...	...	H	1,848	H 5.6	...	...	...	...	Yemen
68.2	73.2	1991	58,300	5.6	...	...	...	...	...	...	H	2,711[20]	H 3.7[20]	H 0.9[20]	...	...	...	Yugoslavia
52.3	55.7	...	...	...	...	...	...	...	...	...		...	H 6.0	...	...	...	...	Zaire
54.4	56.5	...	...	...	...	...	...	...	...	...	H	1,370	H 4.4	H 2.1	...	...	...	Zambia
59.0	62.6	...	...	...	...	...	...	...	...	...		...	H 5.8	...	95.8	...	...	Zimbabwe

and chronic obstructive pulmonary diseases only. [31]Muslims only. [32]1985–90. [33]21 to 30 years of age. [34]Over 31 years of age. [35]Projected rates based on about 10 percent of total deaths. [36]Projected rates based on about 50 percent of total deaths. [37]Average annual rates for the period. [38]Includes Aruba. [39]Over 21 years of age. [40]Reporting areas only (constituting about 60 percent of the total population). [41]Projected rates based on about 45 percent of total deaths. [42]1988–90 average. [43]1993. [44]Projected rates based on about 70 percent of total deaths. [45]Projected rates based on about 35 percent of total deaths. [46]Projected rates based on about 30 percent of total deaths. [47]Of which AIDS, 12.6. [48]Registered events only. [49]Private households only.

National product and accounts

The national product and accounts table furnishes, for most of the countries of the world, breakdowns of (1) gross national product (GNP) and its global and per capita growth rates (1980–91), (2) principal accounting and industrial components of gross domestic product (GDP), (3) recent growth rates of real GDP, and (4) principal elements of each country's balance of payments, including international goods trade, invisibles, and tourism payments.

Measures of national output. The two most commonly used measures of national output (except for the accounting systems of centrally planned economies) are GDP and GNP. Each of these measures represents an aggregate value of goods and services produced by a specific country. The GDP, the more basic of these, is a measure of the total value of goods and services produced entirely within a given country. The GNP, the more comprehensive value, is composed of both domestic production (GDP) *and* the net income from current (short-term) transactions with other countries. When the income received from other countries is greater than payments to them, a country's GNP is greater than its GDP. In theory, if all national accounts could be equilibrated, the global summation of GDP would equal GNP.

In the first section of the table, data are provided for the nominal GNP. ("Nominal" refers to value in current prices for the year indicated and is distinguished from a "real" valuation, which is one adjusted to eliminate the effect of recent inflation [most often] or, occasionally, of deflation between two given dates.) Both the total and per capita values of this product are denominated in U.S. dollars for ease of comparison. Beside these are given figures for average annual growth of total and per capita real GNP. GNP per capita provides a rough measure of annual national income per person, but values should be compared cautiously, as they are subject to a number of distortions, notably of exchange rate, but also of purchasing power parity (the differing ability [by more than an exchange rate] of any two currencies to purchase comparable goods in their respective domestic markets), and in the existence of elements of national production that do not enter the monetary economy in such a way as to be visible to fiscal authorities (*e.g.,* food, clothing, or housing produced and consumed within families or communal groups or services exchanged).

In a number of countries with centrally planned economies, the conventional concept for the aggregated national income/product is net material product (NMP), which includes only material goods and "productive" services. These NMP accounts are not directly comparable to the GDP values presented in this table for market economies. The GDP value is more comprehensive and includes a number of sectors (especially personal and financial services) excluded from the NMP value. Estimated GNPs have been supplied for most countries (including the centrally planned), based either on the country's own, or on external, analysis.

The internal structure of the national product. GDP/GNP values allow comparison of the relative size of national economies, but further information is provided when these aggregates are analyzed according to their component kinds of expenditure, cost components, and industrial sectors of origin.

There are three major domestic components of GDP expenditure: private

National product and accounts

country	gross national product (GNP)					gross domestic product (GDP) by type of expenditure, 1990 (%)					cost components of gross domestic product (GDP), 1990 (%)			
	nominal, 1991 ('000,000 U.S.$)	per capita, 1991 (U.S.$)	average annual growth rates, 1980–91			consumption		gross domestic investment	foreign trade		indirect taxes net of subsidies	consumption of fixed capital	compensation of employees	net operating surplus
			real GNP (%)	population (%)	real GNP per capita (%)	private	government		exports	imports				
Afghanistan	3,100[1]	220[1]	...	0.9	...	...	...	...	...	...	...	...	...	...
Albania	2,700	820	...	1.9	...	73	10	24	—–7—		...	13	62	25
Algeria	52,239	2,020	2.1	2.9	–0.6	50[5]	18[5]	29[5]	16[5]	–14[5]	20[8]	10[8]	40[8]	30[8]
American Samoa	128[6]	2,500[6]	...	3.7	...	...	...	...	...	...	...	...	...	...
Andorra	727[6, 10]	13,550[6, 10]	...	4.9	...	...	...	...	...	...	...	...	...	...
Angola	6,010[5]	620[5]	...	2.7	...	41[5]	35[5]	16[5]	42[5]	–35[5]	9[5]	[11]	43[5]	47[5, 11]
Antigua and Barbuda	355	4,770	4.4	0.0	4.4	70[12]	19[12]	36[12]	75[12]	–100[12]	16[12]	—84[12]—		
Argentina	91,211	2,780	–0.2	1.5	–1.7	—77—		8	23	–8	...	...	...	...
Armenia	7,233	2,150	...	1.0	...	—70[2, 5]—		44[2, 5]	—–14[2, 5]—		...	...	...	...
Aruba	854[6, 10]	13,600[6, 10]	...	1.0	...	66[12]	21[12]	17[12]	—–3[12]—		...	...	...	...
Australia	287,765	16,590	2.8	1.5	1.3	60	17	23	17	–18	12	15	51	22
Austria	157,528	20,380	2.3	0.3	2.0	56	18	25	41	–39	13	12	53	22
Azerbaijan	12,065	1,670	...	1.4	...	—73[2, 5]—		13[2, 5]	—13[2, 5]—		...	...	...	...
Bahamas, The	3,044	11,720	3.3	1.9	1.4	44	14	22	92	–73	16[1]	—	11[1]	73[1]
Bahrain	3,679	6,910	0.1	3.9	–3.8	36	26	31	119	–102	3	16	47	35
Bangladesh	23,449	220	4.2	2.0	2.2	87	9	12	9	–17	...	...	...	...
Barbados	1,711	6,630	1.6	0.3	1.3	64	20	19	49	–52	...	...	...	...
Belarus	32,131	3,110	...	0.6	...	74[2]	2[2]	26[2]	68[2]	–71[2]	...	...	...	...
Belgium	192,370	19,300	2.2	0.1	2.1	62	15	20	71	–68	9	9	52	29
Belize	389	2,050	5.3	2.6	2.7	63	21	32	58	–75	16	7	—77—	
Benin	1,848	380	2.1	3.0	–0.9	87	11	12	19	–28	4[5]	[11]	20[5]	76[5, 11]
Bermuda	1,642[6]	27,790[6]	...	0.8	...	69[5]	12[5]	16[5]	61[5]	–58[5]	...	...	...	...
Bhutan	260	180	9.0	2.2	6.8	54	25	33	30	–42	2[5]	9[5]	—89[5]—	
Bolivia	4,799	650	0.5	2.5	–2.0	70	11	9	29	–20	...	...	...	...
Bosnia and Herzegovina	...	...	...	0.6	...	...	...	...	...	...	...	...	...	...
Botswana	3,335	2,590	9.3	3.4	5.9	31[5]	20[5]	27[5]	62[5]	–41[5]	7[12]	15[12]	28[12]	50[12]
Brazil	447,324	2,920	2.5	2.0	0.5	61	16	22	7	–5	12	—88—		
Brunei	3,500[6,10]	13,890[6,10]	...	3.1	...	...	...	...	...	...	...	...	...	...
Bulgaria	16,316	1,840	1.7	0.1	1.6	67	7	30	—–4—		[19]	14	54	32[19]
Burkina Faso	3,213	350	4.0	3.1	0.9	83	13	20	11	–27	7[8]	—93[8]—		
Burundi	1,210	210	4.3	2.7	1.6	86	16	18	8	–28	12[1]	4[1]	22[1]	63[1]
Cambodia	1,725	200	...	2.9	...	...	...	...	...	...	...	...	...	...
Cameroon	11,320	940	2.1	3.2	–1.1	70	12	16	19	–17	12[22]	5[22]	26[22]	57[22]
Canada	568,765	21,260	3.1	1.2	1.9	60	20	21	25	–26	11	11	57	20
Cape Verde	285	750	4.8	1.3	3.5	76[5]	20[5]	42[5]	14[5]	–53[5]	9[8]	—91[8]—		
Central African Republic	1,218	390	1.2	2.2	–1.0	88	14	11	16	–28	...	...	...	...
Chad	1,212	220	6.3	2.4	3.9	89	23	10	22	–44	8[12]	—92[12]—		
Chile	28,897	2,160	3.4	1.5	1.9	67	10	20	37	–34	13[22]	12[22]	33[22]	42[22]
China	424,012	370	9.4	1.5	7.9	56[2]	9[2]	34[2]	21[2]	–18[2]	...	...	...	...
Colombia	41,922	1,280	3.2	1.8	1.4	65	11	18	20	–15	10	[11]	38	53[11]
Comoros	245	500	2.6	3.4	–0.8	76	30	15	14	–35	8[8]	—92[8]—		
Congo	2,623	1,120	3.1	3.8	–0.7	51	19	16	53	–37	14[5]	19[5]	32[5]	35[5]
Costa Rica	6,156	1,930	3.4	2.9	0.5	62	18	27	35	–41	12	2	51	34
Côte d'Ivoire	8,523	690	0.3	3.9	–3.6	69[5]	16[5]	7[5]	35[5]	–27[5]	19[8]	—81[8]—		
Croatia	24,400[6, 10]	5,110[6, 10]	...	0.4	...	...	...	...	...	...	11	13	62	14
Cuba	17,000	1,580	...	0.9	...	95[2, 5]	9[2, 5]	18[2, 5]	—–21[2, 5]—		...	...	...	...
Cyprus	6,135	8,200	6.0	1.6	4.4	61	14	27	53	–55	9	11	—80—	
Czech Republic[27]	38,427	2,450	0.7	0.2	0.5	47	20	34	31	–32	...	...	...	...
Denmark	121,695	23,660	2.2	0.1	2.1	52	25	18	35	–30	14	9	54	22
Djibouti	340[5, 10]	670[5, 10]	...	3.8	...	71[5]	34[5]	18[5]	47[5]	–70[5]	21[8]	—79[8]—		
Dominica	175	2,440	4.4	–0.4	4.8	64	20	41	50	–75	17	—83—		
Dominican Republic	6,807	950	1.9	2.4	–0.5	82	3	19	27	–31	7	6	—87—	
Ecuador	10,772	1,020	2.0	2.4	–0.4	71	8	22	31	–31	14	[11]	13	73[11]
Egypt	33,068	620	4.5	2.8	1.7	84	12	22	24	–41	7[12]	—93[12]—		
El Salvador	5,697	1,070	1.1	1.4	–0.3	88	11	12	16	–27	6	4	—90—	

consumption (analyzed in greater detail in the "Household budgets and consumption" table), government spending, and gross domestic investment. The fourth, nondomestic, component of GDP expenditure is net foreign trade; values are given for both exports (a positive value) and imports (a negative value, representing obligations to other countries). The sum of these five percentages, excluding statistical discrepancies and rounding, should be 100% of the GDP.

The structure of GDP as accounted by cost components here comprises four general categories: indirect taxes (excise or value-added taxes), net of subsidies; consumption of fixed capital (depreciation); and two income categories: (a) compensation of employees (salaries, wages, etc.) and (b) net operating surplus ("profits," interests, rent, etc.).

The distribution of GDP for ten industrial sectors is aggregated into three major industrial groups:

1. The primary sector, composed of agriculture (including forestry and fishing) and mineral production (including fossil fuels).
2. The secondary sector, composed of manufacturing, construction, and public utilities.
3. The tertiary sector, which includes transportation and communications, trade (wholesale and retail), financial services (including banking, real estate, insurance, and business services), other (community, social, and personal) services, and government services.

Percentages in this section of the table may not add to 100 because the value of each economic sector is calculated as a percentage of the total GDP, which may contain adjustments such as import duties and bank service charges that are not distributed by sector.

Average annual growth rate of real GDP. These columns show average annual growth rates of real product for the decade from 1975 to 1985, as well as for the six years from 1985 to 1991. Real GDP growth rates indicate the change in total output achieved by each country during the periods indicated excluding inflation.

Balance of payments (external account transactions). The external account records the sum (net) of all economic transactions of a current nature between one country and the rest of the world. The account shows a country's net of overseas receipts and obligations, including not only the trade of goods and merchandise but also such invisible items as services, interest and dividends, short- and long-term investments, tourism, transfers to or from overseas residents, etc. Each transaction gives rise either to a foreign claim for payment, recorded as a deficit (*e.g.,* from imports, capital outflows), or a foreign obligation to pay, recorded as a surplus (*e.g.,* from exports, capital inflows) or a domestic claim on another country. Any international transaction automatically creates a deficit in the balance of payments of one country and a surplus in that of another. Values are given in U.S. dollars for comparability.

Tourist trade. Net income or expenditure from tourism (in U.S. dollars for comparability) is often a significant element in a country's balance of payments. Receipts from foreign nationals reflect payments for goods and services from foreign currency resources by tourists in the given country. Expenditures by nationals abroad are also payments for goods and services, but in this case made by the residents of the given country as tourists abroad.

origin of gross domestic product (GDP) by economic sector, 1990 (%)										avg. annual growth rate of real GDP (%)		balance of payments, 1992 (current external transactions; '000,000 U.S.$)			tourist trade, 1991 ('000,000 U.S.$)		country
primary		secondary			tertiary					1975–1985	1985–1991	net transfers		current balance of payments	receipts from foreign nationals	expenditures by nationals abroad	
agriculture	mining	manufacturing	construction	public utilities	transp., communications	trade	financial svcs.	other svcs.	government			goods, merchandise	invisibles				
53[2]	[3]	29[2,3]	6[2]	[3]	4[2]	8[2]	—2[2]—			1.0[2]	−5.3[2,4]	−371[5]	228[5]	−143[5]	1[6]	1[6]	Afghanistan
36[2]	[3]	42[2,3]	6[2]	[3]	3[2]	4[2]	—8[2]—			4.5[2]	0.4[7]	−115[6]	...	...	...	...	Albania
7[5]	19[5]	12[5]	19[5]	2[5]	7[5]	18[5]	—2[5]—		15[5]	6.1	0.1[4]	5,478[9]	−3,111[9]	2,367[9]	64[6]	149[6]	Algeria
...	...	...	...	...	...	...	...	...	...	...	...	−54[6]	...	...	10	...	American Samoa
...	...	...	...	...	...	...	...	...	...	...	...	−1,151[6]	...	...	...	...	Andorra
10[9]	58[9]	3[9]	2[9]	—	2[9]	6[9]	1[9]	—18[9]—		2.5	7.2[7]	1,120[9]	...	...	...	...	Angola
4	2	3	11	4	18	26	22	—18—		4.5	6.1	−289	230	−59	314	18	Antigua and Barbuda
17	3	21	2	5	12	13	8	—19—		−0.0	1.3	−1,684	−6,863	−8,547	2,336	1,739	Argentina
26[2]	[3]	48[2,3]	15[2]	[3]	2[2]	6[2]	—4[2]—			6.7[2]	0.9[2,7]	...	...	...	...	...	Armenia
...	...	...	...	...	...	...	...	...	...	...	12.0[13]	−355	304	51	401	47	Aruba
3	5	15	9	4	8	14	22	18	4	3.0	2.2	3,528	−14,104	−10,576	4,183	3,940	Australia
3	[14]	27[14]	7	3	6	16	17	4	14	2.4	3.0	−10,304	9,601	−703	13,956	7,449	Austria
26[2,9]	[3]	54[2,3,9]	11[2,9]	[3]	3[2,9]	2[2,9]	—4[2,9]—			...	−2.3[2,7]	...	...	...	...	...	Azerbaijan
9	3	24	6	2	5	15	15	—20—		4.5	2.6[4]	−834[9]	654[9]	−180[9]	1,222	205	Bahamas, The
1	22	17	6	2	10	10	13	5	21	4.7	2.3[7]	−193[9]	−545[9]	−738[9]	162	98	Bahrain
37	—	9	6	1	10	8	2	22	4	4.5	4.0	−1,386[9]	1,451[9]	65[9]	9	83	Bangladesh
5[9]	1[9]	7[9]	5[9]	3[9]	7[9]	26[9]	13[9]	3[9]	16[9]	2.3	1.2	−474[9]	444[9]	−30[9]	453	44	Barbados
29[2]	[3]	44[2,3]	12[2]	[3]	5[2]	6[2]	—4[2]—			5.2[2]	3.9[2,4]	...	...	...	...	...	Belarus
2	—	22	6	3	8	—32—		—29—		1.7	3.2	−66[9,15]	4,797[9,15]	4,731[9,15]	3,468	5,543	Belgium
23	1	13	9	3	12	17	11	8	12	2.3	8.9	−104[9]	55[9]	−49[9]	95	8	Belize
36[5]	1[5]	9[5]	3[5]	1[5]	7[5]	17[5]	—11[5]—		10[5]	4.5	1.0[4]	−191[9]	89[9]	−102[9]	29	10	Benin
...	...	...	...	...	...	...	...	...	...	1.8	2.6[4]	−481[6]	447[6]	−34[6]	454	126	Bermuda
45[5]	1[5]	7[5]	8[5]	9[5]	6[5]	6[5]	7[5]	—12[5]—		8.3	7.6[7]	−32[5]	41[5]	9[5]	2[6]	...	Bhutan
21	15	13	3	1	9	13	12	—13—		0.1	2.1	−44[9]	−218[9]	−262[9]	90	63	Bolivia
11[5,16]	[14]	58[5,14,16]	7[5,16]	1[5,16]	6[5,16]	14[5,16]	—3[5,16]—			3.6[17]	0.3[4,17]	...	...	...	...	...	Bosnia and Herzegovina
5	42	4	6	2	3	14	5	2	19	11.7	9.8	147[6]	−11[6]	138[6]	65[6]	39[6]	Botswana
9	2	27	7	3	6	7	25	−4	8	3.8	1.8	10,747[6]	−14,535[6]	−3,788[6]	1,559	1,224	Brazil
2[1]	36[1]	9[1]	3[1]	1[1]	5[1]	12[1]	—33[1]—			3.0	0.2[18]	817[9]	...	...	35[5]	...	Brunei
22[2]	[3]	49[2,3]	8[2]	[3]	9[2]	10[2]	—2[2,20]—			−0.6	−1.3[7]	−768[9]	...	...	320[6]	189[6]	Bulgaria
42[5]	1[5]	16[5]	13[5]	—	4[5]	15[5]	—1[5]—		12[5]	4.1	1.5[7]	−318[9]	214[9]	−104[9]	8	34	Burkina Faso
49[9]	1[9,21]	12[9]	4[9]	[21]	3[9]	9[9]	—2[9]—		11[9]	5.3	3.6	−105[9]	74[9]	−31[9]	4	17	Burundi
...	...	...	...	...	...	...	...	...	...	...	...	−190[5]	...	...	...	...	Cambodia
24[5]	14[5]	13[5]	5[5]	1[5]	6[5]	25[5]	—2[5]—		10[5]	9.0	−3.1[4]	621[1]	−1,050[1]	−429[1]	15	283[1]	Cameroon
2	4	18	7	4	9	11	16	23	6	3,4	2.2	8,666	−31,936	−23,720	5,537	10,526	Canada
20[1]	1[1]	5[1]	11[1]	1[1]	13[1]	25[1]	9[1]	1[1]	10[1]	4.4	6.9[4]	−117[9]	77[9]	−40[9]	...	...	Cape Verde
40	3	10	2	—	—38—					0.5	1.5[4]	−91[6]	2[6]	−89[6]	9[6]	41[6]	Central African Republic
41[5]	—	16[5]	1[5]	1[5]	2[5]	29[5]	—1[5]—		9[5]	−5.0	4.5[4]	−100[9]	20[9]	−80[9]	10	32	Chad
9	7	21	6	3	7	18	—30—			3.5	6.1	751	−1,331	−580	700	409	Chile
28	[3]	39[3]	5	[3]	5	5	—18—			8.0[23]	7.6[23]	8,743[9]	4,529[9]	13,272[9]	2,845	417	China
17	8	21	6	3	9	14	11	5	8	3.8	4.2	2,959[9]	−610[9]	2,349[9]	410	593	Colombia
44[5]	...	4[5]	8[5]	1[5]	4[5]	19[5]	—1[5]—		20[5]	4.2	2.5[4]	−29[9]	20[9]	−9[9]	9	7	Comoros
14[5]	28[5]	6[5]	2[5]	2[5]	14[5]	9[5]	—25[5]—			8.8	0.7[4]	677[9]	−846[9]	−169[9]	7	93	Congo
16	[14]	19[14]	3	3	5	20	12	6	15	2.7	4.0	−207[9]	101[9]	−106[9]	331	149	Costa Rica
36	[24]	20[24]	3[24]	[24]	—44—					3.7	−2.1[4]	1,162[9]	−2,613[9]	−1,451[9]	46	223	Côte d'Ivoire
12[17]	[14]	37[14,17]	8[17]	[25]	10[17,25]	27[17,25]	—6[17,25]—			2.8[17]	−1.7[7,17]	...	...	...	...	...	Croatia
16[5,26]	4[5,26]	39[5,26]	9[5,26]	3[5,26]	8[5,26]	20[5,26]	—1[5,20,26]—			5.7[2]	−1.4[2,14]	−1,557[9]	...	...	300	...	Cuba
7	—	14	10	2	9	21	14	6	11	8.1	5.8	−1,488[9]	1,309[9]	−179[9]	1,026	113	Cyprus
10[5]	[3]	59[3,5]	10[5]	—	5[5]	12[5]	—3[5]—			0.7	2.7[7]	−121[9]	1,029[9]	908[9]	825	393	Czech Republic[27]
4	1	17	5	2	8	12	17	5	19	2.6	1.5	7,119	−2,534	4,585	3,475	3,377	Denmark
3[5]	...	5[5]	6[5]	6[5]	13[5]	34[5]	—3[5]—		30[5]	1.4	1.8[4]	−322[9]	...	...	6[6]	...	Djibouti
21	1	6	6	3	13	11	11	1	15	5.4	4.8	−47[9]	20[9]	−27[9]	28	4[6]	Dominica
15	3	16	8	2	8	14	13	10	10	3.2	1.5	−1,612	1,219	−393	877	154	Dominican Republic
17	17	12	3	2	9	15	11	—15—		4.3	2.3	644[9]	−1,111[9]	−467[9]	189	177	Ecuador
20	[14]	22[14]	5	4	10	—24—		4	11	8.0	4.5	−5,975[9]	7,878[9]	1,903[9]	2,029	225	Egypt
11	—	19	3	2	5	35	8	10	8	−0.4	2.1	−706[9]	493[9]	−213[9]	157	60	El Salvador

National product and accounts (continued)

country	gross national product (GNP)					gross domestic product (GDP) by type of expenditure, 1990 (%)					cost components of gross domestic product (GDP), 1990 (%)			
	nominal, 1991 ('000,000 U.S.$)	per capita, 1991 (U.S.$)	average annual growth rates, 1980–91			consumption		gross domestic invest-ment	foreign trade		indirect taxes net of subsidies	consump-tion of fixed capital	compen-sation of employ-ees	net operating surplus
			real GNP (%)	popu-lation (%)	real GNP per capita (%)	private	govern-ment		exports	imports				
Equatorial Guinea	142	330	...	3.1	...	53	15	31	60	−60	...	...	...	...
Eritrea[28]	...	150	...	2.9	...	...	...	...	...	...	...	...	...	...
Estonia	6,088	3,830	...	0.5	...	65[9]	10[9]	29[9]	—−4[9]—		...	...	...	...
Ethiopia[28]	6,144	120	1.5	2.9	−1.4	70	28	11	11	−20	9[8]	—91[8]—		
Faeroe Islands	662[5, 10]	13,850[5, 10]	...	0.8	...	53[5]	25[5]	19[5]	34[5]	−31[5]	12[8]	[11]	62[8]	26[8, 11]
Fiji	1,377	1,830	1.5	1.4	0.1	70[5]	14[5]	16[5]	58[5]	−58[5]	11[5]	7[5]	41[5]	41[5]
Finland	121,982	24,400	2.9	0.4	2.5	52	21	28	23	−24	12	15	55	17
France	1,167,749	20,600	2.3	0.5	1.8	60	18	22	23	−23	13	13	52	23
French Guiana	179[8]	1,820[8]	...	5.2	...	...	...	...	...	...	...	...	...	...
French Polynesia	3,007[6, 10]	15,260[6, 10]	...	2.7	...	—100—		21	9	−31	...	...	...	...
Gabon	4,419	3,780	−0.9	3.7	−4.6	41	19	22	59	−41	18[5]	14[5]	35[5]	34[5]
Gambia, The	322	360	3.2	3.2	0.0	75	16	21	70	−83	18	10	—72—	
Gaza Strip	380	590	...	3.5	...	152[12]	14[12]	34[12]	47[12]	−148[12]	...	...	...	...
Georgia	9,000	1,640	2.9	0.7	2.2	80[2]	11[2]	19[2]	—−1[2]—		...	...	...	...
Germany[30]	1,516,785	23,650	2.3	0.2	2.1	55	18	21	36	−30	11	12	55	22
Ghana	6,176	400	3.1	2.6	0.5	85	11	12	15	−24	...	...	...	...
Gibraltar	431	15,080	...	−0.2	...	...	...	...	...	...	...	...	...	...
Greece	65,504	6,230	1.6	0.5	1.1	71	21	20	22	−33	12	9	42	37
Greenland	500[1]	9,000[1]	...	0.9	...	...	...	...	...	...	...	...	...	...
Grenada	198	2.180	...	0.2	...	65	20	42	44	−72	...	...	...	...
Guadeloupe	1,170[8]	3,200[8]	...	1.9	...	92[12]	35[12]	21[12]	8[12]	−56[12]	...	...	...	...
Guam	2,000	14,000	...	2.3	...	...	...	...	...	...	...	...	...	...
Guatemala	8,816	930	1.0	2.8	−1.8	84	7	13	20	−24	6	2	—92—	
Guernsey[31]	1,486	25,250	4.8	1.1	3.7	...	...	...	...	...	...	...	...	...
Guinea	2,669	450	...	2.4	...	69	11	17	30	−27	12[8]	—88[8]—		
Guinea-Bissau	194	190	3.3	2.1	1.2	99	13	22	23	−56	13[8]	—87[8]—		
Guyana	233	290	−3.8	0.0	−3.8	63[1]	32[1]	25[1]	82[1]	−103[1]	13	—87—		
Haiti	2,471	370	−0.6	1.9	−2.5	—95—		13	14	−22	10	2	—88—	
Honduras	3,010	570	2.6	3.5	−0.9	72	13	22	34	−40	11	7	43	39
Hong Kong	77,302[10]	13,200[10]	6.9[10]	1.2	5.7[10]	58	8	29	135	−130	5[5]	[11]	49[5]	47[5, 11]
Hungary	28,244	2,690	0.5	−0.3	0.8	62	11	24	32	−29	14	8	54	24
Iceland	5,814	22,580	2.4	1.1	1.3	61	19	19	36	−34	20	12	50	15
India	284,668	330	5.5	2.1	3.4	65	12	24	7	−8	11[5]	10[5]	—79[5]—	
Indonesia	111,409	610	5.8	2.0	3.8	54	9	37	26	−26	7	5	—88—	
Iran	127,366	2,320	2.5	3.7	−1.2	65	11	28	14	−18	3[5]	9[5]	—89[5]—	
Iraq	35,000[5]	1,940[5]	...	3.1	...	56[5]	33[5]	8[5]	27[5]	−24[5]	1[5]	9[5]	28[5]	62[5]
Ireland	37,738	10,780	2.4	0.3	2.1	56	16	20	61	−53	10	10	50	29
Isle of Man	490[1]	7,570[1]	...	0.8	...	...	...	...	...	...	...	...	...	...
Israel	59,128	11,330	3.7	2.3	1.4	63	30	19	35	−46	16	15	49	21
Italy	1,072,198	18,580	2.4	0.1	2.3	62	18	21	19	−20	9	12	45	34
Jamaica	3,365	1,380	1.0	1.2	−0.2	61	15	29	53	−58	15[5]	8[5]	44[5]	33[5]
Japan	3,337,191	26,920	4.3	0.5	3.8	57	9	33	11	−10	7	15	55	24
Jersey	2,884	34,200	...	1.0	...	...	...	...	...	...	...	...	...	...
Jordan	3,881	1,120	...	4.4	...	90	22	20	61	−93	16[8]	8[8]	42[8]	35[8]
Kazakhstan	41,691	2,470	...	1.1	...	...	...	...	...	...	...	...	...	...
Kenya	8,505	340	4.1	4.1	0.0	64	17	24	26	−31	14	[11]	36	50[11]
Kiribati	53	750	...	2.4	...	70[5]	45[5]	31[5]	22[5]	−70[5]	12[12]	12[12]	52[12]	25[12]
Korea, North	22,900	1,040	...	1.8	...	...	...	...	...	...	...	...	...	...
Korea, South	280,800	6,500	10.0	1.2	8.8	53	11	37	31	−32	12	10	46	32
Kuwait	33,089[5]	16,150[5]	...	−10.6	...	54	40	18	45	−57	—	8[8]	34[8]	58[8]
Kyrgyzstan	6,900	1,550	...	1.9	...	61[5]	20[5]	40[5]	—−22[5]—		—	16[5]	50[5]	34[5]
Laos	965	230	...	2.4	...	...	...	...	...	...	...	...	...	...
Latvia	9,193	3,410	...	0.4	...	10[9]	46[9]	34[9]	—10[9]—		...	...	...	...
Lebanon	4,800	1,400	...	0.4	...	110[5]	44[5]	10[5]	32[5]	−96[5]	...	...	...	...
Lesotho	1,053	580	2.7	2.6	0.1	116	16	77	14	−123	19	—81—		
Liberia	984[5]	390[5]	...	3.2	...	55[5]	12[5]	8[5]	44[5]	−23[5]	4[8]	—96[8]—		
Libya	23,333[5]	5,310[5]	...	3.2	...	39[5]	31[5]	25[5]	38[5]	−33[5]	3[22]	6[22]	36[22]	55[22]
Liechtenstein	940[6]	32,790[6]	...	1.2	...	...	...	...	...	...	...	...	...	...
Lithuania	10,220	2,710	...	0.8	...	63	19	30	—−12—		...	...	...	...
Luxembourg	11,761	31,080	4.2	0.6	3.6	57	16	27	98	−99	14	11	65	10
Macau	3,100[10]	6,900[10]	...	3.8	...	34	8	20	83	−45	...	...	...	...
Macedonia	...	...	...	0.6	...	...	...	...	...	...	...	...	...	...
Madagascar	2,560	210	0.5	3.2	−2.7	83	9	17	15	−24	13[8]	—87[8]—		
Malaŵi	1,996	230	3.5	4.4	−0.9	83	15	14	22	−34	10[5]	—90[5]—		
Malaysia	45,787	2,490	5.6	2.6	3.0	54	14	32	78	−78	14	—86—		
Maldives	101	460	10.2	3.4	6.8	59[1]	4[1]	28[1]	—91[1]—		...	...	...	...
Mali	2,412	280	2.5	1.8	0.7	79	15	22	17	−34	8[8]	—92[8]—		
Malta	2,598	6,850	3.5	0.9	2.6	63	18	33	85	−99	12	5	43	40
Marshall Islands	63[5, 10]	1,500[5, 10]	...	4.1	...	...	...	...	...	...	...	...	...	...
Martinique	1,429[8]	4,100[8]	...	1.1	...	83[12]	32[12]	18[12]	11[12]	−44[12]	12[12]	[11]	68[12]	20[11, 12]
Mauritania	1,026	510	0.6	3.0	−2.4	88	10	14	47	−58	13[8]	—87[8]—		
Mauritius	2,623	2,420	7.2	1.2	6.0	66	12	30	67	−75	16	[11]	40	44[11]
Mayotte	134[10]	1,430[10]	...	5.5	...	47	92	3	—−42—		...	...	...	...
Mexico	252,381	2,870	1.5	2.3	−0.8	71	8	22	16	−17	10	10	25	55
Micronesia	150[5]	1,500[5]	...	3.0	...	...	...	...	...	...	...	...	...	...
Moldova	9,529	2,170	...	0.8	...	...	...	...	...	...	...	...	...	...
Monaco	475	16,000	...	1.1	...	...	...	...	...	...	...	...	...	...
Mongolia	2,100[10]	900[10]	...	2.4	...	73	24	30	23	−50	[19]	22	39	40[19]
Morocco	26,451	1,030	4.3	2.6	1.7	64	16	26	25	−31	15[8]	—85[8]—		
Mozambique	1,163	70	−1.1	1.6	−2.7	91	20	36	15	−62	6[8]	—94[8]—		
Myanmar (Burma)	22,200[10]	530[10]	...	2.2	...	—89—		14	3	−5	3	9	44	44
Namibia	2,051	1,120	1.6	3.0	−1.4	56[5]	28[5]	17[5]	55[5]	−56[5]	13[5]	4[5]	44[5]	38[5]
Nauru	90[5]	10,000[5]	...	1.8	...	...	...	...	...	...	...	...	...	...
Nepal	3,453	180	4.7	2.6	2.1	82	11	18	12	−24	7	—93—		
Netherlands, The	278,839	18,560	2.1	0.6	1.5	59	15	21	57	−52	10	11	51	28

origin of gross domestic product (GDP) by economic sector, 1990 (%)										avg. annual growth rate of real GDP (%)		balance of payments, 1992 (current external transactions; '000,000 U.S.$)			tourist trade, 1991 ('000,000 U.S.$)		country
primary		secondary			tertiary					1975–1985	1985–1991	net transfers		current balance of payments	receipts from foreign nationals	expenditures by nationals abroad	
agriculture	mining	manufacturing	construction	public utilities	transp., communications	trade	financial svcs.	other svcs.	government			goods, merchandise	invisibles				
52	[14]	1[14]	4	3	2	7	2	13	12	−6.0	4.2[4]	−24[9]	−1[9]	−25[9]	...	...	Equatorial Guinea
..	...	...	...	...	...	...	...	...	...	...	...	...	...	...	...	...	Eritrea[28]
15[9]	[3]	52[3, 9]	5[9]	[3]	5[9]	6[9]		17[9]		−0.2[29]	−1.6	...	...	...	...	...	Estonia
41	—	11	4	1	7	10	4	7	13	1.6	2.1	−610[6]	326[6]	−284[6]	20	11[6]	Ethiopia[28]
5[5]	1[5]	19[5]	7[5]	2[5]	8[5]	15[5]	19[5]	5[5]	22[5]	2.5	1.4[7]	140[9]	...	...	...	...	Faeroe Islands
19[5]	7[5, 21]	9[5]	4[5]	[21]	10[5]	21[5]		28[5]		1.4	3.0	−118[9]	137[9]	19[9]	211	45	Fiji
6	—	22	10	2	8	11	19	7	18	2.9	1.7	3,851	−8,955	−5,104	1,191	2.634	Finland
6	[14]	19[14]	5	2	6	14	5	24	16	2.3	2.8	−10,139[9]	3,991[9]	−6,148[9]	21,300	12,338	France
...	...	...	...	...	...	...	...	...	...	...	...	618	...	...	...	...	French Guiana
5	[14]	7[14]	6	2	...	23	...	29	29	5.2	5.2[4]	−739	...	...	150	...	French Polynesia
11	48	5	6	2	8	12		7		−2.1	−8.3[4]	1,446[9]	−1,606[9]	−160[9]	8	152	Gabon
24	—	7	6	1	18	37	7	3	12	−0.8	3.3[7]	−31	57	26	26	8[6]	Gambia, The
22[12]	[14]	13[12, 14]	22[14]	[25]			43[12, 25]			2.8	...	−235[8]	219[8]	−16[8]	6[8]	10[8]	Gaza Strip
37	[3]	35[2, 3]	11	[3]	5	6		6		6.1[2, 7]	−4.8[2, 7]	...	...	...	...	...	Georgia
2	3	32	6	...	6	9	12	17	11	2.2	3.2	32,350	−58,340	−25,990	10,947	31,650	Germany[30]
48	2	9	3	2	4	19	4	—	8	0.3	4.8[7]	−470	92	−378	118	13[6]	Ghana
...	...	...	...	...	...	...	...	...	...	...	...	−365[9]	...	...	112[6]	...	Gibraltar
16	1	16	7	3	8	15		8	20	2.8	1.7	−10,112[9]	8,591[9]	−1,521[9]	2,566	1,011	Greece
...	...	...	...	...	...	...	...	...	...	...	...	180[9]	...	...	...	...	Greenland
15	—	6	12	3	15	20	11	4	18	4.9	4.5	−98[9]	59[9]	−39[9]	38[6]	7[6]	Grenada
...	...	...	...	...	...	...	...	...	...	2.3	...	−1,418	...	...	284	...	Guadeloupe
...	...	...	...	...	...	...	...	...	...	...	...	...	...	...	1,093	589[1]	Guam
26	—	15	3	3	8	24	9	6	7	2.2	3.0	−443[9]	259[9]	−184[9]	211	67	Guatemala
...	...	...	...	...	...	...	...	...	...	...	...	...	...	...	151[5]	...	Guernsey[31]
28	24	4	6	1	4	22		11		2.9	3.2[4]	56[9]	...	...	...	...	Guinea
45[5]	—	5[5]	6[5]	1[5]	1[5]	28[5]	6[5]		8[5]	1.7	5.0[4]	−114[9]	...	...	...	...	Guinea-Bissau
22	13	9[32]	5	[32]	6	6	5	2	11	−3.2	−0.6	−41[9]	...	...	30	...	Guyana
34	—	15	5	1	2	17	6	3	12	2.3	0.1	−138[9]	128[9]	−10[9]	46	33	Haiti
23[9]	2[9]	17[9]	4[9]	3[9]	5[9]	13[9]	14[9]	11[9]	7[9]	4.4	3.1	−56[9]	−263[9]	−319[9]	31	37	Honduras
—	—	16	5	2	9	23	30	15		8.9	7.2	−3,920	...	...	5,078	...	Hong Kong
13	3	21	6	4	7	13	7	1	12	0.0	1.7[7]	−55	373	318	1,037	505	Hungary
17	—	14	9	5	8	11	17	7	17	4.1	2.7	−48[9]	−273[9]	−321[9]	116	295	Iceland
31	2	19	6	2	7	13	9	6	6	4.4	5.4	−6,110[6]	−716[6]	−6,826[6]	1,310	425[6]	India
22	15	20	5	1	6	16	7	3	6	6.2	6.3	6,021	−9,700	−3,679	2,515	949	Indonesia
18	5	9	5	1	7	29	13	2	10	1.4	−0.9	101[1]	−1,969[1]	−1,868[1]	62[6]	396[6]	Iran
20	12	10	8	1	8	16	11	14		2.9	5.8[18]	13[9]	...	...	55[6]	...	Iraq
10	[24]	37[24]	[24]	[24]	19		28		6	3.5	4.4	4,169[9]	−2,731[9]	1,438[9]	1,551	1,125	Ireland
3[22]	—	16[22]	10[22]	3[22]	11[22]	12[22]	30[22]	24[22]	8[22]	−1.7	...	...	...	...	36[12]	...	Isle of Man
3	[14]	22[14]	6	3	9	11	24	4	24	3.2	4.4	−5,035	5,121	86	1,306	1,783	Israel
3	[14]	22[14]	6	5	6	19	12	13	13	3.1	2.8	2,410	−27,832	−25,422	19,668	13,300	Italy
5	10	20	13	3	7	22	15	5	9	−1.6	3.5[7]	−406[9]	208[9]	−198[9]	746	54	Jamaica
3	—	31	9	4	6	14[33]	16	16[33]	7	4.4	4.5	132,400	−14,760	117,640	3,435	23,983	Japan
5	—		2				93			...	7.2	...	...	...	526[6]	...	Jersey
7	8	15	6	3	15	9	17	4	20	8.6	−0.1	−1,095[9]	1,505[9]	410[9]	317	281	Jordan
40[2]	[3]	28[2, 3]	15[2]	[3]	9[2]	5[2]		3[2]		2.7[2]	2.1[2, 7]	...	...	...	...	...	Kazakhstan
24	—	10	7	1	6	9	14	1	13	4.9	5.9[4]	−659[9]	428[9]	−231[9]	424	24	Kenya
24[5]	—	2[5]	4[5]	2[5]	14[5]	14[5]	8[5]	3[5]	25[5]	−11.5	0.9[18]	−16[1]	22[1]	6[1]	2	...	Kiribati
...	...	...	...	...	...	...	...	...	...	...	...	−765[9]	...	...	...	...	Korea, North
9	—	29	13	2	7	11	14	7	8	8.0	9.9	−2,146	−2,383	−4,529	3,426	3,784	Korea, South
1[5]	41[5]	14[5]	2[5]	−1[5]	4[5]	8[5]	12[5]	19[5]		−2.4	3.8[18]	549	252	801	123[5]	2,318[5]	Kuwait
36[2, 9]	[3]	45[2, 3, 9]	8[2, 9]	[3]	3[2, 9]		8[2, 9]			4.0[2]	5.0[2, 34]	...	...	...	...	...	Kyrgyzstan
53[9]	—	13[9]	4[9]	2[9]	6[9]	8[9]	3[9]	5[9]	6[9]	...	...	−66[9]	...	...	...	...	Laos
18	[3]	42[3]	7	[3]	9		24			3.4[29]	1.3	...	...	...	...	...	Latvia
9[5]	5[5, 21]	13[5]	3[5]	[21]	4[5]	28[5]		38[5]		−9.4	−22.5[4]	−3,258[9]	...	...	...	...	Lebanon
15	—	13	19	1	4	7	5	8	15	4.7	7.0[7]	−718[9]	782[9]	64[9]	18	11	Lesotho
34[5]	10[5]	7[5]	2[5]	2[5]	7[5]	5[5]	12[5]	3[5]	12[5]	0.0	0.1[4]	63[8]	−181[8]	−118[8]	6[12]	...	Liberia
5[5]	28[5]	8[5]	13[5]	2[5]	6[5]	7[5]	9[5]	1[5]	21[5]	−3.1	−0.5[4]	3,780[6]	−1,577[6]	2,203[6]	6[6]	424[6]	Libya
...	...	...	...	...	...	...	...	...	...	...	...	574[9]	...	...	...	...	Liechtenstein
28	[3]	32[3]	10	[3]	5	6		20		3.9[29]	2.8[7]	...	...	...	...	...	Lithuania
2	—	26	7	2	7	16	13	15	14	2.4	4.3	[15]	[15]	[15]	290[6]	...	Luxembourg
...	...	...	...	...	...	...	...	...	...	...	7.4	−219[9]	...	...	1,643	42	Macau
17[5, 17]	[14]	55[5, 14, 17]	5[5, 17]	1[5, 17]	6[5, 17]	13[5, 17]		3[5, 17]		3.1[17]	1.0[4, 17]	...	...	...	...	...	Macedonia
40[5]	—	12[5]	4[5]	1[5]	8[5]	13[5]	8[5]		14[5]	0.2	2.4[4]	−101[9]	−91[9]	−192[9]	26	32	Madagascar
34	—	13	5	2	6	12	11	4	15	3.1	3.9	44[1]	−97[1]	−53[1]	8[6]	3[6]	Malaŵi
19	10	27	4	2	7	11	10	2	11	6.8	7.1	2,851	−4,578	−1,727	1,530	1,503	Malaysia
24	2	6[32]	9	[32]	6	17	4	24	8	11.5[35]	9.7	−111	−78	−33	87	16	Maldives
46[9]	1[9]	7[9]	4[9]	1[9]	4[9]	16[9]	1[9]	15[9]		1.8	5.6[4]	−93[9]	56[9]	−37[9]	12	60	Mali
3	[36]	27	4[36]	[37]	6	14	14	9	22[37]	6.5	6.1[4]	−599[6]	443[6]	−56[6]	574	140	Malta
...	...	...	...	...	...	...	...	...	...	...	...	...	...	...	...	...	Marshall Islands
...	...	...	...	...	...	...	...	...	...	3.9	...	−1,508	...	...	255	...	Martinique
31[5]	10[5]	6[5]	6[5]	1[5]	11[5]	19[5]	5[5]		14[5]	2.0	2.9[4]	99[5]	−118[5]	−19[5]	15[6]	31[6]	Mauritania
13	—	23	7	2	11	18	12	4	11	4.2	7.1	−223[9]	186[9]	−37[9]	262	110	Mauritius
...	...	...	...	...	...	...	...	...	...	...	...	−83	...	...	...	...	Mayotte
9	2	23	3	1	8	28	11	15		4.1	1.7	−11,063[9]	−2,220[9]	−13,283[9]	4,355	2,146	Mexico
...	...	...	...	...	...	...	...	...	...	...	...	...	...	...	...	...	Micronesia
42[2]	[3]	34[2, 3]	9[2]	[3]	5[2]	9[2]		1[2]		3.8[2]	3.6[2, 7]	...	...	...	...	...	Moldova
...	...	...	...	...	...	...	...	...	...	...	...	...	...	...	...	...	Monaco
20	[3]	34[3]	6	[3]	13	9		18		...	4.1[38]	−80[9]	−31[9]	−111[9]	...	...	Mongolia
16	3	19	5	7	7	13	3	10	12	3.9	4.5	−1,976[9]	1,580[9]	−396[9]	1,052	190	Morocco
37	[14]	23[14]	13	...	10		17			−4.0	2.5	−647[9]	366[9]	−281[9]	...	...	Mozambique
59	1	8	1	—	3	21	—	4		5.8	−1.6	−205[1]	29[1]	−176[1]	13	1	Myanmar (Burma)
15	22	6	2	2	7	12	7	2	21	0.0	2.1[7]	79[5]	−116[5]	−37[5]	...	...	Namibia
...	...	...	...	...	...	...	...	...	...	...	...	...	...	...	...	...	Nauru
54	—	5	7	1	5	5	8	8		3.6	5.2	−482[9]	178[9]	−304[9]	126	38	Nepal
4	3	21	6	2	6	13	17	11	11	1.8	2.7	10,718	−3,970	6,748	4,074	7,886	Netherlands, The

National product and accounts (continued)

country	gross national product (GNP): nominal, 1991 ('000,000 U.S.$)	per capita, 1991 (U.S.$)	average annual growth rates, 1980–91: real GNP (%)	popu-lation (%)	real GNP per capita (%)	gross domestic product (GDP) by type of expenditure, 1990 (%): consumption: private	govern-ment	gross domestic invest-ment	foreign trade: exports	imports	cost components of gross domestic product (GDP), 1990 (%): indirect taxes net of subsidies	consump-tion of fixed capital	compen-sation of employ-ees	net operating surplus
Netherlands Antilles	1,490	7,800	...	1.0	...	70[22]	32[22]	16[22]	67[22]	−84[22]	...	...	...	...
New Caledonia	1,000	6,000	...	1.9	...	45[5]	31[5]	20[5]	32[5]	−29[5]	5[1]	9[1]	47[1]	39[1]
New Zealand	41,626	12,140	1.0	0.8	0.2	63	17	21	27	−28	15	9	45	31
Nicaragua	1,897	340	−1.4	3.4	−4.8	73	29	20	23	−45	...	...	...	...
Niger	2,361	300	−0.9	3.3	−4.2	74	17	13	17	−21	...	...	...	...
Nigeria	34,057	290	1.4	2.1	−0.7	56	4	12	50	−22	1	5	16	78
Northern Mariana Is.	256[10, 12]	12,360[10, 12]	...	9.0	...	...	...	...	...	...	...	...	...	...
Norway	102,885	24,160	2.5	0.4	2.1	51	21	21	44	−37	11	15	52	23
Oman	8,787[6]	5,650[6]	...	4.4	...	27	38	13	53	−31	[19]	[11]	30	70[11, 19]
Pakistan	46,725	400	6.5	3.3	3.2	72	15	19	15	−20	13	6	—82—	
Panama	5,254	2,180	0.3	2.1	−1.8	60	19	17	39	−35	9	9	47	36
Papua New Guinea	3,307	820	1.7	2.2	−0.5	59	25	24	41	−49	11	11	41	37
Paraguay	5,374	1,210	2.3	3.1	−0.8	75	6	23	29	−33	6	11	24	59
Peru	28,295	1,020	−0.4	2.2	−2.6	78	6	16	12	−13	5	6	21	68
Philippines	46,138	740	1.2	2.3	−1.1	72	10	23	28	−33	8	8	35	49
Poland	70,640	1,830	1.2	0.7	0.5	54	7	30	26	−18	...	...	...	...
Portugal	58,451	5,620	3.2	0.1	3.1	63	17	29	36	−45	14	[11]	45	42[11]
Puerto Rico	22,498	6,330	1.8	0.9	0.9	64	15	16	76	−70	5	6	42	46
Qatar	6,968[6]	15,870[6]	...	7.4	...	32[8]	44[8]	14[8]	41[8]	−32[8]	1[12]		———99[12]———	
Réunion	5,245[10]	8,730[10]	...	1.7	...	83[1]	28[1]	29[1]	4[1]	−43[1]	10[1]	[11]	57[1]	33[1, 11]
Romania	31,079	1,340	0.3	0.3	0.0	73	5	34	—−11—		11	13	71	4
Russia	479,546	3,430	...	0.6	...	...	...	...	...	...	...	...	...	...
Rwanda	1,930	260	0.5	3.1	−2.6	82	17	12	8	−19	7[5]	8[5]	25[5]	61[5]
St. Kitts	156	3,960	4.5	−0.3	4.8	73	17	46	50	−86	...	...	...	...
St. Lucia	380	2,500	...	0.8	...	...	...	...	...	...	...	...	...	...
St. Vincent	187	1,730	6.1	0.8	5.3	67	18	31	71	−87	...	...	...	...
San Marino	400[10]	17,000[10]	...	0.8	...	...	...	...	...	...	...	...	...	...
São Tomé and Príncipe	42	350	−1.2	2.2	−3.4	67[5]	48[5]	21[5]	33[5]	−67[5]	...	...	...	...
Saudi Arabia	105,133[6]	7,070[6]	...	4.1	...	47	31	22	38	−37	−0.2[5]	[11]	46[5]	54[5, 11]
Senegal	5,500	720	2.9	2.6	0.3	77	14	13	26	−30	18[8]		———82[8]———	
Seychelles	350[6]	5,110[6]	...	0.9	...	50	27	25	53	−55	21[5]	7[5]	36[5]	36[5]
Sierra Leone	904	210	1.1	2.2	−1.1	85	7	14	20	−25	4[5]	6[5]	15[5]	75[5]
Singapore	39,249	12,890	7.1	1.8	5.3	43	10	37	—9—		...	...	...	...
Slovakia	...	...	...	0.5	...	...	...	...	...	...	...	...	...	...
Slovenia	...	...	...	0.4	...	...	...	...	...	...	...	...	...	...
Solomon Islands	184	560	6.7	3.3	3.4	69[5]	31[5]	33[5]	52[5]	−85[5]	14[8]	7[8]	48[8]	32[8]
Somalia	946[6]	150[6]	...	3.4	...	95[5]	11[5]	40[5]	8[5]	−55[5]	3[8]		———97[8]———	
South Africa	90,953[6]	2,530[6]	...	2.4	...	57	19	19	26	−20	10	16	53	20
Bophuthatswana	...	...	...	...	...	...	...	...	...	...	...	...	...	...
Ciskei	377[22]	490[22]	...	...	...	...	...	...	...	...	...	...	...	...
Transkei	...	...	...	...	...	...	...	...	...	...	...	...	...	...
Venda	...	...	...	...	...	...	...	...	...	...	...	...	...	...
Spain	486,614	12,460	3.2	0.3	2.9	62	15	26	17	−20	8	11	46	35
Sri Lanka	8,665	500	4.0	1.4	2.6	76	10	22	30	−38	14	5	45	37
Sudan, The	10,107[6]	400[6]	...	3.7	...	81[5]	10[5]	15[5]	9[5]	−15[5]	...	...	...	...
Suriname	1,649[6]	3,350[6]	...	1.2	...	53	25	21	28	−28	9	12	46	33
Swaziland	874[6]	1,030[6]	...	2.9	...	73[5]	31[5]	19[5]	74[5]	−97[5]	15[8]	7[8]	45[8]	34[8]
Sweden	218,934	25,490	2.0	0.3	1.7	52	27	21	30	−30	13	11	61	15
Switzerland	225,890	33,510	2.2	0.7	1.5	57	14	29	37	−38	5	11	63	21
Syria	14,234[6]	1,000[6]	...	3.4	...	70	14	15	28	−28	−4	4	—100—	
Taiwan	180,089	8,780	7.9	1.3	6.8	55	18	22	48	−42	11	9	53	28
Tajikistan	5,669	1,050	...	2.9	...	...	...	...	...	...	...	...	...	...
Tanzania	2,424	100	2.0	2.8	−0.8	74	14	48	21	−57	13[5]	3[5]	10[5]	74[5]
Thailand	89,548	1,580	7.8	2.0	5.8	59	10	37	37	−43	14	8	26	52
Togo	1,530	410	1.8	2.9	−1.1	70	19	23	41	−53	21[8]		———79[8]———	
Tonga	110	1,100	...	0.6	...	...	...	...	...	...	...	...	...	...
Trinidad and Tobago	4,525	3,620	−3.9	1.2	−5.1	52	16	17	46	−30	3	10	50	33
Tunisia	12,417	1,510	3.5	2.3	1.2	64	16	27	42	−49	12[5]	11[5]	—78[5]—	
Turkey	103,888	1,820	5.4	2.3	3.1	60	19	24	20	−23	9	6	33	52
Turkmenistan	6,387	1,700	...	2.5	...	...	...	...	...	...	...	...	...	...
Tuvalu	8.8[6, 10]	970[6, 10]	...	1.8	...	...	...	...	...	...	...	...	...	...
Uganda	2,762	160	5.9	2.6	3.3	95[5]	10[5]	24[5]	18[5]	−49[5]	65[12]		———35[12]———	
Ukraine	121,458	2,340	...	0.4	...	...	...	...	...	...	...	...	...	...
United Arab Emirates	32,813	20,130	...	5.9	...	39	16	20	65	−41	−1	13	23	66
United Kingdom	963,696	16,750	2.8	0.2	2.6	64	20	19	24	−27	13	11	58	18
United States	5,686,038	22,560	3.1	1.0	2.1	68	16	17	10	−11	8	12	60	20
Uruguay	8,895	2,860	0.2	0.6	−0.8	68	13	11	27	−19	18	[11]	40	42[11]
Uzbekistan	28,255	1,350	...	2.4	...	...	...	...	...	...	...	...	...	...
Vanuatu	175	1,120	...	2.6	...	63	28	44	46	−77	20[5]	[11]	41[5]	38[5, 11]
Venezuela	52,775	2,610	1.1	2.5	−1.4	62	8	10	39	−20	2	7	32	59
Vietnam	15,000	220	...	2.1	...	...	...	...	...	...	...	...	...	...
Virgin Islands (U.S.)	1,246[8, 10]	11,740[8, 10]	...	0.5	...	...	...	...	...	...	...	...	...	...
West Bank	1,300[6]	1,200[6]	...	2.8	...	97[12]	9[12]	31[12]	21[12]	−57[12]	...	...	...	...
Western Sahara	60[6, 10]	300[6, 10]	...	2.5	...	...	...	...	...	...	...	...	...	...
Western Samoa	156	930	...	0.3	...	...	...	...	...	...	...	...	...	...
Yemen	6,746	540	...	2.7	...	75	27	16	14	−33	9	5	—86—	
Yugoslavia[41]	70,038[6]	2,940[6]	...	...	...	66	18	22	24	−29	16	11	—73—	
Zaire	8,123[6]	220[6]	...	3.3	...	81	12	8	30	−30	...	...	...	...
Zambia	3,394[6]	420[6]	...	3.2	...	63	19	17	37	−37	7	9	57	26
Zimbabwe	6,220	620	3.6	2.8	0.8	58	24	21	31	−33	14		———86———	

[1]1988. [2]Net material product. [3]Manufacturing includes mining and public utilities. [4]1985–89. [5]1989. [6]1990. [7]1985–90. [8]1987. [9]1991. [10]GDP. [11]Net operating surplus includes consumption of fixed capital. [12]1986. [13]1986–91. [14]Manufacturing includes mining. [15]Data refer to the Belgium-Luxembourg Economic Union (BLEU). [16]Gross material product. [17]Social product. [18]1985–88. [19]Net operating surplus includes indirect taxes net of subsidies. [20]Activities in the material sphere not elsewhere specified. [21]Mining includes public utilities. [22]1985. [23]National income. [24]Manufacturing includes mining, construction, and public utilities. [25]Tertiary sector includes public utilities. [26]Global social product. [27]Data refer to former Czechoslovakia. [28]Ethiopia includes

agri-culture	mining	manu-factur-ing	con-struc-tion	public util-ities	transp., commu-nications	trade	finan-cial svcs.	other svcs.	govern-ment	1975–1985	1985–1991	goods, merchan-dise	invisibles	current balance of payments	receipts from foreign nationals	expendi-tures by nationals abroad	country
origin of gross domestic product (GDP) by economic sector, 1990 (%)										avg. annual growth rate of real GDP (%)		balance of payments, 1992 (current external transactions; '000,000 U.S.$)			tourist trade, 1991 ('000,000 U.S.$)		
primary		secondary			tertiary							net transfers					
1[22]	—	13[22]	10[22]	3[22]	12[22]	18[22]	16[22]	6[22]	24[22]	1.9[39]	...	−904[6]	873[6]	−31[6]	484	...	Netherlands Antilles
2[5]	26[5, 21]	5[5]	5[5]	[21]	4[5]	21[5]	—37[5]—			−0.2	...	−518	...	...	150[6]	...	New Caledonia
9	1	18	5	3	8	15	22	4	12	1.6	0.2	2,042[9]	−2,062[9]	−20[9]	1,021	1,408	New Zealand
30	1	16	3	1	4	22	6	4	12	−1.8	−3.5	−518	−177	−695	17	28	Nicaragua
34[5]	10[5, 21]	8[5]	5[5]	[21]	4[5]	15[5]	—24[5]—			1.7	2.1[4]	11[9]	−18[9]	−7[9]	16	40	Niger
39[9]	13[9]	8[9]	2[9]	1[9]	3[9]	13[9]	9[9]	3[9]	9[9]	−0.7	5.4	4,441[9]	−3,238[9]	1,203[9]	39	839	Nigeria
...	...	...	...	...	...	...	...	...	...	...	...	...	...	...	450	...	Northern Mariana Is.
3	15	14	4	4	9	11	9	10	16	4.0	1.6	8,717[9]	−3,778[9]	4,939[9]	1,574	3,207	Norway
3	51	4	3	1	3	11	7	2	16	13.6	3.5[7]	2,969[6]	−1,874[6]	1,095[6]	63	47[6]	Oman
23	1	15	4	3	7	15	6	7	7	6.4	6.1	−2,247[9]	318[9]	−1,929[9]	163	555	Pakistan
11[9]	—	9[9]	3[9]	4[9]	25[9]	12[9]	14[9]	10[9]	12[9]	4.6	0.5	−827[9]	962[9]	135[9]	196	108	Panama
29	12	12	6	2	—16—		—6—		18	1.2	2.6	−23[5]	−332[5]	−355[5]	47	42[5]	Papua New Guinea
28	—	17	5	2	4	29	2	—12—		6.3	3.7	−552[9]	86[9]	−466[9]	145	122	Paraguay
9	2	30	8	1	4	15	—31—			0.6	−1.0	−567	−1,513	−2,080	277	881	Peru
23	2	25	4	2	5	20	7	—12—		2.8	3.7	−4,695	3,696	−999	1,281	61	Philippines
9[2]	[3]	54[2, 3]	11[2]	[3]	5[2]	18[2]	—32[2, 20]—			−0.2	−1.4[7]	−786[9]	−1,566[9]	−2,352[9]	149	143	Poland
6	[14]	29[14]	8	3	6	17	9	8	13	3.1	4.7[7]	−7,848[9]	7,132[9]	−716[9]	3,700	1,027	Portugal
1	—	39	2	3	5	16	15	7	11	3.3	3.2	1,730[9]	−5,131[9]	−3,401[9]	1,445	798	Puerto Rico
1[9]	34[9]	13[9]	4[9]	2[9]	3[9]	6[9]	11[9]	—27[9]—		0.0	...	1,336[9]	...	...	...	...	Qatar
7[5]	2[5, 21]	9[5]	6[5]	[21]	5[5]	15[5]	—54[5]—			5.1	...	−2,180	...	...	140[6]	...	Réunion
18	[3]	48[3]	6	[3]	7	7	2	2	8	−0.1	−2.2[7]	−1,220[9]	36[9]	−1,184[9]	103	114	Romania
18	[3]	48[3]	6	[3]	7	7	2	5	8	3.9[2]	1.2[2, 7]	...	...	...	270[6, 40]	...	Russia
40[5]	—	13[5]	7[5]	—	7[5]	13[5]	8[5]	—8[5]—		5.0	−0.6	−133[9]	99[9]	−34[9]	10[6]	23[6]	Rwanda
8	—	14	12	1	14	24	13	4	17	2.9	6.6	−76[9]	26[9]	−50[9]	74	4	St. Kitts
14	1	8	6	3	17	24	13	4	15	4.6	4.7[13]	−162[9]	81[9]	−81[9]	173	17	St. Lucia
19	—	9	9	5	21	14	11	2	16	6.3	7.1	−45[9]	36[9]	−9[9]	53	7	St. Vincent
...	...	...	...	...	...	...	...	...	...	...	...	...	...	...	...	...	San Marino
29[1]	...	2[1]	4[1]	1[1]	4[1]	17[1]	2[1]	9[1]	23[1]	1.8	1.6[4]	−6[6]	−2[6]	−8[6]	1[6]	2[6]	São Tomé and Príncipe
6	35	9	9	—	6	8	7	3	16	2.8	2.9[4]	22,096[9]	−47,834[9]	−25,738[9]	1,884[6]	2,000[8]	Saudi Arabia
21	[3]	16[3]	3	[3]	9	24	—27—			2.0	4.1[4]	−284[9]	46[9]	−238[9]	171	103	Senegal
4	[14]	9[14]	4	2	44	11	9	3	14	2.5	4.6[4]	−128[9]	132[9]	4[9]	99	12	Seychelles
35	6	7	2	—	13	23	8	1	2	1.4	2.5	−1[6]	−68[6]	−69[6]	19[6]	7[6]	Sierra Leone
—	—	29	5	2	14	17	32	4	7	7.4	7.8	−4,218[9]	8,426[9]	4,208[9]	5,020	2,019	Singapore
9[2]	[14]	62[2, 14]	12[2]	1[2]	5[2]	9[2]	—3[2]—			...	...	...	...	...	...	...	Slovakia
8[5, 17]	[14]	53[5, 14, 17]	9[5, 17]	1[5, 17]	9[5, 17]	18[5, 17]	—3[5, 17]—			3.0[17]	−0.4[4, 17]	...	...	...	...	...	Slovenia
49	—	3	4	1	7	9	3	—24—		6.8	3.4[4]	−8[9]	−29[9]	−37[9]	5	13	Solomon Islands
65[9]	—	4[9]	4[9]	1[9]	6[9]	9[9]	3[9]	2[9]	6[9]	1.4	2.4[4]	−279[5]	122[5]	−157[5]	8[12]	...	Somalia
5	11	26	3	5	8	13	15	1	14	2.6	1.2	6,267[9]	−3,603[9]	2,664[9]	1,046	1,047	South Africa
...	...	...	...		...	...	...	...	...	...	...	...	...	...	...	...	Bophuthatswana
...	...	...	...	...	...	...	...	...	...	...	...	...	...	...	...	...	Ciskei
...	...	...	...	...	...	...	...	...	...	...	...	...	...	...	...	...	Transkei
...	...	...	...	...	...	...	...	...	...	...	...	...	...	...	...	...	Venda
5[5]	[3]	27[3, 5]	8[5]	[3]	—60[5]—					1.7	4.1	−36,131	12,453	−23,678	19,004	4,530	Spain
26	2	15	7	1	10	21	7	4	5	5.3	3.6	−474[9]	206[9]	−268[9]	156	92	Sri Lanka
36[5]	[14]	8[5, 14]	5[5]	2[5]	—38[5]—				12[5]	−0.1	5.8[4]	−597	91	−506	8	12	Sudan, The
10	3	10	7	4	6	19	20	1	17	0.8	0.9[7]	92[6]	−60[6]	32[6]	11	12[6]	Suriname
14[1]	1[1]	20[1]	3[1]	3[1]	6[1]	11[1]	12[1]	3[1]	15[1]	3.6	5.9[4]	−40[9]	49[9]	9[9]	26	20	Swaziland
3	—	22	8	3	7	11	21	—28—		1.6	1.4	6,949	−11,874	−4,925	2,726	6,104	Sweden
4[22]	1[22]	25[22]	8[22]	2[22]	7[22]	17[22]	10[22]	14[22]	11[22]	1.6	2.3	−3,808[9]	13,655[9]	9,847[9]	7,064	5,682	Switzerland
27	14	6	4	−1	9	25	4	2	10	4.5	2.7	2,159[6]	−332[6]	1,827[6]	300	210	Syria
4	—	34	5	3	6	15	19	6	11	8.6	8.5	12,644	−4,747	7,897	2,180	5,678	Taiwan
37[2, 5]	[3]	27[2, 3, 5]	15[2, 5]	[3]	4[2, 5]	—17[2, 5]—				3.7[2]	1.8[2, 7]	...	...	...	...	...	Tajikistan
51[5]	—	8[5]	1[5]	1[5]	6[5]	13[5]	—19[5]—			2.0	3.9	−779[6]	353[6]	−426[6]	95	19[6]	Tanzania
12	4	26	7	2	7	15	9	14	4	6.8	9.9[7]	−5,985[9]	−1,579[9]	−7,564[9]	3,923	1,266	Thailand
35[5]	8[5]	7[5]	4[5]	4[5]	7[5]	23[5]	—3[5]—		10[5]	1.3	4.1[4]	−71[9]	−19[9]	−90[9]	50	48	Togo
34[1]	6[1]	8[1]	3[1]	3[1]	7[1]	23[1]	...	7[1]	8[1]	6.6	...	−36	35	−1	10	2	Tonga
2	30	9	8	2	9	13	10	5	11	2.0	−1.1	541[9]	−558[9]	−17[9]	101	111	Trinidad and Tobago
14	7	15	5	1	6	23	—17—			5.2	3.4	−874[9]	683[9]	−191[9]	685	129	Tunisia
19	1	21	5	2	16	18	3	2	10	3.6	6.0[4]	−8,191	7,248	−943	2,654	592	Turkey
43[2, 5]	[3]	23[2, 3, 5]	18[2, 5]	[3]	6[2, 5]	—9[2, 5]—				1.9[2]	2.7[2, 4]	...	...	...	...	...	Turkmenistan
11[22]	—	2[22]	10[22]	2[22]	1[22]	11[22]	—64[22]—			...	...	4[5]	...	...	0.3	...	Tuvalu
35	[14]	7[14]	7	1	10	21	5	3	10	−1.4	5.5	−298[9]	10[9]	−288[9]	15	18	Uganda
31[2]	[3]	42[2, 3]	10[2]	[3]	6[2]	6[2]	—6[2]—			3.4[2]	1.7[2, 7]	...	...	...	...	...	Ukraine
2	47	7	8	2	5	9	11	2	10	6.9	2.4[7]	8,212[9]	...	...	...	...	United Arab Emirates
1	5[21]	22	8	[21]	7	15	18	6	16	1.8	2.3	−24,621	3,161	−21,460	12,635	18,850	United Kingdom
2[5]	2[5]	19[5]	5[5]	3[5]	6[5]	16[5]	17[5]	19[5]	12[5]	2.9	2.0	−96,280	33,810	−62,470	49,551	39,418	United States
11	—	28	4	3	6	12	13	21	9	0.7	3.4	61[9]	44[9]	105[9]	333	100	Uruguay
42[2, 5]	[3]	26[2, 3, 5]	14[2, 5]	[3]	5[2, 5]	—12[2, 5]—				4.4[2]	3.0[2, 4]	...	...	...	...	...	Uzbekistan
19[5]	—	5[5]	6[5]	2[5]	8[5]	32[5]	—17[5]—		12[5]	5.1	1.7[4]	−59[9]	42[9]	−17[9]	30	1	Vanuatu
5	18	21	5	2	4	16	—19—		9	1.0	4.2	4,791[9]	−3,128[9]	1,663[9]	365	1,011	Venezuela
42[2, 8]	[3]	33[2, 3, 8]	3[2, 8]	[3]	1[2, 8]	19[2, 8]	—3[2, 8, 20]—			3.7[2]	...	−22[9]	...	...	85[6]	...	Vietnam
...	...	...	...	...	...	...	...	...	...	−0.4	...	−1,312[8]	...	...	708	...	Virgin Islands (U.S.)
33[12]	[14]	8[12, 14]	14[12]	[25]	—46[12, 25]—					4.8	...	−391[8]	525[8]	134[8]	10[8]	46[8]	West Bank
...	...	...	...	...	...	...	...	...	...	...	...	...	...	...	...	...	Western Sahara
47[5]	...	13[5]	2[5]	4[5]	4[5]	10[5]	...	9[5]	12[5]	1.3	...	−75[9]	34[9]	−41[9]	18	2	Western Samoa
21	9	9	4	2	8	12	6	1	24	...	...	...	...	...	21	81[5]	Yemen
11	2	26	7	1	10	7	6	—13—		...	...	...	...	...	468	103	Yugoslavia[41]
31[5]	24[5]	1[5]	6[5]	—	1[5]	21[5]	—7[5]—		10[5]	−0.1	0.8[4]	600[6]	−1,243[6]	−643[6]	7[6]	16[6]	Zaire
18	9	32	4	1	5	12	7	—	6	0.2	1.6[7]	566[5]	−749[5]	−183[5]	35	91	Zambia
13	8	26	2	3	8	12	7	14	7	2.4	3.8[7]	501[1]	−384[1]	117[1]	47[6]	58[6]	Zimbabwe

Eritrea. [29]1980–85. [30]Data refer to former West Germany only, except balance of payments and tourism. [31]Excludes Alderney and Sark. [32]Manufacturing includes public utilities. [33]Services includes restaurants and hotels. [34]1978–90. [35]1976–85. [36]Construction includes mining. [37]Government includes public utilities. [38]1984–1990. [39]Includes Aruba. [40]Data refer to the former U.S.S.R. [41]Data refer to the former Socialist Federated Republic of Yugoslavia.

Employment and labour

This table provides international comparisons of the world's national labour forces—giving their size; composition by demographic component and employment status; and structure by industry.

The table focuses on the concept of "economically active population," which the International Labour Organisation (ILO) defines as persons of all ages who are either employed or looking for work. In general, "economically active population" does not include students, persons occupied solely in domestic duties, retired persons, persons living entirely on their own means, and persons wholly dependent on others. Persons engaged in illegal economic activities—smugglers, prostitutes, drug dealers, bootleggers, black marketeers, and others—also fall outside the purview of the ILO definition. Countries differ markedly in their treatment, as part of the labour force, of such groups as members of the armed forces, inmates of institutions, the unemployed (both persons seeking their first job and those previously employed), seasonal and international migrant workers, and persons engaged in informal, subsistence, or part-time economic activities. Some countries include all or most of these groups among the economically active, while others may treat the same groups as inactive.

Three principal structural comparisons of the economically active total are given in the first part of the table: (1) participation rate, or the proportion of the economically active who possess some particular characteristic, is given for women and for those of working age (usually ages 15 to 64), (2) activity rate, the proportion of the total population who *are* economically active, is given for both sexes and as a total, and (3) employment status, usually (and here) grouped as employers, self-employed, employees, family workers (usually unpaid), and others.

Each of these measures indicates certain characteristics in a given national labour market; none should be interpreted in isolation, however, as the meaning of each is influenced by a variety of factors—demographic structure and change, social or religious customs, educational opportunity, sexual differentiation in employment patterns, degree of technological development, and the like. Participation and activity rates, for example, may be high in a particular country because it possesses an older population with few children, hence a higher proportion of working age, or because, despite a young population with many below working age, the economy attracts eligible immigrant workers, themselves almost exclusively of working age. At the same time, low activity and participation rates might be characteristic of a country having a young population with poor employment possibilities or of a country with a good job market distorted by the presence of large numbers of "guest" or contract workers who are not part of the domestic labour force. An illiterate woman in a strongly sex-differentiated labour force is likely to begin and end as a family or

Employment and labour

country	year	economically active population										distribution by economic sector			
		total ('000)	participation rate (%)		activity rate (%)			employment status (%)				agriculture, forestry, fishing		manufacturing; mining, quarrying; public utilities	
			female	ages 15–64	total	male	female	employers, self-employed	employees	unpaid family workers	other	number ('000)	% of econ. active	number ('000)	% of econ. active
Afghanistan	1979	3,941	7.9	49.1	30.3	54.2	4.9	...	...	...	...	2,369	60.1	494	12.5
Albania	1989[3]	1,458	45.8	78.7[4]	45.6	48.0	43.1	...	...	...	...	799	54.8	279	19.1
Algeria	1987	5,341	9.2	44.3	23.6	42.4	4.4	16.8	61.7	2.6	18.9	725	13.6	622	11.6
American Samoa	1990	14.2	41.1	52.6[6]	30.4	34.8	25.7	2.1	92.6	0.2	5.1	0.3	2.3	4.8	33.7
Andorra	1989	25	45.6	74.3	55.1	...	...	...	...	...	...	0.3	1.2	2.7	11.0
Angola	1988	3,936	39.0	61.5[8]	41.5	51.5	31.9	...	...	...	...	2,810	71.4	400[9]	10.2[9]
Antigua and Barbuda	1985	32	40.1	56.2[11, 12]	42.6	53.3	32.9	12.3[13]	69.9[13]	0.6[13]	17.2[13]	2.1[14, 15]	9.0[14, 15]	2.1[14, 15]	9.1[14, 15]
Argentina	1990	12,305	27.9	59.6	38.1	55.4	21.0	25.1[16]	71.2[16]	3.3[16]	0.4[16]	1,201[16]	12.0[16]	2,136[16]	21.3[16]
Armenia	1990	2,044	49.4	79.9[18]	61.3	63.2	59.5	...	...	...	...	117	5.7	453	22.2
Aruba	1991	31.1	42.5	67.1	46.7	54.5	39.0	...	...	...	...	0.2	0.5	2.3	7.3
Australia	1992[21]	8,586	41.8	73.0	49.1	57.3	41.0	14.1	74.5	0.9	10.5	430	5.0	1,431	16.7
Austria	1991[21]	3,607	41.1	68.1	46.1	56.6	36.4	9.9	83.1	3.6	3.4	259	7.2	1,020	28.3
Azerbaijan	1990	3,242	42.6[22]	71.8[18]	45.4	52.1	38.8	...	...	...	...	...	...	...	...
Bahamas, The	1990	114	46.7	75.2	44.9	48.8	41.0	76.5[22]	11.1[22]	0.3[22]	12.1[22]	5.8	5.1	6.4	5.6
Bahrain	1991	226	17.5	66.8	44.6	63.5	18.5	9.5[24]	85.9[24]	0.1[24]	4.6[24]	5	2.3	33	14.6
Bangladesh	1989	50,744	41.4	79.9	46.9	53.2	40.2	29.3	9.4	45.2	16.1	32,569	64.2	7,081	14.0
Barbados	1992[21]	125	48.3	77.3	50.2	54.4	46.4	8.8[14]	76.4[14]	0.2[14]	14.6[14]	6.0	4.8	11.7	9.4
Belarus	1989	5,327	49.0	77.2	52.5	57.2	48.3	...	...	...	...	985[26, 27]	18.9[26, 27]	1,593[26, 27]	30.9[26, 27]
Belgium	1990	4,179	41.6	51.2[28]	41.9	50.1	34.1	12.7	73.9	3.4	10.0	100	2.4	820	19.6
Belize	1991	58.1	26.4	56.1[28]	31.5	45.8	16.8	23.4[29]	55.1[29]	7.5[29]	14.0[29]	18.3	31.4	7.0	12.0
Benin	1988	2,100	47.8	72.5[8]	47.2	50.2	44.3	...	...	...	...	1,310	62.4	173[9]	8.2[9]
Bermuda	1991	35.2	48.2[27]	76.0[12]	59.7[27]	63.5[27]	56.1[27]	7.7[16]	88.6[16]	0.5[16]	3.2[16]	0.6[30]	1.7[30]	1.4[30]	3.9[30]
Bhutan	1985	632	32.9	69.0	44.6	58.0	30.3	...	...	...	...	531[16]	92.5[16]	16[9, 16]	2.8[9, 16]
Bolivia	1990	2,276	23.8	54.5	31.1	48.1	14.6	48.4[32]	34.3[32]	15.8[32]	1.4[32]	869[32]	42.3[32]	263[32]	12.8[32]
Bosnia and Herzegovina	1990[26]	1,026	36.9	...	22.7	...	...	...	...	...	...	39	3.8	519	50.5
Botswana	1991[21]	443	38.4	59.2	33.4	43.1	24.6	6.5	62.5	17.2	13.8	100	22.7	46	10.5
Brazil	1990[21]	64,468	35.5	63.6[28]	43.8	57.5	30.5	26.3	62.3	7.7	3.7	14,181	22.0	10,217	15.9
Brunei	1986	86	30.7	61.6	38.2	51.3	24.2	7.6	85.6	0.7	6.1	3.1	3.5	8.0	9.3
Bulgaria	1985	4,686	47.7	75.7	52.4	55.1	49.6	0.3	98.2	—	1.5	772	16.5	1,778	37.9
Burkina Faso	1988	4,547	46.4	78.1[8]	53.3	57.6	49.1	...	...	...	...	3,869	85.1	223[9]	4.9[9]
Burundi	1991	2,780	52.6	91.4	52.9	51.6	54.2	35.6[33]	5.6[33]	58.4[33]	0.4[33]	2,246[33]	92.9[33]	40[33]	1.6[33]
Cambodia	1992	3,964	55.7	91.2[34]	43.1	41.2	44.7	...	...	...	...	2,454[16]	74.4[16]	220[9, 16]	6.7[9, 16]
Cameroon	1988	4,392	33.8	57.1[8]	41.2	52.5	26.1	60.2[14]	14.6[14]	18.0[14]	7.1[14]	2,901[35]	74.0[35]	180[35]	4.6[35]
Canada	1992[21]	13,797	45.0	75.2	49.7	55.5	44.2	9.0	89.8	0.5	0.8	466	3.4	2,354	17.1
Cape Verde	1990	121	37.1	64.3	35.3	46.9	24.9	24.7	53.7	2.0	19.6	29.9	24.8	6.8	5.7
Central African Republic	1988	1,187	46.8	78.3	48.2	52.2	44.3	75.3	8.0	8.1	8.6	881	74.2	31	2.6
Chad	1988	1,899	21.4	51.0	35.2	56.1	14.8	...	...	...	...	1,452	76.5	124	6.5
Chile	1992[21]	4,990	32.0	58.0	37.5	52.1	23.5	26.2	66.0	3.4	4.4	860	17.2	925	18.5
China	1987[21]	584,569	44.5	76.8[28]	54.7	59.6	49.7	...	...	...	...	414,740	71.0	95,977	16.4
Colombia	1985	9,558	32.8	49.4[36]	34.3	46.6	22.3	...	...	...	...	2,412[16]	28.5[16]	1,231[16]	14.5[16]
Comoros	1988	197	40.6	68.4[8]	45.3	54.2	36.5	47.6[16]	25.6[16]	—26.8[16]—		53[16]	53.3[16]	4.1[16]	4.2[16]
Congo	1984	563	45.6	54.0	29.5	33.0	26.2	64.3	31.4	1.2	3.1	294	52.2	50	8.8
Costa Rica	1992	1,087	29.9	55.6[28]	37.0	52.4	21.9	23.7	72.2	3.4	0.7	259	23.8	219	20.1
Côte d'Ivoire	1988	4,263	32.3	66.6	39.4	52.2	26.0	...	...	...	...	2,451	57.5	433[9]	10.2[9]
Croatia	1991	2,040	42.9	65.2	45.3	53.9	37.4	12.7	73.7	2.0	11.6	341	16.7	571	28.0
Cuba	1989	4,570[32]	36.1[32]	56.9[28, 32]	43.7[32]	55.4[32]	31.7[32]	4.8[24]	94.1[24]	0.2[24]	0.9[24]	721[26]	20.4[26]	768[26]	21.8[26]
Cyprus[37]	1991	280	37.9	73.0	48.2	59.9	36.5	18.1	72.2	6.2	3.5	34	12.3	51	18.1
Czech Republic	1991	5,421	47.6	77.9	52.6	56.8	48.7	2.2	88.7	7.6	1.5	628	11.6	2,021	37.3
Denmark	1991	2,912	46.5	82.4	56.6	61.5	51.8	8.4	89.5	1.7	0.4	161	5.5	609	20.9
Djibouti	1988	230	40.4	67.0[8]	44.9	52.7	36.9	...	...	...	...	176	76.6	21[9]	9.0[9]
Dominica	1989	30.6	41.8	62.3	37.5	47.1	29.3	29.2	50.6	1.9	18.3	7.7	25.2	3.6	11.8
Dominican Republic	1981	1,915	28.9	53.6	33.9	48.1	19.7	36.5	51.3	3.3	8.9	420	22.0	243	12.7
Ecuador	1990	3,360	26.4	55.7	34.8	51.5	18.3	45.7	42.5	4.4	7.4	1,036	30.8	404	12.0
Egypt	1989[21]	16,034	28.8	54.0	30.7	42.8	18.0	26.7	45.7	20.7	6.9	6,335	39.5	2,102	13.1
El Salvador	1980[21]	1,593	34.8	62.4	35.4	47.5	24.0	28.2	59.2	10.9	1.7	637	40.0	262	16.4
Equatorial Guinea	1983	103	35.7	66.7	39.2	52.5	26.9	29.0	16.0	29.9	25.1	59.4	57.9	1.8	1.8
Eritrea[39]	...	...	...	...	...	...	...	...	...	...	...	...	...	...	...
Estonia	1989	856	50.0	79.7	54.7	58.5	51.3	...	...	...	...	100	11.7	270	31.5
Ethiopia[39]	1992	23,518	41.1	70.1	41.3	48.5	34.1	58.5[40]	6.5[40]	34.0[40]	1.0[40]	16,101[40]	88.3[40]	312[40]	1.7[40]
Faeroe Islands	1977	17.6	27.2	64.0	41.9	58.2	23.9	11.9	86.1	...	2.0	3.3	18.8	3.9	21.9

traditional agricultural worker. Loss of working-age men to war, civil violence, or emigration for job opportunities may also affect the structure of a particular labour market.

The distribution of the economically active population by employment status reveals that a large percentage of economically active persons in some less developed countries falls under the heading "employers, self-employed." This occurs because the countries involved have poor, largely agrarian economies in which the average worker is a farmer who tills his own small plot of land. In countries with well-developed economies, "employees" will usually constitute the largest portion of the economically active.

Caution should be exercised when using the economically active data to make intercountry comparisons, as countries often differ in their choices of classification schemes, definitions, and coverage of groups and in their methods of collection and tabulation of data. The population base containing the economically active population, for example, may range, in developing countries, from age 9 or 10 with no upper limit to, in developed countries, age 18 or 19 upward to a usual retirement age of from 55 to 65, with sometimes a different range for each sex. Data on female labour-force participation, in particular, often lack comparability. In many less developed countries, particularly those dominated by the Islamic faith, a cultural bias favouring traditional roles for women results in the undercounting of economically active women. In other less developed countries, particularly those in which subsistence workers are deemed economically active, the role of women may be overstated.

The second major section of the table provides data on the distribution by economic (also conventionally called industrial) sector of the "economically active population." The data usually include such groups as unpaid family workers, members of the armed forces, and the unemployed, the last distributed by industry as far as possible.

The categorization of industrial sectors is based on the divisions listed in the *International Standard Industrial Classification of All Economic Activities.* The "other" category includes persons whose activities were not adequately defined and the unemployed who were not distributable by industrial sector.

A substantial part of the data presented in this table is summarized from various issues of the ILO's *Year Book of Labour Statistics,* which compiles its statistics both from official publications and from information submitted directly by national census and labour authorities. The editors have supplemented and updated ILO statistical data with information from Britannica's holdings of relevant official publications and from direct correspondence with national authorities.

construction		transportation, communications		trade, hotels, restaurants		finance, real estate		public administration, defense		services		other		country
number ('000)	% of econ. active	number ('000)	% of econ. active	number ('000)	% of econ. active	number ('000)	% of econ. active	number ('000)	% of econ. active	number ('000)	% of econ. active	number ('000)	% of econ. active	
51	1.3	66	1.6	138	3.5	[1]	[1]	[1]	[1]	749[1]	19.0[1]	78[2]	2.0[2]	Afghanistan
49	3.4	44	3.0	49	3.3	[1]	[1]	[1]	[1]	220[1]	15.1[1]	17	1.2	Albania
690	12.9	216	4.1	391	7.3	143	2.7	[5]	[5]	1,180[5]	22.1[5]	1,374	25.7	Algeria
1.2	8.3	0.8	5.5	1.8	13.0	0.3	2.1	1.4	10.0	2.8	19.8	0.7[7]	5.1[7]	American Samoa
2.9	11.8	...	...	6.0	24.2	1.3	5.4	2.6	10.3	4.1	16.7	0.1	0.5	Andorra
[9]	[9]	[10]	[10]	[10]	[10]	[10]	[10]	[10]	[10]	726[10]	18.5[10]	—	—	Angola
2.6[14, 15]	11.1[14, 15]	2.6[14, 15]	11.1[14, 15]	5.2[14, 15]	22.4[14, 15]	0.8[14, 15]	3.4[14, 15]	[5]	[5]	7.9[5, 14, 15]	33.9[5, 14, 15]	—	—	Antigua and Barbuda
1,003[16]	10.0[16]	460[16]	4.6[16]	1,702[16]	17.0[16]	396[16]	3.9[16]	[5]	[5]	2,399[5, 16]	23.9[5, 16]	736[17]	7.3[17]	Argentina
162	7.9	88	4.3	88	4.3	18	0.9	8	0.4	41.3	20.2	697[19]	34.1[19]	Armenia
3.2	10.4	2.3	7.5	11.0	35.4	2.4	7.8	[5]	[5]	8.6[5]	27.7[5]	1.1[20]	3.5[20]	Aruba
594	6.9	520	6.1	1,697	19.8	935	10.9	373	4.3	2,189	25.5	418[17]	4.9[17]	Australia
313	8.7	228	6.3	689	19.1	236	6.6	[5]	[5]	822[5]	22.8[5]	40	1.1	Austria
...	...	...	...	...	...	...	...	...	...	...	...	...	...	Azerbaijan
10.8	9.4	8.7	7.6	35.0	30.6	9.0	7.9	[5]	[5]	35.5[5]	31.0[5]	3.2[23]	2.8[23]	Bahamas, The
27	11.8	14	6.1	30	13.2	17	7.6	[5]	[5]	84[5]	37.1[5]	16[20]	7.3[20]	Bahrain
661	1.3	1,278	2.5	4,130	8.1	238	0.5	[5]	[5]	3,439[5]	6.8[5]	1,341[25]	2.6[25]	Bangladesh
7.4	5.9	4.1	3.3	14.2	11.4	4.1	3.3	[5]	[5]	39.1[5]	31.3[5]	38.2[20]	30.5[20]	Barbados
570[26, 27]	11.0[26, 27]	238[26, 27]	4.6[26, 27]	382[26, 27]	7.4[26, 27]	[1]	[1]	[1]	[1]	1,281[1, 26, 27]	25.2[1, 26, 27]	100[26, 27]	2.0[26, 27]	Belarus
236	5.6	257	6.2	634	15.2	328	7.8	[5]	[5]	1,389[5]	33.2[5]	415[20]	9.9[20]	Belgium
4.1	7.0	2.9	5.0	10.0	17.2	1.8	3.1	5.4	9.2	6.0	10.3	2.8	4.8	Belize
[9]	[9]	[10]	[10]	[10]	[10]	[10]	[10]	[10]	[10]	616[10]	29.4[10]	—	—	Benin
3.4	9.7	2.7	7.6	9.5	27.1	4.6	13.0	2.4	6.8	6.4	18.0	4.3[31]	12.1[31]	Bermuda
[9]	[9]	[10]	[10]	[10]	[10]	[10]	[10]	[10]	[10]	27[10, 16]	4.7[10, 16]	—	—	Bhutan
110[32]	5.4[32]	108[32]	5.3[32]	260[32]	12.6[32]	33[32]	1.6[32]	[5]	[5]	375[5, 32]	18.3[5, 32]	36[17, 32]	1.8[17, 32]	Bolivia
75	7.3	69	6.7	131	12.8	39	3.8	[5]	[5]	155[5]	15.1[5]	—	—	Bosnia and Herzegovina
57	12.9	10	2.3	34	7.7	13	3.0	[5]	[5]	103[5]	23.2[5]	79[20]	17.8[20]	Botswana
3,823	5.9	2,440	3.6	7,976	12.4	1,716	2.7	[5]	[5]	21,694[5]	33.7[5]	2,367[7]	3.7[7]	Brazil
9.4	10.9	6.9	8.0	8.0	9.3	4.3	5.0	[5]	[5]	38.6[5]	44.6[5]	8.1[20]	9.3[20]	Brunei
407	8.7	315	6.7	397	8.5	25	0.5	[5]	[5]	993[5]	21.2[5]	1	—	Bulgaria
[9]	[9]	[10]	[10]	[10]	[10]	[10]	[10]	[10]	[10]	455[10]	10.0[10]	—	—	Burkina Faso
15[33]	0.6[33]	6[33]	0.3[33]	21[33]	0.9[33]	1.3[33]	0.1[33]	6[33]	0.2[33]	75[33]	3.1[33]	8[23, 33]	0.3[23, 33]	Burundi
[9]	[9]	[10]	[10]	[10]	[10]	[10]	[10]	[10]	[10]	625[10, 16]	18.9[10, 16]	—	—	Cambodia
67[35]	1.7[35]	52[35]	1.3[35]	154[35]	3.9[35]	8[35]	0.2[35]	[5]	[5]	293[5, 35]	7.5[5, 35]	228[5, 20]	5.8[5, 20]	Cameroon
879	6.4	1,002	7.3	2,412	17.5	809	5.9	[5]	[5]	5,767[5]	41.8[5]	106[7]	0.7[7]	Canada
22.7	18.8	6.1	5.1	12.7	10.6	0.8	0.7	[5]	[5]	17.4[5]	14.4[5]	24.1	20.0	Cape Verde
6	0.5	7	0.6	92	7.8	0.7	0.1	[5]	[5]	70[5]	5.9[5]	100[20]	8.5[20]	Central African Republic
[9]	[9]	[10]	[10]	[10]	[10]	[10]	[10]	[10]	[10]	323[10]	17.0[10]	—	—	Chad
339	6.8	335	6.7	849	17.0	244	4.9	[5]	[5]	1,221[5]	24.5[5]	218[20]	4.4[20]	Chile
13,298	2.3	10,898	1.9	20,785	3.6	1,268	0.2	9,704	1.7	17,414	3.0	487	0.1	China
242[16]	2.9[16]	353[16]	4.2[16]	1,262[16]	14.9[16]	278[16]	3.3[16]	[5]	[5]	1,998[5, 16]	23.6[5, 16]	691[16, 17]	8.2[16, 17]	Colombia
3.3[16]	3.3[16]	2.1[16]	2.1[16]	1.9[16]	1.9[16]	0.2[16]	0.2[16]	2.4[16]	2.4[16]	4.6[16]	4.7[16]	28[16]	27.8[16]	Comoros
25	4.5	29	5.1	67	11.8	3	0.5	[5]	[5]	85[5]	15.1[5]	10	2.0	Congo
66	6.1	50	4.6	180	16.6	39	3.5	[5]	[5]	258[5]	23.8[5]	16[17]	1.5[17]	Costa Rica
[9]	[9]	[10]	[10]	[10]	[10]	[10]	[10]	[10]	[10]	1,377[10]	32.3[10]	—	—	Côte d'Ivoire
93	4.5	112	5.5	223	10.9	58	2.8	104	5.1	204	10.0	329[20]	16.1[20]	Croatia
344[26]	9.8[26]	236[26]	6.7[26]	395[26]	11.2[26]	22[26]	0.6[26]	152[26]	4.3[26]	836[26]	23.7[26]	53[26]	1.5[26]	Cuba
23	8.3	15	5.5	61	21.8	17	6.1	[5]	[5]	54[5]	19.3[5]	24[25]	8.6[25]	Cyprus[37]
412	7.6	366	6.8	551	10.2	[38]	[38]	238	4.4	1,005[38]	18.5[38]	200	3.7	Czech Republic
199	6.8	195	6.7	422	14.5	253	8.7	218	7.5	802	27.6	52[17]	1.8[17]	Denmark
[9]	[9]	[10]	[10]	[10]	[10]	[10]	[10]	[10]	[10]	33[10]	14.4[10]	—	—	Djibouti
2.6	8.5	1.6	5.2	2.9	9.5	0.7	2.3	[5]	[5]	5.7[5]	18.6[5]	5.4[25]	17.6[25]	Dominica
81	4.3	40	2.1	192	10.0	22	1.2	[5]	[5]	363[5]	18.9[5]	553[17]	28.9[17]	Dominican Republic
197	5.9	131	3.9	477	14.2	81	2.4	[5]	[5]	838[5]	24.9[5]	196[17]	5.8[17]	Ecuador
990	6.2	780	4.9	1,340	8.4	255	1.6	[5]	[5]	3,116[5]	19.4[5]	1,115[20]	7.0[20]	Egypt
80	5.0	66	4.1	256	16.1	16	1.0	[5]	[5]	250[5]	15.7[5]	27[23]	1.7[23]	El Salvador
1.9	1.9	1.8	1.7	3.1	3.0	0.4	0.4	[5]	[5]	8.4[5]	8.2[5]	25.8[20]	25.2[20]	Equatorial Guinea
...	...	...	...	...	...	...	...	...	...	...	...	...	...	Eritrea[39]
73	8.5	73	8.5	75	8.8	4	0.5	19	2.2	182	21.3	60	7.0	Estonia
46[40]	0.3[40]	77[40]	0.4[40]	696[40]	3.8[40]	15[40]	0.1[40]	[5]	[5]	933[5, 40]	5.1[5, 40]	56[2, 40]	0.3[2, 40]	Ethiopia[39]
2.0	11.1	1.9	11.1	2.1	11.9	0.3	1.9	[5]	[5]	3.5[5]	20.1[5]	0.6	3.2	Faeroe Islands

Employment and labour (continued)

country	year	economically active population										distribution by economic sector			
		total ('000)	participation rate (%)		activity rate (%)			employment status (%)				agriculture, forestry, fishing		manufacturing; mining, quarrying; public utilities	
			female	ages 15–64	total	male	female	employers, self-employed	employees	unpaid family workers	other	number ('000)	% of econ. active	number ('000)	% of econ. active
Fiji	1986	241	21.2	56.0	33.7	52.4	14.5	33.6	42.2	16.3	7.9	106	44.1	22	9.0
Finland	1992	2,526	46.9	74.2	50.1	54.8	45.8	12.8	84.5	0.7	2.0	203	8.0	520	20.6
France	1991[21]	24,609	43.3	66.9	44.5	51.1	38.3	12.6	77.1	1.0	9.3	1,257	5.1	4,841	19.7
French Guiana	1990	48.7	38.2	67.2	42.4	50.4	33.8	11.2	59.7	5.0	24.1	4[14]	11.4[14]	2[14]	5.9[14]
French Polynesia	1988	75	37.1	64.8	39.9	48.2	30.9	13.0	55.0	4.0	28.0	7.6	10.0	5.4	7.2
Gabon	1988	473	37.6	57.0[8]	43.3	54.8	32.1	...	...	...	...	326	69.0	62[9]	13.1[9]
Gambia, The	1983	326	46.3	78.2	47.3	51.1	43.6	0.5	78.0	14.3	7.1	240	73.7	9	2.9
Gaza Strip	1991	112	2.5	34.3[28]	17.4	33.7	0.9	...	...	...	...	21.5	19.3	10.8[41]	9.6[41]
Georgia	1991	2,514	45.9[22]	90.1[18, 22]	46.4	...	...	...	...	...	...	386	15.3	690[9]	27.4[9]
Germany	1991	39,405	42.3	72.6	50.2	60.0	41.1	7.3	91.4	1.3	—	1,487	3.8	11,898	30.2
Ghana	1984	5,580	51.2	82.5[28]	45.4	44.9	45.8	67.7	15.7	12.2	4.4	3,311	59.3	631	11.3
Gibraltar	1991	14.8	33.4	66.9[28]	53.8	71.9	35.4	6.6[24]	89.7[24]	...	3.6[24]	—	—	1.1	7.5
Greece	1990[21]	4,000	37.1	57.7[32]	39.6[32]	50.8[32]	28.7[32]	32.4	50.6	12.0	5.0	893	22.3	808	20.2
Greenland	1976	21.4	33.4	63.5[28]	43.1	53.0	31.4	12.6	82.5	0.4	4.5	3.2	15.1	3.3	15.3
Grenada	1988	38.9	48.6	72.7[42]	39.9	42.9	37.2	...	...	...	...	5.6	14.3	3.3	8.6
Guadeloupe	1990	172	45.5	66.4	44.5	49.6	39.7	13.2	53.7	2.0	31.1	9.4[43]	7.2[43]	6.8[43]	5.3[43]
Guam	1990	66.1	37.4	75.7[6]	49.7	58.4	39.7	2.4	94.4	0.1	3.1	0.5	0.8	3.5	5.3
Guatemala	1989[21]	2,898	25.5	59.1	33.5	50.8	16.7	32.7	47.6	16.2	3.5	1,416	48.9	405	14.0
Guernsey[44]	1991	30.2	43.2	74.2	51.2	60.6	42.6	13.7	86.3	—	—	2.4	7.8	2.4	7.9
Guinea	1983	1,823	39.4	63.5	39.1	48.7	30.1	36.2	15.6	37.6	10.6	1,424	78.1	27	1.5
Guinea-Bissau	1988	446	41.3	66.9[8]	47.2	57.2	37.8	...	...	...	...	354	79.4	17[9]	3.9[9]
Guyana	1987[45]	270	29.9	60.4	35.7	50.9	21.0	14.3[16]	63.8[16]	1.9[16]	20.0[16]	50[16]	20.4[16]	41[16]	16.8[16]
Haiti	1990	2,679	40.0	64.8	41.1	50.3	32.3	59.1	16.5	10.4	14.0	1,535	57.3	178	6.6
Honduras	1992[21]	1,729	31.2	58.3[28]	34.8	49.0	21.2	36.5	48.7	10.7	4.1	640	37.0	264	15.3
Hong Kong	1992[21]	2,793	36.8	69.2	49.5	61.6	36.9	10.7	86.5	0.9	2.0	19	0.7	671	24.0
Hungary	1992[46]	4,242	46.3	51.2[28]	41.0	45.9	36.6	11.0	86.7	2.3	—	648	15.3	1,227	28.9
Iceland	1990	127	46.6[47]	81.8[47, 48]	56.5[47]	60.1[47]	52.7[47]	...	...	...	...	13	10.4	32	25.2
India	1991	314,904	29.0	60.7[24, 28]	37.6	51.5	22.7	8.8[24]	16.3[24]	3.6[24]	71.3[24]	172,713[24]	66.4[24]	28,846[24]	11.1[24]
Indonesia	1989	75,508	39.9	67.7	42.6	51.2	34.0	42.4	26.2	28.6	2.8	41,284	54.7	7,909	10.5
Iran	1986	12,855	10.3	46.8	26.0	45.6	5.5	36.9	41.5	3.9	17.7	3,209	25.0	1,584	12.3
Iraq	1988	4,127	12.0	45.3	24.7	42.3	6.1	25.4[49]	59.5[49]	11.4[49]	3.7[49]	477	11.6	439	10.6
Ireland	1991	1,334	32.2	59.7	37.8	51.4	24.3	18.2	77.8	1.4	2.6	155	11.6	246	18.4
Isle of Man	1991	33.2	42.3	73.2	47.6	56.9	38.9	15.8	80.1	—	4.1	1.2	3.7	3.9	11.6
Israel	1992[21]	1,858	41.8	58.3	35.5	41.4	29.6	15.0	72.9	0.9	11.2	61	3.3	386	20.8
Italy	1991[21]	24,245	37.1	65.1[50]	42.5	54.9	30.7	21.6	63.8	3.7	10.9	1,823	7.5	4,958	20.4
Jamaica	1992	1,075	47.0	71.6[27, 51]	43.9	46.4	41.4	34.1[52]	47.2[52]	2.7[52]	16.0[52]	247	23.0	113	10.5
Japan	1992	65,780	40.7	71.2	52.9	63.9	42.3	12.8	77.8	6.9	2.4	4,110	6.2	16,080	24.4
Jersey	1991	47.5	43.2	66.9[28]	56.5	66.1	47.5	12.6	84.0	...	3.4	2.2	4.7	3.8	8.0
Jordan	1988	644	11.4	43.2	22.8	39.3	5.3	22.8[33]	67.2[33]	0.8[33]	9.2[33]	33	5.1	55	8.6
Kazakhstan	1992	7,449	54.0[22]	80.4[18, 22]	43.7	...	...	...	...	...	...	1,355	18.2	1,290	17.3
Kenya	1988	9,220	40.0	65.1[8]	39.9	47.9	32.0	...	...	...	...	7,182	77.9	696[9]	7.5[9]
Kiribati	1990	32.6	46.4	75.6[28]	45.1	48.9	41.4	71.9	25.3	...	2.8	23.1	71.0	0.9	2.8
Korea, North	1985	9,084	46.0	75.3	44.6	48.6	40.6	...	...	...	...	3,726[14]	44.1[14]	2,790[9, 14]	33.0[9, 14]
Korea, South	1992[21]	19,385	40.1	63.7	45.4	54.0	36.6	28.1	59.3	10.2	2.4	3,025	15.6	4,894	25.2
Kuwait	1988	730	24.3	61.5	38.9	53.5	21.0	5.9[35]	92.4[35]	0.1[35]	1.5[35]	9	1.3	69	9.4
Kyrgyzstan	1989[26]	1,429	48.6	81.3[18]	33.0	...	...	...	...	...	...	474	33.2	400	28.0
Laos	1985	2,014	45.3	84.2	48.9	53.1	44.6	...	...	...	...	1,393[16]	75.7[16]	130[9, 16]	7.1[9, 16]
Latvia	1991	1,462	50.0[22]	80.0[22]	55.1[22]	59.3[22]	51.5[22]	——95.5——		——4.5——		248	17.0	371	25.4
Lebanon	1988	904	16.6	44.0	26.5	43.9	8.9	...	...	...	...	132[43]	19.1[43]	131[43]	18.9[43]
Lesotho	1986	504	27.0	44.0	31.6	47.3	16.7	16.8	55.7	20.5	7.0	131	25.9	142	28.2
Liberia	1984	704	41.0	56.3	33.5	39.1	27.8	59.1	21.6	14.4	5.0	481	68.3	31	4.4
Libya	1989	994	8.7[32]	37.5[8, 32]	24.9[32]	43.3[32]	4.6[32]	23.7[53]	69.6[53]	4.2[53]	2.6[53]	192	19.2	144	14.5
Liechtenstein	1991	14.7	37.7	70.8	50.0	63.7	37.0	9.1	87.3	3.6	—	0.3	2.4	5.1	34.4
Lithuania	1992	1,869	48.9[22]	76.9[22]	52.4[22]	56.6[22]	48.6[22]	...	...	...	...	343	18.4	594	31.8
Luxembourg	1991[54]	168	36.5	62.5	43.5	56.4	31.2	9.2	85.3	1.1	4.4	5	3.2	26	15.8
Macau	1991[21]	175	415	66.4[55]	50.1	60.2	40.4	9.5	86.3	1.2	3.0	0.1	0.1	57	32.5
Macedonia	1990[26]	507	37.3	...	23.8	...	...	...	...	...	...	42	8.3	224	44.1
Madagascar	1988	4,945	40.8	65.3[8]	44.0	52.5	35.4	...	...	...	...	3,830	77.5	509[9]	10.3
Malawi	1987	3,458	51.0	89.4	43.3	43.9	42.8	4.9	16.2	77.6	1.3	2,968	85.8	114	3.3
Malaysia	1990[21]	6,685	35.5	63.5	37.6	48.2	26.9	25.6[32]	61.9[32]	12.5[32]	—	1,889[32]	30.6[32]	1,059[32]	17.1[32]
Maldives	1990	56	19.9	50.2	26.5	41.3	10.8	39.7	49.3	4.5	6.5	14.1	25.0	9.4	16.6
Mali	1988	2,808	16.5	48.3[8]	31.8	54.8	10.3	...	...	...	...	2,301	82.0	70[9]	2.5[9]
Malta	1990	132	25.4	47.4[55]	37.2	56.1	18.7	14.1[11]	77.4[11]	...	8.5[11]	3	2.5	38	28.8
Marshall Islands	1980	4.4	25.2	30.0[12]	14.3	20.8	7.4	3.3	78.1	0.3	18.4	0.1	1.0	0.4[57]	9.4[57]
Martinique	1990	165	47.5	68.1	45.9	49.8	42.2	9.5	56.9	1.5	32.1	10.4[43]	7.1[43]	7.1[43]	4.9[43]
Mauritania	1988	593	21.8	45.8[8]	31.0	49.1	13.3	...	...	...	...	390	65.7	60[9]	10.2[9]
Mauritius[58]	1991	463	35.2	68.0	44.5	57.9	31.2	12.2[27]	80.1[27]	1.9[27]	5.9[27]	81	17.5	146	31.5
Mayotte	1985	22.3	40.1	68.9	33.4	39.2	27.3	48.0	30.1	13.0	8.9	12.3	55.0	0.9	3.8
Mexico	1991	31,229	30.7	59.9	37.5	53.1	22.6	30.8	54.0	12.7	2.5	8,190	26.2	5,175	16.6
Micronesia	1990	30.5	29.8[16]	60.6	30.3	...	...	2.7[16]	74.4[16]	0.1[16]	22.7[16]	12.7	41.5	1.6	5.2[54]
Moldova	1991	2,070	50.0[22]	86.3[27]	47.4	...	...	...	...	...	...	739	35.7	424	20.5
Monaco	1990	12.6	39.7	...	42.0	53.2	31.8	17.4	75.1	0.3	7.2	—	0.3	2.7	21.8
Mongolia	1990	694	45.5[35]	82.2[35]	46.9[35]	50.9[35]	42.8[35]	...	...	...	...	192	27.6	123	17.8
Morocco	1982	5,999	19.7	48.9	29.3	47.1	11.6	27.1	40.5	17.6	14.8	2,352	39.2	1,016	16.9
Mozambique	1980	5,671	52.4	87.3[28]	48.6	47.6	49.5	44.4[13]	40.0[13]	14.5[13]	1.1[13]	4,755	83.8	347	6.1
Myanmar (Burma)	1989–90[21]	15,701	35.3[11]	64.2[11]	40.2[11]	52.4[11]	28.2[11]	...	...	...	...	10,614[60]	67.6[60]	1,232	7.8
Namibia	1985	477	23.9	55.4	30.8	47.3	14.6	...	...	...	...	185[16]	43.4[16]	93[9, 16]	21.8[9, 16]
Nauru	1977	2.2	...	...	30.5	...	...	...	...	...	...	...	...	...	...
Nepal	1990	8,585	34.7	82.5[43]	45.4	57.5	32.6	86.2[24]	9.1[24]	2.5[24]	2.2[24]	6,244[24]	91.1[24]	37[24]	0.5[24]
Netherlands, The	1991	7,011	39.7	67.6	46.6	56.9	36.5	8.8	82.7	1.5	7.0	293	4.2	1,227	17.5
Netherlands Antilles	1988[21]	73	43.1	59.5[43]	38.5	45.1	32.3	...	...	...	...	0.5	0.7	5.8	8.0
New Caledonia	1989	66	37.5	70.7[50]	40.2	49.1	30.8	16.3	64.3	1.6	17.8	7.8	11.8	6.2	9.3
New Zealand	1992[21]	1,635	43.6	70.8[52]	47.1[52]	53.9[52]	40.6[52]	18.0	70.2	1.1	10.7	159	9.7	255	15.6
Nicaragua	1991	1,386	33.2	62.0[28]	34.7	47.8	22.3	...	...	...	...	415	30.0	208	15.0
Niger	1988[62]	2,316	20.4	55.2	31.9	51.1	13.0	51.4	5.0	40.3	3.3	1,764	76.2	73	3.1

construction		transportation, communications		trade, hotels, restaurants		finance, real estate		public administration, defense		services		other		country
number ('000)	% of econ. active	number ('000)	% of econ. active	number ('000)	% of econ. active	number ('000)	% of econ. active	number ('000)	% of econ. active	number ('000)	% of econ. active	number ('000)	% of econ. active	
12	4.9	13	5.5	26	10.8	6	2.5	[5]	[5]	37[5]	15.2[5]	20[20]	8.2[20]	Fiji
208	8.2	177	7.0	357	14.1	206	8.2	131	5.2	666	26.4	58[23]	2.3[23]	Finland
1,581	6.4	1,405	5.7	3,778	15.4	2,227	9.1	[5]	[5]	6,982[5]	28.4[5]	2,537[20]	10.3[20]	France
3[14]	8.8[14]	1.3[14]	4.2[14]	2[14]	6.2[14]	4[14]	11.3[14]	[5]	[5]	10[5, 14]	31.3[5, 14]	7[14, 20]	20.9[14, 20]	French Guiana
5.5	7.4	2.8	3.7	10.3	13.7	1.2	1.5	[5]	[5]	21.5[5]	28.6[5]	21.1[20]	28.0[20]	French Polynesia
[9]	[9]	[10]	[10]	[10]	[10]	[10]	[10]	[10]	[10]	85[10]	17.9[10]	—	—	Gabon
4	1.3	8	2.5	17	5.1	[1]	[1]	[1]	[1]	22[1]	6.8[1]	25	7.7	Gambia, The
36.0	32.2	5.6	5.0	16.0	14.4	[41]	[41]	11.2	10.0	6.6	5.9	4.1[7, 41]	3.7[7, 41]	Gaza Strip
[9]	[9]	100	4.0	184	7.3	...	...	60	2.4	534	21.2	561	22.3	Georgia
2,503	6.4	2,290	5.8	5,694	14.4	2,763	7.0	[5]	[5]	12,773[5]	32.4[5]	—	—	Germany
65	1.2	123	2.2	792	14.2	27	0.5	98	1.7	376	6.7	158[7]	2.8[7]	Ghana
2.8	19.0	0.7	4.6	3.0	20.0	1.5	10.1	2.6	17.3	3.2	21.6	—	—	Gibraltar
260	6.5	259	6.5	672	16.8	187	4.7	[5]	[5]	721[5]	18.0[5]	201[23]	5.0[23]	Greece
3.1	14.6	1.8	8.6	2.7	12.6	0.3	1.6	[5]	[5]	6.3[5]	29.5[5]	0.6	2.8	Greenland
3.5	9.1	1.7	4.4	5.4	13.9	0.8	2.0	[5]	[5]	5.9[5]	15.3[5]	12.7[20]	32.5[20]	Grenada
8.8[43]	6.8[43]	4.0[43]	3.1[43]	9.6[43]	7.4[43]	18.7[43]	14.5[43]	[5]	[5]	31.4[5, 43]	24.3[5, 43]	40.6[7, 43]	31.4[7, 43]	Guadeloupe
8.0	12.1	4.5	6.8	11.5	17.5	3.9	6.0	17.7	26.7	14.5	21.9	2.0[7]	3.1[7]	Guam
114	3.9	72	2.5	375	12.9	38	1.3	[5]	[5]	417[5]	14.4[5]	60[20]	2.1[20]	Guatemala
3.2	10.5	1.4	4.5	7.4	24.6	5.8	19.3	1.9	6.4	5.3	17.7	0.4	1.3	Guernsey[44]
9	0.5	29	1.6	37	2.0	4	0.2	[5]	[5]	138[5]	7.5[5]	156	8.5	Guinea
[9]	[9]	[10]	[10]	[10]	[10]	[10]	[10]	[10]	[10]	75[10]	16.7[10]	—	—	Guinea-Bissau
7[16]	2.8[16]	9[16]	3.8[16]	15[16]	6.2[16]	3[16]	1.2[16]	30[16]	12.1[16]	29[16]	11.9[16]	61[16, 20]	24.7[16, 20]	Guyana
28	1.0	21	0.8	353	13.2	5	0.2	[5]	[5]	155[5]	5.8[5]	404[20]	15.1[20]	Haiti
72	4.2	52	3.0	282	16.3	30	1.7	[5]	[5]	334[5]	19.3[5]	55[20]	3.2[20]	Honduras
231	8.3	295	10.6	748	26.8	232	8.3	[5]	[5]	542[5]	19.4[5]	55[7]	2.0[7]	Hong Kong
273	6.4	373	8.8	564	13.3	[1]	[1]	[1]	[1]	1,157[1]	27.3[1]	—	—	Hungary
12	9.7	8	6.6	18	14.3	10	8.0	23	17.9	15	12.1	2[7]	1.8[7]	Iceland
3,864[24]	1.5[24]	6,207[24]	2.4[24]	12,638[24]	4.9[24]	1,822[24]	0.7[24]	[5]	[5]	18,515[5, 24]	7.1[5, 24]	15,670[24]	6.0[24]	India
1,829	2.4	2,192	2.9	10,891	14.4	397	0.5	[5]	[5]	8,969[5]	11.7[5]	2,138[20]	2.8[20]	Indonesia
1,207	9.4	631	4.9	876	6.8	114	0.9	[5]	[5]	3,051[5]	23.7[5]	2,183[20]	17.0[20]	Iran
461	11.2	266	6.4	282	6.8	42	1.0	[5]	[5]	2,160[5]	52.3[5]	—	—	Iraq
80	6.0	65	4.9	201	15.0	95	7.1	[5]	[5]	286[5]	21.5[5]	209[23]	15.7[23]	Ireland
3.4	10.3	2.4	7.3	6.1	18.4	4.4	13.1	[5]	[5]	10.4[5]	31.4[5]	1.4[7]	4.1[7]	Isle of Man
121	6.5	109	5.9	245	13.3	180	9.7	[5]	[5]	625[5]	33.7[5]	128[23]	6.9[23]	Israel
1,957	8.1	1,149	4.7	4,660	19.2	1,003	4.1	[5]	[5]	6,042[5]	24.9[5]	2,652[7]	10.9[7]	Italy
59	5.5	36	3.4	172	16.0	44	4.1	[5]	[5]	229[5]	21.3[5]	175[20]	16.3[20]	Jamaica
6,190	9.4	3,850	5.9	14,360	21.8	5,460	8.3	[5]	[5]	14,010[5]	21.3[5]	1,720[20]	2.6[20]	Japan
4.4	9.3	2.4	5.0	6.8	14.4	7.4	15.6	3.1	6.5	15.7	33.1	1.6[20]	3.4[20]	Jersey
51	7.9	52	8.1	76	11.8	18	2.8	[5]	[5]	358[5]	55.6[5]	—	—	Jordan
588	7.9	520	7.0	916	12.3	44	0.6	159	2.1	1,055	14.2	1,522	20.4	Kazakhstan
[9]	[9]	[10]	[10]	[10]	[10]	[10]	[10]	[10]	[10]	1,342[10]	14.6[10]	—	—	Kenya
0.3	1.0	0.9	2.8	1.3	4.1	0.4	1.4	2.1	6.5	2.3	7.0	1.1[20]	3.4[20]	Kiribati
[9]	[9]	[10]	[10]	[10]	[10]	[10]	[10]	[10]	[10]	1,939[10, 14]	22.9[10, 14]	—	—	Korea, North
1,652	8.5	1,008	5.2	4,244	21.9	1,126	5.8	[5]	[5]	2,972[5]	15.3[5]	464[7]	2.4[7]	Korea, South
115	15.7	38	5.2	83	11.4	22	3.0	[5]	[5]	384[5]	52.6[5]	11[2]	1.5[2]	Kuwait
...	...	79	5.5	93	6.5	40	2.8	...	...	288	20.2	55	3.9	Kyrgyzstan
[9]	[9]	[10]	[10]	[10]	[10]	[10]	[10]	[10]	[10]	316[10, 16]	17.2[10, 16]	—	—	Laos
130	8.9	107	7.3	178	12.2	85	5.8	24	1.6	254	17.4	65	4.5	Latvia
43[43]	6.2[43]	48[43]	7.0[43]	115[43]	16.5[43]	24[43]	3.5[43]	[5]	[5]	200[5, 43]	28.8[5, 43]	—	—	Lebanon
28	5.5	8	1.6	24	4.7	2	0.5	[5]	[5]	157[5]	31.1[5]	13	2.6	Lesotho
4	0.6	14	2.0	47	6.7	[1]	[1]	[1]	[1]	63[1]	9.0[1]	64[20]	9.1[20]	Liberia
156	15.7	79	7.9	53	5.3	15	1.5	308	31.0	48	4.8	—	—	Libya
1.2	8.3	0.5	3.1	1.7	11.3	1.1	7.2	0.6	4.1	4.2	28.5	0.1[25]	0.7[25]	Liechtenstein
169	9.1	124	6.6	227	12.2	14	0.8	26	1.4	290	15.5	81	4.3	Lithuania
14	8.4	11	6.3	29	17.5	15	9.2	21	12.8	31	18.7	14[25]	8.1[25]	Luxembourg
15	8.4	8	4.6	37	20.9	6	3.4	[5]	[5]	47[5]	27.1[5]	5[20]	3.1[20]	Macau
48	9.4	26	5.2	64	12.5	14	2.8	[5]	[5]	90[5]	17.7[5]	—	—	Macedonia
[9]	[9]	[10]	[10]	[10]	[10]	[10]	[10]	[10]	[10]	606[10]	12.2[10]	—	—	Madagascar
46	1.4	25	0.7	94	2.7	6	0.2	[5]	[5]	147[5]	4.3[5]	57	1.7	Malaŵi
340[32]	5.5[32]	266[32]	4.3[32]	1,120[32]	18.1[32]	231[32]	3.7[32]	844[32]	13.7[32]	427[32]	6.9[32]	—	—	Malaysia
3.2	5.6	5.3	9.4	8.9	15.7	1.1	1.9	[5]	[5]	11.8[5]	21.0[5]	2.7[56]	4.7[56]	Maldives
[9]	[9]	[10]	[10]	[10]	[10]	[10]	[10]	[10]	[10]	437[10]	15.5[10]	—	—	Mali
6	4.4	9	6.9	13	9.8	5	3.7	[5]	[5]	53[5]	40.0[5]	5[7]	3.8[7]	Malta
0.4	8.4	[57]	[57]	0.5	12.3	—	0.7	0.6	13.4	1.6	36.4	0.8[20]	18.4[20]	Marshall Islands
6.9[43]	4.7[43]	5.9[43]	4.0[43]	12.4[43]	8.5[43]	19.3[43]	13.2[43]	[5]	[5]	32.9[5, 43]	22.6[5, 43]	51.1[7, 43]	35.0[7, 43]	Martinique
[9]	[9]	[10]	[10]	[10]	[10]	[10]	[10]	[10]	[10]	143[10]	24.1[10]	—	—	Mauritania
24	5.2	32	6.9	61	13.2	11	2.4	[5]	[5]	94[5]	20.3[5]	14[20]	3.1[20]	Mauritius[58]
2.0	8.9	0.6	2.6	0.6	2.7	0.9	4.0	[5]	[5]	2.9[5]	13.0[5]	2.3[20]	10.1[20]	Mayotte
1,872	6.0	1,141	3.7	6,150	19.7	1,295	4.1	[5]	[5]	6,527[5]	20.9[5]	880[20]	2.8[20]	Mexico
1.8	6.1	[59]	[59]	[59]	[59]	[59]	[59]	6.3	20.8	3.7[59]	12.1[59]	4.1[7]	13.5[7]	Micronesia
153	7.4	67	3.2	137	6.6	[1]	[1]	[1]	[1]	519[1]	25.1[1]	31	1.5	Moldova
0.7	5.3	...	...	2.5	20.2	1.0	8.0	2.8	22.4	1.9	14.9	0.9[25]	7.1[25]	Monaco
45	6.4	55	7.9	49	7.1	[1]	[1]	[1]	[1]	184[1]	26.5[1]	47[20]	6.7[20]	Mongolia
437	7.3	141	2.3	498	8.3	[38]	[38]	533	8.9	474[38]	7.9[38]	548[2]	9.1[2]	Morocco
42	0.7	7.7	1.4	112	2.0	[1]	[1]	[1]	[1]	243[1]	4.3[1]	95[7]	1.7[7]	Mozambique
174	1.1	385	2.5	1,405	8.9	[1]	[1]	[1]	[1]	956[1]	6.1[1]	935[61]	6.0[61]	Myanmar (Burma)
[9]	[9]	[10]	[10]	[10]	[10]	[10]	[10]	[10]	[10]	148[10, 16]	34.7[10, 16]	—	—	Namibia
...	...	...	...	...	...	...	...	...	...	...	...	...	...	Nauru
2[24]	—	7[24]	0.1[24]	109[24]	1.6[24]	10[24]	0.1[24]	[5]	[5]	314[5, 24]	4.6[5, 24]	127[24]	1.9[24]	Nepal
418	6.0	403	5.7	1,138	16.2	682	9.7	[5]	[5]	2,313[5]	33.0[5]	537[20]	7.7[20]	Netherlands, The
5.4	7.4	4.7	6.4	15.9	21.8	4.6	6.3	[5]	[5]	21.3[5]	29.3[5]	14.7[7]	20.2[7]	Netherlands Antilles
4.5	6.8	3.1	4.7	9.5	14.3	2.5	3.8	[5]	[5]	22.0[5]	33.4[5]	13.5[7]	16.0[7]	New Caledonia
80	4.9	89	5.4	308	18.9	158	9.6	[5]	[5]	416[5]	25.4[5]	171[20]	10.5[20]	New Zealand
30	2.2	43	3.1	196	14.1	25	1.8	98	7.1	184	13.3	188[2]	13.6[2]	Nicaragua
14	0.6	15	0.6	209	9.0	2	0.1	[5]	[5]	123[5]	5.3[5]	117[25]	5.0[25]	Niger

Employment and labour (continued)

country	year	economically active population										distribution by economic sector			
		total ('000)	participation rate (%)		activity rate (%)			employment status (%)				agriculture, forestry, fishing		manufacturing; mining, quarrying; public utilities	
			female	ages 15–64	total	male	female	employers, self-employed	employees	unpaid family workers	other	number ('000)	% of econ. active	number ('000)	% of econ. active
Nigeria	1986[21]	30,766	33.3	58.8	31.1	41.1	20.9	64.6	18.8	10.7	5.9	13,259	43.1	1,401	4.6
Northern Mariana Islands	1990	26.6	43.2	83.3[6]	61.3	66.2	55.9	1.4	96.1	0.2	2.3	0.6	2.3	6.0	22.5
Norway	1992	2,130	45.2	79.9[50]	49.7	55.1	44.5	8.3	84.3	1.2	6.2	114	5.3	353	16.6
Oman	1988	644	6.3	57.2	38.2	60.7	5.9	...	...	...	...	399	62.0	33	5.1
Pakistan	1992–93[21]	33,829	14.2	50.8	28.0	46.4	8.2	41.2	32.4	20.2	6.2	15,034	44.5	4,190	12.4
Panama	1991[21]	859	33.8	60.0[63]	37.4	48.9	25.6	28.4	61.0	4.4	6.2	196	22.9	91	10.6
Papua New Guinea	1980[64]	733	39.8	35.2[8]	24.6	28.3	20.5	72.7	26.4	—	0.9	564	77.0	21	2.9
Paraguay	1982	1,039	19.7	57.5	34.3	54.8	13.6	43.1	37.7	9.2	9.9	446	42.9	129	12.4
Peru	1990	7,435	38.3[65]	54.6[28]	34.5	...	...	39.8[24]	41.8[24]	8.4[24]	10.0[24]	2,497	34.0	969	13.2
Philippines	1992[21]	26,938	37.2	66.5	41.1	51.3	30.7	36.9	40.5	13.9	8.6	10,869	41.5	2,781	10.6
Poland	1992	17,529	45.9	69.5	46.1	51.1	41.4	20.3	60.4	5.6	13.7	3,758	21.4	3,827	21.8
Portugal	1992[21]	4,737	44.3	68.2	48.2	56.2	40.9	22.8	74.5	1.7	1.0	531	11.2	1,184	25.0
Puerto Rico	1993[21]	1,211	39.1	53.7[6]	33.5	42.3	24.1	14.0	84.1	0.7	1.2	35	2.9	217	17.9
Qatar	1988	293	11.2	80.8	53.7	77.3	22.2	1.8[43]	97.7[43]	—	0.5[43]	4.5	1.6	22.0	7.5
Réunion	1990[21]	234	41.1	60.3	39.1	46.8	31.6	8.4	53.1	1.1	37.4	11	4.8	11	4.8
Romania	1992	10,290	44.3	67.2	45.2	51.2	39.3	11.7	82.5	1.5	4.3	2,187	21.3	4,153	40.4
Russia	1991	73,809	48.5[22]	77.1[22]	52.6[22]	57.9[22]	47.9[22]	...	...	...	...	9,970	13.5	20,117	27.3
Rwanda	1989	3,143	53.5	77.6[8, 32]	46.3	44.6	48.0	38.8[66]	7.2[66]	53.8[66]	0.2[66]	2,833	90.1	52	1.7
St. Kitts and Nevis	1980	17.1	41.0	69.5	39.5	48.4	31.2	9.7	78.5	0.4	11.4	4.5	26.1	3.8	22.3
St. Lucia	1980	42.2	39.1	69.9	37.2	47.1	28.0	21.0	55.8	1.6	21.6	10.7	25.5	3.7	8.7
St. Vincent	1980	34.7	36.1	60.9[28]	35.5	46.6	25.0	18.0[13]	82.5[13]	1.5[13]	—	8.9	25.7	2.3	6.6
San Marino	1991	13.3	40.8	72.9	53.3	61.8	44.4	21.7	77.8	0.6	—	0.3	2.2	4.5	33.7
São Tomé and Príncipe	1981	31	32.4	61.1	31.7	43.1	20.4	15.8	79.4	0.1	4.7	16	53.9	1.9	6.2
Saudi Arabia	1988	5,369	3.6	59.1	36.3	54.9	3.6	...	...	...	...	192	3.6	595	11.1
Senegal	1990	2,433	26.0	46.2[8]	33.5	50.9	17.0	...	...	...	...	...	...	...	...
Seychelles	1991	29[22]	42.5[22]	74.3[22]	44.0[22]	50.7[22]	37.3[22]	10.7[24]	76.6[24]	0.3[24]	12.4[24]	2.2[67]	8.8[67]	4.4[9, 67]	17.9[9, 67]
Sierra Leone	1988	1,452	33.1	54.4[8]	36.8	50.2	23.9	...	...	...	...	929	64.0	244[9]	16.8[9]
Singapore	1992[21]	1,620	40.1	69.3	50.2	59.4	40.7	12.3	84.1	0.9	2.7	5	0.3	443	27.3
Slovakia	1991	2,618	46.9	76.0	49.6	54.0	45.5	1.4	87.9	8.2	2.5	365	13.9	867	33.1
Slovenia	1991	946	46.7	66.7	48.1	52.9	43.6	2.2	88.8	1.9	7.1	121	12.8	335	35.4
Solomon Islands	1992[69]	26.8	25.6[43]	24.9[43, 55]	13.7[43]	19.7[43]	7.3[43]	29.6[43]	68.6[43]	—	1.8[43]	6.4	23.7	2.5	9.0
Somalia	1988	2,972	41.2	65.1[8]	43.3	52.8	34.8	...	...	...	...	2,118	71.3	290	9.7
South Africa	1991	11,624	39.4	68.3[35, 50]	37.5	45.5	29.5	7.0	74.8	...	18.2	1,224	10.5	2,361	20.3
Bophuthatswana	1980[70]	333	...	...	25.2	...	...	...	...	...	...	157	47.2	54	16.2
Ciskei	1980[70]	140	...	...	20.5	...	...	...	...	...	...	11	7.9	31	21.9
Transkei	1980[70]	554	...	...	23.8	...	...	...	...	...	...	420	75.9	30	5.4
Venda	1985[70]	67	42.2	31.3	14.6	20.2	10.5	...	...	...	...	9.2	13.8	4.3	6.4
Spain	1992[21]	15,155	36.2	60.0[6]	39.0	51.0	27.6	17.5	71.1	3.9	7.5	1,446	9.5	3,178	21.0
Sri Lanka	1992	5,948	32.7	56.6[28]	40.9	55.3	26.6	24.0	51.5	11.2	13.3	2,380	40.0	711	11.9
Sudan, The	1983[62]	6,343	29.1	57.4	35.1	50.0	20.4	59.2[53]	25.3[53]	9.9[53]	5.6[53]	4,029	63.5	317	5.0
Suriname	1990[21, 71]	99	41.3	59.2	43.8	51.9	35.9	...	...	...	...	2.9	2.9	11.2	11.3
Swaziland	1988	302	39.4	62.8[8]	41.0	50.3	31.9	...	...	...	...	220	73.0	33[9]	11.0[9]
Sweden	1992[21]	4,464	48.0	82.0[6]	51.5	54.2	48.8	8.7	86.1	0.4	4.8	137	3.1	857	19.2
Switzerland	1992	3,573	38.3	62.2[28]	51.5	64.7	38.8	9.7[16]	90.3[16]	...	...	194	5.4	859	24.0
Syria	1991[21]	3,485	18.0	46.7[43]	27.8	44.6	10.2	31.0	49.3	13.0	6.7	917	26.3	471	13.5
Taiwan	1992[21]	8,765	37.7	59.3[28]	42.4	51.2	33.1	22.9	66.8	8.8	1.5	1,065	12.2	2,642	30.1
Tajikistan	1990	2,468	39.0	78.1[18]	46.1	...	...	...	...	...	...	831[26]	42.9[26]	261[26]	13.5[26]
Tanzania	1988	12,003	48.3	74.3[8]	47.4	49.6	45.2	...	...	...	...	9,836	82.0	558[9]	4.7[9]
Thailand	1991[21, 72]	30,805	44.7	78.5[28]	54.0	59.6	48.3	30.5	35.0	25.8	8.7	15,330[60]	49.8[60]	4,315	14.0
Togo	1988	1,334	36.8	61.4[8]	41.1	52.6	29.9	70.3[24]	10.4[24]	11.3[24]	8.0[24]	936	70.2	145[9]	10.9[9]
Tonga	1990	32.0	33.0	57.0	33.6	45.2	22.0	33.7	45.4	16.8	4.1	11.7	36.5	5.1	15.8
Trinidad and Tobago	1991	492	36.0	60.8	39.3	47.3	30.2	17.0	79.2	2.9	0.9	51	10.4	86	17.4
Tunisia	1989	2,361	20.9	52.8	29.8	46.5	12.7	20.9	54.9	7.4	16.8	510	21.6	418	17.7
Turkey	1992[21]	21,184	30.9	58.4[52]	36.2	48.7	22.7	29.4	39.0	27.9	3.7	8,785	41.5	3,440	16.2
Turkmenistan	1991	1,585	52.2[27]	84.2[18]	42.7	...	...	...	...	...	...	675	42.6	168	10.6
Tuvalu	1991	5.9	51.3[33]	85.5	65.3	...	...	0.3[33]	22.2[33]	—77.5[33]—		4.2	68.0	0.1	2.0
Uganda	1988	7,687	41.4	69.5[8]	44.7	52.9	36.7	...	...	...	...	6,307	82.1	404[9]	5.2[9]
Ukraine	1991	24,977	49.2[22]	80.6[22, 50]	50.8[22]	56.0[22]	46.4[22]	...	...	...	...	4,762	19.1	7,769	31.1
United Arab Emirates	1990	690	10.4[32]	69.0[32]	47.0[32]	67.6[32]	12.9[32]	6.8[16]	92.7[16]	0.1[16]	0.5[16]	43	6.3	94	13.6
United Kingdom	1991	28,295	43.0	75.4	49.2	57.7	41.0	11.1	80.8	...	8.1	557	2.0	7,076[9]	25.0[9]
United States	1992[73]	128,548	45.1	74.9	50.4	56.7	44.4	8.0	91.0	0.3	0.8	3,653	2.8	24,005	18.7
Uruguay	1991	1,239	40.7	67.7[51]	44.7	55.7	34.7	23.2	72.5	1.6	2.7	56	4.5	265	21.4
Uzbekistan	1991	8,976	43.8	78.2[18]	43.0	...	...	...	...	...	...	1,977[26]	29.1[26]	1,200[26]	17.6[26]
Vanuatu	1989	67.0	46.3	85.0	47.0	49.0	44.9	...	...	...	...	49.8	74.4	1.0	1.5
Venezuela	1991[21]	7,418	32.2	62.2	37.3	50.1	24.2	28.2	61.1	2.0	8.7	837	11.3	1,346	18.1
Vietnam	1989	30,521	51.7	79.9	47.4	47.0	47.7	...	...	...	...	20,471	67.1	3,390	11.1
Virgin Islands (U.S.)	1990[21]	47.4	47.8	67.5[12]	46.6	50.3	43.1	7.1[16]	86.4[16]	0.3[16]	6.2[16]	0.5[16]	1.2[16]	3.8[16]	10.0[16]
West Bank	1991	200	11.4	39.4[28]	20.9	36.9	4.8	...	...	...	...	39.2	19.6	26.1[41]	13.0[41]
Western Sahara	...	...	...	...	...	...	...	...	...	...	...	...	...	...	...
Western Samoa	1986	45.6	18.8	48.6[24]	29.0	44.5	11.6	21.1[24]	43.5[24]	35.0[24]	0.4[24]	29.0	63.6	2.4	5.4
Yemen	1988	3,029	31.6	52.6	26.4	36.8	16.4	...	...	...	...	2,152	71.1	129	4.3
Yugoslavia	1992	3,352	41.6	...	32.1	...	...	...	...	...	...	128	3.8	1,036	30.9
Zaire	1988	12,869	35.8	57.4[8]	38.1	49.6	27.0	...	...	...	...	8,483	66.9	1,910[9]	15.0[9]
Zambia	1988	2,628	29.3	52.6[8]	33.5	48.0	19.4	22.9[16]	42.5[16]	3.6[16]	31.0[16]	1,833	69.8	286[9]	10.9[9]
Zimbabwe	1986–87	3,260	47.8	76.5[28]	42.1	44.8	39.6	...	...	...	...	2,110	64.7	179	5.5

[1]Services includes finance, real estate and public administration, defense. [2]Unemployed, not previously employed only. [3]Employed persons only. [4]Ages 15–59 (male) and 15–54 (female). [5]Services includes public administration, defense. [6]Ages 16–64. [7]Unemployed only. [8]Over age 10. [9]Manufacturing; mining, quarrying; public utilities includes construction. [10]Services includes transportation, communications; trade, hotels, restaurants; finance, real estate; and public administration, defense. [11]1983. [12]Over age 16. [13]1970. [14]1982. [15]Wage earners and self-employed only. [16]1980. [17]Includes unemployed, not previously employed. [18]Ages 16–59 (male) and 16–54 (female). [19]Includes self-employed and unemployed. [20]Mostly unemployed. [21]Excludes all or some classes or elements of the military. [22]1989. [23]Mostly unemployed, not previously employed. [24]1981. [25]Includes unemployed. [26]State sector only. [27]1990. [28]Over age 15. [29]1983–84. [30]Agriculture includes mining, quarrying. [31]Mostly employees of international companies and unemployed. [32]1988. [33]1979. [34]Ages 16–60. [35]1985. [36]Over age 12. [37]Republic of Cyprus only. [38]Services includes finance, real estate. [39]Ethiopia includes Eritrea. [40]1984. [41]Other includes public utilities and finance, real estate. [42]Ages 15–65. [43]1986. [44]Excludes Alderney and Sark. [45]Data are for

construction		transportation, communications		trade, hotels, restaurants		finance, real estate		public administration, defense		services		other		country
number ('000)	% of econ. active	number ('000)	% of econ. active	number ('000)	% of econ. active	number ('000)	% of econ. active	number ('000)	% of econ. active	number ('000)	% of econ. active	number ('000)	% of econ. active	
546	1.8	1,112	3.6	7,417	24.1	120	0.4	[5]	[5]	4,902[5]	15.9[5]	2,009[20]	6.5[20]	Nigeria
5.8	21.7	1.4	5.3	5.3	19.8	1.0	3.8	1.4	5.3	4.5	16.9	0.6[7]	2.3[7]	Northern Mariana Islands
133	6.2	161	7.6	366	17.2	157	7.4	[5]	[5]	779[5]	36.6[5]	66[23]	3.1[23]	Norway
52	8.0	26	4.0	23	3.6	1	0.2	[5]	[5]	110[5]	17.1[5]	—	—	Oman
2,099	6.2	1,663	4.9	4,198	12.4	283	0.8	[5]	[5]	4,207[5]	12.4[5]	2,146[20]	6.3[20]	Pakistan
34	3.9	54	6.3	167	19.5	34	4.0	[5]	[5]	227[5]	26.4[5]	54[23]	6.3[23]	Panama
22	2.9	1.7	2.4	25	3.4	4	0.6	[5]	[5]	77[5]	10.5[5]	2	0.2	Papua New Guinea
70	6.7	31	2.9	86	8.3	18	1.7	[5]	[5]	174[5]	16.8[5]	86[17]	8.3[17]	Paraguay
272	3.7	323	4.4	1,146	15.6	176	2.4	[5]	[5]	1,961[5]	26.7[5]	—	—	Peru
1,035	4.0	1,221	4.7	3,283	12.5	452	1.7	[5]	[5]	4,254[5]	16.2[5]	2,284[20]	8.7[20]	Philippines
995	5.7	831	4.7	1,636	9.3	204	1.2	[5]	[5]	3,884[5]	22.2[5]	2,394[7]	13.7[7]	Poland
386	8.1	225	4.7	936	19.8	143	3.0	[5]	[5]	1,291[5]	27.3[5]	42[2]	0.9[2]	Portugal
92	7.6	44	3.6	258	21.3	37	3.1	[5]	[5]	513[5]	42.4[5]	15[2]	1.2[2]	Puerto Rico
64.2	22.0	11.9	4.1	34.2	11.7	6.2	2.1	[5]	[5]	149.6[5]	51.1[5]	—	—	Qatar
17	7.1	7	3.1	18	7.7	3	1.3	[5]	[5]	79[5]	33.9[5]	87[20]	37.4[20]	Réunion
579	5.6	617	6.0	694	6.7	57	0.6	[5]	[5]	1,528[5]	14.8[5]	475[23]	4.6[23]	Romania
10,778	14.6	5,750	7.8	5,626	7.6	[38]	[38]	2,479	3.3	14,653[38]	19.9[38]	4,436	6.0	Russia
38	1.2	7	0.2	80	2.5	3	0.1	[5]	[5]	120[5]	3.8[5]	9	0.3	Rwanda
0.4	2.5	0.3	1.6	1.3	7.3	0.8	4.7	1.0	5.7	2.9	17.0	2.2[20]	12.8[20]	St. Kitts and Nevis
2.6	6.3	1.5	3.5	2.8	6.5	0.5	1.1	2.4	5.6	7.9	18.8	10.1[20]	24.0[20]	St. Lucia
3.5	10.2	1.9	5.4	2.6	7.4	0.4	1.0	[5]	[5]	7.6[5]	21.8[5]	7.6	21.9	St. Vincent
1.1	7.9	0.2	1.7	2.2	16.7	0.3	2.2	2.1	15.7	2.1	16.0	0.5[7]	3.7[7]	San Marino
1.8	5.9	1.0	3.4	2.0	6.5	0.2	0.5	2.4	7.8	3.5	11.3	1.4[7]	4.6[7]	São Tomé and Príncipe
1,181	22.0	321	6.0	964	18.0	151	2.8	[5]	[5]	1,965[5]	36.6[5]	—	—	Saudi Arabia
...	...	...	...	...	...	...	...	...	...	...	...	...	...	Senegal
[9]	[9]	[68]	[68]	8.6[67, 68]	35.3[67, 68]	[1]	[1]	[1]	[1]	9.3[1, 67]	38.1[1, 67]	—	—	Seychelles
[9]	[9]	[10]	[10]	[10]	[10]	[10]	[10]	[10]	[10]	280[10]	19.2[10]	—	—	Sierra Leone
103	6.4	158	9.8	356	22.0	171	10.6	[5]	[5]	339[5]	20.9[5]	44[20]	2.7[20]	Singapore
243	9.3	165	6.3	246	9.4	[38]	[38]	99	3.8	498[38]	19.0[38]	135	5.2	Slovakia
42	4.4	53	5.6	103	10.9	44	4.7	[5]	[5]	177[5]	18.7[5]	71[20]	7.5[20]	Slovenia
1.1	4.1	1.4	5.3	3.2	11.9	1.2	4.5	4.3	15.9	6.9	25.6	—	—	Solomon Islands
[9]	[9]	[10]	[10]	[10]	[10]	[10]	[10]	[10]	[10]	565[10]	19.0[10]	—	—	Somalia
526	4.5	497	4.3	1,358	11.7	504	4.3	[5]	[5]	2,641[5]	22.7[5]	2,513[20]	21.6[20]	South Africa
22	6.6	7	2.2	23	6.8	1.2	0.4	[5]	[5]	52[5]	15.7[5]	17	5.0	Bophuthatswana
6	4.1	5	3.8	14	10.0	1.2	0.9	[5]	[5]	33[5]	23.9[5]	38	27.5	Ciskei
15	2.7	4	0.6	11	2.1	1.1	0.2	[5]	[5]	49[5]	8.9[5]	23	4.2	Transkei
7.1	10.7	2.6	3.8	5.4	8.1	1.3	1.9	[5]	[5]	17.4[5]	26.0[5]	19.6	29.3	Venda
1,538	10.1	783	5.2	2,905	19.2	818	5.4	[5]	[5]	3,467[5]	22.9[5]	1,020[23]	6.7[23]	Spain
249	4.2	232	3.9	530	8.9	36	0.6	[5]	[5]	821[5]	13.8[5]	990[20]	16.6[20]	Sri Lanka
139	2.2	215	3.4	294	4.6	21	0.3	[5]	[5]	550[5]	8.7[5]	777[23]	12.3[23]	Sudan, The
3.9	3.9	5.3	5.3	13.8	13.9	2.6	2.6	[5]	[5]	37.2[5]	37.1[5]	22.7[20]	22.9[20]	Suriname
[9]	[9]	[10]	[10]	[10]	[10]	[10]	[10]	[10]	[10]	48[10]	16.0[10]	—	—	Swaziland
273	6.1	305	6.8	604	13.5	399	8.9	[5]	[5]	1,668[5]	37.4[5]	221[20]	5.0[20]	Sweden
320	9.0	215	6.0	713	20.0	374	10.5	[5]	[5]	805[5]	22.5[5]	92[7]	2.6[7]	Switzerland
341	9.8	167	4.8	378	10.9	25	0.7	[5]	[5]	951[5]	27.3[5]	235[7]	6.8[7]	Syria
779	8.9	450	5.1	1,771	20.2	420	4.8	309	3.5	1,196	13.6	132	1.5	Taiwan
161[26]	8.3[26]	65[26]	3.3[26]	145[26]	7.5[26]	...	...	39[26]	2.0[26]	437[26]	22.5[26]	—	—	Tajikistan
[9]	[9]	[10]	[10]	[10]	[10]	[10]	[10]	[10]	[10]	1,608[10]	13.4[10]	—	—	Tanzania
1,866	6.1	900	2.9	3,698	12.0	[1]	[1]	[1]	[1]	3,348[1]	10.9[1]	1,347[20]	4.4[20]	Thailand
[9]	[9]	[10]	[10]	[10]	[10]	[10]	[10]	[10]	[10]	253[10]	18.9[10]	—	—	Togo
1.3	3.9	1.8	5.7	2.6	8.1	1.2	3.7	[5]	[5]	7.1[5]	22.0[5]	1.3[7]	4.2[7]	Tonga
75	15.1	30	6.0	83	16.8	32	6.6	[5]	[5]	135[5]	27.4[5]	1	0.2	Trinidad and Tobago
248	10.5	96	4.1	217	9.2	15	0.7	[5]	[5]	444[5]	18.8[5]	412[20]	17.5[20]	Tunisia
1,049	5.0	798	3.8	2,471	11.7	446	2.1	[5]	[5]	2,539[5]	12.0[5]	1,656[7]	7.8[7]	Turkey
151	9.5	64	4.0	90	5.7	[1]	[1]	[1]	[1]	410[1]	25.9[1]	27	1.7	Turkmenistan
0.2	4.0	0.1	1.0	0.2	4.0	—	—	[5]	4.4[5]	1.3[5]	22.0[5]	—	—	Tuvalu
[9]	[9]	[10]	[10]	[10]	[10]	[10]	[10]	[10]	[10]	976[10]	12.7[10]	—	—	Uganda
2,267	9.1	1,774	7.1	1,863	7.5	[1]	[1]	[1]	[1]	3,888[1]	15.6[1]	2,655	10.6	Ukraine
119	17.3	72	10.4	101	14.7	19	2.7	[5]	[5]	241[5]	35.0[5]	—	—	United Arab Emirates
[9]	[9]	[59]	[59]	[59]	[59]	[59]	[59]	1,931	6.8	16,193[59]	57.2[59]	2,241[7]	7.9[7]	United Kingdom
8,118	6.3	7,018	5.5	26,431[74]	20.6[74]	13,359	10.4	[5]	[5]	44,939[5, 74]	35.0[5, 74]	1,018[23]	0.8[23]	United States
82	6.6	66	5.3	219	17.7	60	4.8	[5]	[5]	459[5]	37.0[5]	32[23]	2.6[23]	Uruguay
714[26]	10.5[26]	251[26]	3.7[26]	462[26]	6.8[26]	[1]	[1]	[1]	[1]	2,067[1, 26]	30.4[1, 26]	129[26]	1.9[26]	Uzbekistan
1.3	1.9	1.0	1.5	2.7	4.1	0.6	1.0	[5]	[5]	7.9[5]	11.8[5]	2.6	3.8	Vanuatu
685	9.2	421	5.7	1,549	20.9	426	5.7	[5]	[5]	2,062[5]	27.8[5]	92[23]	1.2[23]	Venezuela
581	1.9	576	1.9	1,880	6.2	90	0.3	305	1.0	1,374	4.5	1,854[20]	6.1[20]	Vietnam
3.7[16]	9.7[16]	2.8[16]	7.4[16]	9.0[16]	23.8[16]	2.6[16]	6.7[16]	4.1[16]	10.8[16]	9.2[16]	24.2[16]	2.3[7, 16]	6.2[7, 16]	Virgin Islands (U.S.)
50.7	25.3	10.4	5.2	22.6	11.3	[41]	[41]	22.3	11.1	8.4	4.2	20.6[7, 41]	10.3[7, 41]	West Bank
...	...	...	...	...	...	...	...	...	...	...	...	...	...	Western Sahara
0.1	0.1	1.5	3.3	1.7	3.7	0.8	1.8	[5]	[5]	9.4[5]	20.7[5]	0.6	1.4	Western Samoa
178	5.9	90	3.0	84	2.8	4	0.1	[5]	[5]	391[5]	12.9[5]	—	—	Yemen
171	5.1	157	4.7	301	9.0	87	2.6	[5]	[5]	453[5]	13.5[5]	1,020[75]	30.4[75]	Yugoslavia
[9]	[9]	[10]	[10]	[10]	[10]	[10]	[10]	[10]	[10]	2,297[10]	18.1[10]	—	—	Zaire
[9]	[9]	[10]	[10]	[10]	[10]	[10]	[10]	[10]	[10]	509[10]	19.3[10]	—	—	Zambia
51	1.6	76	2.3	128	3.9	24	0.7	[5]	[5]	397[5]	12.2[5]	277[20]	8.5[20]	Zimbabwe

the economically active population ages 15–64 only. [46]Data exclude unemployed. [47]1993. [48]Ages 16–74. [49]1977. [50]Ages 20–64. [51]Ages 14–64. [52]1991. [53]1973. [54]Excludes about 30,000 foreign border workers. [55]Over age 14. [56]Includes unemployed, previously employed. [57]Manufacturing; mining, quarrying; public utilities includes transportation, communications. [58]Island of Mauritius only. [59]Services includes transportation, communications; trade, hotels, restaurants; and finance, real estate. [60]Includes unemployed seasonal agricultural workers. [61]Includes underemployed seasonal nonagricultural workers. [62]Excludes nomadic population. [63]Ages 15–69. [64]Citizens over age 10 involved in money-raising activities only. [65]1985–86. [66]1978. [67]Excludes self-employed and domestic workers. [68]Trade, hotels, restaurants, includes transportation, communications. [69]Wage earners only. [70]Excludes migrant workers in South Africa. [71]Districts of Wanica and Paramaribo only. [72]May survey. [73]Excludes armed forces overseas. [74]Services includes hotels. [75]Private sector 8.1%, unemployed 22.3%.

Agriculture and land use

This table provides data on the structure of national agricultural sectors from the perspective of farms and farmland use. The data are taken mainly from national agricultural censuses and surveys, supplemented by reports of the United Nations Food and Agriculture Organization's (FAO's) *World Census of Agriculture.* Many of these national censuses, of course, are taken under guidelines established by the FAO for the *World Census of Agriculture* programs (the 1990 census is the fifth and will include national censuses taken during the decade 1986–95). It represents a cooperative effort by FAO member countries to collect agricultural data within a general framework that permits international harmonization of concepts and definitions; transfer of technical expertise; and increased effectiveness in the collection, analysis, publication, and policy-related use of such statistics. More than 100 countries were expected to participate in the 1990 census.

All agricultural statistics are subject to quality-control problems, including errors or biases arising from such factors as incomplete or inaccurate lists of holdings, ambiguous questions, respondents who inadvertently or willfully give inaccurate information, failure to record data for all parts of fragmented holdings, respondents' misunderstandings of the definitions of land use and cropping methods, or a failure to report livestock temporarily absent from the holding on public or common pasture land or in transit. Frequently, subjects studied, classificational schemes, and definitions vary from the FAO guidelines (economic planners need different information about a commercial, high-technology, multicrop agricultural sector than they do for a family-subsistence, low-technology, one-crop sector). When a complete census of agriculture is impossible, a sample survey may be taken. This is a limited census of a predetermined number of carefully screened holdings. From these results, nationwide projections may be prepared.

With respect to the first section of the table, number and size of farms, many countries impose a minimum size limit for holdings that may be covered in their census reports, and this cutoff, if not sufficiently low, can result in a substantial undercount of smaller holdings; conversely Soviet-bloc nations formerly published statistics only on state collective or cooperative farms and excluded production from privately held plots of land, even though these often represented a significant fraction of agricultural output.

The land tenure statistics classify farms (a single parcel of land, or holding, or a group of holdings operated as a single farm) according to the rights under which the farmer holds the land or operates the enterprise represented by the farm. Owner-operated includes two types of ownership: outright ownership in which the holder has title and has the right to determine use and transfer of the land; and ownerlike possession in which the holder lacks the legal title but uses it under perpetual lease, hereditary tenure, or leases of 30 years or more with nominal, or no, rent. Farms classed as owner-operated are divided into individual and family, corporate or state, and socialized or collective proprietorships. Rented includes

Agriculture and land use

country	farms (latest census of agriculture)[a]															
	year	number of farms ('000)	size of holding								tenure (% of farms)					
			average (ha)	size class (%)							owner-operated			rented (including share-croppers)	tribal/ com-munal	other[b]
				under 1 ha	1–5 ha	5–10 ha	10–20 ha	20–50 ha	50–200 ha	over 200 ha	individual/ family	corporate/ state	socialized/ collective			
Afghanistan	1981	126[1]	3.5[1]	44.8[1]	35.2[1]			20.0[1]			55.1[1]	—	—	25.1[1]	—	19.8[1]
Albania	1990	0.5[2]	1,182[2, 3]	...	...	...	...	...	...	...	—	100.0		—	—	—
Algeria	1987	899[6]	6.2[6]	1.1[6]	12.7[6]	15.8[6]	21.7[6]	25.6[6]	18.0[6]	5.1[6]	...	...	...	...	...	...
American Samoa	1990	1.1	2.9	44.7[7]	40.0[8]	13.8[9]			1.6[10]		93.9	—	—	2.2	—	3.9
Andorra	—	...	...	...	...	...	...	...	...	...	...	...	...	...	...	...
Angola	1970–71	1,067	3.9	3.3	13.5	9.3	11.3	13.7	19.2	29.7	80.5	1.1	—	—	18.2	0.2
Antigua and Barbuda	1984	2.3	2.1	61.7	33.8	2.9	0.6	0.6	0.4	—	32.1[12]	22.9[12]		40.5[12]	—	4.5[12]
Argentina	1988	421	469	15.1		8.4	14.0[13]	12.0[14]	25.1	25.5	85.1[12]	—	—	8.3[12]	—	6.6[12]
Armenia	1990	...	...	...	...	...	...	...	...	...	...	...	...	...	...	...
Aruba	...	...	...	...	...	...	...	...	...	...	...	...	...	...	...	...
Australia	1991–92	126	3,710			15.1			9.6[16]	75.3[17]	...	...	...	...	...	...
Austria	1990	273	26.4	3.3	32.2	17.8	20.0	21.5	4.6	0.7	38.9	1.5	—	59.5	—	0.1
Azerbaijan	1990	...	...	...	...	...	...	...	...	...	...	...	...	...	...	...
Bahamas, The	1978	4.2	8.5	55.2[7]	30.1[8]	12.3[9]		1.1[18]	0.4[19]	1.0[20]	74.9	0.6	—	4.0	—	20.5
Bahrain	1980	0.8	4.4	19.4	52.9	17.4	8.2	2.0	0.1		37.9	0.1	—	62.0	—	—
Bangladesh	1983–84	10,045	0.9	70.3	27.0[21]	2.5[22]		0.2[23]			62.8	...	...	1.4	...	35.8
Barbados	1969	0.2	95.8	...	...	...	...	...	...	...	...	...	...	...	...	...
Belarus	1990	...	...	...	...	...	...	...	...	...	...	...	...	...	...	...
Belgium	1991	84	16.5	13.9	24.1	14.8	19.1	22.1	6.0		33.4[12]	...	...	65.7[12]	—	0.9[12]
Belize	1974	8.9	26.7		69.4		16.7	8.6	4.4	0.9	43.6	56.4	—	—	—	—
Benin	1983	...	...	...	...	...	...	...	...	...	...	...	...	...	...	...
Bermuda	1990	0.08[26]	3.1[26]	...	...	...	...	...	...	...	...	...	...	...	...	...
Bhutan	1984	160	0.8	51.3[7, 27]	42.9[8, 27]			5.8[27, 28]			...	...	...	...	...	...
Bolivia	1984	315	72.1	25.3	42.1	12.1	6.8	6.1	4.9	2.8	70.3	...	...	2.0	4.3	23.3
Bosnia and Herzegovina[29]	1981	540	...	33.4	48.9	13.7	2.3		0.6		100.0	—	—	—	—	—
Botswana	1990	90.3[30]	5.0	9.1	56.1	26.9		7.9			—	0.4	—	—	99.6	—
Brazil	1985	5,835	64.5	11.1	28.6	13.2	14.0	15.6	12.4	4.9	63.2	—	—	17.9	—	18.4[32]
Brunei	1964	6.3	2.6	44.1[7]	40.4[8]			15.5[28]			52.3	1.0	—	22.0	—	24.7
Bulgaria	1991	2.2[5, 34]	2,467[5, 34]	...	...	...	...	...	...	...	—	84.6[5, 12]	—	15.4[5]	—	—
Burkina Faso	1984	1,860	4.8	...	...	...	...	...	...	...	...	...	...	...	...	...
Burundi	1983	...	...	...	...	...	...	...	...	...	...	...	...	...	...	...
Cambodia	1962[35]	840	3.6	30.7	54.9	10.4	3.4		0.6		...	...	...	...	...	...
Cameroon	1973	926	1.6	42.7	53.8	3.2	0.3	—	—	—	2.4	—	—	5.2	59.5	32.9
Canada	1991	280	242	1.4[7]	3.5[8]		24.2[36]		70.9[37]			63.5		36.5	—	—
Cape Verde	1979	...	...	...	...	...	...	...	...	...	...	...	...	...	...	...
Central African Republic	1974	283	1.7	32.2	65.2	2.5	—	—	—	—	0.3[12]	—	—	0.1[12]	98.6[12]	1.2[12]
Chad	1973	366	2.6	19.7	69.5	10.0	0.8		—	—	...	...	...	...	...	...
Chile	1975–76	306	94.1	16.0	32.5	13.4	12.3	11.8	9.2	4.8		84.0		7.2	8.8	
China	1987	1,650[40]	...	...	...	...	...	...	...	...	—	10.0[41]	90.0[41]	—	—	—
Colombia	1971	1,177	26.3	22.8	36.7	13.6	10.0	8.5	6.3	2.1	68.7	—	—	5.8	4.1	21.4
Comoros	1982	...	...	...	...	...	...	...	...	...	...	...	...	...	...	...
Congo	1986	143[6]	1.4[6]	37.3[6]	62.2[6]	0.5[6]	—	—	—	—	91.7[12]	8.3[12]	—	—	—	—
Costa Rica	1973	82	38.3	23.3	25.5	11.2	10.8	15.2	10.7	3.3	97.9	1.7	—	0.1	—	0.3
Côte d'Ivoire	1975	550	5.0	9.5	54.4	24.9	9.4	1.7	0.1	—	...	...	...	...	...	...
Croatia[29]	1981	569	...	30.7	51.1	14.7	2.3		0.3		100.0	—	—	—	—	—
Cuba	1988	1.8[34]	1,047[34]	...	...	...	...	...	...	...	...	...	...	...	...	...
Cyprus	1985	48.0	3.8	24.4	56.8	15.0	2.9		0.9			79.0		9.4	—	11.6[42]
Czech Republic[43]	1980	1,391	8.1	89.9[44]			9.9[45]		0.2[46]		6.0[12]	30.8[12]	63.2[12]	—	0.6	—
Denmark	1991[47]	77	35.9	2.7		15.2	23.4	37.7	20.9			64.4[2]			35.6[2]	
Djibouti	1987–88	1.2	0.4	*c. 100*	...	...	...	...	...	...	...	...	...	...	...	...
Dominica	1986–88	1.9	...	89[48]		9[49]			2		33	...	...	15	...	52
Dominican Republic	1981	385	6.3	16.0	65.7	8.5	5.4	2.6	1.5	0.3	53.2	18.5	4.5	1.6	—	17.4
Ecuador	1974	517	15.4	27.8	38.8	10.6	8.0	8.2	5.6	0.9	70.3	0.3	—	7.7	7.4	14.3
Egypt	1985	3,546	0.7	95.5[50]	2.4[51]			2.1[52]			...	...	...	...	...	...
El Salvador	1970–71	271	5.4	48.9	37.9	5.8	3.4	2.6	1.2	0.2	41.5	—	—	28.2	6.3	24.1

sharecropping; communal/tribal includes types of customary or traditional arrangements in which title or goods do not change hands. "Other" usually includes farms operated on several parcels of land and held under multiple forms of tenure.

Statistics on types of farms by commodities produced refer to FAO categories. The terms "mainly crops" and "mainly livestock" indicate that more than half of the for-sale production was that indicated.

The section on technology provides some measures of the role modern technology plays in the farm activities of each country (although, of course, irrigation may employ technology developed in ancient times). Ratios referred to area mean area of "arable" (cultivated and cultivable) land, roughly "cropland," less area of permanent crops (see below).

The classification of farmland by economic use is also subject to differing treatment internationally. For purposes of this table, "cropland" comprises: (1) land under temporary crops (those requiring replanting after each harvest), (2) land under permanent crops (those *not* requiring replanting, including tree, bush and shrub, and vine crops), and (3) land temporarily (less than five years) fallow (unused, but capable of being returned to cultivation with no special preparation). "Meadows and pastures" includes land (both permanent and temporary use) whose principal purpose is the raising of animal fodder or forage. "Woodland and forest" includes both natural and planted tracts of timber (*e.g.,* plantings of Christmas trees), whether harvested or not. "Other" comprises: (1) mixed and multiple use lands, (2) residue of farmland holdings not classifiable according to categories listed above (including areas of farm buildings, roads, ornamental gardens, watercourses and flooded land, wasteland, etc.), (3) land not classified by respondents in census, or (4) detail not distinguishable as one of categories above by reason of its summarization in a published source. When "cropland" is indicated to compose 100 percent of farmland, it should usually be understood to mean only that woodland, pasture, etc., were not part of the published data, rather than that those classes of land use do not exist.

Measurements of area are given in hectares (ha; 1 hectare is equal to 2.471 acres). A kilogram (kg) is equal to 2.205 pounds (1 kg/ha = 0.89 lb/ac). The following notes further define the column headings:

a. All properties used wholly or partly for agricultural production. A property need not have agricultural land to be considered a farm; piggeries, hatcheries, and poultry batteries are farms because they engage in agricultural production, *i.e.,* raise livestock and produce livestock products.

b. All forms of tenure not included in the preceding categories. Includes land operated by schools, religious bodies, squatters, seasonally by nomads, and built-on, waste, and similar types of alienation.

... Not available, or no agricultural census or survey ever taken.

— None, less than half the smallest unit shown, or not applicable.

farmland use																	country
activity (% of farms)			technology (latest)				land in farms		land use (%)								
									cropland								
mainly crops	mainly livestock	mixed/ other	tractors (per 1,000 ha)	electricity (% of farms having)	irrigation (% of land irrig.)	artificial fertilizer (kg/ha)	total ('000 ha)	% of total land area	permanent crops	temporary crops	fallow	total cropland	meadows and pastures	woodland and forest	other	
...	...	...	0.1	...	35	7	39,810	61.0	1.8	46.3	51.9	19.9	75.4	4.8	—	Afghanistan
57.9[4]	36.2[4]	5.9[4]	21.7	...	74	158	1,111[5]	40.0[5]	17.8	—82.2—		64.3[5]	35.7[5]	...	...	Albania
...	...	...	12.9	...	5	15	39,701	16.7	7.6	51.0	41.4	19.2	78.3	—	2.5	Algeria
55.7[4]	44.3[4]	—	7.0	38.5	...	...	3.2	16.4	—88.7—		11.3	71.4	5.3	...	23.3	American Samoa
...	...	...	...	...	...	...	...	2.0	...	...	...	...	...	...	...	Andorra
...	...	...	3.5	...	89[11]	7	4,180	3.4	36.8	63.2	—	1.7	82.0	...	16.2	Angola
32.9	44.1	23.0	29.8	...	...	...	2.5	9.0	26.0	57.1	16.9	62.6	36.0	—1.4—		Antigua and Barbuda
10.6[15]	78.9[15]	10.5[15]	8.1	...	7	4	177,437	64.8	4.8	71.5	23.7	15.4	56.4	21.3	6.9	Argentina
...	...	...	27.9	...	63	...	1,300	43.3	...	...	...	38.5	53.8	—	7.7	Armenia
...	...	...	...	...	...	...	...	...	...	...	...	...	...	...	...	Aruba
24.0	58.3	17.7	6.8	...	4	28	466,000	60.7	1.1	—98.9—		10.1		—89.9—		Australia
59.8	—	40.2	243	...	0.3	201	7,217	87.2	5.3	93.5	1.2	20.8	25.9	42.4	10.9	Austria
...	...	...	25.5	...	88	...	4,200	48.3	...	...	...	38.1	52.4	—	9.5	Azerbaijan
...	...	...	9.8	...	10[11]	...	36.2	2.6	23.3	59.9	16.8	23.3	6.9	25.7	44.0	Bahamas, The
...	...	...	...	21.3	100	...	3.5	5.2	50.7	49.3	—	45.9	...	...	54.1	Bahrain
91.3[24]	8.7[24]	—	0.6	...	34	98	9,180	70.5	0.1	99.9	—	89.2	...	0.1	10.7	Bangladesh
...	...	...	18.8	...	...	91	19.8	45.9	...	...	...	13.7		—86.3—		Barbados
...	...	...	20.6	...	2	...	9,300	44.9	...	...	...	65.6	33.3	—	1.1	Belarus
...	2.5[25]	...	144.3	...	0.1	496	1,392	45.6	1.2	98.4	0.4	51.9	45.2	0.5	2.4	Belgium
...	...	...	24.4	...	4	88	233	10.0	13.1	81.1	5.8	36.5	15.9	36.1	11.6	Belize
...	...	...	0.1	...	0.4	2	3,300	29.3	...	...	...	100.0	—	—	—	Benin
...	...	...	22.9	...	...	...	2.4	4.4	18.6	72.9	8.5	91.1	8.9	...	...	Bermuda
...	...	...	...	...	30	1	156	3.4	11.7	—88.3—		100.0	—	—	—	Bhutan
...	...	...	2.5	...	8	3	22,670	20.6	—55.0—		45.0	6.9	47.7	39.0	6.4	Bolivia
...	...	...	...	...	...	...	2,525	49.4	8.9	70.9	20.2	44.2	55.4	—	0.4	Bosnia and Herzegovina[29]
13.6[26]	27.9[26]	58.5[26]	4.6	...	0.1	1	343[31]	5.9[31]	—	100.0[31]	—	83.5[31]	...	...	...	Botswana
80.0[33]	16.2[33]	3.8[33]	10.4	4.1[33]	4	43	376,287	44.5	18.2[31]	66.9[31]	14.9[31]	15.8[31]	47.8[31]	24.2[31]	12.2[31]	Brazil
...	...	...	24.0	...	33	57	16.4	2.8	78.0	22.0	—	54.8	0.1	16.4	28.7	Brunei
54.4[4]	45.6[4]	—	13.2	...	32	195	6,159	55.6	6.3	—93.7—		75.4	24.6	...	...	Bulgaria
...	...	...	3.7	...	0.6	6	8,919	32.6	...	...	...	...	...	...	...	Burkina Faso
...	...	...	0.1	...	7	4	2,388	85.8	—73.8—		26.2	56.7	37.7	5.6	...	Burundi
...	...	...	0.5	...	3	1	2,984	16.5	94.9	3.5	1.6	96.1	—	3.9	—	Cambodia
...	...	...	0.2	...	0.5	6[2]	1,490	3.3	...	...	...	100.0	—	—	—	Cameroon
43.9	42.9	13.2	17.0	...	1.9	47	67,754	7.3	—80.9—		19.1	61.1	6.1	—32.7—		Canada
...	...	...	0.4	...	5	—	25[38]	6.2[38]	20.8[38]	79.1[38]	...	100.0[38]	—	—	—	Cape Verde
...	...	...	0.1	...	...	2	491	0.8	11.8	88.2	—	100.0	—	—	—	Central African Republic
...	...	...	0.05	...	0.3	2	23,877[39]	45.8[39]	50.0[39]	—50.0[39]—		23.7[39]	76.3[39]	...	...	Chad
...	...	...	8.5	...	31	69	28,759	38.0	24.4	36.6	38.9	11.5	42.3	20.7	25.5	Chile
...	...	...	8.5	...	51	261	166,902	17.4	4.1	—95.9—		100.0	—	—	—	China
...	...	...	9.2	...	13	101	30,993	27.0	30.6	27.6	41.8	24.7	56.4	...	18.9	Colombia
...	...	...	...	...	...	...	83	44.3	56.4	—43.6—		100.0	—	—	—	Comoros
6.2[4]	93.8[4]	—	4.9	...	3	3	226	0.7	14.8	85.2	—	100.0	—	—	—	Congo
...	...	...	22.8	...	42	203	3,122	60.0	42.2	57.8	—	15.7	49.9	22.9	11.4	Costa Rica
...	...	...	1.5	...	3	11	2,753	8.6	65.9	34.1	—	100.0	—	—	—	Côte d'Ivoire
...	...	...	...	...	...	...	3,220	57.0	8.8	81.8	9.4	50.4	48.5	—	1.1	Croatia[29]
...	...	...	30.1	...	35	199	8,679	78.3	...	...	...	33.9	32.1	31.9	2.1	Cuba
72.7	27.3	—	129	...	34	144	210	35.6	34.7	54.3	11.0	74.9	—	—25.1—		Cyprus
34.3	24.4	41.3	26.8	100.0	6	314	6,924	54.1	2.6	—97.4—		75.3	24.7	...	...	Czech Republic
49.1	22.4	28.5	62.8	...	17	255	2,770	65.3	...	98.9	...	80.2	19.8	...	...	Denmark
...	...	...	...	...	...	...	6	0.3	...	6.8	...	100.0	—	—	—	Djibouti
...	...	...	12.9	...	...	259	20	26.3	...	...	...	...	...	...	...	Dominica
44.0	56.0	—	2.3	60.0	23	50	2,412	49.8	38.0	40.2	21.8	34.1	51.6	13.0	0.9	Dominican Republic
67.8	12.4	19.8	5.1	...	32	29	7,955	29.6	32.8	51.5	15.7	32.8	32.2	29.0	6.0	Ecuador
...	...	...	26.0	...	116	373	2,731[54]	3.0[54]	3.5[54]	96.5[54]	...	100.0[54]	—	—	—	Egypt
95.3	4.7	—	6.1	...	21	106	1,452	69.0	25.1	58.6	16.4	44.9	38.2	11.6	5.3	El Salvador

Agriculture and land use (continued)

country	farms (latest census of agriculture)[a]															
	year	number of farms ('000)	size of holding								tenure (% of farms)					
			average (ha)	size class (%)							owner-operated			rented (including share-croppers)	tribal/ com-munal	other[b]
				under 1 ha	1–5 ha	5–10 ha	10–20 ha	20–50 ha	50–200 ha	over 200 ha	individual/ family	corporate/ state	socialized/ collective			
Equatorial Guinea	...	...	...	...	...	...	...	...	...	...	...	...	...	...	...	...
Eritrea[53]	—	...	...	...	...	...	...	...	...	...	...	...	...	...	...	...
Estonia	1990	...	...	...	...	...	...	...	...	...	...	...	...	...	...	...
Ethiopia[53]	1976–77	4,893	1.4	49.9	46.5	3.4	0.2	—	—	—	98.4	1.6	—	—	—	—
Faeroe Islands	...	...	...	...	...	...	...	...	...	...	...	...	...	...	...	...
Fiji	1978–79	66	4.2	64.3	20.6	8.1	3.7	2.1	1.2		—	—	—	3.5	95.1	1.4
Finland	1990[55]	199	12.8	—	34.6	21.5	23.9	17.6	2.4		78.6			21.4	—	—
France	1988	1,017	26.6[31]	8.8	18.6	11.0	16.4	28.3	16.9		65.2[41]	—	—	33.5[41]	—	1.2[41]
French Guiana	1988	4.5	4.6	16.5	73.6	6.0	1.5	2.4			...	...	...	...	...	...
French Polynesia	1987	5.6	...	37.7	62.3						36.5	...	...	6.3	...	57.1
Gabon	1975	71	1.0	68.0	32.0		—	—	—	—	81.8	—	—	0.3	5.3	12.5
Gambia, The	1989–90	...	...	...	...	...	...	...	...	...	...	...	...	...	...	...
Gaza Strip	1968	...	...	...	...	...	...	...	...	...	...	...	...	...	...	...
Georgia	1990	...	...	...	...	...	...	...	...	...	...	...	...	...	...	...
Germany	1992[3, 55]	601	28.0	12.4[48]	17.1[56]	16.4	19.5	24.5	10.1		...	—	—	...	—	...
Ghana	1970	805	3.2	36.6	48.7	9.0	3.9	1.8	—	—	...	...	...	...	...	...
Gibraltar	—	...	...	...	...	...	...	...	...	...	...	...	...	...	...	...
Greece	1981	999	3.5	24.7	54.2	15.0	4.7	1.2	0.2		...	...	...	...	...	...
Greenland	—	...	...	...	...	...	...	...	...	...	...	...	...	...	...	...
Grenada	1981	8	1.7	88.3[48]	6.9[58]	3.3[59]	0.7	0.4[18]	0.3[60]		73.2			14.1	—	12.7
Guadeloupe	1988	17	2.8	32.1	58.3	7.0	1.6	0.9			46.6[61]	—	—	19.1[61]	—	34.3[61]
Guam	1987	0.4	15.1	42.2[7]	33.9[8]	19.4[9]		4.6[10]			64.4	—	—	4.3	—	31.3
Guatemala	1979	600	6.8	39.7[63]	49.8[64]	8.2[65]			2.2[66]		74.0[67]			6.3[67]	5.8[67]	13.9[67]
Guernsey	1991	0.102	16.2	6.7[15]	24.0[15]	23.1[15]	46.1[15]		—	—	32.4[2, 12]	—	—	67.6[2, 12]	—	—
Guinea	1984–85[3]	...	2.4	...	...	...	...	...	...	...	...	...	...	...	...	...
Guinea-Bissau	1961	87	3.0	13.4	73.3	10.0	3.0	0.3	—	—	...	...	...	...	...	...
Guyana	1964	...	...	...	...	...	...	...	...	...	...	90.0	...	...	...	10.0
Haiti	1971	617	1.4	58.7	37.5	3.8		—	—	—	66.6	—	—	25.0	—	8.4
Honduras	1974	195	13.5	17.3	46.6	14.5	9.8	7.8	3.3	0.8	99.7	0.1	—	—	0.2	—
Hong Kong	1986	11	0.3	97.5	2.3	0.1	0.1		—	—	9.0			77.0	—	14.0
Hungary	1990	1,412	...	90.0[57]	9.9[57]		0.1[57]				6.8[70]	13.3[70]	74.5[70]	—	—	—
Iceland	1981	7.0	...	15.7	9.3	11.7	23.7	35.8	3.7		...	...	...	...	...	...
India	1976–77	81,569	2.0	54.6	35.8	6.6	2.4	0.5	0.1		92.7	—	—	1.2	—	6.1
Indonesia	1987	19,501[54]	c.1[54]	70.7[54]	29.3[54]						74.8[5]	—[6]	—[6]	3.2[6]	—[6]	22.1[6]
Iran	1982	...	...	...	...	...	...	...	...	...	...	...	...	...	...	...
Iraq	1979	470	13.3	25.9[72]	27.6[73]	23.2[74]	11.5[75]	9.4	1.9[76]	0.5[77]	52.5[11]	—	—	40.9[11]	—	6.6[11]
Ireland	1986	279[33]	25.0[15]	2.7[33]	37.8[33]		52.4[33]		7.1[33]	—	...	...	...	...	...	...
Isle of Man	1987	0.8	59.7	25.8[78]			14.0[79]	18.2[18]	23.4[19]	18.5[20]	72.4	—	—	27.6	—	—
Israel	1981	52	11.3	26.5	57.6	8.3	4.0	2.0	1.8		84.0	—	1.4	—	—	14.6
Italy	1990–91	3,036	7.5	33.0	43.0	11.7	6.7	3.8	1.8		81.5[33]	—	—	6.7[33]	—	11.8[33]
Jamaica	1978–79	184	2.9	32.5[81]	60.7[82]	4.8[59]	0.9	0.4[18]	0.3[19]	0.4[20]	99.5[83]	0.2[83]	—	—	—	0.3[83]
Japan	1990	3,835	1.4	68.5	29.4	2.1					79.4[33]	...	...	...	...	20.6[33]
Jersey	1990	0.6	11.1	45.0[84]		16.4[85]	19.7[86]	19.0[87]			31.4[27]	—	—	68.6[27]	—	—
Jordan	1983	57	6.3	25.3	44.6	15.6	8.6	4.5	1.3	0.1	80.5	—	—	13.1	0.3	6.1
Kazakhstan	1990	...	...	...	...	...	...	...	...	...	...	...	...	...	...	...
Kenya	1976–79[89]	2,750	2.5	65.5	27.3	2.7[90]	4.4[91]				...	...	...	...	...	...
Kiribati	...	...	...	...	...	...	...	...	...	...	...	...	...	...	...	...
Korea, North	...	...	...	...	...	...	...	...	...	...	...	...	...	...	...	...
Korea, South	1990[3]	1,767	1.2	60.8[2]	39.2[2]						82.5[32]	—	—	17.4[33]	—	0.1[33]
Kuwait	1985–86	1.9	2.4	48.6[33]	25.4[33]	10.2[33]	8.7[33]	4.0[33]	3.1[33]	—	95.3	—	—	...	...	4.7
Kyrgyzstan	1990	...	...	...	...	...	...	...	...	...	...	...	...	...	...	...
Laos	1983	...	...	...	...	...	...	...	...	...	...	...	...	...	...	...
Latvia	1990	...	...	...	...	...	...	...	...	...	...	...	...	...	...	...
Lebanon	1970	143	4.3	47.7	44.5		6.5		1.2	0.1	...	...	...	...	...	...
Lesotho	1986	207	2.0[33]	27.0[33]	67.5[33]	5.5[33]		—	—	—	...	...	...	...	...	...
Liberia	1971[92]	122	3.0	52.8	31.0	12.0	3.7		0.5		40.0[12]	—	—	—	43.3[12]	16.7[12]
Libya	1974	144	14.0	12.7	34.1	20.6	17.4	12.0	3.2		...	...	...	...	...	...
Liechtenstein	1990	0.42	8.7	33.8	25.7	10.3	10.8	18.7	0.7		31.7	—	—	24.5	—	43.8
Lithuania	1990	...	...	...	...	...	...	...	...	...	...	...	...	...	...	...
Luxembourg	1992	3.5	36	14.6	11.7	8.3	9.2	23.7	32.6		45.4[12]	...	...	...	...	...
Macau	—	...	...	...	...	...	...	...	...	...	...	...	—	...	...	...
Macedonia[29]	1981	176	...	44.7	43.0	6.7	1.2	0.2			100.0	—	—	—	—	—
Madagascar	1984–85	1,453	1.3	54.8	44.2	1.0	0.2	0.1	0.1		87.3[12]			4.9[12]	...	7.4[12]
Malawi	1980–81[89]	1,136	1.2	54.9	40.1[93]	5.0[94]					...	...	...	...	...	...
Malaysia	1980[89, 95]	920	2.2	...	...	...	...	...	...	...	53.2[33]	18.2[33]	...	19.6[33]	...	9.0[33]
Maldives	1985	...	...	...	...	...	...	...	...	...	...	...	...	...	...	...
Mali	1982–83	562	4.0	20.1	54.1	17.4	8.4			—	96.8[97]	3.2	—	...	—	—
Malta	1983	12	1.1	67.8	30.0	2.0	0.2				16.0	—	—	70.4	—	13.6[42]
Marshall Islands	—	...	...	...	...	...	...	...	...	...	...	...	...	...	...	...
Martinique	1988	16.0	2.3	64.9	28.2	4.0	1.6	1.4			...	...	...	...	...	...
Mauritania	1984–85	100	2.0	49.2	41.0[21]	7.0[59]	2.0	0.5[18]	0.3[60]		68.4	...	—	4.4	10.4	17.0
Mauritius	1980	32.5	1.1	61.3	36.2	1.9	0.3	0.2	0.1		95.8	—	—	4.2	—	—
Mayotte	1987	5.9[54]	1.7[88]	...	...	...	...	...	...	...	...	...	...	...	...	...
Mexico	1970[98]	2,848	49	23.5	39.4	21.1	8.8	2.7	2.9	1.5	97.6			1.0	—	1.5
Micronesia	...	...	...	...	...	...	...	...	...	...	...	...	...	...	...	...
Moldova	1990	...	...	...	...	...	...	...	...	...	...	...	...	...	...	...
Monaco	...	...	...	...	...	...	...	...	...	...	...	...	...	...	...	...
Mongolia	1985	0.3	385,000	...	...	...	...	...	...	...	—	16.0	84.0	—	—	—
Morocco	1985–86	1,900[88]	3.9[88]	29.8[6]	44.0[6]	14.9[6]	7.7[6]	3.0[6]	0.7[6]		...	...	...	...	...	...
Mozambique	1973	1,605	3.1	...	...	...	...	...	...	...	0.2	0.1	—	—	99.7	—
Myanmar (Burma)	1987–88	4,308[99]	2.3[99]	61.2[48, 99]	24.7[58, 99]	11.5[99, 100]	2.5[79, 99]	0.8[10, 99]			...	...	...	...	...	...
Namibia	1983	...	...	...	...	...	...	...	...	...	...	...	...	...	...	...
Nauru	...	...	...	...	...	...	...	...	...	...	...	...	...	...	...	...
Nepal	1981–82	2,194	1.1	66.7	29.9	2.7	0.7				97.5	—	—	1.6	—	0.9
Netherlands, The	1988[47]	130	15.5	10.5	22.3	17.1	21.5	24.4	4.2		31.5[12]		—	12.2[12]	—	56.4[12]

activity (% of farms)			technology (latest)				farmland use									country
							land in farms		land use (%)							
									cropland							
mainly crops	mainly live-stock	mixed/ other	tractors (per 1,000 ha)	electri-city (% of farms having)	irriga-tion (% of land irrig.)	artificial fertilizer (kg/ha)	total ('000 ha)	% of total land area	perma-nent crops	tempo-rary crops	fallow	total crop-land	mead-ows and pastures	wood-land and forest	other	
...	...	...	0.8	...	...	...	...	...	...	...	...	...	...	...	...	Equatorial Guinea
...	...	...	...	...	...	...	...	...	...	...	...	...	...	...	...	Eritrea[53]
...	...	...	18.5	...	...	...	1,400	31.1	...	...	...	78.6	21.4	—	—	Estonia
...	...	...	0.3	...	1	7	6,971	5.7	7.4	76.8	15.8	86.9	9.1	...	4.0	Ethiopia[53]
...	...	...	...	...	...	...	...	...	...	...	...	...	...	...	...	Faeroe Islands
...	...	...	28.4	...	1	96	277	15.2	...	...	...	...	...	...	...	Fiji
52.3	——47.6——		92.7	100.0[33]	3	210	12,338	40.5	0.3[33]	97.6[33]	2.1[33]	18.4	1.0	58.0	22.6	Finland
35.8	37.9	26.3	81.0	...	7	319	33,649[5]	61.8[5]	7.4[5]	90.6[5]	2.0[5]	53.6[5]	34.1[5]	8.2[5]	4.1[5]	France
...	...	...	30.8	...	20	64	24.6	0.3	3.1	53.8	43.0	60.0	40.0	...	...	French Guiana
...	...	...	31.0	...	19.4	33	36.8	10.4	90.0	7.1	2.9	62.0	8.5	1.9	27.6	French Polynesia
...	...	...	5.0	...	...	3	73.0	0.3	...	...	...	...	...	...	...	Gabon
...	...	...	0.2	...	7	11	176.4	16.5	...	100.0	...	100.0	...	...	...	Gambia, The
...	...	...	83.3	...	133	...	19.3	53.2	74.6	25.4	...	100.0	—	—	—	Gaza Strip
...	...	...	31.3	...	59	...	3,200	45.7	...	...	...	25.0	62.5	—	12.5	Georgia
...	...	...	132	...	4	384	19,185[57]	54.9[57]	1.8[57]	——98.2[57]——		61.3[57]	27.4[57]	8.0[57]	3.3[57]	Germany
...	...	...	3.6	...	1	3	2,574	10.8	61.4	38.6	—	100.0	—	—	—	Ghana
...	...	...	...	...	...	4	...	...	...	...	...	...	...	...	...	Gibraltar
...	...	...	75.7	...	42	175	3,546	26.9	29.2	61.1	9.7	98.1	1.9	...	...	Greece
...	c. 100	...	...	...	...	...	...	...	...	...	...	...	...	...	...	Greenland
...	...	...	5.8	...	...	...	13.9	40.2	...	...	...	...	...	...	...	Grenada
...	...	...	42.6	...	13	307	143.4	84.1	16.2	46.7	37.1	33.3	18.6	48.1	...	Guadeloupe
72.2[62]	17.2[62]	10.5[62]	13.3	68.7	...	...	5.3	9.8	——51.2[27]——		48.8[27]	17.8[27]	34.3[27]	——47.9[27]——		Guam
...	...	...	3.0	...	6	66	4,147	38.1	27.6	——72.4——		42.0	27.3	27.2	3.4	Guatemala
...	67.6	...	...	...	...	...	2	26.2	—	100.0	—	10.5	89.5	...	...	Guernsey
...	...	...	0.5	...	4	1	1,600[68]	6.5	...	...	...	...	...	...	...	Guinea
...	...	...	0.6	...	...	3	169	4.7	...	...	...	...	...	...	...	Guinea-Bissau
...	...	...	7.5	...	27	33	10,652	26.2	...	...	...	8.4	91.6	...	...	Guyana
...	...	...	0.4	...	14	4	1,579	57.0	...	...	...	54.4	33.3	12.3	...	Haiti
...	...	...	2.1	...	6	18	2,630	23.5	15.4[69]	34.6[69]	50.0[69]	52.0[69]	48.0[69]	...	...	Honduras
56.3	37.3	6.4	1.2	...	33	100.0[26]	7.3	6.8	7.4	37.0	55.6	100.0	—	—	—	Hong Kong
43.4[4]	44.3[4]	12.3[4]	8.9	...	3	231	8,236	88.5	3.4	96.6	—	60.6	14.4	20.6	4.4	Hungary
...	...	...	1,313	87.0[38]	...	2,529	...	...	...	...	...	...	...	...	...	Iceland
...	...	...	6.0	...	28	69	163,343	49.7	——88.3[71]——		11.7[71]	96.0[71]	1.5[71]	——2.5[71]——		India
86.8[6]	—[6]	13.2[6]	1.8	...	51	110	48,583	25.3	27.0	45.2	27.8	60.7	5.1	18.9	15.3	Indonesia
...	...	...	8.2	...	41	80	104,900	63.8	4.9	62.0	33.2	14.2	85.8	...	...	Iran
87.9	11.2	0.8	6.3	...	49	40	5,732	13.1	3.0	62.4	34.6	87.2	0.7	0.2	11.9	Iraq
...	...	...	180	...	...	741	5,692	82.6	0.5	99.5	...	9.5	69.5	——21.0——		Ireland
...	...	...	...	...	...	...	48	83.3	3.5	——96.5——		12.8	87.2	...	...	Isle of Man
...	...	...	77.1	...	51	252	584	28.2	22.0	——78.0——		70.5	19.1	...	10.4	Israel
...	...	...	162	...	35	151	22,651	77.0	26.3[80]	73.7[80]	...	52.4[80]	21.2[80]	17.1[80]	9.3[80]	Italy
...	...	...	14.8	...	17	116	603[83]	54.8[83]	22.2[83]	72.2[83]	5.6[83]	41.3[83]	21.6[83]	13.5[83]	23.6[83]	Jamaica
80.8[31]	——19.2[31]——		480	...	69	414	5,243	13.9	9.1	——90.9——		95.5	—	—	4.5	Japan
85.1[88]	14.9[88]	—	...	...	...	...	6.5	56.2	——98.9——		1.1	63.4	————36.6————			Jersey
58.2[62, 80]	14.9[62, 80]	26.9[62, 80]	18.6	1.5	20	61	364	4.1	13.3	63.0	23.7	87.7	1.0	0.3	11.0	Jordan
...	...	...	6.2	...	6	...	197,600	72.7	...	...	...	18.0	81.9	—	0.1	Kazakhstan
...	...	...	7.3	...	3	48	6,922	11.9	11.5	——88.5——		71.0	23.8	1.9	3.3	Kenya
...	...	...	...	...	...	...	...	...	...	...	...	...	...	...	...	Kiribati
...	...	...	43.3	...	84	407	...	...	...	...	...	...	...	...	...	Korea, North
82.3[4]	17.7[4]	—	27.5	...	69	454	2,109	21.2	6.7	——93.3——		100.0	—	—	—	Korea, South
36.7	61.8	1.5	24.0	100.0	40	200	44.5	0.3	30.2	69.8	—	100.0	—	—	—	Kuwait
...	...	...	20.1	...	75	...	10,100	51.0	...	...	...	13.9	85.1	—	1.0	Kyrgyzstan
...	...	...	1.0	...	14	2	1,680	7.1	2.3	——97.7——		52.4	47.6	...	...	Laos
...	...	...	27.3	...	...	...	2,500	38.5	...	...	...	68.0	32.0	—	—	Latvia
77.0[62]	8.1[62]	14.9[62]	13.9	...	40	92	275[31]	27.0[31]	36.7[31]	39.7[31]	23.6[31]	100.0[31]	—	—	—	Lebanon
37.3	—	62.7	5.4	...	...	14	372[33]	12.3[33]	—	89.6[33]	10.4[33]	98.8[33]	...	...	1.2[33]	Lesotho
...	...	...	2.6	...	2	7	370[70]	3.8[70]	66.2[70]	33.8[70]	—	98.3[70]	...	1.7[70]	...	Liberia
...	...	...	18.8	...	14	37	8,800[70]	5.1[70]	——33.3[70]——		66.7[70]	20.5[70]	79.5[70]	...	...	Libya
23.9[26]	61.6[26]	14.5[26]	106	...	...	...	3.9	24.2	1.1	——98.9——		39.9	57.5	1.1	1.5	Liechtenstein
...	...	...	21.2	...	...	...	3,400	52.3	...	...	...	67.6	32.4	—	—	Lithuania
25.8	55.7	18.5	155	...	...	...	137	53.1	2.5	97.0	0.5	41.4	50.7	7.2	0.7	Luxembourg
...	...	...	...	...	...	...	...	...	...	...	...	...	...	...	...	Macau
...	...	...	...	...	...	...	1,320	51.3	9.3	65.4	25.3	46.4	53.4	—	1.2	Macedonia[29]
...	...	...	1.1	...	36	2	2,044	3.5	15.4	84.6	—	100.0	—	—	—	Madagascar
22.1	...	77.9	0.8	...	1	23	1,332	14.1	0.2	99.8	—	94.8	...	5.2	...	Malaŵi
...	...	...	11.8[96]	...	33[96]	170[96]	4,100[27]	31.2[27]	84.8[27]	15.2[27]	—	100.0[27]	...	...	...	Malaysia
...	...	...	...	...	...	...	19	63.5	...	...	...	...	...	...	...	Maldives
...	...	...	0.4	...	10	9	2,277	1.8	—	100.0	—	100.0	—	—	—	Mali
...	...	...	37.4	...	8	39	13.0	41.2	5.0	——95.0——		87.5	————12.5————			Malta
...	...	...	...	...	...	...	...	...	...	...	...	...	...	...	...	Marshall Islands
...	...	...	89.0	...	40	945	95.6	86.9	23.2	36.1	40.7	39.8	20.1	40.1	—	Martinique
...	...	...	1.7	...	6	12	194	0.2	—	56.2	43.8	100.0	—	—	—	Mauritania
...	...	...	3.6	...	17	304	171	91.5	5.9	94.1	—	62.2	4.4	33.4	...	Mauritius
...	...	...	...	...	...	...	14.6	39.0	33.3	66.7	—	100.0	—	—	—	Mayotte
83.9	12.9	3.2	7.4	...	22	70	139,868	72.7	6.3	58.1	35.6	16.5	53.3	14.2	16.0	Mexico
61.4[4]	15.7[4]	22.9[4]	7.4	45	0	...	5.8	12.2	——9.3——		90.7	32.9	30.2	——36.9——		Micronesia
...	...	...	27.7	...	16	...	2,500	73.5	...	...	...	68.0	12.0	—	20.0	Moldova
...	...	...	...	...	...	...	...	...	...	...	...	...	...	...	...	Monaco
...	...	...	8.3	...	6	12	124,587	79.6	—	66.8	33.2	0.9	99.1	...	...	Mongolia
...	...	...	4.7	...	14	35	8,062	17.6	6.6	72.9	20.5	100.0	—	—	—	Morocco
...	...	...	2.0	...	4	1	13,626	17.8	——44.9——		55.1	55.0	45.0	...	...	Mozambique
...	...	...	1.0	...	10	8	12,560	18.6	3.0	79.5	17.5	97.0	3.0	...	...	Myanmar (Burma)
...	...	...	4.7	...	0.6	...	662	0.8	0.3	——99.7——		100.0	—	—	—	Namibia
...	...	...	...	...	...	...	...	...	...	...	...	...	...	...	...	Nauru
...	...	...	1.7	...	40	25	2,464	16.7	1.3	97.1	1.6	94.0	1.7	0.6	3.7	Nepal
32.3	54.9	12.9	216	...	63	628	2,012	48.1	3.5	95.8	0.7	44.6	55.4	...	...	Netherlands, The

Agriculture and land use (continued)

country	year	number of farms ('000)	size of holding: average (ha)	size class (%): under 1 ha	1–5 ha	5–10 ha	10–20 ha	20–50 ha	50–200 ha	over 200 ha	tenure (% of farms): owner-operated: individual/family	corporate/state	socialized/collective	rented (including share-croppers)	tribal/communal	other[b]
	farms (latest census of agriculture)[a]															
Netherlands Antilles	...	...	...	...	...	...	...	...	...	...	...	...	...	...	...	...
New Caledonia	1983–84	12.7	23	71.2[48]	13.8[56]	3.7	2.3	2.5	3.8	2.8	...	...	...	...	...	...
New Zealand	1991	80.4	217	—12.5[26]—		10.3[26]	8.4[26]	—46.5[26]—		22.3[26]	85.7[26]	10.9[26]	—	—	—	3.4[26]
Nicaragua	1984	...	...	—26.2—				—30.6—		43.3	62.3[12]	19.3[12]	18.6[12]	—	—	—
Niger	1980[3]	699	4.9	3.8	54.1	37.8		—4.3—			...	...	...	...	...	...
Nigeria	1971	...	...	92.0	7.8	0.2	—	—	—	—	...	...	...	...	...	...
Northern Mariana Is.	1990	0.1	49.1	26.1[101]	35.3[102]	—24.4[9]—		—14.3—			56.3	...	...	23.5	...	20.2
Norway	1989	183	10.2	6.4[51]	11.3[52]	12.7	16.6	23.7	22.2	7.1	—65.4—			34.6	—	—
Oman	1978–79	83	1.0	70.5	25.0	2.8	1.3[103]	0.3[104]	0.1	—	...	...	...	...	...	...
Pakistan	1980	4,070	4.7	17.2	56.2	17.4	6.5	—2.7—			64.1[12]	0.3[12]	—	35.6[12]	—	—
Panama	1991	209	14.2	47.4	25.0	7.6	7.0	7.5	5.0	0.7	28.6	—	—	1.4	—	70.0
Papua New Guinea	1985[105]	0.8	483	—26.8[49]—					28.3[54]	44.9[54]	26.9[12, 54]	71.0[12, 54]	—	2.1[12, 54]	—	—
Paraguay	1981	249	88	8.6	27.4	19.9	22.7	14.5	4.4	2.5	54.5	0.4	—	9.2	—	35.9[32]
Peru	1984	1,574	9.5	24.1	47.7	13.2	6.7	5.5	—2.8—		75.5	—	—	0.8	6.8	16.9
Philippines	1980	3,420	2.6	22.7	63.3	10.5	—3.5—				58.3	—	—	27.4	—	14.3
Poland	1989	3,952	4.8	52.0[48]	19.5[56]	17.5	—10.9—			0.1	76.2[12]	—	23.8[12]	—	—	—
Portugal	1979	784	6.6	44.5	41.9	7.7	3.3	1.5	0.7	0.4	68.1	—	—	8.7	—	23.2
Puerto Rico	1987	20	17.2	—48.7[106]—		19.5[107]	16.7[108]	6.7[109]	—8.3[60]—		—77.5—		—	7.1	—	15.4
Qatar	1990	0.8	7.0	20.5	41.8	18.0	12.6	5.8	—1.4—		...	...	...	...	...	...
Réunion	1988–89	15	4.1	35.6	47.9	12.5	2.7	—1.3—			46.1[6]	—	—	22.5[6]	—	31.4[6]
Romania	1987	4.2[26, 34]	2,700[26, 34]	...	...	...	...	...	...	...	...	13.7[12, 26]	60.8[12, 26]	—	—	25.5[12, 26]
Russia	1990	...	...	...	...	...	...	...	...	...	...	...	...	...	...	...
Rwanda	1984	1,112	1.2	56.8	26.8[110]	—16.4[111]—					50.9	—	—	1.4	—	47.7[42]
St. Kitts and Nevis	1981	...	...	...	...	...	...	...	...	...	46.8[12]	48.0[12]	—	5.2[12]	—	—
St. Lucia	1986	12	2.0	75.9[48]	10.3[58]	4.9[59]	0.9	0.3[18]	0.2[19]	0.4[20]	72.0	—	—	15.5	—	12.5
St. Vincent	1985–86	8[61]	1.8[61]	48.0[61, 81]	40.7[61, 112]	8.5[61, 58]	2.4[9, 61]	—0.5[10, 61]—			62.0[61]	—	—	8.8[61]	—	19.2[61]
San Marino	1975	0.7	7.0	21.3	47.8	—24.7—		5.1	—1.1—		39.9[12]	15.5[12]	—	29.9[12]	—	14.7[12]
São Tomé and Príncipe	1964	11.1	8.7	88.5	9.8	0.7	0.2	0.2	0.2	0.4	77.2	—	—	20.5	—	2.3
Saudi Arabia	1982–83	212	10.1	36.6	35.8	11.3	8.2	5.0	2.6	0.5	85.9	—	—	2.6	—	11.5
Senegal	1976	362	7.0	—99.4—					—0.6—		...	...	0.6	...	...	99.4
Seychelles	1977	4.9	1.5	...	...	...	...	...	...	...	...	...	...	...	...	...
Sierra Leone	1971	286	1.8	38.8	55.0	—6.1—		—0.1—			93.6	—	—	6.4	—	—
Singapore	1973	16	0.8	77.4	22.2	0.3	—0.1—				7.4	—	—	88.8	—	3.8
Slovakia[43]	1991	...	...	...	...	...	...	...	...	...	...	...	...	...	...	...
Slovenia[29]	1981	192	...	31.8	34.0	17.0	11.7	—4.7—			100.0	—	—	—	—	—
Solomon Islands	1975[89]	92	1.0	...	...	...	...	...	...	...	—	—	—	—	100.0	—
Somalia	1984	198	3.6	...	...	...	...	...	...	...	99.9	0.1	—	—	—	—
South Africa	1978	72	1,193	...	...	...	...	...	...	...	...	...	...	...	...	...
Bophuthatswana	1976	...	...	...	...	...	...	...	...	...	...	...	...	...	...	...
Ciskei	1986	...	...	...	...	...	...	...	...	...	...	...	...	...	...	...
Transkei	1976	...	...	...	...	...	...	...	...	...	...	...	...	...	...	...
Venda	1976	53.3	9.3	...	...	...	...	...	...	...	...	...	...	...	...	...
Spain	1982	2,375	18.7	26.4	37.1	14.0	10.2	7.1	3.9	1.3	75.4	...	...	4.0	—	20.6
Sri Lanka	1982	1,817	1.1	77.5[7]	—22.2[113]—		0.1[114]	0.1[18]	—0.1[60]—		77.1[6]	6.4[6]	0.1[6]	14.4[6]	—	2.0[6]
Sudan, The	1982	...	...	...	...	...	...	...	...	...	22.3	2.2	—	28.0	42.0	5.5
Suriname	1981	22	7.5	21.9[83]	61.2[83]	11.1[83]	3.6[83]	1.6[83]	0.3[83]	0.3[83]	20.2[83]	0.9[83]	—	49.5[83]	—	29.4[83]
Swaziland	1972	39	19.5	26.2	60.4	—12.0—				1.4	86.1	—	—	3.4	—	10.5
Sweden	1990[47]	97	29.5	...	15.5	19.7	21.6	27.3	15.0	0.9	47.7[2]	—	—	15.4[2]	—	36.8[2, 42]
Switzerland	1985	119	9.1	23.1	18.7	14.6	27.5	15.2	0.9	—	36.2[31]	—	0.8[31]	58.5[31]	—	4.5[31]
Syria	1988	444	8.9	16.7	36.8[21]	22.8[59]	13.1	8.5	2.0[115]	0.2[116]	65.8[12, 97]	1.8[12]	32.5[12]	...	—	—
Taiwan	1989	723	1.2	72.6	27.4	...	...	...	...	...	86.4	—	—	3.7	—	9.9
Tajikistan	1990	...	...	...	...	...	...	...	...	...	...	...	...	...	...	...
Tanzania	1986–87	3,626	0.9[3]	70.1	28.8	1.0	—0.1—				87.3[61]	—	—	3.6[61]	—	9.1[61]
Thailand	1988	4,877	3.7	14.3	72.0[117]	—13.1[118]—		—0.5[119]—			87.0	—	—	3.6	—	9.3
Togo	1982–83	263	1.5	48.8	38.6[93]	—12.7[94]—					70.7[12]	—	—	21.1[12]	8.2[12]	—
Tonga	1985	10.1	3.3	18.9	67.9	12.7	—	0.5	—	—	—97.2—			—	—	2.8
Trinidad and Tobago	1982	30.6	4.3	35.1	50.7	9.6	4.1	—	0.4	0.1	52.1	—	—	36.5	—	11.4
Tunisia	1988	376	13.6	—45.7—		20.6	17.9	11.4	—4.4—		...	...	...	...	...	...
Turkey	1980	3,651	6.2	15.8	46.3	20.2	11.6	5.3	0.8	—	88.6	—	—	12.1	—	1.2
Turkmenistan	1990	...	...	...	...	...	...	...	...	...	...	...	...	...	...	...
Tuvalu	1976	1.5	1.7	...	...	...	...	...	...	...	99.9	...	...	...	0.1	—
Uganda	1964	1,171	3.9	20.7	59.8	11.2	—8.3—				97.4	—	—	—	—	2.6
Ukraine	1990	...	...	...	...	...	...	...	...	...	...	...	...	...	...	...
United Arab Emirates	1986–87	17.9	2.3	45.4	38.8[121]	—15.9[122]—					...	...	...	...	...	...
United Kingdom	1991	241	107.3[123]	5.8[25, 48]	8.3[25, 56]	12.6[25]	16.4[25]	24.9[25]	26.1[25]	5.8[25]	—73.1[25, 124]—		—	26.9[25, 124]	—	—
United States	1987	2,088	187.0	—8.7[82]—		—19.8[9]—		30.9[125]	22.9[126]	17.7[127]	52.8	6.1	—	11.5	—	29.2
Uruguay	1986	57	280.5	—	9.0	13.0	12.8	16.0	22.8	26.3	—59.1[31]—		—	17.3[31]	—	23.6[31]
Uzbekistan	1990	...	...	...	...	...	...	...	...	...	...	...	...	...	...	...
Vanuatu	1983–84	27	6.9	...	...	...	...	...	...	...	65.3[31]	34.7[31]	—	...	...	...
Venezuela	1984–85	381	82.0	8.3	36.3	15.7	13.0	10.4	9.3	7.1	61.5[41]	...	—	6.1[41]	...	31.3[32, 41]
Vietnam	1991	31[34]	28.0[3]	...	...	...	...	...	...	...	—	—100—		—	—	—
Virgin Islands (U.S.)	1987	0.3	27.0	30.0[128]	30.3[129]	12.0	13.9	6.0	3.7[130]	4.1[131]	75.3	...	—	8.6	—	16.1
West Bank	1965	55	3.4	49.8	34.4	10.6	4.0	1.0	0.2	0.0	7.16	—	—	6.4	—	22.0
Western Sahara	1983	...	...	...	...	...	...	...	...	...	...	...	...	...	...	...
Western Samoa	1989	11	6.1	...	...	...	...	...	...	...	...	...	...	...	86.0	14.0
Yemen[132]	1977–83	591	2.3	57.5	30.9	7.4	3.3	0.8	0.1	—	90.3[12]	—	—	9.4[12]	—	0.3[12]
Yugoslavia	1981	1,198	...	24.7	48.8	19.9	4.4	—0.7—			100.0	—	—	—	—	—
Zaire	1970	2,538	2.3	41.6	57.3	1.0	0.2	—	—	—	4.2	0.1	—	...	95.6	0.1
Zambia	1971	768	3.1	50.5	45.2	—3.8—		—0.5—			...	...	...	...	...	...
Zimbabwe	1974	765	38.7	—16.7[78]—			52.8[135]	29.8[136]	—0.7[17]—		—2.0—		—	—	98.0	—

[1]1967. [2]1989. [3]Cultivated area only. [4]Based on value of output by sector. [5]1987. [6]1973. [7]Less than 1.2 ha. [8]1.2 to 4.0 ha. [9]4.0 to 20 ha. [10]20 ha or more. [11]Percentage of farms having irrigation. [12]Based on area, not number, of holdings. [13]10 to 25 ha. [14]25 to 50 ha. [15]1974. [16]50 to 100 ha. [17]100 ha or more. [18]20 to 40 ha. [19]40 to 61 ha. [20]61 ha or more. [21]1.0 to 4.0 ha. [22]4.0 to 10.1 ha. [23]10.1 ha or more. [24]1977. [25]1988. [26]1985. [27]1982. [28]4 ha or more. [29]Holdings and tenure refer to private plots only; land use 1990. [30]Includes about 21,000 farms without land; distribution by size refers to traditional farms with land only. [31]1980. [32]Almost all squatters. [33]1970. [34]State farms and cooperatives only. [35]Precollectivization. [36]4.0 to 52.2 ha. [37]52.2 ha and over. [38]Irrigated land only. [39]1968. [40]1984. [41]1971. [42]Owned and rented holdings. [43]Data for Czech Republic include Slovakia. [44]Less than 0.5 ha. [45]0.5 to 50 ha. [46]50 to 1,000 ha. [47]Arable area only. [48]Less than 2.0 ha. [49]2.0 to 20 ha. [50]2.1 ha or less. [51]2.1 to 4.2 ha. [52]4.2 ha or more. [53]Data for Ethiopia include Eritrea; values shown for Ethiopia would remain broadly representative for Eritrea. [54]1983. [55]Excludes holdings of less than 1.0 ha. [56]2.0 to 5.0 ha. [57]1991. [58]2.0 to 4.0 ha. [59]4.0 to 10 ha. [60]40 ha or more. [61]1972. [62]Commercial farms only. [63]Less than 0.7 ha. [64]0.7 to 7.1 ha. [65]7.1 to 45 ha. [66]45 ha or more. [67]Excludes holdings of 0.04 ha (500 sq m) or less. [68]1990. [69]1979. [70]1981. [71]Excludes state of Punjab. [72]Less than

activity (% of farms)			technology (latest)				farmland use: land in farms		land use (%): cropland							country
mainly crops	mainly livestock	mixed/other	tractors (per 1,000 ha)	electricity (% of farms having)	irrigation (% of land irrig.)	artificial fertilizer (kg/ha)	total ('000 ha)	% of total land area	permanent crops	temporary crops	fallow	total cropland	meadows and pastures	woodland and forest	other	
...	...	...	2.5	...	...	...	...	...	...	...	...	...	...	...	...	Netherlands Antilles
...	...	...	135	...	...	60	293	15.8	51.7	34.8	13.5	6.5	93.5	...	...	New Caledonia
13.9	65.5	20.6	193	...	73	741	17,450	64.5	13.0[5]	87.0[5]	—	1.9[5]	98.1[5]	...	...	New Zealand
...	...	...	2.4	...	8	28	5,651	47.7	...	...	...	...	...	...	...	Nicaragua
...	...	...	0.08	...	5	1	3,407	2.9	...	...	...	...	...	...	...	Niger
...	...	...	0.4	...	3	12	34,290	37.1	—20.0—		80.0	31.4	27.5	41.1	...	Nigeria
64.3[4]	35.7[4]	—	22	45	...	...	5.8	12.2	...	...	...	32.9	30.2	—36.9—		Northern Mariana Is.
24.3[4]	70.6[4]	3.9[4]	180	...	11	242	20,570	63.5	0.4	98.5	1.0	4.3	0.6	34.2	60.9	Norway
...	...	...	9.2	...	87	111	83	0.3	68.6	31.4	—	49.2		—50.8—		Oman
...	...	...	13.1	...	82	91	19,109	24.0	—83.7—		16.3	93.8	...	0.6	5.6	Pakistan
...	...	...	10.1	0.5[41]	6	58	2,942	39.0	23.7	41.3	35.0	22.2	50.0	24.1	3.6	Panama
...	...	...	30.8	...	...	40	386	0.8	100.0	—	—	33.7	26.4	...	39.9	Papua New Guinea
33.0	—67.0—		7.4	...	3	9	21,941	53.9	4.2	76.6	19.2	12.6	47.5	38.5	1.4	Paraguay
4.9	93.0	2.1	4.9	6.5	37	41	14,893	11.6	24.1	75.9	—	27.1	47.5	19.8	5.6	Peru
98.2	1.5	0.3	2.4	...	35	67	9,034	30.1	57.5	42.5	—	86.3	6.8	—6.9—		Philippines
53.8[4]	46.2[4]	—	82.1	...	0.7	219	18,720	59.9	1.9	—98.1—		78.3	21.7	...	...	Poland
...	...	...	5.9	...	27	73	5,183	56.1	26.1	44.6	29.3	52.6	3.2	34.5	9.7	Portugal
61.0	33.4	5.6	58.8	...	58	...	349	39.3	—70.4—		29.6	28.0	46.4	19.1	6.6	Puerto Rico
50.4[4]	49.6[4]	—	15.8	...	100	230	5.7	0.5	25.2	74.8	—	100.0	—	—	—	Qatar
...	...	...	48.7	...	13	282	212.6	84.4	2.6	44.1	53.3	53.9	4.8	41.3	...	Réunion
...	...	...	14.1	...	34	133	14,759	61.9	4.0	96.0	—	77.9	22.1	—	—	Romania
...	...	...	10.2	...	5	...	213,700	12.5	...	...	...	61.7	37.5	—	0.8	Russia
...	...	...	0.1	...	0.5	1	1,350	51.3	—85.6—		14.4	63.7	10.6	5.2	20.5	Rwanda
...	...	...	27.0	...	...	...	12	45.3	31.5	—68.5—		58.1		—41.9—		St. Kitts and Nevis
25.0[15]	—75.0[15]—		17.4	...	20	...	23	38.0	68.5[15]	—31.5[15]—		57.9[15]	10.2[15]	26.4[15]	5.5[15]	St. Lucia
...	...	...	19.5	...	25	...	17.9	34.8	64.3	16.1	19.6	84.3	15.7	...	...	St. Vincent
...	...	...	...	...	...	...	4.7	76.5	60.9	6.5	32.6	69.2	6	8.2	16.4	San Marino
...	...	...	62.5	...	6	...	96	100.0	99.4	—0.6—		38.3	...	59.7	2.0	São Tomé and Príncipe
...	...	...	0.9	...	41	401	2,135	1.0	4.1	18.7	77.2	88.5		—11.5—		Saudi Arabia
...	...	...	0.2	...	8	2	11,338	59.1	0.1	—99.9—		22.4	77.6	...	...	Senegal
1.8	32.4	65.8	40.0	...	...	...	7.5	27.8	89.6	—10.4—		100.0	—	—	—	Seychelles
50.3	—49.7—		1.1	...	7	1	2,732	38.1	20.7	—79.3—		19.3	80.7	...	...	Sierra Leone
12.5	6.2	81.3	64.0	...	100	5,600	5.6[40]	9.0[40]	75.0	25.0	—	66.7	...	33.3	...	Singapore
...	...	...	14.4	...	...	123	2,448	49.9	3.2	92.1	4.7	67.0	33.0	—	—	Slovakia[43]
...	...	...	...	...	...	...	866	42.8	19.0	80.0	1.0	35.2	64.7	—	0.1	Slovenia[29]
43.4	—56.6—		...	...	...	...	93	3.4	40.0	45.2	14.8	100.0	—	—	—	Solomon Islands
20.0	60.0	20.0	2.1	...	12	3	...	...	...	...	...	...	...	...	...	Somalia
...	...	...	13.5	...	9	59	85,447	70.2	5.9	—94.1—		11.9	79.7	1.3	7.1	South Africa
...	...	...	...	...	1	...	3,839	94.8	...	87.1	...	2.4	97.6	...	...	Bophuthatswana
...	...	...	...	...	—	...	770	95.3	9.7	80.3	—	10.0	90.0	...	...	Ciskei
...	...	...	...	...	3	...	622	14.9	...	...	...	100.0	—	—	—	Transkei
...	...	...	0.3	...	1	4.8	500	64.9	25.4	63.6	11.0	9.2	90.8	...	...	Venda
...	...	...	49.5	...	22	101	44,312	87.8	23.8	55.8	20.4	40.9	12.5	21.7	24.9	Spain
...	...	...	34.7	...	57	111	2,009	30.6	56.4	43.6	—	86.0	1.0	2.7	8.8	Sri Lanka
...	...	...	0.8	...	15	4	31,500	13.3	0.8	88.7	10.5	23.8	76.2	...	...	Sudan, The
33.0[83]	12.5[83]	54.5[83]	22.8	...	100	26	165	1.0	15.0	53.0	32.0	40.4	23.1	19.1	17.4	Suriname
39.7	—60.3—		17.3	...	31	46	766,775	44.6	2.0	81.1	16.9	19.7	60.6	12.0	7.7	Swaziland
17.3[105]	39.5[105]	33.9[105]	65.2	...	4	127	8,253	21.7	...	91.0	9.0	34.8	4.0	50.3	10.9	Sweden
35.5[31]	—64.5[31]—		292	...	6	430	1,203	29.1	6.7	66.2	27.1	36.1	53.4	10.5	...	Switzerland
...	...	...	15.4	...	14	45	6,065	32.8	—77.3—		22.7	91.7	...	...	8.3	Syria
41.9	30.3	27.8	...	...	38	400[88]	2,827	78.5	27.5	72.5	—	31.7	...	65.7	2.4	Taiwan
...	...	...	41.7	...	78	...	4,300	30.1	...	...	...	18.6	76.7	—	4.7	Tajikistan
44.1	4.7	51.2	2.5	...	6	9	7,545[61]	8.5[61]	19.1[61]	72.5[61]	8.4[61]	49.8[61]	10.2[61]	24.7[61]	15.3[61]	Tanzania
...	...	...	8.2	...	22	36	14,178	27.6	13.5	—86.5—		93.8	0.9	2.1	3.2	Thailand
...	...	...	0.6	...	1	8	406	7.1	17.3[24]	—82.7[24]—		71.0[24]	29.0[24]	...	...	Togo
...	—	...	6.8	...	...	2	33	44.5	—62.7—		37.3	81.2	6.7	10.1	1.9	Tonga
63.7[120]	—36.3[120]—		35.5	40.7	30	57	132	25.8	55.9	—44.1—		62.3	4.4	6.1	27.2	Trinidad and Tobago
...	...	...	8.8	...	8	22	9,449	61.1	31.1	48.3	20.6	78.2	21.8	...	...	Tunisia
11.5	2.5	86.0	28.4	...	10	64	30,732	39.9	17.5	71.0	11.5	85.4	7.3	1.7	5.4	Turkey
...	...	...	43.3	...	107	...	35,800	73.4	...	...	...	3.4	96.1	—	0.5	Turkmenistan
...	...	...	...	...	...	...	...	...	...	...	...	...	...	...	...	Tuvalu
...	...	...	0.9	...	0.2	...	2,262	11.3	29.8	70.2	—	100.0	—	—	—	Uganda
...	...	...	12.5	...	7	...	41,400	68.5	...	...	...	80.7	16.9	—	2.4	Ukraine
...	...	...	6.3	...	17	311	17.5[88]	0.2[88]	64.8[88]	18.2[88]	17.1[88]	97.6[88]	...	1.3[88]	1.1[88]	United Arab Emirates
...	...	...	76.3	...	3	376	18,498	75.8	0.7	98.3	1.0	35.8	60.4	—3.8—		United Kingdom
40.7	55.4	3.8	25.6	68.8	10	99	390,316	41.0	1.0	90.5	8.5	46.0	42.5	8.3	3.2	United States
37.1[31]	58.7[31]	4.2[31]	25.7	...	10	54	15,882	90.7	3.1	—96.9—		8.8	85.3	4.2	1.7	Uruguay
...	...	...	41.3	...	91	...	26,600	59.4	...	...	...	16.9	81.2	—	1.9	Uzbekistan
92.2	7.2	0.6	3.8	...	...	...	183	15.0	62.5	3.0	34.5	84.9	15.1	...	...	Vanuatu
27.6	9.0	63.4	15.1	...	6	138	31,278	34.3	19.0[41]	59.0[41]	22.0[41]	13.2[41]	57.0[41]	22.8[41]	7.0[41]	Venezuela
74.5[4]	25.5[4]	—	5.5	...	35	82	9,060	27.4	7.4	—92.6—		100.0	...	...	...	Vietnam
48.3	40.8	10.9	15.4	15.4	...	...	7.2	20.9	18.3	13.7	68.0	10.7	75.3	10.3	3.7	Virgin Islands (U.S.)
...	...	...	14.1[27]	...	5	...	185[31]	31.4[31]	62.2[31]	37.8[31]	—	100.0[31]	—	—	—	West Bank
...	...	...	...	...	...	...	5,002	18.8	—	—	—	—	100.0	...	...	Western Sahara
...	...	...	0.6	...	...	...	70[80]	24.8[80]	71.2[80]	28.8[80]	—	93.8[80]	6.2[80]	...	...	Western Samoa
35.5[12, 133]	56.9[12, 133]	7.6[12, 133]	3.6	...	21	12	1,351	0.1	6.7	69.7	23.6	98.8	...	...	1.2	Yemen[140]
12.7[83, 134]	–87.3[83, 134]–		151	...	2	115	6,238	61.1	8.8	89.3	1.9	65.4	34.0	—	0.6	Yugoslavia
92.3	—9.7—		0.3	...	0.2	1	5,897	2.6	7.7	—92.3—		70.6	20.1	2.0	7.3	Zaire
15.8	9.7	74.5	1.1	...	0.6	15	938	1.3	4.5	—95.5—		14.2	38.1	...	47.7	Zambia
1.8[12, 88]	26.7[12, 88]	71.5[12, 88]	7.5	...	8	53	29,620	76.6	2.5	—97.5—		34.5	65.7	...	...	Zimbabwe

2.5 ha. [73]2.5 to 7.5 ha. [74]7.5 to 12.5 ha. [75]12.5 to 20 ha. [76]50 to 250 ha. [77]250 ha or more. [78]Less than 8.0 ha. [79]8.0 to 20 ha. [80]1975. [81]Less than 0.4 ha. [82]0.4 to 4.0 ha. [83]1969. [84]Less than 4.5 ha. [85]4.5 to 9.0 ha. [86]9.0 to 18 ha. [87]18 ha or more. [88]1978. [89]Excludes large commercial farms. [90]5.0 to 8.0 ha. [91]8.0 ha or more. [92]Excludes temporary rangeland available for agricultural use to subsistence farms. [93]1.0 to 3.0 ha. [94]3.0 ha or more. [95]West Malaysia except as noted. [96]Malaysia. [97]Includes some rented farms. [98]Preliminary 1991 census reported 4,310,000 farms and an average size of 50 ha. [99]Family farms only. [100]4.0 to 8.0 ha. [101]Less than 0.8 ha. [102]0.8 to 4.0 ha. [103]10 to 25 ha. [104]25 to 50 ha. [105]Large holdings only. [106]1.0 to 3.9 ha. [107]3.9 to 7.9 ha. [108]7.9 to 19.7 ha. [109]19.7 to 40 ha. [110]1.0 to 2.0 ha. [111]2.0 ha or more. [112]0.4 to 2.0 ha. [113]1.2 to 12 ha. [114]12 to 20 ha. [115]50 to 300 ha. [116]300 ha or more. [117]1.0 to 6.4 ha. [118]6.4 to 22.4 ha. [119]22.4 ha or more. [120]1963. [121]1.0 to 7.5 ha. [122]7.5 ha or more. [123]Full-time operations only. [124]Excludes Northern Ireland. [125]20 to 72 ha. [126]72 to 202 ha. [127]202 ha or more. [128]Less than 3.0 ha. [129]3.0 to 10 ha. [130]100 to 260 ha. [131]260 ha or more. [132]Former Yemen Arab Republic only. [133]1976. [134]Data refer to Yugoslavia as constituted prior to 1991. [135]8.0 to 16 ha. [136]16 to 100 ha.

Crops and livestock

This table provides comparative data for selected categories of agricultural production for the countries of the world. The data are taken mainly from the United Nations Food and Agriculture Organization's (FAO) annual *Production Yearbook.*

The FAO depends largely on questionnaires supplied to each country for its statistics, but, where no official or semiofficial responses are returned, the FAO makes estimates, using incomplete, unofficial, or other similarly limited data. And, although the FAO provides standardized guidelines upon which many nations have organized their data collection systems and methods, persistent, often traditional, variations in standards of coverage, methodology, and reporting periods reduce the comparability of statistics that *can* be supplied on such forms. FAO data are based on calendar-year periods; that is, data for any particular crop refer to the calendar year in which the harvest (or the bulk of the harvest) occurred.

In spite of the often tragic food shortages in a number of countries in recent years, worldwide agricultural production is probably more often underreported than overreported. Many countries do not report complete domestic production. Some countries, for example, report only crops that are sold commercially and ignore subsistence crops produced for family or communal consumption, or barter; others may limit reporting to production for export only, to holdings above a certain size, or represent a sampling only.

Methodological problems attach to much smaller elements of the agricultural whole, however. The FAO's cereals statistics relate, ideally, to weight or volume of crops harvested for dry grain (excluding cereal crops used for grazing, harvested for hay, or harvested green for food, feed, or silage). Some countries, however, collect the basic data they report to the FAO on sown or cultivated areas instead and calculate production statistics from estimates of yield. Millet and sorghum, which in many European and North American countries are used primarily as livestock or poultry feed, may be reportable by such countries as animal fodder only, while elsewhere many nations use the same grains for human consumption and report them as cereals. Statistics for tropical fruits are frequently not compiled by producing countries, and coverage is not uniform, with some countries reporting only commercial fruits and others including those consumed for subsistence as well. Figures on wild fruits and berries are seldom included

Crops and livestock

country	crops																	
	grains				roots and tubers[a]				pulses[b]				fruits[c]		vegetables[d]			
	production ('000 metric tons)		yield (kg/hectare)		production ('000 metric tons)		yield (kg/hectare)		production ('000 metric tons)		yield (kg/hectare)		production ('000 metric tons)		production ('000 metric tons)			
	1979–81 average	1992	1979–81 average	1992	1979–81 average	1992	1979–81 average	1992	1979–81 average	1992	1979–81 average	1992	1979–81 average	1992	1979–81 average	1992		
Afghanistan	4,060	2,420	1,337	1,105	265	224	14,881	16,842	41	37	989	997	807	614	516	490		
Albania	916	588	2,500	2,736	112	60	6,967	6,667	23	14	493	560	146	129	333	248		
Algeria	1,958	3,219	656	1,012	540	900	6,878	8,182	52	47	431	403	1,197	1,084	824	1,966		
American Samoa	...	...	...	...	3	2	4,116	3,361	...	...	...	...	2	1	...	...		
Andorra	...	...	...	...	...	...	...	...	...	...	...	...	...	...	...	...		
Angola	379	465	533	453	1,820	2,095	3,562	3,816	42	36	385	267	432	425	231	235		
Antigua and Barbuda	—	—	1,809	1,833	—	—	4,673	5,156	...	...	...	...	9	8	1	2		
Argentina	24,457	24,750	2,183	3,026	2,328	3,200	14,087	19,104	239	276	918	1,272	6,258	5,731	2,279	2,834		
Armenia	270	275	1,783	1,905	240	343	12,213	13,720	5,556	—	1	—	407	315	468	472		
Aruba	...	...	...	...	...	...	...	...	...	...	...	...	...	...	...	...		
Australia	21,150	24,939	1,321	1,764	843	1,139	23,413	25,631	192	1,661	912	1,059	2,124	2,608	1,044	1,591		
Austria	4,391	4,310	4,130	5,137	1,356	780	25,387	23,611	23	108	2,876	3,484	951	870	666	452		
Azerbaijan	1,105	1,305	2,253	2,161	142	170	7,359	8,500	2,167	—	9	—	1,647	1,580	852	880		
Bahamas, The	1	1	1,142	1,262	2	2	8,998	9,242	1	1	1,238	1,309	12	12	28	27		
Bahrain	...	...	...	...	—	—	19,048	15,833	—	—	917	1,111	35	23	15	10		
Bangladesh	20,983	28,538	1,938	2,640	1,705	1,850	10,062	10,477	637	506	646	719	1,304	1,358	1,066	1,386		
Barbados	2	2	2,538	2,500	11	7	11,653	8,247	1	1	1,209	1,254	3	3	10	7		
Belarus	4,108	6,340	1,438	2,508	12,672	8,000	16,085	10,453	101	300	496	1,765	510	280	799	850		
Belgium[3]	2,069	2,244	4,861	6,513	1,468	1,800	39,246	36,000	7	19	3,080	3,673	386	658	955	1,567		
Belize	27	27	1,924	1,559	3	4	20,000	21,875	1	2	526	686	72	148	3	5		
Benin	366	541	698	858	1,363	2,139	7,449	9,358	34	57	445	560	142	164	121	233		
Bermuda	...	...	...	...	1	1	9,041	20,636	...	...	...	...	1	—	2	3		
Bhutan	159	106	1,439	1,087	40	55	6,767	10,596	2	2	592	800	29	73	11	10		
Bolivia	663	761	1,183	1,331	1,063	1,298	5,185	6,935	18	31	1,014	1,083	547	940	317	393		
Bosnia and Herzegovina	...	1,348	...	3,634	...	296	...	5,611	—	23	—	985	—	168	—	153		
Botswana	35	15	203	252	7	8	5,513	6,154	19	12	622	400	9	11	16	16		
Brazil	30,805	44,165	1,496	2,138	27,265	26,005	11,570	12,095	2,206	2,832	464	539	18,607	32,279	4,089	5,487		
Brunei	3	1	1,640	1,625	1	1	1,470	2,813	...	...	...	...	5	5	8	8		
Bulgaria	8,130	6,845	3,853	3,506	376	550	10,175	11,458	68	68	984	937	1,975	1,152	2,021	1,404		
Burkina Faso	1,166	2,332	575	850	126	90	8,927	5,696	46	120	1,004	1,003	56	72	155	245		
Burundi	219	309	1,081	1,422	1,052	1,487	6,956	7,622	324	383	941	930	1,164	1,735	151	230		
Cambodia	1,438	2,304	1,056	1,223	178	117	6,569	5,087	17	47	635	1,022	121	254	323	478		
Cameroon	866	905	849	1,160	1,663	1,952	3,994	5,135	105	76	542	514	1,715	1,552	370	459		
Canada	42,730	49,147	2,174	2,450	2,626	3,529	23,818	28,482	199	944	1,577	1,612	697	766	1,747	1,869		
Cape Verde	6	6	465	464	15	10	3,598	3,497	4	—	286	—	12	11	5	11		
Central African Republic	103	74	529	620	1,106	866	3,270	3,481	7	15	556	1,013	163	197	44	64		
Chad	508	915	587	648	424	643	4,505	5,496	59	60	434	435	97	116	59	74		
Chile	1,742	2,901	2,124	4,177	901	1,030	10,262	16,255	171	147	843	1,267	1,657	2,920	1,760	2,093		
China	286,456	400,409	3,027	4,397	144,326	147,898	13,612	15,203	6,648	6,513	1,223	1,478	8,820	23,102	79,707	119,786		
Colombia	3,339	3,674	2,452	2,550	4,144	4,021	11,043	11,959	128	181	604	796	3,905	5,555	1,362	1,435		
Comoros	18	14	1,058	1,298	57	59	3,660	5,327	5	8	1,237	833	36	56	3	4		
Congo	15	27	780	844	679	857	6,685	7,849	5	10	572	838	126	184	33	43		
Costa Rica	337	249	2,498	3,415	45	125	5,764	17,055	12	36	498	563	1,362	2,131	58	135		
Côte d'Ivoire	866	1,191	867	869	3,414	4,096	5,154	5,198	8	8	667	667	1,549	1,678	317	446		
Croatia	...	2,355	...	3,974	...	480	...	7,895	—	26	—	1,057	—	552	—	203		
Cuba	551	404	2,458	2,149	997	813	6,092	5,228	12	25	306	342	810	1,478	466	585		
Cyprus	87	182	1,793	2,980	182	172	23,108	20,023	6	2	1,047	1,149	359	345	101	128		
Czech Republic[4]	9,762	10,319	3,798	4,300	3,388	2,686	16,730	16,183	137	288	1,692	2,375	644	958	1,017	1,125		
Denmark	7,346	7,106	4,040	4,389	913	1,500	26,904	33,782	14	318	3,420	2,607	124	68	263	314		
Djibouti	—	—	833	3,000	...	...	...	...	...	...	...	...	...	...	13	22		
Dominica	—	—	1,427	1,364	26	26	11,085	9,463	—	—	467	450	46	96	7	7		
Dominican Republic	447	576	3,004	4,091	214	347	5,783	6,706	73	135	958	1,481	1,333	1,210	209	266		
Ecuador	686	1,557	1,633	1,961	552	474	9,595	6,260	39	35	547	440	3,769	4,836	243	371		
Egypt	8,134	14,702	4,053	5,869	1,330	2,019	18,336	20,897	283	455	2,000	2,308	2,310	4,798	7,345	9,358		
El Salvador	719	992	1,702	2,039	27	53	12,350	16,561	41	62	850	780	257	316	96	122		
Equatorial Guinea	...	...	...	...	53	82	2,926	2,645	...	...	...	...	11	17	...	...		
Eritrea[5]	...	...	...	...	...	...	...	...	...	...	...	...	...	...	...	...		
Estonia	796	594	1,862	1,325	1,031	648	14,257	14,499	1	—	1,333	1,278	46	24	117	115		
Ethiopia[5]	5,804	7,000	1,186	1,338	1,631	2,074	3,703	3,565	962	815	1,061	881	201	234	501	599		
Faeroe Islands	...	...	...	...	1	2	13,684	...	...	...	...	...	...	...	...	...		

in national reports at all. FAO vegetable statistics include vegetables and melons grown for human consumption only. Some countries do not make this distinction in their reports, and some exclude the production of kitchen gardens and small family plots, although in certain countries, such small-scale production may account for 20 to 40 percent of total output.

Livestock statistics may be distorted by the timing of country reports. Ireland, for example, takes a livestock enumeration in December that is reported the following year and that appears low against data for otherwise comparable countries because of the slaughter and export of animals at the close of the grazing season. It balances this, however, with a June enumeration, when numbers tend to be high. Milk production as defined by the FAO includes whole fresh milk, excluding milk sucked by young animals but including amounts fed by farmers or ranchers to livestock, but national practices vary. Certain countries do not distinguish between milk cows and other cattle, so that yield per dairy cow must be estimated. Some countries do not report egg production statistics (here given in metric tons), and external estimates must be based on the numbers of chickens and reported or assumed egg-laying rates. Other countries report egg production by number, and this must be converted to weight, using conversion factors specific to the makeup by species of national poultry flocks.

Metric system units used in the table may be converted to English system units as follows:

metric tons × 1.1023 = short tons
kilograms × 2.2046 = pounds
kilograms per hectare × 0.8922 = pounds per acre.

The notes that follow, keyed by references in the table headings, provide further definitional information.

a. Includes such crops as potatoes and cassava.
b. Includes beans and peas harvested for dry grain only. Does not include green beans and green peas.
c. Excludes melons.
d. Includes melons, green beans, and green peas.
e. From milk cows only.
f. From chickens only.

livestock														country
cattle		sheep		hogs		chickens		milk[e]				eggs[f]		
stock ('000 head)		stock ('000 head)		stock ('000 head)		stock ('000 head)		production ('000 metric tons)		yield (kg/animal)		production (metric tons)		
1979–81 average	1992	1979–81 average	1992	1979–81 average	1992	1979–81 average	1992	1979–81 average	1992	1979–81 average	1992	1979–81 average	1992	
3,723	1,650	18,667	13,500	...	...	6,000	7,000	552	340	491	430	14,000	14,200	Afghanistan
606	500	1,232	1,000	174	170	3,000	5,000	296	338	1,326	1,300	9,957	11,000	Albania
1,356	1,420	13,111	18,600	4	6	24,000	76,000	514	650	975	970	24,550	135,000	Algeria
...	...	...	...	10	11	49[1]	50[2]	—	—	800	800	34	30	American Samoa
...	...	...	...	...	...	...	...	...	...	...	...	...	...	Andorra
3,117	3,200	225	250	600	810	5,000	6,000	146	148	500	502	3,650	3,900	Angola
14	16	12	13	4	4	62[1]	80[2]	6	6	977	1,058	138	120	Antigua and Barbuda
55,620	50,020	31,473	23,711	3,751	4,770	38,000	58,000	5,311	6,700	1,746	2,343	253,731	327,600	Argentina
766	550	2,242	980	231	200	9,000	9,000	501	300	1,677	1,500	25,367	22,000	Armenia
...	...	...	...	...	...	...	...	...	...	...	...	...	...	Aruba
26,161	23,602	134,871	146,820	2,416	2,758	46,000	59,000	5,598	6,940	2,994	4,260	197,870	211,000	Australia
2,553	2,532	193	323	3,906	3,629	15,000	13,000	3,434	3,300	3,509	3,709	96,804	93,000	Austria
1,765	1,800	5,128	5,088	179	100	17,000	27,000	800	800	1,208	1,143	40,200	49,400	Azerbaijan
4	5	35	40	18	20	1,000	2,000	3	3	1,000	1,000	356	420	Bahamas, The
6	15	7	9	...	...	—	1,000	6	19	2,703	2,629	3,238	2,950	Bahrain
25,053	23,700	750	700	...	...	59,000	62,000	833	770	221	206	39,745	44,000	Bangladesh
23	21	52	56	44	45	1,000	2,000	6	10	1,294	1,300	1,489	1,600	Barbados
6,760	6,600	525	400	4,520	4,700	35,000	50,000	6,082	5,894	2,215	2,563	166,267	189,800	Belarus
3,104	3,313	110	140	5,083	6,565	29,000	36,000	4,042	3,771	3,876	4,442	200,655	180,400	Belgium[3]
50	54	3	4	16	26	—	1,000	4	7	1,021	1,032	1,034	1,450	Belize
810	1,000	972	920	455	750	11,000	25,000	12	16	120	130	7,860	18,000	Benin
1	1	...	...	2	2	56[1]	50[2]	2	1	2,836	2,917	435	500	Bermuda
299	422	10	52	55	74	125[1]	...	26	29	257	257	159	340	Bhutan
4,570	5,779	8,967	7,300	1,553	2,226	7,000	28,000	71	120	1,396	1,412	22,500	57,000	Bolivia
—	826	...	1,287	...	590	...	8,000	...	705	...	1,533	...	20,000	Bosnia and Herzegovina
2,906	2,500	147	250	5	16	1,000	2,000	90	94	350	350	627	792	Botswana
116,645	153,000	18,414	19,500	34,102	33,050	426,000	570,000	11,378	15,500	712	795	765,117	1,455,000	Brazil
3	1	...	...	11	14	1,000	2,000	...	...	...	...	1,787	3,100	Brunei
1,782	1,311	10,358	6,703	3,803	3,010	29,000	36,000	1,843	1,550	2,638	2,981	131,679	88,300	Bulgaria
2,760	4,096	3,200	5,350	198	530	11,000	18,000	81	118	175	175	7,448	16,000	Burkina Faso
614	440	301	370	44	105	3,000	4,000	37	26	350	350	2,356	3,192	Burundi
831	2,274	—	—	205	1,729	3,000	8,000	14	20	170	198	5,400	14,000	Cambodia
3,521	4,730	2,167	3,560	1,139	1,380	8,000	19,000	88	118	500	500	8,400	12,400	Cameroon
13,328	13,002	729	914	9,709	10,395	96,000	118,000	7,354	7,380	4,137	5,348	330,863	317,060	Canada
12	19	1	6	40	86	...	1,000	1	1	500	500	65	400	Cape Verde
1,662	2,700	84	137	243	460	2,000	3,000	23	48	200	222	966	1,341	Central African Republic
4,360	4,507	2,620	2,043	9	14	3,000	4,000	118	121	270	270	2,850	3,780	Chad
3,650	3,461	6,059	6,600	1,068	1,330	18,000	35,000	1,111	1,540	1,561	1,812	66,046	103,938	Chile
52,567	82,760	101,864	111,143	313,660	379,739	860,000	2,179,000	1,143	5,223	1,802	1,564	2,325,749	7,027,500	China
24,110	24,772	2,399	2,553	2,013	2,644	30,000	44,000	2,187	4,214	965	951	176,972	267,350	Colombia
60	47	8	14	...	...	243[1]	362[2]	3	4	500	500	564	640	Comoros
64	69	69	110	28	55	1,000	2,000	1	1	500	500	825	1,200	Congo
2,183	1,707	2	3	223	225	5,000	4,000	318	470	1,067	1,478	16,760	21,185	Costa Rica
664	1,183	1,020	1,200	315	382	17,000	26,000	12	25	110	123	10,253	15,800	Côte d'Ivoire
...	590	...	539	...	1,183	...	13,000	...	645	...	1,864	...	38,700	Croatia
5,166	4,700	356	370	1,417	1,850	24,000	27,000	1,045	856	1,579	1,821	98,936	88,000	Cuba
22	57	290	310	162	285	2,000	3,000	33	113	3,601	4,788	5,309	8,000	Cyprus
4,935	4,325	883	886	7,694	7,139	46,000	48,000	5,830	5,300	3,140	3,369	243,327	260,000	Czech Republic[4]
2,970	2,185	55	160	9,699	10,345	15,000	15,000	5,126	4,600	4,920	6,166	77,130	88,000	Denmark
52	180	452	450	...	...	...	...	...	...	...	...	...	...	Djibouti
7	9	6	8	8	5	98[1]	117[2]	3	5	1,000	1,000	177	158	Dominica
1,918	2,356	65	122	298	750	12,000	30,000	427	350	1,742	1,699	19,267	38,000	Dominican Republic
2,987	4,665	1,148	1,511	3,417	2,434	33,000	59,000	924	1,510	1,446	2,097	43,056	57,000	Ecuador
1,906	3,016	1,791	4,350	20	115	28,000	36,000	648	691	674	658	78,100	127,440	Egypt
1,234	1,276	4	5	455	310	5,000	4,000	268	350	958	1,203	36,822	47,305	El Salvador
4	5	33	36	4	5	120[1]	195[2]	...	...	...	...	116	185	Equatorial Guinea
...	...	...	...	...	...	...	...	...	...	...	...	...	...	Eritrea[5]
821	708	164	143	1,038	799	6,000	5,000	1,149	900	3,633	3,600	29,267	24,100	Estonia
26,000	31,000	23,250	23,200	18	20	52,000	59,000	615	774	197	208	73,140	79,350	Ethiopia[5]
2	2	67	68	...	...	...	...	...	...	...	...	...	...	Faeroe Islands

Crops and livestock (continued)

country	crops															
	grains				roots and tubers[a]				pulses[b]				fruits[c]		vegetables[d]	
	production ('000 metric tons)		yield (kg/hectare)		production ('000 metric tons)		yield (kg/hectare)		production ('000 metric tons)		yield (kg/hectare)		production ('000 metric tons)		production ('000 metric tons)	
	1979–81 average	1992	1979–81 average	1992	1979–81 average	1992	1979–81 average	1992	1979–81 average	1992	1979–81 average	1992	1979–81 average	1992	1979–81 average	1992
Fiji	19	35	2,004	2,338	24	66	7,945	12,524	—	1	540	1,210	11	12	6	13
Finland	2,993	2,803	2,511	3,065	629	673	15,578	19,289	13	29	2,182	1,785	107	88	130	211
France	46,091	60,420	4,700	6,516	6,735	6,495	28,465	35,866	340	3,360	3,304	4,623	14,127	12,495	7,005	7,179
French Guiana	1	26	1,159	4,815	13	18	10,842	10,112	...	...	...	...	2	6	3	16
French Polynesia	...	...	...	...	19	12	12,245	9,200	...	...	...	...	4	10	6	7
Gabon	11	25	1,718	1,736	372	447	6,289	6,964	—	—	528	650	181	265	22	31
Gambia, The	78	123	1,189	1,160	6	6	3,000	3,000	4	4	267	267	4	4	7	8
Gaza Strip	5	1	2,793	529	5	22	18,333	22,000	—	—	3,071	—	200	118	61	100
Georgia	573	459	1,942	1,815	412	200	12,400	10,000	10	—	711	—	1,678	1,090	960	820
Germany	...	34,749	...	5,334	...	10,975	...	30,190	—	209	—	2,102	—	6,530	—	4,224
Ghana	726	970	807	970	3,183	6,200	6,721	6,596	14	20	101	100	966	1,342	299	443
Gibraltar	...	...	...	...	...	...	...	...	...	...	...	...	...	...	...	...
Greece	4,951	5,458	3,090	3,880	1,041	967	16,378	23,245	94	47	1,262	1,415	3,437	4,346	3,636	3,583
Greenland	...	...	...	...	...	...	...	...	...	...	...	...	...	...	...	...
Grenada	—	—	949	1,000	3	4	4,582	5,072	1	1	1,607	1,092	29	22	2	2
Guadeloupe	...	...	...	...	22	21	8,459	10,825	—	—	514	600	115	128	17	26
Guam	—	—	3,000	2,000	2	2	13,756	13,895	...	...	...	...	2	2	2	4
Guatemala	1,117	1,404	1,574	1,902	52	60	3,535	4,798	77	111	844	694	734	830	277	403
Guernsey	...	...	...	...	...	...	...	...	...	...	...	...	...	...	...	...
Guinea	678	1,022	958	883	644	885	7,116	7,437	42	60	646	857	639	942	410	420
Guinea-Bissau	102	171	711	1,458	47	61	5,986	6,778	2	2	971	896	45	67	21	20
Guyana	267	276	2,907	2,894	16	32	6,626	7,273	1	1	487	591	41	69	9	12
Haiti	419	240	1,009	930	689	673	3,778	3,588	90	78	471	495	1,007	792	281	210
Honduras	492	692	1,170	1,350	21	35	4,896	7,945	38	46	517	664	1,650	1,580	95	164
Hong Kong	—	—	1,712	2,000	—	—	25,407	—	...	...	...	...	3	4	189	94
Hungary	13,001	10,435	4,519	4,128	1,507	1,203	15,894	27,843	127	382	1,547	3,023	2,389	1,950	1,841	1,986
Iceland	...	...	...	...	11	11	11,858	11,000	...	...	...	...	...	...	1	2
India	138,182	199,585	1,324	1,969	16,777	21,920	12,926	16,141	10,509	12,850	461	582	20,409	30,037	42,616	56,000
Indonesia	33,605	55,757	2,837	3,908	16,153	19,224	9,054	11,729	352	504	882	1,302	4,941	7,135	2,434	4,722
Iran	8,855	16,602	1,108	1,677	1,284	2,800	14,324	18,666	247	600	799	955	3,235	7,172	4,976	8,135
Iraq	1,803	1,255	832	612	96	195	18,464	16,250	36	25	802	1,104	1,161	1,560	1,880	2,306
Ireland	2,009	2,080	4,733	6,029	822	620	20,799	28,182	—	7	3,444	4,667	22	25	283	234
Isle of Man	...	...	...	...	...	...	...	...	...	...	...	...	...	...	...	...
Israel	239	274	1,840	2,454	201	220	36,551	35,882	8	12	955	1,610	1,913	1,559	762	1,270
Italy	18,025	19,608	3,548	4,651	2,962	2,512	18,274	22,456	321	241	1,335	1,757	20,661	19,820	13,401	14,120
Jamaica	7	4	1,667	1,174	230	287	11,666	13,973	8	7	882	1,048	332	382	104	149
Japan	14,318	14,428	5,252	5,847	5,342	5,612	22,838	25,189	108	144	1,258	1,658	6,330	4,551	15,230	13,737
Jersey	...	...	...	...	...	...	...	...	...	...	...	...	...	...	...	...
Jordan	91	148	570	932	9	59	16,866	25,106	8	14	588	1,032	90	253	437	668
Kazakhstan	26,790	29,427	1,063	1,275	1,918	2,200	10,220	10,377	...	...	...	...	379	205	1,185	1,300
Kenya	2,281	3,019	1,364	1,752	1,257	1,620	7,993	7,941	185	235	430	336	650	969	490	655
Kiribati	...	...	...	...	9	14	8,011	8,889	...	...	...	...	5	5	4	5
Korea, North	9,001	9,872	5,964	6,568	1,909	2,475	12,486	13,026	280	330	849	930	851	1,346	2,636	4,460
Korea, South	8,452	7,873	4,986	5,825	1,653	793	17,787	20,868	56	32	940	1,070	997	2,037	9,070	9,938
Kuwait	—	2	3,087	4,994	—	—	16,934	16,000	...	...	...	...	1	1	36	—
Kyrgyzstan	1,413	1,417	2,452	2,274	272	325	12,348	13,542	2	—	1,000	—	247	128	396	385
Laos	1,056	1,561	1,402	2,499	184	207	10,114	8,458	17	37	1,728	2,224	89	144	184	235
Latvia	859	1,103	1,278	1,528	1,371	1,000	12,979	11,905	7	79	1,167	2,106	106	100	229	236
Lebanon	41	75	1,307	1,893	130	252	16,923	18,534	10	31	968	1,753	704	1,167	347	809
Lesotho	198	88	977	586	6	8	15,526	15,000	8	6	536	283	16	18	21	26
Liberia	254	110	1,251	786	346	351	6,894	6,806	3	3	500	500	121	130	64	71
Libya	225	298	430	658	97	150	6,671	8,108	9	13	1,079	1,130	203	306	527	772
Liechtenstein	...	...	...	...	11	12[7]	18,742	17,974[7]	...	...	...	...	...	...	...	...
Lithuania	1,742	2,198	1,642	1,936	1,832	1,079	13,022	9,465	110	27	31	898	202	118	333	334
Luxembourg[3]	...	...	...	...	...	...	...	...	...	...	...	...	...	...	...	...
Macau	...	...	...	...	4	7	11,174	13,214	—	1	—	—	4	3	2	1
Macedonia	...	...	...	...	...	66	...	5,467	—	17	—	1,332	—	552	—	203
Madagascar	2,178	2,617	1,664	2,000	2,267	3,136	5,704	6,297	53	47	852	806	719	753	283	296
Malawi	1,341	685	1,161	479	562	459	4,458	3,059	204	258	609	575	375	432	212	237
Malaysia	2,061	1,896	2,828	2,784	468	524	8,895	8,934	...	...	...	...	931	1,119	310	308
Maldives	—	—	806	1,000	7	9	5,176	5,143	—	—	600	625	8	10	15	20
Mali	1,064	2,156	790	938	123	145	8,349	8,485	47	61	338	203	13	15	173	261
Malta	8	9	3,252	3,431	21	24	8,948	20,000	1	1	2,333	2,297	11	12	47	53
Marshall Islands	...	...	...	...	...	...	...	...	...	...	...	...	...	...	...	...
Martinique	...	...	...	...	22	26	6,997	9,559	...	...	...	...	178	293	27	22
Mauritania	48	74	384	595	7	6	2,888	1,781	29	19	407	351	15	14	7	11
Mauritius	1	2	2,536	2,889	12	16	17,368	16,431	1	2	491	800	6	8	26	43
Mayotte	...	...	...	...	...	...	...	...	...	...	...	...	...	...	...	...
Mexico	20,692	24,742	2,152	2,438	1,120	1,342	12,906	16,807	1,311	1,040	719	766	7,316	14,199	3,860	5,738
Micronesia	...	...	...	...	...	...	...	...	...	...	...	...	...	...	...	...
Moldova	2,565	2,106	3,221	2,767	324	300	7,969	7,317	53	80	1,463	2,000	1,994	1,370	1,609	1,300
Monaco	...	...	...	...	...	...	...	...	...	...	...	...	...	...	...	...
Mongolia	320	492	573	877	50	76	7,878	9,500	—	3	292	1,000	3	—	26	20
Morocco	3,583	2,954	811	588	503	912	14,169	15,925	229	163	571	351	1,623	2,148	1,320	2,785
Mozambique	649	239	603	176	3,712	3,371	4,194	3,410	59	56	381	215	327	306	184	115
Myanmar (Burma)	12,984	14,340	2,521	2,740	167	230	8,087	9,329	365	642	588	685	838	975	1,872	2,220
Namibia	90	32	468	208	203	220	9,242	7,333	6	7	944	1,000	31	35	28	30
Nauru	...	...	...	...	...	...	...	...	...	...	...	...	...	...	...	...
Nepal	3,640	4,710	1,615	1,783	349	873	5,455	7,704	140	169	536	606	135	500	517	1,000
Netherlands, The	1,280	1,292	5,696	7,454	6,329	7,595	37,752	40,869	24	51	3,145	3,643	535	542	2,527	3,689
Netherlands Antilles	1[1]	2[2]	653[1]	714[2]	...	...	...	...	...	...	...	...	...	...	...	...
New Caledonia	3	1	2,134	1,672	21	22	5,692	5,684	—	—	772	667	9	7	3	6
New Zealand	785	819	4,077	5,203	220	314	26,301	29,725	63	65	2,882	2,345	363	848	382	510
Nicaragua	392	463	1,475	1,591	28	96	9,107	11,901	39	79	576	632	313	330	47	55
Niger	1,702	2,258	440	299	212	253	7,210	7,553	292	608	269	155	37	45	142	251

livestock														country
cattle		sheep		hogs		chickens		milk[e]				eggs[f]		
stock ('000 head)		stock ('000 head)		stock ('000 head)		stock ('000 head)		production ('000 metric tons)		yield (kg/animal)		production (metric tons)		
1979–81 average	1992	1979–81 average	1992	1979–81 average	1992	1979–81 average	1992	1979–81 average	1992	1979–81 average	1992	1979–81 average	1992	
153	160	...	...	14	15	1,000	3,000	54	62	1,701	1,699	1,976	2,050	Fiji
1,747	1,263	107	61	1,430	1,357	9,000	5,000	3,236	2,399	4,572	5,613	77,967	67,500	Finland
23,825	20,928	12,133	10,579	11,472	12,384	177,000	208,000	27,084	25,341	3,707	5,101	849,667	954,000	France
6	20	3	4	6	10	121[1]	100[2]	—	—	2,080	2,143	292	250	French Guiana
8	7	2	—	24	32	—	—	2	2	2,771	2,022	923	1,600	French Polynesia
5	29	105	170	126	164	2,000	2,000	—	1	250	269	1,050	1,500	Gabon
293	400	136	121	10	11	280[1]	1,000	5	7	175	175	402	813	Gambia, The
5	4	15	24	...	...	1,000	3,000	11	6	4,185	4,000	2,265	4,500	Gaza Strip
1,552	1,100	1,961	1,400	926	850	17,000	19,000	643	500	1,055	1,000	35,900	31,900	Georgia
—	17,134	—	2,488	—	26,063	—	121,000	—	28,191	—	5,034	...	954,000	Germany
804	1,400	1,942	2,500	379	500	11,000	12,000	16	27	130	130	12,203	13,515	Ghana
...	...	...	...	...	...	...	...	...	...	...	...	...	...	Gibraltar
929	616	8,040	9,694	944	1,150	30,000	27,000	666	715	1,867	2,344	122,540	142,500	Greece
...	...	20	22	...	...	...	...	...	...	...	...	...	...	Greenland
6	4	14	12	8	7	252[1]	260[2]	1	1	769	800	948	920	Grenada
91	68	3	4	44	54	420[1]	390[2]	1	2	507	513	778	900	Guadeloupe
1	—	...	...	13	4	127[1]	218[2]	...	...	...	...	1,071	680	Guam
1,886	2,097	615	676	737	1,110	14,000	10,000	263	300	749	800	40,590	64,720	Guatemala
4	...	...	...	...	...	...	...	8	...	3,514	...	...	...	Guernsey
1,753	1,800	436	510	39	33	7,000	13,000	41	42	185	185	7,420	14,490	Guinea
290	450	177	250	256	300	—	1,000	9	12	170	170	300	604	Guinea-Bissau
189	225	115	130	115	60	13,000	13,000	13	56	832	933	3,900	4,200	Guyana
1,000	1,300	89	90	1,533	880	5,000	13,000	20	16	229	200	2,943	3,300	Haiti
1,980	2,351	5	8	418	750	5,000	8,000	224	380	538	950	19,093	31,000	Honduras
7	2	...	...	520	175	6,000	5,000	4	1	3,022	2,199	2,737	890	Hong Kong
1,936	1,420	2,960	1,808	8,232	5,993	62,000	36,000	2,559	2,370	3,727	5,043	250,000	228,000	Hungary
60	73	838	700	11	20	247[1]	307[2]	121	110	3,635	3,548	3,000	3,900	Iceland
186,500	192,650	44,987	44,407	9,433	10,500	160,000	410,000	13,420	29,400	530	948	682,000	1,434,000	India
6,502	11,000	4,124	5,900	3,234	7,000	168,000	600,000	79	330	762	1,031	177,767	414,000	Indonesia
5,450	6,900	31,672	45,000	17	...	97,000	170,000	1,125	1,449	700	700	155,333	350,000	Iran
1,630	1,400	10,842	9,000	...	...	26,000	35,000	290	278	750	750	48,362	45,000	Iraq
6,043	6,073	2,374	6,187	1,122	1,134	8,000	9,000	4,729	5,494	3,178	4,027	35,000	34,000	Ireland
...	32[6]	...	147[6]	...	8[6]	...	71[6]	...	...	...	...	...	...	Isle of Man
299	349	243	360	96	70	25,000	23,000	702	998	6,817	9,073	91,675	108,600	Israel
8,697	8,004	9,120	10,435	8,885	8,549	138,000	139,000	10,546	9,800	3,478	3,562	659,163	711,000	Italy
279	320	4	2	210	250	5,000	8,000	48	49	1,000	1,000	15,500	16,500	Jamaica
4,261	5,025	13	31	9,851	10,951	284,000	335,000	6,526	8,300	4,526	5,853	1,998,041	2,586,000	Japan
7	6[7]	...	...	...	...	...	...	...	...	...	...	...	...	Jersey
29	32	950	2,000	...	...	28,000	55,000	18	38	1,000	2,000	19,000	43,000	Jordan
8,349	9,600	34,162	33,908	3,017	3,000	44,000	58,000	4,490	4,948	1,546	1,522	187,867	190,800	Kazakhstan
10,418	11,000	5,100	6,000	89	105	17,000	25,000	958	1,810	460	470	19,896	42,000	Kenya
...	...	...	...	10	9	154[1]	220[2]	...	...	...	...	105	128	Kiribati
945	1,300	292	390	2,100	3,300	18,000	44,000	55	93	2,244	2,385	103,833	160,000	Korea, North
1,634	2,517	6	3	2,153	5,505	41,000	75,000	449	1,740	4,864	6,616	255,786	440,000	Korea, South
17	5	250	297	...	...	9,000	1,000	24	8	2,653	3,300	8,573	600	Kuwait
968	1,200	9,853	9,200	320	300	9,000	13,000	676	900	1,803	1,875	23,283	31,000	Kyrgyzstan
437	993	...	...	1,117	1,561	5,000	9,000	6	11	200	200	22,167	35,000	Laos
1,413	1,383	207	184	1,623	1,246	10,000	10,000	1,668	1,530	2,898	2,879	40,467	40,000	Latvia
64	72	137	230	18	42	19,000	20,000	85	125	2,290	2,778	41,275	60,000	Lebanon
582	536	1,183	1,460	75	75	1,000	1,000	20	24	290	290	789	826	Lesotho
39	38	200	220	103	120	2,000	4,000	1	1	130	130	2,336	4,032	Liberia
164	135	5,046	5,600	...	...	6,000	58,000	63	150	1,499	1,531	16,233	35,750	Libya
6	6	2	3	3	3	43[1]	...	9	14	3,310	4,655	...	...	Liechtenstein
2,195	2,197	61	58	2,568	2,180	13,600	16,000	2,565	2,245	2,955	3,043	54,000	53,200	Lithuania
...	...	...	...	...	...	...	...	...	...	...	...	...	...	Luxembourg[3]
...	...	...	...	3	1	353[1]	450[2]	...	...	...	...	575	650	Macau
—	282	...	2,250	...	171	...	5,000	...	99	...	1,145	...	22,000	Macedonia
10,147	10,276	695	770	1,090	1,493	18,000	23,000	443	475	259	272	12,327	18,220	Madagascar
817	967	84	195	192	238	8,000	9,000	35	40	458	440	10,503	11,330	Malawi
539	720	65	275	1,869	2,800	51,000	155,000	25	30	549	640	131,100	313,200	Malaysia
...	...	...	...	...	...	...	...	...	...	...	...	...	...	Maldives
5,670	5,373	6,247	6,658	48	75	12,000	22,000	139	122	245	245	6,720	11,880	Mali
13	23	5	6	12	107	1,000	1,000	29	24	4,111	3,810	6,256	6,800	Malta
...	...	...	...	...	...	...	...	...	...	...	...	...	...	Marshall Islands
57	35	76	63	37	49	...	...	5	2	754	670	1,500	1,150	Martinique
1,262	1,400	5,166	5,400	...	...	3,000	4,000	85	98	350	350	2,720	4,250	Mauritania
27	34	10	7	7	10	2,000	2,000	25	25	2,500	2,500	2,800	4,300	Mauritius
...	...	...	...	...	...	...	...	...	...	...	...	...	...	Mayotte
27,706	30,157	6,484	6,184	16,895	16,502	177,000	282,000	6,949	7,204	1,284	1,113	636,256	1,160,648	Mexico
...	...	...	...	...	...	...	...	...	...	...	...	...	...	Micronesia
1,138	1,021	1,208	1,189	2,020	1,404	16,000	23,000	1,189	1,200	2,780	3,158	48,633	44,800	Moldova
...	...	...	...	...	...	...	...	...	...	...	...	...	...	Monaco
2,452	2,900	14,261	15,040	32	188	165[1]	300[2]	210	180	355	232	983	1,150	Mongolia
3,362	3,300	15,228	17,000	7	9	24,000	42,000	753	970	640	519	72,900	94,700	Morocco
1,400	1,250	106	118	120	170	17,000	22,000	63	68	170	170	9,400	12,800	Mozambique
8,565	9,470	235	284	2,263	2,514	23,000	25,000	283	431	245	247	31,435	36,608	Myanmar (Burma)
2,403	2,100	4,117	3,000	37	52	...	...	68	70	412	412	113	132	Namibia
...	...	...	...	2	3	3[1]	...	...	...	...	...	8	16	Nauru
6,893	6,246	730	912	375	599	6,000	7,000	190	259	325	372	14,300	17,700	Nepal
5,071	4,876	856	1,954	10,058	13,727	81,000	105,000	11,832	11,876	5,025	6,042	540,409	618,000	Netherlands, The
2	1	8	4	7	3	100[1]	135[2]	1	2	1,262	1,250	517	510	Netherlands Antilles
113	124	4	3	16	39	—	1,000	3	4	600	600	887	1,400	New Caledonia
8,063	8,450	67,393	53,500	433	409	7,000	10,000	6,586	8,140	3,016	2,976	56,855	47,600	New Zealand
2,373	1,673	3	4	625	700	3,000	7,000	225	160	767	632	28,833	26,000	Nicaragua
3,343	1,800	3,007	3,400	31	38	10,000	20,000	97	152	200	400	6,800	8,840	Niger

Crops and livestock (continued)

country	crops															
	grains				roots and tubers[a]				pulses[b]				fruits[c]		vegetables[d]	
	production ('000 metric tons)		yield (kg/hectare)		production ('000 metric tons)		yield (kg/hectare)		production ('000 metric tons)		yield (kg/hectare)		production ('000 metric tons)		production ('000 metric tons)	
	1979–81 average	1992	1979–81 average	1992	1979–81 average	1992	1979–81 average	1992	1979–81 average	1992	1979–81 average	1992	1979–81 average	1992	1979–81 average	1992
Nigeria	7,480	12,583	1,264	1,130	18,926	41,602	8,823	10,742	647	1,600	444	792	2,062	2,732	2,906	3,975
Northern Mariana Islands	...	...	...	...	...	...	...	...	...	...	...	...	...	...	...	...
Norway	1,129	901	3,634	2,722	524	450	25,884	24,590	...	...	...	...	117	118	189	173
Oman	2	2	982	1,591	1	5	13,663	22,979	...	...	...	...	111	197	105	163
Pakistan	17,200	22,078	1,608	1,916	423	866	10,495	11,313	595	709	397	481	2,569	4,070	2,083	3,833
Panama	253	281	1,524	1,745	76	76	8,018	6,230	5	9	443	378	1,208	1,247	44	67
Papua New Guinea	4	3	2,087	1,654	1,125	1,282	7,087	7,231	2	2	500	512	1,327	1,743	286	370
Paraguay	659	803	1,538	1,721	2,080	3,388	13,100	14,646	69	50	803	850	826	779	229	221
Peru	1,422	1,497	1,933	2,465	2,477	1,819	7,574	7,536	111	91	856	903	1,483	1,719	720	940
Philippines	10,942	13,755	1,611	2,067	3,100	2,221	6,632	6,419	37	38	652	790	6,816	7,145	3,477	4,338
Poland	18,466	19,969	2,345	2,400	39,508	23,388	16,808	13,309	216	598	1,232	1,783	1,584	2,389	4,573	4,823
Portugal	1,210	1,275	1,102	1,493	1,141	1,317	8,947	11,523	76	63	228	285	2,055	2,115	1,529	1,781
Puerto Rico	6	—	8,925	5,000	39	24	6,470	6,462	6	2	916	705	296	271	28	46
Qatar	1	4	2,623	3,404	—	—	13,367	6,944	...	...	...	...	7	8	18	30
Réunion	12	13	5,064	6,500	11	19	13,133	12,857	1	1	2,626	1,405	23	52	15	43
Romania	18,109	12,285	2,854	2,130	4,317	2,600	14,728	10,400	115	88	258	973	2,952	2,075	4,168	3,140
Russia	82,466	102,117	1,147	1,745	37,632	37,800	9,962	11,187	2,659	4,500	815	1,452	3,075	2,723	12,696	11,900
Rwanda	271	301	1,134	1,209	1,743	1,530	8,809	5,869	221	218	727	779	2,162	2,961	169	133
St. Kitts and Nevis	...	...	...	...	2	1	3,649	3,316	—	—	1,000	1,000	1	2	1	1
St. Lucia	—	—	703	714	10	11	4,250	4,151	—	—	2,187	2,000	90	149	1	1
St. Vincent and the Grenadines	1	1	3,294	3,311	24	18	8,049	4,727	—	—	913	1,000	35	91	2	3
San Marino	...	...	...	...	...	...	...	...	...	...	...	...	...	...	...	...
São Tomé and Príncipe	1	1	1,538	1,935	14	20	12,701	14,741	...	...	...	...	4	5	3	3
Saudi Arabia	303	4,746	820	4,741	3	50	9,930	20,000	6	7	1,813	1,850	480	713	687	1,423
Senegal	850	857	690	789	43	62	4,344	2,731	21	11	398	318	75	110	82	134
Seychelles	...	...	...	...	—	—	5,000	5,000	...	...	...	...	2	2	1	2
Sierra Leone	542	478	1,249	1,073	124	105	3,315	3,838	31	40	579	658	128	169	153	188
Singapore	...	...	...	...	2	—	11,330	10,000	...	...	...	...	9	—	39	5
Slovakia	...	...	...	...	...	...	...	...	...	...	...	...	...	...	...	...
Slovenia	...	434	...	3,654	...	368	...	12,132	—	9	—	1,167	—	340	—	71
Solomon Islands	13	—	3,513	—	87	111	15,048	17,267	2	3	840	1,250	11	16	5	6
Somalia	305	202	474	497	39	33	10,863	9,623	10	9	494	257	182	156	27	26
South Africa[8]	14,036	4,646	1,896	907	793	1,250	11,435	14,045	110	44	1,051	484	3,139	3,890	1,662	1,792
Bophuthatswana[8]	...	...	...	...	...	...	...	...	...	...	...	...	...	...	...	...
Ciskei[8]	...	...	...	...	...	...	...	...	...	...	...	...	...	...	...	...
Transkei[8]	...	...	...	...	...	...	...	...	...	...	...	...	...	...	...	...
Venda[8]	...	...	...	...	...	...	...	...	...	...	...	...	...	...	...	...
Spain	14,709	14,358	1,986	1,949	5,670	5,314	15,986	19,998	365	186	704	688	12,603	14,524	8,547	10,106
Sri Lanka	2,132	2,285	2,464	2,761	717	441	9,685	8,599	47	71	845	735	1,718	714	535	657
Sudan, The	2,962	5,691	655	800	296	159	3,329	2,960	99	113	1,260	1,077	763	852	795	910
Suriname	258	190	3,972	3,451	3	4	5,301	12,982	—	—	849	750	52	71	6	29
Swaziland	92	58	1,345	981	13	10	1,993	2,000	3	4	576	581	121	136	12	11
Sweden	5,407	3,757	3,595	3,363	1,191	1,144	28,914	29,181	32	67	2,248	2,500	207	190	228	243
Switzerland	843	1,213	4,883	5,983	924	737	37,834	38,995	1	10	3,354	4,016	724	779	306	307
Syria	3,069	4,363	1,156	1,172	279	420	15,302	17,213	180	175	799	793	733	1,496	2,973	1,775
Taiwan	3,565[1]	3,303[2]	4,264[1]	5,272[2]	2,341[1]	5,430[2]	15,146[1]	13,889[2]	32[1]	40[2]	944[1]	1,887[2]	1,639[1]	2,165[2]	2,387[1]	3,531[2]
Tajikistan	285	318	1,295	1,237	152	165	16,926	13,750	6	10	792	1,250	431	250	495	770
Tanzania	3,010	3,538	1,063	1,087	6,158	7,577	9,491	8,289	315	312	454	493	1,953	2,133	973	1,096
Thailand	20,314	22,266	1,910	2,024	15,512	21,348	14,226	14,593	342	485	685	805	6,304	5,788	2,711	2,518
Togo	301	459	729	785	922	884	8,722	7,553	23	24	238	203	41	48	65	178
Tonga	...	...	...	...	91	90	5,934	5,687	...	...	...	...	14	13	7	15
Trinidad and Tobago	13	17	3,167	2,821	20	11	12,206	9,973	4	3	1,638	1,365	57	64	30	16
Tunisia	1,146	2,199	828	1,526	127	218	12,905	12,938	89	102	560	857	518	700	1,044	1,607
Turkey	25,232	30,201	1,869	2,152	2,958	4,501	16,664	22,712	817	1,866	1,140	883	7,682	9,350	13,338	19,054
Turkmenistan	281	780	2,142	2,661	16	32	7,833	6,400	...	...	...	...	90	228	279	360
Tuvalu	...	...	...	...	—	—	...	...	...	...	...	...	—	1	...	...
Uganda	1,171	1,636	1,555	1,433	3,548	5,789	5,823	6,397	252	513	697	756	6,300	8,714	290	400
Ukraine	33,181	35,530	2,208	2,839	18,429	20,427	11,017	13,858	1,551	3,037	1,238	2,406	3,973	2,351	7,773	6,101
United Arab Emirates	3	8	5,608	4,160	2	4	14,558	16,522	...	...	...	...	62	235	130	361
United Kingdom	18,840	22,190	4,791	6,365	6,601	7,882	32,891	43,789	240	718	3,168	3,177	524	547	3,762	4,170
United States	301,405	353,353	4,150	5,360	15,487	19,207	28,933	34,377	1,457	1,222	1,633	1,668	26,531	26,956	25,471	30,438
Uruguay	1,012	1,337	1,644	2,499	197	215	5,497	6,761	5	6	909	981	273	461	172	188
Uzbekistan	2,597	2,185	2,208	1,832	264	335	10,409	7,976	7	—	952	—	1,284	960	2,718	3,750
Vanuatu	1	1	513	538	32	51	19,630	10,200	...	...	...	...	10	19	6	9
Venezuela	1,550	2,027	1,904	2,479	626	722	8,042	8,926	37	58	509	586	2,037	2,666	402	542
Vietnam	12,222	22,165	2,049	3,100	6,284	5,400	6,592	8,227	117	207	558	680	2,584	4,059	2,504	3,929
Virgin Islands (U.S.)	...	...	...	...	...	...	...	...	...	...	...	...	...	...	...	...
West Bank	...	...	...	...	...	...	...	...	...	...	...	...	...	...	...	...
Western Sahara	1[1]	2[2]	708[1]	741[2]	...	...	...	...	...	...	...	...	...	...	...	...
Western Samoa	...	...	...	...	39	41	6,952	6,607	...	...	...	...	53	50	—	1
Yemen	913	811	1,041	1,121	133	165	11,992	11,114	80[10]	75	1,087[10]	1,523	173	319	335	552
Yugoslavia	...	...	...	...	...	711	...	6,464	...	...	...	...	—	1,324	—	987
Zaire	900	1,377	807	758	13,595	19,126	6,901	7,541	155	195	604	621	2,624	3,088	479	569
Zambia	990	600	1,676	768	205	299	3,465	3,839	7	21	340	531	76	97	209	250
Zimbabwe	2,273	505	1,359	428	76	136	3,823	4,510	23	42	566	651	109	140	136	132

livestock														country
cattle		sheep		hogs		chickens		milk[e]				eggs[f]		
stock ('000 head)		stock ('000 head)		stock ('000 head)		stock ('000 head)		production ('000 metric tons)		yield (kg/animal)		production (metric tons)		
1979–81 average	1992	1979–81 average	1992	1979–81 average	1992	1979–81 average	1992	1979–81 average	1992	1979–81 average	1992	1979–81 average	1992	
12,066	15,700	8,022	13,500	1,000	5,328	80,000	135,000	289	370	239	236	180,000	225,000	Nigeria
...	...	...	...	...	...	...	...	...	...	...	...	...	...	Northern Mariana Islands
989	1,011	2,033	2,211	675	749	4,000	4,000	1,926	1,908	5,125	5,608	44,665	55,000	Norway
141	140	114	145	...	...	—	3,000	18	18	420	420	710	6,105	Oman
15,268	17,745	22,580	26,995	...	...	54,000	164,000	2,189	3,788	864	1,058	96,367	230,900	Pakistan
1,425	1,499	...	...	205	257	5,000	9,000	94	127	988	1,134	14,553	12,000	Panama
130	105	2	4	870	1,010	2,000	3,000	—	—	228	100	1,815	3,300	Papua New Guinea
5,966	7,800	387	380	1,090	2,600	12,000	18,000	163	240	1,903	1,905	26,025	36,000	Paraguay
3,958	3,961	14,565	12,079	2,083	2,417	37,000	62,000	796	768	1,298	1,327	59,700	106,700	Peru
1,885	1,656	30	30	7,712	8,032	53,000	63,000	13	16	994	1,032	201,285	292,000	Philippines
12,494	8,221	4,105	1,870	20,343	22,086	77,000	50,000	16,250	12,800	2,778	3,040	488,642	389,000	Poland
1,332	1,370	4,440	5,847	3,367	2,580	17,000	18,000	750	1,547	2,123	3,828	62,008	77,720	Portugal
497	600	6	8	225	202	7,000	13,000	420	391	2,324	400	21,902	19,575	Puerto Rico
9	11	48	132	...	...	1,000	3,000	4	4	1,561	1,521	281	3,500	Qatar
20	19	2	2	61	89	3,000	5,000	5	4	526	444	2,413	3,300	Réunion
6,351	4,355	15,766	13,879	10,926	10,954	92,000	106,000	3,987	2,838	1,914	1,618	323,833	340,000	Romania
58,414	54,677	63,566	52,535	36,218	35,384	507,000	628,000	46,953	46,930	2,113	2,282	2,193,000	2,370,000	Russia
625	610	303	395	124	142	1,000	1,000	61	89	510	600	860	2,600	Rwanda
5	5	14	15	2	2	74[1]	85[2]	...	...	...	...	297	350	St. Kitts and Nevis
10	12	13	16	10	12	128[1]	250[2]	1	1	1,390	1,494	497	540	St. Lucia
8	6	13	12	6	9	139[1]	178[2]	1	2	1,362	1,379	530	595	St. Vincent and the Grenadines
...	...	...	...	...	...	...	...	...	...	...	...	...	...	San Marino
3	4	2	2	2	3	70[1]	100[2]	—	—	170	170	148	172	São Tomé and Príncipe
374	216	2,888	6,008	...	...	19,000	83,000	64	230	443	2,911	41,967	156,800	Saudi Arabia
2,424	2,800	1,966	3,600	180	310	8,000	19,000	87	101	357	360	6,353	12,600	Senegal
3	2	...	...	10	19	109[1]	290[2]	1	—	519	530	811	2,016	Seychelles
349	333	268	275	36	50	4,000	6,000	18	17	250	250	4,669	7,130	Sierra Leone
1	—	...	...	1,017	280	14,000	3,000	...	...	...	...	26,870	15,000	Singapore
...	...	...	...	...	...	...	...	...	...	...	...	...	...	Slovakia
...	484	...	28	...	529	...	12,000	...	352	...	1,706	...	15,800	Slovenia
23	13	...	...	45	54	133[1]	143[2]	1	2	600	940	284	288	Solomon Islands
4,437	1,000	10,467	4,000	9	2	3,000	1,000	477	100	414	357	2,320	800	Somalia
13,647	13,585	31,625	32,110	1,339	1,490	30,000	40,000	2,553	2,390	2,809	2,598	159,952	221,200	South Africa[8]
...	...	...	...	...	...	...	...	...	...	...	...	...	...	Bophuthatswana[8]
...	...	...	...	...	...	...	...	...	...	...	...	...	...	Ciskei[8]
...	...	...	...	...	...	...	...	...	...	...	...	...	...	Transkei[8]
...	...	...	...	...	...	...	...	...	...	...	...	...	...	Venda[8]
4,608	4,924	14,721	24,625	10,392	17,240	51,000	51,000	5,984	5,800	3,255	3,473	665,560	597,400	Spain
1,662	1,568	27	17	71	91	6,000	9,000	182	194	448	309	28,857	45,800	Sri Lanka
18,376	21,600	17,628	22,600	...	...	27,000	35,000	1,352	3,193	500	480	31,745	34,500	Sudan, The
46	95	3	9	19	31	5,000	9,000	7	17	1,209	1,768	2,638	3,050	Suriname
658	753	32	23	17	31	1,000	1,000	36	42	252	271	272	330	Swaziland
1,928	1,774	392	448	2,711	2,280	13,000	12,000	3,452	3,168	5,257	6,016	113,633	112,000	Sweden
2,008	1,783	350	415	2,113	1,706	6,000	6,000	3,653	3,845	4,194	4,917	43,186	36,100	Switzerland
778	762	9,311	15,782	1	1	15,000	16,000	504	775	1,353	2,363	68,759	65,250	Syria
130[1]	134[9]	...	...	3,267[1]	6,674[2]	24,760[1]	76,979[9]	46[1]	203[9]	3,426[1]	4,398[9]	59,462[1]	178,500[2]	Taiwan
1,177	1,400	2,377	2,620	130	100	6,000	6,000	452	475	1,025	950	19,000	18,000	Tajikistan
12,616	13,217	3,754	3,706	160	330	18,000	25,000	374	460	160	158	35,302	50,050	Tanzania
4,228	6,820	25	153	3,344	5,100	60,000	136,000	19	200	1,950	2,000	104,667	448,500	Thailand
229	320	592	1,500	231	800	2,000	7,000	7	9	225	225	1,677	5,980	Togo
10	10	...	...	105	97	121[1]	130[2]	—	—	2,106	1,500	229	280	Tonga
77	60	10	14	59	50	7,000	10,000	6	12	1,169	1,560	7,433	8,000	Trinidad and Tobago
583	636	4,651	6,400	4	6	24,000	41,000	216	418	1,064	1,129	36,383	53,250	Tunisia
15,467	11,973	46,199	40,433	13	10	55,000	139,000	7,737	6,106	1,300	1,300	217,164	390,000	Turkey
606	900	4,277	5,380	159	300	5,000	8,000	311	400	1,372	1,429	13,550	15,000	Turkmenistan
...	...	...	...	6	13	10[1]	21[2]	...	...	...	...	11	12	Tuvalu
5,063	5,100	1,152	1,980	242	880	13,000	20,000	354	446	350	350	10,587	16,000	Uganda
25,433	23,700	8,912	7,332	20,197	17,800	209,000	233,000	21,044	19,000	2,272	2,289	850,167	830,000	Ukraine
26	55	132	275	...	...	2,000	7,000	4	6	446	207	2,533	10,750	United Arab Emirates
13,321	11,623	21,643	28,932	7,856	7,519	116,000	124,000	15,917	14,692	4,755	5,417	834,000	650,900	United Kingdom
112,152	99,559	12,670	10,750	64,045	57,684	1,068,000	1,437,000	58,139	68,966	5,377	7,002	4,116,200	4,175,700	United States
10,965	9,508	19,219	25,702	308	215	6,000	9,000	811	1,100	1,442	1,760	16,903	22,200	Uruguay
3,391	5,100	7,949	9,200	441	700	22,000	34,000	2,123	2,860	1,627	1,634	81,567	90,000	Uzbekistan
91	131	...	...	68	60	131[1]	180[2]	2	3	201	248	237	276	Vanuatu
10,527	14,192	333	525	2,241	1,727	42,000	57,000	1,356	1,485	1,163	1,337	128,745	122,265	Venezuela
1,646	3,135	...	...	9,396	12,140	55,000	80,000	26	40	800	800	55,317	112,200	Vietnam
8	8	4	3	5	3	57[1]	49[2]	3	2	3,477	2,746	196	160	Virgin Islands (U.S.)
...	...	...	...	...	...	...	...	...	...	...	...	...	...	West Bank
...	...	17[1]	25[2]	...	...	...	1,000[2]	...	...	...	...	...	...	Western Sahara
26	31	...	...	80	270	...	...	1	2	1,000	1,000	152	200	Western Samoa
973	1,190	3,002	3,850	...	...	6,000	24,000	79	99	234	251	7,220	17,700	Yemen
...	2,189	...	2,715	...	3,844	...	24,000	...	1,700	...	1,991	...	80,000	Yugoslavia
1,159	1,650	726	920	685	840	15,000	21,000	6	7	827	909	7,247	8,200	Zaire
2,238	3,095	29	63	217	290	18,000	19,000	60	84	300	300	27,893	40,000	Zambia
5,378	4,700	481	580	155	290	9,000	13,000	455	415	431	419	11,100	168,000	Zimbabwe

[1]1975–77. [2]1986. [3]Belgium includes Luxembourg. [4]Data refer to former Czechoslovakia. [5]Ethiopia includes Eritrea. [6]1987. [7]1990. [8]South Africa includes Bophuthatswana, Ciskei, Transkei, and Venda. [9]1991. [10]Former Yemen Arab Republic only.

Extractive industries

Extractive industries are generally defined as those exploiting in situ natural resources and include such activities as mining, forestry, fisheries, and agriculture; the definition is often confined, however, to nonrenewable resources only. For the purposes of this table, agriculture is excluded; it is covered in the two tables immediately preceding.

Extractive industries are divided here into three parts: mining, forestry, and fisheries. These major headings are each divided into two main subheadings, one that treats production and one that treats foreign trade. The production sections are presented in terms of volume except for mining, and the trade sections are presented in terms of U.S. dollars. Volume of production data usually imply output of primary (unprocessed) raw materials only, but, because of the way national statistical information is reported, the data may occasionally include some processed and manufactured materials as well, since these are often indistinguishably associated with the extractive process (sulfur from petroleum extraction, cured or treated lumber, or "processed" fish). This is also the case in the trade sections, where individual national trade nomenclatures may not distinguish some processed and manufactured goods from unprocessed raw materials.

Mining. In the absence of a single international source publication or standard of practice for reporting volume or value of mineral production, single-country sources predominantly have been used to compile mining production figures, supplemented by U.S. Bureau of Mines data, by the United Nations' *Industrial Statistics Yearbook* (2 vol.), and by industry sources, especially *Mining Journal*'s *Mining Annual Review*. Each country has its own methods of classifying mining data, which do not always accord with the principal mineral production categories adopted in this table—namely, "metals," "nonmetals," and "energy." The available data have therefore been adjusted to accord better with the definition of each group. Included in the "metal" category are all ferrous and nonferrous metallic ores, concentrates, and scrap; the "nonmetal" group includes all nonmetallic minerals (stone, clay, precious gems, etc.) except the mineral fuels; the last group, "energy," is composed predominantly of the natural hydrocarbon fuels, though it may also include manufactured gas.

The contribution (value) of each national mineral sector to its country's gross domestic product is given, as is the distribution by group of that contribution (to gross domestic product and to foreign trade), although statistics regarding the value of mineral production are less readily available in country sources than those regarding trade or volume of minerals produced. Figures for value added by mineral output, though not always available, were sought first, as they provide the most consistent standard to compare the importance of minerals both within a particular national economy and among national mineral sectors worldwide. Where value added to the gross domestic product was not available, gross value of production or sales was substituted and the exception footnoted. Figures for value of production are reported here in millions of U.S. dollars to permit comparisons to be made from country to country. Comparisons can also be made as to the relative importance of each mineral group within a given country.

Extractive industries

country	mining														
	% of GDP, 1991	mineral production (value added)					trade (value)								
		year	total ('000,000 U.S.$)	by kind (%)			year	exports				imports			
								total ('000,000 U.S.$)	by kind (%)			total ('000,000 U.S.$)	by kind (%)		
				metals[a]	non-metals[b]	energy[c]			metals[a]	non-metals[b]	energy[c]		metals[a]	non-metals[b]	energy[c]
Afghanistan	...	1988[1]	16.2	—	17.7	82.3	1986	46.6[2]	—	—	100.0[2]	0.3	—	100.0	—
Albania	...	1990	124.4	—32.7—		67.3	...	...	...	...	...	...	...	...	...
Algeria	18.7[3]	1987	9,569.7	—2.4—		97.6	1988	6,081.8	0.4	0.4	99.2	130.3	9.2	26.4	64.4
American Samoa	...	1990	...	—	100.0	—	1989	0.1	100.0	—	—	0.1	—	—	100.0
Andorra	...	...	...	...	...	...	1990	0.3	—	100.0	—	26.9	—	95.1	4.9
Angola	58.2	1989	2,609.0	—	4.9	95.1	1990	2,215.9	—	2.8	97.2	—	—	—	—
Antigua and Barbuda	2.1[3]	1989	3.3	—	100.0	—	1984	—	—	—	—	1.1	—	—	100.0
Argentina	2.3	1990	4,033.2	2.7	3.9	93.4	1989	80.4	27.0	13.9	59.1	567.9	43.2	6.3	50.5
Armenia	...	...	...	...	...	...	...	...	...	...	...	...	...	...	...
Aruba	...	1990	...	—	100.0	—	...	...	...	...	...	...	...	...	...
Australia	5.0[5]	1990–91	14,669.6	37.5[6]	7.1[6]	55.4[6]	1990	8,977.7	32.6	3.9	63.5	1,434.1	8.0	18.4	73.6
Austria	0.3	1989	631.1	6.1	24.5	69.4	1990	354.8	39.0	60.0	1.0	2,820.9	16.0	8.9	75.1
Azerbaijan	...	...	...	...	...	...	1990	620.8	14.9	5.9	79.2	...	...	...	...
Bahamas, The	...	1988[1]	11.3	—	100.0	—	1989	1,850.2	—	0.6	99.4	1,556.7	—	—	100.0
Bahrain	22.1[4]	1990	861.4	—	1.2[7]	98.8[7]	1990	48.2	17.1	82.9	—	1,805.7	0.1	0.9	99.0
Bangladesh	—	1989–90	2.6	—	0.3	99.7	1987	—	—	—	—	211.7	0.2	11.5	88.3
Barbados	0.6	1991	9.3	—	—100.0—		1990	—	—	—	—	6.9	—	37.5	62.5
Belarus	...	...	...	...	...	...	1990	1,177.4	14.2	14.7	71.1	2,180.6	47.8	5.5	46.7
Belgium	0.3	1991	503.7	—	44.6[8]	55.4[8]	1990[9]	8,782.3	5.5	93.0	1.5	17,057.7	14.5	50.9	34.6
Belize	0.9	1991	2.8	—	100.0	—	1986	—	—	—	—	0.9	—	—	100.0
Benin	0.6[4]	1990	14.5[10]	—	—100.0[10]—		1990	22.5	—	—	100.0	...	...	...	...
Bermuda	...	...	...	...	...	...	1990	25.5	0.2	99.8	—	1.7[8]	—	42.0[8]	58.0[8, 11]
Bhutan	0.8[3]	1989	2.2	—	—100.0—		1987	1.5	13.8	85.9	0.3[11, 12]	0.9	—	9.7	90.3[11, 12]
Bolivia	15.3	1990	843.4	—56.5[13]—		43.5[13]	1990	492.9	53.8	0.2	46.0	1.2[7]	—	100.0[7]	—
Bosnia and Herzegovina	...	...	...	...	...	...	...	...	...	...	...	...	...	...	...
Botswana	41.6[5]	1990–91	1,484.5	...	...	...	[14]	...	...	...	...	...	...	...	...
Brazil	1.7	1991	6,079.0	...	...	...	1989	2,962.4	91.1	8.7	0.2	4,749.4	12.6	3.8	83.6
Brunei	36.1[13]	1988	1,068.6[15]	...	...	...	1990	1,783.7	—	—	100.0	13.2	—	100.0	—
Bulgaria	0.4[13]	1988	128.8	...	...	...	...	...	...	...	...	...	...	...	...
Burkina Faso	1.2[3]	1989	24.0	—	100.0	—	1989	—	—	—	—	...	...	...	...
Burundi	0.5[3]	1989	5.0	...	...	...	1990	—	—	—	—	2.6[3]	—	100.0[3]	—
Cambodia	...	1991	...	—	100.0	—	...	...	...	...	...	...	...	...	...
Cameroon	13.9[3]	1989	1,398.0[10]	...	...	...	1989	229.6	—	—	100.0	43.4	82.4	17.6	—
Canada	3.9[4]	1988	21,053.1	32.0	8.2	59.8	1990	15,157.9	27.1	8.2	64.7	7,875.4	19.5	7.1	73.4
Cape Verde	0.6[13]	1988	1.8	—	100.0	—	1989	0.1	—	100.0	—	0.5	—	—	100.0
Central African Republic	2.8[13]	1989	32.0[16]	—100.0[16]—		—	1989	60.7	—	100.0	—	1.0	—	100.0	—
Chad	0.3[3]	1989	3.0	—	100.0	—	1989	6.0	100.0	—	—	...	...	...	...
Chile	7.3	1990	3,086.7	...	...	...	1989	1,213.0[13]	96.1[13]	3.9[13]	—	713.2	0.8	6.0	93.2
China	...	1989	10,951.4	11.2	13.9	74.9	1990	4,990.3	4.2	14.5	81.3	1,549.2	61.3	11.3	27.4
Colombia	7.6[4]	1990	3,666.9	...	...	...	1989	1,603.7	0.1	6.8	93.1	72.4	44.1	55.9	—
Comoros	—[13]	1991	...	—	100.0	—	...	...	...	...	...	...	...	...	...
Congo	27.9[3]	1989	677.7[10]	...	...	...	1986	785.6	1.7	5.9	92.4	3.8	—	100.0	—
Costa Rica	...	1990	3.8	12.8	87.2	—	1987	8.2	100.0	—	—	102.5	—	16.9	83.1
Côte d'Ivoire	2.2[3]	1989	143.0[10]	...	...	...	1985	37.2	6.4	0.9	92.7	313.1	0.2	3.6	96.2
Croatia	...	...	...	...	...	...	...	...	...	...	...	...	...	...	...
Cuba	...	...	...	...	...	...	1987	431.4	83.6	1.8	14.6	1,257.3	—	1.8	98.2
Cyprus	0.3	1990	14.6	4.1	95.9	—	1990	8.5	74.0	26.0	—	139.0	—	10.9	89.1
Czech Republic[18]	...	1990	1,527.6	5.2	7.0	87.8	1987	627.2[12]	2.5	12.1	85.4[12]	7,150.1[11, 12]	8.5	3.0	88.5[11, 12]
Denmark	1.2	1990	1,202.8	—	13.4	86.6	1990	783.9	19.7	16.7	63.6	1,378.1	9.2	9.0	81.8
Djibouti	—[13]	1987	...	—	100.0	—	1989	—	—	—	—	14.6[12]	0.2	9.7	90.1[12]
Dominica	0.7[4]	1990	1.2	—	100.0	—	1989	...	...	...	...	0.7	—	—	100.0
Dominican Republic	3.3	1991	111.5	91.6[1, 19]	8.4[1, 19]	—	1985	1.3	20.8	79.2	—	367.2	14.7	—	85.3
Ecuador	12.0	1990	1,637.5	—5.4[20]—		94.6[12]	1989	1,041.2	—	0.4	99.6	12.1	—	99.8	0.2
Egypt	10.9[3]	1988	1,960.0	0.4	6.7	92.9	1989	574.4	1.0	—	99.0	189.7	18.8	27.7	53.5
El Salvador	0.2	1991	10.1	100.0	—	—	1987	3.6	—	100.0	—	105.4	—	8.1	91.9

Since the data for value of mineral production are obtained mostly from country sources, there is some variation (from a standard calendar year) in the time periods to which the data refer. In addition, the time period for which production data are available does not always correspond with the year for which mineral trade data are available.

The Standard International Trade Classification (SITC), Revision 3, was used to determine the commodity groupings for foreign trade statistics. The actual trade data for these groups is taken largely from the United Nations' *International Trade Statistics Yearbook* (2 vol.) and national sources.

Forestry. Data for the production and trade sections of forestry are based on the Food and Agriculture Organization (FAO) of the United Nations' *Yearbook of Forest Products.* Production of roundwood (all wood obtained in removals from forests) is the principal indicator of the volume of each country's forestry sector; this total is broken down further (as percentages of the roundwood total) into its principal components: fuelwood and charcoal, and industrial roundwood. The latter group was further divided to show its principal component, sawlogs and veneer; lesser categories of industrial roundwood could not be shown for reasons of space. These included pitprops (used in mining, a principal consumer of wood) and pulpwood (used in papermaking and plastics). Value of trade in forest products is given for both imports and exports, although exports alone tend to be the significant indicator for producing countries, while imports of wood are rarely a significant fraction of the trade of most importing countries.

Fisheries. Data for nominal (live weight) catches of fish, crustaceans, mollusks, etc., in all fishing areas (marine areas and inland waters) are taken from the FAO *Yearbook of Fishery Statistics* (*Catches and Landings*). Total catch figures are given in metric tons; the catches in inland waters and marine areas are given as percentages of the total catch, as are the main kinds of catch—fish, crustaceans, and mollusks. The total catch figures exclude marine mammals, such as whales and seals; and such aquatic animal products as corals, sponges, and pearls; but include frogs, turtles, and jellyfish. The subtotals by kind of catch, however, exclude the last group, which do not belong taxonomically to the fish, crustaceans, or mollusks.

Figures for trade in fishery products (including processed products and preparations like oils, meals, and animal feeding stuffs) are taken from the FAO's *Yearbook of Fishery Statistics* (*Fishery Commodities*). Value figures for trade in fish products are given for both imports and exports.

The following notes further define the column headings:

a. Includes ferrous and nonferrous metallic ores, concentrates, and scraps, such as iron ore, bauxite and alumina, copper, zinc, gold (except unwrought or semimanufactured), lead, or uranium.

b. Includes natural fertilizers; stone, sand, and aggregate; and pearls, precious and semiprecious stones, worked and unworked.

c. Includes hydrocarbon solids, liquids, and gases.

1 cubic metre = 35.3147 cubic feet

1 metric ton = 1.1023 short tons

forestry, 1991						fisheries, 1991								country
production of roundwood				trade (value, '000 U.S.$)		catch (nominal)						trade (value, '000 U.S.$)		
total ('000 cubic metres)	fuelwood, charcoal (%)	industrial roundwood (%)		exports	imports	total ('000 metric tons)	by source (%)		by kind of catch (%)			exports	imports	
		total	sawlogs, veneer				marine	inland	fish	crustaceans	mollusks			
6,759	76.7	23.3	12.7	...	1,003	1.5	—	100.0	100.0	—	—	...	...	Afghanistan
2,556	60.9	39.1	39.1	762	2,114	12.0	55.2	44.8	81.1	1.8	17.1	6,987	120	Albania
2,221	87.9	12.1	0.9	...	348,388	80.1	99.5	0.5	95.9	3.2	0.9	1,944	1,714	Algeria
...	...	...	...	...	...	0.1	100.0	—	100.0	—	—	305,947[4]	3,204[4]	American Samoa
...	...	...	...	...	...	—	—	100.0	100.0	—	—	...	...	Andorra
6,593	85.9	14.1	1.0	131	7,960	75.1	90.7	9.3	98.9	0.8	0.3	5,896	49,052	Angola
...	...	...	...	...	...	2.3	100.0	—	91.3	8.7	—	460	1,190	Antigua and Barbuda
10,819	40.0	60.0	23.7	193,376	102,100	640.6	98.3	1.7	92.4	1.4	7.6	448,012	18,763	Argentina
...	...	...	...	...	...	4.5	...	...	...	...	...	...	...	Armenia
...	...	...	...	...	...	0.8	100.0	—	100.0	—	—	160	4,750	Aruba
19,315	15.0	85.0	39.6	471,454	1,215,642	227.3	98.1	1.9	65.2	20.1	14.7	577,592	359,809	Australia
16,759	16.5	83.5	59.2	3,284,526	1,557,628	4.5	—	100.0	100.0	—	—	3,011	161,550	Austria
...	...	...	...	...	...	39.7	...	...	...	...	...	...	...	Azerbaijan
115	—	100.0	13.0	...	26,792	9.2	100.0	—	13.3	82.2	4.5	27,500	6,490	Bahamas, The
—	—	—	—	...	25,252	7.6	100.0	—	78.6	19.6	1.8	3,557	3,540	Bahrain
31,757	97.2	2.8	1.5	...	33,317	892.7	29.0	71.0	90.8	9.2	—	178,932	—	Bangladesh
...	...	...	...	...	15,121	2.7	100.0	—	100.0	—	—	208	6,796	Barbados
...	...	...	...	...	...	15.5	...	...	...	...	...	...	...	Belarus
5,082[9]	11.3[9]	88.7[9]	58.0[9]	1,926,040[9]	3,450,567[9]	40.2	97.9	2.1	95.2	3.6	1.2	227,557[9]	779,104[9]	Belgium
188	67.0	33.0	33.0	1,736	4,791	1.6	99.9	0.1	25.3	60.7	14.0	5,620	500	Belize
5,203	94.6	5.4	0.8	...	1,532	41.0	22.0	78.0	81.2	18.8	—	—	5,129	Benin
...	...	...	...	...	...	0.4	100.0	—	99.3	0.7	—	—	7,465	Bermuda
1,560	82.2	17.8	15.4	10,135	...	1.0	—	100.0	100.0	—	—	...	...	Bhutan
1,632	84.3	15.7	14.9	30,444	4,000	5.4	—	100.0	100.0	—	—	105	2,425	Bolivia
5,379[4]	...	...	...	...	...	3.6[4]	—	100.0[4]	...	...	...	...	...	Bosnia and Herzegovina
1,440	93.8	6.2	—	...	9,415	1.9	—	100.0	100.0	—	—	1,000	6,695	Botswana
264,621	71.9	28.1	14.3	1,472,364	247,118	800.0	73.2	26.8	89.2	10.0	0.8	157,398	180,800	Brazil
295	26.8	73.2	69.8	181	17,206	1.7	93.6	6.4	71.8	27.6	0.6	440	6,780	Brunei
3,638	36.2	63.8	26.1	45,375	101,240	49.9	82.9	17.1	97.0	—	3.0	15,966	602	Bulgaria
8,995	95.5	4.5	—	...	5,477	7.0	—	100.0	100.0	—	—	—	5,560	Burkina Faso
4,343	98.8	1.2	0.1	...	5,460	23.1	—	100.0	100.0	—	—	197	257	Burundi
6,387	86.3	13.7	3.8	18,143	99	111.1	32.8	67.2	91.4	5.8	2.8	...	...	Cambodia
14,637	78.7	21.3	15.6	200,645	120,086	78.0	71.8	28.2	83.8	16.2	—	2,265	22,293	Cameroon
178,049	3.8	96.2	69.3	16,930,896	1,839,979	1,529.8	96.7	3.3	83.7	8.5	7.8	2,168,121	675,242	Canada
...	...	...	...	...	2,320	8.5	100.0	—	99.2	0.7	—	2,380	225	Cape Verde
3,444	88.7	11.3	3.4	15,104	144	13.5	—	100.0	100.0	—	—	—	2,056	Central African Republic
4,141	85.8	14.2	0.1	...	3,700	60.0	—	100.0	100.0	—	—	...	...	Chad
18,817	35.9	64.1	39.3	836,300	77,000	6,002.9	99.9	0.1	97.1	0.5	2.0	1,066,922	5,900	Chile
282,334[17]	68.1[17]	31.9[17]	16.0[17]	828,528[17]	3,904,458[17]	13,135.0	57.9	42.1	77.0	9.9	12.4	1,181,989	438,090	China
19,702	86.4	13.6	9.9	16,787	129,448	108.7	77.0	23.0	88.0	11.6	0.4	117,737	52,100	Colombia
...	...	...	...	...	...	6.5	100.0	—	99.2	0.8	—	—	750	Comoros
3,760	57.1	42.9	22.2	128,514	2,088	45.6	40.3	59.7	99.2	0.8	—	2,600	22,175	Congo
4,201	72.1	27.9	22.4	21,895	80,567	17.9	89.0	11.0	80.2	19.5	0.3	61,609	12,955	Costa Rica
13,061	77.6	22.4	16.4	278,400	28,159	85.2	72.0	28.0	97.4	2.6	—	173,067	114,947	Côte d'Ivoire
4,877[4]	...	...	...	...	...	45.3[4]	77.0[4]	23.0[4]	...	...	...	...	...	Croatia
3,140	80.5	19.5	6.1	1,847	193,411	165.2	86.9	13.1	86.5	9.3	3.8	129,612	15,361	Cuba
56	32.1	67.9	50.0	234	85,015	2.7	97.4	2.6	89.6	0.1	10.3	4,422	26,295	Cyprus
16,477	8.4	91.6	48.7	426,544	106,079	22.5	—	100.0	100.0	—	—	17,034	61,343	Czech Republic[18]
2,300	19.8	80.2	43.9	416,959	1,766,207	1,793.2	98.0	2.0	92.3	0.7	7.0	2,302,299	1,148,255	Denmark
...	...	...	...	...	1,997	0.4	100.0	—	99.7	0.3	—	186	601	Djibouti
...	...	...	...	...	3,901	0.6	100.0	—	100.0	—	—	—	1,310	Dominica
982	99.4	0.6	0.4	...	85,036	17.2	93.7	6.3	68.5	5.8	25.7	620	25,920	Dominican Republic
7,762	86.7	13.3	7.2	26,470	162,868	383.6	99.4	0.6	67.9	31.3	0.8	587,635	5,752	Ecuador
2,300	95.3	4.7	—	...	2,730,043	298.0	27.6	72.4	96.8	2.9	0.3	11,050	73,172	Egypt
4,666	96.9	3.1	1.9	2,725	21,800	11.3	61.5	38.5	73.3	22.0	4.7	14,482	2,325	El Salvador

Extractive industries (continued)

country	mining														
	% of GDP, 1991	mineral production (value added)					trade (value)								
		year	total ('000,000 U.S.$)	by kind (%)			year	exports				imports			
				metals[a]	non-metals[b]	energy[c]		total ('000,000 U.S.$)	by kind (%) metals[a]	non-metals[b]	energy[c]	total ('000,000 U.S.$)	by kind (%) metals[a]	non-metals[b]	energy[c]
Equatorial Guinea	—[13]	...	...	...	...	...	...	...	...	...	...	...	...	...	...
Eritrea[21]	...	...	...	...	...	...	...	...	...	...	...	...	...	...	...
Estonia	...	...	...	...	...	...	...	...	...	...	...	...	...	...	...
Ethiopia[21]	0.2[22]	1989–90	10.5	——100.0——		—	1988	...	...	...	...	91.9	—	4.2	95.8
Faeroe Islands	0.1[13]	1988	1.2	—	—	100.0	1990	2.5	—	100.0	—	0.1	—	100.0	—
Fiji	3.3[3]	1986	17.2	95.2	4.8	—	1988	0.2	99.8	0.2	—	2.6	1.2	42.7	56.1
Finland	0.3[4]	1990	400.7	32.7	67.3	—	1990	165.4	25.3	47.0	27.7	2,992.8	16.8	8.6	74.6
France	0.5[3]	1989	4,733.5	5.6	20.8	73.6	1990	2,409.7	53.9	34.7	11.4	19,617.6	10.1	6.8	83.1
French Guiana	...	1990	...	——100.0——		—	1990	—	—	—	—	2.0	—	—	100.0
French Polynesia	...	...	...	...	...	...	1990	58.8	—	100.0	—	3.9[13]	—	25.5[13]	74.5[13]
Gabon	47.8[4]	1990	1,904.1	20.1[3]	—	79.9[3]	1990	1,020.1	12.7	—	87.3	...	...	...	...
Gambia, The	—	1990–91	—	—	100.0	—	1986	3.3	—	100.0	—	...	...	...	...
Gaza Strip	...	...	...	...	...	...	[24]	[24]	...	...	...	...	...	...	...
Georgia	...	...	...	...	...	...	1990	275.2	74.7	9.9	15.4	547.0	55.8	12.4	31.8
Germany	3.4[3, 25]	1989[25]	11,803.2	0.6	20.0	79.4	1990[25]	4,098.9	41.2	32.9	25.9	24,615.2	19.1	7.4	73.5
Ghana	1.8[4]	1990	109.8	...	...	—	1989	97.6	23.5	76.5	—	...	...	...	...
Gibraltar	...	...	...	...	...	...	1986	1.0	—	100.0	—	0.3	—	100.0	—
Greece	1.5[4]	1989	592.0	14.6	35.8	49.6	1990	313.0	44.2	34.5	21.3	1,242.3	7.6	8.1	84.3
Greenland	...	1990	...	100.0	—	—	1990	—	96.6	3.4	—	2.6	—	100.0	—
Grenada	0.4	1991	0.7	—	100.0	—	1986	—	—	—	—	1.2	—	38.7	61.3
Guadeloupe	...	1991	...	—	100.0	—	1990	1.1	100.0	—	—	2.7	—	—	100.0
Guam	...	1987[1]	2.3	—	100.0	—	1986[26]	—	100.0	—	—	...	...	...	...
Guatemala	0.2	1990	25.3[10]	...	...	...	1989	14.1	—	—	100.0	171.3[27]	—	42.7[27]	57.3[27]
Guernsey	...	...	...	...	...	...	...	...	...	...	...	...	...	...	...
Guinea	23.9[4]	1990	764.5[29]	——100.0[29]——		—	1989	444.4	99.3	0.7	—	0.3[8]	100.0[8]	—	—
Guinea-Bissau	—[3]	1988	0.1	—	100.0	—	1986	1.0	—	100.0	—	...	...	...	...
Guyana	10.8	1991	38.1[30]	——100.0——		—	1989	86.3	97.8	2.2	—	1.1[7]	—	100.0[7]	—
Haiti	—	1991	1.4	100.0	—	—	1989	—	—	—	—	...	...	...	...
Honduras	1.8	1991	45.6	——100.0——		—	1989	—	100.0	—	—	80.0	—	9.8	90.2
Hong Kong	—[4]	1989	27.4	—	100.0	—	1990	1,595.2	18.4	80.6	1.0	2,539.6	4.3	80.4	15.3
Hungary	...	1989	939.5	4.8	4.3	90.9	1990	412.0[12]	33.0	—	67.0[12]	977.4[11, 12]	5.9	5.6	88.5[11, 12]
Iceland	...	1990	...	—	100.0	—	1990	9.8	—	100.0	—	60.8	71.8	19.5	8.7
India	2.2[22]	1989–90	5,194.3	8.7	9.7	81.6	1988	3,718.2	17.8	81.7	0.5	5,320.0	10.3	48.4	41.3
Indonesia	14.5[4]	1990	15,600.2	——6.5[27]——		93.5[27]	1990	10,730.6	5.8	0.6	93.6	1,189.0	24.3	11.9	63.8
Iran	4.6[5]	1989–90	16,995.0[15]	...	...	...	1987	9,417.7	0.1	0.1	99.8	23.9	14.9	24.8	60.3
Iraq	11.8[4]	1989	15,160.6[10]	...	...	...	1986	8,784.3	—	0.4	99.6	4.6	23.5	74.9	1.6
Ireland	...	1988	314.7[31]	33.8	64.7	1.5[31]	1990	460.8	84.8	5.5	9.7	813.3	14.9	7.5	77.6
Isle of Man	...	1991	...	—	100.0	—	...	...	...	...	...	...	...	...	...
Israel	...	1988	267.7	...	...	...	1990	3,757.7	0.3	97.7	2.0	4,275.0	0.1	74.7	25.2
Italy	...	1987	2,473.6	5.9	19.2	74.9	1990	773.7	32.1	50.9	17.0	17,572.2	15.0	7.8	77.2
Jamaica	11.4	1991	397.5	99.2	0.8	—	1989	623.3	99.8	0.2	—	6.6	0.7	—	99.3
Japan	0.2[4]	1988	1,771.4	7.5	36.6	55.9	1990	536.6	34.8	64.3	0.9	60,817.0	15.0	8.6	76.4
Jersey	...	...	...	...	...	...	...	...	...	...	...	...	...	...	...
Jordan	7.7[3]	1990	291.8	—	100.0	—	1988	408.8	4.2	95.8	—	387.5	—	10.5	89.5
Kazakhstan	...	...	...	...	...	...	...	...	...	...	...	...	...	...	...
Kenya	0.2[4]	1990	20.9	...	...	...	1987	24.2	8.6	90.0	1.4	310.2	1.0	1.7	97.3
Kiribati	—	1990	—	...	...	...	1987	0.03	98.6	1.4	—	0.04	—	67.4	32.6
Korea, North	...	...	...	...	...	...	...	...	...	...	...	...	...	...	...
Korea, South	0.5[4]	1989	1,404.4	4.3	32.4	63.3	1990	194.2	23.1	69.2	7.7	11,298.9	20.3	4.5	75.2
Kuwait	40.9[3]	1989	9,441.8	—	—	100.0	1989	4,474.6	0.4	1.1	98.5	48.1	—	54.6	45.4
Kyrgyzstan	...	...	...	...	...	...	...	...	...	...	...	...	...	...	...
Laos	0.3[3]	1990	...	——100.0——		—	...	...	...	...	...	...	...	...	...
Latvia	...	...	...	...	...	...	1990	111.2	58.9	38.0	3.1	607.9	47.2	6.9	45.9
Lebanon	—[27]	...	...	...	...	...	1986	45.8	28.3	71.7	—	28.9	2.2	78.3	19.5
Lesotho	0.4[4]	1990	2.4	—	100.0	—	[14]	...	...	...	...	...	...	...	...
Liberia	3.0[4]	1989	122.3[33]	——100.0[33]——		—	1989	264.0	95.8	4.2	—	...	...	...	...
Libya	27.8[3]	1989	6,873.2	—	...	...	1990	8,682.4	—	—	100.0	6.3[13]	—	100.0[13]	—
Liechtenstein	...	...	...	...	...	...	...	...	...	...	...	...	...	...	...
Lithuania	...	...	...	...	...	...	1990	344.8	4.9	16.9	78.2	927.7	30.0	4.2	65.8
Luxembourg	0.1[4]	1990	8.0	—	100.0	—	[9]	...	...	...	...	...	...	...	...
Macau	...	1990	1.2	—	100.0	—	1989	—	—	—	—	19.2	—	74.5	25.5
Macedonia	...	...	...	...	...	...	...	...	...	...	...	...	...	...	...
Madagascar	0.3[3]	1989	6.0	——100.0——		—	1986	18.0	36.0	64.0	—	2.3	—	58.9	41.1
Malaŵi	...	1986	0.1	—	100.0	—	1985	—	—	—	—	6.1	—	60.5	39.5
Malaysia	9.7[4]	1990	5,922.8	4.5[3]	2.3[3]	93.2[3]	1990	5,038.4	2.7	1.9	95.4	802.7	39.4	25.3	35.3
Maldives	1.9	1991	1.9	—	100.0	—	1990	0.05	100.0	—	—	24.2[12]	0.1	10.3	89.6[12]
Mali	1.5	1991	36.6	——100.0——		—	1990	2.8	—	100.0	—	0.2	—	100.0	—
Malta	...	1988	3.1	—	100.0	—	1989	8.6	69.7	29.5	0.8	23.4	—	39.3	60.7
Marshall Islands	...	...	...	...	...	...	...	...	...	...	...	...	...	...	...
Martinique	...	1991	...	—	100.0	—	1990	1.7	34.1	—	65.9	155.1	—	—	100.0
Mauritania	9.9[3]	1989	76.0	——100.0——		—	1989	180.6	93.5	0.3	6.2	0.3[7]	—	100.0[7]	—
Mauritius	0.1	1991	2.6	—	100.0	—	1987	14.6	—	100.0	—	18.8	0.8	80.2	19.0
Mayotte	...	...	...	...	...	...	...	...	...	...	...	...	...	...	...
Mexico	2.3	1990	6,227.3[12]	22.5	20.3	57.2[12]	1990	9,836.2	3.4	3.3	93.3	722.0	33.0	39.2	27.8
Micronesia	—	—	—	—	—	—	...	...	...	...	...	...	...	...	...
Moldova	...	...	...	...	...	...	1990	75.1	54.4	45.6	—	664.5	40.0	12.6	47.4
Monaco	...	...	...	...	...	...	...	...	...	...	...	...	...	...	...
Mongolia	...	...	...	...	...	...	...	...	...	...	...	...	...	...	...
Morocco	2.7[4]	1990	645.5	——93.6[13]——		6.4[13]	1989	621.6	15.9	84.1	—	959.3	0.2	14.3	85.5
Mozambique	0.2[3]	1989	2.0	0.4[1, 27]	79.7[1, 27]	19.9[1, 27]	1984	1.7	71.6	—	28.4	21.0	—	100.0	—
Myanmar (Burma)	0.8[5]	1990–91	139.8[15]	...	...	...	1989	15.5	56.1	43.9	—	...	...	...	...
Namibia	21.6[4]	1990	408.1	——100.0——		—	1983	593.0	64.0	36.0	—	[14]	[14]	[14]	[14]
Nauru	...	1990	...	—	100.0	—	1987	90.9	—	100.0	—	...	...	...	...
Nepal	0.2[22]	1989–90	3.4	...	...	...	1986	0.4	—	100.0	—	2.7	14.3	85.7	—
Netherlands, The	3.1[3]	1990	6,999.8	—	7.9[13]	92.1[13]	1990	5,351.5	20.3	9.9	69.8	11,943.0	10.5	7.5	82.0

forestry, 1991						fisheries, 1991								country
production of roundwood				trade (value, '000 U.S.$)		catch (nominal)						trade (value, '000 U.S.$)		
total ('000 cubic metres)	fuelwood, charcoal (%)	industrial roundwood (%)		exports	imports	total ('000 metric tons)	by source (%)		by kind of catch (%)			exports	imports	
		total	sawlogs, veneer				marine	inland	fish	crusta-ceans	mollusks			
607	73.6	26.4	26.4	18,700	...	3.5	90.0	10.0	81.5	11.1	3.7	—	1,580	Equatorial Guinea
...	...	...	...	...	...	...	...	...	...	...	...	...	...	Eritrea[21]
...	...	...	...	...	...	317.4	...	...	...	...	...	...	...	Estonia
43,686	96.1	3.9	—	...	4,194	4.5	38.9	61.1	100.0	—	—	—	113	Ethiopia[21]
...	...	...	...	...	...	246.0	100.0	—	93.5	5.2	1.3	407,731	17,099	Faeroe Islands
307	12.1	87.9	86.6	47,506	16,026	31.1	86.9	13.1	78.8	4.4	14.8	33,015	25,700	Fiji
34,091	8.8	91.2	42.0	8,238,230	511,629	82.8	91.1	8.9	100.0	—	—	10,663	128,946	Finland
44,752	23.3	76.7	52.1	3,842,090	6,152,020	812.8	94.3	5.7	63.9	2.6	33.4	925,560[23]	2,925,994[23]	France
254	26.0	74.0	70.5	4,170	2,132	7.3	98.9	1.1	49.1	50.9	—	37,274	3,685	French Guiana
...	...	...	...	...	13,892	2.6	99.4	0.6	96.1	3.6	0.3	370	6,390	French Polynesia
4,286	61.9	38.1	38.1	225,804	5,979	22.0	90.9	9.1	80.8	19.2	—	4,450	12,580	Gabon
940	97.8	2.2	1.5	...	473	23.7	89.5	10.5	90.1	4.4	5.5	5,710	5,310	Gambia, The
...	...	...	...	...	...	0.5	100.0	—	100.0	—	—	...	...	Gaza Strip
...	...	...	...	...	...	104.0[4]	...	...	...	...	...	...	...	Georgia
44,874	10.0	90.0	48.3	6,818,620	12,567,493	300.2	84.4	15.6	84.4	4.7	10.9	715,975	2,114,720	Germany
17,122	90.6	9.4	7.2	93,453	11,455	365.0	84.4	15.6	98.6	0.4	1.0	15,619	31,320	Ghana
...	...	...	...	...	...	—	100.0	—	100.0	—	—	...	...	Gibraltar
2,345	57.6	42.4	23.7	100,202	998,786	149.0	93.2	6.8	88.9	4.0	7.1	86,013	172,982	Greece
—	—	—	—	...	...	113.4	100.0	—	35.5	64.5	—	325,735	5,854	Greenland
...	...	...	...	...	...	2.0	100.0	—	98.0	0.5	0.8	50	1,630	Grenada
17	88.2	11.8	11.8	...	43,252	8.4	99.5	0.5	91.5	2.3	6.0	200	22,009	Guadeloupe
...	...	...	...	...	...	0.8	76.2	23.8	100.0	—	—	...	...	Guam
8,049	98.6	1.4	1.3	19,111	70,028	6.7	55.5	44.5	61.9	37.8	0.3	14,980	2,204	Guatemala
...	...	...	...	...	...	[28]	[28]	[28]	[28]	[28]	[28]	5,703	...	Guernsey
3,988	89.3	10.7	0.4	800	1,056	37.5	90.7	9.3	100.0	—	—	—	4,750	Guinea
569	74.2	25.8	7.0	1,553	200	5.0	96.0	4.0	79.4	20.5	0.1	1,600	420	Guinea-Bissau
175	8.0	92.0	80.0	4,283	1,458	40.8	98.0	2.0	88.5	11.5	—	17,550	—	Guyana
5,957	96.0	4.0	3.8	...	10,187	5.2	93.2	6.8	74.7	17.5	7.8	2,130	4,170	Haiti
6,288	87.5	12.5	11.0	30,921	136,393	21.0	99.1	0.9	22.0	41.9	36.1	59,781	1,161	Honduras
193	100.0	—	—	860,643	1,935,923	230.9	97.4	2.6	90.1	5.3	4.6	641,927	1,236,578	Hong Kong
6,084	42.5	57.5	33.4	135,289	338,684	29.4	—	100.0	100.0	—	—	5,060	17,963	Hungary
—	—	—	—	...	59,293	1,051.4	99.9	0.1	95.2	3.8	1.0	1,280,006	13,981	Iceland
279,801	91.2	8.8	6.6	39,257	399,116	4,036.9	57.9	42.1	92.6	6.6	0.8	570,317	—	India
172,984	83.1	16.9	15.1	3,600,758	295,187	3,186.0	74.7	25.3	88.6	9.1	1.9	1,192,082	47,395	Indonesia
6,792	36.3	63.7	4.7	...	466,731	277.4	70.3	29.7	96.9	2.6	0.5	63,718	12,220	Iran
155	67.7	32.3	12.9	...	117,378	12.0	25.0	75.0	100.0	—	—	...	...	Iraq
1,677	3.0	97.0	62.6	136,239	466,715	240.7	99.7	0.3	88.0	3.5	8.5	308,147	97,985	Ireland
...	...	...	...	...	...	4.6	100.0	—	23.3	2.7	74.0	...	...	Isle of Man
113	11.5	88.5	31.9	25,816	404,877	20.7	16.3	83.7	98.6	1.0	0.4	7,175	88,620	Israel
8,393	51.3	48.7	26.8	1,818,251	6,165,752	548.2	89.7	10.3	56.4	6.4	37.2	249,039[32]	2,689,639[32]	Italy
180	7.2	92.8	59.4	85	66,906	10.4	69.0	31.0	98.7	1.2	—	6,962	27,348	Jamaica
28,272	1.2	98.8	62.4	2,139,035	12,452,561	9,306.8	97.8	2.2	81.8	1.9	15.2	839,200	12,043,577	Japan
...	...	...	...	...	...	2.8[28]	100.0[28]	—[28]	14.4[28]	81.5[28]	4.1[28]	3,052	...	Jersey
9	55.6	44.4	—	9,267	56,086	—	9.1	90.9	100.0	—	—	968	15,017	Jordan
...	...	...	...	...	...	82.7	...	...	...	...	...	...	...	Kazakhstan
36,861	95.1	4.9	1.2	3,621	24,378	198.6	3.7	96.3	99.5	0.4	0.1	24,480	540	Kenya
...	...	...	...	...	...	30.0	100.0	—	85.5	0.7	13.8	235	234	Kiribati
4,737	87.3	12.7	12.7	1,010	4,526	1,700.1	94.1	5.9	100.0	—	—	61,400	—	Korea, North
6,485	69.3	30.7	16.4	506,139	2,611,770	2,515.3	98.8	1.2	61.7	4.4	32.9	1,490,616	568,201	Korea, South
...	...	...	...	6,197	59,830	2.0	100.0	—	60.9	39.1	—	11,200	10,100	Kuwait
...	...	...	...	...	...	1.0	...	...	...	...	...	...	...	Kyrgyzstan
4,340	90.9	9.1	6.7	15,720	950	20.0	—	100.0	100.0	—	—	—	...	Laos
...	...	...	...	...	...	369.9	...	...	...	...	...	...	...	Latvia
481	96.3	3.7	3.7	13	40,872	1.8	94.4	5.6	97.2	1.4	1.4	...	...	Lebanon
631	100.0	—	—	...	4,588	—	—	100.0	100.0	—	—	[14]	[14]	Lesotho
6,134	80.9	19.1	16.4	78,264	2,751	9.6	58.4	41.6	98.8	1.2	—	1,320	8,170	Liberia
645	83.1	16.9	9.8	...	52,016	7.8	100.0	—	99.6	—	0.4	1,120	9,350	Libya
...	...	...	...	...	...	—	—	100.0	100.0	—	—	[34]	[34]	Liechtenstein
...	...	...	...	...	...	317.0	...	...	...	...	...	...	...	Lithuania
[9]	[9]	[9]	[9]	[9]	[9]	—	—	100.0	100.0	—	—	[9]	[9]	Luxembourg
...	...	...	...	1,399	14,677	2.3	100.0	—	58.5	38.8	2.7	6,878	15,022	Macau
1,063[4]	...	...	...	...	...	1.6[4]	—	100.0[4]	...	...	...	...	...	Macedonia
8,335	90.3	9.7	5.6	1,891	3,249	101.0	72.5	27.5	87.6	11.5	0.3	51,912	399	Madagascar
8,515	95.2	4.8	0.9	46	7,650	63.7	—	100.0	100.0	—	—	355	790	Malaŵi
49,327	18.1	81.9	79.2	3,120,337	498,699	620.0	97.7	2.3	75.2	12.7	10.8	264,938	170,478	Malaysia
...	...	...	...	...	3,374	80.7	100.0	—	99.5	—	—	36,969	—	Maldives
5,768	93.6	6.4	0.2	...	1,915	60.0	—	100.0	100.0	—	—	352	1,730	Mali
...	...	...	...	...	37,814	0.7	100.0	—	98.5	0.8	0.7	2,280	18,050	Malta
...	...	...	...	...	...	0.2	100.0	—	100.0	—	—	580	210	Marshall Islands
12	83.3	16.7	16.7	...	33,720	3.6	97.6	2.4	94.8	4.4	—	237	31,095	Martinique
13	61.5	38.5	7.7	...	844	90.0	93.3	6.7	56.2	0.3	43.5	147,156	679	Mauritania
17	17.6	82.4	52.9	...	34,748	18.9	99.7	0.3	97.6	0.5	1.9	20,695	15,406	Mauritius
...	...	...	...	...	...	0.8[7]	...	...	...	...	...	...	...	Mayotte
23,617	67.1	32.9	24.0	133,007	675,751	1,421.9	88.0	12.0	86.8	6.0	7.1	393,493	46,710	Mexico
...	...	...	...	...	...	1.4	99.6	0.4	98.3	0.7	0.5	1,060	293	Micronesia
...	...	...	...	...	...	5.2	...	...	...	...	...	...	...	Moldova
...	...	...	...	...	...	—	100.0	—	100.0	—	—	[23]	[23]	Monaco
2,390	56.5	43.5	43.5	99	1,494	0.1	—	100.0	100.0	—	—	—	2,260	Mongolia
2,549	55.1	44.9	9.9	3,311	238,874	592.9	99.8	0.2	83.3	1.0	15.7	608,919	1,241	Morocco
16,065	93.5	6.5	0.3	686	4,886	34.0	98.5	1.5	81.7	17.7	0.6	61,800	11,140	Mozambique
23,585	77.0	23.0	17.6	148,084	4,721	769.2	77.2	22.8	99.1	0.9	—	26,250	—	Myanmar (Burma)
[35]	[35]	[35]	[35]	[35]	[35]	204.5	100.0	—	99.8	0.2	—	[14]	[14]	Namibia
...	...	...	...	...	...	0.2	100.0	—	100.0	—	—	...	...	Nauru
18,704	96.7	3.3	3.3	224	3,860	16.0	—	100.0	100.0	—	—	...	...	Nepal
1,351	11.2	88.8	39.6	2,432,875	4,399,285	443.1	99.1	0.9	85.4	1.8	11.3	1,356,212	977,450	Netherlands, The

Extractive industries (continued)

country	mining														
	% of GDP, 1991	mineral production (value added)					trade (value)								
		year	total ('000,000 U.S.$)	by kind (%)			year	exports				imports			
				metals[a]	non-metals[b]	energy[c]		total ('000,000 U.S.$)	by kind (%)			total ('000,000 U.S.$)	by kind (%)		
									metals[a]	non-metals[b]	energy[c]		metals[a]	non-metals[b]	energy[c]
Netherlands Antilles	...	1988	7.4	—	100.0	—	1990[36]	257.2	0.1	1.7	98.2	1,451.6	—	0.2	99.8
New Caledonia	23.1[13]	1988	466.8	100.0	—	—	1991	400.0[37]	100.0[37]	—	—	12.8[7, 11]	—	13.3[7]	86.7[7, 11]
New Zealand	1.0[22]	1989–90	471.3	——14.6——		85.4	1990	200.9	16.3	6.1	77.6	782.6	18.8	11.9	69.3
Nicaragua	0.5	1991	16.5	82.2	17.8	—	1986	3.8	100.0	—	—	92.8	—	6.9	93.1
Niger	6.4[3]	1989	131.0	——100.0——		—	1985	164.9	100.0	—	—	—	—	—	—
Nigeria	12.7	1990	10,858.9	—	0.8	99.2	1986	5,451.9	0.2	0.2	99.6	70.3	21.9	78.1	—
Northern Mariana Islands	—	—	—	—	—	—	...	...	...	...	...	...	...	...	...
Norway	14.9[4]	1990	14,217.1	0.6	1.4	98.0	1990	14,991.6	1.7	1.5	96.8	2,001.4	70.3	8.9	20.8
Oman	50.6[4]	1990	5,378.4	—	0.7	99.3	1990	2,531.4	0.3	—	99.7	9.5	—	100.0	—
Pakistan	0.6[5]	1990–91	279.9	—22.0[1, 38]—		78.0[1, 38]	1989	49.2	12.9	30.2	56.9	633.3	19.2	5.1	75.7
Panama	0.1	1991	5.6	——100.0——		—	1989	120.9	4.0	94.6	1.4	121.8	4.7	0.1	95.2
Papua New Guinea	12.1[4]	1990	428.8	100.0	—	—	1988	860.0	100.0	—	—	3.9	—	100.0	—
Paraguay	0.4	1991	22.7	—	100.0	—	1991	0.3	—	100.0	—	64.3	—	27.0	73.0
Peru	2.4	1990	881.2	—48.6[20]—		51.4	1988	731.8	96.8	0.3	2.9	49.4	41.0	24.6	34.4
Philippines	1.5[4]	1990	685.2	75.7	——24.3——		1988	411.5	93.0	1.8	5.2	1,210.6	9.2	5.5	85.3
Poland	...	1990	1,903.5	17.9	17.6	64.5	1989	1,227.4	3.4	23.7	72.9	1,269.9	12.9	11.9	75.2
Portugal	...	1986	129.2	14.4	77.7	7.9	1990	493.6	70.5	29.4	0.1	2,727.6	13.3	5.7	81.0
Puerto Rico	0.1[5]	1990–91	32.0	—	100.0	—	1986[26]	50.7	2.4	95.9	1.7	52.1	0.4	28.8	70.8
Qatar	34.0	1991	2,266.5[15]	...	...	...	1989	2,211.4[12]	0.1	0.3	99.6[12]	49.1[11, 12]	62.8	16.0	21.2[11, 12]
Réunion	...	1991	...	—	100.0	—	1990	0.6	100.0	—	—	10.1	—	—	100.0
Romania	...	1990	1,818.1	1.4	7.3	91.3	...	...	...	...	...	...	...	...	...
Russia[41]	...	1989[1]	90,630.0	21.6	12.4	65.8	1984	52,690.0[42]	10.3	1.4	88.3[42]	10,070.0[42]	59.3	2.7	38.0[42]
Rwanda	0.2[3]	1989	9.9	100.0	—	—	1988	0.5	100.0	—	—	2.6	—	100.0	—
St. Kitts and Nevis	0.7	1991	1.0	—	100.0	—	1988	—	—	—	—	0.6	—	—	100.0
St. Lucia	0.7	1991	2.3	—	100.0	—	1986	—	—	—	—	1.5	—	—	100.0
St. Vincent	0.3	1991	0.4	—	100.0	—	1990	—	—	—	—	1.4	—	—	100.0
San Marino	...	...	...	...	...	...	...	...	...	...	...	...	...	...	...
São Tomé and Príncipe	0.2[7]	1986	0.1	—	100.0	—	1983	—	—	—	—	...	...	...	...
Saudi Arabia	35.5[4]	1990	33,110.8	——1.4——		98.6	1989	20,083.7	0.4	0.6	99.0	190.6	65.6	34.4	—
Senegal	1.3[3]	1989	37.0	—	100.0	—	1990	72.9	3.8	96.2	—	170.6	—	17.8	82.2
Seychelles	...	1989	—	—	100.0	—	1991	—	—	—	—	37.8[12]	—	0.4	99.6[12]
Sierra Leone	6.2[22]	1989–90	45.1	——100.0——		—	1986	112.6	57.0	43.0	—	0.1	—	100.0	—
Singapore	0.2	1991	54.8	—	100.0	—	1990	388.7	49.2	31.8	19.0	7,122.9	2.7	3.3	94.0
Slovakia	...	...	...	...	...	...	...	...	...	...	...	...	...	...	...
Slovenia	...	...	...	...	...	...	...	...	...	...	...	...	...	...	...
Solomon Islands	−0.3[4]	1990	−1.1	——100.0——		—	1988	0.7[44]	100.0[44]	—	—	0.7	—	51.1	48.9
Somalia	0.2	1991	1.0	—	100.0	—	1989	—	—	—	—	...	...	...	...
South Africa	10.7[4]	1989	9,012.6	——86.6——		13.4	1989[14]	4,143.7[45]	33.5	22.6	43.9[45]	193.7[45]	26.0	74.0	—[45]
Bophuthatswana	...	...	...	...	...	...	...	...	...	...	...	...	...	...	...
Ciskei	...	...	...	...	...	...	...	...	...	...	...	...	...	...	...
Transkei	0.1[7]	1986	0.4	...	...	...	...	...	...	...	...	...	...	...	...
Venda	3.9[27]	1987	8.5	—	—	100.0	...	...	...	...	...	...	...	...	...
Spain	1.4[19]	1989	3,057.9	10.5	25.2	64.3	1990	558.4	48.7	47.3	4.0	10,501.9	14.0	4.7	81.3
Sri Lanka	2.4[4]	1990	117.2[46]	—100.0[46]—		—	1987	92.1	10.2	89.8	—	292.2	6.0	12.4	81.6
Sudan, The	0.1[3]	1989	6.0	—100.0—		—	1989	—	—	—	—	...	...	...	...
Suriname	3.3[4]	1989[1]	520.4	96.4	—	3.6	1988	237.4	100.0	—	—	4.4[7]	—	—	100.0[7]
Swaziland	1.1[3]	1989	6.0	...	...	...	1986	17.2	—	70.0	30.0	[14]	[14]	[14]	[14]
Sweden	0.4[4]	1990	888.7	79.5	20.5	—	1990	975.6	81.9	15.0	3.1	3,978.1	12.3	7.2	80.5
Switzerland	1.1[8]	1991	...	—	100.0	—	1990	3,281.7	4.8	95.0	0.2	4,403.6	2.3	77.5	20.2
Syria	12.3[3]	1989	2,054.2[10]	—	—100.0[10]—		1989	814.2	—	—	100.0	122.2	0.7	11.7	87.6
Taiwan	0.4	1991	692.0	—	83.6	16.4	1991	467.2	...	...	...	6,509.6	——35.2——		64.8
Tajikistan	...	...	...	...	...	...	...	...	...	...	...	...	...	...	...
Tanzania	1.0[4]	1990	24.7	...	...	...	1988	8.4	—	100.0	—	113.5	—	24.1	75.9
Thailand	3.6[4]	1990	2,872.8	1.7	69.4	28.9	1988	779.3	7.3	82.0	10.7	1,763.9	18.9	30.8	50.3
Togo	7.5[3]	1989	91.0	—	100.0	—	1989	130.6	—	100.0	—	3.2	—	100.0	—
Tonga	0.8	1988–89	0.5	—	100.0	—	1988	—	—	—	—	0.4	—	33.7	66.3
Trinidad and Tobago	16.0	1991	842.8	—	1.2[13]	98.8[13]	1990	772.1	—	1.0	99.0	180.1	28.4	4.9	66.7
Tunisia	6.8	1990	853.1	——9.1[7]——		90.9[7]	1990	584.0	3.0	6.5	90.5	375.7	3.2	48.4	48.4
Turkey	1.9	1989	1,786.8	11.9	22.0	66.1	1990	376.5	28.4	64.1	7.5	4,940.1	12.3	1.9	85.8
Turkmenistan	...	...	...	...	...	...	...	...	...	...	...	...	...	...	...
Tuvalu	—	1991	—	—	—	—	1986	—	—	—	—	—	—	—	100.0
Uganda	—[3]	1989	0.2	...	...	...	1989	0.4	100.0	—	—	...	...	...	...
Ukraine	...	...	...	...	...	...	1990	7,590.9	80.2	4.5	15.3	10,662.0	35.9	2.7	61.4
United Arab Emirates	39.0[3]	1990	15,782.9[15]	—	—100.0[15]—		1986	9,043.3	0.3	0.1	99.6	33.3	19.7	79.5	0.8
United Kingdom	3.3[27]	1989[1]	23,578.9	—	5.0	95.0	1990	15,142.3	7.5	28.0	64.5	16,721.7	15.8	26.1	58.1
United States	1.7[13]	1988	80,400.0	2.6[27]	6.5[27]	90.9[27]	1990	13,434.6	37.8	23.2	39.0	60,582.4	7.1	9.9	83.0
Uruguay	0.2	1991	17.2	—	100.0	—	1990	3.2	—	100.0	—	219.2	2.7	5.2	92.1
Uzbekistan	...	...	...	...	...	...	...	...	...	...	...	...	...	...	...
Vanuatu	...	1991	—	—	100.0	—	1986	—	—	—	—	0.5	—	38.0	62.0
Venezuela	18.5	1990	11,372.7	2.3	0.9	96.8	1990	9,027.0	1.3	0.1	98.6	186.0	66.1	31.6	2.3
Vietnam	...	...	...	...	...	...	...	...	...	...	...	...	...	...	...
Virgin Islands (U.S.)	...	1987[1]	2.7	—	100.0	—	1986[26]	0.3	18.3	81.7	—	966.5	—	0.2	99.8
West Bank	...	...	...	...	...	...	1986[24]	11.8[24, 47]	...	...	...	...	...	...	...
Western Sahara	...	...	...	...	[48]	...	...	...	...	...	...	...	...	...	...
Western Samoa	—	1991	—	—	—	—	1989	—	—	—	—	...	...	...	...
Yemen	9.1[4]	1990	585.8	—	——100.0——		1985[49]	0.4	—	100.0	—	86.5[12]	—	—	100.0[12]
Yugoslavia	2.1[4, 50]	1989[50]	1,784.2	25.7	16.4	57.9	1990[50]	369.7	90.5	6.5	3.0	3,313.8	8.7	5.3	86.0
Zaire	24.1[3]	1989	1,197.0	...	...	...	1989	324.8	3.5	50.1	46.4	...	...	...	...
Zambia	8.2[4]	1990	352.5	96.1[27]	3.9[27]	—	1989	26.1	—	100.0	—	...	...	...	...
Zimbabwe	8.2[4]	1988	383.5	80.0	——20.0——		1986	75.8	14.0	83.4	2.6	29.0	81.8	18.2	—

[1]Gross value of production (output). [2]1988–89 average. [3]1989. [4]1990. [5]1990–91. [6]1988–89. [7]1986. [8]1985. [9]Belgium includes Luxembourg. [10]Mostly crude petroleum. [11]Includes coke and briquettes. [12]Includes petroleum products. [13]1988. [14]South Africa includes Botswana, Lesotho, Namibia, and Swaziland. [15]Mostly crude petroleum and natural gas. [16]Mostly diamonds, some gold. [17]China includes Taiwan. [18]Data refer to former Czechoslovakia. [19]1984. [20]Includes coal mining. [21]Ethiopia includes Eritrea. [22]1989–90. [23]France includes Monaco. [24]West Bank includes Gaza Strip. [25]Former West Germany only. [26]Trade with the United States only. [27]1987. [28]Jersey includes Guernsey. [29]Mostly bauxite and diamonds. [30]Mostly bauxite. [31]Excludes crude petroleum

forestry, 1991						fisheries, 1991								country
production of roundwood				trade (value, '000 U.S.$)		catch (nominal)						trade (value, '000 U.S.$)		
total ('000 cubic metres)	fuelwood, charcoal (%)	industrial roundwood (%)		exports	imports	total ('000 metric tons)	by source (%)		by kind of catch (%)			exports	imports	
		total	sawlogs, veneer				marine	inland	fish	crusta-ceans	mollusks			
...	...	...	...	...	13,902	1.1	100.0	—	100.0	—	—	281	7,355	Netherlands Antilles
12	—	100.0	91.7	...	9,807	4.9	100.0	—	58.1	13.9	2.7	4,365	3,730	New Caledonia
13,987	0.4	99.6	59.2	884,732	211,874	609.0	99.8	0.2	83.6	0.6	15.7	460,766	37,084	New Zealand
4,182	79.0	21.0	19.8	2,634	6,508	5.7	95.5	4.5	44.1	55.9	—	18,079	1,332	Nicaragua
5,116	93.8	6.2	—	...	4,511	3.2	—	100.0	100.0	—	—	—	1,400	Niger
111,059	92.9	7.1	5.0	11,224	97,556	266.6	65.9	34.1	95.8	4.2	—	15,590	191,460	Nigeria
...	...	...	...	...	...	0.1	100.0	—	98.3	1.7	—	18	...	Northern Mariana Islands
10,987	8.3	91.7	51.9	1,516,504	708,281	2,095.9	100.0	—	97.4	2.4	0.2	2,282,247	307,051	Norway
...	...	...	...	...	46,878	117.8	100.0	—	97.5	0.9	1.6	34,515	3,947	Oman
27,174	91.0	9.0	7.5	...	153,277	515.5	77.5	22.5	92.5	6.4	1.1	110,365	—	Pakistan
1,872	91.2	8.8	5.6	1,010	56,176	147.4	99.8	0.2	89.4	9.3	1.3	74,757[39]	10,610[39]	Panama
8,188	67.6	32.4	30.3	113,800	5,401	25.3	47.5	52.5	90.1	5.9	—	12,470	35,400	Papua New Guinea
8,466	63.3	36.7	31.8	27,568	20,947	13.0	—	100.0	100.0	—	—	92	803	Paraguay
7,912	86.8	13.2	12.0	4,064	109,450	6,944.2	99.6	0.4	98.5	0.2	1.3	491,076	1,000	Peru
38,738	88.5	11.5	4.0	94,200	160,795	2,311.8	73.5	26.5	85.2	4.9	9.7	467,729	96,109	Philippines
17,182	16.6	83.4	45.9	250,484	126,728	457.4	89.5	10.5	90.6	2.1	7.3	188,743	37,450	Poland
11,181	5.3	94.7	35.0	1,209,223	738,293	325.3	99.2	0.8	91.4	0.4	8.6	287,214	757,843	Portugal
...	...	...	...	...	...	2.3	92.3	7.7	82.6	12.6	4.8	[40]	[40]	Puerto Rico
...	...	...	...	...	11,040	8.1	100.0	—	87.6	11.5	0.9	—	2,700	Qatar
36	86.1	13.9	11.1	...	54,776	2.3	99.9	0.1	84.9	13.8	—	9,115	38,095	Réunion
14,769	13.5	86.5	29.7	170,953	79,840	124.9	67.6	32.4	100.0	—	—	330	10,840	Romania
355,400	22.8	77.2	38.6	2,773,316	926,900	9,216.9	88.8	11.2	95.1	2.4	2.4	837,169	46,068	Russia[41]
5,620	95.9	4.1	0.4	...	5,508	3.6	—	100.0	100.0	—	—	—	240	Rwanda
...	...	...	...	...	...	1.8	100.0	—	87.4	12.6	—	150[43]	900[43]	St. Kitts and Nevis
...	...	...	...	...	...	0.9	100.0	—	99.6	0.4	—	—	2,630	St. Lucia
...	...	...	...	...	1,840	7.7	100.0	—	42.9	1.0	56.1	17,077	535	St. Vincent
...	...	...	...	...	...	—	—	100.0	100.0	—	—	[32]	[32]	San Marino
9	—	100.0	100.0	...	...	3.5	100.0	—	99.1	0.1	0.8	...	680	São Tomé and Príncipe
...	...	...	...	...	371,403	43.3	95.4	4.6	93.1	6.9	—	4,068	78,171	Saudi Arabia
5,098	87.9	12.1	0.1	...	31,154	319.7	94.5	5.5	90.3	1.8	7.9	233,400	38,635	Senegal
...	...	...	...	...	...	5.9	100.0	—	98.8	0.4	0.8	16,045	5,372	Seychelles
3,146	96.1	3.9	0.1	52	2,061	50.0	70.0	30.0	92.8	2.0	5.2	10,500	1,460	Sierra Leone
...	...	...	...	633,742	964,198	13.1	99.8	0.2	77.9	11.5	10.6	499,950	460,545	Singapore
...	...	...	...	...	...	...	...	...	...	...	...	...	...	Slovakia
2,435[4]	...	...	...	...	...	6.9[4]	87.2[4]	12.8[4]	...	...	...	...	...	Slovenia
449	30.7	69.3	69.3	34,952	679	69.3	100.0	—	98.5	—	0.1	40,909	179	Solomon Islands
7,326	98.7	1.3	0.4	...	873	16.1	98.1	1.9	95.0	3.1	1.9	9,240	10	Somalia
19,679[35]	36.0[35]	64.0[35]	24.3[35]	381,025[35]	232,252[35]	498.9	99.5	0.5	97.2	0.7	2.1	140,536[14]	143,417[14]	South Africa
...	...	...	...	...	...	...	...	...	...	...	...	...	...	Bophuthatswana
...	...	...	...	...	...	...	...	...	...	...	...	...	...	Ciskei
...	...	...	...	...	...	...	...	...	...	...	...	...	...	Transkei
...	...	...	...	...	...	...	...	...	...	...	...	...	...	Venda
17,272	11.5	88.5	29.3	1,120,466	2,783,990	1,350.0	97.8	2.2	75.7	2.2	22.1	772,651	2,748,305	Spain
9,096	92.9	7.1	0.3	...	75,852	198.1	88.0	12.0	96.9	3.0	0.1	21,477	53,116	Sri Lanka
23,449	90.7	9.3	—	...	9,278	33.3	4.5	95.5	100.0	—	—	100	2,300	Sudan, The
140	12.9	87.1	68.6	552	2,640	4.1	96.3	3.7	73.9	26.1	—	4,480	300	Suriname
2,223	25.2	74.8	14.3	75,171	655	0.1	—	100.0	100.0	—	—	[14]	[14]	Swaziland
51,724	8.6	91.4	43.7	9,872,643	1,168,014	245.0	97.7	2.3	98.0	1.3	0.7	167,623	441,095	Sweden
4,070	17.2	82.8	61.4	1,283,312	2,136,306	4.8	—	100.0	100.0	—	—	7,506[34]	392,668[34]	Switzerland
59	25.4	74.6	42.4	113	52,924	5.5	27.3	72.7	98.8	1.2	—	47	451	Syria
94	20.7	79.3	...	...	...	1,316.7	80.0	20.0	...	...	...	589,980[13]	118,195[13]	Taiwan
...	...	...	...	...	...	3.9	...	...	...	...	...	...	...	Tajikistan
35,545	94.1	5.9	0.9	2,974	13,014	400.3	13.8	86.2	99.4	0.4	0.1	—	—	Tanzania
37,940	92.4	7.6	0.6	135,512	1,210,073	3,065.2	91.2	8.8	76.7	9.9	11.7	2,901,366	1,049,962	Thailand
1,234	84.8	15.2	0.6	...	5,063	12.5	96.6	3.4	100.0	—	—	1,170	18,500	Togo
5	—	100.0	100.0	...	2,027	1.9	100.0	—	100.0	—	—	1,199	364	Tonga
72	30.6	69.4	66.7	458	54,396	10.3	100.0	—	87.5	12.5	—	2,796	5,584	Trinidad and Tobago
3,320	94.9	5.1	0.5	9,257	182,707	90.7	100.0	—	82.6	2.5	14.9	82,156	1,335	Tunisia
15,764	62.1	37.9	23.0	47,679	385,339	364.6	87.1	12.9	92.0	0.6	7.4	60,984	24,768	Turkey
...	...	...	...	...	...	43.0	...	...	...	...	...	...	...	Turkmenistan
...	...	...	...	...	...	0.5	100.0	—	100.0	—	—	...	...	Tuvalu
15,715	87.1	12.9	0.4	...	2,109	254.9	—	100.0	100.0	—	—	...	...	Uganda
...	...	...	...	...	...	900.0	...	...	...	...	...	...	...	Ukraine
...	...	...	...	...	...	92.3	100.0	—	99.9	0.1	—	17,970	16,840	United Arab Emirates
6,409	4.4	95.6	56.1	1,727,240	8,853,400	823.2	97.7	2.3	86.0	5.2	8.8	1,121,885	1,911,905	United Kingdom
495,800	17.3	82.7	50.3	12,478,143	13,466,987	5,473.3	95.0	5.0	75.4	9.3	14.7	3,279,343[40]	5,997,616[40]	United States
3,829	77.6	22.4	15.7	16,826	29,647	143.7	99.7	0.3	98.3	—	1.7	111,738	3,381	Uruguay
...	...	...	...	...	...	27.4	...	...	...	...	...	...	...	Uzbekistan
63	38.1	61.9	61.9	1,021	176	3.2	100.0	—	65.5	9.1	23.8	—	579	Vanuatu
1,290	60.3	39.7	37.7	...	221,163	352.8	94.0	6.0	90.3	3.6	6.1	89,530	4,574	Venezuela
29,525	83.6	16.4	10.0	93,476	12,677	877.0	69.6	30.4	88.0	8.2	3.8	112,816	—	Vietnam
...	...	...	...	...	...	0.9	100.0	—	87.7	8.4	3.9	...	...	Virgin Islands (U.S.)
...	...	...	...	...	...	...	...	...	...	...	...	...	...	West Bank
...	...	...	...	...	...	—	100.0	—	—	—	—	...	...	Western Sahara
131	53.4	46.6	44.3	11	1,476	0.6	100.0	—	99.1	0.4	0.5	110	1,000	Western Samoa
324	100.0	—	—	29	10,499	85.3	99.0	1.0	94.8	2.7	2.5	13,600	2,550	Yemen
4,351[4]	...	...	...	...	...	8.1[4]	5.7[4]	94.3[4]	...	...	...	2,582[50]	33,567[50]	Yugoslavia
40,079	92.7	7.3	1.0	23,886	8,973	160.0	1.3	98.7	100.0	—	—	—	62,760	Zaire
13,719	94.4	5.6	1.9	...	6,000	65.9	—	100.0	100.0	—	—	630	470	Zambia
7,925	79.1	20.9	6.5	7,738	19,407	22.2	—	100.0	100.0	—	—	96	1,129	Zimbabwe

and natural gas. [32]Italy includes San Marino. [33]Mostly iron ore. [34]Switzerland includes Liechtenstein. [35]South Africa includes Namibia. [36]Curaçao and Bonaire only. [37]Mostly nickel. [38]1985–86. [39]Excludes the Free Zone of Colón and the Canal Zone. [40]United States includes Puerto Rico. [41]Data refer to the former U.S.S.R. [42]Includes refined petroleum and electricity. [43]Includes Anguilla. [44]Gold only. [45]Excludes crude petroleum. [46]Mostly precious and semiprecious stones. [47]Exports of stone and marble to Jordan only. [48]Accounts for 5–6% of 1988 phosphate production of Morocco. [49]Former Yemen Arab Republic only. [50]Data refer to former Yugoslavia only.

Manufacturing industries

This table provides a summary of manufacturing activity by industrial sector for the countries of the world, providing figures for total manufacturing value added, as well as the percentage contribution of 29 major branches of manufacturing activity to the gross domestic product. U.S. dollar figures for total value added by manufacturing are given but should be used with caution because of uncertainties with respect to national accounting methods, purchasing power parities, price structures and preferments, exchange rates, and so on, especially for countries having nonconvertible currencies.

Manufacturing activity is classified here according to a modification of the International Standard Industrial Classification (ISIC), revision 2, published by the United Nations. A summary of the 2-, 3-, and 4-digit ISIC codes (groups) defining these 29 sectors follows, providing definitional detail beyond that possible in the column headings.

The collection and publication of national manufacturing data is usually carried out by one of three methods: a full census of manufacturing (usually done every 5 to 10 years for a given country), a periodic survey of manufacturing (usually taken at annual or other regular intervals between censuses), and the onetime sample survey (often limited in geographical, sectoral or size of enterprise coverage). The full census is, naturally, the most complete, but, since up to 10 years may elapse between such censuses, it is sometimes necessary to substitute a survey of more recent date but less complete coverage. In certain instances, in order to provide the most timely data, the estimate series maintained by the United National Industrial Development Organization (UNIDO) in Vienna for its *Industry and Development Global Report* and other studies has been used.

ISIC code(s)		Products manufactured
31		Food, beverages, and tobacco
	311+312	food including prepared animal feeds
	313	alcoholic and nonalcoholic beverages
	314	tobacco manufactures
32		Textiles, wearing apparel, and leather goods
	321	spinning of textile fibres, weaving and finishing of textiles, knitted articles, carpets, rope, etc.
	322	wearing apparel (including leather clothing; excluding knitted articles and footwear)
	323+324	leather products (including footwear; excluding wearing apparel), leather substitutes, and fur products

Manufacturing industries

country	year	total manufacturing value added ('000,000 U.S.$)	(31) food (311+312)	beverages (313)	tobacco manufactures (314)	(32) textiles (exc. wearing apparel) (321)	wearing apparel (322)	leather and fur products (323+324)	(33) wood products (exc. furniture) (331)	wood furniture (332)	(34) paper, paper products (341)	printing and publishing (342)	(35) industrial chemicals (351)	paints, soaps, etc. (352 exc. 3522)	drugs and medicines (3522)
Afghanistan	1988–89[1]	435	18.3	1.9	—	8.0	0.4	16.7	—0.5—		0.9	4.9	4.8	0.2	2.7
Albania	1990[2]	885		—23.9—			—33.2—		—6.5[3]—		[3]	1.1			—7.7—
Algeria	1990	5,821	14.0	3.0	3.5	7.2	6.4	3.4	3.2	1.5	3.8	0.4	0.4	—2.8—	
American Samoa	1990	297	...	...	...	...	...	...	...	...	...	...	...	...	...
Andorra	1989[5]	22	0.6	20.6	—	—	45.9	0.2	—0.4—		2.3	0.7	—	0.2	—
Angola	1989	319	20.0	—12.2—			—11.6—		—3.7—		—0.3—		9.1[6]	[6]	[6]
Antigua and Barbuda	1990	14	...	...	...	...	...	...	...	...	...	...	...	...	...
Argentina	1990	36,987	13.8	3.6	2.1	6.6	1.6	1.6	0.8	0.8	3.0	2.0	6.0	—6.4—	
Armenia	1990[8, 9]	1,923[10]	—9.9—		...	14.7	2.0	15.4	...	...	...	...	3.5[6]	[6]	[6]
Aruba	1982	20	...	...	...	...	...	...	...	...	...	...	...	...	...
Australia	1989–90	52,692	13.2	3.2	0.7	3.1	2.3	0.7	3.2	1.7	2.4	7.6	3.1	3.0	1.3
Austria	1989[11]	25,148	7.1	2.6	4.7	4.2	1.8	0.9	2.3	3.3	4.4	3.8	4.3	1.8	1.7
Azerbaijan	1990[8, 9]	12,166[12]	—38.0—		...		—18.4—		...	...	1.7	...	5.9[6]	[6]	[6]
Bahamas, The	1987[11]	101	18.1	41.6	...	0.2	1.9	—	...	3.7[13]	0.2	12.3	[14]	0.8	11.2
Bahrain	1982[11, 15]	904	...	...	...	...	...	...	...	...	...	...	56.6	...	...
Bangladesh	1988–89[16]	1,476	17.7	0.2	4.9	30.9	8.4	3.3	0.8	0.1	2.3	1.7	10.8	1.6	5.1
Barbados	1990	122	28.1	13.2	1.7	0.8	7.4	—	—	1.7	0.8	9.9	—	—2.5—	
Belarus	1989[8, 9]	39,976[12]	—14.3—		...		—18.1—		—4.7—		...	...	8.7[6]	[6]	[6]
Belgium	1990	43,114	16.7	1.9	0.5	4.9	2.2	0.3	0.8	3.6	2.5	3.4	10.6	—2.8—	
Belize	1990	34	69.8	0.5	4.7	...	8.5	...	1.7	0.9	2.6	0.4	1.4	—0.6—	
Benin	1986	56		—62.5—			—8.8—		—3.4—		—4.0—				—5.5—
Bermuda	1990	173	...	...	...	...	...	...	...	...	...	...	...	...	...
Bhutan	1991[1, 17]	38	10.9	6.9	—	—	—	—	26.0	—	—	—	33.1	—	—
Bolivia	1989[11, 18]	539	13.5	13.3	1.0	0.9	0.3	1.8	2.1	0.1	0.4	2.6	0.4	1.1	1.9
Bosnia and Herzegovina	1989	4,252	8.3	0.9	1.1	3.5	10.5	6.5	—12.0—		3.3	1.0	7.3[19]	[19]	[19]
Botswana	1990	148	38.8	19.0	—	9.5	1.4	0.7	0.7	0.7	2.7	0.7	0.7	—0.7—	
Brazil	1990	118,743	10.6	0.9	0.7	6.9	2.9	3.2	1.0	0.9	3.3	2.1	5.9	—6.0—	
Brunei	1990	582	...	...	...	...	...	...	...	...	...	...	...	...	...
Bulgaria	1990[20]	14,993	14.2	2.3	2.3	7.8	6.1	2.6	1.6	2.4	0.8	0.7	3.3	—3.2—	
Burkina Faso	1990	216	45.4	16.7	0.9	16.2	1.9	3.7	—	1.4	—	0.9	0.9	—	—
Burundi	1990	89	42.0	26.1	12.5	3.4	3.4	—	—	—	—	1.1	3.4	—1.1—	
Cambodia	1988[8, 9]	25[21]		—70.2—		—10.3—		...	...	...	...	...	—	...	—
Cameroon	1990	1,266	29.7	18.7	3.3	9.1	1.1	0.8	5.5	2.3	0.6	1.0	3.3	—4.2—	
Canada	1989[11]	114,620	10.1	2.7	0.7	2.7	2.5	0.5	4.4	1.9	8.6	6.3	4.6	3.3	1.9
Cape Verde	1986[9]	24	—45.5—		8.3	—	...	...	—20.8—		—	...	—	...	...
Central African Republic	1990	51	27.5	13.7	19.6	2.0	—	—	13.7	2.0	—	5.9	2.0	—3.9—	
Chad	1988[9]	98	...	...	...	17.5[23]	—	—	—	—	—	—	—	...	—
Chile	1989[11, 24]	8,484	17.6	3.6	3.2	3.9	1.8	1.7	3.2	0.6	6.9	2.2	2.8	3.9	2.0
China	1990	89,865	5.0	2.7	6.9	11.5	2.3	1.0	0.6	0.5	2.2	1.1	9.8	1.2	2.2
Colombia	1989	7,971	16.1	12.3	2.2	10.2	3.0	1.9	0.7	0.5	3.6	3.0	6.7	—7.1—	
Comoros	1991	11	...	...	—	...	...	...	...	...	—	—	—	—	—
Congo	1990	105	16.3	21.2	4.8	4.8	1.0	3.8	10.6	5.8	1.0	1.0	1.9	—2.9—	
Costa Rica	1990[11]	923	30.9	13.3	3.3	3.3	3.3	1.3	2.3	2.2	4.7	3.5	3.4	3.5	1.6
Côte d'Ivoire	1990	1,481	18.8	4.7	4.4	14.7	0.7	1.2	3.7	1.0	0.6	1.0	1.3	—4.7—	
Croatia	1989	8,364	13.0	2.3	1.1	4.5	7.7	5.7	—6.5—		2.4	1.5	11.0[19]	[19]	[19]
Cuba	1990[20]	6,030	17.1	6.0	43.6	1.8	1.6	1.2	0.9	0.7	0.2	1.3	1.1	—5.0—	
Cyprus[25]	1990	792	12.7	9.6	5.4	4.2	14.3	5.3	5.3	4.6	1.7	4.5	0.4	3.0	0.6
Czech Republic[26]	1990[9]	12,527	7.3	2.1	0.2	6.3	1.8	...	2.3	1.2	2.0	1.0	5.6	0.5	0.9
Denmark	1990[16, 18]	22,978	17.7	3.3	0.9	2.7	1.1	0.3	2.1	2.8	2.7	6.9	4.8	2.1	4.6
Djibouti	1990	68	...	...	—	—	...	...	...	...	—	—	...	...	—
Dominica	1991[16]	10	...	...	—	—	...	—	...	...	—	—	—	...	—
Dominican Republic	1990	1,308	31.6	13.6	5.1	3.4	1.2	3.0	0.2	1.5	2.8	1.7	2.1	—3.4—	
Ecuador	1989[11, 24]	853	28.8	4.2	0.8	10.7	1.4	1.4	1.7	1.4	4.4	3.0	2.6	6.3	2.4
Egypt	1988–89[16, 27]	12,980	22.1	1.8	3.5	15.5	0.6	0.7	0.6	1.4	1.2	1.5	3.1	4.0	2.2
El Salvador	1992[9]	1,209	37.0	14.2	4.4	6.3	4.6	1.5	1.5	2.3[13]	1.6	1.6		—5.5—	
Equatorial Guinea	1990[8]	1.9	27.6	4.1	...	...	2.6	...	...	49.3	...	1.2	...	—13.8—	
Eritrea[28]	...	...	...	...	...	...	...	...	...	...	...	...	...	...	...
Estonia	1990[8, 9]	6,334[10]	—25.8—		...	15.9	4.1	3.3	—8.7—		1.1	...	...	...	...
Ethiopia[28]	1987–88[24]	754	17.4	22.9	7.9	13.0	1.3	5.7	1.0	0.6	0.8	2.4	0.3	—2.9—	
Faeroe Islands	1988[9, 16]	186	50.2[29]	...	...	...	...	...	...	...	...	...	...	...	...

ISIC code(s)		Products manufactured
33		Wood and wood products
	331	sawlogs, wood products (excluding furniture), cane products, and cork products
	332	wood furniture
34		Paper and paper products, printing and publishing
	341	wood pulp, paper, and paper products
	342	printing, publishing, and bookbinding
35		Chemicals and chemical, petroleum, coal, rubber, and plastic products
	351	basic industrial chemicals (including fertilizers, pesticides, and synthetic fibres)
	352 minus 3522	chemical products not elsewhere specified (including paints, varnishes, and soaps and other toiletries)
	3522	drugs and medicines
	353+354	refined petroleum and derivatives of petroleum and coal
	355	rubber products
	356	plastic products (excluding synthetic fibres)
36		Glass, ceramic, and nonmetallic mineral products
	361+362	pottery, china, glass, and glass products
	369	bricks, tiles, cement, cement products, plaster products, etc.

ISIC code(s)		Products manufactured
37		Basic metals
	371	iron and steel
	372	nonferrous basic metals and processed nickel and cobalt
38		Fabricated metal products, machinery and equipment
	381	fabricated metal products (including cutlery, hand tools, fixtures, and structural metal products)
	382 minus 3825	nonelectrical machinery and apparatus not elsewhere specified
	3825	office, computing, and accounting machinery
	383 minus 3832	electrical machinery and apparatus not elsewhere specified
	3832	radio, television, and communications equipment (including electronic parts)
	384 minus 3843	transport equipment not elsewhere specified
	3843	motor vehicles (excluding motorcycles)
	385	professional and scientific equipment; photographic and optical goods; watches and clocks
39		Other manufactured goods
	390	jewelry, musical instruments, sporting goods, artists' equipment, toys, etc.

			(36)		(37)		(38)								(39)	country
refined petroleum and products	rubber products	plastic products	pottery, china, and glass	bricks, tiles, cement, etc.	iron and steel	non-ferrous metals	fabricated metal products	nonelectrical machinery	office equip., computers	electrical equip.	radio, television	transport equip. exc. motor vehicles	motor vehicles	professional equip.	jewelry, musical instruments	
(353+354)	(355)	(356)	(361+362)	(369)	(371)	(372)	(381)	(382 exc. 3825)	(3825)	(383 exc. 3832)	(3832)	(384 exc. 3843)	(3843)	(385)	(390)	
—	—	2.1	1.1		0.4	—	—	—	—	—	—	—	0.1	—	37.1	Afghanistan
			...	3.5	20.1[4]		[4]								4.0	Albania
2.9	0.5	1.0	1.1	8.8	9.9	0.6	9.3	1.6		5.3		7.1		1.0	1.3	Algeria
...	...	...	...	...	...	...	...	...	...	...	...	...	...	...	...	American Samoa
—	0.1	4.6	0.2	0.1	0.8	1.6	—	3.3		14.6		—	—	2.4	1.3	Andorra
20.0	[6]	[6]	11.3		1.9		5.0					4.7		[7]	0.3[7]	Angola
...	...	...	...	...	...	...	...	...	...	...	...	...	...	...	...	Antigua and Barbuda
19.2	1.3	1.2	1.3	3.2	5.5	1.0	5.4	2.8		3.5		6.6		0.4	0.3	Argentina
...	[6]	[6]	...	2.0	...	...	8.7								...	Armenia
...	...	...	...	...	...	...	...	...	...	...	...	...	...	...	...	Aruba
3.2	1.0	3.2	2.2	3.0	4.6	7.1	7.9	4.0		2.0	3.8	3.0	7.7	0.9	0.8	Australia
2.2	1.1	1.6	2.0	4.8	7.6	1.8	7.9	9.8		9.2	2.6	0.9	4.0	0.7	0.9	Austria
9.2	[6]	[6]	...	2.7	3.4		18.7								...	Azerbaijan
−1.9[14]	...	0.8	0.1	0.3	6.4	...	...	...	...	0.9	0.4	...	...	...	3.2	Bahamas, The
35.9	...	...	...	...	...	7.5	...	...	...	...	...	...	...	...	...	Bahrain
0.7	0.6	0.4	0.5	2.1	1.3	...	1.7	0.5		2.4		1.7		—	0.4	Bangladesh
5.0	2.5	2.5	0.8	3.3	—	—	9.1	4.1		4.1		2.5		—	—	Barbados
4.5	[6]	[6]	...	4.0	...	...	38.7								...	Belarus
1.4	0.9	4.3	1.8	2.0	4.6	2.2	7.6	7.7		7.6		6.9		0.4	2.2	Belgium
...	...	...	...	4.9	...	...	1.4	...	...	...	...	2.1	0.4	...	—	Belize
			10.1		—	—	5.0								0.7	Benin
...	...	...	...	...	...	...	...	...	...	...	...	...	...	...	...	Bermuda
—	—	1.8	—	21.2	—	—	—	—	—	—	—	—	—	—	—	Bhutan
50.2	...	1.3	0.5	4.6	—	1.9	1.0	0.1		0.2	—	0.5		0.1	—	Bolivia
−0.7	0.2	[19]	2.4		5.8	7.0	11.6	5.8		6.3		7.1		...	0.3	Bosnia and Herzegovina
—	0.7	—	—	—	—	—	7.5	0.7		0.7		0.7		—	14.3	Botswana
7.2	2.1	2.6	0.9	3.4	7.1	2.3	4.0	8.8		8.5		6.7		1.0	1.1	Brazil
...	...	...	...	...	...	...	...	...	...	...	...	...	...	...	...	Brunei
1.3	2.2	1.4	1.3	2.6	2.0	1.3	3.3	16.7		7.7		4.6		2.0	6.3	Bulgaria
—	1.4	0.9	—	—	0.5	0.5	0.5	0.5		0.5		1.4		—	6.0	Burkina Faso
—	—	—	—	2.3	—	—	4.5	—	—	—	—	—	—	—	—	Burundi
—	...	—	...	...	—	—	...	—	—	—	—	...	—	—	...	Cambodia
0.6	0.7	6.5	1.0	1.1	3.0	3.2	1.2	1.3		0.3		0.7		—	0.8	Cameroon
1.4	1.2	2.5	0.7	2.7	3.7	3.4	5.8	5.6	1.1	3.0	3.6	3.5	9.5	0.8	1.5	Canada
—	—	—	...	...	...	—	[22]	—	—	—	—	10.8[22]	—	—	—	Cape Verde
—	—	—	—	—	—	—	2.0	—	—	—	—	3.9		—	3.9	Central African Republic
—	—	—	—	—	—	—	—	...	—	—	—	...	—	—	...	Chad
6.5	0.8	1.5	0.8	2.2	4.1	22.3	3.7	1.7	—	1.2	0.3	0.4	0.9	0.1	0.2	Chile
3.2	1.8	1.9	6.4		7.3	2.3	3.3	11.3		4.9	3.4	4.4		0.9	1.9	China
1.9	1.6	2.8	2.0	4.5	4.7	0.5	3.3	1.7		3.7		4.2		0.9	1.1	Colombia
—	—	—	—	—	—	—	—	—	—	—	—	—	—	—	—	Comoros
1.9	1.0	1.0	1.9	1.9	—	—	8.7	1.9		1.9		4.8		—	—	Congo
3.6	1.7	3.7	1.5	3.7	...	0.1	2.0	1.4		1.2	2.2	1.0	0.7	...	0.4	Costa Rica
17.3	0.3	—	0.3	1.9	0.2	0.1	4.3	0.2		1.2		15.8		—	1.7	Côte d'Ivoire
4.0	1.0	[19]	3.9		2.1	1.8	7.6	8.4		6.6		8.7		...	0.3	Croatia
...	1.4	1.3	0.5	1.9	0.7	1.1	1.3	2.8		0.9		3.9		0.2	3.5	Cuba
0.9	0.2	3.2	0.5	9.0	—	—	6.6	3.0	—	1.3	—	0.3	0.8	—	2.4	Cyprus[25]
...	1.0	0.4	2.7	3.3	10.1	1.9	4.8	20.7		7.1		7.2		0.7	1.5	Czech Republic[26]
1.4	0.5	2.8	0.8	4.1	1.2	0.3	8.0	13.3		3.0	2.7	4.9		2.7	2.1	Denmark
—	—	...	—	...	—	—	—	—	—	—	—	—	—	—	...	Djibouti
—	—	—	—	...	—	—	...	—	—	...	—	—	—	—	...	Dominica
16.0	0.9	1.6	0.8	3.6	1.8	0.2	3.7	0.5		0.8		0.1		0.2	0.2	Dominican Republic
2.7	1.7	4.0	1.8	6.4	2.3	0.4	4.9	0.3		3.2	0.5	—	1.9	0.4	0.4	Ecuador
3.2	0.4	1.8	1.5	7.4	5.3	8.0	4.0	3.7	—	1.4	0.8	1.4	2.2	0.7	0.1	Egypt
6.0	0.7	...	5.2		2.7		0.9	0.7		1.7		0.3		...	...	El Salvador
...	...	...	...	0.8	...	...	0.6	...	...	...	...	...	...	...	...	Equatorial Guinea
...	...	...	...	...	...	...	...	...	...	...	...	...	...	...	...	Eritrea[28]
2.2	...	...	...	4.5	...	...	18.0								...	Estonia
12.8	1.6	1.5	0.1	2.6	1.5	—	1.6	—	—	0.1		—	1.9	—	—	Ethiopia[28]
...	...	...	...	...	...	...	...	...	...	...	...	21.8[30]	...	...	...	Faeroe Islands

Manufacturing industries (continued)

country	year	total manufacturing value added ('000,000 U.S.$)	(31) food (311+312)	beverages (313)	tobacco manufactures (314)	(32) textiles (exc. wearing apparel) (321)	wearing apparel (322)	leather and fur products (323+324)	(33) wood products (exc. furniture) (331)	wood furniture (332)	(34) paper, paper products (341)	printing and publishing (342)	(35) industrial chemicals (351)	paints, soaps, etc. (352 exc. 3522)	drugs and medicines (3522)
Fiji	1987	118	60.7	—7.1—		—3.8—		0.1	5.6	1.3	2.3	3.5	—	5.2	—
Finland	1990[16, 32]	26,434	9.8	2.5	0.7	1.5	1.6	0.5	4.0	1.9	13.7	8.0	5.2	1.6	1.1
France	1991[33]	216,302	...	...	...	2.2	3.4	1.1	1.8	1.8	2.9	6.4	4.2	4.0	2.1
French Guiana	1989[24]	12	...	...	...	—[34]—			—11.0[34]—		...	...	...	...	...
French Polynesia	1989[9]	174	—26.2—		—	...	...	—	...	...	—	—	—	...	—
Gabon	1989	202	16.4	—29.8—		—2.3—			—16.0—		—3.4—		3.1[6]	[6]	[6]
Gambia, The	1990	16	50.0	14.3	—	—	—	—	—	7.1	—	—	—	—	—
Gaza Strip	1987[9, 36]	84	—15.5—			12.4[37]	16.8	[37]	—13.7[38]—		—[38]—		...	...	...
Georgia	1988[8, 9]	11,879[12]	—36.7—		...	—21.9—			—3.5—		...	...	4.0[6]	[6]	[6]
Germany[39]	1989[11, 18]	428,032	5.0	2.2	2.2	2.3	1.1	0.4	1.1	1.5	2.3	1.9	7.4	3.3	2.1
Ghana	1990	573	9.2	14.5	14.0	6.3	0.2	0.3	13.3	0.7	0.7	1.0	0.3	—5.6—	
Gibraltar	...	...	...	...	...	...	...	...	...	...	...	...	...	...	...
Greece	1989[16, 24]	7,787	13.8	4.9	2.5	12.5	5.5	1.8	1.8	0.9	2.5	2.9	3.1	4.4	2.0
Greenland	1987[40]	125	99.9	—	—	—	—	0.1	—	—	—	—	—	—	—
Grenada	1991[16, 41]	9.0	...	...	...	—	...	—	...	...	—	—	—	...	—
Guadeloupe	1989[24]	59	...	...	—	—[34]—			—30.7[34]—		...	...	...	...	...
Guam	1986	9.1	...	—	—	...	—	—	...	—	...	...	—	—	—
Guatemala	1988[11, 32]	842	24.1	5.3	2.5	6.5	3.2	2.7	1.2	0.6	1.4	4.8	4.9	9.1	6.8
Guernsey	1991[42]	53	—	—	—	—2.9—		—	...	...	—	10.8	—	—	7.3
Guinea	1990	115	...	...	...	...	...	...	...	...	...	...	...	...	...
Guinea-Bissau	1988	11	...	...	...	...	...	...	...	...	...	...	...	...	...
Guyana	1991[43]	41	...	...	...	...	...	...	...	...	...	...	—	...	...
Haiti	1987–88[11]	155	30.7	3.0	4.3	—13.9—			...	...	—	...	—5.9—		
Honduras	1989	589	31.0	9.9	4.6	4.1	2.8	0.9	6.2	1.7	3.3	2.7	0.6	4.1	1.5
Hong Kong	1990	11,841	3.4	1.2	2.1	15.2	20.5	0.9	0.3	0.6	2.3	7.4	—1.8—		
Hungary	1989	7,109	7.4	1.8	0.5	4.6	2.6	1.6	1.0	1.6	1.7	2.0	7.3	0.3	5.3
Iceland	1989[16]	752	44.1	1.6	—	2.8	1.1	0.3	0.1	4.6	1.0	9.8	1.6	1.5	—
India	1987–88[16, 44]	18,335	9.1	1.0	1.8	12.0	0.9	0.8	0.5	0.1	1.6	2.0	7.7	4.4	3.6
Indonesia	1990	12,554	10.2	0.6	9.2	10.9	1.9	0.9	9.8	0.4	2.1	1.2	3.8	—3.9—	
Iran	1987–88[11, 24]	21,130	10.0	2.4	10.9	15.7	1.5	2.3	1.5	0.5	1.0	1.3	2.1	2.7	2.5
Iraq	1990	3,605	7.5	2.9	2.9	5.7	1.1	1.4	0.1	0.4	1.8	1.1	3.9	—9.9—	
Ireland	1989[16, 45]	12,359	20.5	5.0	1.0	2.2	1.5	0.3	1.1	0.6	1.2	3.6	2.8	1.3	11.4
Isle of Man	1985–86[9, 16]	45	—16.9—		...	...	...	...	...	...	...	...	...	...	...
Israel	1988[11, 32]	8,966	13.6	1.5	0.2	3.6	4.0	0.8	1.2	1.5	2.7	4.4	7.4[46]	2.5	1.5
Italy	1990	163,844	5.4	2.1	0.4	7.2	3.4	2.3	1.1	2.0	2.4	4.4	5.8	—4.6—	
Jamaica	1990	615	18.7	12.5	12.4	0.5	2.3	2.3	0.5	3.9	1.8	4.7	7.0	—1.3—	
Japan	1989[47]	872,035	7.6	1.2	0.2	3.2	1.3	0.4	1.6	1.0	2.6	5.3	4.5	2.5	2.9
Jersey	1991	45	...	...	...	...	...	...	...	...	...	...	...	...	...
Jordan	1990[11]	581	10.0	4.9	13.0	3.4	2.2	0.8	—3.0—		3.5	2.1	7.6	2.7	4.6
Kazakhstan	1988[8, 9]	28,438[12]	—16.2—		...	—16.2—			—2.7—		...	...	7.3[6]	[6]	[6]
Kenya	1990[16, 18]	909	27.8	—11.2—		6.0	1.7	1.9	1.8	1.2	4.6	3.0	1.9	5.6	1.8
Kiribati	1988	0.60	...	...	—	—	—	—	...	—	—	—	—	...	—
Korea, North	...	...	...	...	...	...	...	...	...	...	...	...	...	...	...
Korea, South	1989[11, 32]	82,000	5.9	2.1	3.4	8.5	3.8	1.7	0.8	0.9	2.2	2.4	3.5	3.0	2.1
Kuwait	1987	2,878	4.6	0.9	—	0.5	4.0	—	0.4	1.2	0.7	2.0	2.7	—0.7—	
Kyrgyzstan	1991[8, 9]	6,219[12]	—20.9—		...	—31.4—			...	...	2.1	...	...	...	...
Laos	1990	54	...	...	...	...	...	...	...	...	...	...	...	...	...
Latvia	1991[8, 9]	25,318[10]	—26.3—		...	14.9	4.0	4.0	—5.3—		1.9	0.5	7.2[6]	[6]	[6]
Lebanon	1987	483	...	...	...	...	...	...	...	...	...	...	...	...	...
Lesotho	1991[9]	113	—52.4—		...	—32.6—			—1.6—		...	2.3	...	—2.8—	
Liberia	1985[8, 11, 18]	64	10.8	42.7	...	—	—	0.3	—	4.5	0.6	1.3	0.4	—7.2—	
Libya	1989	936	7.4	3.2	8.0	3.2	0.7	7.1	0.4	0.5	0.7	0.7	10.9	—2.0—	
Liechtenstein	...	...	...	...	...	...	...	...	...	...	...	...	...	...	...
Lithuania	1990[8, 9]	12,970[10]	—21.9—		...	14.4	4.1	3.5	—3.3—		1.5	...	3.7[6]	[6]	[6]
Luxembourg	1990	2,006	2.3	3.3	0.6	2.9	—0.7—		0.1	0.1	1.5	1.9	5.2	—1.6—	
Macau	1990[11]	468	1.2	0.9	—	19.6	49.2	2.8	0.3	1.1	0.8	1.9	—	0.4	0.8
Macedonia	1989	2,095	7.3	3.2	6.4	14.3	15.4	6.8	—3.7—		0.9	0.7	7.6[19]	[19]	[19]
Madagascar	1990	134	12.8	12.0	1.5	40.6	1.5	3.0	—	—	3.8	0.7	—	—6.8—	
Malaŵi	1990	133	20.2	9.0	6.7	13.4	1.5	3.0	1.5	0.7	0.7	6.7	3.7	—15.7—	
Malaysia	1989	7,602	21.0	0.9	1.2	2.9	2.4	0.1	5.1	0.5	1.4	1.5	5.5	1.6	0.3
Maldives	1990	5.8	...	...	—	—	...	—	—	...	—	...	—	...	—
Mali	1990	122	13.9	1.6	10.7	41.8	10.7	—	—	—	—	0.8	0.8	—0.8—	
Malta	1988	453	10.4	9.6	1.6	2.5	17.2	2.5	0.4	4.5	1.0	5.5	0.6	—3.1—	
Marshall Islands	1981[1]	0.16	39.7	—	—	—	—	—	—	8.8	—	51.5	—	—	—
Martinique	1989[24]	71	...	...	...	—[34]—			—33.3[34]—		...	...	...	...	...
Mauritania	1989[9]	103	63.1[29]	...	...	...	...	...	...	...	...	...	...	...	...
Mauritius	1990[11]	480	16.7	5.1	1.7	5.9	42.5	1.6	1.0	0.9	0.7	2.5	—4.6—		
Mayotte	1990	...	...	—	—	—	—	—	—	—	—	—	—	—	—
Mexico	1988[11, 51]	30,308	12.4	4.3	2.4	5.3	1.5	1.3	0.9	0.8	2.9	2.2	6.9	3.6	2.7
Micronesia	...	...	...	...	...	...	...	...	...	...	...	...	...	...	...
Moldova	1991[8, 9]	9,858[12]	—32.9—		...	—24.3—			—3.9—		...	...	2.8[6]	[6]	[6]
Monaco	...	...	...	...	...	...	...	...	...	...	...	...	...	...	...
Mongolia	1990[9]	621	—33.1—		...	20.6	6.7	14.5	—6.3—		...	2.1	—16.1—		
Morocco	1990	1,899	19.6	4.1	2.1	12.6	3.1	2.1	2.4	0.4	3.2	2.0	8.7	—5.5—	
Mozambique	1988	292	28.6	9.2	5.4	18.2	4.1	1.4	1.3	0.8	2.9	2.2	0.5	—5.1—	
Myanmar (Burma)	1984–85[9]	731	—38.8—			—9.4—			...	...	...	3.4	...	...	...
Namibia	1990	117	...	...	...	...	...	...	...	...	...	...	...	...	...
Nauru	1989	—	—	—	—	—	—	—	—	—	—	—	—	—	—
Nepal	1989–90[9, 11, 24]	206	14.3	5.9	16.2	16.5	8.4	1.5	1.0	0.5	1.5	0.8	...	4.9	1.1
Netherlands, The	1990	45,140	—20.8—			2.2	0.5	0.3	—1.9—		3.6	7.1	—16.5—		
Netherlands Antilles	1988	78	...	...	...	...	...	...	...	...	...	...	...	...	...
New Caledonia	1988[9]	474	—5.8—			...	...	...	...	...	...	...	...	...	...
New Zealand	1990	7,553	23.8	3.0	0.7	3.3	3.3	1.6	4.9	1.8	6.5	7.5	3.3	—2.9—	
Nicaragua	1991[8, 9, 52]	222	20.5	19.9	11.5	3.5	0.2	4.0	—	0.7	2.6	1.7	—14.0—		
Niger	1991	156	...	...	...	...	...	...	...	...	...	...	...	...	...

refined petroleum and products (353+354)	rubber products (355)	plastic products (356)	(36) pottery, china, and glass (361+362)	bricks, tiles, cement, etc. (369)	(37) iron and steel (371)	non-ferrous metals (372)	(38) fabricated metal products (381)	nonelectrical machinery (382 exc. 3825)	office equip., computers (3825)	electrical equip. (383 exc. 3832)	radio, television (3832)	transport equip. exc. motor vehicles (384 exc. 3843)	motor vehicles (3843)	professional equip. (385)	(39) jewelry, musical instruments (390)	country
—	0.5	1.8	—	2.1[31]	[31]	—	3.1	1.2				1.2	—	—	0.4	Fiji
3.0	0.5	1.5	0.9	4.0	3.2	1.4	6.6	11.1	1.5	3.6	3.3	3.4	1.9	1.3	0.6	Finland
7.6	1.6	3.0	5.3		2.8	2.0	9.8	8.1	2.2	11.4		4.5	8.1	1.9	1.8	France
...	...	...	35		35		79.8[35]	9.2							...	French Guiana
—	...	...	...	...	—	—	41.7								...	French Polynesia
12.8	6	6	6.7		...	...	9.5								...	Gabon
—	—	—	—	—	—	—	—	—	—	—	—	—	—	—	28.6	Gambia, The
...	...	...	...	13.9	20.6[4]		4								...	Gaza Strip
...	6	6	...	5.2	...	...	15.7								...	Georgia
3.7	1.3	3.0	1.2	2.2	4.0	1.5	6.9	13.3	1.8	6.5	7.2	1.5	11.1	1.5	0.5	Germany[39]
14.0	0.7	0.7	0.3	3.3	0.3	11.0	2.1	—	—	0.7		0.5		0.2	—	Ghana
...	...	...	...	...	...	...	...	...	...	...	...	...	...	...	...	Gibraltar
4.1	1.0	2.8	1.3	6.6	3.7	4.3	4.8	1.9	—	3.5	1.0	4.6	0.9	0.2	0.6	Greece
—	—	—	—	—	—	—	—	—	—	—	—	—	—	—	—	Greenland
—	...	—	—	—	—	—	—	—	—	—	—	—	—	—	...	Grenada
—	...	...	35		35		61.4[35]	7.8							...	Guadeloupe
—	—	...	...	...	—	—	—	—	—	—	—	...	—	...	...	Guam
1.1	2.3	3.6	3.4	5.9	3.1	0.1	2.8	0.7	0.1	2.4	0.4	0.1	0.2	0.2	0.5	Guatemala
—	—	11.8	—	2.8	—	—	—	7.7		—	50.2	4.5	—	—	2.0	Guernsey
...	...	...	...	...	...	...	...	...	...	...	...	...	...	...	...	Guinea
...	...	...	...	...	...	...	...	...	...	...	...	...	...	...	...	Guinea-Bissau
—	—	—	—	—	—	—	—	...	—	...	—	—	—	—	...	Guyana
			—	5.1	...	—	23.6							—	13.6	Haiti
1.9	2.2	4.3	0.2	7.0	0.9	0.2	5.0	0.9	—	1.1	0.5	0.2	0.3	0.2	1.6	Honduras
0.1	0.1	6.4	1.0		0.7		6.1	6.5	5.1	1.7	5.5	2.8		4.5	3.7	Hong Kong
3.8	1.4	1.9	2.0	2.8	6.4	4.3	4.0	10.7		4.0	7.5	2.6	3.8	5.1	2.0	Hungary
—	—	2.6	0.4	3.8	2.9	6.9	9.7		—	—	—	2.4		—	2.6	Iceland
6.1	2.2	1.1	0.8	3.9	9.3	1.5	3.0	8.1	0.1	7.0	2.2	3.8	4.2	0.8	0.6	India
15.4	4.1	1.2	0.9	1.8	5.9		5.8	0.9		2.3		6.1		0.1	0.5	Indonesia
1.1	2.1	1.6	1.7	15.3	5.1	1.9	3.9	6.4	0.1	0.8	1.6	0.6	2.9	0.3	0.3	Iran
32.5	0.3	1.0	0.8	16.1	0.5	—	1.8	3.3		3.9		1.2		—	—	Iraq
0.3	0.8	2.0	1.4	3.6	0.7	0.1	2.9	2.9	12.8	2.6	10.8	1.4	0.6	4.0	0.7	Ireland
...	...	...	...	...	...	...	...	...	...	...	...	...	...	...	...	Isle of Man
[46]	0.7	4.3	0.5	2.8	0.9	0.7	13.2	1.7	1.2	2.7	17.5	5.3	0.9	1.5	1.2	Israel
1.3	1.7	3.4	3.2	3.9	5.2	1.4	5.2	12.8		9.0		10.7		0.8	0.3	Italy
7.8	1.5	2.9	1.5	4.1	1.1	—	2.4	1.6		2.1		6.2		—	0.8	Jamaica
0.9	1.2	3.5	1.4	3.0	5.7	1.4	6.8	10.0	3.4	6.4	8.9	1.1	9.1	1.4	1.5	Japan
...	...	...	...	...	...	...	...	...	...	...	...	...	...	...	...	Jersey
9.4	0.2	2.9	1.1	14.6	4.2	1.5	4.0	1.6	—	2.0	—	—	0.1	0.3	0.3	Jordan
...	6	6	...	6.4	...	...	17.5								...	Kazakhstan
0.8	3.6	2.7	0.7	4.6	0.3		7.0[48]	0.6		4.8		2.9	1.4	—	2.2	Kenya
—	—	—	—	—	—	—	...	—	—	—	—	...	—	—	...	Kiribati
...	...	...	...	...	...	...	...	...	...	...	...	...	...	...	...	Korea, North
3.0	3.2	2.7	1.2	3.5	6.1	1.3	5.2	5.9	0.7	9.2	6.0	2.0	6.5	1.3	2.1	Korea, South
70.5	0.1	1.1	0.3	4.0	0.5	—	3.1	1.1	—	0.8	—	0.3	0.1	—	0.4	Kuwait
0.9	...	...	...	4.9	4.7		28.0								...	Kyrgyzstan
...	...	...	...	...	...	...	...	...	...	...	...	...	...	...	...	Laos
0.3	6	6	0.9	3.2	0.9	0.1	4.4	16.6							...	Latvia
...	...	...	...	...	...	...	...	...	...	...	...	...	...	...	...	Lebanon
...	...	...	4.2		1.5	...	...	...	...	...	...	...	...	...	...	Lesotho
—	—	0.6	0.2	20.7	—	—	9.5	0.3		0.7		—	—	—	—	Liberia
30.8	—	0.5	0.1	21.6	—	—	0.3	—	—	—	—	—	—	—	1.9	Libya
...	...	...	...	...	...	...	...	...	...	...	...	...	...	...	...	Liechtenstein
3.3	6	6	...	6.6	...	...	23.9								...	Lithuania
0.2	10.6	2.7	4.4	6.5	32.1	3.1	10.6	6.7		1.5		0.7		0.6	0.1	Luxembourg
—	—	0.6	0.8	—	—	—	1.7	0.3		1.4	0.1	0.8	—	0.8	14.5	Macau
−1.4	0.2	[19]	6.1		5.8	3.7	5.1	2.5		8.1		3.7		...	0.1	Macedonia
6.8	0.7	0.7	—	2.3	—	—	3.8	—	—	2.3		0.7		—	—	Madagascar
—	—	3.7	—	6.0	—	—	3.7	2.2		0.7		0.7		—	—	Malawi
4.5	7.1	1.9	0.6	2.5	4.0	1.3	3.1	2.6	—	2.4	20.2	1.0	3.1	0.8	0.7	Malaysia
—	—	...	—	...	—	—	...	—	—	—	—	...	—	—	...	Maldives
0.8	—	—	—	0.8	—	—	4.1	1.6		1.6		9.8		—	—	Mali
—	3.5	1.8	0.4	2.1	—	[49]	4.0[49]	1.3		2.8	14.1	3.9	—	3.6	3.6	Malta
—	—	—	—	—	—	—	—	—	—	—	—	—	—	—	—	Marshall Islands
...	...	...	35		35		62.7[35]	4.0							...	Martinique
...	...	...	...	...	...	...	...	...	...	...	...	...	...	...	...	Mauritania
—	0.4	1.4	0.1	2.2	3.8[50]		[50]	0.8		1.1		0.6	0.2	2.7	3.3	Mauritius
—	—	—	—	...	—	—	—	—	—	—	—	—	—	—	—	Mayotte
7.3	1.5	2.5	2.8	2.9	4.5	1.5	4.7	2.9	1.0	5.3	2.3	0.5	12.3	0.3	0.6	Mexico
...	...	...	...	...	...	...	...	...	...	...	...	...	...	...	...	Micronesia
...	6	6	...	4.0	1.1		24.7								...	Moldova
...	...	...	...	...	...	...	...	...	...	...	...	...	...	...	...	Monaco
			0.6	7.4	...	...	...	...	...	...	...	...	...	...	...	Mongolia
6.7	1.4	0.7	0.3	10.8	0.6	0.3	6.5	2.0		2.6		2.1		0.1	0.1	Morocco
0.8	2.5	1.2	0.9	2.9	0.8	0.4	2.7	0.8		4.3		2.6		0.1	0.1	Mozambique
...	...	...	...	10.0	...	...	...	1.4		1.1		5.3		...	...	Myanmar (Burma)
...	...	...	...	...	...	...	...	...	...	...	...	...	...	...	...	Namibia
—	—	—	—	—	—	—	—	—	—	—	—	—	—	—	—	Nauru
—	1.0	1.8	...	11.3	3.6	—	2.5	—	—	0.7	0.7	—	—	...	0.8	Nepal
2.6	3.5		3.7		4.2		6.9	7.9		11.7		5.5		0.7	0.4	Netherlands, The
...	...	...	...	...	...	...	...	...	...	...	...	...	...	...	...	Netherlands Antilles
...	...	...	...	...	...	78.1	5.6								...	New Caledonia
3.0	0.9	2.9	1.1	2.3	1.3	3.0	7.5	5.4		3.8		4.4		0.4	1.3	New Zealand
...	0.3	...	7.5		...	—	6.9	1.0				0.2		—	...	Nicaragua
...	...	...	...	...	...	...	...	...	...	...	...	...	...	...	...	Niger

Manufacturing industries (continued)

country	year	total manufacturing value added ('000,000 U.S.$)	(31) food (311+312)	beverages (313)	tobacco manufactures (314)	(32) textiles (exc. wearing apparel) (321)	wearing apparel (322)	leather and fur products (323+324)	(33) wood products (exc. furniture) (331)	wood furniture (332)	(34) paper, paper products (341)	printing and publishing (342)	(35) industrial chemicals (351)	paints, soaps, etc. (352 exc. 3522)	drugs and medicines (3522)
Nigeria	1990	3,612	14.5	9.8	1.7	15.9	0.1	2.8	0.6	0.8	3.1	2.9	0.4	12.4	
Northern Mariana Islands	1987[1,9]	58		3.3		26.0	62.7[53]		...	...	...	1.3	...	...	...
Norway	1991[32]	13,323	11.0	9.2		1.4	0.4	0.2	3.8	1.7	5.0	10.4	5.2	1.4	1.3
Oman	1990[9]	393	...	...	...	...	...	...	...	...	...	...	...	...	...
Pakistan	1990	4,356	14.5	1.7	11.8	16.7	1.1	1.8	0.2	0.1	0.9	1.1	8.6	6.8	
Panama	1990	407	29.7	13.3	6.5	1.3	6.4	1.9	1.9	2.1	5.8	3.1	0.8	7.8	
Papua New Guinea	1989	451	48.4	13.1	4.9	—	0.4	—	11.6	2.0	1.1	2.4	1.1	1.1	
Paraguay	1990	611	26.2	8.2	1.3	5.9	0.3	7.2	17.3	1.6	0.3	4.7	1.5	1.0	
Peru	1990[9]	9,182	22.5	8.9		9.7	5.6	1.3	5.1		1.4	3.5	3.1	3.5	1.7
Philippines	1988[11,24]	6,250	19.3	11.8	6.5	4.6	5.9	0.4	2.9	1.3	2.7	1.3	4.1	4.7	4.7
Poland	1990	23,017	11.3	8.0	1.6	5.3	1.9	1.7	1.4	1.3	1.5	0.7	4.6	1.6	1.3
Portugal	1987[11,56]	7,530	10.9	2.9	2.0	15.7	4.4	3.1	3.5	0.8	7.8	3.6	5.0	3.3	2.0
Puerto Rico	1987[9]	13,709	4.7	9.4	...	0.6	5.0	1.5	0.3	0.6	0.7	2.0	0.8	3.5	38.8
Qatar	1990[24]	819		1.5			0.6		0.8		2.1				81.9
Réunion	1990[9,24]	255	34.8	12.4	—	1.2		—	2.0		1.5	10.4	[58]	3.7	
Romania	1990[9]	16,101	8.4	4.1	0.1	10.0	5.4	3.2	3.6	2.2	1.3	0.4	2.7	1.8	0.6
Russia[60]	1990	502,639[61]	17.1	1.7	0.5	7.4	4.8	1.6	1.3	1.1	0.8	0.8	3.9	1.9	
Rwanda	1990	180	32.6	19.3	8.8	...	...	...	4.4	0.6	1.1	1.1	7.7	—	—
St. Kitts and Nevis	1991[16]	19	...	...	...	...	...	...	...	...	...	...	...	...	...
St. Lucia	1990[8,62]	63	35.7	41.5	...	...	22.8	...	...	...	...	...	...	0.1	...
St. Vincent	1988[9,16]	14	24.9	25.4			10.1		1.9		5.3		...	...	...
San Marino	1978	47		7.2			9.5		5.8		5.0				11.4
São Tomé and Príncipe	1988	0.77	...	...	—	—	...	—	...	...	—	—	—	...	—
Saudi Arabia	1990	14,709	6.2	0.7	1.0	1.5	1.5	0.9	1.5	0.5	1.1	1.1	...	...	...
Senegal	1990	383	35.5	4.4	2.3	12.5	2.9	1.6	0.3	0.3	1.0	2.3	4.7	1.8	
Seychelles	1989	26		79.6			0.6		2.1		6.0				4.1
Sierra Leone	1985–86[24]	43		60.6			0.5		15.8		0.5				4.1
Singapore	1991[24]	13,389	2.7	1.1	0.6	0.6	2.1	0.2	0.4	0.7	1.6	4.4	4.7	6.3	
Slovakia	...	...	...	...	...	...	...	...	...	...	...	...	...	...	...
Slovenia	1989	7,943	8.1	1.7	0.4	5.0	7.8	3.8	6.1		4.1	1.3	11.2[19]	[19]	[19]
Solomon Islands	1990[16,66]	6.7	...	...	...	—	...	—	...	...	—	...	—	—	—
Somalia	1988	18	26.5	4.8	18.7	3.3	0.4	14.0	—	0.1	10.9			6.7	
South Africa	1989[16]	19,984	8.5	4.3	0.6	3.6	2.7	1.8	1.3	1.0	6.4	2.9	5.8	11.0[67]	
Bophuthatswana	1985	120	...	...	...	...	...	...	...	...	...	...	...	...	...
Ciskei	1980[16]	36	...	...	...	...	...	...	...	...	...	...	...	...	...
Transkei	1986[9,16]	49	...	...	...	...	...	...	...	...	...	...	...	...	...
Venda	1985[16]	12		70.7			19.4		4.8		—	—	—	—	—
Spain	1989[16,18]	71,701	12.2	4.3	1.1	4.0	2.3	1.7	2.4	1.6	2.5	4.7	4.6	3.3	2.5
Sri Lanka	1989[11,32]	805	25.9	9.6	15.4	8.2	12.8	2.3	0.7	0.1	1.1	1.1	0.7	2.3	0.3
Sudan, The	1988	354	44.1	2.3	12.7	9.3	0.3	2.5	0.3	0.3	1.7	2.3	0.8	4.0	
Suriname	1989[8,16,62]	348	46.7	20.1	7.1	...	1.8	1.1	5.0	1.1	2.9	1.8	...	6.3	
Swaziland	1988	204	26.5	36.4	—		4.5		2.9		23.3				0.6
Sweden	1990[16,32]	51,431	8.3	1.4	0.5	1.2	0.4	0.2	5.9	1.1	8.8	6.1	3.9	2.0	3.0
Switzerland	1990	58,051	10.3	1.7	0.5	3.0	2.0	0.8	3.9	2.5	2.4	7.3	7.2	7.8	
Syria	1989	1,452		23.5			29.5		5.5		1.4				19.8
Taiwan	1991	61,390	5.3	5.5		7.1	3.4	1.5	1.4		5.2		6.7	2.2	
Tajikistan	1990[8]	4,432[10]	20.0		...		47.8		1.3		...	...	5.2[6]	[6]	[6]
Tanzania	1990	104	18.9	5.7	5.7	17.9	1.9	3.8	1.9	0.9	2.8	4.7	3.8	2.8	
Thailand	1986[9,18,68]	7,653	11.6	14.9	13.2	18.5	2.3	0.3	1.6	1.2	1.9	0.7	1.4	1.0	0.8
Togo	1989[9]	115		50.8			14.1		7.1		3.8				5.9
Tonga	1990[8,9,69]	12		40.0		21.3		...	4.6		10.1	...			8.6
Trinidad and Tobago	1987[24]	423	28.5	9.6	8.0	1.0	2.7	0.8	0.8	1.2	6.1	4.9	0.8		2.2
Tunisia	1990	1,605	7.4	5.7	2.2	5.2	7.5	3.0	1.3	0.9	2.1	1.6	2.9	8.7	
Turkey	1989[11,71]	20,981	9.5	3.0	4.1	11.1	3.2	0.5	0.7	0.3	2.0	1.1	6.1	2.7	2.4
Turkmenistan	1990[8,9]	4,550[10]	15.4		...	38.4	6.2		...	...	1.4	...	4.2[6]	[6]	[6]
Tuvalu	1990	0.3	...	—	—	—	...	—	—	...	—	—	—	...	—
Uganda	1982	406	33.9	11.7	9.4	27.1	2.3	1.3	2.1	0.8	—	—	—	2.5	
Ukraine	1990[8]	165,624[10]	18.7		...	5.2	3.8	1.9	2.9		9.0	...	6.0[6]	[6]	[6]
United Arab Emirates	1990	3,786	...	...	...	...	...	...	...	...	...	...	...	...	...
United Kingdom	1990	203,581	9.2	2.5	0.9	2.6	2.3	0.7	1.3	1.8	3.0	7.5	5.8	2.0	3.1
United States	1991	1,313,829	9.0	2.0	1.9	2.0	2.5	0.3	2.1	1.6	4.4	7.9	5.3	3.2	3.3
Uruguay	1987[11,32]	1,938	16.6	7.7	4.5	10.8	3.3	5.0	0.5	0.2	3.6	2.2	2.1	3.6	3.5
Uzbekistan	1991[8,9]	53,417[10]	14.4		...	38.4	5.5	2.6	1.4		0.3	...	0.2[6]	[6]	[6]
Vanuatu	1985[9]	4.6	33.8	8.8	—		8.7		5.4		17.2		...	...	...
Venezuela	1990[11,32]	12,176•	9.9	4.8	2.2	2.4	1.3	1.1	0.3	0.5	2.3	1.5	3.6	3.6	1.8
Vietnam	1989[72,73]	5,533		28.2			17.7[74]		[75]		[75]	[74]		9.9	
Virgin Islands (U.S.)	...[76]	...	...	...	...	...	...	...	...	...	...	...	...	...	...
West Bank	1987[9,36]	237		40.7		9.8		4.0	5.1		...	...			15.1
Western Sahara	...	...	...	...	...	...	...	...	...	...	...	...	...	...	...
Western Samoa	1990	15	36.0	25.5	19.2	—	...	—	10.7	—	—	—	—	8.6	...
Yemen[77]	1986	540		51.9			8.7		3.9		0.5				9.2
Yugoslavia	1989	12,986	18.1	2.7	0.8	4.9	9.2	4.3	3.8		1.5	1.1	8.7[19]	[19]	[19]
Zaire	1990	94	7.4	32.6	14.7	3.2	2.1	3.2	1.0	1.0	—	1.0	8.4	—	—
Zambia	1990	1,074	8.8	20.8	9.9	6.4	4.1	3.3	2.6	2.1	1.0	2.0	3.8	7.4	
Zimbabwe	1988[16]	2,130	10.4	15.4	4.7	9.5	4.5	3.3	1.6	1.0	2.4	3.1	3.7[46]	4.6	1.3

[1]Gross output in value of sales. [2]State sector only. [3]33 includes 341. [4]37 includes 38. [5]Value of manufactured exports (excluding duty-free reexports). [6]351 includes 352, 355, and 356. [7]390 includes 385. [8]Gross output of production. [9]Percentage breakdown by ISIC category is incomplete. [10]Rubles of former U.S.S.R. [11]In producer's prices. [12]Constant rubles of 1982 of the former U.S.S.R. [13]Includes metal furniture. [14]353 + 354 includes 351. [15]Three largest sectors only. [16]In factor values. [17]Seven major industrial enterprises only. [18]Establishments employing 20 or more persons. [19]351 includes 352 and 356. [20]Excludes petroleum refining. [21]Excludes fabricated metal products. [22]384 minus 3843 includes 381. [23]Cotton fibre only. [24]Establishments employing 10 or more persons. [25]Republic of Cyprus only. [26]Includes Slovakia. [27]Private establishments employing 10 or more persons, and all public establishments. [28]Ethiopia includes Eritrea. [29]Processed fish only. [30]Ship repair only. [31]369 includes 371. [32]Establishments employing five or more persons. [33]Data exclude sector 31. [34]33 includes 32. [35]381 includes 36 and 37. [36]Data refer to "Revenue" (mostly value of sales). [37]321 includes 323 + 324. [38]33 includes 34. [39]Former West Germany only. [40]Value of external sales by public enterprises. [41]Primarily beverages. [42]Value of manufactured exports. [43]Includes public utilities. [44]Establishments with electric power and 10 or more employees, or without electric power and 20 or more employees. [45]Establishments employing

refined petroleum and products (353+354)	rubber products (355)	plastic products (356)	(36) pottery, china, and glass (361+362)	bricks, tiles, cement, etc. (369)	(37) iron and steel (371)	non-ferrous metals (372)	(38) fabricated metal products (381)	nonelectrical machinery (382 exc. 3825)	office equip., computers (3825)	electrical equip. (383 exc. 3832)	radio, television (3832)	transport equip. exc. motor vehicles (384 exc. 3843)	motor vehicles (3843)	professional equip. (385)	(39) jewelry, musical instruments (390)	country
1.1	1.7	2.9	0.5	6.1	0.6	1.9	5.5	1.2		2.1		11.0		—	0.3	Nigeria
…	[53]	[53]	4.9		…	…	…	…	…	…	…	…	…	…	…	Northern Mariana Islands
2.1	0.4	2.0	0.8	2.4	2.4	5.1	5.8	12.4	0.4	3.4	2.6	6.6	1.0	0.8	0.8	Norway
9.5[54]	…	…	…	…	…	…	…	…	…	…	…	…	…	…	…	Oman
7.7	1.1	0.7	0.9	8.0	8.2	—	0.8	2.0		2.6		2.5		0.1	0.3	Pakistan
4.3	0.3	3.9	0.7	3.8	0.4	0.4	3.5	0.3		0.5		0.4		0.4	0.7	Panama
—	—	0.4	0.7	1.6	…	—	6.7	1.3		0.7		2.4		…	…	Papua New Guinea
12.8	—	2.1	0.7	4.2	—	0.5	2.0	0.2		0.2		1.3		0.2	0.5	Paraguay
1.1	1.8		5.2		2.2	15.4	1.5	0.7		2.2		2.1		…	…	Peru
6.2	2.4	1.7	1.7	0.7[55]	3.9	2.3	1.4[48]	0.7	0.1	1.7	4.0	0.9	1.0	0.2	1.0	Philippines
7.2	0.9	1.2	1.5	2.6	8.2	4.1	4.7	11.0	0.3	3.7	2.5	4.6	3.5	0.8	1.1	Poland
2.3[57]	1.1	2.0	3.4	5.4	2.7	0.5	4.4	2.3	0.2	3.3	2.4	1.9	2.6	0.3	0.2	Portugal
1.8	1.1	1.3	0.4		0.5		1.3	1.4	4.2	5.4	7.5	…	…	4.4	0.7	Puerto Rico
			1.3		10.7		1.0								0.1	Qatar
—	—	3.7	3.9[58]	11.7	—	—	10.3	…	…	…	2.3	…	…	…	…	Réunion
2.1	1.4	1.3	1.5	…	…	1.4	5.0	13.5	0.7	5.2		2.8	2.9	2.5	7.6[59]	Romania
4.2	1.1	0.6	1.0	3.5	3.1	1.6	2.3	26.1		3.0		3.8		3.2	3.7	Russia[60]
—	—	—	—	13.3	—	—	9.4	0.6		0.6		0.6		—	…	Rwanda
…	…	…	…	…	…	…	…	…	…	…	…	…	…	…	…	St. Kitts and Nevis
…	…	…	…	…	…	…	…	…	…	…	…	…	…	…	…	St. Lucia
…	…	0.4	…	…	…	…	6.6[63]	…	…	[63]	[63]	…	…	…	…	St. Vincent
			12.3		—	—	26.2	—	—	—	—	—	—	—	22.6	San Marino
—	—	—	…	…	—	—	—	—	—	—	—	—	—	—	—	São Tomé and Príncipe
66.7	…	7.7	—	4.9	0.2	0.1	1.2	0.7		1.0		0.9		…	0.6	Saudi Arabia
6.3	—	—	—	7.8	—	—	8.6	2.9		0.8		4.2		—	—	Senegal
			5.2		—	—	2.4								—	Seychelles
			6.8[64]		[64]		4.1								7.7	Sierra Leone
8.6	0.3	2.7	0.3	1.4	0.7	0.3	6.0	6.1	[65]	4.2	33.8[65]	7.4		1.7	1.2	Singapore
…	…	…	…	…	…	…	…	…	…	…	…	…	…	…	…	Slovakia
0.5	1.9	[19]	3.1		3.4	2.1	7.6	7.5		14.8		8.7		…	0.7	Slovenia
—	—	—	—	—	—	—	—	—	—	—	—	…	—	—	—	Solomon Islands
—	—	10.7	—	2.1	—	0.3	1.5	—	—	—	—	—	—	—	—	Somalia
[67]	1.3	1.9	1.3	3.8	10.0	3.6	6.8	5.6		4.2		1.5	7.0	0.7	2.4	South Africa
…	…	…	…	…	…	…	…	…	…	…	…	…	…	…	…	Bophuthatswana
…	…	…	…	…	…	…	…	…	…	…	…	…	…	…	…	Ciskei
…	…	…	…	…	…	…	…	…	…	…	…	…	…	…	…	Transkei
—	—	—	—	2.2	—	—	2.9	—	—	—	—	—	—	—	—	Venda
2.5	1.8	2.5	1.8	5.0	4.8	1.8	6.1	6.0	0.6	4.0	2.3	2.5	9.8	0.4	0.8	Spain
1.5	4.0	0.5	2.2	3.5	0.5	0.2	1.5	1.5	—	1.1	—	0.9	0.1	—	1.8	Sri Lanka
2.0	2.0	1.1	0.3	1.1	—	4.5	4.0	—	—	2.5		1.7		—	0.3	Sudan, The
—	0.2	0.3	4.2		—	—	—	…	…	…	…	1.0	—	0.2	0.3	Suriname
			2.3		—	—	2.4	0.2					—	—	0.9	Swaziland
3.0	0.8	1.5	0.8	2.2	4.1	1.2	8.6	11.1	1.0	3.4	4.4	2.9	9.7	2.3	0.3	Sweden
2.9	1.2	3.2	1.1	1.6	2.0	1.7	6.7	13.2		10.0		1.8		4.8	0.3	Switzerland
			8.8		0.8		10.6							—	0.1	Syria
8.6	1.4	6.2	3.6		6.5		5.3	4.0		13.7		7.1		1.4	3.9	Taiwan
0.4	[6]	[6]	…	3.5	11.8		10.0								…	Tajikistan
3.8	3.8	0.9	—	1.9	2.8	1.9	4.7	0.9		1.9		5.7		—	0.9	Tanzania
…	5.6	0.3	3.4	4.2	1.4	0.1	3.5	0.3	—	2.3	1.2	0.6	1.6	0.8	…	Thailand
			10.9		2.2	—	4.3	…	…	…	…	…	…	…	…	Togo
			4.4		…	…	10.6	…	…	…	…	…	…	…	…	Tonga
7.6	2.5	2.6	7.0		3.8[70]	—	[70]	—	—	3.2		0.1	4.9	[7]	1.6[7]	Trinidad and Tobago
0.9	0.9	2.4	1.6	15.3	8.9	0.7	9.3	0.2		5.2		5.3		0.1	0.6	Tunisia
15.5	1.7	0.9	3.0	4.4	8.4	2.5	3.1	4.1	—	2.1	2.1	0.7	4.3	0.3	0.3	Turkey
21.7	[6]	[6]	…	6.3	…	…	5.4								…	Turkmenistan
—	—	—	—	…	—	—	—	—	—	—	—	—	—	—	…	Tuvalu
—	—	—	0.7	6.8	1.5	—	—	—	—	—	—	—	—	—	—	Uganda
5.8	[6]	[6]	…	3.5	12.2		30.9								…	Ukraine
…	…	…	…	…	…	…	…	…	…	…	…	…	…	…	…	United Arab Emirates
2.2	1.2	3.2	1.3	3.3	2.3	0.9	5.5	11.7	2.3	4.0	4.9	6.4	5.6	1.4	1.2	United Kingdom
1.8	1.2	2.7	0.9	1.6	2.1	1.4	5.8	7.4	2.1	3.3	4.8	6.0	5.6	6.3	1.5	United States
10.7	3.1	2.2	2.2	1.8	0.9	0.2	3.3	0.7	0.1	2.6	0.5	1.5	5.9	0.1	0.4	Uruguay
4.4	[6]	[6]	…	3.8	5.0		10.1								…	Uzbekistan
…	…	…	…	…	11.1		…	…	…	…	…	…	…	…	…	Vanuatu
39.0	1.1	1.8	1.0	2.4	4.1	6.5	2.8	1.4	—	1.6	0.4	0.1	1.6	0.3	0.5	Venezuela
5.7	…	…	16.8[75]		1.6		15.8								…	Vietnam
…	…	…	…	…	…	…	…	…	…	…	…	…	…	…	…	Virgin Islands (U.S.)
			9.3		7.0[50]		[50]	…	…	…	…	…	…	…	…	West Bank
…	…	…	…	…	…	…	…	…	…	…	…	…	…	…	…	Western Sahara
—	—	—	—	—	—	—	—	—	—	—	—	—	—	—	—	Western Samoa
			15.3		—	—	8.7	—	—	—	—	—	—	—	1.8	Yemen[77]
0.7	2.5	[19]	3.7		2.7	3.3	9.2	7.2		7.5		7.8		…	0.4	Yugoslavia
1.0	—	—	—	1.0	2.1	1.0	2.1	3.2		2.1		3.2		—	9.5	Zaire
0.9	2.3	1.2	0.5	5.5	0.7	0.2	8.8	1.7		1.9		4.0		—	0.1	Zambia
[46]	2.1	3.3	0.6	3.1	11.5	0.6	5.3	1.3		2.3	0.4	0.6	2.7	0.1	0.6	Zimbabwe

three or more persons. [46]351 includes 353+354. [47]Establishments employing four or more persons. [48]Excludes metal furniture. [49]381 includes 372. [50]37 includes 381. [51]Includes production of *maquiladores* (foreign-owned assembly plants). [52]60 large enterprises only. [53]322 and 323+324 includes 355+356. [54]Refined petroleum only. [55]Excludes cement. [56]Some sector data are limited to establishments with 10 or more employees; other coverage may be limited to conform with disclosure rules. [57]Excludes derivatives. [58]361+362 includes 351. [59]Includes waterworks and supply. [60]Data refer to former U.S.S.R. [61]In constant U.S.$ of 1980. [62]Selected industries only. [63]381 includes 383. [64]36 includes 37. [65]3832 includes 3825. [66]Excludes fish processing and sawmilling. [67]352 includes 353+354. [68]Some sector coverage is limited to conform with disclosure rules. [69]Tongatapu Island only. [70]371 includes 381. [71]Private establishments employing 25 or more persons, and all public establishments. [72]Includes electricity. [73]Includes mining. [74]32 includes 342. [75]36 includes 33 and 341. [76]Data withheld for reasons of confidentiality. [77]Former Yemen Arab Republic only.

Energy

This table provides data about the commercial energy supplies (reserves, production, consumption, and trade) of the various countries of the world, together with data about oil pipeline networks and traffic. Many of the data and concepts used in this table are adapted from the United Nations' *Energy Statistics Yearbook*.

Electricity. Total installed electrical power capacity comprises the sum of the rated power capacities of all main and auxiliary generators in a country. "Total installed capacity" (kW) is multiplied by 8,760 hours per year to yield "Total production capacity" (kW-hr).

Production of electricity comprises the total gross production of electricity by publicly or privately owned enterprises and also that generated by industrial establishments for their own use, but usually excludes consumption by the utility itself. Measured in millions of kilowatt-hours (kW-hr), annual production of electricity ranges generally between 50% and 60% of total production capacity. The data are further analyzed by type of generation: fossil fuels, hydroelectric power, and nuclear fuel.

The great majority of the world's electrical and other energy needs are met by the burning of fossil hydrocarbon solids, liquids, and gases, either for thermal generation of electricity or in internal combustion engines. Many renewable and nontraditional sources of energy are being developed worldwide (wood, biogenic gases and liquids, tidal, wave, and wind power, geothermal and photothermal [solar] energy, and so on), but collectively these sources are still negligible in the world's total energy consumption. For this reason only hydroelectric and nuclear generation are considered here separately with fossil fuels.

Trade in electrical energy refers to the transfer of generated electrical output via an international grid. Total electricity consumption (residential and nonresidential) is equal to total electricity requirements less transformation and distribution losses.

Coal. The term coal, as used in the table, comprises all grades of anthracite, bituminous, subbituminous, and lignite that have acquired or may in the future, by reason of new technology or changed market prices, acquire an economic value. These types of coal may be differentiated according to heat content (density) and content of impurities. Most coal reserve data are based on proved recoverable reserves only, of all grades of coal. Exceptions are footnoted, with proved in-place reserves reported only when recoverable reserves are unknown. Production figures include deposits removed from both surface and underground workings as well as quantities used by the producers themselves or issued to the miners. Wastes recovered from mines or nearby preparation plants are excluded from production figures.

Natural gas. This term refers to any combustible gas (usually chiefly methane) of natural origin from underground sources. The data for production cover, to the extent possible, gas obtained from gas fields, petroleum fields, or coal mines that is actually collected and marketed. (Much natural gas in Middle Eastern and North African oil fields is

Energy

country	electricity												coal		
	installed capacity, 1991 ('000 kW)	production, 1991		power source, 1991			trade, 1991		consumption				reserves, latest ('000,000 metric tons)	production, 1991 ('000 metric tons)	consumption, 1991 ('000 metric tons)
		capacity ('000,000 kW-hr)	amount ('000,000 kW-hr)	fossil fuel (%)	hydropower (%)	nuclear fuel (%)	exports ('000,000 kW-hr)	imports ('000,000 kW-hr)	amount, 1991 ('000,000 kW-hr)	per capita, 1991 (kW-hr)	residential, 1990 (%)	nonresidential, 1990 (%)			
Afghanistan	494	4,327	1,015	32.0	68.0	—	—	—	1,015	57	...	...	66	135	135
Albania	720	6,307	2,800	8.9	91.1	—	320	675	3,155	960	...	...	15[1]	1,850	1,930
Algeria	5,369	47,032	17,345	98.3	1.7	—	796	135	16,684	651	...	...	43	15	1,315
American Samoa	33	289	90	100.0	—	—	—	—	90	1,837	27.5[3]	72.5[3]	—	—	...
Andorra	...	...	...	...	...	...	...	...	...	...	...	...	—	—	...
Angola	617	5,405	1,840	26.1	73.9	—	—	—	1,840	193	27.5[2]	72.5[2]	...	—	—
Antigua and Barbuda	26	228	95	100.0	—	—	—	—	95	1,439	42.4[4]	57.6[4]	...	...	...
Argentina	17,469	153,028	54,048	55.2	30.4	14.4	10	885	54,923	1,601	45.9	54.1	130	292	1,317
Armenia	2,810[5]	24,616	9,500	85.0[5]	15.0[5]	—	...	1,699[5]	12,076[5]	3,621[5]	...	...	...	50[5]	570[5]
Aruba	90	788	340	100.0	—	—	—	—	340	5,484	...	...	...	...	...
Australia	35,461	310,638	156,883	89.7	10.3	—	—	—	156,883	9,045	30.1[2]	69.9[2]	90,940	214,030	98,881
Austria	16,779	146,984	51,484	36.4	63.6	—	7,738	8,503	52,249	6,747	23.1[2]	83.4[2]	59	2,081	6,926
Azerbaijan	...	...	23,300	...	...	...	...	...	...	...	...	...	...	...	...
Bahamas, The	401	3,513	965	100.0	—	—	—	—	965	3,712	33.6[4]	66.4[4]	...	—	—
Bahrain	1,040	9,110	3,495	100.0	—	—	—	—	3,495	6,747	...	...	...	...	...
Bangladesh	2,690	23,564	8,930	90.6	9.4	—	—	—	8,930	77	43.8	56.2	1,054[1]	—	162
Barbados	140	1,226	527	100.0	—	—	—	—	527	2,043	33.7	66.3	...	—	—
Belarus	...	...	38,700	...	...	...	...	13,044[5]	51,744	5,029	...	...	...	—	1,500
Belgium	14,097	123,490	71,945	39.1	1.3	59.6	6,845	4,998	70,098	7,020	26.9[8]	73.1[8]	410	634	14,128
Belize	23	201	105	100.0	—	—	—	—	105	541	...	...	...	...	...
Benin	15	131	5	100.0	—	—	—	198	203	43	...	...	...	...	...
Bermuda	140	1,226	513	100.0	—	—	—	—	513	8,274	39.6	60.4	...	—	—
Bhutan	360	3,154	1,580	0.4	99.6	—	1,400	3	183	116	29.2[3]	69.8[3]	...	2	18
Bolivia	633	5,545	2,150	41.2	58.8	—	2	—	2,148	292	76.1	23.9	...	—	—
Bosnia and Herzegovina	3,441[5]	30,140[5]	14,632[5]	79.1[5]	20.9[5]	—	289[5]	858[5]	15,201[5]	3,497[5]	21.8	78.2	...	...	...
Botswana	[10]	[10]	522[10, 11]	[10]	[10]	[10]	[10]	82[10, 11]	[10]	[10]	...	...	3,500	400[8, 10]	[10]
Brazil	54,135	474,223	234,366	6.5	92.9	0.6	8	26,803	261,161	1,723	46.2	53.8	2,359	5,124	16,811
Brunei	382	3,346	1,242	100.0	—	—	—	—	1,242	4,705	55.3[4]	44.7[4]	...	—	—
Bulgaria	11,025	96,579	38,917	59.9	6.2	33.9	1,643	3,716	40,990	4,567	41.2[3]	58.8[3]	3,730	28,451	32,968
Burkina Faso	59	517	157	100.0	—	—	—	—	157	17	...	...	...	...	...
Burundi	43	377	136	1.5	98.5	—	—	23	159	28	...	...	...	...	...
Cambodia	35	307	70	57.1	42.9	—	—	—	70	8	...	...	...	—	—
Cameroon	627	5,493	2,712	2.7	97.3	—	—	—	2,712	229	...	...	...	1	1
Canada	104,631	916,568	507,913	22.5	60.7	16.8	24,522	6,094	489,485	18,134	28.8[4]	71.2[4]	8,623	71,135	50,622
Cape Verde	7	61	36	100.0	—	—	—	—	36	97	...	...	...	—	—
Central African Republic	43	377	96	18.7	81.3	—	—	—	96	31	...	...	4	...	...
Chad	31	272	85	100.0	—	—	—	—	85	15	...	...	...	...	...
Chile	4,809	42,127	19,961	48.7	51.3	—	—	—	19,961	1,491	32.7	67.3	1,181	2,248	3,097
China	146,000	1,278,960	677,550	81.5	18.5	—	260	3,110	680,400	592	7.7	92.3	114,500	1,087,406	1,058,208
Colombia	9,724	85,182	36,661	24.4	75.6	—	—	—	36,661	1,116	69.8	30.2	4,539	23,600	6,553
Comoros	5	44	16	87.5	12.5	—	—	—	16	28	...	...	...	...	...
Congo	118	1,034	482	0.6	99.4	—	—	65	547	238	...	...	...	...	1
Costa Rica	1,054	9,233	3,872	5.8	94.2	—	174	194	3,892	1,250	72.1	27.9	...	...	...
Côte d'Ivoire	1,173	10,275	2,376	32.9	67.1	—	—	—	2,376	191	29.6	70.4	...	...	...
Croatia	3,272[5]	28,660[5]	8,833	34.5	65.5	—	1,215	6,068	11,902	2,485	50.6	49.4	...	146	...
Cuba	3,988	34,935	16,255	99.5	0.5	—	—	—	16,255	1,518	56.0	44.0	...	—	200
Cyprus	471	4,126	2,077	100.0	—	—	—	—	2,077	2,929	77.3	22.7	...	—	15
Czech Republic	21,329[12]	186,842[12]	83,274[12]	67.6[12]	3.8[12]	28.6[12]	6,298[12]	8,107[12]	85,083[12]	5,421[12]	23.6[3, 12]	76.4[3, 12]	5,370[12]	100,334[12]	101,395[12]
Denmark	9,578	83,903	36,303	97.8	0.1	2.1[13]	5,047	3,075	34,331	6,669	32.5[8]	67.5[8]	63[5]	—	13,513
Djibouti	38	333	178	100.0	—	—	—	—	178	393	...	...	...	...	...
Dominica	8	70	31	48.4	51.6	—	—	—	31	431	53.5[4]	46.5[4]	...	...	...
Dominican Republic	1,447	12,676	5,330	84.1	15.9	—	—	—	5,330	728	...	...	...	—	1[11]
Ecuador	2,240	19,622	6,952	27.2	72.8	—	—	—	6,952	644	68.2	31.8	24	...	...
Egypt	13,345	116,902	40,460	75.5	24.5	—	—	—	40,460	754	29.6	70.4	53	—	1,207
El Salvador	740	6,482	2,300	8.9	72.8	18.3[13]	10	12	2,302	436	68.8	31.2	...	...	...

flared [burned] because it is often not economical to capture and market it.) Manufactured gas is generally a by-product of industrial operations such as gasworks, coke ovens, and blast furnaces. It is usually burned at the point of production and rarely enters the marketplace. Production of manufactured gas is, therefore, only reported as a percentage of domestic gas consumption.

Crude petroleum. Crude petroleum is the liquid product obtained from oil wells; the term also includes shale oil, tar sand extract, and field or lease condensate. Production and consumption data in the table refer, so far as possible, to the same year so that the relationship between national production and consumption patterns can be clearly seen; both are given in barrels.

Proved reserves are that oil remaining underground in known fields whose existence has been "proved" by the evaluation of nearby producing wells or by seismic tests in sedimentary strata known to contain crude petroleum, and that is judged recoverable within the limits of present technology and economic conditions (prices). The published proved reserve figures do not necessarily reflect the true reserves of a country, because government authorities or corporations often have political or economic motives for withholding or altering such data.

The estimated exhaustion rate of petroleum reserves is an extrapolated ratio of published proved reserves to the current rate of withdrawal/production. Present world published proved reserves will last about 40 to 45 years at the present rate of withdrawal, but there are large country-to-country variations above or below the average.

Data on petroleum and refined product pipelines are provided because of the great importance to both domestic and international energy markets of this means of bringing these energy sources from their production or transportation points to refineries, intermediate consumption and distribution points, and final consumers. Their traffic may represent a very significant fraction of the total movement of goods within a country. Available data for petroleum pipelines are often incomplete and their basis varies internationally, some countries reporting only international shipments, others reporting domestic shipments of 50 kilometres or more, and so on.

For data in the hydrocarbons portions of the table (coal, natural gas, and petroleum), extensive use has been made of a variety of international sources, such as those of the United Nations, the International Energy Agency (of the Organization for Economic Cooperation and Development), the World Energy Conference (in its *Survey of Energy Resources* [triennial]); the U.S. Department of Energy (especially its *International Energy Annual*); and of various industry surveys, such as those published by the *International Petroleum Encyclopedia*, the *Oil and Gas Journal*, and *World Oil*.

natural gas						crude petroleum							country
published proved reserves, 1993 ('000,000,000 cu m)	production		consumption			reserves, 1993		production, 1992 ('000,000 barrels)	consumption, 1991 ('000,000 barrels)	refining capacity, 1993 ('000 barrels per day)	pipelines (latest)		
	natural gas, 1992 ('000,000 cu m)	manufactured gas, 1991 (% of total gas consumption)	amount, 1991 ('000,000 cu m)	residential, 1990 (%)	nonresidential, 1990 (%)	published proved ('000,000 barrels)	years to exhaust proved reserves				length (km)	traffic ('000,000 metric ton-km)	
99	294	...	1,421	...	...	...	...	—	—	—	...	...	Afghanistan
11	136	...	552	...	...	185	31	6	8	40	200	...	Albania
3,650	52,089	51.2	11,026	26.8[2]	73.2[2]	10,387	25	423	176	530	6,910	...	Algeria
...	...	...	...	...	...	...	...	—	—	—	—	...	American Samoa
...	...	...	...	...	...	...	...	—	—	—	—	—	Andorra
48	566	10.4	167	...	...	1,334	8	172	11	32	179	...	Angola
...	...	...	...	...	...	...	...	—	—	—	—	—	Antigua and Barbuda
674	17,166	10.2	27,661	49.2	50.8	1,630	8	202	174	709	6,990	...	Argentina
...	170[5]	...	4,882[5]	...	...	...	...	—	...	—	...	...	Armenia
...	...	...	...	...	...	...	...	—	[3]	...	—	—	Aruba
2,093	24,231	28.9	17,598	...	...	3,155	16	195	195	698	3,000	...	Australia
16	1,433	18.0	5,711	25.7[2]	74.3[2]	76	10	8	59	210	725	5,319	Austria
170[6]	11,655[7]	...	...	...	...	3,300[6]	38[6]	86[7]	...	406	...	1,705	Azerbaijan
...	—	—	...	...	...	...	...	—	—	—	—	—	Bahamas, The
159	4,783	4.7	5,141	...	...	56	4	15	82	243	72	...	Bahrain
719	5,335	0.2	5,251	34.2	65.8	1.5	1	1.8	9	31	—	—	Bangladesh
0.2	22	...	23	62.6	37.4	6	12	0.5	2	3	—	—	Barbados
...	210[7]	...	15,400[5]	...	...	...	...	14	143[6]	832	...	...	Belarus
—	14[5]	22.5	12,770	43.4[8]	56.6[8]	...	...	—	210[9]	607	1,328	1,011	Belgium
...	...	...	...	...	...	...	...	—	—	—	—	—	Belize
—	...	...	...	...	...	20	14	1.4	—	—	—	—	Benin
...	...	...	...	...	...	...	...	—	—	—	—	—	Bermuda
...	...	...	...	...	...	...	...	—	—	—	—	—	Bhutan
118	3,078	25.4	699	—	100.0	118	15	8	8	45	2,380	...	Bolivia
...	—	...	...	...	...	...	...	—	...	...	—	—	Bosnia and Herzegovina
...	...	[10]	...	...	...	—	...	—	[10]	—	—	—	Botswana
137	3,757	59.7	3,604	—	100.0	3,667	15	238	410	1,403	5,804	...	Brazil
371	8,396	0.8	2,133	...	...	1,130	17	66	0.01	9	553	...	Brunei
7	11	11.5	5,499	...	...	13	43	0.3	32	300	611	...	Bulgaria
...	...	...	...	...	...	...	...	—	—	—	—	—	Burkina Faso
...	...	...	...	...	...	...	...	—	—	—	—	—	Burundi
...	...	...	...	...	...	...	...	—	—	—	—	—	Cambodia
110	—	100.0	...	...	...	326	7	50	5	42	—	—	Cameroon
2,665	122,279	23.0	66,762	20.6[2]	79.4[2]	5,668	11	501	486	1,872	23,564	99,908	Canada
...	...	...	...	...	...	...	...	—	—	—	—	—	Cape Verde
...	...	...	...	...	...	...	...	—	—	—	—	—	Central African Republic
...	...	...	...	...	...	...	...	—	—	—	—	—	Chad
108	1,150	34.4	1,645	23.4	76.6	132	26	5	46	144	1,540	...	Chile
1,274	15,392	49.1	16,033	12.2	87.8	29,600	28	1,061	905	2,200	7,600	...	China
110	4,078	15.2	4,658	12.8	87.2	1,643	10	160	92	264	4,935	...	Colombia
...	...	...	...	...	...	...	...	—	—	—	—	—	Comoros
77	2[7]	58.5	2	...	...	725	12	63	5	21	25	...	Congo
...	—	16.7	—	—	—	...	...	—	3	15	176	...	Costa Rica
99	—	68.0	—	—	—	100	200	0.5	15	69	—	—	Côte d'Ivoire
35	2,061	...	...	...	...	151	15	10	...	143	1,911	3,482	Croatia
2	31[5]	89.5	31	3.4	96.6	128	18	7	50	280	—	—	Cuba
—	—	69.2	—	—	—	...	...	—	6	19	—	—	Cyprus
3	702[12]	23.4[12]	14,419[12]	...	...	9	15	0.6	77[12]	457[12]	2,948[12]	8,902[12]	Czech Republic
101	3,769	18.0	2,085	...	...	715	13	57	64	184	688	1,898	Denmark
...	...	...	...	...	...	...	...	—	—	—	—	—	Djibouti
...	...	...	...	...	...	—	—	—	—	—	—	—	Dominica
—	—	37.5	...	...	...	...	...	—	10	48	104	...	Dominican Republic
112	102	41.2	91	—	—	2,040	17	119	45	147	2,158	...	Ecuador
348	8,917	12.1	7,765	5.3	94.7	3,593	10	346	177	532	1,767	...	Egypt
—	—	55.6	—	—	—	...	...	—	5	15	—	—	El Salvador

Energy (continued)

country	electricity												coal		
	installed capacity, 1991 ('000 kW)	production, 1991		power source, 1991			trade, 1991		consumption				reserves, latest ('000,000 metric tons)	production, 1991 ('000 metric tons)	consumption, 1991 ('000 metric tons)
		capacity ('000,000 kW-hr)	amount ('000,000 kW-hr)	fossil fuel (%)	hydro-power (%)	nuclear fuel (%)	exports ('000,000 kW-hr)	imports ('000,000 kW-hr)	amount, 1991 ('000,000 kW-hr)	per capita, 1991 (kW-hr)	residential, 1990 (%)	non-residential, 1990 (%)			
Equatorial Guinea	5	44	18	88.9	11.1	—	—	—	18	50	...	...	...	...	...
Eritrea	...	...	...	...	...	...	...	...	...	...	...	...	...	...	...
Estonia	...	...	14,627	...	...	...	8,477[5]	1,475[5]	9,856	6,270	...	...	...	...	...
Ethiopia	393	3,443	973	12.4	80.7	6.9[13]	—	—	973	19	...	...	11	—	—
Faeroe Islands	91	797	203	63.1	36.9	—	—	—	203	4,319	...	...	...	—	—
Fiji	200	1,752	472	18.4	81.6	—	—	—	472	645	10.5	89.5	...	—	18
Finland	13,347	116,920	58,137	43.9	22.5	33.6	641	7,931	65,427	13,050	18.6[2]	81.3[2]	...	—	5,626
France	106,879[14]	936,260[14]	454,702[14]	13.5[14]	13.6[14]	72.9[14]	58,746[14]	5,516[14]	401,472[14]	7,044[14]	30.3[8]	69.7[8]	210	12,092[14]	33,283[14]
French Guiana	150	1,314	395	100.0	—	—	—	—	395	3,911	...	58.7[2, 15]	...	...	...
French Polynesia	79	692	275	74.5	25.5	—	—	—	275	1,355	...	...	...	...	...
Gabon	279	2,444	914	22.6	77.4	—	—	—	914	764	55.1	44.9	...	...	...
Gambia, The	13	114	68	100.0	—	—	—	—	68	77	...	...	...	...	...
Gaza Strip	...	...	...	...	...	...	...	...	...	...	...	...	...	...	...
Georgia	...	...	14,200[5]	...	...	...	...	...	...	...	...	...	...	700	...
Germany	123,160	1,078,882	573,752	67.9	3.7	28.4	26,200	27,500	575,052	7,199	26.3[8, 16]	73.7[8, 16]	80,069	458,102	469,095
Ghana	1,187	10,398	6,152	0.7	99.3	—	285	—	5,867	379	...	...	...	—	3
Gibraltar	27	237	82	100.0	—	—	1	—	81	2,613	...	...	...	—	—
Greece	8,912	78,069	35,813	91.1	8.9	—	854	1,498	36,457	3,591	30.6[8]	69.4[8]	3,000	52,695	52,735
Greenland	87	762	215	100.0	—	—	—	—	215	3,839	35.3[17]	64.7[17]	183	...	...
Grenada	9	79	52	100.0	—	—	—	—	52	571	46.8[4]	53.2[4]	...	...	...
Guadeloupe	319	2,794	688	100.0	—	—	—	—	688	1,742	...	32.9[15, 17]	...	...	...
Guam	302	2,646	800	100.0	—	—	—	—	800	5,882	39.7	60.3	...	...	...
Guatemala	696	6,097	2,330	10.3	89.7	—	—	—	2,330	246	27.0[1]	73.0[2]	...	...	...
Guernsey	...	...	227	100.0	...	...	...	...	227	5.108	...	...	...	...	...
Guinea	176	1,542	521	66.2	33.8	—	—	—	521	88	...	...	...	...	...
Guinea-Bissau	11	96	41	100.0	—	—	—	—	41	42	...	...	...	...	...
Guyana	114	999	225	97.8	2.2	—	—	—	225	281	32.5[18]	67.5[18]	...	...	...
Haiti	153	1,340	475	31.6	68.4	—	—	—	475	72	...	...	13[1]	...	...
Honduras	290	2,540	1,105	19.9	80.1	—	2	170	1,273	240	51.7	48.3	21[1]	...	...
Hong Kong	8,387	73,470	31,807	100.0	—	—	3,061	—	28,746	4,996	70.8	29.2	...	—	9,635
Hungary	6,526	57,168	30,039	53.5	0.6	45.9	1,047	8,409	37,401	3,551	30.7[3]	69.3[3]	4,461	16,957	19,872
Iceland	969	8,488	4,494	0.2	93.5	6.3[13]	—	—	4,494	17,486	20.9[2]	79.1[2]	...	—	60
India	79,540	696,770	309,370	76.4	21.8	1.8	100	1,060	310,330	360	45.8	54.2	62,548	224,500	227,921
Indonesia	11,800	103,368	44,660	80.4	19.1	0.5[13]	—	—	44,660	238	55.0	45.0	32,063	13,715	6,610
Iran	18,204	159,467	56,900	88.4	11.6	—	—	—	56,900	949	21.1[11]	78.9[11]	193	1,400	1,800
Iraq	9,000	78,840	20,810	98.5	1.5	—	—	—	20,810	1,114	...	...	...	—	—
Ireland	3,811	33,384	15,147	93.6	6.4	—	—	—	15,147	4,336	41.4[8]	58.6[8]	14	1	3,190
Isle of Man	...	...	188[4]	100.0	—	—	—	—	172[3]	2,530[3]	48.1[8]	51.9[8]	...	...	...
Israel	4,135	36,223	21,320	100.0	—	—	360	—	20,960	4,303	68.4	31.6	...	—	4,049
Italy	57,871[19]	506,950[19]	222,041[19]	78.0[19]	20.5[19]	1.5[4, 19]	372[19]	35,454[19]	257,123[19]	4,452[19]	25.0[8]	75.0[8]	34	961[19]	19,706[19]
Jamaica	732	6,412	2,735	95.2	4.8	—	—	—	2,735	1,120	25.6	74.4	...	—	—
Japan	199,973	1,751,763	888,086	63.9	11.9	24.0	—	—	888,086	7,161	20.8[2]	79.2[2]	844	8,068	117,938
Jersey	...	...	440	...	...	...	...	...	440	6,579	...	...	...	...	...
Jordan	1,048	9,180	3,723	99.8	0.2	—	—	...	3,723	898	60.0	40.0	...	...	...
Kazakhstan	...	...	86,128[5]	...	...	...	...	32,677[5]	118,805[5]	7,040[5]	...	...	25,000	130,315	...
Kenya	829	7,262	3,227	4.9	85.8	9.3[13]	—	134	3,361	138	35.1	64.9	...	—	132
Kiribati	2	18	7	100.0	—	—	—	—	7	97	...	...	...	...	...
Korea, North	9,500	83,220	53,500	40.7	59.3	—	—	—	53,500	2,411	...	...	600	89,000	91,100
Korea, South	24,571	215,242	132,228	53.6	3.8	42.6	—	—	132,228	3,020	34.0	66.0	203	15,058	42,392
Kuwait	6,790	59,480	9,100	100.0	—	—	—	—	9,100	4,362	92.1	7.9	...	...	...
Kyrgyzstan	...	...	14,903	...	...	...	...	...	...	...	...	...	...	2,250	...
Laos	256	2,243	972	4.8	95.2	—	575	14	411	95	...	...	...	1	1
Latvia	...	...	5,600	...	...	...	3,555[5]	7,138[5]	10,230[5]	2,477[5]	...	...	...	—	...
Lebanon	870	7,621	4,750	88.2	11.8	—	—	40	4,790	1,721	...	...	...	—	—
Lesotho	[10]	[10]	[10]	[10]	[10]	[10]	[10]	[10]	[10]	[10]	...	...	...	[10]	[10]
Liberia	332	2,908	450	64.4	35.6	—	—	—	450	169	...	...	...	...	...
Libya	4,100	35,916	19,500	100.0	—	—	—	—	19,500	4,142	...	...	—	—	5
Liechtenstein	[21]	[21]	[21]	[21]	[21]	[21]	[21]	[21]	[21]	[21]	...	...	...	—	[21]
Lithuania	...	...	29,363	98.5[5]	1.5[5]	—	16,513[5]	4,539[5]	16,614	4,423	...	...	...	...	...
Luxembourg	1,238	10,845	1,415	43.6	56.4	—	780	4,500	5,135	13,693	15.3[8]	84.7[8]	...	—	212
Macau	221	1,936	889	100.0	—	—	—	94	983	2,056	75.0[4]	25.0[4]	...	—	—
Macedonia	1,657[5]	14,515[5]	5,755[5]	91.5[5]	8.5[5]	—	52[5]	185[5]	5,888[5]	2,909[5]	27.4	72.6	...	...	...
Madagascar	220	1,927	569	43.8	56.2	—	—	—	569	46	...	...	1,075[1]	—	13
Malaŵi	185	1,621	750	1.9	98.1	—	—	—	750	75	52.8	47.2	12	—	11
Malaysia	6,060	53,086	28,362	84.3	15.7	—	151	128	28,339	1,545	51.6	48.4	4	180	2,203
Maldives	14	123	28	100.0	—	—	—	—	28	127	50.9[3]	49.1[3]	...	...	...
Mali	87	762	276	33.0	67.0	—	—	—	276	29	...	...	—	...	...
Malta	250	2,190	1,100	100.0	—	—	—	—	1,100	3,090	25.1[11]	74.9[11]	...	—	297
Marshall Islands	...	...	...	...	...	...	...	...	...	...	...	...	...	...	...
Martinique	110	964	734	100.0	—	—	—	—	734	2,016	...	40.9[15, 17]	...	...	...
Mauritania	105	920	143	82.5	17.5	—	—	—	143	69	...	...	...	—	6
Mauritius	313	2,742	813	90.8	9.2	—	—	—	813	749	...	...	...	—	66
Mayotte	7	61	15	100.0	...	...	...	...	15	160	...	...	...	...	...
Mexico	29,274	256,440	126,375	74.2	19.2	6.6[13]	2,500	375	124,250	1,440	17.4[11]	82.6[11]	1,720	10,500	10,700
Micronesia	...	...	...	...	...	...	...	...	...	...	...	...	...	...	...
Moldova	...	...	15,690[5]	...	...	...	...	4,471[5]	20,161[5]	4,619[5]	...	...	...	—	4,576[5]
Monaco	[14]	[14]	[14]	[14]	[14]	[14]	[14]	[14]	[14]	[14]	...	...	...	[14]	[14]
Mongolia	901	7,893	3,500	100.0	—	—	—	150	3,650	1,623	29.8[3]	70.2[3]	24,000[1]	7,775	7,175
Morocco	2,434	21,322	9,834	87.5	12.5	—	—	641	9,834	408	66.6	33.4	45	555	1,760
Mozambique	2,358	20,656	490	89.8	10.2	—	—	325	815	56	...	...	240	42	62
Myanmar (Burma)	1,116	9,776	2,400	52.1	47.9	—	—	—	2,400	56	...	59.1[2, 15]	2	83	85
Namibia	[10]	[10]	[10]	[10]	[10]	[10]	[10]	[10]	[10]	[10]	...	...	...	[10]	[10]
Nauru	10	88	29	100.0	—	—	—	—	29	2,900	...	...	...	...	...
Nepal	282	2,470	890	3.0	97.0	—	65	29	854	43	67.3	32.7	...	—	67
Netherlands, The	17,545	153,694	74,252	95.3	0.2	4.5	624	9,778	83,406	5,542	25.0[4]	75.0[4]	497	—	12,282

natural gas						crude petroleum							country
published proved reserves, 1993 ('000,000,000 cu m)	production		consumption			reserves, 1993		production, 1992 ('000,000 barrels)	consumption, 1991 ('000,000 barrels)	refining capacity, 1993 ('000 barrels per day)	pipelines (latest)		
	natural gas, 1992 ('000,000 cu m)	manufactured gas, 1991 (% of total gas consumption)	amount, 1991 ('000,000 cu m)	residential, 1990 (%)	non-residential, 1990 (%)	published proved ('000,000 barrels)	years to exhaust proved reserves				length (km)	traffic ('000,000 metric ton-km)	
37	...	...	...	...	...	4	10	0.4	...	—	—	—	Equatorial Guinea
...	...	...	...	...	...	...	...	...	...	...	...	...	Eritrea
...	...	...	1,521	...	...	...	...	...	...	...	...	...	Estonia
23	—	100.0	—	...	...	...	...	—	5	18	—	—	Ethiopia
...	...	...	...	...	...	...	...	—	—	—	—	—	Faeroe Islands
...	—	...	—	—	—	...	...	—	—	—	—	—	Fiji
—	—	30.9	2,885	0.6[8]	99.4[8]	...	...	—	73	200	—	—	Finland
41	3,356	22.5[14]	33,726[14]	32.4[8]	67.6[8]	166	7	23	555[14]	1,851	7,546	22,969	France
...	...	...	...	...	...	...	...	—	—	—	—	—	French Guiana
...	...	...	...	...	...	...	...	—	—	—	—	—	French Polynesia
11	102	7.6	100	19.7	80.3	768	7	107	8	24	284	...	Gabon
...	...	...	...	...	...	...	...	—	—	—	—	—	Gambia, The
...	...	...	...	...	...	...	...	—	—	—	—	—	Gaza Strip
...	45[7]	...	...	...	...	...	...	0.9	...	106	...	...	Georgia
221	21,127	21.2	88,409	36.6[8, 16]	63.4[8, 16]	225	9	24	667	2,233	7,590	14,136	Germany
—	—	83.5	—	—	—	0.5	...	...	7	27	—	—	Ghana
...	...	...	...	...	...	...	...	—	...	—	—	—	Gibraltar
8	102	97.8	164	...	...	41	8	5	92	396	573	...	Greece
...	...	...	...	...	...	...	...	—	—	—	—	—	Greenland
...	...	...	...	...	...	...	...	—	—	—	—	—	Grenada
...	...	...	...	...	...	...	...	—	—	—	—	—	Guadeloupe
...	—	100.0[5]	—	—	—	...	...	—	—	—	...	...	Guam
0.3	8	9.8	...	...	...	207	104	2	5	16	275	...	Guatemala
...	...	...	...	...	...	...	...	—	—	—	—	—	Guernsey
24[6]	...	...	...	...	...	...	...	—	—	—	—	—	Guinea
...	...	...	...	...	...	...	...	—	—	—	—	—	Guinea-Bissau
...	...	...	...	...	...	...	...	—	—	—	—	—	Guyana
...	...	...	...	...	...	...	...	—	—	—	—	—	Haiti
—	—	33.4	—	—	—	...	...	—	2	14	—	—	Honduras
...	—	68.9	—	—	—	...	...	—	—	—	—	—	Hong Kong
97	4,774	9.1	10,201	14.0[8]	86.0[8]	122	9	14	49	235	1,834	3,367	Hungary
...	...	...	...	...	...	...	...	—	—	—	—	—	Iceland
677	13,796	22.4	10,548	53.7	46.3	5,935	28	211	405	1,047	5,200	...	India
1,374	47,927	22.5	14,697	—	100.0	8,350	15	546	299	860	2,961	...	Indonesia
17,273	26,595	7.5	22,909	—	100.0[4]	61,300	50	1,220	310	1,089	9,800	...	Iran
3,095	1,620	14.5	1,169	...	...	99,840	620	161	100	319	5,075	...	Iraq
20	2,352	4.1	2,241	13.9[8]	86.1[8]	...	...	—	13	56	—	—	Ireland
...	—	...	...	...	...	...	...	—	...	—	—	—	Isle of Man
0.4	23	109.1	26	—	100.0	3	30	0.1	60	221	998	...	Israel
360	16,469	13.4[19]	52,073[19]	45.6[8]	54.4[8]	822	27	31	533[19]	2,420	3,851	8,980	Italy
—	—	37.1	—	—	—	...	...	—	7	32	10	...	Jamaica
27	2,326	40.3	56,716	61.3[8]	38.7[8]	60	10	6	1,432	4,741	406	...	Japan
...	...	...	...	...	...	...	...	—	—	—	—	—	Jersey
6	161	82.0	—	—	—	4	40	0.1	17	100	209	...	Jordan
...	7,885[7]	...	...	...	...	...	...	194[7]	...	390	3,400	22,300	Kazakhstan
—	—	104.0	—	—	—	...	...	—	15	90	483	...	Kenya
...	...	...	...	...	...	...	...	—	—	—	—	—	Kiribati
...	...	...	...	...	...	...	...	—	21	42	37	...	Korea, North
—	—	30.3	3,758	...	...	...	...	—	411	1,147	455	...	Korea, South
1,347	2,648	25.7	451	25.0	75.0	92,428	296	312	40	368	917	...	Kuwait
...	68[6]	...	1,947[6]	...	...	...	...	0.9[6]	...	...	...	...	Kyrgyzstan
...	...	...	...	...	...	...	...	—	—	—	136	...	Laos
...	—	...	...	...	...	...	...	—	...	...	1,555	...	Latvia
—	—	8.0	...	...	...	...	...	—	4	38	72	...	Lebanon
—	—	[10]	—	...	...	...	...	—	[10]	—	—	—	Lesotho
—	—	50.5[20]	—	...	...	...	...	—	—	15	—	—	Liberia
1,233	6,773	7.2	7,306	...	...	38,190	71	538	113	348	4,826	...	Libya
—	—	[21]	[21]	...	...	...	...	—	[21]	—	—	—	Liechtenstein
...	...	...	...	...	...	...	...	...	...	267	...	...	Lithuania
...	—	41.2	521	48.0[8]	52.0[8]	...	...	—	[9]	—	48	...	Luxembourg
...	...	...	...	...	...	...	...	—	—	—	—	—	Macau
...	—	...	...	...	...	...	...	—	...	51	—	—	Macedonia
2	—	50.5	—	...	...	...	...	—	1.4	16	—	—	Madagascar
...	—	—	—	—	—	...	...	—	—	—	—	—	Malaŵi
1,895	20,802	16.9	3,793	6.6	93.4	4,260	19	230	72	263	1,307	...	Malaysia
...	...	...	...	...	...	...	...	—	—	—	—	—	Maldives
...	...	...	...	...	...	...	...	—	—	—	—	—	Mali
—	...	—	...	...	...	...	...	—	—	—	—	—	Malta
...	...	...	...	...	...	...	...	—	—	...	—	—	Marshall Islands
—	—	212.6	...	...	...	...	...	—	4	16	—	—	Martinique
...	...	86.5	...	...	...	...	...	—	6	—	—	—	Mauritania
...	...	...	...	...	...	...	...	—	—	—	—	—	Mauritius
...	...	...	...	...	...	...	...	—	—	—	—	—	Mayotte
1,983	25,499	28.5	25,932	3.9[11]	96.1[11]	51,225	51	1,009	471	1,524	38,350	...	Mexico
...	...	...	...	...	...	...	...	—	—	...	—	—	Micronesia
...	—	...	4,004[5]	...	...	...	...	—	52[5]	...	...	...	Moldova
...	...	[14]	[14]	...	...	...	...	—	[14]	—	—	—	Monaco
...	...	...	...	...	...	...	...	—	—	—	—	—	Mongolia
1	31	36.3	39	—	100.0	2	20	0.1	41	155	362	...	Morocco
65	—	—	—	...	...	...	...	—	—	...	595	...	Mozambique
278	841	0.5	998	—	100.0[4]	100	17	6	7	32	1,343	...	Myanmar (Burma)
147	—	[10]	—	...	...	...	...	—	[10]	—	—	—	Namibia
...	...	...	...	...	...	...	...	—	—	—	—	—	Nauru
...	—	—	—	—	—	...	...	—	—	—	—	—	Nepal
1,929	58,656	15.1	49,850	46.8[4]	53.4[4]	329	14	24	355	1,231	1,383	4,560	Netherlands, The

Energy (continued)

country	electricity												coal		
	installed capacity, 1991 ('000 kW)	production, 1991		power source, 1990			trade, 1991		consumption				reserves, latest ('000,000 metric tons)	pro-duction, 1991 ('000 metric tons)	con-sump-tion, 1991 ('000 metric tons)
		capacity ('000,000 kW-hr)	amount ('000,000 kW-hr)	fossil fuel (%)	hydro-power (%)	nuclear fuel (%)	exports ('000,000 kW-hr)	imports ('000,000 kW-hr)	amount, 1991 ('000,000 kW-hr)	per capita, 1991 (kW-hr)	resi-dential, 1990 (%)	non-resi-dential, 1990 (%)			
Netherlands Antilles	200	1,752	800	100.0	—	—	—	—	800	4,571	...	...	...	...	...
New Caledonia	253	2,216	1,166	70.6	29.4	—	—	—	1,166	6,859	...	...	2	—	176
New Zealand	7,504	65,735	29,556	21.0	73.9	5.1[13]	—	—	29,556	8,635	37.5[4]	62.5[4]	117	2,714	2,314
Nicaragua	395	3,460	1,043	46.5	25.2	28.3[13]	10	200	1,233	324	67.1	32.9	...	...	...
Niger	63	552	168	100.0	—	—	—	188	356	45	50.0	50.0	70	157	157
Nigeria	4,040	35,390	9,955	77.7	22.3	—	100	—	9,855	88	80.4	19.6	190	90	55
Northern Mariana Islands	...	...	...	...	...	...	...	...	...	...	...	...	...	...	...
Norway	27,134	237,694	110,950	0.4	99.6	—	6,039	3,227	108,138	25,373	27.0[2]	73.0[2]	13	339	690
Oman	1,564	13,701	5,548	100.0	—	—	—	—	5,548	3,511	...	...	...	...	...
Pakistan	10,097	88,450	47,334	60.5	38.7	0.8	—	—	47,334	390	64.5	35.5	524	3,054	4,200
Panama	958	8,392	2,907	30.0	70.0	—	64	203	3,046	1,235	26.8[11]	73.2[11]	...	—	177
Papua New Guinea	490	4,292	1,790	74.3	25.7	—	—	—	1,790	452	27.5	72.5	...	...	1
Paraguay	6,500	56,940	29,780	0.1	99.9	—	26,803	3	2,980	678	...	...	...	...	...
Peru	4,137	36,240	14,828	23.6	76.4	—	—	—	14,828	674	35.8	64.2	1,060	140	140
Philippines	6,789	59,472	22,484	51.5	22.9	25.6[13]	—	—	22,484	352	53.0	47.0	263	1,265	2,577
Poland	30,984	271,420	134,696	97.5	2.5	—	9,326	6,708	132,078	3,448	33.5[3]	66.5[3]	41,200	209,782	168,783
Portugal	7,414	64,947	29,871	69.3	30.7	—	1,620	1,712	29,963	3,037	36.4[2]	63.6[2]	36	270	4,381
Puerto Rico	4,230	37,055	15,730	98.2	1.8	—	—	—	15,730	4,416	31.0[11]	69.0[11]	...	—	192
Qatar	1,410	12,352	4,716	100.0	—	—	—	—	4,716	10,718	83.0	17.0	...	...	...
Réunion	175	1,533	923	33.9	66.1	—	—	—	923	1,503	...	...	...	...	...
Romania	22,268	195,068	56,912	75.0	25.0	—	—	7,047	63,959	2,748	23.6[3]	76.4[3]	3,118	32,406	38,405
Russia	213,300[5]	1,868,500[5]	1,068,000	73.7[5]	15.4[5]	10.9[5]	36,300[22]	360[22]	1,068,200[5]	5,856[22]	21.6[3, 22]	78.4[3, 22]	265,582[22]	353,000	395,000
Rwanda	60	526	179	1.1	98.9	—	3	10	186	26	...	...	...	...	...
St. Kitts and Nevis	15	131	40	100.0	—	—	—	—	40	952	...	...	...	...	...
St. Lucia	22	193	105	100.0	—	—	—	—	105	778	26.6[3]	73.4[3]	...	...	...
St. Vincent and the Grenadines	14	123	51	23.5	76.5	—	—	—	51	472	45.3[4]	54.7[4]	...	...	...
San Marino	[19]	[19]	[19]	[19]	[19]	[19]	[19]	[19]	[19]	[19]	...	...	...	[19]	[19]
São Tomé and Príncipe	6	53	15	46.7	53.3	—	—	—	15	124	...	...	...	...	...
Saudi Arabia	18,350	160,746	47,710	100.0	—	—	—	—	47,710	3,101	69.3[17]	30.7[17]	...	...	...
Senegal	231	2,024	756	100.0	—	—	—	—	756	100	...	...	...	...	...
Seychelles	29	254	102	100.0	—	—	—	—	102	1,437	...	...	...	...	...
Sierra Leone	126	1,104	230	100.0	—	—	—	—	230	54	...	...	...	—	—
Singapore	3,500	30,660	16,597	100.0	—	—	—	—	16,597	6,060	48.0	52.0	...	—	2
Slovakia	...	...	22,731	...	...	...	...	...	...	...	...	...	...	4,149	...
Slovenia	2,701[5]	23,660[5]	12,399[5]	38.7[5]	24.0[5]	37.3[5]	29[5]	7[5]	12,377[5]	6,288[5]	18.0	82.0	...	...	...
Solomon Islands	12	105	30	100.0	—	—	—	—	30	91	69.4	30.6	...	...	...
Somalia	60	526	110	100.0	—	—	—	—	110	12	...	...	...	...	...
South Africa	25,854[10]	226,481[10]	169,645[10]	97.0[10]	0.5[10]	2.5[10]	5,936[10]	254	163,963[10]	3,709[10]	...	...	55,333	176,174[10]	133,527[10]
Bophuthatswana	...	...	...	...	...	...	...	...	...	...	...	...	...	...	...
Ciskei	...	...	...	...	...	...	...	...	...	...	...	...	...	...	...
Transkei	...	...	...	...	...	...	...	...	...	...	...	...	...	...	...
Venda	...	...	...	...	...	...	...	...	...	...	...	...	...	...	...
Spain	43,622	382,129	155,704	46.1	18.2	35.7	3,762	3,083	155,025	3,972	16.7[2]	83.2[2]	1,450	33,562	47,659
Sri Lanka	1,289	11,292	3,377	7.7	92.3	—	—	—	3,377	194	65.1	34.9	...	—	1
Sudan, The	500	4,380	1,329	29.4	70.6	—	—	—	1,329	51	...	...	...	—	—
Suriname	415	3,635	1,400	20.4	79.6	—	—	—	1,400	3,256	...	...	...	—	1
Swaziland	[10]	[10]	[10]	[10]	[10]	[10]	[10]	[10]	[10]	[10]	18.7[18]	81.3[18]	999	[10]	[10]
Sweden	34,089	298,620	147,730	4.7	43.1	52.2	7,519	6,224	146,435	17,008	26.4[2]	73.6[2]	1	28	3,563
Switzerland	16,296[21]	142,753[21]	57,802[21]	2.5[21]	57.8[21]	39.7[21]	22,578[21]	19,782[21]	55,006[21]	8,100[21]	26.6[8]	73.4[8]	...	—	396[21]
Syria	3,717	32,561	12,179	48.7	51.3	—	—	—	12,179	951	21.2[8]	78.8[8]	...	—	—
Taiwan	18,383	161,035	89,639	56.1	6.1	37.8	—	—	80,977	3,949	31.2	68.8	100	403	...
Tajikistan	...	...	17,500	...	...	...	...	...	...	...	...	...	...	313	...
Tanzania	439	3,846	901	31.0	69.0	—	—	—	901	33	...	...	200	4	4
Thailand	10,771	94,354	52,486	91.3	8.7	—	40	595	53,041	958	51.0	49.0	999	14,689	14,868
Togo	34	298	60	91.7	8.3	—	—	290	350	96	...	...	...	...	...
Tonga	7	61	22	100.0	—	—	—	—	22	227	...	...	...	...	...
Trinidad and Tobago	1,150	10,074	3,640	100.0	—	—	—	—	3,640	2,910	41.0	59.0	...	—	—
Tunisia	1,414	12,387	5,555	99.2	0.8	—	42	—	5,513	670	42.8	57.2	—	—	12
Turkey	17,207	150,733	60,338	62.1	37.7	0.2[13]	506	759	60,591	1,060	14.2[9]	85.8[9]	7,148	46,178	57,511
Turkmenistan	...	...	17,171	...	...	...	8,834	...	8,337	2,216	...	...	...	...	...
Tuvalu	...	...	...	...	...	...	...	...	...	...	...	...	...	...	...
Uganda	162	1,419	783	0.9	99.1	—	112	—	671	37	...	...	...	...	...
Ukraine	55,600[5]	485,000[5]	279,000	...	...	...	43,900[5]	15,500[5]	248,200[5]	4,782[5]	...	...	...	135,600	...
United Arab Emirates	4,660	40,822	13,790	100.0	—	—	—	—	13,790	8,460	...	...	...	...	...
United Kingdom	70,022	613,393	322,133	76.2	1.9	21.9	15	16,422	338,540	5,860	35.4[8]	64.6[8]	3,800	96,144	108,247
United States	788,312	6,905,613	3,079,085	70.1	9.4	19.9	8,540	30,812	3,101,357	12,281	34.9[8]	65.1[8]	240,561	901,877	806,483
Uruguay	1,795	15,724	7,017	12.9	87.1	—	1,791	—	5,226	1,679	60.6	39.4	...	—	—
Uzbekistan	...	...	57,400[6]	...	...	...	2,157[5]	...	54,800[6]	2,565[6]	...	...	...	6,200[6]	10,400[6]
Vanuatu	11	96	26	100.0	—	—	—	—	26	170	...	...	...	...	...
Venezuela	17,726	155,280	57,150	40.0	60.0	—	—	—	57,150	2,893	42.0	58.0	417	2,696	400
Vietnam	1,645	14,410	8,550	38.3	61.7	—	—	—	8,550	126	36.4[3]	63.6[3]	150	5,000	4,050
Virgin Islands (U.S.)	316	2,768	1,000	100.0	—	—	—	—	1,000	9,346	40.2[4]	59.8[4]	...	—	...
West Bank	...	...	...	...	...	...	...	...	...	...	...	...	...	...	...
Western Sahara	56	491	85	100.0	—	—	—	—	85	354	...	...	...	...	...
Western Samoa	19	166	47	57.4	42.6	—	—	—	47	297	...	...	...	...	...
Yemen	810	7,096	1,750	100.0	—	—	—	—	1,750	145	...	...	1[5]	...	...
Yugoslavia	21,159[23]	185,353[23]	36,488	70.2[23]	24.2[23]	5.6[23]	2,300[23]	3,600[23]	39,453	3,791	26.0	74.0	16,570[23]	40,105	40,410
Zaire	2,831	24,800	6,168	2.6	97.4	—	198	2	5,972	155	...	89.1[2, 15]	600	128	174
Zambia	2,436	21,339	7,775	0.5	99.5	—	1,500	20	6,295	750	31.8	68.2	55	380	375
Zimbabwe	2,038	17,853	9,565	63.1	36.9	—	5	900	10,460	1,019	44.2	55.8	734	5,600	5,575

natural gas						crude petroleum							country
published proved reserves, 1993 ('000,000,000 cu m)	production		consumption			reserves, 1993		production, 1992 ('000,000 barrels)	consumption, 1991 ('000,000 barrels)	refining capacity, 1993 ('000 barrels per day)	pipelines (latest)		
	natural gas, 1992 ('000,000 cu m)	manufactured gas, 1991 (% of total gas consumption)	amount, 1991 ('000,000 cu m)	residential, 1990 (%)	nonresidential, 1990 (%)	published proved ('000,000 barrels)	years to exhaust proved reserves				length (km)	traffic ('000,000 metric ton-km)	
—	—	88.9	...	...	...	...	...	—	71	470	—	—	Netherlands Antilles
...	...	...	...	...	...	...	...	—	—	—	—	—	New Caledonia
89	6,308	7.3	4,227	4.8[4]	95.2[4]	160	12	13	32	84	310	...	New Zealand
—	—	93.7	—	—	—	...	...	—	3	16	56	...	Nicaragua
...	—	—	—	—	—	...	...	—	...	—	—	—	Niger
3,451	4,703	1.3	4,750	—	100.0	18,213	26	704	88	433	5,042	...	Nigeria
...	...	...	...	...	...	...	...	—	—	...	—	—	Northern Mariana Islands
2,756	26,114	49.5	2,049	...	...	16,788	21	800	94	285	53	9,618	Norway
481	3,457	7.4	2,673	...	...	4,740	18	270	25	80	1,300	...	Oman
671	13,470	1.5	12,639	41.5	58.5	147	7	22	52	121	1,135	...	Pakistan
—	—	21.5	60	—	—	...	...	—	8	100	130	...	Panama
402	—	...	—	—	—	146	7	19	—	—	—	—	Papua New Guinea
—	—	31.0	...	...	...	...	...	—	3	8	—	—	Paraguay
199	1,314	32.6	520	61.4	38.6	782	19	42	51	189	800	...	Peru
71	—	59.1	—	—	—	180	30	6	80	278	357	...	Philippines
155	3,617	32.0	10,544	...	...	36	26	1.4	87	333	2,346	17,661	Poland
—	—	57.0	...	...	...	...	...	—	70	294	69	...	Portugal
—	—	100.0	...	...	...	...	...	—	39	127	—	—	Puerto Rico
4,672	9,093	18.9	8,689	—	100.0	4,339	26	167	20	60	235	...	Qatar
...	...	...	...	...	...	...	...	—	...	—	—	—	Réunion
169	25,100	7.2	32,036	...	...	1,245	25	50	114	737	4,229	6,654	Romania
48,677	643,000	8.7[22]	643,000	...	...	156,700	54	2,911	3,700	6,463	68,400	1,240,000	Russia
57	0.2[7]	—	0.1	...	...	...	...	—	—	—	—	—	Rwanda
...	...	...	...	...	...	...	...	—	—	—	—	—	St. Kitts and Nevis
...	...	...	...	...	...	...	...	—	—	—	—	—	St. Lucia
...	...	...	...	...	...	...	...	—	—	—	—	—	St. Vincent and the Grenadines
...	...	[19]	[19]	...	...	...	...	—	[19]	—	—	—	San Marino
...	...	...	...	...	...	...	...	—	—	—	—	—	São Tomé and Príncipe
5,134	32,808	48.2	37,218	9.8[8]	90.2[8]	258,600	87	2,975	534	1,863	6,550	...	Saudi Arabia
—	—	14.3	...	...	...	...	...	—	6	23	—	—	Senegal
...	...	...	...	...	...	...	...	—	—	—	—	—	Seychelles
—	...	...	...	...	...	...	...	—	2	10	—	—	Sierra Leone
—	—	419.3	—	—	—	...	...	—	326	1,029	—	—	Singapore
8	313[7]	...	...	...	...	7	14	0.5	...	...	...	...	Slovakia
...	24[5]	—	...	...	...	...	...	0.02[5]	...	15	593	128	Slovenia
...	—	—	—	—	—	...	...	—	—	—	—	—	Solomon Islands
6	—	...	—	...	...	...	...	—	0.8	10	15	...	Somalia
54	—	100.0[10]	—	...	...	—	...	—	116[10]	431	2,679	...	South Africa
...	...	...	...	...	...	...	...	—	—	—	...	...	Bophuthatswana
...	...	...	...	...	...	...	...	—	—	—	...	...	Ciskei
...	...	...	...	...	...	...	...	—	—	—	...	...	Transkei
...	...	...	...	...	...	...	...	—	—	—	...	...	Venda
20	1,308	42.6	6,438	...	...	23	3	8	396	1,301	2,059	4,664	Spain
—	—	74.1	—	—	—	...	...	—	12	50	62	...	Sri Lanka
85	—	54.5	...	...	...	300	...	...	8	22	815	...	Sudan, The
—	...	...	...	...	...	49	33	1.5	1.2	—	—	—	Suriname
...	...	[10]	...	...	...	...	...	...	[10]	—	—	—	Swaziland
—	—	38.7	466	...	...	...	...	—	125	428	—	—	Sweden
—	—	15.5[21]	2,237[21]	38.3[8]	61.7[8]	...	...	...	34[21]	132	314	1,110	Switzerland
227	3,469	29.1	295	...	...	3,000	16	188	80	237	1,819	...	Syria
68	767	...	...	...	...	4	10	0.4	...	543	615	...	Taiwan
...	93[7]	...	...	...	...	...	...	0.7[7]	...	...	...	...	Tajikistan
116	—	100.0	—	...	...	...	...	...	4	17	982	...	Tanzania
231	8,376	17.6	5,353	—	100.0	242	13	18	87	221	67	...	Thailand
—	...	...	...	...	...	...	...	...	...	—	—	—	Togo
...	...	...	...	...	...	...	...	...	...	—	—	—	Tonga
240	4,635	3.6	5,918	1.8	98.2	541	11	51	41	246	1,051	...	Trinidad and Tobago
85	238	9.1	1,531	9.1	90.9	468	12	38	13	34	883	...	Tunisia
11	201	36.0	3,709	...	...	281	9	30	161	714	4,059	55,492	Turkey
326[6]	84,300[7]	...	9,500	...	...	740[6]	17	43[7]	...	236	...	...	Turkmenistan
...	...	...	...	...	...	...	...	...	...	—	—	—	Tuvalu
...	...	...	...	...	...	...	...	...	...	—	—	—	Uganda
...	28,100[7]	...	...	...	...	...	...	36[7]	...	1,244	...	200,000	Ukraine
5,448	25,516	15.7	20,315	...	...	64,747	77	837	65	193	830	...	United Arab Emirates
610	53,669	15.5	57,474	52.7[8]	47.3[8]	4,554	7	684	591	1,843	3,926	9,836	United Kingdom
4,665	537,542	17.5	606,228	33.4[11]	66.6[11]	22,845	9	2,617	4,921	15,210	275,800	871,618	United States
—	—	87.6	—	—	—	...	...	...	10	29	—	—	Uruguay
...	41,600	...	37,800[6]	...	...	...	...	21	62[6]	173	176	200	Uzbekistan
...	...	...	...	...	...	...	...	...	...	—	—	—	Vanuatu
3,651	22,877	14.2	23,749	9.1	90.9	63,330	73	865	357	1,167	6,850	...	Venezuela
7	711	...	3	...	...	350	9	38	0.3	—	150	...	Vietnam
—	—	125.0	...	...	...	...	...	...	126	545	—	—	Virgin Islands (U.S.)
...	...	...	...	...	...	...	...	...	...	—	—	—	West Bank
...	...	...	...	...	...	...	...	...	...	—	—	—	Western Sahara
...	...	...	...	...	...	...	...	...	...	—	—	—	Western Samoa
429	...	41.7	...	...	...	2,010	29	69	34	115	456	—	Yemen
16	846[7]	20.1[23]	749	...	...	130	19	7	90[23]	444	1,398	894	Yugoslavia
30	—	7.8	—	—	—	187	19	10	3	17	390	...	Zaire
—	—	100.0	—	—	—	...	...	...	4	24	1,724	...	Zambia
...	—	90.6	—	—	—	...	...	...	...	—	8	...	Zimbabwe

[1]Estimated reserves in place. [2]1981. [3]1985. [4]1984. [5]1990. [6]1992. [7]1991. [8]1983. [9]Belgium includes Luxembourg. [10]South Africa includes Botswana, Lesotho, Namibia, and Swaziland. [11]1982. [12]Data refer to former Czechoslovakia. [13]Geothermally generated electricity. [14]France includes Monaco. [15]Transportation and industry only; excludes agricultural, commercial, and public-service sectors. [16]Data refer to former West Germany only. [17]1988. [18]1980. [19]Italy includes San Marino. [20]1989. [21]Switzerland includes Liechtenstein. [22]Data refer to former U.S.S.R. [23]Data refer to Yugoslavia as constituted prior to 1991.

Transportation

This table presents data on the transportation infrastructure of the various countries and dependencies of the world and on their commercial passenger and cargo traffic. Most states have roads and airports, with services corresponding to the prevailing level of economic development. A number of states, however, lack railroads or inland waterways because of either geographic constraints or lack of development capital and technical expertise. Pipelines, one of the oldest means of bulk transport if aqueducts are considered, are today among the most narrowly developed transportation modes worldwide for shipment of bulk materials. Because the principal contemporary application of pipeline technology is to facilitate the shipment of hydrocarbon liquids and gases, coverage of pipelines will be found in the "Energy" table. It is, however, also true that pipelines now find increasing application for slurries of coal or other raw materials.

While the United Nations' *Statistical Yearbook* and *Monthly Bulletin of Statistics* provide much data on infrastructure and traffic and have established basic definitions and classifications for transportation statistics, the number of countries covered is limited. Several commercial publications maintain substantial databases and publishing programs for their particular areas of interest: highway and vehicle statistics are provided by the International Road Federation's annual *World Road Statistics;* the International Union of Railways' *International Railway Statistics* and Jane's *World Railways* provide similar data for railways; Lloyd's *Register of Shipping Statistical Tables* summarizes the world's merchant marine; the *Official Airline Guide,* the International Civil Aviation Organization's *Digest of Statistics: Commercial Air Carriers,* and the International Air Transport Association's *World Air Transport Statistics* have also been used to supplement and update data collected by the UN. Because several of these agencies are commercially or insurance-oriented, their data tend to be more complete, accurate, and timely than those of intergovernmental organizations, which depend on periodic responses to questionnaires or publication of results in official sources. All of these international sources have been extensively supplemented by national statistical sources to provide additional data. Such diversity of sources, however, imposes limitations on the comparability of the statistics from country to country because the basis and completeness of data collection and the frequency and timeliness of analysis and publication may vary greatly. Data shown in italic are from 1988 or earlier.

The categories adopted in the table also have special problems of comparability. Total road length is subject to wide international variation of interpretation, as "roads" can mean anything from mere tracks to highly developed highways. Each country also has individual classifications that differ according to climate, availability of road-building materials, traffic patterns, administrative responsibility, and so on. "Paved roads," by contrast, is a much more tightly definable category, but the proportion of paved to total roads may be distorted by the less comparable total road statistics. Automobile and truck and bus fleet statistics, which are usually

Transportation

country	roads and motor vehicles (latest)								railroads (latest)					
	roads			motor vehicles			cargo		track length		traffic			
	length		paved (percent)	automobiles	trucks and buses	persons per vehicle	short ton-mi ('000,000)	metric ton-km ('000,000)	mi	km	passengers		cargo	
	mi	km									passenger-mi ('000,000)	passenger-km ('000,000)	short ton-mi ('000,000)	metric ton-km ('000,000)
Afghanistan	*11,930*	*19,200*	*47*	31,800	30,900	257	*1,993*	*2,910*	*6*	*10*	...	...	...	...
Albania	4,629	7,450	38	16,000	32,900	68	818.5	1,195	447	720	484.2	779.2	400	584
Algeria	56,000	90,000	70	760,000	510,000	20	9,589	14,000	2,668[2]	4,293[2]	1,859	2,991	1,842	2,690
American Samoa	217	350	43	4,447	445	9.3	...	...	—	—	—	—	—	—
Andorra	167	269	74	34,168	4,033	1.4	...	...	—	—	—	—	—	—
Angola	45,118	72,611	11	120,000	40,000	64	...	...	*1,739*[2]	*2,798*[2]	203	326	1,178	1,720
Antigua and Barbuda	724	1,165	33	13,650	3,550	3.8	...	...	—	—	—	—	—	—
Argentina	*131,338*	*211,369*	*27*	4,088,000	1,512,000	5.7	...	...	*21,198*[2]	*34,115*[2]	6,618	10,651	5,790	8,453
Armenia	4,800	7,700	99	230,100	...	...	780.8	1,140	511	823	199	320	2,861	4,177
Aruba	*236*	*380*	*100*	27,546	655	2.3	...	...	—	—	—	—	—	—
Australia	503,474	810,264	36	7,734,100	1,915,400	1.8	*58,582*	*85,529*	22,050[2, 7]	35,486[2, 7]	*5,800*	*9,300*	36,533	53,338
Austria	77,700	125,000	100	3,100,014	268,577	2.3	*5,949*	*8,685*	4,136	6,657	5,864[7]	9,437[7]	8,362[7]	12,208[7]
Azerbaijan	22,800	36,700	87	235,600	...	...	5,660	8,264	1,299	2,090	3,025	4,869	...	...
Bahamas, The	2,094	3,370	*40*	70,000	15,000	3.0	...	...	—	—	—	—	—	—
Bahrain	1,660	2,671	75	107,657	24,523	3.8	...	...	—	—	—	—	—	—
Bangladesh	120,100	193,283	4	67,000	63,000	850	...	...	1,706[2]	2,746[2]	2,850	4,587	446	651
Barbados	977	1,573	95	39,406	9,318	5.3	...	...	—	—	—	—	—	—
Belarus	29,900	48,100	94	498,700	...	...	15,321	22,369	3,472	5,587	10,268	16,524	56.0	81.7
Belgium	85,672	137,876	97	3,970,317	596,452	2.2	17,794	25,979	2,162[2]	3,479[2]	4,207	6,770	5,584	8,153
Belize	1,600	2,575	13	12,075	2,800	13	...	...	—	—	—	—	—	—
Benin	5,241	8,435	12	22,000	12,000	132	...	...	359	578	*86.7*	*139.6*	*2.7*	*4.0*
Bermuda	120	193	100	19,500	3,500	2.6	...	...	—	—	—	—	—	—
Bhutan	1,600	2,500	72	*2,590*	*1,367*	*348*	...	...	—	—	—	—	—	—
Bolivia	*25,875*	*41,642*	4	265,000	60,000	23	*1,133*	*1,654*	2,264[2]	3,643[2]	244.2	393.0	414.5	605.2
Bosnia and Herzegovina	13,153	21,168	54	438,080	50,578	8.9	2,708	3,954	646	1,039	...	...	...	...
Botswana	11,933	19,204	13	17,000	28,000	27	...	...	551	887	160	257	0.5	0.8
Brazil	1,037,780	1,670,148	10	12,127,562	935,783	11	*178,359*	*260,400*	18,721[2]	30,129[2]	8,431	13,569	82,267	120,108
Brunei	1,397	2,248	49	115,495	13,019	2.0	...	...	12[13]	19[13]	—	—	...	...
Bulgaria	22,947	36,930	92	1,316,644	133,375	6.2	7,596	11,090	4,076	6,560	3,351	5,393	5,314	7,758
Burkina Faso	8,161	13,134	*12*	12,000	13,000	360	...	...	308[2]	495[2]	*422*	*680*	*322*	*470*
Burundi	3,893	6,265	16	13,696	14,027	195	...	...	—	—	—	—	—	—
Cambodia	9,200	14,800	18	*4,000*	*7,100*	*737*	...	...	*403*	*649*	*33.6*	*54.0*	*6.9*	*10.0*
Cameroon	29,950	48,200	7	94,000	82,000	70	*175*	*255*	686[2]	1,104[2]	284	457	514	751
Canada	513,092	825,743	35	12,811,318	3,458,368	1.6	*29,033*	*42,388*	*56,771*	*91,365*	725	1,166	163,978	239,404
Cape Verde	*3,489*	*5,615*	*29*	10,000	5,000	23	...	...	—	—	—	—	—	—
Central African Republic	14,750	23,738	2	10,782	8,051	145	*2.8*	*4.1*	—	—	—	—	—	—
Chad	*24,855*	*40,000*	*1*	8,000	6,000	396	...	...	—	—	—	—	—	—
Chile	49,457	79,593	14	792,950	412,462	11	...	...	2,778[2]	4,470[2]	669	1,076	1,077	1,572
China	646,931	1,041,136	87	1,852,400	4,208,800	190	230,011	335,810	42,261	68,013	195,700	315,000	795,900	1,162,000
Colombia	80,229	129,117	8	936,000	364,000	24	15	22	*2,011*[2]	*3,236*[2]	49.2	79.2	204.3	298.3
Comoros	376	605	*53*	*1,000*	*4,000*	*84*	...	...	—	—	—	—	—	—
Congo	7,919	12,745	10	27,000	15,430	58	*46*	*67*	494	795	270	434	320	467
Costa Rica	22,081	35,536	16	168,814	95,066	12	1,385	2,022	435[2]	700[2]	26.5	42.6	*102.7*	*150.0*
Côte d'Ivoire	*41,900*	*67,500*	*7*	168,000	91,000	45	...	...	410[2]	660[2]	634[15]	1,021[15]	396[15]	578[15]
Croatia	17,012	27,378	81	865,516	72,043	5.1	958.2	1,399	1,519	2,444	1,949	3,137	2,701	3,943
Cuba	*28,928*	*46,555*	*27*	*241,300*	*208,400*	*23*	*1,208*	*1,763*	3,033	4,881	1,880	3,025	937	1,368
Cyprus	6,345	10,211	53	189,701	84,024	2.1	...	...	—	—	—	—	—	—
Czech Republic	34,730	55,892	...	2,435,645	232,703	3.9	5,569[17]	8,131[17]	5,874	9,453	11,969[17]	19,263[17]	20,974	30,622
Denmark	44,125	71,012	100	1,604,638	315,511	2.7	7,100	10,400	1,763	2,838	2,981	4,797	1,273	1,858
Djibouti	1,789	2,879	13	13,000	2,000	34	...	...	66	106	182	293	81.7	119.3
Dominica	*470*	*756*	...	4,696	4,616	7.7	...	...	—	—	—	—	—	—
Dominican Republic	11,000	17,000	17	160,000	110,000	27	...	...	88	142	...	...	...	...
Ecuador	*23,386*	*37,636*	*17*	165,600	207,300	27	*178*	*259*	600[2]	965[2]	51	82	3.4	5.0
Egypt	28,272[19]	45,500[19]	68[19]	826,915	550,649	38	21,394	31,235	5,489	8,831	26,834	43,185	2,166	3,162
El Salvador	7,764	12,495	14	80,000	80,000	34	...	...	374[2]	602[2]	4.9	7.9	25.0	36.5

based upon registration, are relatively accurate, though some countries round off figures, and unregistered vehicles may cause substantial undercount. There is also inconsistent classification of vehicle types; in some countries a vehicle may serve variously as an automobile, a truck, or a bus, or even as all three on certain occasions. Relatively few countries collect and maintain commercial road traffic statistics.

Data on national railway systems are generally given for railway track length rather than the length of routes, which may be multitracked. Siding tracks usually are not included, but some countries fail to distinguish them. The United States data include only class 1 railways, which account for about 94 percent of total track length. Passenger traffic is usually calculated from tickets sold to fare-paying passengers. Such statistics are subject to distortion if there are large numbers of nonpaying passengers, such as military personnel, or if season tickets are sold and not all the allowed journeys are utilized. Railway cargo traffic is calculated by weight hauled multiplied by the length of the journey. Changes in freight load during the journey should be accounted for but sometimes are not, leading to discrepancies.

Merchant fleet and tonnage statistics collected by Lloyd's registry service for vessels over 100 gross tons are quite accurate. Cargo statistics, however, reflect the port and customs requirements of each country and the reporting rules of each country's merchant marine authority (although these, increasingly, reflect the recommendations of the International Maritime Organization); often, however, they are only estimates based on customs declarations and the count of vessels entered and cleared. Even when these elements are reported consistently, further uncertainties may be introduced because of ballast, bunkers, ships' stores, or transshipped goods included in the data.

Airport data are based on scheduled flights reported in the commercial *Official Airline Guide* and are both reliable and current. The comparability of civil air traffic statistics suffers from differing characteristics of the air transportation systems of different countries; data for an entire country may be two to three years behind those for a single airport.

Outside of Europe, where standardization of data on inland waterways is necessitated by the volume of international traffic, comparability of national data declines markedly. Calculations as to both the length of a country's waterway system (or route length of river, lake, and coastal traffic) and the makeup of its stock of commercially significant vessels (those for which data will be collected) are largely determined by the nature and use of the country's hydrographic net—its seasonality, relief profile, depth, access to potential markets—and inevitably differ widely from country to country. Data for coastal or island states may refer to scheduled coastwise or interisland traffic.

merchant marine				air					canals and inland waterways (latest)				country
fleet, 1992 (vessels over 100 gross tons)	total dead-weight tonnage, 1992 ('000)	international cargo (latest)		airports with sched-uled flights, 1993	traffic (latest)				length		cargo		
		loaded metric tons ('000)	off-loaded metric tons ('000)		passengers		cargo		mi	km	short ton-mi ('000,000)	metric ton-km ('000,000)	
					passenger-mi ('000,000)	passenger-km ('000,000)	short ton-mi ('000,000)	metric ton-km ('000,000)					
—	—	—	—	1	121[1]	195[1]	9.9[1]	14.4[1]	750	1,200	...	...	Afghanistan
24	81.0	1,065	664	1	...	...	...	...	27	43	24	35	Albania
149	1,093.4	57,607	14,284	25	1,921[3]	3,092[3]	16.6[3]	24.3[3]	...	...	...	...	Algeria
3	0.1	380	733	3	...	...	...	...	...	...	...	...	American Samoa
—	—	—	—	—	—	—	—	—	—	—	—	—	Andorra
113	123.5	21,102	1,242	16	*606*[4]	*975*[4]	*23.2*[4]	*33.9*[4]	805	1,295	...	...	Angola
292	997.4	28	113	2	121	195	0.1	0.2	...	...	...	...	Antigua and Barbuda
423	1,173.1	33,978	5,820	49	5,019[5]	8,078[5]	120[5]	175[5]	6,800	11,000	*19,326*	*28,215*	Argentina
...	...	...	...	2	3,453	5,557	33.6	49.0	...	...	...	...	Armenia
[6]	[6]	...	...	1	...	...	...	...	...	...	...	...	Aruba
695	3,857.3	262,980	24,723	441	23,019	37,045	1,414	2,065	5,200	8,368	...	...	Australia
26	208.5	*2,538*	*6,607*	6	2,990	4,812	70.2	102.5	277	446	1,253	1,830	Austria
...	...	...	...	1	3,025	4,869	...	...	...	...	...	...	Azerbaijan
1,061	33,081.7	5,920	5,705	24	215	346	0.2	0.3	...	...	...	...	Bahamas, The
87	192.5	13,285	3,512	1	963[8]	1,549[8]	30.3[8]	44.3[8]	...	...	...	...	Bahrain
301	566.8	1,395	9,235	7	1,407	2,264	68	100	5,000	8,046	...	...	Bangladesh
37	84.0	206	538	1	*93*[9]	*149*[9]	*0.8*[10]	*1.1*[10]	...	...	...	...	Barbados
...	...	...	...	1	3,575	5,754	34.0	49.0	...	...	1,236	1,805	Belarus
232	218.5	57,250	100,335	3	3,867	6,223	332.8	485.8	1,269	2,043	3,732	5,448	Belgium
32	45.7	178	241	8	...	...	...	...	513	825	...	...	Belize
12	0.2	92	1,118	1	144.3[11]	232.3[11]	27.0[11]	39.4[11]	...	...	...	...	Benin
94	5,206.5	130	470	1	...	...	...	...	...	...	...	...	Bermuda
—	—	—	—	1	*2.7*	*4.4*	...	...	—	—	—	—	Bhutan
1	15.8	...	...	19	739	1,190	22.7	33.2	6,214	10,000	*90*	*132*	Bolivia
...	...	...	...	1	...	...	...	...	...	...	...	...	Bosnia and Herzegovina
—	—	—	—	6	44.6[12]	71.8[12]	0.4[12]	0.6[12]	...	...	...	...	Botswana
635	9,348.3	168,026	52,570	110	17,294	27,832	1,729	2,525	31,069	50,000	*56,030*	*81,803*	Brazil
51	349.7	13,554	1,325	1	687	1,105	23.8	34.7	130	209	...	...	Brunei
222	1,938.2	5,290	20,080	3	1,863	2,999	29.5	43.0	292	470	0.3	0.5	Bulgaria
—	—	—	—	2	*129.6*	*208.6*	*24.1*	*35.2*	...	...	...	...	Burkina Faso
1	*0.4*	*39*	*182*	1	...	...	...	...	...	...	...	...	Burundi
3	3.8	11	95	1	...	...	...	...	2,300	3,700	...	...	Cambodia
47	39.8	10,081	3,396	5	*349*	*561*	*25*	*37*	1,299	2,090	...	...	Cameroon
1,185	2,896.8	161,140	67,042	106	29,461	47,413	3,569	5,210	1,860	3,000	...	...	Canada
42	30.9	*170*	*490*	7	*76.4*	*122.9*	*1.6*	*2.3*	...	...	...	...	Cape Verde
—	—	—	—	1	144[11]	232[11]	12.1[11]	17.7[11]	500	800	91.1	133	Central African Republic
—	—	—	—	1	144	232	12.1	17.7	1,240	2,000	...	...	Chad
392	854.9	15,942	5,326	16	1,819	2,928	362	529	450	725	*5,629*	*8,218*	Chile
2,390	20,658.0	81,795	72,370	86	24,800	39,900	925	1,350	86,100	138,600	793,979	1,159,190	China
101	403.0	25,950	6,357	63	2,797	4,502	647	945	8,900	14,300	2	3	Colombia
6	3.6	11	104	4	1.9	3.0	...	...	...	...	...	...	Comoros
22	10.8	8,987	736	14	144.3	232.3	27.0	39.4	696	1,120	...	...	Congo
24	8.4	1,605	1,892	13	787.0[14]	1,267[14]	25.5[14]	37.3[14]	454	730	...	...	Costa Rica
51	98.6	4,980	5,168	7	52.4[16]	84.4[16]	5.2[16]	7.6[16]	609	980	...	...	Côte d'Ivoire
203	140.9	...	...	1	...	...	...	...	...	...	80.8	118	Croatia
393	924.6	8,092	15,440	10	1,908	3,070	23.8	34.8	149	240	...	...	Cuba
1,416	36,198.1	2,259	3,560	1	1,302	2,095	22.6	33.0	...	...	...	...	Cyprus
22[17]	446.2[17]	...	...	4	1,459[17]	2,348[17]	39.5[17]	57.7[17]	295[17]	475[17]	2,665[17]	3,891[17]	Czech Republic
456	7,569.1	14,489	31,713	11	2,480[18]	3,991[18]	79.9[18]	116.7[18]	259	417	1,100	1,600	Denmark
10	4.1	414	958	3	...	...	...	...	...	...	...	...	Djibouti
7	3.2	40	63	2	...	...	...	...	...	...	...	...	Dominica
28	10.4	2,550	4,182	5	154.0	247.9	2.7	4.0	...	...	...	...	Dominican Republic
154	504.1	10,445	2,568	14	746.3	1,201	46.6	68.0	932	1,500	...	...	Ecuador
444	1,685.2	102,663	81,720	10	3,250	5,230	90.4	132	2,175	3,500	1,715	2,504	Egypt
15	...	275	1,639	1	662[20]	1,066[20]	3.2[20]	4.6[20]	...	...	...	...	El Salvador

Transportation (continued)

country	roads and motor vehicles (latest)								railroads (latest)					
	roads			motor vehicles			cargo		track length		traffic			
	length		paved (percent)	automobiles	trucks and buses	persons per vehicle	short ton-mi ('000,000)	metric ton-km ('000,000)	mi	km	passengers		cargo	
	mi	km									passenger-mi ('000,000)	passenger-km ('000,000)	short ton-mi ('000,000)	metric ton-km ('000,000)
Equatorial Guinea	1,667	2,682	19	5,500	3,500	40	...	...	—	—	—	—	—	—
Eritrea	...	...	...	...	...	...	...	...	...	...	...	...	...	...
Estonia	9,203	14,811	52	261,086	85,685	4.5	2,610	3,811	638	1,026	791	1,273	4,779	6,977
Ethiopia	17,381	27,972	15	37,799	15,539	984	...	...	486[21]	782[21]	185	297	88	128
Faeroe Islands	269	433	...	12,882	3,214	2.9	...	...	—	—	—	—	—	—
Fiji	2,996	4,821	13	42,012	29,225	10	...	...	370[13]	595[13]	...	...	...	...
Finland	47,649	76,684	61	1,922,541	273,358	2.3	16,300	23,800	3,646[2]	5,867[2]	1,645	2,647	5,230	7,635
France	503,300	810,000	*92*	23,810,000	5,192,000	2.0	101,200	147,700	21,173[2]	34,074[2]	38,618	62,150	35,264	51,484
French Guiana	*706*	*1,137*	*40*	23,520	1,689	4.1	...	...	—	—	—	—	—	—
French Polynesia	584	940	42	37,000	15,000	3.7	...	...	—	—	—	—	—	—
Gabon	*4,286*	*6,898*	*11*	19,000	15,000	33	...	...	414	668	*21*	*34*	*126*	*184*
Gambia, The	1,483	2,386	32	6,500	1,500	109	...	...	—	—	—	—	—	—
Gaza Strip	...	...	...	18,116	3,937	28	...	...	—	—	—	—	—	—
Georgia	21,000	33,900	87	427,400	...	...	4,168	6,085	976	1,570	10.6	17.0	...	...
Germany	386,037	621,267	...	35,512,083	2,764,191	2.1	117,437	171,455	56,397	90,760	40,131	64,585	83,857	122,429
Ghana	22,800	36,700	20	57,897	30,125	160	873	1,275	592[2]	953[2]	172	278	86.9	127
Gibraltar	27	43	100	18,149	2,576	1.4	...	...	—	—	—	—	—	—
Greece	80,800	130,000	79	1,790,939	817,729	3.9	8,457	12,347	1,570[2]	2,527[2]	969.3	1,560	419	612
Greenland	50	80	...	1,619	1,434	18	...	...	—	—	—	—	—	—
Grenada	700	1,127	51	*4,784*	*981*	*16*	...	...	—	—	—	—	—	—
Guadeloupe	1,286	2,069	*80*	*95,962*	*28,134*	*2.7*	...	...	—	—	—	—	—	—
Guam	419	674	100	63,380	22,961	1.6	...	...	—	—	—	—	—	—
Guatemala	8,297	13,352	26	145,000	105,000	37	...	...	570[2]	917[2]	6.3	10.1	29.2	42.7
Guernsey	...	...	...	33,545	6,302	1.6	...	...	—	—	—	—	—	—
Guinea	*17,600*	*28,400*	*4*	13,000	13,000	258	...	...	411[2]	662[2]	...	...	...	...
Guinea-Bissau	2,100	3,500	15	3,200	2,400	170	...	...	—	—	—	—	—	—
Guyana	3,540	5,697	11	24,000	9,000	23	...	...	55[13]	88[13]	...	...	...	...
Haiti	2,485	4,000	15	33,000	22,000	118	...	...	—	—	—	—	—	—
Honduras	7,066	11,371	21	88,982	18,049	44	...	...	583	939	4.8	7.7	20.7	30.2
Hong Kong	969	1,559	100	237,055	155,836	15	...	...	21	34	1,939	3,120	41.0	60.0
Hungary	18,591	29,919	99	2,015,455	225,220	4.6	4,068	5,939	8,200	13,200	6,591	10,607	8,177	11,938
Iceland	7,121	11,460	20	120,862	16,012	1.9	*318*	*464*	—	—	—	—	—	—
India	1,266,000	2,037,000	49	2,391,000	1,396,000	225	*144,000*	*210,000*	38,752[2]	62,366[2]	183,700	295,700	166,200	242,700
Indonesia	165,487	266,326	44	1,372,673	1,533,152	62	*17,000*	*25,000*	4,090	6,583	6,070	9,768	2,375	3,468
Iran	94,130	151,488	34	1,600,000	600,000	26	*46,750*	*68,250*	2,838[2]	4,567[2]	2,953	4,752	5,454	7,963
Iraq	28,305	45,554	84	744,252	295,744	18	...	...	1,484[2]	2,389[2]	271	436	223	326
Ireland	57,369	92,327	94	836,583	152,719	3.6	3,400	5,000	1,749	2,814	761	1,224	403	589
Isle of Man	357	574	58	39,392	4,443	1.5	...	...	37[2]	59[2]	...	...	...	...
Israel	8,266	13,300	100	848,000	165,000	4.9	...	...	357[2]	574[2]	94.9	152.7	710.7	1,038
Italy	188,838	303,906	100	28,200,000	2,521,000	1.9	114,542	167,228	12,176	19,595	30,050	48,361	15,091	22,033
Jamaica	10,212	16,435	29	97,500	18,000	21	...	...	129[2]	208[2]	12.1	19.5	1.7	2.5
Japan	693,206	1,115,609	70	37,076,065	22,936,389	2.1	187,978	274,444	23,690	38,125	240,767	387,478	18,628	27,196
Jersey	...	...	...	59,466	8,005	1.2	...	...	—	—	—	—	—	—
Jordan	3,529	5,680	100	173,077	65,687	14	*19,133*	*27,934*	490[2]	788[2]	*3.7*	*6.0*	338	493
Kazakhstan	102,500	164,900	69	*734,800*	...	...	30,670	44,777	13,200	21,200	12,100	19,400	256.3	374.2
Kenya	38,881	62,573	13	157,166	172,023	76	*134*	*196*	1,885[2]	3,034[2]	451.4	726.5	1,315	1,920
Kiribati	398	640	5	*307*	*130*	*147*	...	...	—	—	—	—	—	—
Korea, North	*14,290*	*23,000*	*2*	...	...	...	...	...	3,122	5,024	...	...	...	...
Korea, South	34,659	55,778	61	2,727,852	1,519,964	10	*5,921*	*8,645*	4,092	6,586	20,796	33,468	9,929	14,496
Kuwait	2,655	4,273	100	499,388	110,663	3.5	...	...	—	—	—	—	—	—
Kyrgyzstan	11,900	19,100	86	*173,800*	...	...	3,858	5,632	490	789	...	...	...	...
Laos	8,757	14,093	24	21,269	14,790	119	36	53	—	—	—	—	—	—
Latvia	37,421	60,224	55	328,436	70,545	6.7	3,327	4,857	1,489	2,397	2,441	3,929	11,465	16,739
Lebanon	*4,579*	*7,370*	*85*	*473,372*	*49,560*	*5.0*	...	...	*259*	*417*	*5.3*	*8.6*	*29*	*42*
Lesotho	2,607	4,195	20	*6,363*	*15,379*	*73*	...	...	1.6	2.6	...	...	...	...
Liberia	*5,011*	*8,064*	*9*	*7,148*	*4,031*	*209*	...	...	*304*[2]	*490*[2]	...	...	*1,746*[13]	*2,549*[13]
Libya	*11,992*	*19,300*	*56*	448,000	322,000	5.3	...	...	—	—	—	—	—	—
Liechtenstein	201	323	...	16,891	1,673	1.5	...	...	12	19	...	...	...	...
Lithuania	27,700	44,500	80	480,804	90,085	6.5	4,808	7,019	1,862	2,996	1,703	2,740	7,765	11,337
Luxembourg	3,167	5,097	99	200,739	20,367	1.8	*164*	*239*	168[2]	271[2]	144	282	488	713
Macau	*60*	*97*	*100*	27,223	5,560	11	...	...	—	—	—	—	—	—
Macedonia	6,581	10,591	48	230,993	22,594	8.0	1,819	2,655	431	693	...	...	...	...
Madagascar	33,700	54,200	10	46,636	33,156	150	*220*	*321*	655[2]	1,054[2]	121.5	195.5	144.0	210.3
Malaŵi	7,590	12,215	22	16,118	17,394	254	—	—	495[2]	797[2]	57.0	91.7	40.5	59.1
Malaysia	32,623	52,501	68	2,000,000	400,000	7.6	...	...	1,381	2,222	1,089[29]	1,752[29]	871.2[29]	1,272[29]
Maldives	...	...	...	623	813	150	...	...	—	—	—	—	—	—
Mali	*11,185*	*18,000*	*8*	22,000	9,000	267	...	...	*401*[2]	*646*[2]	304.2	489.5	187.2	273.3
Malta	990	1,593	91	104,863	19,951	2.8	...	...	—	—	—	—	—	—
Marshall Islands	...	...	...	*763*	*80*	*43*	...	...	—	—	—	—	—	—
Martinique	1,050	1,690	*75*	*135,269*	*7,328*	*2.3*	...	...	—	—	—	—	—	—
Mauritania	4,696	7,558	23	10,000	5,000	133	...	...	428[2]	689[2]	*4.4*	*7.0*	5,393	7,873
Mauritius	1,119	1,801	93	50,016	16,849	16	...	...	—	—	—	—	—	—
Mayotte	*143*	*230*	*49*	*——1,528——*		*40*	...	...	—	—	—	—	—	—
Mexico	150,554	242,294	35	6,819,305	3,063,185	8.5	74,579	108,884	16,363[2]	26,334[2]	2,765	4,450	23,562	34,400
Micronesia	140	226	17	...	...	...	...	...	—	—	—	—	—	—
Moldova	8,738	14,062	86	210,385	14,254	19	4,951	7,229	715	1,150	5,515	8,875	10,279	15,007
Monaco	31	50	100	17,000	3,800	1.4	...	...	1	2	...	...	...	...
Mongolia	*30,600*	*49,200*	*2*	...	...	...	*1,438*	*2,099*	1,445	2,325	359	578	4,082	5,960
Morocco	36,955	59,474	50	669,637	282,945	26	*830*	*1,212*	1,176[2]	1,893[2]	1,387	2,232	3,501	5,112
Mozambique	16,955	27,287	17	*24,700*	*42,180*	*202*	...	...	1,857	2,988	*46.8*	*75.3*	*158.8*	*231.8*
Myanmar (Burma)	*14,579*	*23,463*	*38*	35,000	35,000	611	*71*	*103.7*	1,949[2]	3,137[2]	2,781	4,476	395	576
Namibia	26,570	42,760	11	——122,331——		11	...	...	1,481	2,383	4.0	6.5	820.6	1,198
Nauru	10	16	100	——1,448——		6.3	...	...	3[13]	5[13]	...	...	*4.7*	*6.8*
Nepal	4,599	7,401	41	4,949	3,363	2,259	*984*	*1,437*	33[2]	53[2]	...	...	...	...
Netherlands, The	73,455	118,214	89	5,658,000	797,000	2.4	15,900	23,300	1,727	2,780	7,949	12,792	2,104	3,072

merchant marine				air					canals and inland waterways (latest)				country
fleet, 1992 (vessels over 100 gross tons)	total dead-weight tonnage, 1992 ('000)	international cargo (latest)		airports with sched-uled flights, 1993	traffic (latest)				length		cargo		
		loaded metric tons ('000)	off-loaded metric tons ('000)		passengers		cargo		mi	km	short ton-mi ('000,000)	metric ton-km ('000,000)	
					passenger-mi ('000,000)	passenger-km ('000,000)	short ton-mi ('000,000)	metric ton-km ('000,000)					
3	6.7	110	64	1	*4*	*7*	*0.7*	*1.0*	...	...	...	...	Equatorial Guinea
...	...	...	...	...	...	...	...	...	...	...	...	...	Eritrea
234	680.4	...	...	1	650	1,046	4.1	6.0	...	...	0.7	1.0	Estonia
27	84.3	520	3,014	29	977	1,572	65.2	95.2	...	...	...	...	Ethiopia
191	59.8	388	387	1	...	...	...	...	...	...	...	...	Faeroe Islands
64	60.4	568	625	19	548	882	17.4	25.3	126	203	...	...	Fiji
263	989.3	25,024	32,962	24	6,116	9,842	95.5	139.5	4,148	6,675	2,439	3,560	Finland
729	4,981.0	62,803	163,010	64	20,236[22]	32,567[22]	4,580[22]	6,687[22]	9,278	14,932	4,700	6,800	France
7	0.7	62	359	8	...	...	...	...	286	460	...	...	French Guiana
41	16.5	15	666	36	...	...	...	...	...	...	...	...	French Polynesia
29	30.2	12,828	212	18	276.7	445.3	17.9	26.1	994	1,600	...	...	Gabon
11	2.0	169	212	1	...	...	...	...	250	400	...	...	Gambia, The
—	—	...	...	—	...	...	...	...	—	—	...	...	Gaza Strip
...	...	...	...	1	3,291	5,296	...	...	...	...	...	...	Georgia
1,375	6,832.3	57,595	117,582	40	62,809	101,082	3,064	4,473	4,686	7,541	31,400	45,800	Germany
155	131.0	1,810	2,842	3	253.3	407.6	45.8	66.8	795	1,280	75	110	Ghana
49	1,136.1	5	400	1	...	...	...	...	—	—	...	...	Gibraltar
1,872	45,276.6	21,595	25,189	34	3,848	6,193	78.2	114.2	50	80	*585*	*854*	Greece
82	17.2	298	288	18	*16.3*	*26.3*	*0.23*	*0.34*	...	...	...	...	Greenland
3	0.5	33	59	2	...	...	...	...	...	...	...	...	Grenada
20	4.4	300	1,225	6	...	...	...	...	...	...	...	...	Guadeloupe
5	0.1	92	184	1	...	...	...	...	...	...	...	...	Guam
8	0.4	3,440	1,828	2	142.9	230.0	6.3	9.2	162	260	...	...	Guatemala
—	—	...	...	1	...	...	...	...	...	...	...	...	Guernsey
23	1.7	12,210	712	1	*17.9*	*28.8*	*1.7*	*2.5*	805	1,295	...	...	Guinea
19	1.8	33	263	2	*6*	*9*	*0.7*	*1.0*	...	...	...	...	Guinea-Bissau
82	13.5	1,730	673	1	133	214	1.9	2.8	3,700	6,000	...	...	Guyana
4	0.4	170	704	2	...	...	...	...	60	100	...	...	Haiti
966	1,437.3	1,316	1,002	9	321[23]	516[23]	2.0[23]	3.0[23]	289	465	...	...	Honduras
387	11,688.6	18,778[24]	46,517[24]	1	...	...	...	...	...	...	...	...	Hong Kong
15	134.5	...	...	1	799.5	1,287	5.7	8.3	1,008	1,622	9,902	14,456	Hungary
394	114.9	1,090	1,868	19	1,143	1,840	21.1	30.8	...	...	*58*	*84*	Iceland
888	10,365.9	26,155	46,476	98	10,264	16,518	454	663	10,054	16,180	...	...	India
2,014	3,130.2	91,264	17,532	117	9,270	14,919	315.2	460.2	13,409	21,579	*17,000*	*25,000*	Indonesia
403	8,345.3	113,207	16,719	19	3,391	5,457	59.0	86.1	562	904	...	...	Iran
131	1,578.8	*97,830*	*8,638*	...	*976*	*1,570*	*37.4*	*54.6*	631	1,015	...	...	Iraq
189	208.6	6,367	17,637	10	2,364	3,804	296	432	...	...	...	...	Ireland
101	2,836.5	*6*	*203*	1	115.5	185.9	0.2	0.3	...	...	...	...	Isle of Man
58	723.4	7,920	14,492	7	4,363[25]	7,021[25]	569[25]	831[25]	...	...	...	...	Israel
1,636	10,940.1	44,711	198,860	32	13,482[26]	21,697[26]	1,338[26]	1,953[26]	1,500	2,400	88	129	Italy
12	16.2	8,090	5,120	4	888.6	1,430	14.2	20.8	...	...	...	...	Jamaica
10,091	37,815.8	81,670	714,750	71	59,268	95,383	9,064	13,233	1,100	1,770	167,500	244,546	Japan
—	—	...	...	1	...	...	...	...	...	...	...	...	Jersey
5	113.6	9,633	6,596	2	1,729	2,782	174	254	...	...	*19,202*	*28,035*	Jordan
...	...	...	...	6	7,800	12,600	48.0	70.0	...	...	2,638	3,851	Kazakhstan
29	11.6	2,320	5,689	14	828.3[27]	1,333[27]	82.9[27]	121.1[27]	...	...	...	...	Kenya
7	2.7	15	26	18	5.3	8.6	0.5	0.8	3	5	...	...	Kiribati
100	951.2	635	5,520	1	...	...	...	...	1,400	2,253	...	...	Korea, North
2,138	11,724.9	63,302	145,374	12	12,401	19,957	1,825	2,664	1,000	1,609	*11,382*	*16,617*	Korea, South
209	3,188.5	51,400	4,522	1	1,186	1,908	198	289	...	...	...	...	Kuwait
...	...	...	...	1	2,304	3,708	...	...	...	...	...	...	Kyrgyzstan
1	1.5	—	—	13	*11*	*18*	*1.4*	*2.0*	2,850	4,587	11	16	Laos
261	1,436.9	...	...	1	1,863	2,999	15.1	22.0	...	...	236	344	Latvia
163	438.2	152	1,150	2	934	1,503	16.4	24.0	...	...	...	...	Lebanon
—	—	—	—	1	4.8	7.7	0.2	0.3	—	—	—	—	Lesotho
1,672	97,374.0	14,900	1,520	1	*11*	*17*	*0.07*	*0.1*	...	...	...	...	Liberia
150	1,223.6	55,299	7,586	11	1,223[28]	1,968[28]	7.1[28]	10.3[28]	—	—	...	...	Libya
—	—	—	—	—	—	—	—	—	...	...	...	...	Liechtenstein
52	373.9	...	...	1	569.8	917.0	3.6	5.3	...	...	97	141	Lithuania
54	2,603.6	—	—	1	*79.5*	*128*	*606.9*	*886.1*	23	37	*208*	*304*	Luxembourg
6	0.1	755	3,935	—	—	—	—	—	...	...	...	...	Macau
...	...	...	...	1	...	...	...	...	...	...	...	...	Macedonia
85	82.1	400	1,205	50	319	513	52.5	76.7	...	...	...	...	Madagascar
1	0.3	...	...	4	49	79	9.8	14.3	891	1,434	*6.7*	*9.8*	Malawi
552	2,916.3	66,025	30,083	39	9,276	14,929	506.9	740.1	4,534	7,296	...	...	Malaysia
44	79.0	27	78	1	...	...	...	...	...	...	...	...	Maldives
—	—	—	—	1	*68*	*110*	*0.4*	*0.6*	1,128	1,815	*18*	*27*	Mali
889	17,073.2	178	2,111	1	693	1,116	5.1	7.4	...	...	...	...	Malta
35	4,182.4	*26*	*117*	24	...	...	2.4	3.5	...	...	...	...	Marshall Islands
6	1.1	365	1,051	1	...	...	...	...	...	...	...	...	Martinique
126	23.9	10,037	674	10	*129.6*	*208.6*	*24.1*	*35.2*	...	...	...	...	Mauritania
35	152.2	1,010	1,444	1	898	1,467	124.8	182.3	...	...	...	...	Mauritius
1	1.1	—	—	1	...	...	...	...	...	...	...	...	Mayotte
635	1,495.3	83,135	11,785	54	10,839[30]	17,444[30]	1,182[30]	1,726[30]	1,800	2,900	...	...	Mexico
17	6.9	...	...	4	...	...	...	...	...	...	...	...	Micronesia
...	...	...	...	1	1,461	2,352	13.0	19.0	...	...	163	238	Moldova
1	...	...	...	1	—	—	...	...	...	...	...	...	Monaco
—	—	—	—	1	331	532	7.3	10.6	247	397	*2.9*	*4.3*	Mongolia
492	586.2	20,257	12,454	16	1,700	2,700	24.0	35.0	...	...	*2,622*	*3,828*	Morocco
107	31.6	2,578	3,379	7	344	554	41.5	60.6	2,330	3,750	...	...	Mozambique
144	1,354.0	765	645	20	137.7	221.6	5.6	8.2	7,954	12,800	*236.5*	*345.3*	Myanmar (Burma)
30	5.9	*483*	*260*	11	349.0	561.6	2.3	3.3	...	...	...	...	Namibia
2	5.8	1,650	59	1	*148*[31]	*238*[31]	*1.1*[31]	*1.6*[31]	...	...	...	...	Nauru
—	—	—	—	6	439	706	7.5	11.0	...	...	...	...	Nepal
1,076	4,191.0	96,240	273,840	5	17,135	27,576	1,577	2,303	3,939	6,340	4,436	6,476	Netherlands, The

Transportation (continued)

country	roads and motor vehicles (latest)								railroads (latest)					
	roads			motor vehicles			cargo		track length		traffic			
	length		paved (per-cent)	auto-mobiles	trucks and buses	persons per vehicle	short ton-mi ('000,-000)	metric ton-km ('000,-000)	mi	km	passengers		cargo	
	mi	km									passen-ger-mi ('000,000)	passen-ger-km ('000,000)	short ton-mi ('000,000)	metric ton-km ('000,000)
Netherlands Antilles	525	845	...	55,136	12,511	2.8	...	...	—	—	—	—	—	—
New Caledonia	3,580	5,762	22	50,000	18,000	2.5	...	...	—	—	—	—	—	—
New Zealand	57,764	92,962	73	1,539,809	309,543	1.9	...	...	2,627	4,227	*285*	*458*	1,837	2,682
Nicaragua	*9,319*	*14,997*	*10*	35,000	35,000	57	...	...	186[2]	300[2]	15.8	25.5	46.6	68.0
Niger	6,997	11,258	29	31,427	8,768	192	1,044	1,524	—	—	—	—	—	—
Nigeria	*77,000*	*124,000*	*48*	785,000	625,000	61	...	...	*2,178*	*3,505*	*2,366*	*3,808*	*1,194*	*1,743*
Northern Mariana Islands	186	300	18	16,170	5,602	2.0	...	...	—	—	—	—	—	—
Norway	55,760	89,737	70	1,619,438	390,272	2.1	5,269	7,692	2,502[2]	4,027[2]	1,368	2,201	1,745	2,548
Oman	17,053	27,438	18	96,559	70,231	9.2	...	...	—	—	—	—	—	—
Pakistan	87,040	140,077	46	721,150	200,160	132	...	...	5,453[2]	8,775[2]	11,285	18,161	4,085	5,964
Panama	6,216	10,004	32	150,903	72,744	11	...	...	362[2]	583[2]	0.3	0.6	1.9	2.7
Papua New Guinea	*12,263*	*19,736*	*6*	*17,532*	*29,021*	*76*	...	...	—	—	—	—	—	—
Paraguay	*15,957*	*25,681*	*9*	117,067	3,375	36	...	...	*274*[2]	*441*[2]	*13.5*	*21.8*	*13.6*	*19.8*
Peru	43,460	69,942	11	399,881	235,663	35	...	...	2,157[2]	3,472[2]	198.7	319.8	566.3	826.8
Philippines	99,767	160,560	14	456,606	848,633	48	...	...	658[2]	1,059[2]	113.2	182.1	6.4	9.4
Poland	227,027	365,365	63	6,112,171	1,329,650	5.1	34,000	49,000	16,061	25,848	24,926	40,115	44,621	65,146
Portugal	43,605	70,176	86	1,800,000	648,200	4.0	7,482	10,923	2,229[2]	3,588[2]	3,500	5,700	1,225	1,788
Puerto Rico	*5,810*	*9,351*	*87*	1,315,587	205,565	2.3	...	...	—	—	—	—	—	—
Qatar	*671*	*1,080*	*63*	117,966	55,234	2.9	...	...	—	—	—	—	—	—
Réunion	1,690	2,719	*81*	150,000	50,000	3.1	...	...	*384*[2]	*614*[2]	...	...	...	...
Romania	95,099	153,014	51	1,397,118	332,273	13	19,859	28,994	6,887	11,083	15,800	25,428	25,924	37,848
Russia	549,000	884,000	74	8,964,000	484,000	16	205,045	299,360	99,900	160,800	169,696	273,100	1,698	2,479
Rwanda	8,185	13,173	9	7,868	2,048	697	*140*	*200*	—	—	—	—	—	—
St. Kitts and Nevis	186	300	42	4,000	*700*	*10*	...	...	—	—	—	—	—	—
St. Lucia	500	805	56	7,000	4,000	12	...	...	—	—	—	—	—	—
St. Vincent and the Grenadines	586	943	16	5,350	2,814	13	...	...	—	—	—	—	—	—
San Marino	*147*	*237*	...	21,769	3,559	1.0	...	...	—	—	—	—	—	—
São Tomé and Príncipe	*236*	*380*	*66*	*1,774*	*265*	*41*	...	...	—	—	—	—	—	—
Saudi Arabia	89,897	144,676	43	2,350,000	2,150,000	3.1	...	...	555[2]	893[2]	75.2	121	549	801
Senegal	*8,772*	*14,117*	*27*	90,000	37,000	56	*375*	*547*	562	904	*24.9*	*40.0*	*276.2*	*403.3*
Seychelles	198	319	66	4,700	1,600	11	...	...	—	—	—	—	—	—
Sierra Leone	4,660	7,500	20	29,012	10,173	103	*36*	*53*	*52*	*84*	...	...	...	...
Singapore	1,817	2,924	97	302,824	128,993	6.5	...	...	16	26	...	...	...	...
Slovakia	11,101	17,866	...	906,129	109,106	5.2	...	...	2,275	3,661	...	...	11,818	17,254
Slovenia	9,045	14,553	72	583,923	35,661	3.2	2,645	3,861	849	1,366	...	...	...	...
Solomon Islands	*1,300*	*2,100*	*8*	*1,350*	*2,026*	*84*	...	...	—	—	—	—	—	—
Somalia	*10,697*	*17,215*	*15*	20,000	12,000	234	...	...	—	—	—	—	—	—
South Africa	113,294	182,329	30	3,403,605	1,497,607	6.3	1,053	1,538	13,432[2]	21,617[2]	7,916	12,740	63,713	93,019
Bophuthatswana	3,900	6,300	21	...	...	...	...	...	165	265	...	...	...	...
Ciskei	1,867	3,004	15	...	...	...	...	...	60	96	...	...	...	...
Transkei	*5,591*	*8,998*	*11*	...	...	...	...	...	190	306	...	...	...	...
Venda	1,305	2,100	15	...	...	...	...	...	*8*	*13*	...	...	...	...
Spain	206,271	331,961	99	12,537,099	2,615,033	2.6	102,700	150,000	7,806[2]	12,563[2]	9,462	15,228	7,307	10,668
Sri Lanka	16,126	25,952	81	180,135	146,799	53	3,620	5,285	884[2]	1,423[2]	1,631	2,625	103.6	151.2
Sudan, The	14,000	22,500	9	116,000	57,000	141	...	...	3,029[2]	4,874[2]	311	501	442	646
Suriname	5,687	9,153	29	36,755	14,473	7.9	...	...	*104*	*167*	...	...	...	...
Swaziland	1,740	2,801	26	25,333	8,603	23	...	...	326	525	...	...	*73*	*107*
Sweden	84,419	135,859	72	3,588,600	329,200	2.2	20,000	29,000	6,960	11,202	3,388	5,453	15,219	22,219
Switzerland	44,183	71,106	96	3,085,372	291,457	2.0	4,552	6,646	3,126	5,031	7,695	12,384	5,556	8,112
Syria	19,616	31,569	77	117,570	138,603	46	*1,075*	*1,570*	948[2]	1,525[2]	813	1,308	847	1,236
Taiwan	12,111	19,490	86	3,033,651	751,627	5.5	7,906	11,543	2,858	4,600	5,809	9,349	1,413	2,063
Tajikistan	8,324	13,396	93	209,100	...	...	3,518	5,136	554	891	6,094	9,808	7,617	11,121
Tanzania	51,023	82,114	4	45,000	55,000	244	...	...	2,218	3,569	2,125	3,420	857	1,248
Thailand	44,844	72,170	55	735,326	1,903,220	21	...	...	2,399[2]	3,861[2]	7,965	12,820	2,305	3,365
Togo	4,688	7,545	24	4,920	389	658	...	...	326	525	*68*	*109*	*8*	*11*
Tonga	240	386	76	1,009	2,430	28	...	...	—	—	—	—	—	—
Trinidad and Tobago	*4,906*	*7,895*	*46*	150,196	60,006	5.9	...	...	—	—	—	—	—	—
Tunisia	18,133	29,183	60	321,101	208,596	15	678	990	1,343[2]	2,162[2]	634	1,020	1,242	1,813
Turkey	228,421	367,608	14	1,864,344	756,905	22	42,445	61,969	5,238[2]	8,430[2]	3,892	6,264	5,648	8,246
Turkmenistan	8,300	13,400	86	*170,600*	...	...	3,283	4,793	1,317	2,120	...	...	37.6	54.9
Tuvalu	*5*	*8*	—	...	...	...	...	...	—	—	—	—	—	—
Uganda	*17,605*	*28,332*	22	35,496	14,094	326	...	...	770[2]	1,240[2]	67.7	109	70.5	103
Ukraine	104,998	168,979	94	*2,920,000*	...	...	53,781	78,519	14,167	22,799	44,097	70,968	277,762	405,525
United Arab Emirates	*2,709*	*4,360*	*61*	302,000	157,000	4.1	...	...	—	—	—	—	—	—
United Kingdom	222,472	358,034	100	19,742,000	2,861,000	2.5	93,300	136,200	23,518[44]	37,849[44]	19,919	32,057	10,512	15,347
United States	3,879,322	6,243,163	58	142,955,623	45,416,312	1.3	810,024	1,182,615	172,893	278,245	13,297	21,400	1,180,382	1,723,329
Uruguay	*32,311*	*52,000*	*23*	379,600	49,900	7.2	*500*	*730*	1,865[2]	3,002[2]	*87.4*	*140.6*	139.7	204.0
Uzbekistan	55,431	89,207	83	*790,800*	...	...	15,037	21,954	4,200	6,800	3,300	5,200	48,400	70,600
Vanuatu	*660*	*1,062*	*24*	4,200	2,800	21	...	...	—	—	—	—	—	—
Venezuela	48,174	77,529	34	1,590,000	319,000	10	...	...	226[2]	363[2]	37.3	60.0	32.9	48.0
Vietnam	55,000	88,000	*11*	...	...	...	*1,182*	*1,726*	2,001	3,220	1,189	1,913	580	847
Virgin Islands (U.S.)	532	856	100	49,012	14,176	1.6	...	...	—	—	—	—	—	—
West Bank	...	...	...	*40,033*	*14,324*	*16*	...	...	...	...	...	...	...	...
Western Sahara	3,790	6,100	8	*6,284*	*424*	*20*	...	...	—	—	—	—	—	—
Western Samoa	*1,296*	*2,085*	*19*	2,514	3,048	29	...	...	—	—	—	—	—	—
Yemen	31,980	51,467	9	165,438	237,957	29	...	...	—	—	—	—	—	—
Yugoslavia	28,595	46,019	59	1,406,000	132,100	6.8	14,929[47]	21,796[47]	2,453	3,947	7,178[47]	11,552[47]	16,124[47]	23,541[47]
Zaire	91,031	146,500	12	100,000	90,000	203	...	...	3,193	5,138	162[48]	260[48]	1,186[48]	1,732[48]
Zambia	23,214	37,359	18	100,000	70,000	47	...	...	*1,345*	*2,164*	*472*	*759*	*515*	*752*
Zimbabwe	52,964	85,237	19	178,000	82,000	36	...	...	1,714[2]	2,759[2]	355.1	571.4	3.7	5.4

[1]Bakhtar Afghan Airlines only. [2]Route length. [3]Air Algérie international flights only. [4]TAAG-Angola Airlines only. [5]Aerolineas Argentinas only. [6]Included with Netherlands Antilles. [7]Government railways only. [8]Apportionment of ¼ of international flights of Gulf Air (jointly run by Bahrain, Oman, Qatar, and United Arab Emirates) only. [9]Caribbean Airways only. [10]Caribbean Air Cargo only. [11]Air Afrique only. [12]Air Botswana only. [13]For industrial purposes only. [14]Lasca only. [15]Traffic between Ouagadougou, Burkina Faso, and Abidjan, Côte d'Ivoire. [16]Air Ivoire only. [17]Data refer to former Czechoslovakia. [18]Apportionment of 2/7 of SAS operations only. [19]National roads only. [20]TACA airlines only. [21]Includes 100 km of the Chemin de Fer Djibouti-Ethiopien (CDE) in Djibouti. [22]Air France, UTA, and Air Inter only. [23]TAN and SAHSA airlines only. [24]Includes transshipments. [25]El Al only. [26]Alitalia only. [27]Kenya Airways only. [28]International traffic only. [29]Peninsular

merchant marine: fleet, 1992 (vessels over 100 gross tons)	merchant marine: total deadweight tonnage, 1992 ('000)	international cargo (latest): loaded metric tons ('000)	international cargo (latest): off-loaded metric tons ('000)	air: airports with scheduled flights, 1993	air traffic (latest), passengers: passenger-mi ('000,000)	air traffic (latest), passengers: passenger-km ('000,000)	air traffic (latest), cargo: short ton-mi ('000,000)	air traffic (latest), cargo: metric ton-km ('000,000)	canals and inland waterways (latest), length: mi	canals and inland waterways (latest), length: km	canals and inland waterways (latest), cargo: short ton-mi ('000,000)	canals and inland waterways (latest), cargo: metric ton-km ('000,000)	country
154[32]	1,053.6[32]	13,905[32]	10,462[32]	5	*234*[33]	*377*[33]	*1.2*[33]	*1.8*[33]	...	...	...	...	Netherlands Antilles
17	18.1	1,040	930	10	79.7[34]	128[34]	0.3[34]	0.5[34]	...	...	...	...	New Caledonia
139	279.8	13,060	8,292	36	6,606	10,632	260	380	1,000	1,609	*1,503*	*2,195*	New Zealand
25	1.3	320	1,629	3	68.8	110.7	2.5	3.6	1,379	2,220	...	...	Nicaragua
—	—	—	—	1	*129.6*	*208.6*	*24.1*	*35.2*	186	300	...	...	Niger
271	733.3	80,607	10,812	14	481.4	774.8	14.9	21.7	5,328	8,575	...	...	Nigeria
2	0.9	...	...	3	...	...	...	...	...	...	...	...	Northern Mariana Islands
1,630	2,143.3	75,788	19,077	47	4,415[18]	7,106[18]	536.4[18]	783.1[18]	980	1,577	5,749	8,394	Norway
26	11.7	33,843	2,492	6	1,042[8]	1,676[8]	35.1[8]	51.2[8]	...	...	...	...	Oman
73	513.8	4,214	18,837	35	5,631	9,062	256.0	373.8	...	...	...	...	Pakistan
5,217	79,255.6	1,432	2,204	8	169	272	1.6	2.4	497	800	...	...	Panama
87	40.9	2,463	1,784	101	227	365	8.2	12.0	6,798	10,940	...	...	Papua New Guinea
38	38.5	...	...	1	355	571	2.4	3.5	1,900	3,100	...	...	Paraguay
623	615.6	10,197	5,077	25	1,093	1,759	17.1	25.0	5,300	8,600	...	...	Peru
1,499	13,807.1	16,515	24,635	21	8,010[35]	12,891[35]	213.7[35]	311.9[35]	2,000	3,219	...	...	Philippines
644	4,314.3	29,362	17,915	12	2,230	3,589	30.8	45.0	2,484	3,997	505	737	Poland
326	1,129.3	8,400	19,824	13	4,362	7,020	114.1	166.6	510	820	...	...	Portugal
13	...	...	...	7	...	...	...	...	...	...	...	...	Puerto Rico
65	635.6	18,145	2,588	1	1,042[8]	1,676[8]	35.1[8]	51.2[8]	...	...	...	...	Qatar
7	33.5	293	725	1	...	...	...	...	...	...	...	...	Réunion
439	4,845.5	6,578	33,480	14	2,387	3,842	53.4	78.0	1,071	1,724	1,390	2,030	Romania
4,543	16,592.3	...	...	58	95,132	153,100	2,755	4,022	...	...	146,543	213,949	Russia
—	—	—	—	3	...	...	...	...	...	...	...	...	Rwanda
1	0.6	24	36	2	...	...	...	...	...	...	...	...	St. Kitts and Nevis
7	2.1	150	234	2	...	...	...	...	...	...	...	...	St. Lucia
881	7,044.2	80	125	5	...	...	...	...	...	...	...	...	St. Vincent and the Grenadines
—	—	—	—	—	—	—	—	—	—	—	—	—	San Marino
4	2.3	16	25	2	*3.8*	*6.1*	*0.07*	*0.1*	...	...	...	...	São Tomé and Príncipe
301	1,381.7	214,070	46,437	25	9,984	16,068	418	610	...	...	...	...	Saudi Arabia
183	27.5	2,630	2,837	9	144.3[28]	232.3[28]	27.0[28]	39.4[28]	560	900	...	...	Senegal
9	3.3	7	247	1	...	...	...	...	...	...	...	...	Seychelles
62	18.4	1,802	533	1	*68.3*[36]	*109.9*[36]	*1.4*[36]	*2.0*[36]	500	800	*447*	*652*	Sierra Leone
946	14,929.2	66,343	98,231	1	23,056	37,105	1,579	2,306	...	...	...	...	Singapore
...	...	...	...	4	...	...	...	...	...	...	...	...	Slovakia
11	0.7	...	...	1	359	577	833	1,216	...	...	...	...	Slovenia
33	5.0	278	349	22	117.1[37]	188.4[37]	*0.02*[37]	*0.04*[37]	...	...	...	...	Solomon Islands
28	18.5	324	1,118	...	154	248	1.4	2.0	...	...	...	...	Somalia
219	282.5	82,500	31,840	36	5,201[38]	8,370[38]	131[38]	191[38]	...	...	...	...	South Africa
—	—	—	—	1	—	—	—	—	...	...	...	...	Bophuthatswana
—	—	—	—	1	—	—	—	—	...	...	...	...	Ciskei
—	—	—	—	1	...	...	...	...	...	...	...	...	Transkei
—	—	—	—	1	—	—	—	—	...	...	...	...	Venda
2,190	5,077.3	51,522	115,798	24	16,926	27,240	425.2	620.8	649	1,045	*21,836*[39]	*31,880*[39]	Spain
66	472.6	4,001	8,271	1	2,588	4,165	75.3	109.9	267	430	...	...	Sri Lanka
16	62.2	1,195	3,467	13	317.6[40]	511.1[40]	23.7[40]	34.6[40]	3,300	5,310	...	...	Sudan, The
24	15.7	5,776	1,286	3	*345*[41]	*555*[41]	*15.7*[41]	*23.0*[41]	746	1,200	...	...	Suriname
—	—	—	—	1	25.6	41.2	0.1	0.1	—	—	—	—	Swaziland
664	3,327.7	46,879	57,823	42	4,115[42]	6,622[42]	118[42]	172[42]	1,275	2,052	5,300	7,800	Sweden
24	602.8	...	...	6	10,038	16,154	728.1	1,063	40	65	108	158	Switzerland
94	210.4	15,314	10,333	5	719	1,157	9.9	14.4	418	672	...	...	Syria
649	9,241.3	127,840	204,160	12	20,906	33,645	2,928	4,275	...	...	...	...	Taiwan
...	...	...	...	1	3,214	5,173	22.1	32.3	...	...	...	...	Tajikistan
43	48.5	839	3,240	19	174	280	3.0	4.4	...	...	...	...	Tanzania
351	1,194.5	29,854	30,057	26	12,737	20,498	634.5	926.3	2,300	3,701	...	...	Thailand
8	20.6	850	753	1	20.1	32.3	3.9	5.8	—	—	...	...	Togo
15	13.7	15	104	4	3.7	5.9	0.01	0.02	...	...	...	...	Tonga
53	17.5	9,622	10,961	2	1,944	3,129	10.1	14.8	...	...	...	...	Trinidad and Tobago
77	443.3	10,209	9,472	5	875	1,408	12.2	17.8	...	...	...	...	Tunisia
880	7,114.3	70,955	43,389	24	3,491[43]	5,619[43]	80.1[43]	116.9[43]	750	1,200	*35*	*51*	Turkey
...	...	...	...	1	2,021	3,253	222	324	...	...	...	...	Turkmenistan
6	16.0	...	...	1	...	...	...	...	...	...	...	...	Tuvalu
2	...	...	...	1	41.6	67.0	2.1	3.0	...	...	...	...	Uganda
...	...	...	...	20	10,000	16,100	85.6	125	...	...	7,148	10,436	Ukraine
276	1,491.7	88,153	9,595	4	2,411[8]	3,880[8]	98.6[8]	144[8]	...	...	...	...	United Arab Emirates
1,631	4,687.3	134,126	175,813	53	54,188	87,208	1,636	2,389	1,424	2,291	35,900	52,500	United Kingdom
5,710	25,646.4	381,370[45]	536,089[45]	834	475,430	765,132	12,738	18,597	25,482	41,009	509,158	743,358	United States
93	172.5	710[46]	1,450[46]	7	293	471	1.8	2.6	1,000	1,600	...	...	Uruguay
...	...	...	...	1	6,500	10,500	60,800	88,700	...	...	...	...	Uzbekistan
280	3,259.6	80	55	28	...	...	—	—	...	...	...	...	Vanuatu
271	1,355.4	101,435	17,932	31	3,690	5,939	90.4	132.0	4,400	7,100	...	...	Venezuela
230	872.8	303	1,510	4	*6,363*	*10,240*	*4.1*	*6.0*	11,000	17,702	...	...	Vietnam
1	...	*105.5*	*648.3*	4	...	...	...	...	...	...	...	...	Virgin Islands (U.S.)
—	—	...	...	—	—	—	—	—	...	...	...	...	West Bank
—	—	40	15	1	...	...	...	...	...	...	...	...	Western Sahara
7	6.5	28	68	2	...	...	...	...	...	...	...	...	Western Samoa
40	13.7	1,936	7,829	12	641	1,032	8.0	11.7	...	...	...	...	Yemen
462[47]	5,173.1[47]	8,610[47]	26,423[47]	5	5,375[47]	8,651[47]	92.5[47]	135[47]	1,616[47]	2,600[47]	3,430[47]	5,007[47]	Yugoslavia
27	30.7	2,395	1,453	24	89.6[49]	144.2[49]	14.4[49]	21.0[49]	9,300	15,000	*678*	*990*	Zaire
—	—	—	—	8	200	322	27.3	39.9	1,398	2,250	...	...	Zambia
—	—	—	—	6	491.5	791.0	14.9	21.8	...	...	...	...	Zimbabwe

Malaysia and Singapore. [30]Aeronaves de Mexico and Mexicana only. [31]Air Nauru only. [32]Includes Aruba. [33]Antillean Airlines only. [34]Air Caledonie only. [35]PAL only. [36]Sierra Leone Airlines international traffic only. [37]Solair only. [38]SAA only. [39]Coastal shipping only. [40]Sudan Airways only. [41]Suriname Airways only. [42]Apportionment of 3/7 of SAS operations only. [43]Turkish Airlines only. [44]British Railways only; excludes Northern Ireland. [45]Includes Puerto Rico. [46]Port of Montevideo only. [47]Data refer to Yugoslavia as constituted prior to 1991. [48]Zaire National Railways only. [49]Air Zaire only.

Communications

Virtually all the states of the world have a variety of communications media and services available to their citizens: book publishing and newspapers (although only daily papers are included in this table); postal services; radio and television broadcast systems; telephones; and cinema. Unfortunately, the availability of information about the structure and volume of these national services and sectors often runs behind the capabilities of the services themselves. Certain countries publish no official information; others publish data analyzed according to a variety of fiscal, calendar, religious, or other years; still others, while they possess such data almost simultaneously with the end of the business year, may not see them published except in company or parastatal reports of limited distribution. Even when such data are published in national statistical summaries, it may be only after a delay of up to several years. Figures in italics are from 1988 or earlier.

The data also differ in their completeness and reliability. Figures for book production, for example, generally include all works published in separate bindings except advertising works, timetables, telephone directories, price lists, catalogs of businesses or exhibitions, musical scores, maps, atlases, and the like. The figures include government publications, school texts, theses, offprints, series works, and illustrated works, even those consisting principally of illustrations. Figures refer to works actually published during the year of survey, usually by a registered publisher, and deposited for copyright. A book is defined as a work of 49 or more pages, a pamphlet as a work of from 5 to 48 pages. A work published simultaneously in more than one country is counted as having been published in each. Newspaper statistics are especially difficult to collect and compare. Newspapers continually are founded, cease publication, merge, or change frequency of publication. Data on circulation, sales, and readership are often incomplete, slow to be aggregated at the national level, or regarded as proprietary. In some countries circulation data are virtually nonexistent. In others no daily newspaper exists.

Post office statistics are compiled mainly from the Universal Postal Union's annual summary *Statistique des services postaux*. Postal services, unlike the other media discussed earlier, tend most often to be operated by a single national service, to cover a country completely, and to record traffic data according to broadly similar schemes (although the details of *classes* of mail handled may differ). Some countries do not enumerate domestic traffic or may record only international traffic requiring handling charges.

Data for some kinds of communications apparatus and traffic are relatively

Communications

country	publishing (latest)								daily newspapers (latest)		
	number of titles				number of copies ('000)						
	books		periodicals	pamphlets	books		periodicals	pamphlets	number	total circulation ('000)	circulation per 1,000 population
	total	school textbooks			total	school textbooks					
Afghanistan	1,776	150	*105*	1,019	...	...	...	...	14	180	11
Albania	1,651	...	143	...	8,066	...	3,477	...	2	135	42
Algeria	*551*	*39*	48	*167*	...	...	803	...	10	1,274	51
American Samoa	...	...	...	...	...	...	...	...	—	—	—
Andorra	45	1	*15*	...	...	...	*15*	...	1	3	54
Angola	*14*	...	...	...	*130*	...	...	...	4	115	11
Antigua and Barbuda	...	...	...	...	...	...	...	...	1	6	79
Argentina	*4,836*	...	...	...	...	...	...	...	159	4,000	124
Armenia	817[9]	...	76	[9]	10,100[9]	...	28,800	[9]	82	1,678	496
Aruba	...	...	...	...	...	...	...	...	5	...	...
Australia	*6,644*	*469*	...	*4,319*	...	...	...	...	62	4,200	249
Austria	9,315	...	2,619	990	...	...	...	...	25	2,706	357
Azerbaijan	829[9]	...	91	[9]	12,500[9]	...	49,100	[9]	*154*	*2,900*	*416*
Bahamas, The	...	...	...	...	...	...	...	...	3	35	135
Bahrain	*46*	...	...	...	...	...	...	...	2	29	56
Bangladesh	1,209	...	*41*	...	...	...	*163*	...	52	700	6
Barbados	17	...	52	60	...	...	...	...	2	41	160
Belarus	1,845	65	129	978	47,115	3,772	4,596	7,796	28	2,937	286
Belgium	6,822[9]	...	*12,222*	[9]	...	...	...	...	33	3,000	305
Belize	*12*	...	...	...	*156*	...	...	...	—	—	—
Benin	...	...	...	...	...	...	...	...	1	12	3
Bermuda	...	...	...	...	...	...	...	...	1	18	310
Bhutan	...	...	...	...	...	...	...	...	—	—	—
Bolivia	*365*	...	*106*	*82*	*365*	...	...	*46*	17	400	55
Bosnia and Herzegovina	966	...	92	...	7,540	...	1,887	...	3	149	34
Botswana	*134*	*18*	*20*	*155*	...	...	*153*	...	1	18	14
Brazil	*13,973*	...	*3,782*	*3,675*	...	...	*980*	...	356	8,100	54
Brunei	25	6	*4*	...	56	22	*363*	...	1	10	38
Bulgaria	2,915	890	907	497	40,815	10,617	6,006	6,259	24	4,065	451
Burkina Faso	*4*	...	37	...	*9*	...	24	...	1	3	0.3
Burundi	*37*	*9*	...	*17*	*274*	*229*	...	*174*	1	20	4
Cambodia	...	...	...	...	...	...	...	...	1	25	3
Cameroon	...	...	*58*	...	...	...	*127*	...	1	66	5
Canada	12,750	...	1,503	...	...	...	39,510	...	105	5,115	187
Cape Verde	9	—	...	1	9	—	...	1	—	—	—
Central African Republic	...	...	...	...	...	...	...	...	1	2	0.7
Chad	...	...	*10*	...	...	...	...	...	1	2	0.3
Chile	1,716	...	262	634	...	...	1,015	...	45	6,000	445
China	73,923	11,107	6,078	...	5,387,020	2,657,140	1,840,000	...	44	...	...
Colombia	1,486	214	...	...	...	...	...	...	31	1,441	23
Comoros	...	...	...	...	...	...	...	...	—	—	—
Congo	...	...	3	...	...	...	34	...	5	17	7
Costa Rica	230	1	*274*	14	...	...	*163*	...	4	314	102
Côte d'Ivoire	*46*	*13*	*12*	...	*3,766*	*3,517*	*325*	...	1	90	8
Croatia	2,239	...	352	...	12,220	...	6,357	...	9	636	133
Cuba	1,735	1,043	*108*	464	44,032	21,968	*2,894*	6,501	17	1,315	124
Cyprus	454	59	48	238	750	293	244	482	11	78	111
Czech Republic	7,503[20]	2,614[20]	2,513[20]	1,082[20]	69,545[20]	16,330[20]	60,061[20]	11,956[20]	17	3,788	368
Denmark	7,578	817	210	3,504	...	...	7,906	...	47	1,810	352
Djibouti	...	...	*7*	...	...	...	*6*	...	1	4	8
Dominica	...	...	...	...	...	...	...	...	—	—	—
Dominican Republic	...	...	*277*	...	...	...	...	...	12	230	32
Ecuador	...	...	...	...	...	...	...	...	25	920	87
Egypt	*1,311*	*256*	265	*140*	*20,096*	*14,267*	*2,017*	*2,967*	14	3,000	57
El Salvador	*15*	*6*	...	—	*63*	*21*	...	—	5	457	87
Equatorial Guinea	...	*17*	...	...	...	*17*	...	...	2	2	6
Eritrea[21]	...	...	...	...	...	...	...	...	...	...	...
Estonia	1,654[9]	...	351	[9]	23,300[9]	...	19,000	[9]	111	2,556	1,620
Ethiopia[21]	165	42	*3*	220	...	...	*14*	...	*3*	*42*	*0.8*
Faeroe Islands	148	...	...	...	...	...	...	...	—	—	—

easy to collect; telephones, for example, even mobile, must be installed, and service recorded so that it may be charged. But in most countries radios may be purchased by anyone and turned on whenever desired; car radios are seldom enumerated or licensed separately. As a result, data on distribution and use of radio and television apparatus may be collected in a variety of ways—on the basis of numbers of subscribers, licenses issued, periodic sample surveys, census or housing surveys, or private consumer surveys. Statistics on commercial cinema attendance (usually those of the United Nations Educational, Scientific and Cultural Organization [Unesco] or national data) may refer to a variety of screening facilities, including fixed, mobile, or drive-in facilities.

The *Statistical Yearbook* of Unesco contains extensive data on book publishing, newspapers, radio and television, and cinema that have been collected from standardized questionnaires. The quality and recency of its data, however, depend on the completion and timely return of each questionnaire by national authorities, and response rates depend on a variety of factors. In general, however, response rates for inquiries by international organizations in communications are better than in other fields because these organizations and the responsible authorities in each country must conduct day-to-day business and, hence, have a better ongoing relationship. The commercially published annual *World Radio TV Handbook* (Andrew G. Sennitt, editor) is a valuable source of information on broadcast media and has complete and timely coverage. It depends on data received from broadcasters, but, because some do not respond, local correspondents and monitors are used in many countries, and some unconfirmed or unofficial data are included as estimates. The statistics on telephones are derived mainly from the UN-affiliated International Telecommunication Union's (ITU's) *Yearbook of Common Carrier Telecommunication Statistics* and from a variety of national and regional intergovernmental sources. A number of countries report incomplete telephone data: the national total may exclude figures for some telephone companies, or some portion of the national territory; some countries supply statistics only on telephone exchange lines; some island states report only radio telephones. A number of countries omit data on public coin-box telephones; their statistics thus reflect an undercount.

... Not available.

—None, nil, or not applicable.

post offices, 1991				radio, 1992		television, 1992		telephones, 1991		cinema (latest)		country
number	persons per office	pieces of mail handled ('000)	pieces of mail handled per capita	receivers (all types; '000)	persons per receiver	receivers (all types; '000)	persons per receiver	receivers ('000)	persons per receiver	annual attendance: number ('000,000)	annual attendance: per 1,000 population	
358[1]	41,400[1]	36,981[1, 2]	2.5[1, 2]	1,500	12	100	181	31[3]	443[3]	...	...	Afghanistan
613[4]	5,020[4]	13,763[4]	4.5[4]	210	16	246[5]	13[5]	53	63	6.9	2,160	Albania
2,828[6]	8,840[6]	401,378[6]	16[6]	3,500	7.7	2,000	13	1,103[6]	23[6]	*21.0*	*880*	Algeria
...	...	...	...	20	2.5	8.0	6.2	7.3[7]	5.0[7]	...	...	American Samoa
...	...	3,483[8]	90[8]	10.0	5.7	6.0[1]	8.6[1]	21[6]	2.5[6]	...	...	Andorra
76	145,000	8,793	0.8	450	24	51	210	78	132	*3.2*	*370*	Angola
...	...	...	...	75	0.9	28	2.3	16[6]	4.0[6]	...	...	Antigua and Barbuda
5,047	6,460	449,721[1, 2]	14[1, 2]	21,582	1.5	7,165	4.6	4,622[6]	7.0[6]	25.3	800	Argentina
898[10]	3,840[10]	49,000[11]	14[11]	642[5]	5.6[5]	722[5]	5.0[5]	650	5.3	13.4	4,020	Armenia
...	...	...	...	40	1.7	19	3.6	20	3.4	...	...	Aruba
4,361[6]	3,910[6]	3,493,185[6]	200[6]	20,000	0.9	8,000	2.2	8,046	2.1	39.8	2,360	Australia
2,665[1, 12]	2,860[1, 12]	3,406,656[1]	450[1]	4,700	1.7	2,706	2.9	4,732	1.7	10.2	1,340	Austria
1,821[10]	3,970[10]	538,885	75	3,682[13]	1.9[13]	1,522[5]	4.7[5]	1,174[5]	6.1[5]	31.0	4,290	Azerbaijan
128[1]	1,960[1]	60,526[1]	240[1]	200	1.3	60	4.4	142	1.8	...	...	Bahamas, The
12	41,900	37,250[14]	74[14]	320	1.7	270	2.0	163	3.1	0.6	1,230	Bahrain
7,985[1]	13,100[1]	197,363	1.8	4,500	25	350	316	262	427	*302.3*	*3,000*	Bangladesh
16	15,900	18,311	72	200	1.3	69	3.7	109	2.4	...	...	Barbados
4,264[10]	2,420[10]	1,505,873	146	3,140[5]	3.3[5]	3,122[5]	2.9[5]	1,791	5.8	94.0	9,120	Belarus
1,822	5,480	3,463,458	350	4,521	2.2	4,200	2.4	5,691	1.8	*16.1*	*1,630*	Belgium
112[7]	1,520[7]	3,096[7]	18[7]	100	2.0	27	7.3	20	9.8	...	...	Belize
189	25,700	5,808	1.2	350	14	20	246	18	273	*1.3*	*330*	Benin
16[1]	3,680[1]	18,200[1, 14]	310[1, 14]	100	0.6	30	2.0	54	1.1	*0.2*	*3,630*	Bermuda
84	18,100	3,813	2.5	28	54	0.2[8]	6,180[8]	2.1[1]	669[1]	...	...	Bhutan
201	36,000	13,957	1.9	4,000	1.9	610[5]	12[5]	198	38	4.6	650	Bolivia
656	6,630	128,886	30	733[6]	5.9[6]	629[6]	6.9[6]	727[6]	6.0[6]	4.3	1,000	Bosnia and Herzegovina
165	7,820	30,477	24	1,100	1.2	14	99	58	23	...	...	Botswana
11,645	12,600	3,325,769[15]	23[15]	60,000	2.5	30,000	5.0	14,125[6]	10[6]	*91.3*	*680*	Brazil
13	20,000	9,002	35	100	2.7	67	4.0	53	4.9	*2.3*	*11,900*	Brunei
3,137	2,870	223,852[16]	25[16]	3,000	3.0	3,127	2.9	2,839[17]	3.0[17]	68.0	7,750	Bulgaria
145[6]	62,200[6]	3,552[1, 2]	0.4[1, 2]	200	48	46	209	18[13]	485[13]	*6.0*	*720*	Burkina Faso
33	182,000	4,400	0.7	500	11	4.5	1,260	11	506	*0.1*	*24*	Burundi
...	...	...	...	800	11	70	129	2.9[1]	3,300[1]	...	...	Cambodia
1,595[6]	7,420[6]	...	...	2,000	6.3	15	844	61[13]	185[13]	...	...	Cameroon
16,734[1]	1,570[1]	9,004,547[1, 15]	340[1, 15]	22,600	1.2	17,400	1.6	20,126[4]	1.3[4]	*78.8*	*3,040*	Canada
62	5,970	2,178	5.9	50	6.9	5.0[4]	65[4]	9.1	38	...	...	Cape Verde
53	54,600	...	...	550	5.3	7.5	391	7.3	399	...	...	Central African Republic
88	66,100	4,125	0.7	1,260	4.7	5.0[4]	1,050[4]	8.0[6]	716[6]	...	...	Chad
1,116	12,000	250,264	19	4,250	3.1	2,000	6.7	1,146[6]	11[6]	14.3	1,100	Chile
51,544	22,500	5,210,810[15, 18]	4.5[15, 18]	209,205[6]	5.4[6]	35,000[6]	32[6]	14,990	77	16,878	15,300	China
1,678[6]	19,700[6]	220,456[6]	6.7[6]	34,487	1.0	5,500	6.1	3,795	8.7	*41.0*	*1,290*	Colombia
56	8,930	923[19]	1.8[19]	50	9.9	0.2[6]	2,310[6]	5.3	93	...	...	Comoros
124[6]	18,300[6]	2,582[6, 19]	1.1[6, 19]	250	11	8.5	317	26[1]	86[1]	...	...	Congo
279	8,660	54,443[6]	18[6]	255	12	340	9.2	452	6.9	*0.2*	*76*	Costa Rica
868	13,800	40,642	3.4	1,500	8.6	810	16	153[6]	80[6]	...	...	Côte d'Ivoire
1,087[6]	4,390[6]	232,707	49	761	6.3	1,027[6]	4.6[6]	1,138	4.2	3.1	640	Croatia
903[13]	11,500[13]	116,244[13]	11[13]	2,140	5.1	2,500	4.3	611	18	44.8	4,260	Cuba
783	910	52,172[18, 19]	73[18, 19]	270	2.8	234	3.2	349	1.6	...	...	Cyprus
5,982[20]	2,610[20]	1,537,005[20]	99[20]	2,956[5]	3.5[5]	3,246[5]	3.2[5]	3,246	3.2	36.4	3,530	Czech Republic
1,363	3,790	1,815,100	350	2,235	2.3	2,500	2.1	5,000[6]	1.0[6]	10.3	2,010	Denmark
5[8]	76,600[8]	1,623[8]	4.2[8]	30	19	17	33	14	40	...	...	Djibouti
63[8]	1,210[8]	2,051[8]	27[8]	45	1.6	5.2	14	12	5.8	...	...	Dominica
240	29,900	4,609[4]	0.7[4]	1,150	6.5	728	10	547	14	...	...	Dominican Republic
508	21,200	19,329	1.8	3,000	3.5	900	12	541	20	*10.1*	*1,060*	Ecuador
7,048	8,090	269,097	4.7	14,000	4.0	5,000	11	2,500	22	*30.3*	*620*	Egypt
307	19,200	19,331	3.3	1,935	2.8	501	11	260	21	...	...	El Salvador
20[1]	17,100[1]	...	...	100	3.7	2.5	147	2.0[4]	163[4]	...	...	Equatorial Guinea
...	...	...	...	...	...	...	...	...	...	...	...	Eritrea[21]
...	...	283,000	180	926[1]	1.7[1]	600	2.6	395	3.9	7.3	4,640	Estonia
921	57,000	31,509	0.6	3,300	16	100	541	169	316	...	...	Ethiopia[21]
...	...	...	...	20	2.4	14	3.4	24[22]	2.0[22]	...	500	Faeroe Islands

Communications (continued)

country	publishing (latest)								daily newspapers (latest)		
	number of titles				number of copies ('000)						
	books		periodicals	pamphlets	books		periodicals	pamphlets	number	total circulation ('000)	circulation per 1,000 population
	total	school textbooks			total	school textbooks					
Fiji	*10*	*6*	...	*3*	*20*	*12*	...	*6*	1	27	35
Finland	7,494	558	5,711	2,659	...	...	...	...	66	2,780	559
France	41,720[9]	1,076	2,588	[9]	...	...	118,354	...	79	11,792	210
French Guiana	...	...	*7*	...	...	...	*6*	...	1	1	10
French Polynesia	...	...	...	...	...	...	...	...	2	21	102
Gabon	...	...	...	...	...	...	...	...	1	20	17
Gambia, The	*23*	*2*	10	*19*	*31*	*22*	885	*32*	2	2	2
Gaza Strip	...	...	...	...	...	...	...	...	—	—	—
Georgia	1,659[9]	...	75	[9]	20,100[9]	...	29,700	[9]	147	3,677	671
Germany	71,998	3,810	9,040	...	...	...	332,913	...	354	30,083	424
Ghana	*338*	*27*	121	*12*	...	...	774	...	2	200	13
Gibraltar	...	...	*15*	...	...	...	*4*	...	2	4	133
Greece	3,255[9]	...	*309*	[9]	...	...	...	...	*117*	*1,400*	*140*
Greenland	...	...	...	...	...	...	...	...	—	—	—
Grenada	...	...	...	...	...	...	...	...	—	—	—
Guadeloupe	...	...	*45*	...	...	...	*142*	...	1	20	57
Guam	...	...	...	...	...	...	...	...	1	22	183
Guatemala	...	...	...	...	...	...	...	...	5	190	21
Guernsey	...	...	...	...	...	...	...	...	1	16	277
Guinea	...	...	3	...	...	...	5	...	—	—	—
Guinea-Bissau	...	...	...	...	...	...	...	...	1	6	6
Guyana	9	—	...	37	...	—	...	...	2	80	101
Haiti	188	17	...	83	...	...	...	...	4	45	7
Honduras	...	...	...	...	...	...	...	...	5	199	39
Hong Kong	*3,642*	*538*	617	*2,039*	*27,483*	*7,771*	...	*16,829*	38	3,700	632
Hungary	7,464	1,052	1,201	858	113,112	20,403	15,146	12,629	34	2,460	233
Iceland	1,062	194	562	453	...	...	...	...	6	148	572
India	11,607	210	*19,937*	2,330	...	...	*50,094*	...	2,281	17,000	21
Indonesia	1,211	55	117	307	...	...	4,281	...	64	5,144	28
Iran	6,289	...	318	...	31,565	...	6,166	...	21	1,500	27
Iraq	*82*	...	...	...	*452*	...	...	...	6	650	34
Ireland	*628*	...	*257*	*2,051*	...	...	*2,975*	...	7	591	159
Isle of Man	...	...	...	...	...	...	...	...	—	—	—
Israel	*2,038*	*291*	*807*	*176*	*8,872*	*3,961*	...	...	30	1,200	261
Italy	22,948	1,658	9,121	2,120	207,278	55,193	79,103	13,678	76	6,093	107
Jamaica	*23*	*3*	...	*48*	...	...	...	...	3	155	63
Japan	*36,346*	*1,657*	*2,877*	...	*315,225*	*2,117*	...	...	125	72,524	587
Jersey	...	...	...	...	...	...	...	...	1	24	300
Jordan	...	...	31	...	...	...	43	...	4	225	56
Kazakhstan	2,055[9]	...	88	[9]	28,800[9]	...	33,300	[9]	456	8,622	512
Kenya	343	...	...	5	686	...	...	9	5	350	15
Kiribati	...	...	...	...	...	...	...	...	—	—	—
Korea, North	...	...	...	...	...	...	...	...	11	5,000	230
Korea, South	35,967	3,878	...	3,363	227,073	106,698	...	20,889	39	12,000	280
Kuwait	*749*	...	*73*	*44*	...	...	*257*	...	9	450	221
Kyrgyzstan	936[9]	...	50	[9]	9,700[9]	...	34,400	[9]	128	1,622	367
Laos	79	9	...	30	423	180	...	143	3	14	3
Latvia	1,564[9]	...	243	[9]	20,800[9]	...	68,300	[9]	172	4,396	1,637
Lebanon	...	...	...	...	...	...	...	...	14	320	118
Lesotho	...	...	*2*	...	...	...	*11*	...	4	20	11
Liberia	...	...	...	...	...	...	...	...	8	35	14
Libya	*121*	*20*	...	...	*553*	*180*	...	...	3	70	15
Liechtenstein	...	...	*79*	...	...	...	*220*	...	2	9	307
Lithuania	2,686[9]	...	135	[9]	23,700[9]	...	40,400	[9]	*140*	*2,595*	*712*
Luxembourg	362	13	508	158	...	...	...	...	5	145	389
Macau	...	...	11	...	...	...	...	...	8	240	501
Macedonia	559	...	74	...	1,683	...	347	...	2	52	26
Madagascar	88	20	*121*	58	343	61	*261*	388	5	50	4
Malaŵi	66	5	*14*	75	...	...	*124*	...	1	25	3
Malaysia	4,370	1,409	*1,631*	208	21,526	14,250	*1,689*	1,707	45	2,500	140
Maldives	...	...	*64*	...	...	...	*70*	...	2	2	7
Mali	*160*	*76*	...	...	*92*	*56*	...	...	2	10	1
Malta	337	11	332	123	...	...	...	...	3	54	153
Marshall Islands	...	...	...	...	...	...	...	...	—	—	—
Martinique	...	...	*8*	...	...	...	*17*	...	1	32	92
Mauritania	...	...	...	...	...	...	...	...	1	1	0.5
Mauritius	53	5	48	22	107	17	...	109	7	80	74
Mayotte	...	...	...	...	...	...	...	...	*1*	*12*	*160*
Mexico	3,490	107	178	...	...	...	28,388	...	285	11,237	127
Micronesia	...	...	...	...	...	...	...	...	—	—	—
Moldova	1,277[9]	...	68	[9]	19,800[9]	...	38,400	[9]	*189*	*2,400*	*561*
Monaco	41[9]	...	6	[9]	722[9]	...	8	[9]	1	8	286
Mongolia	193	...	45	524	6,397[9]	...	6,361	[9]	1	162	74
Morocco	...	...	...	...	...	...	...	...	13	320	13
Mozambique	*29*	...	*5*	*37*	*3,130*	...	*2,263*	*360*	2	81	5
Myanmar (Burma)	*673*	...	...	...	...	...	...	...	2	200	5
Namibia	70	10	...	36	...	...	...	...	6	220	124
Nauru	...	...	...	...	...	...	...	...	—	—	—
Nepal	...	122	...	...	...	7,243	...	...	28	150	8
Netherlands, The	13,691	2,119	367	...	...	...	19,283	...	*86*	*4,592*	*311*
Netherlands Antilles	...	...	...	...	...	...	...	...	6	55	293
New Caledonia	*11*	...	*15*	*3*	...	...	*27*	...	1	19	114
New Zealand	*1,601*	*14*	*5,788*	*1,851*	...	...	...	...	35	1,100	324
Nicaragua	*27*	—	...	*14*	*271*	—	...	*192*	6	250	65
Niger	...	...	...	...	...	...	...	...	1	5	0.6

post offices, 1991				radio, 1992		television, 1992		telephones, 1991		cinema (latest)		country
number	persons per office	pieces of mail handled ('000)	pieces of mail handled per capita	receivers (all types; '000)	persons per receiver	receivers (all types; '000)	persons per receiver	receivers ('000)	persons per receiver	annual attendance number ('000,000)	annual attendance per 1,000 population	
265	2,790	20,633	28	450	1.7	10[6]	73[6]	78	9.6	...	...	Fiji
2,075	2,410	1,661,200	330	4,950	1.0	1,900	2.6	3,800	1.3	7.2	1,450	Finland
16,945[23]	3,460[23]	21,867,860[23]	370[23]	49,000	1.2	29,300	2.0	34,346[24]	1.6[24]	118.8	2,110	France
...	...	...	...	44[7]	2.1[7]	6.5	19	31[6]	3.8[6]	...	...	French Guiana
95	1,990	19,429	100	84	2.5	27	7.8	44[4]	4.3[4]	*0.4*	*2,190*	French Polynesia
52[6]	22,500[6]	6,478[2, 6, 19]	5.5[2, 6, 19]	250	5.0	40	31	26[6]	57[6]	*0.1*	*95*	Gabon
...	...	...	...	180	5.1	...	...	9.3[1]	92[1]	...	...	Gambia, The
...	...	...	...	...	...	...	...	...	...	...	...	Gaza Strip
...	...	138,000[6, 11]	25[6, 11]	...	...	...	...	1,047	5.2	47.0	8,680	Georgia
26,135[25]	2,400[25]	17,051,746[25]	270[25]	30,000	2.6	30,500	2.6	45,711[13]	1.7[13]	166.3	2,110	Germany
1,006	15,300	133,176	8.7	3,594	4.2	250	61	79[6]	185[6]	*3.9*	*340*	Ghana
4[6]	7,710[6]	12,699[6]	410[6]	17	1.7	7.5	3.9	18	1.6	*0.17*	*5,830*	Gibraltar
1,254[12]	8,190[12]	433,702	42	4,085	2.5	2,300	4.5	4,980	2.1	...	...	Greece
...	...	...	...	25	2.2	21	2.6	17[1]	3.4[1]	...	...	Greenland
191[12]	450[12]	...	...	80	1.1	30	3.0	27[1]	3.4[1]	...	...	Grenada
...	...	...	...	100	4.0	150	2.7	121[1]	3.2[1]	...	...	Guadeloupe
...	...	...	...	105	1.3	75	1.9	41[13]	3.1[13]	...	...	Guam
594	15,500	95,348	10	400	24	475	20	250[1]	36[1]	*7.7*	*910*	Guatemala
15	3,870	14,685[15]	250[15]	...	...	...	...	60[13]	1.0[13]	...	...	Guernsey
75	80,000	14,383	2.4	130	56	65	111	19	382	*2.6*	*430*	Guinea
24	40,200	339[2, 16, 18]	0.4[2, 16, 18]	35	29	...	...	15	67	...	...	Guinea-Bissau
63[12]	12,700[12]	4,577[2, 14]	5.7[2, 14]	310	2.4	40[5]	19[5]	33[7]	23[7]	*13.0*	*17,200*	Guyana
132	49,100	887,930	140	3,000	2.3	25	271	50[13]	126[13]	*2.1*	*380*	Haiti
...	...	...	...	1,800	2.8	160	31	96	51	...	...	Honduras
164	35,700	927,944	160	2,500	2.3	1,749	3.3	3,455	1.7	58.5	10,290	Hong Kong
3,209	3,220	1,556,785	150	6,000	1.7	4,262	2.4	1,956	5.3	45.8	4,400	Hungary
127	2,040	67,411	260	155	1.7	76	3.4	136	1.9	1.2	4,750	Iceland
148,719	5,680	14,626,630	17	55,000	16	20,000	44	6,021	145	4,300.0	5,150	India
14,884	12,300	580,517	3.2	22,000	8.4	11,000	17	1,505	122	*133.2*	*770*	Indonesia
4,426	13,100	284,731[19]	4.9[19]	12,000	5.0	2,250	26	2,270[6]	25[6]	80.5	1,490	Iran
343[6]	51,800[6]	244,870[6, 19]	14[6, 19]	3,500	5.4	1,000	19	712[6]	25[6]	...	...	Iraq
2,024	1,730	540,000[16, 18]	150[16, 18]	2,000	1.8	1,000	3.5	1,030	3.4	*11.6*	*3,290*	Ireland
34	2,050	30,049	430	...	...	...	...	...	...	...	...	Isle of Man
1,609	3,140	453,100[18]	90[18]	2,250	2.3	1,500	3.5	2,545	2.0	...	...	Israel
14,464[6]	3,990[6]	8,995,333[6]	160[6]	15,000	3.8	17,000	3.4	32,037[6]	1.8[6]	93.8	1,630	Italy
825	2,930	80,147[16, 18]	33[16, 18]	1,500	1.6	484	5.1	192	13	...	...	Jamaica
24,181	5,110	22,723,628	180	97,000	1.3	100,000	1.2	66,636[24]	1.8[24]	143.6	1,170	Japan
23	3,650	47,419	570	...	...	...	...	90[1]	0.9[1]	...	...	Jersey
842[6]	3,760[6]	51,057	16	700	5.2	250	15	350	10	0.9	290	Jordan
5,450[10]	3,100[10]	1,602,917	95	4,188[5]	4.0[5]	4,795[5]	3.5[5]	3,504	4.8	150.0	8,890	Kazakhstan
1,064	21,500	321,057	14	4,200	6.4	260	104	383[6]	66[6]	...	...	Kenya
24[6]	2,990[6]	337[6]	4.7[6]	10.0	7.5	...	...	1.5[13]	46[13]	...	...	Kiribati
...	...	...	...	4,700	4.7	250[5]	87[5]	30[6]	720[6]	*187.4*	*9,560*	Korea, North
3,343	13,000	2,657,967	61	42,000	1.0	8,700	5.0	17,697	2.5	55.3	1,300	Korea, South
54[13]	36,300[13]	115,215[1, 14]	56[1, 14]	1,000	1.4	800	1.5	362[13]	5.5[13]	*0.9*	*480*	Kuwait
1,020[10]	4,350[10]	355,300	80	825[5]	5.4[5]	875[5]	5.1[5]	383	12	32.0	7,190	Kyrgyzstan
209	20,600	4,060	0.9	425	10	32	138	7.3	598	...	...	Laos
1,141[6, 10]	2,350[6, 10]	458,900	170	1,396[5]	1.9[5]	1,200	2.2	836	3.2	19.7	7,340	Latvia
...	...	...	...	2,150	1.3	1,100	2.5	310	9.1	...	...	Lebanon
140[6]	12,600[6]	77,615[6]	44[6]	420	4.4	50	37	21	85	...	...	Lesotho
44[13]	55,400[13]	26,803[1]	11[1]	600	4.6	45	62	28[4]	86[4]	...	...	Liberia
317[12]	14,300[12]	1,707,397[2, 14]	380[2, 14]	1,000	4.4	500	8.9	500[13]	8.0[13]	...	...	Libya
12	2,450	16,236[15]	550[15]	10[6]	2.8[6]	9.8[6]	2.9[6]	17	1.7	...	...	Liechtenstein
...	...	450,900[26]	120[26]	1,420	2.7	1,400	2.7	1,634	2.3	13.9	3,690	Lithuania
106	3,630	145,000	380	230	1.7	101	3.9	192	2.0	0.5	1,330	Luxembourg
20	23,900	11,425	24	250[5]	1.4[5]	70	5.2	128	2.9	*2.7*	*6,400*	Macau
257	7,880	38,401	19	365[6]	5.5[6]	331[6]	6.1[6]	357[6]	5.7[6]	2.1	1,060	Macedonia
9,354	1,240	26,354	2.3	1,500	8.5	130	98	60[6]	203[6]	*3.0*	*280*	Madagascar
263[24]	28,000[24]	113,975[24]	15[24]	1,060	8.9	...	...	55	184	...	...	Malawi
5,053	3,630	824,472	43	3,500	5.3	2,000	9.3	2,023[6]	8.9[6]	41.6	2,400	Malaysia
28	7,970	1,671	7.5	25	9.2	4.8	48	2.5[24]	75[24]	...	...	Maldives
88[6]	92,600[6]	5,660[6]	0.7[6]	150	56	10	846	15[6]	564[6]	...	...	Mali
50	7,140	47,240	130	90	4.0	133	2.7	192	1.9	0.3	860	Malta
...	...	...	...	...	...	...	...	0.8[13]	57[13]	...	...	Marshall Islands
...	...	...	...	60	6.2	65	5.7	159[6]	2.3[6]	*1.1*	*3,150*	Martinique
60	33,700	...	...	300	7.0	1.1	1,920	7.8	268	...	...	Mauritania
113	9,720	34,856	32	250	4.3	138	7.8	75[6]	14[6]	0.9	850	Mauritius
...	...	...	...	30	3.3	3.5	28	3.2[6]	29[6]	...	...	Mayotte
25,679	3,360	857,371	10	16,325	5.2	12,350[5]	6.7[5]	10,838	8.0	*351.0*	*4,500*	Mexico
...	...	...	...	70	1.5	7.0	15	2.8	37	...	...	Micronesia
1,398[10]	3,120[10]	536,331	123	1,421[5]	3.1[5]	1,264[5]	3.5[5]	577	7.6	30.0	6,880	Moldova
...	...	...	...	11	2.8	20	1.5	53	0.6	0.1	3,390	Monaco
424[13]	4,790[13]	12,820[13, 16, 18]	6.3[13, 16, 18]	186	12	120	18	69	31	20.1	9,720	Mongolia
1,297	19,400	184,798	7.3	4,500	5.8	1,210	21	561	46	30.2	1,240	Morocco
160	103,000	1,849	0.1	500	30	35	424	69	211	*4.1*	*300*	Mozambique
1,152	36,200	70,499	1.7	3,200	14	1,000	43	81[13]	501[13]	...	...	Myanmar (Burma)
...	...	...	...	240[6]	5.6[6]	27	53	88	16	...	...	Namibia
1[24]	8,500[24]	168[24]	20[24]	4.0	2.4	...	...	1.5[13]	5.9[13]	...	...	Nauru
3,921	4,710	41,529	2.2	600	33	250	79	67[1]	275[1]	...	...	Nepal
2,624[4]	5,580[4]	6,105,000[1]	410[1]	12,146	1.3	6,000	2.5	10,500	1.4	15.6	1,050	Netherlands, The
16[1]	11,800[1]	17,427[1]	92[1]	125	1.5	35	5.5	50[1]	3.8[1]	...	...	Netherlands Antilles
264	640	18,482[19]	110[19]	90	1.9	36	4.9	31	5.6	*0.2*	*1,260*	New Caledonia
1,242[7]	2,670[7]	838,656[7, 19]	250[7, 19]	3,100	1.1	1,100	3.2	2,403[4]	1.4[4]	...	...	New Zealand
...	...	...	...	880	4.8	210	20	50	81	*5.0*	*1,750*	Nicaragua
64[12]	121,000[12]	3,010	0.4	400	21	25	330	15	541	...	...	Niger

Communications (continued)

country	publishing (latest): number of titles				number of copies ('000)				daily newspapers (latest)		
	books		periodicals	pamphlets	books		periodicals	pamphlets	number	total circulation ('000)	circulation per 1,000 population
	total	school textbooks			total	school textbooks					
Nigeria	900	800	*92*	566	...	...	*495*	...	31	1,700	16
Northern Mariana Islands	...	...	...	...	...	...	...	...	—	—	—
Norway	2,998	...	6,498	714	...	...	...	...	85	2,588	614
Oman	...	...	11	...	...	...	90	...	4	62	41
Pakistan	...	...	*282*	...	...	...	*7,674*	...	237	1,817	15
Panama	...	...	*8*	...	...	...	*18*	...	8	170	70
Papua New Guinea	...	...	...	...	...	...	...	...	2	49	13
Paraguay	...	...	...	...	...	...	...	...	5	165	39
Peru	*359*	*3*	*45*	*122*	...	...	*90*	...	66	1,700	79
Philippines	1,112	142	1,570	...	...	...	9,468	...	47	3,400	54
Poland	8,591	372	3,007	1,651	152,955	36,791	41,194	22,607	67	4,889	127
Portugal	6,527[9]	1,328	937	[9]	26,264[9]	8,500	6,359	[9]	24	390	38
Puerto Rico	...	...	...	...	...	...	...	...	3	456	131
Qatar	448	334	190	73	...	...	120	...	5	80	217
Réunion	*41*	—	...	*32*	...	—	...	...	3	65	109
Romania	1,828	...	435	350	49,562	...	22,675	2,915	65	...	...
Russia	41,234[9]	...	3,681	[9]	1,553,100[9]	...	5,010,200	[9]	4,808	166,000	1,119
Rwanda	*131*	*42*	15	*76*	*746*	*552*	101	*2,109*	1	0.5	0.1
St. Kitts and Nevis	—	—	10	*3*	—	—	43	*3*	—	—	—
St. Lucia	*44*	*25*	...	*19*	*89*	*84*	...	*7*	—	—	—
St. Vincent	...	...	...	...	...	...	...	...	—	—	—
San Marino	...	...	15	...	...	...	...	...	6	2	87
São Tomé and Príncipe	...	...	...	...	...	...	...	...	—	—	—
Saudi Arabia	...	...	*58*	...	...	...	...	...	12	600	42
Senegal	*42*	*8*	*123*	...	*169*	*70*	*381*	...	1	50	7
Seychelles	...	...	*2*	...	...	...	*2*	...	1	3.2	47
Sierra Leone	...	*16*	...	...	...	...	...	...	1	10	2
Singapore	*1,524*	*389*	*1,786*	*403*	*8,947*	*4,081*	...	*2,179*	8	763	280
Slovakia	...	...	...	...	...	...	...	...	12	1,291	246
Slovenia	1,853	...	274	...	6,267	...	7,194	...	3	226	115
Solomon Islands	...	...	...	...	...	...	...	...	—	—	—
Somalia	...	...	...	...	...	...	...	...	1	9	1
South Africa	3,193	254	...	1,757	24,708	9,646	...	6,121	22	1,340	38
Bophuthatswana	...	...	...	...	...	...	...	...	—	—	—
Ciskei	...	...	...	...	...	...	...	...	—	—	—
Transkei	...	...	...	...	...	...	...	...	—	—	—
Venda	...	...	...	...	...	...	...	...	—	—	—
Spain	31,619	3,003	*1,998*	4,620	161,046	35,293	...	23,903	*102*	*3,200*	*82*
Sri Lanka	959	138	*170*	1,496	12,102	9,674	*1,770*	7,589	18	550	32
Sudan, The	...	...	*10*	...	...	...	*136*	...	5	610	24
Suriname	...	...	*22*	...	...	...	*44*	...	2	40	95
Swaziland	...	...	...	...	...	...	...	...	3	10	13
Sweden	9,503	496	*46*	2,531	...	...	*4,947*	...	107	4,499	533
Switzerland	9,153	186	*3,079*	4,686	...	...	...	...	94	3,213	463
Syria	*119*	*1*	...	...	*553*	...	...	...	10	280	22
Taiwan	16,156	...	4,134	...	...	...	...	...	*93*	*4,000*	*202*
Tajikistan	787[9]	...	36	[9]	12,000[9]	...	27,200	[9]	74	1,598	309
Tanzania	127	23	...	45	275	46	...	89	3	200	7
Thailand	7,684	579	1,293	99	...	...	...	...	34	4,000	72
Togo	...	...	...	...	...	...	...	...	1	10	3
Tonga	...	...	...	...	...	...	...	...	1	7	74
Trinidad and Tobago	...	...	...	...	...	...	...	...	4	173	140
Tunisia	293	...	...	...	879	...	...	...	6	300	37
Turkey	5,279	220	1,325	1,012	...	...	1,325	...	399	4,000	72
Turkmenistan	759[9]	...	33	[9]	7,600[9]	...	12,800	[9]	66	1,141	319
Tuvalu	...	...	...	...	...	...	...	...	—	—	—
Uganda	...	...	26	...	...	...	158	...	2	30	2
Ukraine	5,168	193	185	1,878	116,602	28,084	9,957	53,874	127	13,026	251
United Arab Emirates	...	281	80	...	...	4,423	922	...	8	250	157
United Kingdom	*48,897*	*1,346*	*6,408*	*3,964*	...	...	...	...	*104*	*22,494*	*395*
United States	50,000	...	*11,593*	...	...	...	...	...	1,611	62,328	250
Uruguay	386	40	*465*	419	536	60	...	473	30	720	233
Uzbekistan	2,080[9]	...	95	[9]	51,000[9]	...	171,800	[9]	279	6,600	322
Vanuatu	...	...	...	...	...	...	...	...	—	—	—
Venezuela	*996*	*32*	*160*	*206*	...	...	*4,649*	...	54	2,800	142
Vietnam	...	...	...	...	...	...	...	...	5	600	9
Virgin Islands (U.S)	...	...	...	...	...	...	...	...	2	19	166
West Bank	...	...	...	...	...	...	...	...	—	—	—
Western Sahara	...	...	...	...	...	...	...	...	—	—	—
Western Samoa	...	...	...	...	...	...	...	...	—	—	—
Yemen	...	...	...	...	...	...	...	...	5	135	12
Yugoslavia	8,724[28]	1,507[28]	1,361[28]	1,073[28]	39,439[28]	19,238[28]	4,197[28]	4,077[28]	12	1,006	98
Zaire	...	...	*68*	...	...	...	...	...	*7*	*45*	*1*
Zambia	*454*	*215*	...	...	...	...	...	...	2	99	12
Zimbabwe	145	17	28	204	...	...	680	...	2	206	21

[1]1989. [2]Foreign-received and foreign-sent only. [3]1984. [4]1987. [5]1991. [6]1990. [7]1986. [8]1983. [9]Books includes pamphlets. [10]Includes telephone and telegraph offices. [11]Letters sent only. [12]Permanent post offices only. [13]1988. [14]Letters only. [15]Domestic and foreign-sent only. [16]Excludes printed matter. [17]1993. [18]Excludes small packets. [19]Excludes postcards. [20]Data refer to

post offices, 1991				radio, 1992		television, 1992		telephones, 1991		cinema (latest)		country
number	persons per office	pieces of mail handled ('000)	pieces of mail handled per capita	receivers (all types; '000)	persons per receiver	receivers (all types; '000)	persons per receiver	receivers ('000)	persons per receiver	annual attendance: number ('000,000)	annual attendance: per 1,000 population	
3,547	25,000	590,596	6.7	10,000	9.0	4,100[5]	21[5]	722[13]	118[13]	*4.6*	*51*	Nigeria
...	...	...	...	10.5	4.3	4.1	11	4.9[4]	4.4[4]	...	...	Northern Mariana Islands
2,543	1,680	2,019,583	470	3,300	1.3	1,500	2.9	2,579[3]	1.6[3]	12.4	2,930	Norway
76	19,700	27,089[2]	18[2]	900	1.8	1,500	1.1	263	6.1	...	...	Oman
13,413	8,720	710,260[15]	6.1[15]	10,000	13	2,080	63	1,295	95	*25.3*	*230*	Pakistan
268[6]	9,020[6]	18,116	7.8	450	5.6	205	12	273	9.1	...	...	Panama
114[6]	34,200[6]	36,478[2, 6]	9.4[2, 6]	235	16	10	383	63[6]	59[6]	...	...	Papua New Guinea
310	13,800	6,441	1.5	775	5.8	350	13	133	33	...	...	Paraguay
1,317	17,400	30,285	1.3	4,400	5.1	2,000	11	799	28	*33.0*	*1,910*	Peru
2,512	25,000	970,006	15	4,000	16	7,000	9.1	1,097	57	...	...	Philippines
8,041[6]	4,740[6]	977,401	26	10,400	3.7	10,000	3.8	5,480	7.0	69.5	1,830	Poland
7,814	1,260	794,018	81	2,475	4.0	1,770	5.6	3,071	3.2	*16.9*	*1,650*	Portugal
...	...	...	...	2,000	1.8	830	4.3	903	3.9	...	...	Puerto Rico
28	14,300	22,630[2]	56[2]	250	2.1	250	2.1	146	3.5	0.3	710	Qatar
...	...	...	...	150	4.2	91	6.9	168[6]	3.6[6]	...	...	Réunion
4,604	5,040	38,638[2]	1.7[2]	3,000	7.8	4,000	5.8	3,100	7.3	203.4	8,790	Romania
54,457	2,730	21,923,325	150	90,000	1.7	54,200[5]	2.7[5]	24,128	6.1	1,323.0	8,910	Russia
43	184,000	9,972	1.3	630	12	...	...	15	480	*0.3*	*56*	Rwanda
8	5,580	2,836	53	25	1.7	9.5	4.4	9.4[6]	4.6[6]	...	...	St. Kitts and Nevis
58	2,600	5,095	34	90	1.5	25	5.3	24	5.6	...	...	St. Lucia
56	2,300	526[2]	4.1[2]	55	2.0	18	6.1	17[6]	6.4[6]	...	...	St. Vincent
10	2,640	...	...	13[5]	1.9[5]	8.0[6]	2.9[6]	16[13]	1.5[13]	0.02	880	San Marino
11	11,000	226	1.9	31	4.0	...	...	3.1	39	...	...	São Tomé and Príncipe
609[6, 12]	23,200[6, 12]	356,378[6]	25[6]	5,000	3.4	4,500	3.7	1,466	11	...	...	Saudi Arabia
133	52,600	14,210	2.0	850	9.0	61	126	48	157	...	...	Senegal
5	14,000	4,175	60	30	2.4	8.2	8.7	14[13]	4.8[13]	...	...	Seychelles
78	51,300	2,688	0.7	900	4.9	25	175	35	125	...	...	Sierra Leone
675	4,140	502,569	180	800	3.5	550	5.1	1,220[13]	2.2[13]	*30.7*	*20,600*	Singapore
...	...	...	...	1,094[5]	4.8[5]	1,309[5]	4.0[5]	1,305	4.0	13.8	2,630	Slovakia
534	3,690	270,048	140	601[6]	3.3[6]	445[6]	4.4[6]	657[6]	3.0[6]	2.8	1,440	Slovenia
117	2,900	2,164[6, 18]	6.8[6, 18]	38	8.9	...	...	7.0[1]	46[1]	...	...	Solomon Islands
...	...	...	...	400	20	3.0[4]	2,270[4]	8.0[13]	882[13]	...	...	Somalia
...	...	...	...	10,000	3.9	3,445	11	5,208	7.5	26.0	680	South Africa
...	...	...	...	...	...	...	...	36[13]	52[13]	...	...	Bophuthatswana
34[3]	21,500[3]	...	...	...	...	...	...	23[13]	35[13]	...	...	Ciskei
192[7]	15,600[7]	...	...	...	...	6.0[13]	619[13]	7.2[7]	409[7]	...	...	Transkei
...	...	...	...	...	...	...	...	...	...	...	...	Venda
41,833[6]	950[6]	5,608,624[6]	140[6]	12,600	3.1	17,240	2.3	15,477[4]	2.5[4]	78.1	1,970	Spain
3,982	4,340	485,301	28	2,200	7.9	700	25	172	101	*37.2*	*2,270*	Sri Lanka
808[6]	35,000[6]	10,357	0.4	6,000	5.0	250	120	78[13]	343[13]	*13.0*	*600*	Sudan, The
...	...	...	...	250	1.6	43	9.4	54	7.5	...	...	Suriname
70	12,100	18,272	22	65	13	13	66	25[6]	31[6]	...	...	Swaziland
1,978	4,370	1,732,584[14, 27]	200[14, 27]	7,272	1.2	3,750	2.3	7,410[8]	1.1[8]	*18.0*	*2,140*	Sweden
3,739	1,840	4,182,292[18, 19]	610[18, 19]	2,685	2.6	2,200	3.2	6,227	1.1	12.8	1,900	Switzerland
585[1]	20,000[1]	20,857[6]	1.7[6]	2,850	4.5	700	19	708	18	6.9	590	Syria
13,233	1,550	1,754,119	86	13,600[5]	1.5[5]	6,660[5]	3.1[5]	8,243[6]	2.4[6]	64.2	3,200	Taiwan
785[10]	6,920[10]	320,049	59	854[5]	6.4[5]	860[5]	6.3[5]	285	19	30.0	5,520	Tajikistan
846	27,400	92,807	4.0	4,000	6.5	80	323	140[6]	177[6]	1.7	74	Tanzania
4,162	13,700	682,195	12	10,000	5.7	3,300	17	1,553	36	...	...	Thailand
420	8,560	...	...	700	5.3	23	161	21	170	...	...	Togo
...	...	...	...	66	1.5	...	...	5.1	19	...	...	Tonga
242	5,100	22,940	19	700	1.8	250	5.1	234	5.3	...	...	Trinidad and Tobago
695[12]	11,400[12]	134,621[19]	17[19]	1,700	4.9	650	13	464	18	...	...	Tunisia
41,885[12]	1,370[12]	1,076,799	19	7,100	8.3	10,530	5.6	10,150	5.7	*25.8*	*510*	Turkey
580[10]	6,490[10]	244,027	65	823[5]	4.6[5]	705[5]	5.3[5]	279	14	46.0	12,200	Turkmenistan
9[13]	970[13]	88[2, 13]	10[2, 13]	4.0	2.3	...	...	0.23	55	...	...	Tuvalu
307	53,700	14,325	0.9	3,500	4.9	115	150	59	287	...	...	Uganda
17,200[6, 10]	3,020[6, 10]	13,466,000[6]	260[6]	15,000[6]	3.5[6]	17,200[6]	3.0[6]	8,120	6.4	416.0	8,020	Ukraine
190	10,000	106,928	56	420	4.7	170	12	777	2.5	...	...	United Arab Emirates
20,638[6]	2,780[6]	16,412,000[6]	290[6]	70,000	0.8	20,000	2.9	29,518[3]	1.9[3]	94.6	1,650	United Kingdom
39,985	6,350	164,639,561[15]	650[15]	520,000	0.5	215,000	1.2	181,091[3]	1.3[3]	1,132.5	4,580	United States
361[6]	8,570[6]	34,418[6]	11[6]	1,800	1.7	600	5.2	579[6]	5.4[6]	*6.2*	*2,110*	Uruguay
3,800[10]	5,520[10]	1,537,874	73	3,677[5]	5.7[5]	3,308[5]	6.3[5]	1,518	14	126.0	6,010	Uzbekistan
...	...	...	...	20	7.8	1.0[6]	148[6]	3.2[7]	44[7]	...	...	Vanuatu
580	34,000	86,989	4.4	8,100	2.5	3,700	5.5	1,794[6]	11[6]	29.8	1,590	Venezuela
...	...	...	...	6,000	12	2,200	31	116[13]	544[13]	*239.9*	*3,760*	Vietnam
...	...	...	...	90	1.1	32	3.3	59[6]	1.7[6]	...	...	Virgin Islands (U.S.)
...	...	...	...	...	...	...	...	...	...	...	...	West Bank
...	...	...	...	...	...	...	...	...	...	...	...	Western Sahara
45	3,560	3,514[2]	22[2]	75	2.5	6.0[6]	27[6]	5.5[13]	30[13]	...	...	Western Samoa
406[1]	27,700[1]	17,624[1]	1.6[1]	325	37	335[6]	34[6]	136	87	...	...	Yemen
1,548[6]	6,660[6]	474,729[6]	46[6]	1,907[6]	5.4[6]	1,643	6.3	1,839[6]	5.6[6]	8.3	800	Yugoslavia
365[6]	93,500[6]	45,394[6, 19]	1.3[6, 19]	3,400	12	22	1,870	32[13]	1,026[13]	...	...	Zaire
463	16,900	76,475[18, 19]	9.8[18, 19]	1,660	5.0	200	41	105	78	...	...	Zambia
294[6]	31,900[6]	175,141[6]	19[6]	522	19	137	72	313	31	*5.6*	*690*	Zimbabwe

former Czechoslovakia. [21]Ethiopia includes Eritrea. [22]1981. [23]Includes overseas departments and Monaco. [24]1985. [25]Former West Germany only. [26]1992. [27]Domestic only. [28]Data refer to former Socialist Federal Republic of Yugoslavia.

Trade: external

The following table presents comparative data on the international, or foreign, trade of the countries of the world. The table analyzes data for both imports and exports in two ways: (1) into several major commodity groups defined in accordance with the United Nations system called the Standard International Trade Classification (SITC) and (2) by direction of trade for each country with major world trading blocs and partners. These commodity groupings are defined by the SITC code numbers beneath the column headings. The single-digit numbers represent broad SITC categories (in the SITC, called "sections"); the double-digit numbers represent subcategories ("divisions") of the single-digit categories (27 is a subcategory of 2); the three-digit number is a subcategory ("group") of the double-digit (667 is a subcategory of 66). Where a plus or minus sign is used before one of these SITC numbers, the SITC category or subcategory is being added to or subtracted from the aggregate implied by the total of the preceding sections. The SITC commodity aggregations used here are listed in the table at the end of this headnote. The full SITC commodity breakdown—some 3,118 basic headings—is presented in the 1986 United Nations publication *Standard International Trade Classification, Revision 3.*

The SITC was developed by the United Nations through its Statistical Commission as an outgrowth of the need for a standard system of aggregating commodities of external trade to provide international comparability of foreign trade statistics. The United Nations Statistical Commission has defined external merchandise trade as "all goods whose movement into or out of the customs area of a country compiling the statistics adds to or subtracts from the material resources of the country." Goods passing through a country for transport only are excluded, but goods entering for reexport, or deposited (as in a bonded warehouse, or free trade area) for reimport, are included. Statistics in this table refer only to goods and exclude purely financial transactions that are covered in the "Finance" and "National product and accounts" tables.

For purposes of comparability of data, total value of imports and exports is given in this table in U.S. dollars. Conversions from currencies other than rubles are determined according to the average rates for the year for which data are supplied; these are mainly as calculated by the International Monetary Fund (IMF). Ruble conversions to U.S. dollars have been made using an official rate. The commodity categories are given in terms of percentages of the total value of the country's import or export trade (with the exclusions noted above). Value is based on transaction value: for imports, the value at which the goods were purchased by the importer plus the cost of transportation and insurance to the frontier of

Trade: external

country	year	imports												
		total value ('000,000 U.S.$)	Standard International Trade Classification (SITC) categories (%)							direction of trade (%)				
			food and agricultural raw materials (0+1+2 −27−28 +4)	mineral ores and concen- trates (27+28 +667)	fuels and other energy (3)	manufactured goods: total[a] (5+6 −667 +7+8 +9)	of which chemicals and related products (5)	of which machinery and transport equipment (7)	of which other[a] (6−667 +8+9)	from European Economic Community (EEC)[b]	from United States	from Eastern Europe[c]	from Japan	from all other[d]
Afghanistan	1989[1]	821.7	—13.4[2]—		2.7	83.9[3]	2.2	46.2	35.4[3]	6.2[4]	0.5[4]	49.9[4]	9.6[4]	33.8[4]
Albania	1990	446.5	25.7	—24.5—		49.8	9.3	31.0	9.5	37.7[5]	...	27.9	0.1	34.4
Algeria	1991	7,683.3	29.3	0.5	3.3	67.0	9.2	31.1	26.7	61.8	9.9	2.1	4.8	21.3
American Samoa	1989[6]	377.9	65.1	—[2]	7.1	27.8[3]	1.2	6.7	20.0[3]	—	28.0	—	3.9	68.1
Andorra	1987	700.4	—28.3[2]—		3.7	68.0[3]	7.3	19.9	40.8[3]	84.9	2.8	0.2	6.3	5.9
Angola	1991	1,347.0	31.7[7]	0.2[7]	0.8[7]	67.3[7]	12.1[7]	20.9[7]	34.3[7]	65.1[4]	10.5[4]	...	7.8[4]	16.6[4]
Antigua and Barbuda	1984	131.9	24.6	—	25.0	50.4	6.4	21.8	22.2	10.6	37.8	—	—	51.6
Argentina	1990	4,076.7	8.0	6.1	8.3	77.6	27.6	32.0	18.1	25.6	20.1	1.3	4.4	48.6
Armenia	1990[8]	7,969.2	—28.1[2]—		6.5	65.4[3]	7.9	20.9	36.5[3]	...	...	75.2[9]	...	24.8
Aruba	1988	330.9	22.3	0.1	7.6	70.0	8.0	19.7	42.3	22.8	40.7	0.1	3.7	32.8
Australia	1991	40,131.8	6.7	0.8	5.5	87.0	8.8	41.6	36.5	21.1	24.1	0.3	16.9	37.6
Austria	1992	54,047.1	8.0	1.3	5.1	85.6	9.8	39.5	36.3	67.9	4.0	6.5	4.7	17.0
Azerbaijan	1991[8]	6,302.1	—35.0[2]—		8.3	56.7[3]	5.8	18.2	32.7[3]	...	...	80.3[9]	...	19.7
Bahamas, The	1988	2,263.5	10.2	0.1	56.7	33.0	6.4	9.6	17.1	7.7	39.6	1.0	0.6	51.1
Bahrain	1991	4,115.2	8.4	0.2	45.1	46.3	5.9	20.1	20.2	21.8[4]	13.4[4]	...	4.4[4]	60.4[4]
Bangladesh	1991[10]	2,184.7	27.9	5.7	16.0	50.4	8.7	17.2	24.5	12.6	3.6	3.2	7.8	72.8
Barbados	1991	699.6	21.0	0.4	13.7	64.9	10.4	23.0	31.5	17.8	36.1	0.1	6.0	40.0
Belarus	1990[8]	33,787.4	—16.2[2]—		9.7	74.1[3]	12.3	35.1	26.7[3]	...	...	75.1[9]	....	24.9
Belgium[11]	1992	125,122.1	12.9	8.3	7.6	71.2	11.9	25.6	33.7	73.5	4.4	1.6	2.2	18.2
Belize	1986	122.0	27.4	0.1	13.9	58.6	8.4	18.0	32.2	16.5	57.4	0.1	2.4	23.7
Benin	1987	349.3	—34.5[2, 12]—		13.0[2]	52.4[3, 12]	7.4[12]	14.1[12]	31.0[3, 12]	41.1	3.9	1.3	5.6	48.0
Bermuda	1990	540.6[13]	23.3	0.1	8.6	67.9	10.0	20.2	37.8	15.3	59.5	—	5.2	20.0
Bhutan	1983	39.0[14]	14.5	0.3	21.4	63.9	3.4	29.7	30.8	12.0	0.3	—	4.6	83.1[15]
Bolivia	1991	992.4	12.7	0.2	0.8	86.4	11.8	44.1	30.5	15.7	25.9	0.8	12.3	45.2
Bosnia and Herzegovina	1990	1,866.9	...	...	31.6	...	...	...	...	...	...	...	...	...
Botswana	1989	1,966.2	11.4	1.9	4.7	82.0	6.2	38.6	37.3	7.3	1.2	—	0.3	91.1[17]
Brazil	1991	22,976.9	13.9	3.0	23.9	59.2	16.3	28.1	14.8	21.8	23.5	1.7	5.9	47.1
Brunei	1988	743.4	—22.8[2]—		0.9	76.3[3]	6.6	32.8	37.0[3]	18.7	12.6	—	16.0	52.8
Bulgaria	1991	2,700.4	15.2	—58.7[19]—		26.1[20]	5.7	15.8	4.6[20]	20.7	2.9	46.5	0.5	29.4
Burkina Faso	1987	434.3	—25.4[2]—		7.7	66.8[3]	13.5	27.2	26.1[3]	50.8	6.4	0.9	5.0	36.8
Burundi	1989	188.1	10.6	1.4	11.9	76.1	14.9	31.1	30.1	48.3	1.2	4.5	8.1	37.9
Cambodia	1989	215.0[4]	...	...	30.2[21]	...	1.2[21]	36.9[21]	...	1.9[4]	—[4]	96.1[4, 22]	1.7[4]	0.3[4]
Cameroon	1989	1,273.3	16.6	3.4	1.4	78.6	15.2	30.8	32.6	60.8	5.1	0.8	5.7	27.7
Canada	1992	122,479.1	7.8	1.7	4.3	86.1	7.4	50.6	28.2	9.8	65.2	0.3	7.3	17.4
Cape Verde	1989	111.9	35.4	—	6.3	58.4	5.9	24.9	27.6	61.2	4.2	4.5	6.2	23.9
Central African Republic	1989	159.1	20.1	0.7	6.7	72.6	14.0	33.2	25.3	56.7	1.3	0.3	7.6	34.2
Chad	1989	235.0	15.9[25]	0.6[25]	14.2[25]	69.3[25]	16.4[25]	28.8[25]	24.1[25]	43.6[4]	16.5[4]	—[4]	2.1[4]	37.8[4]
Chile	1991	7,452.6	8.4	0.5	14.9	76.3	13.7	37.9	24.7	18.9	21.2	0.8	8.7	50.4
China	1991	63,791.4	11.7	2.0[2]	3.3	83.0[3]	14.5	30.7	37.7[3]	13.2	12.6	4.2	15.7	54.4
Colombia	1991	4,967.0	10.2	1.2	6.0	82.6	24.2	33.2	25.2	18.7	35.0	1.0	10.2	35.1
Comoros	1990	51.6	—47.1[2, 26]—		13.1[26]	39.8[3, 26]	3.5[26]	17.6[26]	18.8[3, 26]	73.0[4]	—[4]	...	5.0[4]	22.1[4]
Congo	1986	578.6	18.9	0.7	1.7	78.7	9.1	35.3	34.3	76.0	5.2	1.1	4.2	13.5
Costa Rica	1991	2,234.6	9.3	0.4	9.4	80.9	17.8	19.4	43.7	9.2	51.3	0.2	5.3	33.9
Côte d'Ivoire	1987	2,241.4	—24.0—		15.0	61.1	13.8	21.3	25.9	56.5	4.4	1.0	5.5	32.6
Croatia	1991	3,828.0	14.3	2.4[2]	17.4	65.9[3]	13.5	21.9	30.5[3]	47.6[5]	3.9	13.9[5]	2.9	31.7
Cuba	1987	7,611.5	14.2	0.3[2]	34.7	50.8[3]	5.8	30.7	14.3[3]	9.8	—	81.6	1.4	7.2
Cyprus	1991	2,620.8	17.9	0.8	10.3	71.1	8.0	28.2	34.9	51.1	7.9	7.9	11.4	21.6
Czech Republic	1991[27]	11,072.0	13.8[28]	2.9[28]	17.3[28]	65.9[28]	9.3[28]	36.9[28]	19.6[28]	32.1	1.8	38.5	1.2	26.4
Denmark	1992	33,632.1	16.4	0.5	6.3	76.8	11.8	29.9	35.2	53.5	5.6	3.2	4.1	33.6
Djibouti	1991	212.3	34.8	1.3	9.2	54.6	7.5	15.6	31.5	45.6	3.7	...	7.2	43.5
Dominica	1990	117.9	—25.7[2]—		6.1	68.3[3]	11.1	26.1	31.1[3]	22.7	33.1	0.2	6.2	37.7
Dominican Republic	1990	2,056.7	13.7[21]	0.3[21]	35.2[21]	50.7[21]	11.7[21]	23.2[21]	15.9[21]	11.8[4]	42.8[4]	—[4]	10.4[4]	35.0[4]
Ecuador	1991	2,327.9	10.3	0.7	1.1	87.9	23.0	40.5	24.4	22.3	31.9	1.5	10.0	34.3
Egypt	1992	8,293.0	35.7	1.8	1.4	61.1	13.0	26.2	21.9	36.3	17.5	3.7	4.3	38.1
El Salvador	1991	884.8	20.2	0.3	12.7	66.8	18.7	23.4	24.6	10.4	41.1	0.1	4.8	43.5
Equatorial Guinea	1991	91.1[4]	—28.6[2, 12]—		20.1[12]	51.3[3, 12]	4.3[12]	25.4[12]	21.6[3, 12]	45.4[4]	14.6[4]	—[4]	0.1[4]	39.9[4]
Eritrea	...	...	...	...	...	...	...	...	...	...	...	...	...	...
Estonia	1991	2,549.8	—15.8[2]—		12.0	72.2[3]	7.3	17.8	47.1[3]	1.4[5]	3.5	85.4[5]	...	9.7
Ethiopia	1990	1,081.4	17.2	0.8	11.9	70.1	10.1	39.7	20.3	44.1[4]	5.4	15.0[4]	6.5	29.0[4]
Faeroe Islands	1991	294.0	28.6	0.7	13.2	57.4	7.9	15.6	33.9	61.1	3.9	1.4	2.3	31.4

the importing country (c.i.f. [cost, insurance, and freight] valuation); for exports, the value at which the goods were sold by the exporter, including the cost of transportation and insurance to bring the goods onto the transporting vehicle at the frontier of the exporting country (f.o.b. [free-on-board] valuation).

The largest part of the information presented here comes from the United Nations' *Commodity Trade Statistics* (including microfiche format) and *International Trade Statistics Yearbook*. These publications, however, cannot always provide the most recent data for all countries listed in this table and must be supplemented by national and regional sources. In some cases where the original data were only available for an alternative trade classification, an approximation has been made of the SITC commodity groupings.

a. Also includes any unallocated commodities.
b. EEC of 12 countries (Belgium, Denmark, France, Germany, Greece, Ireland, Italy, Luxembourg, The Netherlands, Portugal, Spain, and the United Kingdom).
c. Includes Albania, Bulgaria, Czech Republic, Hungary, Poland, Romania, Slovakia, and all republics of the former U.S.S.R. (including republics now regarded as Asian).
d. May include value of trade shown as not available (...) in any of the four preceding columns. May include any unspecified areas or countries.
... Not available.
— None, less than 0.05%, or not applicable.
Detail may not add to 100.0 or indicated subtotals because of rounding.

SITC category codes

code		description
0		food and live animals
1		beverages and tobacco
2		crude materials, inedible, except fuels
	27	crude fertilizers and crude minerals (excluding coal, petroleum, and precious stones)
	28	metalliferous ores and metal scrap
3		mineral fuels, lubricants, and related materials (including coal, petroleum, natural gas, and electric current)
4		animal and vegetable oils, fats, and waxes
5		chemicals and related products not elsewhere specified
6		manufactured goods classified chiefly by material
	667	pearls, precious and semiprecious stones, unworked or worked
7		machinery and transport equipment
8		miscellaneous manufactured articles
9		commodities and transactions not classified elsewhere

exports													country
total value ('000,000 U.S.$)	Standard International Trade Classification (SITC) categories (%)							direction of trade (%)					
	food and agricultural raw materials (0+1+2−27−28+4)	mineral ores and concentrates (27+28+667)	fuels and other energy (3)	manufactured goods: total[a] (5+6−667+7+8+9)	of which chemicals and related products (5)	of which machinery and transport equipment (7)	of which other[a] (6−667+8+9)	to European Economic Community (EEC)[b]	to United States	to Eastern Europe[c]	to Japan	to all other[d]	
235.9	—58.5[2]—		23.6	17.9[3]	...	...	...	12.8[4]	0.6[4]	70.3[4]	0.3[4]	16.0[4]	Afghanistan
267.4	37.9	—46.8—		15.3	1.5	0.8	13.0	23.1[5]	...	38.2	2.1	36.6	Albania
11,790.0	0.5	0.3	96.9	2.3	0.6	0.7	1.0	71.3	17.3	1.4	0.7	9.3	Algeria
307.5	100.0	—	—	—	—	—	—	—	100.0	—	—	—	American Samoa
24.6	—29.6[2]—		—	70.4[3]	7.2	10.9	52.4[3]	99.9	—	—	—	0.1	Andorra
3,427.0	...	5.5	92.1	2.4	...	...	...	32.7[4]	56.6[4]	...	0.1[4]	10.5[4]	Angola
17.6	6.2	—	11.5	82.3	7.5	30.1	44.7	3.4	17.9	—	—	78.7	Antigua and Barbuda
12,351.5	60.2	0.2	8.0	31.6	6.0	5.8	19.8	30.6	13.8	5.6	3.2	46.8	Argentina
6,022.2	—13.5[2]—		0.2	86.3[3]	6.0	23.5	56.7[3]	...	...	97.3[9]	...	2.7	Armenia
30.5	54.0	1.2	0.2	44.5	7.1	7.9	29.5	5.6	22.3	—	—	72.1	Aruba
43,148.1	24.3	8.8	17.0	49.9	2.5	8.8	38.6	12.0	10.3	1.1	27.1	49.5	Australia
44,367.7	6.7	0.8	1.1	91.5	8.6	38.9	43.9	66.1	2.6	9.7	1.5	20.1	Austria
6,983.1	—34.6[2]—		12.8	52.5[3]	9.5	17.3	25.7	...	...	93.9[9]	...	6.1	Azerbaijan
2,163.8	2.8	0.8	77.7	18.7	16.8	0.8	1.2	2.2	79.6	—	2.2	16.0	Bahamas, The
3,513.1	1.0	0.1	80.6	18.3	4.0	1.1	13.2	3.9[4]	2.6[4]	...	11.6[4]	81.9[4]	Bahrain
1,670.5	22.6	—	0.8	76.7	2.8	0.1	73.8	35.1	28.3	6.1	3.4	27.1	Bangladesh
206.2	25.7	0.2	28.4	45.8	12.5	13.1	20.2	17.3	13.6	—	0.3	68.8	Barbados
32,469.6	—10.8[2]—		7.8	81.4[3]	12.7	46.0	22.6	...	...	90.7[9]	...	9.3	Belarus
123,459.9	12.3	7.0	3.5	77.2	14.7	27.0	35.5	75.0	3.9	1.4	1.0	18.7	Belgium[11]
92.6	69.7	—	2.9	27.4	0.9	3.6	23.0	28.4	56.5	1.0	0.1	14.1	Belize
114.0	—50.3[2, 12]—		44.7[12]	5.0[3, 12]	0.3[12]	1.2[12]	3.5[3, 12]	50.4	16.8	0.1	0.9	31.8	Benin
59.7	...	...	...	...	81.7	...	...	33.2	54.8	—	—	11.9	Bermuda
13.9[14]	32.1	—	—	67.9	16.5	—	51.4	0.4	—	—	0.2	99.4[16]	Bhutan
899.8	24.2	27.1	26.8	22.0	0.4	—	21.5	26.5	21.9	—	0.2	51.4	Bolivia
2,056.1	...	...	...	...	9.4	20.8	...	...	...	...	...	...	Bosnia and Herzegovina
2,420.1	5.3	89.1	—	5.6	0.5	2.3	2.8	2.2	0.3	—	0.1	97.5[18]	Botswana
31,621.8	28.3	9.9	1.4	60.4	6.0	18.6	35.8	31.2	20.2	1.2	8.1	39.4	Brazil
1,706.7	—0.9[2]—		97.5	1.6[3]	0.1	0.8	0.7[3]	0.1	2.1	—	65.0	32.8	Brunei
3,432.6	24.1	—10.5[19]—		65.4[20]	11.9	30.6	22.9[20]	15.6	3.4	55.0	0.7	25.4	Bulgaria
155.0	—58.0[2]—		—	42.0[3]	0.5	9.7	31.8[3]	45.5	0.2	—	1.9	52.4	Burkina Faso
77.8	90.0	—	—	10.0	—	—	10.0	79.7[4]	0.8[4]	—[4]	3.6[4]	15.9[4]	Burundi
25.0[4]	82.9[21, 23]	...	...	...	...	...	...	4.0[4]	1.4[4]	78.8[4, 22]	9.2[4]	6.5[4]	Cambodia
1,281.6	54.5	0.2	18.0	27.3	1.6	5.2	20.5	66.6	10.0	1.6	1.5	20.3	Cameroon
134,169.8	17.6	3.0	10.3	69.0	5.3	37.5	26.2	7.1	77.4	0.9	4.6	10.0	Canada
28.1	27.7	0.3	59.8	12.1	0.4	8.6	3.1	10.2	—	—	0.2	89.6[24]	Cape Verde
140.3	54.3	43.2	—	2.5	0.2	0.2	2.0	89.2	0.6	—	—	10.2	Central African Republic
132.8	90.5	0.3[2, 19]	—	9.3[3, 20]	0.5	5.1	3.7[3, 20]	30.3	0.1	—	5.7	63.9	Chad
8,960.1	35.2	13.8	0.5	50.4	3.5	1.2	45.7	32.9	15.5	0.4	18.7	32.5	Chile
71,910.2	14.9	0.9[2]	6.7	77.5[3]	5.3	9.9	62.2[3]	9.4	8.6	2.8	14.3	64.9	China
7,268.6	37.6	2.2	28.8	31.4	4.6	2.7	24.1	25.2	38.8	0.9	3.2	31.9	Colombia
17.9	59.8	—	1.8	38.4	35.3	...	3.1	75.1[4]	19.2[4]	...	2.6[4]	3.1[4]	Comoros
776.9	8.4	1.4	89.1	1.2	0.1	0.5	0.6	41.6	54.2	0.5	0.1	3.5	Congo
1,627.6	65.8	0.1	0.5	33.6	5.1	3.1	25.4	26.8	47.6	0.2	1.3	24.2	Costa Rica
3,109.8	—77.3—		10.9	11.8	2.3	1.5	7.9	63.1	10.5	5.4	0.6	20.3	Côte d'Ivoire
3,292.0	—13.6[2]—		6.8	79.6[3]	12.1	23.4	44.1[3]	60.5[5]	3.6	11.5[5]	...	24.4	Croatia
5,402.1	84.1	6.7[2]	6.8	2.5[3]	0.5	0.6	1.4[3]	10.2	—	81.5	1.4	6.8	Cuba
951.5	36.6	1.2	4.6	57.6	5.3	12.2	40.2	43.4	1.4	4.9	0.3	50.1	Cyprus
10,921.3	7.5[28]	1.3[28]	5.2[28]	86.0[28]	7.6[28]	44.4[28]	34.1[28]	40.6	1.0	32.8	0.6	25.0	Czech Republic
39,549.0	30.0	0.5	4.0	65.5	10.0	26.9	28.6	54.4	4.9	2.9	3.6	34.2	Denmark
17.2	32.1	—	—	67.9	0.3	8.3	59.3	62.6	0.8	...	0.9	35.7	Djibouti
55.0	—65.4[2]—		—	34.6[3]	24.1	0.9	9.5[3]	56.9	10.9	0.2	—	32.0	Dominica
734.5	75.7[29]	0.3[29]	—[29]	24.1[29]	4.0[29]	4.5[29]	15.6[29]	19.6	66.8	—	2.0	11.6	Dominican Republic
2,851.4	56.9	0.1	40.4	2.6	0.5	0.3	1.8	16.9	49.2	0.4	2.2	31.4	Ecuador
3,050.0	14.0	0.4	43.8	41.8	5.3	1.2	35.2	39.3	9.4	6.4	2.4	42.4	Egypt
366.6	56.4	0.1	0.5	43.0	10.0	3.0	30.0	21.4	34.8	0.2	2.7	41.0	El Salvador
36.9[4]	—76.5[2, 12]—		0.2[12]	23.3[3, 12]	0.1[12]	0.5[12]	22.7[3, 12]	95.2[4]	0.7[4]	—[4]	—[4]	4.0[4]	Equatorial Guinea
...	...	...	...	...	...	...	...	...	...	...	...	...	Eritrea
2,920.6	—17.4[2]—		5.2	77.4[3]	11.0	11.6	54.8[3]	...	...	94.7[9]	...	5.3	Estonia
297.5	87.7	—	6.9	5.3	2.0	—	3.3	39.0[4]	10.7	5.5[4]	14.7	30.0[4]	Ethiopia
433.6	94.4	—	—	5.6	0.1	5.4	0.1	77.9	7.1	0.4	3.5	11.1	Faeroe Islands

Trade: external (continued)

country	year	imports												
		total value ('000,000 U.S.$)	Standard International Trade Classification (SITC) categories (%)							direction of trade (%)				
			food and agricultural raw materials (0+1+2 −27−28 +4)	mineral ores and concen-trates (27+28 +667)	fuels and other energy (3)	manufactured goods				from European Economic Community (EEC)[b]	from United States	from Eastern Europe[c]	from Japan	from all other[d]
						total[a] (5+6 −667 +7+8 +9)	of which chemicals and related products (5)	of which machinery and transport equipment (7)	of which other[a] (6−667 +8+9)					
Fiji	1991	651.8	——17.4[2]——		15.2	67.4[3]	7.5	22.5	37.4[3]	4.9	4.3	—	11.4	79.4
Finland	1992	21,205.4	9.5	4.0	12.9	73.7	12.2	33.1	28.3	47.2	6.1	10.2	5.5	31.1
France[31]	1992	238,907.6	12.9	1.2	8.6	77.3	11.0	34.9	31.4	59.6	8.4	2.3	4.1	25.6
French Guiana	1992	718.1	18.1	0.2	8.6	73.0	6.8	34.8	31.4	78.0[4]	3.0	0.1	2.6	16.3[4]
French Polynesia	1988	808.3	20.4	0.2	5.4	74.1	6.4	35.9	31.8	65.2	11.3	0.1	4.4	18.9
Gabon	1990	851.0	18.5[29]	1.0[29]	1.8[29]	78.8[29]	7.5[29]	38.5[29]	32.7[29]	69.6	6.4[4]	0.1	4.9	19.0[4]
Gambia, The	1991	219.6	——36.1[2]——		10.1	53.8[3]	7.8	16.1	30.0[3]	46.3[4]	4.1[4]	4.0[4]	4.1[4]	41.6[4]
Gaza Strip	1990	36.5[33]	...	...	...	...	...	...	...	...	...	...	...	...
Georgia	1991[8]	4,159.1	14.6	...	9.6	75.8	9.6	18.4	47.8	...	...	89.6[9]	...	10.4
Germany	1992	408,238.6	12.9	1.6	7.4	78.0	8.6	34.6	34.9	52.0	6.6	5.5	6.0	29.9
Ghana	1990	1,412.3	——8.0[2, 21]——		29.2[21]	62.8[3, 21]	12.5[21]	26.4[21]	23.9[3, 21]	49.7	10.8	0.8	5.5	33.2
Gibraltar	1988	257.9	——24.4[2]——		20.7	54.9[3]	4.3	21.4	29.2[3]	73.4[35]	5.4[35]	...	10.4[35]	10.8[35]
Greece	1991	21,580.1	17.0	1.1	9.6	72.3	10.4	32.9	29.1	60.3	4.3	4.5	6.6	24.3
Greenland	1992	453.1	20.5	0.3	9.9	69.3	4.2	28.7	36.4	81.2	2.5	0.7	3.2	12.4
Grenada	1987	88.7	——31.7[2]——		5.8	62.5[3]	9.5	23.2	29.8[3]	24.6	26.9	—	7.2	41.3
Guadeloupe	1992	1,548.4	22.6	0.2	5.6	71.6	9.5	29.3	32.8	75.1[4]	4.0	0.2	2.6	18.2[4]
Guam	1983	610.7	16.9	0.1	46.9	36.2	2.3	19.1	14.8	...	23.4	...	19.9	56.6
Guatemala	1991	1,851.3	13.7	0.4	16.7	69.1	20.5	25.8	22.8	13.0	42.6	0.3	6.6	37.5
Guernsey[37]	...	...	...	...	...	...	...	...	...	...	...	...	...	...
Guinea	1990	693.0	—12.8[2, 38]—		13.7[38]	73.5[3, 38]	...	17.0[38]	56.5[3, 38]	67.5[4]	8.8[4]	...	3.9[4]	19.8[4]
Guinea-Bissau	1984	38.7	20.1[39]	2.2[39]	6.2[39]	71.5[39]	5.6[39]	36.4[39]	29.5[39]	52.0	8.8	15.2	0.2	23.8
Guyana	1990	511.4	5.6[29]	0.5[29]	43.2[29]	50.7[29]	9.4[29]	23.2[29]	18.1[29]	26.8[4]	35.1[4]	0.8[4]	5.9[4]	31.4[4]
Haiti	1989[6]	313.7	——32.5[2]——		17.7	49.8[3]	9.2	17.0	23.5[3]	19.3[4]	46.9	0.4[4]	6.8	26.6[4]
Honduras	1992	667.8	13.1	1.2	14.2	71.5	21.3	23.7	26.5	7.1	54.2	0.3	4.8	33.6
Hong Kong	1992	126,419.2	8.2	2.2	1.9	87.7	6.9	31.1	49.7	9.3	7.2	0.1	16.9	66.6
Hungary	1991	11,382.1	9.1	1.9[2]	15.5	73.6[3]	12.4	31.0	30.2[3]	41.1	2.6	22.3	2.7	31.2
Iceland	1991	1,739.0	10.9	3.6	8.3	77.2	8.3	34.1	34.8	52.4	10.4	4.1	7.4	25.8
India	1991[1]	23,799.2	7.2	14.2	27.3	51.3	12.9	17.6	20.7	28.3	10.7	5.4	7.5	48.1
Indonesia	1991	25,868.8	10.2	2.7	9.0	78.1	13.3	45.0	19.9	18.2	13.1	0.6	24.5	43.6
Iran	1989[1]	8,113.0	——19.9[2]——		4.2	75.9[3]	18.7	36.8	20.4[3]	46.1[4]	1.0[4]	3.6[4]	10.2	39.1[4]
Iraq	1989	11,730.0[4]	17.6[40]	0.2[40]	0.3[40]	81.9[40]	7.5[40]	39.8[40]	34.6[40]	31.6[4]	11.0[4]	11.9[4]	4.6[4]	40.9[4]
Ireland	1992	22,478.2	13.1	0.7	5.2	81.0	13.0	35.6	32.4	66.5	14.2	0.8	5.0	13.5
Isle of Man[37]	...	...	...	...	...	...	...	...	...	...	...	...	...	...
Israel	1992	20,247.7	9.0	17.1	7.7	66.2	9.6	31.8	24.8	50.2	17.2	0.9	5.3	26.4
Italy[41]	1992	187,527.4	17.3	1.8	10.3	70.6	11.5	31.9	27.2	58.8	5.2	4.1	2.3	29.5
Jamaica	1991	1,700.7	15.4	0.2	19.1	65.3	13.2	23.2	28.9	10.4	52.4	0.3	7.4	29.4
Japan	1992	233,021.4	23.2	5.0	22.6	49.2	7.4	16.9	24.9	13.5	22.6	1.3	—	62.6
Jersey	1980	537.1	23.9	0.4	9.3	66.5	6.5	24.8	35.2	84.9[42]	...	...	...	15.1
Jordan	1992	3,256.5	22.5	0.5	13.7	63.3	11.1	24.5	27.7	29.4	11.1	5.6	6.0	48.0
Kazakhstan	1991	11,295.0	...	...	...	...	...	...	...	...	...	88.0[9]	...	12.0
Kenya	1988	1,986.7	8.7	0.4	14.6	76.3	17.9	38.5	19.9	47.8	5.0	0.7	12.3	34.2
Kiribati	1991	25.9	38.5	0.1	10.9	50.5	5.5	24.8	20.2	1.5	3.6	—	18.4	76.6
Korea, North	1991	2,280.0	...	...	...	...	...	...	...	2.9[5]	—	37.6[5]	9.8	49.7
Korea, South	1992	81,775.3	12.5	3.3	17.9	66.2	9.4	35.4	21.4	11.7	22.4	1.0	23.8	41.1
Kuwait	1989	6,302.2	20.2	0.4	1.0	78.4	7.5	29.5	41.4	29.9	13.2	1.6	12.9	42.4
Kyrgyzstan	1991[8]	3,654.0	——24.3[2]——		10.4	65.3[3]	9.1	22.5	33.7[3]	...	...	84.2[9]	...	15.8
Laos	1989	250.0[4]	32.1[44]	0.2[44]	11.2[44]	56.4[44]	6.1[44]	25.7[44]	24.7[44]	3.2[4]	0.2[4]	50.8[4]	10.7[4]	35.1[4]
Latvia	1991[8]	3,611.3	—16.9[2, 32]—		9.4[32]	73.7[3, 32]	11.6[32]	31.3[32]	30.9[3, 32]	...	...	88.9	...	11.1
Lebanon	1991	3,748.4[4]	—17.3[2, 29]—		3.6[29]	79.1[3, 29]	7.8[29]	29.3[29]	42.0[3, 29]	46.8[4]	4.9[4]	5.6[4, 5]	3.2[4]	39.6[4]
Lesotho	1990	699.3	23.2[45]	0.4[45]	8.7[45]	67.8[45]	7.4[45]	16.7[45]	43.7[45]	2.5	0.2[4]	—[4]	0.1[4]	97.2[4, 46]
Liberia	1984	363.2	25.5	0.9	19.8	53.9	6.7	26.8	20.5	40.0	22.3	1.1	8.1	28.5
Libya	1988	5,879.2	16.3	0.1	0.3	83.3	7.9	38.9	36.5	56.9	1.1	0.9	11.8	29.3
Liechtenstein	1991	626.4	4.2	0.3[2]	1.0	94.5[3]	6.0	29.1	59.3[3]	...	...	...	...	...
Lithuania	1991	4,996.5	——20.7[2]——		16.7	62.5[3]	10.3	22.5	29.7[3]	2.5	1.5	92.6	0.1	3.3
Luxembourg	1991	8,115.0	11.4	——11.9[2]——		76.7[3]	12.6	32.9	31.2[3]	90.6	2.0	...	1.7	5.7
Macau	1991	1,839.3	13.9	0.6	4.4	81.1	5.2	21.0	54.9	8.1	4.6	0.3	17.4	69.6
Macedonia	1990	1,113.4	...	...	19.1	...	...	7.2	...	...	...	...	...	...
Madagascar	1986	373.6	17.0	0.4	23.1	59.5	11.7	28.8	19.0	48.9	10.7	10.0	6.5	23.8
Malaŵi	1988	409.1	9.1[21]	1.3[21]	13.3[21]	76.3[21]	20.2[21]	29.4[21]	26.8[21]	36.3	5.1	0.9	9.1	48.6
Malaysia	1992	39,924.9	7.6	1.5	4.2	86.8	8.1	54.9	23.7	12.5	15.8	0.4	26.0	45.4
Maldives	1990	137.7	——29.7——		15.8	54.6	4.8	21.7	28.0	13.8[4]	0.2[4]	—[4]	6.5[4]	79.5[4]
Mali	1987	374.1	——22.3[2]——		14.8	62.9[3]	15.0	22.1	25.8[3]	48.8	5.0	0.9	3.3	42.0
Malta	1989	1,494.0	13.4	0.6	6.4	79.6	7.0	40.7	31.8	74.0	3.9	2.1	3.1	16.9
Marshall Islands	1988	33.8	45.5	—[2]	10.7	43.7[3]	2.0	10.8	31.0[3]	—	51.3	—	17.6	31.1
Martinique	1992	1,762.8	20.6	0.2	9.2	70.0	9.7	29.2	31.1	75.0	3.0	0.2	2.4	19.4
Mauritania	1990	639.3	30.6[38]	...	7.0[38]	62.4[38]	...	51.0[38]	11.4[38]	40.9	3.8	...	1.4	53.9
Mauritius	1991	1,574.9	15.4	1.8	8.3	74.5	7.1	24.8	42.6	32.7	2.9	0.3	7.2	56.8
Mayotte	1990	60.2	——22.2——		5.2	72.6	9.9	36.4	26.3	68.7[47]	...	...	...	31.3
Mexico	1990	28,066.3	19.7	2.1	4.1	74.1	11.2	36.8	26.0	15.4	64.7	0.5	3.8	15.7
Micronesia	1988	67.7	——42.0[2]——		6.0	52.0[3]	5.2	13.5	33.2[3]	...	36.2	...	22.0	41.8
Moldova	1990[8]	9,887.5	——12.3[2]——		18.9	68.8[3]	10.2	34.4	24.2[3]	...	...	85.5[9]	...	14.5
Monaco[31]	...	...	...	...	...	...	...	...	...	...	...	...	...	...
Mongolia	1990	828.6	10.8[38]	—33.5[19, 38]—		55.7[20, 38]	7.0[38]	30.2[38]	18.5[20, 38]	5.0[5]	—	87.4	1.1	6.6
Morocco	1991	6,870.4	16.2	4.2	14.5	65.2	10.8	29.7	24.7	55.8	5.8	4.3	2.1	32.0
Mozambique	1988	715.0	——37.3[2]——		8.5	54.2[3]	6.5	33.4	14.3[3]	43.2[4]	7.9	13.7[22]	4.0[4]	31.2[4]
Myanmar (Burma)	1991[1]	612.4[48]	——15.1[2]——		5.7	79.2[3]	8.1	49.0	22.1[3]	11.0	...	1.9	16.5	67.4
Namibia	1989	894.0	...	...	27.5[29]	...	...	25.5[29]	...	...	...	...	...	...
Nauru	1989[49]	13.9	——33.7[2]——		0.4	65.9[3]	2.7	22.3	40.9[3]	...	...	...	...	...
Nepal	1990[10]	404.5	17.1	0.5	12.2	70.1	15.6	23.7	30.8	15.3	1.6	2.8	13.7	66.6
Netherlands, The	1992	134,470.0	16.2	1.5	8.6	73.7	10.6	31.6	31.5	63.6	7.6	1.8	3.5	23.4
Netherlands Antilles	1990[50]	2,145.8	——6.3[2]——		70.4	23.3[3]	3.0	9.7	10.6[3]	15.7[4]	21.3[4]	—[4]	3.5[4]	59.5[4]
New Caledonia	1989	763.9	——17.6[2]——		9.2	73.3[3]	6.2	39.5	27.5[3]	44.1[47]	10.4	...	5.3	40.2
New Zealand	1992	9,205.0	8.4	2.4	6.5	82.6	13.1	39.5	30.0	17.9	19.6	0.1	14.7	47.7
Nicaragua	1986	774.5	12.8	0.8	17.9	68.5	18.3	27.3	23.0	23.7	2.7	37.4	2.5	33.7
Niger	1985	344.5	——41.4[2]——		11.1	47.6[3]	8.1	20.5	19.0[3]	42.1	11.4	0.1	3.8	42.6

exports													country
total value ('000,000 U.S.$)	Standard International Trade Classification (SITC) categories (%)							direction of trade (%)					
	food and agricultural raw materials (0+1+2 −27−28 +4)	mineral ores and concentrates (27+28 +667)	fuels and other energy (3)	manufactured goods				to European Economic Community (EEC)[b]	to United States	to Eastern Europe[c]	to Japan	to all other[d]	
				total[a] (5+6 −667 +7+8 +9)	of which chemicals and related products (5)	of which machinery and transport equipment (7)	of which other[a] (6−667 +8+9)						
450.6	—61.1[2,30]—		—[30]	38.9[3,30]	0.7[30]	0.5[30]	37.6[3,30]	26.2	11.3	—	5.7	56.8	Fiji
23,992.4	10.9	0.6	3.3	85.3	6.7	29.1	49.5	53.2	5.9	6.6	1.3	33.0	Finland
231,940.7	17.1	0.8	2.3	79.8	13.6	39.3	26.9	62.7	6.5	2.1	1.8	26.9	France[31]
102.2	52.9	0.1	—	47.1	0.2	22.3	24.6	46.6[4]	1.7	—	—	51.8[4]	French Guiana
74.7	5.9	31.3	—	62.8	1.6	38.6	22.6	40.0	18.9	—	22.5	18.6	French Polynesia
2,460.5	11.7	10.6[2,19]	74.2	3.6[3,20]	1.7	0.2	1.7[3,20]	46.1	29.7	0.4	4.1	19.7	Gabon
42.2	73.4[32]	0.2[2,19,32]	—[32]	26.4[3,20,32]	—[32]	0.7[32]	25.6[3,20,32]	64.9[4]	1.1[4]	—[4]	22.7[4]	11.3[4]	Gambia, The
12.4[34]	...	...	...	...	...	...	...	...	...	...	...	...	Gaza Strip
3,498.6	34.5	...	...	65.5	3.5	13.7	48.3	...	...	98.0[9]	...	2.0	Georgia
429,789.7	6.5	0.8	1.2	91.5	12.6	49.6	29.2	54.4	6.4	5.6	2.2	31.5	Germany
1,072.3	52.1	21.2[2,19]	3.4	23.3[3,20]	0.1	0.3	22.9[3,20]	63.3[4]	13.1[4]	4.4[4]	5.0[4]	14.3[4]	Ghana
82.1	—8.2[2]—		51.5	40.3[3]	2.8	18.1	19.4[3]	22.2	...	...	...	77.8[36]	Gibraltar
8,647.2	33.2	2.5	8.9	55.4	3.9	4.3	47.2	63.5	5.7	5.0	1.0	24.8	Greece
332.8	94.8	—	1.0	4.2	—	1.7	2.5	90.4	2.3	1.0	3.7	2.7	Greenland
31.6	91.3	—	—	8.7	0.4	—	8.3	64.7	4.8	—	—	30.5	Grenada
136.8	76.6	0.5	0.2	22.6	2.7	14.8	5.0	73.7[4]	0.9	—	—	25.4[4]	Guadeloupe
39.2	23.5	2.7	3.5	70.3	5.6	11.5	53.2	...	24.9	...	4.8	70.4	Guam
1,202.2	69.8	0.3	2.0	27.9	11.0	1.5	15.5	11.2	37.8	—	2.8	48.1	Guatemala
...	...	...	...	...	...	...	...	...	...	...	...	...	Guernsey[37]
788.0	6.3	86.5	—	7.2	—	—	7.2	56.4[4]	20.6[4]	...	1.1[4]	22.0[4]	Guinea
18.9	87.1[39]	0.3[39]	—[39]	12.6[39]	0.3[39]	—[39]	12.3[39]	64.4	—	—	—	35.6	Guinea-Bissau
250.6	40.6	29.2[2,19]	—	30.3[3,20]	3.5	6.7	20.1[3,20]	44.2[4]	19.0[4]	1.9[4]	5.8[4]	29.1[4]	Guyana
160.6	—36.3[2]—		—	63.7[3]	...	...	...	38.7[4]	56.2	0.1[4]	1.2	3.7[4]	Haiti
515.7	84.3	2.8	0.5	12.4	2.1	0.3	10.0	30.0	52.5	0.6	2.5	14.4	Honduras
118,665.0	4.9	1.2	0.8	93.0	5.6	27.3	60.1	15.8	23.0	0.4	5.2	55.5	Hong Kong
10,186.9	28.3	2.2[2]	2.9	66.6[3]	12.6	22.1	31.8[3]	45.8	3.2	19.4	1.7	29.9	Hungary
1,571.5	84.0	0.6	—	15.3	0.1	1.0	14.3	66.8	12.6	0.8	7.9	12.0	Iceland
17,940.2	19.5	20.3	2.9	57.2	7.4	7.4	42.4	27.6	14.7	17.7	9.3	30.7	India
29,142.4	16.4	2.9	38.3	42.3	2.9	2.3	37.1	12.8	12.0	0.4	36.9	37.8	Indonesia
11,830.0	—4.2[2]—		91.4	4.5[3]	—	—	4.5[3]	41.5[4]	0.1[4]	13.8[4]	12.8[4]	31.9[4]	Iran
14,520.0[4]	0.5	—	99.5	—	—	—	—	23.2[4]	16.0[4]	16.6[4]	7.5[4]	36.6[4]	Iraq
28,332.5	26.0	1.5	0.6	71.9	19.1	27.0	25.9	74.3	8.2	0.9	2.9	13.6	Ireland
...	...	...	...	...	...	...	...	...	...	...	...	...	Isle of Man[37]
12,967.3	8.7	29.4	0.6	61.4	14.3	27.5	19.6	34.5	30.5	1.6	5.3	28.1	Israel
177,523.9	8.0	0.3	1.9	89.7	7.8	36.8	45.0	57.8	7.0	3.7	1.9	29.7	Italy[41]
1,074.3	21.9	61.3	1.0	15.8	2.2	2.4	11.3	27.1	32.1	2.6	0.8	37.4	Jamaica
339,649.6	1.1	0.2	0.5	98.3	5.6	70.9	21.7	18.5	28.4	0.6	—	52.5	Japan
209.2	27.6	4.3[43]	—	68.0	1.2	31.1	35.7	67.3[42]	...	...	...	32.7	Jersey
1,220.4	15.5	25.8	0.1	58.6	27.0	10.7	21.0	4.9	1.6	1.3	1.5	90.8	Jordan
8,814.0	...	...	...	...	...	...	...	...	...	85.8[9]	...	14.2	Kazakhstan
1,072.5	70.0	3.4	12.7	13.9	2.9	1.9	9.0	47.6	4.9	0.4	1.4	45.7	Kenya
3.2	81.8	8.6	—	9.6	—	—	9.6	17.5	19.8	—	—	62.7	Kiribati
1,240.0	...	...	...	...	...	...	...	7.3[5]	—	45.4[5]	22.9	24.4	Korea, North
76,631.5	4.1	0.2	2.3	93.4	5.8	42.5	45.1	12.1	23.7	1.1	15.1	48.0	Korea, South
11,476.0	0.7	0.2	91.0	8.2	2.4	2.5	3.3	22.7[4]	8.2[4]	1.3[4]	18.5[4]	49.3[4]	Kuwait
3,647.0	—22.1[2]—		3.6	74.3[3]	1.9	33.2	39.1[3]	...	...	99.4[9]	...	0.6	Kyrgyzstan
120.0[4]	46.5[21]	3.4[21]	50.1[21]	—[21]	—[21]	—[21]	—[21]	2.5[4]	0.6[4]	20.0[4]	5.8[4]	71.1[4]	Laos
4,290.2	—26.2[2,32]—		1.8[32]	72.0[3,32]	12.4[32]	27.9[32]	31.7[3,32]	...	...	97.1	...	2.9	Latvia
490.2[4]	—14.4[2,29]—		—[29]	85.6[3,29]	1.1[29]	18.2[29]	66.2[3,29]	22.7[4]	5.3[4]	3.7[4,5]	0.3[4]	68.0[4]	Lebanon
59.0	—28.4[2]—		—	71.6[3]	1.4	0.4	69.8[3]	16.1	12.4	—	—	71.4	Lesotho
449.1	34.1	64.8	—	1.1	0.1	0.3	0.8	70.7	20.2	1.6	1.3	6.1	Liberia
6,683.2	—	—	93.9	6.1	6.1	—	—	86.8	—	1.8	0.1	11.4	Libya
1,200.2	3.9	—[2]	0.2	95.9[3]	8.1	47.3	40.5[3]	45.4	...	...	...	54.6	Liechtenstein
7,040.7	—37.5[2]—		8.6	53.9[3]	4.3	20.0	29.6[3]	2.3	—	95.9	—	1.8	Lithuania
6,277.2	6.6	—1.1[2]—		92.3[3]	17.6	20.2	54.5[3]	82.4	3.3	...	0.7	13.5	Luxembourg
1,655.3	2.2	—	—	97.8	1.2	3.6	93.0	37.6	31.2	0.2	1.8	29.2	Macau
579.2	...	...	...	...	5.4	14.2	...	...	...	...	...	...	Macedonia
316.6	84.6	5.7	2.2	7.5	1.3	1.9	4.4	59.2	14.8	2.6	10.9	12.4	Madagascar
280.0	95.0[21]	—[21]	—[21]	5.0[21]	0.5[21]	—[21]	4.5[21]	49.5	11.3	0.6	11.8	26.8	Malaŵi
40,624.6	20.8	0.6	12.8	65.8	2.1	43.9	19.8	14.9	18.6	0.2	13.3	53.0	Malaysia
52.6	72.2	0.1	—	27.7	—	—	27.7	25.9	24.4	—	8.5	41.3	Maldives
179.0	—69.0[2]—		—	31.0[3]	...	...	...	9.4	—	12.4	1.0	77.2	Mali
858.0	3.6	1.0	1.8	93.6	1.5	49.7	42.5	73.5	5.4	1.7	0.1	19.3	Malta
2.1	100.0	—	—	—	—	—	—	—[29]	79.4[29]	—[29]	—[29]	20.6[29]	Marshall Islands
254.6	64.3	0.4	17.3	18.0	2.1	8.7	7.3	64.6	0.7	—	—	34.7	Martinique
469.1	47.7	48.6[2,19]	1.9	1.6[3,20]	—	0.3	1.3[3,20]	59.7	5.1[4]	...	19.7	15.5[4]	Mauritania
1,231.3	31.1	2.2	0.3	66.5	0.9	1.9	63.7	78.4	11.8	—	0.3	9.5	Mauritius
6.9	17.9[30]	—[30]	—[30]	82.1[30]	81.3[30]	—[30]	0.8[30]	70.2[21,47]	...	...	...	29.8[21]	Mayotte
26,811.7	13.2	2.4	36.8	47.5	6.8	25.1	15.7	12.6	70.3	0.1	5.6	11.5	Mexico
2.3	87.2	—	—	12.8	...	...	...	...	0.3	...	58.2	41.5	Micronesia
5,028.7	—33.3[2]—		4.1	62.6[3]	5.8	35.3	21.5[3]	...	...	91.9[9]	...	8.1	Moldova
...	...	...	...	...	...	...	...	...	...	...	...	...	Monaco[31]
592.6	39.0[38]	—41.7[19,38]—		15.8[20,38]	...	0.1[38]	15.7[20,38]	4.0[5]	0.1	90.7	1.2	4.0	Mongolia
4,286.9	31.0	11.1	2.5	55.5	20.2	5.8	29.4	62.4	2.5	0.7	5.2	29.2	Morocco
103.0	82.4	7.7[2,19]	1.3	8.7[3,20]	0.3	0.8	7.6[3,20]	28.7[5]	15.5	...	16.6	39.2	Mozambique
389.7[48]	—89.0[2]—		0.3	10.7[3]	0.4	—	10.3[3]	2.8	...	—	7.2	90.0	Myanmar (Burma)
1,020.9	11.0	75.9	...	13.1	...	...	...	...	25.0[45]	...	15.0[45]	60.0[45]	Namibia
80.3	—	99.8	—	0.2	—	—	0.2	...	...	...	...	...	Nauru
149.2	6.1	—	—	93.9	0.1	—	93.8	45.5	32.9	2.7	0.5	18.3	Nepal
139,934.3	25.7	1.1	8.6	64.7	14.2	23.7	26.7	71.2	3.7	1.7	0.8	22.6	Netherlands, The
1,792.7	—0.8[2]—		96.3	2.9[3]	1.4	0.6	0.8[3]	16.1[4]	41.1[4]	—[4]	1.3[4]	41.6[4]	Netherlands Antilles
671.6	—[30]	29.9[30]	—[30]	70.1[30]	—[30]	—[30]	70.1[30]	36.4[47]	6.2	...	28.4	29.0	New Caledonia
9,830.0	63.3	0.5	2.5	33.7	5.8	7.5	20.4	16.2	12.3	0.2	14.9	56.3	New Zealand
233.6	94.2	—	—	5.8	2.5	—	3.3	53.6	—	3.7	16.9	25.8	Nicaragua
209.0	—96.5[2]—		—	3.4[3]	0.3	1.4	1.8[3]	72.9	0.1	—	6.0	21.0	Niger

Trade: external (continued)

country	year	imports: total value ('000,000 U.S.$)	SITC categories (%): food and agricultural raw materials (0+1+2−27−28+4)	mineral ores and concentrates (27+28+667)	fuels and other energy (3)	manufactured goods: total[a] (5+6−667+7+8+9)	of which chemicals and related products (5)	of which machinery and transport equipment (7)	of which other[a] (6−667+8+9)	direction of trade (%): from European Economic Community (EEC)[b]	from United States	from Eastern Europe[c]	from Japan	from all other[d]
Nigeria	1987	3,918.7	12.8	2.7	0.4	84.1	16.9	38.2	29.0	56.4	8.3	5.0	9.0	21.3
Northern Mariana Islands	1989	313.7	16.6	—	19.2	64.1	2.8	28.8	32.6	—	24.6	—	15.5	60.0
Norway	1992	25,909.3	8.6	4.8	3.4	83.1	9.4	37.4	36.4	48.8	8.6	2.4	6.3	33.9
Oman	1990	2,681.3	18.9	0.4	4.0	76.8	6.6	36.2	34.0	27.9	9.4	0.2	17.0	45.5
Pakistan	1992	9,573.0	18.8	2.1	16.3	62.8	15.7	34.8	12.3	25.5	10.5	1.2	14.2	48.7
Panama	1991	1,695.0	10.6	0.3	14.9	74.1	14.3	26.4	33.4	7.3	35.8	0.2	6.8	49.9
Papua New Guinea	1988	1,347.1	17.8	0.3	8.4	73.5	7.2	39.6	26.7	7.9	10.4	—	17.8	63.9
Paraguay	1991	1,460.3	11.3	0.6	11.9	76.1	9.4	42.6	24.1	13.8	15.0	0.5	13.1	57.6
Peru	1990	3,469.2	25.4	1.0[2,19]	12.5	61.2[3,20]	14.6	32.8	13.7[3,20]	15.0	27.7	0.5	2.3	54.5
Philippines	1991	12,855.7	10.6	2.5	14.9	71.9	11.2	25.2	35.5	10.4	20.1	0.8	19.5	49.3
Poland	1990	8,160.0	10.8	3.3	21.9	63.9	8.6	37.5	17.9	42.5	1.6	25.2	2.3	28.3
Portugal	1991	26,112.7	16.2	0.7	9.1	74.0	9.2	36.2	28.6	72.0	3.4	0.4	2.9	21.3
Puerto Rico	1988[10]	11,859.1	19.7	0.6	10.7	69.0	15.6	23.7	29.7	6.5	66.8	0.1	4.9	21.7
Qatar	1990	1,694.9	18.0	2.5	0.7	78.8	5.5	44.8	28.5	42.0	9.5	0.3	14.7	33.6
Réunion	1991	2,133.5	19.0	0.2	5.9	74.9	8.6	34.9	31.4	75.1	5.6	—	2.2	17.0
Romania	1990	9,843.4	11.7	——47.6[19]——		40.7[20]	6.3	23.7	10.6[20]	19.6	4.6	35.9	0.8	39.0
Russia	1992[8]	35,000.0	——14.4[2,32]——		7.0[32]	78.7[3,32]	8.0[32]	47.5[32]	23.1[3,32]	10.9[5,32]	1.4[32]	70.5[32]	1.3[32]	15.9[32]
Rwanda	1988	368.8	10.3	0.7	12.9	76.0	2.8	30.1	43.1	45.8	1.4	1.8	14.5	36.4
St. Kitts and Nevis	1988	93.3	21.0	—	5.5	73.5	7.5	32.0	34.0	21.2	47.4	—	3.8	27.5
St. Lucia	1986	154.8	25.7	0.2	7.7	66.5	12.2	19.8	34.5	24.5	34.1	0.1	6.9	34.4
St. Vincent and the Grenadines	1990	136.1	27.4	0.2[2]	6.1	66.4[3]	11.0	21.7	33.7[3]	25.8	36.0	0.1	3.3	34.8
San Marino[41]	...	...	...	...	...	...	...	...	...	...	...	...	...	...
São Tomé and Príncipe	1988	21.7	——35.2——		6.5	58.3	...	30.5	27.8	63.1[4]	31.3[4]	...	1.1[4]	4.5[4]
Saudi Arabia	1990	24,069.0	14.5	0.8	0.2	84.5	9.3	37.4	37.9	34.1	16.7	0.9	15.3	32.9
Senegal	1990	1,620.4	30.5	1.9	16.0	51.7	9.7	21.3	20.7	56.1	5.3	1.2	3.6	33.7
Seychelles	1991	172.5	21.7	0.1	21.9	56.4	6.0	23.1	27.2	31.4	2.5	0.1	5.2	60.7
Sierra Leone	1992	130.5	——40.4[2]——		10.4	49.2[3]	10.9	18.9	19.4[3]	38.5[4]	11.1[4]	0.8[4]	2.3[4]	47.4[4]
Singapore	1992	72,173.7	7.5	0.6	12.8	79.1	7.5	47.9	23.6	12.7	16.5	0.4	21.1	49.4
Slovakia[53]	1990	3,412.7	——13.6[2]——		18.7	67.7[3]	11.3	42.7	13.7[3]	25.9[5]	...	30.3	0.5	43.3
Slovenia	1991	4,141.0	——13.9[2]——		8.7	77.4[3]	15.7	34.6	27.1[3]	57.2[5]	3.5	11.0[5]	2.2	26.2
Solomon Islands	1989	113.1	——18.2[2]——		9.7	72.1[3]	4.3	36.4	31.4[3]	4.6	2.8	0.1	23.2	69.3
Somalia	1990	403.2[4]	30.3[45]	0.2[45]	4.6[45]	64.9[45]	5.1[45]	37.1[45]	22.7[45]	49.2[4]	3.1[4]	—[4]	2.3[4]	45.3[4]
South Africa[54]	1991	18,797.0	9.5	1.1	0.5[55]	88.8[56]	14.3	43.0	31.5[56]	42.2	12.5[4]	—	9.6	35.7[4]
Bophuthatswana[54]	...	...	...	...	...	...	...	...	...	...	...	...	...	...
Ciskei[54]	...	...	...	...	...	...	...	...	...	...	...	...	...	...
Transkei[54]	...	...	...	...	...	...	...	...	...	...	...	...	...	...
Venda[54]	...	...	...	...	...	...	...	...	...	...	...	...	...	...
Spain	1992	106,400.5	14.6	1.8	10.2	73.4	10.2	37.2	26.0	60.7	7.4	1.5	4.6	25.8
Sri Lanka	1991	3,866.1	19.3	2.4	11.2	67.0	9.3	19.3	38.4	14.7	5.0	1.0	11.7	67.5
Sudan, The	1988	1,060.7	——17.2[2]——		20.8	62.0[3]	10.5	26.9	24.6[3]	31.9	8.9	2.4	3.7	53.2
Suriname	1990	472.0	11.8	1.5	18.0	68.7	21.4	24.7	22.6	29.4	41.0	—	2.8	26.8
Swaziland	1990	666.0	18.3	1.0	15.8	64.9	10.0	23.8	31.2	5.0	0.3	...	0.8	94.0[58]
Sweden	1992	49,870.3	9.5	1.4	8.7	80.3	10.6	36.0	33.8	55.4	8.8	3.1	5.1	27.7
Switzerland[59]	1992	65,722.8	8.7	4.8	4.4	82.2	12.8	30.8	38.6	72.2	6.4	1.0	4.3	16.1
Syria	1989	2,097.5	28.8	0.7[2]	5.9	64.6[3]	16.8	17.6	30.2[3]	43.7	7.9	10.2	4.2	34.1
Taiwan	1992	72,132.4	12.4[38]	2.4[38]	7.9[38]	77.2[38]	12.7[38]	32.9[38]	31.6[38]	13.1	21.9	1.3	30.2	33.4
Tajikistan	1990[8]	5,921.4	——15.5[2]——		20.9	63.6[3]	8.6	27.3	27.8[3]	2.7[5]	0.4	92.4	0.3	4.3
Tanzania	1988	1,495.2	10.5	1.8[2]	10.2	77.4[3]	8.8	45.6	23.0[3]	50.4	2.0	0.6	12.5	34.5
Thailand	1991	37,588.3	10.4	5.7	9.2	74.7	9.6	39.7	25.4	14.0	10.6	1.6	29.4	44.5
Togo	1990	581.4	23.6	0.6	8.3	67.5	12.4	22.6	32.6	56.6	5.3	0.6	4.3	33.2
Tonga	1988	55.2	33.3	0.3	9.7	56.7	6.5	21.9	28.3	1.9	7.6	—	7.6	82.9
Trinidad and Tobago	1991	1,667.0	17.0	3.0	14.7	65.3	12.6	26.0	26.8	15.0	39.6	0.5	5.6	39.2
Tunisia	1991	5,189.1	11.6	3.3	8.2	76.8	9.6	30.4	36.8	71.7	4.8	3.4	2.3	17.8
Turkey	1990	22,300.7	12.6	3.2	20.7	63.5	12.8	31.6	19.2	41.9	10.2	8.7	5.0	34.1
Turkmenistan	1990[8]	4,690.6	——17.4[2]——		7.2	75.4[3]	6.9	46.5	22.0[3]	3.3[5]	0.3	92.5	0.3	3.5
Tuvalu	1989	4.1	——38.2[2]——		12.8	49.0[3]	7.1	12.2	29.6[3]	5.4[45]	1.0[45]	—[45]	3.1[45]	90.6[45]
Uganda	1990	463.0[4]	8.7[26]	0.7[26]	29.6[26]	61.0[26]	11.1[26]	26.8[26]	23.0[26]	46.2[4]	6.2[4]	—[4]	5.8[4]	41.8[4]
Ukraine	1991[8]	36,119.1	——9.0[2,32]——		22.3[32]	68.7[3,32]	8.9[32]	37.6[32]	22.2[3,32]	4.4[5,32]	0.5[32]	89.6[32]	0.4[32]	5.2[32]
United Arab Emirates	1987	7,296.8	19.4	1.1	3.9	75.6	7.0	30.3	38.3	33.2	8.0	0.6	17.1	41.2
United Kingdom[37]	1992	222,177.4	13.6	2.6	5.6	78.3	9.2	37.6	31.4	52.2	10.9	1.2	5.9	29.8
United States[62]	1992	553,496.5	7.6	1.7	10.6	80.1	5.2	42.8	32.0	17.5	—	0.4	18.1	64.0
Uruguay	1991	1,552.1	11.4	1.0	15.7	71.9	18.6	30.4	23.0	17.1	9.9	0.7	3.8	68.6
Uzbekistan	1990[8]	21,006.8	——18.3[2]——		21.1	60.6[3]	7.6	30.2	22.9[3]	2.3[5]	0.3	93.4	0.6	3.4
Vanuatu	1989	67.9	——20.8[2]——		8.1	71.0[3]	6.9	31.1	33.1[3]	4.9[38]	—[38]	—[38]	9.4[38]	85.8[38]
Venezuela	1990	6,363.6	15.5	2.9	3.0	78.5	15.9	40.0	22.7	25.9	46.2	0.2	3.9	23.8
Vietnam	1991	2,194.0	——9.4[2]——		22.9	67.8[3]	16.3	26.1	25.4[3]	11.5[4]	0.2[4]	4.4[4]	10.9[4]	73.0[4]
Virgin Islands (U.S.)	1991	3,118.0	...	...	70.2	...	...	...	...	...	45.6	...	...	...
West Bank	1990	62.1[63]	...	...	...	...	...	...	...	...	...	...	...	...
Western Sahara	...	...	...	...	...	...	...	...	...	...	...	...	...	...
Western Samoa	1989	77.0	24.3[29]	0.3[29]	17.5[29]	57.9[29]	7.4[29]	22.9[29]	27.6[29]	8.7[4]	5.6	—[4]	12.8	72.9[4]
Yemen	1990	1,572.3	44.3	0.2[2]	9.0	46.5[3]	7.1	16.3	23.1[3]	32.1	5.5	5.1	4.1	53.2
Yugoslavia	1991	5,548.6	12.4	1.3	19.0	67.4	13.7	22.7	31.0	43.1	4.2	24.5	2.3	26.0
Zaire	1990	886.1	——20.0[60]——		13.8[60]	66.2[60]	4.4[60]	45.5[60]	16.3[60]	59.1[4]	9.8[4]	0.1[4]	2.7[4]	28.3[4]
Zambia	1990	1,298.0	3.7	1.1[2]	15.2	79.9[3]	12.6	47.0	20.3[3]	35.2	10.1	0.2	6.7	47.8
Zimbabwe	1990	1,852.0	6.3	1.2	15.6	77.0	15.5	37.4	24.1	27.5	11.4	0.7	4.6	55.8

[1]Year ending March. [2]Excluding precious stones, etc. (667). [3]Including precious stones, etc. (667). [4]Estimate, sometimes based solely or partly on trading partners' information. [5]Main countries only. [6]Year ending September 30. [7]1981. [8]Approximate figures based on estimates of foreign trade and of trade between the republics constituting the former U.S.S.R. [9]Other republics of the former U.S.S.R. only. [10]Year ending June 30. [11]Figures for Belgium-Luxembourg Economic Union (Luxembourg is also shown separately). [12]1984. [13]Free-on-board valuation (f.o.b.). [14]1990–91 (year ending June 30): imports $106.4, exports $74.1. [15]Includes 82.1% from India (83.4% in 1990–91). [16]Includes 97.5% to India (89.6% in 1990–91). [17]Includes 87.5% from rest of Customs Union of Southern Africa. [18]Includes 76.4% to Switzerland. [19]Including metals. [20]Excluding metals. [21]1985. [22]Former U.S.S.R. only. [23]Rubber only. [24]Includes ships' bunkers and stores. [25]1975. [26]1976. [27]Data refer to former Czechoslovakia. [28]1989. [29]1983. [30]Domestic exports only. [31]Figures for France include Monaco. [32]1990. [33]Excluding imports from Israel ($380.5 million in 1987). [34]Excluding exports to Israel ($143.2 million in 1987). [35]Excluding petroleum products. [36]Includes 51.5% for ships' bunkers. [37]Figures for United Kingdom include Guernsey, Isle of Man, and Jersey (the latter is also shown separately). [38]1988. [39]1980. [40]1986; commercial imports only (excluding oil companies' imports). [41]Figures for Italy include San Marino. [42]United Kingdom only.

country	exports: total value ('000,000 U.S.$)	SITC: food and agricultural raw materials (0+1+2−27−28+4)	SITC: mineral ores and concentrates (27+28+667)	SITC: fuels and other energy (3)	manufactured goods: total[a] (5+6−667+7+8+9)	manufactured goods: of which chemicals and related products (5)	manufactured goods: of which machinery and transport equipment (7)	manufactured goods: of which other[a] (6−667+8+9)	direction of trade (%): to European Economic Community (EEC)[b]	to United States	to Eastern Europe[c]	to Japan	to all other[d]
Nigeria	7,383.4	3.7	—	95.4	0.9	0.2	—	0.7	41.4	47.0	—	0.1	11.5
Northern Mariana Islands	130.5[51]	...	...	...	...	...	...	100.0	—	—	—	—	100.0
Norway	35,190.0	9.7	1.2	50.2	38.8	6.3	14.2	18.4	67.0	5.4	1.4	1.6	24.5
Oman	5,215.0	1.9	0.2	91.4	6.6	0.3	3.6	2.6	3.5[4]	5.6[4]	—[4]	34.2[4]	56.8[4]
Pakistan	7,370.7	19.5	0.3	1.2	79.0	0.5	0.9	77.7	28.1	12.8	0.4	7.7	51.1
Panama	341.8	74.5	0.7	0.3	24.5	6.2	0.6	17.7	26.9	40.6	—	0.8	31.7
Papua New Guinea	1,453.4	28.7	59.2	0.2	11.9	0.2	2.4	9.3	32.1	3.0	0.9	41.2	22.8
Paraguay	737.0	88.6	0.1	0.1	11.3	3.4	0.2	7.7	32.0	4.7	—	0.5	62.7
Peru	3,230.9	26.3	42.6[2, 19]	10.9	20.2[3, 20]	1.8	1.1	17.2[3, 20]	31.3	22.3	3.4	13.4	29.5
Philippines	8,839.5	20.2	3.7	2.4	73.7	3.4	13.9	56.4	18.6	34.7	0.3	19.9	26.5
Poland	13,626.8	15.8	2.6	10.7	70.9	9.1	26.2	35.5	46.7	2.8	22.1	0.8	27.6
Portugal	16,277.8	13.0	2.8	2.6	81.6	4.7	19.6	57.3	75.4	3.8	0.2	0.9	19.7
Puerto Rico	13,952.8	16.9	1.0	2.2	79.9	39.8	19.7	20.4	3.3	88.0	—	0.1	8.5
Qatar	3,641.2	0.2	0.2	81.5	18.2	10.0	2.0	6.2	2.1[4]	1.4[4]	—[4]	53.8[4]	42.6[4]
Réunion	149.8	79.8	0.4	0.2	19.7	2.2	9.2	8.2	79.9	0.1	—	6.1	13.9
Romania	5,869.9	4.9	——33.7[19]——		61.4[20]	6.5	30.8	24.1[20]	31.4	5.8	34.7	1.6	26.5
Russia	38,100.0	——6.5[2, 32]——		35.2[32]	58.3[3, 32]	7.0[32]	32.7[32]	18.6[3, 32]	9.3[5, 32]	0.3[32]	76.9[32]	0.8[32]	12.6[32]
Rwanda	95.6	98.7	0.5	—	0.8	—	—	0.8	89.8[45]	2.6[45]	—[45]	1.0[45]	6.6[45]
St. Kitts and Nevis	27.4	42.0	—	0.9	57.0	0.1	34.2	22.8	22.3	62.3	—	—	15.4
St. Lucia	82.9	75.6	—	0.1	24.4	0.3	4.7	19.3	69.2	12.1	—	—	18.7
St. Vincent and the Grenadines	82.7	76.1	—[2]	—	23.8[3]	1.6	4.7	17.6[3]	54.6	10.4	—	—	35.0
San Marino[41]	...	...	...	...	...	...	...	...	...	...	...	...	...
São Tomé and Príncipe	11.6	100.0	—	—	—	—	—	—	85.2[5]	10.4[4]	...	—[4]	4.4[4]
Saudi Arabia	44,416.3	0.9	0.4	90.3	8.4	5.7	1.1	1.6	17.7	24.0	0.7	19.0	38.6
Senegal	782.6	55.8	9.3	12.4	22.5	14.9	2.4	5.2	53.3	0.1	—	2.0	44.6
Seychelles	48.7	34.1	0.1	60.6	5.2	—	4.0	1.2	28.9	1.2	—	0.1	69.9[52]
Sierra Leone	149.9	3.2	90.4	...	6.4	...	...	...	46.8	30.6	—	—	22.6
Singapore	63,474.2	7.4	0.5	13.1	79.0	6.5	55.1	17.4	14.9	21.1	0.8	7.6	55.6
Slovakia[53]	2,898.7	——18.7[2]——		19.8	61.5[3]	11.1	31.5	18.9[3]	25.6[5]	...	38.0	0.4	35.9
Slovenia	3,860.0	——7.6[2]——		...	92.4[3]	8.3	38.1	46.0[3]	6.1[5]	4.3	13.1[5]	...	21.5
Solomon Islands	74.8	93.9	0.6	—	5.5	—	—	5.5	28.0	0.1	—	33.2	38.6
Somalia	81.0	97.2	1.1[2, 19]	0.2	1.5[3, 20]	—	0.6	0.9[3, 20]	58.9	0.3[4]	—	0.5	40.3[4]
South Africa[54]	24,164.0	11.2	14.5	6.3	68.1[57]	4.3	5.0	58.9[57]	28.2[4]	6.1[4]	0.1[4]	6.3[4]	59.3[4]
Bophuthatswana[54]	...	...	...	...	...	...	...	...	...	...	...	...	...
Ciskei[54]	...	...	...	...	...	...	...	...	...	...	...	...	...
Transkei[54]	...	...	...	...	...	...	...	...	...	...	...	...	...
Venda[54]	...	...	...	...	...	...	...	...	...	...	...	...	...
Spain	69,086.3	16.7	0.8	3.0	79.4	7.8	43.1	28.5	71.1	4.8	1.3	0.9	21.9
Sri Lanka	2,652.7	34.2	7.1	1.5	57.3	1.0	2.9	53.3	27.6	28.5	0.9	5.0	38.1
Sudan, The	509.1	97.2	0.5	—	2.3	—	—	2.3	31.6	3.2	2.6	11.1	51.4
Suriname	472.6	15.7	74.0	1.2	9.0	—	0.3	8.7	36.9	11.4	—	6.8	45.0
Swaziland	566.2	80.9[30]	3.2[30]	0.9[30]	14.9[30]	0.2[30]	2.1[30]	12.6[30]	24.3[30]	6.9[30]	—[30]	0.7[30]	68.0[30]
Sweden	56,018.7	8.5	1.6	3.2	86.7	9.2	42.7	34.8	55.6	8.3	2.5	2.0	31.5
Switzerland[59]	65,678.3	3.7	4.2	0.1	92.0	23.5	30.5	37.9	58.9	8.5	2.0	3.7	26.8
Syria	3,005.8	15.2	1.5	39.2	44.1	11.8	0.5	31.7	31.9	2.4	41.0	0.1	24.6
Taiwan	81,332.9	6.5[38]	0.2[38]	0.6[38]	92.7[38]	3.5[38]	35.2[38]	54.0[38]	15.2	28.9	0.1	10.9	44.9
Tajikistan	3,417.1	——10.5[2]——		6.5	83.1[3]	4.6	12.3	66.2[3]	4.4[5]	0.2	86.5	0.6	8.4
Tanzania	337.1	77.7	2.2	3.0	17.1	1.0	0.7	15.4	45.9	2.6	1.7	4.6	45.2
Thailand	28,420.9	31.5	3.8	1.0	63.7	2.6	24.0	37.2	20.7	21.3	1.9	18.1	38.0
Togo	267.9	44.5	44.6	—	10.9	0.4	0.7	9.8	40.5	1.1	5.9	0.1	52.4
Tonga	8.2	65.8	—	—	34.2	—	2.2	32.0	0.5	16.4	—	4.4	78.6
Trinidad and Tobago	1,985.0	6.0	0.1	65.3	28.7	16.9	0.9	10.8	9.4	50.0	—	1.3	39.4
Tunisia	3,699.6	15.7	1.1	14.3	68.8	14.0	8.1	46.8	76.6	0.7	2.2	0.3	20.3
Turkey	12,959.4	25.5	2.7	2.3	69.6	5.8	6.6	57.2	53.3	7.5	6.4	1.8	31.0
Turkmenistan	4,936.8	——6.6[2]——		61.7	31.6[3]	5.4	1.3	24.9[3]	0.9[5]	—	97.3	0.1	1.7
Tuvalu	0.1[60]	100.0[45]	—	—	—	—	—	—	—	—	—	—	100.0[61]
Uganda	152.1	98.9	0.1	—	1.1	0.1	0.6	0.3	75.9	8.1[4]	0.4	3.3	12.3[4]
Ukraine	29,192.0	——10.6[2, 32]——		6.9[32]	82.4[3, 32]	7.5[32]	46.4[32]	28.5[3, 32]	4.7[5, 32]	0.2[32]	88.4[32]	0.3[32]	6.4[32]
United Arab Emirates	15,948.0[4]	2.0[45]	0.2[45]	89.9[45]	8.0[45]	0.5[45]	2.5[45]	5.0[45]	9.0[4]	4.1[4]	—[4]	31.1[4]	55.8[4]
United Kingdom[37]	191,185.9	9.1	2.3	6.4	82.2	13.8	40.9	27.5	56.0	11.3	1.5	2.1	29.2
United States[62]	447,330.2	14.1	1.5	2.5	81.9	10.1	48.1	23.8	23.0	—	1.2	10.7	65.1
Uruguay	1,573.8	59.0	0.2	—	40.8	6.5	2.4	31.9	24.7	10.1	4.1	1.3	59.9
Uzbekistan	13,165.8	——7.1[2]——		22.8	70.1[3]	8.4	20.4	41.3[3]	2.7[5]	0.1	92.7	0.8	3.7
Vanuatu	22.1	92.1[30]	—[30]	—[30]	7.9[30]	—[30]	—[30]	7.9[30]	57.5[30]	0.1[30]	—[30]	18.4[30]	24.0[30]
Venezuela	17,227.3	2.5	0.8	81.0	15.7	2.1	1.7	11.9	12.8	51.5	0.1	2.8	32.8
Vietnam	1,970.0	——48.9[2]——		35.6	15.5[3]	0.7	0.1	14.7[3]	9.9[4]	—[4]	8.2[4]	30.6[4]	51.4[4]
Virgin Islands (U.S.)	2,518.4	...	...	90.3[60]	...	...	...	...	...	90.0	...	...	...
West Bank	28.4[64]	...	...	...	...	...	...	...	...	...	...	...	...
Western Sahara	...	...	...	...	...	...	...	...	...	...	...	...	...
Western Samoa	12.8	88.4	—	—	11.6	—	—	11.6	27.6	8.1	—	0.4	63.9
Yemen	693.0	9.8	0.4	88.8	1.0	0.1	—	0.9	36.6	37.2	1.0	1.7	23.4
Yugoslavia	4,704.1	15.9	0.6	4.4	79.1	9.1	19.6	50.3	48.6	4.5	29.1	0.2	17.6
Zaire	999.3	13.2	55.2[2, 19]	12.7	18.9[3, 20]	0.1	0.8	18.0[3, 20]	74.6[4]	12.5[4]	—[4]	1.7[4]	11.2[4]
Zambia	1,350.2	5.3[28]	83.4[2, 19, 28]	0.1[28]	11.3[3, 20, 28]	0.1[28]	0.3[28]	10.9[3, 20, 28]	30.5	1.6	—	31.0	36.8
Zimbabwe	1,470.4	51.3	6.9	0.7	41.1	1.7	3.7	35.7	41.1	6.5	0.6	5.5	46.3

[43]Including coins. [44]1974. [45]1986. [46]Includes 94.1% from rest of Customs Union of Southern Africa. [47]France only. [48]Excluding border trade. [49]Based on trade with Australia and New Zealand only. [50]Curaçao and Bonaire only. [51]All reexports. [52]Includes 61.1% for bunkers. [53]Excluding trade with Czech Republic. [54]Figures for South Africa refer to Customs Union of Southern Africa (includes South Africa, Botswana, Lesotho, Namibia, and Swaziland, also shown separately; also Bophuthatswana, Ciskei, Transkei, and Venda). [55]Excluding crude oil. [56]Including crude oil (included in "unclassified goods" accounting in total for 12.3%). [57]Including gold (included in "unclassified goods" accounting in total for 38.7%). [58]Includes 90.1% from South Africa; this includes imports passing through South Africa in transit, which may have had their origin from other countries. [59]Figures for Switzerland include Liechtenstein. [60]1987. [61]All to the South Pacific region in 1985. [62]Figures for United States include American Samoa, Guam, Puerto Rico, and Virgin Islands (U.S.), also shown separately. [63]Excluding imports from Israel ($580.7 million in 1987). [64]Excluding exports to Israel ($160.5 million in 1987).

Trade: domestic

The following table presents data relating to domestic wholesale and retail trade for the countries of the world. The section on wholesale trade is based for the most part on establishments engaged primarily in selling goods to retailers and distributors for resale or to purchasers who buy for business and farm uses. The retail trade section is based on businesses engaged in selling merchandise for personal or household consumption; restaurants are, when possible, included, hotels excluded.

The data presented here are based on information from a variety of country and international sources. The country sources include statistical abstracts, correspondence, annual reports, and censuses of business and trade.

Because there is no single published source or common international methodology for the compilation of data on wholesale and retail trade, nor a single current year on which, by common agreement, the various national reports would be based, allowance must be made for variations in the meaning and recency of the information provided for any single country and for its comparability internationally. Variations occur in part because of the ways in which countries define wholesale and retail trade; the conventional free-enterprise distinction between wholesale and retail activity (of a single enterprise or an entire national trade sector) may not exist in the business practice of some countries. Variations also exist in the kind and level of detail reported. For example, countries may design surveys differently according to the size (number of employees, sales, surface area) of establishments surveyed, their profitability, or other less direct criteria, such as ownership or location. The depth of analysis to which the data are subjected may also vary. The structure of a national trade sector is also affected by the degree of government involvement, which may range from total control of wholesale distribution in some socialist countries to partial involvement in some strategic sectors, or to relative noninvolvement in fully private trade sectors of capitalist countries. In some smaller countries data may refer to a single trading enterprise.

At the table's extreme left, preceding the year to which the trade data refer, the combined value of the country's wholesale and retail trade as a percentage of gross domestic product or net material product is given. Unless otherwise noted, GDP data include restaurants and exclude hotels.

Both the wholesale and retail sections of the table provide similar detail: establishments or outlets, employees, sales, and derived values for relationships among these measures; the retail section provides an additional breakdown of sales by an end-use classification of retail sales outlets.

Although all sales figures are given in U.S. dollars, the comparability of these dollar figures may differ considerably; for instance, the purchasing power of various national currencies in domestic transactions may bear only a distant relationship to the exchange rate of the same currency in international transactions, especially for countries having nonconvertible currencies. The price of goods may also vary, depending on the degree to which they are subject to direct subsidies and artificial cost controls such as tax, investment, or free-trade preferences by a central government seeking to influence social or economic conditions.

The data on distribution of retail sales by kind of consumer goods may have their origin in several different types of data or analysis. One country

Trade: domestic

country	domestic trade as percentage of GDP, 1990	year	wholesale trade					retail trade		
			establishments[a]	employees[b]	sales[c] (U.S.$'000,000)	employees per establishment	sales per establishment (U.S.$'000)	outlets[a]	employees[b]	sales[c] (U.S.$'000,000)
Afghanistan	7.9[1, 2]	1981–82	...	[3]	...	...	...	...	126,100[3]	...
Albania	4.6	1990	...	[3]	...	...	...	11,741[4]	62,000[3]	1,570[4]
Algeria	17.8[5]	1986	...	[3]	...	...	...	3,600[6, 7]	390,990[1, 3, 8]	16,200
American Samoa	...	1990	177	255	...	...	...	583	1,495	...
Andorra	25.2[9]	1988	...	...	...	...	...	592[10]	7,227	...
Angola	6.1[11]	1973	[3]	...	...	...	...	29,138[3]	...	...
Antigua and Barbuda	24.9[1, 12]	1980	25	350	...	14.0	...	199	1,000	23[13]
Argentina	13.0	1974	45,700	275,000[14]	10,922[15]	6.0[14]	...	445,798[16]	930,000[14, 16]	15,540[13]
Armenia	5.6	1990	...	[3]	...	...	...	...	88,100[3]	...
Aruba	37.2[1, 9]	1990	...	723	...	...	...	...	5,700	[17]
Australia	14.2[18]	1990–91	39,319[19]	361,000[14, 19]	...	9.2[14, 19]	...	160,160[20]	928,500[14, 20]	114,195
Austria	16.4[1]	1991	17,149[5]	191,000	78,920	10.2[5]	3,526[5]	33,601[5]	253,000	38,712
Azerbaijan	2.2[11]	...	...	...	...	...	...	...	...	...
Bahamas, The[21]	26.2[1, 20]	1980	23	1,066	143	46.3	6,235	132	4,059	460[20]
Bahrain	10.2[1, 5]	1983	[3]	[3]	...	[3]	...	255[3]	12,551[3]	1,601
Bangladesh	8.4[1, 2]	1985	...	[3]	...	...	...	271,000	3,610,000[3]	5,500[20]
Barbados	26.3[1, 11]	1990	...	[3]	...	...	...	1,911[22]	20,800[3]	264[13]
Belarus	5.5	1990	...	[3]	...	...	...	...	382,000[3]	...
Belgium	17.3[1, 12]	1984	60,589	160,600	65,110	2.6	1,075	135,534	193,500	20,957
Belize	16.5[1]	1983	...	[3]	...	...	...	...	4,558[3]	33[20]
Benin	19.5[1, 5]	1979	...	...	...	...	...	170[6]	1,910[14, 20]	150[13]
Bermuda	32.8[23]	1985	60[23]	820	...	...	...	310[6, 23]	4,342[14]	116[16, 24]
Bhutan	6.3[1, 5]	1982	...	[3]	...	...	...	...	9,000[3, 4, 14]	...
Bolivia	12.9	1989	...	[3]	...	...	...	...	244,907[3, 4]	1,570[20]
Bosnia and Herzegovina	13.9[5]	1990	...	[3]	18,469[5]	...	...	...	130,914[3]	18,065[5]
Botswana	14.2[18]	1983–84	205	3,500	494[13]	...	...	1,660	10,700	165[13]
Brazil	7.2	1985	44,994	498,280	51,475	11.1	1,144	674,695	3,088,751	65,264
Brunei	12.4[1, 12]	1986	[3]	[3]	...	[3]	...	833[3, 25]	4,261[3, 25]	...
Bulgaria	10.5[1, 26]	1987	...	7,700[27]	...	...	...	41,339[16]	79,820[16]	34,700[16]
Burkina Faso	15.2[5]	1975	...	[3]	...	...	...	...	19,354[3, 14]	...
Burundi	9.1[11]	1986	...	...	...	...	...	...	...	210
Cambodia	...	...	...	...	...	...	...	...	...	...
Cameroon	25.1[1, 5]	1980	...	...	...	...	...	1,312[6]	13,776[14, 20]	1,430[20]
Canada	11.5	1989	...	[3]	169,270[20]	...	...	...	2,428,000[3, 28]	158,920
Cape Verde	28.4[5]	1980	...	[3]	...	...	...	...	3,930[3]	...
Central African Republic	26.4[5]	1989	113	302	...	2.7	...	14,543	23,078	230
Chad	29.5[5]	1983	...	[3]	[3]	...	...	...	1,661[3, 6, 29]	497[3]
Chile	18.1	1983	561[6]	15,300[6]	2,312[6]	27.2[6]	4,121[6]	1,125[16, 20]	21,700[16, 20]	1,403[16, 20]
China	6.4	1991	99,000[5]	1,550,000[14]	...	15.6[14]	...	9,241,000	21,987,000	154,895
Colombia	14.1	1985	...	...	...	...	...	1,110[32]	49,000[32]	8,600[20]
Comoros	12.2[1, 33]	1980	...	[3]	...	...	...	...	1,873[3, 6]	...
Congo	14.4[5]	1984	...	[3]	...	...	...	...	13,240[3]	...
Costa Rica	20.0	1975	332[34]	4,073[34]	35[34]	12.3[34]	104[34]	9,713	26,486	475[35]
Côte d'Ivoire	12.9[5]	1981	...	...	...	...	...	2,023[6]	16,720[6]	1,800[20]
Croatia	3.7	1989	...	...	38,117	...	...	19,882	83,737	39,231
Cuba	20.1[5, 26]	1989	...	...	15,174	...	...	56,916[27]	230,000[8, 14]	8,124
Cyprus	21.3[1]	1989	1,559[24]	13,308	74	5.3[24]	720[24]	8,474[24]	34,112	173
Czech Republic[36]	12.1[10]	1990	63,110[27]	251,000[27]	40,083[27]	4.0[27]	635[27]	62,667[5]	258,127	21,235
Denmark	13.6[11]	1991	22,230	177,106	72,601	8.0	3,266	36,750	211,085	29,872
Djibouti	10.8[20]	1985	28	371[9]	...	...	...	431	1,877[9]	...
Dominica	13.2[1, 11]	1989	...	[3]	...	...	...	...	3,700[3]	790[20]
Dominican Republic	14.3	1983	670	...	3,136	...	4,681	11,220[9]	...	1,259[9]
Ecuador	14.8	1983	402	15,900	1,396	39.6	3,473	501	17,400	2,550[20]
Egypt	24.6[1, 37]	1983–84	2,552	45,500[14]	4,492	18.0[14]	1,760	2,545	55,800[14]	29,700[20]
El Salvador	34.8[1]	1983	396	6,400	1,038	16.2	2,621	1,416	10,700	485

may aggregate sales data by kind of establishment only (this may be perfectly satisfactory in a country of small, independent outlets); another may aggregate data directly by kind of goods (most easily done in a country with well-developed statistical, tax-reporting, and commercial systems). Other countries may find it impolitic to publish data that reflect the poverty of their distribution network or their supply of consumer goods and may aggregate or publish data for only a few sectors: food or nonfood goods, for example. For countries with only a few trading enterprises in a particular sector, detail must often be withheld to preserve the confidentiality of individual businesses.

The notes that follow further define the column headings.

a. The number of establishments or outlets refers to economic units that operate at a single physical location in one principal kind of activity, whether singly owned or part of a multiunit firm. Such units are not necessarily identical with a company or enterprise.
b. Number of employees refers to full-time and part-time paid workers, including salaried managers and officers; it usually excludes owner-operators, partners, vendors, and unpaid relatives.
c. Total sales (also called turnover) includes the value of merchandise sold for cash or credit; amounts received from customers for layaway purchases; receipts from rental or leasing of vehicles, equipment, tools, instruments, etc.; receipts for delivery, installation, maintenance, repair, alteration, storage, and other services.
d. Outlets engaged primarily in the sale of food and nonalcoholic beverages, such as grocery stores, meat and fish markets, and bakeries.
e. Outlets engaged primarily in the sale of clothing and shoes; also includes outlets that sell accessory items, such as millinery, furs, and leather goods.
f. Outlets engaged primarily in the sale of home furnishings, including furniture, draperies, floor coverings, household appliances, and home entertainment equipment.
g. Outlets that primarily serve food and drink, including restaurants, lunchrooms, cafeterias, social caterers, refreshment places, contract feeders, ice cream parlors, and bars and taverns.
h. Outlets engaged primarily in the sale of pharmaceuticals, cosmetics, and perfumes.
i. Outlets engaged primarily in the sale of building materials, hardware, garden supplies, paint, electrical supplies, and farm equipment.
j. Outlets engaged primarily in the sale of motor vehicles, motorcycles, bicycles, and tires, batteries, and other automotive supplies and parts; includes service stations.
k. Outlets engaged in the sale of multiple lines of merchandise, such as department stores, variety stores, and rural general stores.
l. Miscellaneous specialized outlets such as those engaged primarily in the sale of liquors, sporting goods, books, jewelry, photographic and optical goods, gifts, flowers, tobacco products, home fuels, and newspapers.

retail trade (continued)												country
percentage breakdown of sales									employees per outlet	sales per outlet (U.S.$'000)	population per outlet	
food[d]	clothing, shoes[e]	home furnishings[f]	eating, drinking[g]	drugs, pharma-ceuticals[h]	building materials[i]	automobile parts[j]	general merchandise[k]	other[l]				
...	...	...	...	...	...	...	...	...	...	...	...	Afghanistan
62.4				37.6					...	134[4]	277[4]	Albania
...	...	...	...	...	...	...	...	...	5.0[6, 7]	...	5,146[6, 7]	Algeria
...	...	...	...	...	...	...	...	...	...	...	81	American Samoa
...	...	...	...	...	...	...	...	...	3.8[10]	...	39[10]	Andorra
...	...	...	...	...	...	...	...	...	...	...	...	Angola
...	...	...	...	...	...	...	...	...	5.0	100	378	Antigua and Barbuda
...	...	...	...	...	...	...	...	...	2.1[14, 16]	...	58[16]	Argentina
...	...	...	...	...	...	...	...	...	...	...	...	Armenia
...	...	...	...	...	...	...	...	...	...	...	...	Aruba
37.8	8.6	2.9	4.8	4.2	5.8	...	10.9	25.0	5.8[14, 20]	387[20]	100[20]	Australia
33.9[12]	13.5[12]	5.7[12]	...	5.2[12]	...	18.7[12]	8.5[12]	14.5[12]	7.1[5]	857[5]	227[5]	Austria
...	...	...	...	...	...	...	...	...	...	...	...	Azerbaijan
24.4[9]	7.7[9]	7.1[9]	—	3.7[9]	8.4[9]	30.1[9]	7.6[9]	11.0[9]	30.8	1,881	1,026	Bahamas, The[21]
...	...	...	...	...	...	...	...	...	49.2[3]	...	1,507[3]	Bahrain
...	...	...	...	...	...	...	...	...	...	...	...	Bangladesh
...	...	...	...	...	...	...	...	...	...	...	130[22]	Barbados
...	...	...	...	...	...	...	...	...	...	...	...	Belarus
35.1				64.9					1.4	155	73	Belgium
...	...	...	...	...	...	...	...	...	...	...	...	Belize
...	...	...	...	...	...	...	...	...	11.3[14, 20]	...	19,871[20]	Benin
...	...	...	...	...	...	...	...	...	11.0[13, 16]	...	178[6, 23]	Bermuda
...	...	...	...	...	...	...	...	...	...	...	...	Bhutan
...	...	...	...	...	...	...	...	...	...	...	...	Bolivia
...	...	...	...	...	...	...	...	...	...	...	...	Bosnia and Herzegovina
...	...	...	...	...	...	...	...	...	6.4	99.4	604	Botswana
14.8	10.7	6.3	...	4.8	12.8	29.5	17.7	3.6	4.6	98	201	Brazil
...	...	...	...	...	...	...	...	...	5.1[3, 25]	...	279[3, 25]	Brunei
50.9	10.9	3.4	...	5.9	...	...	0.2	28.7	1.9[16]	839[16]	217[16]	Bulgaria
...	...	...	...	...	...	...	...	...	...	...	...	Burkina Faso
...	...	...	...	...	...	...	...	...	...	...	...	Burundi
...	...	...	...	...	...	...	...	...	...	...	...	Cambodia
...	...	...	...	...	...	...	...	...	10.5[6, 14]	...	6,481[6]	Cameroon
23.7	6.3	6.1	...	4.5	...	36.2	10.9	12.3	...	...	...	Canada
...	...	...	...	...	...	...	...	...	...	...	...	Cape Verde
...	...	...	...	...	...	...	...	...	1.6	16	187	Central African Republic
...	...	...	...	...	...	...	...	...	...	...	...	Chad
28.3[9]	[30]	5.0[9]	1.6[9]	5.4[9]	4.7[9]	18.0[9]	17.1[9, 30]	19.9[9]	19.3[16, 20]	1,247[16, 20]	10,210[16, 20]	Chile
55.0	16.4	...	...	4.3	[31]	3.1	13.6[31]	7.6	2.4[14, 16]	17[16]	124[16]	China
...	...	...	...	...	...	...	...	...	44.1[32]	1,522[32]	...	Colombia
...	...	...	...	...	...	...	...	...	...	...	...	Comoros
...	...	...	...	...	...	...	...	...	...	...	...	Congo
37.7	13.5	6.9	...	8.2	7.0	15.1	5.9	5.7	2.7	59	202	Costa Rica
...	...	...	...	...	...	...	...	...	8.3[6]	...	4,257[6]	Côte d'Ivoire
23.0	5.5	2.0	...	...	6.8	17.9	34.6	10.2	4.2	1,973	235	Croatia
35.8	17.2	9.9	...	5.3	0.8	5.1	...	25.9	4.0[8, 14]	184[27]	177[27]	Cuba
9.8	7.6	2.2	46.2	1.6	3.5	11.2	6.4	11.5	1.0[24]	124[24]	77[24]	Cyprus
42.9	15.1	12.8	...	3.6	2.9	10.0	...	12.7	4.2[5]	362[5]	249[5]	Czech Republic[36]
49.8	8.1	3.6	...	3.1	2.6	18.2	1.4	13.2	5.7	813	140	Denmark
...	...	...	...	...	...	...	...	...	...	...	998	Djibouti
...	...	...	...	...	...	...	...	...	...	...	...	Dominica
...	...	...	...	...	...	...	...	...	...	112[9]	519[9]	Dominican Republic
24.2[35]	29.1[35]	8.1[35]	3.0[35]	4.8[35]	4.0[35]	17.8[35]	3.4[35]	5.6[35]	34.7	2,131	79	Ecuador
...	...	...	...	...	...	...	...	...	21.9[14]	1,278	17,756	Egypt
11.9[7, 38]	7.6[7, 38]	16.2[7, 38]	...	7.9[7, 38]	6.3[7, 38]	12.4[7, 38]	28.2[7, 38]	9.5[7, 38]	7.6	342	3,336	El Salvador

Trade: domestic (continued)

country	domestic trade as percentage of GDP, 1990	year	wholesale trade					retail trade		
			establishments[a]	employees[b]	sales[c] (U.S.$'000,000)	employees per establishment	sales per establishment (U.S.$'000)	outlets[a]	employees[b]	sales[c] (U.S.$'000,000)
Equatorial Guinea	8.4[5]	1983	...	36	...	...	...	...	2,701	...
Eritrea[39]	...	...	...	...	...	...	...	...	...	...
Estonia	6.2[5]	1990	...	...	...	...	...	...	70,000	...
Ethiopia[39]	9.6[1, 2]	1984	375[6, 40]	3,200[6, 40]	...	8.5[6, 40]	...	7,416[6, 40]	17,100[6, 40]	273
Faeroe Islands	16.0[12]	1987	78	[3]	19	...	241	430	1,484[1, 3, 35]	38
Fiji	22.8[1, 5]	1988	181	2,289	228	12.6	1,259	660	5,472	271
Finland	11.3[1]	1991	10,001[24]	82,719[24]	46,378	8.3[24]	2,622[24]	39,969[28]	162,621[28]	36,556
France	15.2[11]	1989	192,080	1,105,679	317,219[12]	5.8	1,800[12]	552,945	1,274,477	295,850
French Guiana	17.3[24]	1991	[3]	[3]	...	...	...	1,714	2,737[3, 20]	...
French Polynesia	22.7	1986	[3]	[3]	...	...	...	947[3]	5,038[3]	...
Gabon	12.1[1]	1982	...	[3]	...	...	...	...	12,683[3, 14, 23]	...
Gambia, The	37.0[18]	1983	...	[3]	...	...	...	...	16,551[3]	...
Gaza Strip	...	1986	...	[3]	...	...	...	...	13,400[3]	...
Georgia	5.6	1988	...	[3]	...	...	...	...	172,400[3]	...
Germany[41]	8.7	1989	41,909[20]	1,017,900	458,038	23.6[14, 20]	8,715[20]	168,230[20]	2,251,000	294,579
Ghana	19.0	1983	460[42]	1,100[42]	115[42]	2.4[42]	250[42]	1,500	16,000	252[20]
Gibraltar	...	1991	...	737	...	...	...	...	1,835	...
Greece	12.8[1, 5]	1984	23,218	73,812	...	3.2	...	184,892	301,318	12,263[43]
Greenland	8.0[22]	1991	...	[3]	132	...	...	...	2,214[3, 8]	218
Grenada	20.2[1]	1988	...	[3]	[3]	...	...	...	5,421[3]	6[3, 13]
Guadeloupe	17.0[1, 9]	1989	661[28]	...	...	...	...	3,326	12,866	810
Guam	51.5[9]	1987	94	1,392	245	14.8	1,274	804	7,344	786
Guatemala	24.4	1989	...	[3]	...	...	...	88,200[9]	374,690[3]	1,200[20]
Guernsey	...	1991	...	642	...	...	...	...	2,573	...
Guinea	21.9	1979	...	[3]	...	...	...	...	12,808[3, 42]	...
Guinea-Bissau	27.5[1, 5]	1979	[3]	[3]	...	...	...	685[3, 42]	5,085[3]	44[3, 25]
Guyana	8.6[11]	1980	...	[3]	...	...	...	147[6]	14,690[3]	93[13]
Haiti	17.1[2]	1983	...	[3]	...	...	...	653[6, 33]	303,353[3]	500[20]
Honduras	13.4	1991	...	[3]	...	...	...	...	156,500[3]	401[13]
Hong Kong	22.8	1990	18,240	79,381	15,955	4.4	875	62,539	309,434	25,509
Hungary	12.6	1991	206[9]	122,600[9]	13,121[23]	595[23]	...	153,689	652,300	13,833
Iceland	11.4	1988	1,509[13, 44]	5,132[23]	598[35, 44]	...	...	1,892[44]	9,162[44, 45]	1,502[44]
India	12.5[37]	1980	[3]	[3]	...	...	...	3,132,000[3, 16]	3,615,000[3, 16]	108,300[13]
Indonesia	16.2	1980	[3]	[3]	[3]	[3]	[3]	54,632[3]	85,400[3]	3,451[3]
Iran	28.9[1, 18]	1972–73	18,210	31,688	2,429	1.7	133	218,132	80,055	37,350[20]
Iraq	16.1[1]	1975–76	1,532[25]	2,700[25]	...	1.8[25]	...	77,766[25]	106,800[25]	11,378[13]
Ireland	11.2[1, 8]	1988	3,972	39,101	11,420	9.8	2,875	31,699	89,680	10,952
Isle of Man	12.0[13]	1981	...	775	...	...	...	...	3,146	...
Israel	11.6[1, 5]	1988	17,967	67,300	16,875	3.8	939	43,844	103,100	10,763
Italy	18.7[1]	1983	...	[3]	...	...	...	1,033,725	1,369,200[3]	122,978
Jamaica	21.7[1]	1991	...	[3]	...	...	...	10,150[35]	173,500[3]	1,457[13]
Japan	13.8	1991	475,967	4,773,000[14]	3,209,473	9.4[14]	6,743	1,591,186[16]	6,936,000[14, 16]	1,043,976[16]
Jersey	...	1986	...	855	...	...	...	...	7,046	...
Jordan	9.0[5]	1989	390	2,895	278	7.4	713	32,470	124,929	2,065
Kazakhstan	4.6	1991	...	...	...	...	...	42,168	484,800	...
Kenya	9.5	1985	3,079[8]	27,481	...	13.6	...	5,033[7]	34,628	1,085[13]
Kiribati	13.5[5]	1987	...	[3]	...	...	...	30	1,127[3, 27]	3.8
Korea, North	...	...	...	...	...	...	...	...	...	...
Korea, South	11.3	1990	90,621	502,476	70,389	5.5	777	1,040,490[1]	2,356,800[1]	76,057[1]
Kuwait	8.9[5]	1987	3,124[20]	25,829[20]	3,861	8.3[20]	1,160[20]	14,190	64,429	7,078
Kyrgyzstan	...	1988	...	[3]	...	...	...	...	92,900[3]	...
Laos	10.3[5]	1990	...	...	...	...	...	15,000	...	576
Latvia	13.6	1991	...	...	...	...	...	7,214	95,300	...
Lebanon	34.2[8]	1986	...	[3]	...	...	...	...	114,706[3]	1,662[13]
Lesotho	7.0	...	...	...	...	...	...	...	...	...
Liberia	19.1[1, 5]	1984	...	[3]	...	...	...	...	46,850[3]	115[20]
Libya	6.8[5]	1973	1,126	4,148[14]	...	3.7[14]	...	26,825	44,605[14]	9,205[13]
Liechtenstein	...	1975	67	216	...	3.2	...	228	740	...
Lithuania	...	1991	...	[3]	...	...	...	...	188,600[3]	...
Luxembourg	16.4	1990	1,468	9,616	5,259	6.6	3,582	3,721	16,099	4,191
Macau	...	1991	...	[3]	...	...	...	...	47,706[3]	...
Macedonia	14.4[5]	1990	...	[3]	9,522[5]	...	...	...	65,593[5]	9,238[5]
Madagascar	13.0[5]	1976	1,104	...	...	...	...	1,570	...	696[23]
Malaŵi	10.9[11]	1984	439	23,000	522	52	1,189	500	8,600	127
Malaysia	11.0	1980	19,663	116,200	15,461	5.9	786	95,993	73,000	8,200[20]
Maldives	17.5[1]	1990	...	[3]	...	...	...	...	8,884[3]	5[20]
Mali	15.5[1, 11]	1979	...	[3]	...	...	...	...	5,200[3]	...
Malta	14.4[1]	1983	3	[3]	1.0	...	333	4[20]	11,936[3, 6]	2.3
Marshall Islands	83.7[1, 23]	1988	...	[3]	...	...	...	...	1,394[3]	...
Martinique	19.4[1, 24]	1991	740	[3]	...	...	...	5,489	12,399[3, 20]	234[13]
Mauritania	19.1[1, 5]	1971[6]	23	100	102	4.3	4,445	59	700	103
Mauritius	17.9[1, 11]	1986	[3]	[3]	...	[3]	...	207[1, 3, 6]	10,107[1, 3, 6]	164[1, 3, 6]
Mayotte	...	1983	[3]	[3]	[3]	...	[3]	41[3]	597[3, 8]	27[3]
Mexico	11.0	1988	36,512	[3]	23,506	...	644	713,315	3,875,100[3, 28]	39,810
Micronesia	11.9[13]	1980	...	348[14]	...	...	...	...	489[1, 14]	...
Moldova	9.2	1990	...	[3]	...	...	...	...	148,000[3]	...
Monaco	...	1975	...	273	...	...	...	...	1,439	...
Mongolia	21.7[5]	1983[3, 49]	...	...	...	...	...	4,828	21,100	1,235[27]
Morocco	19.9	1972	...	...	...	...	...	4,000[6]	20,000[6]	5,750[20]
Mozambique	...	1980	...	[3]	...	...	...	...	63,058[3]	...
Myanmar (Burma)	20.6[18]	1983	...	[3]	...	...	...	...	1,405,000[2, 3]	2,116
Namibia	12.4	1977	222	5,035	377	22.7	1,698	1,248	7,569	254
Nauru	...	...	...	...	...	...	...	...	...	...
Nepal	4.8[1, 2]	1983	...	[3]	...	...	...	...	119,000[3, 14, 23]	736
Netherlands, The	16.0[11]	1990	45,600	285,300[8]	171,300	7.1[8]	3,756	81,700	372,700[8]	58,339

retail trade (continued)

percentage breakdown of sales									employees per outlet	sales per outlet (U.S.$'000)	population per outlet	country
food[d]	clothing, shoes[e]	home furnishings[f]	eating, drinking[g]	drugs, pharma-ceuticals[h]	building materials[i]	automobile parts[j]	general merchandise[k]	other[l]				
...	...	...	...	...	...	...	...	...	...	...	...	Equatorial Guinea
...	...	...	...	...	...	...	...	...	...	...	...	Eritrea[39]
...	...	...	...	...	...	...	...	...	...	...	...	Estonia
15.9	45.2	...	...	...	7.9	9.8	10.5	10.7	2.3[6, 40]	27[6, 40]	55,200[6, 40]	Ethiopia[39]
...	...	...	...	...	...	...	...	...	...	89	109	Faeroe Islands
13.8	9.9	5.3	7.6	3.4	11.3	9.7	37.6	1.4	8.3	410	1,089	Fiji
32.9	5.5	1.6	...	3.2	8.1	21.9	13.6	13.2	4.1[28]	1,002[28]	125[28]	Finland
35.6	14.3	15.6	...	4.8	...	15.2	7.7	6.8	2.3	535	109	France
...	...	...	...	...	...	...	...	...	...	...	156	French Guiana
...	...	...	...	...	...	...	...	...	5.3[3]	...	188[3]	French Polynesia
50.5	9.6	...	...	...	33.8	6.1	...	...	...	...	...	Gabon
...	...	...	...	...	...	...	...	...	...	...	...	Gambia, The
...	...	...	...	...	...	...	...	...	...	...	...	Gaza Strip
...	...	...	...	...	...	...	...	...	...	...	...	Georgia
28.5	12.6	7.2	...	7.1	...	17.4	21.9	5.3	12.5[14, 20]	1,322[20]	363[20]	Germany[41]
...	...	...	...	...	...	...	...	...	1.1	108[42]	7,993	Ghana
...	...	...	...	...	...	...	...	...	...	...	...	Gibraltar
60.0[43]	18.1[43]	9.5[43]	...	...	...	...	...	12.4[43]	1.6	...	54	Greece
...	...	...	...	...	...	...	...	...	...	...	...	Greenland
...	...	...	...	...	...	...	...	...	...	...	...	Grenada
...	...	...	...	...	...	...	...	...	...	...	...	Guadeloupe
11.6	10.9	4.9	8.0	0.3	5.2	26.9	3.3	28.9	9.1	978	147	Guam
...	...	...	...	...	...	...	...	...	...	...	83[9]	Guatemala
...	...	...	...	...	...	...	...	...	...	...	...	Guernsey
...	...	...	...	...	...	...	...	...	...	...	...	Guinea
...	...	...	...	...	...	...	...	...	0.8[3, 42]	...	1,080[3, 42]	Guinea-Bissau
9.7	18.9	13.8	4.5	2.8	17.7	18.6	...	14.0	...	743	5,884	Guyana
...	...	...	...	...	...	...	...	...	...	...	7,034[6, 33]	Haiti
...	...	...	...	...	...	...	...	...	...	...	...	Honduras
16.7	10.0	...	21.1	...	...	8.5	...	43.7	4.9	408	91	Hong Kong
28.3	8.2	...	11.6	3.1	16.2	17.0	4.5	11.1	4.2	90	67	Hungary
24.6[42]	8.8[42]	10.1[42]	—	5.6[42]	—	—	31.1[42]	19.8[42]	4.8[44, 45]	794[44]	132[44]	Iceland
...	...	...	...	...	...	...	...	...	1.2[3, 16]	...	219[3, 16]	India
...	...	...	...	...	...	...	...	...	1.6[3]	63[3]	2,681[3]	Indonesia
...	...	...	...	...	...	...	...	...	0.4	...	141	Iran
...	...	...	...	...	...	...	...	...	1.4[25]	...	148[25]	Iraq
40.6	9.1	1.4	10.4	2.9	5.1	21.6	2.8	6.1	2.8	345	112	Ireland
...	...	...	...	...	...	...	...	...	...	...	...	Isle of Man
35.4	12.2	20.0	...	...	...	...	6.2	26.2	2.4	245	103	Israel
50.8	15.1	...	...	3.4	...	...	...	30.7	...	119	55	Italy
...	...	...	...	...	...	...	...	...	...	...	214[35]	Jamaica
29.5	10.6	8.5	—	2.8	...	13.5	14.1	21.0	4.4[14, 16]	656[16]	77.9[16]	Japan
...	...	...	...	...	...	...	...	...	...	...	...	Jersey
21.7	10.2	13.2	...	3.4	11.1	23.3	12.0	5.1	3.8	63	94	Jordan
...	...	...	...	...	...	...	...	...	11.5	...	400	Kazakhstan
...	...	...	...	...	...	...	...	...	7.0	...	4,057[8]	Kenya
...	...	...	...	...	...	...	...	...	...	127	2,226	Kiribati
...	...	...	...	...	...	...	...	...	...	...	...	Korea, North
29.4[22, 46]	13.1[22]	8.9[22]	18.9[22]	5.0[22]	2.4[22]	5.4[22]	1.2[22]	15.6[22]	2.3[1]	73[1]	41[1]	Korea, South
8.2	11.7	16.8	...	1.8	6.5	26.9	15.2	12.9	4.5	499	128	Kuwait
...	...	...	...	...	...	...	...	...	...	...	...	Kyrgyzstan
...	...	...	...	...	...	...	...	...	...	38	278	Laos
...	...	...	...	...	...	...	...	...	...	...	...	Latvia
...	...	...	...	...	...	...	...	...	...	...	...	Lebanon
...	...	...	...	...	...	...	...	...	...	...	...	Lesotho
...	...	...	...	...	...	...	...	...	...	...	...	Liberia
...	...	...	...	...	...	...	...	...	1.7[14]	...	84	Libya
...	...	...	...	...	...	...	...	...	3.2	...	105	Liechtenstein
...	...	...	...	...	...	...	...	...	...	...	...	Lithuania
28.5[46]	11.7	11.5	...	4.2	...	37.1	...	7.0	4.3	1,126	103	Luxembourg
...	...	...	...	...	...	...	...	...	...	...	...	Macau
...	...	...	...	...	...	...	...	...	...	...	...	Macedonia
...	...	...	...	...	...	...	...	...	...	...	4,977	Madagascar
...	...	...	...	...	...	...	...	...	17.2	254	14,196	Malaŵi
32.9[47]	7.3[47]	10.8[47]	...	2.5[47]	1.1[47]	33.3[47, 48]	4.4[47]	7.7[47]	0.8	64	143	Malaysia
...	...	...	...	...	...	...	...	...	...	...	...	Maldives
...	...	...	...	...	...	...	...	...	...	...	...	Mali
...	...	...	...	...	...	...	...	...	...	578[6]	83,378[6]	Malta
...	...	...	...	...	...	...	...	...	...	...	...	Marshall Islands
...	...	...	...	...	...	...	...	...	...	...	68	Martinique
...	...	...	...	...	...	...	...	...	11.9	1,742	20,300	Mauritania
...	...	...	...	...	...	...	...	...	48.8[1, 3, 6]	792[1, 3, 6]	4,976[1, 3, 6]	Mauritius
...	...	...	...	...	...	...	...	...	...	652[3]	1,477[3]	Mayotte
33.8	...	...	...	...	37.0	23.7	...	5.8	...	59	113	Mexico
...	...	...	...	...	...	...	...	...	...	...	...	Micronesia
...	...	...	...	...	...	...	...	...	...	...	...	Moldova
...	...	...	...	...	...	...	...	...	...	...	...	Monaco
...	...	...	...	...	...	...	...	...	4.3	225	372	Mongolia
...	...	...	...	...	...	...	...	...	5.0[6]	...	*c.* 4,000[6]	Morocco
...	...	...	...	...	...	...	...	...	...	...	...	Mozambique
...	...	...	...	...	...	...	...	...	...	...	...	Myanmar (Burma)
31.4	11.9	5.3	...	2.8	1.7	...	41.9	5.0	5.9	196	713	Namibia
...	...	...	...	...	...	...	...	...	...	...	...	Nauru
...	...	...	...	...	...	...	...	...	...	...	...	Nepal
40.5	11.6	12.2	...	2.1	...	5.8	11.2	16.6	4.4[8]	714	183	Netherlands, The

Trade: domestic (continued)

country	domestic trade as percentage of GDP, 1990	year	wholesale trade					retail trade		
			establishments[a]	employees[b]	sales[c] (U.S.$'000,000)	employees per establishment	sales per establishment (U.S.$'000)	outlets[a]	employees[b]	sales[c] (U.S.$'000,000)
Netherlands Antilles	13.6[12]	1988	...	[3]	...	...	...	...	15,890[3]	149[13, 17]
New Caledonia	20.8[12]	1991	...	[3]	...	...	...	1,023	4,995[3]	...
New Zealand	17.1[1, 37]	1992	8,263[50]	76,664[50]	16,295[50]	9.3[50]	1,972[50]	29,961[16, 50]	116,301[16, 50]	16,550
Nicaragua	22.3	1987	...	[3]	...	...	...	20,610[9]	94,600[3]	790[20]
Niger	13.2[1, 5]	...	...	...	...	...	...	...	...	...
Nigeria	13.1[11]	1983[6]	154	16,000	2,220	104	14,415	421	20,000	2,202
Northern Mariana Islands	...	1987	28	187	49	6.7	1,777	383	2,304	155
Norway	11.1[1]	1991	20,865	107,648[45]	58,656	5.2[45]	2,811	39,596	122,103[45]	28,347
Oman	11.4	1990	[3]	[3]	...	...	...	25,840[1, 3, 5]	87,500[3]	2,449[13]
Pakistan	15.0[1]	1983	...	...	...	...	...	276,701[33]	501,773[14, 33]	12,848
Panama	12.1[11]	1982[52]	560	13,115	1,491	23.4	2,662	7,561	15,765[6]	1,334
Papua New Guinea	9.8[5]	1985	...	[3]	...	...	...	...	25,100[3, 35]	669[1]
Paraguay	29.0[1]	1982	...	[3]	...	...	...	...	85,961[3]	2,645[20]
Peru	15.3	1973	4,210	34,100	2,163	8.1	514	103,010	72,200	8,500[20]
Philippines	19.8[1]	1981	20,642	122,717	4,538	5.9	220	279,968	241,872	4,836
Poland	18.3[1, 5, 26]	1991	...	119,600[27, 45]	33,482[27]	...	...	630,000	606,700[27, 45]	43,164
Portugal	17.4	1983	4,522	135,400[14]	9,260	29.9[14]	2,048	4,889	74,400[14]	3,057
Puerto Rico	15.5	1985	2,327	18,000	7,365	7.7	3,165	35,918	127,000	7,206
Qatar	6.3[11]	1990	134	3,801	85	28.4	636	4,956	18,238	1,048[12]
Réunion	17.7[12]	1989	[3]	[3]	...	...	...	6,409[3, 12]	17,689[3]	...
Romania	5.5[1, 12, 26]	1989	...	...	...	...	...	82,035	465,200	19,926
Russia	15.1	...	...	[3]	...	...	...	...	5,545,000[3]	...
Rwanda	18.5[1, 5]	1978	...	[3]	...	...	...	...	8,014[1, 3]	350[20]
St. Kitts and Nevis	23.5[1]	1984	...	[3]	...	...	...	...	940[3]	...
St. Lucia	24.1	1980	...	[3]	...	...	...	...	4,770[1, 3, 14]	...
St. Vincent	14.2[1, 4]	...	...	...	...	...	...	...	...	...
San Marino	...	1992	102[20]	[3]	...	...	...	867[20]	2,232[3]	...
São Tomé and Príncipe	12.5[5]	1981	...	[3]	...	...	...	...	1,994[3]	...
Saudi Arabia	8.1	1991[16]	4,460	31,481[14]	1,354	7.1[14]	304	80,266	174,187[14]	2,292
Senegal	24.5	1987	97[6]	1,843[6]	...	19[6]	...	289[6]	4,964[6]	664[13]
Seychelles	11.3	1985	[3]	[3]	...	[3]	...	131[3]	1,298[3]	...
Sierra Leone	31.8[5]	1983–84	...	[3]	...	...	...	...	7,211[3]	177[13]
Singapore	17.5[1]	1989	21,576	123,560	60,463	5.7	2,802	18,638[16]	74,815[16]	8,477[16]
Slovakia	8.9[26]	...	...	[3]	...	...	...	...	245,629[3]	...
Slovenia	16.2[5]	1990	...	[3]	29,509	...	...	...	97,981[3]	22,738
Solomon Islands	9.0	1991	...	[3]	...	...	...	405[20]	2,849[3]	139[20]
Somalia	9.3	...	...	...	...	...	...	...	...	...
South Africa[53]	13.5[2]	1989	...	...	38,682	...	...	58,100[35]	373,200[35]	22,913
Bophuthatswana[53]	...	1979[3]	...	...	...	...	...	1,248	4,195	110
Ciskei[53]	...	1979[3]	...	...	...	...	...	682	1,632	36
Transkei[53]	...	1977[3]	...	...	...	...	...	...	5,580[14]	...
Venda[53]	...	1978[3]	...	...	...	...	...	485	...	...
Spain	20.5[1, 27]	1984	40,000[22]	...	...	...	...	710,865[22]	1,400,000[22]	54,777
Sri Lanka	21.3[1]	1983[6]	190	15,000	[3]	78.9	...	1,348	44,300	1,116[3, 24]
Sudan, The	12.8[5]	1981	...	...	...	...	...	...	...	3,278
Suriname	18.0[12]	1985	...	[3]	...	...	...	13,000[15]	12,840[3]	110[20]
Swaziland	26.1[1, 5]	1984	67	1,000	...	14.9	...	656	3,700	23[20]
Sweden	10.7	1990	31,960[24]	167,800[24]	37,518[24]	5.2[24]	1,174[24]	61,095	224,228[8]	38,349
Switzerland	17.4[27]	1985	15,019	143,470	...	9.6	...	53,465	259,674	23,620[24]
Syria	22.4[5]	1983	2,827[33]	...	...	...	...	75,865[33]	110,000[14, 33]	7,330[20]
Taiwan	15.3[1]	1987	55,654[13]	169,100	7,572[27]	2.9[13]	101[13]	355,760[13]	181,200	14,291[27]
Tajikistan	17.0[5]	...	...	[3]	...	...	...	...	145,400[3]	...
Tanzania	13.3[1, 5]	1983	...	...	...	...	...	1,620[6]	16,524[6]	3,975[20]
Thailand	15.2	1985[6, 56]	3,290	20,251	3,955	6.2	1,202	8,648	42,508	1,363
Togo	22.6[5]	1980	...	...	...	...	...	181[6]	1,815[6]	112
Tonga	9.8[37]	1976	...	14[14]	...	...	...	...	654[14]	...
Trinidad and Tobago	13.4[1]	1977	124	6,786	509	54.7	4,102	370	15,986	1,670[20]
Tunisia	23.2[1]	1984	...	[3]	...	...	...	...	153,860[3, 27]	2,814
Turkey	17.5[11]	1985	49,428	181,067[14]	18,820	3.7[14]	381	369,133	696,967[14]	21,957
Turkmenistan	...	1990	...	[3]	...	...	...	...	90,000[3]	4,150
Tuvalu	14.9[1]	1979	...	[3]	...	...	...	...	113[3, 14]	...
Uganda	20.5	1977	226	4,100	...	18.1	...	251	3,200	5,285[23]
Ukraine	10.4[5]	1991	...	[3]	...	...	...	...	1,753,000[3, 28]	70,800
United Arab Emirates	10.9[5]	1983	[3]	[3]	...	[3]	...	13,906[1, 3, 42]	121,278[3, 42]	5,910[20]
United Kingdom	14.7[1]	1990[57]	119,000[5]	877,000[5]	388,386[5]	7.4[5]	3,263[5]	349,847	2,476,000	226,280
United States	16.0[5]	1992	469,539[8]	5,609,024[8]	1,790,264[28]	11.9[8]	5,377[8]	1,503,593[8]	17,779,942[8]	1,962,423
Uruguay	11.9	1985	...	[3]	...	...	...	...	139,242[3]	5,397[16, 24]
Uzbekistan	8.7[11]	1991	...	[3]	...	...	...	...	462,000[3]	...
Vanuatu	32.2	1983[58]	18	187[14]	...	10.4[14]	...	256	1,439[14]	...
Venezuela	15.6	1979	...	...	...	...	...	...	161,596	12,345[20]
Vietnam	18.0[11]	1979	2,400[59]	[3]	...	...	...	...	1,724,100[3, 11]	7,485[42]
Virgin Islands (U.S.)	...	1987	84	1,322	211	15.7	2,509	1,311	8,529	703
West Bank	...	1986	...	[3]	...	...	...	...	23,000[3]	...
Western Sahara	...	...	...	...	...	...	...	...	...	...
Western Samoa	11.9[20]	1986	...	[3]	...	...	...	...	842[3]	...
Yemen[60]	11.9[8]	1986	...	[3]	...	...	...	...	201,606[3]	2,195[13]
Yugoslavia	17.7[5, 26]	1992	8,979[28, 61]	50,579[28, 61]	8,671	5.6[28, 61]	569[28, 61]	72,303	244,593[28, 61]	8,958
Zaire	20.7[5]	1981	...	...	...	...	...	3,036[6]	33,398[6]	3,300[13]
Zambia	14.3	1974	494[6]	15,500[6]	977[6]	31.4[6]	1,978[6]	1,636[6]	13,700[6]	768[13]
Zimbabwe	11.5	1990	...	[3]	...	...	...	...	95,400[3]	693[27]

[1]Includes hotels. [2]1989–90. [3]Retail-trade data include wholesale trade. [4]Excludes retail-trade network of the agricultural cooperatives. [5]1989. [6]Data refer to larger establishments only. [7]1971. [8]1987. [9]1982. [10]1972. [11]1991. [12]1988. [13]1983. [14]All persons engaged, including proprietors. [15]1973. [16]Excludes restaurants (eating and drinking establishments). [17]Netherlands Antilles includes Aruba. [18]1990–91. [19]1981–82. [20]1986. [21]Data refer to New Providence Island only. [22]1979. [23]1981. [24]1984. [25]Privately owned establishments only. [26]Percentage of net material product. [27]1985. [28]1990. [29]1976. [30]General merchandise includes clothing and shoes. [31]General merchandise includes building materials. [32]For major cities only. [33]1975. [34]Wholesale selling directly to the public only. [35]1980. [36]Data refer to former Czechoslovakia. [37]1988–89. [38]Selected outlets in urban areas only. [39]Ethiopia includes Eritrea. [40]Excludes Addis Ababa and Asmera.

retail trade (continued)												country
percentage breakdown of sales									employees per outlet	sales per outlet (U.S.$'000)	population per outlet	
food[d]	clothing, shoes[e]	home furnishings[f]	eating, drinking[g]	drugs, pharma-ceuticals[h]	building materials[i]	automobile parts[j]	general merchandise[k]	other[l]				
...	...	...	...	...	...	...	...	...	...	...	...	Netherlands Antilles
...	...	...	...	...	...	...	...	...	...	...	169	New Caledonia
23.7	5.5	6.6	15.1	3.2	2.3	30.8	4.5	8.3	3.9[16, 50]	346[16, 50]	106[16, 50]	New Zealand
...	...	...	...	...	...	...	...	...	...	...	143[9]	Nicaragua
...	...	...	...	...	...	...	...	...	...	...	...	Niger
...	...	...	...	...	...	...	...	...	47.5	5,230	226,615	Nigeria
27.0	[51]	2.3	8.8	...	7.2	[51]	4.7	50.0[51]	6.0	406	56	Northern Mariana Islands
35.2	10.3	7.2	...	...	4.8	26.6	4.2	11.7	3.1[45]	716	108	Norway
...	...	...	...	...	...	...	...	...	...	...	56[1, 3, 5]	Oman
64.0	12.0	4.0	...	...	...	...	...	20.0	1.8[14, 33]	...	273[33]	Pakistan
...	...	...	...	...	...	...	...	...	13.9[6]	176	270	Panama
...	...	...	7.1[1]	...	...	26.0	...	66.9	...	...	...	Papua New Guinea
...	...	...	...	...	...	...	...	...	...	...	...	Paraguay
...	...	...	...	...	...	...	...	...	0.7	20	145	Peru
25.4[46]	12.3	6.7	...	...	11.3	29.5[48]	...	14.8	0.9	17	177	Philippines
31.1[42]	9.9[42]	11.1[42]	...	2.0[42]	4.9[42]	6.7[42]	...	34.3[42]	2.4[27, 44]	68	61	Poland
21.5[43]	14.1[43]	11.2[43]	...	3.3[43]	5.6[43]	35.2[43]	—9.1[43]—		15.3[14]	625	2,047	Portugal
30.5[9]	9.9[9]	4.5[9]	7.5[9]	4.3[9]	5.9[9]	23.2[9]	8.9[9]	5.3[9]	3.5	201	91	Puerto Rico
9.0[12]	9.6[12]	13.2[12]	...	2.7[12]	7.2[12]	29.7[12]	9.1[12]	19.5[12]	3.7	177[12]	98	Qatar
...	...	...	...	...	...	...	...	...	3.4[3, 12]	...	90[3, 12]	Réunion
30.0[35]	10.0[35]	5.9[35]	25.0[35]	1.6[35]	0.8[35]	...	...	26.7[35]	5.7	243	282	Romania
...	...	...	...	...	...	...	...	...	...	...	...	Russia
...	...	...	...	...	...	...	...	...	...	...	...	Rwanda
...	...	...	...	...	...	...	...	...	...	...	...	St. Kitts and Nevis
...	...	...	...	...	...	...	...	...	...	...	...	St. Lucia
...	...	...	...	...	...	...	...	...	...	...	...	St. Vincent
...	...	...	...	...	...	...	...	...	...	...	26[20]	San Marino
...	...	...	...	...	...	...	...	...	...	...	...	São Tomé and Príncipe
...	...	...	...	...	...	...	...	...	2.2[14]	29	201	Saudi Arabia
...	...	...	...	...	...	...	...	...	17.2[6]	...	23,430[6]	Senegal
...	...	...	...	...	...	...	...	...	9.9[3]	...	498[3]	Seychelles
...	...	...	...	...	...	...	...	...	...	...	...	Sierra Leone
1.2[13]	4.3[13]	10.2[13]	10.5[13]	0.7[13]	0.3[13]	22.1[13]	—50.7[13]—		4.0[16]	454[16]	142[16]	Singapore
...	...	...	...	...	...	...	...	...	...	...	...	Slovakia
...	...	...	...	...	...	...	...	...	...	...	...	Slovenia
...	...	...	...	...	...	...	...	...	...	...	...	Solomon Islands
...	...	...	...	...	...	...	...	...	...	...	...	Somalia
43.7	16.5	9.4	3.8	4.0	...	...	14.2	8.4	6.4[35]	383[35]	c. 540[35]	South Africa[53]
...	...	...	...	...	...	...	...	...	3.4	88	1,041	Bophuthatswana[53]
...	...	...	...	...	...	...	...	...	2.4	53	972	Ciskei[53]
...	...	...	...	...	...	...	...	...	...	...	...	Transkei[53]
...	...	...	...	...	...	...	...	...	...	...	621	Venda[53]
39.2	10.5	16.7	...	...	...	4.2[54]	...	29.4	2.0[22]	119[22]	52[22]	Spain
...	...	...	...	...	...	...	...	...	32.9	...	11,436	Sri Lanka
...	...	...	...	...	...	...	...	...	...	...	...	Sudan, The
...	...	...	...	...	...	...	...	...	...	...	...	Suriname
52.5[20]	25.1[20]	22.4[20]	...	...	...	...	...	...	5.6	...	969	Swaziland
42.3[5]	13.7[5]	16.7[5]	...	2.1[5]	...	...	12.5[5]	12.7[5]	3.1[8]	628	140	Sweden
46.4[24]	13.5[24]	...	...	4.0[24]	...	...	...	36.1[24]	4.9	...	122	Switzerland
16.0	2.5	...	...	3.5	12.3	39.5[55]	3.5	22.7	1.4[14, 33]	...	97[33]	Syria
21.5[23]	3.2[23]	8.8[23]	...	4.1[23]	3.1[23]	8.7[23, 48]	3.1[23]	47.5[23]	0.3[13]	33[13]	52[13]	Taiwan
...	...	...	...	...	...	...	...	...	...	...	...	Tajikistan
...	...	...	...	...	...	...	...	...	10.0[6]	...	12,600[6]	Tanzania
2.6	4.0	3.1	3.8	0.9	14.9	36.8	19.8	14.1	4.9	157	5,895	Thailand
...	...	...	...	...	...	...	...	...	10.0[6]	...	15,600[6]	Togo
...	...	...	...	...	...	...	...	...	...	...	...	Tonga
18.6	...	8.5	2.7	...	10.7	28.2	15.3	15.9	43.2	1,467	2,798	Trinidad and Tobago
...	...	...	...	...	...	...	...	...	...	...	...	Tunisia
25.0	11.5	15.3	...	2.4	4.8	32.3	0.8	7.9	1.9	60[14]	136	Turkey
...	...	...	...	...	...	...	...	...	...	...	...	Turkmenistan
...	...	...	...	...	...	...	...	...	...	...	...	Tuvalu
...	...	...	...	...	...	...	...	...	12.7	...	47,200	Uganda
...	...	...	...	...	...	...	...	...	...	...	...	Ukraine
...	...	...	...	...	...	...	...	...	...	...	49[2, 3, 42]	United Arab Emirates
36.4	9.6	5.6	10.0	3.5	9.6	...	17.6	7.7	7.1	647	164	United Kingdom
19.6	5.3	5.4	11.6	3.9	5.2	27.9	12.6	8.5	11.8[8]	912[8]	162[8]	United States
...	...	...	...	...	...	...	...	...	...	...	...	Uruguay
...	...	...	...	...	...	...	...	...	...	...	...	Uzbekistan
...	...	...	...	...	...	...	...	...	5.6[14]	...	484	Vanuatu
50.2	10.1	7.6	...	...	...	5.0	...	27.1	...	...	...	Venezuela
...	...	...	...	...	...	...	...	...	...	...	...	Vietnam
17.6	7.9	6.4	12.0	2.3	4.8	11.4	1.9	35.7	6.5	536	81	Virgin Islands (U.S.)
...	...	...	...	...	...	...	...	...	...	...	...	West Bank
...	...	...	...	...	...	...	...	...	...	...	...	Western Sahara
...	...	...	...	...	...	...	...	...	...	...	...	Western Samoa
...	...	...	...	...	...	...	...	...	...	...	...	Yemen[60]
34.8[28, 61]	16.5[28, 61]	...	...	...	4.9[28, 61]	1.2[28, 61]	...	42.6[28, 61]	3.6[28, 61]	124	145	Yugoslavia
...	...	...	...	...	...	...	...	...	11.0[6]	...	9,676[6]	Zaire
...	...	...	...	...	...	...	...	...	8.4[6]	359[6]	2,873[6]	Zambia
...	...	...	...	...	...	...	...	...	...	...	...	Zimbabwe

[41]Data refer to former West Germany only. [42]1977. [43]1978. [44]Excludes fuels, automobiles, alcohol and tobacco, and building materials. [45]Full-time equivalents. [46]Includes alcohol and tobacco. [47]Peninsular Malaysia only. [48]Includes all fuels. [49]State- and cooperative-owned establishments, including public catering. [50]1982–83. [51]Other includes clothing, shoes, and automobile parts. [52]Excludes Colón Free Trade Zone. [53]South Africa includes Bophuthatswana, Ciskei, Transkei, and Venda. [54]Motor vehicles only. [55]Includes machinery, transport equipment, and petroleum products. [56]Excludes combined wholesale/retail outlets. [57]Great Britain only. [58]Urban establishments only. [59]State sector only. [60]Data refer to former Yemen Arab Republic only. [61]Data refer to the former Socialist Federated Republic of Yugoslavia.

Finance

This table presents major statistical aggregates comprising national financial structure or constituting a basis for certain international financial comparisons. It includes such data as international reserves, money supply, central banking activity and discount rates, commercial (or "deposit money") banking activity, and external indebtedness of the central government. The country models are broadly similar and permit comparison of internal structure and external position at a high level of generalization.

One of the principal financial criteria of the relative economic position of a country is the size of its international reserves. International reserves as represented in this table comprise the sum of a country's (1) reserve position in the International Monetary Fund (IMF), a quota subscribed in the country's own currency, constituting a level up to which transactions may be effected within the IMF system, (2) holdings of foreign exchange, (3) holdings of gold, and (4) holdings of Special Drawing Rights (SDRs; an unconditional credit allocation, within a quota system set by the IMF, of currency needed by a country to maintain stability of foreign exchange transactions or markets). At appropriate accounting intervals these four elements are valued in a single unit of account (the SDR) and summed. The portion of this reserve total comprised by foreign exchange is very significant as an indication of the country's international liquidity (ability to pay its debts immediately in hard, or convertible, currencies). The ratio of external debt to total reserves, however, is less susceptible of interpretation in isolation: a low ratio, for example, may characterize the situation of a country with little need to borrow or of one with substantial debt but also the means to repay it. Much higher ratios, on the other hand, may be manageable, despite small reserves, if a country's export earnings are also high.

The section on money supply for the country, both as a total and as a per capita amount, refers to one particular measure of money in circulation: M1, the sum of money in private sector demand deposit accounts and outside banks in circulation; it is distinguished from a broader measure of supply, M2, which is roughly M1 plus "quasi-money" (the time, savings, and foreign-currency deposits of residents).

The section of the table outlining banking activity and the principal monetary aggregates encompasses both central bank authorities and commercial (deposit) banks. For both, the principal component aggregates are grouped under assets and liabilities. For certain countries, the four principal aggregates under assets and liabilities do not comprise the entire total, and the percentages shown, therefore, may add to less than 100% (occasionally more, when the net of other liabilities [capital, reserves, undistributed profits, checks, and other transit items] is negative, reducing the total against which these percentages are calculated). The items excluded by the choice of categories are the least significant worldwide but may be important locally; they include such items as quasi-money, money seasonally adjusted, unused bank overdrafts, and so on. In the case of the central bank authority, data are also provided for the central bank discount rate, generally the controlling interest rate for banking and commercial activity in the country.

The largest share of assets in the case of both central and commercial

Finance

country	international reserves, 1993[a]			money supply, 1992[b]		central bank authority, 1992[b]								
	total ('000,000 SDRs)	% foreign exchange	ratio of external debt to total reserves, 1991[b]	stock ('000,000,000 national currency)	M1 per capita	assets (%)				liabilities (%)				central bank discount rate, 1993[a]
						claims on government	claims on private sector	claims on banks	claims on foreign assets	reserve money	government deposits	foreign liabilities	capital accounts	
Afghanistan	199[1]	78.4[1]	16.1[2, 3]	351.025[2]	20,500[2]	93.9[2, 4]	0.1[2]	0.5[2]	5.5[2]	73.6[2]	5.3[2]	6.3[2]	3.0[2]	...
Albania	...	...	...	...	...	...	...	...	...	...	...	...	...	...
Algeria	1,325	85.1	15.0	324.5[6]	12,500[6]	41.1[6]	—	44.4[6]	14.5[6]	65.6[6]	2.4[6]	10.0[6]	—	...
American Samoa	...	...	...	...	...	...	...	...	...	...	...	...	...	...
Andorra	...	...	...	...	...	...	...	...	...	...	...	...	...	...
Angola	...	...	...	...	...	...	...	...	...	...	...	...	...	...
Antigua and Barbuda	36	100.0	4.5[3, 7]	0.183	2,850	20.9	—	0.9	78.2	99.9	0.1	—	—	7.0[8]
Argentina	4,769[6]	94.1[6]	6.7	2.706[2]	80[2]	...	...	...	...	...	...	...	...	11[9]
Armenia	...	...	...	...	...	...	...	...	...	...	...	...	...	...
Aruba	128	97.7	...	0.331	4,780	—	—	—	100.0	75.1	7.9	—	19.7	9.5
Australia	7,937	91.6	...	60.292	3,410	42.1	—	—	57.9	60.3	7.8	0.2	—	5.8
Austria	10,087	88.2	...	283.0	35,900	3.4	—	27.5	69.0	73.8	0.1	—	29.8	6.3
Azerbaijan	...	...	...	18.535[6]	2,590[6]	...	...	...	...	...	...	...	...	...
Bahamas, The	143[6]	94.4[6]	3.8[2, 3]	0.365	1,380	48.3	—	0.9	50.8	70.9	4.1	—	29.1	7.3
Bahrain	941	94.0	1.1[2, 3]	0.352	650	—	—	—	100.0	28.2	48.0	3.4	37.6	3.6[10]
Bangladesh	1,520	97.6	9.4	80.442	710	9.0[4]	—	28.8	62.2	58.2	3.0	25.3	4.8	6.5
Barbados	124	100.0	5.5	0.502	1,940	36.5	—	14.5	49.0	57.1	16.7	38.1	5.3	12.0
Belarus	...	...	...	35.985[6]	3,490[6]	...	...	...	...	...	...	...	...	20.0[1]
Belgium	10,660	85.3	...	1,217.0[2]	122,000[2]	6.6	—	—	93.4	54.9	—	—	—	6.3
Belize	30	90.0	2.8	0.126	640	7.7	—	—	92.3	91.8	—	15.3	—	12.0
Benin	146	97.9	6.4	128.2	25,700	19.6	—	34.3	46.1	84.1	7.9	4.9	—	12.5
Bermuda	...	...	...	0.052[2, 11]	870[2, 11]	...	...	...	...	...	...	...	...	...
Bhutan	57[1]	98.2[1]	0.9	0.841	550	—	—	2.1	97.9	60.7	1.0	—	—	8.0[9]
Bolivia	128	68.0	23.2	1.923	250	64.0[4]	—	16.0	20.0	16.4	54.0	17.4	3.4	24.0[1, 9]
Bosnia and Herzegovina	...	...	...	...	...	...	...	...	...	...	...	...	...	...
Botswana	2,823	98.7	0.1	0.607	440	—	—	—	100.0[6]	9.3[6]	55.6[6]	—	19.0[6]	14.5
Brazil	15,049	99.4	10.8	...	...	73.1[4]	—	3.5	23.4	7.3	15.6	44.4	7.0	2,346
Brunei	...	...	...	...	...	...	...	...	...	...	...	...	...	...
Bulgaria	...	...	...	...	...	...	...	...	...	...	...	...	...	...
Burkina Faso	252	94.4	2.5	110.6	11,500	17.9	—	7.9	74.2	83.5	4.4	9.0	—	12.5
Burundi	133	94.7	6.3	23.233[2]	4,390[2]	21.1[4]	0.6	3.8	74.5	29.8	12.4	22.4	20.7	...
Cambodia	...	...	...	...	...	...	...	...	...	...	...	...	...	...
Cameroon	34[1]	70.6[1]	113.4	410.3	32,100	86.7	—	11.2	2.1	43.3	6.0	46.2	0.7	12.0[1]
Canada	9,040	80.5	...	108.0	3,760	50.0	—	—	50.0	96.3	—	—	—	5.0
Cape Verde	60[13]	100.0[13]	...	9.907	28,500	42.7[4]	25.6	1.6	30.0	53.7	4.4	1.1	16.4	4.0[1, 9]
Central African Republic	75[1]	98.7[1]	7.8	52.2	17,600	47.8	—	3.7	48.5	74.2	1.1	18.6	1.7	12.0[1]
Chad	84[6]	69.0[6]	4.6	62.9	10,400	48.8	—	15.2	36.0	74.3	0.7	15.2	1.6	12.0[1]
Chile	7,111	99.0	1.4	937.5	69,800	34.0[4]	1.5	23.7	40.8	51.9	11.9	11.4	21.1	22.1[9]
China	15,444	91.8	1.1	1,171.4	1,000	12.3	7.3	67.2	13.2	91.5	2.3	—	5.2	...
Colombia	4,852[1]	96.8[1]	2.4	4,020.4	119,000	11.6	—	5.7	82.7	50.3	5.1	8.2	6.9	34.7
Comoros	21[2]	100.0[2]	...	9.932[6]	20,300[6]	24.6[6]	—	—	75.4[6]	59.2[6]	7.4[6]	6.0[6]	27.8[6]	...
Congo	3[1]	100.0[1]	697.2	127.6	46,700	88.2	—	8.2	3.6	81.2	4.8	10.9	2.1	12.0[1]
Costa Rica	697	98.4	3.6	79.8[6]	25,500[6]	32.5[4, 6]	—	13.3[6]	54.2[6]	66.9[6]	7.0[6]	92.3[6]	6.5[6]	25.5
Côte d'Ivoire	7	14.3	662.5	498.4	37,900	30.5	—	69.3	0.2	34.6	1.0	62.8	—	12.5
Croatia	...	...	...	...	...	...	...	...	...	...	...	...	...	...
Cuba	...	...	...	...	...	...	...	...	...	...	...	...	...	...
Cyprus	817[1]	94.9[1]	1.1	0.506	870	43.5	—	3.6	52.9	80.1	13.8	3.9	—	6.5
Czech Republic	...	...	...	306.9	29,700	...	...	...	...	...	...	...	...	8.0
Denmark	6,502	92.7	...	256.0	49,500	5.1	1.0	40.0	53.9	28.4	23.3	21.4	—	7.8
Djibouti	59	96.6	1.8	34.981	61,800	—	—	0.3	99.7	82.0	0.8	—	9.7	...
Dominica	14	100.0	5.0	0.086	1,170	33.6	—	—	66.4	87.5	—	12.4	—	6.4[8]
Dominican Republic	374	99.5	7.8	11.047	1,460	23.8	—	16.3	59.9	108.8	—	159.0	4.7	...
Ecuador	422[1]	96.2[1]	10.5	1,333.6[6]	126,000[6]	65.9[4]	1.4	10.2	22.5	75.9	41.1	96.4	3.6	31.1
Egypt	8,343	97.8	6.6	30.832	550	50.7[4]	—	9.0	40.3	31.3	30.8	37.1	—	21.3[6]
El Salvador	365	95.3	6.6	6.284	1,150	50.2[4]	—	13.8	36.1	44.6	10.6	23.5	14.5	16.3[9]

banks is usually either claims on government and government agencies or foreign assets and holdings, though some of the latter, such as the large outstanding loans to socialist and less developed countries, have become the chief liabilities. The chief liability of a central bank is usually reserve money (the currency and notes issued by the bank). When government deposits represent a substantial share, budgetary surpluses have usually been deposited by the central government. Large foreign liabilities imply extensive foreign investment. Among the deposit money banks, loans to the private sector normally represent the largest share of assets; occasionally, a trade- or banking-oriented country such as Belgium or Luxembourg will show major foreign assets. The chief liabilities of these banks will usually be savings deposits. If the country commands a high degree of confidence internationally, foreign liabilities may comprise a substantial share of liabilities.

Because the majority of the world's countries are in the less developed bloc, and because their principal financial concern is often external debt and its service, data are given for outstanding external public and publicly guaranteed long-term debt rather than for total public debt, which is the major concern in the developed countries. For comparability, the data are given in U.S. dollars. The volume of debt by itself does not create external payment problems. If the country's external debt service (interest payments plus principal repayment) needs can be met by a strong, dependable export market, by export of services, or, occasionally, by direct remittances from abroad (by residents working abroad and sending wages home in foreign currencies, for example), no debt problem need exist. Countries whose debt service ratio (total debt service as a percent of exports of goods and services) is relatively high, however, must often base their external borrowing policy on maintenance of domestic conditions of strict efficiency and, sometimes, austerity. The failure to adhere to such policies may lead to eventual crises of financial liquidity, deflation, and slower growth.

Ideally, the data presented here should be obtained by utilizing a single international methodology to provide a universally comparable set of international statistics. No international agency, however, can collect such data for all countries because of differences, both overall and in detail, in national definitions of financial aggregates, in accounting methodology, and in the completeness with which it is possible to survey a country's financial activity. The greater part of the data presented in the table comes from the IMF's *International Financial Statistics* and the World Bank's *World Debt Tables.* These sources are supplemented by other recent data from national, regional, or other international sources. In a few cases the desired data are negligible or unavailable, as noted.

Detailed percentages may not add to 100.0 because of rounding, statistical discrepancy, or nonaccounting of negligible quantities.

— None, less than half the last significant figure, or not applicable.

... Not available.

a. Latest month.

b. Year-end.

deposit money banks, 1992[b]									external public debt outstanding (long-term, disbursed only), 1991							country
assets (%)				liabilities					total ('000,000 U.S.$)	creditors (%)		debt service				
loans to government	loans to private sector	reserves	foreign assets	deposits ('000,000,000 national currency)	composition (%)					official	private	total ('000,000 U.S.$)	repayment (%)		debt service ratio (%)	
					demand depos.	savings depos.	govt. depos.	foreign liabilities					principal	interest		
1.4[2,4]	51.2[2]	31.1[2]	16.3[2]	51.160[2]	35.6[2]	49.4[2,5]	0.5[2]	0.6[2]	5,074[2,3]	...	...	115[2,3]	10.4[2,3]	89.6[2,3]	9.3[2,3]	Afghanistan
...	...	...	...	...	...	...	...	...	176[2,3]	...	...	9[2,3]	22.2[2,3]	77.8[2,3]	2.1[2,3]	Albania
8.3[6]	84.5[6]	1.2[6]	6.0[6]	385.8[6]	34.5[6]	23.4[6]	3.0[6]	43.5[6]	26,557	24.7	75.3	9,664	79.8	20.2	67.3	Algeria
...	...	...	...	...	...	...	...	...	...	...	...	...	...	...	...	American Samoa
...	...	...	...	...	...	...	...	...	...	...	...	...	...	...	...	Andorra
...	...	...	...	...	...	...	...	...	7,370	46.2	53.8	155	74.2	25.8	4.3	Angola
11.2[4]	63.0	10.5	15.3	0.941	12.6	57.3[5]	5.3	19.2	124[3,7]	...	...	10[3,7]	...	...	3.2[3,7]	Antigua and Barbuda
34.2[2]	53.0[2]	6.6[2]	6.2[2]	20.2[2]	2.2[2]	22.2[2,5]	5.7[2]	19.4[2]	45,388	27.3	72.7	5,448	44.6	55.4	36.8	Argentina
...	...	...	...	...	...	...	...	...	...	...	...	...	...	...	...	Armenia
2.8	58.0	11.5	27.7	1.280	19.7	51.8	0.8	20.0	...	...	...	...	...	...	...	Aruba
10.5[4]	82.8	1.3	5.4	331.9	13.2	53.4	1.1	16.5	...	...	...	...	...	...	...	Australia
29.7[4]	46.0	2.1	22.2	3,403.8	4.8	46.0	1.8	25.8	...	...	...	...	...	...	...	Austria
...	...	...	...	...	...	...	...	...	...	...	...	...	...	...	...	Azerbaijan
22.9[4]	84.6	7.0	−14.5	1.443	19.4	70.9[5]	2.0	—	596[2,3]	...	...	387[2,3]	83.5[2,3]	16.5[2,3]	16.8[2,3]	Bahamas, The
7.9	29.0	6.6	56.5	1.776	14.2	45.9	20.4	18.8	1,343[2,3]	...	...	167[2,3]	53.9[2,3]	46.1[2,3]	4.4[2,3]	Bahrain
27.8[4]	56.7	11.2	4.3	326.779	13.0	66.6	8.8	2.7	12,103	98.6	1.4	412	62.9	37.1	14.0	Bangladesh
26.5	56.8	8.0	8.7	2.092	14.6	62.7	6.0	13.7	483	50.1	49.9	131	71.4	28.6	14.0[2]	Barbados
...	...	...	...	...	...	...	...	...	...	...	...	...	...	...	...	Belarus
22.0[2,4]	21.9[2]	0.2[2]	55.9[2]	10,652.2[2]	5.5[2]	17.8[2,5]	—	69.7[2]	...	...	...	...	...	...	...	Belgium
12.1[4]	72.7	10.4	4.8	0.512	14.5	55.7	14.5	6.2	147.8	85.4	14.6	15.7	68.6	31.4	7.1[2]	Belize
3.8	41.8	42.4	11.9	167.5	43.5	28.6	11.8	9.2	1,221	99.0	1.0	28	57.1	42.9	5.7	Benin
...	...	...	...	8.835[2]	...	...	...	...	445[2,3]	...	...	45[2,3]	40.0[2,3]	60.0[2,3]	5.9[2,3]	Bermuda
34.5[4]	19.0	37.0	9.5	2.240	22.1	33.4[5]	8.9	15.9	86.3	81.0	19.0	6.4	67.7	32.3	6.6[2]	Bhutan
—	84.9	11.5	3.6	8.954	11.6	57.7[5]	1.8	8.6	3,523	91.4	8.6	221	51.6	48.4	23.5	Bolivia
...	...	...	...	...	...	...	...	...	...	...	...	...	...	...	...	Bosnia and Herzegovina
3.8[4]	65.7	23.3	7.3	2.010	22.1	63.0	—	2.2	535.9	95.8	4.2	79.5	59.2	40.8	3.4	Botswana
40.3[4,12]	41.4[12]	14.4[12]	3.8[12]	6.694[12]	10.9[12]	12.8[12]	1.4[12]	14.1[12]	87,477	29.5	70.5	7,604	51.4	48.6	21.8	Brazil
14.2[12]		0.5[12]	...	4.928[12]	83.6[12]			...	27[3,7]	...	...	2[3,7]	...	...	0.1[3,7]	Brunei
...	...	...	...	...	...	...	...	...	11,023	23.7	76.3	1,076	74.5	25.5	21.2	Bulgaria
8.7	59.6	23.4	8.3	161.1	25.7	35.2	31.6	7.4	871	99.3	0.7	40	62.5	37.5	5.2[2]	Burkina Faso
18.3[4]	70.0	7.2	4.5	34.203	39.5	32.3	0.6	5.5	898	99.3	0.7	38	68.4	31.6	29.9	Burundi
...	...	...	...	...	...	...	...	...	1,514[2,3]	...	...	30[2,3]	3.3[2,3]	96.7[2,3]	69.8[2,3]	Cambodia
23.4	72.0	1.5	3.1	1,230.0	21.1	27.2	16.1	5.4	5,027	78.8	21.2	306	48.7	51.3	12.9[2]	Cameroon
12.0[4]	75.3	1.2	11.6	495.0	17.1	53.9[5]	0.3	17.7	...	...	...	...	...	...	...	Canada
...	...	...	...	...	...	...	...	...	149.5	98.4	1.6	5.6	64.3	35.7	8.6	Cape Verde
22.8[4]	69.4	1.6	6.2	44.0	20.6	14.2	12.0	9.2	802	97.4	2.6	9	44.4	55.6	4.9	Central African Republic
32.0[4]	51.9	1.5	14.6	58.4	27.1	6.2	14.0	13.4	546.9	97.2	2.8	9.1	48.4	51.6	3.7	Chad
2.6[4]	88.0	6.7	2.7	7,832.5	5.8	58.7[5]	4.6	19.0	10,024	52.7	47.3	2,793	21.3	78.7	24.0	Chile
—	78.6	16.3	5.1	2,918.8	22.9	41.6	—	3.8	50,502	33.7	66.3	7,269	59.5	40.5	10.3	China
5.5	68.3	22.3	3.9	8,030.2	26.9	34.6[5]	7.3	9.4	14,503	58.4	41.6	3,089	61.7	38.3	29.8	Colombia
—	77.6[6]	10.2[6]	12.2[6]	12.400[6]	27.9[6]	47.0[6]	—	12.6[6]	161.4	100.0	—	1.9	10.5	89.5	4.8	Comoros
29.1[4]	60.3	2.0	8.6	218.3	29.6	23.0	8.3	12.1	3,989	81.7	18.3	216	82.4	17.6	19.3	Congo
6.6[4,6]	36.4[6]	49.9[6]	7.1[6]	260.4[6]	17.3[6]	80.9[5,6]	1.4[6]	2.6[6]	3,316	79.9	20.1	341	49.3	50.7	15.1	Costa Rica
18.0	74.6	1.8	5.6	1,259.8	18.6	27.5	5.9	9.8	10,424	71.3	28.7	498	45.2	54.8	13.5	Côte d'Ivoire
...	...	...	...	...	...	...	...	...	...	...	...	...	...	...	...	Croatia
...	...	...	...	...	...	...	...	...	26,231[2,3]	...	...	1,193[2,3]	46.1[2,3]	53.9[2,3]	42.3[2,3]	Cuba
9.2	57.9	14.6	18.3	3.706	7.8	55.7	1.0	26.2	1,513	70.0	30.0	252	60.3	39.7	6.9[2]	Cyprus
...	...	...	...	...	...	...	...	...	5,845[14]	9.0[14]	91.0[14]	1,313[14]	74.9[14]	25.1[14]	9.2[14]	Czech Republic
12.7	50.2	2.0	35.1	813.5	28.2	30.3	—	28.3	...	...	...	...	...	...	...	Denmark
0.6[4]	48.5	1.2	49.7	71.585	30.2	32.1	1.3	21.0	175.5	99.9	0.1	10.0	78.0	22.0	3.5[2]	Djibouti
14.2[4]	59.4	9.3	17.1	0.447	12.3	54.0[5]	6.7	16.8	86.6	100.0	—	4.0	55.0	45.0	3.8[2]	Dominica
7.4[4]	65.4	20.5	6.7	25.631	19.7	52.0	10.8	2.6	3,471	72.3	27.7	180	57.2	42.8	7.7	Dominican Republic
0.5[6]	74.8[6]	19.4[6]	5.3[6]	2,050.1[6]	32.5[6]	34.3[6]	—	4.1[6]	9,952	42.4	57.6	927	51.1	48.9	27.0	Ecuador
41.9[4]	20.9	12.7	24.5	154.099	9.1	56.3[5]	6.6	5.1	36,028	86.5	13.5	1,827	68.3	31.7	12.6	Egypt
4.2	68.0	23.6	4.1	18.028	17.9	66.0[5]	3.0	1.6	2,048	91.2	8.8	224	69.2	30.8	16.1	El Salvador

Finance (continued)

country	international reserves, 1993[a]			money supply, 1992[b]		central bank authority, 1992[b]								
						assets (%)				liabilities (%)				central bank discount rate, 1993[a]
	total ('000,000 SDRs)	% foreign exchange	ratio of external debt to total reserves, 1991[b]	stock ('000,000,000 national currency)	M1 per capita	claims on government	claims on private sector	claims on banks	claims on foreign assets	reserve money	government deposits	foreign liabilities	capital accounts	
Equatorial Guinea	10[1]	40.0[1]	...	3.6	9,600	75.7	—	—	24.3	20.4	0.2	67.3	1.3	12.0[1]
Eritrea[15]	...	...	...	...	...	...	...	...	...	...	...	...	...	...
Estonia	...	...	...	...	...	...	...	...	...	...	...	...	...	...
Ethiopia[15]	180	93.9	53.7	7.142	130	63.3	—	23.2	13.5	67.7	6.5	10.7	5.7	12.0
Faeroe Islands	...	...	...	...	...	...	...	...	...	...	...	...	...	...
Fiji	188	91.5	1.0	0.314	420	—	—	—	100.0	45.5	0.5	—	16.6	6.0
Finland	4,276	91.0	...	134.829	26,700	5.2	6.2	24.7	63.9	80.7	0.2	5.1	14.5	7.0
France	26,735	82.2	...	1,523.0	26,500	12.9	0.5	39.9	46.7	40.2	20.1	22.1	24.7	9.5
French Guiana	...	...	...	5.119	40,600	...	...	...	...	...	...	...	...	...
French Polynesia	...	...	...	46.210	221,000	...	...	...	...	...	...	...	...	...
Gabon	167[1]	98.2[1]	9.0	170.5	136,000	54.4	—	26.2	19.4	59.5	7.5	24.6	1.5	12.0[1]
Gambia, The	47[6]	100.0[6]	4.6	0.435	470	23.1[4]	—	—	76.9	25.7	34.2	39.7	6.4	14.5
Gaza Strip	...	...	...	...	...	...	...	...	...	...	...	...	...	...
Georgia	...	...	...	...	...	...	...	...	...	...	...	...	...	...
Germany	36,636	81.1	...	640.7	7,940	8.8	—	50.5	40.7	84.8	0.1	7.1	—	7.3
Ghana	245	88.2	5.2	360.7	23,400	71.2[4]	—	0.6	28.2	36.0	0.7	76.5	2.1	35.0
Gibraltar	...	...	...	...	...	...	...	...	...	...	...	...	...	...
Greece	3,568	83.7	5.9[2, 3]	2,097.6[6]	204,000[6]	61.9	—	14.5	23.7	31.4	1.1	36.9	—	21.5
Greenland	...	...	...	...	...	...	...	...	...	...	...	...	...	...
Grenada	17	100.0	5.6	0.110	1,210	33.4	—	0.6	66.0	100.0	—	—	—	6.5[8]
Guadeloupe	...	...	...	6.157	14,900	...	...	...	...	...	...	...	...	...
Guam	...	...	...	...	...	...	...	...	...	...	...	...	...	...
Guatemala	551	97.3	2.6	4.193	440	26.0[4]	—	26.5	47.5	241.0	87.9	36.1	7.5	22.6[1]
Guernsey	...	...	...	...	...	...	...	...	...	...	...	...	...	...
Guinea	...	...	...	...	...	...	...	...	...	...	...	...	...	...
Guinea-Bissau	...	...	...	...	...	...	...	...	...	...	...	...	...	...
Guyana	134	100.0	12.5	7.466[6]	9,960[6]	18.8[6]	—	—	81.2[6]	50.7[6]	—	413.5[6]	−9.8[6]	16.3
Haiti	14[1]	57.1[1]	32.8	2.634[7]	410[7]	84.2[4, 7]	8.3[7]	2.1[7]	5.4[7]	67.9[7]	5.5[7]	28.0[7]	6.7[7]	...
Honduras	101	99.0	27.1	2.582	510	39.0[4]	—	28.8	32.2	43.1	22.8	96.7	21.4	26.1[1]
Hong Kong	...	...	...	155.557	26,400	...	...	...	...	...	...	...	...	...
Hungary	3,806[1]	99.9[1]	4.9	549.2[6]	53,100[6]	51.9[6]	0.2[6]	25.6[6]	22.3[6]	49.1[6]	7.3[6]	90.2[6]	—	27.0[6]
Iceland	366	96.7	...	30.050	115,000	16.7	0.9	9.1	73.3	41.4	22.3	1.8	—	12.0
India	5,214	87.7	15.0	1,174.9	1,310	73.2	—	10.3	16.5	80.3	—	8.4	10.6	12.0
Indonesia	8,055	96.2	5.1	28,801.0	154,000	13.6[4]	1.6	25.1	59.7	26.6	30.5	6.1	10.3	11.3[10]
Iran	...	...	...	12,625.7[6]	209,000[6]	91.1[4, 6]	—	2.1[6]	6.8[6]	67.3[6]	15.2[6]	0.7[6]	1.5[6]	...
Iraq	...	...	...	...	...	...	...	...	...	...	...	...	...	...
Ireland	4,766	94.4	...	3.253	920	14.3	—	—	85.7	81.9	25.4	28.4	39.7	8.0
Isle of Man	...	...	...	...	...	...	...	...	...	...	...	...	...	...
Israel	4,211	99.9	2.8[2, 3]	10.336	1,940	29.2	—	31.0	39.8	61.4	32.8	4.1	—	10.9
Italy	20,689	79.5	...	519,530.0[6]	8,993,000[6]	70.7	—	2.9	26.4	76.4	—	2.7	—	10.5
Jamaica	109[1]	100.0[1]	35.4	13.391	5,460	27.0	—	—	73.0	135.6	133.8	109.2	13.1	27.0[8]
Japan	58,611	86.6	...	136,140.0	1,094,000	45.0[4]	—	47.0	8.0	106.7	13.2	—	—	2.5
Jersey	...	...	...	...	...	...	...	...	...	...	...	...	...	...
Jordan	495	93.5	8.7	1.705	460	40.8	—	—	59.2	104.9	8.1	—	—	8.5[1]
Kazakhstan	...	...	...	...	...	...	...	...	...	...	...	...	...	...
Kenya	59	71.2	39.4	31.667[6]	1,200[6]	78.1[6]	—	—	21.9[6]	83.3[6]	—	33.3[6]	7.5[6]	20.4[1]
Kiribati	...	...	...	...	...	...	...	...	...	...	...	...	...	...
Korea, North	...	...	...	...	...	...	...	...	...	...	...	...	...	...
Korea, South	13,401	99.9	1.6	24,586.0	561,000	7.1[4]	—	60.6	32.3	42.9	10.7	0.1	—	5.0
Kuwait	3,175	90.2	0.2[2, 3]	1.076	720	—	—	—	100.0	35.4	56.9	—	13.7	7.5[1]
Kyrgyzstan	...	...	...	...	...	...	...	...	...	...	...	...	...	...
Laos	...	...	...	...	...	...	...	...	...	...	...	...	...	...
Latvia	...	...	...	...	...	...	...	...	...	...	...	...	...	...
Lebanon	1,132	68.9	0.3	1.199	421,000	2.7	1.1	1.9	94.3	17.2	10.5	0.1	0.9	16.0[1]
Lesotho	121	96.7	3.5	0.351	190	21.9	—	1.0	77.1	30.6	55.7	0.9	8.7	15.0
Liberia	6[7]	100.0[7]	...	0.266	100	96.3[4]	1.1	2.5	0.1	28.6	1.0	48.5	6.9	7.7[1, 9]
Libya	4,622[1]	84.4[1]	0.5[2, 3]	4.987	1,110	71.0	0.1	—	28.9	60.5	12.4	—	—	5.0[7]
Liechtenstein	...	...	...	...	...	...	...	...	...	...	...	...	...	...
Lithuania	...	...	...	...	...	...	...	...	...	...	...	...	...	11.0[6]
Luxembourg	...	...	...	81.8	209,000	...	...	...	...	...	...	...	...	6.0[9]
Macau	...	...	...	16.229[6]	44,200[6]	...	...	...	...	...	...	...	...	...
Macedonia	...	...	...	...	...	...	...	...	...	...	...	...	...	...
Madagascar	69[1]	100.0[1]	38.1	915.4	70,300	85.6[4]	—	3.2	11.2	38.9	37.2	222.4	0.7	...
Malaŵi	20	75.0	9.9	0.757	90	81.1[4]	—	—	18.9	47.6	20.6	38.1	—	20.0
Malaysia	12,750[1]	96.8[1]	1.5	27.928[6]	1,520[6]	5.0[6]	—	—	95.0[6]	64.8[6]	18.7[6]	—	—	7.8[1]
Maldives	28	96.4	3.4	0.404[6]	1,800[6]	61.0[6]	—	0.2[6]	38.8[6]	86.4[6]	15.1[6]	2.1[6]	8.2[6]	7.0[6, 10]
Mali	233	95.7	7.5	108.2	12,400	25.5	—	16.4	58.1	90.2	4.1	11.5	—	12.5
Malta	880	93.0	0.1	0.409	1,130	—	—	—	100.0	89.5	3.4	—	—	5.5
Marshall Islands	...	...	...	...	...	...	...	...	...	...	...	...	...	...
Martinique	...	...	...	6.294	16,800	...	...	...	...	...	...	...	...	...
Mauritania	22	100.0	27.8	20.202	9,910	50.1	1.6	21.4	26.9	52.2	16.2	101.6	15.9	7.0
Mauritius	589	95.1	0.9	7.505	6,880	8.6	—	2.6	88.8	64.7	0.1	0.5	2.5	8.3
Mayotte	...	...	...	0.783	7,690	...	...	...	...	...	...	...	...	...
Mexico	13,800[1]	96.9[1]	4.4	122.020	1,370	20.4	0.5	3.1	76.0	57.7	—	23.9	1.6	18.9[10]
Micronesia	...	...	...	...	...	...	...	...	...	...	...	...	...	...
Moldova	...	...	...	...	...	...	...	...	...	...	...	...	...	...
Monaco	...	...	...	...	...	...	...	...	...	...	...	...	...	...
Mongolia	75[1]	49.4[1]	...	7.947[6]	3,680[6]	...	...	...	...	...	...	...	...	...
Morocco	2,357	95.9	6.4	92.080[6]	3,550[6]	23.7[6]	14.7[6]	15.3[6]	46.4[6]	87.2[6]	1.0[6]	10.7[6]	—	...
Mozambique	...	...	...	...	...	21.9[6]	36.8[6]	—	41.3[6]	43.9[6]	17.9[6]	154.2[6]	—	...
Myanmar (Burma)	225	95.6	16.9	30.587[2]	730[2]	80.7[2]	—	16.5[2]	2.8[2]	80.0[2]	—	3.2[2]	—	9.0[6, 9]
Namibia	...	...	...	...	...	...	...	...	...	...	...	...	...	...
Nauru	...	...	...	...	...	...	...	...	...	...	...	...	...	...
Nepal	372	97.0	4.2	17.614[6]	900[6]	46.8	1.2	1.7	50.3	46.7	18.5	8.2	20.8	13.0[1]
Netherlands, The	19,333	87.6	...	135.3	8,870	7.9	—	6.9	85.2	68.1	4.1	—	—	6.3

deposit money banks, 1992[b]									external public debt outstanding (long-term, disbursed only), 1991							country
assets (%)				liabilities					total ('000,000 U.S.$)	creditors (%)		debt service				
					composition (%)								repayment (%)			
loans to government	loans to private sector	reserves	foreign assets	deposits ('000,000,000 national currency)	demand depos.	savings depos.	govt. depos.	foreign liabilities		official	private	total ('000,000 U.S.$)	principal	interest	debt service ratio (%)	
21.6[4]	56.1	10.4	11.8	14.1	13.8	5.7	7.4	5.7	210.0	91.7	8.3	2.3	56.5	43.5	5.7	Equatorial Guinea
...	...	...	...	...	...	...	...	...	...	...	...	...	...	...	...	Eritrea[15]
...	...	...	...	...	...	...	...	...	...	...	...	...	...	...	...	Estonia
52.3[4]	11.6	21.5	14.6	6.584	37.0	39.6	3.7	5.0	3,301	88.9	11.1	125	71.2	28.8	22.9	Ethiopia[15]
...	...	...	...	...	...	...	...	...	...	...	...	...	...	...	...	Faeroe Islands
15.6[4]	65.5	13.7	5.2	1.344	15.7	72.8	0.5	7.8	267.9	94.6	5.4	77.6	72.3	27.7	8.5[2]	Fiji
1.3	74.4	5.1	19.2	587.332	21.4	23.7	1.7	35.9	...	...	...	...	...	...	...	Finland
6.6	65.8	0.3	27.3	10,359.0	13.4	25.1	—	27.9	...	...	...	...	...	...	...	France
...	...	...	...	...	...	...	...	...	62[3,7]	...	...	9[3,7]	...	...	7.4[3,7]	French Guiana
...	...	...	...	...	...	...	...	...	296[2,3]	...	...	21[2,3]	38.1[2,3]	61.9[2,3]	3.3[2,3]	French Polynesia
30.9[4]	61.7	1.8	5.6	373.8	30.4	28.4	8.1	9.9	2,935	76.4	23.6	78	48.7	51.3	5.5[2]	Gabon
28.8[4]	37.7	14.1	19.4	0.591	38.6	51.3	—	2.1	307.3	95.5	4.5	22.9	72.1	27.9	22.1[2]	Gambia, The
...	...	...	...	...	...	...	...	...	...	...	...	...	...	...	...	Gaza Strip
...	...	...	...	...	...	...	...	...	...	...	...	...	...	...	...	Georgia
17.3[4]	65.3	2.7	14.6	4,263.6	10.3	28.0	5.5	10.0	...	...	...	...	...	...	...	Germany
13.6[4]	27.4	26.8	32.2	504.7	34.6	32.7	4.5	12.0	2,958	92.7	7.3	161	62.7	37.3	14.7	Ghana
——39.6[6]——		0.1[6]	—	4,418.2[6]	——39.7[6]——			—	640[2,3]	...	...	89[2,3]	30.3[2,3]	69.7[2,3]	17.0[2,3]	Gibraltar
43.4[6]	31.2[6]	17.8[6]	7.6[6]	9,213.4[6]	6.6[6]	61.0[6]	—	24.4[6]	21,191[2,3]	...	...	3,219[2,3]	44.5[2,3]	55.5[2,3]	16.8[2,3]	Greece
...	...	...	...	...	...	...	...	...	...	...	...	...	...	...	...	Greenland
8.9[4]	64.5	11.3	15.3	0.492	12.9	59.0[5]	3.5	16.3	95.8	97.8	2.2	2.4	45.8	54.2	1.9	Grenada
...	...	...	...	...	...	...	...	...	49[3,7]	...	...	14[3,7]	...	...	6.3[3,7]	Guadeloupe
...	...	...	...	...	...	...	...	...	...	...	...	...	...	...	...	Guam
16.1	61.7	21.8	0.3	10.739	13.7	83.0	0.6	2.4	2,103	82.3	17.7	253	61.7	38.3	15.0	Guatemala
...	...	...	...	...	...	...	...	...	...	...	...	...	...	...	...	Guernsey
...	...	...	...	...	...	...	...	...	2,401	95.9	4.1	121	67.8	32.2	14.4	Guinea
...	...	...	...	...	...	...	...	...	573.7	94.6	5.4	3.9	41.0	59.0	24.9[2]	Guinea-Bissau
36.4[4]	24.1	29.1	10.4	36.192	11.3	67.7	—	5.1	1,554	90.9	9.1	56	37.5	62.5	58.1[2]	Guyana
1.3[7]	60.5[7]	34.8[7]	3.4[7]	2.486[7]	30.9[7]	60.1[7]	—	1.7[7]	609	92.6	7.4	12	50.0	50.0	3.0	Haiti
16.3[4]	67.6	10.1	6.0	6.433	19.8	49.5[5]	10.1	1.5	2,866	90.2	9.8	260	48.5	51.5	24.9	Honduras
...	...	...	...	5,730.1	...	...	...	...	6,794[2,3]	...	...	1,445[2,3]	52.7[2,3]	47.3[2,3]	1.8[2,3]	Hong Kong
9.5[4,6]	54.7[6]	29.7[6]	6.1[6]	1,765.3[6]	15.6[6]	35.1[5,6]	1.0[6]	7.8[6]	19,221	20.1	79.9	3,772	61.9	38.1	30.1	Hungary
10.4	81.7	6.2	1.7	229.331	11.4	54.0	—	19.0	...	...	...	...	...	...	...	Iceland
25.9	61.1	13.0	—	2,878.2	15.4	75.5	—	—	62,842	64.2	35.8	5,988	56.8	43.2	24.6	India
7.5[4]	75.2	9.5	7.8	166,401.0	10.2	54.2[5]	3.9	9.7	48,003	77.5	22.5	6,817	61.2	38.8	20.9	Indonesia
6.4[6]	56.4[6]	36.3[6]	0.9[6]	21,388.9[6]	36.7[6]	62.4[6]	—	0.7[6]	2,736	6.0	94.0	199	87.4	12.6	1.2	Iran
...	...	...	...	...	...	...	...	...	14,301[2,3]	...	...	1,382[2,3]	43.5[2,3]	56.5[2,3]	23.2[2,3]	Iraq
10.6	63.0	2.5	24.0	19.945	8.4	54.7	0.6	19.3	...	...	...	...	...	...	...	Ireland
...	...	...	...	...	...	...	...	...	...	...	...	...	...	...	...	Isle of Man
29.0	48.7	8.5	13.8	209.501	2.9	42.3	7.3	15.3	17,483[2,3]	...	...	2,774[2,3]	55.4[2,3]	44.6[2,3]	21.3[2,3]	Israel
16.0[6]	61.2[6]	12.6[6]	10.2[6]	1,068,320.0[6]	40.4[6]	45.3[6]	—	17.6[6]	...	...	...	...	...	...	...	Italy
20.2[4]	36.2	27.1	16.5	41.062	23.5	50.9	4.4	13.7	3,751	87.2	12.8	566	66.6	33.4	24.0	Jamaica
9.2[4]	78.9	1.0	10.9	716,100.0	13.7	51.8	—	12.4	...	...	...	...	...	...	...	Japan
...	...	...	...	...	...	...	...	...	...	...	...	...	...	...	...	Jersey
7.0	38.3	28.6	26.1	5.542	12.2	40.8	5.3	28.8	7,570	62.9	37.1	583	47.9	52.1	19.1	Jordan
...	...	...	...	...	...	...	...	...	...	...	...	...	...	...	...	Kazakhstan
21.4[4,6]	66.8[6]	9.0[6]	2.7[6]	72.791[6]	26.3[6]	51.9[5,6]	7.3[6]	1.9[6]	4,789	83.6	16.4	522	61.3	38.7	21.9[2]	Kenya
...	...	...	...	...	...	...	...	...	16[3,7]	...	...	0[3,7]	...	...	3.6[3,7]	Kiribati
...	...	...	...	...	...	...	...	...	3,775[2,3]	...	...	270[2,3]	64.8[2,3]	35.2[2,3]	24.8[2,3]	Korea, North
3.0	80.5	10.2	6.3	161,618.0	10.0	44.3[5]	5.0	7.1	22,246	41.1	58.9	3,204	62.7	37.3	6.2[2]	Korea, South
—	80.7	0.7	18.6	7.111	9.2	59.8	0.9	7.9	352[2,3]	...	...	247[2,3]	85.8[2,3]	14.2[2,3]	6.7[2,3]	Kuwait
...	...	...	...	...	...	...	...	...	...	...	...	...	...	...	...	Kyrgyzstan
...	...	...	...	...	...	...	...	...	1,096	100.0	—	8	62.5	37.5	8.3[2]	Laos
...	...	...	...	...	...	...	...	...	...	...	...	...	...	...	...	Latvia
21.5	33.4	4.6	40.5	14,396.6	2.7	73.5[5]	0.7	12.1	576.9	55.0	45.0	104.7	81.9	18.1	...	Lebanon
15.6[4]	35.9	15.4	33.0	0.881	35.4	42.2	4.5	2.8	405.9	93.1	6.9	26.7	62.5	37.5	4.6	Lesotho
2.7[4]	47.9	45.0	4.3	0.320	34.8	48.9	9.3	11.6	1,127	82.7	17.3	—	—	—	—	Liberia
—	59.6	37.5	2.9	4.764	56.5	26.4	3.8	4.4	2,841[2,3]	...	...	458[2,3]	86.7[2,3]	13.3[2,3]	8.9[2,3]	Libya
...	...	...	...	...	...	...	...	...	...	...	...	...	...	...	...	Liechtenstein
...	...	...	...	...	...	...	...	...	...	...	...	...	...	...	...	Lithuania
—	4.4	—	95.6	13,070.8	0.8	10.6	—	81.4	...	...	...	...	...	...	...	Luxembourg
——35.8[6]——		...	60.9[6]	71.313[6]	22.3[6]	35.6[6]	...	31.4[6]	149[2,3]	...	...	21[2,3]	33.3[2,3]	66.7[2,3]	1.4[2,3]	Macau
...	...	...	...	...	...	...	...	...	...	...	...	...	...	...	...	Macedonia
1.4	66.9	17.4	14.3	1,373.0	43.6	20.2	10.1	3.2	3,381	93.1	6.9	114	41.2	58.8	24.4	Madagascar
13.4[4]	67.4	15.9	3.4	1.318	33.7	48.1	—	9.7	1,528	96.7	3.3	102	59.8	40.2	16.4[2]	Malaŵi
9.5[6]	80.3[6]	6.0[6]	4.2[6]	130.593[6]	12.1[6]	47.2[6]	4.7[6]	9.0[6]	16,447	28.3	71.7	2,725	58.9	41.1	6.9	Malaysia
21.2[4,6]	30.8[6]	31.5[6]	16.5[6]	0.803[6]	14.3[6]	37.5[6]	2.7[6]	18.7[6]	77.2	96.2	3.8	6.8	79.4	20.6	3.8	Maldives
1.9	51.9	39.9	6.3	176.9	26.8	27.7	21.0	7.3	2,392	99.5	0.5	11	45.5	54.5	2.1	Mali
7.1	55.2	8.5	29.2	1.102	5.2	75.1	—	5.6	142.2	100.0	—	11.5	66.1	33.9	0.5[7]	Malta
...	...	...	...	...	...	...	...	...	...	...	...	...	...	...	...	Marshall Islands
...	...	...	...	...	...	...	...	...	40[3,7]	...	...	9[3,7]	...	...	2.1[3,7]	Martinique
0.4	85.7	11.1	2.7	46.770	25.6	15.4	4.9	27.1	1,912	96.2	3.8	60	66.7	33.3	12.0	Mauritania
19.1	54.9	18.9	7.1	33.822	10.9	80.4	—	0.2	794	84.1	15.9	100	55.0	45.0	5.7	Mauritius
...	...	...	...	...	...	...	...	...	...	...	...	...	...	...	...	Mayotte
8.4[4]	86.0	1.9	3.7	395.790	20.8	45.6[5]	5.0	15.0	78,456	32.1	69.9	9,378	38.4	61.6	20.7	Mexico
...	...	...	...	...	...	...	...	...	...	...	...	...	...	...	...	Micronesia
...	...	...	...	...	...	...	...	...	...	...	...	...	...	...	...	Moldova
...	...	...	...	...	...	...	...	...	...	...	...	...	...	...	...	Monaco
...	...	...	...	...	...	...	...	...	14,529[2,3]	...	...	287[2,3]	—	100.0[2,3]	190.1[2,3]	Mongolia
...	...	...	...	...	...	...	...	...	20,132	77.2	22.8	2,023	46.5	53.5	24.4	Morocco
17.3[6]	42.1[6]	32.3[6]	8.3[6]	313.900[6]	71.4[6]	6.6[6]	19.6[6]	9.1[6]	4,039	89.2	10.8	33	69.7	30.3	9.0	Mozambique
93.8[4,13]	4.4[13]	1.8[13]	—	64.073[13]	1.6[13]	11.9[5,13]	8.5[13]	15.7[13]	4,557	94.5	5.5	78	37.2	62.8	29.3[7]	Myanmar (Burma)
...	...	...	...	1.961[7]	...	...	...	...	3[3,7]	...	...	0[3,7]	...	...	...	Namibia
...	...	...	...	...	...	...	...	...	181[3,7]	...	...	23[3,7]	...	...	...	Nauru
28.2[4,6]	47.4[6]	8.9[6]	15.5[6]	33.870[6]	12.7[6]	68.6[6]	—	4.5[6]	1,705	94.4	5.6	57	54.4	45.6	11.9	Nepal
12.5[4]	51.1	0.3	36.1	952.4	10.3	35.9[5]	—	31.4	...	...	...	...	...	...	...	Netherlands, The

Finance (continued)

country	international reserves, 1993[a]			money supply, 1992[b]		central bank authority, 1992[b]								
						assets (%)				liabilities (%)				central bank discount rate, 1993[a]
	total ('000,000 SDRs)	% foreign exchange	ratio of external debt to total reserves, 1991[b]	stock ('000,000,000 national currency)	M1 per capita	claims on government	claims on private sector	claims on banks	claims on foreign assets	reserve money	government deposits	foreign liabilities	capital accounts	
Netherlands Antilles	147[1]	87.1[1]	5.5[2, 3]	0.679	3,550	13.3	—	—	86.7	71.3	7.5	—	12.3	6.0
New Caledonia	...	...	...	54.104	304,000	...	...	...	...	...	...	...	...	...
New Zealand	2,228	95.2	...	23.481[6]	6,780[6]	33.3[6]	—	2.8[6]	63.9[6]	18.9[6]	57.4[6]	0.4[6]	—	7.3
Nicaragua	...	...	...	...	...	54.2[12]	—	44.1[12]	1.7[12]	92.3[12]	9.7[12]	20.6[12]	0.1[12]	...
Niger	174	94.8	6.3	71.1	8,490	26.5	—	20.6	52.9	71.3	2.5	19.7	—	12.5
Nigeria	587	95.7	7.4	48.708[6]	550[6]	64.1[6]	1.1[6]	0.7[6]	34.1[6]	26.9[6]	43.0[6]	—	3.2[6]	23.0
Northern Mariana Islands	...	...	...	...	...	...	...	...	...	...	...	...	...	...
Norway	10,306	93.9	...	284.3	66,200	8.4	—	36.9	54.7	25.6	44.9	—	—	7.5
Oman	1,140[1]	95.5[1]	1.4	0.433	260	4.1	—	—	95.9	31.2	26.6	—	22.3	6.3[1, 9]
Pakistan	349	78.5	28.2	371.796	2,820	62.0	—	24.5	13.5	73.2	5.3	16.0	—	10.0
Panama	403	96.3	7.9	0.639	250	58.7[4]	15.0	—	26.3	9.2	70.8	24.1	8.2	...
Papua New Guinea	87	96.6	4.9	0.438	110	54.0	—	—	46.0	32.3	42.0	11.7	39.8	6.4
Paraguay	410[1]	80.2[1]	1.8	920.912	201,000	48.8[4]	0.3	7.9	43.0	54.9	7.0	4.3	15.7	...
Peru	2,254	96.8	5.9	1.608[6]	70[6]	3.8[4, 6]	—	8.5[6]	87.7[6]	59.9[6]	0.1[6]	57.4[6]	4.5[6]	30.6
Philippines	3,613	94.9	7.2	117.5	1,830	33.4[4]	—	9.4	57.2	62.2	72.2	104.3	2.8	7.2
Poland	2,525	96.3	12.1	127,006.0[6]	3,312,000[6]	19.7[4, 6]	—	47.8[6]	32.5[6]	69.6[6]	7.1[6]	14.0[6]	0.6[6]	38.0[1]
Portugal	12,185	93.3	0.9	3,417.3	348,000	8.5[4]	—	0.5	91.0	69.9	14.6	0.1	4.7	13.5
Puerto Rico	...	...	...	...	...	...	...	...	...	...	...	...	...	...
Qatar	532	84.4	0.5[2, 3]	3.990	7,520	—	—	5.1	94.9	70.1	10.8	—	3.2	...
Réunion	...	...	...	10.187	16,200	...	...	...	...	...	...	...	...	...
Romania	651	87.3	0.6	1,011.5	44,400	25.8	—	34.6	39.6	84.3	16.0	46.6	7.3	...
Russia	...	...	...	...	...	...	...	...	...	...	...	...	...	20.0[1]
Rwanda	46	73.9	7.1	22.631	3,030	69.8	0.3	2.3	27.6	33.8	18.0	14.4	20.7	11.0
St. Kitts and Nevis	20	100.0	2.5	0.065	1,530	9.9	—	—	90.1	99.9	0.1	—	—	6.5[8]
St. Lucia	38	97.4	1.4	0.212	1,580	8.4	—	0.5	91.1	97.6	2.4	—	—	7.0[8]
St. Vincent and the Grenadines	23	95.7	2.6	0.091	840	8.5	—	—	91.4	93.8	6.3	—	—	6.5[8]
San Marino	...	...	...	...	...	...	...	...	...	...	...	...	...	...
São Tomé and Príncipe	...	...	...	...	...	...	...	...	...	...	...	...	...	...
Saudi Arabia	5,042	71.6	0.2[2, 3]	101.9[2]	7,070[2]	—	—	—	100.0[2]	24.7[2]	10.5[2]	—	—	...
Senegal	14	78.6	198.4	217.4	27,900	45.9	—	53.2	0.9	51.0	1.1	30.4	—	12.5
Seychelles	22	100.0	5.7	0.293	4,110	59.9	—	1.0	39.1	77.4	16.0	—	3.4	9.5
Sierra Leone	17	82.4	64.1	31.387	7,080	45.6	—	—	54.4	117.6	9.6	981.5	—	55.0[1]
Singapore	29,599	99.5	0.1[2, 3]	18,515	6,500	—	—	—	100.0	20.6	38.1	—	—	2.8[10]
Slovakia	...	...	...	...	...	...	...	...	...	...	...	...	...	...
Slovenia	...	...	...	...	...	...	...	...	...	...	...	...	...	...
Solomon Islands	17	94.1	11.6	0.109	320	36.4	—	—	63.6	36.4	4.2	1.4	44.2	13.5[8]
Somalia	12[7]	100.0[7]	...	139.8[7]	18,900[7]	36.9[4, 7]	—	43.9[7]	19.2[7]	74.2[7]	13.4[7]	238.0[7]	15.1[7]	45.0[2]
South Africa	1,336[1]	82.0[1]	...	49.858[2]	1,320[2]	26.7[2]	—	12.5[2]	60.7[2]	115.9[2]	62.3[2]	6.5[2]	—	13.0
Bophuthatswana	...	...	...	...	...	...	...	...	...	...	...	...	...	...
Ciskei	...	...	...	...	...	...	...	...	...	...	...	...	...	...
Transkei	...	...	...	...	...	...	...	...	...	...	...	...	...	...
Venda	...	...	...	...	...	...	...	...	...	...	...	...	...	...
Spain	29,411	95.0	...	16,900.0	432,000	16.0	—	36.5	47.5	94.8	0.8	—	12.8	11.3
Sri Lanka	767	96.5	8.2	50.057	2,850	51.4	—	5.7	42.9	47.2	2.7	30.9	18.6	17.0
Sudan, The	3	100.0	1,289.3	44,305[6]	1,500[6]	97.3[4, 6]	—	0.9[6]	1.8[6]	87.2[6]	—	83.3[6]	1.0[6]	...
Suriname	2	—	3.4[2, 3]	3.221	7,960	98.1	—	—	1.9	92.7	0.4	2.3	1.5	...
Swaziland	188	95.2	1.5	0.254	300	—	—	1.5	98.5	46.3	29.3	0.8	5.4	11.3
Sweden	14,747	95.3	...	...	...	39.4	—	16.5	44.1	73.1	—	3.4	—	7.0
Switzerland	25,034	85.8	...	86.2	12,400	7.6	—	2.0	90.4	60.4	0.6	—	—	5.0
Syria	173[7]	82.7[7]	...	95.030[7]	7,970[7]	72.4[4, 7]	—	6.8[7]	20.8[7]	63.9[7]	20.1[7]	32.9[7]	0.2[7]	...
Taiwan	60,000	99.2	0.0[2, 3]	2,434.5	117,000	0.5	—	8.9	90.6	53.7	5.2	—	—	5.6
Tajikistan	...	...	...	...	...	...	...	...	...	...	...	...	...	...
Tanzania	278	96.4	28.3	64.126[13]	2,740[13]	39.3[13]	—	49.7[13]	11.0[13]	40.9[13]	—	97.1[13]	—	15.5[7]
Thailand	15,692	97.9	0.8	249.7	4,360	9.2	—	9.0	81.8	37.6	30.6	—	35.2	11.0
Togo	203	99.5	3.1	78.5[6]	21,800[6]	32.5	—	6.5	61.0	73.7	5.0	11.2	—	12.5
Tonga	26	92.3	1.5	0.022	230	19.2	—	—	80.8	96.0	1.0	—	5.0	4.3[9]
Trinidad and Tobago	109	98.2	5.3	2.696	2,110	56.9	—	5.0	38.1	38.3	16.2	27.5	27.4	13.0
Tunisia	407	97.8	8.9	2.894	340	5.7	—	52.3	42.1	65.6	3.4	14.3	4.8	10.8[10]
Turkey	5,383	96.8	7.3	48,768.0[6]	841,000[6]	55.2[4, 6]	—	4.2[6]	40.7[6]	38.8[6]	1.4[6]	55.5[6]	2.3[6]	45.0[1]
Turkmenistan	...	...	...	13.060[6]	4,210[6]	...	...	...	...	...	...	...	...	...
Tuvalu	...	...	...	...	...	...	...	...	...	...	...	...	...	...
Uganda	77	96.1	39.6	...	...	92.1[4, 17]	—	—	7.9[17]	91.0[17]	47.3[17]	69.3[17]	—	26.0
Ukraine	...	...	...	173.4[6]	3,330[6]	...	...	...	...	...	...	...	...	5.4[6]
United Arab Emirates	4,081	94.3	0.6[2, 3]	14.981	7,450	1.9	—	0.2	97.9	60.9	27.7	1.5	7.6	...
United Kingdom	28,342	91.3	...	238.4	4,120	32.9	—	—	67.1	52.8	—	45.1	—	5.0[10]
United States	54,542	55.8	...	1,058.6	4,120	81.6	—	—	18.4	96.6	7.3	1.9	—	3.0
Uruguay	665	87.4	6.2	2.544	810,000	51.2[4]	0.5	18.6	29.7	16.3	33.2	32.3	—	143.5
Uzbekistan	...	...	...	...	...	...	...	...	...	...	...	...	...	...
Vanuatu	30[1]	93.3[1]	1.0	4.377[6]	28,700[6]	—	—	0.2[6]	99.8[6]	45.4[6]	46.1[6]	1.0[6]	13.3[6]	6.0[10]
Venezuela	6,615	88.1	2.2	375.5	18,000	21.7[4]	—	1.3	77.0	29.2	13.2	33.9	7.9	61.0
Vietnam	...	...	...	...	...	...	...	...	...	...	...	...	...	...
Virgin Islands (U.S.)	...	...	...	...	...	...	...	...	...	...	...	...	...	...
West Bank	...	...	...	...	...	...	...	...	...	...	...	...	...	...
Western Sahara	...	...	...	...	...	...	...	...	...	...	...	...	...	...
Western Samoa	43	93.0	1.7	0.038	240	1.2	—	4.1	94.7	44.1	55.7	—	—	5.5[10]
Yemen	...	...	...	...	...	...	...	...	...	...	...	...	...	...
Yugoslavia[18]	1,103[1]	93.9[1]	4.2	...	...	...	...	...	...	...	...	...	...	...
Zaire	119	99.2	49.6	18,056.0[6]	510,000[6]	82.2[6]	0.1[6]	—	17.7[6]	22.1[6]	0.6[6]	62.5[6]	11.3[6]	50.0[7]
Zambia	129[6]	100.0[6]	26.8	22.360[6]	2,780[6]	8.1[6]	2.4[6]	—	89.5[6]	144.5[6]	−186.7[6]	793.2[6]	—	113.9
Zimbabwe	280	93.6	15.3	2.978[6]	310[6]	53.7[4, 6]	—	—	46.3[6]	52.5[6]	—	74.0[6]	—	30.0[1]

deposit money banks, 1992[b]									external public debt outstanding (long-term, disbursed only), 1991							country
assets (%)				liabilities					total ('000,000 U.S.$)	creditors (%)		debt service				
loans to govern-ment	loans to private sector	re-serves	foreign assets	deposits ('000,000,000 national currency)	composition (%)					offi-cial	private	total ('000,000 U.S.$)	repayment (%)		debt service ratio (%)	
					demand depos.	savings depos.	govt. depos.	foreign liabilities					princi-pal	inter-est		
2.9[4]	52.4	3.7	40.9	3.273	13.0	41.8[5]	1.5	39.5	1,331[2,3]	...	...	160[2,3]	45.6[2,3]	54.4[2,3]	10.6[2,3]	Netherlands Antilles
...	...	...	...	...	...	...	...	...	226[2,3]	...	...	33[2,3]	50.0[2,3]	50.0[2,3]	4.7[2,3]	New Caledonia
12.0[6]	79.9[6]	4.5[6]	3.6[6]	64.761[6]	34.5[6]	44.2[6]	—	18.7[6]	...	...	...	...	...	...	...	New Zealand
—	74.7[12]	25.2[12]	0.1[12]	1.044[12]	66.0[12]	18.2[5,12]	8.1[12]	0.2[12]	8,703	74.8	25.2	386	43.5	56.5	110.9	Nicaragua
11.5	51.0	32.1	5.4	138.9	21.4	35.0	16.7	25.7	1,278	98.7	1.3	109	89.9	10.1	28.9	Niger
5.9	46.8	27.3	20.0	99.265	31.3	41.7	3.6	1.3	33,245	56.4	43.6	3,287	32.5	67.5	24.5	Nigeria
...	...	...	...	...	...	...	...	...	...	...	...	...	...	...	...	Northern Mariana Islands
13.9[4]	73.1	0.7	12.3	654.2	38.2	30.3[5]	4.9	11.9	...	...	...	...	...	...	...	Norway
12.7	68.8	4.8	13.7	1.498	13.8	56.2	9.3	2.7	2,270	16.3	83.7	541	71.2	28.8	12.8[2]	Oman
33.6	51.1	9.0	6.3	568.908	35.8	25.2	0.8	20.0	17,632	96.8	3.2	1,472	61.6	38.4	16.5[2]	Pakistan
1.2	26.0	—	72.8	13.338	4.3	20.7	—	63.9	3,939	39.5	60.5	181	40.3	59.7	2.9	Panama
23.2	71.4	1.6	3.8	1.574	18.6	63.1	2.8	7.4	1,601	74.8	25.2	236	66.9	33.1	13.8	Papua New Guinea
—	55.9	16.2	27.9	2,196.666	14.1	61.6	—	3.2	1,779	71.4	28.6	185	58.9	41.1	15.6[2]	Paraguay
24.3[4,6]	38.0[6]	17.2[6]	20.5[6]	4.9[6]	13.3[6]	53.5[5,6]	15.5[6]	5.4[6]	15,080	63.4	36.6	794	57.2	42.8	18.4	Peru
17.2[4]	46.5	17.2	19.1	616.3	5.6	60.3	4.3	12.2	24,530	68.6	31.4	2,787	49.9	50.1	18.8	Philippines
45.9[4,6]	26.6[6]	12.3[6]	15.2[6]	375,766.0[6]	18.7[6]	40.7[5,6]	2.2[6]	4.5[6]	44,057	74.4	25.6	834	45.9	54.1	4.5	Poland
27.4[4]	47.2	15.7	9.7	14,540.8	18.0	42.2	3.3	23.4	19,374	22.0	78.0	5,077	74.5	25.5	18.4	Portugal
...	...	...	...	...	...	...	...	...	...	...	...	...	...	...	...	Puerto Rico
—	67.4	2.9	29.7	26.871	9.9	41.1	18.7	0.8	308[2,3]	...	...	35[2,3]	33.3[2,3]	66.7[2,3]	2.4[2,3]	Qatar
...	...	...	...	...	...	...	...	...	61[2,3]	...	...	9[2,3]	77.8[2,3]	22.2[2,3]	0.5[2,3]	Réunion
7.4	71.7	9.7	11.2	2,666.7	28.2	29.2	13.4	8.0	334	88.3	11.7	29	79.3	20.7	0.6	Romania
...	...	...	...	...	...	...	...	...	54,436[16]	22.7[16]	77.3[16]	12,769[16]	75.1[16]	24.9[16]	...	Russia
22.1[4]	48.6	9.9	19.4	31.482	36.8	45.3	9.4	4.1	780.1	99.7	0.3	19.4	65.5	34.5	13.6	Rwanda
17.2[4]	53.9	9.2	19.7	0.623	6.8	48.6[5]	16.1	19.5	43.5	98.2	1.8	2.5	52.0	48.0	3.2[2]	St. Kitts and Nevis
8.5[4]	68.8	9.7	13.0	1.008	14.7	54.3[5]	15.7	12.1	69.9	97.9	2.1	9.2	62.0	38.0	3.3	St. Lucia
14.1[4]	50.9	12.8	22.2	0.510	12.0	49.0[5]	18.8	15.3	60.3	100.0	—	4.2	59.5	40.5	3.7	St. Vincent and the Grenadines
...	...	...	...	...	...	...	...	...	...	...	...	...	...	...	...	San Marino
...	...	...	...	...	...	...	...	...	147.1	99.9	0.1	1.5	53.3	46.7	28.0[2]	São Tomé and Príncipe
—	42.7	5.2	52.1	204.2	41.1	45.4[5]	0.7	15.9	2,041[2,3]	...	...	676[2,3]	79.7[2,3]	20.3[2,3]	2.7[2,3]	Saudi Arabia
4.3	78.2	13.8	3.7	536.6	19.9	31.2	18.8	8.8	2,838	95.0	5.0	222	59.9	40.1	13.4[2]	Senegal
63.4[4]	14.6	17.4	4.6	1.083	15.7	61.0	4.0	3.3	154.0	81.0	19.0	21.2	69.8	30.2	8.3	Seychelles
10.4[4]	37.6	20.9	31.0	27.271	47.7	38.3	—	—	642	85.5	14.5	3	66.7	33.3	3.9[2]	Sierra Leone
8.4	50.1	3.9	37.6	137.383	7.5	41.6	4.2	35.3	3,481[2,3]	...	...	557[2,3]	40.6[2,3]	59.4[2,3]	1.0[2,3]	Singapore
...	...	...	...	...	...	...	...	...	...	...	...	...	...	...	...	Slovakia
...	...	...	...	...	...	...	...	...	...	...	...	...	...	...	...	Slovenia
55.6	37.5	3.5	3.4	0.192	38.5	57.8	2.2	2.8	99.3	89.1	10.9	11.4	76.3	23.7	9.5	Solomon Islands
−12.4[4,7]	69.3[7]	27.1[7]	16.1[7]	129.6[7]	49.4[7]	13.8[7]	—	—	1,929	98.1	1.9	—	—	—	—	Somalia
7.1[2]	88.5[2]	3.5[2]	0.9[2]	134.074[2]	30.6[2]	53.0[2]	—	5.0[2]	...	...	...	...	...	...	...	South Africa
...	...	...	...	...	...	...	...	...	...	...	...	...	...	...	...	Bophuthatswana
...	...	...	...	...	...	...	...	...	...	...	...	...	...	...	...	Ciskei
...	...	...	...	...	...	...	...	...	...	...	...	...	...	...	...	Transkei
...	...	...	...	...	...	...	...	...	...	...	...	...	...	...	...	Venda
19.0[4]	62.4	7.2	11.4	69,159.0	15.5	40.2	3.9	13.5	...	...	...	...	...	...	...	Spain
18.7[4]	57.2	9.9	14.2	163.934	13.9	48.6	5.5	18.6	5,653	88.9	11.1	289	56.1	43.9	9.4	Sri Lanka
—	42.4[6]	30.4[6]	27.2[6]	33.122[6]	56.5[6]	28.5[6]	5.2[6]	4.8[6]	9,221	82.8	17.2	23	56.5	43.5	4.0	Sudan, The
4.8	53.1	41.3	0.8	4.640	39.2	50.5	0.5	3.6	82[2,3]	...	...	15[2,3]	73.3[2,3]	26.7[2,3]	3.6[2,3]	Suriname
—	64.1	20.7	15.2	1.050	18.8	62.8	8.5	6.1	254.4	98.0	2.0	27.4	64.6	35.4	3.5	Swaziland
4.7	69.0	2.6	23.8	1,383.8	—44.2[5]—		—	39.4	...	...	...	...	...	...	...	Sweden
2.8	70.2	1.0	26.0	803.0	5.1	37.4	—	22.8	...	...	...	...	...	...	...	Switzerland
57.3[4,6]	17.3[6]	13.0[6]	12.5[6]	155.244[6]	27.0[6]	29.2[6]	3.1[6]	5.4[6]	14,932	94.5	5.5	627	79.1	20.9	25.2[2]	Syria
12.3[4]	73.0	11.2	3.5	9,235.8	21.6	58.4	6.0	4.2	2,876[2,3]	...	...	592[2,3]	64.7[2,3]	35.3[2,3]	1.2[2,3]	Taiwan
...	...	...	...	...	...	...	...	...	...	...	...	...	...	...	...	Tajikistan
84.0[4,13]	8.5[13]	5.2[13]	2.4[13]	94.860[13]	34.7[13]	24.9[13]	1.3[13]	84.3[13]	5,786	95.7	4.3	98	66.3	33.7	19.3[2]	Tanzania
5.4[4]	89.0	2.5	3.1	2,419.9	2.7	77.2	3.2	6.9	13,292	63.1	36.9	1,856	61.8	38.2	4.9	Thailand
0.6[6]	53.2[6]	34.8[6]	11.4[6]	212.0[6]	19.4[6]	40.7[6]	23.5[6]	11.2[6]	1,143	95.3	4.7	37	51.4	48.6	5.2	Togo
9.0[4]	38.5	52.5	—	0.081	18.9	37.3	12.8	—	50.2	82.1	17.9	2.9	58.6	41.4	4.9	Tonga
11.7[4]	71.8	12.6	3.9	10.738	17.3	60.8	1.3	2.4	1,817	39.6	60.4	316	54.7	45.3	15.1[2]	Trinidad and Tobago
6.2	86.0	1.5	6.3	8.608	18.1	40.5	—	16.1	7,156	82.1	17.9	1,135	67.2	32.8	18.8	Tunisia
25.8[4,6]	50.3[6]	10.2[6]	13.7[6]	189,402.0[6]	15.7[6]	37.1[6]	10.2[6]	31.8[6]	39,207	47.8	52.2	6,604	59.7	40.3	25.6	Turkey
...	...	...	...	...	...	...	...	...	...	...	...	...	...	...	...	Turkmenistan
...	...	...	...	...	...	...	...	...	...	...	...	...	...	...	...	Tuvalu
12.9[4]	40.2	13.3	36.6	261.359	41.2	22.1	3.1	10.1	2,325	90.0	10.0	92	73.9	26.1	42.2	Uganda
...	...	...	...	...	...	...	...	...	...	...	...	...	...	...	...	Ukraine
8.5[4]	38.7	5.9	47.0	144.500	6.8	37.7	7.8	18.2	1,154[2,3]	...	...	338[2,3]	72.2[2,3]	27.8[2,3]	2.3[2,3]	United Arab Emirates
1.4[4]	50.4	0.5	47.7	1,357.8	16.3	25.0[5]	—	50.3	...	...	...	...	...	...	...	United Kingdom
9.9[4]	81.2	2.7	6.3	4,500.1	16.7	51.4	1.0	8.2	...	...	...	...	...	...	...	United States
6.1[4]	32.4	16.2	45.2	30,325.8	3.8	43.5[5]	3.3	38.3	2,843	35.8	64.2	638	73.4	26.6	26.7	Uruguay
...	...	...	...	...	...	...	...	...	...	...	...	...	...	...	...	Uzbekistan
2.0[4,6]	22.2[6]	3.5[6]	72.3[6]	28.051[6]	11.4[6]	69.7[5,6]	2.2[6]	8.9[6]	38.1	96.9	3.1	1.2	66.7	33.3	1.5[2]	Vanuatu
5.4[4]	61.9	23.6	9.1	1,244.9	19.7	66.4[5]	2.0	3.9	25,189	10.1	89.9	2,312	26.2	73.8	12.6	Venezuela
...	...	...	...	...	...	...	...	...	16,319[2,3]	...	...	429[2,3]	26.1[2,3]	73.9[2,3]	45.3[2,3]	Vietnam
...	...	...	...	...	...	...	...	...	...	...	...	...	...	...	...	Virgin Islands (U.S.)
...	...	...	...	...	...	...	...	...	...	...	...	...	...	...	...	West Bank
...	...	...	...	...	...	...	...	...	...	...	...	...	...	...	...	Western Sahara
3.9[4]	51.1	36.8	8.2	0.139	18.6	58.8	1.4	17.2	112.9	98.9	1.1	4.1	70.7	29.3	5.1	Western Samoa
...	...	...	...	...	...	...	...	...	5,207	97.0	3.0	111	74.8	25.2	5.0	Yemen
...	...	...	...	...	...	...	...	...	11,641	58.3	41.7	2,339	57.8	42.2	12.5	Yugoslavia[18]
0.2[4]	7.1	69.0	23.7	570,680.0	66.5	11.9[5]	2.5	9.7	9,151	90.5	9.5	95	41.1	58.9	5.9[2]	Zaire
22.5[6]	35.7[6]	22.7[6]	19.1[6]	63.005[6]	20.9[6]	41.2[6]	5.0[6]	4.8[6]	4,954	90.1	9.9	483	51.3	48.7	11.5[2]	Zambia
16.4[4,6]	69.4[6]	10.6[6]	3.7[6]	6.801[6]	30.7[6]	40.1[6]	2.8[6]	9.1[6]	2,604	62.8	37.2	465	49.0	51.0	22.6	Zimbabwe

[1]1992. [2]1990. [3]Includes long-term private debt not guaranteed by the government. [4]Includes claims on nonfinancial government (public) enterprises and/or local governments. [5]Includes foreign-currency deposits. [6]1991. [7]1989. [8]Treasury bill rate. [9]Short-term deposit rate. [10]Money market rate. [11]Notes and coins only. [12]1987. [13]1988. [14]Data refer to former Czechoslovakia. [15]Ethiopia includes Eritrea. [16]Data refer to the former U.S.S.R. [17]1986. [18]Data refer to the former Socialist Federal Republic of Yugoslavia.

Housing and construction

The present table summarizes data about the housing stock and the construction industries of the countries of the world. The principal focus is on the elements that are most comparable internationally: the age of the housing (by decade, so far as possible), the legal tenure of the householder, construction of exterior walls, principal physical amenities, sanitary arrangements, and the amount of space both absolutely (total area of the average dwelling in square metres [1 square metre equals 1.20 square yards, or 10.76 square feet]) and relatively (persons per room). The data on construction characterize the industry in terms of: (1) the portion of national gross domestic product (GDP) represented by each country's construction industry, (2) the number of new dwelling units constructed annually, their area, and the rate (in years) required to replace the total national stock of dwellings shown on the extreme left of the table, and (3), for nonresidential construction, the number of buildings or portions of buildings built for nonresidential purposes and their area in square metres.

Because housing patterns differ greatly from country to country, the portion of each country's housing stock for which data are compared was defined as specifically as possible. In general, the numbers refer to permanent, private dwelling units that are usually occupied year-round, whether or not actually occupied on the date of the housing census or survey. That definition implies the exclusion of certain housing that is often part of national housing censuses: vacation homes, second homes occupied less than half the year, collective or communal dwellings, and so on. The housing unit to which the data on tenure refer may be either the individual dwelling or the household, according to the reporting practice of the country concerned.

The data are collected mostly from national housing censuses and surveys. The majority of countries combine the housing census with the population census at five- to ten-year intervals. Some countries, however, can conduct a meaningful housing census only in the capital city or in the few largest cities; others may be able to collect and process data for only a few of the most important housing characteristics even when national coverage is complete. These choices may be dictated by the lack of funding to collect data for the entire country or by the perception, particularly in a tropical, rural country where adequate dwellings can be built by hand, that no urgent housing problem exists. These choices may be complex, however, as

Housing and construction

country	housing stock			decade built (percent)					tenure[c] (percent)			construction of exterior walls (percent)			
	year	dwelling units[a]	median age[b] (years)	1949 or earlier	1950–59	1960–69	1970–79	1980 or later	owned	rented	collective, vacant, other	traditional materials	sawn/framed wood	masonry or cement	other
Afghanistan	1979	3,940,000[1]	...	...	...	...	...	...	55.2	23.5	21.3	...	...	...	...
Albania	1989	385,769[4]	22.6	14.0[5]	20.3[6]	19.0[7]	24.3[8]	22.4[9]	91.2	8.8	—	...	...	...	...
Algeria	1987	3,050,812	...	——51.4[12]——		6.4[13]	18.6	23.6	63.0[14]	24.6[14]	12.4[14]	...	...	...	...
American Samoa	1990	6,959	13.9	4.4	7.5	21.9	22.7	43.5	78.1	21.9	—	4.1[16]	56.3[16]	34.9[16]	4.7[16]
Andorra	1990	...	18.1	18.0	5.7	20.8	——55.5——		...	...	...	...	...	...	...
Angola	...	...	...	...	...	...	...	...	...	...	...	...	...	...	...
Antigua and Barbuda	1970	15,405[19]	11.1	23.3	31.4	46.1	—	—	55.9	40.4	3.7	...	...	...	...
Argentina	1980	10,096,888[18]	21.6	24.0	17.3	22.0	18.3	18.4	67.7	14.8	17.5	6.1	6.7	84.2	3.0
Armenia	1989	559,000[22]	...	...	...	...	...	...	...	...	...	...	...	...	...
Aruba	1991	19,224	27.7	17.0[23]	25.8[24]	12.1	16.8	28.3	70.6	26.7	2.7	—	7.7	90.6	1.7
Australia	1986	6,450,152[18]	26.1[25]	37.9[25]	10.4[25]	18.6[25]	——33.1[25]——		69.1[22]	26.7[22]	5.1[22]	...	...	...	...
Austria	1991	3,393,271	33.8	33.0[5]	14.7[6]	18.1[7]	18.5[8]	15.7[9]	50.0	38.7	11.3	—	5.1[4]	81.9[4]	13.0[4]
Azerbaijan	1989	1,381,000[22]	...	...	...	...	...	...	...	...	...	...	...	...	...
Bahamas, The	1980	54,308	30.7	——54.7——		25.6	——19.7——		51.4	37.4	11.2	4.0[30]	32.3	54.7	9.0
Bahrain	1981	52,810	15.2	58.3	14.5	——27.2——			49.6	30.0	20.4	2.1[28]	—	95.1[28]	2.8[28]
Bangladesh	1981	14,785,048	...	...	...	...	...	...	89.7	5.0	5.3	20.0	11.6	5.0	63.4
Barbados	1990	75,211	19.1	——48.6——			22.9	28.5	76.1	20.4	3.5	0.2	61.2[32]	35.4	3.2
Belarus	1989	2,796,000[22]	...	...	...	...	...	...	...	...	...	...	...	...	...
Belgium	1991	3,748,165	...	37.0[5]	21.5[34]	13.1[35]	18.5[8]	9.9[9]	64.5	34.2	1.3	...	...	...	...
Belize	1980	27,298	...	24.6	30.0		——41.0——		56.1	27.2	16.7	7.5	73.4	14.0	5.1
Benin	1979	612,041	...	...	...	...	...	...	...	...	...	...	...	...	...
Bermuda	1991	22,061	...	——56.0——		15.8	12.0	16.2	43.4	52.4	4.2	—	1.7[16,32]	95.1[16]	3.2[16]
Bhutan	...	...	...	...	...	...	...	...	...	...	...	...	...	...	...
Bolivia	1988	1,318,800	...	...	...	...	...	...	69.1	13.4	17.5	72.3	2.3	21.1	4.2
Bosnia and Herzegovina	1989	...	...	...	...	...	...	...	...	...	...	...	...	...	...
Botswana	1991	276,209	...	...	...	...	...	...	59.2	22.9	17.9	48.7	—	49.3	2.0
Brazil	1990	35,578,857	...	...	...	...	...	...	67.0	17.7	15.3	...	...	...	...
Brunei	1981	28,676	...	...	...	...	...	...	83.8	11.8	4.4	0.2	54.8	36.5	8.5
Bulgaria	1975	3,326,000[20]	17.9	——81.9——		11.1	——7.0——		77.3	22.7	—	...	...	...	...
Burkina Faso	1985	1,274,546[22]	...	...	...	...	...	...	...	...	...	...	...	...	...
Burundi	1979	938,000[44]	...	...	...	...	...	...	98.7	1.1	0.2	...	...	...	...
Cambodia	...	...	...	...	...	...	...	...	...	...	...	...	...	...	...
Cameroon	1976	1,390,896[19]	...	...	...	...	...	...	83.4	11.2	5.4	75.5	13.9	9.5	1.1
Canada	1986	10,079,442[18]	10.5	20.3[5]	20.0[6]	19.4[7]	——40.3[46]——		62.1	37.5	0.5	...	...	...	...
Cape Verde	1980	59,919	...	——68.6——		——31.4——			...	15.4	...	57.7	...	36.5	5.8
Central African Republic	1975	405,399	...	...	...	...	...	...	...	...	...	82.2	7.1	2.5	8.2
Chad	...	...	...	...	...	...	...	...	...	...	...	...	...	...	...
Chile	1982	2,510,275	20.4	——46.2——		21.1	——32.7——		63.1	18.7	18.2	13.0	44.4	41.6	1.0
China	1990	276,947,962	...	...	...	...	...	...	18.5[2,26]	81.5[2,26]	—	...	...	...	...
Colombia	1985	5,266,581	20.6[47]	54.6[47]	26.2[47]	19.2[47]	—	—	67.6	23.6	8.8	16.7	7.0	75.6	0.7
Comoros	1980	81,791	...	5.3	7.7	21.3	——63.7——		87.4	3.1	9.5	73.5	1.8	16.9	7.8
Congo	1984	363,140[22]	...	...	...	...	...	...	61.0	34.6	4.4	15.0	20.0	52.8	12.2
Costa Rica	1984	500,788	...	...	...	...	...	...	65.8	20.7	13.5	1.1	60.1	35.6	3.2
Côte d'Ivoire	1985	1,146,370[48]	...	...	...	...	...	...	...	...	...	...	...	...	...
Croatia	1989	...	...	...	...	...	...	...	...	...	...	...	...	...	...
Cuba	1981	2,363,364	24.6	23.2[49]	21.3[50]	21.6	——25.6——		...	...	...	1.4	37.1	61.5	—
Cyprus	1982	168,588	22.8	——39.9——		15.4	——44.7——		60.0	16.5	23.5	11.9	—	87.6	0.5
Czech Republic	1991	3,705,691	42.4	41.7[5]	10.2[6]	14.5[7]	19.6[8]	14.0[9]	44.7[16]	41.7[16]	13.6[16]	—	32.0[51]	67.1	0.9
Denmark	1991	2,374,970	36.6	44.3	10.0	16.4	18.1	11.2	53.8	44.5	1.7	...	...	...	...
Djibouti	1982	25,000[52]	27.6	...	...	...	...	...	...	...	...	—	73.0[53]	22.5	4.5
Dominica	1970	17,310[22, 25]	...	58.4	16.9	21.1	——3.6——		64.7	26.6	8.7	0.2	88.8	10.2	0.8
Dominican Republic	1981	1,125,785[19]	...	...	...	...	...	...	72.0	17.0	11.0	31.1	31.3	31.0	6.7
Ecuador	1990	2,111,121	...	...	...	...	...	...	68.1	22.6	9.3	32.2	9.3	57.7	0.8
Egypt	1986	9,732,728	...	——37.1[2]——		——62.9[2]——			64.0	27.2	8.8	...	...	...	...
El Salvador	1971	680,456	...	...	...	...	...	...	56.7[54]	22.3[54]	21.0[54]	37.9	9.6	46.9	5.6
Equatorial Guinea	1983	...	...	...	...	...	...	...	...	...	...	...	...	...	...
Eritrea	...	...	...	...	...	...	...	...	...	...	...	...	...	...	...
Estonia	1989	427,000[22]	...	...	...	...	...	...	...	...	...	...	...	...	...
Ethiopia	1984	9,300,000	...	...	...	...	...	...	...	...	...	...	...	...	...
Faeroe Islands	1977	11,172[14]	32.5	——60.1——		21.8	——15.0——		84.5	9.9	5.6	—	43.9	53.5	2.6
Fiji	1986	124,098	...	...	...	...	...	...	74.4	14.6	11.0	9.0	26.4	29.8	34.8
Finland	1990	2,152,938	17.1	——29.6——		16.5	26.4	27.5	71.5	20.5	8.0	14.0[4, 14]	81.8[4, 14]	——4.2[4, 14]——	
France	1990	21,535,677	19.1[40]	——43.5[40, 58]——		11.6[40, 59]	27.3[40, 60]	17.7[40, 61]	54.4	39.6	6.0	...	...	...	...
French Guiana	1990	33,285	...	...	...	23.2[38]	...	...	41.3	——58.7——		29.4	——70.6——		
French Polynesia	1988	39,513	10.8	——11.3——		16.0	27.6	45.1	68.5	21.2	10.3	36.9	15.8	45.2	2.2

planners are always aware that much housing is physically inadequate to protect dwellers from the elements, is disadvantageously placed in relation to tainted or disease-infested water supply or to the outfall of unprocessed sewage, or is built of materials (mud, skins, thatch, etc.) that may harbour pests or disease. In the developed countries, median age and the distribution of physical amenities provide strong indicators of the quality and availability of housing.

The data for the construction industry refer to the most recent year in which a broad range of countries could be surveyed.

The broadest indication of total activity in a national construction industry is its contribution to the national gross domestic product, since that figure, in addition to construction of buildings, also includes civil engineering projects, such as dams, roads and other transportation infrastructure, recreational facilities, irrigation and land reclamation works, and the like. The scope of the data relating to construction of buildings may be limited in several respects. It may be confined to activity capable of being surveyed in the modern or urban sectors only, may be limited to private new construction only or to government and government-financed activity only, or may refer to construction mortgaged or financed through certain organizations only. Depending on national data-collection systems, it usually excludes remodeling of old premises but may include extensions or enlargements of existing buildings. The data for new construction are usually of two principal types: authorized new construction or certification after construction that newly built structures meet building and fire codes and the like. Data for construction completed are naturally more meaningful but are not available for every country, necessitating the substitution of authorized construction data, which are usually available only for areas regulated by certain types of governmental authorities.

The following notes further define the column headings:

a. Data refer to permanent, private dwelling units that are usually occupied year-round, whether or not occupied on the census date.
b. Data are estimates unless specifically provided by a country source.
c. Data may be either for dwellings or for households, depending on country reporting practice.
d. Data may be either for construction completed or for construction authorized, depending on country reporting practice.

physical amenities (percent)			sewage disposal (percent)			space[b]			construction industry (1990)						country
									percent of GDP	new residential[d]			new nonresidential[d]		
piped water	electricity	inside toilet or WC	closed public sewer or septic tank	open public sewer	other	average area (sq m)	rooms per dwelling unit	persons per room		total no. of dwellings	floor area ('000 sq m)	years to replace nat'l stock	number of units	floor area ('000 sq m)	
25.3[2]	66.5[2]	5.5[2]	5.5	77.9	16.6	...	5.5	2.1	5.8[3]	...	...	...	...	...	Afghanistan
33.0	...	21.3	...	...	...	35.7	1.8	2.6	6.4[10, 11]	12,428	...	37.4	...	...	Albania
72.7	73.3[14]	...	51.0[14]	22.8[14]	26.2[14]	...	2.9	2.6	17.3[15]	71,433[15]	...	42.6[15]	...	...	Algeria
96.2	94.4	93.4	68.5	—31.5—		...	4.5	1.6	...	218[17]	...	21.5[17]	...	...	American Samoa
—	...	—	...	—	...	...	...	...	19.9	...	91[16]	...	14[16]	47.5[16]	Andorra
...	...	...	...	...	...	...	...	...	1.9[18]	...	585[16]	...	210[16]	164.5[16]	Angola
85.4	...	...	17.0	—83.0—		...	3.1	...	13.0[20]	764[17]	...	20.2[17]	...	...	Antigua and Barbuda
72.9	86.8	95.1	77.1	—22.9—		...	3.9	1.3	1.9	67,528[21]	...	105.2[11]	...	...	Argentina
...	...	...	...	...	...	...	...	...	14.6	...	1,460[11]	...	...	...	Armenia
97.9	98.7[25]	89.2[25]	...	...	...	...	5.2	0.7	8.2[26]	158[18]	...	94.5[18]	113[18]	...	Aruba
97.1[27]	98.4[28]	92.2[25]	99.0[25]	—1.0[25]—		...	5.1[25]	0.6[25]	8.8[29]	135,456[11]	11,170	43.0[11]	23,340[14]	13,727	Australia
95.0[25]	...	88.7	94.3[25]	—	5.7[25]	85.0	4.3[17]	0.6[17]	7.0	36,553	3,618	92.8	500[14]	100[14]	Austria
...	...	...	...	...	...	...	...	...	10.6[10, 18]	...	2,848	...	...	...	Azerbaijan
63.9	77.9	...	63.2	2.2	34.6	...	4.0	1.2	3.1[17]	1,027[15]	...	52.9[15]	62[15]	...	Bahamas, The
97.5	98.2	...	44.7	...	55.3	...	3.0[20]	2.3[28]	6.5[11]	1,919[17]	...	27.5[17]	1,444[17]	...	Bahrain
56.8	6.6	2.6	1.5	—98.7—		...	2.0	2.9	5.8[31]	300,900[21]	...	49.1	...	...	Bangladesh
94.0	92.6	66.2	66.8	0.4	32.8	...	4.3	0.8	4.8[18]	1,960[17]	...	...	...	...	Barbados
...	...	...	...	...	...	...	...	...	11.8[10]	...	5,490[11, 33]	...	...	[33]	Belarus
99.6	100.0	91.9	62.5[38]	—37.5[38]—		86.3	4.3	0.6	5.8	49,801[11]	31,755[39]	72.3[11]	9,101[11]	52,062[39]	Belgium
60.1	59.4	19.7	21.1	—78.9—		...	...	...	8.6	...	6,185[40]	...	...	...	Belize
...	...	...	...	...	...	...	...	...	4.9[17]	...	...	...	...	...	Benin
97.4[16]	...	96.7[16]	96.7[16]	—3.3[16]—		...	3.2[16]	0.7[16]	4.9[41]	556[11]	...	36.6[11]	...	...	Bermuda
...	...	...	...	...	...	...	...	...	8.4[11]	...	...	...	...	...	Bhutan
60.2	59.3	23.2	22.5	—77.5—		...	...	...	2.7	24,980[11]	...	52.8[11]	...	...	Bolivia
66.2	94.2	53.2	...	...	...	56.0	...	...	7.1[10, 11]	26,568	...	...	...	...	Bosnia and Herzegovina
77.0	5.4[25]	25.4[25]	8.6[25]	20.4[25]	71.0[25]	...	2.6	1.8	5.7[29]	...	96[15]	...	472[14]	132[15]	Botswana
73.4	87.8	...	60.1[17]	—39.9[17]—		...	5.1[16]	0.9[16]	7.0	...	20,090[15]	...	5,017[14]	8,180[15]	Brazil
90.3	64.2	94.2	57.4	—42.6—		...	4.2	1.6	2.6[20]	195[40]	...	147.0[40]	5[40]	...	Brunei
74.6	99.8	33.2	33.2	—67.8—		45.3[42]	2.5[43]	1.1[43]	9.4[10, 20]	62,800[11]	2,844[11]	53.0[11]	...	...	Bulgaria
...	...	...	...	...	...	...	...	...	0.6[15]	...	...	...	...	...	Burkina Faso
11.0	0.6	...	1.6	—98.4—		37.2[26]	2.4[26]	0.6[26]	4.1[18]	...	...	...	...	...	Burundi
...	...	...	...	...	...	...	...	...	5.3[45]	...	...	...	...	...	Cambodia
22.0	5.9	2.2	2.2	70.4	27.6	...	4.1	1.2	6.8[20]	...	230[1]	...	53[1]	51.1[1]	Cameroon
99.8[20]	100.0	99.4[20]	98.9[25]	—1.1—		...	5.7	0.5	6.6	218,304[11]	...	44.0[11]	14,846[14]	...	Canada
7.1	13.7	14.8	—3.4—		96.6	...	1.8	2.8	15.6[17]	...	31[26]	...	3[26]	0.5[26]	Cape Verde
...	...	...	...	...	...	...	...	...	1.8	...	15	...	11	...	Central African Republic
...	...	...	...	...	...	...	...	...	1.6[15]	...	...	...	...	...	Chad
81.4	84.7	...	63.2	36.4	0.4	59.9[20, 42]	3.6	1.3	5.8	78,094[11]	4,495	32.1[11]	...	1,747	Chile
89.4[2, 15]	...	25.2[2, 15]	47.0[2, 15]	—53.0[2, 15]—		37.0[15]	2.2[15]	1.8[15]	5.7	...	862,888	...	...	215,038	China
70.5	78.5	77.9	69.6	—30.4—		...	3.3	1.6	5.7	74,996[15]	5,648[11]	70.2[15]	...	1,994[11]	Colombia
12.9	5.7	...	2.1	—97.9—		33.7	2.5	2.1	9.7[15]	...	...	...	...	...	Comoros
30.5	8.8	16.6	—86.2[2]—		13.8[2]	...	3.7[2]	1.7[2]	1.8[11]	...	...	...	...	...	Congo
86.9	97.3	...	66.5	—33.5—		...	4.0	1.4	3.3	...	760[14]	...	2,868[14]	178[14]	Costa Rica
23.0	39.6	23.9	—68.5—		31.5	...	...	...	2.2[40]	...	...	...	...	...	Côte d'Ivoire
74.5	96.1	62.3	...	...	...	64.1	...	...	6.9[11]	18,565	...	...	...	...	Croatia
74.1	82.9	45.2	60.9	9.3	30.1	71.0[42]	4.1	1.0	9.3[10, 11]	25,344[20]	1,800[20]	93.2[20]	469[14]	1,803[14]	Cuba
100.0	98.1	74.5	95.6	—4.4—		...	4.6	0.8	9.6	6,639[15]	979[15]	25.4[15]	1,103[14]	411[14]	Cyprus
96.9	100.0	88.5	98.1	—1.9—		70.5	2.7	1.0	11.3	...	2,112[18]	...	...	...	Czech Republic
100.0	100.0	99.2[11]	98.6[25]	—1.4[25]—		107.8	3.8	0.6	5.8	25,392[11]	1,736[18]	90.8[11]	6,141[15]	4,509[18]	Denmark
45.0	58.0	82.0	26.0	23.0	51.0	...	1.9	6.9	2.1[17]	...	24.3[15]	...	26[15]	13.7[15]	Djibouti
91.1[1]	...	12.3	12.3	—87.7—		...	2.8	1.7	7.3[18]	...	...	...	...	...	Dominica
64.4	36.7[38]	14.1	52.1[38]	22.6[38]	25.3[38]	...	2.8[38]	1.5[38]	8.5	...	648[15]	...	856[15]	508[15]	Dominican Republic
62.7[19]	77.7[19]	49.6[19]	39.5[19]	25.1[19]	35.4[19]	...	2.8	1.7	3.3	...	3,825[14]	...	596[14]	412.7[14]	Ecuador
73.1	87.0	...	...	...	...	...	3.3	1.5	5.0[29]	183,505[11]	...	53.0[11]	...	...	Egypt
48.0	34.1	6.3[28]	20.0[16]	—80.0[16]—		...	1.5[54]	3.3[54]	2.6	...	341[14]	...	8[14]	0.7[14]	El Salvador
...	...	...	...	...	...	...	...	...	5.6[11]	...	...	...	...	...	Equatorial Guinea
...	...	...	...	...	...	...	...	...	...	...	...	...	...	...	Eritrea
...	...	...	...	...	...	...	...	...	10.9[11]	...	468	...	...	...	Estonia
...	...	...	...	...	...	...	...	2.7[55]	3.6[3]	...	260[56]	...	92[1]	63.3[56]	Ethiopia
99.7	99.5	95.0	89.7	8.1	2.2	...	5.5	1.1	9.0[20]	298[21]	...	37.5[15]	...	...	Faeroe Islands
73.7	48.5	56.0	35.4[57]	—64.6[57]—		...	3.3	1.8	3.6[20]	2,767[15]	24[11]	45.1[15]	105[15]	24[11]	Fiji
95.1	95.9[4, 14]	92.7	96.4	—3.6—		74.2	3.5	0.6	9.7	65,397	5,226	45.4	32,886[27]	34,050[39]	Finland
99.7[20]	...	93.5	73.8[48]	—26.2[48]—		77.0[54]	3.9	0.7	5.0	258,900[18]	...	83.2[18]	...	47,887[20]	France
77.0	86.7	62.0	34.3[26]	—65.7[26]—		...	2.8	1.2	8.2[11, 19]	667[26]	64[26]	31.6[26]	...	28.5[14]	French Guiana
5.4	91.0	78.9	2.0[1]	67.0[1]	31.0[1]	...	3.8	1.3	6.1	700[15]	85[33]	59.3[15]	156[15]	[33]	French Polynesia

Housing and construction (continued)

country	housing stock: year	dwelling units[a]	median age[b] (years)	decade built (percent): 1949 or earlier	1950–59	1960–69	1970–79	1980 or later	tenure[c] (percent): owned	rented	collective, vacant, other	construction of exterior walls (percent): traditional materials	sawn/framed wood	masonry or cement	other
Gabon	1967	15,886[52]	...	...	...	...	...	...	—87.0—		13.0	...	...	...	...
Gambia, The	1983	202,199	...	...	...	...	...	...	63.9	21.9	14.2	82.9	—	12.9	4.2
Gaza Strip	1985	66,819[62]	...	...	...	...	...	...	89.1[63]	7.6[63]	3.3[63]	...	...	...	...
Georgia	1989	1,244,000[22]	...	...	...	...	...	...	...	...	...	...	...	...	...
Germany[64]	1987	27,524,000	...	30.6[58]	15.2[65]	23.6[66]	19.8[67]	10.8[68]	39.0	60.3	0.7	...	...	...	...
Ghana	1984	1,216,677	...	...	...	...	...	...	47.7[48]	25.3[48]	27.0[48]	...	...	...	...
Gibraltar	1991	7,604[19]	25.0	37.3[70]	16.7[71]	15.6[72]	23.0[73]	7.4[74]	15.2	84.8	—	...	...	...	...
Greece	1981	3,999,332	29.2	30.2[5]	27.4[6]	20.7[7]	—21.5—		73.1[75]	26.9[75]	—	...	...	...	...
Greenland	1989	18,401	10.2	11.9[27]	18.8[27]	46.5[27]	—22.8[27]—		39.3[14]	—60.7[14]—		...	...	...	...
Grenada	1970	21,017[25]	18.3	48.0	29.0	22.2	—0.8—		76.5	14.0	9.5	0.4	80.8	17.8	1.0
Guadeloupe	1990	112,478	...	...	...	8.1[75]	...	...	62.6	—37.4—		29.5		—70.5—	
Guam	1990	35,223	15.8	2.3	7.1	19.2	41.5	29.9	45.6	54.4	—	0.0	5.1	85.8	9.1
Guatemala	1981	1,259,598	12.5	—62.0—		10.0	—28.0—		64.7	11.3	24.0	55.6	21.1	19.3	4.0
Guernsey	1991	21,215[19]	...	...	...	...	...	...	68.4	31.6	—	...	...	...	...
Guinea	1983	674,152[22]	...	...	...	...	...	...	...	...	...	...	...	...	...
Guinea-Bissau	1979	123,936	...	...	...	...	...	...	...	...	...	95.7	0.1	2.3	1.9
Guyana	1980	149,734[22]	17.6	—43.5—		19.4	—37.1—		56.1	27.1	16.8	...	74.8	17.1	8.1
Haiti	1982	1,130,795	...	—75.9—			—24.1—		82.9[27]	4.8[27]	12.3[27]	...	...	...	...
Honduras	1988	809,263	12.1[75]	—38.9[75]—		37.8[67]	—23.3[75]—		71.8[75]	16.5[75]	12.7[75]	61.0[75]	26.4[75]	11.7[75]	0.9[75]
Hong Kong	1991	1,580,072	...	—48.1[25]—		13.6[25]	—38.3[25]—		42.6	53.0	4.4	...	...	...	...
Hungary	1990	3,817,000	16.4	32.9[5]	11.8[50]	14.9	23.2	17.2	75.9	23.7	0.4	30.8[40]	14.3[40]	54.8[40]	0.1[40]
Iceland	1984	70,777	25.6	—46.0—		—54.1—			70.3[76]	—29.7[76]—		...	...	71.9[76]	...
India	1981	142,954,921	...	...	...	...	...	...	84.6[28]	15.4[28]	—	...	...	...	...
Indonesia	1980	30,263,273[22]	...	...	...	...	...	...	87.0[28]	5.0[28]	8.0[28]	...	...	...	...
Iran	1986	8,211,375	...	—82.5[27]—			—17.5[27]—		77.0	12.2	9.8	28.8	0.7	69.2	1.3
Iraq	1956	741,000	...	...	...	...	...	...	83.0	12.8	4.2	...	...	...	...
Ireland	1981	1,038,000[18]	47.2	—60.0—		12.8	—26.2—		67.9	20.9	11.2	...	...	...	...
Isle of Man	1981	27,042	...	...	...	...	...	...	62.5	36.5	1.0	...	...	...	...
Israel	1983	1,104,270	...	9.5[77]	—90.5[78]—				72.9	24.6	2.5	...	...	...	...
Italy	1991	19,509,362[22]	19.4[25]	30.8[5]	19.7[34]	27.5[79]	—22.0[46]—		58.9[25]	35.5[25]	5.6[25]	...	...	...	...
Jamaica	1982	517,297[22]	17.0	—33.6—		28.8	—39.6—		46.7	29.5	23.8	7.1	28.4	54.4	10.1
Japan	1988	37,454,000[22]	11.0	7.3[80]	—67.8[81]—		—24.9[46]—		61.4	37.2	1.4	—	73.1	25.5	1.4
Jersey	1991	32,463	...	...	...	...	...	...	49.6	48.0	2.4	...	...	...	...
Jordan	1979	378,815	...	...	...	...	...	...	62.6	30.8	6.6	...	...	...	...
Kazakhstan	1989	3,824,000[22]	...	...	...	...	...	...	...	...	...	...	...	...	...
Kenya	1979	2,956,369[22]	...	...	...	...	...	...	...	...	...	...	...	...	...
Kiribati	1985	10,093[22]	...	...	...	...	...	...	68.2[54]	17.9[54]	13.9[54]	64.4[54]		—35.6[54]—	
Korea, North	1987	4,054,027[22]	...	...	...	...	...	...	...	...	...	...	...	...	...
Korea, South	1990	7,374,000	19.0[16]	26.1[16]	15.8[16]	18.2[16]	—39.2[16]—		83.8[14]	12.8[14]	3.4[14]	11.8[16]	38.8[16]	49.2[16]	0.2[16]
Kuwait	1985	228,781	14.5[16]	—12.2[16]—		38.8[16]	—34.5[16]—		38.2	53.6	8.2	46.5[4]	—	36.5[4]	17.0[4]
Kyrgyzstan	1989	856,000[22]	...	...	...	...	...	...	...	...	...	...	...	...	...
Laos	...	...	...	...	...	...	...	...	...	...	...	...	...	...	...
Latvia	1989	732,000[22]	...	...	...	...	...	...	...	...	...	...	...	...	...
Lebanon	1970	483,908[19]	...	30.1[83]	40.2[84]	—29.4—			...	...	...	...	...	...	...
Lesotho	1986	317,161[19]	...	...	...	...	...	...	...	...	...	...	...	...	...
Liberia	1974[52]	263,333	...	...	...	...	...	...	...	...	...	...	...	...	...
Libya	1984	569,679	...	...	...	...	...	...	62.5[47]	28.0[47]	9.5[47]	...	...	...	...
Liechtenstein	1980	9,336	29.4	27.1[83]	15.0[84]	27.1	—30.8—		53.6	41.7	4.7	...	...	...	...
Lithuania	1991	1,165,700[22]	...	...	...	...	...	...	...	...	...	...	...	...	...
Luxembourg	1991	144,683	33.1	34.5[5]	17.6[6]	12.5[7]	17.8[8]	17.6[9]	66.1	28.3	5.6	...	...	...	...
Macau	1981	45,158	...	...	...	...	...	...	71.8[38]	28.2[38]	—	—	0.5[38]	99.3[38]	0.2[38]
Macedonia	1989	...	...	...	...	...	...	...	...	...	...	...	...	...	...
Madagascar	1975	1,671,473[22]	...	...	...	...	...	...	...	...	...	...	...	...	...
Malaŵi	1977	1,834,118	...	...	...	...	...	...	39.6	—60.4—		...	...	...	...
Malaysia	1991	3,447,597[19]	...	...	...	...	...	...	64.0[16]	23.0[16]	13.0[16]	...	...	...	...
Maldives	1990	37,114	11.6	15.1	7.9	13.7	21.7	41.6	96.4	3.6	—	53.8	2.7	41.1	2.4
Mali	1987	1,366,907	...	...	...	...	...	...	...	...	...	...	...	...	...
Malta	1985	101,509	...	—81.8[86]—		—18.2[87]—			53.9	43.0	3.1	93.0[62]	...	92.9[62]	0.21[62]
Marshall Islands	1980	4,163	...	6.4	13.3	24.7	—55.5—		60.0	33.0	7.0	10.7	63.5	15.9	9.9
Martinique	1990	123,317	...	...	...	...	...	...	60.9	—39.1—		20.4[26]		—79.6[26]—	
Mauritania	1977	246,462[22]	...	...	...	...	...	...	...	...	...	...	...	...	...
Mauritius[88]	1983	191,676	...	—19.7—		24.3[89]	—56.0[90]—		66.0	18.6	15.4	—	4.2	66.8	28.9
Mayotte	1985	13,142	...	...	...	...	...	...	88.1[54]	6.2[54]	5.7[54]	67.7	—16.7—		15.6
Mexico	1990	16,197,802	...	—51.4[16]—		15.4[16]	—33.2[16]—		77.9	14.6	7.5	19.0	8.1	69.5	3.4
Micronesia	1980	11,562	...	3.8	5.2	21.3	—69.7—		51.8	39.2	9.0	6.0	41.8	14.6	37.6
Moldova	1989	1,144,000[22]	...	...	...	...	...	...	...	...	...	...	...	...	...
Monaco	1990	16,122	30.0	—39.5[58]—		13.0[59]	19.7[60]	27.8[91]	23.3	60.5	16.2	...	...	...	...
Mongolia	1969	242,000	...	...	...	...	...	...	100.0	—	—	...	...	...	...
Morocco	1982	3,419,282[22]	...	...	...	...	...	...	40.8[2]	43.7[2]	15.5[2]	24.5	—	73.5	1.8
Mozambique	1980	2,712,439[22]	...	...	...	...	...	...	...	...	...	86.5	2.3	8.3	2.9
Myanmar (Burma)	1983	6,750,884	...	...	...	...	...	...	...	...	...	83.5	14.8	—	1.7
Namibia	...	...	...	...	...	...	...	...	...	...	...	...	...	...	...
Nauru	1977	508[92]	...	—88.6[92]—			—11.4[92]—		11.0[55]	80.6[55]	8.4[55]	...	...	...	...
Nepal	1981	2,585,154[22]	...	...	...	...	...	...	75.3[55]	10.7[55]	14.0[55]	...	...	...	...
Netherlands, The	1990	5,802,400	25.4	28.2	11.8	18.0	21.7	20.3	43.2[14]	56.8[14]	...	...	...	...	...
Netherlands Antilles	1981	41,101	21.0	—49.8—		19.7	—30.5—		45.3	54.7	—	—	21.6	75.7	2.7
New Caledonia	1989	44,047	...	—19.3—		—80.7—			56.4	29.7	13.9	6.4	11.7	61.7	20.2
New Zealand	1991	1,185,396	...	—64.1[25]—		19.2[25]	—16.2[25]—		72.4	22.7	4.9	...	...	...	...
Nicaragua	1971	330,422	...	...	...	...	...	...	64.4	20.3	15.3	30.8	45.6	21.8	1.8
Niger	1988	1,163,424[22]	...	...	...	...	...	...	...	...	...	66.5	...	...	...
Nigeria	1961[52]	92,900	...	...	...	...	...	...	8.0	80.9	11.1	...	...	...	...
Northern Mariana Islands	1990	8,210	...	1.0	2.5	6.4	13.3	76.8	39.5	56.6	3.9	0.0	13.5	66.5	20.0
Norway	1990	1,769,000	25.3	44.1[5]	20.6[6]	17.8[7]	20.7[8]	16.0[9]	80.3	—19.7—		...	...	...	...
Oman	1982	2,469	...	...	...	...	...	...	...	...	...	...	...	...	...
Pakistan[93]	1980	12,587,648[22]	17.2	17.1[83]	36.7[94]	24.9[95]	—21.3[37]—		78.4	7.7	13.9	49.2	2.4	41.4	7.1

physical amenities (percent)			sewage disposal (percent)			space[b]			construction industry (1990)						country
									percent of GDP	new residential[d]			new nonresidential[d]		
piped water	electricity	inside toilet or WC	closed public sewer or septic tank	open public sewer	other	average area (sq m)	rooms per dwelling unit	persons per room		total no. of dwellings	floor area ('000 sq m)	years to replace nat'l stock	number of units	floor area ('000 sq m)	
...	50.5	...	...	...	...	...	3.0	1.3	6.2	...	216[48]	...	75[48]	119.4[48]	Gabon
21.9	...	...	...	...	...	...	2.0	2.0	6.5[29]	...	...	...	14[48]	...	Gambia, The
97.2	93.5	97.3	...	...	...	144.3[42]	2.6	2.5	22.2[15]	1,247[15]	180[15]	53.6[15]	...	31.1[15]	Gaza Strip
...	...	...	...	...	...	...	...	...	11.0	...	1,005[11]	...	...	...	Georgia
100.0	99.7	98.3	97.1[16]	—2.9[16]—		86.1	4.4	0.5	5.6	214,252[11]	4,848	128.5[11]	46,123[15]	35,908	Germany[64]
34.0[69]	...	...	...	...	...	...	...	...	3.1	...	...	...	...	...	Ghana
96.7[25]	100.0[25]	99.2	100.0[25]	—	—	...	3.3	1.1	...	...	...	...	...	...	Gibraltar
81.3[28]	89.0[28]	93.0[28]	...	...	...	138.4[17]	3.3[17]	0.9[28]	6.8	107,034[20]	43,462[11, 39]	37.4[20]	11,471[27]	13,509[11, 39]	Greece
62.7[27]	84.2[27]	39.1[27]	39.1[27]	—60.9[27]—		72.0[42]	2.8	1.1	23.3[16]	255[11]	18[11]	71.1[11]	...	12.3[14]	Greenland
86.5	...	23.0	23.0	—77.0—		...	2.9	1.6	12.1	...	...	...	...	...	Grenada
83.2	89.4	78.2	24.6[26]	—75.4[26]—		...	3.3	1.0	4.7[26]	676[11]	...	126.7[11]	...	166[17]	Guadeloupe
99.2	98.4	97.0	97.0	—3.0—		...	5.0	0.8	7.9[26]	417[15]	...	67.4[15]	500[15]	...	Guam
52.0	37.0	14.3	20.1	3.4	76.5	...	2.4	2.2	2.0[18]	...	495[11, 33]	...	...	[33]	Guatemala
96.5[27]	...	98.8	65.9	—34.1—		...	5.8[17]	0.5[17]	...	165[11]	...	128.6[11]	...	...	Guernsey
...	...	...	...	...	...	...	...	...	5.6	...	...	...	...	...	Guinea
3.7	3.9	25.6	25.8	—74.2—		...	1.4	4.5	1.7[15]	...	...	...	...	...	Guinea-Bissau
38.1	69.0	29.0	10.4	—89.6—		...	2.9	1.8	5.2	...	...	...	56[21]	...	Guyana
12.0[16]	1.1[16]	...	2.0	—98.0—		...	2.2[28]	2.1[28]	5.1[3]	...	...	...	...	...	Haiti
55.0[16]	25.0[16]	13.0[16]	14.4[16]	—85.6[16]—		...	2.4[16]	2.3[16]	4.4[14]	1,442[40]	214[17]	...	148[17]	98[17]	Honduras
85.7[25]	...	69.2[47]	65.4[47]	—34.6[47]—		53.2[28]	3.1[47]	2.8[47]	5.5	67,579[15]	1,814[18]	25.5[15]	303[15]	2,166[18]	Hong Kong
90.1	98.8[40]	75.9	85.5	—14.5—		52.3	2.6	1.0	5.1	50,600[20]	4,353[11]	78.3[20]	3,433[14]	21,886[14, 39]	Hungary
99.1[76]	94.6[76]	93.6[76]	86.5[76]	—13.5[76]—		...	4.8[76]	0.9[76]	8.8	1,728[20]	...	...	649[20]	926.5[39, 41]	Iceland
67.0[47]	53.5[2, 47]	20.0[47]	...	...	...	...	2.0[28]	2.6[28]	5.6[3]	...	...	...	13,908[40]	...	India
11.0	14.2	26.6	22.8[28]	—77.2[28]—		59.0	3.3	1.7[28]	5.5	...	...	...	...	...	Indonesia
73.7	83.7	43.6	...	...	...	60.0[27]	2.8	1.8	5.3[29]	124,891[14]	18,608[14]	65.0[14]	5,235[14]	1,466[14]	Iran
20.8	17.1	...	...	...	...	...	2.4	...	8.0	...	11,521[15]	...	11,799[14]	1,176[15]	Iraq
94.8	94.7[28]	93.0	72.3[28]	—27.7[28]—		...	3.7[14]	1.0[14]	5.0[15]	20,000[18]	5,887	51.9[11]	...	840[17]	Ireland
...	...	96.8	...	...	...	...	...	0.4	9.8[15]	168[15]	...	161.0[15]	...	...	Isle of Man
96.5[28]	96.5[28]	98.8	99.0[75]	—1.0[75]—		149.8[42]	3.0	1.2	5.3[11]	42,640[18]	6,390[18]	25.9[18]	...	1,200[18]	Israel
98.7[25]	99.0[28]	94.0[25]	95.7[28]	—4.3[28]—		85.3[25]	4.0[14]	0.8[25]	5.9	167,076	84,111[39]	105.0[11]	29,235[11]	97,878[39]	Italy
76.9	48.6	35.2	...	...	...	...	2.4[38]	4.3	13.1[18]	4,115	...	125.7	...	...	Jamaica
94.0[1]	...	65.8	61.2[1]	—38.8[1]—		89.9	4.9	0.7	8.8	1,753,260[20]	155,868	21.4[20]	...	127,560	Japan
94.0[82]	...	93.0[25]	96.0[82]	...	...	...	5.0	0.5	...	354[15]	...	82.5[15]	...	...	Jersey
77.2	77.3	55.4[55]	15.7	—84.3—		...	...	...	8.2[11]	6,292[17]	1,709[17]	60.2[17]	820[17]	557[17]	Jordan
...	...	...	...	...	...	...	...	...	15.3	...	7,871[11]	...	...	...	Kazakhstan
...	...	...	...	...	...	...	...	...	6.9	...	136[17]	...	85[17]	184[17]	Kenya
21.3[54]	23.7[54]	15.5[54]	...	...	...	...	...	...	3.9[11]	...	...	...	...	...	Kiribati
...	...	...	...	...	...	...	...	...	...	...	...	...	...	...	Korea, North
44.6	49.9[38]	51.6	...	...	...	81.4	3.4	1.7	12.9	750,000[11]	59,060	9.8[11]	36,801[15]	46,124	Korea, South
53.9[16]	99.5[16]	...	35.9[16]	—64.1[16]—		...	4.0[16]	1.8[16]	2.3[15]	9,735[44]	2,563[11]	23.5[44]	370[15]	416[11]	Kuwait
...	...	...	...	...	...	...	...	...	7.7[18]	...	1,560	...	...	...	Kyrgyzstan
...	...	...	...	...	...	...	...	...	3.7[11]	...	...	...	...	...	Laos
...	...	...	...	...	...	...	...	...	8.0[10]	...	819	...	...	...	Latvia
...	93.4	82.9	...	...	...	...	...	...	4.8[15]	...	4,938[15, 33]	...	...	[33]	Lebanon
...	...	...	...	...	...	...	...	...	18.7	...	...	...	52[17]	...	Lesotho
...	...	...	...	...	...	...	2.3[14]	1.7	2.5[20]	...	...	...	...	...	Liberia
70.1[47]	72.1[47]	40.6[47]	40.6[47]	—59.4[47]—		...	3.3[47]	1.8[47]	12.7[11]	...	...	...	...	...	Libya
96.5	96.6	86.7	90.2	—9.8—		102.0	3.0	1.4	...	...	'360[33]	...	...	312[33]	Liechtenstein
...	...	...	...	...	...	...	...	...	6.2[18]	15,300[19]	1,015[18]	...	...	...	Lithuania
99.4	...	99.4	93.0[38]	—7.0[38]—		114.2	5.4[16]	0.5[16]	7.0	1,940[11]	491	66.1[11]	74[15]	172	Luxembourg
95.7	99.3	68.9	...	...	...	...	3.2[40]	2.5[40]	...	10,581[18]	886[18]	4.3[18]	1,003	406	Macau
72.0	96.4	56.3	...	...	...	68.6	...	...	5.7[11]	10,189	...	...	...	...	Macedonia
...	...	...	...	...	...	...	...	...	3.8[15]	...	24[15]	...	...	8.9[15]	Madagascar
12.4	15.7[62]	33.0[62]	33.0[62]	—67.0[62]—		...	2.1	1.7	4.2[18]	...	...	...	...	...	Malaŵi
65.0[16]	64.4[16]	...	56.4[16]	4.4[16]	39.2[16]	...	2.3[38, 85]	2.6[38, 85]	3.5	...	8,809[17]	...	...	960[17]	Malaysia
...	53.4[14]	...	43.2	—56.8—		...	4.4	1.5	8.7[18]	680[15]	...	54.6[15]	...	...	Maldives
...	...	...	...	...	...	...	...	...	4.0[18]	...	...	...	...	...	Mali
98.0	98.0	98.8	98.0	15.4[62]	6.1[62]	...	3.2[62]	1.3[62]	...	2,132[4, 15]	...	47.6[4, 15]	2,319[17]	...	Malta
46.3	48.9	...	28.6	—71.4—		...	...	...	7.4[25]	...	...	...	...	...	Marshall Islands
94.1	78.0	73.1	41.8[26]	—58.2[26]—		...	3.2	0.9	3.6[26]	1,528[26]	...	55.8[26]	...	56.2[25]	Martinique
...	...	...	...	...	...	...	...	...	7.9[40]	...	...	...	...	...	Mauritania
99.1	93.2	48.9	51.1	—48.9—		...	3.6	1.4	7.0	...	887[18]	...	552[15]	227[18]	Mauritius[88]
27.4[54]	...	4.4	54.7[54]	—45.3[54]—		...	4.1	2.5	...	616[17]	...	21.3[17]	...	...	Mayotte
79.4	87.5	45.0[16]	60.9	2.7	36.4	...	3.4	1.5	3.4	...	...	...	61,386[25]	...	Mexico
40.0	28.3	...	8.0	—92.0—		...	...	...	...	...	...	...	...	...	Micronesia
...	...	...	...	...	...	...	...	...	9.0	...	1,594	...	...	...	Moldova
100.0	100.0	96.2	98.4[48]	—1.6[48]—		...	2.8	0.8	...	...	...	...	...	...	Monaco
0.3	47.5	...	...	...	...	...	...	...	5.8[11]	...	461[17]	...	...	176[17]	Mongolia
30.5	37.2	50.2	...	...	...	...	2.7	2.2	5.5	51,911[17]	2,156[14]	65.9[17]	1,014[14]	457[14]	Morocco
12.7	4.2	...	...	...	...	...	...	...	13.2	...	247[75]	...	...	121[75]	Mozambique
...	...	...	...	...	...	...	...	...	1.3[29]	...	...	...	1,483[11]	...	Myanmar (Burma)
...	...	...	...	...	...	...	...	...	2.3	...	...	...	...	...	Namibia
...	49.2	...	...	...	...	...	3.6[55]	1.6[55]	...	...	...	...	...	...	Nauru
47.7	30.2	6.1	...	...	...	...	3.7	2.0	6.7[3]	...	...	...	...	...	Nepal
100.0	98.0	100.0	90.0[15]	—10.0[15]—		...	4.1[14]	0.7[14]	6.2[11]	97,384[11]	35,616[16, 39]	59.6[11]	15,091[14]	49,968[14, 39]	Netherlands, The
79.6	96.9	79.6	...	...	...	...	4.2	1.0	9.5[20]	547[18]	...	150.2[18]	173[18]	...	Netherlands Antilles
90.1	85.3	70.9	76.7	—23.3—		...	3.3	1.2	4.9[20]	772[18]	46[17]	57.1[18]	1[40]	...	New Caledonia
92.7[28]	...	97.1[28]	...	...	...	126.3[15, 42]	5.6	0.5	3.5[31]	19,092[11]	2,543[15]	61.2[11]	...	3,218[15]	New Zealand
27.9	40.9	19.3	19.2	—80.8—		...	2.2	2.1	3.5	...	43[17]	...	28[40]	19.6[40]	Nicaragua
...	...	...	...	...	...	...	...	...	4.0[11]	...	...	...	...	...	Niger
...	81.3	7.0	...	...	...	...	1.4	3.0	1.9[18]	31,038[26]	...	...	1,592[16]	...	Nigeria
91.0	94.1[16]	79.5	81.7	—18.3—		...	3.6	1.1	...	...	...	...	...	...	Northern Mariana Islands
97.5[38]	...	94.6	86.8[16]	—13.2[16]—		103.5	4.1	0.6	4.2	21,689[18]	2,696[18]	82.2[18]	4,954[14]	2,228[18]	Norway
...	...	...	...	...	...	...	...	...	3.1	1,043[17]	...	...	266[17]	...	Oman
20.3	30.6	25.1	...	...	...	...	1.9	3.3	3.6[29]	...	...	...	...	...	Pakistan[93]

Housing and construction (continued)

country	housing stock: year	dwelling units[a]	median age[b] (years)	decade built (percent): 1949 or earlier	1950–59	1960–69	1970–79	1980 or later	tenure[c] (percent): owned	rented	collective, vacant, other	construction of exterior walls (percent): traditional materials	sawn/framed wood	masonry or cement	other
Panama	1990[96]	524,284[19]	18.0[16]	47.4[16]	12.8[16]	18.1[16]	—21.7[16]—		75.5	15.7	8.8	16.9	—	81.2	1.9
Papua New Guinea	1980	556,519[22]	...	...	...	...	...	...	40.0[48]	—60.0[48]—		...	...	...	...
Paraguay	1982	868,284[97]	21.1	—56.0—		17.0	—27.0—		80.4	10.5	9.1	21.5	29.7	47.6	1.2
Peru	1981	4,049,000[18]	...	—30.9—		—69.1—			68.5	14.8	14.8	47.4	7.0	33.1	12.5
Philippines	1980	11,380,000[22, 99]	...	—78.5[38]—		—21.5[38]—			80.2	12.4	7.4	36.3	33.6	23.8	6.3
Poland	1984	10,789,300[20]	...	35.0[80]	—33.7[81]—		—31.3[46]—		...	...	...	—14.1[54]—		—85.9[54]—	
Portugal	1981	3,235,630	33.7	—53.3—		17.5	—29.2—		56.7	38.8	4.6	—	0.7	61.0	38.3
Puerto Rico	1980	1,188,985[99]	15.8	12.2	15.0	31.6	—41.2—		72.1[99]	27.9[99]	—	—	19.7	77.4	2.9
Qatar	1986	64,543	...	...	...	...	...	...	21.9	72.0	6.1	...	...	...	...
Réunion	1982	157,853[99]	...	...	...	21.2[75]	...	...	54.6	34.5	10.9	...	...	...	...
Romania	1992	7,632,000	...	...	...	...	...	...	78.6	20.8	0.6	...	...	...	...
Russia	1989	40,246,000[22]	...	...	...	...	...	...	...	...	...	...	...	...	...
Rwanda	1978	1,055,950[22]	...	...	...	...	...	...	...	...	...	...	...	...	...
St. Kitts and Nevis	1980	11,615[22]	24.2	—63.5—		17.9	—14.7—		54.7	29.5	15.8	—	75.7[14]	20.8	3.5
St. Lucia	1991	33,079	13.5	—17.0—		12.4	26.0	44.6	72.4	26.8	0.8	—	53.4	46.1	0.5
St. Vincent and the Grenadines	1970	20,290[16, 22]	...	—	...	...	...	...	74.7	16.5	7.9	8.9	64.1	26.1	0.8
San Marino	1979	8,384[99]	...	...	...	...	...	...	73.5	21.9	4.6	...	...	...	...
São Tomé and Príncipe	1981	25,197[22, 100]	...	...	...	...	...	...	...	...	...	...	...	...	...
Saudi Arabia	...	...	...	...	...	...	...	...	...	...	...	...	...	...	...
Senegal	1955[52, 101]	13,000	...	...	...	...	...	...	—84.6—		15.4	...	...	...	...
Seychelles	1987	15,050	...	...	...	...	...	...	63.7	25.1	11.2	1.0	40.0	52.0	7.0
Sierra Leone	...	...	...	...	...	...	...	...	...	...	...	...	...	...	...
Singapore	1980	513,224	...	—63.2—		—36.8—			55.0	39.6	5.4	4.7	—95.3—		
Slovakia	1991	1,617,829	26.9	17.1[5]	17.3[6]	20.3[7]	25.4[8]	19.9[9]	...	...	...	—	38.0[51]	61.4	0.6
Slovenia	1989	...	...	...	...	...	...	...	...	...	...	...	...	...	...
Solomon Islands	1986	43,842[22]	...	...	...	...	...	...	27.4[27]	43.0[27]	29.6[27]	...	...	...	...
Somalia	...	...	...	...	...	...	...	...	...	...	...	...	...	...	...
South Africa	1991	3,599,518[102]	18.6[38]	40.6[38]	24.2[38]	35.2[38]	—	—	54.5	34.0	11.5	...	...	...	...
Bophuthatswana	...	...	...	...	...	...	...	...	...	...	...	...	...	...	...
Ciskei	...	...	...	...	...	...	...	...	...	...	...	...	...	...	...
Transkei	1986	518,896[22]	...	...	...	...	...	...	...	...	...	...	...	...	...
Venda	...	...	...	...	...	...	...	...	...	...	...	...	...	...	...
Spain	1991	11,824,851[19]	39.4[16]	39.2[16, 103]	23.4[16, 104]	18.5[7, 16]	—18.9[16, 46]—		67.5	14.9	17.6	...	...	...	...
Sri Lanka	1981	2,811,406	...	...	...	...	...	...	69.4	10.1	20.5	...	...	...	...
Sudan, The	1966[2]	253,060	...	...	...	...	...	...	59.2	28.3	12.6	76.5	4.4	16.7	2.4
Suriname	1980	77,658	...	—52.4—		—47.6—			...	...	...	38.9[105]	—61.1[105]—		
Swaziland	1986	122,369	...	...	...	...	...	...	...	...	...	65.9	—34.1—		
Sweden	1990	3,830,037	20.0	33.2	14.2	22.4	22.2	10.6	55.9	40.0	4.1	98.7[16]	...	...	...
Switzerland	1980	3,180,835[18]	...	—58.1—		22.6	—19.3—		29.9	67.1	3.0	...	...	...	...
Syria	1987	1,836,195	...	—91.3[38]—		—8.7[38]—			81.6[38]	15.5[38]	2.8[38]	...	...	...	...
Taiwan	1990	4,237,174[19]	17.2	6.1[5]	6.7[6]	15.8[7]	42.6[8]	28.8[9]	78.5	12.8	8.7	...	...	...	...
Tajikistan	1989	799,000[22]	...	...	...	...	...	...	...	...	...	...	...	...	...
Tanzania	1978	3,554,793	...	—17.0—		—83.0—			75.4	19.4	5.2	83.0	—	16.3	0.7
Thailand	1980	12,224,400[22, 99]	...	22.0[38]	25.0[38]	53.0[38]	—	—	83.4	9.1	7.5	15.1	70.0	6.3	8.6
Togo	1958–60[2]	22,274	...	...	...	...	...	...	...	...	...	...	...	...	...
Tonga	1976	15,091[17, 22]	22.5	—59.4[106]—		20.3[107]	—20.3[108]—		85.1	2.5	12.4	35.1	45.4	15.3	4.2
Trinidad and Tobago	1980	314,739[99]	...	—56.3—		14.5	—29.2—		64.6	34.0	1.4	3.3	32.6	53.8	10.3[32]
Tunisia	1984	1,512,300[11]	...	...	...	...	...	...	78.9	12.6	8.5	...	...	...	...
Turkey	1986	10,855,495	8.4	16.2[106]	6.2[109]	19.6[95]	—58.0[37]—		77.2	12.0	10.8	—28.8—		—71.2—	
Turkmenistan	1989	598,000[22]	...	...	...	...	...	...	...	...	...	...	...	...	...
Tuvalu	1979	1,079	...	...	...	...	...	...	81.6	12.1	6.6	64.9	4.2	31.0	—
Uganda	...	...	...	...	...	...	...	...	...	...	...	...	...	...	...
Ukraine	1989	14,057,000[22]	...	...	...	...	...	...	...	...	...	...	...	...	...
United Arab Emirates	1980	153,009	15.0	0.8	1.3	11.4	—86.5—		36.2	45.2	18.6	2.9	7.3	87.3	2.5
United Kingdom[111]	1981	21,897,322[18, 22]	32.6	54.0	13.0	16.6	—16.4—		66.6[11]	33.4[11]	—[11]	...	...	...	...
United States	1990	102,263,678	25.0	32.9[14]	14.0[14]	16.6[14]	—36.5[14]—		64.2	35.8	—	...	...	...	...
Uruguay	1985	852,400	...	...	...	...	...	...	59.0	23.9	17.1	...	...	...	...
Uzbekistan	1989	3,415,000[22]	...	...	...	...	...	...	...	...	...	...	...	...	...
Vanuatu	1979	22,513	...	...	...	...	...	...	40.9[52]	25.7[52]	33.4[52]	61.4	7.7	13.6	17.2
Venezuela	1981	3,534,507[99]	...	...	...	...	...	...	75.1	17.8	7.1	11.8	2.1	78.9	7.2
Vietnam	1989	12,958,041[22]	...	...	...	...	...	...	...	...	...	...	...	...	...
Virgin Islands (U.S.)	1990	39,290	14.7	10.0[16]	8.9[16]	42.7[16]	—38.4[16]—		44.6	55.4	—	...	...	...	...
West Bank	1985	119,165[62]	...	...	...	...	...	...	86.2[63]	11.5[63]	2.3[63]	...	...	...	...
Western Sahara	1982	19,559	...	...	...	...	...	...	32.2[49]	62.3[49]	5.5[49]	...	...	...	...
Western Samoa	1981	33,402	...	...	...	...	...	...	80.1	2.0	17.9	62.3	24.4	8.6	4.7
Yemen[112]	1988[113]	1,701,203	...	...	...	...	...	...	83.9	5.2	10.9	...	...	...	...
Yugoslavia[114]	1981	7,556,000[18]	...	31.1	12.7	26.8	—29.4—		67.1	25.0	7.9	...	—82.6—		17.4
Zaire	1967[52]	168,000	...	...	...	...	...	...	47.4	38.3	14.3	...	...	...	...
Zambia	1980	1,128,356	...	...	...	...	...	...	78.8[115]	21.1[115]	...	...	...	...	...
Zimbabwe	1969	925,581	...	...	...	...	...	...	65.1[102]	32.6[102]	2.3[102]	55.9[116]	—44.1[116]—		

[1]1983. [2]Urban only. [3]1989–90. [4]Data refer to buildings. [5]1945 or earlier. [6]1946–60. [7]1961–70. [8]1971–80. [9]1981 or later. [10]Percentage of net material product. [11]1989. [12]1962 or earlier. [13]1963–69. [14]1985. [15]1987. [16]1980. [17]1986. [18]1991. [19]Occupied dwellings only; may include seasonal and/or temporary housing. [20]1988. [21]Average annual gain in housing stock during intercensal interval. [22]Data refer to households. [23]1939 or earlier. [24]1940–59. [25]1981. [26]1982. [27]1976. [28]1971. [29]1990–91. [30]Stucco. [31]1988–89. [32]Includes wood and brick, and wood and concrete. [33]Residential includes nonresidential. [34]1946–61. [35]1962–70. [36]1971–75. [37]1976 or later. [38]1970. [39]Volume in cubic metres. [40]1984. [41]1983–85 average. [42]Average size of dwelling unit in year to which new dwellings and floor area data refer. [43]1986–87. [44]Data refer to compound dwellings, which usually contain two or three dwelling units each. [45]1966. [46]1971 or later. [47]1973. [48]1975. [49]1934–45. [50]1946–59. [51]Includes prefabricated units. [52]Capital city only. [53]Includes corrugated steel. [54]1978. [55]1961. [56]1987–88. [57]1977. [58]1948 or earlier. [59]1949–61. [60]1962–74. [61]1975 or later. [62]1967. [63]Excludes refugee camps. [64]Former West Germany. [65]1949–57. [66]1958–68. [67]1969–78. [68]1979 or later. [69]1979. [70]1952 or earlier. [71]1953–62.

physical amenities (percent)			sewage disposal (percent)			space[b]			construction industry (1990)						country
									percent of GDP	new residential[d]			new nonresidential[d]		
piped water	electricity	inside toilet or WC	closed public sewer or septic tank	open public sewer	other	average area (sq m)	rooms per dwelling unit	persons per room		total no. of dwellings	floor area ('000 sq m)	years to replace nat'l stock	number of units	floor area ('000 sq m)	
80.7	65.7[16]	74.3[16]	44.2	—55.8—		...	2.8	1.6	3.3[18]	15,149[15]	...	34.6[15]	90[14]	142.5[14]	Panama
50.0	56.0	40.0	...	...	...	...	...	...	5.7	587[17]	...	...	...	...	Papua New Guinea
...	...	26.4	...	...	...	...	2.2[98]	2.4[98]	5.5	...	61[27]	...	2,715[15]	365[15]	Paraguay
73.4	89.5	78.0	58.1	—41.9—		42.4	2.6	2.0	8.1	...	952[17]	...	...	...	Peru
41.4	46.0	35.0	44.1	—55.9—		...	2.4[98]	2.3[98]	4.4	...	3,486[20]	...	2,807[14]	3,222[20]	Philippines
69.7[54]	96.2[54]	41.4[54]	67.0[54]	—33.0[54]—		55.6	3.5	1.1	9.5[10, 11]	189,600[11]	13,856[15]	56.9[11]	62,041[14]	...	Poland
73.4	77.6	67.7	75.5	—24.5—		75.4[11, 42]	5.0[20]	0.8	7.5	33,984[11]	4,198	95.2[11]	5,888[15]	2,045	Portugal
95.2	97.4	89.7	89.6	—10.4—		...	4.8	0.8	2.1[20]	11,710[15]	1,740[15]	82.8[15]	900[14]	41.0[14]	Puerto Rico
...	93.2	...	—50.5—		49.5	...	4.1	1.3	3.9[18]	1,095[15]	391[17]	58.9[15]	258[17]	168[17]	Qatar
70.6	81.6	50.7	52.4	—47.6—		...	3.6	1.2	7.4[20]	8,499[11]	...	16.6[11]	...	...	Réunion
...	48.6[45]	...	12.2[45]	—87.8[45]—		89.6[42]	2.6	1.4	7.3[10, 11]	60,400[11]	5,409[11]	98.6[11]	...	...	Romania
...	...	...	...	...	...	...	...	...	12.7	...	61,694	...	...	...	Russia
...	...	...	...	...	...	...	...	...	6.9[20]	435[40]	60[25]	...	63[40]	34[25]	Rwanda
46.3	57.5	33.5	31.8[39]	—68.2[39]—		...	3.0	1.1	12.2	171[21]	...	68.0[21]	...	...	St. Kitts and Nevis
64.7	72.9	35.7	35.7	—64.3—		...	3.4	1.2	6.0	471[4, 15]	70	57.2[4, 15]	121[17]	18.3	St. Lucia
95.0[1]	...	...	22.0[1]	—78.0[1]—		...	2.8	1.8	8.9	465[15, 33]	88[15, 33]	...	[33]	[33]	St. Vincent and the Grenadines
99.8	100.0	98.3	98.3	—1.7—		...	4.5	0.8	...	128	...	65.5	101	...	San Marino
...	...	...	...	...	...	...	...	...	9.7[15]	...	...	...	...	...	São Tomé and Príncipe
...	...	...	...	...	...	...	...	...	9.1	...	...	...	...	...	Saudi Arabia
87.7	95.9	...	...	...	...	...	2.3	1.5	2.9	...	257[15]	...	34[15]	33[15]	Senegal
77.0	75.8	95.0	33.1[57]	—66.9[57]—		...	4.1	1.1	4.2	4,802[33, 57]	...	...	46[17]	[33]	Seychelles
...	...	...	...	...	...	...	...	...	1.8[20]	...	...	...	...	...	Sierra Leone
90.6[38]	98.3	63.6[38]	63.6[38]	—36.4[38]—		...	1.8[38]	2.5[38]	5.3	14,170	9,222[27]	36.2	992[27]	2,226	Singapore
91.8	...	80.1	87.6	—12.4—		71.7	2.9	1.1	12.0	...	1,147[18]	...	...	...	Slovakia
93.0	98.9	75.3	...	...	...	66.1	...	...	5.9[11]	7,759	...	...	...	...	Slovenia
92.7[27]	79.6[27]	89.2	89.2[27]	—10.8[27]—		10.8[27]	2.3[27]	2.0[27]	4.3	...	...	...	...	...	Solomon Islands
...	...	...	...	...	...	...	...	...	3.8[18]	...	...	...	...	...	Somalia
...	...	...	...	...	...	117.6[42]	3.4[38]	...	3.2	39,266[11]	4,619[11]	34.5[11]	...	1,316[11]	South Africa
...	...	...	...	...	...	...	...	...	...	...	...	...	...	...	Bophuthatswana
...	...	...	...	...	...	...	...	...	...	...	...	...	...	...	Ciskei
...	...	...	...	...	...	...	...	...	...	...	...	...	...	...	Transkei
...	...	...	...	...	...	...	...	...	...	...	...	...	...	...	Venda
98.7	99.2	97.1	87.9[16]	—12.1[16]—		86.6	4.4[38]	...	8.3[11]	281,059	...	43.9	...	...	Spain
18.2	14.9	4.7	4.7	—95.3—		18.6[38]	2.5	2.1	7.4	59,637[17]	...	47.2[17]	...	...	Sri Lanka
63.9	26.4	70.2	2.6	—97.4—		...	2.2	2.5	4.5[31]	...	...	...	...	...	Sudan, The
62.9	82.0	40.4	19.6[105]	—80.4[105]—		...	2.1	1.9	6.0[20]	...	355[14, 39]	...	161[14]	...	Suriname
42.5	11.6	21.4	...	...	...	...	...	...	2.8[20]	...	...	...	28[40]	...	Swaziland
99.0[14]	96.2[16]	98.0	96.3[16]	—3.7[16]—		...	3.4	0.6	7.6	58,426	...	65.6	...	3,818[40]	Sweden
100.0	...	93.3	92.2	—	7.8	86.0	3.8[17]	0.6[17]	7.6[14]	37,597[18]	...	84.6[18]	8,109[17]	...	Switzerland
40.2[1]	41.7[1]	...	36.0[1]	—64.0[1]—		93.0	3.0	2.0	4.3[11]	55,572[15]	2,390[20]	33.0[15]	...	339[20]	Syria
79.4[16]	99.7[16]	94.2[16]	69.3[16]	...	...	30.5	4.1	1.2	4.9	...	32,008[18, 33]	...	...	[33]	Taiwan
...	...	...	...	...	...	...	...	...	14.7	...	1,753	...	...	...	Tajikistan
37.2	6.3	...	...	...	...	...	2.5	1.9	1.5[11]	...	...	...	...	...	Tanzania
29.7[99]	89.3[99]	40.9	40.9[27]	9.8[27]	49.3[27]	...	1.9[27]	...	7.2	...	16,343	...	...	13,499	Thailand
4.1	10.3	...	—	—100.0—		...	1.8	3.4	3.5[20]	...	...	...	...	...	Togo
61.3	20.9	42.3	11.2	—88.8—		...	...	...	5.6[31]	...	...	...	...	...	Tonga
64.3	83.3	41.1	41.0	—59.0—		...	3.3	1.4	7.7	...	211	...	69[17]	27.2	Trinidad and Tobago
26.4	63.4	43.3	69.2[11]	—30.8[11]—		...	1.9	2.4	4.9	34,566[15]	...	43.8[15]	...	...	Tunisia
68.0	56.8	70.6	42.0	52.0	6.0	110.5[42]	2.4[14]	2.2[38]	6.6[11]	250,480[11]	25,692	43.3[11]	3,933[17]	7,477	Turkey
...	...	...	...	...	...	...	...	...	22.7[18]	...	1,787	...	...	...	Turkmenistan
65.4	7.4	37.3	...	...	...	...	...	...	14.6	...	...	...	...	...	Tuvalu
...	...	...	...	...	...	...	...	...	7.2	...	...	...	65[98]	26.8[98]	Uganda
...	...	...	...	...	...	...	...	...	11.2[11]	...	17,464	...	...	...	Ukraine
30.9[110]	24.2[110]	84.5	...	...	...	...	2.8	1.8	9.2[11]	...	...	...	133[40]	...	United Arab Emirates
...	...	99.0	...	...	...	...	5.0[18, 22]	0.5[18, 22]	6.8[18]	206,682[11]	...	109.4[11]	...	...	United Kingdom[111]
98.5	96.9	98.2	99.2	—0.8—		147.1	5.2	0.5	4.8[11]	1,488,000[11]	214,900[17]	68.7[11]	...	140,100[17]	United States
88.9	84.7	73.3	...	92.0	...	...	3.4	1.7	3.5	...	160[14]	...	105[14]	21.4[14]	Uruguay
...	...	...	...	...	...	...	...	...	10.7[18]	...	9,908	...	...	...	Uzbekistan
13.7	11.7	19.1	...	...	...	...	...	...	5.8	...	5.7[17]	...	...	15.3[17]	Vanuatu
85.3	88.6	84.4	71.3	—28.7—		53.5[42]	3.9[28]	1.5[28]	4.9	91,666[17]	4,904[17]	29.5[17]	678[17]	1,067[17]	Venezuela
...	...	...	...	...	...	...	...	...	4.4[18]	...	...	...	53[40]	59.3[40]	Vietnam
96.3[16]	98.1[16]	86.0[16]	93.6[16]	—6.4[16]—		...	4.3	0.6	...	...	...	...	262[16]	...	Virgin Islands (U.S.)
75.2	91.2	90.1	...	...	...	127.2[42]	2.4	2.7	14.1[15]	5,740[15]	730[15]	20.8[15]	...	175.8[15]	West Bank
78.5	95.3	...	...	...	...	...	4.5	1.2	...	...	...	...	...	...	Western Sahara
80.7	37.7	71.0	16.6	—83.4—		...	3.9[27, 101]	1.5[27, 101]	1.9[11]	132[14]	...	...	118[14]	...	Western Samoa
5.7[48]	4.6[48]	...	...	...	...	...	2.0[48]	2.8[48]	11.0[20]	...	1,988[14]	...	...	...	Yemen[112]
67.8	95.7	53.3	...	...	...	60.7	2.6[22]	1.3[22]	6.0[11]	116,236[11]	12,883[11]	65.0[11]	15,522[5]	1,197[11]	Yugoslavia[114]
...	...	...	...	...	...	...	...	...	2.0[20]	...	20[14]	...	73[14]	39[14]	Zaire
12.4[115]	27.5[76]	15.1[115]	...	...	82.3[115]	...	1.9[115]	2.6[115]	3.5	...	...	...	...	...	Zambia
...	9.3[116]	...	...	...	...	...	2.8	1.9	2.2	...	...	...	...	...	Zimbabwe

[72]1963–72. [73]1973–81. [74]1982 or later. [75]1974. [76]1960. [77]1947 or earlier. [78]1948–83. [79]1961–71. [80]1944 or earlier. [81]1945–70. [82]Minimum. [83]1946 or earlier. [84]1947–60. [85]Peninsular Malaysia only. [86]1957 or earlier. [87]1958–67. [88]Excluding Rodrigues and lesser outlying islands. [89]1960–68. [90]1969 or later. [91]1975–82. [92]Dwellings of indigenous population only. [93]Excludes Islāmābad, North-West Frontier, and federally administered tribal areas. [94]1947–65. [95]1966–75. [96]Excludes areas under U.S. military control in the provinces of Panamá and Colón. [97]1992. [98]1972. [99]1990. [100]De jure population. [101]European-style dwellings only. [102]White, Coloured, and Asian dwellings only; excludes Bantu. [103]1940 or earlier. [104]1941–60. [105]1964. [106]1955 or earlier. [107]1956–66. [108]1967 or later. [109]1956–65. [110]1968. [111]Excludes Northern Ireland. [112]Former Yemen Arab Republic only. [113]Combined from 1986 and 1988 census data. [114]Data refer to Yugoslavia as constituted prior to 1991. [115]1969. [116]Bantu dwellings only.

Household budgets and consumption

This table provides international data on household income, on the consumption expenditure of households for goods and services, and on the principal object of such expenditure (in most countries), food consumption (by kind). For purposes of this compilation, income comprises pretax monetary payments and payment in kind. The first part of the table provides data on distribution of income by households and by sources of income; the second part analyzes the largest portion of income use—consumption expenditure. Such expenditure is defined as the purchase of goods and services to satisfy current wants and needs. This definition excludes income expended on taxes, debts, savings and investments, and insurance policies. The third and last part of the table focuses on food, which usually, and often by a wide margin, represents the largest share of consumer spending worldwide. The data provided include daily available calories per capita and consumption of major food groups.

For both sources of income and consumption expenditure, the primary basis of analysis for most countries is the household, an economic unit that can be as small as a single person or as large as an extended family. For some of the countries that do not compile information by household, the table provides data on personal income and personal expenditure—*i.e.,* the income and expenditure of all the individuals constituting a society's households. When no expenditure data at all is available, the table reports the weights of each major class of goods and services making up a given country's consumer (or retail) price index (CPI). The weighting of the components of the CPI usually reflects household spending patterns within the country or its principal urban or rural areas.

The data on distribution of income show, collectively for an entire country, the proportion of total income earned (occasionally, expended) by households constituting the lowest quintile and highest decile (poorest 20% and wealthiest 10%) within the country. These figures show the degree to which either group represents a disproportionate share of poverty or wealth.

The data on sources of income illuminate patterns of economic structure in the gaining of an income. They indicate, for example, that in poor, agrarian countries income often derives largely from self-employment (usually farming) or that in industrial countries, with well-developed systems of salaried employment and social welfare, income derives mainly from wages and salaries and secondarily from transfer payments (*see* note a). Because household sizes and numbers of income earners vary so greatly internationally, and because the frequency and methodology of household and CPI surveys do not permit single-year comparisons for more than a few countries at once, no summary of total *household* income or expenditure was possible. Instead, U.S. dollar figures are supplied for *per capita* private final consumption expenditure (for a single, recent year) that are more comparable internationally and refer to the same date. The figures on distribution of consumption expenditure by end use reveal patterns of personal and family use of disposable income and indicate, inter alia, that in developing countries food may absorb 50% or more of disposable income, while in the larger household budgets of the developed countries, by contrast, food purchases may account for only 20–30% of spending. In either type of country, the cost of transportation often rivals that of housing, once the more basic need. Each category of expenditure betrays similar complexities of local habit, necessity, and aspiration.

The reader should exercise caution when using these data to make inter-country comparisons. Most of the information comes from single-country surveys, which often differ markedly in their coverage of economically or

Household budgets and consumption

country	income (latest)						consumption expenditure						
	percent received by		by source (percent)				per capita private final, U.S.$ 1991	by kind or end use (percent of household or personal budget; latest)					
	lowest 20% of households	highest 10% of households	wages, salaries	self-employment	transfer payments[a]	other[b]		food[c]	housing[d]	clothing[e]	health care	energy, water	education
Afghanistan	...	...	20.7	28.0	8.2	43.1	...	33.9	3.0	...	1.1	0.7	...
Albania	...	...	...	...	...	...	680[1]	...	...	...	...	...	...
Algeria	...	...	...	...	...	...	610	55.7	5.4[2]	9.1	3.1	[2]	[3]
American Samoa	...	...	...	...	...	...	1,877[4]	32.9	20.4[5]	5.2	...	...	0.2
Andorra	...	...	...	...	...	...	...	...	...	...	...	...	...
Angola	...	...	...	...	...	...	420[6]	...	...	...	...	...	...
Antigua and Barbuda	...	...	...	...	...	...	2,170[7]	*42.9*	*23.3*	*7.5*	...	5.5	...
Argentina	*4.4*	*35.2*	...	...	...	...	2,830	38.2	9.3	8.0	7.9	9.0	2.6
Armenia	...	...	74.8	—	25.2	—	3,750[1]	47.3	...	17.4	...	...	...
Aruba	...	...	...	...	...	...	...	26.9	12.6	8.4	2.9	5.6	1.9
Australia	4.8	28.1	58.6	15.2	14.4	11.8	9,900	18.9	18.2	5.6	7.3	2.2	1.6
Austria	*4.0*	*28.7*	55.5	[8]	24.4	20.1[8]	11,610	18.3	13.6	9.5	5.1	4.0	0.3
Azerbaijan	...	...	...	...	...	...	...	...	...	...	...	...	...
Bahamas, The	3.6	32.1	...	...	...	...	3,950[6]	19.8	19.2	7.2	3.4	4.3	7.8
Bahrain	...	...	...	...	...	...	2,800[1]	32.4	21.2	5.9	2.3	2.2	2.3
Bangladesh	9.5[9]	24.6[9]	26.1	50.8	0.5	22.6	170	63.3	8.8	5.9	1.1	8.4	1.2
Barbados	*6.8*	...	...	...	...	...	4,540	*43.2*	*13.1*	*5.1*	...	*6.2*	...
Belarus	...	...	71.6	—	28.4	—	3,650[1]	29.0	2.7	...	...	...	...
Belgium	*7.9*[10]	*21.5*[10]	49.6	10.9	20.7	18.8	12,870	17.5	12.3	7.8	11.2	4.4	[3]
Belize	...	...	*84.1*	—	*15.9*	—	1,350	51.5[11]	2.3	11.1	3.4	6.0	1.5
Benin	*8.0*	*39.0*	26.3	—	73.7	—	320	37.0	10.0	14.0	5.0	2.0	4.0
Bermuda	7.2	24.7	72.2	6.7	2.4	18.7	12,690[12]	20.7[11]	21.8	6.0	6.8	4.5	[3]
Bhutan	...	...	...	...	...	...	100[1]	*72.3*	...	*21.2*	...	*3.7*	...
Bolivia	*4.0*	...	...	...	...	...	570	*41.4*	*12.5*	*9.7*	*4.5*	*0.7*	*1.2*
Bosnia and Herzegovina	...	...	53.2	12.0	18.2	16.6	1,890[1]	44.7	1.6	8.3	3.4	7.8	[3]
Botswana	1.4[9]	49.6[9]	79.5	9.4	5.3	5.8	1,290[6]	39.5[11]	13.3[2]	5.6	2.3	[2]	[3]
Brazil	2.1[13]	51.3[13]	...	...	...	...	1,720	35.0	9.0	10.0	6.0	2.0	5.0
Brunei	...	...	...	...	...	...	...	*45.1*	*5.0*[2]	*6.1*	...	[2]	[3]
Bulgaria	9.7	22.5	58.3	3.8	27.3	10.6	1,350	39.2	0.9	10.1	6.1	2.8	[14]
Burkina Faso	...	...	...	...	...	...	220	38.7[15]	5.1[15]	4.4[15]	5.2[15]	13.7[15]	[3]
Burundi	...	...	...	...	...	...	180	59.6[15]	4.4[15]	11.1[15]	...	5.8[15]	...
Cambodia	...	...	...	...	...	...	...	...	...	...	...	...	...
Cameroon	...	...	34.7	51.3	10.4	3.6	680	24.0	13.0	7.0	12.0	3.0	9.0
Canada	5.7	24.1	64.7	6.8	14.6	14.0	13,270	13.8	23.1[2]	5.5	4.4	[2]	2.8
Cape Verde	...	...	...	...	...	...	880[1]	60.0	8.5	2.5	0.5	4.9	[14]
Central African Republic	...	...	...	...	...	...	360	70.5[15]	0.6[15]	9.5[15]	1.0[15]	6.5[15]	...
Chad	*8.0*	*30.0*	...	...	...	...	210	45.3[15]	...	3.5[15]	11.9[15]	5.8[15]	...
Chile	3.7[13]	48.9[13]	*40.8*	...	*8.0*	*51.2*	1,560	27.9	15.2	22.5	...	...	...
China	6.4[13]	24.6[13]	75.7[17]	—	24.3[17]	—	170	53.8[11, 17]	2.3[17]	13.7[17]	2.2[17]	3.7[17]	2.3[17]
Colombia	4.0[13]	37.1[13]	46.1	36.7	9.6	7.6	820	36.6	8.3	6.0	6.7	2.3	1.7
Comoros	...	...	*25.6*	*64.5*	*8.7*	*1.2*	430[1]	56.0	...	10.0	5.0	14.4	...
Congo	*7.0*	*43.5*	...	...	...	...	680	37.0	6.0	6.0	6.0	3.0	8.0
Costa Rica	4.0[13]	34.1[13]	...	...	...	...	1,090	33.0	8.0	8.0	7.0	1.0	8.0
Côte d'Ivoire	7.3[9]	26.9[9]	44.9	49.9	— 5.2	—	390	39.0	4.0	9.0	9.0	1.0	6.0
Croatia	...	...	40.2	40.8	12.1	6.9	5,050[1]	37.8	2.9	8.6	4.3	7.6	[3]
Cuba	...	...	57.3	...	...	42.7	1,510[6]	26.7	...	...	...	2.5	...
Cyprus	*7.9*[17]	...	...	...	...	...	6,500	23.9	5.9	9.4	3.1	1.2	1.4
Czech Republic	10.0[18, 19]	21.8[18, 19]	71.9	...	10.9	17.2	...	29.5	...	9.9	...	9.9	...
Denmark	3.5	25.6	48.2	33.6	18.2	...	13,130	20.9[11]	21.6	5.4	1.9	6.0	[3]
Djibouti	...	...	*51.6*	*36.0*	*10.5*	*1.9*	1,030[1]	50.3	6.4	1.7	2.4	13.1	...
Dominica	...	...	...	...	...	...	1,800[6]	43.1	16.1	6.5	...	5.4	...
Dominican Republic	4.2[13]	39.6[13]	*41.7*	*31.8*	*1.5*	*25.0*	810	46.0	10.0	3.0	8.0	5.0	3.0
Ecuador	*2.9*	*51.5*	15.9	76.8	4.6	2.7	850	36.0	3.8	11.6	4.1	1.1	[14]
Egypt	*5.8*	*33.2*	...	...	...	...	520	49.0	6.0	11.0	3.0	3.0	6.0
El Salvador	*5.5*[10]	*29.5*[10]	...	...	...	...	960	33.0	5.0	9.0	8.0	2.0	5.0

demographically stratified groups, in sample design, or in the methods employed for collection, classification, and tabulation of data. Further, the reference period of the data varies greatly; while a significant portion of the data is from 1980 or later, information for some countries dates from the 1970s. This older information is typeset in italic. Finally, intercountry comparisons of annual personal consumption expenditure may be misleading because of the distortions of price and purchasing power present when converting a national currency unit into U.S. dollars.

The table's food consumption data include total daily available calories per capita (food supply), which amounts to domestic production and imports minus exports, animal feed, and nonfood uses, and a percentage breakdown of the major food groups that make up food supply.

The data for daily available calories per capita provide a measure of the nutritional adequacy of each nation's food supply. The following list, based on estimates from the United Nations Food and Agriculture Organization (FAO), indicates the regional variation in recommended daily minimum nutritional requirements, which are defined by factors such as climatic ambience, physical activity, and average body weight: Africa (2,320 calories), formerly Centrally Planned Asia (2,300 calories), Far East (2,240 calories), Latin America (2,360 calories), Near East (2,440 calories).

The breakdown of diet by food groups describes the character of a nation's food supply. A typical breakdown for a low-income country might show a diet with heavy intake of vegetable foods, such as cereals, potatoes, or cassava. In the high-income countries, a relatively larger portion of total calories derives from animal products (meat, eggs, and milk). The reader should note that these data refer to total national *supply* and often do not reflect the differences that may exist within a single country.

In compiling this table, Britannica editors rely on both numerous national reports and principal secondary sources such as the World Bank's *World Development Report* (annual), the International Labour Organisation's *Statistical Sources and Methods, vol. 1 Consumer Price Indices* (2nd ed.), the UN's *Yearbook of National Accounts Statistics* (annual) and *National Accounts Statistics: Compendium of Income Distribution Statistics,* and the FAO's *Food Balance Sheets 1988–90.*

The following terms further define the column headings:

a. Includes pensions, family allowances, unemployment payments, remittances from abroad, and social security and related benefits.
b. Includes interest and dividends, rents and royalties, and all other income not reported under the three preceding categories.
c. Includes alcoholic and nonalcoholic beverages and meals away from home when identifiable. Excludes tobacco except as noted.
d. Rent, maintenance of dwellings, and taxes only; excludes energy and water (heat, light, power, and water) and household durables (furniture, appliances, utensils, and household operations), shown separately.
e. Includes footwear.
f. Furniture, appliances, and utensils; usually includes expenditure on household operation.
g. Includes expenditure on cultural activities other than education.
h. May include data not shown separately in preceding categories, including meals away from home (*see* note c).
i. Represents pure fats and oils only.
j. Consists mainly of peas, beans, and lentils; spices; stimulants; alcoholic beverages (when combined with "other"); sugars and honey; and nuts and oilseeds.

				food consumption										country
				daily available calories per capita (1988–90)	percent of total calories (latest) derived from:									
transportation, communications	household durable goods[f]	recreation[g]	personal effects, other[h]		cereals	potatoes, cassava	meat, poultry	fish	eggs, milk	fruits, vegetables	fats, oils[i]	other[j]	
...	...	...	61.3	1,764	75.5	1.2	4.8	—	3.3	2.8	7.9	4.5	Afghanistan
...	...	...	...	2,585	63.4	1.6	5.3	0.2	7.4	3.5	7.7	10.9	Albania
6.7	6.4	3.4[3]	10.2	2,945	55.0	2.5	1.7	0.4	6.5	4.3	14.7	14.9	Algeria
15.1	[5]	1.1	25.1	...	...	...	...	...	...	...	...	...	American Samoa
...	...	...	...	*3,567*	*23.8*	*5.5*	*18.0*	*1.5*	*9.4*	*6.7*	*15.9*	*19.1*	Andorra
...	...	...	...	1,880	32.5	32.4	4.4	3.0	2.8	3.6	9.9	11.2	Angola
10.0	...	...	*10.8*	2,307	26.9	1.0	16.7	3.0	11.0	7.2	13.0	21.2	Antigua and Barbuda
11.6	...	7.5	5.9	3,068	30.9	5.5	18.1	0.3	9.0	4.1	12.8	19.4	Argentina
...	6.6	...	28.7	...	...	...	...	...	...	...	...	...	Armenia
17.4	9.1	3.1	12.1	...	...	...	...	...	...	...	...	...	Aruba
15.1	6.3	7.7	17.1	3,302	24.3	3.0	19.9	0.8	11.1	4.9	13.6	22.4	Australia
16.5	7.9	6.6	18.2	3,486	19.8	3.3	13.7	0.6	10.5	6.6	22.2	23.2	Austria
...	...	...	...	...	...	...	...	...	...	...	...	...	Azerbaijan
18.9	10.2	5.3	3.9	2,776	25.2	1.9	17.4	1.3	7.6	9.6	9.3	27.6	Bahamas, The
8.5	9.8	6.4	9.0	...	...	...	...	...	...	...	...	...	Bahrain
0.9	...	...	10.4	2,038	82.9	1.3	0.5	0.6	1.2	1.1	5.4	6.9	Bangladesh
4.6	*9.6*	...	*16.2*	3,217	28.1	3.9	13.7	2.5	7.4	3.3	13.4	27.7	Barbados
...	...	...	68.3	...	...	...	...	...	...	...	...	...	Belarus
13.6	10.8	6.6[3]	15.8	3,925	19.0	4.7	18.6	1.0	9.1	5.6	21.3	20.7	Belgium
6.5	10.1	2.2	5.4	2,575	32.9	1.9	8.7	0.4	10.9	6.2	11.7	27.3	Belize
14.0	5.0	...	9.0	2,383	35.0	39.0	2.3	0.8	0.9	2.9	7.8	11.3	Benin
17.1	14.7	8.4[3]	6.8	2,960	20.5	2.3	19.7	2.7	8.9	9.5	13.4	23.0	Bermuda
...	*0.7*	...	*2.1*	...	*85.2*	*2.4*	*0.4*	*0.1*	*0.6*	*1.4*	*5.3*	*4.6*	Bhutan
12.5	*8.9*	*3.1*	*5.5*	2,012	41.2	11.2	9.7	0.1	2.5	8.4	9.2	17.6	Bolivia
6.0	4.1	3.5[3]	2.3	...	...	...	...	...	...	...	...	...	Bosnia and Herzegovina
13.1	14.0	8.3[3]	3.9	2,260	62.7	0.8	4.0	0.3	7.1	1.4	5.5	18.2	Botswana
8.0	8.0	...	17.0	2,730	34.4	6.4	6.8	0.4	6.4	5.0	15.0	25.5	Brazil
17.2	*8.3*	*8.9*[3]	*9.4*	2,859	47.6	1.0	11.9	1.6	5.7	4.0	7.0	21.1	Brunei
10.4	5.8	[14]	24.7[14]	3,695	39.6	1.5	10.3	0.4	8.8	5.1	15.2	19.2	Bulgaria
18.6[15]	3.0[15]	2.3[3, 15]	9.0[15]	2,218	71.8	1.4	2.3	0.2	1.4	0.8	4.1	17.6	Burkina Faso
...	6.0[15]	...	13.1[15, 16]	1,947	21.1	29.0	1.0	0.2	0.8	9.6	2.6	35.8	Burundi
...	...	...	...	2,122	83.4	3.1	3.2	0.8	0.4	3.2	1.2	4.8	Cambodia
12.0	3.0	...	17.0	2,208	38.9	15.9	3.5	1.1	1.6	11.8	8.6	18.6	Cameroon
15.2	9.3	8.5	17.4	3,242	22.6	3.4	15.1	1.4	9.9	6.4	18.5	22.7	Canada
8.8	6.9	[14]	7.9[14]	2,780	51.5	5.0	3.7	0.9	3.0	2.4	13.9	19.6	Cape Verde
4.1[15]	0.8[15]	1.3[15]	5.7[15]	1,847	25.6	33.4	7.3	0.5	1.2	5.7	7.3	19.2	Central African Republic
...	...	...	33.5[15]	1,733	50.2	16.3	3.5	1.8	2.8	2.8	5.0	17.3	Chad
6.4	...	...	28.0	2,484	45.7	4.3	8.3	1.4	6.5	5.5	8.6	19.7	Chile
1.4[17]	...	6.0[17]	14.6[17]	2,642	69.7	5.8	8.0	0.6	1.4	2.6	4.7	7.1	China
15.7	6.4	4.5	14.7	2,453	31.4	8.1	7.4	0.2	6.6	9.1	9.9	27.2	Colombia
6.6	...	3.0	5.0	1,760	44.9	17.8	1.7	1.5	1.6	8.9	7.3	16.3	Comoros
15.0	4.0	...	15.0	2,295	18.6	43.9	2.7	3.2	1.0	7.4	11.6	11.6	Congo
8.0	9.0	...	18.0	2,711	35.7	0.8	5.1	0.3	8.8	4.9	13.0	31.3	Costa Rica
10.0	3.0	...	19.0	2,565	36.7	27.2	2.5	1.2	1.4	9.4	9.9	11.6	Côte d'Ivoire
9.3	4.5	4.1[3]	1.5	...	...	...	...	...	...	...	...	...	Croatia
5.4	...	...	65.4	3,129	32.9	4.8	6.5	1.1	7.9	3.8	14.1	29.0	Cuba
15.8	10.1	6.5	22.8	...	*40.0*	*2.5*	*13.7*	*0.4*	*7.9*	*7.0*	*10.1*	*18.4*	Cyprus
...	5.3	...	45.4	3,574[18]	29.9[18]	4.2[18]	13.0[18]	0.5[18]	9.5[18]	4.2[18]	17.5[18]	21.2[18]	Czech Republic
16.4	6.3	10.5[3]	11.0	3,639	20.4	3.6	23.7	2.0	8.7	3.9	17.7	20.1	Denmark
...	1.5	...	24.6	2,363	53.5	0.6	4.1	0.3	6.0	2.8	11.9	20.9	Djibouti
11.6	6.0	...	11.3	2,911	27.9	8.5	8.9	1.0	9.2	9.6	9.3	25.6	Dominica
4.0	8.0	...	13.0	2,310	32.7	3.5	5.2	0.3	5.2	15.2	14.1	23.7	Dominican Republic
12.1	8.0	[14]	23.3[14]	2,399	33.4	3.2	4.8	1.0	6.9	11.1	20.7	19.0	Ecuador
4.0	3.0	...	15.0	3,310	63.2	1.8	2.8	0.4	1.8	6.3	11.1	12.6	Egypt
10.0	7.0	...	21.0	2,331	53.8	0.8	2.3	0.1	6.2	4.5	8.3	24.0	El Salvador

Household budgets and consumption (continued)

country	income (latest)						consumption expenditure						
	percent received by		by source (percent)				per capita private final, U.S.$ 1991	by kind or end use (percent of household or personal budget; latest)					
	lowest 20% of households	highest 10% of households	wages, salaries	self-employment	transfer payments[a]	other[b]		food[c]	housing[d]	clothing[e]	health care	energy, water	education
Equatorial Guinea	...	...	...	...	...	...	380[1]	...	...	...	...	...	...
Eritrea[20]	...	...	...	...	...	...	...	...	...	...	...	...	...
Estonia	...	...	78.2		—21.8—		5,070[1]	45.0	...	...	...	...	...
Ethiopia[20]	8.6[9]	27.5[9]	0.2	79.5	—	20.3	80	49.0	7.0	6.0	3.0	7.0	4.0
Faeroe Islands	...	...	...	...	...	...	...	40.9	11.0	8.0	...	18.9	...
Fiji	*3.7*	*37.8*	*81.5*	*9.1*	—	*9.4*	1,280[1]	31.3	11.9[2]	10.2	2.2	[2]	[3]
Finland	3.7	26.9	65.4	8.4	21.4	4.8	13,630	20.9	14.7	5.4	4.1	3.5	[3]
France	*6.3*	*25.5*	52.7	14.2	27.0	6.2	12,630	18.0	15.4	6.4	9.4	3.7	0.5
French Guiana	...	...	74.6		—25.4—		...	30.0[11]	16.1[2]	6.7	4.4	[2]	[3]
French Polynesia	...	...	63.7	[8]	14.8	21.5[8]	4,310[21]	32.1	...	6.3	1.0	8.1	[3]
Gabon	*3.3*	*54.4*	...	...	...	...	1,660	54.7[11, 15, 22]	13.0[15, 22]	17.5[15, 22]	1.9[15, 22]	...	...
Gambia, The	...	...	...	...	...	...	220[1]	58.0[23]	5.1[23]	17.5[23]	...	5.4[23]	...
Gaza Strip	...	...	...	...	...	...	910[7]	...	...	...	...	...	...
Georgia	...	...	71.4		—28.6—		2,500[1]	38.3	...	14.8	...	0.3	...
Germany	6.8[24]	23.4[24]	57.4[24]	[8]	20.8[24]	21.9[8, 24]	13,350[24]	19.5[24]	16.7[24]	8.1[24]	3.9[24]	4.0[24]	[3]
Ghana	7.0[9]	29.0[9]	41.6[25]	47.1[25]	—	11.3[25]	360	*57.4*	*11.5*[2]	*14.3*	*1.3*	[2]	[3]
Gibraltar	...	...	...	...	...	...	...	39.1[11]	12.6	11.0	...	...	...
Greece	...	...	39.5	[8]	17.5	43.0[8]	4,930	34.3	9.0	8.7	3.8	2.6	0.6
Greenland	...	...	...	...	...	...	...	29.5	8.9	7.6	...	7.1	...
Grenada	...	...	...	...	...	...	1,610	40.7[11]	11.9	5.2	[26]	3.9	[3]
Guadeloupe	...	...	...	...	...	...	4,080[7]	31.6[11]	11.3[2]	9.3	4.6	[2]	[3]
Guam	...	...	...	...	...	...	...	*24.1*	*28.6*	*10.6*	*4.8*	...	...
Guatemala	2.1[13]	46.6[13]	...	...	...	...	840	64.4	16.0[2]	3.1	0.6	[2]	0.3
Guernsey	...	...	...	...	...	...	...	23.7	12.1	7.5	...	8.2	...
Guinea	...	...	...	...	...	...	320	*61.5*	*7.3*[2]	*7.9*	*11.1*	[2]	...
Guinea-Bissau	...	...	...	...	...	...	180	...	...	...	...	...	...
Guyana	...	...	*73.0*	...	*6.3*	*20.7*	240	*42.5*[11]	*21.4*	*8.6*	...	*5.2*	[3]
Haiti	...	...	...	...	...	...	370	*77.9*	*8.3*	*3.2*	...	...	...
Honduras	2.7[13]	47.9[13]	58.3	[8]	1.8	39.9[8]	410	44.5	22.5[2]	9.1	7.0	[2]	[3]
Hong Kong	4.3[19]	37.3[19]	...	...	...	...	7,040	17.8	15.9[2]	20.3	6.1	[2]	1.2
Hungary	10.9[13]	20.8[13]	46.1	11.9	22.4	19.6	1,990	40.7	6.0	7.9	0.9	4.6	0.8
Iceland	4.7	27.3	74.4	3.0	16.6	6.0	15,550	21.1	11.1	10.4	1.7	2.5	0.3
India	8.8[9]	27.1[9]	42.2	39.7	...	18.1	150	49.2	6.5	12.8	2.4	4.6	1.5
Indonesia	8.7[9]	27.9[9]	*42.1*	*41.5*	*2.5*	*13.9*	340	47.5[17]	20.1[2, 17]	5.5[17]	...	[2]	...
Iran	*3.8*	*41.7*	37.4[17]	30.5[17]	—32.1[17]—		1,290	46.7[11]	23.5[2]	12.1	3.4	[2]	[3]
Iraq	*2.1*	...	23.9	33.9	23.0	18.6	1,710[12]	50.2	19.9[2]	10.6	1.6	[2]	[3]
Ireland	4.6	26.5	58.6	13.3	19.9	8.2	6,910	32.6	5.8	7.2	[26]	4.5	[3]
Isle of Man	6.4	26.6	64.1	6.6	16.9	12.4	...	31.0	7.9	7.0	...	11.0	...
Israel	8.4	23.1	87.3[17, 22]	2.2[17, 22]	—10.5[17, 22]—		7,280	25.1[11]	21.7	5.4	...	4.2	...
Italy	6.8	25.3	42.0	28.0	19.6	10.4	12,600	19.3	11.1	10.3	6.4	3.5	[3]
Jamaica	6.0[9]	32.6[9]	63.6	13.9	14.0	8.5	880	35.7	5.7	4.6	2.8	4.9	0.2
Japan	10.9	31.6[27]	58.0	11.6	19.4	11.0	15,300	25.1	5.1	7.3	2.8	5.5	4.3
Jersey	...	...	...	...	...	...	...	*28.3*	*14.9*	*8.3*	...	*6.5*	...
Jordan	...	...	...	...	...	...	920	37.8	6.3[2]	5.5	4.0	[2]	3.3
Kazakhstan	...	...	81.4		—18.6—		...	29.6	2.6	...	...	...	...
Kenya	2.7[9]	45.4[9]	...	...	...	...	200	46.5	10.0	7.7	2.2	2.6	1.0
Kiribati	...	...	*69.7*	*21.4*	*6.0*	*2.9*	370[4]	64.0[11]	1.0	8.0	...	3.6	...
Korea, North	...	...	...	...	...	...	...	46.5[28]	0.6[28]	29.9[28]	...	3.3[28]	...
Korea, South	8.0[17, 29]	24.5[17, 29]	52.3	28.1	13.0	6.7	3,450	36.9[11]	10.0[2]	4.8	7.2	[2]	[3]
Kuwait	...	...	*53.8*	*20.8*	*—25.4—*		3,460	28.1[11]	15.5	8.1	0.7	9.6	[3]
Kyrgyzstan	...	...	71.2		—28.8—		2,370[1]	33.5	2.2	...	...	...	...
Laos	...	...	...	...	...	...	140[6]	...	...	...	...	...	...
Latvia	...	...	63.2	5.3	16.6	14.9	3,950[1]	45.2	...	...	...	...	...
Lebanon	*5.0*	*45.0*	*27.9*	...	*3.0*	*69.1*	780[4]	*42.8*[15]	*16.8*[15]	*8.6*[15]	*7.2*[15]	*4.5*[15]	*3.9*[15]
Lesotho	4.5[13]	45.0[13]	22.4	27.8	44.7	5.1	430	48.0[11]	10.1	16.4	...	...	...
Liberia	*5.3*	...	...	...	...	...	330[6]	*34.4*[15]	*14.9*[15]	*13.8*[15]	...	*5.0*[15]	...
Libya	*10.1*	...	...	...	...	...	2,330[6]	*37.2*[11]	*32.2*[2]	*6.9*	*3.3*	[2]	[3]
Liechtenstein	...	...	92.9[30]	7.1[30]	...	...	...	21.3[11]	18.0	6.6	7.7	4.4	[3]
Lithuania	...	...	66.4	9.7	18.7	5.2	4,360[1]	50.3	...	...	...	...	...
Luxembourg	...	...	88.6	9.1	2.3	—	13,880	13.6	14.4	6.2	7.6	6.4	[3]
Macau	...	...	...	...	...	...	4,160	44.2[11]	22.8	7.3	...	4.8	...
Macedonia	...	...	57.7	17.2	16.2	9.0	1,800[1]	40.6	1.9	7.8	3.0	7.8	[3]
Madagascar	*5.2*	...	*58.8*[15, 31]	*14.1*[15, 31]	—	*27.1*[15, 31]	180	59.0	6.0	6.0	2.0	6.0	4.0
Malaŵi	*10.4*	*40.1*	83.3	6.0	—	11.7	200	30.0	4.0	9.0	4.0	5.0	10.0
Malaysia	4.6[13]	37.9[13]	...	...	...	...	1,420	28.7	10.2[2]	4.3	2.5	[2]	0.6
Maldives	...	...	...	...	...	...	270[6]	...	...	...	...	...	...
Mali	...	...	...	...	...	...	240	57.0	2.0	6.0	2.0	6.0	4.0
Malta	...	...	50.7	17.7	17.6	14.0	4,100[1]	29.1	3.7	7.4	3.6	1.8	0.4
Marshall Islands	...	...	...	...	...	...	...	57.7	15.6[2, 5]	12.0	...	[2]	...
Martinique	...	...	*74.2*	...	...	*25.8*	4,840[7]	32.1[11]	10.6[2]	8.0	5.2	[2]	[3]
Mauritania	...	...	...	...	...	...	410	61.0[15]	24.0[15]	5.2[15]	...	...	...
Mauritius	4.0	46.7	51.7	29.0	11.2	8.1	1,640	50.4[11]	4.0	10.4	3.0	6.4	2.9
Mayotte	...	...	...	...	...	...	...	79.6	—	...	...	7.1	...
Mexico	4.1[13]	39.5[13]	52.4	23.6	5.6	18.4	2,380	35.6[11]	11.2[2]	7.5	4.0	[2]	[3]
Micronesia	...	...	67.2	18.0	...	14.8	...	73.5	...	...	...	...	...
Moldova	...	...	69.1	6.7	12.6	11.6	2,640[1]	...	...	...	...	...	...
Monaco	...	...	...	...	...	...	...	...	...	...	...	...	...
Mongolia	...	...	81.9		—18.1—		780[1]	39.1	5.9[2]	23.4	0.5	[2]	2.9
Morocco	6.6[9]	30.5[9]	...	...	...	...	760	38.0	7.0	11.0	5.0	2.0	8.0
Mozambique	...	...	...	...	...	...	70	...	...	...	...	...	...
Myanmar (Burma)	*8.0*	...	...	...	...	...	500[1]	*49.1*[15]	*10.4*[15]	*15.3*[15]	*2.4*[15]	*4.0*[15]	*5.9*[15]
Namibia	...	...	73.3	0.4	3.4	22.9	900	...	...	...	...	...	...
Nauru	...	...	...	...	...	...	...	...	...	...	...	...	...
Nepal	9.1[9]	25.0[9]	25.1	63.4	—11.5—		120	61.2	17.3	11.7	3.7	...	[3]
Netherlands, The	6.9	23.0	49.5	...	29.0	21.5	11,620	16.6	14.6	6.9	12.5	4.1	0.3

				food consumption									country
				daily available calories per capita (1988–90)	percent of total calories (latest) derived from:								
transportation, communications	household durable goods[f]	recreation[g]	personal effects, other[h]		cereals	potatoes, cassava	meat, poultry	fish	eggs, milk	fruits, vegetables	fats, oils[i]	other[j]	
...	...	...	...	...	...	...	...	...	...	...	...	...	Equatorial Guinea
...	...	...	...	...	...	...	...	...	...	...	...	...	Eritrea[20]
...	...	...	55.0	...	...	...	...	...	...	...	...	...	Estonia
8.0	2.0	...	14.0	1,699	71.5	4.1	3.1	—	2.4	0.8	3.6	14.5	Ethiopia[20]
...	6.6	...	14.6	...	*29.3*	*5.5*	*15.8*	*3.9*	*7.0*	*3.3*	*18.0*	*17.2*	Faeroe Islands
11.3	7.8	4.3[3]	21.0	2,768	38.7	6.1	3.9	3.1	4.6	1.5	14.1	27.9	Fiji
18.4	6.9	10.7[3]	15.4	3,066	23.4	4.9	16.7	1.9	15.4	4.9	12.8	20.0	Finland
16.5	7.9	7.0	15.2	3,593	23.9	3.7	16.0	1.2	12.5	4.9	18.9	18.9	France
17.5	7.9	6.2[3]	11.2	2,805	29.1	4.3	17.0	3.0	7.7	8.7	8.0	22.1	French Guiana
12.2	12.3	6.9[3]	21.1	2,765	36.5	5.2	12.4	2.4	5.1	4.3	11.5	22.7	French Polynesia
6.3[15, 22]	...	...	6.6[15, 22]	2,442	24.4	25.5	6.3	2.1	1.4	14.7	7.9	17.7	Gabon
...	...	...	14.0[23]	2,290	67.2	1.0	2.4	1.3	1.7	1.1	9.7	15.5	Gambia, The
...	...	...	...	...	*50.4*	*1.6*	*4.2*	*0.2*	*4.9*	*9.0*	*13.8*	*15.9*	Gaza Strip
...	5.9	...	40.7	...	...	...	...	...	...	...	...	...	Georgia
17.1[24]	9.2[24]	10.3[3, 24]	11.2[24]	3,522	22.3	4.8	13.9	0.8	10.1	6.0	18.8	23.3	Germany
3.3	*3.8*	*3.9*[3]	*4.5*	2,141	29.0	39.3	1.9	2.5	0.3	8.5	8.6	9.9	Ghana
13.3	10.0	...	14.0	...	...	...	...	...	...	...	...	...	Gibraltar
14.3	8.2	5.0	13.5	3,775	27.7	3.9	12.2	0.8	10.1	9.5	18.4	17.3	Greece
7.7	9.3	12.4	17.5	...	...	...	...	...	...	...	...	...	Greenland
9.1	13.7	4.6[3]	10.9[26]	2,400	26.5	2.4	7.6	2.4	12.3	8.3	10.0	30.6	Grenada
20.5	9.3	4.7[3]	8.7	2,777	34.4	3.3	11.2	3.2	7.5	8.0	11.2	21.3	Guadeloupe
18.0	...	*5.1*	*8.8*	...	...	...	...	...	...	...	...	...	Guam
7.0	5.0	0.9	2.7	2,254	60.5	0.4	1.4	—	2.9	2.1	7.2	25.4	Guatemala
15.7	8.3	...	24.7	...	...	...	...	...	...	...	...	...	Guernsey
5.1	*2.9*	*4.1*	*0.1*	2,243	48.2	13.2	1.5	0.7	1.2	14.4	12.0	8.7	Guinea
...	...	...	...	2,235	63.6	6.1	4.6	0.3	. 1.5	4.2	13,0	6.7	Guinea-Bissau
4.8	*2.9*	*6.4*[3]	*8.2*	2,495	48.4	2.1	4.5	3.0	5.6	5.0	6.9	24.6	Guyana
...	*4.0*	...	*6.6*	2,005	37.4	12.4	3.5	0.3	1.7	9.8	6.1	28.7	Haiti
3.0	8.3	2.4[3]	3.2	2,211	50.9	0.5	2.3	0.3	5.1	6.8	13.3	20.9	Honduras
8.7	11.8	7.8	10.4	2,860	35.4	1.0	16.2	3.0	4.8	4.5	16.2	18.8	Hong Kong
12.9	8.6	5.6	12.1	3,608	29.1	2.8	12.6	0.3	8.8	4.5	20.8	21.1	Hungary
18.6	11.3	8.2	14.9	3,473	27.5	2.7	12.5	5.0	15.8	3.3	10.3	22.9	Iceland
9.6	5.2	1.7	6.5	2,229	63.1	1.8	0.7	0.3	4.8	3.2	7.2	18.9	India
...	2.9[17]	...	24.0	2,605	66.5	6.2	1.3	1.2	0.6	2.3	7.7	14.3	Indonesia
4.6	5.6	1.4[3]	2.7	3,022	62.8	2.1	3.3	0.3	3.2	7.1	10.8	10.3	Iran
6.5	6.7	0.8[3]	3.7	3,092	61.5	0.5	3.5	0.1	3.0	6.4	12.7	12.4	Iraq
13.4	8.0	11.1[3]	17.3[26]	3,951	24.3	6.0	14.8	0.8	14.5	3.6	17.4	18.7	Ireland
14.9	5.7	...	22.5	...	...	...	...	...	...	...	...	...	Isle of Man
4.3	6.7	...	32.6	3,220	31.3	1.9	8.1	1.1	9.6	9.0	19.1	19.9	Israel
12.2	9.5	9.3[3]	18.4	3,498	32.1	2.1	11.0	1.1	8.6	7.4	21.7	15.9	Italy
12.4	5.5	2.1	26.1	2,558	32.6	7.3	6.5	1.4	6.1	7.0	11.5	27.7	Jamaica
9.3	4.1	9.6	26.9	2,921	39.7	2.6	5.6	6.9	6.2	4.4	11.2	23.3	Japan
13.9	*7.1*	...	*21.0*	...	...	...	...	...	...	...	...	...	Jersey
5.8	4.8	2.9	29.6	2,710	51.8	1.0	6.2	0.2	4.6	4.6	11.0	20.9	Jordan
...	...	...	67.8	...	...	...	...	...	...	...	...	...	Kazakhstan
8.4	9.4	3.1	9.1	2,064	52.0	7.4	4.1	0.5	8.4	3.2	6.4	17.9	Kenya
8.0	2.9	...	12.5	2,516	39.0	10.9	3.7	5.7	1.2	5.8	8.2	25.5	Kiribati
...	3.8[28]	...	15.9	2,843	62.1	5.7	3.4	2.6	1.1	5.8	3.3	16.0	Korea, North
10.4	6.1	11.7[3]	12.9	2,826	52.5	0.7	5.2	3.5	2.2	6.9	9.1	19.8	Korea, South
13.7	11.2	5.2[3]	7.9	3,057	36.0	1.2	10.7	0.7	9.5	8.1	15.8	17.9	Kuwait
...	...	...	64.3	...	...	...	...	...	...	...	...	...	Kyrgyzstan
...	...	...	...	2,465	74.7	4.6	7.0	0.4	1.7	2.5	1.9	7.2	Laos
...	...	...	54.8	2,490	...	...	...	...	...	...	...	...	Latvia
5.4[15]	*2.6*[15]	*1.9*[15]	*6.3*[15]	3,142	37.6	3.1	6.0	—	5.9	11.4	15.7	20.3	Lebanon
4.7	11.9	...	8.8	2,121	75.3	0.6	4.2	0.2	1.5	1.7	3.9	12.5	Lesotho
...	*6.1*[15]	...	*25.8*[15]	2,264	46.7	22.6	2.0	1.1	0.5	4.9	14.4	7.7	Liberia
9.4	*4.6*	*8.5*[3]	*2.5*	3,293	45.4	1.7	5.6	0.2	6.7	7.5	16.5	16.3	Libya
13.3	5.8	16.3[3]	6.6	...	...	...	...	...	...	...	...	...	Liechtenstein
...	...	...	49.7	2,110	...	...	...	...	...	...	..	...	Lithuania
18.1	10.0	4.0[3]	19.7	3,925	19.0	4.7	18.6	1.0	9.1	5.6	21.3	20.7	Luxembourg
4.9	2.9	...	13.1	2,295	42.7	2.0	16.0	1.4	4.6	5.3	12.8	15.3	Macau
6.5	4.2	3.3[3]	1.8	...	...	...	...	...	...	...	...	...	Macedonia
4.0	1.0	...	12.0	2,156	55.8	19.2	6.2	0.7	3.3	4.2	3.5	7.1	Madagascar
10.0	3.0	...	25.0	2,048	68.8	4.0	1.5	0.9	0.7	4.6	1.7	17.9	Malaŵi
20.9	7.7	11.0	14.1	2,671	40.3	3.4	7.3	1.7	4.9	3.4	19.2	19.7	Malaysia
...	...	...	...	2,400	52.6	3.9	0.6	12.6	—	4.2	4.8	21.4	Maldives
10.0	1.0	...	12.0	2,259	72.7	1.9	3.3	0.6	4.2	0.8	7.8	8.6	Mali
16.5	9.1	6.9	21.4	3,169	30.1	1.5	10.7	1.0	11.3	6.6	15.9	22.9	Malta
...	5	...	14.7	...	...	...	...	...	...	...	...	...	Marshall Islands
20.7	9.4	5.4[3]	8.6	2,768	31.2	3.7	11.3	2.7	7.7	10.9	11.2	21.2	Martinique
...	...	...	9.8[15]	2,447	54.8	0.4	4.0	0.6	12.5	1.6	8.3	17.9	Mauritania
10.0	6.4	—	6.5	2,897	50.0	1.2	3.7	1.4	6.4	1.5	12.2	23.5	Mauritius
5.4	...	...	7.9	...	...	...	...	...	...	...	...	...	Mayotte
10.9	11.5	5.0[3]	14.3	3,061	46.7	0.7	8.5	0.6	5.8	3.3	12.5	21.8	Mexico
...	...	...	26.5	...	...	...	...	...	...	...	...	...	Micronesia
...	...	...	...	...	...	...	...	...	...	...	...	...	Moldova
...	...	...	...	3,593	23.9	3.7	16.0	1.2	12.5	4.9	18.9	18.9	Monaco
3.5	8.0	0.4	16.2	2,361	46.5	2.0	24.1	0.1	6.4	0.8	6.2	13.8	Mongolia
8.0	5.0	...	16.0	3,031	54.5	1.7	2.1	0.6	1.8	4.4	10.9	24.0	Morocco
...	...	...	...	1,804	32.0	43.3	1.5	0.3	0.7	1.8	12.7	7.7	Mozambique
3.8[15]	*0.5*[15]	*1.1*[15]	*7.5*[15]	2,453	79.5	0.4	1.8	1.0	1.0	2.5	6.3	7.5	Myanmar (Burma)
...	...	...	...	1,968	55.0	15.5	8.1	0.7	3.0	1.7	7.1	8.9	Namibia
...	...	...	...	...	...	...	...	...	...	...	...	...	Nauru
1.2	...	2.9[3]	2.0	2,206	80.9	3.0	1.2	—	4.1	0.9	4.4	5.4	Nepal
11.0	8.5	9.6	16.0	3,078	17.8	5.3	12.2	0.6	13.1	6.1	20.2	24.6	Netherlands, The

Household budgets and consumption (continued)

country	income (latest)						consumption expenditure						
	percent received by		by source (percent)				per capita private final, U.S.$ 1991	by kind or end use (percent of household or personal budget; latest)					
	lowest 20% of households	highest 10% of households	wages, salaries	self-employment	transfer payments[a]	other[b]		food[c]	housing[d]	clothing[e]	health care	energy, water	education
Netherlands Antilles	...	...	...	...	...	...	4,110[12]	21.2[11, 32]	16.8[2, 32]	8.4[32]	2.3[32]	[2]	[3]
New Caledonia	...	...	56.0	21.3	22.7	...	5,410[33]	37.0	15.7	7.0	2.5	0.7	[3]
New Zealand	5.1[19]	28.7[19]	52.1	5.6	21.0	21.3	8,050	16.1	20.0	5.2	6.4	2.4	[3]
Nicaragua	*3.1*[34]	...	...	...	...	...	360	...	...	...	...	...	...
Niger	...	...	...	...	...	...	250	50.5	19.1[5]	7.3	...	...	...
Nigeria	...	...	*36.2*	*49.4*	*4.3*	*10.1*	120	48.0	3.0	5.0	3.0	1.0	4.0
Northern Mariana Islands	...	...	...	...	...	...	...	36.9	7.4	...	3.1	6.3	3.7
Norway	2.6	26.6	59.4	10.0	23.3	7.3	12,660	23.5	13.4	7.7	4.8	6.0	0.5
Oman	...	...	...	...	...	...	2,510	...	...	...	...	...	...
Pakistan	8.4[9]	25.2[9]	22.0	56.0	...	22.0	270	37.0	11.0	6.0	1.0	5.0	1.0
Panama	2.0[13]	42.1[13]	*85.3*	[8]	*9.2*	*5.5*[8]	1,400	34.9	12.6[2]	5.1	3.5	[2]	[3]
Papua New Guinea	...	...	*57.3*	[8]	*1.1*	*41.6*[8]	600	40.9	12.5[5]	6.2	...	4.9	...
Paraguay	...	...	33.9	[8]	2.5	63.6[8]	1,040	48.7	16.4	9.7	3.4	—	1.5
Peru	4.9[9]	35.4[9]	35.7	55.0	5.0	4.3	1,760	31.5[11]	0.8[2]	10.7	4.5	[2]	[3]
Philippines	6.5[9]	32.1[9]	46.1	46.1	3.2	4.6	530	56.4	3.9[2]	3.6	...	[2]	...
Poland	9.2[13]	21.6[13]	34.0	4.3	20.7	41.0	1,190	41.2	2.8	10.9	8.1	1.0	[3]
Portugal	*5.2*	*33.4*	42.6	25.0	21.3	11.1	4,520	34.8	2.0	10.3	4.5	3.0	1.4
Puerto Rico	*3.2*	*34.7*	53.7	7.3	29.3	9.7	5,850	23.0	15.9[2]	8.8	8.2	[2]	3.2
Qatar	...	...	80.8	5.6	...	13.6	3,600[4]	24.5	35.1[5]	9.1	1.0	1.9	4.3
Réunion	*3.1*[19]	*51.4*[19]	—67.5—		29.7	2.8	4,820[33]	29.2[11]	13.0[2]	8.8	4.3	[2]	[3]
Romania	...	...	62.6	—37.4—			690	51.1	16.4[2, 5]	15.7	1.2	[2]	[3]
Russia	...	...	77.7	3.8	13.2	5.3	4,860[1]	34.8	2.7	22.3	...	...	...
Rwanda	9.7[9]	24.6[9]	*16.5*	[8]	*9.5*	*74.0*[8]	180	29.0	9.0	11.0	3.0	6.0	6.0
St. Kitts and Nevis	...	...	...	...	...	...	2,580[1]	*55.6*[11]	*7.6*	*7.5*	...	*6.6*	...
St. Lucia	...	...	...	...	...	...	...	49.6[11]	13.5	6.5	2.3	4.5	[3]
St. Vincent and the Grenadines	...	...	...	...	...	...	1,240[1]	59.8	6.3	7.7	...	6.2	...
San Marino	...	...	...	...	...	...	...	30.4[11]	9.7[2]	8.8	5.1	[2]	[3]
São Tomé and Príncipe	...	...	...	...	...	...	400[1]	...	...	...	...	...	...
Saudi Arabia	...	...	...	...	...	...	2,790	52.2[17, 36]	17.2[17, 36]	6.6[17, 36]	2.1[17, 36]	1.8[17, 36]	1.1[17, 36]
Senegal	*5.5*	*45.4*	51.6[15]	—48.4[15]—			600	49.0	7.0	11.0	2.0	4.0	6.0
Seychelles	4.1	35.6	*77.2*	*3.8*	*3.2*	*15.8*	3,110[1]	53.9	13.6	4.2	0.4	9.1	...
Sierra Leone	*5.6*	*37.8*	27.9	61.6	...	10.5	100	67.7[11]	14.1[2]	2.8	1.1	[2]	[3]
Singapore	5.1	33.5	*75.4*	*18.7*	*2.0*	*3.9*	6,280	17.1	9.2[2]	7.4	4.4	[2]	1.0
Slovakia	...	...	73.2	[8]	11.5	15.3[8]	...	31.9	...	11.8	...	6.6	...
Slovenia	...	...	59.4	14.5	17.5	8.6	5,100[1]	31.3	3.5	8.9	4.2	6.6	[3]
Solomon Islands	...	...	74.1	—25.9—			820[4]	61.0[11, 15]	12.5[2, 5, 15]	4.9[15]	...	[2]	...
Somalia	...	...	...	...	...	...	17[1]	62.3[11, 15]	15.3[15]	5.6[15]	...	4.3[15]	...
South Africa	*1.9*	*39.4*	76.7	[8]	4.4	18.9[8]	1,800	34.3	10.2[2]	7.5	4.8	[2]	0.4
Bophuthatswana	...	...	...	...	...	...	...	...	...	...	...	...	...
Ciskei	...	...	...	...	...	...	...	38.6[11]	10.8	12.2	2.8	...	1.8
Transkei	3.4	43.8	...	...	...	...	...	...	...	...	...	...	...
Venda	...	...	56.2	4.8	32.9	6.1	...	51.2	4.3	11.2	0.5	4.5	1.9
Spain	6.9[10]	24.5[10]	48.1	24.4	19.6	7.9	8,440	21.8[11]	12.6[2]	8.9	3.8	[2]	[3]
Sri Lanka	4.9[13]	43.0[13]	50.3	[8]	8.2	41.5[8]	410	53.0	1.8	6.4	1.6	2.8	1.2
Sudan, The	*4.0*	*34.6*	...	...	...	...	760[1]	63.6	11.5	5.3	4.1	3.8	[3]
Suriname	*9.3*	...	*74.6*	...	*3.2*	*22.2*	2,260[1]	*39.9*[15]	*4.4*[15]	*11.0*[15]	*3.6*[15]	*6.9*[15]	*2.6*[15]
Swaziland	*2.8*	*54.5*	44.4	22.2	12.2	21.2	650[1]	33.5[11]	13.4[2]	6.0	1.8	[2]	[3]
Sweden	5.3	18.6	63.0	7.2	23.5	6.3	14,920	20.0	21.2	7.2	2.6	4.5	0.1
Switzerland	6.0[37]	27.0[37]	64.9	[8]	14.5	20.6[8]	19,550	27.2[11]	15.3	4.8	12.6	4.8	[3]
Syria	*6.0*	...	...	...	...	...	1,630	*48.8*[11]	*17.7*	*9.1*	...	*4.6*	[3]
Taiwan	7.5	38.6[27]	68.3	[8]	3.6	28.1[8]	4,670	27.2	16.4[38]	4.6	5.3	2.9[38]	[3]
Tajikistan	...	...	—75.6—		—24.4—		1,440[1]	...	...	...	...	...	...
Tanzania	2.4[9]	46.5[9]	*33.8*	*59.8*	...	*6.4*	100	53.8[11]	8.6	10.8	4.5	6.6	0.8
Thailand	6.1[9]	35.3[9]	38.8	48.3	0.5	12.4	970	31.8	6.6	13.9	7.0	1.7	0.4
Togo	*8.0*	*30.5*	...	...	...	...	340	*60.9*	*9.9*[2]	*7.7*	*1.6*	[2]	*0.6*
Tonga	...	...	...	...	...	...	...	56.3[11]	10.5	5.6	0.3	2.7	...
Trinidad and Tobago	*2.6*	*33.6*	...	...	...	...	2,690	27.7	22.7	15.5	2.2	1.1	1.5
Tunisia	5.9[9]	30.7[9]	...	...	...	...	1,020	39.0	10.7	6.0	3.0	5.1	1.8
Turkey	*3.5*[10]	*41.5*[10]	24.1	51.4	10.8	13.7	1,100	40.0	6.0	15.0	4.0	7.0	1.0
Turkmenistan	...	...	61.9	—38.1—			2,410[1]	...	...	...	...	...	...
Tuvalu	...	...	*17.9*	*76.1*	...	*6.0*	...	56.0[11]	11.5[5]	7.5	...	...	...
Uganda	8.5[9]	27.2[9]	...	...	...	...	140	57.1[11, 15]	...	5.5[15]	...	7.3[15]	...
Ukraine	...	...	61.2	—38.8—			2,760[1]	41.3	1.7	...	...	...	[3]
United Arab Emirates	...	...	...	...	...	...	8,610	...	...	...	...	...	...
United Kingdom	7.2[10]	19.1[10]	61.9	10.5	15.0	12.6	11,290	18.7	15.4	5.7	1.6	3.9	1.3
United States	3.8	46.9[27, 39]	63.8	8.2	11.9	16.2	15,390	15.0	14.3	5.4	15.5	2.9	[14]
Uruguay	6.0[10, 17]	29.3[10, 17]	53.5	20.8	—30.1—		2,130	39.9	17.6[2]	7.0	9.3	[2]	1.3
Uzbekistan	...	...	48.2	—51.8—			2,150[1]	...	...	...	...	...	...
Vanuatu	...	...	56.7	[8]	7.7	35.6[8]	660[1]	49.9[11]	4.8	7.1	2.7	4.5	0.5
Venezuela	4.8[13]	33.2[13]	...	...	...	...	1,710	42.5[11]	9.4[2]	8.3	[40]	[2]	[3]
Vietnam	...	...	...	...	...	...	...	62.4	2.5	5.0	...	...	2.9
Virgin Islands (U.S.)	...	...	65.7	2.6	13.0	12.7	...	25.3[41]	*24.9*[41]	*5.4*[41]	...	*6.5*[41]	...
West Bank	...	...	...	...	...	...	1,380[7]	...	...	...	...	...	...
Western Sahara	...	...	...	...	...	...	...	...	...	...	...	...	...
Western Samoa	...	...	*49.4*	*22.8*	...	*27.8*	710[1]	58.8	5.1[5]	4.2	...	5.0	...
Yemen	...	...	...	...	...	...	450	...	...	...	...	...	...
Yugoslavia	5.3[13, 42]	27.4[13, 42]	51.5	14.8	17.9	15.8	2,480	43.2[11]	6.7	8.0	3.4	8.1	[3]
Zaire	...	...	...	...	...	...	190	61.7	11.5[2]	9.7	2.6	[2]	[3]
Zambia	*3.4*	*46.4*	79.9	17.8	1.3	1.0	370	36.0	7.0	10.0	8.0	4.0	14.0
Zimbabwe	*3.0*	*55.5*	...	...	...	...	350	30.1[11]	6.5	10.3	7.1	8.9	6.0

[1]1990. [2]Housing includes energy, water. [3]Recreation includes education. [4]1988. [5]Housing includes household durable goods. [6]1989. [7]1986. [8]Other includes self-employment. [9]Data refer to expenditure shares by fractiles of persons. [10]Based on posttax income. [11]Includes tobacco. [12]1985. [13]Data refer to income shares by fractiles of persons. [14]Personal effects, other includes education and recreation. [15]Capital city only. [16]Includes wage taxes. [17]Urban areas only. [18]Data refer to former Czechoslovakia. [19]Based on posttax per capita income. [20]Ethiopia includes Eritrea. [21]1984. [22]Wage earners only. [23]Low-income population in Banjul and Kombo St. Mary only. [24]Former West Germany only. [25]Urban areas of Eastern Region only. [26]Personal effects,

transportation, communications	household durable goods[f]	recreation[g]	personal effects, other[h]	food consumption: daily available calories per capita (1988–90)	percent of total calories (latest) derived from: cereals	potatoes, cassava	meat, poultry	fish	eggs, milk	fruits, vegetables	fats, oils[i]	other[j]	country
23.6[32]	10.2[32]	6.6[3, 32]	10.9[32]	2,681	33.5	3.3	16.0	1.9	9.3	6.6	11.4	18.1	Netherlands Antilles
10.4	11.4	5.4[3]	9.9	2,909	40.2	6.4	10.0	1.2	5.7	4.5	13.1	18.9	New Caledonia
15.7	6.9	7.8[3]	19.4	3,460	22.3	2.8	16.8	1.6	10.8	6.3	16.4	23.0	New Zealand
...	...	...	...	2,234	51.1	1.6	2.1	—	4.7	2.9	8.3	29.3	Nicaragua
...	[5]	...	23.1	2,240	73.9	3.6	2.1	—	2.1	1.1	3.0	14.2	Niger
3.0	6.0	...	27.0	2,199	36.8	34.2	1.3	0.4	0.5	3.3	11.8	11.6	Nigeria
18.2	7.5	4.0	12.9	...	...	...	...	...	...	...	...	...	Northern Mariana Islands
13.3	7.2	8.5	15.0	3,221	27.0	5.3	10.6	4.2	13.2	4.9	16.9	18.0	Norway
...	...	...	...	...	...	...	...	...	...	...	...	...	Oman
13.0	5.0	...	21.0	2,283	58.9	0.4	2.2	0.1	7.3	2.6	13.8	14.6	Pakistan
15.1	8.4	11.7[3]	8.7	2,269	37.7	3.1	7.5	1.3	7.0	6.6	13.8	23.0	Panama
13.0	[5]	...	22.5	2,589	23.0	26.5	5.9	1.9	0.8	24.8	4.8	12.1	Papua New Guinea
4.5	6.2	2.3	7.3	2,684	29.2	17.0	11.7	0.2	4.2	8.0	10.7	19.0	Paraguay
6.8	11.3	11.2[3]	23.2	2,035	42.9	9.3	5.2	1.7	5.2	4.9	7.2	23.7	Peru
4.5	13.0	...	18.6	2,343	56.3	4.5	5.3	3.2	1.9	7.3	5.8	15.7	Philippines
8.9	8.3	15.0[3]	3.8	3,426	33.3	5.8	12.1	0.9	10.8	3.3	15.4	18.4	Poland
15.4	8.6	4.4	15.6	3,342	30.8	5.5	11.9	2.6	6.6	5.8	17.1	19.6	Portugal
14.1	6.7	3.8	16.3	...	...	...	...	...	...	...	...	...	Puerto Rico
13.0	[5]	——11.1——		...	...	...	...	...	...	...	...	...	Qatar
21.2	8.4	6.3[3]	8.7	3,083	47.8	2.3	10.5	1.5	5.3	5.1	10.3	17.2	Réunion
6.6	[5]	4.5[3]	4.5	3,081	44.1	4.0	8.3	0.7	7.9	5.3	13.6	16.0	Romania
...	9.4	...	30.8	3,380[35]	36.8[35]	5.3[35]	10.6[35]	2.1[35]	8.8[35]	3.4[35]	13.2[35]	19.8[35]	Russia
9.0	9.0	...	18.0	1,915	18.0	31.0	1.0	—	1.4	16.0	2.5	30.1	Rwanda
4.3	*9.4*	...	*9.0*	2,435	18.7	3.8	11.3	3.4	7.9	4.2	18.6	32.1	St. Kitts and Nevis
6.3	5.8	3.2[3]	8.3	2,424	26.7	5.7	14.0	1.3	7.7	9.8	11.0	23.8	St. Lucia
3.7	6.6	...	9.7	2,460	34.6	10.6	8.8	0.4	5.2	4.1	7.4	28.9	St. Vincent and the Grenadines
14.5	7.5	8.1[3]	15.9	3,498	32.1	2.1	11.0	1.1	8.6	7.4	21.7	15.9	San Marino
...	...	...	...	2,153	31.3	13.9	1.3	2.5	1.2	2.9	16.4	30.5	São Tomé and Príncipe
4.5[17, 36]	5.9[17, 36]	...	8.6[17, 36]	2,932	49.5	0.8	6.9	0.5	6.7	10.5	11.4	13.6	Saudi Arabia
5.0	2.0	...	12.0	2,323	63.3	1.3	3.7	1.9	2.6	1.2	12.4	13.6	Senegal
6.4	6.6	1.4	4.4	2,356	48.9	1.1	5.3	2.4	5.9	3.5	11.6	21.3	Seychelles
8.2	2.2	1.4[3]	2.6	1,899	52.7	5.8	1.1	1.4	0.8	3.6	21.7	13.0	Sierra Leone
13.7	8.9	14.3	23.9	3,121	41.4	2.3	15.0	1.8	4.8	7.2	5.7	21.9	Singapore
...	4.4	...	45.3	...	...	...	...	...	...	...	...	...	Slovakia
12.8	5.4	5.9[3]	1.0	...	...	...	...	...	...	...	...	...	Slovenia
6.6[15]	[5]	...	15.0[15]	2,277	25.3	36.6	3.6	5.4	0.7	2.9	8.7	16.8	Solomon Islands
...	...	...	12.1[15]	1,873	52.8	0.9	6.6	0.3	21.2	2.2	8.6	7.4	Somalia
15.1	10.7	6.2	10.9	3,134	53.9	1.7	7.6	0.7	4.0	2.4	9.5	20.3	South Africa
...	...	...	...	...	...	...	...	...	...	...	...	...	Bophuthatswana
8.5	7.7	1.2	16.3	...	...	...	...	...	...	...	...	...	Ciskei
...	...	...	...	...	...	...	...	...	...	...	...	...	Transkei
5.4	11.9	0.9	8.2	...	...	...	...	...	...	...	...	...	Venda
15.4	6.6	6.5[3]	24.4	3,472	21.3	5.2	20.0	1.6	8.6	7.3	17.5	18.5	Spain
15.4	5.1	2.4	10.3	2,246	57.5	3.1	0.4	1.4	2.8	4.7	3.8	26.1	Sri Lanka
1.5	5.5	0.7[3]	4.0	2,042	56.0	0.8	4.2	0.1	11.3	3.0	10.6	14.0	Sudan, The
9.5[15]	*12.3*[15]	*5.8*[15]	*4.0*[15]	2,436	52.1	2.0	6.5	0.5	6.2	4.1	9.9	18.8	Suriname
8.8	12.8	3.3[3]	20.4	2,634	53.9	1.1	4.7	—	3.7	3.6	7.5	25.5	Swaziland
18.1	6.4	9.5	10.4	2,976	21.1	4.4	10.1	2.3	15.3	5.5	20.1	21.3	Sweden
11.8	4.3	10.4[3]	8.8	3,508	20.3	2.4	17.6	0.7	12.9	5.8	18.3	22.0	Switzerland
3.8	*5.1*	*3.1*[3]	*7.8*	3,121	53.1	1.4	3.0	—	6.3	7.2	13.1	15.8	Syria
13.2	5.1	17.2[3]	8.1	2,872	36.8	2.5	14.3	1.9	3.1	8.3	14.4	18.7	Taiwan
...	...	...	...	...	...	...	...	...	...	...	...	...	Tajikistan
6.4	6.3	1.6	0.6	2,195	48.5	22.6	2.3	1.2	1.7	6.0	5.0	12.6	Tanzania
11.3	8.0	3.5	15.8	2,280	58.7	1.1	5.0	1.6	1.4	5.6	5.3	21.4	Thailand
8.2	*3.9*	*0.4*	*6.8*	2,269	47.7	29.0	2.3	1.2	0.6	1.8	9.3	8.0	Togo
5.8	10.6	0.5	7.7	2,967	15.7	35.1	12.2	2.0	2.1	4.5	8.0	20.5	Tonga
13.2	8.8	1.4	5.9	2,769	42.1	2.5	5.0	0.5	6.5	3.4	13.1	26.9	Trinidad and Tobago
9.0	11.2	7.1	7.1	3,123	53.0	1.3	2.7	0.6	4.7	5.5	17.6	14.5	Tunisia
5.0	...	...	22.0	3,197	48.4	3.7	2.5	0.4	2.9	8.5	15.8	18.0	Turkey
...	...	...	...	...	...	...	...	...	...	...	...	...	Turkmenistan
10.5	[5]	...	14.5	...	...	...	...	...	...	...	...	...	Tuvalu
5.9[15]	...	...	24.2[15]	2,179	23.5	30.8	2.4	1.1	1.7	17.3	1.8	21.3	Uganda
...	6.8	6.3[3]	43.9	...	...	...	...	...	...	...	...	...	Ukraine
...	...	...	...	3,286	34.6	1.3	11.5	1.4	9.3	14.6	10.8	16.4	United Arab Emirates
17.3	6.5	8.8	20.8	3,270	22.1	6.1	14.7	0.9	11.8	4.5	17.8	22.1	United Kingdom
11.4	7.9	[14]	27.6[14]	3,642	21.7	2.7	14.7	0.8	11.4	5.6	18.1	25.0	United States
10.4	6.3	3.1	5.1	2,668	36.8	3.9	18.3	0.2	13.0	3.7	9.6	14.4	Uruguay
...	...	...	...	...	...	...	...	...	...	...	...	...	Uzbekistan
17.2	2.9	0.9	9.5	2,736	21.7	24.5	12.2	2.2	1.8	3.3	10.4	23.9	Vanuatu
5.1	2.8	4.9[3, 40]	27.0	2,440	36.4	2.0	5.9	1.2	7.4	7.3	16.1	23.6	Venezuela
...	4.6	...	22.6	2,216	72.7	7.5	6.0	0.9	0.5	4.3	1.8	6.2	Vietnam
11.7[41]	*4.3*[41]	...	*21.9*[41]	...	...	...	...	...	...	...	...	...	Virgin Islands (U.S.)
...	...	...	...	...	*44.4*	*1.9*	*6.1*	*0.1*	*6.2*	*11.0*	*12.5*	*17.8*	West Bank
...	...	...	...	...	...	...	...	...	...	...	...	...	Western Sahara
9.0	[5]	...	17.9	*2,469*	*20.1*	*19.1*	*12.0*	*3.6*	*1.2*	*13.2*	*8.4*	*22.4*	Western Samoa
...	...	...	...	2,231	66.9	1.0	3.5	0.4	3.7	3.5	6.5	14.4	Yemen
7.2	4.4	4.1[3]	14.9	3,545[42]	43.2[42]	2.3[42]	8.2[42]	0.2[42]	7.9[42]	3.7[42]	16.9[42]	17.7[42]	Yugoslavia
5.9	4.8	3.8[3]	—	2,129	16.4	55.8	1.8	0.7	0.1	7.7	7.0	10.4	Zaire
5.0	1.0	...	15.0	2,016	75.0	4.8	2.4	0.7	1.3	1.6	3.2	11.0	Zambia
1.1	12.9	0.6	16.5	2,256	59.4	1.4	2.5	0.2	1.5	1.1	9.6	24.3	Zimbabwe

other includes health care. [27]Highest 20 percent. [28]Workers and clerical workers only. [29]Excludes single-person households and self-employed. [30]Earned income only. [31]Malagasy households only. [32]Curaçao and Bonaire only. [33]1987. [34]Rural areas only. [35]Data refer to former U.S.S.R. [36]Middle-income population only. [37]Excludes transfer payments and property income. [38]Housing includes water. [39]Income of highest five percent of households is 18.6 percent. [40]Recreation includes health care. [41]St. Thomas only. [42]Data refer to former Socialist Federal Republic of Yugoslavia.

Health services

The provision of health services in most countries is both a principal determinant of the quality of life and a large and growing sector of the national economy. This table summarizes the basic indicators of health personnel; hospitals, by kind and utilization; mortality rates that are most indicative of general health services; external controls on health (adequacy of food supply and availability of safe drinking water); and sources and amounts of expenditure on health care. Each datum refers more or less directly to the availability or use of a particular health service in a country, and, while each may be an accurate measure at a national level, each may also conceal considerable differences in availability of the particular service to different segments of a population or regions of a country. In the United States, for example, the availability of physicians ranges from about one per 800 persons in the least well-served states to one per 297 in the best-served, with a rate of one per 163 in the national capital. Such disparities are even more pronounced in most other countries, unless the government has made some special effort to achieve a more even distribution of personnel and facilities. In addition, even when trained personnel exist and facilities have been created, the country may lose health professionals via the "brain drain" to foreign countries; or low levels of financial support at the national level may leave facilities underserved; or lack of good transportation may prevent those most in need from reaching a clinic or hospital that could help them.

Definitions and limits of data have been made as specific as possible in the compilation of this table. For example, despite wide variation worldwide in the nature of the qualifying or certifying process that permits an individual to represent himself as a physician, organizations such as the World Health Organization (WHO) try to maintain more consistent international standards for training and qualification. International statistics presented here for "physicians" refer to persons qualified according to WHO standards and exclude traditional health practitioners, whatever the local custom with regard to the designation "doctor." Statistics for health personnel in this table uniformly include all those actually working in the health service field, whether in the actual provision of services or in teaching, administration, research, or other tasks. One group of practitioners for whom this type of guideline works less well is that of midwives, whose training and qualifications vary enormously from country to country but who must be included, as they represent, after nurses, perhaps the largest and most important category of health auxiliary worldwide. The statistics here refer to those midwives working in some kind of institutional setting (a hospital, clinic, community health-care centre, or the like) and exclude rural noninstitutional midwives and traditional birth attendants.

Hospitals also differ considerably worldwide in terms of staffing and services. In this tabulation, the term hospital refers generally to a permanent facility offering inpatient services and/or nursing care and staffed by at least one physician. Establishments offering only outpatient or custodial care are excluded. These statistics are broken down into data for general hospitals (those providing care in more than one specialty), specialized facilities (with care in only one specialty), local medical centres, and rural health-care centres; the last two generally refer to institutions that provide a more limited range of medical or nursing care, often less than full-time. Hospital data are further analyzed into three categories of administrative classification: public, private nonprofit, and private for profit. Statistics on

Health services

country	health personnel							hospitals									
	year	physicians	dentists	nurses	pharmacists	midwives	population per physician	year	number	kinds (%): general	kinds (%): specialized	kinds (%): medical centres	kinds (%): rural	ownership (%): government	ownership (%): private nonprofit	ownership (%): private for profit	hospital beds per 10,000 pop.
Afghanistan	1987	2,957	329	2,135	...	...	4,797	1982	68	66.2	16.2	—	17.6	86.8	13.2	—	5
Albania	1990	5,566[4]	[4]	...	772[5]	9,936[5]	585[4]	1989	895	—17.9—		—82.1—		100.0	—	—	57
Algeria	1990	23,550	7,199	24,700[8]	2,134	3,800[8]	1,062	1988	264[9]	...	...	...	...	...	...	...	25
American Samoa	1989	34	7	140	2	1	1,384	1990	1	100.0	—	—	—	100.0	—	—	27
Andorra	1990	105	...	...	2[10]	...	502	1990	1	100.0	—	—	—	100.0	—	—	23
Angola	1990	662	...	9,145	...	1,237[12]	15,136	1990	58	...	...	...	...	...	...	...	12
Antigua and Barbuda	1988	48	7[5]	207[5]	27[12]	...	1,333	1986	2	50.0	50.0	—	—	100.0	—	—	48[14]
Argentina	1988	96,000	22,500	17,118	681[10]	...	328	1980	3,189	84.2	15.8	—	—	41.9	3.6	54.5	48[5]
Armenia	1991	14,700[4]	[4]	36,200[16]	...	[16]	234[4]	1991	183	...	...	...	...	100.0	...	...	89
Aruba	1991	74	19	515	11	3	910	1991	2	50.0	—	50.0	—	100.0	—	—	39
Australia	1986	36,610	6,310	182,236[16]	10,637	[16]	438	1990	1,071[15]	...	...	...	...	65.5[15]	—34.5[15]—		50
Austria	1992	24,049	3,354	31,920	2,004[18]	825	327	1992	323	39.3	60.7	—	—	...	...	...	95
Azerbaijan	1991	28,100[4]	[4]	69,900[16]	...	[16]	257[4]	1991	749	...	...	...	...	100.0	...	...	99
Bahamas, The	1990	361	31[10]	618[19]	...	...	684	1985	5	60.0	20.0	20.0	—	60.0	—40.0—		40[20]
Bahrain	1991	535	38	1,607	121	...	937	1991	12	58.3	42.7	—	—	75.0	16.7	8.3	23
Bangladesh	1991	21,004	535[5]	9,655	...	7,713	5,264	1991	890	68.9[12]	5.1[12]	23.1[12]	2.9[12]	68.5	—31.5—		3
Barbados	1986	243	25[10]	760[10]	...	436[10]	1,042	1982	11	27.3	18.2	—	54.5	81.8	—	18.2	83[5]
Belarus	1991	41,700[4]	[4]	112,600[16]	...	[16]	246[4]	1991	868	...	...	...	...	100.0	...	...	110
Belgium	1991	33,817	7,135	...	12,335	...	296	1982	531	53.3	46.7	—	—	36.3	—63.7—		97[11]
Belize	1991	96	12	282	15	114	2,021	1991	7	...	...	...	...	100.0	—	—	30
Benin	1986	363	...	1,317[26]	...	323[26]	11,306	1980	131	4.6	9.9	80.9	4.6	87.8	12.2	—	13[27]
Bermuda	1992	59	27	548	36	...	1,022	1989	2	50.0	50.0	—	—	...	...	...	68
Bhutan	1989	157	...	213[14]	18[14]	72[14]	8,969	1989	26	...	...	...	...	...	...	...	7
Bolivia	1987[19]	3,174	1,298	2,319	...	...	2,124	1987[30]	553	—14.8—		27.3	57.9	...	...	...	15
Bosnia and Herzegovina	1989	6,929	1,368	...	781	...	624	1989	...	...	...	...	...	...	...	...	46
Botswana	1990	240	21[14]	2,488	40[14]	...	5,417	1990	30	...	...	...	...	80.0	10.0	10.0	25
Brazil	1988	169,500	28,772[5]	...	6,094[5]	...	848	1985	28,972	15.0	4.6	—80.4—		58.9	—41.1—		37[14]
Brunei	1990	171	30	870	8	173	1,473	1990	8	87.5	—	—	12.5	87.5	—12.5—		35
Bulgaria	1992	27,112	5,699	50,198	2,604	7,007	312	1991	257	74.7	25.3	—	—	...	...	...	103[31]
Burkina Faso	1988	280	17	1,993	104	292	29,914	1988	66	3.0	—	83.4	13.6	100.0	—	—	7[10]
Burundi	1990	168[19]	10[5]	670[19]	29[5]	97[19]	31,777[19]	1988	264	—12.5—		—87.5—		87.5	—12.5—		19[20]
Cambodia	1988	425	...	7,271	130[10]	2,232	18,518	1988	188[30]	...	...	...	...	100.0	—	—	16
Cameroon	1986	833	...	...	...	...	12,540	1988	629	—27.0—		—73.0—		72.3	—27.7—		27[10]
Canada	1989	58,470	13,503[5]	241,955[5]	16,348[5]	...	449	1989	1,079	81.8	16.6	1.6	—	95.8	—	4.2	70
Cape Verde	1987	77	...	186[10]	...	10[10]	4,208	1980	21	9.5	4.8	61.9	23.8	100.0	—	—	19[5]
Central African Republic	1988	154	6	376	19	188	17,292	1988	133	—21.1—		—78.9—		79.7	—20.3—		15
Chad	1980	94	...	...	...	...	47,640	1978	4	100.0	—	—	—	—	—	100.0	8
Chile	1991	14,664	1,319[11, 19]	...	203[11, 19]	1,629[11, 19]	895	1990	220	51.4[27]	19.0[27]	—	29.6[27]	83.2	—16.8—		33
China	1992	1,808,000[35]	...	1,040,000	408,000[36]	59,000[36]	648[35]	1991	63,101	15.6	6.0	—78.4—		100.0	—	—	23
Colombia	1989	29,353	13,815	43,065	...	...	1,061	1983	946	—79.6—		—20.4—		82.1[34]	17.9[34]	—	15[11]
Comoros	1990	42	5	69[16]	3[10]	[16]	11,100	1980	17	17.7	—	23.5	58.8	100.0	—	—	23[27]
Congo	1989	567	...	...	...	...	3,873	1978	473	0.6	0.2	97.3	1.9	94.9	5.1	—	22[11]
Costa Rica	1991	3,123	1,167	4,755	1,260	...	981	1980	39	48.7	28.2	—23.1—		92.3	—	7.7	23[36]
Côte d'Ivoire	1982	502	...	...	...	...	17,847	1988	...	...	...	...	...	...	...	...	9
Croatia	1991	8,964	1,991	...	1,651	...	534	1991	...	...	...	...	...	...	...	...	65
Cuba	1989	34,752	6,482	58,589	650[12]	...	303	1986	261	28.0	—47.1—		24.9	100.0	—	—	71[11]
Cyprus[39]	1990	1,208	431	2,450[11, 16]	93[12]	[16]	476	1989	124[27]	3.2[27]	—89.5[27]—		7.3[27]	12.1[27]	0.8[27]	87.1[27]	60[20]
Czech Republic	1991	32,285	5,904	...	...	...	319	1991	278	60.8	39.2	—	—	100.0	—	—	102
Denmark	1990	14,277	4,562	34,756	1,498[14]	915[8]	360	1991	127[27]	87.4[27]	12.6[27]	—	—	91.3[27]	8.7[27]	—	54
Djibouti	1989	97	10	359[10]	14	175[10]	5,258	1989[30]	13	—69.2—		30.8	—	100.0	...	...	27
Dominica	1990	37	4[14]	273[14, 16]	12	[16]	1,947	1990	10	—30.0—		—70.0—		100.0	—	—	41
Dominican Republic	1990	7,332	689	5,398	129[12]	...	934	1987	103	—44.7—		—55.3—		...	...	...	20
Ecuador	1990	9,785	4,292[10]	14,794[10]	...	...	1,039	1984	337	16.6	7.1	49.6	26.7	...	...	...	17[20]
Egypt	1990	31,312	5,910	44,022	9,774	...	1,698	1982	1,521	32.3	13.2	15.9	38.6	83.1	3.8	13.1	20[11]
El Salvador	1991	4,080	800[14]	4,898[14]	597[10]	1,940	1,322	1989	42	45.2	14.3	40.5	—	69.0	—	31.0	10

number of beds refer to beds that are maintained and staffed on a full-time basis for a succession of inpatients to whom care is provided.

Data on hospital utilization refer to institutions defined as above. Admission and discharge, the two principal points at which statistics are normally collected, are the basis for the data on the amount and distribution of care by kind of facility. The data on numbers of patients exclude babies born during a maternal confinement but include persons who die before being discharged. The bed-occupancy and average length-of-stay statistics depend on the concept of a "patient-day," which is the annual total of daily censuses of inpatients. The bed-occupancy rate is the ratio of total patient-days to potential days based on the number of beds; the average length-of-stay rate is the ratio of total patient-days to total admissions. Bed-occupancy rates may exceed 100% because stays of partial days are counted as full days.

Two measures that give health planners and policy makers an excellent indication of the level of ordinary health care are those for mortality of children under age five and for maternal mortality. The former reflects the probability of a newborn infant dying before age five. The latter refers to deaths attributable to delivery or complications of pregnancy, childbirth, the puerperium (the period immediately following birth), or abortion.

Levels of nutrition and access to safe drinking water are two of the most basic limitations imposed by the physical environment in which health-care activities take place. The nutritional data are based on recommendations of the United Nations' Food and Agriculture Organization for the necessary daily intake (in calories) for a moderately active person of average size in a climate of a particular kind (fewer calories are needed in a hot climate) to remain in average *good* health. Excess intake in the many developed countries ranges to more than 40% above the minimum required to maintain health (the excess usually being construed to diminish, rather than raise, health). The range of deficiency is less dramatic numerically but far more critical to the countries in which deficiencies are chronic, because the deficiencies lead to overall poor health (raising health service needs and costs), to decreased productivity in nearly every area of national economic life, and to the loss of social and economic potential through early mortality. By "safe" water is meant only water that has no substantial quantities of chemical or biological pollutants—*i.e.,* quantities sufficient to cause "immediate" health problems.

Two principal kinds of public health-care finance data are given: health insurance and central government expenditure. The data on insurance refer to public programs only and identify the mandated basis or extent of responsibility for costs or funding required under the relevant law of the principal participants (individuals, employers, and government). Data on public health-care expenditure refer to a consolidated statement of expenditure, budgetary and otherwise, by all elements of the central government but exclude expenditure by other levels of government (state, city, etc.) and parastatal expenditures. In a number of countries significant government expenditures for health-care services are made at these other levels, amounting to 2, 10, and sometimes 20 times the level of central government expenditure. These expenditures may include costs for national health insurance, family-planning programs, and workers' compensation. Expenditures at the national level for social security are excluded.

admissions or discharges							mortality		population with access to safe water (latest) (%)	food supply (% of FAO requirement) 1988–90	financing of public health care, latest year					country
rate per 10,000 pop.	by kinds of hospital (%)				bed occupancy rate (%)	average length of stay (days)	under age 5 per 1,000 live newborn 1991	maternal mortality per 100,000 live births 1989–90			health-care insurance			public health expenditures (% of natl. budget)	public health expenditures per capita (U.S.$)	
	general	specialized	medical centres	rural							indiv. (% of earnings)	employer (% of payroll)	govt. (% of covered earnings)			
76[1]	52.8[1]	46.7[1]	—	0.5[1]	58.0[1]	8[1]	257	640[2]	21	72	—	—	—	...	2[3]	Afghanistan
...	...	...	...	...	...	...	31	...	97	107	—	8.0[6]	[7]	...	26[3]	Albania
568[10]	...	...	...	...	...	...	61	140[2]	68	123	1.5	12.5	—	...	170[3]	Algeria
965	100.0	—	—	—	38.4	4	11[11]	...	...	...	...	...	...	25.5	320	American Samoa
...	...	...	...	...	...	...	...	...	100	...	...	...	...	...	...	Andorra
238	...	...	...	...	44.5[13]	16[13]	292	...	35	80	...	...	...	...	11[3]	Angola
63[15]	...	...	...	...	49.9[15]	7[15]	23	...	100	95	2.5	2.5	—	...	67[3]	Antigua and Barbuda
...	...	...	...	...	...	...	24	48.6[5]	65	116	3.0	5.4	—	3.0	7	Argentina
...	...	...	...	...	...	...	...	34.6	...	...	...	...	...	18.3	150[3]	Armenia
...	...	...	...	...	...	...	...	...	...	...	...	...	...	...	...	Aruba
...	...	...	...	...	...	...	10	4.9[14]	99	124	[17]	—	[7]	12.7	580	Australia
2,559	...	...	...	...	78.2	11	9	6.6	100	133	3.2[17]	3.2[17]	...	12.9	1,070	Austria
...	...	...	...	...	...	...	...	28.6	...	...	...	...	...	9.2	98[3]	Azerbaijan
979[9]	77.0	—23.0—		—	...	...	34[20]	69.3[5]	100	115	1.7[6, 21]	7.1[6, 22]	—	14.6	310	Bahamas, The
1,274[14]	...	...	...	...	80.0[14]	7[14]	18	7.9[7]	100	...	—	—	—	9.2	240	Bahrain
853[5]	...	...	...	...	...	...	133	600[2]	81	88	—	[22, 23]	[24]	4.8	2	Bangladesh
842	93.9	4.6	—	1.5	89.8[9]	34[9]	12	26.7[14]	100	133	0.7	0.7	—	11.9	260	Barbados
...	...	...	...	...	...	...	16[20]	24.8	...	...	...	...	...	18.0	160[3]	Belarus
1,552	91.0	9.0	—	—	85.3	19	10	3.4[12]	100	149	3.7	6.0	...	1.7	130	Belgium
...	...	...	...	...	...	...	29	43.2[25]	75	114	[17]	[17]	[17]	10.6	85	Belize
...	...	...	...	...	...	...	149	160[2]	54	104	—	0.2[28]	—	5.6	3	Benin
1,327	96.6	3.4	—	—	83.0	16	9[20]	...	...	112	[17]	[17]	...	14.5	680	Bermuda
3,796[14, 29]	...	...	...	...	...	...	205	1,310[2]	32	128	...	...	...	4.8	3	Bhutan
...	...	...	...	...	...	...	126	600[2]	53	84	2.0	8.0	—	3.3	4	Bolivia
529[15]	...	...	...	...	82.4[15]	11[15]	...	56.0	...	...	...	...	...	...	...	Bosnia and Herzegovina
...	...	...	...	...	93.1[11]	...	85	200[2]	54	97	—	[17]	—	5.1	51	Botswana
...	...	...	...	...	...	...	67	65.3[12]	97	114	[17]	[17]	[17]	6.7	75	Brazil
1,069[27]	98.5[27]	—	—	1.5[27]	38.0[27]	4[27]	10	...	100	128	...	...	...	3.4	190	Brunei
2,118[27]	...	...	...	...	84.4[27]	16[27]	21	20.9	99	148	—	30.0[6]	[7]	4.8	61	Bulgaria
...	...	...	...	...	...	...	206	810[2]	69	94	—	11.5[32]	—	5.2	2	Burkina Faso
109[8]	...	...	...	...	...	...	181	...	38	84	—	—	—	...	7[3]	Burundi
...	...	...	...	...	...	...	188	500[2]	18	96	—	—	—	...	...	Cambodia
...	...	...	...	...	...	...	126	430[2]	42	95	—	4.2[32]	—	3.4	7	Cameroon
1,677[33]	93.9[33]	6.0[33]	0.1[33]	—	75.7[27]	13[27]	9	4.1	100	122	[17]	[17]	[17]	5.2	250	Canada
...	...	...	...	...	...	...	61	...	71	118	3.0	2.0	...	...	...	Cape Verde
326[10]	...	...	...	...	41.9[10]	7[10]	180	600[2]	26	82	—	3.0[28, 32]	—	5.1	18[3]	Central African Republic
...	...	...	...	...	...	...	213	960[2]	57	73	2.0[28, 32]	4.0[28, 32]	—	3.8	13[3]	Chad
797[5]	84.9[34]	9.3[34]	—	5.8[34]	73.8[5]	8[5]	21	48.3[5]	89	102	[17]	—	...	5.9	30	Chile
460	—60.8—		—39.2—		80.9	16	27	95[2]	74	112	—	[22]	...	...	11[3]	China
385[27]	...	...	...	...	59.3[27]	6[27]	21	77.0[12]	88	106	2.3	4.7	...	6.2	10	Colombia
...	...	...	...	...	...	...	133	50[37]	63	75	...	...	...	7.3	12	Comoros
...	...	...	...	...	...	...	110	900[2]	38	103	—	0.2	—	...	21[3]	Congo
1,192	77.8	16.7	—5.5—		75.7	8	18	18.4[14]	92	121	[17]	9.3	1.3	32.0	150	Costa Rica
...	...	...	...	...	...	...	127	...	76	111	—	0.5[38]	—	4.0	28[3]	Côte d'Ivoire
733[15]	...	...	...	...	83.4[15]	12[15]	...	3.6	...	...	...	...	...	...	...	Croatia
1,619	32.3	—64.2—		3.5	74.4[27]	11[27]	14	38.8[14]	82	135	—	10.0[6, 32]	[7]	...	52[3]	Cuba
729	96.1	1.2	—	2.7	71.6[15]	7[12, 15]	11	...	100	...	[17]	6.0[6]	3.5[6]	6.5	203	Cyprus[39]
1,759	96.1	3.9	—	—	72.2	15	13[40]	7.6[40]	100	145[40]	—	50.0[6, 40]	[7]	0.4[40]	7[40]	Czech Republic
2,109	98.3	1.7	—	—	82.5	8	9	1.6	100	135	—	—	[7]	1.1	110	Denmark
...	...	...	...	...	...	...	161	740[37]	45	...	...	...	...	8.2	21	Djibouti
1,016[41]	...	...	...	...	84.3[41]	8[41]	20	48.2[25]	77	120	3.0[6]	6.8[6]	—	12.9	90	Dominica
488	...	...	...	...	55.3	4	76	93.6[8]	63	102	2.5[6]	7.0[6]	2.5[6]	14.0	16	Dominican Republic
471	...	...	...	...	60.4	8	82	122.9[14]	58	105	[17]	[17]	...	11.0	17	Ecuador
...	...	...	...	...	...	...	85	65.2[5]	73	132	1.0	4.0	—	2.8	14	Egypt
384	59.7	20.4	19.9	—	64.6	6	67	58.8[8]	48	102	2.5	6.3	...	7.7	9	El Salvador

Health services (continued)

country	health personnel: year	physicians	dentists	nurses	pharma-cists	midwives	population per physician	hospitals: year	number	kinds (%): general	specialized	medical centres	rural	ownership (%): government	private non-profit	private for profit	hospital beds per 10,000 pop.
Equatorial Guinea	1987	90	...	...	...	...	3,622	1982	...	...	...	...	...	...	...	...	112
Eritrea[42]	...	...	...	...	...	...	...	...	...	...	...	...	...	...	...	...	...
Estonia	1991	6,005	760	12,030[16]	930	[16]	262	1991	125	...	...	...	...	100.0	...	...	115
Ethiopia[42]	1986–87	1,241	...	12,016[16]	282	[16]	36,660	1986–87	86	32.6[34]	18.6[34]	—	48.8[34]	88.4[34]	9.3[34]	2.3[34]	3
Faeroe Islands	1991	83	42	359	10[14]	17	571	1991	3	33.3	—	—	66.7	100.0	—	—	67
Fiji	1990	300	47	1,651	...	...	2,438	1986	25	...	...	...	...	...	...	...	24[20]
Finland	1991	12,357	4,562	115,848	578[18]	539	406	1990	434	86.9	13.1	—	—	...	...	...	125
France	1990	148,089	37,931	304,480	51,367	10,705	382	1988	3,793	—91.2—			8.8	28.3	—71.7—		126
French Guiana	1990	180	51	521	37	30	644	1987	6	50.0	—	—	50.0	50.0	—50.0—		92
French Polynesia	1989	317	88	477	38	89	607	1981	34	8.8	5.9	52.9	32.4	94.1	—	5.9	70[11]
Gabon	1984	565	...	...	...	...	2,000	1985	105	—26.7—		—73.3—		100.0	—	—	45
Gambia, The	1991	61	...	430[11]	...	...	14,536	1989	7	...	...	...	...	57.1	—42.9—		7[36]
Gaza Strip	1984	250	...	...	...	...	2,000	1991	6	...	...	...	...	...	...	...	13
Georgia	1990	32,100[4]	[4]	64,100[16]	...	[16]	170[4]	1990	422	...	...	...	...	100.0	...	...	110
Germany	1992	251,877	56,342	708,000[16]	42,369	[16]	313	1991	2,411	...	...	...	...	51.5	34.8	13.7	83
Ghana	1989[19]	628	39	11,808	67	1,736	22,452	1991	121	90.9	9.1	—	—	60.3	—39.7—		13
Gibraltar	1991	34	2[14]	302	3[14]	8[14]	921	1991	2	50.0	50.0	—	—	100.0	—	—	78
Greece	1989	33,151	9,628	31,433	7,266[18]	1,638	303	1989	402	46.0	54.0	—	—	...	...	...	51
Greenland	1990	70	29[14]	537[14]	...	13[5]	794	1990	16	6.3	—	—	93.7	100.0	—	—	75
Grenada	1990	56	7	296	28	36	1,617	1982	39	7.7	7.7	69.2	15.4	100.0	...	...	36[20]
Guadeloupe	1990	555	110	1,485	175	107	703	1989	29[8]	...	...	...	...	37.9[8]	—62.1[8]—		84[20]
Guam	1986	147	...	594[16]	...	[16]	823	1982	4	25.0	25.0	50.0	—	50.0	—50.0—		21[47]
Guatemala	1987	3,579	810[10]	9,093[10]	411[10]	...	2,356	1985	...	...	...	...	...	...	...	...	17[5]
Guernsey	1991	77	...	...	...	...	765	1991	1	100.0	—	—	—	100.0	—	—	91[27]
Guinea	1988	672	22	243	261	343	9,732	1988	38	—100.0—		...	...	100.0	—	—	6
Guinea-Bissau	1985	122	13[12]	674	12[12]	111	7,164	1981	17	11.8	—	—	88.2	100.0	—	—	27[12]
Guyana	1989	111	15	854	29	172	6,809	1979	55	20.0	12.7	27.3	40.0	87.3	3.6	9.1	29[5]
Haiti	1989	944	98	2,262[14]	...	...	6,083	1989	87	—77.8[43]—		22.2[43]	—	61.1[43]	—38.9[43]—		8
Honduras	1990	2,900	459[14]	1,001[14]	792[14]	...	1,586	1990	46	59.1[27]	11.4[27]	—	29.5[27]	45.7	—54.3—		12
Hong Kong	1992[48]	6,818	1,565	22,273	784	981	896	1982	71	43.7	15.5	39.4	1.4	50.7	26.8	22.5	46[31]
Hungary	1991	35,069	4,439	51,518[20]	4,652	2,695[20]	295	1991	148	—75.2[49]—		—24.8[49]—		...	...	...	101
Iceland	1990	715	219	1,713	121	197	355	1988	41	56.1	41.5	2.4	—	...	...	...	172
India	1990[48]	365,000	9,598[10]	219,299[5]	...	181,323[5]	2,337	1981	25,452	26.7	0.3	65.8	7.2	71.6	—28.4—		8[36]
Indonesia	1990	25,752	...	98,842[16]	...	[16]	6,861	1992	1,552	...	...	...	...	...	...	...	6
Iran	1992	22,000	4,770	43,291[5]	2,650[26]	2,202[26]	2,685	1982	581	71.1	15.5	9.8	3.6	66.4	13.9	19.7	15[31]
Iraq	1991	9,366	1,577	11,964[20]	1,552	...	1,922	1990	177	72.9	27.1	—	—	...	...	...	18
Ireland	1984	5,180	1,131	25,261	...	...	681	1991[9, 50]	104	81.7	18.3	—	—	100.0	—	—	39
Isle of Man	1988	86	...	...	...	...	745	1986	3	33.3	33.3	—	33.3	100.0	—	—	109[43]
Israel	1987	11,895	2,900[26]	14,785[26]	2,540[26]	12,110[26]	345	1991	192	24.0	76.0	—	—	24.0	39.0	37.0	59
Italy	1989	249,704	3,697[12]	186,335[12, 16]	...	[16]	228	1990	1,900	71.7	28.3	—	—	60.4	—39.6—		72
Jamaica	1991	1,122[5]	238	1,874[19]	57[19]	377[19]	2,095[5]	1991	31	80.6	19.4	—	—	80.6	—19.4—		22
Japan	1990	211,797	74,028	721,403	150,627	22,918	583	1990	10,096	89.2	10.8	—	—	68.6	—31.4—		136
Jersey	1991	88	...	...	...	...	956	1990	6	16.7	83.3	—	—	100.0	—	—	88
Jordan	1990	5,811	1,083	2,439	2,111	513	565	1990	53	...	...	...	...	52.8	—47.2—		18
Kazakhstan	1991	67,600[4]	[4]	196,300[16]	...	[16]	248[4]	1991	1,805	...	...	...	...	100.0	...	...	136
Kenya	1989	3,266	561	25,489	413	...	7,313	1989	558	—47.3—		—52.7—		...	...	...	14
Kiribati	1990	16	1[8]	125[8, 16]	3[8]	[16]	4,483	1982	34	2.9	—	97.1	—	100.0	—	—	43[12]
Korea, North	1989	57,690	...	...	...	...	370	1982	7,924	19.3	12.4	—68.3—		...	...	...	135[11]
Korea, South	1990	42,554	9,619	89,032	37,118	7,643	1,007	1990	924	—60.2—		39.8	—	...	...	...	23
Kuwait	1989	2,949	382	9,764[14]	846	137[14]	695	1988	24	...	...	...	...	66.7	—33.3—		30[11]
Kyrgyzstan	1991	16,400[4]	[4]	47,300[16]	...	[16]	268[4]	1991	331	...	...	...	...	100.0	...	...	122
Laos	1990	1,173	...	6,753[8, 16]	...	[16]	3,555	1990	1,074	0.7	—99.3—			100.0	—	—	25
Latvia	1991	10,696	1,507	16,754	...	...	246	1991	187	...	...	...	...	100.0	...	...	135
Lebanon	1986	3,509	...	...	...	...	771	1982	...	...	...	...	...	...	...	...	38
Lesotho	1987	103	...	...	...	...	15,728	1987	22	90.9	9.1	—	—	54.5	45.5	—	15
Liberia	1985	89	5	908	...	443	24,600	1981	85[34]	...	...	...	...	60.0[34]	—40.0[34]—		15
Libya	1984	5,272	400[26]	5,924[16, 26]	618[26]	[16]	690	1982	64	68.8	31.2	—	—	100.0	—	—	48
Liechtenstein	1991	29	12	...	2	...	1,007	1985	1	...	...	...	...	...	...	...	37
Lithuania	1992	13,764	2,088	78,300	...	4,900	274	1992	199	...	...	...	...	100.0	...	...	118
Luxembourg	1991	780	198[20]	...	316	134	496	1991	32	56.3	43.7	—	—	...	...	...	115
Macau	1991	315	33	653	37	...	1,111	1991	39	5.1	—	94.9	—	30.8	—69.2—		33
Macedonia	1989	4,331	1,094	...	404	...	464	1989	...	...	...	...	...	...	...	...	55
Madagascar	1985	1,189	100	3,323	37	1,638	8,610	1978	749	0.8	1.1	75.7	22.4	100.0	—	—	23[27]
Malaŵi	1984	262	12[26]	2,002[16]	12[26]	[16]	27,094	1987	395	12.2	0.8	—87.0—		59.2	—40.8—		16
Malaysia	1989	6,577	1,401	36,076	815[10]	...	2,638	1989	264	...	...	...	...	38.6	—61.4—		22
Maldives	1990	40	1	137	13[8]	141[8]	5,377	1990	5	20.0	—	80.0	—	100.0	—	—	8
Mali	1983	349	15	2,058	58	305	20,602	1983	162	...	...	...	...	100.0	—	—	6
Malta	1991	805	98	3,905	440	274	444	1991	6	...	...	...	...	...	...	...	93
Marshall Islands	1987	19	2[8]	88	...	...	2,076	1985	2	100.0	—	—	—	100.0	—	—	14
Martinique	1990	623	125	1,456	174	129	580	1989	...	...	...	...	...	...	...	...	99[20]
Mauritania	1988	187	19	920	10	749	10,128	1988	16	...	...	...	...	100.0	—	—	8
Mauritius	1991	1,090	140[20]	2,768[16, 20]	127[20]	[16]	996	1986	19	36.8	21.1	31.6	10.5	89.5	—10.5—		28[36]
Mayotte	1985	9	1	51	1	2	7,427	1985	2	100.0	—	—	—	100.0	—	—	12
Mexico	1987	130,000	4,925	108,486	...	...	600	1991[9]	726	86.0	14.0	...	...	...	...	...	13
Micronesia	1989	32	10	291	10[8]	...	3,247	1985	4	100.0	—	—	—	100.0	—	—	31[11]
Moldova	1991	17,100[4]	[4]	48,200[16]	...	[16]	255[4]	1991	335	...	...	...	...	100.0	...	...	131
Monaco	1990	80	...	...	...	...	366	1982	1	100.0	—	—	—	100.0	—	—	180[20]
Mongolia	1991[19]	6,318	200[12]	7,932[26]	400[12]	...	337	1981	1,659	2.1	5.4	71.9	20.6	100.0	—	—	121[36]
Morocco	1990	5,665	701	22,925	1,697	87	4,415	1990[30]	203	31.0	—	69.0	—	100.0	—	—	11
Mozambique	1988	342	118	3,086	332	1,080	43,536	1988	238	4.2	0.8	84.5	13.5	100.0	—	—	9
Myanmar (Burma)	1991	12,243	1,029	8,811	...	14,281	3,491	1982	614	49.7	2.4	—	47.9	100.0	—	—	6[36]
Namibia	1992	324	51	4,471	70[14]	...	4,594	1992	47	...	...	...	...	91.5	—8.5—		60[14]
Nauru	1980	11	...	...	...	...	700	1980	...	...	...	...	...	...	...	...	250
Nepal	1991	1,196	...	2,950	427[12]	2,379[20]	16,007	1991	111	88.2[34]	11.8[34]	—	—	82.4[34]	17.6[34]	—	2
Netherlands, The	1991	37,461	7,900	...	2,247	1,194	400	1991	249[20]	67.9[20]	32.1[20]	—	—	...	...	...	60

admissions or discharges: rate per 10,000 pop.	by kinds of hospital (%): general	by kinds of hospital (%): specialized	by kinds of hospital (%): medical centres	by kinds of hospital (%): rural	bed occupancy rate (%)	average length of stay (days)	mortality: under age 5 per 1,000 live newborn 1991	mortality: maternal mortality per 100,000 live births 1989–90	population with access to safe water (latest) (%)	food supply (% of FAO requirement) 1988–90	financing of public health care, latest year: health-care insurance: indiv. (% of earnings)	health-care insurance: employer (% of payroll)	health-care insurance: govt. (% of covered earnings)	public health expenditures (% of natl. budget)	public health expenditures per capita (U.S.$)	country
...	...	...	...	...	...	...	202	...	...	...	4.5[6]	21.5[6]	...	...	...	Equatorial Guinea
...	...	...	...	...	...	...	...	...	...	...	...	...	...	...	...	Eritrea[42]
...	...	...	...	...	...	...	...	31.4	...	...	...	...	...	7.6	...	Estonia
...	...	...	...	...	...	...	212	...	19	73	—	—	—	3.4	1	Ethiopia[42]
1,812[12]	76.6[12]	—	—	24.3[12]	60.6	11[12]	...	...	...	...	...	...	...	13.3	1,310	Faeroe Islands
886	...	...	...	...	72.6	7	30	41.1[8]	80	104	—	[22]	—	8.1	43	Fiji
2,237	96.8	3.2	—	—	89.1	18	7	3.2	95	113	1.7	1.5	[7]	11.2	830	Finland
2,243	...	...	...	...	83.0	16	9	8.5	100	143	6.8	12.6	...	15.3	1,100	France
2,060[12, 30]	...	...	...	...	63.4[12, 30]	9[12, 30]	...	129.7[10]	...	124	...	...	...	...	...	French Guiana
1,472	70.9	...	3.2	25.9	51.7	8	...	...	...	104	...	...	...	...	...	French Polynesia
258[43]	...	...	...	...	23.6[43]	13[43]	161	190[2]	68	104	2.5[6]	4.6	—	...	45[3]	Gabon
...	...	...	...	...	...	...	234	1,100[37]	75	100	—	—	—	8.0	8	Gambia, The
1,152	...	...	...	...	83.1	4	...	...	...	...	...	...	...	...	...	Gaza Strip
...	...	...	...	...	...	...	...	54.9	...	...	...	...	...	...	...	Georgia
1,823	...	...	...	...	83.8	15	9	10.3	100	132	6.4[17, 44]	6.4[17, 44]	...	18.1[45]	1,010[45]	Germany
...	...	...	...	...	...	...	137	1,000[2]	57	93	—	...	—	9.0	5	Ghana
1,474	...	...	...	...	41.4	8	...	...	...	...	...	...	...	13.2	640	Gibraltar
1,249	78.4	21.6	—	—	66.0	10	11	4.0	98	151	2.3	4.5	...	10.5	160	Greece
2,450	29.2	—	—	70.8	69.4	8	39[20]	...	...	...	...	...	...	10.5	1,510	Greenland
749[46]	...	...	...	...	...	...	37	65.4[5]	85	99	4.0[6]	4.0[6]	—	15.6	22	Grenada
2,103	75.2	24.8	—	—	83.0	12	...	89.3[26]	...	114	...	...	...	...	...	Guadeloupe
738[47]	97.6[47]	2.4[47]	—	—	78.8[47]	8[47]	15[11]	...	100	...	...	...	...	8.2	320	Guam
284	...	...	...	...	57.7	9	92	92.3[14]	62	103	2.0	7.0	1.5	9.9	11	Guatemala
1,055	100.0	—	—	—	83.9[27]	28[27]	...	—	...	...	...	...	...	21.8	1,020	Guernsey
...	...	...	...	...	...	...	234	800[2]	51	97	1.6	2.4	—	...	19[3]	Guinea
326	59.8	—	—	40.2	57.5	11	242	700[2]	27	97	...	...	...	1.4	4	Guinea-Bissau
...	...	...	...	...	...	...	69	112.1[10]	61	110	4.4[6]	6.6[6]	—	5.7	28	Guyana
123[43]	...	...	...	...	...	...	137	340[2]	36	89	...	...	...	...	30[3]	Haiti
429[34]	75.6[34]	16.7[34]	—	7.7[34]	70.2[34]	8[34]	73	49.9[26]	65	98	2.5	5.0	2.5	9.1	26[3]	Honduras
1,494	93.6	3.2	3.2	—	82.4	8	8	5.7	100	114	—	[22]	—	10.0	250	Hong Kong
2,203	...	...	...	...	74.4	12	17	20.7	98	137	10.0[6]	43.0[6]	[7]	7.9	130	Hungary
2,753	92.0	6.8	1.2	—	92.7	18	7	21.0	100	131	2.0	—	[7]	24.9	1,500	Iceland
...	...	...	...	...	...	...	126	460[2]	86	101	2.3	5.0	...	1.6	1	India
...	...	...	...	...	...	...	86	450[2]	58	121	—	7.0	—	2.4	3	Indonesia
...	...	...	...	...	...	...	62	120[2]	89	125	7.0[6]	20.0[6]	3.0[6]	8.3	240	Iran
645	...	...	...	...	42.4	4	143	120[2]	92	128	5.0[6]	12.0[6]	—	...	...	Iraq
1,478	81.9	18.1	—	—	70.9	7	10	3.8	100	157	1.3	1.3	[7]	13.0	670	Ireland
1,274[43]	83.9[43]	7.0[43]	—	9.1[43]	81.2[43]	25[43]	5[20]	...	...	...	...	...	...	26.0	520	Isle of Man
1,680[15]	...	...	...	...	87.3[15]	5[15]	12	6.9	100	125	5.6	5.0	0.2	3.7	170	Israel
1,535	90.4	9.6	—	—	70.4	12	10	7.7[14]	100	139	1.1	15.4	...	11.3	770	Italy
528[9]	79.4[9]	20.6[9]	—	—	63.6[9, 15]	6[9, 15]	19	102[31]	100	114	2.5[6]	2.5[6]	...	7.8	44	Jamaica
643[27]	97.9[27]	2.1[27]	—	—	83.3[27]	56[27]	6	8.6	100	125	[17]	—	...	...	1,540[3]	Japan
1,718	84.0	16.0	—	—	86.8[26]	24[26]	...	...	...	...	...	...	...	19.9	1,240	Jersey
1,061[12]	93.6[27]	6.4[27]	—	—	61.8[12]	4[12]	46	48[2]	99	110	—	—	—	5.0	22	Jordan
...	...	...	...	...	...	...	...	53.1	...	...	...	...	...	11.5	150[3]	Kazakhstan
...	...	...	...	...	...	...	75	170[2]	30	89	[17]	—	—	5.4	6	Kenya
633	47.6	—	52.4	—	58.0	15	85	...	44	95	—	—	—	13.0	32	Kiribati
...	...	...	...	...	...	...	34	41[2]	100	121	...	...	...	...	...	Korea, North
519[51]	97.8	2.2	—	—	80.6[51]	13[51]	10	9.9	100	120	1.5[21]	1.5[21]	...	1.2	14	Korea, South
1,235	...	...	...	...	71.7[27]	8[27]	17	1.9[5]	100	126	—	—	[52]	7.4	360	Kuwait
...	...	...	...	...	...	...	...	42.6	...	...	...	...	...	13.4	120[3]	Kyrgyzstan
...	...	...	...	...	...	...	148	...	35	111	...	...	...	...	5[3]	Laos
...	...	...	...	...	...	...	...	56.5	...	...	...	...	...	7.3	...	Latvia
...	...	...	...	...	...	...	46	...	92	127	1.5	5.5	...	...	...	Lebanon
221[15]	...	...	...	...	...	...	137	...	48	93	...	...	...	11.5	22	Lesotho
...	...	...	...	...	...	...	200	...	55	98	—	—	—	5.1	6	Liberia
719	...	...	...	...	52.7	13	108	80[2]	94	139	1.5	1.4	2.2	2.7	62	Libya
...	...	...	...	...	...	...	5[20]	...	...	...	...	...	...	...	...	Liechtenstein
1,877	...	...	...	...	...	...	...	22.9	...	...	...	...	...	...	160[3]	Lithuania
1,970	91.7	8.3	—	—	82.2	17	9	20.3	100	149	4.2	4.2	...	2.5	260	Luxembourg
662	...	...	...	...	56.5	10	10[20]	13.2	...	100	...	...	...	...	...	Macau
646[15]	...	...	...	...	58.2[15]	9[15]	...	16.7	...	...	...	...	...	...	...	Macedonia
699[15]	...	...	...	...	57.9[15]	2[15]	173	570[2]	22	95	—	8.3[28, 32]	—	6.6	2	Madagascar
436[8]	...	...	...	...	90.6[8]	8[8]	228	170[2]	56	88	—	—	—	7.4	4	Malaŵi
717[9]	...	...	...	...	...	...	20	59[2]	79	120	—	—	...	...	67[3]	Malaysia
291[8]	...	...	...	...	57.5[8, 53]	5[8, 53]	81	315.6[14]	95	...	...	...	...	9.7	33	Maldives
...	...	...	...	...	...	...	225	2,000[2]	41	96	—	2.0	—	2.1	2	Mali
1,569[27]	...	...	...	...	83.7[27]	19[27]	17	35.8[8]	100	128	8.3[6]	8.3[6]	8.3[6]	7.1	210	Malta
...	...	...	...	...	...	...	...	...	...	...	—	—	—	26.1	120	Marshall Islands
2,127	76.5	23.5	—	—	64.3	11	...	94.8[5]	...	114	...	...	...	...	...	Martinique
...	...	...	...	...	...	...	209	...	66	106	—	2.0	—	2.8	5	Mauritania
1,139[8, 9]	...	...	...	...	84.5[9, 34]	8[9, 34]	28	99.2[5]	95	128	—	—	[52]	8.3	58	Mauritius
778	100.0	—	—	—	74.8	6	...	...	...	...	...	...	...	...	...	Mayotte
403	...	...	...	...	40.3	5	37	65.2[12]	71	131	3.0	8.4	0.6	1.9	10	Mexico
2,171	100.0	—	—	—	...	...	...	...	...	...	—	—	—	...	100	Micronesia
...	...	...	...	...	...	...	...	34.1	...	...	...	...	...	12.2	140[3]	Moldova
2,630	100.0	—	—	—	77.6	14	...	...	100	...	...	...	...	...	...	Monaco
2,508	25.9	33.0	1.1	40.0	89.1	14	82	140[2]	65	97	...	...	...	...	...	Mongolia
238	93.6[49]	—	6.4[49]	—	52.9	9	91	300[2]	61	125	0.2	0.4	—	3.0	7	Morocco
92[15, 34]	...	...	...	...	70.2[15, 34]	9[15, 34]	292	300[2]	24	77	...	...	...	6.6	3	Mozambique
289	75.7	10.1	—	14.2	78.1	9	117	460[2]	31	114	1.0	2.0	1.0	4.6	3	Myanmar (Burma)
...	...	...	...	...	...	...	120	370[2]	...	...	...	...	...	9.7	72	Namibia
...	...	...	...	...	...	...	...	...	...	...	...	...	...	14.2	180	Nauru
54[14]	...	...	...	...	61.5[15, 34]	7[15, 34]	147	830[2]	37	100	—	—	—	4.7	1	Nepal
1,056	97.6	2.4	—	—	79.3	16	8	5.3	100	114	9.9	11.2	...	12.4	1,260	Netherlands, The

Health services (continued)

country	health personnel: year	physicians	dentists	nurses	pharmacists	midwives	population per physician	hospitals: year	number	kinds (%): general	specialized	medical centres	rural	ownership (%): government	private non-profit	private for profit	hospital beds per 10,000 pop.
Netherlands Antilles	1992	273	62	998	31	12	701	1991	11	36.4	36.4	27.2	—	...	...	...	75
New Caledonia	1990	216	64	...	46	38	776	1990	8	12.5	12.5	75.0	—	62.5	—37.5—		62
New Zealand	1992	10,331	1,875[36]	44,780[16, 36]	3,423[36]	[16]	337	1991	344[5]	...	...	...	...	49.7[5]	—50.3[5]—		75
Nicaragua	1991	2,125	310	2,360	...	...	1,882	1985	52	55.1	8.2	36.7	...	...	...	...	12[36]
Niger	1985	160	...	...	...	192	38,500	1979	...	...	...	...	...	...	...	...	6
Nigeria	1986	16,003	899[8]	57,108[8]	3,567[8]	47,052[8]	4,946	1985	11,588	6.6	0.5	—92.9—		81.4	—18.6—		9
Northern Mariana Islands	1986	23	4	103	2	2	1,324	1988	1	100.0	—	—	—	100.0	—	—	19
Norway	1993	14,084	5,124	60,035	3,041[26]	...	305	1991	338	20.7	79.3	—	—	...	...	...	56
Oman	1990	1,579	97	3,944	239	33[26]	969	1989	180	—28.3—		—71.7—		100.0	—	—	26[20]
Pakistan	1990	51,883	2,077	20,034	3,718	15,029	2,364	1991	10,673	—7.6—		—92.4—		88.5	—11.5—		6
Panama	1991	2,831	531	2,458	...	...	871	1991	56	...	...	...	...	86.7[20, 49]	–13.3[20, 49]–		30
Papua New Guinea	1989	361	...	3,241	...	...	9,953	1980	390	5.1	—	53.6	41.2	46.2	53.8	—	42[11]
Paraguay	1991	2,992	195[10]	3,584[10]	...	...	1,470	1991	...	...	...	...	...	...	...	...	12
Peru	1989	21,856	5,331	15,796	6,113	3,437	997	1990	368	...	...	...	...	49.7[14]	—50.3[14]—		16
Philippines	1989	57,270	1,203[14, 19]	12,296[14, 19]	635[8, 19]	10,369[14, 19]	1,039	1988	1,766	...	...	...	...	34.4[8]	—65.6[8]—		15[11]
Poland	1992	82,925	17,544	204,004	16,094	23,763	464	1992	886	77.4	22.6	—	—	...	...	...	68
Portugal	1990	27,608	1,267	29,525[8]	5,656	824[8]	376	1989	621	24.8	13.7	61.5	—	86.3	—13.7—		46
Puerto Rico	1988	9,422	...	...	...	...	349	1988	67	...	...	...	...	...	...	...	39[14]
Qatar	1991	672	92	1,574[19]	144[19]	...	750	1991	3	33.3	66.7	—	—	100.0	—	—	22
Réunion	1992	1,034	278	2,299	227	119	602	1991	...	...	...	...	...	75.3[49]	—24.7[49]—		48
Romania	1991[19]	41,813	6,717	...	6,432[11]	...	549	1990	437[43]	56.8[43]	32.5[43]	—	10.8[43]	...	...	...	94
Russia	1991	657,800[4]	[4]	1,691,700[16]	...	[16]	226[4]	1991	12,711	...	...	...	...	100.0	...	...	135
Rwanda	1985[19]	178	9	559	9	464[26]	33,170	1985[9]	220	—13.6—		—86.4—		100.0	—	—	9
St. Kitts and Nevis	1990	28	5[5]	231[5]	7[8]	...	1,498	1990	4	...	...	...	...	...	...	...	64
St. Lucia	1990	60	12[11]	246[11]	13[10]	...	2,521	1988	6	16.7	16.7	—	66.6	...	...	...	37
St. Vincent	1992	40	6	224	15[10]	...	2,690	1990	9[5]	11.1[5]	22.2[5]	11.1[5]	55.6[5]	88.9[5]	—11.1[5]—		39[5]
San Marino	1987	60	...	...	...	...	375	1987	...	...	...	...	...	...	...	...	66
São Tomé and Príncipe	1987	40	—	344[26]	1[26]	10[26]	2,819	1978	16	12.5	—	87.5	—	...	...	...	63[26]
Saudi Arabia	1990	22,688	1,424[14]	38,434[14, 16]	1,237[14]	[16]	623	1990	285	...	...	...	...	77.5	—22.5—		28
Senegal	1988	407	58	934	200	474	17,072	1984	87	18.4	29.9	51.7	—	100.0	—	—	9[14]
Seychelles	1992	61	11	327	2	...	1,162	1992	7	14.3	14.3	71.4	—	100.0	—	—	58
Sierra Leone	1988	300	18[10]	1,318[10, 16]	14[10]	[16]	13,150	1988	219	—25.6—		—74.4—		...	...	...	10
Singapore	1992	3,962	706	10,633	677	528	711	1992	22	...	...	...	...	54.5	—45.5—		35
Slovakia	1991	16,101	2,623	...	...	...	328	1991	111	72.1	27.9	—	—	100.0	—	—	91
Slovenia	1989	4,071	1,062	...	659	...	481	1989	...	...	...	...	...	...	...	...	72
Solomon Islands	1988	31	15[8]	464	...	...	9,852	1986	8	100.0	—	—	—	75.0	25.0	—	53
Somalia	1986	450	2	1,834	180	556	13,315	1985	...	...	...	...	...	...	...	...	9
South Africa	1991[48]	24,614	3,944	151,631	8,930[20]	...	1,275	1987	737	51.4	——48.6——			...	...	...	49
Bophuthatswana	1989	178	...	6,039	...	...	10,750	1989	216	—5.6—		—94.4—		...	...	...	31
Ciskei	1986[19]	283	7	3,855	10	54	2,714	1986	97	5.2	1.0	92.8	1.0	99.0	1.0	—	41
Transkei	1985	240	...	...	...	...	12,220	1987	31	...	...	...	...	...	...	...	25
Venda	1991	52	...	1,736	...	...	10,710	1991	8	37.5	37.5	25.0	...	...	...	...	31
Spain	1991	153,306	11,249	161,285	37,648	6,250	257	1989	830	54.9	45.1	—	—	42.8	—57.2—		43
Sri Lanka	1991[19]	2,962	301[8]	9,955	...	3,255[8]	5,823	1991[9]	420	...	...	...	...	100.0	—	—	28[20]
Sudan, The	1986[19]	2,405	...	...	...	...	9,439	1981	160	21.9	5.6	—	72.5	...	...	...	9
Suriname	1989	299	22[10]	1,400[10]	...	...	1,346	1980	17	29.4	17.6	47.1	5.9	58.8	29.4	11.8	47[11]
Swaziland	1984	80	13	377[26]	4[26]	...	7,971	1984	23	30.4	8.7	—60.9—		56.5	—43.5—		25
Sweden	1991	21,800	5,000	85,600[16]	5,282	[16]	395	1990	1,000[26]	10.3[26]	89.7[26]	—	—	...	...	...	61
Switzerland	1990	22,000	4,800	...	...	...	311	1983	372	52.7	47.3	—	—	...	...	...	81[20]
Syria	1988	8,420	3,067	10,400	3,313	3,201	1,347	1988	213	80.3	19.7	—	—	23.0	—77.0—		12
Taiwan	1992	24,981	6,560	45,862	18,499	1,439	829	1990	827	...	...	...	...	11.5	—88.5—		44
Tajikistan	1991	14,100[4]	[4]	42,800[16]	...	[16]	392[4]	1991	374	...	...	...	...	100.0	...	...	107
Tanzania	1984	1,065	...	...	...	...	19,775	1982	3,032	4.9	—	87.2	7.9	...	...	...	11[10]
Thailand	1990	12,520	2,285	77,186	4,168	10,796	4,377	1990	1,043	91.9	8.1	—	—	75.6	—24.4—		17
Togo	1988	278	5[10]	1,285	25	348	11,856	1979	65	10.8	4.6	61.5	23.1	96.9	3.1	—	16[14]
Tonga	1989	45	11	266	2	37	2,130	1989	4	...	...	...	...	...	...	...	32
Trinidad and Tobago	1990	802	99	2,565[16]	552	[16]	1,543	1990	31[8]	...	...	...	...	...	...	...	31
Tunisia	1989	4,313	577	10,545	1,264[5]	...	1,834	1991[9]	138	5.8	3.6	—90.6—		100.0	—	—	20
Turkey	1990	50,639	10,514	44,904	15,792	30,415	1,108	1990	857	74.9	8.5	—16.6—		85.4	—14.6—		22
Turkmenistan	1991	13,800[4]	[4]	40,600[16]	...	[16]	276[4]	1991	368	...	...	...	...	100.0	...	...	114
Tuvalu	1990	4	2[5]	31[5]	1[8]	...	2,261	1985	8	11.1	—	—	88.9	100.0	—	—	36
Uganda	1984	700	...	...	...	...	20,300	1981	485	15.5	1.2	83.3	—	84.5	15.5	—	12[11]
Ukraine	1991	228,900[4]	[4]	614,500[16]	...	[16]	226[4]	1991	3,900	...	...	...	...	100.0	...	...	135
United Arab Emirates	1990	2,986	388	7,130	190[8]	...	618	1991	33	...	...	...	...	100.0	—	—	23
United Kingdom	1981	92,172[56]	17,472	182,897	17,589	...	611[56]	1988	2,501[43]	...	...	...	...	100.0	—	—	62[43]
United States	1992	614,000	162,000	1,805,000	198,000	3,000	416	1991	6,738	82.1	17.9	—	—	31.4	50.4	18.2	47
Uruguay	1990	9,061	3,291[14]	1,516[14]	886[14]	616[14]	341	1988	52	—26.9—		—	73.1	100.0	—	—	28
Uzbekistan	1991	75,000[4]	[4]	242,200[16]	...	[16]	282[4]	1991	1,388	...	...	...	...	100.0	...	...	123
Vanuatu	1990	20	...	321	...	...	7,345	1990	21	—23.8—		—76.2—		...	...	...	25
Venezuela	1989	32,616	7,945	52,260	5,615	...	590	1989	544	...	...	...	...	42.8	—57.2—		25
Vietnam	1990	23,300[4]	[4]	83,401[12]	12,100[5]	18,047[12]	2,843[4]	1984	10,768	14.6	6.5	78.9	...	100.0	—	—	25[20]
Virgin Islands (U.S.)	1985	167	...	...	...	...	622	1985	...	...	...	...	...	...	...	...	49
West Bank	1984	510	...	...	...	...	1,535	1991	17	...	...	...	...	...	...	...	14
Western Sahara[57]	1982	11	—	...	2	...	13,000	1982[30]	2	50.0	—	50.0	—	100.0	—	—	9
Western Samoa	1990	44	10[11]	285[11]	...	...	3,584	1984	30	3.3	—	—	96.7	100.0	—	—	39[11]
Yemen	1990	2,708	144	6,430	188	199	4,166	1990	74	...	...	...	...	...	...	...	9
Yugoslavia	1991	25,873[4]	[4]	...	2,651	...	409[4]	1991	...	...	...	...	...	...	...	...	58
Zaire	1985	1,318	...	...	...	...	23,193	1979	942	37.3	38.9	23.8	—	40.9	44.6	14.5	21[8]
Zambia	1984	798	42	5,167	44	1,392	8,437	1987	965	8.2	0.3	19.0	72.5	80.9	19.1	—	29[11]
Zimbabwe	1987	1,243	113	14,369	323	2,512	6,951	1985	1,202	3.7	1.3	—95.0—		72.5	—27.5—		24

[1]Excludes four specialized hospitals. [2]1980–90 UN estimate. [3]May include parastatal expenditures and expenditures at the intermediate and local levels of government and/or the costs of additional services such as national health insurance and family-planning programs. [4]Physicians includes dentists. [5]1987. [6]Includes funds for old-age retirement, incapacitating disability, work injury, and life insurance. [7]Government provides remainder of the cost of benefits. [8]1985. [9]Government hospitals only. [10]1984. [11]1989. [12]1986. [13]Excludes specialized hospitals and medical centres. [14]1988. [15]General hospitals only. [16]Nurses includes midwives. [17]Amounts vary internally. [18]Number of pharmacies. [19]Government-employed health personnel only. [20]1990. [21]Minimum on a graduated scale. [22]Maximum on a graduated scale. [23]Factory and shop workers only. [24]Government provides hospital facilities. [25]1982–87 average. [26]1983. [27]1982. [28]Employed women only. [29]Includes outpatients. [30]Public sector only. [31]1992. [32]Includes family allowances. [33]1978. [34]1980. [35]Includes physicians practicing dentistry and doctors of traditional Chinese medicine

admissions or discharges: rate per 10,000 pop.	by kinds of hospital (%): general	special-ized	medical centres	rural	bed occupancy rate (%)	average length of stay (days)	mortality: under age 5 per 1,000 live newborn 1991	maternal mortality per 100,000 live births 1989–90	population with access to safe water (latest) (%)	food supply (% of FAO requirement) 1988–90	financing of public health care, latest year: health-care insurance: indiv. (% of earnings)	em-ployer (% of payroll)	govt. (% of covered earnings)	public health expenditures (% of natl. budget)	public health expenditures per capita (U.S.$)	country
...	...	...	...	...	...	...	...	...	...	111	...	...	...	6.9	110	Netherlands Antilles
1,165[15]	...	...	...	...	84.8[15]	8[15]	...	...	...	109	...	...	...	...	...	New Caledonia
1,204[9, 50]	...	...	...	...	66.8[9, 50]	9[9, 50]	10	17.4[14]	100	131	—	—	[52]	11.9	540	New Zealand
634	——91.7——		8.3	...	...	...	81	47.1[10]	54	99	4.0	12.5	0.5	14.6	33	Nicaragua
...	...	...	...	...	...	...	218	700[2]	61	95	—	11.0[28, 32]	—	5.2	6	Niger
...	...	...	...	...	...	...	188	800[2]	53	93	6.0[6]	6.0[6]	—	0.8	1	Nigeria
1,550	100.0	—	—	—	54.7	4	...	...	...	...	...	...	...	...	510	Northern Mariana Islands
1,542	90.9	9.1	—	—	82.8	11	8	8.4	100	120	7.8[6]	16.7[6]	[7]	10.3	1,160	Norway
1,226	...	...	...	...	83.0[15]	5[15]	42	...	55	...	...	...	...	5.4	140	Oman
...	...	...	...	...	...	...	134	500[2]	56	99	—	7.0	—	0.7	1	Pakistan
975	...	...	...	...	58.7	7	30	38.2[5]	84	98	1.0	8.0	—	20.5	120	Panama
253[14, 15]	...	...	...	...	...	...	79	900[2]	34	114	—	—	...	9.4	27	Papua New Guinea
...	...	...	...	...	...	...	59	379.5[12]	34	116	9.5[6]	13.0[6]	1.5[6]	4.3	5	Paraguay
416[27]	...	...	...	...	88.2[27]	14[27]	97	88.7[26]	61	87	3.0	6.0	...	5.1	19	Peru
...	...	...	...	...	...	...	46	100[2]	81	104	3.3	4.7	[7]	4.1	6	Philippines
1,281	...	...	...	...	72.2	14	17	12.8	89	131	—	43.0[6]	[7]	10.8	65	Poland
1,006	——94.7——		5.3	—	66.6	11	12	10.3	92	136	11.0[6]	24.5[6]	...	9.0	160	Portugal
1,156	...	...	...	...	66.2	7	16[11]	19.5	...	...	...	...	...	10.7	230	Puerto Rico
1,328[43]	54.3[43]	45.7[43]	—	—	...	...	35	...	100	...	...	...	...	0.8	70	Qatar
2,157	...	...	...	...	79.3	6	...	...	...	136	...	...	...	...	...	Réunion
...	...	...	...	...	...	...	34	155.5[14]	95	116	—	20.0[6, 21]	[7]	9.2	40	Romania
...	...	...	...	...	...	...	31[54]	49.0	100[54]	132[54]	1.0[6, 54]	26.0[6, 54]	[7, 54]	...	160[3]	Russia
85[51]	...	...	...	...	42.8[51]	7[51]	189	210[2]	50	82	—	—	—	4.6	2	Rwanda
1,028[15, 34]	...	...	...	...	58.9[15, 34]	10[15, 34]	43	...	100	101	5.0[6]	5.0[6]	—	12.4	84	St. Kitts and Nevis
955	...	...	...	...	...	...	22	12.4[25]	67	100	5.0[6]	5.0[6]	—	6.3	83	St. Lucia
717[15]	...	...	...	...	64.1[15]	6[15]	26	...	75	102	2.5[6]	3.0[6]	—	15.1	81	St. Vincent
1,435[34]	...	...	...	...	69.5[34]	11[34]	...	...	...	...	...	...	...	...	...	San Marino
1,733	76.1	—	23.9	—	68.7	12	89	76.7[5]	52	92	4.0[6]	6.0[6]	—	...	...	São Tomé and Príncipe
749[34]	...	...	...	...	...	...	43	90[2]	94	121	—	—	—	...	320[3]	Saudi Arabia
...	...	...	...	...	...	...	182	600[2]	47	98	3.0[22]	3.0[22]	—	2.3	7	Senegal
1,559[55]	...	...	...	...	71.0[55]	6[55]	21	...	100	104	5.0[6]	10.0[6, 21]	—	6.5	210	Seychelles
13[15, 34]	...	...	...	...	77.1[15, 34]	18[15, 34]	253	450[2]	36	83	—	—	—	3.6	1	Sierra Leone
1,235	...	...	—	—	73.0[43]	10[43]	10	2.1	100	136	3.0	3.0	[7]	4.6	130	Singapore
1,679	94.9	5.1	—	—	73.2	14	...	...	100	...	...	...	...	...	...	Slovakia
968[15]	...	...	...	...	84.1[15]	10[15]	...	4.3	...	...	...	...	...	...	...	Slovenia
...	...	...	...	...	...	...	...	10[37]	82	86	—	—	—	6.2	14	Solomon Islands
...	...	...	...	...	...	...	211	1,100[2]	37	81	—	—	—	3.2	2	Somalia
1,597	...	...	...	...	71.7	8	72	83[2]	...	128	—	—	[7]	9.7	100	South Africa
...	...	...	...	...	...	...	...	...	...	...	...	...	...	8.0	29	Bophuthatswana
488	...	...	...	...	79.0	16	...	...	...	...	...	...	...	...	...	Ciskei
632[12]	...	...	...	...	...	...	...	...	...	...	...	...	...	...	...	Transkei
1,130[8]	...	...	...	...	102.4[8]	11[8]	...	...	...	...	...	...	...	...	...	Venda
946	...	...	...	...	76.9	12	9	5.0[5]	100	141	4.8[6]	24.0[6]	...	13.7	450	Spain
1,464[20]	...	...	...	...	88.3[27]	6[27]	21	46.5[12]	60	101	—	—	—	4.8	7	Sri Lanka
81[15]	...	...	...	...	...	...	169	550[2]	46	87	—	—	—	1.3	1	Sudan, The
820	83.6	2.4	8.0	6.0	41.6	15	37	31.1[5]	68	108	...	...	...	3.7	49	Suriname
506	...	...	...	...	...	...	113	...	30	114	—	—	—	8.5	30	Swaziland
1,824	...	...	...	...	75.9	9	5	5.2	100	111	—	10.1	[7]	0.8	100	Sweden
1,278	85.9	14.1	—	—	80.8	24	9	6.0	100	130	[17]	—	[7]	13.1	380	Switzerland
474	...	...	...	...	57.9	5	47	140[2]	70	126	—	—	—	1.9	8	Syria
...	...	...	...	...	...	...	8	7.8[36]	...	...	1.4[6]	5.6[6]	2.8[6]	...	...	Taiwan
...	...	...	...	...	...	...	...	38.9	...	...	...	...	...	...	100[3]	Tajikistan
706	66.5	—	13.1	20.4	...	...	178	340[2]	56	94	—	—	...	3.7	1	Tanzania
...	...	...	...	...	...	...	33	71[2]	93	103	1.5	1.5	1.5	7.4	19	Thailand
...	...	...	...	...	...	...	144	420[2]	59	99	—	2.0[28]	—	5.2	6	Togo
718[27]	...	...	...	...	56.8[27]	10[27]	26	...	75	112	...	...	...	6.6	51	Tonga
...	...	...	...	...	...	...	23	63.0[14]	96	114	2.8[6]	5.6[6]	...	8.9	180	Trinidad and Tobago
652[10]	...	...	...	...	65.5[10]	8[10]	58	50[2]	92	131	5.0	15.0	—	6.6	31	Tunisia
568	78.3[43]	19.1[43]	—	2.6[43]	44.1[43]	9[43]	89	150[2]	83	127	5.0	7.0	—	3.0	16	Turkey
...	...	...	...	...	...	...	...	55.2	...	...	...	...	...	9.4	130[3]	Turkmenistan
1,368	40.9	—	—	59.1	51.5[15]	12.2[15]	...	...	...	...	...	...	...	3.1	34	Tuvalu
...	...	...	...	...	...	...	164	300[2]	21	93	—	—	—	5.5	1	Uganda
...	...	...	...	...	...	...	17[20]	3.5	...	...	...	...	...	...	130[3]	Ukraine
1,032[27]	...	...	...	...	69.6[27]	7[27]	29	...	95	136	...	...	...	6.9	140	United Arab Emirates
1,434	...	...	...	...	80.6[12]	15[12]	9	8.1	100	130	2.0[6, 21]	5.0[6, 21]	[7]	13.3	860	United Kingdom
1,330	...	...	...	...	69.1	9	11	8.4[14]	100	138	1.5	1.5	...	13.8	780	United States
392	...	...	...	...	67.4	17	24	25.3	73	101	3.0	4.0	...	4.5	32	Uruguay
...	...	...	...	...	...	...	...	42.8	...	...	...	...	...	...	120[3]	Uzbekistan
912[34]	...	...	...	...	55.0	8[34]	89	...	100	103	—	—	—	6.6	29	Vanuatu
...	...	...	...	...	...	...	43	55.0[5]	90	99	2.0	5.3	1.5[6, 21]	10.0	73	Venezuela
1,587	12.4	8.1	56.6	22.9	80.7	7	52	120[2]	42	103	...	...	...	...	2[3]	Vietnam
...	...	...	...	...	...	...	16[14]	...	...	...	...	...	...	15.7	330	Virgin Islands (U.S.)
831	...	...	...	...	74.2	5	...	...	...	...	...	...	...	...	...	West Bank
226	98.2	—	1.8	—	36.9	5	...	...	...	...	...	...	...	...	...	Western Sahara[57]
823	62.0	—	—	38.0	25.4	7	59	...	83	101	—	—	...	7.1	21	Western Samoa
95[10, 58]	89.0[10, 58]	0.4[10, 58]	—	10.6[10, 58]	73.4[10, 58]	18	182	...	38	...	...	...	...	4.7	13	Yemen
...	...	...	...	...	75.5	...	22[59]	16.8	83[59]	140[59]	8.7[59]	[17]	[17]	...	140[3, 59]	Yugoslavia
474[15]	...	...	...	...	71.6[15]	12[15]	180	800[2]	33	96	—	—	...	0.7	—	Zaire
1,249	——75.7——		——24.3——		68.5	7	200	150[2]	60	87	5.0[6, 22]	5.0[21, 26]	—	7.4	10	Zambia
767	40.8	25.7	——33.5——		64.1	7	88	...	66	94	—	—	—	7.6	20	Zimbabwe

(330,000 in 1991). [36]1991. [37]1980–88 UN estimate. [38]Employed women and workers' wives only; special system for public employees. [39]Republic of Cyprus only. [40]Data refer to former Czechoslovakia. [41]Princess Margaret Hospital only. [42]Ethiopia includes Eritrea. [43]1981. [44]Average contributions. [45]Former West Germany only. [46]Excludes medical centres. [47]1979. [48]Registered personnel; all may not be present and working in the country. [49]Based on bed ownership. [50]Excludes psychiatric hospitals. [51]General and specialized hospitals only. [52]Government provides entire cost of benefits. [53]Central Hospital only. [54]Data refer to former U.S.S.R. [55]Victoria Hospital only. [56]OECD estimate for 1990 is 80,400 physicians (1 per 714 persons). [57]Settlements of Smara, Boujdour, and El Aaiún only. [58]Former Yemen Arab Republic only. [59]Data refer to former Socialist Federal Republic of Yugoslavia.

Social protection

This table summarizes three principal areas of social protective activity for the countries of the world: social security, crime and law enforcement, and military affairs. Because the administrative structure, financing, manning, and scope of institutions and programmed tasks in these fields vary so greatly from country to country, no well-accepted or well-documented body of statistical comparisons exists in international convention to permit objective assessment of any of these subjects, either from the perspective of a single country or internationally. The data provided within any single subject area do, however, represent the most consistent approach to problems of international comparison found in the published literature for that field.

The provision of social security programs to answer specific social needs, for example, is summarized simply in terms of the existence or nonexistence of a specific type of benefit program because of the great complexity of national programs in terms of eligibility, coverage, term, age limits, financing, payments, and so on. Activities connected with a particular type of benefit often take place at more than one governmental level, through more than one agency at the same level, or through a mixture of public and private institutions. The data shown here are summarized from the U.S. Social Security Administration's *Social Security Programs Throughout the World* (biennial). A bullet symbol (●) indicates that a country has at least one program within the defined area; in some cases it may have several. A blank space indicates that no program existed providing the benefit shown; ellipses [...] indicate that no information was available as to whether a program existed.

Data given for social security expenditure as a percentage of total central governmental expenditure are taken from the International Monetary Fund's *Government Finance Statistics Yearbook,* which provides the most comparable analytic series on the consolidated accounts of central governments, governmentally administered social security funds, and independent national agencies, all usually separate accounting entities, through which these services may be provided in a given country.

Data on the finances of social security programs are taken in large part from the International Labour Office's *The Cost of Social Security* (triennial), supplemented by national data sources.

Figures for criminal offenses known to police, usually excluding civil offenses and minor traffic violations, are taken in part from Interpol's *International Crime Statistics* (biennial) and a variety of national sources. Statistics are usually based on the number of offenses reported to police, not the number of offenders apprehended or tried in courts. Attempted offenses are counted as the offense that was attempted. A person identified as having committed multiple offenses is counted only under the most serious offense. Murder refers to all acts involving the voluntary taking of life, including infanticide, but excluding abortion, or involuntary acts such as those normally classified as manslaughter. Assault includes "serious," or aggravated, assault—that involving injury, endangering life, or perpetrated with the use of a dangerous instrument. Burglary involves theft from the premises of another; although Interpol statistics are reported as "breaking and entering," national data may not always distinguish cases of forcible

Social protection

country	social security															
	programs available, 1991					expenditures, 1990 (% of total central govt.)	finances									
							year	receipts					expenditures			
	old-age, invalidity, death[a]	sickness and maternity[b]	work injury[c]	unemployment[d]	family allowances[e]			total ('000,000 natl. cur.)	insured persons (%)	employers (%)	government (%)	other (%)	total ('000,000 natl. cur.)	benefits (%)	administration (%)	other (%)
Afghanistan	●	●	●		●	...	...	...	...	...	...	...	...	...	...	...
Albania	●	●	●		●	...	1990	967.0	—	—	88.8	11.2	1,440.0	99.5	—0.5—	
Algeria	●	●	●		●	...	1987	17,632.0	...	...	...	...	16,378.0	94.1	5.6	0.3
American Samoa	●	...	...	...	...	...	1990	...	...	...	...	...	13.0	100.0	—	—
Andorra	...	...	...	...	...	...	1990	8,809.7	...	...	...	...	5,195.2	89.3	4.5	6.2
Angola	...	...	...	...	...	...	...	...	...	...	...	...	...	...	...	...
Antigua and Barbuda	●	●	●		●	...	1983	13.0	29.2	48.7	—	22.1	4.2	66.1	33.9	—
Argentina	●	●	●		●	35.3[10]	1986	4,994.5	31.3	45.6	19.5	3.6	4,500.2	97.4	2.3	0.3
Armenia	●	●	●		●	...	...	...	...	...	...	...	...	...	...	...
Aruba	●	...	●	...	...	[12]	1988	40.0	...	...	...	...	35.0	...	...	...
Australia	●	●	●	●	●	25.9	1986	24,310.5	1.8	12.5	84.8	0.9	23,896.9	98.8	1.2	—
Austria	●	●	●	●	●	45.4[13]	1986	368,562.0	29.5	46.8	21.2	2.5	361,191.0	96.2	2.4	1.4
Azerbaijan	●	●	●		●	...	...	...	...	...	...	...	...	...	...	...
Bahamas, The	●	●	●			9.3[7]	1986	73.6	26.8	40.7	1.3	31.2	31.8	75.6	23.2	1.2
Bahrain	●		●			2.3[13]	1986	35.8	21.1	42.2	—	36.7	7.6	73.2	19.7	7.1
Bangladesh		●	●	●		9.8[13, 14]	1986	154.3	37.4	41.8	1.4	19.4	57.9	95.8	4.2	—
Barbados	●	●	●	●		19.8[10]	1986	148.0	37.7	39.4	5.6	17.3	129.5	92.9	5.2	1.9
Belarus	●	●	●		●	...	1986	3,199.0	—	—	93.2	6.8	3,199.0	100.0	—	—
Belgium	●	●	●	●	●	41.3[10]	1986	1,347,070.0	24.4	39.7	31.6	4.3	1,322,636.0	94.5	4.3	1.2
Belize	●	●	●			1.0[13]	1986	11.2	9.4	56.4	—	34.2	2.4	52.1	46.2	1.7
Benin	●		●		●	8.7[13, 15]	1986	4,539.2	15.9	78.4	—	5.7	3,906.3	65.5	3.0	1.0
Bermuda	●		●			...	...	...	...	...	...	...	...	...	...	...
Bhutan	...	...	...	...	...	1.0	1990	...	...	...	...	...	26.0[13]	...	...	...
Bolivia	●	●	●		●	16.9	1986	70,737,008.0	25.6	39.4	23.4	11.5	52,958.650.0	82.0	17.6	0.4
Bosnia and Herzegovina	●	●	●	●	●	...	...	...	...	...	...	...	...	...	...	...
Botswana			●			1.0[13]	1988	—	...	...	...	...	33.0[13]	...	...	...
Brazil	●	●	●	●	●	22.7	1986	201,807,600.0	38.5	53.5	3.8	4.2	184,814,900.0	91.7	6.4	1.9
Brunei	●	...	...	...	...	...	1984	...	...	...	...	...	39.5	...	...	...
Bulgaria	●	●	●	●	●	16.7	1986	3,707.4	—	17.8	0.4	—	3,593.0	99.8	0.2	—
Burkina Faso	●		●		●	8.4[7, 13]	1986	8,057.5	15.6	64.3	—	20.1	2,060.4	99.2	—	0.8
Burundi	●		●		●	0.7[16]	1986	1,368.9	30.9	51.1	—	18.0	933.1	82.2	14.8	3.0
Cambodia	...	...	●	...	●	...	...	...	...	...	...	...	...	...	...	...
Cameroon	●		●		●	6.5[10, 13]	1986	56,770.0	14.0	68.2	—	17.8	19,869.0	100.0	—	—
Canada	●	●	●	●	●	28.6[10]	1986	87,538.9	11.7	16.6	61.2	10.5	77,122.0	96.2	2.7	1.1
Cape Verde	●	●	●		●	...	1986	499.9	27.5	62.5	1.5	8.5	210.3	62.3	14.7	23.0
Central African Republic	●		●		●	6.2[3, 13]	1986	4,549.0	9.8	88.5	—	1.7	5,550.0	45.7	13.6	40.7
Chad	●		●		●	1.9[18]	1986	1,221.9	26.3	65.9[13]	—	7.8	841.4	41.4	55.3	3.3
Chile	●	●	●	●	●	29.2[4]	1986	588,205.0	30.1	2.0	48.9	19.0	425,099.0	92.0	7.4	0.6
China	●	●	●	●		...	...	...	...	...	...	...	...	...	...	...
Colombia	●	●	●		●	19.6[3]	1986	169,872.0	21.5	56.5	1.7	20.2	133,837.0	51.6	42.3	6.1
Comoros	...	...	...	...	...	...	1983	40.7	100.0	—	—	—	54.3	17.4	62.3	20.3
Congo	●		●		●	0.4[21]	1983	15,272.8	12.1	80.2	—	7.7	7,256.7	66.6	21.3	12.1
Costa Rica	●	●	●		●	13.8	1986	23,387.4	25.5	49.2	2.7	22.6	18,080.1	81.8	3.8	14.4
Côte d'Ivoire	●		●		●	3.6[3]	1986	40,277.4	13.6	53.1	—	33.3	22,866.5	79.6	14.1	6.3
Croatia	●	●	●	●	●	...	...	...	...	...	...	...	...	...	...	...
Cuba	●	●	●			...	1986	1,887.7	—	41.8	58.2	—	1,887.7	96.4	—	3.6
Cyprus[22]	●	●	●	●	●	18.5	1986	141.6	29.4	39.9	17.2	13.5	81.7	98.5	1.4	0.1
Czech Republic[23]	●	●	●	●	●	21.1	1986	120,692.0	—	3.7	94.5	1.8	120,692.0	99.7	0.3	—
Denmark	●	●	●	●	●	37.7[10]	1986	178,991.9	3.5	8.0	85.7	2.8	174,349.8	97.1	2.9	—
Djibouti	●	...	...	...	●	6.2[13, 17]	1979	1,352.2	...	...	...	...	1,115.7	...	...	...
Dominica	●	●	●			1.4[15]	1986	12.3	22.6	50.9	—	26.5	4.4	68.0	32.0	—
Dominican Republic	●	●	●			4.7[10]	1986	77.9	20.1	72.9	—	6.8	74.3	75.9	24.1	—
Ecuador	●	●	●	●		1.9[10]	1986	101,137.5	16.4	24.3	11.0	48.3	41,625.0	88.1	11.9	—
Egypt	●	●	●	●		12.0[10]	1988	2,633.0	38.6	61.4	—	—	2,596.0	...	...	...
El Salvador	●	●	●			2.2	1986	287.4	23.2	54.0	—	22.8	210.9	75.0	25.0	—

entry. Automobile theft excludes brief use of a car without the owner's permission, "joyriding," and implies intent to deprive the owner of the vehicle permanently. Criminal offense data for certain countries refer to cases disposed of in court, rather than to complaints. Police manpower figures refer, for the most part, to full-time, paid professional staff, excluding clerical support and volunteer staff. Personnel in military service who perform police functions are presumed to be employed in their principal activity, military service.

The figures for military manpower refer to full-time, active-duty military service and exclude reserve, militia, paramilitary, and similar organizations. Because of the difficulties attached to the analysis of data on military manpower and budgets (including problems such as data withheld on national security grounds, or the publication of budgetary data specifically intended to hide actual expenditure, or the complexity of long-term financing of purchases of military matériel [how much was actually spent as opposed to what was committed, offset by nonmilitary transfers, etc.]), extensive use is made of the principal international analytic tools: publications such as those of the International Institute for Strategic Studies (*The Military Balance* and *Strategic Survey*) and the U.S. Arms Control and Disarmament Agency (*World Military Expenditures and Arms Transfers*), both annuals.

The data on military expenditures are from the sources identified above, as well as from the IMF's *Government Finance Statistical Yearbook* and country statistical publications.

The following notes further define the column headings:

a. Programs providing cash payments for *each* of the three types of long-term benefit indicated to persons (1) exceeding a specified working age (usually 50–65, often 5 years earlier for women) who are qualified by a term of covered employment, (2) partially or fully incapacitated for their usual employment by injury or illness, and (3) qualified by their status as spouse, cohabitant, or dependent minor of a qualified person who dies.

b. Programs providing cash payments (jointly, or alternatively, medical services as well) to occupationally qualified persons for *both* of the short-term benefits indicated: (1) illness and (2) maternity.

c. Programs providing cash or medical services to employment-qualified persons who become temporarily or permanently incapacitated (fully or partially) by work-related injury or illness.

d. Programs providing term-limited cash compensation (usually 40–75% of average earnings) to persons qualified by previous employment (of six months minimum, typically) for periods of involuntary unemployment.

e. Programs providing cash payments to families or mothers to mitigate the cost of raising children and to encourage the formation of larger families.

f. A police officer is a full-time, paid professional, performing domestic security functions. Data include administrative staff but exclude clerical employees, volunteers, and members of paramilitary groups.

g. Includes all active-duty personnel, regular and conscript, performing national security functions. Excludes reserves, paramilitary forces, border patrols, and gendarmeries.

crime and law enforcement (latest)						military protection								country
offenses reported to the police per 100,000 population					population per police officer[f]	manpower, 1993[g]		expenditure, 1989				arms trade, 1989 ('000,000 U.S.$)		
total	personal		property			total ('000)	per 1,000 population	total '000,000	per capita	% of central government expenditure	% of GDP or GNP	imports	exports	
	murder	assault	burglary	automobile theft										
...	...	...	...	...	540[1]	[2]	[2]	287[3]	21[3]	64.4[3]	7.7[3]	3,800	0	Afghanistan
...	...	...	...	...	550	73.0	21.3	157	49	11.4[4]	4.1	0	0	Albania
2,080	...	109.0	...	...	840	121.7	4.5	2,313	94	9.0[4]	5.1	575	0	Algeria
5,183	13.1	995.0	696.0	52.4	460	—	[5]	—	—	—	—	...	...	American Samoa
5,430	...	46.0	1,510.0	254.0	220	—	—	...	...	...	...	...	...	Andorra
237	10.9	0.8	...	0.1	14[6]	45.0	4.1	1,127[7]	161[7]	28.8[8]	23.9[7]	750	0	Angola
2,568	...	297.3	844.0	...	120	[9]	[9]	...	...	...	...	...	...	Antigua and Barbuda
637	8.5	0.6	—	110.4	1,270	70.8	2.1	1,854	58	12.0[11]	3.4	40	60	Argentina
363	6.1	7.0	...	...	...	20.0	5.6	...	...	...	...	...	...	Armenia
3,938	37.5	393.1	...	...	...	—	[5]	—	—	—	—	...	...	Aruba
6,773	4.5	369.6	1,962.8	770.6	450	63.2	3.6	6,153	368	9.2	2.3	675	80	Australia
6,007	2.3	1.8	1,151.6	26.7	470	52.0	6.6	1,402	184	2.8	1.1	100	40	Austria
305	...	...	...	...	...	42.6	5.8	...	...	...	...	...	...	Azerbaijan
6,836	52.6	115.8	2,580.4	...	155	0.9	3.2	9[3]	40[3]	2.5[3]	0.5[3]	...	...	Bahamas, The
1,878	0.6	624.3	63.5	...	180	7.2	14.7	196	389	13.1	6.5	50	0	Bahrain
16.8	2.0	2.1	4.4	0.3	2,560	107.0	0.9	323	3	15.1	1.6	120	0	Bangladesh
4,519	11.7	109.0	323.0	13.6	280	[9]	[9]	10	38	1.8	0.6	0	0	Barbados
650	2.9	7.0	...	...	...	102.6	9.9	...	...	...	...	...	...	Belarus
3,338	2.2	120.7	690.9	281.0	640	80.7	8.0	3,881	392	7.2	2.5	220	20	Belgium
1,869	...	573.8	420.2	...	290	0.7	3.2	4[3]	25[3]	4.0[3]	2.0[3]	...	...	Belize
1,234	...	...	...	...	3,250	4.3	0.8	33	7	19.4	2.0	0	0	Benin
7,413	10.8	154.6	2,092.3	...	370	—	[5]	—	—	—	—	...	...	Bermuda
...	...	...	...	...	...	4.0[14]	3.1[14]	...	...	...	...	...	...	Bhutan
...	...	...	...	...	...	33.5	4.3	182	27	25.3	4.0	10	0	Bolivia
558	...	...	...	...	...	60.0	13.6	...	...	...	...	...	...	Bosnia and Herzegovina
6,693	19.5	442.6	411.8	...	750	6.1	4.3	62	52	6.0	2.8	10	0	Botswana
116	...	...	...	...	...	296.7	1.9	5,731[4]	41[4]	2.3[4]	1.3[4]	160	50	Brazil
358	0.4	3.7	113.9	10.8	100	4.4	16.0	305[3]	1,398[3]	24.5[3]	8.1[3]	...	...	Brunei
...	...	...	...	...	...	99.4	11.7	5,885	656	29.7	11.9	290	160	Bulgaria
41	0.2	4.1	—	—	...	8.7	0.9	52[4]	6[4]	17.5[4]	2.1[4]	10	0	Burkina Faso
87	3.3	7.4	...	...	...	7.2	1.3	28	5	14.2	2.6	10	0	Burundi
...	...	...	...	...	1,980	102.0	11.0	...	...	...	...	490	0	Cambodia
...	0.2	0.1	0.2	0.3	1,170	12.1	0.9	148	14	6.6	1.3	5	0	Cameroon
11,442.6	5.7	134.3	1,331.7	382.7	8,640	78.1	2.8	10,840	413	8.8	2.0	190	410	Canada
...	...	...	...	...	110	1.1	3.1	12[17]	47[17]	13.5[17]	11.8[17]	5	0	Cape Verde
135	1.6	22.8	2.7	...	2,740[1]	6.5	2.2	18	6	6.6	1.7	0	0	Central African Republic
...	...	...	...	...	990	25.2	4.1	39[4]	8[4]	45.1[4]	4.3[4]	10	0	Chad
1,347	5.8	107.0	...	11.2	470	91.8	6.8	790	61	16.3[4]	3.4	120	160	Chile
201	1.9	4.1	17.5	...	1,360[19]	3,030.0	2.6	22,330	20	19.1	3.7	110	2,000	China
840	40.5	266.9	...	...	420	140.0	4.1	758	23	16.4	2.1	150	0	Colombia
...	...	...	...	...	960	—	[20]	...	...	...	...	...	...	Comoros
32	1.5	4.7	0.2	0.2	870	10.8	3.9	99[11]	49[11]	12.5[11]	5.1[11]	0	0	Congo
868	5.3	11.1	232.4	23.1	480	7.5	2.3	22	8	1.6	0.5	0	0	Costa Rica
262	2.6	47.9	12.2	19.9	4,640	7.1	0.5	130	11	9.2[4]	1.5	0	0	Côte d'Ivoire
1,087	...	...	...	...	...	103.3	21.4	...	...	...	...	...	...	Croatia
...	...	...	...	...	650	173.5	15.9	1,377	131	10.2	3.9	1,200	5	Cuba
671	3.2	12.3	208.7	2.8	180	10.0	17.1	41	59	3.0	0.9	40	0	Cyprus[22]
1,911	2.0	89.4	621.5	95.7	640	106.5	10.3	8,361	534	21.7	6.8	460	875	Czech Republic[23]
10,270	4.6	163.4	2,382.9	575.9	600	27.7	5.3	2,184	426	5.2	2.2	110	20	Denmark
487	4.8	67.0	14.4	9.8	...	3.9	6.9	27[3]	67[3]	22.4[3]	8.1[3]	...	...	Djibouti
22,432	9.3	47.0	1,025.0	11.0	300	[9]	[9]	...	...	...	...	...	...	Dominica
946	11.9	30.8	154.0	24.8	580	23.2	3.0	52	7	5.0	0.8	5	0	Dominican Republic
333	5.1	4.0	...	4.3	260	58.0	5.3	163	16	11.6	1.7	20	0	Ecuador
3,314	1.6	0.7	...	3.4	580	430.0	7.5	3,499	67	10.7	5.0	600	370	Egypt
...	...	...	...	...	1,000	30.5	5.5	252	48	37.3	4.0	70	0	El Salvador

Social protection (continued)

country	social security: programs available, 1991: old-age, invalidity, death[a]	sickness and maternity[b]	work injury[c]	unemployment[d]	family allowances[e]	expenditures, 1990 (% of total central govt.)	finances: year	receipts: total ('000,000 natl. cur.)	insured persons (%)	employers (%)	government (%)	other (%)	expenditures: total ('000,000 natl. cur.)	benefits (%)	administration (%)	other (%)
Equatorial Guinea	●		●		●	...	1983	43.0	4.7	95.3	—	—	20.0	30.0	70.0	—
Eritrea[25]	...	...	...	...	...	...	...	...	...	...	...	...	...	...	...	...
Estonia	●	●	●	●	●	...	...	90.1	...	...	...	...	...	...	...	...
Ethiopia[25]	●		●			4.1[4]	1986	162.1	32.5	63.2	—	4.2	116.3	98.2	1.8	—
Faeroe Islands	●	...	...	...	●	...	...	...	...	...	...	...	...	...	...	...
Fiji	●		●			4.6	1986	111.6	26.5	26.5	—	47.0	34.4	94.8	5.2	—
Finland	●	●	●	●	●	34.7[13]	1986	90,413.3	8.3	39.7	44.7	7.3	82,164.8	96.8	3.2	—
France	●	●	●	●	●	44.2[10]	1986	1,431,025.0	23.4	50.6	23.0	3.0	1,439,788.7	95.1	4.0	0.9
French Guiana	●	...	●	...	●	...	1987	597.8	...	...	...	...	653.7	...	...	...
French Polynesia	●	...	●	...	●	...	1988	14,902.3	...	...	...	...	13,640.5	...	...	...
Gabon	●		●		●	...	1986	37,788.0	8.3	84.8	—	6.9	42,326.0	80.7	15.1	4.2
Gambia, The	●		●			3.5[27]	1982	—	...	...	...	...	5.6	...	...	...
Gaza Strip	...	...	...	...	...	—	...	...	...	...	...	...	...	...	...	...
Georgia	●	●	●		●	...	...	...	...	...	...	...	...	...	...	...
Germany	●	●	●	●	●	48.5[10, 13]	1986[28]	459,340.0	36.6	35.0	25.8	2.6	451,885.0	97.2	2.8	—
Ghana	●		●			6.4[4]	...	—	...	...	...	...	...	...	...	...
Gibraltar	●	●	...	●	●	...	...	...	...	...	...	...	...	...	...	...
Greece	●	●	●	●	●	28.8[17]	1986	872,503.0	29.4	42.5	21.4	6.7	898,814.0	93.7	6.3	—
Greenland	●	...	...	...	●	...	...	...	...	...	...	...	...	...	...	...
Grenada	●	●				5.0[13, 16]	1986	15.2	27.7	57.9	—	14.4	6.0	91.0	9.0	—
Guadeloupe	●	...	...	...	●	...	1987	3,111.2	...	...	...	...	1,833.5	...	...	...
Guam	●	...	...	...	●	...	1989	...	...	...	...	...	7.3	...	...	...
Guatemala	●	●	●			5.2[10, 13]	1986	209.0	26.9	55.9	—	17.2	134.4	86.0	10.9	3.1
Guernsey	...	...	...	...	...	...	...	...	...	...	...	...	...	...	...	...
Guinea	●	●	●		●	...	1986	269.2	3.0	90.9	—	6.1	268.7	85.2	1.8	13.0
Guinea-Bissau	...	...	...	...	...	8.8[13]	1986	138.0	22.8	63.4	10.3	3.8	61.9	59.6	40.4	—
Guyana	●	●	●			3.7[8]	1986	200.2	17.3	21.4	0.7	60.6	62.1	80.2	18.2	1.6
Haiti	●		●			5.1[3]	1977	60.5	——26.6——		69.9	3.5	52.4	92.7	7.3	—
Honduras	●	●	●			4.5[15]	1986	166.2	23.9	40.8	3.3	32.0	76.8	84.6	15.4	—
Hong Kong	●	●	●			...	1989–90	...	...	...	...	...	4,155.0	87.0	13.0	—
Hungary	●	●	●	●	●	27.7	1986	149,400.0	21.1	78.9	—	—	142,939.0	99.3	0.7	—
Iceland	●	●	●	●	29	3.5[11]	1988	9,413.0	—	21.0	79.0	—	45,577.0	98.1	1.9	—
India	●	●	●			...	1986	87,807.7	9.8	66.9	9.6	13.7	40,362.2	98.4	1.6	—
Indonesia	●	●	●			—	1986	97.9	17.3	58.1	—	24.6	92.2	12.5	19.4	68.1
Iran	●	●	●	●	●	13.7	1986	346,460.0	83.2	0.1	8.2	8.5	167,879.0	43.4	6.3	50.0
Iraq	●	●	●			...	1977	107.8	9.9	55.6	21.9	12.6	71.0	94.0	2.4	3.6
Ireland	●	●	●	●	●	26.2	1986	4,299.6	13.0	24.4	61.7	0.9	4,302.2	95.2	4.7	0.1
Isle of Man	●	●	●	●	●	37.0[30]	1985	...	...	...	...	...	14.4	...	...	...
Israel	●		●	●	●	21.7	1986	6,723.0	23.9	37.3	30.7	8.1	6,146.8	89.9	5.4	4.7
Italy	●	●	●	●	●	28.5[4]	1986	90,646.0	19.5	51.7	17.6	11.2	100,251.0	89.3	2.0	8.7
Jamaica	●	●	●			3.2[16]	1986	330.4	11.8	14.3	36.1	37.8	171.5	93.4	6.0	0.6
Japan	●	●	●	●	●	...	1986	50,525,725.0	27.2	30.6	26.8	15.4	40,145,652.0	94.6	1.7	3.7
Jersey	●	●	●	...	●	9.5	1991	60.9	——63.8——		23.4	12.8	52.8	...	...	...
Jordan	●		●			8.6	1986	53.6	28.7	55.3	—	16.0	9.5	77.4	14.0	8.6
Kazakhstan	●	●	●		●	...	...	...	...	...	...	...	...	...	...	...
Kenya	●		●			0.1	1986	1,660.0	27.7	27.7	1.2	43.4	268.0	85.1	14.9	—
Kiribati	●		●			...	...	...	...	...	...	...	...	...	...	...
Korea, North	...	...	...	...	...	...	...	...	...	...	...	...	...	...	...	...
Korea, South	●		●			7.5	1990	1,286,000.0	31.6	68.4	—	—	2,037,000.0	...	...	...
Kuwait	●					8.5[10]	1986	385.8	6.3	12.4	54.6	26.7	169.5	96.3	3.7	—
Kyrgyzstan	●	●	●		●	...	...	...	...	...	...	...	...	...	...	...
Laos	...	...	●	...	...	...	...	...	...	...	...	...	...	...	...	...
Latvia	●	●	●		●	...	...	...	...	...	...	...	...	...	...	...
Lebanon	●	●	●		●	...	...	...	...	...	...	...	...	...	...	...
Lesotho	...	...	...	...	...	1.6[13]	1988	—	...	...	...	...	5.3	...	...	...
Liberia	●		●		●	1.0[4]	1983	2.9	—	69.0	13.8	17.2	2.6	54.4	45.6	—
Libya	●	●	●			...	1977	192.9	9.1	28.7	58.7	3.5	128.2	96.2	3.2	0.5
Liechtenstein	●	●	●	●	●	...	...	...	...	...	...	...	...	...	...	...
Lithuania	●	●	●		●	...	...	...	...	...	...	...	...	...	...	...
Luxembourg	●	●	●	●	●	44.6	1986	59,427.9	24.7	34.2	34.5	6.6	51,643.0	96.8	2.7	0.5
Macau	●	...	...	...	●	...	1989	89.0	...	...	...	...	93.5	...	...	...
Macedonia	●	●	●	●	●	...	...	...	...	...	...	...	...	...	...	...
Madagascar	●		●		●	2.7[13]	1986	10,288.2	22.2	77.8	—	—	10,075.3	87.0	13.0	—
Malaŵi			●			1.0[7]	1986	—	...	...	...	...	5.4	...	...	...
Malaysia	●		●			3.8[11]	1986	6,304.0	21.6	40.5	2.5	35.4	1,589.3	93.9	6.1	—
Maldives	...	...	...	...	...	1.0	1989	—	...	...	...	...	6.4	...	...	...
Mali	●		●		●	3.0[4]	1986	8,128.8	16.6	74.3	—	9.1	7,924.6	63.7	34.7	1.6
Malta	●	●	●	●	●	31.0	1986	71.6	26.8	33.5	39.7	—	94.0	94.4	5.6	—
Marshall Islands	●	●				...	...	...	...	...	...	...	...	...	...	...
Martinique	●	...	...	...	●	...	1988	2,332.2	...	...	...	...	3,706.2	...	...	...
Mauritania	●		●		●	3.7[15]	1986	584.6	6.3	87.7	—	6.0	583.3	81.8	18.2	—
Mauritius	●		●		●	13.0[13]	1986	993.8	9.6	35.0	37.7	17.7	654.1	95.1	4.1	0.8
Mayotte	...	...	...	...	...	...	...	...	...	...	...	...	...	...	...	...
Mexico	●	●	●			12.3	1986	2,463,649.0	19.6	63.1	5.0	12.3	2,115,574.0	73.6	17.3	9.1
Micronesia	●					...	...	...	...	...	...	...	...	...	...	...
Moldova	●	●	●		●	...	...	...	...	...	...	...	...	...	...	...
Monaco	...	...	...	...	...	...	...	...	...	...	...	...	...	...	...	...
Mongolia	●	●	...	...	●	...	...	...	...	...	...	...	...	...	...	...
Morocco	●	●	●		●	6.9[11, 13]	1986	3,660.7	27.6	41.2	—	31.2	2,506.5	94.5	3.5	1.9
Mozambique	●	...	...	...	...	...	1986	228.2	—	86.2	13.7	0.1	145.0	100.0	—	—
Myanmar (Burma)		●	●			0.2	1986	44.3	19.9	59.6	18.5	2.0	35.9	51.5	15.6	32.9
Namibia	●	...	...	...	...	6.4	...	...	...	...	...	...	...	...	...	...
Nauru	●	●	●	...	●	...	...	...	...	...	...	...	...	...	...	...
Nepal	●		●			0.7[14]	1985	—	...	...	...	...	59.3	...	...	...
Netherlands, The	●	●	●	●	●	34.3	1986	140,734.0	38.0	33.4	15.6	13.0	122,791.0	97.0	3.0	—

crime and law enforcement (latest)						military protection								country
offenses reported to the police per 100,000 population					population per police officer[f]	manpower, 1993[g]		expenditure, 1989				arms trade, 1989 ('000,000 U.S.$)		
total	personal		property			total ('000)	per 1,000 population	total '000,000	per capita	% of central government expenditure	% of GDP or GNP	imports	exports	
	murder	assault	burglary	automobile theft										
...	...	...	...	...	190	1.3	3.4	2[24]	9[24]	21.0[24]	...	10	0	Equatorial Guinea
...	...	...	...	...	...	...	...	...	...	...	...	...	...	Eritrea[25]
1,213	5.6	20.5	...	...	...	2.5	1.6	...	...	...	...	...	...	Estonia
94	6.7	24.8	1.9	...	1,100	[26]	[26]	763	15	30.4	12.8	925	0	Ethiopia[25]
...	...	...	...	...	...	—	[5]	—	—	—	—	...	...	Faeroe Islands
1,915	4.3	31.6	411.1	...	440	3.9	5.1	26	35	8.8[3]	2.2	0	0	Fiji
9,631	0.6	47.2	1,432.6	364.8	640	32.8	6.5	1,788	360	5.3	1.6	20	0	Finland
6,169	4.4	86.5	712.0	519.6	630	411.6	7.1	35,260	628	8.6	3.7	210	2,700	France
...	...	...	...	...	...	—	[5]	—	—	—	—	...	...	French Guiana
...	...	...	...	...	...	—	[5]	—	—	—	—	...	...	French Polynesia
323	2.2	25.3	62.2	20.9	1,290	4.8	3.7	140	132	12.4	4.5	20	0	Gabon
...	...	...	...	...	3,310	0.8	0.8	1	2	2.0	0.7	0	0	Gambia, The
4,355	...	...	...	...	...	—	—	...	...	...	...	...	...	Gaza Strip
...	...	...	...	...	...	—	—	...	...	...	...	...	...	Georgia
7,108[28]	3.9[28]	107.0[28]	1,749.1[28]	115.1[28]	...	408.2	5.0	33,600	544	9.5	2.8	875	1,200	Germany
864	2.0	95.9	4.7	...	620	6.9	0.4	30	2	3.1[4]	0.6	30	0	Ghana
10,039	—	860.2	...	...	170	—	[5]	—	—	—	—	...	...	Gibraltar
3,306	2.0	97.6	265.0	68.4	380	159.3	15.5	3,097	309	13.4	5.9	2,000	0	Greece
10,339	23.5	671.5	924.2	...	340	—	[5]	—	—	—	—	...	...	Greenland
2,679	10.0	880.0	153.0	...	230	[9]	[9]	...	...	...	...	...	...	Grenada
...	...	...	...	...	...	—	[5]	—	—	—	—	...	...	Guadeloupe
9,299	10.1	109.9	700.9	208.1	...	—	[5]	—	—	—	—	...	...	Guam
510	27.4	77.1	27.9	58.1	670	43.9	4.5	131	15	13.0	1.6	10	0	Guatemala
...	...	...	...	...	...	—	[5]	—	—	—	—	...	...	Guernsey
32.4	1.0	0.8	1.3	0.5	1,140	9.7	1.3	27[4]	4[4]	6.7[4]	1.2[4]	10	0	Guinea
...	...	...	...	...	...	9.2	8.9	3[11]	4[11]	4.1[11]	2.4[11]	10	0	Guinea-Bissau
1,980	15.6	28.1	434.7	...	190	2.0	2.6	6	8	3.6	2.7	0	0	Guyana
701	...	...	...	...	400	7.4	1.1	45	8	12.4	1.9	0	0	Haiti
...	9.4	7.7	...	3.3	1,040	16.8	3.3	150	32	15.5	3.2	30	0	Honduras
1,522	2.6	129.9	218.9	37.6	220	—	[5]	—	—	—	—	...	...	Hong Kong
3,287	3.1	66.0	742.9	77.6	710	78.0	7.6	4,064	384	20.1	6.3	30	50	Hungary
1,550	0.9	64.3	704.8	112.8	940	—	—	—	—	—	—	0	0	Iceland
187	3.5	...	19.3	...	820	1,265.0	1.4	8,174	10	13.6	3.1	3,500	0	India
134	0.9	6.2	28.4	6.0	1,340	270.9	1.4	1,510	8	8.2	1.7	90	0	Indonesia
76.6	0.5	47.7	...	...	...	473.0	7.8	21,120[14]	449[14]	34.1[14]	7.9[14]	1,300	0	Iran
91	1.7	21.7	40.8	1.4	140	382.0	19.7	16,710[14]	1,098[14]	50.8[27]	30.7[11]	1,900	60	Iraq
2,476	0.8	2.1	821.5	31.6	310	13.0	3.7	449	128	3.7	1.6	5	0	Ireland
...	...	...	...	...	...	—	[5]	—	—	—	—	...	...	Isle of Man
5,234	2.2	202.5	2,483.0	315.6	210	176.0	32.5	5,745	1,323	25.2	12.8	725	625	Israel
4,358	6.4	33.8	...	546.0	680	344.6	6.0	20,720	360	4.9	2.4	300	60	Italy
1,927	20.9	476.0	305.6	14.8	430	3.4	1.4	36	15	2.2[4]	1.1	5	0	Jamaica
1,397	1.0	15.7	184.3	27.6	480	237.7	1.9	28,410	231	6.0[4]	1.0	1,400	110	Japan
...	...	...	...	...	...	—	[5]	—	—	—	—	...	...	Jersey
625	1.9	13.6	44.4	12.3	630	100.6	26.7	548	175	32.7	12.7	190	5	Jordan
815	...	...	...	...	...	[31]	[31]	...	...	...	...	...	...	Kazakhstan
364	4.2	57.3	63.5	6.6	1,500	24.4	0.9	210	9	9.5	2.7	10	0	Kenya
285	12.4	5.5	73.3	...	330	—	—	...	...	...	...	...	...	Kiribati
...	...	...	...	...	460	1,127.0	49.8	6,000	285	40.7[4]	20.0	525	400	Korea, North
2,637	1.5	42.5	12.3	...	420	633.0	14.4	9,100	213	23.8	4.3	525	400	Korea, South
695	6.6	25.8	66.8	17.1	80	13.7	9.6	1,964	962	19.9	6.2	490	0	Kuwait
581	...	...	...	...	...	12.0	2.7	...	...	...	...	...	...	Kyrgyzstan
...	...	...	...	...	280	37.0	8.2	55[7]	15[7]	21.3[3]	10.5[3]	100	0	Laos
1,292	...	...	...	...	...	5.0	1.9	...	...	...	...	...	...	Latvia
366	13.2	14.1	65.7	67.3	530	41.3	15.9	429[8]	135[8]	20.0[8]	8.2[8]	10	10	Lebanon
1,896	51.1	204.3	201.3	...	1,130	2.0	1.1	11[11]	7[11]	9.4[11]	2.3[11]	0	0	Lesotho
...	...	...	...	...	1,570	—[32]	—[32]	58	23	13.3	4.8	10	0	Liberia
1,007	2.9	5.7	...	...	...	70.0	15.3	3,309	808	29.2	14.9	975	40	Libya
...	...	...	...	...	660	—	[33]	—	—	—	—	...	...	Liechtenstein
991	...	...	...	...	...	9.8	2.6	...	...	...	...	...	...	Lithuania
6,628	2.2	84.1	1,047.3	131.5	730	0.8	2.0	76	200	2.7[4]	0.9	10	5	Luxembourg
1,226	1.8	133.8	152.2	47.4	...	—	[5]	...	...	...	...	...	...	Macau
686	...	...	...	...	...	10.4	5.0	...	...	...	...	...	...	Macedonia
...	...	...	...	...	2,900	21.0	1.6	35	3	28.9	1.5	30	0	Madagascar
1,001	2.6	96.5	15.6	...	1,670	10.4	1.0	35	4	8.2	2.3	5	0	Malaŵi
451	1.9	14.3	97.7	18.4	760	114.5	6.0	1,039	61	10.0	2.9	70	0	Malaysia
2,353	1.9	3.3	36.1	...	35,710	—	—	...	...	...	...	...	...	Maldives
33	—	1.1	3.9	—	160	7.4	0.9	41	5	7.9[4]	2.0	10	10	Mali
2,802	10.4	50.6	1,907.1	367.1	230	1.7	4.6	22	62	2.4	1.1	0	0	Malta
2,273	...	...	...	...	400	—	[34]	—	—	—	—	...	...	Marshall Islands
4,284	7.3	104.6	711.9	101.8	...	—	[5]	—	—	—	—	...	...	Martinique
...	...	...	...	...	710	15.6	7.2	40	22	13.4	4.3	20	0	Mauritania
2,770	2.5	15.1	50.0	...	240	—	—	5	4	0.9	0.2	5	0	Mauritius
...	...	...	...	...	...	—	[5]	—	—	—	—	...	...	Mayotte
108	7.3	30.2	...	...	...	175.0	1.9	875	10	2.3	0.5	20	10	Mexico
...	...	...	...	...	...	—	[34]	—	—	—	—	...	...	Micronesia
...	...	...	...	...	...	9.4	2.2	...	...	...	...	...	...	Moldova
4,614	...	170.2	373.7	140.1	...	—	—	...	...	...	...	...	...	Monaco
...	...	...	...	...	120	21.3	9.4	259	122	...	...	0	0	Mongolia
769	1.5	170.5	...	...	840	195.5	7.4	1,203	48	21.1[11]	5.5	40	0	Morocco
...	...	...	...	...	...	50.0	3.3	107	8	40.7[4]	9.7	120	0	Mozambique
262	4.9	35.5	0.1	50.2	650	286.0	6.4	611	15	24.3[4]	3.7	20	0	Myanmar (Burma)
...	...	...	...	...	...	8.1	5.3	...	...	—	—	...	...	Namibia
...	25.0	400.0	100.0	...	110	—	—	...	...	...	...	...	...	Nauru
29.1	2.2	0.5	0.2	...	1,000	35.0	1.8	33	2	6.2	1.2	0	0	Nepal
7,613	14.8	148.3	2,621.8	181.8	510	74.6	4.9	6,399	431	5.4	2.9	480	140	Netherlands, The

Social protection (continued)

country	social security: programs available, 1991: old-age, invalidity, death[a]	sickness and maternity[b]	work injury[c]	unemployment[d]	family allowances[e]	expenditures, 1990 (% of total central govt.)	finances: year	receipts: total ('000,000 natl. cur.)	insured persons (%)	employers (%)	government (%)	other (%)	expenditures: total ('000,000 natl. cur.)	benefits (%)	administration (%)	other (%)
Netherlands Antilles	●	...	●	●	...	34.8[12]	1990	115.1	100.0	—	—	—	125.5	...	...	...
New Caledonia	...	...	...	...	●	...	1987	15,834.0	...	...	...	...	14,598.0	...	...	...
New Zealand	●	●	●	●	●	31.6[4]	1986	9,645.5	1.6	3.1	92.5	2.9	9,534.5	97.4	2.4	0.2
Nicaragua	●	●	●			3.3[24]	1983	832.9	20.4	53.5	10.4	15.7	427.5	65.5	28.5	6.0
Niger	●		●		●	1.7[13, 24]	1986	12,890.6	12.3	39.2	37.8	10.7	10,032.1	49.0	32.4	18.6
Nigeria	●		●			2.5[37]	1986	108.4	17.9	24.4	—	57.7	17.5	44.7	55.3	—
Northern Mariana Islands	●	...	...	...	...	...	...	...	...	...	...	...	...	...	...	...
Norway	●	●	●	●	●	38.0[13]	1986	157,853.7	17.5	24.6	55.7	2.2	153,249.6	99.0	1.0	—
Oman	...	...	...	...	...	2.4[13]	1990	—	...	...	...	...	38.0[13]	...	...	...
Pakistan	●	●	●			0.2[7]	1986	5,134.8	1.0	10.1	83.6	5.3	4,629.5	98.4	1.2	0.4
Panama	●	●	●			20.1	1986	500.5	30.0	44.9	3.4	21.7	425.9	94.3	5.5	0.2
Papua New Guinea	●		●			0.5[4]	1983	45.0	40.5	32.1	8.0	19.4	9.4	82.3	9.7	8.0
Paraguay	●	●	●			11.7	1988	49,272.0	...	...	...	...	40,588.0	...	...	...
Peru	●	●	●			0.2[8]	1986	7,041,677.0	31.1	68.9	—	—	6,136,672.0	39.5	51.6	8.9
Philippines	●	●	●			1.1	1986	10,705.0	18.6	26.5	—	54.9	4,244.8	86.9	13.1	—
Poland	●	●	●	●	●	...	1986	2,242,443.0	2.6	60.7	35.3	1.4	1,830,162.0	99.2	0.8	—
Portugal	●	●	●	●	●	25.7[4, 13]	1986	494,527.0	24.6	66.0	7.0	2.4	459,353.8	95.4	4.6	—
Puerto Rico	●	●	●	●	●	...	1980	...	...	...	...	...	1,041.3	100.0	—	—
Qatar	...	...	...	...	...	...	1986	80.0	—	—	100.0	—	80.0	100.0	—	—
Réunion	...	...	...	...	...	...	...	...	...	...	...	...	...	...	...	...
Romania	●	●	●	●	●	31.3	1983	72,064.9	—	54.0	46.0	—	63,927.5	100.0	—	—
Russia	●	●	●		●	...	...	...	...	...	...	...	...	...	...	...
Rwanda	●		●			2.9[27]	1986	2,123.8	24.5	41.0	—	34.5	585.9	65.0	35.0	—
St. Kitts and Nevis	●	●	●			9.4[11, 13]	1989	14.3	...	...	...	...	7.9	...	...	...
St. Lucia	●	●	●			...	1986	14.6	28.6	28.6	—	42.8	3.4	61.4	38.6	—
St. Vincent and the Grenadines	●	●	●			2.3[13]	1989	—	...	...	...	...	—	...	...	...
San Marino	●	...	...	●	...	...	1983	51,673.0	12.0	48.7	36.1	3.2	46,179.0	95.7	3.7	0.6
São Tomé and Príncipe	●	●	●			...	1986	46.4	37.7	56.3	—	6.0	23.7	100.0	—	—
Saudi Arabia	●		●			...	...	...	...	...	...	...	...	...	...	...
Senegal	●		●		●	2.6[3, 13]	1986	22,094.0	21.2	69.9	—	8.7	18,827.0	84.8	15.3	—
Seychelles	●	●	●			5.3[16]	1983	69.1	30.1	60.2	—	9.7	42.7	69.6	4.9	25.5
Sierra Leone			●			1.9	1977	10.5	——26.7——		73.3	—	10.0	100.0	—	—
Singapore	●		●			2.1	1986	6,691.0	51.0	23.2	0.1	25.7	5,601.2	71.9	0.4	27.7
Slovakia	...	...	...	...	...	...	...	...	...	...	...	...	...	...	...	...
Slovenia	●	●	●	●	●	...	...	...	...	...	...	...	...	...	...	...
Solomon Islands	●		●			0.6[4]	1986	13.7	27.9	41.8	—	30.3	6.8	40.8	11.5	47.7
Somalia			●			1.7[13, 37]	...	—	...	...	...	...	...	...	...	...
South Africa	●	●	●	●	●	...	1987	976.0	—	100.0	—	—	668.0	...	...	...
Bophuthatswana	...	...	...	...	...	...	...	...	...	...	...	...	...	...	...	...
Ciskei	...	...	...	...	...	...	1984	...	...	...	...	...	21.9	...	...	...
Transkei	...	...	...	...	...	...	...	...	...	...	...	...	...	...	...	...
Venda	...	...	...	...	...	...	...	...	...	...	...	...	...	...	...	...
Spain	●	●	●	●	●	34.7[10]	1986	5,893,481.0	16.4	54.0	27.1	2.5	5,801,152.0	95.0	2.7	2.3
Sri Lanka	●		●			13.2[13]	1986	10,432.8	20.9	24.2	32.2	22.7	4,022.6	98.8	1.1	0.1
Sudan, The	●		●			2.2[27]	1986	42.1	14.3	28.7	—	57.0	8.5	49.4	50.6	—
Suriname	●	...	...	...	●	6.0[7]	1983	125.8	35.8	26.5	36.6	1.1	106.3	98.1	1.9	—
Swaziland	●		●			0.4[13]	1986	10.7	31.4	31.4	—	37.2	3.9	45.8	54.2	—
Sweden	●	●	●	●	●	47.7	1986	318,641.9	1.8	38.5	49.2	10.5	291,962.1	95.9	4.1	—
Switzerland	●	●	●	●	●	49.9[3]	1986	37,602.7	45.1	23.2	26.3	5.4	35,691.2	91.5	2.8	5.7
Syria	●		●			2.0	1989	—	...	...	...	...	1,150.0	...	...	...
Taiwan	●	●	●			13.8	...	...	...	...	...	...	...	...	...	...
Tajikistan	●	●	●		●	...	...	...	...	...	...	...	...	...	...	...
Tanzania	●		●			0.5[14]	1986	1,286.6	26.9	33.7	2.0	37.4	487.7	41.4	55.3	3.3
Thailand			●			3.5	1986	284.8	—	100.0	—	—	246.0	88.8	11.2	—
Togo	●		●		●	6.5[11]	1986	9,588.0	9.3	70.9	—	19.8	4,671.0	70.7	29.3	—
Tonga	...	...	...	...	...	1.0[10]	...	...	...	...	...	...	...	...	...	...
Trinidad and Tobago	●	●	●			5.3[17]	1986	505.4	15.7	31.5	34.9	17.9	383.2	77.1	11.8	11.1
Tunisia	●	●	●	●	●	12.0	1989	325.3	36.9	63.1	—	—	358.3	90.0[16]	6.1[16]	3.9[16]
Turkey	●	●	●			0.6	1986	1,753,294.0	28.2	32.5	15.9	23.4	1,417,940.0	97.1	2.6	0.3
Turkmenistan	●	●	●		●	...	...	...	...	...	...	...	...	...	...	...
Tuvalu	●	...	...	...	...	...	1981	...	...	...	...	...	0.1	67.6	32.4	—
Uganda	●		●			2.1[7]	1986	75.1	44.6	44.6	—	10.8	0.5	100.0	—	—
Ukraine	●	●	●		●	...	1986	16,835.0	—	—	94.7	5.3	16,835.0	100.0	—	—
United Arab Emirates	...	...	...	...	...	3.2[10, 13]	1989	42.0	...	...	...	...	420.0[13]	...	...	...
United Kingdom	●	●	●	●	●	28.3[13]	1986	78,737.0	18.3	23.4	55.1	3.2	76,059.0	95.4	2.9	1.7
United States	●		●	●		20.5	1986	644,464.0	24.5	33.7	30.2	11.6	525,855.0	95.9	3.2	0.9
Uruguay	●	●	●	●	●	50.2[13]	1986	92,849.0	33.3	37.2	24.0	5.4	93,379.0	92.7	6.0	1.3
Uzbekistan	●	●	●		●	...	...	...	...	...	...	...	...	...	...	...
Vanuatu	●					0.9[7]	...	—	...	...	...	...	—	...	...	...
Venezuela	●	●	●	●		6.9[7]	1986	7,457.6	21.3	40.7	12.7	25.3	6,355.7	86.1	14.9	—
Vietnam	●	●	●			...	...	...	...	...	...	...	...	...	...	...
Virgin Islands (U.S.)	●	...	...	●	●	...	...	...	...	...	...	...	...	...	...	...
West Bank	...	...	...	...	...	...	...	...	...	...	...	...	...	...	...	...
Western Sahara	...	...	...	...	...	...	...	...	...	...	...	...	...	...	...	...
Western Samoa	●		●			—	...	—	...	...	...	...	—	...	...	...
Yemen	●	...	...	...	...	—	...	—	...	...	...	...	—	...	...	...
Yugoslavia	●	●	●	●	●	6.0[44]	1986[44]	2,777,651.0	63.3	32.2	3.4	1.1	2,732,679.0	90.3	1.9	7.8
Zaire	●		●		●	0.4[17]	1986	1,238.3	28.6	60.2	—	11.2	1,044.2	27.9	72.1	—
Zambia	●		●			1.5[4]	1986	179.2	28.4	28.4	—	43.2	67.7	40.6	59.4	—
Zimbabwe			●			2.5[11]	1983	167.0	25.9	7.6	64.2	2.3	112.2	93.7	6.2	0.1

[1]Rural areas only. [2]The bulk of the national armed forces disintegrated after the fall of the central government in April 1992, with only the northern corps retaining its integrity. [3]1984. [4]1988. [5]Political dependency; defense is the responsibility of the administering country. [6]Includes civilian militia. [7]1986. [8]1983. [9]Paramilitary unit of a country participating in the U.S.-sponsored Regional Security System, a defense pact among eastern Caribbean states. [10]1989. [11]1987. [12]Netherlands Antilles includes Aruba. [13]Includes welfare. [14]1985. [15]1979. [16]1977. [17]1981. [18]1976. [19]Local officers only. [20]Military defense is the responsibility of France. [21]1971. [22]Republic of Cyprus only. [23]Data refer to former Czechoslovakia, except military manpower, 1993. [24]1980. [25]Ethiopia includes Eritrea. [26]Following the declaration of independence by Eritrea in April 1993, estimated strength of Ethiopian armed forces was some 100,000. [27]1982. [28]Former West Germany. [29]Coverage

crime and law enforcement (latest)						military protection								country
offenses reported to the police per 100,000 population					population per police officer[f]	manpower, 1993[g]		expenditure, 1989				arms trade, 1989 ('000,000 U.S.$)		
total	personal		property			total ('000)	per 1,000 population	total '000,000	per capita	% of central government expenditure	% of GDP or GNP	imports	exports	
	murder	assault	burglary	automobile theft										
5,146[35]	...	317.7	...	...	330	—	[5]	—	—	—	—	...	...	Netherlands Antilles
...	...	...	...	...	...	—	[5]	—	—	—	—	...	...	New Caledonia
13,247	4.1	136.9	2,477.6	1,026.4	630	10.8	3.1	847	258	5.6	2.2	50	0	New Zealand
...	...	...	...	...	90[6]	15.2	3.6	5,225[11]	1,597[14]	26.2[11]	17.2[11]	430	0	Nicaragua
32	0.2	2.5	1.0	0.1	2,350[36]	5.3	6.2	27	3	1.3	7.6	5	0	Niger
312	...	...	...	...	1,140	78.8	0.9	130	1	2.4	0.5	5	20	Nigeria
...	...	...	...	...	...	—	[5]	—	—	—	—	...	...	Northern Mariana Islands
5,563	2.6	44.1	116.4	608.7	660	29.4	6.8	2,925	691	6.9	3.3	340	30	Norway
162	...	...	...	...	430	36.7	21.6	1,552	1,085	41.4	20.3	60	0	Oman
221	5.6	0.1	9.1	4.1	720	577.0	4.5	2,488	22	24.5	6.8	460	20	Pakistan
703	6.1	18.9	...	125.1	180	11.8	4.6	141	59	7.2[4]	3.4	5	0	Panama
750.6	7.9	43.7	96.4	14.4	720	3.8	1.0	48	13	4.0	1.4	40	0	Papua New Guinea
461	10.0	111.6	...	109.1	310	16.5	3.6	61	13	17.6[4]	1.4	0	0	Paraguay
474	12.0	8.9	243.7	...	730	115.0	5.0	2,198[11]	106[11]	24.8[11]	4.9[11]	180	0	Peru
230	30.1	41.8	...	1.2	1,160	106.5	1.6	960	15	12.1	2.2	70	0	Philippines
2,311	2.8	50.5	1,027.7	...	370	287.5	7.5	15,480	410	23.4	8.9	625	400	Poland
805	2.8	6.9	34.5	48.2	660	50.7	5.2	1,457	141	7.5	3.3	60	40	Portugal
5,484	...	...	...	...	380	—	[5]	—	—	—	—	...	...	Puerto Rico
358	3.0	54.7	1.5	7.8	...	9.5	17.6	608[24]	2,638[24]	20.1[11]	9.3[11]	0	0	Qatar
...	...	...	...	...	220	—	[5]	—	—	—	—	...	...	Réunion
276	3.4	3.0	45.7	6.7	...	203.1	8.9	6,916	299	16.9	6.1	20	70	Romania
1,240	10.5	41.3	...	...	...	2,030.0	13.7	...	...	...	...	...	...	Russia
327	6.1	58.9	4.0	...	4,650	5.2	0.7	37[4]	5[4]	10.0[4]	1.6[4]	20	0	Rwanda
15,468	...	...	...	...	300	—[9]	—[9]	...	...	...	...	...	...	St. Kitts and Nevis
4,386	17.0	1,193.0	778.0	...	430	—[9]	—[9]	...	...	...	...	...	...	St. Lucia
3,977	10.3	986.9	...	...	250	—[9]	—[9]	...	...	...	...	...	...	St. Vincent and the Grenadines
...	...	...	...	...	...	—	—	...	...	...	...	...	...	San Marino
558	4.0	...	...	...	400	—	—	1[24]	7[24]	2.5[24]	1.6[24]	5	0	São Tomé and Príncipe
120	0.6	19.2	...	16.9	280	101.0	5.8	14,690	897	38.5	16.0	4,200	5	Saudi Arabia
149	1.0	13.5	5.1	0.3	730	9.7	1.2	90	12	6.3	2.0	5	0	Senegal
4,583	7.4	648.6	1,028.5	...	120	1.1	15.4	8[3]	124[3]	7.4[3]	5.6[3]	...	...	Seychelles
...	...	...	...	...	600	6.2	1.4	6[4]	1[4]	7.0[4]	0.7[4]	0	0	Sierra Leone
1,507	1.5	4.7	126.2	15.9	230	55.5	19.3	1,475	550	18.9	5.1	120	70	Singapore
...	...	...	...	...	...	47.0	8.8	...	...	...	...	...	...	Slovakia
1,930	...	...	...	...	...	15.0	7.5	...	...	...	...	...	...	Slovenia
...	...	...	...	...	620	—	—	...	...	...	...	...	...	Solomon Islands
144	1.5	8.0	31.2	...	540	—[38]	—[38]	43[7]	6[7]	30.0[7]	3.2[7]	30	0	Somalia
...	...	...	...	...	870	67.5	1.6	3,786	98	13.5	4.4	100	0	South Africa
...	...	...	...	...	...	...	...	...	...	...	...	...	...	Bophuthatswana
...	...	...	...	...	...	...	...	...	...	...	...	...	...	Ciskei
...	...	...	...	...	...	...	...	...	...	...	...	...	...	Transkei
...	...	...	...	...	...	...	...	...	...	...	...	...	...	Venda
2,635	2.4	26.2	1,212.0	342.8	580	200.7	5.1	7,775	199	5.7	2.1	750	130	Spain
309	11.6	40.3	57.8	...	860	110.8	6.3	223	13	10.2	3.2	10	0	Sri Lanka
509	30.5	60.3	107.7	6.9	740	72.8	2.9	339	13	11.7[4]	2.2	70	0	Sudan, The
17,819	7.6	1,824.4	...	...	...	1.8	4.4	39	100	7.2	3.0	0	0	Suriname
4,310	87.8	542.0	922.9	...	610	—	—	11	13	5.5	1.7	0	0	Swaziland
14,188	7.0	36.2	1,801.8	879.0	330	64.8	7.4	4,875	574	6.5	2.6	70	575	Sweden
5,275	3.2	50.0	1,076.0	1,504.6[39]	640	1.8	0.3	3,806	568	9.6[4]	2.1	300	600	Switzerland
73	1.6	5.5	27.3	2.2	1,970	408.0	30.5	2,234	186	69.8	11.6	1,000	0	Syria
481	...	...	...	...	720	442.0	21.1	8,060	397	30.3	5.4	430	10	Taiwan
317	2.5	4.6	...	...	...	...	...	...	...	...	...	...	...	Tajikistan
1,250	6.4	0.5	97.3	0.9	1,330	49.5	1.9	110	4	10.0	4.1	40	0	Tanzania
1,449	9.5	21.8	25.0	4.2	530	295.0	5.1	1,843	33	17.7	2.7	240	0	Thailand
11	...	...	...	...	1,970	5.3	1.4	43	12	16.3	3.3	5	0	Togo
1,278	...	...	...	...	330	—	[40]	—	—	—	—	...	...	Tonga
5,335	8.4	164.5	611.3	...	280	2.6	2.0	59	47	4.4	1.6	0	0	Trinidad and Tobago
1,240	2.1	134.0	143.6	11.1	340	35.5	4.2	273	34	7.4	2.8	20	0	Tunisia
134.3	1.7	55.8	...	9.5	1,570	480.0	8.0	3,150	56	17.2	4.1	1,100	0	Turkey
...	...	...	...	...	...	[41]	[41]	...	...	...	...	...	...	Turkmenistan
...	...	...	...	—	290	—	—	...	...	...	...	...	...	Tuvalu
...	...	...	...	...	1,090	60.0	3.4	68[4]	4[4]	20.9[4]	1.5[4]	20	0	Uganda
711	5.4	12.9	...	...	...	438.0	8.4	...	...	...	...	...	...	Ukraine
1,496	1.8	5.4	...	...	140	57.5	28.9	1,471	695	40.7	5.3	850	5	United Arab Emirates
8,986[42]	2.2[42]	353.5[42]	1,991.2[42]	977.4[42]	420	274.8	4.7	34,630	605	12.1	4.2	650	3,000	United Kingdom
5,820	9.4	424.1	1,235.9	657.8	345	1,729.7	6.7	304,100	1,222	25.5	5.8	1,600	11,200	United States
1,027	3.1	70.5	196.9	...	170	24.7	7.8	168[4]	57[4]	12.0[4]	2.2[4]	20	0	Uruguay
420	5.1	15.6	...	...	...	40.0	1.9	...	...	...	...	...	...	Uzbekistan
...	...	...	...	...	450	—	—	...	...	...	...	...	...	Vanuatu
1,158	9.1	155.0	...	155.1	320	75.0	3.6	407	21	5.2	1.0	80	0	Venezuela
...	...	...	...	...	...	857.0	12.2	2,400[7]	39[7]	40.7[7]	19.4[7]	1,300	0	Vietnam
3,798	...	...	...	...	240	—	[5]	—	—	—	—	...	...	Virgin Islands (U.S.)
2,226	...	...	...	...	...	—	—	...	...	...	...	...	...	West Bank
...	...	...	...	...	...	—	[5]	—	—	—	—	...	...	Western Sahara
...	...	...	...	...	...	—	[40]	—	—	—	—	...	...	Western Samoa
...	...	...	...	...	1,940	64.5	5.2	566[4, 43]	84[4, 43]	30.0[4, 43]	9.9[4, 43]	650	0	Yemen
1,135[44]	5.4[44]	35.5[44]	...	...	140[44]	136.5	12.9	2,126[44]	90[44]	53.4[44]	3.6[44]	120[44]	150	Yugoslavia
...	...	...	...	...	910	49.1	1.2	49[4]	1[4]	1.6[4]	0.8[4]	0	0	Zaire
2,088	8.3	17.5	406.8	18.6	540	21.6	2.5	65	8	8.4	1.4	60	0	Zambia
4,276	17.9	192.9	367.5	27.0	750	48.2	4.8	386	38	15.0	6.7	10	0	Zimbabwe

is through tax system. [30]1988–89. [31]Russian-controlled forces on Kazakhstan territory. [32]As a result of civil war, the armed forces of Liberia have ceased to exist. [33]Military defense is the responsibility of Switzerland. [34]Military defense is the responsibility of the United States. [35]Curaçao only. [36]Includes paramilitary forces. [37]1978. [38]Following 1991 revolution, no national armed forces have yet been formed. [39]Includes bicycles and motorcycles. [40]Military defense is the responsibility of New Zealand. [41]Forces under joint Turkmenistan/Russian control. [42]England and Wales. [43]Former Yemen Arab Republic only. [44]Data refer to Yugoslavia as constituted prior to 1991.

Education

This table presents international data on education analyzed to provide maximum comparability among the different educational systems in use among the nations of the world. The principal data are, naturally, numbers of schools, teachers, and students, arranged by four principal levels of education—the first (primary); general second level (secondary); vocational second level; and third level (higher). Whenever possible, data referring to preprimary education programs have been excluded from this compilation. The ratio of students to teachers is calculated for each level. These data are supplemented at each level by a figure for enrollment ratio, an indicator of each country's achieved capability to educate the total number of children potentially educable in the age group usually represented by that level. At the first and second levels this is given as a net enrollment ratio and at the third level as a gross enrollment ratio. Two additional comparative measures are given at the third level: students per 100,000 population and proportion (percentage) of adults age 25 and over who have achieved some level of higher or postsecondary education. Data in this last group are confined as far as possible to those who have completed their educations and are no longer in school. No enrollment ratio is provided for vocational training at the second level because of the great variation worldwide in the academic level at which vocational training takes place, in the need of countries to encourage or direct students into vocational programs (to support national development), and, most particularly, in the age range of students who normally constitute a national vocational system (some will be as young as 14, having just completed a primary cycle; others will be much older).

At each level of education, differences in national statistical practice, in national educational structure, public-private institutional mix, training and deployment of teachers, and timing of cycles of enrollment or completion of particular grades or standards all contribute to the problems of comparability among national educational systems.

Reporting the number of schools in a country is not simply a matter of counting permanent red-brick buildings with classrooms in them. Often the resources of a less developed country are such that temporary or outdoor facilities are all that can be afforded, while in a developed but sparsely settled country students might have to travel 80 km (50 mi) a day to find a classroom with 20 students of the same age, leading to the institution of measures such as traveling teachers, radio or televisual instruction at home under the supervision of parents, or similar systems. According to UNESCO definitions, therefore, a "school" is defined only as "a body of students . . . organized to receive instruction."

Such difficulties also limit the comparability of statistics on numbers of teachers, with the further complications that many at any level must work part-time, or that the institutions in which they work may perform a mixture of functions that do not break down into the tidy categories required by a table of this sort. In certain countries teacher training is confined to higher education, in others as a vocational form of secondary training, and so on. For purposes of this table, teacher training at the secondary level has been treated as vocational education. At the higher level, teacher training is classified as one more specialization in higher education itself.

The number of students may conceal great variation in what each country defines as a particular educational "level." Many countries do, indeed, have a primary system composed of grades 1 through 6 (or 1 through 8)

Education

country	year	first level (primary)					general second level (secondary)					vocational second level[a]	
		schools	teachers[c]	students[d]	student/ teacher ratio	net enroll- ment ratio[b]	schools	teachers[c]	students[d]	student/ teacher ratio	net enroll- ment ratio[b]	schools	teachers[c]
Afghanistan	1989	553	16,756	586,014	35.0	19	819	5,715	271,000	47.4	...	33	556
Albania	1990	1,726	28,796	557,000	19.3	...	47	2,318	68,000	29.3	...	466	7,390
Algeria	1992	13,560	156,937	4,317,018	27.5	88	3,288	127,754	2,171,452	17.0	53	147	6,343
American Samoa	1989	122	461	10,209	22.1	...	7	207	3,097	15.0	...	1	15
Andorra	1991	...	...	...	...	...	12	...	2,303	...	...	6	...
Angola	1990	6,308[5]	32,157[6]	1,041,126	...	66	5,276[5]	5,138	155,257	30.2	10	...	539[7]
Antigua and Barbuda	1992	43	549	10,770	19.6	...	12	353	4,373	12.5	...	1[8]	45[8]
Argentina	1989	21,207	259,579	4,998,963	19.3	...	7,224[9]	262,000[9]	1,862,000[9]	7.1[9]	...	[9]	[9]
Armenia	1992	1,374[11]	54,000[11]	592,000[11]	11.0[11]	...	[11]	[11]	[11]	[11]	...	69	...
Aruba	1990	29	317	6,640	20.9	...	10	166	2,988	18.0	...	16	221
Australia	1991	[13]	95,916[2]	1,786,500	18.4[2]	97	9,980[13]	103,298[2]	1,288,600	12.4[2]	80	234[5, 14]	52,587[5, 14]
Austria	1992	3,389	29,929	380,883	12.7	93	2,045	56,761	431,483	7.6	...	939[2]	18,915[2]
Azerbaijan	1992	4,332[11]	139,000[11]	1,375,000[11]	9.9[11]	...	[11]	[11]	[11]	[11]	...	77	...
Bahamas, The	1991	100[17]	1,409[10]	27,264[17]	20.9[10]	...	37[17]	1,555[10]	23,616[17]	19.1[10]	...	...	...
Bahrain	1992	131[15]	3,673[15]	57,174	16.5[15]	93	35[15]	1,563[15]	27,859	21.2[15]	80	9[15]	707[15]
Bangladesh	1991	48,146	202,847	13,035,000	64.3	65	9,731	110,313	3,662,000	33.2	16	153	1,440
Barbados	1990	104	1,602	29,539	18.4	97	33	1,406	21,259	15.1	80	8[15]	79[15]
Belarus	1990	5,187[11]	123,000[11]	1,489,000[11]	12.1[11]	...	[11]	[11]	[11]	[11]	...	148	...
Belgium	1991	4,584	71,064[6, 15]	744,882	...	99	2,055	114,628[15]	793,599	...	88	397	14,548[15]
Belize	1991	237[20]	1,782[20]	47,146[20]	26.5[20]	...	29	564	7,904	14.0	...	8	...
Benin	1990	2,808	13,180	457,140	34.7	52	151[15]	2,493	72,256	29.0	13	13[15]	687[15]
Bermuda	1990	24	310	5,472	17.7	...	12	331	3,555	10.7	...	[22]	[22]
Bhutan	1990	156	1,757	52,029	29.6	...	31	662	15,984	24.1	...	8	149
Bolivia	1990	12,639[10]	51,763	1,278,775	24.7	79	724[10]	12,434[9]	219,232[9]	17.6[9]	28	47[10]	[9]
Bosnia and Herzegovina	1991	2,205	23,369	539,875	23.1	...	238	9,030	172,063	19.1	...	...	...
Botswana	1991	654	9,708	308,840	31.8	91	169	3,743	68,137	18.2	36	40	759
Brazil	1990	208,934	1,260,501	28,943,619	23.0	88	10,160	243,246	3,198,777	14.4	16	...	...
Brunei	1990	162	2,912	49,611	17.0	...	19	1,713	19,761	11.5	...	6	326
Bulgaria	1993	3,403[11]	72,393[11]	1,027,457[11]	14.2[11]	85	[11]	[11]	[11]	[11]	62	512	18,760
Burkina Faso	1990	2,362	8,572	472,979	55.2	29	113[15]	1,700[15]	82,931	33.7[15]	5	18[5]	341
Burundi	1991	1,342	9,456	633,153	66.9	51	113	2,026	44,207	21.8	3	...	...
Cambodia	1991	4,617	40,821	1,321,573	32.4	...	463	13,105[3]	248,966	24.7[24]	...	13[24]	278[24]
Cameroon	1990	6,549	37,804	1,946,301	51.4	75	388[10]	11,400	366,528	32.2	15	220[10]	6,267
Canada	1993	16,044[11]	298,560[11]	5,285,400[11]	17.7[11]	96	[11]	[11]	[11]	[11]	95	...	...
Cape Verde	1990	367	2,028	67,761	33.4	95	16[10]	238	7,114	29.9	12	3[10]	56[27]
Central African Republic	1991	930	4,004	308,409	77.0	55	46[9]	845[9]	46,989[9]	55.6[9]	...	[9]	[9]
Chad	1990	1,868	7,327	525,165[26]	67.2	38	66[3]	1,422	61,493[26]	38.5	...	25[10]	285[3]
Chile	1989	8,101	55,266	1,987,758	36.0	86	1,694[15]	...	607,709	...	55	1,262[15]	...
China	1991	893,623	6,301,000	143,735,000	22.8	100	85,851	3,090,000	46,835,000	15.2	...	13,497	467,000
Colombia	1991	41,044	143,193	4,310,970	30.1	73	6,134[9, 15]	119,742[9]	2,377,947[9]	19.9[9]	36	[9]	[9]
Comoros	1990	257[15]	1,777[15]	64,737[15]	36.4[15]	55	32[28]	557	14,472	26.0	...	4[28]	41[10]
Congo	1990	1,604	7,704	492,595	63.9	...	238[15]	4,774	165,840	34.7	...	60[15]	1,965[15]
Costa Rica	1990	3,268	13,651	435,205	31.9	87	179	5,808	125,738	21.6	36	77	2,076
Côte d'Ivoire	1992	6,844	39,237	1,447,785	36.9	...	147[29]	9,263[29]	289,510[29]	31.3[29]	...	15	1,947[28]
Croatia	1991	2,074	23,988	434,901	18.1	...	220	12,201	188,305	15.4	...	3	122
Cuba	1990	9,417	71,887	885,500	12.3	95	2,175	108,560	1,073,100	9.9	69	618	30,252
Cyprus[31]	1991	383	3,034	62,962	20.8	100	108[9]	3,735[9]	44,614[9]	11.9[9]	86	[9]	[9]
Czech Republic	1992	4,065	64,072	1,166,000	18.2	...	258	7,050	113,450	16.1	...	507	12,798
Denmark	1992	2,127[32]	59,800[32]	613,329[32]	10.3[32]	...	154[33]	7,500[33]	74,000[33]	9.6[3, 33]	86	204	...
Djibouti	1990	66	707	30,778	43.5	39	32[9]	319[9, 34]	8,912[9]	...	12	[9]	[9]
Dominica	1991	65	439	12,836	29.2	...	9[15]	171[15]	5,030[2]	19.1[15]	...	...	...
Dominican Republic	1990	4,854[34]	21,850[34]	1,032,055[34]	47.2[34]	73	...	9,963[10]	426,962[10]	42.9[10]	...	...	108[10, 35]
Ecuador	1990	16,146[10]	60,608	1,843,819	30.4	...	2,027[9, 10]	36,730[15, 21]	504,481[15, 21]	13.7[15, 21]	...	[9]	16,838[15, 21]
Egypt	1990	14,767[36]	241,119[36]	6,155,100[36]	25.5[36]	...	6,558[36]	155,941[15]	3,123,233[15]	20.0[15]	...	519[37]	72,237
El Salvador	1989	4,160	25,318	1,016,181	40.1	70	468[9]	...	28,370	28.2[9, 15]	15	[9]	...

that passes students on to some kind of postprimary education. But the age of intake, the ability of parents to send their children or to permit them to finish that level, or the need to withdraw the children seasonally for agricultural work all make even a simple enrollment figure difficult to assess in isolation. All of these difficulties are compounded when a country has instruction in more than one language or when its educational establishment is so small that higher, sometimes even secondary, education cannot take place within the country. Enrollment figures in this table may, therefore, include students enrolled outside the country.

Student-teacher ratio, however, usually provides a good measure of the ratio of trained educators to the enrolled educable. In general, at each level of education both students and teachers have been counted on the basis of full-time enrollment or employment, or full-time equivalent when country statistics permit. At the primary and secondary levels, net enrollment ratio is the ratio of the number of children within the usual age group for a particular level who are actually enrolled to the total number of children in that age group (× 100). This ratio is usually less than (occasionally, equal to) 100 and is the most accurate measure of the completeness of enrollment at that particular level. It is not always, however, the best indication of utilization of teaching staff and facilities. Utilization, provided here for higher education only, is best seen in a gross enrollment ratio, which compares total enrollment (of all ages) to the population within the normal age limits for that level. For a country with substantial adult literacy or general educational programs, the difference may be striking: typically, for a less developed country, even one with a good net enrollment ratio of 90 to 95, the gross enrollment ratio may be 20%, 25%, even 30% higher, indicating the heavy use made by the country of facilities and teachers at that level.

Literacy data provided here have been compiled as far as possible from data for the population age 15 and over for the best comparability internationally. Standards as to what constitutes literacy may also differ markedly; sometimes completion of a certain number of years of school is taken to constitute literacy; elsewhere it may mean only the ability to read or write at a minimal level testable by a census taker; in other countries studies have been undertaken to distinguish among degrees of functional literacy. When a country reports an official 100% (or near) literacy rate, it should usually be viewed with caution, as separate studies of "functional" literacy for such a country may indicate 10%, 20%, or even higher rates of inability to read, or write, effectively.

Finally, the data provided for public expenditure on education are complete in that they include all levels of public expenditure (national, state, local) but are incomplete for certain countries in that they do not include data for private expenditure; in some countries this fraction of the educational establishment may be of significant size. Occasionally data for external aid to education may be included in addition to domestic expenditure.

The following notes further define the column headings:

a. Usually includes teacher training at the second level.
b. Latest.
c. Full-time.
d. Full-time; may include students registered in foreign schools.

		third level (higher)							literacy[b]				public expenditure on education (percent of GNP)[b]	country
students[d]	student/ teacher ratio	institutions	teachers[c]	students[d]	student/ teacher ratio	gross enroll- ment ratio[b]	students per 100,000 popula- tion[b]	percent of population age 25 and over with post- secondary education[b]	over age	total (%)	male (%)	female (%)		
8,537	15.4	5	198	1,419	7.5	1.3	115	3.2	15	29.4	44.1	13.9	2.0	Afghanistan
138,000	18.7	8	1,806	27,000	15.0	7.2	680	...	15	100.0	100.0	100.0	...	Albania
127,963	20.2	15[1]	20,562[2]	258,995[2]	12.6[2]	11.8	1,146	0.3	15	57.4	69.8	45.5	9.1	Algeria
139	9.3	2	...	909	...	...	...	12.6	15	95.9	95.6	96.3	8.3	American Samoa
1,455	...	...	...	802[3, 4]	...	...	...	24.9	15	100.0	100.0	100.0	...	Andorra
15,899	...	1[5]	383	6,048	15.8	0.8	65	...	15	41.7	55.6	28.5	7.3	Angola
590[8]	13.1[9]	[8]	[8]	[8]	[8]	...	...	...	15	90.0	...	...	2.5	Antigua and Barbuda
[9]	[9]	1,540[10]	70,000	959,000	13.7	40.8	3,079	6.9	15	95.3	95.5	95.1	1.5	Argentina
40,600	...	14	...	66,100	...	...	...	71.5[12]	...	...	...	...	...	Armenia
2,578	11.7	1	20	180	9.0	...	...	...	15	95.0	...	...	...	Aruba
932,300[3]	...	95[15]	25,916[15]	485,100[2, 16]	16.2[3]	34.5	2,875	21.5	15	99.5	...	...	5.1	Australia
171,164[2]	9.0[2]	88[2]	12,034	212,644	17.7	31.4	2,714	6.0	15	100.0	100.0	100.0	5.4	Austria
60,100	...	18	...	108,000	...	...	...	68.6[12]	...	...	...	...	...	Azerbaijan
...	...	1[18]	300[18]	2,200[18]	7.3[18]	...	...	...	15	95.0	...	...	4.4	Bahamas, The
6,165	10.6[15]	2	561	7,090	12.6	17.5	1,332	3.8	15	77.4	82.1	69.3	5.4	Bahrain
27,891	19.4	997	23,332	767,385	32.9	3.3	310	1.3	15	34.8	45.2	23.7	2.2	Bangladesh
996[15]	12.6[15]	3	153[3]	4,242	8.6[3]	17.3	1,665	3.3	15	98.0[19]	...	...	8.0	Barbados
139,000	...	33	...	184,600	...	...	...	60.2[12]	...	...	...	...	...	Belarus
137,175	...	21	10,517[15]	111,845	...	37.2	2,754	...	...	100.0	100.0	100.0	5.2	Belgium
1,726[21]	...	[8]	[8]	[8]	...	...	...	2.3	15	93.0	...	...	...	Belize
6,879[15]	10.0[15]	13[15]	956	10,873	11.4	2.8	235	...	15	23.4	31.7	15.6	5.1	Benin
[22]	...	1[22]	56[22]	498[22]	8.9[22]	...	...	7.4	15	96.9	96.7	97.0	3.2	Bermuda
1,822	12.2	2	57	519	9.1	0.3	17	...	15	18.0	31.0	9.0	3.7	Bhutan
[9]	[9]	10[10]	3,555[10]	140,890	...	22.8	1,980	6.2	15	77.5	84.7	70.7	2.4	Bolivia
...	...	44	2,801	37,541	13.4	...	...	4.3[23]	10	85.5	96.5	76.7	...	Bosnia and Herzegovina
7,057	9.3	1	370	3,352	9.1	3.0	255	0.9	15	73.6	83.7	65.1	8.1	Botswana
...	...	918	145,585	1,540,080	10.6	11.6	1,064	5.0	15	81.2	81.8	80.6	3.9	Brazil
1,565	4.8	2	214	1,110	5.2	...	...	9.4	15	85.1	90.9	78.7	4.9	Brunei
224,246	11.9	87	21,976	192,270	8.7	31.1	2,092	...	15	95.5	...	...	5.8	Bulgaria
8,055	23.6	2	205	5,675	27.7	0.7	65	3.8	15	18.2	27.9	8.9	2.3	Burkina Faso
...	...	8	436	3,884	8.9	0.7	66	...	15	50.0	60.1	39.8	3.5	Burundi
7,334[24]	26.4[24]	7	180[25]	6,640	13.5[25]	...	...	...	15	48.0	...	...	...	Cambodia
90,633	14.5	5[10]	975[10]	19,586[10]	20.1[10]	3.5	242	...	15	54.1	66.3	42.6	3.3	Cameroon
...	...	270[26]	63,570[26]	856,520[26]	13.5[26]	69.8	5,125	37.4	14	95.6	95.6	95.7	7.4	Canada
752	...	...	...	...	...	—	...	0.5	15	47.4	61.4	38.6	2.9	Cape Verde
[9]	[9]	1[2, 16]	134[2, 16]	2,534[2, 16]	18.9[2, 16]	1.5	118	...	15	37.7	51.8	24.9	2.8	Central African Republic
2,714[26]	15.1[3]	4[10]	141[26]	1,643[26]	11.7[26]	0.8	69	...	15	29.8	42.2	17.9	1.8	Chad
134,301	...	201[15]	15,131[24]	233,148[15]	...	18.8	1,843	7.1	15	93.4	93.5	93.2	2.9	Chile
5,433,000	11.6	1,075	391,000	2,044,000	5.2	1.7	188	1.0	15	77.7	87.0	68.0	2.4	China
[9]	[9]	235[10]	51,725[3]	474,787[3]	9.2[3]	13.7	1,466	...	15	86.7	87.5	85.9	2.9	Colombia
334[10]	14.6[10]	—	32	248	7.8	—	...	0.2	15	46.3	54.2	39.0	6.5	Comoros
20,722[15]	10.5	12[15]	641[15]	10,310[15]	16.1[15]	5.5	470	3.0	15	56.6	70.0	43.9	5.5	Congo
28,593	13.8	4[16]	6,451[16]	57,789[16]	9.0[16]	25.5	2,477	14.2	15	92.8	92.6	93.1	4.6	Costa Rica
3,094	...	1[30]	1,204[1]	19,660[24]	...	2.6	200	...	15	53.8	66.9	40.2	7.0	Côte d'Ivoire
1,839	15.1	54	6,303	66,881	10.6	...	...	6.4[23]	10	98.0	98.9	97.0	...	Croatia
312,000	10.3	35	24,499	242,400	9.9	20.7	2,304	4.2	15	96.0	...	...	6.7	Cuba
[9]	[9]	26[2]	481[2]	6,554	12.2[2]	15.0	935	...	15	94.5	...	...	3.6	Cyprus[31]
191,298	14.9	23	12,762	111,990	8.8	17.7	1,215	5.0	15	100.0	100.0	100.0	4.7	Czech Republic
149,000	...	94[26]	...	126,221[26]	...	31.5	2,466	...	...	100.0	100.0	100.0	7.4	Denmark
[9]	...	—	—	161[24]	—	—	...	...	20	33.7	...	...	2.5	Djibouti
...	...	2[15]	12[3]	68[3]	5.7[3]	...	...	1.7	15	94.4	...	...	5.8	Dominica
3,602[10, 35]	...	7[16]	5,319[16, 26]	86,504[16, 26]	16.3[16, 26]	18.6	1,929	2.3	15	83.3	84.8	81.8	1.5	Dominican Republic
260,850[15, 21]	15.5[15, 21]	21	12,856	206,541	16.1	20.0	1,942	7.6	15	89.8	91.6	88.0	2.7	Ecuador
1,015,809	14.1	12[3, 16]	33,106[16, 36]	656,179[16]	...	19.0	1,698	4.1	15	48.4	62.9	33.8	6.7	Egypt
66,708	[9]	6[2, 16]	2,637[2, 16]	51,277[2, 16]	19.4[2, 16]	17.1	1,564	2.3	15	73.0	76.2	70.0	1.8	El Salvador

Education (continued)

country	year	first level (primary)					general second level (secondary)					vocational second level[a]	
		schools	teachers[c]	students[d]	student/ teacher ratio	net enroll- ment ratio[b]	schools	teachers[c]	students[d]	student/ teacher ratio	net enroll- ment ratio[b]	schools	teachers[c]
Equatorial Guinea	1988	703	1,065	61,009	57.3	...	9	319	9,226	28.9	...	...	...
Eritrea	1990	165[11]	1,782[11]	27,000[11]	15.2[11]	...	[11]	[11]	[11]	[11]	...	...	...
Estonia	1992	690[11]	17,952[2, 11]	223,700[11]	12.7[2, 11]	...	[11]	[11]	[11]	[11]	...	...	...
Ethiopia[38]	1988	8,584[5]	65,993	2,855,846	43.3	28	1,209[5]	21,220	874,000	41.2	...	...	763
Faeroe Islands	1991	67[11]	611[3, 11]	5,440[3]	14.0[3, 11]	...	[11]	[11]	2,979[3]	[11]	...	9[15]	...
Fiji	1990	672[5]	4,272	143,553	33.6	98	140[5]	2,684	52,536	19.6	...	44[5]	369
Finland	1991	4,845[39]	42,601[39]	583,676[39]	13.7[39]	...	464[40]	6,185[40]	101,625[40]	16.4[40]	93	593	...
France	1991	44,131	309,876	4,062,246	13.1	100	11,325[9]	413,304[9]	5,402,300[9]	13.1[9]	83	[9]	[9]
French Guiana	1990	84[15]	...	14,256	...	...	11[15]	...	10,722[9]	...	...	8[15]	...
French Polynesia	1990	278	2,503	44,734	17.9	...	32[9]	1,341[9]	20,159[9]	15.0[9]	...	[9]	[9]
Gabon	1987	992	4,229	195,049	46.1	...	51[7]	1,512	32,922	21.8	...	29[7]	759
Gambia, The	1991	233	2,757	86,101	31.2	53	14	279	6,434	26.1	...	18	477
Gaza Strip	1989	331[11]	4,429[11]	185,410[11]	41.9[11]	...	[11]	[11]	[11]	[11]	...	[11]	[11]
Georgia	1990	3,788[11]	...	924,700[11]	...	...	[11]	...	[11]	...	...	...	...
Germany	1992	42,315[11]	611,338[11]	9,142,565[11]	14.9	89[40]	[11]	[11]	[11]	[11]	85[41]	7,983	100,257
Ghana	1990	9,831	62,859	1,703,074	27.1	...	5,415	45,429	793,388	17.5	...	58	2,317
Gibraltar	1991	21[11]	92[3]	5,308[11]	31.9[3]	...	[11]	124[3]	[11]	...	...	1	29[3]
Greece	1993	7,634[34]	37,549[34]	745,666[34]	19.9[34]	96	2,988	45,794	700,488	15.3	87	695	14,349
Greenland	1990	90[3, 11]	994[11]	7,674	9.1[11]	...	[11]	[11]	1,387	[11]	...	...	...
Grenada	1992	57	763[26]	21,358	26.5[26]	...	18	331[26]	6,834	19.7[26]	...	...	...
Guadeloupe	1991	222	2,069	38,531	18.7	...	86[9]	3,329[9]	51,928[9]	15.6[9]	...	[9]	[9]
Guam	1990	36	850	16,819	19.8	...	24	736	15,733	21.4	...	[42]	176[42]
Guatemala	1990	9,265	36,850	1,270,144	34.5	58	1,877[9]	19,817[9]	291,171[9]	14.7[9]	13	[9]	[9]
Guernsey	1992	22	231	4,469	19.3	...	8	286	3,521	12.3	...	1	228[43]
Guinea	1990	2,442[3]	8,113[3]	310,064[3]	38.2[3]	26	225[15]	4,846	75,674	15.6	7	35[15]	1,130
Guinea-Bissau	1988	632[10]	3,065[10]	79,035	24.6[10]	45	12[5]	824[5]	5,505	7.5[5]	3	4[10]	107
Guyana	1990	423	4,010[3]	118,015[3]	29.4[3]	...	93	...	72,096[3]	...	...	8	176
Haiti	1992	5,625[3]	26,208	1,148,400[2]	47.4[2]	44	...	9,470[9]	184,986[9]	19.5[9]	...	[9]	[9]
Honduras	1991	7,487	25,854	923,902	35.7	91	540	8,517	132,953	15.6	21	5[3]	581[3]
Hong Kong	1993	652	19,346[45]	501,625	26.7[45]	95	494	20,360[45]	461,460	22.5[45]	61	34[2]	2,488[15]
Hungary	1992	3,641	95,300	1,129,300	11.8	90	780	24,017	309,400	12.9	75	317	6,765
Iceland	1992	...	...	25,809	...	...	...	...	29,985	...	...	...	...
India	1991	558,392	1,636,898	99,118,320	60.6	...	219,595	2,331,797	51,381,096	22.0	...	...	...
Indonesia	1991[48]	147,064	1,331,993	26,308,423	19.8	98	28,834	707,987	8,236,018	11.6	38	3,823	108,536
Iran	1991	59,280	339,189	9,369,646	27.6	94	18,445[2]	197,630	4,822,087	24.4	49	1,006[2]	18,643
Iraq	1992	8,875	127,578	3,316,036	26.0	84	2,746	43,937	1,084,715	24.7	39	296	9,957
Ireland	1991	3,437	20,430[49]	543,979	...	88	478	11,550	213,047	18.4	78	350	7,294
Isle of Man	1989	32	240[37]	5,458	...	...	7	276[37]	4,908	...	...	1	...
Israel	1992	1,712	43,461[50]	633,680	16.2	...	781	48,489	437,571	9.0	...	381	...
Italy	1992	22,491	186,397	2,985,398	15.5	...	9,932	109,999	2,154,711	19.6	...	7,952	135,136
Jamaica	1992[34]	788[39]	9,948[39]	389,005[39]	39.1[39]	99	126	8,213	150,966	18.4	59	17	1,018
Japan	1992	24,730	441,000	8,947,000	20.3	100	16,801	567,000	10,256,000	18.1	96	6,679[26]	53,000[26]
Jersey	1990	32	294[10]	5,794	19.2[10]	...	14	372[10]	4,405	12.3[10]	...	1	...
Jordan	1990	2,983	21,073	590,275	28.0	93	622	10,264[3]	357,754	11.5[3]	68	30	2,135
Kazakhstan	1992	8,841[11]	262,600	3,226,400[11]	12.3	...	[11]	[11]	[11]	[11]	...	3,115	...
Kenya	1990	14,691	163,609	5,389,300	32.9	91	2,654	28,056	640,635	22.8	...	24[35]	1,332[3, 35]
Kiribati	1990	104	514	14,709	28.6	...	9	172	2,713	15.8	...	6	75
Korea, North	1987	4,792[5, 11]	...	1,492,000	...	...	[11]	...	2,655,000	...	...	473[5]	...
Korea, South	1992	6,122	138,880	4,560,128	32.8	100	4,274[9]	191,672[9]	4,461,857[9]	23.3[9]	79	[9]	[9]
Kuwait	1992	203[26]	10,310	189,560	18.4	85	315[26]	21,585	270,580	12.5	...	34	617
Kyrgyzstan	1992	1,796	76,000[11]	949,000[11]	12.5[11]	...	1,334	[11]	[11]	[11]	...	48	...
Laos	1990	6,435	19,970	563,734	28.2	69	750	10,048	125,636	12.5	...	139[3]	1,672
Latvia	1992	943[11]	33,712[11]	330,468[11]	9.8[11]	...	[11]	[11]	[11]	[11]	...	57[26]	...
Lebanon	1986	2,130[1]	22,810[1]	399,029	...	...	1,405[1]	21,344[28]	279,849	...	...	181[1]	3,506[7]
Lesotho	1992	1,198	6,685	361,144	54.0	70	179	2,407	46,572	19.3	14	10	227
Liberia	1986	1,651[30]	9,099[30]	80,048	25.0[30]	...	419[30]	1,129[30]	43,273[24]	45.8[30]	...	6[30]	63[30]
Libya	1988	2,744[37]	41,515[7]	974,295	19.0	...	1,555[37]	30,524[7]	389,530	12.2	...	195[37]	3,051[7]
Liechtenstein	1991	14	115	1,892	16.4	...	8	80	1,092	13.6	...	1[3]	74[3]
Lithuania	1993	2,219[11]	43,900[11]	512,411[11]	11.7[11]	...	[11]	[11]	[11]	[11]	...	104	4,638
Luxembourg	1991	...	1,764[2, 34]	26,612[34]	...	85	...	1,922[9, 34]	7,594	...	60	...	[9]
Macau	1991	69	1,088	34,972	32.1	...	21	913	17,601	19.3	...	2	30
Macedonia	1991	1,063	12,987	268,963	20.7	...	90	4,200	74,886	17.8	...	...	...
Madagascar	1990	13,555	37,932	1,512,312	39.9	64	1,142[3]	14,382	331,238	23.0	...	61[15]	1,630
Malaŵi	1990	2,624	20,580	1,325,453	64.4	54	94	1,096	29,326	26.8	2	13	250
Malaysia	1990	6,828	120,025	2,447,206	20.4	...	1,261	69,493	1,335,377	19.2	...	81	3,902
Maldives	1986	243	1,138	41,812	36.7	...	9	291	3,581	12.3	...	10	52
Mali	1991	1,342	7,706	353,694	45.9	19	307	3,061	60,518	19.8	...	...	...
Malta	1991	194	1,455	36,899	25.4	98	43	1,594	25,891	16.2	78	31	710
Marshall Islands	1989	89[5]	538	10,940	20.3	...	7[5]	95	1,862	19.6	...	...	...
Martinique	1989	210	2,004	32,986	16.4	...	75[10]	2,745[9, 10]	31,234	16.5[9, 10]	...	...	[9]
Mauritania	1990	1,214	3,497	155,116	44.4	...	44[5]	1,995	35,758	17.9	...	6[5]	178
Mauritius	1991	279	6,507[2]	129,154	21.1[2]	92	125	3,728[2]	79,327	21.0[2]	...	7	69[1]
Mayotte	1990	88	427	19,078	44.7	...	4	66	2,280	34.5	...	2	17
Mexico	1993	86,636	481,466	14,500,000	30.1	98	25,131	352,865	5,980,000	16.9	44	6,571	77,347
Micronesia	1988	177	1,051[24]	25,139	22.2[24]	...	16	314[24]	5,385	13.2[24]	...	...	...
Moldova	1992	1,654[11]	53,000[11]	725,000[11]	13.6[11]	...	[11]	[11]	[11]	[11]	...	53	...
Monaco	1990	6[10]	735[11]	5,523[11]	7.5[11]	...	3[10]	[11]	[11]	[11]	...	...	...
Mongolia	1991	[13]	[13]	[13]	[13]	94	665[13]	21,900[13]	459,400[13]	21.0[13]	...	44	1,200[3]
Morocco	1991	4,052	87,839	2,483,691	28.3	55	1,080[34]	69,915[34]	1,121,193[34]	16.0[34]	29	562[27]	5,359[27]
Mozambique	1988	3,647[52]	21,410[52]	1,199,669[52]	56.0[52]	41	207[53]	3,422[53]	107,080[53]	31.3[53]	...	32	968
Myanmar (Burma)	1992	36,499	198,909	5,759,700	29.0	...	2,920	67,503	1,316,600	19.5	...	103	2,158
Namibia	1990	1,134[3]	...	313,528	...	64	...	2,534	74,331	29.3	...	9[15]	140[3]
Nauru	1989	3	61	1,367	22.4	...	2	34	629	18.5	...	1	3
Nepal	1991	18,694	74,495	2,884,275	38.7	64	6,124[9]	24,632[9]	773,808[9]	31.4[9]	23	[9]	[9]
Netherlands, The	1992	9,436	99,031[26]	1,518,000	15.7[26]	100	1,189	89,370[26]	673,000	7.7[26]	81	943	18,613[26]

students[d]	student/ teacher ratio	third level (higher): institutions	teachers[c]	students[d]	student/ teacher ratio	gross enroll-ment ratio[b]	students per 100,000 popula-tion[b]	percent of population age 25 and over with post-secondary education[b]	literacy[b]: over age	total (%)	male (%)	female (%)	public expenditure on education (percent of GNP)[b]	country
...	...	5	133	1,542	11.6	6.1	...	1.1	15	62.8	77.8	48.6	1.7	Equatorial Guinea
...	...	...	...	...	...	...	...	...	...	...	...	...	...	Eritrea
23,100[26]	...	10	3,168[26]	25,643	8.2[26]	...	...	...	15	99.7	...	...	...	Estonia
8,243	10.8	11[24]	1,699	31,204	18.4	0.8	70	...	15	4.8	9.3	0.5	4.8	Ethiopia[38]
1,387[15]	...	1	20	100	5.0	...	...	...	15	100.0	100.0	100.0	...	Faeroe Islands
3,290	8.9	5[37]	320[5]	2,211[5]	6.9[5]	4.2	467	3.3	15	87.0	90.0	84.0	5.0	Fiji
164,249	...	20	7,788	110,646	14.2	46.7	3,331	10.9	15	100.0	100.0	100.0	5.8	Finland
[9]	[9]	1,062[3]	53,110	1,698,643	32.0	40.0	3,026	...	...	98.8	98.9	98.7	5.5	France
[9]	...	...	...	...	...	...	...	6.4	16	82.0	82.5	81.3	17.6	French Guiana
[9]	[9]	4[3]	70[3]	701[3]	10.0[3]	...	...	...	15	95.0	94.9	95.0	9.7	French Polynesia
15,352	20.2	1[15, 16]	363[15, 16]	2,896[15, 16]	8.0[15, 16]	4.2	377	...	15	60.7	73.5	48.5	5.7	Gabon
13,966	29.3	9[7]	177[7]	1,489[7]	8.4[7]	—	...	...	15	27.2	39.0	16.0	5.2	Gambia, The
[11]	[11]	1[37]	30[1]	2,387[37]	...	...	...	9.5	...	...	...	...	...	Gaza Strip
...	...	19	...	93,100	...	...	...	72.5[12]	...	...	...	...	...	Georgia
2,448,283	24.4	318	171,025	1,782,739	10.4	33.3[41]	2,810	4.3	15	100.0	100.0	100.0	4.1	Germany
30,221	13.0	3	700	9,274	13.2	1.5	127	3.5	15	60.4	70.0	50.9	3.4	Ghana
772	14.1[5]	—	—	—	—	...	...	...	15	99.0	99.0	99.0	6.0	Gibraltar
290,443	20.2	82[15]	12,760[15]	189,173[15]	14.8[15]	28.9	2,200	7.4	15	93.2	97.6	89.1	2.8	Greece
2,297[3]	...	4	35[10]	200[15]	5.7[10]	...	...	...	15	100.0	100.0	100.0	...	Greenland
...	...	2	91	586	6.4	...	...	1.5	15	85.0	...	...	4.6	Grenada
[9]	[9]	1	...	6,517	...	...	...	5.2	15	90.1	89.7	90.5	14.3	Guadeloupe
1,095[42]	6.2[42]	1	206	2,208	10.7	...	...	34.4	15	96.4	96.4	96.5	8.5	Guam
[9]	[9]	5[3]	4,346[3]	69,532[3]	16.0[3]	8.6	741	3.0	15	60.3	69.7	51.7	1.8	Guatemala
4,952[44]	21.7	—	—	—	—	—	...	...	15	100.0	100.0	100.0	...	Guernsey
10,268	9.1	10[15]	805[16]	6,245[16]	7.8[16]	1.4	122	...	15	24.0	34.9	13.4	1.4	Guinea
825	7.7	...	...	...	...	—	...	...	15	36.5	50.2	24.0	2.8	Guinea-Bissau
5,388	30.6	1[16, 57]	370[16, 45]	2,391[16, 45]	6.5[16, 45]	5.1	587	1.8	15	96.4	97.5	95.4	8.8	Guyana
[9]	[9]	[46]	530[46]	6,475[46]	12.2[46]	1.2	107	0.7	15	53.0	59.1	47.4	1.8	Haiti
47,727	13.7[4]	5	2,740	34,333	12.5	9.1	854	3.3	15	73.1	75.5	70.6	4.6	Honduras
50,782	18.5[15]	12	1,422[15]	68,694	32.4[15]	13.1	1,410	7.1	15	88.1	94.7	80.9	2.7	Hong Kong
204,700	30.2	77	17,477	107,200	6.1	14.5	970	7.0	15	98.9	99.2	98.6	6.1	Hungary
...	...	5[26]	369[26, 47]	5,450[26]	14.0[26, 47]	24.7	2,154	3.7	15	100.0	100.0	100.0	5.4	Iceland
...	...	7,301	...	4,430,000	...	6.7	581	2.5	15	48.2	61.8	33.7	3.2	India
1,352,009	12.5	900[2]	141,094[2]	1,485,894[2]	10.5[2]	8.4	600	1.2	15	77.6	85.6	70.0	0.9	Indonesia
262,745	14.1	44[16]	23,376	312,076	13.4	6.4	566	7.8	15	65.2	73.8	55.8	4.1	Iran
152,903	15.4	20	10,520	197,786	18.8	13.8	1,188	...	15	59.7	69.8	49.3	5.1	Iraq
129,369	17.7	49	3,934[3]	64,098	16.0[3]	26.4	2,308	24.4	15	100.0	100.0	100.0	6.6	Ireland
425[26]	...	...	...	...	...	...	...	...	...	...	...	...	...	Isle of Man
121,601	...	7	6,017[26]	78,640	...	32.8	2,655	23.1	15	91.8	95.0	88.7	6.0	Israel
2,864,885	21.2	82[26]	54,991[26]	1,334,821[26]	24.3[26]	30.7	2,545	4.1	15	97.1	97.8	96.4	5.0	Italy
14,875	14.6	15[3]	1,047[15]	19,173[2]	17.9[15]	4.7	515	2.0	15	98.4	98.2	98.6	5.9	Jamaica
1,242,000[26]	23.4[26]	1,114	150,000	2,817,000	18.8	30.7	2,184	31.7	15	100.0	100.0	100.0	4.7	Japan
283[10]	...	...	...	...	...	...	...	...	15	100.0	100.0	100.0	4.1	Jersey
26,525	12.4	55[3]	3,435	69,389	20.2	26.6	2,006	...	15	80.1	89.3	70.3	4.4	Jordan
1,091,600	...	61	...	288,000	...	...	...	64.0[12]	...	...	...	...	...	Kazakhstan
14,456[35]	13.4[3, 35]	15	...	29,231	...	1.6	135	1.3	15	59.2	69.6	49.2	6.4	Kenya
290	3.9	—	—	54	—	—	...	...	15	90.0	...	...	5.9	Kiribati
220,000	...	281[5]	9,244[1]	301,000	...	...	...	...	15	99.0	...	...	3.7	Korea, North
[9]	[9]	592	46,524	1,588,246	34.1	40.5	3,953	14.2	15	96.3	99.1	93.5	3.6	Korea, South
2,872	4.7	1[3]	1,181[3]	17,988[3]	15.2[3]	17.9	1,384	11.1	15	73.0	77.1	66.7	5.0	Kuwait
42,700	...	12	...	58,000	...	...	...	30.0	...	...	...	...	...	Kyrgyzstan
12,262	7.3	9	698	4,730	6.8	1.4	118	...	15	83.9	92.0	75.8	1.0	Laos
38,100[26]	...	14	...	46,279	...	...	...	...	15	98.0	...	...	...	Latvia
30,407	10.6[7]	18[1]	7,460[7]	70,510[7]	9.5[7]	27.7	2,634	...	15	80.1	87.8	73.1	...	Lebanon
2,167	9.5	1	204	1,421	7.0	4.8	406	0.6	15	73.6	62.4	84.5	4.0	Lesotho
2,322[30]	36.9[30]	3[30]	470[10]	5,095[10]	...	2.5	220	...	15	39.5	49.8	28.8	5.7	Liberia
70,335	10.0	6	1,340[30]	40,365	...	10.1	792	...	15	63.8	75.4	50.4	9.6	Libya
147[3]	...	—	—	—	—	—	...	11.2	15	100.0	100.0	100.0	...	Liechtenstein
42,000	9.1	17	9,003[15]	55,000	7.3[15]	...	...	...	...	...	...	...	...	Lithuania
11,430	...	...	...	4,957	...	3.1	245	...	15	100.0	100.0	100.0	4.4	Luxembourg
388	12.9	9	478	7,037	14.7	...	...	15.9	10	61.3	76.4	46.2	...	Macau
...	...	27	2,101	26,413	12.6	...	...	5.1	10	89.1	94.2	83.8	...	Macedonia
17,674	10.8	3	960	37,046	38.6	3.4	298	...	15	80.2	87.7	72.9	1.9	Madagascar
3,679	14.7	4	235	2,685	11.4	0.7	61	0.2	15	41.6	...	...	3.5	Malaŵi
39,187	10.0	43[3]	10,697[3]	108,845[3]	10.2[3]	7.2	671	1.9	15	78.4	86.5	70.4	5.5	Malaysia
462	8.9	—	—	—	—	—	...	0.4	15	90.4	90.6	90.1	6.9	Maldives
...	...	7	675	5,536[10]	...	0.8	86	0.2	15	32.0	40.8	23.9	3.3	Mali
6,653	9.4	1[2]	244[2]	2,511[2]	10.3[2]	10.5	485	3.9	15	96.0	96.2	95.9	3.8	Malta
...	...	...	...	...	...	...	...	11.4	25	91.2	92.4	90.0	...	Marshall Islands
8,035	[9]	1	40[10]	2,743	30.5[9]	...	...	6.3	15	92.5	91.8	93.2	15.3	Martinique
1,516	8.8	7	270	5,810	21.5	3.6	303	...	15	34.0	47.1	21.4	4.9	Mauritania
587	...	2	382[3]	2,199	5.7[3]	2.1	207	3.6	15	81.8[51]	89.0[51]	74.8[51]	3.5	Mauritius
392	23.1	—	—	—	—	—	...	...	15	31.8	...	...	...	Mayotte
1,076,700	13.9	1,832	128,212	1,256,100	9.8	14.3	1,480	5.3	15	87.3	89.5	85.1	4.1	Mexico
...	...	...	...	920[10]	...	...	...	8.0	15	76.7	67.0	87.2	...	Micronesia
47,200	...	11	...	52,200	...	...	...	55.1[12]	...	...	...	...	...	Moldova
1,218[1]	...	...	...	...	...	...	...	6.8	...	...	...	...	...	Monaco
29,100	17.7[3]	8	1,465	13,829	9.4	21.8	2,297	8.1	10	97.9	...	...	7.0	Mongolia
68,802[27]	12.8[27]	35	7,713	225,001	29.2	10.2	958	0.6	15	49.5	61.3	38.0	7.4	Morocco
10,604	10.9	2	457	2,562	5.6	0.2	16	0.2	15	32.9	45.1	21.3	1.2	Mozambique
26,600	12.3	36	6,416	260,200	40.6	5.4	459	0.1	15	78.5	85.8	71.6	1.9	Myanmar (Burma)
1,666[3]	11.9[3]	...	213[26]	2,507[26]	11.8[26]	...	...	2.0	15	72.5	74.2	70.8	1.6	Namibia
30	10.0	1[54]	...	c. 200[54]	...	...	...	...	15	99.0	...	...	...	Nauru
[9]	[9]	3	4,694[3]	154,528	21.8[3]	6.5	562	6.8	15	37.7	51.7	23.3	2.9	Nepal
505,000	28.0[26]	318	30,952[5]	378,000	...	34.3	2,946	7.2	15	100.0	100.0	100.0	6.5	Netherlands, The

Education (continued)

country	year	first level (primary)					general second level (secondary)					vocational second level[a]	
		schools	teachers[c]	students[d]	student/ teacher ratio	net enroll-ment ratio[b]	schools	teachers[c]	students[d]	student/ teacher ratio	net enroll-ment ratio[b]	schools	teachers[c]
Netherlands Antilles	1989	85[10]	1,231[10]	21,778	17.9[10]	...	23[10]	664[10]	8,698	14.2[10]	...	36[10]	50[5]
New Caledonia	1990	279	1,696	34,242	20.2	...	44	1,685[9]	14,237	12.5[9]	...	29	[9]
New Zealand	1991	2,491[55]	22,186[55]	418,698[55]	18.9	100	337	15,586	230,210	14.8	88	29	4,498[2]
Nicaragua	1991	4,535[6]	20,141[6]	674,045[6]	33.5[6]	75	427[9]	4,188[2, 9]	179,998[9]	...	23	[9]	[9]
Niger	1989	2,097	7,915	317,840	40.1	25	105	2,443	63,379	25.9	6	7	226
Nigeria	1991	35,446	353,600	13,776,854	38.9	...	5,594[15]	141,491	3,123,277	22.1	...	376[15]	15,738[3]
Northern Mariana Islands	1989	18	240	4,882	20.3	...	9[9]	163[9]	2,075[9]	12.7[9]	...	[9]	[9]
Norway	1992	3,389	33,961[26]	467,502	14.0[26]	98	831[9]	20,647[9, 26]	243,558[9]	11.5[9, 26]	85	[9]	[9]
Oman	1990	671	12,344	304,207	24.6	84	128	2,219	36,617	16.5	42	25	728
Pakistan	1991	127,575	218,300	8,856,000	40.6	...	13,604	184,200	3,397,000	18.4	...	930	8,722
Panama	1991	2,683	13,596	349,858	25.7	92	345[9]	9,929[9]	198,138[9]	20.0[9]	48	[9]	[9]
Papua New Guinea	1989	2,692	13,171	417,818	31.7	73	122[5]	2,306	57,676	25.0	...	112[5]	751
Paraguay	1991	4,602	27,490	687,331	25.0	95	...	...	...	...	25	...	9,444[15]
Peru	1991	28,860[2]	138,455	4,053,801	29.3	95	6,462[2]	96,969	1,996,181	20.6	42	1,524[2]	11,289
Philippines	1990	34,382	315,585	10,284,861	32.6	99	5,523	118,805	3,961,639	33.3	54	945	15,386
Poland	1992	18,578	321,500	5,302,700	16.5	98	1,565	26,600	548,800	20.6	76	8,826	89,500
Portugal	1993	11,771	71,788	925,936	12.9	99	1,368	64,479	815,491	12.6	...	220	...
Puerto Rico	1989[34]	1,145	33,357[11]	661,693[11]	19.8[11]	...	315	[11]	[11]	[11]	...	52[5]	...
Qatar	1991[34]	155	2,843	53,050	18.7	87	34	1,015	9,669	9.5	74	3	102
Réunion	1992	360	...	72,744	...	...	95[9]	...	87,834[9, 20]	...	...	[9]	...
Romania	1992	13,985	159,199	2,639,279	16.6	...	1,209	55,013	778,420	14.2	...	1,101	6,619
Russia	1992	69,900[11]	1,516,000[11]	20,936,000[11]	13.8[11]	...	[11]	[11]	[11]	[11]	...	2,605	...
Rwanda	1992	1,724	18,937	1,104,903	58.3	65	192[9]	4,054[9]	62,701[9]	15.5[9]	7	[9]	[9]
St. Kitts and Nevis	1992	31	342	6,978	20.4	...	7	298	4,645	15.6	...	[2]	[35]
St. Lucia	1990	83	1,112	32,636	29.3	...	13	376	6,771	18.0	...	1[8]	...
St. Vincent and the Grenadines	1992	60	1,215	24,134	19.9	...	21	408	7,124	17.5	...	2	...
San Marino	1992	14	218	1,200	5.5	...	3	129	841	6.5	...	...	...
São Tomé and Príncipe	1989	64	559	19,822	35.5	...	11[7]	318	7,446	23.4	...	2[7]	18[57]
Saudi Arabia	1989	8,631	105,937	1,694,394	16.0	62	4,153	52,818	739,088	14.0	33	32[15]	3,295[15]
Senegal	1991	2,458	13,394	708,299	52.9	48	321	4,791[3]	173,490	34.8[3]	13	13	259[3]
Seychelles	1993	25[15]	685	12,851	18.8	...	4[5]	553	7,337	13.3	...	1[5]	190
Sierra Leone	1990	1,795	10,850	367,426	33.9	...	232[3]	5,544	97,049	17.5	...	16[5]	475[5]
Singapore	1991	202	9,843	260,286	26.4	100	186	9,200	185,713	20.2	...	23	1,586
Slovakia	1992	2,415	37,812	716,416	18.9	...	147	3,875	59,347	15.3	...	204	6,343
Slovenia	1991	822	12,402	226,463	18.3	...	145	6,633	94,062	14.2	...	...	...
Solomon Islands	1991	520	2,388	60,259	25.2	...	23[9]	364[9]	6,363[9]	17.5[9]	...	[9]	[9]
Somalia	1987	1,125	8,208	171,830	20.9	11	82	2,109	42,764	20.3	4	21	498
South Africa	1991	20,348[2, 11]	256,256[11]	7,945,386[11]	31.0[11]	...	[11]	[11]	[11]	[11]	...	214[2]	9,922[2]
Bophuthatswana	1986	1,293	10,153[34]	498,585	35.1[34]	...	1,282[34]	16,178[34]	553,848[34]	34.2[34]	...	8[34]	261[34, 35]
Ciskei	1987	545	4,369	200,752	45.9	...	158	1,809	59,414	32.8	...	1	20
Transkei	1987	1,387	12,617	778,825	61.7	...	1,754	10,245	217,842	21.3	...	17[59]	349[59]
Venda	1986	400	4,039	139,822	34.6	...	155	2,081	51,078	24.5	...	1	42
Spain	1990	19,821	135,747	2,961,955	21.8	100	22,633[3]	200,633[3]	3,611,860[3]	18.3[3]	74	2,668[3]	63,236[3]
Sri Lanka	1991	9,527[34]	67,019[34]	2,081,104[34]	31.1[34]	100	9,044	106,792	2,105,959	19.7	...	23	437
Sudan, The	1992	8,501	64,227	2,079,649	32.4	...	5,578[9]	20,024[9]	446,898[9]	22.3[9]	...	[9]	[9]
Suriname	1992	301	2,918	63,083	21.6	100	89	1,684	26,708	15.8	44	64[7]	1,283[7]
Swaziland	1991	523	5,015	183,738	36.6	82	153	2,149	50,676	23.6	...	8	280
Sweden	1993	4,745	93,950	887,323	9.4	100	600[9]	29,585[9]	306,165[9]	10.4[9]	86	[9]	[9]
Switzerland	1992	...	...	414,129	...	...	...	...	393,047	...	...	...	...
Syria	1990	9,524	90,272	2,357,981	26.1	98	2,077	42,623	856,942	20.1	45	238	8,920
Taiwan	1992	2,495	84,304	2,293,444	27.2	...	883	69,206	1,394,463	20.2	...	212	18,000
Tajikistan	1992	3,179[11]	99,000[11]	1,310,000[11]	13.2[11]	...	[11]	[11]	[11]	[11]	...	...	...
Tanzania	1990	10,417[61]	96,850[61]	3,379,000[61]	34.9[61]	47	288[10]	7,863[3]	145,748[3]	18.5[3]	...	63[10]	1,015[3]
Thailand	1989	32,858	365,246	6,496,758	17.8	...	1,437[30]	107,033	1,836,610	17.2	...	1,528[30]	23,525
Togo	1988	2,429[3]	10,426[3]	569,388[3]	54.6[3]	72	358[24]	4,003[10]	103,835	27.1[10]	...	18[10]	357
Tonga	1990	115	689	16,522	24.0	...	57[10]	767	13,877	18.1	...	9	65
Trinidad and Tobago	1991	476	7,473	193,922	25.9	90	100[3]	4,856	96,599	19.9	71	...	...
Tunisia	1992	3,940	51,948	1,426,215	27.5	95	599	25,445	589,674	23.2	23	...	237[15, 35]
Turkey	1991	51,055	225,852	6,861,711	30.4	99	7,185[2]	109,136	2,897,655	26.6	48	2,542[2]	50,265
Turkmenistan	1992	1,791[11]	60,000[11]	842,000[11]	14.0[11]	...	[11]	[11]	[11]	[11]	...	41	...
Tuvalu	1990	11[10]	72	1,485	20.6	100	1[10]	21	314	15.0	...	...	10
Uganda	1989	7,905	75,561	2,632,764	34.8	53	774	13,356	240,334	18.0	...	136	2,081
Ukraine	1992	21,904[11]	543,000[11]	7,102,000[11]	13.1[11]	...	[11]	[11]	[11]	[11]	...	754	...
United Arab Emirates	1990	354[11, 15]	11,921	215,532	18.1	100	[11]	7,614[9]	94,979	12.6	59	9[5]	[9]
United Kingdom	1991[34]	24,135	219,200	4,812,300	21.9	100	4,790	229,100	3,473,300	15.2	78	724[15, 62]	93,000[7, 62]
United States	1991	61,340[34, 55]	1,680,000	33,978,000	20.2	99	20,406[9, 34]	1,072[9]	12,472,000[9]	11.6[9]	81	[9]	[9]
Uruguay	1989	2,735	19,391	359,455	18.5	88	293	13,571[14, 15]	196,851	...	...	95[15]	...
Uzbekistan	1992	...	384,000[11]	4,721,400[11]	13.0[11]	...	...	[11]	[11]	[11]	...	243	...
Vanuatu	1991	267	869	24,952	28.7	...	21[21]	208	3,799	18.3	...	...	...
Venezuela	1991	15,445	199,104	4,052,947	20.4	61	1,517[9]	30,844[9, 15]	281,419[9]	9.1[9]	20	[9]	[9]
Vietnam	1989	14,424[11]	443,000[11]	12,204,000[11]	27.5[11]	91	[11]	[11]	[11]	[11]	...	277	10,700
Virgin Islands (U.S.)	1989[63]	41[10]	965	12,263	12.7	...	10[10]	799	9,741	12.2	...	3[5]	27[5]
West Bank[64]	1990	410	5,458[3]	198,740	34.2[3]	...	...	5,892[10]	108,610	20.1[10]	...	...	170
Western Sahara	1989[34]	27	596	14,794	24.8	...	18	577	9,218	16.0	...	...	...
Western Samoa	1987	164[37]	1,511[65]	40,755	27.0	...	38[1]	492	11,395	23.2	...	4[37]	37
Yemen[66]	1991	7,313[3]	35,350	1,291,372	36.5	...	942[5]	12,106	394,578	32.6	...	73[5]	1,247
Yugoslavia	1992	4,442	51,393	936,469	18.2	79[67]	538	24,977	347,916	13.9	76[67]	...	...
Zaire	1988	10,817	113,468[10]	4,356,416	36.6[10]	60	4,276[9]	49,153[9]	507,944	21.7[9]	17	27	27
Zambia	1989	3,489	32,348[15]	1,446,847	44.1[15]	80	480	5,786[15]	161,349[15]	27.9[15]	15	26	846
Zimbabwe	1992	4,567	60,834	2,306,089	37.9	100	1,518	23,233	657,344	28.3	...	25	1,479

[1]1982. [2]1990. [3]1989. [4]Students registered abroad. [5]1986. [6]Includes preschool. [7]1985. [8]Vocational second level includes third level. [9]General second level includes vocational second level. [10]1987. [11]First level includes second level. [12]Percentage having completed secondary or more. [13]General second level includes first. [14]Includes special education. [15]1988. [16]Universities only. [17]Data exclude 86 combined primary/secondary schools with 12,286 students. [18]College of the Bahamas only. [19]National literacy standard based solely on school attendance. [20]1993. [21]General second level includes teacher training at second level. [22]Third level includes vocational second level. [23]Age 15 and over. [24]1984. [25]University of Phnom Penh only. [26]1991. [27]Excludes teacher training. [28]1981. [29]Data do not include 208 private schools with 107,096 students. [30]1980. [31]Republic of Cyprus only. [32]Includes preschool, primary, and lower secondary (to age 15). [33]Upper-second level only (ages 16–18). [34]Public schools only. [35]Teacher training only. [36]Data exclude 1,147 primary and 1,057 secondary schools, as well as the university, in the al-Azhar education system. [37]1983. [38]Data include Eritrea. [39]Includes lower-secondary students at all-age schools. [40]Excludes lower-secondary students. [41]Former West Germany only. [42]Postsecondary

		third level (higher)							literacy[b]				public expenditure on education (percent of GNP)[b]	country
students[d]	student/ teacher ratio	institutions	teachers[c]	students[d]	student/ teacher ratio	gross enroll- ment ratio[b]	students per 100,000 popula- tion[b]	percent of population age 25 and over with post- secondary education[b]	over age	total (%)	male (%)	female (%)		
6,526	13.0[5]	2[5]	80[5]	578	8.8[5]	...	...	6.4	15	95.0	...	...	2.8	Netherlands Antilles
6,765	[9]	6	141[3]	1,207	9.9[3]	...	...	...	15	57.9	57.4	58.3	13.4	New Caledonia
77,142	12.6[2]	7[16]	3,761[2, 16]	87,973[16]	21.0[2, 16]	40.7	3,591	6.9	15	100.0	100.0	100.0	7.9	New Zealand
[9]	[9]	10	3,469	34,846	10.0	8.4	768	...	15	74.0	...	...	2.6	Nicaragua
2,437	10.8	3[15]	341[56]	4,506[15]	11.1[56]	0.7	60	0.2	15	10.8	16.7	5.4	3.1	Niger
391,583[3]	24.9[3]	...	19,601[3]	307,207[3]	15.7[3]	3.3	282	...	15	42.4	53.8	31.5	1.7	Nigeria
[9]	[9]	1	102	1,097	10.8	...	...	21.9	15	96.3	96.9	95.6	...	Northern Mariana Islands
[9]	[9]	211	7,556[26]	148,865	18.3[26]	42.5	3,384	18.8	15	100.0	100.0	100.0	7.9	Norway
5,596	7.7	5	482	3,925	8.1	5.4	397	...	6	41.0	58.0	24.0	3.7	Oman
108,000	12.4	733	26,050	658,900	25.3	2.8	258	1.9	15	25.6	36.0	15.2	3.4	Pakistan
[9]	[9]	9	3,390	58,625	17.3	21.0	2,114	8.4	15	88.1	88.1	88.2	5.7	Panama
9,331	12.4	2[5]	902	6,397	7.1	1.7	146	...	15	52.0	64.9	37.8	4.7	Papua New Guinea
153,206	17.4[15]	2	2,694[7]	32,884	...	8.3	769	3.4	15	90.1	92.1	88.1	1.0	Paraguay
312,669	27.7	493[2]	44,361	751,234	16.9	35.6	3,450	4.8	15	89.3	95.9	82.6	3.5	Peru
291,600	19.0	810	70,012[15]	1,225,315	22.6[15]	26.5	2,490	15.2	15	88.7	89.9	87.5	3.0	Philippines
1,677,000[26]	18.8[26]	117	63,200	423,500	6.7	21.8	1,418	6.5	15	98.7	99.2	98.3	4.9	Poland
84,932	...	250	30,998	214,403	6.9	18.4	1,525	0.3	15	86.8	86.7	86.9	4.9	Portugal
149,191[5]	...	45	9,045	156,818	17.3	48.1	4,091	18.4	15	89.1	89.7	88.5	8.2	Puerto Rico
877	8.6	1[45]	561[45]	6,548[45]	11.7[45]	24.0	1,848	13.3	15	75.7	76.8	72.5	3.4	Qatar
[9]	...	1[16]	183[16]	6,300[16]	34.4[16]	...	...	4.3	15	78.2	75.9	80.3	15.6	Réunion
430,210	65.0	48	17,615	215,226	12.2	8.6	712	4.6	15	95.8	...	...	3.1	Romania
2,201,000	...	519	...	1,668,000	...	...	...	...	...	...	...	...	7.9	Russia
[9]	[9]	3[7]	646[2]	3,454	5.2[2]	0.6	48	...	15	50.4	49.8	50.9	4.2	Rwanda
189	5.4	1	3	36	12.0	...	...	2.1	15	98.0	...	...	3.0	St. Kitts and Nevis
763[8]	...	[8]	...	[8]	...	...	...	1.3	15	80.0	...	...	7.2	St. Lucia
337	...	...	...	...	...	...	...	1.4	15	85.0	...	...	6.9	St. Vincent and the Grenadines
317	...	...	...	332[4, 10]	...	...	...	...	15	98.0	98.2	97.7	...	San Marino
289	...	...	...	700[4, 37]	...	...	...	0.3	15	54.2	70.2	39.1	4.3	São Tomé and Príncipe
31,354[15]	9.5[15]	82	9,631	115,006	11.9	13.8	1,089	...	15	62.4	73.1	48.1	5.8	Saudi Arabia
6,435	24.6[3]	18	770[16]	18,862	19.3[16]	3.0	253	0.8	15	28.6	38.8	19.4	3.7	Senegal
1,682	8.9	...	...	...	...	...	...	3.1	15	84.2	82.9	85.7	9.1	Seychelles
6,086[5]	12.8[5]	2	600	4,752	7.9	1.3	114	...	15	20.7	30.7	11.3	1.4	Sierra Leone
28,871	18.2	6	4,959	60,373	12.2	7.9	963	3.4	10	90.7	95.7	85.6	3.4	Singapore
99,751	15.7	13	7,873	61,272	7.8	...	...	...	15	100.0	100.0	100.0	...	Slovakia
...	...	28	2,555	33,574	13.1	...	...	5.9[23]	10	99.2	99.3	99.1	...	Slovenia
[9]	[9]	—	—	—	—	...	...	2.6	15	54.1	62.4	44.9	4.7	Solomon Islands
4,809	9.7	1	262[28]	1,692	...	3.0	57	...	10	54.8	60.9	47.9	0.4	Somalia
205,682[2]	20.7[2]	17[16]	31,783	308,297	9.7	...	...	2.3	15	76.4	77.8	75.1	3.8	South Africa
4,939[34]	13.0[34, 35]	1	187	3,282	17.6	...	...	...	15	75.0	...	...	...	Bophuthatswana
174	8.7	3[58]	97[58]	1,677[58]	17.3[58]	...	...	...	15	72.0	...	...	...	Ciskei
6,363[59]	18.2[59]	1	203	3,988	19.6	...	...	...	...	...	...	...	...	Transkei
422	10.0	5	119[24]	5,135	24.0[24]	...	...	...	...	...	...	...	...	Venda
1,234,045[3]	19.5[3]	789[3]	59,135	1,169,141	19.8	33.5	2,981	7.1	15	94.7	97.0	92.5	4.8	Spain
8,908	20.4	8	1,937	31,447	16.2	4.2	400	1.1	15	84.3	88.3	80.1	2.7	Sri Lanka
[9]	[9]	24	1,943	54,345	28.0	2.9	246	...	15	27.1	42.7	11.7	4.0	Sudan, The
15,996[7]	12.5[7]	1[2]	...	2,164[2]	...	9.1	1,025	...	15	94.9	95.1	94.7	9.7	Suriname
772	2.8	1	146	1,705	11.7	5.1	430	...	15	67.0	69.0	65.0	7.2	Swaziland
[9]	[9]	...	27,523[2, 60]	272,718[2]	9.9[2]	32.8	2,281	15.4	15	100.0	100.0	100.0	7.8	Sweden
207,410	...	...	...	143,192	...	27.6	2,118	...	15	100.0	100.0	100.0	4.8	Switzerland
56,094	6.3	44	4,605[10]	203,979	...	19.9	1,737	1.3	15	79.9	89.7	69.3	4.4	Syria
475,852	26.4	123	29,444	612,376	20.8	...	2,225	6.0	15	92.8	96.8	88.2	3.6	Taiwan
...	...	13	...	69,300	...	...	...	62.6[12]	...	...	...	...	...	Tajikistan
13,263[3]	13.1[3]	4[3]	1,206[3]	5,254[3]	4.4[3]	0.2	20	...	15	85.0	...	...	5.8	Tanzania
381,139	16.2	43	52,317	952,012	18.2	16.1	1,734	2.9	15	88.8	93.2	84.5	3.8	Thailand
5,956	16.7	1[16]	276[16]	7,732[16]	26.6[16]	2.6	226	1.3	15	39.1	51.7	27.5	5.2	Togo
872	13.4	1[5]	17[7]	705[7]	41.5[7]	—	...	0.1	15	92.8	92.9	92.8	4.2	Tonga
731	...	1[45]	471[45]	4,541[45]	9.6[45]	6.0	563	2.9	15	96.1	...	...	4.1	Trinidad and Tobago
3,839[15, 35]	16.2	...	3,901[3]	76,097	14.0[3]	8.5	838	3.4	15	65.3	74.2	56.3	6.0	Tunisia
910,487	18.1	387[2]	34,469	749,921	21.8	13.7	1,342	3.9	15	80.7	89.7	71.1	1.8	Turkey
33,700	...	9	...	41,700	...	...	...	65.1[12]	...	...	...	...	...	Turkmenistan
31	3.1	—	—	—	—	—	...	...	15	95.5	95.5	95.5	...	Tuvalu
23,179	11.1	9	934[24]	5,778	8.8[24]	1.0	82	0.1	15	48.3	62.2	34.9	3.4	Uganda
739,200	...	156	...	876,200	...	...	...	29.9	...	...	...	...	...	Ukraine
690	[9]	1[3]	478[3]	7,655[3]	16.0[3]	10.8	642	...	15	73.0	74.5	68.4	1.9	United Arab Emirates
539,718[15, 62]	...	48[16]	49,377[16]	370,254[16]	7.5[16]	25.2	2,063	11.0	15	100.0	100.0	100.0	4.7	United Kingdom
[9]	[9]	3,559	824,000	13,710,000	16.6	74.5	5,608	32.2	15	95.5	95.7	95.3	5.3	United States
56,084	...	2	5,925[15]	63,777	10.5[15]	50.4	3,751	14.8	15	95.0	94.5	95.4	3.3	Uruguay
254,400	...	52	...	337,400	...	...	...	66.9[12]	...	...	...	...	...	Uzbekistan
261	...	1	...	124	...	—	...	...	15	52.9	57.3	47.8	4.4	Vanuatu
[9]	[9]	99	46,137	550,030	11.9	29.1	2,782	7.0	15	92.2	93.5	91.1	4.1	Venezuela
130,000	12.1	103	19,900	122,000	6.1	2.3	214	6.8	15	87.6	93.0	82.8	3.0	Vietnam
775[5]	28.7[5]	1[10]	97[10]	757[10]	8.3[10]	...	...	17.6	15	90.0	...	...	7.5	Virgin Islands (U.S.)
1,595	9.4	4[37]	988[3]	14,434[3]	14.6	...	8.1		...	...	...	...	...	West Bank[64]
...	...	...	...	...	...	...	...	...	...	...	...	...	...	Western Sahara
228	6.2	6[37]	37[37]	562[37]	15.2[37]	...	...	2.0	15	100.0	100.0	100.0	5.9	Western Samoa
26,119	20.9	1[3]	470[3]	23,457[3]	49.9[3]	2.9	274	...	15	38.5	53.3	26.3	6.1	Yemen[66]
...	...	145	11,629	132,814	11.4	18.2[67]	1,374[67]	5.7[23]	10	89.2	95.4	83.2	6.1	Yugoslavia
558,407	[9]	...	3,506	52,800	15.1	1.9	184	...	15	71.8	83.6	60.7	0.9	Zaire
8,218	9.7	2	320	6,247	19.5	2.0	178	0.4	15	72.8	80.8	65.3	2.9	Zambia
27,431	18.5	3	935	11,975	12.8	4.6	508	...	15	76.0	81.5	66.8	8.2	Zimbabwe

associate-degree program only. [43]Includes part-time teachers. [44]Includes part-time students. [45]1992. [46]State University of Haiti only. [47]Based on data for four schools only. [48]Schools under the Department of Education and Culture only. [49]National schools only. [50]Teaching posts financed by the Ministry of Education and Culture only. [51]Island of Mauritius only. [52]Includes Portuguese-language initiation classes. [53]Includes upper primary. [54]University of the South Pacific extension centre. [55]Includes 79 composite schools that provide both primary and secondary education. [56]Université de Niamey and École Nationale d'Administration du Niger only. [57]Vocational teachers only. [58]Excludes the University of Fort Hare. [59]Includes postsecondary teacher training. [60]Includes graduate assistants. [61]Excludes Pemba and Zanzibar. [62]Third-level vocational and teacher training. [63]Excludes 42 private schools with 6,556 students. [64]Excludes East Jerusalem. [65]Includes some secondary teachers. [66]Data are for the former Yemen Arab Republic only. [67]Includes all the territory of former Yugoslavia.

BIBLIOGRAPHY AND SOURCES

The following list indicates the principal sources used in the compilation of *Britannica World Data*. It is by no means a complete list, either for international or for national sources, but is indicative only of the range of materials to which reference has been made in preparing this compilation. For example, in addition to the kinds of works cited below, reference has also been made to the constitution of each country, to the publications of its central or commercial banks, to unpublished information received in correspondence from the countries, and to other more specialized sources.

International Statistical Sources

Asian Development Bank. *Asian Development Outlook* (annual); *Key Indicators of Developing Member Countries of ADB* (annual, with supplements).

Billboard Ltd. *World Radio TV Handbook* (annual).

Caribbean Development Bank. *Annual Report.*

Comité Monétaire de la Zone Franc. *La Zone Franc: Rapport* (annual).

Commonwealth of Independent States. *SNG: Statistichesky Yezhegodnik Strany-Chlen* (*Member States of the CIS: Statistical Yearbook*).

Eastern Caribbean Central Bank. *Report and Statement of Accounts* (annual).

Europa Publications Ltd. *Africa South of the Sahara* (annual); *Eastern Europe and the Commonwealth of Independent States; The Europa Year Book* (2 vol.); *The Far East and Australasia* (annual); *The Middle East and North Africa* (annual).

Food and Agriculture Organization. *Food Balance Sheets; Production Yearbook; Trade Yearbook; World Census of Agriculture* (decennial); *Yearbook of Fishery Statistics* (2 vol.); *Yearbook of Forest Products.*

FT Caribbean. *The Caribbean Handbook* (annual).

Her Majesty's Stationery Office. *The Commonwealth Yearbook.*

Instituts d'Émission d'Outre-Mer et des Départements d'Outre-Mer (France). *Rapport annuel, Bulletin trimestriel* (quarterly).

Inter-American Development Bank. *Economic and Social Progress in Latin America* (annual).

Inter-Parliamentary Union. *Chronicle of Parliamentary Elections and Developments* (annual); *World Directory of Parliaments* (annual).

International Air Transport Association. *World Air Transport Statistics* (annual).

International Bank for Reconstruction and Development/The World Bank. *World Bank Atlas* (annual); *World Debt Tables* (annual); *World Development Report* (annual).

International Civil Aviation Organization. *Civil Aviation Statistics of the World* (annual); *Digest of Statistics.*

International Institute for Strategic Studies. *The Military Balance* (annual).

International Labour Organisation. *Year Book of Labour Statistics; The Cost of Social Security: Basic Tables* (triennial).

International Monetary Fund. *Annual Report on Exchange Arrangements and Exchange Restrictions; Government Finance Statistics Yearbook; International Financial Statistics* (monthly, with supplements and yearbook).

International Road Federation. *World Road Statistics* (annual).

Jane's Publishing Co., Ltd. *Jane's World Railways* (annual).

Lloyd's Register of Shipping. *Lloyd's Register of Shipping: Statistical Tables* (annual).

Longman Group U.K. Ltd. *Keesing's Record of World Events* (monthly).

Macmillan Press Ltd. *The Statesman's Year-Book.*

Middle East Economic Digest Ltd. *Africa Economic Digest* (semimonthly); *Middle East Economic Digest* (semimonthly).

Mining Journal. *Mining Annual Review* (2 vol.).

Nordic Council. *Yearbook of Nordic Statistics.*

Official Airline Guides, Inc. *Official Airline Guide* (monthly).

Organization of Eastern Caribbean States. *Statistical Pocket Digest.*

Organization for Economic Cooperation and Development. *Economic Surveys* (annual); *Financing and External Debt of Developing Countries* (annual); *National Accounts of Developing Countries* (irreg.).

Oxford University Press. *World Christian Encyclopedia* (David B. Barrett, ed. [1982]).

PennWell Publishing Co. *International Petroleum Encyclopedia* (annual).

René Moreux et Cie. *Marchés tropicaux & Méditerranéens* (weekly).

South Pacific Commission. *Key Economic Indicators* (irreg.); *South Pacific Economies: Statistical Summary* (biennial).

United Nations (UN). *Demographic Yearbook; International Trade Statistics Yearbook* (2 vol.); *Energy Statistics Yearbook; Industrial Statistics Yearbook* (2 vol.); *Monthly Bulletin of Statistics; Population Studies* (irreg.); *National Accounts Statistics* (3 vol.; annual); *Population and Vital Statistics Report* (quarterly); *Statistical Yearbook; World Population Prospects 19*** (biennial).

UN: Conference on Trade and Development. *Handbook of International Trade and Development Statistics* (annual); *The Least Developed Countries* (annual).

UN: Economic Commission for Africa. *African Socio-Economic Indicators* (annual); *African Statistical Yearbook* (4 vol.); *Demographic and Related Socio-Economic Data Sheets for ECA Member States* (1986); *Survey of Economic and Social Conditions in Africa* (irreg.).

UN: Economic Commission for Europe. *Annual Bulletin of Housing and Building Statistics for Europe; Annual Bulletin of Transport Statistics for Europe.*

UN: Economic Commission for Latin America. *Economic Survey of Latin America and the Caribbean* (annual); *Statistical Yearbook for Latin America and the Caribbean.*

UN: Economic and Social Commission for Asia and the Pacific. *Foreign Trade Statistics of Asia and the Pacific* (annual); *Statistical Indicators for Asia and the Pacific* (quarterly); *Statistical Yearbook for Asia and the Pacific.*

UN: Economic and Social Commission for Western Asia. *Demographic and Related Socio-Economic Data Sheets* (irreg.); *Population Bulletin* (irreg.); *The Population Situation in the ESCWA Region* (irreg.); *Statistical Abstract of the Region of the Economic and Social Commission for Western Asia* (annual).

UN: Educational, Scientific, and Cultural Organization. *Statistical Yearbook.*

United Nations Industrial Development Organization. *Industry and Development: Global Report* (annual).

United States: Central Intelligence Agency, *The World Factbook* (annual); Dept. of Commerce, *World Population Profile* (irreg.); Dept. of Energy, *International Energy Annual;* Dept. of Health and Human Services, *Social Security Programs Throughout the World* (biennial); Dept. of Interior, *Minerals Yearbook* (3 vol. in 8); Dept. of State, *Background Notes* (irreg.).

Vatican (Central Statistics Office of the Church). *Statistical Yearbook of the Church.*

World Energy Conference. *Survey of Energy Resources* (quinquennial).

World Health Organization. *World Health Statistics Annual; World Health Statistics Quarterly.*

World Tourism Organization. *World Tourism Statistics* (2 vol.; annual).

National Statistical Sources

Afghanistan. *First Seven-Year Economic and Social Development Plan, 1355–1361 (March 1976–March 1983); Preliminary Results of the First Afghan Population Census, 1979*).

Albania. *Population and Housing Census 1989; Statistical Yearbook of Albania.*

Algeria. *Annuaire statistique; Recensement général de la population et de l'habitat, 1987.*

American Samoa. *American Samoa Statistical Digest* (annual); *Population of American Samoa* (ESCAP; Country Monograph Series No. 7.1 [1979]); *1990 Census of Population and Housing* (U.S.).

Andorra. *Estadístiques* (annual); *Recull Estadístic General de la Població Andorra 90.*

Angola. *Angola: an Introductory Economic Review* (A World Bank Country Study [1991]); *Informação Estatística* (annual); *Perfil estatístico de Angola* (annual).

Antigua. *Statistical Yearbook.*

Argentina. *Anuario estadístico de la República Argentina; Boletín estadístico trimestral* (quarterly); *Censo nacional de población y vivienda, 1991; Encuesta permanente de hogares* (irreg.).

Armenia. *Statisticheskii Yezhegodnik Armenii* (Statistical Yearbook of Armenia).

Aruba. *Statistical Yearbook; Third Population and Housing Census October 6, 1991.*

Australia. *Census of Manufacturing Establishments: Summary of Operations by Industry Subdivision, Australia* (annual); *Foreign Trade Australia: Comparative and Summary Tables* (annual); *Monthly Summary of Statistics, Australia; National Income and Expenditure* (annual); *Social Indicators* (irreg.); *Year Book Australia; 1991 Census of Population and Housing.*

Austria. *Grosszählung 1991* (General Census 1991). *Österreichisches Jahrbuch* (annual); *Sozialstatistische Daten* (irreg.); *Statistisches Jahrbuch für die Republik Österreich.*

Azerbaijan. *Economic Review: Armenia* (IMF [1992]); *Narodnoye Khozyaystvo Azerbaydzhanskoy SSR* (National Economy of the Azerbaijan S.S.R. [annual]).

Bahamas, The. *Census of Population and Housing 1990; Quarterly Statistical Summary; Statistical Abstract* (annual); *Vital Statistics Report* (annual).

Bahrain. *Statistical Abstract* (annual); *1981 Census of Bahrain.*

Bangladesh. *Bangladesh Population Census, 1991; Population of Bangladesh* (ESCAP; Country Monograph Series No. 8 [1981]); *Statistical Yearbook of Bangladesh.*

Barbados. *Barbados Economic Report* (annual); *Monthly Digest of Statistics.*

Belarus. *Narodnoye Kozyaystvo Belorusskoy S.S.R.* (National Economy of the Belorussian S.S.R. [annual]).

Belgium. *Annuaire statistique de la Belgique; Recensement de la population et des logements au 1er mars 1991.*

Belize. *Abstract of Statistics* (annual); *Belize Economic Survey* (annual); *Belize Today: Development Plan 1990–94; Labour Force Survey (1983–84); 1991 Population Census: Major Findings.*

Benin. *Annuaire statistique; Recensement des Entreprises 1980* (2 parts); *Recensement général de la population et de l'habitation* (1979).

Bermuda. *Bermuda Digest of Statistics* (annual); *Report of the Manpower Survey* (annual); *The 1991 Census of Population and Housing.*

Bhutan. *Bhutan: Development Planning in a Unique Environment* (A World Bank Country Study [1988]); *Statistical Yearbook of Bhutan* (annual).

Bolivia. *Bolivia en Cifras* (annual); *Censo Nacional de población y vivienda 1992; Compendio Estadístico* (annual); *Estadísticas Económicas* (annual); *Estrategia de Desarrollo Económico y Social 1989–2000; Resumen estadístico* (annual).

Botswana. *National Development Plan 1985–91; 1991 Population and Housing Census.*

Brazil. *Anuário Econômico-Fiscal; Anuário Estatístico do Brasil; Censo Demografico 1991; Comercio Exterior do Brasil* (2 vol.; annual).
Brunei. *Brunei Statistical Yearbook; Population Survey 1986: Demographic Report; Report on the Census of Population, 1981.*
Bulgaria. *Prebroyavaneto na naselenìeto kŭm 4.12.1985 godina* (Census of Population of Dec. 4, 1985); *Statisticheskii godishnikna Republika Bŭlgariya* (Statistical Yearbook of the Republic of Bulgaria).
Burkina Faso. *Annuaire Statistique; Recensement général de la population du 10 au 20 decembre 1985; Statistiques Sociales* (annual).
Burundi. *Annuaire statistique; Recensement général de la population, 1990.*
Cambodia. *Cambodia: A Country Study* (1990); *Intersectoral Basic Needs Assessment Mission to Cambodia* (Unesco; 1991); *Report of the Kampuchea Needs Assessment Study* (UNDP; 1989).
Cameroon. *Note annuelle de statistique; Recensement général de la population et de l'habitat 1987.*
Canada. *Canada Year Book* (biennial); *Census Canada 1991: Population.*
Cape Verde. *Boletim Anual de Estatística; I.º Recenseamento Geral da População e Habìtação—1990.*
Central African Republic. *Annuaire statistique; Economic and Social Development Plan 1986–90; Recensement général de la population 1988.*
Chad. *Annuaire statistique; Chad: a Country Study* (1990).
Chile. *Chile XVI censo nacional de población y V de vivienda, 22 de abril 1992; Compendio estadístico* (annual); *Plan nacional indicativo de desarrollo* (quinquennial).
China, People's Republic of. *China: A Statistics Survey in 19*** (annual); *People's Republic of China Year-Book; Statistical Yearbook of China; 10 Percent Sampling Tabulation on the 1990 Population Census of the People's Republic of China.*
Colombia. *Colombia estadística* (2 vol.; annual); *XV Censo nacional de población y IV de vivienda* (1985).
Comoros. *Plan interimaire de développement économique et sociale (1983–1986); Recensement général de la population et de l'habitat 15 septembre 1980.*
Congo. *Annuaire statistique; Recensement Général de la Population et de l'Habitat de 1984.*
Costa Rica. *Anuario estadístico; Censo de Población 1984; Plan Nacional de Desarrollo, 1986–90* (2 vol.).
Côte d'Ivoire. *Annuaire statistique; La Côte d'Ivoire en chiffres* (irreg.); *L'Économie Ivoirienne* (irreg.); *Enquête permanente aupres des menages: resultats provisoires 1985.*
Croatia. *Census of Population, Households, Dwellings and Farms 31st March 1991; Statistical Yearbook.*
Cuba. *Anuario estadístico; Censo de población y viviendas, 1981; Compendio estadístico de Cuba* (annual); *Cuba Half-Yearly Economic Report.*
Cyprus. *Census of Industrial Production* (annual); *Economic Report* (annual); *Statistical Abstract* (annual).
Czech Republic. *Statistické Přehledy* (Monthly Statistics).
Denmark. *Folke- og boligtaellingen, 1981* (Population and Housing Census); *Statistisk årbog* (Statistical Yearbook).
Djibouti. *Annuaire statistique de Djibouti.*
Dominica. *Statistical Digest* (irreg.).
Dominican Republic. *República Dominicana en cifras* (annual); *VI Censo nacional de población y vivienda, 1981.*
Ecuador. *Encuesta anual de manufactura y minería; Serie estadística* (quinquennial); *Censo de población (V) y de vivienda (IV) 1990.*
Egypt. *Population, Housing, and Establishment Census, 1986; Statistical Yearbook.*
El Salvador. *Anuario estadístico* (8 vol.); *El Salvador en cifras* (annual); *Indicadores Económicos y Sociales* (annual).
Equatorial Guinea. *Censos Nacionales, I de Población y I de Vivienda—4 al 17 de Julio de 1983; Guinea en cifras* (irreg.).
Estonia. *Eesti Statistika Aastaraamat* (Estonia Statistical Yearbook); *Estonia: The Transition to a Market Economy* (1993).
Ethiopia. *Ethiopia 1984 Population and Housing Census; Ethiopia Statistical Abstract* (annual).
Faeroe Islands. *Arbog for Faerøerne* (Yearbook for the Faeroe Islands); *Rigsombudsmanden på Færøerne: Beretning* (annual).
Fiji. *Annual Employment Survey; Census of Industries* (annual); *Current Economic Statistics* (quarterly); *1986 Census of the Population.*
Finland. *Annual Statistics of Agriculture; Economic Survey* (annual); *1985 Population and Housing Census; Statistical Yearbook of Finland.*
France. *Annuaire statistique de la France; Données sociales* (triennial); *Recensement général de la population de 1990; Métropole; Tableaux de l'Economie Française* (annual).
French Guiana. *Recensement général de la population de 1990: logements-population-emplois, 973: Guyane; Tableaux economiques regionaux: Guyane* (annual).
French Polynesia. *Résultats du Recensement Général de la Population de la Polynésie Française, du 6 Septembre 1988; Tableaux de l'economie polynesienne* (irreg.); *Te avei'a: Bulletin d'information statistique* (monthly).
Gabon. *Situation économique, financière et sociale de la République Gabonaise* (annual).
Gambia, The. *Statistical Abstract* (annual?).
Gaza Strip. *Judaea, Samaria, and Gaza Area Statistics Quarterly; Palestinian Statistical Abstract* (annual).
Georgia. *Narodnoye Khozyaystvo Gruzinskoy SSR* (National Economy of the Georgian S.S.R. [annual]).
Germany. *Statistisches Jahrbuch für die Bundesrepublik Deutschland; Volkszählung vom 25. Mai 1987* (Census of Population).
Ghana. *Population Census of Ghana, 1984; Quarterly Digest of Statistics.*
Gibraltar. *Abstract of Statistics* (annual); *Census of Gibraltar, 1991.*
Greece. *Recensement des industries manufacturières: Artisanat, du commerce et autres services* (1978); *Recensement de la population et des habitations, 1991; Statistical Yearbook of Greece.*
Greenland. *Grønland* (annual); *Grønlands befolkning* (Greenland Population [annual]).
Grenada. *Abstract of Statistics* (annual).
Guadeloupe. *Recensement général de la population de 1990: logements-population-emplois, 971: Guadeloupe; Tableaux economiques regionaux: Guadeloupe* (annual).
Guam. *Guam Annual Economic Review; Census '90: Guam.*
Guatemala. *Censos nacionales, 1981: IX de población—IV de habitación.*
Guernsey. *Guernsey Census 1991; Statistical Digest* (annual).
Guinea. *Situation Économique et Conjoncturelle au 31 decembre 1985 et éléments sur la mise en oeuvre de la réform économique au cours du première trimestre 1986.*
Guinea-Bissau. *Boletim Trimestral de Estatística; Recenseamento Geral da População e da Habitação, 16 de Abril de 1979.*
Guyana. *Annual Statistical Abstract.*
Haiti. *Bulletin trimestriel de statistique; Dominican Republic and Haiti: Country Studies* (1991); *Résultats préliminaires du recensement général (Septembre 1982).*
Honduras. *Anuario estadístico; Censo nacional de Población y Vivienda 1988; Honduras en cifras* (annual); *Plan nacional de desarrollo, 1987–90.*
Hong Kong. *Annual Digest of Statistics; Hong Kong* (annual); *Hong Kong 1991 Population Census; Hong Kong in Figures* (annual); *Hong Kong Social and Economic Trends* (irreg.).
Hungary. *Statisztikai évkönyv* (Statistical Yearbook); *1990, Évi népszámlálás* (Census of Population).
Iceland. *Hagtidhindi* (monthly); *Landshagir* (Statistical Abstract of Iceland [irreg.]); *Verslunarskýrslur* (External Trade [annual]).
India. *Census of India, 1991; Economic Survey* (annual); *India: A Reference Annual; Statistical Abstract* (annual).
Indonesia. *Indonesia: An Official Handbook* (1989); *Hasil Sensus penduduk Indonesia, 1990* (Census of Population); *Statistical Yearbook of Indonesia.*
Iran. *National Census of Population and Housing, October 1986; A Statistical Reflection of the Islamic Republic of Iran* (annual); *Statistical Yearbook of the Islamic Republic of Iran.*
Iraq. *Iraq: A Country Study* (1990); *Statistical Abstract* (annual).
Ireland. *Census of Population of Ireland, 1991; National Income and Expenditure* (annual); *Statistical Abstract* (annual).
Isle of Man. *Census Report 1991; Isle of Man Digest of Economic and Social Statistics* (annual).
Israel. *1983 Census of Population and Housing; Statistical Abstract* (annual).
Italy. *Annuario di statistica agraria: Annuario di statistiche demografiche; Annuario di statistiche industriali; Annuario statistico dell'istruzione; Annuario statistico Italiano; Statistiche forestale* (annual); *Statistiche sociali* (1981); *13° Censimento generale della popolazione e delle Abitazioni 20 Ottobre 1991.*
Jamaica. *Economic and Social Survey* (annual); *Statistical Abstract* (annual); *Statistical Yearbook of Jamaica.*
Japan. *Establishment Census of Japan, 1981; Japan Statistical Yearbook; Statistical Indicators on Social Life* (annual); *1990 Population Census of Japan.*
Jersey. *Report of the Census for 1991; Statistical Digest* (annual).
Jordan. *Census 1979; Family Expenditure Survey* (1980); *National Accounts* (irreg.); *Statistical Yearbook.*
Kazakhstan. *Statistichesky Yezhegodnik* (Statistical Yearbook).
Kenya. *Economic Survey* (annual); *Kenya Statistical Digest* (quarterly); *Statistical Abstract* (annual).
Kiribati. *Annual Abstract of Statistics; Kiribati Population Census 1990; Sixth National Development Plan, 1987–1991.*
Korea, North. *North Korea: A Country Study* (1981).
Korea, South. *Korea Statistical Yearbook; Social Indicators in Korea* (irreg.); *The 5th Five-Year Economic and Development Plan, 1982–1986; 1990 Population and Housing Census.*
Kuwait. *Annual Statistical Abstract; Economic Report* (annual); *General Census of Population and Housing and Buildings 1985.*
Kyrgyzstan. *Statistichesky Yezhegodnik Kyrgyzstana* (Statistical Yearbook of Kyrgyzstan).
Latvia. *Latvia: The Transition to a Market Economy* (1993); *Statistical Yearbook of Latvia.*
Lebanon. *Lebanon: A Country Study* (1989).
Lesotho. *Annual Statistical Bulletin; 1986 Population Census.*
Liberia. *Economic Survey* (annual); *1974 Census of Population and Housing.*
Libya. *The Five-Year Development Plan 1981–85; Libya Population Census, 1973; Statistical Abstract for Libya* (annual).
Liechtenstein. *Statistisches Jahrbuch; Volkszählung, 2 Dezember 1980* (Census of Population).
Lithuania. *Lithuania: The Transition to a Market Economy* (1993); *Lithuania's Statistics Yearbook.*
Luxembourg. *Annuaire statistique; Bulletin du STATEC* (monthly); *Recensement général de la population du 31 mars 1991.*
Macau. *Anuário Estatístico; Inquerito Industrial* (annual); *XIII Recenseamento Geral da População, 1991.*
Madagascar. *Recensement général de la population et des habitats, 1975; Situation économique* (annual).
Malaŵi. *Malawi Population and Housing Census, 1987; Malawi Statistical Yearbook; Malawi Yearbook.*
Malaysia. *Fifth Malaysia Plan, 1986–1990; Malaysia Official Year Book; Malaysian Annual Statistical Bulletin; Population and Housing Census of Malaysia 1991.*
Maldives. *National Development Plan 1991–1993; Population and Housing Census of Maldives 1990; Statistical Year Book of Maldives.*
Mali. *Annuaire statistique du Mali; Comptes Economiques du Mali* (annual); *Recensement general de la population et de l'habitat* (*du 1er au 14 avril 1987*).
Malta. *Annual Abstract of Statistics; Census of Industrial Production Report for 19*** (annual); *Malta Year Book* (annual).
Marshall Islands. *Marshall Islands Statistical Abstract* (annual).
Martinique. *Annuaire statistique de la Martinique; Bulletin de statistique* (quarterly); *Recensement de la population de 1990: logements-population-emplois, 972: Martinique; Tableaux economiques regionaux: Martinique* (annual).
Mauritania. *Annuaire Statistique; Mauritania: A Country Study* (1990).
Mauritius. *Annual Digest of Statistics; 1983 Housing and Population Census of Mauritius.*
Mayotte. *Resultats du recensement de la population de la Collectivité territoriale de Mayotte 5 août 1985.*
Mexico. *Anuario estadístico; XI Censo general de población y vivienda, 1990; La Economia Mexicana en Cifras* (1990); *Informe de Gobierno: Estadístico* (annual).
Micronesia. *Second National Development Plan 1992–1996.*
Moldova. *Republica Moldova in Cifre* (annual).
Monaco. *Annuaire Officiel.*
Mongolia. *National Economy of the MPR, 1921–86* (1986; quinquennial?); *The Mongolian People's Republic: Towards a Market Economy* (1991).
Morocco. *Annuaire statistique du Maroc; Economic and Social Development Report, 1981; Recensement général de la population et de l'habitat de 1982.*
Mozambique. *Informação Estatística* (annual); *1º Recenseamento Geral da População, 1980.*

Myanmar (Burma). *Report to the Pyithu Hluttaw on the Financial, Social, and Economic Conditions for 19*** (annual); *1983 Population Census.*
Namibia. *Budget 19**–19*** (annual); *Population Census 1981; Statistical/Economic Review* (annual).
Nepal. *Census of Manufacturing Establishments of Nepal, 1981–82; Economic Survey* (annual); *Population Monograph of Nepal* (1987); *The Seventh Plan (1985–90); Statistical Pocket Book* (irreg.); *Statistical Yearbook of Nepal.*
Netherlands, The. *Statistical Yearbook of the Netherlands; 14e Algemene volkstelling, 28 februari 1971* (14th General Population Census).
Netherlands Antilles. *Tweede Algemene Volks- en Woningtelling Nederlandse Antillen: toestand per 1 Februari 1981; Statistical Yearbook of the Netherlands Antilles.*
New Caledonia. *Annuaire statistique; Enquête socio-économique, 1980–1981; Recensement de la population de la Nouvelle-Calédonie au 4 avril 1989; Tableaux de l'economie Caledonienne* (annual).
New Zealand. *1991 New Zealand Census of Population and Dwellings; New Zealand Official Yearbook.*
Nicaragua. *Anuario estadístico de Nicaragua; Nicaragua: A Country Study* (1982); *Plan Económico, 1987* (irreg.).
Niger. *Annuaire statistique; Les comptes de la nation* (triennial); *Plan de developpement economique et social du Niger 1987–91; 2ème Recensement général de la population 1988.*
Nigeria. *Annual Abstract of Statistics; Fourth National Development Plan* (1981); *Nigeria: A Country Study* (1981).
Norway. *Folke- og boligtelling 1990* (Population and Housing Census); *Industristatistikk* (annual); *Statistisk årbok* (Statistical Yearbook).
Oman. *Statistical Year Book; The Second Five-Year Plan of Development, 1981–1985.*
Pakistan. *Economic Survey* (annual); *Pakistan Statistical Yearbook; Population Census of Pakistan, 1981; Some Socio-Economic Trends* (annual); *10 Years of Pakistan in Statistics, 1972–1982* (1983).
Panama. *Indicadores económicos y sociales* (annual); *Censos nacionales de 1990: IX de población y V de vivienda, 13 de mayo de 1990; Panama en cifras* (annual); *Situacion económica: Cuentas nacionales* (annual); *Situacion económica: Industria* (annual).
Papua New Guinea. *Abstract of Statistics* (quarterly); *National Accounts Statistics—Statistical Bulletin* (quarterly); *Population of Papua New Guinea* (*ESCAP;* Country Monograph Series No. 7.2 [1982]); *Social Indicators of Papua New Guinea, 1980–85; Summary of Statistics* (annual); *1990 National Population Census.*
Paraguay. *Anuario estadístico del Paraguay; Censo nacional de población y viviendas, 1992.*
Peru. *Censos nacionales; VIII de población: III de vivienda, 12 de julio de 1981; Compendio estadístico* (2 vol.; annual); *Informe estadístico* (annual).
Philippines. *Philippine Statistical Yearbook; Philippine Yearbook; 1990 Census of Population and Housing.*
Poland. *Narodowy spis powszechny 1988* (Census of Population); *Rocznik statystyczny* (Statistical Yearbook).
Portugal. *Anuário Estatístico; Estatísticas Agricolas* (annual); *Estatísticas do Comercio Externo* (annual); *Estatísticas Demograficas* (annual); *Estatísticas Industriais* (2 vol.; annual); *Estatísticas Monetarias e Financeiras* (annual); *Recenseamento Agricola, 1979; XIII Recenseamento Geral da População: III Recenseamento Geral da Habitação, 1991.*
Puerto Rico. *Anuario estadístico; Estadisticas socio-economicas* (annual); *Informe económico al gobernador* (Economic Report to the Governor [annual]); *1990 Census of Population and Housing* (U.S.).
Qatar. *Annual Statistical Abstract; Economic Survey of Qatar* (annual); *Qatar Year Book.*
Réunion. *Panorama de l'Économie de la Réunion* (annual); *Recensement général de la population de 1990: logements-population-emploi, 974; Réunion.*
Romania. *Anuarul statistic al României; Population and Housing Census January 7, 1992; Romania Yearbook.*
Russia. *Narodnoye Khozyaystvo Rossiyskoy Federatsii* (National Economy of the Russian Federation [annual]).
Rwanda. *Bulletin de Statistique: Supplement Annuel; IIIème Plan de Developpement Economique, Social et Culturel 1982–86; Recensement General de la Population et de l'Habitat 1991.*
St. Kitts and Nevis. *Annual Digest of Statistics; St. Christopher and Nevis: Economic Report* (World Bank Country Study) (1985).
St. Lucia. *Annual Statistical Digest.*
St. Vincent and the Grenadines. *Digest of Statistics* (annual); *Population and Housing Census 1991.*
San Marino. *Annuario statistico, 1981–84* (4 vol.?; irreg.); *3 Censimento generale dell agricoltura* (1977); *5 Censimento generale della popolazione* (1979).
São Tomé and Príncipe. *1° Recenseamento Geral da População e da Habitação 1981.*
Saudi Arabia. *The Statistical Indicator* (annual); *Statistical Summary* (Saudi Arabian Monetary Agency [annual]); Statistical Year Book.
Senegal. *Le Sénégal en chiffres* (irreg.); *Recensement de la Population et de l'Habitat 1988; Situation économique du Senegal* (annual).
Seychelles. *National Development Plan, 1990–94;* (2 vol.); *Statistical Abstract* (annual); *1987 Census Report.*
Sierra Leone. *Sierra Leone: 12 Years of Economic Achievement and Political Consolidation under the APC and Dr. Siaka Stevens, 1968–80.*
Singapore. *Census of Population, 1980; Report on the Census of Industrial Production* (annual); *Singapore Yearbook; Yearbook of Statistics Singapore.*
Slovakia. *Sčítanie L'udu, Domov a Bytov 1991* (Census of Population, Housing, and Families 1991).
Slovenia. *Statistični Letopis Republike Slovenija* (Statistical Yearbook of the Republic of Slovenia).
Solomon Islands. *Solomon Islands 1986 Population Census; Statistical Bulletin* (irreg.).
Somalia. *Statistical Abstract* (annual).
South Africa. *1991 Population Census; South Africa: Official Yearbook of the Republic of South Africa; South African Statistics* (biennial).
Spain. *Anuario estadístico; Censo de población de 1991.*
Sri Lanka. *Census of Population and Housing, 1981; Report on the Survey on Manufacturing Industries, 1979; Sri Lanka Year Book; Statistical Pocketbook of the Democratic Socialist Republic of Sri Lanka* (annual).
Sudan, The. *Third Population Census, 1983.*
Suriname. *General Population Census 1980; Statistisch Jaarboek van Suriname.*
Swaziland. *Annual Statistical Bulletin; Fourth Five-Year Development Plan (1986/87–90/91 Fiscal Years*); *Report on the 1986 Swaziland Population Census.*
Sweden. *Folk- och bostadsräkningen, 1990* (Population and Housing Census); *Statistisk årsbok för Sverige* (Statistical Abstract of Sweden [annual]).
Switzerland. *Recensement fédéral de la population, 1990; Statistisches Jahrbuch* (Statistical Yearbook).
Syria. *General Census of Housing and Inhabitants, 1981; Statistical Abstract* (annual).
Taiwan. *Industry of Free China* (monthly); *Social Indicators of the Republic of China* (annual); *Statistical Abstract* (annual); *Statistical Yearbook of the Republic of China; Taiwan Statistical Data Book* (annual); *Yearbook of Labor Statistics; 1990 Census of Population and Housing.*
Tajikistan. *Narodnoye Khozyaystvo Tadzhikskoy SSR* (National Economy of the Tadzhik S.S.R. [annual]).
Tanzania. *Tanzania Statistical Abstract* (irreg.); *1978 Population Census.*
Thailand. *Report of the Survey of Business Trade and Services* (biennial); *Foreign Trade Statistics* (monthly); *Report of the Industrial Survey, Whole Kingdom* (biennial); *Report of the Labor Force Survey: Whole Kingdom* (quarterly); *Statistical Handbook of Thailand* (annual); *Statistical Yearbook; 1990 Population and Housing Census.*
Togo. *Annuaire statistique du Togo; Eurostat Country Profile: Togo* (1991); *Plan de développement économique & social, 1981–1985; Recensement Général de la Population et de l'Habitat 1981.*
Tonga. *Population Census, 1986; Sixth Development Plan 1991–95; Statistical Abstract* (irreg.).
Trinidad and Tobago. *Annual Statistical Digest; 1990 Population and Housing Census.*
Tunisia. *Annuaire statistique de la Tunisie; Recensement général de la population et des logements, 30 mars 1984.*
Turkey. *Diş Ticaret İstatistikleri* (Annual Foreign Trade Statistics); *Genel Sanayi ve İşyerleri Sayımı* (Census of Industry and Business Establishments [1980]); *1990 Genel Nüfus Sayımı* (1990 Census of Population); *Genel Tarım Sayımı, 1980* (Census of Agriculture); *İnşaat İstatistikleri* (Construction Statistics [annual]); *Türkiye İstatistik Yilliği* (Statistical Yearbook of Turkey).
Turkmenistan. *Narodnoye Khozyaystvo Turkmenskoy SSR* (National Economy of the Turkmen S.S.R. [annual]).
Ukraine. *Narodne Hospodarstvo Ukrayini u 19** rotsi* (National Economy of Ukraine in the year 19** [annual]).
United Arab Emirates. *Statistical Yearbook* (Abu Dhabi).
United Kingdom. *Annual Abstract of Statistics; Britain: An Official Handbook* (annual); *National Income and Expenditure* (annual); *Census 1991; Report on the Census of Production: Summary Tables* (annual).
United States. *Agricultural Statistics* (annual); *Annual Energy Review; Current Population Reports* (Series P-20, P-23, P-25, P-26, P-27, P-28, P-60); *Digest of Education Statistics* (annual); *Minerals Yearbook* (3 vol.; annual); *National Transportation Statistics* (annual); *Statistical Abstract* (annual); *U.S. Exports: SIC-Based Products* (annual); *U.S. Imports: SIC-Based Products* (annual); *Vital and Health Statistics* (series 1–20); *1987 Census of Construction Industries; 1987 Census of Manufacturing; 1987 Census of Retail Trade; 1987 Census of Wholesale Trade; 1987 Census of Agriculture; 1990 Census of Population and Housing.*
Uruguay. *Anuario Estadístico; Censo General: VI de población: IV de viviendas, Octubre 1985. Encuesta Nacional de Hogares* (annual).
Uzbekistan. *Narodnoye Khozyaystvo Respubliki Uzbekistan v 19** g.* (National Economy of Uzbekistan in the year 19** [annual]).
Vanuatu. *National Population Census 1989; Second National Development Plan 1987–1991* (2 vol.); *Vanuatu Statistical Yearbook.*
Venezuela. *Anuario estadístico; Censo '90; Encuesta de hogares por muestreo* (annual); *Encuesta industrial* (annual).
Vietnam. *Nien Giam Thong Ke* (Statistical Yearbook); *Tong Dieu Tra Dan So Viet Nam—1989* (*Vietnam Population Census—1989*); *Vietnam: a Country Study* (1989).
Virgin Islands of the United States. *Annual Report; Economic Review, 1986; 1990 Census of Population and Housing* (U.S.).
West Bank. *Judaea, Samaria, and Gaza Area Statistics Quarterly; Palestinian Statistical Abstract* (annual).
Western Sahara. *Recensement General de la Population et de l'Habitat* (1982 [Morocco]).
Western Samoa. *Annual Statistical Abstract; Census of Population and Housing,* 1981; *Seventh Development Plan 1992–1994.*
Yemen. *Country Presentation: Republic of Yemen* (1990); *The Yemens: Country Studies* (1986).
Yugoslavia. *Popis stanovištva, domaćinstava, stanova i poljoprivrednih gazdinstava 1991 godine* (Census of Population, Households, Housing, and Agricultural Holdings 1991); *Statistički godišnjak Jugoslavije* (Statistical Yearbook of Yugoslavia).
Zaire. *Annuaire statistique* (irreg.); Conjoncture Economique (semiannual); *Recensement Scientifique de la Population du 1er juillet 1984.*
Zambia. *Country Profile: Zambia 1985; Monthly Digest of Statistics; National Development Plan, 1989–93; 1990 Census of Population, Housing, Agriculture.*
Zimbabwe. *1982 Population Census: Main Demographic Features of the Population of Zimbabwe; Statistical Yearbook.*

Index

This index covers both *Britannica Book of the Year* (cumulative for ten years) and *Britannica World Data.*

Entries in dark type are titles of articles in the *Book of the Year;* an accompanying year in dark type gives the year the reference appears, and the accompanying page number in light type **shows where the article appears. References for previous years are preceded by the year in dark type. For example, "Archaeology 94:**95; **93:**96; **92:**95; **91:**125; **90:**143; **89:**125; **88:**125; **87:**141; **86:**164; **85:**165" **indicates that the article "Archaeology" appeared every year from 1985 through 1994. Other references that appear with a page number but without a year refer to references from the current yearbook.**

Indented entries in light type that follow dark type article titles refer by page number to other places in the text where the subject of the article is discussed. Light type entries that are not indented refer by page number to subjects that are not themselves article titles. Names of people covered in biographies and obituaries are followed by the abbreviation "(biog.)" or "(obit.)" with the year in dark type and a page number in light type, *e.g.,* Ailey, Alvin (obit.) **90:**103, or Reagan, Ronald Wilson (biogs.) **89:**82; **88:**80; **87:**93; **86:**108; **85:**110. In cases where a person has both a biography and an obituary, the words appear as subentries under the main entry and are alphabetized accordingly, *e.g.:*

Berlin, Irving
  biography **89:**66
  obituary **90:**105

References to illustrations are by page number and are preceded by the abbreviation *il.*

The index uses word-by-word alphabetization (treating a word as one or more characters separated by a space from the next word). Names beginning with "Mc" and "Mac" are alphabetized as "Mac"; "St." is treated as "Saint."

A

B

References with dark type numbers refer to the previous years, *e.g.*, **92**:264 for the 1992 edition, page 264.

C

References giving only a page number in light type are for the current edition.

D

H

References giving only a page number in light type are for the current edition.

I

J

References giving only a page number in light type are for the current edition.

K

L

M

N

O

P

References with dark type numbers refer to the previous years, *e.g.*, **92**:264 for the 1992 edition, page 264.

Q

R

T

U

V

W